THE OFFICIAL MUSEUM DIRECTORY®
2021

The 2021 edition of The Official Museum Directory® is published by NRP Direct.

President	R. Brett Grayson
Publisher	Robert Docherty
Sales Manager	April Tann

EDITORIAL

Managing Editor	Eileen Fanning
Content Editor	Linda Hummer
	Patrick O'Dowd

MARKETING

Creative Services Manager	Kathleen F. Stein

Printed and bound in the United States of America

International Standard Book Number: 978-0-87217-087-2
International Standard Serial Number: 0090-6700
Library of Congress Catalog Card Number: 79-144808

OMD ONLINE
The Official Museum Directory

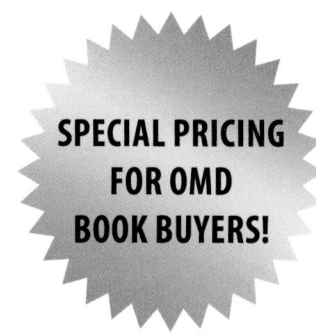
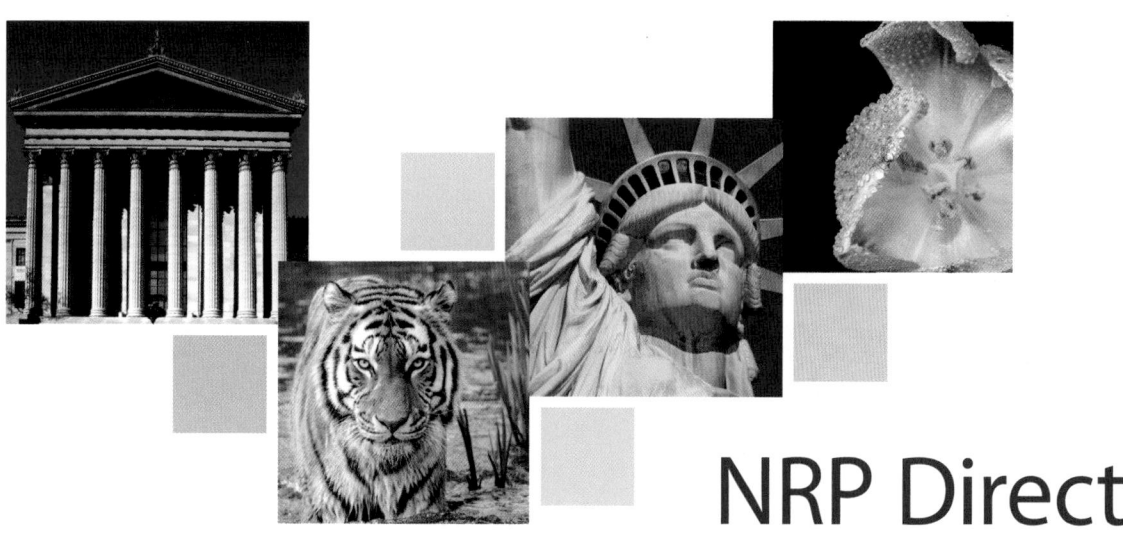

THE OFFICIAL MUSEUM DIRECTORY® 2021

TABLE OF CONTENTS

Visit www.officialmuseumdirectory.com to download additional Personnel and Collection Indices.

Key to Symbols:
Volunteer President [Pres. (V)]
Volunteer Chairman [Chm. (V)]

Traveling Exhibit [(T)]
Telecommunications Device for the Deaf [TDD]
Handicapped Accessible [♿]

THE OFFICIAL MUSEUM DIRECTORY®

NRP Direct takes great pride in presenting the 2021 edition of The Official Museum Directory®. With 51 years of experience in the museum field, we are able to ensure that the OMD is the most comprehensive directory of America's museums, zoos, historic sites, and other related institutions. In this edition you will find a wealth of information on the nation's ever-expanding and influential museum community.

The 2021 Directory contains information on approximately 15,000 museums operating in 87 different fields, ranging from fine arts to historic homes, from zoos to science museums. We are pleased to include information on exhibits along with completely new listings.

The Official Museum Directory® is an invaluable source for museum professionals seeking to contact directors and curators, identify unique collections and locate traveling exhibitions. Library patrons and travelers can discover important local cultural centers and identify educational travel destinations. To provide all users with alternate means of accessing this rich museum content, the directory includes institution and category indices. Additional personnel and collection indices can be found online at www.officialmuseumdirectory.com. The Products & Services section helps readers to locate suppliers who specialize in the museum field.

We hope The Official Museum Directory® will prove to be not only an inspiration but also a valuable tool to help you take full advantage of one of America's truly great national resources – our country's diverse community of museums.

Sincerely,

Robert Docherty
Publisher
NRP Direct
430 Mountain Avenue, Suite 403
New Providence, NJ 07974
844-592-4197
www.officialmuseumdirectory.com

Index to Products & Services Suppliers

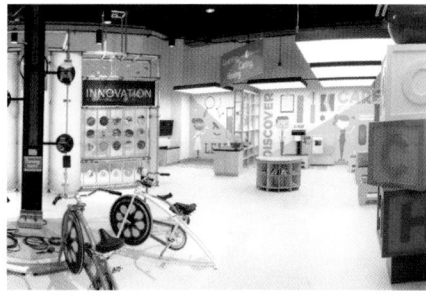

"Lighting Buffalo's Imagination" | Explore & More Children's Museum | Design by Gyroscope

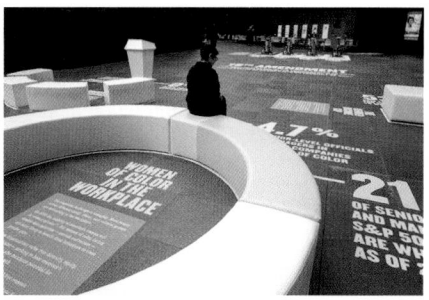

"Seat at the Table- Vision 2020" | Kimmel Center for the Performing Arts | Exhibition Design & Photo by Dome

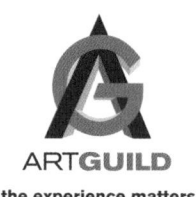

ART GUILD, INC.
300 Wolf Dr.
West Deptford, NJ 08086
Tel: 856-853-7500
E-mail: degner@artguildinc.com
Website: www.artguildinc.com

Type of Business:

Collaborating with designers and museums nationwide, Art Guild's team of museum professionals crafts exceptional exhibit environments, which include archival casework, graphics, interactives, AV/media, and specialty trades. Headquartered in a state-of-the-art 380,000 SF facility in NJ, we employ an expert project management team, experienced craftspeople, and the latest technologies to transform your exhibit concepts into built reality. At Art Guild, the experience always matters.
Contact David M. Egner to learn more about our superlative team.

Personnel:

David M. Egner (Vice President, Museum Services)

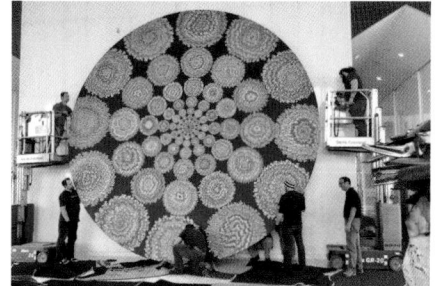

Large and small scale installations

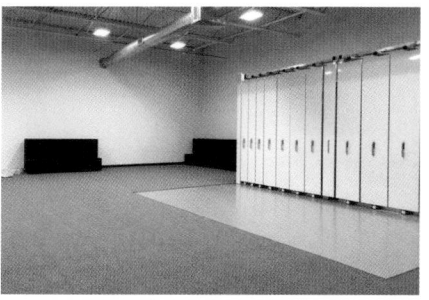

Fine arts storage and customized private vaults

ARTPACK SERVICES, INC.
24650 Crestview Ct.
Farmington Hills, MI 48335-1504
Tel: 248-478-8946; Fax: 248-478-9588
E-mail: info@artpack.com
Website: www.artpack.com

Type of Business:

Artpack was founded in 1981 to provide professional services to museums, auction houses, galleries, corporate and private collectors for fine arts and antiques. We specialize in fine arts storage, custom & museum quality crating and packing, installation, local and long distance shipping including a monthly New York shuttle. Our operations are climate controlled and staff trained to museum standards. Artpack also offers collection/project management and courier services, mount and pedestal fabrication, rigging and conservation services.

Personnel:

Ted Lee Hadfield (President)
Wendy MacGaw (Vice President)

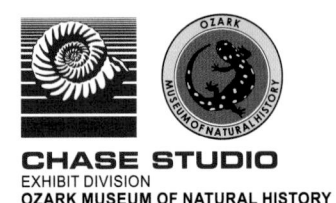

CHASE STUDIO
EXHIBIT DIVISION
OZARK MUSEUM OF NATURAL HISTORY

CHASE STUDIO
205 Wolf Creek Rd.
Cedar Creek, MO 65627
Tel: 417-794-3303; Fax: 417-794-3741
E-mail: chasestudio@chasestudio.com
Website: www.chasestudio.com

Type of Business:
Designers and builders of natural history and environmental science exhibits; paleontological reconstructions, zoological models, botanical reproductions, dioramas and habitat groups, illustrations and mural painting, graphic design, photography, lighting design, fine cabinetwork, taxidermy, research, video production, script writing, exhibit planning and consultation. Exhibits for more than 200 museums worldwide since 1973.

Personnel:
Dr. Terry L. Chase (Director)

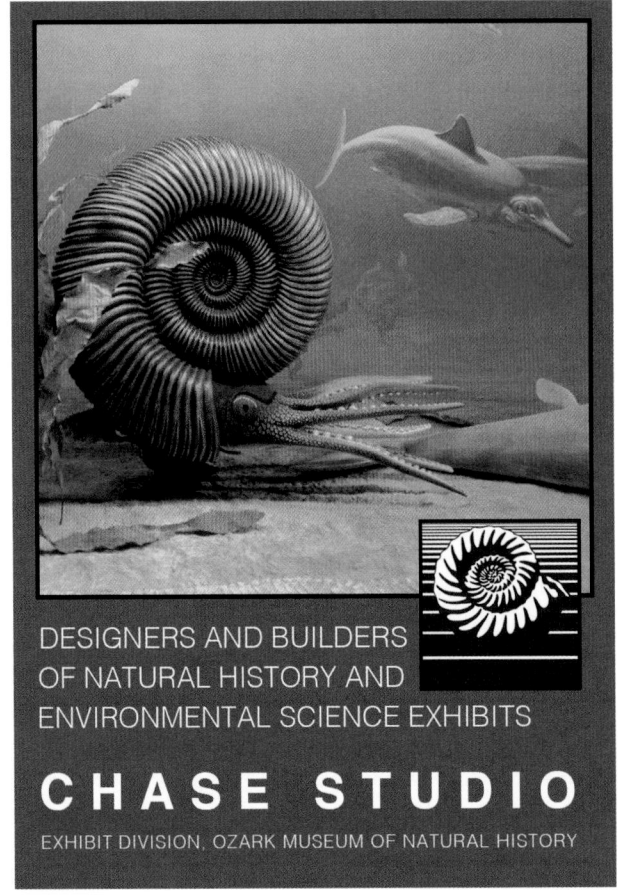

CHRISTIE'S

CHRISTIE'S
20 Rockefeller Plaza
New York, NY 10020
Tel: 212-636-2620; Fax: 212-636-2370
E-mail: MuseumServices@christies.com
Website: www.christies.com

Type of Business:

Christie's is available to assist museums in a variety of areas including: appraising collections, objects and bequests and establishing values for loans; managing sales of major objects and minor collections; assistance with indemnification appraisals; and consulting on buying and selling at auction. We welcome collector circle visits, and our specialists are available for participation in lectures, symposia and scholarly talks.

Personnel:

Allison Whiting (Senior Museum Advisor)
Ben Whine (Development Director, Museums)
Katherine Drake (Associate Museum Services Manager)

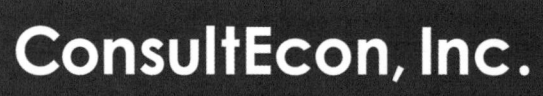

Economic and Management Consultants

CONSULTECON, INC.
545 Concord Ave., Ste. 210
Cambridge, MA 02138
Tel: 617-547-0100; Fax: 617-547-0102
E-mail: info@consultecon.com
Website: www.consultecon.com

Type of Business:

ConsultEcon, Inc. provides services to clients in the areas of project and plan concept development, market and financial evaluation, visitor surveys, economic impact and project implementation. We are dedicated to serving museums and visitor attractions of all sizes and types, and have worked over many years with clients responding to a broad spectrum of issues, ranging from the economics of operations to strategic planning.

Personnel:

Thomas J. Martin (President)
Robert E. Brais (Vice President)
Elena Kazlas (Principal)
James Stevens (Senior Associate)

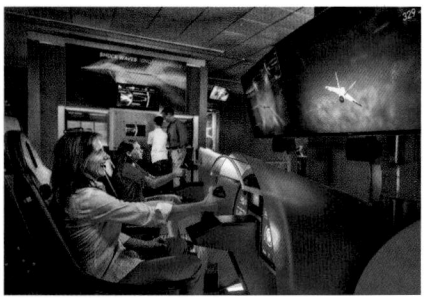

Above and Beyond Traveling Exhibit

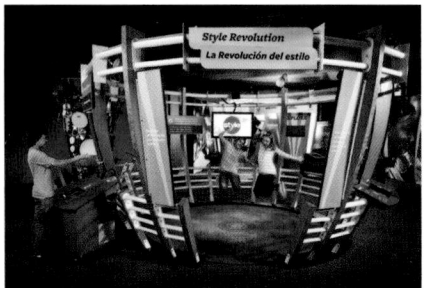

MathAlive! Traveling Exhibit

Evergreen
Exhibitions

EVERGREEN EXHIBITIONS
7979 Broadway, Ste. 107
San Antonio, TX 78209
Tel: 210-582-0015
E-mail: christi@evergreenexhibitions.com
Website: www.evergreenexhibitions.com

Type of Business:
EVERGREEN EXHIBITIONS is a premier provider of interactive educational exhibitions, with 29 years of experience touring science, natural history, art and object exhibitions. Highly respected in the museum community for its commitment and dedication to quality and education, Evergreen Exhibitions delivers immersive experiences to more than 200 natural history museums, science centers and art museums worldwide. TRAVELING EXHIBITIONS include *Vatican Splendors, MathAlive!, Above and Beyond: The Ultimate Flight Exhibition, Leonardo da Vinci: Machines in Motion, Space: A Journey to Our Future, Brain: The World Inside Your Head, Extreme Deep: Mission to the Abyss, Masters of the Night: The True Story of Bats* and *The Robot Zoo*. Evergreen also recently announced its partnership with the Australian Museum in Sydney, adding three exciting new exhibits to its portfolio: *Tyrannosaurs - Meet the Family, Spiders - From Fear to Fascination* and, coming soon, *Sharks*.

Personnel:
Mark Greenberg (President)
Anne Kinsey (Vice President Exhibitions)
Christi Klingelhefer (Venue Sales Manager)

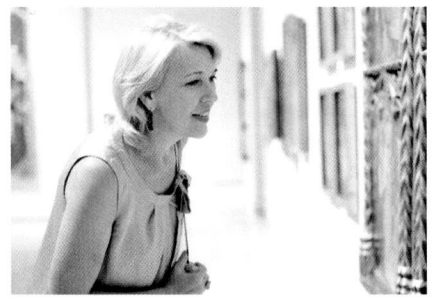

Gallagher, we know it's more than a collection to you. We provide comprehensive insurance solutions, allowing you to show your collection with confidence.

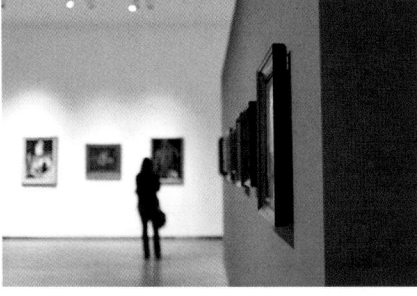

Gallagher has over 100 years combined experience in providing creative risk management solutions to the museum world.

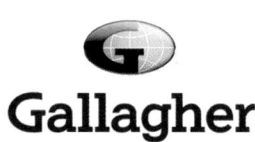

Gallagher

Insurance | Risk Management | Consulting

GALLAGHER
250 Park Ave., 3rd Fl.
New York, NY 10177
Tel: 212-994-7100
E-mail: Ellen_Ross@ajg.com
Website: www.ajg.com/finearts

Type of Business:
Gallagher's Fine Arts insurance and risk management coverages work with the world's premier art institutions and galleries to protect and preserve some of the world's rare valuable objects. Our team of risk management experts possess specialized knowledge and passion for the arts, because working with our fine arts clients requires a curator's eye combined with a risk manager's expertise. Our team has insured all facets of the fine arts industry. We specialize in providing significant guidance and innovative solutions to meet the changing needs of the museum world. Our professional staff provides comprehensive insurance programs in all lines of business, including Fine Arts, Property & Casualty, Cyber, Media. E & O, Title, Workers Compensation and Benefits.

Personnel:
Ellen Ross (Managing Director Fine Arts)

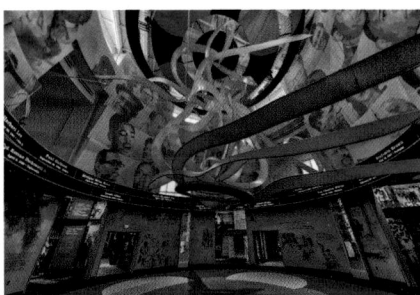

This Little Light of Mine, Mississippi Civil Rights Museum, Jackson, MS

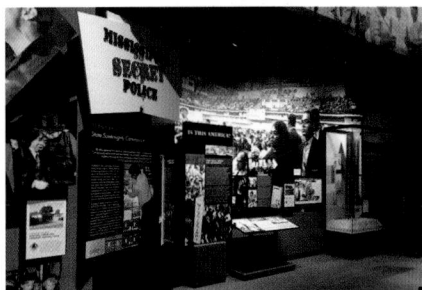

Mississippi's Secret Police interactive, Mississippi Civil Rights Museum, Jackson, MS

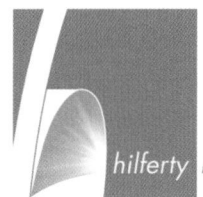

hilferty *museum planning* | *exhibit design*

HILFERTY
14240 State Rte. 550
Athens, OH 45701
Tel: 740-448-3821
Fax: 740-448-2331
E-mail: gha@hilferty.com
Website: www.hilferty.com

Type of Business:
For more than 40 years, Hilferty has provided a full range of interpretive services to museums, visitor centers, nature centers, botanical gardens, historic sites, zoos/aquariums, halls of fame and museums of conscience. We excel at interpretive and facility master planning, concept development and research, label writing, exhibit and graphic design, and producing donor recognition and funding support materials. From social movements to natural sciences, football to physics, presidents to children's gardens, every Hilferty exhibit vividly captures stories that engage visitors' minds and hearts. We approach each project with a unique mix of techniques chosen to best bring the subject to life. Our innovative portfolio spans the spectrum of intimate displays of precious objects, captivating immersive environments, enthralling interactive components, and stunning theatrical presentations. Hilferty creates unforgettable museum experiences.

Personnel:
Gerard Hilferty (President & Creative Director)
Dean Clouse (CEO)

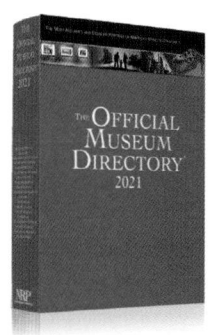

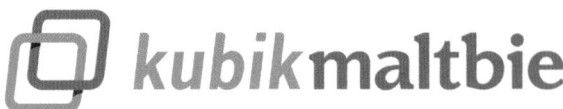

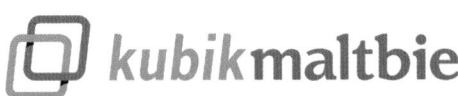

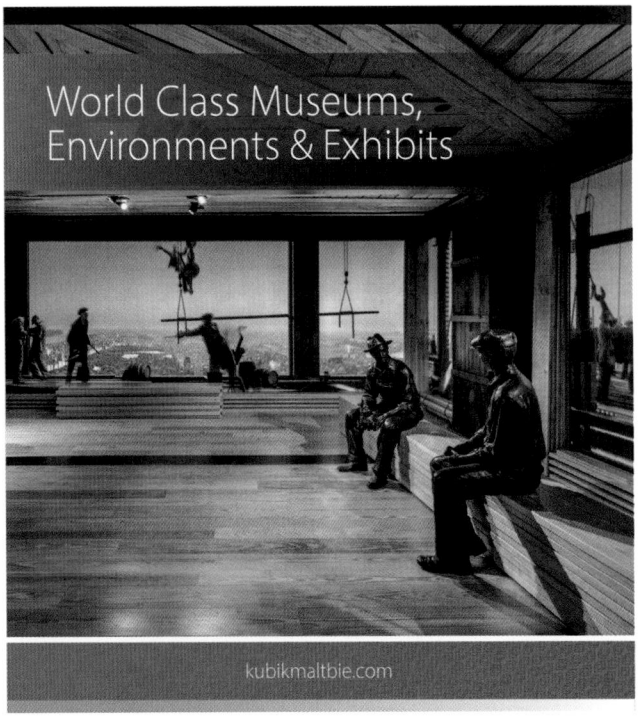

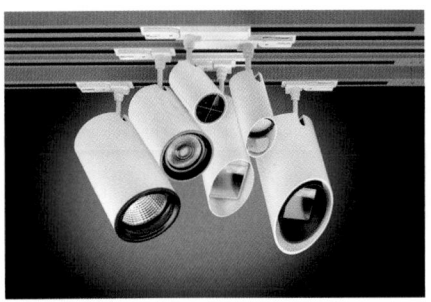

Lighting Services Inc LumeLEX Series

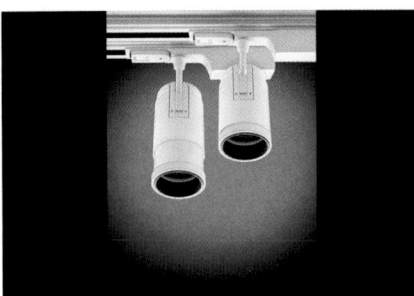

Lighting Services Inc LZ ZOOM Series

Lighting Services Inc LSI

LIGHTING SERVICES INC
2 Holt Dr.
Stony Point, NY 10980
Tel: 800-999-9574 & 845-942-2800
Fax: 845-942-2177
E-mail: Sales@mailLSI.com
Website: www.LightingServicesInc.com

Type of Business:

Lighting Services Inc (LSI) is the premier manufacturer of track, accent, display and LED lighting systems for museum environments. Since 1958, LSI has been dedicated to designing, engineering and manufacturing lighting fixtures of the highest quality. Our reputation for creativity and innovative design, coupled with specification grade products and intelligent personalized service, has made us the manufacturer of choice amongst the most discriminating specifiers of lighting for museums and galleries.

Personnel:

Daniel Gelman (President)

MONADNOCKmedia

MONADNOCK MEDIA, INC.
59 North St.
Hatfield, MA 01038
Tel: 413-247-6447; Fax: 413-247-6448
E-mail: steve@monadnock.org; alan@monadnock.org
Website: www.monadnock.org

Type of Business:

Monadnock Media designs and produces innovative and thought-provoking multimedia and interactive experiences for history, science and culture museums. From master media planning and design through technical systems specifications, production and installation, we work closely with designers and museum staff to come up with compelling and meaningful media installations for entire museums. Our deep commitment to storytelling, combined with our knowledge of technology, result in novel and engaging experiences in every media form: immersive theaters, interactives and interactive environments, multi-player games, and augmented and virtual reality.

Monadnock is known for signature installations that defy categorization.

Personnel:

Alan Hoff (Managing Director)
Steve Bressler (Creative Director)

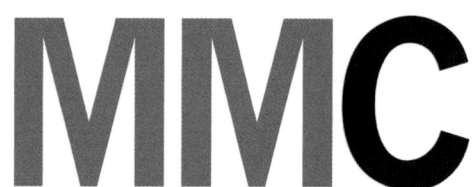

MUSEUM MANAGEMENT CONSULTANTS, INC.
37 Graham St., Suite 110
San Francisco, CA 94129
Tel: 415-982-2288
E-mail: mmc@museum-management.com
Website: www.museum-management.com

Type of Business:

Museum Management Consultants, Inc. (MMC) specializes in organizational assessment, strategic planning, business models, board development, executive search, audience research, and professional coaching. Founded in 1987 and based in San Francisco, MMC has provided consulting services to hundreds of museums and cultural organizations throughout the United States and abroad. MMC's mission is to help our clients thrive in a competitive and changing environment. We help museums accentuate their strengths, address critical issues, and move strategically into the future. MMC supports the highest ethical standards in our relationships with our clients and their communities. We believe every organization is unique in its culture, circumstance, and constituencies, and thus our process is tailored to meet each client's individual needs and objectives.

Personnel:

Adrienne Horn (President)
Stephen Horn (Senior Vice President)
Katie Sevier Potter (Senior Vice President)

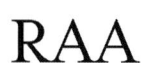

RAA | *Planning Design Media*

RALPH APPELBAUM ASSOCIATES INCORPORATED
88 Pine St.
New York, NY 10005
Tel: 212-334-8200
Fax: 212-334-6214
E-mail: frontdesk@raai.com
Website: www.raai.com

Type of Business:

Exhibition planning and design; masterplanning; media, interactive, website and publication design and production; graphic design and scriptwriting; photo research and acquisition; architectural integration for museum, visitor centers and educational environments worldwide. RAA has a staff of over 200 technology and media specialists, architects, writers, editors, and management personnel operating from studios in New York, London, Beijing, Berlin, Moscow, and Dubai. Across over 800 commissions, the portfolio includes the National Museum of African American History and Culture, Canadian Museum for Human Rights, United States Holocaust Memorial Museum, Fossil Halls and Rose Center for Earth and Space at the American Museum of Natural History, William J. Clinton Presidential Library, National World War I Museum, U.S. Capitol Visitor Center, National Constitution Center, National Museum of Scotland, Jozef Pilsudski Museum, Thomas Edison National Historical Park, Jewish Museum and Tolerance Center, Natural History Museum of Utah, Craig Thomas Discovery Center at Grand Tetons National Park, Smithsonian Arctic Studies Center, London Transport Museum, NASCAR Hall of Fame, Lavazza Museum, the IBM THINK Centennial Exhibition, World Museum Vienna, and the Bernice Pauhai Bishop Museum. On-going projects include the Humboldt Forum, Berlin; Second World War Galleries at the Imperial War Museums, London; Richard Gilder Center for Science, Education, Innovation at the American Museum of Natural History, New York; and the Obama Presidential Center, Chicago.

Personnel:

Ralph Appelbaum (President)
Nicholas Appelbaum (Vice President)
Deborah Wolff (Chief of Staff)
Casey Lynn (Director, Business Development)

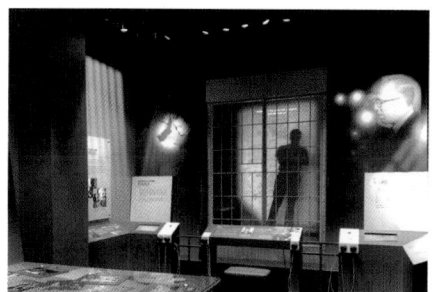

November 1963, University of North Texas at Dallas (Dallas, TX)
Evocative and immersive exhibits interpret the events of the 1963 JFK assassination for a modern visitor.

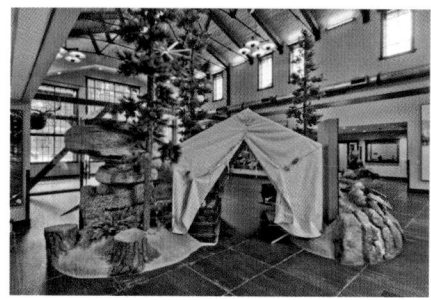

Deadwood Welcome Center (Deadwood, SD)
Exhibits that educate and engage visitors as they plan their stay in historic Deadwood, South Dakota.

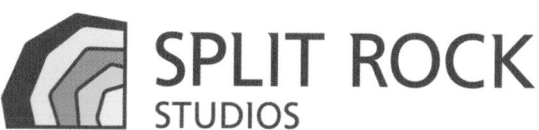

SPLIT ROCK STUDIOS
2071 Gateway Blvd.
St. Paul, MN 55112
Tel: 651-631-2211; 800-433-9599
Fax: 651-631-0707
E-mail: info@splitrockstudios.com
Website: www.splitrockstudios.com

Type of Business:

Split Rock Studios is a full-service Exhibit firm specializing in designing and developing interpretive exhibits for museums and related institutions. We have the in-house capabilities to produce all facets of a major exhibition: Exhibit Design and Development; Custom Exhibit Casework and Furniture; Themed Environments and Dioramas; Hand-Painted Interpretive Murals; Realistic Animal and Human Sculpture; Graphic Design and Production.

Personnel:

James Tordoff
Colin Cook
Isaiah Boehlert

STEPHEN SAITAS DESIGNS
370 Convent Ave., 1A
New York, NY 10031
Tel: 212-388-0997
E-mail: ssaitas@aol.com

Type of Business:

Specializing in museum exhibition design, Stephen Saitas Designs provides services from schematic design through installation supervision for projects ranging from the design of a single pedestal through complete reinstallations of permanent collections. Clients have included museums, galleries, libraries, and historic houses. Since being established in 1982, SSD has planned and designed over 275 installations and exhibitions, and provided related graphic designs, for more than fifty institutions.

Personnel:

Stephen Saitas (Principal)

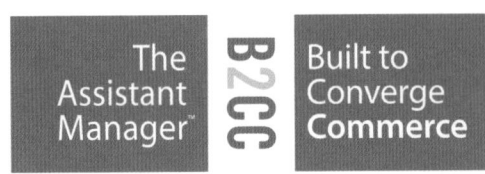

TAM INTELLIWARE, DIV. OF LODE DATA SYSTEMS, INC.

10609 West 159th St.
Orland Park, IL 60467
Tel: 888-843-1476; Fax: 708-460-1253
E-mail: sales@tamretail.com
Website: www.theassistantmanager.com

Type of Business:

The Assistant Manager™ (TAM) is a software application that converges commerce wherever non-profit organizations drive revenue. An application that satisfies the needs of all business units to converge an enterprise's commerce successfully. The mission critical needs of your customer facing POS and dining, digitally facing, and back of the house business units must be met. Our solely developed and proven application provides all that's needed. Easily view 360° of all of your entire enterprise's activity. Eliminate each business unit's reporting efforts from fragmented data stores, manual worksheets, and graphs.

Convergence of commerce immediately plugs these drains on your team's productivity. Our application is modularly deployed; pick the features specifically needed and tailor the configuration to meet current needs and budget. We are more than a software provider; we are a team of always ready (24/7/365), accountable, and ready to help you maximize the use of our application in your organization.

Personnel:

Bruce H. Lode (Executive Vice President of Marketing and Sales)

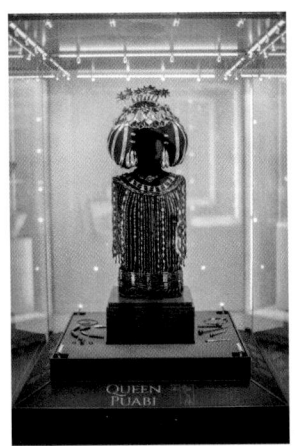

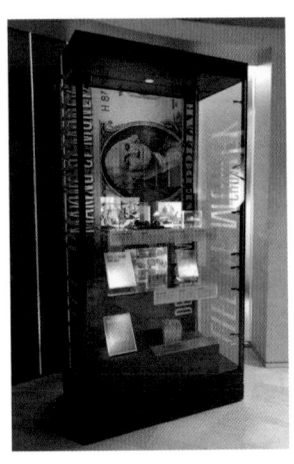

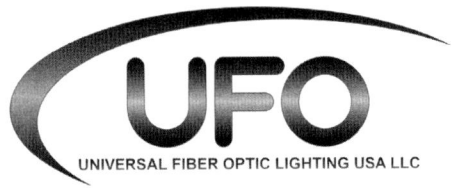

UNIVERSAL FIBER OPTIC LIGHTING USA, LLC

1749 Northgate Blvd.
Sarasota, FL 34234
Tel: 1-800-UFO-5554 & 941-343-8115
Fax: 941-296-7906
E-mail: info@fiberopticlighting.com
Website: www.fiberopticlighting.com

Type of Business:

Universal Fiber Optic Lighting is a premier manufacturer and supplier of complete fiber optic and LED lighting systems for the museum, gallery and conversation sector. We offer a diverse and specialist range of display lighting products that combine functionality and aesthetic form with the inherent safety and easy maintenance that is needed for illuminating historical artifacts and precious objects. Each of our products are designed and manufactured in-house and can be custom-made to suit our clients' specific requirements. We have years of experience in working with high profile lighting designers and case manufacturers, and our lighting systems have been used to illuminate some of the world's most prestigious venues. Examples of our work can be found in the Smithsonian Museum, the Art Gallery of Ontario, the Royal Observatory, Westminster Abbey and in Althorp House where our lighting illuminates the wedding dress worn by Diana, Princess of Wales.

Personnel:

Mr. Patric Dietrich (USA Sales Manager, pdietrich@fiberopticlighting.com)

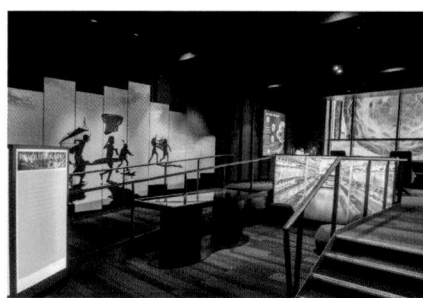

Seattle Children's Research Institute's *Discovery Portal*, Seattle, WA

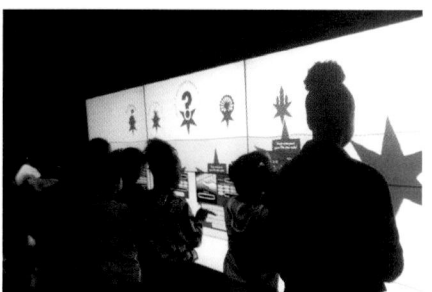

The Fifth Star Challenge interactive touch wall, Chicago History Museum, Chicago, IL

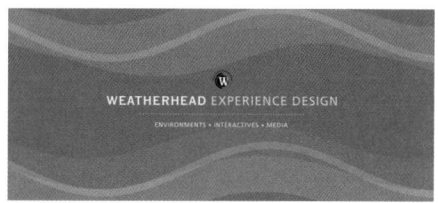

WEATHERHEAD EXPERIENCE DESIGN GROUP, INC.
5221 28th Avenue South
Seattle, WA 98108
Tel: 206-271-4347
E-mail: contact@weatherhead-design.com
Website: www.weatherhead-design.com

Type of Business:

Celebrating 20 years in business this year, WEATHERHEAD Experience Design is the dedicated group of experts behind some of the world's most memorable exhibit experiences. We create imaginative, visitor-centered designs that never fail to captivate, inform and delight - from initial concept, to sophisticated interactives, to multimedia development, straight through to opening day and beyond. Our experience design services include: Exhibit design and development; Interactive development; Multimedia production; Multimedia installations; Media production (film, video, audio).

Personnel:

Andrea K. Weatherhead (Principal)

INSTITUTIONS
BY STATE

ALABAMA
(197 listings)

Alexander City

WELLBORN MUSCLECAR MUSEUM, 124 Broad St., Alexander City, AL 35010-2689. Tel.: 256-329-8474.
E-mail: wellbornmusclecarmuseum@gmail.com
Web Site: www.wellbornmusclecarmuseum.com
Institution Type/Description: Car Museum.
Hours & Admission Prices: Mon.-Fri. 9-5, Sat. 10-4. Adults $10, children 7-17 $6; children 6 & under no charge.

Aliceville

ALICEVILLE MUSEUM, 104 Broad St. NE, Aliceville, AL 35442-2701. Tel.: 205-373-2363. Facebook: Aliceville Museum.
E-mail: museum@nctv.com
Web Site: www.alicevillemuseum.org
Key Personnel: Dir., John Gillum.
Institution Type/Description: Museum & Cultural Arts Center.
Hours & Admission Prices: Tues.-Sat.10-12 & 1-4. Adults $10, senior citizens & military $7, students $5; members no charge. &
Attendance: 3,500 (actual)

Anniston

ANNISTON MUSEUM OF NATURAL HISTORY, 800 Museum Dr., Anniston, AL 36206-2813. Mailing Address: P.O. Box 1587, Anniston, AL 36202-1587. Tel.: 256-237-6766. Fax: 256-237-6776.
E-mail: info@annistonmuseum.org
Web Site: www.annistonmuseum.org
Key Personnel: Exec. Dir., Alan Robison; Chm., Josephine Ayers.
Institution Type/Description: Natural History Museum & Cultural Center.
Hours & Admission Prices: Tues.-Sat. 10-5, Sun. 1-5. Adults $6, senior citizens $5.50, children 4-17 $5; discounts to groups; members and children 3 & under no charge. Closed New Year's Day; Thanksgiving; Christmas. &
Attendance: 73,223 (actual)

BERMAN MUSEUM OF WORLD HISTORY, 840 Museum Dr., Anniston, AL 36206-2813. Mailing Address: P.O. Box 2245, Anniston, AL 36202-2245. Tel.: 256-237-6261. Fax: 256-238-9055.
E-mail: Dford@bermanmuseum.org
Web Site: www.bermanmuseum.org
Key Personnel: Dir., Cheryl Bragg; Coord. Business Devel., David Ford; Mgr. Collections, Robert Lindley; Facilities Mgr., Adam Cleveland.
Institution Type/Description: History Museum.
Hours & Admission Prices: June-Aug. Mon.-Sat. 10-5, Sun. 1-5; Sept.-May Tues.-Sat. 10-5, Sun. 1-5. Adults $5, senior citizens $4, children 4-17 $2.50; discounts to AAA members & active military; children 3 & under and members no charge. Closed New Year's Day; Thanksgiving; Christmas Eve & Day. &
Attendance: 12,250 (actual)

Arab

ARAB HISTORIC VILLAGE, 224 City Park Dr., S.E., Arab, AL 35016-1071. Tel.: 256-586-6397; 256-550-0290.
E-mail: info@arab-chamber.org
Web Site: www.arabcity.org
Institution Type/Description: Historic Village Museum.
Hours & Admission Prices: March-Nov. Thurs.-Fri. 10-3, Sat. 1-4; other times by appointment. No charge.

Ashville

ASHVILLE MUSEUM AND ARCHIVES, 78 6th Ave., Ashville, AL 35953. Mailing Address: P.O. Box 1570, Ashville, AL 35953. Tel.: 205-594-2128.
E-mail: archives@stclairco.com
Institution Type/Description: History Museum.
Hours & Admission Prices: Mon.-Fri. 8-12 & 1-5.

Athens

ALABAMA VETERANS MUSEUM AND ARCHIVES, 100 Pryor St., P.O. Box 1500, Athens, AL 35612. Tel.: 256-771-7578.
Web Site: www.alabamaveteransmuseum.weebly.com

Key Personnel: Dir., Sandy Thompson.
Institution Type/Description: Military Museum.
Hours & Admission Prices: Call for hours. No charge; donations accepted.

ALTAR OF THE NEW TESTAMENT AND FOUNDERS HALL, Athens State Univ., 300 N. Beaty St., Athens, AL 35611. Tel.: 256-233-8100.
E-mail: sara.love@athens.edu
Web Site: www.athens.edu
Institution Type/Description: Religious History Museum.
Hours & Admission Prices: Mon.-Fri. 8-4:30. No charge. &

DONNELL HOUSE, 601 1/2 S. Clinton St., Athens, AL 35612. Mailing Address: P.O. Box 465, Athens, AL 35612. Tel.: 239-249-2211.
E-mail: idaho2@charter.net
Web Site: www.donnellhouse.net
Key Personnel: Pres. (V), Ida Terry.
Institution Type/Description: Historic House Museum: housed in the former home of Rev. Robert Donnell, founder of Cumberland Presbyterian Church; built in 1851. Listed on the National Register of Historic Places.
Hours & Admission Prices: Fri. 1-3; other times by appointment.

LIMESTONE COUNTY HISTORY MUSEUM, 101 N. Houston St., Athens, AL 35611-2540. Mailing Address: P.O. Box 82, Athens, AL 35612. Tel.: 256-233-8770.
E-mail: mail@limestonecountyhistoricalsociety.org
Web Site: limestonecountyhistoricalsociety.org
Key Personnel: Dir., Jackie Leonard; Chm. (V) & Museum Shop Mgr., Rex Lewis.
Institution Type/Description: History Museum: housed in the former home of George S. Houston, attorney, member of U.S. Senate and Governor of Alabama; built in 1835.
Hours & Admission Prices: Mon.-Fri. 10-5. No charge; donations accepted.
Attendance: 700 (estimated)

Atmore

POARCH BAND OF CREEK INDIANS MUSEUM, Mailing Address: 5811 Jack Springs Rd., Atmore, AL 36502. Tel.: 251-368-9136, ext. 2202.
E-mail: amontgomery@pci-nsb.gov
Web Site: www.poarchcreekindians.org/westminster/cultural.html
Key Personnel: Cultural Dir., Karla S. Martin; Museum Coord., Amanda Montgomery; Gift Shop Clerk, Nora Franklin.
Institution Type/Description: Native American Museum.
Hours & Admission Prices: Mon.-Fri. 8-5.

Attalla

TIGERS FOR TOMORROW AT UNTAMED MOUNTAIN, 708 County Rd. 345, Attalla, AL 35954. Tel.: 256-524-4150.
E-mail: untamedmountain@gmail.com
Web Site: www.tigersfortomorrow.org
Institution Type/Description: Animal Preserve.
Hours & Admission Prices: Fri.-Sun. 9-5; other times by appointment. Adults $15, children 3-11 $7.50. &
Attendance: 10,000 (estimated)

Auburn

BIGGIN GALLERY - AUBURN UNIVERSITY, 101 Biggin Hall, 112 S. College St., Auburn, AL 36849. Tel.: 334-844-4373. Fax: 334-844-4024. Facebook: @biggingallery.
E-mail: art@auburn.edu
Web Site: www.cla.auburn.edu/art/galleries/exhibitions
Key Personnel: Gallery & Lectures Coord., Jessye McDowell.
Institution Type/Description: Art Gallery.
Hours & Admission Prices: Mon.-Fri. 7:45-4:45; other times by appointment.

JAN DEMPSEY COMMUNITY ARTS CENTER, 222 E. Drake Ave., Auburn, AL 36830-3918. Tel.: 334-501-2930.
E-mail: webparksrec@auburnalabama.org
Web Site: www.auburnalabama.org/arts
Key Personnel: Cultural Arts Dir., Sara Hand Custer.
Institution Type/Description: Art Museum.
Hours & Admission Prices: Mon.-Fri. 8-5. Closed major holidays. &

JULE COLLINS SMITH MUSEUM OF FINE ART, Auburn University, 901 S. College St., Auburn, AL 36849. Tel.: 334-844-1484. Fax: 334-844-1463.
E-mail: crh0035@auburn.edu
Web Site: jcsm.auburn.edu
Key Personnel: Interim Dir., Andy Tennant; Mgr. Membership, Cindy Cox; Cur., Dennis Harper; Mktg. & Communications, Charlotte Hendrix; Financial Admin., Janice Allen; Cur. Education, Scott Bishop; Devel. Coord., Joshlyn Bess; Preparator, Christopher Carr; Registrar, Danielle Mohr Funderburk.
Institution Type/Description: Art Museum.
Hours & Admission Prices: Tues.-Wed. & Fri.-Sat. 10-4:30, Thurs. 10-8, Sun. 1-4; other times by appointment. Suggested Donation: $5. Closed New Year's Day; Memorial Day; Independence Day; Labor Day; Thanksgiving; Christmas. &
Attendance: 30,000 (actual)

Beatrice

RIKARD'S MILL HISTORICAL PARK, 4116 Hwy. 265 N., Beatrice, AL 36425. Mailing Address: 31 N. Alabama Ave., Monroeville, AL 36460. Tel.: 251-789-2781.
E-mail: mchm@frontiernet.net
Web Site: monroecountymuseum.org/rikards-mill-historical-park
Key Personnel: C.E.O. & Museum Shop Mgr., Nathan Carter; Chm. (V), Clark McKinley.
Institution Type/Description: History Museum: 1845 restored Grist Mill with water-powered turbine.
Hours & Admission Prices: Open to public on the first Thurs., Fri. & Sat. in Nov. &
Attendance: 8,500 (estimated)

Bessemer

BESSEMER HALL OF HISTORY, 1905 Alabama Ave., Bessemer, AL 35020-5009. Tel.: 205-426-1633. Fax: 205-426-1633.
E-mail: bessemerhallofhi@bellsouth.net
Web Site: www.bessemerhallofhistory.org
Key Personnel: Cur., Chris Eiland.
Institution Type/Description: History Museum: housed in the Southern R.R. Depot; built in 1916. Listed on the National Register of Historical Places.
Hours & Admission Prices: Tues.-Sat. 9-3. No charge; donations accepted. Closed Memorial Day; Independence Day. &
Attendance: 6,500 (estimated)

Birmingham

ABROMS-ENGEL INSTITUTE FOR THE VISUAL ARTS, 1221 10th Ave. S., Birmingham, AL 35205. Tel.: 205-975-6436. Facebook: @aeiva.uab; Instagram & Twitter: @AEIVAuab.
E-mail: aeiva@aub.edu
Web Site: www.uab.edu/cas/aeiva
Key Personnel: Cur., John Fields; Registrar Collections, Exhibitions & Programs, Christina McClellan.
Institution Type/Description: Art Museum.
Hours & Admission Prices: Mon.-Fri. 10-6, Sat. noon to 6.

ALABAMA JAZZ HALL OF FAME, Carver Theatre for Performing Arts, 1631 4th Ave. N., Birmingham, AL 35203. Tel.: 205-327-9424. Fax: 205-254-2785. Facebook: @AlabamaJazzHallofFame; Twitter: @JazzHallofFame.
E-mail: leahtuckeronline@gmail.com
Web Site: www.jazzhall.com
Key Personnel: Exec. Dir., Leah Tucker; Admin. Asst., Dr. Leslie Marlow; Dir. Student Jazz Programs, Raymond Reach.
Institution Type/Description: Jazz Museum.
Hours & Admission Prices: Hall of Fame: Tues.-Sat. 10-5. Guided Tours: Tues.-Wed. & Fri. 10-2, Sat. 1-5. Guided Tour: $3; Self-Guided Tour: $2.

ALABAMA MUSEUM OF THE HEALTH SCIENCES, 1700 University Blvd., Birmingham, AL 35294. Mailing Address: UAB Lister Hill Library, 1720 Second Ave. S., Birmingham, AL 35292-0013. Tel.: 205-934-4475. Fax: 205-975-8476.
E-mail: medicalmuseum@uab.edu
Web Site: www.uab.edu/amhs
Key Personnel: Assoc. Prof. & Cur., Stefanie Rookis.
Institution Type/Description: Medical Museum.
Hours & Admission Prices: Closed for renovations. &
Attendance: 3,000 (estimated)

ALABAMA SPORTS HALL OF FAME, Birmingham Jefferson civic Center, 2150 Richard Arrington Jr. Blvd. N., Birmingham, AL 35203-1102. Mailing Address: P.O. Box 10163, Birmingham, AL 35202-0163. Tel.: 205-323-6665. Fax: 205-252-2212. Facebook: @AlabamaSportsHOF.
E-mail: info@ashof.org
Web Site: ashof.org
Key Personnel: Exec. Dir., Scott Myers; Facility Dir., Bill Miller.
Institution Type/Description: Sports Museum.
Hours & Admission Prices: Mon.-Fri. 9-5. Families $14, adults $5, senior citizens 60 & over $4, students $3; discounts to groups of 10 or more.

ARLINGTON ANTEBELLUM HOME & GARDENS, 331 Cotton Ave., S.W., Birmingham, AL 35211. Tel.: 205-780-5656. Fax: 205-788-0585. Facebook: @arlingtonantebellumhomeandgardens.
E-mail: arlingtonantebellumhome@gmail.com
Web Site: www.arlingtonantebellumhomeandgardens.com
Key Personnel: Dir., Steve Moode.
Institution Type/Description: Historic House Museum: housed in the home of Judge William S. Mudd, one of 10 founders of Birmingham; built in 1850.
Hours & Admission Prices: Tues.-Sat. 10-4, Sun. 1-4. Adults $5, students 6-18 $3; discount to groups & AAM members; children under 6 no charge when accompanied by an adult. Closed holidays.
Attendance: 25,000 (estimated)

BIRMINGHAM BOTANICAL GARDENS, 2612 Lane Park Rd., Birmingham, AL 35223-1800. Tel.: 205-414-3950. Fax: 205-414-3966. Facebook: @BirminghamBotanicalGardens; Instagram & Twitter: @bbgardens.
E-mail: bells@bbgardens.org
Web Site: www.bbgardens.org
Key Personnel: Exec. Dir., Tom Underwood; Chair, Beverley Hoyt; C.F.O., Stephanie Banks; Vice Pres. Devel., Penny Hartline; Vice Pres. Education, Henry Hughes; Dir., James Horton; Dist. Horticulture Supvr., Virgil Matthews; Dir. Library Svcs., Hope Long; Public Rels. Coord., Blake Ells; Volunteer Coord., Alice Moore.
Institution Type/Description: Botanical Garden & Herbarium.
Hours & Admission Prices: Gardens: daily dawn to dusk; Garden Center: daily 8-5; Library: Mon.-Fri. 9-4, Sat. 10-4, Sun. 2-5. No charge. Closed city holidays. &
Attendance: 350,000 (estimated)

BIRMINGHAM CIVIL RIGHTS INSTITUTE, 520 16th St., N., Birmingham, AL 35203-1911. Tel.: 205-328-9696, ext. 218, 866-328-9696 (toll free). Fax: 205-323-5219. Facebook: @BCRI.ORG; Twitter: @bhamcivilrights.
E-mail: bcri@bcri.org
Web Site: www.bcri.org
Key Personnel: Pres. & C.E.O., Andrea Taylor; Bd. Chm., Mike Oatridge; Vice Pres. Finance & Operations, Carol Wells; Vice Pres. Institutional Programs, Priscilla Hancock Cooper; Head Archives & Technology, Wayne Coleman; Vice Pres. Education & Exhibitions, Ahmad Ward; Vice Pres. Devel., Jennifer Fields Hall; Devel. Consultant, Patrick Packer; Operations Mgr., LeRoy Simmons; Bldg. & Grounds Supt., David W. Davis; Information Systems Admin., Michael Holland; Gift Store Mgr., Carolyn Cunningham; Coord. Youth Programs, Michelle Craig; Coord. Group Tours, Staci McCloud; Head Communications, Melissa Snow-Clark.
Institution Type/Description: History Museum.
Hours & Admission Prices: Tues.-Sat. 10-5, Sun. 1-5. Adults $15, member adults $10, college students with college ID $6, senior citizens 65 & over and Grades 4-12 outside Jefferson County $5; discount to adult groups of 25 or more, military & AAA members; members & Jefferson County children no charge. Closed major holidays. &
Attendance: 145,000 (actual)

BIRMINGHAM HISTORY CENTER, Pythian Building, 310 18th St., N. Ste. 401, Birmingham, AL 35203-3134. Tel.: 205-202-4146. Fax: 205-202-4146. Facebook: Birmingham History Center; Twitter: @BhamHistoryCtr.
E-mail: bjhm@bham.rr.com
Web Site: www.birminghamhistorycenter.org
Key Personnel: Dir., Jerry R. Desmond.
Institution Type/Description: History Museum.
Hours & Admission Prices: Mon.-Fri. 9-4:30.
Attendance: 5,000 (estimated)

BIRMINGHAM MUSEUM OF ART, 2000 Rev. Abraham Woods Jr. Blvd., Birmingham, AL 35203-2205. Tel.: 205-254-2565. Fax: 205-254-2714. Facebook: @artsbma; Instagram & Twitter: @bhammuseum.

E-mail: marketing@artsbma.org
Web Site: www.artsbma.org
Key Personnel: R. Hugh Daniel Dir., Gail Andrews; C.F.O., Johnny McIntosh; Deputy Dir. & William Cary Hulsey Cur. American Art, Graham C. Boettcher, Ph.D.; Dir. Mktg. & Communications, Cate McCusker Boehm; Objects Conservator, Margaret K. Burnham; Chief Cur. & Marguerite Jones Harbert and John M. Harbert III Cur. Decorative Arts, Anne Forschler-Tarrasch, Ph.D.; Sr. Cur. & Cur. Arts of Africa and the Americas, Emily G. Hanna, Ph.D.; Sr. Cur. & Virginia & William M. Spencer II Cur. Asian Art, Donald A. Wood, Ph.D.; Dir. Devel., Kate Cleveland; Store Mgr., Kristie Allen; Dir. Photography & Visual Svcs., Sean Pathasema; Head Preparator, Priscilla Tapio; Chief Registrar, Rose Wood; Security Chief, J.R. Feagins.
Institution Type/Description: Art Museum.
Hours & Admission Prices: Museum Galleries: Tues.-Sat. 10-5, Sun. noon to 5, 1st Thurs. each month 10-9; Clarence C. Hanson, Jr. Library: by appointment only. No charge; donations accepted. Closed major holidays. &
Attendance: 193,394 (actual)

BIRMINGHAM ZOO, 2630 Cahaba Rd., Birmingham, AL 35223-1154. Tel.: 205-879-0409. Fax: 205-879-9426. Facebook, Twitter.
E-mail: kschmidt@birminghamzoo.com
Web Site: www.birminghamzoo.com
Key Personnel: C.E.O. & Dir., Dr. William R. Foster; Chm. Bd. Dirs., Cissy Jackson; Sr. Vice Pres., Chris Pfefferkorn; C.F.O., Jennie Whitman; Vice Pres. Devel., Karen Carrol; Vice Pres. Education, Roger Torbert; Vice Pres. Sales & Mktg., Kerry Graves; Vice Pres. Operations, Rusty Keene.
Institution Type/Description: Zoo.
Hours & Admission Prices: Winter: daily 9-5; Summer: Mon.-Fri. 9-5, Sat.-Sun. 9-7. Adults $16, active duty military w/ID and seniors 65 & up $14; children 2-12 $11; discounts on Tuesdays; zoo members no charge. Closed Thanksgiving; Christmas. &
Attendance: 574,581 (actual)

DON KRESGE MEMORIAL MUSEUM, 600 N. 18th St., Birmingham, AL 35203-2206. Mailing Address: Alabama Historical Radio Society, P.O. Box 131418, Birmingham, AL 35213. Tel.: 205-967-2000.
E-mail: ahrs2000@gmail.com
Web Site: www.alabamahistoricalradiosociety.org
Key Personnel: Pres., Tom Killian; Vice Pres., Steven Westbrook; Instructor, Robert Frye.
Institution Type/Description: History Museum.
Hours & Admission Prices: Call for hours.

MCWANE SCIENCE CENTER, 200 19th St., N., Birmingham, AL 35203-3117. Tel.: 205-714-8300. Fax: 205-714-8400. Facebook.
E-mail: marketing@mcwane.org
Web Site: www.mcwane.org
Key Personnel: C.E.O., Amy Templeton; Vice Pres. Devel., Miranda Springer; Vice Pres. Exhibits, Lamar Smith.
Institution Type/Description: Science and Technology Center.
Hours & Admission Prices: June-Aug. Mon.-Fri. 9-6, Sat. 10-6, Sun. 12-6; Sept.-May. Mon.-Fri. 9-5, Sat. 10-6, Sun. 12-6. Parking: General Public $5; members no charge. Museum: adults $13, seniors $12, children $9; members no charge. IMAX DMR Movie: adults $10, children $9. IMAX Film: adults $9, seniors & children $8. Combo: adults $18, seniors $16, children $14. ASTC Travel Passport Program. Closed New Year's Day; Easter; Thanksgiving; Christmas Eve & Day. &
Attendance: 500,000 (estimated)

RUFFNER MOUNTAIN NATURE PRESERVE, 1214 81st St. S., Birmingham, AL 35206. Tel.: 205-833-8264. Fax: 205-836-3960. Facebook & Twitter: @ruffnermountain; Instagram @ruffnermt.
E-mail: info@ruffnermountain.org
Web Site: ruffnermountain.org
Key Personnel: Exec. Dir., Carlee Sanford; Pres. Bd. Dirs., Darryl Washington; Wildlife Cur., Chivon Morse; Programs Dir., Christine Harlan; Conservation Technician, Rebecca Rodamar; Conservation Dir., Jaime Nobles; Communications Dir., Daniel DeVaughn; Design & Fab Mgr., Will Fuhrmeister.
Institution Type/Description: Nature Center.
Hours & Admission Prices: Nature Center: Tues.-Sun. 9-5; Trails: daily dawn to dusk. No charge; donations accepted. Closed New Year's Day; Thanksgiving; Christmas Eve & Day. &
Attendance: 30,000 (estimated)

SAMUEL ULLMAN MUSEUM, 2150 15th Ave. S., Birmingham, AL 35205-3920. Tel.: 205-703-0960.
E-mail: executivedirector@jasaweb.org
Web Site: www.uab.edu/ullmanmuseum
Key Personnel: Exec. Dir., Tamara Moriya.
Institution Type/Description: General Museum.

Hours & Admission Prices: By appointment only. No charge; donations accepted.

SLOSS FURNACES NATIONAL HISTORIC LANDMARK, 20 32nd St. N., Birmingham, AL 35222-1236. Tel.: 205-254-2025.
E-mail: info@slossfurnaces.com
Web Site: www.slossfurnaces.com
Key Personnel: Interim Dir. & Cur., Karen Utz; Interim Dir., Opers., Nikitres Frazier; Education Coord., Ty Malugani.
Institution Type/Description: Industrial Museum: c.1882-1970 ironmaking plant including blast furnaces, blowing engines, power house, boilers & related buildings.
Hours & Admission Prices: Tues.-Sat. 10-4, Sun. 12-4. No charge. Closed New Year's Day; Thanksgiving; Christmas. &
Attendance: 200,000 (actual)

SOUTHERN ENVIRONMENTAL CENTER, 900 Arkadelphia Rd., Birmingham, AL 35254. Tel.: 205-226-4934. Twitter: @secbsc; Instagram: @southern_environmental_center.
E-mail: rhazelho@bsc.edu
Web Site: www.bsc.edu/sec
Key Personnel: Dir., Roald Hazelhoff; Asst. Dir. Grants, Liz Taylor.
Institution Type/Description: Environmental Center.
Hours & Admission Prices: By appointment.

SOUTHERN MUSEUM OF FLIGHT, 4343 73rd St. N., Birmingham, AL 35206-3642. Tel.: 205-833-8226. Fax: 205-836-2439. Facebook: @SouthernMuseumofFlight; Twitter: @SMoF1.
E-mail: info@southernmuseumofflight.org
Web Site: www.southernmuseumofflight.org
Key Personnel: Exec. Dir. & Historian, Dr. Brian J. Barsanti; Cur. & Dir. Operations, Wayne Novy; Office Mgr., Daphne Dunn; Restoration Technician, Zachary Edison; Events Mgr., Elizabeth Grady; Education Coord., Melissa C. Morgan; Educator & Special Projects Asst. to Dir., Charles Phillips.
Institution Type/Description: Aviation Transportation Museum.
Hours & Admission Prices: Tues.-Sat. 9:30-4:30. Adults $7, seniors & students $6; active duty military & family and children 3 & under no charge. &
Attendance: 63,247 (actual)

SPACE ONE ELEVEN, 2409 2nd Ave. N., Birmingham, AL 35203. Tel.: 205-328-0553. Fax: 205-254-6176. Facebook, Twitter, Instagram.
E-mail: jannaphillips@spaceoneeleven.org
Web Site: spaceoneeleven.org
Key Personnel: C.E.O. & Co-Founder, Peter Prinz; Dir. Programs, Cheryl Lewis; Arts Education Coord., Janna Phillips.
Institution Type/Description: Art Gallery.
Hours & Admission Prices: Tues.-Fri. 10-12 & 1-5 during exhibitions.

VULCAN PARK AND MUSEUM, 1701 Valley View Dr., Birmingham, AL 35209. Tel.: 205-933-1409. Fax: 205-933-1776. Facebook, Twitter & Instagram: @visitvulcan.
E-mail: info@visitvulcan.com
Web Site: www.visitvulcan.com
Key Personnel: Pres. & CEO, Darlene Negrotto.
Institution Type/Description: History Museum.
Hours & Admission Prices: Museum: Mon.-Sun. 10-6; Tower: daily 10-10. Adults $6, seniors 65 & over and military $5, children 5-12 $4; discounts to groups; children 4 & under no charge. &
Attendance: 160,936 (actual)

Blountsville

BLOUNTSVILLE HISTORICAL PARK, 71406 Main St., Blountsville, AL 35031. Tel.: 205-429-2338. Fax: 205-429-2468.
E-mail: betoka84@yahoo.com
Web Site: www.blountsvillehistoricalsociety.com
Key Personnel: Pres. (V), O.K. Alexander; Contact, Betty Alexander.
Institution Type/Description: History Museum.
Hours & Admission Prices: Thurs.-Sat. 9-3:30; other times by appointment. No charge. &
Attendance: 750 (estimated)

Brewton

THOMAS E. MCMILLAN MUSEUM, Jefferson Davis College, 220 Alco Dr., Brewton, AL 36426. Tel.: 251-809-1528. Fax: 251-809-1527.
E-mail: museum@jdcc.edu
Web Site: museum.jdcc.edu

Key Personnel: Museum Coord., Jerry Simmons; Maintenance Supvr., Don Odom.
Institution Type/Description: History Museum: located near the site of 1830 Leigh plantation.
Hours & Admission Prices: Tues. & Thurs. 9-3; other times by appointment. No charge; donations accepted. Closed New Year's Eve & Day; Memorial Day; Labor Day; Thanksgiving; Christmas week. &
Attendance: 1,000 (estimated)

Bridgeport

BRIDGEPORT DEPOT MUSEUM, 116 Soulard Sq., Bridgeport, AL 35740. Tel.: 256-495-4020. Facebook & Twitter: @bridgeport-depot.
E-mail: bridgeportareahi@bellsouth.net
Web Site: www.bridgeportdepot.com
Key Personnel: Cur., Chris Gunter.
Institution Type/Description: Railroad Depot Museum: housed on the site of the original depot that was destroyed in July 1863 by Confederate forces under C.S. A. Gen. Braxton Bragg; current depot built in 1917.
Hours & Admission Prices: Mon. & Thurs.-Sat. 9-1, Sun. 1-5. No charge.

RUSSELL CAVE NATIONAL MONUMENT, 3729 County Rd. 98, Bridgeport, AL 35740-6825. Tel.: 256-495-2672 x113. Fax: 256-495-9220. Facebook.
Web Site: nps.gov/ruca
Key Personnel: Supt., Stephen Black; Park Ranger, Kenna Graham.
Institution Type/Description: Archaeology Museum.
Hours & Admission Prices: Daily 8-4:30. No charge; donations accepted. Closed New Year's Day; Thanksgiving; Christmas. &
Attendance: 30,000 (estimated)

Calera

HEART OF DIXIE RAILROAD MUSEUM, 1919 Ninth St., Calera, AL 35040. Mailing Address: P.O. Box 727, Calera, AL 35040-0727. Tel.: 205-668-3435. Fax: 205-668-9900.
E-mail: info@hodrrm.org
Web Site: www.hodrrm.org
Key Personnel: Pres., Jim Garnett; Archivist, David Coombs; Treas., James Ketchersid; Museum Shop Mgr., Mark Walker.
Institution Type/Description: Railroad Museum: housed in 1890s wooden railroad station building.
Hours & Admission Prices: Museum: Tues., Thurs. & Sat. 9-4. No charge; donations requested. Train Rides: March to mid-Dec. Sat. Adults $12, children $8; members no charge. Closed major holidays. &
Attendance: 40,000 (estimated)

Centre

CHEROKEE COUNTY HISTORICAL MUSEUM, 101 E. Main St., Centre, AL 35960. Tel.: 256-927-7835. Fax: 256-266-1392.
E-mail: museumatcentre@gmail.com
Web Site: www.museumatcentrealabama.com/
Key Personnel: Dir., David Crum; Chm. (V), Kurt Duryea.
Institution Type/Description: History Museum.
Hours & Admission Prices: Tues.-Fri. 8:30-4. Adults $3; children 6 & under no charge. Closed major holidays.
Attendance: 4,000 (actual)

Chatom

WASHINGTON COUNTY HISTORY MUSEUM, 45 Court St., Chatom, AL 36518. Mailing Address: P.O. Box 233, Chatom, AL 36518-0233. Tel.: 251-847-2052. Facebook: @washcohx.
E-mail: bookworm@millry.net
Key Personnel: Cur., Ashlea Singleton.
Institution Type/Description: History Museum.
Hours & Admission Prices: Mon.-Fri. 8-4:30; guided tours by appointment. No charge. Closed Christmas Eve & Day.

Columbiana

KARL C. HARRISON MUSEUM OF GEORGE WASHINGTON, Mildred B. Harrison Regional Library, 50 Lester St., Columbiana, AL 35051-9477. Tel.: 205-669-8767.
E-mail: info@washingtonmuseum.com
Web Site: www.washingtonmuseum.com
Key Personnel: Cur., Donald Relyea.
Institution Type/Description: History Museum.
Hours & Admission Prices: Mon.-Fri. 10-3. No charge.

SHELBY COUNTY MUSEUM & ARCHIVES, 1854 Old Courthouse Circle, Columbiana, AL 35051. Mailing Address: P.O. Box 457, Columbiana, AL 35051-0457. Tel.: 205-669-3912. Facebook: @shelbycountymuseum.
E-mail: schs1854@bellsouth.net
Web Site: shelbycountymuseum.com
Formerly: Shelby County Historical Society, Inc. Museum & Archives
Key Personnel: Exec. Dir., Jennifer Maier.
Institution Type/Description: Historic Building Museum: built in 1854. Listed on the National Register of Historic Places.
Hours & Admission Prices: Tues.-Fri. 9-3. No charge. Closed holidays.

Cullman

AVE MARIA GROTTO, 1600 St. Bernard Dr., S.E., Cullman, AL 35055-3057. Tel.: 256-734-4110. Fax: 256-737-8768.
Web Site: www.avemariagrotto.com
Key Personnel: Dir. & Museum Shop Mgr., Rev. Bill Ellis; Museum Shop Mgr., Joyce Nix.
Institution Type/Description: Religious History Museum: replicas built by Benedictine Monk, Bro. Joseph Zoettl, O.S.B.
Hours & Admission Prices: Daily 9-5. Adults $7, senior citizens $5, children 6-12 $4.50; discounts to groups; children under 6 no charge. Closed Christmas.
Attendance: 27,564 (actual)

CULLMAN COUNTY MUSEUM, 211 Second Ave., N.E., Cullman, AL 35055-2905. Tel.: 256-739-1258, 800-533-1258. Fax: 256-737-8782.
Web Site: www.cullmancountymuseum.com
Key Personnel: Cur., Elaine L. Fuller.
Institution Type/Description: History Museum: housed in replica of 1873 home of Col. John G. Cullman, founder of Cullman.
Hours & Admission Prices: Mon.-Fri. 9-4, Sun. 1:30-4:30. Adults $5, seniors $4, children under 12 $3; discounts to groups, AAM, AAA & ICOM members; members no charge. Closed New Year's Day; Independence Day; Thanksgiving; Christmas. &
Attendance: 15,000 (estimated)

CULLMAN DEPOT, 301 1st Ave., N.E., Cullman, AL 35055. Mailing Address: 211 2nd Ave., N.E., Cullman, AL 35055-2905. Tel.: 800-533-1258, 256-739-1258. Fax: 256-737-8782.
Web Site: cullmancountymuseum.com
Institution Type/Description: Historic Building: listed on the National and State Registers of Historic Places.
Hours & Admission Prices: Mon.-Fri. 8-4:30. No charge.

Danville

JESSE OWENS MUSEUM, 7019 County Rd. 203, Danville, AL 35619-9053. Mailing Address: 174 County Rd. 241, Moulton, AL 35650. Tel.: 256-974-3636. Fax: 256-615-8777. Facebook.
E-mail: jesseowens1936@charter.net
Web Site: jesseowensmemorialpark.com
Formerly: Jesse Owens Memorial Park and Museum
Key Personnel: Chm. (V) & Pres. (V), Kenneth Brackins; Co Dir., James Pinion; Co Dir. & Museum Shop Mgr., Nancy Pinion; Museum Shop Mgr., Joyce Cole.
Institution Type/Description: History & Sports Museum.
Hours & Admission Prices: Mon.-Sat. 10-4, Sun. 1-4. Admission by donation. Groups: $3 per person. Closed New Year's Day; Thanksgiving; Christmas. &
Attendance: 45,000 (estimated)

Daphne

AMERICAN SPORTS ART MUSEUM AND ARCHIVES, US Sports Academy, One Academy Dr., Daphne, AL 36526-7055. Tel.: 251-626-3303. Fax: 251-621-2527.
E-mail: asama@ussa.edu
Web Site: www.asama.org
Key Personnel: C.E.O., Dr. T.J. Rosandich; Coord. Communications, Leigha Bolton.
Institution Type/Description: Art Museum.
Hours & Admission Prices: Mon.-Fri. 8-4. No charge; donations accepted. &
Attendance: 2,000 (estimated)

OLD DAPHNE METHODIST CHURCH MUSEUM, 405 Dryer Ave., Daphne, AL 36526. Tel.: 251-621-9620.
Web Site: www.daphnemuseumalabama.org
Institution Type/Description: Historic Building: built in 1858.
Hours & Admission Prices: Fri.-Sun. 1-4. No charge. &

Dauphin Island

ESTUARIUM, Dauphin Island Sea Lab, 101 Bienville Blvd., Dauphin Island, AL 36528-4603. Tel.: 251-861-2141. Fax: 251-861-4646.
E-mail: bklein@disl.org
Web Site: estuarium.disl.org
Key Personnel: Exec. Dir., Dr. John Valentine; Mgr., Robert Dixon; Registrar, Sally Brennan; Administrative Asst. to the Dir., Lori Angelo; Administrative Asst. Discovery Hall Programs, Denise Keaton; Reservations, Sara Orescan.
Institution Type/Description: Aquarium.
Hours & Admission Prices: March-Aug. Mon.-Sat. 9-6, Sun. 12-6; Sept.-Feb. Mon.-Sat. 9-5, Sun. 1-5. Adults $7, seniors $6, children 5-18 & students with ID $4; discounts to AAA members, groups, & military. Closed New Year's Day; Easter; Thanksgiving; Christmas. &
Attendance: 66,407 (actual)

Daviston

HORSESHOE BEND NATIONAL MILITARY PARK, 11288 Horseshoe Bend Rd., Daviston, AL 36256-6524. Tel.: 256-234-7111.
Web Site: www.nps.gov/hobe/
Key Personnel: Park Ranger-Interpreter, Ove Jensen.
Institution Type/Description: Historic Site: Horseshoe Bend Battlefield, location of final battle of the Creek Indian War of 1813-1814.
Hours & Admission Prices: Visitor Center: daily 9-4:30. Grounds: daily 8-5. No charge; donations accepted. Closed New Year's Day; Thanksgiving; Christmas. &
Attendance: 111,864 (actual)

Decatur

THE ART GALLERY, JOHN C. CALHOUN STATE COMMUNITY COLLEGE, 6250 U.S. Hwy. 31 N., Fine Arts Bldg., Tanner, AL 35671. Mailing Address: P.O. Box 2216, Decatur, AL 35609-2216. Tel.: 256-306-2695.
E-mail: klv@calhoun.cc.al.us
Web Site: www.calhoun.edu
Key Personnel: C.E.O., Kristine Beadle; Chm., William Godsey; Pres., Dr. Marilyn Beck; Dir., Kathryn Vaughn.
Institution Type/Description: College Art Gallery.
Hours & Admission Prices: Mon.-Fri. 9-5. No charge; donations accepted. &
Attendance: 3,600 (estimated)

BLUE & GRAY MUSEUM OF NORTH ALABAMA, 723 Bank St., Decatur, AL 35601. Tel.: 256-350-4018.
E-mail: info@alabamacivilwarmuseum.com
Web Site: www.alabamacivilwarmuseum.com
Key Personnel: Dir. & C.E.O., Robert L. Sackheim; Museum Shop Mgr., Robert Parham.
Institution Type/Description: Military History Museum.
Hours & Admission Prices: Tues.-Fri. 10-5, Sat. 10-4. Adults $6, students $3; discounts to seniors & groups; pre-school children no charge. &
Attendance: 1,200 (estimated)

CARNEGIE VISUAL ARTS CENTER, 207 Church St., N.E., Decatur, AL 35601-1847. Mailing Address: P.O. Box 1591, Decatur, AL 35602-1591. Tel.: 256-341-0562. Fax: 256-341-0713.
Web Site: carnegiearts.org
Key Personnel: Exec. Dir., Laura Phillips.
Institution Type/Description: Art Center.
Hours & Admission Prices: Tues.-Fri. 10-5, 3rd Sat. 10-2.

COOK'S MUSEUM OF NATURAL SCIENCE, 133 4th Ave., N. E., Decatur, AL 35601-5916. Mailing Address: P.O. Box 2955, Decatur, AL 35602. Tel.: 256-351-4505. Facebook.
E-mail: info@cookmuseum.org
Web Site: www.cookmuseum.org
Key Personnel: Dir., Schelly Corry; Pres. (V), Brian Cook; Museum Shop Mgr., Debbie Moore.
Institution Type/Description: Natural Science Museum.
Hours & Admission Prices: Opening in 2017 &

PRINCESS THEATRE CENTER FOR THE PERFORMING ARTS, 112 Second Ave., N.E., Decatur, AL 35601. Mailing Address: P.O. Box 335, Decatur, AL 35602-0335. Tel.: 256-350-1745. Facebook. Twitter: @princesstheatre.
E-mail: anne@princesstheatre.org

Web Site: www.princesstheatre.org
Key Personnel: Exec. Dir., Anne Scarbrough; Technical Dir., Penny Linville; Bd. Chair, Julia Smeds Roth; Box Office & Patron Mgr., Mary McDonald; Education Dir., Jameel Lewis.
Institution Type/Description: Theatre Museum: housed in a former livery stable in 1887, later turned into a silent film & vaudeville playhouse. Listed on the National Register of Historic Places.
Hours & Admission Prices: Call for hours & admission prices.

WHEELER NATIONAL WILDLIFE REFUGE, 2700 Refuge Headquarters Rd., Decatur, AL 35603. Tel.: 256-350-6639.
E-mail: wheeler@fws.gov
Web Site: www.fws.gov/refuge/wheeler
Institution Type/Description: Wildlife Refuge.
Hours & Admission Prices: March-Sept. Tues.-Sat. 9-4; Oct.-Feb. daily 9-5. No charge.

Demopolis

BLUFF HALL ANTEBELLUM HOUSE MUSEUM, Marengo County Historical Soc., 405 N. Commissioners Ave., Demopolis, AL 36732. Mailing Address: P.O. Box 159, Demopolis, AL 36732-0159. Tel.: 334-289-9644. Facebook: Marengo History.
E-mail: marengohistory@bellsouth.net
Web Site: www.marengocountyhistoricalsociety.com
Institution Type/Description: History Museum: house built in 1832-1850.
Hours & Admission Prices: Tues.-Sat. 10-5, Sun. 2-5. Adults $5, college students $4, students 6-18 $3; discounts to groups of 15 or more; members no charge. Closed New Year's Day; Easter; Independence Day; Thanksgiving; Christmas.
Attendance: 2,800 (estimated)

GAINESWOOD, 805 S. Cedar Ave., Demopolis, AL 36732-2915. Tel.: 334-289-4846.
Web Site: www.gaineswood.org
Key Personnel: Site Dir., Eleanor W. Cunningham; Dir. Collections & Interpretation, Bruce M. Lipscombe; Maintenance, Richard Rand.
Institution Type/Description: Historical Building & Site: housed in the former home of Nathan Bryan Whitfield; built between 1843-1861.
Hours & Admission Prices: Tues.-Fri. 10-4, 1st Sat. 10-2; other times by appointment. Adults $5, youth 6-18 $3; discounts to seniors, military, college students, AAA & groups. Closed state holidays. &
Attendance: 2,732 (actual)

THE LAIRD COTTAGE/GENEVA MERCER MUSEUM, 311 N. Walnut Ave., Demopolis, AL 36732. Tel.: 334-289-0282.
Web Site: www.marengocountyhistoricalsociety.com
Institution Type/Description: Historic House Museum: built in 1870.
Hours & Admission Prices: By appointment.

MARENGO COUNTY HISTORY AND ARCHIVE MUSEUM, 101 N. Walnut Ave., Demopolis, AL 36732. Mailing Address: P.O. Box 1144, Demopolis, AL 36732. Tel.: 334-289-0599.
Web Site: www.marengomuseum.com
Key Personnel: Pres. & Dir., Mary Jones-Fitts.
Institution Type/Description: History Museum.
Hours & Admission Prices: Tues., Thurs. & Sat. 10-2, Wed. by appointment.

Dora

ALABAMA MINING MUSEUM, 120 East St., Dora, AL 35062-4612. Tel.: 205-648-2442.
Key Personnel: Dir., Bonnie Sue Groves.
Institution Type/Description: Mining Museum.
Hours & Admission Prices: Tues.-Sat. 8:30-4; school groups by appointment. No charge; donations accepted. &
Attendance: 20,000 (estimated)

Dothan

DOTHAN AREA BOTANICAL GARDENS, 5130 Headland Ave., Dothan, AL 36303-7691. Tel.: 334-793-3224. Fax: 334-793-5275.
E-mail: info@dabg.com
Web Site: www.dabg.com
Key Personnel: Exec. Dir., Conner Vernon; Pres., Larry Dykes; Vice Pres., Russ Parrish; Groundskeeper, Charles McClendon; Office Mgr., Janie Edmondson.
Institution Type/Description: Botanical Gardens.
Hours & Admission Prices: Summer: daily 7-7; Winter: daily 7-5. No charge. &

G.W. CARVER INTERPRETIVE MUSEUM, 305 N. Foster St., Dothan, AL 36303. Tel.: 334-712-0933.
E-mail: mail@gwcarvermuseum.com
Web Site: www.gwcarvermuseum.com
Institution Type/Description: History Museum.
Hours & Admission Prices: Tues.-Fri. 10-5:30, Sat. 1-5; groups by appointment. Closed holidays & holiday weekends.

LANDMARK PARK, ALABAMA'S OFFICIAL MUSEUM OF AGRICULTURE, 430 Landmark Dr., Dothan, AL 36303. Mailing Address: P.O. Box 6362, Dothan, AL 36302-6362. Tel.: 334-794-3452. Fax: 334-677-7229.
E-mail: parkinfo@landmarkpark.com
Web Site: landmarkparkdothan.com
Key Personnel: Exec. Dir., William M. Holman; Education Dir., Anna Holman; Asst. Dir., Kathie Moore; Dir. Pub. Rels. & Membership, Laura Stakelum.
Institution Type/Description: Living History Museum & Park Complex serving as the Official Museum of Agriculture for the State of Alabama.
Hours & Admission Prices: Mon.-Sat. 9-5, Sun. 12-6. Adults $4, children 3-12 $3; members and children 2 & under no charge. Blue Start Museum program. Closed New Year's Day; Thanksgiving Day; Christmas Day. &
Attendance: 48,600 (actual)

WIREGRASS MUSEUM OF ART, 126 Museum Ave., Dothan, AL 36303-4802. Mailing Address: P.O. Box 1624, Dothan, AL 36302-1624. Tel.: 334-794-3871. Fax: 334-792-9035.
E-mail: director@wiregrassmuseum.org
Web Site: www.wiregrassmuseum.org
Key Personnel: Pres., Jeff Coleman; Exec. Dir., Tara Holman; Dir. Visitor Svcs., Holly Roberts; Dir. Collections & Exhibits, Alison A. Beeson; Art Educator, Lydel Matthews; Art Educator, Jamie Richey; Grants Writer, Amber Hanson; Security & Maintenance, Mike Roberts; Dir. Devel., Tonye Frith; Membership & Administrative Asst., Dana Lemmer.
Institution Type/Description: Art Museum: housed in 1912 electric plant.
Hours & Admission Prices: Tues.-Sat. 10-5. No charge; donations accepted. &
Attendance: 20,000 (actual)

Elberta

BALDWIN COUNTY HERITAGE MUSEUM, 25521 Hwy. 98 East, Elberta, AL 36530. Mailing Address: P.O. Box 356, Elberta, AL 36530-0356. Tel.: 251-986-8375 & 752-8883. Facebook.
E-mail: bchm@gulftel.com
Web Site: www.baldwincountyheritagemuseum.com
Key Personnel: Chm. (V), Ralph Veller; Vice Chm., June Taylor; Chm. (V), Clark Cathey; Clerk, Tammy Kinney.
Institution Type/Description: History Museum.
Hours & Admission Prices: Wed.-Sat. 10-3, 2nd & 4th Sun. 12-5. No charge. Closed all national & state holidays. &
Attendance: 2,700 (estimated)

Eufaula

FENDALL HALL, 917 W. Barbour St., Eufaula, AL 36027. Mailing Address: 468 S. Perry St., P.O. Box 300900, Montgomery, AL 36130-0900. Tel.: 334-687-8469 & 695-6562.
E-mail: fendallhall@gmail.com
Web Site: ahc.alabama.gov; fendallhall.weebly.com
Key Personnel: Dir., Lindsey B. Dudeck.
Institution Type/Description: Historic House Museum: built in 1860.
Hours & Admission Prices: Mon.-Sat. 10-4; other times by appointment. Admission $7; military no charge. Closed state holidays. &

SHORTER MANSION MUSEUM, 340 N. Eufaula Ave., Eufaula, AL 36027-1518. Tel.: 334-687-3793, 888-EUFAULA (383-2852). Fax: 334-687-1836.
E-mail: eufaulaheritageassoc@eufaula.rr.com
Web Site: www.eufaulapilgrimage.com
Key Personnel: Exec. Dir., Pam Snead.
Institution Type/Description: Local History Museum: housed in the former home of Eli Sims Shorter II; built in 1884. Listed on the National Register of Historic Places.
Hours & Admission Prices: Mon.-Sat. 10-4; group tours by appointment. Adults $5, children 5-12 $3; discounts to groups, AAM & AAA members; children under 4 no charge. &
Attendance: 10,000 (actual)

Fairhope

EASTERN SHORE ART CENTER, 401 Oak St., Fairhope, AL 36532-2403. Tel.: 251-928-2228.
E-mail: info@esartcenter.org
Web Site: www.esartcenter.com
Key Personnel: Mng. Dir., C.E.O. & Pres. (V), Kate Fisher.
Institution Type/Description: Art Museum.
Hours & Admission Prices: Tues.-Fri. 10-4, Sat. 10-2. No charge; donations accepted. Closed major holidays. &
Attendance: 20,000 (estimated)

Fayette

FAYETTE ART MUSEUM, 530 N. Temple Ave., Fayette, AL 35555-2211. Tel.: 205-932-8727. Fax: 205-932-8727.
E-mail: fayetteartmuseum@yahoo.com
Web Site: www.fayetteartmuseum.vpweb.com
Key Personnel: Dir. & Cur., Anne Perry-Uhlman.
Institution Type/Description: Art Museum: housed in c.1930 former school building.
Hours & Admission Prices: Mon.-Fri. 9-12 & 1-4; other times by appointment. No charge; donations accepted. &
Attendance: 40,000 (estimated)

Florence

CHILDREN'S MUSEUM OF THE SHOALS, 2810 Darby Dr., Florence, AL 35630-1524. Tel.: 256-765-0500.
E-mail: cmos@shoalschildrensmuseum.org
Key Personnel: Dir., Peggy McCloy.
Institution Type/Description: Children's Museum.
Hours & Admission Prices: Thurs.-Sat. 10-4:30; groups by appointment. Admission 2 & over $5; discounts to groups of 10 or more; children under 2 and ACM & museum members no charge. Closed major holidays. &

FRANK LLOYD WRIGHT ROSENBAUM HOUSE, 601 Riverview Dr., Florence, AL 35630-6026. Mailing Address: P.O. Box 98, Florence, AL 35630. Tel.: 256-718-5050.
Web Site: www.wrightinalabama.com
Key Personnel: Dir., Libby Jordan.
Institution Type/Description: Historic House Museum: designed by Frank Lloyd Wright, c.1939.
Hours & Admission Prices: Tues.-Sat. 10-4, Sun. 1-4. Adults $8, senior citizens, students & children $5; discounts to groups of 10 or more. Closed major holidays.
Attendance: 6,700 (actual)

INDIAN MOUND & MUSEUM, 1028 S. Court St., Florence, AL 35630-6116. Mailing Address: 217 E. Tuscaloosa St., Florence, AL 35630-4724. Tel.: 256-760-6427.
E-mail: ljordan@florenceal.org
Web Site: www.florenceal.org
Key Personnel: Dir., Libby Jordan; Cur., Jim Walden.
Institution Type/Description: History Museum.
Hours & Admission Prices: Temporarily closed for construction of new museum. &
Attendance: 3,500 (estimated)

KENNEDY-DOUGLASS CENTER FOR THE ARTS, 217 E. Tuscaloosa St., Florence, AL 35630-4724. Tel.: 256-760-6379. Fax: 256-760-6382.
E-mail: ljordan@florenceal.org
Web Site: www.florenceal.org
Key Personnel: Dir., Libby Jordan; Program Coord., Mary Nicely; Administrative Asst., Faye Vines.
Institution Type/Description: Art Council: housed in 1917-18 Kennedy-Douglass House.
Hours & Admission Prices: Mon.-Fri. 9-4; other times by appointment. No charge. &
Attendance: 12,000 (estimated)

POPE'S TAVERN MUSEUM, 203 Hermitage Dr., Florence, AL 35630-4667. Mailing Address: 217 E. Tuscaloosa St., Florence, AL 35630-4724. Tel.: 256-760-6439.
E-mail: ljordan@florenceal.org
Web Site: www.florenceal.org
Key Personnel: Dir., Libby Jordan.
Institution Type/Description: Historic House: housed in a former stagecoach stop, tavern & inn; used as a hospital by Confederate & Union forces.

Hours & Admission Prices: Tues.-Sat. 10-4. Adults $2, children $.50. &
Attendance: 2,657 (actual)

W.C. HANDY HOME MUSEUM AND LIBRARY, 620 W. College St., Florence, AL 35630-5360. Mailing Address: 217 Tuscaloosa St., Florence, AL 35630-4724. Tel.: 256-760-6434. Fax: 256-760-6382.
E-mail: ljordan@florenceal.org
Web Site: www.florenceal.org
Key Personnel: Dir., Libby Jordan.
Institution Type/Description: Historic House.
Hours & Admission Prices: Tues.-Sat. 10-4. Adults $2, students $.50. &
Attendance: 3,500 (estimated)

Foley

FOLEY RAILROAD MUSEUM, 125 E. Laurel Ave., Foley, AL 36535. Tel.: 251-943-1818. Fax: 251-971-1819.
E-mail: foleymuseum@gulftel.com
Web Site: www.foleyrailroadmuseum.com
Key Personnel: Exec. Dir., Bonnie Donaldson.
Institution Type/Description: Railroad Museum: housed in the former L & N Railroad Depot; built in 1905.
Hours & Admission Prices: Museum: Mon.-Fri. 10-4, Sat. 10-2. Model Train Exhibit: Tues., Thurs. & Sat. 10-2.

Fort Mitchell

FORT MITCHELL HISTORIC SITE, 561 Hwy. 165, Fort Mitchell, AL 36856. Mailing Address: c/o RCHC, P.O. Box 3411, Phenix City, AL 36868. Tel.: 334-855-1406.
Institution Type/Description: Historic Site: military fort built in 1813. Listed as a National Historic Site.
Hours & Admission Prices: Thurs.-Sat. 10-5, Sun. 1-5. Adults $6, military $5, students $4; children under 5 no charge.

Fort Payne

ALABAMA FAN CLUB AND MUSEUM, 101 Glenn Blvd., S.W., Fort Payne, AL 35967-4963. Tel.: 256-845-1646. Fax: 256-845-5650.
E-mail: info@conwayent.com
Institution Type/Description: Country Music Group Museum.
Hours & Admission Prices: Memorial Day to Labor Day daily 9-6; Sept.-May Wed.-Sat. 9-6, Sun. 1-6.

COOK SOUND STUDIOS, 1419 Scenic Rd. E., Fort Payne, AL 35968. Tel.: 256-845-2286.
Institution Type/Description: Country Music Museum: housed in the studio of Alabama band member, Jeff Cook.
Hours & Admission Prices: By appointment.

FORT PAYNE DEPOT MUSEUM, 105 5th St., N.E., Fort Payne, AL 35967-2455. Mailing Address: P.O. Box 681420, Fort Payne, AL 35968. Tel.: 256-845-5714. Facebook.
E-mail: depotmuseum@bellsouth.net
Web Site: fortpaynedepotmuseum.com
Key Personnel: Chm. (V), Eric Brisendine; Dir., Jessica Harper-Brown.
Institution Type/Description: History Museum: housed in historic Fort Payne railroad depot built by the Alabama Great Southern Railroad in 1891.
Hours & Admission Prices: Wed.-Fri. 10-3, Sun. 2-4. Adults 3, children 7-18 $1; children 6 & under no charge. Closed major holidays.
Attendance: 4,000 (estimated)

Fort Rucker

U.S. ARMY AVIATION MUSEUM, Bldg. 6000 Novosel St, Fort Rucker, AL 36362. Mailing Address: P.O. Box 620610, Fort Rucker, AL 36362-0610. Tel.: 334-598-2508 & 888-Army-Avn.
E-mail: foundation@armyaviationmuseum.org
Web Site: www.armyaviationmuseum.org
Key Personnel: Dir., Robert Mitchell; Cur. Collections, Robert D. Mitchell.
Institution Type/Description: Aviation Technology and Military Museum.
Hours & Admission Prices: Mon.-Fri. 9-4, Sat. 9-3. No charge; donations accepted. Closed New Year's Eve & Day; Thanksgiving; Christmas Eve & Day. &
Attendance: 150,000 (estimated)

Franklin

ALABAMA RIVER MUSEUM, Claiborne Lock & Dam, Alabama River (north of Monroeville), 31 Isaac Creek Rd., Franklin, AL 36444. Mailing Address: 31 N. Alabama Ave., Monroeville, AL 36461. Tel.: 251-575-7433. Fax: 251-575-2513.
E-mail: mchm@frontiernet.net
Web Site: www.monroecountymuseum.org
Formerly: River Heritage Museum
Key Personnel: C.E.O. & Museum Shop Mgr., Stephanie Rogers; Chm. (V), Clark McKinley.
Institution Type/Description: History Museum.
Hours & Admission Prices: Open by appointment only. &

Gadsden

ETOWAH HERITAGE MUSEUM & JERRY B. JONES HISTORICAL RESEARCH LIBRARY, 2829 W. Meighan Blvd., Gadsden, AL 35902. Mailing Address: P.O. Box 8131, Gadsden, AL 35902. Tel.: 256-886-9611. Facebook.
E-mail: etowahhistory@gmail.com
Web Site: www.etowahhistory.com
Key Personnel: Dir., Danny K. Crownover.
Institution Type/Description: Historical Society Museum & Library.
Hours & Admission Prices: Mon. & Tues. 10-4. No charge; donations accepted. Closed holidays. &
Attendance: 10,000 (estimated)

GADSDEN MUSEUM OF ART, 515 Broad St., Gadsden, AL 35901-3719. Tel.: 256-546-7365. Fax: 256-549-4748.
Web Site: gadsdenmuseum.com
Key Personnel: Dir. & Cur., Ray Wetzel; Education Coord., Jill Edwards.
Institution Type/Description: Art & History Museum.
Hours & Admission Prices: Tues.-Sat. 10-5. No charge; donations accepted. &
Attendance: 8,000 (estimated)

MARY G. HARDIN CENTER FOR CULTURAL ARTS, 501 Broad St., Gadsden, AL 35901-3719. Mailing Address: P.O. Box 1507, Gadsden, AL 35902-1507. Tel.: 256-543-2787. Fax: 256-546-7435. Facebook.
E-mail: info@culturalarts.org
Web Site: www.culturalarts.org
Key Personnel: C.E.O. & Exec. Dir., Robert M. Welch; Chm. (V), Catherine Ray; Vice Chm., Bill Heller; Financial Dir., Kay Moore; Deputy Dir., Tom Banks; Dir. Children's Museum & Education, Holly Guinn; School for the Arts, Susie Collins.
Institution Type/Description: Art Center.
Hours & Admission Prices: Mon.-Sat. 10-5, Sun. 1-5. Imagination Place: Mon.-Sat. 10-6, Sun. 1-5. Adults $8; children under 2, members & ASTC reciprocal no charge. Closed Thanksgiving; Christmas. &
Attendance: 84,873 (actual)

Georgiana

HANK WILLIAMS' BOYHOOD HOME & MUSEUM, 127 Rose St., Georgiana, AL 36033. Mailing Address: P.O. Box 310, Georgiana, AL 36033. Tel.: 334-376-2396. Fax: 334-376-9850. Facebook: Hank Williams Sr. Boyhood Home & Museum.
E-mail: cityofgeorgiana@centurytel.net
Key Personnel: Chm. (V), Lynn H. Watson; Museum Shop Mgr., Margaret Gaston.
Institution Type/Description: Historic House Museum: housed in the boyhood home of Hank Williams, Sr.
Hours & Admission Prices: Mon.-Sat. 10-4. Adults $5; discounts to tour groups. &
Attendance: 3,067 (actual)

Gilbertown

CHOCTAW COUNTY HISTORICAL MUSEUM, 40 Melvin Rd., Gilbertown, AL 36908. Mailing Address: P.O. Box 162, Gilbertown, AL 36908-0162. Tel.: 251-843-2501. Facebook: Choctaw County Historical Museum.
E-mail: cchm@millry.net
Key Personnel: Dir., Sandra Jenkins Little; Pres. (V), Gerald A. Little, Jr.; Cur. & Museum Shop Mgr., Danny Roberts.
Institution Type/Description: History Museum.
Hours & Admission Prices: Wed. 9-3:30, Sat. 9-1; other times by appointment. Adults $5, senior citizens $4, students 6-17 $3; discounts to groups; children under 6 & members no charge. Closed on holidays that fall on Wed. or Sat. &
Attendance: 400 (estimated)

Greensboro

MAGNOLIA GROVE-HISTORIC HOUSE MUSEUM, 1002 Hobson St., Greensboro, AL 36744-1414. Tel.: 334-624-8618.
E-mail: magnoliagrove2@yahoo.com
Web Site: www.preserveala.org
Key Personnel: Site Dir., Eleanor W. Cunningham.
Institution Type/Description: Historic House Museum: c.1840 Greek Revival style home built by Isaac Croom. Boyhood home of Rear Admiral Richmond Pearson Hobson, Spanish-American war hero.
Hours & Admission Prices: House: Tues.-Fri. 10-4, 1st Sat. each month 10-2. Grounds: daily. Adults $5, college students $4, children 6-18 $3; discount to AAA, military, seniors & groups. Closed major holidays. &
Attendance: 982 (actual)

SAFE HOUSE BLACK HISTORY MUSEUM, 518 Martin Luther King Dr., Greensboro, AL 36744-2237. Tel.: 334-624-2030 & 624-4228. Fax: 334-624-2036.
E-mail: safehouseblackhi@bellsouth.net
Web Site: www.safehousemuseum.org
Formerly: Hale County Civil Rights
Key Personnel: Dir., David Cooper; Museum Shop Mgr., Theresa Burroughs.
Institution Type/Description: History Museum: housed in the home used to conceal Dr. Martin Luther King Jr. while he organized peaceful resistance protests of segregation in Alabama during the 1960s.
Hours & Admission Prices: By appointment. Adults $5; discounts to seniors, mentally challenged, elementary & high school students.
Attendance: 2,000 (estimated)

Grove Hill

CLARKE COUNTY HISTORICAL MUSEUM, 116 W. Cobb St., Grove Hill, AL 36451. P.O. Box 388, Grove Hill, AL 36451. Tel.: 251-275-8684.
E-mail: museum@clarkemuseum.com
Web Site: www.clarkemuseum.com
Institution Type/Description: History Museum.
Hours & Admission Prices: Mon. 12-4, Tues.-Fri. 10-4, Sat. 10-2.

Gulf Shores

ALABAMA GULF COAST ZOO, 1204 Gulf Shores Pkwy., Gulf Shores, AL 36542-5908. Tel.: 251-968-5732. Fax: 251-967-3358.
E-mail: info@alabamagulfcoastzoo.org
Web Site: www.alabamagulfcoastzoo.org
Key Personnel: Dir., Patti Hall; Gen. Mgr., Kim Dahlgren; Cur., Cyndi Johnson.
Institution Type/Description: Zoo.
Hours & Admission Prices: Daily 9-4. Adults $11, seniors 55 & over $9, children 3-12 $8; children 2 & under no charge. Closed New Year's Day; Thanksgiving; Christmas.

FORT MORGAN MUSEUM, 110 Hwy. 180 W., Gulf Shores, AL 36542-7802. Tel.: 251-540-7127.
Web Site: www.fort-morgan.org
Key Personnel: Dir., Michael Bailey; Education Program Devel., Dylan Tucker; Museum Shop Mgr., Jan Dillon.
Institution Type/Description: Military History Museum.
Hours & Admission Prices: Museum: daily 9-4:30. Fort & Grounds: daily 8-5. Adults $7, seniors $5, children 6-12 $4; discounts to military & veterans; children under 6 no charge. Closed New Year's Day; Thanksgiving; Christmas. &
Attendance: 89,147 (actual)

GULF SHORES MUSEUM, 244 W. 19th Ave., Gulf Shores, AL 36542. Mailing Address: P.O. Box 299, Gulf Shores, AL 36547-0299. Tel.: 251-968-1473.
E-mail: museum@gulfshoresal.gov
Web Site: www.gulfshoresal.gov
Key Personnel: Chm. (V), May Alanko; C.E.O., Wendy Congiardo; Dir., Grant Brown; Museum Admin., Christie Shannon; Docent, Jan Meeks.
Institution Type/Description: History Museum.
Hours & Admission Prices: Tues.-Fri. 10-12 & 1-5, Sat. 10-2. No charge; donations accepted. Closed New Year's Day; Mardi Gras Day; Memorial Day; Independence Day; Labor Day; Veterans Day; Thanksgiving; Christmas Eve & Day. &
Attendance: 4,340 (actual)

Guntersville

GUNTERSVILLE MUSEUM, 1215 Rayburn Ave., Guntersville, AL 35976-1432. Tel.: 256-571-7597. Fax: 256-571-7584.

E-mail: info@guntersvillemuseum.org
Web Site: guntersvillemuseum.org
Key Personnel: Dir., Julie Patton; Chm. Bd., Chris Wright; Pres. (V), Jeannie Wallace.
Institution Type/Description: History Museum & Art Museum: housed in a former military armory for Company E 167th Infantry Division; built in 1936.
Hours & Admission Prices: Tues.-Fri. 10-4, Sat.-Sun. 1-4. No charge; donations accepted. &
Attendance: 6,000 (estimated)

Hanceville

THE EVELYN BURROW MUSEUM, Burrow Center for the Fine and Performing Arts Bldg., 801 Main St., N.W., Hanceville, AL 35077. Mailing Address: P.O. Box 2000, Hanceville, AL 35077. Tel.: 256-352-8458 & 8457, 866-350-9722 (Toll Free).
E-mail: donny.wilson@wallacestate.edu
Web Site: www.burrowmuseum.org
Key Personnel: Dir., Donny Wilson.
Institution Type/Description: Art Museum.
Hours & Admission Prices: Tues.-Fri. 9-5, Sat. 10-2. No charge. &
Attendance: 6,000 (estimated)

Hillsboro

POND SPRING - THE GENERAL JOE WHEELER HOME, 12280 Alabama Hwy. 20, Hillsboro, AL 35643. Tel.: 256-637-8513.
E-mail: pondspringdirector@gmail.com
Web Site: www.generaljoewheelerhome.com
Key Personnel: Dir., Melissa Beasley; Cur., Kara Long; Pres. (V), Dr. Mildred Candle; Museum Shop Mgr., Hollye Raines.
Institution Type/Description: Historic House: housed in the former home of General Joe Wheeler. National Register of Historic Places.
Hours & Admission Prices: Wed.-Sat. 9-4, Sun. 1-5. Adults $8, seniors $5, students $3.
Attendance: 15,000 (estimated)

Huntsville

BURRITT ON THE MOUNTAIN - A LIVING MUSEUM, 3101 Burritt Dr., Huntsville, AL 35801-1142. Tel.: 256-536-2882. Fax: 256-532-1784.
E-mail: bm-recep@huntsvilleal.gov
Web Site: www.burrittonthemountain.com/
Formerly: Burritt Museum & Park
Key Personnel: C.E.O., Leslie Ecklund; C.O.O. & Finance Officer, Pat Robertson; Dir. Education, Tammy Cooney; Mktg. Dir., Elizabeth Jones; Cur. & Historic Park Coord., Stephanie Timberlake.
Institution Type/Description: Historic Village & Museum: housed in a 1935 mansion. Listed on the National Register of Historic Places.
Hours & Admission Prices: April-Oct. Tues.-Sat. 9-5, Sun. 12-5; Nov.-March Tues.-Sat. 10-4, Sun. 12-4. Adults $10, seniors 60 & over $9, children 3-18 $8; discounts to local residents and AAM & AAA members; children 2 & under and members no charge. Closed New Year's Day; Thanksgiving; Christmas Eve & Day. &
Attendance: 100,000 (estimated)

EARLYWORKS FAMILY OF MUSEUMS, 404 Madison St., Huntsville, AL 35801-4203. Tel.: 256-564-8100. Fax: 256-564-8151. Facebook, Twitter, Instagram.
Web Site: www.earlyworks.com
Formerly: EarlyWorks Museums
Key Personnel: Exec. Dir. & C.E.O., Bart Williams; Coord. Volunteers, Andrea Sanchez; Constitution Village Museum Shop Mgr., Lora McGowan.
Institution Type/Description: History Museum.
Hours & Admission Prices: EarlyWorks: Tues.-Sat. 9 am-4 pm. Village: March-Oct. Wed.-Sat. 10-3; Thanksgiving to Dec. 23 5 pm-9 pm. Village Shop: Tues.-Sat. 9-4. Depot: March-Dec. Tues., Thurs. & 2nd Sat. each month 10 am-2 pm. Depot Park & Grounds daily 9-5. EarlyWorks & Alabama Constitution Village: adults $12, senior citizens 55 & over and youth 4-17 $10, children 1-3 $5; discounts to AAM, ACM & veterans and their family members; members & children under one no charge. Depot: Self-Guided Tour: $5 per person; Guided Tour: $10 per person; member and children 1 & under no charge. Closed New Year's Day; Thanksgiving; Christmas Eve & Day. &
Attendance: 150,000 (actual)

HARMONY PARK SAFARI, 431 Cloud's Cove Rd., S.E., Huntsville, AL 35803-6513. Tel.: 256-723-3880, 877-726-4625 (Toll Free).
Web Site: www.harmonyparksafari.com

Institution Type/Description: Nature Preserve.
Hours & Admission Prices: March-Nov. daily 10am to sunset.

HOWARD WEEDEN HOUSE MUSEUM, 300 Gates Ave. S.E., Huntsville, AL 35801-3101. Tel.: 256-536-7718.
E-mail: theweedenhouse@att.net
Web Site: https://weedenhousemuseum.com
Key Personnel: Dir., Beth Hamilton.
Institution Type/Description: History Museum: housed in 1819 Federal style home & birthplace of artist & poet, Maria Howard Weeden.
Hours & Admission Prices: Wed.-Sat. 10:30 a.m.-11:30 a.m. or by appointment. Adults $5, children 12 & under $3 (cash only).

HUNTSVILLE/MADISON COUNTY BOTANICAL GARDEN, 4747 Bob Wallace Ave., Huntsville, AL 35805-3390. Tel.: 256-830-4447 & 877-930-4447 (Toll Free). Fax: 256-830-5314.
E-mail: email@hsvbg.org
Web Site: www.hsvbg.org
Key Personnel: Dir., Paula Steigerwald.
Institution Type/Description: Botanical Garden.
Hours & Admission Prices: May-Sept. Mon.-Wed. & Fri.-Sat. 9-6, Thurs. 9-8, Sun. 12-6; Oct.-April Mon.-Sat. 9-5, Sun. 12-5; groups by appointment. Adults $10, seniors 55 & over and military $8, children 3-18 $5; members and children 2 & under no charge. Closed New Year's Day; Thanksgiving; Christmas.
Attendance: 325,000 (actual)

HUNTSVILLE MUSEUM OF ART, 300 Church St., Huntsville, AL 35801-4910. Tel.: 256-535-4350 & 800-786-9095 (Toll Free). Fax: 256-532-1743.
E-mail: info@hsvmuseum.org
Web Site: hsvmuseum.org
Key Personnel: Exec. Dir., Christopher Madkour; Dir. Curatorial Affairs, Peter J. Baldaia; Cur. Exhibitions & Collections, David Reyes; Dir. Education & Museum Academy, Laura Smith; Dir. Communications, Samantha Nielson; Dir. Devel., Andrea Petroff; Guest Services Mgr., Linda Nagle; Facilities Mgr., Doug Lighton; Events Mgr., Lil Parton; Accountant, Wendy Worley; Museum Shop Mgr., Janell Zesinger.
Institution Type/Description: Art Museum.
Hours & Admission Prices: Tues.-Wed. & Fri.-Sat. 11-5, Thurs. 11-8, Sun. noon-5. Adults $12, seniors, active military & educators $10, children 6 & up & students $5; discounts to groups; members no charge. Closed New Year's Day; Memorial Day; Labor Day; Thanksgiving; Christmas Eve & Day.
Attendance: 77,652 (actual)

NORTH ALABAMA RAILROAD MUSEUM, 694 Chase Rd., Huntsville, AL 35811-1523. Mailing Address: P.O. Box 4163, Huntsville, AL 35815-4163. Tel.: 256-851-6276.
E-mail: narm-mail@comcast.net
Web Site: www.northalabamarailroadmuseum.com
Formerly: North Alabama Railroad Club
Key Personnel: Pres. (V), Joe Slika; Dir., Jimmy Boren; Museum Shop Mgr., Amy Boren.
Institution Type/Description: Railroad Museum.
Hours & Admission Prices: Daily 9-4; groups by appointment. No charge; donations accepted. Train: adults $15, children under 12 $10.
Attendance: 5,000 (estimated)

THE 3 ART GALLERIES AT UAH: UNION GROVE, WILSON HALL, SALMON LIBRARY, Dept. of Art & Art History UAH, Wilson Hall 160-B, Huntsville, AL 35899. Tel.: 256-824-6114. Fax: 256-824-6438.
E-mail: art@uah.edu
Web Site: www.uah.edu/colleges/liberal/art
Key Personnel: Printmaking & Design, Brandon Gardner; Dean, College of Liberal Arts, Glenn Dasher; Painting, Kathryn Jill Johnson; Graphic Design, Keith Jones; Chair, Dept. Art & Art History, Lillian Joyce; Art History, David Stewart; Drawing, Roxie Veasey; Art History, Martha Vines; Staff Asst., Marylyn Coffey; Drawing & Painting, Monique K. Given; Photography, Jose Betancourt; Sculpture, Jimmy Kuehnle.
Institution Type/Description: Union Grove Gallery & Meeting House: housed in 1830s Greek Revival Chapel. Wilson Hall Gallery: Art Dept. Building. Salmon Library Gallery.
Hours & Admission Prices: Union Grove Gallery: Mon.-Fri. 12:30-4:30; other times by appointment. Library Gallery: Mon.-Thurs. 8am-12 midnight, Fri. 8-8, Sat. 9-6, Sun. 1-10. Wilson Hall Gallery: Mon.-Fri. 8:30-5. No charge.
Attendance: 5,000 (estimated)

THE U.S. SPACE & ROCKET CENTER, One Tranquility Base, Huntsville, AL 35805-3371. Tel.: 256-837-3400, 800-637-7223.
Web Site: www.spacecamp.com

Key Personnel: C.E.O., Dr. Deborah Barnhart; C.F.O., Brooke Balch; Vice Pres. Human Resources, Vickie Henderson; Dir. Special Events, Claudia Jones; Dir. Museum Operations, Amber Williams; Mgr. Museum Education, Joseph Vick; Mgr. Theater, Chris Brothers; Museum Shop Mgr., Susan Moore; Coord. Membership, Amanda Gatlin; Volunteer Coord., Bennie Jacks.
Institution Type/Description: Aeronautics & Space Museum.
Hours & Admission Prices: Daily 9-5. General Admission: adults $20, children 5-12 $15; discount to ASTC Passport Program members & AAA members; children 4 & under no charge. Closed New Year's Eve & Day; Thanksgiving; Christmas Eve & Day.
Attendance: 509,006 (actual)

VETERANS MEMORIAL MUSEUM, 2060A Airport Rd., Huntsville, AL 35801-5338. Tel.: 256-883-3737. Fax: 256-883-3912.
E-mail: info@memorialmuseum.org
Web Site: www.memorialmuseum.org
Key Personnel: Dir. & Pres. (V), Randall Withrow.
Institution Type/Description: Military History Museum.
Hours & Admission Prices: Memorial Day to Labor Day Wed.-Sat. 10-5; Sept.-May Wed.-Sat. 10-4; other times by appointment. Adults $5, seniors $4, students $3; military in uniform no charge. Closed New Year's Day; Thanksgiving; Christmas.
Attendance: 3,600 (estimated)

Jacksonville

DR. FRANCIS MEDICAL AND APOTHECARY MUSEUM, 207 Gayle Ave., S.E., Jacksonville, AL 36265-2544. Mailing Address: c/o Jacksonville Public Library, 200 Pelham Rd. S., Jacksonville, AL 36265-2651. Tel.: 256-435-6332. Fax: 256-435-4459.
E-mail: lotsabooks@hotmail.com
Web Site: jacksonvillepubliclibrary.org
Key Personnel: Acting Dir., Barbara Rowell.
Institution Type/Description: Medical Museum: housed in 1850 Antebellum office & apothecary of Dr. Francis.
Hours & Admission Prices: Tues.-Fri. 8-5, Sat. 8-3. Appointment preferred. No charge; donations accepted.
Attendance: 47 (actual)

Lafayette

CHAMBERS COUNTY MUSEUM, 1st Ave. S.W., Lafayette, AL 36862. Mailing Address: P.O. Box 87, Lafayette, AL 36862. Tel.: 334-864-9656 & 7924.
Institution Type/Description: History Museum: housed in the former Central of Georgia railway depot.
Hours & Admission Prices: Wed. 9-12 & 1-4, Sat. 9-12; other times by appointment.

Leeds

BARBER VINTAGE MOTORSPORTS MUSEUM, 6030 Barber Motorsports Pkwy., Leeds, AL 35094-3418. Tel.: 205-699-7275. Fax: 205-702-8700.
E-mail: bvmm@barbermuseum.org
Web Site: www.barbermuseum.org
Key Personnel: Dir., Jeff Ray; Museum Shop Mgr., Brittany Perryman.
Institution Type/Description: Motorsports Museum.
Hours & Admission Prices: April-Sept. Mon.-Sat. 10-6, Sun. 12-6; Oct.-March Mon.-Sat. 10-5, Sun. 12-5. Adults $15, children 4-12 $10; discounts to AAA members; children 3 & under no charge. Closed New Year's Day; Easter; Independence Day; Thanksgiving; Christmas Eve & Day.

Lincoln

INTERNATIONAL MOTORSPORTS HALL OF FAME AND MUSEUM, 3198 Speedway Blvd., Lincoln, AL 35096-6327. Mailing Address: P.O. Box 1018, Talladega, AL 35161-1018. Tel.: 256-362-5002. Fax: 256-315-4565.
Web Site: www.motorsportshalloffame.com
Key Personnel: Exec. Dir., Russell Branham; Mgr. Hall of Fame, Bruce Ramey.
Institution Type/Description: Motorsports Museum.
Hours & Admission Prices: Daily 9-5; extended hours during race weeks at Talladega Superspeedway. Adults $12, students 6-12 $5; discounts to senior citizens, military, policemen & firemen; children 5 & under no charge. Closed New Year's Day; Easter; Thanksgiving; Christmas.
Attendance: 900 (estimated)

Loachapoka

LEE COUNTY HISTORICAL SOCIETY, 6500 Stage Rd., Loachapoka, AL 36865. Mailing Address: P.O. Box 206, Loachapoka, AL 36865-0206. Tel.: 334-887-3007.
Web Site: www.leecountyhistoricalsociety.org
Key Personnel: Pres., Jeannette Frandsen; Vice Pres., Charles Mitchell.
Institution Type/Description: Historical Society Museum.
Hours & Admission Prices: By appointment only. No charge; donations accepted.
Attendance: 6,500 (estimated)

Marion

ALABAMA WOMEN'S HALL OF FAME, Judson College, Howard Bean Hall, 302 Bibb St., Marion, AL 36756-2504. Tel.: 334-683-5100 & 5167. Fax: 334-683-5147.
E-mail: bpoole1@judson.edu
Web Site: www.awhf.org
Key Personnel: Exec. Sec., Bill Mathews.
Institution Type/Description: History Museum.
Hours & Admission Prices: Call for hours. No charge; donations accepted. ♿

McCalla

IRON & STEEL MUSEUM OF ALABAMA, TANNEHILL IRONWORKS HISTORICAL STATE PARK, 12632 Confederate Pkwy., McCalla, AL 35111-2620. Tel.: 205-477-5711. Fax: 205-477-9400. Facebook.
E-mail: tannehillmuseum@bellsouth.net
Web Site: www.Tannehill.org
Key Personnel: C.E.O., John Morrison; Museum Dir., Jennifer Watts; Chm., James S. Day; Business Officer, Lisa Carroll.
Institution Type/Description: Industrial Museum & State Park: located on the c.1839 Tannehill Furnace Site.
Hours & Admission Prices: Museum: Tues.-Fri. 8:30-4:30, Sat. 9-4:30, Sun. 12:30-4:30. Park: daily 7-sunset. Adults $2, children 6-11 and 62 & over $1; members and children 5 & under no charge. ♿
Attendance: 500,000 (actual)

Mobile

ALABAMA CONTEMPORARY ART CENTER, 301 Conti St., Mobile, AL 36602-2714. Mailing Address: P.O. Box 198, Mobile, AL 36601. Tel.: 251-208-5671. Fax: 251-208-5655.
E-mail: cla.sain@cityofmobile.org
Web Site: alabamacontemporary.org
Formerly: Centre for the Living Arts
Key Personnel: Exec. Dir., Amanda Solley.
Institution Type/Description: Contemporary Visual Arts Centre.
Hours & Admission Prices: Wed.-Sat. 11-5, Sun 12-5. Adults $5, students, seniors & educators $3; Fri., members & children under 12 no charge. ♿
Attendance: 122,000 (estimated)

BRAGG-MITCHELL MANSION, 1906 Springhill Ave., Mobile, AL 36607-2304. Tel.: 251-471-6364. Fax: 251-478-300. Facebook.
E-mail: info@braggmitchellmansion.com
Web Site: braggmitchellmansion.com
Institution Type/Description: Historic Mansion: built in 1855.
Hours & Admission Prices: Tues.-Fri. 10-4; tours on the hour; last tour at 3. Adults $10, students 3-12 $5; discounts to groups & AAA members. ♿
Attendance: 3,819 (actual)

GULF COAST EXPLOREUM SCIENCE CENTER, 65 Government St., Mobile, AL 36602-3107. Mailing Address: P.O. Box 1968, Mobile, AL 36633-1968. Tel.: 251-208-6893.
Web Site: www.exploreum.com
Formerly: Gulf Coast Exploreum Museum of Science
Key Personnel: Exec. Dir., Jan McKay; Asst. Dir. Operations & Education, Don Comeaux; Asst. Dir., Toni Webb; Dir. Devel. & Membership, John Goodroe; Dir. Mktg. & Design, Josh Holland.
Institution Type/Description: Science Center.
Hours & Admission Prices: Tues.-Thurs. 9-4, Fri.-Sat. 9-5, Sun. 12-5. Exhibits: adult $12, youth 13-17 $10.50, children 7-12 $10, children 4-6 $5. IMAX: adults $8.75, youth 13-17 $7.25, children 7-12 $6.50, children 4-6 $5. Combo: adults $16, youth 13-17 $15, children 7-12 $13.50, children 4-6 $8; discounts to military; members no charge. Closed Joe Cain Day; Mardi Gras Tuesday; Easter; Thanksgiving; Christmas Eve & Day. ♿
Attendance: 200,000 (actual)

GULFQUEST NATIONAL MARITIME MUSEUM OF THE GULF OF MEXICO CLOSED, 155 S. Water St., Mobile, AL 36602. Tel.: 251-436-8901.
E-mail: info@gulfquest.org
Web Site: www.gulfquest.org
Institution Type/Description: Maritime Museum.
Hours & Admission Prices: Wed.-Fri. 9-4, Sat. 10-5. Adults $14, seniors, college students & active military $13, youth 5-17 $11; children under 5 no charge.

HISTORIC FORT CONDE AND OFFICIAL WELCOME CENTER, 111 S. Royal St., Mobile, AL 36652. Mailing Address: P.O. Box 2068, Mobile, AL 36652. Tel.: 251-208-7569.
E-mail: ron.jamro@historymuseumofmobile.com
Web Site: www.historymuseumofmobile.com
Key Personnel: Dir., Ron Jamro.
Institution Type/Description: History Museum.
Hours & Admission Prices: Mon.-Sat. 9-5, Sun. 1-5. Adults $10, seniors 65 & up, students 18 & up w/ID and active/retired military w/ID $9, children 13-18 $7.50, children 6-12 $5; discounts to AAM, AASLH, AMA & SEMC members; children 5 & under, members no charge.

HISTORIC MOBILE PRESERVATION SOCIETY, 350 Oakleigh Place, Mobile, AL 36604-2910. Tel.: 251-432-6161. Fax: 251-432-8843.
E-mail: hmps@bellsouth.net
Web Site: www.historicmobile.org
Key Personnel: Exec. Dir., Collene Watson; Pres., Herndon Inge, III; Vice Pres., Hodge Alves; Sec., Stacey Killingsworth; Treas., Stephen May.
Institution Type/Description: Historical Preservation Society & Historic Houses.
Hours & Admission Prices: Tues.-Sat. 10-4; other times by appointment. Adults $10, children $5; discounts to groups, senior citizens, AAM & ICOM members; members no charge. Closed most holidays; New Year's Day; Easter; Memorial Day; Independence Day; Labor Day; Thanksgiving; Christmas. ♿
Attendance: 3,800 (estimated)

THE HISTORY MUSEUM OF MOBILE, 111 S. Royal St., Mobile, AL 36602-3101. Tel.: 251-208-7569.
E-mail: ron.jamro@historymuseumofmobile.com
Web Site: www.museumofmobile.com
Key Personnel: Dir., Ron Jamro; Cur. Education, Jennifer Fondren; Registrar, Nick Beeson; Cur. Collections, Lori McDuffie.
Institution Type/Description: History Museum.
Hours & Admission Prices: Museum of Mobile: Mon.-Sat. 9-5, Sun. 1-5. Adults $10, children 13-17 $7.50, children 6-12 $5; discounts to groups; children under 6 no charge. Historic Fort Conde: daily 8:30-4:30. No charge; donations accepted. Phoenix Fire Museum: Tues. & Thurs. 9-5. Closed New Year's Day; Thanksgiving; Christmas; some city holidays. ♿
Attendance: 90,000 (estimated)

MOBILE BOTANICAL GARDENS, 5151 Museum Dr., Mobile, AL 36608-1919. Tel.: 251-342-0555. Facebook.
E-mail: mbg2@bellsouth.net
Web Site: www.mobilebotanicalgardens.org
Formerly: Southern Alabama Botanical & Horticultural Society
Key Personnel: Exec. Dir., Robin Krchak.
Institution Type/Description: Botanical Gardens.
Hours & Admission Prices: Wed.-Sun. 9-4. Adults $5; children 12 & under and MBG & AHSG members no charge. ♿
Attendance: 30,000 (estimated)

MOBILE MEDICAL MUSEUM, 1664 Springhill Ave., Mobile, AL 36604-1405. Tel.: 251-415-1109. Facebook.
E-mail: admin@mobilemedicalmuseum.org
Web Site: www.mobilemedicalmuseum.org
Formerly: Eichold Heustis Medical Museum of the South
Key Personnel: Exec. Dir., Daryn P. Glassbrook, Ph.D.; Pres. (V), Charles B. Rodning, Ph.D., M.D.
Institution Type/Description: Medical History Museum.
Hours & Admission Prices: Tues.-Fri. 10-4 by appointment. Adults $6, seniors 62 & over and students $5, children under 12 $4; discounts to groups; members no charge. ♿
Attendance: 1,000 (actual)

MOBILE MUSEUM OF ART, 4850 Museum Dr., Mobile, AL 36608-1917. Tel.: 251-208-5200 & 5209. Fax: 251-208-5201. Facebook; Twitter; Instagram.
E-mail: glenn.bingham@cityofmobile.org
Web Site: www.MobileMuseumOfArt.com

Key Personnel: Dir., Deborah Velders; Chm. Bd. (V), Tyrone Fenderson; Chief Cur., Paul W. Richelson; Cur. Collections, Kurtis Thomas; Cur. Exhibitions, Donan Klooz; Registrar, Rachel Young.
Institution Type/Description: Art Museum.
Hours & Admission Prices: Tues.-Wed. & Fri.-Sun. 10-5, Thurs. 10-9. Adults $12; discounts to AAM & ICOM members, City of Mobile employees, active military, students, seniors; members & Thurs. no charge. Closed New Year's Day; Memorial Day; Independence Day; Thanksgiving; Christmas. &
Attendance: 33,529 (actual)

THE NATIONAL AFRICAN-AMERICAN ARCHIVES AND MUSEUM, 564 Dr. Martin Luther King Jr. Ave., Mobile, AL 36603. Tel.: 251-433-8511.
E-mail: naaamcc@gmail.com
Key Personnel: Founder & Dir., Delores S. Dees.
Institution Type/Description: History Museum: housed in the former Davis Avenue Branch of the Mobile Public Library, the only library for African-Americans from 1932 to the mid-1960s. Listed on the National Register for Historic Places.
Hours & Admission Prices: Call for hours and admissions.

PHOENIX FIRE MUSEUM, 203 S. Claiborne St., Mobile, AL 36602-2322. Tel.: 251-208-7508.
E-mail: fondrenj@historymuseumofmobile.com
Web Site: museumofmobile.com/phoenix-fire-museum
Institution Type/Description: History Museum: housed in the restored home of Phoenix Volunteer Fire Company No. 6.
Hours & Admission Prices: Tues. & Thurs. 9-5. No charge.

PORTIER HOUSE, 307 Conti St., Mobile, AL 36602. Tel.: 251-434-1565.
Web Site: www.portierhouse.org/
Key Personnel: Group Tours, Bunky Ralph.
Institution Type/Description: Historic House Museum: housed in the former home of Bishop Michael Portier, the first Bishop of Mobile. Listed on the National Register of Historic Places.
Hours & Admission Prices: Call for hours and admissions.

RICHARDS-DAR HOUSE MUSEUM, 256 N. Joachim St., Mobile, AL 36603-6472. Tel.: 251-208-7320.
E-mail: questions@richardsdarhouse.com
Web Site: www.richardsdarhouse.com
Key Personnel: Pres. (V), Susan Tomlinson.
Institution Type/Description: Historic House: built in 1860.
Hours & Admission Prices: Mon.-Fri. 11-3:30, Sat. 10-4, Sun. 1-4. Adults $10, children 5-11 $5; children 4 & under no charge.
Attendance: 4,250 (estimated)

USS ALABAMA BATTLESHIP MEMORIAL PARK, 2703 Battleship Pkwy., Mobile, AL 36601. Mailing Address: P.O. Box 65, Mobile, AL 36601-0065. Tel.: 251-433-2703. Fax: 251-433-2777.
E-mail: btunnell@ussalabama.com
Web Site: www.ussalabama.com
Key Personnel: C.E.O., Maj. Gen. Janet Cobb.
Institution Type/Description: Historic Ship & Military Museum.
Hours & Admission Prices: March-Sept. daily 8-5; Oct.-March daily 8-4. Adults $15, children 6-11 $6; discounts to groups, AARP, AAA & Historic Naval Ships Assoc. members; children under 6 & active duty military personnel no charge. Parking: $5 per vehicle. Closed Christmas. &
Attendance: 414,532 (actual)

Monroeville

MONROE COUNTY HERITAGE MUSEUM, 31 N. Alabama Ave., Monroeville, AL 36460-1818. Tel.: 251-575-7433. Fax: 251-575-2513.
E-mail: mchm@frontiernet.net
Web Site: www.monroecountymuseum.org
Key Personnel: Exec. Dir., Wanda Green; Chm. (V) & Museum Shop Mgr., Robyn Neilsen; Dir. Education, Wanda Green; Dir. Sites & Operations, Nathan Carter; Mgr. Rikard's Mill Museum, Larry Tuberville; Devel. Officer, Gail Deas.
Institution Type/Description: Historic Building: housed in the 1903 Old Monroe County Courthouse; setting for the film To Kill A Mockingbird.
Hours & Admission Prices: June-Sept. Tues.-Fri. 10-4, Sat. 10-2, Oct.-May Tues.-Fri. 10-4, Sat. 10-1. Admission fee for non-members; members no charge. Closed New Year's Day; Martin Luther King Jr. Day; Presidents' Day; Good Friday; Memorial Day; day before Independence Day; Labor Day; Veterans Day; Thanksgiving & day after; Christmas Eve, Day & day after. &
Attendance: 25,000 (estimated)

Montevallo

ALDRICH COAL MINE MUSEUM, 137 Hwy. 203, Montevallo, AL 35115-7105. Tel.: 205-665-2886.
Key Personnel: Owner, Rose Emfinger; Owner, Henry Emfinger.
Institution Type/Description: Coal Mining Museum.
Hours & Admission Prices: Thurs.-Sat. 10-4, Sun. 1-4; other times by appointment. Adults $5, children $3. &

THE AMERICAN VILLAGE, 3727 Hwy. 119 S., Montevallo, AL 35115. Mailing Address: P.O. Box 6, Montevallo, AL 35115-0006. Tel.: 205-665-3535, 877-811-1776 (Toll Free). Fax: 205-665-7577.
E-mail: mpoole@americanvillage.org
Web Site: www.americanvillage.org
Key Personnel: Founder & C.E.O., Tom Walker; Mktg. & Commun., Melanie Poole.
Institution Type/Description: History Museum.
Hours & Admission Prices: Mon.-Fri. 10-4; other times by appointment. &

Montgomery

ALABAMA DEPARTMENT OF ARCHIVES & HISTORY, MUSEUM OF ALABAMA, 624 Washington Ave., Montgomery, AL 36130-3003. Mailing Address: P.O. Box 300100, Montgomery, AL 36130-0100. Tel.: 334-242-4364. Fax: 334-240-3433.
E-mail: tours.archives@archives.alabama.gov
Web Site: www.archives.alabama.gov
Key Personnel: Dir., Steve Murray; Asst. Dir. Government Records, Tracey Berezansky; Collections, Debbie Pendleton.
Institution Type/Description: History Museum.
Hours & Admission Prices: Museum: Mon.-Sat. 8:30-4:30. Archives: Mon.-Sat. 8:30-4:30. Reference Room: Tues.-Fri. 8:30-4:30. No charge. Closed state holidays. &
Attendance: 50,000 (estimated)

ALABAMA STATE CAPITOL, 600 Dexter Ave., Montgomery, AL 36104. Tel.: 334-242-3188. Facebook: @alabamastatecapitoltours.
E-mail: capitoltours@ahc.alabama.gov
Web Site: ahc.alabama.gov/alabama-state-capitol.aspx
Key Personnel: Site Dir., Lisa Franklin.
Institution Type/Description: Historic Building: built in 1851. A National Historic Landmark.
Hours & Admission Prices: Mon.-Fri. 8-4:30, Sat. 9-4. No charge. Closed state holidays. &
Attendance: 100,000 (estimated)

CIVIL RIGHTS MEMORIAL CENTER, 400 Washington Ave., Montgomery, AL 36104. Tel.: 334-956-8200 & 888 414-7752 (Toll Free).
Web Site: civilrightsmemorialcenter.org
Institution Type/Description: History Museum & Memorial.
Hours & Admission Prices: Mon.-Fri. 9-4:30, Sat. 10-4. Adults $2; children no charge.

DEXTER PARSONAGE MUSEUM, 309 S. Jackson St., Montgomery, AL 36104. Tel.: 334-261-3270.
E-mail: dextertour@wowway.com
Web Site: www.dexterkingmemorial.org
Key Personnel: Pres. (V), Rev. Michael F. Thurman.
Institution Type/Description: Historic House Museum: housed in the former home of 12 pastors of the Dexter Avenue King Memorial Baptist Church from 1920-1992. Listed on the National Register of Historic Places.
Hours & Admission Prices: Tours: Tues.-Fri. 10-3, Sat. 10-1; on the hour by reservation only. &

FIRST WHITE HOUSE OF THE CONFEDERACY, 644 Washington Ave., Montgomery, AL 36130-3057. Mailing Address: P.O. Box 1861, Montgomery, AL 36102-1861. Tel.: 334-242-1861.
E-mail: info@firstwhitehouse.org
Web Site: www.firstwhitehouse.org
Key Personnel: Regent, Seibels L. Marshall; Dir., Dr. Robert Wieland; Gift Shop Mgr., Evelyn England.
Institution Type/Description: Historic House Museum: 1832-1835 home of Jefferson Davis & his family in 1861 when Montgomery was the capital of the Confederacy.
Hours & Admission Prices: Mon.-Fri. 8-noon & 1-4:30, Sat. 9-4. No charge; donations accepted. Closed state holidays. &
Attendance: 25,699 (actual)

FREEDOM RIDES MUSEUM, 210 S. Court St., Montgomery, AL 36104. Mailing Address: 468 S. Perry St., P.O. Box 300900, Montgomery, AL 36104. Tel.: 334-414-8647.
E-mail: freedomridesmuseum@gmail.com
Web Site: www.freedomridesmuseum.org
Formerly: Freedom Riders Museum
Key Personnel: Site Dir., Dorothy Walker; Exec. Dir., Frank White.
Institution Type/Description: History Museum: housed in a former Greyhound bus station; built in 1951.
Hours & Admission Prices: Tues.-Sat. 12-4; guided tours by appointment. Adults $5, seniors, military & college students $4, children 6-18 $3. Closed state holidays. &
Attendance: 2,155 (actual)

THE GEORGINE CLARKE ALABAMA ARTIST'S GALLERY, Alabama State Council on the Arts, 201 Monroe St., Montgomery, AL 36104. Mailing Address: Alabama State Council on the Arts, 201 Monroe St., Ste. 110, Montgomery, AL 36130-1800. Tel.: 334-242-4076, ext. 250. Fax: 334-240-3269. Facebook: Alabama State Council on the Arts.
E-mail: staff@arts.alabama.gov
Web Site: arts.alabama.gov
Formerly: Alabama Artist's Gallery
Key Personnel: Dir. Alabama State Council on the Arts, Albert B. Head; Dir. Gallery & Mgr. Visual Arts Program, Elliot Knight.
Institution Type/Description: Art Museum.
Hours & Admission Prices: Mon.-Fri. 8-5. No charge. Closed state holidays. &
Attendance: 10,000 (estimated)

HANK WILLIAMS MUSEUM, 118 Commerce St., Montgomery, AL 36104-2538. Tel.: 334-262-3600.
E-mail: hankwilliamsmuse@bellsouth.net
Web Site: www.thehankwilliamsmuseum.net
Institution Type/Description: History Museum.
Hours & Admission Prices: Mon.-Fri. 9-4:30, Sat. 10-4, Sun. 1-4. Admission 15 & over $10, children 3-14 $3; discounts to groups, military & AAA members; members no charge. &
Attendance: 20,000 (estimated)

HYUNDAI MOTOR MANUFACTURING ALABAMA TOURS, 700 Hyundai Blvd., Montgomery, AL 36105. Tel.: 334-387-8000.
Web Site: hmmausa.com/hmma-tours
Institution Type/Description: Company Museum.
Hours & Admission Prices: By appointment: April-Oct. Mon., Wed. & Fri. 9:30, 12 & 2:30, Thurs. 6:30 pm; Nov.-March Mon., Wed. & Fri. 9:30, 12 & 2:30. Children under 6 not admitted. No charge. Closed Christmas Day & week.

LANDMARKS FOUNDATION/OLD ALABAMA TOWN, 301 Columbus St., Montgomery, AL 36104-2624. Tel.: 334-240-4500, 888-240-1850. Fax: 334-240-4519.
E-mail: c.king@oldalabamatown.com
Web Site: www.oldalabamatown.com
Key Personnel: Exec. Dir., Marion Baab; Cur., Carole King; Dir. Education, Florence Giles; Dir. Mktg., Rosemary Russell; Pres. (V), Sandra Nickel.
Institution Type/Description: Historical & Preservation Society: located in Old Alabama Town Reception Center.
Hours & Admission Prices: Mon.-Sat. 9-4. Adults $10, students 6-18 $5; discount to groups & AAA members; children 5 & under and members no charge. Closed New Year's Day; Thanksgiving; Christmas. &
Attendance: 55,000 (estimated)

MANN WILDLIFE LEARNING MUSEUM, 2301 Coliseum Parkway, Montgomery, AL 36110. Tel.: 334-240-4900 & 625-4905. Fax: 334-240-4916. Facebook: Mann Wildlife Learning Museum.
E-mail: zooinfo@montgomeryal.gov
Web Site: www.montgomeryzoo.com
Key Personnel: Zoo Dir., Doug Goode; Deputy Zoo Dir., Marcia Woodard; Animal Care Mgr., Lisa Peek; Dir. Concessions, Sabrina Townsend; Cur. Education, Jennifer Murphy; Mktg. & Public Rels. Mgr., Sarah McKemey; Mgr. Program Svcs., Steven Pierce; Gift Shop Mgr., Deborah Stewart.
Institution Type/Description: Wildlife Learning Museum
Hours & Admission Prices: Daily 9-5:30. Mann Museum: adults $7, seniors 65 & over and children 3-12 $6. Zoo: adults $15, seniors 65 & over $13, children 3-12 $11. Mann Museum & Zoo: adults $20, seniors 65 & over $18, children 3-12 $15; discounts to groups with two weeks advanced reservation & military; children 2 & under, AAM, AZA & society members no charge. Closed New Year's Day; Thanksgiving; Christmas. &

MONTGOMERY MUSEUM OF FINE ARTS, One Museum Dr., Montgomery, AL 36117-4600. Mailing Address: P.O. Box 230819, Montgomery, AL 36123-0819. Tel.: 334-240-4333. Fax: 334-240-4384.
E-mail: museuminfo@mmfa.org
Web Site: www.mmfa.org
Key Personnel: Dir., Mark M. Johnson; Asst. Dir. Operations, Steve Shuemake; Devel. Officer, Jennifer Eitzmann; Dir. Mktg. & Public Rels., Cynthia Milledge; Cur. Art, Margaret Lynne Ausfeld; Cur. Art, Michael Panhorst; Cur. Art, Jennifer Jankauskas; Asst. Cur. Education, Alice Novak; Registrar, Pamela Bransford; Preparator & Designer, Jeff Dutton; Special Events Coord. & Museum Shop Mgr., Blake Rosen; Museum Shop Mgr., Ward Chesser; Pres. (V), Leslie Sanders.
Institution Type/Description: Art Museum.
Hours & Admission Prices: Tues.-Wed. & Fri.-Sat. 10-5, Thurs. 10-9, Sun. 12-5. No charge; donations accepted. Closed New Year's Day; Veterans Day; Thanksgiving; Christmas. &
Attendance: 143,209 (actual)

THE MOOSEUM, 201 S. Bainbridge St., Montgomery, AL 36104-4332. Tel.: 334-265-1867. Fax: 334-834-5326.
E-mail: info@bamabeef.org
Web Site: www.bamabeef.org/p/about/273
Key Personnel: Coord., Kara Harden.
Institution Type/Description: Children's Museum.
Hours & Admission Prices: Mon.-Fri. 8-12 & 1-4:30 by appointment. No charge; donations accepted. Closed major holidays; special events.
Attendance: 10,000 (estimated)

ROSA PARKS LIBRARY AND MUSEUM, 252 Montgomery St., Montgomery, AL 36104-3527. Tel.: 334-241-8661 & 8615. Fax: 334-241-5435.
E-mail: rosaparks@troy.edu
Web Site: http://www.troy.edu/rosaparks
Institution Type/Description: Library & History Museum.
Hours & Admission Prices: Mon.-Fri. 9-5, Sat. 9-3; groups of 10 or more by appointment. Adults over 12 $5.50, children 12 & under $3.50; discounts to AAA members & Alabama College students. Closed holidays. &
Attendance: 50,095 (actual)

SCOTT & ZELDA FITZGERALD MUSEUM, 919 Felder Ave., Montgomery, AL 36106-1926. Tel.: 334-264-4222. Facebook: The Fitzgerald Museum.
E-mail: thefitzgeraldmuseum@gmail.com
Web Site: www.thefitzgeraldmuseum.org
Key Personnel: Exec. Dir., Sara Powell; Pres. Bd., Dr. Kirk Curnutt.
Institution Type/Description: Literary Museum.
Hours & Admission Prices: Tues.-Sun. 10-3. Suggested Donation: $10. Closed major holidays.
Attendance: 2,784 (estimated)

UNITED STATES AIR FORCE'S ENLISTED HERITAGE HALL, Maxwell-Gunter Air Force Base, 550 McDonald St., Bldg. 1210, Montgomery, AL 36114-3107. Tel.: 334-416-1110.
E-mail: au.ecampussupport@us.af.mil
Web Site: AFEHRI.au.af.mil
Institution Type/Description: Military History Museum.
Hours & Admission Prices: Mon.-Fri. 8-4, Sat. 9-4. Closed holidays.

W.A. GAYLE PLANETARIUM, 1010 Forest Ave., Montgomery, AL 36106-1115. Tel.: 334-625-4799. Facebook: Gayle Planetarium.
E-mail: m01planet@troy.edu
Web Site: troy.edu/planetarium
Key Personnel: Dir. & Museum Shop Mgr., Rick Evans.
Institution Type/Description: Planetarium.
Hours & Admission Prices: Public Shows: Sun. 2pm, Mon.-Thurs. 4pm, 1st & 3rd Sat. 2pm. Admission 5 & over $6.50. School & Group Shows: by appointment. &
Attendance: 30,000 (actual)

Moundville

MOUNDVILLE ARCHAEOLOGICAL PARK, 13075 Moundville Archaeological Park, Moundville, AL 35474-6413. Mailing Address: University of Alabama Museums, P.O. Box 870340, Tuscaloosa, AL 35487-0340. Tel.: 205-371-2234.
E-mail: llrasco@ua.edu
Web Site: moundville.ua.edu

Key Personnel: Dir., Dr. Alexander Benitez; Education Coord., Betsy Irwin; Volunteer Coord., Kenric Minges; Museum Shop Mgr., Janet Wyatt.
Institution Type/Description: Archaeological Site: over two dozen Mississippian mounds and 320-acre park.
Hours & Admission Prices: Park: daily 8-dusk. Museum: call for hours. Adults $8, seniors $7, students & children 5-18 $6; discounts to University of Alabama faculty, staff & students, AAA members & active duty military; children under 5 & Native Americans with tribal membership card no charge. Closed New Year Eve & Day; Easter Sunday; Thanksgiving; Christmas Eve & Day. &
Attendance: 50,000 (estimated)

Normal

STATE BLACK ARCHIVES RESEARCH CENTER AND MUSEUM, AAMU James Hembray Wilson Bldg., 4900 Meridian St. N, Normal, AL 35762. Tel.: 256-372-5846.
E-mail: info@aamu.edu
Web Site: www.aamu.edu
Key Personnel: Dir., Patricia D. Ford.
Institution Type/Description: History Museum.
Hours & Admission Prices: Mon.-Fri. 9-4:30. Adults 12 & over $5, senior citizens $4, children 11 & under $3; discounts to groups; children 5 & under no charge. Closed Martin Luther King Jr. Day; Memorial Day; Independence Day; Labor Day; Thanksgiving; Christmas. &
Attendance: 3,000 (actual)

Northport

KENTUCK MUSEUM ASSOCIATION, INC., 503 Main Ave., Northport, AL 35476-4483. Tel.: 205-758-1257. Fax: 205-758-1258. Facebook: Kentuck Art Center.
E-mail: kentuck@kentuck.org
Web Site: www.kentuck.org
Key Personnel: Exec. Dir., Amy Echols; Pres. Bd. (6/15-6/1/16), Sontonia Stephens; Pres. Bd. (6/16-6/1/17), David Pass; Mgr. Devel., Sherri Warner; Program Mgr., Exa Skinner; Museum Shop Mgr., Curtis Clark.
Institution Type/Description: Art Museum.
Hours & Admission Prices: Tues.-Fri. 9-5, Sat. 10-4:30. No charge; donations accepted. Closed New Year's Day; Memorial Day; Independence Day; Labor Day; Thanksgiving; Christmas.
Attendance: 13,000 (estimated)

Oneonta

BLOUNT COUNTY MEMORIAL MUSEUM, 204 2nd St. N., Oneonta, AL 35121-1740. Mailing Address: P.O. Box 45, Oneonta, AL 35121. Tel.: 205-625-6905. Facebook.
E-mail: arhudy@co.blount.al.us
Web Site: blountmuseum.org
Key Personnel: Dir., Cur. & Museum Shop Mgr., Amy Rhudy.
Institution Type/Description: County History Museum.
Hours & Admission Prices: Tues.-Thurs. 8-5. No charge; donations accepted. &
Attendance: 2,000 (estimated)

Opelika

THE MUSEUM OF EAST ALABAMA, 121 S. 9th St., Opelika, AL 36801-4917. Mailing Address: P.O. Box 3085, Opelika, AL 36803-3085. Tel.: 334-749-2751.
E-mail: museum@eastalabama.org
Web Site: www.eastalabama.org
Key Personnel: Exec. Dir. & Cur., Glenn Buxton; Pres. (V), Jim Hardin; Treas., Elenore Parker.
Institution Type/Description: General Museum.
Hours & Admission Prices: Tues.-Fri. 10-4, Sat. 2-4. No charge; donations accepted. Closed New Year's Day; Memorial Day; Christmas Eve & Day. &
Attendance: 1,386 (estimated)

Orange Beach

ORANGE BEACH INDIAN AND SEA MUSEUM, 25850 John Snook Dr., Orange Beach, AL 36561. Mailing Address: P.O. Box 458, Orange Beach, AL 36561-0458. Tel.: 251-981-8545. Fax: 251-981-6053.
E-mail: jfitz@cityoforangebeach.com
Web Site: obparksandrec.com/artcentermuseum/museum.html
Key Personnel: Museum Guide, Gail Graham.
Institution Type/Description: Historic Building: housed in period schoolhouse.
Hours & Admission Prices: Tues.-Thurs. 9-4; tours by appointment. No charge. &
Attendance: 2,500 (actual)

Pelham

ALABAMA WILDLIFE CENTER, Oak Mountain State Park, 100 Terrace Dr., Pelham, AL 35124-4314. Tel.: 205-663-7930. Fax: 205-682-6867.
E-mail: wildlife@awrc.org
Web Site: www.awrc.org
Formerly: The Wildlife Center
Key Personnel: Chm. (V), Richard Esposito; Exec. Dir., Doug Adair.
Institution Type/Description: Nature & Rehabilitation Center.
Hours & Admission Prices: Daily 9-5. Center: no charge. Park: adults $3, seniors 62 & over and children 6-11 $1; children under 6 no charge. &
Attendance: 10,000 (estimated)

Prattville

AUTAUGA COUNTY HERITAGE ASSOCIATION, 102 E. Main St., Prattville, AL 36067-3114. Tel.: 334-361-0961.
E-mail: director@autaugahistory.org
Web Site: www.autaugahistory.org
Key Personnel: Exec. Dir., Greg Duke; Pres., Louise Jennings.
Institution Type/Description: History Museum.
Hours & Admission Prices: Tues.-Fri. 10-4, Sat. 10-2. No charge; donations accepted. Closed Christmas week. &
Attendance: 1,200 (actual)

Red Bay

RED BAY MUSEUM, 110 4th Ave., S.E., Red Bay, AL 35582. Mailing Address: 400 4th St. S.W., Red Bay, AL 35582. Tel.: 256-356-8758.
E-mail: scottydk@att.net
Web Site: www.redbaymuseum.org
Institution Type/Description: History Museum.
Hours & Admission Prices: Tues. & Thurs. 1:30-4; other times by appointment. Adults $5, students $3; children under 6 no charge.
Attendance: 1,000 (estimated)

Scottsboro

SCOTTSBORO BOYS MUSEUM AND CULTURAL CENTER, 428 W. Willow St., Scottsboro, AL 35768. Mailing Address: P.O. Box 1557, Scottsboro, AL 35768. Tel.: 256-244-1310 & 609-4202.
E-mail: scottsboroboysmuseum@scottsboro.org
Web Site: www.scottsboroboysmuseum.com
Institution Type/Description: History Museum.
Hours & Admission Prices: Call for hours.

SCOTTSBORO JACKSON HERITAGE CENTER, 208 S. Houston St., Scottsboro, AL 35768-4318. Tel.: 256-259-2122. Fax: 256-574-6991. Facebook: Scottsboro-Jackson Heritage Center.
E-mail: heritage@scottsboro.org
Web Site: www.sjhc.us
Key Personnel: Dir., Judi Weaver; Chm. (V), Susan Fisher.
Institution Type/Description: History Museum.
Hours & Admission Prices: Mon.-Fri. 11-4; tours by appointment. No charge; donations accepted. &
Attendance: 1,500 (estimated)

Selma

NATIONAL VOTING RIGHTS MUSEUM AND INSTITUTE, 6 U.S. Hwy. 80 E., Selma, AL 36701. Mailing Address: P.O. Box 1366, Selma, AL 36702-1366. Tel.: 334-526-4340. Fax: 334-418-1991.
E-mail: nvrm1965@gmail.com
Web Site: www.nvrmi.com
Key Personnel: Pres. (V), Rose M. Sanders; Treas., Louretta Wimberly; Interim Dir., Pearlie L. Walker; Chm., Carolyn G. Varner; Chm. (V), Charles Mauldin; Museum Shop Mgr., Lashunda G. Brown; Tour Guide, Sam Walker.
Institution Type/Description: Historical Museum: housed in the former headquarters of the White Citizen's Council of Alabama; located at the foot of the Edmund Pettus Bridge, the site of Bloody Sunday.
Hours & Admission Prices: Mon.-Thurs. 10-4, Fri.-Sun. by appointment only. Adults $6.50, students & seniors 65 & older $4.50; discounts to members, groups and AAM & ICOM members. Closed New Year's Day; Memorial Day; Martin Luther King Jr. Day; Christmas. &
Attendance: 150,000 (estimated)

OLD DEPOT MUSEUM, 4 Martin Luther King St., Selma, AL 36703-3109. Mailing Address: P.O. Box 1392, Selma, AL 36702. Tel.: 334-874-2197.
Institution Type/Description: History Museum.
Hours & Admission Prices: Mon.-Sat. 10-4. Adults $4, seniors $3, college students $2, children $1.

STURDIVANT HALL, 713 Mabry St., Selma, AL 36701-5521. Mailing Address: P.O. Box 1205, Selma, AL 36702-1205. Tel.: 334-872-5626. Fax: 334-872-5626.
E-mail: info@sturdivanthall.com
Key Personnel: Dir., Mary Hansell; Co-Dir., Nancy Gantt; Pres., Anne F. Knight; Museum Shop Mgr., Patty DeBardeleben.
Institution Type/Description: Historic House Museum: 1852 Sturdivant Hall.
Hours & Admission Prices: Tues.-Sat. 10-4. Adults $5, students $2. Closed major holidays. &
Attendance: 17,500 (estimated)

Stevenson

STEVENSON RAILROAD DEPOT MUSEUM, 207 W. Main St., Stevenson, AL 35772-3567. Tel.: 256-437-3012.
E-mail: info@stevensondepotmuseum.com
Key Personnel: Dir., Loretta Barbee.
Institution Type/Description: Historic Building Museum: built in 1872. Listed on the National Register of Historic Places.
Hours & Admission Prices: Mon.-Fri. 8-4. No charge; donations accepted. &
Attendance: 15,000 (estimated)

Summerdale

ALLIGATOR ALLEY, 19950 Hwy. 71, Summerdale, AL 36580. Tel.: 866-994-2867, 251-946-2483. Facebook: Gator Alley Farm.
E-mail: info@gatoralleyfarm.com
Web Site: gatoralleyfarm.com
Key Personnel: Owner, Wes Moore.
Institution Type/Description: Alligator Farm.
Hours & Admission Prices: Thurs.-Tues. 10-5. Adults $10, children 4-12 $8; children under 3 no charge.

Sylacauga

ISABEL ANDERSON COMER MUSEUM & ARTS CENTER, 711 N. Broadway, Sylacauga, AL 35150-2155. Mailing Address: P.O. Box 245, Sylacauga, AL 35150-0245. Tel.: 256-245-4016. Facebook: Comer Museum & Arts Center.
E-mail: comercenter@bellsouth.net
Web Site: comermuseum.weebly.com
Key Personnel: Exec. Dir., Donna Rentfrow; Bd. Pres., Don Smith; Asst. Dir., Linda Pearson.
Institution Type/Description: History & Art Museum.
Hours & Admission Prices: Tues.-Fri. 10-5; other times by appointment. No charge; donations accepted. Closed major holidays. &
Attendance: 14,200 (estimated)

Talladega

JEMISON-CARNEGIE HERITAGE HALL, 200 South St., Talladega, AL 35160. Mailing Address: P.O. Box 1118, Talladega, AL 35161. Tel.: 256-761-1364. Facebook: Heritage Hall.
E-mail: hhmuse@bellsouth.net
Web Site: heritagehallmuseum.org
Key Personnel: Coord. Museum Svcs., Kelly Williams; Pres. (V), George Hartsfield.
Institution Type/Description: Historic Building: housed in the former Talladega Public Library; built in 1906.
Hours & Admission Prices: Tues.-Fri. 10-4. No charge; donations accepted. &
Attendance: 4,000 (estimated)

Theodore

BELLINGRATH GARDENS & HOME, 12401 Bellingrath Gardens Rd., Theodore, AL 36582-8496. Tel.: 251-973-2217 & 800-247-8420. Fax: 251-973-0540.
E-mail: bellingrath@bellingrath.org
Web Site: www.bellingrath.org
Key Personnel: Exec. Dir., William E. Barrick, Ph.D.; Museum Dir., Thomas C. McGehee.
Institution Type/Description: Botanical Garden & Home.

Hours & Admission Prices: Home: daily 9-4. Gardens, Home & River Cruise $27. Gardens & Home: $19. Gardens: $11. Closed Thanksgiving; Christmas. &
Attendance: 169,000 (actual)

Thomasville

KATHRYN TUCKER WINDHAM MUSEUM, Coastal Alabama Community College, Library Bldg., 30755 U.S. Highway 43, Thomasville, AL 36784. Mailing Address: P.O. Box 2000, Thomasville, AL 36784. Tel.: 334-636-9642. Fax: 334-636-1380. Facebook: Kathryn Tucker Windham Museum.
E-mail: deborah.rankins@coastalalabama.edu
Web Site: www.coastalalabama.edu/about/kathryn_tucker_windham_museum
Key Personnel: Asst. Dir. Library Svcs., Deborah Rankins.
Institution Type/Description: History Museum.
Hours & Admission Prices: Mon.-Thurs. 7:30-5, Fri. 7:30-3..

Troy

JOHNSON CENTER FOR THE ARTS, 300 E. Walnut St., Troy, AL 36081-3539. Mailing Address: P.O. Box 863, Troy, AL 36081-0863. Tel.: 334-670-2287. Fax: 334-808-4025.
E-mail: vicki@tpcac.org
Formerly: Troy-Pike Cultural Arts Center
Key Personnel: Exec. Dir., Vicki Gaines Pritchett; Chm. (V), Mack Gibson; Devel. Coord., Wiley B. White; Exhibitions Coord., Walter Black.
Institution Type/Description: Art Museum.
Hours & Admission Prices: Wed.-Fri. 10-5, Sat. 10-3. No charge; donations accepted. Closed holidays. &
Attendance: 800 (estimated)

PIONEER MUSEUM OF ALABAMA, 248 Hwy. 31 N., Troy, AL 36081. Tel.: 334-566-3597.
E-mail: pioneer@troycable.net
Web Site: www.pioneer-museum.org
Formerly: Pike Pioneer Museum
Key Personnel: C.E.O., Jeff Kervin; Dir., Kari Barley.
Institution Type/Description: History Museum.
Hours & Admission Prices: Tues.-Sat. 9-5. Adults $6, seniors 60 & over $5, students $4; discounts to military, AAM & ICOM members; members no charge. Closed major holidays. &
Attendance: 10,000 (actual)

Tuscaloosa

ALABAMA MUSEUM OF NATURAL HISTORY, Smith Hall, University of Alabama Campus, 427 6th Ave., Tuscaloosa, AL 35487. Mailing Address: Box 870340, Tuscaloosa, AL 35487. Tel.: 205-348-7550 & 7551. Fax: 205-348-9292. Facebook: Alabama Museum of Natural History.
E-mail: museum.programs@ua.edu
Web Site: www.almnh.ua.edu
Key Personnel: Education Coord., Allie Sorlie; Museum Dir., Dr. John Friel; Coord. Environmental Education & Programs, Dr. Douglas Phillips; Museum Naturalist, Todd Hester.
Institution Type/Description: Natural History Museum.
Hours & Admission Prices: Smith Hall Museum: Mon.-Sat. 10-4:30. Adults $2, children $1; members no charge. Closed university holidays. &
Attendance: 32,000 (estimated)

BATTLE-FRIEDMAN HOUSE, 1010 Greensboro Ave., Tuscaloosa, AL 35401-2336. Mailing Address: P.O. Box 1665, Tuscaloosa, AL 35403-1665. Tel.: 205-758-6138. Fax: 205-758-8163. Facebook: Battle-Friedman House; Twitter & Pinterest: TuscPreserveSoc.
E-mail: info@historictuscaloosa.org
Web Site: www.historictuscaloosa.org
Key Personnel: Dir., Katherine Richter.
Institution Type/Description: Historic House: built in 1835. Listed on the National Register of Historic Places.
Hours & Admission Prices: Tues.-Fri. 10-12 & 1-4, Sat. by appointment. Admission $5; discounts to groups; children under 12 no charge. Closed major holidays & during scheduled events. &
Attendance: 450 (estimated)

CHILDREN'S HANDS-ON MUSEUM (CHOM), 2213 University Blvd., Tuscaloosa, AL 35401-1541. Tel.: 205-349-4235. Fax: 205-349-4272.
E-mail: info@chomonline.org

Web Site: www.chomonline.org
Key Personnel: Exec. Dir. & Dir. Exhibits, Charlotte Gibson; Chm. (V), Kim S. Hudson; Visitors Svcs. Coord. & Volunteer Coord., Sherie Giles; Membership Coord., LaKesa Grey; Museum Shop Mgr., Pam Hisey.
Institution Type/Description: Children's Museum.
Hours & Admission Prices: Mon.-Fri. 9-5, Sat. 10-4. Admission 3 & over $8, seniors over 60 $6, children 1-3 $5; discounts to groups & scouts; members & children under one no charge. ACM reciprocal members. Holiday or Summer Pass: $36 (3 months). Closed major holidays. &
Attendance: 59,680 (actual)

GORGAS HOUSE MUSEUM, 810 Capstone Dr., University of Alabama, Tuscaloosa, AL 35487. Mailing Address: University of Alabama Museums, Box 870340, Tuscaloosa, AL 35487. Tel.: 205-348-5906 & 7550. Fax: 205-348-9292.
E-mail: gorgashouse@ua.edu
Web Site: gorgashouse.ua.edu
Key Personnel: Dir., Lydia Ellington.
Institution Type/Description: Historic House: built in 1829 as a dining hall for students, home of Josiah & Amelia Gayle Gorgas and family from 1878-1953 & one of four buildings to survive the burning of the campus in 1865 by federal troops.
Hours & Admission Prices: Mon.-Fri. 9-12 & 1-4:30; other times by appointment. Admission $2. University of Alabama students, faculty, staff and alumni with card no charge. Closed university holidays. &
Attendance: 3,236 (actual)

JEMISON-VAN DE GRAAFF MANSION, 1305 Greensboro Ave., Tuscaloosa, AL 35401-2840. Mailing Address: P.O. Box 1216, Tuscaloosa, AL 35403-1216. Tel.: 205-758-2906.
E-mail: jemisonmansion1305@gmail.com
Web Site: www.jemisonmansion.com
Institution Type/Description: Historic House: housed in the former home of Senator Robert Jemison, Jr.; built in 1862.
Hours & Admission Prices: Mon.-Fri. 10-5; groups by appointment. No charge; donations accepted.

MURPHY AFRICAN AMERICAN MUSEUM, 2601 Paul W. Bryant Dr., Tuscaloosa, AL 35401-2214. Tel.: 205-758-2861. Fax: 205-758-8163.
E-mail: jmelton11@comcast.net
Web Site: www.historictuscaloosa.org
Key Personnel: Dir. & Chm. (V), Emma Jean Melton.
Institution Type/Description: History Museum: housed in the home of Tuscaloosa's first licensed black mortician; built c. 1920.
Hours & Admission Prices: Tues.-Fri. 10-3; tours by appointment. No charge; donations accepted. &
Attendance: 3,000 (estimated)

THE OLD TAVERN MUSEUM, 500 28th Ave.-Capitol Park, Tuscaloosa, AL 35401. Mailing Address: P.O. Box 1665, Tuscaloosa, AL 35403-1665. Tel.: 205-758-1998. Fax: 205-758-8163. Facebook: The Old Tavern Museum.
E-mail: info@historictuscaloosa.org
Web Site: www.historictuscaloosa.org
Key Personnel: Exec. Dir., Katherine Richter.
Institution Type/Description: Historic House Museum: 1827 Old Tavern, relocated on Capitol Park, the site of the Capitol Building when Alabama's Capitol was in Tuscaloosa.
Hours & Admission Prices: By appointment only. No charge; donations accepted. Closed major holidays.
Attendance: 200 (estimated)

PAUL W. BRYANT MUSEUM, 300 Paul W. Bryant Dr., Tuscaloosa, AL 35487. Mailing Address: P.O. Box 870385, Tuscaloosa, AL 35487-0385. Tel.: 205-348-4668, 866-772-2327. Fax: 205-348-8883.
E-mail: info@bryantmuseum.com
Web Site: www.bryantmuseum.com
Key Personnel: Dir., Kenneth Gaddy; Visitor Svcs. Coord., Jan Scurlock; Cur., Taylor Watson; Collections Asst., Brad Green; Program Asst., Olivia Arnold; Cashier, Lynn Bobo; Museum Shop Mgr., Melinda Register; Audio Visual Tech, David Mize; Cashier, DiAnne Griffin.
Institution Type/Description: Sport Museum.
Hours & Admission Prices: Daily 9-4; call for holiday hours. Adults $2, senior citizens 60 & over, students and children 6-17 $1; children under 6, alumni & members no charge. Closed major holidays. &
Attendance: 40,000 (estimated)

SARAH MOODY GALLERY OF ART, THE UNIVERSITY OF ALABAMA, 103 Garland Hall, Tuscaloosa, AL 35487. Mailing Address: Box 870270, Tuscaloosa, AL 35487-0270. Tel.: 205-348-1891 & 5967 (art dept.). Fax: 205-348-0287.
E-mail: vrial@art.as.ua.edu
Web Site: art.ua.edu/gallery/smga/
Key Personnel: Dir., Bill Dooley; Exhibitions Coord., Vicki Rial.
Institution Type/Description: Art Gallery.
Hours & Admission Prices: Sept.-June Mon.-Wed. & Fri. 9-4:30, Thurs. 9-8. No charge. Closed university holidays. &
Attendance: 10,000

STILLMAN ART GALLERY, Stillman College, Cordell Wynn Humanities and Fine Arts Center, Tuscaloosa, AL 35403. Mailing Address: P.O. Box 1430, Tuscaloosa, AL 35403-1430. Tel.: 205-248-3404.
E-mail: ldawson@stillman.edu
Web Site: www.stillman.edu
Key Personnel: Asst. Prof. & Dir. Galleries, Leonard Dawson.
Institution Type/Description: Art Gallery.
Hours & Admission Prices: Mon.-Fri. 9-5.

TUSCALOOSA MUSEUM OF ART, 1400 Jack Warner Pkwy, N. E., Tuscaloosa, AL 35404. Mailing Address: 2700 Yacht Club Way, Tuscaloosa, AL 35406-1125. Tel.: 205-562-5280. Fax: 205-562-5012.
E-mail: whawkins@westervelt.com
Web Site: www.tuscaloosamoa.org
Formerly: Westervelt-Warner Museum of American Art
Institution Type/Description: Art Museum.
Hours & Admission Prices: Tues.-Sat. 10-6, Sun. 1-6. Adults $9, seniors 65 & over $8, students 10 years old to college age $7; members no charge. &
Attendance: 15,000 (estimated)

UNIVERSITY OF ALABAMA ARBORETUM, 4801 Arboretum Way, Tuscaloosa, AL 35404-5424. Mailing Address: Box 870344, Tuscaloosa, AL 35487-0344. Tel.: 205-553-3278. Fax: 205-553-3728.
E-mail: ua.arboretum@ua.edu
Web Site: www.arboretum.ua.edu
Key Personnel: Pres. (V), Julia Hartman; Asst. Dir., Mary Jo Modica; Caretaker, Kenneth Robinson.
Institution Type/Description: Arboretum & Botanical Garden.
Hours & Admission Prices: Daily 8am to sunset. No charge; donations accepted. Closed New Year's Day; Thanksgiving; Christmas.
Attendance: 7,000 (estimated)

Tuscumbia

ALABAMA MUSIC HALL OF FAME, 617 Hwy. 72 W., Tuscumbia, AL 35674-8711. Mailing Address: P.O. Box 740405, Tuscumbia, AL 35674-7417. Tel.: 256-381-4417. Fax: 256-248-4817.
E-mail: dconnell@alamhof.org
Web Site: www.alamhof.ocm
Institution Type/Description: Music Museum.
Hours & Admission Prices: Tues.-Sat. 9-5. Adults $10, senior citizens 55 & over & students 13-18 $8, children 6-12 $6; discounts to AAA, military & groups of 10 or more; children 5 & under no charge. Closed New Year's Day; Easter; Thanksgiving & day after; Christmas Eve & Day. &
Attendance: 35,000 (actual)

BELLE MONT MANSION, 1569 Cook Lane, Tuscumbia, AL 35674. Mailing Address: 12280 AL Hwy. 20, Hillsboro, AL 35643-3808. Tel.: 256-381-5052.
E-mail: info@bellemontmansion.org
Web Site: www.bellemontmansion.org
Key Personnel: Dir., Ninon Parker; Mgr., Joy Caitlin Moore.
Institution Type/Description: Historic House: built c. 1828-1832.
Hours & Admission Prices: Wed.-Sat. 10-4; groups by appointment. Adults $6, seniors & military $5, children 6-18 $3; children under 6 no charge. Closed state & federal holidays.
Attendance: 2,000 (actual)

IVY GREEN, BIRTHPLACE OF HELEN KELLER, 300 N. Commons St., W., Tuscumbia, AL 35674-1134. Tel.: 256-383-4066. Fax: 256-383-4068.
E-mail: helenkellerbirthplace@comcast.net

Web Site: helenkellerbirthplace.org
Key Personnel: Mgr., Sue Pilkilton.
Institution Type/Description: Historic House Museum: 1820, birthplace of Helen Keller; main house, birthplace cottage, kitchen, carriage house, memorial gardens.
Hours & Admission Prices: Mon.-Sat. 8:30-4. Adults $6, AAA members & seniors $5, student 5-18 $2; discount to groups; children under 5 no charge. Closed New Year's Day; Easter; Labor Day; Thanksgiving; Christmas Eve, Day & day after. &
Attendance: 35,000

TENNESSEE VALLEY ART CENTER, 511 N. Water St., Tuscumbia, AL 35674-1931. Mailing Address: P.O. Box 474, Tuscumbia, AL 35674-0474. Tel.: 256-383-0533. Fax: 256-383-0535.
E-mail: tvaa@comcast.net
Web Site: www.tvaa.net
Key Personnel: Exec. Dir., Mary Settle Cooney; Asst. Dir., Jim Berryman; Chm. (V), Verna Brennan; Dir. Mktg. & Devel., Kay Brackin; Program Asst., Lori Curtis; Administrative Asst., J.K. Keith McMurtrey.
Institution Type/Description: Art Center.
Hours & Admission Prices: Mon.-Fri. 9-5, Sun. 1-3. Adults $5; members no charge. Closed Easter; Memorial Day; Labor Day; Thanksgiving; Christmas. &
Attendance: 60,000 (actual)

Tuskegee Institute

TUSKEGEE INSTITUTE NATIONAL HISTORIC SITE, 1200 W. Montgomery Rd., Tuskegee Institute, AL 36088. Mailing Address: 1212 W. Montgomery Rd., Tuskegee, AL 36088. Tel.: 334-727-3200. Fax: 334-727-1448. Facebook: @tuskegeenps.
E-mail: shirley_baxter@nps.gov
Web Site: www.nps.gov/tuin
Key Personnel: Supt., Sandy Taylor; Museum Shop Mgr., Shirley Baxter.
Institution Type/Description: History Museum: The George Washington Carver Museum; 1899 The Oaks, home of Booker T. Washington.
Hours & Admission Prices: Tuskegee Institute National Historic Site: daily 9-4:30, George Washington Carver Museum: Mon-Sat. 9-4:30, The Oaks: Tues.-Sat. tours at 9:30, 10:30, 1:30, 2:30 & 3:30. No charge. Closed New Year's Day; Thanksgiving; Christmas. &
Attendance: 490,861 (estimated)

Valley

THE MUSEUM AT THE CANNERY, 61st St., Valley, AL 36854. Mailing Address: P.O. Box 186, Valley, AL 36854. Tel.: 334-756-5228. Fax: 334-756-4922.
Institution Type/Description: History Museum.
Hours & Admission Prices: Call for hours.

Vance

MERCEDES-BENZ VISITOR CENTER AND MUSEUM, 6 Mercedes Dr., Vance, AL 35490-2900. Mailing Address: 1 Mercedes Drive, Vance, AL 35490. Tel.: 888-286-8762 (Toll Free), 205-507-2252.
E-mail: visitorcenter@mbusi.com
Web Site: www.mbusi.com/visitorcenter/vc-museum
Institution Type/Description: Transportation Museum.
Hours & Admission Prices: Visitor Center: Mon.-Fri. 8:30-4. No charge. Plant Tours: Mon. & Wed. 9, 9:15, 12:30 & 12:45 by appointment. Admission $5 per person; MBUSI team members & their families no charge. Children under 12 not admitted on tour. Closed major holidays.

Vinemont

CROOKED CREEK CIVIL WAR MUSEUM, 516 County Rd. 1127, Vinemont, AL 35179. Tel.: 256-739-2741.
Key Personnel: Dir. Pres. (V) & Museum Shop Mgr., Fred Wise; Chm. (V), Mike Wise.
Institution Type/Description: Military Museum: housed on the site of the Crooked Creek Civil War Battle.
Hours & Admission Prices: Daily 9-6. Adults $5.
Attendance: 2,000 (estimated)

ECHOTA CHEROKEE INTERPRETIVE CENTER, 630 County Rd. 1281, Vinemont, AL 35622. Mailing Address: P.O. Box 768, Falkville, AL 35622-0768. Tel.: 256-734-7337.
E-mail: echotacherokeetribe4@yahoo.com
Web Site: echotacherokeetribe.homestead.com

Key Personnel: Principal Chief, Stanley Trimm.
Institution Type/Description: Native American History Center.
Hours & Admission Prices: Mon.-Wed. 8-4, Thurs. 8-12. No charge.

Waterloo

EDITH NEWMAN CULVER MEMORIAL MUSEUM, 501 Main St., Waterloo, AL 35677. Mailing Address: Florence/Lauderdale Tourism, 200 Jim Spain Dr, Florence, AL 35630. Tel.: 256-767-6081.
E-mail: alison@visitflorenceal.com
Web Site: www.visitflorenceal.com/things-to-do/history/
Institution Type/Description: Historic House Museum: built in 1870.
Hours & Admission Prices: May-Oct. Sun. 1-5. &

Wetumpka

FORT TOULOUSE/JACKSON PARK, 2521 W. Fort Toulouse Rd., Wetumpka, AL 36093-1112. Tel.: 334-567-3002.
E-mail: ftjack1@bellsouth.net
Web Site: www.forttoulouse.com
Key Personnel: Park Dir., Ove Jenson; Living History Program Coord. & Archaeologist, Ned Jenkins.
Institution Type/Description: Park & Historic Site.
Hours & Admission Prices: Park: April-Oct. daily 7-7; Nov.-March daily 7-5. Visitor Center: daily 9-4; groups by appointment. Adults $2, children 6-18 $1; discounts to groups. Closed New Year's Day; Thanksgiving; Christmas.

ALASKA

(88 listings)

Anaktuvuk Pass

NORTH SLOPE BOROUGH PLANNING DEPT. - THE SIMON PANEAK MEMORIAL MUSEUM, 341 Mekiana Rd., Anaktuvuk Pass, AK 99721. Mailing Address: P.O. Box 21085, Anaktuvuk Pass, AK 99721-0085. Tel.: 907-661-3413. Facebook: Simon Paneak Memorial Museum.
E-mail: vicky.monahan@north-slope.org
Web Site: north-slope.org
Key Personnel: Cur., Vicky Monahan.
Institution Type/Description: Local History and Ethnographic Museum.
Hours & Admission Prices: Mon.-Fri. 8:30-5. Adults $10. &
Attendance: 800 (estimated)

Anchorage

ALASKA AVIATION MUSEUM, 4721 Aircraft Dr., Anchorage, AK 99502-1080. Tel.: 907-248-5325. Facebook: Alaska Aviation Heritage Museum.
E-mail: admin@alaskaairmuseum.org
Web Site: www.alaskaairmuseum.org
Formerly: Alaska Aviation Heritage Museum
Key Personnel: Exec. Dir., Phyllis Kilgore; Cur., Colls. & Exhibs., Darian La Tocha.
Institution Type/Description: Aeronautics Museum.
Hours & Admission Prices: Tues.-Sat. 10-5. Adults $17, seniors 65 & over & veterans $14, children 5-17 $10; family 2 adults, 3 children $5; children under 5 & members no charge. &
Attendance: 20,000 (actual)

ALASKA BOTANICAL GARDEN, 4601 Campbell Airstrip Rd., Anchorage, AK 99507. Tel.: 907-770-3692.
E-mail: garden@alaskabg.org
Web Site: alaskabg.org
Institution Type/Description: Botanical Garden.
Hours & Admission Prices: See website for hours. Summer: adults $12, seniors, military & students $10, youth 7-17 $8; members & children 6 & under no charge.

ALASKA HERITAGE MUSEUM, 301 W. Northern Lights Blvd., Ste. 103, Anchorage, AK 99503-2652. Tel.: 907-313-7018. Facebook: Wells Fargo.
E-mail: wfmuseum.ak@wellsfargo.com
Web Site: www.wellsfargohistory.com/museums/anchorage/
Formerly: Heritage Library Museum
Institution Type/Description: Alaskan Heritage & Company Museum: housed in the Wells Fargo Rgnl. Corp. Headquarters.

Hours & Admission Prices: Mon.-Fri. 12-4. No charge. Closed bank holidays. ৬

ALASKA JEWISH MUSEUM, 1221 E. 35th Ave., Anchorage, AK 99508-4258. Tel.: 907-770-7021. Fax: 907-279-7890.
E-mail: museum@alaskajewishcampus.org
Web Site: www.alaskajewishmuseum.com
Institution Type/Description: History Museum.
Hours & Admission Prices: mid-Oct. to mid-May Sun.-Thurs. 1-6. Mid-May to mid-Oct. Sun.-Fri. 1-6. Adults $10, seniors, military & students with ID $7, children 3-12 $5.

ALASKA MASONIC LIBRARY AND MUSEUM, 518 E. 14th Ave., Anchorage, AK 99501. Mailing Address: P.O. Box 190668, Anchorage, AK 99519.
Institution Type/Description: Library & History Museum.
Hours & Admission Prices: Call for hours. ৬

ALASKA MUSEUM OF SCIENCE & NATURE, 201 N. Bragaw, Anchorage, AK 99508-1311. Tel.: 907-274-2400. Facebook: Alaska Museum of Science & Nature.
E-mail: akscimuseum1@gmail.com
Web Site: www.alaskamuseum.org
Formerly: Alaska Museum of Natural History
Key Personnel: Mgr. Collections, Sam Winer.
Institution Type/Description: Natural History, Science & Technology Museum.
Hours & Admission Prices: Thurs.-Sat. 10-4. Adults $8, seniors & military with ID $7, youth 3-18 $6; members & children under 3 no charge. Closed New Year's Day, Memorial Day, Independence Day, Thanksgiving & Christmas. ৬
Attendance: 20,000 (actual)

ALASKA NATIVE HERITAGE CENTER, 8800 Heritage Center Dr., Anchorage, AK 99504-6100. Tel.: 907-330-8000; 855-330-8085. Fax: 907-330-8030.
E-mail: aes@alaskanative.net
Web Site: www.alaskanative.net
Key Personnel: Exec. Dir., Emily Edenshaw.
Institution Type/Description: Cultural Center.
Hours & Admission Prices: Mid-May to mid-Sept. daily 9-5; Winter: see website for hours. Adults $28.95, seniors 65 & over $24.95, children 4-17 $18.95; discounts to Alaska residents. ৬
Attendance: 100,000 (estimated)

ALASKA ZOO, 4731 O'Malley Rd., Anchorage, AK 99507-6573. Tel.: 907-346-2133. Fax: 907-346-2673.
E-mail: plampi@alaskazoo.org
Web Site: www.alaskazoo.org
Key Personnel: Exec. Dir., Patrick Lampi; Chief Business Officer, Tristan Thon; Animal Cur., Shannon Jensen.
Institution Type/Description: Zoo.
Hours & Admission Prices: See website for hours. Admission $12; children 2 & under and members no charge. ৬
Attendance: 189,481 (actual)

ANCHORAGE MUSEUM, 625 C St., Anchorage, AK 99501. Tel.: 907-929-9200. Facebook: Anchorage Museum.
E-mail: museum@anchoragemuseum.org
Web Site: www.anchoragemuseum.org
Formerly: Anchorage Museum at Rasmuson Center
Key Personnel: Dir. & C.E.O., Julie Decker; Chief Cur., Francesca DuBrock.
Institution Type/Description: Art, History & Science Museum.
Hours & Admission Prices: May-Sept. Wed.-Sat. 9-6. Winter: see website for hours. Adults $20, residents $17, senior citizens, students & military $15, children 6-12 $10; discounts to AAA, Lifebalance & Reciprocal Museum members; first Fri., members & children 5 & under no charge. ৬
Attendance: 200,000 (estimated)

FRATERNAL ORDER OF ALASKA STATE TROOPERS MUSEUM, 245 W. 5th Ave., Ste. 113, Anchorage, AK 99501. Tel.: 907-279-5050. Facebook: FOAST Law Enforcement Museum.
E-mail: admin@foast.org
Web Site: www.alaskatroopermuseum.com
Key Personnel: Dir., Eugene Harnett.
Institution Type/Description: History Museum.
Hours & Admission Prices: Mon.-Fri. 10-4, Sat. 12-4. Adults $5, military, law enforcement, seniors, youth 12-17 $3; members & children under 12 no charge. ৬
Attendance: 5,500 (actual)

INTERNATIONAL GALLERY OF CONTEMPORARY ART, 427 D St., Anchorage, AK 99501-2325. Tel.: 907-279-1116.
E-mail: igcamanager@igcaalaska.org
Web Site: www.igcaalaska.org
Key Personnel: Mgr., Elissa Meyers.
Institution Type/Description: Art Gallery.
Hours & Admission Prices: Tues.-Sun. 12-4.

THE OSCAR ANDERSON HOUSE MUSEUM, 420 M St., (in Elderberry Park), Anchorage, AK 99501-1929. Tel.: 907-274-2336.
E-mail: akpreservation@gmail.com
Institution Type/Description: Historic House: housed in a bungalow style, one and a half story home, built in 1915.
Hours & Admission Prices: May-Sept. Mon.-Sat. 12-4. Adults 13 & over $10, children, Alaska residents & seniors $5; members no charge.
Attendance: 3,559 (actual)

THE ULU FACTORY TOUR, 211 W. Ship Creek Ave., Anchorage, AK 99501-1603. Tel.: 800-478-3119 (Inside AK); 800-488-5592 (Outside AK). Fax: 907-276-3118.
E-mail: info@theulufactory.com
Web Site: theulufactory.com
Institution Type/Description: Company Museum.
Hours & Admission Prices: See website for hours.

Anvik

ANVIK HISTORICAL SOCIETY AND MUSEUM, Main Rd., Anvik, AK 99558. Mailing Address: P.O. Box 110, Anvik, AK 99558-0110. Tel.: 907-663-6360.
E-mail: donnamac@mcgrathalaska.net
Key Personnel: Dir., Donna MacAlpine.
Institution Type/Description: Historical Society Museum.
Hours & Admission Prices: Summer: by appointment. No charge; donations accepted.
Attendance: 250 (estimated)

Barrow

INUPIAT HERITAGE CENTER, 5421 North Star St., Barrow, AK 99723. Mailing Address: P.O. Box 69, Barrow, AK 99723-0069. Tel.: 907-852-0422.
Web Site: www.north-slope.org
Key Personnel: Dir., Reanne Tupaaq Johnson; Deputy Dir., Colleen Akpik-Lemen; Museum Shop Mgr., Debbie Suvlu.
Institution Type/Description: Heritage Center.
Hours & Admission Prices: mid-May to mid-Sept. Mon.-Fri. 8:30-5. Adults $10, youth 7-17 $5; seniors 60 & over and North Slope residents no charge. ৬
Attendance: 16,260 (actual)

Bethel

YUPIIT PICIRYARAIT CULTURAL CENTER AND MUSEUM, 420 Chief Eddie Hoffman Hwy., Bethel, AK 99559. Mailing Address: P.O. Box 368, Bethel, AK 99559. Tel.: 907-543-1819.
E-mail: tsupport@avcp.org
Web Site: www.alaska.org/detail/yupiit-piciryarait-cultural-center-and-museum
Institution Type/Description: Regional Tribal Museum.
Hours & Admission Prices: Mon.-Fri. 1-4. ৬

Central

CIRCLE DISTRICT MUSEUM, 1275 Mile Steese Hwy., Central, AK 99730. Mailing Address: P.O. Box 1893, Central, AK 99730. Tel.: 907-520-1893.
E-mail: info@steesehighway.org
Web Site: steesehighway.org
Institution Type/Description: History Museum.
Hours & Admission Prices: Memorial Day to Labor Day daily 12-5; Winter: by appointment.

Copper Center

GEORGE I. ASHBY MEMORIAL MUSEUM, Mile 101 Old Richardson Hwy., Copper Center Loop Rd., Copper Center, AK 99573. Mailing Address: P.O. Box 84, Copper Center, AK 99573-0084. Tel.: 907-822-3922.
Institution Type/Description: History Museum.

Hours & Admission Prices: May 15 to Sept. 15 daily 10-5. No charge; donations accepted.
Attendance: 3,448 (actual)

Cordova

CORDOVA HISTORICAL MUSEUM, 622 Main St., Cordova, AK 99574. Tel.: 907-424-6665.
E-mail: curator@cordovamuseum.org
Institution Type/Description: General Museum.
Hours & Admission Prices: Call for hours and admissions. &
Attendance: 12,000 (actual)

ILANKA CULTURAL CENTER, 110 Nicholoff Way, Cordova, AK 99574. Mailing Address: P.O. Box 322, Cordova, AK 99574-1388. Tel.: 907-424-7903. Fax: 907-424-3018.
E-mail: brooke.mallory@eyak-nsn.gov
Web Site: www.nveyak.com
Key Personnel: Deputy Dir., Brooke Mallory.
Institution Type/Description: Cultural Center.
Hours & Admission Prices: Mon.-Fri. 10-5. No charge; donations accepted. Closed holidays. &
Attendance: 2,500 (estimated)

Delta Junction

SULLIVAN ROADHOUSE HISTORICAL MUSEUM, Mile 1422 Alaska Hwy., Delta Junction, AK 99737. Mailing Address: P.O. Box 987, Delta Junction, AK 99737-0987. Tel.: 907-895-5068. Fax: 907-895-5141.
E-mail: deltacc@deltachamber.org
Web Site: www.deltachamber.org
Institution Type/Description: Historic House Museum: built in 1905 by John and Florence Sullivan.
Hours & Admission Prices: See website for hours & admissions.
Attendance: 24,000 (estimated)

Dillingham

SAMUEL K. FOX MUSEUM, 306 D St. West, Dillingham, AK 99576. Mailing Address: P.O. Box 273, Dillingham, AK 99576-0273. Tel.: 907-842-4831.
E-mail: samfoxmuseum@nushtel.net
Web Site: www.alaska.org/detail/samuel-k.-fox-museum
Institution Type/Description: Alaskan Native & Indian Museum.
Hours & Admission Prices: Mon.-Fri. 10-5:30, Sat. 10-2. No charge; donations accepted. &
Attendance: 7,500 (estimated)

Eagle

EAGLE HISTORICAL SOCIETY & MUSEUMS, 3rd & Chamberlain, Eagle, AK 99738. Mailing Address: P.O. Box 23, Eagle, AK 99738-0023. Tel.: 907-547-2325.
E-mail: ehsmdirector@gmail.com
Web Site: www.eaglehistoricalsociety.com
Key Personnel: Dir. & Cur. Education, Donna Westphal.
Institution Type/Description: Local History Museum: housed in 1900 courthouse; 1898 U.S. Army Mule Barn; 1900-1911 U.S. Army Post Fort Egbert all located in the first city incorporated in interior Alaska.
Hours & Admission Prices: Tour: Memorial Day to Labor Day daily 9am; other times by appointment. Adults $7; discounts to AAM & NHA members; members & children under 12 no charge.
Attendance: 6,800 (estimated)

Eagle River

EAGLE RIVER NATURE CENTER, 32750 Eagle River Rd., Eagle River, AK 99577. Tel.: 907-694-2108. Fax: 907-694-2119.
E-mail: info@ernc.org
Web Site: www.ernc.org
Key Personnel: Exec. Dir., Asta Spurgis.
Institution Type/Description: Nature Center.
Hours & Admission Prices: See website for hours and admissions.

Fairbanks

ALASKA HOUSE ART GALLERY, 1003 Cushman St., Fairbanks, AK 99701-4618. Mailing Address: P.O. Box 70501, Fairbanks, AK 99707-0501. Tel.: 907-456-6449.
E-mail: info@thealaskahouse.com
Web Site: www.thealaskahouse.com
Institution Type/Description: Art Gallery: built in 1939.
Hours & Admission Prices: Summer: call for hours.

FAIRBANKS ICE MUSEUM, 500 2nd Ave., Fairbanks, AK 99701-4729. Tel.: 907-451-8222.
E-mail: ice@gci.net
Web Site: www.icemuseum.com
Institution Type/Description: Historic Building: housed in the Lacey Street Theater; built in 1936.
Hours & Admission Prices: May to early Oct. daily 10-8. Adult $15, children 6-14 $10. &
Attendance: 22,526 (estimated)

PIONEER AIR MUSEUM, 2300 Airport Way, Fairbanks, AK 99701. Mailing Address: Box 70437, Fairbanks, AK 99707-0437. Tel.: 907-451-0037.
E-mail: curator@pioneerairmuseum.org
Web Site: www.pioneerairmuseum.org
Formerly: Alaskaland Pioneer Air Museum
Key Personnel: Dir. & Museum Shop Mgr., Peter Haggland; Colls. Mgr., Rita Butteri.
Institution Type/Description: Aeronautics Museum.
Hours & Admission Prices: May 15 to Sept. 15 call for hours. Families of four $8, adults $4; children under 12 no charge.
Attendance: 13,000 (actual)

PIONEER MUSEUM & THE BIG STAMPEDE, Pioneer Park, Bldg. #1, 2300 Airport Way, Fairbanks, AK 99701. Mailing Address: P.O. Box 70176, Fairbanks, AK 99707-0176. Tel.: 907-456-8579.
Web Site: pioneersofalaskafairbanks.org/pioneer-museum
Institution Type/Description: History Museum.
Hours & Admission Prices: March-Memorial Day Fri.-Sun. 1-5; late May to mid-Sept. daily 11-8. Museum: no charge; donations accepted. Big Stampede Show: Memorial Day to Labor Day. Adults $4; youth 6-16 $2; children under 6 no charge. &
Attendance: 19,000 (actual)

UNIVERSITY OF ALASKA MUSEUM OF THE NORTH, 1962 Yukon Dr., Fairbanks, AK 99775-6960. Mailing Address: P.O. Box 756960, Fairbanks, AK 99775-6960. Tel.: 907-474-7505.
E-mail: ua-museum@alaska.edu
Web Site: www.uaf.edu/museum
Key Personnel: Dir., Pat Druckenmiller; Exec. Asst., Emilie Nelson; Cur. Archeology, Josh Reuther, Ph.D.; Cur. Mammalogy, Link E. Olson; Cur. Ornithology, Kevin S. Winker; Cur. Herbarium, Stefanie Ickert-Bond; Cur. Ichthyology & Aquatics, J. Andres Lopez, Ph.D.; Sr. Collections Mgr., Ethnology & History, Angela Linn; Cur. Alaska Center for Documentary Film, Leonard J. Kamerling; Cur. Fine Arts, Mareca Guthrie, M.F.A.; Education & Public Programs Mgr., Jennifer Arseneau; Mktg. & Communications Mgr., Theresa Bakker; Operations Mgr., Kevin May.
Institution Type/Description: Natural History & Art Museum.
Hours & Admission Prices: June-Aug. daily 9-7; Sept.-May Mon.-Sat. 9-5. Adults $16, seniors & veterans $14, Local $12, Alaska active duty military $10, youth 5-12 $9; Univ. Alaska faculty, students, staff & children 4 & under no charge. &
Attendance: 96,016 (actual)

WICKERSHAM HOUSE MUSEUM (TANANA-YUKON HISTORICAL SOCIETY), 535 2nd Ave., Ste. 201, Fairbanks, AK 99701-4770. Mailing Address: P.O. Box 71336, Fairbanks, AK 99707-1336. Tel.: 907-457-6165.
E-mail: tyhs@alaska.net
Web Site: tananayukonhistory.org/our-work/wickersham-house-tours/
Key Personnel: Pres., Ronald Inouye; Treas., Elizabeth Cook.
Institution Type/Description: Historical Society Museum: housed in the Wickersham House Museum, home of Judge James Wickersham & the first frame home completed in the rough gold camp which became Fairbanks, AK.
Hours & Admission Prices: Memorial Day-Labor Day daily 12-8; other times by appointment. No charge; donations accepted. &
Attendance: 11,000 (estimated)

Girdwood

ALASKA WILDLIFE CONSERVATION CENTER, 79 Seward Hwy., Portage, AK 99587. Mailing Address: P.O. Box 949, Girdwood, AK 99587-0949. Tel.: 907-783-2025. Facebook; Twitter; Instagram.
E-mail: info@alaskawildlife.org
Web Site: www.alaskawildlife.org
Key Personnel: Dir., Opers. & Devel., Trish Baker; Cur., Sarah Howard.
Institution Type/Description: Conservation Center.
Hours & Admission Prices: See website for hours. Adults $17, seniors & military $15, Students $13; children 6 & under no charge. Closed New Year's Day; Thanksgiving; Christmas Eve & Day.

Haines

ALASKA INDIAN ARTS, INC., Historic Bldg. #13, Fort Seward, Haines, AK 99827. Mailing Address: P.O. Box 271, Haines, AK 99827-0271. Tel.: 907-766-2160.
E-mail: mail@alaskaindianarts.com
Web Site: www.alaskaindianarts.com
Key Personnel: Exec. Dir., Lee D. Heinmiller.
Institution Type/Description: Indian Living Village Museum.
Hours & Admission Prices: Mon.-Fri. 9-5. No charge; donations accepted. Closed national holidays. &

AMERICAN BALD EAGLE FOUNDATION, 113 Haines Hwy., Haines, AK 99827. Mailing Address: P.O. Box 49, Haines, AK 99827-0049. Tel.: 907-766-3094. Facebook: American Bald Eagle Foundation.
E-mail: info@baldeagles.org
Web Site: www.baldeagles.org
Key Personnel: Exec. Dir., Cheryl McRoberts.
Institution Type/Description: Natural History Museum.
Hours & Admission Prices: Tues.-Sat. 9-4. &
Attendance: 10,000 (estimated)

HAMMER MUSEUM, INC., 108 Main St., Haines, AK 99827. Mailing Address: P.O. Box 702, Haines, AK 99827-0702. Tel.: 907-766-2374.
E-mail: hammer@hammermuseum.org
Web Site: www.hammermuseum.org
Key Personnel: Exec. Dir., Ashleigh Reed.
Institution Type/Description: History Museum.
Hours & Admission Prices: May-Sept. Mon.-Fri. 10-5, Sat. 10-2; other times by appointment. Admission $5; children 12 & under accompanied by an adult no charge.
Attendance: 5,000 (estimated)

SHELDON MUSEUM AND CULTURAL CENTER, INC., 11 Main St., Haines, AK 99827. Mailing Address: P.O. Box 269, Haines, AK 99827-0269. Tel.: 907-766-2366. Fax: 907-766-2368.
E-mail: museumdirector@aptalaska.net
Web Site: sheldonmuseum.org
Key Personnel: Pres. Bd. Trustees (V), Jim Heaton; Dir. & Cur., Helen Alten; Operations Coord., Blythe Carter.
Institution Type/Description: History & ethnographic Tlingit Indian Culture museum.
Hours & Admission Prices: mid-May to mid-Sept. Mon.-Fri. 10-5, Sat.-Sun. 1-4; call for additional hours. Adults $5; discounts for AAM, Museums Alaska & Chilkat Valley Historical Society members; children under 12 no charge. &
Attendance: 13,720 (actual)

Homer

ALASKA ISLANDS AND OCEAN VISITOR CENTER, 95 Sterling Hwy., Homer, AK 99603-7472. Tel.: 907-235-6961.
E-mail: alaskamaritime@fws.gov
Web Site: www.fws.gov/refuge/alaska_maritime
Key Personnel: Mgr. Visitor's Center, Kara Zwickey.
Institution Type/Description: Marine Wildlife Museum.
Hours & Admission Prices: Memorial Day to Labor Day daily 9-5; Sept.-May Tues.-Sat. 12-5. No charge. Closed Federal holidays; New Year's Eve; Christmas Eve. &
Attendance: 60,000 (actual)

BUNNELL STREET ARTS CENTER, 106 W. Bunnell St., Homer, AK 99603-7825. Tel.: 907-235-2662. Facebook: Bunnell Street Arts Center.

E-mail: info@bunnellarts.org
Web Site: www.bunnellarts.org
Key Personnel: Exec. Dir., Adele Person.
Institution Type/Description: Art Gallery.
Hours & Admission Prices: See website for hours. Gallery: no charge; donations accepted.
Attendance: 10,000 (estimated)

FIREWEED GALLERY, 475 E. Pioneer Ave., #A, Homer, AK 99603-7622. Tel.: 907-235-3411.
E-mail: art@fireweedgallery.com
Web Site: www.fireweedgallery.com
Institution Type/Description: Art Gallery.
Hours & Admission Prices: Mon.-Sat. 11-5:30.

PRATT MUSEUM, 3779 Bartlett St., Homer, AK 99603-7579. Tel.: 907-235-8635. Fax: 907-235-2764.
E-mail: info@prattmuseum.org
Web Site: www.prattmuseum.org
Key Personnel: Exec. Dir., Savanna Bradley; Bldg. Mgr., Art Koeninger; Finance & Grants Mgr., Jennifer Bartolowits.
Institution Type/Description: General Museum.
Hours & Admission Prices: Feb.-April & Oct.-Dec. Tues.-Sun. 12-5; mid-May to mid-Sept. daily 10-6. Adults $10, seniors $8, youths 6-18 54; children under 6 & members no charge. &
Attendance: 34,300 (actual)

Hope

HOPE-SUNRISE HISTORICAL AND MINING MUSEUM, 64851 2nd St., Hope, AK 99605. Mailing Address: P.O. Box 88, Hope, AK 99605-0088. Tel.: 907-782-3740.
E-mail: hopehistoricalsociety@gmail.com
Key Personnel: Pres. (V), Diane Olthuis.
Institution Type/Description: History Museum.
Hours & Admission Prices: Memorial Day to Labor Day daily 12-4. No charge; donations accepted.
Attendance: 3,000 (estimated)

Juneau

ALASKA STATE CAPITOL, 120 4th St., Juneau, AK 99801. Tel.: 907-465-3853.
Web Site: www.alaska.org/detail/alaska-state-capitol-building
Institution Type/Description: Government History Museum.
Hours & Admission Prices: See website for hours. No charge.

ALASKA STATE MUSEUM, 395 Whittier St., Juneau, AK 99801-1746. Mailing Address: P.O. Box 110571, Juneau, AK 99811-0571. Tel.: 907-465-2901. Fax: 907-465-2151.
E-mail: addison.field@alaska.gov
Web Site: museums.alaska.gov/asm/asmhome.html
Key Personnel: Chief Cur., Addison Field; Cur. Collections, Steve Henrikson; Conservator, Ellen Carrlee.
Institution Type/Description: General Museum.
Hours & Admission Prices: Summer: daily 9-5; Winter: Tues.-Sat. 10-4. Summer: adults $12, seniors 65 & over $11; active military and youth 18 & under no charge. Winter: adults $7, seniors 65 & over $6; active military and youth 18 & under no charge. Closed holidays. &
Attendance: 60,000 (actual)

HOUSE OF WICKERSHAM STATE HISTORICAL SITE, 213 Seventh St., Juneau, AK 99801-1117. Mailing Address: 400 Willoughby Ave., P.O. Box 111017, Juneau, AK 99801-1783. Tel.: 907-586-9001.
E-mail: dnr.pic@alaska.gov
Web Site: dnr.alaska.gov/parks/aspunits/southeast/wickshp.htm
Institution Type/Description: Historic House: constructed in 1898 by Frank Hammond, a gold mine superintendent. The house was purchased in 1928 by James Wickersham, a judge & delegate to congress. Listed on the National Register of Historic Places.
Hours & Admission Prices: See website for hours. &
Attendance: 1,000 (estimated)

JUNEAU-DOUGLAS CITY MUSEUM, 114 W. 4th St., Juneau, AK 99801-1758. Mailing Address: 155 S. Seward St., Juneau, AK 99801-1332. Tel.: 907-586-3572.
E-mail: museum.info@juneau.org
Web Site: www.juneau.org/library/museum/index.php

Key Personnel: Dir., Beth Weigel; Cur. Collections & Exhibits, Niko Sanguinetti; Cur. Public Progs., Elissa Borges.
Institution Type/Description: Local History & Culture Museum: housed in 1951 library building.
Hours & Admission Prices: June-Sept. Thurs.-Sun. 10-4; Oct.-April Tues.-Sat. 10-4. Summer: adults $6; seniors $5; children 12 & under no charge. Winter: no charge. Closed Thanksgiving; Christmas. &
Attendance: 23,000 (actual)

LAST CHANCE MINING MUSEUM, 1001 Basin Rd., Juneau, AK 99801-1038. Tel.: 907-586-5338.
Institution Type/Description: Historic Building: listed on the National Register of Historic Places.
Hours & Admission Prices: mid-May to late Sept. daily 9:30-12:30 & 3-6:30; other times by appointment. Adults $5.

SEALASKA HERITAGE INSTITUTE (SHI), 105 S. Seward St., Ste. 201, Juneau, AK 99801. Tel.: 907-586-9261. Facebook: SH Institute.
E-mail: heritage@sealaska.com
Web Site: www.sealaskaheritage.org
Key Personnel: Pres., Dr. Rosita Worl.
Institution Type/Description: History Museum.
Hours & Admission Prices: Summer: 9-8, Winter: 10-6. Adults $5; seniors 65 & over and children under 7 no charge.

Kenai

KENAI VISITORS & CULTURAL CENTER, 11471 Kenai Spur Hwy., Kenai, AK 99611-7757. Tel.: 907-283-1991. Fax: 907-283-2230.
E-mail: johna@kenaichamber.org
Web Site: kenaichamber.org/
Key Personnel: Dir., Johna Beech.
Institution Type/Description: History Museum.
Hours & Admission Prices: Mon.-Fri. 9-6, Sat. 10-5, Sun. 12-5. No charge; donations accepted.
Attendance: 50,000 (actual)

Ketchikan

SOUTHEAST ALASKA DISCOVERY CENTER, USDA FOREST SERVICE, 50 Main St., Ketchikan, AK 99901-6559. Tel.: 907-228-6220. Fax: 907-228-6234.
Web Site: www.fs.usda.gov/recarea/tongass/recarea/?recid=78948
Institution Type/Description: History Museum.
Hours & Admission Prices: May-Oct. Mon.-Fri. 8-5, Sat.-Sun. 8-4; Oct.-April Thurs.-Sun. 10-4. Summer: $5, children 15 & under and winter no charge.

TONGASS HISTORICAL MUSEUM, 629 Dock St., Ketchikan, AK 99901-6529. Tel.: 907-225-5600. Facebook.
E-mail: anitam@ktn-ak.us
Web Site: www.ktn-ak.us/tongass-historical-museum
Key Personnel: Dir., Anita Maxwell; Sr. Cur. Collections, Hayley Chambers; Sr. Cur. Colls, Hayley Chambers; Cur. Exhibits, Ryan McHale; Registrar, Erika Brown.
Institution Type/Description: General Museum.
Hours & Admission Prices: Jan.-April Tues.-Sat. 1-5; May-Sept. daily. 8-5. Adults $6, seniors 65 & over $5; locals, active military, winter & children 17 & under no charge. &
Attendance: 30,000 (estimated)

TOTEM HERITAGE CENTER, 601 Deermount, Ketchikan, AK 99901. Mailing Address: 629 Dock St., Ketchikan, AK 99901-6529. Tel.: 907-225-5900. Facebook.
E-mail: anitam@ktn-ak.us
Web Site: www.ktn-ak.us/totem-heritage-center-exhibits
Key Personnel: Dir., Anita Maxwell.
Institution Type/Description: Anthropology, Ethnology & History Museum; Indian Art Center.
Hours & Admission Prices: May to Sept. daily 8-5; Oct. to April Tues.-Sat. 1-5. Adults $6, seniors $5; active military, winter & children 17 & younger no charge. &
Attendance: 33,218 (actual)

Kodiak

ALUTIIQ MUSEUM AND ARCHAEOLOGICAL REPOSITORY, 215 Mission Rd., Ste. 101, Kodiak, AK 99615-7326. Tel.: 844-425-8844.
E-mail: info@alutiiqmuseum.org
Web Site: www.alutiiqmuseum.org
Key Personnel: Exec. Dir., April Laktonen Counceller; Asst. Dir., Rosanne Wilson; Chief Cur., Amy Steffian; Cur. Collections, Marnie Leist.
Institution Type/Description: Archaeology Museum & Ethnographic.
Hours & Admission Prices: Tues.-Fri. 10-4, Sat. 12-4. Adults $7; children 16 & under and members no charge. &
Attendance: 6,500 (estimated)

KODIAK HISTORY MUSEUM, Erskine House, 101 Marine Way, Kodiak, AK 99615-6307. Tel.: 907-486-5920. Facebook: Baranov Museum.
E-mail: director@kodiakhistorymuseum.org
Web Site: kodiakhistorymuseum.org
Key Personnel: Exec. Dir., Sarah Harrington; Cur. Collections, Margaret Greutert; Museum Shop Mgr., Shaira Dungca.
Institution Type/Description: General Museum: housed in c.1800 fur warehouse & offices of Alexander Baranov, chief manager of Russian American Company; after 1867 used by the American Commercial Company; 1911-1948 the W.J. Erskine family home.
Hours & Admission Prices: Tues.-Thurs. & Sat. 10-4, Fri. 12-7. Adults $10; children 12 & under no charge. &
Attendance: 10,000 (estimated)

KODIAK MARITIME MUSEUM, Kodiak, AK 99615. Mailing Address: P.O. Box 1876, Kodiak, AK 99615. Tel.: 907-486-0384. Fax: 907-486-0385.
E-mail: info@kodiakmaritimemuseum.org
Web Site: www.kodiakmaritimemuseum.org
Key Personnel: Exec. Dir., Toby Sullivan.
Institution Type/Description: Maritime Museum.
Hours & Admission Prices: Virtual Museum.

KODIAK MILITARY HISTORY MUSEUM, Fort Abercrombie State Historical Park, 1623 Mill Bay Rd., Kodiak, AK 99615. Mailing Address: 1417B Mill Bay Rd., Kodiak, AK 99615-7505. Tel.: 907-486-7015. Fax: 907-486-5541.
E-mail: jbs@kadiak.org
Web Site: www.kadiak.org/museum/museum.html
Key Personnel: Webmaster, Joe Stevens; Business Mgr., Curt Law.
Institution Type/Description: Military Museum: housed in the WWII Ready Ammunition bunker at Miller Point; a buried concrete structure built in 1942.
Hours & Admission Prices: May & Sept. Sat.-Sun. 1-4; June-Aug. Fri.-Mon. 1-4; other times by appointment.

Metlakatla

DUNCAN COTTAGE MUSEUM, 501 Tait St., Metlakatla, AK 99926. Mailing Address: P.O. Box 8, Metlakatla, AK 99926-0008. Tel.: 907-886-8687.
E-mail: duncancottagemuseum@gmail.com
Web Site: wdcmuseum.weebly.com/
Key Personnel: Dir., Naomi Leask.
Institution Type/Description: Historic House: 1891 seven room cottage that was home of Father Wm. Duncan, English missionary/teacher of the Tsimpshians of Metlakatla, AK.
Hours & Admission Prices: Call for hours & admissions. &
Attendance: 4,000 (estimated)

Nenana

ALFRED STARR NENANA CULTURAL CENTER, 415 Riverfront, Nenana, AK 99760. Mailing Address: P.O. Box 70, Nenana, AK 99760-0070. Tel.: 907-832-5527.
E-mail: nenana1@nenana.net
Institution Type/Description: Cultural Center.
Hours & Admission Prices: Summer: daily 10-6; Winter: by appointment. No charge; donation accepted. &

Nome

CARRIE M. MCLAIN MEMORIAL MUSEUM, 100 W. 7th Ave., Nome, AK 99762. Tel.: 907-443-6630.
E-mail: museum@nomealaska.org

Web Site: www.nomealaska.org/department/index.php?structureid=12
Key Personnel: Dir., Amy Phillips-Chan.
Institution Type/Description: History Museum.
Hours & Admission Prices: Mon.-Thurs. 12-7, Fri.-Sat. 12-6. Adults $4; youth & elders $3; members, Nome residents, youth under 5 & Fri. no charge. &
Attendance: 11,000 (estimated)

Palmer

COLONY HOUSE MUSEUM - PALMER HISTORICAL SOCIETY, 316 E. Elmwood Ave., Palmer, AK 99645-6621. Mailing Address: P.O. Box 1935, Palmer, AK 99645-1935. Tel.: 907-745-1935. Facebook: Palmer Historical Society Alaska.
E-mail: ptownhistory@gmail.com
Web Site: www.palmerhistoricalsociety.org
Key Personnel: Pres. & Sec., Sheri Hamming.
Institution Type/Description: Historic House Museum: housed in an original Colony Farm House built for the New Deal resettlement in 1935.
Hours & Admission Prices: Summer: Tues.- Sat. 10-4; Winter: by appointment only. Adults $2, children 12 & under $1.

MUSK OX FARM & MUSEUM, 12850 E. Archie Rd., Palmer, AK 99645. Mailing Address: P.O. Box 587, Palmer, AK 99645-0587. Tel.: 907-745-4151. Fax: 907-746-4831.
E-mail: info@muskoxfarm.org
Web Site: www.muskoxfarm.org
Key Personnel: Educ. Dir., Dani Biersteker.
Institution Type/Description: Farm History Museum.
Hours & Admission Prices: May-Sept. daily 10-6; Oct. to early May Wed.-Sat. 12-4. Adults $11, seniors $9, children $5.

PALMER MUSEUM OF HISTORY AND ART, 723 S. Valley Way, Palmer, AK 99645-6601. Tel.: 907-746-7668.
E-mail: museuminfo@palmermuseum.org
Web Site: www.palmermuseum.org
Key Personnel: Exec. Dir., Sam Dinges.
Institution Type/Description: History & Art Museum.
Hours & Admission Prices: See website for hours and admissions. &
Attendance: 35,000 (actual)

Petersburg

CLAUSEN MEMORIAL MUSEUM, 203 Fram St., Petersburg, AK 99833. Mailing Address: P.O. Box 708, Petersburg, AK 99833-0708. Tel.: 907-772-3598.
E-mail: clausenmuseum@gmail.com
Web Site: clausenmuseum.com/
Key Personnel: Dir., Cindi Lagoudakis.
Institution Type/Description: History Museum.
Hours & Admission Prices: Summer: Mon.-Sat. 10-5; Winter: Mon.-Fri. 1-5, Sat. 12-5. &
Attendance: 3,902 (actual)

Seward

ALASKA SEALIFE CENTER, 301 Railway Ave., Seward, AK 99664. Mailing Address: P.O. Box 1329, Seward, AK 99664-1329. Tel.: 907-224-6300, 800-224-2525. Fax: 907-224-6320. Facebook: Alaska SeaLife Center.
E-mail: visit@alaskasealife.org
Web Site: www.alaskasealife.org
Key Personnel: Pres. & C.E.O., Tara Riemer, Ph.D.
Institution Type/Description: Marine Wildlife Center.
Hours & Admission Prices: See website for hours. Adults $29.95, military with ID $25.95, children 3-12 $17.95; discounts to groups & Alaska residents; members and children 2 & under no charge. &

CHUGACH MUSEUM AND INSTITUTE OF HISTORY AND ART, Orca Bldg., 3rd & Washington St., Seward, AK 99503. Mailing Address: 3800 Centerpoint Dr., Ste. 601, Anchorage, AK 99503-5826. Tel.: 907-563-8866, ext. 4151. Fax: 907-563-8402.
Institution Type/Description: Culturally Specific.
Hours & Admission Prices: By appointment.

QUTEKCAK CULTURE CENTER, 221 Third Ave., Seward, AK 99664. Mailing Address: P.O. Box 1467, Seward, AK 99664-1467. Tel.: 907-224-3118.
E-mail: tribaladmin@qntak.org
Institution Type/Description: Native Heritage Museum.

Hours & Admission Prices: Call for hours.

RESURRECTION BAY HISTORICAL SOCIETY MUSEUM & SEWARD LIBRARY MUSEUM, 239 6th Ave., Seward, AK 99664. Mailing Address: P.O. Box 55, Seward, AK 99664-0055. Tel.: 907-224-4082.
E-mail: rbhs1903@gmail.com
Web Site: www.cityofseward.us/departments/library-museum
Key Personnel: Dir., Valerie Kingsland; Cur., Elana Yanusz.
Institution Type/Description: Historical Society Museum.
Hours & Admission Prices: Summer: Tues.-Sat. 10-5, Mon. by appointment. Adults 12 & over $4. Winter: Fri.-Sat. 12-5, Mon.-Thurs by appointment. No charge. &
Attendance: 8,942 (actual)

SEWARD COMMUNITY LIBRARY & MUSEUM, 239 6th Ave., Seward, AK 99664. Mailing Address: P.O. Box 2389, Seward, AK 99664. Tel.: 907-224-4082 (Library) & 3902 (Museum).
E-mail: vkingsland@cityofseward.net
Key Personnel: Dir., Valarie Kingsland; Cur., Elana Yanusz; Prog. Coord., Amanda Lyon.
Institution Type/Description: Library & Museum.
Hours & Admission Prices: Library: Summer: Mon. & Fri.-Sat. 10-6, Tues.-Thurs. 10-8; Winter: Mon. & Fri.-Sat. 11-6, Tues.-Thurs. 11-8. Museum: Summer: Tues.-Sat. 10-5; Winter: Fri.-Sat. 12-5; other times by appointment. Summer: $4; children 12 & under, Resurrection Bay Historical Society and winter no charge.

Sitka

ALASKA RAPTOR CENTER, 1000 Raptor Way, Sitka, AK 99835-9302. Tel.: 907-747-8662.
E-mail: members@alaskaraptor.org
Web Site: www.alaskaraptor.org
Key Personnel: Exec. Dir., Jennifer Cross; Avian Dir., Jennifer Cedarleaf.
Institution Type/Description: Environmental Conservation Center.
Hours & Admission Prices: May-Sept. tours daily 8-4, Oct.-April Mon.-Fri. 10-3. Adults $13, children 6-12 $6.; children 5 & under no charge.

RUSSIAN BISHOP'S HOUSE, 201 College Dr., Sitka, AK 99835. Mailing Address: Sitka National Historic Park, 103 Monastery St., Sitka, AK 99835-7617. Tel.: 907-747-0110.
E-mail: nps_sitk_website_contact@nps.gov
Web Site: www.nps.gov/sitk/learn/historyculture/russian-bishops-house.htm
Institution Type/Description: Historic House: the former residence of the Bishop of the Russian Orthodox Church; built in 1842. A National Historic Landmark.
Hours & Admission Prices: Summer: daily; Winter: by appointment.

SHELDON JACKSON MUSEUM, 104 College Dr., Sitka, AK 99835-7657. Tel.: 907-747-8981.
E-mail: jacqueline.fernandez-hamberg@alaska.gov
Web Site: www.museums.state.ak.us
Key Personnel: Cur., Colls, Jackie Hamberg.
Institution Type/Description: Anthropology Museum: housed in the first concrete building built in the territory of Alaska; built in 1895.
Hours & Admission Prices: Summer: daily 9-4:30. Adults $7, seniors $6; Winter: Tues.-Sat. 10-4. Adults $5, seniors $4. Friends of SJM, SLAM & children 18 & under no charge. &
Attendance: 16,000 (actual)

SITKA HISTORICAL SOCIETY, 330 Harbor Dr., Sitka, AK 99835-7553. Tel.: 907-738-3766.
E-mail: HalSpackman@SitkaHistory.org
Web Site: sitkahistory.org
Key Personnel: Dir., Hal Spackman; Cur., Kristy Griffin; Admin., Heidi Nance.
Institution Type/Description: General History Museum.
Hours & Admission Prices: Summer: Mon.-Fri. 9-5; call for weekend hours. &
Attendance: 67,415 (actual)

SITKA NATIONAL HISTORICAL PARK, 106 Metlakatla St., Sitka, AK 99835-7665. Mailing Address: 103 Monastery St., Sitka, AK 99835-7617. Tel.: 907-747-0110.
E-mail: kelsey_lutz@nps.gov
Web Site: www.nps.gov/sitk
Key Personnel: Cur., Kelsey Lutz.
Institution Type/Description: Park Museum & Visitor Center: located near site of 1804 Battle of Sitka, fought between the Tlingit Indians & the Russians.
Hours & Admission Prices: Visitor Center: May-Sept. daily 8:30-4:30; OCt. 1-18 Tues.-Sun. 8-4:30; mid-Oct.-April Tues.-Sat. 9-3. No charge; donations accepted. Closed New Year's Day; Thanksgiving; Christmas. &

Skagway

CORRINGTON'S MUSEUM OF ALASKAN HISTORY, Broadway & 5th, Skagway, AK 99840. Mailing Address: P.O. Box 382, Skagway, AK 99840. Tel.: 907-983-2579.
Institution Type/Description: History Museum.
Hours & Admission Prices: Call for hours. No charge.

KLONDIKE GOLD RUSH NATIONAL HISTORICAL PARK, Second & Broadway, Skagway, AK 99840. Mailing Address: P.O. Box 517, Skagway, AK 99840-0517. Tel.: 907-983-9200. TDD: 907-983-2921.
Web Site: www.nps.gov/klgo
Key Personnel: Supt., Jason Taylor.
Institution Type/Description: Park Museum: housed in c.1898 White Pass & Yukon Route Railroad Depot.
Hours & Admission Prices: Visitor Center: May-Sept. daily 8:30-5:30. Park Museum: Summer daily 8:30-5:30; Winter Mon.-Fri. 8-3. Moore House: May to mid-Sept. daily 10-4:30. &
Attendance: 800,000 (estimated)

SKAGWAY MUSEUM & ARCHIVES, 700 Spring St., Skagway, AK 99840. Mailing Address: P.O. Box 415, Skagway, AK 99840. Tel.: 907-983-2420.
E-mail: info@skagwaymuseum.org
Web Site: https://www.skagway.org/museum
Key Personnel: Dir., Judith Munns.
Institution Type/Description: History Museum: housed in 1899 McCabe College, built by Methodist Church.
Hours & Admission Prices: Call for hours & admissions. &
Attendance: 38,000 (estimated)

Soldotna

SOLDOTNA HISTORICAL SOCIETY AND MUSEUM, Centennial Park Rd., Soldotna, AK 99669. Mailing Address: P.O. Box 1986, Soldotna, AK 99669-1986. Tel.: 907-262-3832.
Key Personnel: Pres., Bobbi O'Neill.
Institution Type/Description: History Museum.
Hours & Admission Prices: May 15-Sept. 15 Tues.-Sat. 10-4, Sun. 12-4. No charge; donations accepted. &
Attendance: 2,270 (actual)

Talkeetna

TALKEETNA HISTORICAL SOCIETY AND MUSEUM, 22248 S. D St., Talkeetna, AK 99676. Mailing Address: P.O. Box 76, Talkeetna, AK 99676-0076. Tel.: 907-733-2487. Facebook: Talkeetna Historical Society.
E-mail: info@talkeetnahistoricalsociety.org
Web Site: www.talkeetnahistoricalsociety.org
Key Personnel: Pres. (V), Sharon Montagnino.
Institution Type/Description: General Museum: housed in the first school house in Talkeetna. Museum Buildings: The Ole Dahl Cabin; The Three German Bachelor's Cabin; The Harry Robb Cabin; Old Railroad Section House; Old Railroad Depot.
Hours & Admission Prices: Summer: daily 10-6; Winter: Sat.-Sun. 11-4, weekdays by appointment only. Adults $5, seniors & military $4; members & children 10 & under no charge. &
Attendance: 14,500 (actual)

Trapper Creek

TRAPPER CREEK MUSEUM, Mile 6 W. of Parks Hwy. on Petersville Rd., Trapper Creek, AK 99683. Mailing Address: P.O. Box 13011, Trapper Creek, AK 99683-0011. Tel.: 907-733-2557.
E-mail: trappercreekmuseum@yahoo.com
Institution Type/Description: History Museum: housed in a log cabin built by the Donaldson family, members of the Michigan 59'ers.
Hours & Admission Prices: Call for hours and admissions.
Attendance: 1,200 (actual)

Unalaska

MUSEUM OF THE ALEUTIANS, 314 Salmon Way, Unalaska, AK 99685. Mailing Address: P.O. Box 648, Unalaska, AK 99685-0648. Tel.: 907-581-5150.
E-mail: museumofthealeutians@gmail.com
Web Site: www.aleutians.org

Key Personnel: Exec. Dir., Virginia Hatfield; Colls. Mgr., Melia Busch; Store Mgr., Megan Dean.
Institution Type/Description: General Museum.
Hours & Admission Prices: Tues.-Sat. 11-4. Adults $7, children 3-12 $3, active military $2; members & children under 3 no charge. &
Attendance: 4,036 (actual)

Valdez

MAXINE & JESSE WHITNEY MUSEUM, 303 Lowe St., Valdez, AK 99686. Mailing Address: P.O. Box 97, Valdez, AK 99686. Tel.: 907-834-1600. Facebook.
E-mail: wgoldstein@alaska.edu
Web Site: www.mjwhitneymuseum.org/
Institution Type/Description: History Museum.
Hours & Admission Prices: Summer: daily 9-7; Winter: by appointment. No charge; donations accepted.

THE VALDEZ MUSEUM & HISTORICAL ARCHIVE ASSOCIATION, INC., 217 Egan Ave., Valdez, AK 99686-0008. Mailing Address: P.O. Box 8, Valdez, AK 99686-0008. Tel.: 907-835-2764 & 5407.
E-mail: info@valdezmuseum.org
Web Site: www.valdezmuseum.org
Key Personnel: Exec. Dir., Patricia Relay; Cur. Collection & Exhibits, Andrew Goldstein; Cur. Education & Public Prog., Faith Revell.
Institution Type/Description: Local History Museum.
Hours & Admission Prices: Winter: Tues.-Sun. 12-5; Summer: daily 9-5. Adults $9, senior citizens 60 & over, military & students 14-17 $7; discounts to groups; members & children under 13 no charge. Closed New Year's Day; Thanksgiving; Christmas. &
Attendance: 20,000 (actual)

Wasilla

DOROTHY G. PAGE MUSEUM, 391 Main St., Wasilla, AK 99654-7021. Tel.: 907-373-9071. Fax: 907-373-9072.
E-mail: museum@ci.wasilla.ak.us
Web Site: www.cityofwasilla.com/museum
Key Personnel: Cur., Bethany Buckingham.
Institution Type/Description: City of Wasilla Museum: housed in 1931 log Wasilla Community Hall.
Hours & Admission Prices: April-Sept. Mon.-Sat. 9-5; Oct.-March Wed.-Fri. 9-5. Adults $3, senior citizens 60 & over $2.50, military $2; fri. & children 12 & under no charge. &
Attendance: 4,702 (actual)

IDITAROD TRAIL SLED DOG RACE MUSEUM, 2100 S. Knik Goose Bay Rd., Wasilla, AK 99654. Mailing Address: P.O. Box 870800, Wasilla, AK 99687-0800. Tel.: 907-376-5155, ext. 108.
Web Site: www.anchorage.net/listings/iditarod-trail-sled-dog-race/36025/
Institution Type/Description: Dog Race Museum.
Hours & Admission Prices: mid-May to mid-Sept. daily 8-7; Winter: Mon.-Fri. 8-5.

INDEPENDENCE MINE STATE HISTORICAL PARK & VISITOR CENTER, 7278 E. Bogard Rd., Wasilla, AK 99654. Tel.: 907-745-2827.
E-mail: dnr.pic@alaska.gov
Institution Type/Description: Park & Visitor Center.
Hours & Admission Prices: mid-June to Labor Day Wed.-Sun. 11-6 call for hours. Guided Tours: adults $6, children 6-12 $3; groups by appointment.

KNIK MUSEUM - WASILLA KNIK HISTORICAL SOCIETY, 10524 S. Knik Goose Bay Rd., Wasilla, AK 99654. Mailing Address: 300 N. Boundary St., Wasilla, AK 99654-7128. Tel.: 907-376-7755.
E-mail: wasillaknikhistoricalsociety@yahoo.com
Web Site: wkhsociety.org
Key Personnel: Pres., Robbin Robbert.
Institution Type/Description: History Museum.
Hours & Admission Prices: June-Oct. Wed.-Sun. 1-6. Adults $3, seniors & children $2; members no charge.
Attendance: 1,000

MUSEUM OF ALASKA TRANSPORTATION & INDUSTRY, INC., 3800 W. Museum Dr., Wasilla, AK 99654. Mailing Address: P.O. Box 870646, Wasilla, AK 99687-0646. Tel.: 907-376-1211.
E-mail: mati@mtaonline.net
Web Site: www.museumofalaska.org/

Key Personnel: Dir., Sherry Jackson; Pres. (V), John Stroup.
Institution Type/Description: Alaskan Industrial History & Transportation Museum.
Hours & Admission Prices: May-Sept. daily 10-5. &
Attendance: 12,000 (estimated)

Wrangell

NOLAN CENTER MUSEUM, 296 Campbell Dr., Wrangell, AK 99929. Mailing Address: P.O. Box 1050, Wrangell, AK 99929-1050. Tel.: 907-874-3770.
E-mail: cyni@nolancenter.org
Web Site: www.nolancenter.org/
Key Personnel: Dir., Cyni Crary.
Institution Type/Description: Natural History Museum.
Hours & Admission Prices: May-Sept. Mon.-Sat. 10-5; Oct.-April Tues.-Sat. 1-5. Adults $5, seniors $3, children 6-12 $2.

WRANGELL MUSEUM, 296 Campbell Dr., Wrangell, AK 99929. Mailing Address: P.O. Box 1050, Wrangell, AK 99929-1050. Tel.: 907-874-3770. Fax: 907-874-3785.
E-mail: museum@wrangell.com
Web Site: www.wrangell.com
Key Personnel: Dir., Terri Henson; Museum Shop Mgr., Marlene Messmer.
Institution Type/Description: General Museum.
Hours & Admission Prices: April-Sept. Mon.-Sat. 10-5; Oct.-March Fri.-Sat. 12-5. Adults $7, seniors $5, children 6-12 & non-local school groups $4; local school groups no charge. Closed New Year's Day; Easter; Memorial Day; Independence Day; Labor Day; Thanksgiving; Christmas. &
Attendance: 8,237 (actual)

ARIZONA

(242 listings)

Ajo

AJO HISTORICAL SOCIETY, 160 S. Mission Rd., Ajo, AZ 85321-2601. Mailing Address: P.O. Box 778, Ajo, AZ 85321. Tel.: 520-387-7105. Facebook: Ajo Museum.
E-mail: walters@tabletoptelephone.com
Web Site: ajomuseum.org
Key Personnel: Pres. (V), G. J. Walters.
Institution Type/Description: Historical Society Museum.
Hours & Admission Prices: Oct.-May daily 12-4. No charge; donations accepted. Closed Thanksgiving; Christmas.
Attendance: 2,403 (actual)

ORGAN PIPE CACTUS NATIONAL MONUMENT MUSEUM, 10 Organ Pipe Dr., Ajo, AZ 85321-9626. Tel.: 520-387-6849. Fax: 520-387-7144.
E-mail: orpi_information@nps.gov
Web Site: www.nps.gov/orpi
Key Personnel: Supt., Brent K. Range.
Institution Type/Description: National Monument.
Hours & Admission Prices: Jan.-March daily 8-5; April-Dec. daily 8:30-4:30. Weekly vehicle admission $12; Golden Eagle, Golden Age & Golden Access Passport holders & children 16 under with adult no charge. Closed Thanksgiving; Christmas.
Attendance: 22,000 (estimated)

Apache Junction

SUPERSTITION MOUNTAIN LOST DUTCHMAN MUSEUM, 4087 N. Apache Trail, Apache Junction, AZ 85119-8409. Mailing Address: P.O. Box 3845, Apache Junction, AZ 85117-3845. Tel.: 480-983-4888. Fax: 480-288-6524.
E-mail: smhsgold@aol.com
Web Site: www.superstitionmountainmuseum.org
Key Personnel: Exec. Dir., Liz Nicklus; Pres., James Geil.
Institution Type/Description: History Museum.
Hours & Admission Prices: Daily 9-4. Adults $5, seniors 55 & over $4; discounts to groups; children under 17 no charge. Closed New Year's Day; Thanksgiving; Christmas. &
Attendance: 50,000 (estimated)

Benson

KARTCHNER CAVERNS STATE PARK, 2980 S. Hwy. 90, Benson, AZ 85602. Mailing Address: P.O. Box 1849, Benson, AZ 85602-1849. Tel.: 520-586-4100. Fax: 520-586-4113.
E-mail: sblack@azstateparks.gov
Web Site: azstateparks.gov
Key Personnel: Dir., Sue Black.
Institution Type/Description: Natural History Museum.
Hours & Admission Prices: April 15 to Oct. 15 daily 8-5; mid-Oct to mid-April daily 7:30-6. Cave Tours: adults $23, youth 7-14 $13. Park Entrance Fee: $7 per vehicle. Closed Christmas. &
Attendance: 140,000 (actual)

SAN PEDRO VALLEY ARTS AND HISTORICAL SOCIETY, 180 S. San Pedro, Benson, AZ 85602. Tel.: 520-586-3134. Facebook.
E-mail: bensonmuseum@gmail.com
Web Site: bensonmuseum.com
Institution Type/Description: Historical Society Museum: housed in a former general store, c.1920.
Hours & Admission Prices: May-July & Sept. Tues.-Sat. 10-2; Oct.-April Tues.-Fri. 10-4, Sat. 10-2.
Attendance: 3,000 (estimated)

Bisbee

BISBEE MINING & HISTORICAL MUSEUM, No. 5 Copper Queen Plaza, Bisbee, AZ 85603. Mailing Address: P.O. Box 14, Bisbee, AZ 85603-0014. Tel.: 520-432-7071 & 7848. Fax: 520-432-7800. Facebook.
E-mail: carrie@bisbeemuseum.org
Web Site: bisbeemuseum.org
Key Personnel: Dir., Carrie Gustavson; Cur. Collections, Annie Larkins.
Institution Type/Description: History Museum: housed in the Old General Office Building of the Phelps Dodge Corp.; National Registered Landmark, a Smithsonian Affiliate.
Hours & Admission Prices: Daily 10-4. Adults $8, senior citizens 60 & over $7, children under 16 $3; discounts to groups of 10 or more; members & local school groups no charge. Closed Thanksgiving; Christmas. &
Attendance: 16,753 (actual)

Bowie

FORT BOWIE NATIONAL HISTORIC SITE, 3500 S. Apache Pass Rd. (13 miles south of Bowie), Bowie, AZ 85605. Mailing Address: P.O. Box 158, Bowie, AZ 85605-0158. Tel.: 520-847-2500, ext. 2. Fax: 520-847-0113.
E-mail: larry_ludwig@nps.gov
Web Site: www.nps.gov/fobo
Key Personnel: Cur., Larry Ludwig.
Institution Type/Description: Historic Site: 1858-1894 ruins of military structures; 1858 Apache Pass Overland Mail Station.
Hours & Admission Prices: Daily 8:15-4:15. No charge. Closed Thanksgiving; Christmas. &
Attendance: 10,000 (actual)

Buckeye

BUCKEYE VALLEY MUSEUM, 116 E. MC 85, Buckeye, AZ 85326. Mailing Address: c/o Buckeye Public Library, 21699 W. Yuma Rd., Ste. 116, Buckeye, AZ 85326. Tel.: 623-349-6315. Fax: 623-349-6310. Facebook.
E-mail: clarson@buckeyeaz.gov
Web Site: www.buckeyeaz.gov/museum
Formerly: Buckeye Museum
Key Personnel: Supvr., Christine Larson.
Institution Type/Description: History Museum.
Hours & Admission Prices: Sept.-May Fri.-Sat. 11-4; groups of 10 or more by appointment. No charge; donations accepted. Closed holidays; Thanksgiving weekend; Christmas weekend.
Attendance: 2,000 (actual)

LAURIDSEN AVIATION MUSEUM, Buckeye Municipal Airport, 3000 S. Palo Verde Rd., Buckeye, AZ 85326. Tel.: 480-586-7312. Fax: 480-575-6954.
E-mail: hans@lauridsenaviaiton museum.com
Web Site: www.lauridsenaviationmuseum.com
Institution Type/Description: Aviation Museum.
Hours & Admission Prices: Call for hours.

Bullhead City

COLORADO RIVER MUSEUM, 2201 Hwy. 68, Bullhead City, AZ 86430. Mailing Address: P.O. Box 1599, Bullhead City, AZ 86430-1599. Tel.: 928-754-3399. Fax: 928-754-3399 (call first). Facebook.
E-mail: crhsmuseum@frontier.net
Web Site: crhsmuseum.com
Institution Type/Description: History Museum.
Hours & Admission Prices: Sept.-May Tues.-Fri. 10-4. Adults $2; discount to Arizona Historical Society members; members no charge. &
Attendance: 2,839 (actual)

Camp Verde

FORT VERDE STATE HISTORIC PARK, 125 E. Holloman, Camp Verde, AZ 86322. Mailing Address: P.O. Box 397, Camp Verde, AZ 86322-0397. Tel.: 928-567-3275. Fax: 928-567-4036. Facebook.
E-mail: sstubler@azstateparks.gov
Web Site: www.azstateparks.com
Key Personnel: Park Mgr., Sheila Stubler.
Institution Type/Description: State Park General Museum: located on site of Fort Verde, Arizona Territory.
Hours & Admission Prices: Visitor Center: daily 8-5. Adults 14 & over $7, children 7-13 $4; discount to groups, veterans & AZ State Park Pass holders; children 6 & under no charge. Closed Christmas. &
Attendance: 20,000 (estimated)

MONTEZUMA CASTLE NATIONAL MONUMENT, 2800 Montezuma Castle Rd., Camp Verde, AZ 86322. Mailing Address: Box 219, Camp Verde, AZ 86322-0219. Tel.: 928-567-3322 & 5276. Fax: 928-567-3597.
E-mail: moca_administration@nps.gov
Web Site: www.nps.gov/moca
Key Personnel: Supvr. Park Ranger, Lucas Hoedl; Chief Ranger, Caleb Kesler.
Institution Type/Description: Pre-historic Museum.
Hours & Admission Prices: June-Aug. daily 8-6; Sept.-May daily 8-5. Adults $10; children 15 & under no charge.
Attendance: 500,000 (estimated)

OUT OF AFRICA WILDLIFE PARK, 3505 W. SR-260, Camp Verde, AZ 86322. Mailing Address: 4020 N. Cherry Rd., Camp Verde, AZ 86322. Tel.: 928-567-2840. Fax: 928-567-2839. Facebook.
E-mail: ashton@outofafricapark.com
Web Site: www.outofafricapark.com
Institution Type/Description: Park Museum.
Hours & Admission Prices: Daily 9:30-5. Adults $33.95, seniors 65 & over $31.95, veterans & active military $22, children 3-12 $18.95; discounts to AAM members; children under 3 no charge. Closed Thanksgiving; Christmas. &
Attendance: 140,000 (actual)

VERDE VALLEY ARCHAEOLOGY CENTER & MUSEUM, 385 S. Main St., Camp Verde, AZ 86322. Tel.: 928-567-0066.
E-mail: center@verdevalleyarchaeology.org
Web Site: www.verdevalleyarchaeology.org/museum
Key Personnel: Exec. Dir., Kenneth Zoll.
Institution Type/Description: Archaeology Museum.
Hours & Admission Prices: Tues.-Sat. 10-4. No charge. Closed major holidays.

Casa Grande

THE MUSEUM OF CASA GRANDE, 110 W. Florence Blvd., Casa Grande, AZ 85122. Tel.: 520-836-2223. Facebook: @cgvhs.
E-mail: info@tmocg.org
Web Site: www.tmocg.org
Formerly: Casa Grande Valley Historical Society and Museum
Key Personnel: Dir., Michael Sirota; Pres. (V), Cathy Kenyon; Vice Pres. (V), Roger Hooper.
Institution Type/Description: History Museum.
Hours & Admission Prices: Sept.-April Thurs.-Sun. 12-4; special tours by appointment. Adults $5, seniors 60 & over $4; children under 16 & members no charge. Closed major holidays. &
Attendance: 2,089 (actual)

Cave Creek

CAVE CREEK MUSEUM, 6140 E. Skyline Dr., Cave Creek, AZ 85327. Mailing Address: P.O. Box 1, Cave Creek, AZ 85327. Tel.: 480-488-2764. Fax: 480-595-0838.
E-mail: info@cavecreekmuseum.com
Web Site: cavecreekmuseum.com
Key Personnel: Dir., Karrie Porter Brace; Pres. (V), Bill Oelman; Administrative Asst., Karen Friend.
Institution Type/Description: History Museum.
Hours & Admission Prices: Oct.-May Wed.-Thurs. & Sat.-Sun. 1-4:30, Fri. 10-4:30. Adults $7, seniors 60 & over and students 12 & over $5; discounts to AAM members; children under 12 no charge. Closed New Year's Eve & Day; Easter; Mother's Day; Memorial Day; Thanksgiving; Christmas Eve & Day. &
Attendance: 8,000 (estimated)

Chandler

ARIZONA RAILWAY MUSEUM, 330 E. Ryan Rd., Chandler, AZ 85224. Mailing Address: P.O. Box 842, Chandler, AZ 85244-0842. Tel.: 480-821-1108.
E-mail: azrymuseum@cox.net
Web Site: www.azrymuseum.org
Key Personnel: Pres., Larry Benedict.
Institution Type/Description: Railway Museum.
Hours & Admission Prices: Labor Day to Memorial Day Sat.-Sun. 12-4; other times by appointment. Work Sessions: Sat. 8am to 12pm. Adult $5, children 2-12 $2; children under 2 and active military no charge.
Attendance: 8,000 (estimated)

CHANDLER MUSEUM, 300 S. Chandler Village Dr., Chandler, AZ 85226. Mailing Address: MS 305, P.O. Box 4008, Chandler, AZ 85244-4008. Tel.: 480-782-2717. Fax: 480-782-2875.
E-mail: jody.crago@chandleraz.gov
Web Site: www.chandlermuseum.org
Key Personnel: Dir., Jody A. Crago; Cur. Education, Tiffani Egnor; Cur. Collections, Nate Meyers.
Institution Type/Description: History Museum.
Hours & Admission Prices: Chandler Museum: Tues.-Sat. 10-4. Tumbleweed Ranch: daily 6-6. No charge for admission. Closed New Year's Day; Martin Luther King Jr. Day; Memorial Day; Independence Day; Labor Day; Veterans Day; Thanksgiving; Christmas. &
Attendance: 15,000 (estimated)

HUHUGAM HERITAGE CENTER, 21359 S. Maricopa Rd., Chandler, AZ 85226. Mailing Address: 4759 N. Maricopa Rd., Chandler, AZ 85226-5203. Tel.: 520-796-3500.
Institution Type/Description: Native American Museum.
Hours & Admission Prices: Wed.-Fri. 10-4; other times by appointment. Adults $6, seniors & students $4, children 6-12 $2; children 5 & under and Native Americans no charge.

VISION GALLERY, 10 E. Chicago St., Chandler, AZ 85225. Mailing Address: P.O. Box 4008, Chandler, AZ 85244-4008. Tel.: 480-782-2695.
E-mail: vision.gallery@chandleraz.gov
Web Site: www.visiongallery.org
Institution Type/Description: Art Gallery.
Hours & Admission Prices: Mon.-Fri. 10-5, Sat. 10-4. No charge; donations accepted. &
Attendance: 10,000 (estimated)

Chinle

CANYON DE CHELLY NATIONAL MONUMENT, 3 mi. east of Chinle, Rte. 7, Chinle, AZ 86503. Mailing Address: P.O. Box 588, Chinle, AZ 86503-0588. Tel.: 928-674-5500. Fax: 928-674-5507.
E-mail: lashanna_deschine@nps.gov
Web Site: www.nps.gov/cach
Key Personnel: Supt., Lloyd Masayumptewa.
Institution Type/Description: Park Museum.
Hours & Admission Prices: Visitor Center: daily 8-5. No charge; donations accepted. Closed New Year's Day; Thanksgiving; Christmas. &
Attendance: 1,000,000 (actual)

Clarkdale

TUZIGOOT NATIONAL MONUMENT, 25 Tuzigoot Rd., Clarkdale, AZ 86324. Mailing Address: P.O. Box 219, Camp Vere, AZ 86322-0219. Tel.: 928-634-5564 & 567-5276. Fax: 928-567-3597. Facebook.
E-mail: MOCA_administration@nps.gov
Web Site: www.nps.gov/tuzi
Key Personnel: Supt., Dorothy FireCloud; Supvr., Caleb Kesler.
Institution Type/Description: Park Museum & Visitor Center: located on the Sinagua Indian ruins.
Hours & Admission Prices: Winter: daily 8-5; Summer: daily 8-6. Adults $10; children 15 & under and senior citizens with Golden Age Passport no charge. Closed New Year's Day; Christmas.

Clifton

GREENLEE COUNTY HISTORICAL SOCIETY, 299 Chase Creek, Clifton, AZ 85533. Mailing Address: P.O. Box 787, Clifton, AZ 85533. Tel.: 602-865-3115. Facebook.
E-mail: greenleecountyhs74@gmail.com
Key Personnel: Pres. (V), Tammy McWhinney; Museum Shop Mgr., Linda Fout.
Institution Type/Description: Historical Society Museum.
Hours & Admission Prices: Tues., Thurs. & Sat. 2-4:30; tours by appointment. No charge; donations accepted.
Attendance: 1,000 (estimated)

Coolidge

CASA GRANDE RUINS NATIONAL MONUMENT, 1100 W. Ruins Dr., Coolidge, AZ 85128. Tel.: 520-723-3172. Fax: 520-723-7209.
Web Site: www.nps.gov/cagr
Key Personnel: Administrative Officer, Diana Mills.
Institution Type/Description: Archaeology & Park Museum: located on Hohokam village site dating to approx. A.D. 500-1450.
Hours & Admission Prices: Daily 9-5. Adults $5; children 15 & under and educational groups no charge. Golden Eagle, Golden Age, Golden Access Passports honored. Closed Thanksgiving; Christmas.
Attendance: 85,000 (actual)

COOLIDGE HISTORICAL SOCIETY, 151 W. Harding Ave., Coolidge, AZ 85228. Mailing Address: P.O. Box 1186, Coolidge, AZ 85228. Tel.: 520-723-3588.
Institution Type/Description: Historical Society Museum.
Hours & Admission Prices: Oct.-April Fri.-Sat. 10-2; other times by appointment.

Cottonwood

VERDE HISTORICAL SOCIETY, CLEMENCEAU HERITAGE MUSEUM, 1 N. Willard, Cottonwood, AZ 86326-3651. Mailing Address: P.O. Box 511, Cottonwood, AZ 86326-0511. Tel.: 928-634-2868.
E-mail: clemenceauheritagem@qwestoffice.net
Web Site: www.clemenceaumuseum.com
Key Personnel: Dir., Helen Killebrew; Pres. (V), & Museum Shop Mgr., Barbara Evans; Chm. (V), Bob Lanning; Treas., Connie Phillips.
Institution Type/Description: Historical Society Museum: housed in 1923-1924 school building.
Hours & Admission Prices: Wed. 9-12, Fri.-Sun. 11-3. No charge; donations accepted. Closed New Year's Day; Easter; Independence Day; Thanksgiving; Christmas.
Attendance: 1,754 (actual)

Douglas

THE DOUGLAS HISTORICAL SOCIETY - DOUGLAS-WILLIAMS HOUSE, 1001 D Ave., Douglas, AZ 85607. Tel.: 520-364-7370. Facebook.
E-mail: info@douglashistoricalsociety.net
Web Site: www.douglasazhistoricalsociety.net
Key Personnel: Dir. & C.E.O., Lavinia C. Spivey.
Institution Type/Description: Historical Society Museum.
Hours & Admission Prices: Wed. & Sat. 12-4; other times by appointment. No charge; donations accepted.
Attendance: 1,000 (estimated)

SLAUGHTER RANCH MUSEUM, 6153 Geronimo Trail, Douglas, AZ 85608. Mailing Address: 12630 N. 103rd Ave., Ste. 214, Sun City, AZ 85351. Tel.: 520-678-7935. Fax: 602-933-3777.
E-mail: slaughterranch.mail@gmail.com
Web Site: www.slaughterranch.com
Key Personnel: C.E.O. (V), Harvey Finks; Education & Historian, Dr. Reba Grandrud.
Institution Type/Description: Historic Site: located on c.1893 John Slaughter Ranch.
Hours & Admission Prices: Wed.-Sun. 9:30-3:30. Adults $5; children no charge. Closed New Year's Day; Christmas.
Attendance: 4,000 (estimated)

Dragoon

THE AMERIND MUSEUM, 2100 N. Amerind Rd., Dragoon, AZ 85609. Mailing Address: P.O. Box 400, Dragoon, AZ 85609-0400. Tel.: 520-586-3666. Fax: 520-586-4679. Facebook, Twitter & Instagram: amerindmuseum.
E-mail: amerind@amerind.org
Web Site: www.amerind.org
Key Personnel: Pres., John H. Davis; Dir., Dr. Christine Szuter; Cur., Dr. Eric Kaldahl; Museum Shop Mgr., Tammy Stansberry.
Institution Type/Description: Archaeology & Ethnology Museum and Art Gallery.
Hours & Admission Prices: Business Office: Mon.-Fri. 8-5. Museum: Tues.-Sun. 10-4. Adults $10, senior citizens $9, children 10-17 $7; members & children under 10 no charge. Closed New Year's Day; Easter; Memorial Day; Independence Day; Labor Day; Thanksgiving; Christmas.
Attendance: 13,000 (actual)

Flagstaff

THE ARBORETUM AT FLAGSTAFF, 4001 S. Woody Mountain Rd., Flagstaff, AZ 86005. Tel.: 928-774-1442. Fax: 928-774-1441.
E-mail: info@thearb.org
Web Site: www.thearb.org
Key Personnel: Dir., Lynne Nemeth; Pres., Ingrid Lee; Dir. Research, Kris Haskins; Dir. Education, Coreen Walsh; Mgr. Finance, Kirsten Mead.
Institution Type/Description: Arboretum.
Hours & Admission Prices: April 15-Oct. Wed.-Mon. 9-5. Guided Tours: daily 11 & 1. Adults $10, seniors & college students $7, children 3-17 $5; dogs $2.50; children under 3 & members no charge.
Attendance: 18,709 (actual)

ARIZONA HISTORICAL SOCIETY - PIONEER MUSEUM, 2340 N. Fort Valley Rd., Flagstaff, AZ 86001-1200. Mailing Address: 949 E. 2nd St., Tucson, AZ 85719-4898. Tel.: 928-774-6272. Fax: 928-774-1596.
E-mail: ahsflagstaff@azhs.gov
Web Site: www.azhs.gov
Key Personnel: Northern Arizona Division Dir., William Peterson, Ph.D.
Institution Type/Description: History Museum.
Hours & Admission Prices: May-Oct. Mon.-Sat. 9-5; Nov.-April Mon.-Sat. 10-4. Adults $6, seniors 65 & over and students $5, youth 7-17 $3; veterans, children 6 & under and members no charge. Closed New Year's Day; Martin Luther King Jr. Day; Presidents' Day; Columbus Day; Veterans Day; Thanksgiving; Christmas.
Attendance: 12,000 (estimated)

COLORADO PLATEAU BIODIVERSITY CENTER, Northern Arizona University, Flagstaff, AZ 86011. Mailing Address: Northern Arizona University, Campus Box 5640, Flagstaff, AZ 86011. Tel.: 928-523-4463. Fax: 928-523-7500.
E-mail: stefan.sommer@nau.edu
Web Site: www.mpcer.nau.edu/cpbc
Key Personnel: Div. Cur. Arthropods, Neil Cobb; Cur. Botany, Dr. Randall Scott; Div. Cur. Botany, Dr. Tina Ayers; Cur. Vertebrates, Dr. Tad Theimer; Cur. Ichthyology, Dr. Linn Montgomery; Div. Cur. Fungi, Dr. Kitty Gehring; Cur. Genetics & Genomics, Dr. Gery Allan; Div. Cur. Paleoecology, Dr. Scott Anderson; Div. Cur. Marine Invertebrates & Molluscs, Dr. Stephen Shuster.
Institution Type/Description: Natural History Museum.
Hours & Admission Prices: No charge; donations accepted.
Attendance: 15,000 (estimated)

LOWELL OBSERVATORY, 1400 W. Mars Hill Rd., Flagstaff, AZ 86001-4499. Tel.: 928-774-3358. Fax: 928-774-6296.
E-mail: mbaker@lowell.edu
Web Site: www.lowell.edu
Key Personnel: Dir., Jeffrey C. Hall; Trustee, Lowell Putnam; Museum Shop Mgr., Diana Weintraub.

Institution Type/Description: Astronomy Museum & Observatory.
Hours & Admission Prices: Call for hours. Adults $15, children 5-17 $8; discounts to AAA members; members & children under 5 no charge. Closed New Year's Eve & Day; Easter; Independence Day; Thanksgiving; Christmas Eve & Day. &
Attendance: 100,000 (estimated)

MUSEUM OF NORTHERN ARIZONA, 3101 N. Fort Valley Rd., Flagstaff, AZ 86001-8348. Tel.: 928-774-5213. Fax: 928-779-1527. Facebook.
E-mail: info@mna.mus.az.us
Web Site: www.musnaz.org
Key Personnel: Dir. & C.E.O., Carrie Heinonen; Dir. Mktg., Cristen Crujido.
Institution Type/Description: History Museum: building built in 1928.
Hours & Admission Prices: Mon.-Sat. 10-5, Sun. 12-5. Adults $12, senior & military $10, students w/ID $7, youth 10-17 & Native Americans $8; children under 10 & members no charge. Closed New Year's Day; Thanksgiving; Christmas. &
Attendance: 60,000 (actual)

NAU ART MUSEUM, Knoles & McMullen Circle, Bldg. #10, N. NAU Campus, Flagstaff, AZ 86011. Mailing Address: P.O. Box 6021, Flagstaff, AZ 86011. Tel.: 928-523-3471. Fax: 928-523-1424.
E-mail: art.museum@nau.edu
Web Site: www4.nau.edu/art_museum
Formerly: Northern Arizona University Art Museum and Galleries
Key Personnel: Dir., George V. Speer.
Institution Type/Description: Art Museum.
Hours & Admission Prices: Museum: Tues.-Sat. 12-5. Beasley Gallery: Mon.-Fri. 11-4. No charge; donations accepted. Closed legal & university holidays. &
Attendance: 40,000 (estimated)

RIORDAN MANSION STATE HISTORIC PARK, 409 W. Riordan Rd., Flagstaff, AZ 86001-6440. Mailing Address: 949 E. 2nd St., Tucson, AZ 85719-4898. Tel.: 928-779-4395. Fax: 928-556-0253.
Web Site: www.azstateparks.com/riordan-mansion
Key Personnel: Riordan Mansion Mgr., Nikki Lober.
Institution Type/Description: Historic Mansion: c.1904 site containing a collection of original Craftsman furnishings.
Hours & Admission Prices: May-Oct. daily 9:30-5; Nov.-April Thurs.-Mon. 10:30-5; guided tours on the hour, reservations recommended. Adults $10, youth 7-13 $5; children under 6 no charge. Closed Thanksgiving; Christmas.
Attendance: 22,000 (estimated)

SUNSET CRATER VOLCANO NATIONAL MONUMENT, 6400 N. U.S. Hwy. 89, Flagstaff, AZ 86004-2759. Tel.: 928-527-0322. Fax: 928-526-4259.
E-mail: kayci_cook@nps.gov
Web Site: www.nps.gov
Key Personnel: Supt., Kayci Cook Collins; Cur., Gwenn Gallenstein.
Institution Type/Description: Park Museum & Visitor Center.
Hours & Admission Prices: May-Oct. daily 8-5; Nov.-May daily 9-5. Admission: $20 per vehicle; $15 per motorcycle; $10 per cyclist or pedestrian. Closed Christmas. &
Attendance: 300,000 (estimated)

WALNUT CANYON NATIONAL MONUMENT, 6400 N. Hwy. 89, Flagstaff, AZ 86004-2759. Tel.: 928-527-0322. Fax: 928-526-4259.
Web Site: www.nps.gov
Key Personnel: Supt., Kayci Cook Collins; Cur., Gwenn Gallenstein.
Institution Type/Description: Park Museum: located on the site of prehistoric Indian ruins of the Sinagua Indian culture.
Hours & Admission Prices: Daily 9-5. Admission: $20 per passenger vehicle, $15 per motorcycle, $10 per cyclist or pedestrian. Closed Christmas. &
Attendance: 150,000 (estimated)

WUPATKI NATIONAL MONUMENT, 6400 N. Hwy. 89, Flagstaff, AZ 86004-2759. Tel.: 928-527-0322. Fax: 928-526-4259.
E-mail: gwenn_gallenstein@nps.gov
Web Site: www.nps.gov
Key Personnel: Supt., Kayci Cook Collins; Cur., Gwenn Gallenstein.
Institution Type/Description: Historic Site: over 2,600 archaeological sites dating from approximately 1100 A.D.; Hopi ancestral homeland.
Hours & Admission Prices: Daily 9-5. Admission: $20 per passenger vehicle, $15 per motorcycle, $10 per cyclist or pedestrian. Closed Christmas. &
Attendance: 300,000 (estimated)

Florence

MCFARLAND STATE HISTORIC PARK, 24 W. Ruggles Ave., Florence, AZ 85232. Mailing Address: P.O. Box 109, Florence, AZ 85232-0109. Tel.: 520-868-5216. Fax: 520-868-9056.
E-mail: cdemille@azstateparks.gov
Web Site: www.co.pinal.az.us/mcfarland
Formerly: McFarland Historical State Park
Key Personnel: Park Mgr., Jessica Licano-Moore.
Institution Type/Description: Park Museum: housed in 1878 Pinal County Courthouse.
Hours & Admission Prices: June-Sept. Mon.-Sat. 9-2; Oct.-May Mon.-Sat. 9-5. Closed Christmas. &
Attendance: 7,500 (estimated)

PINAL COUNTY HISTORICAL SOCIETY AND MUSEUM, 715 S. Main St., Florence, AZ 85132. Mailing Address: P.O. Box 851, Florence, AZ 85132. Tel.: 520-868-4382.
E-mail: pchsmuseum@yahoo.com
Web Site: www.pinalcountyhistoricalmuseum.org
Key Personnel: Pres. (V), Cathy Adam; Museum Mgr., H. Christine Reid; Vice Pres. & Collections, Terri Bonesteel; Treas., Larry Pfeiffer; Recording Sec., Doris Hagemann.
Institution Type/Description: Historical Society Museum.
Hours & Admission Prices: Sept.-July 14 Tues.-Sat. 11-4, Sun. 12-4. Adults $5; discounts to groups of 10 or more; members & children under 18 no charge. Closed New Year's Day; Easter; Independence Day; Thanksgiving; Christmas. &
Attendance: 6,091 (actual)

Fort Apache

NOHWIKE BAGOWA, THE WHITE MOUNTAIN APACHE CULTURAL CENTER AND MUSEUM, Indian Rte. 46, Fort Apache, AZ 85926. Mailing Address: P.O. Box 507, Fort Apache, AZ 85926-0507. Tel.: 928-338-4625. Fax: 928-338-1716.
Web Site: www.wmat.nsn.us
Key Personnel: Dir., Dr. Karl Hoerig; Tribal Chm., Ronnie Lupe.
Institution Type/Description: Historical Museum.
Hours & Admission Prices: Winter: Mon.-Fri. 8-5; Summer: Mon.-Sat. 8-5. Adults $5, students $3; children under 7 & tribal members no charge. Closed major holidays. &
Attendance: 15,203 (actual)

Fort Huachuca

FORT HUACHUCA MUSEUM, Boyd & Grierson Sts., Fort Huachuca, AZ 85613. Mailing Address: IMSW-HUA-PLT, Fort Huachuca, AZ 85613-6000. Tel.: 520-533-3638.
E-mail: curator@huachucamuseum.com
Web Site: www.huachuca.army.mil/site/visitor/index.asp
Key Personnel: Dir., Tim Phillips.
Institution Type/Description: History Museum: housed on 1877 Fort, National Historic Landmark.
Hours & Admission Prices: Tues.-Sat. 9-4. No charge; donations accepted. Closed Federal holidays. &
Attendance: 70,000 (actual)

Fountain Hills

RIVER OF TIME MUSEUM, 12901 N. La Montana Dr., Fountain Hills, AZ 85268-4742. Tel.: 480-837-2612. Fax: 480-836-4292.
E-mail: info@rotmuseum.org
Web Site: rotmuseum.org
Key Personnel: Exec. Dir., Cherie Koss; Pres. (V), Gerry Colbert; Museum Shop Mgr., Sandra Ursini.
Institution Type/Description: History Museum.
Hours & Admission Prices: June-Oct. Thurs.-Sat. 9 to noon; Winter: Tues.-Sat. 1-4; groups by appointment. Adults $5, seniors $4, children 6-12 & students $3; members no charge. &
Attendance: 900

Fredonia

PIPE SPRING NATIONAL MONUMENT VISITOR CENTER AND CULTURAL MUSEUM, 406 N. Pipe Spring Rd., Fredonia, AZ 86022. Mailing Address: HC 65, Box 5, 406 N. Pipe Spring Rd., Fredonia, AZ 86022. Tel.: 928-643-7105.
E-mail: pisp_interpretation@nps.gov
Key Personnel: Zion Natl. Park Forever Project, Susan Garcia.
Institution Type/Description: History Museum.

Hours & Admission Prices: Grounds & Museum: Summer daily 8-5; Winter daily 8:30-4:30. Castle: June-Aug. daily 8-4:30; Sept.-May daily 9-4. Adults $7; children under 15 no charge. Closed Thanksgiving; Christmas. &
Attendance: 50,000 (estimated)

Ganado

HUBBELL TRADING POST NATIONAL HISTORIC SITE, Hwy. 264, Ganado, AZ 86505. Mailing Address: P.O. Box 150, Ganado, AZ 86505-0150. Tel.: 928-755-3475. Fax: 928-755-3405.
E-mail: kathy_tabaha@nps.gov
Web Site: www.nps.gov/hutr/
Key Personnel: Supt., Lloyd Masayumptewa; Museum Cur., Nancy Mahaney; Museum Technician, Kathleen Tabaha; Museum Shop Mgr., Edison Eskeets.
Institution Type/Description: Historic Site.
Hours & Admission Prices: May-Sept. daily 8-6; Oct.-April daily 8-5. No charge. Closed New Year's Day; Thanksgiving; Christmas. &
Attendance: 86,059 (actual)

Gilbert

GILBERT HISTORICAL MUSEUM, 10 S. Gilbert Rd., Gilbert, AZ 85296-1047. Mailing Address: P.O. Box 1484, Gilbert, AZ 85299-1484. Tel.: 480-926-1577. Facebook: Gilbert Historical Museum.
E-mail: info@gilbertmuseum.org
Web Site: www.gilbertmuseum.org
Institution Type/Description: History Museum.
Hours & Admission Prices: Tues.-Sat. 9-4. Adults $6, seniors $5, children 5-12 $3; children under 5 no charge. Closed holidays. &
Attendance: 5,000 (actual)

Glendale

ARIZONA DOLL AND TOY MUSEUM, 5847 W. Myrtle Ave., Glendale, AZ 85301. Tel.: 623-939-6186. Facebook.
E-mail: kathylanford@cox.net
Key Personnel: Pres. (V), Kathleen Lanford; Museum Shop Mgr., Cheryl Fox.
Institution Type/Description: Doll and Toy Museum.
Hours & Admission Prices: Tues.-Sat. 10-4. Adults $5, children $1; discounts to handicapped. Closed holidays. &
Attendance: 7,500 (estimated)

GLENDALE COMMUNITY COLLEGE ART COLLECTION, Art Department, 6000 W. Olive Ave., Glendale, AZ 85302. Tel.: 623-845-3755.
E-mail: pam.hall@gccaz.edu
Web Site: www2.gccaz.edu
Key Personnel: Cur., Darlene Goto.
Institution Type/Description: Art Museum.
Hours & Admission Prices: Fall & Spring Semesters: Mon.-Thurs. 7am-10pm, Fri.-Sat. 7-5; Summer: Mon.-Thurs. 7am-9pm, Sun. 12-5. No charge.

SAHUARO RANCH PARK HISTORIC AREA, 9802 N. 59th Ave., Glendale, AZ 85302-1203. Mailing Address: 5850 W. Glendale Ave., Glendale, AZ 85301-2563. Tel.: 623-930-4200. Fax: 623-915-7587.
E-mail: maborruso@glendaleaz.com
Web Site: www.glendaleaz.com/srpha
Formerly: Historic Sahuaro Ranch
Key Personnel: Coord. Facilities & Events, Paul King; Coord. Historic Education & Outreach, John Akers.
Institution Type/Description: Historic House Museum.
Hours & Admission Prices: June-July Fri.-Sat. 10-2; Sept.-May Wed.-Sat. 10-2, Sun. 12-4. No charge; donations accepted. Closed Federal holidays; Easter. &
Attendance: 50,000 (actual)

SOUTHWEST MUSEUM OF ENGINEERING, COMMUNICATIONS AND COMPUTATION, 5802 W. Palmaire Ave., Glendale, AZ 85301-2442. Tel.: 623-435-1522.
E-mail: info@smecc.org
Web Site: www.smecc.org
Key Personnel: Archivist, Ed Sharpe.
Institution Type/Description: Technology Museum.
Hours & Admission Prices: Tues.-Sat. 12-3; other times by appointment. Call to confirm. No charge.

Globe

BESH-BA-GOWAH ARCHAEOLOGICAL PARK, 1324 Jesse Hayes Rd., Globe, AZ 85501. Mailing Address: 150 N. Pine St., Globe, AZ 85501-2514. Tel.: 928-425-0320. Fax: 928-402-1071. Facebook.
E-mail: beshbagowah@globeaz.gov
Web Site: www.globeaz.gov/visitors/besh-ba-gowah
Key Personnel: Dir., Leana Asberry.
Institution Type/Description: Archaeology Museum & Archaeological Site.
Hours & Admission Prices: July-Sept. Wed.-Sun. 9-4:30; Oct.-June daily 9-4:30. Adults $5, senior citizens 65 & over $4; children 12 & under no charge. Closed New Year's Day; Thanksgiving; Christmas. &
Attendance: 35,000 (estimated)

GILA COUNTY HISTORICAL MUSEUM, 1330 N. Broad St., Globe, AZ 85501. Mailing Address: P.O. Box 2891, Globe, AZ 85502-2891. Tel.: 928-425-7385.
E-mail: museum@gilahistorical.com
Key Personnel: C.E.O., Gary Andress; Acting Dir. & Museum Mgr., Linda Lopey; Treas., Jane Hale; Museum shop Mgr., Vernon Perry.
Institution Type/Description: History Museum: housed in 1920 mine rescue facility.
Hours & Admission Prices: Mon.-Fri. 10-4, Sat. 11-3. No charge; donations accepted. Closed major holidays. &
Attendance: 4,000 (estimated)

Goodyear

BIBLE MUSEUM, Hampton Inn & Suites, 2000 N. Litchfield, Goodyear, AZ 85395-1280. Tel.: 623-536-8614. Fax: 623-536-1414.
E-mail: BibleMuseum@hotmail.com
Institution Type/Description: Religious Museum.
Hours & Admission Prices: Mon.-Fri. 9-4.

Grand Canyon National Park

GRAND CANYON NATIONAL PARK MUSEUM COLLECTION, 2C Albright Ave., Grand Canyon Village, South Rim, Grand Canyon National Park, AZ 86023. Mailing Address: P. O. Box 129, Grand Canyon, AZ 86023-0129. Tel.: 928-638-7769 (Museum) & 7888 (National Park). Fax: 928-638-7490.
E-mail: GRCA_Museum_Collection@nps.gov
Web Site: www.nps.gov/grca/historyculture/collections.htm
Key Personnel: Supt., Christine Lehnertz.
Institution Type/Description: National Park: the Grand Canyon, a deep gorge of the Colorado River measuring 277 mi. long, 1-18 mi. wide & one mile deep.
Hours & Admission Prices: Park: daily 24 hours. Library & Museum: Tues.-Thurs. 8-4:30, Mon. & Fri. by appointment. Park: $15 per person; $30 per vehicle. Annual Pass: $60. &
Attendance: 5,900,000 (estimated)

Greer

BUTTERFLY LODGE MUSEUM, 4 County Rd. 1126, Greer, AZ 85927. Mailing Address: P.O. Box 76, Greer, AZ 85927-0076. Tel.: 928-735-7514.
E-mail: butterflylodgemuseum@gmail.com
Web Site: butterflylodgemuseum.org
Institution Type/Description: History Museum: housed in the home of Western writer, James Willard Schultz and his artist son, Hart Merriam Schultz, also known as Lone Wolf. Listed on the National Register of Historic Places.
Hours & Admission Prices: Memorial Day to Labor Day Thurs.-Sat. 10-5. Adults $2, youth 12-17 $1; children no charge. &

Hereford

CORONADO NATIONAL MEMORIAL, 4101 E. Montezuma Canyon Rd., Hereford, AZ 85615-9376. Tel.: 520-366-5515. Fax: 520-366-5705.
Web Site: www.nps.gov/coro
Institution Type/Description: Park Museum & Visitor Center.
Hours & Admission Prices: Daily 9-5. No charge; donations accepted. Closed Thanksgiving; Christmas. &
Attendance: 26,000 (actual)

Holbrook

NAVAJO COUNTY HISTORICAL SOCIETY MUSEUM, 100 E. Arizona St., Holbrook, AZ 86025-2698. Tel.: 928-524-6558.
E-mail: contact@holbrookazmuseum.org
Web Site: www.holbrookazmuseum.org
Key Personnel: Dir., Jolynn Fox.
Institution Type/Description: History Museum.
Hours & Admission Prices: Daily 8-5. No charge; donations accepted. Closed federal holidays. ⅊
Attendance: 24,917 (estimated)

Jerome

GOLD KING MINING MUSEUM AND GHOST TOWN, Perkinsville Rd., Jerome, AZ 86331. Mailing Address: P.O. Box 125, Jerome, AZ 86331. Tel.: 928-634-0053.
E-mail: info@goldkingmineghosttown.com
Web Site: goldkingmineghosttown.com/index.php/contact/
Institution Type/Description: Mining Museum.
Hours & Admission Prices: Daily 10-5. Closed Thanksgiving; Christmas.

JEROME HISTORICAL SOCIETY MINE MUSEUM, 200 Main St., Jerome, AZ 86331. Mailing Address: P.O. Box 156, Jerome, AZ 86331-0156. Tel.: 928-634-5477. Fax: 928-634-7122.
E-mail: jtomlinson@jeromehistoricalsociety.com
Web Site: www.jeromehistoricalsociety.com
Key Personnel: Pres. (V), Allen Muma.
Institution Type/Description: Historical Society Museum.
Hours & Admission Prices: Daily 9-5. Adults $2, seniors $1; children no charge. ⅊
Attendance: 30,112 (actual)

JEROME STATE HISTORIC PARK, 100 Douglas Rd., Jerome, AZ 86331. Mailing Address: P.O. Box D, Jerome, AZ 86331-0097. Tel.: 928-634-5381. Fax: 928-639-3132.
E-mail: wyeager@azstateparks.gov
Web Site: www.azstateparks.com
Key Personnel: Park Mgr., Wes Yeager.
Institution Type/Description: History & Mining Museum.
Hours & Admission Prices: Daily 8:30-4:45. Adults 14 & over $7, children 7-13 $4; children 6 & under no charge. Closed Christmas. ⅊
Attendance: 70,584 (actual)

Kayenta

KAYENTA VISITOR'S CENTER, Hwy. 160, Kayenta, AZ 86033. Mailing Address: P.O. Box 544, Kayenta, AZ 86033-0544. Tel.: 928-697-3572.
Institution Type/Description: Visitor Center.
Hours & Admission Prices: Call for hours.

Kingman

MOHAVE MUSEUM OF HISTORY AND ARTS, 400 W. Beale, Kingman, AZ 86401-5797. Tel.: 928-753-3195. Fax: 928-718-1562.
E-mail: director@mohavemuseum.org
Web Site: www.mohavemuseum.org
Key Personnel: Dir. & C.E.O., Shannon Rossiter; Pres. (V), William Porter.
Institution Type/Description: History Museum; housing Mohave County history.
Hours & Admission Prices: Mon.-Fri. 9-5, Sat. 1-5. Adults $4, seniors $3; discounts to AAM members; members no charge. Closed New Year's Day; Easter; Memorial Day; Labor Day; Thanksgiving; Christmas. ⅊
Attendance: 30,000 (estimated)

ROUTE 66 MUSEUM, 120 W. Andy Devine Ave., Ste. 7, Kingman, AZ 86401-5807. Tel.: 928-753-9889.
E-mail: rt66mus@okhistory.org
Web Site: www.okhistory.org/sites/route66.php
Institution Type/Description: History Museum; housed in the historical Powerhouse building.
Hours & Admission Prices: Daily 9-5. Adults $4, seniors 60 & over $3; discounts to groups; children under 12 no charge. ⅊

Lake Havasu City

LAKE HAVASU MUSEUM OF HISTORY, 320 London Bridge Rd., Lake Havasu City, AZ 86403-4645. Tel.: 928-854-4938.
E-mail: lhmuseum@npgcable.com

Web Site: www.havasumuseum.com
Key Personnel: Pres. (V), Ed Walker; Exec. Dir., Becky Maxedon.
Institution Type/Description: History Museum.
Hours & Admission Prices: Tues.-Sat. 10-4. Adults $5; members and children 12 & under no charge. Closed New Year's Day; Independence Day; Thanksgiving; Christmas. ⅊
Attendance: 3,500 (actual)

Litchfield Park

WILDLIFE WORLD ZOO & AQUARIUM, 16501 W. Northern, Litchfield Park, AZ 85340-9466. Tel.: 623-935-9453. Fax: 623-935-9499.
E-mail: info@wildlifeworld.com
Web Site: www.wildlifeworld.com
Key Personnel: Dir., Mickey Ollson; Deputy Dir., Jack Ewert; Museum Shop Mgr., Anna Milts.
Institution Type/Description: Zoo & Aquarium.
Hours & Admission Prices: Daily 9-6. Adults $39.95, senior citizens $29.95, children $16.95; discounts to AAM, AZA & ZAA members. ⅊
Attendance: 450,000 (estimated)

Maricopa

AK-CHIN HIM-DAK ECO-MUSEUM, 47685 N. Eco-Museum Rd., Maricopa, AZ 85139. Tel.: 520-568-1350. Fax: 520-568-1351.
E-mail: epeters@ak-chin.nsn.us
Key Personnel: Dir., Elaine Peters.
Institution Type/Description: Cultural History Museum.
Hours & Admission Prices: Mon.-Fri. 10-3, Sat. by appointment only. No charge; donations accepted.

Mesa

ARIZONA COMMEMORATIVE AIR FORCE MUSEUM, Falcon Field, 2017 N. Greenfield Rd., Mesa, AZ 85215. Tel.: 480-924-1940.
E-mail: info@azcaf.org
Web Site: www.azcaf.org
Institution Type/Description: Combat Aviation History Museum.
Hours & Admission Prices: June-Sept. Wed.-Sun. 9-3; Oct.-May daily 10-4. Adults 13 & over $15, seniors 62 & over $12, children 5-12 $5; children under 5, disabled & active veterans no charge. Closed New Year's Day; Thanksgiving; Christmas.

ARIZONA MUSEUM OF NATURAL HISTORY, 53 N. MacDonald St., Mesa, AZ 85201-7325. Tel.: 480-644-2230. Fax: 480-644-3424. Facebook.
E-mail: azmnh.info@mesaaz.gov
Web Site: www.azmnh.org
Formerly: Mesa Southwest Museum
Key Personnel: Dir., Dr. Thomas H. Wilson; Pres. (V), Lynn Johnson; Cur. Natural History, Dr. Robert McCord; Cur. Anthropology, Emily Goble Early; Collections Mgr., Melanie Deer; Coord. Exhibits, Tim Walters; Exhibits Preparator, Mike Keller; Collections Mgr., Gavin McCullough; Cur. Education, Alison Stoltman; Administrative Asst., Sandra Williamson; Museum Graphics/ Multimedia Specialist, Michael Ramos; Museum Shop Mgr., Terri Walters; Volunteer Coord., T.J. Gaudelli; Membership Coord., Heather Jones.
Institution Type/Description: Natural History Museum.
Hours & Admission Prices: Tues.-Fri. 10-5, Sat. 11-5, Sun. 1-5. Adults $12, senior citizens 65 & over $10, students $8; children 3-12 $7; discounts to AAA & AAM members; children 2 & under and members no charge. ⅊
Attendance: 124,229 (actual)

I.D.E.A. MUSEUM, 150 W. Pepper Place, Mesa, AZ 85201-7326. Tel.: 480-644-4332. Fax: 480-644-2466.
E-mail: ideamuseum@mesaaz.gov
Web Site: www.ideamuseum.org
Formerly: Arizona Museum For Youth
Key Personnel: Chm., Jennifer Duff; Exec. Dir., Sunnee D. O'Rork; Cur. Art, Jeffory Morris; Mktg. & Public Rels. Dir., Yvette Armendariz; Exhibits Designer, Rex Witte; Cur. Education, Dena Milliron.
Institution Type/Description: Children's Fine Arts Center.
Hours & Admission Prices: Tues.-Sat. 9-4, Sun. 12-4. Admission $8; discounts to AAM & Association of Children's Museums members; children under 1 & members no charge. ⅊
Attendance: 70,546 (actual)

MESA ARTS CENTER & MESA CONTEMPORARY ARTS MUSEUM, One E. Main St., Mesa, AZ 85211. Mailing Address: P.O. Box 1466, Mesa, AZ 85211-1466. Tel.: 480-644-6560.
E-mail: cindy.ornstein@mesaartscenter.com
Web Site: www.mesaartscenter.com
Key Personnel: Exec. Dir. & Dir. Art & Culture Dept., Cindy Ornstein; Cur., Patty Haberman.
Institution Type/Description: Contemporary Art Museum.
Hours & Admission Prices: Tues.-Wed. & Fri.-Sat. 10-5, Thurs. 10-8, Sun. 12-5. No charge. &

MESA HISTORICAL MUSEUM, 51 E. Main St., Mesa, AZ 85201-1823. Mailing Address: P.O. Box 582, Mesa, AZ 85211-0582. Tel.: 480-835-2286. Facebook, Pinterest, Instagram, Twitter.
E-mail: info@mesamuseum.org
Web Site: www.valleyhistoryinc.com
Key Personnel: Exec. Dir., Tim Sheridan; Chm. Bd. (V), Spencer Morgan.
Institution Type/Description: History Museum
Hours & Admission Prices: Wed.-Sat. 10-4. Adults $5, seniors over 65 $4, youth 3-12 $3; discounts to groups; children under 3 & members no charge. Closed major holidays. &
Attendance: 28,000 (estimated)

WINGSPAN AIR MUSEUM, Superstition Springs Mall, 6555 E. Southern Ave., Ste. 1106, Mesa, AZ 85206. Mailing Address: Wingspan Air Heritage Foundation, P.O. Box 21268, Mesa, AZ 85277. Tel.: 480-924-5543.
E-mail: info@wingspanair.org
Web Site: www.wingspanair.org
Key Personnel: Pres. & Exec. Dir., Jeff Furnari; Dir. Aircraft Collections, Robert Kropp.
Institution Type/Description: Military History Museum.
Hours & Admission Prices: Tues.-Fri. 10-6, Sat. 10-5.

Miami

BULLION PLAZA CULTURAL CENTER & MUSEUM, 150 N. Plaza Circle, Miami, AZ 85539. Mailing Address: P.O. Box 786, Miami, AZ 85539-0786. Tel.: 928-473-3700. Fax: 928-473-9097.
E-mail: az.terr1912@yahoo.com
Web Site: www.bullionplazamuseum.org
Key Personnel: Exec. Dir., Thomas N. Foster; Pres. (V), Joe Sanchez.
Institution Type/Description: Art & History Museum: housed in a former grammar school; built in 1923.
Hours & Admission Prices: Thurs.-Sat. 11-3, Sun. 12-3; other times by appointment. No charge; donations accepted. &
Attendance: 2,000 (estimated)

Mount Lemmon

UNIVERSITY OF ARIZONA MOUNT LEMMON SKYCENTER, 9800 E. Ski Run Rd., Mount Lemmon, AZ 85619. Tel.: 520-626-8792.
E-mail: skycenter@as.arizona.edu
Web Site: www.skycenter.arizona.edu
Key Personnel: Dir., Alan Strauss.
Institution Type/Description: Science Center: located at an altitude of 9,157.
Hours & Admission Prices: By appointment.

Nogales

PIMERIA ALTA HISTORICAL SOCIETY, 136 N. Grand Ave., Nogales, AZ 85621-3211. Mailing Address: P.O. Box 2281, Nogales, AZ 85628-2281. Tel.: 520-287-4621. Fax: 520-287-5201. Facebook.
Key Personnel: Pres., Kathleen Escalada; Project Dir., Sigrid Maitrejean.
Institution Type/Description: Historical Society Museum.
Hours & Admission Prices: Tues.-Sun. 11-4. No charge; donations accepted. Closed New Year's Day; Thanksgiving; Christmas. &
Attendance: 3,359 (actual)

Oracle

ORACLE HISTORICAL SOCIETY, INC. - ACADIA RANCH MUSEUM, 825 E. Mt. Lemmon Hwy., Oracle, AZ 85623. Mailing Address: P.O. Box 10, Oracle, AZ 85623. Tel.: 520-896-9609.
E-mail: oraclehistoricalsociety@gmail.com
Web Site: oraclehistoricalsociety.org
Key Personnel: Pres. (V), Kent Thornell.

Institution Type/Description: Historic Building: housed on the ranch of Edwin S. and Lillian Dodge; built c.1882.
Hours & Admission Prices: Thurs. 4-6, Sat. 1-4; other times by appointment. No charge; donations accepted. &
Attendance: 500 (estimated)

Page

JOHN WESLEY POWELL MEMORIAL MUSEUM, 6 N. Lake Powell Blvd., Page, AZ 86040. Mailing Address: Box 547, Page, AZ 86040-0547. Tel.: 928-645-9496. Fax: 928-645-3412. Facebook: Powell Museum.
E-mail: director@powellmuseum.org
Web Site: www.powellmuseum.org
Key Personnel: Pres. (V), John Mayes; Dir., Billie Wright; Museum Shop Mgr., Vickie Johnston.
Institution Type/Description: History Museum.
Hours & Admission Prices: April-Oct. Mon.-Sat. 9-5; Nov.-March Mon.-Fri. 9-5; call for additional hours. Adults $5, senior citizens 61 & over $3, children 6-13 $1; military & their families during the summer, children 5 & under, museum & Blue Star Museums' members no charge. Closed Thanksgiving; Christmas. &
Attendance: 30,000 (actual)

Parker

BILL WILLIAMS RIVER NATIONAL WILDLIFE REFUGE, 60911 Hwy. 95, Parker, AZ 85344. Mailing Address: P.O. Box 1306, Albuquerque, NM 87103-1306. Tel.: 928-667-4144. Fax: 928-667-3402.
Web Site: www.fws.gov/refuge/bil_williams_river/
Key Personnel: Mgr., Richard Gilbert.
Institution Type/Description: Wildlife Refuge.
Hours & Admission Prices: Visitor Center: Mon.-Fri. 8-4, Sat.-Sun. 10-2. Closed federal holidays.

COLORADO RIVER INDIAN TRIBES MUSEUM, 1007 W. Arizona Ave., Parker, AZ 85344. Mailing Address: 26600 Mohave Rd., Parker, AZ 85344. Tel.: 928-669-8970. Fax: 928-669-1925.
E-mail: wilene.fisher-holt@crit-nsn.gov
Web Site: coloradoriverindiantribes.com
Key Personnel: Dir., Michael Tsosie.
Institution Type/Description: American Indian Museum.
Hours & Admission Prices: Mon.-Fri. 8-5, Sat. 10-3; call for holiday hours. No charge; donations accepted. &
Attendance: 4,000 (estimated)

PARKER AREA HISTORICAL SOCIETY, 1214 California Ave. (Hwy. 95), Parker, AZ 85344-1500. Mailing Address: P.O. Box 1500, Parker, AZ 85344. Tel.: 928-669-8077.
Web Site: www.parkerhistory.org/
Institution Type/Description: Historical Society Museum.
Hours & Admission Prices: Thurs.-Fri. 10-2.

Payson

NORTHERN GILA COUNTY HISTORICAL SOCIETY, INC. - RIM COUNTRY MUSEUM, 700 S. Green Valley Pkwy., Payson, AZ 85541. Mailing Address: P.O. Box 2532, Payson, AZ 85547-2532. Tel.: 928-474-3483. Facebook: @RimCountyMuseumAndZaneGreyCabin.
E-mail: ngchs82@gmail.com
Web Site: www.rimcountrymuseums.com
Key Personnel: Museum Shop Mgr., Betty Berryman; Financial Dir., Nancy Purkey; Pres. & Archivist, Sandy Carson; Security, Peter Bernard.
Institution Type/Description: Cultural History Museum.
Hours & Admission Prices: Mon. & Wed.-Sat. 10-4, Sun. 1-4. Adults $5, seniors 55 & over $4, students 12-18 $3; discounts to groups, military, partnership museum members; members & children under 12 no charge. Closed New Year's Day; Easter; Thanksgiving; Christmas. &
Attendance: 5,500 (estimated)

Peoria

CHALLENGER SPACE CENTER OF ARIZONA, 9617 N. Metro Pkwy. W., Ste. 2214, Phoenix, AZ 85051. Tel.: 623-322-2001 & 2012.
E-mail: information@azchallenger.net
Web Site: www.azchallenger.org
Key Personnel: Exec. Dir., Beverly Swayman.

Institution Type/Description: Space Museum.
Hours & Admission Prices: Temporarily closed for relocation. &

PEORIA ARIZONA HISTORICAL SOCIETY SCHOOL HOUSE & JAIL MUSEUMS, 8322 W. Washington St., Peoria, AZ 85345. Mailing Address: c/o Peoria Arizona Historical Society, P.O. Box 1, Peoria, AZ 85380. Tel.: 623-487-8030.
E-mail: pahsoffice@aol.com
Institution Type/Description: History Museum.
Hours & Admission Prices: Sept.-May Tues., Thurs. & Sat. 10-2; other times by appointment. No charge; donations accepted. &

WEST VALLEY ART MUSEUM, Peoria, AZ 85385. Mailing Address: P.O. Box 6377, Peoria, AZ 85385. Tel.: 623-972-0635.
E-mail: info@wvam.org
Web Site: www.wvam.org
Formerly: West Valley Art Museum-Sun Cities Museum of Art
Institution Type/Description: Art Museum.
Hours & Admission Prices: Temporarily closed. &
Attendance: 5,000 (estimated)

Peridot

SAN CARLOS APACHE CULTURAL CENTER, Hwy. 70 at Milepost 272, Peridot, AZ 85542. Mailing Address: P.O. Box 760, Peridot, AZ 85542-0760. Tel.: 928-475-2894.
Institution Type/Description: Cultural Center.
Hours & Admission Prices: Mon.-Fri. 9-5. Adults $3, seniors $1.50, students $1; children under 12 no charge.
Attendance: 2,497 (actual)

Petrified Forest National Park

PETRIFIED FOREST NATIONAL PARK, One Park Rd., Petrified Forest National Park, AZ 86028-9997. Mailing Address: P.O. Box 2217, Petrified Forest National Park, AZ 86028-2217. Tel.: 928-524-6228, ext. 267. Fax: 928-524-3567.
E-mail: patricia_thompson@nps.gov
Web Site: www.nps.gov
Key Personnel: Supt., Cliff Spencer.
Institution Type/Description: National Park.
Hours & Admission Prices: Call for hours. Car: $10, Bus $5; Golden Eagle, Golden Age & Golden Access passes honored. Closed Christmas. &
Attendance: 580,000 (estimated)

Phoenix

ADOBE MOUNTAIN RAILROAD MUSEUM & DESERT RAILROAD, 23280 N. 43rd Ave., Phoenix, AZ 85310. Mailing Address: 9186 W. Grovers Ave., Peoria, AZ 85382. Tel.: 623-670-1904.
E-mail: jerryoy147@msn.com
Key Personnel: Dir., Jerry Oyler.
Institution Type/Description: Railroad Museum.
Hours & Admission Prices: Sept.-May Sun. 12-4; other times by appointment. No charge; donations accepted. &
Attendance: 4,350 (estimated)

ARIZONA CAPITOL MUSEUM, 1700 W. Washington St., Phoenix, AZ 85007-2812. Tel.: 602-926-3620. Fax: 602-256-7985.
E-mail: capmus@azlibrary.gov
Web Site: www.azlibrary.gov/museum
Key Personnel: Museum Admin., Dorie Hanson; Asst. Admin., Jason Czerwinski; Cur., Stephanie Mahan; Museum Shop Mgr., Ken Judd.
Institution Type/Description: History Museum: housed in restored Capitol Building.
Hours & Admission Prices: September-May Mon.-Fri. 9-4, Sat. 10-2; June-August Mon.-Fri. 9-4. No charge; donations accepted. &
Attendance: 60,000 (actual)

ARIZONA CENTER FOR NATURE CONSERVATION, DBA THE PHOENIX ZOO, 455 N. Galvin Pkwy., Phoenix, AZ 85008-3431. Tel.: 602-286-3800.
Web Site: www.phoenixzoo.org
Formerly: Arizona Zoological Society dba the Phoenix Zoo
Key Personnel: Chm. Bd., Harry A. Papp; C.E.O. & Pres., Norberto J. (Bert) Castro; Exec. Vice Pres. & C.F.O., Bonnie Mendoza; Exec. Vice Pres. Conservation & Education, Ruth Allard; Exec. Vice Pres., Animal Health & Collection, Dr. Gary West, DVM; Vice President, Devel., Lorraine Frias; Vice

Pres. H.R., Christine Lowery-Nunez; Vice Pres. Facilities, Opers. & Construction, Brian T. Skinner.
Institution Type/Description: Zoo.
Hours & Admission Prices: Jan. 10-May & Sept.-Nov. 2 daily 9-5; June-Aug. Mon.-Fri. 7-2, Sat.-Sun. 7-4; Nov. 3-Jan. 9 daily 9-4. Adults $20, senior citizens $17, children $14; discounts to groups; children 2 & under and members no charge. Closed Christmas. &
Attendance: 1,400,000 (estimated)

ARIZONA JEWISH HISTORICAL SOCIETY, 122 E. Culver St., Phoenix, AZ 85004-1720. Tel.: 602-241-7870.
E-mail: lbell@azjhs.org
Web Site: www.azjhs.org
Key Personnel: Exec. Dir., Lawrence Bell, Ph.D.; Assoc. Dir., Jeffrey Schesnol.
Institution Type/Description: Jewish Historical Society.
Hours & Admission Prices: Office hours: 10:30-4.
Attendance: 2,000 (estimated)

ARIZONA MILITARY MUSEUM, Papago Park Military Reservation, 5636 E. McDowell Rd., Phoenix, AZ 85003-2668. Mailing Address: 9014 N. Wealth Rd., Maricopa, AZ 85139. Tel.: 602-267-2676 & 509-8762. Fax: 602-253-3342.
E-mail: joeabo7@gmail.com
Key Personnel: Dir. & Pres. (V), Col. Joseph E. Abodeely, USA (Ret.).
Institution Type/Description: Military Museum.
Hours & Admission Prices: Sept.-June Sat.-Sun. 1-4. No charge; donations accepted. Closed holidays. &
Attendance: 1,200 (estimated)

ARIZONA SCIENCE CENTER, 600 E. Washington, Phoenix, AZ 85004-2394. Tel.: 602-716-2000.
E-mail: robertsonr@azscience.org
Web Site: www.azscience.org
Key Personnel: C.E.O. & Pres., Chevy Humphrey; Chief Finance & Admin. Officer, Dean Briere; Chief of Staff, Carrie Altamirano; Chief Strategy Officer, Kristin Priscella; Chief Learning Officer, Andi Fourlis; Chief Mktg. Officer, Cathy Hall; Vice Pres., Exhibits & Collections, Sari Custer.
Institution Type/Description: Science Center.
Hours & Admission Prices: Daily 10-5. Gen. admission: adults $18, children 3-17 $13; children 2 & under and members no charge. Featured Exhibitions, IMAX & Planetarium: additional fee; discounts to members. Closed Christmas. &
Attendance: 300,000 (actual)

ARIZONA STATE PARKS BOARD, 1300 W. Washington, Phoenix, AZ 85007-2929. Mailing Address: 23751 N. 23rd Ave., Ste. 190, Phoenix, AZ 85085-1863. Tel.: 602-542-4174. Fax: 602-542-4188. Facebook.
E-mail: sblack@azstateparks.gov
Web Site: azstateparks.com
Key Personnel: Exec. Dir., Sue Black; State Historic Preservation Officer, Kathryn Leonard.
Institution Type/Description: Historical Parks, Archaeological Park, Museums & Arboretum.
Hours & Admission Prices: Office: daily 8-5. See website for admissions. &
Attendance: 600,000 (estimated)

BARBARA ANDERSON GIRL SCOUT MUSEUM, Girl Scouts - Arizona Cactus-Pine Council, Inc., 806 N. 3rd St., Ste. 200, Phoenix, AZ 85012. Tel.: 602-452-7000, 800-352-6133. Fax: 602-452-7100.
E-mail: museum@girlscoutsaz.org
Web Site: www.girlscoutsaz.org
Institution Type/Description: Girl Scout Museum.
Hours & Admission Prices: By appointment. No charge; donations accepted. &
Attendance: 400 (estimated)

CHILDREN'S MUSEUM OF PHOENIX, 215 N. 7th St., Phoenix, AZ 85034. Tel.: 602-253-0501.
Web Site: www.childrensmuseumofphoenix.org
Key Personnel: C.E.O., Kate Wells; Dir. Devel., Debra Paine; Dir. Mktg. & Communs., Marion Wiener; Dir. Education & Programs, Kelley Fitzsimmons; Controller, Rachel Johnson; Dir. Visitor Experience, Betsy Ferman.
Institution Type/Description: Children's Museum: housed in the former Monroe School building.
Hours & Admission Prices: Tues.-Sun. 9-4. Admission $11, seniors 62 & over $10; members & children under one no charge.

DEER VALLEY PETROGLYPH PRESERVE, 3711 W. Deer Valley Rd., Phoenix, AZ 85308-2038. Tel.: 623-582-8007. Facebook.
Web Site: shesc.asu.edu/dvpp
Formerly: Deer Valley Rock Art Center
Key Personnel: Admin., Alexandra Brewis Slade; Dir., Richard Toon; Opers. Coord., Elizabeth Gerold.
Institution Type/Description: General Museum.
Hours & Admission Prices: Museum will re-open spring 2017. Adults $7, seniors, military & students $4, children 6-12 $3; discounts to AAA members; members, ASU students and children 5 & under no charge. &
Attendance: 16,000 (actual)

DESERT BOTANICAL GARDEN, 1201 N. Galvin Pkwy., Papago Park, Phoenix, AZ 85008-3437. Tel.: 480-941-1225. Fax: 480-481-8124. TDD: 480-481-8143.
E-mail: contact@dbg.org
Web Site: www.dbg.org
Key Personnel: Exec. Dir., Kenneth J. Schutz; Snr. Dir. Desert Horticulture & Conservation, Dr. Kimberlie McCue; Snr. Dir. Membership & Philanthropy, Beverly Duzik; Dir. Event Svcs., Marcia Flynn; Dir. Horticulture, Tina Wilson; Snr. Dir. Visitor Experience & Community Engagement, Elaine McGinn; C.F.O., Margie Burke; Dir. Facilities & Opers., Halee Williamson; Dir. Mktg. Communs., Dana Terrazas; Dir. Education, Marie Long; Dir. IT, James Gentile; Dir. Exhibits, Lauren Warren; Dir. HR, Jason Neifield.
Institution Type/Description: Botanical Garden.
Hours & Admission Prices: Daily 7-8. Adults $14.95, youth 3-17 $9.95; members & children under 3 no charge. Closed Independence Day; Thanksgiving; Christmas. &
Attendance: 380,259 (actual)

GEORGE WASHINGTON CARVER MUSEUM AND CULTURAL CENTER, 415 E. Grant St., Phoenix, AZ 85004-2659. Mailing Address: P.O. Box 20491, Phoenix, AZ 85036-0491. Tel.: 602-254-7516. Fax: 602-258-7050.
E-mail: info@gwcmccaz.org
Web Site: www.gwcmccaz.org
Key Personnel: Exec. Dir., Princess Crump.
Institution Type/Description: History Museum: housed in Arizona's first Black high school, Phoenix Union Colored High, built in 1926.
Hours & Admission Prices: Feb.-June 1st & 3rd Fri. 3-9.

HALL OF FLAME MUSEUM OF FIREFIGHTING, 6101 E. Van Buren, Phoenix, AZ 85008-3421. Tel.: 602-275-3473. Fax: 602-275-0896.
E-mail: webmaster@halloflame.org
Web Site: www.halloflame.org
Key Personnel: Exec. Dir., Dr. Peter M. Molloy; Pres. (V), George F. Getz; Vice Pres., Bert A. Getz; Vice Pres., Lynn Getz; Sec. & Treas., Michael Olsen; Cur. Public Programs & Education, Mark Moorhead; Restorator, Donald G. Hale; Docent, Grace Deutsch; Volunteer Pres., Ron Deutsch.
Institution Type/Description: History & Fire Fighting Museum.
Hours & Admission Prices: Mon.-Sat. 9-5, Sun. 12-4. Adults $7, senior citizens $6, students 6-17 $5, children 3-5 $2; discount to groups; children under 3 no charge. Closed New Year's Day; Thanksgiving; Christmas. &
Attendance: 35,000 (actual)

HEARD MUSEUM, 2301 N. Central Ave., Phoenix, AZ 85004-1323. Tel.: 602-252-8848. Fax: 602-252-9757. Facebook.
E-mail: contact@heard.org
Web Site: www.heard.org
Key Personnel: Dir. & C.E.O., David Roche; Dir. Curation & Research, Ann E. Marshall, Ph.D.; C.O.O. & Deputy Dir., John Bulla; Dir. Strategic Devel. & Programming, Dan Hagerty; C.F.O., Robin Klung; Guild Pres., Mary Endorf; Head Cur., Diana Pardue; Registrar, Sharon Moore; Dir. Community Engagement, Marcus Monenerkit; Dir. Library & Archives, Mario Nick Klimiades; Dir. Creative & Mktg., Caesar Chaves; Vice Pres. Retail Sales, Bruce McGee.
Institution Type/Description: Native Cultures & Art Museum.
Hours & Admission Prices: Mon.-Sat. 9:30-5, Sun. 11-5. Adults $18, senior citizens 65 & over $13.50, students w/ID & children 6-12 $7.50; discounts to AAM members; children under 6, Native Americans with proof of tribal heritage & members no charge. Closed Easter; Independence Day; Thanksgiving; Christmas. &
Attendance: 200,000 (estimated)

HOUSE OF BROADCASTING RADIO & TELEVISION MUSEUM, 7534 N. 7th St., Phoenix, AZ 85020-4129. Tel.: 602-944-1997. Fax: 602-997-8707. Facebook.
E-mail: pschu@q.com

Web Site: www.houseofbroadcasting.com
Key Personnel: C.E.O. & Pres. (V), Mary Morrison.
Institution Type/Description: Radio & Television History Museum.
Hours & Admission Prices: Temporarily closed for relocation.
Attendance: 150 (estimated)

LISA SETTE GALLERY, 210 E. Catalina Dr., Phoenix, AZ 85012. Tel.: 480-990-7342.
E-mail: sette@lisasettegallery.com
Web Site: www.lisasettegallery.com
Key Personnel: Dir., Lisa Sette; Assoc. Dir., Ashley Rice.
Institution Type/Description: Art Gallery.
Hours & Admission Prices: Tues.-Fri. 10-5, Sat. 12-5; other times by appointment.

MUSICAL INSTRUMENT MUSEUM, 4725 E. Mayo Blvd., Phoenix, AZ 85050. Tel.: 480-478-6000. Fax: 480-471-8690. Facebook.
E-mail: guestservice@mim.org
Web Site: www.mim.org
Key Personnel: Exec. Dir., April Salomon; Deputy Dir. & Chief Cur., Dr. Manuel Jordan; C.F.O. & Bd. Treas., Craig D. Culy; Dir. Education & Public Programs, Brian P. Dredla.
Institution Type/Description: Musical Instrument Museum.
Hours & Admission Prices: Daily 9-5. Adults $20, teens 13-19 $15, children 4-12 $10; discounts to AAM members; members and children 3 & under no charge. Closed Thanksgiving; Christmas. &
Attendance: 200,000 (estimated)

PHOENIX AIRPORT MUSEUM, 3400 Sky Harbor Blvd., Ste. 3300, Phoenix, AZ 85034. Tel.: 602-273-2744. Fax: 602-273-2702. Facebook & Twitter: @PHXSkyHarbor.
E-mail: gary.martelli@phoenix.gov
Web Site: skyharbor.com/museum
Key Personnel: Mgr. & Cur., Gary Martelli.
Institution Type/Description: Arizona Art & Aviation History Museum.
Hours & Admission Prices: Daily 24 hours. No charge. &

PHOENIX ART MUSEUM, 1625 N. Central Ave., Phoenix, AZ 85004-1685. Tel.: 602-257-1880. Fax: 602-253-8662. Facebook; Instagram; Twitter.
E-mail: info@phxart.org
Web Site: www.phxart.org
Key Personnel: Dir. Sybil Harrington & C.E.O., Amada Cruz; C.F.O., Mark Koening; Selig Family Chief Cur., Gilbert Vicario; Cur. Latin American Art, Vanessa Davidson, Ph.D.; Adjunct Cur. American Art, Betsy Fahlman, Ph.D.; Cur. Asian Art, Janet Baker, Ph.D.; Cur. Fashion Design, Dennita Sewell; Registrar, Laura Wenzel; Museum Store Mgr., Jennifer Barnella.
Institution Type/Description: Art Museum.
Hours & Admission Prices: Tues. & Thurs.-Sat. 10-5, Wed. 10-9, Sun. 12-5, 1st Fri. of month 6-10. Adults $23, senior citizens $20, students $18, youth $14; discounts to AAM; members, veterans, active-duty military & children under 6 no charge. &
Attendance: 285,920 (actual)

PHOENIX CENTER FOR THE ARTS, 1202 N. Third St., Phoenix, AZ 85004-1812. Tel.: 602-254-3100. Fax: 602-559-4694.
E-mail: info@phoenixcenterforthearts.org
Web Site: phoenixcenterforthearts.org
Key Personnel: Dir., Joseph Benesh; Deputy Dir., Lauren Henschen.
Institution Type/Description: Art Center.
Hours & Admission Prices: Mon.-Fri. 9-5. No charge. &
Attendance: 35,000 (actual)

PHOENIX POLICE MUSEUM, Historic City Hall, 17 S. 2nd Ave., 1st Fl., Phoenix, AZ 85003. Tel.: 602-534-7278.
E-mail: mike.nikolin@phoenix.gov
Web Site: phoenixpolicemuseum.com
Key Personnel: Exec. Dir., Dennis Garrett.
Institution Type/Description: Police Museum.
Hours & Admission Prices: Mon.-Fri 9-3. No charge; donations accepted. Closed city & federal holidays. &
Attendance: 8,700

PHOENIX TROLLEY MUSEUM/ARIZONA STREET RAILWAY MUSEUM, 25 W. Culver St., Phoenix, AZ 85004. Mailing Address: P.O. Box 13521, Phoenix, AZ 85002. Tel.: 602-254-0307.
E-mail: phoenixtrolley@hotmail.com
Web Site: www.phoenixtrolley.com

Key Personnel: Pres. (V), John Drury.
Institution Type/Description: Railway Museum.
Hours & Admission Prices: Oct.-May Sat. 9-4; other times by appointment.
Attendance: 300 (estimated)

PIONEER ARIZONA LIVING HISTORY VILLAGE & MUSEUM, Mailing Address: 3901 W. Pioneer Rd., Phoenix, AZ 85086-7020. Tel.: 623-465-1052. Fax: 623-465-3901.
E-mail: info@pioneeraz.org
Web Site: pioneeraz.org
Key Personnel: Dir., Joe Villasenor; Pres. (V), C.J. Smith.
Institution Type/Description: Living History Museum Complex.
Hours & Admission Prices: June-Sept. 5 Wed.-Sun. 7-11; Sept. 6-May Wed.-Sun. 9-4. Adults $10, seniors & veterans $8, children under 18 $8; discounts to groups; children under 5 no charge. Guided Tour: $1 extra. Closed Easter; Thanksgiving; Christmas. &
Attendance: 65,000 (estimated)

PUEBLO GRANDE MUSEUM AND ARCHAEOLOGICAL PARK, 4619 E. Washington, Phoenix, AZ 85034-1909. Tel.: 602-495-0901, 877-706-4408 (toll free). Fax: 602-495-5645.
E-mail: pueblo.grande.museum.pks@phoenix.gov
Web Site: www.pueblogrande.com
Institution Type/Description: Archaeological Site Museum.
Hours & Admission Prices: May-Sept. Tues.-Sat. 9-4:45; Oct.-April Mon.-Sat. 9-4:45, Sun. 1-4:45. Adults $6, senior citizens 55 & over $5, children $3; Sun. children 17 & under, members & children under 6 no charge. Closed New Year's Day; Martin Luther King Jr. Day; Independence Day; Labor Day; Thanksgiving; Christmas. &
Attendance: 44,165 (actual)

ROSSON HOUSE MUSEUM AT HERITAGE SQUARE, 7th St. & Monroe, Phoenix, AZ 85004. Mailing Address: 113 N. 6th St., Phoenix, AZ 85004-2328. Tel.: 602-261-8063.
E-mail: director@heritagesquarephx.org
Web Site: heritagesquarephx.org
Key Personnel: Exec. Dir., Michelle Reid.
Institution Type/Description: Historic House Museum: built in 1895.
Hours & Admission Prices: Wed.-Sat. 10-4, Sun. 12-4. Adults $9, seniors, students, active military & AAA members $8, children $4; children 5 & under no charge. Closed New Year's Day; Easter; Memorial Day; Independence Day; Labor Day; Thanksgiving; Christmas Eve & Day. &
Attendance: 8,000 (estimated)

SHEMER ART CENTER & MUSEUM, 5005 E. Camelback Rd., Phoenix, AZ 85018-3015. Tel.: 602-262-4727.
E-mail: info@shemerartcenter.org
Web Site: www.shemerartcenter.org
Key Personnel: Exec. Dir., Shonna James; Artistic Dir., Tess Mosko Scherer; Admin. Asst., Anne Mello.
Institution Type/Description: Art Museum.
Hours & Admission Prices: Tues.-Sat. 10-3. Suggested donations: couple $10, adult 7. Closed New Year's Day; Martin Luther King Jr. Day; Presidents' Day; Cesar Chavez's Birthday; Memorial Day; Independence Day; Labor Day; Veterans Day; Thanksgiving & day after; Christmas. &
Attendance: 25,000 (estimated)

SUNNYSLOPE HISTORICAL SOCIETY MUSEUM, 737 E. Hatcher Rd., Phoenix, AZ 85020-2506. Tel.: 602-331-3150.
E-mail: shsociety1@qwestoffice.net
Web Site: www.sunnyslopehistoricalsociety.org
Key Personnel: Pres., Bobbie Kraver.
Institution Type/Description: History Museum.
Hours & Admission Prices: Thurs.-Sun. 10-3. No charge; donations accepted. &
Attendance: 1,000 (estimated)

WELLS FARGO HISTORY MUSEUM CLOSED, 145 W. Adams St., Phoenix, AZ 85003. Mailing Address: Wells Fargo Historical Services, 420 Montgomery St., MAC-A0101-022, San Francisco, CA 94163. Tel.: 602-378-1852. Fax: 602-378-5174. Facebook: Wells Fargo.
E-mail: phoenix.historymuseum@wellsfargo.com
Web Site: www.wellsfargohistory.com
Key Personnel: Museum Mgr., Connie Whalen; Cur., Amanda Walters.
Institution Type/Description: Company History Museum: housed in Wells Fargo Plaza Bldg.
Hours & Admission Prices: Mon.-Fri. 9-5. No charge. Closed bank holidays. &

Pima

EASTERN ARIZONA MUSEUM AND HISTORICAL SOCIETY OF GRAHAM COUNTY INC., 2 N. Main St., Pima, AZ 85543. Mailing Address: P.O. Box 274, Pima, AZ 85543-0274. Tel.: 928-485-3032.
E-mail: edresbarney@yahoo.com
Web Site: www.easternarizonamuseum.com
Key Personnel: Pres., Nick Bingham; Vice Pres., Shawn Wright; Sec., Anna Jane Jarvis; Dir. & Treas., Edres Barney.
Institution Type/Description: History Museum.
Hours & Admission Prices: Thurs.-Sat. 10-3; other times by appointment. No charge; donations accepted. &
Attendance: 2,400 (estimated)

Pine

PINE-STRAWBERRY MUSEUM, 3886 Hwy. 87, Pine, AZ 85544. Mailing Address: P.O. Box 564, Pine, AZ 85544-0564. Tel.: 928-476-3547.
Institution Type/Description: History Museum.
Hours & Admission Prices: Wed.-Sat. 10-2. Adults $1; children 11 & under no charge. Closed New Year's Day; Easter; Thanksgiving; Christmas. &
Attendance: 2,000 (estimated)

Prescott

HIGHLANDS CENTER FOR NATURAL HISTORY, 1375 S. Walker Rd., Prescott, AZ 86303-6893. Tel.: 928-776-9550. Fax: 928-776-9530.
E-mail: highlands@highlandscenter.org
Web Site: highlandscenter.org
Formerly: Community Nature Center
Key Personnel: Exec. Dir., Dave Irvine.
Institution Type/Description: Nature Center and Botanic Garden.
Hours & Admission Prices: March-Nov. 9-4; Dec.-Feb. 10-3. Charge for classes, special events & programming only; donations accepted. Trails open to the public. &
Attendance: 11,000 (estimated)

PHIPPEN MUSEUM, 4701 Hwy. 89 N., Prescott, AZ 86301-8303. Tel.: 928-778-1385. Fax: 928-778-4524. Facebook: Phippen Museum of Western Art.
E-mail: phippen@phippenartmuseum.org
Web Site: www.phippenartmuseum.org
Key Personnel: Dir., Kim Villalpando; Chm. (V), Kevin Pitts; Mktg. & Communications Mgr., Edd Kellerman; Programming & Volunteer Coord., Brenda Smith; Cur., Mgr. Collections & Museum Shop Mgr., Lynette Tritel; Gallery Mgr. Admin. Asst., Brenda Smith; Bookkeeper, Julie Richardson; Museum Librarian, Linda Phillips; Education Coord. & Programming, Neal McEwen.
Institution Type/Description: Art of the American West Museum.
Hours & Admission Prices: Tues.-Sat. 10-4, Sun. 1-4. Adults $7, students $5; discounts to AAA members; children under 12 & members no charge. Closed New Year's Day; Easter; Thanksgiving; Christmas. &
Attendance: 10,333 (actual)

SHARLOT HALL MUSEUM, 415 W. Gurley St., Prescott, AZ 86301-3691. Tel.: 928-445-3122. Fax: 928-776-9053. Facebook.
E-mail: gails@sharlot.org
Web Site: www.sharlot.org
Key Personnel: Dir., Fred Veil; Pres. (V), Kim Fiuston; Chief Cur., Mick Woodcock.
Institution Type/Description: Regional History Museum.
Hours & Admission Prices: June-Sept. Mon.-Sat. 10-5, Sun. 12-4; Oct.-May Mon.-Sat. 10-4, Sun. 12-4. Adults $7, seniors $6, children 13-17 $3; members and children 18 & under no charge. Closed New Year's Day; Thanksgiving; Christmas. &
Attendance: 30,000 (estimated)

SMOKI MUSEUM - AMERICAN INDIAN ART & CULTURE, 147 N. Arizona, Prescott, AZ 86301-3184. Mailing Address: P.O. Box 10224, Prescott, AZ 86304-0224. Tel.: 928-445-1230.
E-mail: director@smokimuseum.org
Web Site: www.smokimuseum.org
Key Personnel: Dir., Cynthia Gresser; Pres. (V), James Christopher; Vice Pres., Ray Carlson; Treas., Kent Robinson; Museum Shop Mgr., Carol Semplice.
Institution Type/Description: Anthropology Museum.

Hours & Admission Prices: Mon.-Sat. 10-4, Sun. 1-4. Adults $7, seniors $6, students $5; children 12 & under and Native Americans no charge. Closed Easter; Thanksgiving; Christmas. ఉ
Attendance: 6,800 (actual)

THE SPOT...A CHILD'S MUSEUM, 3250 Gateway Blvd., Prescott, AZ 86302. Mailing Address: P.O. Box 3938, Prescott, AZ 86302.
E-mail: president@thespotmuseum.org
Key Personnel: Dir., C.E.O. & Pres. (V), Judy L. Paris; Chmn. (V), Eileen Bond.
Institution Type/Description: Children's Science & Arts Museum.
Hours & Admission Prices: Fri.-Sat. 1-5, Sun. 1:30-4:30. Admission $3. ఉ
Attendance: 2,500 (estimated)

Quartzsite

TYSON'S WELL STAGE STATION MUSEUM, 161 W. Main St., Quartzsite, AZ 85346. Mailing Address: Quartzsite Historical Society, P.O. Box 331, Quartzsite, AZ 85346-0331. Tel.: 928-927-5229.
E-mail: qhs@tds.org
Web Site: www.quartzstemuseum.org
Institution Type/Description: History Museum: housed in a restored adobe stage station built in 1866.
Hours & Admission Prices: April-Oct. Thurs. 9am-12pm; Nov.-March Wed.-Sun. 10-4; other times by appointment. No charge; donations accepted.

Queen Creek

SAN TAN HISTORICAL SOCIETY MUSEUM, 20425 S. Ellsworth Rd., Queen Creek, AZ 85142. Tel.: 480-987-9380.
E-mail: info@santanhistoricalsociety.org
Web Site: www.santanhistoricalsociety.org
Institution Type/Description: Historical Society Museum.
Hours & Admission Prices: Sat. 9-1. No charge.

Roosevelt

TONTO NATIONAL MONUMENT, 26260 N. Arizona Hwy. 188, #2, Roosevelt, AZ 85545. Mailing Address: HC02, Box 4602, Roosevelt, AZ 85545. Tel.: 928-467-2241. Fax: 928-467-2225.
E-mail: TONT_superintendent@nps.gov
Web Site: www.nps.gov/tont
Key Personnel: Supt., Terry Saunders; Park Ranger, Susan Hughes.
Institution Type/Description: Archaeology Museum.
Hours & Admission Prices: Visitor Center & Museum: daily 8-5. Self-Guided Trail: daily 8-4. Adults $3; holders of National Park Pass, Golden Age or Golden Access passes & children under 16 no charge. Closed Christmas. ఉ
Attendance: 80,021 (actual)

Safford

DISCOVERY PARK CAMPUS, 1651 W. Discovery Park Blvd., Safford, AZ 85546-3909. Tel.: 928-428-6260. Fax: 928-428-8081.
E-mail: discoverypark@eac.edu
Web Site: www.eac.edu/discoverypark/
Key Personnel: Dir., Paul Anger.
Institution Type/Description: Science Center.
Hours & Admission Prices: Mon.-Fri. 8-5, Sat. 4pm-9:30pm. No charge; donations accepted. ఉ
Attendance: 7,000 (actual)

GRAHAM COUNTY HISTORICAL SOCIETY, 3430 W. Main st., Thatcher, AZ 85552. Mailing Address: P.O. Box 274, Thatcher, AZ 85552-0274. Tel.: 928-651-6389.
E-mail: brentquinn357@gmail.com
Web Site: www.grahammuseum.org
Key Personnel: Pres., Chris Gibbs; Museum Dir., Tom Down.
Institution Type/Description: Historical Society Museum.
Hours & Admission Prices: Jan.-July & mid-Aug. to mid-Dec. Mon.-Tues. & Sat. 10-4; other times by appointment. No charge; donations accepted. Closed holidays. ఉ
Attendance: 3,500 (actual)

Sahuarita

ASARCO MINERAL DISCOVERY CENTER, 1421 W. Pima Mine Rd., Ste. A, Sahuarita, AZ 85629-8361. Tel.: 520-625-7513 & 8233. Fax: 520-625-4756.

E-mail: amdcinfo@asarco.com
Web Site: www.mineraldiscovery.com
Institution Type/Description: Mineral Museum.
Hours & Admission Prices: May-Sept. Tues.-Fri. 9-3, Sat. 9-5. Mine Tours: Sat. 9:30, 11, 12:30, & 3:30. Exhibits & Theater: no charge. Mine Tour: adults $10, seniors & military $8, children 5-12 $7; children 4 & under no charge. Closed major holidays.

TITAN MISSILE MUSEUM, 1580 W. Duval Mine Rd., Sahuarita, AZ 85629. Mailing Address: 1580 W. Duval Mine Rd., Green Valley, AZ 85614. Tel.: 520-625-7736 & 4598. Fax: 520-625-9845.
E-mail: ymorris@titanmissilemuseum.org
Web Site: www.titanmissilemuseum.org
Key Personnel: Acting Exec. Dir., Yvonne C. Morris; Chm. (V), Count Ferdinand von Galen.
Institution Type/Description: Missile Museum: housed in a former operational Titan II ICBM complex.
Hours & Admission Prices: May-Oct. Sun.-Fri. 9:45-4, Sat. 8:45am-5pm; Nov.-April Sunday-Fri. 9:45-5, Sat. 8:45am-5pm. Adults $10.50, senior citizens & military $9.50, children 5-12 $7; discounts to AAA members; members and children 4 & under no charge. Closed Thanksgiving; Christmas. ఉ
Attendance: 50,000 (estimated)

Saint Johns

APACHE COUNTY HISTORICAL SOCIETY MUSEUM, 180 W. Cleveland, Saint Johns, AZ 85936. Mailing Address: P.O. Box 146, Saint Johns, AZ 85936-0146. Tel.: 928-337-4737 & 480-516-2544.
E-mail: achs.museum@yahoo.com
Institution Type/Description: Historical Society Museum.
Hours & Admission Prices: April-Nov. Tues., Thurs. & Sat. 10-2; other times by appointment.

Saint Michaels

ST. MICHAELS HISTORICAL MUSEUM, 24 Mission Rd., Saint Michaels, AZ 86511. Mailing Address: Navajo Tourism Dept., P. O. Box 663, Window Rock, AZ 86515. Tel.: 928-871-4171.
E-mail: info@discovernavajo.com
Web Site: www.discovernavajo.com
Institution Type/Description: History Museum.
Hours & Admission Prices: Memorial Day to Labor Day Mon.-Fri. 9-5.

San Manuel

SAN MANUEL HISTORICAL SOCIETY, 137 8th Ave., San Manuel, AZ 85631-0742. Mailing Address: P.O. Box 742, San Manuel, AZ 85631-0742.
E-mail: smgranny@q.com
Web Site: www.sanmanuelhistoricalsociety.com
Key Personnel: Dir. & Museum Shop Mgr., Janice L. Rapp; Pres. (V), Francis Winslow.
Institution Type/Description: Historical Society Museum.
Hours & Admission Prices: Tues. & Fri. 10-2, Sat. 10-1.

Scottsdale

AFRICAN AMERICAN MULTICULTURAL MUSEUM, 617 N. Scottsdale Rd., Ste. A, Scottsdale, AZ 85257-4207. Tel.: 480-314-4400.
E-mail: aammuseumaz@gmail.com
Web Site: aammuseum.org
Institution Type/Description: Multicultural Museum.
Hours & Admission Prices: Thurs.-Sat. 1-5; other times by appointment. No charge.

CELEBRATION OF FINE ART, 7900 E. Greenway Rd., Ste. 101, Scottsdale, AZ 85260-1714. Tel.: 480-443-7695. Fax: 480-596-8179.
E-mail: info@celebrateart.com
Web Site: www.celebrateart.com
Institution Type/Description: Art Gallery.
Hours & Admission Prices: mid-Jan. to late March daily 10-6. Adults $10, seniors & military $8; children under 12 no charge.

CONGREGATION BETH ISRAEL'S PLOTKIN JUDAICA MUSEUM, 10460 N. 56th St., Scottsdale, AZ 85253-1133. Tel.: 480-951-0323. Fax: 480-951-7150.

E-mail: library@cbiaz.org
Web Site: cbiaz.org
Key Personnel: Chm. (V) & Librarian, Carol Reynolds.
Institution Type/Description: Religious Antiques Museum: housed in Temple belonging to oldest Jewish Congregation in the Phoenix area.
Hours & Admission Prices: By appointment. Donation: adults $3.50. Closed national & Jewish holidays. &
Attendance: 500 (estimated)

ELLIE & MICHAEL ZIEGLER FIESTA BOWL CENTER & MUSEUM, 7135 E. Camelback Rd. Ste. 190, Scottsdale, AZ 85251. Tel.: 480-350-0900. Fax: 480-350-0915.
E-mail: ktrichel@fiestabowl.org
Web Site: www.fiestabowl.org
Key Personnel: Exec. Dir., Mike Nealy.
Institution Type/Description: Sports Museum.
Hours & Admission Prices: Mon.-Fri. 8:30-5. No charge; donations accepted.

FRANK LLOYD WRIGHT'S TALIESIN WEST, 12621 N. Frank Lloyd Wright Blvd., Scottsdale, AZ 85259. Tel.: 480-860-2700 & 627-5340.
Key Personnel: Pres. & C.E.O., Stuart Graff.
Institution Type/Description: Historic House Museum: housed in the former winter home of Frank Lloyd Wright; built in 1937. A National Historic Landmark.
Hours & Admission Prices: June-Aug. Sun.-Mon. & Thurs. 8:30-2:30, Fri.-Sat. 8:30-7:30; Sept. Fri. 8:30-7:30, Sat.-Thurs. 8:30-5; Oct.-May Fri. 8:30-7, Sat.-Thurs. 8:30-6. Closed Easter; Thanksgiving; Christmas.

GEBERT CONTEMPORARY ART GALLERY, 7160 Main St., Scottsdale, AZ 85251-4316. Tel.: 480-970-3111.
E-mail: gallery@gebertartaz.com
Web Site: gebertartaz.com
Institution Type/Description: Art Gallery.
Hours & Admission Prices: Mon.-Wed. & Fri.-Sat. 10-5, Thurs. 10-9, Sun. 12-4.

HOO-HOOGAM KI MUSEUM, 10005 E. Osborn Rd., Scottsdale, AZ 85256-4019. Tel.: 480-362-6320.
E-mail: huhugamki.museaum@srpmic-nsn.gov
Web Site: www.srpmic-nsn.gov/history-culture/museum.asp
Institution Type/Description: Cultural Heritage Museum.
Hours & Admission Prices: Mon.-Fri. 9:30-4:30. No charge. Closed federal holidays.

THE MARSHALL/LEKAE GALLERY, 7106 E. Main St., Scottsdale, AZ 85251-4316. Tel.: 480-970-3111. Fax: 480-970-0092.
E-mail: email@marshall-lekaegallery.com
Web Site: www.marshall-lekaegallery.com
Institution Type/Description: Art Gallery.
Hours & Admission Prices: Mon.-Wed. & Fri.-Sat. 10-5:30, Thurs. 10-9.

RIVA YARES GALLERY, 3625 N. Bishop Ln., Scottsdale, AZ 85251-5511. Tel.: 480-947-3251. Fax: 480-947-4251.
E-mail: art@rivayaresgallery.com
Web Site: www.rivayaresgallery.com
Institution Type/Description: Art Gallery.
Hours & Admission Prices: Mon.-Sat. 10-5.

SCOTTSDALE HISTORICAL MUSEUM, 7333 E. Scottsdale Mall, Scottsdale, AZ 85251-4414. Mailing Address: Scottsdale Historical Society, P.O. Box 143, Scottsdale, AZ 85252-0143. Tel.: 480-945-4499.
E-mail: info@scottsdalehistory.org
Web Site: www.scottsdalemuseum.com
Institution Type/Description: History Museum.
Hours & Admission Prices: Sept. Wed.-Sat. 10-2; Oct.-May Wed.-Sat. 10-5. No charge; donations accepted. Closed holidays.
Attendance: 25,000 (estimated)

SCOTTSDALE MUSEUM OF CONTEMPORARY ART, 7374 E. Second St., Scottsdale, AZ 85251-5604. Mailing Address: 7380 E. Second St., Scottsdale, AZ 85251-5604. Tel.: 480-874-4666. Fax: 480-874-4655. Facebook, Instagram, Twitter.
E-mail: smoca@sccarts.org
Web Site: www.smoca.org
Key Personnel: Bd. Chm., David Itzkowitz; Acting Dir., Jennifer McCabe; Cur. Programming, Julie Ganas; Exhibit Mgr., Laura Best; Registrar, Carrie Tovar; Curatorial Coord., Keshia Turley.

Institution Type/Description: Modern & contemporary art, architecture & design.
Hours & Admission Prices: Tues.-Wed. & Sun. 12-5, Thurs.-Sat. 12-9. Adults $10, students $7; discounts for AAM & ICOM members; Thurs., Fri.-Sat. 5-9, members & children under 15 no charge. Reciprocal membership benefits available. Closed national holidays. &
Attendance: 45,030 (actual)

WESTERN SPIRIT: SCOTTSDALE'S MUSEUM OF THE WEST, 3830 N. Marshall Way, Scottsdale, AZ 85251. Tel.: 480-686-9539. Facebook: Western Spirit Scottsdale's Museum of the West.
E-mail: info@scottsdalemuseumwest.org
Web Site: scottsdalemuseumwest.org
Key Personnel: Dir. & C.E.O., Mike Fox; Museum Shop Mgr., Jeffrey White.
Institution Type/Description: History Museum.
Hours & Admission Prices: Tues.-Wed. & Fri.-Sat. 9:30-5, Thurs. 9:30-9, Sun. 11-5. Adults $13, seniors 65 & over and active military $11, students & children 6-17 $8; members and children 5 & under no charge. Closed Easter; Memorial Day; Independence Day; Labor Day; Thanksgiving; Christmas. &

Second Mesa

HOPI CULTURAL CENTER, 5 Miles W. of 87 Rte. 264, Second Mesa, AZ 86043. Mailing Address: 5200 E. Cortland Blvd., Ste. E200-7, Flagstaff, AZ 86004. Tel.: 928-734-2401.
E-mail: info@hopiculturalcenter.com
Web Site: www.hopiculturalcenter.com
Key Personnel: Gen. Mgr., Lamar Keevama.
Institution Type/Description: History Museum.
Hours & Admission Prices: Call for hours.

Sedona

SEDONA ARTS CENTER, INC., 15 Art Barn Rd., Sedona, AZ 86336-4249. Mailing Address: P.O. Box 569, Sedona, AZ 86339-0569. Tel.: 928-282-3809, 888-954-4442.
E-mail: sac@sedonaartscenter.com
Web Site: www.sedonaartscenter.com
Key Personnel: Exec. Dir., Vince Fazio.
Institution Type/Description: Art Center.
Hours & Admission Prices: Daily 10-5. No charge; donations accepted. Closed Thanksgiving; Christmas. &
Attendance: 62,000 (actual)

SEDONA HERITAGE MUSEUM, 735 Jordan Rd., Jordan Historical Park, Sedona, AZ 86336. Tel.: 928-282-7038. Fax: 928-282-7038.
E-mail: info@sedonamuseum.org
Institution Type/Description: History Museum: housed in the former farm home of Walter & Ruth Jordan, built in 1930. Listed on the National Register of Historic Places.
Hours & Admission Prices: Daily 11-3; group tours by appointment. Adults $7; members & children under 12 no charge. &
Attendance: 12,000 (actual)

Shonto

NAVAJO NATIONAL MONUMENT, End of U.S. Highway 564, Shonto, AZ 86054. Mailing Address: P.O. Box 7717, Shonto, AZ 86054-7717. Tel.: 928-672-2700. Fax: 928-672-2703.
Web Site: www.nps.gov/nava
Key Personnel: Park Archaeologist, Lloyd Masayumptewa; Admin., Matthew Klozik; WNPA Mgr., Althea James; Supt., Alden Miller.
Institution Type/Description: Archaeological Museum.
Hours & Admission Prices: Visitor Center: May 24-Sept. 13 daily 8-6; Sept. 14-May 22 daily 9-5. No charge. Closed New Year's Day; Christmas. &
Attendance: 89,000 (estimated)

Show Low

SHOW LOW HISTORICAL SOCIETY MUSEUM, 561 E. Deuce of Clubs, Show Low, AZ 85901-4826. Mailing Address: P.O. Box 3468, Show Low, AZ 85902-3468. Tel.: 928-532-7115. Fax: 928-532-7115. Facebook: Show Low Museum.
E-mail: showlowmuseum@cableone.net
Web Site: showlowmuseum.com
Key Personnel: Dir., Clair Thomas; Asst. Dir., Carol Grossheim.
Institution Type/Description: Historical Society Museum.

Hours & Admission Prices: March-Dec. Wed.-Sat. 10-3. No charge; donations accepted. &

Attendance: 4,500 (estimated)

Sierra Vista

HENRY F. HAUSER MUSEUM, Ethel Berger Center, 2950 E. Tacoma St., Sierra Vista, AZ 85635-1352. Mailing Address: 1011 N. Coronado, Sierra Vista, AZ 85635. Tel.: 520-439-2306.

E-mail: nancy.krieski@sierravistaaz.gov
Web Site: www.sierravistaaz.gov
Key Personnel: Cur. & Mgr., Nancy M. Krieski.
Institution Type/Description: History Museum.
Hours & Admission Prices: Mon. & Tues. 10-4, Wed. 10-7, Thurs.-Fri. 10-1, Sat. 11-2. No charge; donations accepted. &

Attendance: 3,000 (estimated)

Snowflake

STINSON PIONEER MUSEUM, 102 S. 1st St., Snowflake, AZ 85937. Mailing Address: 113 N. Main St., Ste. A, Snowflake, AZ 85937. Tel.: 928-536-4331 & 4881.

Institution Type/Description: History Museum.
Hours & Admission Prices: Summer: Mon.-Sat. 10-2; other times by appointment.

Somerton

COCOPAH MUSEUM, County 15 and Avenue G, Somerton, AZ 85350. Tel.: 928-627-1992.

E-mail: museum@cocopah.com
Web Site: www.cocopah.com/museum.html
Institution Type/Description: Native American History Museum.
Hours & Admission Prices: Mon.-Fri. 9-4. No charge; donations accepted.

Springerville

CASA MALPAIS VISITOR CENTER AND MUSEUM, 418 E. Main St., Springerville, AZ 85938-5220. Tel.: 928-333-5375.

E-mail: casa@springervilleaz.gov
Web Site: www.casamalpais.org
Key Personnel: Dir., Lynette Cross.
Institution Type/Description: History Museum.
Hours & Admission Prices: Tues.-Sat. 8-4. Guided Tours: 9am, 11:30am, & 2pm. Adults $10, seniors over 60 $8, students 18 & under $5. Closed for tours Dec., Jan. & Feb.

Attendance: 2,000 (actual)

Sun City

DEL WEBB SUN CITIES MUSEUM, 10801 Oakmont Dr., Sun City, AZ 85351. Tel.: 623-974-2568.

E-mail: scahsm@gmail.com
Web Site: www.delwebbsuncitiesmuseum.org
Institution Type/Description: History Museum.
Hours & Admission Prices: mid-Sept. to mid-May Mon., Wed. & Fri. 1-4; other times by appointment only. No charge; donations accepted.

Superior

BOYCE THOMPSON ARBORETUM, 37615 E. Arboretum Way, Superior, AZ 85173-5100. Tel.: 602-827-3000. Fax: 520-689-5858.

E-mail: msiegwar@cals.arizona.edu
Web Site: arboretum.ag.arizona.edu
Formerly: Boyce Thompson Southwestern Arboretum
Key Personnel: Dir., Dr. S.H. "Sy" Sohmer; Chm. (V) & Pres. (V), Ian Thompson; Museum Shop Mgr., Lynnea Spencer.
Institution Type/Description: Arboretum.
Hours & Admission Prices: Summer: daily 6am-3pm; Oct.-April daily 8-5. Adults $15, children 5-12 $5; discounts to AABGA members; members no charge. Closed Christmas. &

Attendance: 85,000 (estimated)

SUPERIOR HISTORICAL SOCIETY - THE BOB JONES MUSEUM, 300 Main St., Superior, AZ 85173. Mailing Address: P.O. Box 613, Superior, AZ 85173.

Institution Type/Description: History Museum.
Hours & Admission Prices: Fri. 1-4, Sat.-Sun. 10-4. No charge; donations accepted. &

Attendance: 700 (estimated)

WORLD'S SMALLEST MUSEUM, 11 W. U.S. Hwy. 60, Superior, AZ 85173-3429. Tel.: 520-689-5800.

E-mail: sales@smallestmuseum.com
Web Site: www.worldssmallestmuseum.com
Institution Type/Description: General Museum.
Hours & Admission Prices: Wed.-Sun. 8-1:30. No charge; donations accepted. Closed major holidays.

Taylor

TAYLOR/SHUMWAY HERITAGE FOUNDATION, 2 N. Main St., Taylor, AZ 85939. Mailing Address: P.O. Box 566, Taylor, AZ 85939. Tel.: 928-536-6649. Facebook.

E-mail: taylormuseum@frontiernet.net
Formerly: Taylor Pioneer Museum
Key Personnel: Chm. (V), Carmen Shumway; Pres. (V), Lynn Hancock; Museum Shop Mgr., Kathryn Udall.
Institution Type/Description: History Museum.
Hours & Admission Prices: Call for hours. No charge; donations accepted. &

Attendance: 2,043 (actual)

Tempe

AMERICAN HEART ASSOCIATION - HALLE HEART CHILDREN'S MUSEUM, 2929 S. 48th St., Tempe, AZ 85282-3145. Tel.: 602-414-2800. Fax: 602-414-5355.

E-mail: hhcm@heart.org
Web Site: www.hhcm.org
Formerly: Halle Heart Center
Key Personnel: Dir. Programs & Operations, Claudine M. Wessel.
Institution Type/Description: Science & Health Museum.
Hours & Admission Prices: Public Tours: Sept.-July Mon. & Fri. 9-4, Tues.-Thurs. 12-4. Admission $5, seniors 62 & over $4; children 3 & under and members no charge. Closed national holidays. &

Attendance: 28,000 (estimated)

ARIZONA HISTORICAL SOCIETY - AZ HERITAGE CENTER AT PAPAGO PARK, 1300 N. College Ave., Tempe, AZ 85281-1211. Mailing Address: 949 E. 2nd St., Tucson, AZ 85719-4898. Tel.: 480-929-0292. Fax: 480-967-5450.

E-mail: azheritagecenter@azhs.gov
Web Site: www.azhs.gov
Key Personnel: Central Arizona Div. Dir., Tawn Downs; Library & Archives Division Dir., Susan Irwin.
Institution Type/Description: History Museum.
Hours & Admission Prices: Museum: Mon.-Thurs. 10-5, Fri-Sat. 10-4. Adults $12, seniors 65 & over $10, children 7-17 $8; veterans & AHS members no charge. Library: Mon.-Thurs. 10-6, Fri. 9-4. No charge. Closed New Year's Day; Martin Luther King Jr. Day; Presidents' Day; Memorial Day; Independence Day; Labor Day; Columbus Day; Veterans Day; Thanksgiving; Christmas. &

Attendance: 22,500 (estimated)

ARIZONA STATE UNIVERSITY ART MUSEUM, 51 E. 10th St., Tempe, AZ 85287. Mailing Address: Box 872911, Tempe, AZ 85287-2911. Tel.: 480-965-2787. Fax: 480-965-5254.

E-mail: asuartmuseum@asu.edu
Web Site: asuartmuseum.asu.edu
Key Personnel: Dir., Miki Garcia; Sr. Cur., Heather Lineberry; Cur., Julio Cesar Morales.
Institution Type/Description: Art Museum & Gallery.
Hours & Admission Prices: Tues.-Wed. & Fri.-Sat. 11-5, Thurs. 11-8. No charge; donations accepted. Closed federal & state holidays. &

Attendance: 51,000 (actual)

ARIZONA STATE UNIVERSITY LIBRARIES' ARCHIVES AND SPECIAL COLLECTIONS - LUHRS GALLERY, Hayden Library, ASU Main Campus, Tempe, AZ 85287-1006. Mailing Address: P.O. Box 871006, Tempe, AZ 85287-1006. Tel.: 480-954-4925.

E-mail: karrie.porterbrace@asu.edu
Key Personnel: Dir., Karrie Porter Brace.
Institution Type/Description: History Museum.
Hours & Admission Prices: Call for hours. No charge.
Attendance: 75,000 (estimated)

CENTER FOR ARCHAEOLOGY AND SOCIETY INNOVATION GALLERY, Arizona State University, SHESC Bldg. 233, Tempe, AZ 85287-2402. Mailing Address: c/o ASU School of Human Evolution & Social Change, P.O. Box 872402, Tempe, AZ 85287-2402. Tel.: 480-965-6213. Fax: 480-965-7671.
E-mail: richard.toon@asu.edu
Web Site: shesc.asu.edu
Key Personnel: Co-Dir., Richard Toon.
Institution Type/Description: Anthropology Museum.
Hours & Admission Prices: Fall & Spring Semesters: Mon.-Fri. 11-3; Winter & Summer: by appointment. No charge. Closed New Year's Eve & Day; Martin Luther King Jr. Day; Memorial Day; Independence Day; Labor Day; Veterans Day; Thanksgiving; Christmas Day & week. &
Attendance: 3,500 (actual)

CENTER FOR METEORITE STUDIES - ARIZONA STATE UNIVERSITY, ISTB4, Bldg. 75, 2nd Fl., 781 E. Terrace Rd., Tempe, AZ 85287-6004. Mailing Address: P.O. Box 876004, Tempe, AZ 85287-6004. Tel.: 480-965-6511. Fax: 480-965-4907. Twitter: @asumeteorites.
E-mail: meteorites@asu.edu
Web Site: meteorites.asu.edu
Key Personnel: Dir., Meenakshi Wadhwa.
Institution Type/Description: Meteorite Museum.
Hours & Admission Prices: Mon.-Fri. 9-5. No charge; donations accepted. Closed ASU holidays. &
Attendance: 3,600 (estimated)

SALT RIVER PROJECT HISTORY MUSEUM, 1521 N. Project Dr., Tempe, AZ 85281-1206. Tel.: 602-236-5900.
Institution Type/Description: History Museum.
Hours & Admission Prices: Mon.-Fri. 9-4.

SEA LIFE ARIZONA AQUARIUM, 5000 S. Arizona Mills Circle, Ste. 145, Tempe, AZ 85282. Tel.: 877-526-3960. Fax: 480-478-7609.
E-mail: arizonasealife@sealifeus.com
Web Site: www.visitsealife.com/arizona
Institution Type/Description: Aquarium.
Hours & Admission Prices: Mon.-Sat. 10-7:30, Sun. 10-6. Adults 13 & over $18; children 3-12 $13. &

TEMPE HISTORY MUSEUM, 809 E. Southern Ave., Tempe, AZ 85282-5205. Tel.: 480-350-5100. Fax: 480-350-5150. TDD: 480-350-5050.
E-mail: museum@tempe.gov
Web Site: www.tempe.gov/museum
Formerly: Tempe Historical Museum
Key Personnel: Museum Admin., Brenda Abney; Cur. Collections, Josh Roffler; Exhibits Coord., Dan Miller; Cur. History, Jared Smith.
Institution Type/Description: History Museum.
Hours & Admission Prices: Museum: Tues.-Sat. 10-5, Sun. 1-5. Petersen House: open for special events only. No charge; donations accepted. Closed major holidays. &
Attendance: 25,316 (actual)

Tombstone

BIRD CAGE THEATRE MUSEUM, 535 E. Allen St., Tombstone, AZ 85638. Mailing Address: P.O. Box 248, Tombstone, AZ 85638-0248. Tel.: 520-457-3421, 800-457-3423 (Toll Free).
E-mail: tombstonebirdcage@gmail.com
Web Site: www.tombstonebirdcage.com
Institution Type/Description: History Museum: built in the 1880s.
Hours & Admission Prices: Self-Guided Tours: daily 9-6. Adults $12, seniors 60 & over $11, children 8-18 $10. Ghost Tours: daily 6:15pm & 8pm. Call to verify. Admission: $20.

O.K. CORRAL, 326 E. Allen St., Tombstone, AZ 85638. Mailing Address: P.O. Box 367, Tombstone, AZ 85638-0367. Tel.: 520-457-3456. Fax: 520-457-3456.
E-mail: info@ok-corral.com
Web Site: www.okcorral.com
Formerly: Historama
Institution Type/Description: History Museum.
Hours & Admission Prices: Daily 9-5. Adults $10. Closed Thanksgiving; Christmas. &
Attendance: 100,000 (actual)

ROSE TREE MUSEUM, 118 4th St., Tombstone, AZ 85635. Mailing Address: P.O. Box 808, Tombstone, AZ 85638. Tel.: 520-457-3326.
E-mail: info@tombstonerosetree.com
Web Site: tombstonerosetree.com
Institution Type/Description: History Museum: housed in a former hotel; built in 1885.
Hours & Admission Prices: Mid-Feb. to mid-May 9-5; mid-May to mid-Feb. 11-5. Adults $5; discounts to AAM members; youth under 14 no charge. &
Attendance: 20,000 (estimated)

TOMBSTONE COURTHOUSE STATE HISTORIC PARK, 223 E. Toughnut St., Tombstone, AZ 85638. Mailing Address: P.O. Box 216, Tombstone, AZ 85638-0216. Tel.: 520-457-3311. Fax: 520-457-2565. Facebook: Tombstone Courthouse.
E-mail: tombstonecourthouse@tombstonechamber.com
Web Site: www.azstateparks.com
Key Personnel: Dir. & Museum Shop Mgr., Julie Vanderdasson; Chm. (V), Susan Wallace.
Institution Type/Description: Local History Museum: housed in an 1882 Cochise County Courthouse.
Hours & Admission Prices: Daily 9-5 Adults 14 & over $5; youth 7-13 $2; discounts to military; children 6 & under no charge. Closed Christmas. &
Attendance: 59,889 (actual)

TOMBSTONE WESTERN HERITAGE MUSEUM, 6th St. & Fremont St., Tombstone, AZ 85638. Mailing Address: P.O. Box 730, Tombstone, AZ 85638-0730. Tel.: 520-457-3933.
E-mail: silvrldy@yahoo.com
Web Site: thetombstonemuseum.com
Key Personnel: Dir., Marjorie Elliott.
Institution Type/Description: History Museum.
Hours & Admission Prices: Daily 12-5. Adults $7.50, youth 18 & under $5; discounts to active military, families & groups; members & children under 12 no charge. &
Attendance: 2,000 (estimated)

Topawa

TOHONO O'ODHAM NATION CULTURAL CENTER & MUSEUM, Fresnal Canyon Rd., Topawa, AZ 85639. Mailing Address: P.O. Box 837, Sells, AZ 85634-0837. Tel.: 520-383-0211.
E-mail: contactus@tonation-nsn.gov
Web Site: www.himdagki.org
Institution Type/Description: Native American History Museum.
Hours & Admission Prices: Mon.-Sat. 10-4. No charge; donations accepted.

Tuba

EXPLORE NAVAJO INTERACTIVE MUSEUM, 10 N. Main St., Tuba, AZ 86045. Mailing Address: c/o Monument Hospitality Inc., 6677 W. Thunderbolt Rd., Ste. J176, Glendale, AZ 85306. Tel.: 928-640-0684, 800-644-8383.
E-mail: info@explorenavajo.com
Web Site: www.explorenavajo.com
Institution Type/Description: Native American History Museum.
Hours & Admission Prices: Mon.-Sat. 8-6, Sun. 12-6. Adults $9, seniors 65 & over $7, children 7-12 $6; children 6 & under no charge.

Tubac

TUBAC CENTER OF THE ARTS, 9 Plaza Rd., Tubac, AZ 85646-1911. Mailing Address: P.O. Box 1911, Tubac, AZ 85646-1911. Tel.: 520-398-2371. Fax: 520-398-9511.
E-mail: contactus@tubacarts.org
Web Site: tubacarts.org
Key Personnel: Exec. Dir., Karin Topping; Mgr. Exhibitions, Michael Fenlason; Museum Shop Mgr., Bonnie Jaus; Pres. (V), Colin Steffen.
Institution Type/Description: Art Center.
Hours & Admission Prices: Sept.-May Mon.-Sat. 10-4:30. Sun. 12-4:30. Offices: daily. No charge; donations accepted. Closed national holidays. &
Attendance: 39,000 (estimated)

TUBAC PRESIDIO STATE HISTORIC PARK, 1 Burruel St., Tubac, AZ 85646. Mailing Address: P.O. Box 1296, Tubac, AZ 85646-1296. Tel.: 520-398-2252. Fax: 520-398-2685.
E-mail: info@tubacpresidio.org
Web Site: www.tubacpresidio.org

Key Personnel: Dir., Shaw Kinsley.
Institution Type/Description: Park Museum and Visitor Center.
Hours & Admission Prices: Daily 9-5. Adults 14 & over $5, children 7-13 $2; children 6 & under and handicapped no charge. Closed Christmas. ᕳ
Attendance: 14,622 (actual)

Tucson

ARIZONA HISTORICAL SOCIETY - ARIZONA HISTORY MUSEUM, 949 E. 2nd St., Tucson, AZ 85719-4898. Tel.: 520-628-5774. Fax: 520-628-5695.
E-mail: ahstucson@azhs.gov
Web Site: www.azhs.gov
Key Personnel: Exec. Dir., James Burns, Ph.D.; Deputy Dir. & COO, Bill Ponder.
Institution Type/Description: History Museum.
Hours & Admission Prices: Museum: Mon.-Thurs. 9-4, Fri. 9-8, Sat. 11-4. Adults $10, senior citizens 65 & over $8, college student with ID $5, youth 7-17 $4; children 6 & under, veterans and members no charge. Library: Tues.-Fri. 9-4. No charge. Closed New Year's Day; Veterans Day; Thanksgiving; Christmas. ᕳ
Attendance: 20,000 (estimated)

ARIZONA HISTORICAL SOCIETY - DOWNTOWN HISTORY MUSEUM CLOSED, 140 N. Stone Ave., Tucson, AZ 85701. Mailing Address: 949 E. 2nd St., Tucson, AZ 85719-4898. Tel.: 520-770-1473.
E-mail: ahstucson@azhs.gov
Web Site: www.azhs.gov
Key Personnel: Operations Mgr., Eric Gonzales.
Institution Type/Description: History Museum.
Hours & Admission Prices: Wed.-Thurs. 10-4, Fri. 10-3. No charge; donations accepted. Closed New Year's Day; Independence Day; Veterans Day; Thanksgiving; Christmas. ᕳ
Attendance: 2,000 (estimated)

ARIZONA HISTORICAL SOCIETY - FORT LOWELL MUSEUM CLOSED, 2900 N. Craycroft Rd., Tucson, AZ 85712. Mailing Address: 949 E. 2nd St., Tucson, AZ 85719-4898. Tel.: 520-885-3832.
E-mail: ahstucson@azhs.gov
Web Site: www..azhs.gov
Key Personnel: Mgr. Operations, Eric Gonzales.
Institution Type/Description: Military Museum: housed in a reconstructed officer's quarters from a military post active from 1873 to 1891.
Hours & Admission Prices: Thurs.-Sat. 10-4. No charge; donations accepted. Closed New Year's Day; Independence Day; Veterans Day; Thanksgiving; Christmas. ·
Attendance: 2,500 (estimated)

ARIZONA HISTORICAL SOCIETY - SOSA-CARRILLO-FRÉMONT HOUSE MUSEUM, 151 S. Granada Ave., Tucson, AZ 85701. Mailing Address: 949 E. 2nd St., Tucson, AZ 85719-4898. Tel.: 520-882-8607.
E-mail: ahstucson@azhs.gov
Web Site: www.azhs.gov
Key Personnel: Mgr. Operations, Eric Gonzales.
Institution Type/Description: Historic House: housed in the former residence of pioneer families Sosa & Carrillo; also 1881 residence of John C. Fremont, Governor of Arizona Territory.
Hours & Admission Prices: Mon.-Fri. 10-5. No charge; donations accepted. Closed New Year's Day; Martin Luther King Jr. Day; Presidents' Day; Memorial Day; Independence Day; Labor Day; Columbus Day; Veterans Day; Thanksgiving; Christmas. ᕳ
Attendance: 1,000 (estimated)

ARIZONA-SONORA DESERT MUSEUM, 2021 N. Kinney Rd., Tucson, AZ 85743-9719. Tel.: 520-883-1380 & 2702. Fax: 520-883-2500.
E-mail: info@desertmuseum.org
Web Site: www.desertmuseum.org
Key Personnel: Exec. Dir., Craig S. Ivanyi; General Cur., Stephanie Poulin.
Institution Type/Description: Nature Center & Natural History Museum.
Hours & Admission Prices: March-May & Sept. daily 7:30-5; June-Aug. Sun.-Fri. 7:30 am-5pm, Sat. 7:30 am - 10 pm; Oct.-Feb. daily 8:30-5. Adults $21.95, seniors 65 & over $19.95, youth 3-12 $8.95; children under 3 no charge. ᕳ
Attendance: 378,489 (actual)

ARIZONA STATE MUSEUM, University of Arizona, 1013 E. University Blvd., Tucson, AZ 85721. Mailing Address: P.O. Box

210026, Tucson, AZ 85721-0026. Tel.: 520-621-6302 & 6281. Fax: 520-621-2976. Facebook.
E-mail: dfl@email.arizona.edu
Web Site: www.statemuseum.arizona.edu
Key Personnel: Dir., Patrick D. Lyons, Ph.D., RPA; Dir. Mktg. & Membership, Darlene Lizarraga; Head Library, Molly Stothert-Maurer; Head Preservation, Nancy N. Odegaard, Ph.D.; Museum Registrar, Andrew Higgins; Head Community Engagement, Lisa Falk; Head Collections, Suzanne L. Eckert, Ph.D.
Institution Type/Description: Anthropology Museum.
Hours & Admission Prices: Mon.-Sat. 10-5. Adult $5; students, children & museum members no charge. Closed state & national holidays.
Attendance: 34,847 (actual)

CENTER FOR CREATIVE PHOTOGRAPHY, University of Arizona, 1030 N. Olive Rd., Tucson, AZ 85721-0103. Mailing Address: University of Arizona, P.O. Box 210103, Tucson, AZ 85721-0103. Tel.: 520-621-7968. Fax: 520-621-9444.
E-mail: info@ccp.arizona.edu
Web Site: www.creativephotography.org
Key Personnel: Dir., James Burnes; Assoc. Dir., Denise Gose; Archivist, Leslie Squyres; Registrar, Megan Clancy; Assoc. Registrar, Rebecca Drudge; Chief Cur. & Cur. Norton Family, Rebecca Senf; Licensing Mgr., Tammy Carter.
Institution Type/Description: Art Museum.
Hours & Admission Prices: Visit Website for gallery hours. No charge; donations accepted. Closed major holidays. ᕳ
Attendance: 50,000 (estimated)

CHILDREN'S MUSEUM TUCSON, 200 S. Sixth Ave., Tucson, AZ 85701-2109. Mailing Address: P.O. Box 2609, Tucson, AZ 85702-2609. Tel.: 520-792-9985. Fax: 520-792-0639. Facebook, Twitter.
E-mail: tcm@tucsonchildrensmuseum.org
Web Site: www.childrensmuseumtucson.org
Key Personnel: Exec. Dir., Michael Luria; Dir. Devel. & Opers., Autumn Rentmeester; Dir. Mktg., Teresa Truelsem.
Institution Type/Description: Children's Museum.
Hours & Admission Prices: School Year: Tues.-Fri. 9-5, Sat.-Sun. 10-5; Summer: call for hours. Adults $8, second Sat. of Mon $2, children under one & members no charge. ᕳ
Attendance: 161,798 (actual)

CONRAD WILDE GALLERY, 101 W. 6th St., Tucson, AZ 85701. Tel.: 520-622-8997. Fax: 520-622-7988.
E-mail: info@conradwildegallery.com
Web Site: www.conradwildegallery.com
Institution Type/Description: Art Gallery.
Hours & Admission Prices: By appointment.

DAVIS DOMINGUEZ GALLERY, 154 E. 6th St., Tucson, AZ 85705-8321. Tel.: 502-629-9759.
E-mail: info@davisdominguez.com
Web Site: www.davisdominguez.com
Key Personnel: Owner, Candice Davis.
Institution Type/Description: Art Gallery.
Hours & Admission Prices: Tues.-Fri. 11-5, Sat. 11-4. No charge. ᕳ

DEGRAZIA GALLERY IN THE SUN, 6300 N. Swan Rd., Tucson, AZ 85718-3697. Tel.: 520-299-9191, 800-545-2185. Fax: 520-299-1381.
E-mail: cs@degrazia.org
Web Site: www.degrazia.org
Key Personnel: Exec. Dir., Lance Laber; Dir. Collections & Exhibitions, Jim Jenkins; Museum Shop Mgr., Lisa Palmer.
Institution Type/Description: Art Gallery: building listed on the National Register of Historic Places.
Hours & Admission Prices: Daily 10-4. Admission $8; discounts to groups over 20. Closed New Year's Day; Easter; Thanksgiving; Christmas. ᕳ
Attendance: 50,000 (estimated)

DINNERWARE ARTSPACE, 101 W. 6th St., Tucson, AZ 85701. Tel.: 520-869-3166. Facebook: @dinnerweartspace.
E-mail: dinnerwareartspace@gmail.com
Key Personnel: Dir., David Aguirre.
Institution Type/Description: Contemporary Art Space: located in historic downtown Tucson arts district.
Hours & Admission Prices: By appointment. ᕳ
Attendance: 16,000 (actual)

ETHERTON GALLERY, 135 S. Sixth Ave., Tucson, AZ 85701. Tel.: 520-624-7370. Fax: 520-792-4569.
E-mail: info@ethertongallery.com
Web Site: www.ethertongallery.com
Institution Type/Description: Art Gallery.
Hours & Admission Prices: Tues.-Sat. 11-5.

FLANDRAU SCIENCE CENTER AND PLANETARIUM, The University of Arizona, 1601 E. University Blvd., Tucson, AZ 85719. Mailing Address: P.O. Box 210091, Tucson, AZ 85721-0091. Tel.: 520-621-STAR. Fax: 520-621-8451.
E-mail: uascreservations@gmail.com
Web Site: www.flandrau.org
Key Personnel: Dir., William Plant; Facilities Mgr., Neil McSweeney; Technical Mgr., Michael Magee; Program Coord., Roseann Mankel-Stofelano; Education Coord., Noel Hensley.
Institution Type/Description: Science Center, Planetarium & Observatory.
Hours & Admission Prices: Science Center & Planetarium: Mon.-Wed. 10-3, Thurs.-Fri. 10-3 & 6-9, Sat. 10-9, Sun. 1-4. Admission 15 & over $7.50, children 4-14 $5; ASTC members no charge. &
Attendance: 50,000 (estimated)

HISTORY OF PHARMACY MUSEUM, University of Arizona College of Pharmacy, 1703 E. Mabel, Tucson, AZ 85721. Mailing Address: University of Arizona College of Pharmacy, P.O. Box 210202, Tucson, AZ 85721-0202. Tel.: 520-626-1427. Fax: 520-626-4063.
E-mail: stephenhall@pharmacy.arizona.edu
Web Site: www.pharmacy.arizona.edu
Key Personnel: Cur., Stephen Hall.
Institution Type/Description: Pharmacy Museum.
Hours & Admission Prices: Mon.-Fri. 8-5. No charge.

INTERNATIONAL WILDLIFE MUSEUM, 4800 W. Gates Pass Rd., Tucson, AZ 85745-9600. Tel.: 520-629-0100. Fax: 520-618-3538. Facebook: International Wildlife Museum.
E-mail: shanker@safariclub.org
Web Site: www.thewildlifemuseum.org
Key Personnel: Dir., Sue Hanker; Bus. Opers. Mgr., Dan Brooks.
Institution Type/Description: Natural History Museum.
Hours & Admission Prices: Mon.-Fri. 9-5, Sat.-Sun. 11-5. Adults $9, senior citizens & military $7, children 4-12 $4; children 3 & under no charge. ASTC reciprocal membership. Closed Thanksgiving; Christmas. &
Attendance: 48,119 (actual)

JEWISH HISTORY MUSEUM, 564 S. Stone Ave., Tucson, AZ 85701. Mailing Address: P.O. Box 889, Tucson, AZ 85702. Tel.: 520-670-9073. Facebook: Jewish History Museum.
E-mail: museum@jewishhistorymuseum.org
Web Site: www.jewishhistorymuseum.org
Key Personnel: Interim Exec. Dir., Byran Davis; Chm. (V), Dr. Barry Friedman.
Institution Type/Description: History Museum.
Hours & Admission Prices: Wed.-Thurs. & Sat.-Sun. 1-5, Fri. 12-3. Adults $7; discounts to Time Travelers Network; members & students no charge. &

KITT PEAK NATIONAL OBSERVATORY, State Rte. 86 & Rte. 386, Tucson, AZ 85726-6732. Mailing Address: 950 N. Cherry Ave., Tucson, AZ 85719-4933. Tel.: 520-318-8726. Fax: 520-318-8451.
E-mail: kpno@noao.edu
Web Site: www.noao.edu/kpvc
Institution Type/Description: Observatory.
Hours & Admission Prices: Daily 9-3:45. Guided Tours: 10, 11:30 & 1:30. Museum: no charge. Guided Tours: adults $9.75, children $3.25. Closed New Year's Day; Thanksgiving; Christmas. &
Attendance: 60,000 (estimated)

LOUIS CARLOS BERNAL GALLERY, Pima Community College - West Campus, 2202 W. Anklam Rd., Tucson, AZ 85709-0015. Tel.: 520-206-6942. Fax: 520-206-6719.
E-mail: dandres@pima.edu
Web Site: www.pima.edu/cfa
Formerly: Pima Community College Art Gallery
Key Personnel: Dir., David Andres.
Institution Type/Description: Art Gallery.
Hours & Admission Prices: Mon.-Thurs. 10-5, Fri. 10-3; call for confirmation of hours. No charge; donations accepted. Closed all major holidays. &
Attendance: 8,000 (estimated)

THE MINI TIME MACHINE MUSEUM OF MINIATURES, 4455 E. Camp Lowell Dr., Tucson, AZ 85712. Tel.: 520-881-0606. Fax: 520-881-9307.
E-mail: info@theminitimemachine.org
Web Site: www.theminitimemachine.org
Key Personnel: Pres. & Cur., Patricia Arnell; Exec. Dir., Lisa Hastreiter-Lamb.
Institution Type/Description: General Museum.
Hours & Admission Prices: Tues.-Sat. 9-4, Sun. 12-4. Adults $9, seniors 65 & over and military $8, children 4-17 $6; children 3 & under no charge. Closed major holidays. &
Attendance: 40,000 (actual)

OLD PASCUA MUSEUM AND YAQUI CULTURAL CENTER, 856 W. Calle Santa Ana, Tucson, AZ 85705. Tel.: 520-884-8527.
Key Personnel: Dir., Bill Quiroga.
Institution Type/Description: Native American History Museum: housed in a former home built c.1920. Listed on the National Register of Historic Places.
Hours & Admission Prices: Tues.-Sat. 9-1. No charge; donations accepted.

OLD PUEBLO ARCHAEOLOGY CENTER, 2201 W. 44th St., Tucson, AZ 85713-4575. Mailing Address: P.O. Box 40577, Tucson, AZ 85717-0577. Tel.: 520-798-1201.
E-mail: info@oldpueblo.org
Web Site: oldpueblo.org
Key Personnel: Exec. Dir., Allen Dart; Pres. (V), Monica Zappia Young.
Institution Type/Description: Archaeology Education Center.
Hours & Admission Prices: By appointment. &
Attendance: 3,000 (estimated)

OLD TUCSON, 201 S. Kinney Rd., Tucson, AZ 85735. Tel.: 520-883-0100.
E-mail: guestrelations@oldtucson.com
Web Site: oldtucson.com
Institution Type/Description: History Museum: housed on the site where over 300 movies & television productions have been filmed since 1939.
Hours & Admission Prices: See website for seasonal hours. Adults $19.95, children 4-11 $10.95; children 3 & under no charge.

OLD WEST MOVIE POSTER MUSEUM, 1300 N. Stone Ave., Tucson, AZ 85705-7338. Tel.: 520-770-1910.
E-mail: info@flamingohoteltucson.com
Web Site: www.flamingohoteltucson.com
Institution Type/Description: Western Movie Poster Museum.
Hours & Admission Prices: Daily 9-5. Hotel guests no charge.

OTIS CHIDESTER SCOUT MUSEUM OF SOUTHERN ARIZONA, 1937 E. Blacklidge Dr., Tucson, AZ 85719-2847. Tel.: 520-795-9484; 520-326-7669.
E-mail: museum@azscoutmuseum.com
Web Site: www.azscoutmuseum.com
Key Personnel: Pres. (V), James Klein; Cur., Luis Romero.
Institution Type/Description: Scout Museum.
Hours & Admission Prices: By appointment. No charge; donations accepted.
Attendance: 500 (estimated)

PIMA AIR & SPACE MUSEUM, 6000 E. Valencia Rd., Tucson, AZ 85756-9403. Tel.: 520-574-0462. Fax: 520-574-9238. Facebook: Pima Air & Space Museum.
E-mail: yvonnem@pimaair.org
Web Site: www.pimaair.org
Key Personnel: Dir. Titan Missile Museum, Yvonne C. Morris; Chm. (V), Count Ferdinand von Galen; Exec. Dir., Scott Marchand; Cur., James Stemm; Museum Shop Mgr., Beth Barksdale.
Institution Type/Description: Aeronautics & Space Museum & Arizona Aviation Hall of Fame.
Hours & Admission Prices: Pima Air & Space Museum: daily 9-5. Adults $15.50, seniors 62 & over, AAA and military $12.75, children 7-12 $9; children 6 & under and members no charge. &
Attendance: 175,000 (actual)

THE POSTAL HISTORY FOUNDATION, 920 N. First Ave., Tucson, AZ 85719-4818. Tel.: 520-623-6652. Fax: 520-623-3810. Facebook; Twitter.
E-mail: info@phtucson.org
Web Site: www.postalhistoryfoundation.org
Institution Type/Description: Postal History Museum.
Hours & Admission Prices: Mon.-Fri. 8-3. No charge, but donations accepted. &
Attendance: 2,000 (estimated)

REID PARK ZOO, 3400 Zoo Ct., Tucson, AZ 85715. Mailing Address: 1100 S. Randolph Way, Tucson, AZ 85716-5835. Tel.: 520-791-3204. Fax: 520-791-5378.
E-mail: reidzoo@tucsonaz.gov
Web Site: www.tucsonzoo.org
Key Personnel: Admin., Jason Jacobs; Cur. Education, Conservation Programs, Guest Experience & Promotions & Media, Vivian W. VanPeenen.
Institution Type/Description: Zoo.
Hours & Admission Prices: Oct.-May daily 9-4; June-Sept. daily 8-3. Adults $9, senior citizens 62 & over $7, children 2-14 $5; members & children under 2 no charge. Closed Thanksgiving; Christmas. &
Attendance: 525,000 (estimated)

SAGUARO NATIONAL PARK - EASTERN DISTRICT VISITOR CENTER, 3693 S. Old Spanish Trail, Tucson, AZ 85730-5601. Tel.: 520-733-5158. Fax: 520-733-5183.
E-mail: saguaro_information@nps.gov
Web Site: www.nps.gov/sagu
Key Personnel: Supt., Leah McGinnis.
Institution Type/Description: Natural History Museum.
Hours & Admission Prices: Visitor Center: daily 9-5. Park: daily sunrise to sunset. Weekly Pass: $10 vehicles, $5 per person. Closed Christmas. &
Attendance: 2,440,444

SAGUARO NATIONAL PARK - WESTERN DISTRICT VISITOR CENTER, 2700 N. Kinney Rd., Tucson, AZ 85743-9719. Tel.: 520-733-5158.
E-mail: webmaster@saguaronationalpark.com
Web Site: www.saguaronationalpark.com
Institution Type/Description: Natural History Museum.
Hours & Admission Prices: Daily 9-5. Closed Christmas.

SAN XAVIER DEL BAC MISSION, 1950 W. San Xavier Rd., Tucson, AZ 85746-7409. Tel.: 520-294-2624. Fax: 520-294-3438.
E-mail: info@sanxaviermission.org
Web Site: sanxaviermission.org
Institution Type/Description: Church & Religious Museum: built in the late 1700s.
Hours & Admission Prices: Self-Guided Tour: 8:30-4:30. Services: call for hours. No charge; donations accepted. &
Attendance: 2,000 (estimated)

SOUTHERN ARIZONA TRANSPORTATION MUSEUM, 414 N. Toole Ave., Tucson, AZ 85701. Tel.: 520-623-2223.
E-mail: contactus@tucsonhistoricdepot.org
Web Site: tucsonhistoricdepot.org
Key Personnel: Dir., C.E.O. & Chm. (V), Ken Karrels, Ph.D.
Institution Type/Description: Transportation History Museum.
Hours & Admission Prices: Tues.-Thurs. & Sun. 11-3, Fri.-Sat. 10-4. No charge; donations accepted. &
Attendance: 14,100 (actual)

390TH MEMORIAL MUSEUM, 6000 E. Valencia Rd., Tucson, AZ 85756-9403. Tel.: 520-574-0287. Fax: 520-574-3030. Facebook: 390th Memorial Museum Foundation, Inc.
E-mail: museum@390th.org
Web Site: 390th.org
Key Personnel: Dir., Wally Scales.
Institution Type/Description: Military History Museum.
Hours & Admission Prices: Located on the grounds of the Pima Air and Space Museum. Daily 10-4:30. Grounds: fee charged. Memorial Museum: no charge. Closed Thanksgiving; Christmas.
Attendance: 100,000 (estimated)

TOHONO CHUL PARK INC., 7366 N. Paseo del Norte, Tucson, AZ 85704-4415. Tel.: 520-742-6455, ext. 210. Fax: 520-797-1213.
E-mail: info@tohonochul.org
Web Site: www.tohonochulpark.org
Key Personnel: Exec. Dir., Dr. Christine Conte; Dir. Finance & Human Resources, Penny Poynter; Dir. Education & Visitor Svcs., Jo Falls; Volunteer Svcs. Coord., Lauren Malanga; Cur. Exhibitions, James Schaub; Asst. Cur. Exhibitions, Karen Hayes; Dir. Gen. Svcs., Lee Mason; Dir. Retail, Linda Wolfe.
Institution Type/Description: Nature Center.
Hours & Admission Prices: Garden Bistro: daily 8-5. Exhibits, Museum Shops & Greenhouse: daily 9-5; guided tours by appointment. May-Sept. adults $8, seniors 62 & over $6, military & students $4, children 5-12 $2; members and children under 5 no charge. Oct.-April adults $10, seniors 62 & over $8, students & military $5, children 5-12 $3; members & children under 5 no charge. Closed New Year's Day; Independence Day; Thanksgiving; Christmas. &
Attendance: 170,000 (estimated)

TUCSON BOTANICAL GARDENS, 2150 N. Alvernon Way, Tucson, AZ 85712-3199. Tel.: 520-326-9686, ext. 10. Fax: 520-324-0166.
E-mail: info@tucsonbotanical.org
Web Site: www.tucsonbotanical.org
Key Personnel: Exec. Dir., Michelle Conklin; Bd. Pres. (V), John Smith; Dir. Horticulture, Michael Chamberland; Dir. Mktg. & Communications, Melissa D'Auria.
Institution Type/Description: Arboretum & Botanical Garden.
Hours & Admission Prices: Garden: daily 8:30-4:30. Butterfly Magic: daily 9:30-3. Garden: Oct.-April adults $13, seniors, students & military $12, children 4-12 $7.50, members & children under 4 no charge; May-Sept. adults $8, seniors, students & military $7; children 4-12 $4, members & children under 4 no charge. Closed New Year's Day; Independence Day; Thanksgiving; Christmas Eve & Day. &
Attendance: 100,000 (estimated)

TUCSON DESERT ART MUSEUM, 7000 E. Tanque Verde Rd., Tucson, AZ 85715. Tel.: 520-202-3888.
E-mail: mail@tucsondart.org
Web Site: www.tucsondart.org
Institution Type/Description: Art Museum.
Hours & Admission Prices: June & Aug.-Oct. Wed.-Sun. 10-4; Nov.-May daily 10-4. Adults $10; seniors $8, students $6, youth 7-14 $4; members, active military, and Native American with ID no charge. Closed major holidays. &

TUCSON MUSEUM OF ART & HISTORIC BLOCK, 140 N. Main Ave., Tucson, AZ 85701-8290. Tel.: 520-624-2333. Fax: 520-624-7202.
E-mail: info@tucsonmuseumofart.org
Web Site: www.tucsonmuseumofart.org
Key Personnel: C.O.O., Alan Hershowitz; Dir. Account. & HR, Andra Allen; Collections Mgr. & Registrar, Susan Dolan; Mktg. & Digital Content Coord., Jordan Bohannon; Membership & Devel. Assoc., Katherine Beaty; Dir. Devel., Alba Rojas-Sukkar; Chief Cur. & Cur. Modern & Contemporary Art, Julie Sasse; Dir. Communications & External Affairs, Kelly Wiehe; Preparator, David Longwell; Cur. Education & Community Partnerships, Morgan Wells; Chief Bldg., Grounds, & Security, Dave Hopkins, Jr.; Retail Mgr., Justin Germain.
Institution Type/Description: Art Museum.
Hours & Admission Prices: Tues.-Sat. 10-5, Sun. 12-5. Adults $12, senior citizens (65+) $10, youth/student $7; children (12 & under), veterans w/ID & museum members free; discounts to ICOM members; AAM members, first Sun. of month, children under 12 and members no charge. Closed Thanksgiving; Christmas &
Attendance: 237,000 (estimated)

TUCSON RODEO PARADE MUSEUM, 4823 S. Sixth Ave., Tucson, AZ 85714-3004. Mailing Address: P.O. Box 1788, Tucson, AZ 85702-1788. Tel.: 520-294-1280 (Office); 520-294-3636 (Museum).
E-mail: office@tucsonrodeoparade.org
Web Site: www.tucsonrodeoparade.org
Key Personnel: Chm. (V), Diane Culin.
Institution Type/Description: Western Cultural Museum.
Hours & Admission Prices: Jan. 2-March 26 Mon.-Sat. 9:30-3:30. Suggested donation: adults $10, seniors $7. Closed Parade Day. &
Attendance: 5,000 (estimated)

UNIVERSITY OF ARIZONA MINERAL MUSEUM, Univ. of Arizona, Flandrau Science Center, Cherry & University, 1601 E. University Blvd., Tucson, AZ 85721. Mailing Address: P.O. Box 210091, Tucson, AZ 85721-0091. Tel.: 520-621-4227. Fax: 520-621-8451.
E-mail: flandrau@email.arizona.edu
Web Site: www.uamineralmuseum.org
Key Personnel: Cur., Dr. Robert T. Downs.
Institution Type/Description: Mineral Museum.
Hours & Admission Prices: Mon.-Thurs. 9-5, Fri. 9am-10pm, Sat. 10-10, Sun. 12-5. Science Center: Adults $7; children 4-17, seniors, military & college students with ID $5, children 3 & under no charge. Planetarium & Laser Light Show: Adults $7; children 4-17, seniors, military & college students with ID $5, children 3 & under no charge. Closed New Year's Day; Thanksgiving; Christmas. &

THE UNIVERSITY OF ARIZONA MUSEUM OF ART, 1031 N. Olive Rd., Tucson, AZ 85721. Mailing Address: University of Arizona, P.O. Box 210002, Tucson, AZ 85721-0002. Tel.: 520-621-7567 (Main) & 7568 (Mktg./Public Rels.). Fax: 520-621-8770.
E-mail: artmuseum@email.arizona.edu
Web Site: www.artmuseum.arizona.edu

Key Personnel: Deputy Dir. & Acting Head, Jill McCleary; Cur. Exhibitions & Education, Olivia Miller; Registrar, Kristen Schmidt; Program Coord. & Guest Svcs., Angela Telesco; Security Officer, Jim Kushner.
Institution Type/Description: Art Museum.
Hours & Admission Prices: Aug. 11-May 11 Tues.-Fri. 9-4, Sat. 9-5, Sun. 12-5. Adults $8, seniors 65 7 over $6; discounts to AAM members & groups; UA faculty & staff, students with ID, children & members no charge. Closed university holidays. ዿ
Attendance: 24,810 (actual)

UNIVERSITY OF ARIZONA STUDENT UNION GALLERIES, 1303 E. University Blvd., Tucson, AZ 85719. Tel.: 520-621-6142. Fax: 520-621-6930.
E-mail: su-gallery@email.arizona.edu
Web Site: www.union.arizona.edu/involvement/galleries/
Institution Type/Description: Art Gallery.
Hours & Admission Prices: Union Gallery: Mon.-Fri. 10-5; Kachina Gallery: Mon.-Fri. 6:30 a.m. to 10 p.m., Sat.-Sun. 8 a.m. to 10 p.m. No charge. Closed major holidays & installation day. ዿ
Attendance: 11,500 (actual)

WESTERN ARCHEOLOGICAL & CONSERVATION CENTER, 255 N. Commerce Park Loop, Tucson, AZ 85745-2796. Tel.: 520-791-6400. Fax: 520-791-6465.
E-mail: wacc_information@nps.gov
Web Site: www.nps.gov/orgs/1260/index.htm
Key Personnel: Cur., Brenda McLain; Archivist, Khaleel Saba; Objects Conservator, Dana Senge; Registrar, Kim E. Beckwith.
Institution Type/Description: History Museum.
Hours & Admission Prices: Mon.-Fri. 9-3; library & other times by appointment. No charge. Closed federal holidays. ዿ

Tumacacori

TUMACACORI NATIONAL HISTORICAL PARK, 1891 E. Frontage Rd., Tumacacori, AZ 85640. Mailing Address: P.O. Box 8067, Tumacacori, AZ 85640-8067. Tel.: 520-398-2341, ext. 0. Fax: 520-398-9271.
E-mail: jeremy_moss@nps.gov
Web Site: www.nps.gov/tuma
Key Personnel: Supt., Ann Razor; Cur., Jeremy Moss.
Institution Type/Description: National Park, Historic Site and Museum: site 1795 San Jose de Tumacacori Spanish Mission Church, abandoned in 1848; Los Santos Angeles de Guevavi Mission; San Cayetano de Calabazas Mission.
Hours & Admission Prices: Daily 9-5. Adults $3; children under 17, Golden Age, Golden Eagle & annual park pass holders no charge. Closed Thanksgiving; Christmas. ዿ
Attendance: 60,000 (actual)

Vail

COLOSSAL CAVE MOUNTAIN PARK - LA POSTA QUEMADA RANCH MUSEUM, 16721 E. Old Spanish Trail Rd., Vail, AZ 85641. Tel.: 520-647-7275. Fax: 520-647-3299.
E-mail: info@colossalcave.com
Web Site: www.colossalcave.com
Institution Type/Description: History Museum.
Hours & Admission Prices: Sun.-Thurs. 8-5, Fri.-Sat. 8-8. Adults $18, children 5-12 $9; discounts to military; children 4 & under no charge. Closed Thanksgiving; Christmas.

Valentine

KEEPERS OF THE WILD NATURE PARK, 13441 E. Hwy. 66, Valentine, AZ 86437. Tel.: 928-769-1800. Fax: 928-769-1805.
E-mail: info@keepersofthewild.org
Web Site: www.keepersofthewild.org
Key Personnel: Founder & Dir., Jonathan Kraft; Chm. (V), Sandy Jenkins.
Institution Type/Description: Nature Park.
Hours & Admission Prices: Wed.-Mon. 9-5. Adults $20, seniors 65 & over $15, children 12 & under $12; discounts to groups of 20 or more; children under 2 no charge. Closed Tues., Thanksgiving; Christmas. ዿ
Attendance: 15,000 (estimated)

Whiteriver

FORT APACHE HISTORIC PARK AND MUSEUM - KINISHBA RUINS, Fort Apache Indian Reservation, Whiteriver, AZ 85941. Mailing Address: P.O. Box 507, Fort Apache, AZ 85926-0507. Tel.: 928-338-4625.

Institution Type/Description: Native American Museum: listed on the National Register of Historic Places.
Hours & Admission Prices: June-Aug. Mon.-Sat. 8-5; Winter: Mon.-Fri. 8-5. Adults $5, seniors 64 & over and students $3; children under 7 no charge. Closed major holidays.

Wickenburg

DESERT CABALLEROS WESTERN MUSEUM, 21 N. Frontier St., Ste. A, Wickenburg, AZ 85390-3431. Tel.: 928-684-2272. Fax: 928-684-5794. Facebook: desertcaballeroswesternmuseum.
E-mail: info@westernmuseum.org
Web Site: westernmuseum.org
Key Personnel: Exec. Dir., Sandra Harris; Chm. (V), Peter Schweitzer; Deputy Dir. & Cur., Mary Ann Igna; Visitor Experience & Museum Shop Mgr., Marilu Rix; Communications & Membership Mktg. Asst., Amanda Schlueter; Cur. Education, Natalie Olson.
Institution Type/Description: General Museum.
Hours & Admission Prices: June-Aug. Tues.-Sat. 10-5, Sun. 12-4; Sept.-May Mon.-Sat. 10-5, Sun. 12-4. Adults $12, senior citizens over 55 $10; discounts to AAM members; members, active-duty military & guest and youth 18 & under no charge. Closed major holidays. ዿ
Attendance: 74,000 (estimated)

NATURE CONSERVANCY HASSAYAMPA RIVER PRESERVE VISITOR CENTER, 49614 N. U.S. Hwy. 60, Wickenburg, AZ 85390. Mailing Address: 1510 E. Ft. Lowell, Tucson, AZ 85719. Tel.: 928-684-2772. Fax: 928-684-2773.
E-mail: bmccollum@tnc.org
Web Site: www.nature.org
Key Personnel: Mgr., Jessica Bland.
Institution Type/Description: Nature Preserve.
Hours & Admission Prices: mid-May to mid-Sept. Fri.-Sun. 7am-11am; mid-Sept. to mid-May Wed.-Sun. 8-5. Adults $5, members $3; children under 12 no charge. Closed New Year's Eve & Day; Thanksgiving; Christmas Eve & Day.

Willcox

CHIRICAHUA NATIONAL MONUMENT, 12856 E. Rhyolite Creek Rd., Willcox, AZ 85643-4722. Tel.: 520-824-3560. Fax: 520-824-3421.
E-mail: libby_schaaf@nps.gov
Web Site: www.nps.gov/chir
Key Personnel: Park Ranger, Suzanne Moody; Cur., Julena Campbell.
Institution Type/Description: Natural History Museum: located in the visitor center. Faraway Ranch & Stafford Cabin offer historical artifacts.
Hours & Admission Prices: Daily 8-4:30. No charge. ዿ
Attendance: 55,000 (actual)

REX ALLEN ARIZONA COWBOY MUSEUM, 150 N. Railroad Ave., Willcox, AZ 85643-2132. Mailing Address: P.O. Box 142, Wilicox, AZ 85644. Tel.: 520-384-4583. Facebook.
E-mail: info@rexallenmuseum.org
Web Site: www.rexallenmuseum.org
Key Personnel: Chm. (V) & Museum Shop Mgr., Gladys Olsen; Pres. (V), Alfred Telles; Museum Shop Mgr., Phyllis Brooks.
Institution Type/Description: Western Movie & Cowboy Museum.
Hours & Admission Prices: June to Labor Day Mon. 10-1, Tues.-Sat. 11-3; Sept.-May Mon. 10-1, Tues.-Sat. 10-4. Admission $2; children under 10 & members no charge. Closed all major holidays. ዿ
Attendance: 2,400 (estimated)

SULPHUR SPRINGS VALLEY HISTORICAL SOCIETY, 127 E. Maley St., Willcox, AZ 85643-2127. Tel.: 520-384-3971 & 2291.
E-mail: ssvhs@ssvecnet.com
Web Site: ssvhs.weebly.com
Institution Type/Description: Historical Society Museum.
Hours & Admission Prices: Mon.-Sat. 10-4. Family $5, couple $3, adult $2.

Williams

THE GRAND CANYON DEER FARM, 6769 E. Deer Farm Rd., Williams, AZ 86046-8419. Tel.: 928-635-4073. Fax: 928-635-2357.
E-mail: deerfrmr@aol.com
Web Site: www.deerfarm.com
Key Personnel: Owner, Pat George; Owner, Randy George.
Institution Type/Description: Zoo.
Hours & Admission Prices: mid-March to mid-Oct. daily 9-6; mid-Oct. to mid-March daily 10-5. Adults $14, seniors 62 & over $12.50, children 3-13 $8; dis-

counts to groups of 10 or more, military & AAA members; children 2 & under no charge. Closed Thanksgiving; Christmas. &

PLANES OF FAME AIR MUSEUM - GRAND CANYON, 755
Mustang Way, Williams, AZ 86046. Tel.: 928-635-1000. Fax: 928-635-1001.
E-mail: bob.reed@planesoffame.org
Web Site: www.planesoffame.org
Key Personnel: Dir. & C.E.O., Bob Reed; Museum Shop Mgr., LeeAnna Fish.
Institution Type/Description: Military Plane Museum.
Hours & Admission Prices: Daily 9-5. Adults $6.95, children under 12 $1.95; discounts to AAA members; active military, members & children under 5 no charge. Closed Thanksgiving; Christmas.
Attendance: 72,000 (actual)

Window Rock

NAVAJO NATION MUSEUM, Hwy. 264 & Loop Rd., Window
Rock, AZ 86515. Mailing Address: P.O. Box 1840, Window Rock, AZ 86515-1840. Tel.: 928-871-7941. Fax: 928-871-7942.
E-mail: info@navajonationmuseum.org
Web Site: www.navajonationmuseum.org
Key Personnel: Dir., Manuelito Wheeler; Cur, Collections, Clarenda Begay; ASO, Michelle Henry; Archivist, Eunice Kahn; Cultural Specialist, Robert Johnson; Museum Shop Mgr., Tracey Lynch.
Institution Type/Description: Native American Museum.
Hours & Admission Prices: Mon. 8-5, Tues.-Fri. 8-7, Sat. 9-5. Collections & archives by appointment only. No charge; donations accepted. Closed national & tribal holidays. &
Attendance: 106,445 (actual)

NAVAJO NATION ZOO & BOTANICAL PARK, Hwy. 264,
Bldg. 36A, Window Rock, AZ 86515. Mailing Address: P.O. Box 1329, Window Rock, AZ 86515-1480. Tel.: 928-871-6574. Fax: 928-871-6644.
E-mail: dmikesic@navajozoo.org
Institution Type/Description: Zoo & Botanical Park.
Hours & Admission Prices: Mon.-Sat. 10-4:30. No charge. Closed New Year's Day; Christmas.

Winslow

HOMOLOVI STATE PARK, State Route 87 North, (Mile Post
347), Winslow, AZ 86047-9402. Mailing Address: HCR 63 Box 5 (SR87N), Winslow, AZ 86047-9402. Tel.: 928-289-4106. Fax: 928-289-2021. Facebook: Homolovi State Park.
E-mail: kke2@azstateparks.gov
Web Site: www.azstateparks.com
Formerly: Homolovi Ruins State Park
Key Personnel: Mgr., Chad Meunier; Park Ranger II, Kenn Evans, III.
Institution Type/Description: State Park.
Hours & Admission Prices: Prehistoric Ancestral Hopi Sites: daily 8-5 (we do not observe DLS). Star parties and public observatory open 1st Sat. of the month except Aug. & Dec and start at 5 p.m. Admission $7 (4 adults per vehicle), each additional person $3. Campground: $15-$30. Day use area, Museum & Observatory closed Christmas. Camping reservations encouraged. &
Attendance: 26,539 (actual)

METEOR CRATER DISCOVERY CENTER, Interstate 40, Exit
233, Meteor Crater Rd. 5.5 miles S., Winslow, AZ 86047. Mailing Address: P.O. Box 30940, Flagstaff, AZ 86003-0940. Tel.: 928-289-5898. Fax: 928-289-2598.
E-mail: info@meteorcrater.com
Web Site: www.meteorcrater.com
Formerly: Museum of Astrogeology, Meteor Crater
Key Personnel: Pres., Brad Andes.
Institution Type/Description: Astrogeology Museum.
Hours & Admission Prices: Winter: daily 8-5; Summer: daily 7-7. Adults $16, senior citizens 60 & over $15, juniors 6-17 $8; discounts to military & groups; children 5 & under no charge. Closed Christmas. &
Attendance: 213,600 (actual)

OLD TRAILS MUSEUM, 212 N. Kinsley Ave., Winslow, AZ
86047-3618. Tel.: 928-289-5861. Facebook.
E-mail: info@oldtrailsmuseum.org
Web Site: www.oldtrailsmuseum.org
Key Personnel: Dir. & Museum Shop Mgr., Ann-Mary J. Lutzick; Pres. (V), Curtis Hardy.
Institution Type/Description: Historical Society Museum: housed in the 1921 First National Bank Building.

Hours & Admission Prices: Tues.-Sat. 10-3. Groups by appointment. No charge; donations accepted. Closed national holidays.
Attendance: 3,500 (actual)

TINA MION MUSEUM AT LA POSADA HOTEL, 303 E. 2nd
St., 2nd Fl., Winslow, AZ 86047. Tel.: 928-289-4366. Fax: 928-289-3873.
E-mail: info@laposada.org
Web Site: www.tinamion.com
Institution Type/Description: Art Gallery.
Hours & Admission Prices: Daily 8-8.

Yuma

ARIZONA HISTORICAL SOCIETY - SANGUINETTI HOUSE
MUSEUM AND GARDENS, 240 S. Madison Ave., Yuma, AZ 85364-1421. Mailing Address: 949 E. 2nd St., Tucson, AZ 85719-4898. Tel.: 928-782-1841. Fax: 928-783-0680.
E-mail: ahsyuma@azhs.gov
Web Site: www.azhs.gov
Key Personnel: Rio Colorado Division Dir., Yanna Kruse.
Institution Type/Description: History Museum: housed in 1870s residences-Sanguinetti House Museum & Jack Mellon Mercantile.
Hours & Admission Prices: Tues.-Sat. 10-3. Admission $6, seniors 60 & over $5; children 12 & under, veterans and members no charge. Closed New Year's Day; Independence Day; Veterans Day; Thanksgiving; Christmas. &
Attendance: 5,000 (estimated)

CASTLE DOME MINE MUSEUM, 27550 E. County 15th St. N.
Sr4, Yuma, AZ 85365. Tel.: 928-920-3062.
E-mail: castledomemuseum01@gmail.com
Web Site: castledomemuseum.org
Institution Type/Description: Mine Museum: housed on the site of a former mine town built in 1878.
Hours & Admission Prices: Nov.-April daily 10-5. Museum or Trail: adults $6, children 6-12 $3; children under 6 no charge. Museum & Trail: adults $10, children 6-12 $5; children under 6 no charge.

COLORADO RIVER STATE HISTORIC PARK, 201 N. 4th
Ave., Yuma, AZ 85364-2336. Tel.: 928-783-0071. Fax: 928-783-1897.
E-mail: tammy.snook@yumaaz.gov
Web Site: azstateparks.com/colorado-river/
Formerly: Yuma Quartermaster Depot State Historic Park
Key Personnel: Park Mgr., Tammy Snook.
Institution Type/Description: History Museum: housed in a former U.S. Army supply depot during the Indian Wars period and later as the site of the Bureau of Reclamation's Yuma Project Headquarters.
Hours & Admission Prices: June-Sept. Tues.-Sun. 9-4:30; Oct.-May daily 9-4:30; day before Thanksgiving & Christmas Eve 9-2. Adult 14 & up $6, children 7-13 $3; children 6 & under no charge. Closed Thanksgiving; Christmas. &
Attendance: 23,000

KOFA NATIONAL WILDLIFE REFUGE, 9300 E. 28th St.,
Yuma, AZ 85365. Tel.: 928-783-7861. Fax: 928-783-8611.
Institution Type/Description: Wildlife Refuge.
Hours & Admission Prices: Visitor Center: Mon.-Fri. 8-4:30. No charge. Closed federal holidays.

SAIHATI CAMEL FARM, 15672 S. Avenue 1E, Yuma, AZ 85365.
Tel.: 928-627-7511.
Institution Type/Description: Wildlife Farm.
Hours & Admission Prices: Oct.-May Mon.-Sat. 9-5. Adults $8, seniors $6, children 3-12 $5; children 3 & under no charge.

YUMA FINE ARTS ASSOCIATION, Yuma Campus Art Gallery
AB 110, Yuma, AZ 85365. Tel.: 928-317-6060.
E-mail: william.blomquist@azwestern.edu
Key Personnel: Contact, William Blomquist.
Institution Type/Description: Visual Arts Center & Museum.
Hours & Admission Prices: Call for hours. No charge; donations accepted. &
Attendance: 50,000 (estimated)

YUMA TERRITORIAL PRISON STATE HISTORIC PARK,
220 N. Prison Hill Rd., Yuma, AZ 85364-8792. Tel.: 928-783-4771.
E-mail: mike.guertin@yumaaz.gov
Web Site: savetheprison.com
Key Personnel: Park Mgr., Mike Guertin.

Institution Type/Description: General Museum.
Hours & Admission Prices: June-Sept. Thurs.-Mon. 9-5; Oct.-May daily 9-5. Adults 14 & over $8, seniors 62 & over $6, children 7-13 $4; children 6 & under no charge. Closed Thanksgiving; Christmas. &
Attendance: 80,000 (actual)

ARKANSAS

(199 listings)

Altus

ALTUS HERITAGE HOUSE MUSEUM, 106 N. Franklin, Altus, AR 72821. Mailing Address: P.O. Box 197, Altus, AR 72821. Tel.: 479-468-1310.
Institution Type/Description: Historic Building: housed in the former German-American State Bank; c.1800. Listed on the National Register of Historic Places.
Hours & Admission Prices: Call for hours.

Arkadelphia

CLARK COUNTY HISTORICAL MUSEUM, 750 S. 5th St., #1, Arkadelphia, AR 71923-6237. Mailing Address: P.O. Box 516, Arkadelphia, AR 71923-0516. Tel.: 870-230-1360.
E-mail: info@cchmuseum.org
Web Site: www.cchmuseum.org
Institution Type/Description: History Museum.
Hours & Admission Prices: Call for hours.

OUACHITA BAPTIST UNIVERSITY HAMMONS GALLERY, 410 Ouachita St., Arkadelphia, AR 71998. Tel.: 870-245-5129.
Institution Type/Description: Art Gallery.
Hours & Admission Prices: Mon.-Fri. 9-5.

REYNOLDS SCIENCE CENTER PLANETARIUM, 514 N. 12th St., Arkadelphia, AR 71998. Mailing Address: 1100 Henderson St., Arkadelphia, AR 71999. Tel.: 870-230-5006.
E-mail: cordovd@hsu.edu
Web Site: www.hsu.edu/EngineeringPhysics/RSCPlanetarium.html
Institution Type/Description: Planetarium.
Hours & Admission Prices: Call for hours. Adults $3, students $1.

Ashdown

GN & A DEPOT, 180 E. Whitaker, Ashdown, AR 71822-2724. Tel.: 870-898-2758.
E-mail: director@littlerivercounty.org
Web Site: www.littlerivercounty.org
Institution Type/Description: Historic Building: listed on the National Register of Historic Places.
Hours & Admission Prices: Call for hours.

LITTLE RIVER COUNTY COURTHOUSE, 310 N. Second St., Ashdown, AR 71822. Mailing Address: c/o Little River Chamber of Commerce, 180 E. Whitaker St., Ashdown, AR 71822-2724. Tel.: 870-898-5528.
E-mail: director@littlerivercounty.org
Institution Type/Description: Historic Building: built in 1907. Listed on the National Register of Historic Places.
Hours & Admission Prices: Call for hours.

TWO-RIVERS MUSEUM, 5 E. Main St., Ashdown, AR 71822-2825. Tel.: 870-898-5200.
E-mail: trumpet62@hotmail.com
Formerly: Hunter-Coulter Museum
Key Personnel: Dir., Mary Francis McKay; Chm. (V), Wynell Choate.
Institution Type/Description: Historic House Museum: built in 1918 by Henry Westbrook. Listed on the National Register of Historic Places.
Hours & Admission Prices: Mon. 12-3. No charge; donations accepted. &
Attendance: 2,000 (estimated)

Batesville

LYON COLLEGE KRESGE GALLERY, Highland & 22nd Sts., Batesville, AR 72503. Tel.: 870-307-7242.
E-mail: ian.campbell@lyon.edu
Institution Type/Description: Art Gallery.
Hours & Admission Prices: Call for hours.

MARK MARTIN MUSEUM, 1601 Batesville Blvd., Batesville, AR 72501-8372. Mailing Address: P.O. Box 2677, Batesville, AR 72503. Tel.: 870-793-4461.
E-mail: sales@markmartinmerchandise.com
Institution Type/Description: Racing Museum.
Hours & Admission Prices: Call for hours. No charge.

OLD INDEPENDENCE REGIONAL MUSEUM, 380 S. Ninth St., Batesville, AR 72501-5703. Tel.: 870-793-2121. Fax: 870-793-2101.
E-mail: oirm@oirm.org
Web Site: www.oirm.org
Key Personnel: Bd. Pres. (V), Sandy West; Cur. Collections, Twyla Wright; Cur. Exhibits, Dr. Sharon Pittser; Museum Shop Mgr., Claudia Nobles.
Institution Type/Description: History Museum: housed in former National Guard Armory built as a WPA project in 1936 of local sandstone.
Hours & Admission Prices: Tues.-Sat. 9-4:30, Sun. 1:30-4. Adults $3, senior citizens $2, students 6-12 $1; discounts for groups of 10 or more; members & children under 6 no charge. Closed New Year's Day; Easter; Independence Day; Thanksgiving; Christmas. &
Attendance: 6,435 (actual)

Bauxite

BAUXITE MUSEUM, 6706 Benton Rd., Bauxite, AR 72011-9124. Mailing Address: P.O. Box 245, Bauxite, AR 72011-0245. Tel.: 501-557-9858.
Institution Type/Description: History Museum.
Hours & Admission Prices: Wed. 10-2, Sun. 1:30-4; other times by appointment. No charge.

Bella Vista

BELLA VISTA HISTORICAL MUSEUM, 1885 Bella Vista Way, Bella Vista, AR 72714-3810. Tel.: 479-855-2335. Facebook: Bella Vista Historical Museum.
E-mail: info@bellavistamuseum.org
Web Site: www.bellavistamuseum.org
Key Personnel: Co-Pres. (V), Virginia Reynolds; Co-Pres. (V), Xyta Lucas.
Institution Type/Description: History Museum.
Hours & Admission Prices: Wed.-Sun. noon-4; other times by appointment. No charge; donations accepted. &
Attendance: 1,074 (estimated)

Benton

GANN MUSEUM OF SALINE COUNTY, 218 S. Market St., Benton, AR 72015-4304. Tel.: 501-778-5513 & 860-4113.
E-mail: thegannmuseum@live.com
Key Personnel: Chm. (V), Dorcas Holicer; Dir., Elton Fitzhugh.
Institution Type/Description: Historic House: housed in the former medical office of Dr. Dewel Gann, Sr., built in 1896 using bauxite aluminum ore.
Hours & Admission Prices: Memorial Day to Labor Day Tues.-Thurs. 10-4; Sept.-May Tues.-Thurs. 9-3; other times by appointment. No charges, donations accepted.
Attendance: 761 (estimated)

Bentonville

COMPTON GARDENS AND CONFERENCE CENTER, 312 N. Main St., Bentonville, AR 72712. Tel.: 479-254-3870. Fax: 479-254-3871. Facebook; Twitter.
E-mail: officemanager@peelcompton.net
Web Site: www.peelcompton.org
Key Personnel: Exec. Dir., Corrin Troutman.
Institution Type/Description: History Museum.
Hours & Admission Prices: Center: Mon.-Fri. 9:30-3:30. Gardens: dawn to dusk. No charge. &
Attendance: 4,000 (estimated)

CRYSTAL BRIDGES MUSEUM OF AMERICAN ART, 600 Museum Way, Bentonville, AR 72712-4947. Tel.: 479-418-5700. Fax: 479-418-5701. Facebook: Crystal Bridges Museum.
E-mail: info@crystalbridges.org
Web Site: www.crystalbridges.org
Key Personnel: Dir., Rod Bigelow.
Institution Type/Description: Art Museum.
Hours & Admission Prices: Visit Website for hours. No charge. &
Attendance: 600,000 (actual)

MUSEUM OF NATIVE AMERICAN HISTORY, 202 S.W. O St., Bentonville, AR 72712-3641. Tel.: 479-273-2456. Fax: 479-268-6909. Facebook; Twitter; Instagram.
E-mail: monah202@gmail.com
Web Site: www.monah.us
Key Personnel: Dir. & Museum Shop Mgr., Charlotte Buchanan-Yale; Chm (V), David Bogle.
Institution Type/Description: Native American Museum.
Hours & Admission Prices: Mon.-Sat. 9-5. No charge; donations accepted. &
Attendance: 27,000 (estimated)

THE PEEL MANSION MUSEUM & HERITAGE GARDENS, 400 S. Walton Blvd., Bentonville, AR 72712. Mailing Address: 312 N. Main, Bentonville, AR 72712. Tel.: 479-254-3870. Fax: 479-254-3871. Facebook: Peel Compton.
E-mail: officemanager@peelcompton.net
Web Site: www.peelcompton.org/peel/index.htm
Key Personnel: Exec. Dir., Corrin Troutman.
Institution Type/Description: Historic House Museum: housed in 1875 Italianate villa & 1850 log cabin.
Hours & Admission Prices: Gardens: Mon.-Fri. sunrise to sunset. Mansion: Tues.-Sat. 10-3. Mansion: adults $5, children $2 & tax. Gardens: no charge. Closed New Year's Eve & Day; Memorial Day; Independence Day; Labor Day; Christmas Eve, Day & week. &
Attendance: 4,000 (estimated)

SCOTT FAMILY AMAZEUM, 1009 Museum Way, Bentonville, AR 72712. Tel.: 479-696-9280.
E-mail: info@amazeum.org
Web Site: www.amazeum.org
Institution Type/Description: Children's Museum.
Hours & Admission Prices: Mon. & Wed.-Sat. 10-5, Sun. 1-5. Admission $9.50; children under 2 & members no charge. Closed New Year's Day; Thanksgiving; Christmas.

21C MUSEUM HOTEL BENTONVILLE, 200 N.E. A St., Bentonville, AR 72712. Tel.: 479-286-6500.
E-mail: dcastleman@21cMuseum.org
Institution Type/Description: Art Gallery.
Hours & Admission Prices: Daily 24 hours. Video Installations: daily 7am to 1am. No charge.

WAL-MART VISITOR'S CENTER, 105 N. Main St., Bentonville, AR 72712-5341. Tel.: 479-273-1329. Facebook: Walmart Museum.
Web Site: corporate.walmart.com/our-story/heritage/visitor-center
Key Personnel: Sr. Dir. Heritage & Assoc. Mktg., Alan Dranow.
Institution Type/Description: History Museum: birthplace of Wal-Mart.
Hours & Admission Prices: Mon.-Thurs. 8 a.m-9 p.m., Fri.-Sat. 8 a.m.-10 p.m., Sun. 12-5. No charge. &
Attendance: 50,000

Berryville

HERITAGE CENTER MUSEUM, 403 Public Sq., Berryville, AR 72616-0249. Tel.: 870-423-6312.
E-mail: history1880@windstream.net
Web Site: www.rootsweb.com/~arcchs
Key Personnel: Pres., Gordon Hale.
Institution Type/Description: Local History Museum: housed in 1880 Carroll County Court House.
Hours & Admission Prices: Mon.-Fri. 9-4. Family $5, adults $2, children $1; children under 6 no charge. Closed national holidays.
Attendance: 3,000 (estimated)

SAUNDERS MEMORIAL MUSEUM, 113-15 E. Madison St., Berryville, AR 72616-3954. Mailing Address: P.O. Box 227, Berryville, AR 72616. Tel.: 870-423-2563.
Web Site: www.berryville.com
Key Personnel: Mgr., Rose M. Garrett; Chm. (V), Don Rustuhaltz.
Institution Type/Description: Gun & Period Furnishings Museum.
Hours & Admission Prices: April 15 to 1st weekend in Nov. Mon.-Sat. 10:30-5. Adults $5, children under 13 $2.50; discount to groups of 10 & over; children under 6 no charge. Closed holidays. &
Attendance: 3,000 (estimated)

Blytheville

BLYTHEVILLE HERITAGE MUSEUM, 107C Main St., Blytheville, AR 72315-3431. Mailing Address: P.O. Box 234, Blytheville, AR 72316-0234. Tel.: 870-763-2525.
Institution Type/Description: History Museum: housed in the former S. H. Kresse Department Store building. Listed on the National Register of Historic Places.
Hours & Admission Prices: Call for hours.

DELTA GATEWAY MUSEUM, 210 W. Main St., Blytheville, AR 72315. Tel.: 870-824-2346. Fax: 870-824-2347. Facebook: Delta Gateway Museum.
E-mail: lhester43@yahoo.com
Web Site: www.deltagatewaymuseum.org
Key Personnel: Dir., Leslie Hester.
Institution Type/Description: History Museum: housed in the historic Kress Building.
Hours & Admission Prices: Tues.-Fri. 1-5, Sat. 10-4. No charge; donations accepted. Closed federal holidays. &
Attendance: 1,000 (estimated)

Brinkley

CENTRAL DELTA DEPOT MUSEUM, 100 W. Cypress, Brinkley, AR 72021-2809. Tel.: 870-589-2124.
E-mail: billsayger@yahoo.com
Key Personnel: Dir., Bill Sayger; Chm. (V), Laura Bussell; Pres. (V), Catherine Jacques.
Institution Type/Description: History Museum.
Hours & Admission Prices: Mon.-Sat. 9-5, Sun. 1-4. Adults $2, children $1; members no charge. &
Attendance: 1,150 (actual)

Calico Rock

CALICO ROCK MUSEUM & VISITOR CENTER, 104 Main St., Calico Rock, AR 72519. Tel.: 870-297-6100.
E-mail: calicorockmuseum@gmail.com
Web Site: www.calicorockmuseum.com
Key Personnel: Exec. Dir., Gloriaann Sanders; Chm. (V), Steven Mitchell.
Institution Type/Description: Art & History Museum: housed in the E.N. Rand Building; built in 1903.
Hours & Admission Prices: Tues.-Sat. 9-5. No charge; donations accepted. &
Attendance: 21,242 (actual)

Camden

MCCOLLUM-CHIDESTER HOUSE, 926 W. Washington St., Camden, AR 71701-3382. Tel.: 870-836-9243. Facebook: Ouachita County Historical Society.
E-mail: ochs2003@sbcglobal.net
Web Site: ouachitacountyhistoricalsociety.org
Key Personnel: Pres. (V), David Reynolds; Museum Mgr., Becky Davis.
Institution Type/Description: Historic House Museum: built in 1847.
Hours & Admission Prices: Wed.-Sat. 9-4. Adults $5, students $2. Closed major holidays. &
Attendance: 1,200 (estimated)

OUACHITA COUNTY HISTORICAL SOCIETY, 926 Washington St., N.W., Camden, AR 71701-3382. Tel.: 870-836-9243 & 0245.
E-mail: ochs2003@sbcglobal.net
Web Site: ouachitacountyhistoricalsociety.org
Key Personnel: Pres., David Reynolds; Museum Mgr., Becky Davis.
Institution Type/Description: Historical Society Museum.
Hours & Admission Prices: Wed.-Sat. 9-4. Adults $5, students $2. Closed major holidays. &
Attendance: 1,200 (estimated)

Charleston

BELLE MUSEUM & PRESBYTERIAN CHAPEL, 322 E. Main, Charleston, AR 72933. Mailing Address: P.O. Box 261, Charleston, AR 72933-0261.
Key Personnel: Dir., Delbert Ervin; Dir., Mary B. Ervin.
Institution Type/Description: History & Church Museum.
Hours & Admission Prices: May-June call for hours. No charge; donations accepted. &

Clinton

VAN BUREN COUNTY HISTORICAL MUSEUM, 211 3rd St., Clinton, AR 72031. Mailing Address: P.O. Box 1023, Clinton, AR 72031-1023. Tel.: 501-745-4066.
E-mail: museum@artelco.com
Key Personnel: Chm. (V), Carol Hutto; Chm. (V), Charlotte West; Pres. (V), Dortha Borecky.
Institution Type/Description: Historical Museum.
Hours & Admission Prices: Mon.-Thurs. 10-3. No charge; donations accepted. Closed holidays. &
Attendance: 500 (estimated)

Conway

BAUM GALLERY OF FINE ART, 201 Donaghey Ave., Conway, AR 72035-5001. Mailing Address: McAlister 101, Dept. of Art, UCA, 201 Donaghey Ave., Conway, AR 72035. Tel.: 501-450-5793 & 5000. Fax: 501-450-3670.
E-mail: barclaym@uca.edu
Web Site: www.uca.edu/art/baum
Key Personnel: Dir. & Cur., Brian Young.
Institution Type/Description: Art Gallery.
Hours & Admission Prices: July-May Mon.-Wed. & Fri. 10-5, Thurs. 10-7, Sun. for receptions only. No charge. Closed spring break; summer sessions; Christmas break. &
Attendance: 7,500 (actual)

FAULKNER COUNTY MUSEUM, Courthouse Square, 805 Locust St., Conway, AR 72034. Mailing Address: P.O. Box 2442, Conway, AR 72033-2442. Tel.: 501-329-5918.
E-mail: fcm@conwaycorp.net
Web Site: www.faulknercountymuseum.org
Key Personnel: Dir., Lynita Langley-Ware; Chm. (V), Dr. Sondra Gordy.
Institution Type/Description: History Museum.
Hours & Admission Prices: Mon.-Thurs. 9-4; groups by appointment. No charge; donations accepted. &
Attendance: 1,600 (actual)

De Queen

COLLIN RAYE MUSEUM, 607 Haes St., De Queen, AR 71832. Tel.: 870-642-6642.
E-mail: seviercountymuseum@windstream.net
Institution Type/Description: History Museum: housed in the boyhood home of country music star, Collin Raye.
Hours & Admission Prices: By appointment.

SEVIER COUNTY MUSEUM, 717 Walter J. Leeper Dr., De Queen, AR 71832. Tel.: 870-642-6642. Facebook.
E-mail: seviercountymuseum@gmail.com
Web Site: www.seviercountymuseum.com
Formerly: The Sevier County Historical Museum
Key Personnel: Dir., Karen Mills; Bd. Pres., Gary Walker.
Institution Type/Description: History and Education Museum.
Hours & Admission Prices: Tues.-Sat. 12-5. No charge; donations accepted. &
Attendance: 1,500 (estimated)

Des Arc

LOWER WHITE RIVER MUSEUM STATE PARK, 2009 Main St., Des Arc, AR 72040-3135. Tel.: 870-256-3711. Fax: 870-256-9202.
E-mail: lowerwhiterivermuseum@arkansas.com
Web Site: www.arkansasstateparks.com/lowerwhiterivermuseum
Formerly: Prairie County Museum
Key Personnel: Supt., Monica Smith.
Institution Type/Description: History Museum.
Hours & Admission Prices: Tues.-Sat. 8-5, Sun. 1-5. No charge. Closed New Year's Day; Thanksgiving; Christmas Eve & Day. &
Attendance: 2,000 (actual)

Dumas

DESHA COUNTY MUSEUM, Hwy. 161 E., Dumas, AR 71639. Mailing Address: P.O. Box 141, Dumas, AR 71639-0141. Tel.: 870-382-4222.
E-mail: deshacomuseum@yahoo.com
Key Personnel: Bd. Dir., Charlotte Schexnayder; Pres. (V), Martha Clark; Dir., Peggy Chapman.

Institution Type/Description: Historical & Preservation Society.
Hours & Admission Prices: Tues.-Fri. 10-3:30, Sun. 2-4. No charge; donations accepted. &
Attendance: 4,000 (estimated)

Earle

CRITTENDEN COUNTY MUSEUM, 1112 Main St., Earle, AR 72331. Mailing Address: P.O. Box 644, Earle, AR 72331. Tel.: 870-792-7374. Facebook.
E-mail: tammy.berry319@gmail.com
Web Site: www.crittendencountymuseum.com
Key Personnel: Dir., Tamara Berry; Chm. (V), Clara Miller; Pres. (V), Scott Lovelady.
Institution Type/Description: History Museum: housed in the former Missouri Pacific train depot. Listed on the National Register of Historic Places.
Hours & Admission Prices: Call for hours. No charge; donations accepted.
Attendance: 600 (estimated)

El Dorado

SOUTH ARKANSAS ARTS CENTER, 110 E. Fifth St., El Dorado, AR 71730-3822. Tel.: 870-862-5474. Fax: 870-862-4921.
E-mail: info@saac-arts.org
Web Site: saac-arts.org
Key Personnel: Exec. Dir., Jack Wilson.
Institution Type/Description: Art Gallery.
Hours & Admission Prices: Mon.-Fri. 9-5. No charge; donations accepted. Closed holidays. &
Attendance: 30,000 (estimated)

SOUTH ARKANSAS HISTORICAL PRESERVATION SOCIETY & THE NEWTON HOUSE MUSEUM, 510 N. Jackson, El Dorado, AR 71730. Mailing Address: P.O. Box 144, El Dorado, AR 71731-0144. Tel.: 870-862-9890. Fax: 870-863-9893.
Web Site: www.soarkhistory.com
Institution Type/Description: Historical Preservation Society & Historic House: house built c.1849.
Hours & Admission Prices: Mon.-Fri. 10-4. No charge; donations accepted. Closed major holidays.

Eureka Springs

AVIATION CADET MUSEUM, 542 CR 2073, Eureka Springs, AR 72632. Tel.: 479-253-5008.
E-mail: av1cadet@arkansas.net
Web Site: www.aviationcadet.org/home.aspx
Key Personnel: Museum Shop Mgr., E.D. Severe.
Institution Type/Description: Aviation Museum.
Hours & Admission Prices: Tours: April-Oct. Mon.-Fri. 10, 1 & 3, Sat. 1 & 3, Sun. 3pm; other times by appointment. Adults $15, children 6-12 $7.
Attendance: 400 (estimated)

BLUE SPRING HERITAGE CENTER, 1537 CR 210, Eureka Springs, AR 72632. Tel.: 479-253-9244. Fax: 479-253-9256.
E-mail: info@bluespringheritage.com
Web Site: bluespringheritage.com
Institution Type/Description: Heritage Center.
Hours & Admission Prices: mid-March to late Nov. daily 9-6. Adults $9.75, children 6-17 $6.50; children 5 & under no charge. &

CASTLE ROGUE'S MANOR, 124 Spring St., Eureka Springs, AR 72632. Tel.: 800-250-5827.
Web Site: castleroguesmanor.com
Institution Type/Description: Historic House Museum.
Hours & Admission Prices: By appointment. Adults $20; children $10.

EUREKA FINE ART GALLERY, 2 Pine St., Ste. C, Eureka Springs, AR 72632-3105. Tel.: 479-363-6000. Facebook: Eureka Fine Art Gallery.
E-mail: eurekafineartgallery@gmail.com
Web Site: www.eurekafineartgallery.com
Institution Type/Description: Art Gallery.
Hours & Admission Prices: Sun.-Sat. 10-5, Wed. by appointment. No charge.

EUREKA SPRINGS HISTORICAL MUSEUM, 95 S. Main, Eureka Springs, AR 72632-3600. Tel.: 479-253-9417. Facebook: Eureka Springs Historical Museum.
E-mail: info@eurekaspringshistoricalmuseum.org

Web Site: www.eurekaspringshistoricalmuseum.org
Key Personnel: Museum Operations Mgr., Stephanie Stodden; Chm. (V), Gayla Wolfinbarger.
Institution Type/Description: Historic House Museum: housed in the Calif House, 1889.
Hours & Admission Prices: Mon.-Sat. 9:30-4, Sun. 11-4. Self-Guided Tours: adults $5, children 12 & under and members no charge. Closed New Year's Day; Thanksgiving; Christmas.
Attendance: 12,000 (actual)

FAMILY HERITAGE MUSEUM, 338 Onyx Cave Ln., Eureka Springs, AR 72632. Tel.: 479-253-5444 & 5875. Fax: 479-253-7497.
E-mail: muriels@familyheritagemuseum.com
Web Site: www.familyheritagemuseum.com
Formerly: Gay 90's Button & Doll Museum
Key Personnel: Owner & Cur., Muriel H. Schmidt.
Institution Type/Description: Family Heritage Museum.
Hours & Admission Prices: By appointment. No charge; donations accepted. &
Attendance: 500 (estimated)

THE GREAT PASSION PLAY BIBLE MUSEUM, The Great Passion Play, 935 Passion Play Rd., Eureka Springs, AR 72632-9496. Mailing Address: P.O. Box 471, Eureka Springs, AR 72632. Tel.: 479-253-8559. Fax: 479-253-2302.
E-mail: akovalcik@greatpassionplay.com
Key Personnel: Dir., Anne Kovalcik.
Institution Type/Description: Religious Museum.
Hours & Admission Prices: May-Oct. Mon.-Sat. 10-8. Adults $5, children $2.50. &
Attendance: 64,000 (actual)

ONYX CAVE & MUSEUM, 338 Onyx Cave Lane, Eureka Springs, AR 72632-9631. Tel.: 479-253-9321.
Institution Type/Description: Geology Museum.
Hours & Admission Prices: May-Sept. daily 9-4; Oct.-April call for hours. Adults 13 & over $7.50, children 4-12 $3.50; children 3 & under no charge.

QUIGLEY'S CASTLE, 274 Quigley Castle Rd., Eureka Springs, AR 72632-9144. Tel.: 479-253-8311. Facebook: Quigley's Castle.
E-mail: quigleyscastle@gmail.com
Web Site: quigleyscastle.com
Institution Type/Description: Historic House Museum: housed in the former home of Elise & Albert Quigley; built in 1943. Listed on the National Register of Historic Places.
Hours & Admission Prices: April-Oct. Mon.-Wed. & Fri.-Sat. 8:30-5. Adults $7; children 14 & under no charge.

THE ROSALIE, 282 Spring St., Eureka Springs, AR 72632-3152. Tel.: 479-253-7377.
E-mail: info@therosalie.com
Web Site: www.therosalie.com
Key Personnel: Owner, Charles Ragsdell; Owner, Lori Ragsdell.
Institution Type/Description: Historic House: built in 1889 by J. W. Hill owner of local livery & stables, and builder of Eureka Springs phone system.
Hours & Admission Prices: Tours: by appointment. Adults $7.50; children under 6 no charge.
Attendance: 1,000 (estimated)

TURPENTINE CREEK WILDLIFE REFUGE, 239 Turpentine Creek Lane, Eureka Springs, AR 72632-9185. Tel.: 479-253-5841.
E-mail: tigers@turpentinecreek.org
Key Personnel: Cur., Emily McCormack.
Institution Type/Description: Wildlife Refuge.
Hours & Admission Prices: Summer: daily 9-6; Winter: daily 9-5. Adults $20, youth 13-19 $15, children 4-12, seniors & veterans $10; children 3 & under no charge. Closed Christmas.

Fairfield Bay

LOG CABIN MUSEUM, 335 Snead Dr., Fairfield Bay, AR 72088. Mailing Address: P.O. Box 1549, Fairfield Bay, AR 72088. Tel.: 501-581-1638.
Key Personnel: Dir., Marilyn Robertson.
Institution Type/Description: Historic Building: housed in an 1850s log cabin.
Hours & Admission Prices: Mon. 10-2, Thurs. - Sun. 1-4. No charge.

NORTH CENTRAL ARKANSAS ART GALLERY, 110 Lost Creek Parkway, Fairfield Bay, AR 72088. Mailing Address: P.O.

Box 1643, Fairfield Bay, AR 72088. Tel.: 501-884-6100, 501-680-2741.
E-mail: chardon@artelco.com
Web Site: www.ncafae.org/galleries.html
Key Personnel: Dir., Bob Thompson; Volunteer Coord., Charlotte Rierson; Chmn. (V), Joyce Hobbs; Museum Shop Mgr., Wilba Thompson.
Institution Type/Description: Art Gallery.
Hours & Admission Prices: Call for hours. No charge; donations accepted. &
Attendance: 11,158 (estimated)

Fayetteville

ARKANSAS AIR & MILITARY MUSEUM, 4290 S. School Ave., Fayetteville, AR 72701-8008. Tel.: 479-521-4947. Fax: 4791-521-4947.
E-mail: arairmus@aol.com
Web Site: www.arkansasairandmilitary.com
Formerly: Arkansas Air Museum
Key Personnel: Pres., Ray Boudreaux; Vice Pres., Rick Bailey; Treas., James Nicholson; Sec., Rick McKinney; Museum Shop Mgr., Sally Ebbrecht.
Institution Type/Description: Air Museum: housed in WWII era wooden truss hangar; military section housed in 2 additional buildings.
Hours & Admission Prices: Sun.-Fri. 11-4:30, Sat. 10-4:30. Family $20, adults $10, children 6-12 $5; discounts to groups; members no charge. Closed New Year's Day; Thanksgiving; Christmas. &
Attendance: 15,000 (estimated)

BOTANICAL GARDEN OF THE OZARKS, 4703 N. Crossover Rd., Fayetteville, AR 72764. Mailing Address: P.O. Box 10407, Fayetteville, AR 72703-0042. Tel.: 479-750-2620.
E-mail: ctaylor@bgozarks.org
Web Site: www.bgozarks.org
Key Personnel: Exec. Dir., Charlotte Taylor; Pres. (V), Walt Eilers.
Institution Type/Description: Botanical Garden.
Hours & Admission Prices: Daily 9-5. Adults $7, children 5-12 $4; members, children under 5, & Sat. 9-12 Fayetteville residents no charge. Reciprocal admission to AHS members. &
Attendance: 95,000 (estimated)

CLINTON HOUSE MUSEUM, 930 W. Clinton Dr., Fayetteville, AR 72701-4912. Tel.: 479-444-0066, 877-BIL-N-HIL.
E-mail: director@clintonhousemuseum.org
Web Site: www.clintonhousemuseum.org
Key Personnel: Dir., Kate Johnson.
Institution Type/Description: Historic House; housed in the former home of Bill & Hillary Clinton while he was a professor at the University of Arkansas.
Hours & Admission Prices: Mon.-Fri. 8:30-4:30. Adults $8, students $5, children $1; AAM & Blue Star Museum members and active duty military families no charge. &
Attendance: 7,500 (estimated)

FINE ARTS CENTER GALLERY - UNIVERSITY OF ARKANSAS, Fulbright College of Arts and Sciences, 116 Fine Arts Center, Fayetteville, AR 72701. Tel.: 479-575-7987. Fax: 479-575-2062.
E-mail: stk004@uark.edu
Web Site: art.uark.edu/fineartsgallery
Key Personnel: Dir., Shannon Dillard Mitchell.
Institution Type/Description: Art Gallery.
Hours & Admission Prices: Mon.-Fri. 9-5:30, Sun. 2-5. No charge.

HEADQUARTERS HOUSE MUSEUM, 118 E. Dickson St., Fayetteville, AR 72701-4207. Tel.: 479-521-2970.
E-mail: info@washcohistoricalsociety.org
Web Site: www.washcohistoricalsociety.org/hispro
Key Personnel: Pres., Vince Chadick.
Institution Type/Description: History Museum: built in 1853 by Judge Jonas M. Tebbetts, this home served as headquarters for the Federal and Confederate armies during the Civil War.
Hours & Admission Prices: Tours by appointment. Adults $8, children $1; discounts to members. &
Attendance: 4,000 (estimated)

OZARK MILITARY MUSEUM, 4290 S. School Ave., Fayetteville, AR 72701-8008. Tel.: 479-587-1941. Fax: 479-587-0848.
Key Personnel: Dir., Leonard McCandless.
Institution Type/Description: Military Museum.
Hours & Admission Prices: Sun.-Fri. 11-4:30, Sat. 10-4:30.

THE UNIVERSITY MUSEUM COLLECTIONS, University of Arkansas, Biomass Bldg. Rm. 125, Fayetteville, AR 72701-1201. Tel.: 479-575-3456. Fax: 479-575-7464.
E-mail: collectn@uark.edu
Web Site: www.uark.edu/~museinfo/
Key Personnel: Interim Dir., Dr. Jeannine Durdik; Cur. Collections, Dr. Mary Suter; Cur. Zoology, Dr. Nancy G. McCartney.
Institution Type/Description: General Museum.
Hours & Admission Prices: Mon.-Fri. by appointment only. No charge. Closed university holidays. &
Attendance: 200 (estimated)

Fordyce

DALLAS COUNTY MUSEUM, 221 S. Main St., Fordyce, AR 71742. Mailing Address: P.O. Box 703, Fordyce, AR 71742-0703. Tel.: 870-352-5262. Facebook: Dallas County Museum.
E-mail: dcmus@windstream.net
Institution Type/Description: History Museum.
Hours & Admission Prices: Tues.-Fri. 10-4, Sat. 10-2. No charge; donations accepted. Closed most holidays. &

Foreman

NEW ROCKY COMFORT MUSEUM, 3rd & Schuman, Foreman, AR 71836. Mailing Address: P.O. Box 268, Foreman, AR 71836-0268. Tel.: 870-542-7887. Fax: 870-542-6347.
Institution Type/Description: Historic Building: housed in a restored jail; built in 1902.
Hours & Admission Prices: Call for hours.

Forrest City

ST. FRANCIS COUNTY MUSEUM, 603 Front St., Forrest City, AR 72335-3808. Mailing Address: P.O. Box 1332, Forrest City, AR 72336-1332. Tel.: 870-261-1744. Fax: 870-630-1210.
Web Site: www.sfcmuseum.org
Key Personnel: Dir., H. Wayne Parker; Chm. (V), Rush Beavers; Cur., Shelley Gervasi.
Institution Type/Description: Historical & Culturally Specific Museum.
Hours & Admission Prices: Mon.-Fri. 10-5. No charge; donations accepted. &
Attendance: 4,205 (actual)

Fort Smith

CHAFFEE BARBERSHOP MUSEUM AND MUSEUM OF CHAFFEE HISTORY, 7313 Terry St., Fort Smith, AR 72916. Mailing Address: 7020 Taylor Ave., Fort Smith, AR 72916. Tel.: 479-434-6774. Fax: 479-452-4566. Facebook: Chaffee Barber Shop.
E-mail: history@chaffeecrossing.com
Key Personnel: Dir., Joseph H. Chasteen.
Institution Type/Description: Historic Building: housed in a former barbershop.
Hours & Admission Prices: Mon.-Sat. 9-4. No charge; donations accepted. Closed National holidays. &

CLAYTON HOUSE, 514 N. Sixth St., Fort Smith, AR 72901-2006. Tel.: 479-783-3000.
E-mail: claytonhouse@claytonhouse.org
Web Site: claytonhouse.org
Institution Type/Description: Historic House: housed in the former home of District Attorney, William Henry Harrison Clayton; built c.1850. Listed on the National Register of Historic Places.
Hours & Admission Prices: Tues.-Sat. 12-4, Sun. 1-4; other times by appointment. &

FORT SMITH AIR MUSEUM, Fort Smith Regional Airport, 6700 McKennon Blvd., Fort Smith, AR 72903. Mailing Address: 3 Glen Haven Dr., Fort Smith, AR 72901-6837. Tel.: 479-785-1839.
E-mail: whaver@mynewroads.com
Web Site: www.fortsmithairmuseum.com
Key Personnel: Dir., Chm. (V) & Pres. (V), Wayne Haver; Vice Pres., Carl Riggens.
Institution Type/Description: Air Museum.
Hours & Admission Prices: Daily 5:30am-11pm. No charge. &
Attendance: 50,000 (estimated)

FORT SMITH MUSEUM OF HISTORY, 320 Rogers Ave., Fort Smith, AR 72901-1937. Tel.: 479-783-7841. Fax: 479-783-3244.

E-mail: leisa.gramlich@fortsmithmuseum.com
Web Site: www.fortsmithmuseum.com
Key Personnel: C.E.O., Leisa Gramlich; Pres., John Cooley; Museum Shop Mgr., Caroline Speir.
Institution Type/Description: History Museum: housed in 1907 Atkinson-Williams Building.
Hours & Admission Prices: June-Aug. Tues.-Sat. 10-5, Sun. 1-5; Sept.-May Tues.-Sat. 10-5. Adults $5, children 6-15 $2; discounts to groups; Fort Smith public schools, children under 6 & members no charge. Closed holidays. &
Attendance: 20,000 (estimated)

FORT SMITH NATIONAL HISTORIC SITE, 301 Parker Ave., Fort Smith, AR 72901-1938. Mailing Address: P.O. Box 1406, Fort Smith, AR 72902-1406. Tel.: 479-783-3961. Fax: 479-783-5307. TDD: 479-783-3961.
Web Site: www.nps.gov/fosm/
Key Personnel: Supt., Lisa Conard Frost; Chief Interpretation & Resource Mgmt., Michael Groomer; Museum Technician, Emily Lovick; Administrative Officer, Judy Bachler; Facility Mgr., Darin Huggins.
Institution Type/Description: Historic Site: 1817-24 Fort Smith, 1838 regarrisoned at new location, completed larger fort 1849, became the Federal Courthouse and Jail, 1871-1896.
Hours & Admission Prices: Daily 9-5. Individual Seven Day Pass 16 & up $6; educational groups and children 15 & under with adult no charge. Closed New Year's Day; Thanksgiving; Christmas. &
Attendance: 100,000 (estimated)

FORT SMITH REGIONAL ART MUSEUM, 1601 Rogers Ave., Fort Smith, AR 72901. Tel.: 479-784-ARTS (2787). Fax: 479-784-9071.
E-mail: info@fsram.org
Web Site: fsram.org
Formerly: Fort Smith Art Center
Key Personnel: Exec. Dir., Louis Meluso; Gallery Mgr., Casey Seamans; Mktg. Coord., Melissa Conry; Dir. Education, Daleana Vaughan; Education Asst., Natasha Luong.
Institution Type/Description: Art Museum.
Hours & Admission Prices: Tues.-Sat. 11-6, Sun. 1-5. No charge; donations accepted. Closed New Year's Day; Independence Day; Thanksgiving & day after; Christmas Eve & Day. &
Attendance: 14,000 (estimated)

FORT SMITH TROLLEY MUSEUM, 100 S. 4th St., Fort Smith, AR 72901-1947. Tel.: 479-783-0205.
E-mail: info@fstm.org
Web Site: www.fstm.org
Key Personnel: C.E.O. & Pres. (V), Art B. Martin, M.D.; Museum Shop Mgr., Bradley Martin.
Institution Type/Description: History Museum.
Hours & Admission Prices: Museum: Sat. 10-5, Sun. 1-5; other times by appointment. Trolley: May-Oct. Mon.-Sat. 10-5, Sun. 1-5; Nov.-April Sat. 10-5, Sun. 1-5. Museum: no charge; donations accepted. Trolley Rides: adult $2, children $1. &
Attendance: 10,000 (estimated)

JANET HUCKABEE ARKANSAS RIVER VALLEY NATURE CENTER, 8300 Wells Lake Rd., Fort Smith, AR 72916. Tel.: 479-452-3993. Fax: 479-452-1334.
Web Site: www.rivervalleynaturecenter.com
Institution Type/Description: Nature Center.
Hours & Admission Prices: Tues.-Sat. 8:30-4:30, Sun. 1-5. No charge. Closed Easter; Thanksgiving; Christmas.

Garfield

PEA RIDGE NATIONAL MILITARY PARK, 15930 Hwy. 62, Garfield, AR 72732-9532. Tel.: 479-451-8122. Fax: 479-451-0219.
E-mail: peri_interpretation@nps.gov
Web Site: www.nps.gov/peri/
Key Personnel: Park Ranger, Troy Banzhaf; Supt., John Scott; Museum Shop Mgr., Serena Rothfus.
Institution Type/Description: Historical Building: reconstructed Elkhorn Tavern.
Hours & Admission Prices: Daily 8-5. 7 Day Permit: adults 16-61 $5; discounts to NPS passholders; children under 16 no charge. Closed New Year's Day; Thanksgiving; Christmas. &
Attendance: 120,000 (estimated)

Gillett

ARKANSAS POST MUSEUM, 5530 Hwy. 165 S., Gillett, AR 72055-9730. Tel.: 870-548-2634. Fax: 870-548-3003.
E-mail: arkansaspostmuseum@arkansas.gov
Web Site: www.arkansasstateparks.com/arkansaspostmuseum/
Key Personnel: Dir., Christy Murphy.
Institution Type/Description: Local History Museum.
Hours & Admission Prices: Tues.-Sat. & Mon. holidays 8-5, Sun. 1-5. Museum: no charge. Closed New Year's Day; Thanksgiving; Christmas Eve & Day. &
Attendance: 6,000 (actual)

ARKANSAS POST NATIONAL MEMORIAL, 1741 Old Post Rd., Gillett, AR 72055-9733. Tel.: 870-548-2207. Fax: 870-548-2431.
E-mail: arpo_superintendent@nps.gov
Web Site: www.nps.gov/arpo
Key Personnel: Supt., Edward Wood.
Institution Type/Description: History Museum.
Hours & Admission Prices: Park daily 8-dusk. Visitor Center daily 8-5. No charge; donations accepted. Closed New Year's Day; Thanksgiving; Christmas. &
Attendance: 38,180 (actual)

Glenwood

BILLY'S HOUSE OF GUITARS & MUSICAL MUSEUM, 201 Broadway, Glenwood, AR 71943-9200. Tel.: 870-356-4301.
Institution Type/Description: Musical Instruments Museum.
Hours & Admission Prices: Call for hours. No charge; donations accepted.

Gravette

GRAVETTE HISTORICAL MUSEUM, 503 Charlotte St., S.E., Gravette, AR 72736. Mailing Address: P.O. Box 1421, Gravette, AR 72736. Tel.: 479-787-7334. Fax: 479-787-9910.
Key Personnel: Chm. (V), Steve Mitchael; Financial Dir., Michael Von Ree; Museum Shop Mgr., Erin McVittie.
Institution Type/Description: Historical Museum.
Hours & Admission Prices: Tues. & Sat. 12-4; other times by appointment. No charge; donations accepted. Closed New Year's Day; Christmas; Thanksgiving. &
Attendance: 400 (estimated)

Greenbrier

RIDDLE'S ELEPHANT AND WILDLIFE SANCTUARY, Arkansas 25 off U.S. 65 N., Greenbrier, AR 72058. Mailing Address: P.O. Box 715, Greenbrier, AR 72058. Tel.: 501-589-3291. Fax: 501-589-2248.
E-mail: info@elephantsanctuary.org
Web Site: www.elephantsanctuary.org
Key Personnel: Owner, Scott Riddle; Owner, Heidi Riddle.
Institution Type/Description: Wildlife Sanctuary.
Hours & Admission Prices: 1st Sat. each month 11-3.

Greenwood

OLD JAIL MUSEUM, 307 Town Sq., Greenwood, AR 72936. Mailing Address: P.O. Box 523, Greenwood, AR 72936. Tel.: 479-996-6357.
E-mail: info@greenwoodchamber.net
Key Personnel: Pres. (V), Ruth McConnell; Cur., Donna Goldstein; Archivist, Sue Edwards.
Institution Type/Description: History Museum.
Hours & Admission Prices: May-Oct. Thurs.-Sat. 11-3; other times by appointment. No charge; donations accepted.
Attendance: 1,200 (actual)

Gurdon

HOO-HOO INTERNATIONAL FORESTRY MUSEUM, 207 Main St., Gurdon, AR 71743-1237. Mailing Address: P.O. Box 118, Gurdon, AR 71743-0118. Tel.: 870-353-4997, 800-979-9950. Fax: 870-353-4151.
E-mail: info@hoo-hoo.org
Web Site: www.hoo-hoo.org
Key Personnel: Exec. Sec., Beth A. Thomas.
Institution Type/Description: Logging & Lumber Museum.
Hours & Admission Prices: Mon.-Fri. 9-4. No charge.

Hamburg

ASHLEY COUNTY MUSEUM, 302 N. Cherry St., Hamburg, AR 71646. Mailing Address: P.O. Box 27, Hamburg, AR 71646-0027. Tel.: 870-853-2244.
E-mail: info@ashleycountymuseum.com
Web Site: www.ashleycountymuseum.com
Institution Type/Description: Historic House Museum: housed in the former home of David E. Watson; built in 1918. Listed on the National Register of Historic Places.
Hours & Admission Prices: Tues. 10-3; other times by appointment.

Hardy

GOOD OLD DAYS VINTAGE MOTORCAR MUSEUM, INC., 301 W. Main St., Hardy, AR 72542. Mailing Address: P.O. Box 311, Hardy, AR 72542-0311. Tel.: 870-856-4884. Fax: 870-856-4884.
E-mail: esutherland@tenn.plast.com
Key Personnel: Dir., Ernest E. Sutherland.
Institution Type/Description: Automobile Museum.
Hours & Admission Prices: Mon.-Fri. 9:30-4, Sat. 9-4:30, Sun. 12-5. Adults $10, children 12 & under $5; discounts to groups and museum, AAM & ICOM members. Closed Thanksgiving; Christmas. &
Attendance: 4,500 (estimated)

Harrison

BOONE COUNTY HERITAGE MUSEUM, 124 S. Cherry St., Harrison, AR 72601-5024. Mailing Address: P.O. Box 1094, Harrison, AR 72602-1094. Tel.: 870-741-3312.
E-mail: bchm@windstream.net
Web Site: www.bchrs.org
Key Personnel: Pres. (V), John Berry; Dir., Roz Slavik.
Institution Type/Description: History Museum.
Hours & Admission Prices: March-Nov. Mon.-Fri. 10-4; Dec.-Feb. Thurs. 10-4. Adults $2. Closed holidays.

BUFFALO NATIONAL RIVER, 402 N. Walnut St. Ste. #136, Harrison, AR 72601-3622. Tel.: 870-365-2700. Fax: 870-365-2701.
E-mail: buff_information@nps.gov
Web Site: www.nps.gov/buff/index.htm
Key Personnel: Supt., Kevin G. Cheri.
Institution Type/Description: National Park.
Hours & Admission Prices: Daily 8:30-4:30. No charge. Closed federal holidays except Memorial Day, Independence Day & Labor Day. &
Attendance: 1,000,000 (actual)

MARINE CORPS LEGACY MUSEUM, 127 Rush St., Harrison, AR 72601. Mailing Address: P.O. Box 2654, Harrison, AR 72602-2654. Tel.: 870-743-1680.
E-mail: mclm@windstream.net
Institution Type/Description: Military History Museum.
Hours & Admission Prices: Tues.-Sat. 10-5.

Heber Springs

OLMSTEAD FUNERAL & HISTORICAL MUSEUM, 108 S. 4th St., Heber Springs, AR 72543-3810. Mailing Address: 601 W. Main St., Heber Springs, AR 72543. Tel.: 501-362-2422 & 250-3890.
E-mail: mail@olmstead.cc
Web Site: www.olmstead.cc/museum.htm
Institution Type/Description: History Museum.
Hours & Admission Prices: Call for appointment.

Helena

DELTA CULTURAL CENTER, 141 Cherry St., Helena, AR 72342-3501. Tel.: 870-338-4350, 800-358-0972. Fax: 870-338-4358.
E-mail: info@deltaculturalcenter.com
Web Site: www.deltaculturalcenter.com
Key Personnel: Dir., Katie Harrington; Chm. Policy Advisory Bd., Emma Petty; Museum Shop Mgr., Kathleen Randall.
Institution Type/Description: Cultural Center: housed in the former St. Louis & Iron Mountain Railroad Depot; c.1912.

Hours & Admission Prices: Tues.-Sat. 9-5. No charge; donations accepted. Closed New Year's Day; Thanksgiving; Christmas Eve & Day. &
Attendance: 26,988 (actual)

HELENA MUSEUM OF PHILLIPS COUNTY, 623 Pecan St., Helena, AR 72342-3298. Mailing Address: P.O. Box 38, Helena, AR 72342. Tel.: 870-338-7790. Fax: 870-338-7732. Facebook: Helena Museum.
E-mail: helenamuseum@gmail.com
Web Site: www.helenamuseum.com
Key Personnel: Dir., Shane Williams; Pres. (V), Joe Ann Hargraves; Vice Pres. (V), Riley Porter; Sec., Jeanie Turley; Treas., Walter Morris, Jr.
Institution Type/Description: History Museum.
Hours & Admission Prices: Wed.-Sat. 10-4. No charge; donations accepted. Closed New Year's Day; Memorial Day; Independence Day; Labor Day; Thanksgiving; Christmas Day & two days after. &
Attendance: 3,463 (actual)

PILLOW-THOMPSON HOUSE, 718 Perry St., Helena, AR 72342-3134. Mailing Address: P.O. Box 785, Helena, AR 72342-0785. Tel.: 870-338-8535.
E-mail: dussery@pccua.edu
Institution Type/Description: Historic House: built in 1896.
Hours & Admission Prices: Wed.-Sat. 10-4; groups by appointment. No charge. Closed New Year's Day; Easter; Thanksgiving; Christmas.

Hope

CLINTON BIRTHPLACE HOME, 117 S. Hervey St., Hope, AR 71801-4208. Mailing Address: P.O. Box 1925, Hope, AR 71802-1925. Tel.: 870-777-4455. Fax: 870-722-6929.
E-mail: clinton@arkansas.net
Web Site: www.clintonbirthplace.com
Key Personnel: Dir., Martha Berryman.
Institution Type/Description: Historic House: housed in the boyhood home of President William Jefferson Clinton. Listed on the National Register of Historic Places.
Hours & Admission Prices: Daily 9-4:30; groups by appointment. No charge.

HOPE VISITOR CENTER AND MUSEUM, 100 E. Division St., Hope, AR 71801. Mailing Address: P.O. Box 596, Hope, AR 71802-0596. Tel.: 870-722-2580.
E-mail: vic-depot@hopearkansas.net
Web Site: www.hopearkansas.net
Institution Type/Description: History Museum: housed in the former Iron Mountain/Missouri Pacific Railroad Depot; built in 1912.
Hours & Admission Prices: Call for hours. No charge; donations accepted. &

KLIPSCH HERITAGE MUSEUM ASSOCIATION, INC., 136 Hempstead 278, Hope, AR 71801. Mailing Address: P.O. Box 280, Hope, AR 71801. Tel.: 833-794-5287.
E-mail: contact@klipschmuseum.org
Web Site: www.klipschmuseum.org
Institution Type/Description: History Museum.
Hours & Admission Prices: Wed.-Fri. 10-2 by appointment. Adults $5, seniors, children, & college students $3.

Hot Springs

THE FINE ARTS CENTER OF HOT SPRINGS, 626 Central Ave., Hot Springs, AR 71901-5331. Mailing Address: P.O. Box 6263, Hot Springs, AR 71902-6263. Tel.: 501-624-0489.
E-mail: info@hsfac.org
Key Personnel: Exec. Dir., Donna Dunnahoe; Pres. (V), Bob Dion.
Institution Type/Description: Art Gallery.
Hours & Admission Prices: Mon.-Sat. 10-5. No charge, but donations accepted.
Attendance: 16,000 (estimated)

GANGSTER MUSEUM OF AMERICA, 510 Central Ave., Hot Springs, AR 71901. Tel.: 501-318-1717.
E-mail: director@tgmoa.com
Web Site: www.tgmoa.com
Key Personnel: Dir., Robert Raines.
Institution Type/Description: History Museum.
Hours & Admission Prices: Sun.-Thurs. 10-5, Fri.-Sat. 10-6. Adults $12, seniors $11, children 8-12 $6; children under 8 no charge.

GARVAN WOODLAND GARDENS, 550 Arkridge Rd., Hot Springs, AR 71913-8729. Mailing Address: P.O. Box 22240, Hot Springs, AR 71903-2240. Tel.: 501-262-9300, 800-366-4664.
E-mail: gardeninfo@garvangardens.org
Web Site: www.garvangardens.org
Key Personnel: Dir. Mktg., Sherre Freeman.
Institution Type/Description: Gardens.
Hours & Admission Prices: Feb.-March & Oct-Nov. 21. daily 10-5; Nov. 22-Dec. 12-9, April-Sept. daily 9-8. Adults $10, children 6-12 $5, children 5 & under free; discounts to groups of 20 or more. Closed New Year's Day; Thanksgiving; Christmas. &
Attendance: 140,516 (actual)

HOT SPRINGS NATIONAL PARK VISITOR CENTER, 369 Central Ave., Bathhouse Row, Hot Springs, AR 71901-3525. Mailing Address: 101 Reserve St., Hot Springs, AR 71901. Tel.: 501-620-6715. Fax: 501-624-3458. TDD: 501-623-2308; Facebook: Hot Springs National Park.
E-mail: hosp_park_information@nps.gov
Web Site: www.nps.gov/hosp
Key Personnel: Supt., Laura A. Miller; Supvr. Interpreter, Margaret Daly; Interpreter & Museum Shop Coord., Nalissala Allen; Interpreter & Volunteer Coord., Rachel Winters; Museum Cur., Tom Hill; Museum Shop Mgr., Eastern National, Melissa Haus.
Institution Type/Description: History Building.
Hours & Admission Prices: Daily 9-5. No charge; donations accepted. Closed New Year's Day; Thanksgiving; Christmas. &
Attendance: 272,291 (actual)

JOSEPHINE TUSSAUD WAX MUSEUM, 250 Central Ave., Hot Springs, AR 71901. Tel.: 501-623-5836.
Institution Type/Description: Wax Museum.
Hours & Admission Prices: Summer: Sun.-Thurs. 9-8, Fri.-Sat. 9-9; Winter: Mon.-Thurs. 9:30-5, Fri.-Sat. 9:30-8, Sun. 9:30-5.

MID-AMERICA SCIENCE MUSEUM, 500 Mid America Blvd., Hot Springs, AR 71913-8412. Tel.: 501-767-3461, 800-632-0583 (Arkansas). Fax: 501-767-1170.
E-mail: info@midamericamuseum.org
Web Site: www.midamericamuseum.org
Key Personnel: Exec. Dir., Andy Marquart; Museum Shop Mgr., Noreen Killen.
Institution Type/Description: General Museum.
Hours & Admission Prices: Winter: Tues.-Sun. 10-5; Summer: daily 9:30-6. Adults $9, children 3-12 $7; discount to AAM & ASTC members; members & children under 3 no charge. Closed New Year's Day; Thanksgiving; Christmas Eve & Day. &
Attendance: 89,151 (actual)

Jacksonport

JACKSONPORT STATE PARK, 205 Avenue St., Jacksonport, AR 72075. Mailing Address: 205 Avenue St., Newport, AR 72112-8771. Tel.: 870-523-2143. Fax: 870-523-4620.
E-mail: jacksonport@arkansas.com
Web Site: www.arkansasstateparks.com/jacksonport
Formerly: Jacksonport State Park Courthouse Museum
Key Personnel: Supt., Mark Ballard.
Institution Type/Description: Historic Museum: 1872 Courthouse.
Hours & Admission Prices: Please call for hours. No charge, donations accepted & requested. Closed New Year's Day; Thanksgiving; Christmas Eve & Day. &
Attendance: 2,100 (actual)

Jacksonville

JACKSONVILLE MUSEUM OF MILITARY HISTORY, 100 Veterans' Circle, Jacksonville, AR 72076-4344. Tel.: 501-241-1943. Fax: 501-241-1944.
E-mail: jaxmilmuseum@gmail.com
Web Site: www.jaxmilitarymuseum.org
Key Personnel: Pres. (V), Joan Zumwalt; Dir., Danna Kay Duggar.
Institution Type/Description: Military History Museum.
Hours & Admission Prices: Mon.-Sat. 9-5. Adults $3, seniors & military $2, students $1; members no charge. Closed holidays. &
Attendance: 4,765 (estimated)

Jasper

BRADLEY HOUSE MUSEUM, 403 Clark St., Jasper, AR 72641. Mailing Address: P.O. Box 360, Jasper, AR 72641-0360. Tel.: 870-446-6247. Facebook: Bradley House Museum.
E-mail: history@rittonteam.com
Web Site: www.newtoncountyar.com
Key Personnel: Dir. & Museum Shop Mgr., Donna Dodson; Pres. (V), Thomas Niswouger.
Institution Type/Description: Historic House Museum: housed in the c.1900 home of Dr. W.A. Bradley.
Hours & Admission Prices: April-Oct. Tues.-Thurs. 11-4; Nov.-Dec. Tues. 11-4. No charge; donations accepted. Closed Independence Day.
Attendance: 500 (estimated)

HILARY JONES WILDLIFE MUSEUM, 4208 Hwy. 7 N., Jasper, AR 72641. Mailing Address: P.O. Box 277, Jasper, AR 72641-0277. Tel.: 870-446-6180.
E-mail: newtoncoinfo@ritternet.com
Institution Type/Description: Wildlife Museum.
Hours & Admission Prices: Daily 9-5.

Jonesboro

ARKANSAS STATE UNIVERSITY ART GALLERY, 114 S. Caraway Rd., Jonesboro, AR 72467. Mailing Address: P.O. Box 1920, State University, AR 72467-1920. Tel.: 870-972-3050. Fax: 870-972-3932.
E-mail: csteele@astate.edu
Web Site: www.finearts.astate.edu/
Key Personnel: Chm. Gallery Committee, Tom Chaffee; Gallery Committee, Gayle Pendergrass.
Institution Type/Description: University Art Gallery.
Hours & Admission Prices: Fine Arts Gallery: Mon.-Fri. 10-5. Bradbury Gallery: Tues.-Sat. 12-5, Sun. 2-5. No charge. Closed holidays.
Attendance: 3,600 (estimated)

ARKANSAS STATE UNIVERSITY MUSEUM, Museum Bldg., 320 U Loop West, Jonesboro, AR 72401. Mailing Address: P.O. Box 490, State University, AR 72467-0490. Tel.: 870-972-2074. Fax: 870-972-2793. Facebook: Arkansas State University Museum.
E-mail: mallen@astate.edu
Web Site: www.museum.astate.edu
Key Personnel: Exec. Dir., Dr. Marti L. Allen; Cur. Education, Jill Kary; Cur., Elisabeth Engel, M.A.; Office Mgr., Valerie Ponder.
Institution Type/Description: History & Culture Museum.
Hours & Admission Prices: Mon. & Wed.-Fri. 9-5, Tues. 9-7, Sat.10-5. No charge; donations accepted. Closed national holidays.
Attendance: 70,000 (estimated)

FORREST L. WOOD CROWLEY'S RIDGE NATURE CENTER, 600 E. Lawson Rd., Jonesboro, AR 72404. Tel.: 870-933-6787. Fax: 870-932-4582.
E-mail: lee.elkins@agfc.ar.gov
Web Site: www.crowleysridge.org
Institution Type/Description: Nature Center.
Hours & Admission Prices: Tues.-Sat. 8:30-4:30, Sun. 1-5. No charge. Closed major holidays.

Lake Village

OUR LADY OF THE LAKE CHURCH MUSEUM, 314 S. Lakeshore Dr., Lake Village, AR 71653. Tel.: 870-265-5439.
E-mail: frtheophilus@yahoo.com
Web Site: ourladyofthelake.us
Institution Type/Description: Religious Museum.
Hours & Admission Prices: Call for hours.

Lepanto

MUSEUM LEPANTO USA, 310 S. Greenwood, Lepanto, AR 72354. Mailing Address: P.O. Box 418, Lepanto, AR 72354. Tel.: 870-475-6166. Fax: 870-475-2384.
Key Personnel: Dir. & Pres. (V), Judy Bradford; Chm. (v), Mack Howington.
Institution Type/Description: Historic Building: housed in a 1915 bank building.
Hours & Admission Prices: Wed. & Fri. 1-4; other times by appointment. No charge, donations accepted.

Leslie

OZARK HERITAGE ARTS CENTER & MUSEUM, 410 Oak St., Leslie, AR 72645. Mailing Address: P.O. Box 217, Leslie, AR 72645-0217. Tel.: 870-447-2500. Fax: 870-447-2528.
E-mail: ohac@windstream.net
Key Personnel: Exec. Dir., Gary Hall.
Institution Type/Description: History Museum.
Hours & Admission Prices: April-Dec. Tues.-Sat. 10-4. No charge.

Lincoln

ARKANSAS COUNTRY DOCTOR MUSEUM, 107 & 109 N. Starr Ave., Lincoln, AR 72744. Mailing Address: P.O. Box 1004, Lincoln, AR 72744-1004. Tel.: 479-824-4307. Fax: 479-824-4307.
E-mail: countrydoc@pgtc.com
Web Site: www.drmuseum.net
Key Personnel: Pres., Roy Horne; Vice Pres., Mike Allen; Treas. & Security, Jerry Leach; Museum Shop Mgr., Diana Hale; Sec., Carolyn McDonald.
Institution Type/Description: Country Doctor Museum.
Hours & Admission Prices: Feb. 20-Dec. 11 Wed.-Sat. 1-4; other times by appointment. No charge; donations accepted. Closed Independence Day.
Attendance: 625 (estimated)

Little Rock

THE ARKANSAS ARTS CENTER, 501 E. 9th St., Little Rock, AR 72202. Mailing Address: P.O. Box 2137, Little Rock, AR 72203-2137. Tel.: 501-372-4000. Fax: 501-375-8053.
E-mail: showell@arkansasartscenter.org
Web Site: www.arkansasartscenter.org
Key Personnel: Exec. Dir., Todd A. Herman, Ph.D.; Chm. (V), Mary Ellen Irons; Pres. (V), J. Shepherd Russell; Chief Cur. & Cur. Contemporary Craft, Brian Lang; Cur. Drawings, Ann Prentice Wagner, PhD; Deputy Dir. & C.F.O., Laine Harber; Dir. Education & Programs, Rana Edgar; Registrar, Katie Hall; Dir. Devel., Kelly Fleming; Dir. Children's Theatre, Bradley Anderson; State Svcs., Jessica Wright; Museum Shop Mgr., Kim White.
Institution Type/Description: Art Museum.
Hours & Admission Prices: Tues.-Sat. 10-5, Sun. 11-5. No charge, suggested donation $5; discount to AAM members; members no charge. Closed major holidays.
Attendance: 327,833 (actual)

ARKANSAS GAME AND FISH COMMISSION, 2 Natural Resources Dr., Little Rock, AR 72205-1572. Tel.: 501-223-6300, 800-364-4263. Fax: 501-223-6465.
E-mail: askagfc@agfc.state.ar.us
Web Site: www.agfc.com
Key Personnel: Dir., Mike Knoedl.
Institution Type/Description: Zoology Museum.
Hours & Admission Prices: Mon.-Fri. 8-4:30. No charge.

ARKANSAS STATE CAPITOL, Visitor Center, 500 Woodlane St., Little Rock, AR 72201. Tel.: 501-682-5080.
E-mail: scheduling@sos.arkansas.gov
Institution Type/Description: Historic Building: built 1899-1915.
Hours & Admission Prices: Guided Tours: Mon.-Fri. 9-3. No charge.

BARTON ROCK AND ROLL MUSEUM, 2600 Howard St., Little Rock, AR 72207. Tel.: 501-372-8341.
E-mail: info@arkansasstatefair.com
Institution Type/Description: History Museum.
Hours & Admission Prices: By appointment.

EMOBA - ERNIE'S MUSEUM OF BLACK ARKANSAS, 1208 Louisiana, Little Rock, AR 72214. Tel.: 501-372-0018.
Key Personnel: Founder & Dir., Ernie Dodson.
Institution Type/Description: Black History Museum.
Hours & Admission Prices: Feb.-Sept. by appointment only.

ESSE PURSE MUSEUM, 1510 Main St., Little Rock, AR 72202. Mailing Address: P.O. Box 165070, Little Rock, AR 72216. Tel.: 501-916-9022.
E-mail: info@essepursemuseum.com
Web Site: essepursemuseum.com
Key Personnel: Dir. & Owner, Anita Davis; Dir., Ally Weaver.
Institution Type/Description: Social History Museum.

Hours & Admission Prices: Tues.-Sun. 11-4, Sun. 11-3. Adults $10, seniors 60 & over, children 6-18 and military $8; discounts to groups; children under 6 no charge. Closed holidays. &

FIREHOUSE HOSTEL AND MUSEUM, 1201 Commerce St., Little Rock, AR 72202. Mailing Address: P.O. Box 2753, Little Rock, AR 72203. Tel.: 501-476-0294.
E-mail: firehousehostel@sbcglobal.net
Web Site: firehousehostel.org
Institution Type/Description: Historic Building: housed in the former Old Fire Station Number Two; built in 1917.
Hours & Admission Prices: Call for hours.

HEARNE FINE ART, 1001 Wright Ave., Ste. C, Little Rock, AR 72206. Tel.: 501-372-6822. Fax: 501-372-7133.
E-mail: info@hearnefineart.com
Web Site: hearnefineart.com
Institution Type/Description: Art Gallery.
Hours & Admission Prices: Mon.-Thurs. 9-5, Fri. 9-6, Sat. 11-6; other times by appointment.

HISTORIC ARKANSAS MUSEUM, 200 E. Third St., Little Rock, AR 72201-1608. Tel.: 501-324-9351. Fax: 501-324-9345. Facebook: Historic Arkansas Museum; TDD: 501-324-9811.
E-mail: info@historicarkansas.org
Web Site: www.historicarkansas.org
Formerly: Arkansas Territorial Restoration
Key Personnel: Interim Museum Dir., Donna Uptigrove; Dir. Community Engagement, Ellen Korenblat; Dir. Volunteers & Membership, Tricia Spione; Registrar, Lark Buckingham; Cur. Exhibits, Cary Voss; Arkansas Made Researcher, Victoria Chandler; Museum Shop Mgr., Paige James; education Coord., Joleen Linson; Public Use Coord., Sherry Stevenson.
Institution Type/Description: History Museum.
Hours & Admission Prices: Mon.-Sat. 10-4, Sun. 1-4. Galleries: no charge. Tour: Adults $2.50, senior citizens $1.50, children $1; discount to AAM members; members no charge. Closed New Year's Day; Easter; Thanksgiving; Christmas Eve & Day. &
Attendance: 60,000 (estimated)

HISTORICAL RESOURCES AND MUSEUM SERVICES, Arkansas State Parks, One Capitol Mall, Little Rock, AR 72201-1013. Tel.: 501-682-3603. Fax: 501-682-0081.
Web Site: arkansasstateparks.com
Institution Type/Description: State Agency for Museum Services.
Hours & Admission Prices: Business Office: Mon.-Fri. 8-5. &

LITTLE ROCK CENTRAL HIGH SCHOOL NATIONAL HISTORIC SITE, 2120 Daisy L. Gaston Bates Dr., Little Rock, AR 72202. Tel.: 501-374-1957. Fax: 501-396-3001.
E-mail: CHSC_visitor_center@nps.gov
Web Site: www.nps.gov/chsc/
Formerly: Central High Museum & Visitor Center
Key Personnel: Supt., Robin White.
Institution Type/Description: National Historic Site.
Hours & Admission Prices: National Park visitor hours daily 9-4:30. No charge; donations accepted. Closed New Year's Day; Thanksgiving; Christmas. &
Attendance: 150,000 (actual)

LITTLE ROCK ZOOLOGICAL GARDENS, 1 Zoo Dr., Little Rock, AR 72205-5401. Tel.: 501-666-2406. Fax: 501-666-7040. TDD: 501-399-3451.
E-mail: mblakely@littlerock.org
Web Site: www.littlerockzoo.com
Key Personnel: Dir., Michael E. Blakely; Museum Shop Mgr., Barbara Brown.
Institution Type/Description: Zoo.
Hours & Admission Prices: Summer: daily 9-5; Winter: daily 9-4:30. Adults $12.95, seniors 60 & over and military $10.95, children 1-12 $9.95; discounts to AZA institutions & groups with reservation; zoo members & children under one no charge. Closed New Year's Day; Thanksgiving; Christmas. &
Attendance: 283,768 (actual)

MACARTHUR MUSEUM OF ARKANSAS MILITARY HISTORY, Tower Building of the Little Rock Arsenal, 503 E. Ninth St., Little Rock, AR 72202-3997. Tel.: 501-376-4602.
E-mail: macarthur@littlerock.gov
Web Site: www.arkmilitaryheritage.com
Key Personnel: Exec. Dir., Stephan McAteer.
Institution Type/Description: Military History Museum: birthplace of General Douglas MacArthur.

Hours & Admission Prices: Mon.-Sat. 9-4, Sun. 1-4. No charge. Closed New Year's Day; Thanksgiving; Christmas Eve & Day. &
Attendance: 28,000 (estimated)

MOSAIC TEMPLARS CULTURAL CENTER, 501 W. 9th St., Little Rock, AR 72201-4111. Mailing Address: 1500 Tower Bldg., 323 Center St., Little Rock, AR 72201-2603. Tel.: 501-683-3593.
E-mail: info@mosaictemplarscenter.com
Web Site: www.mosaictemplarscenter.com
Key Personnel: Dir., Sericia Cole; Museum Shop Mgr., Phyllis Brown.
Institution Type/Description: African American History Museum.
Hours & Admission Prices: Call for hours.

MUSEUM OF DISCOVERY, 500 President Clinton Ave., Ste. 150, Little Rock, AR 72201-1757. Tel.: 501-396-7050, ext. 200. Fax: 501-396-7054.
E-mail: info@museumofdiscovery.org
Web Site: www.amod.org
Formerly: Museum of Discovery: Arkansas Museum of Science and History
Key Personnel: C.E.O., Kelley Bass.
Institution Type/Description: Science & Technology Museum.
Hours & Admission Prices: Tues.-Sat. 9-5, Sun. 1-5. Adults $10, seniors 60 & over, teachers, Little Rock city employees & military $8, children under 12 months no charge. Closed New Year's Day; Easter; Thanksgiving; Christmas Eve & Day. &
Attendance: 103,103 (actual)

OLD STATE HOUSE MUSEUM, 300 W. Markham St., Little Rock, AR 72201-1423. Tel.: 501-324-9685. Fax: 501-324-9688. Facebook: Old State House Museum.
E-mail: info@oldstatehouse.com
Web Site: www.oldstatehouse.com
Formerly: The Old State House
Key Personnel: Dir., Bill Gatewood; Historic Sites Mgr., Ed Garretson; Dir. Devel., Brooke Malloy; Deputy Dir., Brendetta Murrell; Dir. Public Rels., Matt Rowe; Dir. Education, Georganne Sisco; Dir. Exhibits, Gail Stephens; Cur., JoEllen Maack; Museum Shop Mgr., David Kennedy.
Institution Type/Description: History Museum: built 1833-1842, first state capitol (1836-1911).
Hours & Admission Prices: Mon.-Sat. 9-5, Sun. 1-5. No charge; donations accepted. Closed New Year's Day; Thanksgiving; Christmas Eve & Day. &
Attendance: 52,866 (actual)

PINNACLE MOUNTAIN STATE PARK, 11901 Pinnacle Valley Rd., Little Rock, AR 72223-5173. Tel.: 501-868-5806. Fax: 501-868-5018.
E-mail: pinnaclemountain@arkansas.com
Web Site: www.arkansasstateparks.com
Key Personnel: Park Supt., Ron Salley.
Institution Type/Description: Environmental Education Center.
Hours & Admission Prices: Visitor Center: daily 8-5. No charge. Visitor Center: closed New Year's Day; Thanksgiving; Christmas. &
Attendance: 515,666 (actual)

UNIVERSITY OF ARKANSAS AT LITTLE ROCK ART DEPARTMENT GALLERY I & II & III, 2801 S. University Ave., Little Rock, AR 72204-1000. Tel.: 501-569-3182. Fax: 501-683-7022.
E-mail: becushman@ualr.edu
Web Site: ualr.edu/art/index.php/home/gallery/
Key Personnel: Coord., Brad Cushman; Gallery Asst., Nathan Larson.
Institution Type/Description: University Art Gallery.
Hours & Admission Prices: Sept. to mid-May Mon.-Fri. 9-5, Sat. 10-1, Sun. 2-5; Summer: Mon.-Fri. 9-5. No charge. Closed spring break week; Christmas week; University holidays. &
Attendance: 6,000 (estimated)

WILLIAM J. CLINTON PRESIDENTIAL LIBRARY & MUSEUM, 1200 President Clinton Ave., Little Rock, AR 72201-1749. Tel.: 501-372-4242. Fax: 501-244-2883.
E-mail: clinton.library@nara.gov
Web Site: www.clintonlibrary.gov
Key Personnel: Dir., Terri Garner; Education, Kathleen Pate; Registrar, Joseph Angemi; Cur., Christine Mouw; Deputy Dir., Kurt Senn; Museum Shop Mgr., Connie Fails; Security, Steve Samford.
Institution Type/Description: Presidential History Museum.
Hours & Admission Prices: Mon.-Sat. 9-5, Sun. 1-5. Adults 18-61 $7, college students, retired military and senior citizens 62 & over $5, children 6-17 $3; children under 6, school groups w/reservation, active duty, military reservists,

National Guard, UACS faculty & staff no charge. Closed New Year's Day; Thanksgiving; Christmas. &

Attendance: 300,000 (actual)

WITT STEPHENS JR. CENTRAL ARKANSAS NATURE CENTER, 602 President Clinton Ave., Little Rock, AR 72201. Tel.: 501-907-0636. Fax: 501-907-0638.

Web Site: www.centralarkansasnaturecenter.com

Institution Type/Description: Nature Center.

Hours & Admission Prices: Tues.-Sat. 8:30-4:30, Sun. 1-5. No charge. Closed major holidays.

Lonoke

LONOKE COUNTY MUSEUM, 215 E. Front St., Lonoke, AR 72086. Mailing Address: P.O. Box 873, Lonoke, AR 72086. Tel.: 501-676-6750.

E-mail: lonokecomuseum@yahoo.com

Key Personnel: Dir., Sherryl Miller.

Institution Type/Description: History Museum.

Hours & Admission Prices: Wed.-Thurs. 8-4; other times by appointment. No charge; donations accepted. Closed major holidays.

Lowell

LOWELL HISTORICAL MUSEUM, 304 Jackson Pl., Lowell, AR 72745. Tel.: 479-770-0191.

E-mail: museumdirector@lowellarkansas.gov

Key Personnel: Dir., Liz Estes.

Institution Type/Description: History Museum.

Hours & Admission Prices: Mon.-Thurs. 9-3, Sat. 10-4. No charge; donations accepted. Closed most holidays. &

Attendance: 1,461 (actual)

Magazine

EVANS MUSEUM, 6335 N. Arkansas 109, Magazine, AR 72943. Tel.: 479-963-3987.

Institution Type/Description: History Museum.

Hours & Admission Prices: Tues.-Fri. 11-4; other times by appointment.

Malvern

HOT SPRING COUNTY MUSEUM - THE 1891 BOYLE HOUSE/1876 LOG CABIN/1868 LOG CABIN, 302 E. Third St., Malvern, AR 72104-3912. Mailing Address: 1712 Texas St., Malvern, AR 72104-6323. Tel.: 501-337-4775.

E-mail: janiswest@hughes.net

Key Personnel: Dir., Commission Chm. (V) & Pres. (V), Janis West; Cur. & Business Officer, Brandon Nesbit; Museum Shop Mgr., Virginia Cardin.

Institution Type/Description: History Museum.

Hours & Admission Prices: Wed.-Fri. 12:30-4:30; group & school tours by appointment. No charge; donations accepted. Closed holidays. &

Attendance: 1,500 (estimated)

Mammoth Spring

MAMMOTH SPRING STATE PARK, DEPOT MUSEUM, 17 Hwy. 63 N., Mammoth Spring, AR 72554-0036. Mailing Address: P.O. Box 36, Mammoth Spring, AR 72554-0036. Tel.: 870-625-7364. Fax: 870-625-3255.

E-mail: mammothspring@arkansas.com

Web Site: www.arkansasstateparks.com

Key Personnel: Park Supt., Dave Jackson.

Institution Type/Description: History Museum: housed in 1886 Frisco Railroad depot.

Hours & Admission Prices: Tues.-Sat. 8-5, Sun. 1-5. No charge; donations accepted. &

Attendance: 300,000 (actual)

Marianna

MARIANNA-LEE COUNTY MUSEUM ASSOC. INC., 67 W. Main St., Marianna, AR 72360-2243. Mailing Address: 60 McCulloch, Marianna, AR 72360-2030. Tel.: 870-295-2439.

Key Personnel: Cur., Suzy Keasler.

Institution Type/Description: Museum Association: housed in 1910 Marianna Elks Club.

Hours & Admission Prices: Mon.-Sat. by appointment. No charge; donations accepted. Closed major holidays.

Marked Tree

MARKED TREE DELTA AREA MUSEUM, 308 Frisco St., Marked Tree, AR 72365. Mailing Address: P.O. Box 106, Marked Tree, AR 72365-0106. Tel.: 870-358-4998.

E-mail: barbara_adams@asun.edu

Web Site: www.markedtreechamber.org

Institution Type/Description: History Museum.

Hours & Admission Prices: Wed.-Fri. 1-4:30, Sat. 9:30-12:30, Sun. 1-4.

Maynard

MAYNARD PIONEER MUSEUM & PARK, Hwy. 328 W., Maynard, AR 72444. Mailing Address: P.O. Box 486, Maynard, AR 72444-0486. Tel.: 870-647-2701. Fax: 870-647-2701. Facebook: Maynard Pioneer Museum & Park.

E-mail: maynardcityhall@centurytel.net

Key Personnel: Chm., Wyle Greer.

Institution Type/Description: History Museum.

Hours & Admission Prices: May-Oct. 1 Mon.-Fri. 8-3 by appointment. No charge; donations accepted. Closed Memorial Day.

Attendance: 7,000 (estimated)

McGehee

WWII JAPANESE AMERICAN INTERNMENT MUSEUM, 100 S. Railroad St., McGehee, AR 71654. Mailing Address: P.O. Box 1263, McGehee, AR 71654. Tel.: 870-222-9168.

Institution Type/Description: History Museum.

Hours & Admission Prices: Tues.-Sat. 10-5. No charge.

McNeil

LOGOLY STATE PARK, County Rd. 47 (Logoly Rd.), McNeil, AR 71752. Mailing Address: P.O. Box 245, McNeil, AR 71752-0245. Tel.: 870-695-3561. Fax: 870-695-3729.

E-mail: logoly@arkansas.com

Web Site: www.arkansasstateparks.com

Key Personnel: Supt., Jim Gann; Interpretive Naturalist, Barley Park; Museum Shop Mgr., Pat Swearingen.

Institution Type/Description: Park Museum & Nature Center.

Hours & Admission Prices: Park: daily 8am to one hour after sunset. Visitors Center: May-Oct. daily 8-5; Nov.-April Mon.-Fri. 8-5, Sat.-Sun. 1-5. No charge. &

Attendance: 25,000 (actual)

Mena

MENA ART GALLERY, 607 Mena St., Mena, AR 71953. Mailing Address: P.O. Box 871, Mena, AR 71953-0871. Tel.: 479-394-3880. Facebook: Mena Art Gallery.

E-mail: email@menaartgallery.org

Web Site: www.menaartgallery.org

Formerly: Southwest Artists, Inc.

Key Personnel: Dir., Julie Vande Zande; Chm. (V), Rick Chrisman.

Institution Type/Description: Art Gallery.

Hours & Admission Prices: Gallery: Wed.-Sat. 10-3. Art Day: Tues. 11-2. No charge; donations accepted. &

Monticello

DREW COUNTY HISTORICAL MUSEUM, 404 S. Main, Monticello, AR 71655-4818. Tel.: 870-367-7446.

Key Personnel: Dir., Sheilla Lampkin.

Institution Type/Description: History Museum.

Hours & Admission Prices: Fri. 1-5, Sat.-Sun. 2-5. No charge; donations accepted. Closed New Year's Day; Thanksgiving; Christmas. &

Attendance: 2,500 (estimated)

TURNER NEAL MUSEUM OF NATURAL HISTORY AND POMEROY PLANETARIUM, University of Arkansas at Monticello, Science Center, 397 University Dr., Monticello, AR 71656. Mailing Address: P.O. Box 3480, Monticello, AR 71656. Tel.: 870-460-1016.

E-mail: edson@uamont.edu

Key Personnel: Dir. Museum, Dr. Jim Edson; Dir. Planetarium, Joe Guenter.

Institution Type/Description: Natural History.
Hours & Admission Prices: Academic Year: Mon.-Fri. call for hours; other times by appointment.

Morrilton

CONWAY COUNTY HISTORICAL PRESERVATION ASSOCIATION, INC. - MORRILTON DEPOT MUSEUM, 101 E. Railroad Ave., Morrilton, AR 72110. Mailing Address: P.O. Box 417, Morrilton, AR 72110. Tel.: 501-354-4347. Facebook: Morrilton Depot Museum.
E-mail: morriltondepotmuseum@yahoo.com
Web Site: www.morrliltondepotmuseum.com
Key Personnel: Pres. (V), Carl Imhauser.
Institution Type/Description: History Museum.
Hours & Admission Prices: Fri.-Sat. 10-2; other times by appointment. No charge; donations accepted. &
Attendance: 1,500 (estimated)

THE MUSEUM OF AUTOMOBILES, Petit Jean Mountain, 8 Jones Lane, Morrilton, AR 72110-9353. Tel.: 501-727-5427. Fax: 501-727-6482.
E-mail: info@museumofautos.com
Web Site: www.museumofautos.com
Key Personnel: Dir., Buddy Hoelzeman; Pres. (V), Raymond Harrill.
Institution Type/Description: Antique Automobile Museum.
Hours & Admission Prices: Daily 10-5. Adults $10, seniors 65 & over $9, children 6-17 $5; discounts for groups of 15 & over; members & children under 6 with parents no charge. Closed Christmas. &
Attendance: 16,000 (actual)

RIALTO COMMUNITY ARTS CENTER - THE GALLERY, 215 E. Broadway, Morrilton, AR 72110-3403. Mailing Address: P.O. Box 176, Morrilton, AR 72110. Tel.: 501-477-9955.
E-mail: director@rialtoartscenter.com
Web Site: www.rialtoartscenter.com/thegallery.html
Institution Type/Description: Art Gallery.
Hours & Admission Prices: Fri.-Sat. 11-2.

Mount Ida

HERITAGE HOUSE MUSEUM OF MONTGOMERY COUNTY, 819 Luzerne St., Mount Ida, AR 71957. Mailing Address: P.O. Box 1362, Mount Ida, AR 71957-1362. Tel.: 870-867-4422.
E-mail: museum@hhmmc.org
Web Site: hhmmc.org
Key Personnel: Dir., Emilie Kinney; Pres. (V) & Museum Shop Mgr., Betty Prince; Treas., Richard Ray.
Institution Type/Description: History Museum.
Hours & Admission Prices: Mon.-Wed. & Fri. 9-4, Sat.-Sun. 1-4. No charge; donations accepted. Closed New Year's Eve & Day; Thanksgiving Eve & Day; Christmas Eve & Day. &
Attendance: 1,550 (estimated)

Mountain View

THE OZARK FOLK CENTER, 1032 Park Ave., Mountain View, AR 72560-6008. Tel.: 870-269-3851. Fax: 870-269-2909.
E-mail: ozarkfolkcenter@arkansas.com
Web Site: www.ozarkfolkcenter.com
Key Personnel: Lodge Mgr., Debra Miller; Accountant, Melody Miller; Public Information Officer, John Morrow; Museum Shop Mgr., Donna Nichols.
Institution Type/Description: Folk Arts Center.
Hours & Admission Prices: Craft Village: mid-April to mid-Nov. Tues.-Sun. 10-5. Music Theater: mid-April to mid-Nov. Thurs.-Sat. 7 pm; Music or Craft Village: adults $12, children $7; discount to groups. One Day Combo: adults $19.50, children 6-12 $10.25. 3-Day Combo adults $45, children $25. Season & Family Passes available. &
Attendance: 160,000 (estimated)

STONE COUNTY MUSEUM, 204 School Ave., Mountain View, AR 72560. Mailing Address: Stone County Historical Society, P.O. Box 210, Mountain View, AR 72560. Tel.: 870-269-4101.
E-mail: stonecountyhistoricalsociety@gmail.com
Web Site: heritageofstone.wordpress.com/museum/
Institution Type/Description: History Museum; built in 1895.
Hours & Admission Prices: Call for hours.

Murfreesboro

CRATER OF DIAMONDS STATE PARK MUSEUM, 209 State Park Road, Murfreesboro, AR 71958-8947. Tel.: 870-285-3113. Fax: 870-285-4169.
E-mail: crater@arkansas.com
Web Site: www.craterofdiamondsstatepark.com
Key Personnel: Park Supt., James Howell; Asst. Supt., Bill Henderson; Park Ranger, Matt Briley; Gift Shop Mgr., Debbie Wright; Park Interpreter, Waymon Cox; Park Interpreter, Margaret Jenks.
Institution Type/Description: Park Interpretative Museum.
Hours & Admission Prices: Memorial Day-Labor Day daily 8-8; Sept.-May daily 8-5. Park: no charge. Diamond Mine: adults $8, children 6-12 $5; discounts to groups of 15 or more; children under 6 no charge. Closed New Year's Day; Thanksgiving; Christmas. &
Attendance: 154,609 (actual)

KA-DO-HA INDIAN VILLAGE MUSEUM, 281 Kadoha Rd., Murfreesboro, AR 71958. Mailing Address: P.O. Box 669, Murfreesboro, AR 71958-0669. Tel.: 870-285-4167. Fax: 870-285-4118.
E-mail: info@kadoha.com
Web Site: www.kadoha.com
Key Personnel: Owner, C.E.O. & Public Rels. Dir., Jack Bonds; Business Officer, Cur. & Gift Shop Mgr., JoAnn Copeland.
Institution Type/Description: Archaeology Museum: housed on 1,000 A.D. Moundbuilder Village & ceremonial center.
Hours & Admission Prices: Summer: daily 9-6; Winter: daily 9-5. Adults $8, children 6-13 $4; discounts to AAM & ICOM members. Closed Thanksgiving; Christmas.
Attendance: 10,000 (estimated)

Newport

E. BOB JACKSON MEMORIAL MUSEUM OF FUNERAL SERVICES, 1900 Block Malcolm Ave., Newport, AR 72112. Tel.: 870-523-5822. Fax: 870-523-4640.
E-mail: jmaris@jacksonsfh.com
Web Site: jacksonsfh.com
Institution Type/Description: History Museum.
Hours & Admission Prices: By appointment.

North Little Rock

ARKANSAS INLAND MARITIME MUSEUM, 120 Riverfront Park Dr., North Little Rock, AR 72114. Tel.: 501-371-8320. Fax: 501-244-9794. Facebook: Arkansas Inland Maritime Museum.
E-mail: info@aimmuseum.org
Web Site: www.aimmuseum.org
Institution Type/Description: Maritime Museum.
Hours & Admission Prices: Spring: Friday-Sat. 10-6, Sun. 1-6. Museum: adults $2. Museum & Submarine: adults $7.50, children 12 & under $5, military and seniors 62 & over $5. Submarine tour not recommended for children under 5. Picture tour of submarine available. &

ARKANSAS NATIONAL GUARD MUSEUM, Camp J.T. Robinson, Bldg. 6400 Box 58, North Little Rock, AR 72199. Tel.: 501-212-5215. Fax: 501-212-5228.
E-mail: raymond.d.screws.nfg@mail.mil
Web Site: www.arngmuseum.com
Key Personnel: Dir., Dr. Raymond D. Screws; Chm. (V), Gen. Keith Klemmer.
Institution Type/Description: Military Museum.
Hours & Admission Prices: Mon.-Fri. 8-3, 1st Sat.-Sun. of month 8-3; call to confirm. ID required for day pass. No charge; donations accepted. &
Attendance: 2,000

ARKANSAS SPORTS HALL OF FAME, Verizon Arena, #3 Verizon Arena Way, North Little Rock, AR 72114. Tel.: 501-663-4328.
E-mail: tcjohnson@arksportshalloffame.org
Web Site: www.arksportshalloffame.org
Institution Type/Description: Sports Museum.
Hours & Admission Prices: Mon.-Sat. 10-4:30. Adults $6, seniors 62 & over $4, children 6-17 $3; discounts to active military & groups of 15 or more; children under 6 no charge.

Ozark

OZARK AREA DEPOT MUSEUM, 103 E. River St., Ozark, AR 72949. Tel.: 479-667-5015.
Institution Type/Description: Historic Building: housed in a former Missouri-Pacific/Union Pacific depot; built in 1911. Listed on the National Register of Historic Places.
Hours & Admission Prices: Call for hours.

Paragould

GREENE COUNTY MUSEUM OF PARAGOULD, 130 S. 14th St., Paragould, AR 72450. Tel.: 870-215-2407.
E-mail: greenecountymuseum@gmail.com
Web Site: www.greenecountymuseum.com
Institution Type/Description: History Museum.
Hours & Admission Prices: Call for hours.

Paris

ARKANSAS HISTORIC WINE MUSEUM, 101 N. Carbon City Rd., Paris, AR 72855-4630. Tel.: 479-963-3990.
E-mail: cowie@cswnet.com
Web Site: www.cowiewinecellars.com
Key Personnel: Dir. (V), Robert G. Cowie.
Institution Type/Description: Historic Wine Museum: housed at Cowie Wine Cellars three miles west of Paris.
Hours & Admission Prices: Mon.-Sat. 10-6, Sun. 12-6. Adults $2. &
Attendance: 3,200 (estimated)

LOGAN COUNTY MUSEUM, 202 N. Vine St., Paris, AR 72855-3222. Tel.: 479-963-3936. Fax: 479-963-3936.
E-mail: logancomuseum@centurytel.net
Web Site: logancountymuseum.com
Key Personnel: Admin., Jeanne S. Reynolds; Pres. (V), Susan Johnson.
Institution Type/Description: History Museum: housed in 1903 former Logan County Jail.
Hours & Admission Prices: Tues.-Sat. 12-4. No charge; donations accepted. Tour Groups: adults $3 for hanging reenactment. Closed most federal holidays.
Attendance: 3,000 (actual)

PARIS-LOGAN COUNTY COAL MINERS MEMORIAL & MUSEUM, 804 S. Elm St., Paris, AR 72855. Tel.: 479-963-6463.
E-mail: parislogancoal@gmail.com
Institution Type/Description: History Museum.
Hours & Admission Prices: Thurs.-Mon. 11-5. No charge.

Perryville

PERRY COUNTY HISTORICAL MUSEUM, 408 Main St., Perryville, AR 72126. Mailing Address: P.O. Box 1128, Perryville, AR 72126. Tel.: 501-889-2855.
E-mail: information@perrycountyhistoricalmuseum.org
Web Site: www.perrycountyhistoricalmuseum.org
Institution Type/Description: History Museum.
Hours & Admission Prices: Call for hours. No charge; donations accepted. &
Attendance: 300 (estimated)

Piggott

HEMINGWAY-PFEIFFER MUSEUM AND EDUCATIONAL CENTER, 1021 W. Cherry St., Piggott, AR 72454-1419. Tel.: 870-598-3487. Fax: 870-598-1037.
E-mail: rhawkins@astate.edu
Web Site: hemingway.astate.edu/
Key Personnel: Asst. Dir. & Facilities Mgr., Dr. Ruth Hawkins; Asst. Dir. & Facilities Mgr., Diana Sanders; Education Coord., Deanna Dismukes; Administrative Asst., Johnna Redman; Tour Guide & Housekeeper, Karen Trout.
Institution Type/Description: Historic House & Barn: listed on the National Historic Register.
Hours & Admission Prices: Mon.-Fri. 9-4, Sat. 1-3. Suggested Donation: adults $5, seniors $3. Closed New Year's Eve & Day; Memorial Day; Labor Day; Thanksgiving; Christmas Eve & Day. &
Attendance: 3,170

MATILDA AND KARL PFEIFFER MUSEUM AND STUDY CENTER, 1071 Heritage Park Dr., Piggott, AR 72454. Tel.: 870-598-3228.

E-mail: pfeifferfnd@centurytel.net
Web Site: www.pfeifferfoundation.com
Institution Type/Description: History Museum: home built early 1930s.
Hours & Admission Prices: Tues.-Fri. 9-4, Sat. 11-4; groups of 10 or more by appointment. No charge; donations accepted. Closed major holidays.

Pine Bluff

ARKANSAS ENTERTAINERS HALL OF FAME, One Convention Center Plaza, Pine Bluff, AR 71601-5067. Tel.: 800-536-7660. Fax: 870-850-2105.
E-mail: pbinfo@pinebluff.com
Web Site: www.arkansasentertainershalloffame.com
Institution Type/Description: Hall of Fame.
Hours & Admission Prices: Mon.-Fri. 9-5, Sat.-Sun. call for hours. No charge; donations accepted. &
Attendance: 25,000 (estimated)

ARKANSAS RAILROAD MUSEUM, 1700 Port Rd., Pine Bluff, AR 71601-4663. Mailing Address: P.O. Box 2044, Pine Bluff, AR 71613-2044. Tel.: 870-535-8819.
E-mail: info@arkansasrailroadmuseum.org
Web Site: arkansasrailroadmuseum.org
Institution Type/Description: Railroad Museum.
Hours & Admission Prices: Mon.-Sat. 9-2. No charge; donations accepted. &
Attendance: 12,000 (estimated)

THE ARTS & SCIENCE CENTER FOR SOUTHEAST ARKANSAS, 701 Main St., Pine Bluff, AR 71601-4903. Tel.: 870-536-3375.
E-mail: info@asc701.org
Web Site: www.asc701.org
Key Personnel: Exec. Dir., Dr. Lenore Shoults.
Institution Type/Description: Arts Cultural Center.
Hours & Admission Prices: Tues.-Fri. 10-5, Sat. 1-4. No charge, donations accepted. Closed New Year's Day; Easter; Independence Day; Thanksgiving; Christmas Eve & Day; for detailed information on closings visit Website. &
Attendance: 37,595 (estimated)

GOVERNOR MIKE HUCKABEE DELTA RIVERS NATURE CENTER, 1400 Black Dog Rd., Pine Bluff, AR 71611. Mailing Address: P.O. Box 8074, Pine Bluff, AR 71611. Tel.: 870-534-0011. Fax: 870-534-4422.
E-mail: info@deltarivers.com
Web Site: www.deltarivers.com
Institution Type/Description: Nature Center.
Hours & Admission Prices: Center: year round Tues.-Sat. 8:30-4:30, Sun. 1-5. Trails: daily dawn to dusk. No charge; donations accepted. Closed New Year's Day, Easter, Thanksgiving, Christmas. &
Attendance: 40,000 (estimated)

LEEDEL MOOREHEAD-GRAHAM FINE ARTS GALLERY, 1200 N. University, Pine Bluff, AR 71601-2799. Mailing Address: Mail Slot 4925, Pine Bluff, AR 71601. Tel.: 870-575-8236. Fax: 870-575-4636.
E-mail: gaines_c@uapb.edu
Web Site: www.uapb.edu
Key Personnel: Chm., Henri Linton.
Institution Type/Description: Art Museum.
Hours & Admission Prices: Mon.-Fri. 8:30-4:30. No charge. Closed school holidays.
Attendance: 5,000 (estimated)

UNIVERSITY OF ARKANSAS MUSEUM AND CULTURAL CENTER, 1200 N. University Dr., Pine Bluff, AR 71601. Mailing Address: 1200 N. University Dr., Mailbox 4925, Pine Bluff, AR 71601. Tel.: 870-575-8232.
E-mail: museum@uapb.edu
Web Site: www.uapb.edu
Institution Type/Description: History Museum.
Hours & Admission Prices: Call for hours.

Pine Ridge/Oden

LUM & ABNER MUSEUM & JOT 'EM DOWN STORE, 4562 Hwy. 88 W., (9 miles W. of Oden), Pine Ridge/Oden, AR 71961-8056. Mailing Address: General Delivery, Pine Ridge, AR 71966. Tel.: 870-326-4442.

E-mail: kmstucker@earthlink.net
Web Site: lum-abner.com
Key Personnel: Co-Dir. & Owner, Noah Lon Stucker; Co-Dir. & Owner, Kathryn Moore Stucker.
Institution Type/Description: History Museum: housed in c.1904 & 1909 general merchandise stores, on which the Lum & Abner radio program 1931-55 was based.
Hours & Admission Prices: mid-March to Nov. Tues.-Sat. 9-4, Sun. 12-4; Dec. to mid-March Mon.-Sat. 10-2. No charge; donations accepted.

Pocahontas

RANDOLPH COUNTY HERITAGE MUSEUM, 106 E. Everett St., Pocahontas, AR 72455-3309. Tel.: 870-892-4056. Fax: 870-892-4056.
E-mail: kpmuseum@hotmail.com
Web Site: www.randolphcomuseum.org
Key Personnel: Pres. (V), Museum Admin., & Museum Shop Mgr., Karen Parish; Chm. (V), Bill Carroll.
Institution Type/Description: Historical Museum.
Hours & Admission Prices: Mon., Wed. & Fri. 10-4. No charge; donations accepted.

Pottsville

POTTS INN MUSEUM, Town Square, Pottsville, AR 72801. Mailing Address: 6368 SR 247, Pottsville, AR 72858-8952. Tel.: 479-968-8369.
E-mail: pottsinn@gmail.com
Web Site: www.pottsinnmuseum.com
Key Personnel: Chm. Bd., Charles Oates; Treas., Kelly Vanes.
Institution Type/Description: Preservation Project: housed in 1850-1858 nine-room home & stage stop of Kirkbride Potts.
Hours & Admission Prices: Wed.-Sun. 1-5. Adults $3, children $1; discounts to AAM members.
Attendance: 1,900 (estimated)

Powhatan

POWHATAN HISTORIC STATE PARK, 4414 Arkansas 25 S., Powhatan, AR 72458. Mailing Address: P.O. Box 93, Powhatan, AR 72458. Tel.: 870-878-6765. Fax: 870-878-6319.
E-mail: pwhatan@arkansas.com
Web Site: www.arkansasstateparks.com/powhatancourthouse
Institution Type/Description: State Park & Historic Buildings: listed on the National Register of Historic Places.
Hours & Admission Prices: Tues.-Sat. 8-5, Sun. 1-5. Family $15, adults $5, children 6-12 $3; discounts to groups of 15 or more. Closed New Year's Day; Thanksgiving; Christmas Eve & Day.

Prairie Grove

PRAIRIE GROVE BATTLEFIELD STATE PARK, 506 E. Douglas St., Prairie Grove, AR 72753-2731. Tel.: 479-846-2990. Fax: 479-846-4035.
E-mail: prairiegrove@arkansas.com
Web Site: www.arkansasstateparks.com/prairiegrovebattlefield/
Key Personnel: Supt., Susan Adkins; Registrar, Alan Thompson; Museum Shop Mgr., Holly Cherry.
Institution Type/Description: Civil War Park Museum: located on site of Dec. 7, 1862, Battle of Prairie Grove.
Hours & Admission Prices: Daily 8-5. No charge; donations accepted. Closed New Year's Day; Thanksgiving; Christmas Eve & Day. &
Attendance: 200,000 (actual)

Prescott

NEVADA COUNTY DEPOT AND MUSEUM, 403 W. 1st St. S., Prescott, AR 71857-2067. Tel.: 870-887-5821. Facebook.
E-mail: curator@depotmuseum.org
Web Site: www.depotmuseum.org
Key Personnel: Cur. & Exec. Dir., Ken Petre.
Institution Type/Description: History Museum.
Hours & Admission Prices: Tues.-Fri. 10-4; tours & groups by appointment. No charge; donations accepted. Closed holidays. &
Attendance: 445 (actual)

Rogers

HOBBS PARK VISITOR CENTER, 21392 E. Hwy. 12, Rogers, AR 72756-8183. Mailing Address: P.O. Box 709, Rogers, AR 72757-0709. Tel.: 479-789-2380.
E-mail: hobbs.statepark@arkansas.gov
Institution Type/Description: Park Museum & Visitor Center.
Hours & Admission Prices: Call for hours.

ROGERS DAISY AIRGUN MUSEUM, 202 W. Walnut St., Rogers, AR 72756-6665. Tel.: 479-986-6873. Fax: 479-986-6875.
E-mail: info@daisymuseum.com
Web Site: www.daisymuseum.com
Formerly: Daisy International Air Gun Museum
Institution Type/Description: Air Gun Museum.
Hours & Admission Prices: Mon.-Sat. 9-5. Adults $2; children 16 & under no charge. Closed major holidays. &

ROGERS HISTORICAL MUSEUM, 322 S. Second St., Rogers, AR 72756-4512. Tel.: 479-621-1154. Fax: 479-621-1155.
E-mail: museum@rogersarkansas.com
Web Site: www.rogershistoricalmuseum.org
Key Personnel: Dir., John Burroughs; Asst. Dir. & Cur. Collections, Terrilyn Wendling; Chm., Kathleen Dickerson; Collections Mgr., Jennifer Kick; Cur. Education, Robert Rousey; Operations Coord., Jennifer Sweet; Foundation Exec. Dir., Tara Worth; Education Asst., Ashley Sayers; Adult Programs Educator, Monte Harris.
Institution Type/Description: Historical Building: c.1895 five-room Hawkins House.
Hours & Admission Prices: Mon.-Sat. 10-5. No charge; donations accepted. Closed major holidays. &
Attendance: 23,400 (actual)

WAR EAGLE CAVERN, 21494 Cavern Rd., Rogers, AR 72756-7493. Tel.: 479-789-2909.
E-mail: wareaglecavern@gmail.com
Web Site: www.wareaglecavern.com
Institution Type/Description: Geology Museum.
Hours & Admission Prices: Mon.-Sat. 9:30-5, Sun. 12-5. Adults $15, children 4-11 $9; children 3 & under no charge.

Russellville

ARKANSAS RIVER VALLEY ARTS CENTER, 1001 E. B St., Russellville, AR 72801-4252. Mailing Address: P.O. Box 2112, Russellville, AR 72811-2112. Tel.: 479-968-2452. Fax: 479-968-5015. Facebook: Arkansas River Valley Arts Center.
E-mail: artscenter@centurytel.net
Web Site: www.arvartscenter.org
Key Personnel: Exec. Dir., Betty LaGrone; Pres. (V), Emory Molitor; Chm. (V), John Gale; Admin. Asst., Phala Harrison; Teaching Artist, Winston J. Taylor.
Institution Type/Description: Art Gallery.
Hours & Admission Prices: Mon.-Thurs. 10-5, Fri. 10-4; other times by appointment. No charge. Closed national holidays. &
Attendance: 2,000 (estimated)

ARKANSAS TECH UNIVERSITY MUSEUM, 1502 N. El Paso Ave./Techionery, Russellville, AR 72801-8816. Tel.: 479-964-0826. Fax: 479-964-0872. Facebook: Arkansas Tech University Museum.
E-mail: jstewartabernathy@atu.edu
Web Site: www.atu.edu/museum
Formerly: Arkansas Tech Museum
Key Personnel: Museum Dir., Judith C. Stewart-Abernathy; Cur., Theresa Jureka Johnson.
Institution Type/Description: History Museum.
Hours & Admission Prices: Tues.-Thurs. 8:30-4:30; other times by appointment. No charge; donations accepted. Closed during university breaks. &
Attendance: 3,838 (actual)

Scott

PLANTATION AGRICULTURE MUSEUM - ARKANSAS STATE PARK, 4815 Hwy. 161 S., Scott, AR 72142. Mailing Address: P.O. Box 87, Scott, AR 72142-0087. Tel.: 501-961-1409. Fax: 501-961-1579.
E-mail: plantationagrimuseum@arkansas.com
Web Site: www.arkansasstateparks.com

Key Personnel: Dir., Linda Goza; Cur., Randy Noah; Museum Interpreter, Lydia Leatherwood; Museum Shop Mgr., Margaret Ellis.
Institution Type/Description: History Museum: housed in c.1912 general store.
Hours & Admission Prices: Tues.-Sat. 8-5, Sun. 1-5. No charge; donations accepted. Closed New Year's Day; Thanksgiving; Christmas Eve & Day. &
Attendance: 7,200 (estimated)

TOLTEC MOUNDS ARCHEOLOGICAL STATE PARK, 490 Toltec Mounds Rd., Scott, AR 72142. Tel.: 501-961-9442. Fax: 501-961-9221.
E-mail: toltecmounds@arkansas.com
Web Site: www.arkansasstateparks.com
Key Personnel: Dir. Toltec Research Station, Dr. Julie Markin; Supt., James Wilborn; Park Interpreter, Robin Gabe; Park Interpreter, Amy Griffin; Museum Shop Mgr., Keryn Cantrell.
Institution Type/Description: Archaeological Site.
Hours & Admission Prices: Mon. holidays & Tues.-Sat. 8-5, Sun. 12-5. Tram Tours: adults $5, children 6-12 $4. Walking Tours: adults $3, children 6-12 $2; discounts to groups of 15 or more & schools with reservations; children under 6 no charge. Closed New Year's Day; Thanksgiving; Christmas Eve & Day. &
Attendance: 30,000 (actual)

Sheridan

GRANT COUNTY MUSEUM, 521 Shackleford Rd., Sheridan, AR 72150-7074. Tel.: 870-942-4496. Fax: 870-917-2248.
E-mail: museum4@windstream.net
Web Site: www.grantcountymuseumar.com
Key Personnel: Chm. (V), Mary Beth Glover-Wilson; Dir., D.J. Wallace; Financial Dir., Noka Emerson; Magazine Editor, Lindsey Stanton.
Institution Type/Description: History Museum.
Hours & Admission Prices: Tues.-Sat. 9-4; other times by appointment. No charge; donations accepted. Closed legal holidays. &
Attendance: 10,000 (estimated)

Siloam Springs

SAGER CREEK ARTS CENTER, 301 E. Twin Springs, Siloam Springs, AR 72761. Mailing Address: P.O. Box 1127, Siloam Springs, AR 72761. Tel.: 479-524-4000. Fax: 479-524-5713.
Institution Type/Description: Art Gallery.
Hours & Admission Prices: Call for hours.

SILOAM SPRINGS MUSEUM, 112 N. Maxwell, Siloam Springs, AR 72761-3174. Mailing Address: P.O. Box 1164, Siloam Springs, AR 72761-1164. Tel.: 479-524-4011.
E-mail: ssmuseum@centurytel.net
Web Site: www.siloamspringsmuseum.com
Key Personnel: Dir. & C.E.O., Donald Warden; Pres. (V), Bill Osgood.
Institution Type/Description: History Museum: housed in 1950 church.
Hours & Admission Prices: Tues.-Sat. 10-5; other times by appointment. No charge; donations accepted. Closed major holidays. &
Attendance: 2,194 (estimated)

Smackover

ARKANSAS MUSEUM OF NATURAL RESOURCES, 3853 Smackover Hwy., Smackover, AR 71762-9575. Tel.: 870-725-2877. Fax: 870-725-2161.
E-mail: museum@amnr.org
Web Site: amnr.org
Key Personnel: Chm. (V), Phoebe Sellers; Dir., Pam Beasley; Exhibit Specialist, Rhonda Millican; Dir. Education & Research, Shelly Franques; Registrar, Sheri Neely; Cur., Van Zbinden; Museum Shop Mgr., Beth Hooks.
Institution Type/Description: History & Technology Museum.
Hours & Admission Prices: Mon.-Sat. 8-5, Sun. 1-5. No charge; donations accepted. Closed New Year's Day; Thanksgiving; Christmas. &
Attendance: 24,326 (actual)

Springdale

ARTS CENTER OF THE OZARKS, 214 S. Main St., Springdale, AR 72764-4446. Tel.: 479-751-5441.
E-mail: info@acozarks.org
Web Site: www.acozarks.org
Institution Type/Description: Art Gallery.
Hours & Admission Prices: Tues.-Fri. 10-5, Sat. 10-3.

SHILOH MUSEUM OF OZARK HISTORY, 118 W. Johnson Ave., Springdale, AR 72764-4313. Tel.: 479-750-8165. Fax: 479-756-7732. Facebook: Shiloh Museum of Ozark History.
E-mail: shiloh@springdalear.gov
Web Site: www.shilohmuseum.org
Key Personnel: Dir., Allyn Lord; Pres. Bd. Trustees, April Rusch; Collections Mgr., Carolyn Reno; Outreach Coord., Susan Young; Exhibit Mgr., Curtis Morris; Education Coord., Judy Costello; Education Asst., Carly Squyres; Library Asst., Rachel Whitaker; Photo Archivist, Marie Demeroukas; Collections & Education Asst., Aaron Loehndorf; Photographer, Kris Johnson; Maintenance, Marty Powers; Museum Shop Mgr., Kathy Plume.
Institution Type/Description: History Museum.
Hours & Admission Prices: Mon.-Sat. 10-5. No charge; donations accepted. Closed New Year's Day; Thanksgiving; Christmas Eve & Day. &
Attendance: 51,235 (actual)

Stuttgart

MUSEUM OF THE ARKANSAS GRAND PRAIRIE, 921 E. 4th St., Stuttgart, AR 72160-4558. Tel.: 870-673-7001. Fax: 870-673-3959.
E-mail: ontheprairiebayou@yahoo.com
Web Site: www.stuttgartmuseum.org
Formerly: Stuttgart Agricultural Museum
Key Personnel: Dir., Melanie Baden; Chm. Bd. Trustees, Bruce Martin; Chm. (V), Beth Hopson; Vice Chm., Garland Demden; Sec., Jean Pollard; Financial Chm., Richard Bell; Cur. Collections, Gena Seidenschwarz; Cur. Restoration-Furniture, Kenneth Bull; Cur. Farm Equip. & Furniture, Jim Gingerich; Educational Dir., Ann Prislovsky; Gen. Asst. & Museum Shop Mgr., Frances Camp.
Institution Type/Description: Agriculture Museum.
Hours & Admission Prices: Tues.-Fri. 8-4, Sat. 10-4. No charge; donations accepted. Closed Easter; legal holidays. &
Attendance: 13,146 (actual)

Texarkana

FOUR STATES AUTO MUSEUM, 217 Laurel St., Texarkana, AR 71854-6051. Tel.: 870-772-2886.
E-mail: fourstatesautomuseum@gmail.com
Web Site: www.fourstatesautomuseum.org
Formerly: Tex Ark Antique Auto Museum
Key Personnel: Dir. & Pres. (V), Paul Taylor; Treas., Scott Shirk.
Institution Type/Description: Transportation Museum.
Hours & Admission Prices: Sat. 10-4, Sun. 1-4. No charge; donations accepted.
Attendance: 5,000 (estimated)

LINDSAY RAILROAD MUSEUM, 202 E. Broad St., Texarkana, AR 71854. Mailing Address: c/o Texarkana Museums System, P. O. Box 2343, Texarkana, TX 75504. Tel.: 903-748-1235.
E-mail: info@texarkanabroadstreetgalleries.com
Web Site: lindsayrailroadmuseumintexarkana.com
Key Personnel: Bd. Pres., Velvet Hall Cool.
Institution Type/Description: Railroad Museum.
Hours & Admission Prices: Thurs. 1-7, Sat. 11-3. Admission $5.

Tontitown

TONTITOWN HISTORICAL MUSEUM, 257 E. Henri de Tonti Blvd., Tontitown, AR 72770. Mailing Address: P.O. Box 144, Tontitown, AR 72770-0144. Tel.: 479-361-2498 & 2700.
E-mail: bcortiana@cox.net
Web Site: www.tontitown.com
Key Personnel: Cur., Charlotte Piazza.
Institution Type/Description: History Museum: housed in the former home of two original settlers, sisters Mary and Zelinda Bastianelli.
Hours & Admission Prices: June-Oct. Sat.-Sun. 1-4; other times by appointment. Extended hours during Tontitown Grape Festival. No charge; donations accepted.

Van Buren

BOB BURNS MUSEUM & RIVER VALLEY MUSEUM OF VAN BUREN, 813 Main St., Old Frisco Depot, Van Buren, AR 72956-4315. Mailing Address: P.O. Box 1518, Van Buren, AR 72957-1518. Tel.: 479-474-6164, 800-332-5889. Fax: 501-474-5084.
E-mail: vanburen@vanburen.org
Web Site: www.vanburen.org
Key Personnel: Dir., Maryl Koeth.

Institution Type/Description: Historical Building: 1901 Frisco Depot.
Hours & Admission Prices: April-Nov. Mon.-Fri. 8:30-5, Sat. 9-5; Dec.-March Mon.-Fri. 8:30-5. No Charge; donations accepted. &
Attendance: 30,000 (estimated)

CENTER FOR ART & EDUCATION, 104 N. 13th St., Van Buren, AR 72956-4512. Tel.: 479-474-7767. Facebook: Center for Art & Education.
E-mail: info@art-ed.org
Web Site: www.art-ed.org
Key Personnel: Exec. Dir., Jane Owen; Pres. (V), Lisa Huckelberry.
Institution Type/Description: Art Gallery.
Hours & Admission Prices: Tues.-Fri. 10-4. No charge; donations accepted.
Attendance: 2,500 (actual)

Waldron

BLYTHE'S SCOTT COUNTY MUSEUM, 1205 N. Main St., Waldron, AR 72958. Tel.: 479-637-3730. Fax: 479-637-4461.
E-mail: blythe.gary1@gmail.com
Web Site: blythemuseumar.com
Institution Type/Description: History Museum.
Hours & Admission Prices: Call for hours.

Walnut Ridge

WINGS OF HONOR MUSEUM AKA WALNUT RIDGE ARMY FLYING SCHOOL MUSEUM, INC., 70 S. Beacon Rd., Walnut Ridge, AR 72476. Tel.: 800-584-5575.
E-mail: harold@bscn.com
Web Site: wingsofhonor.org
Key Personnel: Pres. (V), Harold Johnson; Education, Sue Whitmire; Public Rels., Brett Cooper; Treas., Carolyn Propst; Cur. & Museum Shop Mgr., Judy Wilson.
Institution Type/Description: Military History Museum: housed on the site of the former WWII Walnut Ridge Army Flying School then used as the Warbird Disposal Operation facility, and later the USAF 725th Radar Squadron was stationed here.
Hours & Admission Prices: Mon.-Sat. 9-5, Sun. 2-5. No charge; donations accepted. Closed New Year's Day; Thanksgiving; Christmas. &
Attendance: 3,500 (actual)

Warren

BRADLEY COUNTY HISTORICAL MUSEUM, 200 W. Ash St., Warren, AR 71671-2602. Mailing Address: P.O. Box 311, Warren, AR 71671-0311. Tel.: 870-226-5457.
E-mail: jmldevco@sbcglobal.net
Institution Type/Description: History Museum: housed in the John Wilson Martin House, c.1857.
Hours & Admission Prices: Call for hours. No charge; donations accepted. &
Attendance: 800 (estimated)

Washington

HISTORIC WASHINGTON STATE PARK, 103 Franklin St., Washington, AR 71862. Mailing Address: P.O. Box 129, Washington, AR 71862-0129. Tel.: 870-983-2684. Fax: 870-983-2736.
E-mail: historicwashington@arkansas.com
Web Site: www.historicwashingtonstatepark.com
Key Personnel: Supt., Brandon Owen.
Institution Type/Description: History Museum: located in 1824 town.
Hours & Admission Prices: Daily 8-5. No charge. Guided walking tour of historic sites: adults $8, children 6-12 $4; discounts to groups of 20 or more with advance notice. Closed New Year's Day; Thanksgiving; Christmas. &
Attendance: 100,000 (estimated)

SOUTHWEST ARKANSAS REGIONAL ARCHIVES (SARA), 201 Highway 195, Washington, AR 71862. Mailing Address: P.O. Box 134, Washington, AR 71862-0134. Tel.: 870-983-2633. Fax: 870-983-2636.
E-mail: southwest.archives@arkansas.gov
Web Site: www.archives.arkansas.gov
Key Personnel: Dir. & State Historian, Dr. Lisa K. Speer; Archival Mgr., Melissa A. Nesbitt; Archival Asst., Joshua P. Fischer.
Institution Type/Description: Archives & Research Institute: housed in former Washington Elementary School.
Hours & Admission Prices: Tues.-Sat. 8-4:30. No charge; donations accepted. Closed state holidays. &
Attendance: 1,000 (estimated)

Wilson

HAMPSON ARCHEOLOGICAL MUSEUM STATE PARK, #2 Lake Dr., Wilson, AR 72395. Mailing Address: P.O. Box 156, Wilson, AR 72395-0156. Tel.: 870-655-8622.
E-mail: hampsonarcheologicalmuseum@arkansas.com
Web Site: www.arkansasstateparks.com/hampsonmuseum
Key Personnel: Park Supt., Tess Pruett.
Institution Type/Description: Archaeology Museum.
Hours & Admission Prices: Tues.-Sat. 8-5, Sun. 1-5. Museum: no charge; donations accepted. Closed New Year's Day; Thanksgiving; Christmas Eve & Day. &
Attendance: 5,100 (estimated)

Wynne

CROSS COUNTY MUSEUM & ARCHIVES, 711 E. Union, Wynne, AR 72396-3029. Mailing Address: P.O. Box 943, Wynne, AR 72396-0943. Tel.: 870-238-4100. Fax: 870-238-4100.
E-mail: crossmuseum@sbcglobal.net
Web Site: crosscountymuseum.com
Formerly: Cross County Historical Society
Key Personnel: Pres., Charlie L. Brown; Bd., Michelle Slabaugh.
Institution Type/Description: Historical Society Museum.
Hours & Admission Prices: Mon.-Fri. 10-4. No charge; donations accepted. &
Attendance: 1,000 (estimated)

CALIFORNIA

(1128 listings)

Acton

SHAMBALA PRESERVE, 6867 Soledad Canyon, Acton, CA 93510-2221. Mailing Address: P.O. Box 189, Acton, CA 93510-0189. Tel.: 661-268-0380. Fax: 661-268-8809.
E-mail: info@shambala.org
Institution Type/Description: Wildlife Preserve.
Hours & Admission Prices: Safaris: one Sat.-Sun. a month by appointment. Adults 18 & over $50; children under 18 not admitted.

Agoura Hills

REYES ADOBE HISTORICAL SITE, 30400 Rainbow Crest Dr., Agoura Hills, CA 91301. Mailing Address: 29900 Ladyface Ct., Agoura Hills, CA 91301. Tel.: 818-597-7361, 805-643-2504.
E-mail: xruwhiu@ci.agoura-hills.ca.us
Web Site: www.agourahillsrec.org
Institution Type/Description: Historic House: built c.1850.
Hours & Admission Prices: Tues. 10-2, 2nd & 4th Sat. of month 1-4. Adults $3, seniors $2, children 5-12 $1; children under 5 no charge.

Alameda

ALAMEDA MUSEUM, 2324 Alameda Ave., Alameda, CA 94501. Tel.: 510-521-1233.
E-mail: info@alamedamuseum.org
Web Site: alamedamuseum.org
Institution Type/Description: History Museum.
Hours & Admission Prices: Wed.-Fri. & Sun. 1:30-4, Sat. 11-4. No charge; donations accepted. &

ALAMEDA NAVAL AIR MUSEUM, 2151 Ferry Point Rd., Bldg. 77 at Alameda Point, Alameda, CA 94501. Tel.: 510-522-4262.
E-mail: backtothe40s@gmail.com
Key Personnel: Pres. (V), Larry Pirack; Museum Shop Mgr., Robbie DiLeo.
Institution Type/Description: Military History Museum.
Hours & Admission Prices: Sat.-Sun. 10-4; groups by appointment. Adults 12 & over $7; discounts for AAM & ICOM members; members & children under 12 no charge. &

MEYERS HOUSE & GARDEN, 2021 Alameda Ave., Alameda, CA 94501. Tel.: 510-521-1247.
E-mail: info@alamedamuseum.org
Institution Type/Description: Historic House Museum: built in 1897.
Hours & Admission Prices: 4th Sat. of the month 1-4. Admission $5 per person.

USS HORNET - SEA, AIR & SPACE MUSEUM, 707 W. Hornet Ave., Alameda, CA 94501-5006. Mailing Address: P.O. Box 460,

Alameda, CA 94501-9560. Tel.: 510-521-8448. Fax: 510-521-8327.
E-mail: info@uss-hornet.org
Web Site: www.uss-hornet.org
Key Personnel: Exec. Dir., Jill Rapposelli; Chm. (V), Ray Fortney; Dir. Aircraft & Museum Operations, Rich Thom; Dir. Museum Collections & Exhibitions, Holly Gallagher; Museum Shop Mgr., Carrie Santell.
Institution Type/Description: Air, Sea, & Space Museum. A National & State Historic Landmark.
Hours & Admission Prices: Daily 10-5. Adults $20, seniors 65 & over, military & students $15, youth 5-17 $10; discounts to Time Travelers; members and children 4 & under no charge. Closed New Year's Day; Thanksgiving; Christmas. &
Attendance: 63,000 (estimated)

Aliso Viejo

SOKA UNIVERSITY - FOUNDERS HALL ART GALLERY, 1 University Dr., Aliso Viejo, CA 92656-8081. Tel.: 949-480-4081. Fax: 949-480-4260. Facebook: Soka University of America.
E-mail: info@soka.edu
Web Site: www.soka.edu
Key Personnel: Chair, Wendy Harder.
Institution Type/Description: Art Gallery.
Hours & Admission Prices: Mon.-Fri. 9-5. No charge. &

Alleghany

UNDERGROUND GOLD MINERS MUSEUM, 356 Main St., Alleghany, CA 95910-9998. Mailing Address: P.O. Box 907, Alleghany, CA 95910-0907. Tel.: 530-287-3330 & 3223. Fax: 530-287-3455.
E-mail: info@undergroundgold.com
Web Site: undergroundgold.com
Key Personnel: C.E.O. & Museum Shop Mgr., Rae Bell Arbogast; Pres. (V), David Scinto, C.P.A.; Education, Raymond Wittkopp.
Institution Type/Description: Mining Museum.
Hours & Admission Prices: Memorial Day to Labor Day by appointment & special events. Adults $2. &
Attendance: 1,000 (estimated)

Allensworth

COLONEL ALLENSWORTH STATE HISTORIC PARK, 4011Grant Dr., Allensworth, CA 93219. Mailing Address: Star Rte. 1, Box 148, Earlimart, CA 93219-9710. Tel.: 661-849-3433. Fax: 661-849-4013.
E-mail: sptomey@parks.ca.gov
Key Personnel: State Park Interpreter III, Steven M. Ptomey.
Institution Type/Description: Park Museum & Interpretive Center: located on the site of 1908 town of Allensworth, created to be a place where black people could live & work without racial prejudice.
Hours & Admission Prices: Park: 8-sunset. Visitor Center: daily 10-4; call for holiday hours. House Museum: by appointment only. Camping Fee: Night $20, Day $6; discounts to seniors & disabled. &

Alpine

ALPINE HISTORICAL & CONSERVATION SOCIETY, 2116 Tavern Rd., Alpine, CA 91901. Mailing Address: P.O. Box 382, Alpine, CA 91903-0382. Tel.: 619-659-8740.
E-mail: info@alpinehistory.org
Web Site: www.alpinehistory.org
Key Personnel: Pres. (V), Tom Myers.
Institution Type/Description: Historical Society Museum.
Hours & Admission Prices: last Sat.-Sun. each month 2-4; tours by appointment. No charge; donations accepted. Time Travelers & Reciprocal Membership Network. &
Attendance: 500 (estimated)

Altadena

THE BUNNY MUSEUM, 2605 N. Lake Ave., Altadena, CA 91001. Tel.: 626-798-8848. Facebook; Twitter.
E-mail: sila88@aol.com
Web Site: www.thebunnymuseum.com
Key Personnel: Dir. & Museum Shop Mgr., Candace Frazee; Pres. & C.E.O., Steve Lubanski.
Institution Type/Description: History Museum.

Hours & Admission Prices: Mon.-Sat. 12-6, Sun. 12-5. Adults 13 & over $12, seniors 65 & over and military with ID $10, children 5 & over $8; members & children 4 & under no charge. &
Attendance: 5,000

Alturas

MODOC COUNTY HISTORICAL MUSEUM, 600 S. Main St., Alturas, CA 96101-4117. Tel.: 530-233-2944. Facebook: @ModocHistory.
E-mail: modoccountyhistoricalsociety@yahoo.com
Key Personnel: Dir. & Museum Shop Mgr., Paula Murphy.
Institution Type/Description: Modoc County History Museum.
Hours & Admission Prices: May-Oct. Tues.-Sat. 10-4. Adults $2; discounts to members; children 16 & under no charge. &
Attendance: 6,000 (estimated)

Amador City

AMADOR/WHITNEY, 14170 Hwy. 49, Amador City, CA 95601. Mailing Address: P.O. Box 181, Amador City, CA 95601-0181. Tel.: 209-267-9310. Fax: 209-267-9310.
E-mail: cityclerk@amadorcity.net
Web Site: www.amador-city.com/amador_museum
Key Personnel: Dir., Joyce Davidson.
Institution Type/Description: History Museum.
Hours & Admission Prices: Fri.-Sun. 12-4. No charge; donations accepted.

Anaheim

ANAHEIM HERITAGE CENTER, Anaheim Public Library, 241 S. Anaheim Blvd., Anaheim, CA 92805. Tel.: 714-765-6453. Fax: 714-765-6469.
E-mail: jnewell@anaheim.net
Web Site: www.anaheim.net/library
Formerly: Elizabeth J. Schultz/Anaheim History Room
Key Personnel: Library Branch Mgr. Heritage Svcs., Jane K. Newell.
Institution Type/Description: History Museum.
Hours & Admission Prices: Mon. 12-9, Tues.-Fri. 11-6. No charge.
Attendance: 1,529 (actual)

MOTHER COLONY HOUSE MUSEUM, 414 N. West St., Anaheim, CA 92801-5953. Mailing Address: Anaheim Heritage Center at the Museum, 241 s. Anaheim Blvd., Anaheim, CA 92805. Tel.: 714-765-6453.
Web Site: www.anaheimcolony.com/m_colony.htm
Key Personnel: Museum Mgr., Jane Newell.
Institution Type/Description: Historic House Museum: State Historical Landmark.
Hours & Admission Prices: Call for appointment. No charge; donations accepted. Closed major holidays

MUZEO MUSEUM AND CULTURAL CENTER, 241 S. Anaheim Blvd., Anaheim, CA 92805-3821. Tel.: 714-956-8936.
E-mail: info@muzeo.org
Web Site: www.muzeo.org
Formerly: MUZEO
Key Personnel: Dir., Daniel Finley; Chm. (V), Curt Pringle; Museum Shop Mgr., Patricia Davis.
Institution Type/Description: History Museum.
Hours & Admission Prices: Daily 10-5. Adults $13, children 3-12 $9; discounts to seniors; members no charge. Closed New Year's Day; Thanksgiving; Christmas. &
Attendance: 12,000 (estimated)

OAK CANYON NATURE CENTER, 6700 E. Walnut Canyon Rd., Anaheim, CA 92807-4948. Mailing Address: 200 S. Anaheim Blvd., #433, Anaheim, CA 92805-3820. Tel.: 714-998-8380.
E-mail: ocnc@anaheim.net
Web Site: www.anaheim.net/1096/Oak-Canyon-Nature-Center
Institution Type/Description: Nature Center.
Hours & Admission Prices: Park Grounds & Trails: daily sunrise to sunset. Interpretive Center: Sat.-Sun. 10-4. Suggested donation: $2. &
Attendance: 100,000 (estimated)

Angels Camp

ANGELS CAMP MUSEUM, 753 S. Main St., Angels Camp, CA 95222. Mailing Address: P.O. Box 667, Angels Camp, CA 95222. Tel.: 209-736-2963. Fax: 209-736-0709.

E-mail: kimberlyarth@angelscamp.gov
Web Site: www.angelscamp.gov/museum
Formerly: Angels Camp Museum & Carriage House
Key Personnel: Dir., Kimberly Arth.
Institution Type/Description: History Museum.
Hours & Admission Prices: Mon., Wed.-Sat. 10-4. Adults $7, children $3, children under 4 & members free.
Attendance: 7,952 (actual)

Antioch

ANTIOCH HISTORICAL SOCIETY MUSEUM, 1500 W. Fourth St., Antioch, CA 94509-1046. Tel.: 925-757-1326.
Web Site: www.antiochhistoricalmuseum.org
Key Personnel: Pres. (V), Bob Martin.
Institution Type/Description: Historical Society Museum: housed in the former Riverview Union High School; built in 1911. Listed on the National Register of Historical Places.
Hours & Admission Prices: early Jan. to late Dec. Wed. & Sat. 1-4. No charge; donations accepted. Closed holidays; New Year's Eve & Day; Christmas Eve, Day & week. ♿
Attendance: 4,500 (estimated)

Apple Valley

VICTOR VALLEY MUSEUM, 11873 Apple Valley Rd., Apple Valley, CA 92308-3670. Tel.: 760-240-2111. Fax: 760-240-5290. Facebook: Victor Valley Museum.
E-mail: jennifer.reynolds@sbcm.sbcounty.gov
Key Personnel: Facility Mgr., Rhonda Almager; Dir., Melissa Russo.
Institution Type/Description: Natural History Museum.
Hours & Admission Prices: Wed.-Sat. 10-4, Sun. 1-4. Adults $5, seniors & military $4, students & children $2.50; children under 5 no charge. Closed New Year's Day; Thanksgiving; Christmas. ♿
Attendance: 5,000 (estimated)

Aptos

CABRILLO GALLERY, 6500 Soquel Dr., Bldg. 1000, Rm. 1002, Aptos, CA 95003-3119. Tel.: 831-479-6308. Fax: 831-479-5045.
E-mail: gallery@cabrillo.edu
Web Site: www.cabrillo.edu/services/artgallery
Key Personnel: Gallery Dir., Tobin Keller; Asst. Dir., Rose Sellery.
Institution Type/Description: Art Museum.
Hours & Admission Prices: Spring & Fall Mon.-Tues. 9-4 & 7-9, Wed.-Fri. 9-4. Adults $2, youth 12-17 $1; children no charge. ♿
Attendance: 5,000

Arcadia

THE ARBORETUM LOS ANGELES COUNTY ARBORETUM & BOTANIC GARDEN, 301 N. Baldwin Ave., Arcadia, CA 91007-2697. Tel.: 626-821-3222. Fax: 626-445-1217.
Web Site: www.arboretum.org
Formerly: The Arboretum of Los Angeles County
Key Personnel: C.E.O., Richard Schulhof; Pres. (V), Dan Foliart; Librarian, Susan Eubank; Media, Nancy Yoshihara; Museum Shop Mgr., Rosemary Bullen.
Institution Type/Description: Arboretum: located on the site of Santa Anita Rancho.
Hours & Admission Prices: Daily 9-4:30. Adults $9, seniors & students $6, children 5-12 $4; children under 5 & members no charge. Closed Christmas. ♿
Attendance: 300,000 (actual)

THE GILB MUSEUM OF ARCADIA HERITAGE, 380 W. Huntington Dr., Arcadia, CA 91007. Mailing Address: P.O. Box 60021, Arcadia, CA 91066-6021. Tel.: 626-574-5440. Fax: 626-821-9057. Facebook.
E-mail: dhicks@arcadiaca.gov
Web Site: www.arcadiaca.gov/museum
Formerly: Ruth and Charles Gilb Arcadia Historical Museum
Key Personnel: Dir., Darlene Bradley; Cur., Dana Hicks, Ph.D.
Institution Type/Description: History, Art & Culture Museum.
Hours & Admission Prices: Tues.-Sat. 10-12 & 1-4. No charge; donations accepted. Closed national holidays. ♿
Attendance: 5,600 (actual)

Arcata

HUMBOLDT STATE UNIVERSITY NATURAL HISTORY MUSEUM, 1242 G. St., Arcata, CA 95521-5820. Tel.: 707-826-4479. Fax: 707-826-3201. Facebook: Humboldt State University Natural History Museum.
E-mail: natmus@humboldt.edu
Web Site: www.humboldt.edu/natmus
Key Personnel: Museum Dir., Jeffrey White; Museum Mgr., Julie Van Sickle.
Institution Type/Description: University Natural History Museum.
Hours & Admission Prices: Tues.-Sat. 10-5. Family $10, adults $3, children over 3 $2; ASTC & museum members no charge. Closed New Year's Day; Memorial Day; Independence Day; Labor Day; Thanksgiving; Christmas. ♿
Attendance: 18,500 (estimated)

REESE BULLEN GALLERY, Humboldt State University, 1 Harpst St., Arcata, CA 95521-8222. Tel.: 707-826-5802. Fax: 707-826-3628.
Web Site: www.humboldt.edu
Key Personnel: Chm. & Gallery Dir., Martin Morgan; Dir. Asst., Nancy Clark.
Institution Type/Description: University Art Gallery
Hours & Admission Prices: Sept.-May Mon.-Fri. 11-4. Closed university holidays & semester breaks. ♿
Attendance: 5,400 (actual)

Arroyo Grande

SOUTH COUNTY HISTORICAL SOCIETY, 134 Mason St., Arroyo Grande, CA 93420. Mailing Address: P.O. Box 633, Arroyo Grande, CA 93421-0633. Tel.: 805-489-8282.
E-mail: schs76@sbcglobal.net
Web Site: southcountyhistory.org
Formerly: Paulding History House
Key Personnel: Chm. (V), Joe Swigert; Pres. (V), Kirk Scott.
Institution Type/Description: Historical Society Museum.
Hours & Admission Prices: Heritage Square Museums: Sat. 12-3, Sun. 1-4. Paulding History House: 1st Sat. 12-3. Patricia Loomis History Library Mon.-Fri. 1-5. No charge; donations accepted. Closed New Year's Day; Christmas. ♿
Attendance: 10,000 (estimated)

Atascadero

CHARLES PADDOCK ZOO, Morro Rd., Hwy. 41, W., Atascadero, CA 93422. Mailing Address: 9305 Pismo Ave., Atascadero, CA 93422-4939. Tel.: 805-461-5080. Fax: 805-461-7625.
E-mail: zoo@atascadero.org
Web Site: charlespaddockzoo.org
Key Personnel: C.E.O., Alan G. Baker; Pres. Friends of the Charles Paddock Zoo, Steve Robinson.
Institution Type/Description: Zoo.
Hours & Admission Prices: Summer: daily 10-5; Winter: daily 10-4. Adults 12 & over $5, senior citizens 65 & over $4.25, youth 3-11 $4; AZA members & children under 3 no charge. Closed Thanksgiving; Christmas. ♿
Attendance: 60,000 (estimated)

Atwater

CASTLE AIR MUSEUM, 5050 Santa Fe Dr., Atwater, CA 95301-5154. Tel.: 209-723-2178 & 2182. Fax: 209-723-0323.
E-mail: castleairwater@gmail.com
Web Site: www.castleairmuseum.org
Key Personnel: C.E.O., Joe Pruzzo; Chm. Bd., John Sundgren; Financial Dir., Michael Rosado; Sec., Marcelo Paz; Museum Shop Mgr., Janie Sundgren.
Institution Type/Description: Military & Aviation History Museum.
Hours & Admission Prices: April-Sept. daily 9-5; Oct.-March daily 10-4. Adults $10, seniors 60 & up and youth 6-17 $8; active duty, children under 5, & members no charge. Closed New Year's Day; Easter; Thanksgiving; Christmas Eve & Day. ♿
Attendance: 30,000 (actual)

Auburn

BERNHARD MUSEUM COMPLEX, 291 Auburn-Folsom Rd., Auburn, CA 95603-5039. Mailing Address: 101 Maple St., Auburn, CA 95603-5026. Tel.: 530-889-6500. Fax: 530-889-6510.
E-mail: museums@placer.ca.gov
Web Site: www.placer.ca.gov/museum
Key Personnel: Dir., Melanie Barton.
Institution Type/Description: History Museum.
Hours & Admission Prices: Tues.-Sun. 11-4. Closed holidays. No charge; donations accepted. ♿

PLACER COUNTY MUSEUMS, 101 Maple St., Auburn, CA 95603-5026. Tel.: 530-889-6500. Fax: 530-823-3406.

E-mail: mbarton@placer.ca.gov
Web Site: www.placer.ca.gov/museum
Key Personnel: Museum Admin., Ralph Gibson; Cur. Collections, Kasia Woroniecka; Exhibit Preparator, Jason Adair.
Institution Type/Description: History Museum.
Hours & Admission Prices: Gold Country & Bernhard: Tues.-Sun. 11-4. Placer County: daily 10-4. Griffith Quarry: Sat.-Sun. 12-4. Forest Hill & Gold Drift: Memorial Day-Labor Day Wed. & Sat.-Sun. 12-4. No charge; donations accepted. &
Attendance: 55,000 (actual)

Avalon

CATALINA ISLAND MUSEUM, INC., 217 Metropole Ave., Casino Bldg., Avalon, CA 90704. Mailing Address: P.O. Box 366, Avalon, CA 90704-0366. Tel.: 310-510-2414.
E-mail: info@catalinamuseum.org
Web Site: www.catalinamuseum.org
Key Personnel: Exec. Dir., Julie Perlin Lee; Devel. Coord., Lydia Dixon; Dir. Mktg. & Public Rels., Gail Fornasiere; Asst. Cur., Jessica Zumberge.
Institution Type/Description: History and Art Museum.
Hours & Admission Prices: Daily 10-5. Adults $17, seniors & military $15, students with vaild ID $15; discounts to groups of 15 or more; children under 16 & members no charge. Closed New Year's Day; Independence Day; Thanksgiving; Christmas.
Attendance: 55,000 (estimated)

Bakersfield

BAKERSFIELD MUSEUM OF ART, 1930 R St., Bakersfield, CA 93301-4815. Tel.: 661-323-7219. Fax: 661-323-7266.
E-mail: info@bmoa.org
Web Site: www.bmoa.org
Key Personnel: Exec. Dir., Amy Smith; Chief Cur., Rachel Magnus.
Institution Type/Description: Art Museum.
Hours & Admission Prices: Tues.-Sat. 10-4. Adults $10, seniors & students $5; discounts to AAM members; children 5 & under and members no charge. Closed New Year's Day; Martin Luther King Day; Easter; Memorial Day; Independence Day; Labor Day; Thanksgiving; Christmas. &
Attendance: 25,000 (estimated)

BUENA VISTA MUSEUM OF NATURAL HISTORY, 2018 Chester Ave., Bakersfield, CA 93301-4420. Tel.: 661-324-6350. Fax: 661-324-7522.
E-mail: bvmnh@sharktoothhill.com
Web Site: www.sharktoothhill.org
Key Personnel: Exec. Dir., Koral Hancharick.
Institution Type/Description: Natural History Museum.
Hours & Admission Prices: Thurs.-Sat. 10-4, Sun. 12-4, call to confirm; other times by appointment. Adults $7, senior citizens, children & students $4; discounts to groups of 20 or more; children 5 & under no charge. Closed major holidays.

CALIFORNIA LIVING MUSEUM CALM, 10500 Alfred Harrell Hwy., Bakersfield, CA 93306-9654. Tel.: 661-872-2256. Fax: 661-872-2205.
E-mail: toanspach@kern.org
Web Site: www.calmzoo.org
Key Personnel: Dir., Tom Anspach; Zoo Mgr., Lana Fain; Zoo Cur., Don Richardson.
Institution Type/Description: Zoo.
Hours & Admission Prices: Feb.-Oct. daily 9-5; Nov.-Jan. daily 9-4. Adults $9, seniors $7, children 3-12 $5; discounts to groups; children under 3 & members no charge. Closed New Year's Day; Easter; Thanksgiving; Christmas Eve & Day. &

CALIFORNIA STATE UNIVERSITY, BAKERSFIELD, TODD MADIGAN GALLERY, 9001 Stockdale Hwy., 15FA, Bakersfield, CA 93311-1099. Tel.: 661-654-2238. Fax: 661-654-2539.
E-mail: csubpublicaffairs@csub.edu
Web Site: www.csub.edu/art/gallery
Key Personnel: Dir., Joey Kotting.
Institution Type/Description: Art Gallery.
Hours & Admission Prices: Academic Year: Tues.-Thurs. 1-6, Sat. 1-5. Closed university breaks & holidays.

KERN COUNTY MUSEUM, 3801 Chester Ave., Bakersfield, CA 93301-1345. Tel.: 661-852-5000. Fax: 661-322-6415.
E-mail: info@kerncountymuseum.org
Web Site: kerncountymuseum.org

Key Personnel: Exec. Dir., Mike McCoy; Chair, Joseph Hughes; Cur. Collections, Lori Wear; Dir. Facilities, Ed Pearson; Dir. Education, Stephanie Love; Dir. Finance & Human Resources, Brigitt Sakai.
Institution Type/Description: History Museum.
Hours & Admission Prices: Mon.-Sat. & holidays 10-5, Sun. 12-5; ticket office closes daily at 3. Adults $10, senior citizens over 60 & teens $9, children 6-12 $8, children 3-5 $7; children under 3 & members no charge. Closed New Year's Eve & Day; Easter; Independence Day; Thanksgiving; Christmas Eve & Day. &
Attendance: 75,000 (actual)

Banning

GILMAN HISTORIC RANCH AND WAGON MUSEUM, 1901 W. Wilson St., Banning, CA 92220. Tel.: 951-922-9200.
E-mail: sbangle@rivcoparks.org
Web Site: riversidecountyparks.org
Key Personnel: Scott Bangle.
Institution Type/Description: History Museum; housed in the homestead ranch of James Marshall Gilman.
Hours & Admission Prices: Call for hours.

MALKI MUSEUM, 11795 Malki Rd., Morongo Indian Reservation, Banning, CA 92220. Mailing Address: P.O. Box 578, Banning, CA 92220-0017. Tel.: 951-849-7289. Fax: 951-849-3549. Facebook: Malki Museum.
E-mail: malkimuseummail@gmail.com
Web Site: www.malkimuseum.org
Key Personnel: Co-Dir., Jasmin Gonzalez; Co-Dir., Amanda Castro; Pres., Daniel McCarthy; Vice Pres., Loren Sisquoc; Treas., Elaine Mathews.
Institution Type/Description: Native American Museum.
Hours & Admission Prices: Tues.-Sat. 10-4. No charge; donations accepted. &
Attendance: 2,000 (estimated)

Barstow

BARSTOW ROUTE 66 MOTHER ROAD MUSEUM, Historic Harvey House, 681 N. First Ave., Barstow, CA 92311-2201. Tel.: 760-255-1890, 877-997-8366. Fax: 760-256-6776.
E-mail: barstowmuseum@yahoo.com
Web Site: www.route66museum.com
Key Personnel: Mgr., Cur. & Museum Shop Mgr., Debra Hodkin; Historian & Pres. (V), Bill Tomlinson.
Institution Type/Description: History Museum.
Hours & Admission Prices: Fri.-Sun. 10-4; other times by appointment. No charge; donations accepted. &
Attendance: 15,000 (estimated)

MOJAVE RIVER VALLEY MUSEUM, 270 E. Virginia Way, Barstow, CA 92311-3923. Tel.: 760-256-5452.
E-mail: mrvm@verizon.net
Web Site: www.mojaverivervalleymuseum.org
Key Personnel: Pres., Bob Hilburn; Vice Pres., Dave Romero.
Institution Type/Description: History Museum.
Hours & Admission Prices: Daily 11-4. No charge. Closed Christmas.

WESTERN AMERICA RAILROAD MUSEUM - WARM, 685 N. First St., Barstow, CA 92311. Mailing Address: P.O. Box 703, Barstow, CA 92312-0703. Tel.: 760-256-WARM.
E-mail: warm95@verizon.net
Web Site: www.barstowrailmuseum.org
Institution Type/Description: Railroad Museum.
Hours & Admission Prices: Fri.-Sun. 11-4. No charge; donations accepted. &

Bel Air

MARJORIE AND HERMAN PLATT ART GALLERY - AMERICAN JEWISH UNIVERSITY, Familian Campus, 15600 Mulholland Dr., Bel Air, CA 90077. Tel.: 888-853-6763, 310-476-9777.
E-mail: arts@aju.edu
Web Site: www.ajula.edu
Institution Type/Description: Art Gallery.
Hours & Admission Prices: Call for hours.

SONDRA & MARVIN SMALLEY SCULPTURE GARDEN, American Jewish University, 15600 Mulholland Dr., Bel Air, CA 90077-1519. Tel.: 310-476-9777.
Institution Type/Description: Art Museum.
Hours & Admission Prices: Daily. No charge.

Bellflower

COUNTY OF LOS ANGELES FIRE MUSEUM, 9834 Flora Vista St., Bellflower, CA 90706. Tel.: 562-925-0234. Facebook: Los Angeles County Fire Museum.
E-mail: info@lacountyfiremuseum.com
Web Site: www.lacountyfiremuseum.com
Key Personnel: Dir., Paul Schneider.
Institution Type/Description: Fire-Fighting Museum.
Hours & Admission Prices: 1st Sat. each month by appointment. No charge; donations accepted. &
Attendance: 1,400 (estimated)

Belmont

THE WIEGAND GALLERY, Notre Dame de Namur University, 1500 Ralston Ave., Belmont, CA 94002-1908. Tel.: 650-508-3595. Fax: 650-508-3488.
E-mail: artgallery@ndnu.edu
Web Site: www.wiegandgallery.org
Key Personnel: Dir., Robert Poplack; Art Chm., Betty Friedman; Gallery Coord., Sheila Longacre.
Institution Type/Description: University Art Gallery.
Hours & Admission Prices: Sept.-May Tues.-Fri. 9-4. No charge; donations accepted. Closed Thanksgiving; Christmas. &
Attendance: 3,600

Benicia

BENICIA FIRE MUSEUM, 900 E. 2nd St., Benicia, CA 94510-3349. Mailing Address: P.O. Box 1251, Benicia, CA 94510-4251. Tel.: 707-745-1688.
E-mail: Benicia-firemuseum@pacbell.net
Institution Type/Description: Fire-Fighting Museum.
Hours & Admission Prices: 1st three Sun. of month 1-4; other times by appointment. No charge; donations accepted.

BENICIA HISTORICAL MUSEUM, 2024 Camel Rd., Benicia, CA 94510-2339. Mailing Address: 2060 Camel Rd., Benicia, CA 94510-2339. Tel.: 707-745-5435. Fax: 707-745-5869.
E-mail: info@beniciahistoricalmuseum.org
Web Site: beniciahistoricalmuseum.org
Formerly: Benicia Historical Museum and Cultural Foundation (Camel Barn Museum)
Key Personnel: Exec. Dir., Elizabeth d'Huart; Chm. (V), Louise Martin; Bd. Pres. (V), Dr. James Lessenger; Cur., Beverly Phelan; Coord. Elementary Education, Susan Sullivan; Museum Shop Mgr., Toni Haughey.
Institution Type/Description: Local History Museum; housed in 1853-1857 U.S. Army Arsenal; actively used until 1964. Buildings listed on the National Register of Historic Places.
Hours & Admission Prices: Wed.-Sun. 1-4. Adults $5, seniors & students $3; discounts to groups of 30 or more, CAM & AASLH members; children under 7 & members no charge. Closed New Year's Day; Easter; Mother's Day; Father's Day; Thanksgiving; Christmas.
Attendance: 15,500 (estimated)

FISCHER-HANLON HOUSE, 135 West G St., Benicia, CA 94510-3114. Mailing Address: P.O. Box 404, Benicia, CA 94510. Tel.: 707-745-3385.
E-mail: robin.lancaster@hotmail.com
Web Site: beniciastateparksassoc.org
Key Personnel: Dir. & Pres. (V), Carol Berman; Chm. (V) & Museum Shop Mgr., Robin Lancaster.
Institution Type/Description: History Museum.
Hours & Admission Prices: House: Sat.-Sun. 12-3:30. Garden: Wed.-Sun. 10-5. Adults $3, children $2. &
Attendance: 6,000 (estimated)

Berkeley

THE BADE MUSEUM OF BIBLICAL ARCHAEOLOGY, 1798 Scenic Ave., Berkeley, CA 94709-1323. Tel.: 510-849-8286. Fax: 510-845-8948. Facebook.
E-mail: bade@psr.edu
Web Site: psr.edu/about/centers-and-affiliates/bade/
Formerly: The Bade Institute of Biblical Archaeology and The Howell Bible Collection
Key Personnel: Museum Dir., Dr. Aaron Brody.
Institution Type/Description: Archaeological Museum.

Hours & Admission Prices: Mon. 10-2; other times by appointment. No charge; donations accepted. &

BERKELEY ART CENTER, 1275 Walnut St., Berkeley, CA 94709-1406. Tel.: 510-644-6893. Fax: 510-540-0343.
E-mail: info@berkeleyartcenter.org
Web Site: www.berkeleyartcenter.org
Key Personnel: Gallery Dir., Ann Trinca; Gallery Asst., Katie Hayes; Bd. Pres., Dennis Markham.
Institution Type/Description: Art Gallery.
Hours & Admission Prices: Wed.-Sun. 11-5. No admis fee. Closed holidays. &
Attendance: 12,400 (actual)

BERKELEY HISTORICAL SOCIETY AND THE BERKELEY HISTORY CENTER, Veterans Memorial Bldg., 1931 Center St., Berkeley, CA 94701. Mailing Address: BHS, P.O. Box 1190, Berkeley, CA 94701. Tel.: 510-848-0181.
E-mail: info@berkeleyhistoricalsociety.org
Web Site: berkeleyhistoricalsociety.org
Key Personnel: Museum Mgr., John Aronovici; Co-Pres (V), Tonya Staros; Co-Pres (V), Jeanine-Lin Castello.
Institution Type/Description: History Museum.
Hours & Admission Prices: Thurs.-Sat. 1-4. No charge; donations accepted. &
Attendance: 3,000 (estimated)

BERKELEY ROSE GARDEN, 1200 Euclid Ave., Berkeley, CA 94708. Mailing Address: 2180 Milvia St., Berkeley, CA 94704-1122. Tel.: 510-981-6700. Fax: 510-981-6710.
E-mail: parks@ci.berkeley.ca.us
Web Site: www.ci.berkeley.ca.us/parks/parkspages/berkeleyrosegarden.html
Institution Type/Description: Rose Garden.
Hours & Admission Prices: Dawn to dusk. No charge.

HABITOT CHILDREN'S MUSEUM, 2065 Kittredge St., Berkeley, CA 94704-1404. Mailing Address: PMB 326, 1563 Solano Ave., Berkeley, CA 94707. Tel.: 510-647-1111. Fax: 510-647-1110.
E-mail: habitot@lmi.net
Web Site: www.habitot.org
Key Personnel: Dir., Gina Moreland; Devel. & Mktg. Mgr., Lauren Levin.
Institution Type/Description: Children's Museum.
Hours & Admission Prices: April-Sept. Mon.-Thurs. 9:30-12:30, Fri.-Sat. 9:30-4:30; Oct.-March Mon.-Thurs. 9:30-12:30, Fri.-Sun. 9:30-4:30. Admission $10; discounts to seniors, disabled & AAA members; members & children under one no charge. ACM reciprocal admission. Closed New Year's Day; Easter; Memorial Day; Independence Day; Labor Day; Thanksgiving; Christmas Eve & Day. &
Attendance: 60,000 (estimated)

KALA ART INSTITUTE GALLERY, 2990 San Pablo Ave., Berkeley, CA 94702. Tel.: 510-841-7000. Fax: 510-540-6914.
E-mail: kala@kala.org
Web Site: www.kala.org/mission.html
Key Personnel: Exec. Dir. & Co Founder, Archana Horsting; Artistic Dir. & Co Founder, Yuzo Nakano.
Institution Type/Description: Art Gallery.
Hours & Admission Prices: Tues.-Fri. 12-5, Sat. 12-4:30. Cl. Sun. & Mon. No charge; donations accepted. &

LACIS MUSEUM OF LACE & TEXTILES, 2982 Adeline St., Berkeley, CA 94703-2503. Mailing Address: 3163 Adeline St., Berkeley, CA 94703-2401. Tel.: 510-843-7290. Fax: 510-843-5018.
E-mail: jules@lacismuseum.org
Web Site: lacismuseum.org
Key Personnel: Dir., Jules Kliot; C.E.O., Starnie Johnson; Museum Shop Mgr., Erin Algeo.
Institution Type/Description: Lace & Textile Museum.
Hours & Admission Prices: Mon.-Sat. 12-6. Adults $2; members no charge. &
Attendance: 5,000 (estimated)

LAWRENCE HALL OF SCIENCE, University of California, Berkeley, 1 Centennial Dr., #5200, Berkeley, CA 94720-5200. Tel.: 510-642-5132. Fax: 510-642-1055. Facebook: Lawrence Hall of Science.
E-mail: laurenfrieband@gmail.com
Web Site: www.lawrencehallofscience.org
Key Personnel: Dir., Dr. Elizabeth K. Stage; Deputy Dir., Susan Gregory; Dir. Center for Leadership in Science Teaching, Craig Strang; Dir. Center for Research Evaluation & Assessment, Rena Dorph; Dir. Resource Management,

Flori Ramos; Dir. Center for Curriculum Devel. & Implementation, Jacquey Barber; Dir. Exhibits, Brooke Smith; Dir. Center for Mathematics Excellence & Equity, Harold Asturias; Human Resources Mgr., Sandra Colonna; Museum Shop Mgr., Seth Harthun; Mgr. Visitor Programs, Sue Guevara.
Institution Type/Description: Science & Technology Center.
Hours & Admission Prices: Wed.-Sun. 10-5. Adults $12, youth 7-18, full-time students, disabled and senior citizens 62 & over and children 3-6 $10; discounts to groups, ACM & ASTC members; UC Berkeley students, children under 3 & members no charge. Closed Thanksgiving; Christmas. &
Attendance: 200,000 (estimated)

THE MAGNES COLLECTION OF JEWISH ART AND LIFE, UC Berkeley, 2121 Allston Way, Berkeley, CA 94720. Tel.: 510-643-2526. Facebook: The Magnes.
E-mail: magnes@berkeley.edu
Web Site: www.magnes.berkeley.edu
Formerly: Judah L. Magnes Museum
Key Personnel: Dir., George Breslauer; Cur., Francesco Spagnolo, Ph.D.; Registrar, Exhibitions Coord. & Rights Mgr., Julie Franklin; Asst. Cur., Zoe Lewin; Coord. Programs & Events, Lisa Davis; Asst. Cur., Shir Kochavi; Asst. Registrar, Rebecca Hisiger; Preparator, Ernest Jolly.
Institution Type/Description: Judaica Museum.
Hours & Admission Prices: Call for hours. No charge; donations accepted. &

MUSEUM OF PALEONTOLOGY, 1101 Valley Life Sciences Bldg., University of California, Berkeley, CA 94720. Mailing Address: MC: 4780, 1101 Valley Life Sciences Bldg., University of California, Berkeley, CA 94720. Tel.: 510-642-1821. Fax: 510-642-1822.
E-mail: ldwhite@berkeley.edu
Web Site: www.ucmp.berkeley.edu
Key Personnel: Cur., David R. Lindberg; Cur., Jere Lipps; Cur., William B. Berry; Cur., Carole S. Hickman; Cur., Kevin Padian; Cur., Walter Alvarez; Cur., Roger Byrne; Cur., William A. Clemens; Cur., James W. Valentine; Cur., Tim White; Cur., Lynn Ingram; Cur., Roy Caldwell; Principal Museum Scientist, Mark B. Goodwin; Museum Scientist, Pat Holroyd; Museum Scientist, Diane Erwin; Museum Scientist, Kenneth L. Finger; Museum Rels., Judy Scotchmoor; Museum Rels., David K. Smith; Webmaster, Josh Frankel; Museum Preparator, Jane Mason.
Institution Type/Description: Paleontology Museum.
Hours & Admission Prices: Call for hours. No charge; donations accepted. Closed national holidays. &
Attendance: 15,000 (estimated)

PHOEBE APPERSON HEARST MUSEUM OF ANTHROPOLOGY, 103 Kroeber Hall, University of California, Berkeley, CA 94720. Tel.: 510-642-3682. Fax: 510-642-6271.
E-mail: pahma-admin@berkeley.edu
Web Site: hearstmuseum.berkeley.edu
Key Personnel: Acting Dir., Benjamin Porter, Ph.D.
Institution Type/Description: Anthropology Museum.
Hours & Admission Prices: Wed., Fri. & Sun. 11-5, Thurs. 11-8, Sat. 10-6. Adults $6, non UC students and seniors 65 & over $3; UC Berkeley students, faculty & staff and youth under 18 no charge. &
Attendance: 15,000 (estimated)

TILDEN NATURE AREA ENVIRONMENTAL EDUCATION CENTER, 600 Canon Dr., Berkeley, CA 94708-1162. Tel.: 510-544-2233.
E-mail: tnarea@ebparks.org
Web Site: www.ebparks.org/parks/vc/tna
Institution Type/Description: Nature Center.
Hours & Admission Prices: Nature Area: daily 5am-10pm. Environmental Education Center: Tues.-Sun. 10-4:30. Little Farm: daily 8:30-4. Closed New Year's Day; Thanksgiving; Christmas. &

UNIVERSITY & JEPSON HERBARIA, University of California, 1001 Valley Life Sciences Bldg., #2465, Berkeley, CA 94720. Tel.: 510-642-2465 & 643-7008. Fax: 510-643-5390.
E-mail: smarkos@berkeley.edu
Web Site: ucjeps.berkeley.edu
Key Personnel: Dir., Prof. Brent Mishler; Research Botanist, Ingrid Jordon-Thaden; Cur. Pteridophytes, Dr. Alan R. Smith; Cur. Compositae, Dr. John L. Strother; Cur. Western North American Flora, Dr. Barbara Ertter; Cur. Jepson Herbarium, Bruce G. Baldwin.
Institution Type/Description: Herbaria.
Hours & Admission Prices: Mon.-Fri. 8-12 & 1-5. No charge. Closed university holidays.
Attendance: 500 (estimated)

UNIVERSITY OF CALIFORNIA BERKELEY ART MUSEUM AND PACIFIC FILM ARCHIVE, 2155 Center St., Berkeley, CA 94720. Mailing Address: 2120 Oxford St., #2250, Berkeley, CA 94720. Tel.: 510-642-0808. Fax: 510-642-4889. TDD: 510-642-8734.
E-mail: bampfa@berkeley.edu
Web Site: bampfa.org
Key Personnel: Pres. Bd. Trustees, Noel Nellis; Dir., Lawrence Rinder; C.A.O., Richard Tellinghuisen; Security & Operations Admin., Maria Cisneros; Sr. Film Cur., Susan Oxtoby; Film Cur., Kathy Geritz; Film Collection Cur., Mona Nagai; Dir. Education & Academic Rels., Sherry Goodman; Dir. Registration, Lisa Calden; Sales & Admissions Mgr., Jim Sugarman; Dir. Business Svcs., Rebecca Hoag; Sr. Cur. Asian Art, Julia White; Cur. Contemporary & Modern Art and Phyllis C. Wattis MATRIX, Apsara DiQuinzio; Dir. Devel., Louise Gregory; Chief Preparator, Kelly Bennett.
Institution Type/Description: Art Museum.
Hours & Admission Prices: Wed.-Sun. 11-7. Galleries: adults $14, non-UC Berkeley students, seniors 65 & over & disabled persons, $12; discounts to AAM & ICOM members; BAMPFA members, UC Berkeley students, staff, students & faculty and 18 & under with adult no charge. Osher Theater: general admission $12, UC Berkeley faculty & staff, non-UC Berkeley students, seniors 65 & over and disabled persons $8, BAMPFA members & UC Berkeley students $7. Galleries & Theater: closed university holidays. &
Attendance: 150,000 (estimated)

UNIVERSITY OF CALIFORNIA BOTANICAL GARDEN, 200 Centennial Dr., Berkeley, CA 94720-5045. Tel.: 510-643-2755 & 642-0849. Fax: 510-642-5045.
E-mail: garden@berkeley.edu
Web Site: botanicalgarden.berkeley.edu
Key Personnel: Dir., Eric Siegel; Chm. (V), Jim Landau; Assoc. Dir. Education, Christine Manoux; Horticulturist & Green House Collections, Corina Rieder; Volunteer & Tour Coord., Perry Hall; Dir. Devel., Nadean Lindberg; Cur., Holly Forbes; Retail Coordr., Nancy Rosenlund.
Institution Type/Description: Botanical Garden.
Hours & Admission Prices: Daily 9-5; closed 1st Tues. each month. Adults $12, seniors 65 & over $10, non-UCB students $10, juniors 7-17 $7; UC faculty, students & staff, children under 6 and 1st Thurs. of month no charge. Closed New Year's Eve & Day; Martin Luther King Jr. Day; Thanksgiving; Christmas Eve & Day. &
Attendance: 40,000 (actual)

Beverly Hills

ACADEMY MUSEUM OF MOTION PICTURE, 6067 Wilshire Blvd., Beverly Hills, CA 90036. Mailing Address: c/o Academy Headquarters, 8949 Wilshire Blvd., Beverly Hills, CA 90211. Tel.: 310-247-3000.
E-mail: academymuseum@oscars.org
Web Site: www.oscars.org/museum
Key Personnel: Dir., Kerry Brougher.
Institution Type/Description: Motion Picture Museum.
Hours & Admission Prices: Currently under construction.

CALIFORNIA MUSEUM OF ANCIENT ART, Beverly Hills, CA 90213-3515. Mailing Address: P.O. Box 10515, Beverly Hills, CA 90213-3515. Tel.: 818-762-5500.
E-mail: cmaa@att.net
Web Site: cmaa-museum.org
Key Personnel: Pres., John D. Hofbauer; Dir. & Cur., Jerome Berman; C.F.O., Richard Gerber; Sec., Talma Zelitzki.
Institution Type/Description: Near Eastern Art & Archaeology Museum.
Hours & Admission Prices: Temporarily closed. Call for more information.

GAGOSIAN GALLERY, 456 N. Camden Dr., Beverly Hills, CA 90210. Tel.: 310-271-9400. Fax: 310-271-9420.
E-mail: losangeles@gagosian.com
Web Site: www.gagosian.com
Institution Type/Description: Art Gallery.
Hours & Admission Prices: Mon.-Sat. 10-6.

GREYSTONE MANSION & GARDENS, 905 Loma Vista Dr., Beverly Hills, CA 90210. Mailing Address: 221 N. Figueroa St., Ste. 350, Los Angeles, 90012. Tel.: 310-285-6830.
E-mail: kbuhagiar@beverlyhills.org
Web Site: www.beverlyhills.org/greystone
Institution Type/Description: Historic Mansion: completed in 1928. Listed on the National Register of Historic Places.

Hours & Admission Prices: Grounds: mid-March to early Nov. daily 10-6; early Nov. to mid-March daily 10-5. Mansion & Garden Tours: Dec.-April 1st Sat. each month by appointment.

THE PALEY CENTER FOR MEDIA, 465 N. Beverly Dr., Beverly Hills, CA 90210-4601. Tel.: 310-786-1000.
E-mail: mlevy@lippingroup.com
Web Site: www.paleycenter.org
Formerly: The Museum of Television & Radio
Key Personnel: Pres. & C.E.O., Maureen J. Reidy; Chief Programming Officer, Diane Lewis.
Institution Type/Description: Communication Museum.
Hours & Admission Prices: Wed.-Sun. 12-6. No charge; donations accepted. ♿

VIRGINIA ROBINSON GARDENS, 1008 Elden Way, Beverly Hills, CA 90210-2805. Tel.: 310-276-5367. Fax: 310-276-5352.
E-mail: visit@robinsongardens.org
Web Site: www.robinsongardens.org
Key Personnel: Supt., Timothy Lindsay; Pres. (V), Kerstin Royce; Museum Shop Mgr., Kathleen Huckland.
Institution Type/Description: Historic House & Gardens: 1911 Mediterranean Classic Revival home owned by Mr. and Mrs. Harry Winchester Robinson, heirs to the J.W. Robinson department stores empire.
Hours & Admission Prices: Guided Tours: Tues.-Fri. 10 & 1 by appointment. Adults $11, seniors 62 & over and students $6, children 5-12 $4.
Attendance: 2,000 (estimated)

Big Bear City

BIG BEAR SOLAR OBSERVATORY, 40386 N. Shore Lane, Big Bear City, CA 92314-9672. Tel.: 909-866-5791. Fax: 909-866-4240.
E-mail: pgoode@bbso.njit.edu
Web Site: www.bbso.njit.edu
Key Personnel: Professor & Dir., Phil Goode.
Institution Type/Description: Observatory.
Hours & Admission Prices: By appointment.

BIG BEAR VALLEY HISTORICAL MUSEUM, 800 B Greenway, Big Bear City, CA 92314. Mailing Address: P.O. Box 513, Big Bear City, CA 92314-0513. Tel.: 909-585-8100.
E-mail: historybigbear@gmail.com
Web Site: www.bigbearhistory.org
Key Personnel: Cur., Kim Sweet; Pres. (V), Jim Weyant; Museum Shop Mgr., Cheryl Furniss.
Institution Type/Description: History Museum.
Hours & Admission Prices: Wed. & Sat.-Sun. 10-4. Adults 14 & over $5. ♿
Attendance: 4,000 (actual)

Bishop

LAWS RAILROAD MUSEUM AND HISTORICAL SITE, Silver Canyon Rd., Bishop, CA 93514. Mailing Address: P.O. Box 363, Bishop, CA 93515-0363. Tel.: 760-873-5950.
E-mail: lawsmuseum@aol.com
Web Site: www.lawsmuseum.org
Key Personnel: C.E.O., Admin. & Museum Shop Mgr., Barbara Moss; Chm. (V), Max Cox.
Institution Type/Description: Railroad Museum Complex: housed in 1883 Laws Railroad Depot & 28 other buildings.
Hours & Admission Prices: Daily 10-4. Suggested Donation: adults $5; members no charge. Closed New Year's Day; Easter; Thanksgiving; Christmas. ♿
Attendance: 20,000 (actual)

Blairsden

PLUMAS-EUREKA STATE PARK, 310 Johnsville Rd., Blairsden, CA 96103-9744. Tel.: 530-836-2380. Fax: 530-836-0498.
E-mail: info@parks.ca.gov
Web Site: www.parks.ca.gov
Key Personnel: Ranger, Scott Elliott.
Institution Type/Description: Historic Site: High Sierra Mining Town.
Hours & Admission Prices: Summer: daily 8-4:30; Winter: call for hours. Campgrounds: $20 per night. Museum: no charge; donations accepted.
Attendance: 40,000

Bolinas

BOLINAS MUSEUM, 48 Wharf Rd., Bolinas, CA 94924. Mailing Address: P.O. Box 450, Bolinas, CA 94924-0450. Tel.: 415-868-0330. Fax: 415-868-0607.
E-mail: info@bolinasmuseum.org
Web Site: bolinasmuseum.org
Key Personnel: Dir., Jennifer A. Gately; Pres., Kirsten Walker; Treas., Terry Donohue.
Institution Type/Description: Art & History Museum.
Hours & Admission Prices: Fri. 1-5, Sat.-Sun. 12-5. No charge; donations accepted. Closed New Year's Day; Thanksgiving; Christmas. ♿
Attendance: 18,000 (estimated)

Bonita

BONITA MUSEUM AND CULTURAL CENTER, 4355 Bonita Rd., Bonita, CA 91902-1351. Tel.: 619-267-5141. Fax: 619-267-2143.
E-mail: bonitamuseum@sbcglobal.net
Web Site: www.bonitahistoricalsociety.org
Key Personnel: Exec. Dir., Julie Gay; Pres. (V), Tom Pocklington; Treas., Barbara Scott.
Institution Type/Description: History & Art Museum.
Hours & Admission Prices: Wed.-Sat. 10-4. No charge; donations accepted. Closed New Year's Day; Independence Day; Thanksgiving; Christmas. ♿
Attendance: 7,000 (estimated)

Boonville

ANDERSON VALLEY HISTORICAL SOCIETY MUSEUM, 12340 Hwy. 128, Boonville, CA 95415. Mailing Address: P.O. Box 676, Boonville, CA 95415-0676. Tel.: 707-895-3207.
E-mail: sherihansen1@aol.com
Web Site: www.andersonvalleymuseum.org
Key Personnel: Pres. (V), Jim Hill.
Institution Type/Description: Historical Society Museum.
Hours & Admission Prices: Feb.-Nov. Sat.-Sun. 1-4. No charge; donations accepted.
Attendance: 600 (estimated)

Boron

COLONEL VERNON P. SAXON JR. AEROSPACE MUSEUM, 26922 Twenty Mule Team Rd., Boron, CA 93516. Tel.: 760-762-6600.
E-mail: director@saxonaerospacemuseum.com
Institution Type/Description: Aerospace History Museum.
Hours & Admission Prices: Daily 10-4; groups of 10 or more by appointment. Closed New Year's Day; Thanksgiving; Christmas.

Borrego Springs

ANZA-BORREGO DESERT STATE PARK, 200 Palm Cyn Dr., Borrego Springs, CA 92004-5005. Mailing Address: P.O. Box 2001, Borrego Springs, CA 92004-2001. Tel.: 760-767-4205. Fax: 760-767-3427.
E-mail: stheriault@parks.ca.gov
Web Site: www.parks.ca.gov/default.asp?page_ID=638
Key Personnel: Supt., Gail Sevrens; Exec. Dir. Foundation, Linda Carson; Mgr. VC, Sally Theriault; Museum Shop Mgr., Kelley Jorgensen.
Institution Type/Description: Archaeology & Paleontology Museum: housed inside a subterranean structure, natural face rock without windows.
Hours & Admission Prices: Visitor center: June-Sept. Sat.-Sun. & holidays 9-5; Oct.-May daily 9-5 No charge; donations accepted; day use fee $8 per vehicle for campgrounds. ♿
Attendance: 175,774 (actual)

Boulder Creek

BIG BASIN REDWOODS STATE PARK, 21600 Big Basin Way, Boulder Creek, CA 95006-9064. Tel.: 831-338-8861. Fax: 831-338-8863.
E-mail: alex.takone@parks.ca.gov
Web Site: bigbasin.org
Key Personnel: Ranger, Alex Takone.
Institution Type/Description: Natural History Museum & State Park.

Hours & Admission Prices: Daily 6am-10pm. Entrance Fee: $10 per vehicle, senior citizens per vehicle $9, disabled per vehicle w/CA State Park Disabled Discount Pass $5. State annual park passes accepted. &
Attendance: 750,000 (estimated)

SAN LORENZO VALLEY MUSEUM, 12547 Hwy. 9, Boulder Creek, CA 95006. Mailing Address: P.O. Box 576, Boulder Creek, CA 95006-0576. Tel.: 831-338-8382. Fax: 831-338-8382.
E-mail: slvhm@cruzio.com
Web Site: www.slvmuseum.com
Key Personnel: Exec. Dir. & Museum Shop Mgr., Lynda Phillips; Pres. (V), Lisa Robinson.
Institution Type/Description: History Museum.
Hours & Admission Prices: Wed. & Fri.-Sun. 12-4; other times by appointment. No charge; donations accepted.

Brea

BREA MUSEUM AND HISTORICAL SOCIETY, City Hall Park, Brea Blvd. & Elm St., Brea, CA 92821. Mailing Address: 425 S. Brea Blvd., Brea, CA 92821. Tel.: 714-256-2283.
E-mail: info@breamuseum.org
Web Site: www.breamuseum.org
Key Personnel: Dir., Susan Hall Nguyen.
Institution Type/Description: History Museum.
Hours & Admission Prices: Thurs. 2-5, Sat. 10-3:. No charge; donations accepted.
Attendance: 646 (actual)

CITY OF BREA ART GALLERY, Brea Civic & Cultural Center, Plaza Level, 1 Civic Center Cir., Brea, CA 92821-5732. Tel.: 714-990-7730. Fax: 714-990-7736.
E-mail: breagallery@cityofbrea.net
Web Site: www.breagallery.com
Key Personnel: Gallery Dir., Heather Bowling; Exhibitions Coord., Ariana Foster; Gallery Asst., Katie Chidester.
Institution Type/Description: Art Exhibit Area.
Hours & Admission Prices: Wed.-Sun. 12-5. Adults $3; discounts to AAM members; members, children under 12 no charge. Closed holidays. &
Attendance: 20,000 (actual)

OLINDA HISTORIC MUSEUM AND PARK, 4025 Santa Fe Rd., Brea, CA 92821. Mailing Address: 1 Civic Center Circle, Brea, CA 92821-5792. Tel.: 714-671-4447.
Institution Type/Description: Historic Site.
Hours & Admission Prices: Daily 9-4; tours by appointment. No charge.

Brentwood

EAST CONTRA COSTA MUSEUM, 3890 Sellers Ave., Brentwood, CA 94513. Mailing Address: P.O. Box 202, Brentwood, CA 94513-0202. Tel.: 925-625-3553.
E-mail: ecchs@eastcontracostahistory.org
Web Site: www.eastcontracostahistory.org/about/contact/
Institution Type/Description: History Museum.
Hours & Admission Prices: April-Oct. Sat. & 3rd Sun. of month 2-4.

Bridgeport

BODIE STATE HISTORIC PARK, SR 270, Bridgeport, CA 93517. Mailing Address: P.O. Box 515, Bridgeport, CA 93517-0515. Tel.: 760-647-6445. Fax: 760-647-6486.
E-mail: info@bodiefoundation.org
Web Site: www.bodiefoundation.org
Key Personnel: Supervising Ranger, Joshua Heitzmann.
Institution Type/Description: Historic Site: 1849-1932 Gold Rush Mining Boom Town.
Hours & Admission Prices: Park: Summer: daily 9-6; Winter: daily 9-4. Museum: May 15-Oct. daily 9-5. Adults $8, children 17 & under $5; children 3 & under no charge. &
Attendance: 145,000 (estimated)

Buena Park

BUENA PARK HISTORICAL SOCIETY, 6631 Beach Blvd., Buena Park, CA 90621-2904. Tel.: 714-562-3570.
E-mail: info@historicalsociety.org
Web Site: www.historicalsociety.org
Key Personnel: Pres. (V), Art Brown; Cur., Dean O. Dixon.
Institution Type/Description: Historic House Museum.

Hours & Admission Prices: Thurs. 10:30-2:30, 2nd Sun. of month 1-4. No charge; donations accepted. &
Attendance: 684 (actual)

Burlingame

BURLINGAME MUSEUM OF PEZ & CLASSIC TOY MUSEUM, 214 California Dr., Burlingame, CA 94010-4113. Tel.: 650-347-2301. Fax: 650-347-3840.
E-mail: gary@spectrumnet.com
Web Site: www.burlingamepezmuseum.com
Key Personnel: C.E.O., Gary R. Doss; Museum Shop Mgr., Nancy Doss.
Institution Type/Description: General Museum.
Hours & Admission Prices: Tues.-Sat. 10-6. Adults $3, senior citizens 65 & over and children 4-12 $1; children 3 & under and 1st Thurs. of month no charge. Closed major holidays.

PENINSULA MUSEUM OF ART, 1777 California Dr., Burlingame, CA 94010. Tel.: 650-692-2133.
E-mail: peninsulamuseum@gmail.com
Web Site: www.peninsulamuseum.org
Key Personnel: Chm. (V) & Exec. Dir. (V), Ruth Waters; Permanent Collection, Ann Dinapoli; Public Rels., Christina Chahal; Treas., Arabella Decker; Museum Shop Mgr., Nancee McDonnell.
Institution Type/Description: Art Museum.
Hours & Admission Prices: Wed.-Sun. 11-5. No charge. Closed New Year's Day; Independence Day; Thanksgiving; Christmas. &
Attendance: 5,750 (estimated)

Burney

MCARTHUR-BURNEY FALLS MEMORIAL STATE PARK, 24898 Hwy. 89, Burney, CA 96013-9626. Mailing Address: MBF Interpretive Association, P.O. Box 777, Burney, CA 96013. Tel.: 530-335-2777.
E-mail: webmaster@burneyfallspark.org
Web Site: www.burney-falls.com
Key Personnel: Pres., MBFIA, Bill Cummings.
Institution Type/Description: Park Museum & Visitor Center.
Hours & Admission Prices: Daily sunrise-sunset.

Calabasas

LEONIS ADOBE MUSEUM, 23537 Calabasas Rd., Calabasas, CA 91302-1311. Tel.: 818-222-6511. Fax: 818-222-0862.
E-mail: info@leonisadobemuseum.org
Web Site: www.leonisadobemuseum.org
Key Personnel: Dir., Diane Ramadan; Pres. (V), Don Adams.
Institution Type/Description: Historic House & Gardens: housed in the former home of Miguel Leonis; c.1880.
Hours & Admission Prices: Wed.-Fri. & Sun. 1-4, Sat. 10-4. Suggested Donations: adults $4, senior citizens $3, children under 12 $1. Closed New Year's Day; Thanksgiving; Christmas Eve & Day. &
Attendance: 20,000 (estimated)

Calistoga

PETRIFIED FOREST MUSEUM, 4100 Petrified Forest Rd., Calistoga, CA 94515-9527. Tel.: 707-942-6667.
E-mail: manager@petrifiedforest.org
Web Site: www.petrifiedforest.org
Institution Type/Description: Forest Museum.
Hours & Admission Prices: Summer: daily 9-7; Winter: daily 8-5; call to confirm. Adults $6, seniors over 60 & children 12-17 $5, children 6-11 $3.

SHARPSTEEN MUSEUM, 1311 Washington St., Calistoga, CA 94515-1441. Mailing Address: P.O. Box 573, Calistoga, CA 94515-0573. Tel.: 707-942-5911 & 5916 (Mon.-Fri.). Fax: 707-942-6325.
E-mail: sharpsteenmuseum@att.net
Web Site: sharpsteen-museum.org
Institution Type/Description: Historical Society Museum: adjacent to the museum is one of Sam Brannan's original cottages.
Hours & Admission Prices: Daily 11-4. No charge; donations accepted. Closed Thanksgiving; Christmas. &
Attendance: 14,500 (estimated)

Camarillo

COMMEMORATIVE AIR FORCE SOUTHERN CALIFORNIA WING'S WWII AVIATION MUSEUM, Camarillo Airport, 455 Aviation Dr., Camarillo, CA 93010. Tel.: 805-482-0064.
E-mail: museum@cafsocal.com
Web Site: www.cafsocal.com/join/contact/
Institution Type/Description: Military History Museum.
Hours & Admission Prices: Tues.-Sun. 10-4. Suggested Donations: adults $7, students 11-18 $4, children 6-10 $3; children under 6 & active military no charge.

STUDIO CHANNEL ISLANDS ART CENTER, 2222 Ventura Blvd., Camarillo, CA 93010. Tel.: 805-383-1368.
E-mail: sciartcenter@verizon.net
Web Site: www.studiochannelislands.org
Key Personnel: Exec. Dir., Karin Geiger.
Institution Type/Description: Art Gallery.
Hours & Admission Prices: Tues. 11-3, Wed.-Fri. 11-5, Sat. 10-3. No charge. &

Camp Pendleton

MARINE CORPS MECHANIZED MUSEUM, 2612 Vandegrift Blvd., Camp Pendleton, CA 92055-5021. Tel.: 760-725-5758. Fax: 760-725-5727.
E-mail: mcbcampen_history@usmc.mil
Web Site: www.themech.org
Formerly: Camp Pendleton Museums
Key Personnel: Museum Officer, Faye Jonason; Chm. (V), Lt. Col. Paul Durrance, USMC (Ret.); Pres. Historical Society, Col. Richard Rothwell, USMC (Ret.).
Institution Type/Description: Military Museum.
Hours & Admission Prices: Mon.-Thurs. 8-3:30, Fri. 8-1. Tours: by appointment; email or call: 760-725-0770. Entrance to base requires proof of insurance, registration & current ID. Closed for Marine special liberty. No charge; donations accepted. &
Attendance: 6,000 (estimated)

Campbell

CAMPBELL HISTORICAL MUSEUM & AINSLEY HOUSE, 51 N. Central Ave., Campbell, CA 95008-2015. Tel.: 408-866-2119 & 2757. Fax: 408-866-2795.
E-mail: juliec@cityofcampbell.com
Web Site: www.cityofcampbell.com/museum/index.htm
Institution Type/Description: History Museum: housed in 1951 Fire station which served as the city's first office; 1925 Tudor revival; Carriage House serves as visitor center & museum store.
Hours & Admission Prices: Historical Museum: Thurs.-Sun. 12-4. Admission $2. Ainsley House: March-Dec. 20. Docent Tour: adults $8, senior citizens $6, children 7-17 $4; discounts to AAM members; members no charge. Combination tickets available. Closed major holidays. &
Attendance: 6,935 (actual)

Campo

PACIFIC SOUTHWEST RAILWAY MUSEUM - LIVING HISTORY & TRAIN OPERATION CENTER, 750 Depot St., Campo, CA 91906. Mailing Address: 4695 Nebo Dr., La Mesa, CA 91941-5259. Tel.: 619-465-PSRM (7776).
E-mail: support@sdrm.org
Web Site: www.psrm.org
Key Personnel: Pres. (V), Diana Hyatt; Museum Shop Mgr., Heather Wright.
Institution Type/Description: Railroad Museum.
Hours & Admission Prices: mid-Jan. to Father's Day & Nov. 1st to Thanksgiving Sat.-Sun. 9-5; June to Labor Day Sat. 12-7, Sun. 10-3; Sept. to Halloween Sat.-Sun. 9-5; late Nov. to Christmas Fri.-Sat. 3-9. Admission $5; members no charge. Closed Christmas. &
Attendance: 12,750 (estimated)

Canoga Park

CANOGA-OWENSMOUTH HISTORICAL MUSEUM, Canoga Park Community Center, 7248 Owensmouth Ave., Canoga Park, CA 91303-1529. Tel.: 818-340-3696 & 346-5252.
Institution Type/Description: History Museum.
Hours & Admission Prices: 2nd & 4th Sun. of month 2-4; other times by appointment. No charge.
Attendance: 250 (estimated)

ORCUTT RANCH, 23600 Roscoe Blvd., Canoga Park, CA 91304-3057. Tel.: 818-346-7449.
Web Site: www.laparks.org/dos/horticulture/orcuttranch.htm
Institution Type/Description: Historic House: home of William Warren Orcutt & his wife Mary Logan Orcutt, c.1926. Los Angeles Historic-Cultural Monument.
Hours & Admission Prices: Museum: daily sunrise to sunset. Orchards: July call for hours.

Capitola

CAPITOLA HISTORICAL MUSEUM, 410 Capitola Ave., Capitola, CA 95010-3318. Tel.: 831-464-0322. Facebook: Capitola Historical Museum.
E-mail: capitolamuseum@gmail.com
Web Site: www.capitolamuseum.org
Key Personnel: Dir., Frank Perry; Pres. (V), Niels Kisling.
Institution Type/Description: General Museum.
Hours & Admission Prices: Wed. & Fri.-Sun. 12-4; other time by appointment. No charge. &
Attendance: 7,982 (actual)

Carlsbad

GIA (GEMOLOGICAL INSTITUTE OF AMERICA), 5345 Armada Dr., Carlsbad, CA 92008-4602. Tel.: 760-603-4157. Fax: 760-603-4056.
E-mail: terri.ottaway@gia.edu
Web Site: www.gia.edu
Key Personnel: Cur., Terri Ottaway; Project Mgr. & Exhibit Devel., McKenzie Santimer.
Institution Type/Description: General Museum.
Hours & Admission Prices: By appointment. No charge. Closed New Year's Day; Presidents' Day; Memorial Day; Independence Day; Labor Day; Thanksgiving; Christmas.
Attendance: 10,000 (estimated)

MUSEUM OF MAKING MUSIC, A DIVISION OF THE NAMM FOUNDATION, 5790 Armada Dr., Carlsbad, CA 92008-4608. Tel.: 760-438-5996. Fax: 760-438-8964.
E-mail: museum@museumofmakingmusic.org
Web Site: www.museumofmakingmusic.org
Key Personnel: Exec. Dir., Carolyn Grant; C.E.O. & Pres., Joe Lamond; Museum Shop Mgr., Allison Hargis.
Institution Type/Description: Musical Instruments Museum.
Hours & Admission Prices: Tues.-Sun. 10-5. Adults $10, senior citizens, students & active duty military $7; discounts to AAM & ICOM members; members and children 3 & under no charge. &
Attendance: 40,000 (actual)

Carmel

CARMEL HERITAGE SOCIETY'S FIRST MURPHY HOUSE, Lincoln & Sixth, Carmel, CA 93921. Mailing Address: Carmel Heritage Society, P.O. Box 701, Carmel, CA 93921-0701. Tel.: 831-624-4447. Fax: 831-624-1970.
E-mail: info@carmelheritage.org
Web Site: www.carmelheritage.org
Key Personnel: Pres., Dawn Dull.
Institution Type/Description: Historical House Museum.
Hours & Admission Prices: House: Wed.-Sun. 1-4. Society Office: Mon.-Thurs. 10-2. No charge.

CENTER FOR PHOTOGRAPHIC ART, San Carlos & 9th Sts., Carmel, CA 93921. Mailing Address: P.O. Box 1100, Carmel, CA 93921-1100. Tel.: 831-625-5181. Fax: 831-625-5199.
E-mail: info@photography.org
Web Site: www.photography.org/index.html
Formerly: Friends of Photography
Key Personnel: Exec. Dir., Nicole Garzino.
Institution Type/Description: Photography Museum.
Hours & Admission Prices: Tues.-Sun. 1-5. No charge; donations accepted. Closed New Year's Day; Thanksgiving; Christmas. &
Attendance: 4,000 (actual)

MISSION SAN CARLOS BORROMEO DEL RIO CARMELO, 3080 Rio Rd., Carmel, CA 93923. Tel.: 831-624-1271, ext. 210. Fax: 831-624-0658.
E-mail: stephanie.haney@carmelmission.org
Web Site: www.carmelmission.org
Key Personnel: Cur., Richard J. Menn.
Institution Type/Description: History Museum.

Hours & Admission Prices: Mon.-Sat. 9:30-5, Sun. 10:30-5. Adults $6.50, seniors $4, children 7 & up $2; children under 6 no charge.

WESTON GALLERY, Sixth Ave. & Dolores, Carmel, CA 93921. Mailing Address: P.O. Box 655, Carmel, CA 93921. Tel.: 831-624-4453. Fax: 831-624-7190.
E-mail: info@westongallery.com
Web Site: www.westongallery.com
Institution Type/Description: Art Gallery.
Hours & Admission Prices: Tues.-Sun. 10:30-5:30. No charge.

WINFIELD GALLERY, Dolores between Ocean & 7th, Carmel, CA 93921. Mailing Address: P.O. Box 7393, Carmel, CA 93921. Tel.: 831-624-3369, 800-289-1950 (Toll Free). Fax: 831-624-5618.
E-mail: chris@winfieldgallery.com
Web Site: www.winfieldgallery.com
Institution Type/Description: Art Gallery.
Hours & Admission Prices: Mon.-Sat. 11-5, Sun. 12-5.

Carmichael

EFFIE YEAW NATURE CENTER, 2850 San Lorenzo Way, Carmichael, CA 95608. Mailing Address: P.O. Box 579, Carmichael, CA 95609-0579. Tel.: 916-489-4918. Fax: 916-489-4983.
E-mail: info@sacnaturecenter.net
Web Site: www.sacnaturecenter.net
Key Personnel: Exec. Dir., Paul Tebbel; Pres., Joey Johnson; Volunteer Coord., Jamie Washington; Exhibit Dir. and Dir. Funding & Devel., Betty Cooper; Maidu Cultural Heritage Program, Brena Seck.
Institution Type/Description: Nature Center.
Hours & Admission Prices: Feb.-Oct. Tues.-Sun. 9-5; Nov.-Jan. Tues.-Sun. 9-4. No charge; donations accepted. Closed New Year's Day; Thanksgiving; Christmas.
Attendance: 83,800 (actual)

Carpinteria

CARPINTERIA VALLEY HISTORICAL SOCIETY & MUSEUM OF HISTORY, 956 Maple Ave., Carpinteria, CA 93013-2021. Tel.: 805-684-3112. Fax: 805-684-4721.
E-mail: info@carpinteriahistoricalmuseum.org
Web Site: www.carpinteriahistoricalmuseum.org
Key Personnel: Pres., Dorothy Thielges; Dir. & Cur., David W. Griggs.
Institution Type/Description: Local History Museum.
Hours & Admission Prices: Tues.-Sat. 1-4. No charge; donations requested.
Attendance: 10,000 (estimated)

Carson

THE INTERNATIONAL PRINTING MUSEUM, 315 W. Torrance Blvd., Carson, CA 90745. Tel.: 310-515-7166. Fax: 310-515-8266. Facebook: @printmuseum.
E-mail: mail@printmuseum.org
Web Site: www.printmuseum.org
Formerly: The Printing Museum
Key Personnel: Founding Cur. & Exec. Dir., Mark Barbour; Pres., Bd. Trustees, Dan Freeland; Mus. Mgr., Sara Halpert; Theater Mgr., Phil Soinski.
Institution Type/Description: Print & Typography Museum.
Hours & Admission Prices: Sat. 10-4. By appointment Tues.-Fri. Adults $10, students, seniors & members $8; preschool children no charge.
Attendance: 20,000 (estimated)

UNIVERSITY ART GALLERY, CSU DOMINGUEZ HILLS, 1000 E. Victoria St., Carson, CA 90747. Tel.: 310-243-3334 & 3310.
E-mail: kzimmerer@csudh.edu
Web Site: www.cah.csudh.edu/artgallery
Key Personnel: Dir., Kathy Zimmerer.
Institution Type/Description: University Art Gallery.
Hours & Admission Prices: Sept.-May Mon.-Thurs. 10-4. No charge; donations accepted. Closed academic holidays: Christmas break; spring break.
Attendance: 10,000 (estimated)

Cathedral City

S.C.R.A.P. GALLERY, 31855 Date Palm Dr., #3-110, Cathedral City, CA 92234-3100. Tel.: 760-863-7777. Fax: 760-863-8973. Facebook: SCRAP Gallery.

E-mail: karen@scrapgallery.org
Web Site: www.scrapgallery.org
Key Personnel: Exec. Dir., Karen Riley; Pres. (V), Marilyn Glassman; Treas., Donna Pease.
Institution Type/Description: Art Museum.
Hours & Admission Prices: Sept.-July Mon.-Fri. 9-5, Sat. special hours monthly. No charge. Closed major holidays.
Attendance: 270,000 (actual)

Chatsworth

HOMESTEAD ACRE AND THE HILL-PALMER HOUSE, 10385 Shadow Oak Dr., Chatsworth, CA 91311-2063. Tel.: 818-882-5614.
E-mail: chatsmimi@aol.com
Web Site: www.laparks.org
Institution Type/Description: Historic House Museum.
Hours & Admission Prices: 1st Sun. each month 1-4.

VALLEY RELICS MUSEUM, 21630 Marilla St., Chatsworth, CA 91311. Tel.: 818-678-4934.
E-mail: info@valleyrelics.org
Web Site: valleyrelics.org
Institution Type/Description: History Museum.
Hours & Admission Prices: Sat. 10-3; other times by appointment.

Cherry Valley

EDWARD-DEAN MUSEUM & GARDENS, 9401 Oak Glen Rd., Cherry Valley, CA 92223-3799. Tel.: 951-845-2626. Fax: 951-845-2628.
E-mail: edm-events@rivcoeda.org
Web Site: www.edward-deanmuseum.org
Formerly: Edward-Dean Museum of Decorative Arts
Institution Type/Description: Historic House Museum.
Hours & Admission Prices: Thurs.-Sat. 10-5. Adults $5; children 12 & under and members no charge. Closed national holidays.

Chico

BIDWELL MANSION STATE HISTORIC PARK, 525 Esplanade, Chico, CA 95926-3996. Tel.: 530-895-6144. Fax: 530-895-6699. Facebook: Bidwell Mansion State Historic Park.
Key Personnel: Unit Supvr., Denise Rist.
Institution Type/Description: Historic House: 1868 three-story Victorian Italian villa country estate, home of Gen. & Mrs. John Bidwell.
Hours & Admission Prices: Sat.-Mon. 11-5; call to confirm. Adults 18 & over $6, children 5-17 $3; members and children 4 & under no charge. Closed New Year's Day; Thanksgiving; Christmas.
Attendance: 35,000

CENTERVILLE SCHOOL HOUSE, 13548 Centerville Rd., Chico, CA 95928. Tel.: 530-893-9667.
Institution Type/Description: Historic Building: housed in the first Centerville School; built in 1872.
Hours & Admission Prices: Sat.-Sun. 1-4.

CHICO AIR MUSEUM, 165 Ryan Ave., Chico, CA 95973. Tel.: 530-345-6468. Facebook.
E-mail: chicoairmuseum@digitalpath.net
Web Site: www.chicoairmuseum.org
Key Personnel: Pres., Brian Baldridge; Museum Shop Mgr., John Forbery.
Institution Type/Description: Aviation History Museum.
Hours & Admission Prices: Fri.-Sun. 9-4. No charge; donations accepted.
Attendance: 7,000 (estimated)

CHICO CHILDREN'S MUSEUM, 325 Main St., Chico, CA 95928. Tel.: 530-809-1492.
Web Site: www.chicochildrensmuseum.org
Key Personnel: Exec. Dir., Leslie Amani; Oper., Tamara Maxey.
Institution Type/Description: Children's Museum.
Hours & Admission Prices: Tues.-Sat. 10-5, Sun. 12-5. Admission 2 & over $9.

CHICO CREEK NATURE CENTER, 1968 E. 8th St., Chico, CA 95928-4110. Tel.: 530-891-4671.
E-mail: info@bidwellpark.org
Web Site: bidwellpark.org
Key Personnel: Dir., Caitlin Reilly; Pres. (V), Bill Beckett.
Institution Type/Description: Nature Center.

Hours & Admission Prices: Living Animal Museum: Wed.-Sat. 11-3. Suggested Donation: adults $4, children $2. Closed New Year's Day; Easter; Independence Day; Thanksgiving; Christmas. &
Attendance: 40,000 (estimated)

CHICO MUSEUM, 141 Salem St., Chico, CA 95926. Mailing Address: P.O. Box 4116, Chico, CA 95926. Tel.: 530-891-4336 & 892-1525.
E-mail: director.chicomuseum@farwestheritage.org
Web Site: www.chicomuseum.org
Key Personnel: Mgr. & Pres. (V), Sara Smallhouse; Pres. (V), Susan Donohue; Treas., Jack Thorpe.
Institution Type/Description: History Museum: housed in 1904 Queen Anne & Romanesque Revival style Carnegie Library.
Hours & Admission Prices: Thurs.-Sun. 11-4. No charge; donations accepted. Closed New Year's Day; Easter; Independence Day; Thanksgiving; Christmas Eve & Day. &
Attendance: 6,500 (actual)

COLMAN MEMORIAL COMMUNITY MUSEUM, 13548 Centerville Rd., Chico, CA 95928. Tel.: 530-893-9667.
E-mail: Fthorne@digitalpath.net
Institution Type/Description: History Museum.
Hours & Admission Prices: Sat.-Sun. 1-4. No charge; donations accepted.

GATEWAY SCIENCE MUSEUM - CALIFORNIA STATE UNIVERSITY, 625 Esplanade, Chico, CA 95929-0545. Mailing Address: 400 W. 1st St., Chico, CA 95929-0545. Tel.: 530-898-4121. Facebook.
E-mail: gateway@csuchico.edu
Web Site: gatewayscience.org
Key Personnel: Dir., Dr. Renee Renner.
Institution Type/Description: Science Museum.
Hours & Admission Prices: Wed.-Sun. 12-5. Adults $7, students w/ID & children 3-17 $5; members no charge. ASTC Passport Program. &
Attendance: 20,000 (estimated)

JANET TURNER PRINT MUSEUM, California State University, Chico, 400 W. 1st St., Chico, CA 95929-0820. Tel.: 530-898-4476. Fax: 530-898-5581.
E-mail: csullivan@csuchico.edu
Web Site: www.theturner.org
Key Personnel: Cur. & Head Archives, Catherine Sullivan; Asst. Collection Mgr., Adria Crossen Davis.
Institution Type/Description: Fine Art Print Gallery & Museum Archive.
Hours & Admission Prices: Sept.-May Mon.-Fri. 11-4 during exhibitions; other times by appointment. No charge; donations accepted. Closed spring break; Thanksgiving break; Christmas break. &
Attendance: 5,500 (estimated)

NATIONAL YO-YO MUSEUM, 320 Broadway, Chico, CA 95928-5322. Tel.: 530-893-0545, ext. 4.
E-mail: info@nationalyoyo.org
Web Site: www.nationalyoyo.org/museum/index.htm
Institution Type/Description: Toy Museum.
Hours & Admission Prices: Mon.-Sat. 10-6, Sun. 12-5; groups by appointment.

1078 GALLERY, 1710 Park Ave., Chico, CA 95928. Tel.: 530-433-1043. Facebook.
E-mail: info@1078gallery.org
Web Site: 1078gallery.org
Institution Type/Description: Art Gallery.
Hours & Admission Prices: Thurs.-Sat. 12-4.

VALENE L. SMITH MUSEUM OF ANTHROPOLOGY, California State University, Chico, Chico, CA 95929-0400. Tel.: 530-898-5397. Fax: 530-898-6143.
E-mail: anthromuseum@csuchico.edu
Web Site: www.csuchico.edu/anth/museum
Key Personnel: Dir., Dr. Georgia Fox; Cur., Adrienne Scott; Asst. Cur., Heather McCafferty.
Institution Type/Description: University Anthropology Museum.
Hours & Admission Prices: Sept.-Oct. & Dec.-July Tues.-Sat. 11-3. Office: Summer Mon.-Thurs. 12-4. No charge; donations accepted. &
Attendance: 5,000 (actual)

China Lake

THE CHINA LAKE MUSEUM OF NAVAL ARMAMENT & TECHNOLOGY, 1 Pearl Harbor Way, China Lake, CA 93555-2803. Mailing Address: P.O. Box 217, Ridgecrest, CA 93556-0217. Tel.: 760-939-3105. Fax: 760-939-0564.
E-mail: chinalakemuseum@mediacombb.net
Web Site: www.chinalakemuseum.org
Formerly: U.S. Naval Museum of Armament & Technology
Key Personnel: Pres., Alice Campbell; Treas., Chris Toftner; Devel., Pat Connell.
Institution Type/Description: Military Museum.
Hours & Admission Prices: Mon.-Sat. 10-4. No charge; donations accepted. Closed federal holidays. &
Attendance: 8,500 (actual)

Chino

CHINO'S OLD SCHOOLHOUSE MUSEUM, 5493 "B" St., Chino, CA 91710-4241. Mailing Address: P.O. Box 972, Chino, CA 91708-0972. Tel.: 909-627-6464.
E-mail: schoolhousemuseum@cityofchino.org
Web Site: www.cityofchino.org
Institution Type/Description: History Museum: Chino's first schoolhouse built in 1888.
Hours & Admission Prices: Temporarily closed.

PLANES OF FAME AIR MUSEUM, 7000 Merrill Ave. #17, Chino, CA 91710-9085. Tel.: 909-597-3722. Facebook: Planes of Fame Air Museum.
E-mail: karen.hinton@planesoffame.org
Web Site: planesoffame.org
Key Personnel: Pres., Steve Hinton; Dir. Devel., Karen Hinton.
Institution Type/Description: Aircraft Museum.
Hours & Admission Prices: Sun.-Fri. 10-5, Sat. 9-5. Adults $11, seniors 65 & up and veterans $10, children 5-12 $4; discounts to AAA members; children under 5, active duty military, police & firefighters and members no charge. Closed Thanksgiving; Christmas. &
Attendance: 50,000 (actual)

YANKS AIR MUSEUM, Mailing Address: 7000 Merrill Ave., Hangar A270, P.O. Box 35, Chino, CA 91710-9091. Tel.: 909-597-1735.
E-mail: christen@yanksair.com
Web Site: www.yanksair.com
Formerly: Yankee Air Corps
Key Personnel: Dir., Christen Wright; C.E.O., Charles Nichols; Museum Shop Mgr., Tiffany Agard; Curator/Historian, James Noriega.
Institution Type/Description: Aviation Museum.
Hours & Admission Prices: Tues.-Sun. 9-4. Adults $16, seniors 65 & over $15, children 5-11 $5; children 4 & under and members no charge. Closed holidays. &

YORBA AND SLAUGHTER FAMILIES ADOBE, 17127 Pomona Rincon Rd., Chino, CA 91708-9285. Mailing Address: c/o San Bernardino Co. Museums, 2024 Orange Tree Lane, Redlands, CA 92374. Tel.: 909-597-8332 & 307-2669. Fax: 909-307-0539.
E-mail: rmckernan@sbcm.sbcounty.gov
Web Site: www.sbcountymuseum.org
Formerly: Yorba-Slaughter Adobe Museum
Key Personnel: Dir., Robert McKernan; Site Mgr., Karen Buma; Cur., Michele Nielsen.
Institution Type/Description: Local History and Historic House Museum: housed in c.1853 Adobe home.
Hours & Admission Prices: Tues.-Sat. 10-3. Adults $5, seniors & military $4, students & children under fee no charge. Closed New Year's Day; Thanksgiving; Christmas.
Attendance: 1,000 (estimated)

Chiriaco Summit

GENERAL PATTON MEMORIAL MUSEUM, 62510 Chiriaco Rd., Chiriaco Summit, CA 92201-8203. Tel.: 760-227-3483. Fax: 760-227-3483.
E-mail: info@generalpattonmuseum.com
Web Site: www.generalpattonmuseum.com
Key Personnel: Pres. (V), Margit F. Chiriaco-Rusche.
Institution Type/Description: Military Museum: located near former headquarters of World War II Desert Training Areas.

Hours & Admission Prices: Daily 9:30-4:30. Adults $6, seniors $4.50, children $1.50; American Legion, V.F.W. members and active-duty military no charge. Closed Thanksgiving; Christmas. ♿
Attendance: 73,500 (actual)

Chula Vista

LIVING COAST DISCOVERY CENTER, 1000 Gunpowder Point Dr., Chula Vista, CA 91910-8222. Tel.: 619-409-5900. Fax: 619-409-5910. Facebook: Living Coast Discovery Center.
E-mail: info@thelivingcoast.org
Web Site: www.thelivingcoast.org
Formerly: Chula Vista Nature Center
Key Personnel: Exec. Dir., Ben Vallejos; Chm. (V), Susan Fuller; Dir. Communications & Guest Experience, Sherry Lankston; Dir. Devel., Lori Coons; Dir. Education, Amanda Grant-Stout; Field Trip & Volunteer Mgr., Tina Matthias; Mgr. Animal Care, Lindsay Bradshaw; Mgr. Devel., Jessica LaFave.
Institution Type/Description: Aquarium Zoo; located on the Sweetwater Marsh National Wildlife Refuge.
Hours & Admission Prices: Daily 10-5. Adults $14, seniors 65 & over, children 4-17, & students w/I.D. $9; discount to groups & military; children 3 & under and members no charge. Closed Thanksgiving; Christmas. ♿
Attendance: 70,000 (actual)

City of Industry

WORKMAN & TEMPLE FAMILY HOMESTEAD MUSEUM, 15415 E. Don Julian Rd., City of Industry, CA 91745-1029. Tel.: 626-968-8492. Fax: 626-968-2048. Facebook: Workman & Temple Family Homestead Museum.
E-mail: info@homesteadmuseum.org
Web Site: www.homesteadmuseum.org
Key Personnel: Dir., Paul Spitzzeri; Dir. Public Programs, Alexandra Rasic; Facilities Coord., Robert Barron; Operations Mgr., Steven Dugan; Programs Mgr., Gennie Truelock.
Institution Type/Description: Historic Buildings Museum & Site; located on the site of the Rancho la Puente.
Hours & Admission Prices: Wed.-Sun. 1-4; group tours by appointment. No charge; donations accepted. Closed major holidays. ♿
Attendance: 15,000 (estimated)

Claremont

CLAREMONT MUSEUM OF ART CLOSED, 200 W. First St., Claremont, CA 91711-1136. Mailing Address: P.O. Box 1136, Claremont, CA 91711-1136. Tel.: 909-621-3200.
E-mail: info@claremontmuseum.org
Web Site: www.claremontmuseum.org
Key Personnel: Pres. (V), Sany Baldonado.
Institution Type/Description: Art Museum.
Hours & Admission Prices: Adults $5, children under 18 no charge; donations accepted.

CLARK HUMANITIES MUSEUM-STUDY, Humanities Bldg., Scripps College, Claremont, CA 91711-3905. Mailing Address: Scripps College, 1030 Columbia Ave., Claremont, CA 91711-3905. Tel.: 909-607-3606. Fax: 909-607-7143.
E-mail: ehaskell@scrippscollege.edu
Key Personnel: Chm. Museum Committee, Dr. Eric T. Haskell; Dir., Candida Jaquez; Admin. Asst., Linda DeChaine.
Institution Type/Description: General Museum.
Hours & Admission Prices: Mon.-Fri. 9-12:30 & 1:30-5. No charge. ♿

PETTERSON MUSEUM OF INTERCULTURAL ART, 730 Plymouth Rd., Claremont, CA 91711. Mailing Address: 625 Mayflower Rd., Claremont, CA 91711-4222. Tel.: 909-399-5544. Fax: 909-399-5508.
E-mail: cgil@pilgrimplace.org
Web Site: www.pilgrimplace.org
Key Personnel: Dir., Bill Cunitz; Pres. (V), Gail Duggan; Cur., Carol Bowdoin Gil.
Institution Type/Description: International Folk & Fine Art Museum.
Hours & Admission Prices: Guided Tours: Fri.-Sun. 2-4 or by appointment. No charge; donations accepted. Closed Easter; Thanksgiving; Christmas. ♿
Attendance: 1,500 (estimated)

PITZER COLLEGE ART GALLERIES, Pitzer College, 1050 N. Mills Ave., Claremont, CA 91711-6101. Tel.: 909-607-3143.
E-mail: pitzer_galleries@pitzer.edu
Web Site: www.pitzer.edu/galleries
Key Personnel: Dir., Ciara Ennis.

Institution Type/Description: Art Gallery.
Hours & Admission Prices: Tues.-Fri. 12-5; other times by appointment. No charge. ♿

POMONA COLLEGE MUSEUM OF ART, 330 N. College Ave., Claremont, CA 91711-4401. Mailing Address: 333 N. College Way, Claremont, CA 91711-4429. Tel.: 909-621-8283 & 8000. Fax: 909-621-8989.
E-mail: kathleen_howe@pomona.edu
Web Site: www.pomona.edu/museum
Key Personnel: Dir., Kathleen Howe; Assoc. Dir. & Registrar, Steve Comba; Sr. Cur., Rebecca McGrew; Cur. Academic Programming, Terri Geis; Administrative Asst., Barbara Coldiron; Preparator, Gary Murphy; Security & Information Officer, Anne Merten.
Institution Type/Description: College Art Museum.
Hours & Admission Prices: Sept.-May Tues.-Fri. 12-5, Sat.-Sun. 1-5. No charge. Closed school & national holidays.
Attendance: 10,770 (actual)

RANCHO SANTA ANA BOTANIC GARDEN, 1500 N. College Ave., Claremont, CA 91711-3157. Tel.: 909-625-8767 ext. 200. Fax: 909-626-7670.
E-mail: info@rsabg.org
Web Site: www.rsabg.org
Key Personnel: Chm. Bd. Trustees, Thomas C. Brayton; Exec. Dir. & Judith B. Friend Dir. Research, Lucinda McDade; C.F.O., Kristine Crosby; Interim Dir. Advancement, Karina Chappell; Dir. Visitor Experience, David Bryant; Dir. Conservation Programs, Naomi Fraga; Dir. Horticulture, Peter Evans.
Institution Type/Description: Botanical Garden.
Hours & Admission Prices: Daily 8-5. Adults $10, seniors & students with ID $6, children 3-12 $4; children under 3 & members no charge. Closed New Year's Day; Independence Day; Thanksgiving; Christmas. ♿
Attendance: 80,000 (estimated)

THE RAYMOND M. ALF MUSEUM OF PALEONTOLOGY, 1175 W. Baseline Rd., Claremont, CA 91711-2146. Tel.: 909-624-2798. Fax: 909-624-2798.
E-mail: dlofgren@webb.org
Web Site: www.alfmuseum.org
Key Personnel: Dir., Donald Lofgren, Ph.D.; Dir. Outreach, Kathy Sanders; Cur., Andrew Farke.
Institution Type/Description: Paleontology Museum.
Hours & Admission Prices: June-Aug. Mon.-Fri. 8-12 & 1-4; Sept.-May Mon.-Fri. 8-12 & 1-4, Sat. 1-4; groups by appointment. Admission $6; children 4 & under no charge. ♿
Attendance: 20,000 (actual)

RUTH CHANDLER WILLIAMSON GALLERY, SCRIPPS COLLEGE, 1030 Colombia Ave., Claremont, CA 91711-3905. Tel.: 909-607-3397 & 4690. Fax: 909-607-4691.
E-mail: mmacnaug@scrippscollege.edu
Web Site: www.scrippscollege.edu/dept/gallery
Key Personnel: Dir., Mary Davis MacNaughton; Asst., Colleen Saloman; Registrar & Preparator, Kirk Delman; Data Specialist, Patricia Yu.
Institution Type/Description: College Art Gallery.
Hours & Admission Prices: Wed.-Sun. 1-5. No charge. Closed school & national holidays. ♿
Attendance: 5,200 (estimated)

Clayton

CLAYTON HISTORICAL SOCIETY, 6101 Main St., Clayton, CA 94517-1201. Mailing Address: P.O. Box 94, Clayton, CA 94517-0094. Tel.: 925-672-0240.
E-mail: chp@claytonhistoric.org
Web Site: www.claytonhistoric.org
Institution Type/Description: Historical Society Museum.
Hours & Admission Prices: Wed. 2-4 & 6-8, Sun. 2-4; groups by appointment.

Clovis

CLOVIS BIG DRY CREEK HISTORICAL MUSEUM, 401 Pollasky Ave., (at 4th St.), Clovis, CA 93612-1141. Tel.: 559-297-8033. Fax: 559-297-8882.
E-mail: pbos@clovis-museum.com
Web Site: www.clovis-museum.com
Key Personnel: Pres. & Cur., Peggy Bos.
Institution Type/Description: History Museum; site of the historic 1924 bank robbery.

Hours & Admission Prices: Tues.-Sat. 10-2; other times by appointment. No charge; donations accepted. ⅃
Attendance: 10,101 (actual)

Coalinga

R.C. BAKER MEMORIAL MUSEUM, INC., 297 W. Elm St., Coalinga, CA 93210-1923. Tel.: 559-935-1914.
Key Personnel: Chm. (V), Tim Jordan; Pres. (V), Ruben Velize; Cur., Suzanne Jordan.
Institution Type/Description: History Museum.
Hours & Admission Prices: Mon.-Fri. 10-12 & 1-5., Sat. 11-5, Sun. 1-5. No charge; donations accepted. Closed legal holidays.
Attendance: 2,500 (estimated)

Coarsegold

COARSEGOLD HISTORIC MUSEUM, 31899 Hwy. 41, Coarsegold, CA 93614. Mailing Address: P.O. Box 117, Coarsegold, CA 93614-0117. Tel.: 559-642-4448. Fax: 559-642-4246. Facebook.
E-mail: chs@sti.net
Web Site: coarsegoldhistoricalsociety.com
Formerly: Willow Glen Museum
Key Personnel: Dir. Museum, Linda Core; Pres. (V), Jack Good; Chm. (V), Kay Good.
Institution Type/Description: History Museum.
Hours & Admission Prices: April-Oct. Thurs.-Sat.10-2, Sun. 12-4, Mon. 9-11:30. No charge; donations accepted. ⅃
Attendance: 700 (estimated)

Colfax

COLFAX AREA HISTORICAL SOCIETY - DEPOT MUSEUM, 99 Railroad St., Colfax, CA 95713. Mailing Address: P.O. Box 185, Colfax, CA 95713-0185. Tel.: 530-346-8599.
E-mail: info@colfaxhistory.org
Web Site: www.colfaxhistory.org
Formerly: Colfax Heritage Museum
Key Personnel: Dir., Chris Miller; Pres. (V), Swend Miller; Museum Shop Mgr., Irene Allen.
Institution Type/Description: Historical Society Museum.
Hours & Admission Prices: Daily 10-3. No charge; donations accepted. Closed New Year's Day; Easter; Independence Day; Thanksgiving; Christmas. ⅃
Attendance: 10,887 (actual)

Coloma

MARSHALL GOLD DISCOVERY STATE HISTORIC PARK, 310 Back St., Coloma, CA 95613. Mailing Address: P.O. Box 265, Coloma, CA 95613-0265. Tel.: 530-622-3470. Fax: 530-622-3472.
E-mail: marshallgold@parks.ca.gov
Web Site: www.parks.ca.gov
Key Personnel: Park Supt., Jeremy McReynolds.
Institution Type/Description: Gold Rush History Museum: located near the site of the discovery of gold in 1848.
Hours & Admission Prices: March-Oct. Tues.-Sun. 10-4; Nov.-Feb. Tues.-Sun. 10-3. Park $8 per car, $7 seniors; members no charge. Closed New Year's Day; Thanksgiving; Christmas. ⅃
Attendance: 250,000 (estimated)

Colton

AGUA MANSA PIONEER MEMORIAL CEMETERY, 2001 W. Agua Mansa Rd., Colton, CA 92324-3388. Mailing Address: c/o San Bernardino Co. Museums, 2024 Orange Tree Lane, Redlands, CA 92374. Tel.: 909-307-2669. Fax: 909-307-0539.
E-mail: rmckernan@sbcm.sbcounty.gov
Web Site: www.sbcountymuseum.org
Key Personnel: Dir., Robert McKernan; Cur., Michele Nielsen; Docent, Jason Bowe.
Institution Type/Description: Historic Site & Museum: 1854 cemetery.
Hours & Admission Prices: Fri. 12-3, Sat. 11-3, 1st Sun. of month 12-2. No charge; donations requested. Closed New Year's Day; Thanksgiving; Christmas. ⅃
Attendance: 2,300 (actual)

COLTON AREA MUSEUM & HISTORICAL SOCIETY, 380 N. La Cadena Dr., Colton, CA 92324-2928. Mailing Address: P.O. Box 1648, Colton, CA 92324-0851. Tel.: 909-824-8814 & 783-8817. Fax: 909-783-9241.

E-mail: info@coltonmuseum.net
Web Site: www.coltonmuseum.net
Formerly: Colton Area Museum
Key Personnel: Pres. (V), Michael L. Murphy; Museum Shop Mgr., Pam Gregory.
Institution Type/Description: History Museum & Historic Site: housed in 1908 Andrew Carnegie Library building.
Hours & Admission Prices: Wed. & Fri. 1-4, Sat. 11-2; tours by appointment. No charge; donations accepted. Closed major holidays. ⅃
Attendance: 1,000 (estimated)

Columbia

COLUMBIA STATE HISTORIC PARK, 11255 Jackson St., Columbia, CA 95310-9425. Tel.: 209-536-2916. Fax: 209-532-5064.
E-mail: info@parks.ca.gov
Web Site: www.parks.ca.gov
Key Personnel: Sector Supt., Greg Martin.
Institution Type/Description: State Park Museum.
Hours & Admission Prices: Daily 10-5. No charge. Closed Thanksgiving; Christmas. ⅃
Attendance: 467,000 (estimated)

Corona

CORONA HERITAGE PARK & MUSEUM, 510 W. Foothill Pkwy., Corona, CA 92882. Tel.: 951-898-0687.
E-mail: tom@alignarc.com
Web Site: www.coronaheritage.org
Institution Type/Description: History Museum.
Hours & Admission Prices: Tues.-Sat. 10-2. No charge; donations accepted.

FENDER MUSEUM OF MUSIC AND THE ARTS, 815 W. 6th St., Corona, CA 92882. Tel.: 951-735-2440. Fax: 951-735-2576. Facebook: Kids Rock Free.
E-mail: info@kidsrockfree.org
Web Site: kidsrockfree.org
Key Personnel: Bd. Pres., George Guayante; Exec Dir., Pamela Hogan.
Institution Type/Description: Music & Art Museum.
Hours & Admission Prices: Open to groups of 20 or more by appointment. Tour Package 1: $5. Tour Package 2: $10. ⅃
Attendance: 1,000 (estimated)

Corona del Mar

SHERMAN GARDENS, 2647 E. Coast Hwy., Corona del Mar, CA 92625-2103. Tel.: 949-673-2261. Fax: 949-675-5458.
E-mail: info@slgardens.org
Web Site: www.slgardens.org
Key Personnel: C.E.O., Donald Haskell; Pres. (V), Micky Pearlman; Library Dir., Dr. William O. Hendricks; Garden Dir., Wade Roberts; Business Officer, D.T. Daniels; Sales Shop Mgr., Peggy Schmidt.
Institution Type/Description: Historic Research Institute & Botanical Garden.
Hours & Admission Prices: Gardens: daily 10:30-4. Library: Tues.-Thurs. 9-4:30. Tours: adults $3, children $1; Mon., children 11 & under and members no charge. Closed New Year's Day; Thanksgiving; Christmas. ⅃
Attendance: 64,500 (actual)

Coronado

CORONADO HISTORICAL ASSOCIATION - MUSEUM OF HISTORY AND ART, 1100 Orange Ave., Coronado, CA 92118. Tel.: 619-435-7242; 866-599-7242.
E-mail: info@coronadohistory.org
Web Site: coronadohistory.org
Key Personnel: Pres. (V), Jane Braun; Museum Dir., Christine Stokes; Registrar, Stephanie Washburn.
Hours & Admission Prices: Mon.-Fri. 9-5, Sat.-Sun. 10-5. No charge; donations accepted.
Attendance: 86,500 (estimated)

Costa Mesa

COSTA MESA HISTORICAL SOCIETY & MUSEUM, 1870 Anaheim Ave., Costa Mesa, CA 92628. Mailing Address: P.O. Box 1764, Costa Mesa, CA 92628-1764. Tel.: 949-631-5918.
E-mail: cmhistory@sbcglobal.net
Web Site: costamesahistory.org
Formerly: Diego Sepulveda Adobe Estancia

Key Personnel: Pres. (V), B. Palazzola; Vice Pres., Terry Shaw; Treas., Susan Weeks; Sec., Gladys Refakes.
Institution Type/Description: History Museum.
Hours & Admission Prices: Adobe Tours: 1st & 3rd Sat. 12-4; other times by appointment. CMHS Headquarters & Museum: Thurs.-Fri. 10-3; other times by appointment. No charge; donations accepted.
Attendance: 350 (estimated)

Coulterville

NORTHERN MARIPOSA HISTORY CENTER, 10301 Hwy. 49, Coulterville, CA 95311. Tel.: 209-878-3015.
E-mail: info@coultervillehistorycenter.org
Web Site: coultervillehistorycenter.org
Institution Type/Description: History Museum.
Hours & Admission Prices: Wed.-Sun. 10-4; group tours by appointment.

Covina

H.H. DORJE CHANG BUDDHA III CULTURAL AND ART MUSEUM, 170 E. School St., Covina, CA 91723. Tel.: 626-281-6378. Fax: 626-281-3243.
E-mail: info@hhdcb3cam.org
Web Site: www.hhdcb3cam.org
Institution Type/Description: Cultural and Art Museum.
Hours & Admission Prices: Tues.-Sat. 10-5, Sun. 9:30-12. Closed New Year's Day; Independence Day; Thanksgiving; Christmas.

Crescent City

DEL NORTE COUNTY HISTORICAL SOCIETY, 577 H St., Crescent City, CA 95531-3743. Tel.: 707-464-3922. Fax: 707-464-7186.
E-mail: manager@delnortehistory.org
Web Site: www.delnortehistory.org
Key Personnel: Pres., Sean Smith; Vice Pres., Harlan Watkins.
Institution Type/Description: Historical Society & Maritime Museum: housed in 1926 County Hall of Records, Jail & Sheriff's office; Battery Point Lighthouse c.1856.
Hours & Admission Prices: Main Museum: May 15-Sept. 30 Mon.-Sat. 10-4; Oct.-May 14 Mon. & Sat. 10-4. Requested Donation: adults $3, children 5-17 $1. Lighthouse: April-Sept. daily 10-4 (tide permitting); Oct.-March Sat.-Sun. 10-4 (tide permitting). Adults $3, children 17 & under $1; members & children 4 and under no charge. Research: $5 per hour (by volunteer); $2 per hour (own research).
Attendance: 10,270 (actual)

REDWOOD NATIONAL AND STATE PARKS, 1111 Second St., Crescent City, CA 95531-4123. Tel.: 707-465-7335. Fax: 707-464-1812.
E-mail: redw_superintendent@nps.gov
Web Site: www.nps.gov/redw
Formerly: Redwood National Park
Key Personnel: Supt., Stephen Prokop.
Institution Type/Description: National Park.
Hours & Admission Prices: Open daily; Park Visitor & Information Centers: call or visit website for hours. No charge; donations accepted. Closed New Year's Day; Thanksgiving; Christmas. &
Attendance: 500,000 (estimated)

Culver City

CENTER FOR THE STUDY OF POLITICAL GRAPHICS (CSPG), 3916 Sepulveda Blvd., Ste. 103 & 104, Culver City, CA 90230. Tel.: 310-397-3100. Fax: 310-397-9305. Facebook, Instagram.
E-mail: admin@politicalgraphics.org
Web Site: www.politicalgraphics.org
Key Personnel: Exec. Dir. & Founder, Carol A. Wells; Archivist, Emily Sulzer; Office & Social Media Mgr., Jerri Allyn.
Institution Type/Description: Political Graphics Museum.
Hours & Admission Prices: Mon.-Fri. 9-6; other times by appointment. No charge; donations accepted. Closed holidays. &
Attendance: 3,500 (actual)

MAYME A. CLAYTON LIBRARY & MUSEUM, 4130 Overland Ave., Culver City, CA 90230-3734. Tel.: 310-202-1647. Fax: 310-202-5464.
E-mail: info@claytonmuseum.org
Web Site: www.claytonmuseum.org

Institution Type/Description: History Museum & Library.
Hours & Admission Prices: Tues.-Sat. 10:30-4.

MUSEUM OF JURASSIC TECHNOLOGY, 9341 Venice Blvd., Culver City, CA 90232-2621. Tel.: 310-836-6131.
E-mail: info@mjt.org
Web Site: www.mjt.org
Key Personnel: Museum Dir., David Wilson.
Institution Type/Description: Natural History Museum.
Hours & Admission Prices: Thurs. 2-8, Fri.-Sun. 12-6. Suggested Admission: adults $8, students & seniors $5; members and children 12 & under no charge. Closed New Year's Day; Thanksgiving; Christmas.
Attendance: 25,000 (estimated)

STAR ECO STATION, 10101 Jefferson Blvd., Culver City, CA 90232-3519. Tel.: 310-842-8060. Fax: 310-842-8245.
E-mail: ecostation@starinc.org
Web Site: www.ecostation.org
Key Personnel: Pres. & Exec. Dir., Katya Bozzi; Vice Pres. & Co-Founder, Erick Bozzi, II.
Institution Type/Description: Environmental Science Museum.
Hours & Admission Prices: Sat.-Sun. 10-4; other times by appointment. Adults $8, senior citizens 65 and over $7, children $6; children under 2 & members no charge. Closed New Year's Eve & Day; Easter; Independence Day; Thanksgiving; Christmas Eve & Day. &
Attendance: 100,000 (estimated)

THE WENDE MUSEUM, 5741 Buckingham Pkwy., Ste. E, Culver City, CA 90230-6520. Tel.: 310-216-1600. Fax: 310-216-1609. Facebook.
E-mail: info@wendemuseum.org
Web Site: www.wendemuseum.org
Key Personnel: Dir., Justinian Jampol.
Institution Type/Description: Art, History & Cultural Museum.
Hours & Admission Prices: Museum: Fri. 10-5. Vault Tour: 11:30-2. Wed.-Thurs. by appointment. No charge; donations accepted. Closed national holidays.
Attendance: 2,500 (estimated)

Cupertino

CALIFORNIA HISTORY CENTER & FOUNDATION, 21250 Stevens Creek Blvd., Cupertino, CA 95014-5702. Tel.: 408-864-8712.
E-mail: info@calhistory.org
Web Site: www.deanza.edu/califhistory
Key Personnel: Dir., Tom Izu; Staff & Curatorial Asst., Azha Simmons; Librarian & Archivist, Lisa Christiansen.
Institution Type/Description: History Museum.
Hours & Admission Prices: Sept.-June Tues.-Thurs. 9:30-12 & 1-4, Fri. by appointment. Center: no charge. Library: $5 daily; students & members no charge.
Attendance: 1,800 (estimated)

CUPERTINO HISTORICAL SOCIETY & MUSEUM, Quinlan Community Center, 10185 N. Stelling Rd., Cupertino, CA 95014-5732. Tel.: 408-973-1495.
E-mail: jennifer@cupertinohistoricalsociety.org
Web Site: www.cupertinohistoricalsociety.org
Key Personnel: Exec. Dir., Jennifer Furlong.
Institution Type/Description: Historical Society Museum.
Hours & Admission Prices: Wed.-Sat. 10-4. No charge, donation accepted. &
Attendance: 3,000 (actual)

EUPHRAT MUSEUM OF ART, De Anza College, 21250 Stevens Creek Blvd., Cupertino, CA 95014-5702. Tel.: 408-864-8836. Fax: 408-864-8738.
E-mail: rindfleischjanet@fhda.edu
Web Site: www.deanza.edu/euphrat
Key Personnel: Exec. Dir., Marie Fox Ellison; Dir., Jan Rindfleisch; Co Pres., Margaret Kung; Co Pres., Helen Lewis; Education, Diana Argabrite.
Institution Type/Description: Art Museum.
Hours & Admission Prices: late Sept. to mid-June Mon.-Thurs. 10-4; groups by appointment. No charge; donations accepted. &
Attendance: 10,000 (estimated)

FUJITSU PLANETARIUM AT DE ANZA COLLEGE, De Anza College, 21250 Stevens Creek Blvd., Cupertino, CA 95014-5797. Tel.: 408-864-8814.
E-mail: planetarium@deanza.edu
Web Site: www.planetarium.deanza.edu

Formerly: Minolta Planetarium
Institution Type/Description: Planetarium.
Hours & Admission Prices: Field Trips: Mon.-Fri. mornings. See website for Public Astronomy & Laser Light Show information. &

Dana Point

OCEAN INSTITUTE, 24200 Dana Point Harbor Dr., Dana Point, CA 92629-2723. Tel.: 949-496-2274. Fax: 949-496-4296. Facebook: Ocean Institute.
E-mail: oi@ocean-institute.org
Web Site: www.ocean-institute.org
Formerly: Orange County Marine Institute
Key Personnel: Pres., Dori Moorehead.
Institution Type/Description: Marine Science & Maritime History Center.
Hours & Admission Prices: Mon.-Fri. 10-4, Sat.-Sun. 10-3. Mon.-Fri.: adults $5; members no charge. Sat.-Sun.: adults $10, seniors and children 12 & under $7.50; members & children under 2 no charge. Closed major holidays. &
Attendance: 165,000 (estimated)

Danville

BLACKHAWK MUSEUM, 3700 Blackhawk Plaza Cir., Danville, CA 94506-4652. Tel.: 925-736-2280. Fax: 925-736-4818. Facebook: Blackhawk Museum.
E-mail: museum@blackhawkmuseum.org
Web Site: www.blackhawkmuseum.org
Formerly: Blackhawk Automotive Museum
Key Personnel: C.E.O. & Pres., Don Williams; Exec. Dir., Timothy P. McGrane; Programs Dir., Nora Wagner; Mktg. & Memberships, Jon Snyder.
Institution Type/Description: Automobile & History Museum.
Hours & Admission Prices: Wed.-Sun. 10-5. Adults $15, senior citizens 65 & up, military veterans & students w/I.D. $10; discounts to groups; active military personnel & children under 6 no charge. Closed New Year's Day; Thanksgiving; Christmas. &
Attendance: 75,000 (actual)

EUGENE O'NEILL NATIONAL HISTORIC SITE, Danville, CA 94526-0280. Mailing Address: P.O. Box 280, Danville, CA 94526-0280. Tel.: 925-838-0249 & 943-1531. Fax: 925-838-9471.
E-mail: euon_interpretation@nps.gov
Web Site: www.nps.gov/euon
Key Personnel: Chm. (V), Randy Harabin; Dir., Morgan Smith; Museum Shop Mgr., Nancy Pierce.
Institution Type/Description: National Historic Site: Tao House was the home of playwright Eugene O'Neill from 1937 to 1944.
Hours & Admission Prices: Wed.-Fri. & Sun. 10 & 2 by reservation only, Sat. 10, 12 & 2. No charge; donations accepted. &
Attendance: 3,475 (actual)

Davis

DAVIS ARTS CENTER, 1919 F St., Davis, CA 95616-1163. Mailing Address: P.O. Box 4340, Davis, CA 95617-4340. Tel.: 530-756-4100. Fax: 530-756-3041. Facebook.
E-mail: office@davisartscenter.org
Web Site: www.davisartscenter.org
Key Personnel: Dir., Stacie Frerichs.
Institution Type/Description: Art Center.
Hours & Admission Prices: Mon.-Thurs. 9:30-7, Fri. 9:30-5, Sat. 10-3. No charge. Closed New Year's Eve & Day; Memorial Day; Independence Day; Labor Day; Christmas Day & week. &
Attendance: 40,000 (estimated)

EXPLORIT SCIENCE CENTER, 3141 5th St., Davis, CA 95618-6534. Tel.: 530-756-0191.
E-mail: explorit@explorit.org
Web Site: www.explorit.org
Key Personnel: Pres. (V), Dr. Sheila Allen.
Institution Type/Description: Hands-On Science Center.
Hours & Admission Prices: Wed. & Fri.-Sun. 1-5. Admission $5; discounts to ASTC travel passport program members/Reciprocal admission program; members, teachers, children under 2 no charge. Closed New Year's Day; Memorial Day; Independence Day; Labor Day; Thanksgiving; Christmas. &
Attendance: 80,000 (actual)

HATTIE WEBER MUSEUM OF DAVIS, 445 C St., Davis, CA 95616-4102. Tel.: 530-758-5637 & 753-5959.
E-mail: rddd@dcn.org
Web Site: www.dcn.davis.ca.us/go/hattie

Key Personnel: Dir., Dennis Dingemans.
Institution Type/Description: History Museum.
Hours & Admission Prices: Wed. & Sat. 10-4; other times by appointment. No charge; donations accepted. &
Attendance: 2,800 (actual)

JAN SHREM AND MARIA MANETTI SHREM MUSEUM OF ART, UC Davis, One Shields Ave., Davis, CA 95616. Tel.: 530-752-8500.
E-mail: manettishrem@ucdavis.edu
Institution Type/Description: Art Gallery.
Hours & Admission Prices: Tues.-Wed. & Fri. 12-6, Thurs. 12-10, Sat.-Sun. 11-5. No charge.

JOHN NATSOULAS CENTER FOR THE ARTS, 521 1st St., Davis, CA 95616. Tel.: 530-756-3938. Fax: 530-756-3961.
E-mail: art@natsoulas.com
Web Site: www.natsoulas.com
Institution Type/Description: Art Gallery.
Hours & Admission Prices: Wed.-Thurs. 11-5, Fri. 11-10, Sat.-Sun. 12-5.

PENCE GALLERY, 212 D St., Davis, CA 95616-4513. Tel.: 530-758-3370. Fax: 530-758-4670.
E-mail: penceassistant@sbcglobal.net
Web Site: www.pencegallery.org
Key Personnel: Dir., Natalie Nelson; Asst. Dir., Eileen Hendren; Pres., Sue Smith; Preparator, Tim Barrera; Museum Shop Mgr., Cindy Ruff.
Institution Type/Description: Art Association Gallery.
Hours & Admission Prices: Tues.-Sun. 11:30-5, 1st Fri. each month 7pm-10pm, 2nd Fri. each month 6pm-9pm. Tickets: 1st Fri. 7pm-10pm $10. Closed major holidays. &
Attendance: 17,900 (estimated)

QUAIL RIDGE WILDERNESS CONSERVANCY, 25344 County Rd. 95, Davis, CA 95616. Tel.: 530-219-4477. Fax: 530-758-1316.
E-mail: quailrid@quailridge.org
Web Site: www.quailridge.org
Key Personnel: Exec. Dir., Frank W. Maurer.
Institution Type/Description: Conservancy.
Hours & Admission Prices: Call for hours.

R.M. BOHART MUSEUM OF ENTOMOLOGY, Dept. of Entomology & Nematology, University of California, One Shields Ave., Davis, CA 95616-8584. Tel.: 530-752-0493. Fax: 530-752-9464.
E-mail: bohart@ucdavis.edu
Web Site: bohart.ucdavis.edu
Key Personnel: Dir., Lynn S. Kimsey; Cur., Phil Ward; Collection Mgr., Steve Heydon; Museum Shop Mgr., M.F. Keller.
Institution Type/Description: Entomology Museum.
Hours & Admission Prices: Mon.-Thurs. 8-5. No charge; donations accepted. Closed holidays. &
Attendance: 4,000 (actual)

RICHARD L. NELSON GALLERY & THE FINE ARTS COLLECTION, UC DAVIS, Nelson Hall, Old Davis Rd., Davis, CA 95616-5270. Mailing Address: One Shields Ave., Davis, CA 95616. Tel.: 530-752-8500. Fax: 530-754-9112. Facebook: Nelson Gallery.
E-mail: nelsongallery@ucdavis.edu
Web Site: nelsongallery.ucdavis.edu
Key Personnel: Dir., Rachel Teague; Preparator, Kyle Monhollen; Registrar & Collections Mgr., Robin Bernhard; Asst. to the Dir., Katrina Wong.
Institution Type/Description: Art Gallery & Museum.
Hours & Admission Prices: Sat.-Thurs. 11-5; other times by appointment. No charge; donations accepted. Closed Martin Luther King Jr. Day; Presidents' Day; Independence Day; Thanksgiving; Christmas. &
Attendance: 7,000 (actual)

UC DAVIS ARBORETUM, Valley Oak Cottage (TB-32), La Rue Rd., UC Davis, Davis, CA 95616. Mailing Address: One Shields Ave., Davis, CA 95616-5200. Tel.: 530-752-4880. Fax: 530-752-5796.
E-mail: arboretum@ucdavis.edu
Web Site: arboretum.ucdavis.edu
Key Personnel: Dir., Kathleen Socolofsky; Dir. Planning & Collections, Mary T. Burke; Cur., Mia Ingolia; Supt. Emeritus, Warren G. Roberts; Dir. Horticulture, Ellen Zagory; Asst. Dir., Carmia Feldman; Asst. Dir. Horticulture, Emily

Griswold; GIS Project Mgr., Brian Morgan; Academic Coord., Elaine Fingerett; Administrative & Gifts Mgr., Judy Hayes.
Institution Type/Description: Arboretum.
Hours & Admission Prices: Gardens: daily 24 hours. Office: Mon.-Fri. 8-5. No charge. ♿
Attendance: 250,000 (estimated)

UC DAVIS DESIGN MUSEUM, Cruess Hall, One Shields Ave., Davis, CA 95616-5200. Tel.: 530-752-6150. Fax: 530-752-1392.
E-mail: designmuseum@ucdavis.edu
Web Site: www.designmuseum.ucdavis.edu
Formerly: University of California Design Museum
Key Personnel: Dir., Timothy McNeil.
Institution Type/Description: Design Museum.
Hours & Admission Prices: Mon.-Fri. 12-4, Sun. 2-4. No charge; donations accepted. Closed holidays & holiday weekends; university breaks. ♿
Attendance: 2,000 (estimated)

U.S. BICYCLING HALL OF FAME, 303 3rd St., Davis, CA 95616-4590. Tel.: 530-341-3263.
E-mail: info@usbhof.org
Web Site: usbhof.org
Key Personnel: Pres. Bd., Bob Bowen.
Institution Type/Description: Hall of Fame & Bicycling History Museum.
Hours & Admission Prices: Call for hours. Admission $5. ♿

Death Valley

DEATH VALLEY NATIONAL PARK VISITOR CENTER AND MUSEUMS, Death Valley National Park, Hwy. 190, Death Valley, CA 92328. Mailing Address: P.O. Box 579, Death Valley, CA 92328-0579. Tel.: 760-786-3200. Fax: 760-786-3246. TDD: 760-786-2471.
E-mail: blair_davenport@nps.gov
Web Site: www.nps.gov/deva
Formerly: Death Valley Visitor Center and Museums
Key Personnel: Supt., Kathy Billings.
Institution Type/Description: Park Visitor Center, Museum & Historic House.
Hours & Admission Prices: Furnace Creek Visitor Center: daily 8-5; Scotty's Castle Visitor Center: daily 8-5. Tour bus $25-$200, individual vehicles $20, walk-ins & bike-ins $10. Scotty's Castle: Adults $11, seniors (62 & over) $9, children (6-15) & adults with disabilities $6; discounts to Golden Age, Golden Eagle, & Golden Access card holders; children under 6 no charge. ♿
Attendance: 1,000,000 (estimated)

Delano

DELANO HERITAGE PARK, 330 Lexington, Delano, CA 93215-3602. Tel.: 661-725-6730. Fax: 661-725-2344.
E-mail: heritagepark1@aol.com
Key Personnel: Pres. (V), Peter Finocchiaro.
Institution Type/Description: Park Museum.
Hours & Admission Prices: Temporarily closed. Tours by appointment; guided tours for groups. No charge; donations accepted. ♿
Attendance: 1,750 (estimated)

Desert Hot Springs

CABOT'S PUEBLO MUSEUM FOUNDATION, 67-616 E. Desert View Ave., Desert Hot Springs, CA 92240. Mailing Address: P.O. Box 104, Desert Hot Springs, CA 92240-0104. Tel.: 760-329-7610. Fax: 760-329-2738.
E-mail: ginger.ridgway@cabotsmuseum.org
Web Site: www.cabotsmuseum.org
Formerly: Cabot's Pueblo Museum
Key Personnel: Dir., Ginger Ridgway; Pres. (V), Mike Chedester; Museum Shop Mgr., Dean Krumme.
Institution Type/Description: Historic House Museum; housed in the former pueblo-style home of Cabot Yerxa.
Hours & Admission Prices: Winter: Tues.-Sun. 9-4, adults $15, military, seniors & children 6-12 $13; Summer: Wed.-Sat. 9-1. Guided Tours: adults $10, military, seniors & children 6-12 $5. Closed major holidays.
Attendance: 9,323 (actual)

Dinuba

ALTA DISTRICT HISTORICAL SOCIETY - DEPOT MUSEUM, 289 S. "K" St., Dinuba, CA 93618. Mailing Address: P.O. Box 254, Dinuba, CA 93618. Tel.: 559-591-2144. Fax: 559-591-2144.
E-mail: altahistorical@yahoo.com
Institution Type/Description: Historical Society Museum; housed in the former Dinuba Southern Pacific Depot; built in 1888.
Hours & Admission Prices: Tues.-Wed. by appointment. No charge; donations accepted.

Donner Pass

WESTERN SKISPORT MUSEUM, Interstate 80 Boreal Ridge Ski Area, Donner Pass, CA 95728. Mailing Address: P.O. Box 729, Soda Springs, CA 95728-0729. Tel.: 530-426-3313, ext. 101. Fax: 530-426-3501.
E-mail: bclark@inc.auburnskiclub.org
Web Site: www.auburnskiclub.org
Key Personnel: Dir., Bill Clark.
Institution Type/Description: Ski History Museum.
Hours & Admission Prices: Winter: Fri.-Sun. 10-4; call for extended hours. No charge; donations accepted. ♿
Attendance: 5,000 (estimated)

Downey

COLUMBIA MEMORIAL SPACE CENTER, 12400 Columbia Way, Downey, CA 90242. Tel.: 562-231-1200. Fax: 562-231-1206.
E-mail: bdickow@downeyspacecenter.org
Web Site: www.columbiaspacescience.org
Key Personnel: Exec. Dir., Benjamin Dickow; Center Supvr., Sandra Valencia; Center Suprvr., Sarah Medina.
Institution Type/Description: Space Museum.
Hours & Admission Prices: Tues.-Sat. 10-5. Adults $5, with ID: seniors 65 & over, teachers, veterans $3; discounts to groups of 15 or more; members, ASTC members and children 3 & under no charge. ♿
Attendance: 39,604 (actual)

DOWNEY HISTORICAL SOCIETY, 12540 Rives Ave., Downey, CA 90241. Mailing Address: P.O. Box 554, Downey, CA 90241. Tel.: 562-862-2777.
E-mail: downeyhistorycenter@gmail.com
Institution Type/Description: Historical Society Museum.
Hours & Admission Prices: Wed.-Thurs. & 3rd Sat. of the month 10-2.

Downieville

DOWNIEVILLE MUSEUM, 330 Main St., Downieville, CA 95936. Mailing Address: P.O. Box 1, Downieville, CA 95936. Tel.: 530-289-3506.
E-mail: hangman@jps.net
Key Personnel: Dir. & Chm. (V), Earlene Folsom; Treas., Lee Adams; Volunteer, Liz Fisher; Paid Staff, Donald McIntosh; Volunteer, L. Adams, III; Volunteer, Jane Hallman; Volunteer, David Marshall.
Institution Type/Description: General Museum; housed in 1852 store.
Hours & Admission Prices: May to mid-Oct. Mon.-Fri. 11-4, Sat.-Sun. 10-5. Suggested Donation: adults $1.
Attendance: 6,500 (actual)

Duarte

DUARTE HISTORICAL SOCIETY AND MUSEUM, 777 Encanto Pkwy., Duarte, CA 91010. Mailing Address: P.O. Box 263, Duarte, CA 91009-0263. Tel.: 626-357-9419. famheller@msn.com.
E-mail: famheller@msn.com
Web Site: www.duartehistory.org
Key Personnel: Pres. (V), Claudia Heller.
Institution Type/Description: History Museum.
Hours & Admission Prices: 1st & 3rd Wed. of the month 1-3, Sat. 1-4. No charge; donations accepted. Closed holidays.
Attendance: 1,200 (actual)

THE JUSTICE PRIVATE AUTOMOTIVE COLLECTION, 2734 Huntington Dr., Duarte, CA 91010-2301. Tel.: 626-359-9174. Fax: 626-357-2550. Facebook: @justiceprivateautomotivecollection.
E-mail: museum@justicebrothers.com
Web Site: www.justiceprivatecollection.com
Formerly: Justice Brothers Racing Museum and Private Collection
Key Personnel: C.E.O. & Pres., Ed Justice, Jr.; Museum Shop Mgr., Caitlin Justice.
Institution Type/Description: Racing Museum.
Hours & Admission Prices: Mon.-Fri. 9-5. No charge. Closed business holidays. ♿

Durham

PATRICK RANCH MUSEUM, 10381 Midway, Durham, CA 95938. Tel.: 530-892-1525 & 342-4359. Facebook.
E-mail: karen@patrickranchmuseum.org
Web Site: www.farwestheritage.org & www.patrickranchmuseum.org
Key Personnel: Pres. (V), Susan Donohue; Mgr., Karen Lobach; Treas., Jack Thorpe; Office Mgr., Valerie Wolfe.
Institution Type/Description: History Museum.
Hours & Admission Prices: Sat.-Sun. 11-3. Home Tour: $5. Visitor Center: no charge. &

Eagle Rock

EAGLE ROCK VALLEY HISTORICAL SOCIETY, The Center for the Arts, Eagle Rock, 2225 Colorado Blvd., Eagle Rock, CA 90041. Tel.: 323-257-1357.
E-mail: webmaster@eaglerockhistory.org
Web Site: eaglerockhistory.org
Institution Type/Description: Historical Society Museum.
Hours & Admission Prices: Sat. 10 to noon.

Edwards AFB

AIR FORCE FLIGHT TEST MUSEUM, 405 S. Rosamond Blvd., Edwards AFB, CA 93524. Mailing Address: 412 TW/MU, 405 S. Rosamond Blvd., Edwards AFB, CA 93524. Tel.: 661-277-8050 & 3510 (Public Rels.). Fax: 805-277-8051.
E-mail: museum@edwards.af.mil
Web Site: www.edwardsmuseum.org
Key Personnel: Dir. & Cur., George Welsh.
Institution Type/Description: Aeronautics Museum.
Hours & Admission Prices: Tues.-Sat. 9-5. No charge; donations accepted. Closed federal holidays. &
Attendance: 33,000 (actual)

El Cajon

COMMEMORATIVE AIR FORCE AIR GROUP ONE MUSEUM, Gillespie Field, 1905 N. Marshall Ave., Hangar #6, El Cajon, CA 92020. Mailing Address: 1921 N. Marshall Ave., Hangar #13, El Cajon, CA 92020. Tel.: 619-259-5541.
E-mail: airgroupone@gmail.com
Web Site: www.ag1caf.org
Key Personnel: Air Show Chm., Robert Simon; Wing Leader, Jim McGarvie; Museum Shop Mgr., Dave Hanson.
Institution Type/Description: Military History Museum.
Hours & Admission Prices: Call for hours. No charge; donations accepted.
Attendance: 500 (estimated)

GROSSMONT COLLEGE HYDE ART GALLERY, Physical/ Mailing Address: 8800 Grossmont College Dr., Bldg. 25, El Cajon, CA 92020. Tel.: 619-644-7299. Fax: 619-644-7922. Facebook, Instagram.
E-mail: alex.decosta@gccd.edu
Web Site: hydeartgallery.com
Key Personnel: Dir. & Cur., Alex DeCosta; Professor, Jennifer Bennett; Art Dept. Chm., Marion De Koning.
Institution Type/Description: Art Gallery.
Hours & Admission Prices: Mon.-Thurs. 10-6, Fri. by appointment. No charge. Closed all legal holidays. &
Attendance: 12,000 (estimated)

HERITAGE OF THE AMERICAS MUSEUM, 12110 Cuyamaca College Dr., W., El Cajon, CA 92019-4317. Tel.: 619-670-5194. Fax: 844-210-7423.
E-mail: hofam@sbcglobal.net
Web Site: www.heritageoftheamericasmuseum.org
Key Personnel: Exec. Dir., Kathleen Oatsvall; Chm. (V), Ronald Raymond.
Institution Type/Description: History Museum.
Hours & Admission Prices: Tues.-Fri. 10-4, Sat. 12-4. Adults $3, senior citizens $2; discount to AAM, ICOM & AAA members; youths under 17 & accompanied by an adult & members no charge. &
Attendance: 20,000 (actual)

KNOX HOUSE MUSEUM, 280 N. Magnolia Ave., El Cajon, CA 92020-3906. Mailing Address: P.O. Box 1973, El Cajon, CA 92022-1973. Tel.: 619-444-3800.
E-mail: info@knoxmuseum.org

Web Site: www.elcajonhistory.org
Key Personnel: Pres. (V), Carla L. Nowak.
Institution Type/Description: Historical House Museum: built in 1876.
Hours & Admission Prices: Tours: Sat. 11-2. No charge; donations accepted.

TAYLOR FACTORY TOUR, 1980 Gillespie Way, El Cajon, CA 92020. Tel.: 800-943-6782; 619-258-1207.
Web Site: taylorguitars.com
Institution Type/Description: Company Museum.
Hours & Admission Prices: Visitor Center: Mon.-Fri. 10-4. Factory Tours: Mon.-Fri. 1 pm; groups of 10 or more by appointment. No charge. Closed national holidays.

El Monte

EL MONTE HISTORICAL SOCIETY MUSEUM, 3150 Tyler Ave., El Monte, CA 91731-3354. Mailing Address: 3150 N. Tyler, El Monte, CA 91731-3354. Tel.: 626-444-3813 & 580-2232. Fax: 626-444-8142.
E-mail: museum@elmonteca.gov
Key Personnel: Cur., Donna Crippen.
Institution Type/Description: History Museum.
Hours & Admission Prices: Tues.-Fri. 10-4; tours by appointment. No charge; donations requested. Closed national holidays. &

El Segundo

AUTOMOBILE DRIVING MUSEUM, 610 Lairport St., El Segundo, CA 90245-5004. Tel.: 310-909-0950. Fax: 310-658-5286.
E-mail: tomz@theadm.org
Web Site: www.theadm.org
Key Personnel: Pres. (V) & Cur., Earl Rubenstein; Pres. (V), Mitch Feinstein; C.E.O., Tom Zimmerman; Operations, Jodee Hulsebus.
Institution Type/Description: Transportation Museum.
Hours & Admission Prices: Tues.-Sun. 10-4. No charge; $10 donations accepted. Closed holidays. &
Attendance: 6,000 (estimated)

Encinitas

ENCINITAS HISTORICAL SOCIETY, 390 W. F St., Encinitas, CA 92024. Tel.: 760-942-9066.
E-mail: info@encinitashistoricalsociety.org
Web Site: encinitashistoricalsociety.org
Key Personnel: Pres., Carolyn Cope; Vice Pres., Dayna Donatelli; Sec., Connie McIntire; Treas., Pam Walker.
Institution Type/Description: Historical Society Museum: housed in a one-room schoolhouse; built in 1883.
Hours & Admission Prices: Fri.-Sat. 1-4. No charge; donations accepted. Closed holidays.

LUX ART INSTITUTE, 1550 S. El Camino Real, Encinitas, CA 92024-4908. Tel.: 760-436-6611. Fax: 760-436-1400.
E-mail: info@luxartinstitute.org
Web Site: www.luxartinstitute.org
Key Personnel: Dir., Reesey Shaw; Chm. (V), Wally Dieckmann; Museum Shop Mgr., Grace Chen; Museum Shop Mgr., Farrah Emammi.
Institution Type/Description: Art Museum.
Hours & Admission Prices: Thurs.-Fri. 1-5, Sat. 11-5. Adults $5; discounts to AAM members; members & under 21 no charge. &
Attendance: 1,800 (estimated)

SAN DIEGO BOTANIC GARDEN, 230 Quail Gardens Dr., Encinitas, CA 92024-2707. Mailing Address: P.O. Box 230005, Encinitas, CA 92023-0005. Tel.: 760-436-3036. Fax: 760-632-0917. Facebook.
E-mail: info@sdbgarden.org
Web Site: www.sdbgarden.org
Formerly: Quail Botanical Gardens
Key Personnel: Pres. & C.E.O., Julian Duval; Bd. Chm., Sharon May-Low; Dir. Operations, Ian Cole; Garden Shop Mgr., Jill Gardner.
Institution Type/Description: Botanical Garden.
Hours & Admission Prices: Daily 9-5. Adults $14, seniors, students & military $10, children 3-12 $8; children under 2 no charge. Parking: $2. &
Attendance: 250,000 (estimated)

SAN DIEGUITO HERITAGE MUSEUM, 450 Quail Gardens Dr., Encinitas, CA 92024-2711. Tel.: 760-632-9711. Fax: 760-632-5695.
E-mail: barb@sdheritage.org
Web Site: www.sdheritage.org
Key Personnel: Exec. Dir., Barb Grice; Pres., Ralph Stone.
Institution Type/Description: History Museum.
Hours & Admission Prices: Thurs.-Sun. 12-4. Adults $4, students & seniors $3; young children, military & members no charge. Closed holidays. Ꝺ
Attendance: 9,000 (estimated)

Escondido

CALIFORNIA CENTER FOR THE ARTS, ESCONDIDO MUSEUM, 340 N. Escondido Blvd., Escondido, CA 92025-2600. Tel.: 760-839-4120. Fax: 760-739-0205.
Web Site: www.artcenter.org
Key Personnel: Exec. Dir., Jerry Van Leeuwen.
Institution Type/Description: Art Museum.
Hours & Admission Prices: Tues.-Sat. 10-5, Sun. 1-5. Adults $8, senior citizens & students $5, students $3; discounts to groups, AAM & ICOM members; children 12 & under, military and members no charge. Closed major holidays. Ꝺ
Attendance: 8,200 (actual)

DEER PARK ESCONDIDO WINERY & AUTO MUSEUM, 29013 Champagne Blvd., Escondido, CA 92026-6002. Tel.: 760-749-1666.
E-mail: mail@deerparkwine.com
Web Site: www.deerparkwine.com
Key Personnel: Owner, Clark Knapp.
Institution Type/Description: Winery & Automobile Museum.
Hours & Admission Prices: Summer: Fri.-Sun. 10-5; Winter: Fri.-Sun. 10-4; call to confirm. Adults $10, seniors 55 & over, AAA members and active military $9; discounts to groups of 10 or more; children 9 & under no charge. Closed holidays.
Attendance: 75,000 (actual)

ESCONDIDO CHILDREN'S MUSEUM DBA SAN DIEGO CHILDREN'S DISCOVERY MUSEUM, 320 N. Broadway, Escondido, CA 92025-2716. Tel.: 760-233-7755. Fax: 760-888-1934.
E-mail: info@sdcdm.org
Web Site: www.sdcdm.org
Key Personnel: Exec. Dir., Javier Guerrero; Exec. Dir. Asst., Rebecca Greene; Mktg. & Events Mgr., Rebecca Greene; Operations & Store Mgr., Kristen Hawkes; Museum Education & Program Mgr., Lindy Villa; Devel. Mgr., Wendy Taylor; Exhibit Mgr., Bill Schmidt.
Institution Type/Description: Children's Museum.
Hours & Admission Prices: Mon.-Sun. 9:30-4:30. Admission $6; discounts to military, educators & special needs children; members & children under one no charge. Closed New Year's Day; Easter; Memorial Day; Independence Day; Labor Day; Thanksgiving; Christmas.

ESCONDIDO HISTORY CENTER, 321 N. Broadway, Escondido, CA 92025-2704. Mailing Address: P.O. Box 263, Escondido, CA 92033-0263. Tel.: 760-743-8207. Fax: 760-743-8267. Facebook: Escondido History Center.
E-mail: barker@escondidohistory.org
Web Site: www.escondidohistory.org
Formerly: Heritage Walk Museum
Key Personnel: Pres., Rod McLeod; Exec. Dir., Wendy Barker; Treas., Bob Johnson; Registrar, Marie Tuck.
Institution Type/Description: Local History Museum: housed in 1894 library & 1888 Santa Fe Railroad Depot; 1890 Victorian house, barn & working blacksmith shop; railroad car with model train layout.
Hours & Admission Prices: Office: Tues., Wed., Thurs. & Sat. 10-4. Museum: Tues.-Sat. 1-4. Suggested Donations: adults $3, children $1; members no charge. Closed holidays. Ꝺ
Attendance: 18,000 (estimated)

LAWRENCE WELK MUSEUM, 8860 Lawrence Welk Dr., Escondido, CA 92026-6403. Tel.: 760-749-3000, ext. 22146.
E-mail: box.office@welktheatre.com
Web Site: www.welktheatresandiego.com
Institution Type/Description: History Museum.
Hours & Admission Prices: Daily 10-5; call to verify. No charge.

SAN DIEGO ARCHAEOLOGICAL CENTER, 16666 San Pasqual Valley Rd., Escondido, CA 92027-7001. Tel.: 760-291-0370. Fax: 760-291-0371.
E-mail: info@sandiegoarchaeology.org
Web Site: www.sandiegoarchaeology.org
Key Personnel: Dir., Cindy Stankowski, M.A.; Pres. (V), Robert Case; Collections Mgr., Ad Muniz, Ph.D.; Public Archaeology Dir., Stephanie Sandoval; Mktg. & Devel. Coord., Cheryl Castro.
Institution Type/Description: Archaeology Museum.
Hours & Admission Prices: Mon.-Fri. 9-4, Sat. 10-2. Suggested Donation: family $5, individual $2. Closed New Year's Day; Thanksgiving; Christmas.
Attendance: 5,000 (actual)

SAN DIEGO CHILDREN'S DISCOVERY MUSEUM, 320 N. Broadway Blvd., Escondido, CA 92025. Tel.: 760-233-7755.
Institution Type/Description: Children's Museum.
Hours & Admission Prices: Tues.-Sun. 10-4. Admission 12 months & over $5; discounts to military & disabled; children under one no charge. Closed New Year's Day; Easter; Memorial Day; Labor Day; Thanksgiving; Christmas Eve & Day.

SAN DIEGO ZOO SAFARI PARK, 15500 San Pasqual Valley Rd., Escondido, CA 92027-7017. Mailing Address: P.O. Box 120551, San Diego, CA 92112-0551. Tel.: 760-738-5018 & 747-8702. Fax: 760-746-7081.
Web Site: www.sdzsafaripark.org
Formerly: San Diego Zoo's Wild Animal Park
Key Personnel: Pres. & C.E.O., Douglas Meyers; C.O.O., Matthew Musella; C.F.O., Paula Brock; Chief Devel. & Membership Officer, Mark Stuart; Safari Park Dir., Robert M. McClure; Chief Conservation & Research Officer, Allison Alberts, Ph.D.; Chief Life Sciences Officer, Robert J. Weiss, Ph.D.; Corp. Dir. Animal Health, Donald Janssen, D.V.M.; Corp. Dir. Mktg., Ted Molter; Chief HR Officer, Tim Mulligan; Chief Technology Officer, Robert Erhardt.
Institution Type/Description: Wildlife Preserve.
Hours & Admission Prices: Jan.-June & Sept.-Dec. 9-5; July & Aug. 9-7; hours may vary & subject to change. Adults $48, children 3-11 $38; discounts to qualifying groups; members and children 2 & under no charge. Ꝺ
Attendance: 1,500,000 (estimated)

Eureka

CLARKE HISTORICAL MUSEUM, 240 E St., Eureka, CA 95501-0433. Tel.: 707-443-1947. Fax: 707-443-0290. Facebook: Clarke Historical Museum.
E-mail: clarkehistorical@att.net
Web Site: www.clarkemuseum.org
Formerly: Clarke Memorial Museum, Inc.
Key Personnel: Dir. & Cur., Ben Brown; Pres. (V), Roy Sheppard; Treas., Wendy Wahlund; Office & Events Mgr. & Museum Shop Mgr., Jacqui Langeland; Registrar, Art Barab; Registrar, Jerab Pino; Pres. (V), Ray Sheppard; Museum Shop Mgr., Amber Mitchel.
Institution Type/Description: Regional History Museum.
Hours & Admission Prices: Suggested donation: Individual $5, Family $10. Ꝺ
Attendance: 16,000 (actual)

COLLEGE OF THE REDWOODS ART GALLERY, 7351 Tompkins Hill Rd., Creative Arts Bldg., Eureka, CA 95501-9300. Tel.: 707-476-4558 & 4137.
E-mail: cindy-hooper@redwoods.edu
Web Site: www.redwoods.edu/departments/art/gallery/index.htm
Key Personnel: Dir., Charissa Schulze; Head Art Dept., Cindy Hooper.
Institution Type/Description: Art Gallery.
Hours & Admission Prices: Call for hours. No charge. Closed during academic breaks.
Attendance: 2,500 (estimated)

THE DISCOVERY MUSEUM, 612 G St., Ste. 102, Eureka, CA 95501. Tel.: 707-443-9694. Fax: 707-443-7242.
E-mail: info@discovery-museum.org
Web Site: www.discovery-museum.org
Key Personnel: Exec. Dir., Grace Hamaker.
Institution Type/Description: Children's Museum.
Hours & Admission Prices: Tues.-Sat. 10-4, Sun. 12-4. Admission 2 & over $5; members & children under 2 no charge.

GROSS-WELLS BARNUM HOUSE - HUMBOLDT COUNTY HISTORICAL SOCIETY, 703 8th St., Eureka, CA 95502. Tel.: 707-445-4342. Fax: 707-445-4146.
E-mail: info@humboldthistory.org
Web Site: www.humboldthistory.org

Institution Type/Description: Historical Society Museum: housed in the former home of Helen Wells Barnum; built in 1902.
Hours & Admission Prices: Tues.-Wed. & Fri. 12-4, Thurs. 4-8.

HUMBOLDT ARTS COUNCIL/MORRIS GRAVES MUSEUM OF ART, 636 F St., Eureka, CA 95501-1012. Tel.: 707-442-0278. Fax: 707-442-2040.
E-mail: jemima@humboldtarts.org
Web Site: www.humboldtarts.org
Key Personnel: Pres. (V) & C.E.O., Sally Arnot; Cur., Jemima J. Harr.
Institution Type/Description: Art Museum.
Hours & Admission Prices: Wed.-Sun. 12-5. No charge; donations accepted. Closed New Year's Day; Easter; Independence Day; Thanksgiving; Christmas.
Attendance: 26,000 (actual)

HUMBOLDT BOTANICAL GARDEN, 7707 Tompkins Hill Rd., Eureka, CA 95503. Mailing Address: P.O. Box 6117, Eureka, CA 95502. Tel.: 707-442-5139. Fax: 707-442-6634.
E-mail: susantissot@hbgf.org
Web Site: www.hbgf.org
Key Personnel: Exec. Dir., Susan Tissot.
Institution Type/Description: Botanical Garden.
Hours & Admission Prices: April-Oct. Wed.-Sun. 10-4; Nov.-March Wed.-Sat. 10-2, Sun. 11-3; other times by appointment. Adults $8, children 6-17, seniors, & active military $5; children 5 & under no charge.

WOODEN SCULPTURE GARDEN OF ROMANO GABRIEL, 315 Second St., Eureka, CA 95502-1354. Mailing Address: Eureka Heritage Society, P.O. Box 1354, Eureka, CA 95502-1354. Tel.: 707-445-8775 & 442-8937.
E-mail: info@eurekaheritage.org
Web Site: eurekaheritage.org
Institution Type/Description: Folk Art Museum.
Hours & Admission Prices: Call for hours.

Fair Oaks

FAIR OAKS HISTORICAL SOCIETY, 10340 Fair Oaks Blvd, Fair Oaks, CA 95628. Mailing Address: P.O. Box 2044, Fair Oaks, CA 95628-2044. Tel.: 916-961-6561. fairoakshistory1@gmail.com.
E-mail: webhost@fairoakshistory.org
Web Site: fairoakshistory.org
Key Personnel: Pres. (V), Joe Dobrowolski.
Institution Type/Description: Historical Society Museum.
Hours & Admission Prices: Wed.-Sun. 10-4. No charge; donations accepted. &
Attendance: 520 (actual)

Fairfax

MARIN MUSEUM OF BICYCLING AND MOUNTAIN BIKE HALL OF FAME, 1966 Sir Francis Drake Blvd., Fairfax, CA 94930. Tel.: 415-450-8000. Fax: 415-483-7102.
Web Site: mmbhof.org
Institution Type/Description: Sports Museum.
Hours & Admission Prices: mid-Jan. to Dec. Thurs.-Sun. 11-5. Adults $10; seniors, military & disabled $8; youth 12-17 $5; children 6-11 $3; children 5 & under, museum members & Hall of Fame inductees no charge. Closed New Year's Day; Thanksgiving; Christmas Eve & Day.

Fairfield

JELLY BELLY CANDY COMPANY FACTORY TOURS, 1 Jelly Belly Ln., Fairfield, CA 94533. Tel.: 800-522-3267.
Web Site: jellybelly.com
Institution Type/Description: Company History & Tours.
Hours & Admission Prices: Visitor Center daily 9-5. Factory Tours: daily 9:15-4. Self-Guided Tour: no charge. Guided Tour: $39 for groups of 1-6; by appointment. Closed New Year's Day; Easter; Thanksgiving; Christmas. &

Fall River Mills

FORT CROOK HISTORICAL MUSEUM, 43030 Fort Crook Museum Ave., Fall River Mills, CA 96028. Mailing Address: Box 397, Fall River Mills, CA 96028-0397. Tel.: 530-336-5110.
E-mail: fortcrook@frontiernet.net
Web Site: www.fortcrook.com
Key Personnel: Pres., Larry Burns; Cur., Sharon Hamblin; Museum Shop Mgr., Debbie Lakey.

Institution Type/Description: General Museum.
Hours & Admission Prices: May-Oct. Tues.-Sun. 12-4; other times by appointment. No charge; donations accepted.
Attendance: 3,200 (estimated)

Fallbrook

FALLBROOK HISTORICAL SOCIETY, 1730 S. Hill St., Fallbrook, CA 92028. Mailing Address: P.O. Box 1375, Fallbrook, CA 92088-1375. Tel.: 760-723-4125. Facebook.
E-mail: roymoosa@att.net
Key Personnel: Pres. (V), Roy Moosa.
Institution Type/Description: Historical Society Museum.
Hours & Admission Prices: Sun. & Thurs. 1-4. No charge. &

Felicity

MUSEUM OF HISTORY IN GRANITE, Two Center of the World Plaza, Felicity, CA 92283-7777. Tel.: 760-572-0100. Fax: 760-572-3000.
E-mail: museumforever@gmail.com
Web Site: historyingranite.org
Key Personnel: Chm. (V), Jacques Andre Istel; Treas., Felicia Lee; Museum Shop Mgr., Debra Pavey.
Institution Type/Description: History Museum.
Hours & Admission Prices: Outdoor Exhibits: daily. Shop & Restaurant: Thanksgiving to Easter. Adults $5. &
Attendance: 10,000 (estimated)

Felton

BIGFOOT DISCOVERY MUSEUM, 5497 Hwy. 9, Felton, CA 95018. Tel.: 831-335-4478.
Key Personnel: Cur., Michael Rugg.
Institution Type/Description: General Museum.
Hours & Admission Prices: Wed.-Mon. 11-6. No charge; donations accepted.

Ferndale

FERN COTTAGE FOUNDATION, 2121 Centerville Rd., Ferndale, CA 95536-1286. Mailing Address: P.O. Box 1286, Ferndale, CA 95536-1286. Tel.: 707-786-4835. Facebook.
E-mail: info@ferncottage.org
Web Site: www.ferncottage.org
Key Personnel: Chm., Amy Whitlatch.
Institution Type/Description: Historic House Museum: Russ family farm house, built in 1866.
Hours & Admission Prices: Tours: Thurs.-Sat. 11, 12, 1 & 2. Adults $10.

FERNDALE MUSEUM, 515 Shaw Ave., Ferndale, CA 95536. Mailing Address: P.O. Box 431, Ferndale, CA 95536-0431. Tel.: 707-786-4466.
E-mail: ferndalemuseum@gmail.com
Web Site: www.ferndale-museum.org
Key Personnel: Dir., Don Andersen; Pres (V), Kirk Gothier.
Institution Type/Description: History Museum.
Hours & Admission Prices: Feb.-May & Oct.-Dec. Wed.-Sat. 11-4, Sun. 1-4; June-Sept. Tues.-Sat. 11-4, Sun. 1-4. Adults $1; members no charge. &
Attendance: 3,000 (actual)

Fillmore

FILLMORE HISTORICAL MUSEUM, INC., 350 Main St., Fillmore, CA 93015-2040. Mailing Address: P.O. Box 314, Fillmore, CA 93016-0314. Tel.: 805-524-0948. Fax: 805-524-0516.
E-mail: fillmore.museum@sbcglobal.net
Web Site: fillmorehistoricalmuseum.com
Key Personnel: Dir., Chair (V) & Research Librarian, Martha Gentry; Chm. (V), Jack Stethem.
Institution Type/Description: General Historical Museum.
Hours & Admission Prices: Tues.-Fri. 10-4, Sat. 10:30-3. No charge; donations accepted.
Attendance: 4,402 (estimated)

Firebaugh

HERITAGE OF EAGLES AIR MUSEUM, Eagle Field, 11163 N. Eagle Ave., Firebaugh, CA 93622. Mailing Address: 5543 Mint Rd., Dos Palos, CA 93620. Tel.: 209-364-6132.
Web Site: www.b25.net/museum/hpages/museum.html
Institution Type/Description: Military History Museum: housed on the Eagle Field Army Air Forces Training Base; built in 1942.
Hours & Admission Prices: Call for hours.

Folsom

THE FOLSOM CITY ZOO SANCTUARY, 403 Stafford St., Folsom, CA 95630-2643. Tel.: 916-351-3527.
E-mail: kbanyard@folsom.ca.us
Web Site: www.folsom.ca.us/depts/parks_n_recreation/zoo.asp
Key Personnel: Zoo Mgr., Jocelyn Smeltzer; Zoo Education, Vicki Valentine.
Institution Type/Description: Zoo.
Hours & Admission Prices: June-Aug. Tues.-Sun. 9-3; Sept.-May Tues.-Sun. 10-4. Adults 13 & over $5, senior citizens 55 & over and children 2-12 $4; children under 2 no charge.

FOLSOM, EL DORADO & SACRAMENTO HISTORICAL RAILROAD ASSOCIATION, 198 Wood St., Folsom, CA 95630. Tel.: 916-985-6001.
E-mail: feds@fedshra.org
Web Site: www.fedshra.org
Key Personnel: Pres. (V), Bill Anderson.
Institution Type/Description: History Museum.
Hours & Admission Prices: Sat.-Sun. 11-4. Adults $2.

FOLSOM HISTORY MUSEUM, 823 Sutter St., Folsom, CA 95630-2440. Tel.: 916-985-2707. Fax: 916-985-7288.
E-mail: info@folsomhistorymuseum.org
Web Site: www.folsomhistorymuseum.org
Key Personnel: C.E.O. & Dir., Mary Mast; Chm. (V), Patrick Maxfield; Museum Shop Mgr., Pam Conrad.
Institution Type/Description: Historical Society Museum: site of Pony Express terminus from June 1860 to October 1861; Wells Fargo Assay Office, 1860-1871.
Hours & Admission Prices: Memorial Day to Labor Day daily 11-4; Sept.-May Tues.-Sun. 11-4. Research: by appointment. Adults $4, youth $2; members no charge. Closed New Year's Day; Easter; Mother's Day; Thanksgiving; Christmas. &
Attendance: 18,500 (estimated)

Fontana

MARY VAGLE NATURE CENTER, 11501 Cypress Ave., Fontana, CA 92337. Mailing Address: Community Services, 16860 Valencia Ave., Fontana, CA 92335. Tel.: 909-349-6994.
E-mail: rdean@fontana.org
Web Site: www.fontana.org/index.aspx?NID=196
Key Personnel: Community Services Coord., Rick Dean.
Institution Type/Description: Nature Center.
Hours & Admission Prices: Wed.-Sun. 12-5. No charge; donations accepted. Closed Federal holidays.

Foresthill

FORESTHILL DIVIDE MUSEUM, 24601 Harrison St., Foresthill, CA 95631. Mailing Address: The Forest Hill Divide Historical Society, P.O. Box 646, Foresthill, CA 95631-0646. Tel.: 530-367-3988.
E-mail: placerhistorical@gmail.com
Web Site: mmoffet.mystarband.net/museum.htm
Institution Type/Description: History Museum.
Hours & Admission Prices: mid-May to mid-Oct. Sat.-Sun. & major holidays 12-4. No charge; donations accepted.

Fort Bragg

THE GUEST HOUSE MUSEUM, 343 N. Main St., Fort Bragg, CA 95437. Mailing Address: P.O. Box 71, Fort Bragg, CA 95437-0071. Tel.: 707-964-4251 & 2404.
E-mail: dmaki@mcn.org
Web Site: www.fortbragghistory.org
Key Personnel: C.E.O. & Pres. (V), Mark Ruedrich; Museum Shop Mgr., David Maki.
Institution Type/Description: Logging & Lumber Museum: housed in 1892 C.R. Johnson Home and later Union Lumber Company's guest house from 1912-1969.
Hours & Admission Prices: June-Oct. Mon.-Fri. 11-2, Sat.-Sun. 10-4; Nov.-May Thurs.-Sun. 11-2. No charge; donations accepted. Closed New Year's Day; Thanksgiving; Christmas.
Attendance: 8,500 (estimated)

MENDOCINO COAST BOTANICAL GARDENS, 18220 N. Hwy. 1, Fort Bragg, CA 95437-8773. Tel.: 707-964-4352. Fax: 707-964-3114. Facebook.
E-mail: info@gardenbythesea.org
Web Site: www.gardenbythesea.org
Key Personnel: Exec. Dir., Molly Barker; Museum Shop Mgr., Sarah Flowers.
Institution Type/Description: Botanic Garden.
Hours & Admission Prices: March-Oct. daily 9-5; Nov.-Feb. daily 9-4. Adults 18 & over $14, seniors 65 & over $10, juniors 5-17 $5; children 4 & under and members no charge. American Horticultural Society Reciprocal admissions program. Closed Thanksgiving; Christmas.
Attendance: 71,000 (actual)

TRIANGLE TATTOO & MUSEUM, 356 B. N. Main St., Fort Bragg, CA 95437-3406. Tel.: 707-964-8814. Facebook: Triangle Tattoo.
E-mail: chinchilla@triangletattoo.com
Web Site: www.triangletattoo.com
Key Personnel: Chm. (V), Mr. G; Museum Shop Mgr., Madame Chinchilla.
Institution Type/Description: Tattoo History Museum.
Hours & Admission Prices: Daily 12-6. No charge; donations accepted. Closed Christmas.
Attendance: 10,000 (estimated)

Fort Jones

FORT JONES MUSEUM, 11913 Main St., Fort Jones, CA 96032. Mailing Address: P.O. Box 428, Fort Jones, CA 96032-0428. Tel.: 530-468-5568.
E-mail: fjmuseum@sisqtel.net
Web Site: fortjonesmuseum.com
Key Personnel: Dir., Cecelia Reuter; Chm. (V), Brenda Mendenhall; Mayor, Tom McCulley; City Clerk, Linda Romaine.
Institution Type/Description: Historical Museum.
Hours & Admission Prices: Memorial Day to Labor Day Mon.-Fri. 10-4, Sat. 11-3; other times by appointment. No charge; donations accepted. &
Attendance: 3,000 (estimated)

Fortuna

CHAPMAN'S GEM AND MINERAL MUSEUM, Hwy. 101, Fortuna, CA 95540. Mailing Address: P.O. Box 32, Carlotta, CA 95528-0032. Tel.: 707-725-2714.
Web Site: www.chapmansgemandmineralshop.com
Key Personnel: Co Owner, Lyle Brown; Co Owner, Sharon Brown.
Institution Type/Description: Gem & Mineral Museum.
Hours & Admission Prices: Daily 10-5. No charge; donations accepted. Closed New Year's Day; Easter; Thanksgiving; Christmas. &
Attendance: 125,000 (estimated)

FORTUNA DEPOT MUSEUM, 3 Park St., Fortuna, CA 95540-2461. Tel.: 707-725-7645.
E-mail: fortunamuseum@ci.fortuna.ca.us
Web Site: friendlyfortuna.com
Key Personnel: Chm. Bd. Dirs., Susan J.P. O'Hara; Cur., Dr. Alex Service.
Institution Type/Description: History Museum.
Hours & Admission Prices: June-Aug. daily 12-4:30; Sept.-May Thurs.-Sun. 12-4:30. No charge; donations accepted. &
Attendance: 3,000 (estimated)

Fremont

ARDENWOOD HISTORIC FARM, 34600 Ardenwood Blvd., Fremont, CA 94555-3645. Tel.: 510-791-4196.
E-mail: Lindsey@ardenwoodevents.com
Web Site: www.ebparks.org/parks/arden.htm
Institution Type/Description: Living History Museum.
Hours & Admission Prices: Tues.-Sun. 10-4. April to late Nov. Tues.-Wed. & Sat.: adults $3, children 4-17 $2, Thurs.-Fri. & Sun.: adults $6, seniors 62 & over $5, children 4-17 $4; children under 4 no charge; late Nov. to March Tues.-Sun. adults $3, children $2; children under 4 no charge. Closed Thanksgiving; Christmas. &

LOUIE-MEAGER ART GALLERY, Louie Meager Art Gallery, Ohlone College, 43600 Mission Blvd., Fremont, CA 94539. Tel.: 510-659-6176. Fax: 510-659-6188.
E-mail: kmencher@ohlone.edu
Key Personnel: Dir. & Cur., Kenney Mencher.
Institution Type/Description: College Art Gallery.
Hours & Admission Prices: Mon.-Tues. & Thurs.-Fri. 12-3, Wed. by appointment. No charge. Closed campus holidays & breaks.

MUSEUM OF LOCAL HISTORY, 190 Anza St., Fremont, CA 94539-5802. Tel.: 510-623-7907.
E-mail: info@museumoflocalhistory.org
Institution Type/Description: History Museum.
Hours & Admission Prices: Wed., Fri. & 2nd Sat.-Sun. of month 10-4; groups by appointment.

NILES DEPOT MUSEUM, 37592 Niles Blvd., Fremont, CA 94536. Mailing Address: Niles Depot Historical Foundation, P.O. Box 2716, Fremont, CA 94536-0716. Tel.: 510-797-4449. Facebook: Niles Depot.
E-mail: museum@nilesdepot.org
Web Site: www.nilesdepot.org
Key Personnel: Pres., Rick Zem; Dir., Tom Nelson.
Institution Type/Description: Railroad Museum: housed in 1901 Southern Pacific Depot.
Hours & Admission Prices: Fri. 7:30 p.m. to 9:30 p.m. & Sun. 10-4. No charge; donations accepted. &
Attendance: 4,000 (estimated)

OLD MISSION SAN JOSE, 43300 Mission Blvd., Fremont, CA 94539-5829. Mailing Address: P.O. Box 3159, Fremont, CA 94539-0315. Tel.: 510-657-1797. Fax: 510-651-8332.
E-mail: dmferenz@aol.com
Web Site: missionsanjose.org
Formerly: Mission San Jose Chapel and Museum
Key Personnel: Admin., Dolores Ferenz.
Institution Type/Description: History Museum.
Hours & Admission Prices: Daily 10-5. Adults $5, student $3. Closed New Year's Day; Easter; Thanksgiving; Christmas. &
Attendance: 40,000 (estimated)

Fresno

ARTE AMERICAS, 1630 Van Ness Ave., Fresno, CA 93721-1129. Tel.: 559-266-2623. Fax: 559-268-6130.
E-mail: grace@arteamericas.org
Web Site: www.arteamericas.org
Key Personnel: Dir., Grace Solis; Asst. Dir., Mary Ellen G. Clay; Program Dir., Diana Hernandez; Cur., Kristen Sierra.
Institution Type/Description: Art Museum.
Hours & Admission Prices: Tues.-Wed. & Fri.-Sat. 11-5, Thurs. 11-8. Adults $3, senior citizens & students $2; members & children under 5 no charge.

COKE HALLOWELL CENTER FOR RIVER STUDIES, 11605 Old Friant Rd., Fresno, CA 93730-9701. Tel.: 559-433-3190. Fax: 559-433-0634.
E-mail: jsalimbene@riverparkway.org
Web Site: www.riverparkway.org/rivercenter.asp
Key Personnel: Exec. Dir., Dave Koehler.
Institution Type/Description: Natural History Museum.
Hours & Admission Prices: Ranch House: Fri.-Sun. 11-3; other times by appointment. Grounds: daily 8-5.

THE DISCOVERY CENTER, 1937 N. Winery Ave., Fresno, CA 93703-2828. Mailing Address: 1944 N. Winery, Fresno, CA 93703-2829. Tel.: 559-251-5533. Fax: 559-251-5531.
E-mail: office@thediscoverycenter.net
Web Site: www.thediscoverycenter.net
Key Personnel: C.E.O., Roni Weil; Exec. Dir., Janet Berry; Sec., Karen Perkins.
Institution Type/Description: Participatory, Natural History & Natural Science Museum.
Hours & Admission Prices: Mon.-Fri. 9-5, Sat. 10-4. No charge; donations accepted. Closed New Year's Day; Easter; Independence Day; Thanksgiving; Christmas. &
Attendance: 35,000 (estimated)

DOWNING PLANETARIUM, 5320 N. Maple Ave. M/S DP132, California State University, Fresno, Fresno, CA 93740-8006. Tel.: 559-278-4121. Fax: 559-278-4070.
E-mail: stevenwh@csufresno.edu
Web Site: www.downing-planetarium.org
Institution Type/Description: Planetarium.
Hours & Admission Prices: Call for hours.
Attendance: 24,000

FORESTIERE UNDERGROUND GARDENS, 5021 W. Shaw Ave., Fresno, CA 93722-5026. Mailing Address: P.O. Box 1062, Wilton, CA 95693. Tel.: 559-271-0734.
E-mail: tours@undergroundgardens.com
Web Site: www.undergroundgardens.com
Key Personnel: Dir. & Museum Shop Mgr., Valery Forestiere; C.E.O., Lyn Kosewski.
Institution Type/Description: General Museum: Baldassare Forestiere spent 40 years sculpting this underground complex using only hand tools.
Hours & Admission Prices: Tours: March & Nov. Sat.-Sun. 11-2; April-May & Sept.-Oct. Wed.-Sun. 11-2; Memorial Day to Labor Day Wed.-Sun. 10-4. Adults $14, seniors 60 & over $12, children 5-17 $7; children 4 & under no charge.

FRESNO ART MUSEUM CLOSED, 2233 N. First St., Fresno, CA 93703-2364. Tel.: 559-441-4221. Fax: 559-441-4227. Facebook: Fresno Art Museum.
E-mail: info@fresnoartmuseum.org
Web Site: www.fresnoartmuseum.org
Formerly: Fresno Art Center
Key Personnel: Assoc. Dir., Eva Torres; Assoc. Cur., Kristina Hornback; Coord. Membership, Craig Hamilton Arnold; Coord. Education, Susan Yost-Filgate; Art Instructor, Eliana Saucedo; Art Instructor, Leslie Batty; Art Instructor, Scott Macaulay; Mgr. Office & Facilities, Debbie Horton; Receptionist, Betty Peralta; Maintenance & Security, Frank Alvarado; Security, Cesar Soto; Facility Rental Coord., Natasha Mendoza; Security, Irene Alvarado.
Institution Type/Description: Modern & Contemporary Art Museum.
Hours & Admission Prices: Thurs.-Sun. 11-5. Adults, seniors & students $5; discounts to AAM, WMG & NARM members; members & children under 5 no charge. Closed national holidays. &
Attendance: 21,000 (estimated)

FRESNO CITY AND COUNTY HISTORICAL SOCIETY, 7160 W. Kearney Blvd., Fresno, CA 93706-9520. Tel.: 559-441-0862. Fax: 559-441-1372.
E-mail: frhistsoc@aol.com
Web Site: www.valleyhistory.org
Key Personnel: Exec. Dir., Jill Moffat.
Institution Type/Description: Historical Society Museum.
Hours & Admission Prices: Fri.-Sun. 1, 2 & 3; call to confirm. Adults $5, seniors 60 & over and students 13-17 $4, children 3-12 $3; members & children under 3 no charge.

GALLERY 25, 2223 S. Van Ness Ave., Fresno, CA 93721-3430. Tel.: 559-264-4092. Facebook: Gallery 25.
Web Site: gallery25.org
Key Personnel: Dir., Barbara Van Arnam.
Institution Type/Description: Art Gallery.
Hours & Admission Prices: Fri.-Sun. 1-4. No charge.
Attendance: 3,000 (estimated)

KEARNEY MANSION MUSEUM, 7160 W. Kearney Blvd., Fresno, CA 93706-9520. Tel.: 559-441-0862. Fax: 559-441-1372.
E-mail: frhistsoc@aol.com
Web Site: www.valleyhistory.org
Key Personnel: Exec. Dir., Jill Moffat; Pres. (V), John Boogaert; Dir. Public Rels., Christina Perryman; Archivist, Maria Ortiz; Cur. Collections & Education Coord., Sharon Hiigel; Tour Coord. & Museum Shop Mgr., Amy Lawrence; Bookkeeper & Membership, Barbara James Higgins; Oral History Coord., Ruth Lang.
Institution Type/Description: Historic Site Museum: housed in 1900 original Kearney Mansion.
Hours & Admission Prices: By appointment. Closed New Year's Day; Easter; Independence Day; Thanksgiving; Christmas. &
Attendance: 9,023 (actual)

MEUX HOME MUSEUM, 1007 R St., Fresno, CA 93721-1312. Mailing Address: P.O. Box 70, Fresno, CA 93707-0070. Tel.: 559-233-8007. Fax: 559-233-2331.
E-mail: meauhomemuseum@gmail.com
Web Site: www.meux.mus.ca.us
Key Personnel: Pres., Bob Flynn; Vice Pres., Colleen Sethre; Interim Treas., Jan Stafford.
Institution Type/Description: Historic House: 1888 Victorian house.

Hours & Admission Prices: Feb.-Dec. Fri.-Sun. 12-3; private & school tours during week. Adults $5, students $4, children $3; special events rates vary. Closed holidays. &
Attendance: 30,000 (estimated)

SIMONIAN FARMS, 2629 S. Clovis Ave., Fresno, CA 93725-9307. Tel.: 559-237-2294. Fax: 559-441-1198.
E-mail: simonian@lightspeed.net
Web Site: www.simonianfarms.com
Institution Type/Description: Farm Museum.
Hours & Admission Prices: No charge. &

VETERANS MEMORIAL MUSEUM, "HOME OF THE LEGION OF VALOR", 2425 Fresno St., Fresno, CA 93721-1841. Tel.: 559-498-0510.
E-mail: fresnovetsmuseum@yahoo.com
Web Site: www.fresnovetsmuseum.com
Formerly: Legion of Valor Veterans Museum
Key Personnel: Dir. & C.E.O., Robert E. Specht; Chm. (V), Judy Jones; Deputy Dir., Mike Harris; Museum Shop Mgr., Raymond Lee.
Institution Type/Description: Military Museum.
Hours & Admission Prices: Mon.-Sat. 10-3. No charge; donations accepted. &
Attendance: 15,000 (estimated)

Friant

MILLERTON COURTHOUSE, Department of Parks & Recreation, 5290 Millerton Rd., Friant, CA 93626. Tel.: 559-822-2225. Fax: 209-822-2319.
Institution Type/Description: Historic Building Museum.
Hours & Admission Prices: June-Sept. Sat. 10-6. Courthouse: no charge. Parking: fee charged.

Fullerton

ANTHROPOLOGY TEACHING MUSEUM, CALIFORNIA STATE UNIVERSITY, FULLERTON, 800 N. State College Blvd., Fullerton, CA 92834-6846. Mailing Address: Dept. of Anthropology, Cal-State Univ., Fullerton, P.O. Box 6846, Fullerton, CA 92834-6846. Tel.: 657-278-3626. Fax: 657-278-5001.
E-mail: anthropology@exchange.fullerton.edu
Web Site: www.anthro.fullerton.edu
Key Personnel: Coord. Administrative Support, Debra Redsteer; Dept. Chm., Dr. Mitch Avila; Evolutionary Coord., Dr. John Bock; Cultural Coord., Dr. Barbra Erickson; Archaeology Coord., Dr. Carl Wendt.
Institution Type/Description: Anthropology Museum.
Hours & Admission Prices: School Year: Mon.-Thurs. & by appointment; School Vacation: holidays & weekends by appointment. No charge; donations accepted. &

BEGOVICH GALLERY, CALIFORNIA STATE UNIVERSITY, FULLERTON, 800 N. State College Blvd., Visual Arts Center, Fullerton, CA 92831. Mailing Address: 800 N. State College Blvd., Fullerton, CA 92831. Tel.: 657-278-7750. Fax: 657-278-8191.
E-mail: mmcgee@fullerton.edu
Web Site: www.fullerton.edu/arts/art
Formerly: Main Art Gallery
Key Personnel: Gallery Dir., Mike McGee; Asst. Dir., Jacqueline Bunge; Preparator & Technical Asst., Marty Lorigan.
Institution Type/Description: University Art Gallery.
Hours & Admission Prices: Mon.-Thurs. 12-4, Sat. 12-2, call to confirm. No charge; donations accepted. Closed national holidays. &

THE FULLERTON ARBORETUM, 1900 Associated Rd., Fullerton, CA 92831-1659. Mailing Address: c/o California State University, Fullerton, P.O. Box 6850, Fullerton, CA 92834-6850. Tel.: 657-278-3407. Fax: 657-278-7066.
E-mail: farboretum@fullerton.edu
Web Site: www.fullertonarboretum.org
Key Personnel: Dir., Gregory T. Dyment; Pres. Fullerton Arboretum Commission, Frank Mumford; Pres. Friends of the Fullerton Arboretum (V), Kathie Kingett.
Institution Type/Description: Arboretum & Historic House: 1894 home & office of Dr. George Clark, moved to site of the Gilman Ranch, where first Valencia oranges grown in Orange County were planted.
Hours & Admission Prices: Arboretum: daily 8-4:30. Heritage House: Sat.-Sun. 2-4; other times by appointment. No charge; donations accepted. Closed New Year's Day; Thanksgiving; Christmas. &
Attendance: 120,000 (estimated)

FULLERTON COLLEGE ART GALLERY, 321 E. Chapman Ave., Bldg. 1000, Fullerton, CA 92832-2011. Tel.: 714-992-7329. Fax: 714-992-7320.
E-mail: kjohnson@fullcoll.edu
Web Site: art.fullcoll.edu
Key Personnel: Dir., Beth Solomon Marino.
Institution Type/Description: Art Gallery.
Hours & Admission Prices: Mon. & Wed.-Thurs. 10-2, Tues. 10-2 & 5-7.

FULLERTON MUSEUM CENTER, 301 N. Pomona Ave., Fullerton, CA 92832-1927. Tel.: 714-738-6545. Fax: 714-738-3124.
E-mail: danniellem@ci.fullerton.ca.us
Web Site: www.cityoffullerton.com/depts/museum
Key Personnel: C.E.O., Ed Malkowicz; Dir., Dannielle Mauk; Museum Shop Mgr., Kelly Chidester; Museum Operations Asst., Elvia Taylor.
Institution Type/Description: General Museum.
Hours & Admission Prices: Tues.-Wed. & Fri.-Sun. 12-4, Thurs. 12-8. Adults $4, senior citizens & students $3, children 6-12 $1; discounts for AAM & ICOM members; children 5 & under and members no charge. &
Attendance: 30,000 (estimated)

MUCKENTHALER CULTURAL CENTER AND MANSION MUSEUM, 1201 W. Malvern Ave., Fullerton, CA 92833-2429. Tel.: 714-738-6595, ext. 103. Fax: 714-738-6366. Facebook: the Muckenthaler.
E-mail: info@themuck.org
Web Site: www.themuck.org
Key Personnel: Exec. Dir., Zoot Velasco; Pres. (V), Frederic Ouwelem, Jr.; Museum Shop Mgr., Britt Sullivan.
Institution Type/Description: Cultural Center: housed in 1923 home of Walter Muckenthaler.
Hours & Admission Prices: Wed. & Fri.-Sun. 12-4, Thurs. 12-4 & 6-9. No charge; donations accepted. Closed holidays. &
Attendance: 28,800 (estimated)

THE MUSEUM OF TEACHING AND LEARNING, 1111 E. Commonwealth, Unit C, Fullerton, CA 92831. Mailing Address: P. O. Box 3820, Fullerton, CA 92834-3820.
E-mail: nagel@csulb.edu
Institution Type/Description: Education History Museum.
Hours & Admission Prices: By appointment.

Garden Grove

GARDEN GROVE HISTORICAL SOCIETY, 12174 Euclid St., Garden Grove, CA 92840. Mailing Address: P.O. Box 4297, Garden Grove, CA 92842-4297. Tel.: 714-530-8871. Fax: 714-534-2611.
E-mail: gardengrovehistsoc@att.net
Key Personnel: Pres., Terry Thomas; Vice Pres., Megan Galway; Treas., Lollie Beauchamp.
Institution Type/Description: Historic House Museum: building completed 1892 by E.G. Ware, one of the first pioneers of Garden Grove.
Hours & Admission Prices: 1st & 3rd Sun. of month 1:30; other times by appointment. Suggested Donation: adults $5, students under 18 $1.
Attendance: 925 (actual)

Gardena

CARROLL SHELBY AUTOMOTIVE MUSEUM, 19021 S. Figueroa St., Gardena, CA 90248. Tel.: 310-327-5072. Fax: 310-538-0419.
Web Site: www.shelby.com
Institution Type/Description: Automobile Museum.
Hours & Admission Prices: Call for hours.

Gilroy

CITY OF GILROY MUSEUM, 195 Fifth St., Gilroy, CA 95020-5703. Tel.: 408-846-0446. Fax: 408-847-5604.
E-mail: gilroy.museum@ci.gilroy.ca.us
Web Site: www.ci.gilroy.ca.us
Formerly: Gilroy Historical Museum
Key Personnel: Supvr., Cathy Mirelez.
Institution Type/Description: Local History Museum: housed in 1910 Carnegie Library.
Hours & Admission Prices: Tues. & Thurs. 10-5, Wed. by appointment, 1st Sat. of month 10-2. Call for admission information. Closed New Year's Day; Presidents'

Day; Memorial Day; Independence Day; Labor Day; Veterans Day; Thanksgiving; Christmas.
Attendance: 2,415 (actual)

Glen Ellen

JACK LONDON STATE HISTORIC PARK, 2400 London Ranch Rd., Glen Ellen, CA 95442-9749. Tel.: 707-938-5216. Fax: 707-938-5216.
E-mail: tvanwyck@jacklondonpark.com
Web Site: www.jacklondonpark.com
Key Personnel: Dir., Tjiska Van Wyk; Chm. (V), Chuck Levine; Museum Cur., Carol Dodge; Museum Shop Mgr., Michele Milne.
Institution Type/Description: State Park Museum.
Hours & Admission Prices: Park & Museum: Fri.-Mon. 10-5. Cottage: Sat.-Sun. 12-4. Admission per car $10, senior citizens 62 & over $7. Closed Christmas. &
Attendance: 70,000 (estimated)

Glendale

BRAND LIBRARY & ART CENTER, 1601 W. Mountain St., Glendale, CA 91201-1200. Tel.: 818-548-2051. Fax: 818-548-5079.
E-mail: info@brandlibrary.org
Web Site: www.brandlibrary.org
Key Personnel: Sr. Library Supvr., Alyssa Resnick; Librarian, Cathy Billings.
Institution Type/Description: Library & Art Center.
Hours & Admission Prices: Tues. & Thurs. 1-9, Wed. 1-6, Fri.-Sat. 1-5. No charge; donations accepted. &
Attendance; 130,000

CASA ADOBE DE SAN RAFAEL, 1330 Dorothy Dr., Glendale, CA 91202-1610. Mailing Address: City of Glendale, 613 E. Broadway, Rm. 120, Glendale, CA 91206-4391. Tel.: 818-248-8151.
Key Personnel: Dir., Onnig Bulanikian.
Institution Type/Description: Historic Building Museum: Early Mexican-American heritage.
Hours & Admission Prices: Daily 8 to dusk. Guided Tours: Sept.-June first Sun. of month 1-3; July & Aug. every Sun. 1-3. Group tours by appointment. No charge. &
Attendance: 2,750 (estimated)

CATALINA VERDUGO ADOBE, 2211 Bonita Dr., Glendale, CA 91208. Tel.: 818-244-2841.
Institution Type/Description: Historic Building: housed in the former home of the Verdugo family; c.1828.
Hours & Admission Prices: Park: daily 8 am to dusk. Adobe Guided Tours: by appointment.

DOCTORS' HOUSE MUSEUM, Brand Park, 1601 W. Mountain Ave., Glendale, CA 91201-1200. Mailing Address: c/o The Glendale Historical Society, P.O. Box 4173, Glendale, CA 91202. Tel.: 818-548-2147.
E-mail: tghs@glendalehistorical.org
Web Site: www.glendalehistorical.org/doctors.html
Key Personnel: Dir., Sonia Montejano.
Institution Type/Description: History Museum.
Hours & Admission Prices: Tours: Sun. 2-4, last tour at 3:40. Adults 16 & up $2; members no charge. Closed New Year's Day; Easter; Mothers Day; Fathers Day; month of July; Christmas; very rainy days.

FOREST LAWN MUSEUM, 1712 S. Glendale Ave., Glendale, CA 91205-3320. Tel.: 800-204-3131. Fax: 323-551-5329. Facebook: Forest Lawn.
E-mail: museum@forestlawn.com
Web Site: forestlawn.com
Key Personnel: Chm. (V) & C.E.O., Darin Drabing; Museum Dir., Ana Pescador.
Institution Type/Description: Art Museum.
Hours & Admission Prices: Tues.-Sun. 10-5. No charge. &
Attendance: 50,000 (estimated)

GLENDALE FIRE DEPARTMENT MUSEUM, Fire Station 21, 421 Oak St., Glendale, CA 91204. Tel.: 818-548-4810.
Institution Type/Description: Firefighting History Museum.
Hours & Admission Prices: By appointment.

MUSEUM OF NEON ART, P.O. Box 631, Glendale, CA 91209. Tel.: 213-489-9918. Fax: 213-489-9932.
E-mail: info@neonmona.org
Web Site: www.neonmona.org
Key Personnel: Exec. Dir., Kim Koga.
Institution Type/Description: Neon, Electric & Kinetic Art Museum.
Hours & Admission Prices: Temporarily closed. &
Attendance: 6,000 (actual)

Goffs

GOFFS SCHOOLHOUSE & CULTURAL CENTER, 37198 Lanfair Rd., Goffs, CA 92332. Mailing Address: 37198 Lanfair Rd., Essex, CA 92332-9786. Tel.: 760-733-4482.
E-mail: info@mdhca.org
Institution Type/Description: Historic Building: built in 1914.
Hours & Admission Prices: Oct.-June Sat.-Mon. 9-4.

Goleta

RANCHO LA PATERA & STOW HOUSE (GOLETA VALLEY HISTORICAL SOCIETY), 304 N. Los Carneros Rd., Goleta, CA 93117-1502. Tel.: 805-681-7217 & 7216. Fax: 805-681-7217.
E-mail: info@goletahistory.com
Web Site: goletahistory.org
Key Personnel: Exec. Dir., Amanda DeLucia; Education, Lisa Scoggins; Coord. Events, Dacia Harwood; Cur., Wes Hensley.
Institution Type/Description: Historical Society Museum: housed in c.1872 Rancho la Patera Stow House ranch.
Hours & Admission Prices: Sat.-Sun. 1-4; hours vary for special events. Museum no charge. House Tour: $5, children under 12 no charge. Closed New Year's Day; Christmas. &
Attendance: 25,000 (estimated)

SOUTH COAST RAILROAD MUSEUM AT GOLETA DEPOT, 300 N. Los Carneros Rd., Goleta, CA 93117-1502. Tel.: 805-964-3540. Fax: 805-964-3549.
E-mail: director@goletadepot.org
Web Site: www.goletadepot.org
Key Personnel: Pres., Bruce Morden.
Institution Type/Description: Railroad Museum: housed in 1901 Southern Pacific railroad depot.
Hours & Admission Prices: Fri.-Sun. 1-4. Donation Requested: adults $1. Closed New Year's Eve & Day; Easter; Thanksgiving; Christmas Eve, Day & week. &
Attendance: 22,000 (estimated)

Grass Valley

GRASS VALLEY MUSEUM, 410 S. Church St., Grass Valley, CA 95945-6722. Tel.: 530-272-4725.
E-mail: stjcc@nccn.net & saintjosephsculturalcenter@gmail.com
Web Site: www.saintjosephsculturalcenter.org
Key Personnel: Dir., Joseph Guida.
Institution Type/Description: History Museum: housed in the former orphanage used during Gold Rush times; established by Father William Dalton in 1865 for children orphaned by mining accidents.
Hours & Admission Prices: April 16-Dec. 18 Wed.-Sat. 12:30-3:30; other times by appointment. No charge; donations accepted.
Attendance: 175 (estimated)

LOLA MONTEZ HOME, 248 Mill St., Grass Valley, CA 95945-6712. Mailing Address: 128 E. Main St., Grass Valley, CA 95945. Tel.: 530-273-4667.
Institution Type/Description: History Museum.
Hours & Admission Prices: Mon.-Fri. 9-5. No charge; donations accepted.

Gridley

GRIDLEY MUSEUM, 601 Kentucky St., Gridley, CA 95948. Tel.: 530-846-4482. Facebook: Gridley Museum.
E-mail: gridleymuseum@gmail.com
Web Site: gridleymuseum.com
Key Personnel: Dir., Ruth Ann King; Chm. (V), Robert Trueax.
Institution Type/Description: History Museum: house in c.1909 Veatch Building.
Hours & Admission Prices: Tues.-Fri. 10-2. No charge; donations accepted.

Groveland

GROVELAND YOSEMITE GATEWAY MUSEUM, 18990 Main St., Groveland, CA 95321-9442. Mailing Address: P.O. Box 180, Big Oak Flat, CA 95305. Tel.: 209-962-0300.
E-mail: grovelandmuseum@mlode.com
Web Site: www.grovelandmuseum.org
Key Personnel: Pres., Dodie Harte; Cur., Robert D. Oakley; Museum Shop Mgr., Carrie Carter; Museum Shop Mgr., Bruce Carter.
Institution Type/Description: History Museum.
Hours & Admission Prices: Daily 1-4:30. No charge; donations accepted. &
Attendance: 25,000 (estimated)

Guadalupe

THE DUNES CENTER, 1065 Guadalupe St., Guadalupe, CA 93434. Tel.: 805-343-2455. Fax: 805-343-0442.
E-mail: admin@dunescenter.org
Web Site: dunescenter.org
Institution Type/Description: General Museum.
Hours & Admission Prices: Wed.-Sun. 10-4; other times by appointment. Adults $5; children 12 & under no charge.

Gualala

DOLPHIN GALLERY, 39225 Hwy. One, Gualala, CA 95445. Mailing Address: P.O. Box 244, Gualala, CA 95445. Tel.: 707-884-3896.
E-mail: dolphin@gualalaarts.org
Web Site: gualalaarts.org/dolphin-gallery
Key Personnel: Mgr., Sharon Nickodem; Exhibitions, Nancy Kyle.
Institution Type/Description: Art Gallery.
Hours & Admission Prices: Daily 10-5. Closed Thanksgiving; Christmas.

GUALALA ARTS CENTER, 46501 Old State Hwy., Gualala, CA 95445. Mailing Address: P.O. Box 244, Gualala, CA 95445. Tel.: 707-884-1138. Fax: 707-884-3038.
E-mail: info@gualalaarts.org
Web Site: www.gualalaarts.org
Institution Type/Description: Art Gallery.
Hours & Admission Prices: Mon.-Fri. 9-4, Sat.-Sun. 12-4. No charge; donations accepted.

Gustine

GUSTINE MUSEUM, 397 Fourth St., Hwy. 33, Gustine, CA 95322-1131. Mailing Address: 803 Laurel Ave., Gustine, CA 95322. Tel.: 209-854-2344 & 3120 (Business Office).
E-mail: gustinemuseum@gustinehistoricalsociety.org
Web Site: gustinehistoricalsociety.org
Key Personnel: Dir. & Museum Shop Mgr., Kim Stadter; C.E.O., Patricia S. Snoke; Pres. (V), David Perry.
Institution Type/Description: History Museum.
Hours & Admission Prices: Thurs. & Sun. 1-4. No charge; donations accepted. Closed all holidays. &
Attendance: 1,000 (estimated)

Hacienda Heights

YOUTH SCIENCE CENTER, Bixby Elementary School, 16446 Wedgeworth Dr., Hacienda Heights, CA 91745. Mailing Address: P.O. Box 5723, Hacienda Heights, CA 91745-0723. Tel.: 626-854-9825. Facebook: Youth Science Center.
E-mail: ysc@youthsciencecenter.org
Web Site: www.youthsciencecenter.org
Key Personnel: Chm. (V), Ron Chong; Museum Shop Mgr., Diana Padilla.
Institution Type/Description: Science Center.
Hours & Admission Prices: Sept.-May Mon, Wed. & Fri. No charge; donations accepted.
Attendance: 2,000 (estimated)

Half Moon Bay

COASTAL ARTS LEAGUE MUSEUM, 300 Main St., Ste. 3, Half Moon Bay, CA 94019-1742. Tel.: 650-726-6335.
E-mail: coastalartsleague@gmail.com
Web Site: www.coastalartsleague.com
Key Personnel: Pres. (V), Randall Reid; Museum Shop Mgr., Patricia Dailey, M.D.; Chm. (V), Membership, Patricia E. Keefe.
Institution Type/Description: Art Museum.

Hours & Admission Prices: Thurs.-Mon. 11-5. No charge; donations accepted. &
Attendance: 3,500 (estimated)

THE JAMES JOHNSTON HOUSE, 110 Higgins Canyon Rd., Half Moon Bay, CA 94019. Mailing Address: P.O. Box 789, Half Moon Bay, CA 94019. Tel.: 650-726-0329.
E-mail: events@johnstonhouse.org
Web Site: www.johnstonhouse.org
Institution Type/Description: Historic House Museum: built 1853-1855. Listed on the National Register of Historic Places.
Hours & Admission Prices: Jan.-Sept. 3rd Sat. each month 11-3.

Hanford

CLARK CENTER FOR JAPANESE ART AND CULTURE, 15770 Tenth Ave., Hanford, CA 93230-9533. Tel.: 559-582-4915. Fax: 559-582-9546.
E-mail: info@ccjac.org
Web Site: www.ccjac.org
Formerly: The Ruth & Sherman Lee Institute for Japanese Art
Key Personnel: Dir., Dr. Andreas Marks; Chm. (V), Richard L. Schafer.
Institution Type/Description: Art Museum.
Hours & Admission Prices: Sept.-July Tues.-Sat. 12:30-5. Adults $5; discounts to children 12 & under and students; members no charge. Closed major holidays. &
Attendance: 5,000 (estimated)

HANFORD CARNEGIE MUSEUM CLOSED, 109 E. 8th St., Hanford, CA 93230-3933. Tel.: 559-584-1367.
E-mail: hanfordcarnegie@gmail.com
Key Personnel: Pres. (V), Jennifer Riordan; Dir, Robert Van Wagoner.
Institution Type/Description: History Museum.
Hours & Admission Prices: Wed.-Sat. 10-2. Adults $3, children, students & seniors $1; members no charge.
Attendance: 2,750 (estimated)

TAOIST TEMPLE AND MUSEUM, 12 China Alley, Hanford, CA 93230. Mailing Address: P.O. Box 728, Hanford, CA 93232-0728. Tel.: 559-582-4508.
Key Personnel: Pres. (V), Arianne Wing; Museum Shop Mgr., Camille Wing.
Institution Type/Description: History Museum.
Hours & Admission Prices: Call for hours. No charge; donations accepted.
Attendance: 1,271 (estimated)

Hayward

C.E. SMITH MUSEUM OF ANTHROPOLOGY, CSU East Bay, Hayward, CA 94542-3039. Tel.: 510-885-3168 & 3104. Fax: 510-885-3353.
E-mail: marjorie.rhodesousley@csueastbay.edu
Web Site: class.csueastbay.edu/anthropologymuseum/
Key Personnel: Dir. & Cur., Dr. Henry Gilbert.
Institution Type/Description: Anthropology Museum.
Hours & Admission Prices: Mon.-Fri. 11-4 during exhibits. No charge; donations accepted. Closed federal holidays; university holidays. &
Attendance: 2,000 (estimated)

HAYWARD AREA HISTORICAL SOCIETY, 22380 Foothill Blvd., Hayward, CA 94541-5113. Tel.: 510-581-0223. Fax: 510-581-0217.
E-mail: info@haywardareahistory.org
Web Site: www.haywardareahistory.org
Key Personnel: Exec. Dir., A.T. Stephens; Pres., Georgiandra Ostarello; Cur. & Archivist, Diane Curry; Assoc. Archivist, John Christian; Collections & Historic Properties Manager, Heather Farquhar; Membership & Mktg. Mgr,, Marcess Owings; Education & Volunteer Mgr., Bria Reiniger; Visitor Services Asst., Dillon Harrison; Collections & Historic Properties Mgr., Gretta Stimson.
Institution Type/Description: Historical Society.
Hours & Admission Prices: Wed.-Sun. 10-4. Adults $5, seniors & students $3; discounts to museum professionals & military; children 4 & under and members no charge. Closed major holidays. &
Attendance: 25,000 (actual)

MCCONAGHY HOUSE, 18701 Hesperian Blvd., Hayward, CA 94541-2247. Mailing Address: 22380 Foothill Blvd., Hayward, CA 94541-5113. Tel.: 510-581-0223. Fax: 510-581-0217.
E-mail: info@haywardareahistory.org
Web Site: www.haywardareahistory.org
Key Personnel: Exec. Dir., A.T. Stephens; Pres. (V), Georgiandra Ostarelllo; Cur., Diane Curry; Assoc. Archivist, John Christian; Collections & Historic Properties

Mgr., Heather Farguhar; Membership & Mktg. Mgr., Marcess Owings; Education & Volunteer Mgr., Bria Reiniger; Visitor Services Asst., Dillon Harrison; Collections & Historic Properties Asst., Gretta Stimson.

Institution Type/Description: Historic Home: 1886 Victorian farmhouse depicting the lifestyle of one of the area's first pioneer families.

Hours & Admission Prices: First weekend of the month 11-4. Adults $5, senior citizens & students $3; discounts to museum professionals & military; children 4 & under & HAHS members no charge. Closed New Year's Day; Thanksgiving; Christmas.

Attendance: 4,583 (actual)

MEEK MANSION, 240 Hampton Rd., Hayward, CA 94541. Mailing Address: c/o Haywood Area Historical Society, 22380 Foothill Blvd., Hayward, CA 94541. Tel.: 510-581-0223. Fax: 510-581-0217.

E-mail: info@haywardareahistory.org
Web Site: www.haywardareahistory.org
Key Personnel: Exec. Dir., AT Stephens.
Institution Type/Description: Historic House Museum: housed in the former home of William Meek; built in 1869. Listed on the National Register of Historic Places.
Hours & Admission Prices: By appointment.

SULPHUR CREEK NATURE CENTER, 1801 D St., Hayward, CA 94541-4434. Tel.: 510-881-6747. Fax: 510-888-0129. Facebook: Sulphur Creek Nature Center.

E-mail: nature@haywardrec.org
Web Site: www.haywardrec.org
Key Personnel: Coord., Wendy Winsted.
Institution Type/Description: Nature Center.
Hours & Admission Prices: Daily 10-5. No charge; donations accepted. Closed New Year's Day; Martin Luther King Jr. Day; Veterans Day; Thanksgiving & day after; Christmas Eve & Day.
Attendance: 40,000 (actual)

SUN GALLERY, 1015 E St., Hayward, CA 94541-5210. Tel.: 510-581-4050. Fax: 510-581-3384.

E-mail: sungallery@comcast.net
Web Site: sungallery.org
Key Personnel: Dir., Dorsi Diaz; Pres. (V), Orlando Somoza.
Institution Type/Description: Visual Arts Center.
Hours & Admission Prices: Thurs.-Sun. 11-5. No charge; donations accepted. Closed major holidays. &

Attendance: 5,000 (estimated)

Healdsburg

HEALDSBURG MUSEUM, 221 Matheson St., Healdsburg, CA 95448. Mailing Address: P.O. Box 952, Healdsburg, CA 95448-0952. Tel.: 707-431-3325. Fax: 707-473-4471.

E-mail: info@healdsburgmuseum.org
Web Site: www.healdsburgmuseum.org
Key Personnel: Cur., Holly Hoods.
Institution Type/Description: History Museum.
Hours & Admission Prices: Museum: Weds.-Sun. 11-4. Research Archives: Thurs.-Sat. 11-4 by appointment. No charge.

TILE HERITAGE FOUNDATION, Healdsburg, CA 95448. Mailing Address: Box 1850, Healdsburg, CA 95448-1850. Tel.: 707-431-8453. Fax: 707-431-8455. Facebook: Tile Heritage Foundation.

E-mail: foundation@tileheritage.org
Web Site: www.tileheritage.org
Key Personnel: Pres., Joseph A. Taylor; Exec. Dir., Sheila A. Menzies.
Institution Type/Description: Art Foundation: for the research & preservation of ceramic surfaces.
Hours & Admission Prices: Mon.-Sat. 10-4 by appointment only. No charge; donations accepted. Closed Easter; Independence Day; Thanksgiving; Christmas week. &

Hemet

FINGERPRINTS YOUTH MUSEUM, 123 S. Carmalita St., Hemet, CA 92543-4210. Mailing Address: 418 E. Florida Ave., Hemet, CA 92543-4210. Tel.: 951-765-1223. Fax: 951-652-0064.

E-mail: director@fingerprintsyouthmuseum.com
Web Site: www.fingerprintsmuseum.com
Formerly: The KidZone Riverside County Youth Museum
Institution Type/Description: Children's Museum.

Hours & Admission Prices: Winter: Tues.-Fri. 11-5, Sat. 9-5; Summer: Tues.-Sat. 9-5. Admission $5, seniors 55 & over $4; members & children under 2 no charge. &

Attendance: 10,000 (actual)

HEMET MUSEUM, Santa Fe Depot/State & Florida, Hemet, CA 92543. Mailing Address: 1126 Griffith Way, Hemet, CA 92543. Tel.: 951-929-4409 & 5885.

E-mail: info@hemetmuseum.com
Web Site: www.hemetmuseum.org
Key Personnel: Cur.8, Anne B. Jennings; Museum Shop Mgr., Virginia Sisk.
Institution Type/Description: History Museum: housed in 1898 freight house of the historic Santa Fe Depot.
Hours & Admission Prices: Sept.-July Tues.-Sun. 11-3. No charge; donations accepted. Closed New Year's Day; Independence Day; Labor Day; Thanksgiving; Christmas. &

Attendance: 4,510 (actual)

WESTERN SCIENCE CENTER, 2345 Searl Pkwy., Hemet, CA 92543-9706. Tel.: 951-791-0033. Fax: 951-791-0032.

E-mail: bmarshall@westerncentermuseum.org
Web Site: westerncentermuseum.org
Formerly: Western Center for Archaeology and Paleontology
Key Personnel: Exec. Dir., Alton Dooley, Ph.D.
Institution Type/Description: Archaeology & Paleontology Museum.
Hours & Admission Prices: Tues.-Sun. 10-5. Adults $8, seniors 62 & over and students 13-22 $6.50, youth 5-12 $6; members, military and children 4 & under no charge. &

Attendance: 45,000 (actual)

Hermosa Beach

HERMOSA BEACH HISTORICAL SOCIETY, 710 Pier Ave., Hermosa Beach, CA 90254-3940. Tel.: 310-318-9421.

E-mail: hermosabeachmuseum@gmail.com
Web Site: www.hermosabeachhistoricalsociety.org
Key Personnel: Cur. & Mgr., Christopher Ueberlhor.
Institution Type/Description: Historical Society Museum.
Hours & Admission Prices: Wed. 10-12, Sat.-Sun. 2-4. No charge; donations accepted. Closed holidays.

Hollister

SAN BENITO COUNTY HISTORICAL SOCIETY MUSEUM, 498 5th St., Hollister, CA 95023-3841. Tel.: 831-635-0335.

E-mail: info@sbchistoricalsociety.org
Web Site: sbchistoricalsociety.org
Key Personnel: Pres., Sharlene VanRooy.
Institution Type/Description: History Museum.
Hours & Admission Prices: Historical Society Museum: by appointment. No charge; donations accepted. Historical Village: daily dawn to dusk. Parking fee: $3.

Attendance: 475 (estimated)

Hollywood

HOLLYWOOD GUINNESS WORLD RECORDS MUSEUM, 6764 Hollywood Blvd., Hollywood, CA 90028-4622. Tel.: 323-463-6433. Fax: 323-462-3953. Facebook.

E-mail: hollywood@hollywoodwax.com
Web Site: www.guinnessmuseumhollywood.com
Key Personnel: Gen. Mgr., Mike Eggert; Corp. Communications Dir., Aileen Stein; Partner, Tej Sundher.
Institution Type/Description: Guinness Book of World Records Museum: housed c.1913 Hollywood's first movie theatre.
Hours & Admission Prices: Sun.-Thurs. 9 am to midnight, Fri.-Sat. 9 am-1 am. Adults 12 & over $20.99, children 4-11 $10.99; discounts to groups of 15 or more; children under 4 no charge. &

Attendance: (estimated)

HOLLYWOOD HERITAGE MUSEUM, 2100 Highland Ave., Hollywood, CA 90068-3241. Mailing Address: P.O. Box 2586, Hollywood, CA 90078-2586. Tel.: 323-874-2276 & 4005.

E-mail: rikalad@aol.com
Web Site: www.hollywoodheritage.org
Formerly: Hollywood Studio Museum
Key Personnel: Dir., Cur. & Museum Shop Mgr., George Kiel; Pres. (V), Richard Adkins.
Institution Type/Description: Early Hollywood History & Heritage Museum: housed in restored 1895 barn which was adapted for use as a film studio in

Hollywood in 1912; became Paramount Studios in 1916; state historic landmark in 1955.
Hours & Admission Prices: Wed.-Sun. 12-4. Adults $7, children under 12 & members no charge. Closed New Year's Day; Thanksgiving; Christmas. &
Attendance: 2,000 (estimated)

HOLLYWOOD MUSEUM, 1660 N. Highland Ave., Hollywood, CA 90028-6121. Tel.: 323-464-7776. Fax: 323-464-3777.
E-mail: info@thehollywoodmuseum.com
Web Site: www.thehollywoodmuseum.com
Key Personnel: Volunteer Chm., Donelle Dadigan.
Institution Type/Description: Movie History Museum: housed in the landmark Max Factor building.
Hours & Admission Prices: Wed.-Sun. 10-5. Adults $15, seniors & students under 21 $12, children under 5 $5. &

HOLLYWOOD WAX MUSEUM, INC., 6767 Hollywood Blvd., Hollywood, CA 90028-4623. Tel.: 323-462-5991.
E-mail: hollywood@hollywoodwax.com
Web Site: www.hollywoodwaxmuseum.com
Key Personnel: Gen. Mgr., Mike Eggert.
Institution Type/Description: Wax Museum: housed in c.1929 former Embassy Club.
Hours & Admission Prices: Sun.-Thurs. 9am-midnight, Fri.-Sat. 9am-1am. Adults $22.99, children 4-11 $12.99; children under 4 no charge.
Attendance: 130,000 (estimated)

LOS ANGELES FIRE DEPARTMENT MUSEUM AND MEMORIAL, 1355 N. Cahuenga Blvd., Hollywood, CA 90028. Tel.: 323-464-2727. Fax: 323-464-7401.
E-mail: lafdhsmuseum@msn.com
Web Site: lafdmuseum.org/museum_hollywood
Institution Type/Description: Firefighting History Museum.
Hours & Admission Prices: Sat. 10-4.

MUSEUM OF DEATH, 6031 Hollywood Blvd., Hollywood, CA 90028. Tel.: 323-466-8011.
Web Site: museumofdeath.net
Institution Type/Description: General Museum.
Hours & Admission Prices: Sun.-Thurs. 10-8, Fri. 10-9, Sat. 10-10. Adults $17.

Hoopa

HOOPA VALLEY TRIBAL MUSEUM, Hwy. 96, Hoopa, CA 95546. Mailing Address: P.O. Box 1348, Hoopa, CA 95546-1348. Tel.: 530-625-4110.
E-mail: museum@hoopa-nsn.gov
Web Site: bss.sfsu.edu/calstudies/hupa/hoopa.htm
Key Personnel: Dir., Silis-chi-tawn Jackson.
Institution Type/Description: Tribal Museum.
Hours & Admission Prices: Mon.-Fri. 8-12 & 1-5, Sat. 10-12 & 1-4. Village Tours: $10 per person, groups of 6 or more $50.
Attendance: 2,518 (actual)

Huntington Beach

BOLSA CHICA CONSERVANCY, 3842 Warner Ave., Huntington Beach, CA 92649-4263. Tel.: 714-846-1114. Fax: 714-846-4065. Facebook: Bolsa Chica Conservancy.
E-mail: info@bolsachica.org
Web Site: bolsachica.org
Key Personnel: Exec. Dir., Grace Adams.
Institution Type/Description: Conservatory.
Hours & Admission Prices: Daily 9-4.

FINE ARTS GALLERY AT GOLDEN WEST COLLEGE, 15744 Goldenwest Street, Huntington Beach, CA 92647-2748. Tel.: 714-895-8772.
E-mail: dhudson@gwc.cccd.edu
Web Site: www.goldenwestcollege.edu/gallery
Institution Type/Description: Art Museum.
Hours & Admission Prices: Mon.-Fri. 10-4.

HUNTINGTON BEACH ART CENTER, 538 Main St., Huntington Beach, CA 92648. Tel.: 714-374-1650. Fax: 714-374-5304.
E-mail: artcenterstaff@surfcity-hb.org
Web Site: www.huntingtonbeachartcenter.org
Institution Type/Description: Art Gallery.

Hours & Admission Prices: Tues.-Thurs. 12-8, Fri. 12-6, Sat. 12-5.

INTERNATIONAL SURFING MUSEUM, 411 Olive Ave., Huntington Beach, CA 92648. Mailing Address: P.O. Box 782, Huntington Beach, CA 92648-0782. Tel.: 714-960-3483. Fax: 714-960-1434. TDD: 714-960-3483.
E-mail: info@surfingmuseum.org
Web Site: www.surfingmuseum.org
Formerly: Huntington Beach International Surfing Museum
Key Personnel: Dir., At-Large, Diana Dehm; Chm., Brett Barnes; Vice Chm., Peter Townend; Sec., Michelle Junez; Financial Business Admin., Paul Taylor; Treas. & Museum Shop Mgr., Tom Gibbons.
Institution Type/Description: Surfing Museum: housed in restored Art Deco building.
Hours & Admission Prices: Mon.-Fri. 12-5, Sat.-Sun. 11-6. No charge; donations accepted. Closed New Year's Day; Christmas. &
Attendance: 10,000 (estimated)

NEWLAND HOUSE MUSEUM, 19820 Beach Blvd., Huntington Beach, CA 92648. Tel.: 714-962-5777.
Institution Type/Description: Historic House Museum: housed in the former home of William & Mary Newland; built in 1898.
Hours & Admission Prices: Sat.-Sun. 12-4. Requested Donation: $2. Closed holidays.

Idyllwild

IDYLLWILD AREA HISTORICAL SOCIETY, 54470 N. Circle Dr., Idyllwild, CA 92549. Mailing Address: P.O. Box 3320, Idyllwild, CA 92549-3320. Tel.: 951-659-2717.
E-mail: info@idyllwildhistory.org
Web Site: www.idyllwildhistory.org
Key Personnel: Pres. (V), Marlene Pierce; Shop. Mgr., Nancy Borchers.
Institution Type/Description: Historical Society Museum.
Hours & Admission Prices: late June to Labor Day Fri.-Sun. 11-4; Sept. to late June Sat.-Sun. 11-4. No charge; donations accepted. Closed Christmas. &
Attendance: 4,228 (actual)

IDYLLWILD NATURE CENTER, 25225 Hwy. 243, Idyllwild, CA 92549. Mailing Address: c/o Riverside County Parks, 4600 Crestmore Rd., Jurupa Valley, CA 92509. Tel.: 951-659-3850.
E-mail: parks-web@rivcoparks.org
Web Site: www.rivcoparks.org
Institution Type/Description: Nature Center.
Hours & Admission Prices: Tues.-Sun. 9-4:30. Adults $3, children 2-11 $2; children under 2 no charge.

Imperial

PIONEERS' MUSEUM, 373 E. Aten Rd., Imperial, CA 92251-9653. Tel.: 760-352-3211. Fax: 760-352-5411. Facebook: Imperial County Historical Society.
E-mail: curator@pioneersmuseum.net
Web Site: pioneersparkmuseum.net
Key Personnel: C.E.O., L. Housouer; Pres., Greg Smith; Vice Pres., Jurg Hueberger.
Institution Type/Description: History Museum.
Hours & Admission Prices: Tues.-Sat. 10-4, Sun. 12-5. Adults 13 & over $6, seniors over 65 $5, children 6-12 $3; members & children under 6 no charge. &
Attendance: 2,000 (estimated)

Independence

EASTERN CALIFORNIA MUSEUM, 155 N. Grant St., Independence, CA 93526. Mailing Address: P.O. Box 206, Independence, CA 93526-0206. Tel.: 760-878-0364 & 0258. Fax: 760-878-0412. Facebook: Eastern California Museum.
E-mail: ecmuseum@inyocounty.us
Web Site: inyocounty.us/ecmuseum/index.html
Key Personnel: Museum Svcs. Admin., Jon Klusmire; Cur., Roberta Harlan; Museum Shop Mgr., Heather Todd.
Institution Type/Description: Local & Natural History Museum.
Hours & Admission Prices: Daily 10-5. No charge; donations accepted. Closed New Year's Day; Easter; Thanksgiving; Christmas. &
Attendance: 10,000 (actual)

Indio

COACHELLA VALLEY HISTORICAL SOCIETY MUSEUM AND CULTURAL CENTER, 82616 Miles Ave., Indio, CA 92201-4228. Tel.: 760-342-6651. Fax: 760-863-5232. Facebook; Twitter.
E-mail: info@cvhm.org
Web Site: www.cvhm.org
Key Personnel: Pres. & Interim Exec. Dir., Karen Hawkesworth; Office Mgr., Janice Woodside.
Institution Type/Description: History Museum: 1926 adobe house built by Dr. Harry Smiley, known as Smiley Place.
Hours & Admission Prices: Thurs.-Sat. 10-4, Sun. 1-4. Adults $3, senior citizens & students $2, children 6-12 $1; AAM members, children under 5 & members no charge. Closed holidays.
Attendance: 4,000 (actual)

Irvine

BEALL CENTER FOR ART + TECHNOLOGY, 712 Arts Plaza, Claire Trevor School of the Arts, UC Irvine, Irvine, CA 92697-2775. Tel.: 949-824-6206. Fax: 949-824-2450. Facebook, Snapchat, Twitter, Instagram.
E-mail: beallcenter@uci.edu
Web Site: beallcenter.uci.edu
Formerly: University of California Art Gallery and Beall Center for Art and Technology
Key Personnel: Mgr. Programs, Catlin Moore; Assoc. Dir., David Familian.
Institution Type/Description: Art Museum.
Hours & Admission Prices: Tues.-Sat. 12-6. No charge; donations accepted. Closed New Year's Day; Easter; Christmas Eve & Day; university breaks. &
Attendance: 10,000

IRVINE FINE ARTS CENTER, 14321 Yale Ave., Irvine, CA 92604-1901. Tel.: 949-724-6880. Fax: 949-552-2137. Facebook: Irvine Fine Arts Center.
E-mail: rmcgraw@cityofirvine.org
Web Site: www.cityofirvine.org/depts/cs/finearts
Key Personnel: Dir., Wendy Shields.
Institution Type/Description: Arts & Crafts Museum.
Hours & Admission Prices: Mon.-Thurs. 10-9, Fri. 10-5, Sat. 9-5. No charge. &

IRVINE HISTORICAL MUSEUM, 5 San Joaquin, Irvine, CA 92612. Tel.: 949-786-4112. Facebook: Irvine Historical Museum.
E-mail: gadaniels@cox.net
Web Site: www.irvineranchhistory.com
Key Personnel: Pres. (V), Gail Daniels; Museum Shop Mgr., Anne D. Johnson.
Institution Type/Description: Historical Society Museum.
Hours & Admission Prices: Tues. & Sun. 1-4; other times by appointment. No charge; donations accepted. Closed holidays.
Attendance: 200 (estimated)

THE IRVINE MUSEUM, 18881 Von Karman Ave., Ste. 100, Irvine, CA 92612-6541. Tel.: 949-476-0294. Fax: 949-476-2437.
E-mail: sternj1@uci.edu
Web Site: irvinemuseumcollection.uci.edu
Key Personnel: Exec. Dir., Mr. Jean Stern; Museum Shop Mgr., Don Bridges.
Institution Type/Description: Art Museum.
Hours & Admission Prices: Tues.-Sat. 11-5. No charge. Closed major holidays. &
Attendance: 19,442 (actual)

PRETEND CITY CHILDREN'S MUSEUM, 29 Hubble, Irvine, CA 92618. Tel.: 949-428-3900.
E-mail: info@pretendcity.org
Web Site: www.pretendcity.org
Key Personnel: Dir., Sandra Boton, R.N., J.D.
Institution Type/Description: Children's Museum.
Hours & Admission Prices: Mon. 10-1, Tues.-Sun. 10-5. Admission $12.50, military $8; one & under no charge. &
Attendance: 195,000

UNIVERSITY OF CALIFORNIA IRVINE ARBORETUM, University of California, North Campus Dr. & Jamboree Rd., Irvine, CA 92697. Tel.: 949-824-5833. Fax: 949-824-6146.
E-mail: pabowler@uci.edu
Web Site: arboretum.bio.uci.edu
Key Personnel: Dir., Dr. Peter Bowler.
Institution Type/Description: Arboretum.

Hours & Admission Prices: Mon.-Sat. 9-3. No charge; donations accepted. Closed holidays.
Attendance: 14,100

Jackson

AMADOR COUNTY MUSEUM, 225 Church St., Jackson, CA 95642-2303. Mailing Address: 810 Court St., Jackson, CA 95642-2132. Tel.: 209-223-6386. Fax: 209-223-0749.
E-mail: museum@volcano.net
Key Personnel: Cur. & Museum Shop Mgr., Georgia Fox.
Institution Type/Description: General Museum: housed in c.1859 house.
Hours & Admission Prices: Museum: Feb.-Nov. Wed.-Sun. 10-4. Kennedy Gold Mine Model Tours: Sat.-Sun. 11-3 on the hour; group tours by reservation. Mine Model Tours: $2. Museum: no charge; donations accepted. &
Attendance: 9,000 (estimated)

Jenner

FORT ROSS STATE HISTORIC PARK VISITOR CENTER AND MUSEUM, 19005 Coast Hwy. One, Jenner, CA 95450. Tel.: 707-847-3437.
E-mail: info@fortross.org
Web Site: www.fortross.org
Key Personnel: Opers. Mgr., Sarjan Holt; Pres. & C.E.O., Sarah Sweedler; Museum Shop Mgr., Sondra Hunter.
Institution Type/Description: History Museum.
Hours & Admission Prices: Call for hours. Park: adults $8 per car, seniors $7 per car. Museum: no charge. Closed Thanksgiving; Christmas. &
Attendance: 200,000 (estimated)

Jolon

MISSION SAN ANTONIO DE PADUA, 1 Mission Rd., Jolon, CA 93928. Mailing Address: P.O. Box 803, Jolon, CA 93928-0803. Tel.: 831-385-4478. Fax: 831-386-9332.
E-mail: office@missionsanantonio.net
Web Site: www.missionsanantonio.net
Formerly: San Antonio Mission
Key Personnel: Admin., Joan Steele; Gift Shop Mgr., Ms. Franki Grau.
Institution Type/Description: Historic Museum: restored old San Antonio Mission.
Hours & Admission Prices: Daily 10-4. Adult $5, active military, seniors 55 & over and children under 12 $3. Closed New Year's Day; Easter; Independence Day; Thanksgiving; Christmas Eve & Day.
Attendance: 20,000 (estimated)

Julian

JULIAN HISTORICAL SOCIETY, 2133 Fourth St., Julian, CA 92036. Mailing Address: P.O. Box 513, Julian, CA 92036. Tel.: 760-765-0436.
Institution Type/Description: Historical Society Museum: housed in a former one-room schoolhouse; built in 1888.
Hours & Admission Prices: Call for hours.

JULIAN PIONEER MUSEUM, 2811 Washington St., Julian, CA 92036. Mailing Address: P.O. Box 511, Julian, CA 92036-0511. Tel.: 760-765-0227.
E-mail: info@julianpioneermuseum.org
Web Site: julianpioneermuseum.org
Institution Type/Description: History Museum.
Hours & Admission Prices: Call for hours.

Kentfield

COLLEGE OF MARIN FINE ART GALLERY, 835 College Ave, Kentfield, CA 94904. Tel.: 415-485-9494.
E-mail: WWEST@MARIN.EDU
Formerly: Marin Community College Art Gallery
Key Personnel: Dir., Duane Aten.
Institution Type/Description: Art Museum.
Hours & Admission Prices: Call for hours.

Kernville

KERN RIVER VALLEY HISTORICAL SOCIETY MUSEUM, 49 Big Blue Rd., Kernville, CA 93238. Mailing Address: P.O. Box 651, Kernville, CA 93238-0651. Tel.: 760-376-6683.
E-mail: info@krvhistoricalsociety.org

Web Site: www.krvhistoricalsociety.org/museum.htm
Key Personnel: Pres., Ron Bolyard; Cur., Jon Partin.
Institution Type/Description: Historical Society Museum.
Hours & Admission Prices: Thurs.-Sun. 10-4; other times by appointment. No charge; donations accepted. ♿

King City

MONTEREY COUNTY AGRICULTURAL & RURAL LIFE MUSEUM, San Lorenzo County Park, 1160 Broadway, King City, CA 93930. Mailing Address: P.O. Box 644, King City, CA 93930. Tel.: 831-385-8020. Fax: 831-386-0178. Facebook: mcarlm.
E-mail: info@mcarlm.org
Web Site: www.mcarlm.org
Key Personnel: Dir., Jessica Potts; Pres. (V), Jim Spring.
Institution Type/Description: History Museum.
Hours & Admission Prices: Barn: Tues.-Fri. 10-4. House, Schoolhouse, Depot, & Blacksmith Shop: Fri. 12-4, Sat.-Sun. 11-4. House of Irrigation: by appointment. Museum: no charge. Park: Mon.-Fri. $6 per car, Sat.-Sun. $8 per car. Closed New Year's Eve & Day; Thanksgiving; Christmas Eve & Day. ♿
Attendance: 6,120 (actual)

Kingsburg

KINGSBURG HISTORICAL PARK, 2321 Sierra St., Kingsburg, CA 93631. Mailing Address: P.O. Box 282, Kingsburg, CA 93631-1457.
Web Site: www.kingsburghistoricalpark.org
Key Personnel: Pres. (V), Gary Nelson.
Institution Type/Description: History Museum.
Hours & Admission Prices: Feb.-Nov. Thurs.-Sat. 1-4. Family $6, adults $3, children under 12 $.50; discounts to groups of 25 or more; members no charge. ♿
Attendance: 700 (estimated)

Klamath

END OF THE TRAIL MUSEUM, 15500 Hwy. 101 N., Klamath, CA 95548-9351. Mailing Address: P.O. Box 96, Klamath, CA 95548-0096. Tel.: 707-482-2251.
E-mail: tofm@treesofmystery.net
Web Site: treesofmystery.net
Key Personnel: Museum Shop Mgr., Debbie Thompson.
Institution Type/Description: Native American History Museum.
Hours & Admission Prices: No charge. Closed Christmas. ♿
Attendance: 300,000

La Canada Flintridge

DESCANSO GARDENS, 1418 Descanso Dr., La Canada Flintridge, CA 91011-3102. Tel.: 818-949-4200. Facebook: Descanso Gardens.
E-mail: dbrown@descansogardens.org
Web Site: www.descansogardens.org
Key Personnel: Exec. Dir., David R. Brown; C.O.O., Juliann Rooke.
Institution Type/Description: Botanical Garden: housed on the former estate of E. Manchester Boddy; c.1930s.
Hours & Admission Prices: Daily 9-4:30. Adults $9, senior citizens & students $6, children 5-12 $4; guild members & children under 5 no charge. Closed Christmas Day. ♿
Attendance: 350,000 (estimated)

LANTERMAN HOUSE, 4420 Encinas Dr., La Canada Flintridge, CA 91011-3113. Tel.: 818-790-1421. Fax: 818-952-8450.
E-mail: mpatton.lanterman@gmail.com
Web Site: lantermanfoundation.org
Key Personnel: Exec. Dir., Melissa Patton; Pres. (V), Robert Moses.
Institution Type/Description: Historic House: c.1915.
Hours & Admission Prices: Sept.-July Tues., Thurs. and 1st & 3rd Sun. of month 1-4; group and school tours available Tues.-Thurs. 10-12. Adults $5, seniors & students $3; discounts to AAM members; children under 12 no charge. Closed holidays. ♿
Attendance: 3,000 (actual)

MOUNT WILSON OBSERVATORY & MUSEUM, Mt. Wilson Rd., La Canada Flintridge, CA 91011. Mailing Address: P.O. Box 94146, Pasadena, CA 91109-4146. Tel.: 404-413-5484. Fax: 404-413-5481. Facebook: @WilsonObs; Twitter: @MtWilsonObs.
E-mail: mtwilsontelescopes@gmail.com
Web Site: www.mtwilson.edu

Key Personnel: C.E.O., Mr. Samuel D. Hale; Dir., Dr. Thomas Meneghini; Supt., Ms. Magdalena Moran; STEM Educational Programs, Ms. Jessica Rodriguez; Telescope Reservation Coord., Ms. Shelley Bonus; Mgr., Cosmic Cafe, Ms. Lauren Manwaring.
Institution Type/Description: Science Museum.
Hours & Admission Prices: Museum & Grounds: daily 10-5 in good weather; Guided Tours: weekends 1pm; Telescope Viewing Sessions: by appointment.

La Habra

CHILDREN'S MUSEUM AT LA HABRA, 301 S. Euclid, La Habra, CA 90631-5412. Tel.: 562-383-4236.
E-mail: museumstaff@lahabracity.com
Web Site: www.lhcm.org
Key Personnel: Exec. Dir., Roy Mueller; Asst. Dir., Maria Tinajero-Dowdle; Cur. Exhibits & Educ., Lisa Reckon; Visitor Services Coord., Jennifer Andrade.
Institution Type/Description: Children's Museum: housed in a renovated 1923 Mission Style Union Pacific Railroad Depot.
Hours & Admission Prices: Tues.-Fri. 10-4, Sat. 10-5, Sun. 1-5. Admission $12, La Habra residents $11; children under 2 no charge. Closed major holidays. ♿
Attendance: 100,000 (actual)

La Jolla

ATHENAEUM MUSIC & ARTS LIBRARY, 1008 Wall St., La Jolla, CA 92037-4418. Tel.: 858-454-5872. Fax: 858-454-5835.
E-mail: athdir@pacbell.net
Web Site: ljathenaeum.org
Key Personnel: Dir., Erika Torri.
Institution Type/Description: Art Gallery & Library.
Hours & Admission Prices: Tues. & Thurs.-Sat. 10-5:30, Wed. 10-8:30.

BIRCH AQUARIUM AT SCRIPPS, SCRIPPS INSTITUTION OF OCEANOGRAPHY, UNIVERSITY OF CALIFORNIA, SAN DIEGO, 2300 Expedition Way, La Jolla, CA 92037. Mailing Address: 9500 Gilman Dr., #0207, La Jolla, CA 92093-0207. Tel.: 858-534-5301. Fax: 858-534-7114.
E-mail: heiock@ucsd.edu
Web Site: aquarium.ucsd.edu
Key Personnel: Exec. Dir., Nigella Hillgarth, Ph.D.; Cur. Aquarium, Fernando Nosratpour; Mgr. Mktg., Jessica Crawford; Head Facilities, Mick Curzon; Dir. Operations, Patrick Helbling; Dir. Education, Kristin Evans; Dir. Special Events, Barbara Ramsey; Mgr. Membership, Paula Smith; Mgr. Finance, Ken Steitz; Mgr. Museum Shop, Susan Malk; Mgr. Exhibits, Charles Langsett; Program Scientist, Cheryl Peach; Program Scientist, Debbie Zmarzly.
Institution Type/Description: Aquarium-Museum.
Hours & Admission Prices: Daily 9-5. Adults $14, military $12, seniors 60 & over and college students with ID $10, children 3-17 $9.50; children under 2 & members no charge. ♿
Attendance: 400,000 (estimated)

GOTTHELF ART GALLERY, Lawrence Family Jewish Community Center, 4126 Executive Dr., La Jolla, CA 92037. Tel.: 858-362-1114.
E-mail: gallery@lfjcc.org
Web Site: www.sdcjc.org/gag
Key Personnel: Dir., Wendy Sabin-Lasker.
Institution Type/Description: Art Gallery.
Hours & Admission Prices: Sun.-Fri. 9-5. No charge; donations accepted. ♿

JOSEPH BELLOWS GALLERY, 7661 Girard Ave., La Jolla, CA 92037. Tel.: 858-456-5620. Fax: 858-456-5621.
E-mail: info@josephbellows.com
Web Site: www.josephbellows.com
Key Personnel: Dir., Joseph Bellows; Dir., Carol Lee Brosseau.
Institution Type/Description: Art Gallery.
Hours & Admission Prices: Tues.-Sat. 10-5.

LA JOLLA ART ASSOCIATION GALLERY, 8100 Paseo del Ocaso, Ste. B, La Jolla, CA 92037-3115. Tel.: 858-459-1196.
E-mail: rmarksart@gmail.com
Web Site: www.lajollaart.org
Formerly: Village Gallery
Key Personnel: Gallery Dir., Gwen Nobil; Dir. Exhibitions, Carrie Barton.
Institution Type/Description: Art Museum.
Hours & Admission Prices: Daily 11-5. No charge; donations accepted.

LA JOLLA HISTORICAL SOCIETY - WISTERIA COTTAGE GALLERY, 780 Prospect St., La Jolla, CA 92037-4211. Mailing Address: P.O. Box 2085, La Jolla, CA 92038-2085. Tel.: 858-459-5335. Fax: 858-459-0226. Facebook: La Jolla Historical Society.
E-mail: info@lajollahistory.org
Web Site: www.lajollahistory.org
Key Personnel: Exec. Dir., Heath Fox.
Institution Type/Description: Historical Society Museum: housed in Wisteria Cottage; built in 1904.
Hours & Admission Prices: Mon.-Fri. 10-4 by appointment. No charge; donations accepted. &
Attendance: 3,000 (estimated)

MUSEUM OF CONTEMPORARY ART SAN DIEGO, 700 Prospect St., La Jolla, CA 92037-4291. Tel.: 858-454-3541. Fax: 858-454-6985.
E-mail: info@mcasd.org
Web Site: www.mcasd.org
Key Personnel: The David C. Copley Dir. & C.E.O., Hugh M. Davies, Ph.D.; Deputy Dir. & C.F.O., Charles E. Castle; Deputy Dir. Art & Programs, Kathryn Kanjo; Advancement Dir., Elizabeth Yang-Hellewell; Communications & Mktg. Mgr., Leah Straub; Graphic Design Mgr., Alex Devereaux; Hospitality & Events Mgr., Eric Reichman; Mgr. Retail Operations, Shannel Smith; Security Mgr., David Mesa.
Institution Type/Description: Art Museum.
Hours & Admission Prices: Daily 11-5. Adults $10, senior citizens & students $5; discounts to AAM & ICOM members; military and their families, 25 & under and members no charge. Admission valid for 7 days at all MCASD locations. Closed New Year's Day; Thanksgiving; Christmas. &
Attendance: 167,000 (estimated)

STUART COLLECTION, University of California, San Diego, 105 Pepper Canyon Hall, La Jolla, CA 92093-0010. Mailing Address: UCSD 0010, 9500 Gilman Dr., La Jolla, CA 92093-0010. Tel.: 858-534-2117. Fax: 858-534-9713.
E-mail: mbeebe@ucsd.edu
Web Site: stuartcollection.ucsd.edu
Key Personnel: Dir., Mary L. Beebe; Projects Mgr., Mathieu Gregoire; Office Mgr., Jane Peterson.
Institution Type/Description: University Art Collection.
Hours & Admission Prices: Daily 24 hours. No charge; donations accepted. &
Attendance: 500,000 (estimated)

TASENDE GALLERY, 820 Prospect St., La Jolla, CA 92037. Tel.: 858-454-3691. Fax: 858-454-0589.
E-mail: info@tasendegallery.com
Web Site: www.tasendegallery.com
Institution Type/Description: Art Gallery.
Hours & Admission Prices: Tues.-Fri. 10-6, Sat. 11-5.

La Mesa

HORSELESS CARRIAGE FOUNDATION & AUTOMOTIVE RESEARCH LIBRARY, 8186 Center St., Ste. F, La Mesa, CA 91942-2959. Mailing Address: P.O. Box 369, La Mesa, CA 91944-0369. Tel.: 619-464-0301. Fax: 619-464-0301.
E-mail: research@hcfi.org
Web Site: www.hcfi.org
Key Personnel: C.E.O. & Pres. (V), Greg Long, II; Chm. (V), Exec. Dir. & Archivist, D.A. "Mac" MacPherson; Vice Pres., Roberta Watkins; Treas., Gordon McGregor.
Institution Type/Description: Research Library.
Hours & Admission Prices: Jan. to mid-Dec. Tues.-Fri. 9-4. No charge; donations accepted. Closed major holidays. &
Attendance: 100 (estimated)

LA MESA DEPOT MUSEUM, 4695 Nebo Dr., La Mesa, CA 91941-5259. Tel.: 619-465-PSRM (7776).
E-mail: support@sdrm.org
Web Site: www.psrm.org
Key Personnel: Pres. (V), Diana Hyatt; Museum Coord. (V), Richard Pennick.
Institution Type/Description: Restored 1915 railway depot.
Hours & Admission Prices: Sat. 1-4; other times by appointment. No charge; donations accepted. &
Attendance: 1,000 (estimated)

LA MESA HISTORICAL SOCIETY - MCKINNEY HOUSE MUSEUM AND ARCHIVES, 8369 University Ave., La Mesa,

CA 91941. Mailing Address: P.O. Box 882, La Mesa, CA 91944. Tel.: 619-466-0197.
E-mail: information@lamesahistoricalsociety.com
Web Site: lamesahistory.com
Key Personnel: Pres. (V), James D. Newlan.
Institution Type/Description: Historical Society Museum: house built in 1908.
Hours & Admission Prices: 1st & 3rd Sat. 1-4. No charge; donations accepted.

La Puente

LA PUENTE VALLEY HISTORICAL SOCIETY, INC., 15900 E. Main St., La Puente, CA 91744-4719. Mailing Address: P.O. Box 522, La Puente, CA 91747-0522. Tel.: 626-855-1500. Fax: 626-855-4626.
E-mail: info@lpvhistoricalsociety.org
Key Personnel: Mgr., Carol Hamilton; Pres., Patricia McIntosh; Chm. (V), Lynda Glover; Vice Pres., C. Hamilton; Sec., C. Halstead; Treas., James Rutledge.
Institution Type/Description: Local History Museum: housed in the home of John Rowland; built in 1855.
Hours & Admission Prices: Rowland & Dibble Museum: by appointment. Heritage Room: Thurs. 1-4. No charge; donations accepted. Closed holidays. &
Attendance: 1,900 (estimated)

La Quinta

LA QUINTA MUSEUM, 77-885 Avenida Montezuma, La Quinta, CA 92253. Tel.: 760-777-7170.
E-mail: laquintamuseum@gmail.com
Web Site: www.playinlaquinta.com
Institution Type/Description: History & Cultural Arts Museum.
Hours & Admission Prices: Tues.-Sat. 10-4.

Laguna Beach

LAGUNA ART MUSEUM, 307 Cliff Dr., Laguna Beach, CA 92651-1696. Tel.: 949-494-8971. Fax: 949-494-1530. Facebook: @LagunaMuseum; Twitter & Instagram: @LagunaArtMuseum.
E-mail: elee@lagunaartmuseum.org
Web Site: www.lagunaartmuseum.org
Key Personnel: Dir., Dr. Malcolm Warner; Museum Shop Mgr., Arabella Cant; Pres. (V), Robert Hayden, III.
Institution Type/Description: Art Museum.
Hours & Admission Prices: Thurs. 11-9, Fri.-Tues. 11-5. Adults $7, students, seniors & active military $5; discounts to AAM & ICOM members; children under 12 & museum members no charge. &
Attendance: 50,000 (estimated)

LAGUNA BEACH HISTORICAL SOCIETY - MURPHY-SMITH BUNGALOW, 278 Ocean Ave., Laguna Beach, CA 92651. Tel.: 949-497-6834.
E-mail: info@lagunabeachhistory.org
Key Personnel: Pres. (V), Gregg DeNicola, M.D.
Institution Type/Description: Historical Society Museum.
Hours & Admission Prices: Fri.-Sun. 1-4. No charge; donations accepted.
Attendance: 1,000 (estimated)

Lake Arrowhead

MOUNTAIN SKIES ASTRONOMICAL SOCIETY & SCIENCE CENTER, 2001 Observatory Way, Lake Arrowhead, CA 92352. Mailing Address: P.O. Box 1169, Lake Arrowhead, CA 92352-1169. Tel.: 909-336-1699.
E-mail: stargazersmail@mountain-skies.org
Web Site: www.mountain-skies.org
Key Personnel: Dir. & On-Site Astrophysicist, Lorann Parker, D.Sc., Ph.D.
Institution Type/Description: Science Center & Observatory.
Hours & Admission Prices: Fri. 11-2, Sat. 11-2 on SkyQuest Public Program days. Call for information. &

Lake Elsinore

LEHS MUSEUM & RESEARCH LIBRARY, 183 N. Main St., Lake Elsinore, CA 92530-4005. Mailing Address: Lake Elsinore Historical Society, P.O. Box 84, Lake Elsinore, CA 92531-0084. Tel.: 951-678-1537.
Institution Type/Description: Historical Society Museum & Library.
Hours & Admission Prices: By appointment.

LAKE ELSINORE MUSEUM, 106 S. Main St., Lake Elsinore, CA 92530-4109. Mailing Address: Lake Elsinore Historical Society, P. O. Box 84, Lake Elsinore, CA 92531-0084. Tel.: 951-245-4986.
E-mail: info@lakeelsinorehistoricalsociety.org
Institution Type/Description: History Museum.
Hours & Admission Prices: Sat.-Sun. 11-3.

Lakeport

LAKE COUNTY HISTORIC COURTHOUSE MUSEUM, 255 N. Main St., Lakeport, CA 95453. Mailing Address: 255 N. Forbes St., Lakeport, CA 95453-4790. Tel.: 707-263-4555. Fax: 707-263-7918.
E-mail: museum@lakecountyca.gov
Web Site: www.lakecounty.com/things/museums.html
Formerly: Lake County Museum
Institution Type/Description: History Museum: housed in 1871 Lake County Courthouse.
Hours & Admission Prices: Sun. 12-4, Wed.-Sat. 10-4. No charge; donations accepted. Closed most holidays.
Attendance: 6,000 (actual)

Lakeside

BARONA CULTURAL CENTER AND MUSEUM, 1095 Barona Rd., Lakeside, CA 92040-1541. Tel.: 619-443-7003, ext. 219. Fax: 619-443-0173.
E-mail: museum@baronamuseum.org
Web Site: www.baronamuseum.org
Key Personnel: Dir. & Cur., Laurie Egan-Hedley; Collections Mgr., Therese Chung; Visitor Svcs. Coord., Sabrina Landis; Librarian & Archivist, Charla Wilson; Museum Educator, Mallory Genauer; Asst. Cur., Jennifer Stone; Museum Asst., Vanessa Welch.
Institution Type/Description: History Museum.
Hours & Admission Prices: Tues.-Fri. 12-5, Sat. 10-4. No charge.
Attendance: 10,000 (estimated)

LAKESIDE HISTORICAL SOCIETY & MUSEUM, 12418 Parkside St., Lakeside, CA 92040. Mailing Address: 9906 Maine Ave., Lakeside, CA 92040. Tel.: 619-561-1886. Facebook: Lakeside Historical Society & Museum.
E-mail: info@lakesidehistory.org
Web Site: www.lakesidehistory.org
Institution Type/Description: History Museum.
Hours & Admission Prices: Sat. 11-3; other times by appointment.

Lancaster

ANTELOPE VALLEY CALIFORNIA POPPY RESERVE, 15101 W. Lancaster Rd., Lancaster, CA 93536-9733. Mailing Address: 15701 E. Ave. M, Lancaster, CA 93535. Tel.: 661-946-6092 (office) & 724-1180 (reserve). Fax: 661-946-6116.
E-mail: mdic@parks.ca.gov
Web Site: www.parks.ca.gov
Key Personnel: District Supt., Kathy Weatherman; Pres. & Coop Assoc., Margaret Rhyne; Museum Shop Mgr., Pat Treadwell.
Institution Type/Description: Nature Center.
Hours & Admission Prices: Visitor Center: call for hours. Reserve: mid-March to mid-May. $10 per vehicle, senior citizens 62 & over $9; Small Bus: $50; Large Bus $100.
Attendance: 44,913 (actual)

ANTELOPE VALLEY INDIAN MUSEUM, 15701 E. Ave. M, Lancaster, CA 93535-7059. Tel.: 661-946-3055 & 6900. Fax: 661-946-6116. Facebook.
E-mail: peggy.ronning@parks.ca.gov
Web Site: www.avim.parks.ca.gov
Key Personnel: Cur., Peggy Ronning; Coop. Assoc. & Museum Shop Mgr., Susan Martin.
Institution Type/Description: American Indian Cultural Museum.
Hours & Admission Prices: Sat.-Sun. 11-4. Adults $3. Closed Christmas.
Attendance: 6,831 (actual)

LANCASTER MUSEUM OF ART & HISTORY (MOAH), 665 W. Lancaster Blvd., Lancaster, CA 93534-3226. Mailing Address: 44933 N. Fern Ave., Lancaster, CA 93534-2461. Tel.: 661-723-6250. Fax: 661-723-6260. Facebook: Lancaster Museum of Art & History (MOAH).

E-mail: moah@cityoflancasterca.org
Web Site: www.lancastermoah.org
Formerly: Lancaster Museum Art Gallery (LMAG)
Key Personnel: Dir. Parks Recreation & Arts, Ronda Perez; Mgr. & Cur., Andi Campognone; Museum Supvr. II, Angela Riley.
Institution Type/Description: Art & History Museum.
Hours & Admission Prices: Tues.-Wed. & Fri.-Sun. 11-6, Thurs. 11-8. Suggested Donation: adults $5, students & seniors $3; children under 6 no charge. Closed New Year's Day; Easter; Memorial Day; Independence Day; Labor Day; Thanksgiving; Christmas.
Attendance: 20,000 (estimated)

WESTERN HOTEL/MUSEUM, 557 W. Lancaster Blvd., Lancaster, CA 93534-2533. Mailing Address: 44933 N. Fern Ave., Lancaster, CA 93534-2461. Tel.: 661-723-6250. Fax: 661-723-6260.
E-mail: moah@cityoflancasterca.org
Web Site: www.lancastermoah.org
Key Personnel: Dir., Ronda Perez; Cur., Andi Campognone.
Institution Type/Description: History Museum: c.1880s hotel.
Hours & Admission Prices: 2nd & 4th Fri.-Sat. 11-4. No charge; donations accepted. Closed holidays.
Attendance: 2,000 (estimated)

Lebec

FORT TEJON STATE HISTORIC PARK, 4201 Fort Tejon Rd., Lebec, CA 93243. Mailing Address: P.O. Box 895, Lebec, CA 93243-0895. Tel.: 661-248-6692. Fax: 661-248-8373.
Web Site: www.parks.ca.gov
Key Personnel: Park Supt., Stephen Bylin; Interpreter, Sean T. Malis.
Institution Type/Description: State Historic Park: site of 1854-64 U.S. Army fort.
Hours & Admission Prices: Park: daily 9-4. Park: adults $2; children 16 & under no charge. Special Events: adults $5, children $3. Closed New Year's Day; Thanksgiving; Christmas.
Attendance: 85,000 (estimated)

Lemoore

SARAH A. MOONEY MEMORIAL MUSEUM, 542 W. 'D' St., Lemoore, CA 93245. Mailing Address: P.O. Box 413, Lemoore, CA 93245-0413. Tel.: 559-925-0321.
E-mail: staff@lemoorechamber.com
Web Site: www.lemoore.com/sammm.htm
Institution Type/Description: Historic House Museum: built in 1893.
Hours & Admission Prices: Call for hours. No charge; donations accepted.

Livermore

THE CARNEGIE MUSEUM, 2155 Third St., Livermore, CA 94551. Mailing Address: P.O. Box 961, Livermore, CA 94551-0961. Tel.: 925-449-9927.
E-mail: info@carnegieam.org
Institution Type/Description: Historic House Museum.
Hours & Admission Prices: Wed.-Sun. 11:30-4.

Lodi

MICKE GROVE ZOO, 11793 N. Micke Grove Rd., Lodi, CA 95240-9426. Tel.: 209-331-3010. Fax: 209-331-7271.
E-mail: info@.mgzoo.com
Web Site: www.mgzoo.com
Key Personnel: Cur., Avanti Mallapur.
Institution Type/Description: Zoo.
Hours & Admission Prices: Daily 10-5. Adults 14 & up $5, children 3-13 $3; children 2 & under no charge. Closed Christmas Day.
Attendance: 200,000 (estimated)

SAN JOAQUIN COUNTY HISTORICAL MUSEUM, 11793 N. Micke Grove Rd., Lodi, CA 95240-9426. Mailing Address: P.O. Box 30, Lodi, CA 95241-0030. Tel.: 209-331-2055. Fax: 209-331-2057. Facebook.
E-mail: info@sanjoaquinhistory.org
Web Site: www.sanjoaquinhistory.org
Key Personnel: Exec. Dir., David R. Stuart; Pres. (V), Michael Machado; Collections & Exhibits Mgr., Julie Blood; Mgr. Education & Visitors Svcs. and Museum Shop Mgr., Robin Wood; Archivist, Ignacio Sanchez-Alonso; Administrative Mgr., Ute Gampp; Bookkeeper, Judy Rodman; Maintenance Supvr., Mike Mason.
Institution Type/Description: Regional History Museum.

Hours & Admission Prices: Summer: Wed.-Sun. 10-4; Winter: Wed.-Sun. 11-4; guided tours by appointment. Adults $5, senior citizens & teens $4, children 6-12 $2; San Joaquin County Historical Society members no charge. Closed New Year's Day; Martin Luther King, Jr. Day; Presidents' Day; Memorial Day; Independence Day; Labor Day; Veterans Day; Thanksgiving & day after; Christmas. &
Attendance: 50,000 (estimated)

WORLD OF WONDERS SCIENCE MUSEUM, 2 N. Sacramento St., Lodi, CA 95240. Tel.: 209-368-0969. Fax: 209-369-1290. Facebook: World of Wonders Science Museum.
E-mail: info@wowsciencemuseum.org
Web Site: www.wowsciencemuseum.org
Key Personnel: Pres. (V), Sally Snyde.
Institution Type/Description: Science Museum.
Hours & Admission Prices: Wed.-Mon. 10-5. Adults $7, seniors 60 & over $6, children 2-17 $5; teachers w/ID no charge. &
Attendance: 60,000 (actual)

Loleta

THE ARTISAN CHEESE FACTORY TOUR, 252 Loleta Dr., Loleta, CA 95551. Tel.: 707-733-5470.
E-mail: info@artisancheesefactory.com
Web Site: artisancheesefactory.com
Institution Type/Description: Company Museum.
Hours & Admission Prices: Sun. 9-5.

WIYOT HERITAGE CENTER, 1000 Wiyot Dr., Loleta, CA 95551. Tel.: 707-733-5055, 800-388-7633. Fax: 707-733-5601.
E-mail: ted@wiyot.us
Web Site: wiyot.us/contact
Key Personnel: Cultural Dir., Helene Rouvier.
Institution Type/Description: Heritage Center.
Hours & Admission Prices: Mon.-Fri. 8-5. Closed holidays.

Lomita

LOMITA RAILROAD MUSEUM, 2137 W. 250th St., Lomita, CA 90717-2217. Mailing Address: P.O. Box 339, Lomita, CA 90717-0339. Tel.: 310-326-6255. Fax: 310-326-0690.
E-mail: c.harding@lomitacity.com
Web Site: www.lomita-rr.org
Key Personnel: Dir., Cameron Harding; Chm. (V) & Pres. (V), Susan Deuer; Museum Shop Mgr., Julie Klarin.
Institution Type/Description: Railroad Museum.
Hours & Admission Prices: Thurs.-Sun. 10-5. Adults $4, children under 12 $2. Closed Thanksgiving; Christmas.
Attendance: 6,000 (actual)

Lompoc

LA PURISIMA MISSION STATE HISTORIC PARK, 2295 Purisima Rd., Lompoc, CA 93436-9647. Tel.: 805-733-3713. Fax: 805-733-2497.
E-mail: lpminfo@parks.ca.gov
Web Site: www.lapurisimamission.org
Key Personnel: Chm. (V), Robert Wilson; Museum Shop Mgr., Audrey Bowman.
Institution Type/Description: History Museum: housed in 1813-1821 restored adobe buildings.
Hours & Admission Prices: Daily 9-5. $4 per vehicle. Closed New Year's Day; Thanksgiving; Christmas. &
Attendance: 200,000 (actual)

LOMPOC MUSEUM, 200 S. H St., Lompoc, CA 93436-7297. Tel.: 805-736-3888. Facebook: Lompoc Museum.
E-mail: lompocmuseum@gmail.com
Web Site: www.lompocmuseum.org
Key Personnel: Dir. & Cur. Anthropology, Dr. Lisa A. Renken; Pres. (V), Wynn Clevenger; Administrative Asst., Angie Pasquini.
Institution Type/Description: Anthropology Museum: housed in 1910 Carnegie Library Building.
Hours & Admission Prices: Tues.-Fri. 1-5, Sat.-Sun. 1-4. Suggested Donation: adults $1; children & members no charge. Closed New Year's Day; Easter; Independence Day; Thanksgiving; Christmas.
Attendance: 4,000 (actual)

LOMPOC VALLEY HISTORICAL SOCIETY, INC., 207 N. L St., Lompoc, CA 93436-5901. Mailing Address: P.O. Box 88,

Lompoc, CA 93438-0088. Tel.: 805-735-4626. Facebook: Lompoc Valley Historical Society.
E-mail: myra@best1.net
Web Site: lompochistory.org
Key Personnel: Pres., Karen Paaske; 1st Vice Pres., Ardeane Eckert; Corresponding Sec., Jan Webb; Recording Sec., Debbie Manfrina; Treas., Jeannette Miller Wynne; Newsletter Editor, Julie McLaughlin.
Institution Type/Description: Historical Society Museum: housed in 1875 Fabing-McKay-Spanne House.
Hours & Admission Prices: Mon. & Thurs. 8:30-11, 4th Sat. each month 10-1; special tours by appointment. No charge; donations accepted. Closed major holidays.
Attendance: 500 (estimated)

Lone Pine

MUSEUM OF WESTERN FILM HISTORY, 701 S. Main St., Lone Pine, CA 93545. Mailing Address: P.O. Box 111, Lone Pine, CA 93545-0111. Tel.: 760-876-9909.
E-mail: wrangler@museumofwesternfilmhistory.org
Web Site: museumofwesternfilmhistory.org
Formerly: The Beverly & Jim Rogers Museum of Lone Pine Film History
Key Personnel: Dir., Robert Sigman.
Institution Type/Description: History Museum.
Hours & Admission Prices: Mon.-Sat. 10-5, Sun. 10-4. Suggested donation $5; active duty military & children 12 & under no charge.
Attendance: 25,000 (estimated)

Long Beach

AMERICAN MUSEUM OF STRAW ART, 2324 Snowden Ave., Long Beach, CA 90815-2234. Tel.: 562-431-3540. Fax: 562-598-0457.
E-mail: curator@strawartmuseum.org
Web Site: www.strawartmuseum.org
Key Personnel: Dir. & Cur., Morgyn Owens-Celli; Archivist, Carol Thompson; Devel., Bob McCashey.
Institution Type/Description: Decorative & Folk Art Museum.
Hours & Admission Prices: Temporarily closed.

AQUARIUM OF THE PACIFIC, 100 Aquarium Way, Long Beach, CA 90802-8126. Tel.: 562-590-3100. Fax: 562-951-1629. Facebook: Aquarium of the Pacific.
E-mail: aquariumofpacific@lbaop.org
Web Site: www.aquariumofpacific.org
Formerly: Long Beach Aquarium of the Pacific
Key Personnel: Pres. & C.E.O., Jerry Schubel; Chm. (V), John Molina; Vice Pres. Finance & C.F.O., Anthony Brown; Vice Pres. Govt. Rels. & Special Projects and Corporate Sec., Barbara Long; Vice Pres. Communications & Mktg., Cecile Fisher; Vice Pres. Devel., Christopher Clinton Conway; Dir. Education, David Bader; Vice Pres. Human Resources, Kathie Nirschl; Facilities, Tom Vantress; Dir. Retail, Jeff Spofford; Vice Pres. Husbandry, Perry Hampton; Vice Pres. Operations, John Rouse; Dir. Public Rels., Marilyn Podilla.
Institution Type/Description: Aquarium.
Hours & Admission Prices: Daily 9-6. Adults $25.95, seniors 62 & over $22.95, children 3-11 $14.95. &
Attendance: 1,500,000 (actual)

CALIFORNIA STATE UNIVERSITY, LONG BEACH, UNIVERSITY ART MUSEUM, 1250 Bellflower Blvd., Long Beach, CA 90840-0004. Tel.: 562-985-5761. Fax: 562-985-7602.
E-mail: kaplan@csulb.edu
Web Site: www.csulb.edu/uam
Key Personnel: Dir., Chris Scoates; Pres. (V), Michael Davis; Assoc. Dir., Ilee Kaplan; Cur. Education, Brian Trimble; Registrar & Cur. Collections, Angela Barker; Dir. Publications & Public Rels., Amanda Fruta.
Institution Type/Description: University Art Museum.
Hours & Admission Prices: Summer: Tues.-Sat. 12-5; Sept.-May Tues.-Wed. & Fri. 12-5, Thurs. 12-8. Adults $4; discounts to AAM members; students & staff of CSULB and members no charge. Closed university holidays. &
Attendance: 60,000 (estimated)

EARL BURNS MILLER JAPANESE GARDEN, California State University Long Beach, Earl Warren Dr., Long Beach, CA 90840. Mailing Address: California State University Long Beach, 1250 Bellflower Blvd., BAC Rm. 203, Long Beach, CA 90840. Tel.: 562-985-5930 & 8889.
E-mail: jgcoordinators@csulb.edu
Web Site: www.csulb.edu/~jgarden
Key Personnel: Dir., Jeanette Schelin.

Institution Type/Description: Japanese-style Garden.
Hours & Admission Prices: Tues.-Fri. 8-3:30. Sun. 12-4; call to confirm; groups of 10 or more by appointment. No charge; donations accepted. Closed spring & winter break; Independence Day; Thanksgiving & weekend after. ♿
Attendance: 75,000 (estimated)

EL DORADO NATURE CENTER, 7550 E. Spring St., Long Beach, CA 90815-1698. Tel.: 562-570-1745 & 1748. Fax: 562-570-8530.
E-mail: meaghan.o'neill@longbeach.gov
Web Site: www.lbparks.org
Key Personnel: Supervising Park Naturalist, Meaghan O'Neill.
Institution Type/Description: Nature Center.
Hours & Admission Prices: Trail: Tues.-Sun. 8-5. Museum: Tues.-Fri. 10-4, Sat.-Sun. 8:30-4. Parking: Mon.-Fri. $5 per car; Sat.-Sun. $7 per car, holidays $8 per car, school buses $27, commercial buses $32. Closed Christmas. ♿
Attendance: 150,000 (estimated)

HISTORICAL SOCIETY OF LONG BEACH, 4260 Atlantic Ave., Long Beach, CA 90807. Tel.: 562-424-2220. Facebook.
E-mail: julieb@hslb.org
Web Site: www.hslb.org
Key Personnel: Exec. Dir., Julie Bartolotto.
Institution Type/Description: Historical Society Museum.
Hours & Admission Prices: Tues.-Wed. & Fri. 1-5, Thurs. 1-7, Sat. 11-5. Suggested Donation: $5. ♿
Attendance: 5,000 (estimated)

LONG BEACH FIRE MUSEUM, Old Station 10, 1445 Peterson Ave., Long Beach, CA 90813-2325.
E-mail: lbfdmuseum@verizon.net
Web Site: www.lbfdm.org
Key Personnel: Cur., Herb Bramley.
Institution Type/Description: Fire-Fighting Museum.
Hours & Admission Prices: Wed. 8am-12pm, 2nd Sat. of month 10-3; other times by appointment. No charge.

LONG BEACH MUSEUM OF ART, 2300 E. Ocean Blvd., Long Beach, CA 90803-2442. Tel.: 562-439-2119. Fax: 562-439-3587. Facebook: Long Beach Museum of Art.
E-mail: ronn@lbma.org
Web Site: www.lbma.org
Key Personnel: Dir., Ronald C. Nelson.
Institution Type/Description: Art Museum.
Hours & Admission Prices: Thurs. 11-8, Fri.-Sun. 11-5. Adults $7, students & seniors over 62 $6; discounts to AAM & ICOM members; members, children under 12 & Fri. no charge. Closed New Year's Day; Independence Day; Thanksgiving; Christmas. ♿

MUSEUM OF LATIN AMERICAN ART, 628 Alamitos Ave., Long Beach, CA 90802-1513. Tel.: 562-437-1689. Fax: 562-216-4190.
E-mail: info@molaa.org
Web Site: www.molaa.org
Key Personnel: Co. Chm., Mike Deovlet; Co. Chm., Burke Gumbiner; Vice Chm., Dr. Robert Braun; Pres. & CEO, Stuart Ashman; Vice Pres. Operations, Lee Gumbiner; Vice Pres. Devel. & Mktg., Gina Adams; Vice Pres. Finance & Retail, Christopher Gordon; Dir. Communications, Susan Golden.
Institution Type/Description: Art Museum.
Hours & Admission Prices: Wed. & Fri.-Sun. 11-5, Thurs. 11-9. Adults $9, seniors & students $6; children under 12 & members no charge. Closed New Year's Day; Thanksgiving; Christmas. ♿
Attendance: 55,000 (actual)

PACIFIC ISLAND ETHNIC ART MUSEUM, 695 Alamitos Ave., Long Beach, CA 90802-1514. Tel.: 562-216-4170. Fax: 562-435-3052.
E-mail: info@pieam.org
Web Site: www.pieam.org
Institution Type/Description: Art Museum.
Hours & Admission Prices: Wed.-Sun. 11-5. Adults $5, students & seniors over 62 $3; members & children under 12 no charge. Closed New Year's Day; Independence Day; Thanksgiving; Christmas.

THE QUEEN MARY, 1126 Queens Hwy., Long Beach, CA 90802-6390. Tel.: 877-847-2132.
E-mail: foundation@queenmary.com
Web Site: www.queenmary.com
Institution Type/Description: Maritime Museum: located aboard the Queen Mary, retired British ocean liner.

Hours & Admission Prices: Closed for renovations.
Attendance: 1,300,000 (actual)

RANCHO LOS ALAMITOS HISTORIC RANCH & GARDENS, 6400 E. Bixby Hill Rd., Long Beach, CA 90815-4706. Tel.: 562-431-3541. Fax: 562-430-9694. Facebook: Rancho Los Alamitos.
E-mail: info@rancholosalamitos.org
Web Site: www.rancholosalamitos.org
Key Personnel: Exec. Dir., Pamela Seager; Historic Gardens Assoc., Janet Brown; Cur., Pamela Young Lee; Museum Shop Mgr., Duane Mills.
Institution Type/Description: Historic Site Museum: Native American site; ranch house built c.1800-1933; adobe is part of the 1790 300,000-acre Manuel Nieto land grant.
Hours & Admission Prices: Wed.-Sun. 1-5. No charge; donations accepted. Closed national holidays. ♿
Attendance: 32,000 (estimated)

RANCHO LOS CERRITOS HISTORIC SITE, 4600 Virginia Rd., Long Beach, CA 90807-1916. Tel.: 562-206-2040. Fax: 562-206-2049.
E-mail: ellenc@rancholoscerritos.org
Web Site: www.rancholoscerritos.org
Key Personnel: Exec. Dir., Ellen Calomiris; Education Dir., Meighan Maguire; Horticulturist, Marie Barnidge-McIntyre; Museum Shop Mgr., Cheryl Bryan; Pres. Foundation (V), William Lorbeer.
Institution Type/Description: Historic Site Museum: located on 1790 Spanish land grant to Manuel Nieto; 2-story adobe constructed 1844 and remodeled in 1930.
Hours & Admission Prices: Guided Tours: Wed.-Sun. 1-5. Garden Tours: Sat.-Sun. 2:30. No charge; donations accepted. Closed holidays. ♿
Attendance: 25,000 (estimated)

Los Altos

LOS ALTOS HISTORY MUSEUM AKA ASSOCIATION OF THE LOS ALTOS HISTORICAL MUSEUM, 51 S. San Antonio Rd., Los Altos, CA 94022-3056. Tel.: 650-948-9427. Fax: 650-559-0268. Facebook: Los Altos History.
E-mail: hello@losaltoshistory.org
Web Site: www.losaltoshistory.org
Key Personnel: Exec. Dir., Laura Bajuk, E.D.; Pres. (V), Marilyn Henderson; Treas. (V), Julia Lovin; Museum Shop Mgr., Vicki Holman.
Institution Type/Description: History Museum.
Hours & Admission Prices: Thurs.-Sun. 12-4. No charge; donations accepted; discounts to AAM & California Assn. of Museum members. Closed New Year's Day; Easter; Independence Day; Thanksgiving; Christmas. ♿
Attendance: 22,169 (actual)

Los Angeles

A + D ARCHITECTURE AND DESIGN MUSEUM - LOS ANGELES, 900 E. 4th St., Los Angeles, CA 90013-1804. Tel.: 213-346-9734. Fax: 323-937-0278. Facebook: A Plus D LA.
E-mail: info@aplusd.org
Web Site: www.aplusd.org
Key Personnel: Exec. Dir., Dora Epstein Jones; Pres. (V), Eric Stulte, AIA; Asst. Dir., Iryna Stein.
Institution Type/Description: Architecture & Design Museum.
Hours & Admission Prices: Tues.-Fri. 11-5, Sat.-Sun. 12-6. Adults $7, students & seniors $5; discounts to ICOM & AAM members; members no charge. ♿

ACE MUSEUM, 400 S. La Brea Ave., Los Angeles, CA 90036-3524. Mailing Address: 5514 Wilshire Blvd., 2nd Fl., Los Angeles, CA 90036. Tel.: 323-965-8200.
E-mail: acemuseum@acemuseum.org
Web Site: www.acemuseum.org
Institution Type/Description: Art Gallery.
Hours & Admission Prices: Closed for renovations through May 2018. ♿

THE AFRICAN AMERICAN FIREFIGHTER MUSEUM, 1401 S. Central Ave., Los Angeles, CA 90021. Tel.: 213-744-1730. Fax: 213-744-1731. Facebook: @AAFFMUSEUM.
E-mail: aaffmuseum@sbcglobal.net
Web Site: www.aaffmuseum.org
Key Personnel: Pres. Bd. Dirs., David Spence; Vice Pres. Bd. Dirs., Michelle Banks.
Institution Type/Description: Fire-Fighting History Museum.
Hours & Admission Prices: Sun. 1-4, Tues. & Thurs. 10-2. No charge; donations accepted. Closed New Year's Day; Thanksgiving; Christmas. ♿
Attendance: 772 (actual)

THE AMERICAN FILM INSTITUTE, 2021 N. Western Ave., Los Angeles, CA 90027-1625. Tel.: 323-856-7600. Fax: 323-467-4578.
E-mail: information@afi.com
Web Site: www.afi.com
Key Personnel: Pres. & C.E.O., Bob Gazzale; Chm. Bd. Directors, Robert A. Daly; Chm. Bd. Trustees, Sir Howard Stringer.
Institution Type/Description: National Arts Organization: a national trust dedicated to preserving the heritage of film & television & presenting the moving image as an art form.
Hours & Admission Prices: Call for hours and prices. Library: Mon.-Fri. 9-6 no charge to use library. &

AUTRY MUSEUM OF THE AMERICAN WEST, 4700 Western Heritage Way, Los Angeles, CA 90027-1462. Tel.: 323-667-2000. Fax: 323-660-5721. Facebook: Autry National Center.
E-mail: communications@theautry.org
Web Site: www.theautry.org
Formerly: Autry National Center of the American West
Key Personnel: Pres. & C.E.O., W. Richard West, Jr.; Chm. Bd. Trustees, Marshall McKay; Vice Pres. Communications & Mktg., Maren Dougherty.
Institution Type/Description: Western History & Culture Museum.
Hours & Admission Prices: The Autry in Griffith Park: Tues.-Fri. 10-4, Sat.-Sun. 11-5. Adults $10, senior citizens & students $6, children 3-12 $4; discounts to groups, AAM, ICOM & AAA members; military personnel, veterans, peace officers, park rangers, 2nd Tues. of month & members no charge. Historic Southwest Museum Mt. Washington Campus: Sat. 10-4. No charge. Closed Independence Day; Labor Day; Thanksgiving; Christmas Day. &
Attendance: 162,000 (actual)

AVILA ADOBE AT EL PUEBLO, 10 E. Olvera St., Los Angeles, CA 90012-2921. Mailing Address: 125 El Paseo de la Plaza, History Dept. Ste. 400, Los Angeles, CA 90012. Tel.: 213-628-1274. Facebook, Instagram & Twitter: @elpueblola.
E-mail: eptours@lacity.org
Web Site: www.elpueblo.lacity.org
Formerly: Avila Adobe
Key Personnel: Gen. Mgr., Christopher P. Espinosa.
Institution Type/Description: Historic House Museum: housed in c.1818 home of Don Francisco Avila; also served as headquarters for Commodore Robert Stockton during the Mexican American War.
Hours & Admission Prices: Daily 9-4. No charge; donations accepted. &

BATTLESHIP IOWA MUSEUM, 250 S. Harbor Blvd., Berth 87, Los Angeles, CA 90731. Tel.: 877-446-9261.
E-mail: marketing@labattleship.com
Web Site: www.pacificbattleship.com
Key Personnel: Pres. & CEO, Jonathan Williams; Chm. (V), Jeff Lamberti; Museum Shop Mgr., Anthony Cornejo.
Institution Type/Description: Military Museum: housed on a Navy battleship; built early 1940.
Hours & Admission Prices: Daily 10-5. Admission $19.95; members no charge. Closed Thanksgiving; Christmas.

BEN MALTZ GALLERY AT OTIS COLLEGE OF ART AND DESIGN, 9045 Lincoln Blvd., Los Angeles, CA 90045-3505. Tel.: 310-665-6905 & 6800. Fax: 310-665-6908.
E-mail: galleryinfo@otis.edu
Web Site: www.otis.edu/benmaltzgallery
Formerly: OTIS Gallery, OTIS College of Art and Design
Key Personnel: Dir., Galleries & Exhibitions, Kate McNamara; Exhibitions Coord. & Registrar, Jinger Heffner; Mgr. & Outreach Coord., Kathy MacPherson.
Institution Type/Description: Art Gallery.
Hours & Admission Prices: Jan. to mid-Dec. Tues.-Wed. & Fri.-Sat. 10-5, Thurs. 10-7. No charge. Closed New Year's Day; Martin Luther King Jr. weekend; Presidents' Day weekend; Memorial Day weekend; Labor Day weekend; Thanksgiving weekend. &
Attendance: 16,000 (estimated)

BETA MAIN, 114 W. 4th St., Los Angeles, CA 90013. Tel.: 213-986-8500. Facebook, Twitter, Instagram.
Web Site: themainmuseum.org
Key Personnel: Dir., Allison Agsten; Deputy Dir., Alex Capriotti; Co Founder, Tom Gilmore; Co Founder, Jerri Perrone; Curatorial Assoc., Monica Rodriguez.
Institution Type/Description: Art Museum.
Hours & Admission Prices: Wed.-Sun. 12-7. No charge.

THE BROAD, 221 S. Grand Ave., Los Angeles, CA 90012. Tel.: 213-232-6200. Facebook, Instagram, Twitter.
E-mail: info@thebroad.org
Web Site: www.thebroad.org

Key Personnel: Dir., Joanne Heyler; Assoc. Dir. Museum Opers., Jeannine Guido.
Institution Type/Description: Art Museum.
Hours & Admission Prices: Tues.-Wed. 11-5, Thurs.-Fri. 11-8, Sat. 10-8, Sun. 10-6. No charge. Closed Thanksgiving; Christmas. &
Attendance: 823,216 (actual)

CALIFORNIA AFRICAN AMERICAN MUSEUM, 600 State Dr., Exposition Park, Los Angeles, CA 90037-1267. Tel.: 213-744-7432. Fax: 213-744-2050. Facebook, Instagram & Twitter: @CAAMinLA.
E-mail: reception@caamuseum.org
Web Site: www.caamuseum.org
Key Personnel: Exec. Dir., George O. Davis; Chm. Bd., Todd Hawkins; Deputy Dir. & Chief Cur., Naima J. Keith; Museum Cur., Sonia Brown; Exhibit Design Supvr., Edward Garcia; Program Mgr. Visual Arts, Mar Hollingsworth; Program Mgr. Visual Arts, Vida L. Brown; Cur. History, Tyree Boyd; Research Librarian, Denise L. McIver.
Institution Type/Description: African American Culture Museum.
Hours & Admission Prices: Tues.-Sat. 10-5, Sun. 11-5. No charge; donations accepted. Parking $10. Closed New Year's Day; Thanksgiving; Christmas. &
Attendance: 75,000 (estimated)

CALIFORNIA SCIENCE CENTER, 700 Exposition Park Dr., Los Angeles, CA 90037. Tel.: 323-724-3623. Facebook: @CaliforniaScienceCenter; Twitter: @casciencecenter.
E-mail: 4info@cscmail.org
Web Site: www.californiasciencecenter.org
Formerly: California Museum of Science and Industry
Key Personnel: Pres. & C.E.O., Jeffrey Rudolph; Sr. Vice Pres. & Chief Opers. Officer, Laurie Sowd; Sr. Vice Pres. & Chief Advancement Officer, Alyson Goodall; Deputy Dir. Exhibits, Diane Perlov, Ph.D.; C.F.O., Cynthia Pygin; Sr. Dir. Education, Gretchen Bazela; Deputy Dir. Admin., Cheryl Tateishi; Chm. (V), Raul Anaya.
Institution Type/Description: Science and Technology Museum.
Hours & Admission Prices: Daily 10-5. Closed New Year's Day; Thanksgiving; Christmas. &
Attendance: 2,400,000 (estimated)

CALIFORNIA STATE UNIVERSITY, LOS ANGELES, LUCKMAN GALLERY, 5151 State University Dr., Los Angeles, CA 90032-8116. Tel.: 323-343-6600. Fax: 323-343-6423.
E-mail: luckmangallery@luckmanarts.org
Web Site: www.luckmanarts.org
Key Personnel: Exec. Dir., Wendy Baker.
Institution Type/Description: Art Gallery.
Hours & Admission Prices: Mon.-Thurs. & Sat. 12-5.

CHINESE AMERICAN MUSEUM, 425 N. Los Angeles St., Los Angeles, CA 90012-2939. Mailing Address: 125 Paseo de la Plaza, Ste. 300, Los Angeles, CA 90012. Tel.: 213-485-8567. Fax: 213-473-4224.
E-mail: office@camla.org
Web Site: camla.org
Key Personnel: Interim Exec. Dir., Jeffrey Shapiro; Exhibition Coord. & Collections Mgr., Kim Zarate; Admin. & Donor Rels. Asst., Kenneth Chan.
Institution Type/Description: Chinese American Museum.
Hours & Admission Prices: Tues.-Sun. 10-3. Adults $3, seniors 60 & up & students with I.D. $2; members no charge. Closed New Year's Day; Thanksgiving Day; Christmas Day. &

CORITA ART CENTER, 5515 Franklin Ave., Los Angeles, CA 90028-5901. Tel.: 323-450-4650. Fax: 323-466-2150. Facebook: @coritaartcenter.
E-mail: info@corita.org
Web Site: www.corita.org
Key Personnel: Dir., Ray Smith; Mgr. Collections, Keri Marken.
Institution Type/Description: Art Museum.
Hours & Admission Prices: Mon.-Fri. 10-4; original artwork sales by appointment only. No charge; donations accepted. Closed New Year's week; Christmas week; national holidays. &
Attendance: 500 (estimated)

COUTURIER GALLERY, 166 N. La Brea Ave., Los Angeles, CA 90036. Tel.: 323-933-5557. Fax: 323-933-2357.
E-mail: cg@couriergallery.com
Web Site: couriergallery.com
Key Personnel: Dir., Darrel Couturier.
Institution Type/Description: Art Gallery.
Hours & Admission Prices: Tues.-Sat. 11-5. No charge.

CRAFT AND FOLK ART MUSEUM - CAFAM, 5814 Wilshire Blvd., Los Angeles, CA 90036-4501. Tel.: 323-937-4230.
E-mail: info@cafam.org
Web Site: www.cafam.org
Key Personnel: C.E.O. & Dir., Suzanne Isken; Museum Shop Mgr., Adrienne Parker.
Institution Type/Description: Art Museum.
Hours & Admission Prices: Tues.-Fri. 11-5, Sat.-Sun. 12-6. Adults $7, students & senior citizens $5; discounts to AAM members; members, children under 10 & every Sun. no charge. Closed New Year's Day; Easter; Independence Day; Thanksgiving; Christmas. &
Attendance: 20,000 (estimated)

EL PUEBLO HISTORICAL MONUMENT, 125 Paseo de la Plaza, Ste. 400, Los Angeles, CA 90012-2959. Tel.: 213-485-6855. Fax: 213-485-0428. Facebook: El Pueblo LA.
E-mail: chris.espinosa@lacity.org
Web Site: www.elpueblo.lacity.org
Key Personnel: Gen. Mgr., Christopher Espinosa; Asst. Gen. Mgr., Lisa Sarno.
Institution Type/Description: Historic District & Museum Complex.
Hours & Admission Prices: Avila Adobe & Visitors Center: daily 9-4. Plaza Firehouse Museum & Chinese American Museum Tues.-Sun. 10-3. For tour reservations call 213-628-1274. &
Attendance: 260,000 (actual)

FIDM MUSEUM AND LIBRARY, INC., 919 S. Grand Ave., Los Angeles, CA 90015-1421. Tel.: 213-623-5821. Fax: 213-624-7617.
E-mail: info@fidmmuseum.org
Web Site: www.fidmmuseum.org
Key Personnel: Dir., Barbara Bundy; Pres., Tonian Hohberg; Treas., Annie Johnson; Cur., Kevin L. Jones; Assoc. Cur., Christina Johnson; Public Rels., Shirley Wilson; Registrar, Meghan Hansen; Security, Todd Anderson; Museum Shop Mgr., Judy Yaras.
Institution Type/Description: Costume Museum.
Hours & Admission Prices: Feb. to mid-Dec. daily call for hours. No charge; donations accepted. Closed major holidays. &
Attendance: 80,000 (estimated)

FERNDELL NATURE MUSEUM, 5375 Red Oak Dr., Los Angeles, CA 90068-2531. Tel.: 323-666-5046.
Institution Type/Description: Nature Museum.
Hours & Admission Prices: Daily 6am-10pm.

FLIGHT PATH MUSEUM, LAX Imperial Terminal, 6661 W. Imperial Hwy., Los Angeles, CA 90045. Tel.: 424-646-7284. Facebook: @flightpathmuseum; Twitter: @flightpathlax.
E-mail: flightpathguides@lawa.org
Web Site: flightpathmuseum.com
Formerly: Flight Path Learning Center & Museum
Key Personnel: Pres. & Chair, Lynne Adelman; Exec. Dir., Shawna McLean.
Institution Type/Description: Aviation History Museum.
Hours & Admission Prices: Tues.-Sat. 10-3. No charge. Closed national holidays.

FOWLER MUSEUM AT UCLA, W. Sunset Blvd. & Westwood Plaza, 1586 Fowler Bldg., Los Angeles, CA 90095-1549. Mailing Address: Box 951549, Los Angeles, CA 90095-1549, Tel.: 310-825-4361 & 206-7004. Fax: 310-206-7007. Facebook.
E-mail: fowlerws@arts.ucla.edu
Web Site: www.fowler.ucla.edu
Formerly: UCLA Fowler Museum of Cultural History
Key Personnel: Dir., Marla C. Berns; Deputy Dir., David Blair; Exec. Asst., Sophie Livsey; Dir. Exhibitions, Sebastian Clough; Sr. Cur. Southeast Asian & Pacific Arts, Joanna Barrkman; Dir. Education, Terri Geis; Cur. Archaeology, Wendy Teeter; Cur. Latin American & Caribbean Popular Arts, Patrick Polk; Dir. Registration & Collections Mgmt., Rachel Raynor; Dir. Publications, Daniel Brauer; Dir. Devel., Kris Lewis; Dir. Photography, Don Cole; Project Mgr. Exhibitions, Bridget DuLong; Curatorial & Research Assoc., Gassia Armenian; Mgr. Collections, Isabella Kelly-Ramirez; Coord. Membership, Lori LaVelle; Events & Visitor Svcs. Mgr., Sophia Neveu; Head Conservation, Christian de Brer; Dir. Communications & Engagement, Erin Connors; Head Digital Media, Gene McHugh; Coord. Human Resources, Roberto Salazar; Cur. Public Programs, Greg Sandoval; Museum Shop Mgr., Kathy DiGenova.
Institution Type/Description: Cultural History Museum.
Hours & Admission Prices: Office: Mon.-Fri. 8:30-5. Gallery: Wed. 12-8, Thurs.-Sun. 12-5. No charge; donations accepted. Closed university holidays. &
Attendance: 60,000 (actual)

GEORGE J. DOIZAKI GALLERY, Japanese American Cultural & Community Center, 244 S. San Pedro St., Ste. 505, Los Angeles, CA 90012-3856. Tel.: 213-628-2725. Fax: 213-617-8576.
E-mail: info@jaccc.org
Web Site: www.jaccc.org
Key Personnel: Dir., Chris Alhara; Artistic Dir., Hirokazu Kosaka.
Institution Type/Description: Art Gallery.
Hours & Admission Prices: Tues.-Fri. 12-5, Sat.-Sun. 11-4. No charge; donations accepted.

GRAMMY MUSEUM AT L.A. LIVE, 800 W. Olympic Blvd., Ste. A245, Los Angeles, CA 90015-1366. Tel.: 213-765-6800. Fax: 213-765-6801. Facebook; Twitter.
E-mail: admin@grammymuseum.org
Web Site: grammymuseum.org
Key Personnel: Exec. Dir., Bob Santelli; Deputy Dir., Rita George; Dir. Education, Kate Nader; Dir. Public Programming & Artist Rels., Lynne Sheridan; Dir. Special Projects, Stacie Takaoka Fidler; Retail Mgr., Eric Walsh.
Institution Type/Description: Music History Museum.
Hours & Admission Prices: Mon.-Fri. 10:30-6:30, Sat. & Sun. 10-6:30. Adults $12.95, seniors 65 & up and college students with I.D. $11.95, youth 6-17 & military with I.D. $10.95; discounts to AAA members; children under 5 & members no charge. &
Attendance: 140,000 (estimated)

GRIER MUSSER MUSEUM, 403 S. Bonnie Brae St., Los Angeles, CA 90057-3009. Tel.: 213-413-1814.
E-mail: griermusser@hotmail.com
Web Site: griermussermuseum.org
Key Personnel: Dir., Susan Tejada.
Institution Type/Description: Antiques Museum; housed in c.1898 Queen Ann Victorian house.
Hours & Admission Prices: Wed.-Sat. 12-4, call for reservations. Adults $10, senior citizens & students $7, children $5; discounts to groups, families and AAM & ICOM members. Closed most holidays.
Attendance: 500 (actual)

GRIFFITH OBSERVATORY, 2800 E. Observatory Rd., Los Angeles, CA 90027-1299. Tel.: 213-473-0800.
E-mail: inquires@griffithmedia.org
Web Site: www.griffithobservatory.org
Key Personnel: Dir., Dr. Edwin C. Krupp; Pres. Friends Of The Observatory, Richard Semler.
Institution Type/Description: Public Observatory, Planetarium & Astronomy Museum.
Hours & Admission Prices: Tues.-Fri. 12-10, Sat.-Sun. 10-10; hours are subject to change. Open Tues. in summer & school breaks. Oschin Planetarium: adults $7, seniors & students $5, children 5-12 $3; discounts to members. Closed Thanksgiving; Christmas. &
Attendance: 1,400,000 (actual)

GRUNWALD CENTER FOR THE GRAPHIC ARTS, HAMMER MUSEUM, 10899 Wilshire Blvd., Los Angeles, CA 90024-4343. Tel.: 310-443-7076. Fax: 310-443-7099. TDD: 310-443-7094.
E-mail: info@hammer.ucla.edu
Web Site: www.hammer.ucla.edu
Formerly: Grunwald Center for the Graphic Arts, UCLA Hammer Museum of Art and Cultural Center
Key Personnel: Dir. & Chief Cur., Cynthia Burlingham; Conservation Technician, Maureen McGee; Preparator, Lynne Blaikie; Curatorial Assoc., Leslie Cozzi; Assoc. Registrar, Susan Chin.
Institution Type/Description: Art Museum & Study Center.
Hours & Admission Prices: Grunwald Center Study Room: Mon.-Fri. 10-4, by appointment only. No charge. &

HAMMER MUSEUM, 10899 Wilshire Blvd., Los Angeles, CA 90024. Tel.: 310-443-7000. Fax: 310-443-7099.
E-mail: info@hammer.ucla.edu
Web Site: hammer.ucla.edu
Key Personnel: Dir., Ann Philbin; Chair, Marcy Carsey; Dir. Registration & Collections Mgmt., Portland McCormick; Dir. Finance, Hilary Fahlsing; Dir. Administration, Lindsay Martin; Chief Communications Officer, Gia Storm; Sr. Communications & Mktg. Mgr., Mitch Marr; Dir. Public Programs, Claudia Bestor; Dir. Operations, Henry Clancy; Chief Cur., Connie Butler; Museum Shop Mgr., Sara Beattie.
Institution Type/Description: Art Museum.
Hours & Admission Prices: Tues.-Fri. 11-8, Sat.-Sun. 11-5. No charge. Closed New Year's Day; Independence Day; Thanksgiving; Christmas. &
Attendance: 200,000 (estimated)

HANCOCK MEMORIAL MUSEUM, 850 W. 37Th St., University Park Campus, Los Angeles, CA 90089-0189. Tel.: 213-740-5900. Fax: 213-740-2343.
E-mail: specol@usc.edu
Web Site: https://libraries.usc.edu
Key Personnel: Cur., Melinda Hayes.
Institution Type/Description: History Museum: housed in four rooms dismantled from the original Hancock mansion.
Hours & Admission Prices: By appointment.

HERITAGE SQUARE MUSEUM, 3800 Homer St., Los Angeles, CA 90031-1530. Tel.: 323-225-2700. Fax: 323-225-2725. Facebook: Heritage Square Museum.
E-mail: administrator@heritagesquare.org
Web Site: www.heritagesquare.org
Key Personnel: Pres., Pauline Prinz; Dir. Administration & Operations, Jessica Rivas Acuna; Devel. Assoc., Isabella Shirinyan; Museum Shop Mgr., Bernadette Basurto; Administrative Asst., Kim Kirui.
Institution Type/Description: History Museum.
Hours & Admission Prices: Fri.-Sun. 11:30-4:30, tours at 12, 1, 2, & 3. Adults $10, senior citizens $8, children 6-12 $5; discounts to AAA & Time Travelers members; members no charge. Closed New Year's Day; Thanksgiving; Christmas.
Attendance: 12,000 (estimated)

HOLLYWOOD BOWL MUSEUM, 2301 N. Highland Ave., Los Angeles, CA 90068-2742. Tel.: 323-850-2000.
E-mail: kwelch@laphil.org
Web Site: www.hollywoodbowl.com
Key Personnel: Dir. Archives & Hollywood Bowl, Dr. Ljiljana Grubisic.
Institution Type/Description: Music & Performing Arts Museum.
Hours & Admission Prices: July-Sept. 18 Tues.-Sat. 10-8; Sept. 19-June Tues.-Fri. 10-5, Sat. by appointment. No charge. Closed New Year's Day; Thanksgiving; Christmas.
Attendance: 27,000 (actual)

INSTITUTE OF CONTEMPORARY ART, LOS ANGELES (ICA LA), 1717 E. Seventh St., Los Angeles, CA 90021. Mailing Address: 238 S. Mission Rd., Los Angeles, CA 90033.
E-mail: info@theicala.org
Web Site: www.theicala.org
Formerly: Santa Monica Museum of Art
Key Personnel: Exec. Dir., Elsa Longhauser.
Institution Type/Description: Contemporary Art Museum.
Hours & Admission Prices: Tues.-Sat. 11-6. Suggested Donations: adults $5, artists, senior citizens & students $3; members no charge. Closed legal holidays.
Attendance: (estimated)

THE J. PAUL GETTY MUSEUM, 1200 Getty Center Dr., Los Angeles, CA 90049-1687. Tel.: 310-440-7330; 310-440-7305 (TDD). Fax: 310-440-7751. Facebook, Instagram & Twitter: @gettymuseum.
E-mail: gettymuseum@getty.edu
Web Site: www.getty.edu
Key Personnel: Dir., Timothy Potts; Assoc. Dir., Collections, Richard Rand; Assoc. Dir., Exhibitions, Carolyn Marsden-Smith; Asst. Dir. Public Affairs, John Giurini; Vice Pres., Devel., Janet McKillop; Head, Administration, Robin Weissberger; Sr. Cur., Paintings & Head, Curatorial Affairs, Davide Gasparotto; Sr. Cur., Antiquities, Jeffrey Spier; Sr. Cur., Drawings, Julian Brooks; Sr. Cur., Manuscripts, Beth Morrison; Sr. Cur., Photographs, Jim Ganz; Sr. Cur., Sculpture & Decorative Arts, Anne-Lise Desmas; Sr. Conservator, Antiquities Conservation, Susanne Gänsicke; Sr. Conservator, Decorative Arts & Sculpture Conservation, Jane Bassett; Sr. Conservator, Paintings Conservation, Ulrich Birkmaier; Sr. Conservator, Paper Conservation, Marc Harnly; Chief Registrar, Betsy Severance; Head, Design, Jessica Harden; Head, Education, Keishia Gu; Head, Perparations, Kevin Marshall; Head, Public Programs, Laura Kishi; Head, Interpretive Content, Erik Bertellotti; Head, Collection Information & Access, Brenda Podemski; Publisher, Kara Kirk; Head, Merchandise Devel. & Retail Opers., Thomas Stewart.
Institution Type/Description: Art Museum.
Hours & Admission Prices: Getty Center Museum: Tues.-Fri. & Sun. 10-5:30, Sat. 10-9; extended summer hours. Getty Villa Museum: Wed.-Mon. 10-5 ticket required. Museum: no charge. Villa: no charge; advance timed-entry ticket required. Parking: $20 visit to one or both locations on same day; $15 after 3 p.m. Closed New Year's Day; Independence Day; Thanksgiving; Christmas.
Attendance: 1,783,832 (actual)

JAPANESE AMERICAN NATIONAL MUSEUM, Mailing Address: 100 N. Central Ave., Los Angeles, CA 90012. Tel.: 213-625-0414. Fax: 213-625-1770.
E-mail: mediarelations@janm.org

Web Site: www.janm.org
Key Personnel: Pres. & C.E.O., Ann Burroughs; Chm. (V), Hon. Norman Y. Mineta.
Institution Type/Description: History Museum.
Hours & Admission Prices: Tues.-Wed. & Fri.-Sun. 11-5, Thurs. 12-8. Adults $12, seniors 62 & over, students w/I.D. & youth 6-17 $6; discounts to groups & AAM and ICOM members; Thurs. 5-8 & every 3rd Thurs. of month, members, children 5 & under no charge. Closed New Year's Day; Independence Day; Thanksgiving; Christmas.
Attendance: 82,500 (estimated)

KOHN GALLERY, 1227 N. Highland Ave., Los Angeles, CA 90038-1206. Tel.: 323-658-8088. Fax: 323-658-8068.
E-mail: info@kohngallery.com
Web Site: www.kohngallery.com
Key Personnel: Dir., Samantha Glaser.
Institution Type/Description: Art Gallery.
Hours & Admission Prices: Tues.-Fri. 10-6, Sat. 11-6.

KOREAN AMERICAN NATIONAL MUSEUM, 3727 W. 6th St., Ste. 519, Los Angeles, CA 90020-5110. Tel.: 213-388-4229. Fax: 213-381-1288.
E-mail: info@kamuseum.org
Web Site: www.kamuseum.org
Key Personnel: Exec. Dir., Shinae Yoon.
Institution Type/Description: Korean American Museum.
Hours & Admission Prices: Call for hours.

LA PLAZA DE CULTURA Y ARTES, 501 N. Main St., Los Angeles, CA 90012. Tel.: 213-542-6200, 888-488-8083.
E-mail: info@lapca.org
Web Site: http://lapca.org/
Key Personnel: C.E.O., John Echeveste.
Institution Type/Description: History Museum.
Hours & Admission Prices: Wed.-Mon. 12-7. No charge; donations accepted. Closed New Year's Day; Thanksgiving; Christmas.
Attendance: 100,000 (estimated)

LABAND ART GALLERY, LOYOLA MARYMOUNT UNIVERSITY, One LMU Dr., MS 8346, Los Angeles, CA 90045-2650. Tel.: 310-338-2880. Fax: 310-338-6024. Facebook.
E-mail: labandinfo@lmu.edu
Web Site: cfa.lmu.edu/laband
Key Personnel: Dir. & Cur., Karen Rapp.
Institution Type/Description: University Art Gallery.
Hours & Admission Prices: mid-Sept. to May Tues.-Wed. & Fri.-Sat. 11-4, Thurs. 2-7. No charge; donations accepted.
Attendance: 3,877 (actual)

LACE (LOS ANGELES CONTEMPORARY EXHIBITIONS), 6522 Hollywood Blvd., Los Angeles, CA 90028-6210. Tel.: 323-957-1777.
E-mail: info@welcometolace.org
Web Site: www.welcometolace.org
Key Personnel: Pres., William Moreno; Exec. Dir., Sarah Russin; Bd. Member, Kathie Foley-Meyer; Bd. Member, Jackie Sharp; Bd. Member, Jeff Cain.
Institution Type/Description: Visual Arts Center
Hours & Admission Prices: Wed.-Sun. 12-6. No charge; donations accepted.
Attendance: 15,000 (actual)

LATINO MUSEUM OF HISTORY, ART AND CULTURE, 201 N. Los Angeles St., Los Angeles, CA 90012. Tel.: 213-626-7600. Fax: 213-626-3830.
E-mail: apescador@thelatinomuseum.org
Web Site: www.thelatinomuseum.org
Institution Type/Description: Latino History Museum.
Hours & Admission Prices: Thurs.-Tues. 10-4. Adults $6, students & senior citizens $5; members no charge.

THE LOS ANGELES ART ASSOCIATION/GALLERY 825, 825 N. La Cienega Blvd., Los Angeles, CA 90069-4707. Tel.: 310-652-8272. Fax: 310-652-9251.
E-mail: gallery825@laaa.org
Web Site: www.laaa.org
Key Personnel: Exec. Dir., Peter Mays.
Institution Type/Description: Southern California Art Gallery/Association.
Hours & Admission Prices: Tues.-Sat. 10-5. No charge; donations accepted. Closed New Year's Day; Easter; Independence Day; Thanksgiving; Christmas.
Attendance: 5,000 (estimated)

LOS ANGELES (CENTRAL) PUBLIC LIBRARY, 630 W. Fifth St., Los Angeles, CA 90071-2002. Tel.: 213-228-7000 & 7470; 800-735-2922 (TDD). Fax: 213-228-7069. Twitter: @laplcentral.
Web Site: www.lapl.org
Key Personnel: Central Library Dir., Kren Malone; Programming & Outreach Mgr., Joyce Cooper; Research & Special Collections Mgmt., Ani Boyadjian.
Institution Type/Description: Library with Collections.
Hours & Admission Prices: Mon.-Thurs. 10-8, Fri.-Sat. 9:30-5:30, Sun. 1-5. No charge. Closed national & state holidays. &
Attendance: 2,140,620 (actual)

LOS ANGELES COUNTY MUSEUM OF ART, 5905 Wilshire Blvd., Los Angeles, CA 90036-4598. Tel.: 323-857-6000. Fax: 323-857-6214. Facebook & Twitter: @LACMA.
E-mail: publicinfo@lacma.org
Web Site: www.lacma.org
Key Personnel: C.E.O. & Wallis Annenberg Dir., Michael Govan; Co-Chair Bd., Elaine P. Wynn; Co-Chair Bd., Tony P. Ressler; Sr. Vice Pres. Devel. & Audience Strategy, Melissa Bomes; Sr. Vice Pres. Education & Public Programs, Naima Keith; Sr. Vice Pres. Administration, Gen. Counsel & Sec., Fred Goldstein; Deputy Dir. Exhibitions & Planning, Zoe Kahr; Dir. Program for Art of the Ancient Americas, Diana Magaloni; C.F.O., Ann Rowland; Sr. Deputy Dir. Art Administration & Collections, Nancy Thomas; C.O.O., Diana Vesga.
Institution Type/Description: Art Museum.
Hours & Admission Prices: Mon., Tues. & Thurs. 11-5, Fri. 11-8, Sat.-Sun. 10-7. Adults $25, senior citizens 65 & up and students w/I.D. $21; discounts to LA County residents and AAM & ICOM members; members and children 17 & under no charge. Closed Thanksgiving; Christmas. &
Attendance: 1,400,000 (estimated)

LOS ANGELES MUNICIPAL ART GALLERY - BARNSDALL ART PARK, 4800 Hollywood Blvd., Los Angeles, CA 90027-5302. Tel.: 323-644-6269; 213-660-4254 (TDD). Fax: 323-644-6271. Facebook, Instagram & Twitter: @LAMAGBarnsdall;.
E-mail: lamag@lacity.org
Web Site: www.lamag.org
Key Personnel: Dir., Isabelle Lutterodt; Exhibition Preparator, John Weston; Museum Education, Marta Feinstein; Museum Education/Exhibitions, Gabriel Cifarelli; Cur., Ciara Moloney; Cur., Steven Wong.
Institution Type/Description: Contemporary Art Gallery.
Hours & Admission Prices: No charge; donations accepted. Closed municipal, state & federal holidays. &
Attendance: 50,000 (actual)

LOS ANGELES MUSEUM OF THE HOLOCAUST, 100 The Grove Dr., Los Angeles, CA 90036. Tel.: 323-651-3704.
E-mail: info@lamoth.org
Web Site: www.lamoth.org
Key Personnel: Exec. Dir., Beth Kean; Dir. Operations, Lisa Barnet; Dir. of Education, Jordanna Gessler.
Institution Type/Description: Holocaust History Museum.
Hours & Admission Prices: Fri. 10-2, Sat.-Thurs. 10-5. No charge; donations accepted. Closed New Yea's Day; first day of Passover; first day of Rosh Hashanah; Yom Kippur; Thanksgiving; Christmas. &
Attendance: 63,000 (actual)

LOS ANGELES POLICE MUSEUM, 6045 York Blvd., Los Angeles, CA 90042-3503. Tel.: 323-344-9445. Fax: 323-344-9516. Facebook & Instagram: @LosAngelesPoliceMuseum.
E-mail: info@lapolicemuseum.org
Web Site: www.lapolicemuseum.org
Formerly: Los Angeles Police Historical Society & Museum
Key Personnel: Exec Dir., David Fryar; Immediate Past Chm., Robert Taylor; Museum Mgr., Meesha Walden.
Institution Type/Description: Police History Museum.
Hours & Admission Prices: Mon.-Fri. 10-4, 3rd Sat. each month 9-3. Adults $9, senior citizens over 62 $8; members & groups of less than 5 children under 12 no charge. &
Attendance: 6,722 (actual)

THE LOS ANGELES ZOO AND BOTANICAL GARDENS, 5333 Zoo Dr., Los Angeles, CA 90027-1451. Tel.: 323-644-4200. Fax: 323-662-9786.
E-mail: info@lazoo.org
Web Site: www.lazoo.org
Key Personnel: Pres. Greater LA Zoo Assoc., Karen B. Winnick; Zoo Dir., John R. Lewis; Asst. Gen. Mgr., Denise Verret; Vice Pres. Mktg. & Communications, Kait Hilliard; Visitor Svcs. & Gen. Mgr., Greg Edgar; Dir. Research, Dr. Cathleen Cox; Museum Shop Mgr., Denise Demont.
Institution Type/Description: Zoo.
Hours & Admission Prices: Daily 10-5. Adults 13 & over $20, seniors 62 & over $17, children 2-12 $15; discounts to groups; members & children under 2 no charge. Closed Christmas. &
Attendance: 1,600,000 (actual)

LUMMIS HOME: EL ALISAL, 200 E. Ave. 43, Los Angeles, CA 90031. Mailing Address: 221 N. Figueroa St., Ste. 350, Los Angeles, CA 90012. Tel.: 818-243-6488. Fax: 818-243-6447.
E-mail: RAP.PublicInfo@lacity.org
Formerly: Historical Society of Southern California - Lummis Home: El Alisal
Institution Type/Description: Historic House: housed in the former home of author & Indian rights activist, Charles F. Lummis; built from 1896-1910. Listed on the National Register of Historical Places.
Hours & Admission Prices: Sat.-Sun. 10-3. No charge. &

MILDRED E. MATHIAS BOTANICAL GARDEN, University of California, 777 S. Tiverton Ave., Los Angeles, CA 90095. Mailing Address: UCLA, Box 951606, Los Angeles, CA 90095. Tel.: 310-825-3620 & 1260 (office). Facebook: Mildred E. Mathias Botanical Garden; Instagram: @uclabotanical.
E-mail: rundel@biology.ucla.edu
Web Site: www.botgard.ucla.edu.
Key Personnel: Dir., Dr. Phil Rundel.
Institution Type/Description: Arboretum; Botanical Garden-Herbarium.
Hours & Admission Prices: Mon.-Fri. 8-5, Sat. 8-4. No charge; donations accepted. Closed university holidays. &
Attendance: 36,000

MUSEUM EDUCATION & TOURS PROGRAM FOR HOLLYHOCK HOUSE, Barnsdall Park, 4800 Hollywood Blvd., Los Angeles, CA 90027-5302. Tel.: 323-913-4030. Fax: 323-913-4032.
E-mail: hollyhock-house@sbcglobal.net
Web Site: barnsdall.org
Key Personnel: Dir. Education, Sara L. Cannon; Cur. Historic Site, Jeffrey Herr.
Institution Type/Description: History Museum: home of oil heiress Aline Barnsdall designed by architect Frank Lloyd Wright, c.1919.
Hours & Admission Prices: Fri.-Sun. 12:30, 1:30, 2:30 & 3:30. Adults 17 & up $2; discounts to AAM & ICOM members; conservancy & trust members and youth under 17 no charge.
Attendance: 11,000 (actual)

THE MUSEUM OF AFRICAN AMERICAN ART, Baldwin Hills Crenshaw Plaza, Macy's 3rd Fl., 4005 Crenshaw Blvd., Los Angeles, CA 90008-2534. Tel.: 323-294-7071. Fax: 323-294-7084.
E-mail: info@maaala.org
Web Site: www.maaala.org
Key Personnel: Pres. (V), Belinda Fontenot-Jamerson.
Institution Type/Description: African American Art Museum.
Hours & Admission Prices: Thurs.-Sat. 11-6, Sun. 12-5. No charge; donations accepted. &
Attendance: 1,500 (estimated)

MUSEUM OF BROKEN RELATIONSHIPS, 6751 Hollywood Blvd., Los Angeles, CA 90028. Tel.: 323-892-1200.
E-mail: Museum@Brokenships.LA
Web Site: brokenships.la/visit
Institution Type/Description: General Museum.
Hours & Admission Prices: Mon. 11-5, Tues.-Wed. 11-7, Thurs. 10-8, Fri.-Sat. 10-9, Sun. 11-8. Adults $18, seniors 65 & over and students $15.

THE MUSEUM OF CONTEMPORARY ART, LOS ANGELES, 250 S. Grand Ave., Los Angeles, CA 90012-3021. Tel.: 213-626-6222; 213-626-6222 (TDD). Fax: 213-620-8674. Facebook, Instagram & Twitter: @MOCAlosangeles;.
E-mail: info@moca.org
Web Site: www.moca.org
Key Personnel: Co-Chair (V), Maurice Marciano; Co-Chair (V), Lilly Tartikoff; Pres. (V), Maria Seferian; Dir., Philippe Vergne; C.F.O. & C.O.O., Michael Harrison; Chief Cur., Helen Molesworth; Chief Communications Officer, Sarah L. Stifler; Dir. Visitor Engagement, Catherine Arias; Dir. Exhibition Mgmt., Jill Davis; Dir. Individual Giving, Brooke Devenney; Sr. Cur., Bennett Simpson; Dir. Retail Opers., Andrea Urban; Dir. Exhibition Production, MOCA Grand Ave. & MOCA Pacific Design Center, Patrick Weber; Dir. Opers., Woody Schofield, Jr.; Asst. Cur., Lanka Tattersall.
Institution Type/Description: Art Museum.

Hours & Admission Prices: MOCA Grand Avenue: Mon., Wed. & Fri. 11-6, Thurs. 11-8, Sat.-Sun. 11-5. Adults $12, students & seniors $7; discounts to AAM & ICOM members; children under 12, Thurs. 5-8 & members no charge. &
Attendance: 236,000 (actual)

MUSEUM OF TOLERANCE, 9786 W. Pico Blvd., Los Angeles, CA 90035-4720. Tel.: 310-772-2505. Fax: 310-553-4521. Facebook: Museum of Tolerance; Twitter: @musoftolerance.
E-mail: info@museumoftolerance.com
Web Site: www.museumoftolerance.com
Key Personnel: Founder & Dean, Rabbi Marvin Hier; Assoc. Dir., Rabbi Abraham Cooper; Exec. Dir., Rabbi Meyer H. May; Museum Dir., Liebe Geft; C.F.O. & C.A.O., Susan Burden; Dir. Membership Devel., Marlene F. Hier; Dir. Public Rels., Avra Shapiro; Dir. Communications, Michele E. Alkin; Dir. Media Projects, Richard Trank; Dir. Major Gifts, Janice Prager.
Institution Type/Description: Holocaust & Human Rights Museum.
Hours & Admission Prices: Museum of Tolerance: Sun.-Fri. 10-5. Adults $15.50, seniors 62 & up $12.50, youth 5-18 & students w/ID 11.50. Anne Frank Exhibit: Sun.-Wed. 10-6:30, Thurs. 10-9:30, Fri. 10-5. Adults $15.50, seniors 62 & up $12.50, youth 5-18 & students w/ID 11.50. Discounts to AAM & ICOM members; members no charge. Closed Jewish holidays; New Year's Day; Independence Day; Labor Day; Thanksgiving Day; Christmas Day. &
Attendance: 250,000 (estimated)

NATIONAL MUSEUM OF ANIMALS & SOCIETY, 4302 Melrose Ave., Los Angeles, CA 90029. Mailing Address: P.O. Box 26483, Los Angeles, CA 90026-0483. Tel.: 323-928-2652.
E-mail: info@museumofanimals.org
Web Site: www.museumofanimals.org
Institution Type/Description: Art Museum.
Hours & Admission Prices: Closed for relocation.

NATURAL HISTORY MUSEUM OF LOS ANGELES COUNTY, 900 Exposition Blvd., Los Angeles, CA 90007-4057. Tel.: 213-763-3466. Fax: 213-743-4843. Facebook, Instagram & Twitter: @nhmla.
E-mail: info@nhm.org
Web Site: www.nhm.org
Key Personnel: Pres. & Dir., Dr. Lori Bettison-Varga; Chm. Bd., Paul G. Haaga, Jr.; Chief Deputy Dir., Dawn McDivitt; C.F.O., Gretchen Humbert; Sr. Vice Pres. Research & Collections and Dir. Dinosaur Inst., Dr. Luis M. Chiappe; Vice Pres. Exhibitions, Gretchen Baker; Vice Pres. Education & Programs, Su Oh.
Institution Type/Description: Natural History Museum.
Hours & Admission Prices: Daily 9:30-5. Adults $12, college students with ID, youth 13-17 & seniors $9, children 3-12 $5; children under 3, California teachers with valid school ID & members no charge. Closed New Year's Day; Independence Day; Thanksgiving; Christmas. &
Attendance: 650,000 (estimated)

OLD PLAZA FIREHOUSE AT EL PUEBLO, 501 N. Los Angeles St., Los Angeles, CA 90013. Mailing Address: El Pueblo de Los Angeles Historical Monument, 125 Paseo de la Plaza, Ste. 400, Los Angeles, CA 90012. Tel.: 213-625-3741. Facebook: Old Plaza Firehouse at El Pueblo.
E-mail: eptours@lacity.org
Web Site: www.elpueblo.lacity.org
Formerly: Old Plaza Firehouse
Key Personnel: Gen. Mgr., Christopher P. Espinosa.
Institution Type/Description: Firefighting History Museum: housed in a former firehouse; built in 1884.
Hours & Admission Prices: Tues.-Sun. 10-3. No charge; donations accepted.

PAGE MUSEUM AT THE LA BREA TAR PITS, 5801 Wilshire Blvd., Los Angeles, CA 90036. Tel.: 213-763-3499.
E-mail: info@tarpits.org
Web Site: www.tarpits.org
Key Personnel: Chief Cur., Dr. John Harris; Cur. Ornithology, Dr. Kenneth Campbell; Mgr. Collections, Aisling Farrell; Curatorial Asst., Gary Takeuchi; Archivist, Cathy McNassor.
Institution Type/Description: History Museum.
Hours & Admission Prices: Daily 9:30-5. Adults $12, youth 13-17, seniors 62 & over, and college students $9, children 3-12 $5; members, children 2 & under and military no charge. Closed New Year's Day; Independence Day; Thanksgiving; Christmas.

PETER MENDENHALL GALLERY, 6150 Wilshire Blvd., Space 8, Los Angeles, CA 90048. Tel.: 323-936-0061. Fax: 323-936-0288.
E-mail: info@petermendenhallgallery.com
Web Site: www.petermendenhallgallery.com

Institution Type/Description: Art Gallery.
Hours & Admission Prices: Tues.-Sat. 11-6.

PETERSEN AUTOMOTIVE MUSEUM, 6060 Wilshire Blvd., Los Angeles, CA 90036-3605. Tel.: 323-964-6356 & 6357. Fax: 323-930-6642.
E-mail: info@petersen.org
Web Site: petersen.org
Key Personnel: Exec. Dir., Terry Karges; Chm. (V), Steven E. Young; Cur., Leslie Kendall; Membership, Paul Moritz; Special Events, Mandy Hanlon; Museum Shop Mgr., Gregg Guenthard.
Institution Type/Description: Automotive Museum.
Hours & Admission Prices: Daily 10-6. Adults $16, senior citizens 62 & up and students 13-17 or w/ID $13, children 3-12 $8; discounts to AAA members; children under 3 & members no charge. &
Attendance: 180,000 (estimated)

PLAZA DE LA RAZA, INC. & BOATHOUSE GALLERY, 3540 N. Mission Rd., Los Angeles, CA 90031-3195. Tel.: 323-223-2475. Fax: 323-223-1804.
E-mail: info@plazadelaraza.org
Web Site: www.plazadelaraza.org
Key Personnel: Exec. Dir., Rose Marie Cano; Chm. (V), Armando G. Ramirez; Dir. Education, Maria Jimenez-Torres; Museum Shop Mgr., Rosalie Portillo; Coord., Kay Rosser; Dir. Devel., Tomas J. Benitez; Dir. Mktg., Melissa Richardson Banks.
Institution Type/Description: Art Museum: housed in historic boathouse gallery.
Hours & Admission Prices: Mon.-Fri. 10-5, Sat. 10-2. Suggested Donations: adults $3, children $1. Closed Columbus Day; Veterans Day; Thanksgiving. &

PSYCHIATRY: AN INDUSTRY OF DEATH MUSEUM, 6616 Sunset Blvd., Los Angeles, CA 90028-7104. Tel.: 323-467-4242, 800-869-2247.
E-mail: humanrights@cchr.org
Web Site: www.cchr.org
Institution Type/Description: Psychiatry Museum.
Hours & Admission Prices: Mon.-Fri. 10-9, Sat.-Sun. 10-6. No charge.

ROSAMUND FELSEN GALLERY, 1923 S. Santa Fe Ave., #100, Los Angeles, CA 90021-2917. Tel.: 818-649-1995/213-999-9903. Facebook & Instagram: @rosamundfelsengallery.
E-mail: info@rosamundfelsen.com
Web Site: www.rosamundfelsen.com
Key Personnel: Dir., Rosamund Felsen; Operations Mgr., A. Chau.
Institution Type/Description: Art Gallery.
Hours & Admission Prices: Tues.-Sat. 10-5:30. No charge. &

SEPULVEDA HOUSE AT EL PUEBLO, 12 Olvera St., El Pueblo de Los Angeles, Los Angeles, CA 90012-2921. Tel.: 213-624-7300. Facebook, Instagram & Twitter: @elpueblola.
E-mail: eptours@lacity.org
Web Site: elpueblo.lacity.org
Formerly: Sepulveda House
Key Personnel: Gen. Mgr., Christopher P. Espinosa.
Institution Type/Description: Historic House Museum: housed in former boardinghouse, built in 1887.
Hours & Admission Prices: Tues.-Sun. 10-3. No charge; donations accepted. &

SKIRBALL CULTURAL CENTER, 2701 N. Sepulveda Blvd., Los Angeles, CA 90049-6833. Tel.: 310-440-4500. Fax: 310-440-4595.
E-mail: info@skirball.org
Web Site: www.skirball.org
Key Personnel: Pres. & C.E.O., Uri D. Herscher; Museum Dir., Robert Kirschner; Vice Pres. & Dir. Education, Sheri Bernstein; Cur., Erin Clancey; Dir. Mktg., Jennifer Caballero; Mgr. Membership, Sabrina Wurf.
Institution Type/Description: Art & History Museum.
Hours & Admission Prices: Tues.-Fri. 12-5, Sat.-Sun. 10-5. Adults $10, students w/ ID & seniors 65 & up $7, children 2-12 $5; discounts to AAM members & museum professionals w/ID; Thursdays, children under 2 & members no charge. Closed national & Jewish holidays. &
Attendance: 500,000 (actual)

TRAVEL TOWN TRANSPORTATION MUSEUM, 5200 Zoo Dr., Los Angeles, CA 90027-1472. Mailing Address: P.O. Box 39846 Griffith Station, Los Angeles, CA 90039. Tel.: 323-662-5874. Fax: 818-243-0041.
E-mail: nancy.officialmuseumdirectory2018@traveltown.org
Web Site: www.traveltown.org
Key Personnel: Dir., Nancy Gneier; Asst. Dir., Thomas W. Breckner.

Institution Type/Description: Transportation Museum: located on the site of the Civilian Conservation Corp. camp, which was used as a P.O.W. camp during World War II.
Hours & Admission Prices: Mon.-Fri. 10-4, Sat.-Sun. & holidays 10-5. No charge; donations accepted. Closed Christmas. &
Attendance: 350,000 (estimated)

USC FISHER MUSEUM OF ART, 823 Exposition Blvd., Los Angeles, CA 90089-0292. Mailing Address: 823 Exposition Blvd. # HAR MC 126, Los Angeles, CA 90089-0292. Tel.: 213-740-4561. Fax: 213-740-7676.
E-mail: fmoa@usc.edu
Web Site: fisher.usc.edu
Key Personnel: Dir., Dr. Selma Holo; Assoc. Dir., Kay Allen; Administrative Asst., Raphael Gatchalian; Education & Programs Coord., Ani Mnatsakanyan; Collections Mgr. & Registrar, Stephanie Kowalick; Chief Preparator, Juan Rojas.
Institution Type/Description: University Art Museum.
Hours & Admission Prices: Tues.-Fri. 12-5, Sat. 12-4, during exhibitions. No charge. &
Attendance: 20,000 (estimated)

VELVETERIA, 711 New High St., Los Angeles, CA 90012. Tel.: 626-714-8545.
E-mail: velveteriala@gmail.com
Web Site: velveteria.com
Key Personnel: Owner, Caren Anderson; Owner, Carl Baldwin.
Institution Type/Description: Art Museum.
Hours & Admission Prices: Wed.-Mon. 11-6; other times by appointment. Admission $10.

WATTS TOWERS ARTS CENTER & CHARLES MINGUS YOUTH ARTS CENTER, 1727 E. 107th St., Los Angeles, CA 90002-3621. Tel.: 213-847-4646 & 485-1795. Fax: 323-564-7030.
E-mail: watts.towers1@lacity.org
Web Site: wattstowers.org
Key Personnel: Dir., Rosie Lee Hooks.
Institution Type/Description: Arts Center & Gallery.
Hours & Admission Prices: Watts Towers Arts Center: Tues.-Sat. 10-4, Sun. 12-4. Tours: adults $7, seniors $3; military and children under 12 no charge. Simon Rodia's Watts Towers: Sat. 10-4, Sun. 12-4. Tours: Thurs.-Fri. 11-3, Sat. 10:30-3, Sun. 12:30-3; please call for information. Closed New Year's Day; Christmas. &
Attendance: 25,000 (estimated)

WELLS FARGO HISTORY MUSEUM CLOSED, 333 S. Grand Ave., Los Angeles, CA 90071-1504. Mailing Address: Wells Fargo Historical Services, 420 Montgomery St., MAC A0101-022, San Francisco, CA 94163. Tel.: 213-253-7166. Fax: 213-680-2269. Facebook, Instagram & Twitter: @wellsfargo.
E-mail: wfmuseum.la@wellsfargo.com
Web Site: www.wellsfargohistory.com
Key Personnel: Museum Mgr., Juan Colato; Cur., Ileana Bonilla.
Institution Type/Description: Company History Museum: housed in downtown Los Angeles Wells Fargo Ctr.
Hours & Admission Prices: Mon.-Fri. 9-5. No charge. Closed bank holidays. &

ZIMMER CHILDREN'S MUSEUM, 6505 Wilshire Blvd., Ste. 100, Los Angeles, CA 90048-4908. Tel.: 323-761-8984. Fax: 323-761-8990. Facebook: Zimmer Children's Museum.
E-mail: info@zimmermuseum.org
Web Site: www.zimmermuseum.org
Formerly: Zimmer Children's Museum of Jewish Community Centers of Greater Los Angeles
Key Personnel: C.E.O., Esther Netter; Assoc. Dir. Play & Learning, Belinda Vong; Visitor Experience Mgr., Sasha Karlova; Devel. & Communications Mgr., Christy Moody; Mng. Dir., Amy Shapiro; Accounting & H.R. Mgr., Jennifer Noguera.
Institution Type/Description: Children's Museum.
Hours & Admission Prices: Mon.-Thurs. 10-5, Fri. 10-4, Sun. 12:30-4:30. Admission $7.50; discounts to groups and ACM members; members, children under 1 & grandparents on Thurs. no charge. Closed all national & Jewish holidays; holiday Sundays. &
Attendance: 80,961 (actual)

Los Banos

MILLIKEN MUSEUM, 905 Pacheco Blvd., Los Banos, CA 93635. Mailing Address: P.O. Box 2294, Los Banos, CA 93635-2294. Tel.: 209-826-5505.

E-mail: millikenmuseum@att.net
Formerly: Ralph Milliken Museum
Key Personnel: Chm. (V) & Sec., Dan Nelson.
Institution Type/Description: Cultural Museum.
Hours & Admission Prices: Tues.-Sun. 1-4; special tours by arrangement. No charge; donations accepted.
Attendance: 1,000 (estimated)

Los Gatos

LOS GATOS MUSEUMS ART GALLERY, 24 N. Santa Cruz Ave., Los Gatos, CA 95030. Tel.: 408-354-4530.
Institution Type/Description: Art Gallery.
Hours & Admission Prices: Tues.-Fri. 10-5:30, Sat. 10-5, Sun. 11-3.

NEW MUSEUM LOS GATOS (NUMU), 106 E. Main St., Los Gatos, CA 95030. Mailing Address: P.O. Box 1904, Los Gatos, CA 95031. Tel.: 408-354-2646. Facebook.
E-mail: operations@numulosgastos.org
Web Site: numulosgatos.org
Key Personnel: Exec. Dir., Lisa Coscino; Pres., Barney Davidge.
Institution Type/Description: Art, History, Innovation & Bay Area Museum.
Hours & Admission Prices: Wed. 1-5, Thurs. 11-8, Fri.-Sun. 11-5. Adults $10; seniors, students & military $6; members and children 18 & under no charge. Closed holidays. &
Attendance: 15,000 (actual)

Madera

MADERA COUNTY MUSEUM, 210 W. Yosemite Ave., Madera, CA 93637. Mailing Address: Madera County Historical Society, P. O. Box 150, Madera, CA 93639-0150. Tel.: 559-673-0291. Fax: 559-673-0742.
E-mail: mchs210@gmail.com
Web Site: www.maderahistory.org
Key Personnel: Pres. (V), Sheryl Berry; Cur., Karen Elmore; Museum Shop Mgr., Terri De La Guerra.
Institution Type/Description: General Museum: housed in the 1900, first Madera County Court House.
Hours & Admission Prices: Early Dec. to late Nov. Sat.-Sun. 1-4. No charge; donations accepted. Closed New Year's Day; Easter; Mother's Day; Father's Day; Christmas; some summer days.
Attendance: 1,379 (actual)

Malibu

FREDERICK R. WEISMAN MUSEUM OF ART, Pepperdine University, 24255 Pacific Coast Hwy., Malibu, CA 90263-3999. Tel.: 310-506-7257. Fax: 310-506-4556.
E-mail: michael.zakian@pepperdine.edu
Web Site: arts.pepperdine.edu/museum/
Key Personnel: Dir., Michael Zakian.
Institution Type/Description: University Art Museum.
Hours & Admission Prices: Tues.-Sun. 11-5. No charge. Closed New Year's Eve, Day & week; Memorial Day; Independence Day; Labor Day; Thanksgiving; Christmas Day & week. &
Attendance: 20,000 (estimated)

MALIBU ADAMSON HOUSE FOUNDATION, 23200 Pacific Coast Hwy., Malibu, CA 90265-4937. Mailing Address: P.O. Box 291, Malibu, CA 90265-0291. Tel.: 310-456-8432 & 1770.
E-mail: info@adamsonhouse.org
Web Site: www.adamsonhouse.org
Formerly: Historic Adamson House & Museum and Malibu Lagoon Museum
Key Personnel: Dir., Linus Kojelis; Pres. (V), Lynette Brody; Dir., Devel. & Membership, Nidra Winger.
Institution Type/Description: Historic House & Museum; botanical gardens.
Hours & Admission Prices: Wed.-Sat. 11-3, last house tour 2; groups of 10 & over by appointment only. Adults $7; members no charge. Reciprocal admission to docents of other organizations. Closed holidays. &
Attendance: 50,000 (estimated)

Mammoth Lakes

DEVILS POSTPILE NATIONAL MONUMENT, Mammoth Lakes, CA 93546. Mailing Address: P.O. Box 3999, Mammoth Lakes, CA 93546-3999. Tel.: 760-934-2289. Fax: 760-934-4780.
Web Site: nps.gov/depo
Key Personnel: Park Supt., Deanna Dulen.
Institution Type/Description: Park Museum.

Hours & Admission Prices: May-Oct. daily 9-5 weather permitting. Adult $7, child 3-15 $4; not to exceed $20 per carload. Park Camping: daily.

MAMMOTH SKI MUSEUM, 100 College Pkwy., Mammoth Lakes, CA 93546. Mailing Address: P.O. Box 1815, Mammoth Lakes, CA 93546. Tel.: 760-934-6592 & 3781.
E-mail: info@mammothskimuseum.org
Web Site: www.mammothskimuseum.org
Key Personnel: Dir. & Cur., Kendra Knight.
Institution Type/Description: Ski Museum.
Hours & Admission Prices: Wed.-Sat. 10-5. Adults $5; discounts to AAM members; members no charge. &
Attendance: 1,000

Manhattan Beach

OCEANOGRAPHIC TEACHING STATION INC. - ROUNDHOUSE MARINE STUDIES LAB & AQUARIUM, Manhattan Beach Pier, Manhattan Beach, CA 90266. Mailing Address: P.O. Box 1, Manhattan Beach, CA 90267. Tel.: 310-379-8117. Fax: 310-937-9366.
E-mail: roundhouse.aquarium@verizon.net
Web Site: www.roundhouseaquarium.org
Key Personnel: Pres. OTS Bd. (V), Matt Friedman; Treas., Chuck Milam; Dir. Aquarium, Eric Martin; Dir. Aquarium, Valerie Hill.
Institution Type/Description: Aquarium.
Hours & Admission Prices: Mon.-Fri. 3pm to sunset, Sat.-Sun. 10am to sunset. No charge; donations accepted. Closed New Year's Day; Thanksgiving; Christmas.
Attendance: 49,900 (estimated)

Manteca

MANTECA HISTORICAL SOCIETY AND MUSEUM, 600 W. Yosemite Ave., Manteca, CA 95337-5402. Mailing Address: P.O. Box 907, Manteca, CA 95336-1137. Tel.: 209-825-3021.
E-mail: info.mantecamuseum@gmail.com
Web Site: www.mantecamuseum.org
Key Personnel: Dir., Clancy Rogers.
Institution Type/Description: Historical Society Museum.
Hours & Admission Prices: Tues.-Wed. 1-3, Thurs. & Sun. 1-4; groups by appointment. No charge. &
Attendance: 70,000 (estimated)

Mariposa

CALIFORNIA STATE MINING & MINERAL MUSEUM, 5005 Fairgrounds Dr., Mariposa, CA 95338. Mailing Address: P.O. Box 1192, Mariposa, CA 95338-1192. Tel.: 209-742-7625. Fax: 209-966-3597.
E-mail: mineralmuseum@sierratel.com
Web Site: www.parks.ca.gov
Key Personnel: Acting Dir., Darci Moore.
Institution Type/Description: Mineralogy Museum.
Hours & Admission Prices: May-Sept. Thurs.-Sun. 10-5; Oct.-April Thurs.-Sun. 10-4. Adults $4; children 12 & under no charge. Closed New Year's Day; Thanksgiving; Christmas. &
Attendance: 15,229 (actual)

MARIPOSA MUSEUM AND HISTORY CENTER INC., 5119 Jessie St., Mariposa, CA 95338. Mailing Address: P.O. Box 606, Mariposa, CA 95338-0606. Tel.: 209-966-2924.
E-mail: mmhc@sti.net
Web Site: www.mariposamuseum.com
Key Personnel: Pres. (V), Mike Wenrich; Tour Dir., Janine Clark; Museum Shop Mgr., Phyllis I. Faust-Stephens.
Institution Type/Description: Historical Society Museum.
Hours & Admission Prices: Daily 10-4. Adults $5; under 18 & members no charge. Closed New Year's Eve & Day; Thanksgiving; Christmas Eve & Day. &
Attendance: 11,124 (actual)

Markleeville

ALPINE COUNTY MUSEUM, 135 School St., Markleeville, CA 96120. Mailing Address: P.O. Box 517, Markleeville, CA 96120-0517. Tel.: 530-694-2317. Fax: 530-694-1087. www.alpinecounty-museum.org.
E-mail: alpinemuseum@yahoo.com
Web Site: www.co.alpine.ca.us/dept/museum/museum.htm

Key Personnel: Cur., James Boyd; Pres., Historical Society, Tom Sweeney.
Institution Type/Description: History Museum.
Hours & Admission Prices: Memorial Day to Oct. Thurs.-Mon. 11-4. No charge; donations accepted. &
Attendance: 5,000 (actual)

Martinez

CONTRA COSTA COUNTY HISTORICAL SOCIETY'S HISTORY CENTER, 724 Escobar St., Martinez, CA 94553. Tel.: 925-229-1042. Fax: 925-229-1772. Facebook: CoCo History.
E-mail: info@cocohistory.com
Web Site: www.cocohistory.com
Institution Type/Description: Historical Society Museum.
Hours & Admission Prices: Tues.-Thurs. 9-4, 3rd Sat. of the month 10-2.

JOHN MUIR NATIONAL HISTORIC SITE, 4202 Alhambra Ave., Martinez, CA 94553-3826. Tel.: 925-228-8860. Fax: 925-228-8192.
E-mail: JOMU_interpretation@nps.gov
Web Site: www.nps.gov/jomu
Institution Type/Description: Historic Site.
Hours & Admission Prices: Daily 10-5. No charge. Closed New Year's Day; Thanksgiving; Christmas. &
Attendance: 39,826 (actual)

MARTINEZ MUSEUM, 1005 Escobar, Martinez, CA 94553. Mailing Address: P.O. Box 14, Martinez, CA 94553. Tel.: 510-228-8160.
E-mail: webmaster@martinezhistory.org
Web Site: martinezhistory.org
Key Personnel: Dir., Andrea Blachman; Pres., John Curtis.
Institution Type/Description: History Museum.
Hours & Admission Prices: Tues. & Thurs. 11:30-3, Sun. 1-4. No charge; donations accepted.
Attendance: 1,700 (actual)

Marysville

CHINESE-AMERICAN MUSEUM OF NORTHERN CALIFORNIA, 232 1st St., Marysville, CA 95901-6002. Tel.: 510-710-2342.
E-mail: brianltom@gmail.com
Institution Type/Description: Historic Building Museum: built in 1858.
Hours & Admission Prices: 1st Sat. of the month 12-4. No charge.

MARY AARON MEMORIAL MUSEUM, 704 D St., Marysville, CA 95901-5319. Mailing Address: P.O. Box 1759, Marysville, CA 95901. Tel.: 530-743-1004. Facebook: Mary Aaron Museum.
E-mail: maryaaronmuseum@gmail.com
Web Site: www.maryaaronmuseum.com
Key Personnel: Dir., Diane Barbaccia; Pres. (V), Peppie Schrader.
Institution Type/Description: Historic House Museum: built in 1855.
Hours & Admission Prices: 1st Sat. of the month 1-4; other times by appointment. No charge; donations accepted.
Attendance: 800 (estimated)

MUSEUM OF THE FORGOTTEN WARRIORS, 5865 A Rd., Marysville, CA 95901-8017. Tel.: 530-742-3090.
E-mail: cws21779@aol.com
Web Site: museumoftheforgottenwarriors.org
Institution Type/Description: Military Museum.
Hours & Admission Prices: Thurs. 7pm-9pm, Sat. 10-3; other times by appointment. Call for holiday hours. No charge.

McClellan

AEROSPACE MUSEUM OF CALIFORNIA, 3200 Freedom Park Dr., McClellan, CA 95652-2432. Tel.: 916-643-3192. Fax: 916-643-0389.
E-mail: roxanneyonn@comcast.net
Web Site: www.aerospaceca.org
Key Personnel: Exec. Dir., Roxanne Yonn; Pres. (V), James W. Hopp, Maj. Gen. USAF (Ret.); Museum Shop Mgr., Katie Ferguson.
Institution Type/Description: Aviation & Aerospace Museum.
Hours & Admission Prices: Tues.-Sat. 9-5, Sun. 10-5. Adults $8; seniors 65 & over and youth 13-18 $6, children 6-12 $5; active military and children 5 & under no charge. &
Attendance: 75,000 (estimated)

Mecca

INTERNATIONAL BANANA MUSEUM, 98775 State Hwy. 111, Mecca, CA 92254. Tel.: 619-840-1429. Facebook.
E-mail: ibmbigbanana@aol.com
Web Site: www.internationalbananamuseum.com
Institution Type/Description: General Museum.
Hours & Admission Prices: Fri.-Sun. 1-6.

Mendocino

FORD HOUSE VISITOR CENTER AND MUSEUM, 735 Main St., Mendocino, CA 95460. Mailing Address: P.O. Box 1387, Mendocino, CA 95460-1387. Tel.: 707-937-5397. Facebook: Ford House Visitor Center and Museum.
E-mail: fordhouse@mcn.org
Web Site: www.mendoparks.org
Key Personnel: Mgr., Jenny Heckeroth.
Institution Type/Description: History Museum: house built in 1854. Listed on the National Register of Historic Places.
Hours & Admission Prices: Daily 11-4. Suggested Donation: $2-$5. &
Attendance: 25,000 (estimated)

KELLEY HOUSE MUSEUM, 45007 Albion St., Mendocino, CA 95460. Mailing Address: P.O. Box 922, Mendocino, CA 95460-0922. Tel.: 707-937-5791. Facebook.
E-mail: info@kelleyhousemuseum.org
Web Site: www.kelleyhousemuseum.org
Key Personnel: Exec. Dir., Anne Cooper; Pres. (V), Steven Smith.
Institution Type/Description: Historical Society Museum: 1861 Kelley House.
Hours & Admission Prices: Museum: Fri.-Mon. 11-3; walking tours Sat.-Sun. 11, Research Office: by appointment. Tours: $10 per person. Museum: no charge; donations accepted. Closed New Year's Day; Thanksgiving; Christmas. &
Attendance: 3,500 (estimated)

MENDOCINO ART CENTER, 45200 Little Lake St. at Kasten St., P.O. Box 765, Mendocino, CA 95460-0765. Tel.: 707-937-5818, 800-653-3328. Fax: 707-937-4625.
E-mail: MACBOARD@MCN.ORG
Web Site: www.mendocinoartcenter.org
Key Personnel: Exec. Dir., Lindsay Shields.
Institution Type/Description: Art Gallery.
Hours & Admission Prices: Daily 10-5.

Merced

APPLEGATE PARK ZOO, 1045 W. 25th St., Merced, CA 95340-3500. Mailing Address: 678 W. 18th St., Merced, CA 95340-4721. Tel.: 209-385-6840. Fax: 209-384-5805.
E-mail: johnsonl@cityofmerced.org
Web Site: www.cityofmerced.org
Key Personnel: Dir. Parks & Community Svcs., Mike Conway; Pres. (V), Marlene Murphy; Recreation Supvr., Lindsey Johnson; Lead Zookeeper, Donna McDowell.
Institution Type/Description: Zoo.
Hours & Admission Prices: March-Oct. daily 10-5; Nov.-Dec. daily 10-4. Admission $3, children 5-15 $2, seniors 62 & up $1.50; discounts to AZA, AAZK & reciprocal institution members; museum members, Merced Zoological Society members, & children under 5 no charge. Closed New Year's Day; Thanksgiving; Christmas. &
Attendance: 52,000 (estimated)

MERCED AGRICULTURE MUSEUM, 4498 E. Hwy. 140, Merced, CA 95340-9388. Tel.: 209-723-2451.
Key Personnel: Dir., Bob Olavars; C.E.O., Greg Wellman; Museum Shop Mgr., Judy Carey; Chm. (V), Cathy Krumm; Pres. (V), Charles Parish.
Institution Type/Description: Agriculture Museum.
Hours & Admission Prices: Tues.-Sun. 8-5. No charge; donations accepted. &
Attendance: 480 (estimated)

MERCED COUNTY COURTHOUSE MUSEUM, 21st and N Sts., Merced, CA 95340-3790. Tel.: 209-723-2401. Fax: 209-723-8029. Facebook: Merced County Courthouse Museum.
E-mail: mercedmuseum@sbcglobal.net
Web Site: www.mercedmuseum.org
Key Personnel: C.E.O. & Dir., Sarah Lim; Pres., Carlene Cunningham; Financial Dir., Grey Roberts; Sec., John Hofmann; Museum Shop Mgr., Ann Carson.
Institution Type/Description: Local History Museum: 1875 Italianate style Courthouse.

Hours & Admission Prices: Wed.-Sun. 1-4. No charge; donations accepted. Closed New Year's Eve & Day; Easter; Independence Day; Thanksgiving; Christmas Eve & Day. &
Attendance: 8,000 (estimated)

Mill Valley

MUIR WOODS NATIONAL MONUMENT, 1 Muir Woods Rd., Mill Valley, CA 94941-2696. Tel.: 415-388-2595 & 2596. Fax: 415-389-6957.
E-mail: goga_muwo_socialmedia@nps.gov
Web Site: www.nps.gov/muwo
Key Personnel: Supt., Brian O'Neill.
Institution Type/Description: National Park.
Hours & Admission Prices: Daily 8 to sunset. Adults 16 & over $7; children 15 & under, Golden Eagle and Access Passes no charge. &
Attendance: 1,446,256 (estimated)

Millbrae

THE MILLBRAE MUSEUM, 450 Poplar Ave., Millbrae, CA 94030. Mailing Address: Millbrae Historical Society, P.O. Box 511, Millbrae, CA 94030. Tel.: 650-692-5786.
Institution Type/Description: Historic House Museum: built in 1895.
Hours & Admission Prices: Call for hours.

MILLBRAE TRAIN STATION, California Dr. at Murchison Dr., Millbrae, CA 94030. Mailing Address: Millbrae Historical Society, P.O. Box 511, Millbrae, CA 94030. Tel.: 650-333-1136.
Web Site: www.millbraehs.org
Institution Type/Description: Historic Building: built in 1907.
Hours & Admission Prices: Sat. 10-2; other times by appointment. Adults $2; members no charge. &

Milpitas

SAN FRANCISCO BAY BIRD OBSERVATORY, 524 Valley Way, Milpitas, CA 95035-4106. Tel.: 408-946-6548. Fax: 408-946-9279. Facebook: San Francisco Bay Bird Observatory.
E-mail: outreach@sfbbo.org
Web Site: www.sfbbo.org
Key Personnel: Exec. Dir., Cat Burns.
Institution Type/Description: Bird Conservatory.
Hours & Admission Prices: Call for hours.

Mission Hills

HISTORICAL MUSEUM-ARCHIVAL CENTER, 15151 San Fernando Mission Blvd., Mission Hills, CA 91345-1109. Tel.: 818-365-1501. Fax: 818-361-3276.
E-mail: info@archivalcenter.com
Key Personnel: Archivist, Kevin Feeney, A.C.D.A.
Institution Type/Description: Museum & Archival Center: located on the grounds of the San Fernando Mission.
Hours & Admission Prices: Mon. & Thurs. 1-3; other times by appointment. No charge. Closed national holidays. &

SAN FERNANDO MISSION, 15151 San Fernando Mission Blvd., Mission Hills, CA 91345-1109. Tel.: 818-361-0186. Fax: 818-361-3276.
Key Personnel: Admin., Msgr. Francis J. Weber; Chm., Archbishop Jose H. Gomez; Dir. & Business Mgr., Kevin Feeney; Sales Shop Mgr., Monica Mejorado.
Institution Type/Description: Museums & Mission Complex: founded in 1797 by Fray Fermin Lasuen and later restored.
Hours & Admission Prices: Daily 9-4:30. Adults $5, children 7-15 $3; children under 7 no charge. Closed Thanksgiving; Christmas. &

SAN FERNANDO VALLEY HISTORICAL SOCIETY, INC., 10940 Sepulveda Blvd., Mission Hills, CA 91346. Mailing Address: P.O. Box 7039, Mission Hills, CA 91346-7039. Tel.: 818-365-7810. Fax: 818-365-7810.
E-mail: sfvhs@verizon.net
Web Site: sfvhs.com
Key Personnel: Pres. (V), Ron Van Deest.
Institution Type/Description: History Museum.

Hours & Admission Prices: Mon. 10-4; 3rd Sun. of month 1-4; tours by appointment. No charge; donations accepted. Closed New Year's Day; Easter; Thanksgiving; Christmas.
Attendance: 300 (estimated)

Mission Viejo

CALIFORNIA FIRE MUSEUM, 24861 El Cortijo Ln., Mission Viejo, CA 92691-5232. Tel.: 949-916-5019.
E-mail: forsythd@cox.net
Web Site: www.cafiremuseum.org
Institution Type/Description: Firefighting History Museum.
Hours & Admission Prices: Call for hours.

Modesto

GREAT VALLEY MUSEUM, 2201 Blue Gum Ave., Modesto, CA 95358. Tel.: 209-575-6196. Fax: 209-575-6466. Facebook.
E-mail: gum@mjc.edu
Web Site: www.mjc.edu/gum
Formerly: Great Valley Museum of Natural History
Key Personnel: Dir., Arnold Chavez; Museum Specialist, Molly Flemate.
Institution Type/Description: Natural History, Science & Planetarium Museum.
Hours & Admission Prices: Tues.-Sat 9-4. Admission: museum $3-$5, planetarium $4-$6; discounts for members & Beagle Backer Snoopy Plate. ♿
Attendance: 25,000 (estimated)

HILLIER AIR MUSEUM, Modesto Airport, Hangar 7, 700 Tioga Dr., Modesto, CA 95354. Tel.: 209-526-8297 & 985-9000.
E-mail: tomhillier@msn.com
Web Site: hillierairmuseum.com
Key Personnel: Museum Shop Mgr., Jack Avery.
Institution Type/Description: Aviation Museum.
Hours & Admission Prices: 2nd Sat. each month 9-noon. No charge.

MCHENRY MUSEUM, 1402 I St., Modesto, CA 95354-1032. Tel.: 209-577-5366. Fax: 209-491-4407.
E-mail: museum@mchenrymuseum.org
Web Site: www.mchenrymuseum.org
Key Personnel: Cultural Svcs. Mgr., Wayne A. Mathes; Exhibit Designer, Laura Mesa; Museum Shop Mgr., Anne Hatheway; Museum Shop Mgr., Donnelle Dilbeck.
Institution Type/Description: History Museum: housed in 1911 library building.
Hours & Admission Prices: Tues.-Sun. 12-4. No charge; donations accepted. Closed New Year's Day; Easter; Thanksgiving; Christmas. ♿
Attendance: 25,000 (estimated)

Modjeska Canyon

ARDEN - THE HELENA MODJESKA HISTORIC HOUSE & GARDENS, 29042 Modjeska Canyon Rd., Modjeska Canyon, CA 92676-9793. Tel.: 949-923-2230. Fax: 949-855-6321.
E-mail: ardenmodjeska@ocparks.com
Web Site: www.ocparks.com/modjeskahouse/
Institution Type/Description: Historic House Museum: housed in the home of Polish American Shakespearean actress, Madame Helena Modjeska.
Hours & Admission Prices: Jan.-Nov. 1st & 3rd Tues. and 2nd & 4th Sat. by appointment only. Admission $5. ♿
Attendance: 3,600 (actual)

Moffett Field

MOFFETT FIELD HISTORICAL SOCIETY & MUSEUM, Bldg. 126 Severyns Ave., Moffett Field, CA 94035-0016. Mailing Address: P.O. Box 16, Moffett Field, CA 94035-0016. Tel.: 650-964-4024. Fax: 650-964-4028. Facebook: Moffett Field Historical Society Museum.
E-mail: moffettmuseum@sbcglobal.net
Web Site: www.moffettfieldmuseum.org
Institution Type/Description: Military Aviation History Museum.
Hours & Admission Prices: Wed.-Sat. 10-2. Adults $8, seniors $5, active & reserve military members and children 12 & under no charge. ♿
Attendance: 5,000 (actual)

Montebello

JUAN MATIAS SANCHEZ ADOBE, 946 Adobe Ave., Montebello, CA 90640. Tel.: 323-887-4592.
E-mail: gbrougher@sbcglobal.net
Key Personnel: Cur., Bud Sanchez.
Institution Type/Description: Historic House Museum: built in 1844 by Dona Maria Casilda de Lobo.
Hours & Admission Prices: Wed. & Sat.-Sun. 1-4. No charge. ♿
Attendance: 200 (estimated)

Montecito

GANNA WALSKA LOTUSLAND, 695 Ashley Rd., Montecito, CA 93108. Tel.: 805-969-9990. Fax: 805-969-4423.
E-mail: bcraig@lotusland.org
Web Site: www.lotusland.org
Key Personnel: Exec. Dir., Gwen L. Stauffer; Pres. (V), Connie Pearcy; Museum Shop Mgr., Karen Kester.
Institution Type/Description: Botanic Garden: housed on a 37-acre estate.
Hours & Admission Prices: Guided Tours: Feb. 15-Nov. 15 Wed.-Sat, 10 am & 1:30 pm by appointment. Adults $50; members no charge. ♿
Attendance: 15,000 (actual)

Monterey

COLTON HALL MUSEUM AND OLD MONTEREY JAIL, City Hall, 570 Pacific St., Monterey, CA 93940. Tel.: 831-646-5640. Fax: 831-646-3422.
E-mail: museumpt@monterey.org
Web Site: www.monterey.org/museums/city-museums
Key Personnel: Dir. & Cultural Arts & Archives Mgr., Dennis Copeland; Cultural Arts Asst., Chalet Booker; Museum Admin. Asst., Claire Rygg.
Institution Type/Description: History Museum: Colton Hall, site of 1849 California Constitutional Convention.
Hours & Admission Prices: Daily 10-4. No charge. Closed New Year's Day; Thanksgiving; Christmas.
Attendance: 18,000 (actual)

GREEN CHALK CONTEMPORARY, 616 Lighthouse Ave., Monterey, CA 93940-1100. Mailing Address: 701 Hawthorne, Monterey, CA 93940-1100. Tel.: 202-253-4507. Fax: 831-747-1088.
E-mail: antongallery@aol.com
Web Site: www.greenchalkcontemporary.com
Formerly: Anton Gallery
Key Personnel: Dir., Gail Enns.
Institution Type/Description: Art Gallery.
Hours & Admission Prices: Tues.-Sat. 12-5. No charge; donations accepted.
Attendance: 1,000 (estimated)

MONTEREY BAY AQUARIUM, 886 Cannery Row, Monterey, CA 93940-1085. Tel.: 831-648-4800. Fax: 831-648-4810.
Web Site: www.montereybayaquarium.org
Key Personnel: Exec. Dir., Julie Packard; Chm. (V), Steve Neal; C.O.O., Cynthia Vernon; Chief Devel. Officer, Cristina Fekeci; Chief Mktg. Officer, Mimi Hahn; Chief Human Resources Officer, Teresa Merry; C.F.O., Troy Grande; Chief Conservation and Science Officer, Margaret Spring.
Institution Type/Description: Aquarium: on former site of Hovden Cannery.
Hours & Admission Prices: Daily 10-5; see website for seasonal hours. Adults $49.95. seniors 65 & over and students 13-17 $39.95, children 3-12 $29.95; discounts to military & groups; members & children under 3 no charge. Closed Christmas. ♿
Attendance: 1,800,000 (actual)

MONTEREY FIRE DEPARTMENT HISTORICAL MUSEUM, 582 Hawthorn St., Monterey, CA 93940. Tel.: 831-646-3900.
E-mail: ventimig@ci.monterey.ca.us
Institution Type/Description: Firefighting History Museum.
Hours & Admission Prices: By appointment.

MONTEREY HISTORY AND ART ASSOCIATION, 5 Custom House Plaza, Monterey, CA 93940-2430. Tel.: 831-372-2608. Fax: 831-655-3054.
E-mail: info@montereyhistory.org
Web Site: www.montereyhistory.org
Key Personnel: Exec. Dir., John N. Bailey; Pres. (V), William D. Curtis; Museum Shop Mgr., Christy O'Neil.
Institution Type/Description: Maritime Museum & History Center.
Hours & Admission Prices: Mayo Hayes O'Donnell Library: Wed. & Fri.-Sun. 1-4. No charge. Maritime Museum of Monterey: Thurs.-Tues. 10-5. No charge. Closed New Year's Day; Thanksgiving; Christmas. ♿
Attendance: 60,000 (estimated)

MONTEREY MUSEUM OF ART, 559 Pacific St., Monterey, CA 93940-2805. Tel.: 831-372-5477. Fax: 831-372-5680.

E-mail: info@montereyart.org
Web Site: www.montereyart.org
Institution Type/Description: Art Museum.
Hours & Admission Prices: Thurs.-Mon. 11-5. Adults $10, students & military w/ ID $5; discounts to NARM members; members & children under 12 no charge. Closed New Year's Day; Thanksgiving; Christmas. &
Attendance: 38,500 (actual)

MONTEREY STATE HISTORIC PARK, 20 Custom House Plaza, Monterey, CA 93940-2430. Mailing Address: California Dept. of Parks & Recreation, 2211 Garden Rd., Monterey, CA 93940-5317. Tel.: 831-649-7118. Fax: 831-647-6236.
E-mail: info@parks.ca.gov
Web Site: www.parks.ca.gov
Key Personnel: Dist. Cur., Kris N. Quist; Museum Cur. I, Monterey State Historic Park, Corrine Mendoza.
Institution Type/Description: State Historic Park Museum: consisting of 12 buildings, gardens & sites in Monterey.
Hours & Admission Prices: May-Sept. daily 9-5; Oct.-April 10-4. No charge. Closed New Year's Day; Thanksgiving; Christmas. &
Attendance: 180,000

MONTEREY STATE HISTORIC PARK/ROBERT LOUIS STEVENSON HOUSE, 530 Houston St., Monterey, CA 93940-3226. Mailing Address: 20 Custom House Plaza, Monterey, CA 93940. Tel.: 831-649-7118. Fax: 831-647-6236.
E-mail: info@parks.ca.gov
Web Site: www.historicmonterey.org
Key Personnel: Cur., Kris N. Quist; Guide Supvr., Stephanie Price; District Supt., Dennis Hanson.
Institution Type/Description: Historic House: hotel in which Robert Louis Stevenson stayed in 1879, located in Monterey State Historic Park.
Hours & Admission Prices: Daily 8-4. No charge. Closed New Year's Day; Thanksgiving; Christmas. &
Attendance: 25,000

MUSEUM OF MONTEREY, 5 Custom House Plaza, Monterey, CA 93940-2430. Tel.: 831-372-2608. Fax: 831-655-3054.
E-mail: info@montereyhistory.org
Web Site: www.museumofmonterey.org
Formerly: Maritime Museum of Monterey
Key Personnel: Exec. Dir., Mark Baer; Pres. (V), Christine Sinnott; Registrar, Deborah Silguero; Business Mgr. & Museum Shop Mgr., Maya Freedman.
Institution Type/Description: Local History & Art Museum.
Hours & Admission Prices: Tues.-Sun. 10-5. Adults $5; members no charge. Closed Thanksgiving; Christmas. &
Attendance: 73,500 (estimated)

MY MUSEUM, 425 Washington St., Monterey, CA 93940-3023. Tel.: 831-649-6444. Fax: 831-649-1304.
E-mail: info@mymuseum.org
Web Site: www.mymuseum.org
Key Personnel: Exec. Dir., Lauren Cohen; Pres., Kandis Malfyt; Vice Pres., Debra Panelli.
Institution Type/Description: Children's Museum.
Hours & Admission Prices: Tues.-Sat. 10-5, Sun. 12-5. Admission $8; children under 2 no charge. Closed New Year's Day; Easter; Independence Day; Thanksgiving; Christmas.

Monterey Park

EAST LOS ANGELES COLLEGE VINCENT PRICE ART MUSEUM, 1301 Avenida Cesar Chavez, Monterey Park, CA 91754-6099. Tel.: 323-265-8841. Fax: 323-260-8173.
E-mail: vincentpricemuseum@elac.edu
Web Site: vincentpriceartmuseum.org
Key Personnel: Chm. (V), Julie Silliman.
Institution Type/Description: Art Museum.
Hours & Admission Prices: Tues.-Wed., Fri. & 2nd Sat. each month 12-4, Thurs. 12-7. No charge. Closed campus holidays. &
Attendance: 12,000 (actual)

MONTEREY PARK HISTORICAL MUSEUM, 781 S. Orange Ave., Monterey Park, CA 91754. Mailing Address: P.O. Box 272, Monterey Park, CA 91754. Tel.: 626-307-1267.
Institution Type/Description: History Museum.
Hours & Admission Prices: Sat.-Sun. call for hours. No charge.

Moraga

ST. MARY'S COLLEGE MUSEUM OF ART, 1928 St. Mary's Rd., Moraga, CA 94556-2744. Mailing Address: P.O. Box 5110, Moraga, CA 94575-5110. Tel.: 925-631-4379. Fax: 925-376-5128.
E-mail: cbrewste@stmarys-ca.edu
Web Site: www.stmarys-ca.edu/museum
Formerly: Hearst Art Gallery, St. Mary's College
Key Personnel: Dir., Carrie Brewster; Registrar & Collections Mgr., Julie Armistead; Public Programming & Gallery Mgr., Kyla Tynes; Preparator, Jim Whiteaker.
Institution Type/Description: College Art Museum.
Hours & Admission Prices: Wed.-Sun. 11-4:30. Suggested Donation $5; discount to AAM members; members, military and youth 18 & under no charge. Blue Star Museum. Closed major holidays & between exhibitions. &
Attendance: 13,500 (estimated)

Morgan Hill

MORGAN HILL MUSEUM, Villa Mira Monte, 17860 Monterey St., Morgan Hill, CA 95038. Mailing Address: Morgan Hill Historical Society, P.O. Box 1258, Morgan Hill, CA 95038. Tel.: 408-779-5755.
E-mail: ksullivan@morganhillhistoricalsociety.com
Key Personnel: Pres. (V), Kathy Sullivan.
Institution Type/Description: History Museum: housed in a 1911 farmer's house.
Hours & Admission Prices: Fri. 1-3, Sat. 10-1. No charge; donations accepted. &
Attendance: 600 (estimated)

Morro Bay

MORRO BAY AQUARIUM, 595 Embarcadero, Morro Bay, CA 93442-2217. Tel.: 805-772-7647.
Web Site: www.morrobay.com/morrobayaquarium
Institution Type/Description: Aquarium.
Hours & Admission Prices: Daily 9:30-5. Closing permanently Sept. 2018.

MORRO BAY NATIONAL ESTUARY NATURE CENTER, 601 Embarcadero, Morro Bay, CA 93442. Tel.: 805-772-3834. Fax: 805-772-4162.
E-mail: staff@mbnep.org
Web Site: www.mbnep.org
Institution Type/Description: Nature Center.
Hours & Admission Prices: Daily 10-6. No charge.
Attendance: 37,500

MORRO BAY STATE PARK MUSEUM OF NATURAL HISTORY, 20 State Park Rd., Morro Bay, CA 93442-2430. Tel.: 805-772-2694, ext. 105. Fax: 805-772-7129.
E-mail: rouvaishyana@hearstcastle.com
Web Site: ccnha.org
Key Personnel: Chm. (V), Celeste Royer; CCNHA Exec. Dir., Mary Golden.
Institution Type/Description: Natural History Museum.
Hours & Admission Prices: Daily 10-5. Adults $3; discounts for State Park Pass holders; members, children 16 & under and school groups with reservation no charge. Closed New Year's Day; Thanksgiving; Christmas. &
Attendance: 60,000 (actual)

Mount Shasta

MT. SHASTA SISSON MUSEUM, #1 N. Old Stage Rd., Mount Shasta, CA 96067-9701. Tel.: 530-926-5508. Facebook: Mt. Shasta Sisson Museum.
E-mail: museum@mtshastamuseum.com
Web Site: www.mtshastamuseum.com
Formerly: Sisson Hatchery Museum
Key Personnel: Dir., Jean Nels; Pres., Jim McChesney; Treas., Griff Bloodhart; Chm (V), Judie Cockburn; Museum Shop Mgr., Linda Siegel.
Institution Type/Description: History Museum.
Hours & Admission Prices: April-May Fri.-Sun. 10-4; Memorial Day-Labor Day daily 10-4; Sept. daily 1-4; Oct.-Dec. 10 Fri.-Sun. 1-4. Adults $1; members no charge. Closed New Year's Day; Easter; Thanksgiving; Christmas Eve & Day. &
Attendance: 17,500 (actual)

Mountain View

COMPUTER HISTORY MUSEUM, 1401 N. Shoreline Blvd., Mountain View, CA 94043-1311. Tel.: 650-810-1010. Fax: 650-810-1055.

Web Site: www.computerhistory.org
Key Personnel: Chm. Bd., Len J. Shustek; Pres. & C.E.O., John Hollar; C.F.O., George Holmes; Vice Pres. Operations, Gary Matsushita; Vice Pres. Education, Lauren Silver; Vice Pres. Programming & Business, Carol Stiglic; Vice Pres. Collections & Exhibitions, Kirsten Tashev; Assoc. Vice Pres. Devel., Pamela Gesme Miller; Sr. Cur., Dag Spicer; Retail Mgr., Sandra Shu-Lee; Assoc. Dir. Mktg., Carina Sweet.
Institution Type/Description: History Museum.
Hours & Admission Prices: Wed., Thurs., Sat. & Sun. 10-5; Fri. 10-9, Adults $15, active military, seniors 65 & up & students $12; children 12 & under & members no charge. &
Attendance: 75,000 (actual)

Murphys

OLD TIMERS MUSEUM CLOSED, 470 Main St., Murphys, CA 95247. Mailing Address: P.O. Box 94, Murphys, CA 95247-0094. Tel.: 209-728-1160.
E-mail: murphysotm@gmail.com
Web Site: www.murphysoldtimersmuseum.com
Key Personnel: Dir. & Pres., Ron Fillmore; Treas., Chloe Shufelt.
Institution Type/Description: Historic Building Museum.
Hours & Admission Prices: Fri.-Sun. 12-4; other times by appointment. No charge; donations accepted. &
Attendance: 15,000 (estimated)

Napa

DI ROSA, 5200 Sonoma Hwy., Napa, CA 94559-9761. Tel.: 707-226-5991. Fax: 707-255-8934. Facebook.
E-mail: kristin@dirosaart.org
Web Site: www.dirosaart.org
Formerly: The di Rosa Preserve: Art & Nature
Key Personnel: Dir., Robert Stein; Museum Shop Mgr., Kristin Baird.
Institution Type/Description: Contemporary Art Museum & Sculpture Park.
Hours & Admission Prices: Wed.-Sun. 10-4. Adults $5-$15; discounts to NARM, seniors 65 & over, students and educators; members no charge. Closed New Year's Day; Martin Luther King Jr. Day; Presidents' Day; Memorial Day; Independence Day; Labor Day; Veterans Day; Thanksgiving; Christmas Eve & Day. &
Attendance: 16,758 (actual)

NAPA COUNTY HISTORICAL SOCIETY, 1219 First St., Napa, CA 94559-2929. Mailing Address: P.O. Box 10527, Napa, CA 94581-2527. Tel.: 707-224-1739.
E-mail: director@napahistory.org
Web Site: www.napahistory.org
Key Personnel: Dir., Kristie Sheppard.
Institution Type/Description: Historical Society Museum.
Hours & Admission Prices: By appointment. No charge; donations accepted. &
Attendance: 3,000

Needles

HAVASU NATIONAL WILDLIFE REFUGE, 317 Mesquite Ave., Needles, CA 92363. Tel.: 760-326-3853.
Institution Type/Description: Wildlife Refuge.
Hours & Admission Prices: Call for hours.

Nevada City

MINERS FOUNDRY CULTURAL CENTER, 325 Spring St., Nevada City, CA 95959-2420. Mailing Address: P.O. Box 1991, Nevada City, CA 95959-1940. Tel.: 530-265-5040.
E-mail: info@minersfoundry.org
Web Site: www.minersfoundry.org
Key Personnel: Exec. Dir., Gretchen Bond; Events Coord., Kat Kress.
Institution Type/Description: Mining Museum: site of the Pelton wheel.
Hours & Admission Prices: Tues.-Fri. 9-4; docent tours available by appointment. No charge; donations accepted. &
Attendance: 50,000 (estimated)

NEVADA COUNTY HISTORICAL SOCIETY, INC., 161 Nevada City Hwy., Nevada City, CA 95959-3110. Tel.: 530-264-7569.
E-mail: info@nevadacountyhistory.org
Web Site: www.nevadacountyhistory.org
Key Personnel: Librarian, Searls Historic Library, Pat Chestnut; Dir. Railroad Museum, Madelyn Helling; Dir. Firehouse Museum, Wally Hagaman; Dir. Mining Museum, Rudy Cisar.
Institution Type/Description: Historical Society Museums.

Hours & Admission Prices: Firehouse Museum: May-Oct. Tues.-Sun. 1-4; other times by appointment. Mining Museum: May-Oct. Tues.-Sat. 10-4, sun. 12-4; other times by appointment. Railroad Museum: May-Oct. Fri.- Tues. 10-4; Nov.-April Sat.-Sun. 10-4. Searls Memorial Library: Mon.-Sat. 1-4; other times by appointment. Closed New Year's Day; Thanksgiving; Christmas. &
Attendance: 2,000 (estimated)

Newbury Park

SATWIWA NATIVE AMERICAN INDIAN CULTURE CENTER, 4126 Potrero Rd., Newbury Park, CA 91320-5239. Mailing Address: 401 W. Hillcrest Dr., Thousand Oaks, CA 91360-4223. Tel.: 805-370-2301.
E-mail: samo_interpretation@nps.gov
Web Site: www.nps.gov/samo
Key Personnel: Museum Shop Mgr., Razsa Cruz.
Institution Type/Description: Native American Museum.
Hours & Admission Prices: Sat.-Sun. 9-5. No charge; donations accepted. &
Attendance: 12,000 (estimated)

STAGECOACH INN MUSEUM COMPLEX, 51 S. Ventu Park Rd., Newbury Park, CA 91320-3943. Tel.: 805-498-9441. Fax: 805-498-6375.
E-mail: stagecoach@stagecoachmuseum.org
Web Site: www.stagecoachmuseum.org
Key Personnel: Pres., Jim Gilmore; Dir., Sandra Hildebrandt; Cur. Education, Jackie Pizitz; Cur. History, Miriam Sprankling.
Institution Type/Description: History Museum: housed in 1876 Grand Union Hotel.
Hours & Admission Prices: Wed.-Sun. 1-4. Adults $5, senior citizens & youth 13-21 $4, children 5-12 $2; members & children under 5 no charge. Closed New Year's Day; Easter; Thanksgiving; Christmas. &
Attendance: 10,902 (actual)

Newhall

PLACERITA CANYON NATURE CENTER, 19152 Placerita Canyon Rd., Newhall, CA 91321. Tel.: 661-259-7721.
E-mail: ron@placerita.org
Institution Type/Description: Nature Center.
Hours & Admission Prices: Tues.-Sun. 9-5.

WILLIAM S. HART COUNTY PARK & MUSEUM, 24151 Newhall Ave., Newhall, CA 91321-2908. Tel.: 661-254-4584. Fax: 661-254-6499. Facebook: William S. Hart Park and Museum.
E-mail: information@hartmuseum.org
Web Site: www.hartmuseum.org
Key Personnel: Dir. Natural History Museum, Dr. Jane Pisano; Park Supt., Norman Phillips; Volunteer Coord., Rachel Barnes; Gift Store Mgr., Becki Basham; Admin., Margi Bertram.
Institution Type/Description: Historic Building & Site: 1927 home of silent film star William S. Hart.
Hours & Admission Prices: Museum: mid-June to Labor Day Wed.-Sun. 11-3:30; Sept. to mid-June 10-12:30. Park: mid-June to Labor Day daily 8-6; Sept. to mid-June daily 8-5. No charge; donations accepted. Closed New Year's Day; Thanksgiving; Christmas. &
Attendance: 35,000 (actual)

Newport Beach

EXPLOROCEAN/NEWPORT HARBOR NAUTICAL MUSEUM, 600 E. Bay Ave., Newport Beach, CA 92661. Tel.: 949-675-8915.
E-mail: contactus@discoverycube.org
Web Site: www.explorocean.org
Formerly: Newport Harbor Nautical Museum
Institution Type/Description: Nautical Museum.
Hours & Admission Prices: Sun.-Thurs. 11-3, Fri.-Sat. 11-6, Sun. 11-5. Adults 13 & over $4, youth 4-12 $2; members, active military and children 3 & under no charge. &
Attendance: 42,000 (actual)

ORANGE COUNTY MUSEUM OF ART, 850 San Clemente Dr., Newport Beach, CA 92660-6399. Tel.: 949-759-1122. Fax: 949-759-5623.
E-mail: info@ocma.net
Web Site: www.ocma.net
Key Personnel: Dir. & C.E.O., Todd D. Smith; Chm. & Pres., Craig W. Wells; Deputy Dir. External Affairs, Kirsten Schmidt.
Institution Type/Description: Visual Art Museum.

Hours & Admission Prices: Wed., Sat. & Sun. 11-5, Thurs. & Fri. 11-8. Adults $10, seniors & students $7.50; discounts to AAA & AAM members; members, children under 12 & Fridays no charge. Closed Easter; Independence Day; Thanksgiving; Christmas. &

Attendance: 40,000 (actual)

Nipomo

DANA ADOBE, 671 S. Oakglen Ave., Nipomo, CA 93444-9009. Tel.: 805-929-5679. Facebook.

E-mail: dana@danaadobe.org

Web Site: danaadobe.org

Key Personnel: Exec. Dir., Marina Washburn; Pres. (V), Rudy Stowell; Museum Shop Mgr., Helen Daurio.

Institution Type/Description: Historic Home & Rancho; History Museum.

Hours & Admission Prices: Sat. 10-1, Sun. 1-4. Adults $5; members & students no charge. &

Attendance: 5,000 (estimated)

North Fork

SIERRA MONO INDIAN MUSEUM, 33103 Rd. 228, North Fork, CA 93643-9442. Tel.: 559-877-2115. Fax: 559-877-6515. Facebook.

E-mail: monomuseum@gmail.com

Web Site: www.sierramonomuseum.org

Key Personnel: Dir. & Museum Shop Mgr., Cindy Greenwood; Pres. (V), Kelly Marshall; Chm. (V), Sharon Carter.

Institution Type/Description: Native American Museum.

Hours & Admission Prices: Tues.-Sat. 10-3. Suggested Donation: adults $7, seniors & children $5; discounts to AAM members. &

Attendance: 5,000 (estimated)

North Hollywood

CAMPO DE CAHUENGA, 3919 Lankershim Blvd., North Hollywood, CA 91604-3419. Mailing Address: P.O. Box 956, North Hollywood, CA 91603-0956. Tel.: 818-762-3998, ext. 2. Fax: 818-762-2734.

E-mail: campodecahuenga1847@hotmail.com

Web Site: www.campodecahuenga.com

Institution Type/Description: History Museum: site of the signing of the Treaty of Cahuenga in 1847.

Hours & Admission Prices: 1st & 3rd Sat. each month 12-4. Closed holidays.

THE PORTAL OF THE FOLDED WINGS SHRINE TO AVIATION AND MUSEUM, 10621 Victory Blvd., North Hollywood, CA 91606-3918. Tel.: 818-763-9121. Fax: 818-763-3801.

Web Site: www.portalofthefoldedwings.com

Institution Type/Description: Memorial Park: 75 ft. tall structure of marble, mosaic, & sculpted figures; built in 1924. Listed on the National Register of Historic Places.

Hours & Admission Prices: Tours: 1st Sun. of each month 1-3; other times by appointment. No charge. &

Attendance: 2,000 (estimated)

Northridge

ART GALLERIES, CALIFORNIA STATE UNIVERSITY, NORTHRIDGE, 18111 Nordhoff St., Northridge, CA 91330-8299. Tel.: 818-677-2226 (gallery) & 2156 (office). Fax: 818-677-5910. Facebook, Instagram.

E-mail: erika.ostrander@csun.edu

Web Site: www.csun.edu/artgalleries/

Key Personnel: Dir., Jim Sweeters; Office Mgr., Erika Ostrander.

Institution Type/Description: University Art Gallery.

Hours & Admission Prices: June-Aug. Mon.-Fri. 12-4; Sept.-May Mon.-Wed. & Fri.-Sat. 12-4, Thurs. 12-8. No charge; donations accepted. Closed holidays. &

Attendance: 32,000 (estimated)

CAL STATE NORTHRIDGE BOTANIC GARDEN, Biology Dept., 18111 Nordhoff St. - MC 8303, Northridge, CA 91330. Tel.: 818-677-3496. Fax: 818-677-2034.

E-mail: botanicgarden@csun.edu

Web Site: www.csun.edu/botanicgarden

Key Personnel: Chm. (V), Brenda Kanno.

Institution Type/Description: Botanical Garden.

Hours & Admission Prices: Mon.-Fri. 8-4:45. No charge. Closed holidays. &

Attendance: 10,000 (estimated)

THE MUSEUM OF THE SAN FERNANDO VALLEY, 18860 Nordhoff St., Ste. 204, Northridge, CA 91324-3885. Tel.: 818-347-9665.

E-mail: info@themuseumsfv.org

Web Site: www.themuseumsfv.org

Institution Type/Description: History Museum.

Hours & Admission Prices: Tues. 1-8, Thurs. & Sat. 1-6. No charge; donations accepted. &

Norwalk

HARGITT HOUSE, 12426 Mapledale, Norwalk, CA 90650-6026. Mailing Address: 12700 Norwalk Blvd., Rm. 10, Norwalk, CA 90650. Tel.: 562-864-9663 & 929-5566.

Institution Type/Description: Historic House Museum: housed in the home of Charles & Ida Hargitt, built in 1891 by the D.D. Johnston family.

Hours & Admission Prices: 1st & 3rd Sun. of month 1-4.

Novato

HAMILTON FIELD HISTORY MUSEUM, 555 Hangar Ave., Novato, CA 94947. Tel.: 415-382-8614. Fax: 415-382-8610.

E-mail: hamilton_museum@at.net

Web Site: novatohistory.org

Key Personnel: Contact Mgr., Ray Dwelly; Museum Shop Mgr., Pat Johnstone.

Institution Type/Description: History Museum: housed on a former air base; operational from 1935-1974; first as an Army Air Corps field and later for the U.S. Air Force.

Hours & Admission Prices: Wed.-Thurs. & Sat. 12-4; other times by appointment. No charge; donations accepted. Closed holidays. &

Attendance: 2,460 (actual)

MUSEUM OF THE AMERICAN INDIAN, 2200 Novato Blvd., (in Miwok Park), Novato, CA 94947-2079. Mailing Address: P.O. Box 864, Novato, CA 94948. Tel.: 415-897-4064. Fax: 415-892-7804. Facebook: Museum of the American Indian.

E-mail: office@marinindian.com

Web Site: marinindian.com

Formerly: Marin Museum Society

Key Personnel: Pres. (V), Doug Fryday; Dir. Education, Alicia Retes; Archaeologist, Teresa Saltzman.

Institution Type/Description: Archaeological & Anthropological Museum: located on prehistoric site once occupied by Coast Miwok Indians.

Hours & Admission Prices: Museum: Fri.-Sun. 12:30-4:30. Tours: Tues.-Sun by appointment.

Attendance: 10,000 (estimated)

NOVATO HISTORY MUSEUM, 815 De Long Ave., Novato, CA 94945-7005. Mailing Address: Novato Historical Guild, P.O. Box 1296, Novato, CA 94948. Tel.: 415-897-4320.

E-mail: NHG1850@yahoo.com

Web Site: www.novato.org/museum

Key Personnel: Pres. (V), Susan Magnone; Museum Shop Mgr., Pat Johnstone.

Institution Type/Description: History Museum: located in 1850 Postmaster's House, a Greek Revival two-story farmhouse typical of the era.

Hours & Admission Prices: Wed.-Thurs. & Sat. 12-4; other times by appointment. No charge; donations accepted. Closed major holidays. &

Attendance: 2,500 (estimated)

Oak Glen

HISTORIC OAK GLEN SCHOOLHOUSE, 11911 S. Oak Glen Rd., Oak Glen, CA 92399-9488. Tel.: 909-797-1691. Facebook: Oak Glen School House Museum.

E-mail: oakglenschoolmuseum@gmail.com

Formerly: Oak Glen School House Museum

Key Personnel: Dir., Diane Elder.

Institution Type/Description: History Museum.

Hours & Admission Prices: Sept. to Thanksgiving Wed.-Sun. 12-4; Dec.-Aug. Sat.-Sun. 12-4; other times by appointment. No charge; donations accepted. Blue Star Museum.

Attendance: 5,000 (estimated)

Oakdale

OAKDALE COWBOY MUSEUM, 355 E. F St., Oakdale, CA 95361-4084. Mailing Address: P.O. Box 1155, Oakdale, CA 95361-1155. Tel.: 209-847-5163. Fax: 209-847-4183.

E-mail: karen@oakdalecowboymuseum.org

Web Site: www.oakdalecowboymuseum.org
Key Personnel: Museum Asst. & Museum Shop Mgr., Karen Serpa.
Institution Type/Description: Cowboy History Museum.
Hours & Admission Prices: Mon.-Sat. 10-4. Adults $1; members no charge. Closed holidays. &
Attendance: 5,000 (actual)

OAKDALE MUSEUM & HISTORY CENTER, 212 W. F St., Oakdale, CA 95361. Mailing Address: P.O. Box 2212, Oakdale, CA 95361. Tel.: 209-844-5161. Facebook: Oakdale Museum.
E-mail: oakdaleheritage@yahoo.com
Web Site: oakdalemuseum.org
Key Personnel: Pres. (V), Barbara Torres.
Institution Type/Description: Local History Museum: housed in 1869 residence.
Hours & Admission Prices: Wed.-Thurs. 1-4, Sat. 10-4. No charge; donations accepted. Closed holidays. &
Attendance: 2,500 (estimated)

Oakhurst

CHILDREN'S MUSEUM OF THE SIERRA CLOSED, 49269 Golden Oak Dr., Ste. 104, Oakhurst, CA 93644-9477. Tel.: 559-658-5656. Fax: 559-658-5656.
E-mail: cmos@sti.net
Web Site: www.childrensmuseumofthesierra.com
Key Personnel: Dir. & Chm. (V), Jim Elliott; Education, Donna Marks; Public Rels., Ronda Clarke; Treas. & Cur., Jim Elliott; Registrar, Angelo Pizelo; Museum Shop Mgr., Lian Rausch.
Institution Type/Description: Children's Museum.
Hours & Admission Prices: July-Aug. Tues.-Sat. 10-5; Sept.-June Tues.-Sat. 10-4, Sun. 1-4. Adults $6, seniors 60 & over $4; discounts to groups; children under 2 no charge. Closed Mother's Day; major holidays. &
Attendance: 11,000 (actual)

FRESNO FLATS HISTORIC VILLAGE AND PARK, 49777 Rd. 427, Oakhurst, CA 93644. Mailing Address: P.O. Box 451, Oakhurst, CA 93644-0451. Tel.: 559-683-6570. Fax: 559-658-2161.
E-mail: fresnoflatsmuseum@sti.net
Web Site: fresnoflatsmuseum.org
Key Personnel: Pres. (V), Mary Lou Finley.
Institution Type/Description: History Museum.
Hours & Admission Prices: Museum: Tues.-Sun. 10-3. Library: by appointment. Grounds: daily dawn to dusk. No charge; donations accepted. &
Attendance: 3,000 (estimated)

KING VINTAGE CLOTHING MUSEUM, 40680 Hwy. 41, Oakhurst, CA 93644. Mailing Address: P.O. Box 303, Oakhurst, CA 93644-0303. Tel.: 559-658-6999. Fax: 559-683-3094.
E-mail: kingvintagemuseum@sti.net
Web Site: www.kingvintagemuseum.org
Key Personnel: Chm. (V), Toni Lagunoff; Museum Shop Mgr., Mary Ann Hutcherson.
Institution Type/Description: History Museum.
Hours & Admission Prices: Wed.-Sat. 11-5, Sun. 1-4. Adults $3. &
Attendance: 925 (estimated)

Oakland

AFRICAN-AMERICAN MUSEUM AND LIBRARY AT OAKLAND, 659 14th St., Oakland, CA 94612-1242. Tel.: 510-637-0200. Fax: 510-637-0204. TDD: 510-652-8634.
E-mail: eanswers@oaklandlibrary.org
Web Site: www.oaklandlibrary.org
Key Personnel: C.E.O. & Pres. Trustees (V), Melvin Terry; Cur. & Museum Mgr., Rick Moss; Museum Cur. Asst., Erica L. Watkins; Librarian, Veronica L. Lee; Librarian, Linda Jolivet.
Institution Type/Description: African-American History Museum.
Hours & Admission Prices: Tues.-Sat. 12-5:30. &

BONSAI GARDEN AT LAKE MERRITT, 650 Bellevue Ave., Oakland, CA 94610. Mailing Address: P.O. Box 16176, Oakland, CA 94610-6176. Tel.: 510-763-8409.
E-mail: joembyrd@gsbf-lakemerritt.org
Web Site: www.gsbf-lakemerritt.org
Key Personnel: Chm. (V), Joe Byrd.
Institution Type/Description: Garden.

Hours & Admission Prices: Tues.-Fri. 11-3, Sat. 10-4, Sun. 12-4; call to confirm. No charge; donations accepted. Closed New Year's Day; Thanksgiving; Christmas. &
Attendance: 35,000 (actual)

THE CAMRON-STANFORD HOUSE PRESERVATION ASSOCIATION, 1418 Lakeside Dr., Oakland, CA 94612-4307. Tel.: 510-444-1876 & 874-7802 (office). Fax: 510-874-7803.
E-mail: pelican@cshouse.org
Web Site: www.cshouse.org
Key Personnel: Vice Pres. Collections & House Committee, Frankie Rhodes; Vice Pres. (V) House Administrative, Elaine O. Oldham; Consulting Cur., Wayne Mathes.
Institution Type/Description: Historic House & Preservation Project: 1876 four-story Victorian House, former Oakland Museum.
Hours & Admission Prices: 3rd Wed. of month 1-5. Adults $5, senior citizens $4, juniors 12-18 $3; children under 12, school tours and 1st Sun. no charge.
Attendance: 500 (estimated)

CHABOT SPACE & SCIENCE CENTER, 10000 Skyline Blvd., Oakland, CA 94619-2450. Tel.: 510-336-7373. Fax: 510-336-7491.
E-mail: visit@chabotspace.org
Web Site: www.chabotspace.org
Formerly: Chabot Observatory & Science Center
Key Personnel: C.E.O. & Dir., Adam Tobin; Chm. (V), Michael Levi; Museum Shop Mgr., Lara Miranda.
Institution Type/Description: Science Center.
Hours & Admission Prices: Summer: Tues.-Thurs. & Sun. 10-5, Fri.-Sat. 10-10; Winter: Wed.-Thurs. & Sun. 10-5, Fri.-Sat. 10-10. Telescope Viewing: dusk to 10:30. Adults $18, youth $12.95; discounts to military; children under 3 & members no charge. ASTC reciprocal member's program. Closed Thanksgiving; Christmas. &
Attendance: 177,000 (actual)

COHEN-BRAY HOUSE, 1440 29th Ave., Oakland, CA 94601-2309. Tel.: 510-536-1703.
E-mail: cohenbrayhouse@gmail.com
Institution Type/Description: Historic House Museum.
Hours & Admission Prices: 4th Sun. of month 2pm by appointment.

DUNSMUIR HELLMAN HISTORIC ESTATE, 2960 Peralta Oaks Ct., Oakland, CA 94605-5320. Tel.: 510-615-5555. Fax: 510-562-8294.
E-mail: dcooper@oaklandnet.com
Web Site: www.dunsmuir-hellman.org
Key Personnel: Estate Mgr., Deborah Cooper.
Institution Type/Description: Historic Estate: a 37-room Neoclassical Revival mansion built in 1899.
Hours & Admission Prices: Grounds: Tues.-Fri. 11-4. Closed public holidays. Mansion Tours: April-Sept. Wed. 11am. Adults $5, seniors & children $4.
Attendance: 65,125 (actual)

JUNIOR CENTER OF ART AND SCIENCE, Lakeside Park, 558 Bellevue Ave., Oakland, CA 94610-5026. Tel.: 510-839-5777. Fax: 510-839-8102.
E-mail: jrcenter@sbcglobal.net
Web Site: www.juniorcenter.org
Key Personnel: Exec. Dir., Dominique Enriquez; C.E.O. & Pres. (V), Joel Hart; Cur., Daniel McClain.
Institution Type/Description: Children's Museum.
Hours & Admission Prices: Summer: Mon.-Fri. 8:30-4:30; Academic Year: Tues.-Fri. 10-6, Sat. 10-3; see website for holiday hours. No charge; donations accepted. &

KENNEDY ART CENTER GALLERY AT HOLY NAMES UNIVERSITY, 3500 Mountain Blvd., Oakland, CA 94619-1627. Tel.: 510-436-1457.
Institution Type/Description: Art Gallery.
Hours & Admission Prices: Sat.-Sun. 12-5; other times by appointment.

MERRITT MUSEUM OF ANTHROPOLOGY, 12500 Campus Dr., Library Bldg., Oakland, CA 94619-3107. Tel.: 510-436-2607. Fax: 415-922-0905.
E-mail: apowell@peralta.edu
Web Site: www.merritt.edu/wp/anthr/anthropology-museum/
Key Personnel: Dir., Dr. Barbara Joans; Cur. Conservation, Leslie Fleming; Cur. & Museum Assoc., Lisa Valcenier.
Institution Type/Description: Anthropology Museum.

Hours & Admission Prices: Mon.-Thurs. 7:45-7, Fri. 7:45-3. No charge. Closed academic holidays. &

Attendance: 300 (estimated)

MILLS COLLEGE ART MUSEUM, 5000 MacArthur Blvd., Oakland, CA 94613-1302. Tel.: 510-430-2164. Fax: 510-430-3168.
E-mail: mcam@mills.edu
Web Site: mcam.mills.edu
Key Personnel: Dir., Dr. Stephanie Hanor; Mgr. Exhibitions & Collections, Eli Thorne; Program Dir., Jayna Swartzman-Brosky.
Institution Type/Description: College Art Gallery.
Hours & Admission Prices: Tues. & Thurs.-Sun. 11-4, Wed. 11-7:30. No charge; donations accepted. &
Attendance: 10,100 (actual)

MUSEUM OF CHILDREN'S ART - MOCHA, 1625 Clay St., Ste. 100, Oakland, CA 94612-1564. Tel.: 510-465-8770. Fax: 510-465-0772.
E-mail: hello@mocha.org
Web Site: mocha.org
Institution Type/Description: Children's Museum.
Hours & Admission Prices: Tues.-Fri. 10-3, Sat.-Sun. 12-4.

OAKLAND AVIATION MUSEUM, 8252 Earhart Rd., Oakland, CA 94621-4548. Tel.: 510-638-7100.
E-mail: oamdirector@att.net
Web Site: www.oaklandaviationmuseum.org
Formerly: Western Aerospace Museum
Key Personnel: Dir. Operations, Ian Wright; Pres., John Horton.
Institution Type/Description: Aviation History Museum: housed in 1939 Boeing School of Aeronautics hangar on historic Oakland Airport, North Field.
Hours & Admission Prices: Wed.-Sun. 10-4. Adults $10, senior citizens 55 & over $9, teens 13-18 $7, children 6-12 $5; discounts to groups & Time Travelers; children 5 & under and members no charge. Closed New Year's Eve & Day; Thanksgiving; Christmas Eve & Day. &
Attendance: 7,000 (estimated)

OAKLAND MUSEUM OF CALIFORNIA, 1000 Oak St. (at 10th St.), Oakland, CA 94607-4892. Tel.: 510-318-8400, 888-625-6873 (Toll Free); 510-451-3322 (TTY). Facebook: Oakland Museum of California.
E-mail: equist@museumca.org
Web Site: www.museumca.org
Key Personnel: Chm., Paul Pervere; Dir. & C.E.O., Lori Fogarty; Assoc. Dir. Retail & Product Devel., Michael Silverman; Asst. Dir. Visitor Strategy, Emily Quist; Mktg. Mgr., Charlotte Patterson; Event Services Mgr., Catherine Kitz; Facilities Mgr., Lisa Llewellyn; Accountant, Joan Perry.
Institution Type/Description: Regional Multidisciplinary Museum.
Hours & Admission Prices: Wed.-Thurs. 11-5, Fri. 11-9, Sat.-Sun. 10-6. Adults $15.95, seniors & students $10.95, youth 9-17 $6.95; discounts to non-Oakland school groups, AAM members & Fri. 5-9; children 8 & under & members no charge. Closed New Year's Day; Independence Day; Thanksgiving; Christmas. &
Attendance: 135,000 (actual)

OAKLAND ZOO, 9777 Golf Links Rd., Oakland, CA 94605-4925. Mailing Address: P.O. Box 5238, Oakland, CA 94605-0238. Tel.: 510-632-9525, ext. 132. Fax: 510-635-5719. Facebook: Oak Zoo.
E-mail: nancy@oaklandzoo.org
Web Site: www.oaklandzoo.org
Key Personnel: Pres. & C.E.O., Dr. Joel J. Parrott, D.V.M.; C.F.O., Nik Dehejia; Dir. Animal Care, Conservation & Research, Colleen Kinzley; Mng. Dir., Nancy Filippi; Dir. Education, Bo DeLong; Volunteer Programs Mgr., Lisa O'Dwyer; Sr. Mgr. Events, Amber Frisbie; Dir. Devel., Sara Becker; Dir. Park Svcs., Bob Westfall; Mgr. Retail, Moe Perez.
Institution Type/Description: Adult & Children's Zoo.
Hours & Admission Prices: Daily 10-4. Adults 15-55 $17.75, seniors & children $13.75; discounts to groups; members & seniors 80 & up no charge. Parking: bus $12, car $10. Closed Thanksgiving; Christmas. &
Attendance: 830,000 (estimated)

THE PARDEE HOME MUSEUM, 672 11th St., Oakland, CA 94607-3651. Tel.: 510-444-2187.
E-mail: info@pardeehome.org
Web Site: www.pardeehome.org
Key Personnel: Chm. (V), Cynthia Foster; Chm. (V), Dr. Ron Bachman; Pres. (V), Ann Brown; Museum Shop Mgr., Maria Vermiglio.
Institution Type/Description: Historic House: c.1868 former residence of Gov. George Pardee.

Hours & Admission Prices: Tours: Wed. & 2nd Sat. of month at 10:30, 2nd Sun. of month at 2; groups by appointment. Adults $10; children under 12 & members no charge. Tour & High Tea: $25. &
Attendance: 905 (actual)

PEERLESS COFFEE & TEA COMPANY MUSEUM, 260 Oak St., Oakland, CA 94607-4587. Tel.: 800-310-KONA, 410-763-1763. Fax: 510-763-5026.
E-mail: sonja@peerlesscoffee.com
Web Site: www.peerlesscoffee.com
Key Personnel: Pres. & Cur., Sonja Vukasin.
Institution Type/Description: Company Museum: company founded in 1924.
Hours & Admission Prices: Mon.-Fri. 10-4; groups by appointment. No charge. &

PERALTA HOUSE MUSEUM - PERALTA HACIENDA HISTORICAL PARK, 2465 34th Ave., Oakland, CA 94601. Mailing Address: P.O. Box 7172, Oakland, CA 94601. Tel.: 510-532-9142. Fax: 510-535-4842. Facebook.
E-mail: info@peraltahacienda.org
Web Site: www.peraltahacienda.org
Key Personnel: Exec. Dir., Holly Alonso.
Institution Type/Description: Historic House Museum: built in 1870. Listed on the National Register of Historic Places.
Hours & Admission Prices: Wed.-Sun. 2:30-5:30. Guided Tours: 2:30 & 4. Adults $5; members and children 10 & under no charge. &
Attendance: 40,000 (estimated)

PRO ARTS, 150 Frank H. Ogawa Plaza, Oakland, CA 94612. Tel.: 510-763-4361. Fax: 510-763-9470. Facebook: Pro Arts.
E-mail: info@proartsgallery.org
Web Site: www.proartsgallery.org
Key Personnel: Exec. Dir., Natalia Mount.
Institution Type/Description: Art Gallery.
Hours & Admission Prices: Tues.-Fri. 10-5, Sat. 11-4. No charge; donations accepted. &

ROTARY NATURE CENTER, 600 Bellevue Ave., Oakland, CA 94610-5000. Tel.: 510-238-3739. Fax: 510-238-7962.
E-mail: sbenavidez@oaklandnet.com
Web Site: www.lakemerritt.org
Key Personnel: Supervising Naturalist, Stephanie Benavidez.
Institution Type/Description: Natural History Museum.
Hours & Admission Prices: Daily & holidays 10-5. Feedings 3:30pm. No charge; donations accepted. &
Attendance: 35,000 (estimated)

Oceanside

CALIFORNIA SURF MUSEUM, 312 Pier View Way, Oceanside, CA 92054. Tel.: 760-721-6876.
E-mail: csm@surfmuseum.org
Web Site: www.surfmuseum.org
Key Personnel: Pres. (V), Jim Kempton; Operations & Museum Shop Mgr., Camille Cacas.
Institution Type/Description: Surf Museum.
Hours & Admission Prices: Thurs. 10-8, Fri.-Wed. 10-4. Adults $5, seniors 62 & over, military with ID and students with ID $3; members & 1st Tues. each month no charge. &
Attendance: 30,000 (actual)

MISSION SAN LUIS REY MUSEUM, 4050 Mission Ave., Oceanside, CA 92057-6402. Tel.: 760-757-3651. Fax: 760-757-4613.
E-mail: museumdesk@sanluisrey.org
Web Site: www.sanluisrey.org
Key Personnel: Admin., Edward Gabarra; Exec. Dir., Rev. David Gaa, O.F.M.; Historic Church & Museum Coord., Raffaella Avolio; Museum Assoc. & Tour Coord., Beverly Perna.
Institution Type/Description: Historic Building & Site: 1798 San Luis Rey Mission.
Hours & Admission Prices: Mon.-Fri. 9:30-5; Sat-Sun. 10-5. Adult $4, students 6-18 & retreatants $3; children under 6 & active military no charge. Behind the Scenes Guided Tours: adults $12. Closed New Year's Day; Easter; Thanksgiving; Christmas. &
Attendance: 55,000 (actual)

OCEANSIDE MUSEUM OF ART, 704 Pier View Way, Oceanside, CA 92054-2802. Tel.: 760-435-3720. Fax: 760-966-5819.
E-mail: danielle@oma-online.org
Web Site: oma-online.org

Key Personnel: Exec. Dir., Daniel Foster; Dir. Exhibitions & Collections, Danielle Susalla Deery; Mgr. Facilities, Lissette Guzman; Mgr. Programs, Mitzi Summers; Membership Mgr., Teresa Ellis; Deputy Dir., Tara Smith; Education Coord., Julia Fister; Graphic Designer & Weekend Supvr., Erika Koga; Museum Shop Mgr., Nancy Bergmann.
Institution Type/Description: Art Museum.
Hours & Admission Prices: Tues.-Sat. 10-4, Sun. 1-4. Adults $8; discounts to AAM & ICOM members; museum staff members, members, students, and active military & their dependents, 1st Sun. each month no charge. Closed major holidays. ⑆
Attendance: 53,000 (actual)

Ocotillo

IMPERIAL VALLEY DESERT MUSEUM, 11 Frontage Rd., Ocotillo, CA 92259. Mailing Address: P.O. Box 430, Ocotillo, CA 92259.
E-mail: ivdmuseum@gmail.com
Formerly: Imperial Valley College Desert Museum
Key Personnel: Dir., Dr. Neal V. Hitch.
Institution Type/Description: History Museum.
Hours & Admission Prices: Wed.-Sun. 10-4. Admission $5. ⑆
Attendance: 13,000

Ojai

BEATRICE WOOD CENTER FOR THE ARTS, 8560 Ojai-Santa Paula Rd., Ojai, CA 93023-9351. Tel.: 805-646-3381. Fax: 805-646-0560.
E-mail: beatricewoodcenter@gmail.com
Web Site: www.beatricewood.com
Key Personnel: Dir., Kevin Wallace.
Institution Type/Description: Art Gallery.
Hours & Admission Prices: Fri.-Sun. 11-5.

OJAI VALLEY MUSEUM, 130 W. Ojai Ave., Ojai, CA 93023-3212. Mailing Address: P.O. Box 204, Ojai, CA 93024-0204. Tel.: 805-640-1390.
E-mail: info@ojaivalleymuseum.org
Web Site: www.ojaivalleymuseum.org
Formerly: Ojai Valley Museum of History and Art
Key Personnel: Museum Dir., Wendy Barker; Administrative Assoc., Nerina Nall.
Institution Type/Description: Ojai History, Art & Culture Museum.
Hours & Admission Prices: Tues.-Sat. 10-4, Sun. 12-4. Suggested Donation: adults $5, children 6-18 $1; discounts to NARM members; members & children under 6 no charge. Closed New Year's Day; Independence Day; Thanksgiving; Christmas. ⑆
Attendance: 10,000 (estimated)

Old Sacramento

OLD SACRAMENTO STATE HISTORIC PARK, 111 I St., Old Sacramento, CA 95814-2204. Tel.: 916-445-7387. Fax: 916-327-5655. TDD: 916-324-2667.
E-mail: library.csrm@parks.ca.gov
Web Site: www.csrmf.org
Key Personnel: Dir., Paul J. Hammond; Librarian, Cara Vandall; Historian, Kyle Wyatt; Maintenance Chief, Tim Gellinde.
Institution Type/Description: State Park Museum: located in Old Sacramento State Historic Park.
Hours & Admission Prices: Daily 10-5. Call for schedule of activities. No charge. Closed New Year's Day; Thanksgiving; Christmas. ⑆
Attendance: 60,000 (estimated)

Ontario

CHAFFEY COMMUNITY MUSEUM OF ART, 217 S. Lemon Ave., Ontario, CA 91761. Tel.: 909-463-3733. Facebook: Chaffey Community Museum of Art.
E-mail: info@chaffeymuseum.org
Web Site: www.chaffeymuseum.org
Key Personnel: Chm. (V), Nancy DeDiemar.
Institution Type/Description: Art Museum.
Hours & Admission Prices: Thurs.-Sun. 12-4. No charge; donations accepted. ⑆
Attendance: 5,100 (actual)

GRABER OLIVE HOUSE MUSEUM, 315 E. 4th St., Ontario, CA 91764-2709. Mailing Address: P.O. Box 511, Ontario, CA 91762-8511. Tel.: 909-983-1761, 800-996-5483. Fax: 909-984-2180.
E-mail: info@graberolives.com

Web Site: www.graberolives.com
Key Personnel: C.E.O. & Dir., Clifford C. Graber, II.
Institution Type/Description: Historic House Museum: housed in the home of the Graber Family, growers & producers of Graber Olives since 1894.
Hours & Admission Prices: Daily 9:30-5:30; group tours by appointment. No charge. Closed major holidays. ⑆

ONTARIO MUSEUM OF HISTORY & ART, 225 S. Euclid Ave., Ontario, CA 91762-3812. Tel.: 909-395-2510. Fax: 909-983-8978.
E-mail: museuminfo@ontarioca.gov
Web Site: www.ontarioca.gov/museum
Formerly: Museum of History & Art, Ontario
Key Personnel: Pres. Bd., Chris Kueng; Dir., John Worden; Pres. (V) Museum Assoc., Sherry Glab; Cur. Collections, Michelle Sifuentes; Cur. Education, Rebecca Horta; Office Asst., Loretha Nwosu; Asst. Cur., Leslie Matamoros; Gallery Attendant, Irene Gapido.
Institution Type/Description: Local History & Art Museum.
Hours & Admission Prices: Thurs.-Sun. 12-4. No charge; donations accepted. Closed New Year's Eve & Day; Easter; Memorial Day; Christmas. ⑆
Attendance: 15,000 (estimated)

Orange

CHAPMAN UNIVERSITY GUGGENHEIM GALLERY, One University Dr., Moulton Center, Orange, CA 92866-1005. Tel.: 714-997-6815.
Key Personnel: Coord., Marcus Herse.
Institution Type/Description: Art Gallery.
Hours & Admission Prices: Call for hours.

Oroville

BOLT'S ANTIQUE TOOL MUSEUM, 1650 Broderick St., Oroville, CA 95965-4809. Mailing Address: 1735 Montgomery St., Oroville, CA 95965-4820. Tel.: 530-538-2415. Fax: 530-538-2417.
E-mail: boltmuseum@cityoforoville.org
Key Personnel: Chm. (V), Bud Bolt; Museum Shop Mgr., Laila Bolt.
Institution Type/Description: Tool Museum.
Hours & Admission Prices: Tues.-Sun. 11:45-3:45. Adults $3, AAA members & groups of 15 or more $2.50; children under 12 no charge. Closed national holidays. ⑆
Attendance: 1,902 (actual)

BUTTE COUNTY HISTORICAL SOCIETY MUSEUMS, 1749 Spencer Ave., Oroville, CA 95965. Mailing Address: P.O. Box 2195, Oroville, CA 95965. Tel.: 530-533-9418.
E-mail: buttehistory@sbcglobal.net
Web Site: www.buttecountyhistoricalsociety.org
Key Personnel: Dir., Lucy Sperlin; Chm. (V), Nancy Brower; Pres. (V), Dixie Hargrove; Museum Shop Mgr., Shirley Miller.
Institution Type/Description: Historical Society Museum.
Hours & Admission Prices: Fri. 9-12, Sat. 11-3; other times by appointment. No charge; donations accepted. ⑆
Attendance: 2,000 (estimated)

BUTTE COUNTY PIONEER MEMORIAL MUSEUM, 2332 Montgomery St., Oroville, CA 95965-4924. Mailing Address: 1735 Montgomery St., Oroville, CA 95965-4820. Tel.: 530-538-2415. Fax: 530-538-2417.
E-mail: info@cityoforoville.org
Web Site: www.cityoforoville.org/pioneermuseum.html
Institution Type/Description: History Museum.
Hours & Admission Prices: Feb. 2-Dec. 14 Fri.-Sun. 12-4. Adults $3, AAA members & groups of 15 or more $2.50; children under 12 no charge.
Attendance: 1,000 (estimated)

C.F. LOTT HISTORIC HOME, 1067 Montgomery St., Oroville, CA 95965. Mailing Address: 1735 Montgomery St., Oroville, CA 95965-4820. Tel.: 530-538-2415. Fax: 530-538-2417.
E-mail: info@cityoforoville.org
Web Site: www.cityoforoville.org/cflotthome.html
Institution Type/Description: History Museum.
Hours & Admission Prices: Feb.-Dec. 14 Sun.-Mon. & Fri. 11:30-3:30. Adults $3; discounts to AAA members & groups of 15 or more.
Attendance: 891 (actual)

MILITARY MUSEUM OF BUTTE COUNTY, 4514 Pacific Heights Rd., Oroville, CA 95965-9266. Tel.: 530-534-9956. Fax: 530-534-1170.

Web Site: surpluscity.com/mmbc/index.html
Institution Type/Description: Military History Museum.
Hours & Admission Prices: Mon.-Sat. 8-6. No charge.

OROVILLE CHINESE TEMPLE COMPLEX & MUSEUM,
1500 Broderick St., Oroville, CA 95965-4871. Mailing Address:
1735 Montgomery St., Oroville, CA 95965-4820. Tel.: 530-538-
2415. Fax: 530-538-2417.
E-mail: info@cityoforoville.org
Web Site: www.cityoforoville.org/chinesetemple.html
Institution Type/Description: Religious Museum: 1863 Chinese Temple.
Hours & Admission Prices: Feb.-Dec. 15 daily 12-4; groups by appointment. Adults
$3, AAA members & groups of 15 or more $2.50; children under 12 no charge.
Attendance: 4,886 (actual)

Oxnard

CARNEGIE ART MUSEUM, 424 S. C St., Oxnard, CA 93030-
5944. Tel.: 805-385-8157 & 8179. Fax: 805-483-3654.
E-mail: lisa.horan@oxnard.org
Web Site: www.carnegieam.org
Key Personnel: Dir., Suzanne Bellah; Cur. Education, Martha Jimenez; Pres. (V),
Steve L. Kinney.
Institution Type/Description: Art Museum: housed in 1906 former library & city
hall.
Hours & Admission Prices: Thurs.-Sat. 10-5, Sun. 1-5. Adults $4, students $3,
senior citizens $2, children 6-16 $1; discounts to AAM & WMG members;
members & children under 6 no charge. Closed holidays.
Attendance: 20,000 (estimated)

CHANNEL ISLANDS MARITIME MUSEUM, 3900 Bluefin Cir.,
Oxnard, CA 93035. Tel.: 805-984-6260. Fax: 805-984-5970.
E-mail: office@cimmvc.org
Web Site: www.channelislandsmaritimemuseum.org
Formerly: Ventura County Maritime Museum, Inc.
Key Personnel: Exec. Dir., Julia Chambers.
Institution Type/Description: Maritime Museum.
Hours & Admission Prices: Daily 11-5. Adults $5, seniors $4, children $2. Closed
New Year's Eve & Day; Thanksgiving; Christmas.
Attendance: 20,000 (actual)

MULLIN AUTOMOTIVE MUSEUM, 1421 Emerson Ave.,
Oxnard, CA 93033. Tel.: 805-385-5400. Fax: 805-385-5422.
E-mail: info@mullinautomotivemuseum.com
Web Site: www.mullinautomotivemuseum.com
Institution Type/Description: Transportation Museum.
Hours & Admission Prices: 2nd & 4th Sat. 10-3. Semi-private tours: Tues. at 10 &
Thurs. at 11. Adults $40. Reservations required.

MURPHY AUTO MUSEUM, 2230 Statham Blvd., Oxnard, CA
93033. Tel.: 805-487-4333. Fax: 805-487-4441.
E-mail: info@murphyautomuseum.org
Web Site: murphyautomuseum.org
Key Personnel: Dir. & C.E.O., David Neel.
Institution Type/Description: Auto Museum.
Hours & Admission Prices: Sat.-Sun. 10-4; other times by appointment. Adults $9;
members no charge. Closed New Year's Day; Thanksgiving; Christmas.
Attendance: 5,230 (estimated)

Pacific Grove

**HERITAGE SOCIETY OF PACIFIC GROVE - KETCHAM'S
1891 BARN,** 605 Laurel Ave., Pacific Grove, CA 93950. Mailing
Address: P.O. Box 1007, Pacific Grove, CA 93950. Tel.: 831-372-
2898.
E-mail: info@pacificgroveheritage.org
Web Site: www.pacificgroveheritage.org
Key Personnel: Pres. (V), Steve Honegger.
Institution Type/Description: History Museum.
Hours & Admission Prices: Sat. 1-4. No charge; donations accepted.
Attendance: 1,000 (estimated)

PACIFIC GROVE ART CENTER ASSOCIATES, INC., 568
Lighthouse Ave., Pacific Grove, CA 93950-2624. Mailing
Address: P.O. Box 633, Pacific Grove, CA 93950-0633. Tel.: 831-
375-2208. Fax: 831-375-2208.
E-mail: pgart@mbay.net
Web Site: www.pgartcenter.org

Key Personnel: Pres., Johnny Aliotti; Dir., Alana Puryear; Preparator, Mark Davy;
Preparator, Kait Kent.
Institution Type/Description: Art Center.
Hours & Admission Prices: Wed.-Sat. 12-5, Sun. 1-4. No charge; donations
accepted. Closed legal holidays.
Attendance: 16,000 (actual)

PACIFIC GROVE MUSEUM OF NATURAL HISTORY, 165
Forest Ave., Pacific Grove, CA 93950-2698. Tel.: 831-648-5716.
Fax: 831-648-5755.
E-mail: admin@pgmuseum.org
Web Site: www.pgmuseum.org
Key Personnel: Dir., Jeanette Kihs; Pres. (V), Chris Hasegawa; Cur., Annie
Holdren; Museum Store Mgr., Beverly Bruno.
Institution Type/Description: Natural History Museum.
Hours & Admission Prices: Tues.-Sun. 10-5. Adults $8.95, youth 4-18, students w/
I.D. & military $5.95; members, Monterey County residents & school field trips
no charge. Closed major holidays.
Attendance: 51,785 (actual)

POINT PINOS LIGHTHOUSE, 80 Asilomar Ave., Pacific Grove,
CA 93950. Tel.: 831-646-3176. Facebook.
E-mail: info@pointpinoslighthouse.org
Web Site: pointpinoslighthouse.org
Institution Type/Description: Historic Lighthouse: built in 1854. Listed on the
National Register of Historic Places.
Hours & Admission Prices: Thurs.-Mon. 1-4; groups by appointment. Adults $4,
children 6-17 $2; children under 6 no charge.

Pacific Palisades

THE GETTY VILLA, 17985 Pacific Coast Hwy., Pacific Palisades,
CA 90272. Mailing Address: 1200 Getty Center Dr., Los Angeles,
CA 90049. Tel.: 310-440-7300.
E-mail: visitorservices@getty.edu
Web Site: www.getty.edu/visit
Institution Type/Description: History Museum.
Hours & Admission Prices: Wed.-Mon. 10-5; advanced time-entry ticket required.
No charge; Parking: $15. Closed New Year's Day; Thanksgiving; Christmas.

WILL ROGERS STATE HISTORIC PARK, 1501 Will Rogers
State Park Rd., Pacific Palisades, CA 90272-3941. Tel.: 310-454-
8212, ext. 104. Fax: 310-459-2031.
E-mail: rnicholas@parks.ca.gov
Web Site: www.ugf.edu/aboutugf/galerietrinitas
Key Personnel: District Supt., Ron Schafer; Topanga Supt., Lynette Hernandez;
Museum Cur., Rochelle Nicholas-Booth.
Institution Type/Description: Historic Building & Site Museum: housed in 1924-
1935 original home of Will Rogers.
Hours & Admission Prices: Park: 8 am to sunset. House Tours: Thurs.-Fri. 11-3,
Sat.-Sun. 10-4. Visitor Center: Thurs.-Sun. 10:30-5:30. Parking: adults $12,
seniors $11. Tours: closed New Year's Day; Thanksgiving; Christmas.
Attendance: 230,000 (estimated)

Pacifica

SANCHEZ ADOBE HISTORIC SITE, 1000 Linda Mar Blvd.,
Pacifica, CA 94044-3545. Tel.: 650-359-1462. Fax: 650-359-1462.
E-mail: sanchezadobe@historysmc.org
Web Site: www.historysmc.org/sanchez.html
Key Personnel: Pres., Mitch Postel; Deputy Dir., Carmen Blair; Site Mgr., Becky
Christ; Site Mgr., Chris Thatcher.
Institution Type/Description: Historic House Site: historic rancho built 1842-46 site
of Mission Dolores farming outpost (1783-1828); Pruristac village site for
Ohlone Indians.
Hours & Admission Prices: Tues.-Thurs. 10-4, Sat.-Sun. 1-5. No charge; donations
accepted. Closed legal holidays.
Attendance: 7,280

Paicines

PINNACLES NATIONAL MONUMENT, 5000 Hwy. 146,
Paicines, CA 95043-9770. Tel.: 831-389-4486, ext. 233. Fax: 831-
389-4489.
E-mail: veronica_johnson@nps.gov
Web Site: www.nps.gov
Key Personnel: Supt., Karen Beppler-Dorn; Volunteer Coord., Veronica Johnson;
Museum Shop Mgr., Linda Regan.
Institution Type/Description: Natural History Museum.

Hours & Admission Prices: Winter: daily 7:30-6; Summer: daily 7:30-8. Vehicle $5 for 7 days; Walk-in $3 for 7 days; children under 16 & educational groups with advanced waiver no charge. Visitor Center: daily 9:30-5. &
Attendance: 171,000 (estimated)

Pala

SAN ANTONIO DE PALA ASISTENCIA, 3015 Mission Rd., Pala, CA 92059. Mailing Address: P.O. Box 70, Pala, CA 92059-0070. Tel.: 760-742-3317. Fax: 760-742-3040.
Web Site: missionsanantonio.org
Institution Type/Description: History Museum: housed in a sub-mission of Mission San Luis Rey de Francia.
Hours & Admission Prices: Office & Store: Tues.-Fri. 9:30-4:30, Sat. 9:30-3, Sun. 9:30-1. Mass: Mon.-Fri. 8am, Sat. 5pm, Sun. 8am & 11:30 (English), 11am (Spanish). Closed Thanksgiving; Christmas.

Palm Desert

COLLEGE OF THE DESERT - WALTER N. MARKS CENTER FOR THE ARTS, 43-500 Monterey Ave., Palm Desert, CA 92260. Tel.: 760-346-8041.
E-mail: marksartcenter@gmail.com
Institution Type/Description: Art Gallery.
Hours & Admission Prices: Call for hours.

IMAGO GALLERIES, 45-450 Hwy. 74, Palm Desert, CA 92260. Tel.: 760-776-9890. Facebook: @ImagoGalleries.
E-mail: info@imagogalleries.com
Web Site: www.imagogalleries.com
Key Personnel: Dir., Leisa Austin.
Institution Type/Description: Art Gallery.
Hours & Admission Prices: Tues.-Sat. 11-5; other times by appointment. No charge.
&

THE LIVING DESERT, 47900 Portola Ave., Palm Desert, CA 92260-6156. Tel.: 760-346-5694, ext. 2102. Fax: 760-568-9685.
E-mail: amonroe@livingdesert.org
Web Site: livingdesert.org
Key Personnel: C.E.O. & Pres., Mr. Allen Monroe; Chm. Bd., Roger Snoble; Chm. (V), Ann Schaffner; Dir. Conservation, Peter Siminski; Dir. Accounting, Dwight Middendorf; Dir. Park Svcs., Kerry Graves; Dir. Devel., Jan Hawkins; Dir. Facilities Mgmt., Bert Buxbaum; Cur. Garden Dept., Kirk Anderson; Dir. Education, Mike Chedester; Dir. Animal Programs, RoxAnna Breitigan; Museum Shop Mgr., Diane Startzel.
Institution Type/Description: Zoo & Gardens.
Hours & Admission Prices: June-Sept. daily 8-1:30 (last admission 1pm); Oct.-May daily 9-5 (last admission 4pm). Adults $19.95, AAA, military & seniors 62 & over $17.95, children (3-12) $9.95; discounts to AZA members, groups & schools; children under 3 & members no charge. Closed Christmas Day. &
Attendance: 405,624 (actual)

Palm Springs

AGUA CALIENTE CULTURAL MUSEUM, 219 S. Palm Canyon Dr., Palm Springs, CA 92262-6310. Mailing Address: 901 E. Tahquitz Canyon Way, Ste. C-204, Palm Springs, CA 92262-6757. Tel.: 760-778-1079. Fax: 760-322-7724.
E-mail: cstansberry@accmuseum.org
Web Site: www.accmuseum.org
Key Personnel: Pres. & Chm. (V), Mildred Browne; Archivist, Cara Stansberry; Museum Interpreter, Tina Richey; Museum Interpreter, Ursula Cripps; Museum Interpreter, Tom Cole; Museum Interpreter, Don Karvelis; Office Mgr. & Museum Shop Mgr., Jackie Bagnall.
Institution Type/Description: History Museum.
Hours & Admission Prices: Memorial Day to Labor Day Fri.-Sun. 10-5; Sept.-May Wed.-Sun. 10-5. No charge; donations accepted. Closed New Year's Day; Thanksgiving; Christmas.
Attendance: 20,000 (estimated)

MOORTEN BOTANICAL GARDEN AND CACTARIUM, 1701 S. Palm Canyon Dr., Palm Springs, CA 92264-8936. Tel.: 760-327-6555.
E-mail: clarkmoorten@yahoo.com
Key Personnel: Exec. Dir., C.E.O. & Cur., Clark Moorten.
Institution Type/Description: Botanical Garden.
Hours & Admission Prices: Mon.-Sat. 9-4:30, Sun. 10-4. Adults $3, children age 5-15 $1.50; children under 5 no charge.

PALM SPRINGS AIR MUSEUM, 745 N. Gene Autry Trail, Palm Springs, CA 92262-5464. Tel.: 760-778-6262, ext. 223. Fax: 760-482-1880.
E-mail: fred@palmspringsairmuseum.org
Web Site: www.palmspringsairmuseum.org
Key Personnel: Dir., Fred Bell.
Institution Type/Description: Air Museum.
Hours & Admission Prices: Daily 10-5. Adults $16, seniors 65 & over, military and youth 13-17 $14, children 6-12 $9; members & children under 6 no charge. Closed Thanksgiving; Christmas.
Attendance: 90,000 (actual)

PALM SPRINGS ART MUSEUM, 101 Museum Dr., Palm Springs, CA 92262-5659. Tel.: 760-322-4800. Fax: 760-327-5069.
E-mail: info@psmuseum.org
Web Site: www.psmuseum.org
Formerly: Palm Springs Desert Museum, Inc.
Key Personnel: Chm., Harold J. Meyerman; The JoAnn McGrath Exec. Dir., Elizabeth Armstrong; The Donna & Cargill Macmillan Jr. Dir. Art, Daniell Cornell; Dir. Education & Public Programs, Keri Jhaveri; The Dorothy & Harold J. Meyerman Dir. Devel., Greg Polzin; Deputy Dir. & C.F.O., Jeb Bonner; Dir. Operations, Debra Preston; Dir. HR, Nikki Talley; Membership Services Mgr., MarJon Hudson.
Institution Type/Description: Art Museum.
Hours & Admission Prices: Tues.-Wed. & Fri.-Sun. 10-5, Thurs. 12-8. Adults $12.50, seniors 62 & over $10.50, students $5; discounts to CAM, WMA, AAM, ICOM & AAMD members; active duty military & their families, NARM, members & Thurs. 4-8 no charge. Closed major holidays. &
Attendance: 175,000 (actual)

RUDDY'S 1930S GENERAL STORE MUSEUM, 221 S. Palm Canyon Dr., Palm Springs, CA 92262-6310. Tel.: 760-327-2156.
Institution Type/Description: History Museum.
Hours & Admission Prices: July-Sept. Sat.-Sun. 10-4; Oct.-June Thurs.-Sun. 10-4. Adults $.95; children under 12 no charge.

VILLAGE GREEN HERITAGE CENTER, 221 S. Palm Canyon Dr., Palm Springs, CA 92262-6310. Mailing Address: P.O. Box 1498, Palm Springs, CA 92263-1498. Tel.: 760-323-8297. Fax: 760-320-2561.
E-mail: pshistoricalsociety@gmail.com
Web Site: pshistoricalsociety.org
Institution Type/Description: Historical Society Museum.
Hours & Admission Prices: Sept.-May 28 Mon.-Sat. 10-5, Sun. 11-4. Suggested Donation: $1.

Palmdale

BLACKBIRD AIRPARK MUSEUM, 2503 E. Avenue P, Palmdale, CA 93550. Mailing Address: 405 S. Rosamond Blvd., Edwards Air Force Base, CA 93524. Tel.: 661-277-8050.
E-mail: fthf@antelecom.net
Web Site: afftcmuseum.org/visit/blackbird-airpark/
Institution Type/Description: Air Force Flight Test Center Museum.
Hours & Admission Prices: Fri.-Sun. 10-5. No charge; donations accepted.
Attendance: 12,000 (estimated)

JOE DAVIES HERITAGE AIRPARK AT PALMDALE PLANT 42, 2001 E. Ave. P, Palmdale, CA 93550. Mailing Address: 38260 10th St. E., Palmdale, CA 93550. Tel.: 661-267-5300. Facebook: Joe Davies Airpark at Plant 42.
E-mail: kwhiteside@cityofpalmdale.org
Web Site: www.cityofpalmdale.org/airpark
Formerly: Plant 42 Palmdale Airpark
Key Personnel: Dir., Kathleen Dewhurst-Whiteside.
Institution Type/Description: Military History Museum.
Hours & Admission Prices: Fri.-Sun. 11-4. No charge; donations accepted. Closed New Year's Eve & Day; Christmas week. &
Attendance: 16,800 (actual)

Palo Alto

FOSTER ART & WILDERNESS FOUNDATION, 940 Commercial St., Palo Alto, CA 94303. Tel.: 650-209-7181.
E-mail: info@thefoster.org
Web Site: www.thefoster.org
Institution Type/Description: Art Gallery.
Hours & Admission Prices: Tues. 11am, 3rd Sat. each month 11am; other times by appointment.

MUSEUM OF AMERICAN HERITAGE, 351 Homer Ave., Palo Alto, CA 94301-2727. Mailing Address: P.O. Box 1731, Palo Alto, CA 94302-1731. Tel.: 650-321-1004. Fax: 650-473-6950. Facebook: MOAHPA.
E-mail: mail@moah.org
Web Site: www.moah.org
Key Personnel: Exec. Dir., Allison Wong.
Institution Type/Description: Technology Museum.
Hours & Admission Prices: Fri.-Sun. 11-4. No charge.
Attendance: 20,000 (estimated)

PALO ALTO ART CENTER, 1313 Newell Rd., Palo Alto, CA 94303-2909. Tel.: 650-329-2366. Fax: 650-326-6165. Facebook: Palo Alto Art Center.
E-mail: artcenter@cityofpaloalto.org
Web Site: www.cityofpaloalto.org/artcenter
Key Personnel: Dir., Karen Kienzle; Chm. (V), Marsha Pugsley; Studio Supvr., Fanny Retsek; Operations & Mktg. Mgr., Rebecca Barbee; Volunteer Coord., Grace Abusharkh; Museum Shop Mgr., Elizabeth Evans; Mktg., Ken Heiman; Preparator, Keith Southern.
Institution Type/Description: Visual Art Center.
Hours & Admission Prices: Tues-Wed. & Fri.-Sat. 10-5, Thurs. 10-9, Sun. 1-5. No charge; donations accepted. &
Attendance: 90,000 (actual)

PALO ALTO JUNIOR MUSEUM AND ZOO, 1451 Middlefield Rd., Palo Alto, CA 94301-3351. Tel.: 650-329-2111. Fax: 650-473-1965.
E-mail: alex.hamilton@cityofpaloalto.org
Web Site: www.cityofpaloalto.org
Key Personnel: Dir., John Aikin; Pres. (V), Aletha Coleman; Zoo Cur., Robert Steele; Dir. Education, Alex Hamilton; Exhibits Cur., Tina Keagan; Receptionist, Ines Thiessen.
Institution Type/Description: Children's Museum & Zoo.
Hours & Admission Prices: Tues.-Sat. 10-5, Sun. 1-4. No charge; donations accepted. Closed state & federal holidays; day after Thanksgiving. &
Attendance: 140,000 (estimated)

Palomar Mountain

PALOMAR OBSERVATORY, 35899 Canfield Rd., Palomar Mountain, CA 92060-0200. Tel.: 760-742-2119.
E-mail: palomar-info@astro.caltech.edu
Web Site: www.astro.caltech.edu/palomarnew
Institution Type/Description: Observatory.
Hours & Admission Prices: early March to early Nov. daily 9-4; early Nov. to early March daily 9-3. Closed Christmas Eve & Day.

Palos Verdes Peninsula

SOUTH COAST BOTANIC GARDEN, 26300 Crenshaw Blvd., Palos Verdes Peninsula, CA 90274-2515. Tel.: 310-544-1948. Facebook.
E-mail: info@southcoastbotanicgarden.org
Web Site: www.southcoastbotanicgarden.org
Key Personnel: Bd. Pres., Peter Olpe; C.E.O., Adrienne L. Nakashima; Garden Supt., Tanya E. Finney.
Institution Type/Description: Botanical Garden.
Hours & Admission Prices: Daily 9-5. Adults $9, seniors 62 & over and students $6, children 5-12 $4; children 4 & under no charge. Closed Christmas.
Attendance: 130,000

Paradise

GOLD NUGGET MUSEUM AND HISTORY ACTIVITY CENTER, 502 Pearson Rd., Paradise, CA 95969-5114. Mailing Address: P.O. Box 949, Paradise, CA 95967-0949. Tel.: 530-872-8722. Fax: 530-872-1050. Facebook: Gold Nugget Museum.
E-mail: info@goldnuggetmuseum.com
Web Site: goldnuggetmuseum.com
Institution Type/Description: History Museum.
Hours & Admission Prices: Wed.-Sun. 12-4. No charge; donations accepted. &
Attendance: 15,000 (estimated)

PARADISE DEPOT MUSEUM, Black Olive & Pearson, Paradise, CA 95969. Mailing Address: P. O. Box 949, Paradise, CA 95967. Tel.: 530-872-8722. Fax: 530-872-1050.
E-mail: info@goldnuggetmuseum.com
Web Site: goldnuggetmuseum.com

Key Personnel: Exec. Dir., Joan Dresser.
Institution Type/Description: Historic Building: built in 1904.
Hours & Admission Prices: Sat.-Sun. 12-4. No charge; donations accepted.

Pasadena

ALYCE DE ROULET WILLIAMSON GALLERY, Art Center College of Design, 1700 Lida St., Pasadena, CA 91103. Tel.: 626-396-2446 & 2397. Fax: 626-405-9104.
E-mail: stephen.nowlin@artcenter.edu
Web Site: www.williamsongallery.net
Key Personnel: Dir., Stephen Nowlin.
Institution Type/Description: Art Gallery.
Hours & Admission Prices: Tues.-Thurs. & Sat.-Sun. 12-5, Fri. 12-9. Closed holidays. No charge.
Attendance: 15,000 (estimated)

ARMORY CENTER FOR THE ARTS, 145 N. Raymond Ave., Pasadena, CA 91103. Tel.: 626-792-5101. Fax: 626-449-0139.
E-mail: information@armoryarts.org
Web Site: www.armoryarts.org
Key Personnel: Dir., Irene Tsatsos.
Institution Type/Description: Art Gallery.
Hours & Admission Prices: Tues.-Sun. 12-5. Suggested Donation: adults $5; seniors, students & members no charge.

EATON CANYON NATURE CENTER, 1750 N. Altadena Dr., Pasadena, CA 91107. Tel.: 626-398-5420.
E-mail: eatoncanyon.conservation@gmail.com
Institution Type/Description: Nature Center.
Hours & Admission Prices: Sunrise to sunset Tues.-Sun. 9-5. Closed New Year's Day; Thanksgiving; Christmas.

THE GAMBLE HOUSE, 4 Westmoreland Pl., Pasadena, CA 91103-3593. Tel.: 626-793-3334. Fax: 626-577-7547.
E-mail: gamblehs@usc.edu
Web Site: www.gamblehouse.org
Key Personnel: Dir., Edward R. Bosley; Museum Shop Mgr., Bryan Gonzales.
Institution Type/Description: Historic House Museum: house & decorative arts designed by architects Greene & Greene.
Hours & Admission Prices: Guided Tours: Thurs.-Sun. 12-4; last tour begins at 3. Adults $12.50, seniors 65 & over and students $10; discounts to National Historic Trust members; members & children under 12 no charge. Brown Bag Tours: Tues. 12:15 & 12:45. Adults $5. Closed national holidays. &
Attendance: 25,000 (estimated)

KIDSPACE CHILDREN'S MUSEUM, 480 N. Arroyo Blvd., Pasadena, CA 91103-3269. Tel.: 626-449-9144. Fax: 626-449-9985.
E-mail: info@kidspacemuseum.org
Web Site: www.kidspacemuseum.org
Key Personnel: C.E.O., Michael Shanklin; Chm., Kris Popovich; Chief Devel. Officer, Christine Franke; C.O.O., Mary Ann Viviano; Chief Program Officer, Peter Crabbe; Asst. Dir. Operations, Susan Cardosi-Albert; Mktg. Mgr., Kristen Payne; Asst. Dir. Exhibits, Lauren Kaye; Asst. Dir. Programs, Marco Calderon.
Institution Type/Description: Children's Participatory Museum.
Hours & Admission Prices: March-Sept. Mon-Fri. 9:30-5, Sat.-Sun. 10-5; Sept.-March Tues.-Fri. 9:30-5, Sat.-Sun. 10-5. Admission $13; members & children under one no charge. Closed New Year's Day; Independence Day; Thanksgiving; Christmas Day. &
Attendance: 289,871 (actual)

NORTON SIMON MUSEUM, 411 W. Colorado Blvd., Pasadena, CA 91105-1825. Tel.: 626-449-6840. Fax: 626-796-4978. Facebook: Norton Simon Museum.
E-mail: info@nortonsimon.org
Web Site: www.nortonsimon.org
Formerly: Pasadena Art Museum
Key Personnel: Pres., Walter W. Timoshuk; Chief Cur., Carol Togneri; Cur., Gloria Williams Sander; Assoc. Cur., Emily Talbot; Asst. Cur., Stephanie Rozman; Registrar, Lisa Escovedo; Colls. Mgr., Jacqui Chambers; Dir. External Affairs, Leslie Denk; Exec. Admin., Sally Swaney; Security, Nels Ortlund; Museum Shop Mgr., Andrew Uchin.
Institution Type/Description: Art Museum.
Hours & Admission Prices: Mon., Wed.-Thurs. 12-5, Fri.-Sat. 11-8, Sun. 11-5. Adults $15, seniors $12; discounts to AAM & ICOM members; members & students no charge. Closed Rose Parade Day; Thanksgiving; Christmas. &
Attendance: 200,000 (estimated)

PASADENA MUSEUM OF CALIFORNIA ART CLOSED, 490 E. Union St., Pasadena, CA 91101-1790. Mailing Address: 495 E. Colorado Blvd., Pasadena, CA 91101-2024. Tel.: 626-568-3665. Fax: 626-568-3674.
E-mail: info@pmcaonline.org
Web Site: www.pmcaonline.org
Key Personnel: Exec. Dir., Susana Smith Bautista, PhD; Education & Engagement Coord., Leah Clancy; Lead Preparator & Special Projects Mgr., Emmett Clements; Bookstore Assoc., Mehrnoosh Eskandari; Exhibition Designer, Sergio Gomez; Dir. Exhibitions, Sarah Mitchell; Finance Mgr., Natalie Moreno-Cason; Dir. Development, Mark Stenroos.
Institution Type/Description: Art Museum.
Hours & Admission Prices: Wed.-Sun. 12-5. Adults $7, senior citizens & students $5; Free admission for members & children under 12 on 1st Fri. of month, 3rd Thurs. 5-9. Closed Mon. & Tues.;New Year's Day; Independence Day; Thanksgiving; Christmas. &
Attendance: 28,000 (estimated)

PASADENA MUSEUM OF HISTORY, 470 W. Walnut St., Pasadena, CA 91103-3562. Tel.: 626-577-1660. Fax: 626-577-1662.
E-mail: info@pasadenahistory.org
Web Site: www.pasadenahistory.org
Formerly: Pasadena Historical Museum
Key Personnel: Exec. Dir., Jeannette O'Malley; Pres., Laura Thompson; Dir. Exhibitions & Public Programming, Ardis Willwerth; Archivist, Laura Verlaque; Coord. Membership, Michelle Turner; Coord. Visitor Svcs. & Volunteers, Emily Leiserson; Museum Shop Mgr., Katie Brandon.
Institution Type/Description: Historic House Museum: 1906 Pasadena home belonging to the Fenyes Family & descendants; mansion served as Finnish consulate.
Hours & Admission Prices: History Center & Store: Wed.-Sun. 12-5. Library & Archives: Wed.-Sun. 1-4. Fenyes Mansion Tours: Fri.-Sun. 1:30 & 3. General $5, Mansion Tours $4; discounts to seniors, students & AAM members; children under 12 no charge. &
Attendance: 10,712 (actual)

TOURNAMENT HOUSE AND WRIGLEY GARDENS, 391 S. Orange Grove Blvd., Pasadena, CA 91184-0002. Tel.: 626-449-4100. Fax: 626-449-9066.
E-mail: rosepr@rosemail.org
Web Site: www.tournamentofroses.com/aboutus/house.asp
Institution Type/Description: Historic House Museum: housed in former home of chewing gum manufacturer William Wrigley, Jr.
Hours & Admission Prices: Feb.-Aug. House: Thurs. 2-4. Gardens: daily.

USC PACIFIC ASIA MUSEUM, 46 N. Los Robles Ave., Pasadena, CA 91101-2071. Tel.: 626-449-2742, ext. 0. Fax: 626-449-2754. Facebook & Instagram: Pacific Asia Museum; Twitter: USCPAM.
E-mail: info@pacificasiamuseum.org
Web Site: www.pacificasiamuseum.org
Key Personnel: Exec. Dir., Christina Yu Yu, Ph.D.; Chm. (V), Katherine Murray-Morse; Registrar, Annie Lee; Cur., Yeonsoo Chee; Head Mktg. & Communication, Nathalia Morales-Evanks; Head Education & Public Programs, Michael Fritzen; Dir. Public Programs, Susana Smith-Bautista; Volunteer Coord., Becky Sun.
Institution Type/Description: Museum of Asian and Pacific Island Art: housed in a Chinese Imperial Palace style building; built in 1924.
Hours & Admission Prices: Wed.-Sun. 10-6. Adults $10, seniors & students $7; USC faculty, staff & students and members no charge. Closed New Year's Eve & Day; Independence Day; Thanksgiving; Christmas. &
Attendance: 53,275 (actual)

Paso Robles

ESTRELLA WARBIRDS MUSEUM, 4251 Dry Creek Rd., Paso Robles, CA 93446. Tel.: 805-238-3897 & 227-0440.
E-mail: webmaster@ewarbirds.org
Web Site: www.ewarbirds.org
Institution Type/Description: Military History Museum.
Hours & Admission Prices: Thurs.-Sun. 10-4. Adults $10, seniors 60 & over $8, children 6-12 $5; members & children under 6 no charge. &
Attendance: 7,886 (actual)

PASO ROBLES ART ASSOCIATION, 1130 Pine St., Paso Robles, CA 93446-2219. Mailing Address: P.O. Box 2219, Paso Robles, CA 93447-2219. Tel.: 805-238-5473.
E-mail: info@pasoroblesart.com
Web Site: www.pasoroblesart.org
Formerly: Call-Booth House Gallery

Key Personnel: Pres. (V), Barbara Brogan.
Institution Type/Description: Art Association.
Hours & Admission Prices: Wed.-Sun. 11-3. No charge; donations accepted. &

PASO ROBLES CHILDREN'S MUSEUM, 623 13th St., Paso Robles, CA 93446. Tel.: 805-238-7432. Facebook.
E-mail: jennifer@pasokids.org
Web Site: www.pasokids.org
Key Personnel: Jennifer Cloward.
Institution Type/Description: Children's Museum.
Hours & Admission Prices: Sun. & Thurs.-Fri. 11-4, Wed. & Sat. 10-4. Adults $7, children 1-13 $6, seniors 65 & over $5; members no charge. &
Attendance: 20,000 (estimated)

Perris

DORA NELSON AFRICAN AMERICAN ART & HISTORY MUSEUM, 316 E. 7th St., Perris, CA 92570. Tel.: 310-740-5315.
Institution Type/Description: History Museum.
Hours & Admission Prices: Call for hours.

LAKE PERRIS REGIONAL INDIAN MUSEUM (HOME OF THE WIND), 17801 Lake Perris Dr., Perris, CA 92571-8400. Tel.: 951-940-5657. Fax: 951-657-0077.
Key Personnel: Park Supt., John Rowe.
Institution Type/Description: Park & Museum.
Hours & Admission Prices: Museum: Fri. 10-2, Sat.-Sun. 10-4; groups by appointment. Museum: no charge; donations accepted. Park: entrance fee charged. &
Attendance: 12,000 (actual)

ORANGE EMPIRE RAILWAY MUSEUM, 2201 S. A St., Perris, CA 92570-9318. Mailing Address: P.O. Box 548, Perris, CA 92572-0548. Tel.: 951-943-3020. Fax: 951-943-2676. Facebook: Orange Empire Railway Museum.
E-mail: info@oerm.org
Web Site: www.oerm.org
Key Personnel: C.E.O. & Pres. (V), Joseph Fuller; Chm. (V), Fred Nicas; Div. Mgr. Visitor Experience, Donna Zanin.
Institution Type/Description: Railway Museum: on the historical Santa Fe line from Riverside to San Diego.
Hours & Admission Prices: Daily 9-5. Museum: no charge except for gated events. Weekend Rides: adults $12, children 5-11 $8; discounts to Assoc. of Railway Museums members; children under 5 no charge. Closed Thanksgiving; Christmas. &
Attendance: 40,000 (estimated)

PERRIS VALLEY HISTORICAL MUSEUM, 120 4th St., Perris, CA 92570. Mailing Address: P.O. Box 343, Perris, CA 92572. Tel.: 951-657-0274.
E-mail: info@perrismuseum.com
Web Site: perrismuseum.com
Key Personnel: Pres. (V), Quinn Hawley.
Institution Type/Description: Historic Building Museum: housed in the Santa Fe Depot; built in 1892.
Hours & Admission Prices: Thurs.-Sun. 12-4. No charge. &
Attendance: 1,000 (estimated)

Pescadero

ANO NUEVO STATE RESERVE, 1 New Years Creek Rd., Pescadero, CA 94060. Mailing Address: 303 Big Trees Park Rd., Felton, CA 95018-9660. Tel.: 650-879-2025. Fax: 650-879-2031.
E-mail: info@parks.ca.gov
Web Site: www.parks.ca.gov
Key Personnel: Supervising Ranger, Gary Strachan.
Institution Type/Description: Historic Building & Park Museum: housed in c.1880 Dickerman Dairy Barn.
Hours & Admission Prices: Daily 8:30-4:30. Auto regular $10, auto senior $9. Guided Walks: Dec. 15 to March 31 daily 8:45-2:45. Per ticket $7; children 3 & under no charge. &
Attendance: 105,000

PIGEON POINT LIGHT STATION, 210 Pigeon Point Rd., Hwy. 1, Pescadero, CA 94060. Mailing Address: 1 New Years Creek Rd., Pescadero, CA 94060. Tel.: 650-879-2120. Facebook.
E-mail: info@parks.ca.gov
Web Site: parks.ca.gov
Institution Type/Description: Lighthouse: built in 1872.

Hours & Admission Prices: June-Aug. daily 10-4; Sept.-May Thurs.-Mon.10-4. Tours: daily 1 pm.

Petaluma

GALLERY BERGELLI, 103 H St., Petaluma, CA 94952-5125. Tel.: 415-945-9454. Facebook: Gallery Bergelli.
E-mail: gallery@bergelli.com
Web Site: www.bergelli.com
Institution Type/Description: Art Gallery.
Hours & Admission Prices: Thurs.-Fri. 10-4, Sat.-Sun. 11-4. No charge.

PETALUMA ADOBE STATE HISTORIC PARK, 3325 Adobe Rd., Petaluma, CA 94954. Tel.: 707-762-4871. Fax: 707-762-4871.
E-mail: petaluma.adobe@parks.ca.gov
Web Site: www.petalumaadobe.com
Institution Type/Description: Historic Building: 1836 Vallejo's adobe ranch headquarters.
Hours & Admission Prices: Tues.-Wed. 10-5. Adults 17 & over $3; children 6-16 $2; members no charge. Closed New Year's Day; Thanksgiving; Christmas.
Attendance: 8,700 (actual)

PETALUMA HISTORICAL LIBRARY AND MUSEUM, 20 Fourth St., Petaluma, CA 94952-3004. Tel.: 707-778-4398. Fax: 707-762-3923. Facebook & Twitter: @PetalumaMuseum.
E-mail: pmuseum.info@petalumamuseum.com
Web Site: petalumamuseum.com
Key Personnel: Chmn. (V), Kit Schlich; Pres. (V), Harvy Nieuwboer.
Institution Type/Description: History Museum.
Hours & Admission Prices: Museum: Thurs.-Sat. 10-4, Sun. 12-3; other times by appointment; Hoppy Hopkins Research Library: Mon. & Thurs. 1-4. No charge; suggested donation $5; NARM members & military no charge. Closed holidays.
Attendance: 15,000 (actual)

PETALUMA WILDLIFE AND NATURAL SCIENCE MUSEUM, 201 Fair St., Petaluma, CA 94952-2594. Tel.: 707-778-4787. Fax: 707-778-4603.
E-mail: info@petalumawildlifemuseum.com
Web Site: www.petalumawildlifemuseum.com
Formerly: Wildlife Museum at Petaluma High School
Key Personnel: Exec. Dir., Neal Ramus; Pres., George Grossi.
Institution Type/Description: Wildlife & Natural Science Museum.
Hours & Admission Prices: Sat. 11-3, call to confirm. Admission $5; children 5 & under no charge. Closed major holidays.
Attendance: 3,171 (actual)

Piercy

CONFUSION HILL GRAVITY HOUSE, 75001 N. Hwy. 101, Piercy, CA 95587-8805. Tel.: 707-925-6456. Fax: 707-925-6477.
E-mail: confusion@asis.com
Web Site: www.confusionhill.com
Key Personnel: Owner & Operator, Doug Campbell; Owner & Operator, Carol Campbell.
Institution Type/Description: Logging Museum.
Hours & Admission Prices: House: May-Sept. daily 9-6; Oct.-April daily 9-5. Adults $5, children 4-12 $4; children 3 & under no charge. Train Ride: June-Sept. daily 10-5. Rides: adults $8.50, children 4-12 $6.50; children 3 & under no charge.
Attendance: 20,000 (estimated)

Piru

RANCHO CAMULOS MUSEUM, Rte. 126, Piru, CA 93040. Mailing Address: P.O. Box 308, Piru, CA 93040-0308. Tel.: 805-521-1501.
E-mail: info@ranchocamulos.org
Web Site: www.ranchocamulos.org
Key Personnel: Dir., Susan Falck.
Institution Type/Description: Historic Site: listed on the National Register of Historic Places; a National Historic Landmark.
Hours & Admission Prices: Sun. 1-4; other times by appointment. Adults $5; members no charge.
Attendance: 4,500 (estimated)

Pittsburg

LOS MEDANOS COLLEGE ART GALLERY, 2700 E. Leland Rd., Pittsburg, CA 94565-5197. Tel.: 925-439-2181, ext. 3493.

E-mail: jpettite@losmedanos.edu
Web Site: www.losmedanos.edu/art/gal.aspxtm
Key Personnel: Dir., Judi Pettite; Cur., Dawn Black.
Institution Type/Description: Art Gallery.
Hours & Admission Prices: Tues.-Thurs. 12:30-2:30 & 6:30-8:30. No charge.

Placentia

GEORGE KEY RANCH, 625 W. Bastanchury Rd., Placentia, CA 92870-2230. Tel.: 714-973-3190 & 3191.
E-mail: keyranch@ocparks.com
Web Site: www.ocparks.com/keyranch
Institution Type/Description: Historic House Museum.
Hours & Admission Prices: June-April Tues.-Fri. 12:30-4:30, 1st Sat. each month 2-4.

Placerville

EL DORADO COUNTY HISTORICAL MUSEUM, 104 Placerville Dr. Fairgrounds, Placerville, CA 95667-3910. Tel.: 530-621-5865. Fax: 530-621-6644.
E-mail: museum@co.el-dorado.ca.us
Web Site: www.co.el-dorado.ca.us/museum
Key Personnel: Museum Admin., Mary Cory.
Institution Type/Description: History Museum.
Hours & Admission Prices: Wed.-Sat. 10-4, Sun. 12-4; call for extended hours. No charge; donations accepted. Closed holidays.
Attendance: 20,000 (actual)

Pleasanton

MUSEUM ON MAIN, 603 Main St., Pleasanton, CA 94566-6603. Tel.: 925-462-2766. Fax: 925-462-2779.
E-mail: info@museumonmain.org
Web Site: www.museumonmain.org
Formerly: Amador-Livermore Valley Historical Society
Key Personnel: Exec. Dir., Jim DeMersman; Pres. (V), Roz Wright; Dir. Education, Sarah Schaefer; Cur., Ken MacLennan; Office Mgr., Bonnie Fitzpatrick.
Institution Type/Description: General Museum: housed in c.1914 Town Hall.
Hours & Admission Prices: Tues.-Sat. 10-4, Sun. 1-4. No charge; donations accepted.
Attendance: 21,263 (actual)

Point Arena

POINT ARENA LIGHTHOUSE AND MUSEUM, 45500 Lighthouse Rd., Point Arena, CA 95468. Mailing Address: P.O. Box 11, Point Arena, CA 95468-0011. Tel.: 877-725-4448, 707-882-2777. Fax: 707-882-2111. Facebook: Point Arena Lighthouse.
E-mail: palight@mcn.org
Web Site: www.pointarenalighthouse.com
Key Personnel: Exec. Dir., Mark Hancock; Chm. (V), Nicolas Epanchin.
Institution Type/Description: Lighthouse & History Museum.
Hours & Admission Prices: Winter: daily 10-3:30. Adults $7.50, children $1; members no charge.
Attendance: 40,000 (estimated)

Point Reyes

POINT REYES NATIONAL SEASHORE, 1 Bear Valley Rd., Point Reyes, CA 94956-9703. Tel.: 415-464-5100 & 5125 (Curator). Fax: 415-464-663-8132.
E-mail: carola_derooy@nps.gov
Web Site: www.nps.gov/pore
Key Personnel: Park Supt., Cicely Muldoon.
Institution Type/Description: Natural & Cultural Museum.
Hours & Admission Prices: Bear Valley Visitor Center: Mon.-Fri. 10-5, Sat.-Sun. & holidays 9-5. Ken Patrick Visitor Center: Sat.-Sun. & holidays 10-5. Lighthouse & Lighthouse Visitor Center: see website for 2016 hours). Library & Study collection: Mon.-Fri. 8-4:30, by appointment only. No charge; donations accepted.
Attendance: 500,000 (actual)

Point Richmond

GOLDEN STATE MODEL RAILROAD MUSEUM, 900-A Dornan Dr., Point Richmond, CA 94801-4126. Tel.: 510-234-4884 (recorded message only).
E-mail: info@gsmrm.org
Web Site: www.gsmrm.org

Key Personnel: Gen. Mgr. & Museum Shop Mgr., David Illich.
Institution Type/Description: Model Railroad Museum.
Hours & Admission Prices: April-Dec. Sat.-Sun. 12-5. Train operations only on Sun. Family $10, adults $5, seniors & children 4-11 $3; discounts to Contra Costa Library members; members, Wed. 11-3 & Sat. no charge. &
Attendance: 7,161 (actual)

Pomona

ADOBE DE PALOMARES, 491 E. Arrow Hwy., Pomona, CA 91767-2264. Mailing Address: Historical Society of Pomona Valley, 585 E. Holt Ave., Pomona, CA 91767. Tel.: 909-620-0264, 909-623-2198.
E-mail: pomonahistorical@verizon.net
Web Site: www.pomonahistorical.org/palomares
Institution Type/Description: Historic House Museum.
Hours & Admission Prices: Sun. 2-5. No charge. Closed Easter; Memorial Day; Labor Day; Thanksgiving.

AMERICAN MUSEUM OF CERAMIC ART, 399 N. Garey Ave., Pomona, CA 91767-5431. Tel.: 909-865-3146. Fax: 909-629-1067. Facebook: American Museum of Ceramic Art.
E-mail: frontdesk@amoca.org
Web Site: www.amoca.org
Key Personnel: Dir., Beth Ann Gerstein; Pres., Don Pattison; Devel. Consultant, Carolyn Wagner; Studio Dir., Heidi Kreitchet.
Institution Type/Description: Art Museum.
Hours & Admission Prices: Wed.-Sat. 12-5, 2nd Sat. of month 12-9. Adults $7, senior citizens & students $4; discounts to AAM & ICOM members; members no charge. Closed New Year's Day; Thanksgiving; Christmas Eve & Day. &
Attendance: 15,000 (estimated)

THE DA CENTER FOR THE ARTS, 252-D S. Main St., Pomona, CA 91766. Tel.: 909-397-9716. Fax: 909-629-8697. Facebook: The dA Center for the Arts.
E-mail: daartcenter@gmail.com
Web Site: www.dacenter.org
Key Personnel: Dir., Margaret Aichele; Pres. (V), Chris Toovey.
Institution Type/Description: Art Gallery.
Hours & Admission Prices: Wed.-Sat. 12-4. Artwalk: 2nd Sat. of month 5-9. No charge; donations accepted. &
Attendance: 20,000 (estimated)

DONALD B. HUNTLEY ART GALLERY, California State Polytechnic Univ., Pomona, 3801 W. Temple Ave., Univ. Library, 4th Fl., Pomona, CA 91768. Tel.: 909-979-5556.
E-mail: polycentric@cpp.edu
Hours & Admission Prices: Call for hours.

LA CASA PRIMERA DE RANCHO SAN JOSE, 1569 N. Park Ave., Pomona, CA 91768-1835. Mailing Address: Historical Society of Pomona Valley, 585 E. Holt Ave., Pomona, CA 91767. Tel.: 909-623-2198.
Web Site: www.laokay.com/lacasaprimera.htm
Institution Type/Description: History Museum.
Hours & Admission Prices: Sun. 2-5. Closed Easter weekend; Memorial Day weekend; Labor Day weekend; Thanksgiving and weekend after.

LATINO ART MUSEUM, 281 S. Thomas St., Ste. 105 & 104, Pomona, CA 91766-1750. Tel.: 909-620-6009. Facebook.
E-mail: latinoartmuseum0@gmail.com
Web Site: www.latinoartmuseum.org
Key Personnel: Dir. & C.E.O., Graciela H. Nardi.
Institution Type/Description: Art Museum.
Hours & Admission Prices: Wed.-Sat. 3:30-6:30, 2nd & last Sat. each month 3:30-9:30. No charge; donations accepted. &
Attendance: 500 (estimated)

RAIL GIANTS TRAIN MUSEUM, Los Angeles County Fairgrounds, Fairplex Child Devel. Ctr., 1101 W. McKinley, Pomona, CA 91769. Mailing Address: P.O. Box 2250, Pomona, CA 91769-2250. Tel.: 909-623-0190.
E-mail: railgiants@gmail.com
Web Site: www.railgiants.org
Formerly: Southern California Chapter Railway & Locomotive Historical Society
Key Personnel: Chm. (V), Robert Shatsnider; Pres. (V), Paul Guercio; Membership, Steve McFerson; Museum Shop Mgr., Shelley Hunter.
Institution Type/Description: Railroad Historical Society Museum.

Hours & Admission Prices: 2nd Sat.-Sun. each month 10-4; other times by appointment. Open during the Los Angeles County Fair until 9 pm. No charge; donations accepted.
Attendance: 30,000 (estimated)

SCA PROJECT GALLERY, 281 S. Thomas St., #104, Pomona, CA 91766-1750. Tel.: 909-865-0252.
E-mail: scaprojectgallery@gmail.com
Web Site: www.scaprojectgallery.com
Institution Type/Description: Art Gallery.
Hours & Admission Prices: Thurs.-Sat. 12-4, 2nd Sat. each month 12-9.

W. KEITH AND JANET KELLOGG UNIVERSITY ART GALLERY, California State Polytechnic Univ., Pomona, 3801 W. Temple Ave., Pomona, CA 91768. Tel.: 909-869-4302.
Institution Type/Description: Art Gallery.
Hours & Admission Prices: Academic Year: Mon.-Tues. 4-8, Wed.-Thurs. & Sat.-Sun. 12-4. Parking; Mon.-Fri. $5, Sat.-Sun. $3. Closed university breaks & holidays.

WALLY PARKS NHRA MOTORSPORTS MUSEUM, Fairplex Gate 1, 1101 W. McKinley Ave., Bldg. 3A, Pomona, CA 91768-1639. Tel.: 909-622-2133. Fax: 909-622-1206.
E-mail: themuseum@nhra.com
Web Site: www.museum.nhra.com
Key Personnel: Exec. Dir., Tony Thacker; Cur., Greg Sharp; Mgr. Mktg. & Advertising, Rose Dickinson; Coord. Museum Svcs., Sheri Watson.
Institution Type/Description: Motorsports and Transportation Museum.
Hours & Admission Prices: Wed.-Sun. 10-5. Adults $8, seniors 60 & over and juniors 6-15 $6; discount to AAA members; children under 5 no charge. Closed New Year's Day; Memorial Day; Independence Day; Thanksgiving; Christmas. &
Attendance: 100,000

Port Hueneme

U.S. NAVY SEABEE MUSEUM, 99 23rd Ave., Port Hueneme, CA 93043. Mailing Address: Naval Base Ventura County Bldg. 100, 1001 Addor St., Port Hueneme, CA 93043. Tel.: 805-982-5165. Fax: 805-982-5595. Facebook: Seabee Museum.
E-mail: seabeemuseum@navy.mil
Web Site: www.history.navy.mil
Formerly: U.S. Navy Civil Engineer Corps/Seabee Museum
Key Personnel: Dir., Lara Glodbille; Public Rels. Mgr., Aramis X. Ramirez; Cur., Kimberlyn Crowell; Archivist, Gina Nichols.
Institution Type/Description: Military History Museum.
Hours & Admission Prices: Mon.-Sat. 9-4. No charge. Closed federal holidays. &
Attendance: 15,000 (estimated)

Porterville

PORTERVILLE HISTORICAL MUSEUM, 257 N. D St., Porterville, CA 93257-3622. Tel.: 559-784-2053. Fax: 559-784-4009.
E-mail: portervillemuseum@gmail.com
Web Site: portervillemuseum.org
Key Personnel: Dir. & Pres., Rick Struble; Dir., Bruno Huerta; Treas., Wayne Foltz; Sec., Judy Kover; Cur., Sheila Pickrell.
Institution Type/Description: History Museum: housed in c.1913 Southern Pacific Railroad passenger depot.
Hours & Admission Prices: Summer: Thurs.-Sat. 9-3; Winter: Thurs.-Sat. 10-4. Adults $5, students 6-12 $1; discounts to Friends of the Museum; members & children under 6 no charge. Closed New Year's Day; Fair Week; Thanksgiving; Christmas. &
Attendance: 2,100 (estimated)

ZALUD HOUSE, 393 N. Hockett St., Porterville, CA 93257-3639. Mailing Address: 291 N. Main, Porterville, CA 93257-3737. Tel.: 559-782-7548. Fax: 559-791-7854.
E-mail: dmoore@ci.porterville.ca.us
Key Personnel: C.E.O., Donnie Moore; Cur., Heather Raymond.
Institution Type/Description: Historic House: built in 1892.
Hours & Admission Prices: Feb.-Dec. Wed.-Sat. 10-4, Sun. 2-4. Adults $2, children $.50. Closed Easter; Independence Day; Thanksgiving; Christmas. &
Attendance: 2,888 (actual)

Portola

WESTERN PACIFIC RAILROAD MUSEUM, 700 Western Pacific Way, Portola, CA 96122-8636. Mailing Address: P.O. Box 608, Portola, CA 96122-0608. Tel.: 530-832-4131. Fax: 530-832-1854.
E-mail: info@wplives.org
Web Site: www.wplives.org
Formerly: Portola Railroad Museum
Key Personnel: Pres., Rod McClure; Membership, Eugene Vicknair.
Institution Type/Description: Railroad Museum: former Western Pacific shop & service facility.
Hours & Admission Prices: March & Nov. daily 11-4; April-Oct. daily 10-5. Train Rides: Memorial Day to Labor Day. Adults $8, children $4; members no charge.
Attendance: 10,000 (estimated)

Quincy

PLUMAS COUNTY MUSEUM, 500 Jackson St., Quincy, CA 95971-9412. Tel.: 530-283-6320.
E-mail: pcmuseum@psln.com
Web Site: wwwplumasmuseum.org
Key Personnel: Dir. & C.E.O., Scott J. Lawson; Chm. (V) Bd. Dir., Bill Tantau; Pres. (V) Bd. Trustees & Chm. (V), Don Clark.
Institution Type/Description: Historical Museum.
Hours & Admission Prices: Tues.-Sat. 10-4. Adults $2, children 12-17 $1; children under 12 & members no charge. Closed major holidays Oct.-April. &
Attendance: 6,000 (actual)

Ramona

CLASSIC ROTORS, Ramona Airport, 2690 Montecito Rd., Ramona, CA 92065-1638. Tel.: 760-650-9257.
E-mail: communications@rotors.org
Web Site: www.classicrotors.org
Institution Type/Description: Helicopter Museum.
Hours & Admission Prices: Fri.-Mon. 10-4, Tues.-Thurs. by appointment. No charge, donations accepted.

GUY B. WOODWARD MUSEUM, 645 Main St., Ramona, CA 92065-2043. Mailing Address: Ramona Pioneer Historical Society, P.O. Box 625, Ramona, CA 92065. Tel.: 760-789-7644.
E-mail: info@woodwardmuseum.org
Web Site: www.woodwardmuseum.org
Key Personnel: Pres., Judy Nachazel.
Institution Type/Description: History Museum.
Hours & Admission Prices: Thurs.-Sun. 1-4; other times by appointment.

Rancho Cordova

SACRAMENTO CHILDREN'S MUSEUM, 2701 Prospect Park, Rancho Cordova, CA 95670. Tel.: 916-638-7228. Fax: 916-638-7245.
E-mail: info@sackid.org
Web Site: www.sackids.org
Key Personnel: Dir., Sharon Stone Smith.
Institution Type/Description: Children's Museum.
Hours & Admission Prices: Tues.-Sat. 9-5, Sun. 12-5. Admission $7. &
Attendance: 100,000 (actual)

Rancho Cucamonga

CASA DE RANCHO CUCAMONGA, 8810 Hemlock St., Rancho Cucamonga, CA 91730-2319. Tel.: 909-989-4970.
Institution Type/Description: Historic House Museum.
Hours & Admission Prices: Tues.-Sat. 10-3. No charge; donations requested.

JOHN RAINS HOUSE, 8810 Hemlock Ave., Rancho Cucamonga, CA 91730-2319. Mailing Address: c/o San Bernardino Co. Museums, 2024 Orange Tree Lane, Redlands, CA 92374. Tel.: 909-989-4970 & 307-2669. Fax: 909-307-0539.
E-mail: rmckernan@sbcm.sbcounty.gov
Web Site: www.sbcountymuseum.org
Formerly: Casa de Rancho Cucamonga
Key Personnel: Dir., Robert McKernan; Site Mgr., Pam Strunk; Cur., Michele Nielsen.
Institution Type/Description: Historic House Museum: housed in c.1860 John & Merced Rains home.

Hours & Admission Prices: Tues.-Sat. 10-3. No charge; donations accepted. Closed New Year's Day; Thanksgiving; Christmas. &
Attendance: 3,500 (actual)

WIGNALL MUSEUM OF CONTEMPORARY ART, Chaffey College, 5885 Haven Ave., Rancho Cucamonga, CA 91737-3002. Tel.: 909-652-6492. Fax: 909-652-6491.
E-mail: wignall.staff@chaffey.edu
Web Site: www.chaffey.edu/wignall
Key Personnel: Dir. & Cur., Rebecca Trawick; Asst. Cur., Roman Stollenwerk.
Institution Type/Description: Contemporary art.
Hours & Admission Prices: Aug.-May Mon.-Thurs. 10-4, Sat. 12-4. No charge; donations accepted. Closed college holidays. &
Attendance: 5,000 (actual)

Rancho Mirage

CHILDREN'S DISCOVERY MUSEUM OF THE DESERT, 71-701 Gerald Ford Dr., Rancho Mirage, CA 92270-1934. Tel.: 760-321-0602. Fax: 760-321-1605.
E-mail: jmiller@cdmod.org
Web Site: www.cdmod.org
Key Personnel: Pres., Amir Afsar; C.E.O., Carol E. Scott; Dir. Operations, Cary Alvarez; Dir. Museum Advancement, Kyle Pong; Assoc. Dir. Education, Emily Culhan; Museum Shop Mgr. & Visitors Svcs., Debra Aiello.
Institution Type/Description: Children's Museum.
Hours & Admission Prices: Jan.-April daily 10-5; May-Dec. Tues.-Sun. 10-5. Admission 2 & over $8; members, ACM reciprocal members & children under 2 no charge. Closed New Year's Day; Easter; Memorial Day; Independence Day; Labor Day; Thanksgiving; Christmas. &
Attendance: 70,000 (actual)

SUNNYLANDS CENTER & GARDENS, 37977 Bob Hope Dr., Rancho Mirage, CA 92270. Mailing Address: The Annenberg Retreat at Sunnylands, 71231 Tamarisk Lane, Rancho Mirage, CA 92270. Tel.: 760-202-2222.
E-mail: contact@sunnylands.org
Web Site: sunnylands.org
Key Personnel: Dir., Janice Lyle, Ph.D.; Pres., The Annenberg Foundation Trust at Sunnylands, David J. Lane; Retail Mgr., James Campbell.
Institution Type/Description: Historic House Museum: housed in the former winter residence of Walter and Leonore Annenberg.
Hours & Admission Prices: Center & Gardens: Sept. 22-June 2 Thurs.-Sun. 8:30-4. No charge. House Tours: by appointment; children under 10 not admitted. Adults $48. &
Attendance: 97,648 (actual)

Rancho Palos Verdes

PALOS VERDES ART CENTER, 5504 W. Crestridge, Rancho Palos Verdes, CA 90275. Tel.: 310-541-2479. Fax: 310-541-9520.
E-mail: info@pvartcenter.org
Web Site: www.pvartcenter.org
Key Personnel: C.E.O., Robert A. Yassin; Chm. (V), Loren DeRoy; Pres. (V), Nancy Cumming; Dir. Exhibits, Scott Canty; Administrative Dir., Ann Willens; Dir. Publicity, Julia Parton; Dir. Education, Gail Phinney; Coord. Education, Angela Hoffman.
Institution Type/Description: Art Gallery.
Hours & Admission Prices: Galleries: Mon.-Sat. 10-4, Sun. 1-4. No charge; donations accepted. Closed New Year's Day; President's Day; Memorial Day; Independence Day; Labor Day; Thanksgiving; Christmas. &
Attendance: 80,000 (estimated)

POINT VICENTE LIGHTHOUSE, 31550 Palos Verdes Dr., W., Rancho Palos Verdes, CA 90275. Tel.: 310-541-0334.
Institution Type/Description: Historic Lighthouse: built in 1926. Listed on the National Registry of Historic Sites.
Hours & Admission Prices: Tower & Museum: 2nd Sat. each month 10-3; children under 7 not allowed in tower. No charge.

Rancho Santa Fe

RANCHO SANTA FE ART GUILD, 6004 Paseo Delicias, Rancho Santa Fe, CA 92067. Mailing Address: P.O. Box 773, Rancho Santa Fe, CA 92067-0773. Tel.: 858-759-3545.
E-mail: rsfartguild@gmail.com
Web Site: ranchosantafeartguild.org
Institution Type/Description: Art Gallery.
Hours & Admission Prices: Tues.-Sat. 11-4:30.

Randsburg

RANDSBURG DESERT MUSEUM, 161 Butte Ave., Randsburg, CA 93554. Mailing Address: P.O. Box 307, Randsburg, CA 93554-0307. Tel.: 760-371-0965.
E-mail: hafdog@aol.com
Web Site: randdesertmuseum.com
Key Personnel: Dir., J. Bart Parker; Pres. (V), John Hamlin.
Institution Type/Description: General Museum.
Hours & Admission Prices: Sat.-Sun. 10-5; other times by appointment. No charge; donations accepted.
Attendance: 2,500 (estimated)

Red Bluff

KELLY-GRIGGS HOUSE MUSEUM, 311 Washington St., Red Bluff, CA 96080-3430. Mailing Address: P.O. Box 9082, Red Bluff, CA 96080-6068. Tel.: 530-527-1129.
E-mail: kellygriggsmus@gmail.com
Web Site: www.kellygriggsmuseum.org
Key Personnel: C.E.O. & Pres. (V), Sharon Wilson.
Institution Type/Description: Local History Museum: housed in 1880 Victorian home.
Hours & Admission Prices: Thurs.-Sun. 1-4; groups by appointment. No charge; donations accepted. Closed New Year's Day; Easter; Independence Day; Thanksgiving; Christmas.
Attendance: 3,500 (estimated)

WILLIAM B. IDE ADOBE STATE HISTORIC PARK, 21659 Adobe Rd., Red Bluff, CA 96080-9392. Tel.: 530-529-8599. Fax: 530-529-8598. Facebook.
E-mail: jennifer.pooley@parks.ca.gov
Web Site: www.parks.ca.gov/?page_id=458
Key Personnel: Interpreter, Jennifer Pooley; Park Aide, Greg Harris.
Institution Type/Description: Park & Historic Homestead: 1850 adobe cabin, memorial to William B. Ide, president of the California Republic.
Hours & Admission Prices: Park: daily sunrise to sunset; Visitor Center: Fri.-Sun. 10-4. $6 per vehicle; discount to seniors; POWs & disabled veterans, California State Parks Assn. members and Golden Poppy Vehicle Day Pass & California Day Pass users no charge. Closed New Year's Day; Thanksgiving; Christmas. ♿
Attendance: 30,000 (estimated)

Redding

BEHRENS-EATON DISPLAY MUSEUM, 1939 Butte St., Redding, CA 96001-1613. Tel.: 530-241-3454.
E-mail: eaton@c-zone.net
Institution Type/Description: History Museum.
Hours & Admission Prices: Tues.-Wed. 10-4, Sat. 1-4. No charge; donations accepted. Closed holidays.
Attendance: 300

BEHRENS-EATON HOUSE MUSEUM, 1520 West St., Redding, CA 96001-1624. Mailing Address: 1939 Butte St., Redding, CA 96001-1613. Tel.: 530-241-3454.
E-mail: behrenseaton@gmail.com
Web Site: eatonhousemuseum.org
Institution Type/Description: Historic House Museum: housed in the home of Charles Behrens, Sheriff of Shasta County and grandfather of Judge Richard Behrens Eaton; built in 1895.
Hours & Admission Prices: Tues.-Wed. 10-4, Sat. 1-4. No charge; donations accepted. Closed holidays. ♿

SHASTA HISTORICAL SOCIETY, 1449 Market St., Redding, CA 96001. Tel.: 530-243-3720. Facebook.
E-mail: shs@shastahistorical.org
Web Site: shastahistorical.org
Key Personnel: Exec. Dir., Patricia Lord; Pres. (V), Mike Dahl.
Institution Type/Description: Historical Society Museum.
Hours & Admission Prices: Mon.-Fri. 10-4. No charge.

TURTLE BAY EXPLORATION PARK, 844 Sundial Bridge Dr., Redding, CA 96001. Mailing Address: 1335 Arboretum Dr., Ste. A, Redding, CA 96003-3628. Tel.: 530-243-8850, 800-887-8532. Fax: 530-243-8898. Facebook: Turtle Bay Exploration Park.
E-mail: info@turtlebay.org
Web Site: www.turtlebay.org
Formerly: Turtle Bay Museums & Arboretum on the River

Key Personnel: C.E.O., Mike Warren; Chm. Trustees (V), Randall Hempling; Exhibits Mgr., Julia Cronin; Public Rels. Mgr. & Mktg., Cristy Kidd; Visitor Svcs. Mgr., Carrian Harwig.
Institution Type/Description: History, Art & Nature Museum.
Hours & Admission Prices: May-Labor Day Mon.-Sat. 9-5, Sun. 10-5. Labor Day-April Wed.-Sat. 9-4, Sun. 10-4. Adults $16, seniors 65 & over and children 4-12 $12; discounts to ASTC members; members and children 3 & under no charge. ♿
Attendance: 145,000 (estimated)

Redlands

ASISTENCIA: SAN GABRIEL MISSION OUTPOST, 26930 Barton Rd., Redlands, CA 92373-4312. Mailing Address: c/o San Bernardino Co. Museums, 2024 Orange Tree Lane, Redlands, CA 92374. Tel.: 909-793-5402 & 307-2669. Fax: 909-307-0539.
E-mail: rmckernan@sbcm.sbcounty.gov
Web Site: sbcountymuseum.org
Key Personnel: Dir., Robert McKernan; Site Mgr., Mark Turpin; Cur., Michele Nielsen.
Institution Type/Description: History Museum: 1930s early California mission style ranch buildings.
Hours & Admission Prices: Tues.-Sat. 10-3. No charge; donations accepted. Closed New Year's Day; Thanksgiving; Christmas.
Attendance: 8,500 (actual)

HISTORICAL GLASS MUSEUM FOUNDATION, 1157 N. Orange St., Redlands, CA 92374-3218. Mailing Address: P.O. Box 9195, Redlands, CA 92375-2395. Tel.: 909-798-0868.
E-mail: historicalglassmuseum@gmail.com
Web Site: historicalglassmuseum.com
Key Personnel: Pres. (V), Joann Tortarolo.
Institution Type/Description: Historical American Glass Museum.
Hours & Admission Prices: Sat.-Sun. 12-4. Suggested Donation: adults $3; members no charge. Closed major holidays.

KIMBERLY CREST HOUSE & GARDENS, 1325 Prospect Dr., Redlands, CA 92373-7049. Tel.: 909-792-2111. Fax: 909-798-1716.
E-mail: info@kimberlycrest.org
Web Site: www.kimberlycrest.org
Key Personnel: Exec. Dir., Tonja Blakenship.
Institution Type/Description: Historic Site: housed in an 1897 French chateau-style house & carriage house, formal 1909 Italian gardens and citrus grove.
Hours & Admission Prices: Thurs.-Sat. 1-4. Suggested Donation: adults $10, seniors & students $8, children 6-12 $5; discounts AAM & ICOM members; children 5 & under no charge. Closed major holidays. ♿
Attendance: 13,000 (estimated)

LINCOLN MEMORIAL SHRINE, 125 W. Vine St., Redlands, CA 92373-4761. Tel.: 909-798-7632 (administrative) & 7636 (museum desk). Fax: 909-798-7566.
E-mail: heritage@akspl.org
Web Site: www.lincolnshrine.org
Key Personnel: Dir., Donald McCue; Assoc. Archivist & Museum Shop Mgr., Maria Carrillo; Pres., Library Bd. Trustees, William Hatfield; Cur., Nathan D. Gonzales.
Institution Type/Description: History Museum.
Hours & Admission Prices: Feb. 12 & Tues.-Sun. 1-5, special hours by appointment. No charge; donations accepted. Closed holidays. ♿
Attendance: 17,000 (estimated)

SAN BERNARDINO COUNTY MUSEUM, 2024 Orange Tree Lane, Redlands, CA 92374-4560. Tel.: 909-798-8608. Fax: 909-307-0539.
E-mail: museum@sbcounty.gov
Web Site: www.sbcounty.gov/museum
Key Personnel: Dir., Melissa A. Russo; Museum Education Services, Carolina Zataray; Cur. History, Jennifer Dickerson; Cur. Visitor Engagement & Exhibits, David Myers; Cur. Anthropology, Tamara Serrao-Leiva; Cur. Earth Sciences, Ian Gilbert; Cur. Integrated Sciences, Jessika Vazquez; Media Specialist, Jennifer Reynolds.
Institution Type/Description: General Museum.
Hours & Admission Prices: Tues.-Sun. 9-5. Adults $10, seniors & active duty military $8, student w/I.D. $7, child 5-12 $5; discounts to AAM & AAA members; child under 5 & members no charge. Closed New Year's Day; Thanksgiving; Christmas. ♿
Attendance: 55,000 (actual)

Redwood City

LATHROP HOUSE, 627 Hamilton St., Redwood City, CA 94063. Mailing Address: P.O. Box 1273, Redwood City, CA 94064-1273. Tel.: 650-365-5564.
Institution Type/Description: Historic House: built in 1863. Listed on the National Register of Historic Places.
Hours & Admission Prices: Sept.-July Wed. & 3rd Sat. each month 11-3. No charge; donations accepted.

MARINE SCIENCE INSTITUTE, 500 Discovery Pkwy., Redwood City, CA 94063-4746. Tel.: 650-364-2760. Fax: 650-364-0416.
E-mail: gail@sfbaymsi.org
Web Site: www.sfbaymsi.org
Key Personnel: Exec. Dir., Marilou S. Seiff.
Institution Type/Description: Marine Science Museum.
Hours & Admission Prices: Call for hours.

SAN MATEO COUNTY HISTORICAL ASSOCIATION AND MUSEUM, 2200 Broadway, Redwood City, CA 94063-1639. Tel.: 650-299-0104. Fax: 650-299-0141.
E-mail: info@historysmc.org
Web Site: www.historysmc.org
Key Personnel: Pres., Mitchell Postel; Chm. Bd. Dirs., Mark Jamison; Archival Collections Specialist, Debra Peterson; Cur., Dana Neitzel; Deputy Dir., Carmen Blair; Assoc. Dir. Education, Dawn Distasio; Site Mgr., Becky Christ; Site Mgr., Elizabeth Crowley.
Institution Type/Description: San Mateo County History Museum.
Hours & Admission Prices: Tues.-Sun. 10-4. Adults $6, seniors 62 and over & students with ID $4; discounts to Time Travelers, AAM & NARM members; members & children under 5 no charge. &
Attendance: 58,729 (actual)

Reedley

MENNONITE QUILTING CENTER, 1012 G St., Reedley, CA 93654-2936. Tel.: 559-638-3560.
E-mail: quiltcenter@mcc.org
Web Site: mennonitequiltcenter.org
Institution Type/Description: Quilt Museum.
Hours & Admission Prices: Mon.-Fri. 10-5, Sat. 10-4; groups of 10 or more by appointment. No charge; donations accepted. Closed holidays.

REEDLEY MUSEUM, 1752 10th St., Reedley, CA 93654-2933. Mailing Address: P.O. Box 877, Reedley, CA 93654. Tel.: 559-638-1913.
E-mail: nicole.zieba@reedley.ca.gov
Institution Type/Description: History Museum.
Hours & Admission Prices: Tues. 10-12, Sat. 9:30-12. Adults $1; students & children under 18 no charge

Represa

RETIRED CORRECTIONAL PEACE OFFICERS MUSEUM AT FOLSOM PRISON, 312 3rd St., Represa, CA 95671. Tel.: 916-985-2561, ext. 4589.
E-mail: jbrown@folsomprisonmuseum.org
Web Site: www.folsomprisonmuseum.org
Key Personnel: Operations Mgr., Jim Brown.
Institution Type/Description: History Museum: housed in an old prison house, c.1898.
Hours & Admission Prices: Daily 10-4. Adults $2; school groups, law enforcement & military no charge. Closed New Year's Day; Thanksgiving; Christmas.
Attendance: 10,000 (actual)

Rialto

RIALTO HISTORICAL SOCIETY, 201-205 N. Riverside Ave., Rialto, CA 92376. Mailing Address: P.O. Box 413, Rialto, CA 92377-0413. Tel.: 909-875-1750 & 1175.
Web Site: www.rialtohistoricalsociety.org
Key Personnel: Pres., Jean Randall; Vice Pres., Jo Elliott; Treas., Helen McCain; Sec., Judy Roberts; Historian, John Adams; Corresponding Sec., Shirley Knowles; Computer Technician, Richard McInnis.
Institution Type/Description: Historical Society Museum: adjacent to historic church building.
Hours & Admission Prices: Wed. 2-4, Sat. 10-2; other times by appointment. No charge; donations accepted. Closed holidays.
Attendance: 400 (estimated)

Richmond

RICHMOND ART CENTER, 2540 Barrett Ave., Richmond, CA 94804-1600. Tel.: 510-620-6772. Fax: 510-620-6771.
E-mail: admin@therac.org
Web Site: www.therac.org
Key Personnel: Pres. (V), Andi Biren; Exec. Dir., Richard Ambrose; Dir. On-site Education, Kato Jaworski.
Institution Type/Description: Art Center.
Hours & Admission Prices: Tues.-Sat. 11-5. No charge; donations accepted. &
Attendance: 20,000 (estimated)

RICHMOND MUSEUM OF HISTORY, 400 Nevin Ave., Richmond, CA 94801-3017. Mailing Address: P.O. Box 1267, Richmond, CA 94802-0267. Tel.: 510-235-7387.
E-mail: info@richmondmuseumofhistory.org
Web Site: www.richmondmuseum.org
Key Personnel: Pres., C.E.O. (V) & Programs, Lois H. Boyle; Cur., Melinda McCrary.
Institution Type/Description: History Museum.
Hours & Admission Prices: Wed.-Sun. 1-4. Adults $2, seniors & students $1; children & members no charge. Closed legal holidays. &
Attendance: 2,900 (estimated)

Ridgecrest

MATURANGO MUSEUM OF THE INDIAN WELLS VALLEY, 100 E. Las Flores, Ridgecrest, CA 93555-3654. Tel.: 760-375-6900. Fax: 760-375-0479.
E-mail: info@maturango.org
Web Site: www.maturango.org
Key Personnel: C.E.O. & Dir., Deborah Benson; Bd. Pres., Jerry Bradley; Coord. Art Gallery, Andrea Pelch; Account Mgr. & C.F.O., Julie Stephens; Cur. Natural History, Sherry Brubaker; Cur. Archaeology, Alexander K. Rogers; Cur. History, Elaine Wiley; Membership, Fran Van Valkenburgh; Coord. Education, Nora Nuckles; Coord. Petroglyph Tour, Linda Saholt; Museum Shop Mgr., Maureen Goff.
Institution Type/Description: Cultural and Natural History.
Hours & Admission Prices: Daily 10-5. Adults $5, seniors & children $3; children under 6 & members no charge. Reciprocal admission to members. ASTC member. Closed New Year's Day, Easter; Memorial Day; Independence Day, Labor Day, Thanksgiving, Christmas. &
Attendance: 24,119 (actual)

Rio Vista

RIO VISTA MUSEUM, 16 N. Front St., Rio Vista, CA 94571-1837. Tel.: 707-374-5169.
E-mail: riovistamuseum@yahoo.com
Web Site: riovistamuseum.com
Institution Type/Description: History Museum.
Hours & Admission Prices: Sat.-Sun. 1:30-4:30.

Riverside

BOTANIC GARDENS - UNIVERSITY OF CALIFORNIA RIVERSIDE, 900 University Ave., Riverside, CA 92521-0124. Tel.: 951-784-6962. Fax: 951-827-4437.
E-mail: ucrbg@ucr.edu
Web Site: www.gardens.ucr.edu
Key Personnel: Dir., J.G. Waines.
Institution Type/Description: Botanic Garden.
Hours & Admission Prices: Daily 8-5. Suggested Donation: $5; discounts to American Horticulture Society & RASP. Closed New Year's Day; Independence Day; Thanksgiving; Christmas. &
Attendance: 40,000 (estimated)

JENSEN-ALVARADO HISTORIC RANCH & MUSEUM, 4307 Briggs St., Riverside, CA 92519. Tel.: 951-369-6055.
Web Site: www.riversidecountyparks.org
Institution Type/Description: Historic Building: housed on the former ranch of retired sea captain Cornelius Jensen and his wife Mercedes Alvarado; built c.1880.
Hours & Admission Prices: Mon.-Fri. by appointment. Adults $3, children 3-12 $2.

JURUPA MOUNTAINS DISCOVERY CENTER, 7621 Granite Hill Dr., Riverside, CA 92509-1299. Tel.: 951-685-5818. Fax: 951-685-1240.
E-mail: info@jmdc.org
Formerly: Jurupa Mountains Cultural Center

Key Personnel: Exec. Dir., Wes Andree; Pres., Michael Rankin.
Institution Type/Description: Earth Science Museum.
Hours & Admission Prices: Center & Earth Science Museum: Tues.-Sat. 8-5. Adults $3, teens $2, children 6-12 $1. Public Tours: Sat. 9 & 12. Pre-arranged Group Tours: Tues.-Sat. 8-5, Sun. 12-5. Groups: $8-$12 per person; discounts to members. Closed New Year's Eve & Day; Thanksgiving & day after; Christmas Eve & Day. &
Attendance: 20,000 (estimated)

MARCH FIELD AIR MUSEUM, 22550 Van Buren Blvd., Riverside, CA 92518-2400. Mailing Address: P.O. Box 6463, March ARB, CA 92518-0394. Tel.: 951-902-5949. Facebook: March Field Air Museum.
E-mail: info@marchfield.org
Web Site: www.marchfield.org
Key Personnel: Exec. Dir., Paul Hammond; Bd. Pres. (V), Jamil Dada; Dir. Collections & Exhibits, Jeff Houlihan; Collections Mgr., Sterling Jenson; Venue Rentals Mgr., Denise Stephenson; Dir. Operations, Greg Kuster; Dir. Devel., Valerie Hunter.
Institution Type/Description: Military Aviation History.
Hours & Admission Prices: Tues.-Sun. 10-5. Adults $10, children 5-11 $5; active military, children under 5 & members no charge. Open select Mon. holidays. Closed New Year's Day; Thanksgiving; Christmas. &
Attendance: 56,000 (actual)

MISSION INN FOUNDATION/MUSEUM, 3696 Main St., Riverside, CA 92501-2839. Tel.: 951-781-8241 & 788-9556. Fax: 951-341-6574.
E-mail: info@missioninnmuseum.com
Web Site: www.missioninnmuseum.com
Key Personnel: Exec. Dir., John Worden.
Institution Type/Description: Historic House & Site: restored turn-of-the-century resort hotel now a national historic landmark.
Hours & Admission Prices: Museum: daily 9:30-4:30. Tours: Mon.-Fri. 10, 11:30. 2, & 4, Sat.-Sun. 10, 11:30, 1:30, 2:30, & 4. Museum: $2. Tours: adults $13, children under 12 no charge. Closed Easter; Mother's Day; Thanksgiving; Christmas.
Attendance: 45,000 (actual)

RIVERSIDE ART MUSEUM, 3425 Mission Inn Ave., Riverside, CA 92501-3368. Tel.: 951-684-7111. Fax: 951-684-7332. Facebook.
E-mail: facilityrentals@riversideartmuseum.org
Web Site: www.riversideartmuseum.org
Key Personnel: Exec. Dir., Drew Oberjuerge; Fin. Mgr., Shannon Kane; Art Education Dir., Nicole Tartoni; Permanent Collections & Exhibit Liaison, Kathryn Poindexter; Communications, Ai M. Kelley; Visitor Services, Katie Hernandez; Consultant Cur., Peter Frank.
Institution Type/Description: Art Museum: housed in 1929 building, designed by Julia Morgan, architect for Hearst Castle.
Hours & Admission Prices: Tues.-Sat. 10-4, Sun. 12-4. Adults $5, students, educators and seniors 65 & over $3; military families w/ID, members & children 12 and under no charge. Closed holidays. &
Attendance: 70,000 (estimated)

RIVERSIDE COMMUNITY COLLEGE ART GALLERY, 4800 Magnolia Ave., Quad Room 140, Riverside, CA 92506-1201. Tel.: 951-222-8358. Fax: 909-222-8740.
E-mail: julia.buckley@rcc.edu
Web Site: academic.rcc.edu/art/exhibitions.jsp
Key Personnel: Coord. Art Gallery, Leslie A. Brown.
Institution Type/Description: Art Gallery.
Hours & Admission Prices: Mon.-Wed. & Fri. 10-3, Thurs. 10-3 & 5:30-8.

RIVERSIDE HERITAGE HOUSE, 8193 Magnolia Ave., Riverside, CA 92504-3409. Mailing Address: 3580 Mission Inn Ave., Riverside, CA 92501-3321. Tel.: 951-826-5273.
Web Site: www.riversideca.gov/museum/heritage.asp
Institution Type/Description: Historic House Museum.
Hours & Admission Prices: Sept.-June Fri.-Sun. 12-3:30. Suggested Donations: adults $5. Closed federal holidays.

RIVERSIDE METROPOLITAN MUSEUM, 3580 Mission Inn Ave., Riverside, CA 92501-3321. Tel.: 951-826-5273. Fax: 951-369-4970.
E-mail: smundy@riversideca.gov
Web Site: www.riversideca.gov
Formerly: Riverside Municipal Museum
Key Personnel: Museum & Cultural Affairs Dir., Sarah Mundy; Chm. Bd. (V), Chuck Wilson; RMA Pres. (V), Peggy Barnhart.

Institution Type/Description: Natural History Museum.
Hours & Admission Prices: Museum: Tues.-Fri. 9-5, Sat. 10-5, Sun. 11-5. Heritage House: Sept.-June Fri.-Sun. 12-3:30; groups by appointment. No charge; donations requested. Closed major holidays. &
Attendance: 75,000 (estimated)

SHERMAN INDIAN MUSEUM, 9010 Magnolia Ave., Riverside, CA 92503-4431. Tel.: 951-276-6719.
E-mail: lsisquoc@charter.net
Web Site: www.shermanindianmuseum.org
Key Personnel: Cur., Lorene Sisquoc.
Institution Type/Description: Native American Museum.
Hours & Admission Prices: Tues.-Thurs. 1-4:30 by appointment.

SWEENEY ART GALLERY, UNIVERSITY OF CALIFORNIA, 3824 Main St., Riverside, CA 92501. Tel.: 951-827-4787.
E-mail: krapp@pop.ucr.edu
Web Site: sweeney.ucr.edu
Key Personnel: Dir., Tyler Stallings.
Institution Type/Description: University Art Gallery.
Hours & Admission Prices: Call for hours. Closed major holidays. &
Attendance: 7,500 (estimated)

UCR CALIFORNIA MUSEUM OF PHOTOGRAPHY, 3824 Main St., Riverside, CA 92501-3624. Tel.: 951-827-4787. Fax: 951-827-4797. Facebook: UCR Artsblock.
E-mail: emily.papavero@ucr.edu
Web Site: www.cmp.ucr.edu/
Key Personnel: Exec. Dir., Tyler Stallings; Assoc. Dir., Emily Papavero; Admin. Mgr., Trudy Cohen; Cur., Joanna Szupinska-Myers; Cur. Collections, Leigh Gleason; Curatorial Asst., Kathryn Poindexter; Exhibition Designer, Zaid Yousef; Preparator, Riri Nguyen.
Institution Type/Description: Photography Museum.
Hours & Admission Prices: Tues.-Sat. 12-5. Adults $3; members, students with ID, children & seniors no charge. Closed New Year's Day; Thanksgiving; Christmas. &
Attendance: 35,000 (estimated)

WORLD MUSEUM OF NATURAL HISTORY, La Sierra Univ., 4500 Riverwalk Pkwy., Riverside, CA 92505-3344. Tel.: 951-785-2500 (Mon.-Thurs.); 2209 (Sat.). Fax: 951-785-2426.
E-mail: advancement@lasierra.edu
Web Site: www.lasierra.edu/wmnh
Key Personnel: C.E.O. & Pres. La Sierra Univ., Randal Wisbey; Cur., Kristina Reed; Cur., Dr. Billy Hankins; Cur., Dr. Virchel Wood.
Institution Type/Description: Natural History Museum.
Hours & Admission Prices: Sat. 2-5; other times by appointment. No charge; donations accepted. &
Attendance: 8,000 (estimated)

Rohnert Park

UNIVERSITY ART GALLERY, SONOMA STATE UNIVERSITY, 1801 E. Cotati Ave., Rohnert Park, CA 94928-3609. Tel.: 707-664-2295. Fax: 707-664-4333.
E-mail: carla.stone@sonoma.edu
Web Site: www.sonoma.edu/artgallery/
Key Personnel: Dir., Michael Schwager; Exhibition Coord., Carla Stone.
Institution Type/Description: Art Gallery.
Hours & Admission Prices: Sept.-May Tues.-Fri. 11-4, Sat.-Sun. 12-4. No charge. Closed holidays. &
Attendance: 2,000 (estimated)

Roseville

MAIDU MUSEUM AND HISTORIC SITE, 1970 Johnson Ranch Dr., Roseville, CA 95661-3749. Tel.: 916-774-5934. Fax: 916-772-6161. TDD: 916-774-5220.
E-mail: mmurphy@roseville.ca.us
Web Site: www.roseville.ca.us/indianmuseum
Formerly: Maidu Interpretive Center
Key Personnel: Dir., Mark Murphy; Education, Heidi Frantz; Museum Shop Mgr., Isabella Zaia; Historic Site Restoration Coord., Linda Maurer; Security, Rich Douglas.
Institution Type/Description: Historic Site: listed on the National Register of Historic Places.
Hours & Admission Prices: Mon.-Fri. 9-4, Sat. 9-1. Adults $4.50, children & seniors $4; discounts to groups. Closed major holidays. &
Attendance: 34,500 (actual)

ROSEVILLE HISTORICAL SOCIETY'S CARNEGIE MUSEUM, 557 Lincoln St., Roseville, CA 95678. Tel.: 916-773-3003.
E-mail: carnegie@surewest.net
Web Site: www.rosevillehistorical.org
Institution Type/Description: History Museum: housed in the former Carnegie Library building; built in 1912.
Hours & Admission Prices: Mon.-Fri. 12-4; other times by appointment.

ROSEVILLE UTILITY EXPLORATION CENTER, 1501 Pleasant Gove Blvd., Roseville, CA 95747. Tel.: 916-746-1550.
E-mail: ruec@roseville.ca.us
Web Site: www.roseville.ca.us/explore
Key Personnel: Dir., Rachel Tooker.
Institution Type/Description: Environmental Preservation Museum.
Hours & Admission Prices: Tues.-Sat. 10-5. No charge. &
Attendance: 36,444 (actual)

Sacramento

CALIFORNIA AUTOMOBILE MUSEUM, 2200 Front St., Sacramento, CA 95818-1107. Tel.: 916-442-6802. Fax: 916-442-2646. Facebook, Twitter, Instagram.
E-mail: pr@calautomuseum.org
Web Site: www.calautomuseum.org
Formerly: Towe Auto Museum
Key Personnel: Exec. Dir., Delta Pick Mello; Pres., Tupper Hull; Vice Pres., Chris Lemmon; Cur., Carly Starr.
Institution Type/Description: Transportation Museum.
Hours & Admission Prices: Wed.-Mon. 10-5, 3rd Thurs. each month 10-8. Adults $9, senior citizens 65 & over and military $8, youth 5-18 $4; discounts to NARM members; children 4 & under, members, ROAM, military on Veterans Day & Memorial Day no charge. Closed New Year's Day; Easter; Thanksgiving; Christmas. &
Attendance: 60,066 (actual)

THE CALIFORNIA MUSEUM, 1020 O St., Sacramento, CA 95814-5704. Tel.: 916-653-7524. Fax: 916-653-0314. Facebook, Instagram, Twitter.
E-mail: museuminfo@californiamuseum.org
Web Site: www.californiamuseum.org
Formerly: California State History Museum
Key Personnel: Exec. Dir., Amanda Meeker; Chm., Richard Costigan, III.
Institution Type/Description: General Museum.
Hours & Admission Prices: Tues.-Sat. 10-5, Sun. 12-5. Adults $9, senior citizens & students $7.50, children 6 -17 $6.50; discounts to AAM members & groups; members and children 5 & under no charge. Closed New Year's Eve & Day; Independence Day; Thanksgiving; Christmas Eve & Day. &
Attendance: 65,000 (actual)

CALIFORNIA STATE CAPITOL MUSEUM, 10th & L Streets, Rm. B-27, Sacramento, CA 95814. Tel.: 916-324-0333. Fax: 916-445-3628. TDD: 916-324-2092.
E-mail: capitol@parks.ca.gov
Web Site: www.capitolmuseum.ca.gov, www.parks.ca.gov
Key Personnel: Museum Dir., Casey Hayden.
Institution Type/Description: Historic Building Museum: c.1860-1874 restored California State Capitol.
Hours & Admission Prices: Tours: daily 9-4. No charge. Closed New Year's Day; Thanksgiving; Christmas. &
Attendance: 513,000 (estimated)

CALIFORNIA STATE RAILROAD MUSEUM, 125 I St., Sacramento, CA 95814-2265. Mailing Address: 111 I St., Sacramento, CA 95814-2265. Tel.: 916-323-9280. Fax: 916-327-5655.
E-mail: rrmuseuminfo@parks.ca.gov
Web Site: www.csrmf.org
Key Personnel: Pres. & C.E.O., Cheryl Marcell; Finance Dir., Shell Mercurio; Retail Operations Dir., Tom Grenache; Programs Mgr., Sam Mello; Events Mgr., Melanie Koch; Communications & Mktg. Coord., Lori Hanley.
Institution Type/Description: Railroad Museum: in Old Sacramento State Historic Park.
Hours & Admission Prices: Daily 10-5. Adults $10, children 6-17 $5; discounts to North American Reciprocal Museums; children under 6 & members no charge. Closed New Year's Day; Thanksgiving; Christmas. &
Attendance: 525,000 (estimated)

CENTER FOR SACRAMENTO HISTORY, 551 Sequoia Pacific Blvd., Sacramento, CA 95811-0229. Tel.: 916-808-7072. Fax: 916-808-7582.
E-mail: chs@cityofsacramento.org
Web Site: www.centerforsacramentohistory.org
Formerly: Sacramento Archives and Museum Collection Center
Key Personnel: Mgr., Marcia Eymann; Archivist, Dylan McDonald; Cur. History, Veronica Kandl.
Institution Type/Description: Historic Agency.
Hours & Admission Prices: Wed. 4-7:45, Thurs.-Fri. 8:15-12; by appointment. No charge; donations accepted. Closed city holidays. &
Attendance: 5,000 (estimated)

CROCKER ART MUSEUM, 216 O St., Sacramento, CA 95814-5399. Tel.: 916-808-7000; 888-877-5379 (TTY CA Relay). Fax: 916-808-7372.
E-mail: cam@crockerartmuseum.org
Web Site: www.crockerartmuseum.org
Key Personnel: Dir., Lial A. Jones; Assoc. Dir. & Cur., Scott Shields; Dir. Finance, David Separovich.
Institution Type/Description: Art Museum: housed in 1872 E.B. Crocker Art Gallery; Crocker Mansion Wing; Teel Family Pavilion.
Hours & Admission Prices: Tues.-Wed. & Fri.-Sun. 10-5, Thurs. 10-9; Mon. Holiday's call for hours. Adults $10, senior citizens $8, college & youth 7-17 $5; discounts to AAM members; members & children 6 and under no charge. Closed New Year's Day; Thanksgiving; Christmas. &
Attendance: 259,738 (actual)

GOVERNOR'S MANSION STATE HISTORIC PARK, 1526 H St., Sacramento, CA 95814-2005. Mailing Address: 800 N St., Sacramento, CA 95814-4808. Tel.: 916-323-3047. Fax: 916-322-4775.
Web Site: www.parks.ca.gov/governorsmansion
Key Personnel: Dir. California State Parks, Lisa Mangat.
Institution Type/Description: Historic House Museum: housed in Victorian mansion, built in 1877.
Hours & Admission Prices: Closed to the public. &
Attendance: 39,078 (estimated)

GREGORY KONDOS GALLERY, Sacramento City College - FA9, 3835 Freeport Blvd., Sacramento, CA 95822-1318. Tel.: 916-558-2559.
E-mail: stevens@scc.losrios.edu
Web Site: www.scc.losrios.edu/kondos
Key Personnel: Dir. & Cur., Michael Stevens; Dir. & Cur., Suzanne Adan.
Institution Type/Description: Art Gallery.
Hours & Admission Prices: Mon.-Thurs. 12-4, Fri. 12-3.

LA RAZA/GALERIA POSADA, 2700 Front St. Ste. A, Sacramento, CA 95818-1121. Tel.: 916-446-5133. Fax: 916-446-1324.
E-mail: larazagaleria@gmail.com
Web Site: www.thelatinocenter.com
Key Personnel: Dir., Marie Acosta; Chm. (V), George Raya; Gallery Coord., Roberto Lopez.
Institution Type/Description: Art Center & Museum: housed in the Heilbron Mansion, a Victorian landmark.
Hours & Admission Prices: Wed.-Sat. 12-6, 2nd Sat. of month 12-9. Suggested Donation: $5. Closed Easter; Thanksgiving; Christmas. &
Attendance: 25,000 (estimated)

OLD SACRAMENTO SCHOOLHOUSE MUSEUM, 1200 Front St., Sacramento, CA 95814-3247. Mailing Address: 5325 Ridgefield Ave., Carmichael, CA 95608-2109. Tel.: 916-483-8818.
E-mail: info@oldsacschoolhouse.org
Web Site: www.scoe.net/oldsacschoolhouse
Key Personnel: Pres. (V), Suzanne Hicklin.
Institution Type/Description: History Museum.
Hours & Admission Prices: Mon.-Sat. 10-4, Sun. 12-4. No charge; donations accepted. &
Attendance: 50,000 (estimated)

POWERHOUSE SCIENCE CENTER, Discovery Museum, 3615 Auburn Blvd., Sacramento, CA 95821-2097. Tel.: 916-674-5000. Fax: 916-808-3925.
E-mail: info@powerhousesc.org
Web Site: powerhousesc.org
Formerly: Discovery Museum, Sacramento Museum of History, Science and Technology

Key Personnel: Pres. (V), Michele Wong; Interim Dir., Harry Laswell; Deputy Dir., Rita Mukherjee Hoffstadt; Dir., Finance & Opers., John Lowe; Science Content Devel. & Planetarium Coord., David Mues; Dir., Mktg. & Devel., Shahnaz Van Deventer; Flight Dir., Christopher Kyle; Flight Dir., Caitlin Everhart.
Institution Type/Description: Science & Space Museum.
Hours & Admission Prices: Daily 10-4:30. Adults 18 & over $8, seniors 60 & over & children 4-17 $7; discounts to ASTC & NARM reciprocal members. Closed New Year's Day; Independence Day; Thanksgiving; Christmas. &
Attendance: 120,000 (actual)

ROBERT ELSE GALLERY, California State University Sacramento, 6000 'J' St., Kadema Hall, First Fl., Sacramento, CA 95819-2605. Tel.: 916-278-6166.
E-mail: art@csus.edu
Web Site: www.csus.edu/galleries/else.html
Institution Type/Description: Art Gallery.
Hours & Admission Prices: Academic Year: Mon.-Fri. 12-4:30. No charge.

SACRAMENTO ZOO, 3930 W. Land Park, Sacramento, CA 95822-1123. Tel.: 916-808-5885. Fax: 916-264-5887.
E-mail: info@saczoo.org
Web Site: www.saczoo.org
Key Personnel: Exec. Dir., Kyle Burks; C.F.O., Robert Churchill; Dir. Education, Ann Geiger; Dir. External Affairs, Lesley Kirrene; Dir. Devel., Lisa Clement; Veterinarian, Ray Wack; Dir. Facilities, Anthony Bailey; Gen. Mgr., Gifts & Concessions, Doug Richter.
Institution Type/Description: Zoo.
Hours & Admission Prices: Feb.-Oct. daily 9-5; Nov.-Jan. daily 10-5. Zoo: adults $11.75, seniors 65 & over $11, children 2-11 $7.75; children under 2 no charge. Zoo & Fairyland Combination: Mon.-Fri. adults $16, seniors 65 & over $15.50, children 2-11 $12. Sat.-Sun. adults $17, seniors $16.50, children 2-11 $13; children under 2 no charge. Closed Thanksgiving; Christmas. &
Attendance: 500,000 (estimated)

SIERRA SACRAMENTO VALLEY MEDICAL SOCIETY MUSEUM OF MEDICAL HISTORY, 5380 Elvas Ave., Ste. 101, Sacramento, CA 95819-2300. Tel.: 916-452-2671. Fax: 916-452-2690.
E-mail: info@ssvms.org
Web Site: www.ssvms.org/museum.aspx
Key Personnel: Chm. (V) & Cur., Dr. Bob LaPerriere.
Institution Type/Description: Medical History Museum.
Hours & Admission Prices: Mon.-Fri. 9-4. No charge; donations accepted. Closed holidays. &
Attendance: 1,000 (estimated)

STATE INDIAN MUSEUM, 2618 K St., Sacramento, CA 95816-5104. Tel.: 916-324-0971. Fax: 916-322-1561.
E-mail: connie.mcgough@parks.ca.gov
Web Site: www.parks.ca.gov/indianmuseum
Key Personnel: Interpretive Svcs. & Museum Shop Mgr., Connie McGough.
Institution Type/Description: California Native American Cultural & Historical Museum.
Hours & Admission Prices: Daily 10-5. Adults 18 & up $3, youth 6-17 $2; children 5 & under no charge. Closed New Year's Day; Thanksgiving; Christmas. &
Attendance: 40,000 (estimated)

SUTTER'S FORT STATE HISTORIC PARK, 2701 L St., Sacramento, CA 95816-5613. Mailing Address: California State Parks, P.O. Box 942896, Sacramento, CA 94296. Tel.: 916-445-4422. Fax: 916-442-8613.
E-mail: info@parks.ca.gov
Web Site: www.parks.ca.gov/suttersfort
Key Personnel: Cur., Nancy Jenner; Volunteer Coord., Crista Sykes.
Institution Type/Description: State Park Museum.
Hours & Admission Prices: Daily 10-5. Adults $5, youth 6-17 $3; children 5 & under no charge. Closed New Year's Day; Thanksgiving; Christmas. &
Attendance: 200,000 (estimated)

WELLS FARGO HISTORY MUSEUM CLOSED, Old Sacramento State Historic Park, 1000 Second St., Sacramento, CA 95814-3202. Mailing Address: Wells Fargo Historical Services, 420 Montgomery St., MAC-A0101-022, San Francisco, CA 94163. Tel.: 916-440-4263. Fax: 916-498-0302. Facebook: Wells Fargo.
E-mail: historicalservices@wellsfargo.com
Web Site: www.wellsfargohistory.com
Key Personnel: Museum Mgr., Michael Shanahan; Cur., Martha Blakney.
Institution Type/Description: Company History Museum: located in Old Sacramento State Historic Park.

Hours & Admission Prices: Memorial Day to Labor Day daily 10-6; Sept.-May daily 10-5. No charge. Closed bank holidays. &

WELLS FARGO HISTORY MUSEUM, 400 Capitol Mall, Sacramento, CA 95814-4407. Mailing Address: Wells Fargo Historical Services, 420 Montgomery St., MAC-A0101-022, San Francisco, CA 94163. Tel.: 916-440-4161. Fax: 916-492-2931. Facebook.
E-mail: historicalservices@wellsfargo.com
Web Site: www.wellsfargohistory.com
Key Personnel: Museum Mgr., Michael Shanahan.
Institution Type/Description: Company History Museum: housed in the Wells Fargo Ctr.
Hours & Admission Prices: Tues.-Sat. 10-4. No charge. Closed New Year's Day; Independence Day; Thanksgiving; Christmas. &

Saint Helena

BALE GRIST MILL STATE HISTORIC PARK, 3369 St. Helena Hwy. N., Saint Helena, CA 94515. Mailing Address: 3801 St. Helena Hwy. N., Calistoga, CA 94515-9617. Tel.: 707-942-4575. Fax: 707-942-9560.
E-mail: sjones@parks.ca.gov
Web Site: www.napavalleystateparks.org
Key Personnel: Supvr., Sandy Jones.
Institution Type/Description: History Museum: housed in a grist mill built in 1844-47.
Hours & Admission Prices: Park: daily. Buildings: Sat.-Sun. 10-5. School Tours: Tues. by appointment. Adults $3, children $2; children under 6 no charge. Closed major holidays. &
Attendance: 16,000 (actual)

ROBERT LOUIS STEVENSON MUSEUM, 1490 Library Lane, Saint Helena, CA 94574-1143. Mailing Address: P.O. Box 23, Saint Helena, CA 94574. Tel.: 707-963-3757. Fax: 707-963-0917.
E-mail: director@stevensonmuseum.org
Web Site: www.stevensonmuseum.org
Formerly: Robert Louis Stevenson Silverado Museum
Key Personnel: Chm. (V), Gerry Working; Exec. Dir., Barrett Dahl.
Institution Type/Description: History & Literary Museum.
Hours & Admission Prices: Tues.-Sat. 12-4; other times by appointment. No charge; donations accepted. Closed New Year's Day; Easter; Independence Day; Memorial Day; Thanksgiving; Christmas. &
Attendance: 4,000 (estimated)

ST. HELENA HISTORICAL SOCIETY, St. Helena Public Library, Saint Helena, CA 94574. Mailing Address: P.O. Box 87, Saint Helena, CA 94574-0087. Tel.: 707-967-5502.
E-mail: shstory@shstory.org
Web Site: www.shstory.org
Key Personnel: Pres., Skip Lane.
Institution Type/Description: Historical Society Museum.
Hours & Admission Prices: Mon.-Fri. 9-5.

Salinas

BORONDA ADOBE HISTORY CENTER, 333 Boronda Rd., Salinas, CA 93907. Mailing Address: c/o Monterey County Historical Society, P.O. Box 3576, Salinas, CA 93912-3576. Tel.: 831-757-8085.
E-mail: mchs@redshift.com
Web Site: mchsmuseum.com
Institution Type/Description: History Museum: adobe built in 1844.
Hours & Admission Prices: Tours: Mon.-Fri. 10-2. Office: Mon.-Fri. 9-3.

HARVEY-BAKER HOUSE, Salinas Transportation Center, Salinas, CA 93901. Mailing Address: Monterey County Historical Society, P.O. Box 3576, Salinas, CA 93912-3576. Tel.: 831-424-7155.
Institution Type/Description: Historic House Museum: housed in the home of Isaac Harvey, the first mayor of Salinas, built in 1868.
Hours & Admission Prices: 1st Sun. of month 1-4; other times by appointment. No charge.

JOSE EUSEBIO BORONDA ADOBE, 333 Boronda Rd., Salinas, CA 93907-1808. Mailing Address: P.O. Box 3576, Salinas, CA 93912-3576. Tel.: 831-757-8085.
E-mail: mchs@redshift.com
Institution Type/Description: Historic House Museum: built in the 1840s.

Hours & Admission Prices: Mon.-Fri. 10-3.

NATIONAL STEINBECK CENTER, 1 Main St., Salinas, CA 93901-3436. Tel.: 831-796-3833. Fax: 831-796-3828. Facebook: National Steinbeck Center; Instagram & Twitter @steinbeckcenter.
E-mail: eric@steinbeck.org
Web Site: www.steinbeck.org
Key Personnel: Dir., Dr. Susan Shillinglaw; Chm. (V), Chris Steinbruner; Museum Shop Mgr., Jesse Banda.
Institution Type/Description: Literary, Agriculture & Art Museum.
Hours & Admission Prices: Daily 10-5. Adults $14.95, seniors $8.95, youth 13-17 $7.95, children $5.95; discounts to AAA members; members and children 5 & under no charge. Closed New Year's Day; Thanksgiving; Christmas.
Attendance: 50,000 (estimated)

THE STEINBECK HOUSE, 132 Central Ave., Salinas, CA 93901-2651. Tel.: 831-424-2735. Fax: 831-757-5806.
E-mail: steinbeckhouse@sbcglobal.net
Web Site: steinbeckhouse.com
Institution Type/Description: Historic House Museum: housed in the birthplace & boyhood home of author John Steinbeck; built in 1897. A National Historical Monument.
Hours & Admission Prices: By appointment. Adults $5, students, retired military & seniors $3; active military & children under 6 no charge.

Samoa

HUMBOLDT BAY MARITIME MUSEUM, Hwy. 255, Samoa, CA 95564. Mailing Address: P.O. Box 282, Samoa, CA 95564-0282. Tel.: 707-444-9440.
E-mail: intrepid52315@gmail.com
Web Site: www.humboldtbaymaritimemuseum.com
Key Personnel: Chm., Joshua Smith; Operations, Dalene Zerlang; Museum Shop Mgr., Jeffry Hood.
Institution Type/Description: Maritime Museum.
Hours & Admission Prices: Tues.-Wed. & Fri.-Sat. 11-4. No charge; donations accepted.
Attendance: 2,500 (estimated)

SAMOA COOKHOUSE & LOGGING MUSEUM, 908 Vance Ave., Samoa, CA 95564. Mailing Address: 710 E. St., Ste. 136, Eureka, CA 95501-1853. Tel.: 707-442-1659. Fax: 707-442-1699.
Web Site: www.samoacookhouse.net/samoa-cookhouse-museum.html
Key Personnel: Mgr., Jeff Brustman; Asst. Mgr., Sharon Nichols.
Institution Type/Description: Lumber & Logging Industry Museum.
Hours & Admission Prices: Daily 7am-8pm. No charge.

San Andreas

CALAVERAS COUNTY ARCHIVES, 891 Mountain Ranch Rd., San Andreas, CA 95249-9713.
E-mail: archives@goldrush.com
Key Personnel: Archivist, Shannon Van Zant.
Institution Type/Description: County History Museum.
Hours & Admission Prices: Office: Tues. & Thurs. 9-3. Research: June to late Aug. Tues. & Thurs. 9-3; other times by appointment. Research $10 per hour.

CALAVERAS COUNTY HISTORICAL SOCIETY MUSEUM, 30 N. Main St., San Andreas, CA 95249. Mailing Address: P.O. Box 721, San Andreas, CA 95249-0721. Tel.: 209-754-4658 & 1058. Fax: 209-754-1086.
E-mail: cchs@goldrush.com
Web Site: www.calaverascohistorical.com
Key Personnel: Pres. Calaveras Historical Society, Donna Shannon; Cur., Karen Nicholson.
Institution Type/Description: County History Museum.
Hours & Admission Prices: Daily 10-4. Adults $3, senior citizens $2, children under 12 $1; discounts to student groups; members no charge. Closed New Year's Day; Easter; Christmas.
Attendance: 3,000 (estimated)

RED BARN MUSEUM, Government Center, 891 Mountain Ranch Rd., San Andreas, CA 95249-9713. Mailing Address: Calaveras County Historical Society, P.O. Box 721, San Andreas, CA 95249. Tel.: 209-754-0800. Fax: 209-754-1086.
E-mail: cchs@goldrush.com
Web Site: www.calaverascohistorical.com
Key Personnel: Cur., Rosemary Faulkner.

Institution Type/Description: Historic Building: housed in the former dairy barn of the old County Hospital.
Hours & Admission Prices: Thurs.-Sun. 10-4. Adults $3, senior citizens 60 & over $2, children under 12 $1; members no charge. Closed New Year's Day; Easter; Christmas.

San Bernardino

CALIFORNIA DEPARTMENT OF FORESTRY AND FIRE PROTECTION MUSEUM, 3800 Sierra Way, San Bernardino, CA 92405. Tel.: 909-881-6984.
E-mail: cdfmuseum@yahoo.com
Key Personnel: Mgr., Jarrel B. Glover.
Institution Type/Description: History Museum.
Hours & Admission Prices: Sat. 10-2. Closed holidays.

ROBERT AND FRANCES FULLERTON MUSEUM OF ART (RAFFMA), CALIFORNIA STATE UNIVERSITY, SAN BERNARDINO, 5500 University Pkwy., San Bernardino, CA 92407-2318. Tel.: 909-537-7373. Fax: 909-537-7068.
E-mail: raffma@csusb.edu
Web Site: raffma.csusb.edu
Key Personnel: Pres. University, Dr. Tomas Morales; Dir. & Cur., Eva Kirsch; Pres. Advisory Bd., Eri Yasuhara; Diana Nieto.
Institution Type/Description: University Art Museum.
Hours & Admission Prices: Sept.-July Mon.-Wed. & Sat. 10-5, Thurs. 11-7. Suggested Donation: $3. Parking: $6. Closed major holidays.
Attendance: 10,000 (estimated)

SAN BERNARDINO HISTORICAL AND PIONEER SOCIETY - HERITAGE HOUSE, 796 N. "D" St., San Bernardino, CA 92402. Mailing Address: P.O. Box 875, San Bernardino, CA 92402. Tel.: 909-885-2204.
E-mail: sbhistoricalsociety@mac.com
Web Site: www.sbhistoricalsociety.com
Key Personnel: Pres. (V), Steve Shaw.
Institution Type/Description: Historical Society Museum: house built in 1891.
Hours & Admission Prices: Sat. 10-2. No charge; donations accepted.

San Carlos

HILLER AVIATION INSTITUTE, 601 Skyway Rd., San Carlos, CA 94070-2702. Tel.: 650-654-0200. Fax: 650-654-0220.
E-mail: museum@hiller.org
Web Site: www.hiller.org
Key Personnel: C.E.O. & Pres., Jeffery Bass; Chm. (V), Steve Hiller; Vice Pres. Devel., Bernadette Mellott, MPA; Vice Pres. Mktg., Willie Turner; Dir. Volunteers and Exhibits, James Lichtenstein; Education Programs Mgr., Jon Welte; Private Events Mgr., Lanie Agulay; Registrar, Katie McGee; Dir. Merchandising & Retail, Duncan Chadwick.
Institution Type/Description: Aviation Museum & Research Center: housed at the historic San Carlos Airport.
Hours & Admission Prices: Daily 10-5. Adults $11, senior citizens 65 & over and youth 5-17 $7; discounts to groups of 15 or more; members & children under 5 no charge. Closed New Year's Day; Easter; Thanksgiving; Christmas; occasional special event.
Attendance: 84,000 (actual)

San Clemente

SURFING HERITAGE AND CULTURE CENTER, 110 Calle Iglesia, San Clemente, CA 92672. Tel.: 949-388-0313.
E-mail: barry@surfingheritage.org
Web Site: www.surfingheritage.org
Institution Type/Description: Sports Museum.
Hours & Admission Prices: Mon.-Sat. 11-4; groups by appointment.

San Diego

CABRILLO NATIONAL MONUMENT, 1800 Cabrillo Memorial Dr., San Diego, CA 92106-3601. Tel.: 619-523-4285. Fax: 619-226-6311.
Web Site: www.nps.gov/cabr/
Key Personnel: Supt., Andrea Compton.
Institution Type/Description: Historic Site: commemorating the exploration of California coast & San Diego Bay by Juan Rodriguez Cabrillo in 1542.
Hours & Admission Prices: Daily 9-5. $5 per vehicle, $3 per person; children under 16, seniors over 61, disabled U.S. citizens, members with annual Cabrillo,

Golden Age, Golden Access, America the Beautiful Interagency, Senior or Access Pass no charge. Closed Thanksgiving; Christmas. &
Attendance: 886,620 (actual)

CENTRO CULTURAL DE LA RAZA, 2004 Park Blvd., San Diego, CA 92101. Mailing Address: 2125 Park Blvd., San Diego, CA 92101. Tel.: 619-235-6135.
E-mail: thecentro@att.net
Web Site: centroculturaldelaraza.com
Institution Type/Description: Art Gallery.
Hours & Admission Prices: Tues.-Sun. 12-4.

FLYING LEATHERNECK AVIATION MUSEUM CLOSED, 4203 Anderson Ave., San Diego, CA 92145. Mailing Address: P. O. Box 45316, San Diego, CA 92145-2008. Tel.: 877-359-8762. Fax: 858-693-0037. Facebook, Twitter.
Web Site: www.flyingleathernecks.org
Key Personnel: Dir., Ed Downum; Chm. (V), Dick Miller; Cur., Steve Smith; Retail Mgr., Ginger Raaka.
Institution Type/Description: U.S. Marine Corps Aviation Museum.
Hours & Admission Prices: Tues.-Sun. 9-3:30. No charge; donations accepted. &
Attendance: 30,000 (actual)

GASLAMP MUSEUM AT THE DAVIS-HORTON HOUSE HOME OF THE GASLAMP QUARTER HISTORICAL FOUNDATION, 410 Island Ave., San Diego, CA 92101-6925. Tel.: 619-233-4692. Facebook: Gaslamp Museum.
E-mail: info@gaslampfoundatoin.org
Web Site: www.gaslampfoundation.org
Formerly: William Heath Davis Home
Key Personnel: Exec. Dir., Catalina Preskill; Pres. (V), William English; Mgr. Museum Operations, Rhiannon Luna.
Institution Type/Description: Historic House & Museum: built in 1850. Listed on the National Register of Historic Places.
Hours & Admission Prices: Tues.-Sat. 10-4:30, Sun. 12-3:30. Self-Guided Tour: adults $5. Audio Tour: adults $10, seniors & active military $8, students $5; children under 7 no charge. Gaslamp Quarter Walking Tours: Thurs. 1pm & Sat. 11am. Closed New Year's Day; Easter; Memorial Day; Independence Day; Thanksgiving; Christmas. &
Attendance: 30,000 (estimated)

JAPANESE FRIENDSHIP GARDEN SOCIETY OF SAN DIEGO, 2215 Pan American Rd. E., San Diego, CA 92101-1656. Mailing Address: 2125 Park Blvd., Ste. #2, San Diego, CA 92101. Tel.: 619-232-2721. Fax: 619-239-1340.
E-mail: jfgsd@niwa.org
Web Site: www.niwa.org
Key Personnel: Exec. Dir., Luanne Kanzawa; Pres. (V), Dennis Otsuji; Operations Asst., Marisa Rodriguez; Registrar & Exhibit Coord., Emiko Scudder; Private Events Coord., Christina Zakimi; Event & Mktg. Coord., Jon Oslo; Membership & Fund Devel. Coord., Gerrymelyn Casupang; Program Coord., Frederic Hewett; Volunteer & Outreach Coord., Sara Shah; Head Gardener, Benancio Carreno.
Institution Type/Description: Japanese Gardens.
Hours & Admission Prices: Mon.-Fri. 10-5, Sat.-Sun. 10-4:30. Adults $8, seniors, students & military $7; children 6 & under and members no charge. Closed New Year's Day; Thanksgiving; Christmas Day. &
Attendance: 120,000 (estimated)

JUNIPERO SERRA MUSEUM/SAN DIEGO HISTORY CENTER, 2727 Presidio Dr., Presidio Park, San Diego, CA 92103. Mailing Address: 1649 El Prado, Ste. 3, San Diego, CA 92101-1664. Tel.: 619-232-6203. Facebook.
E-mail: ahendrickson@sandiegohistory.org
Web Site: www.sandiegohistory.org
Formerly: Junipero Serra Museum/San Diego Historical Society
Key Personnel: Exec. Dir., William Lawrence; Pres., Thompson Fetter; Archivist, Renato Rodriguez; Museum Shop Mgr., Manuel Aguilar.
Institution Type/Description: History Museum: housed in a mission-style 1929 structure constructed to commemorate the site where Father Junipero Serra & Captain Gaspar de Portola established the first mission and military outpost on the west coast of the U.S. & Canada.
Hours & Admission Prices: Memorial Day to Labor Day Fri.-Mon. 10-5; Sept.-May Sat.-Sun. 10-4. Suggested Donations: $5-$10; Time Travelers, reciprocal organizations & members no charge. Closed Thanksgiving; Christmas.
Attendance: 10,000 (estimated)

MARINE CORPS RECRUIT DEPOT MUSEUM, SAN DIEGO, Day Hall, Bldg. 26, (on Cuba Ave.), San Diego, CA 92140. Mailing Address: 1600 Henderson Ave., Suite 212, Mail: AC/S G-3, San Diego, CA 92140. Tel.: 619-524-6719. Fax: 619-524-0076.
E-mail: info@corpshistory.org
Web Site: www.corpshistory.org
Key Personnel: Dir., Barbara S. McCurtis; Education Specialist, Joanie Schwarz-Wetter; Historian, Ellen Guillemette; Exhibits Specialist, Chuck Archuleta; Military Specialist, Vincent Gonzalez.
Institution Type/Description: Military Museum.
Hours & Admission Prices: Mon. 8:30-3, Tues.-Sat. 8:30-4. Photo ID required for admittance. No charge; donations accepted. Closed federal holidays. &
Attendance: 175,000 (actual)

MARITIME MUSEUM OF SAN DIEGO, 1492 N. Harbor Dr., San Diego, CA 92101-3309. Tel.: 619-234-9154. Fax: 619-234-8345.
E-mail: taranto@sdmaritime.org
Web Site: www.sdmaritime.org
Key Personnel: Pres. & C.E.O., Raymond E. Ashley; Dir. Devel., Kelli Lewis; Marine Operations Dir., Jim Davis; Public Events Media, Robyn Gallant; Controller, Kitty Chisholm; Collections Mgr., Kevin Sheehan; Volunteer & Tour Coord., Jeff Loman; Education Dir., Jacob Keeton; Collections Mgr., Kevin Sheehan; Vice Pres. Operations, Susan Sirota.
Institution Type/Description: Maritime Museum: housed aboard ten ships.
Hours & Admission Prices: Daily 9-8. Adults $16, senior citizens & military $13, children 3-12 $8; discounts to groups and HNSA members; children under 3 & members no charge. &
Attendance: 143,500 (actual)

MINGEI INTERNATIONAL MUSEUM, 1439 El Prado, Balboa Park, Plaza de Panama, San Diego, CA 92101. Tel.: 619-239-0003. Fax: 619-239-0605.
E-mail: mingei@mingei.org
Web Site: www.mingei.org
Key Personnel: Dir., Rob Sidner; Chair (V) Bd. Trustees, Courtenay McGowen; Dir. Exhibitions & Chief Cur., Christine Hietbrink; Deputy Dir. & Chief Advancement Officer, Jessica Hanson York; Sr. Education & Outreach Mgr., Johanna Benson; Sr. Devel. Mgr., Caroline Nordquist; Membership & Mktg. Mgr., Claire McKee; Mgr. Collections & Registration, Barbara Hanson Forsyth; Library & Digital Asset Mgr., Kristi Ehrig-Burgess; Visitor Experience Mgr., Jill DeDominicis; Cafe Mgr., Holly Utsunomiya; Security & Facilities Mgr., Reggie Cabanilla.
Institution Type/Description: International Folk Art, Craft & Design Museum.
Hours & Admission Prices: Tues.-Sun. 10-5. Adults $10, seniors 62 & up, youth 6-17, students w/I.D. & military w/I.D. $7; discounts to groups; members & children under 6 no charge. Closed national holidays. &
Attendance: 108,000 (estimated)

MISSION SAN DIEGO DE ALCALA, 10818 San Diego Mission Rd., San Diego, CA 92108-2498. Tel.: 619-283-7319. Fax: 619-283-7762.
E-mail: info@missionsandiego.com
Web Site: www.missionsandiego.com
Key Personnel: Pastor, Rev. Peter M. Escalante; Assoc. Pastor, Rev. Billy Zondler; Historian, Anthony Tarantino; Business Mgr., Pat Schmitzer; Gift Shop Mgr., Rhonda Sosa.
Institution Type/Description: Historic Site Museum.
Hours & Admission Prices: Daily 9-4:45. Suggested Donation: adults $3, seniors $2, children $1. Closed Thanksgiving; Christmas. &
Attendance: 75,000 (estimated)

MUSEUM OF CONTEMPORARY ART SAN DIEGO - DOWNTOWN, 1100 & 1100 Kettner Blvd., San Diego, CA 92101. Mailing Address: 700 Prospect St., La Jolla, CA 92037-4291. Tel.: 858-454-3541. Fax: 619-814-4670.
E-mail: info@mcasd.org
Web Site: www.mcasd.org
Key Personnel: Dir. & CEO, Kathryn Kanjo; Pres. Bd. Trustees, Dr. Peter C. Farrell; Vice Pres., Maryanne Pfister; Deputy Dir. & CFO, Charles E. Castle; Sr. Cur., Jill Dawsey; Communications & Mktg. Mgr., Leah Straub; Registrar, Tom Callas.
Institution Type/Description: Art Museum.
Hours & Admission Prices: Thurs.-Tues. 11-5, third Thurs. 11-7. Adults $10, senior citizens & military $5; discounts to AAM & ICOM members; 25 & under and members no charge. Closed New Year's Day; Thanksgiving; Christmas. Admission valid for 7 days at all MCASD locations. &
Attendance: 168,000 (estimated)

MUSEUM OF PHOTOGRAPHIC ARTS, 1649 El Prado, San Diego, CA 92101. Tel.: 619-238-7559. Fax: 619-238-8777.

E-mail: info@mopa.org
Web Site: www.mopa.org
Key Personnel: Exec. Dir., Deborah Klochko; Pres. Bd., Larry Friedman; Deputy Dir., Vivienne Esrig; Operations Mgr., John Hogan; Accounting Mgr., Debra Rosacker, CPA; Special Events Mgr., Melissa Pfeiffer; Visitor Rels. Mgr., Kristie Taylor; Dir. Devel. Operations, Selina Castillo Hudgins; Dir. Education & Innovation, Joaquin Ortiz.
Institution Type/Description: Photographic Arts.
Hours & Admission Prices: Tues.-Sun. 10-5; docent tours by appointment. Adults $8, seniors & retired military $7; students w/I.D. $6; discounts to AAM & ICOM members; children 12 and under, active military, members, & San Diego residents on 2nd Tues. each month no charge. Closed New Year's Day; Martin Luther King Day; Thanksgiving; Christmas Day. ♿
Attendance: 95,830 (estimated)

MUSEUM OF SAN DIEGO HISTORY AND RESEARCH LIBRARY, 1649 El Prado, Ste. 3, San Diego, CA 92101-1664. Tel.: 619-232-6203, ext. 109. Fax: 619-232-6297.
E-mail: angela.sieckman@sandiegohistory.org
Web Site: www.sandiegohistory.org
Formerly: San Diego Historical Society Museum and Research Archives
Key Personnel: Dir., David Kahn; Bd. Pres. (V), Robert Adelizzi; Museum Shop Mgr., Trina Brewer.
Institution Type/Description: History Museum & Research Archives.
Hours & Admission Prices: Museum: daily 10-5. Adults $5, seniors, students & military with ID $4, children 6-17 $2; discounts to groups & AAM members; members & children under 6 no charge. Research Library: Mon.-Fri. 9:30-1. Adults $8, seniors $6, children $4; children under 6 no charge. Closed New Year's Day; Thanksgiving; Christmas Eve & Day. ♿
Attendance: 25,200 (actual)

NEW AMERICANS MUSEUM CLOSED, 2825 Dewey Rd., Ste. 102, San Diego, CA 92106. Tel.: 619-756-7707.
E-mail: contactus@namuseum.org
Web Site: www.newamericansmuseum.org
Formerly: New Americans Immigration Museum & Learning Center
Key Personnel: Exec. Dir., Linda Caballero Sotelo; Founder, Deborah Szekely; Dir. Operations, Celia C.J. Solis; Exec. Asst. to Exec. Dir. & Grants Coord., Polly E. Toledo; Facilities & IT, Martin Caballero; Gallery Attendant, Oral History Coord. & Graphic Designer, Timothy J. Allnutt.
Institution Type/Description: Cultural Center.
Hours & Admission Prices: Wed.-Fri. 10-4, Sat.-Sun. 11-3. No charge; donations accepted. Closed major holidays. ♿

THE NEW CHILDREN'S MUSEUM, 200 W. Island Ave., San Diego, CA 92101-6850. Tel.: 619-233-8792. Fax: 619-233-8796. Facebook; Instagram; Twitter.
E-mail: info@thinkplaycreate.org
Web Site: www.thinkplaycreate.org
Formerly: Children's Museum/Museo de Los Ninos San Diego
Key Personnel: Exec. Dir., Judy Forrester; Vice Pres. Mktg. & Communication, Kerri Fox; Deputy Museum Dir., Tomoko Kuta.
Institution Type/Description: Children's Museum.
Hours & Admission Prices: See website for hours. Admission $15.50; members and children under one no charge.
Attendance: 180,000 (estimated)

OLD POINT LOMA LIGHTHOUSE, 1800 Cabrillo Memorial Dr., San Diego, CA 92106. Tel.: 619-557-5450. Fax: 619-226-6311.
Web Site: nps.go
Institution Type/Description: Historic Building: built 1854.
Hours & Admission Prices: Daily 9-5.

OLD TOWN SAN DIEGO STATE HISTORIC PARK, 4002 Wallace St., San Diego, CA 92110-2743. Mailing Address: 4477 Pacific Hwy., San Diego, CA 92110-3136. Tel.: 619-220-5422. Fax: 619-220-7387.
E-mail: info@parks.ca.gov
Web Site: www.parks.ca.gov/oldtownsandiego
Institution Type/Description: State Park Museum.
Hours & Admission Prices: Daily 10-5. No charge; donations accepted. Closed New Year's Day; Thanksgiving; Christmas. ♿
Attendance: 6,000,000 (estimated)

RANCHO BERNARDO HISTORICAL SOCIETY, Bernardo Winery, 13330 Paseo Del Verano Norte, San Diego, CA 92128. Mailing Address: P.O. Box 27314, San Diego, CA 92198-7314. Tel.: 858-775-5788.
E-mail: rbhistory1@gmail.com
Web Site: www.rbhistoricalsociety.org

Institution Type/Description: History Museum.
Hours & Admission Prices: Tues. 10-12, Fri. 10-3, Sat.-Sun. 1-4; other times by appointment.

REUBEN H. FLEET SCIENCE CENTER, 1875 El Prado, Balboa Park, San Diego, CA 92101-1625. Mailing Address: P.O. Box 33303, San Diego, CA 92163-3303. Tel.: 619-238-1233. Fax: 619-685-5771. TDD: 619-685-5744.
E-mail: ssnyder@rhfleet.org
Web Site: www.rhfleet.org
Key Personnel: C.E.O., Dr. Steven L. Snyder; Dir. HR & Training, Candi Freed; Dir. Institutional Engagement, Julie Schardin; Dir. Education, Kris Mooney; Dir. Exhibitions, Paul Siboroski; Dir. Mktg. & Communications, Wendy M. Grant; Dir. Individual Philanthropy, Jennifer Richard; Dir. Business Operations, Robin Long.
Institution Type/Description: Science Center & IMAX Dome Theater.
Hours & Admission Prices: Mon.-Thurs. 10-5, Fri.-Sun. Adults $19.95, seniors 65 & over $17.95, juniors 3-12 $16.95; discounts to military, teachers, San Diego residents & members. ♿
Attendance: 426,576 (estimated)

SAN DIEGO AIR & SPACE MUSEUM, 2001 Pan American Plaza, San Diego, CA 92101-1636. Tel.: 619-234-8291, ext. 100. Fax: 619-233-4526. Facebook, Twitter & Flickr: SDASM.
E-mail: info@sdasm.org
Web Site: www.sandiegoairandspace.org
Formerly: San Diego Aerospace Museum
Key Personnel: Pres. & C.E.O., James Kidrick; Dir. Mktg., David Neville.
Institution Type/Description: History Museum.
Hours & Admission Prices: Winter: daily 10-4:30; Summer: extended hours. Adults 12 & over $19.50, seniors, students & retired military $16.50, youth 3-11 $10.50; discounts to groups, AAM & Smithsonian Institution Museum of Flight members; children under 3, active military, & members no charge. Closed Thanksgiving; Christmas. ♿
Attendance: 175,000 (actual)

SAN DIEGO AUTOMOTIVE MUSEUM, 2080 Pan American Plaza, Balboa Park, San Diego, CA 92101-1636. Tel.: 619-231-2886. Fax: 619-231-9869.
E-mail: info@sdautomuseum.org
Web Site: www.sdautomuseum.org
Key Personnel: Exec. Dir., Paula Brandes; Dir. Education, Pandora Paul; Office & HR Mgr., Faye Levy.
Institution Type/Description: Transportation Museum: housed in a structure built in 1935 for the Pan American Exposition as the California State Building.
Hours & Admission Prices: Daily 10-5. Adults $9, senior citizens 65 & over and active military w/ID $6, students $5, children 6-15 $4; children under 6 & members no charge. Closed New Year's Day; Thanksgiving; Christmas. ♿
Attendance: 100,000 (estimated)

SAN DIEGO CHINESE HISTORICAL MUSEUM, 404 Third Ave., San Diego, CA 92101-6803. Tel.: 619-338-9888. Fax: 619-338-9889. Facebook: San Diego Chinese Historical Museum.
E-mail: info@sdchm.org
Web Site: www.sdchm.org
Key Personnel: Dir., Tiffany Wai-Ying Beres; Chm. (V), Michael Yee; Education, Kathleen Dang.
Institution Type/Description: Culturally Specific.
Hours & Admission Prices: Tues.-Sat. 10:30-4, Sun. 12-4. Adults $5; members & children under 12 no charge. Closed New Year's Day; Independence Day; Thanksgiving; Christmas. ♿
Attendance: 9,800 (estimated)

SAN DIEGO FIREHOUSE MUSEUM, 1572 Columbia St., San Diego, CA 92101-2913. Tel.: 619-232-3473. Facebook: San Diego Firehouse Museum.
E-mail: sdfirehousemuseum@gmail.com
Web Site: www.sandiegofirehousemuseum.org
Institution Type/Description: Fire-Fighting Museum.
Hours & Admission Prices: Thurs.-Fri. 10-2, Sat.-Sun. 10-4. Adults $3, seniors & children $2.

SAN DIEGO HALL OF CHAMPIONS SPORTS MUSEUM, 2131 Pan American Plaza, Balboa Park, San Diego, CA 92101-1683. Tel.: 619-234-2544. Fax: 619-234-4543.
E-mail: info@sdhoc.com
Web Site: www.sdhoc.com
Key Personnel: Dir., Drew Moser; Chm. (V), Ron Fowler.
Institution Type/Description: Sports Museum & Breitbard Hall of Fame: housed in the Federal Building in Balboa Park.

Hours & Admission Prices: Daily 10-4:30. Adults $8, senior citizens, military & students with ID $6, children 7-17 $4; discounts to AAM & ICOM members; members & children under 7 no charge. Closed New Year's Day; Thanksgiving; Christmas. ♿

Attendance: 25,000 (estimated)

SAN DIEGO MESA COLLEGE ART GALLERY, 7250 Mesa College Dr., D101, San Diego, CA 92111-4998. Tel.: 619-388-2829.

E-mail: amoctezu@sdccd.edu

Institution Type/Description: Art Gallery.

Hours & Admission Prices: Academic Year: Mon.-Tues. 11-4, Wed.-Thurs. 1-8; other times by appointment. Closed school holidays & breaks; Thanksgiving.

SAN DIEGO MODEL RAILROAD MUSEUM, INC., 1649 El Prado, Ste. 4, San Diego, CA 92101-1664. Tel.: 619-696-0199. Fax: 619-696-0239. Facebook: Model Railroad Museum.

E-mail: info@sdmrm.org

Web Site: www.sdmrm.org

Key Personnel: Pres., Jon Everett; Exec. Dir., Anthony Ridenhour; Operations & Programs Mgr., Polly E. Toledo; Education Mgr., Bonnie Neptune; Devel. & Communications Mgr., Ana C. Penagos; Museum Shop Mgr., Veronique Rotsart.

Institution Type/Description: Model Railroad & Railroad History Museum: housed on site of 1915 Panama-California Exposition in the Casa de Balboa building.

Hours & Admission Prices: Museum: Tues.-Fri. 11-4, Sat.-Sun. 11-5; guided tours by appointment. Library: see website for hours. Adults $10, senior citizens 65 & over $7, military $5, students $4.50, children 6-14 $2; discounts to CAM, Assoc. of RR Museums & SD Inter-Museum Promotion Council members; members, San Diego county residents 1st Tues. of month & children under 5 no charge. Closed Thanksgiving; Christmas. ♿

Attendance: 140,509 (actual)

SAN DIEGO MUSEUM OF ART, Balboa Park, 1450 El Prado, San Diego, CA 92101. Mailing Address: P.O. Box 122107, San Diego, CA 92112-2107. Tel.: 619-232-7931. Fax: 619-232-9367. Facebook.

E-mail: info@sdmart.org

Web Site: www.sdmart.org

Key Personnel: Exec. Dir., Roxana Velasquez; Deputy Dir. Curatorial Affairs & Education, Anita Feldman; C.O.O., Dieter Fenkart-Froeschl; Pres. (V), Harvey White.

Institution Type/Description: Art Museum: housed in a Spanish plateresque-style building located on the site of the Panama/California International Exposition.

Hours & Admission Prices: Summer: Mon.-Tues. & Thurs.-Sat. 10-5, Sun. noon-5; Winter: Tues.-Sun. 10-5. Adults $15, military and seniors 65 & over $10, students $8; discounts to ICOM members; members and children 17 & under no charge. Closed New Year's Day; Thanksgiving; Christmas. ♿

Attendance: 360,000 (actual)

SAN DIEGO MUSEUM OF MAN, 1350 El Prado, Balboa Park, San Diego, CA 92101-1681. Tel.: 619-239-2001. Fax: 619-239-2749.

E-mail: museumofman@museumofman.org

Web Site: www.museumofman.org

Key Personnel: C.E.O., Micah D. Parzen; Chm., George Ramirez; Deputy Dir., Ben Garcia; Chief Devel. Officer, Hope Carlson; C.F.O., Tabitha McMahon; Foundation and Government Relations Officer, James Hadden; Mktg. & Communications Mgr., Shannon Fowler; Dir. Education & Public Engagement, Jason Porter; Dir. Exhibit Devel., Emily Anderson; Dir. Collections, Kelly hyberger; Lead Visitor Relations Associate, Ariel Baumbaugh; Lead Security Officer, Samantha Darling.

Institution Type/Description: Anthropology Museum.

Hours & Admission Prices: Daily 10-5. Adults $12.50, seniors 62 & up & active or retired military w/I.D. $8, students 13-17 & college students w/I.D. $8, children/youth 3-12 $6; discounts to AAM & ICOM members; members & children under 3 no charge. Closed Thanksgiving Day; Christmas Day. ♿

Attendance: 156,106 (actual)

SAN DIEGO NATURAL HISTORY MUSEUM, 1788 El Prado, Balboa Pk., San Diego, CA 92101. Mailing Address: P.O. Box 121390, San Diego, CA 92112-1390. Tel.: 619-232-3821. Fax: 619-232-0248. Facebook: San Diego Natural History Museum.

E-mail: customerservice@sdnhm.org

Web Site: www.sdnhm.org

Key Personnel: Pres. & C.E.O., Judy Gradwohl; Bd. Chm., Anita Busquets; Vice Pres. Institutional Advancement, Eowyn Bates; Vice Pres., C.F.O. & C.O.O., Susan Loveall; Vice Pres. Research & Public Programs, Michael Wall; Cur. Paleontology, Tom Demere, Ph.D.; Cur. Herpetology, Bradford Hollingsworth, Ph.D.; Cur. Botany, Jon P. Rebman, Ph.D.; Cur. Birds & Mammals, Philip Unitt;

Dir. Research Library & Registrar, Margaret Dykens; Sr. Dir. Operations, Josh Culver; Sr. Dir. Communications, Rebecca Handelsman; Sr. Dir. Public Programs, Beth Redmond-Jones; Controller, Ghia Santos.

Institution Type/Description: Natural History Museum

Hours & Admission Prices: Daily 10-5. Adults $19, seniors 62 & over, military & college students w/ID $17, youth 7-17 $14, child 3-6 $11; discounts to groups; children 2 & under, members & San Diego County residents w/ID on the first Tues. of month no charge. Closed Thanksgiving; Christmas Day. ♿

Attendance: 380,160 (actual)

SAN DIEGO ZOO, 2920 Zoo Dr., San Diego, CA 92101-1693. Mailing Address: P.O. Box 120551, San Diego, CA 92112-0551. Tel.: 619-231-1515. Fax: 619-557-3970.

E-mail: publicrelations@sandiegozoo.org

Web Site: zoo.sandiegozoo.org

Key Personnel: C.E.O. & Pres., Douglas G. Myers; C.O.O., Shawn Dixon; C.F.O., Paula Brock; Chief Devel. & Membership Officer, Mark Stuart; Zoo Dir., Dwight Scott; Zoo Safari Park Dir., Robert M. McClure; Chief Conservation & Research Officer, Allison Alberts, Ph.D.; Chief Life Sciences Officer, Robert J. Wiese, Ph.D.; Corp. Dir. Animal Health, Nadine Lamberski, D.V.M.; Chief Mktg. Officer, Ted Molter; Chief Technology Officer, Robert Erhardt.

Institution Type/Description: Zoo & Botanical Garden.

Hours & Admission Prices: Zoo: Winter daily 9-5; Spring daily 9-6; Summer daily 9-9; Fall 9-6; hours may vary & subject to change. Safari Park: Jan.-June & Sept.-Dec. 9-5; July & Aug. 9-7; hours may vary & subject to change. Adults 12 & over $54, children 3-11 $44; discounts to groups; children under 3 & members no charge. ♿

Attendance: 3,200,000 (actual)

SEAWORLD SAN DIEGO, 500 SeaWorld Dr., San Diego, CA 92109-7904. Tel.: 800-257-4268. Fax: 619-226-3996.

Web Site: seaworldparks.com

Institution Type/Description: Aquarium, Marine Museum and Oceanarium.

Hours & Admission Prices: Visit website for information. ♿

Attendance: 4,000,000

THOMAS WHALEY HOUSE MUSEUM, 2476 San Diego Ave., San Diego, CA 92110-2730. Tel.: 619-297-7511. Fax: 619-291-3576.

E-mail: sohosandiego@aol.com

Web Site: www.whaleyhouse.org

Key Personnel: Exec. Dir., Bruce Coons; Education & Communs. Dir., Alana Coons; Admin. Mgr., Accts. Mgr., Historian, Dean Glass.

Institution Type/Description: House Museum.

Hours & Admission Prices: Summer: daily 10-9:30. Non-Summer: Sun.-Tues. 10-4:30, Thurs.-Sat. 10-9:30. Daytime Admission: adults $8, seniors 65 & over and children 6-12 $6; children 5 & under no charge. Evening Admission (5-9:30): adults $13, seniors 65 & over and children 6-12 $8. Closed Thanksgiving; Christmas. ♿

Attendance: 120,000 (estimated)

TIMKEN MUSEUM OF ART, 1500 El Prado, Balboa Park, San Diego, CA 92101-1620. Mailing Address: 2550 Fifth Ave., Ste. 500, San Diego, CA 92103. Tel.: 619-239-5548. Fax: 619-531-9640. Facebook: Timken Museum of Art.

E-mail: info@timkenmuseum.org

Web Site: www.timkenmuseum.org

Key Personnel: Exec. Dir., Megan Pogue; Controller, Eric Bockstahler; Dir. Operations, Holly Martin-Bollard; Dir. Education, Kristina Rosenberg; Deputy Dir. Devel. & Endowment, Laurie Hawkins.

Institution Type/Description: Art Museum.

Hours & Admission Prices: Tues.-Sat. 10-4:30, Sun. 12-4:30. No charge; donations accepted. Closed legal holidays. ♿

Attendance: 200,000 (actual)

USS MIDWAY MUSEUM, 910 N. Harbor Dr., San Diego, CA 92101-5811. Tel.: 619-544-9600. Fax: 619-544-9188. Facebook, Instagram, Twitter.

E-mail: smcgaugh@midway.org

Web Site: www.midway.org

Formerly: San Diego Aircraft Carrier Museum

Key Personnel: Pres. & C.E.O., Mac McLaughlin; C.F.O., Phillip Hamilton; Dir. Education, Sara Hanscom; Dir. Opers., Mark Berlin; Cur., Dave Hanson; Dir. Mktg., David Koontz; Gift Shop Mgr., Bryan Morano.

Institution Type/Description: Military Museum.

Hours & Admission Prices: Daily 10-4; groups of 15 or more by appointment. Adults $26, seniors 62 & over $22, students 13-17 $18, youth 6-12 $12; veterans $10; children 5 & under, active military, law enforcement & firefighters no charge. Closed Thanksgiving; Christmas.

UNIVERSITY ART GALLERY SAN DIEGO STATE UNIVERSITY, 5500 Campanile Dr., San Diego, CA 92182-0003. Mailing Address: School of Art, Design & Art History, San Diego, CA 92182. Tel.: 619-594-5171. Fax: 619-594-1217.
E-mail: artgallery@sdsu.edu
Web Site: art.sdsu.edu/about-us/our-galleries
Key Personnel: Dir., Tina Yapelli.
Institution Type/Description: University Art Gallery.
Hours & Admission Prices: Sept.-May Mon.-Thurs. & Sat. 12-4. No charge; donations accepted. Closed holidays. &
Attendance: 5,000 (estimated)

UNIVERSITY GALLERIES: THE HOEHN FAMILY GALLERIES & PRINT STUDY ROOM/FINE ART GALLERIES AT THE INSTITUTE FOR PEACE & JUSTICE/THE DAVID W. MAY GALLERY, University of San Diego Founders Hall 102, 5998 Alcala Park, San Diego, CA 92110. Mailing Address: Dept. of Art, Architecture & Art History, Univ. of San Diego, 5998 Alcala Park, San Diego, CA 92110. Tel.: 619-260-7516 (Hoehn) & 4238 (May). Fax: 619-849-8237.
E-mail: kpowers@sandiego.edu
Web Site: www.sandiego.edu/galleries
Formerly: Anthropology Museum, Founder's Gallery University of San Diego
Key Personnel: Dir., Dr. Alana Cordy-Collins; Mgr. Collections, Joyce Antorietto.
Institution Type/Description: Anthropology Museum.
Hours & Admission Prices: Tues. & Thurs.-Fri. 1-3; other times by appointment. No charge. Closed university holidays. &
Attendance: 200 (estimated)

VILLA MONTEZUMA MUSEUM AKA JESSE SHEPARD/ FRANCIS GRIERSON HOUSE, 1925 K St., San Diego, CA 92102-3828. Mailing Address: 657 20th St., San Diego, CA 92102-2810. Tel.: 619-255-9367.
E-mail: fovm@villamontezumamuseum.org
Web Site: www.villamontezumamuseum.org
Key Personnel: Chm., Louise Torio.
Institution Type/Description: Historic House Museum: housed in the former home of musician & spiritualist Jesse Shepard also known as metaphysical author Francis Grierson; built in 1887. Listed on the National Register of Historic Places.
Hours & Admission Prices: Tours: March 23, June 1, Aug. 17 & Oct. 19. No charge.

WELLS FARGO HISTORY MUSEUM CLOSED, 2733 San Diego Ave., San Diego, CA 92110-2731. Mailing Address: Wells Fargo Historical Services, 420 Montgomery St., MAC-A0101-022, San Diego, CA 94163. Tel.: 619-238-3929. Fax: 619-298-8209. Facebook: Wells Fargo.
E-mail: historicalservices@wellsfargo.com
Web Site: www.wellsfargohistory.com
Key Personnel: Museum Mgr., Casey (William) Gill; Cur., Liam Richards.
Institution Type/Description: Company History Museum: housed in Colorado House, Old Town San Diego State Historic Park.
Hours & Admission Prices: Memorial Day to Labor Day daily 10-6; Sept.-May daily 10-5. No charge. Closed New Year's Day; Thanksgiving; Christmas. &

WOMEN'S MUSEUM OF CALIFORNIA, 2730 Historic Decatur Rd., Barracks 16, San Diego, CA 92106. Tel.: 619-233-7963.
E-mail: info@womensmuseumca.org
Web Site: womensmuseumca.org
Institution Type/Description: Women's History Museum.
Hours & Admission Prices: Museum: Wed.-Sun. 12-4. Library: by appointment.

San Dimas

PACIFIC RAILROAD SOCIETY MUSEUM, 210 W. Bonita Ave., San Dimas, CA 91773. Tel.: 909-394-0616. Facebook.
E-mail: info@pacificrailroadsociety.org
Web Site: pacificrailroadsociety.org
Key Personnel: Dir. & Museum Shop Mgr., David B. Housh; Pres. (V), Virginia Grupp.
Institution Type/Description: Railroad Museum & Library.
Hours & Admission Prices: Mon. & Wed. 12-5, Sat. 10-4; groups by appointment. No charge; donations accepted. &
Attendance: 3,000 (estimated)

San Fernando

LOPEZ ADOBE, 1100 Pico St., San Fernando, CA 91340-3514. Mailing Address: 117 Macheil St., San Fernando, CA 91340-2911. Tel.: 818-898-1290.
E-mail: info@sfcity.org
Web Site: www.sfcity.org
Institution Type/Description: History Museum: structure built in 1882. Listed on the National Register of Historic Places.
Hours & Admission Prices: 4th Sun. of month 1-4. &

San Francisco

ACADEMY OF ART COLLEGE GALLERIES, 625 Sutter St., San Francisco, CA 94105. Mailing Address: 79 New Montgomery St., San Francisco, CA 94105. Tel.: 415-274-2229. Fax: 415-263-8819.
E-mail: info@academyart.edu
Web Site: www.academyart.edu/aboutus/gallery.asp
Institution Type/Description: Art Gallery.
Hours & Admission Prices: Sutter St. Galleries: Mon.-Fri. 10-6, Sat. 10-5. Bush St. Gallery: Mon.-Fri. 9-6, Sat. 10-5.

ALEXANDER F. MORRISON PLANETARIUM, 55 Music Concourse Dr., San Francisco, CA 94118-4503. Tel.: 415-379-8000. Facebook: Morrison Planetarium.
E-mail: info@calacademy.org
Web Site: www.calacademy.org
Key Personnel: Exec. Dir., Jonathan Foley, Ph.D.; Chief Public Engagement Officer, Roberts-Wilson Dean of Education, Elizabeth Babcock, Ph.D.; CFO, Mike McGee; Chief Revenue & Mktg. Officer, Melissa Felder; Chief Philanthropy Officer, Janet Harris; COO, Ike Kwon; Chief of Science, Harry W. & Diana V. Hind Dean of Science & Research Collections, Shannon Bennet, Ph. D.; Chief HR Officer, Raul del Barco.
Institution Type/Description: Planetarium: housed in Natural History Museum.
Hours & Admission Prices: Mon.-Sat. 9:30-5, Sun. 11-5. Adults $34.95, seniors 65 & over, college students and youth 12-17 $29.95, children 4-11 $24.95; children 3 & under no charge. Thurs NightLife 21 & over ID required 6-10pm members $12, non-members $15. $12Closed Thanksgiving; Christmas. &
Attendance: 140,000 (estimated)

AMERICAN BOOKBINDERS MUSEUM, 355 Clementina St., San Francisco, CA 94103-4104. Tel.: 415-824-9754.
E-mail: info@bookbindersmuseum.org
Web Site: www.bookbindersmuseum.org
Key Personnel: Founder, Tim James.
Institution Type/Description: History Museum.
Hours & Admission Prices: Tues.-Sat. 10-4. Adults $10, seniors & youth $8. Closed Memorial Day; Independence Day; Labor Day; Thanksgiving Day; Christmas Eve & Day; New Year's Eve & Day. &

AQUARIUM OF THE BAY, The Embarcadero at Beach St., San Francisco, CA 94133. Tel.: 415-623-5300. Fax: 415-623-5324.
E-mail: info@bayecotarium.org
Web Site: https://bayecotarium.org/about/aquarium-of-the-bay/
Key Personnel: Dir. Mktg. & Communications, Nora Weber; Dir. Education & Conservation, Christina Slager; Dir. Sales & Events, Cathy Tolentino.
Institution Type/Description: Aquarium.
Hours & Admission Prices: June 17-Sept. 3 daily 9-8; Sept. 4-June 16 daily 10-6. Family of 4 $80, adults 13-64 $26.95, seniors $21.95, children 4-12 $16.95; children 3 & under no charge. Closed Christmas.
Attendance: 500,000 (estimated)

ASIAN ART MUSEUM OF SAN FRANCISCO, CHONG-MOON LEE CENTER FOR ASIAN ART AND CULTURE, 200 Larkin St., San Francisco, CA 94102-4734. Tel.: 415-581-3500. Fax: 415-581-4700. Facebook, Twitter.
Web Site: www.asianart.org
Formerly: Asian Art Museum of San Francisco, The Avery Brundage Collection
Key Personnel: Dir., Jay Xu; Deputy Dir. Art Programs, Dr. Robert Mintz; Dir. Communications & Business Devel., Tim Hallman.
Institution Type/Description: Art Museum.
Hours & Admission Prices: early Feb. to Sept. Tues.-Wed. & Fri.-Sun. 10-5, Thurs. 10-9; Oct.-Feb. 8 Tues.-Sun. 10-5. Adults $15, seniors, youth & college students $10; discounts to AAM & ICOM members; children 12 & under and members no charge. Closed New Year's Day; Thanksgiving; Christmas. &
Attendance: 262,482 (actual)

CCA WATTIS INSTITUTE FOR CONTEMPORARY ARTS, 360 Kansas St., San Francisco, CA 94103. Mailing Address: 1111 Eight St., San Francisco, CA 94107. Tel.: 415-355-9670. Fax: 415-355-9676. Facebook, Instagram & Twitter: @wattisarts.
E-mail: wattis@cca.edu
Web Site: www.wattis.org
Key Personnel: Dir. & Chief Cur., Anthony Huberman; Cur. & Head, Programs, Kim Nguyen; Operations Coord., Addy Rabinovitch.
Institution Type/Description: Art Gallery.
Hours & Admission Prices: Logan Center Galleries: Tues.-Fri. 12-7, Sat. 12-5. No charge; donations accepted. Closed major holidays; during installation. &
Attendance: 28,000 (estimated)

CALIFORNIA ACADEMY OF SCIENCES, Golden Gate Park, 55 Music Concourse Dr., San Francisco, CA 94118-4503. Tel.: 415-379-8000. Facebook, Instagram, Twitter.
E-mail: info@calacademy.org
Web Site: www.calacademy.org
Key Personnel: Exec. Dir. & William R. and Gretchen B. Kimball Chair, Dr. Scott D. Sampson; Chief Public Engagement Officer & Robert-Wilson Dean Education, Elizabeth Babcock, Ph.D.; Chief of Science & Harry & Diana V. Hind Dean Science & Research Collections, Shannon Bennett, Ph.D.; Chief Human Resources Officer, Raul del Barco; Chief Revenue & Mktg. Officer, Melissa Felder; C.O.O. & Head Government Affairs, Ike Kwon; C.F.O., Mike McGee; Interim Chief Philanthropy Officer, Rebecca Schuett.
Institution Type/Description: Natural History Museum, Aquarium & Planetarium.
Hours & Admission Prices: Mon.-Sat. 9:30-5, Sun. 11-5. Adults $39.95, senior citizens 65 & up, students & youth 12-17 $34.95, children 4-11 $29.95; children 3 & under no charge. Closed Thanksgiving; Christmas. &
Attendance: 1,500,000 (actual)

CALIFORNIA HISTORICAL SOCIETY, 678 Mission St., San Francisco, CA 94105-4014. Tel.: 415-357-1848. Fax: 415-357-1850. Facebook, Instagram, Twitter.
E-mail: info@calhist.org
Web Site: www.calhist.org
Key Personnel: Exec. Dir. & CEO, Anthea M. Hartig, Ph.D.; Dir. Finance, Pamela Garcia; Acting Dir. HR, Sherry Jordana, SHRM-SCP.
Institution Type/Description: Historical Society Museum.
Hours & Admission Prices: Gallery: Tues.-Sun. 11-5. Library: Wed.-Fri. 1-5. Suggested Donations: $5; members & children no charge. Closed New Year's Day; Martin Luther King Jr. Day; Presidents' Day; Memorial Day; Independence Day; Labor Day; Thanksgiving & day after; Christmas. &
Attendance: 12,000 (estimated)

CARTOON ART MUSEUM, 781 Beach St., San Francisco, CA 94109-1254. Mailing Address: P.O. Box 566, San Francisco, CA 94104-0566. Tel.: 415-227-8666. Fax: 415-243-8666. Facebook & Instagram: @cartoonartmuseum; Twitter: @cartoonart.
E-mail: office@cartoonart.org
Web Site: www.cartoonart.org
Key Personnel: Exec. Dir., Summerlea Kashar; Chm., Ron Evans; Cur., Andrew Farago; Program Coord., Nina Taylor Kester.
Institution Type/Description: Cartoon Art Museum.
Hours & Admission Prices: Thurs.-Tues. 11-5. Adults $10, San Francisco Residents $7, Students, Teens, Seniors, Military, Educators (w/ID) $6, kids 6-12 $4; kids 5 & under and members no charge. &
Attendance: 35,000 (estimated)

CHILDREN'S CREATIVITY MUSEUM, 221 Fourth St., San Francisco, CA 94103-3116. Tel.: 415-820-3320. Facebook; Twitter; Instagram.
E-mail: info@creativity.org
Web Site: www.creativity.org
Formerly: Zeum
Key Personnel: Exec. Dir., Carol Tang, Ph.D.; Dir. External Affairs, Ms. Pat Kilduff; Dir. Finance & Operations, Christine Fitzsimmons.
Institution Type/Description: Children's Museum.
Hours & Admission Prices: Summer: Tues.-Sun. 10-4; Sept.-June Wed.-Sun. 10-4. Admission $12.95; discounts to ASTC members; children under 2 and members no charge; participates in Museums for All, Discover & Go and Blue Star Museums programs. &
Attendance: 100,000 (estimated)

CHINESE CULTURE CENTER OF SAN FRANCISCO, 750 Kearny St., 3rd. Fl., San Francisco, CA 94108-1809. Tel.: 415-986-1822. Fax: 415-986-2825.
E-mail: info@c-c-c.org
Web Site: www.c-c-c.org

Key Personnel: Exec. Dir., Mabel Teng; Cur. & Artistic Dir., Abby Chen; Dir. Communs., Jenny Leung; Dir. Education & Engagement, Darin Ow-Wing.
Institution Type/Description: Art Gallery.
Hours & Admission Prices: Wed.-Sun 11-4. No charge; donations accepted. Closed major holidays. &
Attendance: 65,000 (estimated)

CHINESE HISTORICAL SOCIETY OF AMERICA, 965 Clay St., San Francisco, CA 94108-1527. Tel.: 415-391-1188. Facebook; Instagram; Twitter.
E-mail: info@chsa.org
Web Site: www.chsa.org
Key Personnel: Interim Exec. Dir., Jane D. Chin; Pres., Hoyt Zia.
Institution Type/Description: Chinese Historical Society.
Hours & Admission Prices: Wed.-Sun. 11-4. Adults $15, children 3-17, college students with valid ID & seniors 65 & over $10, children 12 & under with adult admission no charge. Closed holidays.

THE CONTEMPORARY JEWISH MUSEUM, 736 Mission St., San Francisco, CA 94103-3113. Tel.: 415-655-7800. Facebook.
E-mail: info@thecjm.org
Web Site: www.thecjm.org
Key Personnel: Exec. Dir., Lori Starr.
Institution Type/Description: Art Museum & Center.
Hours & Admission Prices: Mon.-Tues. & Fri.-Sun. 11-5, Thurs. 11-8. Adults $14, seniors & students $12, Thurs. after 5p.m. $5; youth 18 & under and members no charge. Closed New Year's Day; 1st day of Passover; Independence Day; 1st day of Rosh Hashanah; Yom Kippur; Thanksgiving. &
Attendance: 125,000 (estimated)

THE EXPLORATORIUM, Pier 15, Embarcadero at Green St., San Francisco, CA 94111. Mailing Address: Pier 17, Ste. 100, San Francisco, CA 94111-1456. Tel.: 415-528-4360.
E-mail: media@exploratorium.edu
Web Site: www.exploratorium.edu
Key Personnel: Exec. Dir., Chris Flink; Chm. Bd. Trustee (V), George W. Cogan; Exec. Assoc. Dir. & Dir. Laboratory, Robert J. Semper; C.O.O., Laura Zander; Dir. Exhibits & Media Studio, Thomas Rockwell; Dir. Mktg., Membership & Frontline, Julie Nunn.
Institution Type/Description: Science Museum & Center.
Hours & Admission Prices: Tues.-Sun. 10-5. Thurs. adults 18 & over only 6-10. Adults $29.95; members no charge. Visit website for holiday hours & free admission days. &
Attendance: 854,325 (actual)

FINE ARTS MUSEUMS OF SAN FRANCISCO, DE YOUNG MUSEUM, Golden Gate Park, 50 Hagiwara Tea Garden Dr., San Francisco, CA 94118-4502. Tel.: 415-750-3600. Facebook, Instagram & Twitter: @deyoungmuseum.
E-mail: contact@famsf.org
Web Site: www.deyoung.famsf.org
Formerly: M. H. de Young Memorial Museum
Key Personnel: Dir. & CEO, Max Hollein; Dir. Mktg. & Communications, Linda Butler; Chief Admin. Cur. & Founding Cur. Photography, Julian Cox.
Institution Type/Description: Fine Arts Museum.
Hours & Admission Prices: Tues.-Sun. 9:30-5:15. Adults $15, seniors over 65 $10, college students with valid ID $6; members & youth 17 & under no charge. Closed Thanksgiving; Christmas. &
Attendance: 1,200,000 (estimated)

FINE ARTS MUSEUMS OF SAN FRANCISCO, LEGION OF HONOR, Legion of Honor, 100 34th Ave., San Francisco, CA 94121-1677. Mailing Address: deYoung Museum, 50 Hagiwara Tea Garden Dr., San Francisco, CA 94118-4502. Tel.: 415-750-3600. Facebook, Instagram & Twitter: @legionofhonor.
E-mail: contact@famsf.org
Web Site: legionofhonor.famsf.org
Key Personnel: Dir., Thomas P. Campbell; Chief Cur. & Founding Cur., Julian Cox.
Institution Type/Description: Fine Arts Museum.
Hours & Admission Prices: Tues.-Sun. 9:30-5:15. Adults $15, seniors 65 & up $12, students w/ ID $6; members and children 17 & under no charge. Closed New Year's Day; Independence Day; Thanksgiving; Christmas. &
Attendance: 893,939 (actual)

500 CAPP STREET FOUNDATION - DAVID IRELAND HOUSE, 500 Capp St., San Francisco, CA 94110. Tel.: 415-872-9240.
E-mail: tours@500cappstreet.org
Web Site: www.500cappstreet.org

Institution Type/Description: Art Gallery.
Hours & Admission Prices: By appointment.

FORT POINT NATIONAL HISTORIC SITE, Presidio of San Francisco, Bldg. 989, Marine Dr., San Francisco, CA 94129. Mailing Address: Fort Mason, Bldg. 201, San Francisco, CA 94123-1307. Tel.: 415-556-1693.
Web Site: www.nps.gov/fopo
Institution Type/Description: Historic Site: c.1853-1861 Fort Point which is the only third system fort on the west coast.
Hours & Admission Prices: See website for hour. No charge; donations accepted. Closed New Year's Day; Thanksgiving; Christmas. &
Attendance: 300,000

GOLDEN GATE NATIONAL RECREATION AREA, Fort Mason, Bldg. 201, San Francisco, CA 94123-0022. Tel.: 415-561-4700.
E-mail: susan_ewing_haley@nps.gov
Web Site: www.nps.gov/goga/
Key Personnel: Museum Specialist, Lulu Chye; Supervisory Museum Cur., Susan Ewing Haley; Registrar, Amanda Williford.
Institution Type/Description: Park Museum: area includes Muir Woods National Monument & Fort Point National Historic Site.
Hours & Admission Prices: Daily 10-5. No charge; donations accepted. Closed New Year's Day; Thanksgiving; Christmas. &
Attendance: 13,803,382 (estimated)

HAAS-LILIENTHAL HOUSE, 2007 Franklin St., San Francisco, CA 94109-2909. Tel.: 415-441-3000. Fax: 415-441-3015. Facebook, Instagram & Twitter: @sfheritage.
E-mail: info@sfheritage.org
Web Site: www.sfheritage.org
Key Personnel: Pres. & C.E.O., Mike Buhler; House Mgr., Heather Kraft; Finance & Operations Mgr., Jane Orr; Museum & Volunteer Coord., Pam Larson.
Institution Type/Description: Historic House: c.1886 Queen Anne style Victorian.
Hours & Admission Prices: Wed. & Sat. 12-3, Sun. 11-4. Adults $8, children 6-12 & senior citizens $5; discount to AAA & Travel with Visa members; members & children under 6 no charge.
Attendance: 6,000 (estimated)

HENRY WILSON COIL MASONIC LIBRARY & MUSEUM, 1111 California St., San Francisco, CA 94108-2252. Tel.: 415-292-9137.
E-mail: akendall@freemason.org
Web Site: masonicheritage.org
Institution Type/Description: History Museum.
Hours & Admission Prices: Library: by appointment. No charge.

INTERNATIONAL ART MUSEUM OF AMERICA, 1023 Market St., San Francisco, CA 94103. Mailing Address: 1025 Market St., San Francisco, 94103. Tel.: 415-376-6344. Fax: 415-255-9415. Facebook.
E-mail: lhuang@internationalartmuseum.org
Web Site: www.internationalartmuseum.org; www.iamasf.org
Key Personnel: Dir. Museum Opers., Loretta Huang, Ph.D.; Chm. (V), Dr. Wu Ching-Kuo; Pres. (V), Dr. Yu-Hua Shou Zhi Wang; Store Assoc., Ayanna Madison.
Institution Type/Description: Art Museum.
Hours & Admission Prices: Tues.-Sun. 10-5. Admission $15; seniors 65+, military & students $10, children under 12 no charge. Closed New Year's Eve; New Year's Day; Independence Day; Thanksgiving & day after; Christmas Eve & Day. &
Attendance: 40,000 (estimated)

INTERNATIONAL MUSEUM OF WOMEN, Mailing Address: 222 Sutter St., Ste. 500, San Francisco, CA 94108. Tel.: 415-248-4800. Fax: 415-543-4668.
E-mail: advocacy-info@globalfundforwomen.org
Web Site: exhibitions.globalfundforwomen.org
Key Personnel: COO, Clare Winterton; Head of Advocacy, Exec. Producer, Catherine King.
Institution Type/Description: Virtual Women's Museum.
Hours & Admission Prices: Online museum.

LEVI STRAUSS & COMPANY VISITOR CENTER, 1155 Battery St., San Francisco, CA 94111. Tel.: 415-501-6000.
Web Site: www.levistrauss.com
Institution Type/Description: Company Museum.

MARY AND CARTER THACHER GALLERY AT THE UNIVERSITY OF SAN FRANCISCO, Gleeson Library Geschke Center, 2130 Fulton St., San Francisco, CA 94117-1080. Tel.: 415-422-5178.
E-mail: thachergallery@usfca.edu
Key Personnel: Dir., Glori Simmons; Gallery Mgr., Nell Herbert.
Institution Type/Description: Art Gallery.
Hours & Admission Prices: Daily 12-6.

THE MEXICAN MUSEUM, Fort Mason Center, Marina Blvd., Bldg. D., San Francisco, CA 94123. Tel.: 415-202-9700. Facebook: @themexicanmuseum; Instagram & Twitter: @sfmexicanmuseum.
E-mail: info@mexicanmuseum.org
Web Site: mexicanmuseum.org
Key Personnel: CEO, Dr. Edgar De Sola; Registrar, Morgan Schlesinger; Museum Opers. Mgr., Vanessa Moreno; Museum Admin., Guadalupe Ochoa.
Institution Type/Description: Fine Arts Museum.
Hours & Admission Prices: Thurs.-Sun. 12-4. No charge; donations accepted. Closed New Year's Day; Martin Luther King Jr. Day; Presidents' Day; Memorial Day; Independence Day; Labor Day; Columbus Day; Veterans Day; Thanksgiving; Christmas. &
Attendance: 6,432 (estimated)

MILITARY INTELLIGENCE SERVICE HISTORIC LEARNING CENTER, 640 Old Mason St., San Francisco, CA 94129. Mailing Address: NJAHS, 1684 Post St., San Francisco, CA 94115. Tel.: 415-921-5007.
E-mail: njahs@njahs.org
Web Site: www.njahs.org/640
Key Personnel: Exec. Dir., Rosalyn Tonai.
Institution Type/Description: Historic Site & Gallery.
Hours & Admission Prices: Sat.-Sun. 12-5. Adults $10; members, veterans and children 12 & under no charge. Closed holidays. &
Attendance: 2,000 (estimated)

MISSION CULTURAL CENTER FOR LATINO ARTS, 2868 Mission St., San Francisco, CA 94110-3908. Tel.: 415-821-1155. Fax: 415-648-0933.
E-mail: info@missionculturalcenter.org
Web Site: www.missionculturalcenter.org
Key Personnel: Exec. Dir., Jennie E. Rodriguez; Multimedia Coord., Maria Hernandez; Events & Media, Arturo Mendez; Mission Grafica Coord., Marsha Shaw; Facilities, Claudia Abrego; Gallery, Angelica A. Rodriguez.
Institution Type/Description: Civic Art, Cultural Center.
Hours & Admission Prices: Tues.-Sat. 10-5. Closed holidays. &
Attendance: 20,000 (estimated)

MISSION SAN FRANCISCO DE ASIS (MISSION DOLORES), 3321 Sixteenth St., San Francisco, CA 94114-1712. Tel.: 415-621-8203.
E-mail: chochenyo@aol.com
Key Personnel: Cur., Andrew A. Galvan.
Institution Type/Description: Historic Building: c.1791.
Hours & Admission Prices: May-Oct. daily 9-4:30; Nov.-April 9-4. Adults $7, seniors & students $5. Closed New Year's Day; Easter; Thanksgiving; Christmas.

MODERNISM, 724 Ellis St., San Francisco, CA 94109. Mailing Address: 601 Van Ness Ave., Ste. E619, San Francisco, CA 94102. Tel.: 415-541-0461. Fax: 415-541-0425.
E-mail: info@modernisminc.com
Web Site: www.modernisminc.com
Key Personnel: Owner, Martin Muller.
Institution Type/Description: Art Gallery.
Hours & Admission Prices: Tues.-Sat. 10-5:30.

THE MUSEE MECANIQUE, Pier 45 Fisherman's Wharf, San Francisco, CA 94133. Tel.: 415-346-2000. Facebook.
E-mail: helpmemuseemecanique@gmail.com
Web Site: museemecanique.net
Key Personnel: Owner, Daniel Galand Zelinsky.
Institution Type/Description: General Museum.
Hours & Admission Prices: Mon.-Fri. 10-7, Sat.-Sun. & holidays 10-8. No charge. &

MUSEO ITALO AMERICANO, Ft. Mason Center, 2 Marina Blvd., Bldg. C, San Francisco, CA 94123-1301. Tel.: 415-673-2200. Fax: 415-673-2292. Facebook; Twitter.
E-mail: info@sfmuseo.org
Web Site: www.sfmuseo.org
Key Personnel: Mng. Dir., Paola Bagnatori; Asst. Mng. Dir., Susan Filippo; Cur., Mary Serventi Steiner; Asst. Cur. & Communs. Dir., Bianca Friundi.
Institution Type/Description: Contemporary Italian, Italian-American Art Museum & Italian Cultural Center.
Hours & Admission Prices: Tues.-Sun. 12-4; Mon. by appointment. No charge; donations accepted. Closed holidays. &
Attendance: 8,450 (actual)

MUSEUM OF RUSSIAN CULTURE, 2450 Sutter St., San Francisco, CA 94115-3016. Tel.: 415-921-4082. Fax: 415-921-4082.
E-mail: contact@mrcsf.org
Key Personnel: Pres., Nicholas Koretsky; Vice Pres., Yevs Franquien.
Institution Type/Description: Ethnic History Museum.
Hours & Admission Prices: Wed. & Sat. 10:30-2:30. No charge. Closed holidays.
Attendance: 300 (estimated)

MUSEUM OF THE AFRICAN DIASPORA, 685 Mission St., San Francisco, CA 94105-4126. Tel.: 415-358-7200. Facebook: @moadsanfrancisco; Instagram: @moad_sf; Twitter: @MoADsf;.
E-mail: linda@moadsf.org
Web Site: www.moadsf.org
Key Personnel: Exec. Dir., Linda Harrison; Vice Chm. Bd., Deborah Santana; C.F.O., Linda Spain de Bruin; Dir. Special Events, Suzy Drell; Dir. Education, Demetri Broxton; Dir. Exhibitions & Curatorial Affairs, Emily A. Kuhlmann; Dir. Public Programs, Elizabeth Gessel, Ph.D.; Dir. Mktg. & Communs., Mark Sabb; Exec. Asst. & Opers. Mgr., Jasmine Brown.
Institution Type/Description: Art Museum.
Hours & Admission Prices: Wed.-Sat. 11-6, Sun. 12-5. Adults $10, seniors & students $5; children 12 & under and members no charge. Closed New Year's Eve & Day; Memorial Day, Independence Day; Labor Day; Thanksgiving Weekend; Christmas Eve & Day.
Attendance: 85,000 (actual)

MUSEUM OF VISION, 655 Beach St., San Francisco, CA 94109-1342. Tel.: 415-561-8500. Fax: 415-561-8533.
E-mail: museum@aao.org
Web Site: www.museumofvision.org
Formerly: Museum of Vision Foundation of the American Academy of Ophthalmology
Key Personnel: Dir. Museum of Vision, Jenny Benjamin.
Institution Type/Description: Medical History Museum.
Hours & Admission Prices: Mon.-Fri. 10-5. Tours by appointment only. No charge; donations accepted. Closed national holidays. &
Attendance: 300 (estimated)

NATIONAL JAPANESE AMERICAN HISTORICAL SOCIETY, 1684 Post St., San Francisco, CA 94115-3604. Tel.: 415-921-5007. Fax: 415-921-5087.
E-mail: njahs@njahs.org
Web Site: www.njahs.org
Key Personnel: Exec. Dir., Rosalyn Tonai.
Institution Type/Description: Historical Society Museum & Peace Gallery.
Hours & Admission Prices: Mon.-Fri. & 1st Sat. of month 12-5. No charge; donations accepted.

NATIONAL LIBERTY SHIP MEMORIAL/S.S. JEREMIAH O'BRIEN, 45 Pier, Ste. 4A, San Francisco, CA 94133-1818. Tel.: 415-544-0100. Fax: 415-544-9890. Facebook: @ssjeremiahobrien.
E-mail: liberty@ssjeremiahobrien.org
Web Site: www.ssjeremiahobrien.org
Key Personnel: Chm. & CEO, Roger Franz; Exec. Dir., Matt Lasher; Events Coord., Kyle Day.
Institution Type/Description: Merchant Marine Ship Museum and U.S. Naval Armed Guard; built in 1943.
Hours & Admission Prices: Daily 9-4. Adults $20, seniors $12, juniors 5-12 & US active military $10; discounts to AAM & ICOM members; members & children under 4 no charge. Closed New Year's Day; Thanksgiving; Christmas.
Attendance: 52,500 (actual)

OCTAGON HOUSE, 2645 Gough St., San Francisco, CA 94123-4402. Tel.: 415-441-7512.
E-mail: info@nscda-ca.org
Web Site: nscda-ca.org/octagon-house

Institution Type/Description: Historic House: octagonal in shape, used as a family residence until the late 1920s. Listed on the National Register of Historic Places.
Hours & Admission Prices: Feb.-Dec. 2nd Sun. & 2nd and 4th Thurs. 12-3. Guided Tours: adults $8. Admission: no charge; donations accepted. Closed legal holidays.
Attendance: 1,249

PRESIDIO HISTORICAL ASSOCIATION, 1031 Franklin St., San Francisco, CA 94109. Mailing Address: P.O. Box 29163, San Francisco, CA 94129-0163. Tel.: 415-359-9910. Fax: 415-359-9910.
E-mail: presidio-assoc@att.net
Web Site: www.presidioassociation.org
Key Personnel: Pres. (V), Lucia Bogatay; Vice Pres. (V), Paul Wermer; Treas., Dorothy Janson; Sec., Mike Brassington.
Institution Type/Description: Historical Society.
Hours & Admission Prices: By appointment only.

RANDALL MUSEUM, Mission Art Center, 745 Treat Ave., San Francisco, CA 94110. Tel.: 415-554-9600. Fax: 415-554-9609.
E-mail: info@randallmuseum.org
Web Site: www.randallmuseum.org
Key Personnel: Exec. Dir., Chris Boettcher; Dir. Devel., Traci McCollister; Cur. Science, Nancy Ellis; Environmental Arts Program Coord., Julie Dodd Tetzlaff.
Institution Type/Description: Community Museum.
Hours & Admission Prices: Tues.-Sat. 10-5. No charge; donations accepted. Closed New Year's Day; Independence Day; Veterans Day; Thanksgiving & day after; Christmas.
Attendance: 85,000 (estimated)

SFO MUSEUM - SAN FRANCISCO INTERNATIONAL AIRPORT, San Francisco International Airport, San Francisco, CA 94128. Mailing Address: P.O. Box 8097, San Francisco, CA 94128-8097. Tel.: 650-821-6700. Fax: 650-821-6777. Facebook, Instagram & Twitter: @SFOMuseum.
E-mail: curator@flysfo.com
Web Site: www.flysfo.com
Formerly: San Francisco Airport Museums
Key Personnel: Pres. Airport Commission, Larry Mazzola; Dir. Airport, Ivar C. Satero; Dir. & Chief Cur., Blake Summers; Asst. Dir. Exhibitions, Timothy O'Brien; Asst. Dir. Aviation, John Hill; Cur. Exhibition Design, Kelvin Godshall; Cur. Registration, Barbara Geib; Cur.-in-Charge Collections Management, Julie Takata; Cur.-in-Charge Museum Affairs, Megan Callan.
Institution Type/Description: History Museum: housed in 20 exhibition sites throughout the airport.
Hours & Admission Prices: Airport Terminals: daily twenty-four hours a day. No charge. Aviation Library & Museum: daily 10-4:30. No charge. &
Attendance: 5,100,000 (estimated)

SAN FRANCISCO AFRICAN AMERICAN HISTORICAL AND CULTURAL SOCIETY, INC., 762 Fulton St., 2nd Fl., San Francisco, CA 94102-4119. Tel.: 415-292-6172. Facebook.
E-mail: info@sfaahcs.org
Web Site: www.sfaahcs.org
Key Personnel: Exec. Dir., W. E. Hoskins; Pres. & Chm. Bd. Dirs., Alfred W. Williams; Treas. & Systems Administrator, Ellis C. Joseph.
Institution Type/Description: African American Cultural Center.
Hours & Admission Prices: Tues.-Sat. 1-5. No charge; donations accepted. Closed New Year's Eve & Day; Memorial Day; Independence Day; Labor Day; Thanksgiving; Christmas. &
Attendance: 55,000

SAN FRANCISCO ART INSTITUTE - WALTER & MCBEAN GALLERIES, 800 Chestnut St., San Francisco, CA 94133-2299. Tel.: 415-771-7020.
E-mail: exhibitions@sfai.edu
Web Site: www.sfai.edu
Key Personnel: Vice Pres. Exhibitions & Public Programs, Hesse McGraw; Asst. Cur. & Exhibitions Mgr., Katie Hood Morgan; Chief Preparator, Robin Beard; Academic Technical Dir., Benjamin Ashlock.
Institution Type/Description: Art Museum.
Hours & Admission Prices: Tues. 11-7, Wed.-Sat. 11-6. No charge; donations accepted. Closed holidays. &
Attendance: 20,000 (estimated)

SAN FRANCISCO BOTANICAL GARDEN, 1199 9th Ave., San Francisco, CA 94122-2370. Tel.: 415-661-1316.
E-mail: info@sfbg.org
Web Site: www.sfbg.org

Key Personnel: Exec. Dir., Stephanie Linder; Garden Dir., Matthew Stephens; Curator, Ryan Guillou; C.F.O., Matthew Ayotte; Dir. Learning & Engagement, Jessa Barzelay; Dir. Visitor Exp. & Mktg., Brendan Lange; Dir. Youth Education, Annette Huddle.
Institution Type/Description: Arboretum & Botanical Gardens.
Hours & Admission Prices: Winter & Fall: daily 7:30-6; Spring & Summer: daily 7:30-7. Families $20, adults weekend $12, adults weekdays $9, seniors 65 & up and youth 12-17 $7, children 5-11 $3; SF residents, children 4 & under, daily 7:30-9 a.m., 2nd Tues. of month, New Year's Day, Thanksgiving, Christmas Day & members no charge. &
Attendance: 500,000 (estimated)

SAN FRANCISCO CAMERAWORK, 1011 Market St., 2nd Fl., San Francisco, CA 94103. Tel.: 415-487-1011.
E-mail: info@sfcamerawork.org
Web Site: www.sfcamerawork.org
Key Personnel: Dir., Heather Snider; Gallery Mgr., Kristina Graber.
Institution Type/Description: Photography Museum.
Hours & Admission Prices: Tues.-Fri. 12-6, Sat. 12-5. No charge; donations accepted. Closed national holidays.
Attendance: 30,000 (estimated)

SAN FRANCISCO FIRE DEPARTMENT MUSEUM, 655 Presidio Ave., San Francisco, CA 94115-2424. Mailing Address: 1152 Oak St., San Francisco, CA 94117. Tel.: 415-558-3546 & 431-4682.
E-mail: info@guardiansofthecity.org
Web Site: www.guardiansofthecity.org/sffd/index.html
Key Personnel: Chief Dept., Joanne Hayes-White.
Institution Type/Description: Fire Museum.
Hours & Admission Prices: Thurs.-Sun. 1-4 by appointment. No charge; donations accepted. &

SAN FRANCISCO MARITIME NATIONAL HISTORICAL PARK, 2 Marina Blvd., Fort Mason Center, Building E, 2nd Fl., San Francisco, CA 94123. Tel.: 415-561-7000. Fax: 415-556-1624. Facebook.
E-mail: kevin_hendricks@nps.gov
Web Site: www.nps.gov/safr
Formerly: San Francisco Maritime Museum
Key Personnel: Supt. & Dir., Kevin Hendricks.
Institution Type/Description: Maritime Museum Complex.
Hours & Admission Prices: Visitor Center: daily 9:30-5. Maritime Museum: daily 10-4. No charge. Ships: adults $10; children 15 & under no charge. Maritime Research Center: Mon.-Fri. 1-4 by appointment. No charge. Hyde Street Pier: daily 9:30-5. Municipal Pier: daily dusk-dawn. &
Attendance: 4,224,898 (actual)

SAN FRANCISCO MARITIME NATIONAL HISTORICAL PARK & USS PAMPANITO, 2905 Hyde St., San Francisco, CA 94109. Mailing Address: 2 Marina Blvd., Bldg. E, 2nd Fl., San Francisco, CA 94123. Tel.: 415-561-7000. Fax: 415-556-1624.
Web Site: www.nps.gov/safr
Key Personnel: Supt., Kevin Hendricks.
Institution Type/Description: Maritime Museum: housed on a WWII Balao class Fleet submarine.
Hours & Admission Prices: June-Aug. daily 9:30-5:30; Sept.-May daily 9:30-5. Adults $16, seniors 62 & over $12, junior 6-12 $10; discounts to groups & active military; children 5 & under no charge. Closed New Year's Day; Thanksgiving; Christmas.

SAN FRANCISCO MUSEUM OF CRAFT + DESIGN, 2569 Third St., San Francisco, CA 94107. Tel.: 415-773-0303, 877-487-3623. Fax: 415-773-0306. Facebook: Museum of Craft and Design.
E-mail: info@sfmcd.org
Web Site: www.sfmcd.org
Formerly: Museum of Craft and Design
Institution Type/Description: Art Museum.
Hours & Admission Prices: Tues.-Sat. 11-6, Sun. 12-5. Adults $8; NARM, Blue Start & museum members no charge. Closed New Year's Day; Thanksgiving; Christmas.
Attendance: 15,000 (estimated)

SAN FRANCISCO MUSEUM OF MODERN ART, 151 Third St., San Francisco, CA 94103-3159. Tel.: 415-357-4000. Facebook, Instagram & Twitter: @sfmoma.
E-mail: visit@sfmoma.org
Web Site: www.sfmoma.org
Key Personnel: Helen & Charles Schwab Dir., Neal Benezra; Deputy Museum Dir. Admin. & Fin., Janet alberti; Deputy Museum Dir. Curatorial Affairs, Ruth

Berson; Deputy Museum Dir. External Rels., Nan Keeton; Sr. Cur. Photography, Clement Cheroux; Elise S. Haas Sr. Cur. Painting & Sculpture, Gary Garrels; Leanne & George Roberts Cur. Education & Public Practice, Dominic Willsdon; Dir. Collections & Conservation, Jill Sterrett; Dir. Mktg. & Communications, Jennifer Northrop; Dir. Museum Store, Jana Machin.
Institution Type/Description: Art Museum.
Hours & Admission Prices: Thurs. 10-9, Fri.-Tues. 10-5. Adults $25, seniors 65 & over $22, youth 19-24 with ID $19; members & children 18 & under no charge. Closed Thanksgiving; Christmas. &
Attendance: 550,000 (estimated)

SAN FRANCISCO ZOO, Sloat Blvd. at Great Hwy., San Francisco, CA 94132. Mailing Address: 1 Zoo Rd., San Francisco, CA 94132. Tel.: 415-753-7080. Fax: 415-681-2039.
E-mail: webmaster@sfzoo.org
Web Site: www.sfzoo.org
Formerly: San Francisco Zoological Gardens
Institution Type/Description: Zoo.
Hours & Admission Prices: Daily & holidays 10-4. Adults $19, senior citizens 65 & over $16, youth 4-14 $13; discounts to San Francisco residents; AZA reciprocating zoos, children 3 & under, members & children's zoo no charge. &
Attendance: 1,000,000 (estimated)

THE SOCIETY OF CALIFORNIA PIONEERS MUSEUM AND LIBRARY, 101 Montgomery St., Ste. 150, The Presidio of San Francisco, San Francisco, CA 94129-1718. Tel.: 415-957-1849. Facebook.
E-mail: info@californiapioneers.org
Web Site: californiapioneers.org
Key Personnel: Mgn. Dir., Mercedes M. Devine; Pres. (V), David Cebalo; Education & Gallery Mgr., John Hogan; Bookkeeper, Lorna Buehler; Dir. Library & Archives, Patricia Keats; Membership Svcs. Coord. & Asst. to the Mng. Dir., Lacey Lieberthal.
Institution Type/Description: Art & History Museum.
Hours & Admission Prices: Wed.-Sun. 10-5; see website to confirm. No charge. Closed New Year's Eve & Day; Martin Luther King Jr. Day; Presidents' Day; Memorial Day; Independence Day; Labor Day; Veterans Day; Thanksgiving & day after; Christmas Eve, Day & week. &
Attendance: 4,500 (estimated)

SOUTHERN EXPOSURE GALLERY - SOEX, 3030 20th St., San Francisco, CA 94110. Tel.: 415-863-2141. Fax: 415-738-8018.
E-mail: communications@soex.org
Web Site: www.soex.org
Key Personnel: Exec. Dir., Patricia Maloney.
Institution Type/Description: Art Gallery.
Hours & Admission Prices: Gallery: Tues.-Sat. 12-6. Office: Mon.-Fri. 10-6.

STEINHART AQUARIUM, 55 Music Concourse Dr., San Francisco, CA 94118. Tel.: 415-379-8000. Fax: 415-379-5704. Facebook.
E-mail: aquarium@calacademy.org
Web Site: www.calacademy.org
Key Personnel: Exec. Dir., California Academy of Sciences, Jonathan Foley, Ph.D.
Institution Type/Description: Aquarium.
Hours & Admission Prices: Mon.-Sat. 9:30-5, Sun. 11-5. Adults $34.95, seniors, students & youth 12-17 $29.95, children 4-11 $24.95; children 3 & under no charge. Closed Thanksgiving; Christmas. &
Attendance: 1,400,000 (actual)

TENDERLOIN MUSEUM, 398 Eddy St., San Francisco, CA 94102. Tel.: 415-351-1912.
E-mail: info@tenderloinmuseum.org
Web Site: tenderloinmuseum.org
Institution Type/Description: History Museum.
Hours & Admission Prices: Tues.-Sun. 10-5. Adults $10; students, youth 13-21 & seniors $6; children 12 & under no charge. Closed New Year's Day; Easter; Independence Day; Thanksgiving; Christmas.

THE VIRTUAL MUSEUM OF THE CITY OF SAN FRANCISCO, San Francisco, CA 94116. Mailing Address: PMB 423, 945 Taraval St., San Francisco, CA 94116.
E-mail: curator@sfmuseum.org
Web Site: www.sfmuseum.org
Key Personnel: Dir. & Founder, Richard Hansen.
Institution Type/Description: Virtual History Museum.
Hours & Admission Prices: Daily.

THE WALT DISNEY FAMILY MUSEUM, 104 Montgomery St., The Presidio, San Francisco, CA 94129-1718. Tel.: 415-345-6800. Facebook.
E-mail: info@wdfmuseum.org
Web Site: www.waltdisney.org
Key Personnel: Exec. Dir., Kirsten Komoroske; Bd. Pres., Ron Miller.
Institution Type/Description: Walt Disney Family History Museum.
Hours & Admission Prices: Wed.-Mon. 10-6. Adults $25, seniors & students with valid ID $20, youth 6-17 $15; active & retired military & families, children under 5 & members no charge. Closed New Year's Day; Thanksgiving; Christmas. &
Attendance: 120,000 (actual)

WELLS FARGO HISTORY MUSEUM, Wells Fargo Bank, Historical Services, 420 Montgomery St., MAC-A0101-022, San Francisco, CA 94163. Tel.: 415-396-2619 & 4157. Fax: 415-975-7430. Facebook: Wells Fargo.
E-mail: historicalservices@wellsfargo.com
Web Site: www.wellsfargohistory.com
Key Personnel: Mgr. Museum, Julian Torres.
Institution Type/Description: Company History Museum: located in Wells Fargo Bank's corporate headquarters.
Hours & Admission Prices: Mon.-Fri. 9-5. No charge. Closed bank holidays. &

YERBA BUENA CENTER FOR THE ARTS, 701 Mission St., San Francisco, CA 94103-3138. Tel.: 415-978-2700.
E-mail: hello@ybca.org
Web Site: www.ybca.org
Key Personnel: C.E.O., Deborah Cullinan; C.O.O., Scott Rowitz; Chief Devel. Officer, Charles Ward; Chief Program & Pedagogy, Marc Bamuthi Joseph; Chief Mktg., Jennifer Martindale; Chief Civic Engagement, Jonathan Moscone.
Institution Type/Description: Arts Center.
Hours & Admission Prices: Tues.-Sun. 11-6. Adults $10, senior citizens, students, teachers & non-profit employees, KQED members, public transit riders, library card holders $9; members no charge. &
Attendance: 200,000 (actual)

San Gabriel

HAYES HOUSE & MUSEUM - SAN GABRIEL HISTORICAL ASSOCIATION, 546 W. Broadway, San Gabriel, CA 91776. Tel.: 626-308-3223.
Web Site: www.sghistorical.org/index.html
Institution Type/Description: History Museum.
Hours & Admission Prices: 1st Sat. of the month 1-4; groups by appointment.

SAN GABRIEL MISSION MUSEUM, 428 S. Mission Dr., San Gabriel, CA 91776-1252. Tel.: 626-457-3035. Fax: 626-282-5308.
E-mail: alsgm1@aol.com
Key Personnel: Business Mgr., Alfred Sanchez; Cur., Helen Nelson.
Institution Type/Description: Religious Museum: fourth in a chain of 21 California Missions founded Sept. 8, 1771, site of San Gabriel Mission.
Hours & Admission Prices: Daily 9-4:30. Adults $5, seniors 62 & over $4, youth 6-17 $2; discounts to inner schools; no charge to clergy & religious. Closed Good Friday noon, Easter, Independence Day, Thanksgiving, Christmas.
Attendance: 50,000 (estimated)

San Jacinto

MT. SAN JACINTO COLLEGE FINE ART GALLERY, 1499 N. State St., San Jacinto, CA 92583. Tel.: 951-487-3585 & 3586.
E-mail: jknuth@msjc.edu
Web Site: www.msjc.edu/artgallery
Key Personnel: Gallery Mgr., Royce Bunyard.
Institution Type/Description: Art Gallery.
Hours & Admission Prices: Mon.-Thurs. 8-4; other times by appointment.
Attendance: 1,500 (estimated)

SAN JACINTO MUSEUM, 695 Ash St., San Jacinto, CA 92583. Mailing Address: P.O. Box 922, San Jacinto, CA 92581-0922. Tel.: 951-654-4952. Fax: 909-654-9270.
E-mail: silynnpeterson@gmail.com
Web Site: www.ci.san-jacinto.ca.us
Key Personnel: Asst., Betty Jo Dunham.
Institution Type/Description: History Museum.
Hours & Admission Prices: Fri.-Sun. 11-4. No charge; donations accepted. Closed New Year's Day; Thanksgiving; Christmas. &
Attendance: 3,000 (actual)

San Jose

BRANDENBURG HISTORICAL GOLF MUSEUM, 23600 McKean Rd., San Jose, CA 95141. Mailing Address: 1122 Willow St. #200, San Jose, CA 95125. Tel.: 408-323-7814.
E-mail: cinnabarhills@cinnabarhills.com
Web Site: brandenburg.properties.com/brandenburggolfmuseum
Institution Type/Description: Golf Museum.
Hours & Admission Prices: Tues.-Fri. 9-5. No charge. &
Attendance: 100,000 (estimated)

CHILDREN'S DISCOVERY MUSEUM OF SAN JOSE, 180 Woz Way, San Jose, CA 95110-2780. Tel.: 408-298-5437. Fax: 408-298-6826.
E-mail: contactus@cdm.org
Web Site: www.cdm.org
Key Personnel: Exec. Dir., Marilee Jennings; Chm. Bd. of Dir. (V), Dan Amend; Vice Chm. Bd. of Dir., Kevan Krysler; Dir. Administration & Finance, Susan Clark; Dir. Education & Programs, Jenni Martin; Dir. Devel. & Mktg., Patricia Narciso; Dir. Information & Compliance, Cheryl Blumenthal.
Institution Type/Description: Children's Museum: housed in Ricardo Legorreta-designed structure.
Hours & Admission Prices: Tues.-Sat. 10-5, Sun. 12-5; call for holiday hours. Admission $15, senior citizens 60 & up $14; members and infants under one no charge. Closed Thanksgiving and Christmas. &
Attendance: 419,790 (actual)

CHINESE CULTURAL GARDEN/OVERFELT GARDENS, 368 Educational Park Dr., San Jose, CA 95133-1711. Mailing Address: Overfelt Gardens c/o Prusch Farms Park, 647 S. King Rd., San Jose, CA 95116-3557. Tel.: 408-251-3323. Fax: 408-251-2865.
E-mail: sylvia@chineseculturalgarden.org
Web Site: chineseculturalgarden.org
Key Personnel: Program Dir., Sylvia Lowe; Park Ranger, Will Bick; Gardener, Sheila Strand; Docent, Pauline Lowe.
Institution Type/Description: General Museum.
Hours & Admission Prices: Tues.-Sun. 10 to sunset. No charge.

HAPPY HOLLOW PARK & ZOO, 748 Story Rd., San Jose, CA 95112. Mailing Address: 1300 Senter Rd., San Jose, CA 95112-2520. Tel.: 408-794-7596.
E-mail: info@happyhollow.org
Web Site: happyhollow.org
Key Personnel: Gen Mgr., Shannon Himer.
Institution Type/Description: Zoo.
Hours & Admission Prices: Call for hours. Admission $12.95, seniors 70 & over $9.95; discounts to groups; children one & under no charge. &
Attendance: 337,123 (actual)

HISTORY SAN JOSE, 1650 Senter Rd., San Jose, CA 95112-2599. Tel.: 408-287-2290. Fax: 408-287-2291.
E-mail: abray@historysanjose.org
Web Site: www.historysanjose.org
Key Personnel: Pres. & C.E.O., Alida Bray; Chm. Bd., Jack Frazer; Dir. Operations & HR, Barbara Johnson; Dir. Devel., Michelle Powers; Dir. Events, Juanita Lara; Dir. Education & Community Engagement, Wendy Abelmann; Finance Mgr., Maggie Williams; Sr. Accountant, Rene Foronda; Cur. Library & Archives, Catherine Mills; Cur. Collections, Ken Middlebrook; Exec. Asst., Dayna Grabeklis.
Institution Type/Description: History Museum.
Hours & Admission Prices: History Park: Mon.-Fri. noon-5, Sat. & Sun. 11-5. No charge, except during special events. Closed New Year's Day; Martin Luther King Jr. Day; Presidents' Day; Memorial Day; Independence Day; Labor Day; Thanksgiving & day after; Christmas Eve & Day. &
Attendance: 100,000 (actual)

NATALIE & JAMES THOMPSON ART GALLERY, Department of Art and Art History, San Jose, CA 95192-0089. Mailing Address: One Washington Sq., San Jose, CA 95192-0289. Tel.: 408-924-4320 & 4327. Fax: 408-924-4326. Facebook: Natalie & James Thompson Art Gallery.
E-mail: thompsongallery@sjsu.edu
Web Site: www.sjsu.edu
Formerly: San Jose State University Art Galleries
Key Personnel: Gallery Dir., Jo Farb Hernandez.
Institution Type/Description: University Art Gallery.
Hours & Admission Prices: Sept.-May Mon. & Wed.-Fri. 10-4, Tues. 10-4 & 6-7:30. No charge; donations accepted. Closed semester breaks; national holidays. &
Attendance: 15,000 (actual)

NEW ALMADEN QUICKSILVER MINING MUSEUM, 21350 Almaden Rd., San Jose, CA 95120-4306. Tel.: 408-323-1107. Fax: 408-323-0943.
Key Personnel: Museum Mgr. & Museum Shop Mgr., Julie Lee.
Institution Type/Description: Mining Museum.
Hours & Admission Prices: July-Aug. Fri.-Sun. 10-4; Sept.-June Fri. 12-4, Sat.-Sun. 10-4; other times by appointment. No charge; donations accepted. Closed New Year's Day; Thanksgiving; Christmas. &
Attendance: 7,500 (estimated)

PORTUGUESE HISTORICAL MUSEUM, 1650 Senter Rd., San Jose, CA 95112-2599. Mailing Address: Portuguese Heritage Society of California, P.O. Box 18277, San Jose, CA 95158. Tel.: 408-644-1407.
E-mail: faial2000@yahoo.com
Web Site: www.portuguesemuseum.org
Key Personnel: Bd. Pres., Antonino Pascoal.
Institution Type/Description: Cultural History Museum.
Hours & Admission Prices: Sat.-Sun. 12-4; other times by appointment. No charge. &
Attendance: 7,000 (estimated)

ROSICRUCIAN EGYPTIAN MUSEUM, 1660 Park Ave., San Jose, CA 95126. Mailing Address: 1342 Naglee Ave., San Jose, CA 95126. Tel.: 408-947-3600 & 3636. Fax: 408-947-3638.
E-mail: info@egyptianmuseum.org
Web Site: www.egyptianmuseum.org
Key Personnel: Dir., Julie Scott; Cur., Dennis Hauck.
Institution Type/Description: Egyptian History Museum.
Hours & Admission Prices: Wed.-Fri. 9-5, Sat.-Sun. 10-6. Adults $9, students with ID & senior citizens $7, children 5-10 $5; discounts to military, KQED, AAM & AAA members; children 4 & under & members no charge. Planetarium Showtimes: Mon.-Fri. 2, Sat.-Sun. 2 & 3:30. Closed major holidays.
Attendance: 100,000 (actual)

SAN JOSE FIRE MUSEUM, 1661 Senter Rd., Bldg. D1, San Jose, CA 95112. Tel.: 408-998-6184. Fax: 408-287-0401.
E-mail: macmhalain@yahoo.com
Web Site: www.sjfivemuseum.org
Key Personnel: Pres. (V), John A. McMillan.
Institution Type/Description: Firefighting History Museum.
Hours & Admission Prices: By appointment. No charge; donations accepted.
Attendance: 800 (estimated)

SAN JOSE INSTITUTE OF CONTEMPORARY ART, 560 S. 1st St., San Jose, CA 95113-2806. Tel.: 408-283-8155. Fax: 408-283-8157.
E-mail: info@sjica.org
Web Site: www.sjica.org
Key Personnel: Dir., Cathy Kimball.
Institution Type/Description: Art Gallery.
Hours & Admission Prices: Tues.-Fri. 10-5, Sat. 12-5. No charge; donations accepted.

SAN JOSE MUSEUM OF ART, 110 S. Market St., San Jose, CA 95113-2383. Tel.: 408-271-6840 & 6880. Fax: 408-294-2977. Facebook: San Jose Museum of Art.
E-mail: info@sjmusart.org
Web Site: sjmusart.org
Key Personnel: Exec. Dir., Susan Krane; Pres. (V), Hildy Shandell; Dep. Dir. Curatorial Affairs, Susan Sayre-Batton; Treas., William Faulkner; Dir. Mktg. & Communications, Sherrill Ingalls; Cur. Education, Jeff Bordona; Assoc. Cur., Rory Padeken; Chief Design & Installation, Richard Karson; Facilities Mgr., John Renzel; Museum Store Mgr., Pat Downward.
Institution Type/Description: Contemporary Art Museum.
Hours & Admission Prices: Tues.-Sun.11-5. Adults $10; discounts to AAM & ICOM members; members no charge. Closed New Year's Day; Thanksgiving; Christmas. &
Attendance: 102,098 (actual)

SAN JOSE MUSEUM OF QUILTS & TEXTILES, 520 S. First St., San Jose, CA 95113-2806. Tel.: 408-971-0323, ext. 16. Fax: 408-971-7226.
E-mail: jane@sjquiltmuseum.org
Web Site: www.sjquiltmuseum.org
Key Personnel: Bd. Pres., Marie Strait; Dir., Christine Jeffers; Museum Shop Mgr., Sofia Motamedi; Educational Outreach, Sylvia Carroll.
Institution Type/Description: Quilt & Textile Museum

Hours & Admission Prices: Tues.-Wed. & Fri.-Sun. 10-5, Thurs. 10-8. Adults $8; discounts to AAM members; children 12 & under and members no charge. Closed major holidays. &
Attendance: 20,000 (estimated)

THE TECH MUSEUM OF INNOVATION, 201 S. Market St., San Jose, CA 95113-2008. Tel.: 408-294-8324. Fax: 408-279-7167.
E-mail: info@thetech.org
Web Site: www.thetech.org
Key Personnel: Pres. & C.E.O., Tim Ritchie; Chm., Christopher S. DiGiorgio; C.F.O., Harvard Sung; Vice Pres. Opers., Bill Bailor; Vice Pres. Devel., Maria Pappas; Vice Pres. Education, Gretchen Walker; Vice Pres. The Tech Awards, David Whitman; Vice Pres. Media & Community, Rachel Wilner; Vice Pres. Info. Systems, Charles Pearson.
Institution Type/Description: Science & Technology Museum.
Hours & Admission Prices: Daily 10-5. Adults $21, students, seniors 65 & up & children 3-17 $16; discounts to AAA members, active-duty military & veterans & groups; members no charge. Closed Thanksgiving Day; Christmas Day. &
Attendance: 400,000 (actual)

YOUTH SCIENCE INSTITUTE, Penitencia Creek Rd., San Jose, CA 95127. Mailing Address: 296 Garden Hill Dr., Los Gatos, CA 95032-7669. Tel.: 408-258-4322. Fax: 408-358-3683.
E-mail: info@ysi-ca.org
Web Site: www.ysi-ca.org
Key Personnel: Exec. Dir., Susane Mulcahy; Pres. (V), Mark Lohbeck; Administrative Asst., Marion Blair; YSI Center Mgr. Sanborn & Animal Cur. Sanborn, Laura Weiss; Animal Cur. Alum Rock, Dorothy Johnson; Dir. Education, Bonnie Lemat.
Institution Type/Description: Children's Natural History Museum & Nature Center.
Hours & Admission Prices: Summer: Tues.-Sun. 12-4:30; School Groups: Mon.-Fri. 9-5. Alum Rock: adults $1, children $.50. Sanborn & Vasona locations donations accepted. &
Attendance: 70,000 (estimated)

San Juan Bautista

OLD MISSION SAN JUAN BAUTISTA VISITOR CENTER, 406 Second St., San Juan Bautista, CA 95045. Mailing Address: P.O. Box 400, San Juan Bautista, CA 95045-0400. Tel.: 831-623-2127 & 4528. Fax: 831-623-2433.
E-mail: ann@oldmissionsjb.org
Web Site: www.oldmissionsjb.org
Key Personnel: Pastor, Rev. Jim Henry; Business Mgr., Ann McMahon; Visitor Center & Museum Shop Mgr., Ana Silva.
Institution Type/Description: Historic Site: one of the original California missions founded by Franciscan Fathers.
Hours & Admission Prices: Office: Mon.-Fri. 9-12 & 1-4. Gift Shop/Visitor Center: daily 9:30-4:30. Suggested Donations: adults $2, students & seniors $1. Closed New Year's Day; Good Friday; Thanksgiving; Christmas. &

SAN JUAN BAUTISTA HISTORICAL SOCIETY LUCK MUSEUM, Monterey St., San Juan Bautista, CA 95045. Mailing Address: P.O. Box 1, San Juan Bautista, CA 95045. Tel.: 831-623-2001.
E-mail: sjbhistoricalsociety@gmail.com
Web Site: www.san-juan-bautista.ca.us/history
Institution Type/Description: Historical Society Museum: housed in the former filling station owned by Carl Luck.
Hours & Admission Prices: Sat. 10-4; other times by appointment.

SAN JUAN BAUTISTA STATE HISTORIC PARK, 2nd St., Washington & Mariposa Sts., San Juan Bautista, CA 95045-0787. Mailing Address: P.O. Box 787, San Juan Bautista, CA 95045-0787. Tel.: 831-623-4881. Fax: 831-623-4612.
E-mail: anita.combs@parks.ca.gov
Web Site: www.parks.ca.gov/sjbshp
Key Personnel: Supt., Stuart Organo; Pres. (V), Bob Cable; Chm. (V), Nikki Combs; Cur., Kris N. Quist; Chief Interpreter, Pat Clark-Gray; Museum Shop Mgr., Joanna McMahon.
Institution Type/Description: State Historic Park: located next to a Franciscan mission.
Hours & Admission Prices: Daily 10-4:30. Adults $3; children 16 & under no charge. Closed New Year's Day; Thanksgiving; Christmas. &
Attendance: 114,838 (actual)

San Juan Capistrano

MISSION SAN JUAN CAPISTRANO HISTORIC LANDMARK AND MUSEUM, 26801 Ortega Hwy., San Juan Capistrano, CA 92675-2601. Tel.: 949-234-1300. Fax: 949-493-8747. Facebook: Mission San Juan Capistrano, CA.
E-mail: mlawrence-adams@missionsjc.com
Web Site: www.missionsjc.com
Key Personnel: Exec. Dir., Mechelle Lawrence-Adams; Devel. & Mktg., Barb Beier; Museum Registrar, Jennifer Ring.
Institution Type/Description: Historic & Archaeological Site and Museum.
Hours & Admission Prices: Daily 9-5. Adults $9, seniors 60+ $8, children 4-11 $6; children 3 & under no charge. Members free except certain special events. Audio tours free with paid admission or membership . Closed Thanksgiving; Christmas.
Attendance: 300,000 (estimated)

San Leandro

SAN LEANDRO HISTORIC RAILWAY SOCIETY, 1302 Orchard Ave., San Leandro, CA 94577. Tel.: 510-569-2490.
E-mail: info@www.slhrs.org
Web Site: www.slhrs.org
Institution Type/Description: History Museum: housed in a Southern Pacific Railroad Station; c.1898.
Hours & Admission Prices: Tues. 7:30pm-9pm, Sat. 9-1. No charge.
Attendance: 1,200 (estimated)

San Luis Obispo

DALLIDET ADOBE AND GARDENS, 1185 Pacific St., San Luis Obispo, CA 93401-3301. Tel.: 805-543-6762. Fax: 805-783-2919.
E-mail: info@historycenterslo.org
Web Site: www.slochs.org/dalliet.asp
Key Personnel: Exec. Dir., Kimberly Alfaro.
Institution Type/Description: History Museum.
Hours & Admission Prices: Fri. 10-4, 2nd Sun. of month 1-4; call to confirm.

H.J. MIOSSI ART GALLERY, Hwy. 1, Rm. 7170, San Luis Obispo, CA 93403. Mailing Address: P.O. Box 8106, San Luis Obispo, CA 93403-8106. Tel.: 805-546-3939. Fax: 805-546-3100.
E-mail: emma_saperstein@cuesta.edu
Web Site: www.cuesta.edu/student/forstudents/artgallery
Formerly: Cuesta College Art Gallery
Key Personnel: Cur. Fine Arts, Margaret Korisheli; Gallery Coord., Emma Saperstein.
Institution Type/Description: Art Gallery.
Hours & Admission Prices: June & July Mon.-Thurs. 12-4 or by appointment; Aug.-May Mon.-Fri. 12-4 or by appointment. No charge; donations accepted. &
Attendance: 1,000 (estimated)

HISTORY CENTER OF SAN LUIS OBISPO COUNTY, 696 Monterey St., San Luis Obispo, CA 93401-3515. Tel.: 805-543-0638.
E-mail: eva@historycenterslo.org
Web Site: www.historycenterslo.org
Formerly: San Luis Obispo County Historical Society & Museum
Key Personnel: Pres. (V), Julie Moore; Cur. & Dir., Eva Ulz; Collections Mgr., Cindy Lambert; Archivist, Aimee Armour-Avant; Community Engagement, Alicia Hightower; Weekend Mgr., Leon Koenen.
Institution Type/Description: History Museum.
Hours & Admission Prices: Wed.-Mon. 10-4; other times by appointment. Suggested Donation $5. Closed New Year's Day; Easter; Memorial Day; Labor Day; Thanksgiving; Christmas. &
Attendance: 20,388 (actual)

MISSION SAN LUIS OBISPO DE TOLOSA, Old Mission Parish, 751 Palm St., San Luis Obispo, CA 93401-3521. Tel.: 805-781-8220 & 543-6850 (gift shop). Fax: 805-781-8214.
E-mail: office@oldmissionslo.org
Web Site: www.missionsanluisobispo.org
Key Personnel: Pastor, Rev. Russell Brown; Mgr. Gift Shop & Museum, Minerva Soto.
Institution Type/Description: Religious & History Museum: 1772 Mission San Luis Obispo de Tolosa.
Hours & Admission Prices: Weekdays 7 & 12:10, Sat. 7-5:30 vigil, Sun. in English: 7, 9, 11 & 6, in Spanish: 12:30 & 7:30. Suggested Donation: $2; fee for private group tours. Closed New Year's Day; Easter; Thanksgiving; Christmas. &
Attendance: 200,000 (estimated)

SAN LUIS OBISPO CHILDREN'S MUSEUM, 1010 Nipomo St., San Luis Obispo, CA 93401. Tel.: 805-544-KIDS. Fax: 805-545-5875.
E-mail: info@slocm.org
Web Site: www.slocm.org
Institution Type/Description: Children's Museum.
Hours & Admission Prices: Winter: Tues.-Wed. 10-3, Thurs.-Sat. 10-5, Sun. 1-5; Summer: Mon.-Wed. 10-3, Thurs.-Sat. 10-5, Sun. 1-5. Admission $8, seniors 60 & over $5; discounts to groups, military families & ACN reciprocal members; children under 2 no charge.
Attendance: 50,000 (estimated)

SAN LUIS OBISPO MUSEUM OF ART, 1010 Broad St., San Luis Obispo, CA 93401-3505. Mailing Address: P.O. Box 813, San Luis Obispo, CA 93406. Tel.: 805-543-8562. Fax: 805-543-4518.
E-mail: office@sloma.org
Web Site: sloma.org
Formerly: San Luis Obispo Art Center
Key Personnel: Dir., Karen M. Kile; Pres. (V), Roger Carmody; Museum Shop Mgr., Wendy Walter.
Institution Type/Description: Art Museum.
Hours & Admission Prices: July 4 to Labor Day daily 11-5; Sept.-July 3 Wed.-Mon. 11-5. No charge; donations accepted. Closed New Year's Day; Easter; Independence Day; Labor Day; Christmas. &
Attendance: 54,000 (estimated)

San Marcos

BOEHM GALLERY, 1140 W. Mission Rd., San Marcos, CA 92069-1415. Tel.: 760-744-1150, ext. 2304. Fax: 760-744-8123.
E-mail: jbigfeather@palomar.edu
Web Site: www.palomar.edu/art/BoehmGallery.html
Key Personnel: Dir., Joanna Bigfeather; Pres. Palomar College, Robert Deegan; Librarian, Daniel Arnsan; Dir. Public Rels., Mike Norton.
Institution Type/Description: Art Gallery.
Hours & Admission Prices: Mon.-Tues. 10-4, Thurs. 10-7, Fri. 10-2. No charge; donations accepted. Closed school holidays. &
Attendance: 6,500 (actual)

San Marino

THE HUNTINGTON LIBRARY, ART COLLECTIONS, AND BOTANICAL GARDENS, 1151 Oxford Rd., San Marino, CA 91108-1218. Tel.: 626-405-2140 & 2100. Fax: 626-405-0225.
E-mail: publicinformation@huntington.org
Web Site: www.huntington.org
Key Personnel: Dir. Art Collections, Kevin Salatino; Dir. Botanical Gardens, James P. Folsom.
Institution Type/Description: Library, Art Gallery & Botanical Gardens.
Hours & Admission Prices: Memorial Day to Labor Day Wed.-Mon. 10:30-4:30; Winter: Mon. & Wed.-Fri. 12-4:30, Sat.-Sun. 10:30-4:30. Adults $23-$25, seniors & youth 12-18 $19-$21, children 4-11 $10; children under 4 & members no charge. Closed New Year's Day; Independence Day; Thanksgiving; Christmas Eve & Day. &
Attendance: 609,000 (actual)

OLD MILL MUSEUM, EL MOLINO VIEJO - OLD MILL FOUNDATION, 1120 Old Mill Rd., San Marino, CA 91108-1840. Tel.: 626-449-5458. Fax: 626-449-1057.
E-mail: oldmill@sbcglobal.net
Web Site: old-mill.org
Key Personnel: Pres., John Quinn; Vice Pres., Mary King Sikora.
Institution Type/Description: History Museum.
Hours & Admission Prices: Tues.-Sun. 1-4. No charge; donations accepted. Closed holidays.

San Martin

WINGS OF HISTORY AIR MUSEUM, 12777 Murphy Ave., San Martin, CA 95046-0495. Mailing Address: P.O. Box 495, San Martin, CA 95046-0495. Tel.: 408-683-2290.
E-mail: wohoffice@sbcglobal.net
Web Site: wingsofhistory.org
Formerly: California Antique Aircraft Museum
Key Personnel: C.E.O., Pres. & Chm., Ed Stricker; Volunteers, Lia Peterson; Prop Maker, Gerie Kindred; Restoration & Cur., Jerry Impellezzeri; Office Mgr., Tours & Docents, Susan Talbot; Sponsorship, Merle Ensign; Museum Shop Mgr., Sita Kern; Librarian, Norm Zimmerman.
Institution Type/Description: Aeronautics Museum.

Hours & Admission Prices: Tues. & Thurs. 10-3, Sat.-Sun. 11-4; other times by appointment. Donation Encouraged: adults $10, seniors & teens $7; children 6-12 $5; children under 6, active military & members no charge. Closed New Year's Day; Easter; July 4; Thanksgiving; Christmas. &
Attendance: 2,000 (estimated)

San Mateo

CURIODYSSEY, 1651 Coyote Point Dr., San Mateo, CA 94401-1097. Tel.: 650-342-7755. Fax: 650-342-7853.
E-mail: info@curiodyssey.org
Web Site: www.curiodyssey.org
Formerly: Coyote Point Museum
Key Personnel: Exec. Dir., Rachel Meyer; Dir. Wildlife, Nikii Finch-Morales; Exec. Asst., Sofia Puchner; Museum Shop Mgr., Melvin Buzon.
Institution Type/Description: Science Center and zoo.
Hours & Admission Prices: Tues.-Sun. 10-5. Adults $9, seniors over 62 & students 13-17 $7, children 2-12 $6; discounts to AZA, KQED, AAA, ASTC & museum members. Closed New Year's Day; Thanksgiving; Christmas Eve & Day. &
Attendance: 138,250 (actual)

SAN MATEO ARBORETUM SOCIETY, INC., 101 9th Ave., San Mateo, CA 94401-4202. Tel.: 650-579-0536. Fax: 650-343-8416.
E-mail: info@sanmateoarboretum.org
Web Site: www.sanmateoarboretum.org
Key Personnel: Pres. (V), Brian Silk; Treas., Jack Bennett.
Institution Type/Description: Arboretum: housed in 1874 Kohl Pump House.
Hours & Admission Prices: Green House: Tues. & Thurs. 10-2, Sun. 10am to noon. Japanese Garden: daily 9-4. No charge; donations accepted. &
Attendance: 200 (estimated)

San Miguel

MISSION SAN MIGUEL, 775 Mission St., San Miguel, CA 93451. Mailing Address: P.O. Box 69, San Miguel, CA 93451-0069. Tel.: 805-467-3256. Fax: 805-467-2448.
E-mail: giftshop@missionsanmiguel.org
Web Site: www.missionsanmiguel.org
Key Personnel: Dir., Max Hottle, O.F.M.
Institution Type/Description: Religious Museum: housed in 1797 Mission.
Hours & Admission Prices: Mission: daily 10-4:30; Mass: Sun. 7 & 11. No charge; donations accepted. Closed New Year's Day; Easter; Thanksgiving; Christmas. &
Attendance: 30,000 (estimated)

RIOS-CALEDONIA ADOBE, 700 S. Mission St., San Miguel, CA 93451. Mailing Address: P.O. Box 326, San Miguel, CA 93451-0326. Tel.: 805-467-3357. Facebook: @RiosCaledoniaAdobe.
E-mail: hermanjah11@yahoo.com
Web Site: rios-caledoniaadobe.org
Key Personnel: Pres. (V), Gary McMaster; Admin., Joyce A. Herman.
Institution Type/Description: Historic House Museum: built in 1835.
Hours & Admission Prices: Fri.-Sun. 11-4. No charge.

San Pablo

ALVARADO ADOBE & THE BLUME HOUSE, 13831 San Pablo Ave., San Pablo, CA 94806-3703. Tel.: 510-215-3046.
Web Site: www.ci.san-pablo.ca.us/main/museums.htm
Key Personnel: Pres. (V), Victor T. Manning.
Institution Type/Description: Alvarado Adobe: reconstructed home of California Governor Juan Bautista Alvarado, 1848-1882. Blume House: 1905 farm house.
Hours & Admission Prices: 2nd & 4th Sun. each month 12-4; other times by appointment. No charge; donations accepted. &
Attendance: 240 (estimated)

San Pedro

ANGELS GATE CULTURAL CENTER, 3601 S. Gaffey St., San Pedro, CA 90731-6969. Tel.: 310-519-0936. Fax: 310-519-8698.
E-mail: info@angelsgateart.org
Web Site: www.angelsgateart.org
Key Personnel: Exec. Dir., Amy Eriksen.
Institution Type/Description: Art Museum.
Hours & Admission Prices: Gallery: Tues.-Sat. 11-5. Office: Mon.-Fri. 10-5:30. No charge; donations accepted.

CABRILLO MARINE AQUARIUM, 3720 Stephen M. White Dr., San Pedro, CA 90731-7012. Tel.: 310-548-7562. Fax: 310-548-2649.

E-mail: mike.schaadt@lacity.org
Web Site: www.cabrillomarineaquarium.org
Formerly: Cabrillo Marine Museum
Key Personnel: Dir., CMA, Mike Schaadt; Exec. Dir., Friends of CMA, Caroline Brady.
Institution Type/Description: Aquarium & Marine Museum.
Hours & Admission Prices: Tues.-Fri. 12-5, Sat.-Sun. 10-5. Suggested Donations: adults $5, students, senior citizens & children $1. Beach Parking: $1 per hour for each car. Closed Thanksgiving; Christmas. &
Attendance: 280,000 (estimated)

FORT MACARTHUR MUSEUM, 3601 S. Gaffey St., San Pedro, CA 90731-6969. Mailing Address: Fort MacArthur Museum Assn., P.O. Box 268, San Pedro, CA 90731. Tel.: 310-548-2631. Fax: 310-241-0847.
E-mail: director@ftmac.org
Web Site: www.ftmac.org
Key Personnel: Dir. & Cur., Stephen R. Nelson.
Institution Type/Description: Military History Museum.
Hours & Admission Prices: Tues., Thurs. & Sat.-Sun. 12-5. Requested Donation: $3 per person. &
Attendance: 35,000 (estimated)

HARBOR MUSEUM OLD FIRE STATION 36, 638 Beacon St., San Pedro, CA 90731. Tel.: 323-464-2727.
E-mail: info@lafdmuseum.org
Web Site: lafdmuseum.org/museum_sanpedro
Institution Type/Description: Firefighting History Museum.
Hours & Admission Prices: Sat. 10-3.

LOS ANGELES MARITIME MUSEUM, Berth 84, (foot of 6th St.), San Pedro, CA 90731. Tel.: 310-548-7618. Fax: 310-832-6537. Facebook: LA Maritime Museum.
E-mail: info@lamaritimemuseum.org
Web Site: www.lamaritimemuseum.org
Key Personnel: Dir., Marifrances Trivelli; Registrar, Lucy Ruggirello.
Institution Type/Description: Maritime Museum: housed in 1941 former Los Angeles Municipal Ferry Building, built in Art Deco style.
Hours & Admission Prices: Tues.-Sun. 10-5; last admission at 4:30. Adults $5, seniors $3, children $1; discounts AAM & ICOM members; members, Council of American Maritime Museum members & school groups no charge. Closed holidays. &
Attendance: 75,000 (estimated)

MULLER HOUSE MUSEUM, 1542 S. Beacon St., San Pedro, CA 90731-4849. Mailing Address: San Pedro Bay Historical Society, P.O. Box 1568, San Pedro, CA 90731. Tel.: 310-831-1788.
E-mail: sanpedrohistory@gmail.com
Web Site: www.sanpedrochamber.com/champint/mulrhsmu.htm
Key Personnel: Pres. (V), Frank Anderson.
Institution Type/Description: Historic House Museum: built in 1899.
Hours & Admission Prices: Sun. 1-4; other times by appointment. No charge; donations accepted. Closed holidays.

POINT FERMIN LIGHTHOUSE, 807 W. Paseo del Mar, San Pedro, CA 90731-7131. Tel.: 310-241-0684. Fax: 310-241-0732.
E-mail: kristen.heather@lacity.org
Web Site: www.pointferminlighthouse.org
Key Personnel: Cur., Kristen Heather.
Institution Type/Description: Lighthouse & Museum.
Hours & Admission Prices: Tues.-Sun. 1-4. No charge; donations accepted. Closed holidays; special events.
Attendance: 15,000 (actual)

SOUTH BAY CONTEMPORARY, 401 S. Mesa St., 3rd Level, San Pedro, CA 90731. Tel.: 310-429-0973.
E-mail: southbaycontemporary@gmail.com
Web Site: southbaycontemporary.org
Institution Type/Description: Art Gallery.
Hours & Admission Prices: Thurs.-Sat. 1-5; call to confirm.

San Rafael

FALKIRK CULTURAL CENTER, 1408 Mission Ave., San Rafael, CA 94901-1971. Mailing Address: P.O. Box 151560, San Rafael, CA 94915-1560. Tel.: 415-485-3328. Fax: 415-485-3404.
E-mail: jane.lange@ci.san-rafael.ca.us
Web Site: www.falkirkculturalcenter.org

Key Personnel: Dir., Jane Lange; Cur., Beth Goldberg; Pres. (V), Margaret Farley; Public Programs & Public Rels., Cory Bytof.
Institution Type/Description: Contemporary Arts Center: housed in the former home of Robert Dollar; built in 1888. Listed on the National Registry of Historic Places.
Hours & Admission Prices: Mon.-Fri. 1-5, Sat. 10-1. No charge; donations requested. Closed legal holidays. &
Attendance: 35,000 (estimated)

MISSION SAN RAFAEL ARCANGEL, 1104 Fifth Ave., San ·Rafael, CA 94901-2916. Tel.: 415-454-8141, ext. 12. Fax: 415-454-8193.
E-mail: tbrunner@saintraphael.com
Web Site: www.saintraphael.com
Key Personnel: Cur., Theresa Brunner; Museum Shop Mgr., Helen Bernardoni.
Institution Type/Description: History Museum.
Hours & Admission Prices: Sun.-Mon. & Wed.-Fri. 11-4. No charge. &

WILDCARE, 76 Albert Park Lane, San Rafael, CA 94901-3929. Tel.: 415-453-1000.
E-mail: info@wildcarebayarea.org
Web Site: www.wildcarebayarea.org
Key Personnel: Exec. Dir., Karen Wilson.
Institution Type/Description: Natural History Museum.
Hours & Admission Prices: Daily 9-5. No charge; donations accepted.

San Simeon

HEARST CASTLE, 750 Hearst Castle Rd., San Simeon, CA 93452-9740. Tel.: 805-927-2020. Fax: 805-927-2031. TDD: 800-274-7275.
E-mail: visitorinfo@hearstcastle.com
Web Site: www.hearstcastle.com
Formerly: Hearst Castle-Hearst San Simeon State Historical Monument
Key Personnel: District Supt., Brooke Gutierrez; Museum Dir., Mary L. Levkoff.
Institution Type/Description: Historic House.
Hours & Admission Prices: March-Sept. daily 8-6, Oct.-Feb. Mon.-Fri. 9-5, Sat. & Sun. 9-3. Grand Room, Upstairs Suites and Cottages & Kitchens Tours: adults $25, children 5-12 $12; Evening Tours: adults $36, children 5-12 $18. Closed New Year's Day; Thanksgiving; Christmas. &
Attendance: 860,000 (actual)

Sanger

SANGER DEPOT MUSEUM, 1700 7th St., Sanger, CA 93657-2804. Mailing Address: P.O. Box 44, Sanger, CA 93657-0044. Tel.: 559-875-2848.
E-mail: sangerdepotmuseum@gmail.com
Web Site: www.sangerdepotmuseum.com
Key Personnel: Pres. (V), James Walton.
Institution Type/Description: History Museum.
Hours & Admission Prices: Fri. 9:30-12:30, Sun. 1-4. Adults $1, children $.25.

Santa Ana

BOWERS MUSEUM, 2002 N. Main St., Santa Ana, CA 92706-2776. Tel.: 714-567-3600. Fax: 714-567-3603.
E-mail: pkeller@bowers.org
Web Site: www.bowers.org
Key Personnel: Pres., Peter C. Keller, Ph.D.; Chm. Bd., Anne Shih; Sr. Dir. Education, Emily Mahon.
Institution Type/Description: Art & Cultural Arts Museum.
Hours & Admission Prices: Museum: Tues.-Sun. 10-4. Weekdays: adults $13, seniors & students $10; Weekends: adults $15, seniors & students $12; discounts to AAM, ICOM & WMA members; children under 12 & members no charge. Kidseum: Sat.-Sun. 10-4. Admission $6; under 2 & members no charge. Closed New Year's Day; Independence Day; Thanksgiving; Christmas Day. &
Attendance: 132,300 (actual)

CALIFORNIA STATE UNIVERSITY, FULLERTON, GRAND CENTRAL ART CENTER, 125 N. Broadway, Santa Ana, CA 92701-8237. Tel.: 714-567-7233. Fax: 714-558-4145.
E-mail: grandcentral@fullerton.edu
Web Site: www.grandcentralartcenter.com
Key Personnel: Dir., John D. Spiak.
Institution Type/Description: Art Gallery.
Hours & Admission Prices: Tues.-Thurs. & Sun. 11-4, Fri.-Sat. 11-7. No charge; donations accepted. &

DISCOVERY CUBE ORANGE COUNTY, 2500 N. Main St., Santa Ana, CA 92705-6600. Tel.: 714-542-2823. Fax: 714-542-2828.
E-mail: contactus@discoverycube.org
Web Site: www.discoverycube.org
Formerly: Discovery Science Center
Key Personnel: Pres., Joe Adams; Chm. (V), Rick Baily; Vice Pres. Sales & Strategic Devel., Sean Fitzgerald; Vice Pres. Finance & C.F.O., Mike McGee; Vice Pres. Operations, Kellee Preston; Vice Pres. Mktg. & Communications, Michael Wheeler; Vice Pres. Education, Janet Yamaguchi; Vice Pres. Devel., Brie Griset Smith.
Institution Type/Description: Science Center.
Hours & Admission Prices: Daily 10-5. Adults $17.95, seniors 62 & up $14.95, children 3-14 $12.95; members and children 2 & under no charge. Closed Thanksgiving; Christmas. &
Attendance: 440,000 (actual)

DR. HOWE-WAFFLE HOUSE AND MEDICAL MUSEUM, 120 Civic Center Dr., W., Santa Ana, CA 92701-7505. Tel.: 714-547-9645.
E-mail: sahps@sahps.org
Web Site: www.santaanahistory.com/house.html
Key Personnel: Chm. & Pres. (V), Alison Young.
Institution Type/Description: Historic House & Medical Museum: home built in 1889 by Orange County physicians, Alvin & Willella Howe.
Hours & Admission Prices: Feb., April, June, Aug.-Sept. & Dec. 1st Sat. of month 12-4. Adults $5; discounts to members.
Attendance: 3,000 (estimated)

HERITAGE MUSEUM OF ORANGE COUNTY - KELLOGG HOUSE, 3101 W. Harvard St., Santa Ana, CA 92704. Tel.: 714-540-0404. Fax: 714-540-1932.
E-mail: info@heritagemuseumoc.org
Web Site: heritagemuseumoc.org
Key Personnel: Interim Exec. Dir., Kevin Cabrera.
Institution Type/Description: Historic House Museum: housed in the former home of Hiram Clay Kellogg; built in 1898.
Hours & Admission Prices: Fri. 1-5, Sat. 9-1:30, Sun. 11-3; other times by appointment. Adults $5, seniors & children $4; discounts to AAA members.

KIDSEUM, 1802 N. Main St., Santa Ana, CA 92706. Tel.: 714-480-1520.
E-mail: membership@bowers.org
Institution Type/Description: Children's Museum.
Hours & Admission Prices: Call for hours. Children 2 & over $10; children under 2 & members no charge.

LYON AIR MUSEUM, 19300 Ike Jones Rd., Santa Ana, CA 92707. Tel.: 714-210-4585. Fax: 714-210-4588. Facebook: Lyon Museum 1.
E-mail: info@lyonairmuseum.org
Web Site: www.lyonairmuseum.org
Key Personnel: Museum Coord., Jade Nguyen.
Institution Type/Description: Military History Museum.
Hours & Admission Prices: Daily 10-4. Adults $12, seniors & veterans $9, children 5-17 $6; discounts to groups; children under 5 no charge. Closed Christmas & Thanksgiving.
Attendance: 30,000 (estimated)

OLD COURTHOUSE MUSEUM, 211 W. Santa Ana Blvd., Santa Ana, CA 92701-7554. Tel.: 714-834-6605 & 973-6607. Fax: 714-834-2280.
E-mail: marshall.duell@ocparks.com
Web Site: www.ocparks.com
Key Personnel: Cur., Marshall Duell; Education Coord., Donna Brietfeller.
Institution Type/Description: County History Museum: housed in 1901 Richardsonian Romanesque style county courthouse.
Hours & Admission Prices: Mon.-Fri. 9-5. No charge. Closed state holidays. &
Attendance: 18,000 (estimated)

SANTA ANA COLLEGE ART GALLERY, 1530 W. 17th St., Santa Ana, CA 92706-3398. Tel.: 714-564-5615. Fax: 714-564-5629.
E-mail: mccabe_caroline@sac.edu
Web Site: www.sac.edu/art
Key Personnel: Dir., Phillip Marquez; Coord. Gallery, Caroline McCabe.
Institution Type/Description: College Art Gallery.
Hours & Admission Prices: Santa Ana College Main Art Gallery: School Year: Mon.-Wed. 10-2, Thurs. 10-2 & 6:30pm-8:30pm. No charge; donations accepted. Closed holidays; spring, summer & winter breaks. SAC Arts at the

Santora: Fri. 12-4, 1st Sat. each month 7pm-10pm. No charge; donations accepted. Closed holidays; spring & winter break. &
Attendance: 15,000 (estimated)

SANTA ANA ZOO, 1801 E. Chestnut Ave., Santa Ana, CA 92701-5001. Tel.: 714-647-6575. Fax: 714-953-7401.
E-mail: kyamaguchi@santa-ana.org
Web Site: santaanazoo.org
Key Personnel: Dir., Kent Yamaguchi; Cur., Ray Cosper; Registrar, Ethan Fisher; Education Specialist, Lauren Bergh.
Institution Type/Description: Zoo.
Hours & Admission Prices: Daily 10-5; last ticket sold 1 hour before closing. Adults $10, senior citizens 60 & over and children 3-12 $7; children 2 & under & FOSAZ members no charge. Closed New Year's Eve; Thanksgiving; Christmas Day. &
Attendance: 268,878 (actual)

Santa Barbara

ART, DESIGN & ARCHITECTURE MUSEUM UC, SANTA BARBARA, University of California, Santa Barbara, Rm. 1626 Art Bldg., Santa Barbara, CA 93106-7130. Tel.: 805-893-2951. Fax: 805-893-3013. Facebook: ADA Museum.
E-mail: lgarcia@museum.ucsb.edu
Web Site: www.museum.ucsb.edu
Formerly: University Art Museum, Santa Barbara
Key Personnel: Dir., Bruce Robertson; Cur. Exhibitions, Elyse A. Gonzales; Designer, Mehmet Dogu; Asst. Designer, Todd Anderson; ADC Cur., Jocelyn Gibbs; Project Archivist (ADC), Alexandra Adler.
Institution Type/Description: Art Museum.
Hours & Admission Prices: Wed.-Sun. 12-5. No charge; donations accepted. Closed major holidays. &
Attendance: 50,000 (estimated)

CARRIAGE AND WESTERN ART MUSEUM, 129 Castillo St., Santa Barbara, CA 93101-5725. Mailing Address: P.O. Box 1587, Santa Barbara, CA 93102-1587. Tel.: 805-962-2353.
Web Site: www.carriagemuseum.org
Key Personnel: Pres. (V), Peter Georgi; Museum Shop Mgr., Tom Peterson.
Institution Type/Description: History Museum.
Hours & Admission Prices: Mon.-Fri. 9-3; groups by appointment. No charge; donations accepted. &
Attendance: 26,000 (estimated)

CASA DEL HERRERO, 1387 E. Valley Rd., Santa Barbara, CA 93108-1202. Mailing Address: P.O. Box 5612, Santa Barbara, CA 93150-5612. Tel.: 805-565-5653. Fax: 805-969-2371.
E-mail: info@casadelherrero.com
Web Site: www.casadelherrero.com
Formerly: The Casa del Herrero Foundation
Key Personnel: Dir., Molly Barker; Devel., Olga Rogers; Volunteer Dir., Susannah Gordon.
Institution Type/Description: Historic House Museum: former home of George Fox Steedman designed by architect George Washington Smith, built in 1925. National Historic Landmark.
Hours & Admission Prices: Public Tours: Wed. & Sat. 10 & 2. Group Tours: Tues.-Sat. 10 & 2 by appointment. Adults $20; discounts to National Trust for Historic Preservation; members no charge. Children under 10 not admitted. Closed New Year's Day; national holidays.
Attendance: 3,225 (estimated)

HISTORIC SANTA BARBARA COURTHOUSE, 1100 Anacapa St., Santa Barbara, CA 93101-2099. Mailing Address: City of Santa Barbara Planning Division, P.O. Box 1990, Santa Barbara, CA 93102-1990. Tel.: 805-962-6464.
E-mail: info@santabarbaracourthouse.org
Web Site: www.santabarbaracourthouse.org
Institution Type/Description: History Museum.
Hours & Admission Prices: Museum: Mon.-Fri. 8-5, Sat.-Sun. 10-4:30. Tours: Mon-Fri 10:30 & 2, Sat & Sun 2. No charge; donations accepted. Closed Christmas.

LA CASA DE LA RAZA, CESAR E. CHAVEZ CENTER, 601 E. Montecito, Santa Barbara, CA 93103. Tel.: 805-956-8581.
E-mail: manuelL@lacasadelaraza.org
Web Site: www.lacasadelaraza.org
Institution Type/Description: Cultural Center.
Hours & Admission Prices: Call for hours. No charge.

MOXI, THE WOLF MUSEUM OF EXPLORATION + INNOVATION, 125 State St., Santa Barbara, CA 93101. Mailing Address: P.O. Box 4808, Santa Barbara, CA 93140. Tel.: 805-708-2282.
E-mail: info@moxi.org
Web Site: www.moxi.org
Key Personnel: Exec. Dir., Sheila Cushman; Mgr. Mktg. & Communications, Martha Swanson.
Institution Type/Description: Science Museum.
Hours & Admission Prices: Daily 10-5. Adults $14, children 3-12 $10; members and children 2 & under no charge. Closed Thanksgiving; Christmas.

OLD MISSION SANTA BARBARA MUSEUM, 2201 Laguna St., Santa Barbara, CA 93105-3611. Tel.: 805-682-6067. Fax: 805-687-7841 & 6067.
E-mail: museumtours@sboldmission.org
Web Site: www.santabarbaramission.org
Formerly: Santa Barbara Mission Museum
Key Personnel: Museum Dir., Kristina W. Foss; Tour Administrator, Laura Foss; Gift Shop Mgr., Jean Cota; Museum Shop Mgr., JoAnn Cota.
Institution Type/Description: Mission Museum.
Hours & Admission Prices: Daily 9-4:15. Adults 18-64 $8, seniors 65 & up $6, youth 5-17 $3; discounts to active duty military; children under 4 no charge. Closed Easter; Thanksgiving; Christmas. &

SANTA BARBARA BOTANIC GARDEN, 1212 Mission Canyon Rd., Santa Barbara, CA 93105-2199. Tel.: 805-682-4726. Fax: 805-563-0352.
E-mail: info@sbbg.org
Web Site: www.sbbg.org
Formerly: The Botanic Garden at Santa Barbara and Ojai
Key Personnel: Chm. Bd. Trustees, James O. Koopmans; Exec. Dir., Steve Windhager; Dir. Conservation & Research, Denise Knapp; Dir. Devel. & Communications, Nina Dunbar; Dir. Horticulture, Betsy Collins; Dir. Education, Frederique Lavoipierre; Visitor Services Mgr., Barbara Backlund; Museum Shop Mgr., Stacy Bloodworth.
Institution Type/Description: Arboretum/Botanical Garden: located at site of Old Mission Dam & Aqueduct.
Hours & Admission Prices: March-Oct. daily 9-6; Nov.-Feb. daily 9-5. Adults $10, seniors 60 & over, youth 13-17, college students & active military $8, children 2-12 $6; discounts to AAM members; members, uniformed military & children under 2 no charge. Closed New Year's Day; Thanksgiving; Christmas Eve & Day; occasional special events.
Attendance: 96,000 (actual)

SANTA BARBARA CONTEMPORARY ARTS FORUM, 653 Paseo Nuevo, Santa Barbara, CA 93101-3392. Tel.: 805-966-5373. Fax: 805-962-1421.
E-mail: lmermel@sbcaf.org
Web Site: www.sbcaf.org
Key Personnel: Exec. Dir., Miki Garcia; Communications Coord., Lauren Mermel; Dir. Operations, Margie Yahyavi.
Institution Type/Description: Contemporary Arts Center.
Hours & Admission Prices: Tues.-Sat. 11-5, Sun. 12-5. No charge; donations accepted. &

THE SANTA BARBARA HISTORICAL MUSEUM, 136 E. De la Guerra St., Santa Barbara, CA 93101-2205. Tel.: 805-966-1601. Fax: 805-966-1603.
E-mail: media@sbhistorical.org
Web Site: sbhistorical.org
Key Personnel: Pres., Bd. Trustees, Sharon Bradford; Exec. Dir., Lynn Bittner; Acting Collections Mgr., Cherie Summers; Dir. Research, Michael Redmon; Dir. Mktg. & Events, Dacia Harwood; Dir. Membership, Jeanne M. Buchanan; Museum Tech. & Dir. Education, Adela Lua; Visitor Svcs. Coord., Lauren Trujillo.
Institution Type/Description: Local History Museum.
Hours & Admission Prices: Tues.-Sat. 10-5, Sun. 12-5. Suggested Donation: general $7, seniors $5. Closed New Year's Day; Easter; Memorial Day; Independence Day; Thanksgiving; Christmas. &
Attendance: 30,000 (estimated)

SANTA BARBARA MARITIME MUSEUM, 113 Harbor Way, Ste. 190, Santa Barbara, CA 93109-2344. Tel.: 805-962-8404. Fax: 805-962-7634.
E-mail: museum@sbmm.org
Web Site: www.sbmm.org
Key Personnel: Pres., Gail Anikouchine; Exec. Dir., Greg Gorga; Vice Pres., Don Barthelmess; Deputy Dir., Emily Falke.
Institution Type/Description: Maritime Museum.

Hours & Admission Prices: Memorial Day-Labor Day Thurs.-Tues. 10-6; Sept.-May Thurs.-Tues. 10-5. Adults $7, seniors, students, youth 6-17 $4, children 1-5 $2; members, CAMM & AASLH members no charge. Closed New Year's Day; Thanksgiving; Christmas. &
Attendance: 28,000 (actual)

SANTA BARBARA MUSEUM OF ART, 1130 State St., Santa Barbara, CA 93101-2746. Tel.: 805-963-4364. Fax: 805-966-6840.
E-mail: info@sbma.net
Web Site: www.sbma.net
Key Personnel: Chm. Bd. Trustees (V), John C. Bishop; Robert & Mercedes Eichholz Dir. & C.E.O., Larry J. Feinberg; C.F.O., James Hutchinson; Dir. Devel., Barbara Ben-Horin; Dir. Education, Patsy Hicks; Dir. Facilities & Installations, John Coplin; Dir. HR, Margot Dement; Dir. IT, Joseph Price; Asst. Dir. & Chief Cur., Eik Kahng; Elizabeth Atkins Cur. Asian Art, Susan Shin-tsu Tai; Cur. Contemporary Art, Julie Joyce; Registrar, Sandy Davis; Retail & Visitor Services Mgr., John Reilly; Public Rels. Mgr., Katrina Carl.
Institution Type/Description: Art Museum.
Hours & Admission Prices: Tues., Wed, Fri-Sun. 11-5, Thurs. 11-8. Adults $10, seniors, youth 6-17 & students w/I.D. $6; discounts to AAM & ICOM members; active US military & their families, museum members, Santa Barbara County students (K-college) & teachers (K-12) and children under 6 no charge. Closed some holidays. &
Attendance: 150,000 (estimated)

SANTA BARBARA MUSEUM OF NATURAL HISTORY, 2559 Puesta del Sol, Santa Barbara, CA 93105-2998. Tel.: 805-682-4711. Fax: 805-569-3170.
E-mail: info@sbnature2.org
Web Site: www.sbnature.org
Key Personnel: Pres. & C.E.O., Luke Swetland; C.O.O., Diane E. Wondolowski; Dir. Devel., Caroline Grange; Dir. Mktg., Briana Sapp Tivey; Dir. Visitor Svcs., Amy Carpenter; Dir. Exhibits, Frank Hein; Dir. Education, Justin Canty; Volunteer Mgr., Rebecca Fagan-Coulter; Information Systems Mgr., Phillip Morones; Membership Mgr., Leana Orsua; Cur. Collections & Research, Dr. Henry Chaney; Librarian, Terri Sheridan.
Institution Type/Description: Natural History Museum.
Hours & Admission Prices: Daily 10-5. Adults $12, seniors 65 & up and teens 13-17 $8, children 2-12 $7; discounts to groups, ASTC & AAM members; children under 2 & members no charge. Closed New Year's Day; last Saturday in June; Thanksgiving Day; Christmas Day. &
Attendance: 212,000 (estimated)

SANTA BARBARA MUSEUM OF NATURAL HISTORY SEA CENTER, 211 Stearns Wharf, Santa Barbara, CA 93101. Tel.: 805-962-2526.
E-mail: lswetland@sbnature2.org
Web Site: www.sbnature.org/seacenter
Formerly: Ty Warner Sea Center
Key Personnel: Sr. Mgr., Richard Smalldon; Volunteer Mgr., Shalina Peterson; Programs Coord., Ed Sweeney; School & Teacher Services Coord., Steve Keller.
Institution Type/Description: Aquarium & Marine Museum.
Hours & Admission Prices: Daily 10-5. Adults $9, seniors 65 & over and youth 13-17 $8, children 2-12 $7; children under 2 & members no charge. Closed New Year's Day; Thanksgiving; Christmas.
Attendance: 212,000 (estimated)

SANTA BARBARA ORCHID ESTATE, 1250 Orchid Dr., Santa Barbara, CA 93111-2914. Tel.: 805-967-1284, 800-553-3387. Fax: 805-683-3405.
E-mail: sboe@sborchid.com
Web Site: www.sborchid.com
Institution Type/Description: Orchid Estate.
Hours & Admission Prices: Mon.-Sat. 8-4:30, Sun. 11-4. Closed New Year's Day; Presidents' Day; Easter; Memorial Day; Independence Day; Labor Day; Thanksgiving; Christmas.

SANTA BARBARA TRUST FOR HISTORIC PRESERVATION, 123 E. Canon Perdido, Santa Barbara, CA 93101-2215. Tel.: 805-965-0093. Fax: 805-568-1999.
E-mail: docjj@silcom.com
Web Site: www.sbthp.org
Key Personnel: Dir., Dr. Jarrell Jackman; Chm. (V), Terease Chin; Treas., Elliot Brownlee; Devel. & Public Rels., Christa Clark Jones; Education, Melissa Chatfield; Cur., Anne Peterson; Archivist, Madison Lowery; Museum Shop Mgr., Marguerite Williams.
Institution Type/Description: Historic Buildings: El Presidio de Santa Barbara State Historic Park - adobe fort built by the Spanish as they colonized California in the late 18th century. Casa de la Guerra - adobe house, home of early 19th century commandant of El Presidio.

Hours & Admission Prices: El Presidio: daily 10:30-4:30. Casa de la Guerra: Thurs.-Sun. 12-4. Adults $5; discounts to seniors & AAM members; members no charge. Closed Thanksgiving; Christmas. &
Attendance: 20,000 (actual)

SANTA BARBARA ZOOLOGICAL GARDENS, 500 Ninos Dr., Santa Barbara, CA 93103-3798. Tel.: 805-962-5339. Fax: 805-962-1673. Facebook: Santa Barbara Zoo.
E-mail: zooinfo@sbzoo.org
Web Site: www.sbzoo.org
Key Personnel: C.E.O., Richard Block.
Institution Type/Description: Zoo.
Hours & Admission Prices: Daily 10-5, Thanksgiving 10-3:30. Adults 13-64 $15, children 2-12 $10, senior citizens 65 & up $12; discounts to AZA members; children under 2 & members no charge. Christmas Eve & Day; check website for changes. &
Attendance: 431,753 (actual)

UNIVERSITY OF CALIFORNIA, SANTA BARBARA - WOMEN'S CENTER ART GALLERY, Student Resource Bldg., 1st Fl., Santa Barbara, CA 93106-7190. Tel.: 805-893-3778. Fax: 805-893-3289.
E-mail: kim.equinoa@sa.ucsb.edu
Web Site: wgse.sa.ucsb.edu/art-gallery
Institution Type/Description: Art Gallery.
Hours & Admission Prices: Mon.-Thurs. 9-9, Fri. 9-5.

WESTMONT RIDLEY - TREE MUSEUM OF ART, 955 La Paz Rd., Santa Barbara, CA 93108-1099. Tel.: 805-565-6162. Fax: 805-565-7161.
E-mail: museum@westmont.edu
Web Site: www.westmontmuseum.org
Formerly: Reynolds Gallery at Westmont College
Key Personnel: Dir., Judy L. Larson, Ph.D.
Institution Type/Description: Art Museum.
Hours & Admission Prices: Mon.-Fri. 10-4, Sat. 11-5. No charge. Closed college holidays. &
Attendance: 5,000 (actual)

Santa Clara

DE SAISSET MUSEUM, SANTA CLARA UNIVERSITY, 500 El Camino Real, Santa Clara, CA 95053. Tel.: 408-554-4528. Fax: 408-554-7840.
E-mail: desaissetmuseum@scu.edu
Web Site: www.scu.edu/desaisset
Key Personnel: Dir., Rebecca M. Schapp; Asst. Dir., Lauren Baines; Exhibition Project Coord., Chris Sicat; Collections Mgr., Morgan Schlesinger; Sr. Admin. Asst., Megan Watt.
Institution Type/Description: Art & History Museum.
Hours & Admission Prices: Tues.-Sun. 11-4. No charge; donations accepted. Closed national holidays; Martin Luther King Jr. Day; Good Friday; Thanksgiving weekend; between exhibitions. &
Attendance: 10,500 (estimated)

EDWARD PETERMAN MUSEUM OF RAILROAD HISTORY, 1005 Railroad Ave., Santa Clara, CA 95050-4319. Tel.: 408-243-3969.
E-mail: info@sbhrs.org
Web Site: www.sbhrs.org
Key Personnel: C.E.O., Robert Marshall; Pres. (V), Michael Steckwell.
Institution Type/Description: History Museum: housed in the Santa Clara Depot; built in 1863.
Hours & Admission Prices: Tues. 6pm-9pm, Sat. 10-3. No charge; donations accepted. &
Attendance: 5,000 (estimated)

INTEL MUSEUM, Robert Noyce Bldg., 2200 Mission College Blvd., Santa Clara, CA 95054. Tel.: 408-765-5050.
E-mail: museum@intel.com
Web Site: www.intel.com/museum
Institution Type/Description: Corporate History, Science & Technology Museum.
Hours & Admission Prices: Mon.-Fri. 9-6, Sat. 10-5. No charge. Closed New Year's Day; Washington's Birthday; Memorial Day; Independence Day; Labor Day; Thanksgiving; Christmas. &
Attendance: 116,847 (actual)

TRITON MUSEUM OF ART, 1505 Warburton Ave., Santa Clara, CA 95050-3791. Tel.: 408-247-3754. Fax: 408-247-3796.

E-mail: staff@tritonmuseum.org
Web Site: www.tritonmuseum.org
Key Personnel: Exec. Dir., Jill Meyers; Pres. (V), Jeff Bramscreiber; Registrar & Assoc. Cur., Stephanie Learmonth; Chief Cur., Preston Metcalf.
Institution Type/Description: Art Museum & Center.
Hours & Admission Prices: Tues.-Sat. 11-5, Sun. 12-4. No charge; donations accepted. Closed national holidays. &
Attendance: 40,000 (estimated)

Santa Cruz

ELOISE PICKARD SMITH GALLERY, Cowell College, University of California, Santa Cruz, CA 95064. Tel.: 831-459-2953.
Web Site: cowell.ucsc.edu/smith.gallery/main.php
Key Personnel: Cur., Joan Blackmer.
Institution Type/Description: Art Gallery.
Hours & Admission Prices: Tues.-Sun. 11-4. &
Attendance: 3,200

MARY PORTER SESNON ART GALLERY, UC Santa Cruz, Porter College, Santa Cruz, CA 95064. Mailing Address: Porter Faculty Svcs., Porter College, UC Santa Cruz, Santa Cruz, CA 95064. Tel.: 831-459-3606. Fax: 831-459-3535.
E-mail: sgraham@ucsc.edu
Web Site: arts.ucsc.edu/sesnon
Key Personnel: Dir. & Cur., Shelby Graham; Gallery Mgr. & Asst. Cur., Mark Shunney.
Institution Type/Description: Art Gallery.
Hours & Admission Prices: Sept.-June 15 Tues.-Sat. 12-5. No charge; donations accepted. &
Attendance: 3,500 (estimated)

MISSION SANTA CRUZ, 130 Emmet St., Santa Cruz, CA 95060. Mailing Address: 210 High St., Santa Cruz, CA 95060. Tel.: 831-426-5686. Fax: 831-423-1043.
E-mail: info@parks.ca.gov
Key Personnel: Dir., Betty Pedrazzi, I.H.M.
Institution Type/Description: Religious Museum.
Hours & Admission Prices: Tues.-Sat. 10-4, Sun. 10-2. No charge; donations accepted. Closed holidays.

MUSEUM OF ART AND HISTORY AT THE MCPHERSON CENTER, 705 Front St., Santa Cruz, CA 95060-4508. Tel.: 831-429-1964. Fax: 831-429-1954.
E-mail: director@santacruzmah.org
Web Site: www.santacruzmah.org
Key Personnel: Exec. Dir., Nina Simon; Dir. Exhibitions, Susan Leask; Cur. Education, Ashley Carniglia; Administrative Mgr., Nicole Campbell; Dir. Membership, Karen Bush; Mgr. Visitors & Volunteers, Diana Kapsner; Cur. History & Registrar, Marla Novo; Program Assoc., Emily Hope Dobkin; Dir. Community Programs, Stacey Marie Garcia.
Institution Type/Description: Museum of Art & History, Archives Library on Site.
Hours & Admission Prices: Tues.-Sun. 11-5. Adults $5, students 18 and over & senior citizens $4; members, students under 18 & children under 12 no charge. Closed legal holidays. &
Attendance: 36,000 (estimated)

SANTA CRUZ ART LEAGUE, INC., 526 Broadway, Santa Cruz, CA 95060-4622. Tel.: 831-426-5787.
E-mail: doreen@scal.org
Web Site: www.scal.org
Key Personnel: Pres. (V), T. Mike Walker; Administrative Dir., Doreen Davis.
Institution Type/Description: Art Gallery.
Hours & Admission Prices: Wed.-Sat. 12-5, Sun. 12-4. No charge; donations accepted. &
Attendance: 20,000

UC SANTA CRUZ ARBORETUM, University of California, 1156 High St., Santa Cruz, CA 95064-1077. Tel.: 831-502-2998. Fax: 831-502-2323. Facebook: UCSC Arboretum.
E-mail: arboretum@ucsc.edu
Web Site: arboretum.ucsc.edu
Key Personnel: Exec. Dir., Martin Quigley, Ph.D.; Pres. (V), Andrea Jesse; Chm. (V), Katie Cordes; Cur. of New Zealand Collection, Thomas Sauceda; Office Mgr., Theresa Milam; Cur. Australian Collection, Melinda Kralj; Cur. Native Collection, Rick Flores.
Institution Type/Description: Arboretum & Botanical Gardens.

Hours & Admission Prices: Daily 9-5. Adults $5, children 2-17 $2; members no charge. &
Attendance: 21,000 (actual)

Santa Fe Springs

HATHAWAY RANCH MUSEUM, 11901 E. Florence Ave., Santa Fe Springs, CA 90670-4494. Tel.: 562-777-3444. Fax: 562-945-1892.
E-mail: hathawayranch@gmail.com
Web Site: hathawayranch.org
Key Personnel: C.E.O. & Exec. Dir., Francine Rippy; Pres. Bd., Virginia Boles.
Institution Type/Description: History Museum.
Hours & Admission Prices: Mon.-Tues. & Thurs. 11-4, Fri.-Sun. & group tours by appointment. No charge; donations accepted. Closed major holidays.
Attendance: 1,200 (estimated)

Santa Margarita

SANTA MARGARITA RANCH HOUSE NATIONAL HISTORIC SITE, 9000 Yerba Buena Ave., Santa Margarita, CA 93453. Mailing Address: c/o Camp Pendleton Historical Society, P.O. Box 5497, Oceanside, CA 92052. Tel.: 760-725-5758. Fax: 760-725-5727.
E-mail: mcbcampen_history@usmc.mil
Web Site: www.pendleton.usmc.mil
Key Personnel: Dir., Faye Jonason; Chm. (V), Lt. Col. Paul Durrance, USMC (Ret.); Pres. Historical Society, Col. Richard Rothwell, USMC (Ret.).
Institution Type/Description: National Historic House Site.
Hours & Admission Prices: Tours: by appointment. Entry to base requires current proof of insurance, registration & ID. No charge; donations accepted. Closed for Marine Special Liberty. &
Attendance: 6,000 (estimated)

Santa Maria

THE NATURAL HISTORY MUSEUM OF SANTA MARIA, 412 S. McClelland, Santa Maria, CA 93454-5117. Mailing Address: P. O. Box 5254, Santa Maria, CA 93456-5254. Tel.: 805-614-0806. Fax: 805-614-0806.
E-mail: naturalhistroy.santamaria@verizon.net
Web Site: www.naturalhistorysantamaria.org
Formerly: Samuel J. Perry Natural History Museum
Key Personnel: Pres., Lora Carter; Chm. (V), Bill Decker; Sec., Laura Dias; Treas., Tahir Masood.
Institution Type/Description: Natural History Museum: housed in the historic Hart Home.
Hours & Admission Prices: Wed.-Sat. 11-4, Sun. 1-4. No charge; donations accepted. Closed holidays. &
Attendance: 4,850 (actual)

SANTA MARIA MUSEUM OF FLIGHT, INC., 3015 Airpark Dr., Santa Maria, CA 93455-1821. Tel.: 805-922-8758. Fax: 805-922-8958.
E-mail: smmof@msn.com
Web Site: www.smmof.org
Key Personnel: Pres., Michael Geddry, Sr.; Registrar, Dan Mahoney; Museum Shop Mgr., Tom Reedy.
Institution Type/Description: Aeronautics Museum.
Hours & Admission Prices: Fri.-Sun. 10-4; groups & other times by appointment. Adults $5, seniors $4, children 12-17 & college students $3, children 7-11 $2; school tours $1; members, military & their dependents no charge. Closed New Year's Day; Christmas. &
Attendance: 10,000 (estimated)

SANTA MARIA VALLEY DISCOVERY MUSEUM, 705 S. McClelland St., Santa Maria, CA 93454-5122. Tel.: 805-928-8414.
E-mail: programs@smvdiscoverymuseum.org
Web Site: www.smvdiscoverymuseum.org
Institution Type/Description: Children's Museum.
Hours & Admission Prices: Tues.-Sat. 10-5, Sun. 12-4. Admission $6 per person; members & children under 2 no charge. &
Attendance: 30,000 (actual)

SANTA MARIA VALLEY HISTORICAL MUSEUM, 616 S. Broadway, Santa Maria, CA 93454-5111. Tel.: 805-922-3130.
E-mail: smvhsmuseum@outlook.com
Web Site: www.smvrhm.org
Formerly: Santa Maria Valley Historical Society, Inc.

Key Personnel: Pres., E.J. Zematitis; Museum Dir., Lucinda Ransick; Sec., Jim Enos.
Institution Type/Description: General Museum: housed in building constructed on site of c.1900 1st municipal water works.
Hours & Admission Prices: Tues.-Sat. 12-5. No charge; donations accepted. &
Attendance: 4,320 (estimated)

Santa Monica

ANGELS ATTIC MUSEUM, 516 Colorado Ave., Santa Monica, CA 90401. Tel.: 310-394-8331. Fax: 310-656-6865.
E-mail: info@angelsattic.com
Web Site: www.angelsattic.com
Key Personnel: Museum Dir., Nicole Dickerson; Dir., Eleanor La Vove; Museum Shop Mgr., Susan Baker.
Institution Type/Description: Toy & Doll Museum: housed in a c.1895 Queen Anne Victorian House.
Hours & Admission Prices: Thurs.-Sun. 12:30-4:30. Adults $6.50; discounts to seniors & children under 12. &
Attendance: 5,000 (estimated)

CALIFORNIA HERITAGE MUSEUM, 2612 Main St., Santa Monica, CA 90405-4002. Tel.: 310-392-8537. Facebook: California Heritage Museum.
E-mail: calmuseum@earthlink.net
Web Site: californiaheritagemuseum.org
Key Personnel: Dir., Tobi Smith.
Institution Type/Description: Fine Art & Decorative Art Museum.
Hours & Admission Prices: Wed.-Sun. 11-4. Adults $10, senior citizens & students $5; children under 12, military, veterans & members no charge. Closed major holidays &
Attendance: 17,500 (estimated)

FIRST INDEPENDENT GALLERY, Bergamot Station G6, 2525 Michigan Ave., Santa Monica, CA 90404. Tel.: 310-829-0345. Fax: 310-829-7612.
E-mail: fig@figgallery.com
Web Site: www.figgallery.com
Institution Type/Description: Art Gallery.
Hours & Admission Prices: Wed.-Sat. 11-5; other times by appointment.

SANTA MONICA HISTORY MUSEUM, 1350 7th St., Santa Monica, CA 90401. Mailing Address: P.O. Box 3059, Santa Monica, CA 90408-3059. Tel.: 310-395-2298. Fax: 310-395-2290 (call first).
E-mail: info@smhistory.org
Web Site: www.santamonicahistory.org
Key Personnel: Pres. & C.E.O., Louise Gabriel; Chm. (V), Richard Bandini Johnson; Museum Shop Mgr., Danielle Lewis.
Institution Type/Description: History Museum.
Hours & Admission Prices: Tues. & Thurs. 12-8, Wed. 10-4, Fri-Sat. 11-5. Adults $5, seniors & students $3; discounts to AAM members; children 12 & under and members no charge. &
Attendance: 2,000 (actual)

SANTA MONICA PIER AQUARIUM, 1600 Ocean Front Walk, Santa Monica, CA 90401. Tel.: 310-393-6149.
E-mail: info@santamonica.com
Web Site: www.healthebay.org/smpa
Institution Type/Description: Aquarium.
Hours & Admission Prices: April-Aug. Tues.-Fri. 2-6, Sat.-Sun. 12:30-6; Sept.-March Tues.-Fri. 2-5, Sat.-Sun. 12:30-5. Adults 12 & over $5; discounts to groups; children under 12 no charge.
Attendance: 85,000 (actual)

Santa Paula

AGRICULTURE MUSEUM, 926 Railroad Ave., Santa Paula, CA 93060. Tel.: 805-525-3100. Fax: 805-525-0484.
E-mail: ebrokaw@venturamuseum.org
Web Site: venturamuseum.org
Institution Type/Description: Agriculture Museum.
Hours & Admission Prices: Wed.-Sun. 10-4. Adults $5, seniors, students & AAA members $3, children 6-17 $1; children 5 & under no charge.

AVIATION MUSEUM OF SANTA PAULA, 800 E. Santa Maria St., #E, Santa Paula, CA 93060. Tel.: 805-525-1109.
E-mail: amszp@verizon.net
Web Site: www.aviationmuseumofsantapaula.org
Key Personnel: Museum Shop Mgr., Theresa Marvel.

Institution Type/Description: History Museum.
Hours & Admission Prices: Call for hours. No charge; donations accepted. &
Attendance: 18,000 (estimated)

CALIFORNIA OIL MUSEUM, 1001 E. Main St., Santa Paula, CA 93060-2809. Mailing Address: P.O. Box 48, Santa Paula, CA 93061-0048. Tel.: 805-933-0076. Fax: 805-933-0096. Facebook: California Oil Museum.
E-mail: info@caolimuseum.org
Web Site: www.caoilmuseum.org
Formerly: Santa Paula Union Oil Museum
Institution Type/Description: California Oil History & Earth Science Museum.
Hours & Admission Prices: Museum: Wed.-Sun. 10-4. Guided Tours: by appointment. Suggested donation: $4. Closed major holidays.
Attendance: 12,000 (actual)

SANTA PAULA ART MUSEUM, 117 N. 10th St., Santa Paula, CA 93060-2877. Tel.: 805-525-5554.
E-mail: info@santapaulaartmuseum.org
Key Personnel: Exec. Dir., Jennifer Heighton.
Institution Type/Description: Art Museum.
Hours & Admission Prices: Wed.-Sat. 10-4, Sun. 12-4. Adults $4, seniors $3; members & students no charge. &
Attendance: 5,000 (estimated)

Santa Rosa

CALIFORNIA INDIAN MUSEUM & CULTURAL CENTER, 5250 Aero Dr., Santa Rosa, CA 95403-8069. Tel.: 707-579-3004. Fax: 707-579-9019.
E-mail: CIMandCC@aol.com
Web Site: www.cimcc.org
Key Personnel: Pres. (Pomo), Andrew Maisel; Vice Pres., Jerry Burroni; Exec. Dir., Nicole Myers-Lim; Project Mgr., David Lim; Devel. Specialist, Carol Oliva; Administrative Asst., Ramona Cruz.
Institution Type/Description: Indian Museum.
Hours & Admission Prices: Mon.-Fri. 9-5. No charge; donations accepted.

CHARLES M. SCHULZ MUSEUM AND RESEARCH CENTER, 2301 Hardies Lane, Santa Rosa, CA 95403-2668. Tel.: 707-579-4452. Fax: 707-579-4436. Facebook: Schulz Museum.
E-mail: inquiries@schulzmuseum.org
Web Site: schulzmuseum.org
Key Personnel: Dir., Karen Johnson; Pres. (V), Jean F. Schulz; Mktg. Dir., Gina Huntsinger; Education Dir., Jessica Ruskin; Collections Mgr., Dinah Houghtaling; Exhibitions Mgr., Lauren Faulkner.
Institution Type/Description: Art Museum.
Hours & Admission Prices: Memorial Day to Labor Day Mon.-Fri. 11-5, Sat.-Sun. 10-5; Labor Day to Memorial Day Mon. & Wed.-Fri. 11-5, Sat.-Sun. 10-5. Adults $12, seniors $8, youth & students $5; discounts to AAM, CAM, AAA & WMA members; members and youth under 3 no charge. Closed New Year's Day; Easter; Independence Day; Thanksgiving; Christmas Eve & Day. &
Attendance: 80,000 (actual)

CHILDREN'S MUSEUM OF SONOMA COUNTY, 1835 W. Steele Ln., Santa Rosa, CA 95403-2628. Mailing Address: P.O. Box 12323, Santa Rosa, CA 95406-2323. Tel.: 707-308-4351. Fax: 707-658-1981.
E-mail: info@cmosc.org
Web Site: cmosc.org
Key Personnel: Founder & C.E.O., Collette Michaud; Chm. (V), Michael Kasper; C.F.O., Douglas Kay; Dir. Programs, Lauren Hodge; Dir. Devel., Cyndi Yoxall; Office Mgr., Janice Vink.
Institution Type/Description: Children's Museum.
Hours & Admission Prices: Call for hours. Adults & children $12, babies under 12 months & members no charge, seniors (62+) & military adults with ID $9; ACM reciprocal memberships with card and ID $6 (limit up to 6 people), EBT cardholders with card and ID $2 (limit up to 6 people, including the cardholder).
Attendance: 150,000 (estimated)

LUTHER BURBANK HOME & GARDENS, Santa Rosa Ave. at Sonoma Ave., Santa Rosa, CA 95402. Mailing Address: 100 Santa Rosa Ave., Rm. 10, Santa Rosa, CA 95404-4957. Tel.: 707-524-5445. Fax: 707-524-5827.
E-mail: burbankhome@lutherburbank.org
Web Site: www.lutherburbank.org
Key Personnel: Vice Chm., Daniel Flock; Chm. (V), Claire Borges; Treas., Toni Hower; Archivist, Rebecca Baker; Museum Shop Mgr., Sharlene McCaw.
Institution Type/Description: Historic House & Garden: 1884 Luther Burbank Home; 1889 greenhouse.

Hours & Admission Prices: April-Oct. Tues.-Sun. 10-3:30; groups & children's tours by appointment. Guided tours $7; Friends of Luther Burbank & cell phone audio tours no charge. Gardens: daily 8am to dusk. No charge. &
Attendance: 75,000 (actual)

MUSEUMS OF SONOMA COUNTY - THE HISTORY MUSEUM OF SONOMA COUNTY & THE ART MUSEUM OF SONOMA COUNTY, 425 Seventh St., Santa Rosa, CA 95401-5233. Tel.: 707-579-1500. Fax: 707-579-4849. Facebook: Museums of Sonoma County.
E-mail: info@museumsc.org
Web Site: www.sonomacountymuseum.org
Key Personnel: Exec. Dir., Diane Evans; Chm. (V), Henry Beaumont; Mgr. Operations, Katie Azanza; Cur. Exhibitions, Eric Stanley; Community Outreach & Volunteer Coord., Cynthia Leung.
Institution Type/Description: Art & History Museum.
Hours & Admission Prices: Tues.-Sun. 11-5. Adults $10, seniors, students & disabled $7; discounts to NARM members; children under 12, school groups, and museum, AAM & ICOM members no charge. Closed New Year's Day; Presidents' Day; Memorial Day; Independence Day; Labor Day; Thanksgiving; Christmas. &
Attendance: 25,000 (estimated)

PACIFIC COAST AIR MUSEUM, One Air Museum Way, Santa Rosa, CA 95403. Tel.: 707-575-7900. Fax: 707-545-2813.
E-mail: director@pacificcoastairmuseum.org
Web Site: www.pacificcoastairmuseum.org
Key Personnel: Pres. (V), Lynn Hunt; Dir. Operations., Christina Olds; Dir. Mktg., Doug Clay; Gift Shop Mgr., Mike Lynch.
Institution Type/Description: Aircraft Museum.
Hours & Admission Prices: Tues., Thurs. & Sat.-Sun. 10-4. Adults $9, seniors 65 & over $7, child 6-17 $5; discount to California Assoc. of Museums; active & retired military and children 5 & under no charge. Closed New Year's Day; Thanksgiving; Christmas. &
Attendance: 23,569 (actual)

ROBERT F. AGRELLA ART GALLERY, 1501 Mendocino Ave., Santa Rosa, CA 95401-4395. Tel.: 707-527-4298.
E-mail: rbreth@santarosa.edu
Web Site: www.santarosa.edu/art-gallery/index.shtml
Formerly: Santa Rosa Jr. College Art Gallery
Key Personnel: Dir., Renata Breth.
Institution Type/Description: College Art Gallery.
Hours & Admission Prices: Mon.-Thurs. 10-4, Sat. 12-4. No charge; donations accepted. Closed summers & all school holidays.

SAFARI WEST WILDLIFE PRESERVE, 3115 Porter Creek Rd., Santa Rosa, CA 95404-9655. Tel.: 707-579-2551, 800-626-2695. Fax: 707-579-8777.
E-mail: safariwest@safariwest.com
Web Site: www.safariwest.com
Key Personnel: Founder, C.E.O. & Pres, Peter Lang; Gen. Dir., Nancy Lang; Dir. Mktg. & Communications, Aphrodite Caserta; Dir., Mark DeWitt.
Institution Type/Description: Wildlife Preserve.
Hours & Admission Prices: Tours: 9am, 10am, 1pm, 2pm & 4pm by appointment. Adults $68, youth 3-12 $30, children 1-2 $10.

SANTA ROSA JUNIOR COLLEGE MUSEUM, 1501 Mendocino Ave., Santa Rosa, CA 95401-4332. Tel.: 707-527-4479. Fax: 707-524-1861.
E-mail: museum@santarosa.edu
Web Site: museum.santarosa.edu
Formerly: Jesse Peter Native American Art Museum.
Key Personnel: Dir., Theresa Molino; Exhibit Coord., Christine Vasquez.
Institution Type/Description: Multicultural Museum.
Hours & Admission Prices: Mon.-Fri. 9-12 & 1-4:30. No charge; donations accepted. Closed summers & all school holidays & breaks. &
Attendance: 17,000 (actual)

Santa Ynez

SANTA YNEZ VALLEY HISTORICAL MUSEUM, 3596 Sagunto St., Santa Ynez, CA 93460-9110. Mailing Address: P.O. Box 181, Santa Ynez, CA 93460-0181. Tel.: 805-688-7889. Fax: 805-688-1109.
E-mail: syvm@verizon.net
Web Site: www.santaynezmuseum.org
Key Personnel: Exec. Dir., Chris Bashforth; Pres., Randy Jones; Cur. Carriage House, Christopher McCarthy.
Institution Type/Description: History Museum.

Hours & Admission Prices: Wed.-Sun. 12-4. Adults $4; members and children 16 & under no charge. Closed major holidays. &
Attendance: 10,000 (estimated)

Santa Ysabel

MISSION SANTA YSABEL, 23013 Hwy. 79, Santa Ysabel, CA 92070. Mailing Address: P.O. Box 129, Santa Ysabel, CA 92070-0129. Tel.: 760-765-0810.
Institution Type/Description: Indian Museum.
Hours & Admission Prices: Daily 8-3. No charge; donations accepted.

Santee

CREATION AND EARTH HISTORY MUSEUM, 10946 Woodside Ave., N., Santee, CA 92071-3272. Mailing Address: Life and Light Foundation, 9336 Abraham Way, Santee, CA 92071-2861. Tel.: 619-599-1104.
E-mail: jayson.payne@creationsd.org
Web Site: www.creationsd.org
Formerly: ICR Museum of Creation & Earth History
Key Personnel: Dir., Jayson Payne; C.E.O., John Van Duzer; Pres., Tom Cantor.
Institution Type/Description: Earth History & Science Museum.
Hours & Admission Prices: Mon.-Sat. 10-6, Sun. 1-6. Adults $8, military & seniors $6, children 5-12 $3; discounts on Groupon; members no charge. Guided Tours: $39. Closed New Year's Day; Thanksgiving & day after; Christmas Eve & Day. &
Attendance: 32,000 (estimated)

Saratoga

HAKONE ESTATE AND GARDENS, 21000 Big Basin Way, Saratoga, CA 95070-5755. Mailing Address: Hakone Foundation, P.O. Box 2324, Saratoga, CA 95070. Tel.: 408-741-4994. Fax: 408-741-4993. Facebook: Saratoga Hakone.
E-mail: public-relations@hakone.com
Web Site: www.hakone.us
Key Personnel: Exec. Dir., Shozo Kagoshima; Pres. of Bd. (V), Ann Waltonsmith; Japanese Garden Specialist, Jabob Kellner; Event Mgr., Tony Barbatti.
Institution Type/Description: Japanese-style Gardens.
Hours & Admission Prices: Mon.-Fri. 10-5, Sat.-Sun. 11-5. Adults $8, seniors 65 & up and students 5-17 w/ID $6; children 4 & under and members no charge. Closed New Year's Day; Christmas Day.

MONTALVO ARTS CENTER, 15400 Montalvo Rd., Saratoga, CA 95070-6327. Mailing Address: P.O. Box 158, Saratoga, CA 95071-0158. Tel.: 408-961-5800. Fax: 408-961-5850.
Web Site: www.montalvoarts.org
Key Personnel: Exec. Dir., Angela McConnell; Pres. (V), Cathie Thermond; Dir. Mktg. & Communications, Diane Maxwell.
Institution Type/Description: Art Museum, Arboretum & Historic House/Site.
Hours & Admission Prices: Park & Grounds: daily 9-5. Gallery: Thurs.-Sun. 11-3. No charge, donations accepted. Closed New Year's Day; Thanksgiving; Christmas. &
Attendance: 250,000 (estimated)

YOUTH SCIENCE INSTITUTE, SANBORN NATURE CENTER, 16055 Sanborn Rd., Sanborn-Skyline Park, Saratoga, CA 95070-9746. Mailing Address: Youth Science Institute, 296 Garden Hill Dr., Los Gatos, CA 95032-7669. Tel.: 408-867-6940 ext. 27.
E-mail: sanborn@ysi-ca.org
Web Site: www.ysi-ca.org
Key Personnel: Exec. Dir., Diane Riccio.
Institution Type/Description: Youth & Science Museum.
Hours & Admission Prices: Open all year, by appointment only. No charge; donations accepted. Closed New Year's Day; Thanksgiving; Christmas. &
Attendance: 16,500 (estimated)

Sausalito

BAY AREA DISCOVERY MUSEUM, Fort Baker, 557 McReynolds Rd., Sausalito, CA 94965-2601. Tel.: 415-339-3900. Fax: 415-339-3901. Facebook: Bay Area Discovery Museum.
E-mail: contact@badm.org
Web Site: www.baykidsmuseum.org
Key Personnel: C.E.O., Karyn Flynn; Chair, Victoria Barret; C.F.O., Michelle Martinez; Vice Pres. Education Strategy, Elizabeth Rood; Vice Pres. External Rels., Brandy Vause; Assoc. Dir. Communications & Mktg., Amber Whiteside;

Dir. Operations & Facilities Mgmt., Scott Dahlman; Sr. Mgr. Visitor Services, Mark Giberson.
Institution Type/Description: Children's Museum.
Hours & Admission Prices: Tues.-Fri. 9-4, Sat. & Sun. 9-5. General $13.95, seniors and children 6-12 months $12.95; discounts to AAM, ACM, ASTC & CAA members; members & children under 6 months no charge. &
Attendance: 300,000 (actual)

SAN FRANCISCO BAY MODEL VISITOR CENTER, 2100 Bridgeway, Sausalito, CA 94965-1764. Tel.: 415-289-3007. Fax: 415-289-3004.
E-mail: steve@codeadvisors.com
Web Site: www.spn.usace.army.mil/bmvc/
Key Personnel: Chm. (V), Steve Machtinger; Park Mgr., Chris Gallagher.
Institution Type/Description: Park Museum: located within the Bay Model Regional Visitor Center, an hydraulic testing facility.
Hours & Admission Prices: Winter: Tues.-Sat. 9-4; Summer: Tues.-Fri. 9-4, Sat.-Sun. & holidays 10-5. No charge, donations accepted. &
Attendance: 117,059 (actual)

Scotts Valley

CANEPA MOTORSPORTS MUSEUM, 4900 Scotts Valley Dr., Scotts Valley, CA 95066. Tel.: 831-430-9940.
E-mail: info@canepa.com
Web Site: www.canepa.com
Institution Type/Description: Motorsports Museum.
Hours & Admission Prices: Mon.-Sat. 10-5.

Seal Beach

SEAL BEACH HISTORICAL SOCIETY/RED CAR MUSEUM, Electric Ave. & Main, Seal Beach, CA 90470. Mailing Address: P.O. Box 152, Seal Beach, CA 90740-0152. Tel.: 562-453-9762. Facebook.
E-mail: sbhsredcarmuseum@gmail.com
Web Site: www.sbhs-redcarmuseum.com
Key Personnel: Dir., Marie Antos; Pres. (V), Monique Atwood.
Institution Type/Description: Historic Train Car: a roving machine shop used to troubleshoot problems along the Pacific Electric LA-Newport Line; built in 1925.
Hours & Admission Prices: 2nd & 4th Sat. 12-3. No charge; donations accepted.
Attendance: 1,000 (estimated)

Sebastopol

WEST COUNTY MUSEUM, 261 S. Main St., Sebastopol, CA 95472. Tel.: 707-829-6711.
E-mail: raeswanson3710@sbcglobal.net
Web Site: www.sebastopol-farm-museum.org
Key Personnel: Dir., Jan King.
Institution Type/Description: History Museum: housed in the former Petaluma and Santa Rosa Electric Railway Depot; built in 1917.
Hours & Admission Prices: Thurs.-Sun. 1-4. No charge; donations accepted.
Attendance: 5,000 (estimated)

Shafter

MINTER FIELD AIR MUSEUM, 401 Vultee St., P.O. Box 445, Shafter, CA 93263-0445. Tel.: 661-393-0291. Facebook: @MinterFieldAirMuseum.
E-mail: mfam@minterfieldairmuseum.com
Web Site: www.minterfieldairmuseum.com
Key Personnel: Chm. Bd., Ronald Pierce; Vice Chm. Bd., Maj. Gen. James T. Whitehead, Jr., USAF (Ret); Vice Chm. Bd., Sam Kisselburg.
Institution Type/Description: Military Aeronautics Museum.
Hours & Admission Prices: Fri.-Sat. 10-2; other times by appointment. No charge; donations accepted. Closed most holidays. &
Attendance: 12,000 (estimated)

SHAFTER DEPOT MUSEUM, 150 Central Valley Hwy., Shafter, CA 93263-2002. Mailing Address: Shafter Historical Society, P.O. Box 1088, Shafter, CA 93263-1088. Tel.: 661-746-4423. Fax: 661-746-1620.
E-mail: hwfarms@sbcglobal.net
Key Personnel: Cur., Stan Wilson; Pres. (V), Helen Goede.
Institution Type/Description: History Museum
Hours & Admission Prices: Sat. 10-2; other times by appointment. No charge; donations accepted. &
Attendance: 900 (estimated)

Shasta

SHASTA STATE HISTORIC PARK, 15312 Hwy. 299 W., Shasta, CA 96087. Mailing Address: P.O. Box 2430, Shasta, CA 96087-2430. Tel.: 530-225-2065. Fax: 530-225-2038.
E-mail: lmartin@parks.ca.gov
Key Personnel: Cur., Lori Martin.
Institution Type/Description: State Park Museum.
Hours & Admission Prices: Thurs.-Sun. 10-5. Adults $3, children 17 & under $2. Closed New Year's Day; Thanksgiving; Christmas.
Attendance: 36,000 (actual)

Shoshone

SHOSHONE MUSEUM, 118 Hwy. 127, Shoshone, CA 92384. Mailing Address: P.O. Box 38, Shoshone, CA 92384-0038. Tel.: 760-852-4524. Facebook: Shoshone Museum.
E-mail: shoshonemuseum@gmail.com
Web Site: shoshonemuseum.org
Key Personnel: Pres. (V), Susan Sorrells.
Institution Type/Description: Historic Building: built in Greenwater in 1906, moved to Zabriskie & later to its present location where it served as a store & gas station.
Hours & Admission Prices: Wed.-Mon. 9-3. No charge; donations accepted. Closed Federal holidays. &
Attendance: 12,000 (actual)

Sierra City

SIERRA COUNTY HISTORICAL SOCIETY (KENTUCKY MINE MUSEUM), 100 Kentucky Mine Rd., Sierra City, CA 96125. Mailing Address: P.O. Box 260, Sierra City, CA 96125-0260. Tel.: 530-862-1310. Facebook.
E-mail: museum@sierracountyhistory.org
Web Site: www.sierracountyhistory.org
Key Personnel: Cur., Dianne Bruns; Pres., Mary Nourse; Vice Pres., Ernie Teague; Chm. Membership, Don Yegge; Treas., William Copren; Caretaker, Toni Strine.
Institution Type/Description: History Museum.
Hours & Admission Prices: Memorial Day to Labor Day Wed.-Sun. 10-4. Adults $1. Guided Tours: adults $7, children 17 & under $3.50; members & children under 6 no charge.
Attendance: 2,000 (estimated)

Silverado

TUCKER WILDLIFE SANCTUARY, 29322 Modjeska Canyon Rd., Silverado, CA 92676-9784. Tel.: 714-649-2760. Fax: 714-649-2760.
E-mail: kcornell@exchange.fullerton.edu
Web Site: www.tuckerwildlife.org
Key Personnel: Dir., Karon Cornell; Site Mgr., Marcella Gilchrist.
Institution Type/Description: Wildlife Sanctuary.
Hours & Admission Prices: Tues.-Sun. 9-4. Suggested Donation: $3 per person. Naturalist Guided Group Tours: $6 per person. Closed major holidays. &
Attendance: 30,000

Simi Valley

R.P. STRATHEARN HISTORICAL PARK AND MUSEUM, 137 Strathearn Place, Simi Valley, CA 93065-1605. Mailing Address: P.O. Box 940461, Simi Valley, CA 93094-0461. Tel.: 805-526-6453. Fax: 805-526-6462. Facebook: Strathearn Park.
E-mail: simimuseum@sbcglobal.net
Web Site: www.simihistory.com
Key Personnel: Dir., Patricia Havens; Pres. (V), Georgia Trumble.
Institution Type/Description: Historic Buildings.
Hours & Admission Prices: Tours: Wed.-Fri. 1 pm, Sat.-Sun. 1-4. Park: Mon.-Fri. 9-3. Requested Donation: adults $3; members and children 17 & under no charge. Closed Easter; Christmas.
Attendance: 6,000 (estimated)

RONALD REAGAN PRESIDENTIAL LIBRARY AND MUSEUM, 40 Presidential Dr., Simi Valley, CA 93065-0699. Tel.: 800-410-8354. Fax: 805-577-4074.
E-mail: info@reaganfoundation.org
Web Site: www.reaganlibrary.com
Key Personnel: Dir., R. Duke Blackwood; Registrar, Jennifer Torres; Gift Shop Mgr., Carolyn Mente.
Institution Type/Description: Presidential Library.

Hours & Admission Prices: Daily 10-5. Please visit website for admission prices. Closed New Year's Day; Thanksgiving; Christmas. &
Attendance: 400,000 (actual)

SANTA SUSANA DEPOT, 6503 Katherine Rd., Simi Valley, CA 93063-4786. Tel.: 805-581-3462.
E-mail: checkmate0072002@yahoo.com
Institution Type/Description: Historic Building: built by the Southern Pacific Railroad in 1903.
Hours & Admission Prices: Sat.-Sun. 1-4. Closed major holidays.
Attendance: 3,200

Soledad

MISSION NUESTRA SENORA DE LA SOLEDAD, 36641 Fort Romie Rd., Soledad, CA 93960. Mailing Address: P.O. Box 515, Soledad, CA 93960-0515. Tel.: 831-678-2586.
Web Site: missionsoledad.com
Key Personnel: Chm. (V) & Museum Shop Mgr., Kristen Dow; Pres. (V), Carlene Bell.
Institution Type/Description: Historical Religious Museum: a national historic register state landmark.
Hours & Admission Prices: Daily 10-4. Mass: 1st Sun. of month. No charge; donations requested. Closed New Year's Day; Easter; Independence Day; Thanksgiving; Christmas.
Attendance: 16,000 (estimated)

Solvang

ELVERHOJ MUSEUM OF HISTORY AND ART, 1624 Elverhoy Way, Solvang, CA 93463-2704. Mailing Address: P.O. Box 769, Solvang, CA 93464-0769. Tel.: 805-686-1211. Fax: 805-686-1822.
E-mail: info@elverhoj.org
Web Site: www.elverhoj.org
Key Personnel: C.E.O., Esther Jacobsen Bates.
Institution Type/Description: History. Danish Culture and Art Museum.
Hours & Admission Prices: Wed.-Sun. 11-4. No charge; suggested donation $5. Closed New Year's Day; Easter; Thanksgiving; Christmas Eve & Day. &
Attendance: 20,000 (actual)

HANS CHRISTIAN ANDERSEN MUSEUM, 1680 Mission Dr., Solvang, CA 93463-3602. Tel.: 805-688-2052.
E-mail: mail@bookloftsolvang.com
Key Personnel: Dir., Katheryn Mullina.
Institution Type/Description: General Museum.
Hours & Admission Prices: Daily 10-5; groups by appointment.
Attendance: 12,000 (estimated)

OLD MISSION SANTA INES, 1760 Mission Dr., Solvang, CA 93463-2625. Mailing Address: P.O. Box 408, Solvang, CA 93464-0408. Tel.: 805-688-4815. Fax: 805-686-4468.
E-mail: sheila.benedict@missionsantaines.org
Web Site: www.missionsantaines.org
Key Personnel: Archives, Sheila Benedict; Gift Shop Mgr., Sonia De Luna; Pastor, Fr. Michael Elshoff, O.F.M.Cap.; Assoc. Pastor, Fr. James Johnson, O.F.M.Cap.
Institution Type/Description: Historic Site & Historic Building: 1804 Old Mission Santa Ines.
Hours & Admission Prices: Winter & Summer: daily 9-4:30. Docent tours: $6, adults $5; discounts for groups; children under 12 no charge. Closed New Year's Day; Easter; Thanksgiving; Christmas. &
Attendance: 50,000 (estimated)

WILDLING MUSEUM OF ART & NATURE, 1511 B Mission Dr., Solvang, CA 93463. Tel.: 805-688-1082. Fax: 805-686-8339.
E-mail: info@wildlingmuseum.org
Web Site: www.wildlingmuseum.org
Formerly: Wildling Art Museum
Key Personnel: Exec. Dir., Stacey A. Otte; Pres. (V), Suzi Schomer; Treas., David Gledhill; Asst. Dir., Katie Pearson; Office Mgr., Laura Carloni.
Institution Type/Description: Art Museum.
Hours & Admission Prices: Wed.-Sun. 11-5. Adults $5, children 16 & under, AAM, ICOM & museum members no charge. Closed New Year's Day; Thanksgiving; Christmas. &
Attendance: 10,500 (actual)

Sonoma

SONOMA STATE HISTORIC PARK, 363 3rd St., W., Sonoma, CA 95476-5632. Tel.: 707-938-1519. Fax: 707-938-1406.
Web Site: www.parks.ca.gov

Key Personnel: Mission Guide, Jackie Barros; Chm. (V), Jennifer Hanson; Pres. (V), Rick Arent; State Park Ranger, Vince Anibale; Museum Cur., Carol A. Dodge; Museum Shop Mgr., Sue Vargas.
Institution Type/Description: State Historic Park Museum Complex.
Hours & Admission Prices: Daily 10-5. Adults $3, children 6-17 $2. Closed New Year's Eve. & Day; Thanksgiving; Christmas.
Attendance: 602,398 (actual)

SONOMA VALLEY HISTORICAL SOCIETY/DEPOT PARK MUSEUM, 270 First St., W., Sonoma, CA 95476. Mailing Address: P.O. Box 861, Sonoma, CA 95476-0861. Tel.: 707-938-1762.
E-mail: depotparkmuseum@comcast.net
Web Site: www.depotparkmuseum.org
Key Personnel: Pres., Carol Page; Mgr. & Dir., Sandi Hansen; Cur., Victoria Blackwell; Museum Shop Mgr., Debbie Nye.
Institution Type/Description: Art & History Museum.
Hours & Admission Prices: Fri.-Sun. 1-4. No charge; donations accepted. Closed some holidays. &
Attendance: 3,000 (estimated)

SONOMA VALLEY MUSEUM OF ART, 551 Broadway, Sonoma, CA 95476-6601. Mailing Address: P.O. Box 322, Sonoma, CA 95476-0322. Tel.: 707-939-7862. Fax: 707-939-1080.
E-mail: admin@svma.org
Web Site: www.svma.org
Key Personnel: Exec. Dir., Kate Eilertsen; Bd. Pres., Douglas Wilson.
Institution Type/Description: Art Museum.
Hours & Admission Prices: Wed.-Sun. 11-5 during exhibitions. Adults $5; discounts to groups of 15 or more and NARM, AAM & ICOM members; members, students K-12 & Sun. no charge. Closed New Year's Day; Presidents' Day; Memorial Day; Independence Day; Labor Day; Thanksgiving; Christmas. &
Attendance: 15,000 (actual)

Sonora

TUOLUMNE COUNTY MUSEUM & HISTORY CENTER, 158 W. Bradford Ave., Sonora, CA 95370-4920. Tel.: 209-532-1317.
E-mail: info@tchistory.org
Web Site: tchistory.org
Key Personnel: Chm. (V), John Brunskill.
Institution Type/Description: Historic Building: housed in a former jail built in 1857 and rebuilt in 1865 after being destroyed by a fire that killed the inmate who allegedly started it. Listed on the National Register of Historic Places.
Hours & Admission Prices: Call for hours. No charge; donations accepted.
Attendance: 1,500 (estimated)

South Lake Tahoe

LAKE TAHOE HISTORICAL SOCIETY & MUSEUM, 3058 Lake Tahoe Blvd., South Lake Tahoe, CA 96150-7810. Mailing Address: P.O. Box 18501, South Lake Tahoe, CA 96151-8501. Tel.: 530-541-5458.
E-mail: laketahoemuseum@att.net
Web Site: laketahoemuseum.org
Key Personnel: Chm. (V), Diane L. Johnson; Pres. (V), Catherine Whelan; Museum Shop Mgr., Kim Copel.
Institution Type/Description: Historical Society Museum.
Hours & Admission Prices: Memorial Day to Labor Day Wed.-Sun. 11-3. No charge; donations accepted.
Attendance: 2,640 (actual)

Stanford

ANDERSON COLLECTION AT STANFORD UNIVERSITY, 314 Lomita Dr., Stanford, CA 94305-5060. Tel.: 650-724-6184. Fax: 650-721-6105. Facebook: Anderson Collection Stanford University.
E-mail: aimees@stanford.edu
Web Site: anderson.stanford.edu
Key Personnel: Dir., Jason Linetzky.
Institution Type/Description: Art Museum.
Hours & Admission Prices: Wed. & Fri.-Mon. 11-5; Thurs. 11-8. No charge; donations accepted. &
Attendance: 90,000 (estimated)

CANTOR ARTS CENTER, STANFORD UNIVERSITY, 328 Lomita Drive at Museum Way, Stanford, CA 94305-5060. Tel.:

650-723-4177. Fax: 650-725-0464. Facebook: @CantorArtsCenter; Twitter: @cantorarts.
E-mail: agass@stanford.edu
Web Site: museum.stanford.edu
Formerly: Iris & B. Gerald Cantor Center for Visual Arts at Stanford University
Key Personnel: Chief Cur. & Assoc. Dir. Exhibits & Collections, Ali Gass; Cur. Prints, Drawings & Photographs, Elizabeth Mitchell; Adjunct Cur. Architecture & Design, Wim de Wit; Exhibition Registrar, Katie Clifford.
Institution Type/Description: Art Museum.
Hours & Admission Prices: Wed., Fri., Sat. Sun., Mon. 11-5, Thurs. 11-8. No charge; donations accepted. Closed Thanksgiving; Christmas. &
Attendance: 269,427 (estimated)

Stinson Beach

AUDUBON CANYON RANCH, 4900 Shoreline Hwy. One., Stinson Beach, CA 94970. Tel.: 415-868-9244. Fax: 415-868-1699.
E-mail: acr@egret.org
Web Site: www.egret.org
Key Personnel: Exec. Dir., John Petersen; Pres. Bd., Judy Prokupek; Treas., Bill Richardson; Museum Shop Mgr., Yvonne Pierce.
Institution Type/Description: Nature Center.
Hours & Admission Prices: April-July Sat.-Sun. & holidays 10-4, Tues.-Fri. by appointment. No charge; donations accepted. &
Attendance: 20,000 (estimated)

Stockton

ALAN SHORT GALLERY, 928 E. Rose St., Stockton, CA 95202-1849. Mailing Address: c/o DDSO, 5051 47th Ave., Sacramento, CA 95824-4036. Tel.: 209-462-8208 & 948-5759. Fax: 209-948-9042.
E-mail: asc@ddso.org
Web Site: www.ddso.org
Institution Type/Description: Art Museum.
Hours & Admission Prices: Daily 8-4. No charge; donations accepted. Closed national holidays

CHILDREN'S MUSEUM OF STOCKTON, 402 W. Weber Ave., Stockton, CA 95203-3108. Tel.: 209-465-4386. Fax: 209-465-4394.
E-mail: yremlinger@gmail.com
Web Site: www.childrensmuseumstockton.org
Key Personnel: Bd. Pres., Diane Batres; Dir., Yvette Remlinger.
Institution Type/Description: Children's Museum.
Hours & Admission Prices: Wed.-Fri. 9-4, Sat. 10-5, Sun. 12-5. Admission $6; discounts to school groups; children under one & members no charge. Closed New Year's Day; Thanksgiving; Christmas Eve & Day. &
Attendance: 60,000 (estimated)

THE HAGGIN MUSEUM, 1201 N. Pershing Ave., Stockton, CA 95203-1604. Tel.: 209-940-6311. Fax: 209-462-1404.
E-mail: info@hagginmuseum.org
Web Site: www.hagginmuseum.org
Key Personnel: Dir. Devel., Susan Obert; Cur. Education, Lisa Cooperman; Registrar, Erin Hicks; Museum Store Mgr., Lisa Falls; Coord. Membership & Mktg., Kristen Anema; Admin. Asst., Merylene Merengo.
Institution Type/Description: Art & History Museum.
Hours & Admission Prices: Wed.-Fri. 1:30-5, 1st & 3rd Thurs. each month 1:30-9, Sat.-Sun. 12-5. Adults $8, seniors $7, youth 10-17 $5; discounts to AAM & ICOM members; members & children under 10 no charge. Closed New Year's Day & day after; Easter; Independence Day; Thanksgiving & day after; Christmas Eve & Day. &
Attendance: 45,000 (estimated)

THE HERBARIUM OF THE UNIVERSITY OF THE PACIFIC, Classroom Bldg., Stockton, CA 95211. Mailing Address: Dept. Biological Sciences, Univ. of the Pacific, Stockton, CA 95211. Tel.: 209-946-2181. Fax: 209-946-3022.
E-mail: mbrunell@pacific.edu
Key Personnel: Cur., Mark Brunell.
Institution Type/Description: Herbarium.
Hours & Admission Prices: Mon.-Fri. 8-5. No charge; donations accepted. Closed university holidays. &

HOLT-ATHERTON SPECIAL COLLECTIONS, University of the Pacific Library, 3601 Pacific Ave., Stockton, CA 95211. Tel.: 209-946-2431 & 2404. Fax: 209-946-2942.

E-mail: trichards@pacific.edu
Web Site: library.pacific.edu/ha
Key Personnel: Archivist, Michael Wurtz; Special Collections Asst., Trish Richards.
Institution Type/Description: History Museum.
Hours & Admission Prices: Mon.-Fri. 10-5. Closed New Year's Eve & Day; Christmas Eve & Day.

STOCKTON FIELD AVIATION MUSEUM, 7430 C.E. Dixon St., Stockton, CA 95206. Tel.: 209-982-0273. Fax: 209-982-4832.
E-mail: museum@twinbeech.com
Web Site: www.twinbeech.com/STOCKTON_FIELD_PAGE.htm
Institution Type/Description: Aviation History Museum.
Hours & Admission Prices: Mon.-Fri. 8:30-5 by appointment. No charge, donations accepted. Closed holidays.

Suisun City

THE WESTERN RAILWAY MUSEUM, 5848 State Hwy. 12, Suisun City, CA 94585-9641. Tel.: 707-374-2978. Fax: 707-374-6742.
E-mail: info@wrm.org
Web Site: www.wrm.org
Key Personnel: C.E.O. & Chm. (V), John Haviland; Treas., Bob Towar; Gen. Mgr., Erika Hunt; Sec., Leanne Styczinski.
Institution Type/Description: Transportation Museum.
Hours & Admission Prices: Memorial Day-Labor Day Wed.-Sun. 10:30-5; Sept.-May Sat.-Sun. 10:30-5. Adults $10, seniors $9, children 2-14 $7; discounts to CAM & AAM members; members no charge. &
Attendance: 25,000 (actual)

Sunnyvale

THE LACE MUSEUM, 552 S. Murphy Ave., Sunnyvale, CA 94086-6116. Tel.: 408-730-4695.
E-mail: lacemuseum@gmail.com
Web Site: www.thelacemuseum.org
Key Personnel: C.E.O., Chm. (V) & Museum Shop Mgr., Suzanne Meyer.
Institution Type/Description: Lace Museum.
Hours & Admission Prices: Tues.-Sat. 11-4; tours by appointment. No charge; donations accepted. Private Tours: $3 per person. Closed New Year's Day; Thanksgiving & two days after; Christmas. &
Attendance: 3,500 (estimated)

SUNNYVALE HISTORICAL SOCIETY AND MUSEUM ASSOCIATION, 570 E. Remington Dr., Sunnyvale, CA 94087-2652. Mailing Address: P.O. Box 61301, Sunnyvale, CA 94088-1301. Tel.: 408-749-0220. Fax: 408-732-4726. Facebook: Sunnyvale Museum.
E-mail: info@heritageparkmuseum.org
Web Site: www.heritageparkmuseum.org
Key Personnel: Pres., Jim Reynolds; Vice Pres., Leslie Lawton; Dir., Laura Babcock; Museum Shop Mgr., Margaret Lawson.
Institution Type/Description: History Museum.
Hours & Admission Prices: Tues., Thurs. & Sun. 12-4; other times by appointment. No charge; donations accepted. Closed national holidays. &
Attendance: 6,000 (estimated)

Sunol

GOLDEN GATE RAILROAD MUSEUM, Niles Canyon Railway, Brightside Yard, 5550 Niles Canyon Rd., Sunol, CA 94586. Mailing Address: 1755 E. Bayshore Rd., Ste. 19A, Redwood City, CA 94063-4153. Tel.: 650-365-2472. Fax: 650-385-2473.
E-mail: 2472info@ggrm.org
Web Site: www.ggrm.org
Key Personnel: Pres. (V), Dave Hensarling; Mgr. Operations, Dave Roth; Treas., Ronald Vane.
Institution Type/Description: Railroad Museum; housed within the former U.S. Navy Hunters Point Shipyard.
Hours & Admission Prices: Call for details on hours and admissions.

Susanville

LASSEN HISTORICAL MUSEUM, 75 N. Weatherlow St., Susanville, CA 96130. Mailing Address: P.O. Box 321, Susanville, CA 96130-0321. Tel.: 530-257-3292.
E-mail: info@cityofsusanville.org
Key Personnel: Pres., Tony Jonas.
Institution Type/Description: Regional History Museum.

Hours & Admission Prices: Summer: Mon.-Fri. 10-4, Sat. 11-3; Winter: Tues.-Thurs. & Sat. 10-2; other times by appointment. No charge; donations accepted.

Sylmar

NETHERCUTT COLLECTION, 15151 Bledsoe St., Sylmar, CA 91342. Tel.: 818-364-6464. Fax: 818-364-6466.
E-mail: info@nethercuttcollection.org
Web Site: www.nethercuttcollection.org
Institution Type/Description: Automobile & Musical Instrument Museum.
Hours & Admission Prices: Thurs.-Sat. 10-1:30 by appointment. No charge. Closed New Year's Eve & Day; Memorial Day weekend; Independence Day; Labor Day weekend; Thanksgiving weekend; Christmas Eve, Day & week.

Taft

WEST KERN OIL MUSEUM, 1168 Wood St., Taft, CA 93268-4336. Mailing Address: P.O. Box 491, Taft, CA 93268-0491. Tel.: 661-765-6664. Fax: 661-765-9175.
E-mail: wkom491@gmail.com
Web Site: www.westkern-oilmuseum.org
Key Personnel: Dir., Jan McCall; Chm. (V), Michael McCormick; Pres. (V), Lane Frank.
Institution Type/Description: Oil History Museum.
Hours & Admission Prices: Thurs.-Sat. 10-4, Sun. 1-4. No charge; donations accepted. Closed New Year's Day; Thanksgiving; Christmas.
Attendance: 1,057 (estimated)

Tahoe City

GATEKEEPER'S MUSEUM & WATSON CABIN MUSEUM, 130 W. Lake Blvd., Tahoe City, CA 96145. Mailing Address: P.O. Box 6141, Tahoe City, CA 96145-6141. Tel.: 530-583-1762. Fax: 530-583-8992.
E-mail: info@northtahoemuseums.org
Web Site: www.northtahoemuseums.org
Formerly: Gatekeeper's Museum & Marion Steinbach Indian Basket Museum
Key Personnel: Museum Coord., Javier Rodriguez; Pres. (V), Nileta Morton; Vice Pres. Finance, Jim Phelan; Vice Pres. Governance, Carol Shaw; Vice Pres. Devel., Trudy Lesem.
Institution Type/Description: Historical Society Museum: site of prehistoric summer camping site & Washoe camp site.
Hours & Admission Prices: June-Sept. Wed.-Mon. 10-5; Oct.-May Fri.-Sat. 10-4; other times by appointment. Adults $5, seniors citizens 65 & over $4; discounts to active military; children under 12 & members no charge.
Attendance: 30,000 (estimated)

TAHOE MARITIME MUSEUM CLOSED, 401 W. Lake Blvd., Tahoe City, CA 96145. Mailing Address: P.O. Box 1907, Tahoe City, CA 96145. Tel.: 530-583-9283. Fax: 530-583-9283.
E-mail: info@tahoemaritime.org
Web Site: www.tahoemaritime.org
Key Personnel: Exec. Dir., Lora Nadolski; Pres. (V), Dave Olson.
Institution Type/Description: Maritime Museum.
Hours & Admission Prices: June-Oct. Thurs.-Tues. 10-5; Nov.-May Fri.-Sun. 10-4:30. Adults $5; members & children under 12 no charge.

Tahoma

PINE LODGE - HELLMAN EHRMAN ESTATE, Ed Z'berg Sugar Pine Point State Park, 7585/7595 Hwy. 89, Tahoma, CA 96142. Mailing Address: California State Parks, Sierra District HQ, P.O. Box 266, Tahoma, CA 96142-0266. Tel.: 530-525-5055. Fax: 530-525-3380.
E-mail: natalie.davenport@perks.ca.gov
Web Site: www.parks.ca.gov
Key Personnel: Sector Supt., Scott Elliott; Museum Cur. II, Natalie E. Davenport.
Institution Type/Description: History Museum.
Hours & Admission Prices: Mansion: Memorial Day to Sept. daily 11-3:30. Tours: adults $10, students $8; children 6 & under no charge. Parking: adults $10, seniors 62 & over $9.
Attendance: 6,508 (estimated)

VIKINGSHOLM, Emerald Bay State Park, 11001 Hwy. 89, Tahoma, CA 96142. Mailing Address: California State Parks, Sierra District HQ, P.O. Box 266, Tahoma, CA 96142-0266. Tel.: 530-525-5055. Fax: 530-525-3380.
E-mail: natalie.davenport@parks.ca.gov

Web Site: www.parks.ca.gov
Key Personnel: Sector Supt., Scott Elliott; Museum Cur. II, Natalie Davenport.
Institution Type/Description: History Museum.
Hours & Admission Prices: Memorial Day to Sept. daily 10-4, tours on the half hour. Adults $10, students $8; children 6 & under no charge. Parking: adults $10, seniors 62 & over $9.
Attendance: 18,474 (estimated)

Taylorsville

INDIAN VALLEY MUSEUM, 4288 Cemetery St., Taylorsville, CA 95983. Mailing Address: P.O. Box 194, Taylorsville, CA 95983-0194. Tel.: 530-284-1046. Facebook: Indian Valley Museum.
E-mail: ivmuseum@yahoo.com
Web Site: indianvalleychamber.snappages.com/indian-valley-museum.htm
Key Personnel: Pres., Dave Wilson; Museum Shop Mgr., Katherine Iglesias.
Institution Type/Description: History Museum.
Hours & Admission Prices: Memorial Day to Oct. Sat.-Sun. 1-4; other times by appointment. No charge; donations accepted.
Attendance: 1,000 (estimated)

Tehachapi

MOURNING CLOAK RANCH AND BOTANICAL GARDENS, 22101 Old Town Rd., Tehachapi, CA 93561-8886. Tel.: 661-822-1661. Fax: 661-822-5062.
Institution Type/Description: Botanical Garden.
Hours & Admission Prices: May-Oct. Mon.-Sat. 10-3.

TEHACHAPI MUSEUM, 310 S. Green St., Tehachapi, CA 93561. Mailing Address: P.O. Box 54, Tehachapi, CA 93581. Tel.: 661-822-8152.
E-mail: info@tehachapimuseum.org
Web Site: www.tehachapimuseum.org
Key Personnel: Pres., Charles White.
Institution Type/Description: History Museum: housed in the former Kern County Library; built in 1931.
Hours & Admission Prices: Fri.-Sun. 12-4.

Tehama

TEHAMA COUNTY MUSEUM, 275 C St., Tehama, CA 96090-0275. Mailing Address: P.O. Box 275, Tehama, CA 96090-0275. Tel.: 530-384-2595.
E-mail: tcmuse@tehama.net
Web Site: tehamacountymuseum.org
Institution Type/Description: History Museum.
Hours & Admission Prices: Fri.-Sun. 1-4. No charge; donations accepted.

Temecula

PENNYPICKLE'S WORKSHOP, 42081 Main St., Temecula, CA 92590-2769. Tel.: 951-308-6376. Twitter: @profpennypickle.
E-mail: phineas@pennypickles.org
Web Site: www.pennypickles.org
Formerly: Imagination Workshop - Temecula Children's Museum
Key Personnel: Founder & Exec. Dir., Pat Comerchero; Mgr., Izzy Kunert.
Institution Type/Description: Science-Based Children's Museum.
Hours & Admission Prices: Tues.-Thurs. & Sat. Session 1: 10-12, Session 2: 12:30-2:30, Session 3: 3-5, Fri. Session 1: 10-12, Session 2: 12:30-2:30, Session 3: 3-5, Session 4: 5:30-7:30, Sun. Session 1: 12:30-2:30, Session 2: 3-5. Admission 24 months & over $5; discounts to groups of 25 & more.
Attendance: 50,000 (estimated)

TEMECULA VALLEY MUSEUM, 28314 Mercedes St., Temecula, CA 92590-1837. Tel.: 951-694-6455. Fax: 951-506-6871.
E-mail: tracy.frick@cityoftemecula.org
Web Site: www.temeculamuseum.org
Key Personnel: Museum Svcs. Mgr., Tracy Frick; Pres., Kelsey Stricker; Sec., Dale Garcia; Treas., Marianne Byers; Museum Shop Mgr., Jo Ann Lamb.
Institution Type/Description: History Museum.
Hours & Admission Prices: Tues.-Sat. 10-4, Sun. 1-4. Suggested Donation: family $10, single $5.
Attendance: 19,008 (actual)

Thousand Oaks

CHUMASH INDIAN MUSEUM, 3290 Lang Ranch Pkwy., Thousand Oaks, CA 91362. Tel.: 805-492-8076. Fax: 805-492-8096.
E-mail: chumashindianmuseum@verizon.net
Web Site: www.chumashindianmuseum.com
Formerly: Ashbrook Chumas Interpretive Center
Key Personnel: Dir., Alfred Mazza; C.E.O., Miles Lang; Museum Shop Mgr., Gray Wolf.
Institution Type/Description: Native American Museum.
Hours & Admission Prices: Thurs.-Sun. 12-5. Adults $5, seniors & children $3; discounts to AAM & ICOM members. Closed major holidays. 占
Attendance: 18,000 (estimated)

CONEJO VALLEY ART MUSEUM, Janss Market Pl., Ste. 193C, Thousand Oaks, CA 91358-0616. Mailing Address: P.O. Box 1616, Thousand Oaks, CA 91358-0616. Tel.: 805-492-8778. Fax: 805-492-7677. TDD: 805-492-7677.
E-mail: dessornes@earthlink.net
Web Site: conejovalleyartmuseum.com
Institution Type/Description: Art Museum.
Hours & Admission Prices: Call for hours. 占
Attendance: 12,000 (estimated)

CONEJO VALLEY BOTANIC GARDEN, 400 W. Gainsborough Rd., Thousand Oaks, CA 91360-2423. Tel.: 805-494-7630.
E-mail: conejogarden@hotmail.com
Web Site: conejogarden.org
Institution Type/Description: Botanic Garden.
Hours & Admission Prices: Daily 7-5. No charge. Closed New Year's Eve & Day; Easter; Independence Day; Thanksgiving; Christmas Eve & Day.

FRED KAVLI THEATRE GALLERY, 2100 Thousand Oaks Blvd., Thousand Oaks, CA 91362. Tel.: 805-449-2767.
E-mail: bneal@toaks.org
Web Site: civicartsplaza.com/galleries
Institution Type/Description: Art Gallery.
Hours & Admission Prices: By appointment or may be viewed by patrons that attend events at the theatre.

SANTA MONICA MOUNTAINS NATIONAL RECREATION AREA, 401 W. Hillcrest Dr., Thousand Oaks, CA 91360-4223. Tel.: 805-370-2300.
E-mail: samo_interpretation@nps.gov
Web Site: www.nps.gov/samo/
Key Personnel: Supt., David Szymanski; Archeologist, Gary Brown.
Institution Type/Description: National Park: Collections consist of natural history specimens, local archaeological & historical artifacts and park archives. Satwiwa Native American Indian Culture Center.
Hours & Admission Prices: Visitor Center: Mon.-Sat. 8-5. Park Site: daily. No charge. Closed major holidays. 占
Attendance: 76 (actual)

WILLIAM ROLLAND GALLERY OF FINE ART - CALIFORNIA LUTHERAN UNIVERSITY, 160 Overton Ct., Thousand Oaks, CA 91360. Mailing Address: 60 W. Olsen Rd., #1700, Thousand Oaks, CA 91360. Tel.: 805-493-3697.
E-mail: rollandgallery@callutheran.edu
Web Site: www.callutheran.edu/rolland
Institution Type/Description: Art Gallery.
Hours & Admission Prices: Call for hours.

Three Rivers

SEQUOIA AND KINGS CANYON NATIONAL PARKS, 47050 Generals Hwy., Three Rivers, CA 93271-9599. Tel.: 559-565-3136. Fax: 559-565-3744.
E-mail: seki_interpretation@nps.gov
Web Site: www.nps.gov/seki
Key Personnel: Chief Park Interpreter, Colleen Bathe; Museum Technician, Ward Eldredge.
Institution Type/Description: Park Museum & Visitor Centers: located at Ash Mountain, Lodgepole & Grant Grove.
Hours & Admission Prices: See website for hours. Visitor Centers: no charge; donations accepted. Parks: fee charged. 占

Tiburon

ANGEL ISLAND STATE PARK, Tiburon, CA 94920. Mailing Address: P.O. Box 318, Tiburon, CA 94920-0318. Tel.: 415-435-5390. Fax: 415-435-0850. Facebook: Angel Island State Park.
E-mail: tours.angelisland@parks.ca.gov
Web Site: www.parks.ca.gov/angelisland
Formerly: U.S. Immigration Station
Institution Type/Description: Historic Buildings & Sites.
Hours & Admission Prices: 8am to sunset, call to confirm. Park entrance fee included in price of ferry ticket; discounts to school groups K-12. 占
Attendance: 175,000 (estimated)

BELVEDERE-TIBURON LANDMARKS SOCIETY, 1550 Tiburon Blvd., Ste. M, Tiburon, CA 94920. Tel.: 415-435-1853.
E-mail: lmsoffice@sbcglobal.net
Web Site: landmarkssociety.com
Key Personnel: Exec. Dir., Alan Brune.
Institution Type/Description: Old St. Hilary's: Preservation Project & Museum: housed in 1888 Carpenter Gothic style church with wildflower preserve. China Cabin: restored social hall of the SS Tiburon, 1866-1886.
Hours & Admission Prices: April-Oct. Wed. & Sat.-Sun. 1-4; other times by appointment. No charge; donations accepted. Charge for group tours off hours. 占
Attendance: 3,500 (estimated)

OLD ST. HILARY'S LANDMARK & WILDFLOWER PRESERVE, 201 Esperanza, Tiburon, CA 94920. Mailing Address: 1550 Tiburon Blvd., Ste. M, Tiburon, CA 94920-2529. Tel.: 415-435-1853.
E-mail: lmsoffice@sbcglobal.net
Web Site: landmarkssociety.com
Formerly: Old St. Hilary's Church Museum & St. Hilary's Preserve
Key Personnel: Exec. Dir., Alan Brune.
Institution Type/Description: Historical Museum: housed in a 19th-century Carpenter Gothic-style church, built in 1888.
Hours & Admission Prices: April-Oct. Wed. & Sun. 1-4. No charge; donations accepted. 占
Attendance: 500 (estimated)

Tomales

TOMALES REGIONAL HISTORY CENTER, 26701 State Hwy. #1, Tomales, CA 94971. Mailing Address: P.O. Box 262, Tomales, CA 94971-0262. Tel.: 707-878-9443.
E-mail: info@tomaleshistory.com
Web Site: tomaleshistory.com
Key Personnel: Bd. Pres., Liz Mitchell; Cur., Ginny Mackenzie Magan; Museum Shop Mgr., Nancy Conzett.
Institution Type/Description: History Center.
Hours & Admission Prices: Fri.-Sun. 1-4; other times by appointment. No charge; donations accepted. Closed major holidays. 占

Torrance

CALIFORNIA MUSEUM OF FINE ART, 1421 Marcelina Ave., Torrance, CA 90501. Tel.: 323-908-8909. Facebook: California Museum of Fine Art.
E-mail: calmusefineart@gmail.com
Web Site: www.californiamuseumoffineart.com
Key Personnel: Dir., Dali Higa; C.E.O., Brian Higa.
Institution Type/Description: Art Museum.
Hours & Admission Prices: By appointment only. No charge. 占
Attendance: 1,500 (estimated)

TORRANCE ART MUSEUM, 3320 Civic Center Dr. N., Torrance, CA 90503-5016. Tel.: 310-618-6340. Fax: 310-618-2399.
E-mail: jramos@torranceca.gov
Web Site: www.torranceartmuseum.com
Key Personnel: Dir. & Head Cur., Max Presneill; Asst. Cur., Jason Ramos; Preparator, Jon Flack; Volunteer Coord., Regina Taylor.
Institution Type/Description: Art Museum.
Hours & Admission Prices: Tues.-Sat. 11-5. No charge; donations accepted. Closed New Year's Day; Memorial Day; Armed Forces Day; Independence Day; Labor Day; Thanksgiving & day after; Christmas week. 占
Attendance: 6,821 (actual)

TORRANCE HISTORICAL SOCIETY & MUSEUM, 1345 Post Ave., Torrance, CA 90501-2621. Tel.: 310-328-5392.
E-mail: museum@torrancehistoricalsociety.org

Web Site: www.torrancehistoricalsociety.org
Key Personnel: Dir., Janet Payne; Pres (V), Jamie Ruth Watson.
Institution Type/Description: Historical Society Museum; housed in the city's first main library; built in 1936.
Hours & Admission Prices: Wed.-Thurs. & Sun. 1-4 & by appointment for special tours & research. No charge; donations accepted. Closed legal holidays. &
Attendance: 5,000 (actual)

TOYOTA USA AUTOMOBILE MUSEUM, 19600 Van Ness Ave., Torrance, CA 90501. Tel.: 310-468-8726 & 4728. Fax: 310-351-5353.
E-mail: susan_sanborn@toyota.com
Web Site: www.toyotausamuseum.com
Key Personnel: Cur., Susan Sanborn.
Institution Type/Description: Company History Museum.
Hours & Admission Prices: By appointment.

WESTERN MUSEUM OF FLIGHT, 3315 Airport Dr., Red Baron #3, Torrance, CA 90505-6152. Tel.: 310-326-9544. Fax: 310-326-9556.
E-mail: info@wmof.com
Web Site: www.wmof.com
Key Personnel: Pres., Cindy Macha Skjonsby.
Institution Type/Description: Aviation History Museum.
Hours & Admission Prices: Tues.-Sun. 10-3. Adults $3; members & children under 12 no charge.

Tracy

TRACY HISTORICAL MUSEUM, 1141 Adam St., Tracy, CA 95376-3506. Mailing Address: P.O. Box 117, Tracy, CA 95378. Tel.: 209-832-7278.
E-mail: tracymuseum@sbcglobal.net
Web Site: www.tracymuseum.org
Formerly: West Side Pioneer Association of Tracy
Key Personnel: Dir. & Pres. (V), Larry Gamino.
Institution Type/Description: History Museum; housed in the former Tracy Post Office building; built in 1937.
Hours & Admission Prices: June-Sept. Sat. 10-2, Sun. 1-4, Mon. 9-2. No charge. Closed most major holidays. &
Attendance: 1,000 (estimated)

Travis AFB

TRAVIS HERITAGE CENTER, 461 Burgan Blvd., Bldg. 80, Travis AFB, CA 94535. Tel.: 707-424-5605.
E-mail: heritagecenter1214@live.com
Web Site: www.travisairmuseum.org
Formerly: Travis Air Museum a k a Jimmy Doolittle Air and Space Museum
Institution Type/Description: Military Museum.
Hours & Admission Prices: Guided Tours: DoD ID: Tues.-Sat. 9-5, Sun. 12-5. General Public: Tues. & Sat. 9-3, Sun. 12-5. No Charge. Closed federal holidays.
Attendance: 12,000 (estimated)

Trinidad

STONE LAGOON RED SCHOOLHOUSE MUSEUM AT REDWOOD TRAILS, 265 Idlewood Lane, Trinidad, CA 95570-9641. Mailing Address: 265 Redwood Trails Cir., P.O. Box 1240, Trinidad, CA 95570. Tel.: 707-488-2061.
E-mail: info@rv4fun.com
Institution Type/Description: Historic Building; housed in former one-room schoolhouse, c.1894.
Hours & Admission Prices: Memorial Day to Labor Day. No charge.

TRINIDAD MUSEUM, 400 Janis Court at Patricks Point Dr., Trinidad, CA 95570. Mailing Address: P.O. Box 1126, Trinidad, CA 95570. Tel.: 707-677-3883 & 3816.
E-mail: baycity@sonic.net
Web Site: www.trinidadmuseum.org
Key Personnel: Pres. (V) & Museum Shop Mgr., Patti Fleschner.
Institution Type/Description: Historic House Museum; housed in the former Sangster-Watkins-Underwood home; c.1900.
Hours & Admission Prices: Thurs.-Sun. 12:30-4. No charge; donations accepted.
Attendance: 4,000 (estimated)

Truckee

DONNER MEMORIAL STATE PARK AND EMIGRANT TRAIL MUSEUM, 12593 Donner Pass Rd., Ste. 9, Truckee, CA 96161-3856. Tel.: 530-582-7892. Fax: 530-550-2347.
E-mail: donner.museum@parks.ca.gov
Web Site: www.parks.ca.gov
Key Personnel: Unit Supervising Ranger, Don Schmidt; Ranger, Mike Rominger; Cur., Judith K. Polanich.
Institution Type/Description: Historic Site & Museum.
Hours & Admission Prices: Daily 9-4. Museum: no charge; donations accepted. Closed New Year's Day; Thanksgiving; Christmas. No winter camping. &
Attendance: 75,000 (actual)

KIDZONE MUSEUM, 11711 Donner Pass Rd., Truckee, CA 96161-4954. Tel.: 530-587-5437.
E-mail: info@kidzonemuseum.org
Web Site: www.kidzonemuseum.org
Key Personnel: Exec. Dir., Carol Meagher.
Institution Type/Description: Children's Museum.
Hours & Admission Prices: Winter: Tues.-Fri. 10-5, Sat.-Sun. 10-3. Children & adults $8; discounts to ACM Assoc. members; children under one no charge. &
Attendance: 30,000 (actual)

TRUCKEE RAILROAD MUSEUM, 10075 Donner Pass Rd., Truckee, CA 96161. Mailing Address: P.O. Box 3838, Truckee, CA 96160.
E-mail: info@truckeedonnerrailroadsociety.com
Web Site: www.truckeedonnerrailroadsociety.com
Key Personnel: Chm. (V), Don Davis; Pres. (V), Jim Hood; Museum Shop Mgr., Bob Bell.
Institution Type/Description: History Museum; housed in a Southern Pacific Railroad caboose.
Hours & Admission Prices: Sat.-Sun. 10-4. No charge; donations accepted. &
Attendance: 4,892 (estimated)

TRUCKEE'S OLD JAIL MUSEUM, Jibbom & Spring Sts., Truckee, CA 96160. Mailing Address: P.O. Box 893, Truckee, CA 96160-0893. Tel.: 530-582-0893.
E-mail: info@truckeehistory.org
Web Site: www.truckeehistory.org
Formerly: Truckee-Donner Historical Society Jail Museum
Key Personnel: Cur. & Coord. Special Group Tours, Chelsea Walterscheid.
Institution Type/Description: Historic Building; served as jailhouse from 1875 to 1964.
Hours & Admission Prices: Memorial Day-Sept. Sat.-Sun. 11-4; group tours by appointment. Requested Donation: $2.

Tujunga

BOLTON HALL MUSEUM, 10110 Commerce Ave., Tujunga, CA 91042-2313. Mailing Address: P.O. Box 203, Tujunga, CA 91043-0203. Tel.: 818-352-3420.
E-mail: littlelanders@verizon.net
Web Site: www.littlelandershistoricalsociety.org
Key Personnel: Pres. (V), Herrold Egger.
Institution Type/Description: Community Historic Museum.
Hours & Admission Prices: Sun. & Tues. 1-4. No charge; donations accepted. &
Attendance: 1,500 (estimated)

Tulare

INTERNATIONAL AGRI-CENTER ANTIQUE FARM EQUIPMENT MUSEUM AND AGVENTURES LEARNING CENTER, 4500 S. Laspina St., Tulare, CA 93274-9165. Tel.: 559-688-1030. Fax: 559-686-5527. Facebook: International Agri-Center.
E-mail: kerissa@farmshow.org
Web Site: www.internationalagricenter.org
Key Personnel: C.E.O., Jerry Sinift.
Institution Type/Description: Agriculture Museum.
Hours & Admission Prices: Daily. No charge; donations accepted. &
Attendance: 10,000 (estimated)

TULARE HISTORICAL MUSEUM, 444 W. Tulare Ave., Tulare, CA 93274-3831. Tel.: 559-686-2074. Fax: 559-686-9295. Facebook: Tulare Historical Museum.
E-mail: info@tularehistoricalmuseum.org
Web Site: www.tularehistoricalmuseum.org

Key Personnel: Exec. Dir. & Cur., Christopher Harrell; Pres., Joe Terri; Docent Coord., Ron Vaughan.
Institution Type/Description: History Museum.
Hours & Admission Prices: June-Aug. Thurs.-Sat. 10-4; Sept.-May Thurs.-Sat. 10-4, 3rd Sun. of month 12:30-4. Adults $6, senior citizens $4, students $3; discounts to AAA members; members, children under 5 & 3rd Sun. Sept.-May no charge. Closed New Year's Day; Easter; Mother's Day; Father's Day; Independence Day; Thanksgiving & day after; Christmas & day after. &
Attendance: 4,000 (estimated)

Tulelake

LAVA BEDS NATIONAL MONUMENT, 1 Indian Wells Headquarters, Tulelake, CA 96134. Mailing Address: P.O. Box 1240, Tulelake, CA 96134-1240. Tel.: 530-667-8101. Fax: 530-667-2737.
E-mail: labe_interpretation@nps.gov
Web Site: www.nps.gov/labe/
Key Personnel: Supt., Mike Reynolds.
Institution Type/Description: History/Natural History Museum.
Hours & Admission Prices: Memorial Day to Labor Day daily 8-6; Sept.-May daily 8:30-5. Monument: $10 per car; federal lands pass holders no charge. Annual Pass: $20. &
Attendance: 100,000 (estimated)

Tustin

MARCONI AUTOMOTIVE MUSEUM, 1302 Industrial Dr., Tustin, CA 92780-6416. Tel.: 714-258-3001. Fax: 714-258-9117. Facebook: @MarconiAutomotiveMuseum; Twitter & Instagram: @MarconiMuseum.
E-mail: mhanover@marconimuseum.org
Web Site: www.marconimuseum.org
Key Personnel: C.E.O., Priscilla "Bo" Marconi; Exec. Dir., Missy Hanover; Operations Mgr., Todd Offosen; Museum Shop Mgr., Victor Contreras.
Institution Type/Description: Automobile Museum.
Hours & Admission Prices: Mon.-Fri. 9-4:30 by appointment. Donation: adults $5; children 12 & under no charge. Closed major holidays. &
Attendance: 3,000 (estimated)

Twentynine Palms

JOSHUA TREE NATIONAL PARK, 74485 National Park Dr., Twentynine Palms, CA 92277-3597. Tel.: 760-367-5500 & 5502. Fax: 760-367-6392.
E-mail: patty-gerhardt@nps.gov
Web Site: www.nps.gov/jotr
Formerly: Twentynine Palms Oasis Visitor Center, Joshua Tree National Park
Key Personnel: Superintendent, David Smith.
Institution Type/Description: Park Museum.
Hours & Admission Prices: Park: daily. Joshua Tree Visitor Center: daily 8-5. Oasis Visitor Center: daily 8:30-5. Cottonwood Visitor Center: daily 8:30-4. Black Rock Nature Center: Oct.-May Fri. 12-8, Sat.-Thurs. 8-4. Park entrance fees: 7-day vehicle permit $20, 7-day single entry permit $10. &
Attendance: 1,256,928 (actual)

Ukiah

GRACE HUDSON MUSEUM & SUN HOUSE, 431 S. Main St., Ukiah, CA 95482-4923. Tel.: 707-467-2836. Fax: 707-467-2835.
E-mail: info@gracehudsonmuseum.org
Web Site: www.gracehudsonmuseum.org
Key Personnel: Chm. (V), Paige Poulos; Dir., Sherrie Smith-Ferri; Cur., Marvin Schenck; Museum Shop Mgr., Marian Scalmanini; Registrar, Karen Holmes.
Institution Type/Description: Historic House: 1911 home of Dr. John W. Hudson & Artist Grace Carpenter Hudson.
Hours & Admission Prices: Wed.-Sat. 10-4:30, Sun. 12-4:30. Family $10, adults $4, students & seniors $3; discount to NARM, AAM & ICOM members; members no charge. Closed holidays. &
Attendance: 11,000 (actual)

HELD-POAGE MEMORIAL HOME AND RESEARCH LIBRARY, 603 W. Perkins St., Ukiah, CA 95482-4726. Tel.: 707-462-6969.
E-mail: mchs@pacific.net
Institution Type/Description: Historical Society Museum: housed in 1903 Queen Ann Victorian home of William D. L. Held.
Hours & Admission Prices: Wed.-Fri. 1-4; other times by appointment. No charge; donations accepted. &
Attendance: 600 (estimated)

Upland

COOPER REGIONAL HISTORY MUSEUM, 217 A St., Upland, CA 91786-6024. Mailing Address: P.O. Box 772, Upland, CA 91785-0772. Tel.: 909-982-8010.
E-mail: lola@coopermuseum.org
Web Site: www.coopermuseum.org
Key Personnel: Exec. Dir., Marilyn Anderson; Pres., David W. Stevens.
Institution Type/Description: History Museum.
Hours & Admission Prices: Fri. 1-4, Sat.-Sun. 11-5. No charge; donations accepted. Closed national holidays. &
Attendance: 5,000 (actual)

UPLAND FIRE COMPANY MUSEUM, 151 East "D" St., Upland, CA 91786. Mailing Address: Fire Administration, 475 N. 2nd Ave., Upland, CA 91786. Tel.: 909-931-4180. Fax: 909-931-4196.
E-mail: dcorbin@ci.upland.ca.us
Institution Type/Description: Fire Company Museum.
Hours & Admission Prices: Call for hours.

Vacaville

MOWERS-GOHEEN MUSEUM - PENA ADOBE HISTORICAL SOCIETY, Pena Adobe Park, Pena Adobe Rd., Vacaville, CA 95687. Mailing Address: c/o 618 E. Main St., Vacaville, CA 95688. Tel.: 707-449-6126.
E-mail: penaadobe@gmail.com
Institution Type/Description: Historical Society Museum.
Hours & Admission Prices: Call for hours.

VACAVILLE MUSEUM, 213 Buck Ave., Vacaville, CA 95688-3835. Tel.: 707-447-4513. Fax: 707-447-2661.
E-mail: vacamuseum@sbcglobal.net
Web Site: vacavillemuseum.org
Key Personnel: Dir., Shawn Lum; Cur. Collections, Annie Farley; Cur. Exhibits, Philip Nollar; Registrar, Heidi Casebolt; Office Mgr., Sheri Ware.
Institution Type/Description: History Museum.
Hours & Admission Prices: Wed.-Sun. 1-4:30. Adults $3, children & students $2; discounts to AAM & ICOM members; CAM & WMA members no charge. Closed holidays. &
Attendance: 10,000 (estimated)

Vallejo

MARE ISLAND MUSEUM, 1100 Railroad Ave., Vallejo, CA 94592. Tel.: 707-557-4646 & 644-4746.
E-mail: mareislandhistoricpark@gmail.com
Web Site: www.mareislandmuseum.org
Institution Type/Description: Historic Building: housed in a former pipe shop where metal parts were made for ships in the Navy Shipyard; built in 1854.
Hours & Admission Prices: Mon.-Fri. 10-2, 1st & 3rd Sat.-Sun. each month 10-4. Adults $5; active military no charge.

SIX FLAGS DISCOVERY KINGDOM, 2001 Marine World Pkwy., Vallejo, CA 94589-4001. Tel.: 707-644-4000. Fax: 707-644-0241. TDD: 707-643-6769.
Web Site: www.sixflags.com
Formerly: Six Flags Marine World
Key Personnel: Gen. Mgr., Rick McCurley; Dir. Mktg., Dwayne McNeil; Mgr. Merchandise & Museum Shop Mgr., Mike Southern; Supvr. Education, Terran Rosenberg; Mgr. Oceanarium, Kathy France; Dir. Opers., Tim Ready; Show Productions, David Miller; Mgr. Public Rels., Jeff Jouett; Dir. Animal Operations, David Blasko.
Institution Type/Description: Wildlife Theme Park.
Hours & Admission Prices: Memorial Day to Labor Day Mon.-Thurs. 10-8, Fri.-Sun. 10-9. Adults $44.99, senior citizens $26.99, children 4-12 $29.99; discounts to groups; children 2 & under no charge. &
Attendance: 1,950,000 (actual)

VALLEJO NAVAL & HISTORICAL MUSEUM, 734 Marin St., Vallejo, CA 94590-5992. Tel.: 707-643-0077. Fax: 707-643-2443.
E-mail: valmuse@pacbell.net
Web Site: www.vallejomuseum.org
Key Personnel: Dir., James E. Kern; Pres., Christine Dunn.
Institution Type/Description: Historical Museum: located in Vallejo's Old City Hall.
Hours & Admission Prices: Tues.-Fri. 12-4, Sat. 10-4. Adults $5, seniors & students 12-17 $3; discounts to AAM & ICOM members; members & children under 12 no charge. Closed holidays. &
Attendance: 9,000 (estimated)

Valley Center

RINCON BAND OF LUISENO INDIANS TRIBAL MUSEUM, 1 W. Tribal Rd., Valley Center, CA 92082. Tel.: 760-297-2635.
E-mail: museum@rincontribe.org
Formerly: Rincon Band of Luiseno Indians' Museum
Institution Type/Description: Native American Museum.
Hours & Admission Prices: Mon.-Fri. 2-5. ♿

Valley Glen

LOS ANGELES VALLEY COLLEGE ART GALLERY, 5800 Fulton Ave., Valley Glen, CA 91401-4062. Tel.: 818-778-5536.
E-mail: nagyj@lavc.edu
Web Site: www.lavc.edu/arts/artgallery.html
Institution Type/Description: Art Gallery.
Hours & Admission Prices: Mon.-Thurs. 11-5.

Van Nuys

THE JAPANESE GARDEN, 6100 Woodley Ave., Van Nuys, CA 91406-6450. Tel.: 818-756-8166. Fax: 818-756-9648.
E-mail: betty.ethridge@lacity.org
Web Site: www.thejapanesegarden.com
Key Personnel: Dir., Gene Greene; Chm. (V) & Museum Shop Mgr., Jan Abrams; Landscape Architect, Patrick Rigney; Technician, Julius Luna; Office Mgr., Betty Ethridge; Tour Desk Staff, Lori Stewart.
Institution Type/Description: Cultural Garden.
Hours & Admission Prices: Mon.-Thurs. 11-4, Sun. 10-4. Tours: Mon.-Thurs. 9:30, 10 & 10:30. Adults $5, children under 10 and seniors 62 & over $3; members no charge. Special events admission varies. Participates in American Horticultural Society reciprocal admission program (except for special events). Closed holidays. ♿
Attendance: 13,316 (actual)

Ventura

ALBINGER ARCHEOLOGICAL MUSEUM, 113 E. Main St., Ventura, CA 93001-2606. Tel.: 805-648-5823.
E-mail: jscott@ci.ventura.ca.us
Web Site: www.albingermuseum.org
Key Personnel: Mgr., Jeanne Scott.
Institution Type/Description: Archaeology Museum.
Hours & Admission Prices: Call for hours. ♿
Attendance: 12,000

CHANNEL ISLANDS NATIONAL PARK, ROBERT J. LAGOMARSINO VISITOR CENTER, 1901 Spinnaker Dr., Ventura, CA 93001-4354. Tel.: 805-658-5730. Fax: 805-658-5799.
E-mail: chris_interpretation@nps.gov
Web Site: www.nps.gov/chis
Key Personnel: Supt., Russell E. Galipeau, Jr.; Chief Interpretation, Yvonne Menard.
Institution Type/Description: National Park & Museum; Natural History Museum.
Hours & Admission Prices: Daily 8:30-5. Park: no charge; donations accepted. Closed Thanksgiving; Christmas. ♿
Attendance: 321,492 (actual)

MISSION SAN BUENAVENTURA MUSEUM, 225 E. Main St., Ventura, CA 93001-2622. Mailing Address: 211 E. Main St., Ventura, CA 93001-2691. Tel.: 805-643-4496. Fax: 805-643-7831.
E-mail: mission@sanbuenaventuramission.org
Web Site: www.sanbuenaventuramission.org
Key Personnel: Pastor, Rev. Thomas Elewaut; Gift Shop Mgr., Veronica Basoco.
Institution Type/Description: Historical Museum: housed in 1782 San Buenaventura Mission, founded by Saint Junipero Serra.
Hours & Admission Prices: Mon.-Sat. 10-5, Sun. 10-4. Museum: adults $4, seniors $3, children $1; discounts to groups & museum of Ventura County. Mass schedule: daily 7:30 am, Sat. 5:30 pm, 7:30 pm (Spanish), Sun. 7:30, 9, 10:30, 12:15 (Spanish). Closed New Year's Day; Easter; Thanksgiving; Christmas. ♿
Attendance: 18,500 (estimated)

MUSEUM OF VENTURA COUNTY, 100 E. Main St., Ventura, CA 93001-2828. Tel.: 805-653-0323. Fax: 805-653-5900. Facebook: Museum of Ventura County.
E-mail: mfreedman@venturamuseum.org
Web Site: www.venturamuseum.org
Formerly: Ventura County Museum of History & Art
Key Personnel: Pres. Bd. Dir. (V), Richard Pidduck; Co-Pres. Docent Council (V), Linda Kimbroug; Co-Pres. docent Council (V), Kathy Sisson; Exec. Dir., Myron

Freedman; Librarian, Charles Johnson; Dir. Education, Wendy VanHorn; Cur. Collections, Anna Rios Bermudez; Dir. Devel., Robin C. Woodworth; Mktg. Coord., Holly Raftery; Museum Shop Mgr., Linden Royce.
Institution Type/Description: History & Art Museum.
Hours & Admission Prices: Tues.-Sun. 11-5. Museum: adults $4, seniors & students w/ID $3, children 6-17 $1; MVC members & children 5 & younger no charge. Closed New Year's Day; Thanksgiving; Christmas. ♿
Attendance: 65,000 (actual)

ORTEGA ADOBE, 215 W. Main St., Ventura, CA 93001. Mailing Address: P.O. Box 99, Ventura, CA 93002-0099. Tel.: 805-658-4728.
E-mail: greyes@cityofventura.net
Web Site: www.ventura.com/points_of_interest/ortegaadobe
Institution Type/Description: History Museum: built in 1857 by Miguel Emigdio Ortega.
Hours & Admission Prices: Daily 9-4 by appointment. No charge.

VENTURA COUNTY MUSEUM OF HISTORY AND ART, 100 E. Main St., Ventura, CA 93001-2607. Tel.: 805-653-0323.
E-mail: ebrokaw@venturamuseum.org
Web Site: venturamuseum.org
Key Personnel: Interim Dir., Elena Brokaw.
Institution Type/Description: History & Art Museum.
Hours & Admission Prices: Tues.-Thurs. & Sat.-Sun. 11-6, Fri. 11-8. Adults $4, seniors $3, children 6-17 $1; members & children under 6 no charge.

Victorville

CALIFORNIA ROUTE 66 MUSEUM, 16825 S. D St., Victorville, CA 92395-3207. Tel.: 760-951-0436. Fax: 760-951-0509.
E-mail: cart66musm@gmail.com
Web Site: califrt66museum.org
Formerly: Old Town Victorville Heritage Preservation, Inc. dba California Route 66 Museum
Key Personnel: Chm. (V) & Pres. (V), Sue Bridges; Museum Shop Mgr., Patti Bridges.
Institution Type/Description: History Museum.
Hours & Admission Prices: Thurs.-Mon. 10-4, Sun. 11-3; other times by appointment. No charge; donations accepted; purchase discounts to veterans; $50 deposit for off-day tours. Closed Memorial Day; Independence Day; Labor Day; Thanksgiving; Christmas. ♿
Attendance: 15,500 (actual)

VICTORVILLE FIRE DEPARTMENT MUSEUM, 15620 8th St., Victorville, CA 92392. Mailing Address: 14343 Civic Dr., P.O. Box 5001, Victorville, CA 92392-5001. Tel.: 760-955-5229.
E-mail: engine373@earthlink.net
Key Personnel: Cur., Greg Coon.
Institution Type/Description: Firefighting History Museum.
Hours & Admission Prices: Sat. 9-12 by appointment. No charge; donations accepted.

Visalia

IMAGINEU CHILDREN'S MUSEUM, 210 N. Tipton St., Visalia, CA 93292. Mailing Address: P.O. Box 688, Visalia, CA 93279-0688. Tel.: 559-733-5975 & 0735. Fax: 559-733-0871. Facebook: ImagineU Children's Museum.
E-mail: info@imagineumuseum.org
Web Site: www.imagineumuseum.org
Key Personnel: Pres., Cheryl Christman; Dir., Peter Sodhy.
Institution Type/Description: Children's Museum.
Hours & Admission Prices: Mon.-Fri. 10-5:30, Sat.-Sun. 12-4. Admission $8; children under 1 & members no charge. ♿
Attendance: 60,000 (estimated)

TULARE COUNTY MUSEUM AT MOONEY GROVE PARK, 27000 S. Mooney Blvd., Visalia, CA 93277-9341. Mailing Address: 5953 S. Mooney Blvd., Visalia, CA 93277. Tel.: 559-733-6616. Fax: 559-635-4896. Facebook: Tulare County Museum.
E-mail: aking1@co.tulare.ca.us
Web Site: tularecountymuseum.org
Key Personnel: Dir. & Cur., Amy King.
Institution Type/Description: History Museum.
Hours & Admission Prices: Summer: Thurs.-Mon. 10-4; Winter: Mon. & Thurs.-Fri. 10-4, Sat.-Sun. 12-4. Mooney Grove Park March-Oct. Sat.-Sun. $6 per car; admission to museum included in park entrance fee. Closed New Year's Eve & Day; Thanksgiving; Christmas Eve & Day. ♿
Attendance: 125,000 (actual)

Vista

ANTIQUE GAS & STEAM ENGINE MUSEUM, INC., 2040 N. Santa Fe Ave., Vista, CA 92083-1534. Tel.: 760-941-1791. Fax: 760-941-0690.
E-mail: rod_agsem@yahoo.com
Web Site: www.agsem.com
Key Personnel: C.E.O., Jeanette Stevens; Dir., Rod Groenewold; Museum Shop Mgr., Glenda Garrison.
Institution Type/Description: Agriculture & Industrial Museum Complex: located on 40 acres of farm land.
Hours & Admission Prices: Daily 10-4. Adults $3. Closed Christmas. &
Attendance: 55,000 (estimated)

VISTA HISTORICAL MUSEUM, 2317 Old Foothill Dr., Vista, CA 92084. Mailing Address: P.O. Box 1032, Vista, CA 92085-1032. Tel.: 760-630-0444. Fax: 760-295-9993.
E-mail: vhm67@1882.sdcoxmail.com
Web Site: www.vistahistoricalsociety.com
Key Personnel: Pres. (V), Carolyn Chiriboga; Dir. & Museum Shop Mgr., Jack Larimer; Financial Dir., Michele Moxley; Devel., Sharon Larimer.
Institution Type/Description: Historical Museum.
Hours & Admission Prices: Wed.-Fri. 1st & 2nd Sat. each month 10-2:30. No charge; donations accepted. &
Attendance: 1,000 (estimated)

Walnut

THE MT. SAN ANTONIO COLLEGE WILDLIFE SANCTUARY, 1100 N. Grand Ave., Walnut, CA 91789. Tel.: 909-594-5611, ext. 4794.
E-mail: marketing@mtsac.edu
Institution Type/Description: Wildlife Sanctuary.
Hours & Admission Prices: Tours: Tues. & Thurs. 9am, 10am, 11am, 2pm, 3pm, & 4pm.

Walnut Creek

BEDFORD GALLERY AT THE DEAN LESHER REGIONAL CENTER FOR THE ARTS, 1601 Civic Dr., Walnut Creek, CA 94596-4299. Tel.: 925-295-1417. Fax: 925-295-1486.
E-mail: lederer@bedfordgallery.org
Web Site: www.bedfordgallery.org
Key Personnel: Dir. Cultural & Community Svcs., Gary Pokorny; Cur., Carrie Lederer; Preparator, Erik Mortensen.
Institution Type/Description: Municipal Art Gallery.
Hours & Admission Prices: Tues.-Wed. & Sun. 12-5, Thurs.-Sat. 12-5 & 6-8. Adults $5, students 17 & under $3; children under 12 no charge. Closed national holidays. &
Attendance: 45,000

LINDSAY WILDLIFE MUSEUM, 1931 First Ave., Walnut Creek, CA 94597-2540. Tel.: 925-935-1978. Fax: 925-935-8015.
E-mail: lbehr@wildlife-museum.org
Web Site: www.wildlife-museum.org
Key Personnel: Pres., Kramer Klabau; Exec. Dir., Loren Behr; Cur. Live Collections, Michele Setter; Financial Dir., Suzie Mahaffay; Dir. Wildlife Rehabilitation, Susan Heckly; Dir. Veterinary Svcs. & Research, Shannon Riggs, D.V.M.; Dir. Operations, Chris Bernard; Dir. Education, Patti Harris; Cur. Natural History & Dir. Operations, Marty Buxton; Museum Shop Mgr., Christine Garcia.
Institution Type/Description: Natural History Museum.
Hours & Admission Prices: Jan.-June 15 Thurs.-Fri. 12-5, Sat.-Sun. 10-5; June 16-Aug. Wed.-Sun. 10-5; Sept.-Dec. Wed.-Fri. 12-5, Sat.-Sun. 10-5. Adults $7, senior citizens 65 & over $6, children 2-17 $5; discount to AAM, ASTC reciprocal members & groups of 15-35; members & children under 2 no charge. Closed Independence Day; Thanksgiving; Christmas. &
Attendance: 102,542 (actual)

SHADELANDS RANCH HISTORICAL MUSEUM, 2660 Ygnacio Valley Rd., Walnut Creek, CA 94598. Tel.: 925-935-7871.
E-mail: wcshadelands@sbcglobal.net
Web Site: www.walnutcreekhistory.info
Institution Type/Description: History Museum: housed in the former home of pioneer Hiram Penniman; built in 1903. National Register of Historic Places.
Hours & Admission Prices: early Feb. to Oct. Wed. & Sun. 1-4; groups of 10 or more by appointment. Adults $3, students 6-17 $1; members & children under 6 no charge.

Walnut Grove

SACRAMENTO RIVER DELTA HISTORICAL SOCIETY RESOURCE CENTER, The Jean Harvie Community Center, 14273 River Rd., Walnut Grove, CA 95690. Mailing Address: P.O. Box 293, Walnut Grove, CA 95690.
E-mail: srdhshs@gmail.com
Web Site: www.srdhs.org/
Institution Type/Description: Historical Society Museum: center built in 1924.
Hours & Admission Prices: Tues. by appointment.

Wasco

WASCO HISTORICAL SOCIETY MUSEUM, 918 6th St., Wasco, CA 93280-1902. Mailing Address: P.O. Box 186, Wasco, CA 93280-0186.
E-mail: bob@paulfarms.net
Key Personnel: Pres. (V), Bob Ellis.
Institution Type/Description: Historical Society Museum.
Hours & Admission Prices: Call for hours. No charge. &

Watsonville

ELKHORN SLOUGH NATIONAL ESTUARINE RESEARCH, 1700 Elkhorn Rd., Watsonville, CA 95076-9218. Tel.: 831-728-2822. Fax: 831-728-1056.
E-mail: info@elkhornslough.org
Web Site: www.elkhornslough.org
Key Personnel: Reserve Mgr., Dave Feliz.
Institution Type/Description: Natural History Museum.
Hours & Admission Prices: Wed.-Sun. 9-5. No charge.

PAJARO VALLEY HISTORICAL ASSOCIATION, 332 E. Beach St., Watsonville, CA 95076. Mailing Address: P.O. Box 623, Watsonville, CA 95077-0623. Tel.: 831-722-0305. Fax: 831-722-5501. Facebook: Pajaro Valley Historical Association.
E-mail: info@pajarovalleyhistory.org
Web Site: www.pajarovalleyhistory.org
Key Personnel: Pres., Judy Nielsen; Sec., Luann Lauresen; Treas., Ralph Jacobs; Office Admin., Jodi Frensley.
Institution Type/Description: History Museum: housed in the Bockius-Orr House.
Hours & Admission Prices: Tues.-Thurs. 11-3. No charge; donations accepted. Closed New Year's Eve, Day & week; Thanksgiving week; Christmas Eve, Day & week. &
Attendance: 750 (estimated)

Weaverville

J.J. JACKSON MEMORIAL MUSEUM, 780 Main St., Weaverville, CA 96093. Mailing Address: P.O. Box 333, Weaverville, CA 96093-0333. Tel.: 530-623-5211. Fax: 530-623-5053.
E-mail: jake@trinitymuseum.org
Web Site: www.trinitymuseum.org
Key Personnel: Dir., Dero Forslund; Pres., George Chapman; Museum Shop Mgr., Pat Williams.
Institution Type/Description: History Museum & Research Center.
Hours & Admission Prices: Jan.-March Tues.-Sat. 12-4; April & Nov.-Dec. daily 12-4; May-Oct. daily 10-5. Adults $2. &
Attendance: 11,750 (actual)

WEAVERVILLE JOSS HOUSE, State Historic Park, 630 Main St., Weaverville, CA 96093. Mailing Address: P.O. Box 1217, Weaverville, CA 96093-1217. Tel.: 530-623-5284.
E-mail: paula@weavervillejosshouse.org
Web Site: www.parks.ca.gov
Key Personnel: Historic Monument Guide, Jack Frost.
Institution Type/Description: Historic Building: housed in a Chinese temple; built in 1874.
Hours & Admission Prices: Thurs.-Sun. 10-5. Adults $3, children 6-17 $2.
Attendance: 20,000

Weed

LIVING MEMORIAL SCULPTURE GARDEN, Hwy. 97, Weed, CA 96094. Mailing Address: P.O. Box 301, Weed, CA 96094-0301. Tel.: 530-842-2477.
Web Site: weedlmsg.org
Key Personnel: Pres. (V), Suzanne Breceda.

Institution Type/Description: War Memorial Sculpture Garden.
Hours & Admission Prices: Daily sunrise-sunset. No charge.
Attendance: 6,000 (estimated)

Weott

HUMBOLDT REDWOODS STATE PARK VISITOR CENTER,
17119 State Rte. 254, Weott, CA 95571. Mailing Address: P.O.
Box 276, Weott, CA 95571-0276. Tel.: 707-946-2263. Fax: 707-
946-2618.
E-mail: vc@humboldtredwoods.org
Web Site: www.humboldtredwoods.org
Key Personnel: State Park Liaison, Greg Hall; Chm. (V), Alan Aiken; Exec. Dir.,
Sophia Eckert; Mgr., Deborah Gardner; Dist. Supt., Victor Bjelajac.
Institution Type/Description: Park Museum & Visitor Center.
Hours & Admission Prices: April-Sept. daily 8-5; Oct.-March daily 9-4. No charge;
donations accepted.
Attendance: 87,254 (actual)

West Covina

HURST RANCH HISTORICAL FOUNDATION, 1227 S. Orange
Ave., West Covina, CA 91790-3320. Tel.: 626-813-0116. Fax:
626-919-1133.
E-mail: info@hurstranch.com
Web Site: www.hurstranch.com
Institution Type/Description: History Museum.
Hours & Admission Prices: By appointment. $5 per person. &
Attendance: 1,600 (estimated)

West Hollywood

**MAK CENTER FOR ART AND ARCHITECTURE AT THE
SCHINDLER HOUSE,** 835 N. Kings Rd., West Hollywood, CA
90069-5409. Tel.: 323-651-1510, ext. 5 & ext. 10. Fax: 323-651-
2340.
E-mail: office@makcenter.org
Web Site: www.makcenter.org
Key Personnel: Dir., Kimberli Meyer; Asst. Programs Coord., Janet Owen;
Museum Shop Mgr., Angelica Fuentes.
Institution Type/Description: Center for Art & Architecture: R.M. Schindler's land-
mark Kings Road House/Studio (1921-22)
Hours & Admission Prices: Wed.-Sun. 11-6. Adults $7, seniors & students $6;
members & children under 12 no charge. Closed New Year's Day; Independence
Day; Labor Day; Christmas. &
Attendance: 9,400 (actual)

Whiskeytown

**WHISKEYTOWN   UNIT,   WHISKEYTOWN-SHASTA-
TRINITY NATIONAL RECREATION AREA,** Hwy. 299 W.,
Whiskeytown, CA 96095-0188. Mailing Address: P.O. Box 188,
Whiskeytown, CA 96095-0188. Tel.: 530-242-3400 & 246-1225.
Fax: 530-246-5154. Facebook: Whiskeytown National Recreation
Area.
Web Site: www.nps.gov/whis
Key Personnel: Supt., Jim F. Milestone.
Institution Type/Description: Anthropology, History Museum: located in former
gold rush area. Tower House Historic District is on the National Register of
Historic Places.
Hours & Admission Prices: Recreation Area: daily 10-4. Visitor Center: daily 10-4.
Park Headquarter Mon.-Fri. 8-4:30. Vehicle Pass: annual $40, weekly $10, daily
$5; Golden Age, Golden Access & Golden Eagle Passport members no charge.
Closed New Year's Day; Thanksgiving; Christmas. &
Attendance: 715,000 (estimated)

Whittier

JONATHAN BAILEY HOME, 13421 E. Camilla St., Whittier, CA
90601-4608. Mailing Address: Whittier Historical Society, 6755
Newlin Ave., Whittier, CA 90601. Tel.: 562-945-3871. Fax: 562-
945-9106.
E-mail: info@whittiermuseum.org
Web Site: www.whittiermuseum.org
Key Personnel: Dir., Tim Traeger; Archival Asst., Kyle Smith.
Institution Type/Description: History Museum.
Hours & Admission Prices: Guided Tours: Sun. 1-4. School tours/group tours by
appointment only Tues.-Fri. 9:30 - 3. No charge; donations accepted.

LOS ANGELES COUNTY SHERIFFS' MUSEUM, 11515 S.
Colima Rd., Bldg. B, Whittier, CA 90604. Tel.: 562-946-7859.
E-mail: shbforthewebsite@lasd.org
Web Site: www.lasheriffsmuseum.lasd.org
Institution Type/Description: Law Enforcement Museum.
Hours & Admission Prices: Mon.-Fri. 9-4 by appointment. Closed holidays.

WHITTIER MUSEUM, 6755 Newlin Ave., Whittier, CA 90601.
Tel.: 562-945-3871. Facebook, Twitter, Pinterest & Instagram:
Whittier Museum.
E-mail: info@whittiermuseum.org
Web Site: www.whittiermuseum.org
Key Personnel: Dir., Tim Traeger; Pres. (V), Stephanie Butler; Archives & Office
Mgr., Kyle Smith.
Institution Type/Description: History Museum.
Hours & Admission Prices: Office: Tues.-Fri. 9-4. No charge; donations accepted.
Public Tours: Fri.-Sat. 1-4. School/Group Tours: Tues.-Fri. 9:30-3 by appoint-
ment only. Archives: by appointment only. Non-members $25 per hour; mem-
bers no charge. &
Attendance: 4,000 (estimated)

Williams

SACRAMENTO VALLEY MUSEUM, 1491 E St., Williams, CA
95987. Mailing Address: P.O. Box 1437, Williams, CA 95987-
1437. Tel.: 530-473-2978. Fax: 530-473-2978. Facebook.
E-mail: sacvalleymuseum@frontiernet.net
Web Site: www.sacvalleymuseum.org
Key Personnel: Dir., Kathy Manor; Asst. Cur., Sajit Singh.
Institution Type/Description: History Museum: former building of Williams Union
High School, built in 1911.
Hours & Admission Prices: mid-March to Oct. Thurs.-Sat. 10-4; other times & tours
by appointment. Admission fees for groups. Individual admission no charge;
donations accepted.
Attendance: 1,500 (estimated)

Willits

MENDOCINO COUNTY MUSEUM, 400 E. Commercial St.,
Willits, CA 95490-3204. Tel.: 707-459-2736. Fax: 707-459-7836.
Facebook: Mendocino Museum.
E-mail: info@mendocinomuseum.org
Web Site: www.mendocinomuseum.org
Key Personnel: C.E.O. & Dir., Alison Glassey.
Institution Type/Description: History & Railroad Museum.
Hours & Admission Prices: Wed.-Sun. 10-4:30. Adults $4. Closed most holidays. &

Willow Creek

WILLOW CREEK - CHINA FLAT MUSEUM, 38949 Hwy. 299,
Willow Creek, CA 95573. Mailing Address: P.O. Box 102, Willow
Creek, CA 95573-0102. Tel.: 530-629-2653.
Web Site: bigfootcountry.net
Institution Type/Description: History Museum.
Hours & Admission Prices: May-Sept. Wed.-Sun. 10-4; Oct. Fri.-Sun. 10-4. No
charge; donations accepted. &
Attendance: 7,300 (actual)

Willows

WILLOWS MUSEUM, 336 W. Walnut St., Willows, CA 95988-
2819. Tel.: 530-934-5644.
Key Personnel: Chm. (V), Ray Crabtree.
Institution Type/Description: History Museum.
Hours & Admission Prices: Thurs. & Sat.-Sun. 1-4; other times by appointment. No
charge; donations accepted.
Attendance: 800 (estimated)

Wilmington

BANNING MUSEUM, 401 E. M St., Wilmington, CA 90744-2610.
Mailing Address: P.O. Box 397, Wilmington, CA 90748-0397.
Tel.: 310-548-7777. Fax: 310-548-2644.
E-mail: info@thebanningmuseum.org
Web Site: www.thebanningmuseum.org
Key Personnel: Dir., Michael Sanborn.
Institution Type/Description: History Museum: 1864 Greek Revival home of
Phineas Banning.
Hours & Admission Prices: Tours: Tues.-Thurs. 12:30, 1:30 & 2:30, Sat.-Sun.
12:30, 1:30, 2:30 & 3:30; groups of 10 or more by appointment. Requested

Donation: adults $5, children under 12 $1. Closed Easter; Memorial Day; Independence Day; Labor Day; Columbus Day; Veterans Day; Thanksgiving; Christmas.
Attendance: 22,000 (actual)

DRUM BARRACKS CIVIL WAR MUSEUM, 1052 Banning Blvd., Wilmington, CA 90744-4604. Tel.: 310-548-7509. Fax: 310-548-2946.
E-mail: susan.ogle@lacity.org
Web Site: www.drumbarracks.org
Key Personnel: Dir., Susan Ogle.
Institution Type/Description: History Museum.
Hours & Admission Prices: Tours: Tues.-Thurs. 10 & 11:30, Sat.-Sun. 11:30 & 1. Requested Donation: adults $5; discounts to AAA members. Closed New Year's Day; Good Friday; Easter; Memorial Day; Independence Day; Labor Day; Thanksgiving; Christmas.
Attendance: 8,600 (actual)

Woodland

CALIFORNIA AGRICULTURE MUSEUM, 1962 Hays Ln., Woodland, CA 95776. Tel.: 530-666-9700. Fax: 530-666-9712. Facebook.
E-mail: lorili@aghistory.org
Web Site: www.californiaagmuseum.org
Formerly: Heidrick Ag History Center
Key Personnel: Exec. Dir. & C.E.O., Lorili Ostman.
Institution Type/Description: Agriculture Museum.
Hours & Admission Prices: Summer: Wed.-Sat. 10-5, Sun. 10-4; Winter: call for hours. Adults $10, seniors 65 & over and veterans $8, students $7, children 6-12 $5; discounts to NARM members; members & children under 5 no charge.
Attendance: 40,000 (estimated)

Woodside

FILOLI CENTER, 86 Canada Rd., Woodside, CA 94062-4144. Tel.: 650-364-8300. Fax: 650-367-0724. Facebook: Filoli Estate.
E-mail: friends@filoli.org; info@filoli.org
Web Site: www.filoli.org
Key Personnel: Pres. (V), Heidi Brown; Dir., Cynthia D'Agosta; Museum Shop Mgr., Linda Fujimoto; Cur., Julie DeVere.
Institution Type/Description: Formal Garden, Historic House & Nature Preserve: 1915-1917 residence designed by Willis J. Polk for William B. Bourn, II; gardens designed by Bruce Porter.
Hours & Admission Prices: mid-Feb. to late Oct. Tues.-Sat. 10-3:30, Sun. 11-3:30; call for tour schedule & reservations Tel.: 650-364-8300, ext. 507. Feb.-May: adults $20, seniors $17, students $10; June-Oct.: adults $18, seniors $15, students $8; discounts to National Trust for Historic Preservation; children 4 & under and members no charge. Additional fee for special events. Closed Federal holidays. &
Attendance: 102,235 (actual)

WOODSIDE STORE HISTORIC SITE, 3300 Tripp Rd., Woodside, CA 94062-3632. Tel.: 650-851-7615.
E-mail: woodsidestore@historysmc.org
Key Personnel: Pres., Mitchell P. Postel; Chm., Mark Jamison; Deputy Dir., Carmen Blair; Site Mgr., Elizabeth Crowley.
Institution Type/Description: Historic Building: c.1854 general store.
Hours & Admission Prices: Tues. & Thurs. 10-4, Sat.-Sun. 12-4. No charge; donations accepted. Closed national holidays. &

Yermo

CALICO GHOST TOWN AND THE LANE HOUSE & MUSEUM, 36600 Ghost Town Rd., Yermo, CA 92398. Mailing Address: P.O. Box 638, Yermo, CA 92398-0638. Tel.: 760-254-3679. Fax: 760-254-2047.
E-mail: calicotown@parks.sbcounty.gov
Web Site: www.calicotown.com
Institution Type/Description: History Museum.
Hours & Admission Prices: Town: daily 9-5. House & Museum: daily 10-4; other times by appointment. Adults $6, youth 6-15 $3; children 5 & under no charge.

Yorba Linda

RICHARD NIXON LIBRARY & BIRTHPLACE, 18001 Yorba Linda Blvd., Yorba Linda, CA 92886-3949. Tel.: 714-993-5075. Fax: 714-528-0544.
E-mail: rexjht@msn.com
Web Site: www.nixonlibraryfoundation.org

Institution Type/Description: History Museum.
Hours & Admission Prices: Mon.-Sat. 10-5, Sun. 11-5. Adult 12 & over $11.95, seniors 62 & over $8.50, students $6.95, children 7-11 $4.75; children 6 & under no charge. Closed Thanksgiving; Christmas.

Yosemite National Park

THE ANSEL ADAMS GALLERY, Village Mall, Yosemite National Park, CA 95389. Mailing Address: P.O. Box 455, Yosemite Village, CA 95389. Tel.: 209-372-4413. Fax: 209-372-4714. Facebook: The Ansel Adams Gallery.
E-mail: yosemite@anseladams.com
Web Site: www.anseladams.com
Key Personnel: Pres., Matthew Adams.
Institution Type/Description: Art Gallery.
Hours & Admission Prices: Daily 9-5.

YOSEMITE NATIONAL PARK, Yosemite National Park, CA 95389. Mailing Address: P.O. Box 577, Yosemite, CA 95389-0577. Tel.: 209-372-0281. Fax: 209-372-0255.
E-mail: yose_museum@nps.gov
Web Site: www.nps.gov/yose
Key Personnel: Chief Cur., Barbara L. Beroza; Archivist, Paul Rogers; Cur. Collections, Greg Cox; Research Librarian, Virginia Sanchez; Registrar, Sara Hay.
Institution Type/Description: National Park and Historic Museum Building.
Hours & Admission Prices: Park: daily. Park Visitor Centers, Museums, Historic Buildings & Cemeteries: call or visit website for hours. $30 per vehicle, $20 per motorcycle, $15 per guest on foot, bicycle or horseback. &
Attendance: 485,000 (estimated)

Yountville

MA(I)SONRY NAPA VALLEY ART GALLERIES, 6711 Washington St., Yountville, CA 94599-1310. Tel.: 707-944-0889. Fax: 707-944-0880.
E-mail: mail@maisonry.com
Web Site: www.maisonry.com
Institution Type/Description: Art Gallery.
Hours & Admission Prices: Call for hours.

NAPA VALLEY MUSEUM, 55 Presidents Circle, Yountville, CA 94599. Mailing Address: P.O. Box 3567, Yountville, CA 94599-3567. Tel.: 707-944-0500. Fax: 707-945-0500.
E-mail: kristie@napavalleymuseum.org
Web Site: www.napavalleymuseum.org
Key Personnel: Exec. Dir., Kristie Sheppard.
Institution Type/Description: Local History, Art & Natural Science Museum.
Hours & Admission Prices: Tues.-Sun. 10-4. Adults $5, senior citizens $3.50, youth $2.50; members no charge. Closed major holidays. &
Attendance: 20,000 (estimated)

Yreka

SISKIYOU COUNTY MUSEUM, 910 S. Main St., Yreka, CA 96097-3373. Tel.: 530-842-3836.
E-mail: scmuseum@co.siskiyou.ca.us
Web Site: www.co.siskiyou.ca.us/page/siskiyou-county-museum
Key Personnel: Dir., Lisa Gioia.
Institution Type/Description: Local History Museum.
Hours & Admission Prices: Tues.-Sat. 9-3. Adults $3, children 6-12 $1; children 5 & under no charge. Closed national, state & county holidays. &
Attendance: 3,000 (estimated)

Yuba City

COMMUNITY MEMORIAL MUSEUM OF SUTTER COUNTY, 1333 Butte House Rd., Yuba City, CA 95993-2301. Tel.: 530-822-7141. Fax: 530-822-7291.
E-mail: museum@syix.com
Web Site: www.co.sutter.ca.us/
Key Personnel: Dir. & Cur., Jessica Hougen; Asst. Cur., Sharyl Simmons.
Institution Type/Description: History Museum.
Hours & Admission Prices: Wed.-Fri. 9-5, Sat. 12-4. No charge; donations accepted. Closed New Year's Day; Thanksgiving; Christmas. &
Attendance: 7,000 (actual)

Yucaipa

MOUSLEY MUSEUM OF YUCAIPA HISTORY, 35308 Panorama Dr., Yucaipa, CA 92399-3532. Mailing Address: P.O. Box 297, Yucaipa, CA 92399-0297. Tel.: 909-790-4685. Fax: 909-790-4685.
E-mail: yucaipahistory@verizon.net
Web Site: www.yucaipahistory.org
Key Personnel: Pres., Claire Teeters; Pres., Harry Birkbeck; Vice Pres., Bob Rippy; Vice Pres., Jack Curtright.
Institution Type/Description: Local History Museum.
Hours & Admission Prices: Wed. 5-9, Sat. 10-3. No charge; donations accepted. &
Attendance: 1,000 (actual)

YUCAIPA ADOBE, 32183 Kentucky St., Yucaipa, CA 92399-1768. Mailing Address: 2024 Orange Tree Ln., Redlands, CA 92374. Tel.: 909-795-3485 & 307-2669. Fax: 909-307-0539.
E-mail: rmckernan@sbcm.sbcounty.gov
Web Site: www.sbcountymuseum.org
Key Personnel: Dir., Robert McKernan; Site Mgr., Tony Webb; Cur., Michele Nielsen.
Institution Type/Description: Local History and Historic House Museum: housed in late 1850s adobe house.
Hours & Admission Prices: Tues.-Sat. 10-3. No charge; donations suggested. Closed New Year's Day; Thanksgiving; Christmas.
Attendance: 500 (actual)

Yucca Valley

HI-DESERT NATURE MUSEUM, 57116 29 Palms Hwy., Yucca Valley, CA 92284-2930. Tel.: 760-369-7212. Fax: 760-369-1605. Facebook: @theHDNM.
E-mail: museum@yucca-valley.org
Web Site: www.hidesertnaturemuseum.org
Key Personnel: Museum Program Supvr., Stefanie Ritter; Museum Registrar & Exhibits Coord., Vanessa Cantu.
Institution Type/Description: Natural History Museum.
Hours & Admission Prices: Thurs.-Sat. 10-5. No charge; donations accepted. Closed holidays. &
Attendance: 34,180 (actual)

COLORADO

(287 listings)

Alamosa

ADAMS STATE UNIVERSITY LUTHER BEAN MUSEUM, Richardson Hall, #256, Alamosa, CO 81101. Mailing Address: 208 Edgemont Blvd., Alamosa, CO 81101. Tel.: 719-587-7151, 800-824-6494. Fax: 719-587-7522.
E-mail: lutherbean@adams.edu
Web Site: adams.edu/lutherbean
Key Personnel: Interim Pres., Dr. Matt Nehring; Collections Mgr., Tawney Beeker; Administration, Linda Relyea; Security, Andrew MacPherson.
Institution Type/Description: Anthropology, Ethnology Indian & History Museum.
Hours & Admission Prices: Mon.-Fri. 1-5; other times by appointment only. No charge; donations accepted. Closed New Year's Eve & Day; Memorial Day; Labor Day; Thanksgiving; Christmas Eve, Day & week; national holidays. &
Attendance: 500 (estimated)

SAN LUIS VALLEY MUSEUM, 401 Hunt Ave., Alamosa, CO 81101. Mailing Address: P.O. Box 1593, Alamosa, CO 81101-1593. Tel.: 719-587-0667.
E-mail: sanluisvalleymuseum@yahoo.com
Formerly: San Luis History Center
Key Personnel: Chm. (V), Dorothy M. Brandt; Office Mgr. & Museum Shop Mgr., Joyce Gunn.
Institution Type/Description: History Museum.
Hours & Admission Prices: Tues.-Sat. 10-4; other times by appointment. Adults $2; students, teachers, retired/active-duty military or veterans & members no charge. &
Attendance: 1,800 (estimated)

Arvada

ARVADA CENTER FOR THE ARTS AND HUMANITIES, 6901 Wadsworth Blvd., Arvada, CO 80003-3499. Tel.: 720-898-7200. Fax: 720-898-7217.
E-mail: galleries@arvadacenter.org

Web Site: www.arvadacenter.org
Key Personnel: Dir. Galleries & Cur., Collin Parson; Exhibition Mgr. & Registrar, Kristin Bueb.
Institution Type/Description: Art and History Museum.
Hours & Admission Prices: Mon.-Fri. 9-6, Sat. 10-5, Sun. 1-5. No charge; donations accepted. Closed New Year's Day; Memorial Day; Independence Day; Labor Day; Thanksgiving; Christmas. &
Attendance: 350,000 (estimated)

ARVADA FLOUR MILL, 5580 Old Wadsworth Blvd., Arvada, CO 80002-3104. Mailing Address: Arvada Historical Society, 7307 Grandview Ave., Arvada, CO 80002. Tel.: 303-431-1261.
E-mail: info@arvadahistory.org
Institution Type/Description: Historic Building: restored flour mill; built in 1926. Listed on the National Register of Historic Places.
Hours & Admission Prices: By appointment. Adults $1.50, children 12 & under $.50.

ARVADA HISTORICAL SOCIETY, 7307 Grandview Ave., Arvada, CO 80002-2507. Tel.: 303-431-1261.
E-mail: info@arvadahistory.org
Web Site: www.arvadahistory.org
Institution Type/Description: Historical Society Museum.
Hours & Admission Prices: Tues.-Sat. 11-3.

Aspen

ASPEN ART MUSEUM, 637 E. Hyman Ave., Aspen, CO 81611. Tel.: 970-925-8050. Fax: 970-925-8054. Facebook: Aspen Art Museum.
E-mail: info@aspenartmuseum.org
Web Site: www.aspenartmuseum.org
Key Personnel: C.E.O. & Dir. Nancy and Bob Magoon, Heidi Zuckerman.
Institution Type/Description: Contemporary Art Museum & non-collecting.
Hours & Admission Prices: Tues.-Sun. 10-6. No charge; donations accepted. Closed New Year's Day; Thanksgiving; Christmas. &
Attendance: 82,435 (actual)

ASPEN HISTORICAL SOCIETY, 620 W. Bleeker St., Aspen, CO 81611-1230. Tel.: 970-925-3721. Fax: 970-925-5347.
E-mail: info@aspenhistory.org
Web Site: www.aspenhistory.org
Formerly: Heritage Aspen
Key Personnel: Pres. (V), Kelly Murphy; Dir., Georgia Hanson; Vice Pres., Cur. Collections, Lisa Hancock; Vice Pres., Education & Programming, Nina Gabianelli.
Institution Type/Description: Historic Home: housed in Wheeler-Stallard House, built in 1888.
Hours & Admission Prices: Summer: Tues.-Sat. 11-5; Winter: Tues.-Fri. 1-5. Adults $10, seniors $8; children 18 & under and members no charge. Closed Christmas. &
Attendance: 25,000 (estimated)

BALDWIN GALLERY, 209 S. Galena St., Aspen, CO 81611. Tel.: 970-920-9797. Fax: 970-920-1821. Facebook.
E-mail: baldwingallery@baldwingallery.com
Web Site: www.artnet.com/baldwin.html
Key Personnel: Dir., Richard Edwards.
Institution Type/Description: Art Gallery.
Hours & Admission Prices: Mon.-Sat. 10-6, Sun. 12-5.

RED BRICK CENTER FOR THE ARTS, 110 E. Hallam St., Aspen, CO 81611-1458. Tel.: 970-429-2777. Fax: 970-920-5700.
E-mail: info@aspenart.org
Web Site: www.aspenart.org
Key Personnel: Exec. Dir., Angie Callen.
Institution Type/Description: Art Gallery.
Hours & Admission Prices: Mon.-Fri. 10-6.

Aurora

AURORA HISTORY MUSEUM, 15051 E. Alameda Pkwy., Aurora, CO 80012-1554. Tel.: 303-739-6660. Fax: 303-739-6657. Facebook.
E-mail: museum@auroragov.org
Web Site: www.auroramuseum.org
Key Personnel: Dir., T. Scott Williams; Cur. Exhibits, Christopher Shackelford; Cur. Collections, Jennifer Cronk; Cur. Education, Jessica Lira; Visitor Svcs. Mgr., Stephanie Thornton-Kneas; Historic Preservation Specialist, Drake Brownfield.

Institution Type/Description: History Museum.
Hours & Admission Prices: Museum: Tues.-Fri. 9-4, Sat.-Sun. 11-4; call for Gully Homestead and Centennial House hours. No Charge. Closed holidays. &
Attendance: 30,000 (actual)

PLAINS CONSERVATION CENTER, 21901 E. Hampden Ave., Aurora, CO 80013-5000. Tel.: 303-326-8380. Fax: 303-693-3379.
E-mail: nature@auroragov.org
Web Site: www.plainscenter.org
Key Personnel: Exec. Dir., Tudi Arneill.
Institution Type/Description: General Museum.
Hours & Admission Prices: Summer: Mon.-Fri. 9-2, Sat.-Sun. 9-7; Winter: Mon.-Fri. 9-2, Sat.-Sun. 9-5. No charge. Closed New Year's Day; Christmas. &
Attendance: 20,000 (actual)

Basalt

ANN KOROLOGOS GALLERY, 211 Midland Ave., Basalt, CO 81621. Tel.: 970-927-9668.
E-mail: art@korologosgallery.com
Web Site: www.korologosgallery.com
Formerly: Basalt Gallery
Key Personnel: Owner, Ann M. Korologos; Dir. Mktg., Leslie Blanton; Gallery Mgr., Caroline Iles.
Institution Type/Description: Art Gallery.
Hours & Admission Prices: Call for hours. No charge. &

Berthoud

LITTLE THOMPSON VALLEY PIONEER MUSEUM, 224 Mountain Ave., Berthoud, CO 80513. Tel.: 970-532-2147.
E-mail: ltvpm@berthoudhistoricalsociety.org
Web Site: www.berthoudhistoricalsociety.org
Key Personnel: Pres. (V), Mark French.
Institution Type/Description: History Museum.
Hours & Admission Prices: Wed.-Sun. 1-5; other times by appointment.
Attendance: 1,500 (actual)

Boulder

BOULDER MUSEUM OF CONTEMPORARY ART, 1750 13th St., Boulder, CO 80302-6226. Tel.: 303-443-2122. Fax: 303-447-1633. Facebook.
E-mail: info@bmoca.org
Web Site: www.bmoca.org
Key Personnel: Exec. Dir., David Dadone.
Institution Type/Description: Contemporary Art Museum.
Hours & Admission Prices: Tues.-Sun. 11-5. Admission $1; discounts to AAM & ICOM members; MOD/CO, NARM members & children under 12 no charge. &
Attendance: 30,000 (estimated)

CU ART MUSEUM - UNIVERSITY OF COLORADO AT BOULDER, VAC, 1085 18th St., 318 UCB, Boulder, CO 80309. Tel.: 303-492-8300. Fax: 303-492-1977.
E-mail: sandra.firmin@colorado.edu
Web Site: www.colorado.edu/cuartmuseum
Key Personnel: Dir., Sandra Q. Firmin; Chair, Jennifer Constable; Dir. Mktg. & Membership, Jessica Brunecky; Mgr. Collections, Maggie Mazzullo; Mgr. Exhibitions, Stephen Martonis.
Institution Type/Description: Art Gallery.
Hours & Admission Prices: See website for hours. No charge; donations accepted. &
Attendance: 15,000 (actual)

CU HERITAGE CENTER, University of Colorado, Boulder Campus, 3rd Fl. Old Main, 1600 Pleasant St., Boulder, CO 80302. Mailing Address: Campus Box 459, Boulder, CO 80309. Tel.: 303-492-6329. Fax: 303-492-1244.
E-mail: allyson.smith@colorado.edu
Web Site: cuheritage.edu
Key Personnel: Dir., Allyson Smith; Cur. History & Collections, Mona Lambrecht.
Institution Type/Description: History Museum.
Hours & Admission Prices: Mon.-Fri. 10-5. No charge; donations accepted. Closed all university holidays. &
Attendance: 26,300 (actual)

CELESTIAL SEASONINGS, 4600 Sleepytime Dr., Boulder, CO 80301. Tel.: 303-581-1266.
Web Site: celestialseasonings.com
Institution Type/Description: Company History Museum.

Hours & Admission Prices: Tour Center: Mon.-Sat. 9-5, Sun. 10-4. Factory Tour: Mon.-Sat. 10-4, Sun. 11-3; children 5 & over allowed on tour. No charge. Closed New Year's Day; Easter; Memorial Day; Independence Day; Labor Day; Thanksgiving; Christmas.

THE DAIRY CENTER FOR THE ARTS, 2590 Walnut St., Boulder, CO 80302-5700. Tel.: 303-440-7826. Fax: 303-440-7104.
E-mail: bill@thedairy.org
Web Site: www.thedairy.org
Key Personnel: Exec. Dir., Bill Obermeier; Pres., Richard Polk; Dir. Programming, Deven Shaff; Dir. Devel., Beth Smith.
Institution Type/Description: Art Gallery.
Hours & Admission Prices: Daily 8:30-11. Closed holidays. &
Attendance: 200,000 (estimated)

LEANIN' TREE MUSEUM OF WESTERN ART CLOSED, 6055 Longbow Dr., Boulder, CO 80301-3296. Mailing Address: Box 9500, Boulder, CO 80301-9500. Tel.: 303-530-1442, 800-777-8716.
E-mail: artmuseum@leanintree.com
Web Site: www.leanintreemuseum.com
Key Personnel: C.E.O. & Pres., Thomas E. Trumble; Dir. & Chm., Edward P. Trumble.
Institution Type/Description: Art Museum of the American West.
Hours & Admission Prices: Tours: Mon.-Fri. 10, 11, 1, 2. Gift Shop: Mon.-Fri. 9-5. No charge. Closed national holidays. &
Attendance: 50,000 (actual)

MUSEUM OF BOULDER, 2205 Broadway, Boulder, CO 80302-7224. Tel.: 303-449-3464. Fax: 303-938-8322.
E-mail: info@boulderhistory.org
Web Site: www.boulderhistorymuseum.org
Formerly: Boulder History Museum
Key Personnel: Exec. Dir. & C.E.O., Nancy Geyer; Assoc. Dir. Programs, Carol Taylor; Cur. Education, Emily Zinn.
Institution Type/Description: History Museum: housed in the Harbeck-Bergheim house built in 1899.
Hours & Admission Prices: Call for hours. Adults $6, seniors $4, children & students $3; discounts to AAM, ICOM & NARM members; members & children under 5 no charge. Closed major holidays. &
Attendance: 10,000 (actual)

SHELBY AMERICAN COLLECTION, 5020 Chaparral Ct., Boulder, CO 80301-3351. Mailing Address: P.O. Box 19228, Boulder, CO 80308-2228. Tel.: 303-516-9565. Fax: 303-447-1380.
E-mail: info@shelbyamericancollection.org
Web Site: www.shelbyamericancollection.org
Key Personnel: Pres., Steven B. Volk.
Institution Type/Description: Automotive Museum.
Hours & Admission Prices: Sat. 10-4; groups & clubs by appointment. Adults $5; children 12 & under no charge. &
Attendance: 3,000 (estimated)

UNIVERSITY OF COLORADO MUSEUM OF NATURAL HISTORY, Henderson Bldg., 218 UCB, 15th & Broadway, Boulder, CO 80309-0218. Tel.: 303-492-6892 & 6297. Fax: 303-492-4195.
E-mail: cumuseum@colorado.edu
Web Site: cumuseum.colorado.edu
Key Personnel: Dir. & Prof. Biology, J. Patrick Kociolek; Collections Mgr. Botany, Tim Hogan; Collections Mgr. Botany, Dina Clark; Cur. Paleontology & Assoc. Prof. Geological Sciences, Dr. Karen Chin; Cur. & Prof. Anthropology, Dr. Stephen Lekson; Cur. Entomology & Prof. Biology, M. Deane Bowers; Collections Mgr. Entomology, Virginia Scott; Dir. Museum & Field Studies Prog. and Cur. Vertebrate Paleontology, Dr. Jaelyn Eberle; Cur. Botany, Dr. Erin Tripp; Collections Mgr. Zoology, Emily Braker; Cur. Invertebrates, Dr. Jingchun Li; Cur. Vertebrate Zoology & Asst. Prof. Biology, Dr. Christy McCain; Media Coord., Jennifer Dillon; Sr. Educator, Jim Hakala; Museum & Field Studies Graduate Program Coord., Janet Bensko; Visitor Svcs. Coord., Samantha Eads; Asst. to Dir., Susanna Drogsvold; Collection Mgr. Anthropology, Christina Cain; Collection Mgr. Invertebrate Paleontology, Dr. Talia Karim.
Institution Type/Description: Natural History & Anthropology Museum.
Hours & Admission Prices: Mon.-Fri. 9-5, Sat. 9-4, Sun. 10-4. Suggested Donation: adults $3, seniors & children 6-18 $1; children under 6 and CU students, faculty & staff no charge. Closed university holidays; New Year's Day; Easter; Independence Day; Thanksgiving; Christmas. &
Attendance: 50,000 (estimated)

Breckenridge

BARNEY FORD HOUSE MUSEUM, 111 E. Washington Ave., Breckenridge, CO 80424. Mailing Address: P.O. Box 2460, Breckenridge, CO 80424-2460. Tel.: 970-453-9767. Fax: 970-547-5813.
E-mail: info@breckheritage.com
Web Site: www.breckheritage.com
Key Personnel: Dir., Larissa O'Neil.
Institution Type/Description: Historic House: former home of Barney L. Ford, an escaped slave who became a prominent entrepreneur and Black civil rights pioneer in Colorado; built in 1882.
Hours & Admission Prices: Open year-round with seasonal schedules. See website for hours. No charge; donations accepted.
Attendance: 10,566 (actual)

MOUNTAIN TOP CHILDREN'S MUSEUM, 605 S. Park Ave., Breckenridge, CO 80424. Mailing Address: P.O. Box 4359, Breckenridge, CO 80424-4359. Tel.: 970-453-7878. Facebook: Mountain Top Children's Museum.
E-mail: mtntopmuseum@gmail.com
Web Site: www.mtntopmuseum.org
Key Personnel: Exec. Dir., Laura Horvath; Asst. Dir., Bethany Boland; Pres. (V), Kelley da Silva; Chm. (V), Amy Hurwitch; Chm. (V), Alison Earnest; Chm. (V), Kelly Smith; Member-at-Large, Jim Myers; Member-at-Large, Kelly Brady; Member-at-Large, Ken Robertson; Member-at-Large, Kimberly Eytel.
Institution Type/Description: Children's Museum.
Hours & Admission Prices: April 20-May 18 & Sept. 4-Dec. 12 Fri.-Mon. 10-4:30; Dec. 12-April 20 daily 10-4:30. Children $7, adults $5; children under one & seniors no charge. Closed New Year's Day; Independence Day; Christmas. &
Attendance: 10,000 (actual)

RED, WHITE & BLUE FIRE MUSEUM, 308 N. Main St., Breckenridge, CO 80424. Mailing Address: P.O. Box 710, Breckenridge, CO 80424. Tel.: 970-453-2474. Fax: 970-453-1350.
E-mail: rwbfd@rwbfire.org
Web Site: www.rwbfire.org
Institution Type/Description: Firefighting History Museum.
Hours & Admission Prices: Call for hours.

Brighton

ADAMS COUNTY HISTORICAL SOCIETY MUSEUM, 9601 Henderson Rd., Brighton, CO 80601-8127. Tel.: 303-659-7103.
E-mail: adamscountymuseum@gmail.com
Web Site: adamscountymuseum.com
Key Personnel: Dir., Tammy Kranz; Pres., Cliff Lushbough; Sec., Sharon Popish; Treas., Richard Hoffman.
Institution Type/Description: Historical Society Museum.
Hours & Admission Prices: Tues.-Sat. 10-4. Guided Tours: adults $4, seniors & children under 12 $3. Closed Thanksgiving. &
Attendance: 13,860 (actual)

Broomfield

BROOMFIELD DEPOT MUSEUM, 2201 W. 10th Ave., Broomfield, CO 80020-6713. Mailing Address: 3 Community Park Rd., Broomfield, CO 80020-3781. Tel.: 303-466-3663.
E-mail: jainlay-conley@broomfield.org
Web Site: www.broomfield.org
Institution Type/Description: History Museum.
Hours & Admission Prices: Sun. 2-4. No charge; donations accepted. Closed holidays.

BROOMFIELD VETERANS MEMORIAL MUSEUM, 12 Garden Center, Ste. 230, Broomfield, CO 80020-7036. Tel.: 303-460-6801.
E-mail: michaelfellows1@msn.com
Key Personnel: Pres. (V), Michael Fellows.
Institution Type/Description: Military Museum.
Hours & Admission Prices: Tues. 7pm-9pm, Sat. 1-4; other times by appointment. No charge; donations accepted.
Attendance: 600

Brush

BRUSH AREA MUSEUM AND CULTURAL CENTER, 314 S. Clayton St., Brush, CO 80723. Mailing Address: P.O. Box 341, Brush, CO 80723-0341. Tel.: 970-842-5280.
E-mail: engineer@kci.net

Institution Type/Description: History Museum: housed in the former Knearl School building; built in 1910.
Hours & Admission Prices: Fri.-Sat. 10-4, Sun. 1-4; other times by appointment.

Buena Vista

BUENA VISTA HERITAGE MUSEUM, 506 E. Main St., Buena Vista, CO 81211. Mailing Address: P.O. Box 1414, Buena Vista, CO 81211-1414. Tel.: 719-395-8458.
E-mail: buenavistaheritage@msn.com
Web Site: www.buenavistaheritage.org
Key Personnel: Dir., Tom Tomson; Pres. (V), George Barnet.
Institution Type/Description: History Museum.
Hours & Admission Prices: Memorial Day to Sept. Mon.-Sat. 10-5, Sun. 12-5. Adults $5, youth 6-18 $1; Colorado Day, children 5 & under and members no charge. &
Attendance: 3,500 (actual)

Burlington

OLD TOWN MUSEUM, 420 S. 14th St., Burlington, CO 80807-2300. Tel.: 719-346-7382, 800-288-1334. Fax: 719-346-7169.
E-mail: nikki.wall@burlingtoncoco.com
Web Site: burlingtoncolo.com
Key Personnel: Dir., Nikki Wall; Asst. Dir., George Robben; Museum Shop Mgr., Vi Clark.
Institution Type/Description: History Museum.
Hours & Admission Prices: Mon.-Sat. 9-5, Sun. 12-5. &
Attendance: 15,000 (estimated)

Canon City

MUSEUM OF COLORADO PRISONS, 201 N. 1st St., Canon City, CO 81212-3219. Tel.: 719-269-3015. Fax: 719-269-9148.
E-mail: kellison@prisonmuseum.org
Web Site: www.prisonmuseum.org
Key Personnel: Dir., M. Kay Ellison.
Institution Type/Description: Prison Museum.
Hours & Admission Prices: May & Sept. to mid-Oct. daily 10-5; Memorial Day to Labor Day daily 8:30-6; mid-Oct. to April Wed.-Sun. 10-5; other times by appointment. Adults $7, seniors 65 & over $6, youth 6-12 $5; discounts to AAA members, Dept. of Corrections & active military. Closed New Year's Day; Easter; Thanksgiving; Christmas. &
Attendance: 15,000 (actual)

ROYAL GORGE REGIONAL MUSEUM & HISTORY CENTER, 612 Royal Gorge Blvd., Canon City, CO 81212-3751. Mailing Address: P.O. Box 1460, Canon City, CO 81215-1460. Tel.: 719-269-9036.
E-mail: historycenter@canoncity.org
Web Site: rgmhc.org
Formerly: Canon City Municipal Museum
Key Personnel: Dir., Lisa Studts.
Institution Type/Description: History Museum.
Hours & Admission Prices: Wed.-Sat. 10-4. No charge; donations accepted. Closed major holidays. &

Carbondale

MT. SOPRIS HISTORICAL MUSEUM, 499 Weant Blvd., Carbondale, CO 81623. Mailing Address: P.O. Box 2, Carbondale, CO 81623-0002. Tel.: 970-963-7041.
E-mail: mtsoprishistoricalsociety@yahoo.com
Web Site: mtsoprishistoricalsociety.org
Key Personnel: Dir., Beth White; Pres. (V), Jeannie Perry.
Institution Type/Description: History Museum: housed in a cabin built by homesteaders in the late 1800s.
Hours & Admission Prices: Call for hours & admission prices.
Attendance: 500 (estimated)

QUINTENZ GALLERY, 417 Main St., Carbondale, CO 81623. Tel.: 970-429-8666.
E-mail: dq@quintenzgallery.com
Web Site: quintenzgallery.com
Key Personnel: Dir., Txell Pedragosa; Cur. & Art Consultant, David Floria.
Institution Type/Description: Art Gallery.
Hours & Admission Prices: Mon.-Sat. 10-6, Sun. 12-5; other times by appointment.

Castle Rock

CASTLE ROCK MUSEUM AND HISTORICAL SOCIETY, 420 Elbert St., Castle Rock, CO 80104. Tel.: 303-814-3164.
E-mail: Museum@CastleRockHistoricalSociety.org
Institution Type/Description: Historical Society Museum.
Hours & Admission Prices: Wed.-Fri. 12-5, Sat. 11-4. No charge.

Centennial

GAMMA PHI BETA INTERNATIONAL HEADQUARTERS & MUSEUM, 12737 E. Euclid Dr., Centennial, CO 80111-6445. Tel.: 303-799-1874. Fax: 303-799-1876.
E-mail: gammaphibeta@gammaphibeta.org
Web Site: www.gammaphibeta.org
Institution Type/Description: History Museum.
Hours & Admission Prices: Mon.-Fri. 8-4:30. No charge.

Central City

CENTRAL CITY OPERA HOUSE ASSOCIATION, 124 Eureka St., Central City, CO 80427. Mailing Address: 400 S. Colorado Blvd., Ste. 530, Denver, CO 80246-1253. Tel.: 303-292-6500. Fax: 303-292-4958.
Web Site: www.centralcityopera.org
Key Personnel: Gen. & Artistic Dir., Pelham G. Pearce; Music Dir., John Baril; Artistic Dir. Emeritus, John Moriarty; Dir. & Admin. Bofils-Stanton Artists Training Prog., Michael Ehrman.
Institution Type/Description: Historic Opera House & Teller House Hotel Museum; built in 1878. A National Historic Landmark.
Hours & Admission Prices: Call for hours & admissions. Closed major holidays. &
Attendance: 20,000 (estimated)

GILPIN HISTORY MUSEUM, 228 E. High St., Central City, CO 80427. Mailing Address: P.O. Box 247, Central City, CO 80427-0247. Tel.: 303-582-5283.
E-mail: gilpinhistory@live.com
Web Site: www.gilpinhistory.org
Key Personnel: Exec. Dir., James Prochaska.
Institution Type/Description: Historical Society Museum: housed in c.1870 Gilpin County Public School.
Hours & Admission Prices: Memorial Day to Labor Day daily 11-4. Adults $5; discounts to AAM members; senior citizens, children under 12 & members no charge.
Attendance: 1,200 (actual)

Clark

HAHNS PEAK AREA HISTORICAL SOCIETY AND SCHOOL HOUSE, Main St., Hahns Peak Village, Clark, CO 80428-9999. Mailing Address: P.O. Box 803, Clark, CO 80428-0803. Tel.: 970-879-7291.
E-mail: maeardley@msn.com
Web Site: www.hahnspeakhistoric.com
Key Personnel: Pres. (V) & Cur., Marge Eardley; Treas., Shelley Stanford.
Institution Type/Description: History Museum: located on the site of the first permanent settlement in Routt County & N.W. Colorado.
Hours & Admission Prices: June-Sept. daily 12-4. No charge; donations accepted.
Attendance: 1,500 (estimated)

Colorado Springs

AMERICAN NUMISMATIC ASSOCIATION MONEY MUSEUM, 818 N. Cascade Ave., Colorado Springs, CO 80903-3279. Tel.: 719-482-9828. Fax: 719-634-4085.
E-mail: museum@money.org
Web Site: www.money.org
Formerly: Museum of the American Numismatic Association
Key Personnel: Pres., Gary Adkins; Exec. Dir., Kim Kiick; Museum Dir. & Cur., Douglas Mudd; Controller, Carol Shuman; Treas., Larry Baber; Mktg. & Communications Dir., Deborah Muelheisen; Library Mgr., David Sklow; Collections Mgr., Andy Dickes.
Institution Type/Description: Numismatic Museum.
Hours & Admission Prices: Tues.-Sat. 10:30-5; groups by appointment. Adults $5; seniors, active military & students $4; discounts to groups; members & 3rd Sat. each month no charge. Closed federal holidays. &
Attendance: 23,000 (actual)

CHEYENNE MOUNTAIN ZOOLOGICAL PARK, 4250 Cheyenne Mountain Zoo Rd., Colorado Springs, CO 80906-5755. Tel.: 719-633-9925. Fax: 719-633-2254.
E-mail: info@cmzoo.org
Web Site: www.cmzoo.org
Key Personnel: Pres. & C.E.O., Bob Chastain.
Institution Type/Description: Zoo.
Hours & Admission Prices: Daily 9-5. May to Labor Day: adults $17.25, seniors 65 & over $15.25, children 3-11 $12.25; Sept.-April adults $14.25, seniors 65 & over $12.25, children 3-11 $10.25; discounts to AZA & AAA members & military; members and children 2 & under no charge. &
Attendance: 575,000 (actual)

COLORADO SPRINGS FINE ARTS CENTER (TAYLOR MUSEUM), 30 W. Dale St., Colorado Springs, CO 80903-3210. Tel.: 719-634-5581. Fax: 719-634-0570.
E-mail: info@csfineartscenter.org
Web Site: www.csfineartscenter.org
Key Personnel: Dir., Erin Hannan; Museum Dir., Rebecca Tucker; Dir. Devel., Erin Hannan; Dir. Bemis School of Art, Tara Thomas; Dir. Performing Arts, Scott R. C. Levy; Dir. Mktg. & Communications, Dori Mitchell.
Institution Type/Description: Art Museum.
Hours & Admission Prices: Sat.-Thurs. 10-5, Fri. & theatre nights 10-7:30. Variable pricing for non-members; members, children 4 & under & museum employees with ID no charge. Closed holidays. &
Attendance: 200,000 (estimated)

COLORADO SPRINGS MUSEUM, 215 S. Tejon St., Colorado Springs, CO 80903-2206. Tel.: 719-385-5990. Fax: 719-385-5645.
E-mail: cosmuseum@springsgov.com
Web Site: www.cspm.org
Key Personnel: Dir., Matt Mayberry; Cur. History, Leah Davis Witherow; Museum Shop Mgr., Carol Denning.
Institution Type/Description: History Museum: housed in the former El Paso County Courthouse, 1903.
Hours & Admission Prices: Tues.-Sat. 10-5. No charge; donations accepted. Closed city holidays. &
Attendance: 55,818 (actual)

DR. LESTER L. WILLIAMS FIRE MUSEUM, 375 Printers Pkwy., Colorado Springs, CO 80901. Mailing Address: P.O. Box 119, Colorado Springs, CO 80901-0119. Tel.: 719-385-5950.
Web Site: williamsfiremuseum.com
Key Personnel: Pres. (V), Roy Manuszak.
Institution Type/Description: History Museum.
Hours & Admission Prices: Mon.-Fri. 8-5. No charge; donations accepted.
Attendance: 2,000 (estimated)

EL POMAR PENROSE HERITAGE MUSEUM, 11 Lake Cir., Colorado Springs, CO 80906. Mailing Address: 10 Lake Cir., Colorado Springs, CO 80906. Tel.: 719-577-7065.
E-mail: jcampbell@elpomar.org
Web Site: elpomar.org
Key Personnel: Chm. & C.E.O., William J. Hybel; Cur., Jason J. Campbell.
Institution Type/Description: Transportation Museum.
Hours & Admission Prices: Mon.-Sat. 9-5, Sun. 1-5. No charge. Closed New Year's Day; Easter; Thanksgiving; Christmas. &
Attendance: 13,000 (estimated)

GALLERY OF CONTEMPORARY ART, UNIVERSITY OF COLORADO, COLORADO SPRINGS, 1420 Austin Bluffs Pkwy., Colorado Springs, CO 80918-3733. Tel.: 719-255-3504. Fax: 719-262-3183. TDD: 262-3621.
E-mail: gallery@uccs.edu
Web Site: www.galleryuccs.org
Key Personnel: Dir., Daisy McGowan.
Institution Type/Description: Art Museum & Center.
Hours & Admission Prices: Tues.-Fri. 12-6; other times by appointment. No charge; donations accepted. Closed major holidays. &
Attendance: 28,000 (estimated)

GARDEN OF THE GODS VISITOR & NATURE CENTER, 1805 N. 30th St., Colorado Springs, CO 80904-1247. Tel.: 719-634-6666. Fax: 719-634-0094.
Web Site: www.gardenofgods.com
Institution Type/Description: Nature Center.
Hours & Admission Prices: Park: May-Oct. daily 5am-11pm; Nov.-April daily 5am-9pm. Visitor Center: Memorial Day to Labor Day daily 8-8; Winter: daily 9-5. No charge.

GHOST TOWN MUSEUM, 400 S. 21st St., Colorado Springs, CO 80904-3755. Tel.: 719-634-0696.
E-mail: history@ghosttownmuseum.com
Web Site: www.ghosttownmuseum.com
Institution Type/Description: History Museum.
Hours & Admission Prices: June-Aug. Mon.-Sat. 9-6, Sun. 10-6; Sept.-May daily 10-5. Adults $7.50, children 6-16 $5; children under 6 no charge. ♿

MAY NATURAL HISTORY MUSEUM, 710 Rock Creek Canyon Rd., Colorado Springs, CO 80926-9799. Tel.: 719-576-0450. Fax: 719-576-3644. Facebook: @maybugmuseum.
E-mail: reservations@goldeneaglecg.com
Web Site: www.coloradospringsbugmuseum.com
Formerly: May Natural History Museum and Museum of Space Exploration
Key Personnel: Caretaker, R.J. Steer; Caretaker, Carrie York.
Institution Type/Description: Natural History, Entomology.
Hours & Admission Prices: May-Sept. daily 9-6; Oct.-April by appointment. Adults $6, seniors 60 & over $5, children 6-12 $4; discounts to schools, senior citizens & AAA members; children under 6 with family no charge. ♿
Attendance: 35,000 (estimated)

MCALLISTER HOUSE MUSEUM, 423 N. Cascade Ave., Colorado Springs, CO 80903-3391. Tel.: 719-635-7925.
E-mail: mcallister.curator@gmail.com
Web Site: www.mcallisterhouse.org
Key Personnel: Chair, Terry Thatcher; Cur., Owanah Wick.
Institution Type/Description: Historic House: c.1873 Major Henry McAllister Home.
Hours & Admission Prices: Feb.-April & Sept.-Dec. Thurs.-Sat. 10-4; May-Aug. Tues.-Sat. 10-4. Adults $5, seniors, students & members $4, children 6-12 $3; children under 6 no charge. Closed major holidays.
Attendance: 3,000 (estimated)

THE NATIONAL MUSEUM OF WORLD WAR II AVIATION, 755 Aviation Way, Colorado Springs, CO 80916. Tel.: 719-637-7559.
Web Site: www.worldwariiaviation.org
Institution Type/Description: Military History Museum.
Hours & Admission Prices: Tours: Tues., Thurs. & Sat. 10-4 by appointment. Adults $12, military $10, seniors $8, children 4-12 $8; discounts for pre-paid tickets; WWII veteran no charge. Closed Thanksgiving; Christmas.

OLD COLORADO CITY HISTORICAL SOCIETY, One South 24th St., Colorado Springs, CO 80904-3319. Tel.: 719-636-1225. Facebook: Old Colorado City Historical Society.
E-mail: info@occhs.org
Web Site: www.occhs.org
Key Personnel: Pres., Sharon Swint.
Institution Type/Description: Historical Society Museum.
Hours & Admission Prices: Tues.-Sat. 11-4. Programs: adults $5; members no charge. Closed holidays. ♿

PRO RODEO HALL OF FAME & MUSEUM OF THE AMERICAN COWBOY, 101 Pro Rodeo Dr., Colorado Springs, CO 80919-2396. Tel.: 719-528-4764. Fax: 719-264-4914. Facebook: Pro Rodeo Hall of Fame & Museum of the American Cowboy.
E-mail: ksturman@prorodeo.com
Web Site: www.prorodeohalloffame.com
Formerly: Pro Rodeo Hall of Champions
Key Personnel: Bd. Pres., Karl Stressman; Dir., Kent L. Sturman; Mktg. & Events Coord., Sara Tadken; Collections & Exhibits Coord., Megan Winterfeldt.
Institution Type/Description: Rodeo & Cowboy History Museum.
Hours & Admission Prices: May-Aug. daily 9-5; Sept.-April Wed.-Sun. 9-5. Adults $8, seniors $7, children 6-12 $5; discount to groups of 15 or more, school groups & military; members and children 5 & under no charge. Closed New Year's Eve & Day; Easter; Independence Day; Thanksgiving; Christmas Eve & Day. ♿
Attendance: 25,000 (actual)

ROCK LEDGE RANCH HISTORIC SITE, 3105 Gateway Rd., Colorado Springs, CO 80904. Mailing Address: 1401 Recreation Way, Colorado Springs, CO 80905-1024. Tel.: 719-578-6777. Fax: 719-578-6965.
E-mail: info@rockledgeranch.com
Web Site: rockledgeranch.com
Key Personnel: Mgr., Andy Morris.
Institution Type/Description: Historic Site: listed on the National Register of Historic Places.

Hours & Admission Prices: June to August Wed.-Sat. 10-5; special events throughout the year. Adults $6, seniors 55 & over and students 13-18 $4; youth 6-12 $2; discounts to groups; children under 6 no charge. ♿
Attendance: 74,000 (actual)

SEVEN FALLS, 6 Lake Ave., Colorado Springs, CO 80906-2919. Tel.: 719-632-0765, 855-923-7272. Fax: 719-632-0781.
E-mail: sevenfalls@broadmoor.com
Web Site: www.sevenfalls.com
Institution Type/Description: Natural History Museum.
Hours & Admission Prices: Seasonal hours: call for information. Adults $14, children $8; children under 2 no charge.

SPACE FOUNDATION DISCOVERY CENTER, 4425 Arrowswest Dr., Colorado Springs, CO 80907. Tel.: 719-576-8000, 800-691-4000.
E-mail: media@spacefoundation.org
Web Site: www.spacefoundation.org
Institution Type/Description: Science Center.
Hours & Admission Prices: June to mid-Aug. Mon.-Sat. 10-5; mid-Aug. to May Tues.-Sat. 10-2. Adults $10, seniors 65 & over and college students $7.50, children 4-17 $4.50, children 2-3 $1; discounts to military; children under 2 no charge.

U.S. OLYMPIC VISITOR CENTER, 1 Olympic Plaza, Colorado Springs, CO 80909. Tel.: 719-866-4618.
E-mail: csotc.visitorcenter@usoc.org
Web Site: www.teamusa.org/tours
Key Personnel: Venues Mgr., Mike Beagley.
Institution Type/Description: Sports Museum.
Hours & Admission Prices: Tours: Summer Mon.-Sat. 9-4:30, Sun. 11-4; Winter Mon.-Sat. 9-4. Adults $12, seniors & military $10, children $8. Closed New Years Day; Easter; Independence Day; Thanksgiving; Christmas Eve & Day.
Attendance: 140,000 (estimated)

WESTERN MUSEUM OF MINING & INDUSTRY, 225 N. Gate Blvd., Colorado Springs, CO 80921-3002. Tel.: 719-488-0880, 800-752-6558. Fax: 719-488-9261. Facebook.
E-mail: info@wmmi.org
Web Site: www.wmmi.org
Key Personnel: Exec. Dir., Richard Sauers; Museum Mgr., Grant Dewey; Mktg. & Communications Coord., Danica Cox; Volunteer Coord., Ryan Ramder.
Institution Type/Description: Mining & Technology History Museum.
Hours & Admission Prices: Mon.-Sat. 9-4, guided tours at 10 & 1. Adults $10, military & AAA members $9, seniors & students $8, children 4-12 $6; discounts to AAM & ICOM members; children under 3 w/ paid adult & members no charge. ♿
Attendance: 20,000 (actual)

WORLD FIGURE SKATING MUSEUM & HALL OF FAME, 20 First St., Colorado Springs, CO 80906-3624. Tel.: 719-635-5200. Fax: 719-635-9548.
E-mail: information@worldskatingmuseum.org
Web Site: www.worldskatingmuseum.org
Key Personnel: Dir. Communications, Barb Reichert; Archivist, Karen Cover.
Institution Type/Description: Sports Museum.
Hours & Admission Prices: Tues.-Fri. 10-4. Adults $5, seniors 60 & over $3; discounts to military & AAA members; children 5 & under and U.S. Figure Skating members no charge. Closed New Year's Eve & Day; Memorial Day; Independence Day; Labor Day; Thanksgiving; Christmas; postal & bank holidays. ♿
Attendance: 7,500 (estimated)

Cortez

CORTEZ CULTURAL CENTER, 25 N. Market St., Cortez, CO 81321-3212. Tel.: 970-565-1151. Fax: 970-565-4075. Facebook: Cortez Cultural Center.
E-mail: info@cortezculturalcenter.org
Web Site: www.cortezculturalcenter.org
Key Personnel: Exec. Dir., Rebecca Levy; Pres. (V), Holly Tatnall.
Institution Type/Description: Native American Museum.
Hours & Admission Prices: Memorial Day to Labor Day. Mon.-Sat. 10-9; Sept.-June Mon.-Sat. 10-5. No charge; donations accepted.
Attendance: 8,000 (estimated)

CROW CANYON ARCHAEOLOGICAL CENTER, 23390 County Rd. K, Cortez, CO 81321-9408. Tel.: 970-565-8975. Fax: 970-565-4859.

E-mail: info@crowcanyon.org
Web Site: www.crowcanyon.org
Key Personnel: Pres. & C.E.O., Elizabeth Perry; Dir. Archaeology, Susan Ryan.
Institution Type/Description: Archaeological Center.
Hours & Admission Prices: April-Oct. Mon.-Fri. 8-5. No charge. Day Tour: May 27-Sept. 8:30-4:30. Adults $60, children 10-17 $35; children under 10 not admitted. &
Attendance: 3,000 (estimated)

NOTAH DINEH MUSEUM, 345 W. Main, Cortez, CO 81321-3132. Tel.: 800-444-2024.
E-mail: notah@fone.net
Key Personnel: Owner, Greg Leighton.
Institution Type/Description: Native American Museum.
Hours & Admission Prices: Mon.-Sat. 9-6:30.

Craig

MUSEUM OF NORTHWEST COLORADO, 590 Yampa Ave., Craig, CO 81625-2612. Tel.: 970-824-6360. Fax: 970-824-1098.
E-mail: ddavidson@moffatcounty.net
Web Site: www.museumnwco.org
Key Personnel: Dir., Dan Davidson; Pres. (V), Delaine Voloshin; Asst. Dir., Jan Gerber.
Institution Type/Description: Local History Museum.
Hours & Admission Prices: Mon.-Sat. 9-5. No charge; donations accepted. &
Attendance: 16,500 (actual)

WYMAN MUSEUM, 94350 E. Hwy. 40, Craig, CO 81625. Mailing Address: P.O. Box 339, Craig, CO 81626-0339. Tel.: 970-824-6346. Fax: 970-824-5890. Facebook: Lou Wyman.
E-mail: wymanmuseum@earthlink.net
Web Site: wymanmuseum.com
Key Personnel: Co Dir., Lou Wyman; Co Dir., Paula Wyman; Chm. (V), Al Shepherd; Museum Shop Mgr., Nicky Boulger.
Institution Type/Description: Living History Museum.
Hours & Admission Prices: Mon.-Fri. 9-5, Sat.-Sun. 11-4. No charge; donations accepted. Closed major holidays. &
Attendance: 10,395 (actual)

Creede

CREEDE UNDERGROUND MINING MUSEUM, 503 Forest Service Rd. #9, Creede, CO 81130. Mailing Address: P.O. Box 422, Creede, CO 81130-0422. Tel.: 719-658-0811.
E-mail: creedeminingmuseum@hotmail.com
Key Personnel: Museum Shop Mgr., Ricky Brown; Museum Shop Mgr., Dianna Brown.
Institution Type/Description: Mining Museum.
Hours & Admission Prices: Memorial Day to Labor Day daily 10-4; Fall & Spring Mon.-Fri. 10-3. Tour: $15 per person.

Crested Butte

CENTER FOR THE ARTS PIPER GALLERY, 606 6th St., Crested Butte, CO 81224-1819. Mailing Address: P.O. Box 1819, Crested Butte, CO 81224-1819. Tel.: 970-349-7487. Fax: 970-349-5626.
E-mail: jenny@crestedbuttearts.org
Web Site: www.crestedbuttearts.org
Key Personnel: Exec. Dir., Jenny Birnie; Pres. (V), Gail Digale.
Institution Type/Description: Art Gallery.
Hours & Admission Prices: Call for hours.
Attendance: 20,500 (estimated)

CRESTED BUTTE MOUNTAIN HERITAGE MUSEUM, 331 Elk Ave., Crested Butte, CO 81224. Mailing Address: P.O. Box 2480, Crested Butte, CO 81224-2480. Tel.: 970-349-1880. Facebook.
E-mail: museum@crestedbutte.cc
Web Site: www.crestedbuttemuseum.com
Key Personnel: C.E.O., Shelley Popke; Pres. (V), Clif Barnhart; Museum Shop Mgr., Mary Haskell.
Institution Type/Description: History Museum.
Hours & Admission Prices: Summer: daily 10-8; Winter: daily 12-6; Spring & Fall: call for hours. Adults $5, inactive duty military $3; discounts to AAM & ICOM members; active duty military, AASLH & museum members no charge. &
Attendance: 46,123 (actual)

Cripple Creek

CRIPPLE CREEK DISTRICT MUSEUM, INC., 500 E. Bennett Ave., Cripple Creek, CO 80813. Mailing Address: P.O. Box 1210, Cripple Creek, CO 80813-1210. Tel.: 719-689-9540 & 2634. Facebook.
E-mail: contactus@cripplecreekmuseum.com
Web Site: www.cripplecreekmuseum.com
Key Personnel: Dir., Kathy Reynolds; Pres., Ike Hern; Bd. Member, Georganna Peiffer.
Institution Type/Description: Historic Buildings.
Hours & Admission Prices: May-Oct. 15 daily 10-5; Oct. 16-April Sat.-Sun. 10-5. Adults $7, military $5; discounts to groups; members and children 12 & under no charge. Closed Thanksgiving; Christmas. &
Attendance: 15,000 (actual)

MOLLIE KATHLEEN GOLD MINE, 9388 U.S. Hwy. 67, Cripple Creek, CO 80813. Mailing Address: P.O. Box 339, Cripple Creek, CO 80813-0339. Tel.: 719-689-2466.
E-mail: molliegold@rmi.net
Web Site: www.goldminetours.com
Institution Type/Description: Mining Museum.
Hours & Admission Prices: April 2-May 14 & Oct. daily 10-4; May 15-Sept. 15 daily 9-5; Sept. 16-Sept. 30 daily 10-5. Adults $18, children 3-12 $10; children 2 & under no charge.

Del Norte

RIO GRANDE COUNTY MUSEUM AND CULTURAL CENTER, 580 Oak St., Del Norte, CO 81132-2210. Tel.: 719-657-2847.
E-mail: rgmuseum@riograndecounty.org
Web Site: museumtrail.org/RioGrandeCountyMuseum.asp
Key Personnel: Dir., Louise Colville.
Institution Type/Description: History Museum.
Hours & Admission Prices: Tues.-Fri. 10-4, Sat. 10-2. Admission $2; members no charge.

Delta

DELTA COUNTY MUSEUM, 251 Meeker St., Delta, CO 81416-1914. Tel.: 970-874-8721.
E-mail: deltamuseum@aol.com
Key Personnel: Chm. (V) & Pres. (V), Keith Lucy; Cur., James K. Wetzel.
Institution Type/Description: History Museum.
Hours & Admission Prices: May-Sept. Tues.-Fri. 10-4; Oct.-April Tues. & Wed. 10-4. Adults $2, seniors $1; children under 12 with adult & members no charge. Closed legal holidays. &
Attendance: 3,500 (estimated)

FORT UNCOMPAHGRE HISTORY MUSEUM, 205 Gunnison River Dr., Delta, CO 81416-1847. Mailing Address: 360 Main St., Delta, CO 81416-1837. Tel.: 970-874-8349. Fax: 970-874-1353.
E-mail: wilma@cityofdelta.net
Web Site: www.cityofdelta.net
Key Personnel: C.E.O., Wilma Erven; Cur., Ken Reyher.
Institution Type/Description: General Museum.
Hours & Admission Prices: April-May & Sept.-Nov. Mon.-Sat. 8-5. Admission $3.50. Closed major holidays. &
Attendance: 3,000 (estimated)

Denver

AMERICAN MUSEUM OF WESTERN ART - ANSCHUTZ COLLECTION, 1727 Tremont Pl., Denver, CO 80202. Tel.: 303-293-2000. Facebook.
E-mail: info@anschutzcollection.org
Web Site: www.anschutzcollection.org
Institution Type/Description: Art Museum.
Hours & Admission Prices: Mon. & Wed. 10-4:30. Tours: 10 & 1.. Guided Tours: adults $10, seniors & students $7. Self-Guided Tours: $5 per person.

BLACK AMERICAN WEST MUSEUM & HERITAGE CENTER, 3091 California St., Denver, CO 80205-3044. Tel.: 303-482-2242. Fax: 303-382-1981.
E-mail: info@blackamericanwestmuseum.com
Web Site: www.blackamericanwestmuseum.org
Institution Type/Description: History Museum: located in the home of Dr. Justina L. Ford, the first Black female physician in Colorado.

Hours & Admission Prices: June-Aug. Tues.-Sat. 10-5; Sept.-May Tues.-Sat. 10-2. Adults $10, senior citizens over 65 $9, students $8, children 6-11 $7; children 5 & under and members no charge. Closed New Year's Day; Easter; Memorial Day; Independence Day; Labor Day; Thanksgiving; Christmas. &
Attendance: 12,500 (estimated)

BYERS-EVANS HOUSE MUSEUM, 1310 Bannock St., Denver, CO 80204-2719. Tel.: 303-620-4933.
E-mail: jillian.allison@state.co.us
Web Site: www.byersevanshousemuseum.org
Key Personnel: Dir., Jillian Allison.
Institution Type/Description: Historic House: 1883 Italianate style home.
Hours & Admission Prices: Mon.-Sat. 10-4. Adults $6, senior citizens & students $5, children 6-12 $4; discounts to AAM members; members & children under 6 no charge. Closed state holidays. &
Attendance: 12,000 (estimated)

CHILDREN'S MUSEUM OF DENVER AT MARSICO CAMPUS, 2121 Children's Museum Dr., Denver, CO 80211-5200. Tel.: 303-433-7444. Fax: 303-433-9520. Facebook, Youtube; Instagram.
E-mail: information@cmdenver.org
Web Site: www.mychildsmuseum.org
Formerly: Children's Museum of Denver
Key Personnel: Pres. & C.E.O., Mike Yankovich; Chm. Bd., Jim Schoeffler; C.O.O., Gretchen Kerr; Vice Pres. Devel. & Communications, Amy Burt; C.F.O., Cyndi Kerins.
Institution Type/Description: Children's Museum.
Hours & Admission Prices: Mon.-Tues. & Thurs.-Fri. 9-4, Wed. 9-7:30, Sat.-Sun. 10-5. Admission 2-59 $13, senior citizens 60 & over & children one-year old $11; discounts to AAM members; children under one & members no charge. Closed New Year's Day; Easter; Thanksgiving; Christmas Eve & Day. &
Attendance: 502,143 (actual)

CLYFFORD STILL MUSEUM, 1250 Bannock St., Denver, CO 80204-3631. Tel.: 720-354-4880.
E-mail: info@clyffordstillmuseum.org
Web Site: clyffordstillmuseum.org
Key Personnel: Dir., Dean Sobel; Chm. (V), Christopher Hunt.
Institution Type/Description: Art Gallery.
Hours & Admission Prices: Tues.-Thurs. & Sat.-Sun. 10-5, Fri. 10-8. Adults $10, seniors 65 & over $8, teachers, students & college students with valid ID $6; discounts to groups; Fri. 5-8, 1st Sat. of month, last Fri. of month & youth under 18 no charge. Closed New Year's Day; Thanksgiving; Christmas. &
Attendance: 42,685 (actual)

COLORADO SPORTS HALL OF FAME, Sports Authority Field at Mile High, 1701 Bryant St., Ste. 500, Denver, CO 80204. Tel.: 720-258-3888. Fax: 303-244-1003.
E-mail: laura@coloradosports.org
Web Site: www.coloradosports.org
Key Personnel: C.E.O., Tom Lawrence; Mktg. & Tour Dir., Kate Becker.
Institution Type/Description: Sports Museum.
Hours & Admission Prices: June-Aug. Mon.-Sat. 10-2; Sept.-May Thurs.-Sat. 10-2. Tours: adults $20, seniors & children 6-12 $15; discounts to groups of 25 & up; children 5 & under with adult no charge. Closed day before home games. &
Attendance: 20,000 (estimated)

COLORADO STATE CAPITOL, 200 E. Colfax Ave., Denver, CO 80203-1776. Tel.: 303-866-2604.
Web Site: leg.colorado.gov/visit-learn
Institution Type/Description: Historic Building: built in the 1890s.
Hours & Admission Prices: Mon.-Fri. 10-3; reservations for groups & those with special needs. No charge. Closed most legal holidays. &

CORE NEW ART SPACE, 900 Santa Fe Dr., Denver, CO 80204-3937. Tel.: 303-297-8428.
E-mail: art@corenewartspace.com
Web Site: www.coreartspace.com
Institution Type/Description: Art Gallery.
Hours & Admission Prices: Thurs. & Sat. 12-6, Fri. 12-9, Sun. 1-4. No charge.
Attendance: 15,000 (estimated)

DAVID B. SMITH GALLERY, 1543 A Wazee St., Denver, CO 80202. Tel.: 303-893-4234.
E-mail: info@davidbsmithgallery.com
Web Site: www.davidbsmithgallery.com
Institution Type/Description: Art Gallery.
Hours & Admission Prices: Wed.-Fri. 12-6, Sat. 12-5; other times by appointment.

DENVER ART MUSEUM, 100 W. 14th Ave. Pkwy., Denver, CO 80204-2788. Tel.: 720-865-5000. Fax: 720-913-0001. Facebook.
Web Site: www.denverartmuseum.org
Key Personnel: Chm., J. Landis Martin; Frederick & Jan Mayer Dir., Christoph Henrich; Deputy Dir. & Chief Mktg. Officer, Andrea Fulton; Deputy Dir. & C.F.O., Curtis Woitte.
Institution Type/Description: Art Museum.
Hours & Admission Prices: Museum: Tues.-Thurs. & Sat.-Sun. 10-5, Fri. 10-8. Library: by appointment; located in the administrative annex. Adults in-state $10, out-of-state $13, senior citizens & students in-state $8, out-of-state $10; children 18 & under, 1st Sat of month and members no charge. Closed Memorial Day; LaborDay; Thanksgiving; Christmas. &
Attendance: 866,000 (estimated)

DENVER BOTANIC GARDENS, INC., 1007 York St., Denver, CO 80206-3014. Mailing Address: 909 York St., Denver, CO 80206. Tel.: 720-865-3500 & 3501. Fax: 720-865-3682. Facebook; Instagram; Twitter.
E-mail: exhibits@botanicgardens.org
Web Site: botanicgardens.org
Key Personnel: C.E.O., Brian Vogt; C.F.O., John Calderhead; Dir. Membership, Visitor & Volunteer Svcs., Mary Bradley; Dir. Events, Sara Buys; Dir. Education, Matthew Cole; Dir. Exhibitions, Art & Interpretation, Lisa Eldred; Dir. Devel., Johanna Kelly; Dir. Horticulture, Sarada Krishnan, Ph.D.; Dir. Research & Conservation, Jennifer Ramp; Dir. Mktg. & Social Responsibility, Jennifer Riley-Chetwynd; Dir. Chatfield Farms, Larry Vickerman; Museum Shop Mgr., Randy Geist.
Institution Type/Description: Botanical Gardens & Arboretum.
Hours & Admission Prices: Call for hours. Adults $12.50, seniors 65 & over and military $9.50, students & children 3-15 $9; discounts to ICOM & AAM members; members and children 2 & under no charge. Closed New Year's Day; Thanksgiving; Christmas. &
Attendance: 1,042,763 (actual)

THE DENVER CENTER FOR THE PERFORMING ARTS, 1101 13th St., Denver, CO 80204. Tel.: 303-893-4000.
E-mail: info@dcpa.org
Web Site: www.denvercenter.org
Key Personnel: Chm., Daniel L. Ritchie; Pres. & C.E.O., Janice Sinden; C.F.O., Vicky Miles; Exec. Dir., Broadway, John Ekeberg.
Institution Type/Description: History Museum.
Hours & Admission Prices: Mon.-Sat. 10-8, Sun. 10-6. Closed major holidays.
Attendance: 685,375 (actual)

DENVER FIREFIGHTERS MUSEUM, 1326 Tremont Pl., Denver, CO 80204-2120. Tel.: 303-892-1436. Fax: 303-893-4835.
E-mail: info@denverfirefightersmuseum.org
Web Site: www.denverfirefightersmuseum.org
Key Personnel: Exec. Dir. & Chief Cur., Winifred Ferrill; Pres. (V), Robert Vallero; Sec., James F. Stillman; Museum Shop Mgr., Tiffany DeBaca.
Institution Type/Description: History Museum.
Hours & Admission Prices: Mon.-Sat. 10-4. Adults $7, senior citizens & students $6, children 2-12 $4; discounts to groups & AAM members; children under 2 & members no charge. &
Attendance: 35,000 (actual)

DENVER MUSEUM OF MINIATURES, DOLLS AND TOYS, 1880 Gaylord St., Denver, CO 80206-1211. Tel.: 303-322-1053. Fax: 303-322-3407.
E-mail: director@dmmdt.org
Web Site: www.dmmdt.org
Key Personnel: Dir., Wendy Littlepage; Asst. Dir. Education & Collections, Kelly Wulf.
Institution Type/Description: Miniatures, Dolls & Toys Museum.
Hours & Admission Prices: Wed.-Sat. 10-4, Sun. 1-4. Adults $6, senior citizens 62 & over $5, children 5-16 $4; discounts to groups; children under 5 no charge. Closed major holidays. &
Attendance: 7,809 (actual)

DENVER MUSEUM OF NATURE & SCIENCE, 2001 Colorado Blvd., Denver, CO 80205-5798. Tel.: 303-370-6000.
E-mail: guestservices@dmns.org
Web Site: www.dmns.org
Formerly: Denver Museum of Natural History
Key Personnel: Pres. & C.E.O., George Sparks; Vice Pres. Finance & Business Operations, Ed Scholz; Vice Pres. Visitor Experience, Mary Hacking; Vice Pres. Partnerships & Programs, Nancy Walsh; Vice Pres. Devel., Serena Bruzgo.
Institution Type/Description: Natural History Museum.
Hours & Admission Prices: Museum: daily 9-5. Adults $16.95 seniors 65 & over $13.95, juniors 3-18 $11.95; members no charge. IMAX: adults $9.95, juniors 3-18 and seniors 65 & over $7.95; discounts to museum members. Museum &

IMAX Combination: adults $23.95, seniors 65 & over $19.95; juniors 3-18 $17.95; discounts to museum members. Additional packages available. Closed Christmas. &
Attendance: 1,252,300 (actual)

DENVER ZOOLOGICAL FOUNDATION, 2300 Steele St., Denver, CO 80205-4899. Tel.: 720-337-1400. Fax: 720-337-1401.
E-mail: guestcare@denverzoo.org
Web Site: www.denverzoo.org
Key Personnel: Interim Pres., Denny O'Malley; C.F.O., Charlie Wright; Chief Devel. Officer, Chris Harvey.
Institution Type/Description: Zoo.
Hours & Admission Prices: March-Oct. daily 9-6. Adults $17, seniors 65 & over $14, children 3-11 $12; children 2 & under no charge. Nov.-Feb. daily 10-5. Adults $13, seniors 65 & over $11, children 3-11 $9; children 2 & under no charge. &
Attendance: 1,989,956 (estimated)

DOWNTOWN AQUARIUM, 700 Water St., Denver, CO 80211-5210. Tel.: 303-561-4450.
E-mail: spieper@ldry.com
Web Site: www.aquariumrestaurants.com
Institution Type/Description: Aquarium.
Hours & Admission Prices: Sun.-Thurs. 10-9, Fri.-Sat. 10-9:30. Adults 12-64 $19.50, seniors 65 & over $18.50, children 3-11 $13.50; children 2 & under no charge.

EMMANUEL GALLERY, Auraria Campus, 1205 10th St., Denver, CO 80204. Mailing Address: Auraria Campus, Campus Box 162, P.O. Box 173364, Denver, CO 80217-3364. Tel.: 303-315-7431. Facebook.
E-mail: emmanuelgallery@ucdenver.edu
Web Site: www.emmanuelgallery.org
Key Personnel: Dir. & Cur., Jeff Lambson.
Institution Type/Description: Art Gallery.
Hours & Admission Prices: Temporarily closed. To reopen mid-2017. No charge.
Attendance: 10,000 (actual)

FORNEY MUSEUM OF TRANSPORTATION, 4303 Brighton Blvd., Denver, CO 80216-3702. Tel.: 303-297-1113. Fax: 303-297-3113.
E-mail: director@forneymuseum.org
Web Site: www.forneymuseum.org
Formerly: Colorado Museum of Transportation
Key Personnel: Dir., Christof Kheim.
Institution Type/Description: Transportation Museum.
Hours & Admission Prices: Mon.-Sat. 10-5, Sun. 12-5. Adults 13-64 $11, seniors 65 & over $9, child 3-12 $5; discounts to disabled, military, AAA, AAM & AAAM members; children under 3 & members no charge. Closed New Year's Eve & Day; Easter; Independence Day; Thanksgiving; Christmas Eve & Day. &
Attendance: 30,000 (estimated)

FOUR MILE HISTORIC PARK, 715 S. Forest St., Denver, CO 80246-2324. Tel.: 720-865-0800. Fax: 720-865-0801. Facebook: Four Mile Historic Park.
E-mail: info@fourmilepark.org
Web Site: www.fourmilepark.org
Key Personnel: Exec. Dir., Laura Hiniker; Chm. (V), Karen Hone; Artifact Mgr., Bonnie Bowman; Dir. Educational Programs, Paul Reimer; Site Mgr., Kate Moreland; Bookkeeper, Raissa Shafer.
Institution Type/Description: Historic Site: 1859 & 1883 Four Mile House, log house, which served as stage stop, wayside inn, tavern & farmhouse.
Hours & Admission Prices: April-Sept. Wed.-Fri. 12-4, Sat.-Sun. 10-4; Oct.-March Wed.-Sun. 12-4. Adults $5, senior citizens 65 & over & military with ID $4, youth 7-17 $3; discount to AAA & National Trust members; members and children 6 & under no charge. Closed New Year's Day; Thanksgiving; Christmas. &
Attendance: 47,000 (actual)

GRANT-HUMPHREYS MANSION, 770 Pennsylvania St., Denver, CO 80203-3619. Tel.: 303-894-2505. Fax: 303-894-2508.
E-mail: rentalsghm@chs.state.co.us
Web Site: www.granthumphreysmansion.org
Key Personnel: Exec. Dir., Steve Turner.
Institution Type/Description: Historic House Museum: 1902 Beaux-Arts style home.
Hours & Admission Prices: Call for an appointment. &
Attendance: 20,000 (estimated)

HISTORY COLORADO, THE COLORADO HISTORICAL SOCIETY, 1200 Broadway, Denver, CO 80203-2109. Tel.: 303-447-8679.
E-mail: agata.hardin@state.co.us
Web Site: www.historycolorado.org
Key Personnel: Exec. Dir., Steve Turner.
Institution Type/Description: Historical Society Museum.
Hours & Admission Prices: History Colorado Center: daily 10-5. Library: Wed.-Sat. 10-2. Adults $14, students 16-22 and senior citizens 65 & over $12, children 5-15 $8; children 4 & under no charge. Closed New Year's Day; Thanksgiving; Christmas. &
Attendance: 229,509 (actual)

KIRKLAND MUSEUM OF FINE & DECORATIVE ART, 12th & Bannock, Denver, CO 80203. Mailing Address: 1311 Pearl St., Denver, CO 80203-2518. Tel.: 303-832-8576. Fax: 303-832-8404.
E-mail: info@kirklandmuseum.org
Web Site: www.kirklandmuseum.org
Formerly: Vance Kirkland Museum
Key Personnel: Founding Dir. & Cur., Hugh Grant; Deputy Dir., Gerald Horner; Mgr. Collections & Deputy Cur., Christopher Herron; Communications Mgr. & Historian, Maya Wright; Volunteer Coord., Megan Sullivan; Mktg. & Community Rels. Mgr., Renee Albiston; Admissions & Membership Coord., Caitlin Barrett; Collections Coord., Rebecca Gates; Collections Asst., Rebecca Goodrum; Librarian, Lily Baird.
Institution Type/Description: Art Museum: housed in a 1910-1911 commercial art building, which was inaugurated as The Student's School of Art by artist Henry Read; the building was later acquired by Colorado painter Vance Kirkland, who used the structure as the Kirkland School of Art from 1932-1946 & continued to paint at this location until his death in 1981.
Hours & Admission Prices: Temporarily closed until fall 2017. &
Attendance: 14,426 (actual)

METROPOLITAN STATE COLLEGE OF DENVER/CENTER FOR VISUAL ART, 965 Santa Fe Dr., Denver, CO 80204. Tel.: 303-294-5207. Fax: 303-294-5210.
E-mail: cva@msudenver.edu
Web Site: www.msudenver.edu/cva
Key Personnel: Exec. Dir., Deanne Pytlinski; Mng. Dir. & Cur., Cecily Cullen; Education Dir., Talya Dornbush; General Mgr., Jenna Miles; Communs. Mgr., Gina Yrrizarry; Asst. Gallery Mgr., Hannah Emmons.
Institution Type/Description: Art Gallery.
Hours & Admission Prices: Tues.-Fri. 11-6, Sat. 12-5. No charge; donations accepted. &
Attendance: 15,000 (actual)

MIZEL MUSEUM, 400 S. Kearney St., Denver, CO 80224-1238. Tel.: 303-394-9993. Facebook.
E-mail: details@mizelmuseum.org
Web Site: www.mizelmuseum.org
Key Personnel: Founding Bd. Member, Courtney Mizel; Pres. & C.E.O., Melanie Pearlman; Mng. Dir., Georgina Kolber; Dir. Education, Penny Nisso; Assoc. Programs Mgr., Heather Olsen.
Institution Type/Description: Cultural Museum.
Hours & Admission Prices: Call for appointment. Closed Jewish holidays. &
Attendance: 135,000 (actual)

MOLLY BROWN HOUSE MUSEUM, 1340 Pennsylvania St., Denver, CO 80203-2417. Tel.: 303-832-4092, ext. 16. Fax: 303-832-2340.
E-mail: admin@mollybrown.org
Web Site: www.mollybrown.org
Key Personnel: Exec. Dir. Historic Denver, Annie Levinsky; Cur. Collections, Stephanie McGuire; Museum Dir., Andrea Malcomb.
Institution Type/Description: Historical & Preservation Society.
Hours & Admission Prices: June 15-Aug. 15 Mon.-Sat. 9:30-3:30, Sun. 12-3:30; mid-Aug. to mid-June Tues.-Sat. 10-3:30, Sun. 12-3:30. Adults $11, senior citizens 65 & over, military and college students $9, children 6-12 $7; discounts to AAM members; NAARM, NT & museum members no charge. Closed major holidays. &
Attendance: 53,404 (actual)

MUSEO DE LAS AMERICAS, 861 Santa Fe Dr., Denver, CO 80204-4344. Tel.: 303-571-4401. Fax: 303-607-9761.
E-mail: guestservices@museo.org
Web Site: www.museo.org
Key Personnel: Exec. Dir., Maruca Salazar; Pres. Bd., Olga Garcia; Operations, Claudia Moran; Dir. Educ., Maruquita Salazar; Public Rels., Brent Bulger; Devel., Juliana Fajardo; Guest Svcs. & Membership Coord., Aaron Fisher.
Institution Type/Description: Art & History Museum.

Hours & Admission Prices: Tues.-Fri. 10-5, Sat.-Sun. 12-5. Adults $5, students and seniors 65 & over $3; discounts to AAM members; members & children under 13 no charge. Closed New Year's Day; Independence Day; Thanksgiving; Christmas. ♿
Attendance: 30,000 (actual)

MUSEUM OF ANTHROPOLOGY, UNIVERSITY OF DENVER, 2000 Asbury Ave., Sturm Hall, Rm 102, Denver, CO 80208. Tel.: 303-871-2687.
E-mail: ckreps@du.edu
Web Site: www.du.edu/duma/duma.html
Key Personnel: Dir., Dr. Christina Kreps; Cur. Collections, Ms. Brook Rohde; Cur. Archaeology, Dr. Bonnie Clark; Cur. Ethnology, Richard Clemmer-Smith; Cur. Digital Anthropology, Estaban M. Gomez.
Institution Type/Description: Anthropology Museum.
Hours & Admission Prices: Sept.-June Mon.-Fri. 9-4; other times by appointment. No charge. Closed university holidays. ♿
Attendance: 1,000 (estimated)

MUSEUM OF CONTEMPORARY ART DENVER, 1485 Delgany, Denver, CO 80202-1100. Tel.: 303-298-7554.
E-mail: admin@mcadenver.org
Web Site: www.mcadenver.org
Key Personnel: Dir. & Chief Animator, Adam Lerner.
Institution Type/Description: Art Museum.
Hours & Admission Prices: Tues.-Thurs. 12-7, Fri. 12-9, Sat.-Sun. 10-5. Adults $8, students, military, and seniors 65 & over $5; children under 18 no charge. ♿

NATIONAL BALLPARK MUSEUM / B'S BALLPARK MUSEUM, 1940 Blake St. #101, Denver, CO 80202. Tel.: 303-974-5835.
E-mail: info@ballparkmuseum.com
Web Site: www. ballparkmuseum.com
Formerly: B's Ballpark Museum
Key Personnel: Dir. & Pres., Bruce S. Hellerstein.
Institution Type/Description: Baseball Ballpark Museum.
Hours & Admission Prices: Tues.-Fri. 12-5:30, Sat. 11-5:30; other times by appointment. Adults $10, senior citizens 65 and over & children 6-12 $5; active military & children under 6 no charge.
Attendance: 400 (estimated)

PIRATE: CONTEMPORARY ART, 3655 Navajo St., Denver, CO 80211. Tel.: 303-909-5748.
E-mail: info@pirateonline.org
Web Site: www.pirateartonline.org
Institution Type/Description: Art Gallery.
Hours & Admission Prices: Fri. 6pm-10pm, Sat. 12-6, Sun. 12-5; other times by appointment. No charge. ♿

RED ROCKS AMPHITHEATRE & VISITOR CENTER, 18300 W. Alameda Pkwy., Denver, CO 80465. Tel.: 720-865-2494.
E-mail: redrocksguestservices@denvergov.org
Web Site: redrocksonline.com
Institution Type/Description: History Museum.
Hours & Admission Prices: Visitor Center: April-Oct. 7am-7pm; Nov.-March 8-4. No charge.

ROBISCHON GALLERY, 1740 Wazee St., Denver, CO 80202. Tel.: 303-298-7788. Fax: 303-298-7799.
E-mail: mail@robischongallery.com
Web Site: robischongallery.com
Key Personnel: Owner & Dir., Jim Robischon; Owner & Dir., Jennifer Doran; Gallery Mgr. & Registrar, Debra Malik Demosthenes.
Institution Type/Description: Art Gallery.
Hours & Admission Prices: Tues.-Fri. 11-6, Sat. 12-5.

RULE GALLERY, 530 Santa Fe Dr., Denver, CO 80204. Tel.: 303-800-6776.
E-mail: info@rulegallery.com
Web Site: www.rulegallery.com
Key Personnel: Dir., Valerie Santerli.
Institution Type/Description: Art Gallery.
Hours & Admission Prices: Tues.-Fri. 12-6, Sat. 12-5.

SPARK GALLERY, 900 Santa Fe Dr., Ste. #1, Denver, CO 80204-3937. Tel.: 720-889-2200.
Web Site: www.sparkgallery.com
Key Personnel: Co-Dir., Leo Franco; Co-Dir., Kate McGuinnes.
Institution Type/Description: Art Gallery.

Hours & Admission Prices: Thurs. & Sat. 12-5, Fri. 12-9, Sun. 1-4.

STILES AFRICAN AMERICAN HERITAGE CENTER, INC., 2607 Glenarm Place, Denver, CO 80205-3151. Tel.: 303-294-0597. Fax: 303-294-0597.
E-mail: grace@stilesheritagecenter.org
Web Site: www.stilesheritagecenter.org
Key Personnel: Dir., Grace L. Stiles.
Institution Type/Description: Heritage Center.
Hours & Admission Prices: Mon., Wed. & Fri. 11-3; other times by appointment. ♿
Attendance: 250 (estimated)

UNIVERSITY OF DENVER, SCHOOL OF ART & ART HISTORY, VICKI MYHREN GALLERY, 2121 E. Asbury Ave., Denver, CO 80210. Tel.: 303-871-3716. Fax: 303-871-4112. Facebook; Instagram.
E-mail: galleryinfo@du.edu
Web Site: www.du.edu/vmgallery
Key Personnel: Dir., Dan Jacobs.
Institution Type/Description: University Art Gallery.
Hours & Admission Prices: Tues.-Wed., Fri.-Sun. 12-5, Thurs. 12-7. No charge. Closed university holidays. ♿

WALKER FINE ART, 300 W. 11th Ave. #A, Denver, CO 80204. Tel.: 303-355-8955. Fax: 303-623-0553.
E-mail: info@walkerfineart.com
Key Personnel: Dir., Bobbi Walker; Gallery Mgr., Dariya Bryant; Administrative Mgr., Abbey Arlt.
Institution Type/Description: Contemporary Art Gallery.
Hours & Admission Prices: Tues.-Sat. 12-6, 1st Fri. each month 12-9; other times by appointment. No charge. ♿

WINGS OVER THE ROCKIES AIR & SPACE MUSEUM, 7711 E. Academy Blvd., Denver, CO 80230-6929. Tel.: 303-360-5360. Fax: 303-360-5328. Facebook.
E-mail: info@wingsmuseum.org
Web Site: wingsmuseum.org
Key Personnel: Pres. & C.E.O., Maj. Gen. John L. Barry, USAF (Ret); C.F.O., Jeff Weule; Cur., Matthew Burchette; Dir. Visitor Svcs., Kyle Grissinger; Mktg. Dir., Ben Theune; Dir. Education, Rob Stannard.
Institution Type/Description: Air & Space Museum; housed in 1930s WWII-era hangar.
Hours & Admission Prices: Mon.-Sat. 10-5, Sun. 12-5. Adults $12.50, seniors 65 & over, veterans and active military $9, children 4-16 $6; children 3 & under no charge. ♿
Attendance: 77,000 (estimated)

Dillon

DILLON SCHOOLHOUSE MUSEUM, 403 La Bonte St., Dillon, CO 80435. Mailing Address: c/o Summit Historical Society, P.O. Box 143, Dillon, CO 80435. Tel.: 970-468-2207.
E-mail: mail@summithistorical.org
Web Site: www.summithistorical.org
Institution Type/Description: Historic Building: originally used as a schoolhouse until 1910 when it became a church; built in 1883.
Hours & Admission Prices: Call for hours.

SUMMIT HISTORICAL SOCIETY, 403 LaBonte St., Dillon, CO 80435. Mailing Address: P.O. Box 143, Dillon, CO 80435-0143. Tel.: 970-453-9022. Facebook: Summit Historical Society.
E-mail: mail@summithistorical.org
Web Site: www.summithistorical.org
Key Personnel: Pres. (V), Dr. Sandra Mather; Vice Pres., Jim Cox; Treas., John Ebright; Dir., Rick Hague; Dir., Ray Smith.; Dir., Linda Kelly; Dir., Polly Koch; Dir., Becky Ravick.
Institution Type/Description: Historical Society Museums: 1883 Dillon schoolhouse, 1885 Lula Myers Cabin & 1936 honeymoon cabin.
Hours & Admission Prices: Hours & admissions vary. ♿
Attendance: 5,000 (estimated)

Dolores

BUREAU OF LAND MANAGEMENT - ANASAZI HERITAGE CENTER - CANYONS OF THE ANCIENTS NATIONAL MONUMENT, 27501 Hwy. 184, Dolores, CO 81323-9217. Tel.: 970-882-5600. Fax: 970-882-7035.
E-mail: rene_farias@blm.gov
Web Site: www.co.blm.gov/ahc

Key Personnel: Mgr., Marietta Eaton.
Institution Type/Description: Archaeology Museum.
Hours & Admission Prices: March-Oct. daily 9-5; Nov.-Feb. daily 10-4. March-Oct. adults $3; Nov.-Feb. no charge. America the Beautiful passes accepted. Closed New Year's Day; Thanksgiving; Christmas. &
Attendance: 22,066 (actual)

Durango

ANIMAS MUSEUM, 3065 W. 2nd Ave., Durango, CO 81301-4209. Mailing Address: P.O. Box 3384, Durango, CO 81302-3384. Tel.: 970-259-2402.
E-mail: animasmuseum@frontier.net
Web Site: www.animasmuseum.org
Key Personnel: Dir., Jeff Hutchinson; Mgr. Collections, Amber Lark.
Institution Type/Description: Historical Society Museum: housed in the former 1904 Animas City School building, a 3-story sandstone structure; a c.1870s hand hewn log cabin is also located on the grounds.
Hours & Admission Prices: May-Oct. Mon.-Sat. 10-5; Nov.-April Tues.-Sat. 10-4. Adults $5, senior citizens $4, children 7-12 $2; discounts to groups; children 6 and under & members no charge. &
Attendance: 8,230 (estimated)

BARBARA CONRAD GALLERY - DURANGO ARTS CENTER, 802 E. Second Ave., Durango, CO 81301-5426. Tel.: 970-259-2606. Fax: 970-259-6571.
E-mail: info@durangoarts.org
Web Site: durangoarts.org/barbara-conrad-gallery/
Key Personnel: Exec. Dir., Sheri Rochford; Pres. (V), Terry Swan; Museum Shop Mgr., Mary Puller.
Institution Type/Description: Art Gallery.
Hours & Admission Prices: Tues.-Sat. 10-5. No charge; donations accepted. &
Attendance: 30,000 (estimated)

CENTER OF SOUTHWEST STUDIES/FORT LEWIS COLLEGE, 1000 Rim Dr., Durango, CO 81301-3911. Tel.: 970-247-7456. Fax: 970-247-7422.
E-mail: stisdale@fortlewis.edu
Web Site: swcenter.fortlewis.edu
Key Personnel: Dir., Shelby Tisdale; FLC Pres., Dene Thomas; Cur., Jeanne Brako; Archivist, Nik Kendziorski; Business & Public Rels. Mgr., Julie Tapley Booth; Librarian, Lara Aase.
Institution Type/Description: Art Museum.
Hours & Admission Prices: Gallery: Mon.-Fri. 1-4, Sat. 12-4. No charge; donations accepted. Closed state & federal holidays. &
Attendance: 20,000 (estimated)

DURANGO & SILVERTON NARROW GAUGE RAILROAD & MUSEUM, 479 Main Ave., Durango, CO 81301. Tel.: 970-247-2733, 877-872-4607.
E-mail: Mgowin@durangotrain.com
Web Site: www.durangotrain.com
Institution Type/Description: History Museum: housed in a former railroad depot; built in 1882.
Hours & Admission Prices: Call for hours.

DURANGO DISCOVERY MUSEUM, 1333 Camino Del Rio, Durango, CO 81301. Tel.: 970-259-9234.
E-mail: info@durangodiscovery.org
Web Site: www.durangodiscovery.org
Formerly: Children's Museum of Durango
Key Personnel: Exec. Dir., Chris Cable.
Institution Type/Description: Science Museum.
Hours & Admission Prices: Wed.-Sat. 10-5, Sun. 1-5. Adults $9.50; children 2 and under & members no charge.

THE STRATER HOTEL, 699 Main Ave., Durango, CO 81301-5423. Tel.: 970-247-4431. Fax: 970-259-2208.
E-mail: mthom@strater.com
Web Site: www.strater.com
Key Personnel: C.E.O., Rod Barker.
Institution Type/Description: Historic Building: c.1887 operative Victorian hotel & saloon.
Hours & Admission Prices: Call for tour hours. No charge; donations accepted.
Attendance: 50,000 (estimated)

Eads

KIOWA COUNTY HISTORICAL MUSEUM, 1313 Maine St., Eads, CO 81036. Mailing Address: P.O. Box 100, Eads, CO 81036. Tel.: 719-438-5810 & 5847.
E-mail: plroper@plainsonline.net
Web Site: www.kiowacountycolo.com/museum.htm
Institution Type/Description: Historical Society Museum.
Hours & Admission Prices: Memorial Day to mid-Sept. Mon.-Sat. 1-4:30; other times by appointment.

Eaton

A.J. EATON HOUSE MUSEUM, 207 Elm Ave., Eaton, CO 80615-3428. Tel.: 970-454-2456. Facebook: Historical Eaton.
E-mail: roger_jordan58@msn.com
Key Personnel: Pres. (V), Art Meyer.
Institution Type/Description: Historic House Museum: housed in the former home of A.J. Eaton.
Hours & Admission Prices: Tues., Thurs. & Sat. 2-4. No charge; donations accepted.
Attendance: 328 (actual)

ANTIQUE WASHING MACHINE MUSEUM, 35901 WCR 31, Eaton, CO 80615. Tel.: 970-454-1856.
E-mail: lee@oldewash.com
Web Site: www.oldewash.com
Institution Type/Description: Washing Machine Museum.
Hours & Admission Prices: By appointment only.
Attendance: 1,500 (estimated)

Englewood

THE MUSEUM OF OUTDOOR ARTS, 1000 Englewood Pkwy., Ste. #2-230, Englewood, CO 80110-2373. Tel.: 303-806-0444, ext. 301. Fax: 303-806-0504.
E-mail: thayes@moaonline.org
Web Site: www.moaonline.org
Key Personnel: Pres. & Exec. Dir., Cynthia Madden Leitner; Administrative Dir., Tatum Hayes; Program Dir., Timothy Vacca; Project Dir., Schuyler Madden; Outreach Coord., Jessica Brack.
Institution Type/Description: Art Museum.
Hours & Admission Prices: Gallery: Tues.-Thurs. 10-5, Fri. 10-4, Sat. 11-4; guided tours by arrangement. No charge; donations accepted. Closed federal holidays. &
Attendance: 250,000 (estimated)

Erie

SPIRIT OF FLIGHT CENTER & MUSEUM, 2650 S. Main St., Bldg. A, Erie, CO 80516. Tel.: 303-460-1156.
E-mail: info@spiritofflight.com
Web Site: spiritofflight.com
Institution Type/Description: Aviation History Museum.
Hours & Admission Prices: Mon.-Fri. 10-2; other times by appointment. Suggested Donation: $5.

Estes Park

ENOS MILLS CABIN MUSEUM & GALLERY, 6760 Hwy. 7, Estes Park, CO 80517-6404. Tel.: 970-586-4706.
E-mail: enosmillscbn@earthlink.net
Institution Type/Description: Historic House Museum: built in 1885 by 15 year old Kansan Enos A. Mills. Listed on the National Register of Historic Places.
Hours & Admission Prices: By appointment. No charge; donations accepted.

ESTES PARK MUSEUM, 200 4th St., Estes Park, CO 80517-6339. Tel.: 970-586-6256. Fax: 970-577-3768.
E-mail: dfortini@estes.org
Web Site: www.estes.org/museum
Formerly: Estes Park Area Historical Museum
Key Personnel: Pres. Friends Bd., Nancy Thomas; Cur. Education, Alicia Mittelman; Cur. Collection, Naomi Gerakios; Dir. & Cur. Exhibits, Derek Fortini; Museum Shop Mgr., Elaine Hunt-Downey.
Institution Type/Description: History Museum.
Hours & Admission Prices: May-Oct. Mon.-Sat. 10-5, Sun. 1-5; Nov.-April Fri.-Sat. 10-5, Sun. 1-5. No charge; donations accepted. Closed major holidays. &
Attendance: 20,312 (actual)

MACGREGOR RANCH, 180 MacGregor Lane, Estes Park, CO 80517. Mailing Address: P.O. Box 4675, Estes Park, CO 80517-4675. Tel.: 970-586-3749. Fax: 970-586-1092. Facebook: MacGregor Ranch.
E-mail: office@macgregorranch.org
Web Site: www.macgregorranch.org
Institution Type/Description: Historic House Museum: housed in the MacGregor family home, c.1896. Listed on the National Register of Historic Places.
Hours & Admission Prices: June-Aug. Tues.-Fri. 10-4; other times by appointment. Adults $5; children no charge.
Attendance: 2,700 (estimated)

RELIANCE FIRE MUSEUM, 460 Elm Rd., Estes Park, CO 80517. Tel.: 970-577-1953.
E-mail: reliancefiremuseum@gmail.com
Web Site: www.reliancefiremuseum.org
Institution Type/Description: Firefighting History Museum.
Hours & Admission Prices: Call for hours.

ROCKY MOUNTAIN NATIONAL PARK, 1000 Highway 36, Estes Park, CO 80517-8311. Tel.: 970-586-1222; 970-586-1319 (TTY).
Web Site: www.nps.gov/romo
Key Personnel: Supt., Vaughn Baker.
Institution Type/Description: Cultural & Natural History Museum.
Hours & Admission Prices: Open 24 hours a day year-round. 7-day vehicle entrance fee $30, single day use pass $20, 7-day individual entrance fee $15; Martin Luther King, Jr. Day, National Park Week, National Park Service Birthday, Public Lands Day & Veterans Day Weekend no charge.
Attendance: 4,500,000 (estimated)

STANLEY STEAMCAR MUSEUM, 333 Wonderview Ave., Estes Park, CO 80517. Tel.: 970-577-4110 & 800-976-1377. Fax: 970-577-1924.
E-mail: estespark@stanleymuseum.org
Key Personnel: Dir., Donald Hoke.
Institution Type/Description: Transportation Museum.
Hours & Admission Prices: June-Oct. daily 10-5; Nov.-May Wed.-Mon. 10-5; by appointment. No charge; donations accepted.

Evergreen

HIWAN HOMESTEAD MUSEUM, 4208 S. Timbervale Dr., Evergreen, CO 80439-8456. Mailing Address: 700 Jefferson County Pkwy., Ste. 100, Golden, CO 80401-6025. Tel.: 720-497-7650. Fax: 303-670-7746.
E-mail: jsteinle@jeffco.us
Web Site: jeffco.us/open-space/parks/hiwan-homestead-museum
Key Personnel: Dir., Tom Hoby; Admin., John Steinle.
Institution Type/Description: History Museum & Heritage Center: housed in 1880s 25-room log mansion, Camp Neosho, later renamed Hiwan Ranch.
Hours & Admission Prices: Jan. 8-May & Sept.-Dec. Tues.-Sun. 12-5; June-Aug. Tues.-Sun. 11-5. No charge; donations accepted.
Attendance: 11,986 (actual)

HUMPHREY HISTORY PARK & MUSEUM, 620 Soda Creek Rd., Evergreen, CO 80439-9263. Tel.: 303-674-5429. Facebook.
E-mail: angela@hmpm.org
Web Site: www.hmpm.org
Formerly: Humphrey Memorial Park & Museum
Key Personnel: Exec. Dir., Angela Rayne.
Institution Type/Description: History Museum.
Hours & Admission Prices: Memorial Day to Labor Day Tues.-Sat. 10-4. Guided Tours: adults $7, seniors $6, children 2-12 $5; discounts to AAM & ICOM members.
Attendance: 1,400 (actual)

Fairplay

SOUTH PARK CITY MUSEUM, 100 4th, Fairplay, CO 80440-0634. Mailing Address: P.O. Box 634, Fairplay, CO 80440-0634. Tel.: 719-836-2387. Fax: 719-836-9855.
E-mail: southparkhistorical@gmail.com
Web Site: www.southparkcity.org
Key Personnel: Finance Officer, Nancy Kreiling; Admin., Cindy Huelsman; Pres. (V), Harley Hamilton; Cur., Carol Davis.
Institution Type/Description: Historic Village Museum: located on the site of a Colorado mining town.

Hours & Admission Prices: mid-May to late May daily 10-5; Memorial Day-Labor Day daily 9-7; Sept. to mid-Oct. daily 10-6. Adults $10, senior citizens 65 & over $9, children 6-12 $4; discounts to members of Time Travelers affiliated institutions AAM, ICOM, AAA members & groups; Park county students, members, handicapped & children under 6 no charge.
Attendance: 14,738 (actual)

Fleming

FLEMING HISTORICAL SOCIETY, Heritage Museum Park, Fleming, CO 80728. Mailing Address: P.O. Box 444, Fleming, CO 80728-0351. Tel.: 970-265-2591 & 3611.
E-mail: ntatencio@kcl.net
Key Personnel: Dir., C.E.O. & Pres. (V), Tom Atencio.
Institution Type/Description: Historical Society Museum.
Hours & Admission Prices: Summer: by appointment. No charge; donations accepted.
Attendance: 300 (estimated)

Florence

FLORENCE PIONEER MUSEUM, 100 E. Front St., Florence, CO 81226. Mailing Address: P.O. Box 131, Florence, CO 81226. Tel.: 719-784-1904.
E-mail: martylamm@wildblue.net
Web Site: www.florencepioneermuseum.org
Formerly: Price Pioneer Museum
Key Personnel: Pres., Richard Upton; Treas., Dale Johns; Sec., Marty Lamm; Museum Cur., Roberta Miller.
Institution Type/Description: Pioneer Museum: housed in 1894 building.
Hours & Admission Prices: mid-May to Oct. Tues.-Sat. 1-4; other times by appointment. Adults $2.
Attendance: 1,500 (estimated)

Florissant

FLORISSANT FOSSIL BEDS NATIONAL MONUMENT, 15807 Teller County Rd. #1, Florissant, CO 80816. Mailing Address: P.O. Box 185, Florissant, CO 80816-0185. Tel.: 719-748-3253. Fax: 719-748-3164.
E-mail: keith.payne@nps.gov
Web Site: www.nps.gov/flfo
Key Personnel: Supt., Keith Payne; Paleontologist, Dr. Herbert W. Meyer; Lead Interpreter & Volunteer Coord., Jeff Wolin; Museum Technician, Conni O'Connor.
Institution Type/Description: Historic House Museum.
Hours & Admission Prices: Park: Memorial Day to Labor Day daily 8-6; Sept.-May daily 9-5. Adults $7, children 15 & under no charge. Closed New Year's Day; Thanksgiving; Christmas.
Attendance: 62,000 (actual)

Fort Collins

AVENIR MUSEUM OF DESIGN AND MERCHANDISING, 216 E. Lake St., Fort Collins, CO 80523-1574. Mailing Address: Colorado State University, 1574 Campus Delivery, Fort Collins, CO 80523-1574. Tel.: 970-491-1983. Fax: 970-491-4376.
E-mail: avenir.museum@colostate.edu
Web Site: www.dm.chhs.colostate.edu/museum
Formerly: Gustafson Gallery/Design & Merchandising
Key Personnel: Cur., Doreen Beard.
Institution Type/Description: Costume, Textiles & Interior Furnishings Museum.
Hours & Admission Prices: Mon.-Fri. 11-5. No charge. Closed Thanksgiving; Christmas; CSU holidays.
Attendance: 5,000 (estimated)

AVERY HOUSE AND POUDRE LANDMARKS FOUNDATION, 328 W. Mountain Ave., Fort Collins, CO 80521-2702. Mailing Address: 108 N. Meldrum St., Fort Collins, CO 80521. Tel.: 970-221-0533.
E-mail: poudrelandmarks@gmail.com
Web Site: poudrelandmarks.org
Key Personnel: Chm. (V) Friends of Water Works, Bill Miller; Chm. (V) Avery House Historic District Guild, Lynda Lloyd; Pres. (V), Doug Ernest.
Institution Type/Description: Historic House: former home of Franklin Avery, founder of the First National Bank; built in 1879. Listed on the National Register of Historic Places.
Hours & Admission Prices: Sat.-Sun. 1-4. No charge; donations requested. Closed New Year's Day; Christmas.
Attendance: 3,123 (actual)

BEE FAMILY CENTENNIAL FARM MUSEUM, 4320 E. County Rd., 58, Fort Collins, CO 80524-9326. Tel.: 970-482-9168. Facebook: Bee Family Farm.
E-mail: info@beefamilyfarm.com
Web Site: www.beefamilyfarm.org
Key Personnel: Chm. (V) & Museum Shop Mgr., Liz Harrison.
Institution Type/Description: Farm Museum.
Hours & Admission Prices: May-Oct. Fri.-Sat. 9-4; other times by appointment. Adults $7, seniors 60 & over $5, children 3-12 $3; members no charge. &
Attendance: 1,200 (estimated)

BUDWEISER TOUR CENTER, 2351 Busch Dr., Fort Collins, CO 80524. Tel.: 970-490-4691.
E-mail: fortcollinsbrewerytour@budwisertours.com
Web Site: www.budwisertours.com
Institution Type/Description: Company Museum.
Hours & Admission Prices: Tours: Sun.-Mon. & Thurs. 11-4. The Biergarten: Sun.-Mon. & Wed.-Thurs. 11-6, Fri.-Sat. 11-8. No charge.

CURFMAN GALLERY, Colorado State University, Fort Collins, CO 80523. Mailing Address: 8033 Campus Delivery, Lory Student Center, Colorado State University, Fort Collins, CO 80523. Tel.: 970-491-2810. Fax: 970-491-3746. Facebook.
E-mail: lsc_artsmanager@mail.colostate.edu
Web Site: www.curfman.colostate.edu
Institution Type/Description: Exhibit Area & Gallery.
Hours & Admission Prices: Academic Year: Mon.-Sat. 10-7; Summer: Tues.-Sat. 12-5. No charge; donations accepted. Closed university holidays. &
Attendance: 35,000 (estimated)

FORT COLLINS MUSEUM & DISCOVERY SCIENCE CENTER, 408 Mason Ct., Fort Collins, CO 80524-4421. Tel.: 970-221-6738. Fax: 970-416-2236.
E-mail: ascott@fcgov.com
Web Site: fcmdsc.org
Key Personnel: Co Exec. Dir., Cheryl Donaldson; Co Exec. Dir., Donna Jared; Assoc. Dir., Brent Carmack; Assoc. Dir., Jason Wolvington; Dir. Devel., Michael Allison; Cur. Collections, Linda Moore.
Institution Type/Description: History Museum: housed in historic Carnegie library.
Hours & Admission Prices: Tues.-Wed. & Fri.-Sun. 10-5, Thurs. 10-8. Adults $9.50, seniors & students $7, children 3-12 $6; members and children 2 & under no charge. Closed national holidays. &
Attendance: 40,000 (actual)

GREGORY ALLICAR MUSEUM OF ART, COLORADO STATE UNIVERSITY, 1400 Remington St., Fort Collins, CO 80523-1778. Mailing Address: Colorado State Univ., Campus Box 1778, Fort Collins, CO 80523-1778. Tel.: 970-491-1989.
E-mail: linda.frickman@colostate.edu
Web Site: www.artmuseum.colostate.edu
Formerly: University Art Museum
Key Personnel: Dir., Linda Frickman; Chief Preparator & Opers. Mgr., Keith Jentzsch; Collections Mgr., Suzanne Hale.
Institution Type/Description: University Art Museum.
Hours & Admission Prices: Tues.-Sat. 11-7. No charge; donations accepted. Closed university holidays; fall, spring & winter breaks. &
Attendance: 15,000 (actual)

MUSEUM OF ART FORT COLLINS, INC., 201 S. College Ave., Ste. 101, Fort Collins, CO 80524-3182. Tel.: 970-482-2787. Fax: 970-482-0804.
E-mail: info@moafc.org
Web Site: www.moafc.org
Key Personnel: Chm. (V) & Pres. (V), David Prosser; Exec. Dir., Lisa Hatchadoorian.
Institution Type/Description: Art Museum.
Hours & Admission Prices: Wed.-Fri. 10-5, Sat.-Sun. 12-5. Adults $5, students & seniors $4; discounts to AAM & NARM members, students & seniors; members no charge. Special Exhibits: adults $8. Closed holidays. &
Attendance: 19,000 (actual)

Fort Garland

FORT GARLAND MUSEUM, 29477 Hwy. 159, Fort Garland, CO 81133. Mailing Address: P.O. Box 368, Fort Garland, CO 81133-0368. Tel.: 719-379-3512. Fax: 719-379-3479. Facebook.
E-mail: anita.mcdaniel@state.co.us
Web Site: www.fortgarlandmuseumfriends.org; www.coloradohistroy.org
Formerly: Old Fort Garland

Key Personnel: Dir., Anita McDaniel.
Institution Type/Description: Military Museum: housed in c.1858-1883 Fort Garland.
Hours & Admission Prices: March to Oct. daily 9-5; Nov.-Dec. Wed.-Sat. 10-4; other times by appointment. Adults $5, senior citizens $4.50, children $3.50; discounts to AAM members; children under 6, active military & C.H.S. members no charge. Closed Thanksgiving; Christmas. &
Attendance: 15,000 (actual)

Fort Morgan

FORT MORGAN MUSEUM, 414 Main St., City Park, Fort Morgan, CO 80701. Mailing Address: P.O. Box 100, Fort Morgan, CO 80701. Tel.: 970-542-4011 & 4006. Fax: 970-542-4012.
E-mail: bmack@cityoffortmorgan.com
Web Site: www.cityoffortmorgan.com/museum
Key Personnel: Dir., Chandra McCoy; Cur., Brian C. Mack.
Institution Type/Description: General Museum.
Hours & Admission Prices: Mon. 9-6, Tues.-Thurs. 9-8, Fri.-Sat. 9-5. Research Room: Mon. 9-6, Tues.-Thurs. 9-8, Fri.-Sat. 9-5. No charge; donations accepted. Closed national holidays. &
Attendance: 13,500 (estimated)

Fraser

COZENS RANCH MUSEUM, 77849 U.S. Hwy. 40, Fraser, CO 80442. Tel.: 970-726-5488. Fax: 970-725-0129.
E-mail: cozens@qwestoffice.net
Web Site: www.grandcountymuseum.com
Key Personnel: Dir., Don Woster.
Institution Type/Description: Historic House: 1874 ranch built by William & Mary Cozens, among the first homesteaders to ranch in the Fraser Valley.
Hours & Admission Prices: Memorial Day to Labor Day Tues.-Sat. 10-5; Sept.-May Wed.-Sat. 10-4. Adults $6, senior citizens $5, children 6-17 $3; discounts to groups; children under 5 & members no charge. &
Attendance: 1,836 (actual)

Frisco

FRISCO HISTORIC PARK & MUSEUM, 120 Main St., Frisco, CO 80443. Mailing Address: P.O. Box 4100, Frisco, CO 80443-4100. Tel.: 970-668-3428. Fax: 970-668-0694.
E-mail: simoneb@townoffrisco.com
Web Site: www.townoffrisco.com
Formerly: Frisco Historical Society
Key Personnel: Museum Mgr., Simone Belz.
Institution Type/Description: History Museum: located in c.1900 Frisco Schoolhouse Museum.
Hours & Admission Prices: Tues.-Sun. 10-5. No charge; donations accepted. Closed Thanksgiving; Christmas. &
Attendance: 35,000 (estimated)

Fruita

COLORADO NATIONAL MONUMENT, 1750 Rim Rock Rd., Fruita, CO 81521. Tel.: 970-858-3617 ext. 360. Fax: 970-858-0372.
E-mail: colm_info@nps.gov
Web Site: www.nps.gov/colm
Key Personnel: Supt., Ken Mabery.
Institution Type/Description: Park Museum.
Hours & Admission Prices: Monument: daily 24 hours. Visitor Center: daily 9-5. 7-day vehicle $10, 7-day motorcycle & individual $5; Visitor Center no charge. Closed Christmas. &
Attendance: 385,000 (estimated)

DINOSAUR JOURNEY, 550 Jurassic Court, Fruita, CO 81521-7707. Mailing Address: P.O. Box 20,000, Grand Junction, CO 81502-5020. Tel.: 970-858-7282. Fax: 970-858-3532.
E-mail: djfront@westcomuseum.org
Web Site: www.dinosaurjourney.org
Key Personnel: Exec. Dir., Peter Booth; Cur. Paleontology, Julia McHugh.
Institution Type/Description: Dinosaur Museum.
Hours & Admission Prices: May-Sept. daily 9-5; Oct.-April Mon.-Sat. 10-4, Sun. 12-4. Family $25, adults $9, seniors $7, children $5; members no charge. Closed New Year's Day; Thanksgiving; Christmas.

Gateway

GATEWAY COLORADO AUTOMOBILE MUSEUM, 43224 Hwy. 141, Gateway, CO 81522. Mailing Address: P.O. Box 339, Gateway, CO 81522-0339. Tel.: 970-931-2895.
Key Personnel: Exec. Dir., Preston Patterson.
Institution Type/Description: Automobile Museum.
Hours & Admission Prices: Sun.-Mon. 10-5, Tues.-Sat. 10-7. Adults $9, seniors 65 & over $7, youth 6-12 $5; discounts to groups; children 5 & under and members no charge. Closed Thanksgiving; Christmas.

Georgetown

GEORGETOWN ENERGY MUSEUM, 600 Griffith St., Georgetown, CO 80444. Mailing Address: 600 Griffith St., P.O. Box 398, Georgetown, CO 80444-0398. Tel.: 303-569-3557.
E-mail: gtnem@juno.com
Web Site: georgetownenergymuseum.org
Institution Type/Description: History Museum: housed in fully functioning and operational hydroelectric generating plant.
Hours & Admission Prices: Memorial Day to Oct. 1 Mon.-Sat. 11-4, Sun. 12-4; other times by appointment; groups by appointment. No charge; donations accepted.

HAMILL HOUSE MUSEUM, 305 Argentine, Georgetown, CO 80444. Mailing Address: P.O. Box 667, Georgetown, CO 80444-0667. Tel.: 303-569-2840.
E-mail: preservation@historicgeorgetown.org
Web Site: www.historicgeorgetown.org
Formerly: Historic Georgetown Inc.
Key Personnel: Exec. Dir., Nancy Hale; Dir. Membership, Sherrie Lichtenwalner.
Institution Type/Description: Historic Houses Museum: located in the Georgetown-Silver Plume Historic District.
Hours & Admission Prices: Hamill House: June-Sept. daily 10-4; Winter: call for hours. Adults $7, seniors & students $5; discounts for AAA, Colorado Historical Society members & groups of 10 or more; member no charge. Closed New Year's Day; Thanksgiving; Christmas.
Attendance: 1,000 (estimated)

HOTEL DE PARIS MUSEUM, 409 6th St., Georgetown, CO 80444. Mailing Address: P.O. Box 746, Georgetown, CO 80444-0746. Tel.: 303-569-2311. Facebook: Hotel de Paris Museum.
E-mail: kevin.kuharic@hoteldeparismuseum.org
Web Site: www.hoteldeparismuseum.org
Key Personnel: Chm. (V), Mary Riddle Clark; Pres. (V), Ann Moore; Exec. Dir., Kevin Kuharic.
Institution Type/Description: Historic Building Museum: built in 1875.
Hours & Admission Prices: Memorial Day weekend to Sept. Mon.-Sat. 10-5, Sun. 12-5; Oct.-Dec. 9. Sat. 10-5, Sun. 12-5. General admission $7; discounts to AAA & National Trust for Historic Preservation. Blue Star Museums May 28 to Sept. 3. Active military (up to 5 family members) no charge.
Attendance: 7,000 (actual)

Glenwood Springs

FRONTIER HISTORICAL SOCIETY AND MUSEUM, 1001 Colorado Avenue, Glenwood Springs, CO 81601-3319. Tel.: 970-945-4448. Facebook.
E-mail: history@rof.net
Web Site: www.glenwoodhistory.com
Key Personnel: Exec. Dir., Cindy Hines.
Institution Type/Description: General Museum.
Hours & Admission Prices: May-Oct. Mon.-Sat. 10-4; Nov.-April Mon. & Thurs.-Sat. 1-4. Adults $4, senior citizens $3, children 12 & under $2; discounts to groups; members no charge. Closed New Year's Day; Memorial Day; Independence Day; Labor Day; Thanksgiving; Christmas.
Attendance: 3,513 (actual)

GLENWOOD RAILROAD MUSEUM, 413 7th St., Glenwood Springs, CO 81601-3442. Tel.: 970-945-7044.
E-mail: janandpat@sopris.net
Web Site: www.glenwoodrailroadmuseum.org
Key Personnel: Gen. Mgr. & Museum Shop Mgr., Jan Girardot; Cur., Dick Helmke.
Institution Type/Description: Railroad Museum: housed in the historic Glenwood Springs Railroad Station; built in 1904.
Hours & Admission Prices: Fri.-Mon. 11-3. Adults $1; members no charge.

GLENWOOD SPRINGS CENTER FOR THE ARTS, 601 E. Sixth St., Glenwood Springs, CO 81601. Tel.: 970-945-2414.
E-mail: info@glenwoodarts.org

Institution Type/Description: Art Gallery.
Hours & Admission Prices: Call for hours.

Golden

BRADFORD WASHBURN AMERICAN MOUNTAINEERING MUSEUM, 710 10th St., Golden, CO 80401. Tel.: 303-996-2755.
E-mail: info@americanmountaineeringcenter.org
Web Site: www.mountaineeringmuseum.org
Key Personnel: Dir., Devyn Studer.
Institution Type/Description: Mountaineering Museum.
Hours & Admission Prices: Mon.-Tues. & Thurs.-Fri. 10-4, Wed. 10-6, Sat. 12-5; other times by appointment. Adults $7, children 6-16 $3; discounts to groups of 8 or more; children 5 & under and members no charge.

BUFFALO BILL MUSEUM & GRAVE, 987 1/2 Lookout Mountain Rd., Golden, CO 80401-9646. Tel.: 303-526-0747 & 0744. Fax: 303-526-0197.
E-mail: buffalobill.museum@ci.denver.co.us
Web Site: www.buffalobill.org
Formerly: Buffalo Bill Memorial Museum
Key Personnel: Dir., Steve Friesen; Educational Programs Coord., Betsy Martinson.
Institution Type/Description: History Museum: Founded by Johnny Baker, a close friend of Buffalo Bill & an important member of Buffalo Bill's Wild West Show.
Hours & Admission Prices: May-Oct. daily 9-5; Nov.-April Tues.-Sun. 9-5. Adults $5, seniors 65 & over $4, children 6-15 $1; AAM members with membership card & children under 6 no charge.
Attendance: 72,851 (actual)

CLEAR CREEK HISTORY PARK, 1020 11th St., Golden, CO 80401. Mailing Address: 923 10th St., Golden, CO 80401. Tel.: 303-278-3557. Fax: 303-278-8916.
Web Site: www.clearcreekhistorypark.org
Key Personnel: Exec. Dir., Shannon Voirol.
Institution Type/Description: Living History Park.
Hours & Admission Prices: May & Sept. Sat. 10-4:30; June-Aug. Tues.-Sat. 10-4:30, Sun. 11-3; Oct.-April groups by appointment. Adults $3, seniors $2.50, youth $2; discounts to AASLH & AAM members; children 5 & under and members no charge. Closed major holidays.
Attendance: 9,610

COLORADO RAILROAD MUSEUM, 17155 W. 44th Ave., Golden, CO 80403-1621. Tel.: 303-279-4591, 800-365-6263. Fax: 303-279-4229. Facebook.
E-mail: info@crrm.org
Web Site: coloradorailroadmuseum.org
Key Personnel: Exec. Dir., Donald Tallman; Business Mgr., Bonnie Prater; Cur. Rolling Stock & Equipment, Jeff Taylor; Cur. Education & Exhibits, Elizabeth Nosek; Cur. Collections, Stephanie Gilmore; Mgr. Communications, Chad Knasinski; Guest Svcs. Mgr. & Buyer, Andrea Bestor.
Institution Type/Description: Railroad Museum.
Hours & Admission Prices: Daily 9-5. Adults $10, senior citizens $8, children under 16 $5; discount to AAM members; members no charge. Closed New Year's Day; Thanksgiving; Christmas.
Attendance: 100,000 (actual)

COLORADO SCHOOL OF MINES GEOLOGY MUSEUM, General Research Lab Bldg., 1310 Maple St., Golden, CO 80401-1887. Tel.: 303-273-3815.
E-mail: geomuseum@mines.edu
Web Site: www.mines.edu/academic/geology/museum
Key Personnel: Interim Dir., Nicholas Iwanicki.
Institution Type/Description: Geology & Mineralogy Museum.
Hours & Admission Prices: Mon.-Sat. 9-4, Sun. 1-4; guided tours by appointment. Closed New Year's Day; Easter; Memorial Day; Independence Day; Thanksgiving; Christmas; CSM school holidays.
Attendance: 16,000 (estimated)

COORS BREWERY TOUR, 1221 Ford St., Golden, CO 80401. Tel.: 800-642-6116, 303-277-2337.
Institution Type/Description: Company Museum.
Hours & Admission Prices: Memorial Day to Labor Day Mon.-Sat. 10-4, Sun. 12-4; Sept.-May Thurs.-Mon. 10-4, Sun. 12-4. No charge. Closed New Year's Eve & Day; Easter; Memorial Day; Independence Day; Thanksgiving & day after; Christmas Eve & Day.

FOOTHILLS ART CENTER, 809 15th St., Golden, CO 80401-1813. Tel.: 303-279-3922.
E-mail: info@foothillsartcenter.org

Web Site: www.foothillsartcenter.org
Key Personnel: Exec. Dir., Reilly Sanborn; Cur., Michael Chavez.
Institution Type/Description: Art Museum.
Hours & Admission Prices: Mon.-Fri. 10-5, Sat. 12-5; call to confirm. Adults $5, seniors $3; members, children & students no charge.

GOLDEN HISTORY MUSEUMS, 923 10th St., Golden, CO 80401-1112. Tel.: 303-278-3557. Fax: 303-278-8916.
E-mail: nrichie@goldenhistorymuseums.org
Web Site: www.goldenhistorymuseums.org
Formerly: Astor House Museum
Key Personnel: Dir., Nathan Richie.
Institution Type/Description: Historic House Museum: housed in c.1867 Astor House hotel.
Hours & Admission Prices: Wed.-Mon. 10-4:30. Astor House & Golden History Center: adults $5. Astor House: adults $3; members and children 6 & under no charge. Closed major holidays. ﾖ
Attendance: 13,300 (actual)

GOLDEN OLDY CYCLERY & SUSTAINABILITY, 17224 W. 17th Place, Golden, CO 80401-2509. Tel.: 720-497-1100.
E-mail: oldbike2@comcast.net
Web Site: www.goldenoldy.org
Key Personnel: Dir., C.E.O. & Chm. (V), Steve Stevens.
Institution Type/Description: Bicycle & Living Museum of Sustainability.
Hours & Admission Prices: Call for hours. No charge, donations accepted.
Attendance: 1,100 (estimated)

ROCKY MOUNTAIN QUILT MUSEUM, 200 Violet St., Ste. 150 (Admin. & Library), Golden, CO 80401. Mailing Address: 200 Violet St., Ste. 140 (Gallery), Golden, CO 80401. Tel.: 303-277-0377 (Gallery); 215-9001 (Admin. & Library). Facebook.
E-mail: rmqm@rmqm.org
Web Site: www.rmqm.org
Key Personnel: Exec. Dir., Karen Roxburgh; Pres. (V), Cindy Harp.
Institution Type/Description: Quilt Museum.
Hours & Admission Prices: Mon.-Sat. 10-5, Sun. 11-5. Adults $8, seniors $7, children, students & military $4; discounts to groups of 10 or more; group escort no charge. Closed New Year's Day; Thanksgiving; Christmas. ﾖ
Attendance: 12,000 (actual)

Grand Junction

BROWN CYCLE MUSEUM, 549 Main St., Grand Junction, CO 81501. Tel.: 970-245-7939. Facebook.
E-mail: info@browncycles.com
Web Site: browncycles.com
Institution Type/Description: Bicycle Museum.
Hours & Admission Prices: April-Sept. Mon.-Sat. 9-6, Sun. 11-2; Oct.-March Mon.-Sat. 9-6; tours by appointment. No charge.

CROSS ORCHARDS HISTORIC FARM, 3073 F Rd., Grand Junction, CO 81504. Mailing Address: P.O. Box 20000, Grand Junction, CO 81502-5020. Tel.: 970-434-9814. Fax: 970-242-3960.
Institution Type/Description: Historic Site: housed on an early 1900s apple orchard. National Register of Historic Sites & Places.
Hours & Admission Prices: April 10 to mid-Oct. Tues.-Sat. 9-4. Adults $4, seniors $3, children $2.50.

MUSEUMS OF WESTERN COLORADO, 462 Ute Ave., Grand Junction, CO 81501-2516. Mailing Address: P.O. Box 20000, Grand Junction, CO 81502-5020. Tel.: 970-242-0971. Fax: 970-242-3960.
E-mail: chatch@westcomuseum.org
Web Site: www.museumofwesternco.org
Key Personnel: Exec. Dir., Peter M. Booth; Chm. Bd. & Pres., Laurena Mayne Davis; Cur. Paleontology, Dr. John R. Foster; Cur. History & Dir. Western Investigations Team, David Bailey; Cur. Collections & Registrar, Zebulon Miracle; Asst. Dir. Operations, Kay Fiegel; Dir. Lloyd Files Research Library & Cur. Archives, Michael Menard; Business Mgr., Erik Vliek; Facilities Mgr., Don Kerven; Membership, Ronna Lee Sharpe; Museum Shop Mgr., Jen McCallaugh.
Institution Type/Description: Cultural & Natural History Museum.
Hours & Admission Prices: History Museum: Winter: Mon.-Sat. 10-4; Summer: Mon.-Sat. 9-5, Sun. 12-4. Family $20, adults $7, seniors $6, children $4. Cross Orchards Living History Site: no charge. Dinosaur Journey: Summer daily 9-5; Winter Mon.-Sat. 10-5, Sun. 12-4. Family $25, adults $9, seniors $7, children $5. ﾖ
Attendance: 105,000 (estimated)

WESTERN COLORADO CENTER FOR THE ARTS DBA THE ART CENTER, 1803 N. 7th St., Grand Junction, CO 81501-3009. Tel.: 970-243-7337. Fax: 970-243-2482.
E-mail: info@gjartcenter.org
Web Site: www.gjartcenter.org
Key Personnel: Dir., Cheryl McNab; Pres. (V), Robbie Breax; Museum Shop Mgr., Carolyn Gillette.
Institution Type/Description: Art Gallery.
Hours & Admission Prices: Tues.-Sat. 9-4. Adults $3; members, children under 12 & Tues. no charge.
Attendance: 30,000 (estimated)

Grand Lake

GRAND LAKE AREA HISTORICAL SOCIETY, 407 Pitkin St., Grand Lake, CO 80447-0656. Mailing Address: Box 656, Grand Lake, CO 80447-0656. Tel.: 970-627-9644. Facebook.
E-mail: info@grandlakehistory.org
Web Site: www.grandlakehistory.org
Key Personnel: Pres., Jim Cervenka.
Institution Type/Description: Historical Society Museum.
Hours & Admission Prices: Memorial Day to Labor Day daily 11-5; Sept. Sat.-Sun. 11-5; tours & other times by appointment. Adults $5; children 12 & under and members no charge. ﾖ
Attendance: 5,500 (actual)

Greeley

CENTENNIAL VILLAGE MUSEUM: LIVING HISTORY EXPERIENCE, 1475 A St., Greeley, CO 80631-2185. Mailing Address: 714 8th St, Greeley, CO 80631-3910. Tel.: 970-350-9220. Fax: 970-350-9570.
E-mail: museums@greeleygov.com
Web Site: www.centennialvillagemuseum.com
Formerly: Centennial Village Museum
Key Personnel: Mgr., Daniel Perry; Cur. Historic Sites, Scott Chartier; Devel. Cur., Peggy Ford Waldo; Cur. Exhibits, Nicole Famiglietti; Educator & Event Coord., Sarah Lester; Registrar, JoAnna Luth Stull; Facility Maintenance Mgr., Barry Alvarado.
Institution Type/Description: Living History Museum.
Hours & Admission Prices: Memorial Day weekend-Labor Day weekend Fri. & Sat. 10-4, Sun. 12-4. Family $18, adult $8, senior citizens 60+ $6, children 3-17 $5. ﾖ
Attendance: 23,000 (estimated)

COLORADO MODELRAILROAD MUSEUM, 680 10th St., Greeley, CO 80631. Tel.: 970-392-2934. Facebook.
E-mail: tours@cmrm.org; susan@cmrm.org
Web Site: www.cmrm.org
Formerly: Greeley Freight Station Museum
Key Personnel: Directing Mgr., Tim McMahon; Exec. Dir., Michelle Kempema.
Institution Type/Description: Railroad & Hobby Museum.
Hours & Admission Prices: June-Aug. Wed.-Sat. 10-4, Sun. 1-4; Sept.-May Fri.-Sat. 10-4, Sun. 1-4. Adults $10, seniors 65 & over $8, children 4-12 $5; discounts to members & military; children 3 & under no charge.
Attendance: 18,000 (estimated)

GREELEY HISTORY MUSEUM, 714 8th Street, Greeley, CO 80631-3910. Tel.: 970-350-9220. Fax: 970-350-9570.
E-mail: museums@greeleygov.com
Web Site: www.greeleymuseums.com
Formerly: Municipal Archives
Key Personnel: Mgr., Daniel Perry; Educator & Event Coord., Sarah Lester; Cur. Exhibits, Nicole Famiglietti; Cur. Collections, Sarah Saxe; Registrar, JoAnna Luth Stull; Collections Specialist, Katie Ross; Devel. Cur., Peggy Ford Waldo.
Institution Type/Description: History Museum.
Hours & Admission Prices: Wed.-Sat. 10-4, Sun. 12-4. Family $15, adults $5, seniors 60 & over and children 3-17 $3; children under 3 no charge. ﾖ
Attendance: 6,000 (estimated)

MARIANI GALLERY, UNIVERSITY OF NORTHERN COLORADO, 8th Ave. & 18th St., Greeley, CO 80639. Mailing Address: School of Visual Arts Galleries, Campus Box 30, Guggenheim Hall University of Northern CO, Greeley, CO 80639. Tel.: 970-351-2184. Fax: 970-351-2299.
E-mail: pvainfo@unco.edu
Web Site: arts.unco.edu/art/galleries
Key Personnel: Dir., Joan Shannon-Miller.
Institution Type/Description: University Art Gallery.

Hours & Admission Prices: Sept.-May Mon.-Tues. & Thurs.-Fri. 10-3, Wed. 1-6. No charge. &
Attendance: 2,500 (estimated)

MEEKER HOME MUSEUM, 1324 9th Ave., Greeley, CO 80631-4608. Mailing Address: 714 8th St., Greeley, CO 80631-3910. Tel.: 970-350-9220. Fax: 970-350-9570.
E-mail: museums@greeleygov.com
Web Site: www.greeleymuseums.com
Key Personnel: Mgr., Daniel Perry; Cur. Historic Sites, Scott Chartier; Facility Maintenance Mgr., Barry Alvarado; Cur. Exhibits, Nicole Famiglietti; Registrar, JoAnna Luth Stull.
Institution Type/Description: Historic House: 1870 home of Nathan C. Meeker, founder of Greeley and his family.
Hours & Admission Prices: By appointment only. Family $15, adults $5, seniors 60 & over and children 3-17 $3. &
Attendance: 400 (actual)

WHITE PLUMB FARM LEARNING CENTER, 955 39th Ave., Greeley, CO 80634-1549. Mailing Address: 714 8th St., Greeley, CO 80631-3910. Tel.: 970-350-9220. Fax: 970-350-9570.
E-mail: museums@greeleygov.com
Web Site: www.greeleymuseums.com
Key Personnel: Mgr., Daniel Perry; Cur. Historic Sites, Scott Chartier; Facility Maintenance Mgr., Barry Alvarado.
Institution Type/Description: Historic Farm Museum.
Hours & Admission Prices: Special Event Days: call for information. Rentals: Indoor & outdoor options, call for details. &
Attendance: 1,000 (estimated)

Gunnison

GUNNISON ARTS CENTER, 102 S. Main St., Gunnison, CO 81230. Mailing Address: P.O. Box 1772, Gunnison, CO 81230-1772. Tel.: 970-641-4029.
E-mail: carlie@gunnisonartscenter.org
Web Site: www.gunnisonartscenter.org
Key Personnel: Exec. Dir., Carlie Kenton; Gallery Dir., Alysa VandenHeuvel.
Institution Type/Description: Art Center.
Hours & Admission Prices: Tues.-Fri. 10-6, Sat. 10-4. No charge.

GUNNISON COUNTY PIONEER AND HISTORICAL SOCIETY, S. Adams St. & Hwy. 50, Gunnison, CO 81230. Mailing Address: P.O. Box 824, Gunnison, CO 81230-0824. Tel.: 970-641-4530.
E-mail: info@gunnisonpioneermuseum.com
Key Personnel: C.E.O. & Pres., C.J. Miller.
Institution Type/Description: Historical Society Museum.
Hours & Admission Prices: Memorial Day to Sept. Mon.-Sat. 9-5, Sun. 11-5. Adults $7, children 6-12 $3; discounts to groups of 10 or more.
Attendance: 5,000 (actual)

Holyoke

PHILLIPS COUNTY MUSEUM, 109 S. Campbell Ave., Holyoke, CO 80734-1501. Tel.: 970-854-2129.
E-mail: pcmuseum@pctelcom.coop
Key Personnel: Pres., Peggy Davis; Sec., Carrie Anderson; Treas., Carol Haynes.
Institution Type/Description: Historical Society Museum.
Hours & Admission Prices: Memorial Day to Labor Day Sun. 2-4:30, Wed. 2-4; other times by appointment. No charge; donations accepted. &
Attendance: 500 (estimated)

Hot Sulphur Springs

GRAND COUNTY MUSEUM/PIONEER VILLAGE MUSEUM, 110 E. Byers, Hot Sulphur Springs, CO 80451. Mailing Address: P. O. Box 165, Hot Sulphur Springs, CO 80451-0165. Tel.: 970-725-3939. Fax: 970-725-0129.
E-mail: serena@grandcountyhistory.org
Web Site: www.grandcountymuseum.com
Institution Type/Description: History Museum: housed in c.1924 school house.
Hours & Admission Prices: Summer: Wed.-Sun. 10-4; Winter: Wed.-Sat. 10-4. Adults $6, senior citizens 62 & over $5, students $3; members & children under 5 no charge. &
Attendance: 2,350 (actual)

Hugo

LINCOLN COUNTY MUSEUM, 617 Third Ave., Hugo, CO 80821. Mailing Address: P.O. Box 124, Hugo, CO 80821-0124. Tel.: 719-740-0106. Fax: 719-743-2447.
E-mail: twbndee@yahoo.com
Formerly: Hedlund House Museum
Key Personnel: Pres., Dee Ann Blevins; Contact, Terry Blevins.
Institution Type/Description: History Museum: located on c.1880 site of the homestead of Hugo's founder.
Hours & Admission Prices: Memorial Day to Labor Day Sat. 10-6, Sun. 1-5; other times by appointment. No charge; donations accepted.
Attendance: 100 (estimated)

Idaho Springs

ARGO GOLD MINE & MILL MUSEUM, 2350 Riverside Dr., Idaho Springs, CO 80452. Mailing Address: P.O. Box 1990, Idaho Springs, CO 80452-1990. Tel.: 303-567-2421. Fax: 303-567-9304.
E-mail: info@historicargotours.com
Web Site: www.historicargotours.com
Key Personnel: C.E.O., James N. Maxwell; Dir., Robert N. Maxwell.
Institution Type/Description: Mining & Milling Museum: housed in 1913 six-story Argo Gold Mill.
Hours & Admission Prices: mid-April to mid-Oct. Wed.-Mon. 10-6; Winter: by appointment. Adults $23, children 5-10 $16; discounts to AAA, AAM, ICOM members & groups of 25 or more with reservation; children 4 & under no charge.
Attendance: 15,000 (estimated)

THE HERITAGE MUSEUM, 2060 Miner St., Idaho Springs, CO 80452-1318. Mailing Address: P.O. Box 1318, Idaho Springs, CO 80452-1318. Tel.: 303-567-4382.
E-mail: njohnson.historicidahosprings@gmail.com
Web Site: www.historicidahosprings.com
Key Personnel: Pres. (V), Rick Wells; Dir., Nancy Johnson; Museum Shop Mgr., Susan Helm; Exec. Asst., Nancy Johnson.
Institution Type/Description: History Museum.
Hours & Admission Prices: Summer hours: daily 9-5. Winter hours: daily 9-4:30No charge; donations accepted. Closed New Year's Day; Easter; Thanksgiving; Christmas.
Attendance: 50,000 (estimated)

UNDERHILL MUSEUM, 1416 Miner St., Idaho Springs, CO 80452-1318. Mailing Address: P.O. Box 1318, Idaho Springs, CO 80452-1318. Tel.: 303-567-4382. Fax: 303-567-9188.
E-mail: njohnson.historicidahosprings@gmail.com
Web Site: www.historicidahosprings.com
Key Personnel: Pres. (V), Rick Wells; Exec. Dir., Nancy Johnson; Museum Shop Mgr., Bonnie Hammett.
Institution Type/Description: Historic House & Mining Engineer Office: housed in the former home & office of college professor & U.S. Mineral Surveyor, James Underhill; built in 1912.
Hours & Admission Prices: Memorial Day to Sept. 10:30-4. No charge; donations accepted. &
Attendance: 3,619 (actual)

Ignacio

SOUTHERN UTE CULTURAL CENTER AND MUSEUM, 503 Ouray Dr., Ignacio, CO 81137. Mailing Address: Box 737 MS #95, Ignacio, CO 81137-0737. Tel.: 970-563-9583; 970-563-9538 (for hours). Fax: 970-563-4641. Facebook: Southern Ute Cultural Center and Museum.
E-mail: info@succm.org
Web Site: www.sucm.org
Key Personnel: Acting Exec. Dir., Shirley Cloud-Lane; Chm., Robert Burch.
Institution Type/Description: Native American History & Ethnology Museum: located on Southern Ute Indian reservation.
Hours & Admission Prices: Memorial Day to Labor Day Tues.-Fri. 9-4:30, Sat. 10-4. Sun. 12-4; Sept.-May Tues.-Fri. 9-4:30; call to confirm. Adults $7, seniors over 65 $4, children 3-14 $3; Ute tribal members no charge. &
Attendance: 15,000 (estimated)

Julesburg

DEPOT MUSEUM, 201 W. 1st St., Julesburg, CO 80737. Mailing Address: Fort Sedgwick Historical Society, 114 E. 1st St., Julesburg, CO 80737. Tel.: 970-474-2264.
E-mail: history@kci.net

Formerly: Pioneer Museum
Key Personnel: Pres. (V), Doris Heath; Vice Pres., Dallas Williams.
Institution Type/Description: History Museum: housed in the Union Pacific Railroad Depot; built in 1930. Listed on National Register of Historical Places.
Hours & Admission Prices: Memorial Day to Labor Day Tues.-Sat. 10-4, Sun. 1-4; other times by appointment. Adults $1, children under 12 $.50; school groups & members no charge. Closed national holidays. &
Attendance: 350 (actual)

FORT SEDGWICK MUSEUM, 114 E. 1st St., Julesburg, CO 80737. Mailing Address: Fort Sedgwick Historical Society, 114 E. 1st St., Julesburg, CO 80737. Tel.: 970-474-2061.
E-mail: history@kci.net
Formerly: Fort Sedgwick Museum & Archives
Key Personnel: Pres. (V), Doris Heath; Vice Pres., Dallas Williams.
Institution Type/Description: History Museum.
Hours & Admission Prices: Memorial Day to Labor Day Tues.-Sat. 10-4, Sun. 1-4; Sept.-May Tues.-Fri. 9-1. Adults $1, children $.50; members no charge. Closed national holidays. &
Attendance: 523 (actual)

HIPPODROME THEATRE, 215 Cedar St., Julesburg, CO 80737-1521. Tel.: 970-474-9977. Fax: 970-474-9977.
E-mail: hippo@pctelcom.coop
Web Site: www.rivertrailonline.org/users/hippodrome
Institution Type/Description: Historic Building: housed in a functioning movie theater; built in 1919.
Hours & Admission Prices: Shows: Fri.-Sat. 7:30pm, Sun. 2pm & 6pm. Admission $4; children 3 & under no charge. &

Keenesburg

THE WILD ANIMAL SANCTUARY, 1946 WCR 53, Keenesburg, CO 80643. Tel.: 303-536-0118.
E-mail: information@wildlife-sanctuary.org
Institution Type/Description: Wildlife Sanctuary.
Hours & Admission Prices: Daily 9 to sunset. Adults $15, children 3-12 $7.50.

Kiowa

ELBERT COUNTY HISTORICAL SOCIETY AND MUSEUM, 515 Comanche St., Hwy. 86, Kiowa, CO 80117. Mailing Address: P.O. Box 43, Kiowa, CO 80117-0043.
Web Site: www.elbertcountymuseum.org
Institution Type/Description: History Museum.
Hours & Admission Prices: Memorial Day to Labor Day Thurs.-Sun. 1-4. No charge; donations accepted.
Attendance: 750 (estimated)

Kit Carson

KIT CARSON HISTORICAL SOCIETY, 202 W. Hwy. 287, Kit Carson, CO 80825. Mailing Address: P.O. Box 67, Kit Carson, CO 80825-0067. Tel.: 719-962-3306.
E-mail: webmaster@rebeltec.net
Web Site: www.kcdr1.org
Key Personnel: C.E.O., Carl Randel; Pres. (V), Penny McPherson; Vice Pres. & Dir., Victor Gibbs; Dir. & Treas., Ronald White; Dir., Polly Johnson; Dir., Deb Dwyer; Dir. & Sec., Charles Oswald; Dir., Marilyn Bullock.
Institution Type/Description: History Museum.
Hours & Admission Prices: May & Sept. Sat.-Sun. 9-5; Memorial Day-Labor Day daily 9-5. No charge; donations accepted. &
Attendance: 877 (actual)

La Junta

BENT'S OLD FORT NATIONAL HISTORIC SITE, 35110 Hwy. 194 E., La Junta, CO 81050-9523. Tel.: 719-383-5010. Fax: 719-383-2129.
E-mail: beol_interpretation@nps.gov
Web Site: www.nps.gov/beol
Key Personnel: Supt., Alexa Roberts; Cur., Rhonda Brewer; Museum Shop Mgr., Karla Linenberger.
Institution Type/Description: Living History Museum.
Hours & Admission Prices: June-Aug. daily 8-5:30; Sept.-May daily 9-4. Adults $3, children 6-12 $2; children under 6 no charge; America the Beautiful passes honored. Closed New Year's Day; Thanksgiving; Christmas.
Attendance: 25,815 (actual)

KOSHARE INDIAN MUSEUM, INC., 115 W. 18th St., La Junta, CO 81050-3302. Mailing Address: P.O. Box 580, La Junta, CO 81050-0580. Tel.: 719-384-4411. Fax: 719-384-8836.
E-mail: kiva.clerk@ojc.edu
Web Site: koshare.org
Key Personnel: Program Dir. & Cur., Jeremy Manyik.
Institution Type/Description: Indian Art & Artifacts Museum.
Hours & Admission Prices: June-Aug. Sun.-Fri. 12-5, Sat. 12-10; Sept.-May Wed.-Sun. 12-5. Adults $5, seniors & students $3; members and children 6 & under no charge. Interpretive Indian Dances: mid-June to Aug. Sat. 7:30pm; Dec. 27-Jan. 4 call for hours. Show: adults $8, children 3-18 $5. Closed major holidays. &
Attendance: 24,000 (estimated)

OTERO MUSEUM ASSOCIATION, 218 Anderson Ave., La Junta, CO 81050-0223. Mailing Address: P.O. Box 223, La Junta, CO 81050-0223. Tel.: 719-384-7500. Fax: 719-384-7500.
E-mail: oteromuseum@centurytel.net
Web Site: www.oteromuseum.org
Key Personnel: Chm. (V), Roy Fitch; Treas., Dona Aldea.
Institution Type/Description: General Museum.
Hours & Admission Prices: June-Sept. Mon.-Sat. 1-5; other times by appointment only. Adults $5; children 12 & under no charge.
Attendance: 2,750 (estimated)

La Veta

FRANCISCO FORT MUSEUM, 306 S. Main St., La Veta, CO 81055. Mailing Address: P.O. Box 263, La Veta, CO 81055-0263. Tel.: 719-742-5501.
E-mail: museumdirector@townoflaveta-co.gov
Web Site: franciscofort.org
Key Personnel: Dir., Bob Kennemer; Pres., Ed Smith; Contact, Peggy Arnold-Hoobler.
Institution Type/Description: Historical Society Museum: housed on 1862 adobe fort and other historic buildings.
Hours & Admission Prices: Memorial Day to Labor Day Tues.-Sat. 10-4; other times by appointment. Admission 12 & over $5, seniors & military $4. &
Attendance: 4,000 (estimated)

Lafayette

LAFAYETTE MINERS MUSEUM, 108 E. Simpson St., Lafayette, CO 80026-2322. Tel.: 303-665-7030.
E-mail: minersmuseum@cityoflafayette.com
Key Personnel: Cur., Claudia Lund.
Institution Type/Description: Coal Mining Museum: housed in c.1892 Lewis House. Listed on the National Register of Historic Places.
Hours & Admission Prices: Thurs. & Sat. 2-4; tours by appointment. No charge; donations accepted. Closed holidays. &
Attendance: 1,800 (actual)

WOW! CHILDREN'S MUSEUM (WORLD OF WONDER), 110 N. Harrison Ave., Lafayette, CO 80026-2336. Tel.: 303-604-2424.
E-mail: jennifer@wowchildrensmuseum.org
Web Site: www.wowmuseum.com
Key Personnel: Co-Founder & Exec. Dir., Lisa Atallah; Mgr., Susan Rasmussen; Mgr. Mktg., Katie MacDonald.
Institution Type/Description: Children's Museum.
Hours & Admission Prices: Tues.-Fri. 9-5, Sat. 10-6, Sun. 12-4. Toddler Hour (children 5 & under): Tues.-Wed. 9am-10am. Children 1-11 $9; discounts to groups; adults, members & children under one no charge. Closed New Year's Day; Easter; Memorial Day; Independence Day; Labor Day; Thanksgiving; Christmas Eve & Day.

Lake City

HINSDALE COUNTY HISTORICAL SOCIETY MUSEUM, 130 N. Silver St., Lake City, CO 81235. Mailing Address: P.O. Box 353, Lake City, CO 81235. Tel.: 970-944-2050.
E-mail: info@lakecitymuseum.com
Web Site: lakecitymuseum.com
Institution Type/Description: History Museum.
Hours & Admission Prices: Summer: Mon.-Sat. 10-5; other times by appointment. Adults $4, children 8-15 $2; children 7 & under no charge.
Attendance: 2,000 (actual)

Lakewood

LAKEWOOD'S HERITAGE CENTER, 801 S. Yarrow St., Lakewood, CO 80226-4372. Tel.: 303-987-7850. Fax: 303-987-7851. TDD: 303-987-4862.
E-mail: jefmur@lakewood.org
Web Site: www.lakewood.org
Key Personnel: HCA Mgr., Michelle Nierling; Admin., Jeffrey Murray; Office Mgr., Julie Elam; Volunteer Coord., Karla Grahn; Mktg. Coord., Allison Scheck.
Institution Type/Description: History Museum.
Hours & Admission Prices: Tues.-Sat. 10-4. Adults $5, seniors citizens $4, youth $3; discounts to AAM members; children 3 & under members no charge. Closed holidays. &
Attendance: 45,238 (actual)

ROBERT H. JOHNSON PLANETARIUM, 200 Kipling St., Lakewood, CO 80226-1046. Mailing Address: Mandalay Middle School, 9651 N. Pierce St., Westminster, CO 80021. Tel.: 303-982-7278. Fax: 303-982-7277.
Formerly: Jefferson County Schools Planetarium
Key Personnel: Dir., Kathy Miller; Coord. Scheduling, Lisa Delameter.
Institution Type/Description: Planetarium & Observatories.
Hours & Admission Prices: Call for hours. &
Attendance: 32,000

ROCKY MOUNTAIN COLLEGE OF ART + DESIGN GALLERIES, 1600 Pierce Ave., Lakewood, CO 80214-1897. Tel.: 800-888-ARTS. Fax: 303-759-4970. Facebook.
E-mail: cstell@rmead.edu
Web Site: www.rmcad.edu/exhibitions
Formerly: The Philip J. Steele Gallery
Key Personnel: C.E.O., Maria Puzziferro; Cur., Cortney Stell.
Institution Type/Description: College Art Gallery: Philip J. Steele Gallery.
Hours & Admission Prices: Mon.-Fri. 11-4. No charge. Closed New Year's Day; Independence Day; Labor Day; Thanksgiving; Christmas.

Lamar

BIG TIMBERS MUSEUM, 7515 US Hwy. 50, Lamar, CO 81052. Mailing Address: P.O. Box 362, Lamar, CO 81052-0362. Tel.: 719-336-2472. Fax: 719-336-2472.
E-mail: bigtimbers@prowerscounty.net
Web Site: www.bigtimbersmuseum.org
Key Personnel: Cur., Kathleen Scranton.
Institution Type/Description: History Museum: housed in the original AT&T Co. repeater station.
Hours & Admission Prices: June-Aug. Tues.-Sat. 10-5; Sept.-May Tues.-Sat. 1-4. Family $5, adults $3. Closed New Year's Day; Good Friday; Thanksgiving; Christmas.
Attendance: 1,300 (actual)

Las Animas

JOHN W. RAWLINGS HERITAGE CENTER & MUSEUM, 560 Bent Ave., Las Animas, CO 81054. Mailing Address: P.O. Box 68, Las Animas, CO 81054-0068. Tel.: 719-456-6066. Facebook: Pioneer Historical Society of Bent County.
E-mail: bentctyheritage@centurytel.net
Web Site: bentcounty.org
Formerly: Kit Carson Museum
Institution Type/Description: General Museum.
Hours & Admission Prices: Mon.-Fri. 12-4:30. Adults $3; discounts to groups of 10 or more. &
Attendance: 1,000 (actual)

Leadville

HEALY HOUSE-DEXTER CABIN, 912 Harrison Ave., Leadville, CO 80461-3321. Tel.: 719-486-0487. Fax: 719-486-2557.
E-mail: maureen.scanlon@state.co.us
Web Site: www.historycolorado.org
Key Personnel: C.E.O., Ed Nichols.
Institution Type/Description: Historic Buildings.
Hours & Admission Prices: mid-May to Oct. daily 10-4:30; other times tours by appointment. Adults $6, senior citizens $5.50, children 6-16 $4.50; discounts to AAM members, school & group tours; children under 6 & members no charge.
Attendance: 8,000

HERITAGE MUSEUM & GALLERY, 102 E. Ninth St., Leadville, CO 80461-3302. Mailing Address: P.O. Box 962, Leadville, CO 80461-0962. Tel.: 719-486-1878.
Key Personnel: Pres., Ray Stamps.
Institution Type/Description: History Museums: located in Historic Leadville District.
Hours & Admission Prices: Memorial Day to Sept. daily 10-5. Adults $7. &
Attendance: 9,000 (actual)

THE HISTORICAL TABOR OPERA HOUSE, 308 Harrison Ave., Leadville, CO 80461-3612. Tel.: 719-486-8409.
E-mail: info@taboroperahouse.net
Web Site: www.taboroperahouse.net
Key Personnel: House & Tours Mgr., Tammy Taber.
Institution Type/Description: Historic Theater Museum: listed on the National Register of Historic Places.
Hours & Admission Prices: House: late May to Sept. Tues.-Fri. 11-5, Sat.-Sun. 10:30-5:30. Adults $10, seniors, veterans & students $8; discounts to AAA, groups & military; children 10 & under no charge. &

HOUSE WITH THE EYE MUSEUM, 127 W. Fourth St., Leadville, CO 80461-3629. Mailing Address: P.O. Box 911, Leadville, CO 80461-0911. Tel.: 719-486-0708. Facebook.
Key Personnel: Cur., Barbara M. Bost.
Institution Type/Description: Historic House Museum: 1879 House with the Eye, built by noted French architect Robitaille for his bride; features a gingerbread front & hand-crafted wainscoting.
Hours & Admission Prices: June-Labor Day daily 10-4. Adults $5, senior citizens $4; discounts to AAM & ICOM members.

MATCHLESS MINE AND BABY DOE'S CABIN, E. 7th St., Leadville, CO 80461-3403. Mailing Address: P.O. Box 981, Leadville, CO 80461-0981. Tel.: 719-486-1229. Fax: 719-486-3927. Facebook: National Mining Hall of Fame & Museum.
E-mail: director@mininghalloffame.org
Web Site: www.mininghalloffame.org
Formerly: Matchless Mine Museum
Key Personnel: Exec. Dir., Stephen L. Whittington; Chm. (V), Frank McAllister.
Institution Type/Description: Historic Mine Site.
Hours & Admission Prices: Memorial Day to Sept. daily 12-5. Guided Tours: 1pm, 2pm & 3pm. Guided Tours: adults $12, students $10. Self-Guided Tours: adults $6, students $5; discounts to groups, schools, AAA, Blue Star & AARP members; members, children under 6, AAM, NARM, active military & Boy Scouts working on or have earned the Mining in Society merit badge no charge.
Attendance: 4,246 (actual)

NATIONAL MINING HALL OF FAME & MUSEUM, 120 W. 9th St., Leadville, CO 80461-3403. Mailing Address: P.O. Box 981, Leadville, CO 80461-0981. Tel.: 719-486-1229. Fax: 719-486-3927. Facebook.
E-mail: director@mininghalloffame.org
Web Site: www.mininghalloffame.org
Key Personnel: Exec. Dir., Stephen L. Whittington; Chm. (V), Frank McAllister.
Institution Type/Description: Mining Museum.
Hours & Admission Prices: May-Oct. daily 9-5; Nov.-April Tues.-Sun. 9-5. Adults $12, students $10; discounts to AAA, AARP & Blue Star members, groups and schools; members, children under 6, AAM & NARM members, Boy Scouts working on or have earned the Mining in Society merit badge & active military no charge. Closed New Year's Day; Thanksgiving; Christmas. &
Attendance: 19,548 (actual)

TABOR HOME, 116 E. 5th St., Leadville, CO 80461. Mailing Address: c/o Lake County Tourism Panel, P.O. Box 964, Leadville, CO 80461. Tel.: 719-486-3900, 855-488-1222.
Web Site: www.visitleadvilleco.com
Institution Type/Description: Historic House Museum: housed in the former home of Horace Tabor and his wife Augusta until 1881.
Hours & Admission Prices: Call for hours.

TEMPLE ISRAEL SYNAGOGUE AND MUSEUM, 201 W. 4th St., Leadville, CO 80461. Mailing Address: 208 W. 8th, Leadville, CO 80461. Tel.: 719-486-3625.
Institution Type/Description: Historic Building: built in 1884.
Hours & Admission Prices: mid-May to Oct. daily 10:30-6; other times by appointment.

Limon

LIMON HERITAGE MUSEUM, 899 First St., Limon, CO 80828. Mailing Address: P.O. Box 341, Limon, CO 80828-0341. Tel.: 719-775-9418. Fax: 719-775-8808. Facebook: Limon Heritage Museum.
E-mail: limonmuseum@hotmail.com
Web Site: limonmuseum.com
Key Personnel: C.E.O. & Dir., Tony Wernsman; Dir., Kevin Pickerill; Mgr. Operations, Mary Andersen; Education & Devel., Lucille Reimer; Treas. & Registrar, Barbara Berry.
Institution Type/Description: History Museum.
Hours & Admission Prices: Memorial Day-Labor Day Mon.-Sat. 1-8, Sun. 1-4. No charge; donations accepted. &
Attendance: 5,000 (estimated)

Littleton

COLORADO GALLERY OF THE ARTS/ARAPAHOE COMMUNITY COLLEGE, 5900 S. Santa Fe Dr., 1st Fl. Annex Bldg., Littleton, CO 80120-1801. Tel.: 303-797-5649.
E-mail: marketing@arapahoe.edu
Key Personnel: Gallery Coord., Trish Sangelo.
Institution Type/Description: Art Gallery.
Hours & Admission Prices: Mon. & Wed.-Fri. 12-5, Tues. 12-7; other times by appointment. No charge. Closed holidays. &
Attendance: 14,000

LITTLETON MUSEUM, 6028 S. Gallup St., Littleton, CO 80120-2703. Tel.: 303-795-3950. Fax: 303-730-9818. Facebook: Littleton Museum.
E-mail: tnimz@littletongov.org
Web Site: www.littletongov.org/museum
Formerly: Littleton Historical Museum
Key Personnel: Dir., Tim Nimz; Chm. (V), Amy Fischer; Cur. Exhibits, Bill Hastings; Cur. Collections, Terri White; Admin. Coord. & Museum Shop Mgr., Becky Kosma; Cur. Education & Interpretation, Suellen Winstead.
Institution Type/Description: General Museum: history museum & living history farms.
Hours & Admission Prices: Tues.-Fri. 8-5, Sat. 10-5, Sun. 1-5. No charge; donations accepted. Closed holidays. &
Attendance: 143,488 (actual)

Longmont

BOULDER COUNTY PARKS AND OPEN SPACE CULTURAL HISTORY PROGRAM, 8348 Ute Hwy. 66, Longmont, CO 80503-9232. Mailing Address: 5201 St. Vrain Rd., Longmont, CO 80503. Tel.: 303-776-8848. Fax: 303-776-3322.
E-mail: skippen@bouldercounty.org
Web Site: www.bouldercounty.org/os/culture/pages/default.aspx
Formerly: Agricultural Heritage Center at the Lohr-McIntosh Farm
Institution Type/Description: History Museum & Historic Buildings.
Hours & Admission Prices: See website for each location. No charge.

LONGMONT MUSEUM, 400 Quail Rd., Longmont, CO 80501-8989. Tel.: 303-651-8374. Fax: 303-774-4780. Facebook: Longmont Museum.
E-mail: kim.manajek@longmontcolorado.gov
Web Site: www.longmontmuseum.org
Key Personnel: Dir., Wesley Jessup; Bd. Chm., Bryan Bowles; Bd. Vice Chm., Richard Luke; Cur. Exhibits, Jared Thompson; Cur. Education, Ann Macca; Registrar, Heather Thorwald; Mgr. Mktg. & Devel., Joan Harrold; Cur. Research & Information, Erik Mason; Coord. Discovery Days, Elaine Waterman; Art in Public Places Admin., Lauren Greenfield; Mgr. Auditorium, Amy Kaiser; Museum Asst., Joann McCoy; Museum Shop Mgr., Christina Mehler.
Institution Type/Description: Regional History Museum.
Hours & Admission Prices: Mon.-Sat. 9-5, Sun. 1-5. Adults $8, children $5; discounts to NARM; members & children 3 & under no charge. Closed holidays. &
Attendance: 62,024 (actual)

Louisville

LOUISVILLE HISTORICAL MUSEUM, 1001 Main St., Louisville, CO 80027-1725. Mailing Address: City Hall, 749 Main St., Louisville, CO 80027. Tel.: 303-665-9048.
E-mail: museum@louisvilleco.gov
Key Personnel: Museum Coord., Bridget Bacon.
Institution Type/Description: History Museum.
Hours & Admission Prices: Tues.-Wed. & Sat. 10-3.

Loveland

BENSON SCULPTURE GARDEN, 2908 Aspen Dr., Loveland, CO 80538. Mailing Address: P.O. Box 7006, Loveland, CO 80537-0006. Tel.: 970-663-2940. Fax: 970-669-7390.
E-mail: lhpac@sculptureinthepark.org
Web Site: www.sculptureinthepark.org
Institution Type/Description: Sculpture Garden.
Hours & Admission Prices: Daily dawn to dusk.

LOVELAND MUSEUM GALLERY, 503 N. Lincoln Ave., Loveland, CO 80537-5619. Tel.: 970-962-2410. Fax: 970-962-2910.
E-mail: maureen.corey@cityofloveland.org
Web Site: www.lovelandmuseumgallery.org
Key Personnel: C.E.O. & Dir. Curatorial Svcs., Susan P. Ison; Pres. Historical Society (V), Mike Perry; Cur. Education, Jenni Dobson; Cur. History, Jennifer Cousino; Cur. Art, Maureen Corey; Public Art Mgr., Suzanne Janssen; Exhibits Preparator, Quinn Johnson; Administrative Specialist, Mary Shada; Coord. Mktg., Kim Akeley-Charron; Registrar, Robert Hoot; Graphic Designer, Michelle Standiford.
Institution Type/Description: Art and History Museum.
Hours & Admission Prices: Tues.-Wed. & Fri. 10-5, Thurs. 10-9, Sat. 10-4, Sun. 12-4. No charge; donations accepted. Closed New Year's Day; Independence Day; Thanksgiving & day after; Christmas. &
Attendance: 52,000 (estimated)

TIMBERLANE FARM MUSEUM, 2306 E. First St., Loveland, CO 80537-5906. Tel.: 970-646-2875. Fax: 970-663-7364.
Web Site: www.timberlanefarmmuseum.org
Key Personnel: Mgr., Dean Schilling; Cur., Teri Johnson.
Institution Type/Description: Farm Museum.
Hours & Admission Prices: Tues.-Sun. 9-4. No charge; donations accepted. Closed major holidays. &

Lyons

THE LYONS REDSTONE MUSEUM, 340 High St., Lyons, CO 80540. Mailing Address: P.O. Box 9, Lyons, CO 80540-0009. Tel.: 303-823-5925 & 5271. Fax: 303-823-8257.
E-mail: lavern921@aol.com
Web Site: lyonsredstonemuseum.com
Key Personnel: Dir. & Museum Shop Mgr., Terri Weir; C.E.O. & Pres. (V), Lavern M. Johnson; Chm. (V), Monique Sawyer Lang; Vice Pres., Jerry L. Johnson; Deputy Dir., Maxine Harkalis; Historic Asst., Calvin Schilling.
Institution Type/Description: History Museum: housed in c.1881 school building.
Hours & Admission Prices: May Sat. 9:30-4:30, Sun. 12:30-4:30, June-Sept. Mon.-Sat. 9:30-4:30, Sun. 12:30-4:30. No charge, donations accepted.
Attendance: 2,600 (estimated)

Manassa

JACK DEMPSEY MUSEUM AND PARK, 412 Main St., Manassa, CO 81141. Mailing Address: P.O. Box 130, Manassa, CO 81141-0130. Tel.: 719-843-5207.
E-mail: mchale45@yahoo.com
Web Site: www.museumtrail.org/jack-dempsey-museum.html
Institution Type/Description: History Museum: housed in the cabin where heavyweight boxing champion, Jack Dempsey was born.
Hours & Admission Prices: Memorial Day to Labor Day Tues.-Sat. 10-5. No charge; donations accepted. &
Attendance: 2,000 (estimated)

Manitou Springs

CAVE OF THE WINDS, 100 Cave of the Winds Rd., Manitou Springs, CO 80829. Mailing Address: P.O. Box 826, Manitou Springs, CO 80829-0826. Tel.: 719-685-5444. Fax: 719-685-1712.
E-mail: info@caveofthewinds.com
Web Site: caveofthewinds.com
Institution Type/Description: Natural History Museum.
Hours & Admission Prices: Summer daily 9-9; Winter: daily 10-5. Adults $18, children 6-11 $9; children 5 & under no charge.

CLIFF DWELLINGS MUSEUM, U.S. Hwy. 24, 10 Cliff Dwellings Rd., Manitou Springs, CO 80829. Mailing Address: P.O. Box 272, Manitou Springs, CO 80829-0272. Tel.: 719-685-5242 & 800-354-9971.
E-mail: info@cliffdwellingsmuseum.com

Web Site: www.cliffdwellingsmuseum.com
Key Personnel: Dir., Michele Hefner.
Institution Type/Description: Natural History Museum.
Hours & Admission Prices: March-April & Sept.-Oct. daily 9-5; May-Aug. daily 9-6; Nov. daily 9-4; Dec.-Feb. daily 10-4. Adults 12 & over $10, children $7.50; discounts to groups; adults 100 & over, persons in wheelchairs and children 6 & under no charge. Closed Thanksgiving; Christmas.
Attendance: 100,000 (estimated)

GARDEN OF THE GODS TRADING POST, 324 Beckers Lane, Manitou Springs, CO 80829. Tel.: 800-874-4515, 719-685-9045.
E-mail: webmail@ggtp.cc
Web Site: www.gardenofthegodstradingpost.com
Institution Type/Description: Art Gallery.
Hours & Admission Prices: Summer: daily 8-8; Winter: daily 9-5. Closed Thanksgiving; Christmas.

MIRAMONT CASTLE MUSEUM, 9 Capitol Hill Ave., Manitou Springs, CO 80829-1618. Tel.: 719-685-1011, 888-685-1011. Fax: 719-685-1985.
E-mail: miramontcastle@yahoo.com
Web Site: www.miramontcastle.org
Key Personnel: Treas. & Museum Shop Mgr., Peggie Yager.
Institution Type/Description: Historic Building Museum: built in 1895.
Hours & Admission Prices: Memorial Day to Labor Day daily 9-5; Sept.-May Tues.-Sun. 10-4; groups by appointment. Adults $8, seniors over 59 $7, children 6-12 $5; active military, children under 6 & members no charge. &
Attendance: 34,943 (actual)

Meeker

THE WHITE RIVER MUSEUM, 565 Park St., Meeker, CO 81641. Mailing Address: Rio Blanco County Historical Society, P.O. Box 413, Meeker, CO 81641-0413. Tel.: 970-878-9982.
E-mail: info@rbchistory.org
Web Site: www.rioblancocounty.org
Key Personnel: Pres. (V), Ellene Meece; Museum Shop Mgr., Sandra Shimko.
Institution Type/Description: History Museum; housed in 1880 Officer's Quarters for military cantonment.
Hours & Admission Prices: May-Sept. Mon.-Sat. 9-5, Sun. 12-5; Oct.-April Mon.-Sat. 10-4, Sun. 12-4. No charge; donations accepted. Closed New Year's Day; Easter; Mother's Day; Father's Day; Thanksgiving; Christmas. &
Attendance: 3,500 (estimated)

Mesa Verde National Park

MESA VERDE NATIONAL PARK MUSEUM, Mesa Verde National Park, CO 81330. Mailing Address: P.O. Box 8, Mesa Verde National Park, CO 81330-0008. Tel.: 970-529-4600. Fax: 970-529-4637.
E-mail: meve_general_information@nps.gov
Web Site: www.nps.gov/meve
Key Personnel: Supt., Cliff Spencer.
Institution Type/Description: Park Museum: archaeological & ethnographic exhibits; ancestral Puebloan archaeological sites dating from AD 550-1300.
Hours & Admission Prices: Park: open daily. Mesa Verde Visitor Center & Chapin Mesa Archeological Museum: please call or visit Website for seasonal hours. Park: Summer $20 per car; Winter $15 per car. Seasonal guided tours of Cliff Palace, Balcony House & Long House $4 per person. &
Attendance: 623,000 (estimated)

Monte Vista

MONTE VISTA HISTORICAL SOCIETY HISTORY CENTER, 110 Jefferson St., Monte Vista, CO 81144-1700. Mailing Address: P.O. Box 323, Monte Vista, CO 81144-0323. Tel.: 719-849-9320.
E-mail: mvhs123@msn.com
Key Personnel: Pres. (V), Peg Schall.
Institution Type/Description: History Museum.
Hours & Admission Prices: May-Sept. Tues.-Wed. 11-3; Winter: by appointment. No charge; donations accepted. &
Attendance: 10 (estimated)

TRANSPORTATION OF THE WEST MUSEUM, 916 First Ave., Monte Vista, CO 81144-1445. Mailing Address: P.O. Box 323, Monte Vista, CO 81144-0323. Tel.: 719-849-9320.
E-mail: mvhs123@msn.com
Key Personnel: Pres. (V), Peg Schall.
Institution Type/Description: Transportation Museum.

Hours & Admission Prices: May-Sept. Thurs.-Fri. 11-3; other times by appointment. No charge; donations accepted. &
Attendance: 150 (actual)

Montrose

MONTROSE COUNTY HISTORICAL MUSEUM, 21 N. Rio Grande, Montrose, CO 81401-3467. Mailing Address: P.O. Box 1882, Montrose, CO 81402-1882. Tel.: 970-249-2085. Facebook.
E-mail: info@montrosehistory.org
Web Site: www.montrosehistory.org
Key Personnel: Pres. (V), Zilla May Brown; Treas., Stephen Gray; Sec., Kathy Kennedy; Cur., Sally Johnson.
Institution Type/Description: Historical Society Museum: housed in c.1912 Denver & Rio Grande Western Depot.
Hours & Admission Prices: May-Sept. Mon.-Fri. 9-5, Sat. 10-2. Adults $6, students $2; members no charge. Closed holidays. &
Attendance: 3,500 (actual)

UTE INDIAN MUSEUM/MONTROSE VISITOR CENTER, 17253 Chipeta Dr., Montrose, CO 81403-4748. Tel.: 970-249-3098. Fax: 970-252-8741.
E-mail: cj.brafford@state.co.us
Key Personnel: C.E.O. & Museum Shop Mgr., C.J. Brafford.
Institution Type/Description: Indian History Museum: located on the site of Chief Ouray, leader of the Uncompahgre Utes.
Hours & Admission Prices: Jan.-June Tues.-Sat. 9-4; July-Oct. Mon.-Sat. 9-4:30, Sun. 11-4:30; Nov.-Dec. Mon.-Sat. 9-4:30. Adults $4.50, seniors over 65 $4, students 6-16 $2; members & children under 6 no charge. Closed New Year's Day; Thanksgiving; Christmas. &
Attendance: 17,000 (actual)

Morrison

MORRISON NATURAL HISTORY MUSEUM, 501 Colorado Hwy. 8, Morrison, CO 80465. Mailing Address: P.O. Box 564, Morrison, CO 80465-0564. Tel.: 303-697-1873. Fax: 303-697-8752.
E-mail: info@mnhm.org
Key Personnel: Dir., Matthew T. Mossbrucker.
Institution Type/Description: Natural History Museum.
Hours & Admission Prices: Daily 10-4. Admission 12 & over $8, children 3-11 $6; children 2 & under no charge. Closed New Year's Day; Easter; Thanksgiving; Christmas Eve & Day.

Mosca

GREAT SAND DUNES NATIONAL PARK AND PRESERVE, 11999 Hwy. 150, Mosca, CO 81146-9502. Tel.: 719-378-6300 & 6399. Fax: 719-378-6360.
E-mail: patrick_myers@nps.gov
Key Personnel: Supt., Lisa Carrico; Resource Mgmt., Fred Bruch; Cur., Phyllis Pineda Bovin.
Institution Type/Description: Park Museum.
Hours & Admission Prices: Visitor Center: Summer: daily 8:30-6; Spring & Fall daily 9-5; Winter: daily 9-4:30. Adults 16 & over $3; children no charge.

Naturita

RIMROCKER HISTORICAL SOCIETY OF WEST MONTROSE COUNTY AND MUSEUM, 411 W. 2nd Avenue, Naturita, CO 81422. Mailing Address: P.O. Box 913, Nucla, CO 81424-0913. Tel.: 970-865-2100. Facebook: Rimrocker Historical Society.
E-mail: rimrocker@nntcwireless.net
Key Personnel: Chm. (V), Sharon Johannsen; Pres. (V), Jane Thompson.
Institution Type/Description: Historical Society Museum: housed in Old Naturita Elementary School House.
Hours & Admission Prices: June-Labor Day Tues.-Sat. 2-4; Winter: Wed. 2-4. No charge; donations accepted. &
Attendance: 450 (estimated)

Nunn

DRYLANDERS MUSEUM, 755 3rd St., Nunn, CO 80648. Tel.: 970-897-3125 (summer) 2671 (winter).
Institution Type/Description: History Museum.
Hours & Admission Prices: Summer: Sat.-Sun. 1-4; other times by appointment.

Ouray

OURAY COUNTY HISTORICAL SOCIETY MUSEUM, 420 6th Ave., Ouray, CO 81427. Mailing Address: P.O. Box 151, Ouray, CO 81427-0151. Tel.: 970-325-4576.
E-mail: ochs@ouraynet.com
Institution Type/Description: Historical Society Museum: housed in the former St. Joseph's Miners' Hospital; built in 1886.
Hours & Admission Prices: mid-April to mid-May & Oct. to week before Thanksgiving Thurs.-Sat. 10-4:30; mid-May to Sept. Mon.-Sat. 10-4:30, Sun. 12-4:30; other times by appointment. Adults $6, children 6-12 $1; discounts to groups; members & children under 6 no charge.

Pagosa Springs

FRED HARMAN ART MUSEUM, 85 Harman Park Dr., Pagosa Springs, CO 81147. Mailing Address: P.O. Box 192, Pagosa Springs, CO 81147-0192. Tel.: 970-731-5785. Fax: 970-731-4832.
E-mail: info@harmanartmuseum.com
Web Site: www.harmanartmuseum.com
Key Personnel: C.E.O. & Cur., Fred C. Harman, III; Chm. (V), John Cramer; Financial Dir. & Treas., Marilyn Harris; Devel., Membership & Museum Shop Mgr., Norma Harman; Security, Lee Ligon.
Institution Type/Description: Art Museum: home of Fred Harman, artist & cartoonist, creator of the Red Ryder & Little Beaver comics; one of the founders of the Cowboy Artists of America.
Hours & Admission Prices: May to Oct. Mon.-Sat., 10:30-5. Adults $3; members no charge. Closed Thanksgiving; Christmas. &
Attendance: 1,900 (actual)

Palmer Lake

LUCRETIA VAILE MUSEUM, 66 Lower Glenway St., Palmer Lake, CO 80133. Mailing Address: Palmer Lake Historical Society, P.O. Box 662, Palmer Lake, CO 80133-0662. Tel.: 719-559-0837.
Web Site: www.palmerdividehistory.org
Key Personnel: Dir., Roger Davis.
Institution Type/Description: Historical Society Museum.
Hours & Admission Prices: June-Aug. Wed. 1-4, Sat. 10-2; Sept.-May Wed. 1-3, Sat. 10-2. No charge; donations accepted. Closed national holidays. &
Attendance: 750 (estimated)

Parker

WILDLIFE EXPERIENCE MUSEUM, 10035 Peoria St., Parker, CO 80134-9600. Tel.: 720-488-3300.
E-mail: info@twexp.org
Web Site: www.thewildlifeexperience.org
Institution Type/Description: Natural History Museum.
Hours & Admission Prices: Daily 9:30-5. Adults $10, seniors 60 & over $9, children 3-12 $6; discounts to groups; children under 3 no charge. Additional fee for theater & shows. Closed Thanksgiving; Christmas.

Peterson Air Force Base

PETERSON AIR & SPACE MUSEUM, 21st Space Wing/MU, 150 E. Ent Ave., Peterson Air Force Base, CO 80914-1303. Tel.: 719-556-4915. Fax: 719-556-8509. Facebook.
E-mail: 21sw.mu@us.af.mil
Web Site: www.petemuseum.org
Institution Type/Description: Military Museum.
Hours & Admission Prices: Tues.-Sat., 9-4. No charge; donations accepted. Closed federal holidays. &
Attendance: 14,000 (estimated)

Platteville

FORT VASQUEZ MUSEUM, 13412 U.S. Hwy. 85, Platteville, CO 80651-8017. Tel.: 970-785-2832.
E-mail: brittany.gutierrez@state.co.us
Web Site: www.coloradohistory.org
Institution Type/Description: Fur Trade and Native American Museum: reconstructed adobe fort on site of original 1835 trading post. Fort Vasquez trading post archaeological site and the Works Progress Administration adobe fort are listed in the National Register of Historic Places.
Hours & Admission Prices: April-Sept. daily 10-4. Oct.-March Wed.-Sun. 10-4. Adults $3, seniors $2.50, students 7-16 $2; children 6 & under no charge. Closed New Year's Day; Thanksgiving; Christmas. &
Attendance: 4,301 (actual)

Pueblo

COLORADO MENTAL HEALTH INSTITUTE AT PUEBLO MUSEUM, 13th & Francisco Sts., Pueblo, CO 81003. Mailing Address: 1600 W. 24th St., Pueblo, CO 81003-1411. Tel.: 719-543-2012.
E-mail: info@cmhipmuseum.org
Web Site: www.cmhipmuseum.org
Key Personnel: Dir., Bob Mitchell; Asst. Dir., Nell Mitchell.
Institution Type/Description: Psychiatry Museum: listed on the National Register of Historic Places.
Hours & Admission Prices: Tues. 10-4; other times by appointment. No charge.

EL PUEBLO HISTORY MUSEUM, 301 N. Union, Pueblo, CO 81003-4266. Tel.: 719-583-0453. Fax: 719-583-8214.
E-mail: deborah.espinosa@chs.state.co.us
Web Site: www.coloradohistory.org
Key Personnel: Dir., Deborah Espinosa; Administrative Asst., Kathleen Byers; Education Coord., Kathleen Eriksen; Trades, Truman Pooler.
Institution Type/Description: Historical Society Museum.
Hours & Admission Prices: Mon.-Sat. 10-4, Sun. 12-4. Adults $5, seniors 65 & over, military and students $4; discounts to AAM members; children under 6 no charge. Closed major holidays. &
Attendance: 23,000 (actual)

HOSE CO. NO. 3 FIRE MUSEUM, 116 Broadway Ave., Pueblo, CO 81003. Mailing Address: 116 N. Main St., Pueblo, CO 81003. Tel.: 719-821-1273. Fax: 719-553-2831. Facebook: Hose Co. No. 3 Fire Museum.
E-mail: gmmpf@hotmail.com
Web Site: hosecono3.com
Key Personnel: Chm. (V) & Dir., Gary M. Micheli; Pres. (V), Mark Pickerel.
Institution Type/Description: Firefighting History Museum.
Hours & Admission Prices: Call for hours. No charge; donations accepted.
Attendance: 738 (actual)

INFOZONE NEWS MUSEUM, 100 E. Abriendo Ave., Pueblo, CO 81004-4232. Tel.: 719-553-0205.
E-mail: maria.tucker@pueblolibrary.org
Web Site: www.pueblolibrary.org
Key Personnel: Dir., Maria Sanchez-Tucker.
Institution Type/Description: History Museum.
Hours & Admission Prices: Mon.-Thurs. 9-9, Fri.-Sat. 9-6, Sun. 1-5. No charge. &
Attendance: 30,000 (actual)

PUEBLO ART GUILD AND GALLERY, 1500 N. Santa Fe, Pueblo, CO 81003-3700. Tel.: 719-543-2455.
E-mail: pag_enews@q.com
Web Site: www.puebloartguild.com
Key Personnel: Pres., Freda Moore.
Institution Type/Description: Art Gallery: housed in the historic boathouse in Mineral Palace Park.
Hours & Admission Prices: Spring, Summer & Fall Wed.-Sun. 12-4. Winter: call for hours. No charge; donations accepted. Closed most holidays.

PUEBLO COUNTY HISTORICAL SOCIETY MUSEUM AND EDWARD H. BROADHEAD LIBRARY, 203 W. "B" St., Pueblo, CO 81003-3403. Tel.: 719-543-6772.
E-mail: info@pueblohistory.org
Web Site: www.pueblohistory.org
Key Personnel: Pres. (V), Joan Mihalick; Museum Shop Mgr., Joe Mahaney.
Institution Type/Description: Historical Society Museum & Library.
Hours & Admission Prices: Tues.-Sat. 10-4. Adult $6, seniors, students with ID & military $5, children 6-12 $4; members no charge. Closed holidays. &
Attendance: 4,000 (estimated)

PUEBLO WEISBROD AIRCRAFT MUSEUM, 31001 Magnuson Ave., Pueblo, CO 81001-4822. Tel.: 719-948-9219. Fax: 719-948-2437.
E-mail: phas@pwam.org
Web Site: www.pwam.org
Formerly: International B-24 Museum
Key Personnel: Pres., Don Blehm; Vice Pres., Ralph Decker.
Institution Type/Description: Aircraft & Military History Museum.
Hours & Admission Prices: Mon.-Sat. 10-4, Sun. 1-4. Adults $7; military with proper ID no charge. &
Attendance: 18,000 (actual)

PUEBLO ZOO, 3455 Nuckolls Ave., Pueblo, CO 81005-1234. Tel.: 719-561-1452, ext. 100. Fax: 719-561-8686.
E-mail: akrause@pueblozoo.org
Web Site: www.pueblozoo.org
Key Personnel: Exec. Dir., Abigail Krause; Pres., Janet Fieldman; Cur., Ashley Bowen; Mktg., Vikki Graston; Education, Heather Dewey; Museum Shop Mgr., Carol Ecker.
Institution Type/Description: Zoo.
Hours & Admission Prices: May-Sept. daily 9-5; Oct.-April Mon.-Sat. 9-4, Sun. 12-4. Adults $12, children 3-12 $10; discounts to groups & AZA members; members & children under 3 no charge. Closed New Year's Day; Thanksgiving; Christmas. &
Attendance: 86,457 (actual)

ROSEMOUNT MUSEUM, 419 W. 14th St., Pueblo, CO 81003-2707. Tel.: 719-545-5290. Fax: 719-545-5291.
E-mail: ddarrow@rosemount.org
Web Site: www.rosemount.org
Key Personnel: C.E.O. & Exec. Dir., Deb Darrow; Pres., Kathlyn Thatcher Vail; Collections Mgr. & Housekeeping, Susan Kittinger; Maintenance & Groundskeeper, Roger Cain; Museum Shop Mgr., Patricia Bedard.
Institution Type/Description: Historic House Museum: housed in an 1893 Victorian mansion, the John A. Thatcher residence; Henry Hudson Holly, architect.
Hours & Admission Prices: Feb.-Dec. Tues.-Sat. 10-3:30. Adults $8, senior citizens $6, groups of 10 or more scheduled in advance $5 per person, children 6-18 $4; discounts active military; members & children under 6 no charge. Closed holidays.
Attendance: 7,000 (actual)

SANGRE DE CRISTO ARTS CENTER & CONFERENCE CENTER, 210 N. Santa Fe Ave., Pueblo, CO 81003-4133. Tel.: 719-295-7200. Fax: 719-295-7230.
E-mail: mail@sdc-arts.org
Web Site: www.sdc-arts.org
Formerly: Sangre de Cristo Arts Center & Buell Children's Museum
Key Personnel: C.E.O., Dr. Jim Richerson; Cur. Visual Arts, LuDel Walter; Artistic Dir. School of Dance, Nan Wainwright; Membership, Adele McCanless; Museum Shop Mgr., Jade Lopez.
Institution Type/Description: Arts Center & Children's Museum.
Hours & Admission Prices: Arts Center & Children's Museum: Wed.-Sat. 11-4, Sun 12-4. Adults $8, children, military & seniors $6; discounts to military & AAM members; members no charge. Office: Mon.-Sat. 9-5, Sun. 12-4. Closed legal holidays. &
Attendance: 222,000 (actual)

SOUTHEASTERN COLORADO HERITAGE CENTER AND MUSEUM D.B.A. PUEBLO HERITAGE MUSEUM, 201 W. B St., Pueblo, CO 81003-3403. Tel.: 719-295-1517. Fax: 719-295-0040.
E-mail: info@theheritagecenter.us
Web Site: www.theheritagecenter.us
Key Personnel: Museum Coord., Fran Reed.
Institution Type/Description: History Museum: listed on the National Register of Historic Buildings.
Hours & Admission Prices: Tues.-Sat. 10-4. Adults $5, seniors 55 & over and active duty military w/ID $4, children 6-12 $3; children 5 & under and SCHC members no charge. Closed New Year's Day; Independence Day; Thanksgiving & day after; Christmas. &
Attendance: 9,000 (estimated)

Rangely

RANGELY OUTDOOR MUSEUM, 150 Kennedy Dr., Rangely, CO 81648-3503. Mailing Address: Rangely Museum Society, P.O. Box 131, Rangely, CO 81648. Tel.: 970-675-2612.
E-mail: ramuseum@quikus.com
Formerly: Rangely Museum
Key Personnel: Dir., Brenda Hopson; Pres. (V), Tom Collins.
Institution Type/Description: History Museum.
Hours & Admission Prices: April-May & Sept.-Oct. Fri.-Sat. 10-4, Sun. 12-4; June-Aug. Mon.-Sat. 10-4, Sun. 12-4; other times by appointment. No charge; donations accepted.

Ridgway

RIDGWAY RAILROAD MUSEUM, US Hwy. 550 & Colorado State Hwy. 62, Ridgway, CO 81432. Mailing Address: P.O. Box 588, Ridgway, CO 81432-0588. Tel.: 970-626-4239.
E-mail: ridgwayrailroadmuseum@ouraynet.com
Web Site: www.ridgwayrailroadmuseum.org

Key Personnel: Pres. (V), Karl Schaeffer.
Institution Type/Description: Railroad Museum.
Hours & Admission Prices: May & Oct.-Nov. daily 10-3; June-Sept. daily 9-5; Dec.-April by appointment. No charge; donations accepted.
Attendance: 7,500 (actual)

Rifle

RIFLE CREEK MUSEUM, 337 East Ave., Rifle, CO 81650-2333. Mailing Address: P.O. Box 1882, Rifle, CO 81650-1882. Tel.: 970-625-4862.
E-mail: retractcec@gmail.com
Key Personnel: Pres. (V), Cecil Waldron; Vice Pres., Kathy Runia; Sec., Betty Waldron; Treas., Lynn Roe.
Institution Type/Description: General Museum.
Hours & Admission Prices: May-Oct. Mon.-Fri. 10-4; other times by appointment. Adults $5, senior citizens $4, children 6-12 $3; children 5 & under and members no charge. &
Attendance: 2,500 (estimated)

Rocky Ford

ROCKY FORD HISTORICAL MUSEUM, 1005 Sycamore Ave., Rocky Ford, CO 81067. Tel.: 719-254-6737.
E-mail: rfmuseum@centurytel.net
Key Personnel: Cur., William B. Hodges, Jr.
Institution Type/Description: General Museum: housed in the form Carnegie Library; built in 1909.
Hours & Admission Prices: Memorial Day to Labor Day Tues.-Fri. 1-5, Sat. 10 to noon; Sept.-May Wed. 1-5; other times by appointment. No charge; donations accepted. &
Attendance: 700 (estimated)

Saguache

HAZARD HOUSE MUSEUM, 735 Pitkin Ave., Saguache, CO 81149. Mailing Address: P.O. Box 569, Saguache, CO 81149. Tel.: 719-655-6550.
Key Personnel: Dir., Trish Gilbert.
Institution Type/Description: History Museum: housed in a 1908 Museum.
Hours & Admission Prices: Memorial Day to 3rd week of Sept. daily 9-4. Adults $2, children under 12 $1; discounts to groups of 40 or more.

SAGUACHE COUNTY MUSEUM, 405 8th St., Saguache, CO 81149. Mailing Address: P.O. Box 569, Saguache, CO 81149-0569. Tel.: 719-655-2557. Facebook.
E-mail: dorraine@fairpoint.net
Web Site: www.museumtrail.org
Key Personnel: C.E.O., Dorraine Gasseling.
Institution Type/Description: Pioneer Museum & National Historic Site.
Hours & Admission Prices: Memorial Day-Labor Day daily 9-4. Adults $7, children under 12 $1; discounts to groups of 50 or more; members no charge. &
Attendance: 1,424 (actual)

Salida

SALIDA MUSEUM, 406 1/2 W. Rainbow Blvd., Salida, CO 81201-2236. Tel.: 719-539-7483. Facebook.
E-mail: salidamuseum@gmail.com
Web Site: www.salidamuseum.org
Key Personnel: Museum Shop Mgr., Bob Campbell.
Institution Type/Description: General Museum.
Hours & Admission Prices: Memorial Day to Labor Day daily 11-5; tours by appointment; Sept.-May Sat.-Sun. 1-5. Adults $5, seniors $3, children 7-17 $1; children under 7 & members no charge. &
Attendance: 500 (estimated)

Silt

SILT HISTORICAL SOCIETY, 707 Orchid Ave., Silt, CO 81652. Mailing Address: P.O. Box 401, Silt, CO 81652-0401. Tel.: 970-876-5801.
E-mail: silthistorical@yahoo.com
Web Site: www.silthistoricalpark.com
Key Personnel: Pres. Bd., Bill Smith.
Institution Type/Description: Living History Museum.
Hours & Admission Prices: May-Oct. Tues.-Sat. 12-5. No charge; donations accepted. &
Attendance: 3,000 (estimated)

Silver Cliff

SILVER CLIFF MUSEUM, 612 E. Main, Silver Cliff, CO 81252. Mailing Address: P.O. Box 154, Silver Cliff, CO 81252-0154. Tel.: 719-783-2615.
E-mail: silvercliftown@centurytel.net
Key Personnel: Cur., Dorothy L. Urban; Chm. (V), Carol Franta.
Institution Type/Description: General Museum.
Hours & Admission Prices: Memorial Day to Labor Day. Sat.-Sun. 1-4; other times by appointment. No charge; donations accepted.
Attendance: 310 (actual)

Silver Plume

GEORGE ROWE MUSEUM AT THE SILVER PLUME SCHOOLHOUSE, 315 Main St., Silver Plume, CO 80476. Mailing Address: P.O. Box 935, Silver Plume, CO 80476-0935. Tel.: 303-569-2562.
Key Personnel: Chm. (V), Judith Caldwell.
Institution Type/Description: History Museum.
Hours & Admission Prices: Memorial Day to Labor Day daily 12-5; Sept. Sat.-Sun. 12-5. Adults $4, seniors $1.50, children $1; members & Silver Plume residents no charge.
Attendance: 1,210 (actual)

Silverton

SAN JUAN COUNTY HISTORICAL SOCIETY MUSEUM, 1557 Greene, Silverton, CO 81433. Mailing Address: P.O. Box 154, Silverton, CO 81433-0154. Tel.: 970-387-5838 & 5609. Fax: 970-387-5144.
E-mail: bevrich@frontier.net
Web Site: sanjuancountyhistoricalsociety.org
Key Personnel: Chm. (V), Beverly Rich; Treas. & Sec., Scott Fetchenhier; Museum Shop Mgr., Judy Zimmerman.
Institution Type/Description: Local History Museum.
Hours & Admission Prices: Memorial Day-Sept. daily 9-5; Oct. daily 10-3. Mayflower Gold Mill: Memorial Day-Sept. 30 daily 10-4:30. Tours on half hour: adults $8, children 5-12 $3; discounts to groups; members & children under 5 no charge.
Attendance: 14,000 (estimated)

Snowmass Village

ANDERSON RANCH ARTS CENTER, 5263 Owl Creek Rd., Snowmass Village, CO 81615. Mailing Address: P.O. Box 5598, Snowmass Village, CO 81615-5598. Tel.: 970-923-3181. Fax: 970-923-3871. Facebook; Twitter; Instagram; YouTube.
E-mail: info@andersonranch.org
Web Site: www.andersonranch.org
Key Personnel: Exec. Dir., Nancy Wilhelms; Museum Shop Mgr., Jessica Cerise.
Institution Type/Description: Art School & Gallery.
Hours & Admission Prices: Mon.-Fri. 9-5. No charge.
Attendance: 5,000

Steamboat Springs

STEAMBOAT ART MUSEUM, 807 Lincoln Ave., Steamboat Springs, CO 80487. Mailing Address: P.O. Box 883434, Steamboat Springs, CO 80488-3434. Tel.: 970-870-1755.
E-mail: sam@steamboatartmuseum.org
Web Site: www.steamboatartmuseum.org
Key Personnel: Pres. (V), Rod Hanna; Exec. Dir., Berse Grassby; Museum Shop Mgr., Susie Pace.
Institution Type/Description: Art Museum: housed in an historic bank building.
Hours & Admission Prices: Tues.-Sat. 11-6. No charge; donations accepted.
Attendance: 10,256 (actual)

TREAD OF PIONEERS MUSEUM, 800 Oak St., Steamboat Springs, CO 80477. Mailing Address: P.O. Box 772372, Steamboat Springs, CO 80477-2372. Tel.: 970-879-2214. Fax: 970-879-6109.
E-mail: topmuseum@springsips.com
Web Site: www.treadofpioneers.org
Key Personnel: Dir., Candice Bannister; Cur., Katie Adams; Museum Shop Mgr., Tamra Monahan.
Institution Type/Description: Local History Museum.
Hours & Admission Prices: Tues.-Sat. 11-5; call for seasonal extended hours. Adults $5, senior citizens $4, children 6-12 $1; discounts to AAA members; members & Routt County residents no charge.
Attendance: 10,000 (estimated)

Sterling

OVERLAND TRAIL MUSEUM, 110 Overland Trail, Sterling, CO 80751. Mailing Address: Box 4000, Sterling, CO 80751-0400. Tel.: 970-522-3895.
E-mail: krich@sterlingcolo.com
Web Site: www.sterlingcolo.com
Key Personnel: Cur., Kay L. Brigham Rich; Asst., Janet Bigler; Asst., Perry Johnson.
Institution Type/Description: General Museum: located on the site of the Overland Trail, near the Valley Station of Ben Holladay Stage line.
Hours & Admission Prices: April-Oct. Mon.-Sat. 9-5, Sun. 1-5, Holidays 10-5; Nov.-March Tues.-Sat. 10-4. Adults $1.50-$3.
Attendance: 14,000 (estimated)

Strasburg

COMANCHE CROSSING HISTORICAL SOCIETY & MUSEUM, 56060 E. Colfax Ave., Strasburg, CO 80136. Mailing Address: P.O. Box 647, Strasburg, CO 80136-0647. Tel.: 303-622-4322.
E-mail: csmith80136@tds.net
Web Site: cchscolorado.com
Key Personnel: Pres., Tracy Morgan; Treas., Karen Tangeman; Cur., Clifford Smith; Museum Shop Mgr., Marilee Gillock.
Institution Type/Description: Historical Society Museum: Comanche Crossing is the location where the first continuous chain of rails was completed by the Kansas Pacific Railroad, Aug. 15, 1870.
Hours & Admission Prices: June-Aug. daily 1-4; other times by appointment. No charge; donations accepted.
Attendance: 800 (estimated)

Telluride

TELLURIDE GALLERY OF FINE ART, 130 E. Colorado Ave., P.O. Box 1900, Telluride, CO 81435. Tel.: 970-728-3300. Fax: 775-320-3646.
E-mail: info@telluridegallery.com
Web Site: www.telluridegallery.com
Institution Type/Description: Art Gallery.
Hours & Admission Prices: mid-Nov. to mid-Oct. Tues.-Sat. 10-7, Sun.-Mon. 12-6.

TELLURIDE HISTORICAL MUSEUM, 201 W. Gregory Ave., Telluride, CO 81435. Mailing Address: P.O. Box 1597, Telluride, CO 81435-1597. Tel.: 970-728-3344. Fax: 970-728-6757.
E-mail: museum@telluridecolorado.net
Web Site: www.telluridemuseum.org
Key Personnel: Exec. Dir., Kiernan Lannon; Mgr. Collections, Kathy Rohrer; Pres., Danny Craft.
Institution Type/Description: General Museum: housed in 1896 community hospital building.
Hours & Admission Prices: June-Oct. Mon.-Sat. 11-5, Sun. 1-5; Dec. to early April Tues.-Sat. 11-5. Adults $5, seniors & students $3; discounts to AAM members; children 5 & under & members no charge. Closed major holidays.
Attendance: 6,000 (estimated)

Trinidad

ARTHUR ROY MITCHELL MEMORIAL MUSEUM, 150 E. Main St., Trinidad, CO 81082-2709. Mailing Address: P.O. Box 95, Trinidad, CO 81082-0095. Tel.: 719-846-4224. Fax: 719-846-2004.
E-mail: mitchellmuseum@qwestoffice.net
Web Site: armitchell.org
Key Personnel: Exec. Dir., Allyson Sheumaker.
Institution Type/Description: Art Museum: housed in c.1906 building.
Hours & Admission Prices: Thurs.-Sat. 10-5; other times by appointment. Adult $3; members & children under 12 no charge.
Attendance: 3,500 (actual)

LOUDEN-HENRITZE ARCHAEOLOGY MUSEUM, Trinidad State Junior College, 600 Prospect St., Trinidad, CO 81082-2356. Tel.: 719-846-5508. Fax: 719-846-5050. Facebook.
E-mail: loretta.martin@trinidadstate.edu
Web Site: www.trinidadstate.edu/museum
Key Personnel: Dir., Loretta Martin.
Institution Type/Description: Natural History Museum.
Hours & Admission Prices: Summer: Mon.-Fri. 10-4; groups by appointment; call for additional hours. No charge. Closed national & state holidays.
Attendance: 2,322 (actual)

USAFA

U.S. AIR FORCE ACADEMY VISITOR CENTER, 2346 Academy Dr., USAFA, CO 80840-9401. Tel.: 719-333-2025. Fax: 719-333-4402.
E-mail: pa.comrel@usafa.edu
Web Site: usafa.af.mil
Key Personnel: Bldg. Mgr., Larry Wells.
Institution Type/Description: Military Museum.
Hours & Admission Prices: Daily 9-5. No charge. Closed New Year's Eve & Day; Thanksgiving; Christmas Eve & Day. &
Attendance: 430,506 (actual)

Vail

COLORADO SKI & SNOWBOARD MUSEUM AND HALL OF FAME, 231 S. Frontage Rd. E., Level 3-Vail Village Transportation Center, Vail, CO 81657. Tel.: 970-476-1876.
E-mail: skimuseum@gmail.com
Web Site: www.skimuseum.net
Key Personnel: Exec. Dir., Susie Tjossem; Chm., Jamie Duke; Cur., Dana Mathios; Museum Shop Mgr., Pam Gross.
Institution Type/Description: Ski and Snowboard History Museum.
Hours & Admission Prices: Tues.-Sun. 10-6. No charge; donations accepted. Closed Thanksgiving; Christmas. &
Attendance: 60,000 (estimated)

Victor

VICTOR LOWELL THOMAS MUSEUM, 3rd St. & Victor Ave., Victor, CO 80860. Mailing Address: P.O. Box 238, Victor, CO 80860-0238. Tel.: 719-689-5509.
E-mail: museum@victorcolorado.com
Web Site: victorcolorado.com
Key Personnel: Pres. (V), Ruth Zalewski; Museum Shop Mgr., Cindy Slane.
Institution Type/Description: History Museum: built in 1899.
Hours & Admission Prices: Memorial Day to Labor Day daily 9:30-5:30; Sept. Fri.-Mon. 10-5; Oct. to late Dec. Sat.-Sun. 10-5. Adults $7, seniors 60 & over $6, children 12 & under $5; discounts to groups of 20 or over.
Attendance: 10,000 (actual)

Walsenburg

HUERFANO COUNTY HISTORICAL SOCIETY, INCLUDING THE WALSENBURG MINING MUSEUM & FT. FRANCISCO MUSEUM OF LA VETA, 112 W. 5th St., Walsenburg, CO 81089-1941. Mailing Address: P.O. Box 134, Walsenburg, CO 81089-0134. Tel.: 719-738-1992. Fax: 719-738-6218.
E-mail: director@franciscofort.org
Key Personnel: Dir. Walsenberg, Margaret Gleisberg; Museum Shop Mgr., Marge Figal.
Institution Type/Description: Mining Museum: housed in c.1896 jail building.
Hours & Admission Prices: Walsenburg Mining Museum: May-Sept. Mon.-Fri. 10-4, Sat. 10-1. Adults $2, teens $1; children under 12 no charge. Ft. Francisco Museum: Mon.-Sat. 10-4, Sun. 1-4. Adults $6, children & seniors $3.
Attendance: 1,500 (estimated)

Westminster

BOWLES HOUSE MUSEUM - WESTMINSTER HISTORICAL SOCIETY, 3924 W. 72nd Ave., Westminster, CO 80031. Mailing Address: P.O. Box 492, Westminster, CO 80036-0492. Tel.: 303-430-7929.
E-mail: westminstercohistory@gmail.com
Web Site: westminstercohistory.com
Key Personnel: Dir., Elaine Egan; Pres. (V), Linda Graybeal.
Institution Type/Description: Historical Society Museum: housed in the former home of Edward Bruce Bowles; built in 1871. Listed on the National Register of Historic Places.
Hours & Admission Prices: See website for information on tours; other times by appointment. No charge; donations accepted.

BUTTERFLY PAVILION, 6252 W. 104th Ave., Westminster, CO 80020-4107. Tel.: 303-469-5441. Fax: 303-657-5944. Facebook: Butterfly Pavilion; Instagram: @butterflypavilion; Twitter: @b_flypavilion.
E-mail: marketing@butterflies.org
Web Site: www.butterflies.org

Key Personnel: C.E.O., Patrick Tennyson; Museum Shop Mgr., Kimm Damor.
Institution Type/Description: Tropical Conservatory.
Hours & Admission Prices: Daily 9-5. Adults $11, seniors 65 & over $9, children 2-12 $6; children under 2 no charge. Closed Thanksgiving; Christmas. &
Attendance: 250,000 (actual)

Wheat Ridge

WHEAT RIDGE HISTORIC PARK, 4610 Robb St., Wheat Ridge, CO 80033-2537. Mailing Address: P.O. Box 1833, Wheat Ridge, CO 80034-1833. Tel.: 303-421-9111. Fax: 303-467-0023.
Web Site: www.wheatridgehistoricalsociety.org
Formerly: Wheat Ridge Soddy
Key Personnel: Pres. (V), Claudia Worth; Vice Pres.., Charlotte Whetsel; Museum Shop Mgr., Jane Harvey.
Institution Type/Description: History Museum.
Hours & Admission Prices: Fri. 10-3; other times by appointment. Np charge, but donations accepted. Closed national holidays. &
Attendance: 3,100 (estimated)

Windsor

WINDSOR MUSEUM, 6th St. & Ash St., Windsor, CO 80550. Mailing Address: 301 Walnut St., Windsor, CO 80550. Tel.: 970-674-2443. Fax: 970-674-2456.
E-mail: cknight@windsorgov.com
Web Site: www.windsorgov.com
Key Personnel: Mgr. Arts & Heritage, Carrie Knight; Cur., Elizabeth Handwerk Kurt.
Institution Type/Description: History Museum.
Hours & Admission Prices: Memorial Day to Labor Day Tues.-Sat. 1-4. No charge; donations accepted.
Attendance: 5,000 (estimated)

Woodland Park

ROCKY MOUNTAIN DINOSAUR RESOURCE CENTER, 201 S. Fairview St., Woodland Park, CO 80863-1154. Tel.: 719-686-1820. Fax: 719-686-1399. Facebook: Rocky Mountain Dinosaur Resource Center.
E-mail: info@rmdrc.com
Web Site: www.rmdrc.com
Key Personnel: Dir. & Pres., J.J. Triebold.
Institution Type/Description: Paleontology Museum.
Hours & Admission Prices: Mon.-Sat. 9-6, Sun. 10-5. Adults $11.50; members no charge. Closed New Year's Day; Easter; Thanksgiving; Christmas. &

Wray

WRAY MUSEUM, 205 E. Third St., Wray, CO 80758-1106. Mailing Address: P.O. Box 161, Wray, CO 80758-0161. Tel.: 970-332-5063. Facebook.
E-mail: wraymuseum@cityofwray.org
Web Site: www.cityofwray.org
Key Personnel: Dir., Ardith Hendrix.
Institution Type/Description: History Museum.
Hours & Admission Prices: Tues.-Sat. 12-4. Adults $1, seniors & children under 5 $.50; members no charge. &
Attendance: 2,000 (actual)

CONNECTICUT

(347 listings)

Ansonia

ANSONIA NATURE & RECREATION CENTER, 10 Deerfield Ln., Ansonia, CT 06401. Tel.: 203-736-1053. Fax: 203-734-1672.
E-mail: ansnaturectr@ansonicct.org
Web Site: ansonianaturecenter.org
Key Personnel: Dir., Alison M Rubelmann.
Institution Type/Description: Nature Center.
Hours & Admission Prices: Park: sunrise to sundown. Center: daily 9-5. No charge; donations accepted. Closed New Year's Day; Thanksgiving; Christmas.
Attendance: 10,000 (estimated)

DERBY HISTORICAL SOCIETY & GENERAL DAVID HUMPHREYS' HOUSE, 37 Elm St., Ansonia, CT 06401-3312.

Mailing Address: P.O. Box 331, Derby, CT 06418-0331. Tel.: 203-735-1908.
E-mail: info@derbyhistorical.org
Web Site: www.derbyhistorical.org/humphrey.htm
Institution Type/Description: Historic House: built in 1698.
Hours & Admission Prices: Mon.-Fri. 1-4. Adults $5, seniors & students $3; children under 8 no charge.
Attendance: 2,000 (estimated)

Avon

THE AVON HISTORICAL SOCIETY, INC., 8 E. Main St., Avon, CT 06001. Mailing Address: P.O. Box 448, Avon, CT 06001-0448. Tel.: 860-678-7621.
E-mail: info@avonhistoricalsociety.org
Web Site: www.avonhistoricalsociety.org
Key Personnel: Pres., Terri Wilson; Vice Pres., Helaine Bertsch.
Institution Type/Description: Historical Society Museum; housed in four 19th century buildings: two schoolhouses, one farmhouse & one barn.
Hours & Admission Prices: Pine Grove Schoolhouse: June-Oct. Sun. 2-4. Derrin House: June-Oct. Sun. 2-4. Library: Tues. & Thurs. 2-4; other times by appointment. No charge; donations accepted.
Attendance: 200 (estimated)

FARMINGTON VALLEY ARTS CENTER (FVAC), 25 Arts Center Lane, Avon, CT 06001-3746. Tel.: 860-678-1867. Facebook.
E-mail: info@artsfvac.org
Web Site: www.artsfvac.org
Key Personnel: Pres. (V), Roy David; Administrative Dir., Sandy Buerkles.
Institution Type/Description: Arts Center.
Hours & Admission Prices: Call for hours. No charge.
Attendance: 3,000 (estimated)

THE LIVING MUSEUM OF AVON, 8 E. Main St., Avon, CT 06001. Mailing Address: P.O. Box 448, Avon, CT 06001. Tel.: 860-678-7621.
E-mail: ahs.mail.1830@sbcglobal.net
Institution Type/Description: History Museum: housed in a 19th-century schoolhouse.
Hours & Admission Prices: June-Sept. by appointment. No charge; donations accepted.

Bethel

BETHEL HISTORICAL FIRE FIGHTING MUSEUM, 36 South St., Bethel, CT 06801. Tel.: 203-794-8521.
Institution Type/Description: Fire Fighting Museum.
Hours & Admission Prices: By appointment.

Bethlehem

ABBEY OF REGINA LAUDIS, 273 Flanders Rd., Bethlehem, CT 06751. Tel.: 203-266-7727.
Web Site: abbeyofreginalaudis.org
Institution Type/Description: Religious Museum: housed on a 450 acre working farm.
Hours & Admission Prices: Creche: Easter Sunday to Jan. 6th daily 10-4. No charge.

BELLAMY-FERRIDAY HOUSE & GARDEN, 9 Main St. N., Bethlehem, CT 06751. Mailing Address: P.O. Box 181, Bethlehem, CT 06751. Tel.: 203-266-7596.
E-mail: bellamy.ferriday@ctlandmarks.org
Web Site: www.ctlandmarks.org
Institution Type/Description: Historic House: built in 1754.
Hours & Admission Prices: May-Aug. Wed. & Fri.-Sun. 11-4; Sept. to Columbus Day Sat.-Sun. 11-4; groups by appointment. Adults $7, students and seniors 65 & over $6, children 6-18 $4; members & children under 6 no charge.
Attendance: 1,500 (actual)

OLD BETHLEHEM HISTORICAL SOCIETY, 4 Main St. N., Bethlehem, CT 06751. Mailing Address: P.O. Box 132, Bethlehem, CT 06751-0132. Tel.: 203-266-5196.
E-mail: oldbethlem@bethlehemct.org
Key Personnel: Pres. (V), Carol Ann Brown.
Institution Type/Description: Historical Society Museum.
Hours & Admission Prices: June-Aug. Sun. 1-4; other times by appointment. No charge; donations accepted. Closed holidays.

Bloomfield

THE 4-H EDUCATION CENTER AT AUER FARM, 158 Auer Farm Rd., Bloomfield, CT 06002. Tel.: 860-242-7144. Fax: 860-243-0005.
E-mail: info@auerfarm.org
Web Site: www.auerfarm.org
Institution Type/Description: Science & Agricultural Museum: housed on a 120-acre farm.
Hours & Admission Prices: Call for hours.

WINTONBURY HISTORICAL SOCIETY, 151-153 School St., Bloomfield, CT 06002-2718. Mailing Address: 151-153 School St., P.O. Box 7454, Bloomfield, CT 06002. Tel.: 860-243-1531.
E-mail: wintonbursociety@att.net
Web Site: www.bloomfieldcthistory.org
Key Personnel: Pres., William Weissenburger.
Institution Type/Description: Historic Building: built c.1796. Listed on the National Register of Historic Places.
Hours & Admission Prices: May 15-Oct. 15 Sun. 1-4. No charge; donations accepted.
Attendance: 300 (estimated)

Branford

BRANFORD HISTORICAL SOCIETY - HARRISON HOUSE, 124 Main St., Branford, CT 06405-3523. Mailing Address: P.O. Box 504, Branford, CT 06405-0504. Tel.: 203-488-4828.
E-mail: info@branfordhistoricalsociety.org
Web Site: www.branfordhistoricalsociety.org
Key Personnel: Pres. (V), Matt Radulski.
Institution Type/Description: Historic House: c.1724 restored by architect J. Frederick Kelly.
Hours & Admission Prices: June-Sept. Sat. 1-4; other times by appointment. No charge; donations accepted.
Attendance: 125 (estimated)

Bridgeport

THE BARNUM MUSEUM, 820 Main St., Bridgeport, CT 06604-4912. Tel.: 203-331-1104. Fax: 203-331-0079. Facebook, Twitter.
E-mail: info@barnum-museum.org
Web Site: www.barnum-museum.org
Key Personnel: Exec. Dir., Kathleen Maher; Cur., Adrienne Saint Pierre; Business Mgr., John Temple Swing.
Institution Type/Description: History Museum: housed in original 1893 structure.
Hours & Admission Prices: June-Sept. Thurs.-Sat. 11-3; Oct.-May Thurs.-Fri. 11-3. No charge; donations accepted.
Attendance: 25,000 (estimated)

CITY LIGHTS GALLERY, 265 Golden Hill St., Bridgeport, CT 06604. Tel.: 203-334-7748.
E-mail: citygallerybpt@gmail.com
Web Site: www.citylightsgallery.org
Key Personnel: Exec. Dir., Suzanne Kachmar.
Institution Type/Description: Art Gallery.
Hours & Admission Prices: Wed.-Fri. 11:30-5, Sat. 12-4; other times by appointment. No charge.

CONNECTICUT'S BEARDSLEY ZOO, 1875 Noble Ave., Bridgeport, CT 06610-1646. Tel.: 203-394-6569. Fax: 203-394-6566.
E-mail: info@beardsleyzoo.org
Web Site: www.beardsleyzoo.org
Key Personnel: Zoo Dir., Gregg Dancho; Dir. Animal Care & Operations, Don Goff; Museum Shop Mgr., Rose Ryan.
Institution Type/Description: Zoo.
Hours & Admission Prices: Daily 9-4. Adults $16, children 3-11 $13, seniors 62 & over $12; discount to groups; children under 3, AZA & zoo members no charge. Closed New Year's Day; Thanksgiving; Christmas.
Attendance: 262,000 (estimated)

THE DISCOVERY MUSEUM, INC., 4450 Park Ave., Bridgeport, CT 06604-1098. Tel.: 203-372-3521. Fax: 203-374-1929.
E-mail: info@discoverymuseum.org
Web Site: www.discoverymuseum.org
Formerly: Museum of Art, Science & Industry
Key Personnel: Exec. Dir., Bill Finch.
Institution Type/Description: Science Museum & Planetarium.

Hours & Admission Prices: July-Aug. daily 10-5; Sept.-June Tues.-Sun. 10-5. Museum & Planetarium: adults $11, children 3-17, senior citizens & students with ID $9; discounts to ASTC members; members & children under 2 no charge. Closed New Year's Day; Easter; Memorial Day; Independence Day; Labor Day; Thanksgiving; Christmas. &
Attendance: 59,344 (actual)

HOUSATONIC MUSEUM OF ART, 900 Lafayette Blvd., Bridgeport, CT 06604-4704. Tel.: 203-332-5052. Fax: 203-332-5123.
E-mail: rzella@housatonic.edu
Web Site: www2.housatonic.edu/artmuseum
Key Personnel: Dir. & Cur., Robbin Zella.
Institution Type/Description: College Museum.
Hours & Admission Prices: June-Aug. Mon.-Wed. & Fri. 8:30-5:30, Thurs. 8:30-7; Sept.-May Mon.-Wed. & Fri. 8:30-5:30, Thurs. 8:30-7, Sat. 9-3, Sun. 12-4. No charge; donations accepted. &
Attendance: 10,000 (estimated)

Bristol

AMERICAN CLOCK AND WATCH MUSEUM, INC., 100 Maple St., Bristol, CT 06010-5092. Tel.: 860-583-6070. Fax: 860-583-1862.
E-mail: info@clockmuseum.org
Web Site: www.clockandwatchmuseum.org
Key Personnel: Exec. Dir., Patti Philippon; Office Mgr., Jill Godbout; Dir. Interpretation, Colleen Nicastro.
Institution Type/Description: Horological Museum: housed in 1801 Miles Lewis House & 1956 Ebenezer Barnes Wing & 1987 Edward Ingraham Wing.
Hours & Admission Prices: April-Nov. daily 10-5; Dec.-March Fri.-Sun. 10-5; other times by appointment only. Families $15, adults $6, senior citizens $5, children 8-17 $3; discounts to groups; members and children 7 & under no charge. Closed New Year's Day; Easter; Thanksgiving; Christmas Eve & Day. &
Attendance: 5,532 (actual)

BRISTOL HISTORICAL SOCIETY, 98 Summer St., Bristol, CT 06010. Mailing Address: P.O. Box 1393, Bristol, CT 06011-1393. Tel.: 860-583-6309.
E-mail: president@bristolhistoricalsociety.org
Web Site: bristolhistoricalsociety.org
Key Personnel: Pres., Mike Saman.
Institution Type/Description: Historical Society Museum.
Hours & Admission Prices: Wed. & Sat. 10-2; other times by appointment.

HARRY C. BARNES MEMORIAL NATURE CENTER, 175 Shrub Rd., Bristol, CT 06010. Mailing Address: ELCCT, 501 Wolcott Rd., Bristol, CT 06010. Tel.: 860-583-1234.
Web Site: elcct.org
Key Personnel: Exec. Dir., Scott E. Heth.
Institution Type/Description: Nature Center.
Hours & Admission Prices: Thurs.-Sat. 10-4, Sun. 12-4. No charge.

IMAGINE NATION, A MUSEUM EARLY LEARNING CENTER, One Pleasant St., Bristol, CT 06010-6254. Tel.: 860-314-1400. Fax: 860-584-3608. Facebook.
E-mail: info@imaginenation.org
Web Site: www.imaginenation.org
Key Personnel: Dir., Coral Richardson; C.E.O., Michael Suchopar; Dir. Devel., Doreen Stickney.
Institution Type/Description: Children's Museum.
Hours & Admission Prices: Jan.-March Wed.-Sat. 9:30-5, Sun. 11-5; July & Aug. Tues.-Sat. 9:30-5. Admission $7; members & children under one no charge. Special Events: admission prices vary. Closed New Year's Day; Thanksgiving; Christmas. &
Attendance: 25,000 (actual)

INDIAN ROCK NATURE PRESERVE, 501 Wolcott Rd., Bristol, CT 06010. Tel.: 860-583-1234.
Web Site: elcct.org
Institution Type/Description: Nature Preserve.
Hours & Admission Prices: Call for hours.

THE NEW ENGLAND CAROUSEL MUSEUM, 95 Riverside Ave., Bristol, CT 06010-6390. Tel.: 860-585-5411. Fax: 860-314-0483.
E-mail: info@thecarouselmuseum.org
Web Site: thecarouselmuseum.org

Key Personnel: Exec. Dir., Louise L. DeMars; Education Coord., Lori Little; Museum Mgr., Morgan Urgo; Visitor Svcs., Elaine Lipton.
Institution Type/Description: Carousel Museum: housed in a restored hosiery factory.
Hours & Admission Prices: Wed.-Sat. 10-5, Sun. 12-5. Adults $6, senior citizens $5.50, children 4-14 $3.50, children 1-3 $2; discounts to groups, AAM, AAA, ICOM, Lets Go Arts & Chamber of Commerce members; members no charge. Closed New Year's Day; Easter; Independence Day; Labor Day; Thanksgiving; Christmas. &
Attendance: 10,745 (actual)

WITCH'S DUNGEON CLASSIC MOVIE MUSEUM, 90 Battle St., Bristol, CT 06010. Tel.: 860-583-8306.
E-mail: tdickau@sbc.global.net
Web Site: www.preservehollywood.org/DungeonWebNew
Key Personnel: Owner, Cortlandt Hull.
Institution Type/Description: Movie Museum.
Hours & Admission Prices: Call for hours.

Brookfield

BROOKFIELD CRAFT CENTER, 286 Whisconier Rd., Brookfield, CT 06804. Mailing Address: P.O. Box 122, Brookfield, CT 06804-0122. Tel.: 203-775-4526. Fax: 203-740-7815.
E-mail: info@brookfieldcraft.org
Web Site: www.brookfieldcraft.org
Key Personnel: Exec. Dir., Howard Lasser.
Institution Type/Description: Craft Gallery: housed in 1780 old grist mill.
Hours & Admission Prices: Tues.-Fri. 12-5, Sat. 11-5, Sun. 12-4; call to confirm. No charge; donations accepted. Closed major holidays.
Attendance: 5,000 (estimated)

BROOKFIELD MUSEUM AND HISTORICAL SOCIETY, 165 Whisconier Rd., Brookfield, CT 06804. Mailing Address: P.O. Box 5231, Brookfield, CT 06804-5231. Tel.: 203-740-8140.
E-mail: brookfieldhistsoc@snet.net
Web Site: www.brookfieldcthistory.org
Key Personnel: Pres. (V), Robert Brown; Vice Pres., John Furlong; Museum Shop Mgr., Eleanor Loesch.
Institution Type/Description: Local History Museum.
Hours & Admission Prices: Sat. 12-4; other times by appointment. No charge; donations accepted. &
Attendance: 2,300 (estimated)

Brooklyn

BROOKLYN HISTORICAL SOCIETY & MUSEUM AND DANIEL PUTNAM TYLER LAW OFFICE, 25 Canterbury Rd., Brooklyn, CT 06234. Tel.: 860-774-7728.
Web Site: www.brooklynct.org
Key Personnel: Cur., Elaine R. Knowlton.
Institution Type/Description: History Museum.
Hours & Admission Prices: late May to early Oct. Wed. & Sun. 1-5; other times by appointment. No charge; donations accepted.
Attendance: 384 (actual)

Burlington

LAMOTHE'S SUGAR HOUSE, 89 Stone Rd., Burlington, CT 06013. Tel.: 860-675-5043.
E-mail: lamothes.sugar.house@snet.net
Web Site: www.lamothesugarhouse.com
Institution Type/Description: History Museum.
Hours & Admission Prices: Tours: mid-Feb. to March Sat.-Sun. 1-4:30; groups by appointment.

SESSIONS WOODS WILDLIFE MANAGEMENT AREA & CONSERVATION EDUCATION CENTER, 341 Milford St., Burlington, CT 06013-1550. Mailing Address: P.O. Box 1550, Burlington, CT 06013-1550. Tel.: 860-675-8130.
E-mail: laura.rogers-castro@ct.gov
Institution Type/Description: Nature Center.
Hours & Admission Prices: Exhibits: Mon.-Fri. 8:30-4. Trails: sunrise to sunset.

Canaan

NEW ENGLAND ACCORDION MUSEUM, 17 Margaret Lane, Canaan, CT 06018. Tel.: 860-833-1374. Facebook.

E-mail: ramunni@comcast.net
Web Site: newenglndaccordionconnectionandmuseumcompany.com
Key Personnel: Owner, Paul Ramunni.
Institution Type/Description: Musical Instrument Museum.
Hours & Admission Prices: By appointment only. No charge; donations accepted.

Canterbury

PRUDENCE CRANDALL MUSEUM, 1 S. Canterbury Rd., Canterbury, CT 06331-0058. Mailing Address: P.O. Box 34, Canterbury, CT 06331. Tel.: 860-546-7800. Fax: 860-546-7803. Facebook.
E-mail: friends@friendsofprudencecrandallmuseum.org
Web Site: www.cultureandtourism.org
Institution Type/Description: Historic House & Site: housed in 1805 Prudence Crandall House.
Hours & Admission Prices: See website for current hours. Adults $6, senior citizens, college students & youth $4; children 5 & under no charge. Closed major holidays. &
Attendance: 2,500 (actual)

Canton

GALLERY ON THE GREEN, 5 Canton Green Rd., Canton, CT 06019. Mailing Address: P.O. Box 281, Canton, CT 06019. Tel.: 860-693-4102.
E-mail: cantonartists@att.net
Institution Type/Description: Art Gallery: housed in a c.1790 schoolhouse.
Hours & Admission Prices: Fri.-Sun. 1-5.

ROARING BROOK NATURE CENTER, 70 Gracey Rd., Canton, CT 06019-2113. Tel.: 860-693-0263.
E-mail: rbnc@thechildrensmuseumct.org
Web Site: ww.roaringbrook.org
Institution Type/Description: Nature Center.
Hours & Admission Prices: July-Aug. Mon.-Sat. 10-5, Sun. 1-5; Sept.-June Tues.-Sat. 10-5, Sun. 1-5. Adults $7, seniors $6, children $5; members no charge.

Cheshire

THE BARKER CHARACTER, COMIC AND CARTOON MUSEUM, 1188 Highland Ave. (Rte. 10), Cheshire, CT 06410-1624. Tel.: 203-699-3822.
E-mail: museum@barkeranimation.com
Web Site: www.barkermuseum.com
Key Personnel: Owners, Herbert Barker; Owners, Gloria Barker; Dir. & Cur., Judy Fuerst.
Institution Type/Description: General Museum.
Hours & Admission Prices: Summer: Wed.-Sat. 11-5; Winter Wed.-Sat. 12-4; group tours for ages 8 & over by appointment. Adults $5, seniors over 65 $4, children 17 & under $3; discounts to Blue Star Museum members; children 3 & under no charge. Closed holidays. &
Attendance: 20,000 (estimated)

Clinton

STANTON HOUSE, 63 E. Main St., Clinton, CT 06413-2036. Tel.: 860-669-2132.
E-mail: curator@stantonhousect.com
Web Site: www.stantonhousect.com/
Key Personnel: Cur., David Perrelli.
Institution Type/Description: Historic House: 1789 Stanton House.
Hours & Admission Prices: By appointment. No charge; donations requested.
Attendance: 1,200 (estimated)

Collinsville

CANTON HISTORICAL MUSEUM, 11 Front St., Collinsville, CT 06019-3118. Tel.: 860-693-2793. Fax: 860-693-2793. Facebook.
E-mail: cantonmuseum@gmail.com
Web Site: www.cantonmuseum.org
Key Personnel: Pres. (V), Paul J. Therrien; Museum Shop Mgr., Curt Edgar.
Institution Type/Description: History Museum: housed in c.1865 building used for finishing agricultural plows.
Hours & Admission Prices: May-Nov. Fri.-Sun. 1-4; Dec.-April Sat.-Sun. 1-4. Adults $4, seniors $3, children 6-16 $1; children under 5 no charge. Closed Easter; Christmas.
Attendance: 2,000 (actual)

Cos Cob

GREENWICH HISTORICAL SOCIETY AKA BUSH-HOLLEY HISTORIC SITE, 39 Strickland Rd., Cos Cob, CT 06807-2727. Tel.: 203-869-6899, ext. 10. Fax: 203-861-9720.
E-mail: mcouture@hstg.org
Web Site: www.hstg.org
Key Personnel: Exec. Dir. & C.E.O., Debra Mecky; Chm., Davidde Strackbein; Museum Shop Mgr., Michele Couture.
Institution Type/Description: History Museum: includes Bush-Holley House, a National Historic Landmark; site of Connecticut's first art colony.
Hours & Admission Prices: Library & Archives: Wed. 10-4; other times by appointment. Bush Holley House & Museum: Jan.-Feb. Sat.-Sun. 12-4; March-Dec. Wed.-Sun. 12-4. House Tours: 1, 2 & 3. Adults $10, senior citizens & students $8; discounts to AAM members; children under 18 & museum members no charge. Closed New Year's Day; Easter; Independence Day; Thanksgiving; Christmas. &
Attendance: 15,000 (actual)

Coventry

THE MUSEUM OF CONNECTICUT GLASS, 290 N. River Rd., Coventry, CT 06238. Mailing Address: 27 Plank Ln., Glastonbury, CT 06033-2523. Tel.: 860-633-2944.
E-mail: noel.tomas@glassmuseum.org
Web Site: www.glassmuseum.org
Key Personnel: Pres. & C.O.O., Noel Tomas.
Institution Type/Description: History Museum: housed in the former home of Capt. John Turner; c.1813.
Hours & Admission Prices: By appointment.

NATHAN HALE HOMESTEAD MUSEUM, 2299 South St., Coventry, CT 06238. Mailing Address: P.O. Box 760, Coventry, CT 06238-0760. Tel.: 860-742-6917.
E-mail: hale@ctlandmarks.org
Web Site: www.ctlandmarks.org
Key Personnel: Exec. Dir., Sheryl Hack; Site Admin., Anne Marie Charland.
Institution Type/Description: History Museum: site of Capt. Nathan Hale's birth in 1755; Hale family built present structure in 1776 & moved in a month after Nathan's death.
Hours & Admission Prices: May & Oct. Sat.-Sun. 12-4; June-Sept. Thurs.-Sun. 12-4, Sun. 11-4. Family $20, adults $12, seniors & students $10, children 6-18 $5; discounts to teachers and AAM & AAA members; members & children under 6 no charge. &
Attendance: 8,000 (estimated)

STRONG PORTER MUSEUM - COVENTRY HISTORICAL SOCIETY, 2382 South St., Coventry, CT 06238. Mailing Address: P.O. Box 534, Coventry, CT 06238. Tel.: 860-742-3054.
E-mail: info@ctcoventryhistoricalsociety.org
Web Site: www.ctcoventryhistoricalsociety.org
Key Personnel: Pres. (V), James Murphy.
Institution Type/Description: Historical Society Museum: housed in the former farmhouse of Aaron Strong; built in 1730. Listed on the National Register of Historic Places.
Hours & Admission Prices: June to mid-Oct. Sun. 12-3. No charge; donations accepted.
Attendance: 500 (estimated)

Danbury

THE DANBURY MUSEUM & HISTORICAL SOCIETY, 43 Main St., Danbury, CT 06810-8011. Tel.: 203-743-5200. Fax: 203-743-1131.
E-mail: info@danburymuseum.org
Web Site: www.danburymuseum.org
Key Personnel: Exec. Dir. & Museum Shop Mgr., Brigid Guertin; Pres., Robert Young.
Institution Type/Description: History Museum.
Hours & Admission Prices: Tours: Tues.-Sat. 10-3. Exhibits: Tues.-Sat. 10-4. Research: by appointment. Tours: adults $10, senior citizens & students $6; children under 5 no charge. &
Attendance: 4,000 (estimated)

DANBURY RAILWAY MUSEUM, 120 White St., Danbury, CT 06810-6642. Mailing Address: P.O. Box 90, Danbury, CT 06813-0090. Tel.: 203-778-8337. Fax: 203-778-1836. Facebook.
E-mail: info@danburyrail.org
Web Site: www.danburyrailwaymuseum.org
Key Personnel: Pres., Stan Madyda; Museum Shop Mgr., Patty Osmer.

Institution Type/Description: Railway Museum.
Hours & Admission Prices: June-Aug. Mon.-Fri. 10-4, Sat. 10-5, Sun. 12-5; Sept.-May Wed.-Sat. 10-4, Sun. 12-4. Admission 3 & over $7; children under 3 & members no charge. Closed most holiday.
Attendance: 20,000 (estimated)

Danielson

KILLINGLY HISTORICAL AND GENEALOGICAL SOCIETY, INC., 196 Main St., Danielson, CT 06239-2823. Mailing Address: P.O. Box 265, Danielson, CT 06239-0265. Tel.: 860-779-7250. Facebook.
E-mail: info@killinglyhistorical.org
Web Site: www.killinglyhistorical.org
Formerly: Killingly Historical Society
Key Personnel: Dir., Elaine Tenis.
Institution Type/Description: History Museum.
Hours & Admission Prices: Wed.-Sat. 10-4. No charge; donations accepted.
Attendance: 250 (estimated)

Darien

BATES-SCOFIELD HOMESTEAD, THE DARIEN HISTORICAL SOCIETY, 45 Old King's Hwy., N., Darien, CT 06820-4607. Tel.: 203-655-9233. Fax: 203-656-3892.
E-mail: info@ukremer@darienhistorical.org
Web Site: www.darienhistorical.org
Key Personnel: Exec. Dir., Maggie McIntire, Jr.; Pres. (V), Robert Pascal, Jr.; Cur. Costume, Babs White; Cur. History, Ken Reiss.
Institution Type/Description: Historic House: housed in c.1736 structure.
Hours & Admission Prices: Tues.-Thurs. 12-5, Sun. 12-3. Suggested Donation: adults $5; children 6 & under and members no charge. Closed major holidays.
Attendance: 4,000 (estimated)

DARIEN NATURE CENTER, 120 Brookside Rd., Darien, CT 06820. Tel.: 203-655-7459.
E-mail: info@dariennaturecenter.org
Institution Type/Description: Nature Center.
Hours & Admission Prices: Mon.-Fri. 9-4, Sat. 9-1.

Deep River

STONE HOUSE, 245 Main St., P.O. Box 151, Deep River, CT 06417-2055. Tel.: 860-526-5811 & 1449. Facebook.
E-mail: info@deepriverhistoricalsociety.org
Web Site: deepriverhistoricalsociety.org
Key Personnel: Pres. (V), Jeffrey D. Hostetler.
Institution Type/Description: Historic House: built in 1840.
Hours & Admission Prices: Tues. & Thurs. 10 to noon.

Derby

KELLOGG ENVIRONMENTAL CENTER, 500 Hawthorne Ave., Derby, CT 06418. Tel.: 203-734-2513.
E-mail: donna.kingston@po.state.ct.us
Key Personnel: Environmental Educator, Susan Quincy; Environmental Educator, Susan Robinson .
Institution Type/Description: Science Center.
Hours & Admission Prices: Tues.-Sat. 9-4:30.

OSBORNE HOMESTEAD MUSEUM, 500 Hawthorne Ave., Derby, CT 06418-1020. Tel.: 203-734-2513. Fax: 203-922-7833.
E-mail: susan.d.robinson@ct.gov
Web Site: www.ct.gov/deep/kellogg
Key Personnel: Dir., Diane Joy; Cur., Susan Robinson.
Institution Type/Description: History Museum: housed in the former estate of Frances Osborne Kellogg, an accomplished businesswomen & conservationist who was dedicated to preserving land for future generations.
Hours & Admission Prices: May-Oct. Thurs.-Fri. 10-3, Sat. 10-4, Sun. 12-4. No charge; donations accepted.

East Canaan

BECKLEY FURNACE, 140 Lower Rd., East Canaan, CT 06024. Mailing Address: FOBF, Inc., P.O. Box 383, East Canaan, CT 06024. Tel.: 860-837-0270. Facebook.
Web Site: beckleyfurnace.org
Institution Type/Description: Historic Building: built in 1846. Listed on the National Register of Historic Places.

Hours & Admission Prices: Daily 8am to sunset. Guided Tours: Summer: Sat. 10-2. No charge.
Attendance: 3,500 (estimated)

East Granby

OLD NEW-GATE PRISON AND COPPER MINE, 115 Newgate Rd., East Granby, CT 06026-9545. Tel.: 860-653-3563. Fax: 860-844-2142.
E-mail: newgate.museum@ct.gov
Web Site: www.cultureandtourism.org
Key Personnel: Museum Asst., Morgan Bengel; Dir. Operations, Elizabeth Shapiro.
Institution Type/Description: History Museum: abandoned underground copper mine used as first state prison from 1773 to 1827.
Hours & Admission Prices: July 14-Oct. 29 Fri. 1-5, Sat.-Sun. 10-5, Mon. 10-1. Adults $6; discounts to schools; children 12 & under no charge. ♿
Attendance: 18,114 (actual)

East Haddam

ALLEGRA FARM & HORSE-DRAWN CARRIAGE AND SLEIGH MUSEUM, 69 Lake Hayward Town Rd., East Haddam, CT 06415. Mailing Address: P.O. Box 455, East Haddam, CT 06423-0455. Tel.: 860-537-8861.
E-mail: info@allegrafarm.com
Institution Type/Description: Transportation Museum.
Hours & Admission Prices: By appointment.

GILLETTE CASTLE STATE PARK, 67 River Rd., East Haddam, CT 06423-1462. Tel.: 860-526-2336. Fax: 860-424-4070.
E-mail: dep.stateparks@ct.gov
Web Site: www.ct.gov/dep
Key Personnel: Park Supvr., Scott Dawley.
Institution Type/Description: Historic Building: housed in a twenty four room mansion built for actor, director, & playwright, William Hooker Gillette, c.1914.
Hours & Admission Prices: Park: daily 8am to sunset. No charge. Castle: Memorial Day to Columbus Day daily 10-5. Adults $6, children 6-12 $2; children under 6 no charge.
Attendance: 225,000 (estimated)

NATHAN HALE SCHOOLHOUSE IN EAST HADDAM, 29 Main St., Rte. 149, East Haddam, CT 06423. Mailing Address: Connecticut SAR, P.O. Box 411, East Haddam, CT 06423.
Web Site: www.connecticutsar.org
Key Personnel: Property Steward, David Packard.
Institution Type/Description: Historic Building: housed in the former schoolhouse where Nathan Hale was schoolmaster; built in 1750.
Hours & Admission Prices: May-Oct. Wed.-Sun. 12-4; call to confirm. No charge; donations accepted.
Attendance: 1,000 (actual)

East Hampton

CHATHAM HISTORICAL SOCIETY OF EAST HAMPTON, 6 Bevin Blvd., East Hampton, CT 06424. Mailing Address: 60 Colchester Ave., East Hampton, CT 06424. Tel.: 860-267-8953.
E-mail: podskoch@comcast.net
Institution Type/Description: Historical Society Museum.
Hours & Admission Prices: 1st Sun. each month 2-4; other times by appointment. No charge; donations accepted. ♿
Attendance: 500 (estimated)

East Hartford

EDWARD E. KING MUSEUM, Raymond Library, 840 Main St., East Hartford, CT 06108-3128. Tel.: 860-289-6429.
E-mail: jpannone@easthartfordct.gov
Key Personnel: Dir. Cultural Assets/Reference Librarian, Jason Pannone.
Institution Type/Description: History Museum.
Hours & Admission Prices: Mon.-Thurs. 9-8. Fri.-Sat. 9-5. No charge. ♿

HISTORICAL SOCIETY OF EAST HARTFORD, Martin Park, 307 Burnside Ave., East Hartford, CT 06108. Mailing Address: P. O. Box 380166, East Hartford, CT 06138-0166. Tel.: 860-568-2884 & 528-0716.
E-mail: hseh@hseh.org
Web Site: www.hseh.org
Key Personnel: Dir., Ruth Shapleigh-Brown; Pres. (V), Craig R. Johnson; Vice Pres. (V), Bette Daraskevich.

Institution Type/Description: Historical Society Museum.
Hours & Admission Prices: Guided Tours: June-Aug. Sun. 1-4. No charge; donations accepted.

East Haven

SHORE LINE TROLLEY MUSEUM, 17 River St., East Haven, CT 06512-2519. Tel.: 203-467-6927. Fax: 203-467-7635.
E-mail: info@shorelinetrolley.org
Web Site: www.shorelinetrolley.org
Formerly: Branford Trolley Museum
Key Personnel: Exec. Dir. & C.E.O., John Proto; Chm. (V), Peter Callahan; Pres., Wayne Sandford; Dir. Vehicle Collection Management, Denis Pacelli; Archivist, Michael Schreiber.
Institution Type/Description: Transportation: Technology & Operating Railway Museum.
Hours & Admission Prices: Memorial Day to Labor Day Tues.-sun. 10:30-4:30. Adults $10, senior citizens & children 2-15 $7; discounts to groups, ICOM, AAA & ARM members; children under 2 & members no charge. &
Attendance: 24,435 (actual)

East Windsor

CONNECTICUT FIRE MUSEUM, 58 North Rd. (Rte. 140), East Windsor, CT 06088. Mailing Address: P.O. Box 297, East Windsor, CT 06088-0297. Tel.: 860-627-6540. Fax: 860-627-6510.
E-mail: ctfiremuseum@hotmail.com
Web Site: ct-trolley.org/firemuseum
Key Personnel: Pres. (V), Bert Johanson; Treas., Devel. & Museum Shop Mgr., Alan Walker.
Institution Type/Description: Fire-Fighting Museum.
Hours & Admission Prices: Memorial Day-Labor Day Mon. & Wed.-Sat. 10-4, Sun. 12-4; Sept.-Oct. Sat. 10-4, Sun. 12-4. Adults $9.50, senior citizens $8.50, children $6.
Attendance: 18,520 (actual)

CONNECTICUT TROLLEY MUSEUM, 58 North Rd., East Windsor, CT 06088. Mailing Address: P.O. Box 360, East Windsor, CT 06088-0360. Tel.: 860-627-6540. Fax: 860-627-6510.
E-mail: office@ceraweb.org
Web Site: www.ct-trolley.org
Key Personnel: Pres. (V), Galen Semprebon; Chm. (V), Ted Coppola; Business Mgr., Gina Maria Alimberti; Museum Shop Mgr., John Pelletier.
Institution Type/Description: Trolley Museum.
Hours & Admission Prices: March 24-June 10 & Sept. 8-Sept. 30 Sat.-Sun. 10-4:30; June 16-Sept. 3 Wed.-Mon. 10-4:30; see website for additional hours. Adults $10, senior citizens 62 & up $9, children 4-12 $7; discounts to AAA, MTA, ALA & ARM members & museum members with ID; children under 4 no charge. Closed Thanksgiving; Christmas.
Attendance: 20,000 (estimated)

SCANTIC ACADEMY MUSEUM, EAST WINDSOR HISTORICAL SOCIETY, INC., 115 Scantic Rd., Rte. 191, East Windsor, CT 06088-9737. Tel.: 860-623-5327.
E-mail: eastwindsorhistory@gmail.com
Web Site: eastwindsorhistory.wordpress.com
Key Personnel: Pres. (V), Michael Hunt; Treas., Larry Tribble; Sec., Jessica Bottomley.
Institution Type/Description: General Museum: housed in 1817 Scantic Academy Building.
Hours & Admission Prices: Sat. 9-12; other times by appointment. No charge; donations accepted. &
Attendance: 150 (estimated)

Ellington

NELLIE MCKNIGHT MUSEUM - ELLINGTON HISTORICAL SOCIETY, 70 Main St., Ellington, CT 06029. Mailing Address: P. O. Box 73, Ellington, CT 06029. Tel.: 860-875-7160 & 5804.
Key Personnel: Cur., Nancy Long.
Institution Type/Description: Historical Society Museum: housed in a former farm house owned by Nellie McKnight.
Hours & Admission Prices: June-Aug. Thurs. 1-4. No charge; donations accepted.

Enfield

MARTHA A. PARSONS HOUSE MUSEUM, 1387 Enfield St., Enfield, CT 06082-5524. Mailing Address: Enfield Historical Society, P.O. Box 586, Enfield, CT 06083-0586. Tel.: 860-745-6064.

E-mail: questions@enfieldhistoricalsociety.org
Web Site: www.enfieldhistoricalsociety.org
Institution Type/Description: Historic House Museum: built in 1782 by John Meacham.
Hours & Admission Prices: May-Oct. Sun. 2-4:30; other times by appointment. No charge.'

OLD TOWN HALL MUSEUM, 1294 Enfield St., Enfield, CT 06082-4928. Mailing Address: Enfield Historical Society, P.O. Box 586, Enfield, CT 06083. Tel.: 860-745-1729.
E-mail: questions@enfieldhistoricalsociety.org
Web Site: www.enfieldhistoricalsociety.org
Institution Type/Description: Historic Building: housed in the former meeting house of the First Ecclesiastical Society; c.1774. Listed on the National Register of Historic Places.
Hours & Admission Prices: May-Oct. Sun. 2-4:30; other times by appointment. No charge. Closed major holidays.
Attendance: 700 (estimated)

Essex

CONNECTICUT RIVER MUSEUM, 67 Main St., Essex, CT 06426-1150. Tel.: 860-767-8269. Fax: 860-767-7028.
E-mail: cdobbs@ctrivermuseum.org
Web Site: www.ctrivermuseum.org
Key Personnel: Exec. Dir., Jerry Roberts; Cur., Amy Trout; Chm. Bd. Trustees, Tim Boyd; Front Desk & Shop Mgr., Helen Davis; Business Mgr., Joan Meek; Dir. Education, Jennifer White-Dobbs.
Institution Type/Description: Maritime & River Museum: housed in 1878 wooden warehouse.
Hours & Admission Prices: Tues.-Sun. 10-5. Adults $8, senior citizens, students, & AAA members $7, children $5; discounts to AAM members; children under 6 & members no charge. &
Attendance: 16,000 (actual)

ESSEX HISTORICAL SOCIETY, INC., 22 Prospect St., Essex, CT 06426-1021. Mailing Address: P.O. Box 123, Essex, CT 06426-0123. Tel.: 860-767-0681.
E-mail: ehs@essexhistory.net
Web Site: essexhistory.org
Key Personnel: Pres. (V), Hank McInerney; Dir., Melissa Josefiak.
Institution Type/Description: History Museum.
Hours & Admission Prices: Research Center: Tues. 9:30 to noon. Pratt House: June-Sept. Fri.-Sun. 1-4; other times by appointment. No charge; donations accepted.
Attendance: 400 (estimated)

Fairfield

CONNECTICUT AUDUBON BIRDCRAFT MUSEUM, 314 Unquowa Rd., Fairfield, CT 06824-5018. Tel.: 203-259-0416. Fax: 203-259-1344.
E-mail: birdcraft@ctaudubon.org
Web Site: www.ctaudubon.org
Key Personnel: Exec. Dir., Patrick Comins; Museum Shop Mgr., Jane Guenther.
Institution Type/Description: Natural Science & Ornithology Museum: founded in 1914 by Mabel Osgood Wright, who played a major role in establishing the American conservation movement.
Hours & Admission Prices: Mon.-Fri. 9-1; other times by appointment. Adults $2, children $1; discounts to Connecticut Ornithological Assoc. members; members no charge. Closed major holidays. &
Attendance: 9,000 (actual)

CONNECTICUT AUDUBON SOCIETY OF FAIRFIELD, 2325 Burr St., Fairfield, CT 06824-1806. Tel.: 203-259-6305. Fax: 203-254-7365.
E-mail: bmucci@ctaudubon.org
Web Site: www.ctaudubon.org
Key Personnel: Chm. (V), Peter Kunkel; Dir. Education, Michelle Eckman; Mgr. Communications, Liza Hickey.
Institution Type/Description: Nature Center.
Hours & Admission Prices: Mon.-Sat. 10-3. Adults $2, children $1; members no charge. Closed major holidays. &
Attendance: 12,000 (actual)

FAIRFIELD MUSEUM AND HISTORY CENTER, 370 Beach Rd., Fairfield, CT 06824-6639. Tel.: 203-259-1598. Fax: 203-255-2716.
E-mail: info@fairfieldhs.org
Web Site: www.fairfieldhistory.org

Formerly: Fairfield Historical Society
Key Personnel: Exec. Dir., Michael A. Jehle; Pres., Tom Kreitler; Dir. Education, Christine Jewell; Prog. & Volunteer Coord., Walter Matis.
Institution Type/Description: History Museum & Library.
Hours & Admission Prices: Museum: daily 10-4. Library: Tues.-Fri. 10-4, Sat. 12-4. Adults, seniors & students 6-22 $3; discounts to AAM members; children 5 & under and members no charge. Closed Independence Day; Thanksgiving; Christmas. ♿
Attendance: 20,600 (estimated)

FAIRFIELD UNIVERSITY ART MUSEUM, 1073 N. Benson Rd., Fairfield, CT 06824. Tel.: 203-254-4000, ext. 4046. Fax: 203-249-5529. Facebook; Twitter; Instagram.
E-mail: museum@fairfield.edu
Web Site: www.fairfield.edu/museum
Formerly: Bellarmine Museum of Art
Key Personnel: Dir. & Chief Cur., Linda Wolk-Simon; Asst. Dir., Carey Mack Weber; Museum Asst., Lauren Williams.
Institution Type/Description: Art Museum.
Hours & Admission Prices: Academic Year: Bellarmine Hall: Tues.-Sat. 11-4. Walsh Gallery: Wed.-Sat. 12-4. No charge; donations accepted. Closed university & national holidays. ♿
Attendance: 7,000 (actual)

OGDEN HOUSE & GARDENS, 1520 Bronson Rd., Fairfield, CT 06824. Mailing Address: c/o Fairfield Historical Society, 370 Beach Rd., Fairfield, CT 06824. Tel.: 203-259-1598.
E-mail: info@fairfieldhs.org
Web Site: www.fairfieldhistory.org/visit/ogden-house/
Institution Type/Description: Historic House Museum: built in 1750. Listed on the National Register of Historic Places.
Hours & Admission Prices: June-Sept. Sun. 1-4. Adults $3; members no charge.

Falls Village

FALLS VILLAGE-CANAAN HISTORICAL SOCIETY, 44 Railroad St., Falls Village, CT 06031. Mailing Address: P.O. Box 206, Falls Village, CT 06031-0206. Tel.: 860-824-8226. Facebook.
E-mail: fvchs8226@gmail.com
Web Site: www.fallsvillage-canaanhistoricalsociety.org
Key Personnel: Pres. (V), Richard Heinz; Cur. South Canaan Meeting House, Cheryl Aeschliman; Cur. Falls Village Depot, Mary Margaret Cortesi; Cur. Beebe Hill Schoolhouse, Lillian Lovitt.
Institution Type/Description: Historical Society Museum.
Hours & Admission Prices: Tues. 9 am to noon; other times by appointment. No charge; donations accepted. ♿
Attendance: 175 (estimated)

Farmington

BARNES-FRANKLIN GALLERY, 271 Scott Swamp Rd., Farmington, CT 06032. Tel.: 860-255-3500.
E-mail: wkluba@tunxis.edu
Web Site: www.tunxis.edu/campus-resources/barnes-franklin-gallery
Institution Type/Description: Art Gallery.
Hours & Admission Prices: Mon.-Thurs. 9-8; other times by appointment.

HILL-STEAD MUSEUM, 35 Mountain Rd., Farmington, CT 06032-2304. Tel.: 860-677-4787. Fax: 860-677-0174. Facebook, Instagram, Twitter.
E-mail: info@hillstead.org
Web Site: www.hillstead.org
Key Personnel: Exec. Dir. & C.E.O., Susan Ballek; Cur. & Dir. Interpretation & Programs, Melanie Bourbeau; Pres. Bd. Governors, William H. Watson; Visitor Svcs. Mgr., Michele LaBonte; Dir. Operations, David Perbeck; Asst. to the Exec. Dir., Holly Maynard.
Institution Type/Description: Historic House Museum: fine art collection amidst furnishings of intact 1901 Colonial Revival home designed by Theodate Pope Riddle in collaboration with McKim, Mead & White. History Sunken Garden based on c.1920 plan by Beatrix Farrand.
Hours & Admission Prices: Tues.-Sun. 10-4. Adults $16, seniors $14, students $12, children 6-12 $8; discounts for AAA members; members & children under 6 no charge. Closed Easter; Independence Day; Thanksgiving; Christmas. ♿
Attendance: 38,000 (estimated)

STANLEY-WHITMAN HOUSE, FARMINGTON, 37 High St., Farmington, CT 06032-2314. Tel.: 860-677-9222. Fax: 860-677-7758.
E-mail: lisa@stanleywhitman.org
Web Site: www.stanleywhitman.org
Key Personnel: Exec. Dir., Andy Verzosa.
Institution Type/Description: Historic House Museum: c.1719-1772 Stanley-Whitman House; interpretation of 18th-century Farmington.
Hours & Admission Prices: Wed.-Sun. 10-4. Adults $7, senior citizens 63 & over $5, students 6-18 $4; discounts to AAA & New England Museum Assoc. members; children under 6, Greater Hartford Assoc. of Historic Houses & museum members no charge. Closed national holidays. ♿
Attendance: 12,000 (estimated)

Franklin

BLUE SLOPE COUNTRY MUSEUM, 138 Blue Hill Rd., Franklin, CT 06254-1601. Tel.: 860-642-6413.
E-mail: museum@blueslope.com
Web Site: www.blueslope.com/museum.huml
Key Personnel: Dir., Sandy Staebner.
Institution Type/Description: History Museum.
Hours & Admission Prices: By appointment. Discounts to AAM members.
Attendance: 2,541 (actual)

DR. ASHBEL WOODWARD HOUSE MUSEUM, 387 Route 32, Franklin, CT 06254. Mailing Address: c/o Museum Commission Board, 7 Meetinghouse Hill, Franklin, CT 06254. Tel.: 860-642-1988.
Key Personnel: Chm., Alden Miner.
Institution Type/Description: Historic House Museum: housed in the former home of town physician & Civil War veteran Dr. Ashbel Woodward; built in 1835. Listed on the National Register of Historic Places.
Hours & Admission Prices: Call for hours.

Gales Ferry

NATHAN LESTER HOUSE, 153 Vinegar Hill Rd., Gales Ferry, CT 06335. Tel.: 860-464-8540.
E-mail: nathanlesterhouse@gmail.com
Web Site: ledyardhistory.org/nathan-lester-house
Institution Type/Description: Historic House: housed in an 18th century farmhouse.
Hours & Admission Prices: House: Memorial Day to Labor Day Tues. & Thurs. 2-4, Sat.-Sun. 1-4:30; other times by appointment. Grounds: daily. No charge; donations accepted.

Gaylordsville

GAYLORDSVILLE HISTORICAL SOCIETY - THE LITTLE RED SCHOOLHOUSE, 56 Gaylord Rd., Gaylordsville, CT 06755. Mailing Address: P.O. Box 25, Gaylordsville, CT 06755. Tel.: 860-350-0300.
E-mail: webmaster@gaylordsville.org
Web Site: www.gaylordsville.org
Institution Type/Description: Historical Society Museum: housed in a one room schoolhouse; built in 1740.
Hours & Admission Prices: Red Schoolhouse & Brown's Forge: July-Aug. Sun. 2-4. No charge; donations accepted.
Attendance: 350 (estimated)

Glastonbury

CONNECTICUT AUDUBON SOCIETY CENTER AT GLASTONBURY, 1361 Main St., Glastonbury, CT 06033-3105. Tel.: 860-633-8402. Fax: 860-657-4228.
E-mail: cbartholomew@ctaudubon.org
Web Site: www.ctaudubon.org
Formerly: Holland Brook Nature Center
Key Personnel: Dir., Kate Reamer; Pres., Alex Brash.
Institution Type/Description: Nature Center.
Hours & Admission Prices: Center: Mon.-Fri. 10-4:30, Sat. 10-3. No charge; donations accepted. ♿
Attendance: 6,000 (estimated)

HISTORICAL SOCIETY OF GLASTONBURY INC., 1944 Main St., Glastonbury, CT 06033-2901. Mailing Address: P.O. Box 46, Glastonbury, CT 06033-0046. Tel.: 860-633-6890. Fax: 860-633-6890. Facebook.
E-mail: hsglastonbury@sbcglobal.net
Web Site: www.hsgct.org
Key Personnel: Exec. Dir., James Bennett; Cur., Linda Scarduzio; Librarian, Phylis Reed.
Institution Type/Description: Historical Society Museum: housed in c.1840 Old Town Hall.

Hours & Admission Prices: Welles-Shipman-Ward: Summer Tues. 1-4. Adults $5. Museum on the Green: Mon.-Tues. & Thurs. 9-4, 3rd Sun. each month 1-4; other times by appointment. No charge; donations accepted. Closed national holidays.
Attendance: 3,800 (estimated)

Goshen

ACTION WILDLIFE FOUNDATION, 337 Torrington Rd., Rte. 4, Goshen, CT 06756-2031. Tel.: 860-482-4465; 491-9191. Fax: 860-482-8337.
E-mail: info@actionwildlife.org
Web Site: www.actionwildlife.org
Key Personnel: Museum Dir., Jim Mazzarelli; Animal Mgr., Sue Tracy; Sec., Julie Mazzarelli.
Institution Type/Description: Foundation.
Hours & Admission Prices: Spring to Fall daily 10-5. Adults $11, children under 12 $7. &

GOSHEN HISTORICAL SOCIETY, 21 Old Middle St., Goshen, CT 06756. Mailing Address: P.O. Box 457, Goshen, CT 06756-0457. Tel.: 860-491-9610 & 3129.
E-mail: jvnkuq@juno.com
Web Site: goshenhistoricalct.org
Key Personnel: Pres. (V), Henrietta C. Horvay.
Institution Type/Description: History Museum.
Hours & Admission Prices: April-Nov. Tues. 10 am to noon; other times by appointment only. No charge; donations accepted. &
Attendance: 300 (estimated)

Granby

SALMON BROOK HISTORICAL SOCIETY, INC., 208 Salmon Brook St., Granby, CT 06035. Mailing Address: P.O. Box 840, Granby, CT 06035-0840. Tel.: 860-653-9713.
E-mail: claun@cox.net
Web Site: www.salmonbrookhistorical.org
Key Personnel: Pres. (V), Richard Zlotnick.
Institution Type/Description: History Museum: housed in c.1732 Abijah Rowe House.
Hours & Admission Prices: House: June-Sept. Sun. 2-4; other times by appointment. Adults $5, children $2; members no charge. Library: Tues. & Thurs. 9 am to noon; other times by appointment. Closed Independence Day; Labor Day weekend.
Attendance: 600 (estimated)

Greenwich

AUDUBON GREENWICH, 613 Riversville Rd., Greenwich, CT 06831-2624. Tel.: 203-869-5272. Fax: 203-869-4437.
E-mail: greenwich_center@audubon.org
Web Site: greenwich.audubon.org
Key Personnel: Center Dir., Michelle Frankel; Asst. Center Dir., Eli Schaffer; Environmental Education Specialist, James Flynn; Sr. Naturalist & Environmental Education, Ted Gilman.
Institution Type/Description: Nature Center.
Hours & Admission Prices: Daily 10-5. Adults $6, children & senior citizens over 62 $3; discount to AAM members; members no charge. &
Attendance: 30,000 (estimated)

BENDHEIM GALLERY, 299 Greenwich Ave., Greenwich, CT 06830-6504. Tel.: 203-862-6750. Fax: 203-862-6753.
E-mail: gallery@greenwicharts.org
Web Site: www.greenwicharts.org/index.asp
Key Personnel: Exec. Dir., Tatiana Mori; Pres. (V), Barbara Collier.
Institution Type/Description: Art Gallery.
Hours & Admission Prices: July-Aug. Tues.-Fri. 10-4, Sat. 12-4; Sept.-June Tues.-Fri. 10-4, Sat.-Sun. 12-4. No charge. &
Attendance: 50,000 (estimated)

BRUCE MUSEUM, 1 Museum Dr., Greenwich, CT 06830-7157. Tel.: 203-869-0376. Fax: 203-869-0963. Facebook, Instagram, Twitter.
E-mail: info@brucemuseum.org
Web Site: www.brucemuseum.org
Formerly: Bruce Museum of Arts and Science
Key Personnel: Exec. Dir., Peter C. Sutton, Ph.D.; Dir. Mktg. & Communications, Scott Smith; Cur. Science, Daniel Ksepka; Dir. Devel., Whitney Rosenberg; Dir. Exhibits, Anne von Stuelpnagel; Dir. Finance, Bill Ference; Registrar, Kirsten Reinhardt; Museum Shop Mgr., Justine Matteis; Mgr. Volunteers, Mary Ann Lendenmann.

Institution Type/Description: Art, Science & Natural History.
Hours & Admission Prices: Tues.-Sun.10-5. Adults $10, students & senior citizens $8; discounts to AAM & ASTC members; children under 5, members & Tues. no charge. Closed New Year's Day; Easter; Independence Day; Labor Day; Thanksgiving; Christmas. &
Attendance: 71,282 (actual)

PUTNAM COTTAGE, 243 E. Putnam Ave., Greenwich, CT 06830-4808. Tel.: 203-869-9697.
E-mail: info@putnamcottage.org
Web Site: www.putnamcottage.org
Key Personnel: Museum Shop Mgr., Mrs. Sally Bretschger.
Institution Type/Description: History Museum: housed in c.1700 Knapps Tavern. A National Historic Site.
Hours & Admission Prices: By appointment. Closed holidays.
Attendance: 300 (estimated)

Groton

ALEXEY VON SCHLIPPE GALLERY OF ART, 1084 Shennecossett Rd., Groton, CT 06340. Tel.: 860-405-9052.
E-mail: julia.pavone@uconn.edu
Web Site: www.averypointarts.uconn.edu
Key Personnel: Dir. & Cur., Julia Pavone.
Institution Type/Description: Art Gallery.
Hours & Admission Prices: Wed.-Sun. 12-4.

AVERY-COPP MUSEUM, 154 Thames St., Groton, CT 06340-3631. Mailing Address: P.O. Box 7011, Groton, CT 06340-7011. Tel.: 860-445-1637 & 449-1596. Fax: 860-405-1154.
E-mail: averycopphouse@sbcglobal.net
Web Site: averycopphouse.com/index.html
Key Personnel: Dir., Leslie Evans.
Institution Type/Description: Historic House Museum: built c.1800.
Hours & Admission Prices: By appointment. Adults $4, youth 12-18 & students $2; children under 12 no charge.

EBENEZER AVERY HOUSE, Fort Griswold Battlefield State Park, 57 Fort St., Groton, CT 06340. Mailing Address: Avery Memorial Association, P.O. Box 7245, Groton, CT 06340-7245. Tel.: 860-446-9257. Facebook.
E-mail: sglantiere@aol.com
Web Site: averymemorialassociation.com
Key Personnel: Museum Shop Mgr., Stephanie Lantiere.
Institution Type/Description: Historic House Museum: built in 1750.
Hours & Admission Prices: Memorial Day to Labor Day Fri.-Sun. 12-4. No charge; donations accepted.
Attendance: 1,000 (estimated)

SUBMARINE FORCE MUSEUM AND HISTORIC SHIP NAUTILUS, 1 Crystal Lake Rd., Groton, CT 06349-5571. Mailing Address: P.O. Box 571, Groton, CT 06349-5571. Tel.: 860-694-3174, 800-343-0079. Fax: 860-694-4150. Facebook.
Web Site: www.ussnautilus.org
Key Personnel: Officer-in-Charge, Lt. Commander Bradley Boyd; Exec. Dir., Gretchen Marion; Dir. Education, Eury Cantillo; Museum Shop Mgr., Heather Henderson.
Institution Type/Description: Naval Museum: housed on USS Nautilus submarine & adjacent museum.
Hours & Admission Prices: Museum: May-Oct. Wed.-Mon. 9-5; Nov.-April Wed.-Mon. 9-4. Library: Mon.-Fri. by appointment only. No charge. Closed New Year's Day; Thanksgiving; Christmas. &
Attendance: 129,394 (actual)

Guilford

HENRY WHITFIELD STATE HISTORICAL MUSEUM, 248 Old Whitfield St., Guilford, CT 06437-3459. Tel.: 203-453-2457. Fax: 203-453-7544. Facebook.
E-mail: whitfieldmuseum@ct.gov
Web Site: www.cultureandtourism.org
Key Personnel: Cur., Michael A. McBride; Cur., Michelle Parrish; State Historic Preservation Officer, Daniel Forrest; Guide, Chris Collins.
Institution Type/Description: National Historic Landmark: 1639 oldest building in Connecticut, oldest stone house in New England; first state-owned museum in Connecticut (1899), colonial revival restorations by Norman Isham in 1902-1904 & J. Frederick Kelly in the 1930s.
Hours & Admission Prices: See website for current hours. Adults $8, seniors $6, youth $5; children 5 & under no charge. Closed major holidays. &
Attendance: 5,000 (actual)

THE HYLAND HOUSE, 84 Boston St., Guilford, CT 06437-2874. Mailing Address: P.O. Box 229, Guilford, CT 06437-0229. Tel.: 203-453-9477 & 3850. Faceboo.
E-mail: info@hylandhouse.org
Web Site: www.hylandhouse.org
Key Personnel: Pres., Grace Zimmer; Treas., Mairi Graham Bryan; Dir., Pamela Besse; Dir., Sandra Flatow; House Mgr., Katherine Frydenborg.
Institution Type/Description: General Museum.
Hours & Admission Prices: June-Sept. Fri.-Sat. 11-4, Sun. 12-4. No charge.
Attendance: 1,000 (estimated)

THE THOMAS GRISWOLD HOUSE AND MUSEUM, 171 Boston St., Guilford, CT 06437. Mailing Address: P.O. Box 363, Guilford, CT 06437-0363. Tel.: 203-453-3176.
E-mail: info@guilfordkeepingsociety.com
Web Site: guilfordkeepingsociety.com
Key Personnel: Dir., Patricia Lovelace; Programs, Robert Donahue.
Institution Type/Description: Historic House: built in 1774.
Hours & Admission Prices: June-Sept. Tues.-Sun. 11-4; other times for pre-arranged groups. Adults & students $2; discounts to NEMA members & groups; children & members no charge.
Attendance: 1,500 (estimated)

Haddam

HADDAM HISTORICAL SOCIETY - THANKFUL ARNOLD HOUSE, 14 Hayden Hill Rd., Haddam, CT 06438. Mailing Address: P.O. Box 97, Haddam, CT 06438-0097. Tel.: 860-345-2400.
E-mail: contact@haddamhistory.org
Web Site: www.haddamhistory.org
Key Personnel: Dir., Elizabeth Malloy; Pres. (V), R. Dianne McHutchison.
Institution Type/Description: Historic House Museum: built between 1794 and 1810.
Hours & Admission Prices: Memorial Day to Columbus Day Wed. 9-3, Thurs. 2-8, Fri. 12-3, Sun. 1-4; Oct.-May Wed. 9-3, Thurs. 2-8, Fri. 12-3. No charge; donations accepted.
Attendance: 1,500 (estimated)

Hamden

ELI WHITNEY MUSEUM, INC., 915 Whitney Ave., Hamden, CT 06517-4036. Tel.: 203-777-1833. Fax: 203-777-1229.
E-mail: dc@eliwhitney.org
Web Site: www.eliwhitney.org
Key Personnel: Dir., William Brown; Assoc. Dir. Design, Sally Hill; Sr. Shop Mgr., Ryan Paxton.
Institution Type/Description: Experimental Learning Workshop & Museum.
Hours & Admission Prices: Memorial Day to Labor Day daily 11-4; Sept.-May Wed.-Fri. & Sun. 12-5, Sat. 10-3. No charge; donations accepted. Closed Easter; Christmas.
Attendance: 48,000 (estimated)

HAMDEN HISTORICAL SOCIETY, INC., 105 Mt. Carmel Ave., Hamden, CT 06518. Mailing Address: P.O. Box 5512, Hamden, CT 06518-0512. Tel.: 203-288-0017.
E-mail: hamdenhistoricalsociety@wordpress.com
Key Personnel: Museum Shop Mgr., Lois Casey.
Institution Type/Description: History Museum: housed in 1792 Jonathan Dickerman House.
Hours & Admission Prices: Temporarily closed due to storm damage.
Attendance: 400 (estimated)

IRELAND'S GREAT HUNGER MUSEUM, 3011 Whitney Ave., Hamden, CT 06518. Tel.: 203-582-6574.
E-mail: claire.puzarne@qu.edu
Web Site: ighm.nfshost.com
Key Personnel: Interim Dir., Claire Puzarne.
Institution Type/Description: History Museum.
Hours & Admission Prices: Wed. & Fri.-Sat. 10-5, Thurs. 10-7, Sun. 1-5. Self-Guided Tours: no charge. Guided Tours: $50-$100; school groups no charge. Closed Good Friday; Easter; Memorial Day; Independence Day; Thanksgiving; Christmas Eve & Day.

Hampton

GOODWIN FOREST CONSERVATION EDUCATION CENTER, 23 Potter Rd., Hampton, CT 06247-3616. Tel.: 860-

455-9534. Fax: 860-455-9857. Facebook: Goodwin Forest Conservation Education Center.
E-mail: bbernard@ctwoodlands.org
Web Site: www.ct.gov/dep/goodwin
Key Personnel: Dir. Forest & Programs, Jim Parda.
Institution Type/Description: Conservation Center.
Hours & Admission Prices: Call for hours. No charge; donations accepted.
Attendance: 10,000 (estimated)

TRAIL WOOD: THE EDWIN WAY TEALE MEMORIAL SANCTUARY, 93 Kenyon Rd., Hampton, CT 06274. Tel.: 860-928-4948.
Institution Type/Description: Historic House: housed in the former home of Pulitzer Prize-winning author Edwin Way Teale & his wife.
Hours & Admission Prices: House: by appointment. Grounds: daily dawn to dusk. No charge.

Hartford

BUTLER-MCCOOK HOUSE AND GARDEN, 396 Main St., Hartford, CT 06103-3001. Tel.: 860-522-1806. Fax: 860-249-4907.
E-mail: butler.mccook@ctlandmarks.org
Web Site: www.ctlandmarks.org
Key Personnel: Dir., Sheryl Hack.
Institution Type/Description: Historic House.
Hours & Admission Prices: Garden: daily sunrise to sunset. House: May-Sept. Thurs.-Sun. 12-4; Oct.-Dec. Sat.-Sun. 12-4; groups by appointment. Adults $7, senior citizens, students & teachers $6, children 6-18 $4; discounts to groups of 15 or more; members & children under 6 no charge.

CHARTER OAK CULTURAL CENTER, 21 Charter Oak Ave., Hartford, CT 06106-1801. Tel.: 860-310-2580. Fax: 860-524-8014.
E-mail: yashiras@charteroakcenter.org
Web Site: www.charteroakcenter.org
Key Personnel: Administrative Coord., Yashira Santiago.
Institution Type/Description: Cultural Art Center.
Hours & Admission Prices: July-Aug. Tues.-Fri. 10-4; Sept.-June Mon.-Fri. 10-4; other times be appointment. No charge; donations accepted.

CLARE GALLERY, Franciscan Center for Urban Ministry, 285 Church St., Hartford, CT 06103. Tel.: 860-756-4034. Fax: 860-249-6487.
Web Site: hartford.com/clare-gallery/
Key Personnel: Pastoral Assoc., Patricia Curtis.
Institution Type/Description: Art Gallery.
Hours & Admission Prices: Mon.-Thurs. 8:30-7, Fri. 8:30-4:30, Sat. 9-4, Sun. 9-11:30. No charge.

CONNECTICUT HISTORICAL SOCIETY, 1 Elizabeth St., Hartford, CT 06105-2292. Tel.: 860-236-5621. Fax: 860-236-2664.
E-mail: ask_us@chs.org
Web Site: www.chs.org
Key Personnel: C.E.O., Robert Kret; Chief Cur., Ilene Frank; C.F.O., Kevin Hughes; Chief Advancement Officer, Richard Tuchman.
Institution Type/Description: Historical Society Museum & Library.
Hours & Admission Prices: Museum: Tues.-Thurs. 12-5, Fri.-Sat. 9-5. Library & Research: Tues.-Thurs. 12-5, Fri.-Sat. 9-5. Museum: adults $12, senior citizens $10, students $8; discount to AAM members; children 5 & under and members no charge. Closed New Year's Day; Independence Day; Thanksgiving; Christmas.
Attendance: 60,000 (estimated)

CONNECTICUT LANDMARKS, 59 S. Prospect St., Hartford, CT 06106-1901. Tel.: 860-247-8996. Fax: 860-249-4907.
E-mail: info@ctlandmarks.org
Web Site: www.ctlandmarks.org
Formerly: The Antiquarian and Landmarks Society, Inc.
Key Personnel: Exec. Dir., Sheryl N. Hack; Mktg. & Devel. Assoc., Jamie-Lynn Fontaine Connell; Property Mgr., Joseph Pukas.
Institution Type/Description: Historic Houses & Historic Site concerned with Connecticut's Social History.
Hours & Admission Prices: Call or see website for hours. Adults $7, students, teachers & seniors $6, children 6-18 $4; discounts to groups of 10 or more, New England Museum Assoc. & AAM members; members & children under 6 no charge.
Attendance: 20,000 (estimated)

CONNECTICUT SCIENCE CENTER, 250 Columbus Blvd., Hartford, CT 06103-2802. Tel.: 860-SCIENCE (724-3623).
E-mail: tshirer@CTScienceCenter.org

Web Site: www.ctsciencecenter.org
Key Personnel: Pres. & C.E.O., Matt Fleury; Dir. Mtkg. & Public Relations, Tracy Shirer.
Institution Type/Description: Science Center.
Hours & Admission Prices: July-Aug. daily 10-5; Sept.-June Tues.-Sun. 10-5. Adults $21.95, senior citizens 65 & over $19.95; youth 3-17 $14.95; members & children under 3 no charge. Closed Thanksgiving; Christmas. &
Attendance: 325,000 (actual)

CONNECTICUT SUPREME COURT, External Affairs Div., Connecticut Judicial Branch, 231 Capitol Ave., Hartford, CT 06160. Tel.: 860-757-2200. Fax: 860-757-2215.
Web Site: www.jud.state.ct.us/external/news/SupCtTour.html
Key Personnel: Exec. Asst., Elizabeth I. Hanes.
Institution Type/Description: Historic Building: built from 1908-1910.
Hours & Admission Prices: Mon.-Fri. by appointment.

CONNECTICUT'S OLD STATE HOUSE, 800 Main St., Hartford, CT 06103-2301. Tel.: 860-522-6766. Fax: 860-522-2812.
E-mail: ctoldstatehouse@cga.ct.gov
Web Site: www.ctoldstatehouse.com
Key Personnel: Exec. Dir., Sally Whipple; Head Public Programs & History Day, Rebecca Taber-Conover.
Institution Type/Description: Historic Federal Building: built in 1796, designed by Charles Bulfinch; site of first meeting house, George Washington's meeting with Comte de Rochambeau and the French troops; first Amistad Trial.
Hours & Admission Prices: July 4 to Columbus Day Tues.-Sat. 10-5; Oct.-July 3 Mon.-Fri. 10-5. Guided Tours: adults $6, senior citizens, students & children 6-17 $3; children 5 & under no charge. Closed major holidays. &
Attendance: 32,368 (actual)

GOVERNOR'S RESIDENCE, 990 Prospect Ave., Hartford, CT 06105-1102. Mailing Address: Office of the Governor, State of Connecticut, 990 Prospect Ave., Hartford, CT 06105-1102. Tel.: 860-524-7355.
Institution Type/Description: Historic Building: built in 1909.
Hours & Admission Prices: Guided Tours: by appointment.

HARRIET BEECHER STOWE CENTER, 77 Forest St., Hartford, CT 06105-3296. Tel.: 860-522-9258. Fax: 860-522-9259.
E-mail: info@stowecenter.org
Web Site: www.harrietbeecherstowecenter.org
Key Personnel: Exec. Dir., Briann Greenfield; Chm., Susan Johnson; Collections Mgr., Beth Burgess; Dir. Education & Visitor Svcs., Shannon Burke; Visitor Svcs. Mgr., Anita Durkin; Dir. Mktg., Vivian Nabeta.
Institution Type/Description: Historic Buildings: housed in the home of activist author Harriet Beecher Stowe; located on Nook Farm, the 19th-century neighborhood where Mark Twain, Isabella Beecher Hooker & William H. Gillette also resided.
Hours & Admission Prices: Mon.-Sat. 9:30-5, Sun. 12-5. Adult $16, seniors 65 & over & students over 17 $14; children 5-16 $10; discounts to museum professionals, groups & AAM members; children under 5 & members no charge. Closed New Year's Day; Easter; Independence Day; Thanksgiving; Christmas Eve & Day.
Attendance: 25,739 (actual)

INSTITUTE OF LIVING MUSEUM - MYTHS, MINDS, AND MEDICINE, 80 Seymour St., Commons Bldg., 2nd Fl., Hartford, CT 06102. Tel.: 860-545-7665; 860-545-7716.
E-mail: paula.rego@hhchealth.org
Institution Type/Description: Science Museum.
Hours & Admission Prices: Mon.-Fri. 9-5.

THE MARK TWAIN HOUSE & MUSEUM, 351 Farmington Ave., Hartford, CT 06105-4401. Tel.: 860-247-0998. Fax: 860-278-8148. Facebook, Twitter.
E-mail: info@marktwainhouse.org
Web Site: www.marktwainhouse.org
Key Personnel: Exec. Dir., Pieter Roos; Dir. Mktg. & Public Relations, Jennifer LaRue; Dir. Education, Dr. James Golden; Dir. Mgr., Ilana Stollmna.
Institution Type/Description: Historic Building: Mark Twain House, author's home 1874-1891 designed by Edward Tuckerman Potter; Alfred M. Thorp & decorated by Louis C. Tiffany and Associated Artists in 1881.
Hours & Admission Prices: Jan.-Feb. Wed.-Mon. 9:30-5:30; March-Dec. daily 9:30-5:30; specialty tours & group tours by appointment. Adults $20, seniors $18, children 6-16 $12; discounts to AAM members & groups of 10 or more; children under 6 & members no charge. Closed New Year's Day; Easter; Independence Day; Thanksgiving; Christmas Eve & Day. &
Attendance: 67,855 (actual)

MUSEUM OF CONNECTICUT HISTORY, Connecticut State Library, 231 Capitol Ave., Hartford, CT 06106-1569. Tel.: 860-757-6535. Fax: 860-757-6521.
Web Site: www.museumofcthistory.org
Key Personnel: Cur. Education, Patrick Smith; Cur. Collections, Dave Corrigan.
Institution Type/Description: History Museum.
Hours & Admission Prices: Mon.-Fri. 9-4, Sat. 9-2. No charge. Closed state holidays. &
Attendance: 25,000 (actual)

PUMP HOUSE GALLERY, Bushnell Park, 60 Elm St., Hartford, CT 06123. Mailing Address: P.O. Box 230778, Hartford, CT 06123-0778. Tel.: 860-757-9526.
E-mail: manager@bushnellpark.org
Web Site: www.bushnellpark.org
Institution Type/Description: Historic Building: housed in a working Tudor-style pump house, part of the Connecticut River Flood Control Project; built in 1947.
Hours & Admission Prices: Tues.-Sat. 11-2. No charge.

REAL ART WAYS, 56 Arbor St., Hartford, CT 06106-1228. Tel.: 860-232-1006. Fax: 860-233-6691.
E-mail: info@realartways.org
Web Site: www.realartways.org
Key Personnel: Exec. Dir., Will K. Wilkins.
Institution Type/Description: Art Gallery.
Hours & Admission Prices: Daily 12:30-9; other times by appointment. Suggested Donation: $3; members no charge. &

STATE CAPITOL, HARTFORD, CONNECTICUT, 210 Capitol Ave., Hartford, CT 06106-1535. Tel.: 860-240-0222. Fax: 860-240-8627.
E-mail: capitol.tours@cga.ct.gov
Web Site: www.cga.ct.gov/capitoltours
Key Personnel: Dir., Kimberly Fabrizio.
Institution Type/Description: Historic Building.
Hours & Admission Prices: One-hour Tour: July-Aug. Mon.-Fri. 9:15, 10:15, 11:15, 12:15, 1:15 & 2:15; Sept.-June Mon.-Fri. 9:15, 10:15, 11:15, 12:15 & 1:15. No charge. Closed state & national holidays; Christmas week. &
Attendance: 30,228 (actual)

WADSWORTH ATHENEUM MUSEUM OF ART, 600 Main St., Hartford, CT 06103-2990. Tel.: 860-278-2670. Fax: 860-527-0803. Facebook, Twitter.
E-mail: info@wadsworthatheneum.org
Web Site: www.thewadsworth.org
Formerly: Wadsworth Atheneum
Key Personnel: Dir. & C.E.O., Thomas J. Loughman; Bd. Pres. (V), William R. Peelle, Jr.; C.F.O., Cindy J. Martinez; Exec. Admin., Jennifer Bordiere; Senior Cur. and Charles C. & Eleanor Lamont Cunningham Cur. European Decorative Arts, Linda Roth; Dir. Museum Svcs., Cecil Adams; Dir. Education Georgette Auerbach Koopman, Anne Butler Rice; Dir., Mktg. & Communs., Kim Hugo; Dir., Human Resources & Spec. Initiatives, Michael Dudich.
Institution Type/Description: Art Museum.
Hours & Admission Prices: Museum: Wed.-Fri. 11-5, Sat.-Sun. 10-5. Adults $15, senior citizens 62 & over $12, students 18 & over with ID $5; discounts to AAM members & veterans; youth under 18, Hartford residents & members no charge. Library: Wed.-Thurs. 11-5, Sat. 12-4. Closed New Year's Day; Independence Day; Thanksgiving; Christmas. &
Attendance: 100,000 (estimated)

WIDENER GALLERY, AUSTIN ARTS CENTER, TRINITY COLLEGE, 300 Summit St., Hartford, CT 06106-3100. Mailing Address: 300 Summit St., Hallden Hall - Fine Arts, Hartford, CT 06106. Tel.: 860-297-5232 & 2199. Fax: 860-297-5349.
E-mail: austinartsinfo@trincoll.edu
Web Site: www.trincoll.edu/Arts/Pages/AustinArtsCenter.aspx
Key Personnel: Cur., Felice Caivano.
Institution Type/Description: College Gallery.
Hours & Admission Prices: Academic Year: Mon.-Sat. 1-6. No charge. Closed academic holidays & recesses.

Higganum

HADDAM SHAD MUSEUM, 212 Saybrook Rd., Higganum, CT 06441. Mailing Address: 82 Clarkhurst Rd., Haddam Neck, CT 06424-3001. Tel.: 860-267-0388.
E-mail: u16576@snet.net
Web Site: www.haddamshadmuseum.com

Key Personnel: Dir., Dr. Joseph Zaientz; Volunteer, Lenny Kochinowski; Volunteer, David Roberts; Volunteer, John Calhoun.
Institution Type/Description: History Museum.
Hours & Admission Prices: mid-April to mid-June Sun. 10-3. No charge.
Attendance: 100 (estimated)

Ivoryton

MUSEUM OF FIFE AND DRUM, 62 N. Main St., Ivoryton, CT 06442-0277. Mailing Address: P.O. Box 277, Ivoryton, CT 06442-0277. Tel.: 860-767-2237. Fax: 860-767-9765. Facebook.
E-mail: companyhq@companyoffifeanddrum.org
Web Site: www.companyoffifeanddrum.org
Key Personnel: Pres. (V) & Public Rels., Kevin Brown; Vice Pres., Mark Logsdon; 2nd Vice Pres. & Security, Scott Mitchell; Treas., Kristen Livoti; Cur. & Archivist, Marty Sampson; Museum Shop Mgr., Roberta Armstead.
Institution Type/Description: Musical Instruments Museum.
Hours & Admission Prices: June 30-Labor Day Sat.-Sun. 1-5 by appointment only. Adults $5, youth 12-17 & seniors 60 and over $3; members & children 12 and under no charge. &
Attendance: 1,150 (estimated)

Kensington

BERLIN HISTORICAL SOCIETY, 305 Main St., Kensington, CT 06037. Mailing Address: P.O. Box 8192, Kensington, CT 06037. Tel.: 860-828-5114.
E-mail: berlincthistorical@gmail.com
Web Site: berlincthistorical.org
Institution Type/Description: Historical Society Museum.
Hours & Admission Prices: April-Dec. Sat. 1-4; other times by appointment.

NEW BRITAIN YOUTH MUSEUM AT HUNGERFORD PARK, 191 Farmington Ave., Kensington, CT 06037-1220. Tel.: 860-827-9064 & 225-3020. Fax: 860-827-1266.
E-mail: marketing@newbritainyouthmuseum.org
Web Site: newbritainyouthmuseum.org
Key Personnel: Dir., Ann F. Peabody; Chm. (V), Christopher LaSaracina.
Institution Type/Description: Children's Museum & Nature Center.
Hours & Admission Prices: Tues.-Sat. 10-4:30. Admission $6; children under 2 no charge. Closed major holidays. &
Attendance: 23,732 (actual)

Kent

CONNECTICUT ANTIQUE MACHINERY ASSOCIATION MUSEUM, 31 Kent-Cornwall Rd., Kent, CT 06757. Mailing Address: P.O. Box 425, Kent, CT 06757. Tel.: 860-927-0050. Fax: 860-927-0050.
E-mail: camainfo@ctamachinery.com
Web Site: www.ctamachinery.com
Key Personnel: Dir. & Pres. (V), John Pawloski; Museum Shop Mgr., John Stauffer.
Institution Type/Description: History Museum.
Hours & Admission Prices: May-Oct. Wed.-Sun. 10-4; other times by appointment. No charge; donations requested. &
Attendance: 15,000 (estimated)

ERIC SLOANE MUSEUM & KENT IRON FURNACE, 31 Kent Cornwall Rd., Rte. 7, Kent, CT 06757. Mailing Address: P.O. Box 917, Kent, CT 06757-0917. Tel.: 860-927-3849. Fax: 860-927-2152. Facebook: Eric Sloane Museum.
E-mail: ericsloane.museum@ct.gov
Web Site: www.cultureandtourism.org
Formerly: Sloane-Stanley Museum and Kent Furnace
Key Personnel: Museum Dir., Karin Peterson; Museum Asst., Barbara Russ.
Institution Type/Description: Early American Tools & Implements Museum: located on the site of the ruins of Kent Iron Furnace.
Hours & Admission Prices: See website for hours. Adults $8, senior citizens 60 & over and college students $6, children 6-17 $5; discounts to school groups; children 5 & under no charge.
Attendance: 3,000 (actual)

THE KENT ART ASSOCIATION, 21 S. Main St., Kent, CT 06757. Mailing Address: P.O. Box 202, Kent, CT 06757-0202. Tel.: 860-927-3989. Fax: 860-927-4218.
E-mail: kent.art.assoc@snet.net
Web Site: www.kentart.org
Key Personnel: Pres. (V), Carolyn Fisher; Exec. Dir., Davia Kennedy Fink.
Institution Type/Description: Art Museum.

Hours & Admission Prices: Call for hours. No charge; donations accepted.
Attendance: 5,000 (estimated)

Lebanon

BEAUMONT HOMESTEAD, 844 Trumbull Hwy., Lebanon, CT 06249. Mailing Address: Lebanon Historical Society, P.O. Box 151, Lebanon, CT 06249-0151. Tel.: 860-642-6579. Fax: 860-642-6583.
E-mail: museum@historyoflebanon.org
Web Site: www.historyoflebanon.org
Formerly: William Beaumont Birthplace
Key Personnel: Dir., Donna K. Baron.
Institution Type/Description: Historic House Museum: housed in the childhood home of Dr. William Beaumont.
Hours & Admission Prices: mid-May to Columbus Day Sat. 12-4; other times by appointment. No charge; donations accepted.
Attendance: 325 (estimated)

GOVERNOR JONATHAN TRUMBULL HOUSE & WADSWORTH STABLE MUSEUMS, 169 W. Town St., Lebanon, CT 06249-1550. Mailing Address: Connecticut Daughters of the American Revolution, P.O. Box 54, Lebanon, CT 06249-0054. Tel.: 860-642-7558.
E-mail: info@govtrumbullhousedar.org
Web Site: www.govtrumbullhouse.dar.org
Key Personnel: Chm. (V), Cecelia Messier.
Institution Type/Description: Historic House Museum: built c.1740. Listed on the National Registry of Historic Places.
Hours & Admission Prices: House: temporarily closed. Wadsworth Stable: call for hours. No charge; donations accepted.
Attendance: 900 (estimated)

JONATHAN TRUMBULL JR. HOUSE MUSEUM, 780 Trumbull Hwy., Lebanon, CT 06249-1523. Mailing Address: c/o Town Hall, 579 Exeter Rd., Lebanon, CT 06249. Tel.: 860-642-6100. Fax: 860-642-7716.
E-mail: WebsiteAdministrator@Lebanonct.gov
Web Site: www.lebanontownhall.org/trumbulljuniormuseum.htm
Institution Type/Description: Historic House Museum: housed in the home of Jonathan Trumball, Jr., son of Connecticut's Revolutionary War Governor who served as Gen. George Washington's secretary and later Connecticut's governor from 1797-1809; house built c.1769. Listed on the National Register of Historic Places.
Hours & Admission Prices: mid-May to Columbus Day Sat.-Sun. 12-4. No charge. &

LEBANON HISTORICAL SOCIETY, 856 Trumbull Hwy., Lebanon, CT 06249-1546. Mailing Address: P.O. Box 151, Lebanon, CT 06249. Tel.: 860-642-6579. Fax: 860-642-6583.
E-mail: museum@historyoflebanon.org
Web Site: www.historyoflebanon.org
Key Personnel: Dir., Donna K. Baron.
Institution Type/Description: Historical Society Museum.
Hours & Admission Prices: Wed.-Sat. 12-4. No charge; donations accepted. &

REVOLUTIONARY WAR OFFICE, 149 W. Town St., Lebanon, CT 06249. Mailing Address: CT Sons of American Revolution, P. O. Box 411, East Haddon, CT 06423.
E-mail: info@connecticutsar.org
Web Site: www.connecticutsar.org
Institution Type/Description: History Museum: housed in the building where Gov. Jonathan Trumbull held meetings during the Revolutionary War; built in 1727. Listed on the National Register of Historic Places.
Hours & Admission Prices: Memorial Day to Labor Day Sat.-Sun. 12-4. No charge.
Attendance: 1,000 (actual)

Litchfield

LITCHFIELD HISTORICAL SOCIETY AND MUSEUM, 7 South St., On-the-Green, Litchfield, CT 06759. Mailing Address: P.O. Box 385, Litchfield, CT 06759-0385. Tel.: 860-567-4501. Fax: 860-567-3565.
E-mail: director@litchfieldhistoricalsociety.org
Web Site: www.litchfieldhistoricalsociety.org
Key Personnel: Dir., Catherine Keene Fields; Librarian & Archivist, Linda Hocking; Museum Shop Mgr., Kate Zullo; Cur. Education, Linda Loveday.
Institution Type/Description: Historical Society Museum & Historic House: Tapping Reeve House & Law School, America's first law school.

Hours & Admission Prices: Museum & Tapping Reeve House: mid-April to Nov. Tues.-Sat. 11-5, Sun. 1-5. Adults $5, senior citizens & students $3 (combined admission to Reeve House, Law School & Museum); AAM & museum members no charge. &
Attendance: 13,000 (estimated)

LIVINGSTON RIPLEY WATERFOWL CONSERVANCY, 55 Duck Pond Rd., Litchfield, CT 06759. Mailing Address: P.O. Box 210, Litchfield, CT 06759. Tel.: 860-567-2062. Fax: 860-567-4369.
E-mail: info@lrwc.net
Web Site: www.lrwc.net
Institution Type/Description: Conservancy.
Hours & Admission Prices: April-Nov. Fri.-Sun. 10-4. Adults $10, seniors $8, children 4-14 $5; children 3 & under and members no charge.

TOPSMEAD STATE FOREST, Buell Rd., Litchfield, CT 06759. Mailing Address: P.O. Box 1081, Litchfield, CT 06759. Tel.: 860-567-5694.
Institution Type/Description: Historic House Museum: housed in the former summer estate of Miss Edith Morton Chase, daughter of Alice Morton Chase and Henry Sabin Chase, the first President of Chase Brass and Copper Company in Waterbury; built in 1923.
Hours & Admission Prices: June-Oct. 2nd & 4th Sat.-Sun. 12-5. &

WHITE MEMORIAL CONSERVATION CENTER, INC., 80 Whitehall Rd., Litchfield, CT 06759-3914. Mailing Address: P.O. Box 368, Litchfield, CT 06759-0368. Tel.: 860-567-0857. Fax: 860-567-2611.
E-mail: info@whitememorialcc.org
Web Site: whitememorialcc.org
Key Personnel: Exec. Dir., Keith R. Cudworth; Dir. Administration & Devel., Gerri Griswold; Pres., Arthur Hill Diedrick; Dir. Education, Carrie Szwed; Dir. Research, James Fischer; Museum Shop Mgr., Lois Melaragno.
Institution Type/Description: Natural History Museum: located on 4,000-acre preserve of the White Memorial Foundation.
Hours & Admission Prices: Museum: Tues.-Sat. 9-5, Sun. 12-5. Suggested Donations: adults $6, children $3; members no charge. Guided Tours up to 25 people $75. Closed major holidays. &
Attendance: 16,100 (actual)

Madison

MADISON HISTORICAL SOCIETY, Lee Academy, 14 Meetinghouse Ln., Madison, CT 06443. Mailing Address: P.O. Box 17, Madison, CT 06443-0017. Tel.: 203-245-4567.
E-mail: contact@madisonhistory.org
Web Site: www.madisoncthistorical.org
Key Personnel: Pres. (V), James Matteson.
Institution Type/Description: History Museum: housed in c.1785 Allis-Bushnell House.
Hours & Admission Prices: Call for hours. No charge; donations accepted.
Attendance: 500 (estimated)

MEIGS POINT NATURE CENTER, Hammonasset Beach State Park, 1288 Boston Post Rd., Madison, CT 06443. Mailing Address: P.O. Box 271, Madison, CT 06443. Tel.: 203-245-8743, 860-462-9643. Fax: 203-245-9201.
E-mail: rangermpnc@gmail.com
Web Site: www.meigspointnaturecenter.org
Institution Type/Description: Nature Center.
Hours & Admission Prices: April-Oct. Tues.-Sun. 10-5; Nov.-March Tues.-Sun. 10-4. No charge; donations accepted. &
Attendance: 25,000 (actual)

Manchester

THE FIRE MUSEUM, 230 Pine St., Manchester, CT 06040-5829. Tel.: 860-649-9436.
E-mail: thefiremuseum@att.net
Web Site: www.thefiremuseum.org
Key Personnel: Pres. (V), Wayne Crossman; Museum Shop Mgr., Lucy Crossman.
Institution Type/Description: Fire Museum: housed in a former fire station; built in 1901.
Hours & Admission Prices: mid-April to mid-Nov. Fri.-Sat. 12-4; other times by appointment. Suggested Donation: adults $4, seniors, youth 12-16 & firefighters $2, children 6-12 $1; children under 6 no charge.
Attendance: 1,000 (actual)

HANS WEISS NEWSPACE GALLERY, Manchester Community College, Great Path, MS#19, Manchester, CT 06040. Tel.: 860-512-3000.
E-mail: sclassen-sullivan@mcc.commnet.edu
Web Site: www.mcc.commnet.edu/students/life/newspace.php
Institution Type/Description: Art Gallery.
Hours & Admission Prices: Mon.-Fri. 11-8, Sat. 12-5.

LUTZ CHILDREN'S MUSEUM, 247 S. Main St., Manchester, CT 06040-6561. Tel.: 860-643-0949.
E-mail: reckert@lutzmuseum.org
Web Site: www.lutzmuseum.org
Key Personnel: Dir., Bob Eckert; Pres. (V), Kristen Addabbo; Volunteer Coord., Leslie Strano; Visitor Svcs., Lucas Pierson.
Institution Type/Description: Children's Museum.
Hours & Admission Prices: Tues.-Fri. 9-5, Sat.-Sun. 12-5; Nature Trails dawn to dusk. Admission $6; members no charge. Closed some holidays. &
Attendance: 30,000 (estimated)

MANCHESTER HISTORICAL SOCIETY, 175 Pine St., Manchester History Center, Manchester, CT 06040-5921. Tel.: 860-647-9983.
E-mail: info@manchesterhistory.org
Web Site: www.manchesterhistory.org
Institution Type/Description: Historical Society
Hours & Admission Prices: Mon.-Fri. 10-2. No charge; donation requested. Closed legal holidays. &
Attendance: 1,200 (actual)

OLD MANCHESTER MUSEUM, 126 Cedar St., Manchester, CT 06040-5839. Mailing Address: Manchester Historical Society, 175 Pine St., Manchester, CT 06040. Tel.: 860-647-9983.
E-mail: info@manchesterhistory.org
Web Site: www.manchesterhistory.org
Key Personnel: Exec. Dir., Eileen Sweeney.
Institution Type/Description: History Museum: housed in c.1859 school house.
Hours & Admission Prices: Sat. 10-4, Sun. 1-4; other times by appointment. Donation: adults $5; discounts to AAM members; members no charge. Closed holidays. &
Attendance: 1,500 (actual)

WICKHAM PARK AVIARY AND NATURE CENTER, 1329 W. Middle Tpke., Manchester, CT 06040. Tel.: 860-528-0856. Fax: 860-528-5156.
E-mail: info@wickhampark.org
Web Site: www.wickhampark.org
Key Personnel: Dir., Jeffrey Maron.
Institution Type/Description: Nature Center.
Hours & Admission Prices: April-Oct. daily 9:30 to sunset. Vehicle Fee: Mon.-Fri. $5, Sat.-Sun. $7. &
Attendance: 200,000 (estimated)

Mashantucket

MASHANTUCKET PEQUOT MUSEUM AND RESEARCH CENTER, 110 Pequot Trail, Mashantucket, CT 06338-3180. Mailing Address: P.O. Box 3180, Mashantucket, CT 06338-3180. Tel.: 800-411-9671, 860-396-6945. Fax: 860-396-7013. Facebook: Pequot Museum.
E-mail: bkingsland@mptn-nsn.gov
Web Site: www.pequotmuseum.org
Key Personnel: Interim Dir., Travis Williams; Interim Dir., Dale Merrill; Mgr. Finance, Randy Banker; Education, Kimberly Shockley; Museum Shop Mgr., Heather Montey.
Institution Type/Description: Native American Museum.
Hours & Admission Prices: April-Oct. Wed.-Sat. 9-5; Nov. Tues.-Sat. 9-5. Adults $20, senior citizens 55 & over and college students $15, children 6-17 $12; discounts to AAM members & groups; members & children under 6 no charge. Closed New Year's Eve & Day; Thanksgiving Eve & Day; Christmas Eve & Day. &
Attendance: 60,000 (estimated)

Meriden

CONNECTICUT STATE POLICE MUSEUM AND EDUCATIONAL CENTER, State Police Mulcahy Complex, 294 Colony St., Bldg. #7, Meriden, CT 06450-0899. Tel.: 203-440-3858.
Web Site: www.cspmuseum.org

Institution Type/Description: Police Museum.
Hours & Admission Prices: Fri. 12:30-3:30, Sat. 12-4; other times by appointment. No charge; donations accepted.

GALLERY 53, 53 Colony St., Meriden, CT 06451-3210. Tel.: 203-235-5347.
E-mail: gallery53ct@gmail.com
Web Site: www.gallery53.org
Institution Type/Description: Art Gallery.
Hours & Admission Prices: Tues.-Fri. 12-4, Sat. 10-2, Sun. 12-3. No charge.

MERIDEN HISTORICAL SOCIETY, INC., 1090 Hanover St., Morehouse Research Center, Meriden, CT 06451-6207. Mailing Address: P.O. Box 3005, Meriden, CT 06450-9305. Tel.: 203-639-1913.
E-mail: meridenhistoricalsociety@gmail.com
Web Site: www.meridenhistoricalsociety.org
Key Personnel: C.E.O. & Pres. (V), Ruth Borsuk; Treas., Sherwin Borsuk; Cur., Allen Weathers; Sec., Christina Ruel.
Institution Type/Description: Local History Museum & Research Library: museum housed in 1760 Andrews Homestead; Meriden Historical Society Museum: 424 W. Main St., Meriden, CT 06451; Research Library: 1090 Hanover Rd., South Meriden, CT 06451.
Hours & Admission Prices: Research Center: Wed. 1:30-4; Andrews Homestead Museum: May & Oct. Sun. 12:30-4; tours by appointment. No charge; donations accepted. Closed holidays.
Attendance: 250 (estimated)

SOLOMON GOFFE HOUSE, 677 N. Colony St., Meriden, CT 06450. Mailing Address: 1176 N. Colony St., Meriden, CT 06450. Tel.: 203-235-2192. Facebook.
Institution Type/Description: Historic House Museum: built in 1711. A National Historic Landmark.
Hours & Admission Prices: April-Nov. 1st Sun. each month 1:30-4:30; other times by appointment. Admission $2.

Middletown

DAVISON ART CENTER, WESLEYAN UNIVERSITY, 301 High St., Middletown, CT 06459-0487. Tel.: 860-685-2500. Fax: 860-685-2501.
E-mail: crogan@wesleyan.edu
Web Site: www.wesleyan.edu/dac
Key Personnel: Gallery Supvr., Aidan Earle; Cur., Miya Tokumitsu; Mgr. Museum Information Svcs. & Registrar Collections, Robert Lancefield.
Institution Type/Description: Art Museum: housed in c.1838-40 Alsop House, a pre-Civil War mansion.
Hours & Admission Prices: Sept.-May Tues.-Sun. 12-4. No charge; donations accepted. Closed holidays; academic vacations. &
Attendance: 3,000 (actual)

EZRA AND CECILE ZILKHA GALLERY, Center for the Arts, Wesleyan University, 283 Washington Terr., Middletown, CT 06459. Mailing Address: Wesleyan University, 283 Washington Terr., Middletown, CT 06459. Tel.: 860-685-3283. Fax: 860-685-2061.
Web Site: wesleyan.edu/cfa
Key Personnel: Assoc. Dir., Sarah Curran.
Institution Type/Description: Art Gallery.
Hours & Admission Prices: Tues.-Wed. & Fri.-Sun. 12-5, Thurs. 12-7. No charge. Closed holidays; during academic recess. &
Attendance: 9,500 (actual)

KIDCITY CHILDREN'S MUSEUM, 119 Washington St., Middletown, CT 06457-2817. Tel.: 860-347-0495.
E-mail: info@kidcitymuseum.com
Web Site: www.kidcitymuseum.com
Key Personnel: Exec. Dir., Jennifer Alexander.
Institution Type/Description: Children's Museum.
Hours & Admission Prices: Sun.-Tues. 11-5, Wed.-Sat. 9-5. Admission $10; children under one no charge. Closed New Year's Day; Easter; Thanksgiving; Christmas. &

MANSFIELD FREEMAN CENTER FOR EAST ASIAN STUDIES - WESLEYAN UNIVERSITY, 343 Washington Ter., Middletown, CT 06459. Tel.: 860-685-2330. Fax: 860-685-2331.
E-mail: samorrell56@gmail.com
Key Personnel: Dir., Stephen Angle; Cur., Patrick Dowdey; Program Coord., Ann Gertz.

Institution Type/Description: East Asian Cultural Center: housed in a late Victorian shingle-style home; built in 1905.
Hours & Admission Prices: Tues.-Sun. 12-4. Closed academic holidays.

MIDDLESEX COUNTY HISTORICAL SOCIETY, 151 Main St., Middletown, CT 06457-3423. Tel.: 860-346-0746. Fax: 860-346-0746.
E-mail: middlesexhistory@wesleyan.edu
Web Site: mchsct.org
Key Personnel: Dir., Deborah D. Shapiro; Pres., Joseph Samolis.
Institution Type/Description: Historical Society Museum: housed in General Mansfield house; c.1817.
Hours & Admission Prices: Museum: Winter Mon.-Thurs. & 1st Sat. of month 10-2; Summer Tues.-Thurs. 10-2, 1st Sat. each month 10-2. Research: Mon.-Thurs. 10-2 by appointment. Adults $5; discount to AAM members; members no charge. Closed holidays & holiday weekends.
Attendance: 1,800 (estimated)

MIDDLETOWN SPORTS HALL OF FAME AND MUSEUM, 58 Bernie O'Rourke Dr., Middletown, CT 06457. Tel.: 860-347-9575. Facebook.
Institution Type/Description: Sports Museum.
Hours & Admission Prices: Mon.-Fri. 9:30 to noon; other times by appointment.

WADSWORTH MANSION AT LONG HILL, 421 Wadsworth St., Middletown, CT 06457. Tel.: 860-347-1064.
E-mail: events@wadsworthmansion.com
Web Site: www.wadsworthmansion.com
Institution Type/Description: Historic House Museum.
Hours & Admission Prices: Tours: Wed. 2-4.

Milford

MILFORD HISTORICAL SOCIETY, 34 High St., Milford, CT 06460-4732. Mailing Address: P.O. Box 337, Milford, CT 06460-0337. Tel.: 203-874-2664. Facebook.
E-mail: info@milfordhistoricalsociety.org
Web Site: www.milfordhistoricalsociety.org
Formerly: Eells-Stow House, Milford Historical Society
Key Personnel: Dir., Sandra Elgee; Museum Shop Mgr., Barbara Arndt.
Institution Type/Description: General Museum.
Hours & Admission Prices: June to mid-Oct. Sat.-Sun. 1-4; other times by appointment. No charge; donations accepted. &
Attendance: 2,000 (estimated)

Monroe

MONROE HISTORICAL SOCIETY, 31 Great Ring Rd., Monroe, CT 06468-1328. Mailing Address: P.O. Box 212, Monroe, CT 06468-0212. Tel.: 203-261-1383.
E-mail: society@monroecthistory.org
Web Site: www.monroehistoricsociety.org
Key Personnel: Pres. (V), Nancy Zorena; Chm. (V), Karen Cardi; Vice Pres., Vida Stone.
Institution Type/Description: General Museum.
Hours & Admission Prices: By appointment. No charge; donations accepted.
Attendance: 1,500 (estimated)

WEBB MOUNTAIN DISCOVERY ZONE, 52 Webb Cir., Monroe, CT 06468. Tel.: 203-556-9737. Facebook: Webb Mountain Discovery Zone.
E-mail: info@webbdiscoveryzone.org
Web Site: webbmountaindiscoveryzone.com
Institution Type/Description: Nature Center.
Hours & Admission Prices: Call for hours.

Moodus

AMASA DAY HOUSE MUSEUM, 33 Plains Rd., Moodus, CT 06469. Mailing Address: c/o CT Landmarks, 59 S. Prospect St., Hartford, CT 06106. Tel.: 860-247-8996, ext. 12.
E-mail: info@ctlandmarks.org
Web Site: www.ctlandmarks.org
Key Personnel: Exec. Dir., Sheryl Hack.
Institution Type/Description: Historic House: built in 1816.
Hours & Admission Prices: Temporarily closed.

Morris

JAMES MORRIS MUSEUM, 4 North St., Morris, CT 06763. Tel.: 860-567-5036.
Institution Type/Description: History Museum.
Hours & Admission Prices: Call for hours.

Mystic

DENISON HOMESTEAD MUSEUM - PEQUOTSEPOS MANOR, 120 Pequotsepos Rd., Mystic, CT 06355. Tel.: 860-536-9248. Fax: 860-536-9248.
E-mail: membership@denisonsociety.org
Web Site: www.denisonhomestead.org
Key Personnel: Homestead Mgr., Julie Soto.
Institution Type/Description: Historic House Museum: housed in the former home of Captain George Denison; built in 1717. Listed on the National Register of Historic Places.
Hours & Admission Prices: June-Oct., Mon. & Fri.-Sat. 12-4. Adults $5, seniors & students $4, children $2; discounts to active military; members & children under 6 no charge.

DENISON PEQUOTSEPOS NATURE CENTER, 109 Pequotsepos Rd., Mystic, CT 06355-3045. Mailing Address: P.O. Box 122, Mystic, CT 06355-0122. Tel.: 860-536-1216. Fax: 860-536-2983.
E-mail: info@dpnc.org
Web Site: www.dpnc.org
Key Personnel: Exec. Dir., Margaret L. Jones; Pres. (V), Hilary Hardaway; Dir. Finance, Kevin Metivier; Dir. Education, Kim Hargrave.
Institution Type/Description: Natural Science & Environmental Education.
Hours & Admission Prices: Mon.-Sat. 9-5, Sun. 10-4. Adults $8, seniors & children under 12 $5; discounts to military, ANCA & AAA members. Closed New Year's Day; Easter; Thanksgiving; Christmas.
Attendance: 50,000 (estimated)

MYSTIC AQUARIUM, 55 Coogan Blvd., Mystic, CT 06355-1997. Tel.: 860-572-5955. Fax: 860-572-5969.
E-mail: info@mysticaquarium.org
Web Site: www.mysticaquarium.org
Key Personnel: Pres. & C.E.O., Dr. Stephen Coan; Exec. Vice Pres. & C.O.O., Larry Rivarde; Chm. Bd. (V), George M. Milne, Jr., Ph.D.; Senior Vice Pres. & C.F.O., Robert Constable; C.F.O., Denise H. Armstrong; Sr. Vice Pres. Facilities, Keith P. Sorensen; Sr. Vice Pres. Advancement, Debra Neuman; Vice Pres. Education & Public Conservation Programs, Kelly E. Matis; Sr. Vice Pres. Membership & Guest Svcs., Jackie Almeida; Sr. Vice Pres. Mission Programs, Katie Cubina.
Institution Type/Description: Aquarium & Marine Museum.
Hours & Admission Prices: March & Sept. 8-Nov. daily 9-4:50; April to Labor Day daily 9-5:50; Dec.-Feb. daily 10-4:50. Adults $37.99, seniors 60 & up $32.99, youth 13-17 $31.99, children 3-12 $27.99; members and children 2 & under no charge. Closed Thanksgiving; Christmas.
Attendance: 700,000 (estimated)

MYSTIC MUSEUM OF ART, 9 Water St., Mystic, CT 06355-2592. Tel.: 860-536-7601. Fax: 860-536-0610. Facebook.
E-mail: eneenan@mysticmuseumofart.org
Web Site: www.mysticmuseumofart.org
Formerly: Mystic Arts Center
Key Personnel: Exec. Dir., George G. King; Pres., Alex Bancroft; Treas., Michele Kirk; Treas., Bill Middleton.
Institution Type/Description: Art Museum Center.
Hours & Admission Prices: Jan.-April Tues.-Sun. 11-5; May-Dec. daily 11-5. Suggested Donation: adults $3. Closed New Year's Day; Easter; Thanksgiving; Christmas Eve & Day.
Attendance: 20,000 (estimated)

MYSTIC SEAPORT MUSEUM, 75 Greenmanville Ave., Mystic, CT 06355-0990. Mailing Address: P.O. Box 6000, Mystic, CT 06355-0990. Tel.: 860-572-0711. Fax: 860-572-5326. TDD: 860-572-5319.
E-mail: info@mysticseaport.org
Web Site: www.mysticseaport.org
Key Personnel: Pres., Stephen C. White; Chm. Bd., J. Barclay Collins; C.O.O., Susan Funk; C.F.O., David Patten; Vice Pres., Curatorial Affairs, Nicholas Bell; Sr. Vice Pres., Advancement, Laura Hopkins; Vice Pres., Watercraft, Chris Gasiorek; Dir. Communications, Daniel McFadden; Dir. Facilities Management, Ken Wilson; Dir. Shipyard, Quentin Snediker; Cur. Photography & Dir. Intellectual Property, Mary Anne Stets; Dir. Security & Administrative Svcs., Mark Dulin; Vice Pres., Colls. Research & Dir. Library, Paul J. O'Pecko.

Institution Type/Description: Maritime History.
Hours & Admission Prices: Ships & Exhibits: see website for seasonal hours. Adults 18-64 $28.95, seniors 65 & over $26.95, youths 13-17 $24.95, children 3-12 $18.95; discounts to AAA members, military & students; tots 2 & under no charge. Closed Thanksgiving; Christmas Eve & Day.
Attendance: 259,000 (actual)

Naugatuck

NAUGATUCK HISTORICAL SOCIETY, 195 Water St., Naugatuck, CT 06770-2826. Mailing Address: P.O. Box 317, Naugatuck, CT 06770-0317. Tel.: 203-729-9039.
E-mail: naugatuckhistory@sbcglobal.net
Web Site: www.naugatuckhistory.com
Key Personnel: Pres. (V), Ken Hanks; Museum Shop Mgr., Mary Doback.
Institution Type/Description: Historical Society Museum: housed an historic railroad station.
Hours & Admission Prices: Wed.-Fri. 12-4, 1st Thurs. each month 12-4 & 6-8, Sat. 10-2; other times by appointment. Adults $2, children & student $1.50; active military & their families and members no charge.
Attendance: 1,500 (estimated)

New Britain

CENTRAL CONNECTICUT STATE UNIVERSITY ART GALLERIES, University Galleries, Maloney Hall, S.T. Chen Fine Arts Center, 1615 Stanley St., New Britain, CT 06050-2439. Tel.: 860-832-2620 & 2633. Fax: 860-832-2634.
E-mail: rodiamond2@yahoo.com
Web Site: www.art.ccsu.edu/gallery.html
Formerly: Museum of Central Connecticut State University
Key Personnel: Co Dir., Sean Gallagher; Co Dir., Mark Strathy.
Institution Type/Description: Art Museum.
Hours & Admission Prices: Mon.-Fri. 1-4. No charge; donations accepted.
Attendance: 3,000 (estimated)

COPERNICAN OBSERVATORY & PLANETARIUM, 1615 Stanley St., Central CT State University, New Britain, CT 06053. Tel.: 860-832-3399.
E-mail: larsen@ccsu.edu
Web Site: web.ccsu.edu/astronomy
Institution Type/Description: Planetarium.
Hours & Admission Prices: Shows: Fri.-Sat. 8:30 pm. Children's Shows: Fri. 7 pm, Sat. 1:30. No charge. Closed state holidays.

NEW BRITAIN INDUSTRIAL MUSEUM, 59 W. Main St., New Britain, CT 06051. Tel.: 860-832-8654. Facebook, Twitter.
E-mail: newbritainim@gmail.com
Web Site: nbindustrial.org
Key Personnel: Chm., Randall Judd.
Institution Type/Description: Industrial Museum.
Hours & Admission Prices: Wed. 12-4, Thurs.-Fri. 2-4, Sat. 10-4. No charge; donations accepted.
Attendance: 1,200 (actual)

NEW BRITAIN MUSEUM OF AMERICAN ART, 56 Lexington St., New Britain, CT 06052-1412. Tel.: 860-229-0257. Fax: 860-229-3445.
E-mail: nbmaa@nbmaa.org
Web Site: www.nbmaa.org
Key Personnel: Chm. (V), John N. Howard; Dir. & C.E.O., Min Jung Kim; Dir. Finance, Thomas Bell; Dir. Education, Cynthia Cormier; Devel. Assoc., Jenna Lucas; Mgr. Facilities & Security, Paul Grzyb; Collections Mgr., Keith Gervase; Mktg. & Design Mgr., Melissa Nardiello; Sr. Mgr., Visitor Experience Programs, Jeffrey Mainville; Museum Shop Mgr., Laura Van Dine.
Institution Type/Description: Art Museum.
Hours & Admission Prices: Sun., Tues.-Wed. & Fri. 11-5, Thurs. 11-8, Sat. 10-5. Adults $15, seniors $12, youth 13-17 & students $10; discounts to AAM & ICOM members; members, children under 12, & Sat. 10 to noon no charge. Closed New Year's Day; Independence Day; Thanksgiving & day after; Christmas.
Attendance: 75,459 (actual)

NEW BRITAIN PUBLIC LIBRARY - LOCAL HISTORY ROOM, 20 High St., New Britain, CT 06051. Tel.: 860-224-3155, ext. 125.
E-mail: nbpllhr@nbpl.info
Web Site: www.nbpl.info/localhistory.html
Institution Type/Description: Local History Library.

Hours & Admission Prices: Mon. & Wed. 9-2, Tues. & Thurs. 2-4, Fri.-Sat. by appointment.

NEW BRITAIN YOUTH MUSEUM, 30 High St., New Britain, CT 06051-4227. Tel.: 860-225-3020. Fax: 860-229-4982.
E-mail: nbymdwtn@sbcglobal.net
Web Site: www.newbritainyouthmuseum.org
Key Personnel: Acting Dir., Ann F. Peabody; Chm. Bd., Christopher LaSaracina; Programs & Education, Lisette Velasquez; Mktg. & Special Events, Donna M. Veach.
Institution Type/Description: Children's Museum & Nature Center.
Hours & Admission Prices: Museum: Fall/Winter/Spring: Tues.-Sat. 10:30-4:30; Summer: Mon.-Fri. 10-4. Admission: $2. New Britain Youth Museum, Hungerford Park: Tues.-Sat. 10-5. Adults $2; children under 2 no charge. Closed federal & state holidays. ठ
Attendance: 42,850 (actual)

New Canaan

NEW CANAAN HISTORICAL SOCIETY, 13 Oenoke Ridge, New Canaan, CT 06840-4195. Tel.: 203-966-1776. Fax: 203-972-5917.
E-mail: info@nchistory.org
Web Site: www.nchistory.org
Key Personnel: Exec. Dir., Nancy Geary; Pres. (V), Mark Markiewitz; Librarian Archivist, Micheal Murphy; Asst. Dir., Donna Dearth.
Institution Type/Description: History Museum.
Hours & Admission Prices: Library: Tues.-Fri. 9:30-4:30, Sat. 9:30-12:30. Museums: call for hours. Donations Requested: $5 per person. Closed Easter; Memorial Day; Independence Day; Thanksgiving; Christmas. ठ
Attendance: 5,000 (estimated)

NEW CANAAN NATURE CENTER, 144 Oenoke Ridge, New Canaan, CT 06840-4198. Tel.: 203-966-9577. Fax: 203-966-6536.
Web Site: www.newcanaannature.org
Key Personnel: Exec. Dir., Laura Heckman.
Institution Type/Description: Nature Center.
Hours & Admission Prices: Grounds: daily dawn to dusk. Visitor Center: Mon.-Sat. 9-4. No charge; donation accepted. Closed major holidays. ठ
Attendance: 70,000 (estimated)

PHILIP JOHNSON GLASS HOUSE, Visitor Center, 199 Elm St., New Canaan, CT 06840-5328. Tel.: 203-594-9884.
E-mail: contact@theglasshouse.org
Web Site: theglasshouse.org
Key Personnel: Cur. & Collections Mgr., Irene Shum Allen.
Institution Type/Description: Architecture Museum.
Hours & Admission Prices: Tours: April-Oct. 10:30 & 2:30 by appointment. Admission 10 & over $30-$45; not recommended for children under 10.

SILVERMINE ARTS CENTER, 1037 Silvermine Rd., New Canaan, CT 06840-4398. Tel.: 203-966-9700. Fax: 203-966-2763.
E-mail: silvermine@silvermineart.org
Web Site: www.silvermineart.org
Formerly: Silvermine Guild Arts Center
Key Personnel: Gallery Dir., Roger Mudre; Chm. (V), Rose-Marie Fox; Dir. Operations, Barbara Linarducci; Dir. Silvermine School of Art, Anne Connell.
Institution Type/Description: Contemporary Art Gallery.
Hours & Admission Prices: Mon.-Thurs. & Sat. 12-5, Sun. 1-5. No charge; donations accepted. Closed New Year's Day; Easter; Independence Day; Thanksgiving; Christmas. ठ
Attendance: 12,000 (estimated)

New Hartford

NEW HARTFORD HISTORICAL SOCIETY, 537 Main St., New Hartford, CT 06057. Mailing Address: P.O. Box 41, New Hartford, CT 06057-0041. Tel.: 860-379-6894.
E-mail: newhartfordhistory@att.net
Web Site: www.newhartfordcthistory.org
Key Personnel: Chm. (V) & Pres. (V), Patrick Casey.
Institution Type/Description: Historical Society Museum.
Hours & Admission Prices: Wed. 7pm-9pm by appointment. No charge; donations accepted.
Attendance: 100 (estimated)

New Haven

BEINECKE RARE BOOK & MANUSCRIPT LIBRARY, 121 Wall St., New Haven, CT 06511. Tel.: 203-432-2977. Fax: 203-432-4047.

E-mail: beinecke.library@yale.edu
Web Site: beinecke.library.yale.edu
Institution Type/Description: Library.
Hours & Admission Prices: By appointment.

CONNECTICUT CHILDREN'S MUSEUM, 22 Wall St., New Haven, CT 06511-6528. Tel.: 203-562-5437. Fax: 203-787-9414.
E-mail: info@childrensbuilding.org
Web Site: childrensbuilding.org
Key Personnel: Dir., Sandra Malmquist.
Institution Type/Description: Children's Museum.
Hours & Admission Prices: Educational Field Trips: Tues.-Thurs. by appointment. General Public: Fri.-Sat. 12-5. Admission $7.50. ठ

CONNECTICUT WOMEN'S HALL OF FAME, Schwarts Hall, Southern Connecticut State Univ., 320 Fitch St., New Haven, CT 06515. Tel.: 203-392-9007. Fax: 203-392-9012.
E-mail: kathryn@cwhf.org
Web Site: www.cwhf.org
Key Personnel: Exec. Dir., Kathryn Gloor.
Institution Type/Description: Hall of Fame.
Hours & Admission Prices: Call for hours.

ETHNIC HERITAGE CENTER, Southern Connecticut State Univ., 270 Fitch St., New Haven, CT 06515. Tel.: 203-392-6126. Fax: 203-392-5140.
E-mail: ethnicheritagecenter270@yahoo.com
Web Site: ethnicheritagecenter.org
Institution Type/Description: History Museum.
Hours & Admission Prices: Tues.-Thurs. 9-3, Fri. 9-12, Sun. 2-4.

HARVEY CUSHING/JOHN HAY WHITNEY MEDICAL LIBRARY, HISTORICAL LIBRARY, 333 Cedar St., New Haven, CT 06510-3206. Mailing Address: P.O. Box 208014, New Haven, CT 06520-8014. Tel.: 203-737-5352. Fax: 203-785-5636.
E-mail: askyalemedicallibrary@yale.edu
Web Site: www.med.yale.edu/library/historical/
Key Personnel: Dir., John Gallagher.
Institution Type/Description: Medical Library.
Hours & Admission Prices: Library Public Hours: Mon.-Fri. 10am to noon & 1-4:30; call for additional hours. No charge. Closed New Year's Day; Independence Day; Thanksgiving; Christmas. ठ

JEWISH HISTORICAL SOCIETY OF GREATER NEW HAVEN, INC., Southern Connecticut State Univ., Ethnic Heritage Center, 270 Fitch St., New Haven, CT 06515. Mailing Address: P. O. Box 3251, New Haven, CT 06515. Tel.: 203-392-6125. Fax: 203-392-5140.
E-mail: jhsgnh@yahoo.com
Web Site: jhsgnh.org
Key Personnel: Pres., Robert Pierce Forbes.
Institution Type/Description: Jewish History Museum.
Hours & Admission Prices: Mon.-Fri. 8:30 to noon; other times by appointment. No charge; donations accepted. ठ

KNIGHTS OF COLUMBUS MUSEUM, One State St., New Haven, CT 06511-6702. Tel.: 203-865-0400 & 0320. Fax: 203-865-0351.
E-mail: kathy.cogan@kofc.org
Web Site: www.kofcmuseum.org
Key Personnel: Supreme Knight & C.E.O., Carl A. Anderson; Dir., Kathy Cogan; Cur. & Registrar, Bethany Sheffer; Archivist, VivianLea Solek; Dir. Education, Outreach & Visitor Svcs., Peter Sonski; Museum Shop Mgr., Olga Lapaeva; Administrative Asst., Erica Ruzbarsky.
Institution Type/Description: History Museum; Catholic Fraternal Society.
Hours & Admission Prices: Daily 10-5; groups by appointment. No charge; donations accepted. Closed Good Friday; Thanksgiving; Christmas Eve & Day. ठ
Attendance: 25,000 (actual)

NEW HAVEN MUSEUM, 114 Whitney Ave., New Haven, CT 06510-1238. Tel.: 203-562-4183. Fax: 203-562-2002. Facebook: New Haven Museum.
E-mail: info@newhavenmuseum.org
Web Site: www.newhavenmuseum.org
Formerly: New Haven Museum & Historical Society
Key Personnel: Exec. Dir., Margaret Anne Tockarshewsky.
Institution Type/Description: History Museum.
Hours & Admission Prices: Tues.-Fri. 10-5, Sat. 12-5. Adults $4, senior citizens $3, students 6-17 $2; discounts to NEMA & AAM members; AAA with coupon,

children under 12 & members no charge. Closed New Year's Day; Martin Luther King Day; Presidents' Day; Memorial Day; Independence Day; Labor Day; Thanksgiving; Christmas. &
Attendance: 10,000 (estimated)

PARDEE-MORRIS HOUSE, 325 Lighthouse Rd., New Haven, CT 06512. Mailing Address: 114 Whitney Ave., New Haven, CT 06510. Tel.: 203-562-4183. Fax: 203-562-2002. Facebook: New Haven Museum.
E-mail: info@newhavenmuseum.org
Web Site: newhavenmuseum.org
Institution Type/Description: Historic House: housed in the former farmhouse of Amos Morris.
Hours & Admission Prices: June-Aug. Sun. 12-4; call for additional hours for special programs. No charge; donations accepted.
Attendance: 1,000 (actual)

PEABODY MUSEUM OF NATURAL HISTORY, Yale University, 170 Whitney Ave., New Haven, CT 06511-8118. Mailing Address: P.O. Box 208118, New Haven, CT 06520-8118. Tel.: 203-432-3738. Fax: 203-432-6575. Facebook.
E-mail: peabody.director@yale.edu
Web Site: www.peabody.yale.edu
Key Personnel: Dir., David Skelly; Chief of Staff, Susan Rodrigues; Dir. Collections & Research, Tim White; Asst. Dir. Devel., Christopher Renton; Dir. Finance & Admin., Jonathan Rohner; Dir. Student Programs, David Heiser; Dir. Public Programs, Chris Norris; Dir. Devel., Monty Shepardson; Project Dir., Carol DeNatale.
Institution Type/Description: University Natural History Museum.
Hours & Admission Prices: Tues.-Sat. 10-5, Sun. 12-5. Adults $10, senior citizens 65 & over $8, children 3-18, discounts to Blue Star Museum members Memorial Day to Labor Day, Friends of Museum Associates, and AAM, ASTC & ICOM members; members, children under 3, and Yale Univ. faculty & students w/ID no charge. Closed New Year's Day; Easter; Independence Day; Thanksgiving; Christmas Eve & Day. &
Attendance: 130,000 (estimated)

WEST ROCK NATURE CENTER, 1080 Wintergreen Ave., New Haven, CT 06515. Mailing Address: c/o Dept. Parks, Recreation & Trees, 720 Edgewood Ave., New Haven, CT 06515. Tel.: 203-946-6559.
E-mail: jmilone@newhavenct.gov
Web Site: www.newhavenct.gov/gov/depts/parks/our_parks/west_rock.htm
Key Personnel: Ranger, Joe Milone; Outdoor Adventure Coord., Martin Torresquintero.
Institution Type/Description: Nature Center.
Hours & Admission Prices: Daily sunrise to sunset. No charge; donations accepted. Closed city holidays.
Attendance: 20,000 (estimated)

YALE CENTER FOR BRITISH ART, 1080 Chapel St., New Haven, CT 06510-2302. Mailing Address: P.O. Box 208280, New Haven, CT 06520-8280. Tel.: 203-432-2800, 877-BRIT-ART. Fax: 203-432-4538. Facebook, Twitter, Instagram.
E-mail: ycba.info@yale.edu
Web Site: britishart.yale.edu
Key Personnel: Dir., Amy Meyers; Deputy Dir., Constance Clement; Deputy Dir. Finance & Administration, Rebecca Sender; Deputy Dir. Advancement & External Affairs, Beth Miller; Deputy Dir. Collections, Scott Wilcox; Deputy Dir. Research, Exhibitions & Publications, and Cur. Sculpture, Martina Droth; Chief Cur. Art Collections, Matthew Hargraves; Sr. Curatorial Asst., Rare Books & Manuscripts, Laura Callery; Sr. Cur. Education, Linda Friedlaender; Asst. Museum Shop Mgr., Anissa Pellegrino; Head Conservator Works on Paper, Soyeon Choi; Sr. Assoc. Communications & Mktg., Ronnie Rysz; Head Exhibitions & Publications & Asst. Cur. Seventeenth Century Paintings, Nathan Flis; Chief Librarian, Kraig Binkowski; Chief Registrar, Corey Myers; Chief Conservator, Mark Aronson; C.O.O., Paul Harding; Security Chief, Albert Wise, Jr.; Special Events & Advancement Coord., Kristin Dwyer.
Institution Type/Description: Art Museum.
Hours & Admission Prices: Tues.-Sat. 10-5, Sun. 12-5. No charge. Closed New Year's Day; Independence Day; Thanksgiving; Christmas Eve & Day. &
Attendance: 86,000 (estimated)

YALE MARSH BOTANICAL GARDEN, 265 Mansfield St., New Haven, CT 06511. Tel.: 203-432-6320.
E-mail: michael.donoghue@yale.edu
Web Site: marshbotanicalgarden.yale.edu
Key Personnel: Dir., Michael Donoghue.
Institution Type/Description: Botanical Garden.

Hours & Admission Prices: Tours: Tues. & Thurs. 10am, 11am. & 2pm by appointment; call for additional hours. Greenhouses: Tues.-Fri. 9-5.

YALE UNIVERSITY ART GALLERY, 1111 Chapel St., New Haven, CT 06510-2300. Mailing Address: P.O. Box 208271, New Haven, CT 06520-8271. Tel.: 203-432-0600. Fax: 203-432-9523. Facebook; Twitter; Instagram; YouTube.
E-mail: artgalleryinfo@yale.edu
Web Site: artgallery.yale.edu
Key Personnel: Dir., Jock Reynolds.
Institution Type/Description: Art Museum.
Hours & Admission Prices: July-Aug. Tues.-Fri. 10-5, Sat.-Sun. 11-5; Sept.-June Tues.-Wed. & Fri. 10-5, Thurs. 10-8, Sat.-Sun. 11-5. No charge; donations accepted. Closed major holidays. &
Attendance: 221,000 (estimated)

YALE UNIVERSITY COLLECTION OF MUSICAL INSTRUMENTS, 15 Hillhouse Ave., New Haven, CT 06511-6823. Mailing Address: P.O. Box 208278, New Haven, CT 06520-8278. Tel.: 203-432-0822. Fax: 203-432-8342.
E-mail: musinst@yale.edu
Web Site: collection.yale.edu
Key Personnel: Dir., William Purvis; Cur., Susan E. Thompson.
Institution Type/Description: Musical Instruments Museum.
Hours & Admission Prices: Sept.-July Tues.-Fri. 1-4, Sun. 1-5. No charge; donations accepted. Closed university recesses, summer & national holidays.

New London

CONNECTICUT COLLEGE ARBORETUM, 270 Mohegan Ave., New London, CT 06320-4150. Mailing Address: Campus Box 5201, 270 Mohegan Ave., New London, CT 06320. Tel.: 860-439-5020 & 5060. Fax: 860-439-5482. Facebook, Instagram, Twitter.
E-mail: arbor@conncoll.edu
Web Site: arboretum.conncoll.edu
Key Personnel: Interim Dir., Maggie Redfern; Arboretum Horticulturist, Leigh S. Knuttel; Cur. & Information Resource Mgr., Mary Villa; Senior Groundsperson, Bryan Goulet; Groundsperson, Kraig Clark; Administrative Asst., Christine Donovan.
Institution Type/Description: Arboretum.
Hours & Admission Prices: Arboretum: daily dawn to dusk. Office: Mon.-Fri. 8:30-4:30. No charge.
Attendance: 12,000 (estimated)

GROTON MONUMENT AND MONUMENT HOUSE MUSEUM, Fort Griswold Battlefield State Park, 90 Walbach St., New London, CT 06320. Mailing Address: P.O. Box 7032, Groton, CT 06340. Tel.: 860-445-1729.
E-mail: info@fortgriswold.org
Web Site: fortgriswold.org
Institution Type/Description: History Museum.
Hours & Admission Prices: Memorial Day to Labor Day daily 9-5. No charge.

HEMPSTED HOUSES, 11 Hempstead St., New London, CT 06320. Tel.: 860-443-7949. Fax: 860-249-4907.
E-mail: hempsted@ctlandmarks.org
Web Site: www.ctlandmarks.org
Key Personnel: Dir., Sheryl Hack.
Institution Type/Description: Historic Houses.
Hours & Admission Prices: May-Oct. call for hours; groups by appointment. Adults $7, senior citizens, teachers, & students $6, children 6-18 $4; discount to families; children under 6 no charge.

LYMAN ALLYN ART MUSEUM, 625 Williams St., New London, CT 06320-4199. Tel.: 860-443-2545. Fax: 860-443-2060.
E-mail: info@lymanallyn.org
Web Site: www.lymanallyn.org
Key Personnel: Dir., Samuel Quigley.
Institution Type/Description: Art Museum.
Hours & Admission Prices: Tues.-Sat. 10-5, Sun. 1-5. Adults $10, seniors & students over 18 $7, students under 18 $5; members, children 12 & under and New London residents no charge. Closed major holidays. &
Attendance: 20,000 (actual)

NATHAN HALE SCHOOLHOUSE IN NEW LONDON, 19 Atlantic St., New London, CT 06320. Mailing Address: Connecticut SAR, P.O. Box 411, East Haddam, CT 06423. Tel.: 860-873-3399.

E-mail: info@connecticutsar.org
Web Site: www.connecticutsar.org
Institution Type/Description: Historic Building: housed in the former schoolhouse where Nathan Hale was schoolmaster from 1774-1775.
Hours & Admission Prices: May-Oct. Wed.-Sun. 11-4. No charge; donations accepted.
Attendance: 3,500 (actual)

NEW LONDON COUNTY HISTORICAL SOCIETY, 11 Blinman St., New London, CT 06320-5677. Tel.: 860-443-1209. Fax: 860-443-1209. Facebook.
E-mail: info@nlchs.org
Web Site: www.nlhistory.org
Key Personnel: Exec. Dir., Steve Manuel; Pres., Joseph J. Selinger.
Institution Type/Description: Historic House Museum: housed in the 1756 Shaw Mansion, used as Connecticut's Naval Office during the Revolution.
Hours & Admission Prices: Tours: Thurs. 1-4; other time by appointment. Research: by appointment only. Adults $5, senior citizens $4, children under 12 $2; discounts to AAM & NEMA members and groups of 10 or more; members no charge. Closed national holidays; Thanksgiving; Christmas. &
Attendance: 3,100 (estimated)

U.S. COAST GUARD MUSEUM, U.S. Coast Guard Academy, 78 Howard St., Ste. A, New London, CT 06320-4195. Tel.: 860-444-8511. Fax: 860-701-6700.
E-mail: info@coastguardmuseum.org
Web Site: www.coastguardmuseum.org
Institution Type/Description: Maritime Museum.
Hours & Admission Prices: early Jan. to May & Sept. to mid-Dec. Mon.-Fri. 9-4, Sat. 10-4, Sun. 1-4; Summer: Mon.-Fri. 9-4, 1st & 3rd Sat. 10-4. No charge; donations accepted. Government-issued photo identification needed to enter campus. Closed federal holidays; winter break. &
Attendance: 25,000 (actual)

New Milford

MOTHER EARTH GALLERY & MINING COMPANY, 499 Danbury Rd., New Milford, CT 06776-4359. Tel.: 203-775-6272. Fax: 203-775-5620.
E-mail: motherearthbrookfield@gmail.com
Web Site: www.motherearthcrystals.com
Institution Type/Description: Mining Museum.
Hours & Admission Prices: Mon. & Wed.-Sat. 10-6, Sun. 12-5. Closed New Year's Day; Thanksgiving; Christmas.
Attendance: 6,000

THE NEW MILFORD HISTORICAL SOCIETY AND MUSEUM, 6 Aspetuck Ave., New Milford, CT 06776. Mailing Address: P.O. Box 359, New Milford, CT 06776-0359. Tel.: 860-354-3069.
E-mail: nmhistorical@gmail.com
Web Site: www.nmhistorical.org
Key Personnel: Pres. Bd. Trustees (V), Justin Krul; Cur., Lisa D. Roush; Sec., Anita Regan.
Institution Type/Description: Historical Society Museum.
Hours & Admission Prices: Tues.-Fri. 12-3, Sat. 11-2; other times by appointment. Adults $5; discounts to students; members no charge. Closed legal holidays. &

Newington

AMERICAN RADIO RELAY LEAGUE, 225 Main St., Newington, CT 06111. Tel.: 860-594-0200. Fax: 860-594-0259.
E-mail: hq@arrl.org
Web Site: www.arrl.org
Institution Type/Description: Amateur Radio History.
Hours & Admission Prices: Mon.-Fri. 8-5; groups by appointment.

ENOCH KELSEY HOUSE, 1702 Main St., Newington, CT 06111-3938. Tel.: 860-667-0545.
E-mail: NGTNheritage@aol.com
Web Site: www.newingtonhistoricalsociety.org/index.htm
Key Personnel: Dir., Dorothy Abbott.
Institution Type/Description: Historic House Museum: home built by Enoch Kelsey & his son David, c.1799.
Hours & Admission Prices: April-Nov. 1st & 3rd Sun. of month 1-3. Closed holidays.

KELLOGG-EDDY HOUSE AND MUSEUM, 679 Willard Ave., Newington, CT 06111-2615. Tel.: 860-666-7118.

E-mail: NGTNheritage@aol.com
Web Site: www.newingtonhistoricalsociety.org/index.htm
Key Personnel: Exec. Dir., Dorothy Abbott.
Institution Type/Description: Historic House Museum: housed in the former home of General Martin Kellogg, built in 1808.
Hours & Admission Prices: April-Nov. 1st Sun. of month 1-3. Closed holidays.

Niantic

CHILDREN'S MUSEUM OF SOUTHEASTERN CONNECTICUT, 409 Main St., Niantic, CT 06357-3103. Tel.: 860-691-1111. Fax: 860-691-1194.
E-mail: pclaffey@childrensmuseumsect.org
Web Site: childrensmuseumsect.org
Key Personnel: Exec. Dir., Holly Cheeseman; Pres. (V), John Schweizer; Education Coord., Donna Dione; Mktg., Rita Rivera.
Institution Type/Description: Children's Museum.
Hours & Admission Prices: Tues.-Sat. 9:30-4:30, Sun. 12-4:30. Admission $8; discount to groups of 10 or more; members no charge. Closed Easter, Memorial Day, Independence Day, Labor Day, Thanksgiving, Christmas. &
Attendance: 40,000 (actual)

EAST LYME HISTORICAL SOCIETY/THOMAS LEE HOUSE, 228 W. Main St., Niantic, CT 06357. Mailing Address: P.O. Box 112, East Lyme, CT 06333-0112. Tel.: 860-739-9660. Fax: 860-444-6661.
E-mail: info@eastlymehistoricalsociety.org
Web Site: www.eastlymehistoricalsociety.org
Key Personnel: Pres., Norman B. Peck, III; Treas. & Museum Shop Mgr., Elizabeth Kuchta.
Institution Type/Description: Historical Society Museum.
Hours & Admission Prices: mid-June to Labor Day Wed.-Sun. 1-4; other times by appointment. No charge; donations accepted.
Attendance: 500 (estimated)

THOMAS AVERY HOUSE A/K/A SMITH-HARRIS HOUSE, 33 Society Rd., Niantic, CT 06357. Mailing Address: Friends of the Smith-Harris House, P.O. Box 6, Niantic, CT 06357. Tel.: 860-739-0761.
E-mail: curator@smithharris.org
Institution Type/Description: Historic House Museum: housed in the former home of early settlers, Christopher Avery and Nehemiah Smith; built in 1845.
Hours & Admission Prices: June-Aug. Fri.-Sun. 12-4; other times by appointment. No charge; donations accepted. Closed Independence Day.

Noank

NOANK HISTORICAL SOCIETY, INC., 17 Sylvan St., Noank, CT 06340-5742. Mailing Address: P.O. Box 9454, Noank, CT 06340-9454. Tel.: 860-536-3021 & 3029.
E-mail: noankhist@sbcglobal.net
Web Site: www.noankhistoricalsociety.org
Key Personnel: Pres., Deborah Bates; Cur., Mary Anderson; Historian, Arnold Crossman; Treas., Steven Anderson.
Institution Type/Description: History Museum: housed in c.1847 mercantile building.
Hours & Admission Prices: July to Columbus Day Wed. & Sat.-Sun. 2-5; other times by appointment. No charge; donations accepted.
Attendance: 1,000 (estimated)

Norfolk

NORFOLK HISTORICAL MUSEUM, 13 Village Green, Norfolk, CT 06058. Mailing Address: P.O. Box 288, Norfolk, CT 06058-0288. Tel.: 860-542-5761.
E-mail: info@norfolkhistoricalsociety.org
Web Site: www.norfolkhistoricalsociety.org
Key Personnel: Dir., Barry Webber; Cur., Ann Havemeyer.
Institution Type/Description: Historical Society Museum.
Hours & Admission Prices: June-Oct. 7 Sat.-Sun. 1-4; other times by appointment. No charge; donations accepted. &

North Canaan

DOUGLAS LIBRARY AND C.H. PEASE MUSEUM, 108 Main St., North Canaan, CT 06018. Tel.: 860-824-7863.
E-mail: douglaslibrary@comcast.net
Web Site: www.douglaslibrarycanaan.org/index.html
Institution Type/Description: Library & History Museum.
Hours & Admission Prices: Mon. 1:30-8, Wed. & Fri. 10-8, Sat. 10-1. No charge.

North Haven

NORTH HAVEN HISTORICAL SOCIETY, 27 Broadway, North Haven, CT 06473-2302. Tel.: 203-239-7722.
E-mail: nhhistsoc@gmail.com
Web Site: www.northhavenhistoricalsociety.wordpress.com
Key Personnel: Pres., Patricia Buonopane; Vice Pres., Ann Clark; Treas., Walter Brockett.
Institution Type/Description: History Museum.
Hours & Admission Prices: July-Aug. Thurs. 3-6; Sept.-June Tues. & Thurs. 3-6. Closed New Year's Eve & Day; Christmas Eve, Day & week.

North Stonington

NORTH STONINGTON HISTORICAL SOCIETY - STEPHEN MAIN HOMESTEAD, 1 Wyassup Rd., North Stonington, CT 06359-1322. Mailing Address: P.O. Box 134, North Stonington, CT 06359. Tel.: 860-535-9448.
E-mail: gchase1@comcast.net
Web Site: nostonhistoricalsociety.homestead.com
Key Personnel: Pres., Frank Eppinger; Contact Person, Gladys Chase.
Institution Type/Description: Historical Society Museum: house built in 1781.
Hours & Admission Prices: Tues. 2-4. No charge; donations accepted. &

Norwalk

ART GALLERY AT NORWALK COMMUNITY COLLEGE, 188 Richards Ave., Norwalk, CT 06854. Tel.: 203-857-7000.
Institution Type/Description: Art Gallery.
Hours & Admission Prices: Mon.-Thurs. 9-9, Fri. 9-4, Sat. 9-12. No charge. Closed holidays.

CENTER FOR CONTEMPORARY PRINTMAKING, Mathews Park, 299 West Ave., Norwalk, CT 06850-4002. Tel.: 203-899-7999. Fax: 203-899-7997.
E-mail: info@contemprints.org
Web Site: www.contemprints.org
Key Personnel: Interim Exec. Dir., Kimberly G. Henrikson.
Institution Type/Description: Printmaking Museum.
Hours & Admission Prices: Mon.-Sat. 9-5, Sun. 12-5. No charge; donations accepted. &
Attendance: 15,000 (estimated)

LOCKWOOD-MATHEWS MANSION MUSEUM, 295 West Ave., Norwalk, CT 06850-4002. Tel.: 203-838-9799. Fax: 203-838-1434.
E-mail: info@lockwoodmathewsmansion.com
Web Site: www.lockwoodmathewsmansion.com
Key Personnel: Exec. Dir., Susan Gilgore; Chm. (V), Patsy Brescia.
Institution Type/Description: Historic House Museum: c.1868 Elm Park Home.
Hours & Admission Prices: Guided Tours: early April to early Jan. Wed.-Sun. 12, 1, 2 & 3. Adults $10, senior citizens $8, students $6; discount to National Preservation Trust members; children under 8 & members no charge. Closed major holidays. &
Attendance: 23,000 (estimated)

THE MARITIME AQUARIUM AT NORWALK, 10 N. Water St., Norwalk, CT 06854-2228. Tel.: 203-852-0700, ext. 2248. Fax: 203-838-5416.
E-mail: marketing@maritimeaquarium.org
Web Site: www.maritimeaquarium.org
Institution Type/Description: Aquarium: housed in 19th-century iron works foundry.
Hours & Admission Prices: July to Labor Day daily 10-6; Sept.-June daily 10-5. Aquarium: adults $24.95, seniors 65 & over $22.95, youth 3-12 $17.95; children 3 & under & members no charge. Closed Thanksgiving; Christmas. &
Attendance: 500,000 (estimated)

NORWALK HISTORICAL SOCIETY, 141 E. Ave., Norwalk, CT 06851. Mailing Address: P.O. Box 1640, Norwalk, CT 06852. Tel.: 203-846-0525.
E-mail: info@norwalkhistoricalsociety.org
Web Site: norwalkhistoricalsociety.org
Institution Type/Description: Historical Society Museum.
Hours & Admission Prices: Wed.-Sat. 12-4.

SHEFFIELD ISLAND LIGHTHOUSE, Seaport Dock (Ferry Svc.), 10 N. Water St., Norwalk, CT 06854. Mailing Address: Norwalk Seaport Association, 132 Water St., 06854, CT 06854. Tel.: 203-838-9444. Fax: 203-855-1017.
E-mail: info@seaport.org
Web Site: seaport.org
Key Personnel: Pres., Vincent Scicchitano.
Institution Type/Description: Historic Lighthouse: housed on Sheffield Island; built in 1868.
Hours & Admission Prices: Ferry Service: May-Sept. call for schedule. Adults $22, seniors $20, children 4-12 $12, children 3 & under $5; discounts to AAM members.
Attendance: 5,000 (estimated)

SONO SWITCH TOWER MUSEUM, 77 Washington St., Norwalk, CT 06854-3086. Tel.: 203-246-6958.
E-mail: info@westctnrhs.org
Institution Type/Description: Historic Building: built in 1896.
Hours & Admission Prices: May-Oct. Sat.-Sun. 12-5. No charge; donations accepted.

STEPPING STONES MUSEUM FOR CHILDREN, 303 West Ave., Mathews Park, Norwalk, CT 06850-4002. Tel.: 203-899-0606, ext. 264. Fax: 203-899-0530. Facebook.
E-mail: info@steppingstonesmuseum.org
Web Site: www.steppingstonesmuseum.org
Key Personnel: C.E.O. & Pres., Rhonda Kiest; Dir. Strategic Initiatives, William E. Jeffries, III; Dir. Education, Kim Kuta Dring; Mktg. Mgr., Kathy Labieniec.
Institution Type/Description: Children's Museum.
Hours & Admission Prices: Sept.-May Tues.-Sun. 10-5; Memorial Day to Labor Day daily 10-5. Adults & children $15, seniors $10; members & children under 1 no charge. Closed New Year's Day; Easter; Thanksgiving; Christmas. &
Attendance: 235,000 (actual)

Norwich

FAITH TRUMBULL CHAPTER, DAUGHTERS OF THE AMERICAN REVOLUTION, INC., MUSEUM AND CHAPTER HOUSE, 42 Rockwell St., Norwich, CT 06360-3537. Tel.: 860-887-8737.
E-mail: website@ctdar.org
Key Personnel: Regent, Stephanie Davis; Cur., Marianne Vanden Bout.
Institution Type/Description: Historical Society Museum.
Hours & Admission Prices: Sat. 1-4; other times by appointment. No charge; donations accepted. Closed holidays.

THE LEFFINGWELL HOUSE MUSEUM, 348 Washington St., Norwich, CT 06360-2444. Mailing Address: Society of the Founders of Norwich, CT, Inc., P.O. Box 62, Norwich, CT 06360. Tel.: 860-889-9440.
E-mail: info@leffingwellhousemuseum.org
Web Site: www.leffingwellhousemuseum.org
Institution Type/Description: Historic House Museum: 1675-1715-1760 The Leffingwell Inn.
Hours & Admission Prices: April-Oct. Sat. 11-4. Adults $5, children under 12 & senior citizens $4; members no charge on regular tour days.
Attendance: 1,500 (estimated)

THE SLATER MEMORIAL MUSEUM - NORWICH FREE ACADEMY, 108 Crescent St., Norwich, CT 06360-3556. Tel.: 860-887-2506 & 425-5560. Fax: 860-885-0379.
E-mail: museum@nfaschool.org
Web Site: www.slatermuseum.org
Key Personnel: Dir., Vivian F. Zoe; Asst. Dir., Erika Williams; Admin. Asst., Sheena Emma.
Institution Type/Description: Art Museum: housed in an historic building designed by Worcester architect, Stephen Earle c.1886; located on the campus of the Norwich Free Academy.
Hours & Admission Prices: Tues.-Fri. 9-4, Sat.-Sun. 1-4. Adults $3, seniors & students $2; discounts to CT Art Trail, NEMA, AAM & ICOM members; members no charge. Closed holidays. &
Attendance: 12,000 (estimated)

Oakdale

GENIUS MUSEUM AT NATURE'S ART VILLAGE, 1650 Hartford New London Turnpike, Oakdale, CT 06370. Tel.: 860-443-4367. Fax: 860-443-0253. Facebook.
E-mail: info@naturesartvillage.com
Web Site: naturesartvillage.com
Formerly: The Dinosaur Place at Nature's Art

Institution Type/Description: History Museum.
Hours & Admission Prices: Call for hours & admissions. &

Old Lyme

FLORENCE GRISWOLD MUSEUM, 96 Lyme St., Old Lyme, CT 06371-1426. Tel.: 860-434-5542. Fax: 860-434-9778 (administrative offices). Facebook: Florence Griswold Museum.
E-mail: jeff@flogris.org
Web Site: www.florencegriswoldmuseum.org
Key Personnel: Dir., Rebekah Beaulieu, Ph.D.; Dir. Devel., Janie Stanley; Dir. Education & Outreach, David Rau; Museum Educator, Julie Riggs; Business Mgr., Therese Kus; Membership Coord., Nathaniel Green; Registrar, Nicole Wholean; Asst. to Dir., Donna Carlson; Cur., Amy Kurtz Lansing; Asst. Cur., Ben Colman; Dir. Mktg., Tammi Amaya Flynn; Dir. Finance, Fred Cote; Coord. Devel. Office, Sarah Layton; Visitor Svcs. Coord. & Museum Shop Mgr., Matt Greene; Mktg. Assoc., Cheryl Poirier.
Institution Type/Description: Art Museum.
Hours & Admission Prices: Tues.-Sat. 10-5, Sun. 1-5. Adults $10, seniors $9, students with ID $8; discounts to NEMA, AAA, ICOM & AAM members; children under 12 & members no charge. &
Attendance: 64,687 (actual)

Old Saybrook

GENERAL WILLIAM HART HOUSE, 350 Main St., Old Saybrook, CT 06475. Mailing Address: P.O. Box 4, Old Saybrook, CT 06475. Tel.: 860-395-1635 & 388-2622.
E-mail: contact@saybrookhistory.org
Institution Type/Description: Historic House Museum: built in 1767. Listed on the National Register of Historic Places.
Hours & Admission Prices: June-Aug. daily 1-4; other times by appointment.

Orange

PEZ VISITOR CENTER, 35 Prindle Hill Rd., Orange, CT 06477. Tel.: 203-298-0201. Facebook, Twitter, Instagram.
E-mail: jeff@pezcandyinc.com
Web Site: us.pez.com
Institution Type/Description: Candy Company Visitor Center.
Hours & Admission Prices: Mon.-Sat. 10-6, Sun. 12-5. Adults $5, seniors 60 & over and children 3-12 $4; discounts to groups; children under 3 no charge.

Plainville

PLAINVILLE HISTORICAL SOCIETY, 29 Pierce St., Plainville, CT 06062-2207. Tel.: 860-747-6577.
E-mail: membership@plainvillehistory.org
Institution Type/Description: Historical Society Museum.
Hours & Admission Prices: By appointment.

PLAINVILLE LIBRARY MUSEUM, 56 E. Main St., Plainville, CT 06062. Tel.: 860-793-1446 (Adult) 1450 (Children). Fax: 860-793-2241.
E-mail: dlord@libraryconnection.info
Web Site: www.ctmuseumquest.com
Key Personnel: Dir., Doug Lord.
Institution Type/Description: Library.
Hours & Admission Prices: July-Aug. Mon.-Wed. 10-9, Thurs 10-8, Fri. 10-5; Sept.-June Mon.-Wed. 10-9, Thurs. 10-8, Fri.-Sat. 10-5. No charge. &
Attendance: 125,754 (actual)

Pleasant Valley

THE PEOPLES STATE FOREST NATURE MUSEUM, Peoples State Forest, 106 E. River Rd., Barkhamsted, CT 06063. Mailing Address: P.O. Box 1, Pleasant Valley, CT 06063. Tel.: 860-379-2469.
E-mail: psfmuseum@gmail.com
Web Site: peoplesstateforestmuseum.org
Formerly: Stone Museum.
Key Personnel: Naturalist, Janet Bumstead.
Institution Type/Description: Historic Building: built in 1934.
Hours & Admission Prices: Memorial Day to June & Sept. to Columbus Day Sun.; July-Aug. Sat.-Sun.

Pomfret Center

CAS GRASSLAND BIRD CONSERVATION CENTER AT POMFRET, 218 Day Rd., Pomfret Center, CT 06259. Mailing Address: P.O. Box 11, Pomfret Center, CT 06259. Tel.: 860-928-4948.
E-mail: pomfret@ctaudubon.org
Key Personnel: Dir., Sarah Heminway.
Institution Type/Description: Bird Sanctuary.
Hours & Admission Prices: Center: Mon.-Fri. 9-4, Sat.-Sun. 12-4. Bafflin Sanctuary & Trail Wood Sanctuary: daily dawn to dusk.

Portland

RUTH CALLANDER HOUSE MUSEUM - THE PORTLAND HISTORICAL SOCIETY, 492 Main St., Portland, CT 06480-0098. Mailing Address: P.O. Box 98, Portland, CT 06480-0098.
E-mail: portlandhistsoc@yahoo.com
Web Site: portlandhistsoc.com
Institution Type/Description: Historical Society Museum: house built in 1715.
Hours & Admission Prices: Call for hours.

Ridgefield

THE ALDRICH CONTEMPORARY ART MUSEUM, 258 Main St., Ridgefield, CT 06877-4935. Tel.: 203-438-4519. Fax: 203-438-0198.
E-mail: general@aldrichart.org
Web Site: www.aldrichart.org
Key Personnel: Chm., Eric Diefenbach; Interim Co Dir., Richard Klein; Interim Co Dir., Tracy Moore.
Institution Type/Description: Contemporary Art Museum.
Hours & Admission Prices: Sun.-Mon. & Wed.-Fri. 12-5, Sat. 10-5. Adults $10, senior citizens and students 13 & over $5; discount to AAM members; children 12 & under, & members no charge. Closed New Year's Day; Thanksgiving; Christmas. &
Attendance: 33,000 (estimated)

KEELER TAVERN MUSEUM, 132 Main St., Ridgefield, CT 06877-4931. Tel.: 203-438-5485 & 431-0815. Fax: 203-438-9953.
E-mail: info@keelertavernmuseum.org
Key Personnel: Pres., Hilary Micalizzi; 1st Vice Pres., Rhonda Hill; Treas., M. Shen-Zhuang Chien; Exec. Dir., Hildegard Grob.
Institution Type/Description: Historic Building Museum.
Hours & Admission Prices: Feb.-Dec. Wed. & Sat.-Sun. 1-4; other times by appointment. Adults $8, senior citizens & children $5; members no charge. Closed New Year's Day; Easter; Memorial Day, Independence Day; Thanksgiving, Christmas.
Attendance: 10,000 (estimated)

RIDGEFIELD HISTORICAL SOCIETY, 4 Sunset Lane, Ridgefield, CT 06877-4643. Tel.: 203-438-5821.
E-mail: ridgefieldhistory@sbcglobal.net
Web Site: www.ridgefieldhistoricalsociety.org
Institution Type/Description: Historical Society Museum.
Hours & Admission Prices: Tues.-Thurs. 1-5; other times by appointment.

Riverton

GREENWOOD GLASS BLOWING STUDIO GALLERY & SCHOOL, 3 Robertsville Rd., Riverton, CT 06065. Mailing Address: P.O. Box 242, Riverton, CT 06065. Tel.: 860-738-9464.
E-mail: peter@petergreenwood.com
Web Site: www.petergreenwood.com
Institution Type/Description: Art Gallery: housed in historic Union Church; built in 1829.
Hours & Admission Prices: Tues.-Sat. 9-5 by appointment. No charge.
Attendance: 3,000 (estimated)

Rocky Hill

ACADEMY HALL MUSEUM OF THE ROCKY HILL HISTORICAL SOCIETY, INC., 785 Old Main St., Rocky Hill, CT 06067-1519. Mailing Address: P.O. Box 185, Rocky Hill, CT 06067-0185. Tel.: 860-563-6704. Fax: 860-563-6704.
E-mail: inforhhistory@gmail.com
Web Site: rhhistory.org
Key Personnel: Pres., Ed Chiucarello.
Institution Type/Description: History Museum: housed in 1803 schoolhouse.

Hours & Admission Prices: Tues. 10-12, Sat. 12:30-3; other times by appointment. No charge. &
Attendance: 340 (actual)

DINOSAUR STATE PARK, 400 West St., Rocky Hill, CT 06067-3506. Tel.: 860-529-5816. Fax: 860-257-1405.
E-mail: info@dinosaurstatepark.org
Web Site: www.ct.gov/deep/dinosaurstatepark
Key Personnel: Dir., Meg Enkler.
Institution Type/Description: State Park.
Hours & Admission Prices: Exhibit Center: Tues.-Sun. 9-4. Park: daily 9-4:30. Trails: daily 9-4. Exhibit Center: adults 13 & over $6; youth 6-12 $2; children 5 & under no charge. Closed New Year's Day; Thanksgiving; Christmas. &
Attendance: 53,000 (estimated)

Rowayton

ROWAYTON ARTS CENTER, 145 Rowayton Ave., Rowayton, CT 06853-1444. Tel.: 203-866-2744. Fax: 203-866-1123.
E-mail: rowart@snet.net
Web Site: www.rowaytonartscenter.org
Key Personnel: Pres., Steve Mernick; Dir. Education, Suzy Aubrey.
Institution Type/Description: Art Center.
Hours & Admission Prices: June-Aug. Tues.-Fri. 11-5, Sat.-Sun. 11-2; Sept.-May Tues.-Fri. 11-5, Sat. 11-2. No charge; donations accepted. Closed Thanksgiving; Christmas.
Attendance: 700 (estimated)

Scotland

D'ELIA ANTIQUE TOOL MUSEUM, 21 Brook Rd., Scotland, CT 06264. Mailing Address: P.O. Box 164, Scotland, CT 06264-0164. Tel.: 860-456-1516.
E-mail: info@deliatoolmuseum.com
Web Site: www.deliatoolmuseum.com
Institution Type/Description: Tool Museum.
Hours & Admission Prices: June-Aug. Sun. 10-3.

HUNTINGTON HOMESTEAD, 36 Huntington Rd., Scotland, CT 06264-2209. Mailing Address: P.O. Box 231, Scotland, CT 06264-0231. Tel.: 860-456-8381.
E-mail: info@huntingtonhomestead.org
Web Site: huntingtonhomestead.org
Institution Type/Description: Historic House: the birthplace of Samuel Huntington, a signer of the Declaration of Independence.
Hours & Admission Prices: May-Oct. 1st & 3rd Sat. each month 11-3. No charge; donations accepted.

Sharon

SHARON AUDUBON CENTER, 325 Cornwall Bridge Rd., Sharon, CT 06069-2512. Tel.: 860-364-0520. Fax: 860-364-5792.
E-mail: sheth@audubon.org
Web Site: www.audubon.org/local/sanctuary/sharon
Key Personnel: Dir., Eileen Fielding; Land Mgr., Mike Dudek; Mgr. Education Programs, Wendy Miller; Wildlife Rehabilitation & Outreach Coord., Sunny Kellner.
Institution Type/Description: Nature Center.
Hours & Admission Prices: Trails: dawn-dusk. Tues.-Sat. 9-5, Sun. 1-5. Adults $3, children under 12 & seniors $1.50; discounts to National Audubon Society members; members no charge. Closed holidays. &
Attendance: 10,000 (estimated)

SHARON HISTORICAL SOCIETY - GAY HOYT HOUSE, 18 Main St., Sharon, CT 06069-2052. Mailing Address: P.O. Box 511, Sharon, CT 06069-0511. Tel.: 860-364-5688. Facebook: Sharon Historical Society.
E-mail: director@sharonhist.org
Web Site: www.sharonhist.org
Key Personnel: Exec. Dir., Jennifer Owens; Treas., Allen Reiser; Cur., Marge Smith.
Institution Type/Description: Historical Society Museum: house built in 1775.
Hours & Admission Prices: Wed.-Fri. 12-4, Sat. 10-2; other times by appointment. No charge. Closed New Year's Day; Thanksgiving; Christmas Day & week. &
Attendance: 1,200 (estimated)

Shelton

SHELTON HISTORICAL SOCIETY, 70 Ripton Rd., Shelton, CT 06484. Mailing Address: P.O. Box 2155, Shelton, CT 06484. Tel.: 203-929-7963.
E-mail: sheltonhistoricalcenter@gmail.com
Web Site: www.sheltonhistoricalsociety.org
Formerly: Huntington Historical Society
Institution Type/Description: Historical Society Museum.
Hours & Admission Prices: Call for hours.
Attendance: 2,000 (estimated)

Sherman

THE SHERMAN HISTORICAL SOCIETY, INC. - NORTHROP HOUSE MUSEUM OF LOCAL HISTORY, 10 Rte. 37 Center, Sherman, CT 06784-1503. Tel.: 860-350-3475 (store) & 354-3083 (office). Facebook.
E-mail: office@shermanhistoricalsociety.org
Web Site: www.shermanhistoricalsociety.org
Key Personnel: Pres. (V), Sue Moga; Cur., Gloria Thorne; Museum Shop Mgr., Moira Kelly.
Institution Type/Description: Local History Museum: built in 1829.
Hours & Admission Prices: Museum & shop: April-Dec. Thurs.-Sun. 12-4. No charge; donations accepted. Closed holidays. &
Attendance: 2,500 (estimated)

Simsbury

SIMSBURY HISTORICAL SOCIETY, PHELPS TAVERN MUSEUM, 800 Hopmeadow St., Simsbury, CT 06070-1825. Mailing Address: P.O. Box 2, Simsbury, CT 06070-0002. Tel.: 860-658-2500. Fax: 860-651-4354.
E-mail: info@simsburyhistory.org
Web Site: www.simsburyhistory.org
Institution Type/Description: History Museum.
Hours & Admission Prices: Tours: Tues.-Sat. 12-4. Adults $6, senior citizens over 65 $5, children 6-17 $4; discount to groups & AAA members; members and children 5 & under no charge. Library & Archives: Thurs.-Sat. 12-4. Closed federal holidays.
Attendance: 3,800 (actual)

STRATTON BROOK STATE PARK NATURE CENTER, 149 Farms Village Rd., Simsbury, CT 06070. Mailing Address: c/o Penwood, 57 Gun Mill Rd., Bloomfield, CT 06002. Tel.: 860-651-1091.
E-mail: deep.stateparks@ct.gov
Institution Type/Description: Nature Center: built by the Civilian Conservation Corps in 1935. Listed on the National Register of Historic Places.
Hours & Admission Prices: Memorial Day to Labor Day Fri.-Mon. 10:30-4:30; Sept. to Columbus Day Sat.-Sun. 10:30-4:30. No charge.

Somers

SOMERS HISTORICAL SOCIETY MUSEUM, 11 Battle St., Somers, CT 06071. Mailing Address: P.O. Box 652, Somers, CT 06071. Tel.: 860-749-6437.
Institution Type/Description: Historical Society Museum: housed in the former public library; built in 1896.
Hours & Admission Prices: Call for hours. No charge; donations accepted.

South Glastonbury

WELLES SHIPMAN WARD HOUSE, 972 Main St., South Glastonbury, CT 06073. Mailing Address: P.O. Box 46, Glastonbury, CT 06033. Tel.: 860-633-6890.
E-mail: hsglastonbury@sbcglobal.net
Web Site: www.hsgct.org
Key Personnel: Dir., James Bennett.
Institution Type/Description: Historic House Museum: built c.1755.
Hours & Admission Prices: Summer: Tues. 1-4. Adults $5; members no charge.
Attendance: 3,000 (estimated)

South Windsor

SOUTH WINDSOR HISTORICAL SOCIETY, 771 Ellington Rd., Rte. 74, South Windsor, CT 06074. Mailing Address: P.O. Box 216, South Windsor, CT 06074-0216.
E-mail: rivard.brian071@gmail.com

Web Site: southwindsorhistory.org/wordpress
Institution Type/Description: Historical Society Museum.
Hours & Admission Prices: April-June & Sept.-Nov. 1st Sun. of month 1-4; July-Aug. Tues. & Thurs. 12-4, 1st Sun. of month 1-4. No charge; donations accepted.

WOOD MEMORIAL LIBRARY AND MUSEUM, 783 Main St., South Windsor, CT 06074. Mailing Address: P.O. Box 131, South Windsor, CT 06074. Tel.: 860-289-1783. Facebook: Wood Memorial Library Museum.
E-mail: director@woodmemoriallibrary.org
Web Site: www.woodmemoriallibrary.org
Key Personnel: Exec. Dir., Carolyn Venne; Dir. Communications, Jessica Vogelgesang.
Institution Type/Description: Library.
Hours & Admission Prices: Mon. 10-5, Thurs. 10-8, 2nd Sat. each month 10-1; other times by appointment. &

Southbury

AUDUBON CENTER AT BENT OF THE RIVER, 185 E. Flat Hill Rd., Southbury, CT 06488-1151. Tel.: 203-264-5098. Fax: 203-264-6332.
E-mail: bentoftheriver@audubon.org
Web Site: bentoftheriver.audubon.org
Key Personnel: Dir., Leslie Kane.
Institution Type/Description: Wildlife Sanctuary.
Hours & Admission Prices: Center: Mon.-Fri. 9-5. Trails: daily sunrise to sunset. No charge; donations accepted. &
Attendance: 5,600 (estimated)

Southington

THE BARNES MUSEUM, 85 N. Main St., Southington, CT 06489-2518. Tel.: 860-628-5426. Fax: 860-628-0488.
E-mail: secondom@southington.org
Web Site: barnesmuseum.wordpress.com
Key Personnel: Exec. Dir., Kristi Sadowski; Cur., Marie Secondo.
Institution Type/Description: History Museum.
Hours & Admission Prices: July-Aug. Mon.-Wed. & Fri. 1-5, Thurs. 1-7; late Sept. to June Mon.-Wed., Fri., 1st & last Sat. of month 1-5, Thurs. 1-7. Adults $8, seniors $6, students $4; children 5 & under no charge.
Attendance: 6,500 (actual)

Stafford Springs

AMERICAN MUSEUM OF AVIATION, 21 Clearview Dr., Stafford Springs, CT 06076. Tel.: 860-208-3095.
E-mail: info@AmericanMuseumofAviation.org
Web Site: www.americanmuseumofaviation.org
Formerly: Propliners of America
Key Personnel: Pres. (V) & Founder, William Bradshaw.
Institution Type/Description: Aviation History Museum.
Hours & Admission Prices: By appointment. No charge; donations accepted. &
Attendance: 420,000 (actual)

NORTHEAST STATES CIVILIAN CONSERVATION CORPS MUSEUM, 166 Chestnut Hill Rd., Stafford Springs, CT 06076-4007. Tel.: 860-684-3013.
E-mail: nescccmuseum@aol.com
Institution Type/Description: Historic House Museum: housed in the original Civilian Conservation Corps camp building; c.1935.
Hours & Admission Prices: By appointment. No charge. &

Stamford

BARTLETT ARBORETUM & GARDENS, 151 Brookdale Rd., Stamford, CT 06903-4199. Tel.: 203-883-4052; 322-6971.
E-mail: jvontrapp@bartlettarboretum.org
Web Site: bartlettarboretum.org
Formerly: Bartlett Arboretum, University of Connecticut
Key Personnel: C.E.O., Jane von Trapp; Chair (V), Polly O'Brien.
Institution Type/Description: Arboretum, Herbarium & Library.
Hours & Admission Prices: Grounds: daily dawn to dusk. Office: Mon.-Fri. 9-4. No charge; donations accepted.
Attendance: 20,000 (estimated)

MUSEUM OF BLACK WWII HISTORY, Stamford, CT 06906. Mailing Address: 71 Plymouth Rd., Stamford, CT 06906. Tel.: 203-348-6810.
E-mail: brucebird@blackww2museum.org
Key Personnel: Founder & Cur., Bruce Bird.
Institution Type/Description: History Museum.
Hours & Admission Prices: Feb. 5 to late Nov. Thurs.-Mon. 10-5; other times by appointment. Adults $5, veterans, seniors over 65 & students $3.
Attendance: 350 (estimated)

RICHARD AND HINDA ROSENTHAL GALLERY, Rich Forum, 307 Atlantic St., Stamford, CT 06901-3506. Mailing Address: 61 Atlantic St., Stamford, CT 06901-3506. Tel.: 203-358-2305.
Institution Type/Description: Art Gallery.
Hours & Admission Prices: Call for hours.

SACKLER ART GALLERY, Palace Theatre, 61 Atlantic St., Stamford, CT 06901-2403. Tel.: 203-358-2305.
E-mail: publicaffairsAsia@si.edu
Institution Type/Description: Art Gallery: housed in a former vaudeville theatre; built in 1927.
Hours & Admission Prices: Call for hours.

SOUNDWATERS COASTAL EDUCATION CENTER, Cove Island Park, 1281 Cove Rd., Stamford, CT 06902-5457. Tel.: 203-323-1978. Fax: 203-967-8306.
E-mail: connect@soundwaters.org
Key Personnel: Exec. Dir., Leigh Shemitz, Ph.D.
Institution Type/Description: Education Center.
Hours & Admission Prices: Memorial Day to Labor Day Tues.-Sat. 10-5. No charge.

STAMFORD HISTORICAL SOCIETY, INC., 1508 High Ridge Rd., Stamford, CT 06903-4107. Tel.: 203-329-1183. Fax: 203-322-1607. Facebook.
E-mail: administrator@stamfordhistory.org
Web Site: www.stamfordhistory.org
Key Personnel: Exec. Dir., Thomas Zoubek, Ph.D.; Chm. (V), Marshall Millsap.
Institution Type/Description: History & Decorative Arts Museum.
Hours & Admission Prices: Museum: Thurs.-Sat. 10-4. Hoyt-Barnum House: Thurs.-Fri. 11, 12, 1:30, 2:30, Sat. 1:30 & 2:30. Adults $5, members $2, children $1; discounts to AAM, ICOM & NEMA members. Closed New Year's Day; Thanksgiving; Christmas. &
Attendance: 10,000 (estimated)

STAMFORD MUSEUM & NATURE CENTER, 39 Scofieldtown Rd., Stamford, CT 06903-4096. Tel.: 203-322-1646. Fax: 203-322-0408. Facebook: @stamfordmuseum.
E-mail: info@stamfordmuseum.org
Web Site: www.stamfordmuseum.org
Key Personnel: Exec. Dir., Melissa H. Mulrooney; Dir. Finance, William King; Cur. Collections, Jillian Casey; Dir. Mktg., Susan Klein; Visitor Svcs., Sam Naring.
Institution Type/Description: General Museum.
Hours & Admission Prices: Mon.-Sat. & holidays 9-5, Sun. 11-5. Adults $10, senior citizens $8, students 18 & over $6, children 4-17 $5; children 3 & under and members no charge. Observatory: Summer: Fri. 8:30 pm-10:30 pm; Winter: Fri. 8 pm-10 pm. Adults $5, children $3. Closed New Year's Day; Independence Day; Thanksgiving; Christmas. &
Attendance: 200,000 (actual)

UKRAINIAN MUSEUM & LIBRARY, 161 Glenbrook Rd., Stamford, CT 06902-3002. Tel.: 203-323-8866. Fax: 203-357-7681.
E-mail: ukrmulrec@optonline.net
Web Site: ukrainianmuseumlibrary.org
Key Personnel: Dir., John M. Terlecky.
Institution Type/Description: Culturally Specific.
Hours & Admission Prices: Wed.-Fri. 1-5; other times by appointment. No charge; donations accepted. Closed major holidays. &
Attendance: 4,000 (estimated)

Stonington

CAPTAIN NATHANIEL B. PALMER HOUSE - HOME OF THE DISCOVERER OF ANTARCTICA AKA PINE POINT AND THE PALMER-LOPER HOUSE, 40 Palmer St.,

Stonington, CT 06378-1014. Mailing Address: The Stonington Historical Society, Inc., P.O. Box 103, Stonington, CT 06378. Tel.: 860-535-8445, ext. 10.
E-mail: director@stoningtonhistory.org
Web Site: www.stoningtonhistory.org/palmer
Key Personnel: Pres. Stonington Historical Society (V), Michael E. Schefers; Exec. Dir., Elizabeth Wood; Treas., Kirby Williams.
Institution Type/Description: History Museum.
Hours & Admission Prices: May-Oct. Fri.-Mon. 1-5. Palmer House & Old Lighthouse Museum: adults $10, seniors $8, students $6; members & children under 6 no charge.
Attendance: 3,500 (estimated)

OLD LIGHTHOUSE MUSEUM - STONINGTON HISTORICAL SOCIETY, 7 Water St., Stonington, CT 06378-1422. Mailing Address: P.O. Box 103, Stonington, CT 06378-0103. Tel.: 860-535-1440.
E-mail: director@stoningtonhistory.org
Web Site: www.stoningtonhistory.org
Formerly: Stonington Harbor Lighthouse
Key Personnel: Exec. Dir. Stonington Historical Society, Elizabeth Wood.
Institution Type/Description: Historic Site Museum.
Hours & Admission Prices: May-Nov. Thurs.-Tues. 10-5; other times by appointment. Adults $9; discounts to NEMA members; members no charge. Admission includes Capt. Palmer House.
Attendance: 8,500 (actual)

Storrs

THE BALLARD INSTITUTE & MUSEUM OF PUPPETRY, 1 Royce Cir., Ste. 101B, Storrs, CT 06268. Tel.: 860-486-8580.
E-mail: bimp@uconn.edu
Web Site: www.bimp.uconn.edu
Key Personnel: Dir., Dr. John Bell.
Institution Type/Description: Puppetry Museum.
Hours & Admission Prices: Tues.-Sun. 11-7. Suggested Donations: $5.

CONNECTICUT STATE MUSEUM OF NATURAL HISTORY AND CONNECTICUT ARCHAEOLOGY CENTER, University of Connecticut, Unit 4023, 2019 Hillside Rd., Storrs, CT 06269. Tel.: 860-486-4460. Fax: 860-486-0827.
E-mail: csmnhinfo@uconn.edu
Web Site: www.cac.uconn.edu
Key Personnel: Dir., Dr. Janine Caira; Assoc. Dir., Leanne Kennedy Harty; Coord. Public Information, David C. Colberg; Exhibits Planner, Collin Harty.
Institution Type/Description: Natural History Museum.
Hours & Admission Prices: Mon.-Fri. 10-4. No charge; donations accepted. Closed holidays.
Attendance: 90,000 (actual)

J. ROBERT DONNELLY HUSKY HERITAGE SPORTS MUSEUM, UConn Alumni Center, 2384 Alumni Dr., Unit-3053, Storrs, CT 06269. Tel.: 888-822-5861.
E-mail: ucaa@uconn.edu
Web Site: www.uconnhuskies.com/trads/museum.html
Formerly: Alumni Center - Husky Heritage Sports Museum
Key Personnel: Exec. Dir., Lisa Lewis; Center Mgr., Julie Sweeney.
Institution Type/Description: Sports Museum.
Hours & Admission Prices: Mon.-Fri. 8-5. No charge.

MANSFIELD HISTORICAL SOCIETY MUSEUM, 954 Storrs Rd., Storrs, CT 06268-2611. Mailing Address: P.O. Box 145, Storrs, CT 06268-0145. Tel.: 860-429-6575.
E-mail: mansfieldhistorical@snet.net
Web Site: mansfieldct-history.org
Key Personnel: Pres., David Landry; Dir., Ann Galonska; Treas., Anne Greineder.
Institution Type/Description: History Museum: housed in former Mansfield Town Office building & adjacent Town Hall c.1843.
Hours & Admission Prices: June-Sept. Sat.-Sun. 1:30-4:30.
Attendance: 1,000 (estimated)

UNIVERSITY OF CONNECTICUT ANIMAL BARNS, George White Bldg., Dept. of Animal Science, 3636 Horsebarn Hill Rd. Ext., Storrs, CT 06269-4040. Tel.: 860-486-2413.
Institution Type/Description: Animal Barns.
Hours & Admission Prices: Daily 10-4.

UNIVERSITY OF CONNECTICUT CONTEMPORARY ART GALLERIES, Art & Art History Bldg., 830 Bolton Rd., Storrs, CT 06269. Tel.: 860-486-3930.
E-mail: cag@uconn.edu
Web Site: contemporaryartgalleries.uconn.edu
Institution Type/Description: Art Gallery.
Hours & Admission Prices: Mon.-Fri. 10-4, Sun. 1-4. Closed holidays & academic breaks.

THE WILLIAM BENTON MUSEUM OF ART, University of Connecticut, 245 Glenbrook Rd. U-3140, Storrs, CT 06269-3140. Tel.: 860-486-4520. Fax: 860-486-0234. Facebook: Benton Museum.
E-mail: karen.somer@uconn.edu
Web Site: www.benton.uconn.edu
Key Personnel: Exec. Dir., Nancy Stula; Operations & Programs, Karen Sommer; Preparator, Kerry Smith; Visitor Svcs. Coord., Samantha Smith.
Institution Type/Description: Art Museum.
Hours & Admission Prices: Tues.-Fri. 10-4:30, Sat.-Sun. 1-4:30. No charge; donations accepted. Closed between some exhibitions; national holidays.
Attendance: 38,000 (estimated)

Stratford

BOOTHE MEMORIAL PARK AND MUSEUM, 5800 Main St. - Putney, Stratford, CT 06614. Mailing Address: P.O. Box 902, Stratford, CT 06615-0902. Tel.: 203-381-2046.
E-mail: friendsofboothe@yahoo.com
Web Site: boothememorialpark.org
Key Personnel: Dir. Friends of Boothe Park, Bessie Burton; CEO & Pres. (V), Dr. Virginia Harris.
Institution Type/Description: Americana.
Hours & Admission Prices: Museum: June-Oct. 1 Tues.-Fri. 11-1, Sat.-Sun. 1-4. Grounds: daily. No charge; donations accepted.
Attendance: 10,000 (estimated)

MERRITT PARKWAY MUSEUM, Ryder's Landing Shopping Ctr., 6580 Main St., Stratford, CT 06614-1605. Mailing Address: Merritt Parkway Conservancy, P.O. Box 17072, Stamford, CT 06907. Tel.: 203-661-3255.
E-mail: jill@merrittparkway.org
Web Site: merrittparkway.org/pages/project_mp_museum.asp#
Institution Type/Description: History Museum.
Hours & Admission Prices: Mon.-Fri. 9-5.

NATIONAL HELICOPTER MUSEUM, INC., 2480 Main St., Stratford, CT 06615-5940. Mailing Address: P.O. Box 775, Stratford, CT 06615-0775. Tel.: 203-375-8857.
E-mail: raymond.jankowich@gmail.com
Web Site: www.nationalhelicoptermuseum.org
Key Personnel: Dir., Raymond E. Jankowich, M.D.; Pres. (V), Ken Pike; Chm. (V) & Museum Shop Mgr., Gale Whittemore.
Institution Type/Description: Helicopter Museum.
Hours & Admission Prices: Memorial Day to mid-Oct. Wed.-Sun. 1-4. No charge; donations accepted.
Attendance: 1,400 (actual)

PERRY HOUSE VISITORS CENTER, 1128 W. Broad St., Stratford, CT 06615. Tel.: 203-377-3779. Fax: 203-386-0035. Facebook.
E-mail: info@perryhousestratford.org
Web Site: perryhousestratford.org
Institution Type/Description: Historic House: built c.1690.
Hours & Admission Prices: Mon.-Tues. 9:30-3, Thurs. & Sat. 9-12. No charge.

THE STRATFORD HISTORICAL SOCIETY & CATHARINE B. MITCHELL MUSEUM, 967 Academy Hill, Stratford, CT 06615-0382. Mailing Address: P.O. Box 382, Stratford, CT 06615-0382. Tel.: 203-378-0630. Fax: 203-378-2562.
E-mail: judsonhousestfd@aol.com
Web Site: www.stratfordhistoricalsociety.org
Key Personnel: Cur., Carol Lovell; Archivist, Gloria Duggan.
Institution Type/Description: Historical Society Museum: housed in 1750 Capt. David Judson Home, located on the original common of 1639.
Hours & Admission Prices: June-Oct. Sun. 12-4. Adults $7, seniors $5, student $3; members & children under 5 no charge.
Attendance: 1,000 (estimated)

Suffield

THE KING HOUSE MUSEUM, 232 S. Main St., Suffield, CT 06078. Mailing Address: P.O. Box 893, Suffield, CT 06078-0893. Tel.: 860-668-5256.
Web Site: www.suffieldhistoricalsociety.org/kinghouse.htm
Key Personnel: Pres. (V), Edward W. Chase, III; Cur., Lester Smith.
Institution Type/Description: Historic House Museum: built in 1764.
Hours & Admission Prices: May-Sept. Wed. & Sat. 1-4; other times by appointment. No charge; donations accepted.
Attendance: 600 (estimated)

PHELPS-HATHEWAY HOUSE, 55 S. Main St., Suffield, CT 06078. Tel.: 860-668-0055. Fax: 860-249-4907.
E-mail: phelps.hatheway@ctlandmarks.org
Web Site: www.ctlandmarks.org
Key Personnel: Dir., Sheryl Hack.
Institution Type/Description: Historic House Museum.
Hours & Admission Prices: mid-May to mid-Oct. call for hours; groups by appointment. Adults $10; senior citizens, teachers & students $8, children 6-18 $5; discounts to groups; members & children under 6 no charge.

Terryville

LOCK MUSEUM OF AMERICA, INC., 230 Main St., Rte. 6, Terryville, CT 06786-5900. Mailing Address: P.O. Box 104, Terryville, CT 06786-0104. Tel.: 860-589-6359. Fax: 860-589-6359 (call first).
E-mail: tlockmuseum@gmail.com
Web Site: www.lockmuseum.com/
Key Personnel: Pres. & Asst. Cur., Thomas Hennessy, Jr.; Sec. & Librarian, Reggie Murawski.
Institution Type/Description: Lock Museum: located on the site of the original offices of the Eagle Lock Co., built in 1859.
Hours & Admission Prices: May-Oct. Tues.-Fri. 1:30-4:30; other times by appointment. Admission $4.
Attendance: 1,000 (estimated)

Thomaston

RAILROAD MUSEUM OF NEW ENGLAND, 242 E. Main St., Thomaston, CT 06787-0400. Mailing Address: P.O. Box 400, Thomaston, CT 06787-0400. Tel.: 860-283-7245. Fax: 860-283-7245.
E-mail: info@rmne.org
Web Site: www.rmne.org
Key Personnel: Pres., Celeste Echlin.
Institution Type/Description: History Museum: housed in the New England Thomaston Station; built in 1881.
Hours & Admission Prices: Train Rides: see website for schedule.

Thompson

THOMPSON MUSEUM AT THE ELLEN LARNED MEMORIAL BUILDING, Historic Thompson Common, Rte. 193, Thompson, CT 06277. Mailing Address: P.O. Box 47, Thompson, CT 06277. Tel.: 860-923-3776.
E-mail: jiamartino@charter.net
Web Site: www.thompsonhistorical.org
Institution Type/Description: Historical Society Museum; housed in a former library building; built in 1902.
Hours & Admission Prices: May-June & Sept.-Nov. 1st Sat. each month 11-2; other times by appointment. No charge; donations accepted.
Attendance: 350 (estimated)

Tolland

DANIEL BENTON HOMESTEAD, Metcalf Rd., Tolland, CT 06084. Mailing Address: P.O. Box 107, Tolland, CT 06084-0107. Tel.: 860-974-1875.
E-mail: tolland.historical@snet.net
Web Site: www.tollandhistorical.org/danielbentonhomestead
Key Personnel: Museum Dir., Gail W. White.
Institution Type/Description: Historic Building: 1720 house.
Hours & Admission Prices: mid July to Oct. Sun. 1-4; other times by appointment. Donation $2. Closed Labor Day.

HICKS-STEARNS FAMILY MUSEUM, 42 Tolland Green, Tolland, CT 06084-3042. Mailing Address: P.O. Box 278, Tolland, CT 06084. Tel.: 860-875-7552.
Key Personnel: Co Dir., Beatrice White-Ramirez; Co Dir., Teresa A. Gerry.
Institution Type/Description: Historic House Museum.
Hours & Admission Prices: mid-May to mid-Oct. Sun. & Wed. 1-4; other times by appointment. No charge; donations accepted.

OLD TOLLAND COUNTY COURT HOUSE, 53 Tolland Green, Tolland, CT 06084. Mailing Address: P.O. Box 107, Tolland, CT 06084-0107. Tel.: 860-870-9599. Fax: 860-870-4689.
E-mail: society@tollandhistorical.org
Web Site: www.tollandhistorical.org
Key Personnel: Dir., Ni-Ni Reinard.
Institution Type/Description: Historic Building: built in 1822.
Hours & Admission Prices: May-Oct. Call for hours.

TOLLAND HISTORICAL SOCIETY - OLD TOLLAND COUNTY JAIL & MUSEUM, 52 Tolland Green, Tolland, CT 06084. Mailing Address: P.O. Box 107, Tolland, CT 06084-0107. Tel.: 860-870-9599. Fax: 860-870-4689.
E-mail: society@tollandhistorical.org
Web Site: www.tollandhistorical.org
Key Personnel: Dir. & Pres., Kathy Bach.
Institution Type/Description: Historic Society Museum: housed in old jail cell block & jailer's home.
Hours & Admission Prices: June-Sept. Sun. 1-4; other times by appointment. No charge; donations accepted.
Attendance: 3,030 (actual)

Torrington

ARTWELL GALLERY, 504 Essex Ct., Torrington, CT 06790-2864. Tel.: 860-805-5898. Fax: 860-492-5122.
E-mail: artwell@sbcglobal.net
Web Site: artwellgallery.org
Key Personnel: Exec. Dir., Michael Yurgeles.
Institution Type/Description: Art Gallery.
Hours & Admission Prices: Wed.-Sat. 12-5. No charge; donations accepted.
Attendance: 3,000 (estimated)

KIDSPLAY CHILDREN'S MUSEUM, 61 Main St., Torrington, CT 06790. Tel.: 860-618-7700. Facebook: KidsPlay Museum.
E-mail: info@kidsplaymuseum.org
Web Site: www.kidsplaymuseum.org
Key Personnel: Dir., Eileen Marriott.
Institution Type/Description: Children's Museum.
Hours & Admission Prices: Wed.-Sat. 10-4. Admission $6; discounts to ACM members; children under one no charge.

TORRINGTON HISTORICAL SOCIETY, INC., 192 Main St., Torrington, CT 06790-5201. Tel.: 860-482-8260.
E-mail: torringtonhistorical@snet.net
Web Site: www.torringtonhistoricalsociety.org
Key Personnel: Exec. Dir., Mark McEachern; Pres. (V), David R. Bennett; Cur., Gail Kruppa; Archivist, Carol Clapp.
Institution Type/Description: Local History Museum.
Hours & Admission Prices: House & History Museum: April 15-Oct. Tues.-Sat. 12-4. Library: Tues.-Fri. 1-4. House Museum: adults $5. History Museum: adults $2; discounts to AAM members; members no charge. Closed legal holidays.
Attendance: 4,500 (estimated)

Trumbull

TRUMBULL HISTORICAL SOCIETY MUSEUM AND RESEARCH LIBRARY, 1856 Huntington Tpke., Trumbull, CT 06611. Mailing Address: P.O. Box 312, Trumbull, CT 06611-0312. Tel.: 203-377-6620. Facebook.
E-mail: trumbullhistory@gmail.com
Web Site: trumbullhistory.org
Institution Type/Description: Historical Society Museum & Library.
Hours & Admission Prices: 1st & 3rd Sun. of month 2-4. No charge; donations accepted.

TRUMBULL NATURE & ARTS CENTER, 7115 Main St., Rte. 25, Trumbull, CT 06611. Mailing Address: Patrons of TNAC, Inc., P.O. Box 110438, Trumbull, CT 06611-0438. Tel.: 203-452-4421.
E-mail: info@trumbullnatureandartscenter.org
Institution Type/Description: Nature Center.

Hours & Admission Prices: Call for hours.

Uncasville

TANTAQUIDGEON INDIAN MUSEUM, Rte. 32, 1819 Norwich-New London Rd., Uncasville, CT 06382-1320. Tel.: 860-848-3985. Fax: 860-862-6025.
E-mail: museum@moheganmail.com
Key Personnel: Exec. Dir., Melissa Tantaquidgeon Zobel; Cur., Stacy Dufresne.
Institution Type/Description: Indian Museum.
Hours & Admission Prices: May-Nov. Tues.-Fri. 10-3. No charge. Closed holidays. &

Unionville

UNIONVILLE MUSEUM, 15 School St., Unionville, CT 06085-1029. Tel.: 860-673-2231.
E-mail: unionville@unionvillemuseum.org
Web Site: unionvillemuseum.org
Institution Type/Description: History Museum: housed in the restored Andrew Carnegie free public library building, c.1917.
Hours & Admission Prices: Wed. & Sat.-Sun. 2-4. No charge; donations accepted.

Vernon

NEW ENGLAND CIVIL WAR MUSEUM, 14 Park Pl., Vernon Memorial Hall, 2nd Fl, Vernon, CT 06066-3291. Tel.: 860-870-3563.
E-mail: necwm@hotmail.com
Web Site: www.newenglandcivilwarmuseum.com
Key Personnel: Exec. Dir., Matt Reardon; Librarian & Cur., Jerry Caroon; Librarian & Cur., Alex Oliphant.
Institution Type/Description: Civil War Museum.
Hours & Admission Prices: mid-July to mid-Aug. Sun. 12-3, Thurs. 12-4; mid-Aug. to mid-July Sun. 12-3; other times by appointment. No charge; donations accepted. &
Attendance: 1,200 (actual)

VERNON HISTORICAL SOCIETY MUSEUM, 734 Hartford Turnpike, Vernon, CT 06066-5127. Mailing Address: P.O. Box 2055, Vernon, CT 06066-1455. Tel.: 860-875-4326.
E-mail: vernonhs@sbcglobal.net
Web Site: vernonhistoricalsoc.org
Key Personnel: Dir., Jean Luddy; Pres. (V), Tara Remillard.
Institution Type/Description: Historical Society Museum.
Hours & Admission Prices: Thurs. & 2nd and 4th Sun. of month 2-4. No charge; donations accepted. &
Attendance: 300 (estimated)

Wallingford

PETERS RAILROAD MUSEUM, 49 Parkview Rd., Wallingford, CT 06492. Tel.: 203-269-1788.
Institution Type/Description: Railroad Museum.
Hours & Admission Prices: By appointment.

WALLINGFORD HISTORICAL SOCIETY, INC., 180 S. Main St., Wallingford, CT 06492-4217. Mailing Address: P.O. Box 73, Wallingford, CT 06492-0073. Tel.: 203-294-1996.
E-mail: lbertekap-wallingfordhistoricalsociety@yahoo.com
Key Personnel: Pres. (V), Raymond A. Chappell; 1st Vice Pres., Robert Beaumont.
Institution Type/Description: General Museum: housed in 1759 Parsons House.
Hours & Admission Prices: Memorial Day to Labor Day Sun. 2-4:30; other times by appointment. No charge.
Attendance: 900 (estimated)

Washington

GUNN HISTORICAL MUSEUM, 5 Wykeham Rd., Washington, CT 06793. Mailing Address: P.O. Box 1414, Washington, CT 06793-0273. Tel.: 860-868-7756. Fax: 860-868-7247.
E-mail: gunnmuseum@sbcglobal.net
Web Site: www.gunnlibrary.org
Formerly: Gunn Memorial Library and Museum
Key Personnel: Cur., Stephen Bartkus; Mgr. Operations, Lisa Breese.
Institution Type/Description: General Museum: housed in 1781 building.
Hours & Admission Prices: Closed until early 2019.
Attendance: 5,000 (actual)

THE INSTITUTE FOR AMERICAN INDIAN STUDIES (IAIS), 38 Curtis Rd., Washington, CT 06793-0260. Mailing Address: P.O. Box 1260, Washington, CT 06793-0260. Tel.: 860-868-0518. Fax: 860-868-1649. Facebook.
E-mail: general@iaismuseum.org
Web Site: iaismuseum.org
Key Personnel: Exec. Dir., Chris Combs; Chm., Edward White; Archaeologist, Dir. Research & Collections, Lucianne Lavin, Ph.D.; Asst. Exec. Dir., Colleen Swift; Educational Programs & Gift Shop, Darlene Kascak.
Institution Type/Description: American Indian Culture & Archaeology Museum.
Hours & Admission Prices: Wed.-Sat. 10-5, Sun. 12-5. Adults $10, seniors $8, children 3-12 $6; discounts to NEMA & AAM members; members & active military no charge. Closed New Year's Day; Easter; Memorial Day; Independence Day; Labor Day; Thanksgiving; Christmas. &
Attendance: 60,000 (actual)

Waterbury

THE MATTATUCK MUSEUM, 144 W. Main St., Waterbury, CT 06702-1298. Tel.: 203-753-0381, ext. 10. Fax: 203-756-6283.
E-mail: info@mattatuckmuseum.org
Web Site: www.mattatuckmuseum.org
Key Personnel: Exec. Dir., Robert Burns; Cur., Cynthia Roznoy, Ph.D.; Mgr. Collections, Wayne Eldred; Dir. Finance, Janice Shambor, CPA; Dir. Operations & Mktg., Stephanie Harris; Dir. Devel., Cyndi Tolosa.
Institution Type/Description: History & Art Museum: housed in renovated Masonic Temple.
Hours & Admission Prices: Tues.-Sat. 10-5, Sun. 12-5. Adults $7, seniors $6; members & children under 16 no charge. Closed major holidays. &
Attendance: 45,000 (actual)

Waterford

HARKNESS MEMORIAL STATE PARK, 275 Great Neck Rd., Waterford, CT 06385-3895. Tel.: 860-443-5725. Fax: 860-441-6151.
E-mail: docent@harkness.com
Web Site: www.ct.gov/dep
Institution Type/Description: Park Museum: 1906 Eolia, summer residence of the Edward S. Harkness family. The estate & mansion are located near the confluence of the Thames River & Long Island Sound on the promontory, Goshen Point.
Hours & Admission Prices: Grounds: daily 8am to sunset. In-State cars Mon.-Fri. $5, Sat.-Sun. & holidays $7; out-of-state cars Mon.-Fri. $7, Sat.-Sun. & holidays $10. Season Pass: CT residents $50; Out of State residents $75. Mansion Tours: Memorial to Labor Day Sat.-Sun. & holidays 10-2. No charge; donations accepted. &

Watertown

WATERTOWN HISTORICAL SOCIETY, INC., 22 DeForest St., Watertown, CT 06795-2116. Mailing Address: P.O. Box 853, Watertown, CT 06795. Tel.: 860-274-1050. Facebook.
E-mail: watertownctmuseum@sbcglobal.net
Web Site: www.watertownhistoricalsociety.org
Key Personnel: Vice Pres., Jan J. Guidess; Treas., Kendra Scapeccia.
Institution Type/Description: Local History Museum: housed in 1846 building.
Hours & Admission Prices: Museum; temporarily closed. Old Nova Scotia Schoolhouse: by appointment.
Attendance: 300 (estimated)

West Hartford

AMERICAN SCHOOL FOR THE DEAF MUSEUM & ARCHIVES, 139 N. Main St., West Hartford, CT 06107. Tel.: 860-570-2353. Fax: 860-570-1823. Facebook: American School for the Deaf.
E-mail: elizabeth.whitty@asd-1817.org
Web Site: www.asd-1817.org
Key Personnel: Exec. Dir., Jeffrey S. Bravin; Dir. Institutional Advancement, Liz Whittly; Museum Shop Mgr., Brad Moseley.
Institution Type/Description: History Museum.
Hours & Admission Prices: Tues. 9am-11am, Thurs. 1-3; other times by appointment. No charge; donations accepted. Closed school holidays.
Attendance: 225 (estimated)

ART MUSEUM, UNIVERSITY OF SAINT JOSEPH, 1678 Asylum Ave., West Hartford, CT 06117-2791. Tel.: 860-231-5399. Facebook.
E-mail: artmuseum@usj.edu

Web Site: www.usj.edu/artmuseum
Formerly: Saint Joseph College Art Gallery
Key Personnel: Dir. & Cur., Ann H. Sievers; Collection Mgr. & Registrar, Rochelle L. R. Oakley.
Institution Type/Description: Art Museum.
Hours & Admission Prices: Tues.-Wed. & Fri.-Sat. 11-4, Thurs. 11-7, Sun. 1-4. No charge. Closed national holidays. ᕫ
Attendance: 5,000 (estimated)

CHASE FAMILY GALLERY, 335 Bloomfield Ave., West Hartford, CT 06117. Tel.: 860-236-4571. Fax: 860-233-0802.
E-mail: thejcc@mandelljcc.org
Key Personnel: Exec. Dir., David Jacobs.
Institution Type/Description: Art Gallery.
Hours & Admission Prices: Call for hours.

THE CHILDREN'S MUSEUM, 950 Trout Brook Dr., West Hartford, CT 06119-1492. Tel.: 860-231-2824. Fax: 860-232-0705. Facebook.
E-mail: info@thechildrensmuseumct.org
Web Site: www.thechildrensmuseumct.org
Formerly: Science Center of Connecticut
Key Personnel: Exec. Dir., Michael Werle; Chm. (V), Peter Stevens; Dir. Opers., Beth Weller; Dir. Roaring Brook Nature Ctr., Jay Kaplan.
Institution Type/Description: Children's Museum.
Hours & Admission Prices: Summer: Mon.-Sat. 9-4, Sun. 11-4; Winter: Tues.-Sat. 9-4, Sun. 11-4. Adults $14.75, children & senior citizens 62 & up $13.75; discounts to ASTC & ACM reciprocal members; children under 2 no charge. Closed Easter; Memorial Day; Independence Day; Labor Day; Thanksgiving; Christmas Eve & Day.
Attendance: 210,000 (estimated)

JOSELOFF GALLERY, HARTFORD ART SCHOOL, UNIVERSITY OF HARTFORD, 200 Bloomfield Ave., West Hartford, CT 06117-1545. Tel.: 860-768-4090.
E-mail: joseloff@hartford.edu
Web Site: hartford.edu/galleries
Key Personnel: Dir. & Cur., Ricardo Reyes.
Institution Type/Description: Art Gallery.
Hours & Admission Prices: Tues.-Wed. 1-6, Thurs. 1-7, Fri.-Sun. 1-5. No charge; donations accepted. Closed major university & national holidays. ᕫ
Attendance: 10,000 (estimated)

NOAH WEBSTER HOUSE/WEST HARTFORD HISTORICAL SOCIETY, 227 S. Main St., West Hartford, CT 06107-3430. Tel.: 860-521-5362. Fax: 860-521-4036.
E-mail: comments@noahwebsterhouse.org
Web Site: www.noahwebsterhouse.org
Formerly: Noah Webster House Museum of West Hartford History
Key Personnel: Exec. Dir., Jennifer DiCola Matos; Cur., Sheila Daley; Coord. Education, Beth Sweeney; Mgr. Public Programs, Sophie Huget.
Institution Type/Description: History Museum: housed in 18th-century Noah Webster House.
Hours & Admission Prices: Daily 1-4. Adults $8, seniors $6, children 6-18 $5; discounts for groups, AAM, NEMA, & GHAHHM members; children 5 & under and members no charge. Closed national holidays. ᕫ
Attendance: 17,500 (actual)

SARAH WHITMAN HOOKER HOMESTEAD, 1237 New Britain Ave., West Hartford, CT 06110-2404. Mailing Address: c/o 11 Dodge Dr., West Hartford, CT 06107. Tel.: 860-785-9549.
E-mail: fransson1701@att.net
Web Site: sarahwhitmanhooker.com
Institution Type/Description: Historic House Museum: built c.1720.
Hours & Admission Prices: By appointment. Adult $7, children under 13 $3.50.

SHERMAN MUSEUM OF JEWISH CIVILIZATION - UNIVERSITY OF HARTFORD, Mortensen Library, Harry Jack Gray Center, West Hartford, CT 06117. Tel.: 860-768-4964. Fax: 860-768-5044.
E-mail: freund@hartford.edu
Web Site: uhaweb.hartford.edu/greenberg-center
Key Personnel: Dir., Marc Epstein.
Institution Type/Description: History Museum.
Hours & Admission Prices: Call for hours. No charge. ᕫ

WESTMOOR PARK EDUCATION CENTER, 119 Flagg Rd., West Hartford, CT 06119. Tel.: 860-561-8260. Fax: 860-236-3815.
E-mail: westmoorpark@westhartfordct.gov

Web Site: westmoorpark.com
Institution Type/Description: Park & Education Center.
Hours & Admission Prices: Office: Mon.-Fri. 9-4:30. Farm: daily 9-4. Grounds: daily dawn to dusk. No charge; donations accepted. ᕫ
Attendance: 105,000 (estimated)

West Haven

SAVIN ROCK MUSEUM, 6 Rock St., West Haven, CT 06516-5846. Mailing Address: 355 Main St., West Haven, CT 06516. Tel.: 203-937-3666.
Web Site: www.savinrockmuseum.com
Key Personnel: Cur., Harold Hartmann.
Institution Type/Description: History Museum.
Hours & Admission Prices: April 5-Sept. 14 Tues. 9am-12pm, Wed. & Fri. 1-4, Sat.-Sun. 4-7; Sept. 17-Dec. 21 Wed. & Fri.-Sun. 1-4. Adults $4, seniors & children under 12 $2.

WARD-HEITMANN HOUSE MUSEUM, 277 Elm St., West Haven, CT 06516. Mailing Address: P.O. Box 573, West Haven, CT 06516. Tel.: 203-937-9823. Fax: 203-937-9823.
E-mail: wardheitmann@sbcglobal.net
Web Site: www.wardheitmann.org
Key Personnel: Pres. (V), Michael Weber.
Institution Type/Description: Historic House Museum: built c.1684. Listed on the National Register of Historic Places.
Hours & Admission Prices: By appointment. Adults $5; discounts to students; members no charge.
Attendance: 950 (estimated)

West Redding

HIGHSTEAD ARBORETUM, 127 Lonetown Rd., West Redding, CT 06896. Tel.: 203-938-8809.
E-mail: info@highstead.net
Web Site: highsteadarboretum.org/programs/Art_Exhibition.shtml
Institution Type/Description: Arboretum.
Hours & Admission Prices: By appointment.

NEW POND FARM, 101 Marchant Rd., West Redding, CT 06896. Tel.: 203-938-2117. Fax: 203-938-9593.
E-mail: info@newpondfarm.org
Web Site: www.newpondfarm.org
Key Personnel: Exec. Dir., Ann Taylor.
Institution Type/Description: Working Farm: 102-acre property.
Hours & Admission Prices: Learning Center: daily 9-5. Dairy Annex: daily 7-7.

West Simsbury

FLAMIG FARM, 7 Shingle Mill Rd., West Simsbury, CT 06092-2311. Tel.: 860-658-5070.
E-mail: info@flamigfarm.com
Web Site: flamigfarm.com
Institution Type/Description: Farm & Educational Center.
Hours & Admission Prices: April-Nov. Daily 9-5. Admission $6 per person; seniors over 80 no charge.

Westbrook

MILITARY HISTORIANS, HEADQUARTERS & MUSEUM, 24 Westbrook Pl., Westbrook, CT 06498-3902. Tel.: 860-399-9460.
E-mail: military.historians@snet.net
Formerly: The Company of Military Historians Headquarters and Museum
Key Personnel: Admin., Maj. William R. Reid; Cur. Uniforms, Insignia & Photos, Earl Vincent; Librarian, Charles W. Reid.
Institution Type/Description: Military Uniform Museum.
Hours & Admission Prices: Tues.-Thurs. 8-1; other times by appointment. No charge, donations accepted.

STEWART B. MCKINNEY NATIONAL WILDLIFE REFUGE, 733 Old Clinton Rd., Westbrook, CT 06498-1760. Tel.: 860-399-2513. Fax: 860-399-2515. Facebook.
E-mail: shaun_roche@fws.gov
Web Site: www.fws.gov/northeast/mckinney
Key Personnel: Mgr., Richard Potvin.
Institution Type/Description: Wildlife Refuge.
Hours & Admission Prices: Daily sunrise to sunset. No charge.

Weston

WESTON HISTORICAL SOCIETY, 104 Weston Rd., Weston, CT
06883. Mailing Address: P.O. Box 1092, Weston, CT 06883-0092.
Tel.: 203-226-1804. Facebook.
E-mail: info@westonhistoricalsociety.org
Web Site: www.westonhistoricalsociety.org
Formerly: The Coley Homestead & Barn Museum
Key Personnel: Pres., Pamela Kersey; Dir., Marianne Frisch.
Institution Type/Description: Historical Society Museum: housed in an historic
house & barn, c.1841.
Hours & Admission Prices: Call for hours. No charge; donations accepted. &
Attendance: 5,000 (estimated)

Westport

EARTHPLACE - THE NATURE DISCOVERY CENTER, 10
Woodside Lane, Westport, CT 06880-2322. Tel.: 203-227-7253.
Fax: 203-227-8909.
E-mail: info@earthplace.org
Web Site: www.earthplace.org
Formerly: Nature Center for Environmental Activities, Inc.
Key Personnel: Exec. Dir., Tony McDowell.
Institution Type/Description: Natural History Museum & Environmental Studies
Center.
Hours & Admission Prices: Mon.-Sat. 9-5, Sun. 1-4. Adults $7, seniors 62 & over
and children 1-12 $5; members no charge. Closed New Year's Day; Easter;
Memorial Day; Independence Day; Labor Day; Thanksgiving; Christmas. &
Attendance: 70,000 (estimated)

SHERWOOD ISLAND STATE PARK NATURE CENTER,
Sherwood Island Connector, Westport, CT 06881. Mailing
Address: P.O. Box 544, Westport, CT 06881. Tel.: 203-226-6983.
E-mail: sherwoodislandnaturecenter@gmail.com
Key Personnel: Supvr., Jim Beschle.
Institution Type/Description: Nature Center.
Hours & Admission Prices: Wed.-Sun. 10-4.

WESTPORT ARTS CENTER, 51 Riverside Ave., Westport, CT
06880. Tel.: 203-222-7070.
E-mail: info@westportartscenter.org
Web Site: www.westportartscenter.org
Key Personnel: Dir., Nancy Heller; C.E.O., Lance Lundberg.
Institution Type/Description: Art Gallery.
Hours & Admission Prices: Mon.-Fri. 10-4, Sat.-Sun. 12-4. No charge. &

WESTPORT HISTORICAL SOCIETY, 25 Avery Place, Westport,
CT 06880-3215. Tel.: 203-222-1424. Fax: 203-221-0981.
Facebook.
E-mail: sgold@westporthistory.org
Web Site: westporthistory.org
Key Personnel: Exec. Dir., Ramin Ganeshram; Asst. Dir., Barbara Peck.
Institution Type/Description: History Museum.
Hours & Admission Prices: Tues.-Sat. 10-4. Adults $5, students & seniors $3; mem-
bers and children 10 & under no charge. &
Attendance: 5,000 (estimated)

**WESTPORT OBSERVATORY - THE WESTPORT
ASTRONOMICAL SOCIETY,** 182 Bayberry Lane, Westport,
CT 06880. Tel.: 203-293-8759.
E-mail: observatory@was-ct.org
Formerly: Rolnick Observatory
Institution Type/Description: Observatory.
Hours & Admission Prices: Wed. 8pm-10pm. No charge.

Wethersfield

BUTTOLPH-WILLIAMS HOUSE, 249 Broad St., Wethersfield,
CT 06109. Mailing Address: 211 Main St., Wethersfield, CT
06109-2339. Tel.: 860-529-0612. Fax: 860-529-0460.
E-mail: info@webb-deane-stevens.org
Institution Type/Description: Historic House: built c.1711.
Hours & Admission Prices: April & Nov. Sat. 10-4, sun. 1-4; May-Oct. Mon. &
Wed.-Sat. 10-4, Sun. 1-4. Adults $6, seniors 60 & over, student, & children 5-18
$5; members no charge. Closed Memorial Day; Independence Day; Labor Day.

ELEANOR BUCK WOLF NATURE CENTER, 156 Prospect St.,
Wethersfield, CT 06109. Tel.: 860-721-2980.
E-mail: nature.center@wethersfieldct.gov

Institution Type/Description: Nature Center.
Hours & Admission Prices: Tues.-Sat. 10-5. Suggested Donation: $3. &

THE WEBB-DEANE-STEVENS MUSEUM, 211 Main St.,
Wethersfield, CT 06109-2339. Tel.: 860-529-0612. Fax: 860-571-
8636.
E-mail: info@webb-deane-stevens.org
Web Site: www.webb-deane-stevens.org
Key Personnel: Exec. Dir., Charles T. Lyle; Dir. Education, Cindy Riccio; Rentals,
Katie Sullivan.
Institution Type/Description: Historic Houses: restored 18th-century houses.
Hours & Admission Prices: April & Nov. Sat. 10-4, Sun. 1-4; May-Oct. Wed.-Mon.
10-4, Sun. 1-4; other times by appointment. Closed Memorial Day;
Independence Day; Labor Day. &
Attendance: 12,500 (actual)

WETHERSFIELD HISTORICAL SOCIETY, 150 Main St.,
Wethersfield, CT 06109-3126. Tel.: 860-529-7656. Fax: 860-563-
2609.
E-mail: society@wethersfieldhistory.org
Web Site: www.wethhist.org
Key Personnel: Exec. Dir., Amy Northrop Wittorff; Pres., Elaine St. Onge; Vice
Pres., Beverly Lucas.
Institution Type/Description: History Museum.
Hours & Admission Prices: Old Academy & Research Library: Tues.-Fri. 10-4 &
by appointment. No charge. Wethersfield Museum at Keeney Memorial: Tues.-
Sat. 10-4, Sun. 1-4. Hurlbut-Dunham House: Memorial Day to 1st weekend in
Oct. & 1st 3 weekends in Dec. Sat.-Sun. 1-4. Cove Warehouse: Memorial Day
to 1st weekend in Oct. Sat.-Sun. 1-4. No charge; donations accepted. &
Attendance: 23,308 (actual)

Willimantic

CONNECTICUT EASTERN RAILROAD MUSEUM, 55 Bridge
St., Willimantic, CT 06226. Mailing Address: P.O. Box 665,
Willimantic, CT 06226-0665. Tel.: 860-456-9999. Facebook.
E-mail: info@cteastrrmuseum.org
Web Site: www.cteastrrmuseum.org
Key Personnel: Pres. (V), Mark F. Granville; Museum Shop Mgr., M. Jean
Lambert.
Institution Type/Description: Railroad Museum.
Hours & Admission Prices: May-Oct. Sat. 10-4, Sun. 12-4; other times by appoint-
ment. Adults $7, children 8-12 $3; discounts to groups; members & children
under 8 no charge.
Attendance: 1,200 (actual)

**WINDHAM TEXTILE AND HISTORY MUSEUM (THE MILL
MUSEUM),** 411 Main St., Willimantic, CT 06226-3173. Tel.:
860-456-2178.
E-mail: themillmuseum@gmail.com
Web Site: www.millmuseum.org
Key Personnel: Exec. Dir., Jamie Eves.
Institution Type/Description: Textile & History Museum: located in 1877 buildings
built as a company store & library for the Willimantic Linen Company.
Hours & Admission Prices: Fri.-Sun. 10-4. Adults $7, senior citizens & students $5;
discounts to groups, AAM & ICOM members; children & members no charge.
Closed Easter; Independence Day; Christmas. &
Attendance: 7,000 (estimated)

Wilton

WEIR FARM NATIONAL HISTORIC SITE, 735 Nod Hill Rd.,
Wilton, CT 06897-1309. Tel.: 203-834-1896. Fax: 203-834-2421.
E-mail: wefa_interpretation@nps.gov
Web Site: www.nps.gov/wefa/
Key Personnel: Supt., Linda Cook.
Institution Type/Description: Historic Site: comprised of 60 acres of J. Alden Weir's
farm (1852-1919) in Branchville, CT. Listed on the National Register of Historic
Places.
Hours & Admission Prices: Visitor Center: May-Oct. Wed.-Sun. 10-4; Grounds:
daily dawn to dusk. House Tours: May-Oct. Wed.-Sun. 11, 1, 2, & 3. No charge;
donations accepted. Closed New Year's Day; Thanksgiving; Christmas.
Attendance: 17,000 (actual)

WILTON HISTORICAL SOCIETY, INC., 224 Danbury Rd.,
Wilton, CT 06897-6000. Tel.: 203-762-7257. Fax: 203-762-3297.
E-mail: info@wiltonhistorical.org
Web Site: www.wiltonhistorical.org
Key Personnel: Co Dir., Kim Mellin; Co Dir., Allison Sanders.
Institution Type/Description: Historical Society Museum.

Hours & Admission Prices: Tues.-Sat. 10-4. Adults $5; members no charge. &
Attendance: 8,000 (estimated)

WOODCOCK NATURE CENTER, 56 Deer Run Rd., Wilton, CT 06897. Tel.: 203-762-7280.
E-mail: wnc@woodcocknaturecenter.org
Web Site: woodcocknaturecenter.org
Key Personnel: Exec. Dir., Lenore Eggleston Herbst.
Institution Type/Description: Nature Center.
Hours & Admission Prices: Center: Summer: Mon.-Fri. 9-4; Winter: Mon.-Fri. 9-4, Sat. call for hours. Trails: daily dawn to dusk. No charge; donations accepted.

Windsor

LUDDY/TAYLOR CONNECTICUT VALLEY TOBACCO MUSEUM, Northwest Park, 135 Lang Rd., Windsor, CT 06095. Tel.: 860-285-1888. Facebook.
E-mail: tobaccomuseum@townofwindsorct.com
Web Site: www.tobaccohistsoc.org
Key Personnel: Dir., Brianna E. Dunlap.
Institution Type/Description: History Museum.
Hours & Admission Prices: March to mid-Dec. Tues.-Thurs. & Sat. 12-4. No charge; donations accepted. $5 for groups of 10 or more. &
Attendance: 1,200 (estimated)

MERCY GALLERY, 261 Broad St., Windsor, CT 06095-3028. Tel.: 860-688-5165.
E-mail: jane@windsorcc.org
Institution Type/Description: Art Gallery.
Hours & Admission Prices: Winter: Mon., Wed. & Fri. 11-4, Tues. & Thurs. 11-4 & 7:45 pm-9:45 pm, Sun. 1-4; other times by appointment.

NORTHWEST PARK & NATURE CENTER, 145 Lang Rd., Windsor, CT 06095. Tel.: 860-285-1886.
E-mail: northwestpark@townofwindsorct.com
Web Site: northwestpark.org
Institution Type/Description: Nature Center.
Hours & Admission Prices: Mon.-Sat. 8:30-4:30, Sun. 1-4. No charge. &

OLIVER ELLSWORTH HOMESTEAD AND MUSEUM, 778 Palisado Ave., Windsor, CT 06095-2097. Mailing Address: P.O. Box 791, Windsor, CT 06095-0791. Tel.: 860-688-8717.
E-mail: website@ctdar.org
Web Site: www.ellsworthhomesteaddar.org
Key Personnel: Chm. (V), Jean E. Kelsey; Pres. (V), Jennie May Rehnberg.
Institution Type/Description: Historic House Museum: built in 1781.
Hours & Admission Prices: May 15-Oct. 15 Fri.-Sat. 12-4, Sun. 1-4; tours by appointment. Adults $5; children 12 & under no charge. Closed major holidays.
Attendance: 1,000 (estimated)

VINTAGE RADIO AND COMMUNICATIONS MUSEUM OF CONNECTICUT, 115 Pierson Lane, Windsor, CT 06095. Mailing Address: P.O. Box 894, Windsor, CT 06095. Tel.: 860-683-2903. Facebook: Vintage Radio and Communications Museum of Connecticut.
E-mail: radioclctr@aol.com
Web Site: vrcmct.org
Key Personnel: Dir., John C. Ellsworth.
Institution Type/Description: History Museum.
Hours & Admission Prices: Thurs.-Fri. 10-3, Sat. 10-5, Sun. 1-4; groups by appointment. Adults $10, seniors 60 & over $7, students $5; children under 5 no charge.

WINDSOR ART CENTER, 40 Mechanic St., Windsor, CT 06095. Tel.: 860-688-2528.
E-mail: info@windsorartcenter.org
Web Site: ww.windsorartcenter.org
Key Personnel: Exec. Dir., Amanda Pawlik.
Institution Type/Description: Art Gallery: housed in the former freight house.
Hours & Admission Prices: Thurs. 6pm-8pm, Sat. 10-4, Sun. 11-4. No charge.

WINDSOR HISTORICAL SOCIETY, 96 Palisado Ave., Windsor, CT 06095. Tel.: 860-688-3813. Fax: 860-657-1633.
E-mail: info@windsorhistoricalsociety.org
Web Site: www.windsorhistoricalsociety.org
Key Personnel: Exec. Dir., Christine Ermenc.
Institution Type/Description: History Museum.

Hours & Admission Prices: Wed.-Sat. 11-4 with historic house tours at 11 & 1. Adults $8, seniors & students $6; society members & children under 12 no charge. &
Attendance: 6,471 (actual)

Windsor Locks

NEW ENGLAND AIR MUSEUM, Bradley International Airport, 36 Perimeter Rd., Windsor Locks, CT 06096-1069. Tel.: 860-623-3305. Fax: 860-627-2820.
E-mail: staff@neam.org
Web Site: www.neam.org
Key Personnel: Interim Dir., Debbie Reed.
Institution Type/Description: Aeronautics Museum.
Hours & Admission Prices: Memorial Day to Labor Day daily 10-5; Sept.-May Tues.-Sun. 10-5. Adults $15, senior citizens $14, children 4-14 $10; discounts to groups; CAHA members and children 3 & under no charge. Closed New Year's Day; Easter; Thanksgiving; Christmas. &
Attendance: 64,916 (actual)

NODEN-REED FARM MUSEUM, 58 West St., Windsor Locks, CT 06096-1808. Tel.: 860-627-9212. Facebook.
E-mail: nodenreedmuseum@gmail.com
Web Site: windsorlockshistorical.org
Key Personnel: Dir., Rose Horan; Cur., James Anderson.
Institution Type/Description: History Museum: housed in Victorian farmhouse. Listed on National Register of Historical Places.
Hours & Admission Prices: May-Oct. Sun. 1-5. No charge; donations accepted. Closed holiday weekends.
Attendance: 200 (estimated)

Winsted

AMERICAN MUSEUM OF TORT LAW, 654 Main St., Winsted, CT 06098. Tel.: 860-379-0505. Fax: 860-379-0235. Facebook.
E-mail: sara@tortmuseum.org
Web Site: www.tortmuseum.org
Key Personnel: Exec. Dir., Richard L. Newman; Pres., Ralph Nader; Asst. Dir., Sara Nowak.
Institution Type/Description: History Museum.
Hours & Admission Prices: April-Dec. Wed.-Mon. 10:30-5; other times by appointment. Adults $7, seniors & students $5; children under 10 no charge. &

Woodbridge

AMITY AND WOODBRIDGE HISTORICAL SOCIETY, 1907 Litchfield Turnpike, Woodbridge, CT 06525. Tel.: 203-387-2823.
E-mail: donaldmenzies@sbcglobal.net
Web Site: www.woodbridgehistory.org
Key Personnel: C.E.O. & Pres., Donald Menzies.
Institution Type/Description: Local History & Historical Society Museum: housed in Thomas Darling House.
Hours & Admission Prices: By appointment. No charge; donations accepted.
Attendance: 200 (estimated)

Woodbury

FLANDERS NATURE CENTER & LAND TRUST, 596 Flanders Rd., Woodbury, CT 06798-1718. Mailing Address: 5 Church Hill Rd., Woodbury, 06798. Tel.: 203-263-3711. Fax: 203-263-2214.
E-mail: flanders@flandersnaturecenter.org
Web Site: www.flandersnaturecenter.org
Key Personnel: Exec. Dir., Arthur S. Milnor.
Institution Type/Description: Nature Center.
Hours & Admission Prices: Daily dawn to dusk. No charge.

THE GLEBE HOUSE MUSEUM AND GERTRUDE JEKYLL GARDEN, 49 Hollow Rd., Woodbury, CT 06798. Mailing Address: P.O. Box 245, Woodbury, CT 06798-0245. Tel.: 203-263-2855. Facebook.
E-mail: office@glebehousemuseum.org
Web Site: www.glebehousemuseum.org
Key Personnel: Dir., Lorianne Witte.
Institution Type/Description: Historic Building: c.1750 The Glebe House, birthplace of American Episcopacy.
Hours & Admission Prices: May to mid-Oct. Wed.-Sun. 1-4; other times by appointment only. Adults $7, children $2; members no charge.
Attendance: 5,000 (estimated)

Woodstock

ROSELAND COTTAGE, 556 Rte. 169, Woodstock, CT 06281-2344. Mailing Address: P.O. Box 186, Woodstock, CT 06281. Tel.: 860-928-4074. Facebook.
E-mail: roselandcottage@historicnewengland.org
Web Site: www.historicnewengland.org
Key Personnel: Site Mgr., Laurie Masciandaro.
Institution Type/Description: Historic House: 1846 Gothic Revival cottage.
Hours & Admission Prices: June-Oct. 15 Wed.-Sun. 11-4; tours on the hour. Adults $10, seniors $9, students $5; members no charge. Closed Independence Day; Columbus Day. &
Attendance: 15,882 (actual)

WOODSTOCK HISTORICAL SOCIETY, INC., 523 Rte. 169, Woodstock, CT 06281. Mailing Address: P.O. Box 65, Woodstock, CT 06281-0065. Tel.: 860-928-1035.
E-mail: woodstockhist@att.net
Web Site: www.woodstockhistoricalsociety.org
Key Personnel: Pres. (V), Gail White.
Institution Type/Description: Historical Society Museum.
Hours & Admission Prices: April-Oct. Sun. 11-4. No charge; donations accepted. Closed major holidays. &
Attendance: 200 (estimated)

DELAWARE

(80 listings)

Arden

ARDEN CRAFT SHOP MUSEUM, 1807 Millers Rd., Ste. A, Arden, DE 19810-4052. Tel.: 302-475-3060.
E-mail: ardencraftshopmuseum@gmail.com
Web Site: www.ardencraftshopmuseum.com
Key Personnel: Chm. (V), Lisa Mullinax.
Institution Type/Description: Art Museum.
Hours & Admission Prices: Sun. 1-3, Wed. 7:30pm-9pm. No charge; donations accepted or requested. &
Attendance: 300 (estimated)

Bear

WHALE WALLOW NATURE CENTER - LUMS POND STATE PARK, 1068 Howell School Rd., Bear, DE 19701. Tel.: 302-368-6989. Fax: 302-368-6971.
E-mail: Mike.Moyer@state.de.us
Web Site: www.destateparks.com/park/lums-pond/
Institution Type/Description: Nature Center.
Hours & Admission Prices: Park: daily 8am to sunset. Center: Memorial Day to Labor Day daily 12-6.

Bridgeville

BRIDGEVILLE HISTORICAL SOCIETY, 102 S. Williams St., Bridgeville, DE 19933. Mailing Address: P.O. Box 306, Bridgeville, DE 19933-0336. Tel.: 302-337-7600.
E-mail: hehzoo@aol.com
Key Personnel: Dir., Mike Collison; Pres., Howard E. Hardesty.
Institution Type/Description: Historical Society: building built in 1911. Listed on the National Register of Historic Places.
Hours & Admission Prices: By appointment. No charge.
Attendance: 312 (actual)

Christiana

CHRISTIANA FIRE COMPANY MUSEUM, 2 E. Main St., Christiana, DE 19702. Tel.: 302-737-2433.
Institution Type/Description: Fire Company Museum.
Hours & Admission Prices: By appointment.

Claymont

ROBINSON HOUSE, 1 Naamans Rd., Claymont, DE 19703-2701. Tel.: 302-792-0285.
E-mail: info@robinsonhousede.org
Web Site: www.robinsonhousede.org
Key Personnel: Pres., Frances West.
Institution Type/Description: Historic House Museum.
Hours & Admission Prices: By appointment.

Delaware City

FORT DELAWARE SOCIETY, 2711 Staff Lane, Ft. Dupont State Park, Delaware City, DE 19706. Mailing Address: P.O. Box 553, Delaware City, DE 19706-0553. Tel.: 302-834-1630. Fax: 302-834-1630.
E-mail: society@fortdelaware.org
Web Site: www.fortdelaware.org
Key Personnel: Pres. (V), David P. Price; Chm. (V), William G. Robelen, IV.
Institution Type/Description: Military & Park Museum Complex: located in c.1859 former barracks of Civil War Fort Delaware on Pea Patch Island, accessible by boat only.
Hours & Admission Prices: mid-June to Sept. Wed.-Sun. & holidays 10-6. Boat Fee: adults $11, children $6; discounts to senior citizens & active military. &
Attendance: 25,000 (actual)

Dover

BIGGS MUSEUM OF AMERICAN ART, 406 Federal St., Dover, DE 19901-3615. Mailing Address: P.O. Box 711, Dover, DE 19903-0711. Tel.: 302-674-2111. Fax: 302-674-5133.
E-mail: cguerin@biggsmuseum.org
Web Site: www.biggsmuseum.org
Formerly: Sewell C. Biggs Museum of American Art
Key Personnel: Dir., Guerin Danko; Chm. (V), Marcia P. Dewitt; Asst. Dir. & Office Mgr., Amanda Feusner; Museum Mgr., Ellen Arthur; Cur., Ryan Grover; Cur. Ed Fellow, Regina Lynch; Mktg. & Devel. Mgr., Stephanie Fitzpatrick.
Institution Type/Description: American Art Museum.
Hours & Admission Prices: Tues.-Sat. 9-4:30, Sun. 1:30-4:30. Adults $10, seniors 60 & up $8; members no charge. Closed New Year's Day; Easter; Thanksgiving; Christmas. &
Attendance: 20,000 (estimated)

DELAWARE AGRICULTURAL MUSEUM AND VILLAGE, 866 N. Dupont Hwy., Dover, DE 19901-2012. Tel.: 302-734-1618. Fax: 302-734-0457.
E-mail: damv@verizon.net
Web Site: www.agriculturalmuseum.org
Key Personnel: Pres., Richard Bergold; Dir., Di Rafter; Mgr. Maintenance, Michael Grimes.
Institution Type/Description: Museum of Rural Life and Agricultural History and Technology.
Hours & Admission Prices: Tues.-Sat. 10-3. Adults $6, senior citizens 65 & over $4, youth 4-17 $3; discounts for groups, AAA members & Time Travelers; members & children under 3 no charge. Closed New Year's Day; Easter; Thanksgiving; Christmas. &
Attendance: 17,000 (estimated)

DELAWARE DIVISION OF HISTORICAL & CULTURAL AFFAIRS, 21 The Green, Dover, DE 19901-3611. Tel.: 302-736-7400. Fax: 302-739-5660.
Web Site: history.delaware.gov
Formerly: Delaware State Museums
Key Personnel: Dir., Timothy Slavin; Deputy Dir., Suzanne Savery; Cur. Archaeology, Paul Nasca; Cur. Collections, Ann M. Baker Horsey; Collections Mgr., Marian Carpenter; Site Supvr. Dover, Nena Todd; Site Supvr. John Dickinson Plantation, Gloria Henry; Site Supvr. Zwaanendael Museum, Bridget Warner.
Institution Type/Description: State Historical Agency & Museums: Old State House: c.1792; Johnson Victrola Museum; Buena Vista: 1845-47, home of John M. Clayton now used as a conference center; Old New Castle Courthouse: located on the Green laid out by Peter Stuyvesant in 1655; in 1776 the Declaration of Independence & the first Constitution of Delaware were approved; John Dickinson Plantation, c.1740, historic house, with reconstructed Afro-American tenant house & farm buildings, boyhood home of John Dickinson who wrote, Letters from a Farmer in Pennsylvania, & signed Articles of Confederation & U.S. Constitution; Zwaanendael Museum, housed in a 1931 adaptation of the Old Town Hall in Hoorn, Holland. Monuments: Cooch's Bridge Monument commemorating September 3, 1777 skirmish with British; DeVries Monument commemorating landing of the Dutch in 1631, the first settlement in Delaware.
Hours & Admission Prices: New Castle Courthouse: Tues.-Sat. 10-4:30, Sun. 1:30-4:30. Johnson Victrola Museum Wed.-Sat. 9-4:30. Historic Old State House: Mon.-Sat. 9-4:30, Sun. 1:30-4:30. John Dickinson Plantation: April-Sept. Sun. 1:30-4:30; Oct.-March Tues.-Sat. 10:30-4:30. Zwaanendael: April-Oct. Tues.-Sat. 10-4:30, Sun. 1:30-4:30. No charge; donations accepted. Closed state holidays. For specific information on tour arrangements, call First State Heritage Park Visitor Center, 121 M.L.K. Jr. Blvd., Dover, DE. Tel: 302-744-5055. &
Attendance: 100,000 (estimated)

DELAWARE PUBLIC ARCHIVES, 121 Duke of York St., Dover, DE 19901-3638. Tel.: 302-744-5000. Fax: 302-739-2578.
Web Site: www.archives.delaware.gov
Key Personnel: Dir., Stephen Marz, C.A.
Institution Type/Description: Archives.
Hours & Admission Prices: Mon.-Fri. 8-4:15, 1st Sat. of month 9-4:45. No charge. Closed state holidays. &

DELAWARE STATE CAPITOL, Court St., Dover, DE 19901. Mailing Address: P.O. Box 1401, Dover, DE 19901. Tel.: 302-739-9194.
Institution Type/Description: Historic Building: built in 1931.
Hours & Admission Prices: Tours: Mon.-Fri. 10-1, 1st Sat. each month 9-4:30. No charge. Closed New Year's Day; Thanksgiving; Christmas.

DELAWARE STATE POLICE MUSEUM, 1425 N. DuPont Hwy., Dover, DE 19901. Mailing Address: P.O. Box 430, Dover, DE 19903-0430. Tel.: 302-739-7700. Fax: 302-739-5993. Facebook: @dspmuseum.
E-mail: dsp_museum@state.de.us
Web Site: www.dspmuseum.com
Key Personnel: Dir., Maj. Kevin McDerby, (Ret.); Pres., Capt. Gregory Sallo, (Ret.); Vice Pres., Maj. Joan Miller, (Ret.); Treas., Maj. Paul R. Kane; Sec., Capt. John A. Campanella.
Institution Type/Description: Police Museum.
Hours & Admission Prices: Mon.-Fri. 9-3, 3rd Sat. of month 11-3; other times by appointment. No charge.
Attendance: 4,000

FIRST STATE HERITAGE PARK WELCOME CENTER, First State Heritage Park Welcome Center, 121 Duke of York St., Dover, DE 19901. Tel.: 302-739-5055.
Web Site: history.delaware.gov/
Formerly: First State Heritage Park Welcome Center and Galleries
Key Personnel: Dir., Sarah Zimmerman.
Institution Type/Description: History Museum & Visitor's Center.
Hours & Admission Prices: Mon.-Sat. 8-4:30, Sun. 1:30-4:30, State holidays 9-4:30; groups by appointment. No charge. Closed New Year's Day; Easter; Christmas. &

JOHN DICKINSON PLANTATION, 340 Kitts Hummock Rd., Dover, DE 19901-7016. Tel.: 302-739-3277. Fax: 302-739-3173. Facebook: John Dickinson Plantation.
E-mail: gloria.henry@state.de.us
Web Site: www.history.delaware.gov
Key Personnel: Supvr., Gloria Henry; Dir., Timothy Slavin.
Institution Type/Description: History Museum.
Hours & Admission Prices: April-Sept. Tues.-Sat. 10-4:30, Sun. 1:30-4:30; Oct.-March Tues.-Sat. 10-4:30. No charge; donations accepted. Closed New Year's Day; Thanksgiving; Christmas. &
Attendance: 11,000 (actual)

JOHNSON VICTROLA MUSEUM, 375 S. New St., Dover, DE 19901. Mailing Address: First State Heritage Park Welcome Center, 121 Duke of York St., Dover, DE 19901. Tel.: 302-739-3262.
E-mail: bridget.warner@state.de.us
Web Site: history.delaware.gov/museums/jvm/jvm_main.shtml
Key Personnel: Dir., Tim Slavin; Site Supvr., Nena Todd.
Institution Type/Description: Technology Museum: Eldridge Reeves Johnson, founder of the Victor Talking Machine Company in 1901, later known as RCA.
Hours & Admission Prices: Wed.-Sat. 9-4:30; groups by appointment. No charge; donations accepted. Closed New Year's Day; Easter; Christmas. Open most state holidays.

THE OLD STATE HOUSE, 25 The Green, Dover, DE 19901. Mailing Address: First State Heritage Park Welcome Center, 121 Duke of York St., Dover, DE 19901. Tel.: 302-744-5054 & 739-9194. Fax: 302-739-3943.
E-mail: suzanne.savery@state.de.us
Web Site: history.delaware.gov/museums/sh/sh_main.shtml
Key Personnel: Dir., Tim Slavin; Site Supvr., Nena Todd.
Institution Type/Description: Historic Site: housed in the restored capitol building; built in 1792.
Hours & Admission Prices: Tues.-Sat. & state holidays 9-4:30, Sun. 1:30-4:30; groups by appointment. No charge; donations accepted. Closed New Year's Day; Easter; Christmas. &

Dover AFB

AIR MOBILITY COMMAND MUSEUM, 1301 Heritage Rd., Dover AFB, DE 19902-5301. Tel.: 302-677-5938 & 5939. Fax: 302-677-5940.
E-mail: amcmuseum@us.af.mil
Web Site: www.amcmuseum.org
Key Personnel: C.E.O., Michael D. Leister; Pres., Donald Sloan; Operations Mgr., John Taylor; Archivist, Harry Heist; Education, Dick Caldwell; Registrar & Collections Mgr., Deborah Sellars; Museum Shop Mgr., Keith Kreisher.
Institution Type/Description: Military Museum: housed in a WWII hanger.
Hours & Admission Prices: Tues.-Sun. 9-4. No charge; donations accepted. Closed federal holidays. &
Attendance: 84,000 (actual)

Fenwick Island

DISCOVERSEA SHIPWRECK MUSEUM, 708 Coastal Hwy., Fenwick Island, DE 19944. Tel.: 302-539-9366, 888-743-5524. Fax: 302-539-1285.
E-mail: dsmuseum@aol.com
Web Site: www.discoversea.com
Key Personnel: Dir., Dale W. Clifton, Jr.
Institution Type/Description: Maritime History Museum.
Hours & Admission Prices: April-May & Oct.-Dec. Sat.-Sun. 11-3:30; June-Aug. daily 11-7; Sept. daily 11-3:30; groups by appointment. No charge; donations accepted.

FENWICK ISLAND LIGHTHOUSE & MUSEUM, Rt. 54, Fenwick Island, DE 19944. Mailing Address: New Friends of the Fenwick Island Lighthouse, P.O. Box 1001, Selbyville, DE 19975. Tel.: 302-436-8100.
E-mail: info@fenwickislandlighthouse.org
Web Site: www.fenwickislandlighthouse.org
Key Personnel: Pres., Winnie Lewis; Vice Pres., Kathy Lesperanch; Sec., Donna Schwartz; Treas., Tracy Lewis.
Institution Type/Description: Historic Lighthouse: built in 1858.
Hours & Admission Prices: May to Columbus Day: Thurs.-Tues. No charge; donations accepted.

Frederica

BARRATT'S CHAPEL AND MUSEUM, 6362 Bay Rd., Frederica, DE 19946-1505. Tel.: 302-335-5544. Fax: 302-335-5750.
E-mail: barratts@aol.com
Web Site: barrattschapel.org
Key Personnel: Dir., Kenyon Camper; Cur., Barb Duffin; Conference Historian, Rev. Philip Lawtor.
Institution Type/Description: Religious Museum.
Hours & Admission Prices: Sat.-Sun. 1:30-4:30; groups & other times by appointment. No charge; donations accepted. &
Attendance: 4,007 (actual)

Georgetown

DELAWARE AVIATION MUSEUM, 21781 Aviation Ave, Georgetown, DE 19947-2016. Tel.: 443-458-8926.
E-mail: info@delawareaviationmuseum.org
Web Site: delawareaviationmuseum.org
Institution Type/Description: Aviation Museum.
Hours & Admission Prices: Sat.-Sun. 10-4

ELSIE WILLIAMS DOLL COLLECTION, 21179 College Dr., Georgetown, DE 19947-0610. Tel.: 302-259-6150.
E-mail: treasures@dtcc.edu
Key Personnel: Dir., Robert Hearn.
Institution Type/Description: Doll Museum.
Hours & Admission Prices: Mon.-Thurs. 8am-10pm, Fri. 8-4:30, Sat. 8-1. No charge. Closed major holidays; Christmas break. &

MARVEL CARRIAGE MUSEUM, 510 S. Bedford St., Georgetown, DE 19947-1852. Tel.: 302-855-9660.
E-mail: marvelmuseum@juno.com
Web Site: www.marvelmuseum.com
Formerly: Nutter D. Marvel Museum
Key Personnel: Sec., Rosalie Walls.
Institution Type/Description: Historic Buildings.
Hours & Admission Prices: By appointment.

OLD SUSSEX COUNTY COURTHOUSE, 10 S. Bedford St., Georgetown, DE 19947-1852. Mailing Address: Georgetown Historical Society, 510 S. Bedford St., Georgetown, DE 19947. Tel.: 302-855-9660.
Institution Type/Description: Historic Building: built in 1791.
Hours & Admission Prices: 1st Wed. of month; other times by appointment.

TREASURES OF THE SEA EXHIBIT, Delaware Technical Community College, Owens, 21179 College Dr., Georgetown, DE 19947. Tel.: 302-259-6150. Facebook: Treasures of the Sea Exhibit.
E-mail: treasures@dtcc.edu
Web Site: www.treasuresofthesea.org
Key Personnel: Dir., Mark Brainard; Education, Registrar & Museum Shop Mgr., Susan Doering; Public Rels., Christine Gillian; Security, William Wood.
Institution Type/Description: Maritime Museum.
Hours & Admission Prices: mid-Jan. to mid-Dec. Mon., Wed. & Fri. 10-4, Sat. 10-2; other times by appointment. Adults $3, senior citizens $2.50, active military, veterans & students $1; discounts to WHYY & AAA members; children 4 & under no charge. Closed major holidays; Christmas break. ⅍
Attendance: 3,000 (estimated)

Greenville

SOMERVILLE MANNING GALLERY, Brecks Mill, 2nd Fl., 101 Stone Block Row, Greenville, DE 19807. Tel.: 302-652-0271. Fax: 302-652-1946.
E-mail: info@somervillemanning.com
Institution Type/Description: Art Gallery.
Hours & Admission Prices: Winter: Tues.-Sat. 10-5; Summer: Mon.-Fri. 10-5, Sat. 11-3; other times by appointment.

Harrington

GREATER HARRINGTON HISTORICAL SOCIETY, 108 Fleming St., Harrington, DE 19952-1145. Tel.: 302-398-3698.
E-mail: societyharringtonhistorical@yahoo.com
Formerly: Harrington Railroad Museum
Key Personnel: Dir. & Pres. (V), M. Jean Miller; Chm. (V), Viva Poore.
Institution Type/Description: History Museum.
Hours & Admission Prices: By appointment. No charge; donations accepted.
Attendance: 1,200 (estimated)

MESSICK AGRICULTURE MUSEUM, 325 Walt Messick Rd., Taylor and Messick, Inc., Harrington, DE 19952-3300. Tel.: 302-398-3729. Fax: 302-398-4732.
E-mail: taylormessick@taylormessick.com
Web Site: www.taylormessick.com
Institution Type/Description: Agriculture Museum.
Hours & Admission Prices: Mon.-Fri. 7:30-4. No charge; donations accepted.

Hockessin

ASHLAND NATURE CENTER OF DELAWARE NATURE SOCIETY, 3511 Barley Mill Rd., Hockessin, DE 19707-9393. Mailing Address: P.O. Box 700, Hockessin, DE 19707-0700. Tel.: 302-239-2334. Fax: 302-239-2473.
E-mail: dnsinfo@delawarenaturesociety.org
Web Site: www.delawarenaturesociety.org
Key Personnel: Exec. Dir., Michael E. Riska.
Institution Type/Description: Nature Center.
Hours & Admission Prices: Grounds & Trails: dawn to dusk. Visitor Center: daily 8:30-4:30. Trail: $2; ANCA & society members no charge. Closed holidays. ⅍
Attendance: 80,000 (estimated)

MT. CUBA CENTER, 3120 Barley Mill Rd., Hockessin, DE 19707. Tel.: 302-239-4244. Fax: 302-239-5366.
E-mail: info@mtcubacenter.org
Web Site: www.mtcubacenter.org
Institution Type/Description: Horticultural Center.
Hours & Admission Prices: April 18 to Nov. Fri.-Sat. 10-4; other times by appointment. Adults $6, youth 6-16 $3; discounts to groups; children under 6 no charge.
Attendance: 7,000 (actual)

Laurel

BALD CYPRESS NATURE CENTER, Trap Pond State Park, 33587 Baldcypress Lane, Laurel, DE 19956-2988. Tel.: 302-875-5163. Fax: 302-875-2697.
E-mail: Trappondnaturecenter@state.de.us
Web Site: destateparks.com
Institution Type/Description: Nature Center.
Hours & Admission Prices: Daily 8 to sunset.

Lewes

THE LEWES HISTORICAL SOCIETY, 110 Shipcarpenter St., Lewes, DE 19958-1210. Tel.: 302-645-7670. Fax: 302-645-2375. Facebook: Lewes Historical Society.
E-mail: info@historiclewes.org
Web Site: www.historiclewes.org
Key Personnel: Exec. Dir., Mike DiPaolo.
Institution Type/Description: History Museum.
Hours & Admission Prices: May to early Oct. Sun.-Sat. 11-4. Adults $5-$10; members & children under 12 no charge.
Attendance: 60,000 (estimated)

PACKARD REATH GALLERY, 142 Second St., Ste. 2A, Lewes, DE 19958-1396. Tel.: 302-644-7513.
Institution Type/Description: Art Gallery.
Hours & Admission Prices: Daily 11-5.

SEASIDE NATURE CENTER - CAPE HENLOPEN STATE PARK, 15099 Cape Henlopen Dr., Lewes, DE 19958-3153. Tel.: 302-645-8983. Fax: 302-645-1146.
E-mail: linda.vansant@state.de.us
Web Site: www.destateparks.com
Institution Type/Description: Nature Center.
Hours & Admission Prices: Center: day after Labor Day to mid-June daily 9-4; mid-June to Labor Day daily 9-5. Park: daily 8am to sunset.

ZWAANENDAEL MUSEUM, 102 Kings Hwy., Lewes, DE 19958. Mailing Address: 21 The Green, Dover, DE 19901-3611. Tel.: 302-645-1148.
E-mail: bridget.warner@st.de.us
Web Site: history.delaware.gov/museums/zm/zm_main.shtml
Key Personnel: Site Supvr., Bridget Warner; Dir., Timothy Slavin.
Institution Type/Description: Historic Building: built in 1931.
Hours & Admission Prices: April-Oct. Tues.-Sat. 10-4:30, Sun. 1:30-4:30; Nov.-March Wed.-Sat. 10-4:30. No charge; donations accepted. Closed state holidays.

Middletown

GILBERT W. PERRY JR. CENTER FOR THE ARTS, 51 W. Main St., Middletown, DE 19709. Tel.: 302-444-0332.
E-mail: info@thegibby.com
Web Site: www.thegibby.com
Institution Type/Description: Art Gallery.
Hours & Admission Prices: Call for hours.

Milford

ABBOTT'S MILL NATURE CENTER, 15411 Abbott's Pond Rd., Milford, DE 19963-3549. Tel.: 302-422-0847. Fax: 302-422-1849.
E-mail: dnsinfo@delawarenaturesociety.org
Web Site: www.delawarenaturesociety.org/abbotts.html
Key Personnel: Exec. Dir., Brian Winslow.
Institution Type/Description: Nature Center.
Hours & Admission Prices: Mon.-Fri. 9-4; other times by appointment.
Attendance: 10,000 (estimated)

DUPONT NATURE CENTER, 2992 Lighthouse Rd., Milford, DE 19963. Tel.: 302-422-1329.
Web Site: www.dnrec.delaware.gov
Institution Type/Description: Nature Center.
Hours & Admission Prices: April-Sept. Tues.-Sun. 10-4; Oct.-March Mon.-Fri. 10-4. No charge; donations accepted. ⅍

MILFORD HISTORICAL SOCIETY, 501 N.W. Front St., Milford, DE 19963-1015. Mailing Address: P.O. Box 352, Milford, DE 19963-0352. Tel.: 302-422-3115.
E-mail: parsonthorne@gmail.com

Formerly: Parson Thorne Mansion
Institution Type/Description: Historic House Museum: housed in the former home of Milford's founder, Parson Sydenham Thorne; built c.1735. Listed on the National Register of Historic Places.
Hours & Admission Prices: Call for hours.
Attendance: 1,000

MILFORD MUSEUM, 121 S. Walnut St., Milford, DE 19963-1955. Tel.: 302-424-1080.
E-mail: claudia@milforddemuseum.org
Web Site: www.milforddemuseum.org
Key Personnel: Chm., Charles Hammond; Dir., Claudia Leister; Dir. Public Rels., Al Lauckner; Sec., Barbara Jones.
Institution Type/Description: Local History Museum: housed in c.1910 Federal style brick building.
Hours & Admission Prices: Tues.-Sat. 10-3:30, Sun. 1-3:30; groups by appointment. No charge; donations accepted. Closed New Year's Day; Easter; Independence Day; Christmas. &
Attendance: 3,000 (estimated)

Millsboro

MILLSBORO ART LEAGUE, 203 Main St., Millsboro, DE 19966. Tel.: 302-934-6440.
E-mail: millsboroartleague@gmail.com
Web Site: www.millsboroartleague.com
Institution Type/Description: Art Gallery.
Hours & Admission Prices: Fri.-Sat. 11-3, Sun. 1-3.

NANTICOKE INDIAN MUSEUM, 27073 John J. Williams Hwy., Millsboro, DE 19966-4642. Tel.: 302-945-7022.
E-mail: nanticok@verizon.net
Web Site: www.nanticokeindians.org
Institution Type/Description: History Museum.
Hours & Admission Prices: Jan.-March Thurs.-Sat. 10-4, Sun. 12-4; April-Dec. Tues.-Sat. 10-4, Sun. 12-4. Adults $3, children $1.

Milton

MILTON HISTORICAL SOCIETY AND MUSEUM, 210 Union St., Milton, DE 19968-1620. Mailing Address: P.O. Box 112, Milton, DE 19968-0112. Tel.: 302-684-1010. Facebook: Milton Historical Society DE.
E-mail: info@historicmilton.org
Web Site: www.historicmilton.org
Formerly: Lydia B. Cannon Museum
Key Personnel: Dir., Allison Schell; Pres., John Bushey.
Institution Type/Description: History Museum: housed in the newly restored 1857 Methodist Church.
Hours & Admission Prices: Wed.-Sat. 11-4; other times by appointment. No charge; donations accepted. Closed federal holidays. &
Attendance: 10,150 (actual)

PRIME HOOK NATIONAL WILDLIFE REFUGE, 11978 Turkle Pond Rd., Milton, DE 19968-3759. Tel.: 302-684-8419. Fax: 302-684-8504.
E-mail: fw5rw_phnwr@fws.gov
Web Site: www.fws.gov/northeast/primehook
Institution Type/Description: Wildlife Refuge.
Hours & Admission Prices: Refuge: daily sunrise to sunset. Visitor Contact Station & Store: Mon.-Fri. 7:30-4. Visitor Center: April-Nov. Sat.-Sun. 9-4.

New Castle

BELLANCA AIRFIELD MUSEUM AND DELAWARE AVIATION HALL OF FAME, Rte. 273 & Centerpoint Blvd., New Castle, DE 19720. Mailing Address: Friends of Bellanca Airfield, P.O. Box 267, New Castle, DE 19720-0267.
E-mail: contact@friendsofbellanca.org
Web Site: www.friendsofbellanca.org
Institution Type/Description: History Museum: housed in Bellanca airfield, aircraft plant, & service hangar; built in 1928 by aviation pioneer Giuseppe Bellanca & Henry B. duPont
Hours & Admission Prices: Daily 11-3. No charge; donations accepted.

NEW CASTLE COURT HOUSE MUSEUM, 211 Delaware St., New Castle, DE 19720-4815. Tel.: 302-323-4453. Fax: 302-323-5319.
E-mail: cynthia.snyder@state.de.us

Web Site: history.delaware.gov
Institution Type/Description: Historic Site.
Hours & Admission Prices: Tues.-Sat. 10-3:30, Sun. 1:30-4:30. No charge; donations accepted. Closed state holidays. &
Attendance: 14,000 (actual)

NEW CASTLE HISTORICAL SOCIETY, 30 Market St., New Castle, DE 19720-4830. Tel.: 302-322-2794. Fax: 302-322-8923.
E-mail: nchistorical@aol.com
Web Site: www.newcastlehistory.org
Key Personnel: Dir., Michael Connolly; Pres. (V), Richard R. Cooch; Coord. Education, Bruce Dalleo.
Institution Type/Description: Historical Society Museum.
Hours & Admission Prices: April-Dec. Tues.-Sat. 11-4, Sun. 1-4. Amstel House or Dutch House: adults $4, children under 12 $1.50. Combination Tickets: adults $7, children 2-12 $2.50; children under 6 & members no charge. Old Library Museum Sat.-Sun. 1-4. No charge. Closed national holidays.
Attendance: 10,500 (actual)

OLD LIBRARY MUSEUM, 40 E. 3rd St., New Castle, DE 19720. Mailing Address: 2 E. 4th St., New Castle, DE 19720-5014. Tel.: 302-322-2794. Fax: 302-322-8923.
E-mail: nchistorical@aol.com
Web Site: www.newcastlehistory.org
Institution Type/Description: Historic Building: housed in a hexagonal brick structure; built in 1892.
Hours & Admission Prices: May-Dec. Sat.-Sun. 1-4.

READ HOUSE & GARDENS, 42 The Strand, New Castle, DE 19720-4826. Tel.: 302-322-8411. Fax: 302-322-8557.
Web Site: www.dehistory.org
Institution Type/Description: Historic House: built in 1801 by George Read Jr., the son of one of Delaware's signers of the Declaration of Independence.
Hours & Admission Prices: April-Dec. Wed.-Fri. & Sun. 11-4, Sat. 10-4. Adults $7, senior citizens over 65, military, & students 13-21 $6; discounts to groups; members & children under 6 no charge. Closed major holidays.
Attendance: 12,000 (estimated)

Newark

CHAMBERS HOUSE NATURE CENTER AT WHITE CLAY CREEK STATE PARK, 1475 Creek Rd., Newark, DE 19711. Mailing Address: 425 Wedgewood Rd., Newark, DE 19711-2123. Tel.: 302-368-6560 & 6900. Fax: 302-368-6901.
E-mail: angerl.burns@state.de.us
Web Site: http://www.destateparks.com
Institution Type/Description: Nature Center.
Hours & Admission Prices: May-Oct. Sat.-Sun. 11-4. No charge; donations accepted. &
Attendance: 1,200 (estimated)

HALE BYRNES HOUSE, 606 Stanton Christiana Rd., Newark, DE 19713-2109. Tel.: 302-998-3792.
E-mail: halebyrneshouse@aol.com
Web Site: www.halebyrnes.org
Key Personnel: Resident Property Mgr. & Cur., Ralph Burdick; Resident Property Mgr. & Cur., Kim Burdick.
Institution Type/Description: Historic House: housed in the building used as a meeting place for General George Washington & his staff between the Battle of Cooch's Bridge in Delaware and the Battle of Brandywine in Pennsylvania in 1777; built in 1750. Listed on the National Register of Historic Places.
Hours & Admission Prices: April-Dec. 1st Wed. each month 12-3; other times by appointment. No charge; donations accepted.

IRON HILL SCIENCE CENTER & MUSEUM, 1115 Robert L. Melson Ln., Newark, DE 19702. Tel.: 302-368-5703. Fax: 302-369-4287.
E-mail: director@ironhill-museum.org
Web Site: ironhillsciencecenter.org
Key Personnel: Mng. Dir., Maureen Zieber; Pres., Joshua Martin; Educational Asst., Cherie Keenan; Bd. Member, Robin Broomall.
Institution Type/Description: Natural History Museum.
Hours & Admission Prices: Tues.-Fri. 10-5. Adults $2. &
Attendance: 6,000 (estimated)

UNIVERSITY MUSEUMS, UNIVERSITY OF DELAWARE, 30 N. College Ave., 208 Mechanical Hall, Newark, DE 19716. Tel.: 302-831-8037. Fax: 302-831-8057.
E-mail: jat@udel.edu

Web Site: library.udel.edu/special/
Key Personnel: Dir., Janis A. Tomlinson, Ph.D.; Mgr. Collections, Janet Broske; Cur. Mineralogical Collection, Sharon L. Fitzgerald, Ph.D.; Preparator, Brian Kamen.
Institution Type/Description: Old College Gallery: housed in 1832 first major Greek Revival structure in the state. Mechanical Hall: renovated 1898 building.
Hours & Admission Prices: Sept.-May Wed. & Fri.-Sun. 12-5, Thurs. 12-8. No charge; donations accepted. Closed during installation; university holidays; semester breaks. &
Attendance: 6,500 (actual)

Odessa

HISTORIC HOUSES OF ODESSA, 209 Main St., Odessa, DE 19730. Mailing Address: P.O. Box 697, Odessa, DE 19730-0697. Tel.: 302-378-4119. Fax: 302-378-4050.
E-mail: info@historicodessa.org
Web Site: www.historicodessa.org
Institution Type/Description: Historic Houses.
Hours & Admission Prices: March-Dec. Tues.-Sat. 10-4:30, Sun. 1-4:30. Adults $10, students $8; discounts to members; children under 6 no charge. Closed Easter; Independence Day; Thanksgiving; Christmas Eve & Day.

Port Penn

PORT PENN INTERPRETIVE CENTER, Rte. 9 & Rd. 2, Port Penn, DE 19731. Mailing Address: P.O. Box 170, Delaware City, DE 19706. Tel.: 302-836-2533.
Web Site: www.destateparks.com/park/fort-delaware/port-penn.asp
Institution Type/Description: History Museum: housed in a former schoolhouse; built in 1886.
Hours & Admission Prices: Memorial Day to Labor Day Fri.-Sun. 10-4; groups by appointment. No charge; donations accepted. &
Attendance: 200 (estimated)

Rehoboth Beach

INDIAN RIVER LIFE-SAVING STATION, 25039 Coastal Hwy., Rehoboth Beach, DE 19971. Tel.: 302-227-6991. Fax: 302-227-6438. Facebook: IRLSS.
E-mail: martina.adams@state.de.us
Web Site: www.destateparks.com
Key Personnel: Dir., Laura Scharle.
Institution Type/Description: Historic Building: built in 1876. Listed on the National Register of Historic Places.
Hours & Admission Prices: Daily 8am to sunset. Adults $4, seniors 62 & up $3, children 6-12 $2; children 5 & under no charge.
Attendance: 22,100

REHOBOTH ART LEAGUE, INC., 12 Dodds Lane, Rehoboth Beach, DE 19971-1668. Tel.: 302-227-8408. Fax: 302-227-4121.
E-mail: info@rehobothartleague.org
Web Site: www.rehobothartleague.org
Institution Type/Description: Historic Buildings & Art League: one gallery & studio in c.1740s homestead, two galleries & a studio located on 3 1/2 acres of formal & informal gardens.
Hours & Admission Prices: Jan.-March Tues.-Sat. 10-4, Sun. 12-4; April-Dec. Mon.-Sat. 10-4, Sun. 12-4. No charge; donations accepted. Closed New Year's Day; Easter; Thanksgiving; Christmas. &
Attendance: 13,000 (estimated)

REHOBOTH BEACH MUSEUM, 511 Rehoboth Ave., Rehoboth Beach, DE 19971. Tel.: 302-227-7310.
E-mail: rbhistoricalsociety@verizon.net
Web Site: rehobothbeachmuseum.org
Institution Type/Description: History Museum.
Hours & Admission Prices: Memorial Day to Labor Day Mon.-Fri. 10-4, Sat.-Sun. 11-3; Sept.-May Mon. & Thurs.-Fri. 10-4, Sat.-Sun. 11-3.

Seaford

GOVERNOR ROSS PLANTATION, 23669 Ross Station Rd., Seaford, DE 19973-5754. Mailing Address: 203 High St., Seaford, DE 19973-3909. Tel.: 302-628-9500. Fax: 302-628-2984. Facebook.
E-mail: seafordsociety@verizon.net
Web Site: www.seafordhistoricalsociety.com
Key Personnel: Pres. (V), Maria Heyssel; Plantation Mgr., Margaret Alexander.
Institution Type/Description: Historic House & Historical Society Museum: c.1860 Italian Villa style home built by Delaware Governor William Ross.

Hours & Admission Prices: Sat.-Sun. 1-4; other times by appointment. Adults $7; members & children under 12 no charge. Closed state holidays. &
Attendance: 6,000 (actual)

SEAFORD MUSEUM, 203 High St., Seaford, DE 19973-3909. Tel.: 302-628-9828. Fax: 302-628-2984. Facebook.
E-mail: seafordsociety@verizon.net
Web Site: www.seafordhistoricalsociety.com
Key Personnel: Pres., Maria Heyssel; Exec. Dir., Amanda R. Goebel; Museum Office Mgr., Phyllis A. Williams.
Institution Type/Description: History Museum: housed in the former post office; built in 1930s.
Hours & Admission Prices: Wed.-Thurs. & Sat. 12-4, Sun. 1-4. Adults $7; members & children under 12 no charge. Closed holidays. &
Attendance: 2,000 (actual)

Smyrna

BOMBAY HOOK NATIONAL WILDLIFE REFUGE, 2591 Whitehall Neck Rd., Smyrna, DE 19977-2912. Tel.: 302-653-9345. Fax: 302-653-0684.
E-mail: fw5rw_bhnwr@fws.gov
Web Site: www.fws.gov/northeast/bombayhook
Key Personnel: Mgr., Michael Stroeh.
Institution Type/Description: Wildlife Refuge.
Hours & Admission Prices: Refuge: daily sunrise to sunset. Visitor's Center: March-May & Sept.-Nov. Mon.-Fri. 8-4, Sat.-Sun. 9-5; June-Aug. & Dec.-Feb. Mon.-Fri. 8-4.

SMYRNA MUSEUM, 11 S. Main St., Smyrna, DE 19977-1430. Mailing Address: P.O. Box 335, Smyrna, DE 19977-0335. Tel.: 302-653-1320. Fax: 302-653-8844.
Key Personnel: Pres., Brooks Keen.
Institution Type/Description: History Museum; 1790's buildings.
Hours & Admission Prices: Tues., Thurs. & Sat. 10-1; other times by appointment. No charge; donations accepted.
Attendance: 1,206 (actual)

Wilmington

BELLEVUE HALL MANSION - BELLEVUE STATE PARK, 800 Carr Rd., Wilmington, DE 19809-2163. Tel.: 302-761-6952. Fax: 302-761-4685.
E-mail: judi.jeffers@state.de.us
Web Site: www.destateparks.com/park/bellevue/bellevue-hall.asp
Institution Type/Description: Historic House.
Hours & Admission Prices: Park: daily 8am to sunset. Mansion: by appointment.

BRANDYWINE CREEK NATURE CENTER, 41 Adams Dam Rd., Wilmington, DE 19807. Mailing Address: P.O. Box 3782, Greenville, DE 19807-0782. Tel.: 302-655-5740.
Institution Type/Description: Nature Center.
Hours & Admission Prices: Daily 8am to sunset.

BRANDYWINE ZOO, 1001 N. Park Dr., Wilmington, DE 19802-3801. Tel.: 302-571-7747. Fax: 302-571-7787.
E-mail: Education@Brandywinezoo.org
Web Site: www.brandywinezoo.org
Key Personnel: Society Exec. Dir., Mike Allen; Cur. Education, Jacque Williamson; Asst. Cur. Education, Melody Whitaker.
Institution Type/Description: Zoo.
Hours & Admission Prices: Daily 10-4. May-Sept. adults $7, senior citizens & children 3-17 $5; Oct.-April adults $5, senior citizens $4, children 3-17 $3; discount to groups; members & children under 3 no charge. &
Attendance: 90,000 (estimated)

DELAWARE ART MUSEUM, 2301 Kentmere Pkwy., Wilmington, DE 19806-2096. Tel.: 302-571-9590. Fax: 302-571-0220.
E-mail: info@delart.org
Web Site: www.delart.org
Key Personnel: Exec. Dir. C.E.O., Samuel D. Sweet; Chief Cur., Heather Campbell Coyle.
Institution Type/Description: Art Museum.
Hours & Admission Prices: Wed.-Sat. 10-4, Sun. 12-4. Adults $12, seniors $10, students & youth $6; discounts to AAM members; members, children 6 & under and Sun. no charge. &
Attendance: 70,000 (actual)

DELAWARE CHILDREN'S MUSEUM, 550 Justison St., Wilmington, DE 19801-5142. Tel.: 302-654-2340.
Web Site: delawarechildrensmuseum.org
Institution Type/Description: Children's Museum.
Hours & Admission Prices: Call for hours & admission prices.

THE DELAWARE CONTEMPORARY, 200 S. Madison St., Wilmington, DE 19801-5100. Tel.: 302-656-6466. Fax: 302-656-6944. Facebook & Instagram: @DEContemporary.
E-mail: info@decontemporary.org
Web Site: www.decontemporary.org
Formerly: Delaware Center for the Contemporary Arts
Key Personnel: Exec. Dir, Joseph J. Gonzalez; Chair, Georgia Coats; Treas., Pat Toman; Assoc. Dir. Administration, Helen Page; Interim Gretchen Hupfel Cur. Contemporary Art, Katherine Page; Dir. Education, Jennifer Polillo; Dir. Special Events, Meagan Mika; Mktg. Mgr., Tatiana Michels.
Institution Type/Description: Art Museum.
Hours & Admission Prices: Tues. & Sun. 12-5, Wed. 12-7. Thurs.-Sat. 10-5. Suggested donation: adults $10, children $5. Closed major holidays. &
Attendance: 18,000 (estimated)

DELAWARE DIVISION OF THE ARTS MEZZANINE GALLERY, Carvel State Office Bldg., 820 N. French St., Wilmington, DE 19801. Tel.: 302-577-8278. Fax: 302-577-6561.
E-mail: delarts@state.de.us
Web Site: www.artsdel.org
Institution Type/Description: Art Gallery.
Hours & Admission Prices: Mon.-Fri. 8-4:30. No charge. Closed state holidays. &

DELAWARE HISTORICAL SOCIETY, 505 N. Market St., Wilmington, DE 19801-3091. Tel.: 302-655-7161. Fax: 302-655-7844.
E-mail: deinfo@dehistory.org
Web Site: www.dehistory.org
Formerly: Historical Society of Delaware
Key Personnel: Exec. Dir., Dr. David W. Young; Bd. Chair, Margaret L. Laird; Chief Cur., Leigh Rifenburg.
Institution Type/Description: Historic House & History Museum.
Hours & Admission Prices: Library: Mon. 11-7, Tues. & Thurs. 9am-1pm, Fri. 9-5. No charge. Delaware History Museum & Center for African American Heritage: Wed.-Sat. 11-4. Adults $6, senior citizens, students & military $5, youth 3-18 $4; children 2 & under no charge. Read House & Gardens: April-Dec. Wed.-Fri. & Sun. 11-4, Sat. 10-4. Adults $8, senior citizens, students & military $6; discounts to groups & AAM members; members & children under 10 no charge. Closed Federal holidays.
Attendance: 40,000 (actual)

DELAWARE MUSEUM OF NATURAL HISTORY, 4840 Kennett Pike, Wilmington, DE 19807-1827. Mailing Address: P.O. Box 3937, Wilmington, DE 19807-0937. Tel.: 302-658-9111. Fax: 302-658-2610.
E-mail: info@delmnh.org
Web Site: www.delmnh.org
Key Personnel: Exec. Dir., Halsey Spruance; Pres. Bd., Richard F. Cairns; Dir. Collections & Cur. Birds, Dr. Jean Woods; Cur. Mollusks, Dr. Liz Shea; Dir. Pub. Programming, Jill Karlson; Controller, Michele Harvey; Dir. Devel., Darcie Martin; Dir. HR & Visitor Svcs., Terri Reed.
Institution Type/Description: Natural History Museum.
Hours & Admission Prices: Mon.-Sat. 9:30-4:30, Sun. 12-4:30. Adults $9, seniors $8, children 3-17 $7; discounts to groups & ASTC members; children under 3 & members no charge. Closed New Year's Day; Thanksgiving; Christmas. &
Attendance: 57,913 (actual)

DELAWARE SPORTS MUSEUM AND HALL OF FAME, Frawley Stadium, Entrance on 1st Base Side, 801 Shipyard Dr., Wilmington, DE 19801. Tel.: 302-425-3263. Fax: 302-425-3713.
E-mail: desports@windstream.net
Web Site: www.desports.org
Key Personnel: Exec. Dir., Don Voltz; Pres. (V), Marty Walsh.
Institution Type/Description: Sports Museum.
Hours & Admission Prices: April-Oct. Tues.-Sat. 12-5; groups & other times by appointment. Adults $4, seniors over 50 $3; youth 13-19 $2; children 12 & under, Hall of Fame inductees & members no charge. &

HAGLEY MUSEUM AND LIBRARY, 298 Buck Rd. E., Wilmington, DE 19807-0630. Mailing Address: P.O. Box 3630, Wilmington, DE 19807-0630. Tel.: 302-658-2400. Fax: 302-658-0568. Facebook: Hagley Museum and Library.
E-mail: askhagley@hagley.org

Web Site: www.hagley.org
Key Personnel: Exec. Dir., David A. Cole, Ph.D.; Dir. Museum & Audience Engagement, Jill MacKenzie; Andrew W. Mellon Cur., Kevin Martin; Cur. Collections & Exhibitions, Debra Hughes; Dir. Library Svcs., Erik Rau; Dir. Personnel Support & Svcs., Yvonne Dalton; Deputy Dir. & C.F.O., Jeanne Belk; Chief Cur. Library Collections, Lynn Catanese; Objects Conservator, Ebenezer Kotei; Store Mgr., Carole Katchur; Cur. Mechanical Exhibitions, John McCoy; Dir. Preservation, Bldgs. & Grounds, Susan Maynard.
Institution Type/Description: History & Technology Museum: located on the original site of DuPont powder yards c.1802-1921.
Hours & Admission Prices: Daily 9:30-4:30. Adults $14, seniors & students $10, children 6-14 $5; discounts to AAM, ICOM, AASLH & ASTC members; children under 6 no charge. Closed Thanksgiving; Christmas. &
Attendance: 62,000 (actual)

LOMBARDY HALL, 1611 Concord Pike, Wilmington, DE 19803. Mailing Address: PO Box 7036, Wilmington, DE 19803. Tel.: 302-229-3770. Fax: 302-478-3828.
E-mail: tmartz@comcast.net
Web Site: www.lomhallfdn.org
Institution Type/Description: Historic House: housed in the former home of Gunning Bedford, Jr., Grand Master of the Grand Lodge of Delaware; 1806-1809.
Hours & Admission Prices: Open by appointment.

MUSEUM OF BUSINESS HISTORY AND TECHNOLOGY, 1200 Philadelphia Pike, Wilmington, DE 19809-2040. Tel.: 302-798-2100.
E-mail: tarusso@mbht.com
Web Site: www.mbht.org
Key Personnel: Dir., C.E.O. & Chm. (V), Thomas A. Russo, Sr.
Institution Type/Description: History Museum.
Hours & Admission Prices: By appointment. No charge; donations accepted. &

NEMOURS ESTATE, 850 Alapocas Dr., Wilmington, DE 19803. Mailing Address: 1600 Rockland Rd., Wilmington, DE 19803-3607. Tel.: 800-651-6912. Fax: 302-651-6933.
E-mail: tours@nemours.org
Web Site: www.nemoursmansion.org
Key Personnel: Exec. Dir., John C. Rumm, Ph.D.
Institution Type/Description: Historic House & Gardens: housed in 1910 Louis XVI-style chateau.
Hours & Admission Prices: May-Dec. Tues.-Sat. 10-5, Sun. 12-5. Family (2 adults & up to 4 children) $40, Adults $18, senior, active military & student with valid ID $16, groups of 15 or more $15 per person (reservations recommended), children 5-16 $8; children 4 & under no charge. Season passes available. Closed New Year's Eve & Day; Thanksgiving; Christmas Eve & Day. &
Attendance: 22,000 (estimated)

OLD SWEDES HISTORIC SITE, 606 Church St., Wilmington, DE 19801-4421. Tel.: 302-652-5629. Fax: 302-652-8615.
E-mail: info@oldswedes.org
Web Site: www.oldswedes.org
Formerly: Holy Trinity (Old Swedes) Church & Hendrickson House Museum
Key Personnel: Pres. (V), Mitchell D. Houser; Exec. Dir., Rebecca L. Wilson.
Institution Type/Description: Historic Site.
Hours & Admission Prices: March Wed.-Fri. 1-4, Sat. 10-4; April Dec. Wed.-Sat. 10-4; other times by appointment. Adults $4; discounts to members; children & members no charge. Closed New Year Day; Independence Day; Thanksgiving & day after; Christmas Eve & Day. &
Attendance: 4,000 (estimated)

ROCKWOOD PARK & MUSEUM, 4651 Washington St. Extension, Wilmington, DE 19808. Mailing Address: 610 Shipley Rd., Wilmington, DE 19809-3609. Tel.: 302-761-4340. Fax: 302-761-4345. Facebook; Twitter: @RockwoodMuseum.
E-mail: pnord@nccde.org
Web Site: www.rockwood.org
Key Personnel: Dir., Philip Nord; Horticulturist, Dena Kirk.
Institution Type/Description: Historic House & Museum Gallery: English Victorian Mansion & grounds.
Hours & Admission Prices: Museum: Wed.-Sun. 10-3. Grounds: daily 7-10. Adults $10, children 2-12 $4; discounts to AAM & ICOM members and New Castle, DE residents; children under 2 no charge. Closed major holidays.
Attendance: 15,000 (estimated)

Winterthur

WINTERTHUR MUSEUM, GARDEN & LIBRARY, 5105 Kennett Pike, Winterthur, DE 19735. Tel.: 302-888-4600, 800-448-3883. Fax: 302-888-4820. TDD: 302-888-4907.
E-mail: tourinfo@winterthur.org
Web Site: www.winterthur.org
Formerly: Winterthur Museum & Country Estate
Key Personnel: Dir., Dr. David P. Roselle.
Institution Type/Description: Decorative Arts & Cultural History Museum: housed in 1839 building with additions in the 1920s, 1930s, 1950s & 1990s.
Hours & Admission Prices: Tues.-Sun. 10-5; call for additional hours during Yuletide. Adults $20, students with valid ID & seniors $18, children 2-11 $5; discounts to groups by advance arrangement, AAM, ICOM, MAAM & AAMD members; members & children under 2 no charge. Closed Thanksgiving; Christmas. &
Attendance: 110,840 (actual)

Yorklyn

MARSHALL STEAM MUSEUM, 3000 Creek Rd., Yorklyn, DE 19736. Mailing Address: Friends of Auburn Heights Inc., P.O. Box 61, Yorklyn, DE 19736-0061. Tel.: 800-349-2134, 302-239-2385.
E-mail: admin@auburnheights.org
Web Site: www.auburnheights.org
Formerly: Auburn Heights Preserve
Key Personnel: Dir., Susan Randolph; Pres. (V), J. Stephen Bryce.
Institution Type/Description: Historic House: housed in the Marshall family home & carriage house. Listed on the National Register of Historic Places.
Hours & Admission Prices: Steamin' Days: June-Nov. 1st Sun. each month.

DISTRICT OF COLUMBIA

(117 listings)

Fort McNair

U.S. ARMY CENTER OF MILITARY HISTORY, MUSEUMS DIVISION, 102 Fourth Ave., Fort McNair, DC 20319-5058. Tel.: 202-685-2441. Fax: 202-685-2113.
E-mail: charles.h.cureton.civ@mail.mil
Web Site: www.history.army.mil
Key Personnel: Dir. Army Museums, Dr. Charles H. Cureton.
Institution Type/Description: History Museum and Military Museums.
Hours & Admission Prices: Library: Mon.-Fri. 9-4. No charge. &

Washington

ADDISON/RIPLEY FINE ART, 1670 Wisconsin Ave., N.W., Washington, DC 20007. Tel.: 202-338-5180. Fax: 202-338-2341.
E-mail: info@addisonripleyfineart.com
Web Site: www.addisonripleyfineart.com
Key Personnel: Owner, Sylvia Ripley; Owner, Christopher Addison; Dir., Romy Silverstein.
Institution Type/Description: Art Gallery.
Hours & Admission Prices: Tues.-Sat. 11-5:30; other times by appointment. No charge.
Attendance: 4,000 (estimated)

AFRICAN AMERICAN CIVIL WAR MUSEUM, 1925 Vermont Ave., N.W., Washington, DC 20001. Tel.: 202-667-2667.
E-mail: info@afroamcivilwar.org
Web Site: afroamcivilwar.org
Key Personnel: Dir., Dr. Frank Smith, Jr.; Educ. Dir., Dawn Chitty; Opers. Mgr., Edwin Gasaway.
Institution Type/Description: History Museum.
Hours & Admission Prices: Tues.-Fri. 10-6:30, Sat. 10-4, Sun. 12-4. No charge; donations accepted.
Attendance: 100,000 (actual)

AMERICAN UNIVERSITY MUSEUM AT THE KATZEN ARTS CENTER, 4400 Massachusetts Ave., N.W., Washington, DC 20016-8301. Tel.: 202-885-1300. Fax: 202-885-1140. Facebook: American University Museum.
E-mail: museum@american.edu
Web Site: www.american.edu/museum
Formerly: Watkins Gallery, American University
Key Personnel: Dir. & Cur., Jack Rasmussen; Assoc. Dir., Kristi-Anne Shaer; Registrar, Carla Galfano; Preparator, Kevin Runyon; Mktg. & Publications

Specialist, Elizabeth Cowgill; Mgr. Museum Operations & Visitor Svcs., Sharon Christiansen.
Institution Type/Description: Art Museum.
Hours & Admission Prices: Tues.-Sun. 11-4. No charge. &

ANACOSTIA COMMUNITY MUSEUM, SMITHSONIAN INSTITUTION, 1901 Fort Pl., S.E., Washington, DC 20020. Mailing Address: P.O. Box 37012, Washington, DC 20013-7012. Tel.: 202-633-4820. Fax: 202-287-3183. TDD: 202-357-1729.
E-mail: acminfo@si.edu
Web Site: anacostia.si.edu
Formerly: Anacostia Museum and Center for African American History & Culture
Key Personnel: Dir., Melanie A. Adams, PhD; Cur., Alcione Amos; Advancement Dir., Katelynd Anderson; Dir. Education & Outreach, Paul Perry; Collection Mgr., Miriam Doutriaux; Public Affairs Specialist, Marcia Baird Burris.
Institution Type/Description: Family & Community History Museum.
Hours & Admission Prices: Daily 10-5. No charge; donations accepted. Closed Christmas. &
Attendance: 28,000 (estimated)

ANDERSON HOUSE - THE AMERICAN REVOLUTION INSTITUTE OF THE SOCIETY OF THE CINCINNATI, 2118 Massachusetts Ave., N.W., Washington, DC 20008-3640. Tel.: 202-785-2040. Fax: 202-785-0729.
E-mail: admin@societyofthecincinnati.org
Web Site: www.societyofthecincinnati.org
Key Personnel: Exec. Dir., Jack D. Warren, Jr.; Deputy Dir. & Cur., Emily Schulz Parsons; Dir. Library, Ellen McCallister Clark; Coord. Museum Visitor Svcs., Caren A. Pauley; Mgr. Museum Education, Kendall Casey.
Institution Type/Description: Historic House Museum: housed in 1902-1905 Anderson House, a Neoclassical mansion designed by Little & Browne of Boston.
Hours & Admission Prices: Museum: Tues.-Sat. 10-4, Sun 12-4. Library: Mon.-Fri. 10-4 by appointment only. No charge; donations accepted. Closed legal holidays & during society meetings. &
Attendance: 14,079 (actual)

THE ANN LOEB BRONFMAN GALLERY, 1529 16th St., N.W., Washington, DC 20036. Tel.: 202-518-9400 & 777-3208. Fax: 202-518-9420.
E-mail: emilyj@edcjcc.org
Web Site: washingtondcjcc.org
Key Personnel: Deputy Exec. Dir., Adina Kanefeld.
Institution Type/Description: Art Gallery.
Hours & Admission Prices: Sun.-Thurs. 10-10, Fri. 10-4. No charge.

ARCHIVES OF AMERICAN ART, SMITHSONIAN INSTITUTION, 750 9th Street, N.W., Ste. 2200, Washington, DC 20001. Mailing Address: P.O. Box 37012, MRC 937, Washington, DC 20013-7012. Tel.: 202-633-7940. Fax: 202-633-7994.
E-mail: aaaemref@si.edu
Web Site: www.aaa.si.edu
Key Personnel: Dir., Kate Haw; Deputy Dir., Liza Kirwin; Assoc. Dir. Advancement, Melissa Rollenhagen; Advancement Asst., Zoe Herrmann; Registrar, Susan Cary; Head Collections Processing, Erin Kinhart; Head Digital Opers., Karen Weiss; Digital Experience Mgr., Michelle Herman.
Institution Type/Description: Research Institution.
Hours & Admission Prices: Manuscript Reading Room: Mon.-Fri. 9:30-noon & 1-4:30 by appointment only. Microfilm Reading Room: Mon.-Fri. 9-5. Lawrence A. Fleishman Gallery: daily 11:30-7. No charge. Closed federal holidays. &
Attendance: 555 (estimated)

ART MUSEUM OF THE AMERICAS, OAS, 201 18th St., N.W., Washington, DC 20006-5606. Mailing Address: 1889 F St., N.W., Washington, DC 20006-4401. Tel.: 202-458-6016 & 6019. Fax: 202-458-6021.
E-mail: artmus@oas.org
Web Site: www.museum.oas.org
Key Personnel: Coord. Education, Adriana Opsina; Cur. Permanent Collection, Maria Leyva; Cur. Temporary Exhibits, Fabian Goncalves Borrega; Public & Media Rels., Gregory Svitil; Administrative, Charo Marroquin.
Institution Type/Description: Latin American Contemporary Art Collection.
Hours & Admission Prices: Tues.-Sun. 10-5. No charge; donations accepted. Closed major holidays; Good Friday.

ARTS CLUB OF WASHINGTON, 2017 I St., N.W., Washington, DC 20006-1804. Tel.: 202-331-7282. Fax: 202-857-3678.
E-mail: membership@artsclubofwashington.org
Web Site: www.artsclubofwashington.org

Key Personnel: Gen. Mgr., Yann Henrotte; Business Mgr., Shelly Gardiner.
Institution Type/Description: Art Gallery: housed in 1802 home of President James Monroe.
Hours & Admission Prices: Sept.-July Tues.-Fri. 10-5, Sat. 10-2. No charge; donations accepted.

BUREAU OF ENGRAVING & PRINTING, Department of the Treasury, 14th and C Sts., S.W., Washington, DC 20228. Tel.: 202-874-4000, 202-874-2330 (public tours).
E-mail: moneyfactory.info@bep.gov
Web Site: www.moneyfactory.gov/home.html
Key Personnel: Dir., Leonard R. Olijar.
Institution Type/Description: History Museum.
Hours & Admission Prices: Call for hours.

CIA MUSEUM, Washington, DC 20505. Mailing Address: Central Intelligence Agency, Office of Public Affairs, Washington, DC 20505. Tel.: 703-482-0623. Fax: 703-482-1739.
Web Site: www.cia.gov
Institution Type/Description: Virtual History Museum.
Hours & Admission Prices: Daily.

CHRISTIAN HEURICH HOUSE MUSEUM, 1307 New Hampshire Ave., N.W., Ste. 300, Washington, DC 20036-1537. Tel.: 202-429-1894.
E-mail: info@heurichhouse.org
Web Site: http://www.heurichhouse.org/
Institution Type/Description: Historic House Museum: housed in the home of local brewer Christian Heurich; built in 1894. Listed on the National Register of Historic Places.
Hours & Admission Prices: Thurs.-Fri. 11:30 & 1, Sat. 11:30, 1 & 2:30; other times by appointment. Suggested Donation: $5 per person.

DAUGHTERS OF THE AMERICAN REVOLUTION MUSEUM, 1776 D St., N.W., Washington, DC 20006-5392. Tel.: 202-879-3241. Fax: 202-628-0820.
E-mail: museum@dar.org
Web Site: www.dar.org/museum
Key Personnel: Museum Dir. & Chief Cur., Diane L. Dunkley; Chm. (V), Beverly D. West; Cur. Education, Raina Boyd; Asst. Cur. Education, Kendall Casey; Cur. Collections, Olive Graffam; Cur. Furnishings, Patrick Sheary; Cur. Textiles & Costumes, Alden O'Brien; Collections Mgr., Anne Ruta; Assoc. Registrar, Stephanie Livingston; Museum Shop Mgr., Beverly Cihan.
Institution Type/Description: Decorative Arts & History Museum: housed in 1904 Memorial Continental Hall.
Hours & Admission Prices: Museum: Mon.-Fri. 9:30-4, Sat. 9-5, Period Room Tours: Mon.-Fri. 10-3, Sat. 9-4:30. Call to confirm hours. No charge; donations accepted. Closed major holidays. &
Attendance: 27,000 (estimated)

DC FIRE & EMS MUSEUM, 439 New Jersey Ave., N.W., Washington, DC 20001. Tel.: 202-673-1709, 202-439-1936 (cell).
E-mail: dcfems.museum@dc.gov
Key Personnel: Exec. Dir., Walter Gold; Cur. & Museum Mgr., Mark Tennyson.
Institution Type/Description: Firefighting History Museum: housed in active fire station; built in 1916.
Hours & Admission Prices: Mon.-Fri. 10:30-3. No charge; donations accepted. &
Attendance: 1,000 (actual)

DECATUR HOUSE MUSEUM, 748 Jackson Pl., N.W., Washington, DC 20006-4912. Mailing Address: 1610 H St., N.W., Washington, DC 20006-4907. Tel.: 202-842-0920. Fax: 202-842-0030.
E-mail: decatur_house@nthp.org
Web Site: www.decaturhouse.org
Key Personnel: Exec. Dir., Cynthia B. Malinick; Chm. (V), Thomas R. Pickering; Dir. Special Events, Arioth Harrison; Dir. Public Rels. & Mktg., Mame Croze; Museum Shop Mgr., Rosemary Rudd Cohen.
Institution Type/Description: Historic House Museum: 1819 Commodore Stephen Decatur House, designed by B. Latrobe.
Hours & Admission Prices: Tues.-Sat. 10-5, Sun. 12-4. Suggested Donation: adult $5. Closed New Year's Day; Thanksgiving; Christmas. &
Attendance: 25,000 (estimated)

DEPARTMENT OF THE TREASURY, Office of the Curator, Rm. 1225, 15th & Pennsylvania N.W., Dept. of the Treasury, Washington, DC 20220. Mailing Address: 1500 Pennsylvania Ave., N.W., Washington, DC 20220-0002. Tel.: 202-622-1250. Fax: 202-622-2294.

E-mail: richard.cote@do.treas.gov
Web Site: www.treasury.gov
Key Personnel: Cur., Richard Cote; Asst. Cur., Guy Munsch.
Institution Type/Description: Architecture Museum: 1836-1869 U.S. Treasury Building.
Hours & Admission Prices: Tours: Sat. 9, 9:45, 10:30 & 11:15 by appointment only through your congressional office. &

DIPLOMATIC RECEPTION ROOMS, DEPARTMENT OF STATE, M/FA, Rm. 8213, 2201 C St., N.W., Washington, DC 20520. Tel.: 202-647-1990. Fax: 202-647-3428.
E-mail: TourOffice@state.gov
Web Site: www.state.gov/m/drr
Key Personnel: Dir. & Cur., Marcee F. Craighill; Mgr. Collections, Virginia B. Hart; Project Coord., Brianne Brophy; Program Operations Specialist, Jessica A. Wallace.
Institution Type/Description: National Agency.
Hours & Admission Prices: By appointment: Mon.-Fri. 9:30, 10:30, 2:45. Fine Arts Tour: recommended age is 12 & up; photo ID required for adults. No charge; donations accepted. For reservations call or fax 90 days in advance: Department of State, Washington, DC 20520. Tel.: 202-647-3241. Web: https://reception-tours.state.gov. TDD: 202-736-4474; Fax: 202-736-4232. &

DISTRICT OF COLUMBIA ARTS CENTER, 2438 18th St., N.W., Washington, DC 20009-2004. Tel.: 202-462-7833. Fax: 419-821-9622. Facebook: District of Columbia Arts Center.
E-mail: info@dcartcenter.org
Web Site: www.dcartscenter.org
Key Personnel: Dir., B. Stanley; Chm. (V), Bruce Kogod; Pres. (V), Jay Bothwell.
Institution Type/Description: Visual & Performing Arts Center.
Hours & Admission Prices: Wed.-Sun. 2-7 & during theater performances. No charge.
Attendance: 4,000 (estimated)

DUMBARTON HOUSE, 2715 Q St., N.W., Washington, DC 20007-3071. Tel.: 202-337-2288. Fax: 202-337-0348. Facebook: Dumbarton House.
E-mail: info@dumbartonhouse.org
Web Site: www.dumbartonhouse.org
Key Personnel: Chm. (V), Jane Boylin; Pres. (V), Marcy M. Moody; Exec. Dir., Karen L. Daly; Museum Cur., Scott S. Scholz; Mgr. Education, Stephanie Boyle.
Institution Type/Description: Historic House: c.1800.
Hours & Admission Prices: Tues.-Sun. 11-3. Adults $5; discounts to AAA members; AAM, NSCDA & museum members, school groups & students w/ID no charge. Closed Christmas Eve; most national holidays. &
Attendance: 18,000 (estimated)

DUMBARTON OAKS RESEARCH LIBRARY & COLLECTION, 1703 32nd St., N.W., Washington, DC 20007-2961. Tel.: 202-339-6960. Fax: 202-625-0283.
E-mail: museum@doaks.org
Web Site: www.doaks.org
Key Personnel: Dir., Prof. Jan Ziolkowski; Dir. Pre-Columbian Studies, Colin McEwan; Dir. Studies in Landscape Architecture, John Beardsley; Dir. Byzantine Studies, Elena Boeck; Dir. Museum, Gudrun Buehl; Mgr. Image Collection & Fieldwork Archives, Bettina Smith; Mgr. House Collection & Archivist, James Carder; Dir. Gardens & Grounds, Gail Griffin; Museum Shop Mgr., Patti Sheer.
Institution Type/Description: Library & Art Museum.
Hours & Admission Prices: Museum: Tues.-Sun. 11:30-5:30. No charge. Gardens: April-Oct. Tues.-Sun. 2-6; Nov.-March Tues.-Sun. 2-5. Adults $10, seniors 60 & up $8; students & children 12 & under $5. Closed national holidays. &
Attendance: 38,000 (estimated)

FEDERAL RESERVE BOARD, 20th & C Sts., N.W., Washington, DC 20551. Fax: 202-736-5680.
E-mail: finearts@frb.gov
Web Site: www.federalreserve.gov/finearts
Key Personnel: Dir., Stephen Bennett Phillips; Chm. (V), Leatrice Eagle; Collections Asst., Rhonda Gray-Young; Fine Arts Program Asst., Nicolette Pisha.
Institution Type/Description: Art Gallery: housed in a 1935-37 building by Paul Philippe Cret.
Hours & Admission Prices: Mon.-Fri. 10-3:30 by appointment. Please email finearts@frb.gov. No charge. Closed federal holidays. &

FLASHPOINT, 916 G St., N.W., Washington, DC 20001-4565. Tel.: 202-315-1305. Fax: 202-315-1303.
E-mail: travis@culturaldc.org

Web Site: www.culturaldc.org
Key Personnel: Interim Deputy Director & Director of Artistic Programs, Jenny McConnell Frederick.
Institution Type/Description: Art Gallery.
Hours & Admission Prices: Call for hours. &

FOLGER SHAKESPEARE LIBRARY, 201 E. Capitol St., S.E., Washington, DC 20003-1094. Tel.: 202-544-4600. Fax: 202-544-4623.
E-mail: info@folger.edu
Web Site: www.folger.edu
Key Personnel: Dir., Michael Witmore; Chm. (V), Paul T. Ruxin; Dir. Research, Louis Cohen; Librarian, Daniel DeSimone; Reference Librarian, Dr. Georgianna Ziegler; Dir. Public Programs, Janet Griffin; Dir. Devel., Essence Newhoff; Museum Shop Mgr., Matthew Frederick; Controller, Howard Parks; Head External Rels., Garland Scott.
Institution Type/Description: Private Independent Research Library.
Hours & Admission Prices: Library: Mon.-Fri. 8:45-4:45, Sat. 9-12 & 1-4:30. Exhibits Gallery: Mon.-Sat. 10-5, Sun. 12-5. No charge; donations accepted. Closed federal holidays. &
Attendance: 200,000 (estimated)

FORD'S THEATRE NATIONAL HISTORIC SITE (LINCOLN MUSEUM), 511 10th St., N.W., Washington, DC 20004. Tel.: 202-426-6924. Fax: 202-426-1845.
Web Site: www.nps.gov/foth/
Key Personnel: Supt., William Cheek.
Institution Type/Description: Historic Site & History Museum.
Hours & Admission Prices: Ford's Theatre: daily 9-5; The Peterson House: daily 9:30-5:50. No charge, but a ticket is required. Closed Christmas.
Attendance: 1,029,000 (actual)

FREDERICK DOUGLASS NATIONAL HISTORIC SITE, 1411 W Street, S.E., Washington, DC 20020-4813. Mailing Address: c/o National Parks-East, 1411 W. St., S.E., Washington, DC 20020. Tel.: 202-426-5961. Fax: 202-426-0880. TDD: 202-540-9217.
E-mail: kamal_mcclarin@nps.gov
Web Site: www.cr.nps.gov/csd/exhibits/douglass
Key Personnel: Rgnl. Dir., Peggy O'Dell; Dir., Jon Jarvis; Park Supt., Gopaul Noojbail; Cur., Ka'mal McClarin.
Institution Type/Description: Historic Site.
Hours & Admission Prices: April-Oct. daily 9-5; Nov.-March daily 9-4. No charge; donations accepted. Closed New Year's Day; Thanksgiving; Christmas.
Attendance: 33,000 (actual)

FREER GALLERY OF ART AND ARTHUR M. SACKLER GALLERY, SMITHSONIAN INSTITUTION, 1050 Independence Ave., S.W., (and Jefferson Dr. at 12th St., S.W.), Washington, DC 20013-7012. Mailing Address: P.O. Box 37012, MRC 707, Washington, DC 20013-7012. Tel.: 202-633-1000; 202-633-5285 (TTY). Fax: 202-357-4911.
E-mail: publicaffairsasia@si.edu
Web Site: asia.si.edu
Key Personnel: The Dame Jillian Sackler Dir., Chase F. Robinson; Interim Deputy Dir. Collections & Research, Massumeh Farhad, Ph.D.; Deputy Dir. Opers. & External Affairs, Lori Duggan Gold; Cur. South and Southeast Asian Art, Debra Diamond; Cur. Ancient Chinese Art, Keith Wilson; Assoc. Cur. Chinese Painting & Calligraphy, Stephen Allee; Asst. Cur. Contemporary Asian Art, Carol Huh.
Institution Type/Description: Asian Art Museum.
Hours & Admission Prices: Daily 10-5:30. No charge. Closed Christmas. &
Attendance: 688,593 (estimated)

GALLAUDET UNIVERSITY MUSEUM, Chapel Hall, 800 Florida Ave., N.E., Washington, DC 20002. Mailing Address: Gate House, 800 Florida Ave., N.E., Washington, 20002. Tel.: 202-250-2235.
E-mail: museum@gallaudet.edu
Web Site: www.gallaudet.edu/museum
Key Personnel: Mgr., Meredith Peruzzi.
Institution Type/Description: History Museum.
Hours & Admission Prices: Academic year: Mon.-Fri. 10-4; summer: Mon. & Fri. 10-4, Tues.-Thurs. by appointment. No charge; donations accepted. &

THE GEORGE WASHINGTON UNIVERSITY MUSEUM AND THE TEXTILE MUSEUM, 701 21st St., Washington, DC 20052. Tel.: 202-994-5200.
E-mail: museuminfo@gwu.edu
Web Site: museum.gwu.edu
Key Personnel: Dir., John Wetenhall.

Institution Type/Description: Art & Textile Museum.
Hours & Admission Prices: Mon., Wed-Fri. 11:30-6:30, Sat. 10-5, Sun. 1-5. Suggested Donation $8; members, children & current GW students, faculty & staff no charge. Closed university holidays. &

GEORGETOWN UNIVERSITY ART COLLECTION, Georgetown University, Healy Hall, Room #107, 3700 O St., N. W., Washington, DC 20057-1174. Mailing Address: Georgetown Univ., Lauinger Library, Special Collections, 5th Fl., 3700 O St., N.W., Washington, DC 20057-1174. Tel.: 202-687-1469. Fax: 202-687-7501.
E-mail: artcollection@georgetown.edu
Web Site: www.library.georgetown.edu/dept/speccoll/guac/
Key Personnel: Cur. Art, LuLen Walker; Asst. Cur., Christen Runge; Head Special Collections, John Buchtel.
Institution Type/Description: Art and History Museum: housed in 1879 Healy Hall on the Georgetown University campus.
Hours & Admission Prices: Check website for hours. No charge. &

GERMAN-AMERICAN HERITAGE MUSEUM, 719 6th St., N. W., Washington, DC 20001. Tel.: 202-467-5000. Fax: 202-467-5440.
E-mail: info@gahmusa.org
Web Site: www.gahmusa.org
Key Personnel: Dir., Erika Harms.
Institution Type/Description: History Museum.
Hours & Admission Prices: Tues.-Fri. 11-5, Sat. 12-5. Adults $7, students $5; members & children under 12 no charge. &
Attendance: 1,200 (estimated)

HILLWOOD ESTATE, MUSEUM & GARDENS, 4155 Linnean Ave., N.W., Washington, DC 20008-3806. Tel.: 202-686-8500. Fax: 202-966-7846.
E-mail: kphelan@hillwoodmuseum.org
Web Site: www.hillwoodmuseum.org
Key Personnel: C.E.O. & Exec. Dir., Kate Markert; Chm. (V) & Pres. (V) Bd., Ellen MacNeille Charles; C.O.O. & Dir. Interpretation & Visitor Svcs., Angie Dodson; Dir. Collections & Chief Cur., Liana Paredes; Head Exhibitions & Collections Management, Lawrence Waung; Cur. American Material Culture & Historian, Estella Chung; Asst. Cur. Costumes & Textiles, Howard Kurtz; Assoc. Cur. 19th Century Art, Wilfried Zeisler; Chief Art Librarian & Archives Mgr., Kristen Regina; Head Interpretation, Audra Kelly; Mgr. Youth Audiences, Rebecca Singer; Mgr. Adult Audiences, Erin Lourie; Interpretation Volunteer Mgr., Lisa Leyh; Horticulture Volunteer Coord. & Horticulturist, Bill Johnson; Dir. Mktg. & Communications, Lynn Rossotti; Head Visitor Svcs., Katy Albertson; Visitor Svcs. Coord., Lauren Strack; Group Tours & Special Events Coord., Amy Luna Knox; Head Merchandising, Lauren Salazar; Dir. Human Resources, Michael Dudich; Dir. Devel., Judith Paska; Dir. Finance & Admin. and C.F.O., Douglas Rose; Dir. Facilities, Don Rogers; Dir. Horticulture, Brian Barr.
Institution Type/Description: Decorative Art Museum: housed in Washington residence of Marjorie Merriweather Post, founder of Hillwood Museum & Gardens Foundation.
Hours & Admission Prices: Museum: Feb.-Dec. Tues.-Sat. 10-5. Office: Mon.-Fri. 9-5. Estate Donation: adults $15, seniors $12, students $10, children 6-18 $5; discounts to AAM & ICOM members. Closed national holidays. &
Attendance: 64,199 (actual)

HIRSHHORN MUSEUM AND SCULPTURE GARDEN, SMITHSONIAN INSTITUTION, Independence Ave. at Seventh St., S.W., Washington, DC 20560. Mailing Address: P.O. Box 37012, MRC Code 350, Washington, DC 20013-7012. Tel.: 202-633-1000 & 4674. Fax: 202-633-8835. TDD: 202-357-1729.
E-mail: sawyerd@si.edu
Web Site: hirshhorn.si.edu
Key Personnel: Dir., Melissa Chiu; Deputy Dir., Jaya Kaveeshwar; Chief Cur., Stephane Aquin.
Institution Type/Description: Art Museum.
Hours & Admission Prices: Museum: daily 10-5:30. Plaza: daily 7:30-5:30. Garden: daily 7:30-dusk. No charge; donations accepted. Closed Christmas. &
Attendance: 659,000 (estimated)

HISTORICAL SOCIETY OF WASHINGTON, DC, 801 K St., N. W., (@ Mt. Vernon Sq.), Washington, DC 20001-3746. Tel.: 202-249-3955. Facebook; Twitter; Instagram.
E-mail: info@dchistory.org
Web Site: www.dchistory.org
Key Personnel: Exec. Dir., John Suau.
Institution Type/Description: Historical Society Museum.

Hours & Admission Prices: Library: Tues.-Fri. 10-4 by appointment. Exhibit: Tues.-Fri. 10-4. No charge. Closed New Year's Day; Thanksgiving; Christmas. &

HOUSE OF THE TEMPLE, 1733 16th St., N.W., Washington, DC 20009-3103. Tel.: 202-232-3579. Fax: 202-464-0487.
E-mail: hcalloway@scottishrite.org
Web Site: www.scottishrite.org
Formerly: The Supreme Council
Key Personnel: C.E.O., Ronald A. Seale; Librarian, Joan Sansbury; Archivist, Art de Hoyos; Asst. Librarian, Larissa Watkins; Cur., Heather K. Calloway; Museum Shop Mgr., Morgan Corr.
Institution Type/Description: Masonic/Fraternal Museum.
Hours & Admission Prices: Mon.-Thurs. 10-4. Adults 18 & over $8, students 18 & over and seniors 60 & over $3; discounts to groups of 10 or more; members no charge. Closed Federal holidays.
Attendance: 15,000 (estimated)

HOWARD UNIVERSITY GALLERY OF ART, 2455 Sixth St., N. W., Fine Arts Bldg., Rm. 1025, Washington, DC 20059. Mailing Address: 2455 Sixth St., N.W., Ste. 1004, Washington, DC 20059. Tel.: 202-806-7070. Fax: 202-806-6503.
E-mail: geverett@howard.edu
Web Site: art.howard.edu/gallery-art
Key Personnel: Dir. Howard Univ. Gallery of Art, Dr. Gwendolyn H. Everett; Asst. Dir., Scott Baker; Registrar, Eileen Johnston.
Institution Type/Description: Art Gallery.
Hours & Admission Prices: Winter: Mon.-Fri. 9:30-5, Sun. 12-4. Summer: Mon.-Fri. 9:30-4:30, Sun. call for hours. No charge; donations accepted. Closed national holidays. &

HOWARD UNIVERSITY MUSEUM, MOORLAND SPINGARN RESEARCH CENTER, 500 Howard Pl., N.W., Rm. 203, Washington, DC 20059. Tel.: 202-806-7275. Fax: 202-806-5903.
E-mail: rballard@howard.edu
Web Site: http://library.howard.edu/MSRC
Institution Type/Description: Black History Museum.
Hours & Admission Prices: Mon.-Fri. 9-4:30. No charge. &

IDB CULTURAL CENTER, 1300 New York Ave., N.W., Washington, DC 20577. Tel.: 202-623-3654. Fax: 202-623-1420.
E-mail: mifcontact@iadb.org
Web Site: www.iadb.org/exhibitions
Institution Type/Description: Art Gallery.
Hours & Admission Prices: Mon.-Fri. 11-6. No charge.
Attendance: 5,000 (estimated)

INDIAN ARTS AND CRAFTS BOARD, 1849 C St., N.W., Rm. 2528, MIB, U.S. Dept. Interior, Washington, DC 20240. Tel.: 202-208-3773. Fax: 202-208-5196.
E-mail: iacb@ios.doi.gov
Web Site: www.doi.gov/iacb
Key Personnel: Dir., Meridith Stanton.
Institution Type/Description: American Indian & Alaska Native Arts Museum.
Hours & Admission Prices: Mon.-Fri. 7:45-4:15. No charge. Closed national holidays. &

INTERNATIONAL SPY MUSEUM, 800 F St., N.W., Washington, DC 20004-1505. Tel.: 202-393-7798. Fax: 202-393-7797.
E-mail: aabrell@spymuseum.org
Web Site: www.spymuseum.org
Key Personnel: Exec. Dir., E. Peter Earnest; Media Rels., Aliza Bran.
Institution Type/Description: Spy Museum.
Hours & Admission Prices: Daily 10am. Adults $21.95, seniors 65 & over, military and law enforcement $15.95, youth 7-11 $14.95; children 6 & under no charge. Operation Spy: adults 12 & over $14.95. Spy in the City: $14.95. Closed Thanksgiving; Christmas. &

JOHN F. KENNEDY CENTER FOR THE PERFORMING ARTS, 2700 F St., N.W., Washington, DC 20566. Tel.: 202-416-8340; 202-416-8524 (TTY).
E-mail: PublicRelations@kennedy-center.org
Web Site: www.kennedy-center.org
Institution Type/Description: Performing Arts Center & History Museum.
Hours & Admission Prices: Tours: Mon.-Fri. 10-5, Sat.-Sun. 10-1. No charge. &

KENILWORTH PARK AND AQUATIC GARDENS, 1550 Anacostia Ave., N.E., Washington, DC 20019-2028. Mailing Address: 1900 Anacostia Dr., S.E., Washington, DC 20020-6722. Tel.: 202-426-6905. Fax: 202-426-5991.
Web Site: www.nps.gov/keaq/index.htm
Key Personnel: Park Supt., Gopaul Noojibail; Park Ranger, Kate Bucco; Gardener Foreman, Doug Rowley.
Institution Type/Description: Aquatic Garden.
Hours & Admission Prices: Grounds: daily 8 am to dusk. Aquatic Garden: April-Oct. 9-5; Nov.-March daily 8-4. No charge. Closed New Year's Day; Thanksgiving; Christmas. &
Attendance: 75,000 (estimated)

THE KREEGER MUSEUM, 2401 Foxhall Rd., N.W., Washington, DC 20007-1149. Tel.: 202-337-3050. Fax: 202-337-3051. Facebook: The Kreeger Museum.
E-mail: publicrelations@kreegermuseum.org
Web Site: www.kreegermuseum.org
Key Personnel: Dir., Helen Chason; Financial Officer, Basil Arendse; Head Mktg. & Public Rels., Membership, Beth Shook; Head Education, David Hawkins; Head Visitor Svcs. & Docent Management, Joanna Baker.
Institution Type/Description: Art Museum: housed in the former residence of Carmen & David Lloyd Kreeger; designed by Philip Johnson.
Hours & Admission Prices: Sept.-July Fri.-Sat. 10-4. Tours: Tues.-Thurs. 10:30 & 1:30 by appointment. Adults $10, seniors 65 & over and student $7; discounts to museum professionals, NARM members; members no charge. Closed New Year's Eve & Day; Martin Luther King Jr. Day; Presidents' Day; Memorial Day; Independence Day; Labor Day; Columbus Day; Thanksgiving & day after; Christmas Eve & Day. &
Attendance: 10,000 (estimated)

LAOGAI MUSEUM, 1901 18th St., N.W., Washington, DC 20009. Tel.: 202-408-8302 (office) & 730-9308 (museum). Fax: 888-301-1851. Facebook: Laogai Museum, Twitter: LaogaiMuseum.
E-mail: museum@laogai.org
Web Site: www.laogaimuseum.org/
Key Personnel: Dir., Harry Wu.
Institution Type/Description: History Museum.
Hours & Admission Prices: Daily 10-6. No charge; donations accepted. Closed federal holidays.

LIBRARY OF CONGRESS, 101 Independence Ave., S.E., Washington, DC 20540-0002. Tel.: 202-707-5000 (general) & 8000 (visitor information). Fax: 202-707-1714.
E-mail: libofc@loc.gov
Web Site: www.loc.gov
Key Personnel: Librarian of Congress, Carla Hayden.
Institution Type/Description: National library with collections housed in the Thomas Jefferson Building, constructed between 1889-1897; the James Madison Memorial Building, constructed between 1970-1981; & the 1939 John Adams Building.
Hours & Admission Prices: Exhibition Halls: Mon.-Fri. 8:30-9:30, Sat. 8:30-5. General Reading Rooms: call 201-707-6400 for various hours. No charge. Closed all federal government holidays. &
Attendance: 1,600,000 (estimated)

LIBRARY OF THE SUPREME COUNCIL, 33 DEGREES, 1733 16th St., N.W., Washington, DC 20009-3103. Tel.: 202-232-3579. Fax: 202-464-0487.
E-mail: jsansbury@srmason-sj.org
Web Site: www.srmason-sj.org
Key Personnel: Sovereign Grand Commander, Ronald A. Seale; Cur. & Librarian, Joan Sansbury; Archivist & Historian, Art de Hoyos; Asst. Librarian, Larissa Watkins; Dir. Special Programs, Heather Calloway.
Institution Type/Description: Masonic & Americanism Museum.
Hours & Admission Prices: Mon.-Thurs. 8-5. No charge; donations accepted. Closed federal holidays. &
Attendance: 3,600 (estimated)

LILLIAN AND ALBERT SMALL JEWISH MUSEUM, Physical/ Mailing Address: 701 4th St., N.W., Ste. 200, Washington, DC 20001-2607. Tel.: 202-789-0900. Fax: 202-789-0485. Facebook & Twitter: JHSGW.
E-mail: info@jhsgw.org
Web Site: www.jhsgw.org
Key Personnel: Exec. Dir., Kara Blond; Pres. (V), Russell Smith.
Institution Type/Description: Historical Society Museum: housed in the 1876 Historic Adas Israel Synagogue, the first structure built in Washington, DC as a Jewish house of worship.

Hours & Admission Prices: Mon., Tues. & Thurs. 1-4; tours of historic 1876 synagogue offered by advanced reservation Tues.-Fri. 12:30 & 2:30. No charge; donations accepted. Closed major Jewish holidays & federal holidays.
Attendance: 1,745 (estimated)

LINCOLN MEMORIAL, W. Potomac Park @ 23rd St., N.W., Washington, DC 20024. Mailing Address: National Mall & Memorial Parks, 900 Ohio Dr., S.W., Washington, DC 20242-0002. Tel.: 202-426-6841.
Web Site: www.nps.gov/linc
Key Personnel: Supt. National Mall & Memorial, Gay Vietzke.
Institution Type/Description: Historic Building: built in 1917 & dedicated in 1922 to honor the 16th president of the United States, Abraham Lincoln.
Hours & Admission Prices: Memorial open 24 hours. Park Rangers on duty: daily 9:30am-10pm. No charge. &

LINDA K. JORDAN GALLERY, GALLAUDET UNIVERSITY, Washburn Arts Bldg. #127, 800 Florida Ave., N.E., Washington, DC 20002-3600. Tel.: 202-651-5480. Fax: 202-651-5618.
E-mail: patricia.hill@gallaudet.edu
Key Personnel: Acting Chm., Dr. Stephen Weiner.
Institution Type/Description: Art Gallery.
Hours & Admission Prices: Call for hours.

THE LUTHER W. BRADY ART GALLERY, 805 21st St., N.W., Washington, DC 20052-0029. Tel.: 202-994-1525. Fax: 202-994-1632.
E-mail: lutherbradyart@gmail.com
Web Site: www.gwu.edu/~bradyart
Formerly: The George Washington University Art Gallery
Key Personnel: Dir. University Art Galleries, Lenore D. Miller; Asst. Dir., Olivia Kohler.
Institution Type/Description: Art Gallery.
Hours & Admission Prices: Tues.-Fri. 10-5. No charge. Closed during school breaks, summer & national holidays. &
Attendance: 3,500 (estimated)

MADAME TUSSAUDS WASHINGTON D.C., 1001 F St., Washington, DC 20004. Tel.: 202-942-7303. Fax: 202-942-7319. Facebook: Madame Tussauds DC.
E-mail: info@madametussaudsdc.com
Web Site: www.madametussaudsdc.com
Institution Type/Description: Wax Museum.
Hours & Admission Prices: mid-April to early Sept. Sun.-Fri. 10-6, Sat. 10-8; early Sept. to mid-April Sun.-Thurs. 10-6, Fri.-Sat. 10-8. Adults $20, seniors 60 & over $18, children 3-12 $15; discounts to groups; children 2 & under no charge.

MARIAN KOSHLAND SCIENCE MUSEUM, 525 E. St., N.W., Washington, DC 20001. Mailing Address: The National Academies, 500 5th St., N.W., Washington, DC 20001-2736. Tel.: 202-334-1201. Fax: 202-334-1548.
E-mail: ksm@nas.edu
Web Site: www.koshlandsciencemuseum.org
Key Personnel: Dir., Patrice Legro; Chair, May Barenbaum; Operations & Museum Shop Mgr., Johann Yurgen; Financial & Administrative Officer, Lisa Alston; Deputy Dir., Erika Shugart; Community Outreach, Amy Shaw.
Institution Type/Description: Science Museum.
Hours & Admission Prices: Wed.-Mon. 10-6. Adults $7, active military & students $5. Closed New Year's Day; Thanksgiving; Christmas. &
Attendance: 30,000 (actual)

MARY MCLEOD BETHUNE COUNCIL HOUSE NATIONAL HISTORIC SITE, 1318 Vermont Ave., N.W., Washington, DC 20005-3607. Tel.: 202-673-2402. Fax: 202-673-2414.
Web Site: www.nps.gov/mamc
Key Personnel: Supt., Alex Romero; Deputy Supt., Gopaul Noojibail; District Mgr., Joy Kinard; Archivist, Kenneth Chandler; Park Guide, Jamie Euken; Park Guide, Veronica Quiguango; Museum Shop Mgr., Margaret Miles.
Institution Type/Description: Historic House.
Hours & Admission Prices: Mon.-Sat. 9-5. No charge, donations accepted. Closed New Year's Day; Thanksgiving; Christmas.
Attendance: 8,631 (actual)

MAURINE LITTLETON GALLERY, 1667 Wisconsin Ave., N. W., Washington, DC 20007. Tel.: 202-333-9307. Fax: 202-342-2004.
E-mail: info@littletongallery.com
Web Site: www.littletongallery.com
Key Personnel: Dir., Maurine Littleton.

Institution Type/Description: Art Gallery.
Hours & Admission Prices: Tues.-Sat. 11-6; other times by appointment.

MERIDIAN INTERNATIONAL CENTER, Physical/Mailing Address: 1630 Crescent Pl., N.W., Washington, DC 20009-4004. Tel.: 202-667-6800. Fax: 202-939-5512.
E-mail: info@meridian.org
Web Site: www.meridian.org
Formerly: Meridian International Center-Cafritz Galleries
Key Personnel: Pres. & C.E.O., Ambassador Stuart W. Holliday; Chm. (V), Jim Blanchard; Vice Pres. for the Arts, Dr. Curtis Sandberg; Dir. Exhibitions, Terry Harvey.
Institution Type/Description: International Arts & Cultural Center.
Hours & Admission Prices: Wed.-Sun. 2-5. No charge; donations accepted. Closed major holidays. &
Attendance: 25,000 (estimated)

MID-ATLANTIC ASSOCIATION OF MUSEUMS, 1025 Thomas Jefferson St., N.W., Ste. 500W, Washington, DC 20007-5224. Tel.: 202-452-8040. Fax: 202-833-3636.
E-mail: admin@midatlanticmuseums.org
Web Site: www.midatlanticmuseums.org
Key Personnel: Exec. Dir., Graham Hauck.
Institution Type/Description: Museum Service Organization.
Hours & Admission Prices: Mon.-Fri. 9-5. Closed national holidays.
Attendance: 400

MUSEUM OF CULTURES & HERITAGES OF AMERICA (MOCHA), P.O. Box 53067, Washington, DC 20009. Tel.: 202-550-5048.
E-mail: mochamuseum@gmail.com
Web Site: mochamuseumdc.org
Key Personnel: Co-Founder, Exec. Dir. & Chief Cur., W. Marc Zuver.
Institution Type/Description: Art Museum.
Hours & Admission Prices: See website for updates on touring exhibits, educational programs & admissions.

MUSEUM OF POLISH ART AND CULTURE, 2025 "O" St., N. W., Washington, DC 20036-5913. Tel.: 202-785-2320.
E-mail: bbernhardt@thekf.org
Web Site: www.thekf.org
Formerly: The American Center of Polish Culture
Key Personnel: Dir., Barbara Bernhardt.
Institution Type/Description: Cultural History Museum.
Hours & Admission Prices: Mon.-Fri. 10-4. No charge; donations accepted.
Attendance: 1,000 (estimated)

MUSEUM OF THE BIBLE, 400 4th St. S.W., Washington, DC 20024. Mailing Address: P.O. Box 15479, Washington, DC 20003-0479. Tel.: 855-554-5300.
E-mail: customerservice@mbible.org
Web Site: museumofthebible.org
Key Personnel: Dir. Collections, David Trobisch.
Institution Type/Description: Religious History Museum.
Hours & Admission Prices: Mon.-Sat. 10-7, Sun. 10-6. Closed New Year's Day; Thanksgiving; Christmas. &

NATIONAL ACADEMY OF SCIENCES, 2101 Constitution Ave., N.W., Washington, DC 20418-0006. Mailing Address: 500 5th St., N.W., Ste. 1, Washington, DC 20001-2737. Tel.: 202-334-2436. Fax: 202-334-1690. Facebook: National Academy of Sciences.
E-mail: cpnas@nas.edu
Web Site: www.cpnas.org
Key Personnel: Dir., Mr. J.D. Talasek; Sr. Program Assoc., Ms. Alana Quinn.
Institution Type/Description: Art & Science Museum.
Hours & Admission Prices: Mon.-Fri. 9-5. No charge. Closed New Year's Day; Martin Luther King Jr. Day; Presidents' Day; Memorial Day; Independence Day; Labor Day; Thanksgiving & day after; Christmas Eve & Day. &
Attendance: 5,000 (estimated)

NATIONAL AIR AND SPACE MUSEUM, SMITHSONIAN INSTITUTION, 655 Jefferson Dr., SW, Washington, DC 20560. Mailing Address: P.O. Box 37012, Washington, DC 20013-7012. Tel.: 202-633-2214. Fax: 202-633-8174.
E-mail: info@si.edu
Web Site: airandspace.si.edu
Key Personnel: John and Adrienne Mars Dir., Ellen Stofan; Deputy Dir., Christopher Browne; Chief Cur., Peter Jakab; Assoc. Dir. Collections, Archives & Logistics, Rick Flansburg; Assoc. Dir. External Affairs, Meg Caulk; Brot-

Kahn Weil Dir. Education, Beth Crownover; Dir. Advancement, Laura Gleason; Asst. Dir. Business Opers. & Tech., Stephanie A. Brinley; Asst. Dir. Exhibits, Francisco Torres.
Institution Type/Description: Aeronautics & Space Museum.
Hours & Admission Prices: Daily 10-5:30. No charge; donations accepted. Closed Christmas. &
Attendance: 7,500,000 (estimated)

NATIONAL ARCHIVES FOUNDATION, 700 Pennsylvania Ave., N.W., Washington, DC 20408-0002. Mailing Address: 700 Pennsylvania Ave., N.W., Rm. G-12, Washington, DC 20408. Tel.: 202-357-5946. Fax: 202-357-5926. Facebook, Twitter, Instagram & Tumblr: @archivesfoundation.
E-mail: museumprograms@nara.gov
Web Site: archivesfoundation.org
Formerly: National Archives and Records Administration
Key Personnel: Archivist, David F. Ferriero; Chair, A'Lelia Bundles; Exec. Dir. Foundation, Patrick M Madden; Dir. Exhibits, Lisa Royse; Dir. Retail Operations, Angela Catigano; Museum Shop Mgr., Eric Green.
Institution Type/Description: History Museum: housed in the National Archives building; built 1931-1935.
Hours & Admission Prices: Daily 10-5:30. No charge. Research Rooms: Mon. & Wed. 8:45-5, Tues. & Thurs.-Fri. 8:45-9, Sat. 8:45-4:45. Closed Thanksgiving; Christmas. &
Attendance: 1,000,000 (estimated)

NATIONAL BUILDING MUSEUM, 401 F St., N.W., Washington, DC 20001-2637. Tel.: 202-272-2448, ext. 3109. Fax: 202-272-2564. Facebook: National Building Museum.
E-mail: brodgers@nbm.org
Web Site: www.nbm.org
Key Personnel: Exec. Dir. & Pres., Chase W. Rynd; Chm. (V), Gary Haney; C.O. O., Betsy May-Salazar; Vice Pres. Exhibitions & Collections, Cathy Crane Frankel; Vice Pres. Mktg. & Communications, Brett Rodgers; Vice Pres. Visitor Svcs., Jamee Telford; Dir. Finance & Controller, Diane Beckham; Dir. Special Events, Chris Frame; Museum Shop Mgr., Michael Higdon; Exec. Asst., Tom Buck.
Institution Type/Description: Architecture Museum.
Hours & Admission Prices: Mon.-Sat. 10-5, Sun. 11-5. Exhibitions: Adults $10, youth 3-17, students with ID and seniors 60 & over $7; discounts to AAM & ICOM members; military & their families between Memorial Day & Labor Day, members and children 2 & under no charge. Building Zone: adults $3. Closed Thanksgiving; Christmas. &
Attendance: 500,000 (estimated)

NATIONAL GALLERY OF ART, 6th St. & Constitution Ave., N.W., Washington, DC 20565. Mailing Address: 2000B S. Club Dr., Landover, MD 20785. Tel.: 202-737-4215. Facebook; Twitter; Instagram; Pinterest; Youtube.
E-mail: d-lenoir@nga.gov
Web Site: www.nga.gov
Key Personnel: Dir., Kaywin Feldman, III; Pres. (V), Mitchell P. Rales; Chm. (V), Sharon Percy Rockefeller; Deputy Dir. & Chief Cur., Franklin W. Kelly; Admin., Darrell R. Willson; Treas., William McClure; Sec. & Gen. Counsel, Nancy Robinson Breuer; Dean, Center for Advanced Study in Visual Arts, Elizabeth Cropper; Cur. Northern Baroque Paintings, Arthur K. Wheelock, Jr.; Cur. Italian Paintings, David Alan Brown; Cur. Northern Renaissance Paintings, John Hand; Cur. Early European Sculpture, Alison Luchs; Cur. Modern & Head, Contemporary Art, Harry Cooper; Sr. Cur. & Head Dept. Photographs, Sarah Greenough; Cur. Special Projects in Modern Art, Lynne Cooke; A.W. Mellon Sr. Cur. Prints & Drawings, Andrew C. Robison; Asst. Cur. Old Master Prints, Amy Johnston; Cur. & Head Old Master Drawings, Margaret Morgan Grasselli; Cur. & Head Modern Prints & Drawings, Judith Brodie; Cur. & Head Dept., Sculpture & Decorative Arts, C.D. Dickerson; Cur. & Head Dept., American & British Paintings, Nancy Anderson; Chief of Conservation, Mervin Richard; Sr. Conservator & Head Painting Conservation, Jay Krueger; Head Paper Conservation, Kimberly Schenck; Sr. Conservator & Head Object Conservation, Shelley Sturman; Sr. Conservator & Head Textile Conservation, Julia Burke; Head Scientific Research Dept., Barbara Berrie; Exec. Librarian, Neal T. Turtell; Chief Library Image Collections, Gregory P.J. Most; Chief Exhibitions, D. Dodge Thompson; Sr. Cur. & Chief Design, Mark Leithauser; Head Education, Lynn Russell; Head Film Programs, Margaret Parsons; Editor in Chief, Publishing Office, Judy Metro; Chief Registrar, Sally Freitag; Chief Imaging & Visual Svcs., Alan Newman; Head Digital Imaging Svcs., Peter Dueker; Head Visual Svcs., Barbara Bernard; Chief Protocol & Special Events, Carol W. Kelley; Chief Devel. & Corporate Rels. Officer, Christine M. Myers; Chief Press & Public Information Officer, Anabeth Guthrie; Acting Personnel Officer, Doug Goodell; Chief Horticulture Svcs., Cynthia Kaufmann; Deputy Chief Admin. Visitor Svcs., Elizabeth Thomas; Chief Gallery Shop Div., David Krol; Congressional Liaison Officer & Dir. Special Projects, Delia Scott.
Institution Type/Description: Art Museum.

Hours & Admission Prices: Mon.-Sat. 10-5, Sun. 11-6. No charge. Closed New Year's Day; Christmas. &
Attendance: 4,800,000 (estimated)

NATIONAL GEOGRAPHIC MUSEUM, National Geographic Society, 1145 17th St., N.W., Washington, DC 20036. Tel.: 202-857-7700. Fax: 202-857-5864. TDD: 202-857-7198.
E-mail: ngtickets@ngs.org
Web Site: events/nationalgeographic.com/national-geographic-museum
Key Personnel: Vice Pres. Exhibitions, Kathryn Keane.
Institution Type/Description: General Museum.
Hours & Admission Prices: Daily 10-6. Adults $15, subscribers, seniors, students & military $12, children 5-12 $10; children under 5 & annual pass members no charge. Fee charged for special exhibitions. Closed Christmas. &
Attendance: 144,742 (actual)

NATIONAL GUARD MEMORIAL MUSEUM, One Massachusetts Ave., N.W., Washington, DC 20001. Tel.: 202-408-5890. Fax: 202-682-1641.
E-mail: ngaus@ngaus.org
Web Site: www.ngaus.org/national-guard-memorial-museum
Institution Type/Description: History Museum.
Hours & Admission Prices: Mon.-Fri. 9-4. No charge; donations accepted. &
Attendance: 2,500 (estimated)

NATIONAL LIBRARY OF EDUCATION, 400 Maryland Ave., S.W., Washington, DC 20202. Tel.: 202-205-5015; 202-205-7561 (TTY).
E-mail: contact.ies@ed.gov
Web Site: ies.ed.gov/ncee/projects/nle/
Institution Type/Description: Education Library.
Hours & Admission Prices: Mon.-Fri. 9-5 by appointment. Closed federal holidays.

THE NATIONAL MUSEUM OF AFRICAN AMERICAN HISTORY AND CULTURE, SMITHSONIAN INSTITUTION, 1400 Constitution Ave., N.W., Washington, DC 20013. Mailing Address: P.O. Box 37012, MRC 509, Washington, DC 20013-7012. Tel.: 844-750-3012.
E-mail: nmaahcinfo@si.edu
Web Site: www.nmaahc.si.edu
Key Personnel: Dir., Lonnie G. Bunch, III.
Institution Type/Description: History Museum.
Hours & Admission Prices: Daily 10-5:30. No charge; Timed Entry Pass necessary to enter museum. Closed Christmas Day.
Attendance: 1,400,000

NATIONAL MUSEUM OF AFRICAN ART, SMITHSONIAN INSTITUTION, 950 Independence Ave., S.W., Washington, DC 20560-0006. Mailing Address: P.O. Box 37012, Washington, DC 20013-7012. Tel.: 202-633-4600. Fax: 202-357-4879.
E-mail: nmafaweb@si.edu
Web Site: africa.si.edu
Key Personnel: Dir., Augustus Casely-Hayford.
Institution Type/Description: Art Museum.
Hours & Admission Prices: Daily 10-5:30. No charge. Closed Christmas. &
Attendance: 159,000 (estimated)

NATIONAL MUSEUM OF AMERICAN HISTORY, SMITHSONIAN INSTITUTION, 1400 Constitution Ave., N.W., Washington, DC 20560. Mailing Address: P.O. Box 37012, Washington, DC 20013-7012. Tel.: 202-633-1000; 202-633-5285 (TTY). Fax: 202-633-8053.
E-mail: info@si.edu
Web Site: americanhistory.si.edu
Key Personnel: Dir. Elizabeth MacMillan, Anthea M. Hartig, Ph.D.; Assoc. Dir. External Affairs, Maggie Webster; Assoc. Dir. Building Renovation & Exhibition Services, Pedro Colon; Assoc. Dir. Audience Engagement, Amy Bartow-Melia; Dir. Communications & Mktg., Melinda Machado; Dir. Special Initiatives, Magdalena Mieri; Dir. Emeritus, Arthur Molella.
Institution Type/Description: American History & Technology Museum.
Hours & Admission Prices: Daily 10-5:30. No charge; donations accepted. Closed Christmas. &
Attendance: 3,800,000 (estimated)

NATIONAL MUSEUM OF AMERICAN JEWISH MILITARY HISTORY, 1811 R St., N.W., Washington, DC 20009-1603. Tel.: 202-265-6280. Fax: 202-462-3192.
E-mail: nmajmh@nmajmh.org

Web Site: www.nmajmh.org
Key Personnel: Natl. Exec. Dir., Col. Herb Rosenbleeth; Pres. (V), Norman Rosenshein; Dir. Operations, Larry Richardson.
Institution Type/Description: National Museum of American Jewish Military History.
Hours & Admission Prices: Mon.-Fri. 9-5, Sun. by appointment only. No charge; donations accepted. Closed federal & Jewish holidays. &
Attendance: 3,000 (estimated)

THE NATIONAL MUSEUM OF CATHOLIC ART & LIBRARY, 1500 Massachusetts Ave., N.W., Ste. 122, Washington, DC 20005-1800. Tel.: 917-750-0014, 202-450-5707.
E-mail: info@nmcah.org
Web Site: www.nmcal.org/
Key Personnel: Pres. & Exec. Dir., Christina Cox; Chief Cur. Art, Mariavelia Savino.
Institution Type/Description: Religious Art & Christian History Museum.
Hours & Admission Prices: Closed for relocation. &
Attendance: 10,000 (estimated)

NATIONAL MUSEUM OF NATURAL HISTORY, SMITHSONIAN INSTITUTION, 1000 Constitution Ave., N.W., Washington, DC 20560. Mailing Address: P.O. Box 37012, Washington, DC 20013-7012. Tel.: 202-633-1000. Twitter.
E-mail: naturalexperience@si.edu
Web Site: naturalhistory.si.edu
Key Personnel: Sant Dir., Dr. Kirk Johnson; Chm. (V), Paula Kerger; Deputy Dir., Ian Owens; Assoc. Dir. Devel., Dr. Sandra Lovinguth; Assoc. Dir. Science, Rebecca Johnson; Asst. Dir. Exhibitions, Mike Lawrence; Asst. Dir. Collections, Carol Butler; Asst. Dir. Communications, Jim Wood; Asst. Dir. Education & Outreach, Donna Tuggle; Acting Assoc. Dir. Facilities & Operations, Chun-Hsi Wong; Acting Assoc. Dir. of Ops., HR, & Fin., Matt McDermott; Asst. Dir. Science Program Administration, Dr. Wendy Wiswall.
Institution Type/Description: Natural History Museum.
Hours & Admission Prices: Daily 10-5:30. No charge; donations accepted. Closed Christmas. &
Attendance: 7,100,000 (actual)

NATIONAL MUSEUM OF THE AMERICAN INDIAN, SMITHSONIAN INSTITUTION, 4th St. and Independence Ave., S.W., National Mall, Washington, DC 20024. Mailing Address: P.O. Box 37012, Washington, DC 20013-7012. Tel.: 202-633-6700. Fax: 202-633-6921.
E-mail: nmai-info@si.edu
Web Site: nmai.si.edu
Key Personnel: Dir., Kevin Gover; Dir. Public Affairs, Eileen Maxwell.
Institution Type/Description: Native American Museum.
Hours & Admission Prices: Daily 10-5:30; groups of 10 or more by appointment. No charge. Closed Christmas. &
Attendance: 1,100,000 (estimated)

NATIONAL MUSEUM OF THE UNITED STATES NAVY, 805 Kidder Breese St., S.E., Washington, DC 20374-5060. Tel.: 202-685-0528 & 0589. Fax: 202-433-8200. Facebook; Twitter.
E-mail: navymuseum@navy.mil
Web Site: www.history.navy.mil
Key Personnel: Head Cur., Navy Art Gallery, Gale Munro; Historian & Cur., Gordon Calhoun; Collections Mgr., Wes Schwenk.
Institution Type/Description: Naval History Museum: housed in the former Breech Mechanism Shop of the old Naval Gun Factory.
Hours & Admission Prices: Mon.-Fri. 9-4, Sat. 10-4. No charge; donations accepted. Closed holidays. &
Attendance: 215,000 (actual)

NATIONAL MUSEUM OF WOMEN IN THE ARTS, 1250 New York Ave., N.W., Washington, DC 20005-3970. Tel.: 202-783-5000. Fax: 202-393-3235. Facebook, Twitter.
E-mail: media@nmwa.org
Web Site: nmwa.org
Key Personnel: C.E.O. & Dir., Dr. Susan Fisher Sterling; Chm. (V), Wilhelmina Cole Holladay; Pres. (V), Martha Dippell; Dir. Education, Deborah Gaston; Deputy Dir. Art, Programs & Public Engagement and Chief Cur., Kathryn Wat; Registrar, Catherine Bade; Dir. Library & Research Center, Lynora Williams; Dir. National & International Outreach, Ilene Gutman; Dir. Retail Operations, Adriana Regalado; Dir. Public Programs, Melani Douglas.
Institution Type/Description: Art Museum: housed in 1908 second Renaissance revival style structure.
Hours & Admission Prices: Museum: Mon.-Sat. 10-5, Sun. 12-5. Adults $10, seniors & students w/ID $8; discounts to AAM members; children under 18 &

members no charge. Library: Mon.-Fri. 10-noon & 1-5. Closed New Year's Day; Thanksgiving; Christmas. &
Attendance: 131,201 (actual)

NATIONAL PARK SERVICE, 1201 Eye St., N.W. 2265, Washington, DC 20005-5905. Tel.: 202-354-2000. Fax: 202-371-6757.
E-mail: ronald_wilson@nps.gov
Web Site: www.nps.gov/history/museum/
Key Personnel: Chief Cur., Ronald C. Wilson; Museum Registrar, Kathleen Byrne; Museum Cur., Joan Bacharach; Sr. Cur. Natural History, Greg McDonald; Archivist, John W. Roberts.
Institution Type/Description: National Park Service.
Hours & Admission Prices: Offices: Mon.-Fri. 7:45-4:15. Closed national holidays. &

NATIONAL PARK SERVICE - PEIRCE BARN, 5200 Glover Rd., N.W., Washington, DC 20015. Tel.: 202-895-6222. Fax: 202-895-6230.
E-mail: ricardo_perez@nps.gov
Web Site: www.nps.gov/rocr
Formerly: Peirce Mill and Peirce Barn
Key Personnel: Park Supt., Adrienne Coleman; Park Ranger, Ricardo Perez.
Institution Type/Description: Historic Building: c.1820 Grist Mill & Peirce Mill located in Rock Creek Park.
Hours & Admission Prices: Mill & Barn by appointment. Research Facility: by appointment only. Closed federal holidays.

NATIONAL PORTRAIT GALLERY, SMITHSONIAN INSTITUTION, Eighth & F Sts., N.W., Donald W. Reynolds Center for American Art & Portraiture, Washington, DC 20001. Mailing Address: P.O. Box 37012, Victor Bldg., Ste. 410, MRC-973, Washington, DC 20013-7012. Tel.: 202-633-8300; 202-633-5285 (TTY).
E-mail: npgnews@si.edu
Web Site: www.npg.si.edu
Key Personnel: Dir., Kim Sajet; Chief Cur. & Cur. Painting & Sculpture, Brandon Brame Fortune.
Institution Type/Description: Art & History Museum: housed in c.1840, former U. S. Patent Office building.
Hours & Admission Prices: Daily 11:30-7. No charge. Closed Christmas. &
Attendance: 1,600,000 (estimated)

NATIONAL POSTAL MUSEUM, SMITHSONIAN INSTITUTION, 2 Massachusetts Ave., N.E., Washington, DC 20002. Mailing Address: P.O. Box 37012, MRC 570, Washington, DC 20013-7012. Tel.: 202-633-5555. Fax: 202-633-9393.
E-mail: npm@npm.si.edu
Web Site: postalmuseum.si.edu.
Key Personnel: Dir., Elliot Gruber; Collections, Katie Burke; Preservation, Scott Devine; Public Rels., Marty Emery; Curatorial, Lynn Heidelbaugh; Collections, Beth Heydt; Education, Motoko Hioki; Preservation, Rebecca Kennedy; Web Team, Bill Lommel; Curatorial, Calvin Mitchell; External Affairs, Hannah Trumball; Curatorial, Daniel A. Piazza; Curatorial, Nancy Pope; Collections, Patricia Raynor; Library, Baasil Wilder; Collections, Ted Wilson.
Institution Type/Description: Postal History Museum: housed in 1914 Old City Post Office Building.
Hours & Admission Prices: Daily 10-5:30. No charge; donations accepted. Closed Christmas. &
Attendance: 398,000 (actual)

NATIONAL SOCIETY OF THE CHILDREN OF THE AMERICAN REVOLUTION MUSEUM, 1776 D St., N.W., Rm. 224, Washington, DC 20006-5303. Tel.: 202-638-3153. Fax: 202-737-3162.
E-mail: hq@nscar.org
Web Site: www.nscar.org
Key Personnel: National Pres., Nancy Ehmcke.
Institution Type/Description: History Museum.
Hours & Admission Prices: Mon.-Sat. 8:30-4. No charge; donations accepted.

NATIONAL TRUST FOR HISTORIC PRESERVATION, The Watergate Office Building, 2600 Virginia Ave., Ste. 1100, Washington, DC 20037. Tel.: 202-588-6000. Fax: 202-588-6038.
E-mail: info@savingplaces.org
Web Site: savingplaces.org
Key Personnel: Pres. & C.E.O., Stephanie Meeks; Chief of Staff, Tabitha Almquist; Chief Preservation Officer, David J. Brown; Chief Devel. Officer, Robert Lee

Bull, Jr.; Chief Legal Officer, Paul Edmondson; Chief Mktg. Officer, Amy Maniatis; Chief Financial & Administrative Officer, Carla Washinko.
Institution Type/Description: Historical Society.
Hours & Admission Prices: See individual listings for their hours & admission fees.
Attendance: 809,204 (actual)

NATIONAL WWII MEMORIAL, 1750 Independence Ave., S.W., Washington, DC 20006. Mailing Address: National Park Service, 900 Ohio Dr., S.W., Washington, DC 20242-0002. Tel.: 202-619-7222, 800-639-4992.
E-mail: wwll.customerservice@oaktreesys.com
Web Site: www.wwiimemorial.com
Institution Type/Description: Military Memorial.
Hours & Admission Prices: Daily 24 hrs. Rangers on duty to answer questions daily 9:30-11:30.

NATIONAL ZOOLOGICAL PARK, SMITHSONIAN INSTITUTION, 3001 Connecticut Ave., N.W., Washington, DC 20008-2598. Mailing Address: P.O. Box 37012, MRC 5516, Washington, DC 20013-7012. Tel.: 202-633-4888. Fax: 202-673-4607.
Web Site: nationalzoo.si.edu
Key Personnel: Acting Dir. Smithsonian National Zoo, Steven Monfort; Deputy Dir. Smithsonian Conservation Biology Institute, Wiliam Pitt, Ph.D.; Deputy Dir. Smithsonian's National Zoo, Brandie Smith, Ph.D.; Exec. Dir., Friends of the National Zoo (FONZ), Lynn Mento; Assoc. Dir. Communication, Pamela Baker-Masson; Assoc. Dir., Office of Advancement, Virginia Kromm; Assoc. Dir. Office of Advancement, Virginia Kromm; Assoc. Dir. Finance & Business Development, Ginna Newton.
Institution Type/Description: Zoological Park.
Hours & Admission Prices: Exhibit Buildings: Summer daily 9-6; Winter daily 9-4. Grounds: Summer daily 8-7; Winter daily 8-5. Visitor Center: Summer daily 8-6; Winter daily 8-4. No charge; donations accepted. Parking: $25. Closed Christmas. &
Attendance: 2,700,000 (estimated)

THE OCTAGON MUSEUM, 1799 New York Ave., N.W., Washington, DC 20006-5207. Mailing Address: 1735 New York Ave., N.W., Washington, DC 20006. Tel.: 202-638-3221. Fax: 202-626-7420.
E-mail: octagonmuseum@aia.org
Web Site: www.octagonmuseum.org
Key Personnel: Dir., Mgr., Teresa Martinez; Assoc., Margaret Phalen.
Institution Type/Description: Architecture Museum & Historic House: 1799-1801 Federal townhouse built for Colonel John Tayloe III, based on designs by Dr. William Thornton, served as first temporary White House during the winter of 1814-1815 for President James & Dolley Madison; the Treaty of Ghent was signed there, ending the War of 1812.
Hours & Admission Prices: Thurs.-Sat. 1-4. No charge; donations accepted. Closed Thanksgiving; Christmas; New Year's Day.
Attendance: 4,000 (actual)

THE OLD STONE HOUSE, 3051 M St., N.W. (Georgetown), Washington, DC 20007-3702. Mailing Address: 3545 Williamsburg Lane, N.W., Washington, DC 20008. Tel.: 202-426-6851. Fax: 202-895-6015. TDD: 202-426-0125.
E-mail: tara_morrison@nps.gov
Web Site: www.nps.gov/olst
Key Personnel: Supt., Tara Morrison; Park Ranger, Ron Harvey.
Institution Type/Description: Historic Building: 1765 pre-Revolutionary building located in the Georgetown area of the District of Columbia.
Hours & Admission Prices: Wed.-Sun. 11-6; groups by appointment. No charge; donations accepted. Closed federal holidays. &
Attendance: 70,000 (actual)

PENTAGON, 1400 Defense Pentagon, Washington, DC 20301-1400. Tel.: 703-571-3343.
Web Site: pentagontours.osd.mil
Institution Type/Description: Department of Defense Headquarters.
Hours & Admission Prices: Tours: Mon.-Thurs. 10-4, Fri. 12-4 by appointment. Tours scheduled through website. Visitors 18 & over must present a valid form of identification. &
Attendance: 106,000

THE PHILLIPS COLLECTION, 1600 21st St., N.W., Washington, DC 20009-1090. Tel.: 202-387-2151. Fax: 202-387-2436. blog. phillipscollection.org.
E-mail: info@phillipscollection.org

Web Site: www.phillipscollection.org
Key Personnel: Dir., Dorothy Kosinski; Chm. Bd. Trustees (V), Dani Levinas; Vice Chm., Lindsay Ellenbogen; Vice Chm., Scott Spector; Sec., Carol Melton; Treas., George D. Suwyegert, Jr.; C.O.O., Susan J. Nichols; Deputy Dir. Curatorial & Academic Affairs, Klaus Ottmann; Cur. Modern & Contemporary Art, Vesela Sretenovic; Cur., Elsa Smithgall; Asst. Cur., Sue Behrends Frank; Dir. Budgeting & Reporting, Cheryl Nichols; Installations Mgr., William Koberg; Dir. Music, Caroline Mousset; Chief Registrar, Joseph Holbach; Librarian, Karen Schneider; Assoc Registrar Exhibitions, Trish Waters; Chief Information Officer, Darci Vanderhoff; Dir. of Education, Suzanne Wright; Dir. Human Resources, Angela Gillespie; Museum Shop Mgr., Pete Bernal.
Institution Type/Description: Art Museum: housed in the former residence of Duncan Phillips family, 1897 Georgian Revival home.
Hours & Admission Prices: Tues.-Wed. & Fri.-Sat. 10-5, Thurs. 10-8:30, Sun. 12-7. Concerts: Oct.-May Sun. 4pm. Adults $12; members no charge. Closed New Year's Day; Independence Day; Thanksgiving; Christmas Eve & Day. &
Attendance: 150,000 (estimated)

PRESIDENT LINCOLN'S COTTAGE, 140 Rock Creek Church Rd., N.W., (at Upshur St. N.W.), Washington, DC 20011. Mailing Address: AFRH-W 558, 3700 N. Capitol St., N.W., Washington, DC 20011-8400. Tel.: 202-829-0436, ext. 31231. Fax: 202-829-0437. Facebook: Lincolns Cottage.
E-mail: lincolnscottage@savingplaces.org
Web Site: www.lincolncottage.org
Key Personnel: Dir., Erin Carlson Mast; Exec. Asst., Zach Klitzman; Assoc. Dir. Devel., Nora Cobo; Mktg. & Membership Coord., Curtis Harris; Assoc. Dir. Programs, Callie Hawkins; Events Coord., Sahand Miraminy; Progs. Coord., Michelle Martz; Museum Store Coord., Jamie Cooper; Preservation Mgr., Jeffrey Larry.
Institution Type/Description: Historic House: the summer home of Lincoln and his family during his presidency.
Hours & Admission Prices: Mon.-Sat. 9:30-4:30, Sun. 10:30-4:30. Adults $15, students 6-12 $5; discounts to members, military & groups; children under 6 no charge. Closed New Year's Day; Thanksgiving; Christmas. &
Attendance: 32,000 (actual)

THE PRESIDENT WOODROW WILSON HOUSE, 2340 S St., N.W., Washington, DC 20008-4016. Tel.: 202-387-4062. Fax: 202-483-1466.
E-mail: jpucher@woodrowwilsonhouse.org
Web Site: www.woodrowwilsonhouse.org
Key Personnel: Chm. (V), Linna Barnes; Mgr. Business & Operations, John Pucher; Cur., Carrie Villar; Mktg. & Events Mgr., Sarah Andrews.
Institution Type/Description: Historic House Museum: housed in the former home of President Wilson.
Hours & Admission Prices: Wed.-Sun. 10-4. Adults $10, senior citizens $8, students $5; discounts to AAA, AAM, & National Trust members and general museum staff; members & children under 12 no charge. Closed major holidays. &
Attendance: 12,062 (actual)

PROVISIONS LIBRARY, 5813 Nevada Ave., N.W. #1100, Washington, DC 20015-2547. Tel.: 202-670-7768. Fax: 202-232-1651.
E-mail: provisionslibrary@gmail.com
Web Site: www.provisionslibrary.org
Key Personnel: Exec. Dir. & Cur., Donald Russell; Chm. (V), Ethelbert Miller.
Institution Type/Description: Library & Art Museum.
Hours & Admission Prices: Tues.-Fri. 12-5. No charge; donations accepted. &
Attendance: 25,000 (estimated)

RAILS-TO-TRAILS CONSERVANCY, The Duke Ellington Building, 2121 Ward Ct., NW, 5th Fl., Washington, DC 20037-1247. Tel.: 202-331-9696. Fax: 202-331-9680.
E-mail: brandi@railstotrails.org
Web Site: www.railtrails.org
Key Personnel: Pres., Keith Laughlin; Chm. (V), Joe Louis Barrow, Jr.
Institution Type/Description: National Agency.
Hours & Admission Prices: Mon.-Fri. 9-5. No charge. Closed federal holidays. &

RENWICK GALLERY, SMITHSONIAN INSTITUTION, Pennsylvania Ave. at 17th St., N.W., Washington, DC 20006. Mailing Address: MRC 510 Box 37012, Washington, DC 20013-7012. Tel.: 202-633-7970. Facebook & Twitter: @americanart; Instagram: @americanartmuseum.
E-mail: americanartrenwick@si.edu
Web Site: renwick.americanart.si.edu
Key Personnel: The Margaret and Terry Stent Dir., Stephanie Stebich; Chief Admin., Robyn Kennedy; Lloyd Herman Cur. of Craft, Nora Atkinson; Exhibits

Specialist, Jim Baxter; The Fleur & Charles Bresler Cur.-in-Charge, Nicholas Bell; Deputy Chief Opers., Fern Bleckner; Mktg. Specialist, Amy Hutchins.
Institution Type/Description: American Crafts Museum.
Hours & Admission Prices: Daily 10-5:30. No charge. Closed Christmas. &
Attendance: 2,200,000 (estimated)

THE RESTAURANT MUSEUM, Washington, DC 20005. Mailing Address: 1330 Massachusetts Ave., Washington, DC 20005. Tel.: 202-479-2572.
E-mail: info@therestaurantmuseum.com
Web Site: therestaurantmuseum.com
Key Personnel: Dir., William Wooby; Public Rels., Jennifer Leupo.
Institution Type/Description: Virtual History Museum.
Hours & Admission Prices: Online museum.

ROCK CREEK PARK NATURE CENTER AND PLANETARIUM, 5200 Glover Rd., N.W., Washington, DC 20015-1095. Mailing Address: 3545 Williamsburg Lane, N.W., Washington, DC 20008-1207. Tel.: 202-895-6004. Fax: 202-895-6015. TDD: 202-426-6829.
Web Site: www.nps.gov/rocr
Formerly: Rock Creek Nature Center
Key Personnel: Park Supt., Tara Morrison.
Institution Type/Description: Nature Center.
Hours & Admission Prices: Wed.-Sun. 9-5. No charge; donations accepted. Closed New Year's Day; Thanksgiving; Christmas. &
Attendance: 35,000 (actual)

SAINT JOHN PAUL II NATIONAL SHRINE, 3900 Harewood Rd., N.E., Washington, DC 20017-1505. Tel.: 202-635-5400. Fax: 202-635-5411.
E-mail: info@jp2shrine.org
Web Site: www.jp2shrine.org
Formerly: Pope John Paul II Cultural Center
Key Personnel: Exec. Dir., Patrick E. Kelly; Priest-in-Residence, Fr. Jonathan Kalisch, OP; Dir. Research, Dr. Jem Sullivan.
Institution Type/Description: Cultural Center.
Hours & Admission Prices: Shrine & Exhibit Mon.-Sat. 10-5; Gift Shop Mon.-Fri. 11-2. Suggested Donations: families $15, individuals $5, seniors & students $4; discounts to members. Closed Federal holidays. &
Attendance: 29,000 (estimated)

SECURITIES AND EXCHANGE COMMISSION HISTORICAL SOCIETY, Washington, DC 20004-2514. Mailing Address: 1101 Pennsylvania Ave., N.W., Ste. 600, Washington, DC 20004-2514. Tel.: 202-756-5015. Fax: 202-756-5014.
E-mail: c.rosati@sechistorical.org
Web Site: www.sechistorical.org
Key Personnel: Exec. Dir., Jane Cobb.
Institution Type/Description: Virtual Museum.
Hours & Admission Prices: Online access only.

SEWALL-BELMONT HOUSE AND MUSEUM, 144 Constitution Ave., N.E., Washington, DC 20002-5608. Tel.: 202-546-1210.
E-mail: info@sewallbelmont.org
Web Site: www.nationalwomansparty.org
Key Personnel: Exec. Dir., Jennifer Krafchik.
Institution Type/Description: Women's History Museum: housed in c.1800 structure later added on, 1800 residence of Albert Gallatin 1801-1813 and 1929-1972 office & home of Alice Paul, founder of the National Woman's Party & author of the ERA.
Hours & Admission Prices: See website for hours. Tours: $5 per person. Closed holidays. &
Attendance: 15,000 (estimated)

SMITHSONIAN AMERICAN ART MUSEUM, SMITHSONIAN INSTITUTION, 8th & F Streets N.W., Washington, DC 20006. Mailing Address: P.O. Box 37012, MRC 970, Washington, DC 20013-7012. Tel.: 202-633-7970. Fax: 202-633-8535.
E-mail: americanartinfo@si.edu
Web Site: www.americanart.si.edu
Formerly: National Museum of American Art
Key Personnel: The Margaret and Terry Stent Dir., Stephanie Stebich; Chief Cur., Virginia Mecklenburg; Consulting Sr. Cur. Film & Media Arts, John G. Hanhardt; Sr. Cur. Painting & Sculpture, Eleanor Jones Harvey; McEvoy Family Cur. Photography, John Jacob; Cur. Sculpture, Karen Lemmy; Cur. Latino Art, E. Carmen Ramos; Cur. Folk & Self-Taught Art, Leslie Umberger; Chief External Affairs, Jo Ann Gillula; Public Affairs Officer, Laura Baptiste.

Institution Type/Description: Art Museum: housed in 1836 Old Patent Office Building.
Hours & Admission Prices: Daily 11:30-7. No charge. Closed Christmas. &
Attendance: 1,200,000 (actual)

SMITHSONIAN INSTITUTION BUILDING (THE CASTLE), SMITHSONIAN INSTITUTION, 1000 Jefferson Dr., S.W., Washington, DC 20560-0009. Mailing Address: P.O. Box 37012, Washington, DC 20013-7012. Tel.: 202-633-1000; 202-633-5285 (TTY).
E-mail: info@si.edu
Web Site: www.si.edu
Key Personnel: Sec., Lonnie G, Bunch; Under Sec. for Admin., Mike McCarthy; General Counsel, Judith E. Leonard; Chief of Staff to the Bd. of Regents, Porter N. Wilkinson.
Institution Type/Description: National Museum.
Hours & Admission Prices: Daily 8:30-5:30. Visitor Center: daily 8:30-5:30. No charge (except Cooper-Hewitt). Closed Christmas. &
Attendance: 1,100,000 (estimated)

SMITHSONIAN LATINO CENTER, Mailing Address: P.O. Box 37012, MRC 512, Washington, DC 20013-7012. Mailing Address: 600 Maryland Ave., S.W., Washington, DC 20024. Tel.: 202-633-1240. Fax: 202-633-1132.
E-mail: AldabaA@si.edu
Web Site: latino.si.edu
Key Personnel: Dir., Eduardo Diaz; Assoc. to Dir. & Programs, Adrian Aldaba; Project Mgr., Rebecca Looney; Program Mgr., Diana C. Bossa Bastidas; Administrative Officer, LaWand Morgan; New Media & Technology Dir., Melissa Carrillo; Advancement Officer, Jennifer Pichardo; Senior Communications Officer, David L. Coronado; Digital Media Mgr., Jose Ralat; Community Engagement & Volunteer Coord., Natalia M. Febo; Asst. Gallery Mgr., Lola Ramírez; Mgmt. Support Specialist, Gail Holmes; Advancement Assoc., Sarah Sosa-Acevedo; Education Program Mgr., Emily Key; Exhibitions & Public Programs Dir., Ranald Woodman.
Institution Type/Description: Latino Cultural Center.
Hours & Admission Prices: Virtual Museum.

STUDIO GALLERY, 2108 R St., N.W., Washington, DC 20008. Tel.: 202-232-8734.
E-mail: info@studiogallerydc.com
Web Site: www.studiogallerydc.com
Key Personnel: Dir., Lana Shaindlin; Co-Dir., Camila Rondon.
Institution Type/Description: Art Gallery.
Hours & Admission Prices: Wed.-Thurs. 1-7, Fri. 1-8, Sat. 1-6. No charge.
Attendance: 3,000 (estimated)

THE SUPREME COURT OF THE UNITED STATES, Office of the Curator, One First St., N.E., Washington, DC 20543. Tel.: 202-479-3000.
E-mail: curator@supremecourt.gov
Web Site: www.supremecourt.gov
Key Personnel: Cur., Catherine E. Fitts; Photographer, Steve Petteway.
Institution Type/Description: Historic Agency & Building.
Hours & Admission Prices: Mon.-Fri. 9-4:30. Courtroom lectures every hour on the half-hour 9:30-3:30 when court is not sitting. No charge. Closed federal holidays. &
Attendance: 300,000 (estimated)

TOUCHSTONE GALLERY, 901 New York Ave., N.W., Washington, DC 20001-6435. Tel.: 202-347-2787.
E-mail: info@touchstonegallery.com
Web Site: www.touchstonegallery.com
Key Personnel: Dir., Ksenia Grishkova; Pres., Carolyn Johnson.
Institution Type/Description: Art Gallery.
Hours & Admission Prices: Wed.-Fri. 11-6, Sat.-Sun. 12-5. No charge. &
Attendance: 15,000 (estimated)

TUDOR PLACE HISTORIC HOUSE & GARDEN, 1644 31st St., N.W., Washington, DC 20007-2924. Tel.: 202-965-0400, ext. 100. Fax: 202-965-0164. Facebook: Tudor Place Historic House & Garden.
E-mail: info@tudorplace.org
Web Site: tudorplace.org
Key Personnel: Pres. Bd. of Trustees, Thomas E. Crocker; Exec. Dir., Mark Hudson; Mgr. Collections, Kristin Barrow; Cur., Grant Quertermous.
Institution Type/Description: Historic House & Garden: architecture inspired by designs of Dr. William Thornton, first architect of the U.S. Capitol; completed 1816.

Hours & Admission Prices: Feb.-Dec. Tues.-Sat. 10, 11, 12, 1, 2, 3, Sun. 12, 1, 2, 3. House & Garden Tours: adults $10, seniors, students & military $8; discounts to AAA, NTHP & AAM members; members & children under 4 no charge. Garden only: $3 per person. Closed New Year's Day; Easter; Memorial Day; Independence Day; Labor Day; Thanksgiving; Dec. 23-26.
Attendance: 20,000 (estimated)

U.S. CAPITOL HISTORICAL SOCIETY, 200 Maryland Ave., N. E., Washington, DC 20002-5724. Tel.: 202-543-8919, 800-887-9318. Fax: 202-544-8244.
E-mail: uschs@uschs.org
Web Site: www.uschs.org
Key Personnel: Pres., Ronald A. Sarasin; Chm. (V), Hon. E. Thomas Colman; Vice Pres. Membership & Devel., Laura McCulty Stepp; Dir. Finance & Administration, Peter McGuire; Dir. Historical Programs, Lauren E. Borchard; Chief Historian, William C. diGiacomantonio; Vice Pres. Merchandising, Diana Wailes.
Institution Type/Description: Historical Society Museum.
Hours & Admission Prices: Daily 9-4:30. No charge; donations accepted. Closed holidays. &
Attendance: 8,000,000 (estimated)

U.S. NATIONAL ARBORETUM, 3501 New York Ave., N.E., Washington, DC 20002-1958. Tel.: 202-245-2726. Fax: 202-245-4575.
Web Site: www.usna.usda.gov
Key Personnel: Dir., Dr. Richard Olsen.
Institution Type/Description: Arboretum.
Hours & Admission Prices: Arboretum: daily 8-5. Visitor Center: daily 8-4:30. National Bonsai & Penjing Museum daily 10-4. No charge; donations accepted. Closed Christmas. &
Attendance: 600,000 (estimated)

U.S. NAVY MEMORIAL FOUNDATION AND NAVAL HERITAGE CENTER, 701 Pennsylvania Ave., N.W., Suite 123, Washington, DC 20004-2688. Tel.: 202-737-2300, ext. 710 & 725. Fax: 202-737-2308.
E-mail: library@lonesailor.org
Web Site: www.navymemorial.org
Key Personnel: C.E.O. & Pres., Rear Admiral Frank Thorp, IV, USN, (Ret.); Chm. (V), Admiral John C. Harvey, Jr., USN, (Ret.); Treas., Edward Walker, USN, (Ret.); Exec. Vice Pres. & C.O.O., Cindy McCalip; Cur., Registrar & Educator, Mark T. Weber; Museum Shop Mgr., Colin Masso.
Institution Type/Description: Naval Museum.
Hours & Admission Prices: Daily 9:30-5. No charge; donations accepted. Closed New Year's Day; Thanksgiving; Christmas. &
Attendance: 100,000 (estimated)

UNITED STATES BOTANIC GARDEN, 100 Maryland Ave., S. W., Washington, DC 20001. Mailing Address: 245 First St., S.W., Washington, DC 20515. Tel.: 202-225-8333. Fax: 202-225-1561. Facebook: usbotanicgarden.
E-mail: usbg@aoc.gov
Web Site: www.usbg.gov
Key Personnel: Exec. Dir., Saharah Moon Chapotin, Ph.D.; Deputy Exec. Dir., Susan Pell, Ph.D.
Institution Type/Description: Botanical Garden.
Hours & Admission Prices: Conservatory: daily 10-5. No charge. &
Attendance: 1,300,000 (estimated)

UNITED STATES CAPITOL, Capitol Visitors Center, 1st St., N.E., Washington, DC 20515. Tel.: 202-226-8000. Fax: 202-228-4602.
E-mail: mcohen@aoc.gov
Web Site: www.aoc.gov
Key Personnel: Acting Architect of the Capitol, Steven T. Ayers, AIA; Cur., Dr. Michele Cohen; Photo Branch, Michael Dunn; Registrar, Pamela Violante McConnell.
Institution Type/Description: National Agency & Art Museum.
Hours & Admission Prices: Tours: by appointment through the Advance Reservations System or the office of one of your Senators or Representatives. No charge. Closed New Year's Day; Inauguration Day; Thanksgiving; Christmas. &

UNITED STATES DEPARTMENT OF THE INTERIOR MUSEUM, 1849 C St., N.W., Washington, DC 20240. Tel.: 202-208-4743. Fax: 202-208-1535. Facebook; Twitter.
E-mail: diana_ziegler@nbc.gov
Web Site: www.doi.gov/interiormuseum
Key Personnel: Museum Specialist, Tamura Moore.
Institution Type/Description: General Museum.

Hours & Admission Prices: Mon.-Fri. 8:30-4:30. No charge. Photo ID required for adults. &
Attendance: 30,000 (estimated)

UNITED STATES HOLOCAUST MEMORIAL MUSEUM, 100 Raoul Wallenberg Pl., S.W., Washington, DC 20024-2126. Tel.: 202-488-0400. Fax: 202-488-2690. TDD: 202-488-0406.
E-mail: visitorsmail@ushmm.org
Web Site: www.ushmm.org
Key Personnel: Dir. United States Holocaust Memorial Museum, Sara J. Bloomfield; Chm. United States Holocaust Memorial Council, Howard M. Lorber; Vice Chm. United States Holocaust Memorial Council, Allan M. Holt; Chief Program Officer, Sarah Ogilvie; Dir. Collections, Michael Grunberger; Chief Devel. Officer, Jordan Tannenbaum; C.F.O., Polly Povejsil Heath; Chief Information Officer, Joseph Kraus; Dir. Levine Institute Holocaust Education, Michael Abramowitz; Interim Dir. Mandel Ctr. for Advanced Holocaust Studies, Wendy Lower; Chief Mktg. Officer, Lorna Miles; Dir. Museum Operations & Administration, Tanell Coleman; Dir. Simon-Skjodt Ctr. for the Prevention of Genocide, Cameron Hudson.
Institution Type/Description: History Museum.
Hours & Admission Prices: Daily 10-5:20. No charge; donations accepted. Closed Yom Kippur; Christmas. &

UNITED STATES SENATE COMMISSION ON ART, Rm. S-411, U.S. Capitol Bldg., Washington, DC 20510. Tel.: 202-224-2955. Fax: 202-224-8799.
E-mail: curator@sec.senate.gov
Web Site: www.senate.gov
Key Personnel: Cur., Melinda K. Smith; Assoc. Cur., Alexander "Sasha" Lourie; Museum Specialist, Richard L. Doerner; Registrar, Theresa Malanum; Curatorial Asst., Amy Elizabeth Burton.
Institution Type/Description: Preservation Projects: c.1850 Old Senate & Old Supreme Court Chambers & other historic areas of the U.S. Capitol Building & exhibits.
Hours & Admission Prices: Daily 9-4:30. No charge. Closed New Year's Day; Thanksgiving; Christmas. &
Attendance: 1,500,000 (estimated)

WASHINGTON NATIONAL CATHEDRAL, 3101 Wisconsin Ave., N.W., Washington, DC 20016-5000. Tel.: 202-537-6200. Fax: 202-364-6611.
E-mail: info@cathedral.org
Web Site: www.nationalcathedral.org
Key Personnel: Dir. Visitor Prog., Charles E. Fulcher, Jr.
Institution Type/Description: Religious Institution: housed in a Gothic cathedral.
Hours & Admission Prices: Winter: Sun.-Fri. 10-5:30, Sat. 10-4; Summer: call for extended hours; groups by appointment. Adult $12, youth 5-17, senior 65 & over, students with ID & active military or veteran $8; children under 5 no charge. &
Attendance: 500,000 (actual)

THE WHITE HOUSE, 1600 Pennsylvania Ave., N.W., Washington, DC 20502. Mailing Address: President's Park, 1100 Ohio Dr., S. W., Washington, DC 20242. Tel.: 202-456-7041.
Web Site: www.whitehouse.gov
Key Personnel: Dir. Visitor's Office, Ellie Schafer; Cur., William G. Allman.
Institution Type/Description: Historic House Museum: 1792-1800, The White House.
Hours & Admission Prices: Please call 202-456-7041 for information. White House Visitor Center & Ellipse Visitor Pavilion Complex: daily 7:30-4. Tours: Tues.-Thurs. 7:30-11, Fri. 7:30-12, Sat. 7:30-1, registration required through visitor's member of Congress at least 21 days in advance. No charge. Closed New Year's Day; Thanksgiving; Christmas Day. &

THE WHITE HOUSE HISTORICAL ASSOCIATION, 1610 H St., N.W., Washington, DC 20006. Mailing Address: P.O. Box 27624, Washington, 20038. Tel.: 202-737-8292. Fax: 202-789-0440.
E-mail: webmaster@whha.org
Web Site: www.whitehousehistory.org
Key Personnel: Chm. (V), Frederick J. Ryan, Jr.; Pres., Stewart D. McLaurin; Treas., John T. Behrendt; Devel. & Mktg., Rhett Wilson; Registrar, John Botello; Education, Dr. Curtis Sandberg; Public Rels., Lara Kline; Cur., John Botello; Archivist, Stephanie Tuszynski; Museum Shop Mgr., Gina Sherman; Security, Rodney Winter.
Institution Type/Description: Historical Association.
Hours & Admission Prices: Office: Mon.-Fri. 9-5. Exhibitions: Mon.-Sat. 10-3. No charge; donations accepted. Closed Federal holidays.
Attendance: 15,071 (actual)

ZENITH GALLERY, 1429 Iris St., N.W., Washington, DC 20012. Tel.: 202-783-2963.
E-mail: art@zenithgallery.com
Web Site: www.zenithgallery.com
Key Personnel: Founder & Dir., Margery Goldberg.
Institution Type/Description: Art Gallery.
Hours & Admission Prices: Wed.-Sat. 12-6; other times by appointment.

FLORIDA
(448 listings)

Anna Maria Island

ANNA MARIA ISLAND HISTORICAL MUSEUM, 402 Pine Ave., Anna Maria Island, FL 34216. Mailing Address: P.O. Box 4315, Anna Maria, FL 34216-4315. Tel.: 941-778-0492.
E-mail: amihs415@gmail.com
Web Site: www.amihs.org
Institution Type/Description: History Museum.
Hours & Admission Prices: Memorial Day to Labor Day Tues.-Thurs. & Sat. 10-12; Sept.-May Tues.-Thurs. & Sat. 10-3. No charge.

Apalachicola

JOHN GORRIE MUSEUM STATE PARK, 46 6th St. & Avenue D, Apalachicola, FL 32320. Mailing Address: P.O. Box 267, Apalachicola, FL 32329-0267. Tel.: 850-653-9347.
E-mail: josh.hodson@dep.state.fl.us
Web Site: www.floridastateparks.org/JohnGorrieMuseum/
Key Personnel: Dir. Florida Park Service, Eric Draper; Park Mgr., Josh Hodson.
Institution Type/Description: History Museum.
Hours & Admission Prices: Thurs.-Mon. 9-5. Admission $2; children 5 & under no charge. Closed New Year's Day; Thanksgiving; Christmas. &
Attendance: 3,600 (actual)

RANEY HOUSE MUSEUM - APALACHICOLA AREA HISTORICAL SOCIETY, 128 Market St., Apalachicola, FL 32320. Mailing Address: P.O. Box 75, Apalachicola, FL 32329. Tel.: 850-653-4321.
E-mail: aahs.raney@gmail.com
Web Site: aahs.wildapricot.org
Key Personnel: Pres., Bill Spohrer.
Institution Type/Description: Historical Society Museum: housed in the former home of the Raney family; built in 1838.
Hours & Admission Prices: By appointment.

Apopka

MUSEUM OF THE APOPKANS, 122 E. 5th St., Apopka, FL 32703-5314. Tel.: 407-703-1707. Fax: 407-703-1773.
E-mail: apopkamuseum@yahoo.com
Web Site: apopkamuseum.org
Institution Type/Description: History Museum.
Hours & Admission Prices: Tues.-Fri. noon-5; other times by appointment. No charge; donations accepted. &
Attendance: 3,000 (estimated)

Avon Park

AVON PARK DEPOT MUSEUM, 3 N. Museum Ave., Avon Park, FL 33825-3153. Tel.: 863-453-3525.
E-mail: apmuseum@centurylink.net
Web Site: www.avonparkdepotmuseum.com
Formerly: Seaboard Airline Railroad Station
Key Personnel: Dir. Chm. (V), Elaine Levey; Pres. (V), Ricky Nelms; Vice Pres. (V), Kathy Johnson.
Institution Type/Description: History Museum.
Hours & Admission Prices: Wed.-Fri. 10-3. No charge; donations accepted. &
Attendance: 2,500 (estimated)

SOUTH FLORIDA COMMUNITY COLLEGE MUSEUM OF FLORIDA ART AND CULTURE, 600 W. College Dr., Avon Park, FL 33825-9356. Tel.: 863-784-7240.
E-mail: stepem@southflorida.edu
Web Site: www.mofac.org
Institution Type/Description: Art Museum.
Hours & Admission Prices: Sept.-May Wed.-Fri. 12:30-4:30. No charge. &

Barberville

BARBERVILLE PIONEER SETTLEMENT, 1776 Lightfoot Ln., Barberville, FL 32105. Mailing Address: P.O. Box 6, Barberville, FL 32105-0006. Tel.: 386-749-2959. Fax: 386-749-2087. Facebook.
E-mail: info@pioneersettlement.org
Web Site: www.pioneersettlement.org
Formerly: Pioneer Settlement for the Creative Arts
Key Personnel: Exec. Dir., Debra West; Coord. Special Events, Shiloh Thomas.
Institution Type/Description: Cultural Heritage Museum.
Hours & Admission Prices: Mon.-Sat. 9-4. Adults $6, children 6-12 $4; discounts to rack card holders; members & children under 5 no charge. Closed major holidays. &
Attendance: 65,000

Bartow

POLK COUNTY HISTORICAL MUSEUM, 100 E. Main St., Bartow, FL 33830-4629. Tel.: 863-534-4386. Fax: 863-534-4387.
E-mail: museum@polk-county.net
Web Site: www.polkcountymuseum.org
Key Personnel: Dir., Tom Muir; Museum Asst., Maria Trippe.
Institution Type/Description: History Museum.
Hours & Admission Prices: Tues.-Fri. 9-5, Sat. 9-3. No charge; donations accepted. Closed New Year's Day; Martin Luther King Jr. Day; Memorial Day; Independence Day; Labor Day; Veterans Day; Thanksgiving weekend; Christmas. &
Attendance: 28,000 (estimated)

Bay Lake

DISNEY'S ANIMAL KINGDOM THEME PARK, 1200 N. Savannah Circle E., Bay Lake, FL 32830. Mailing Address: P.O. Box 10000, Lake Buena Vista, FL 32830-1000. Tel.: 407-939-2468. Fax: 407-939-6240.
E-mail: jackie.ogden@disney.com
Web Site: www.disneyworld.com
Key Personnel: Vice Pres., Jacqueline J. Ogden, Ph.D.; Vice Pres., Michael Colglazier; Administrative Asst., Donna McKiernan; Administrative Asst., Jill Martin; Dir. Animal Opers., Mark R. Penning, BVSc; Dir. Dept. of Animal Health, Scott P. Terrell, D.V.M., Dipl. A.C.V.P.; Dir. Education & Science, Jill Mellen, Ph.D.; Mgr. Animals, Science, & Environment, Heather Eberhart; Sr. Research Biologist, Tamara Bettinger, Ph.D.; Dir. Conservation, Anne Savage, Ph.D.; Cur. Education, Kathy Lehnhardt; Cur. Education, Allyson Atkins; Animal Records & Regulatory Affairs Mgr., Lynn S. McDuffie; Veterinarian, Natalie Mylniczenko, D.V.M., Dipl. A.C.Z.M.; Veterinary Svcs. Operations Mgr., Elizabeth C. Nolan, D.V.M., Dipl. A.C.Z.M.; Veterinary Svcs. Operations Mgr., Don Neiffer, V.M.D., Dipl. A.C.Z.M.; Veterinarian, Greg Fleming, D.V.M., Dipl. A.C.Z.M.; Veterinarian, Deidre Fontenot, D.V.M.; Animal Operations Mgr., Pagani Forest Exploration Trail (R) & Maharajah Jungle Trek (R), Chelle Plasse; Animal Operations Mgr., Savannahs, Joe Christman; Dir. Animal Operations, Matt Hohne; Asst. Animal Operations Mgr., Rafiki's Planet Watch, Andre J. Daneault; Animal Operations Mgr., Rafiki's Planet Watch, Jerry Brown; Animal Operations Mgr. Disney's Animal Kingdom Lodge, Greg Peccie; Asst. Animal Operations Mgr., Savannahs, Sam Berner; Asst. Animal Operations Mgr., Disney's Animal Lodge, Steve Metzler; Asst. Animal Operations Mgr., Pagani Forest Exploration Trail (R) & Maharajah Jungle Trek (R), Jay Therien; Veterinary Pathologist, Carlos Rodriguez, D.V.M.; Nutritionist, Eduardo V. Valdes, Ph.D.; Gen. Mgr. Park Operations, Tim Sypko; Gen. Mgr. Food & Beverage, Maryann Smith; Dir. Engineering Svcs., Kevin C. Shultz; Mgr. Horticulture Svcs., Wendy Andrew; Animal Operations Mgr., Behavioral Husbandry, Marty MacPhee; Mgr. Human Resources, Park Ops Line of Business, Jeanette Dennis; Gen. Mgr. Merchandise, Robert Kelley.
Institution Type/Description: Zoological Park.
Hours & Admission Prices: Summer: 9-8; Winter 9-5. Adults $94.79, children 3-9 $88.40. &
Attendance: 10,920,000 (estimated)

Boca Grande

PORT BOCA GRANDE LIGHTHOUSE & MUSEUM, Gasparilla Island State Park, Boca Grande, FL 33921. Mailing Address: P.O. Box 637, Boca Grande, FL 33921-0637. Tel.: 941-964-0060. Facebook.
E-mail: infoatblps@gmail.com
Web Site: www.barrierislandparkssociety.org
Formerly: Boca Grand Lighthouse Museum and Visitors Center
Key Personnel: Dir., Sharon McKenzie; Pres. (V), Linden Hustedt; Museum Shop Mgr., Jennifer Summers.
Institution Type/Description: History Museum.

Hours & Admission Prices: June-July & Sept.-Oct. Wed.-Sat. 10-4, Sun. 12-4; Nov.-May Mon.-Sat. 10-4, Sun. 12-4. No charge; donations accepted. Closed New Year's Day; Martin Luther King Jr. Day; Easter; Memorial Day; Independence Day; Labor Day; Thanksgiving; Christmas. &
Attendance: 32,000 (actual)

Boca Raton

BOCA RATON CHILDREN'S MUSEUM CLOSED, 498 Crawford Blvd., Boca Raton, FL 33432-3752. Tel.: 561-368-6875. Fax: 561-948-0306.
E-mail: info@cmboca.org
Web Site: www.cmboca.org
Key Personnel: Exec. Dir., Dr. Denise St. Patrick-Bell; Program Mgr., Victoria Mancilla; Coord. Education, Erin Simpson Krar; Coord. Operations, Jayne Morrison; Coord. Mktg., Sandy Manning.
Institution Type/Description: Children's Museum: housed in c.1912 unaltered wooden structure.
Hours & Admission Prices: Mon.-Sat. 10-5; groups by appointment. $5 per person; infants & members no charge. Closed New Year's Day; Memorial Day; Independence Day; Labor Day; Thanksgiving; Christmas. &
Attendance: 50,000 (estimated)

BOCA RATON HISTORY MUSEUM, 71 N. Federal Hwy., Boca Raton, FL 33432-3919. Tel.: 561-395-6766, ext. 306. Fax: 561-395-4049.
E-mail: info@bocahistory.org
Web Site: www.bocahistory.org
Formerly: Boca Raton Historical Society
Key Personnel: Dir., Mary Csar; Cur., Susan Gillis; Educator, Laurie Lynn Jones.
Institution Type/Description: Historical Society Museum.
Hours & Admission Prices: Mon.-Fri. 10-4. Adults $5; members no charge. Closed state holidays. &
Attendance: 25,000 (estimated)

BOCA RATON MUSEUM OF ART, Director, 501 Plaza Real, Boca Raton, FL 33432-3982. Tel.: 561-392-2500, ext. 200. Fax: 561-391-6410.
E-mail: info@bocamuseum.org
Web Site: www.bocamuseum.org
Key Personnel: Chair, Jody Harrison Grass; Exec. Dir., Irvin Lippman; Museum Shop Mgr., Aylin Tito.
Institution Type/Description: Art Museum.
Hours & Admission Prices: Tues., Wed. & Fri. 10-5, Thurs. 10-8, Sat.-Sun. 12-5. Adults $12, senior citizens 65 & over $10; discounts to groups & AAM members; children 12 & under, students with ID & members no charge. Admission may change for special exhibits. Closed major holidays. &
Attendance: 200,000 (estimated)

CHILDREN'S SCIENCE EXPLORIUM, 300 S. Military Trail, Boca Raton, FL 33486-4302. Tel.: 561-347-3912. Fax: 561-347-3910.
E-mail: explorium@myboca.us
Web Site: www.scienceexplorium.org
Key Personnel: Science Center Cur., Kate Lasher; Coord. Exhibits, Harry Robelen.
Institution Type/Description: Children's Science Museum.
Hours & Admission Prices: Mon.-Fri. 9-6, Sat.-Sun. & holidays 10-5. No charge; $5 donation requested. Closed New Year's Day; Thanksgiving; Christmas. &
Attendance: 167,123 (estimated)

UNIVERSITY GALLERIES, FLORIDA ATLANTIC UNIVERSITY, 777 Glades Rd., Boca Raton, FL 33431-6496. Tel.: 561-297-2966 & 2661.
E-mail: wfaulds@fau.edu
Web Site: www.fau.edu/galleries
Key Personnel: Dir., W. Rod Faulds.
Institution Type/Description: Contemporary Art Museums & Galleries.
Hours & Admission Prices: Ritter Art Gallery & Schmidt Center Gallery: Academic Year: Tues.-Fri. 1-4, Sat. 1-5; Summer Tues.-Fri. 1-4, Sat. by appointment. No charge; donations accepted. &
Attendance: 15,000 (actual)

Bonifay

ROYAL AIR MUSEUM, 1893 Tri County Airport Rd., Bonifay, FL 32425. Tel.: 850-999-7004.
E-mail: jpinto@royalairmuseum.org
Institution Type/Description: Aviation Museum.
Hours & Admission Prices: Tues.-Fri. 9-5, Sat.-Sun. 1-5. Closed New Year's Day; Thanksgiving; Christmas.

Bonita Springs

CENTERS FOR THE ARTS BONITA SPRINGS, 26100 Old 41 Rd., Bonita Springs, FL 34135-8613. Tel.: 239-495-8989. Fax: 239-495-3999.
E-mail: cfabs@artsbonita.org
Web Site: www.artcenterbonita.org
Formerly: Art League of Bonita Springs
Key Personnel: Pres., Susan Bridges; Bd. Chm., Jacqueline McCurdy.
Institution Type/Description: Art Museum.
Hours & Admission Prices: Mon.-Fri. 10-5, Sat. 9-5. No charge; donations accepted. Closed New Year's Day; Christmas. &
Attendance: 85,000 (estimated)

Bowling Green

PAYNES CREEK HISTORIC STATE PARK, 888 Lake Branch Rd., Bowling Green, FL 33834-4078. Tel.: 863-375-4717. Fax: 863-375-4510.
E-mail: jackson.mosley@dep.state.fl.us
Web Site: www.floridastateparks.org
Formerly: Paynes Creek State Historic Site
Key Personnel: Park Mgr., Jacks Mosley; Park Ranger, Ray N. Gilmore; Pres. (V) & Park Ranger, Sam Hale.
Institution Type/Description: Historic Site: located near c.1850 Ft. Chokonikla, Seminole Indian War Fort Visitor Center.
Hours & Admission Prices: Daily 8am to sundown. $3 per vehicle. &
Attendance: 31,000 (estimated)

Boynton Beach

SCHOOLHOUSE CHILDREN'S MUSEUM & LEARNING CENTER, 129 E. Ocean Ave., Boynton Beach, FL 33435-4536. Tel.: 561-742-6780. Fax: 561-742-6781.
E-mail: info@schoolhousemuseum.org
Web Site: www.schoolhousemuseum.org
Key Personnel: Dir., Suzanne Ross; Pres. (V), Jim Guilbeault; Program Mgr., Linda Abbott.
Institution Type/Description: Children's Museum.
Hours & Admission Prices: Tues.-Sat. 10-5. Adults $5, grandparents $4.50, children 1-17 $5; discounts to groups of 10 or more & ACM members; members no charge. &
Attendance: 34,783 (actual)

Bradenton

ARTCENTER MANATEE, 209 9th St., W., Bradenton, FL 34205-8627. Tel.: 941-746-2862. Fax: 941-746-2319.
E-mail: acm@artcentermanatee.org
Web Site: www.artcentermanatee.org
Formerly: Art League of Manatee County
Key Personnel: Exec. Dir., Carla Nierman; Pres. (V), Marianne Barnebey.
Institution Type/Description: Arts Center.
Hours & Admission Prices: Mon. & Fri. 9-5, Tues.-Thurs. 9-6. No charge; donations accepted. Closed New Year's Eve & Day; Memorial Day; Independence Day; Labor Day; Thanksgiving; Christmas Eve & Day. &
Attendance: 30,000 (estimated)

DESOTO NATIONAL MEMORIAL, 8300 DeSoto Memorial Hwy., Bradenton, FL 34209. Mailing Address: P.O. Box 15390, Bradenton, FL 34280-5390. Tel.: 941-792-0458, ext. 105. Fax: 941-792-5094.
E-mail: deso_ranger_activities@nps.gov
Web Site: www.nps.gov/deso/
Key Personnel: Park Ranger, Ben Sims.
Institution Type/Description: Park Museum.
Hours & Admission Prices: Visitor Center: daily 9-5. History Camp: mid-Dec. to mid-April daily 10-4, call to confirm. No charge; donations accepted. Closed New Year's Day; Thanksgiving; Christmas. &
Attendance: 275,505 (actual)

MANATEE VILLAGE HISTORICAL PARK, 1404 Manatee Ave. E., Bradenton, FL 34208-1360. Tel.: 941-741-4075. Fax: 941-708-5924. Facebook: Manatee Historical Park.
E-mail: phaedra.carter@manateeclerk.com
Web Site: www.manateevillage.org
Key Personnel: Suprv., Phaedra Carter; Chm., Hinning Bolanos; Museum Shop Mgr., Liz Boling.
Institution Type/Description: Local History Museum.

Hours & Admission Prices: Mon.-Fri. & 2nd & 4th Sat. each month 9-4. No charge; donations accepted. Closed holidays. &

Attendance: 11,000 (estimated)

SOUTH FLORIDA MUSEUM, BISHOP PLANETARIUM & PARKER MANATEE AQUARIUM, 201 10th St., W., Bradenton, FL 34205-8635. Mailing Address: P.O. Box 9265, Bradenton, FL 34206-9265. Tel.: 941-746-4131. Fax: 941-747-2556.

E-mail: info@southfloridamuseum.org

Web Site: www.southfloridamuseum.org

Key Personnel: C.E.O., Brynne Anne Besio; Pres. (V), Jeanie Kirkpatrick; Provost & C.O.O., Jeff Rodgers; Aquarium Dir. Living Collections, Marilyn Margold; Community Engagement Dir., Martha Wells; Facility Dir., Jack Balkan; Exhibitions Dir. & Chief Cur., Matt Woodside; Museum Store & Visitor Services Dir., Ellen Ferraro; Communications Mgr., Jessica Schubick.

Institution Type/Description: General Museum & Planetarium.

Hours & Admission Prices: Jan.-April & July Mon.-Sat. 10-5, Sun. noon-5; May-June & Aug.-Dec. Tues.-Sat. 10-5, Sun. noon-5. Adult $19, senior 65 & over $17, children 4-12 $14; discounts to groups; ASTC & museum members and children under 4 w/paying adult no charge. Closed New Year's Day; Thanksgiving; Christmas. &

Attendance: 85,000 (estimated)

Bristol

TORREYA STATE PARK, 2576 N.W. Torreya Park Rd., Bristol, FL 32321-2203. Tel.: 850-643-2674. Fax: 850-643-2987.

E-mail: steven.cutshaw@dep.state.fl.us

Web Site: www.floridastateparks.org/torreya

Key Personnel: Park Mgr., Steve Cutshaw.

Institution Type/Description: Park & Historic House Museum.

Hours & Admission Prices: Park: 8 am to sunset. House Tours: Mon.-Fri. 10am, Sat.-Sun. & state holidays 10am, 2pm & 4pm. Adults $3, children 12 & under $2; children under 6 no charge.

Brooksville

HERNANDO HERITAGE MUSEUM, 601 Museum Ct., Brooksville, FL 34601-2631. Tel.: 352-799-0129.

E-mail: info@hernandohistoricalmuseumassoc.com

Web Site: hernandohistoricalmuseumassoc.com/index.htm

Institution Type/Description: Historic House Museum: built c.1856. Listed on the National Register of Historic Places.

Hours & Admission Prices: Tues.-Sat. 12-3. Suggested Donation: adults $5, children $2; students & scouts no charge. &

Attendance: 35,000 (estimated)

Bushnell

DADE BATTLEFIELD HISTORIC STATE PARK, 7200 County Rd. 603, S. Battlefield Dr., Bushnell, FL 33513-3538. Tel.: 352-793-4781. Fax: 352-793-4230.

E-mail: FSP.Feedback@dep.state.fl.us

Web Site: www.floridastateparks.org

Formerly: Dade Battlefield State Historic Site

Key Personnel: Park Mgr., Bill Gruber; Park Ranger, Chuck Wicks; Park Ranger, George Webb.

Institution Type/Description: Historic Site and Park Museum: site of a battle between Seminole & US soldiers on Dec. 28, 1835.

Hours & Admission Prices: Visitor Center & Museum: daily 9-5. Grounds: daily 8am to sunset. $3 per vehicle, $2 bicycles & walk-ins. Bus fee $40 or $1 per person. &

Attendance: 30,000 (estimated)

Cape Canaveral

AIR FORCE SPACE AND MISSILE HISTORY CENTER, 100 Space Port Way, Cape Canaveral, FL 32920.

E-mail: media@afspacemuseum.org

Web Site: www.afspacemuseum.org

Hours & Admission Prices: Tues.-Fri. 9-2, Sat. 9-5, Sun. 12-4. No charge. Closed New Year's Day; Thanksgiving; Christmas.

Cape Coral

CAPE CORAL HISTORICAL MUSEUM, 544 Cultural Park Blvd., Cape Coral, FL 33990-1212. Mailing Address: P.O. Box 150637, Cape Coral, FL 33915-0637. Tel.: 239-772-7037. Fax: 239-573-7518.

E-mail: capecoralmuseum@outlook.com

Web Site: www.capecoralhistoricalmuseum.org

Key Personnel: C.E.O. & Cur., Shalla Ashworth; Pres. (V), Bonnie Potter; Vice Pres., Barbara Peet; Museum Shop Mgr., Rusty Williamson.

Institution Type/Description: History Museum.

Hours & Admission Prices: Sept.-June Wed.-Thurs. 1-4, Sat. 10-2. Suggested Donation: adults $5. Closed holidays. &

Attendance: 1,500 (estimated)

SOUTHWEST FLORIDA MILITARY MUSEUM & LIBRARY CLOSED, 4820 Leonard St., Cape Coral, FL 33904. Tel.: 239-541-8704. Fax: 239-541-8711.

E-mail: veterans-foundation2@hotmail.com

Web Site: swfmm.org

Key Personnel: Dir., Sonia Raymond; Pres. (V), Ralph A. Santillo.

Institution Type/Description: Military History Museum.

Hours & Admission Prices: Mon.-Fri. 9-5, Sat. 9-4. No charge; donations accepted. &

Attendance: 30,000 (actual)

Carrabelle

CAMP GORDON JOHNSTON MUSEUM, 1873 U.S. Hwy. 98 W., Carrabelle, FL 32322. Mailing Address: P.O. Box 1334, Carrabelle, FL 32322. Tel.: 850-697-8575. Facebook.

E-mail: museum@campgordonjohnston.com

Web Site: campgordonjohnston.com

Key Personnel: Dir., Linda Minichiello; Pres., Anthony Minichiello.

Institution Type/Description: World War II Museum.

Hours & Admission Prices: Mon.-Thurs. 1-4, Fri. 12-4, Sat. 10-2. No charge. &

Attendance: 7,000 (actual)

Cedar Key

CEDAR KEY HISTORICAL SOCIETY MUSEUM, 609 2nd St., Cedar Key, FL 32625. Mailing Address: P.O. Box 222, Cedar Key, FL 32625-0222. Tel.: 352-543-5549. Facebook.

E-mail: ckhsm.dir@gmail.com

Web Site: cedarkeymuseum.com

Key Personnel: Exec. Dir., Anna Hodges.

Institution Type/Description: Historical Society Museum: housed in c.1871 former private residence.

Hours & Admission Prices: Sun.-Fri. 1-4, Sat. 11-4. Adults $2, children over 12 $1; members no charge. Closed Christmas. &

Attendance: 9,000

CEDAR KEY MUSEUM STATE PARK, 12231 S.W. 166 Court, Cedar Key, FL 32625-6200. Tel.: 352-543-5350.

E-mail: christopher.camargo@dep.state.fl.us

Web Site: www.floridastateparks.org

Key Personnel: Dir. Florida Park Svc., Donald Forgione; Park Ranger, Charles Neese; Park Mgr., Kristin Ebersol.

Institution Type/Description: State Museum.

Hours & Admission Prices: Thurs.-Mon. 10-5. Admission $2. Closed Christmas. &

Attendance: 20,408 (actual)

Chokoloskee

TED SMALLWOOD'S STORE, INC., 360 Mamie St., Chokoloskee, FL 34138. Mailing Address: P.O. Box 310, Chokoloskee, FL 34138-0367. Tel.: 239-695-2989. Fax: 239-695-4454.

E-mail: lynn@smallwoodstore.com

Web Site: www.smallwoodstore.com

Key Personnel: Exec. Dir., Ms. Lynn Smallwood McMillin.

Institution Type/Description: History Museum: housed in 1906 Indian Trading Post.

Hours & Admission Prices: May 2-Nov. Fri.-Tues. 10-4; Dec.-May 1 daily 10-5. Adults $5, senior citizens $2.50; discounts to groups of 10 or more; children under 12 no charge. Closed Thanksgiving; Christmas Eve & Day.

Attendance: 32,000 (estimated)

Christmas

FORT CHRISTMAS HISTORICAL PARK, 1300 Fort Christmas Rd., Christmas, FL 32709-9427. Mailing Address: Orange County Parks & Recreation, 4801 W. Colonial Dr., Orlando, FL 32808. Tel.: 407-254-9310.

E-mail: parks@ocfl.net

Web Site: www.orangecountyfl.net

Key Personnel: Historic Site Supvr., Joseph Adams.

Institution Type/Description: History Museum.
Hours & Admission Prices: Park: Summer: daily 8-8; Winter: daily 8-6. Fort & Homes: Tues.-Sun. 9-4. No charge; donations accepted. Closed holidays. &
Attendance: 123,775 (estimated)

JUNGLE ADVENTURES NATURE ANIMAL PARK, 26205 E. Colonial Dr., Christmas, FL 32709. Tel.: 407-568-2885, 877-424-2867 (Toll Free). Fax: 407-568-0038.
E-mail: jungleadv@aol.com
Web Site: www.jungleadventures.com
Institution Type/Description: Nature Park.
Hours & Admission Prices: Daily 9:30-5:30. Adults $25.95, seniors 60 & over $22.95, children 3-11 $17.95; discounts to groups of 15 or more; children under 3 no charge.

Clearwater

CLEARWATER MARINE AQUARIUM, 249 Windward Passage, Clearwater, FL 33767-2244. Tel.: 727-441-1790, ext. 240 & 227. Fax: 727-445-1139.
E-mail: fdame@cmaquarium.org
Web Site: www.seewinter.com
Key Personnel: C.E.O., David Yates; Chm., John Draheim; Vice Chm., Paul Auslander; Sec., Linda Griffin-Keliher; Treas., Brent Howie; Exec. Vice Pres. & C.O.O., Frank Dame.
Institution Type/Description: Aquarium & Marine Museum.
Hours & Admission Prices: Daily 9-6. Adults $21.95, seniors $19.95, children 3-12 $16.95; discounts to FAA & AAA members & groups; children under 3 & members no charge. Closed Thanksgiving; Christmas. &
Attendance: 790,000 (estimated)

MOCCASIN LAKE NATURE PARK, AN ENVIRONMENTAL & ENERGY EDUCATION CENTER, 2750 Park Trail Lane, Clearwater, FL 33759-2602. Tel.: 727-793-2976. Fax: 727-793-2978. TDD: 727-562-4833.
E-mail: cliff.norris@myclearwater.com
Web Site: www.myclearwater.com
Key Personnel: Nature Park Supvr., Cliff Norris; Nature Park Programmer, Lloyd Simmons.
Institution Type/Description: Nature Center & Conservation Area; Alternative Energy Demonstration Center.
Hours & Admission Prices: Call for hours. Nonresidents adults $3, Clearwater Residents adults $2; children under 3 no charge. Closed city holidays. &
Attendance: 51,000 (actual)

Clewiston

AH-TAH-THI-KI MUSEUM, Big Cypress Seminole Indian Reservation, 34725 W. Boundary Rd., Clewiston, FL 33440. Mailing Address: 30290 Josie Billie Hwy., PMB 1003, Clewiston, FL 33440. Tel.: 863-902-1113. Fax: 863-902-1117.
E-mail: paulbackhouse@semtribe.com
Web Site: www.ahtahthiki.com
Key Personnel: Museum Dir. & THPO, Dr. Paul Backhouse; Asst. Dir., Dr. Kate Macuen; Collections Mgr., Tara Backhouse; Office Mgr., Rebecca Crum; Museum Shop Mgr., Rebecca Petrie; Facilities Mgr., David Higgins; Visitor Svcs. & Devel. Mgr., Carrie Dilley.
Institution Type/Description: Tribal Museum.
Hours & Admission Prices: Daily 9-5. Adults $10, senior citizens, students & military with ID $7.50; discounts to Time Travelers, AAM & NARM members & groups; children 4 & under and Seminole Tribal & museum members no charge. Closed New Year's Day; Martin Luther King Jr. Day; Labor Day; Thanksgiving Day; Christmas. &
Attendance: 17,000 (actual)

CLEWISTON MUSEUM, INC., 109 Central Ave., Clewiston, FL 33440-3701. Tel.: 863-983-2870.
E-mail: clewistonmuseum@embarqmail.com
Web Site: www.clewistonmuseum.org
Key Personnel: Dir., Butch Wilson.
Institution Type/Description: Heritage & History Museum: housed in c.1928 Clewiston News Building.
Hours & Admission Prices: Mon.-Fri. 9-4; other times by appointment. Adults $4, seniors $3, students $2, discounts to groups. Closed major holidays. &
Attendance: 2,300 (estimated)

Cocoa

ASTRONAUT MEMORIAL PLANETARIUM AND OBSERVATORY, Brevard Community College, 1519 Clearlake Rd., Cocoa, FL 32922-6598. Tel.: 321-433-7373. Fax: 321-433-7646.
E-mail: leslies@brevardcc.edu
Web Site: www.brevardcc.edu/planet
Key Personnel: Dir., Mark Howard; Assoc. Dir., Suzanne Leslie.
Institution Type/Description: Astronomy Museum.
Hours & Admission Prices: Exhibit Halls: Wed. 1:30-4:30. Fri.-Sat. 6:30pm-10:30pm. Public Shows: Wed. 2 & 3, Fri.-Sat. 7pm, 8pm & 9pm. Observatory: Fri.-Sat. dusk-10pm. Single Show: adults $7, seniors, students, & military $6, children 12 & under $4. Planetarium & Movie: adults $11, seniors, students, & military $9, children 12 & under $7. Planetarium, Movie, & Laser: admission $16. &
Attendance: 40,000 (estimated)

BREVARD MUSEUM OF HISTORY AND NATURAL SCIENCE, 2201 Michigan Ave., Cocoa, FL 32926-5618. Tel.: 321-632-1830 & 1920. Facebook: Brevard Museum of History & Natural Science.
E-mail: bruce.piatek@myfloridahistory.org
Web Site: www.brevardmuseum.com
Key Personnel: C.E.O. & Dir., Bruce Piatek.
Institution Type/Description: History & Natural Science Museum.
Hours & Admission Prices: June-Aug. Thurs.-Sat. 10-4; Sept.-May Tues.-Sat. 10-4. Adults $6, seniors $5.50, college students $5, children 5-16 $4.50; members no charge. Closed New Year's Day; Easter; Thanksgiving; Christmas Eve & Day. &
Attendance: 8,000 (estimated)

FLORIDA HISTORICAL SOCIETY, 435 Brevard Ave., Cocoa, FL 32922-7901. Tel.: 321-690-1971. Fax: 321-690-4388.
E-mail: archivist@myfloridahistory.org
Web Site: myfloridahistory.org
Key Personnel: Exec. Dir., Benjamin Brotemarkle; C.O.O., Ben DiBiasi; C.F.O., Deanna Runyan; Dir. Media Production, Jon White; Museum Mgr. Brevard Museum of History & Natural Science, Holly Baker; Membership & Publications Coord., Dorothy Dickey; Development & Fundraising Coord., Delores Spearman.
Institution Type/Description: Historical Society Museum.
Hours & Admission Prices: Library: Tues.-Sat. 10-4:30. No charge; donations accepted. &

Coconut Grove

THE BARNACLE HISTORIC STATE PARK, 3485 Main Hwy., Coconut Grove, FL 33133-5915. Tel.: 305-442-6866. Fax: 305-442-6872.
E-mail: katrina.boler@dep.state.fl.us
Web Site: www.floridastateparks.org/TheBarnacle
Key Personnel: Park Mgr., Katrina A. Boler; Park Svcs. Specialist, Jessica Cabral.
Institution Type/Description: Historic House.
Hours & Admission Prices: Park: Wed.-Mon. 9-5. Admission $2; children 5 7 under no charge. House Tours: 10, 11:30, 1 & 2:30. Group Tours: Mon. & Wed.-Fri. by appointment. Tours: adults 13 & over $3, children 6-12 $1; children 5 & under no charge. Closed New Year's Day; Thanksgiving; Christmas. &
Attendance: 57,157 (estimated)

Coral Gables

CORAL GABLES MUSEUM, 285 Aragon Ave., Coral Gables, FL 33134. Tel.: 305-603-8067.
E-mail: info@coralgablesmuseum.org
Web Site: www.coralgablesmuseum.org
Key Personnel: Chm. (V), George Kakouris; Dir., Arva Moore Parks.
Institution Type/Description: Civic Arts Museum.
Hours & Admission Prices: Tues.-Thurs. 12-6, Fri. 12-8, Sat. 11-5, Sun. 12-5. Adults $7; member no charge. &
Attendance: 7,000 (estimated)

FAIRCHILD TROPICAL BOTANIC GARDEN, 10901 Old Cutler Rd., Coral Gables, FL 33156-4296. Tel.: 305-667-1651. Fax: 305-661-8953.
E-mail: contactus@fairchildgarden.org
Web Site: www.fairchildgarden.org
Key Personnel: Dir., Carl E. Lewis, Ph.D.; Dir. Collections, Brett Jestrow, Ph.D.
Institution Type/Description: Botanical Garden.

Hours & Admission Prices: Daily 9:30-4:30. Adults $25, seniors $18, student with valid school ID $16, children 6-17 $12; children 5 & under & members no charge. Closed Christmas. &
Attendance: 146,388 (actual)

THE LATIN AMERICAN ART MUSEUM, 2206 S.W. Eighth St., Miami, FL 33135. Tel.: 305-644-1127. Fax: 305-261-6996.
Formerly: Florida Museum of Hispanic and Latin American Art
Key Personnel: Dir., Raul Oyuela.
Institution Type/Description: Art Museum.
Hours & Admission Prices: Sun. & Tues.-Fri. 11-5, Sat. 11-4.

LOWE ART MUSEUM, UNIVERSITY OF MIAMI, 1301 Stanford Dr., Coral Gables, FL 33146-2099. Tel.: 305-284-3535. Fax: 305-284-2024.
E-mail: msh119@miami.edu
Web Site: www.lowemuseum.org
Key Personnel: Dir. & Chief Cur., Jill Deupi; Adjunct Cur. African Art., Marcilene Wittmer; Adjunct Cur. Renaissance, Perri L. Roberts; Dir. Membership, Yina Balarezo-Badenjki; Assoc. Preparator, Darren Price; Cur. Education, Jodi Sypher; Receptionist, Janie Graulich; Head Security, Maria Milhomme; Office Mgr., Lorraine Stassun; Coord. School Programs, Hope Torrents; Registrar, Natasha Cuervo; Asst. to Registrar, Julie Berlin; Preparator, Alessia Lewitt; Communications Specialist, Raymond Mathews; Environmental Svcs. Tech, Diana Mazo-Maza.
Institution Type/Description: Art Museum.
Hours & Admission Prices: Tues.-Sat. 10-4, Sun. 12-4. Adults $10, senior citizens & students $5; discounts to AAM & ICOM members; children under 12 & members no charge. Closed major holidays. &
Attendance: 41,235 (actual)

Coral Springs

CORAL SPRINGS MUSEUM OF ART, 2855 Coral Springs Dr., Coral Springs, FL 33065-3825. Tel.: 954-340-5000. Fax: 954-346-4424.
E-mail: jandrews@coralsprings.org
Web Site: www.coralspringsmuseum.org
Key Personnel: Exec. Dir., Julia Black Andrews; Pres. (V), Michael Monas.
Institution Type/Description: Art Museum.
Hours & Admission Prices: Mon.-Sat. 10-5. Adults $6, seniors $5, students $3; children under 5, members & 1st Wed. each month no charge. Closed major holidays. &
Attendance: 329,059 (estimated)

Cortez

FLORIDA MARITIME MUSEUM, 4415 119th St. W., Cortez, FL 34215. Mailing Address: P.O. Box 100, Cortez, FL 34215. Tel.: 941-708-6120.
Key Personnel: Supvr., Kristin Sweeting.
Institution Type/Description: Maritime History Museum: housed in a former schoolhouse; built in 1912.
Hours & Admission Prices: Tues.-Sat. 9-4. No charge; donations accepted.

Cross Creek

MARJORIE KINNAN RAWLINGS HISTORIC STATE PARK, 18700 S. County Rd. 325, Cross Creek, FL 32640-8403. Tel.: 352-466-3672 & 9273. Fax: 352-466-4743.
E-mail: valerie.rivers@dep.state.fl.us
Web Site: www.floridastateparks.org
Formerly: Marjorie Kinnan Rawlings State Historic Site
Key Personnel: Park Mgr., Valerie Rivers.
Institution Type/Description: Historic House Museum: c.1930's citrus farm & home of Marjorie Kinnan Rawlings, a rambling Cracker farmhouse. A National Historic Landmark.
Hours & Admission Prices: Grounds: daily 9-5. $3 per car. House Tours: Oct.-July Thurs.-Sun. 10-4. Adults $3, children 6-12 $2; children under 6 no charge. Closed: Thanksgiving; Christmas. &
Attendance: 25,000

Crystal River

COASTAL HERITAGE MUSEUM, 532 Citrus Ave., Crystal River, FL 34428-4017. Tel.: 352-212-8390.
E-mail: crcoastalmuseum@aol.com
Web Site: coastalheritagemuseum.com
Formerly: The Museum of Citrus County History-Coastal Heritage
Key Personnel: Chm. (V), Sharon Padgett.

Institution Type/Description: Local History Museum: housed in 1939 old City Hall.
Hours & Admission Prices: Aug.-June Tues.-Sat. 10-2. No charge, donations accepted. Closed holidays. &
Attendance: 4,500 (actual)

CRYSTAL RIVER ARCHAEOLOGICAL STATE PARK, 3400 N. Museum Pt., Crystal River, FL 34428-6207. Mailing Address: 3266 N. Sailboat Ave., Crystal River, FL 34428. Tel.: 352-795-3817. Fax: 352-795-6061.
E-mail: FSP.FEEDBACK@DEP.STATE.FL.US
Web Site: floridastateparks.org
Key Personnel: Park Mgr., John Lakich; Dir., Donald Forgione; Pres. (V), John Roberts; Park Ranger & Museum Shop Mgr., Kirrin Peart.
Institution Type/Description: State Park Museum.
Hours & Admission Prices: Museum: Thurs.-Mon. 9-5. Park: daily 8am to sundown. Park Entrance: car: $3; motorcycle & pedestrian $2. &
Attendance: 21,000 (estimated)

Dade City

PIONEER FLORIDA MUSEUM ASSOCIATION, INC., 15602 Pioneer Museum Rd., Dade City, FL 33523. Mailing Address: P.O. Box 335, Dade City, FL 33526-0355. Tel.: 352-567-0262. Fax: 352-567-1262.
E-mail: curator@pioneerfloridamuseum.org
Web Site: www.pioneerfloridamuseum.org
Key Personnel: Pres., Stephanie Black.
Institution Type/Description: Pioneer Museum.
Hours & Admission Prices: Tues.-Sat. 10-5; group tours by appointment. Adults $8, seniors 55 & over $6, students 6-18 $4; members and children 5 & under no charge. Closed major holidays. &
Attendance: 20,000 (estimated)

Dania Beach

HOLOCAUST DOCUMENTATION & EDUCATION CENTER, INC., 303 N. Federal Hwy., Dania Beach, FL 33004-2807. Tel.: 954-929-5690. Fax: 954-929-5635.
E-mail: assistant@hdec.org
Web Site: www.hdec.org
Key Personnel: Exec. Vice Pres., Rositta E. Kenigsberg; Pres. (V), Harry A. (Hap) Levy.
Institution Type/Description: Holocaust Educational Resource Center.
Hours & Admission Prices: By appointment. No charge. Closed national & Jewish holidays. &

Davie

BUEHLER PLANETARIUM AND OBSERVATORY, Broward College, 3501 Davie Rd., Davie, FL 33314-1604. Tel.: 954-201-6681. Fax: 954-201-6316.
E-mail: webmaster@broward.edu
Web Site: www.iloveplanets.com
Institution Type/Description: Planetarium & Observatory.
Hours & Admission Prices: Observatory: Wed. & Fri.-Sat. 8pm-10pm. No charge.

FLAMINGO GARDENS, EVERGLADES WILDLIFE SANCTUARY, 3750 Flamingo Rd., Davie, FL 33330-1698. Tel.: 954-473-2955. Fax: 954-473-1738. Facebook: Flamingo Gardens, Everglades Wildlife Sanctuary.
E-mail: admin@flamingogardens.org
Web Site: www.flamingogardens.org
Key Personnel: Exec. Dir., Stan W. Wood.
Institution Type/Description: Wildlife Sanctuary & Historic Home: housed in the former residence of founders Floyd L. & Jane Wray, built in 1933.
Hours & Admission Prices: Daily 9:30-5; ticket booth closes at 4. Adults $19.95, children 3-11 $12.95; discounts to seniors, students, military, & groups; members no charge. Closed Thanksgiving; Christmas. &
Attendance: 125,000 (actual)

OLD DAVIE SCHOOL HISTORICAL MUSEUM, 6650 Griffin Rd., Davie, FL 33314-4331. Tel.: 954-797-1044. Fax: 954-797-1047.
E-mail: director@olddavieschool.org
Web Site: www.olddavieschool.org
Key Personnel: Exec. Dir., Leslie Schroeder; Pres., Kaylee McCall Correa; Education, Kim Weismantle.

Institution Type/Description: History Museum: housed in a 1918 two-story masonry school building designed by August Geiger. Listed on the National Register of Historic Places.
Hours & Admission Prices: Tues.-Sat. 10-4. Adults $10, seniors & children 5-12 $7; discounts to AAM & ICOM members. Closed New Year's Day; Memorial Day; Independence Day; Labor Day; Thanksgiving; Christmas. &
Attendance: 14,000 (estimated)

ROSEMARY DUFFY LARSON GALLERY AT BROWARD COLLEGE, A. HUGH ADAMS CAMPUS, 3501 S.W. Davie Rd., Bldg. 3, Davie, FL 33314-1604. Tel.: 954-201-6984. Fax: 954-201-6518.
E-mail: cgallery@broward.edu
Formerly: Fine Arts Gallery at Broward College, A. Hugh Adams Campus
Institution Type/Description: Art Gallery.
Hours & Admission Prices: Mon.-Tues. & Thurs.-Fri. 9-3, Wed. 2-8. No charge. &
Attendance: 1,600 (estimated)

YOUNG AT ART MUSEUM CLOSED, 751 S.W. 121st Ave., Ste. 1, Davie, FL 33325-3804. Tel.: 954-424-0085, ext. 23. Fax: 954-370-5057. Facebook: Young At Art Museum.
E-mail: mperrino@youngatartmuseum.org
Web Site: www.youngatartmuseum.org
Key Personnel: Exec. Dir. & C.E.O., Mindy Shrago; Chm. Bd. (V), David DiPietro; Dir. Finance, Dana McLean.
Institution Type/Description: Art Museum.
Hours & Admission Prices: Mon.-Thurs. 10-5, Fri.-Sat. 10-6, Sun. 11-5. Admission one & over $14; military families $11, seniors $12; discounts to groups; members no charge. ACM reciprocal admission to Family Premium & above members. Closed New Year's Day; Easter; Thanksgiving; Christmas. &
Attendance: 200,000 (actual)

Daytona Beach

DAYTONA INTERNATIONAL SPEEDWAY/TOURS, 1801 W. International Speedway Blvd., Daytona Beach, FL 32114-6833. Tel.: 386-681-6640. Fax: 386-681-4078. Facebook; Twitter; Instagram.
E-mail: dkurtz@iscmotorsports.com
Web Site: www.daytonainternationalspeedway.com
Formerly: Daytona 500 Experience
Institution Type/Description: Racing History Museum.
Hours & Admission Prices: Hours & Prices include Motorsports Hall of Fame of America. Daily 9-5; call for extended hours. All Access Tour: adults $25, children 6-12 $19; children under 5 no charge. Speedway Tour: adults $18, children 6-12 $12; children under 5 no charge. Closed Thanksgiving; Christmas. &
Attendance: 101,000 (estimated)

DR. MARY MCLEOD BETHUNE HOME & MUSEUM - MARY MCLEOD BETHUNE FOUNDATION, Bethune-Cookman Univ., 640 Dr. Mary McLeod Bethune Blvd., Daytona Beach, FL 32114. Tel.: 386-481-2121.
E-mail: mmbfoundation@cookman.edu
Institution Type/Description: Historic House: housed in the former home of founder & first president of Bethune-Cookman College; built in 1915.
Hours & Admission Prices: Mon.-Fri. 10-3, Sat. by appointment. No charge; donations accepted. Closed New Year's Eve; Martin Luther King Jr. Day; Independence Day; Labor Day; Thanksgiving; Christmas; University breaks.

HALIFAX HISTORICAL SOCIETY MUSEUM & GIFT SHOP, 252 S. Beach St., Daytona Beach, FL 32114-4407. Tel.: 386-255-6976.
E-mail: mail@halifaxhistorical.org
Web Site: www.halifaxhistorical.org
Key Personnel: Museum Dir., Fayn LeVeille; Pres., Warren Trager; 1st Vice Pres., Matt Romanik; 2nd Vice Pres., Dr. Michael Link; 3rd Vice Pres., Sara Glover, Esq.; Recording Sec., Ruth Trager; Corresponding Sec., ElizabethAlma McMillan; Treas., Elizabeth Beecher.
Institution Type/Description: Local History Museum.
Hours & Admission Prices: Tues.-Fri. 10:30-4:30, Sat. 10-4. Adults $7, children 12 & under $1; members no charge. Thurs. admission by donation. Research: $10 a day in museum; volunteer researcher on staff $20 per hour. Closed major holidays. &
Attendance: 5,000 (estimated)

MOTORSPORTS HALL OF FAME OF AMERICA, 1801 W. International Speedway Blvd., Daytona Beach, FL 32114-6833. Tel.: 248-349-7223. Twitter.
E-mail: info@mshf.com

Web Site: www.mshf.com
Formerly: Motorsports Museum & Hall of Fame
Institution Type/Description: History Museum: located inside the Daytona International Speedway.
Hours & Admission Prices: Hours & Prices include Daytona International Speedway tours. Daily 9-5; call for extended hours. All Access Tour: adults $25, children 6-12 $19; children under 5 no charge. Speedway Tour: adults $18, children 6-12 $12; children under 5 no charge. Closed Thanksgiving; Christmas. &

MUSEUM OF ARTS & SCIENCES, 352 South Nova Rd., Daytona Beach, FL 32114-4597. Tel.: 386-255-0285. Fax: 386-255-5040.
E-mail: info@moas.org
Web Site: www.moas.org
Key Personnel: Exec. Dir., Andrew Sandall; Dir. Finance, Steve Conklin; Dir. Devel., Stephanie Mason-Teague; Dir. Mktg. & Public Relations, Jenelle Codianne; Guest Relations Mgr., Patti Nikolla; Membership Coord., Monica Mitry; Chief Cur., Ruth Grim; Cur. Exhibits, Eric Mauk.
Institution Type/Description: General Museum.
Hours & Admission Prices: Mon.-Sat. & holidays 10-5, Sun. 11-5. Adults $12.95, seniors & students $10.95, children 6-17 $6.95; discounts to groups, AAM, ICOM, HIA & SEMC members; children 5 & under and members no charge. Closed New Year's Day; Thanksgiving; Christmas. &
Attendance: 138,000 (actual)

SOUTHEAST MUSEUM OF PHOTOGRAPHY, Daytona State College, 1200 W. International Speedway Blvd., Bldg. 1200, Daytona Beach, FL 32114. Mailing Address: P.O. Box 2811, Daytona Beach, FL 32120-2811. Tel.: 386-506-4475 & 3350. Fax: 386-506-4487. TDD: 386-506-3023.
E-mail: romnesj@daytonastate.edu
Web Site: www.SMPonline.org
Key Personnel: Dir., James Pearson; Registrar, Alexis Rogers; Cur. Education, Christina Katsolis.
Institution Type/Description: Photography Museum.
Hours & Admission Prices: Jan. 12-July 30 & Aug. 18-Dec. 16 Tues. & Thurs.-Fri. 11-5, Wed. 11-7, Sat.-Sun. 1-5. No charge; donations accepted. Closed Daytona 500 weekend; Easter; DSC spring break; Independence Day; Thanksgiving & weekend after; Christmas Eve, Day & week. &
Attendance: 60,000 (actual)

DeLand

AFRICAN AMERICAN MUSEUM OF THE ARTS, 325 S. Clara Ave., DeLand, FL 32720-5884. Mailing Address: P.O. Box 1319, Deland, FL 32721-1319. Tel.: 386-736-4004. Fax: 386-736-4088.
E-mail: art@africanmuseumdeland.org
Web Site: www.africanmuseumdeland.org
Key Personnel: Exec. Dir., Mary Allen; Pres. (V), Jefferson Pendleton.
Institution Type/Description: Art Museum.
Hours & Admission Prices: Thurs.-Sat. 10-4. No charge; donations accepted. &
Attendance: 5,000 (estimated)

DELAND NAVAL AIR STATION MUSEUM, 910 Biscayne Blvd., DeLand, FL 32724-2009. Tel.: 386-738-4149. Fax: 386-738-5405.
E-mail: dnas.museum.org@gmail.com
Web Site: www.delandnavalairmuseum.org
Key Personnel: Pres., Harold Bradeen.
Institution Type/Description: Military Museum.
Hours & Admission Prices: Museum: Wed-Sun. 12-4. Annex: closed. No charge; donations accepted. &
Attendance: 1,200 (estimated)

THE GILLESPIE MUSEUM - STETSON UNIVERSITY, 234 E. Michigan Ave., DeLand, FL 32724-3539. Mailing Address: Stetson University, 421 N. Woodland Blvd., Unit 8403, DeLand, FL 32723. Tel.: 386-822-7330. Fax: 386-822-7328.
E-mail: gillespie@stetson.edu
Web Site: www.gillespiemuseum.stetson.edu
Formerly: Gillespie Museum of Minerals, Stetson University
Key Personnel: Dir., Karen Cole, Ph.D.; Cur., Bruce Bradeen, Ph.D.; Admin. Asst., Stacy Junkins.
Institution Type/Description: Earth & Environmental Science Museum.
Hours & Admission Prices: Tues.-Fri. 10-4; see website for additional hours. Adults $2, seniors & students $1; discounts to groups & ASTC members; members no charge. Closed national & university holidays. &
Attendance: 6,000 (estimated)

HENRY A. DELAND HOUSE MUSEUM, 137 W. Michigan Ave., DeLand, FL 32720-3418. Tel.: 386-740-6813. Fax: 386-740-6813.
E-mail: delandhouse@msn.com

Web Site: www.delandhouse.com
Institution Type/Description: Historic House: housed in the former home of DeLand's first attorney, Arthur George Hamlin; built in 1886.
Hours & Admission Prices: Tues.-Sat. 12-3; other times by appointment. Admission $5.

HOMER AND DOLLY HAND ART CENTER AT STETSON UNIVERSITY, 139 E. Michigan Ave., DeLand, FL 32720. Mailing Address: 421 N. Woodland Blvd., Unit 8423, DeLand, FL 32723. Tel.: 386-822-7270 & 7271.
E-mail: seules@stetson.edu
Web Site: www2.stetson.edu/handartcenter
Key Personnel: Dir., Tonya Cribb Curran.
Institution Type/Description: Art Gallery.
Hours & Admission Prices: Academic Year: Mon.-Wed. & Fri. 11-4, Thurs. 11-6, Sat. 12-4. No charge. Closed national holidays; university breaks. ♿
Attendance: 5,017 (actual)

MEMORIAL HOSPITAL MUSEUMS, 230 N. Stone St., DeLand, FL 32720-4010. Tel.: 386-740-5800.
E-mail: delandhouse@msn.com
Institution Type/Description: Hospital Museum: listed on the National Register of Historic Buildings.
Hours & Admission Prices: Wed.-Sat. 10-3. No charge; donations accepted. ♿
Attendance: 500 (estimated)

MUSEUM OF ART - DELAND, 600 N. Woodland Blvd., DeLand, FL 32720-3447. Tel.: 386-734-4371. Fax: 386-734-7697.
E-mail: dansberger@moartdeland.org
Web Site: www.moartdeland.org
Formerly: Museum of Florida Art
Key Personnel: C.E.O., George Bolge; Pres. (V), Gen. Lee Downer, (Retired); Dir. Finance & Operations, Dorothy Dansberger; Dir. Mktg., Shonna Green; Cur. Art & Exhibition, David Fithian; Cur. Education, Pam Coffman; Dir. Devel., Pattie Pardee; Guest Svcs., Suzi Tanner; Downtown Gallery & Store Mgr., Teri Peaden; Registrar, Tariq Gibran.
Institution Type/Description: Art Museum.
Hours & Admission Prices: Tues.-Sat. 10-4, Sun. 1-4. Adults $5; discounts to Southeastern & North American Reciprocal Membership members, children under 12, members & staff no charge. Closed national holidays. ♿
Attendance: 30,000 (estimated)

ROBERT M. CONRAD RESEARCH AND EDUCATIONAL CENTER, 137 W. Michigan Ave., DeLand, FL 32720-3418. Tel.: 386-740-6813. delandhouse@msn.com.
E-mail: delandhouse@msn.com
Web Site: www.delandhouse.com
Key Personnel: Exec. Dir., Tom Roberts.
Institution Type/Description: History Museum.
Hours & Admission Prices: Tues.-Sat. 12-4; other times by appointment.

Deerfield Beach

DEERFIELD BEACH HISTORICAL SOCIETY, 380 E. Hillsboro Blvd., Deerfield Beach, FL 33441-3540. Mailing Address: P.O. Box 755, Deerfield Beach, FL 33443-0755. Tel.: 954-429-0378. Fax: 954-429-0378. Facebook: Deerfield Beach Historical Society.
E-mail: elilly707@aol.com
Web Site: www.deerfield-history.org
Key Personnel: Pres., Emily M. Lilly; Vice Pres., Judith Stanich; Sec., Lyn Cacella; Treas., Dave Noderer.
Institution Type/Description: History Museum.
Hours & Admission Prices: Sat. 10-2; other times by appointment. Suggested Donation: $2; discounts to AAM members. ♿
Attendance: 500 (estimated)

SOUTH FLORIDA RAILWAY MUSEUM, 1300 W. Hillsboro Blvd., Deerfield Beach, FL 33442-1716. Tel.: 954-698-6620. Fax: 561-790-4191.
E-mail: sfrm.org@gmail.com
Web Site: www.sfrm.org/
Key Personnel: Pres., Vic Zarzycki; Dir., Richard Bretone.
Institution Type/Description: Transportation Museum.
Hours & Admission Prices: Call for information.

Delray Beach

CASON COTTAGE HOUSE MUSEUM, 5 N.E. 1st St., Delray Beach, FL 33444-3707. Tel.: 561-243-0223 & 243-2577.
E-mail: info@db-hs.org
Institution Type/Description: Historic House Museum: housed in the home of Rev. John R. Cason, a community leader & Methodist minister; built in 1915.
Hours & Admission Prices: Nov.-April Thurs.-Sat. 11-3. Adults $5; children under 16 no charge.. ♿

CORNELL MUSEUM OF ART & AMERICAN CULTURE, 51 N. Swinton Ave., Delray Beach, FL 33444-2631. Tel.: 561-243-7922. Fax: 561-243-7018.
E-mail: gadams@delraycenterforthearts.org
Web Site: www.delraycenterforthearts.org
Key Personnel: Dir. Museum, Gloria Rejune Adams; Bd. Pres., Scott Porten; Pres. & C.E.O., Joe Gillie.
Institution Type/Description: Art History Museum: housed in 1913 building.
Hours & Admission Prices: June-Oct. Tues.-Sat. 10:30-4:30; Nov.-May Tues.-Sat. 10:30-4:30, Sun. 1-4:30. Adults $10, seniors 65 & over $6, students 13-21 with ID $4, children 4-12 $2; discounts to Florida Trust members; children under 3 & members no charge. Closed New Year's Day; Good Friday; Easter; Memorial Day; Independence Day; Labor Day; Thanksgiving; Christmas Eve & Day. ♿
Attendance: 50,000 (actual)

THE MORIKAMI MUSEUM AND JAPANESE GARDENS, 4000 Morikami Park Rd., Delray Beach, FL 33446-2305. Tel.: 561-495-0233.
E-mail: morikami@pbcgov.org
Web Site: www.morikami.org
Key Personnel: Park Admin., Bonnie White LeMay; Pres. Bd. Trustees, Dudley Omura; Cur. Education, Wendy Lo; Chief Cur. & Cultural Dir., Tamara Joy; Volunteer Coord., Diane Valentini; Dir. Mktg. & Events, Kizzy Sanchez Sherven; Resource Supervisor, Heather Grzybek; School Programs Specialist, Beth Kawazura; Cur. Japanese Art, Susanna Brooks; Cur. Collections, Veljko Dujin; Mgr. Membership, Sharyn Samuels; Coord. Youth & Outreach Education, Jaclyn DeMarzo; Museum Shop Mgr., Susan Keller.
Institution Type/Description: Ethnology Museum specializing in Japanese culture.
Hours & Admission Prices: Museum: Tues.-Sun. 10-5. Adults $15, seniors $13, college students $11, children 6-17 $9; discounts to groups of 15 or more and AAM & ICOM members; members & children under 6 no charge. Park: daily sunrise to sundown. No charge. Closed New Year's Day; Easter; Independence Day; Thanksgiving; Christmas. ♿
Attendance: 180,000 (actual)

MUSEUM OF LIFESTYLE & FASHION HISTORY, 322 N.E. 2nd Ave., Delray Beach, FL 33482. Mailing Address: P.O. Box 6127, Delray Beach, FL 33482-6127. Tel.: 561-243-2662. Fax: 561-495-8785.
E-mail: info@mlfhmuseum.org
Web Site: mlfhmuseum.org
Institution Type/Description: General Museum.
Hours & Admission Prices: Temporarily closed.

SILVERBALL MUSEUM, 19 N.E. 3rd Ave., Delray Beach, FL 33483. Tel.: 561-266-3294. Facebook.
Web Site: silverballmuseum.com
Institution Type/Description: General Museum.
Hours & Admission Prices: Daily 11 am - 2 am; call to confirm.

SPADY CULTURAL HERITAGE MUSEUM, 170 N.W. 5th Ave., Delray Beach, FL 33444-2653. Tel.: 561-279-8883.
E-mail: cfjones@spadymuseum.org
Web Site: www.spadymuseum.com/
Key Personnel: Exec. Dir., Daisy Fulton; Museum Dir., Charlene Jones; Educator, Brandy Brownlee.
Institution Type/Description: Cultural Heritage Museum: housed in the former home of Solomon D. Spady, a prominent African American educator & community leader in Delray Beach from 1922-1957.
Hours & Admission Prices: Mon.-Fri. 11-4, Sat. by appointment. Adults $5; members no charge.

Doral

MUSEUM OF THE AMERICAS, 2500 N.W. 79th Ave., Ste. 172, Doral, FL 33122-1071. Tel.: 305-599-8088 & 8089.
E-mail: americasmuseum@aol.com
Web Site: www.museumamericas.org
Key Personnel: Dir., Raul M. Oyuela.
Institution Type/Description: Art Museum.
Hours & Admission Prices: Tues.-Fri. 11-5, Sat. 11-4. No charge.

Dunedin

DUNEDIN FINE ART CENTER, 1143 Michigan Blvd., Dunedin, FL 34698-2799. Tel.: 727-298-3322.
E-mail: gabissett@dfac.org
Web Site: www.dfac.org
Key Personnel: Exec. Dir., George Ann Bissett, C.F.R.E.; Pres. (V), Amy Heimlich; Museum Shop Mgr., Michele DeMattio.
Institution Type/Description: Art Center.
Hours & Admission Prices: Mon.-Fri. 10-5, Sat. 10-2, Sun. 1-4. Adults $4, senior citizens $3; discounts to AAM & ICOM members; children 2 & under and members no charge; donations accepted. &
Attendance: 158,000 (estimated)

DUNEDIN HISTORY MUSEUM, 349 Main St., Dunedin, FL 34698-5700. Mailing Address: P.O. Box 2393, Dunedin, FL 34697-2393. Tel.: 727-736-1176. Facebook.
E-mail: info@dunedinmuseum.org
Web Site: www.dunedinmuseum.org
Key Personnel: Pres., Blair Kooi; Exec. Dir., Vincent Luisi; Dir. Operations, Carol Cortright; Cur., David Knupp.
Institution Type/Description: Local History Museum: housed in 1923 Atlantic Coastline Passenger Station; The Old Freight Warehouse, adjacent to Passenger Station.
Hours & Admission Prices: Tues.-Sat. 10-4. Adults $5, seniors 65 & over, teachers, military and children 12-17 $3; children under 12 & members no charge. &
Attendance: 14,500 (actual)

Eatonville

ZORA NEALE HURSTON NATIONAL MUSEUM OF FINE ARTS, 227 E. Kennedy Blvd., Eatonville, FL 32751-5303. Tel.: 407-647-3307. Fax: 407-539-2192.
E-mail: info@zorafestival.com
Web Site: www.zoranealehurstonmuseum.com
Key Personnel: Exec. Dir., N.Y. Nathiri.
Institution Type/Description: Art Museum.
Hours & Admission Prices: Call for hours and tour information. No charge; donations accepted.

Eglin Air Force Base

AIR FORCE ARMAMENT MUSEUM, 100 Museum St., Eglin Air Force Base, FL 32542-1497. Tel.: 850-651-1808 & 882-4062. Fax: 850-882-3990.
E-mail: info@afarmamentmuseum.com
Web Site: www.afarmamentmuseum.com
Key Personnel: Dir., George Jones; Museum Specialist, John "Chuck" Yeager.
Institution Type/Description: Military Museum.
Hours & Admission Prices: Mon.-Sat. 9:30-4:30. No charge; donations accepted. Closed federal holidays. &
Attendance: 123,000 (estimated)

Ellenton

THE JUDAH P. BENJAMIN CONFEDERATE MEMORIAL AT GAMBLE PLANTATION HISTORIC STATE PARK, 3708 Patten Ave., Ellenton, FL 34222-2152. Tel.: 941-723-4536. Fax: 941-723-4538.
E-mail: DEPNEWS@dep.state.fl.us
Web Site: www.floridastateparks.org
Key Personnel: Park Mgr., Kevin Kiser.
Institution Type/Description: Historic House: 1840-60 plantation home of Robert Gamble. 1844-1865, Gamble Mansion, the main house of the Gamble sugar plantation; Greek revival vernacular construction.
Hours & Admission Prices: Visitor Center: Thurs.-Mon. 8-5. Park Grounds: daily 8am-sunset. Tours: Thurs.-Mon. 9:30, 10:30 & 1, 2, 3, & 4. Adults $6, children 6-12 $4; under 6 no charge.
Attendance: 56,000 (estimated)

Estero

KORESHAN STATE HISTORIC SITE, 3800 Corkscrew Rd., Estero, FL 33928-1919. Tel.: 239-992-0311.
E-mail: andrew.tetlow@dep.state.fl.us
Web Site: www.floridastateparks.org/koreshan/
Key Personnel: Cur., Andrew Tetlow.
Institution Type/Description: Historic Building Complex: 1894-1982 utopian settlement.

Hours & Admission Prices: Daily 8 to sundown. Adults $5 per vehicle; members no charge. &
Attendance: 50,000 (estimated)

Eustis

EUSTIS HISTORICAL MUSEUM, INC., 536 N. Bay St., Eustis, FL 32726-3439. Tel.: 352-483-0046. Facebook: Eustis Historical Museum.
E-mail: eustismuseum@gmail.com
Key Personnel: Pres., Sue Hooper; Treas., John Blankenship; Cur., Gary Marshall; Historian, Louise Carter; Public Rels., Robin Richter.
Institution Type/Description: Historic House Museum: housed in the residence of G.D. Clifford, an early settler.
Hours & Admission Prices: Fri. & Sat. 1-5. No charge; donations accepted. Closed New Year's Day; Christmas. &
Attendance: 10,000 (estimated)

LAKE EUSTIS MUSEUM OF ART, 1 W. Orange Ave., Eustis, FL 32726. Tel.: 352-483-2900.
E-mail: lake.eustis.art.museum@gmail.com
Web Site: www.lakeeustisartmuseum.org
Key Personnel: Asst. Dir., Krysta L. Smith; Pres. (V), Lou Buigas.
Institution Type/Description: Fine Art Museum.
Hours & Admission Prices: Tues.-Fri. 10-4, Sat. 12-4. Suggested Donation: adults $5, seniors $3; discount to NARM members; members no charge. Closed major holidays. &
Attendance: 6,000 (actual)

Fernandina Beach

AMELIA ISLAND MUSEUM OF HISTORY, 233 S. Third St., Fernandina Beach, FL 32034-4210. Tel.: 904-261-7378. Fax: 904-261-9701.
E-mail: info@ameliamuseum.org
Web Site: www.ameliamuseum.org
Key Personnel: Exec. Dir., Phyllis Davis; Cur., Gray Ederfield; Road Scholar Coord., Brenda Brubeck; Mgr. Collections, Teen Peterson; Museum Shop Mgr., Kathy Maier.
Institution Type/Description: History Museum: housed in c.1937 Nassau County Jail building.
Hours & Admission Prices: Mon.-Sat. 10-4, Sun. 1-4. Museum & Spoken History Tour: 11am & 2pm. Adults $8, students & military $5. Centre Street Historic District Tours: Sept.-June Fri.-Sat.; Summer: call for hours. Admission $10. Ghost Tours: Fri. 6pm. Admission $10. Closed all major holidays. &
Attendance: 35,000 (actual)

FORT CLINCH STATE PARK, 2601 Atlantic Ave., Fernandina Beach, FL 32034-2203. Tel.: 904-277-7274. Fax: 904-277-7225.
E-mail: depnews@dep.state.fl.us
Web Site: www.floridastateparks.org
Key Personnel: Park Mgr., Peter Scalco.
Institution Type/Description: Historic Building: 1864 restored Fort Clinch.
Hours & Admission Prices: Visitor Center: daily 9-4:30. Park: daily 8am to sundown. $6 per vehicle up to 8 persons. Fort: daily 9-5. $2 per person over 6. Fort: evening programs $3 per person over 6. &
Attendance: 214,630 (estimated)

Flagler Beach

BULOW PLANTATION RUINS HISTORIC STATE PARK, 3501 S. Old Kings Rd. S., 9 mi. S.E. of Bunnell State Rd. 5, Flagler Beach, FL 32136-4339. Tel.: 386-517-2084.
E-mail: fsp.feedback@dep.state.fl.us
Web Site: www.floridastateparks.org/park/bulow-plantation
Key Personnel: Head Ranger, Nicky Makouski; Park Mgr., Benny Woodham.
Institution Type/Description: History Museum: interpretive center.
Hours & Admission Prices: Thurs.-Mon. 9-5. $3 per vehicle, $1 bicycles & walk-ins. Canoe Rentals: $10 hr., $40 day. Pavilion Rental: $30 plus tax. &

Fort Lauderdale

BONNET HOUSE MUSEUM & GARDENS, 900 N. Birch Rd., Fort Lauderdale, FL 33304-3326. Tel.: 954-563-5393. Fax: 954-561-4174. TDD: 954-563-5393.
E-mail: karenbeard@bonnethouse.org
Web Site: bonnethouse.org
Key Personnel: C.E.O., Karen L. Beard; Bd. Chm. (V), Diana Silvagni; Dir. Devel., Patrick Shavloske; Dir. Mktg., Monica Estevez; Dir. Education & Volunteer

Programs, Linda Schaller; Cur., Denyse Cunningham; Museum Shop Mgr., Dianne Ennis.

Institution Type/Description: Historic House: house built in 1920; property consists of 35 acres from the Atlantic Ocean to the Intracoastal Waterway. Listed on the National Register of Historic Places.

Hours & Admission Prices: Tours: Tues.-Sun. 9-4. Adults $20, children 6-12 $ 16, gardens only $10, tram tour $2; discounts to groups and AAM & AAA members; members & children under 6 no charge. Closed New Year's Day; Thanksgiving; Christmas. &

Attendance: 72,000 (estimated)

FORT LAUDERDALE FIRE AND SAFETY MUSEUM, 1022 W. Las Olas Blvd., Fort Lauderdale, FL 33312. Tel.: 954-763-1005.

E-mail: info@fortlauderdalefiremuseum.com

Web Site: www.fortlauderdalefiremuseum.com

Institution Type/Description: Firefighting History Museum: housed in Fire Station 3; built in 1927.

Hours & Admission Prices: Sat. 9 to noon, Sun. 12-4. Programs by appointment. No charge; donations accepted.

FORT LAUDERDALE HISTORICAL SOCIETY, 231 S.W. 2nd Ave., Fort Lauderdale, FL 33301-1825. Tel.: 954-463-4431.

E-mail: info@flhc.org

Web Site: historyfortlauderdale.org

Key Personnel: Pres., Art Bengochea; Exec. Dir., Patricia Zeiler; Cur. Collections, Lisa Lopez; Cur. Exhibitions, Tara Chadwick; Operations Mgr., Kamal Khan.

Institution Type/Description: Historical Society Museum. History Museum, King Cromartie House Museum, Schoolhouse Museum, Hoch Research Library.

Hours & Admission Prices: Museum: Mon.-Fri. 12-4, Sat. & Sun. 9:30-4. Archives: Mon.-Fri. 9-5. Adults $10-$15; members no charge. Closed major holidays. &

Attendance: 97,000 (estimated)

HISTORIC STRANAHAN HOUSE MUSEUM, 335 S.E. 6th Ave., Fort Lauderdale, FL 33301-2256. Tel.: 954-524-4736. Facebook; Twitter; Instagram; Youtube; Pinterest; Flickr.

E-mail: director@stranahanhouse.org

Web Site: www.stranahanhouse.org

Formerly: Stranahan House, Inc.

Key Personnel: Exec. Dir., April Kirk; Pres., Doug Smith; Sec., Christine Yates; Treas., Gene Harvey; Education Coord., Melanie Claros Rodriguez; Records & Collection Mgr., Deborah Wood; Caretaker, John Della Cerra; Museum Shop Mgr., Merry Wajda; Guest Svcs., David Greig; Weddings, Lindsay Romagnoli.

Institution Type/Description: Historic Building & Site.

Hours & Admission Prices: Guided Tours: daily 1, 2, & 3. Adults $12, seniors $11, students $7; special rates available for large groups (reservations required); members no charge. Closed some holidays. &

Attendance: 30,000 (estimated)

INTERNATIONAL SWIMMING HALL OF FAME, INC., One Hall of Fame Dr., Fort Lauderdale, FL 33316-1694. Tel.: 954-462-6536. Fax: 954-525-4031.

E-mail: lauriem@ishof.org

Web Site: www.ishof.org

Key Personnel: C.E.O., Bruce Wigo, Ed.D.; Dir. Operations & Pro Shop Mgr., Laurie Marchwinski.

Institution Type/Description: Aquatic Sports Museum.

Hours & Admission Prices: Mon.-Fri. 9-5, Sat. 9-2. Adults $8, seniors $6, children $4; discounts to groups of 10 or more; children under 12 & members no charge. &

Attendance: 50,000 (estimated)

MUSEUM OF ART/FORT LAUDERDALE, One E. Las Olas Blvd., Fort Lauderdale, FL 33301-1807. Tel.: 954-525-5500. Fax: 954-524-6011.

E-mail: info@moafl.org

Web Site: www.moafl.org

Formerly: Museum of Art, Inc.

Key Personnel: Dir. & Chief Cur., Bonnie Clearwater.

Institution Type/Description: Art Museum.

Hours & Admission Prices: Tues.-Sat. 11-5, Thurs. 11-8, Sun. 12-5. Adults $12, senior citizens 65 & over & military $8, students 13-17 & college students with ID $5; members, children 12 & under, NSU students, faculty & staff no charge. Special exhibit hours & prices may vary. Closed New Year's Day; Independence Day; Thanksgiving; Christmas. &

Attendance: 100,000 (estimated)

MUSEUM OF DISCOVERY AND SCIENCE, 401 S.W. Second St., Fort Lauderdale, FL 33312-1707. Tel.: 954-467-6637, ext. 311. Fax: 954-467-0046.

E-mail: kcavendish@mods.net

Web Site: www.mods.org

Key Personnel: C.E.O. & Pres., Kim L. Cavendish; Chm. (V), Ken Stiles; Vice Pres. Finance & C.F.O., Joe Majors; Vice Pres. Devel., Meredith Feder; Bldg. Supt., Ilija Nikolorski; Vice Pres. Mktg. & Communications, Marlene Janetos; Dir. Programs & Exhibits, Joe Cytacki; Museum Shop Mgr., Kevin Stradtner.

Institution Type/Description: Science Center & Park.

Hours & Admission Prices: Mon.-Sat. 10-5, Sun. 12-6. Exhibits: adults $16; ASTC & members no charge. IMAX: adults $9; discounts to members & ASTC members. Exhibits & IMAX: adults $21, seniors $19, children $16. &

Attendance: 456,091 (actual)

MY JEWISH DISCOVERY PLACE CHILDREN'S MUSEUM, 6501 W. Sunrise Blvd., Fort Lauderdale, FL 33313-6036. Tel.: 954-792-6700. Fax: 954-792-4839. Facebook.

E-mail: dgraw@sorefjcc.org

Web Site: sorefjcc.org

Key Personnel: C.E.O. & Exec. Dir., Donald Graw.

Institution Type/Description: Children's Museum.

Hours & Admission Prices: Mon.-Fri. 10-4. Admission 2 & over $5; discounts to AAM & ICOM members; one adult accompanied by child no charge.

Attendance: 1,500 (estimated)

NAVAL AIR STATION FORT LAUDERDALE MUSEUM, 4000 W. Perimeter Rd., Fort Lauderdale, FL 33315. Tel.: 954-359-4400.

E-mail: allanmcelhiney@yahoo.com

Web Site: www.nasflmuseum.com

Institution Type/Description: History Museum.

Hours & Admission Prices: Thurs. & Sat.-Sun. 11:30-3:30.

OLD DILLARD MUSEUM, 1009 N.W. 4th St., Fort Lauderdale, FL 33311-8935. Tel.: 754-322-8828. Fax: 754-322-8824.

E-mail: derek.davis@browardschools.com

Web Site: www.broward.k12.Fl.us/olddillardmuseum

Key Personnel: Dir., Derek Davis; Pres. (V), Patricia G. West.

Institution Type/Description: History Museum: housed in a former school for Black children.

Hours & Admission Prices: Mon.-Fri. 11-4; groups by appointment. No charge; donations accepted.

Attendance: 5,148 (actual)

TERRAMAR VISITORS CENTER - HUGH TAYLOR BIRCH STATE PARK, 3109 E. Sunrise Blvd., Fort Lauderdale, FL 33304-3313. Tel.: 954-564-4521. Fax: 954-762-3737.

E-mail: info@friendsoffloridastateparks.org

Institution Type/Description: History Museum: housed in the former home of Chicago attorney, Hugh Taylor Birch; built in 1940.

Hours & Admission Prices: Call for hours.

Fort Myers

BOB RAUSCHENBERG GALLERY AT EDISON STATE COLLEGE, 8099 College Pkwy., Fort Myers, FL 33919. Tel.: 239-489-9313. Fax: 239-489-9482.

E-mail: jdellinger@edison.edu

Web Site: bobrauschenberggallery.com

Key Personnel: Dir., Jade Dellinger.

Institution Type/Description: College Art Gallery.

Hours & Admission Prices: Mon.-Fri. 10-4, Sat. 11-3. No charge; donations accepted. Closed holidays. &

Attendance: 10,000 (actual)

CALUSA NATURE CENTER AND PLANETARIUM, 3450 Ortiz Ave., Fort Myers, FL 33905-7811. Tel.: 239-275-3435. Fax: 239-275-9016.

E-mail: webmaster@calusanature.org

Web Site: www.calusanature.org

Key Personnel: Exec. Dir., Mary Rawl; Pres., Phillip Fowler.

Institution Type/Description: Nature Center.

Hours & Admission Prices: Mon.-Sat. 10-4, Sun. 11-4. Adults $10, seniors $9, children 3-12 $5; discount to groups, members and children 2 & under no charge. &

Attendance: 60,000 (estimated)

EDISON & FORD WINTER ESTATES, 2350 McGregor Blvd., Fort Myers, FL 33901-3315. Mailing Address: P.O. Box 2368, Fort Myers, FL 33902-2368. Tel.: 239-334-7419. Fax: 239-332-6684. Facebook, Twitter, Instagram: @EdisonFordFL.

E-mail: info@edisonfordwinterestates.org

Web Site: www.edisonfordwinterestates.org

Key Personnel: C.E.O. & Pres., Chris Pendleton; C.F.O., Tom Hottovy; Vice Pres. Interpretation, Mike Cosden; Vice Pres. Community & Visitor Rels., Lisa S. Buttoni; Museum Store Mgr., Patti Wensel.
Institution Type/Description: History & Science Museum.
Hours & Admission Prices: Daily 9-5:30. Complete Estate Tour: adults $20, teens 13-19 $15; children 6-12 $11; children 5 & under no charge. Historian Tour: adults $30; teens 13-19 $25, children 6-12 $18; discounts to members; children 5 & under no charge. Museum & Laboratory: adults $15, teens 13-19 $12, children 6-12 $8; children 5 & under no charge. Additional tours & discounts available. Closed Thanksgiving; Christmas. &
Attendance: 250,000 (actual)

FLORIDA GULF COAST UNIVERSITY ART GALLERY, 10501 FGCU Blvd. S., FGCU Library, Fort Myers, FL 32965-6565. Tel.: 239-590-1894. Fax: 239-590-7270.

E-mail: asturdiv@fgcu.edu
Web Site: artgallery.fgcu.edu
Key Personnel: Gallery Dir., John Losuito; Gallery Coord., Anica Sturdivant; Preparator & Studio Mgr., Stephen R. Coe.
Institution Type/Description: Art Museum.
Hours & Admission Prices: Mon.-Fri. 10-4, Thurs. 10-7, Sat. 11-2; other times by appointment. No charge; donations accepted. &
Attendance: 10,000

IMAGINARIUM SCIENCE CENTER, 2000 Cranford Ave., Fort Myers, FL 33916-4006. Tel.: 239-321-7420. Fax: 239-344-5915.

E-mail: imag@cityftmyers.com
Web Site: i-sci.org
Formerly: Imaginarium Hands On Museum and Aquarium
Key Personnel: Exec. Dir., Matt Johnson; Deputy Dir., Shelby Baucom; Exhibits & Facilities Mgr., Tom Dahlheimer; STEM Program Coord., Sarah von Williamsen; Office Mgr., Janet Middel.
Institution Type/Description: Science & Technology Center/Museum: housed in 1938 historic building.
Hours & Admission Prices: Tues.-Sat. 10-5, Sun. noon-5. Adults $12, seniors 55 & up $10, students w/I.D. $8; discounts for ASTC members; museum members & children 2 & under no charge. Closed Thanksgiving; Christmas. &
Attendance: 90,000 (actual)

SOUTHWEST FLORIDA MUSEUM OF HISTORY, 2031 Jackson St., Fort Myers, FL 33901. Tel.: 239-321-7430. Fax: 239-344-5914.

E-mail: museuminfo@cityftmyers.com
Web Site: www.swflmuseumofhistory.com
Formerly: Fort Myers Historical Museum
Key Personnel: Gen. Mgr., Matthew H. Johnson; Business Mgr., Shelby Baucom; Public Rels. & Mktg. Mgr., Helena Finnegan; Education Asst., Pam Miner; Visitors Svc., Chuck Smith; Museum Clerk, Gerri Reaves.
Institution Type/Description: Regional History Museum: housed in 1924 ACL Railroad Depot.
Hours & Admission Prices: Tues.-Sat. 10-5. Adults $9.50, seniors $8.50, students $5; discounts to AAA, AAM & ICOM members; children under 3 & members no charge. Closed all major holidays. &
Attendance: 11,000 (actual)

Fort Pierce

A.E. BACKUS MUSEUM OF ART, 500 N. Indian River Dr., Fort Pierce, FL 34950-3080. Tel.: 772-465-0630. Fax: 772-468-6204. Facebook.

E-mail: info@backusmuseum.com
Web Site: www.backusmuseum.com
Key Personnel: Dir., Kathleen P. Fredrick.
Institution Type/Description: Art Museum.
Hours & Admission Prices: Wed.-Sat. 10-4, Sun. 12-4. Adults $5; discounts AARP members; NARM & museum members, children, students & active military no charge.
Attendance: 28,000 (estimated)

HEATHCOTE BOTANICAL GARDENS, INC., 210 Savannah Rd., Fort Pierce, FL 34982-3447. Tel.: 772-464-4672. Fax: 772-464-2676.

E-mail: info@heathcotebotanicalgardens.org
Web Site: www.heathcotebotanicalgardens.org
Key Personnel: Exec. Dir., Cynthia Warren; Pres. & Chm. (V), Cris Adams; Vice Pres., Henry Onitveros; Treas., Thomas Jefferson.
Institution Type/Description: Botanical Garden.
Hours & Admission Prices: May-Oct. Tues.-Fri. 9-5, Sat. 10-4; Nov.-April Tues.-Fri. 9-5, Sat. 10-4, Sun. noon to 4. Adults $6, seniors $5, children 6-12 $2; dis-

counts to groups; children under 6, members & AHS reciprocal members no charge. Closed major holidays. &
Attendance: 18,000 (estimated)

MANATEE OBSERVATION & EDUCATION CENTER, 480 N. Indian River Dr., Fort Pierce, FL 34950. Tel.: 772-429-6266.

E-mail: manatee@manateeeducationcenter.org
Web Site: www.manateeeducationcenter.org
Key Personnel: Mgr. & Lead Cur., Rachel Tennant; Volunteer Program Coord., Patricia Parker; Education Coord., Erin Lomax; Mktg. & Museum Shop Mgr., Meredith Bennett.
Institution Type/Description: Environmental Education Center: housed on the waterfront of the Indian River Lagoon.
Hours & Admission Prices: July-Sept. Thurs.-Sat. 10-5; Oct.-June Tues.-Sat. 10-5, Sun. 12-4. Admission $1; members & children under 6 no charge. Closed New Year's Day; Easter; Independence Day; Thanksgiving; Christmas. &
Attendance: 45,000 (estimated)

NATIONAL NAVY UDT-SEAL MUSEUM, 3300 N. Hwy. A1A, North Hutchinson Island, Fort Pierce, FL 34949-8520. Tel.: 772-595-5845. Fax: 772-595-5847.

E-mail: udtsealm@bellsouth.net
Web Site: www.navysealmuseum.com
Key Personnel: Pres. (V), Willard Snyder; Cur., Ruth McSween; Dir. Mktg. & Media, Rolf Snyder; Education Coord., Suzi Howard; Funds Mgr., Marisa Moffett.
Institution Type/Description: Military Museum: located on the 1943-1946, site where the Navy first trained Frog Men (Underwater Demolition Teams).
Hours & Admission Prices: Jan.-April Mon.-Sat. 10-4; May-Dec. Tues.-Sat. 10-4, Sun. 12-4. Adults $6, children 6-12 $3; discounts to groups; members & children under 5 no charge. Closed New Year's Eve & Day; Martin Luther King Jr. Day; Presidents' Day; Easter; Memorial Day; Independence Day; Labor Day; Thanksgiving & day after; Christmas Eve & Day. &
Attendance: 30,000 (estimated)

ST. LUCIE COUNTY REGIONAL HISTORY CENTER, 414 Seaway Dr., Fort Pierce, FL 34949-3138. Tel.: 772-462-1795. Fax: 772-462-1877.

E-mail: quatraroh@stlucieco.org
Web Site: www.st-lucie.lib.fl.us/museum
Formerly: St. Lucie County Historical Museum
Key Personnel: Dir., Matthew Baum; Pres. (V), Nancy Bennett.
Institution Type/Description: History Museum.
Hours & Admission Prices: Wed.-Sat. 10-4, Sun. 1-4; guided tours by appointment. Adults $4, seniors $3.50, students with ID $2.50, children $1.50. Closed county holidays. &
Attendance: 15,000 (actual)

Fort Walton Beach

CITY OF FORT WALTON BEACH HERITAGE PARK & CULTURAL CENTER, 139 Miracle Strip Pkwy., S.E., Fort Walton Beach, FL 32548-5817. Tel.: 850-833-9595. Fax: 850-833-9675.

E-mail: gmeyer@fwb.org
Web Site: www.fwb.org
Formerly: Indian Temple Mound Museum
Key Personnel: Mgr., Gail Lynn Meyer; Coord. Programming, Michael Weech; Coord. Operations, Sarah Faison.
Institution Type/Description: Heritage Park & Cultural Center: Fort Walton Temple Mound National Historic Landmark.
Hours & Admission Prices: Indian Temple Mounds Museum: June-Aug. Mon.-Sat. 10-4:30; Sept.-May Mon.-Fri. 12-4:30, Sat. 10-4:30. Historic Buildings: June-Aug. Mon.-Sat. 12-4; Sept.-May Mon.-Sat. 1-3. Adults 18 & over $5, seniors 55 & over & military with ID $4.50, children 4-17 $3; discounts to groups of 12 or more; children 3 & under no charge. Closed major holidays. &
Attendance: 20,000 (estimated)

EMERALD COAST SCIENCE CENTER, 31 Memorial Pkwy., S. W., Fort Walton Beach, FL 32548-6534. Tel.: 850-664-1261. Facebook: Emerald Coast Science Center.

E-mail: business-office@ecscience.org
Web Site: www.ecscience.org
Key Personnel: Exec. Dir., Diane Fraser; Museum Coord., Lisa Parkinson.
Institution Type/Description: Science Center.
Hours & Admission Prices: Labor Day to May Wed.-Sat. 10-4, June-Aug. Mon.-Sat. 10-4; other times by appointment. Adults $9, seniors 65 & over $8, children $7; discounts to groups of 15 or more & military; ASTC & museum members and children 2 & under no charge. Closed New Year's Day; Independence Day; Thanksgiving; Christmas.
Attendance: 20,000 (actual)

GULFARIUM MARINE ADVENTURE PARK, 1010 Miracle Strip Pkwy., S.E., Fort Walton Beach, FL 32548. Tel.: 850-243-9046, 800-247-8575. Fax: 850-244-5809. Facebook; Gulfarium Marine Adventure Park.
E-mail: info@gulfarium.com
Web Site: www.gulfarium.com
Formerly: Florida's Gulfarium
Institution Type/Description: Aquarium.
Hours & Admission Prices: Adult $23.95, senior $22.95, children 3-12 $15.95; discounts to Florida residents & military; children 2 & under no charge.

Gainesville

FLORIDA MUSEUM OF NATURAL HISTORY, S.W. 34th St. & Hull Rd., Gainesville, FL 32611. Mailing Address: P.O. Box 117800, Gainesville, FL 32611-7800. Tel.: 352-846-2000 & 392-1721. Fax: 352-392-8783 & 846-0253.
E-mail: museuminfo@flmnh.ufl.edu
Web Site: flmnh.ufl.edu
Formerly: Florida State Museum
Key Personnel: Dir. & Cur. Invertebrate Paleontology, Dr. Douglas S. Jones; Assoc. Dir., Beverly Sensbach; Dir. Exhibits & Public Programs, Darcie MacMahon; Asst. Dir. Budget & Human Resources, Darlene Novak; Dept. Chair & Cur. Mammalogy, Dr. David Reed; Dir. Devel., Marie Emmerson; Asst. Dir. Mktg. & Public Rels., Paul Ramey; Assoc. Cur. Informatics, Dr. Robert Guralnick; Assoc. Cur. Vertebrate Paleontology, Dr. Jonathan I. Bloch; Asst. Cur. Herbarium, Dr. Nico Cellinese; Distinguished Research Cur., Spanish Colonial Archaeology, Dr. Kathleen A. Deagan; Assoc. Scientist & Program Dir. Center for Science Learning, Dr. Betty A. Dunckel; Assoc. Cur. Environmental Archaeology, Dr. Katherine F. Emery; Dir. McGuire Center for Lepidoptera & Biodiversity, Dr. Jaret Daniels; Cur. Caribbean Archaeology, Dr. William F. Keegan; Cur. Vertebrate Paleontology, Dr. Bruce J. MacFadden; Cur. Paleobotany, Dr. Steven R. Manchester; Cur. FL Archaeology, Dr. William H. Marquardt; Cur. Latin American Art & Archaeology, Dr. Susan Milbrath; Cur. Lepidoptera, Dr. Jacqueline Y. Miller; Cur. Herpetology, Dr. Max A. Nickerson; Cur. Ichthyology, Dr. Lawrence Page; Cur. Marine Malacology, Dr. Gustav Paulay; Cur. Ornithology, Dr. David W. Steadman; Cur. Historical Archaeology, Dr. Charles Cobb; Ordway Professor, Dr. Scott K. Robinson; Distinguished Professor, Molecular Systematics & Evolutionary Genetics, Dr. Pamela S. Soltis; Cur. Malacology, Dr. Gustav Paulay; Asst. Scientist FL Archaeology, Dr. Karen J. Walker; Cur. Botany & Keeper of the Herbarium, Dr. Norris H. Williams; Assoc. Cur., Dr. David Blackburn; Assoc. Cur. Lepidoptera, Dr. Keith R. Willmott; Asst. Cur. FL Archaeology, Dr. Neill Wallis; Museum Shop Mgr., Stacey Crandall.
Institution Type/Description: Natural History Museum.
Hours & Admission Prices: Mon.-Sat. 10-5, Sun. 1-5. Permanent Exhibits: no charge. Butterfly Rainforest & Special Exhibits: call for admission prices. Closed Thanksgiving; Christmas Eve & Day. ♿
Attendance: 208,776 (actual)

HARN MUSEUM OF ART, University of Florida, 3259 Hull Rd., Gainesville, FL 32611-2700. Mailing Address: P.O. Box 14425, Gainesville, FL 32604. Tel.: 352-392-9826. Fax: 352-392-3892.
E-mail: twroath@harn.ufl.edu
Web Site: www.harn.ufl.edu
Key Personnel: Dir., Lee Anne Chesterfield, Ph.D.; Dir. Finance & Operations, Mary B. Yawn; Dir. Mktg. & Public Rels., Tami Wroath; Dir. Devel., Kelly C. Harvey; Dir. Education & Cur. Academic Programs, Eric Segal; Chief Cur. & Cur. Modern Art, Dulce Roman; Cofrin Cur. Asian Art, Jason Steuber; Cur. African Art, Susan Cooksey; Museum Shop Mgr., Megan O'Brien.
Institution Type/Description: Art Museum.
Hours & Admission Prices: Tues.-Fri. 11-5, Sat. 10-5, Sun. 1-5. No charge; donations accepted. Closed New Year's Day; Martin Luther King Jr. Day; Memorial Day; Independence Day; Labor Day; Veterans Day; Thanksgiving & day after; Christmas. ♿
Attendance: 96,300 (actual)

HISTORIC HAILE HOMESTEAD AT KANAPAHA PLANTATION, 8500 S.W. Archer Rd., Gainesville, FL 32608. Mailing Address: Historic Haile Homestead, Inc., 4941 S.W. 91st Terrace, Ste. 101, Gainesville, FL 32608-9106. Tel.: 352-336-9096. Facebook.
E-mail: hailedocent@yahoo.com
Web Site: www.hailehomestead.org
Key Personnel: Pres. (V), Karen A. Kirkman.
Institution Type/Description: Historic House Museum: housed in the home of cotton plantation owner, Thomas Evans Haile & his family, known as Talking Walls; built in 1856. Listed on the National Register of Historic Places.
Hours & Admission Prices: Sat. 10-2, Sun. 12-4; other times by appointment. Adults $5; discounts to members; children under 12 no charge. ♿
Attendance: 3,000 (estimated)

KANAPAHA BOTANICAL GARDENS, 4700 S.W. 58th Dr., Gainesville, FL 32608-0808. Tel.: 352-372-4981. Fax: 352-372-5892. Facebook.
E-mail: kbotanical@gmail.com
Web Site: www.kanapaha.org
Institution Type/Description: Botanical Gardens.
Hours & Admission Prices: Mon.-Wed. & Fri. 9-5, Sat.-Sun. 9am to dusk or 7pm (whichever comes 1st). Adults $8, children 5-13 $4; discounts to groups; children under 5 no charge. Closed Christmas.

MATHESON HISTORY MUSEUM, 513 E. University Ave., Gainesville, FL 32601-5451. Tel.: 352-378-2280. Fax: 352-378-1246. Facebook: @MathesonHistoryMuseum; Instagram & Twitter: @mathesonmuseum.
E-mail: info@mathesonmuseum.org
Web Site: www.mathesonmuseum.org
Formerly: Alachua County Historic Trust: Matheson Museum, Inc.
Key Personnel: Exec. Dir., Dr. Peggy McDonald; Pres. (V), Dr. Anita Spring; Mktg. Dir., Joanna Grey Talbot; Cur. Collections, Kaitlyn Hof-Mahoney.
Institution Type/Description: History Museum.
Hours & Admission Prices: Museum: Tues.-Sat. 11-4. Library & Archives: by appointment. No charge; donations accepted. Closed New Year's Day; Martin Luther King Jr. Day; Memorial Day; Independence Day; Labor Day; Thanksgiving & day after; Christmas Eve, Day & day after. ♿
Attendance: 19,000 (estimated)

MORNINGSIDE NATURE CENTER, 3540 E. University Ave., Gainesville, FL 32641-6057. Mailing Address: Div. Cultural Affairs, Station 30/P.O. Box 490, Gainesville, FL 32627. Tel.: 352-334-2170. Fax: 352-334-2248.
E-mail: info@visitgainesville.com
Key Personnel: Dir. Parks, Recreation & Cultural Affairs, Steve Phillips; Nature & Culture Mgr., Linda Demetropoulos.
Institution Type/Description: Nature Center: includes working turn-of-the-century farm & five relocated buildings of historic significance for architecture & time period.
Hours & Admission Prices: Tues.-Sat. 9-4:30. Closed New Year's Day; Thanksgiving; Christmas. ♿
Attendance: 30,000 (estimated)

SANTA FE COLLEGE TEACHING ZOO, 3000 N.W. 83rd St., Gainesville, FL 32606-6200. Tel.: 352-395-5601. Fax: 352-395-7365. Facebook: SF Teaching Zoo.
E-mail: haley.sivils@sfcollege.edu
Web Site: www.sfcollege.edu/zoo
Formerly: Santa Fe Community College Teaching Zoo
Key Personnel: Zoo Dir., Jonathan Miot; Chm., Vertigo Moody; Pres., Jackson Sasser; Zoo Cur., Kathleen Coyne-Russell; Advisor, Bobbi Cabaret; Asst. Professor, Shawntal Abram; CIT Conservation Education Specialist, Jade Salamone.
Institution Type/Description: Zoo.
Hours & Admission Prices: Self-Guided Tours: daily 9-2. Guided Tours: Mon.-Fri. 9:30, 10:30 & 11:30 by appointment. Adults $6, seniors 60 & over, UF students and children 4-12 $5; SF students & staff and children under 3 no charge. Closed Thanksgiving; Christmas Eve & Day. ♿
Attendance: 53,065 (actual)

SANTA FE GALLERY, 3000 N.W. 83rd St., Bldg. M-147, Gainesville, FL 32606-6210. Tel.: 352-395-5464. Fax: 352-395-4432.
E-mail: kyle.novak@sfcollege.edu
Web Site: www.sfcollege.edu/finearts/gallery/
Key Personnel: Gallery Mgr., Kyle Novak.
Institution Type/Description: Art Gallery.
Hours & Admission Prices: Mon.-Fri. 10-4. No charge; donations accepted. Closed all college holidays & breaks. ♿
Attendance: 10,000

THOMAS CENTER GALLERIES, 302 N.E. 6th Ave., Gainesville, FL 32601-5476. Mailing Address: P.O. Box 490, Station 30, Gainesville, FL 32627. Tel.: 352-393-8532. Fax: 352-334-2146.
E-mail: etlingrh@cityofgainesville.org
Web Site: www.historicthomascenter.org
Key Personnel: Mgr. Cultural Affairs, Russell Etling.
Institution Type/Description: Art Gallery.
Hours & Admission Prices: Mon.-Fri. 8-5, Sat.-Sun. 1-4. No charge. Closed city holidays; New Year's Day; Independence Day; Thanksgiving; Christmas. ♿
Attendance: 10,000 (estimated)

UNIVERSITY GALLERY, University of Florida, 400 S.W. 13th St., Fine Arts Bldg. B, Gainesville, FL 32611. Mailing Address: P. O. Box 115803, University of Florida, Gainesville, FL 32611-5803. Tel.: 352-273-3041. Fax: 352-846-0266.
E-mail: amyv@ufl.edu
Web Site: www.arts.ufl.edu/galleries
Key Personnel: Dir., Amy Vigilante.
Institution Type/Description: Contemporary Art Gallery.
Hours & Admission Prices: Aug. 24-April 26 Tues. 10-6, Wed. & Fri. 10-5, Thurs. 10-7, Sat. 12-4. No charge; donations accepted. Closed academic & national holidays. &
Attendance: 5,000 (estimated)

Geneva

MUSEUM OF GENEVA HISTORY, 165 First St., Geneva, FL 32732. Mailing Address: Geneva Historical & Genealogical Society, Inc., P.O. Box 91, Geneva, FL 32732-0091. Tel.: 407-349-5697.
E-mail: genevahgs@aol.com
Web Site: www.usgennet.orgh/usa/fl/county/seminole/Geneva/
Key Personnel: Dir., Mary Jo Martin.
Institution Type/Description: History Museum.
Hours & Admission Prices: 2nd & 4th Sun. each month 2-4; other times by appointment. No charge; donations accepted. Closed Mother's Day. &
Attendance: 1,000 (estimated)

Green Cove Springs

MILITARY MUSEUM OF NORTH FLORIDA, One Bunker Ave., Green Cove Springs, FL 32043. Tel.: 904-410-0781. Facebook.
E-mail: militarymuseumnf@aol.com
Web Site: www.militarymuseumofnorthflorida.com
Key Personnel: Exec. Dir., David Kersey.
Institution Type/Description: Military Museum.
Hours & Admission Prices: Thurs.-Sat. 10-3, Sun. 12-4. No charge; donations accepted. &
Attendance: 1,900 (estimated)

Gulf Breeze

THE GULF BREEZE ZOO, 5701 Gulf Breeze Pkwy., Gulf Breeze, FL 32563-9553. Tel.: 850-932-2229. Fax: 850-932-8575.
E-mail: web@gbzoo.com
Web Site: www.gulfbreezezoo.org
Formerly: The Zoo
Key Personnel: Dir., Steve Jagielski.
Institution Type/Description: Zoo & Botanical Garden.
Hours & Admission Prices: Oct.-Feb. daily 9-4; March-May 22 & Sept. 8- Sept. 30 daily 9-5; May 23-Sept. 7 daily 9-6. Adults 13-64 $15.95, senior citizens 65 & over $14.95, children 2-12 $11.95; discounts to groups, military with ID; children under 3 no charge. Closed Thanksgiving; Christmas. &
Attendance: 175,000

GULF ISLANDS NATIONAL SEASHORE, 1801 Gulf Breeze Pkwy., Gulf Breeze, FL 32563-5000. Tel.: 850-934-2600. Fax: 850-932-9654.
E-mail: guis_information@nps.gov
Web Site: www.nps.gov/guis/
Key Personnel: Supt., Daniel R. Brown; Chief of Resource Education, Susan Teel; Cultural Resources Program Mgr., David Ogden; Contract Specialist, Evans Ward.
Institution Type/Description: National Park & Historic District; barrier islands stretch from Cat Island in Mississippi, 240 kilometers (160 miles) eastward to the far end of Santa Rosa Island in Florida.
Hours & Admission Prices: Entrance fees collected at Perdido Key & Ft. Pickens. All centers & facilities no charge. Closed New Year's Day; Thanksgiving; Christmas. &

Hollywood

ART AND CULTURE CENTER OF HOLLYWOOD, 1650 Harrison St., Hollywood, FL 33020-6806. Tel.: 954-921-3274. Fax: 954-921-3273. Facebook.
E-mail: info@artandculturecenter.org
Web Site: www.artandculturecenter.org
Key Personnel: C.E.O. & Exec. Dir., Joy Satterlee; Chm. (V), John Stengel; Finance Mgr., Elizabeth Veszi; Deputy Dir., Susan Rakes; Technical Dir., Joseph Popejoy; Mgr. Theater, Chad Harris; Dir. Devel., Jeff Rusnak; Visitor

Svcs. Coord., Bailey Simmons; Communications, Leo Sarmiento; Cur. Exhibitions, Laura Marsh.
Institution Type/Description: Multi-disciplinary Arts Center
Hours & Admission Prices: Tues.-Fri. 10-5, Sat.-Sun. 12-4. Adults $7, seniors & students $4; discounts to groups of 10 or more; Miami-Dade & Broward teachers, firefighters, police, members and children 3 & under no charge. Closed New Year's Day; Easter; Independence Day; Thanksgiving; Christmas. &
Attendance: 49,383 (actual)

Homeland

HOMELAND HERITAGE PARK, 249 Church Ave., Homeland, FL 33847. Mailing Address: P.O. Box 122, Homeland, FL 33847. Tel.: 863-534-3766. Fax: 863-519-8665. Facebook.
E-mail: curtislaubach@polk-county.net
Key Personnel: Dir., Gary Hacking; Coord., Curtis Laubach.
Institution Type/Description: Historical Park, Sites & Buildings.
Hours & Admission Prices: Mon.-Fri. 8-5. No charge. &
Attendance: 15,000 (estimated)

Homestead

BISCAYNE NATIONAL PARK, 9700 S.W. 328th St., Homestead, FL 33033-5634. Tel.: 305-230-1144. Fax: 305-230-1190. Facebook.
E-mail: bisc_information@nps.gov
Web Site: www.nps.gov/bisc
Key Personnel: Supt., Brian Carlstrom; Public Information Officer, Matt Johnson.
Institution Type/Description: National Park & Nature Center.
Hours & Admission Prices: Convoy Point Grounds: daily 7-5:30. Dante Fascell Visitor Center: daily 9-5. No charge. Call 305-230-7275 for information. &
Attendance: 500,000 (estimated)

EVERGLADES NATIONAL PARK, 40001 State Rd. 9336, Homestead, FL 33034-6733. Tel.: 305-242-7826 & 7700. Fax: 305-242-7711. TDD: 305-242-7826.
E-mail: nancy_russell@nps.gov
Web Site: www.nps.gov/ever
Key Personnel: Supt., Pedro Ramos.
Institution Type/Description: National Park; pre & early settlement, southern Florida.
Hours & Admission Prices: Visitor Center: mid-April to mid-Dec. daily 9-5; mid-Dec. to mid-April daily 8-5. Park: $20 per car; senior citizens with Golden Age Passport no charge. &
Attendance: 1,000,000 (estimated)

Hutchinson Island

ELLIOTT MUSEUM, 825 N.E. Ocean Blvd., Hutchinson Island, FL 34996. Tel.: 772-225-1961. Fax: 772-225-2333.
E-mail: info@elliottmuseumfl.org
Web Site: www.elliottmuseumfl.org.
Key Personnel: Chm. (V), Walter Woods; Dir., Jennifer Esler; Dir. Devel., Diane Kimes; Dir. Finance, Amy Martin; Cur., Janel Hendrix.
Institution Type/Description: General Museum.
Hours & Admission Prices: Call for hours. Adults $14, seniors $12, children $6; children under 2 no charge. &
Attendance: 50,000 (estimated)

Indian Rocks Beach

GULF BEACH ART CENTER, 1515 Bay Palm Blvd., Indian Rocks Beach, FL 33785-2827. Tel.: 727-596-4331. Fax: 727-596-4331. Facebook, Twitter, Instagram.
E-mail: arts1515@gmail.com
Web Site: beachartcenter.org
Key Personnel: Exec. Dir., Anna Kuhlman; Pres. (V), Lynda Hamlett.
Institution Type/Description: Art Gallery & School.
Hours & Admission Prices: Mon.-Fri. 9-4. No charge. Closed major holidays. &

Inverness

THE OLD COURTHOUSE HERITAGE MUSEUM, One Courthouse Square, Inverness, FL 34450-4808. Tel.: 352-341-6429. Fax: 352-341-6445.
E-mail: csociety@tampabay.rr.com
Web Site: www.citruscountyhistoricalsociety.org
Formerly: The Museum of Citrus County History-Old Courthouse
Institution Type/Description: History Museum; housed in 1912 Old Courthouse. Listed on the National Register of Historic Places.

Hours & Admission Prices: Museum: Mon.-Fri. 10-4. Historical Resource: Mon.-Fri. 10-5. No charge; donations accepted. &
Attendance: 20,000 (estimated)

Islamorada

FLORIDA KEYS HISTORY AND DISCOVERY CENTER, 82100 Overseas Hwy., MM82, Islamorada, FL 33036. Mailing Address: P.O. Box 1124, Islamorada, FL 33036. Tel.: 305-922-2237. Facebook.
E-mail: info@keysdiscovery.com
Web Site: www.keysdiscovery.com
Key Personnel: Exec. Dir., Jill Miranda Baker; Pres., Richard Russell; Cur., Brad Bertelli.
Institution Type/Description: History Museum.
Hours & Admission Prices: Thurs.-Sun. 10-5. Adults $12, seniors & active military $10; discounts to Time Travelers members; children 13 & under and members no charge. &
Attendance: 7,500 (estimated)

HISTORY OF DIVING MUSEUM, 82990 Overseas Hwy., Islamorada, FL 33036-3600. Tel.: 305-664-9737. Facebook.
E-mail: info@divingmuseum.org
Web Site: www.divingmuseum.org
Formerly: Florida Keys History of Diving Museum
Key Personnel: Pres. Bd., Dr. Sally E. Bauer; Dir., Lisa Mongelia; Community Outreach Coord., Emily Kovacs; Mgr. Collections & Exhibits, Joshua Thacker; Museum Store Mgr., Joanne Birdsall.
Institution Type/Description: Diving Museum.
Hours & Admission Prices: Daily 10-5. Adults $12, seniors & veterans $11, college students $9, children 6-11 $6; discount to AAM & ICOM members; members, active military and children 5 & under no charge. Closed New Year's Day; Thanksgiving; Christmas. &
Attendance: 10,000 (estimated)

Jacksonville

ALEXANDER BREST GALLERY, 2800 University Blvd. N., Phillips Fine Arts Bldg., Jacksonville, FL 32211-3321. Tel.: 904-256-7677. Facebook.
E-mail: jbenedi@ju.edu
Web Site: www.ju.edu
Key Personnel: Dir., Jim Benedict.
Institution Type/Description: University Art Galleries.
Hours & Admission Prices: Mon.-Fri. 9-4:30, Sat. 12-5. No charge. Closed Memorial Day; Independence Day; Labor Day; Veterans Day; Thanksgiving; Christmas. &
Attendance: 12,000 (estimated)

CUMMER MUSEUM OF ART & GARDENS, 829 Riverside Ave., Jacksonville, FL 32204-3336. Tel.: 904-356-6857. Fax: 904-353-4101.
E-mail: kzimmerman@cummermuseum.org
Web Site: www.cummermuseum.org.
Key Personnel: Acting Dir., Holly Keris; Dir. Finance, Susan Surber; Dir. Education, Lynn Norris; Dir. Advancement, Lori Ann Whittington; Registrar, Kristen Zimmerman; Dir. Opers., Lisa Kaspar; Dir. Events & Progs., Cara Bowyer.
Institution Type/Description: Art Museum & Gardens.
Hours & Admission Prices: Tues. 10-9, Wed.-Sat. 10-4, Sun. 12-4. Adults $10, senior citizens, military & students $6; children 5 & under, members, Bank of America & Merrill Lynch cardholders, college students Tues.-Fri., Tues. 4-9, first Sat. each month, military Memorial Day to Labor Day no charge. Closed major holidays. &
Attendance: 164,496 (actual)

DINSMORE HISTORICAL MUSEUM, 7330 Civic Club Dr., Jacksonville, FL 32219. Tel.: 904-527-3952.
E-mail: dinsmorehistoricalmuseum@gmail.com
Web Site: www.dinsmorehistoricalmuseum.org
Institution Type/Description: History Museum.
Hours & Admission Prices: Sun. 1-3. No charge; donations accepted.

FLORIDA STATE COLLEGE AT JACKSONVILLE, KENT CAMPUS ART GALLERY, 3939 Roosevelt Blvd., Jacksonville, FL 32205-8946. Tel.: 904-381-3400.
E-mail: sallen@fscj.edu
Key Personnel: Coord., Sid Allen.
Institution Type/Description: Art Museum.

Hours & Admission Prices: Hours vary by exhibit. No charge. Closed holidays. &
Attendance: 1,200 (estimated)

JACKSONVILLE FIRE MUSEUM, 1406 Gator Bowl Blvd., Jacksonville, FL 32202-1310. Tel.: 904-630-0618. Fax: 904-630-4202.
E-mail: ashleycd@coj.net
Web Site: www.jacksonvillefiremuseum.com
Key Personnel: Dir., Martin Senterfitt; Cur. & Admin., Ashley Charboneau-DiPaolo.
Institution Type/Description: Fire Museum: housed in a historic fire station constructed in 1902. Listed on the National Registered Historical Building.
Hours & Admission Prices: Tues.-Sat. 9-4; groups by appointment. No charge; donations accepted.
Attendance: 60,000 (estimated)

JACKSONVILLE ZOO AND GARDENS, 370 Zoo Pkwy., Jacksonville, FL 32218-5799. Tel.: 904-757-4463, ext. 210. Fax: 904-757-4315. Facebook: Jacksonville Zoo and Gardens.
E-mail: wesleyj@jacksonvillezoo.org
Web Site: www.jacksonvillezoo.org
Formerly: Jacksonville Zoological Gardens
Key Personnel: Dir. & C.E.O., Tony Vecchio; Chmn (V), Jed Davis; Museum Shop Mgr., Janet Johnson; Volunteer, J. Baker.
Institution Type/Description: Zoo and Garden.
Hours & Admission Prices: Mon.-Fri. 9-5, Sat.-Sun. 9-6. Adults $17.95, seniors 65 & over $15.95, children 3-12 $12.95; discounts to groups, military, AAA & zoo members; members and children 2 & under no charge. Closed Christmas. &
Attendance: 1,000,000 (estimated)

KINGSLEY PLANTATION, 11676 Palmetto Ave., Jacksonville, FL 32226-2449. Mailing Address: 13165 Mt. Pleasant Rd., Jacksonville, FL 32225-1227. Tel.: 904-251-3537. Fax: 904-251-3577. Facebook: @TimucuanPreserveNPS; Twitter & Instagram @TimucuanNPS.
E-mail: timu_interpretation@nps.gov
Web Site: www.nps.gov/timu
Key Personnel: Supt., Chris Hughes; Chief of Interpretation, Brian Loadholtz; Museum Cur., Anne Lewellen.
Institution Type/Description: Historic Site.
Hours & Admission Prices: Daily 9-5. No charge; donations accepted. Closed New Year's Day; Thanksgiving; Christmas. &
Attendance: 82,000 (estimated)

MANDARIN MUSEUM AND HISTORICAL SOCIETY, 11964 Mandarin Rd., Walter Jones Historical Park, Jacksonville, FL 32223-1339. Tel.: 904-268-0784. Facebook.
E-mail: mandarinmuseum@bellsouth.net
Web Site: mandarinmuseum.net
Key Personnel: Pres., Sandra Arpen.
Institution Type/Description: Historic Buildings & Park.
Hours & Admission Prices: Museum: Sat. 9-4. Park: daily sunrise to sunset. Historic 1911 Store & Post Office: 1st Sat. each month 12-4. No charge; donations accepted. Closed holidays. &
Attendance: 13,000 (actual)

MUSEUM OF CONTEMPORARY ART JACKSONVILLE, (MOCA JACKSONVILLE), 333 N. Laura St., Jacksonville, FL 32202-3505. Tel.: 904-366-6911. Facebook; Instagram; Twitter.
E-mail: hellomoca@unf.edu
Web Site: mocajacksonville.unf.edu/default.aspx
Formerly: Jacksonville Museum of Modern Art
Key Personnel: Dir., Caitlin Doherty; Deputy Dir., Ben Thompson; Cur., Jaime DeSimone; Creative Dir., Casie Simpson; Assoc. Dir. Devel., Sarah Hande.
Institution Type/Description: Contemporary Art Museum.
Hours & Admission Prices: Tues.-Wed. & Fri.-Sat. 11-5, Thurs. 11-9, Sun. 12-5. Adults $8, senior citizens 65 & over, students, military and children 2-2 $5; UNF students, children under 2 & 1st Wed. of month ArtWalk 5pm-9pm no charge. Closed New Year's Day; Martin Luther King Day; Presidents' Day; Memorial Day; Independence Day; Labor Day; Veterans Day; Thanksgiving; Christmas Eve & Day. &
Attendance: 78,474 (actual)

MUSEUM OF SCIENCE & HISTORY OF JACKSONVILLE, 1025 Museum Cir., Jacksonville, FL 32207-9053. Tel.: 904-396-6674.
Web Site: www.themosh.org
Key Personnel: Exec. Dir., Maria Hane; Dir. Opers, Mike Hornsby; Dir. Visitor Experience, Paul Wenglowsky; Dir. Bryan-Gooding Planetarium & School Prog., Eddie Whisler.

Institution Type/Description: Science & History Museum/Planetarium.
Hours & Admission Prices: Mon.-Thurs. 10-5, Fri. 10-8, Sat. 10-6, Sun. 12-5. Adults $12.50, youth, young adults, student, teacher, seniors 55 & over and military $10, children 3-12 $6; children 2 & under, member children 3 & under, member youth, members no charge. Closed major holidays. &
Attendance: 145,000 (actual)

MUSEUM OF SOUTHERN HISTORY, 4304 Herschel St., Jacksonville, FL 32210-2210. Tel.: 904-388-3574. Facebook.
E-mail: southernmuseum@outlook.com
Web Site: www.museumsouthernhistory.com
Key Personnel: Chm. Bd., Ben Willingham; Chm. (V), James Shillinglaw.
Institution Type/Description: General Museum.
Hours & Admission Prices: Tues.-Sat. 10-4. Adults $3; children 16 & under no charge. Closed holidays. &
Attendance: 7,000 (estimated)

RITZ THEATRE AND MUSEUM, 829 N. David St., Jacksonville, FL 32202-4734. Tel.: 904-802-2011. Fax: 904-632-5553.
E-mail: carola@coj.net
Web Site: www.ritzjacksonville.com
Formerly: Ritz Theatre & LaVilla Museum
Key Personnel: Dir., Stacy Aubrey; Museum Admin., Lydia P. Stewart.
Institution Type/Description: History Museum.
Hours & Admission Prices: Tues.-Fri. 10-4, Sat. 10-2. Adults 18-64 $8, senior citizens 65 & over &students $5; children under 3 no charge. &
Attendance: 6,500 (actual)

TIMUCUAN ECOLOGICAL AND HISTORIC PRESERVE AND FORT CAROLINE NATIONAL MEMORIAL, 12713 Fort Caroline Rd., Jacksonville, FL 32225-1240. Mailing Address: 13165 Mt. Pleasant Rd., Jacksonville, FL 32225-1227. Tel.: 904-641-7155. Fax: 904-641-3798. Facebook, Twitter, Instagram.
E-mail: timu_interpretation@nps.gov
Web Site: www.nps.gov/timu
Key Personnel: Supt., Chris Hughes; Chief Interpretation, Brian Loadholtz; Museum Cur., Anne R. Lewellen.
Institution Type/Description: Historic & Natural History Museum.
Hours & Admission Prices: Daily 9-5. No charge; donations accepted. Closed New Year's Day; Thanksgiving; Christmas. &
Attendance: 1,000,000 (estimated)

Jacksonville Beach

BEACHES MUSEUM & HISTORY PARK, 381 Beach Blvd., Jacksonville Beach, FL 32250-5539. Tel.: 904-241-5657. Fax: 904-241-6243.
E-mail: director@beachesmuseum.org
Web Site: www.beachesmuseum.org
Key Personnel: Exec. Dir., Christine Hoffman; Pres. (V), Jack Schmidt.
Institution Type/Description: History Museum.
Hours & Admission Prices: Tues.-Sat. 10-4, Sun. 12-4. Archives: by appointment. No charge. &
Attendance: 12,000 (actual)

Jay

JAY HISTORICAL SOCIETY & MUSEUM, 3946 Hwy. 4, Jay, FL 32565. Tel.: 850-675-6122.
E-mail: jayhistoricalsociety@gmail.com
Web Site: www.jayhistoricalsociety.org
Institution Type/Description: Historical Society Museum.
Hours & Admission Prices: Fri. 10-3; other times by appointment.

Jensen Beach

THE CHILDREN'S MUSEUM OF THE TREASURE COAST, 1707 N.E. Indian River Dr., Jensen Beach, FL 34957. Mailing Address: P.O. Box 2147, Stuart, FL 34995. Tel.: 772-225-7575. Fax: 772-225-7506.
E-mail: marketing@childrensmuseumtc.org
Web Site: www.childrensmuseumtc.org
Key Personnel: Exec. Dir., Tammy Calabria.
Institution Type/Description: Children's Museum.
Hours & Admission Prices: Tues.-Wed. & Sat. 10-4, Thurs.-Fri. 10-5, Sun. 12-4. Admission 3 & over $8.50 per person, children 1-2 yrs. $4.25; discounts to military & ACM reciprocal members; members & children under one no charge. Closed New Year's Eve & Day; Easter; Independence Day; Thanksgiving; Christmas Eve & Day. &
Attendance: 60,000 (actual)

FPL ENERGY ENCOUNTER, 6501 S. Ocean Dr., Jensen Beach, FL 34957-2041. Tel.: 772-468-4111. Fax: 772-467-7565.
E-mail: energy_encounter@fpl.com
Web Site: www.fpl.com/learning/energy_encounter
Key Personnel: Mgr., Vicki Spencer.
Institution Type/Description: General Museum.
Hours & Admission Prices: Call for hours.
Attendance: 25,000 (actual)

Juno Beach

LOGGERHEAD MARINELIFE CENTER, 14200 U.S. Hwy. 1, Loggerhead Park, Juno Beach, FL 33408-1406. Tel.: 561-627-8280. Fax: 561-627-8305. Facebook.
E-mail: info@marinelife.org
Web Site: www.marinelife.org
Formerly: Marinelife Center of Juno Beach
Key Personnel: Pres. & C.E.O., Jack E. Lighton; Chm. Bd. (V), Raymond E. Graziotto; Chief Conservation Officer, Tommy Cutt; Dir. Retail Operations, Kate Fratalia; Dir. Finance, Caitlin Farmer; Assoc. Dir. Mktg. & Communications, Tom Longo; Assoc. Dir. Research, Justin Perrault, Ph.D.; Staff Veterinarian/Dir. Research & Rehabilitation, Charles A. Manire, D.V.M.; Devel. Mgr., Veronica Clinton; Capital Campaign Dir., Lynne Wells; Sr. Dir. Campus Operations, Tim Hannon.
Institution Type/Description: Sea Turtle Hospital & Marine Museum.
Hours & Admission Prices: Daily 10-5. No charge; donations accepted. Closed New Year's Day; Easter; Thanksgiving; Christmas. &
Attendance: 350,000 (actual)

Jupiter

LOXAHATCHEE RIVER HISTORICAL SOCIETY - JUPITER INLET LIGHTHOUSE AND MUSEUM, 500 Captain Armour's Way, Jupiter, FL 33469-3508. Tel.: 561-747-8380. Fax: 561-575-3292. Facebook: Jupiter Inlet Lighthouse Museum, Twitter: Jupiter LH.
E-mail: visit@jupiterlighthouse.org
Web Site: www.jupiterlighthouse.org
Key Personnel: Chm., Charles Jamieson; Pres. & C.E.O., Jamie Stuve; Dir. Mktg. & Communications, Kathleen Glover.
Institution Type/Description: General History Museum; lighthouse & historic homes.
Hours & Admission Prices: Jan.-April daily 10-5; May-Dec. Tues.-Sun. 10-5, last lighthouse tour 4pm. Adults $12, seniors $10, children 6-18 $6; discounts to groups & AAM members; children under 5 & under, active military and members no charge. Closed some major holidays. &
Attendance: 79,752 (actual)

Kennedy Space Center

NASA KENNEDY SPACE CENTER, DNPS/S.R. 405, Kennedy Space Center, FL 32899. Tel.: 855-433-4223. Facebook: @KenedySpaceCenterVisitorComplex; Twitter: @ExploreSpaceKSC.
Web Site: www.kennedyspacecenter.com
Key Personnel: C.O.O., Therrin Protze.
Institution Type/Description: Space Museum.
Hours & Admission Prices: Visitors Center: Jan. to mid-March, April 9-July 1 & Aug. 13-Dec. 20 daily 9-6; mid-March to April 8 & July-Aug. 12 daily 9-7; see website for additional hours. Visitor Complex: adults $57, seniors $50, children 3-11 $47. Closed Christmas; occasional launch days.

Key Biscayne

BILL BAGGS CAPE FLORIDA STATE PARK, 1200 S. Crandon Blvd., Key Biscayne, FL 33149-2795. Tel.: 305-361-5811.
E-mail: david.foster@dep.stste.fl.us
Web Site: www.floridastateparks.org
Key Personnel: Park Supt., David Foster.
Institution Type/Description: Historic Building: c.1825 restored Lighthouse; reconstruction of Keeper's house.
Hours & Admission Prices: Daily 8am to sunset. $8 per vehicle, $4 per single occupant vehicle or motorcycle, $2 per pedestrian or bicyclist.
Attendance: 700,000 (estimated)

Key West

AUDUBON HOUSE & TROPICAL GARDENS, 205 Whitehead St., Key West, FL 33040-6522. Tel.: 305-294-2116. Fax: 305-294-4513.

E-mail: audubonhouse@audubonhouse.org
Web Site: www.audubonhouse.com
Key Personnel: Pres. (V), Louis Wolfson, III; Operations Mgr., John Dell; Public Rels. & Mktg., Laura McKenna.
Institution Type/Description: Historic House Museum & Tropical Gardens: early 19th-century home of Capt. John H. Geiger which commemorates John James Audubon's visit to Key West in 1832.
Hours & Admission Prices: Call or see website for information.
Attendance: 40,000 (actual)

DONKEY MILK HOUSE, HISTORIC HOME, 613 Eaton St., Key West, FL 33040-6802. Tel.: 305-296-1866. Fax: 305-296-0922.
Institution Type/Description: Historic House: located in 1866 10-room mansion; tropical version of Classic Revival architecture containing rare 19th-century interior detailing, including 1890 Italian decorated ceilings; home of U.S. Marshall Williams & family for over 120 years.
Hours & Admission Prices: Tours by appointment. Adults $5, senior citizens & members $4, students $2.50; discounts to AAM & ICOM members; children under 12 no charge. &

DRY TORTUGAS NATIONAL PARK, Key West, FL 33041. Mailing Address: P.O. Box 6208, Key West, FL 33041-6208. Tel.: 305-242-7700. Fax: 305-242-7711.
E-mail: ever_reception@nps.gov
Web Site: www.nps.gov/drto
Key Personnel: Public Affairs Officer, Richard Cook.
Institution Type/Description: National Park & Preservation Project: c.1846 Fort Jefferson, third order coastal defense.
Hours & Admission Prices: Daily 8-5. Park Entrance: $5. Access to island available from Key West by chartered boat or commercial seaplane. &
Attendance: 95,000

ERNEST HEMINGWAY HOUSE MUSEUM, 907 Whitehead St., Key West, FL 33040-7473. Tel.: 305-294-1136. Fax: 305-294-2755.
E-mail: info@hemingwayhome.com
Web Site: www.hemingwayhome.com
Key Personnel: Gen. Mgr., Jacque Sands; Pres. & C.E.O., Michael A. Morawski; Dir. Events, Anna Morawski; Museum Shop Mgr., Melanie Mosher.
Institution Type/Description: Historic House: 1931-1961 Ernest Hemingway Home, built in Spanish Colonial Style of native rock hewn from the grounds.
Hours & Admission Prices: Daily 9-5. Adults $14, children 6-12 $6; discounts to military & groups; children 5 & under no charge. &
Attendance: 415,244 (actual)

FORT EAST MARTELLO MUSEUM, 3501 S. Roosevelt Blvd., Key West, FL 33040-5209. Mailing Address: 281 Front St., Key West, FL 33040-8313. Tel.: 305-296-3913.
E-mail: kwahs@kwahs.org
Web Site: www.kwahs.org
Key Personnel: Exec. Dir., Michael Gieda; Pres., Shirrel Rhoades.
Institution Type/Description: Historical Museum and Art Gallery: housed in 1861 brick fort.
Hours & Admission Prices: Call or see website for information. &
Attendance: 38,955 (actual)

FORT ZACHARY TAYLOR HISTORIC STATE PARK, 601 Howard England Way, Key West, FL 33040-8396. Tel.: 305-292-6713. Fax: 305-292-6881.
E-mail: david.foster@dep.state.fl.us
Web Site: www.floridastateparks.org/forttaylor
Key Personnel: Park Mgr., David Foster.
Institution Type/Description: History Museum.
Hours & Admission Prices: Park: 8 am to sunset. Museum Tours: daily 12-5. Vehicle (up to 8 passengers): $6.50 per car, Walk-ins $2.50 per person; children under 6 no charge. &
Attendance: 389,000 (actual)

HARRY S. TRUMAN LITTLE WHITE HOUSE MUSEUM, 111 Front St., Key West, FL 33040-8311. Tel.: 305-294-9911. Fax: 305-294-9988. Facebook.
E-mail: bwolz@trumanlittlewhitehouse.com
Web Site: www.trumanlittlewhitehouse.com
Key Personnel: Exec. Dir. & C.F.O., Robert J. Wolz.
Institution Type/Description: Historic House: built in 1890 as the Navy Base Commander home, and used by Presidents Taft, Truman, Eisenhower, John F. Kennedy, Carter & Clinton.
Hours & Admission Prices: Daily 9-4:30. Adults $21.45, seniors $19.30, youth 5-12 $10.75; discounts to Florida Assoc. of Museums; children under 5 no charge. &
Attendance: 67,000 (actual)

KEY WEST ART AND HISTORICAL SOCIETY & CUSTOM HOUSE MUSEUM, 281 Front St., Key West, FL 33040-8313. Tel.: 305-295-6616. Fax: 305-295-6649.
E-mail: kwahs@kwahs.org
Web Site: www.kwahs.org
Key Personnel: Exec. Dir., Michael F. Gieda; Pres., Shirrel Rhoades; Financial Mgr., Addie Unuvar; Membership Coord., Kim Livingston; Cur., Cori Convertito, Ph.D.; Dir. Retail Operations, Daniel Ayers; Asst. Dir. Retail operations, Lynn Clark; Dir. Education, Adele Williams; Mgr. Operations, Shawn Cowles.
Institution Type/Description: Art & History Museum: housed in c.1891 Custom House.
Hours & Admission Prices: Daily 9:30-4:30. Adults $10, seniors $9, children & students $5; discount to AAA members & local residents; members & children under 6 no charge. Closed Christmas. &
Attendance: 76,635 (actual)

KEY WEST LIGHTHOUSE & KEEPERS QUARTERS MUSEUM, 938 Whitehead St., Key West, FL 33040-7423. Mailing Address: 281 Front St., Key West, FL 33040. Tel.: 305-294-0012.
E-mail: kwahs@kwahs.org
Web Site: www.kwahs.org
Key Personnel: Exec. Dir., Michael Gieda; Pres., Shirrel Rhoades.
Institution Type/Description: General Museum: housed in 1887 lighthouse keepers home & 1846 lighthouse museum.
Hours & Admission Prices: Daily & holidays 9:30-4:30; call to confirm. Adults $10, seniors 62 & up $9, children 6 & up and students $5; discounts to groups, AAA members, & local residents; children under 6 & members no charge. Closed Christmas. &
Attendance: 92,321 (actual)

KEY WEST SHIPWRECK TREASURES MUSEUM, 1 Whitehead St., Key West, FL 33040-6634. Tel.: 305-292-8990. Fax: 305-292-1617.
E-mail: shipwreck@historictours.com
Web Site: www.keywestshipwreck.com
Formerly: Key West Shipwreck Historeum Museum
Institution Type/Description: Historic Ship Museum.
Hours & Admission Prices: Daily 9:40-5. Adults $14, students, seniors & military $12, children 4-12 $6; children 3 & under no charge. &

KEY WEST TROPICAL FOREST & BOTANICAL GARDEN, 5210 College Rd., Key West, FL 33040-4302. Tel.: 305-296-1504. Fax: 305-296-2242.
E-mail: kwbgs@kwbgs.org
Web Site: www.kwbgs.org
Key Personnel: Exec. Dir., Misha D. McRAE; Pres., Bernhard Rasch.
Institution Type/Description: Botanical Garden.
Hours & Admission Prices: Daily 10-4. Adults $7, military & seniors $5; members & children under 12 no charge. Closed New Year's Day; Thanksgiving; Christmas. &
Attendance: 25,000 (actual)

MEL FISHER MARITIME HERITAGE SOCIETY, 200 Greene St., Key West, FL 33040-6516. Tel.: 305-294-2633, ext. 15. Fax: 305-294-5671.
E-mail: info@melfisher.org
Web Site: www.melfisher.org
Key Personnel: Dir., Rebecca J. Tomlinson, Ph.D.
Institution Type/Description: Maritime Museum.
Hours & Admission Prices: Mon.-Fri. 8:30-5, Sat.-Sun. 9:30-5. Adults $15, students $12.50, children $5; discounts to groups, AAM members, Monroe County residents, & Florida Assoc. of Museums members; members no charge. &
Attendance: 221,743 (actual)

THE OLDEST HOUSE & GARDEN MUSEUM, 322 Duval St., Key West, FL 33040. Mailing Address: P.O. Box 689, Key West, FL 33041-0689. Tel.: 305-294-9501. Fax: 305-294-4509. Facebook: Oldest House & Garden Key West.
E-mail: oirf@oirf.org
Web Site: www.oirf.org
Key Personnel: Admin., Teri Beard; Pres., Kelly Friend.
Institution Type/Description: Historic House Museum: housed in c.1829 Conch House, home of local sea captain & wrecker.
Hours & Admission Prices: Mon.-Tues. & Thurs.-Sat. 10-4. No charge; donations accepted. &
Attendance: 4,288 (actual)

RIPLEY'S BELIEVE IT OR NOT! MUSEUM, 108 Duval St., Key West, FL 33040-6506. Tel.: 305-293-9939. Fax: 305-293-9709.
E-mail: keywest@ripleys.com
Web Site: www.ripleys.com
Institution Type/Description: General Museum.
Hours & Admission Prices: Daily 10 am-9 pm. Adults $16.99, children 5-12 $9.99; discounts to groups of 6 or more; children 4 & under no charge. ♿
Attendance: 86,000 (actual)

Key West Naval Air Station

NATIONAL NAVAL AVIATION MUSEUM, 1878 S. Blue Angel Pkwy., Key West Naval Air Station, FL 32508. Mailing Address: 1750 Radford Blvd., Ste. B, Naval Air Station, Pensacola, FL 32508-5402. Tel.: 850-452-3604. Fax: 850-452-3296. Facebook: @NationalAviationMuseum; Twitter: @NavalMuseum.
E-mail: namfoffice@navalaviationmuseum.org
Web Site: www.navalaviationmuseum.org
Key Personnel: Chm. Bd. Dirs., Adm. Mark F. Fitzgerald, USN (Ret.); Pres. & C.E.O., Lt. Gen. Duane D. Thiessen, USMC (Ret.); C.F.O., Chief of Staff & Treas., Bill Bowers; Museum Dir., Capt. Sterling Gilliam, USN (Ret.); Exec. Dir. Strategic Devel., Michele Sweigert; Dir. Mktg., Malerie Shelton; Dir. Devel. Opers., Stephanie Pugh; Dir. Events & Administration, Leslie Geiger; Gen. Mgr. Museum Support Co., Fred Geiger.
Institution Type/Description: Naval Aviation Museum.
Hours & Admission Prices: Daily 9-5. No charge; donations accepted. Closed New Year's Day; Thanksgiving; Christmas. ♿
Attendance: 814,000 (estimated)

Kissimmee

MUSEUM OF MILITARY HISTORY, 5210 W. Irlo Bronson Memorial Hwy., Kissimmee, FL 34746. Tel.: 407-507-3894. Fax: 407-507-3894. Facebook: Museum of Military History.
E-mail: militarymuseum1@gmail.com
Web Site: museumofmilitaryhistory.com
Formerly: Veterans Tribute and Museum of Osceola County, Inc.
Key Personnel: C.E.O. & Chm. (V), Donald Smith; Historian, Rick Brumby.
Institution Type/Description: Military Museum.
Hours & Admission Prices: Tues.-Sun. 10-6. Adults $7, seniors $6, students & veterans $5; 100% disabled veterans $4; discounts to AAM & ICOM members. Closed New Year's Day; Thanksgiving; Christmas. ♿
Attendance: 10,000 (actual)

OSCEOLA CENTER FOR THE ARTS, 2411 E. Irlo Bronson Memorial Hwy., Kissimmee, FL 34744-5430. Tel.: 407-846-6257. Fax: 407-846-7902.
E-mail: emoore@ocfta.com
Web Site: www.ocfta.com
Key Personnel: Exec. Dir., Brandon Arrington; Pres. (V), Don Miers.
Institution Type/Description: Art Gallery.
Hours & Admission Prices: Tues.-Fri. 10-5. Art Gallery: no charge. Closed national holidays. ♿
Attendance: 11,000 (estimated)

PIONEER VILLAGE & MUSEUM - OSCEOLA COUNTY HISTORICAL SOCIETY, 2491 Babb Rd., Kissimmee, FL 34746. Mailing Address: 4155 W. Vine St., Kissimmee, FL 34746. Tel.: 407-396-8644.
E-mail: rachel@osceolahistory.org
Web Site: osceolahistory.org
Institution Type/Description: Historical Society Museum.
Hours & Admission Prices: Village: Thurs.-Sun. 10-4. Grounds: Tues.-Fri. 9-5. Adults $5, children 6-12 $2; children 5 & under and members no charge.

WARBIRD ADVENTURES & THE KISSIMMEE AIR MUSEUM, Kissimmee Gateway Airport, 233 N. Hoagland Blvd., Kissimmee, FL 34741-4531. Tel.: 407-870-7366, 800-386-1593. Fax: 407-870-2295.
E-mail: fly@warbirdadventures.com
Web Site: www.warbirdadventures.com/air_museum
Institution Type/Description: Military History Museum.
Hours & Admission Prices: Mon.-Sat. 9-5. Adults $12, seniors & military $11, children 6-12 $6; children under 6 no charge. ♿
Attendance: 5,000 (estimated)

LaBelle

LABELLE HERITAGE MUSEUM, 360 N Bridge St., CSR-29 N., LaBelle, FL 33935. Mailing Address: P.O. Box 2846, LaBelle, FL 33975-2846. Tel.: 863-674-0034.
E-mail: labelleheritagemuseum@comcast.net
Key Personnel: Museum Shop Mgr., Jeannie Horlacher.
Institution Type/Description: Historical Museum.
Hours & Admission Prices: June-Aug. Mon.-Tues. 9-12, Thurs.-Fri. 1-4; Sept.-May Mon.-Tues. & Sat. 9-12, Thurs.-Fri. 1-4; other times by appointment; closed all major holidays. Admission $3; members & children under 6 no charge. ♿
Attendance: 500 (estimated)

Lake City

LAKE CITY COLUMBIA COUNTY HISTORICAL MUSEUM, INC., 157 S.E. Hernando Ave., Lake City, FL 32025-4428. Mailing Address: P.O. Box 3276, Lake City, FL 32056-3276. Tel.: 386-755-9096. Fax: 904-755-6605.
E-mail: lakecitymuseum@yahoo.com
Key Personnel: Dir. & Cur., Pat McAlhany.
Institution Type/Description: History Museum: located in a Historic House.
Hours & Admission Prices: Thurs. & Sat. 10-1. No charge; donations accepted. Closed New Year's Day; Easter; Independence Day; Christmas. ♿
Attendance: 3,000 (estimated)

Lake Wales

BOK TOWER GARDENS, 1151 Tower Blvd., Lake Wales, FL 33853-3470. Tel.: 863-676-1408. Fax: 863-676-6770. Facebook: Bok Tower Gardens.
Web Site: boktowergardens.org
Formerly: Historic Bok Sanctuary
Key Personnel: Pres., David Price; Interim Controller, Steve Jolley; Mktg. & Public Rels. Dir., Brian Ososky; Dir. Retail, Sandra Dent; Dir. Horticulture, Greg Kramer.
Institution Type/Description: Botanical Garden.
Hours & Admission Prices: Daily 8-6. Adults $12, children 5-12 $3; discount to groups; children under 5, AABGA members & members no charge. ♿
Attendance: 130,000 (estimated)

LAKE WALES DEPOT MUSEUM & CULTURAL CENTER, 325 S. Scenic Hwy., Lake Wales, FL 33853-3873. Tel.: 863-678-5160. Fax: 863-678-1842.
E-mail: lakewalesdepot@gmail.com
Web Site: www.cityoflakewales.com
Key Personnel: Dir., Mimi Reid Hardman.
Institution Type/Description: Local History Museum: housed in 1928 ACL & Seaboard Coastline Railroad Depot.
Hours & Admission Prices: Mon.-Fri. 9-5, Sat. 10-4. No charge; donations accepted. Closed major holidays. ♿
Attendance: 20,000 (estimated)

POLK STATE LAKE WALES ARTS CENTER, 1099 State Rd. 60 E., Lake Wales, FL 33853-4208. Mailing Address: Lake Wales Art Council, Inc., P.O. Box 608, Lake Wales, FL 33859-0608. Tel.: 863-676-8426. Fax: 863-676-1117.
E-mail: info@lw-arts.org
Web Site: lakewalesartscouncil.org
Key Personnel: Exec. Admin., Jean M. Donaldson.
Institution Type/Description: Arts Gallery: housed in the Spanish Mission-style building formerly the Holy Spirit Catholic Church; built 1927.
Hours & Admission Prices: Mon.-Fri. 9-4. No charge.

Lake Worth

LAKE WORTH HISTORICAL MUSEUM, 414 Lake Ave., Lake Worth, FL 33460-3807. Tel.: 561-533-7354. Fax: 561-586-1750.
E-mail: lwlibrary@lakeworth.org
Web Site: www.lakeworth.org
Formerly: Museum of the City of Lake Worth
Key Personnel: Library Svcs. Mgr., Vickie Joslin.
Institution Type/Description: History Museum.
Hours & Admission Prices: Wed.-Sat. 1-4; tours by appointment. No charge, donations accepted.

NATIONAL MUSEUM OF POLO AND HALL OF FAME, INC., 9011 Lake Worth Rd., Lake Worth, FL 33467-3617. Tel.: 561-969-3210. Fax: 561-964-8299.

E-mail: polomuseum@att.net
Web Site: www.polomuseum.com
Key Personnel: Exec. Dir., George DuPont, Jr.; Dir. Devel., Brenda Lynn.
Institution Type/Description: Polo Sports History & Hall of Fame.
Hours & Admission Prices: Jan.-April Mon.-Fri. 10-4, Sat. 10-2; May-Dec. Mon.-Fri. 10-4; other times by appointment. No charge; donations accepted. ♿

Lakeland

AEROSPACE DISCOVERY AT FLORIDA AIR MUSEUM, 4175 Medulla Rd., Lakeland, FL 33811-1249. Tel.: 863-904-6833. Fax: 863-648-9264.
E-mail: fly-info@flysnf.org
Web Site: flysnf.org
Formerly: Florida Air Museum At Sun 'n Fun
Key Personnel: Exec. Dir., Robb Williams; Pres. & C.E.O., John Leenhouts; Museum Shop Mgr., Susan Highley.
Institution Type/Description: Aviation Museum.
Hours & Admission Prices: Mon.-Sat. 10-4, Sun. 12-4. Adults $12, senior citizens $10, youth 8-17 $8; ASTC reciprocal program; children 7 & under and members no charge. Closed New Year's Day; Easter; Christmas; Mondays in June, July & Aug. ♿
Attendance: 150,000 (estimated)

EXPLORATIONS V CHILDREN'S MUSEUM, 109 N. Kentucky Ave., Lakeland, FL 33801-5044. Tel.: 863-687-3869.
E-mail: info@explorationsv.com
Web Site: explorationsv.com
Institution Type/Description: Children's Museum.
Hours & Admission Prices: Mon.-Sat. 9-5:30. Admission 2 & over $9, seniors $4.50; discounts to AAA members, seniors & military; children 1 & under and members no charge. Closed major holidays. ♿
Attendance: 90,232

POLK MUSEUM OF ART, 800 E. Palmetto St., Lakeland, FL 33801-5529. Tel.: 863-688-7743. Fax: 863-688-2611.
E-mail: corologas@polkmuseumofart.org
Web Site: www.polkmuseumofart.org
Key Personnel: Exec. Dir., Claire Orologas; Deputy Dir., Palemeschia "Pal" Rivers Powell; Dir. Operations, Gregory Mills; Museum Shop Mgr., Terry Aulisio.
Institution Type/Description: Art Museum.
Hours & Admission Prices: June to Labor Day Tues.-Sat. 10-5; Sept.-May Tues.-Sat. 10-5, Sun. 1-5. No charge. Closed holidays. ♿
Attendance: 140,000 (estimated)

Largo

THE ARMED FORCES HISTORY MUSEUM, 2050 34th Way N., Largo, FL 33771-4094. Tel.: 727-539-8371. Fax: 727-524-4967. Facebook: Armed Forces History Museum.
E-mail: info@armedforcesmuseum.com
Web Site: www.armedforcesmuseum.com
Formerly: The Armed Forces Military Museum
Key Personnel: Dir. & C.E.O., John J. Piazza, Sr.; Dir. Mktg., Cindy Bosselmann; Museum Shop Mgr., Kathy Weed.
Institution Type/Description: Military & History Museum.
Hours & Admission Prices: Tues.-Sat. 10-4, Sun. 12-4. Adults $17.95, seniors 65 & over and veterans $14.95, teens 13-17 $12.95, children 4-12 $9.95; discounts to AAA members & groups of 10 or more; members, children 3 & under and active & retired military with ID no charge. Closed major holidays. ♿

HERITAGE VILLAGE, 11909-125 St., N., Largo, FL 33774-3611. Tel.: 727-582-2123. Fax: 727-582-2211.
E-mail: ebabb@pinellascounty.org
Web Site: www.pinellascounty.org/heritage
Key Personnel: Operations Mgr., Ellen Babb; Museum Interpreter, Paige W. Noel.
Institution Type/Description: Living History Museum.
Hours & Admission Prices: Wed.-Sat. 10-4, Sun. 1-4. No charge; donations accepted. Closed holidays. ♿
Attendance: 200,000 (estimated)

Leesburg

LEESBURG CENTER FOR THE ARTS, 429 W. Magnolia St., Leesburg, FL 34749. Mailing Address: P.O. Box 492857, Leesburg, FL 34749-2857. Tel.: 352-365-0232. Fax: 352-315-1152.
E-mail: director@leesburgcenterforthearts.com
Web Site: www.leesburgcenterforthearts.com
Institution Type/Description: Art Gallery.

Hours & Admission Prices: Call for hours.

Live Oak

SUWANNEE COUNTY HISTORICAL MUSEUM, 208 N. Ohio Ave., Live Oak, FL 32064-2455. Tel.: 386-362-1776.
E-mail: suwanneemuseum@yahoo.com
Web Site: suwanneemuseum.org
Key Personnel: Exec. Dir. & Cur., Randy S. Torrance.
Institution Type/Description: History Museum.
Hours & Admission Prices: Tues.-Sat. 9-12 & 1-3. No charge; donations accepted.

Loxahatchee

LION COUNTRY SAFARI, 2003 Lion Country Safari Rd., Loxahatchee, FL 33470-3977. Tel.: 561-793-1084. Fax: 561-793-9603.
E-mail: sales@lioncountrysafari.com
Web Site: www.lioncountrysafari.com
Key Personnel: Dir. Wildlife, Terry Wolf; Cur. Education, Rhonda Beitmen; Public Rels. & Dir. Mktg., Jennifer Berthume; Coord. Mktg., Esther Sierra.
Institution Type/Description: Zoo; safari drive-through.
Hours & Admission Prices: Mon.-Fri. 10-5, last car admitted at 4; Sat.-Sun. & holidays 9:30-5:30. Admission 10-64 $35, seniors 65 & over $31.50, children 3-9 $26; children 2 & under no charge. Parking: $8 per vehicle. Annual Pass: regular 10-64 $75, senior 65 & over $67, children 3-9 $60; 20% discount on additional guests.

Madison

NORTH FLORIDA COMMUNITY COLLEGE ART GALLERY, 325 N.W. Turner Davis Dr., Ste. A, Madison, FL 32340-1611. Tel.: 850-973-1642. Fax: 850-973-9288.
E-mail: bardenl@nfcc.edu
Institution Type/Description: College Art Gallery.
Hours & Admission Prices: Mon.-Fri. 10-12 & 1-3; Sun. special openings. No charge. ♿

Maitland

ART & HISTORY MUSEUMS - MAITLAND, 231 W. Packwood Ave., Maitland, FL 32751-5596. Tel.: 407-539-2181. Fax: 888-316-5729. Facebook: art & History Museums - Maitland.
E-mail: info@artandhistory.org
Web Site: artandhistory.org
Formerly: Maitland Art Center; Research Studio, Maitland Art Center; and Maitland Historical Society
Key Personnel: Exec. Dir. & C.E.O., Mark Harmon; Pres. Bd., Elisha Gonzalez Bonnewitz; Chief Cur., Rebecca Sexton-Larson; Dir. Mktg., Rae Ward.
Institution Type/Description: Art & History Museums.
Hours & Admission Prices: Art Center Galleries: Tues.-Sun. 11-4. History Museums: Thurs.-Sun. 11-4. Waterhouse Residence Museum & Carpentry Shop Museum: Sat.-Sun. 11-4. Grounds: daily 11-4. Packwood Ave.: Adults $6, seniors 65 & over, children 5-17 & Maitland Residents $5, Maitland Seniors & Students $4. Lake Lily Campus: Adults $3, Maitland Residents $2.50, Seniors 65 & over and children 5-17 $2, Maitland Seniors & Students $1.50; 2nd Thurs. of the month for Maitland Residents, children 4 & under and members no charge. Closed major holidays. ♿
Attendance: 55,000 (actual)

HOLOCAUST MEMORIAL RESOURCE AND EDUCATION CENTER OF FLORIDA, INC., 851 N. Maitland Ave., Maitland, FL 32751-4461. Tel.: 407-628-0555, ext. 284. Fax: 407-628-1079.
E-mail: info@holocaustedu.org
Web Site: www.holocaustedu.org
Key Personnel: Exec. Dir., Pam Kancher; Chm. (V), Tess Wise; Pres. (V), Ellen Wise Lang; Devel. Mgr., Raychel Cesaro; Education, Mitchell Bloomer; Coord. Communications, Mandy Richardson.
Institution Type/Description: History Museum.
Hours & Admission Prices: Mon.-Thurs. 9-4, Fri. 9-1, Sun. 1-4. No charge; donations accepted. Closed Jewish holidays; national holidays. ♿
Attendance: 20,000 (estimated)

Marathon

CRANE POINT MUSEUM & NATURE CENTER, 5550 Overseas Hwy., Marathon, FL 33050-2713. Tel.: 305-743-3900 & 9100 (museum). Fax: 305-743-8172. Facebook: Crane Point Museum & Nature Center.
E-mail: cranepointmuseum@gmail.com

Web Site: www.cranepoint.net
Key Personnel: C.O.O., Charlotte Quinn.
Institution Type/Description: Natural History Museum.
Hours & Admission Prices: Mon.-Sat. 9-5, Sun. 12-5. Adults $14.95, seniors & military $12.95, children 6-12 $9.95; discounts to groups; children under 6 & members no charge. Closed Easter; Thanksgiving; Christmas. &
Attendance: 30,000 (actual)

Marco Island

MARCO ISLAND HISTORICAL SOCIETY, 180 S. Heathwood Dr., Marco Island, FL 34145-2010. Mailing Address: P.O. Box 2282, Marco Island, FL 34146-2282. Tel.: 239-389-6447. Facebook: marcoislandhistoricalsociety.
E-mail: themihs@aol.com
Web Site: www.themihs.com
Key Personnel: Pres., Darcie Guerin; Pres. (V), Thomas M. Wagor; Cur. Collections, Austin Bell; Museum Shop Mgr., Lori Wagor.
Institution Type/Description: Historical Society Museum.
Hours & Admission Prices: Tues.-Sat. 9-4. No charge.

Melbourne

BREVARD ZOO, 8225 N. Wickham Rd., Melbourne, FL 32940. Tel.: 321-254-9453. Fax: 321-259-5966.
E-mail: admin@brevardzoo.org
Web Site: www.brevardzoo.org
Institution Type/Description: Zoo.
Hours & Admission Prices: Daily 9:30-5. Adults $13.50, seniors $12.50, children 2-12 $10; discounts to groups; children under 2 no charge. Closed Thanksgiving; Christmas.

FLORIDA INSTITUTE OF TECHNOLOGY BOTANICAL GARDEN, Florida Tech, 150 W. University Blvd., Melbourne, FL 32901-6982. Tel.: 321-674-8962. Fax: 321-674-7257.
E-mail: garden@fit.edu
Web Site: garden.fit.edu
Key Personnel: Horticulturalist & Mgr. Grounds, Holly Chichester.
Institution Type/Description: Botanical Gardens.
Hours & Admission Prices: Daily sunrise to sunset.

FOOSANER ART MUSEUM CLOSED, 1463 Highland Ave., Melbourne, FL 32935-6562. Tel.: 321-674-8916. Fax: 321-242-0798.
E-mail: info@foosanerartmuseum.org
Web Site: foosanerartmuseum.org
Formerly: Brevard Art Museum
Key Personnel: Exec. Dir. & Chief Cur. University Museums, Carla Funk; Cur. Education, Kathie Elias; Dir. Collections, Sarah Smith; Mgr. Security & Exhibitions, Jose Marquez; Mgr. Visitor Svcs., Tina Murray.
Institution Type/Description: Art Museum.
Hours & Admission Prices: Wed.-Sat. 10-4. No charge. Closed major holidays. &
Attendance: 70,000 (estimated)

LIBERTY BELL MEMORIAL MUSEUM, 1601 Oak St., Melbourne, FL 32901. Tel.: 321-727-1776.
E-mail: franck@honoramerica.org
Web Site: honoramerica.org
Key Personnel: Exec. Dir., Franck Kaiser.
Institution Type/Description: History Museum.
Hours & Admission Prices: Tues.-Fri. 10-4, Sat. 10-2. No charge; donations accepted; closed all major holidays. &
Attendance: 15,000

Miami

BAY OF PIGS MUSEUM & LIBRARY, 1821 S.W. 9th St., Miami, FL 33135-5101. Tel.: 305-649-4719. Fax: 305-649-8719.
E-mail: brigada2506@gmail.com
Web Site: bayofpigs2506.com
Key Personnel: C.E.O., Cur. & Museum Shop Mgr., Esteban Bovo; Chm. (V), Felix Rodrigue; Pres. (V), Humberto Diaz Arguelles; Museum Shop Mgr., Andres Manso; Museum Shop Mgr., Vincente Blanco-Capote.
Institution Type/Description: History Museum.
Hours & Admission Prices: Mon.-Fri. 10-9, Sat. 10-2; other times by appointment. No charge; donations accepted. &
Attendance: 2,000 (estimated)

BLACK HERITAGE MUSEUM, 15801 S.W. 102nd Ave., Miami, FL 33157-1653. Tel.: 786-287-1157.

E-mail: blkhermu@yahoo.com
Key Personnel: Pres., Priscilla G. Stephens Kruize.
Institution Type/Description: Cultural Arts & History Museum.
Hours & Admission Prices: Call for hours; groups by appointment. No charge; donations accepted. Closed New Year's Day; Easter; Christmas. &
Attendance: 4,010

CORAL CASTLE MUSEUM, 28655 S. Dixie Hwy., Miami, FL 33033. Tel.: 305-248-6345. Facebook: @CoralCastleMuseum.
E-mail: lauramaye@coralcastle.com
Web Site: coralcastle.com
Key Personnel: Dir. Mgmt., Mktg. & Sales, Laura Maye.
Institution Type/Description: Historic Building: built by Edward Leedskalnin from 1923-1951. Listed on the National Register of Historic Places.
Hours & Admission Prices: Sun.-Thurs. 8-6, Fri.-Sat. 8-8. Adults $15, senior citizens 65 & up $12, children 7-12 $7; discounts to groups; children under 6 no charge.

DEERING ESTATE AT CUTLER, 16701 S.W. 72nd Ave., Miami, FL 33157-2500. Tel.: 305-235-1668. Fax: 305-254-5866. Facebook, Instagram, Twitter.
E-mail: mpettit@deeringestate.org
Web Site: www.deeringestate.org
Key Personnel: Dir., Jennifer Tisthammer; Business Mgr., Eileen Cahill; Learning Programs Mgr., Chris Bumpus; Historic Preservation & Curatorial Mgr., Bethany Gray; Cultural Programs Coord., Kim Yantis; Special Events Coord., Jenna Noordhoek; Mktg. Specialist, Cathy Guerra; Exec. Dir., Deering Estate Foundation, Mary Pettit.
Institution Type/Description: Historic Estate.
Hours & Admission Prices: Daily 10-5. Adults $12, youth 4-14 $7; discounts to groups; members no charge. Closed Thanksgiving; Christmas. &

EMERSON DORSCH, 5900 NW 2nd Ave., Miami, FL 33127. Tel.: 305-576-1278. Facebook: @EmersonDorsch.
E-mail: info@emersondorsch.com
Web Site: www.emersondorsch.com
Key Personnel: Founder, Brook Dorsch; Cur., Tyler Emerson-Dorsch.
Institution Type/Description: Art Gallery.
Hours & Admission Prices: Call for hours & admissions. &

GOLD COAST RAILROAD MUSEUM, INC., 12450 S.W. 152nd St., Miami, FL 33177-1402. Tel.: 305-253-0063. Facebook: @GoldCoastRailroad; Instagram: @gcrmrailroad; Twitter: @Goldcoast_RR.
E-mail: webmaster@gcrm.org
Web Site: www.gcrm.org
Key Personnel: Exec. Dir., Connie Greer.
Institution Type/Description: Railroad Museum: located on historic NAS RICHMOND, second largest Airship Naval Base World War II.
Hours & Admission Prices: Mon.-Fri. 10-4, Sat. & sun. 11-4. Adults $8, children 2-12 $6. Closed Christmas; New Year's Day. &
Attendance: 120,000 (estimated)

HAITIAN HERITAGE MUSEUM, 4141 N.E. 2nd Ave., Ste. 105C, Miami, FL 33137. Tel.: 305-371-5988. Fax: 305-432-3792. Facebook & Instagram: @haitianheritagemuseum; Twitter: @HaitianMuseum.
E-mail: hhmeveline@comcast.net
Web Site: www.haitianheritagemuseum.org
Key Personnel: Exec. Dir., Eveline Pierre; Dir. Operations, Serge Rodriguez.
Institution Type/Description: Heritage Museum.
Hours & Admission Prices: Tues.-Fri. 10-5; other times by appointment.

HISTORYMIAMI, 101 W. Flagler St., Miami, FL 33130-1504. Tel.: 305-375-1492. Fax: 305-375-1609. Facebook: @HistoryMiami360.
E-mail: e.info@historymiami.org
Web Site: www.historymiami.org
Formerly: Historical Museum of Southern Florida
Key Personnel: Dir., Jorge Zamanillo; Chm., Michael Weiser; C.F.O., Roxanne Cappello; Vice Pres. Curatorial Affairs, Michael Knoll; Vice Pres. Education, Tina Menendez.
Institution Type/Description: History Museum.
Hours & Admission Prices: Tues.-Sat. 10-5, Sun. 12-5; call to confirm. Adults $10, seniors & students $8, children 6-12 $5; discounts to AAM & ICOM members; children under 6 & members no charge. Closed New Year's Day; Martin Luther King Jr. Day; Presidents' Day; Memorial Day; Independence Day; Labor Day; Columbus Day; Veterans Day; Thanksgiving; Christmas. &
Attendance: 83,000 (estimated)

JUNGLE ISLAND, 1111 Parrot Jungle Trail, Miami, FL 33132-1611. Tel.: 305-400-7000. Fax: 305-400-7291. Facebook, Instagram & Twitter: @jungleisland.
E-mail: guestrelations@jungleisland.com
Web Site: www.jungleisland.com
Formerly: Parrot Jungle Island
Key Personnel: Pres., John Dunlop.
Institution Type/Description: Zoological Park.
Hours & Admission Prices: Mon.-Fri. 10-5., Sat. & Sun 10-6. Adults $34.95, children $26.95; discounts to groups, AAM members & contracted travel agents. Annual Pass: adults $79.95, children $71.95. ঌ
Attendance: 400,000 (estimated)

MCD MUSEUM OF ART & DESIGN, 620 Biscayne Blvd., Miami, FL 33132. Tel.: 305-237-7700.
E-mail: museum@mdc.edu
Web Site: www.mdcmoad.org
Key Personnel: Exec. Dir. & Chief Cur., Rina Carvajal.
Institution Type/Description: Art Museum.
Hours & Admission Prices: Wed.-Thurs. 12-5, Fri. 1:30-5. No charge; donations accepted. ঌ

MIAMI CHILDREN'S MUSEUM, 980 MacArthur Causeway, Miami, FL 33132-1604. Tel.: 305-373-5437. Fax: 305-373-5431. Facebook: @miami.childrens.museum; Instagram: @miamichildrensmuseum; Twitter: @MiChiMu.
E-mail: info@miamichildrensmuseum.org
Web Site: www.miamichildrensmuseum.org
Key Personnel: C.E.O., Deborah Spiegelman; C.F.O., Tanya Reid; Chief Business Devel. Officer, Belissa Alvarez; Chief Innovation & Experiences Officer, Lucia Williams; Dir. Devel. & Special Events, Hannah Hausman; Dir. Education, Betty Perez; Dir. Facilities, John Laurence; Dir. Mktg., PR & Sales, Cristina Rodriguez.
Institution Type/Description: Children's Museum.
Hours & Admission Prices: Daily 10-6. Admission $20, Florida Residents $15; military personnel & veterans, children under 1 & members no charge. Closed Thanksgiving; Christmas. ঌ
Attendance: 430,000 (estimated)

MIAMI DADE COLLEGE KENDALL GALLERY, Martin & Pat Fine Center for the Arts, 11011 S.W. 104th St., Miami, FL 33176. Tel.: 305-237-7700.
E-mail: abustama@mdc.edu
Web Site: www.mdc.edu/kendall/art
Key Personnel: Dir. Visual Resources Ctr., Angela Bustamante.
Institution Type/Description: Art Gallery.
Hours & Admission Prices: Mon. 8-4:30, Tues. 8am-11:30am Wed. 10-4:30, Thurs. 8am to noon, Fri. noon to 4. No charge. ঌ
Attendance: 9,500 (estimated)

MIAMI DADE COLLEGE MUSEUM OF ART + DESIGN, 600 Biscayne Blvd., Miami, FL 33132. Tel.: 305-237-7700.
E-mail: museum@mdc.edu
Web Site: www.mdcmoad.org
Key Personnel: Exec. Dir. & Chief Cur., Rina Carvajal; Dir. Campos Galleries, Wanda Texon; Assoc. Dir. Museum Affairs, Jessica Brodsky; Membership & Events Coord., Elizabeth Buege; Registrar, Vickie Pierre; Collections Specialist, Patricia Duany; Lead Preparator, Robert Perez; Volunteer Coord., Sierra Manno; Tour Coord., Cristie Alfonso; Museum Exhibitions Coord., William Iverson.
Institution Type/Description: Art Museum.
Hours & Admission Prices: Closed for renovations until Spring 2018.

MIAMI SEAQUARIUM, 4400 Rickenbacker Causeway, Miami, FL 33149-1095. Tel.: 305-361-5705. Fax: 305-365-0075. Facebook & Twitter: @MiamiSeaquarium.
E-mail: pr@msq.cc
Web Site: www.miamiseaquarium.com
Key Personnel: Gen. Mgr., Andrew Hertz; Veterinarian, Maya Rodriguez, D.V.M.; Financial Dir., Sherryl Moody; Dir. Operations, Charles Gaudio; Museum Shop Mgr., Rosa White.
Institution Type/Description: Aquarium.
Hours & Admission Prices: See website or call for hours. Daily: adults $45.99, children 3-9 $35.99; discounts to senior citizens, military, AAA & AAM members. Annual Pass: adult $59.99, children 3-9 $49.99. Parking: $10. ঌ
Attendance: 500,000

N'NAMDI CONTEMPORARY MIAMI, 177 N.W. 23rd St., Miami, FL 33127. Tel.: 786-332-4736. Facebook: @NNamdiContemporary; Twitter: @nnamdimiami.
E-mail: nncontemporary@gmail.com

Web Site: nnamdicontemporary.com
Key Personnel: Dir., Jumaane N'Namdi.
Institution Type/Description: Art Gallery.
Hours & Admission Prices: Daily 11-6.

PATRICIA & PHILLIP FROST ART MUSEUM, FIU Modesto Maidique Campus, 10975 S.W. 17th St., Miami, FL 33199. Tel.: 305-348-2890. Fax: 305-348-2762. Facebook, Instagram & Twitter: @frostartmuseum;.
E-mail: artinfo@fiu.edu
Web Site: www.thefrost.fiu.edu
Formerly: The Art Museum at Florida International University
Key Personnel: Dir., Dr. Jordana Pomeroy; Cur., Klaudio Rodriguez; Chief Registrar, Debbye Taylor; Education Cur., Miriam Machado; Dir. Devel., Ana Martinez; Bldg. Operations Mgr., Julio Alvarez.
Institution Type/Description: Art Museum.
Hours & Admission Prices: Tues.-Sat. 10-5, Sun. 12-5. No charge; donations accepted. Closed holidays. ঌ
Attendance: 112,000 (estimated)

PEREZ ART MUSEUM MIAMI, 1103 Biscayne Blvd., Miami, FL 33132-1758. Tel.: 305-375-3000. Fax: 305-375-1725. Facebook: @perezartmuseummiami; Twitter: @pamm.
E-mail: info@pamm.org
Web Site: pamm.org
Formerly: Miami Art Museum
Key Personnel: Pres., Gail S. Meyers; Chm., Aaron Podhurst; Dir., Franklin Sirmans; Dir. Membership & Devel. Operations, Angela Oxenberg; Deputy Dir. Mktg. & Public Engagement, Christina Boomer Vazquez.
Institution Type/Description: Art Museum.
Hours & Admission Prices: Mon., Tues. & Fri.-Sun. 10-6, Thurs. 10-9. Adults $16, youth 7-18 & seniors/students w/ID $12; discounts to AAM, ICOM & AAA members; active U.S. military with ID, members & children under 6 no charge. ঌ
Attendance: 62,500 (estimated)

RUBELL FAMILY COLLECTION, 95 N.W. 29th St., Miami, FL 33127. Tel.: 305-573-6090. Fax: 305-573-6023. Facebook: @rubellfamilycollection; Instagram: @rubellcollection; Twitter: @RubellMiami.
E-mail: info@rfc.museum
Web Site: rfc.museum
Key Personnel: Dir., Juan Roselione-Valadez; Collection Mgr., William Vargas; Archivist & Assoc. Registrar, Laura Randall; Visitor Svcs., Lucy Cai.
Institution Type/Description: Art Gallery.
Hours & Admission Prices: By appointment. Adults $10; students & seniors $5; youth under 18 & veterans no charge.

VIZCAYA MUSEUM AND GARDENS, 3251 S. Miami Ave., Miami, FL 33129-2897. Tel.: 305-250-9133, ext. 8452. Fax: 305-285-2004. TDD: 800-955-8771; Facebook.
E-mail: vizcayainformation@vizcaya.org
Web Site: www.vizcaya.org
Key Personnel: Exec. Dir., Joel M. Hoffman.
Institution Type/Description: Historic House: 1916 European-Inspired Villa, Gardens & 11-building village on 50 acres of grounds, formerly the estate of International Harvester Executive James Deering.
Hours & Admission Prices: Thurs.-Mon. 9:30-4:30; call or see website to confirm. Adults $18, children 6-12 $8; children 5 & under, AAM members and members no charge. Closed Thanksgiving; Christmas. ঌ
Attendance: 231,000 (actual)

WINGS OVER MIAMI AIR MUSEUM, Miami Executive Airport, 14710 S.W. 128 St., Miami, FL 33196-2002. Tel.: 305-233-5197. Facebook & Twitter: @WingsOverMiami.
Web Site: www.wingsovermiami.com
Key Personnel: Pres. (V), Fred E. Schlafly; Sec. & Legal Counsel, Larry Ploucha; Treas., Timothy Schmelzer.
Institution Type/Description: Aeronautics Museum: located inside Kendall-Tamiami Executive Airport.
Hours & Admission Prices: Wed.-Sun. 10-5. Adults $10, senior citizens 60 & up $7, children 12 & under $6; discounts to groups, AAA, ICOM & AAM members; members no charge. Closed Thanksgiving; Christmas. ঌ
Attendance: 5,500 (estimated)

ZOO MIAMI, One Zoo Blvd., 12400 S.W. 152nd St., Miami, FL 33177-1402. Tel.: 305-251-0400. Fax: 305-378-6381. Facebook, Instagram & Twitter: @zoomiami.
E-mail: info@zsf.org
Web Site: www.zoomiami.org

Formerly: Miami Metrozoo
Key Personnel: Chm. (V) Zoo Miami Foundation, James A. Kushlan, Ph.D.; Pres. & C.E.O. Zoo Miami Foundation, William W. Moore; Dir. Zoo Miami, Carol Kruse; Dir. Mktg. & Integrated Communications, Cindy Castelblanco; Dir. Education & Volunteer Svcs., Gregory Koch, Ph.D.; Dir. Membership Svcs., Carlos ' Simoes.
Institution Type/Description: Zoo.
Hours & Admission Prices: Daily 9:30-5:30 (gates close at 4). Adults $21.95, children 3-12 $17.95; discounts to military, seniors 65 & up, groups & Miami-Dade County employees; children 2 & under and members no charge. &
Attendance: 810,998 (actual)

Miami Beach

ARTCENTER/SOUTH FLORIDA, 924 Lincoln Rd., Miami Beach, FL 33139-2602. Mailing Address: 924 Lincoln Rd,. Ste. 205, Miami Beach, FL 37139. Tel.: 305-674-8278. Fax: 305-674-8772. Facebook: artCenter/South Florida.
E-mail: email@artcentersf.org
Web Site: www.artcentersf.org
Key Personnel: C.E.O. & Exec. Dir., Maria Del Valle; Chm., Kim Kovel; Artistic Dir., Natalia Zuluaga; Dir. Outreach, Tammy Key Johnston; Controller, Patricia Leder.
Institution Type/Description: Cultural Center
Hours & Admission Prices: Mon.-Thurs. 12-8, Fri.-Sat. 11-10, Sun. 11-9. No charge; donations accepted. &
Attendance: 54,800 (actual)

BASS MUSEUM OF ART, 2100 Collins Ave., Miami Beach, FL 33139. Tel.: 305-673-7530. Fax: 305-673-7062.
E-mail: info@bassmuseum.org
Web Site: www.bassmuseum.org
Key Personnel: Exec. Dir., Silvia Karman Cubina; Chm. (V) & Pres. (V), George Lindemann; Deputy Dir., Jean Ortega; Dir. External Affairs, Megan Riley; Dir. Education, Kylee Crook; Devel. Assoc., Daphna Starr; Registrar & Exhibitions Coord., Sherry Zambrano; Dir. Education, Kylee Crook; Chief Preparator & Exhibition Technician, Jan Galliardt; Mgr. Operations, T.J. Black; Sr. Guest Svcs. Assoc., Gabrielle Peters.
Institution Type/Description: Art Museum.
Hours & Admission Prices: Wed.-Sun. 10-5. Adults $10, senior citizens, students & youth 13-18 $5; discounts to AAM & ICOM members; Miami Beach residents, members and children 12 & under no charge. Call for list of reciprocal memberships. Additional charge for special exhibitions. Closed holidays. &
Attendance: 40,000 (estimated)

JEWISH MUSEUM OF FLORIDA - FIU, 301 Washington Ave., Miami Beach, FL 33139-6965. Tel.: 305-672-5044. Fax: 305-672-5933. Facebook: Jewish Museum of Florida.
E-mail: director@jewishmuseum.com
Web Site: www.jewishmuseum.com
Key Personnel: Exec. Dir. & Chief Cur., Jo Ann Arnowitz; Pres., Elliot Stone; Founding Exec. Dir., Marcia Jo Zerivitz; Designer, Ira Newman; Education, Chaim Lieberperson; Membership, Nancy Doyle Cohen; Devel., Nancy Rachman; Museum Shop Mgr., Eva Shvedova; Fiscal Administrator & Grants Mgr., Irene Warner; Registrar, Todd Bothel; Coord. Administrative Svcs., Roberta Gordon; Asst. Cur., Jacqueline Goldstein.
Institution Type/Description: Jewish History of Florida Museum: housed in a 1936 art deco-style building which served as a synagogue with Moorish copper dome & 80 stained-glass windows & 1929 first synagogue on Miami Beach.
Hours & Admission Prices: Tues.-Sun. 10-5. Adults $6, senior citizens & students $5, children $2.50; discounts to groups, AAM, AAA & PBS members; children under 6, members & Sat. no charge. Closed New Year's Day; Memorial Day; Independence Day; Labor Day; Thanksgiving; Jewish holidays. &
Attendance: 47,000 (actual)

MIAMI BEACH BOTANICAL GARDEN, 2000 Convention Center Dr., Miami Beach, FL 33139-1806. Tel.: 305-673-7256. Facebook.
E-mail: cbrown@mbgarden.org
Web Site: www.mbgarden.org
Key Personnel: Exec. Dir., Cindy Brown.
Institution Type/Description: Botanical Garden.
Hours & Admission Prices: Tues.-Sun. 9-5. No charge. &

THE WOLFSONIAN-FLORIDA INTERNATIONAL UNIVERSITY, 1001 Washington Ave., Miami Beach, FL 33139-5017. Tel.: 305-531-1001. Fax: 305-531-2133.
E-mail: info@thewolf.fiu.edu
Web Site: www.wolfsonian.org
Key Personnel: Pres. (V), Ray E. Marchman; Deputy Dir. Curatorial Affairs, Sharon Misdea; Registrar, Kimberly Bergen; Exhibition Designer, Richard

Miltner; Asst. Dir. Mktg., Member Rels. & New Media, Ian Rand; Chief Librarian, Francis X. Luca; Museum Shop Mgr., Paola La Rivera.
Institution Type/Description: Art, Design, Decorative Arts & Architecture Museum: housed in restored building in the historic Art Deco District.
Hours & Admission Prices: Academic Year: Mon.-Tues., Thurs. & Sat. 10-6, Fri. 10-9, Sun. 12-6; Summer: call for hours. Adults $12, seniors, students & children 6-18 $8; discounts to AAM & ICOM members; Wolfsonian members, Fri. 6pm-9pm, children under 6 and students, faculty & staff of state university system of Florida no charge. &
Attendance: 35,000 (estimated)

WORLD EROTIC ART MUSEUM, 1205 Washington Ave., Miami Beach, FL 33139-4613. Tel.: 305-532-9336. Fax: 305-695-1209.
E-mail: info@weam.com
Web Site: www.weam.com
Key Personnel: Dir., Pres. (V) & Cur., Naomi Wilzig; Public Rels., Robert G. Harbour; Gen. Mgr., Geovanni Gonzalez; Art Dir., Helmut Schuster.
Institution Type/Description: Art Museum.
Hours & Admission Prices: Mon.-Thurs. 11-10, Fri.-Sun. 11am to midnight; children not admitted. Adults $15, senior citizens $14, students $13.50; discounts to groups of 10 or more; members no charge. Closed New Year's Day; Thanksgiving; Christmas. &
Attendance: 5,000 (estimated)

Miami Gardens

ST. THOMAS UNIVERSITY LIBRARY, 16401 N.W. 37th Ave., Miami Gardens, FL 33054-6313. Tel.: 305-628-6668 & 6769. Fax: 305-628-6666.
E-mail: ltreadwell@stu.edu
Web Site: www.stu.edu/Library/tabid/395/Default.aspx
Key Personnel: Dir., Larry Treadwell, IV.
Institution Type/Description: Library.
Hours & Admission Prices: University Library: Mon.-Thurs. 8am-11pm, Fri. 8-5, Sat. 9-5, Sun. 2-10 by appointment. Archives & Museum: Mon.-Thurs. 10-6, Fri. 10-5, Sat. by appointment. Closed major holidays.

Micanopy

MICANOPY HISTORICAL SOCIETY MUSEUM, Cholokka Blvd. at Bay St., Micanopy, FL 32667-4112. Mailing Address: P. O. Box 462, Micanopy, FL 32667-0462. Tel.: 352-466-3200.
E-mail: micanopymuseum@aol.com
Web Site: micanopyhistoricalsociety.com
Key Personnel: Dir., Melanie Barr; Treas., Jean Stream.
Institution Type/Description: History Museum.
Hours & Admission Prices: Daily 1-4. Suggested Donation: $2; discounts to AAM members. Closed New Year's Day; Thanksgiving; Christmas. &
Attendance: 5,558 (actual)

Milton

ARCADIA MILL ARCHAEOLOGICAL SITE, 5709 Mill Pond Lane, Milton, FL 32583-1788. Tel.: 850-626-3084.
E-mail: asams@uwf.edu
Web Site: www.historicpensacola.org/arcadia.cfm
Key Personnel: Site Mgr., Adrianne Sams; Museum Education Coord., Roy Oberto.
Institution Type/Description: Historic Archaeological Site: housed in a mid-19th century industrial complex.
Hours & Admission Prices: Tues.-Sat. 10-4. No charge; donations accepted. Closed New Year's Day; Independence Day; Veterans Day; Thanksgiving & day after; day after Christmas. &
Attendance: 15,000 (estimated)

WEST FLORIDA RAILROAD MUSEUM, 5003 Henry St., Milton, FL 32570-6790. Mailing Address: P.O. Box 770, Milton, FL 32572-0770. Tel.: 850-623-3645.
E-mail: conductor@wfrm.org
Institution Type/Description: Railroad History Museum.
Hours & Admission Prices: Fri.-Sat. 10-3; other times by appointment. No charge; donations accepted. &

Mount Dora

MOUNT DORA CENTER FOR THE ARTS, 138 E. 5th Ave., Mount Dora, FL 32757-5573. Tel.: 352-383-0880. Fax: 352-383-7753.
E-mail: center@mountdoracenterforthearts.org
Web Site: www.mountdoracenterforthearts.org
Key Personnel: Exec. Co-Chair, Nancy Zinkofsky; Pres. (V), Ozell Ward.

Institution Type/Description: Art Center.
Hours & Admission Prices: Mon.-Fri. 10-4, Sat. 10-2. No charge; donations accepted. Closed major holidays. &
Attendance: 35,000 (actual)

MOUNT DORA HISTORY MUSEUM, 450 Royellou Lane, Mount Dora, FL 32757-5554. Mailing Address: P.O. Box 1166, Mount Dora, FL 32756-1166. Tel.: 352-383-0006.
E-mail: mountdorahistory@gmail.com
Web Site: www.mountdorahistoricalsociety.org
Formerly: Royellou Museum
Key Personnel: Museum Mgr., Carolyn M. Green.
Institution Type/Description: History Museum: housed in the old city jail built in 1923.
Hours & Admission Prices: Tues.-Sun. 1-4. Suggested Donations: adults $2, children $1; children under 5 no charge. Closed Thanksgiving; Christmas. &
Attendance: 2,031 (actual)

Mulberry

MULBERRY PHOSPHATE MUSEUM, 101 S.E. 1st St., Mulberry, FL 33860-3169. Mailing Address: P.O. Box 707, Mulberry, FL 33860-0707. Tel.: 863-425-2823. Fax: 863-425-0188. Facebook.
E-mail: cyoung@cityofmulberryfl.com
Web Site: www.mulberryphosphatemuseum.org
Key Personnel: Dir., Chelsea Young; Museum Asst., Elly South; Museum Asst., Jackie Marcucci.
Institution Type/Description: Natural History Museum: housed in c.1899 Mulberry Train Depot.
Hours & Admission Prices: Tues.-Sat. 9-5. No charge; donations accepted. Closed New Year's Day; Memorial Day; Independence Day; Thanksgiving; Christmas. &
Attendance: 9,000 (actual)

Naples

ARTIS-NAPLES, THE BAKER MUSEUM, 5833 Pelican Bay Blvd., Naples, FL 34108-2740. Tel.: 239-254-2620. Fax: 239-254-2753. Facebook.
E-mail: info@artisnaples.org
Web Site: www.artisnaples.org
Formerly: Patty and Jay Baker Naples Museum of Art, Philharmonic Center for the Arts
Key Personnel: Museum Dir. & Chief Cur., Frank Verpoorten; C.E.O. & Pres., Kathleen van Bergen; Chm. (V), Jay Baker; Registrar, Jacqueline Zorn; Dir. Curatorial Affairs, Gisela Carbonell; C.F.O., Perre Edwards; Vice Pres. Devel., Tiffany Heck; Patron Services, Elise Guarino; Asst. Registrar, Carla McCambridge; Cur. Education, Jessica Wozniak; Vice Pres. Mktg., Ashley Mirakian; Vice Pres. Artistic Operations, David Filner; Chief HR Officer, Tammy Read; Art Handler, Chris Smith; Exec. Asst. to the Dir. & Chief Cur., Amanda Plummer; Curatorial Research Assoc., Silvia Perea.
Institution Type/Description: Fine Arts Museum.
Hours & Admission Prices: Sept. 6-July 23 Tues.-Sat. 10-4, Sun. 12-4. Adults $10, students with I.D. $5; children 17 & under, NARM, AAM members & museum members no charge. Closed New Year's Day; Thanksgiving; Christmas. &
Attendance: 44,923 (estimated)

COLLIER COUNTY MUSEUM, 3331 Tamiami Trail E., Naples, FL 34112-4901. Tel.: 239-252-8476. Fax: 239-252-8580. Facebook: Collier County Museum.
E-mail: museums@colliergov.net
Web Site: www.colliermuseums.com
Key Personnel: C.E.O., Ron D. Jamro; Cur., Jennifer Guida; Mgr., Timothy England; Mgr., Lisa Marciano; Museum Asst., Martha Hutcheson; Museum Asst., Jon Nickerson; Special Events & Mktg. Coord., Christina Apkarian; Museum Asst., Pamela Miner; Volunteer Coord., Elsie Collado; Administrative Asst., Wanda Bieschke; Mgr., Jennifer Perry.
Institution Type/Description: History Museum.
Hours & Admission Prices: Mon.-Sat. 9-4. No charge; donations accepted. Closed national & county holidays. &
Attendance: 75,000 (estimated)

CONSERVANCY OF SOUTHWEST FLORIDA NATURE CENTER, 1450 Merrihue Dr., Naples, FL 34102-3449. Tel.: 239-262-0304. Fax: 239-262-0672.
E-mail: info@conservancy.org
Web Site: www.conservancy.org
Key Personnel: Pres. & C.E.O., Rob Moher.
Institution Type/Description: Nature Center.

Hours & Admission Prices: Jan.-April daily 9:30-4:30; May-Dec. Mon.-Sat. 9:30-4:30. Adults $14.95, children 3-11 $9.95; discounts to ANCA members; members and children 2 & under no charge. &

GOLISANO CHILDREN'S MUSEUM OF NAPLES, 15080 Livingston Rd., Naples, FL 34109. Tel.: 239-514-0084. Fax: 239-260-1616.
E-mail: info@cmon.org
Web Site: www.cmon.org
Key Personnel: Exec. Dir., Karysia Demarest; Dir. Play & Learning, Beth Housewert.
Institution Type/Description: Children's Museum.
Hours & Admission Prices: Mon.-Tues. & Thurs.-Sat. 10-5, Sun. 11-4. $10; discounts to ACM members; children under one no charge. &
Attendance: 150,000 (actual)

HOLOCAUST MUSEUM OF SOUTHWEST FLORIDA, 4760 Tamiami Trail N., Ste. 7, Naples, FL 34103-3065. Tel.: 239-263-9200. Fax: 239-263-9500.
E-mail: info@holocaustmuseumswfl.org
Key Personnel: Pres. & C.E.O., Susan L. Suarez.
Institution Type/Description: History Museum.
Hours & Admission Prices: Jan.-April Tues.-Fri. 12:30-5, Sat.-Sun. 1-4; May-June & Oct.-Dec. Tues.-Sun. 1-4; July-Sept. Tues.-Sat. 1-4. Adults $10, students 12-18 $5; members & children under 12 no charge. Closed public holidays. &
Attendance: 8,300 (actual)

MARIANNE FRIEDLAND GALLERY, 359 Broad Ave. S., Naples, FL 34102. Tel.: 239-262-3484.
E-mail: mfgallery@aol.com
Web Site: www.mariannefriedlandglry.com
Institution Type/Description: Art Gallery.
Hours & Admission Prices: Mon.-Sat. 10-5; other times by appointment. No charge. &

THE NAPLES ART ASSOCIATION, 585 Park St., Naples, FL 34102-6611. Tel.: 239-262-6517. Fax: 239-262-5404. Facebook: @NaplesArtAssociation.
E-mail: info@naplesart.org
Web Site: www.naplesart.org
Key Personnel: Dir. & C.E.O., Aimee Schlehr; Pres., Andrew Sroka; Cur., Jack O'Brien; Volunteer Coord., Amy Kessler; Education Coodr., Lynn Bozumato; Outdoor Shows Mgr., Don DeMichele; Gift Shop Mgr., Nancy Baxter.
Institution Type/Description: Community Art Center.
Hours & Admission Prices: Gallery: Mon.-Fri. 10-4; call for seasonal hours. Administration Office: Mon.-Fri. 9-4. No charge; donations accepted. Gift Shop: discounts to NARM & ROAM members. Closed Easter; Memorial Day; Independence Day; Labor Day; Thanksgiving; Christmas. &
Attendance: 50,000 (estimated)

NAPLES BACKYARD HISTORY OLD NAPLES MUSEUM, 1170 Third St., S., Ste. C111, Naples, FL 34102. Tel.: 239-774-2978.
Web Site: www.naplesbackyardhistory.net
Institution Type/Description: History Museum.
Hours & Admission Prices: Thurs. 5-8; other times by appointment.

NAPLES BOTANICAL GARDEN, 4820 Bayshore Dr., Naples, FL 34112-7344. Tel.: 239-643-7275. Fax: 239-649-7306.
E-mail: info@naplesgarden.org
Web Site: www.naplesgarden.org
Key Personnel: Bd. Chm., Thomas D. McCann; C.F.O., Theresa Perkins; Dir. Visitor Svcs., Paula Braida.
Institution Type/Description: Botanical Garden.
Hours & Admission Prices: Tues. 8-5, Wed.-Mon. 9-5. Adults $14.95, children 4-14 $9.95; children 3 & under and members no charge. &
Attendance: 200,000 (actual)

NAPLES ZOO AT CARIBBEAN GARDENS, 1590 Goodlette-Frank Rd., Naples, FL 34102-5260. Tel.: 239-262-5409.
E-mail: info@napleszoo.org
Web Site: www.napleszoo.com
Key Personnel: Chm., Denny Glass.
Institution Type/Description: Zoo.
Hours & Admission Prices: Daily 9-5. Adults $22.95, seniors 65 & over $21.95, children 3-12 $14.95; discounts to active military; members and children 2 & under no charge.

New Port Richey

WEST PASCO HISTORICAL SOCIETY MUSEUM AND LIBRARY, 6431 Circle Blvd., New Port Richey, FL 34652-2360. Tel.: 727-847-0680.
E-mail: westpascohistoricalsociety@gmail.com
Web Site: westpascohistoricalsociety.org
Key Personnel: Chm. (V), Bob Hubach; Corresponding Sec., Diane Faulkner; Recording Sec., Kelly Hackman; Treas., Ann James.
Institution Type/Description: Historical Society Museum: housed in 1913 two-room schoolhouse.
Hours & Admission Prices: Fri.-Sat. 1-4. No charge; donations accepted. Closed legal holidays. &
Attendance: 3,500 (estimated)

New Smyrna Beach

ATLANTIC CENTER FOR THE ARTS, INC., 1414 Art Center Ave., New Smyrna Beach, FL 32168-5560. Tel.: 386-427-6975. Fax: 386-427-5669.
E-mail: program@atlanticcenterforthearts.org
Web Site: www.atlanticcenterforthearts.org
Key Personnel: Exec. Dir., Nancy Lowden Norman; Dir. Mktg. & Membership, Kathryn Peterson.
Institution Type/Description: Art Center & Gallery.
Hours & Admission Prices: Tues.-Fri. 10-4, Sat. 10-2. No charge; donations accepted. Closed Martin Luther King Jr. Day; Presidents' Day; Memorial Day; Independence Day; Labor Day; Thanksgiving & day after; Christmas week. &
Attendance: 5,000 (estimated)

Newberry

DUDLEY FARM HISTORIC STATE PARK, 18730 W. Newberry Rd., Newberry, FL 32669-2192. Tel.: 352-472-1142.
E-mail: dudley@gvlhistorichomes.org
Web Site: www.floridastateparks.org/dudleyfarm
Institution Type/Description: Historic Farmstead.
Hours & Admission Prices: Wed.-Sun. 9-5. Admission $5.

Niceville

MATTIE KELLY ARTS CENTER GALLERIES AT NORTHWEST FLORIDA STATE COLLEGE, 100 College Blvd., Niceville, FL 32578-1347. Tel.: 850-729-6044. Fax: 850-729-5286. Facebook: Mattie Kelly Arts Center Gallery.
E-mail: artgalleries@nwfsc.edu
Web Site: www.mattiekellyartscenter.org
Formerly: Mattie Kelly Arts Center at Okaloosa-Walton College
Key Personnel: Dir., Jeanette Shires; Gallery Dir., K.C. Williams.
Institution Type/Description: College Art Museum.
Hours & Admission Prices: Mon.-Fri. 10-4. No charge. Closed holidays. &
Attendance: 15,300 (estimated)

North Miami

MUSEUM OF CONTEMPORARY ART, NORTH MIAMI, Joan Lehman Bldg., 770 N.E. 125th St., North Miami, FL 33161-5654. Tel.: 305-893-6211. Fax: 305-891-1472.
E-mail: info@mocanomi.org
Web Site: mocanomi.org
Key Personnel: Interim Dir., Natasha Colebrook-Williams; Chm. (V), Frederic Marq; Asst. Dir., Alan Waufle; Asst. Dir. Education & International Programs, Adrienne von Lates; Public Programs Mgr., Tiffany G. Madera; Finance Mgr., Renee Bennett; Buildings Mgr., William Miranda.
Institution Type/Description: Visual Contemporary Art.
Hours & Admission Prices: Tues.-Fri. & Sun. 11-5, Sat. 1-9. Adults $5, seniors & students $3; North Miami residents & city employees, children under 12, veterans & members no charge. Closed Thanksgiving; Christmas. &
Attendance: 82,300 (actual)

North Miami Beach

ANCIENT SPANISH MONASTERY, 16711 W. Dixie Hwy., North Miami Beach, FL 33160-3714. Tel.: 305-945-1461. Fax: 305-945-6986.
E-mail: info@spanishmonastery.com
Web Site: www.spanishmonastery.com
Key Personnel: Exec. Admin. & C.E.O., Dr. Gregory Mansfield; Bd. Pres. (V), Dr. Janie Greenleaf; Museum Shop Mgr., Carolina Del Vecchio; Administrator, Melanie Veizaga.
Institution Type/Description: Art Museum: housed in The Cloister and Refectory, reconstruction of monastery, built in 1133 (12th century) in Segovia, Spain, with original stones brought to United States by William Randolph Hearst.
Hours & Admission Prices: Mon.-Sat. 10-4:30, Sun. 11-4:30. Adults 12-55 $10, senior citizens 55 & over and students 12 & under $5; discounts to AAM & ICOM members; children under 5 & U.S. military (in uniform or with ID) & families no charge. Closed federal holidays.
Attendance: 50,000 (estimated)

North Palm Beach

JOHN D. MACARTHUR BEACH STATE PARK & NATURE CENTER, 10900 Jack Nicklaus Dr., North Palm Beach, FL 33408-3440. Tel.: 561-624-6950 & 6952. Facebook: @macarthurbeach.
E-mail: friends@macarthurbeach.org
Web Site: www.macarthurbeach.org
Key Personnel: Exec. Dir., Cheryl A. Houghtelin.
Institution Type/Description: Park & Nature Center.
Hours & Admission Prices: Nature Center: daily 9-5. Park: daily 8 to sunset. Entrance Fee: $5 per vehicle. &
Attendance: 155,000

Ocala

APPLETON MUSEUM OF ART, 4333 E. Silver Springs Blvd., Ocala, FL 34470-5001. Tel.: 352-291-4455. Fax: 352-291-4460. Facebook: Appleton Museum.
E-mail: appletonmuseum@cf.edu
Web Site: www.appletonmuseum.org
Key Personnel: Dir., Cindi Morrison; Coord. Finance Svcs., Kathleen Balboni; Cur., Ruth Grim; Mgr. Membership & Events, Colleen Harper; Registrar, David Reutter; Coord. Facilities, Russell Days; Staff Asst. III, Joyce Orme; Asst. Dir., Victoria Billig; Graphic Design, Web & Pub. Rels., Jen Boys.
Institution Type/Description: Fine Arts Museum.
Hours & Admission Prices: Tues.-Sat. 10-5, Sun. 12-5. Adults $8, seniors and educators $6, youth 10-18 $4; discounts to AAA, active military & their families, students, teachers, & seniors, children 9 & under, military & their family and members no charge. Reciprocal memberships with other museums. Closed New Year's Day; Thanksgiving; Christmas. &
Attendance: 50,000 (actual)

CF WEBBER CENTER GALLERY, 3001 S.W. College Rd., Ocala, FL 34474-4415. Tel.: 352-873-5800. Fax: 352-873-5886.
E-mail: bjornh@cf.edu
Web Site: www.cf.edu
Key Personnel: Dir. Visual & Performing, Dr. Jennifer Fryns.
Institution Type/Description: Art Museum.
Hours & Admission Prices: Mon.-Fri. 10-4. No charge; donations accepted. Closed college holidays. &
Attendance: 9,000 (estimated)

THE DISCOVERY CENTER, 701 N.E. Sanchez Ave., Ocala, FL 34470. Tel.: 352-401-3900. Fax: 352-368-5514.
E-mail: discovery@ocalafl.org
Web Site: www.mydiscoverycenter.org
Formerly: Discovery Science and Outdoor Center
Key Personnel: Cultural Arts & Science Div. Head, Laura Walker.
Institution Type/Description: Science Center.
Hours & Admission Prices: Tues.-Fri. 9-5, Sat. 10-3. Office: Mon.-Fri. 9-5. Programs: by appointment. Admission $6; children 2 & under no charge. &
Attendance: 25,000 (estimated)

DON GARLITS MUSEUM OF DRAG RACING INC., 13700 S. W. 16th Ave., Ocala, FL 34473-3970. Tel.: 352-245-8661, 877-271-3278 (toll-free). Fax: 352-245-6895. Facebook: Don Garlits Museum of Drag Racing Inc..
E-mail: donna@garlits.com
Web Site: www.garlits.com
Key Personnel: C.E.O. & Chm., Donald G. Garlits; Gen. Mgr. & C.F.O., Chuck Keppel; Admin. Asst., Allyson Dearth.
Institution Type/Description: Drag Racing & Antique Cars & Tools Museum.
Hours & Admission Prices: Daily 9-5. Adults $20, senior citizens, military, college students & teens $15, children 5-12 $10; discounts to groups of 10 or more & AAA members; children under 5 no charge. Closed Thanksgiving; Christmas. &
Attendance: 75,000 (estimated)

SILVER RIVER MUSEUM & ENVIRONMENTAL EDUCATION CENTER, 1445 N.E. 58th Ave., Ocala, FL 34470-1189. Tel.: 352-236-5401. Fax: 352-236-7142.

E-mail: scott.mitchell@marion.k12.fl.us
Web Site: www.silverrivermuseum.com
Key Personnel: Dir., Cur. & Public Rels., Scott Mitchell.
Institution Type/Description: History & Natural History of Florida Museum.
Hours & Admission Prices: Student Tours: Mon.-Fri. General Public: Sat.-Sun. 9-5. Adults $2; children 6 & under no charge. ♿
Attendance: 20,000 (estimated)

Ochopee

BIG CYPRESS NATIONAL PRESERVE, Oasis Visitors Center, 52105 Tamiami Trail E., Ochopee, FL 34141. Mailing Address: 33100 Tamiami Trail, E., Ochopee, FL 34141. Tel.: 239-695-2000. Fax: 239-695-3901.
E-mail: ARDRIANNA_MCLANE@NPS.GOV
Web Site: nps.gov/bicy
Key Personnel: Supt., Tamara Whittington.
Institution Type/Description: National Park & Visitor Center.
Hours & Admission Prices: Oasis Visitor Center: daily 9-4:30. No charge. Closed Christmas. ♿

Orlando

ANITA S. WOOTEN GALLERY AT VALENCIA COLLEGE EAST CAMPUS, 701 N. Econlockhatchee Trail, MC 3 - 2, Orlando, FL 32825. Tel.: 407-582-2298. Fax: 407-582-8917. Facebook: Anita S. Wooten Gallery.
E-mail: agonzalez325@valenciacollege.edu
Web Site: valenciacollege.edu/artsandentertainment/gallery
Key Personnel: Dir., Jackie Otto-Miller.
Institution Type/Description: Art Museum.
Hours & Admission Prices: Winter: Mon.-Fri. 8:30-4:30; Summer: Mon.-Thurs. 8:30-4:30, Fri. 8:30am-12pm. No charge. ♿
Attendance: 18,000 (estimated)

HARRY P. LEU GARDENS, 1920 N. Forest Ave., Orlando, FL 32803-1537. Tel.: 407-246-2620. Fax: 407-246-2849.
E-mail: robert.bowden@cityoforlando.net
Web Site: www.leugardens.org
Key Personnel: Dir., Robert E. Bowden; Membership, Colin Worley; Mktg., Tracy Micciche; Museum Shop Mgr., Mimi Maldonado.
Institution Type/Description: Botanical Garden.
Hours & Admission Prices: Gardens: daily 9-5. House: temporarily closed. Adults $10, children 4-17 $5; discounts to groups; members and children 3 & under no charge. Closed Christmas. ♿
Attendance: 135,000 (actual)

THE MENNELLO MUSEUM OF AMERICAN ART, 900 E. Princeton St., Orlando, FL 32803-1437. Tel.: 407-246-4278. Fax: 407-246-4329.
E-mail: mennellomuseum@cityoforlando.net
Web Site: www.mennellomuseum.com
Key Personnel: C.E.O., Shannon Fitzgerald; Chm. (V), Michael Mennello; Museum Shop Mgr., Christine Vasquez.
Institution Type/Description: American Art Museum.
Hours & Admission Prices: Tues.-Sat. 10:30-4:30, Sun. 12-4:30. Adults $5, seniors $4, students $1; discounts to SARM & SERM members; active military, members & children under 12 no charge. Blue Star Museum. Closed major holidays. ♿
Attendance: 27,000 (actual)

ORANGE COUNTY REGIONAL HISTORY CENTER, 65 E. Central Blvd., Orlando, FL 32801-2401. Tel.: 407-836-8500. Fax: 407-836-8550.
E-mail: michael.perkins@ocfl.net
Web Site: www.thehistorycenter.org
Formerly: Orange County Historical Museum
Key Personnel: Exec. Dir., Michael Perkins.
Institution Type/Description: Local Central Florida History & American History (12,000 years ago to the present).
Hours & Admission Prices: Mon.-Sat. 10-5, Sun. 12-5. Adults $9, seniors 60 & over $7, children 3-12 $6; discounts to AAM members & Orange County employees; children under 3, members & regional Florida teachers no charge. Closed county holidays. ♿
Attendance: 100,000 (actual)

ORLANDO MUSEUM OF ART, 2416 N. Mills Ave., Orlando, FL 32803-1483. Tel.: 407-896-4231. Fax: 407-896-9920.
E-mail: info@omart.org
Web Site: www.omart.org

Key Personnel: Interim Exec. Dir., Dr. Luder Whitlock; Chm. Bd., Francine Newberg; Chief Operations, Stu Worobetz; Dir. Education, Jane Ferry; Cur., Hansen Mulford; Registrar, Tiffany Recicar; Facility Rentals, Jonathan Von Villas.
Institution Type/Description: Art Museum.
Hours & Admission Prices: Tues.-Fri. 10-4, Sat.-Sun. 12-4. Adults $15, groups of 10 or more $13, seniors 65 & over $8, college students & children 4-17 $5; discount AAM members; military, children 3 & under and members no charge. Closed national holidays. ♿
Attendance: 135,000 (actual)

ORLANDO SCIENCE CENTER, INC., 777 E. Princeton St., Orlando, FL 32803. Tel.: 407-514-2000. Fax: 407-514-2277.
E-mail: gservices@osc.org
Web Site: www.osc.org
Key Personnel: Pres. & C.E.O., JoAnn Newman.
Institution Type/Description: Science & Technology Center.
Hours & Admission Prices: Thurs.-Tues. 10-5. Adults $20.95, students and seniors 55 & over $18.95, children 3-11 $14.95; discounts to active military, ASTC members, reciprocal participants & corporate sponsor employees; members and children 2 & under no charge. Closed Thanksgiving; Christmas. ♿
Attendance: 390,000 (actual)

RIPLEY'S BELIEVE IT OR NOT! MUSEUM, 8201 International Dr., Orlando, FL 32819-9326. Tel.: 407-363-4418 & 351-5803. Fax: 407-345-0803.
E-mail: haggadone@ripleys.com
Web Site: www.ripleys.com/orlando
Institution Type/Description: General Museum.
Hours & Admission Prices: Daily 9am to midnight. Adults $21.99, children 3-11 $14.99; discounts to groups of 10 or more, AAM & ICOM members. ♿

TERRACE GALLERY-CITY OF ORLANDO, City Hall, 400 S. Orange Ave., Orlando, FL 32801-3360. Mailing Address: City Hall, P.O. Box 4990, Orlando, FL 32802-4990. Tel.: 407-246-4279. Fax: 407-246-3434.
E-mail: charles.beasley@cityoforlando.net
Web Site: www.cityoforlando.net/arts
Key Personnel: Public Art Coord. & Collections Reg., C. Keith Beasley.
Institution Type/Description: Art Gallery.
Hours & Admission Prices: Terrace Gallery: Mon.-Fri. 8-9, Sat.-Sun. 12-5. No charge. Mayor's Gallery: Mon.-Fri. 8-5. No charge. Garden House Gallery: daily 9-5. Adults $5, children $1. ♿
Attendance: 35,000 (estimated)

UNIVERSITY OF CENTRAL FLORIDA ART GALLERY, Visual Arts Bldg. #51, Orlando, FL 32816. Mailing Address: P.O. Box 161342, Orlando, FL 32816-1342. Tel.: 407-823-5470 & 3161. Fax: 407-823-6470. Facebook.
E-mail: gallery@ucf.edu
Key Personnel: Dir., Diane Daugherty.
Institution Type/Description: Art Museum.
Hours & Admission Prices: Mon.-Fri. 10-5. No charge.
Attendance: 7,000 (estimated)

WYCLIFFE DISCOVERY CENTER, 11221 John Wycliffe Blvd., Orlando, FL 32832-7013. Mailing Address: P.O. Box 628200, Orlando, FL 32862-8200. Tel.: 407-852-3626. Fax: 407-852-3781.
Web Site: www.wycliffe.org/wordspring
Formerly: WordSpring Discovery Center
Key Personnel: Dir., Patricia Cox; Mgr. Events, Brian Shaffer; Mgr. Education Program, Dorcas Winfrey; Museum Shop Mgr., Tim Holloran.
Institution Type/Description: Religious Museum.
Hours & Admission Prices: Mon.-Fri. 9-4, Sat. & holidays call for hours. Adults $8, seniors $7, children grades 1-12 $6; discounts to groups; children under 6 no charge. ♿
Attendance: 15,000 (actual)

Ormond Beach

ORMOND MEMORIAL ART MUSEUM & GARDEN, 78 E. Granada Blvd., Ormond Beach, FL 32176-6534. Tel.: 386-676-3347. Fax: 386-676-3244.
E-mail: omam78e@aol.com
Web Site: www.ormondartmuseum.org
Key Personnel: Dir., Susan Richmond.
Institution Type/Description: Art Museum & Botanical Garden: the museum is located in a four-acre botanical garden.

Hours & Admission Prices: Mon.-Fri. 10-4, Sat.-Sun. 12-4. Suggested Donation: $2. Closed New Year's Day; Good Friday; Easter; Memorial Day; Independence Day; Labor Day; Thanksgiving; Christmas. &

Attendance: 18,000 (estimated)

Osprey

HISTORIC SPANISH POINT, 337 N. Tamiami Trail, Osprey, FL 34229-8911. Mailing Address: P.O. Box 846, Osprey, FL 34229-0846. Tel.: 941-966-5214. Fax: 941-966-1355. Facebook: Historic Spanish Point.

E-mail: john@historicspanishpoint.org

Web Site: www.historicspanishpoint.org

Key Personnel: Chm. (V), Peg Kapustiack; C.E.O. & Exec. Dir., John D. Mason; Pres. (V), Todd Stainbrook; Deputy Dir., Kara Pallin; Site Horticulturist, Nancy Paul.

Institution Type/Description: Historic Site.

Hours & Admission Prices: Mon.-Sat. 9-5, Sun. 12-5. Adults $12, seniors $10, children $5; children under 5, NARM & members no charge. Closed Easter; Thanksgiving; Christmas. &

Attendance: 30,000 (estimated)

Palatka

RAVINE GARDENS STATE PARK, 1600 Twigg St., Palatka, FL 32177-5637. Tel.: 386-329-3721. Fax: 386-329-3718.

E-mail: alfred.bea@dep.state.fl.us

Web Site: www.floridastateparks.org/ravinegardens/default.cfm

Key Personnel: Park Mgr., Nathan Sommons.

Institution Type/Description: Botanical Garden.

Hours & Admission Prices: Daily 8-sunset. Cars with up to 8 people $5, motorcycles & single occupant cars $4, bicycles & walk-ins $2; children under 6 no charge. Annual park passes available. &

Attendance: 145,963 (actual)

Palm Beach

FLAGLER MUSEUM, One Whitehall Way, Palm Beach, FL 33480. Mailing Address: P.O. Box 969, Palm Beach, FL 33480-0969. Tel.: 561-655-2833. Fax: 561-655-2826. Facebook: FlaglerMuseum.

E-mail: mail@flaglermuseum.us

Web Site: www.flaglermuseum.us

Formerly: Henry Morrison Flagler Museum

Key Personnel: Exec. Dir., Erin Manning; C.F.O., Rudina Toro; Chief Cur., Tracy Kamerer; Dir. Public Affairs, David Carson; Dir. Member & Visitor Svcs., Allison Goff; Facility Mgr., William Fallacaro; Museum Store & Cafe Mgr., Kristen Cahill.

Institution Type/Description: Historic House: Whitehall, 1902 Gilded Age estate of Henry Morrison Flagler.

Hours & Admission Prices: Tues.-Sat. 10-5, Sun. 12-5; call or see website to confirm. Adults $18, youth 13-17 $10, children 6-12 $3; discount to groups; children under 6, members & AAM members no charge. Closed New Year's Day; Thanksgiving; Christmas. &

Attendance: 85,000 (actual)

THE SOCIETY OF THE FOUR ARTS, 2 Four Arts Plaza, Palm Beach, FL 33480-4102. Tel.: 561-655-7227 & 7226. Fax: 561-655-7233.

E-mail: contactus@fourarts.org

Web Site: www.fourarts.org

Institution Type/Description: General Museum.

Hours & Admission Prices: O'Keefe Gallery: Dec. to mid-April Mon.-Sat. 10-5, Sun. 1-5. Exhibits: $5. Children's Art Gallery: May-July & Sept.-Oct. Mon.-Fri. 10-4:45; Nov.-April Mon.-Fri. 10-4:45, Sat. 10-12:45. Metropolitan Operas: $27. National Theatre of London: $25. Bolshoi Ballet: $20; Evening Concerts: $40-$45. Sunday Concerts: $20. Films: $5. Discounts to AAM members & groups. Closed New Year's Day; Easter; Thanksgiving; Christmas. Children's Library: May-July & Sept.-Oct. Mon.-Fri. 10-4:45; Nov.-April Mon.-Fri. 10-4:45, Sat. 10-12:45. Closed New Year's Eve, Day & two days after; Presidents' Day; Memorial Day; Independence Day & day before; 3 days after Thanksgiving; Christmas Eve, Day & two days after. Adult Library: June-Oct. Mon.-Fri. 10-5; Nov.-May Mon.-Fri. 10-5, Sat. 10-1. Closed New Year's Eve, Day & two days after; Presidents' Day; Memorial Day; Independence Day & day before; Thanksgiving & three days after; Christmas Eve, Day & two days after. Dixon Education Bldg.: June-Sept. Tues.-Thurs. 10-5; Oct.-May Mon.-Fri. 10-5. Closed New Year's Eve, Day & day after; Presidents' Day; Memorial Day; Independence Day & day before; Labor Day; Columbus Day; two days after Thanksgiving; Christmas Eve, Day & day after. Sculpture & Botanical Gardens: daily 10-5 (weather permitting). Closed major holidays. Call to confirm hours. &

Attendance: 111,464 (estimated)

Palm Coast

FLORIDA AGRICULTURAL MUSEUM, 7900 Old Kings Rd. N., Palm Coast, FL 32137-8285. Tel.: 386-446-7630. Fax: 386-446-7631.

E-mail: info@myagmuseum.com

Web Site: www.floridaagmuseum.org

Key Personnel: C.E.O., Bruce J. Piatek; Chm. (V), Tom Torrence; Trustee, Doyle Conner; Trustee, Ben Hill Griffin, III; Trustee, Brenda Tucker Boyd; Trustee & Chmn., Michael Kenney; Trustee, William Livingston; Trustee, Louis Parrish; Trustee, Clark Bailey; Trustee, Frank Ford; Trustee, Rudy Bradley; C.E.O. & Exec. Dir., Andrew P. Morrow; Trustee, Ron Brame; Trustee, Chery Flood; Trustee, Howard Griffin; Trustee, T. Jeffrey McCullough; Trustee, Nathan McLaughlin; Trustee, Rick Piagno; Trustee, Joe Siegmeister; Trustee, Wendy Smith; Trustee, Cathy Vogel; Trustee, Michael Waldron.

Institution Type/Description: Agriculture Museum.

Hours & Admission Prices: Wed.-Sun. 9-5. Adults $9, children 5-12 $6; members & children under 5 no charge. &

Attendance: 20,000 (estimated)

THE LILLYWHITE FAMILY MUSEUM, Niblick's Reach, Hammock Dunes, 4 Riviera Pl., Palm Coast, FL 32137-2270. Tel.: 386-446-3679. Fax: 386-446-3679.

E-mail: jwlillywhite@mac.com

Web Site: www.thelillywhitefamilymuseum.com

Key Personnel: Dir. & Cur., John W. Lillywhite; Chm. (V), Elisabet G. Wauters-Lillywhite.

Institution Type/Description: Family Sports History Museum.

Hours & Admission Prices: Mon.-Fri. 9-1 by appointment only. No charge; donations accepted. Closed holidays.

Attendance: 300 (estimated)

Palm Harbor

PALM HARBOR MUSEUM, 2043 Curlew Rd., Palm Harbor, FL 34683-6820. Tel.: 727-724-3054. Facebook: Palm Harbor Museum.

E-mail: palmharbormuseum@outlook.com

Web Site: palmharbormuseum.com

Formerly: North Pinellas Historical Museum

Key Personnel: Exec. Consultant, Colin Bissett.

Institution Type/Description: History Museum.

Hours & Admission Prices: Mon. & Sat. 10-4; groups of 10 or more by appointment. No charge; donations accepted. Closed New Year's Day; Thanksgiving; Christmas. &

Attendance: 900 (estimated)

Panama City

GULF COAST STATE COLLEGE AMELIA CENTER GALLERY, 5230 W. Hwy. 98, Panama City, FL 32401-1041. Tel.: 850-769-1551, ext. 4874.

E-mail: pamromin@gulfcoast.edu

Web Site: www.gulfcoast.edu/arts/art/gallery

Formerly: Gulf Coast Community College Art Gallery

Key Personnel: Gallery Dir., Pavel Amromin.

Institution Type/Description: Art Gallery.

Hours & Admission Prices: Mon.-Thurs. 10-4. No charge.

PANAMA CITY CENTRE OF THE ARTS, 19 E. 4th St., Panama City, FL 32401-3106. Tel.: 850-640-3670. Fax: 850-785-9248. Facebook; Twitter.

E-mail: info@centerforartspc.com

Web Site: centerfortheartspc.com

Formerly: Visual Arts Center of Northwest Florida

Key Personnel: Dir., Kim Griffin White.

Institution Type/Description: Art Gallery; 1925 former city courthouse, jail & fire station.

Hours & Admission Prices: Tues.-Sat. 10-5. No charge; donations accepted. Closed New Year's Eve & Day; Christmas. &

Attendance: 10,078 (actual)

SCIENCE AND DISCOVERY CENTER OF NORTHWEST FLORIDA, 308 Airport Rd., Panama City, FL 32405-4610. Tel.: 850-769-6128. Fax: 850-769-6129.

E-mail: sdc@nwfl.org

Web Site: scienceanddiscoverycenter.org

Formerly: The Junior Museum of Bay County

Key Personnel: Exec. Dir., Rae Cotton; Dir. Education, Mickey Busby; Admin., Sarah Sapp.

Institution Type/Description: Children's Museum.
Hours & Admission Prices: Tues.-Sat. 10-5, Sun. 12-5. Adults $7, children, seniors & military $6; discounts to groups; teachers & members no charge. Closed major holidays. ৬
Attendance: 27,000 (actual)

Panama City Beach

MAN IN THE SEA MUSEUM, 17314 Panama City Beach Pkwy., Panama City Beach, FL 32413-6038. Tel.: 850-235-4101. Fax: 850-235-4101.
E-mail: info@maninthesea.org
Web Site: www.maninthesea.org
Formerly: The Museum of Man In the Sea, Inc.
Key Personnel: Mgr., Leslie Baker.
Institution Type/Description: History & Science Museum.
Hours & Admission Prices: Tues.-Sat. 10-5. Adults $7, seniors 65 & over $5.50, youth 6-17 $5; members and children 5 & under no charge. Closed New Year's Day; Thanksgiving; Christmas. ৬
Attendance: 30,080 (actual)

Parrish

FLORIDA RAILROAD MUSEUM, INC., 12210 83rd St. E., Parrish, FL 34219. Mailing Address: P.O. Box 355, Parrish, FL 34219-0355. Tel.: 941-776-0906. Fax: 941-917-0081.
Web Site: www.frrm.org
Formerly: Florida Gulf Coast Railroad Museum
Key Personnel: Pres. (V), Steven Wonderly.
Institution Type/Description: Railroad Museum.
Hours & Admission Prices: Train rides: Sat.-Sun. 11 & 2. Adults $14, children $10, extra charge for special events, please visit website for special event dates; members & children under 3 no charge. Closed New Year's Day; Easter; Christmas.
Attendance: 45,000 (estimated)

Patrick Air Force Base

AIR FORCE SPACE AND MISSILE MUSEUM, 191 Museum Cir., Patrick Air Force Base, FL 32925-2535. Tel.: 321-853-9171.
E-mail: feedback@afspacemuseum.org
Institution Type/Description: Space Museum.
Hours & Admission Prices: Call for hours.

Pembroke Pines

THE ART GALLERY, BROWARD COMMUNITY COLLEGE SOUTH CAMPUS, 7200 Pines Blvd., Bldg. 69, Pembroke Pines, FL 33024-7225. Tel.: 954-210-8895. Fax: 954-201-8934.
E-mail: jfoster@broward.edu
Web Site: www.broward.edu/locations/south/artgallery
Key Personnel: Dir., Dr. Kyra Belan.
Institution Type/Description: Art Gallery.
Hours & Admission Prices: Mon.-Fri. 10-2. No charge.

Pensacola

ANNA LAMAR SWITZER CENTER FOR VISUAL ARTS, Pensacola State College, 1000 College Blvd., Pensacola, FL 32504-8910. Tel.: 850-484-2554 & 2550. Fax: 850-484-2564.
E-mail: vspencer@pensacolastate.org
Web Site: www.pensacolastate.edu/visarts
Formerly: Visual Arts Gallery
Key Personnel: Dir., Vivian L. Spencer.
Institution Type/Description: College Art Museum.
Hours & Admission Prices: Sept.-May Mon.-Thurs. 8 am-9pm, Fri. 8-4. No charge. Closed holidays. ৬
Attendance: 58,000 (actual)

HISTORIC PENSACOLA VILLAGE, 120 Church St., Pensacola, FL 32502-5941. Mailing Address: P.O. Box 12866, Pensacola, FL 32591-2866. Tel.: 850-595-5985, ext. 100. Fax: 850-595-5989. Facebook: Historic Pensacola Village.
E-mail: roverton@uwf.edu
Web Site: www.historicpensacola.org
Key Personnel: Exec. Dir., Robert Overton, Jr.; Special Events Coord., Casey Campbell; Archivist, Jacquelyn Wilson; Dir. Education, Sheyna Marcey; Educator, Jim McMillen; Historic Preservationist, Ross Pristera; Museum Shop Mgr., Wendi Davis.
Institution Type/Description: Historic Houses & Buildings.

Hours & Admission Prices: Village: Tues.-Sat. 10-4. Adults $6, children $3; discounts to senior citizens, AAM & ICOM members, groups over 20 & military personnel; members no charge. Closed New Year's Eve & Day; Martin Luther King Jr. Day; Memorial Day; Independence Day; Labor Day; Veterans Day; Thanksgiving & day after; Christmas Eve, Day & week. ৬
Attendance: 13,351 (actual)

PENSACOLA CHILDREN'S MUSEUM, 115 E. Zaragoza St., Pensacola, FL 32502. Mailing Address: P.O. Box 12866, Pensacola, FL 32591-2866. Tel.: 850-595-1559. Fax: 850-595-5989. Facebook: Pensacola Children's Museum.
E-mail: roverton@uwf.edu
Web Site: www.historicpensacola.org
Key Personnel: Exec. Dir., Malinda Horton; Dir. Education, Sheyna Marcey; Cur. Exhibits, Gale Messerschmidt; Educator, Jim McMillen; Museum Shop Mgr., Wendi Davis.
Institution Type/Description: Children's Museum.
Hours & Admission Prices: Tues.-Sat. 10-4. Admission $3; children under one & members no charge. Closed New Year's Day; Martin Luther King Jr. Day; Memorial Day; Independence Day; Labor Day; Veterans Day; Thanksgiving & day after; Christmas.
Attendance: 18,939

PENSACOLA HISTORICAL SOCIETY, 120 Church St., Pensacola, FL 32502-5941. Tel.: 850-595-5840. Fax: 850-595-5989. Facebook.
E-mail: roverton@uwf.edu
Web Site: historicpensacola.org
Key Personnel: Exec. Dir., Robert Overton, Jr.; Historic Preservationist, Ross Pristera; Chief Cur., Lowell Bassett; Archivist, Jacki Wilson; Museum Shop Mgr., Wendi Davis.
Institution Type/Description: Resource Center & Archives.
Hours & Admission Prices: Resource Center: Tues.-Fri. 10-4. Resource Center: $5.50 per day; members no charge. Closed state & university holidays. ৬
Attendance: 7,404 (actual)

PENSACOLA LIGHTHOUSE & MUSEUM, 2081 Radford Blvd., Pensacola, FL 32508. Tel.: 850-393-1561. Facebook; Instagram.
E-mail: info@PensacolaLighthouse.org
Web Site: www.pensacolalighthouse.org/
Key Personnel: Exec. Dir., Jon Hill; Cur., Jessica Morgan; Operations Mgr., Glenda King.
Institution Type/Description: Maritime & History Museum. Listed on the National Register of Historic Places.
Hours & Admission Prices: Daily 9-5. Adults $7, children 12 & under, military and seniors 65 & over $4.

PENSACOLA MUSEUM OF ART, 407 S. Jefferson St., Pensacola, FL 32502-5901. Tel.: 850-432-6247. Fax: 850-469-1532. Facebook.
E-mail: mhartshorn@pensacolamuseum.org
Web Site: www.pensacolamuseum.org
Key Personnel: Exec. Dir., Raven Holloway; Dir. Communications & Events, Mary Hartshorn; Dir. Education & Membership, Cortlandt Glover; Dir. Curatorial Affairs, Alexis Leader.
Institution Type/Description: Art Museum: housed in 1908 old city jail.
Hours & Admission Prices: Tues.-Thurs. 10-5, Fri.-Sat. 10-7, Sun. 12-4. Adults $7, students, military & seniors $5; members & children 6 & under no charge. Closed New Year's Day; Martin Luther King Day; Easter; Memorial Day; Independence Day; Labor Day; Veteran's Day; Thanksgiving Day; Christmas Eve & Day. ৬
Attendance: 80,000 (estimated)

T.T. WENTWORTH, JR. FLORIDA STATE MUSEUM, 330 S. Jefferson St., Pensacola, FL 32502-5943. Mailing Address: P.O. Box 12866, Pensacola, FL 32591-2866. Tel.: 850-595-5985, ext. 100. Fax: 850-595-5989. Facebook.
E-mail: roverton@uwf.edu
Web Site: www.historicpensacola.org
Key Personnel: Exec. Dir., Robert Overton, Jr.; Dir. Education, Sheyna Marcey; Museum Shop Mgr., Wendy Davis.
Institution Type/Description: Historic Building: housed in the former Pensacola City Hall building.
Hours & Admission Prices: Tues.-Thurs. 10-4, Fri.-Sat. 10-7, Sun. 12-4. No charge; donations accepted. Closed New Year's Day; Martin Luther King Jr. Day; Memorial Day; Independence Day; Labor Day; Veterans Day; Thanksgiving & day after; Christmas. ৬
Attendance: 22,916 (actual)

UNIVERSITY OF WEST FLORIDA ART GALLERY, 11000 University Pkwy., Bldg. 82, Pensacola, FL 32514-5750. Tel.: 850-474-2696. Fax: 850-474-2043.
E-mail: artgallery@uwf.edu
Web Site: uwf.edu/art
Key Personnel: Gallery Dir., Nick Croghan.
Institution Type/Description: University Art Gallery.
Hours & Admission Prices: Mon.-Fri. 10-5, during school year. No charge, donations accepted. Closed Easter; Memorial Day; Independence Day; Veterans Day; Thanksgiving. &
Attendance: 14,000 (actual)

WEST FLORIDA HISTORIC PRESERVATION, INC., 120 Church St., Pensacola, FL 32502-5941. Mailing Address: P.O. Box 12866, Pensacola, FL 32591-2866. Tel.: 850-595-5985. Fax: 850-595-5989. Facebook: West Florida Historic Preservation, Inc..
E-mail: roverton@uwf.edu
Web Site: www.historicpensacola.org
Formerly: Historic Pensacola Preservation Board
Key Personnel: Interim Exec. Dir., Malinda Horton; Bd. Pres. (V), Jerry Maygarden; Museum Shop Mgr., Wendi Davis; C.O.O., Robert Overton; Historic Preservationist, Ross Pristera; Cur. Exhibits, Gale Messerschmidt; Registrar, Carolyn Prime; Archivist, Jacquelyn Wilson; Dir. Education, Sheyna Marcey; Educator, Jim McMillen; Coord. Special Events, Casey Campbell; Living History Coord., Ryan Arvay.
Institution Type/Description: Preservation Society.
Hours & Admission Prices: Offices & Archives: Mon.-Fri. 8-4:30. Research: Tues.-Fri. Research: $5.50 per day; discounts to AAM & ICOM members; members no charge. Closed New Year's Eve & Day; Martin Luther King Jr. Day; Memorial Day; Independence Day; Labor Day; Veterans Day; Thanksgiving & day after; Christmas Eve, Day & week. &
Attendance: 49,707 (actual)

Perry

FOREST CAPITAL STATE MUSEUM, S. U.S. Hwy. 19, 204 Forest Park Dr, Perry, FL 32348-6320. Tel.: 850-584-3227. Fax: 850-584-3488.
E-mail: info@friendsoffloridastateparks.org
Web Site: www.floridastateparks.org
Institution Type/Description: Logging & Lumber Museum: Timber Industry Museum & Forestry including c.1865 Pioneer-Cracker Homestead.
Hours & Admission Prices: Thurs.-Mon. 9-5. Adults $2; children 5 & under & Florida public school groups no charge. Closed New Year's Day; Thanksgiving; Christmas. &
Attendance: 7,000 (estimated)

Pine Island Center

MUSEUM OF THE ISLANDS, 5728 Sesame, Pine Island Center, FL 33956. Mailing Address: P.O. Box 305, Saint James City, FL 33956-0305. Tel.: 239-283-1525.
E-mail: info@museumoftheislands.com
Web Site: www.museumoftheislands.com
Key Personnel: Museum Shop Mgr., Barbara "Bobbie" Mahaffey.
Institution Type/Description: General Museum.
Hours & Admission Prices: May-Oct., Tues., Thurs. & Sat. 11-3; Nov.-April Tues.-Sat. 11-3, Sun. 1-4; groups by appointment. Adults $2, children $1. Closed Easter; Thanksgiving; Christmas. &
Attendance: 8,000 (estimated)

Plant City

DINOSAUR WORLD, 5145 Harvey Tew Rd., Plant City, FL 33565. Tel.: 813-717-9865. Fax: 813-707-9776.
E-mail: info@dinosaurworld.com
Web Site: dinosaurworld.com
Institution Type/Description: Natural History Museum.
Hours & Admission Prices: Daily 9-5. Adults $16.95, seniors over 60 $14.95, children 3-12 $11.95; discounts to groups & military dependents; children under 3 & active military no charge.

EAST HILLSBOROUGH HISTORICAL SOCIETY, INC., 605 N. Collins St., Plant City, FL 33563-3321. Tel.: 813-757-9226.
E-mail: gcenter@tampabay.rr.com
Web Site: http://www.rootsweb.com/~flqgbac
Formerly: 1914 Plant City High School Community Center
Key Personnel: Pres. (V) & Archivist, Shelby Bender.
Institution Type/Description: Pioneer Heritage Museum: housed in c.1914 high school bldg.

Hours & Admission Prices: Pioneer Museum: call for hours. Quintilla Geer Bruton Archives Center: Tues. 10-5, Wed.-Sat. 1-5, evenings by appointment. No charge; donations accepted. &
Attendance: 10,000 (estimated)

PLANT CITY PHOTO ARCHIVES & HISTORY CENTER, 106 S. Evers St., Plant City, FL 33563-5412. Tel.: 813-754-1578.
E-mail: info@plantcityphotoarchives.org
Web Site: www.plantcityphotoarchives.org
Key Personnel: Dir., Gilbert V. Gott; Pres. (V), Edward M. Verner.
Institution Type/Description: History Museum.
Hours & Admission Prices: Mon.-Thurs. 9-7. No charge; donations accepted. Closed major holidays. &
Attendance: 5,000 (estimated)

Plantation

PLANTATION HISTORICAL MUSEUM, 511 N. Fig Tree Lane, Plantation, FL 33317-1849. Tel.: 954-797-2722. Fax: 954-797-2717.
E-mail: jfeeney@plantation.org
Web Site: www.plantation.org/Museum/index.html
Key Personnel: Cur., John Feeney; Museum Asst. Lauren Bhaggan.
Institution Type/Description: Local History Museum.
Hours & Admission Prices: Tues., Thurs. & Sat. 10-12 & 1-4:30, Fri. 12-4:30; groups by appointment on Tues. & Thurs. No charge. Closed national holidays. &
Attendance: 16,000 (estimated)

Point Washington

EDEN STATE GARDENS AND MANSION, 181 Eden Garden Rd., Point Washington, FL 32459. Tel.: 850-267-8320.
E-mail: baym12@aol.com
Key Personnel: Pres. (V), Bailey Miller.
Institution Type/Description: Historic House: housed in the former home of William Henry Wesley, founder of a timber company; built in 1890.
Hours & Admission Prices: Tours: Thurs.-Mon. Adults $4. &
Attendance: 60,000 (estimated)

Polk City

AMERICAN WATER SKI EDUCATIONAL FOUNDATION, 1251 Holy Cow Rd., Polk City, FL 33868-8200. Tel.: 863-324-2472. Fax: 863-324-3996.
E-mail: awsefhalloffame@cs.com
Web Site: waterskihalloffame.com
Key Personnel: Exec. Dir., Tracy Mattes; Chm., Mark Overbye; Pres., Paul Chapin; Treas., Teri Larson Jones.
Institution Type/Description: Waterski Sports Museum.
Hours & Admission Prices: Temporarily closed. &
Attendance: 10,000 (estimated)

FANTASY OF FLIGHT, 1400 Broadway Blvd., S.E., Polk City, FL 33868-9109. Tel.: 863-984-3500.
E-mail: btaylor@fantasyofflight.com
Web Site: www.fantasyofflight.com
Key Personnel: Owner, Kermit Weeks.
Institution Type/Description: Aircraft Museum.
Hours & Admission Prices: Daily 10-5. Adults $28.95, children 6-15 $14.95; discounts to groups & military; children 4 & under no charge. Closed Thanksgiving; Christmas.

Pompano Beach

ELY EDUCATIONAL MUSEUM, Founders Park, 217 N.E. 4th Ave., Pompano Beach, FL 33060. Mailing Address: c/o Pompano Beach Historical Society, P.O. Box 154, Pompano Beach, FL 33061. Tel.: 954-782-3015.
Institution Type/Description: Historic House Museum: housed in the former home of Blanche and Joseph Ely.
Hours & Admission Prices: Call for hours.

KESTER COTTAGES - POMPANO BEACH HISTORICAL SOCIETY, 220 N.E. 3rd Ave., Pompano Beach, FL 33060. Mailing Address: P.O. Box 154, Pompano Beach, FL 33061. Tel.: 954-782-3015.
E-mail: info@pampanohistory.com

Institution Type/Description: History Museum: housed in cottages built in the 1930s.
Hours & Admission Prices: Call for hours.

POMPANO FIRE MUSEUM, 219 N.E. 4th Ave., Pompano Beach, FL 33060. Mailing Address: 217 N.E. 4 Ave., Pompano Beach, FL 33060. Tel.: 954-782-3015 & 553-0772. Facebook.
E-mail: robwillrob@outlook.com
Web Site: pompanofiremuseum.com
Formerly: Old Pompano Fire Station
Key Personnel: Dir., Robert W. Brantley, Jr.
Institution Type/Description: Historic Building: housed in the city's first fire station; built in 1925.
Hours & Admission Prices: Call for hours. No charge; donations accepted.
Attendance: 400 (estimated)

SAMPLE-MCDOUGALD HOUSE, 450 N.E. 10th St., Pompano Beach, FL 33060. Mailing Address: P.O. Box 1599, Pompano Beach, FL 33061. Tel.: 754-307-5446. Facebook.
E-mail: lee@samplemcdougald.org
Web Site: www.samplemcdougald.org
Key Personnel: Exec. Dir., Jennifer D'hollander; Mgr., Lee Waldo.
Institution Type/Description: Historic House Museum: built in 1916. Listed on the National Register of Historic Places.
Hours & Admission Prices: Call for hours. Adults $5.

Ponce Inlet

MARINE SCIENCE CENTER, 100 Lighthouse Dr., Ponce Inlet, FL 32127-7325. Tel.: 386-304-5545.
E-mail: mbrothers@co.volusia.fl.us
Web Site: www.marinesciencecenter.com
Institution Type/Description: Science Center.
Hours & Admission Prices: Tues.-Sat. 10-4, Sun. 12-4. Adults 13 & over $5, seniors $4, youth 3-12 $2; children under 3 no charge. Closed New Year's Day; Martin Luther King Jr. Day; Thanksgiving; Christmas.

PONCE DELEON INLET LIGHTHOUSE PRESERVATION ASSOCIATION, INC., 4931 S. Peninsula Dr., Ponce Inlet, FL 32127-7301. Tel.: 386-761-1821. Fax: 386-761-3121.
E-mail: lighthouse@ponceinlet.org
Web Site: www.ponceinlet.org
Key Personnel: Exec. Dir., Ed Gunn; Pres., Chris Belcher; Dir. Operations, Mike Bennett; Cur., Ellen Henry; Program Mgr., Mary Wentzel.
Institution Type/Description: History Museum, Historic Site & National Historic Landmark.
Hours & Admission Prices: Memorial Day to Labor Day daily 10-9; Sept.-May daily 10-6. Adults $6.95, children $1.95; members & children under 2 no charge. Closed Thanksgiving; Christmas.
Attendance: 159,399 (actual)

Ponte Vedra Beach

MARIAL MUSEUM OF SACRED ART, The Gallery at Christ Episcopal Church, 400 San Juan Dr., Ponte Vedra Beach, FL 32082-2838. Tel.: 904-285-6127.
Web Site: www.marialmuseum.org
Institution Type/Description: Art Gallery.
Hours & Admission Prices: Call for hours.

Port Saint Joe

CONSTITUTION CONVENTION MUSEUM STATE PARK, 200 Allen Memorial Way, Port Saint Joe, FL 32456-2342. Tel.: 850-229-8029, 850-227-1327. Fax: 850-227-1488.
E-mail: mark.knapke@dep.state.fl.us
Web Site: www.floridastateparks.org/constitutionconvention/
Formerly: Constitution Convention State Museum
Key Personnel: Park Mgr., Mark Knapke; Asst. Mgr., Danny Kemp; Park Ranger, William Wilkinson; Park Ranger, JoAnna Lindsey.
Institution Type/Description: History Museum: site of the Constitution Convention for the Territory of FL.
Hours & Admission Prices: Visitor Center: Thurs.-Mon. 9-12 & 1-5. Adults $2; children 4 & under no charge. Closed New Year's Day; Thanksgiving; Christmas.
Attendance: 3,500 (estimated)

Punta Gorda

CHARLOTTE COUNTY HISTORICAL CENTER, 514 E. Grace St., Punta Gorda, FL 33950-6121. Tel.: 941-629-7278. Fax: 941-743-3917. Facebook.
E-mail: historicalcenter@charlottefl.com
Web Site: charlottecountyfl.com/historical
Formerly: Florida Adventure Museum of Charlotte County
Key Personnel: Historian, Linda Roberts.
Institution Type/Description: General Museum.
Hours & Admission Prices: Tues.-Fri. 1-5, Sat. 10-3. Adults $2, children $1; museum, ASTC & CCHC Society members no charge. Closed holidays.
Attendance: 9,000 (actual)

MILITARY HERITAGE MUSEUM, 1200 W. Retta Esplanade, Unit 48, Punta Gorda, FL 33950-5325. Tel.: 941-575-9002.
E-mail: info@freedomisntfree.org
Web Site: www.freedomisntfree.org
Key Personnel: Exec. Dir., Kim Lovejoy Ross; Pres. (V), Dr. Kathleen Roth.
Institution Type/Description: Military Heritage Museum.
Hours & Admission Prices: Summer: Mon.-Sat. 10-6, Sun. 12-6; Winter: call for extended hours. No charge; donations accepted.
Attendance: 63,649 (actual)

Quincy

GADSDEN ARTS CENTER & MUSEUM, 13 N. Madison, Quincy, FL 32351-2409. Tel.: 850-875-4866. Fax: 850-627-8606.
E-mail: grace@gadsdenarts.org
Web Site: www.gadsdenarts.org
Key Personnel: Exec. Dir., Grace B. Robinson; Pres., Ranie Thompson; Cur., Angela Barry; Dir. Education, Anissa Ford.
Institution Type/Description: Fine Arts Museum.
Hours & Admission Prices: Tues.-Sat. 1-5. Suggested Admission $5; discounts to AAM, ROAM & NARM members; members & children no charge. Closed holidays.
Attendance: 18,000 (estimated)

Safety Harbor

SAFETY HARBOR MUSEUM OF REGIONAL HISTORY, 329 Bayshore Blvd. S., Safety Harbor, FL 34695-4053. Tel.: 727-724-1562. Fax: 727-725-9938.
E-mail: logles@cityofsafetyharbor.com
Institution Type/Description: Florida & Regional History Museum.
Hours & Admission Prices: Tues.-Fri. 9-3:30; other times by appointment. Adults $4, seniors $3; discounts to AAA members; children under 7 & members no charge. Closed major holidays.
Attendance: 8,783 (actual)

Saint Augustine

CASTILLO DE SAN MARCOS NATIONAL MONUMENT, One S. Castillo Dr., Saint Augustine, FL 32084-3252. Tel.: 904-829-6506. Fax: 904-823-9388.
E-mail: casa_ranger_activities@nps.gov
Web Site: www.nps.gov/casa
Key Personnel: Supt., Gordon J. Wilson.
Institution Type/Description: Park Museum: housed in 1672-95 restored Spanish Castillo de San Marcos.
Hours & Admission Prices: Daily 8:45-5:15; last admission is at 5. Seven consecutive day pass: adults 16 & over $7; children under 16 no charge; Golden Access & Age Passport, Castillo Annual Pass, Interagency Access, annual, military & senior passes no charge. Closed Thanksgiving; Christmas.

CRISP-ELLERT ART MUSEUM - FLAGLER COLLEGE, 48 Sevilla St., Saint Augustine, FL 32084. Mailing Address: 74 King St., Saint Augustine, FL 32084. Tel.: 904-826-8530.
E-mail: crispellert@flagler.edu
Web Site: www.flagler.edu/crispellert
Key Personnel: Dir., Julie Dickover.
Institution Type/Description: Art Museum.
Hours & Admission Prices: Academic Year: Mon.-Fri. 10-4, Sat. 12-4; Summer: Tues.-Fri. 10-4. No charge.

DE MESA-SANCHEZ HOUSE, 43 St. George St., Saint Augustine, FL 32085. Mailing Address: c/o Colonial Quarter, LLC, 12 S. Castillo Dr., Saint Augustine, FL 32084. Tel.: 904-819-1444.
Institution Type/Description: Historic House Museum.
Hours & Admission Prices: Call for hours.

FORT MATANZAS NATIONAL MONUMENT, 8635 A1A S., Unit A, Saint Augustine, FL 32080-8400. Tel.: 904-471-0116 & 829-6506, ext. 227 (Headquarters). Fax: 904-471-7605.
E-mail: linda_chandler@nps.gov
Web Site: www.nps.gov/foma
Key Personnel: Supt., Gordon Wilson.
Institution Type/Description: Park Museum: Site of first European battle for control of New World.
Hours & Admission Prices: Daily 9-5:30. Ferry: 9:30-4:30. No charge for admission. Cooperative association with National Park Service. Closed Thanksgiving; Christmas. ♿
Attendance: 700,000 (actual)

GOVERNMENT HOUSE MUSEUM, 48 King St., Saint Augustine, FL 32085. Tel.: 904-823-2212.
E-mail: staugustineinfo@admin.ufl.edu
Web Site: www.staugustine.ufl.edu/govHouse.html
Institution Type/Description: Historic House Museum.
Hours & Admission Prices: Daily 10-5. Adults $7.99, children 5-12 $5.99.

LIGHTNER MUSEUM, City Hall, Museum Complex, 75 King St., Saint Augustine, FL 32084. Mailing Address: P.O. Box 334, Saint Augustine, FL 32085-0334. Tel.: 904-824-2874. Fax: 904-824-2712.
E-mail: info@lightnermuseum.org
Web Site: www.lightnermuseum.org
Key Personnel: C.E.O., Robert W. Harper, III; Chm. (V), David C. Drysdale; Cur., Barry W. Myers, Jr.; Visitor Svcs., Toni Franklin; Museum Shop Mgr., Janice Phelan.
Institution Type/Description: General Museum: housed in 1887 Alcazar Hotel.
Hours & Admission Prices: Daily 9-5. Adults $10, active military with ID $6; college students with ID & youth 12-18 $5 students $5; discount to groups, military & AAM members; children under 12 with adult no charge. Closed Christmas. ♿
Attendance: 126,832 (actual)

OLDEST HOUSE MUSEUM COMPLEX, 14 St. Francis St., Saint Augustine, FL 32084-5047. Mailing Address: 271 Charlotte St., Saint Augustine, FL 32084-5033. Tel.: 904-824-2872. Fax: 904-824-2569.
E-mail: sahsdirector@bellsouth.net
Web Site: www.oldesthouse.org
Key Personnel: C.E.O., Dr. Susan R. Parker; Pres. (V), Dr. Kathleen Deagan; Office Mgr., Magen Wilson.
Institution Type/Description: Historic Houses, Military Museum & Ornamental Garden.
Hours & Admission Prices: Daily 9-5. Adults $8, seniors $7, students & adult tours $4; discounts to groups & military; members & children under 6 no charge. Closed Easter; Thanksgiving; Christmas. ♿
Attendance: 40,000 (estimated)

OLDEST STORE MUSEUM, 167 San Marco Ave., Saint Augustine, FL 32084-3269. Tel.: 904-829-9729.
Institution Type/Description: History Museum: housed in a former 1908 general store.
Hours & Admission Prices: Daily 8:30-4:30. Adults $10.64, children 6-12 $6.38; children under 6 no charge. Closed Christmas.

THE PENA-PECK HOUSE MUSEUM - WOMAN'S EXCHANGE OF ST. AUGUSTINE, INC., 143 St. George St., Saint Augustine, FL 32084-3642. Tel.: 904-829-5064. Facebook.
E-mail: info@penapeckhouse.com
Web Site: penapeckhouse.com
Key Personnel: Pres. (V), Nancy Russell; Museum Shop Co-Mgr., Val Roeseler; Museum Shop Co Mgr., Louise Coward.
Institution Type/Description: Historic House: housed in the former home royal Spanish treasurer, Juan Estevan de Pena, built in 1750; second story added by Dr. Seth & Sarah Lay Peck in 1837.
Hours & Admission Prices: Tours: Sun.-Fri. 12:30-4, Sat. 10:30-4. Shop: Mon.-Sat. 10:30-5, Sun. 12:30-5. No charge; donations requested. Closed most major holidays.
Attendance: 5,000 (estimated)

PONCE DE LEON'S FOUNTAIN OF YOUTH ARCHAEOLOGICAL PARK, 11 Magnolia Ave., Saint Augustine, FL 32084. Tel.: 800-356-8222, 904-829-3168. Fax: 904-829-1529.
E-mail: fountain@aug.com
Web Site: www.fountainofyouthflorida.com
Formerly: Fountain of Youth

Key Personnel: Dir. & C.E.O., John W. Fraser; Chm. (V), Kit Keating; Museum Shop Mgr., Rose Fieldhouse.
Institution Type/Description: History Museum.
Hours & Admission Prices: Daily 9-5. Adults $15, seniors over 60 $14, children 6-12 $9; discounts to groups, active military & AAA members; children under 6 no charge. Closed Christmas. ♿
Attendance: 195,000 (actual)

POTTER'S WAX MUSEUM, 31 Orange St., Saint Augustine, FL 32084-3634. Mailing Address: Historic Tours of America, Inc., 201 Front St., Ste. 224, Key West, FL 33040. Tel.: 904-829-9056.
E-mail: potterswaxmuseum@yahoo.com
Web Site: www.potterswax.com
Key Personnel: Dir., Kimber Ponce.
Institution Type/Description: Wax Museum.
Hours & Admission Prices: Daily 9-6. Adults $10, seniors 55 & over $9, children 6-12 $7; discount to local, military & AAA members; children 5 & under no charge.
Attendance: 60,000 (estimated)

RIPLEY'S BELIEVE IT OR NOT! MUSEUM, 19 San Marco Ave., Saint Augustine, FL 32084-3278. Tel.: 904-824-1606.
E-mail: staugustine@ripleys.com
Web Site: staugustine.ripleys.com
Key Personnel: Mgr., Ed Shaffer.
Institution Type/Description: General Museum.
Hours & Admission Prices: Daily 9-8. Adults 12 & over $14.99, senior citizens 55 & over $12.26, children 5-11 $7.99; children under 5 no charge.

ST. AUGUSTINE ALLIGATOR FARM ZOOLOGICAL PARK, 999 Anastasia Blvd., Saint Augustine, FL 32080-4619. Tel.: 904-824-3337.
E-mail: Jbrueggen@alligatorfarm.com
Web Site: www.alligatorfarm.com
Key Personnel: Dir., John Brueggen; Education, Trevor Mia.
Institution Type/Description: Zoological Park.
Hours & Admission Prices: Daily 9-5. Adults $22.95, children 3-11 $11.95; discounts to seniors, groups, AAM, ICOM & AAA members; members no charge. ♿
Attendance: 213,000 (estimated)

ST. AUGUSTINE ART ASSOCIATION, 22 Marine St., Saint Augustine, FL 32084-4438. Tel.: 904-824-2310. Fax: 904-824-0716.
E-mail: info@staaa.org
Web Site: www.staaa.org
Key Personnel: Exec. Dir., Elyse Brady.
Institution Type/Description: Art Museum.
Hours & Admission Prices: Tues.-Sat. 12-4, Sun. 2-5. No charge; donations accepted. Closed holidays. ♿

ST. AUGUSTINE LIGHTHOUSE AND MARITIME MUSEUM, INC., 81 Lighthouse Ave., Saint Augustine, FL 32080-4650. Tel.: 904-829-0745. Fax: 904-808-1248. Facebook.
E-mail: info@staugustinelighthouse.org
Web Site: www.staugustinelighthouse.org
Formerly: First Light Maritime Society - St. Augustine Lighthouse & Museum, Inc.
Key Personnel: Exec. Dir., Kathy Allen Fleming; Chm. (V), Peter Spiller; Deputy Dir., Rick Cain; Dir. Collections, Interpretations, Brenda Swann; Dir. Sales, Lee Capitano; Volunteer & Event Mgr., Loni Wellman; Dir. Museum Advancement, Michelle Adams; Museum Shop Mgr., Sam Andrews.
Institution Type/Description: Maritime & History Museum: National Register site.
Hours & Admission Prices: Winter: daily 9-6; Summer: call for extended hours. Adults $12.95; discounts to St. Johns County School District students, seniors & active military; members no charge. Closed Thanksgiving; Christmas Eve & Day. ♿
Attendance: 217,000 (actual)

ST. AUGUSTINE PIRATE & TREASURE MUSEUM, 12 S. Castillo Dr., Saint Augustine, FL 32084. Tel.: 877-467-5863.
E-mail: sknott@piratesoul.com
Web Site: www.piratesoul.com
Formerly: Pirate Soul Museum
Key Personnel: Exec. Dir., Cindy Stavely; Museum Shop Mgr., Tracy King.
Institution Type/Description: History Museum.
Hours & Admission Prices: Daily 10-7. Adults $14.99, seniors & military $11.99, children $7.99. ♿

ST. PHOTIOS GREEK ORTHODOX NATIONAL SHRINE, 41 St. George St., Saint Augustine, FL 32084-1960. Mailing Address: P.O. Box 1960, Saint Augustine, FL 32085. Tel.: 904-829-8205. Fax: 904-829-8707.
E-mail: phillier@stphotios.com
Key Personnel: Exec. Dir., Polexeni M. Hillier; Chm. (V), Archbishop Demetrios; Pres. (V), Metropolitan Alexios of Atlanta; 1st Vice Pres. (V), Dr. Manuel Tissura; Shrine Mgr., Gina Bingman; Museum Shop Mgr., Eugenia Mercado; Museum Shop Mgr., Jenny Harker.
Institution Type/Description: History Museum: housed in 1740 Avero House. Listed on the National Register of Historic Places.
Hours & Admission Prices: Mon.-Sat. 9-5, Sun. 12-6. No charge; donations accepted. Closed New Year's Day; Greek Orthodox Easter; Independence Day; Thanksgiving; Christmas. &
Attendance: 100,000 (estimated)

WORLD GOLF HALL OF FAME & MUSEUM, One World Golf Pl., Saint Augustine, FL 32092-2724. Tel.: 904-940-4000. Fax: 904-940-4391. Facebook: Golf Hall of Fame.
E-mail: info@wghof.org
Web Site: www.worldgolfhalloffame.org
Key Personnel: Pres., Jack Peter; Collections, Brodie Waters; Sr. Dir. Education & Mktg., Angela Ivey.
Institution Type/Description: Sports Museum.
Hours & Admission Prices: Mon.-Sat. 10-6, Sun. 12-6. Adults $20.95, seniors, military & FL residents $19.95, students 13 & over $10, children 5-12 $5; children 4 & under no charge. IMAX Documentaries: additional $5-$10. Closed Thanksgiving; Christmas. &
Attendance: 200,000 (estimated)

XIMENEZ-FATIO HOUSE MUSEUM, 20 Aviles St., Saint Augustine, FL 32084-4442. Mailing Address: 28 Cadiz St., Saint Augustine, FL 32084. Tel.: 904-829-3575.
E-mail: xf@bellsouth.net
Web Site: www.ximenezfatiohouse.org
Key Personnel: Exec. Dir., Julia Gatlin; Pres. (V), La Grange Gippe.
Institution Type/Description: Historic House Museum.
Hours & Admission Prices: Wed.-Sat. 11-4. Family $15, adults $6, senior, students 6-17 & military $4. &
Attendance: 7,000 (actual)

Saint George Island

ST. GEORGE ISLAND VISITOR CENTER AND LIGHTHOUSE MUSEUM, 2 E. Gulf Beach Dr., Saint George Island, FL 32328-2883. Tel.: 888-927-7744.
E-mail: ExecDirector@apalachicolabay.org
Web Site: www.seestgeorgeisland.com
Institution Type/Description: Maritime History Museum.
Hours & Admission Prices: Visitor Center: Fri.-Wed. 10-5. Lighthouse Tours: March-Oct. Mon.-Wed. & Fri.-Sat. 10-5, Sun. 12-5; Nov.-Feb. Fri.-Wed. 12-5. Adults $5, children 16 & under $3; Lighthouse Assn. members & children 6 and under no charge.

Saint Marks

ST. MARKS NATIONAL WILDLIFE REFUGE VISITOR CENTER, 1255 Lighthouse Rd., Saint Marks, FL 32355. Mailing Address: P.O. Box 68, Saint Marks, FL 32355-0068. Tel.: 850-925-6121. Fax: 850-925-6930. Facebook: SMSVNWRS.
E-mail: saintmarks@fws.gov
Web Site: www.fws.gov/saintmarks
Key Personnel: Refuge Mgr., Terry Peacock; Chm. (V), David Moody; Pres. (V), Mary Smallwood; Museum Shop Mgr., Joanne Harrington.
Institution Type/Description: Wildlife Refuge.
Hours & Admission Prices: Refuge: daily sunrise to sunset. Visitor Center: Mon.-Fri. 8-4, Sat.-Sun. 10-5. Refuge: $5 per car; Federal Recreation Fee passes accepted. Visitor Center: no charge. Closed Thanksgiving; Christmas. &
Attendance: 308,000 (estimated)

SAN MARCOS DE APALACHE HISTORIC STATE PARK, 148 Old Fort Rd., Saint Marks, FL 32355-0027. Mailing Address: 3600 Indian Mounds Rd., Tallahassee, FL 32303-2300. Tel.: 850-922-6007. Fax: 850-488-0366.
E-mail: rob.lacy@dep.state.fl.us
Web Site: www.floridastateparks.org
Key Personnel: Park Mgr., Rob Lacy; Administrative Asst., Leeanne Chandler.
Institution Type/Description: State History Museum: museum built on the foundation of the Civil War-era Marine Hospital.

Hours & Admission Prices: Thurs.-Mon. 9-5. Adults $2; children under 6 no charge. Closed New Year's Day; Thanksgiving; Christmas. &
Attendance: 15,000 (estimated)

Saint Petersburg

THE DALI MUSEUM, One Dali Blvd., Saint Petersburg, FL 33701. Tel.: 727-823-3767. Fax: 727-894-6068. Facebook: @thedalimuseum; Instagram: @dalimuseum; Twitter: @TheDali.
E-mail: info@thedali.org
Web Site: thedali.org
Formerly: Salvador Dali Museum
Key Personnel: Deputy Dir. & Cur. Collections, Joan R. Kropf; Cur. Education, Peter Tush; Dir. Mktg., Beth Bell; Dir. Sales & Merchandise, Dianne Birmingham; Co Dir. Visitor Experience, Pam Whiteaker; Membership & Group Sales Dir., Jim Nixon.
Institution Type/Description: Art Museum.
Hours & Admission Prices: Thurs.-Fri. 10-8, Wed. & Sat.-Sun. 10-6. Adults $25, senior citizens 65 & over $23, children 13-17 & college students $18, children 6-12 $10; discounts to AAA, AAM & ICOM members, Hospitality Industry Association (H.I.A.) and Florida Attraction members with proper I.D.; children 5 & under and members no charge. Closed Thanksgiving; Christmas. &
Attendance: 210,000 (estimated)

FLORIDA CRAFTART, 501 Central Ave., Saint Petersburg, FL 33701. Tel.: 727-821-7391. Fax: 727-822-4294.
E-mail: info@floridacraftsmen.net
Web Site: www.floridacraftsmen.net
Formerly: Florida Craftsmen Gallery
Key Personnel: Exec. Dir., Katie Deits.
Institution Type/Description: Art Gallery.
Hours & Admission Prices: Mon.-Sat. 10-5:30, Sun. 12-5..

FLORIDA HOLOCAUST MUSEUM, 55 5th St., S., Saint Petersburg, FL 33701-4146. Tel.: 727-820-0100, 800-960-7448. Fax: 727-821-8435. Facebook & Instagram: @thefhm; Twitter: @flholocaustmus.
E-mail: info@thefhm.org
Web Site: www.thefhm.org
Key Personnel: Exec. Dir., Elizabeth Gelman; Cur. Exhibitions & Collections, Erin Blankenship.
Institution Type/Description: History Museum.
Hours & Admission Prices: Daily 10-5 (last admission 30 minutes before closing); call for additional hours. Adults $16, senior citizens 65 & over $14, college students $10, students under 18 $8; active military, children 6 & under and members no charge. Closed New Year's Day; Martin Luther King Jr. Day; Easter; Rosh Hashanah; Yom Kippur; Thanksgiving; Christmas. &
Attendance: 100,000 (actual)

GREAT EXPLORATIONS CHILDREN'S MUSEUM, 1925 Fourth St. N., Saint Petersburg, FL 33704-4307. Tel.: 727-821-8992. Fax: 727-823-7287. Facebook: GreatExKids.
E-mail: ahowell@greatex.org
Web Site: www.greatex.org
Key Personnel: C.E.O., Angeline Howell; C.O.O., Alan Kahle; Controller, Laurel Ginn.
Institution Type/Description: Children's Museum.
Hours & Admission Prices: Mon.-Sat. 10-4:30, Sun. 12-4:30; see website for additional fall hours. Admission 1-54 $10, seniors 55 & over $9; discounts for military, teachers, and AAM, AAA & ACM members; members no charge. Reciprocal members with ASTC, NARM & local attractions. &
Attendance: 177,347 (actual)

MOREAN ARTS CENTER, 719 Central Ave., Saint Petersburg, FL 33701-3627. Tel.: 727-822-7872. Fax: 727-821-0516.
E-mail: amanda@moreanartscenter.org
Web Site: www.moreanartscenter.org
Formerly: The Arts Center
Key Personnel: Exec. Dir., Michael Killoren; Cur., Amanda Cooper.
Institution Type/Description: Art Museum.
Hours & Admission Prices: Mon.-Sat. 9-5, Sun. 12-5. No charge. Closed Thanksgiving; Christmas.

MUSEUM OF AMERICAN ARTS & CRAFTS MOVEMENT, 355 Fourth St. N., Saint Petersburg, FL 33701. Tel.: 727-943-9900.
Institution Type/Description: Art & History Museum.
Hours & Admission Prices: Opening summer 2019.

MUSEUM OF FINE ARTS, ST. PETERSBURG, 255 Beach Dr., N.E., Saint Petersburg, FL 33701-3498. Tel.: 727-896-2667. Fax: 727-894-4638. Facebook, Twitter, Instagram.
E-mail: srobertson@mfastpete.org
Web Site: mfastpete.org
Key Personnel: Bd. Chm. & Pres., Mark T. Mahaffey; Exec. Dir., Kristen A. Shepherd; Hazel and William Hough Chief Cur., Dr. Jerry N. Smith; Dir. Devel., Daryl DeBerry; Dir. Mktg., Susan Robertson; Registrar, Ashley Burke; Cur. Public Programs, Anna Alexander Glenn; Assoc. Cur. Public Programs, Mary Szaroleta; Cur. of Contemporary Art, Katherine Pill; Curatorial Asst., Stephanie Chill; Mgr. of Curatorial Affairs & Communications, Bridget Bryson; C.F.O., Diana Waters; Sr. Preparator, Dimitri Lykoudis; Preparator, Jorge Valenzuela; Dir. Public Rels., David O. Connelly; Mgr. Visitor Svcs., Billy Summer; Mgr. Museum Store, Audrie Ranon; Asst. Store Mgr., Jeff Surrena; Member Svcs. Mgr., Dr. Teresa Wilkins; Membership & Volunteer Coord., Rachel Gaddoni; Devel. Assoc., Amanda Bonanno; Exec. Asst., Vicki Sofranko; Dir. Operations, J.P. Fatseas; Donor Devel. Mgr., Margaret Murray; Curatorial Admin & Mgr. Photographic Collections, Robin O'Dell.
Institution Type/Description: Art Museum.
Hours & Admission Prices: Mon.-Wed. & Fri.-Sat. 10-5, Thurs. 10-8, Sun. 12-5. Adults $17, senior citizens 65 & over and military $15, college students & children 7-18 $10; Thurs. after 5pm $5; discounts to students, groups of 10 or more & AAM members; MFA members and children 6 & under no charge. Closed Thanksgiving; Christmas. &
Attendance: 146,634 (actual)

MUSEUM OF MOTHERHOOD - M.O.M., Mailing Address: 538 28th St. N., Saint Petersburg, FL 33713. Tel.: 212-452-9816, 877-711-6667. Facebook: MOM Museum.
E-mail: mommuseum@gmail.com
Web Site: www.mommuseum.org
Key Personnel: Exec. Dir., Joy Rose; Chair, Zena Marpet; Devel., Cara-Leigh Battaglia; Education, Lynn Kuechle.
Institution Type/Description: History Museum.
Hours & Admission Prices: Tues.-Sun. 10:45-6:30. No charge; donations accepted.
Attendance: 6,500 (actual)

NATIONAL COMEDY HALL OF FAME, Saint Petersburg, FL 33742-0492. Mailing Address: P.O. Box 20492, Saint Petersburg, FL 33742-0492.
E-mail: comedyhall@aol.com
Web Site: comedyhall.com
Key Personnel: Exec. Dir., Tony Belmont.
Institution Type/Description: Comedy Museum.
Hours & Admission Prices: Temporarily closed for relocation.

THE PIER AQUARIUM, 250 Eighth Ave., S.E., Saint Petersburg, FL 33701-3503. Mailing Address: 244 2nd Ave., Ste. 203, Saint Petersburg, FL 33701-3306. Tel.: 727-895-7437. Fax: 727-894-1212.
E-mail: info@pieraquarium.org
Web Site: www.pieraquarium.org
Institution Type/Description: Aquarium.
Hours & Admission Prices: Mon.-Sat. 10-8, Sun. 12-6. Adults $5, students 7 & over and seniors 65 & over $4; children under 6 & members no charge. Tampa Bay Touch Tank: daily 1-4. Shark Feeding: daily 3pm. &
Attendance: 65,000 (actual)

RANSOM VISUAL ARTS CENTER, Eckerd College, 4200 54th Ave. S., Saint Petersburg, FL 33711-4744. Tel.: 727-864-8340 & 8342.
E-mail: support@mutualart.com
Web Site: www.eckerd.edu/tour/index.php?f=arts3
Key Personnel: Dir., Arthur Skinner.
Institution Type/Description: Art Center.
Hours & Admission Prices: Mon.-Fri. 10-4:30. No charge.

ST. PETERSBURG MUSEUM OF HISTORY, 335 Second Ave., N.E., Saint Petersburg, FL 33701-3501. Tel.: 727-894-1052, ext. 207. Fax: 727-823-7276.
E-mail: george.banez@stpetemuseumofhistory.org
Web Site: www.spmoh.org
Key Personnel: Exec. Dir., Rui Farias; Dir. Education & Cur., Nevin Sitler; Archivist, Amy Anderson; Guest Svcs. & Events Mgr., Caitlin Grimes.
Institution Type/Description: History Museum.
Hours & Admission Prices: Mon.-Sat. 10-5, Sun. 12-5. Adults $15, seniors $12, children 7-17, teachers, students, military & veterans $9; discounts to students, seniors & teachers; members & children 6 & under no charge &
Attendance: 35,000 (actual)

THE SCIENCE CENTER OF PINELLAS COUNTY, 7701 22nd Ave., N., Saint Petersburg, FL 33710-3899. Tel.: 727-384-0027. Fax: 727-343-5729.
E-mail: info@steic.org
Web Site: www.steic.org
Key Personnel: Dir., Joseph S. Cuenco.
Institution Type/Description: Science Center.
Hours & Admission Prices: Mon.-Fri. 9-4, Sat. special events. Adults $5; discounts to ASTC & FAM members; members no charge. Closed New Year's Day; Thanksgiving; Christmas. &
Attendance: 52,000 (estimated)

TED WILLIAMS MUSEUM AND HITTERS HALL OF FAME, c/o Tropicana Field, One Tropicana Dr., Saint Petersburg, FL 33705-1703. Tel.: 888-326-7297.
E-mail: info@tedwilliamsmuseum.com
Web Site: www.tedwilliamsmuseum.com
Key Personnel: Exec. Dir., Dave McCarthy.
Institution Type/Description: Sports Museum.
Hours & Admission Prices: Two hours before all Rays home games through the 6th inning for game ticket purchasers.

Sanderson

OLUSTEE BATTLEFIELD HISTORIC STATE PARK, 5890 Battlefield Trail Rd., Sanderson, FL 32087. Tel.: 386-758-0400.
E-mail: olusteecso@yahoo.com
Web Site: www.battleofolustee.org
Key Personnel: Park Mgr., Benjamin Faure; Park Ranger, Francis J. Loughran.
Institution Type/Description: State Historic Site & Military Museum.
Hours & Admission Prices: Park: Daily: 8-5. Visitor Center: daily 9-5. No charge; donations accepted; (except for special events). Closed Thanksgiving; Christmas. &

Sanford

CENTRAL FLORIDA ZOO & BOTANICAL GARDENS, 3755 W. Seminole Blvd., Sanford, FL 32771. Mailing Address: P.O. Box 470309, Lake Monroe, FL 32747-0309. Tel.: 407-323-4450, ext. 100. Fax: 407-321-0900.
E-mail: information@centralfloridazoo.org
Web Site: www.centralfloridazoo.org
Key Personnel: Pres. & C.E.O., Dr. Philip Flynn, III; Chm. (V), Charles Davis; C.F.O., Chuck Grimes; Vice Pres. Education, Stephanie Williams; Vice Pres. Operations, David Tetzlaff.
Institution Type/Description: Zoo.
Hours & Admission Prices: Daily 9-5. Adults $19.50, seniors $15.95, children 3-12 $13.75; discounts to groups, military & AAA members; children 2 & under and members no charge. Closed Thanksgiving; Christmas. &
Attendance: 308,000 (actual)

MUSEUM OF SEMINOLE COUNTY HISTORY, 300 Bush Blvd., Sanford, FL 32773-6135. Tel.: 407-665-2489. Fax: 407-665-5220. Facebook.
E-mail: blloyd@seminolecountyfl.gov
Web Site: www.seminolecountyfl.gov/museum
Key Personnel: Museum Coord., Bennett Lloyd.
Institution Type/Description: History Museum.
Hours & Admission Prices: Tues.-Fri. 1-5, Sat. 9-1. Adults $3, children 4-18 $1; children under 4 no charge. Closed New Year's Day; Martin Luther King Jr. Day; Memorial Day; Independence Day; Labor Day; Veterans Day; Thanksgiving & day after; Christmas. &
Attendance: 3,000 (actual)

SANFORD MUSEUM, 520 E. First St., Sanford, FL 32771-1410. Mailing Address: P.O. Box 1788, Sanford, FL 32772-1788. Tel.: 407-688-5198. Fax: 407-688-5125.
E-mail: sanfordmuseum@sanfordfl.gov
Web Site: www.sanfordfl.gov
Formerly: Henry Shelton Sanford Memorial Library & Museum
Key Personnel: Cur., Alicia Clarke.
Institution Type/Description: Museum, Research Library & Archives.
Hours & Admission Prices: Tues.-Fri. 11-4, Sat. 1-4; other times by appointment; No charge; donations accepted. Closed federal holidays; day after Thanksgiving. &
Attendance: 3,000 (estimated)

Sanibel

THE BAILEY-MATTHEWS NATIONAL SHELL MUSEUM,
3075 Sanibel-Captiva Rd., Sanibel, FL 33957-3111. Mailing
Address: P.O. Box 1580, Sanibel, FL 33957-1580. Tel.: 239-395-
2233, 888-679-6450 (toll free). Fax: 239-395-6706.
E-mail: dhipschman@shellmuseum.org
Web Site: www.shellmuseum.org
Key Personnel: Dir., Dorrie Hipschman; Cur., Jose H. Leal, Ph.D.; Museum Store
Mgr., Gretchen Falk.
Institution Type/Description: Natural History Museum.
Hours & Admission Prices: Daily 10-5. Adults $18, youth 12-17 $9, children 5-11
$7; discounts to AAM members; children under 5, active military & members no
charge. Closed major holidays. &
Attendance: 60,000 (actual)

SANIBEL-CAPTIVA CONSERVATION FOUNDATION, INC.,
3333 Sanibel-Captiva Rd., Sanibel, FL 33957-3100. Mailing
Address: P.O. Box 839, Sanibel, FL 33957-0839. Tel.: 239-472-
2329. Fax: 239-472-6421.
E-mail: sccf@sccf.org
Web Site: www.sccf.org
Key Personnel: C.E.O., A. Erick Lindblad; Mgr. Native Plant Nursery, Jenny
Evans; Dir. Marine Lab, Dr. Eric Milbrandt.
Institution Type/Description: Land Trust; Nature Center.
Hours & Admission Prices: June-Sept. Mon.-Fri. 8:30-3; May-Oct. Mon.-Fri. 8:30-
4; Dec.-April Mon.-Fri. 8:30-4, Sat. 10-3. Native Plant Nursery: May-Nov.
Mon.-Fri. 8:30-5; Dec.-April Mon.-Fri. 8:30-5, Sat. 10-3. Adults $3; members &
children under 17 no charge. Closed New Year's Day; Memorial Day;
Independence Day; Labor Day; Thanksgiving; Christmas. &
Attendance: 15,000 (estimated)

Sarasota

ART CENTER SARASOTA, INC, 707 N. Tamiami Tr., Sarasota,
FL 34236-4050. Tel.: 941-365-2032. Fax: 941-366-0585.
E-mail: artsarasota@aol.com
Web Site: www.artsarasota.org
Formerly: Sarasota Visual Arts Center
Key Personnel: Exec. Dir., Lisa Berger.
Institution Type/Description: Art Gallery.
Hours & Admission Prices: Mon.-Sat. 10-4. Suggested Donation: adults $3. Closed
on all major holidays. &
Attendance: 15,000 (estimated)

**BIDWELL-WOOD HOUSE - HISTORICAL SOCIETY OF
SARASOTA COUNTY,** 1260 12th St., Sarasota, FL 34236.
Mailing Address: P.O. Box 1632, Sarasota, 34234. Tel.: 941-264-
9076.
E-mail: hsosc1@gmail.com
Web Site: www.hsosc.org
Institution Type/Description: Historical Society Museum: built in 1882.
Hours & Admission Prices: Call for hours. No charge; donations accepted.

CROWLEY MUSEUM & NATURE CENTER, 16405 Myakka
Rd., Sarasota, FL 34240-9192. Tel.: 941-322-1000. Fax: 941-322-
1000. Facebook: @Crowleyfl.
E-mail: info@crowleyfl.org
Web Site: www.crowleyfl.org
Key Personnel: Pres., Dixie Resnick; Vice Pres., Dean Crolwey; Treas., Philip Nye;
Sec., Ruby Jo Brew; Groundskeeper, Jeff Scarborough.
Institution Type/Description: History Museum, Historic Building & Nature Center.
Hours & Admission Prices: June-Sept. Sat.-Sun. 10-5; Oct.-May Thurs.-Sun., 10-5.
Adults $5, children 3-12 $2; members & active military no charge. Closed New
Year's Day; Independence Day; Thanksgiving; Christmas. &
Attendance: 8,500 (estimated)

JOHN AND MABLE RINGLING MUSEUM OF ART, 5401 Bay
Shore Rd., Sarasota, FL 34243-2161. Tel.: 941-359-5700. Fax:
941-359-7704. TDD: 941-359-5700.
E-mail: info@ringling.org
Web Site: www.ringling.org
Key Personnel: Exec. Dir., Steven High.
Institution Type/Description: Art Museum & Estate.
Hours & Admission Prices: Thurs. 10-8, Fri.-Wed. 10-5. Adults $25, seniors 65 &
over $23, college students & children 6-17 $5; discounts to groups, teachers,
military & AAM members; members and children 5 & under no charge. Closed
New Year's Day; Thanksgiving; Christmas. &
Attendance: 360,000 (estimated)

MARIE SELBY BOTANICAL GARDENS, INC., 811 S. Palm
Ave., Sarasota, FL 34236-7995. Tel.: 941-366-5731. Fax: 941-366-
9807.
E-mail: marketing@selby.org
Web Site: www.selby.org
Key Personnel: Pres. & C.E.O., Jennifer O. Rominiecki; Dir. Mktg., Mischa Kirby,
APR; Museum Shop Mgr., John McAllister.
Institution Type/Description: Arboretum & Botanical Garden: original building &
gardens of Marie & William Selby.
Hours & Admission Prices: Daily 10-5. Adults $20, children 4-17 $10; children 3 &
under and members no charge. Closed Christmas. &
Attendance: 200,000 (actual)

MARIETTA MUSEUM OF ART & WHIMSY, 2121 N. Tamiami
Tr., Sarasota, FL 34234. Tel.: 941-364-3399.
E-mail: info@whimsymuseum.org
Web Site: www.whimsymuseum.org
Key Personnel: Dir. & Cur., Marietta Lee.
Institution Type/Description: Art Museum.
Hours & Admission Prices: Oct. 30-May 28 Thurs.-Sat. 1-4. Closed major holidays.
&
Attendance: 14,000 (actual)

MOTE MARINE LABORATORY/AQUARIUM, 1600 Ken
Thompson Pkwy., Sarasota, FL 34236-1096. Tel.: 941-388-4441,
ext. 332. Fax: 941-388-4312. Facebook.
E-mail: info@mote.org
Web Site: www.mote.org
Formerly: Cape Haze Marine Laboratory
Key Personnel: Pres. & C.E.O., Dr. Michael P. Crosby.
Institution Type/Description: Marine Laboratory Museum.
Hours & Admission Prices: Daily 10-5. Adults $22, children 3-12 $16; children 2 &
under and members no charge. &
Attendance: 352,000 (actual)

**RINGLING COLLEGE OF ART AND DESIGN, GALLERIES
AND EXHIBITIONS,** 2700 N. Tamiami Trail, Sarasota, FL
34234-5895. Tel.: 941-359-7563. Fax: 941-309-1969.
E-mail: selby@ringling.edu
Web Site: www.ringling.edu/selbygallery
Formerly: Selby Gallery
Key Personnel: Interim Dir., Laura Avery; Interim Asst. Dir., Tim Jaeger; Cur.,
Mark Ormond.
Institution Type/Description: Art Museum.
Hours & Admission Prices: Mon. & Wed.-Sat. 10-4, Tues. 10-7. No charge; dona-
tions accepted. Closed school holidays. &
Attendance: 28,000 (actual)

SARASOTA CLASSIC CAR MUSEUM, 5500 N. Tamiami Trail,
Sarasota, FL 34243-2199. Tel.: 941-355-6228.
E-mail: info@sarasotacarmuseum.org
Web Site: www.sarasotacarmuseum.org
Key Personnel: Pres., Martin Godbey.
Institution Type/Description: Classic Car Museum.
Hours & Admission Prices: Daily 9-6. Adults 13-61 $9.85, seniors 62 & over $8.50,
children 6-12 $6.50; discounts to groups; children 5 & under no charge. Annual
Passes: adults $20, senior citizens $18, children $14, college students $12.
Closed Christmas. &
Attendance: 42,000 (estimated)

THE TURNER MUSEUM, 930 N. Tamiami Trail, Sarasota, FL
34236-4070. Tel.: 941-365-1649. Fax: 941-343-8320.
E-mail: turnermuseum@gmail.com
Web Site: jmwturnermuseum.org
Formerly: J.M.W. Turner Museum, Inc.
Key Personnel: Dir., Isis Marina Graham; Trustee Turner Museum Endowment
Fund, Douglass Montrose-Graem; Treas., Michael R. Pender, Jr., CPA;
Webmaster, Ben Gallaher; Fulfillment, Rachel Gallaher.
Institution Type/Description: Art Center.
Hours & Admission Prices: Temporarily closed for relocation. &
Attendance: 100,000 (estimated)

Sebring

CHILDREN'S MUSEUM OF THE HIGHLANDS, 219 N.
Ridgewood Dr., Sebring, FL 33870-7204. Mailing Address: P.O.
Box 1243, Sebring, FL 33871-1243. Tel.: 863-385-5437.
E-mail: cheryl@childrensmuseumhighlands.com
Web Site: www.childrensmuseumhighlands.com
Key Personnel: Dir., Cheryl Matthews.

Institution Type/Description: Children's Museum.
Hours & Admission Prices: Closed for renovations.
Attendance: 20,000 (estimated)

HIGHLANDS ART LEAGUE, 351 W. Center Ave., Sebring, FL 33870-7931. Mailing Address: 1989 Lakeview Dr., Sebring, FL 33870-7931. Tel.: 863-385-6682. Fax: 863-385-6611.
E-mail: manager@highlandsartleague.org
Web Site: www.highlandsartleague.org
Formerly: Highlands Museum Of The Arts
Key Personnel: Cur., Ginger Adelsone.
Institution Type/Description: Art Museum: located in the Alan Altvater Civic Complex.
Hours & Admission Prices: Mon.-Fri. 10-4. No charge; donations accepted. Closed major holidays.
Attendance: 1,500 (estimated)

HIGHLANDS HAMMOCK STATE PARK/CIVILIAN CONSERVATION CORPS MUSEUM, 5931 Hammock Rd., Sebring, FL 33872-7408. Tel.: 863-386-6094. Fax: 863-386-6095.
E-mail: dorothy.l.harris@dep.state.fl.us
Web Site: www.floridastateparks.org
Key Personnel: Park Mgr., Steven Dale; Asst. Park Mgr., Brian Pinson.
Institution Type/Description: Park Museum: housed in 1930s building constructed of heavy native timbers, lumber cut & fabricated on site by the Civilian Conservation Corps.
Hours & Admission Prices: Daily 8am to sunset. Park entrance fee: $6 per vehicle (2-8 passengers), $4 per vehicle (1 passenger), pedestrians & bicycles $2. Call ranger station for tour bus rates. Entrance to museum is included in regular entrance fees. Museum hours: daily 9-4. Annual State Park Entrance Pass available. ♿
Attendance: 15,000 (estimated)

SEBRING HISTORICAL SOCIETY, 321 W. Center Ave., Sebring, FL 33870. Tel.: 863-471-2522.
E-mail: info@sebringhistoricalsociety.org
Web Site: www.sebringhistoricalsociety.org
Institution Type/Description: Historical Society Museum.
Hours & Admission Prices: Mon.-Thurs. 10-3.

St. Augustine

SPANISH MILITARY HOSPITAL MUSEUM, 3 Aviles St., St. Augustine, FL 32084. Tel.: 904-342-7730.
E-mail: info@smhmuseum.com
Web Site: spanishmilitaryhospitalmuseum.com
Institution Type/Description: Medical History Museum.
Hours & Admission Prices: Daily 9-5; groups by appointment. Closed Christmas.

Stuart

FLORIDA OCEANOGRAPHIC COASTAL CENTER, 890 N.E. Ocean Blvd., Hutchinson Island, Stuart, FL 34996-1627. Tel.: 772-225-0505.
E-mail: info@floridaocean.org
Web Site: www.floridaocean.org
Formerly: Coastal Science Center at Hutchinson Island
Key Personnel: Exec. Dir., Mark Perry.
Institution Type/Description: Maritime Museum.
Hours & Admission Prices: Mon.-Sat. 10-5, Sun. 12-4. Adults $12, children 3-12 $6; discounts to active military; children under 3 & members no charge. Closed New Year's Day; Easter; Thanksgiving; Christmas. ♿
Attendance: 50,000 (estimated)

HOUSE OF REFUGE MUSEUM, 301 S.E. MacArthur Blvd., Stuart, FL 34996. Tel.: 772-225-1875. Fax: 772-225-2333.
Web Site: www.houseofrefugefl.org
Formerly: Gilbert's Bar House of Refuge
Key Personnel: Pres. & C.E.O., Jennifer Esler; Dir. Finance, Amy Martin.
Institution Type/Description: Historic House Museum: four room furnished house representing the period 1890-1904. National Register of Historic Places.
Hours & Admission Prices: Mon.-Sat. 10-4, Sun. 1-4. Adults $8, seniors $6, children 2-12 $3; children under 5 no charge. Closed major holidays. ♿
Attendance: 17,000

STUART HERITAGE MUSEUM, 161 S.W. Flagler Ave., Stuart, FL 34994-2139. Tel.: 772-220-4600. Fax: 772-781-3716.
E-mail: stuartheritage1@yahoo.com
Key Personnel: Exec. Dir., Mary Walton Jones; Mgr., Betty Hardwick.
Institution Type/Description: Local County History Museum: built in 1901.

Hours & Admission Prices: Daily 10-3. No charge; donations accepted. Closed New Year's Day; Thanksgiving; Christmas. ♿
Attendance: 4,995 (actual)

Tallahassee

ALFRED B. MACLAY GARDENS STATE PARK, 3540 Thomasville Rd., Tallahassee, FL 32309-3413. Tel.: 850-487-4556 & 4115. Fax: 850-487-8808.
E-mail: ginger.nichols@dep.state.fl.us
Web Site: www.floridastateparks.org/maclay
Key Personnel: Park Mgr., Sasha Craft.
Institution Type/Description: Historic House Museum & Gardens: c.1909 Maclay House.
Hours & Admission Prices: Maclay House & Gardens: daily 9-5. Park: 8am to sundown. House & Gardens: Jan.-April adults $6, children under 12 $3. Park & Gardens: May-Dec. $6 per car (8 people); park fee includes gardens; bicyclers, walkers, extra persons in vehicle $2 per person; members 1st Sat. of each month no charge. ♿
Attendance: 159,000 (actual)

CHALLENGER LEARNING CENTER, 200 S. Duval St., Tallahassee, FL 32301. Tel.: 850-645-7796. Fax: 850-645-7784.
Institution Type/Description: Science Center.
Hours & Admission Prices: Call for hours & admission prices.

FLORIDA ASSOCIATION OF MUSEUMS, 459 Cedar Hill Rd., Tallahassee, FL 32312-1046. Mailing Address: P.O. Box 10951, Tallahassee, FL 32302-2951. Tel.: 850-222-6028. Fax: 850-222-6112.
E-mail: fam@flamuseums.org
Web Site: www.flamuseums.org
Key Personnel: Exec. Dir., Malinda Horton.
Institution Type/Description: State Museum Association.
Hours & Admission Prices: Call for hours.

FLORIDA STATE UNIVERSITY MUSEUM OF FINE ARTS, 530 W. Call St., 250 Fine Arts Bldg., Tallahassee, FL 32306-1140. Mailing Address: P.O. Box 3061140, Tallahassee, FL 32306-1140. Tel.: 850-644-6836. Fax: 850-644-7229.
E-mail: pmclane@fsu.edu
Web Site: www.mofa.fsu.edu
Key Personnel: Dir., Preston McLane.
Institution Type/Description: Art Museum.
Hours & Admission Prices: May-Aug. Mon.-Fri. 9-4; Sept.-April Mon.-Fri. 9-4, Sat.-Sun. 1-4. No charge; donations accepted. Closed university holidays. ♿
Attendance: 33,780 (actual)

FLORIDA'S HISTORIC CAPITOL MUSEUM, 400 S. Monroe St., Tallahassee, FL 32399-6536. Mailing Address: Room B-06, Development Office, 400 S. Monroe St., Tallahassee, FL 32399-1100. Tel.: 850-487-1902. Fax: 850-410-2233.
E-mail: info@flhistoriccapitol.gov
Web Site: www.flhistoriccapitol.gov
Key Personnel: Museum Coord., Tiffany Baker.
Institution Type/Description: History Museum.
Hours & Admission Prices: Mon.-Fri. 9-4:30, Sat. 10-4:30, Sun. & holidays 12-4:30. No charge; donations accepted. Closed Thanksgiving; Christmas.

FOSTER-TANNER FINE ARTS GALLERY, Florida A&M University, Foster Tanner Arts Bldg., 1630 Pinder Dr., Tallahassee, FL 32307. Mailing Address: Dept. of Visual Arts, Humanities & Theatre, 515 Orr Dr., Tucker Hall 208, Tallahassee, FL 32307. Tel.: 850-599-8755. Fax: 850-599-8417.
E-mail: fostertannergallery@famu.edu
Web Site: www.famu.edu
Key Personnel: Dir. & Gallery Coord., Aja Roache.
Institution Type/Description: Art Museum.
Hours & Admission Prices: Jan. 3-Dec. 13 Mon.-Fri. 11-5. No charge; donations accepted.

GOODWOOD MUSEUM AND GARDENS, 1600 Miccosukee Rd., Tallahassee, FL 32308-5166. Tel.: 850-877-4202. Fax: 850-877-3090. Facebook.
E-mail: goodwood@goodwoodmuseum.org
Web Site: www.goodwoodmuseum.org
Key Personnel: Co Exec. Dir., Jennifer Humayon; Co Exec. Dir., Nancy Morgan; Chm. (V), Rose Rodriguez.

Institution Type/Description: Historic House: built c.1840.

Hours & Admission Prices: House: Mon.-Fri. 10, 11:30, 1 & 2:30, Sat. 10, 11:30, 1; groups by appointment. Adults $12, seniors, students & active military $10, children 6-12 $6; discounts to groups of 10 or more; NARM members no charge. Gardens: Mon.-Fri. 9-5, Sat. 10-2. Gardens: no charge. Closed New Year's Eve & Day; Memorial Day; Labor Day; Thanksgiving; Christmas Eve & Day. &

Attendance: 35,000 (estimated)

KNOTT HOUSE MUSEUM, 301 E. Park Ave., Tallahassee, FL 32301-1513. Tel.: 850-922-2459 & 245-6400. Fax: 850-413-7261. Facebook: @museumoffloridahistory.

E-mail: beatrice.cotellis@dos.myflorida.com

Web Site: www.museumoffloridahistory.com/knotthouse

Key Personnel: Site Mgr., Beatrice Cotellis; Educator, Brianna Simmons; Educator, Lydia Nabors.

Institution Type/Description: History Museum: housed in 1843 colonial revival house.

Hours & Admission Prices: Sept.-July Tours: Wed.-Fri. 1, 2 & 3, Sat. on the hour from 10-3. No charge; donations accepted. Group Tours: $1 per person. Closed Thanksgiving; Christmas. &

Attendance: 5,000 (estimated)

LAKE JACKSON MOUNDS ARCHAEOLOGICAL STATE PARK, 3600 Indian Mounds Rd., Tallahassee, FL 32303-2300. Tel.: 850-922-6007. Fax: 850-488-0366.

E-mail: rob.lacy@dep.state.fl.us

Web Site: www.floridastateparks.org

Key Personnel: Park Mgr., Rob Lacy; Administrative Asst., Leeanne Chandler.

Institution Type/Description: Archaeological Site: 1200-1500 ceremonial center of the Fort Walton period.

Hours & Admission Prices: Daily 8-sunset. Cars: $3; pedestrians & bikers $2; donations accepted. &

Attendance: 16,464 (estimated)

LEMOYNE CENTER FOR THE VISUAL ARTS, 125 N. Gadsden St., Tallahassee, FL 32301-1507. Tel.: 850-222-8800. Fax: 850-224-2714.

E-mail: director@lemoyne.org

Web Site: www.lemoyne.org

Formerly: LeMoyne Art Foundation, Inc.

Key Personnel: Exec. Dir., Hillary Brett; Pres. (V), Kelly Dozier; Vice Pres., Eva B. Armstrong; Volunteer Coord. & Museum Shop Mgr., Betty Bayes Lessinger; Dir. Education, Anna Myers; Education Coord., Amanda Wilke; Education Coord., Jennifer Infinger; Cur., Lesley Marchessault; Events Coord., Sheri Sanderson.

Institution Type/Description: Art Center: housed in 1852 wooden structure used as hospital during Civil War.

Hours & Admission Prices: Tues.-Sat. 10-5. Adults $2; discounts to AAM & ICOM members; students & members no charge. Fees charged only for special exhibits. Closed major holidays. &

Attendance: 115,000 (estimated)

MEEK-EATON BLACK ARCHIVES RESEARCH CENTER & MUSEUM, 445 Gamble St., Florida A&M Univ., Tallahassee, FL 32307. Tel.: 850-599-3020. Fax: 850-561-2604.

E-mail: blackarchives@famu.edu

Web Site: www.famu.edu/blackarchives

Formerly: Southeastern Regional Black Archives Research Center and Museum

Key Personnel: Dir., Nashid Madyun, D.M.

Institution Type/Description: History Museum: housed in the Carnegie Library; built in 1907. Listed on the National Register of Historic Places.

Hours & Admission Prices: Mon.-Fri. 10-5, Sat. 12-4. No charge. &

Attendance: 150,000 (estimated)

MISSION SAN LUIS, 2100 W. Tennessee St., Tallahassee, FL 32304-3119. Tel.: 850-245-6406. Fax: 850-488-6186. Facebook: Mission San Luis.

E-mail: info@missionsanluis.org

Web Site: www.missionsanluis.org

Key Personnel: Chm. (V), Hon. Curt Kiser; Museum Shop Mgr., Janelle Willingham.

Institution Type/Description: History Museum.

Hours & Admission Prices: Tues.-Sun. 10-4. Adults $5, seniors 65 & over $3, children 6-17 $2; discounts to AAM & ICOM members; children under six, active military & members no charge. Closed New Year's Day; Easter; Independence Day; Thanksgiving; Christmas Eve & Day. &

Attendance: 57,706 (actual)

MUSEUM OF FLORIDA HISTORY, 500 S. Bronough St., Tallahassee, FL 32399-0250. Tel.: 850-245-6400. Fax: 850-245-6433. Facebook.

E-mail: lisa.barton@dos.myflorida.com

Web Site: www.museumoffloridahistory.com

Key Personnel: Bur. Chief, Lisa Barton; Cur. Educ. & Pub. Engagement, Trampas Alderman; Cur. Research & Collections, Lea Ellen Thornton; Cur. Design & Fabrication, Drew Ericson; Devel. & Finance, Thomas Robinson; Museum Shop Mgr., Kaitlin Silcox.

Institution Type/Description: History Museum.

Hours & Admission Prices: Mon.-Fri. 9-4:30, Sat. 10-4:30, Sun. & holidays 12-4:30. No charge; donations accepted. Closed Thanksgiving; Christmas. &

Attendance: 55,668 (actual)

RILEY HOUSE MUSEUM OF AFRICAN AMERICAN HISTORY & CULTURE, 419 E. Jefferson St., Tallahassee, FL 32301-1817. Tel.: 850-681-7881. Fax: 850-386-4368.

E-mail: staff@rileymuseum.org

Web Site: www.rileymuseum.org; www.faahph.org

Key Personnel: Chair, Annie S. Harris; Program Coord., Catiana Foster; Dir. Education, Paige Lee.

Institution Type/Description: Historic House Museum: housed in home of John Gilmore Riley, first African American principal of Lincoln High School in Tallahassee, Florida; built in 1890.

Hours & Admission Prices: Jan. 3-Dec. 21 Mon.-Thurs. 10-4, Fri.-Sat. 10-2; groups by appointment. Adults $2, members $1.50. Closed New Year's Day; Martin Luther King, Jr. Day; Easter weekend; Memorial Day; Independence Day; Veterans Day; Thanksgiving & day before. &

Attendance: 8,002 (actual)

TALLAHASSEE AUTOMOBILE MUSEUM, 6800 Mahan Dr., Tallahassee, FL 32308-1402. Mailing Address: P.O. Box 120, Hosford, FL 32334-0120. Tel.: 850-942-0137. Fax: 850-576-8500.

E-mail: cars@tacm.com

Web Site: www.tacm.com

Formerly: Antique Car Museum

Institution Type/Description: Automobile & Collectibles Museum.

Hours & Admission Prices: Mon.-Fri. 8-5, Sat. 10-5, Sun. 12-5; Thanksgiving & Christmas by appointment. Adults $16, 2 adults $13.50, students $10.75, children 5-9 $7.50; discounts to groups. Train Museum: $6 per person. &

Attendance: 7,509 (actual)

TALLAHASSEE MUSEUM, 3945 Museum Dr., Tallahassee, FL 32310-6325. Tel.: 850-575-8684. Fax: 850-574-8243.

E-mail: rdaws@tallahasseemuseum.org

Web Site: www.tallahasseemuseum.org

Formerly: Tallahassee Museum of History and Natural Science

Key Personnel: C.E.O. & Pres., Russell S. Daws; Chmn. (V), Michael Carter; Vice Pres. & C.O.O., Rebekka Wade; Dir. Education, Natasha Hartsfield; Chief Cur., Linda Deaton; Cur. Animals, Mike Jones; Facilities Mgr., Mike Sullivan; Museum Shop Mgr., Chris Lindsay.

Institution Type/Description: General Museum.

Hours & Admission Prices: Mon.-Sat. 9-5, Sun. 11-5. Adults $11.50, seniors & college students $11, children 4-15 $8.50; discounts to groups and AAM & FAM members; members and children 3 & under no charge. Closed New Year's Day; Thanksgiving; Christmas Eve & Day. &

Attendance: 155,000 (actual)

Tampa

AMERICAN VICTORY MARINERS MEMORIAL & MUSEUM SHIP, 705 Channelside Dr., Tampa, FL 33602-5600. Tel.: 813-228-8766.

E-mail: marketing@americanvictory.org

Web Site: www.americanvictory.org

Key Personnel: Pres., Bill Kuzmick; Dir. Mktg. & Public Rels., Cindy Dion.

Institution Type/Description: Maritime History Museum: housed on a 1940s-era merchant cargo ship.

Hours & Admission Prices: Sun.-Mon. 12-5; Tues.-Sat. 10-5, Sun. 12-5. Adults $10, veterans & seniors 65 & over $8, children 4-12 $5; children 3 & under no charge.

Attendance: 60,000 (estimated)

BIG CAT RESCUE, 12802 Easy St., Tampa, FL 33625-3702. Tel.: 813-920-4130. Fax: 866-571-4523.

E-mail: info@bigcatrescue.org

Web Site: www.bigcatrescue.org

Institution Type/Description: Wildlife Refuge.

Hours & Admission Prices: By appointment.

CRACKER COUNTRY, 4800 N. Hwy. 301, Tampa, FL 33680. Mailing Address: P.O. Box 11766, Tampa, FL 33680-1766. Tel.: 813-627-4225. Fax: 813-740-3518. Facebook.
E-mail: cindy.horton@floridastatefair.com
Web Site: www.crackercountry.org
Key Personnel: Museum Dir., Cindy Horton; Museum Programs Mgr., Jennifer Wanecski; Facilities Maintenance Cur., Ron Tarlton; Cultural Commerce Supvr., Linda Mahoney.
Institution Type/Description: Historic Village & Museum: 12 turn-of-the-century buildings, 1870-1912, located on the Florida State Fairgrounds in a section known as Cracker Country.
Hours & Admission Prices: Grade School Tours: March-May & Sept.-Dec. Tues.-Fri. $7 per student. General admission: adults $7, seniors & children 6-12 $6, children 5 & under no charge. &
Attendance: 200,000 (estimated)

FLORIDA AQUARIUM, 701 Channelside Dr., Tampa, FL 33602-5614. Tel.: 813-273-4000.
E-mail: moreinfo@flaquarium.com
Web Site: www.flaquarium.org
Institution Type/Description: Aquarium.
Hours & Admission Prices: Daily 9:30-5. Adults $21.95, seniors 60 & over $18.95, children under 12 $16.95; children 2 & under no charge. Closed Thanksgiving; Christmas.

FLORIDA MUSEUM OF PHOTOGRAPHIC ARTS, 400 N. Ashley Dr., C200, Tampa, FL 33602. Tel.: 813-221-2222.
E-mail: info@fmopa.org
Web Site: www.fmopa.org
Formerly: Tampa Gallery of Photographic Art
Key Personnel: Exec. Dir., Zora Carrier; Exhibitions & Development Mgr., Anna Castellano; Mgr. Education & Outreach, Kassandra Collett; Mgr. Communications & Devel., Caitlyn Boza.
Institution Type/Description: Art Museum.
Hours & Admission Prices: Mon.-Thurs. 11-6, Fri. 11-7, Sat.-Sun. 12-5. Adults $10, students, military & seniors $8; discounts to NARM & Southeastern Reciprocal members; members no charge. Closed New Year's Day; Independence Day; Thanksgiving; Christmas. &
Attendance: 10,000 (estimated)

GLAZER CHILDREN'S MUSEUM, 110 W. Gasparilla Plaza, Tampa, FL 33602. Tel.: 813-443-3861. Fax: 813-443-3841. Facebook: Glazer Children's Museum.
E-mail: info@glazermuseum.org
Web Site: www.glazermuseum.org
Key Personnel: Pres. & C.E.O., Jennifer Stancil; Chief Operating Officer, Kristen Nieves.
Institution Type/Description: Children's Museum.
Hours & Admission Prices: Mon.-Fri. 10-5, Sat. 10-6, Sun. 1-6. Adults $15, military & seniors $12.50, children $9.50; children under one no charge. Closed New Year's Day; Easter; Thanksgiving; Christmas. &

HENRY B. PLANT MUSEUM, 401 W. Kennedy Blvd., Tampa, FL 33606-1450. Tel.: 813-258-7301. Fax: 813-258-7272.
E-mail: czinober@ut.edu
Web Site: www.plantmuseum.com
Key Personnel: Exec. Dir., Cynthia Gandee Zinober; Pres. (V), Ronald E. Walker; Cur. Education, Heather Trubee; Cur. & Registrar, Susan Carter; Operations & Membership, Scott Waltz; Museum Store Mgr., Dale Guenther; Museum Rels., Lindsay Huban; Curatorial Asst., Nora Armstrong.
Institution Type/Description: History & Decorative Arts Museum: housed in 1891 Tampa Bay Hotel.
Hours & Admission Prices: Tues.-Sat. 10-5, Sun. 12-5. Adults $10; discounts to SE museums; members no charge. Closed Thanksgiving; Christmas. &
Attendance: 55,000 (estimated)

MOSI (MUSEUM OF SCIENCE & INDUSTRY), 4801 E. Fowler Ave., Tampa, FL 33617-2099. Tel.: 813-987-6000. Fax: 813-987-6310. Facebook & Twitter: @mositampa.
E-mail: megan.haskins@mosi.org
Web Site: www.mosi.org
Formerly: Museum of Science & Industry
Key Personnel: Chm. (V), Mike Schultz; C.O.O., Vicki Ahrens; Vice Pres. Museum Operations, Anthonette Carregal; Vice Pres. Facilities, Donald D. Toeller; Dir. Devel., Jeff Hoberg; Dir. Grants & Research, Mary Dillon; Dir. Mktg., Amy Groves; Vice Pres. Human Resources, Kelly Currington; Volunteer Mgr., Danny Lott; Communications Dir., Grayson Kamm; Museum Shop Mgr., David Bowes.
Institution Type/Description: Science, Industry & Technology Center.

Hours & Admission Prices: Closed for renovations until Nov. 2017. Adults $26.95, seniors 60 & over $25.95, children 3-12 $20.95; discounts for ACM members; members, ASTC members and children 2 & under no charge. &
Attendance: 596,485 (actual)

SCARFONE/HARTLEY GALLERY, 310 N. Blvd., Tampa, FL 33606-1403. Mailing Address: 401 W. Kennedy, Tampa, FL 33606-1450. Tel.: 813-253-6217. Fax: 813-258-7497.
E-mail: dcowden@ut.edu
Web Site: www.ut.edu
Key Personnel: Dir., Jocelyn Boigenzahn.
Institution Type/Description: Fine Arts Gallery.
Hours & Admission Prices: Aug.-May Tues.-Fri. 10-4, Sat. 1-4. No charge; donations accepted. Closed national holidays. &
Attendance: 12,000 (estimated)

TAMPA BAY HISTORY CENTER, INC., 801 Old Water St., Tampa, FL 33602-5418. Tel.: 813-228-0097. Fax: 813-223-7021.
E-mail: info@tampabayhistorycenter.org
Web Site: www.tampabayhistorycenter.org
Key Personnel: Chm., R. James Robbins, Jr.; Pres. & C.E.O., C.J. Roberts; Dir. Devel., Lisa Richardson; Cur., Rodney Kite Powell; Cur. Education, Nancy Dalence; Dir. Mktg., Manny Leto; Mgr. Collections, Malerie Dorman; Dir. Financial Operations, Maria Steijlen; Mgr. Admin. Svcs., Judy Miller; Museum Shop & Visitor Svcs. Supvr., Jennifer Wilhelm; Assoc. Dir. Advancement, Andrea Gallagher Nalls.
Institution Type/Description: History Museum.
Hours & Admission Prices: Daily 10-5. Adults $12.95; discounts to FAM & ICOM members; AAM members & members no charge. Closed Thanksgiving; Christmas. &
Attendance: 85,000 (estimated)

TAMPA FIREFIGHTERS MUSEUM, 720 E. Zack St., Tampa, FL 33602. Tel.: 813-964-6862.
E-mail: tampafiremuseum@gmail.com
Institution Type/Description: Firefighting History Museum: housed in the former fire headquarters of the Tampa Fire Department; built in 1911.
Hours & Admission Prices: Tues.-Sun. 10-2. &

TAMPA MUSEUM OF ART, 120 W. Gasparilla Plaza, Tampa, FL 33602. Tel.: 813-274-8130. Fax: 813-274-8732.
E-mail: michael.tomor@tampamuseum.org
Web Site: tampamuseum.org
Key Personnel: Chm. (V), Debra Williams; Exec. Dir., Michael Tomor, Ph.D.; Assoc. Dir. Devel., Julia Gorzka Freeman; Dir. Finance, Jesus G. Romo; Chief Cur. & Richard E. Perry Cur. of Greek & Roman Art, Seth D. Pevnick; Exhibitions & Collections Mgr., Amanda Seadler; Museum Store Mgr., Sue Gauthier; Public Rels. Specialist, Nancy Seijas-Kipnis.
Institution Type/Description: Art Museum.
Hours & Admission Prices: Mon.-Thurs. 11-7, Fri. 11-8, Sat.-Sun. 11-5. Adults $15, seniors & active military $7.50; students $5; children 6 & under & members no charge. Closed Thanksgiving & Christmas Day. &
Attendance: 85,000 (estimated)

UNIVERSITY OF SOUTH FLORIDA BOTANICAL GARDEN, 4202 E. Fowler Ave., NES 107, Tampa, FL 33620-9951. Tel.: 813-974-2329. Fax: 813-974-4808. Facebook.
E-mail: lwalker@usf.edu
Web Site: gardens.usf.edu
Key Personnel: Dir., Laurie Walker; Coord. Special Events, Kim Hutton; Sr. Groundskeeper, Kevin Slaughter.
Institution Type/Description: Botanical Garden.
Hours & Admission Prices: Mon.-Fri. 9-5, Sat. 9-4, Sun. 12-4. Adults $5, seniors 60 & over $4, youth 6-13 $3, students $1; USFBG members, American Horticulture Society Reciprocal Program members, & children under 6 no charge. Closed major holidays.

UNIVERSITY OF SOUTH FLORIDA CONTEMPORARY ART MUSEUM, 3821 USF Holly Dr., Tampa, FL 33620. Mailing Address: 4202 E. Fowler Ave., CAM101, Tampa, FL 33620-7360. Tel.: 813-974-4133. Fax: 813-974-5130. Facebook: USFCAMfan.
E-mail: caminfo@arts.usf.edu
Web Site: www.usfcam.usf.edu/CAM/cam_about.html
Key Personnel: Dir., Margaret A. Miller; Deputy Dir., Noel Smith; Collections Cur., Peter Foe; Exhibitions Designer, Tony Palms; Chief Preparator, Vince Kral; New Media Cur., Don Michael Fuller; Cur. Latin American & Caribbean Art & Cur. Education, Noel Smith; Collection Asst., Eric Jonas; Cur. Art in Health, Delores Coe; Cur. Public Art & Social Practice, Sarah Howard; Exhibitions Mgr. & Registrar, Shannon Annis; Program Coord., Amy Allison; Security, David Waterman.

Institution Type/Description: Contemporary Art Museum.
Hours & Admission Prices: Museum: Mon.-Wed. & Fri. 10-5, Thurs. 10-8, , Sat. 1-4. No charge. Closed university holidays. &
Attendance: 58,000 (estimated)

YBOR CITY MUSEUM STATE PARK, 1818 Ninth Ave. E., Tampa, FL 33605-3818. Tel.: 813-247-6323. Fax: 813-233-3343.
E-mail: douglas.kinder@dep.state.fl.us
Web Site: www.ybormuseum.org
Formerly: Ybor City State Museum
Key Personnel: Pres. & C.E.O., Chantal Hevia.
Institution Type/Description: Industrial Museum: 1923 Bakery Building; original brick commercial ovens. Complex also contains c.1895 restored & furnished house, originally rented to workers.
Hours & Admission Prices: Wed.-Sun. 9-5. LaCasita: daily 10-3 depending on docent availability. Adults $4; children under 6 no charge. Closed New Year's Day; Thanksgiving; Christmas. &
Attendance: 29,714 (estimated)

ZOOTAMPA AT LOWRY PARK, 1101 W. Sligh Ave., Tampa, FL 33604-5958. Tel.: 813-935-8552. Fax: 813-935-9486.
E-mail: information@lowryparkzoo.org
Web Site: www.lowryparkzoo.org
Key Personnel: Chm., Bob Rasmussen; Exec. Dir. & C.E.O., Joseph Couceiro; Dir., Retail, Kim Gefre.
Institution Type/Description: Zoo.
Hours & Admission Prices: Daily 9:30-5. Adults $34.95, youth 3-1 $25.95; discounts to AZA member & groups; members no charge. Closed Thanksgiving; Christmas. &
Attendance: 848,798 (actual)

Tarpon Springs

LEEPA-RATTNER MUSEUM OF ART AT ST. PETERSBURG COLLEGE, 600 Klosterman Rd., Tarpon Springs, FL 34689-1299. Mailing Address: P.O. Box 1545, Tarpon Springs, FL 34688-1545. Tel.: 727-712-5762. Fax: 727-712-5223. Facebook.
E-mail: lrma@spcollege.edu
Web Site: www.spcollege.edu/museum
Key Personnel: Dir., Ann Larsen; Chm. Bd. Dirs., William Schumacher; Cur., Cristina McCormack.
Institution Type/Description: Art Museum.
Hours & Admission Prices: Tues.-Wed. & Sat. 10-5, Fri. 10-4, Thurs. 10-8, Sun. 1-5. Adults $6, seniors $4; Sun. admission by donation; children, students, members & military no charge. &
Attendance: 35,000 (actual)

SAFFORD HOUSE HISTORIC HOUSE MUSEUM, 23 Parkin Court, Tarpon Springs, FL 34689-3235. Tel.: 727-937-1130. Fax: 727-938-2429.
E-mail: tbucuvalas@ctsfl.us
Web Site: www.tarponarts.org/info_venues_safford.html
Key Personnel: Cur., Tina Bucuvalas.
Institution Type/Description: Historic House Museum: home of Anson P.K. Safford from 1883-1891.
Hours & Admission Prices: Wed. & Fri. 11-3. Adults $5; discounts to Florida Association of Museums; children under 18 no charge. Closed New Year's Day; Epiphany (Jan. 6); President's Day; Memorial Day; Independence Day; Labor Day; Veteran's Day; Thanksgiving & day after; Christmas Eve & Day. &
Attendance: 986 (actual)

TARPON SPRINGS AREA HISTORICAL SOCIETY - DEPOT MUSEUM, 160 E. Tarpon Ave., Tarpon Springs, FL 34689-3452. Tel.: 727-943-4624.
E-mail: tarpon.historical@verizon.net
Key Personnel: Depot Coord., Renee Sousa; Pres., Ed Hoffman, Ph.D.
Institution Type/Description: Historical Society Museum.
Hours & Admission Prices: Tues.-Sat. 11:30-4. No charge; donations accepted. Closed New Year's Day; Memorial Day; Independence Day; Thanksgiving; Christmas. &
Attendance: 4,670 (actual)

TARPON SPRINGS CULTURAL CENTER, 324 Pine St., Tarpon Springs, FL 34689-4004. Tel.: 727-942-5605. Fax: 727-938-2429.
E-mail: bpoteat1@ci.tarpon-springs.fl.us
Key Personnel: Dir., Diane Wood.
Institution Type/Description: Cultural Center: housed in a c.1915 city hall, national register listed building.

Hours & Admission Prices: Mon.-Fri. 9-4, Sat. 12-4. No charge; donations accepted. Closed New Year's Day; Independence Day; Veterans Day; Thanksgiving; Christmas. &
Attendance: 6,726 (actual)

TARPON SPRINGS HERITAGE MUSEUM, 100 Beekman Lane, Tarpon Springs, FL 34689-3555. Mailing Address: P.O. Box 5004, Tarpon Springs, FL 34688-5004. Tel.: 727-937-0686 & 0699. Fax: 727-937-0657.
E-mail: info@tarponarts.org
Web Site: www.tarponarts.org
Key Personnel: Dir., Diane Wood.
Institution Type/Description: History Museum.
Hours & Admission Prices: Mon.-Fri. 10-4. Adults $5; members & children no charge. Closed public holidays. &
Attendance: 2,377 (actual)

Tavares

LAKE COUNTY HISTORICAL SOCIETY AND MUSEUM, Lake County Historic Courthouse, 317 W. Main St., Tavares, FL 32778-3813. Mailing Address: P.O. Box 7800, Tavares, FL 32778-7800. Tel.: 352-343-9890. Fax: 352-343-9814.
E-mail: lakecounty1887@yahoo.com
Key Personnel: Dir., Cur. & Office Mgr., Lavonda Morris.
Institution Type/Description: County Museum.
Hours & Admission Prices: Mon.-Fri. 8:30-5. No charge. &
Attendance: 5,000 (estimated)

Tequesta

LIGHTHOUSE ARTCENTER, Gallery Square North, 373 Tequesta Dr., Tequesta, FL 33469-3027. Tel.: 561-746-3101.
E-mail: info@lighthousearts.org
Web Site: www.lighthousearts.org
Formerly: Lighthouse Center for the Arts
Key Personnel: C.E.O./C.F.O., Nancy Politsch; Cur., Janeen Mason.
Institution Type/Description: Art Gallery.
Hours & Admission Prices: Mon.-Fri. 10-4, Sat. 10-2. Adults $5; members no charge. &
Attendance: 50,000 (estimated)

Titusville

AMERICAN POLICE HALL OF FAME AND MUSEUM, 6350 Horizon Dr., Titusville, FL 32780-8002. Tel.: 321-264-0911. Fax: 321-264-0033.
E-mail: barrys@aphf.org
Web Site: aphf.org
Key Personnel: C.E.O., Barry Shepherd; C.F.O., Brent Shepherd; Pres. (V), Jack Rinchich; Museum Shop Mgr., Lori Shepherd.
Institution Type/Description: Police Museum.
Hours & Admission Prices: Daily 10-6. Adults $13, members $9, seniors, military, & children 4-12 $8, law enforcement $2; discounts to AAA members & military; family survivors no charge. Closed New Year's Day; Memorial Day; Independence Day; Labor Day; Thanksgiving; Christmas. &
Attendance: 50,000 (actual)

AMERICAN SPACE MUSEUM, 308 Pine St., Titusville, FL 32796. Tel.: 321-264-0434. Fax: 321-264-0767. Facebook: @SpaceWalkOfFame.
E-mail: info@americanspacemuseum.org
Web Site: www.americanspacemuseum.org
Formerly: U.S. Space Walk of Fame Museum
Key Personnel: Exec. Dir., Karan Conklin.
Institution Type/Description: Space History Museum.
Hours & Admission Prices: Mon.-Sat. 10-5. Adult, $10, senior & military $8, children 13 to 18 years $5, children 12 & under no charge.
Attendance: 6,000 (estimated)

NORTH BREVARD HISTORICAL MUSEUM, 301 S. Washington Ave., Titusville, FL 32796-3539. Mailing Address: P. O. Box 5265, Titusville, FL 32783-5265. Tel.: 321-269-3658.
E-mail: amattingly@cfl.rr.com
Web Site: www.nbbd.com/godo/history
Key Personnel: Pres. (V), Betty J. Mattingly.
Institution Type/Description: Historical Museum.
Hours & Admission Prices: Tues.-Sat. 10-3. No charge; donations accepted.
Attendance: 2,500 (estimated)

VALIANT AIR COMMAND WARBIRD AIR MUSEUM, 6600 Tico Rd., Titusville, FL 32780-8009. Tel.: 321-268-1941. Fax: 321-268-5969. Facebook.
E-mail: info@vacwarbirds.net
Web Site: www.valiantaircommand.com
Key Personnel: Commander, Lloyd Morris.
Institution Type/Description: Aviation History Museum.
Hours & Admission Prices: Daily 9-5. Adults $20, senior citizens & military $18, children 4-12 $5; discounts to groups. Closed New Year's Day; Thanksgiving; Christmas.
Attendance: 60,000 (estimated)

Valparaiso

HERITAGE MUSEUM OF NORTHWEST FLORIDA, 115 Westview Ave., Valparaiso, FL 32580-1387. Tel.: 850-678-2615. Fax: 850-678-4547. Facebook: Heritage Museum of Northwest Florida.
E-mail: info@heritage-museum.org
Web Site: heritage-museum.org
Key Personnel: Museum Mgr., Gina Marini; Ex Officio, Gordon King; Ex Officio, Steve Czonstke.
Institution Type/Description: History Museum.
Hours & Admission Prices: Tues.-Sat. 10-4. Adults $5, seniors & military $4, children $3; members & children under 4 no charge.
Attendance: 20,000 (estimated)

Venice

VENICE ART CENTER, 390 Nokomis Ave. S., Venice, FL 34285-2416. Tel.: 941-485-7136. Fax: 941-484-4361.
E-mail: info@veniceartcenter.com
Web Site: www.veniceartcenter.com
Key Personnel: Exec. Dir., Mary Moscatelli.
Institution Type/Description: Art Center.
Hours & Admission Prices: Summer: Mon.-Fri. 9-5; Winter: Mon.-Sat. 9-5.

VENICE MUSEUM AND ARCHIVES, 351 S. Nassau St., Venice, FL 34285. Tel.: 941-486-2487.
E-mail: jwatson@venicegov.com
Web Site: www.venicemuseum.org
Institution Type/Description: History Museum.
Hours & Admission Prices: Mon.-Wed. 10-4; other times by appointment.

Vero Beach

THE HERITAGE CENTER AND INDIAN RIVER CITRUS MUSEUM, 2140 14th Ave., Vero Beach, FL 32960-3432. Tel.: 772-770-2263. Fax: 772-770-2131.
E-mail: info@veroheritage.org
Web Site: www.veroheritage.org
Key Personnel: Exec. Dir., Alex Soares; Pres. (V), Nicki Maslin.
Institution Type/Description: History Museum.
Hours & Admission Prices: Tues.-Fri. 10-4. No charge; donations accepted. Closed New Year's Eve & Day; Christmas Day & week.
Attendance: 3,000 (estimated)

MCKEE BOTANICAL GARDEN, 350 U.S. Hwy. 1, Vero Beach, FL 32962-2906. Tel.: 772-794-0601. Fax: 772-794-0602. Facebook: @McKeeGarden.
E-mail: info@mckeegarden.org
Web Site: www.mckeegarden.org
Key Personnel: Pres., Matthew McManus; Dir., Christine Hobart; Museum Shop Mgr., Gail Galbraith.
Institution Type/Description: Botanical Garden: listed on the National Register of Historic Places.
Hours & Admission Prices: Tues.-Sat. 10-5, Sun. 12-5. Adults $12, seniors $11, children $8; reciprocal admission to American Horticultural Society; members no charge. Closed major holidays.
Attendance: 61,500 (actual)

MCLARTY TREASURE MUSEUM, 13180 Highway N. 1A, Part of the Sebastian Inlet State Park, Vero Beach, FL 32963-9400. Tel.: 772-589-2147. Fax: 321-984-4854.
E-mail: fsp.feedback@dep.state.fl.us
Web Site: www.floridastateparks.org/park/sebastian-inlet
Institution Type/Description: History and Film Museum: built on 1715 site of Spanish salvage campsite adjacent to shipwreck in Atlantic Ocean.

Hours & Admission Prices: Daily 10-4; last film showing 3:15. Admission $2 per person; children under 6 no charge.
Attendance: 25,000 (actual)

VERO BEACH MUSEUM OF ART, INC., 3001 Riverside Park Dr., Vero Beach, FL 32963-1874. Tel.: 772-231-0707. Fax: 772-231-0938. Facebook: Vero Beach Museum of Art; Instagram & Twitter: @verobeachmuseum.
E-mail: info@verobeachmuseum.org
Web Site: www.verobeachmuseum.org
Key Personnel: Chm. Bd., Sandra L. Rolf; Exec. Dir., Brady Roberts; Dir. Devel., Robyn P. Orzel; Dir. Finance, Caridad Weber; Dir. Mktg. & Communications, Sophie Bentham Wood; Exhibitions & Collections Mgr., Dana Twersky; Dir. Security, James Nelson; Asst. to Exec. Dir., Bonnie Wetherell.
Institution Type/Description: Art Museum.
Hours & Admission Prices: Memorial Day to Labor Day Tues.-Sat. 10-4:30, Sun. 1-4:30; Sept.-May Mon.-Sat. 10-4:30, Sun. 1-4:30. Adults $10, seniors $9, students $5; discounts to groups and AAM & ICOM members; members, active military, and children 17 & under no charge. Closed New Year's Day; Easter; Memorial Day; Independence Day; Labor Day; Thanksgiving; Christmas.
Attendance: 78,000 (actual)

Weirsdale

GRAND OAKS RESORT & MUSEUM, 3000 Marion County Rd., Weirsdale, FL 32195-5168. Tel.: 352-750-5500. Fax: 352-750-3342. Facebook.
E-mail: laureen@thegrandoaks.com
Web Site: www.thegrandoaks.com
Formerly: Florida Carriage Museum and Resort
Key Personnel: Dir., C.E.O. & Chm., Thomas Warriner; Business Mgr., Laureen Oliver.
Institution Type/Description: Transportation Museum.
Hours & Admission Prices: Tues.-Sat. 10-4, Sun. 12-4; groups by appointment. Adults $11, students 5-18 $5; children 4 & under no charge. Closed holidays.
Attendance: 10,000 (estimated)

West Palm Beach

THE ARMORY ART CENTER, 1700 Parker Ave., West Palm Beach, FL 33401-7042. Tel.: 561-832-1776. Fax: 561-832-0191.
E-mail: sandra.coombs@armoryart.org
Web Site: www.armoryart.org
Formerly: The Robert & Mary Montgomery Armory Art Center
Key Personnel: C.E.O., Sandra B. Coombs; Chm., James Swope; Pres., Stephen Rabb; Dir. Mktg., Kati Erickson; Dir. Education, Talya Lerman.
Institution Type/Description: Art Center: housed in Historic Palm Beach County National Guard Armory.
Hours & Admission Prices: Mon.-Sat. 9-4. Receptions: no charge. Closed New Year's Day; Memorial Day; Independence Day; Labor Day; Thanksgiving; Christmas.
Attendance: 25,000 (actual)

HISTORICAL SOCIETY OF PALM BEACH COUNTY, 300 N. Dixie Hwy., West Palm Beach, FL 33401-4605. Mailing Address: P.O. Box 4364, West Palm Beach, FL 33402-4364. Tel.: 561-832-4164. Fax: 561-832-7965. Facebook: HSPBC.
E-mail: info@historicalsocietypbc.org
Web Site: www.historicalsocietypbc.org
Key Personnel: C.E.O. & Pres., Jeremy W. Johnson; Chm., Grier Pressly, III; Chief Cur., Debi Murray; Cur. Collections, Benjamen Salata; Research Dir., Nick Golubov; Membership Assoc., Lise Steinhauer; Office Mgr., Sharon Poss; Dir. Mktg. & Special Events, Jillian Markwith; Dir. Advancement & Communications, Holly Finch.
Institution Type/Description: History Museum.
Hours & Admission Prices: Museum: Tues.-Sat. 10-5. No charge; donations accepted. Research by appointment. Research Fee $20; discounts to AAM & ICOM members; members no charge.
Attendance: 60,000 (actual)

MOUNTS BOTANICAL GARDEN, 531 N. Military Trail, West Palm Beach, FL 33415-1311. Mailing Address: 559 N. Military Trail, West Palm Beach, FL 33415. Tel.: 561-233-1757. Fax: 561-233-1723. Facebook: Mounts Botanical Garden.
E-mail: mountsbotanical@pbcgov.org
Web Site: www.mounts.org
Key Personnel: Dir., Allen Sistrunk; Pres. (V), Mike Zimmerman.
Institution Type/Description: Botanical Garden.

Hours & Admission Prices: Mon.-Sat. 8-4, Sun. 12-4. Suggested Donation: $5. Closed New Year's Day; Thanksgiving; Christmas Eve & Day.
Attendance: 60,000 (estimated)

NORTON MUSEUM OF ART, 1450 S. Dixie Hwy., West Palm Beach, FL 33401. Tel.: 561-832-5196. Fax: 561-659-4689.
E-mail: info@norton.org
Web Site: www.norton.org
Key Personnel: Exec. Dir., Elliot Bostwick Davis; Deputy Dir., Sam Ankerson; C.F.O., John Safranek; Dir. Human Resources, Natasha Oilar; Cur. Education, Glenn Tomlinson; Cur. Chinese Art, Laurie Barnes; Sr. Registrar, Pamela Parry; Dir. Communications, Scott Benarde.
Institution Type/Description: Art Museum.
Hours & Admission Prices: Mon.-Tues., Thurs. & Sat. 10-5, Fri. 10-10, Sun. 11-5. Adults $18, seniors 60 & over $15, students $5; children 12 & under, Florida educators, active military, members & Fri.-Sat. no charge. Closed major holidays. &
Attendance: 100,000 (actual)

PALM BEACH PHOTOGRAPHIC CENTRE, 415 Clematis St., West Palm Beach, FL 33401-5319. Tel.: 561-253-2600. Facebook, Twitter, Instagram.
E-mail: info@workshop.org
Web Site: www.workshop.org
Key Personnel: Exec. Dir., Fatima NeJame; Mng. Dir., Art NeJame.
Institution Type/Description: Photography Museum.
Hours & Admission Prices: Mon.-Thurs. 10-6, Fri.-Sat. 10-5.

PALM BEACH ZOO, 1301 Summit Blvd., West Palm Beach, FL 33405-3035. Tel.: 561-547-9453. Fax: 561-585-6085.
E-mail: info@palmbeachzoo.org
Web Site: www.palmbeachzoo.org
Key Personnel: C.E.O. & Pres., Margo McKnight; C.O.O., Casey A. Coy; C.F.O., Kathleen Breland; Dir. Wildlife Care & Conservation, Janet L. Steele; Dir. Education & Sustainability, Kristen M. Cytacki; Dir. Animal Health, Dr. Genevieve Dumonceaux.
Institution Type/Description: Zoo.
Hours & Admission Prices: Daily 9-5. Adults $22.95, senior citizens 60 & over $20.95, children 3-12 $16.95; discounts to groups; children under 2 & zoo members no charge. Closed Thanksgiving; Christmas. &
Attendance: 250,000 (estimated)

SOUTH FLORIDA SCIENCE CENTER & AQUARIUM, INC., 4801 Dreher Trail N., West Palm Beach, FL 33405-3017. Tel.: 561-832-1988. Fax: 561-833-0551.
E-mail: media@sfsm.org
Web Site: www.sfsciencecenter.org
Formerly: South Florida Science Museum
Key Personnel: C.E.O., Lew Crampton; Chm. Bd., Matthew Lorentzen; C.O.O., Kate Arrizza; Dir. Devel., Marcy Hoffman; Dir. Events, Kristina Holt; Dir. Operations, Jeff Gourdouze; Aquarium Curator, Rebecca Shearer; Museum Shop Mgr., Lila Klix.
Institution Type/Description: Science Center.
Hours & Admission Prices: Mon.-Fri. 9-5, Sat.-Sun. 10-6. Adults $16.95, seniors $14.95, children 3-12 $12.95; children under 3 & members no charge. Call for information on Planetarium & Laser Light shows. Closed Thanksgiving; Christmas. &
Attendance: 117,000 (actual)

YESTERYEAR VILLAGE, 9067 Southern Blvd., South Florida Fairgrounds, West Palm Beach, FL 33411-3625. Mailing Address: P.O. Box 210367, West Palm Beach, FL 33421-0367. Tel.: 561-790-5232, 800-640-3247. Fax: 561-753-2124.
E-mail: paige@southfloridafair.com
Web Site: www.southfloridafair.com
Key Personnel: Mgr., Paige Poole.
Institution Type/Description: History Museum.
Hours & Admission Prices: Thurs.-Sat. 10-4; other times by appointment. Tours: adults $10, seniors $7, children 5-11 $5; children 5 & under no charge. &

White Springs

STEPHEN FOSTER FOLK CULTURE CENTER STATE PARK, 11016 Lillian Saunders Dr., White Springs, FL 32096-0435. Mailing Address: P.O. Drawer G, White Springs, FL 32096-0435. Tel.: 386-397-2733. Fax: 386-397-4262. www.stephenfostercso.org.
E-mail: andrea.thomas@dep.state.fl.us
Web Site: www.floridastateparks.org/stephenfoster

Key Personnel: Park Mgr., Manny Perez; Asst. Park Mgr., Stephanie McClain; Museum Docent, Pat Cromer; Events Supvr., Elaine McGrath.
Institution Type/Description: Folk Culture Museum: located on the Suwannee River at White Springs, FL.
Hours & Admission Prices: Park: daily 8-sunset. $5 per vehicle (up to 8 people), $2 per person over 8; motorcoach rates available. Museum & Tower; daily 9-5. &
Attendance: 100,000 (estimated)

Wilton Manors

WORLD AIDS MUSEUM AND EDUCATIONAL CENTER, 1201 N.E. 26th St., Wilton Manors, FL 33305. Tel.: 954-390-0550. Facebook.
E-mail: info@worldaidsmuseum.org
Web Site: worldaidsmuseum.org
Key Personnel: Founder, Steve Stagon; CEO, Dr. Requel Lopes, AP.
Institution Type/Description: History Museum.
Hours & Admission Prices: Tues.-Sat. 12-6. &

Winter Garden

CENTRAL FLORIDA RAILROAD MUSEUM, 101 S. Boyd St., Winter Garden, FL 34787-3500. Mailing Address: P.O. Box 770567, Winter Garden, FL 34777-0567. Tel.: 407-656-0559.
E-mail: info@cfrhs.org
Web Site: www.cfrhs.org/
Key Personnel: Pres. (V), Phil Cross; Cur., Ken Murdock; Museum Shop Mgr., Irv Lipscomb; Pres. (V), Jerry Honetor.
Institution Type/Description: Historical Railroad Museum.
Hours & Admission Prices: Daily 1-5. No charge; donations accepted.
Attendance: 10,000 (estimated)

WINTER GARDEN HERITAGE MUSEUM, 1 N. Main St., Winter Garden, FL 34787-2824. Mailing Address: P.O. Box 770657, Winter Garden, FL 34777-0657. Tel.: 407-656-3244. Fax: 407-656-0110. Facebook, Instagram.
E-mail: museum@wghf.org
Web Site: www.wghf.org
Key Personnel: Dir., Cynthia Cardona.
Institution Type/Description: Heritage History Museum.
Hours & Admission Prices: Daily 1-5. No charge; donations accepted.
Attendance: 20,000 (estimated)

Winter Park

ALBIN POLASEK MUSEUM AND SCULPTURE GARDENS, 633 Osceola Ave., Winter Park, FL 32789-4429. Tel.: 407-647-6294. Fax: 407-647-0410.
E-mail: info@polasek.org
Web Site: www.polasek.org/
Key Personnel: Dir., Debbie Komanski; Pres. (V), Rob Sharpstein.
Institution Type/Description: Art Museum.
Hours & Admission Prices: Tues.-Sat. 10-4, Sun. 1-4; groups by appointment. Adults $5, seniors $4, students $3; discounts to American Horticultural Society; members & children under 12 no charge. &
Attendance: 35,000 (estimated)

THE CHARLES HOSMER MORSE MUSEUM OF AMERICAN ART, 445 N. Park Ave., Winter Park, FL 32789-3212. Tel.: 407-645-5311 & 5316. Fax: 407-647-1284. Facebook, Twitter, Instagram & Pinterest: @morsemuseum.
E-mail: information@morsemuseum.org
Web Site: www.morsemuseum.org
Key Personnel: Dir., Dr. Laurence J. Ruggiero; Cur. & Collections Mgr., Jennifer Thalheimer; Cur., Donna Climenhage; Cur. Education, Betsy Peters; Dir. Public Affairs, Catherine Hinman; Visitor Svcs. Mgr., Amy Roviaro; Bldg. Mgr., Tom Mobley; Museum Shop Mgr., Ava Maxwell.
Institution Type/Description: American Art Museum.
Hours & Admission Prices: May-Oct. Tues.-Sat. 9:30-4, Sun. 1-4; Nov.-April Tues.-Thurs. & Sat. 9:30-4, Fri. 9:30-8, Sun. 1-4; guided tours by appointment. Adults $6, seniors $5, students $1; discounts to museum professionals; children 12 and under, Fri. 4-8 & members no charge. Closed New Year's Day; Memorial Day; Labor Day; Thanksgiving; Christmas. &
Attendance: 76,757 (actual)

CREALDE SCHOOL OF ART - ALICE & WILLIAM JENKINS GALLERY, 600 St. Andrews Blvd., Winter Park, FL 32792. Tel.: 407-671-1886. Fax: 407-671-0311.
E-mail: rberrie@crealde.org
Web Site: www.crealde.org/galleries.html

Key Personnel: Exec. Dir., Peter Schreyer.
Institution Type/Description: Art Gallery.
Hours & Admission Prices: Mon.-Thurs. 9-4, Fri.-Sat. 9-1. No charge; donations accepted. ⅃

THE GEORGE D. AND HARRIET W. CORNELL FINE ARTS MUSEUM, Rollins College, 1000 Holt Ave., Winter Park, FL 32789-4499. Tel.: 407-646-2526. Fax: 407-646-2524. Facebook: Cornell Fine Arts Museum.
E-mail: stodd@rollins.edu
Web Site: www.rollins.edu/cfam
Key Personnel: Bruce A. Beal Dir., Ena Heller, Ph.D.; Bd. Chmn., Randy Robertson; Exec. Asst., Sandy Todd; Collections & Exhibs. Mgr., Austin Reeves; Curator, Amy Galpin, Ph.D.; Education Coord., Louise Buyo; Membership & Guest Relations, Dina Mack; Dir. Devel., Dana Thomas; Dale Montgomery Fellow, Rangsook Yoon, Ph.D.
Institution Type/Description: Art Museum.
Hours & Admission Prices: Tues.-Fri. 10-4, Sat.-Sun. 12-5. No charge; donations accepted. Closed major holidays. ⅃
Attendance: 25,000 (estimated)

HANNIBAL SQUARE HERITAGE CENTER, 642 W. New England Ave., Winter Park, FL 32789. Tel.: 407-539-2680.
Web Site: www.crealde.org/heritage_center_gallery.html
Institution Type/Description: Art Gallery.
Hours & Admission Prices: Tues.-Thurs. 12-4, Fri. 12-5, Sat. 10-2. No charge.

SHOWALTER HUGHES COMMUNITY GALLERY, 600 St. Andrews Blvd., Winter Park, FL 32792. Tel.: 407-671-1886.
E-mail: pschreyer@crealde.org
Web Site: www.crealde.org
Institution Type/Description: Art Gallery.
Hours & Admission Prices: Mon.-Thurs. 9-4, Fri.-Sat. 9-1. No charge, donations accepted.

Zephyrhills

ZEPHYRHILLS DEPOT MUSEUM, 39110 South Ave., Zephyrhills, FL 33542-5255. Tel.: 813-780-0067.
E-mail: afigart@ci.zephyrhills.fl.us
Web Site: www.ci.zephyrhills.fl.us
Key Personnel: Dir., Andrea Figart.
Institution Type/Description: History Museum: housed in the restored 1927 Atlantic Coast Line Railroad Depot.
Hours & Admission Prices: Thurs.-Fri. 9-1, Sat. 9-12. No charge. ⅃
Attendance: 1,200 (estimated)

Zolfo Springs

CRACKER TRAIL MUSEUM, 2822 Museum Dr., Zolfo Springs, FL 33890-9433. Tel.: 863-473-5076. Facebook.
E-mail: judith.george@hardeecounty.net
Web Site: www.hardeecounty.net
Key Personnel: Cur., Judith George; Dir. Facilities, Daniel Weeks.
Institution Type/Description: Park Museum.
Hours & Admission Prices: Mon.-Fri. 9-5. Adults $2; children under 5 no charge. ⅃
Attendance: 6,809 (actual)

GEORGIA

(347 listings)

Albany

ALBANY CIVIL RIGHTS INSTITUTE, 326 Whitney Ave., Albany, GA 31701-2861. Mailing Address: P.O. Box 6036, Albany, GA 31706-6036. Tel.: 229-432-1698. Fax: 229-432-2150.
E-mail: iturner@acrmm.org
Web Site: www.albanycivilrightsinstitute.org
Formerly: Albany Civil Rights Movement Museum at Old Mt. Zion Church
Key Personnel: Dir., W. Frank Wilson; Pres. (V), Kenneth Cutts; Admin., Irene L. Turner.
Institution Type/Description: History Museum.
Hours & Admission Prices: Tues.-Sat. 10-4. Adults $6, senior citizens, students 5th-12th grade, military & college students $5, children 1st-4th grade $3, pre-school $2; discounts to groups of 20 or more; members & children under 4 no charge. Closed holidays. ⅃
Attendance: 6,500 (actual)

ALBANY MUSEUM OF ART, 311 Meadowlark Dr., Albany, GA 31707-5704. Tel.: 229-439-8400. Fax: 229-439-1332. Facebook, Twitter, Instagram, Pinterest.
E-mail: info@albanymuseum.com
Web Site: www.albanymuseum.com
Key Personnel: Exec. Dir., Paula Williams; Pres. Bd. Trustees, Ripley Bell, Jr.; Membership & Finance Mgr., Veronica Parrish; Special Event Mgr., Savannah Hughes; Interim Exhibitions Mgr., Michael Mallard; Dir. Education & Public Programming, Chloe Hinton.
Institution Type/Description: Art Museum.
Hours & Admission Prices: Tues.-Sat. 10-5. No charge; donations accepted. Closed major holidays. ⅃
Attendance: 20,000 (estimated)

CHEHAW PARK, 105 Chehaw Park Rd., Albany, GA 31701-1260. Tel.: 229-430-5275. Fax: 229-430-3035.
E-mail: info@chehaw.org
Web Site: www.chehaw.org
Formerly: Chehaw Wild Animal Park
Key Personnel: Dir., Doug Porter.
Institution Type/Description: Zoo.
Hours & Admission Prices: Park: adults $3, seniors 62 & over, military and children 4-12 $2. Zoo: adults 13-61 $7.85, seniors 62 & over $6.85, military & children 4-12 $5.10; discounts to AZA members; children 3 & under no charge. Train: $3; children under 2 no charge. ⅃

FLINT RIVER QUARIUM, 101 Pine Ave., Albany, GA 31701-2593. Mailing Address: 117 Pine Ave., Albany, GA 31701-2593. Tel.: 229-639-2650. Fax: 229-639-2707.
E-mail: vchurchman@flintriverquarium.com
Web Site: www.flintriverquarium.com
Key Personnel: Dir., Scott W. Loehr; Chm. (V), Emily McAfee; Devel. & Public Rels., Wendy Bellacomo; Education, Melissa Martin; Cur., Richard Brown; Accounts Mgr., Vonda Hancock; Operations Mgr., Kathy Batson; Imagination Theater Mgr., Vashion Milledge; Membership & Guest Svcs. Mgr., Vicki Churchman; Aquarist, Kelly Putnam; Aquarist, Melissa Scott; Aquarist, Amanda Margraves; Museum Shop Mgr., Claudia Durham.
Institution Type/Description: Natural Science Museum.
Hours & Admission Prices: Mon.-Fri. 9-5, Sat. 10-6, Sun. 1-5. Adults $9, senior citizens $8, children $6, students $4.50; discounts to groups of 15 or more; members no charge. Closed Thanksgiving; Christmas. ⅃
Attendance: 66,285 (actual)

THRONATEESKA HERITAGE CENTER, 100 W. Roosevelt Ave., Albany, GA 31701-2325. Tel.: 229-432-6955. Fax: 229-435-1572.
E-mail: info@heritagecenter.org
Web Site: www.heritagecenter.org
Key Personnel: C.E.O. & Exec. Dir., Tommy Gregors.
Institution Type/Description: History Museum.
Hours & Admission Prices: Museums: Thurs.-Sat. 10-4; other times by appointment. No charge. Planetarium: Thurs.-Sat. 10-4. Shows: 10:30, 11:30, 1, 2, & 4. Admission $5; discount to groups of 10 or more; children 3 & under and members no charge. Closed New Year's Day; Martin Luther King Jr. Day; Memorial Day; Labor Day; Thanksgiving; Christmas. ⅃
Attendance: 25,418 (actual)

Alpharetta

MANSELL HOUSE AND GARDENS, 1835 Old Milton Pkwy., Alpharetta, GA 30009. Tel.: 770-475-4663.
E-mail: info@alpharettahistoricalsociety.org
Institution Type/Description: Historic House Museum: built in 1912.
Hours & Admission Prices: Mon. 11-2, Wed. & Fri. 10-2; other times by appointment.

Americus

RYLANDER THEATER, 310 W. Lamar St., Americus, GA 31709-3543. Mailing Address: P.O. Box 864, Americus, GA 31709-0864. Tel.: 912-931-0001. Fax: 912-928-2466.
E-mail: rylanderboxoffice@gmail.com
Web Site: www.rylander.org
Key Personnel: Mng. Dir., Heather Stanley; Tour Dir., Kent Sole.
Institution Type/Description: Historic Building: restored working theatre built in 1921.
Hours & Admission Prices: Tours: by appointment. Performances: call for hours. Closed New Year's Day & day after; Memorial Day; Independence Day; Thanksgiving & day after; Christmas Eve, Day & day after.

Andersonville

ANDERSONVILLE NATIONAL HISTORIC SITE, 496 Cemetery Rd., Andersonville, GA 31711-4040. Tel.: 229-924-0343. Fax: 229-924-1086.
E-mail: charles_sellars@nps.gov
Web Site: www.nps.gov/ande
Key Personnel: Supt., Charles Sellars; Chief of Admin., Karen Barry.
Institution Type/Description: National Park & Historic Site: Civil War P.O.W. camp.
Hours & Admission Prices: Visitors Center: daily 9-4:30. Park: daily 8-5. No charge. Visitor Center: closed New Year's Day; Thanksgiving; Christmas. &
Attendance: 150,000 (estimated)

Athens

CHURCH-WADDEL-BRUMBY HOUSE MUSEUM & ATHENS WELCOME CENTER, 280 E. Dougherty St., Athens, GA 30601-2611. Tel.: 706-353-1820. Fax: 706-353-1770.
E-mail: director@athenswelcomecenter.com
Web Site: www.athenswelcomecenter.com
Key Personnel: Dir. & Museum Mgr., Evelyn Reece.
Institution Type/Description: Historic House: housed in c.1820 Church-Waddel-Brumby House.
Hours & Admission Prices: Mon.-Sat. 10-5, Sun. 12-5. No charge; donations accepted. Closed New Year's Day; Thanksgiving; Christmas. No charge; donations accepted. &
Attendance: 13,000 (actual)

CIRCLE GALLERY/COLLEGE OF ENVIRONMENT & DESIGN - UNIVERSITY OF GEORGIA, 285 S. Jackson St., Athens, GA 30602. Mailing Address: 121 Jackson St. Bldg., Athens, GA 30602. Tel.: 706-542-8292. Fax: 706-542-4485.
E-mail: mtufts@uga.edu
Web Site: www.sed.uga.edu/gallery
Formerly: SED Gallery/School of Environmental Design - University of Georgia
Key Personnel: Gallery Dir., Melissa Tufts.
Institution Type/Description: General Museum.
Hours & Admission Prices: Academic Year: Mon.-Fri. 9-6; Summer: by appointment. No charge. Closed holidays. &
Attendance: 2,500 (estimated)

GEORGIA MUSEUM OF ART, UNIVERSITY OF GEORGIA, 90 Carlton St., Athens, GA 30602-1502. Tel.: 706-542-4662. Fax: 706-542-1051. Facebook: Georgia Museum of Art.
E-mail: mlachow@uga.edu
Web Site: www.georgiamuseum.org
Key Personnel: Dir., William U. Eiland; Deputy Dir., Annelies Mondi; Chm. (V), Alan F. Rothchild; Pres. Friends of the Museum, Cyndy Harbold; Coord. Public Rels., Michael Lachowski; Chief Preparator, Todd Rivers; Dir. Devel., Heather Malcolm; Dir. Communications, Hillary Brown; Cur. Decorative Arts, Dale Couch; Cur. Pierre Daura, Lynn Boland; Cur. American Art, Sarah Kate Gillespie; Assoc. Cur. Education, Callan Steinmann; Assoc. Cur. Education, Sage Kincaid; Business Mgr., Lisa Conley; Head Registrar, Tricia Miller; Cur. Larry D. & Brenda A. Thompson African American and African Diasporic Art, Dr. Shawnya Harris; Art Handler, Larry Forte; Museum Shop Mgr., Amy Miller.
Institution Type/Description: Art Museum.
Hours & Admission Prices: Tues.-Wed. & Fri.-Sat. 10-5, Thurs. 10-9, Sun. 1-5. No charge; donations accepted. &
Attendance: 80,000 (actual)

GEORGIA MUSEUM OF NATURAL HISTORY, Natural History Bldg., University of Georgia, Athens, GA 30602-1882. Tel.: 706-542-1663. Fax: 706-542-3920.
E-mail: musinfo@uga.edu
Web Site: museum.nhm.uga.edu
Key Personnel: Dir. & Cur. Zoology, Byron J. Freeman, Ph.D.; Cur. Zooarchaeology, Dr. Elizabeth Reitz; Cur. Mineralogy, Dr. Paul Schroeder; Cur. Botany, Dr. Wendy Zomlefer; Cur. Entomology, Dr. Joseph McHugh; Cur. Economic Geology, Dr. Doug Crowe.
Institution Type/Description: Natural History Museum.
Hours & Admission Prices: Mon.-Fri. 10-4. No charge. Closed holidays. &
Attendance: 10,000 (estimated)

LYNDON HOUSE ARTS CENTER, 293 Hoyt St., Athens, GA 30601-2648. Tel.: 706-613-3623. Fax: 706-613-3627.
E-mail: claire.benson@athensclarkecounty.com
Web Site: lyndonhouseartsfoundation.wordpress.com
Key Personnel: Dir., Claire Benson; Cur., Nancy Lukasiewicz; Pres. (V) Lyndon House Arts Foundation, Lou Kudon; Museum Shop Mgr., Celia Brooks.

Institution Type/Description: Art Center: c.1850 Ware-Lyndon House, originally built by Dr. Edward R. Ware & later sold to Dr. Edward Smith Lyndon.
Hours & Admission Prices: Tues. & Thurs. 12-9, Wed. & Fri.-Sat. 9-5. No charge; donations accepted. Closed Thanksgiving; Christmas. &
Attendance: 70,000 (actual)

THE STATE BOTANICAL GARDEN OF GEORGIA, 2450 S. Milledge Ave., Athens, GA 30605-1674. Tel.: 706-542-1244. Fax: 706-542-3091.
E-mail: garden@uga.edu
Web Site: www.botgarden.uga.edu
Key Personnel: Chm. (V) Advisory Bd., Stephen Reichert; Pres. (V) Friends of the Garden, Karen Radde; Dir. Research, Dr. James Affolter; Dir. Education, Anne Shenk; Dir. Finance, John Graham; Visitor Center Mgr., William Tonks; Museum Shop Mgr., Mike Sikes; Information Specialist, Connie Cottingham; Coord. Plant Conservation, Jennifer Ceska; Horticulturist, Shelly Prescott; Volunteer Coord., Andrea Fischer; Office Admin., Shene Stroud.
Institution Type/Description: University Botanical Garden.
Hours & Admission Prices: Grounds: April-Sept. daily 8-8; Oct.-March daily 8-6. Visitor Center: Tues.-Sat. 9-4:30, Sun. 11:30-4:30. Cafe: Tues.-Fri. 11-2, Sat.-Sun. 11:30-3. No charge; donations accepted. Closed University holidays. &
Attendance: 230,000 (estimated)

T.R.R. COBB HOUSE, 175 Hill St., Athens, GA 30601. Tel.: 706-369-3513. Fax: 706-354-1054.
E-mail: sthomas@trrrcobbhouse.org
Key Personnel: Cur., Sam Thomas.
Institution Type/Description: Historic House Museum: housed in the former home of lawyer & Confederate Army officer Thomas Cobb.
Hours & Admission Prices: Tues.-Sat. 10-4. Suggested Donation: adults $2; children & students no charge. Closed holidays.

TAYLOR-GRADY HOUSE, 634 Prince Ave., Athens, GA 30601-2453. Tel.: 706-549-8688. Facebook.
E-mail: athensjl@gmail.com
Web Site: www.taylorgradyhouse.com
Key Personnel: Dir., Elizabeth Elliott.
Institution Type/Description: Historic House Museum: 1845 Henry W. Grady Home.
Hours & Admission Prices: Mon., Wed. & Fri. 9-3, Tues. & Thurs. 12-4; call to confirm. Admission $3. Closed holidays. &
Attendance: 5,000 (estimated)

Atlanta

THE APEX MUSEUM, 135 Auburn Ave., N.E., Atlanta, GA 30303-2567. Tel.: 404-523-2739. Fax: 404-523-3248 (call first).
E-mail: info@apexmuseum.org
Web Site: www.apexmuseum.org
Key Personnel: Pres. & Founder, Dan Moore, Sr.
Institution Type/Description: History Museum & Building: 1910 John Wesley Dobbs Building, former School Book Depository; entity of the Sweet Auburn historic Freedom Walk.
Hours & Admission Prices: Tues.-Sat. 10-5. Adults $7, senior citizens 55 & over and students $5; discounts to groups; members & children under 4 no charge. &
Attendance: 65,000 (actual)

AMERICAN BAPTIST HISTORICAL SOCIETY, 2930 Flowers Rd. S., Atlanta, GA 30341. Mailing Address: 3001 Mercer University Dr., Atlanta, GA 30341. Tel.: 678-547-6680.
E-mail: abhsoffice@abhsarchives.org
Web Site: abhsarchives.org/index.shtml
Key Personnel: Exec. Dir., Rev. Dr. Priscilla E. Eppinger.
Institution Type/Description: Research Library.
Hours & Admission Prices: By appointment. &

ATLANTA BOTANICAL GARDEN, 1345 Piedmont Ave., N.E., Atlanta, GA 30309-3366. Tel.: 404-876-5859. Fax: 404-876-7472.
E-mail: info@atlantabg.org
Web Site: www.atlantabg.org
Key Personnel: Pres. & C.E.O., Mary Pat Matheson; C.O.O., Arthur Fix; C.F.O., Gary Doubrava; Vice Pres. Horticulture & Collections, Amanda Bennett; Vice Pres. Mktg., Jessica Boatright; Vice Pres. Conservation & Research, Emily Coffey; Vice Pres. Programs, Tracy McClendon; Vice Pres. Institutional Advancement, Leslie Myers.
Institution Type/Description: Arboretum & Botanical Garden.
Hours & Admission Prices: Tues.-Sun. 9-9, check website for detailed hours. Adults $21.95, children 3-12 $18.95; members & children under 3 no charge. Closed New Year's Day; Thanksgiving; Christmas. &
Attendance: 525,000 (actual)

ATLANTA CONTEMPORARY ART CENTER, 535 Means St. N. W., Atlanta, GA 30318-5729. Tel.: 404-688-1970.
E-mail: support@atlantacontemporary.org
Web Site: www.thecontemporary.org
Formerly: Nexus Contemporary Art Center
Key Personnel: Bd. Chm., Randy Gue; Exec. Dir., Veronica Kessenich.
Institution Type/Description: Contemporary Art Center
Hours & Admission Prices: Tues.-Wed. & Fri.-Sat. 11-5, Thurs. 11-8, Sun. 12-4. No charge. &
Attendance: 7,000 (estimated)

ATLANTA HISTORY CENTER, Lloyd and Mary Ann Whitaker Cyclorama Bldg., 130 W. Paces Ferry Rd., N.W., Atlanta, GA 30305-1380. Tel.: 404-814-4000. Fax: 404-814-2041. TDD: 404-814-4000; Facebook.
E-mail: hhardwick@atlantahistorycenter.com
Web Site: www.atlantahistorycenter.com
Formerly: Atlanta Historical Society
Key Personnel: C.E.O. & Pres., Sheffield Hale; Chief Mission Officer & Exec. Vice Pres., Michael Rose; Vice Pres. Operations, Sean Thorndike; Vice Pres. Public Programs, Kate Whitman; Vice Pres. Devel., Cheri Snyder; Vice Pres. Properties, Jackson McQuigg; Vice Pres. Mktg., Hillary Hardwick; Museum Shop Mgr., Michael Mims.
Institution Type/Description: History Museum.
Hours & Admission Prices: Museum: Mon.-Sat. 10-5:30, Sun. 12-5:30. Kenan Research Center: Wed.-Sat. 10-5. Adults $16.50, students 13 & over and seniors 65 & over $13, youth 4-12 $11; discounts to groups, ICOM & AAM members; members & children under 4 no charge. Additional charge for some special events. Admission included access to Margaret Mitchell House. Closed New Year's Day; Thanksgiving; Christmas Eve & Day. &
Attendance: 235,000 (actual)

BRAVES MUSEUM & HALL OF FAME/TURNER FIELD TOURS, 755 Hank Aaron Dr., Atlanta, GA 30315-1120. Tel.: 404-614-2310. Fax: 404-614-1423.
E-mail: suntrustparktours@braves.com
Web Site: braves.com/tours
Key Personnel: Dir., Carolyn Serra.
Institution Type/Description: Sports Museum.
Hours & Admission Prices: April-Sept. Mon.-Sat. 9-3, Sun. 1-3; Oct.-March Mon.-Sat. 10-2. Call for admission fees. &

CALLANWOLDE FINE ARTS CENTER, 980 Briarcliff Rd., N.E., Atlanta, GA 30306-2650. Tel.: 404-872-5338. Fax: 404-872-5175.
E-mail: info@callanwolde.org
Web Site: www.callanwolde.org
Key Personnel: Exec. Dir., Peggy Still-Johnson; Dir. Arts Education, Steve Cole.
Institution Type/Description: Arts Center: housed in 1917-1920 Callanwolde, home of Charles Howard Candler, son of Asa Candler of Coca-Cola fame.
Hours & Admission Prices: Mon.-Fri. 10-8, Sat. 10-3. No charge. Closed legal holidays. &
Attendance: 25,000 (estimated)

CENTENNIAL OLYMPIC PARK VISITOR CENTER, 265 Park Ave. West, N.W., Atlanta, GA 30313-1591. Mailing Address: c/o Georgia World Congress Center, 285 Andrew Young International Blvd., NW, Atlanta, GA 30313-1591. Tel.: 404-223-4412 & 222-7275. Fax: 404-223-4499.
E-mail: info@centennialpark.com
Web Site: www.centennialpark.com
Key Personnel: Sr. Prog. Coord., Greg Knight; Visitor Center & Volunteer Coord., Jennifer Tinker; Sr. Exec. Asst., Lisa Stock; Opers. Supvr., Keith Zachery.
Institution Type/Description: Memorial Park & Visitor Center.
Hours & Admission Prices: Daily 7am-11pm. No charge. &
Attendance: 3,000,000 (estimated)

CENTER FOR PUPPETRY ARTS, 1404 Spring St., N.W., Atlanta, GA 30309-2820. Tel.: 404-873-3089. Fax: 404-873-9907.
E-mail: info@puppet.org
Web Site: www.puppet.org
Key Personnel: Exec. Dir., Vincent Anthony; Administration & HR, Lisa Rhodes; Production, Kristin Haverty; Museum Shop Mgr., Debi Zamoscinski.
Institution Type/Description: Puppetry Museum.
Hours & Admission Prices: Tues.-Fri. 9-5, Sat. 10-5, Sun. 12-5. Museum: admission $8.25; discounts to groups, AAM & ICOM members; children under 2 & members no charge. Museum, Show & Workshop: adults $16, members $9. Closed New Year's Day; Easter; Memorial Day; Independence Day; Labor Day; Thanksgiving; Christmas. &
Attendance: 65,000 (estimated)

CHATTAHOOCHEE RIVER NATIONAL RECREATION AREA, 1978 Island Ford Pkwy., Atlanta, GA 30350-3432. Tel.: 678-538-1200. Fax: 770-399-8087. Facebook: Chattahoochee River National Recreation Area.
Web Site: www.nps.gov/chat
Key Personnel: Supt., Bill Cox; Chief Park Ranger, Scott M. Pfeninger.
Institution Type/Description: Natural & Cultural Area.
Hours & Admission Prices: Daily 9-5. No charge. Entrance Fee: daily $3, annual $35. Closed Christmas. &
Attendance: 3,200,000 (actual)

CLARK ATLANTA UNIVERSITY ART MUSEUM, Mailing Address: 223 James P. Brawley Dr., S.W., Trevor Arnett Hall, 2nd Level, Atlanta, GA 30314-4358. Tel.: 404-880-6644. Fax: 404-880-6968. Facebook.
E-mail: mpoole@cau.edu
Web Site: www.cau.edu/art-galleries
Key Personnel: Dir., Maurita Poole, Ph.D.; Asst. Cur., Dimond Mason.
Institution Type/Description: Art Galleries.
Hours & Admission Prices: Tues.-Fri. 11-4. No charge; donations accepted. &
Attendance: 10,000 (estimated)

COLLEGE FOOTBALL HALL OF FAME, 250 Marietta St., N. W., Atlanta, GA 30313. Tel.: 404-880-4800.
E-mail: info@cfbhall.com
Web Site: www.cfbhall.com
Key Personnel: Vice Pres. Finance & Admin., Mark Petersen.
Institution Type/Description: Sports Museum.
Hours & Admission Prices: Sun.-Fri. 10-5, Sat. 9-6. Adults $19.99, seniors 65 & over, military, and students $17.99, children 3-12 $16.99; children under 3 no charge. Closed Thanksgiving; Christmas. &

DAVID J. SENCER CDC MUSEUM, 1600 Clifton Rd., N.E., (at CDC Pkwy. -MS A14), Atlanta, GA 30329-4018. Tel.: 404-639-0830. Fax: 404-639-0834. Facebook: CDC Museum.
E-mail: museum@cdc.gov
Web Site: www.cdc.gov/museum
Formerly: CDC/Global Health Odyssey Museum
Key Personnel: Dir., Judy M. Gantt; Collections Mgr., Mary Hilpertshauser; Dir. Education, Trudi Ellerman; Cur., Louise E. Shaw.
Institution Type/Description: Medical Museum.
Hours & Admission Prices: Mon.-Wed. & Fri. 9-5, Thurs. 9-7. No charge. Closed federal holidays &
Attendance: 90,000 (actual)

DELTA FLIGHT MUSEUM, Delta World Headquarters, 1060 Delta Blvd., B-914, Atlanta, GA 30354. Tel.: 404-715-7886 (Office) & 773-1219 (Store). Fax: 404-715-2037. Facebook.
E-mail: museum.delta@delta.com
Web Site: www.deltamuseum.org
Formerly: Delta Air Transport Heritage Museum
Key Personnel: Dir. Operations, Tiffany Meng; Dir. Archives, Marie Force; Museum Shop Mgr., Judy Bean.
Institution Type/Description: Corporate History Museum.
Hours & Admission Prices: Mon.-Tues. & Thurs.-Sat. 10-4:30, Sun. 12-4:30. Admission $12.50, seniors $10, youth 5-17 $7; discounts to AAM, ICOM, AASLH, SAA & SGA members; children 4 & under no charge. &
Attendance: 25,000 (estimated)

DEWBERRY GALLERY OF SCAD, 1545 Peachtree St., Ste. 225, Atlanta, GA 30309. Tel.: 404-815-2931.
E-mail: contact@scad.edu
Web Site: www.scad.edu/exhibitions/galleries
Institution Type/Description: Art Gallery.
Hours & Admission Prices: Tues.-Fri. 1-6. No charge.

FEDERAL RESERVE BANK OF ATLANTA, VISITOR'S CENTER AND MONETARY MUSEUM, 1000 Peachtree St., N. E., Atlanta, GA 30309-4470. Tel.: 404-498-8764. Fax: 404-498-8050.
E-mail: amy.hennessy@atl.frb.org
Web Site: www.frbatlanta.org/about/tours/museum.cfm
Formerly: Atlanta Visitor's Center and Monetary Museum
Key Personnel: Dir., Amy Hennessy.
Institution Type/Description: Money Museum.
Hours & Admission Prices: Self-Guided Tours: Mon.-Fri. 9-4; guided tours by appointment. No charge.
Attendance: 20,000 (actual)

FERNBANK MUSEUM OF NATURAL HISTORY, 767 Clifton Rd., N.E., Atlanta, GA 30307-1274. Tel.: 404-929-6300 & 6400 (tickets). Fax: 404-929-6405 & 6406.
E-mail: guest.services@fernbankmuseum.org
Web Site: www.fernbankmuseum.org
Key Personnel: C.E.O. & Pres., Jennifer Grant Warner; Vice Pres. Devel., Leslie Marlowe.
Institution Type/Description: Natural History Museum.
Hours & Admission Prices: Daily 10-5. Museum: adults $18, senior citizens $17, children 3-12 $16, children 2 & under & members no charge, discount to groups & ASTC members; members no charge. IMAX: adults $13, seniors $12, children 3-12 $11, members $8, children 2 & under no charge. Closed Thanksgiving; Christmas. &
Attendance: 402,412 (actual)

FERNBANK SCIENCE CENTER, 156 Heaton Park Dr., N.E., Atlanta, GA 30307-1398. Tel.: 678-874-7102. Fax: 678-874-7110.
E-mail: fernbank@fernbank.edu
Web Site: www.fernbank.edu
Key Personnel: Dir., Douglas J. Hrabe.
Institution Type/Description: Science Museum, Planetarium & Observatory.
Hours & Admission Prices: Exhibits: Mon.-Wed. 12-5, Thurs.-Fri. 12-9, Sat. 10-5; groups by appointment. Library: Mon.-Fri. 12-5, Sat. 10-5. Museum: no charge. Planetarium: adults $7, students & seniors $5; discounts to AAM & ICOM members; members no charge. &
Attendance: 300,000 (estimated)

FOX THEATRE, 660 Peachtree St., N.E., Atlanta, GA 30308-1929. Tel.: 404-881-2100 & 855-285-8499. Fax: 404-872-2972.
E-mail: boxoffice@foxtheatre.org
Web Site: foxtheatre.org
Key Personnel: Pres. & C.E.O., Allan C. Vella.
Institution Type/Description: Historic Building: built c.1920. A National Historic Landmark.
Hours & Admission Prices: Tours by appointment: Mon. & Wed.-Thurs. 10am, Sat. 10am & 11am. Adults $18, seniors $15, children 10 & under $5.

THE GALLERY AT CHASTAIN ARTS CENTER, 135 W. Wieuca Rd., N.W., Atlanta, GA 30342. Tel.: 404-252-2927. Fax: 404-851-1270.
E-mail: chastainarts@atlanta.gov
Web Site: www.ocaatlanta.com/chastain
Institution Type/Description: Art Gallery.
Hours & Admission Prices: Mon. 9:30-5:30, Tues.-Fri. 9:30-9:30, Sat. 9:30-2:30.

GALLERY 1600 - SCAD ATLANTA, 1600 Peachtree St., Bldg. A, 2nd Fl., Atlanta, GA 30309. Tel.: 404-815-2931.
Web Site: www.scad.edu/exhibitions/galleries
Institution Type/Description: Art Gallery.
Hours & Admission Prices: Mon.-Fri. 8:30-5:30. No charge.

GEORGIA AQUARIUM, 225 Baker St., N.W., Atlanta, GA 30313-1809. Tel.: 404-581-4000. Facebook.
E-mail: visitorservices@georgiaaquarium.org
Web Site: www.georgiaaquarium.org
Key Personnel: Chm. & C.E.O., Mike Leven.
Institution Type/Description: Aquarium.
Hours & Admission Prices: See website for hours & admission prices. &
Attendance: 2,032,592 (actual)

GEORGIA CAPITOL MUSEUM, 206 Washington St., Atlanta, GA 30334. Mailing Address: 2 Martin Luther King Dr., Ste. 820, Atlanta, GA 30334-9000. Tel.: 404-656-2846; 463-4536 (tours). Fax: 404-657-3801.
Web Site: www.libs.uga.edu/capitolmuseum
Institution Type/Description: General Museum.
Hours & Admission Prices: Mon.-Fri. 8-5 by appointment. No charge. Closed legal holidays. &
Attendance: 60,000 (estimated)

GEORGIA STATE UNIVERSITY SCHOOL OF ART & DESIGN GALLERY, 10 Peachtree Center Ave., Atlanta, GA 30303-3003. Mailing Address: P.O. Box 4107, Atlanta, GA 30302-4107. Tel.: 404-413-5230. Fax: 404-651-1779.
E-mail: artgallery@gsu.edu
Web Site: artdesign.gsu.edu/artgallery
Key Personnel: Dir., Cynthia Farnell; Cur. Visual Resources, Ann England.
Institution Type/Description: University Art Gallery.

Hours & Admission Prices: Call for hours. No charge. Closed school holidays; New Year's Day; Independence Day; Labor Day; Thanksgiving. &
Attendance: 6,000 (estimated)

GOVERNOR'S MANSION, 391 W. Paces Ferry Rd., N.W., Atlanta, GA 30305-1001. Tel.: 404-261-1776. Fax: 404-231-8621.
E-mail: mansionevents@gov.state.ga.us
Web Site: www.mansion.georgia.gov
Key Personnel: Dir., Joy Forth.
Institution Type/Description: Historic Home: home of current Governor Nathan Deal.
Hours & Admission Prices: Tours: Tues.-Thurs. 10-11:30 am; groups by appointment. No charge.

HAMMONDS HOUSE MUSEUM, 503 Peeples St., S.W., Atlanta, GA 30310-1815. Tel.: 404-612-0500. Fax: 404-752-8733.
E-mail: business@hammondshouse.org
Web Site: hammondshouse.org
Key Personnel: Interim Exec. Dir., Leatrice Ellzy; Cur., Tracy Murrell; Exec. Asst., Audrey M. Johnson; Facilities Mgr., Wendell Hurst.
Institution Type/Description: Art Museum: former home of late Dr. Otis Thrash Hammonds, built around 1872.
Hours & Admission Prices: Wed.-Fri. 10-6, Sat.-Sun. 1-5. Adults $4, senior citizens, students & children $2; members no charge. Closed national holidays. &
Attendance: 10,000

THE HERNDON HOME, 587 University Pl., N.W., Atlanta, GA 30314-4126. Tel.: 404-581-9813. Fax: 404-588-0239.
E-mail: hhinfo@herndonhome.org
Web Site: www.herndonhome.org
Key Personnel: Dir. Programs, Julissa J. White-Smith; Chief Docent, Roberta Phillips.
Institution Type/Description: Historic Home: former home of the Alonzo Herndon family, built in 1910. A National Historic Landmark.
Hours & Admission Prices: Tours: Tues. & Thurs. 10-4; group tours by appointment. Adults $10, seniors, students & active military $7.

HIGH MUSEUM OF ART, 1280 Peachtree St., N.E., Atlanta, GA 30309-3549. Tel.: 404-733-4400. Fax: 404-733-4450.
E-mail: highmuseum@high.org
Web Site: www.high.org
Key Personnel: Dir., Randall Suffolk; Chm. (V), Charles Abney; C.O.O., Philip Verre; C.F.O., Rhonda Matheison; Dir. Exhibitions, Amy Simon; Wieland Family Cur. Modern & Contemporary Art, Michael Rooks; Merrie & Dan Boone Cur. Folk & Self-Taught Art, Katherine Jentleson; Fred and Rita Richman Cur. African Art, Carol Thompson; Margaret and Terry Stent Cur. American Art, Stephanie Heydt; Cur. Decorative Arts & Design, Sarah Schleuning; Eleanor McDonald Storza Dir. Education, Virginia Shearer; Shannon Landing Amos Head Museum Interpretation, Julia Forbes; Head School & Teacher Svcs., Kate McLeod; Exhibitions Designer, Jim Waters; Dir. Devel., Allison Chance; Wine Auction Mgr., Steven Hargrove; Mgr. Public Rels., Marci Tate-Davis; Registrar, Frances Francis; Mgr. Creative Svcs., Angela Jaeger; Controller, Marzell Graham; Mgr. Facilities & Logistics, Kevin Streiter; Head Retail Operations, Sylvia Roberts; Museum Shop Mgr., Patricia Sampson; Chief Security, Stanley Gray.
Institution Type/Description: Art Museum.
Hours & Admission Prices: Tues.-Thurs. & Sat. 10-5, Fri. 10-9, Sun. 12-5. Admission $14.50, discounts to groups of 15 or more; children under 6 & members no charge. Closed New Year's Day; Martin Luther King, Jr. Day; Independence Day; Labor Day; Thanksgiving; Christmas. Friday Night Jazz 3rd Fri. each month 6-10pm. &
Attendance: 400,000 (estimated)

HISTORIC OAKLAND CEMETERY, Historic Oakland Foundation, 248 Oakland Ave., S.E., Atlanta, GA 30312-2220. Tel.: 404-688-2107. Fax: 404-658-6092.
E-mail: info@oaklandcemetery.com
Web Site: www.oaklandcemetery.com
Key Personnel: Exec. Dir., David S. Moore; Visitors Center & Museum Shop Mgr., Tim Wright.
Institution Type/Description: Historical Society: office is located in the 1899 Bell Tower building (Norman).
Hours & Admission Prices: Office: Mon.-Fri. 9-5. Tours: April-Oct. Sat. & Sun. 10am, 2, 4 & 6:30pm, Nov.-March Sat.-Sun. 2pm; other times by appointment. Cemetery no charge. Walking Tours: family $28, adults $12, seniors, students & children $6; members and children 6 & under no charge. &
Attendance: 65,000 (estimated)

IMAGINE IT! THE CHILDREN'S MUSEUM OF ATLANTA, 275 Centennial Olympic Park Dr., N.W., Atlanta, GA 30313-1827. Tel.: 404-659-5437. Fax: 404-223-3675.

E-mail: askme@childrensmuseumatlanta.org
Web Site: www.imagineit-cma.org
Key Personnel: Exec. Dir., Jane Turner.
Institution Type/Description: Children's Museum.
Hours & Admission Prices: Mon.-Tues. & Thurs.-Fri. 10-4, Sat.-Sun. 10-5. Admission $14.95, military $11.95; children under one & members no charge. Closed Thanksgiving; Christmas.
Attendance: 207,000 (estimated)

JIMMY CARTER PRESIDENTIAL LIBRARY AND MUSEUM, 441 Freedom Pkwy., Atlanta, GA 30307-1497. Tel.: 404-865-7100. Fax: 404-865-7102. Facebook.
E-mail: carter.library@nara.gov
Web Site: www.jimmycarterlibrary.gov
Key Personnel: Dir., Dr. Meredith Evans; Deputy Dir., David Stanhope; Cur., Sylvia Naguib; Museum Shop Mgr., James E. Stewart.
Institution Type/Description: Presidential Library.
Hours & Admission Prices: Museum: Mon.-Sat. 9-4:45, Sun. 12-4:45. Adults $8, senior citizens, students & military $6; discounts to AAM members; children under 16 & members no charge. Research Library: Mon.-Fri. 8:30-4:30. Closed New Year's Day; Thanksgiving; Christmas.
Attendance: 82,757 (actual)

THE MARGARET MITCHELL HOUSE, 979 Crescent Ave. N.E., Atlanta, GA 30309. Tel.: 404-249-7015. Facebook.
Web Site: www.atlantahistorycenter.com
Key Personnel: Pres. & C.E.O., Atlanta History Center, Sheffield Hale.
Institution Type/Description: Historic House: the former home of Margaret Mitchell where she wrote the Pulitzer prize-winning novel, Gone With The Wind.
Hours & Admission Prices: Mon.-Sat. 11-4, Sun. 1-4. Adults $13, seniors 65 & over and students 13-18 with ID $10, children 4-12 $5.50 Center & House: adults $21.50, seniors 65 & over and students 13-18 $18, youth 4-12 $9. Closed New Year's Day; Thanksgiving; Christmas Eve & Day.

MARTIN LUTHER KING, JR. CENTER FOR NONVIOLENT SOCIAL CHANGE, INC., 449 Auburn Ave., N.E., Atlanta, GA 30312-1503. Tel.: 404-526-8900. Fax: 404-526-8932. Facebook & Twitter: @thekingcenter.
E-mail: information@thekingcenter.org
Web Site: www.thekingcenter.org
Key Personnel: C.E.O., Dr. Bernice A. King.
Institution Type/Description: History Museum, Educational Center & Archives: located at the Martin Luther King, Jr. National Historic Site.
Hours & Admission Prices: Memorial Day to Labor Day daily 9-6; Sept-May daily 9-5. No charge; donations accepted. Closed New Year's Day; Thanksgiving; Christmas Eve & Day.
Attendance: 1,000,000 (estimated)

MARTIN LUTHER KING, JR. NATIONAL HISTORIC SITE AND PRESERVATION DISTRICT, Mailing Address: 450 Auburn Ave., N.E., Atlanta, GA 30312-1504. Tel.: 404-331-5190. Fax: 404-730-3112.
E-mail: judy_forte@nps.gov
Web Site: www.nps.gov/malu
Key Personnel: Supt., Judy Forte; Chief Ranger, Clark Moore; Chief Interpretation, Rebecca Karcher; Cur., Leah Berry.
Institution Type/Description: Historic Site & District: neighborhood in which Dr. Martin Luther King, Jr. grew up, includes birthplace, boyhood home, church & gravesite.
Hours & Admission Prices: Daily tours. No charge; donations accepted. Closed New Year's Day; Thanksgiving; Christmas.
Attendance: 900,000 (actual)

MICHAEL C. CARLOS MUSEUM, Emory University, 571 S. Kilgo Cir., Atlanta, GA 30322. Tel.: 404-727-4282 & 0573. Fax: 404-727-4292. TDD: 404-727-8017.
E-mail: jadanie@emory.edu
Web Site: www.carlos.emory.edu
Key Personnel: Dir., Bonnie Speed; Assoc. Dir., Catherine Howett Smith.
Institution Type/Description: Art & Archaeology Museum.
Hours & Admission Prices: Tues.-Fri. 10-4, Sat. 10-5, Sun. 12-5. Suggested Donation: adults $8, students, seniors & children 6-17 $6; discounts to AAM & ICOM members; members and children 5 & under no charge.
Attendance: 100,000 (estimated)

THE MUSEUM OF CONTEMPORARY ART OF GEORGIA (MOCA GA), 75 Bennett St. N.W., Ste. A2, Atlanta, GA 30309-1275. Tel.: 404-367-8700. Fax: 404-367-1477. Facebook: MOCAGA.
E-mail: info@mocaga.org

Web Site: www.mocaga.org
Key Personnel: C.E.O. & Dir., Annette Cone-Skelton; Chm. (V), Philip Babb.
Institution Type/Description: Art Museum.
Hours & Admission Prices: MOCA GA: Tues.-Sat. 11-5. Adults $8; seniors & students $5; discounts to NARM members; active military & members no charge. Closed New Year's Day; Martin Luther King Jr. Day; Memorial Day; Independence Day; Labor Day; Thanksgiving; Christmas.
Attendance: 10,000 (estimated)

MUSEUM OF DESIGN ATLANTA, 1315 Peachtree St., Atlanta, GA 30309. Tel.: 404-979-6455. Fax: 404-521-9311.
E-mail: info@museumofdesign.org
Web Site: www.museumofdesign.org
Formerly: Atlanta International Museum of Art and Design
Key Personnel: Exec. Dir., Laura Flusche. Ph.D.; Assoc. Dir., Clare Timmerman.
Institution Type/Description: Design Museum.
Hours & Admission Prices: Tues.-Sat. 11-5. Adults $10; members no charge.
Attendance: 15,000 (estimated)

NATIONAL CENTER FOR CIVIL AND HUMAN RIGHTS, 100 Ivan Allen Jr. Blvd., Atlanta, GA 30313. Mailing Address: 250 Williams St., Ste. 2322, Atlanta, GA 30303. Tel.: 678-999-8990. Facebook; Twitter; Instagram.
E-mail: marketing@civilandhumanrights.org
Web Site: civilandhumanrights.org
Institution Type/Description: History Museum.
Hours & Admission Prices: Mon.-Sat. 10-5, Sun. 12-5. Adults $19.99, students, seniors, & military $17.99, youth 7-12 $15.99; discounts to groups; children 6 & under no charge.

NATIONAL MUSEUM OF COMMERCIAL AVIATION, 727 Airline Museum Way, Atlanta, GA 30354. Mailing Address: 5442 Frontage Rd., Ste. 110, Forest Park, GA 30297. Tel.: 404-675-9266.
E-mail: info@nationalairlinemuseum.com
Web Site: www.nationalairlinemuseum.com
Institution Type/Description: Aviation Museum.
Hours & Admission Prices: Call for information.

NATIONAL MUSEUM OF DECORATIVE PAINTING, 1406 Woodmont Ln., Atlanta, GA 30318. Mailing Address: P.O. Box 250025, Atlanta, GA 30325. Tel.: 404-351-1151.
E-mail: info@dpmuseum.org
Web Site: dpmuseum.org
Institution Type/Description: Art Museum.
Hours & Admission Prices: By appointment. No charge; donations accepted.
Attendance: 600 (estimated)

OGLETHORPE UNIVERSITY MUSEUM OF ART, 4 Lowry Hall, 3rd Floor, 4484 Peachtree Rd., N.E., Atlanta, GA 30319-2797. Tel.: 404-364-8555. Fax: 404-364-8556. Facebook: Oglethorpe University Museum of Art.
E-mail: epeterson1@oglethorpe.edu
Web Site: museum.oglethorpe.edu
Key Personnel: Dir., Elizabeth Peterson; Cur. Collections, John Daniel Tilford.
Institution Type/Description: University Museum.
Hours & Admission Prices: Tues.-Sun. 12-5. Adults $5; groups of 10 or more $3 per person; children under 12 & members no charge. Closed major holidays; University holidays; New Year's week; Christmas week.
Attendance: 8,000 (actual)

PARKS, RECREATION & HISTORIC SITES DIVISION, GEORGIA DEPT. OF NATURAL RESOURCES, 2 Martin Luther King Jr. Dr. E., Ste. 1252, Atlanta, GA 30334-9000. Tel.: 404-656-3500. Fax: 404-651-5871.
E-mail: Becky.Kelley@dnr.ga.gov
Web Site: www.gastateparks.org
Key Personnel: Commissioner, Mark Williams; Dir., Becky Kelley.
Institution Type/Description: State Historic Agency.
Hours & Admission Prices: Mon.-Fri. 8-6, Sat.-Sun. 9-5. Roosevelt's Little White House: adults $12, seniors $10, children 6-17 $7; children under 6 $2. Parking $2. Closed Thanksgiving; Christmas.
Attendance: 2,356,821 (actual)

RHODES HALL, 1516 Peachtree St., N.W., Atlanta, GA 30309-2908. Tel.: 404-885-7800. Fax: 404-875-2205.
E-mail: events@georgiatrust.org
Web Site: www.georgiatrust.org/historic_sites/rhodes_hall.htm

Institution Type/Description: Historic House: former home of Rhodes Furniture founder, Amos Rhodes.

Hours & Admission Prices: Sat. 10-2; tours on the hour. Behind-the Scenes Tour: adults $7; discounts to AAM members. 1st Floor Tour: adults $5; discounts to senior citizens, students & children 6-12; Georgia Trust members & children under 6 no charge. Closed major holidays. &

Attendance: 7,500 (estimated)

ROBERT C. WILLIAMS PAPER MUSEUM, Institute of Paper Science & Technology, 500 10th St., N.W., Atlanta, GA 30332. Mailing Address: Institute of Paper Science & Technology, Mail Code 0620, Georgia Tech, Atlanta, GA 30332-0620. Tel.: 404-894-7840. Fax: 404-894-4778.

E-mail: teri.williams@ipst.gatech.edu

Web Site: www.ipst.gatech.edu/amp

Formerly: Robert C. Williams American Museum of Papermaking at Georgia Tech

Key Personnel: Dir., Teri Williams; Museum Coord., Jerushia Graham; Cur. Education, Virginia Howell.

Institution Type/Description: History, Art & Technology Museum.

Hours & Admission Prices: Mon.-Fri. 9-5. No charge; donations requested. Closed holidays. &

Attendance: 25,000 (estimated)

THE SALVATION ARMY SOUTHERN HISTORICAL CENTER & MUSEUM, 1032 Metropolitan Pkwy., S.W., Atlanta, GA 30310-3488. Tel.: 404-752-7578 & 753-4166. Fax: 404-753-1932.

E-mail: historical.center@uss.salvationarmy.org

Web Site: www.salvationarmyhistory.org

Key Personnel: Dir. & Archivist, Michael Nagy; Museum & Archival Asst., Andrea Troxclair.

Institution Type/Description: Religious Museum.

Hours & Admission Prices: By appointment. No charge; donations accepted. Closed New Year's Day; Good Friday; Easter; Memorial Day; Independence Day; Labor Day; Thanksgiving; Christmas. &

Attendance: 794 (actual)

SCAD FASH MUSEUM OF FASHION + FILM, 1600 Peachtree St., Atlanta, GA 30309. Tel.: 404-253-3132. Facebook, Instagram & Twitter: @SCADFASH.

E-mail: scadfash@scad.edu

Web Site: www.scadfash.org

Key Personnel: Exec. Dir., Alexandra Sachs; Dir. Fashion Exhibitions, Rafael Gomes.

Institution Type/Description: Fashion Gallery.

Hours & Admission Prices: Sun. noon to 5, Tues., Wed., Fri. & Sat. 10-5, Thurs. 10-8. Family $20, general $10, seniors & military $8, college students w/ID & SCAD alumni $5; members & children under 14 no charge.

SOUTH ARTS, 1800 Peachtree St., N.W., Ste. 808, Atlanta, GA 30309-2512. Tel.: 404-874-7244. Fax: 404-873-2148. TDD: 404-876-6240.

E-mail: mbosarge@southarts.org

Web Site: www.southarts.org

Key Personnel: Exec. Dir., Suzette Surkamer; Sr. Dir. Film & Traditional Arts, Teresa Hollingsworth.

Institution Type/Description: A regional arts agency dedicated to providing leadership & support to affect positive change in the arts throughout the south.

Hours & Admission Prices: Mon.-Fri. 9-5. No charge. &

Attendance: 100,000 (estimated)

SPELMAN COLLEGE MUSEUM OF FINE ART, 350 Spelman Lane, Box 1526, Atlanta, GA 30314. Mailing Address: P.O. Box 1526, Atlanta, GA 30314. Tel.: 404-270-5607. Fax: 404-270-5980.

E-mail: museum@spelman.edu

Web Site: museum.spelman.edu

Key Personnel: Dir., Andrea Barnwell Brownlee, Ph.D.; Cur. Collections, Anne Collins Smith.

Institution Type/Description: Art Museum.

Hours & Admission Prices: Tues.-Fri. 10-4, Sat. 12-4. Suggested Donation: $3 per person Closed Good Friday; all federal holidays & Spelman College breaks. &

Attendance: 7,000 (estimated)

SPRUILL GALLERY, 4681 Ashford-Dunwoody Rd., Atlanta, GA 30338. Tel.: 770-394-4019. Fax: 770-394-6179. www.spruillgallery.blogspot.com.

E-mail: gallery@spruillarts.org

Web Site: www.spruillarts.org

Formerly: Spruill Center for the Arts Gallery

Key Personnel: C.E.O., Robert Kinsey; Community Leader, Beth Saxe; Dir., Jennifer Price.

Institution Type/Description: Art Museum.

Hours & Admission Prices: Tues.-Sat. 11-6. No charge; donations accepted. Closed Memorial Day; Independence Day; Labor Day; Thanksgiving. &

Attendance: 25,000 (estimated)

TROIS GALLERY - SCAD ATLANTA, 1600 Peachtree St., Bldg. A, 4th Fl., Atlanta, GA 30309. Tel.: 404-815-2931.

E-mail: contact@scad.edu

Web Site: www.scad.edu/exhibitions/galleries

Institution Type/Description: Art Gallery.

Hours & Admission Prices: Mon.-Fri. 8:30-5:30. No charge.

VSA ARTS OF GEORGIA - ARTS FOR ALL GALLERY, 415 Plasters Ave., N.E., Ste. 100, Atlanta, GA 30324. Tel.: 404-221-1270. Fax: 404-221-1984.

E-mail: administrator@vsaartsga.org

Web Site: www.vsaartsga.org

Key Personnel: Interim Exec. Dir., Debra L. Elovich.

Institution Type/Description: Art Gallery.

Hours & Admission Prices: Tues.-Fri. 11-5, Sat. 12-5 No charge; donations accepted. Closed major holidays. &

Attendance: 6,400 (estimated)

THE WILLIAM BREMAN JEWISH HERITAGE MUSEUM, 1440 Spring St., N.W., Atlanta, GA 30309-2832. Tel.: 678-222-3700. Fax: 404-881-4009.

E-mail: info@thebreman.org

Web Site: www.thebreman.org

Formerly: The Breman Jewish Heritage & Holocaust Museum

Key Personnel: Acting Dir., Ghila Sanders; Dir. Cuba Family Archives, Jeremy Katz; Interim Dir. Weinberg Center for Holocaust Educ., Rabbi Joe Prass; Dir. Mktg. & Communications, David Schendowich; Dir. Membership & Visitor Svcs., Rachel Katz.

Institution Type/Description: Jewish Heritage Museum.

Hours & Admission Prices: Sun.-Thurs. 10-5, Fri. 10-4. Adults $12, senior citizens 62 & over $8, students $6, children 3-6 $4; discount to groups; children under 3 & members no charge. Closed New Year's Day; Independence Day; Thanksgiving; Jewish Holy Days. &

Attendance: 39,000 (estimated)

WORLD OF COCA-COLA PAVILION, 121 Baker St., N.W., Atlanta, GA 30313-1807. Tel.: 404-676-5151; 800-676-2653.

E-mail: cokestore@worldofcoca-cola.com

Web Site: www.worldofcoca-cola.com

Institution Type/Description: History Museum.

Hours & Admission Prices: Call for hours. Adults $17, seniors 65 & over $15, youth 3-12 $12; children 2 & under no charge. Closed Thanksgiving; Christmas.

WREN'S NEST, 1050 Ralph David Abernathy Blvd., S.W., Atlanta, GA 30310-1812. Tel.: 404-753-7735. Fax: 404-753-8535.

E-mail: info@wrensnestonline.com

Web Site: www.wrensnestonline.com

Key Personnel: Exec. Dir., Sue Gilman; Dir. Programs, Kalin Thomas.

Institution Type/Description: Historic House: 1881 home of Joel Chandler Harris, creator of Uncle Remus & chronicler of stories about Br'er Rabbit.

Hours & Admission Prices: Tues.-Sat. 10-2:30. Storytelling: Sat. 1pm. Adults $8, senior citizens & teens $7, children 4-12 $5; discounts for groups & AAM members; members no charge. Closed major holidays. &

Attendance: 9,850 (estimated)

ZOO ATLANTA, 800 Cherokee Ave., S.E., Atlanta, GA 30315-1470. Mailing Address: 800 Cherokee Ave., S.E., Ste. A, Atlanta, GA 30315-1470. Tel.: 404-624-5600.

E-mail: guestexperience@zooatlanta.org

Web Site: www.zooatlanta.org

Institution Type/Description: Zoo.

Hours & Admission Prices: March 11-Nov. 5 Mon.-Fri. 9:30-5:30, Sat.-Sun. 9:30-6:30; Nov. 6-March 10 daily 9:30-5:30. Adults $25.99, seniors $21.99, children 3-11 $17.99; discounts to groups, military & reciprocal members; members and children 2 & under no charge. Closed Thanksgiving; Christmas. &

Attendance: 710,000 (actual)

Augusta

AUGUSTA MUSEUM OF HISTORY, 560 Reynolds St., Augusta, GA 30901-1430. Tel.: 706-722-8454. Fax: 706-724-5192.

E-mail: amh@augustamuseum.org

Web Site: www.augustamuseum.org

Formerly: Augusta Richmond County Museum
Key Personnel: Exec. Dir., Nancy J. Glaser; Operations Mgr., Holly Faircloth; Exhibit Mgr., Larry Graham; Education Mgr., Harvee White; Registrar, Natalie Thompson; Visitor Svcs., W. Keith Bates; Bldgs. & Grounds, Larry Taylor.
Institution Type/Description: History Museum presenting the past of Augusta, Georgia and surrounding counties in Georgia and South Carolina.
Hours & Admission Prices: Museum: Thurs.-Sat. 10-5, Sun. 1-5. House: Tues.-Fri. by appointment, Sat. 10-5. Museum: adults $4, seniors 65 & over $3, children 6-18 $2; discounts to AAM & ICOM members; children 5 & under and members no charge. House: adults $2, children $1; children under 5 no charge. Regional & national reciprocal membership programs. &
Attendance: 35,000 (estimated)

BOYHOOD HOME OF PRESIDENT WOODROW WILSON,
419 Seventh St., Augusta, GA 30901-2317. Mailing Address: P.O. Box 37, Augusta, GA 30903-0037. Tel.: 706-722-9828. Fax: 706-724-3083.
E-mail: erick@historicaugusta.org
Web Site: www.wilsonboyhoodhome.org
Key Personnel: Exec. Dir., Erick D. Montgomery; Pres. (V), Becky Smith; Museum Shop Mgr., Stephanie Herzberg.
Institution Type/Description: Historic House Museum: childhood home of President Woodrow Wilson 1860-1870.
Hours & Admission Prices: Thurs.-Sat. 10-4 on the hour. Adults $5, senior citizens $4, students $3; discounts to groups. Closed New Year's Day; Thanksgiving; Christmas. &
Attendance: 3,500 (estimated)

GERTRUDE HERBERT INSTITUTE OF ART, 506 Telfair St.,
Augusta, GA 30901-2310. Tel.: 706-722-5495. Fax: 706-722-3670.
E-mail: ghia@ghia.org
Web Site: ghia.org
Key Personnel: Exec. Dir., Heather Williams.
Institution Type/Description: Art Museum.
Hours & Admission Prices: Tues.-Fri. 10-5, Sat. by appointment. No charge; donations accepted. Closed holidays; New Year's Eve & Day; Independence Day; Thanksgiving; Christmas Eve, Day & week. &
Attendance: 20,000 (estimated)

LUCY CRAFT LANEY MUSEUM OF BLACK HISTORY AND CONFERENCE CENTER, 1116 Phillips St., Augusta, GA
30901-2724. Tel.: 706-724-3576. Fax: 706-724-3576.
E-mail: info@lucycraftlaneymuseum.com
Web Site: www.lucycraftlaneymuseum.com
Key Personnel: Exec. Dir., Christine Miller-Betts.
Institution Type/Description: Art History Museum.
Hours & Admission Prices: Tues.-Fri. 9-5, Sat. 10-4; other times by appointment. Adults $5, senior citizens $3, students & children $2; discounts to military & seniors. Closed holidays. &
Attendance: 9,000 (estimated)

MEADOW GARDEN - THE HISTORIC FARM HOME OF GEORGE WALTON, 1320 Independence Dr., Augusta, GA
30901-1038. Tel.: 706-724-4174.
E-mail: meadowgarden@att.net
Web Site: www.historicmeadowgarden.org
Key Personnel: Mgr., Susan Jackson; Chm. (V), Virginia Nicholson; State Regent, Virginia Lingelbach.
Institution Type/Description: Historic House: 1792-1804 residence of George Walton, youngest Georgia signer of the Declaration of Independence.
Hours & Admission Prices: Mon.-Fri. 10-4, Sat. by appointment. Adults $5, seniors $4, students K-12 $1; discount to military and groups of 10 & over. &
Attendance: 1,368 (actual)

MORRIS MUSEUM OF ART, One Tenth St., Augusta, GA 30901-
1134. Tel.: 706-724-7501. Fax: 706-724-7612.
E-mail: kgrogan@themorris.org
Web Site: www.themorris.org
Key Personnel: Exec. Dir. & Cur., Kevin Grogan; Chm. (V), William S. Morris, III; Dir. Devel., Phyllis Giddens; Special Events Coord., Lauren Land; Coord. Membership Svcs., Jenna Blitch; Mktg. & Public Rels. Dir., Nicole McLeod; Cur. Education, Matt Porter; Mgr. Educational Programs & Engagement, Chelsea Stutz; Asst. Education Programs, Jason Walter; Visitor Service Coord., Kara Exum; Creative Dir., Todd Beasley; Registrar, Stacey Thompson; Asst. Registrar, Stacey Gawal; Preparator & Exhibition Designer, Dwayne Clark; Senior Guard, Frank Lozito; Security Officer, William Lay; Security Officer, Richard Bohn; Museum Store Clerk, Kim Grimes; Finance Officer, Mary Gadson; Archivist & Librarian, Cary Wilkins; Asst. Librarian, Jacob Vaz; Museum Store Mgr., Christy Love; Museum Store Asst. Mgr., Diane Maloney; Office Mgr., Brenda Hall; Consulting Editor, Keith Claussen.
Institution Type/Description: Art Museum.

Hours & Admission Prices: Tues.-Sat. 10-5, Sun. 12:30-5. Adults $5, senior citizens, military & students $3; discounts to groups, AAM, ICOM, SEMC, GAMG & Southeastern Art Museum Directors' Forum Members (SEAMD); children under 12, members & Sunday no charge. Closed New Year's Day; Easter; Independence Day; Thanksgiving; Christmas. &
Attendance: 36,000 (actual)

SACRED HEART CULTURAL CENTER, 1301 Greene St.,
Augusta, GA 30901. Tel.: 706-826-4700.
E-mail: sfenst@knology.net
Web Site: www.sacredheartaugusta.org
Key Personnel: Exec. Dir., Sandra Fenstermacher; Rental Coord., Rachel Gregory; Museum Shop Mgr., Judy Evans.
Institution Type/Description: Cultural Center.
Hours & Admission Prices: Mon.-Fri. 9-5; other times by appointment. No charge; donations accepted.

1797 EZEKIEL HARRIS HOUSE, 1822 Broad St., Augusta, GA
30904-3918. Mailing Address: 560 Reynolds St., Augusta, GA 30901. Tel.: 706-722-8454. Fax: 706-724-5192.
E-mail: amh@augustamuseum.org
Web Site: www.augustamuseum.org/harris.htm
Key Personnel: Dir., Nancy J. Glaser; Pres. (V), Karla Leeper.
Institution Type/Description: Historic House: 1797 Ezekiel Harris House.
Hours & Admission Prices: Tues.-Sat. 10-5, Sun. 1-5. Adults $4, seniors $3, children 6-18 $2; discounts to AAM & ICOM members; members and children 5 & under no charge. Closed New Year's Day; Martin Luther King Jr. Day; Presidents' Day; Memorial Day; Independence Day; Labor Day; Thanksgiving; Christmas Eve. & Day.
Attendance: 2,000 (actual)

Bainbridge

FIREHOUSE CENTER & GALLERY, 119 W. Water St.,
Bainbridge, GA 39817-3693. Mailing Address: P.O. Box 35, Bainbridge, GA 39818-0035. Tel.: 229-243-1010.
Institution Type/Description: Art Museum.
Hours & Admission Prices: Mon.-Fri. 12-4, Sat.-Sun. 1-5; groups by appointment.

Blairsville

MISTY MOUNTAIN TRAIN MUSEUM, 16 Misty Mountain Ln.,
Blairsville, GA 30512. Tel.: 706-400-2085.
Web Site: www.mistymtnmodelrailroad.com
Institution Type/Description: Model Railroad Museum.
Hours & Admission Prices: Temporarily closed.

UNION COUNTY HISTORICAL SOCIETY MUSEUM, 3 Town
Square, Blairsville, GA 30512. Mailing Address: P.O. Box 35, Blairsville, GA 30514-0035. Tel.: 706-745-5493. Fax: 706-781-1899. Facebook: Union County Historical Society Museum.
E-mail: history1@windstream.net
Web Site: unioncountyhistory.org
Key Personnel: Pres. (V), William Akins; Vice Pres., Alan Denmon; Treas., Lewis McAfee; Admin., Edie Rich; Museum Shop Mgr., Frances Partin.
Institution Type/Description: Historical Society Museum: housed in old Union County Courthouse.
Hours & Admission Prices: May-Nov. Mon.-Sat. 10-4; Dec.-April Mon.-Fri. 10-4. No charge; donations accepted. Closed New Year's Day; Martin Luther King Jr. Day; Labor Day; Christmas. &
Attendance: 10,000 (estimated)

Blakely

KOLOMOKI MOUNDS STATE PARK MUSEUM, Off U.S.
Hwy. 27, follow signs for park, 205 Indian Mounds Rd., Blakely, GA 39823-4460. Tel.: 229-724-2150. Fax: 229-724-2152.
E-mail: kolomoki_park@dnr.state.ga.us
Web Site: www.gastateparks.org
Key Personnel: Park Mgr., Matt Bruner; Interpreter & Museum Shop Mgr., Billy Adams.
Institution Type/Description: Historic Site: 13th-century Indian burial mound & village site.
Hours & Admission Prices: Museum: daily 8-5. Historic Sites: adults $5, seniors $4, youth 6-17 $3.50; discounts to groups; children under 6 no charge. Closed Christmas. &
Attendance: 20,000 (actual)

Brunswick

HOFWYL-BROADFIELD PLANTATION STATE HISTORIC SITE, 5556 U.S. Hwy. 17 N., Brunswick, GA 31525-4651. Tel.: 912-264-7333. Fax: 912-262-3346.
Web Site: www.gastateparks.org/info/hofwyl/
Key Personnel: Site Mgr., Bill Giles; Park Ranger (Interpretation), Faye Cowart; Park Ranger (Interpretation), Andy Beckman.
Institution Type/Description: Historic House: c.1850 Hofwyl-Broadfield Plantation.
Hours & Admission Prices: Wed.-Sun. 9-5. Adults $8, senior citizens 62 & over $7, youth 6-17 $5; discount to groups; children under 6 no charge. Closed New Year's Day; Thanksgiving; Christmas. &
Attendance: 25,000 (actual)

Buckhead

STEFFEN THOMAS MUSEUM OF ART, 4200 Bethany Rd., Buckhead, GA 30625-1729. Tel.: 706-342-7557. Fax: 706-342-4348.
E-mail: info@steffenthomas.org
Web Site: www.steffenthomas.org
Key Personnel: Acting Dir. & Arts Outreach Program Coord., Lisa Conner; Pres., Nancy Vaughan; Vice Pres., Preston Small; Sec. & Treas., Betty Straw Brown; Office Administration, P. Tommany; Visitor Svcs., Sadie Carter; Visitor Svcs., Ashley Myers.
Institution Type/Description: Visual Arts Museum.
Hours & Admission Prices: Tues.-Sat. 11-4. Adults $5, senior citizens & students $3; members & children under 6 no charge. Closed New Year's Day; Martin Luther King, Jr. Day; Memorial Day; Independence Day; Labor Day; Thanksgiving Day; Christmas. &
Attendance: 5,000 (actual)

Buford

GWINNETT ENVIRONMENTAL AND HERITAGE CENTER, 2020 Clean Water Dr., Buford, GA 30519. Tel.: 770-904-3500. Fax: 770-932-3041.
E-mail: info@gwinnettehc.org
Web Site: gwinnettehc.org
Institution Type/Description: Science & History Center.
Hours & Admission Prices: Center: Mon.-Sat. 9-4, last Sun. each month 1-5. Trails: daily dawn to dusk. Adults $7.50, seniors 55 & over and students 13-22 $5.50, children 3-12 $3.50; children 2 & under and members no charge. Closed Thanksgiving; Christmas Eve & Day.

Calhoun

NEW ECHOTA STATE HISTORIC SITE, 1211 Chatsworth Hwy., N.E., Calhoun, GA 30701. Tel.: 706-624-1321. Fax: 706-624-1324.
E-mail: becky.kelley@dnr.ga.gov
Web Site: www.gastateparks.org
Formerly: New Echota State Historical Society
Key Personnel: Supt., David Gomez.
Institution Type/Description: Preservation Project: 1825 capital town of Cherokee Nation.
Hours & Admission Prices: Thurs.-Sat. 9-5. Self-Guided Tours: Thurs.-Sat. Adults $6.50, seniors 62 & over $6, youth 6-17 $5; children under 6 $2; discount to AAA & AAM members and groups. Closed New Year's Day; Thanksgiving; Christmas. &
Attendance: 20,000 (estimated)

ROLAND HAYES MUSEUM, 212 S. Wall St., Calhoun, GA 30701-2499. Tel.: 706-629-2599. Fax: 706-602-2599.
E-mail: info@harrisartscenter.com
Web Site: www.harrisartscenter.com/harris-arts-center/roland-hayes
Key Personnel: Dir. Harris Arts Center, Jennifer Dudley.
Institution Type/Description: History Museum.
Hours & Admission Prices: Mon. 10-6, Tues.-Thurs. 10-4, Fri.-Sat. 10-2. No charge.

Canton

CHEROKEE COUNTY HISTORY MUSEUM & VISITOR CENTER, 100 North St., Ste. 140, Canton, GA 30114. Mailing Address: P.O. Box 1287, Canton, GA 30169. Tel.: 770-345-3288. Fax: 770-345-3289.
E-mail: sjoyner@rockbarn.org
Web Site: www.rockbarn.org
Formerly: Historic Cherokee County Courthouse

Institution Type/Description: Historical Society Museum.
Hours & Admission Prices: Call for hours. No charge; donations accepted.

Cartersville

BARTOW HISTORY MUSEUM, 4 E. Church St., Cartersville, GA 30120-3331. Tel.: 770-382-3818. Fax: 770-383-9314.
E-mail: treyg@bartowhistorymuseum.org
Web Site: www.bartowhistorymuseum.org
Key Personnel: Dir., Trey Gaines; Education Coord., Charity Chastain; Museum Shop Mgr., Elaine Popham.
Institution Type/Description: History Museum.
Hours & Admission Prices: Mon.-Sat. 10-5. Adults $5.50, seniors & students $4.50; active military & members no charge. Southeastern Reciprocal Membership Program. Closed major holidays. &
Attendance: 10,575 (actual)

BOOTH WESTERN ART MUSEUM, 501 N. Museum Dr., Cartersville, GA 30120-3272. Mailing Address: P.O. Box 3070, Cartersville, GA 30120-1702. Tel.: 770-387-1300. Fax: 770-387-1319. Facebook; Twitter; Instagram; Youtube.
E-mail: marketing@boothmuseum.org
Web Site: www.boothmuseum.org
Key Personnel: Dir., Seth Hopkins; Devel., Diane Homesley; Education, Patty Petrey Dees; Mktg., Tom Shinall; Deputy Dir. Opers., Cathy Lee Eckert; Registrar, Nikki Morris; Cur., Lisa Wheeler; Librarian & Archivist, Liz Gentry; Museum Shop Mgr., Gina Windsor; Security, Macra Adair.
Institution Type/Description: Art Museum.
Hours & Admission Prices: Tues.-Wed. & Fri.-Sat. 10-5, Thurs. 10-8, Sun. 1-5. Adults $10, seniors 65 & over $8, students $7; discounts to groups of 10 or more; military, children 12 & under and members no charge. &
Attendance: 47,556 (actual)

ETOWAH INDIAN MOUNDS HISTORICAL SITE, 813 Indian Mounds Rd., S.W., Cartersville, GA 30120-6415. Tel.: 770-387-3747. Fax: 770-387-3972. Facebook.
E-mail: etowah_mounds@dnr.state.ga.us
Web Site: www.gastateparks.org/info/etowah
Key Personnel: Cur., Keith Bailey.
Institution Type/Description: Archaeology Museum.
Hours & Admission Prices: Tues.-Sat. 9-5. Adults $6, seniors $5, youth 6-17 $4, children under 6 $2; discount to school groups of 15 or more. Closed New Year's Day; Thanksgiving; Christmas. &
Attendance: 50,000 (actual)

EUHARLEE COVERED BRIDGE AND HISTORIC MUSEUM, 33 Covered Bridge Rd., Cartersville, GA 30120. Tel.: 770-607-2017.
E-mail: kodom@euharlee.com
Web Site: www.euharleehistory.org
Key Personnel: Chm. (V), Jean G. Cowart.
Institution Type/Description: Historic Site: bridge built in 1886 by Washington W. King, a black contractor. Listed on the National Register of Historic Places.
Hours & Admission Prices: Museum: Wed.-Sat. 10-4, Sun. 2-4. No charge; donations accepted. &
Attendance: 2,000 (actual)

HISTORIC DEPOT AT FRIENDSHIP PLAZA, One Friendship Plaza, Cartersville, GA 30120-3570. Mailing Address: P.O. Box 200397, Cartersville, GA 30120. Tel.: 770-387-1357, 800-733-2280.
E-mail: ddainfo@downtowncartersville.org
Web Site: www.downtowncartersville.org
Institution Type/Description: Historic Building: built in 1854.
Hours & Admission Prices: Mon.-Fri. 9-5, Sat. 11-2, Sun. 1:30-4:30. &

ROSE LAWN MUSEUM, 224 W. Cherokee Ave., Cartersville, GA 30120-3004. Tel.: 770-387-5162. Fax: 770-386-1527.
E-mail: roselawnga@comcast.net
Web Site: www.roselawnmuseum.com
Key Personnel: Dir., Jane Drew; Commissioner, Steve Taylor.
Institution Type/Description: Historic House: c.1880 Victorian mansion, former home of evangelist Samuel Porter Jones.
Hours & Admission Prices: Tues.-Fri. 10-12 & 1-5; other times by appointment. Adults $5, students $2. Closed holidays. &
Attendance: 10,000 (actual)

TELLUS SCIENCE MUSEUM, 100 Tellus Dr., Cartersville, GA 30120. Mailing Address: P.O. Box 3663, Cartersville, GA 30120-1712. Tel.: 770-606-5700. Fax: 770-386-0600.
E-mail: info@tellusmuseum.org
Web Site: www.tellusmuseum.org
Formerly: Tellus: Northwest Georgia Science Museum
Institution Type/Description: Science Museum.
Hours & Admission Prices: Daily 10-5. Adults $14, seniors 65 & over $12, children 3-17 & students with ID $10; active military & members no charge. Planetarium show $3.50. &
Attendance: 200,000 (estimated)

Cedartown

THE POLK COUNTY HISTORICAL SOCIETY, 117 West Ave., Cedartown, GA 30125. Mailing Address: P.O. Box 203, Cedartown, GA 30125-0203. Tel.: 770-748-4828 & 749-0073.
E-mail: pchsmuseum@outlook.com
Web Site: polkhist.com
Key Personnel: Cur., Greg Gray.
Institution Type/Description: Historical Society Museum: housed in 1921 former Hawke's Children's Library.
Hours & Admission Prices: Thurs.-Sat. 11-4. Adults 12 & over $3; discounts to groups; members & children under 12 no charge.
Attendance: 300 (estimated)

Chatsworth

CHIEF VANN HOUSE HISTORIC SITE, 82 Hwy. 225 N., Chatsworth, GA 30705-6331. Tel.: 706-695-2598. Fax: 706-517-4255.
E-mail: vann_house_park@dnr.state.ga.us
Web Site: www.gastateparks.org
Key Personnel: Museum Shop Mgr. & Site Supvr., Jeff Stancil.
Institution Type/Description: Historic House Museum: housed c.1804 Vann House.
Hours & Admission Prices: Thurs.-Sat. 9-5, Sun. 1-5. Adults $6.50, seniors $6, youth 6-17 $5.50; discounts to groups; children 5 & under and members no charge. Closed New Year's Day; Thanksgiving; Christmas. &
Attendance: 12,000 (actual)

FORT MOUNTAIN STATE PARK, 181 Fort Mountain Park Rd., Chatsworth, GA 30705-6669. Tel.: 706-422-1932. Fax: 706-422-1930.
Web Site: www.gastateparks.org
Key Personnel: Supt., Brian Ensley.
Institution Type/Description: State Park.
Hours & Admission Prices: Park: daily 7am-10pm. Office: daily 8-5. Parking $5.

Clarkesville

THE MAULDIN HOUSE, MILLINERY SHOP AND BIG HOLLY CABIN, 458 Jefferson St., Clarkesville, GA 30523. Mailing Address: P.O. Box 21, Clarkesville, GA 30523. Tel.: 706-754-2220. Fax: 706-754-2231.
E-mail: mbhorton@clarkesvillega.com
Web Site: www.clarksvillega.com
Institution Type/Description: History Museum.
Hours & Admission Prices: Mon.-Fri. 8-5; other times by appointment. No charge; donations accepted. &
Attendance: 6,000 (estimated)

Cleveland

BABYLAND GENERAL HOSPITAL/CABBAGE PATCH KIDS, 300 N.O.K. Dr., Cleveland, GA 30528. Tel.: 706-865-2171. Facebook; Twitter.
Web Site: cabbagepatchkids.com
Institution Type/Description: Company Museum.
Hours & Admission Prices: Mon.-Sat. 9-5, Sun. 10-5. No charge. Closed major holidays.

WHITE COUNTY HISTORICAL SOCIETY, White County Court House, Cleveland, GA 30528. Mailing Address: P.O. Box 1139, Cleveland, GA 30528-0022. Tel.: 706-865-3225.
E-mail: wchsga@outlook.com
Key Personnel: Pres., Mark S. Johnson; Vice Pres., Emory Jones; Treas., Judy Lovell; Museum Shop Mgr., Norma Holeman.
Institution Type/Description: Local History Museum.

Hours & Admission Prices: Thurs.-Sat. 10-3. No charge; donations accepted. &
Attendance: 800 (estimated)

Columbus

COCA-COLA SPACE SCIENCE CENTER, 701 Front Ave., Columbus, GA 31901-2925. Tel.: 706-649-1477. Fax: 706-649-1478.
E-mail: info@ccssc.org
Web Site: www.ccssc.org
Key Personnel: Exec. Dir., Dr. Shawn Cruzen; Asst. Dir., Wanja Ngugi; Dir. Challenger Learning Center, Scott Norman; Dir. Planetarium, Lance Tankersley; Coord. Visitor Svcs., Dutch Cummings.
Institution Type/Description: Science Center.
Hours & Admission Prices: Mon.-Fri. 10-4, Sat. 10:30-6. Adults $6, military & seniors $5, children $4, CSU ID card holders $3; discounts to ASTC members. &
Attendance: 35,000 (estimated)

THE COLUMBUS MUSEUM, 1251 Wynnton Rd., Columbus, GA 31906-2899. Tel.: 706-748-2562. Fax: 706-748-2570.
E-mail: information@columbusmuseum.com
Web Site: www.columbusmuseum.com
Key Personnel: Dir., Marianne Richter; Asst. to Dir., Patricia Butts; Mgr. Collections, Aimee Brooks; Cur. History & Exhibitions Mgr., Rebecca Bush; Coord. Community Outreach, Kennan Ducey; Coord. Youth & Family Programs, Jessamy South; Dir. Education, Lucy Kacir; Dir. Devel., Carmen Overton; Mgr. Membership, Hillary Scalmanini; Dir. Mktg. & Public Rels., Bridgette Russell; Devel. Asst., Morgan Wilson; Deputy Dir. Operations, Kimberly Beck; Museum Shop Mgr., Brooke Starling; Security Chief, Rick McGowan; Security Deputy, Alfred Johnson; Security Deputy, Larry Hunter.
Institution Type/Description: Art & History Museum.
Hours & Admission Prices: Tues.-Wed. & Fri.-Sat. 10-5, Thurs. 10-8, Sun. 1-5. No charge; donations accepted. Closed legal holidays. &
Attendance: 65,000 (estimated)

HISTORIC COLUMBUS FOUNDATION, INC., 1440 Second Ave., Columbus, GA 31901-2124. Mailing Address: P.O. Box 5312, Columbus, GA 31906-0312. Tel.: 706-322-0756. Fax: 706-576-4760.
E-mail: hcfinc@historiccolumbus.com
Web Site: www.historiccolumbus.com
Key Personnel: Bd. Chm., George G. Flowers; Pres., Jack P. Jenkins; Exec. Dir., Elizabeth K. Barker; Dir. Finance & Admin., Debbie Lipscomb; Dir. Planning & Prog., Justin Krieg; Dir. Cultural Outreach, Callie Hecht.
Institution Type/Description: Historic Foundation: five house museums including c.1870 first brick house in original residential part of city.
Hours & Admission Prices: By appointment.
Attendance: 3,000 (estimated)

HISTORIC WESTVILLE, INC., 3557 S. Lumpkin Rd., Columbus, GA 31903. Tel.: 706-940-0057. Fax: 229-838-4000. Facebook.
E-mail: info@westville.org
Web Site: www.westville.org
Formerly: Westville Historic Handicrafts
Key Personnel: Dir. Mktg. & Publications, Darby Britto; Dir. Devel., Royce Ann Adkins; Mgr. Collections & Archaeologist, Gillian Wong.
Institution Type/Description: Historic Village Museum: thirty-four buildings & houses c.1850.
Hours & Admission Prices: Wed.-Sat. 9-4, Sun. 12-5. Adults $10, senior citizens, college students & military $8, children K-12 $5; discounts to groups, AAM & ALHFAM members; members & Pre-K students no charge. Closed New Year's Eve & Day; Thanksgiving; Christmas. &
Attendance: 13,000 (estimated)

NATIONAL CIVIL WAR NAVAL MUSEUM AT PORT COLUMBUS, 1002 Victory Dr., Columbus, GA 31901-3429. Tel.: 706-327-9798. Fax: 706-324-7225. Facebook; Twitter.
E-mail: director@portcolumbus.org
Web Site: www.portcolumbus.org
Key Personnel: Exec. Dir., Holly Wait.
Institution Type/Description: Naval Museum.
Hours & Admission Prices: Mon.-Sat. 10-4:30, Sun. 12:30-4:30. Adults $8, military and seniors 65 & over $7, students $6; members and children 6 & under no charge. Closed New Year's Day; Easter; Thanksgiving; Christmas. &
Attendance: 28,000 (actual)

NATIONAL INFANTRY MUSEUM, 1775 Legacy Way, Columbus, GA 31903. Tel.: 706-545-2958. Fax: 706-545-5158.
Web Site: www.infantry.army.mil/museum

Key Personnel: Dir., Scott A. D. Daubert.
Institution Type/Description: Military History Museum.
Hours & Admission Prices: Tues.-Sat. 9-5, Sun. 11-5. Suggested Donation: $5. &

Attendance: 77,493 (actual)

THE RIVER MARKET ANTIQUES & LUNCHBOX MUSEUM,
3218 Hamilton Rd., Columbus, GA 31904. Tel.: 706-653-6240.
Web Site: therivermarketantiques.com
Key Personnel: Contact, Allen Woodall.
Institution Type/Description: Lunchbox Museum.
Hours & Admission Prices: Mon.-Sat. 10-6.

Conyers

MONASTERY OF THE HOLY SPIRIT HERITAGE CENTER AND MUSEUM, 2625 Hwy. 212 S.W., Conyers, GA 30094. Tel.: 770-483-8705 & 760-0959.
Web Site: trappist.net
Institution Type/Description: Religious Museum.
Hours & Admission Prices: Mon.-Sat. 10-4:30. No charge; donations accepted. Closed New Year's Day; Easter; Memorial Day; Independence Day; Labor Day; Thanksgiving; Christmas.

Cordele

GEORGIA VETERANS MEMORIAL MUSEUM, 2459-A Hwy. 280 W., Cordele, GA 31015-9511. Tel.: 229-276-2371. Fax: 229-276-2711.
E-mail: a.sayles@gavetspark.com
Web Site: www.gastateparks.com
Key Personnel: Mgr., James Bell.
Institution Type/Description: Military Museum.
Hours & Admission Prices: Daily 8-5. Museum: no charge; donations accepted. Park: $5 per vehicle. Closed Thanksgiving & Christmas. &
Attendance: 3,403 (actual)

Cornelia

LOUDERMILK BOARDING HOUSE MUSEUM & EVERYTHING ELVIS MUSEUM, 271 Foreacre St., Cornelia, GA 30531-3659. Tel.: 706-778-2001. Facebook: Loudermilk Boarding House Museum.
E-mail: elvisqueen@windstream.net
Web Site: bigefest.com
Key Personnel: Dir. & Museum Shop Mgr., Joni Mabe.
Institution Type/Description: History Museum: housed in the former home of Robert Loudermilk and his wife, Phanettia Henderson; built in 1908.
Hours & Admission Prices: Fri.-Sat. 10-5. Admission $10; children under 6 no charge.

Crawfordville

CONFEDERATE MUSEUM, 456 Alexander St., Crawfordville, GA 30631-2903. Mailing Address: P.O. Box 310, Crawfordville, GA 30631-0310. Tel.: 706-456-2221 (Museum) & 2602 (Park Office). Fax: 706-456-2396.
Key Personnel: Dir., Andre McLenton.
Institution Type/Description: History Museum.
Hours & Admission Prices: Tues.-Sun. 10-5. Adults $4, senior citizens $3.50, children 6-18 $2; discounts to groups; children 5 & under no charge. Closed New Year's Day; Thanksgiving; Christmas. &
Attendance: 92,000

Dahlonega

DAHLONEGA GOLD MUSEUM STATE HISTORIC SITE, #1 Public Square, Dahlonega, GA 30533-1210. Tel.: 706-864-2257. Fax: 706-864-8370.
E-mail: dahlonega@dnr.state.ga.us
Web Site: www.gastateparks.org
Formerly: Historic Lumpkin County Courthouse
Key Personnel: Site Mgr., David Foot; Interpretive Ranger, Teresa Krummel; Interpretive Ranger, Robin Glass.
Institution Type/Description: Historic Building: housed in c.1836 Lumpkin County Courthouse.
Hours & Admission Prices: Mon.-Sat. 9-4:45, Sun. 10-4:45. Adults $8.50, senior citizens 62 & over $8, children 6-17 $6; discount to groups with reservation; children 6 & under no charge. Annual Pass available. Closed New Year's Day; Thanksgiving; Christmas. &
Attendance: 60,000 (actual)

Dallas

PAULDING COUNTY HISTORICAL SOCIETY & MUSEUM,
295 N. Johnston St., Dallas, GA 30132-3603. Mailing Address: P. O. Box 333, Dallas, GA 30132. Tel.: 770-505-3485.
E-mail: pchsminc@gmail.com
Institution Type/Description: Historical Society Museum.
Hours & Admission Prices: Thurs. 12-4. Adults $2, children $1.

Dalton

CREATIVE ARTS GUILD, 520 W. Waugh St., Dalton, GA 30720-3474. Tel.: 706-278-0168. Fax: 706-278-6996.
E-mail: terryt@creativeartsguild.org
Web Site: www.creativeartsguild.org
Key Personnel: Dir. Guild Ctr., Jessie Fincher; Dir. Gallery, Savannah Thomas.
Institution Type/Description: Art Commission & Gallery.
Hours & Admission Prices: Tues.-Thurs. 10-6, Fri. 10-4. Galleries: Sat. 9am-12pm; other times by appointment. No charge; donations accepted. Closed New Year's Day; Memorial Day; Independence Day; Labor Day; Thanksgiving; Christmas. &
Attendance: 200,000

PRATERS MILL FOUNDATION, 5845 Hwy. 2, Dalton, GA 30721-1282. Mailing Address: P.O. Drawer H, Varnell, GA 30756-1008. Tel.: 706-694-6455. Fax: 706-694-8413. Facebook: Praters Mill.
E-mail: pratersmill@pratersmill.org
Web Site: www.pratersmill.org
Key Personnel: Exec. Dir., Elaine Watkins; Fair Dir., Mikey Sims.
Institution Type/Description: Historic Site Museum: housed in c.1855 grist mill & c.1898 Prater's Country Store.
Hours & Admission Prices: Grounds: sunrise to sunset. No charge. Group Tours: by appointment. Adults $7. Country Fair: adults $7; discounts to tour groups; children under 12 no charge.
Attendance: 10,000 (estimated)

WHITFIELD-MURRAY HISTORICAL SOCIETY, 715 Chattanooga Ave., Dalton, GA 30720-8804. Mailing Address: P.O. Box 6180, Dalton, GA 30722-6180. Tel.: 706-278-0217. Facebook: @WhitfieldMurrayHistoricalSociety.
E-mail: wmhs@optilink.us
Web Site: whitfield-murrayhistoricalsociety.org
Formerly: Crown Gardens and Archives
Key Personnel: Exec. Dir., Vallarie Pratt; Pres., Timothy Howard.
Institution Type/Description: Preservation Project & Historic Building: c.1890 Crown Cotton Mill office building located in the Crown Mill Historic District; 1848 Blunt House; 1908 Wright Hotel-Chatsworth; 1840 John Hamilton House-Chatsworth Depot; Historic Huff House-Dalton; Old Spring Place Methodist Church-Spring Place.
Hours & Admission Prices: Mon.-Fri. 10-4, Sat. by appointment. Crown Gardens: no charge; donations accepted. Hamilton House & Blunt House: no charge; donations accepted. Closed New Year's Day; Martin Luther King, Jr. Day; Memorial Day; Independence Day week; Labor Day; Thanksgiving; Christmas week. &
Attendance: 7,000 (estimated)

Darien

FORT KING GEORGE STATE HISTORIC SITE, 302 McIntosh Rd., S.E., Darien, GA 31305. Mailing Address: P.O. Box 711, Darien, GA 31305-0711. Tel.: 912-437-4770. Fax: 912-437-5479. Facebook.
E-mail: fortkinggeorge.shs@dnr.state.ga.us
Web Site: www.gastateparks.org/fortkinggeorge
Key Personnel: Historic Site Mgr., Valarie Ikhwan; Interpreter, Jason Baker; Museum Shop Mgr., Andrea Spicey.
Institution Type/Description: History Museum & Historic Site.
Hours & Admission Prices: Tues.-Sun. 9-5. Adults $7.50, senior citizens $7, youth $4.50; discount to groups of 15 or more; children under 6 no charge. Closed New Year's Day; Thanksgiving; Christmas. &
Attendance: 15,000 (estimated)

Decatur

DALTON GALLERIES, Agnes Scott College, Dana Fine Arts Bldg., 141 E. College Ave., Decatur, GA 30030-5361. Tel.: 404-471-5361. Fax: 404-471-5369.
E-mail: daltongallery@agnesscott.edu
Web Site: daltongallery.agnesscott.edu

Institution Type/Description: Art Gallery.
Hours & Admission Prices: During academic school year: Mon.-Fri. 10-4:30, Sat.-Sun.12-4. No charge. &
Attendance: 1,500 (estimated)

DEKALB HISTORY CENTER MUSEUM, 101 E. Court Sq., Decatur, GA 30030-2544. Tel.: 404-373-1088. Fax: 404-373-8287.
E-mail: info@dekalbhistory.org
Web Site: www.dekalbhistory.org
Formerly: DeKalb Historical Society Museum
Key Personnel: Exec. Dir., Melissa Forgey; Treas., John Hewitt.
Institution Type/Description: History Museum: housed in the Old Courthouse on Decatur Square.
Hours & Admission Prices: Museum: call for hours. Swanton House & Biffle Cabin: open by appointment. Closed county & national holidays. &
Attendance: 3,600 (estimated)

Demorest

JOHNNY MIZE ATHLETIC CENTER AND MUSEUM, 280 Laurel Ave., Demorest, GA 30535. Tel.: 706-778-3000.
Institution Type/Description: Sports Museum.
Hours & Admission Prices: Mon.-Fri. 9-5. No charge.

MASON-SCHARFENSTEIN MUSEUM OF ART - PIEDMONT COLLEGE, 567 Georgia St., Demorest, GA 30535. Tel.: 800-277-7020.
E-mail: museum@piedmont.edu
Web Site: www.piedmont.edu/art/gallery.html
Institution Type/Description: Art Gallery.
Hours & Admission Prices: Call for hours.

Douglas

HERITAGE STATION MUSEUM, 219 W. Ward St., Douglas, GA 31533-3501. Tel.: 912-389-3461. Fax: 912-389-3446. Facebook: @CCHistoricalSociety.
E-mail: cchs@cityofdouglas.com
Key Personnel: Pres. (V), Mgr. & Dir., Carol Morgan.
Institution Type/Description: History Museum.
Hours & Admission Prices: Thurs. & Fri. 10-4, Sat. 10-2. $1. &
Attendance: 680 (actual)

WORLD WAR II FLIGHT TRAINING MUSEUM, 3 Airport Cir., Douglas, GA 31534. Tel.: 912-383-9111.
E-mail: douglas63rd@windstream.net
Web Site: www.wwiiflighttraining.org
Institution Type/Description: Military History Museum.
Hours & Admission Prices: Fri.-Sat. 11-4.

Douglasville

CULTURAL ARTS COUNCIL OF DOUGLASVILLE - DOUGLAS COUNTY, 8652 Campbellton St., Douglasville, GA 30134-1825. Mailing Address: P.O. Box 2018, Douglasville, GA 30133-2018. Tel.: 770-949-2787. Fax: 770-949-5946. Facebook: @cac.dville; Twitter: @artsdouglas.
E-mail: cultureom@earthlink.net
Web Site: www.artsdouglas.org
Key Personnel: Exec. Dir., Davina Grace Hill.
Institution Type/Description: Cultural Arts Center: housed in the historic Roberts/Mozley house, built in 1901. Listed on the National Register of Historic Places.
Hours & Admission Prices: Jan. 3-Dec. 21 Mon.-Fri. 9-5. No charge; donations accepted. &
Attendance: 15,000 (actual)

DOUGLAS COUNTY MUSEUM OF HISTORY AND ART, 6754 W. Broad St., Old Douglas County Courthouse, Douglasville, GA 30134-1711. Tel.: 770-949-4090.
E-mail: info@douglascountymuseum.com
Web Site: douglascountymuseum.com
Institution Type/Description: History Museum: housed in the Old Douglas County Courthouse.
Hours & Admission Prices: Tues.-Fri. 10-5, Sat. 10-3. No charge.

Dublin

DUBLIN-LAURENS MUSEUM, 311 Academy Ave., Dublin, GA 31021-5219. Mailing Address: P.O. Box 1461, Dublin, GA 31040-1461. Tel.: 478-272-9242.
E-mail: museum@laurenshistory.org
Key Personnel: Dir., Scott Thompson, Sr.
Institution Type/Description: Historical Society Museum: housed in 1904 restored Carnegie Library.
Hours & Admission Prices: Tues.-Fri. 1-4:30; other times by appointment. No charge; donations accepted. &
Attendance: 4,000 (estimated)

Duluth

GWINNETT COUNTY PARKS & RECREATION - MCDANIEL FARM PARK, 3251 McDaniel Rd., Duluth, GA 30096-4605. Mailing Address: 75 Langley Dr., Lawrenceville, GA 30045-6936. Tel.: 770-814-4920. Fax: 770-814-4922.
E-mail: mark.patterson@gwinnettcounty.com
Web Site: www.gwinnettcounty.com
Formerly: Lanier Museum of Natural History
Key Personnel: Dir., Dr. Mark A. Patterson.
Institution Type/Description: Historic Site.
Hours & Admission Prices: Fri.-Sat. 10-4, Sun. 12-4. Admission $1; discounts to AAM & ICOM members; members & Gwinnett History Museum members no charge.
Attendance: 40,000 (estimated)

JACQUELINE CASEY HUDGENS CENTER FOR THE ARTS, 6400 Sugarloaf Pkwy., Bldg. 300, Duluth, GA 30097-7419. Tel.: 770-623-6002. Fax: 770-623-3555.
E-mail: info@thehudgens.org
Web Site: www.thehudgens.org
Formerly: Gwinnett Fine Arts Center
Key Personnel: Bd. Chm., Stan Hall; Exec. Dir., Teresa Osborn; Dir. Mktg., Kelly Olson; Dir. Education, Angela Nichols.
Institution Type/Description: Art Museum.
Hours & Admission Prices: Tues.-Sat. 10-5. Adults $5, seniors & students $3; children 2 & under no charge. Closed New Year's Day; Martin Luther King Jr. Day; Memorial Day; Independence Day; Labor Day; Thanksgiving; Christmas. &
Attendance: 45,000 (estimated)

SOUTHEASTERN RAILWAY MUSEUM, 3595 Buford Hwy., Duluth, GA 30096. Mailing Address: P.O. Box 1267, Duluth, GA 30096-0023. Tel.: 770-476-2013. Fax: 770-573-3754.
E-mail: admin@southeasternrailwaymuseum.org
Web Site: www.srmduluth.org
Key Personnel: Admin., Randy Pirkle.
Institution Type/Description: Railway Museum.
Hours & Admission Prices: Jan.-Feb. Thurs.-Sat. 10-5; March-May & Aug.-Dec. Wed.-Sat. 10-5; June-July Tues.-Sat. 10-5. Adults $10, seniors 65 & over $8, children 2-12 $7; discounts to groups & NRHS members; children under 2 no charge. &
Attendance: 15,150 (actual)

East Point

EAST POINT HISTORICAL SOCIETY, 1685 Norman Berry Dr., East Point, GA 30344. Mailing Address: P.O. Box 90675, East Point, GA 30364-0675. Tel.: 404-767-4656.
E-mail: ephistoricalsociety@gmail.com
Web Site: www.eastpoinths.org
Institution Type/Description: Historical Society Museum.
Hours & Admission Prices: Thurs. 1-4, Sat. 11-3. No charge.

Eatonton

UNCLE REMUS MUSEUM, 214 Oak St., Eatonton, GA 31024. Mailing Address: P.O. Box 3184, Eatonton, GA 31024-3184. Tel.: 706-485-6856.
Web Site: www.uncleremusmuseum.org/contact/
Key Personnel: C.E.O., J. Marshal; Dir. & Museum Shop Mgr., Lanelle Frost; Pres. (V), Mona Betzel.
Institution Type/Description: History Museum: housed in a former slave cabin, c.1820.
Hours & Admission Prices: March to mid-Nov. Mon.-Sat. 10-5, Sun. 2-5; mid-Nov. to Feb. Mon. & Wed.-Sat. 10-5. Adults $2, children 8 & under $1. Closed New Year's Day; Mother's Day; Independence Day; Christmas. &
Attendance: 12,000 (estimated)

Elberton

ELBERTON GRANITE MUSEUM & EXHIBIT, 1 Granite Plaza, Elberton, GA 30635. Mailing Address: P.O. Box 640, Elberton, GA 30635-0640. Tel.: 706-283-2551. Fax: 706-283-6380.
E-mail: granite@egaonline.com
Key Personnel: Exec. Vice Pres. & Dir., Christopher J. Kubas.
Institution Type/Description: Granite Museum.
Hours & Admission Prices: Mon.-Sat. 2-5; call for additional hours. No charge. Closed holidays.
Attendance: 1,280 (actual)

Ellijay

GILMER ARTS, 207 Dalton St., Ellijay, GA 30540-9000. Tel.: 706-635-5605.
E-mail: gilmerarts@gilmerarts.org
Web Site: www.gilmerarts.org
Institution Type/Description: Art Association.
Hours & Admission Prices: Mon.-Fri. 10-5. No charge.
Attendance: 500 (estimated)

Fairburn

OLD CAMPBELL COUNTY MUSEUM, Intersection of E. Broad St. & Cole St., Fairburn, GA 30213. Mailing Address: c/o OCCHS, P.O. Box 463, Fairburn, GA 30213-0342. Tel.: 770-548-9181.
E-mail: info@oldcampbellcountyhistoricalsociety.com
Web Site: www.oldcampbellcountyhistoricalsociety.com/homepage.html
Key Personnel: Dir., Nancy Cornell; Pres. (V), Stan Jones.
Institution Type/Description: Historical Society Museum.
Hours & Admission Prices: Tues. 11-4; other times by appointment. No charge; donations accepted. &
Attendance: 1,000 (estimated)

Fairmount

SUNRISE PLANETARIUM & SCIENCE MUSEUM, 1427 Slate Mine Rd., Fairmount, GA 30139-2835. Tel.: 706-337-3394.
E-mail: info@campsunrise.com
Web Site: campsunrise.com
Institution Type/Description: Planetarium & Science Museum.
Hours & Admission Prices: Available for groups by appointment. No charge; donations accepted.

Fargo

STEPHEN C. FOSTER STATE PARK, 17515 Hwy. 177, Fargo, GA 31631-5004. Tel.: 912-637-5274. Fax: 912-637-5587.
E-mail: Becky.Kelley@dnr.ga.gov
Web Site: www.gastateparks.org/info/scfoster
Key Personnel: Mgr., Bryan Gray.
Institution Type/Description: State Park Museum.
Hours & Admission Prices: Park: 7am-10pm. Suwannee River Center: Temporarily closed. Office: Fall & Winter: daily 8-5; Spring & Summer: daily 7-6. National Park Pass: $5 per vehicle. Boat tours: adults $10, children $6; children under 4 no charge. Closed Christmas. &
Attendance: 65,000 (estimated)

Fayetteville

HOLLIDAY-DORSEY-FIFE MUSEUM, 140 Lanier Ave., W., Fayetteville, GA 30214-1606. Tel.: 770-716-5332. Fax: 770-460-3906.
E-mail: manager@hdfhouse.com
Web Site: hdfhouse.com
Key Personnel: House Mgr. & Museum Shop Mgr., Nicole Gilbert; Dir., Brian Wismer; Chm. (V), Debi Riddle.
Institution Type/Description: History Museum.
Hours & Admission Prices: Thurs.-Sat. 10-3. Adults $5, senior citizens, students & military $4.
Attendance: 500 (estimated)

Fitzgerald

BLUE AND GRAY MUSEUM, 116 N. Johnston St., Fitzgerald, GA 31750-2476. Tel.: 229-426-5069; 800-386-4642. Fax: 229-426-5069.
E-mail: bgmuseum@mchsi.com
Key Personnel: Dir., Aaron Benefield.

Institution Type/Description: History Museum.
Hours & Admission Prices: Tues.-Sat. 10-4, Sun. 1-5. Adults $5, students $2; discounts to AAM members, seniors & groups of 10 or morel; members no charge. Closed New Year's Day; Memorial Day; Independence Day; Labor Day; Thanksgiving & day after; Christmas. &
Attendance: 1,396 (estimated)

Flovilla

INDIAN SPRINGS STATE PARK MUSEUM, Hwy. 42, 5 mi. S. of Jackson, Flovilla, GA 30216. Mailing Address: 678 Lake Clark Rd., Flovilla, GA 30216-2309. Tel.: 770-504-2277. Fax: 770-504-2178.
E-mail: becky.kelley@dnr.ga.gov
Web Site: www.georgiastateparks.org
Key Personnel: Mgr., Ken Lalumiere.
Institution Type/Description: History Museum.
Hours & Admission Prices: Memorial Day-Labor Day Sat.-Sun. 12-4. Museum: no charge. Parking $5. &
Attendance: 400,000 (actual)

Flowery Branch

FLOWERY BRANCH DEPOT MUSEUM, 5517 Main St., Flowery Branch, GA 30542. Tel.: 770-967-6472.
Institution Type/Description: History Museum: housed in the former Flowery Branch train depot; built in 1890.
Hours & Admission Prices: Sat. 11-3.

Fort Gaines

SUTTONS CORNER FRONTIER STORE MUSEUM, 115 S. Washington St., Fort Gaines, GA 39851. Mailing Address: 105 N. Washington St., Ste. 1, Fort Gaines, GA 39851. Tel.: 229-221-2502.
E-mail: karen@suttonscorner.org
Key Personnel: Cur., Karen Klear.
Institution Type/Description: History Museum: housed in a former country store; built c.1850.
Hours & Admission Prices: Fri. -Sat. 10-3 by appointment. No charge; donations accepted. Closed Thanksgiving; Christmas. &
Attendance: 300 (estimated)

Fort Gordon

U.S. ARMY SIGNAL CORPS MUSEUM, 504 Chamberlain Ave., Bldg. 29807, Fort Gordon, GA 30905-5735. Tel.: 706-791-2818 & 3856. Fax: 706-791-6069.
E-mail: atzh-pom-m@gordon.army.mil
Key Personnel: Dir., Robert Anzuoni.
Institution Type/Description: Military/Science & Technology Museum.
Hours & Admission Prices: Tues.-Fri. 8-4, Sat. 10-4. No charge; donations accepted. Closed federal holidays. &
Attendance: 34,000 (actual)

Fort Oglethorpe

CHICKAMAUGA AND CHATTANOOGA NATIONAL MILITARY PARK, 3370 LaFayette Rd., Fort Oglethorpe, GA 30742. Mailing Address: P.O. Box 2128, Fort Oglethorpe, GA 30742-0128. Tel.: 706-866-9241.
Web Site: www.nps.gov/chch
Institution Type/Description: Military Museum.
Hours & Admission Prices: Chickamauga Battlefield Visitor Center: daily 8:30-5. Lookout Mountain Battlefield Visitor Center: daily 8:30-5. Point Park: daily 8:30 to sunset. No charge; donations accepted. Closed New Year's Day; Christmas. &
Attendance: 900,000 (actual)

6TH CAVALRY MUSEUM, #6 Barnhardt Circle, Fort Oglethorpe, GA 30742-3646. Mailing Address: P.O. Box 2011, Fort Oglethorpe, GA 30742-0011. Tel.: 706-861-2860.
E-mail: info@6thcavalrymuseum.com
Web Site: www.6thcavalrymuseum.com
Key Personnel: Exec. Dir., Christine McKeever.
Institution Type/Description: Military History Museum: listed on the National Register of Historic Places.
Hours & Admission Prices: Tues.-Sat. 10-4. Families $10, adults $5, students $3; discounts to groups; children 5 & under no charge. Closed holidays.
Attendance: 5,000 (estimated)

Fort Stewart

FORT STEWART MUSEUM, 2022 Frank Cochran Dr., Bldg. T904, Fort Stewart, GA 31314-4936. Tel.: 912-767-7885. Fax: 912-767-2121.
E-mail: walter.meeks@stewart.army.mil
Key Personnel: Dir., Walter W. Meeks, III.
Institution Type/Description: Military Museum.
Hours & Admission Prices: Temporarily closed for renovations.
Attendance: 45,036 (actual)

Fort Valley

A.L. FETTERMAN EDUCATIONAL MUSEUM, Massee Lane Gardens, 100 Massee Lane, Fort Valley, GA 31030-6974. Tel.: 478-967-2358. Fax: 478-967-2083.
E-mail: crichard@americancamellias.org
Web Site: www.americancamellias.org
Key Personnel: Exec. Dir., Celeste Richard; Pres., Don Bergamini; Museum Shop Mgr., Stefanie Turner.
Institution Type/Description: Library & Porcelain Museum.
Hours & Admission Prices: Tues.-Sat. 10-4:30, Sun. 1-4:30. Adults $5, seniors 65 & over $4; ACS members & children under 12 no charge. Closed national holidays.
Attendance: 22,500 (estimated)

MASSEE LANE GARDENS, HOME OF AMERICAN CAMELLIA SOCIETY, 100 Massee Lane, Fort Valley, GA 31030-6974. Tel.: 478-967-2358. Fax: 478-967-2083. Facebook.
E-mail: crichard@americancamellias.org
Web Site: www.americancamellias.org
Key Personnel: Operations Mgr., Celeste Richard; Museum Shop Mgr., Leisa Dortch.
Institution Type/Description: Horticultural Society.
Hours & Admission Prices: Feb. Mon.-Sat. 10-4:30, Sun. 1-4:30; March-Jan. Tues.-Sat. 10-4:30, Sun. 1-4:30. Adults $5, senior $4; discounts to groups, AAA, AAM & ICOM members; children under 12 & members no charge.
Attendance: 35,000 (estimated)

Gainesville

BRENAU UNIVERSITY GALLERIES, BRENAU UNIVERSITY, 500 Washington St., S.E., Gainesville, GA 30501-3697. Tel.: 770-534-6263 (gallery). Fax: 770-538-4599.
E-mail: gallery@brenau.edu
Web Site: galleries.brenau.edu
Key Personnel: Dir., Nichole Rawlings; University Pres., Ed Schrader; Gallery Mgr., Allison Lauricella.
Institution Type/Description: University Art Gallery: four gallery spaces are located on the main floor of the Simmons Visual Arts Center, a recently renovated 1914 structure; outside the balcony area of Brenau's c.1880s restored Pearce Auditorium; in the John S. Burd Center for the Performing Arts; and in the Brenau University Downtown Center.
Hours & Admission Prices: Sellars Gallery & President's Gallery: Mon.-Thurs. 10-4. Leo Castelli Gallery: by appointment. Manhattan Gallery: Mon.-Fri. 9-5. No charge. Closed university holidays.
Attendance: 26,000 (estimated)

ELACHEE NATURE SCIENCE CENTER, 2125 Elachee Dr., Gainesville, GA 30504-7158. Tel.: 770-535-1976. Fax: 770-535-2302.
E-mail: elachee@elachee.org
Web Site: www.elachee.org
Key Personnel: Pres. & C.E.O., Andrea Timpone; Pres., R.K. Whitehead; Education, Peter Gordon; Devel. & Public Rels., Lavon Callahan; Museum Shop Mgr., Judy Stock.
Institution Type/Description: Nature Science Center.
Hours & Admission Prices: April-Nov. Mon.-Sat. 10-5; Dec.-March Mon.-Fri. 10-3. Adults $5, children 2-12 $3; discounts to ANCA members; members & children under 2 no charge. Closed New Year's Day; Thanksgiving; Christmas.
Attendance: 70,000 (estimated)

INTERACTIVE NEIGHBORHOOD FOR KIDS, 999 Chestnut St., S.E., Ste. 11, Gainesville, GA 30501-6962. Tel.: 770-536-1900. Fax: 770-536-5459. Facebook: INK for Kids.
E-mail: info@inkfun.org
Web Site: www.inkfun.org
Key Personnel: Exec. Dir., Mandy Volpe; Chm. (V), Alan Wayne.
Institution Type/Description: Children's Museum.

Hours & Admission Prices: Mon.-Sat. 10-5. Admission $8; discounts Sun. 1-5.
Attendance: 70,000 (actual)

NORTHEAST GEORGIA HISTORY CENTER AT BRENAU UNIVERSITY, 322 Academy St., N.E., Gainesville, GA 30501. Mailing Address: P.O. Box 1451, Gainesville, GA 30503-1451. Tel.: 770-297-5900. Fax: 770-297-5933.
E-mail: historycenter@brenau.edu
Web Site: www.negahc.org
Formerly: Georgia Mountains History Museum at Brenau University
Key Personnel: C.E.O., Glen Kyle; Pres. (V), Dr. Patricia Burd.
Institution Type/Description: History Museum.
Hours & Admission Prices: Tues.-Sat. 10-4. Adults $6, senior citizens & military $5, students $4; discounts to AAA members; members no charge. Closed New Year's Day; Independence Day; Christmas.
Attendance: 6,000 (actual)

QUINLAN VISUAL ARTS CENTER, 514 Green St., N.E., Gainesville, GA 30501-3314. Tel.: 770-536-2575. Fax: 678-343-2738. Facebook: Quinlan Visual Arts Center.
E-mail: info@qvac.org
Web Site: www.qvac.org
Key Personnel: Exec. Dir., Amanda McClure; Asst. Dir., Paula E. Lindner; Admin., Margaret Tingley.
Institution Type/Description: Arts Center.
Hours & Admission Prices: Mon.-Fri. 9-5, Sat. 10-4. No charge; donations accepted. Closed Memorial Day; Independence Day; Labor Day; Thanksgiving; Christmas.
Attendance: 9,000 (estimated)

Glennville

THE GLENNVILLE - TATTNALL MUSEUM, 211 S. Tillman St., Glennville, GA 30427-1737. Mailing Address: c/o City of Glennville, 134 S. Veterans Blvd., Glennville, GA 30427. Tel.: 912-654-3756. Fax: 912-538-3156.
Web Site: www.glennvillega.com/Museum.html
Key Personnel: Museum Bd. Chm., Dane Bazemore.
Institution Type/Description: Art, Science & History Museum.
Hours & Admission Prices: Mon.-Thurs. 8am-9pm. Closed national holidays.

Grovetown

GROVETOWN MUSEUM, 106 W. Robinson Ave., Grovetown, GA 30813. Tel.: 706-863-1867.
Institution Type/Description: History Museum.
Hours & Admission Prices: Thurs.-Fri. 10-4, Sat. 1-4.

Harlem

LAUREL & HARDY MUSEUM, 250 N. Louisville St., Harlem, GA 30814. Mailing Address: P.O. Box 99, Harlem, GA 30814. Tel.: 888-288-9108, 706-556-0401.
E-mail: museum@harlemga.org
Institution Type/Description: History Museum: birthplace of Oliver Hardy.
Hours & Admission Prices: Tues.-Sat. 10-4.

Hartwell

HART COUNTY HISTORICAL MUSEUM - TEASLEY-HOLLAND HOUSE, 31 E. Howell St., Hartwell, GA 30643. Tel.: 706-376-6330.
E-mail: hartmuseum@scrtc.com
Web Site: www.hartcountymuseum.org/
Institution Type/Description: History Museum: housed in the former home of Isham Asbury Teasley; built in 1880.
Hours & Admission Prices: Mon.-Fri. 8:30-5. No charge.

Hawkinsville

HAWKINSVILLE/PULASKI COUNTY ARTS COUNCIL, 100 Lumpkin St., Hawkinsville, GA 31036-1518. Mailing Address: 42 Lumpkin St., Hawkinsville, GA 31036. Tel.: 912-783-1884. Fax: 912-783-2333.
E-mail: ArtsCouncil@cstel.net
Web Site: www.hawkinsvilleoperahouse.com
Key Personnel: Office Mgr., Julianna Stewart.
Institution Type/Description: Art Gallery.
Hours & Admission Prices: Tours: Mon.-Fri. 10-4.

Hiawassee

BRASSTOWN BALD VISITOR CENTER, 2941 State Hwy. 180, Hiawassee, GA 30546. Mailing Address: 2042 Hwy. 515 W., Blairsville, GA 30512-3773. Tel.: 706-745-6928 & 896-2556. Fax: 706-745-7494.
E-mail: vcmorris@fs.fed.us
Web Site: www.fs.fed.us/conf
Key Personnel: Resource Asst., Alison Koopman; Recreation Program Mgr., Valencia Morris.
Institution Type/Description: Park Museum: located within the Chattahoochee National Forest.
Hours & Admission Prices: mid-April to May Sat.-Sun. 10-5; Memorial Day to Veterans Day daily 10-5. Parking & Shuttle Ride: 16 & over $5; discounts to seniors, Golden Age Pass & Interagency Access Pass holders. Center: No charge; donations accepted. &
Attendance: 75,000 (estimated)

Jefferson

CRAWFORD W. LONG MUSEUM, 28 College St., Jefferson, GA 30549-1036. Tel.: 706-367-5307.
E-mail: info@crawfordlong.org
Web Site: www.crawfordlong.org
Key Personnel: Mgr., Vicki Starnes; Pres. (V), Jana Cleveland; Guest Svcs. Coord., Karen Jaskoski.
Institution Type/Description: Medical Museum, History Museum & Historic Building & Site.
Hours & Admission Prices: Tues.-Fri. 10-5, Sat. 10-4. Adults $5, senior citizens $4, students $3; discounts to military; children 5 & under no charge. Closed on major holidays. &
Attendance: 2,286 (actual)

Jekyll Island

THE GEORGIA SEA TURTLE CENTER, 214 Stable Rd., Jekyll Island, GA 31527-0844. Tel.: 912-635-4444.
E-mail: georgiaseaturtlecenter@jekyllisland.com
Web Site: www.georgiaseaturtlecenter.org
Key Personnel: Dir. & Veterinarian, Terry Norton; Coord. Research, Kimberly Andrews; Coord. Education, Katie Higgins; Educator, Kristen Lee; Educator, Kira Sterns.
Institution Type/Description: Marine Museum.
Hours & Admission Prices: March-Nov. Mon. 10-2, Tues.-Sun. 9-5; Dec.-Feb. Tues.-Sun. 9-5. Adults 13 & over $7, senior citizens 65 & over $6, children 4-12 $5; children 3 & under no charge. Closed New Year's Day; Christmas Eve & Day.

JEKYLL ISLAND MUSEUM, 100 Stable Rd., Jekyll Island, GA 31527-0870. Mailing Address: 381 Riverview Dr., Jekyll Island, GA 31527-0874. Tel.: 912-635-4036. Fax: 912-635-4420.
E-mail: bpiatek@jekyllisland.com
Web Site: www.jekyllisland.com
Key Personnel: Dir., Bruce J. Piatek; Cur., Gretchen Greminger; Programming, Andrea Marroquin; Tours, Shirley Martin.
Institution Type/Description: Historic Site & Preservation Project.
Hours & Admission Prices: Daily 9-5. Passport to the Century Tour: two period furniture restored cottages. Adults $16, students 7-15 $7; children 6 & under no charge. Call for tour hours. Closed New Year's Day; Christmas. &
Attendance: 37,246 (actual)

Johns Creek

AUTREY MILL NATURE PRESERVE & HERITAGE CENTER, 9770 Autrey Mill Rd., Johns Creek, GA 30022-7168. Tel.: 678-366-3511. Fax: 678-366-3512.
E-mail: events@autreymill.org
Web Site: autreymill.org
Key Personnel: Dir., Ben Team; Heritage & Events, Claudette Lopez; Office Asst., Michael Hanff.
Institution Type/Description: Nature Preserve.
Hours & Admission Prices: Park: daily 8am to dusk. Visitor Center: Mon.-Sat. 10-4. No charge; donations accepted.
Attendance: 12,000 (estimated)

Jonesboro

ROAD TO TARA MUSEUM, 104 N. Main St., Jonesboro, GA 30236-8315. Tel.: 770-478-4800, 800-662-7829. Fax: 770-478-1888.

E-mail: info@visitscarlett.com
Web Site: visitscarlett.com/roadtotaramuseum.html
Key Personnel: Dir., Frenda Turner; Museum Shop Mgr., Julie Bustamante; Chm. (V), Linda Summerlin.
Institution Type/Description: History Museum: housed in 1867 Historic Train Depot.
Hours & Admission Prices: Mon.-Fri. 8:30-5:30, Sat. 10-4. Adults $7, senior citizens & children $6.
Attendance: 13,000 (actual)

STATELY OAKS PLANTATION, 100 Carriage Lane, Jonesboro, GA 30236. Mailing Address: P.O. Box 922, Jonesboro, GA 30237-0922. Tel.: 770-473-0197. Fax: 770-473-9855.
E-mail: statelyoaks@historicaljonesboro.org
Web Site: historicaljonesboro.org
Key Personnel: Pres., Mary Q. Bruce.
Institution Type/Description: Historic House.
Hours & Admission Prices: Mon.-Sat. 10-4. Adults $12, senior citizens 55 & over and military with ID $9, children under 11 & retired military $6. &
Attendance: 5,000 (estimated)

Juliette

JARRELL PLANTATION GEORGIA STATE HISTORIC SITE, 711 Jarrell Plantation Rd., Juliette, GA 31046-2525. Tel.: 478-986-5172. Fax: 478-986-5919.
E-mail: jarrell.plantation.park@dnr.state.ga.us
Web Site: gastateparks.org
Key Personnel: Dir., Ken Lalumiere; Ranger, Bretta Perkins.
Institution Type/Description: Living Farm Historic Site.
Hours & Admission Prices: Thurs.-Sun. 9-5. Adults $6.50, seniors $6, youth 6-17 $4; discount to groups & Friends of Georgia State Parks & Historic Sites members; children under 6 no charge. Closed New Year's Day; Thanksgiving; Christmas.
Attendance: 5,000 (estimated)

Kennesaw

BERNARD A. ZUCKERMAN MUSEUM OF ART, 492 Prillaman Way, #3104, Kennesaw, GA 30144-5591. Tel.: 770-499-3223. Fax: 770-499-3345. Facebook.
E-mail: zma@kennesaw.edu
Web Site: zuckerman.kennesaw.edu
Formerly: Kennesaw State University Art Museum & Galleries
Key Personnel: Dir., Justin Rabideau.
Institution Type/Description: Art Museum.
Hours & Admission Prices: Tues.-Thurs. & Sat. 11-4. No charge; donations accepted. Closed university & public holidays. &
Attendance: 26,000 (actual)

KENNESAW MOUNTAIN NATIONAL BATTLEFIELD PARK, 900 Kennesaw Mountain Dr., Kennesaw, GA 30152-4854. Tel.: 770-427-4686. Fax: 770-528-8398. Facebook: Kennesaw Mountain National Battlefield Park.
E-mail: kemo_superintendent@nps.gov
Web Site: www.nps.gov/kemo
Key Personnel: Park Supt., Nancy Walther; Chief Interpretation, Marjorie Thomas; Cur., Amanda K. Corman; Museum Shop Mgr., Dan Beard.
Institution Type/Description: Civil War History Museum: located on the site of a Civil War battlefield.
Hours & Admission Prices: Park: March-Oct. daily 6:30 am-8:30 pm; Nov.-Feb. daily 6:30 am-6:30 pm. Visitor Center: daily 9-5. Center: no charge; donations accepted. Shuttle Service Fee: adults 12 & over $3, children 6-11 $1.50; America the Beautiful - The National Parks & Federal Recreational Land Pass holders and children 5 & under no charge. Visitor Center: closed New Year's Day; Thanksgiving; Christmas. &
Attendance: 2,100,000 (estimated)

MUSEUM OF HISTORY AND HOLOCAUST EDUCATION, Kennesaw State Univ. Center, 3333 Busbee Dr., Kennesaw, GA 30144. Mailing Address: 1000 Chastain Rd., MD 3308, Kennesaw, GA 30144-5588. Tel.: 678-797-2083. Fax: 770-420-4432.
E-mail: mhhe@kennesaw.edu
Web Site: www.kennesaw.edu/historymuseum
Institution Type/Description: History Museum.
Hours & Admission Prices: Mon.-Fri. 10-5; groups by appointment. Closed during university holidays & breaks.

SMITH-GILBERT GARDENS, 2382 Pine Mountain Rd., Kennesaw, GA 30152. Tel.: 770-919-0248.

E-mail: aparsons@kennesaw-ga.gov
Key Personnel: Dir. Operations, Susan Schroeder.
Institution Type/Description: Botanical Garden.
Hours & Admission Prices: Tues.-Sat. 9-4; other times by appointment. Adults $7, seniors & active military $6, children 6-12 $5; children 5 & under no charge.

THE SOUTHERN MUSEUM OF CIVIL WAR AND LOCOMOTIVE HISTORY, 2829 Cherokee St., Kennesaw, GA 30144-2823. Tel.: 770-427-2117. Fax: 770-421-8485.

E-mail: rbanz@kennesaw.ga.gov
Web Site: www.southernmuseum.org
Formerly: Kennesaw Civil War Museum
Key Personnel: Exec. Dir., Dr. Richard Banz; Cur., Jane Smith; Archivist, Sallie Loy; Dir. Operations, Dena Bush.
Institution Type/Description: Civil War & Train Museum: located on the site where the Great Locomotive chase began.
Hours & Admission Prices: Mon.-Sat. 9-5, Sun. 11-6. Adults $7.50, senior citizens $6.50, children 4-12 $5.50; members & children under 3 no charge. Closed Easter; Thanksgiving; Christmas Eve & Day. &
Attendance: 50,000 (estimated)

Kingsland

KINGSLAND DEPOT, 200 E. King Ave., Kingsland, GA 31548. Tel.: 912-673-1890.

Institution Type/Description: Historic Building & Welcome Center: housed in a former railroad depot; built c.1920. The OWN Network & BBC America rented the depot to be their Lovetown USA Headquarters from Feb. 14 to March 14, 2012. Oprah Winfrey filmed the opening for Remembering Whitney: The Oprah Interview in the Kingsland Depot.
Hours & Admission Prices: Mon.-Fri. 8-5.

Kingston

KINGSTON WOMAN'S HISTORY CLUB MUSEUM, 13 E. Main St., N.W., Kingston, GA 30145-2307. Mailing Address: P.O. Box 261, Kingston, GA 30145-0261. Tel.: 770-546-3116.

Institution Type/Description: History Museum.
Hours & Admission Prices: Sat.-Sun. 1-4; other times by appointment. No charge; donations accepted.

LaFayette

THE MARSH HOUSE, 308 N. Main St., LaFayette, GA 30728-2422. Mailing Address: P.O. Box 722, LaFayette, GA 30728-0722. Tel.: 706-638-5187. Facebook: The Marsh House of Lafayette.

E-mail: stephaniewardlaw1@hotmail.com
Web Site: marshhouseoflafayette.com
Key Personnel: Pres., Stephanie Wardlaw; Recording Sec., Dr. David P. Boyle; Docent Training, Jennie Chandler.
Institution Type/Description: Historic House: built in 1836.
Hours & Admission Prices: Tours by appointment. Adults $5; discounts to AAM members. &
Attendance: 500 (estimated)

LaGrange

HILLS AND DALES ESTATE, 1916 Hills and Dales Dr., LaGrange, GA 30240-2958. Mailing Address: P.O. Box 790, LaGrange, GA 30241-0014. Tel.: 706-882-3242. Fax: 706-882-3464. Facebook: Hills and Dales Estate.

E-mail: cwood@hillsanddales.org
Web Site: www.hillsanddales.org
Key Personnel: Exec. Dir., Carleton Wood; Pres. Foundation, H. Speer Burdette, III; Treas. Foundation, Esther S. Rainey; Museum Shop Mgr., Carrie Mills.
Institution Type/Description: Historic House Museum: housed in the former home of textile magnate Fuller E. Callaway Sr. and his family.
Hours & Admission Prices: March-June Tues.-Sat. 10-6, Sun. 1-6; July-Feb. Tues.-Sat. 10-5. Adults $15, students $7. Closed major holidays. &
Attendance: 10,000 (actual)

LAGRANGE ART MUSEUM, 112 Lafayette Pkwy., LaGrange, GA 30240-3209. Tel.: 706-882-3267. Fax: 706-882-2878.

E-mail: art@lagrangeartmuseum.org
Web Site: www.lagrangeartmuseum.org
Formerly: Chattahoochee Valley Art Museum
Institution Type/Description: Art Museum: housed in 1892 Victorian structure, originally a county jail.

Hours & Admission Prices: Tues.-Fri. 9-5, 3rd Sat. 1-4, Mon. by appointment. Suggested Donation: adults $5; Troup County residents no charge. Closed New Year's Day; Memorial Day; Independence Day; Thanksgiving; Christmas. &
Attendance: 8,152 (actual)

LAMAR DODD ART CENTER, LAGRANGE COLLEGE, 302 Forrest Ave., LaGrange, GA 30240. Mailing Address: 601 Broad St., LaGrange, GA 30240-2955. Tel.: 706-880-8211. Fax: 706-880-8007.

E-mail: dmarrin@lagrange.edu
Web Site: lagrange.edu/academics/art/lamar.dodd.htm
Key Personnel: Dir., John Lawrence.
Institution Type/Description: College Art Museum.
Hours & Admission Prices: Academic Year: Mon.-Fri. 8:30-4:30. No charge. &
Attendance: 20,000 (estimated)

LEGACY MUSEUM ON MAIN; A HISTORY MUSEUM FOR WEST GEORGIA, 136 Main St., LaGrange, GA 30240-3218. Mailing Address: P.O. Box 1051, LaGrange, GA 30241-0019. Tel.: 706-884-1828. Fax: 706-884-1840. Facebook: Troup County Archives.

E-mail: info@trouparchives.org
Web Site: www.trouparchives.org
Key Personnel: Interim Dir. & Historian, Clark Johnson; Archivist & Asst. Dir., Shannon Gavin-Harris; Historian, F.C. Johnson, III; Museum & Office Mgr., Cindy Pendleton.
Institution Type/Description: History Museum.
Hours & Admission Prices: Mon.-Fri. 9-5, Sat. 10-4. No charge; donations accepted. Closed federal holidays. &
Attendance: 4,680 (actual)

Lawrenceville

GWINNETT HISTORICAL SOCIETY, 185 Crogan St., Lawrenceville, GA 30046-0261. Mailing Address: P.O. Box 261, Lawrenceville, GA 30046-0261. Tel.: 770-822-5174.

E-mail: ghs@gwinnetths.org
Web Site: www.gwinnetths.org
Key Personnel: Co-Pres., Beverly Paff; Co-Pres., Betty Walbington; Librarian, Harriett Nicholls; Corresponding Sec., Frances Johnson; Recording Sec., Vickie Watkins.
Institution Type/Description: Historical Society Museum.
Hours & Admission Prices: Mon.- Fri. 10-2. No charge; donations accepted. &
Attendance: 1,600 (estimated)

GWINNETT HISTORY MUSEUM, Lawrenceville Female Seminary Bldg., 455 S. Perry St., S.W., Lawrenceville, GA 30045-4836. Tel.: 770-822-5178. Fax: 770-237-5612.

E-mail: gwinnetthistorymuseum@gwinnettcounty.com
Key Personnel: Dir., Jennifer Collins; Outreach Coord., Kim Elmore; Outreach Coord., Jillian Waters Griffin.
Institution Type/Description: History Museum: housed on the second floor of the c.1854 Lawrenceville Female Seminary, an all-girls school. Listed on the National Register of Historic Places.
Hours & Admission Prices: Closed for renovations until Winter 2017.
Attendance: 12,000 (estimated)

GWINNETT VETERANS MEMORIAL MUSEUM, 185 Crogan St., Rm. 118, Lawrenceville, GA 30045. Mailing Address: P.O. Box 166, Snellville, GA 30078. Tel.: 770-985-0901 & 921-1326.

E-mail: topchief@earthlink.net
Web Site: vetmemorialmuseum.tripod.com
Institution Type/Description: Military History Museum: housed in the historic Gwinnett County Courthouse.
Hours & Admission Prices: Mon.-Fri. 10-4, Sat. 10-2. No charge; donations accepted.

Leslie

GEORGIA RURAL TELEPHONE MUSEUM, 135 Bailey Ave., Leslie, GA 31764-2601. Mailing Address: P.O. Box 187, Leslie, GA 31764-0187. Tel.: 229-874-4786.

Institution Type/Description: Telephone Museum: housed in renovated 1920s cotton warehouse.
Hours & Admission Prices: Mon.-Fri. 9-3:30. Adults $5, seniors $4, children $2; discounts to groups. Closed Memorial Day; Independence Day; Labor Day; Thanksgiving & day after; Christmas Eve & Day.

Lilburn

BAPS SHRI SWAMINARAYAN MANDIR, 460 Rockbridge Rd., N.W., Lilburn, GA 30047. Tel.: 678-906-2277. Fax: 678-906-2984.
E-mail: info.atlanta@usa.baps.org
Web Site: atlanta.baps.org
Institution Type/Description: Religious Museum.
Hours & Admission Prices: Mandir: daily 9-6; groups by appointment. Sacred Shrines: daily 9-10:30, 11:15-12, & 4-6. No charge.

Lincolnton

ELIJAH CLARK MEMORIAL MUSEUM, 2959 McCormick Hwy., Lincolnton, GA 30817-3909. Tel.: 706-359-3458. Fax: 706-359-5856. Facebook: Friends of Elijah Clark.
Web Site: gastateparks.org/info/elijah
Key Personnel: Dir., Nelson S. Noble.
Institution Type/Description: State Park Museum: housed in replica of the house of Elijah Clark.
Hours & Admission Prices: April-Nov. Sat.-Sun. 9-5; other times by appointment. No charge.

Lithia Springs

SWEETWATER CREEK STATE PARK, 1750 Mount Vernon Rd., Lithia Springs, GA 30122-3501. Mailing Address: P.O. Box 816, Lithia Springs, GA 30122-0816. Tel.: 770-732-5871. Fax: 770-732-5874.
E-mail: sweetwater_creek.park@dnr.state.ga.us
Web Site: gastateparks.org
Key Personnel: Park Mgr., Brad Ballard.
Institution Type/Description: State Park: located at the site of the ruins of an 1849 textile mill burned in Gen. Sherman's Atlanta Campaign.
Hours & Admission Prices: Park: daily 7am to sunset. Visitor Center & Museum: daily 9-5. No charge. Parking: $5. &
Attendance: 200,000 (estimated)

Lumpkin

BEDINGFIELD INN MUSEUM, 353 Cotton St. on The Square, Lumpkin, GA 31815. Mailing Address: P.O. Box 818, Lumpkin, GA 31815-0818. Tel.: 229-838-6804. Fax: 229-838-6134.
E-mail: schc@sowega.net
Key Personnel: Dir. & Pres. (V), Sally P. Long; Museum Shop Mgr., Joanne Brazler.
Institution Type/Description: Historic Building Museum: 1836 Stagecoach Inn.
Hours & Admission Prices: Fri.-Sat. 10-4; other times by appointment. Adult $5, children $2; members no charge.
Attendance: 500 (estimated)

PROVIDENCE CANYON STATE PARK, 8930 Canyon Rd., Lumpkin, GA 31815. Tel.: 229-838-6202, 800-864-7275 (reservations).
Web Site: www.gastateparks.org
Key Personnel: Mgr., Joy L. Joyner.
Institution Type/Description: State Park Natural History Museum.
Hours & Admission Prices: Park: mid-Sept. to mid-April daily 7-6; mid-April to mid-Sept. 7am-9pm. Visitor Center: Mon.-Thurs. 9-5, Fri.-Sun. 8-5. Parking: $5. &
Attendance: 90,000 (actual)

Mableton

MABLE HOUSE COMPLEX, 5239 Floyd Rd., Mableton, GA 30126. Tel.: 770-819-3285 & 7765.
Institution Type/Description: Historic House Museum: housed in the former home of Robert Mable; built in 1843. Listed on the National Register of Historic Places.
Hours & Admission Prices: June-Sept. Thurs. 8:30-12:30.

Macon

THE ALLMAN BROTHERS BAND MUSEUM AT THE BIG HOUSE, 2321 Vineville Ave., Macon, GA 31208. Mailing Address: The Big House Foundation, P.O. Box 4291, Macon, GA 31208-4291. Tel.: 478-741-5551.
E-mail: info@thebighousemuseum.org
Web Site: www.thebighousemuseum.org

Key Personnel: Dir., Robert R. Schneck; Chm. (V), Brown Edwards; Office Mgr., Maggie Johnson; Dir. Collections & Merchandise, Richard Brent.
Institution Type/Description: Band History Museum.
Hours & Admission Prices: Thurs.-Sun. 11-6. Adults $10, students, seniors, military & groups of 10 or more $8, children under 6 & members no charge. &
Attendance: 10,000 (estimated)

THE CANNONBALL HOUSE, 856 Mulberry St., Macon, GA 31201-6755. Tel.: 478-745-5982. Fax: 478-745-5944. Facebook: Cannonball House.
E-mail: cbhinfo@yahoo.com
Web Site: www.cannonballhouse.org
Key Personnel: Dir., Nicole Thurston; Pres. (V), James Bass.
Institution Type/Description: History Museum: c.1853.
Hours & Admission Prices: Summer: Mon.-Sat. 10-5, Sun. by appointment; Winter: Mon.-Sat. 11-5. Adults $6, military and senior citizens 65 & over $5, students $3; discounts to AAA members & groups of 15 or more; children 6 & under and members no charge. Closed most major holidays.
Attendance: 10,000 (estimated)

GEORGIA MUSIC HALL OF FAME, 200 Martin Luther King Jr. Blvd., Macon, GA 31201-3490. Mailing Address: 75 5th St. N.W., Ste 1200, Atlanta, GA 30308-1020. Tel.: 888-GA-ROCKS, 478-751-3334. Fax: 478-751-3100.
E-mail: ccreekmore@georgia.org
Web Site: www.georgiamusic.org
Key Personnel: Dir., Lisa Love; Chm., Eugene C. Dunwody, Jr.; Cur., Joseph Johnson; Music Store Coord., Melvina Spence; Public Rels. & Event Mgr., Katie Roberts; Asst. Cur. & Educator, Kristin Veline; Visitor Svcs. Mgr., Mary Stansfield; Visitor Svcs. Coord. & Volunteer Coord., Steven Fulbright; Administrative Operations Coord., Cissie Creekmore; Mgr. Facilities, A.B. Goel.
Institution Type/Description: Music Museum.
Hours & Admission Prices: Tues.-Sat. 9-5. Adults $8, senior citizens, students, tour & family groups $6, children $3.50; discounts to AAA members; members no charge. Closed New Year's Day; Thanksgiving; Christmas & day after. &
Attendance: 45,000 (estimated)

GEORGIA SPORTS HALL OF FAME, 301 Cherry St., Macon, GA 31201-3398. Mailing Address: P.O. Box 4644, Macon, GA 31208-4644. Tel.: 478-752-1585, ext. 100. Fax: 478-752-1587.
E-mail: jimm@gshf.org
Web Site: www.gshf.org
Key Personnel: Dir. & Devel., Ben Sapp; Chm., Paul Holmes, Jr.; Treas., Gwen Arrington; Museum Shop Mgr., Candice Barca; Museum Shop Sr. Assoc., Courtney Freeman; Rental Coord., Eric Thomas.
Institution Type/Description: State Agency.
Hours & Admission Prices: Tues.-Sat. 9-5. Adults $8, senior citizens, students & military with ID $6, children $3.50; discounts to groups & AAA members; members no charge. Closed New Year's Day; Easter; Thanksgiving; Christmas & day after. &
Attendance: 13,560 (actual)

HAY HOUSE MUSEUM, 934 Georgia Ave., Macon, GA 31201-6708. Tel.: 478-742-8155. Fax: 478-745-4277. Facebook: hayhousemacon.
E-mail: jposton@georgiatrust.org
Web Site: www.georgiatrust.org; hayhousemacon.org
Key Personnel: Jonathan Poston.
Institution Type/Description: Historic House: 1855-59 Italian Renaissance Revival Mansion.
Hours & Admission Prices: Mon.-Sat. 10-4, Sun. 1-4. Adults $11, seniors & military $10, students $7; discounts to AAA members; children under 6 & members no charge. Closed major holidays. &
Attendance: 16,752 (actual)

HISTORIC MACON FOUNDATION, INC. - SIDNEY LANIER COTTAGE HOUSE MUSEUM, Sidney Lanier Cottage, 935 High St., Macon, GA 31201. Mailing Address: P.O. Box 13358, Macon, GA 31208-3358. Tel.: 478-743-3851 & 742-5084.
E-mail: bturner@historicmacon.org
Web Site: www.historicmacon.org
Formerly: Middle Georgia Historical Society, Inc.
Key Personnel: Exec. Dir., Josh Rogers; Dir. SLC, Janis I. Haley; Dir. Finance, Cantey Ayres.
Institution Type/Description: Historic Site: c.1840 birthplace of poet Sidney Lanier.
Hours & Admission Prices: Thurs.-Sat. 10-4; groups by appointment. Adults $5, seniors $4, children 6-18 $3; discounts to AAA members, groups of 10 or more & military; members no charge. Closed major holidays. &
Attendance: 10,000 (estimated)

MUSEUM OF ARTS AND SCIENCES, 4182 Forsyth Rd., Macon, GA 31210-4869. Tel.: 478-477-3232. Fax: 478-477-3251. Facebook: MASMacon.
E-mail: lfisher@masmacon.com
Web Site: www.masmacon.org
Key Personnel: Dir., Susan Welsh; Operations Dir., Lisa Gant Fisher; Bd. Pres., Julia Wood; Cur. Education, Susan Mays; Cur. Science, Paul Fisher; Museum Shop Mgr., Beth Fisher.
Institution Type/Description: General Museum.
Hours & Admission Prices: Museum: Tues.-Sat. 10-5, Sun. 1-5. Adults $10, seniors (62+) $8; students w/ID $7, children 3-17 $5, children under 3 no charge; discounts to military w/ID; members no charge. Planetarium Programs: Tues.-Fri. 11:30 & 4, Sat. 11:30, 2 & 4, Sun. 2 & 4. Mini-Zoo Programs: Sun. & Tues.-Fri. 3 p.m., Sat. 1 & 3. Closed New Year's Day; Easter; Memorial Day; Independence Day; Labor Day; Thanksgiving; Christmas Eve & Day. &
Attendance: 64,567 (actual)

OCMULGEE MOUNDS NATIONAL HISTORIC PARK, 1207 Emery Hwy., Macon, GA 31217-4320. Tel.: 478-752-8257, ext. 210. Fax: 478-752-8259.
E-mail: ocmu_superintendent@nps.gov
Web Site: www.nps.gov/ocmu
Institution Type/Description: Park Museum.
Hours & Admission Prices: Visitor Center: daily 9-5. No charge; donations accepted. Closed New Year's Day; Christmas. &
Attendance: 170,000 (actual)

TUBMAN AFRICAN AMERICAN MUSEUM, 310 Cherry St., Macon, GA 31201-0515. Mailing Address: P.O. Box 6671, Macon, GA 31208-6671. Tel.: 478-743-8544. Fax: 478-743-9063.
E-mail: guestservices@tubmanmuseum.com
Web Site: www.tubmanmuseum.com
Key Personnel: Bd. Chm., Billy Pitts; Bd. Vice Chm., Morris Butler; Exec. Dir., Andy Ambrose; C.F.O., Barrie Miller-Howard; IT & Office Mgr., Adra Dudley; Dir. Exhibitions, Jeff Bruce; Dir. Education, Trenda Byrd; Guest Services Coord., Patricia Stephens.
Institution Type/Description: History Museum.
Hours & Admission Prices: Tues.-Fri. 9-5, Sat. 11-5. Adults $10, seniors & military with ID $8, children $4; discounts to AAM & ICOM members; museum members no charge. Closed New Year's Day; Memorial Day; Independence Day; Thanksgiving; Christmas. &
Attendance: 57,372 (actual)

Madison

MADISON-MORGAN CULTURAL CENTER, 434 S. Main St., Madison, GA 30650-1640. Tel.: 706-342-4743. Fax: 706-342-1154. Facebook: Madison Morgan Cultural Center.
E-mail: tdickinson@mmcc-arts.org
Web Site: www.mmcc-arts.org
Key Personnel: Dir., Kim Brown; Chm., David Buck; Vice Chm., Chris Vambert; Dir. Devel. & Special Events, Erin Garrett; Dir. Mktg., Theresa Dickinson; Performance Dir., Rebecca Bonas; Dir. Visitor Svcs., Box Office & Membership, Deanna Lamar.
Institution Type/Description: Multi-disciplinary Cultural Center; housed in the 1895 Madison Graded School, in Madison Historic District.
Hours & Admission Prices: Tues.-Sat. 10-5, Sun. 2-5. Adults $5, seniors $4, students $3; discounts to groups of 20 or more; children under 6, museum & AAM members no charge. Closed New Year's Day; Memorial Day; Independence Day; Labor Day; Thanksgiving; Christmas Eve & Day. &
Attendance: 20,000 (estimated)

MADISON MUSEUM OF FINE ART, 300 Hancock St., Madison, GA 30650-1305. Mailing Address: P.O. Box 814, Madison, GA 30650. Tel.: 706-485-4530.
E-mail: mbechtell@prodigy.net
Web Site: madisonmuseum.org
Key Personnel: C.E.O., Pres. (V) & Dir., Michele L. Bechtell; Sec., Sean Gallagher; Treas., Henry C. Ransom.
Institution Type/Description: Visual Art History Museum.
Hours & Admission Prices: Mon.-Sat. 1-5. No charge; donations accepted. &
Attendance: 5,000 (estimated)

MORGAN COUNTY AFRICAN AMERICAN MUSEUM, 156 Academy St., Madison, GA 30650-1202. Tel.: 706-342-9191.
Institution Type/Description: History Museum.
Hours & Admission Prices: Tues.-Sat. 10-4. Adults $5, students $3.

ROGERS HOUSE & ROSE COTTAGE, 179 E. Jefferson, Madison, GA 30650-1361. Mailing Address: c/o City of Madison, P.O. Box 32, Madison, GA 30650. Tel.: 706-343-0190.
Institution Type/Description: Historic Houses.
Hours & Admission Prices: Mon.-Sat. 10-4:30, Sun. 1:30-4:30.

Marietta

BRUMBY HALL & GARDENS, 500 Powder Springs St., Marietta, GA 30064. Tel.: 770-427-2500.
Institution Type/Description: Historic House Museum; housed in the former home of Colonel Arnoldus V. Brumby; built in 1851.
Hours & Admission Prices: By appointment.

COBB COUNTY YOUTH MUSEUM, 649 Cheatham Hill Dr., Marietta, GA 30064-5512. Mailing Address: P.O. Box 78, Marietta, GA 30061-0078. Tel.: 770-427-2563. Fax: 770-427-1060. Facebook: The Youth Museum.
E-mail: youthmuseum@aol.com
Web Site: www.theyouthmuseum.org
Key Personnel: Pres., Leah Pharr; Pres. Elect, Mark Justice; Dir., Anita S. Barton; Administrative Asst. & Museum Shop Mgr., Eleanor Watson; Administrative Asst., Terri Fritz.
Institution Type/Description: Youth Museum.
Hours & Admission Prices: Tours: Sept.-May Mon.-Fri. 9:30-1:30 by appointment. Admission $12; two teachers per group no charge. Closed school holidays. &
Attendance: 13,000 (estimated)

GONE WITH THE WIND MOVIE MUSEUM, 18 Whitlock Ave., Marietta, GA 30064-2346. Tel.: 770-794-5576.
E-mail: csutherland@mariettaga.gov
Web Site: www.mariettaga.gov/gwtw/
Key Personnel: Dir., Connie Sutherland.
Institution Type/Description: Movie Museum.
Hours & Admission Prices: Mon.-Sat. 10-5. Adults $7, seniors & students $6; discounts to groups of 15 or more.

MARIETTA/COBB MUSEUM OF ART, 30 Atlanta St., S.E., Marietta, GA 30060-1975. Tel.: 770-528-1444. Fax: 770-528-1440.
E-mail: smacaulaymcma@bellsouth.net
Web Site: www.mariettacobbartmuseum.org
Key Personnel: Exec. Dir., Sally Macaulay; Chm., Ray Worden; Dir. Operations, Jennifer Sucher Fox; Dir. Education, Allison Frink; Cur., Kelsey Moran; Mktg. Coord., Wanda Davis.
Institution Type/Description: Fine Art Museum; housed in 1909 Greek Revival Post Office Building.
Hours & Admission Prices: Tues.-Fri. 11-5, Sat. 11-4, Sun. 1-4. Adults $8, students & senior citizens $5; discounts to groups, AAA, AAM & ICOM members; members & children under 6 no charge. Closed major holidays. &
Attendance: 75,000 (estimated)

MARIETTA FIRE MUSEUM, 112 Haynes St., Fire Station #1, Marietta, GA 30060-1973. Tel.: 770-794-5491.
E-mail: kblair@mariettaga.gov
Web Site: mariettafire.com/189/Fire-Museum
Institution Type/Description: Fire-Fighting Museum.
Hours & Admission Prices: Mon.-Fri. 8-5, Sat.-Sun. by appointment. No charge.

MARIETTA MUSEUM OF HISTORY, 1 Depot St., Marietta, GA 30060-1905. Tel.: 770-794-5710. Fax: 770-794-5733. Facebook, Twitter & Instagram: @mariettamuseum.
E-mail: info@mariettahistory.org
Web Site: www.mariettahistory.org
Key Personnel: Interim Dir., Jan Galt; Cur. Exhibits & Education, Amy Reed; Reg. & Membership Mgr., Christa McCay.
Institution Type/Description: History Museum.
Hours & Admission Prices: Mon.-Sat. 10-4. Adults $7, seniors & students $5; active military with ID, members & children under 5 no charge. Closed New Year's Day; Easter; Memorial Day; Independence Day; Labor Day; Thanksgiving; Christmas. &
Attendance: 13,000 (actual)

WILLIAM ROOT HOUSE AND GARDEN, N. Marietta Loop & Polk St., Marietta, GA 30060. Mailing Address: 145 Denmead St., Marietta, GA 30060-1934. Tel.: 770-426-4982. Fax: 770-499-9540.
E-mail: executive.director@cobblandmarks.com
Web Site: roothousemuseum.com

Formerly: The Root House Museum
Key Personnel: Dir., Trevor Beemon; Chm., Abbie Parks; Cur., Rick Dreger.
Institution Type/Description: Historic House Museum: built c.1845.
Hours & Admission Prices: Wed.-Sat. 11-4. Adults $7, senior citizens & students $6, children 6-17 $5; members no charge. &
Attendance: 6,000 (estimated)

McDonough

THE BROWN HOUSE - THE GENEALOGICAL SOCIETY OF HENRY & CLAYTON COUNTIES, INC., 71 Macon St., McDonough, GA 30253. Mailing Address: P.O. Box 1296, McDonough, GA 30253-1296. Tel.: 770-954-1456.
E-mail: genealsoc@bellsouth.net
Institution Type/Description: Genealogical Society: housed in the former home of Revolutionary War soldier, Andrew Brown, c.1820. Listed on the National Register of Historic Places.
Hours & Admission Prices: Jan. to mid-Dec. Wed. & Fri. 10-3. Closed holidays.

HISTORICAL VETERANS MUSEUM & HISTORIC PARK, 101 Lake Dow Rd., McDonough, GA 30252. Tel.: 770-288-7300.
Institution Type/Description: Military History Museum.
Hours & Admission Prices: Museum: Mon.-Sat. 10-3; other times by appointment. Park Tours: by appointment. No charge; donations accepted.

Midway

DORCESTER ACADEMY MUSEUM OF AFRICAN-AMERICAN HISTORY, 8787 E. Oglethorpe Hwy., Midway, GA 31320. Mailing Address: P.O. Box 51, Midway, GA 31320-0051. Tel.: 912-884-2347.
E-mail: doracad1@coastalnow.net
Web Site: dorchesteracademy.com
Key Personnel: Dir., Deborah Robinson; C.E.O., William Austin.
Institution Type/Description: History Museum.
Hours & Admission Prices: Tues.-Fri. 11-2, Sat.-Sun. 2-4. No charge; donations accepted.
Attendance: 1,000 (estimated)

FORT MORRIS STATE HISTORIC SITE, 2559 Fort Morris Rd., Midway, GA 31320-6205. Tel.: 912-884-5999. Fax: 912-884-5285.
E-mail: fortmorris@coastalnow.net
Web Site: gastateparks.org
Key Personnel: Site Mgr., Arthur C. Edgar, Jr.
Institution Type/Description: Military Museum.
Hours & Admission Prices: Thurs.-Sat. & holidays 9-5. Adults $4.50, senior citizens $4, youth 6-18 $3; children under 5 no charge. Group Tours: adults $3.25, youth 6-18 $2.50, children 5 & under $1. Closed New Year's Day; Thanksgiving; Christmas. &
Attendance: 13,000 (estimated)

MIDWAY MUSEUM, INC., 491 N. Coastal Hwy., Midway, GA 31320. Mailing Address: P.O. Box 195, Midway, GA 31320-0195. Tel.: 912-884-5837. Facebook: @midwaymuseum.
E-mail: midwaymuseum@yahoo.com
Web Site: themidwaymuseum.org
Key Personnel: Treas., Tina Ladson.
Institution Type/Description: History Museum.
Hours & Admission Prices: Tues.-Sat. 10-4; groups by appointment. Adults $10, senior citizens $8, children $5; discounts to groups & DAC members; children under 6 no charge. Closed holidays.
Attendance: 50,000 (estimated)

SEABROOK VILLAGE, 660 Trade Hill Rd., Midway, GA 31320-6215. Tel.: 912-884-7008. Fax: 912-884-3046.
E-mail: seabrookvillage@yahoo.com
Web Site: seabrookvillage.org
Key Personnel: Administrative Mgr., Florence Tate-Roberts; Pres. (V), Jolonda Greene.
Institution Type/Description: History Museum.
Hours & Admission Prices: Tues.-Sat. 10-2. Self-Guided Tours: adults $5, children under 12 $3; discounts to active military, military reserve, AASLH, Coastal Museum Assoc., groups & AAM members; members & children under 6 no charge. Closed holidays. &
Attendance: 2,500 (estimated)

Milledgeville

BLACKBRIDGE GALLERY - GEORGIA COLLEGE & STATE UNIVERSITY DEPARTMENT OF ART, 209 Blackbridge Hall, Milledgeville, GA 31061. Mailing Address: Campus Box 94, Milledgeville, GA 31061. Tel.: 478-445-4572.
E-mail: anna.leavitt@gcsu.edu
Web Site: www.gcsu.edu/art/blackbridgegallery.htm
Key Personnel: Dir., Carlos M. Herrera.
Institution Type/Description: Art Gallery.
Hours & Admission Prices: Mon.-Fri. 9-5.

GEORGIA COLLEGE AND STATE UNIVERSITY MUSEUM, 221 N. Clarke St., Milledgeville, GA 31061. Mailing Address: Campus Box 43, Milledgeville, GA 31061. Tel.: 478-445-4391. Fax: 478-445-6847.
E-mail: museum@gcsu.edu
Web Site: library.gcsu.edu/museum
Formerly: Museum & Archives of Georgia Education
Key Personnel: Cur., Shannon Morris; Dean, Dr. Rachel Schipper.
Institution Type/Description: History Museum.
Hours & Admission Prices: Mon.-Sat. 10-4; other times by appointment. No charge; donations accepted. &
Attendance: 2,500 (estimated)

GEORGIA COLLEGE NATURAL HISTORY MUSEUM, Herty Hall, 1st Fl., W. Montgomery & N. Wilkinson Sts., Milledgeville, GA 31061. Mailing Address: Dept. of Biological & Environmental Sciences, Campus Box 081, Milledgeville, GA 31061. Tel.: 478-445-2395.
E-mail: nhm@gcsu.edu
Web Site: www.gcsu.edu/nhm
Institution Type/Description: Natural History Museum & Planetarium.
Hours & Admission Prices: Mon.-Fri. 8-4. No charge. Closed holidays. &
Attendance: 8,000 (estimated)

GEORGIA'S OLD CAPITAL MUSEUM, 201 E. Greene St., Milledgeville, GA 31061. Mailing Address: P.O. Box 1177, Milledgeville, GA 31059-1177. Tel.: 478-453-1803. Fax: 478-453-4813.
E-mail: info@oldcapitalmuseum.org
Web Site: www.oldcapitalmuseum.org
Key Personnel: Exec. Dir., Dr. Amy Wright.
Institution Type/Description: History Museum.
Hours & Admission Prices: Tues.-Fri. 10-4, Sat. 12-4. No charge; donations accepted. Closed legal holidays.
Attendance: 9,500 (actual)

JOHN MARLOR ARTS CENTER - ALLIED ARTS, 201 N. Wayne St., Milledgeville, GA 31061-3437. Tel.: 478-452-3950. Fax: 478-452-5321.
E-mail: alliedarts@milledgevillealliedarts.com
Web Site: milledgevillealliedarts.com
Formerly: John Marlor Arts Center
Key Personnel: Exec. Dir., Randy Cannon.
Institution Type/Description: Art Center: housed in home built by John Marlor in 1830.
Hours & Admission Prices: Mon.-Fri. 9-4:30. No charge; donations accepted. &
Attendance: 1,500 (estimated)

OLD GOVERNOR'S MANSION - GEORGIA COLLEGE & STATE UNIVERSITY, 231 W. Hancock St., Milledgeville, GA 31061. Tel.: 478-445-4545.
E-mail: matt.davis@gcsu.edu
Web Site: www.gcsu.edu/mansion
Key Personnel: Dir., Matthew S. Davis.
Institution Type/Description: Historic Building: housed in the residence of Georgia's Governors; built in 1839.
Hours & Admission Prices: Tues.-Sat. 10-4, Sun. 2-4; groups by appointment. Adults $10, senior citizens $7, students $2; children under 6 and GCSU faculty, staff & students no charge. Closed holidays.

STETSON-SANFORD HOUSE, 601 W. Hancock St., Milledgeville, GA 31061-3215. Mailing Address: 201 E. Green St., Milledgeville, GA 31061-3519. Tel.: 800-653-1804. Fax: 478-453-4813.
E-mail: sally@oldcapitalmuseum.org
Web Site: www.oldcapitalmuseum.org

Institution Type/Description: Historic House Museum: housed in a former hotel built for George T. Brown; purchased by merchant Daniel B. Stetson in 1857 whose daughter Elizabeth married Judge Daniel B. Sanford, Clerk of the Secession Convention.
Hours & Admission Prices: House: Thurs.-Sat. with CVB Trolley Tour; other times by appointment. Museum: Tues.-Fri. 10-4, Sat. 12-4. Museum: adults $5.50, seniors $4.50, students $2.25. Closed major holidays.

Mitchell

HAMBURG STATE PARK MUSEUM, 6071 Hamburg State Park Rd., Mitchell, GA 30820-2999. Mailing Address: P.O. Box 310, Crawfordville, GA 30631-0310. Tel.: 478-552-2393, 800-864-7275.
E-mail: friendsofhamburg@gmail.com
Web Site: gastateparks.org/info/hamburg
Key Personnel: Park Ranger, Earvin Cordry.
Institution Type/Description: Industrial Museum: housed in 1920 water turbine powered gin & milling complex.
Hours & Admission Prices: Park: daily 7am-10pm. Museum: daily 8-5. No charge. Parking: $3; Wed. no charge. Closed Thanksgiving; Christmas.
Attendance: 3,500 (estimated)

Moreland

OLD MILL MUSEUM, 7 Main St., Moreland, GA 30259. Mailing Address: P.O. Box 128, Moreland, GA 30259-0128. Tel.: 770-254-2627. Fax: 770-254-2628.
Institution Type/Description: History Museum.
Hours & Admission Prices: Sat.-Sun. 1-4; other times by appointment. No charge; donations accepted.

Moultrie

COLQUITT COUNTY ARTS CENTER, 401 7th Ave., S.W., Moultrie, GA 31768-4633. Tel.: 912-985-1922. Fax: 912-890-6746.
E-mail: info@colquittcountyarts.com
Key Personnel: Exec. Dir., Jeffery Ophime.
Institution Type/Description: Arts Center: housed in the former Moultrie High School.
Hours & Admission Prices: Mon.-Fri. 10-5:30, Sat. 10-2.

MUSEUM OF COLQUITT COUNTY HISTORY, 500 4th Ave., S.E., Moultrie, GA 31788. Mailing Address: P.O. Box 86, Moultrie, GA 31776-0086. Tel.: 229-890-1626.
E-mail: olreb@moultriega.net
Institution Type/Description: History Museum.
Hours & Admission Prices: Fri.-Sat. 10-5, Sun. 2-5; other times by appointment. No charge; donations accepted.

Mountain City

THE FOXFIRE MUSEUM & HERITAGE CENTER, 98 Foxfire Lane, Mountain City, GA 30562. Mailing Address: P.O. Box 541, Mountain City, GA 30562-0541. Tel.: 706-746-5828. Fax: 706-746-5829. Facebook: The Foxfire Museum & Heritage Center.
E-mail: foxfire@foxfire.org
Web Site: www.foxfire.org
Key Personnel: Interim Dir., Barry Stiles; Chm. (V), Hunter Moorman; Museum Shop Mgr., Paulette Carpenter.
Institution Type/Description: Appalachian Historic Buildings.
Hours & Admission Prices: Mon.-Sat. 8:30-4:30; groups & guided tours by appointment. Self-Guided Tour: adults 11 & up $6, children 7-10 $3; discounts to AAA & AARP members; children 6 & under no charge. Closed Thanksgiving; Christmas.
Attendance: 13,500 (actual)

Nelson

PICKENS COUNTY MARBLE MUSEUM, 1985 Kennesaw Ave., Nelson, GA 30151. Tel.: 770-735-2211.
Institution Type/Description: History Museum.
Hours & Admission Prices: Mon.-Fri. 9-4. No charge; donations accepted.

Newnan

NEWNAN-COWETA HISTORICAL SOCIETY - MALE ACADEMY MUSEUM, 30 Temple Ave., Corner of Temple Ave. & College St., Newnan, GA 30263-2066. Mailing Address: P.O. Box 1001, Newnan, GA 30264. Tel.: 770-251-0207. Fax: 770-683-0208.
E-mail: wjeffbishop@newnancowetahistoricalsociety.com
Web Site: newnancowetahistoricalsociety.net
Key Personnel: Dir., Jeff Bishop; Curation Specialist, Jessie Merrell.
Institution Type/Description: Historical Society Museum.
Hours & Admission Prices: Tues.-Sat. 10-12 & 1-3; other times by appointment. Adults $5, students $3, seniors 60 & over & children 4-12 $2; discounts to groups; children 3 & under & NCHS no charge.

Norcross

BLUE MOON CYCLE'S BMW & EUROPEAN MOTORCYCLE MUSEUM, 752 W. Peachtree St., Norcross, GA 30071-1866. Tel.: 770-447-6945. Fax: 770-447-5798. Facebook: Blue Moon Cycle.
E-mail: generalinfo@bluemooncycle.com
Web Site: www.bluemooncycle.com
Institution Type/Description: Motorcycle Museum.
Hours & Admission Prices: Tues.-Fri. 9-5. No charge.

Palmetto

PALMETTO TRAIN DEPOT MUSEUM, 549 Main St., Palmetto, GA 30268-1241. Mailing Address: c/o City of Palmetto, P.O. Box 190, Palmetto, GA 30268. Tel.: 770-463-3377.
E-mail: info@citypalmetto.com
Web Site: www.citypalmetto.com
Institution Type/Description: Historic Building: housed in a former train depot; built in early 1900s.
Hours & Admission Prices: Tues. & Thurs. 10-2. No charge.

Peachtree City

CAF DIXIE WING MUSEUM, 1200 Echo Ct., Peachtree City, GA 30269. Tel.: 678-364-1110.
Web Site: dw.squawk1200.net
Key Personnel: Dir. & Museum Shop Mgr., Billy G. Baldwin.
Institution Type/Description: Military Museum.
Hours & Admission Prices: Tues., Thurs. & Sat. 9-4; other times by appointment. No charge; donations accepted. Closed major holidays.
Attendance: 1,100 (estimated)

Pine Mountain

CALLAWAY GARDENS, 17800 U.S. Hwy. 27, Pine Mountain, GA 31822-2000. Mailing Address: P.O. Box 2000, Pine Mountain, GA 31822-2000. Tel.: 844-873-3543. Fax: 706-663-5068. Facebook: @CallawayGardens.
E-mail: info@callawaygardens.com
Web Site: www.callawaygardens.com
Key Personnel: Pres. & C.E.O., William R. Doyle; Dir. Mktg. & Public Rels., Rachel Crumbley.
Institution Type/Description: Arboretum/Botanical Garden.
Hours & Admission Prices: Labor Day to March 13 daily 9-5; March 19 to Sept. daily 9-6. Fantasy in Lights 5-10. Adults $20, seniors $15, children 6-12 $10; discounts to groups & AABGA members; members and children 5 & under no charge.
Attendance: 700,000 (actual)

Plains

JIMMY CARTER NATIONAL HISTORIC SITE, 300 N. Bond St., Plains, GA 31780-5562. Tel.: 229-824-4104. Fax: 229-824-3441. Facebook: Jimmy Carter NHS.
E-mail: kevin_bartley@nps.gov
Web Site: www.nps.gov/jica
Key Personnel: Chief Vis. Svcs., Beth Wright; Interdisciplinary Cultural Resources Specialist, Kevin Bartley.
Institution Type/Description: Presidential Museums.
Hours & Admission Prices: Plains High School Museum: daily 9-5. Plains Depot - 1976 Carter Presidential Campaign Headquarters Museum: daily 9-4:30. Jimmy Carter Boyhood Farm Museum: daily 10-5. No charge; donations accepted. Closed New Year's Day; Thanksgiving; Christmas.
Attendance: 65,000 (estimated)

Pooler

NATIONAL MUSEUM OF THE MIGHTY EIGHTH AIR FORCE, 175 Bourne Ave., Pooler, GA 31322-9516. Mailing Address: P.O. Box 1992, Savannah, GA 31402-1992. Tel.: 912-748-8888. Fax: 912-748-0209.
E-mail: development@mightyeighth.org
Web Site: mightyeighth.org
Key Personnel: C.E.O. & Pres., Henry Skipper; Devel. Dir., Meghan Lowe; Research Center Dir., Vivian Rogers-Price; Dir. Education & Dir. Volunteers, Heather Thies; Dir. Mktg., Pearl Fyderek; Dir. Finance, Dir. Personnel & Memorial Gardens Coord., Pam Vining; Museum Store Mgr. & Visitor Svcs. Coord., Felice Stelljes; Facility Manager, Bruce Johnson; Dir., Meetings, Tours & Special Events, Holly Kirkpatrick; E-Commerce, Tameka Ford; Membership Coord., Shirley Carter; Special Events Assoc., Christa Smith.
Institution Type/Description: Military History Museum.
Hours & Admission Prices: Daily 9-5. Adults $10, senior citizens, AARP & AAA members & retired military $9, children 6-12 & active duty military $6; discounts to groups; WWII veterans & children under 6 no charge. Closed New Year's Day; Easter; Thanksgiving; Christmas. &
Attendance: 84,222 (actual)

Powder Springs

SEVEN SPRINGS MUSEUM AT THE BODIFORD HOUSE, 4355 Marietta St., Powder Springs, GA 30127. Mailing Address: P. O. Box 2005, Powder Springs, GA 30127. Tel.: 678-626-0799. Fax: 770-943-1136.
E-mail: 7springsmuseum@att.net
Institution Type/Description: Historical Society Museum.
Hours & Admission Prices: Wed. 10 to noon, Sat. 12-4, Sun. 1-4.

Riceboro

GEECHEE KUNDA CULTURAL ARTS CENTER AND MUSEUM, 622 Ways Temple Rd., Riceboro, GA 31323-4307. Tel.: 912-884-4440.
E-mail: jim@bacote.com
Web Site: www.geecheekunda.com
Institution Type/Description: History Museum.
Hours & Admission Prices: Tues.-Sat. 10-4. No charge; donations accepted. Closed Federal holidays.

Richmond Hill

FORT MCALLISTER, 3894 Fort McAllister Rd., Richmond Hill, GA 31324-4862. Tel.: 912-727-2339; 800-864-7275. Fax: 912-727-3614.
E-mail: ftmcallr@coastalnow.net
Web Site: www.fortmcallister.org
Key Personnel: Park Mgr., Daniel Brown.
Institution Type/Description: Preservation Project: located on the site of 1861 Confederate fort.
Hours & Admission Prices: Park daily 7 am-10 pm. Historic Site: daily 8-5. Adults $9, seniors $8, children $5; discounts to groups; children under 5 no charge. Closed Thanksgiving; Christmas. &
Attendance: 140,000 (estimated)

RICHMOND HILL HISTORY MUSEUM, 11460 Ford Ave., Richmond Hill, GA 31324. Mailing Address: P.O. Box 381, Richmond Hill, GA 31324. Tel.: 912-756-3697. Facebook: Richmond Hill GA Historical Society.
E-mail: richmondhillhistoricalsociety@gmail.com
Web Site: www.richmondhillmuseum.com
Institution Type/Description: Historical Society Museum: housed in the former Henry Ford Kindergarten.
Hours & Admission Prices: Wed.-Sat. 10-3. No charge; donations accepted. Closed holidays. &

Rincon

GEORGIA SALZBURGER SOCIETY MUSEUM, 2980 Ebenezer Rd., Rincon, GA 31326-3716. Tel.: 912-754-7001 & 655-4555.
E-mail: info@georgiasalzburgers.com
Web Site: www.georgiasalzburgers.com
Key Personnel: Cur., Patsy Zeigler; Asst. Cur., Robert Peavy.
Institution Type/Description: General Museum.
Hours & Admission Prices: Sat.-Sun. 3-5; other times by appointment. No charge; donations accepted. &
Attendance: 950 (estimated)

Ringgold

OLD STONE CHURCH MUSEUM, GA Hwy. #2, Ringgold, GA 30736. Mailing Address: CCHS P.O. Box 113, Ringgold, GA 30736-0113. Tel.: 706-935-5232.
Institution Type/Description: Historic Building: housed in a former church built c.1849.
Hours & Admission Prices: Thurs.-Sun. 1-5. No charge; donations accepted.

Rome

CHIEFTAINS MUSEUM/MAJOR RIDGE HOME, 501 Riverside Pkwy., Rome, GA 30161-0373. Mailing Address: P.O. Box 373, Rome, GA 30162-0373. Tel.: 706-291-9494. Fax: 706-291-2410.
E-mail: chmuseum@bellsouth.net
Web Site: www.chieftainsmuseum.org
Key Personnel: Dir., Heather Shores.
Institution Type/Description: History Museum: housed in early 19th-century log cabin, expanded in 1828, to a plantation house belonging to Cherokee leader Major Ridge.
Hours & Admission Prices: Wed.-Sat. 10-5. Adults $5, senior citizens 62 & over $3, students $2; discounts to AAM members, groups & school tours; members & Cherokee Nation registered members no charge. Closed major holidays. &
Attendance: 6,000 (actual)

OAK HILL AND THE MARTHA BERRY MUSEUM, 24 Veterans Memorial Hwy., Rome, GA 30161. Mailing Address: P. O. Box 490189, Mount Berry, GA 30149-0189. Tel.: 706-368-6789, 800-220-5504. Fax: 706-368-6787.
E-mail: oakhill@berry.edu
Web Site: www.berry.edu/oakhill
Key Personnel: Asst. Dir., Rebecca Roberts; Coord. Mktg., Patrice Shannon; Mgr. Operations & Museum Shop Mgr., Cheli Rouse; Ground Mgr., Kristin McNully; Horticulturalist, Heather Miller; Museum Asst., Rebecca Henry.
Institution Type/Description: Historic House Museum: home and gardens of Martha Berry, Berry College founder. History Museum: maps the evolution of Berry College from an industrial and agricultural school to a liberal arts college.
Hours & Admission Prices: Mon.-Sat. 10-5. Adults $5, children $3, tours & family group rates $4 per person; discounts to AAA members & senior citizens. Closed New Year's Day, Martin Luther King Jr. Day; Easter; Memorial Day; Independence Day; Labor Day; Christmas week. &
Attendance: 15,000 (estimated)

ROME AREA HISTORY MUSEUM, 305 Broad St., Rome, GA 30161-3005. Tel.: 706-235-8051. Fax: 706-235-6631.
E-mail: leighb@romehistorymuseum.org
Web Site: www.romehistorymuseum.org
Key Personnel: Dir., Leigh Barba; Chm. (V). Gardner Wright; Pres. Bd., Janet Byington; Archivist, Russell McClanahan; Exec. Asst., Donna Shaw.
Institution Type/Description: History Museum.
Hours & Admission Prices: Wed.-Fri. 10-4, Sat. 11-2. No charge. Closed New Year's Day; Independence Day; Labor Day; Thanksgiving; Christmas Eve & Day. &
Attendance: 12,407 (actual)

Rossville

THE CHIEF JOHN ROSS HOUSE ASSOC., 200 E. Lake Ave., Rossville, GA 30741. Mailing Address: 826 Chickamauga Ave., Rossville, GA 30741-1407. Tel.: 706-861-3954 & 866-5171. Fax: 706-861-3967.
E-mail: kawasaki826@comcast.net
Key Personnel: C.E.O. & Pres., W. Larry Rose.
Institution Type/Description: Historic House: 1797 two-story log house of Chief John Ross with ties to the Great Locomotive Chase of 1862 & strategic site used during the Battle of Chickamauga and Missionary Ridge in 1863.
Hours & Admission Prices: June-Aug. 15 Thurs.-Sat. 10-2; groups of 12 or more at other times by appointment. Adults $2; children under 12 no charge. &
Attendance: 400 (actual)

Roswell

ARCHIBALD SMITH PLANTATION HOME, 935 Alpharetta St., Roswell, GA 30075-3827. Tel.: 770-641-3978. Fax: 770-641-3974.
E-mail: cdouglas@roswellgov.com
Key Personnel: Dir., Chuck Douglas.
Institution Type/Description: History Museum.

Hours & Admission Prices: Mon.-Sat. 10-3, Sun. 1-3. Adults $8, seniors 65 & over $7, students & children 6-18 $6; discounts to AAA members; members & children under 6 no charge. Closed major holidays. &

Attendance: 14,000 (actual)

BARRINGTON HALL, 535 Barrington Dr., Roswell, GA 30075. Tel.: 678-639-7500, 770-225-2457.

E-mail: RWINEBARGER@ROSWELLGOV.COM

Institution Type/Description: Historic House Museum: housed in the former home of Roswell co-founder, Barrington King, c.1842. Listed on the National Register of Historic Places.

Hours & Admission Prices: Mon.-Sat. 10-3, Sun. 1-3. Adults $8, seniors 65 & over $7, children 6-12 $6; discounts to groups & AAA members; children under 6 no charge. Closed National holidays.

BULLOCH HALL, 180 Bulloch Ave., Roswell, GA 30075-4420. Mailing Address: P.O. Box 1309, Roswell, GA 30077-1309. Tel.: 770-992-1731 & 1951. Fax: 770-587-1840.

E-mail: info@bullochhall.org

Web Site: www.bullochhall.org

Key Personnel: Site Coord., Pam Billingsley; Asst. Site Coord., Jenny Goldemund; Dir. Education, Gwen Koehler; Museum Shop Mgr., Chris Anthis.

Institution Type/Description: Historic House: c.1839 Antebellum Greek Revival House & Cottage.

Hours & Admission Prices: Mon.-Sat. 10-3, Sun. 1-3; tours on the hour. Adults $8, seniors $7, children 6-18 $6; members & children under 6 no charge. Closed New Year's Eve & Day; Martin Luther King Jr. Day; Easter; Memorial Day; Independence Day; Labor Day; Thanksgiving; Christmas Eve & Day. &

Attendance: 11,000 (estimated)

CHATTAHOOCHEE NATURE CENTER, 9135 Willeo Rd., Roswell, GA 30075-4723. Mailing Address: P.O. Box 769769, Roswell, GA 30076-8228. Tel.: 770-992-2055.

E-mail: marketing@chattnaturecenter.org

Institution Type/Description: Nature Center.

Hours & Admission Prices: Mon.-Sat. 10-5, Sun. 12-5. Adults $10, seniors 65 & over and children 13-18 $7, children 3-12 $6; children 2 & under no charge. Closed New Year's Day; Thanksgiving; Christmas Eve & Day.

ROSWELL FIRE & RESCUE MUSEUM, 1002 Alpharetta St., Roswell, GA 30075-3661. Mailing Address: 1810 Hembree Rd., Alpharetta, GA 30009. Tel.: 770-641-3730.

E-mail: fire@roswellgov.com

Web Site: www.roswellgov.com/index.aspx?NID=208

Key Personnel: Fire Chief, Ricky Burnette.

Institution Type/Description: Fire-Fighting Museum.

Hours & Admission Prices: Call for hours. No charge. &

Attendance: 500 (estimated)

ROSWELL VISUAL ARTS CENTER & GALLERY, 10495 Woodstock Rd., Roswell, GA 30075-2941. Mailing Address: 38 Hill St., Ste. 100, Roswell, GA 30075. Tel.: 770-594-6122. Fax: 770-594-6529.

E-mail: rrpd@ci.roswell.ga.us

Web Site: www.roswellgov.com

Institution Type/Description: Art Gallery.

Hours & Admission Prices: Mon.-Fri. 9:30-6, Sat. 9-1. Roswell Art Center West: Wed.-Sat. 10-6. No charge. &

TEACHING MUSEUM NORTH, 793 Mimosa Blvd., Roswell, GA 30075. Tel.: 770-552-6339.

E-mail: museum@fultonschools.org

Web Site: www.fultonschools.org

Institution Type/Description: History Museum.

Hours & Admission Prices: Mon.-Fri. 8-4; other times by appointment.

Royston

TY COBB MUSEUM, 461 Cook St., Royston, GA 30662-4003. Tel.: 706-245-1825. Fax: 706-245-1831. Facebook: Ty Cobb Museum; Twitter: @tycobbmuseum.

E-mail: jridgway@csg-ga.net

Web Site: www.tycobbmuseum.org

Key Personnel: Dir. & Museum Shop Mgr., Julie Ridgway; C.E.O., Matt McRee.

Institution Type/Description: Sports Museum.

Hours & Admission Prices: Mon.-Fri. 9-4, Sat. 10-4; call to confirm. Adults $5, seniors 62 & over $4, students $3; discounts to groups of 10 or more and AAM

& ICOM members; children under 5, active duty military & members w/ID no charge. &

Attendance: 3,700 (estimated)

Saint Marys

CUMBERLAND ISLAND NATIONAL SEASHORE - MAINLAND MUSEUM, Physical/Mailing Address: 101 Wheeler St., Saint Marys, GA 31558-8421. Tel.: 912-882-4336. Fax: 912-882-6284.

E-mail: cumberlandislandreservations@gmail.com

Web Site: www.nps.gov/cuis

Key Personnel: Supt., Gary Ingram.

Institution Type/Description: Historical Museum.

Hours & Admission Prices: Museum: daily 1-4. Visitor Center: daily 8-4. Ferry: March-Nov. daily 9 am & 11:45 am; Dec.-Feb. Mon. & Thurs.-Sun. 9 am & 11:45 am. Call for reservations 877-860-6787. &

Attendance: 40,000 (estimated)

ORANGE HALL, 311 Osborne St., Saint Marys, GA 31568. Tel.: 912-576-3644.

Web Site: www.orangehallstmarys.org

Institution Type/Description: Historic House Museum: c.1820.

Hours & Admission Prices: Daily call for hours.

ST. MARYS FILM MUSEUM, 1000 Osborne St., Saint Marys, GA 31558. Mailing Address: Coastal Georgia Film Alliance, 511 Osborne St., Saint Marys, GA 31558. Tel.: 912-576-5488.

E-mail: info@coastalgeorgiafilm.org

Web Site: www.coastalgeorgiafilm.org

Institution Type/Description: Film Museum.

Hours & Admission Prices: Mon.-Sat. 9-5.

ST. MARYS SUBMARINE MUSEUM, 102 St. Marys St. W., Saint Marys, GA 31558-4945. Tel.: 912-882-2782. Fax: 912-882-2748.

E-mail: submus@tds.net

Web Site: www.stmaryssubmuseum.com

Key Personnel: Pres., Doug Cooper; Museum Shop Mgr., John Crouse.

Institution Type/Description: Military & Submarine Museum.

Hours & Admission Prices: Tues.-Sat. 10-5, Sun. 12-5. Adults $5, senior citizens 63& over and military $4, children 6-18 $3; children under 6 & members no charge. Closed New Year's Eve, Day & week; Easter; Thanksgiving; Christmas week. &

Attendance: 10,000 (estimated)

Saint Simons Island

THE ARTHUR J. MOORE METHODIST MUSEUM, 100 Arthur Moore Dr., Saint Simons Island, GA 31522. Mailing Address: P.O. Box 24081, Saint Simons Island, GA 31522-7081. Tel.: 912-638-4050. Fax: 912-638-9050.

E-mail: director@mooremuseum.org

Web Site: www.mooremethodistmuseum.org

Key Personnel: Cur. & Archivist, Anne Packard; Asst. Archivist, Cindy Angelich.

Institution Type/Description: Religious Museum: near the site of Oglethorpe, John and Charles Wesley's activities in 1736.

Hours & Admission Prices: Mon.-Sat. 10-4. No charge; donations accepted. Closed New Year's Day; Independence Day; Thanksgiving; Christmas. &

Attendance: 10,000 (actual)

COASTAL GEORGIA HISTORICAL SOCIETY - ST. SIMONS ISLAND LIGHTHOUSE MUSEUM, THE MARITIME CENTER AT THE HISTORIC COAST GUARD STATION, 610 Beachview Dr., Saint Simons Island, GA 31522-4821. Mailing Address: P.O. Box 21136, Saint Simons Island, GA 31522-0636. Tel.: 912-638-4666. Fax: 912-638-6609.

E-mail: adminoffice@saintsimonslighthouse.org

Web Site: saintsimonslighthouse.org

Formerly: A.W. Jones Heritage Center and St. Simons Island Lighthouse Museum - Coastal Georgia Historical Society

Key Personnel: Exec. Dir., Sherri Jones; Cur., Mimi Rogers.

Institution Type/Description: Local History Museum; Lighthouse Museum.

Hours & Admission Prices: Mon.-Sat. 10-5, Sun. 1:30-5. Adults $12, children 6-12 $5; discounts to groups; military, children under 6 & members no charge. (Admission prices include all museums & venues). Closed New Year's Day; Easter; Thanksgiving; Christmas Eve & Day. &

Attendance: 100,000 (actual)

FORT FREDERICA NATIONAL MONUMENT, 6515 Frederica Rd., Saint Simons Island, GA 31522. Tel.: 912-638-3639. Fax: 912-634-5357.
E-mail: denise_spear@nps.gov
Web Site: www.nps.gov/fofr
Institution Type/Description: Park Museum.
Hours & Admission Prices: Visitor Center: daily 9-5. No charge. Closed New Year's Day; Thanksgiving; Christmas. &
Attendance: 292,505 (actual)

GLYNN VISUAL ARTS, 106 Island Dr., Saint Simons Island, GA 31522-3780. Tel.: 912-638-8770.
E-mail: info@glynnvisualarts.org
Web Site: www.glynnvisualarts.org
Formerly: The Glynn Art Association, Inc.
Key Personnel: Dir., Susan Ryles; Pres. (V), Sue Cansler; Vice Pres., Deborah Wright.
Institution Type/Description: Art Gallery.
Hours & Admission Prices: Mon.-Fri. 9-5, Sat. call for hours. No charge; donations accepted. Closed New Year's Day; Independence Day; Labor Day; Thanksgiving; Christmas. &
Attendance: 10,000 (estimated)

MARITIME CENTER - COASTAL GEORGIA HISTORICAL SOCIETY, 4201 First St., Saint Simons Island, GA 31522-3902. Tel.: 912-638-4666. Fax: 912-638-6609. Facebook: Maritime Center at the Historic Coast Guard Station.
E-mail: ssi1872@comcast.net
Web Site: saintsimonslighthouse.org
Formerly: Maritime Museum at Historic Coast Guard Station
Key Personnel: Dir., Sherri Jones; Pres., Anne Stembler; Public Rels., Leigh Ann Stroud; Cur., Ellen Rogers; Museum Shop Mgr., Curt Smith.
Institution Type/Description: Coast Guard & Natural History Museum: housed in a lighthouse & keeper's dwelling; built in 1872.
Hours & Admission Prices: Mon.-Sat. 10-5, Sun. 1:30-5. Adults $12, children 6-12 $5; children under 6 & members no charge. (Admission prices include all museums & venues.) Closed New Year's Day; Easter; Thanksgiving; Christmas Eve & Day. &
Attendance: 40,000 (estimated)

MILDRED HUIE PLANTATION & LANDMARK MUSEUM, 1819 Frederica Rd., Saint Simons Island, GA 31522. Mailing Address: P.O. Box 30841, Sea Island, GA 31561. Tel.: 912-638-3057.
E-mail: medhouse1819@gmail.com
Formerly: Mildred Huie Museum
Key Personnel: C.E.O., Mildred Huie Wilcox; Cur., Jeanine Gehringer.
Institution Type/Description: Art Museum: housed in the Mediterranean House; built in 1929.
Hours & Admission Prices: Fri.-Sun. 1-5; other times by appointment. No charge; donations accepted. &
Attendance: 150 (estimated)

Sandersville

THE BROWN HOUSE MUSEUM, 268 N. Harris St., Sandersville, GA 31082. Mailing Address: P.O. Box 6088, Sandersville, GA 31082-6088. Tel.: 478-552-1965 & 2963.
E-mail: fcveal@yahoo.com
Key Personnel: Dir., Frances C. Veal; Pres. Society, Layne Kilchens.
Institution Type/Description: History Museum: housed in c.1850 house, headquarters for General Sherman in 1864.
Hours & Admission Prices: Tues. & Thurs-Fri. 2-5, Sat. 10-3; other times by appointment. No charge; donations accepted. Closed holidays. &
Attendance: 1,000 (estimated)

THE CHARLES EDWARD CHOATE EXHIBIT, 131 W. Haynes St., Ste. B, Sandersville, GA 31082-1737. Tel.: 478-552-3288. Fax: 478-552-1449.
E-mail: chamber@washingtoncountyga.com
Web Site: www.washingtoncounty-ga.com
Institution Type/Description: Art Museum.
Hours & Admission Prices: Mon.-Fri. 9-12 & 1-5. No charge. Closed holidays. &
Attendance: 50 (estimated)

GENEALOGY RESEARCH CENTER AND OLD JAIL MUSEUM, 129 Jones St., Sandersville, GA 31082-1768. Mailing Address: P.O. Box 6088, Sandersville, GA 31082-6088. Tel.: 478-552-6965.

E-mail: genealogyresearch@att.net
Web Site: www.rootsweb.com/gawashin/genweb/
Formerly: Washington County Museum
Key Personnel: Dir. & Chm. (V), Loretta Cato.
Institution Type/Description: History Museum: housed in c.1891 sheriffs' house with attached jail.
Hours & Admission Prices: Tues. & Thurs.-Fri. 2-5, St. 10-3. No charge; donations accepted. Closed holidays. &
Attendance: 400 (estimated)

Sandy Springs

ABERNATHY ARTS CENTER, 254 Johnson Ferry Rd., N.W., Sandy Springs, GA 30328. Tel.: 404-613-6172. Fax: 404-303-6135. Facebook: Abernathy Arts Center.
E-mail: joanna.strickland@fultoncountyga.gov
Web Site: www.fultonarts.org/index.php/art-centers/ abernathy-arts-center
Institution Type/Description: Art Gallery.
Hours & Admission Prices: Tues.-Fri. 9-5, Sat. 9-2. No charge. &

GEORGIA COMMISSION ON THE HOLOCAUST, 5920 Roswell Rd., Ste. 209, Sandy Springs, GA 30328. Tel.: 770-206-1558.
Web Site: www.holocaust.georgia.gov
Institution Type/Description: History Museum.
Hours & Admission Prices: Tues.-Thurs. 10-4, Fri. 10-2, Sat.-Sun. 12-4. No charge.

SANDY SPRINGS HISTORIC SITE & MUSEUM, 6075 Sandy Springs Cir., Sandy Springs, GA 30328-3841. Mailing Address: c/o Heritage Sandy Springs, 6110 Bluestone Rd., Sandy Springs, GA 30328. Tel.: 404-851-9111. Fax: 404-851-9807.
E-mail: information@heritagesandysprings.org
Web Site: heritagesandysprings.org
Key Personnel: Exec. Dir., Carol Thompson.
Institution Type/Description: Historic House: housed in the Williams-Payne house; built in 1869.
Hours & Admission Prices: House: by appointment. Park: daily dawn to 8pm. No charge.

Sautee

SAUTEE-NACOOCHEE CENTER, 283 Hwy. 255 N., Sautee, GA 30571-2606. Mailing Address: P.O. Box 460, Sautee, GA 30571-0460. Tel.: 706-878-3300. Fax: 706-878-1395.
E-mail: cbrooks@snca.org
Web Site: www.snca.org
Formerly: Sautee-Nacoochee Community Association
Key Personnel: C.E.O. & Dir., Kathy Blandin, Ph.D.; Chm., Bob Prim; Cur., Sam Schultz; Cur. Folk Pottery, John Burrison; Dir. Folk Pottery Museum, Chris Brooks.
Institution Type/Description: Art & History Museum.
Hours & Admission Prices: Office: Mon.-Fri. 9-5. Museum & Gallery: Sat. 10-5, Sun. 1-5. Adults $5; members no charge. &
Attendance: 22,300 (estimated)

Savannah

ALEXANDER HALL GALLERY - SAVANNAH COLLEGE OF ART AND DESIGN, 668 Indian St., Savannah, GA 31401-1105. Tel.: 912-525-4727. Fax: 912-525-4952.
E-mail: contact@scad.edu
Web Site: www.scad.edu/exhibitions/galleries
Institution Type/Description: Art Gallery.
Hours & Admission Prices: Mon.-Fri. 9-5. No charge.

ANDREW LOW HOUSE, 329 Abercorn St., Savannah, GA 31401-4634. Tel.: 912-233-6854. Fax: 912-233-9239. Facebook: Andrew Low House.
E-mail: sbohlin@andrewlowhouse.com
Web Site: www.andrewlowhouse.com
Key Personnel: Chm., Rebecca Moore; Pres., Mrs. Jay Daniels Schwartz; Dir., Stephen Bohlin; Registrar, Jessica Estes; Museum Shop Mgr., Marla Denmark.
Institution Type/Description: Historic Site: housed in the former home of Andrew Low, a wealthy Savannah cotton factor.
Hours & Admission Prices: mid-Jan. to Dec. Mon.-Sat. 10-4, Sun. 12-4. Adults $10, students & children $6; discounts to military, groups of 10 or more, AAA, AAM, AARP, AASCH & NARM members; members no charge. Closed Labor Day; Thanksgiving; Christmas.
Attendance: 40,609 (actual)

ARCHIVES MUSEUM, TEMPLE MICKVE ISRAEL, 20 Wayne St. (Tour Entrance), Savannah, GA 31401. Mailing Address: P.O. Box 816, Savannah, GA 31402-0816. Tel.: 912-233-1547. Fax: 912-233-3086.
E-mail: info@mickveisrael.org
Web Site: www.mickveisrael.org
Key Personnel: Rabbi, Robert Haas; Exec. Dir., Jennifer Rich; Gift Shop Mgr., Glenda McNew.
Institution Type/Description: Religious Museum: housed in c.1876 Gothic style, Congregation Mickve Israel Synagogue.
Hours & Admission Prices: Mon.-Fri. 10-1 & 2-4, call to confirm. Adults $5; children under 12 & members no charge. Closed holidays.
Attendance: 8,000 (estimated)

DAVENPORT HOUSE MUSEUM, 324 E. State St., Savannah, GA 31401-3411. Tel.: 912-236-8097. Fax: 912-233-7938. Facebook.
E-mail: info@davenporthousemuseum.org
Web Site: davenporthousemuseum.org
Key Personnel: Pres. (V) & C.E.O. Historic Savannah Foundation, Daniel Carey; Dir., Jamie Credle; Museum Collection Officer, Jeff Freeman; Museum Shop Mgr., Gaye Kurmas.
Institution Type/Description: Historic House Museum.
Hours & Admission Prices: Mon.-Sat. 10-4, Sun. 1-4; tours on the half hour; special and group tours available upon request. Adults $9, students 6-17 $5; discount to museum employees & volunteers, AAA, Coastal Museum Assoc. members & National Trust Partner Place members; members & children under 6 no charge. Closed New Year's Day; St. Patrick's Day; Thanksgiving; Christmas.
Attendance: 36,155 (actual)

FIRST AFRICAN BAPTIST CHURCH & MUSEUM, 23 Montgomery St., Savannah, GA 31401-2429. Tel.: 912-233-6597. Fax: 912-234-7950.
Institution Type/Description: Religious Museum.
Hours & Admission Prices: Mon.-Fri. 10-4; other times by appointment. Adults $8, seniors & students $6.
Attendance: 10,000 (estimated)

FLANNERY O'CONNOR CHILDHOOD HOME, 207 E. Charlton St., Savannah, GA 31401-4605. Tel.: 912-233-6014. Facebook: Flannery O'Connor Childhood Home.
E-mail: flanneryoconnorhome@gmail.com
Web Site: www.flanneryoconnorhome.org
Key Personnel: Mng. Dir., Jared Hall.
Institution Type/Description: Historic House: housed in the childhood home of author, Flannery O'Connor.
Hours & Admission Prices: Fri.-Wed. 1-4. Adults $6, students $5; members and youth 15 & under no charge. Closed major holidays.
Attendance: 2,349 (actual)

FORT PULASKI NATIONAL MONUMENT, U.S. Hwy. 80 E., Savannah, GA 31410. Mailing Address: P.O. Box 30757, Savannah, GA 31410-0757. Tel.: 912-786-5787. Fax: 912-786-6023.
E-mail: randy_wester@nps.gov
Web Site: www.nps.gov/fopu/
Key Personnel: Supt., Randall Wester.
Institution Type/Description: History Museum & Park.
Hours & Admission Prices: Labor Day-Memorial Day daily 9-5; call for extended summer hours. Adult 16 & over $5; children 15 & under no charge. Golden Age, Eagle & National Park Pass accepted. Closed Thanksgiving; Christmas.
Attendance: 400,000 (estimated)

GEORGIA HISTORICAL SOCIETY, 501 Whitaker St., Savannah, GA 31401-4889. Tel.: 912-651-2125. Fax: 912-651-2831.
E-mail: ghs@georgiahistory.com
Web Site: www.georgiahistory.com
Key Personnel: C.E.O. & Pres., Dr. W. Todd Groce; Chm., Thomas M. Holder; Exec. Vice Pres., Laura Garcia-Culler; Sr. Historian, Dr. Stan Deaton; Dir. Comms., Patricia Meagher.
Institution Type/Description: Historical Society Museum: housed in 1874-1875 building designed by Detlief Lienau.
Hours & Admission Prices: Wed.-Fri. 12-5, 1st & 3rd Sat. each month 10-5. Adults $5; members no charge. Closed national & state holidays.
Attendance: 35,000 (actual)

GEORGIA STATE RAILROAD MUSEUM, 655 Louisville Rd., Savannah, GA 31401. Tel.: 912-651-6823.
E-mail: admin@chsgeorgia.org
Web Site: www.chsgeorgia.org/railroad-museum.html

Institution Type/Description: Railroad History Museum: A National Historic Landmark.
Hours & Admission Prices: Call for hours.

GIRL SCOUT FIRST HEADQUARTERS MUSEUM, 330 Drayton St., Savannah, GA 31401-4433. Tel.: 888-223-3883.
E-mail: gshg@gshg.org
Web Site: www.gshg.org/en/our-council/girl-scout-first-headquarters.html
Institution Type/Description: Girl Scout History Museum: housed in the former carriage house to the Andrew Low House, built in 1848. Girl Scout founder, Juliette Low converted building into Girl Scout Headquarters in 1912.
Hours & Admission Prices: Mon.-Tues. & Thurs.-Sat. 10-4.

GREEN-MELDRIM HOUSE MUSEUM, 14 W. Macon St., Savannah, GA 13401. Mailing Address: c/o St. John's Church, 1 W. Macon St., Savannah, GA 31401. Tel.: 912-233-3845.
Web Site: www.stjohnssav.org/green-meldrim-house
Institution Type/Description: Historic House Museum: housed in the former home of Charles Green who offered General William T. Sherman the use of his home as headquarters during the Civil War in 1864.
Hours & Admission Prices: Tues. & Thurs.-Fri. 10-4, Sat. 10-1. Guided tours: adults $10, students $5.

GUTSTEIN GALLERY - SAVANNAH COLLEGE OF ART AND DESIGN, 201 E. Broughton St., Savannah, GA 31401-3401. Mailing Address: P.O. Box 3146, Savannah, GA 31402-3146. Tel.: 912-525-4735. Fax: 912-525-4952.
E-mail: exhibitions@scad.edu
Web Site: www.scad.edu
Key Personnel: Exec. Dir., Laurie Ann Farrell.
Institution Type/Description: Art Museum.
Hours & Admission Prices: Mon.-Fri. 10-6, Sat. 12-5. No charge; donations accepted.
Attendance: 25,000 (estimated)

HALL STREET GALLERY - SAVANNAH COLLEGE OF ART AND DESIGN, 668 Indian St., Savannah, GA 31401. Tel.: 912-525-4727.
E-mail: scadmoa@scad.edu
Web Site: www.scadmoa.org/art/scad-museums-and-galleries
Institution Type/Description: Art Gallery.
Hours & Admission Prices: Mon.-Fri. 10-5. No charge.

JEPSON CENTER FOR THE ARTS, 207 W. York St., Savannah, GA 31401. Mailing Address: P.O. Box 10081, Savannah, GA 31412-0221. Tel.: 912-790-8800.
E-mail: info@telfair.org
Web Site: www.telfair.org/visit/jepson
Institution Type/Description: Contemporary Art Center.
Hours & Admission Prices: Sun.-Mon. 12-5, Tues.-Sat. 10-5. Adults $20, seniors 65 & over and military $18, student K-College $5; discounts to AAA members; members & children under 5 no charge. Closed New Year's Day; Martin Luther King, Jr. Day; St. Patrick's Day; Easter; Labor Day; Thanksgiving; Christmas.

JULIETTE GORDON LOW BIRTHPLACE, 10 E. Oglethorpe Ave., Savannah, GA 31401-3707. Tel.: 912-233-4501; TDD: 912-233-4501. Fax: 912-233-4659.
E-mail: info@juliettegordonlowbirthplace.org
Web Site: www.girlscouts.org/birthplace
Key Personnel: Exec. Dir., Lisa Junkin Lopez; Assoc. Dir., Sherryl Lang.
Institution Type/Description: Historic House Museum: 1818-1821 Wayne-Gordon House.
Hours & Admission Prices: mid-Jan. to Feb. & Nov.-Dec. Mon.-Tues. & Thurs.-Sat. 10-4, Sun. 11-4; March-Oct. Mon.-Sat. 10-4, Sun. 11-4. Adults $8; Girl Scout adults & students 6-20 $7, Girl Scouts 6-18 $6; children 5 & under no charge. Closed New Year's Day; St. Patrick's Day; Easter; Thanksgiving; Christmas Eve & Day.
Attendance: 65,000 (actual)

KING-TISDELL COTTAGE - MUSEUM OF BLACK HISTORY, 514 E. Huntingdon St., Savannah, GA 31401-5115. Mailing Address: Beach Institute, 502 E. Harris St., Savannah, GA 31401. Tel.: 912-234-8000. Fax: 912-234-8001.
E-mail: kingtisdell@bellsouth.net
Web Site: www.kingtisdell.org
Institution Type/Description: Historic House Museum: housed in an 1896 Victorian cottage.
Hours & Admission Prices: Mon.-Fri. 12-5, Sat.-Sun. 1-4. Adults $1.50, children $.75; discounts to groups. Closed holidays.

MASSIE SCHOOL, 207 E. Gordon St., Savannah, GA 31401-5003. Tel.: 912-395-5070. Fax: 912-201-5224.
E-mail: steve.smith@sccpss.com
Web Site: www.massieschool.com
Formerly: Massie Heritage Center
Key Personnel: Dir., Candy Lowe; Pres. (V), Emma Adler; Museum Shop Mgr., Sandee Lipsitz.
Institution Type/Description: Heritage Center.
Hours & Admission Prices: Mon.-Sat. 10-4, Sun. 12-4; groups by appointment. Guided Tours: adults $8, children 5-12 $3; members no charge. Self-Guided Tours: adults $5, children 5-12 $3; discounts to NTHP members; children under 4 & members no charge. Closed holidays. &

MERCER WILLIAMS HOUSE MUSEUM, 429 Bull St., Monterey Square, Savannah, GA 31401. Tel.: 912-236-6352, 877-430-6352 (toll free). Fax: 912-238-3993.
E-mail: mercerwilliamshouse@mercerhouse.com
Web Site: www.mercerhouse.com/home.htm
Institution Type/Description: Historic House Museum: housed in the former home of John Wilder; built c.1868.
Hours & Admission Prices: Mon.-Sat. 10:30-4:10, Sun. 12-4. Adults $12.50, students $8.

OATLAND ISLAND WILDLIFE CENTER, 711 Sandtown Rd., Savannah, GA 31410-1019. Tel.: 912-395-1212 & 1500. Fax: 912-898-3983.
E-mail: annie.quinting@sccpss.com
Web Site: www.oatlandisland.org
Formerly: Oatland Island Education Center
Key Personnel: Dir., Heather Merbs; Education, Pam Keener; Education, Annie Quinting; Education, Max McKelvey; Administrative Sec., Courtney Moncnef; Naturalist, Pam Hewatt.
Institution Type/Description: Environmental Education Nature Center.
Hours & Admission Prices: Daily 10-4. Adults $5, seniors, children 4-17 & military $3; members no charge. Closed New Year's Day; Thanksgiving; Christmas Eve & Day. &
Attendance: 67,080 (actual)

OLD FORT JACKSON, 1 Ft. Jackson Rd., Savannah, GA 31404-1039. Tel.: 912-232-3945. Fax: 912-236-5126.
E-mail: oldfortjackson@chsgeorgia.org
Web Site: www.chsgeorgia.org/jackson
Key Personnel: Site Mgr., Marty Liebschner.
Institution Type/Description: American Military Museum.
Hours & Admission Prices: Daily 9-5. Adults $7, children 2-12 $4; discounts to AAA & CHS members. Closed New Year's Day; Thanksgiving; Christmas. &
Attendance: 75,000 (estimated)

OWENS-THOMAS HOUSE, 124 Abercorn St., Savannah, GA 31401-3732. Mailing Address: P.O. Box 10081, Savannah, GA 31412-0281. Tel.: 912-233-9743.
E-mail: info@telfair.org
Institution Type/Description: Historic House Museum: housed in a home designed by architect, William Jay; c.1819.
Hours & Admission Prices: Tues.-Sat. 10-5, Sun.-Mon. 12-5. Closed New Year's Day; Martin Luther King Jr. Day; St. Patrick's Day; Easter; Labor Day; Thanksgiving; Christmas.

PINNACLE GALLERY - SAVANNAH COLLEGE OF ART AND DESIGN, 320 E. Liberty St., Savannah, GA 31401. Tel.: 912-525-4950.
E-mail: contact@scad.edu
Web Site: www.scadexhibitions.com
Institution Type/Description: Art Gallery.
Hours & Admission Prices: Mon.-Fri. 9-5:30, Sat. 10-5, Sun. 1-4.

RALPH MARK GILBERT CIVIL RIGHTS MUSEUM, 460 Martin Luther King, Jr. Blvd., Savannah, GA 31401-4800. Mailing Address: P.O. Box 13130, Savannah, GA 31416-0130. Tel.: 912-777-6099. Facebook: Ralph Mark Gilbert Civil Rights Museum, Inc..
Institution Type/Description: History Museum: named in honor of the late Dr. Ralph Mark Gilbert, father of Savannah's civil rights movement & NAACP leader.
Hours & Admission Prices: Tues.-Sat. 9-5. Museum Tours: adults $8, senior citizens 65 & over $6, students $4; discounts to groups of 10 or more; members no charge.

ROUNDHOUSE RAILROAD MUSEUM, 601 W. Harris St., Savannah, GA 31401-3193. Tel.: 912-651-6823. Fax: 912-651-3194.
Institution Type/Description: Railroad Museum: A National Historic Landmark.
Hours & Admission Prices: Call for hours & admission prices.

SCAD MUSEUM OF ART, 601 Turner Blvd., Savannah, GA 31401-4242. Mailing Address: P.O. Box 3146, Savannah, GA 31402-3146. Tel.: 912-525-7191. Facebook: SCAD Museum of Art.
E-mail: scadmoa@scad.edu
Web Site: www.scadmoa.org
Key Personnel: Dir. Museum Operations, Sean McGee.
Institution Type/Description: Art Museum.
Hours & Admission Prices: Tues.,Wed., Fri. & Sat. 10-5, Thurs. 10-8, Sun. 12-5. Family $20, adults $10, senior & military $8, high school students, college students & SCAD alumni $5; members & children under 14 no charge. &
Attendance: 45,000 (estimated)

SAVANNAH BOTANICAL GARDENS, 1388 Eisenhower Dr., Savannah, GA 31406. Tel.: 912-355-3883.
E-mail: sacgc@att.net
Web Site: www.savannahbotanical.org
Institution Type/Description: Botanical Garden.
Hours & Admission Prices: Mon.-Sat. 8-8, Sun. 8am-8:45pm. Garden: fee may be charged for groups of 10 or more.

SAVANNAH COLLEGE OF ART & DESIGN GALLERIES - ATLANTA, 601 Turner Blvd., Savannah, GA 31401. Mailing Address: P.O. Box 3146, Savannah, GA 31402. Tel.: 912-525-7191.
E-mail: scadmoa@scad.edu
Web Site: www.scadmoa.org/art/scad-galleries
Formerly: Atlanta College of Art
Key Personnel: Pres. & Founder, Paula S. Wallace.
Institution Type/Description: Art Gallery.
Hours & Admission Prices: Mon.-Fri. 8:30-5:30. No charge; donations accepted. Closed holidays. &
Attendance: 12,000 (estimated)

SAVANNAH HISTORY MUSEUM, 303 Martin Luther King Jr. Blvd., Savannah, GA 31401-4217. Tel.: 912-651-6825 & 238-1779.
Web Site: www.chsgeorgia.org/shm/
Institution Type/Description: History Museum: housed in the old Central of Georgia Railway passenger shed, built 1850-1860s.
Hours & Admission Prices: Mon.-Fri. 8:30-5, Sat.-Sun. 9-5. Adults $7, children 2-12 $4. Closed New Year's Day; Thanksgiving; Christmas.

SAVANNAH - OGEECHEE CANAL MUSEUM & NATURE CENTER, 681 Fort Argyle Rd., Savannah, GA 31419-9239. Tel.: 912-748-8068.
E-mail: info@savannahogeecheecanalsociety.com
Web Site: www.savannahogeecheecanal society.org
Key Personnel: Pres. (V), Steve Elkins; Museum Shop Mgr., Chica Arndt.
Institution Type/Description: History Museum & Nature Center.
Hours & Admission Prices: Call for hours. Adults $2, children 5-12 $1; members no charge.
Attendance: 2,500 (estimated)

SHIPS OF THE SEA MARITIME MUSEUM/WILLIAM SCARBROUGH HOUSE AND GARDENS, 41 Martin Luther King Blvd., Savannah, GA 31401-2435. Tel.: 912-232-1511. Fax: 912-234-7363.
E-mail: contact@shipsofthesea.org
Web Site: www.shipsofthesea.org
Key Personnel: Dir., Tony Pizzo; Cur. Exhibits & Education, Wendy Melton; Mgr. Communication & Events, Michelle Riley.
Institution Type/Description: Maritime Museum.
Hours & Admission Prices: Tues.-Sun. 10-5 (last admission 4:15). Family $20, adults $8.50, senior citizens, students, AAA, & military $6.50; discounts to AAM members & groups of 10 or more. Closed New Year's Eve & Day; St. Patrick's Day; Easter; Thanksgiving; Christmas Eve & Day. &
Attendance: 20,000 (estimated)

TELFAIR ACADEMY, Telfair Academy of Arts & Sciences, 121 Barnard St., Savannah, GA 31401. Mailing Address: P.O. Box

10081, Savannah, GA 31412-0281. Tel.: 912-232-1177, ext. 16. Fax: 912-232-6954.
E-mail: info@telfair.org
Web Site: www.telfair.org
Formerly: Telfair Museum of Art
Key Personnel: Dir. & C.E.O., Robin Nicholson; Registrar, Jessica M. Estes; Designer & Preparator, Milutin Pavlovic; Sr. Cur. Education, Harry H. DeLorme; Exec. Asst. to Dir., Margo Jackson; Operations Mgr. Owens-Thomas House Store, Stacy Palmer; Chief Cur., Courtney McNeil; Deputy Dir. Devel., Molly Taylor; Dir. Annual Giving, Catherine Renner; Designer & Preparator, Heath Ritch; Dir. Retail Operations, Lisa Ocampo; Dir. Special Events, Lesley Hail; Lead Interpreter, Lilith Logan; Tourism Rels. & Sales Mgr., Ginger Graham.
Institution Type/Description: Art Museum & Historic House: housed in 1819 Regency mansion.
Hours & Admission Prices: Museum of Art: Sun.-Mon. 12-5, Tues.-Sat. 10-5. Family $40, adults $20, senior citizens & military $18, students 13-15 $15, children 6-12 $5; discounts to AAA, AAM & ICOM members; members no charge. NARM Reciprocal Museum Program. Closed holidays. &
Attendance: 177,611 (actual)

THE UGA MARINE EXTENSION SERVICE - MARINE EDUCATION CENTER & AQUARIUM, 30 Ocean Science Circle, Savannah, GA 31411. Tel.: 912-598-2496. Fax: 912-598-2302.
E-mail: fish@uga.edu
Web Site: www.marex.uga.edu/aquarium
Key Personnel: Dir., Mark Risse; Assoc. Dir., Anne Lindsay.
Institution Type/Description: Aquarium.
Hours & Admission Prices: Mon.-Fri. 9-4, Sat. 10-5. Adults 13 & over $6, seniors 55 & over, military and children 3-12 $3; children under 2 no charge. Season Passes available. &
Attendance: 25,000 (estimated)

WORMSLOE STATE HISTORIC SITE, 7601 Skidaway Rd., Savannah, GA 31406-6449. Tel.: 912-353-3023. Fax: 912-353-3023.
E-mail: wormsloe@bellsouth.net
Web Site: www.gastateparks.org
Key Personnel: Mgr., Chris Floyd.
Institution Type/Description: Historic Site: ruins of 1739 fortified house.
Hours & Admission Prices: Daily 9-5; groups by appointment. Adults $10, senior citizens 62 & over $9, children 6-17 $4.50, children under 6 $. Closed Thanksgiving; Christmas. &
Attendance: 100,000 (estimated)

Senoia

THE BUGGY SHOP MUSEUM, 74 Main St., Senoia, GA 30276. Mailing Address: P.O. Box 310, Senoia, GA 30276. Tel.: 770-253-1018.
E-mail: buggyshopsenoia@aol.com
Institution Type/Description: History Museum.
Hours & Admission Prices: April-Oct. 3rd Sat.-Sun. each month 1-4. No charge; donations accepted.

Smyrna

SMYRNA MUSEUM OF HISTORY, 2861 Atlanta Rd., S.E., Smyrna, GA 30080-3657. Tel.: 770-435-7549 & 431-2858.
E-mail: imharoldsmith@gmail.com
Web Site: smyrnahistory.org
Key Personnel: Dir., Harold Smith.
Institution Type/Description: Historical Society Museum.
Hours & Admission Prices: Tues.-Sat. 10-4; other times by appointment. No charge; donations accepted. &

Springfield

HISTORIC EFFINGHAM SOCIETY - THE EFFINGHAM MUSEUM AND LIVING HISTORY SITE, 1002 Pine St., Springfield, GA 31329. Mailing Address: P.O. Box 999, Springfield, GA 31329. Tel.: 912-754-2170.
E-mail: histeffingham@aol.com
Web Site: www.historiceffinghamsociety.org
Formerly: Effingham Old Jail Museum
Key Personnel: Pres. & Dir., Thomas Hodgson; Vice Pres., David Seitz; Docent & Sec., Betty Renfro; Museum Shop Mgr., Beverly Poole.
Institution Type/Description: History Museum & Living History Site.

Hours & Admission Prices: Tues.-Fri. 9-3, Sat.-Sun. by appointment. Adults $5, seniors & military $4, students 6-18 $3; members & children under 6 no charge. &
Attendance: 1,000 (actual)

Statesboro

GEORGIA SOUTHERN UNIVERSITY MUSEUM, 2142 Southern Dr., Statesboro, GA 30458. Mailing Address: P.O. Box 8061, Statesboro, GA 30460-1000. Tel.: 912-478-5444. Fax: 912-478-0729.
E-mail: btharp@georgiasouthern.edu
Web Site: www.georgiasouthern.edu/museum
Key Personnel: Dir., Dr. Brent W. Tharp; Asst. Dir., Debbie Gleason; Visitor Svcs. Coord., Billy Tyson; Cur. Education, Ruby Ashley; Cur. Paleontology, Dr. Kathlyn Smith.
Institution Type/Description: University Museum.
Hours & Admission Prices: Tues.-Fri. 9-5, Sat.-Sun. 2-5. Admission $2; discounts to AAM, Coastal Museum Assn. & Ga. Assn. of Museums & Galleries members; GSU students, members and children 3 & under no charge. Closed university holidays. &
Attendance: 20,000 (estimated)

Stockbridge

PANOLA MOUNTAIN STATE CONSERVATION PARK, 2600 Hwy. 155, S.W., Stockbridge, GA 30281-5250. Tel.: 770-389-7801. Fax: 770-389-7925.
E-mail: panola_mountain@mail.dnr.state.ga.us
Web Site: www.gastateparks.org/info/panolamt
Institution Type/Description: State Conservation Park.
Hours & Admission Prices: Park: daily 7am to dusk. Nature Center: Thurs.-Tues. 8:30-5. Parking: $5. Annual Pass: $30. &
Attendance: 201,000 (actual)

Stone Mountain

ART STATION, 5384 Manor Dr., Stone Mountain, GA 30083-3067. Mailing Address: P.O. Box 1998, Stone Mountain, GA 30086. Tel.: 770-469-1105.
E-mail: info@artstation.org
Web Site: www.artstation.org
Key Personnel: Founder, Pres. & Artistic Dir., David Thomas; Museum Shop Mgr., Bill E. Leavell.
Institution Type/Description: Art Museum.
Hours & Admission Prices: Tues.-Fri. 10-5, Sat. 10-3. No charge; donations accepted. &
Attendance: 5,000 (estimated)

GEORGIA'S STONE MOUNTAIN PARK, 1000 Robert E. Lee Blvd., Stone Mountain, GA 30083. Mailing Address: P.O. Box 778, Stone Mountain, GA 30086-0778. Tel.: 770-498-5690. Fax: 770-498-5735. TDD: 770-498-5702 (available through switchboard).
E-mail: smpmarketing@stonemountainpark.com
Web Site: www.stonemountainpark.com
Key Personnel: Gen. Mgr., Gerald Rakestraw.
Institution Type/Description: General Museum.
Hours & Admission Prices: Visitors Center: daily 8:30-5:30. One Day Adventure Pass: adults 12 & up $26, senior & military $23, children 3-11 $21. Closed Christmas. &
Attendance: 6,000,000 (actual)

Suwanee

CHI PHI GREEK LIFE MUSEUM, 1160 Satellite Blvd., Suwanee, GA 30024. Tel.: 800-849-1824.
E-mail: museum@greeklifemuseum.org
Web Site: www.greeklifemuseum.org
Key Personnel: Sr. Dir. Devel., Elizabeth Vaughn, C.F.R.E.
Institution Type/Description: History Museum.
Hours & Admission Prices: By appointment.

Tallapoosa

WEST GEORGIA MUSEUM OF TALLAPOOSA, 185 Mann St., Tallapoosa, GA 30176. Mailing Address: P.O. Box 725, Tallapoosa, GA 30176-0725. Tel.: 770-574-3125. Facebook: West Georgia Museum of Tallapoosa.

E-mail: westgeorgiamuseum@gmail.com
Web Site: westgeorgiamuseum.com
Key Personnel: Dir., Mildred McElroy; Chm. (V), Bud Jones.
Institution Type/Description: History Museum.
Hours & Admission Prices: Mon.-Fri. 9-4, Sat. 10-3. Adults $2, children $1.
Attendance: 2,000 (estimated)

Thomasville

BIRDSONG NATURE CENTER, 2106 Meridian Rd., Thomasville, GA 31792-0417. Tel.: 229-377-4408, 800-953-BIRD (2473). Fax: 229-377-8723.
E-mail: birdsong@birdsongnaturecenter.org
Web Site: www.birdsongnaturecenter.org
Key Personnel: Exec. Dir., Kathleen D. Brady.
Institution Type/Description: Nature Center: former plantation; farmhouse & 1880s barn.
Hours & Admission Prices: Wed. & Fri.-Sat. 9-5, Sun. 1-5; groups by appointment. Adults $5, children $2.50; discount to groups; Association of Nature Center Administrators members no charge. Closed New Year's Day; Christmas.
Attendance: 3,700 (actual)

JACK HADLEY BLACK HISTORY MUSEUM, 214 Alexander St., Thomasville, GA 31792-4996. Tel.: 229-226-5029. Fax: 229-226-5084. Facebook: Jack Hadley Black History Museum.
E-mail: jackhadleyblackhistorymuseum@rose.net
Web Site: www.jackhadleyblackhistorymuseum.com
Key Personnel: Dir., C.E.O., Pres. (V), James "Jack" Hadley.
Institution Type/Description: Black History Museum.
Hours & Admission Prices: Tues.-Fri. 10-5, Sat. 11-4. Adults $5, children & college students $3; discounts to groups. Closed New Year's Day; Thanksgiving; Christmas Eve & Day. &
Attendance: 1,698 (actual)

LAPHAM-PATTERSON HOUSE, 626 N. Dawson St., Thomasville, GA 31792-4449. Mailing Address: Thomas County Historical Society, 725 N. Dawson St., Thomasville, GA 31792. Tel.: 229-226-7664.
E-mail: anne@thomascountyhistory.org
Key Personnel: C.E.O. & Cur., Cheryl Walters; Interpretive Ranger, Voncile Jones; Chm. (V), John Wood.
Institution Type/Description: Historic House: c.1884 Lapham-Patterson House, Victorian home.
Hours & Admission Prices: Temporarily closed. &
Attendance: 5,000 (actual)

PEBBLE HILL PLANTATION, 1251 U.S. 319 S., Tallahassee Rd., Thomasville, GA 31792. Mailing Address: P.O. Box 830, Thomasville, GA 31799-0830. Tel.: 229-226-2344. Fax: 229-227-0095.
E-mail: wwhite@pebblehill.com
Web Site: www.pebblehill.com
Key Personnel: Chm. (V), Warren Bicknell; Gen. Mgr., Wallace Goodman.
Institution Type/Description: Historic Site, Buildings & Art Gallery.
Hours & Admission Prices: Tues.-Sat. 10-5, Sun. 1-5; last tour of the Main House begins at 4. Gate: adults $5, children 2-12 $2. House: adults $10, children 6-12 $4; children under 6 not admitted; discounts to groups of 18 & up with advance reservations. Closed New Year's Day; Thanksgiving; Christmas Eve & Day. &
Attendance: 20,000 (estimated)

POWER OF THE PAST AVIATION MUSEUM, 882 Airport Rd., Thomasville, GA 31757. Mailing Address: 432 Colton Ave, Thomasville, GA 31792. Tel.: 229-226-3010.
E-mail: ljdekle@rose.net
Web Site: powerofthepast.org
Key Personnel: Dir., James Dekle; Chm. (V), John Dekle.
Institution Type/Description: Aviation History Museum.
Hours & Admission Prices: Sun. 2-6; other times by appointment. No charge; donations accepted.
Attendance: 1,000 (estimated)

THOMAS COUNTY MUSEUM OF HISTORY, 725 N. Dawson St., Thomasville, GA 31792-4452. Tel.: 229-226-7664. Fax: 229-226-7466.
E-mail: history@rose.net
Web Site: www.thomascountyhistory.org
Institution Type/Description: History Museum.
Hours & Admission Prices: Sept. to mid-Aug. Mon.-Sat. 10-12 & 2-5; other times by appointment. Adults $5, students $1; discounts to groups; members no

charge. Closed New Year's Eve & Day; Independence Day; Thanksgiving; Christmas Eve & Day.

THOMASVILLE CULTURAL CENTER, INC., 600 E. Washington St., Thomasville, GA 31792-4648. Mailing Address: P.O. Box 2177, Thomasville, GA 31799-2177. Tel.: 229-226-0588. Fax: 229-226-0599.
E-mail: info@thomasvilleculturalcenter.org
Web Site: www.thomasvilleculturalcenter.org
Key Personnel: C.E.O. & Exec. Dir., Tricia Collins; Pres. (V), Peggy Rich; Dir. Devel., Susan O'Neal; Dir. Finance, Kelly Swan; Dir. Education & Outreach, Mary Oglesby; Coord. Visual Arts, Amy Wheeler; Member Svcs. & Communications Coord., Rachael Fink; Dir. PWAF, Sharlene Celaya Cannon; Asst. Dir. PWAF, Holly Jarvis; Mgr. Bldg. & Grounds, Herbert Brinson; Administrative Asst., Casie Vela.
Institution Type/Description: Cultural Center: housed in 1915 East Side School.
Hours & Admission Prices: Office: Tues.-Fri. 9-5. Gallery: Tues.-Fri. 9-5, Sat. 1-5. No charge; donations accepted. Closed New Year's Eve & Day; Martin Luther King Jr. Day; Easter; Memorial Day; Independence Day; Labor Day; Thanksgiving; Christmas Eve & Day. &
Attendance: 63,781 (estimated)

Thomson

HICKORY HILL, 502 Hickory Hill Dr., Thomson, GA 30824-7655. Tel.: 706-595-7777, 877-595-9777 (toll free). Fax: 706-595-7177. Facebook: Hickory Hill House Museum.
E-mail: mzupan@hickory-hill.org
Web Site: www.hickory-hill.org
Key Personnel: Pres., Tad Brown; Chm. (V), Byron Attridge; Cur., Michelle Zupan.
Institution Type/Description: Historic House Museum: housed in the home of Thomas E. Watson.
Hours & Admission Prices: Mon.-Fri. 10-5. Adults $3, senior citizens $2, children $1; discounts AASLH, AAM & ICOM members and groups. Closed major holidays; Hickory Hill Forum. &
Attendance: 4,800 (estimated)

MAC ON MAIN ART GALLERY AND STUDIO, 107 Main St., Thomson, GA 30824. Tel.: 706-699-1804.
Web Site: maconmainartgallery.com/contact-us
Institution Type/Description: Art Gallery.
Hours & Admission Prices: Tues.-Thurs. 11-5, Fri. 10-4.

MCDUFFIE MUSEUM, 121 Main St., Thomson, GA 30824. Tel.: 706-595-9923.
E-mail: info@mcduffiemuseum.com
Web Site: www.mcduffiemuseum.com
Institution Type/Description: History Museum.
Hours & Admission Prices: Tues.-Sat. 12-5.

Tifton

GEORGIA MUSEUM OF AGRICULTURE & HISTORIC VILLAGE AT ABAC, 1392 Whiddon Mill Rd., (I-75, Exit 63B), Tifton, GA 31793-7800. Tel.: 229-391-5205; 800-733-3653. Fax: 229-391-5201. Facebook.
E-mail: abacinfo@abac.edu
Web Site: www.gma.abac.edu
Formerly: Agrirama, Georgia's Living History Museum & Village
Key Personnel: Dir., Paul Willis; Mktg., Garrett Boone.
Institution Type/Description: 19th-Century Living History Museum.
Hours & Admission Prices: Tues.-Fri. 9-3. Adults $7, senior citizens $6, children 5-16 $4; discounts to military & groups of 20 or more; children 4 & under no charge. Sat. 9-4. Adults $10, seniors $8, children 5-16 $5; children 4 & under no charge. Steam Train: Sat. 9-4. Store: Mon.-Sat. 9-5. Closed New Year's Eve & Day; Labor Day; Thanksgiving; Christmas Day & week. &
Attendance: 40,000 (actual)

Toccoa

CURRAHEE MILITARY MUSEUM, 160 N. Alexander St., Toccoa, GA 30577. Tel.: 706-282-5055.
E-mail: contact@toccoahistory.com
Web Site: www.toccoahistory.com
Institution Type/Description: Military History Museum.
Hours & Admission Prices: Mon.-Sat. 10-4, Sun. 1-4. Closed New Year's Eve & Day; Christmas Eve & Day.

Tunnel Hill

WESTERN & ATLANTIC RAILROAD TUNNEL AND MUSEUM, 215 Clisby Austin Rd., Tunnel Hill, GA 30755. Mailing Address: P.O. Box 6177, Dalton, GA 30722-6177. Tel.: 706-876-1571.
E-mail: ejohns@visitdaltonga.com
Formerly: Tunnel Hill Heritage Center Museum & Historic W & A Railroad Tunnel
Key Personnel: Mgr., Erin Johns.
Institution Type/Description: History Museum.
Hours & Admission Prices: Mon.-Sat. 9-5. Deluxe Tour $10, Standard Tour $6; children under 5 no charge. Closed New Year's Day; Thanksgiving Day; Christmas Day. &
Attendance: 5,000 (actual)

Tybee Island

TYBEE ISLAND LIGHT STATION AND TYBEE MUSEUM, 30 Meddin Dr., Tybee Island, GA 31328-9733. Mailing Address: P.O. Box 366, Tybee Island, GA 31328-0366. Tel.: 912-786-5801. Fax: 912-786-6538.
E-mail: tybeelighthouse@yahoo.com
Web Site: www.tybeelighthouse.org
Formerly: Tybee Museum and Lighthouse
Key Personnel: Exec. Dir. Tybee Island Historical Society, Sarah Jones.
Institution Type/Description: History Museum: housed in old Spanish-American War Coastal Defense Battery; c.1867 Tybee Island lighthouse & cottages.
Hours & Admission Prices: Wed.-Mon. 9-5:30; other times by appointment. Adults $9, seniors, military & children 6-17 $7; children under 6 no charge. Last ticket sold at 4:30. Closed New Year's Day; St. Patrick's Day; Thanksgiving; Christmas.
Attendance: 100,000 (actual)

Valdosta

THE CRESCENT, VALDOSTA GARDEN CENTER, INC., 904 N. Patterson St., Valdosta, GA 31601-4531. Mailing Address: P.O. Box 2423, Valdosta, GA 31604-2423. Tel.: 229-244-6747. Fax: 912-242-1005.
E-mail: thecrescent1898@gmail.com
Institution Type/Description: Nature Center & Historic House: 1898 mansion, home of former U.S. Sen. William S. West.
Hours & Admission Prices: Mon.-Fri. 2-5; other times by appointment when not rented. No charge; donations accepted. &
Attendance: 4,286 (actual)

LOWNDES COUNTY HISTORICAL SOCIETY AND MUSEUM, 305 W. Central Ave., Valdosta, GA 31601-5404. Mailing Address: P.O. Box 56, Valdosta, GA 31603-0056. Tel.: 229-247-4780. Fax: 229-247-2840.
E-mail: history@valdostamuseum.com
Web Site: www.valdostamuseum.org
Key Personnel: Exec. Dir., Donald O. Davis; Pres., Patsy Giles; Financial Dir., Redden Hart.
Institution Type/Description: History Museum: housed in 1913 Carnegie Library.
Hours & Admission Prices: Mon.-Fri. 10-5, Sat. 10-2. No charge; donations accepted. Closed New Year's Day; Sat. before Easter; Memorial Day; Independence Day; Labor Day; Thanksgiving; Christmas to New Year's Day. &
Attendance: 26,000 (actual)

VALDOSTA STATE UNIVERSITY FINE ARTS GALLERY, Fine Arts Bldg., Rm 1070A - 1st Fl., Valdosta, GA 31698. Mailing Address: 1500 N. Patterson St., Valdosta, GA 31698. Tel.: 229-333-5835. Fax: 229-259-5121.
E-mail: apearce@valdosta.edu
Web Site: valdosta.edu/art
Key Personnel: Gallery Dir., Julie Bowland.
Institution Type/Description: Art Gallery.
Hours & Admission Prices: Mon.-Thurs. 8:30-5:30, Fri. 8:30-3. No charge; donations accepted. Closed school holidays. &
Attendance: 10,000

Vidalia

ALTAMA MUSEUM OF ART & HISTORY, 611 Jackson St., Vidalia, GA 30474-4721. Mailing Address: P.O. Box 33, Vidalia, GA 30475-0033. Tel.: 912-537-1911. Facebook: @AltamaMuseum.

E-mail: altama@bellsouth.net
Key Personnel: Dir., Jennifer Martinez.
Institution Type/Description: Art and History Museum: housed in 1911 Brazell House.
Hours & Admission Prices: Mid-Sept. to Mid-May Thurs.-Sat. 10-3, Sun. 1-3 & by advance appt. No charge; donations accepted. Closed for national holidays. &

Warm Springs

ART IN MOTION VINTAGE MOTORCYCLE MUSEUM, 78 Lil Sturgis St., Warm Springs, GA 31830. Mailing Address: 31 Red Bud Trail, Newman, GA 30263. Tel.: 770-502-0028, 678-296-3326.
E-mail: presto434343@yahoo.com
Web Site: prestonopportunities.com
Key Personnel: Dir., Preston Evans.
Institution Type/Description: Motorcycle Museum.
Hours & Admission Prices: Fri.-Sat. 11-6, Sun. 1-6; other times by appointment. Adults $5-$12.
Attendance: 5,000 (estimated)

ROOSEVELT'S LITTLE WHITE HOUSE STATE HISTORIC SITE, 401 Little White House Rd., Warm Springs, GA 31830-2157. Tel.: 706-655-5870. Fax: 706-655-5872.
E-mail: Becky.Kelley@dnr.ga.gov
Web Site: www.gastateparks.org
Key Personnel: Site Mgr., Robin Glass; Asst. Mgr., Mary F. Thrash; Museum Shop Mgr., Diane Crane.
Institution Type/Description: Historic Buildings Museum: 1932 Georgia home of Pres. Roosevelt, where he died April 12, 1945.
Hours & Admission Prices: Daily 9-4:45. Adults $12, seniors 62 & over $10, children 6-17 $7, children under 6 $2; discount to groups of 15 or more. Closed New Year's Day; Thanksgiving; Christmas. &
Attendance: 100,000 (estimated)

Warner Robins

MUSEUM OF AVIATION AT ROBINS AIR FORCE BASE, GA, 1942 Heritage Blvd., Robins AFB, Warner Robins, GA 31099. Tel.: 478-926-6870. Fax: 478-926-5566.
E-mail: kenneth.emery@robins.af.mil
Web Site: www.museumofaviation.org
Key Personnel: Dir., Kenneth Emery; Cur., Mike Rowland.
Institution Type/Description: Aviation Museum.
Hours & Admission Prices: Daily 9-5. No charge; donations accepted. Closed New Year's Day; Easter; Thanksgiving; Christmas. &
Attendance: 400,000 (estimated)

Warrenton

MUSEUM OF CULTURAL HERITAGE, 46 S. Norwood St., Warrenton, GA 30828. Tel.: 706-465-9604.
Institution Type/Description: History Museum: housed in the former East Warrenton Depot.
Hours & Admission Prices: Mon.-Fri. 10-4. No charge.

Warthen

WARTHEN OLD JAIL, 7616 Hwy. 15 N., Warthen, GA 31094. Mailing Address: c/o Washington County Chamber of Commerce, 131-B W. Haynes St., Sanderson, GA 31082. Tel.: 478-552-3288.
E-mail: genealogyresearch@att.net
Web Site: www.washingtoncountyga.com
Institution Type/Description: Historic Building: housed in a former wooden jail. Listed on the National Register of Historic Places.
Hours & Admission Prices: Mon.-Fri. 9-5. No charge.

Washington

CALLAWAY PLANTATION, 2160 Lexington Rd., Washington, GA 30673-3310. Tel.: 706-678-7060. Fax: 706-678-7060.
E-mail: callaway@washingtongeorgia.net
Key Personnel: Dir., David Van Hart; Museum Shop Mgr., Olivia Jackson.
Institution Type/Description: Historic House Museum.
Hours & Admission Prices: Tues.-Sat. 10-5, Sun. by appointment. Call for admission prices. Closed major holidays. &
Attendance: 6,000 (estimated)

ROBERT TOOMBS HOUSE, 216 E. Robert Toombs Ave., Washington, GA 30673-2037. Tel.: 706-678-2226.
E-mail: roberttoombshouse16@live.com
Web Site: www.gastateparks.org
Key Personnel: Site Mgr., Marcia Campbell.
Institution Type/Description: Historic House Museum.
Hours & Admission Prices: Tues.-Sat. 10-4. Adults 13 & over $5, children 6-12 $3, children 3-5 $1; discount to groups; children under 3 no charge. Closed New Year's Day; Thanksgiving; Christmas.
Attendance: 2,600 (estimated)

WASHINGTON HISTORICAL MUSEUM, 308 E. Robert Toombs Ave., Washington, GA 30673-2038. Tel.: 706-678-2105. Fax: 706-678-3752.
E-mail: historical@washingtonwilkes.org
Key Personnel: Cur., Stephanie Macchia.
Institution Type/Description: Historical Museum: 1836 Barnett-Slaton House, built by Albert Gallatin Semmes. Listed on the National Register of Historic Places.
Hours & Admission Prices: Tues.-Sat. 10-5; groups by appointment. Adults $7, children $5; discount to groups of 15 or more. Closed major holidays. &
Attendance: 2,400 (actual)

Watkinsville

EAGLE TAVERN MUSEUM, 26 N. Main St., Watkinsville, GA 30677. Tel.: 706-769-5197. Fax: 706-310-1682.
E-mail: welcomecenter@oconee.ga.us
Web Site: visitoconee.com
Key Personnel: Dir. Tourism & Cur., Peggy Holcomb.
Institution Type/Description: Historic Building: tavern stage coach stop.
Hours & Admission Prices: Tours: Tues.-Fri. 10-4. Adults & seniors $2, children 6-15 $1; children under 6 no charge. &
Attendance: 7,000 (actual)

Waycross

OKEFENOKEE HERITAGE CENTER, 1460 N. Augusta Ave., Waycross, GA 31503-4954. Tel.: 912-285-4260. Fax: 912-283-2858. Facebook.
E-mail: okeheritage@gmail.com
Web Site: www.okefenokeeheritagecenter.org
Key Personnel: Dir. & Cur., Steven Bean; Museum Shop Mgr., Betty Callahan.
Institution Type/Description: History Museum/Art Center.
Hours & Admission Prices: Tues.-Sat. 9-2. Adults $5, seniors, veterans & children under 12 $3; children under 5 no charge. Closed New Year's Day; Thanksgiving; Christmas. &
Attendance: 13,000 (estimated)

SOUTHERN FOREST WORLD, 1440 N. Augusta Ave., Waycross, GA 31503-4954. Tel.: 912-285-4056. Fax: 912-285-4056.
E-mail: southernforestworld@gmail.com
Web Site: www.southernforestworld.org
Institution Type/Description: Forestry Museum.
Hours & Admission Prices: Tues.-Sat. 9-2; groups by appointment. Adults 19 & above $5, students 6-17 $4; children 5 & under & members no charge. Closed major holidays. &
Attendance: 6,000 (estimated)

Waynesboro

BURKE COUNTY MUSEUM, 536 Liberty St., Waynesboro, GA 30830. Mailing Address: Burke County Board of Commissioners, P.O. Box 89, Waynesboro, GA 30830. Tel.: 706-437-9557.
E-mail: l.carter-chambers@burkecounty-ga.gov
Web Site: www.burkecounty-ga.gov
Key Personnel: Cur., Robert L. Hammond.
Institution Type/Description: History Museum.
Hours & Admission Prices: Mon.-Fri. 8-4, Sat.-Sun. & holidays by appointment.

Williamson

CANDLER FIELD MUSEUM - PEACH STATE AERODROME, 349 Jonathan's Roost Rd., Williamson, GA 30292. Tel.: 770-467-9490.
E-mail: info@candlerfield.com
Key Personnel: Owner, Ron Alexander.
Institution Type/Description: Airport History Museum.
Hours & Admission Prices: Tues.-Sun.

Winder

BARROW COUNTY HISTORICAL SOCIETY AND MUSEUM, 94 E. Athens St., Winder, GA 30680. Mailing Address: P.O. Box 277, Winder, GA 30680. Tel.: 770-307-1183.
E-mail: bchistorical@gmail.com
Institution Type/Description: Historical Society Museum: housed in the former Barrow County jail; built in 1915. Listed on the National Register of Historic Places.
Hours & Admission Prices: Mon.-Fri. 1-4.

FORT YARGO STATE PARK, 210 S. Broad St., Winder, GA 30680-2059. Tel.: 770-867-3489. Fax: 770-867-7517.
E-mail: fort_yargo_park@dnr.state.ga.us
Web Site: www.gastateparks.org
Institution Type/Description: Historic Building: restored blockhouse used during the Creek Indian Wars.
Hours & Admission Prices: Park: daily 7am-10pm. Office: daily 8-5. Old Fort Tours: by appointment. Park Pass: daily $5 per vehicle. Annual $50 per vehicle, senior citizens $25. &
Attendance: 400,000

Winterville

CARTER-COILE COUNTRY DOCTORS MUSEUM, 111 Marigold Ln., Winterville, GA 30683. Mailing Address: P.O. Box 306, Winterville, GA 30683-0306. Tel.: 706-742-8600. Fax: 706-742-5476.
E-mail: winterville@charter.net
Web Site: www.cityofwinterville.com/doctor_museum.html
Key Personnel: Municipal Clerk, Wendy Bond.
Institution Type/Description: Medical Museum: housed in 1874 frame building used as an office for Dr. Warren Carter & Dr. Frank Coile.
Hours & Admission Prices: 1st Sat. each month 10-2. Historians & researchers by appointment. Call for special event openings.

Woodstock

AIR ACRES MUSEUM, 2115 Jep Wheeler Rd., Woodstock, GA 30188-6520. Tel.: 770-517-6090.
Institution Type/Description: Military Aircraft Museum.
Hours & Admission Prices: Tues.-Sat.

HAWAII

(100 listings)

Captain Cook

AMY B.H. GREENWELL ETHNOBOTANICAL GARDEN, 82-6160 Mamalahoa Hwy., Captain Cook, HI 96704. Mailing Address: P.O. Box 1053, Captain Cook, HI 96704-1053. Tel.: 808-323-3318. Fax: 808-323-2394.
E-mail: pvandyke@bishopmuseum.org
Web Site: www.bishopmuseum.org/greenwell
Key Personnel: Mgr., Peter Van Dyke; Cur., Brian Kiyabu.
Institution Type/Description: Botanical Garden.
Hours & Admission Prices: Tues.-Sun. 9-4. Adults $7, members $5; discounts to AAM members. Closed New Year's Day; Presidents' Day; Memorial Day; King Kamehameha Day; Independence Day; Labor Day; Thanksgiving & day after; Christmas.
Attendance: 12,040 (estimated)

KONA COFFEE LIVING HISTORY FARM, 82-6199 Mamalahoa Hwy., Captain Cook, HI 96704. Mailing Address: P.O. Box 398, Captain Cook, HI 96704. Tel.: 808-323-2006. Fax: 808-323-2398.
E-mail: coffeefarm@konahistorical.org
Web Site: www.konahistorical.org
Key Personnel: Dir., Joy Holland.
Institution Type/Description: Living History Farm: established in 1913. Listed on the National Register of Historic Places.
Hours & Admission Prices: Mon.-Fri. 10-2; last tour begins at 1pm. Adults $15, senior citizens $13, children $5; members no charge.

Ewa

HAWAIIAN RAILWAY SOCIETY, 91-1001 Renton Rd., Ewa, HI 96706. Mailing Address: P.O. Box 60369, Ewa, HI 96706. Tel.: 808-681-5461.

E-mail: info@hawaiianrailway.com
Web Site: hawaiianrailway.com
Key Personnel: Dir., Steve Vendt.
Institution Type/Description: Railroad History Museum.
Hours & Admission Prices: Train Rides: Sun. 1 & 3, Sat. 3; other times by appointment. Adults $15, children 2-12 and seniors 62 & over $10; children under 2 no charge. Closed Christmas Eve & Day. &
Attendance: 20,000 (estimated)

Fort DeRussy

U.S. ARMY MUSEUM OF HAWAII, 2131 Kalia Rd., Fort DeRussy, HI 90830. Mailing Address: P.O. Box 8064, Honolulu, HI 96830. Tel.: 808-942-0318.
E-mail: hams1execdir@hawaiiantel.net
Web Site: hiarmymuseumsoc.org
Institution Type/Description: Military History Museum: housed in Battery Randolph, a Taft Period coast artillery battery; located at Fort DeRussy, one of the earliest military posts established by the U.S. Army in Hawaii; owned & operated by U.S. Army Garrison, Hawaii.
Hours & Admission Prices: Tues.-Sun. 9-4:15. No charge; donations accepted. &
Attendance: 100,000 (estimated)

Haleiwa

WAIMEA VALLEY BOTANICAL GARDEN, 59-864 Kamehameha Hwy., Haleiwa, HI 96712-9406. Tel.: 808-638-7766. Fax: 808-638-7776.
E-mail: jhoh@waimeavalley.net
Web Site: waimeavalley.net
Formerly: Waimea Arboretum and Botanical Garden; Waimea Valley Audubon Center
Key Personnel: Exec. Dir., Richard Pezzulo.
Institution Type/Description: Living Plant Museum, Arboretum & Botanical Garden.
Hours & Admission Prices: June to Labor Day daily 9-5:30; Sept.-May daily 9-5. Adults $16.95, senior & student $12.95; children 4-12 $8.95; discounts to Hawaii residents, groups & military. Closed Thanksgiving; Christmas. &
Attendance: 250,000 (estimated)

Hana, Maui

HANA CULTURAL CENTER, 4974 Ua Kea Rd., Hana, Maui, HI 96713. Mailing Address: P.O. Box 27, Hana, Maui, HI 96713-0027. Tel.: 808-248-8622. Fax: 808-248-7898.
E-mail: mail@hanaculturalcenter.org
Web Site: www.hanaculturalcenter.org
Key Personnel: Gen. Mgr., Meiling Hoopai; Pres.(V), Patricia Eason; Vice Pres. (V), Harolen Kaiwi.
Institution Type/Description: Cultural Center.
Hours & Admission Prices: Mon.-Fri. 10-4. Adults $3; members no charge. Closed New Year's Day; Easter; Thanksgiving; Christmas. &
Attendance: 26,510 (estimated)

Hanalei

WAIOLI MISSION HOUSE MUSEUM, 4050 Nawiliwili Rd., Hanalei, HI 96714. Mailing Address: c/o Waioli Corporation, P.O. Box 1631, Lihue, HI 96766-5631. Tel.: 808-245-3202. Fax: 808-245-7988.
E-mail: tours@grovefarm.org
Web Site: grovefarm.org
Key Personnel: Caretaker, Barbara Kennedy; Caretaker, Roger Kennedy.
Institution Type/Description: Historic House: housed in an 1837 missionary house. Listed on the National Register of Historic Places.
Hours & Admission Prices: Guided Tours: Tues., Thurs. & Sat. 9-3.

Hawaii Volcanoes National Park

HAWAII VOLCANOES NATIONAL PARK, KILAUEA VISITOR CENTER, Headquarters Bldg. #1, Crater Rim Dr., Hawaii Volcanoes National Park, HI 96718. Mailing Address: P.O. Box 52, Hawaii National Park, HI 96718-0052. Tel.: 808-985-6000. Fax: 808-985-6004.
Web Site: www.nps.gov/havo/
Key Personnel: Park Superintendent, Cindy Orlando.
Institution Type/Description: Visitor Center.
Hours & Admission Prices: Park open 24 hours. Kilauea Visitor Center: daily 9-5. Jaggar Museum: daily 10-8. 7-day vehicle entrance fee $15, 7-day individual entrance fee $8; Martin Luther King, Jr. Day, National Park Week, Hawai'i Volcanoes National Park Cultural Festival, National Park Service Day, National Public Lands Day & Veterans Day Weekend no charge. &
Attendance: 1,500,000 (estimated)

Hilo

HAWAII MUSEUM OF CONTEMPORARY ART, 141 Kalakaua St., Hilo, HI 96720-2807. Tel.: 808-961-5711.
E-mail: admin@ehcc.org
Web Site: www.ehcc.org
Formerly: East Hawaii Cultural Center
Key Personnel: Bd. Pres. & Museum Dir., Lourdan Kimbrell.
Institution Type/Description: Art Gallery.
Hours & Admission Prices: Tues.-Thurs. 9-4, Fri.-Sat. 10-7. No charge; donations accepted.

IMILOA ASTRONOMY CENTER, 600 Imiloa Place, Hilo, HI 96720. Tel.: 808-969-9703 & 9700. Fax: 808-969-9748.
E-mail: info@imiloahawaii.org
Web Site: www.imiloahawaii.org
Key Personnel: Dir., Kaiu Kimura.
Institution Type/Description: Astronomy Museum.
Hours & Admission Prices: Tues.-Sun. 9-5. Adults $19, children 5-12 $12, seniors & military $17; children 4 & under no charge. Closed New Year's Day; Thanksgiving; Christmas.
Attendance: 42,000 (actual)

LYMAN MUSEUM, 276 Haili St., Hilo, HI 96720-2978. Tel.: 808-935-5021. Fax: 808-969-7685. Facebook: Lyman Museum.
E-mail: info@lymanmuseum.org
Web Site: www.lymanmuseum.org
Key Personnel: Chmn. (V), Richard Henderson; Dir., Barbara Moir.
Institution Type/Description: General Museum: depicting the natural & cultural history of Hawaii.
Hours & Admission Prices: Mon.-Sat. 10-4:30. Adults $10, senior citizens $8, children 6-17 $3; discounts to AAA, AASLH & Hawaii Museums Association members; members no charge. Closed New Year's Day; Memorial Day; Independence Day; Labor Day; Thanksgiving; Christmas. &
Attendance: 14,000 (actual)

NANI MAU GARDENS, 421 Makalika St., Hilo, HI 96720-5899. Tel.: 808-959-3500. Fax: 808-959-3501.
E-mail: mark@nanimaugarden.com
Web Site: www.nanimaugardens.com
Institution Type/Description: Gardens.
Hours & Admission Prices: Daily 10-3. Gardens: adults $10, Kamaaina $7, seniors & children 4-10 $5. Garden & Tram Tour: adults $17, children 4-10 $10.

PACIFIC TSUNAMI MUSEUM, 130 Kamehameha Ave., Hilo, HI 96720-2833. Mailing Address: P.O. Box 806, Hilo, HI 96720. Tel.: 808-935-0926. Fax: 808-935-0842. Facebook.
E-mail: tsunami@tsunami.org
Web Site: www.tsunami.org
Key Personnel: Exec. Dir., Marlene Murray; Cur. & Archivist, Barbara J. Muffler; Administrative Asst., Kini Gonzalez.
Institution Type/Description: Natural History Museum.
Hours & Admission Prices: Tues.-Sat. 10-4. Adults $8, senior citizens & Kama'aina $7, children 6-17 $4; members and children 5 & under no charge. Closed New Year's Day; Independence Day; Thanksgiving; Christmas Eve & Day. &
Attendance: 17,194 (actual)

PANAEWA RAINFOREST ZOO & GARDENS, 800 Stainback Hwy., Hilo, HI 96720. Mailing Address: Friends of the Zoo, P.O. Box 738, Kea'au, HI 96749-0738. Tel.: 808-959-9233. Fax: 808-961-8411.
E-mail: foz@hilozoo.com
Web Site: www.hilozoo.com
Key Personnel: Dir., Pam Mizuno.
Institution Type/Description: Zoo.
Hours & Admission Prices: Daily 9-4. Petting Zoo: Sat. 1:30-2:30. No charge. Closed New Year's Day; Christmas.

WAILOA CENTER, 200 Piopio St., Wailoa State Park, Hilo, HI 96720. Tel.: 808-933-0416.
E-mail: wailoa@yahoo.com
Web Site: www.wailoacenter.com
Formerly: Wailoa Arts & Cultural Center
Key Personnel: Dir., Codie M. King.
Institution Type/Description: Art Museum.

Hours & Admission Prices: Mon.-Fri. 8:30-4:30. No charge; donations accepted. Closed state holidays. &

Attendance: 30,000 (estimated)

Holualoa

HULA DADDY KONA COFFEE FARM AND VISITOR CENTER, 74-4944 Mamalahoa Hwy., Holualoa, HI 96725. Tel.: 808-327-9744.

Web Site: huladaddy.com/visitor-center
Institution Type/Description: Company Tours.
Hours & Admission Prices: Mon.-Fri. 10-4. Tours: by appointment. Closed major holidays.

Honolulu

BATTLESHIP MISSOURI MEMORIAL, Historic Ford Island, Pearl Harbor, 63 Cowpens St., Honolulu, HI 96818-5006. Mailing Address: USS Missouri Memorial Assoc., Inc., P.O. Box 879, Aiea, HI 96701. Tel.: 808-455-1600, 877-644-4896 (toll free).

E-mail: mightymo@ussmissouri.org
Web Site: www.ussmissouri.com
Key Personnel: Pres. & C.E.O., Michael A. Carr; Cur., Mike Weidenbach.
Institution Type/Description: Military Museum: housed on the USS Missouri, built in 1941.
Hours & Admission Prices: See website for hours. General admission: adults $27, children 4-12 $13. Closed New Year's Day; Thanksgiving; Christmas.

BERNICE PAUAHI BISHOP HERITAGE CENTER, THE KAMEHAMEHA SCHOOLS, 1887 Makuakane St., Honolulu, HI 96817-1800. Tel.: 808-842-8635. Fax: 808-842-8603.

E-mail: heritagecenter@ksbc.edu
Key Personnel: Cur., Nu'u Atkins.
Institution Type/Description: Heritage Center: school founded by Bernice Pauahi Bishop & her husband, Charles Reed Bishop.
Hours & Admission Prices: Mon.-Fri. 9-2 by appointment.

BISHOP MUSEUM, 1525 Bernice St., Honolulu, HI 96817-2704. Tel.: 808-847-3511. Facebook.

E-mail: webmaster@bishopmuseum.org
Web Site: www.bishopmuseum.org
Key Personnel: Pres. & C.E.O., Linda Lee Kuuleilani Farm.
Institution Type/Description: Cultural & Natural History Museum.
Hours & Admission Prices: Daily 9-5. Adult $22.95, senior citizens 65 & over $19.95, youth 4-12 $14.95; discounts for Kama'aina & military; members and children 4 & under no charge. Closed Thanksgiving; Christmas. &
Attendance: 327,967 (actual)

DORIS DUKE FOUNDATION FOR ISLAMIC ART - SHANGRI LA, 4055 Papu Circle, Honolulu, HI 96816. Tel.: 808-734-1941. Fax: 808-732-4361.

E-mail: shangrilahawaii@ddcf.org
Web Site: www.shangrilahawaii.org
Institution Type/Description: Art & History Museum: housed in the seasonal home of Doris Duke; built in 1937.
Hours & Admission Prices: Wed.-Sat. by appointment only. Out-of-State $25; In-State $20. &
Attendance: 13,312 (actual)

EAST-WEST CENTER, 1601 East-West Rd., Honolulu, HI 96848-1601. Tel.: 808-944-7111.

E-mail: ewccontact@eastwestcenter.org
Web Site: www.eastwestcenter.org
Key Personnel: Cur., Michael Schuster, Ph.D.
Institution Type/Description: General Museum.
Hours & Admission Prices: Mon.-Fri. 8-5, Sun. 12-4. No charge; donations accepted. Closed federal holidays. &
Attendance: 6,000

442ND VETERANS CLUB ARCHIVES, Mailing Address: 933 Wiliwili St., Apt. 102, Honolulu, HI 96826-2766. Tel.: 808-945-0032. Fax: 808-949-0032.

Formerly: 442nd Veterans Archives & Learning Center
Institution Type/Description: Military Museum.
Hours & Admission Prices: Mon.-Fri. 9-2 by appointment. No charge; donations accepted. Closed Federal, State & local holidays.

HAROLD L. LYON ARBORETUM, 3860 Manoa Rd., Honolulu, HI 96822-1198. Tel.: 808-988-0456.

Web Site: www.hawaii.edu/lyonarboretum
Key Personnel: Fiscal Officer, Destin Shigano.
Institution Type/Description: Botanical Garden & Arboretum.
Hours & Admission Prices: Mon.-Fri. 9-4, Sat. 9-3. Requested Donation: $5 per person. Closed federal holidays. &
Attendance: 30,000 (estimated)

HAWAII CHILDREN'S DISCOVERY CENTER, 111 Ohe St., Honolulu, HI 96813-5517. Tel.: 808-524-5437. Fax: 808-524-5400.

E-mail: info@discoverycenterhawaii.org
Web Site: www.discoverycenterhawaii.org
Key Personnel: Chm. (V), Loretta Yajima.
Institution Type/Description: Children's Museum.
Hours & Admission Prices: Tues.-Fri. 9-1, Sat.-Sun. 10-3. Admission $12; Kama'aina & military with ID $10, seniors 62 & over with ID $8, children under one & members no charge. Closed New Year's Day; Easter; Labor Day week; Thanksgiving; Christmas. &

HAWAII STATE CAPITOL, 415 S. Beretania St., Honolulu, HI 96813-2477. Mailing Address: 415 S. Beretania St., Rm 415, Honolulu, HI 96813-2407. Tel.: 808-586-0221. Fax: 808-586-0046.

Web Site: governor.hawaii.gov/hawaii-state-capitol-tours
Institution Type/Description: History Museum.
Hours & Admission Prices: Mon.-Fri. 8:30-3:30. Guided Tours: see website. No charge. Closed holidays.

HAWAII STATE FOUNDATION ON CULTURE & THE ARTS AND HAWAII STATE ART MUSEUM, 250 S. Hotel St., 2nd Fl., Honolulu, HI 96813-2831. Tel.: 808-586-0300. Fax: 808-586-0308. Facebook, Instagram, Twitter.

Web Site: www.hawaii.gov/sfca
Key Personnel: Exec. Dir., Jonathan Johnson.
Institution Type/Description: Art Museum.
Hours & Admission Prices: Tues.-Sat. 10-4. No charge. Closed Good Friday; Independence Day; Statehood Day; Veterans Day; Thanksgiving. &
Attendance: 30,000

HAWAIIAN HISTORICAL SOCIETY, 560 Kawaiaha'o St., Honolulu, HI 96813-5023. Tel.: 808-537-6271.

E-mail: hhsoffice@hawaiianhistory.org
Web Site: www.hawaiianhistory.org
Key Personnel: Exec. Dir., Jennifer L. Higa.
Institution Type/Description: Historical Society Museum.
Hours & Admission Prices: Tues.-Fri. 10-4. No charge.

HAWAIIAN MISSION HOUSES HISTORIC SITE AND ARCHIVES, 553 S. King St., Honolulu, HI 96813-3002. Tel.: 808-447-3910. Fax: 808-545-2280.

E-mail: info@missionhouses.org
Web Site: www.missionhouses.org
Formerly: Mission Houses Museum
Key Personnel: Interim Exec. Dir., Richard Kennedy; Cur. Archives & Librarian, John Barker; Dir. Devel. & Society Rels. Dir., Mary Ann Alexander Lentz; Cur. Public Programs, Mike Smola; Cur. Object Collections, Elizabeth Pooloa; Volunteer Coord. & Program Asst., Po'ai Lincoln; Gift Shop & Facilities Rentals Coord., Dianne Ching; Exec. Asst., Lisa Solomine; Controller, Gabriela Bonilla; Communications Specialist, Bonnie Louise Judd.
Institution Type/Description: Historic House Museum.
Hours & Admission Prices: Tues.-Sat. 10-4. Adults $10, Kama'aina, military & seniors 65 & over $8, students 6 to college $6; members no charge. Closed New Year's Eve & Day; Martin Luther King Jr. Day; Presidents' Day; Prince Jonah Kuhio Day; Memorial Day; Independence Day; Statehood Day; Labor Day; Discoverer's Day; Thanksgiving; Christmas Eve & Day.
Attendance: 22,000 (estimated)

HONOLULU BOTANICAL GARDENS, Mailing Address: 50 N. Vineyard Blvd., Honolulu, HI 96817-3759. Tel.: 808-522-7066.

E-mail: hbg@honolulu.gov
Web Site: www.honolulu.gov/parks/hbg
Key Personnel: Dir., Michele K. Nekota; Deputy Dir., Jeanne C. Ishikawa.
Institution Type/Description: Botanical Gardens.
Hours & Admission Prices: Foster, Ho'omaluhia & Wahiawa daily 9-4. Lili'uokalani daily 7-5. Koko Crater daily sunrise to sunset. Foster: adults $5, Hawaii residents $3, students 6-12 $1; children 5 & under no charge. Ho'omaluhia, Wahiawa, Lili'uokalani & Koko Crater no charge. Closed New Year's Day; Christmas. &
Attendance: 204,998 (estimated)

HONOLULU MUSEUM OF ART, 900 S. Beretania St., Honolulu, HI 96814-1495. Tel.: 808-532-8700. Fax: 808-532-8787.
E-mail: info@honolulumuseum.org
Web Site: www.honolulumuseum.org
Formerly: Honolulu Academy of Arts
Key Personnel: Dir., Sean O'Harrow; Chm. (V), Violet S.W. Loo; Dir. Finance, Tania Ginoza; Dir. Devel., Cara Mazzei; Dir. Communications, Lesa Griffith; Cur. Asian Art, Shawn Eichman; Mgr. Textiles, Sara Oka; Cur. European & American Art, Theresa Papanikolas; Dir. Tour & Docent Programs, Betsy Robb; Dir. Honolulu Museum of Art School, Vince Hazen; Theater Mgr., Taylour Chang; Cur. Contemporary Art, Jay Jensen; Cur. Arts of Hawaii, Healoha Johnson; Registrar, Collections, Pauline Sugino; Registrar, Exhibitions, Cynthia Low; Volunteer Svc. Coord., Micah Vargas; Visitor Information Center Mgr., Kim Hutchison; Head Operational Svcs., Eric Walden; Museum Shop Mgr., Cori Mackie; Librarian, Sachi Kawaiaea.
Institution Type/Description: Art Museum: housed in c.1927 building designed by Bertram G. Goodhue Associates.
Hours & Admission Prices: Tues.-Sat. 10-4:30, Sun. 1-5. Adults $10; discounts to ICOM members; children under 17, members, first Wed. & 3rd Sun. each month and July 31 no charge. Admission also includes entry to Spalding House. Closed New Year's Day; Independence Day; Labor Day; Thanksgiving; Christmas. &
Attendance: 250,000 (estimated)

HONOLULU MUSEUM OF ART SPALDING HOUSE, 2411 Makiki Heights Dr., Honolulu, HI 96822-2547. Tel.: 808-526-1322.
E-mail: info@honolulumuseum.org
Web Site: honolulumuseum.org/11981-contemporary_museum_spalding_house
Formerly: The Contemporary Museum
Key Personnel: Dir., Sean O'Harrow.
Institution Type/Description: Art Museum.
Hours & Admission Prices: Tues.-Sat. 10-4, Sun. 12-4. Adults $10; children under 17 & members no charge. Admission also includes same day entry to Honolulu Museum of Art, 900 Beretania St. Closed New Year's Day; Independence Day; Thanksgiving; Christmas. &
Attendance: 25,000 (estimated)

HONOLULU POLICE DEPARTMENT LAW ENFORCEMENT MUSEUM, 801 S. Beretania St., Honolulu, HI 96813-5790. Tel.: 808-723-3111.
Web Site: www.honolulupd.org/community/index.php?page=museum
Institution Type/Description: History Museum.
Hours & Admission Prices: Mon.-Fri. 9-3. No charge. Closed state & federal holidays. &
Attendance: 8,100 (estimated)

HONOLULU ZOO, 151 Kapahulu Ave., Honolulu, HI 96815-4096. Tel.: 808-971-7171.
E-mail: info@honoluluzoo.org
Web Site: honoluluzoo.org
Institution Type/Description: Zoo.
Hours & Admission Prices: Daily 9-4:30. Adults 13 & over $14, children 3-12 $6, US & Kama'aina military: adults $8, children 3-12 $4. Closed Christmas. &
Attendance: 667,981 (actual)

IOLANI PALACE, 364 S. King St., Honolulu, HI 96813-2900. Mailing Address: P.O. Box 2259, Honolulu, HI 96804-2259. Tel.: 808-522-0822. Fax: 808-532-1051.
Web Site: www.iolanipalace.org
Key Personnel: Exec. Dir., Kippen de Alba Chu; Dir. Curation & Education, Teresa Valencia; Dir. Devel., Pomai Toledo.
Institution Type/Description: Historic Building: Iolani Palace c.1882 erected as state residence for Hawaii's last king, Kalakaua; Iolani Barracks c.1871 housed Royal Guard; Coronation Pavilion c.1883; 11-acre grounds with many original plantings.
Hours & Admission Prices: Palace: Mon.-Sat. 9-4. Guided Tours: Tues.-Thurs. 9-10, Fri.-Sat. 9-11:15; reservations required. Adults $21.75, children 5-12 $6; children 4 & under no charge. Audio Tours: Mon. 9-4, Tues.-Thurs. 10:30-4, Fri.-Sat. 12-4. Adults $14.75, children 5-12 $6; discounts to groups. Basement Gallery: adults $5, children 5-12 $3. Closed New Year's Eve & Day; Presidents Day; Memorial Day; Independence Day; Labor Day; Thanksgiving; Christmas. &
Attendance: 103,744 (actual)

JAPANESE CULTURAL CENTER OF HAWAII, 2454 S. Beretania St., Honolulu, HI 96826-1524. Tel.: 808-945-7633.
E-mail: info@jcch.com
Web Site: www.jcch.com
Key Personnel: Exec. Dir., C.E.O. & Pres., Carole Hayashino; Gift Shop Mgr., Kendrick Yoshida.
Institution Type/Description: History Museum.

Hours & Admission Prices: Gallery & Gift Shop: Mon.-Fri. 10-4, Sat. 9-2. Adults $7; discounts to Kama'aina, military, senior citizens & school groups. Parking validated. &
Attendance: 15,000 (estimated)

JOHN YOUNG MUSEUM OF ART, Univ. of Hawaii at Manoa, Krauss Hall, 2500 Dole St., Honolulu, HI 96822-2349. Tel.: 808-956-7198.
E-mail: gallery@hawaii.edu
Web Site: hawaii.edu/johnyoung-museum
Institution Type/Description: Art Museum.
Hours & Admission Prices: Call for hours. No charge; donations accepted.

KING KAMEHAMEHA V JUDICIARY HISTORY CENTER, 417 S. King St., Honolulu, HI 96813-2943. Tel.: 808-539-4999. Fax: 808-539-4996.
E-mail: info@jhchawaii.net
Web Site: www.jhchawaii.net
Key Personnel: Exec. Dir., Matt Mattice.
Institution Type/Description: History Museum: housed in Ali'iolani Hale (1874), the Hawaii Supreme Court Building.
Hours & Admission Prices: Mon.-Fri. 8-4; group & school tours by appointment. No charge; donations accepted. Closed state & federal holidays. &
Attendance: 58,565 (estimated)

MANOA HERITAGE CENTER, 2859 Manoa Rd., Honolulu, HI 96822-1752. Tel.: 808-988-1287.
E-mail: contact@manoaheritagecenter.org
Web Site: www.manoaheritagecenter.org
Key Personnel: Educ. Dir., Jenny Engle.
Institution Type/Description: History Museum: listed on the National Register of Historic Places.
Hours & Admission Prices: Mon.-Fri. 9:30-2:30 by appointment. Adults $7; seniors & military $4; children & students no charge.

MOANALUA GARDENS FOUNDATION, 1414 Dillingham Blvd., Ste. 211, Honolulu, HI 96819-1796. Tel.: 808-839-5334. Fax: 808-839-3658.
E-mail: info@moanaluagardensfoundation.org
Web Site: moanaluagardensfoundation.org
Key Personnel: Exec. Dir., Alexander Jamile.
Institution Type/Description: Historic Foundation.
Hours & Admission Prices: By reservation: Mon.-Tues. & Fri. 8-4, Wed.-Thurs. 8:30-1. Fees for guided tours, lectures & trips. Requested donations for Prince Lot Hula Festival. Closed state holidays.

PACIFIC AVIATION MUSEUM PEARL HARBOR, Historic Ford Island, 319 Lexington Blvd., Honolulu, HI 96818-5004. Tel.: 808-441-1000. Fax: 808-441-1019. Facebook: @PacificAviationMuseum.
E-mail: reservations@pacificaviationmuseum.org
Web Site: www.pacificaviationmuseum.org
Key Personnel: Exec. Dir. Operations, Kenneth H. DeHoff, Jr.; Exec. Dir. Devel., Elissa Lines; Dir. Mktg., Anne Murata; Dir. Devel., Carol Greene; Dir. Education, Shauna Tonkin, Ph.D.; Historian, Burl Burlingame.
Institution Type/Description: Aviation Museum.
Hours & Admission Prices: Daily 8-5. Adults $25, children 4-12 $12; discounts to military, Kama'aina & school groups; members & children under 4 no charge. Closed New Year's Day; Thanksgiving; Christmas. &
Attendance: 150,000

QUEEN EMMA SUMMER PALACE, 2913 Pali Hwy., Honolulu, HI 96817-1417. Tel.: 808-595-3167.
E-mail: info@daughtersofhawaii.org
Web Site: www.daughtersofhawaii.org
Key Personnel: Regent, Bonnie Rice.
Institution Type/Description: Historic House Museum: c.1847, the summer retreat of Queen Emma of Hawaii from 1857-1885, King Kamehameha IV & their son, Prince Albert Edward. Listed on the National Historic Registry.
Hours & Admission Prices: Mon.-Sat. 9-4, Sun. 10-3. Adults $10, senior citizens $8, youth 5-17 $1; discounts to groups; members no charge. Closed holidays. &
Attendance: 14,144 (estimated)

ROYAL MAUSOLEUM STATE MONUMENT, 2261 Nuuanu Ave., Honolulu, HI 96817-1713. Tel.: 808-587-0300.
Web Site: hawaiistateparks.org/parks/oahu/royal-mausoleum-state-monument
Institution Type/Description: Historic Building: burial site of the Kamehameha & Kalakaua royal families; built in 1865.
Hours & Admission Prices: Mon.-Fri. 8-4 No charge.

USS BOWFIN SUBMARINE MUSEUM & PARK, 11 Arizona Memorial Dr., Honolulu, HI 96818-3104. Tel.: 808-423-1341. Fax: 808-422-5201.
E-mail: info@bowfin.org
Web Site: www.bowfin.org
Institution Type/Description: Military Museum.
Hours & Admission Prices: Daily 7-5. Submarine & Museum (Digital Audio Tours): adults $12, military & Kama'aina $8, children 4-12 $5; Museum: adults $5, children $3; members & children under 4 no charge. (Children under 4 not permitted on submarine for safety reasons). Closed New Year's Day; Thanksgiving; Christmas.
Attendance: 306,731 (actual)

UNIVERSITY OF HAWAI'I ART GALLERY, 2535 McCarthy Mall, Honolulu, HI 96822-2233. Tel.: 808-956-6888. Fax: 808-956-9659.
E-mail: gallery@hawaii.edu
Web Site: www.hawaii.edu/artgallery
Key Personnel: Assoc. Dir., Sharon Tasaka.
Institution Type/Description: Art Museum.
Hours & Admission Prices: late Aug. to mid-May Mon.-Fri. 10-4, Sun. 12-4. No charge; donations accepted. Closed holidays.
Attendance: 50,000 (estimated)

WAIKIKI AQUARIUM, 2777 Kalakaua Ave., Honolulu, HI 96815-4027. Tel.: 808-923-9741. Facebook.
E-mail: director@waquarium.org
Web Site: www.waquarium.org
Institution Type/Description: Marine Aquarium.
Hours & Admission Prices: Daily 9-5. Adults $12, Kama'aina & military $8, seniors 65 & over, juniors 5-12 $5; children 4 & under and FOWA members no charge. Closed Marathon Day; Christmas.
Attendance: 290,479 (actual)

WASHINGTON PLACE, 320 S. Beretania St., Honolulu, HI 96813-2420. Tel.: 808-536-8040.
Institution Type/Description: Historic House: built in 1847 by Capt. John Dominis; home of Queen Lili'uokalani, Hawaii's last monarch & daughter in-law of Dominis.
Hours & Admission Prices: Tours: Thurs. by appointment. No charge; donations accepted. Closed holidays.
Attendance: 9,000 (estimated)

WORLD WAR II VALOR IN THE PACIFIC NATIONAL MEMORIAL, 1 Arizona Memorial Pl., Honolulu, HI 96818. Mailing Address: 1845 Wasp Blvd. Bldg. #176, Honolulu, HI 96818. Tel.: 808-422-3399. Fax: 808-725-6161.
Web Site: nps.gov/valr
Formerly: USS Arizona Memorial
Key Personnel: Superintendent, Jacqueline Ashwell.
Institution Type/Description: Park Visitor Center & Military Museum; Historic Site & World War II Memorial Museum.
Hours & Admission Prices: Pearl Harbor Visitor Center: daily 7-5; USS Arizona Tours: daily 7:30-3. No charge; donations accepted. Closed New Year's Day; Thanksgiving Day; Christmas Day.
Attendance: 1,420,000

Kahului

MAUI ARTS AND CULTURAL CENTER, One Cameron Way, Kahului, HI 96732-1137. Tel.: 808-242-2787. Fax: 808-244-4665.
E-mail: art@mauiarts.org
Web Site: www.mauiarts.org
Key Personnel: Pres. & C.E.O., Art Vento; Gallery Dir., Neida Bangerter.
Institution Type/Description: Art Gallery.
Hours & Admission Prices: Mon.-Fri. 9-5. No charge.

Kailua-Kona

DAUGHTERS OF HAWAII - HULIHEE PALACE, 75-5718 Ali'i Dr., Kailua-Kona, HI 96740-1702. Tel.: 808-329-1877. Fax: 808-329-1321.
E-mail: info@daughtersofhawaii.org
Web Site: www.daughtersofhawaii.org
Formerly: Hulihee Palace
Key Personnel: Sr. Docent, Jolee Chip.
Institution Type/Description: Historic House Museum: c.1838 vacation residence for Hawaiian royalty, built by Gov. Kuakini, recently restored to the Kalakaua period.

Hours & Admission Prices: Museum: Mon.-Sat. 9-4, Sun. 10-3; guided tours by appointment. Gift Shop: Mon.-Sat. 9:30-4. Adults $10, senior citizens, military & Kama'aina $8, children 5-17 $1. Closed holidays.
Attendance: 26,000 (actual)

ORIGINAL HAWAIIAN CHOCOLATE PLANTATION & FACTORY, 78-6772 Makenawai St., Kailua-Kona, HI 96740. Tel.: 808-322-2626 & 888-447-2626. Fax: 808-322-6737.
E-mail: info@ohcf.us
Web Site: www.ohcf.us
Institution Type/Description: Chocolate Plantation & Factory.
Hours & Admission Prices: Tours: Wed. 9am, Fri. 9am & 11am by appointment. Adults $20; children under 12 no charge. Store: Tues.-Fri. 10-3.

Kalaheo

KAUAI COFFEE ESTATE, 870 Halewili Rd., Kalaheo, HI 96741. Tel.: 808-335-0813.
E-mail: ddomingo@kauaicoffee.com
Web Site: kauaicoffee.com
Institution Type/Description: Company Tour.
Hours & Admission Prices: Guided Tours: daily 12, 2 & 4.

NATIONAL TROPICAL BOTANICAL GARDEN, 3530 Papalina Rd., Kalaheo, HI 96741-9599. Tel.: 808-332-7324, ext. 203. Fax: 808-332-9765.
E-mail: administration@ntbg.org
Web Site: www.ntbg.org
Key Personnel: C.E.O. & Dir., Chipper Wichman; Museum Shop Mgr., Gwen Silva.
Institution Type/Description: Tropical Botanical Garden.
Hours & Admission Prices: Reservations required. Allerton (guided), McBryde (guided), call 808-742-2623; Limahuli Garden (self guided), call 808-826-1053; Kahanu Garden (self guided), call 808-248-8912; The Kampong (self-guided), call 305-442-7169. Call for admission fees. Closed holidays.
Attendance: 96,000 (estimated)

Kalaupapa

KALAUPAPA NATIONAL HISTORICAL PARK, 7 Puahi St., Kalaupapa, HI 96742. Mailing Address: P.O. Box 2222, Kalaupapa, HI 96742-0040. Tel.: 808-567-6802. Fax: 808-567-6729.
E-mail: t_scott_williams@nps.gov
Web Site: www.nps.gov/kala/gov
Key Personnel: Supt., Erika Stein Espaniola; Cur., T. Scott Williams; Museum Technician, Kirk Dietz; Museum Technician, Kellie M. Ellis.
Institution Type/Description: National Park: site of the 1886-present Molokai Island leprosy settlement.
Hours & Admission Prices: Park: Mon.-Fri. 7-3:30. Tours: Mon.-Sat. Call Damien Tours, 808-567-6171, for tour of the park.

Kamuela

ANNA RANCH HERITAGE CENTER, 65-1480 Kawaihae Rd., Kamuela, HI 96743-8554. Tel.: 808-885-4426. Facebook; Instagram.
E-mail: info@annaranch.org
Web Site: www.annaranch.org
Key Personnel: Programs Mgr., Maka Wiggins.
Institution Type/Description: Historic House: former home of Anna Leialoha Lindsey Perry-Fiske. Listed on the Hawaii State Register of Historic Places.
Hours & Admission Prices: Tues.-Fri. 10-3; guided home tours at 10 & 1 by appointment. Admission $10; discount to Kama'aina residents. Closed most major holidays.
Attendance: 850 (estimated)

PARKER RANCH HISTORIC HOMES & GARDENS, 66-1304 Mamalahoa Highway, Kamuela, HI 96743-8433. Tel.: 808-885-7311. Fax: 808-885-5602. Facebook: @parkerranchhawaii; Twitter: @parker_ranch; Instagram: @parker_ranch_hawaii.
E-mail: info@parkerranch.com
Web Site: www.parkerranch.com
Key Personnel: C.E.O., Neil T. Kuyper.
Institution Type/Description: Historic Homes: housed in Mana Hale, the home of founder John Palmer Parker and Puuopelu, the Parker Hawaiian Victorian Estate from 1879 to 1992.
Hours & Admission Prices: Self Guided Tours: Mon.-Fri. 8-4. No charge.
Attendance: 200

Kaneohe

GALLERY IOLANI AT WINDWARD COMMUNITY COLLEGE, 45-720 Keaahala Rd., Kaneohe, HI 96744. Tel.: 808-236-9155.
E-mail: galleryiolani@gmail.com
Web Site: gallery.windward.hawaii.edu
Key Personnel: Dir., Antoinette Martin.
Institution Type/Description: Art Gallery.
Hours & Admission Prices: Mon.-Tues. 1-5 & 6-8, Wed.-Fri. & Sun. 1-5.

HAWAII PACIFIC UNIVERSITY GALLERY, 45-045 Kamehameha Hwy., Kaneohe, HI 96744-5221. Tel.: 808-544-0228. Fax: 808-544-9340.
E-mail: cla@hpu.edu
Web Site: www.hpu.edu
Key Personnel: Pres., John Y. Gotanda, J.D.; Chm., Richard C. Hunter; Cur., Sanit Khewhok.
Institution Type/Description: Art Gallery.
Hours & Admission Prices: Mon.-Sat. 8-5. No charge. Closed New Year's Eve & Day; Thanksgiving; Christmas. &
Attendance: 7,000 (estimated)

SENATOR FONG'S PLANTATION & GARDENS, 47-285 Pulama Rd., Kaneohe, HI 96744-5026. Tel.: 808-239-6775. Fax: 808-239-6469.
E-mail: info@fonggarden.com
Web Site: www.fonggarden.com
Key Personnel: Mgr., Patsy Fong.
Institution Type/Description: Plantation & Garden Museum.
Hours & Admission Prices: Sun.-Fri. 10-2:30. Tours: 10:30am & 1pm. Adults $14.50, seniors $13, children 5-12 $9; discounts to military, AAA members & groups. Closed New Year's Day; Christmas.

Kapaa

LYDGATE FARMS HAWAIIAN CHOCOLATE FARM, 5730 Olohena Rd., Kapaa, HI 96746. Tel.: 808-821-1857. Facebook.
E-mail: info@lydgatefarms.com
Web Site: lydgatefarms.com
Institution Type/Description: Chocolate Farm.
Hours & Admission Prices: Tour: Mon.-Fri. 9-12. Adults $95; children 12 & under no charge.

Kapolei

HAWAII MUSEUM OF FLYING DBA NAVAL AIR MUSEUM BARBERS POINT, Bldg. 1792, 91-1299 A Midway St., Kalaeloa Airport, Kapolei, HI 96707. Mailing Address: P.O. Box 75253, Kapolei, HI 96707-0253. Tel.: 808-682-3982. Fax: 808-682-3983.
E-mail: info@nambp.org
Web Site: www.nambarberspoint.org
Institution Type/Description: Military History Museum.
Hours & Admission Prices: Tues.-Fri. 8-3:30, Sat.-Sun. 1-4:30 by appointment. Donation: adults $15, seniors $10, children under 18 $8.

Kawaihae

HAMAKUA MACADAMIA NUT COMPANY VISITOR CENTER, 61-3251 Maluokalani St., Kawaihae, HI 96743. Mailing Address: P.O. Box 44715, Kamuela, HI 96743. Tel.: 888-643-6688 & 808-882-1690.
E-mail: macnutstore@gmail.com
Web Site: hawnnut.com/visitor-center
Institution Type/Description: Company Visitor Center & Store.
Hours & Admission Prices: Daily 9-5:30. Closed New Year's Day; Thanksgiving; Christmas.

PUUKOHOLA HEIAU NATIONAL HISTORIC SITE, 62-3601 Kawaihae Rd., Kawaihae, HI 96743-9720. Tel.: 808-882-7218. Fax: 808-882-1215.
Web Site: www.nps.gov/puhe
Key Personnel: Supt., Daniel Kawaiaea.
Institution Type/Description: Park Museum: ruins of Puukohola Heiau, Temple on the Hill of the Puukohola Whale, war temple built 1790-1791 by King Kamehameha the Great.
Hours & Admission Prices: Daily 8-4:45. No charge. &
Attendance: 256,639 (actual)

Kealakekua

KONA HISTORICAL SOCIETY - H.N. GREENWELL STORE, 81-6551 Mamalahoa Hwy., Kealakekua, HI 96750. Mailing Address: Kona Historical Society, P.O. Box 398, Captain Cook, HI 96704-0398. Tel.: 808-323-3222. Fax: 808-323-2398.
E-mail: khs@konahistorical.org
Web Site: www.konahistorical.org
Key Personnel: Exec. Dir., Joy Holland; Pres. (V), Allen Wall.
Institution Type/Description: Historical Society Museum: housed in a restored general store; built c.1875. Listed on the National Register of Historic Places.
Hours & Admission Prices: Mon. & Thurs. 10-2. H.N. Greenwell Store: adults $7, children 5-12 $3; discounts to seniors, military & AAA members. &
Attendance: 6,000

KONA JOE COFFEE PLANTATION TOUR, 79-7346 Mamalohoa Hwy., Kealakekua, HI 96750. Tel.: 808-322-2100. Fax: 808-322-9800.
E-mail: sales@konajoe.com
Web Site: konajoe.com
Hours & Admission Prices: Tours: daily 8-5; groups of 6 or more by appointment. &

Kekaha

KOKEE NATURAL HISTORY MUSEUM, Kokee State Park, 15 mile marker, Hwy. 550, Kekaha, HI 96752. Mailing Address: P.O. Box 100, Kekaha, Kauai, HI 96752-0100. Tel.: 808-335-9975. Fax: 808-335-6131.
E-mail: kokeemuseum@earthlink.net
Web Site: www.kokee.org
Key Personnel: Exec. Dir., Marsha Erickson.
Institution Type/Description: Natural History Museum.
Hours & Admission Prices: Daily 9-4. No charge; donations accepted. &
Attendance: 95,595 (estimated)

Kilauea

KAAKAANIU PLANTATION TOURS, 11 Larson Beach Rd., Kilauea, HI 96754. Tel.: 888-882-6664.
Web Site: realnoni.com
Institution Type/Description: Plantation Tours.
Hours & Admission Prices: Tours: Mon., Wed. & Fri. 10 am by appointment. No charge.

KILAUEA POINT NATIONAL WILDLIFE REFUGE, Kilauea Point, Kilauea, HI 96754. Mailing Address: P.O. Box 1128, Kilauea, HI 96754-1128. Tel.: 808-828-1413. Fax: 808-828-6634.
E-mail: jennifer_waipa@fws.gov
Web Site: www.fws.gov/refuge/kilauea_point/
Institution Type/Description: Wildlife Refuge.
Hours & Admission Prices: Tues.-Sat. 10-4.

Kualapua

MOLOKAI MUSEUM AND CULTURAL CENTER, Kala'e Hwy., Mile Marker 4, Kualapuu, HI 96757. Mailing Address: P.O. Box 269, Kualapua, HI 96757-0269. Tel.: 808-567-6436. Fax: 808-567-6624.
Key Personnel: Exec. Dir., Noelani Keliikipi.
Institution Type/Description: Historic Site: housed on the site of the former R.W. Meyer Sugar Mill, built in 1878. Listed on the National Register of Historic Places.
Hours & Admission Prices: Mon.-Sat. 10-2. Adults $2.50, students 5-18 $1. Closed New Year's Day; Thanksgiving; Christmas.

Kula

OCEAN VODKA ORGANIC FARM AND DISTILLERY, 4051 Omaopio Rd., Kula, HI 96790. Tel.: 808-877-0009 & 866-776-2326. Fax: 808-877-8797. Facebook; Twitter.
E-mail: info@oceanvodka.com
Web Site: oceanvodka.com/our-tours
Institution Type/Description: Farm & Distillery.
Hours & Admission Prices: Tours: daily 9:30-4. Closed Independence Day.

Kurtistown

FUKU-BONSAI CULTURAL CENTER & HAWAII STATE BONSAI REPOSITORY, 17-856 Olaa Rd., Kurtistown, HI 96760. Mailing Address: P.O. Box 6000, Kurtistown, HI 96760-6000. Tel.: 808-982-9880. Fax: 808-982-9883.
E-mail: david.f@fukubonsai.com
Web Site: www.fukubonsai.com
Institution Type/Description: Nature Center.
Hours & Admission Prices: Mon.-Sat. 8-4. No charge; donations accepted.

Lahaina

LAHAINA RESTORATION FOUNDATION, 120 Dickenson St., Lahaina, HI 96761-1224. Tel.: 808-661-3262. Fax: 808-661-9309.
E-mail: info@lahainarestoration.org
Web Site: www.lahainarestoration.org
Key Personnel: Exec. Dir., Theo Morrison.
Institution Type/Description: History Museums.
Hours & Admission Prices: Daily 10-4. Adults $7; members & children no charge. Closed Easter; Thanksgiving; Christmas. &
Attendance: 240,000 (estimated)

WHALERS VILLAGE MUSEUM, 2435 Ka'anapali Pkwy., Bldg. H-14, Lahaina, HI 96761-1980. Tel.: 808-661-4567. Fax: 808-661-5854.
E-mail: info@whalersvillage.com
Web Site: www.whalersvillage.com/museum/museum.htm
Institution Type/Description: Whaling Museum.
Hours & Admission Prices: Currently closed for renovations.

Laie

POLYNESIAN CULTURAL CENTER, 55-370 Kamehameha Hwy., Laie, HI 96762-1113. Tel.: 800-367-7060. Fax: 808-293-3022.
E-mail: customercare@polynesia.com
Web Site: www.polynesia.com
Institution Type/Description: Cultural Center.
Hours & Admission Prices: Mon.-Sat. 11:45-9. Call for admission prices. Closed Thanksgiving; Christmas. &

Lanai City

LANAI CULTURE & HERITAGE CENTER, 730 Lanai Ave., Ste. 118, Lanai City, HI 96763. Mailing Address: P.O. Box 631500, Lanai City, HI 96763-1305. Tel.: 808-565-7177.
E-mail: mikala@lanaichc.org
Web Site: www.lanaichc.org
Key Personnel: Exec. Dir., Kepa Maly.
Institution Type/Description: History Museum.
Hours & Admission Prices: Mon.-Fri. 8:30-3:30; groups by appointment. No charge; donations accepted.

Laupahoehoe

LAUPAHOEHOE TRAIN MUSEUM, 36-2377 Mamalahoa Hwy., Laupahoehoe, HI 96764. Mailing Address: P.O. Box 358, Laupahoehoe, HI 96764-0358. Tel.: 808-962-6300. Fax: 808-963-6957.
E-mail: thetrainmuseum@yahoo.com
Web Site: www.thetrainmuseum.com
Key Personnel: Treas., Doug Connors.
Institution Type/Description: History Museum.
Hours & Admission Prices: Thurs.-Sun. 10-5; other times & groups by appointment. Family $15, adults $6, seniors $5, children $3; discounts to AAM members. Closed holidays. &
Attendance: 7,000 (estimated)

Lihue

GROVE FARM MUSEUM, 4050 Nawiliwili Rd., Lihue, HI 96766. Mailing Address: P.O. Box 1631, Lihue, Kauai, HI 96766. Tel.: 808-245-3202. Fax: 808-245-7988.
E-mail: tours@grovefarm.org
Web Site: grovefarm.org
Key Personnel: Dir., Paul Horner; Cur., Moises Madayag.
Institution Type/Description: Sugar Plantation: listed on the National Register of Historic Places.

Hours & Admission Prices: Mon. & Wed.-Thurs. 10am & 1pm by appointment. Adults $20, children 5-12 $10.

KAUAI HISTORICAL SOCIETY, 4396 Rice St., Ste. 101, Lihue, HI 96766-1371. Mailing Address: P.O. Box 1778, Lihue, HI 96766-5778. Tel.: 808-245-3373. Fax: 808-245-8693.
E-mail: info@kauaihistoricalsociety.org
Web Site: www.kauaihistoricalsociety.org
Institution Type/Description: Historical Society Museum & Archive.
Hours & Admission Prices: Office: Mon.-Tues. & Thurs.-Fri. 10-4. Archives: by appointment. No charge; donations accepted.

KAUAI MUSEUM, 4428 Rice St., Lihue, HI 96766. Tel.: 808-245-6931. Fax: 808-245-6864.
E-mail: secretary@kauaimuseum.org
Web Site: kauaimuseum.org
Key Personnel: Dir., Chucky boy Chock.
Institution Type/Description: History & Art Museum: housed in early 20th-century Wilcox building designed by Hart Wood.
Hours & Admission Prices: Mon.-Sat. 9-4. Adults $15, seniors 65 & over $12, youths 8-17 $10; children 7 & under no charge. Closed New Year's Day; Memorial Day; Independence Day; Labor Day; Thanksgiving; Christmas. &
Attendance: 25,175 (estimated)

KILOHANA PLANTATION, 3-2087 Kaumualii Hwy., Lihue, HI 96766-9505. Mailing Address: P.O. Box 3121, Lihue, HI 96766-6121. Tel.: 808-245-5608. Fax: 808-245-7818.
E-mail: kilohana@hawaiilink.net
Web Site: www.kauaikilohana.com
Institution Type/Description: Historic House: housed in the former home of sugar baron, Gaylord Parke Wilcox; built in 1936.
Hours & Admission Prices: Mon.-Sat. 10-9:30, Sun. 9:30-3. No charge. &

Makawao

HUI NO'EAU VISUAL ARTS CENTER, 2841 Baldwin Ave., Makawao, HI 96768-9642. Tel.: 808-572-6560. Fax: 808-572-2750.
E-mail: info@huinoeau.com
Web Site: huinoeau.com
Key Personnel: Exec. Dir., Caroline Killhour; Devel., Membership & Mktg., Erin Wooldridge; Registrar, Jessica Hoecker; Program Dir., Anne-Marie Forsythe; Sr. Program Mgr., Lana Coryell.
Institution Type/Description: Visual Arts Center: housed in 1917 Mediterranean-style home.
Hours & Admission Prices: Daily 9-4. No charge; donations accepted. &
Attendance: 30,000 (estimated)

MAUI PINEAPPLE TOURS, 883 Haliimaile Rd., Makawao, HI 96768. Tel.: 808-665-5491.
Web Site: mauipineappletour.com
Institution Type/Description: Pineapple Plantation.
Hours & Admission Prices: Tours: daily 9:30, 11:45 & 1:30. Adults $65, children 5-12 $55; children under 2 not admitted.

Mountain View

HILO COFFEE MILL & FARM TOURS, 17-995 Volcano Hwy., Mountain View, HI 96771. Mailing Address: P.O. Box 486, Kurtistown, HI 96760. Tel.: 808-968-1333.
Web Site: hilocoffeemill.com/tours.aspx
Institution Type/Description: Company Museum.
Hours & Admission Prices: Store: Tues.-Sat. 8-4:30. Tours: Tues. & Sat. by appointment.

Paauilo

THE HAWAIIAN VANILLA CO., 43-2007 Paauilo Mauka Rd., Paauilo, HI 96776. Tel.: 808-776-1771. Facebook.
Web Site: hawaiianvanilla.com
Institution Type/Description: Company Museum.
Hours & Admission Prices: Gallery: Mon.-Fri. 10-3. Vanilla Luncheon & Tour: Mon.-Fri. 12:30 by appointment. Adults $55, children under 12 $30; children under 3 no charge. Farm Tour: Mon.-Fri. 1 pm by appointment. Admission $25.

Paia

MAUI CRAFTS GUILD, 120 Hana Hwy., Paia, HI 96779. Mailing Address: P.O. Box 790609, Paia, HI 96779-0609. Tel.: 808-579-9697. Fax: 808-579-8694. Facebook.
E-mail: info@mauicraftsguild.com
Web Site: www.mauicraftsguild.com
Institution Type/Description: Art Museum.
Hours & Admission Prices: Daily 10-6.

Papaikou

HAWAII TROPICAL BOTANICAL GARDEN, 27-717 Old Mamalahoa Hwy., Papaikou, HI 96781-7746. Mailing Address: P.O. Box 80, Papaikou, HI 96781-0080. Tel.: 808-964-5233. Fax: 808-964-1338. Facebook: Hawaii Tropical Botanical Garden.
E-mail: htbg@ilhawaii.net
Web Site: www.hawaiigarden.com
Key Personnel: Dir., David C. Tan.
Institution Type/Description: Botanical Garden.
Hours & Admission Prices: Garden: daily 9-5. Gift Shop: daily 8:30-5. Adults $20, children 6-16 $5; children under 6 no charge. Closed New Year's Day; Independence Day; Thanksgiving; Christmas.
Attendance: 80,000 (estimated)

Puunene

ALEXANDER & BALDWIN SUGAR MUSEUM, 3957 Hansen Rd., Puunene, HI 96784. Mailing Address: P.O. Box 125, Puunene, HI 96784-0125. Tel.: 808-871-8058. Fax: 808-871-4321.
E-mail: sugarmus@maui.net
Web Site: sugarmuseum.com
Key Personnel: Dir., Roslyn Lightfoot.
Institution Type/Description: Agriculture Museum: housed in 1902 former sugar factory superintendent's residence, located across the way from Hawaii's largest sugar mill.
Hours & Admission Prices: Daily 9:30-4. Adults $7, seniors $5, children 6-12 $2; children 5 & under no charge. Closed New Year's Day; Easter; Thanksgiving; Christmas. &
Attendance: 35,000 (estimated)

Volcano

VOLCANO ART CENTER GALLERY, 19-4074 Old Volcano Rd., Volcano, HI 96785. Mailing Address: P.O. Box 129, Volcano, HI 96785-0129. Tel.: 808-967-7565. Fax: 808-967-7511.
E-mail: gallery@volcanoartcenter.org
Web Site: www.volcanoartcenter.org
Key Personnel: Exec. Dir., Michael A. Nelson; Gallery Mgr., Emily Catey Weiss; Bd. Chm. (V), William Hamilton.
Institution Type/Description: Cultural Center & Gallery: housed in a hotel built in 1877.
Hours & Admission Prices: Daily 9-5. No charge; donations accepted. Closed Christmas. &
Attendance: 100,000 (estimated)

Wahiawa

TROPIC LIGHTNING MUSEUM, Bldg. #361, Waianae Ave., Schofield Barracks, Wahiawa, HI 96786. Mailing Address: Directorate of Plans, Training, Mobilization & Security, 745 Wright Ave., Bldg. 107, Wheeler Army Airfield, Schofield Barracks, Wahiawa, HI 96786. Tel.: 808-655-0438.
Key Personnel: Cur., Kathleen Ramsden.
Institution Type/Description: Military History Museum.
Hours & Admission Prices: Tues.-Sat. 10-4. No charge; donations accepted. Closed holidays. &
Attendance: 14,000 (estimated)

Wailuku

HAWAII NATURE CENTER, 875 Iao Valley Rd., Wailuki, HI 96793. Mailing Address: 2131 Makiki Heights Dr., Honolulu, HI 96822. Tel.: 808-955-0100; 244-6500. Fax: 808-955-0116.
E-mail: hncinfo@hawaiinaturecenter.org
Web Site: www.hawaiinaturecenter.org
Key Personnel: Exec. Dir., Jeeyun Lee.
Institution Type/Description: Interactive Nature Museum.

Hours & Admission Prices: Mon.-Fri. 12-4, Sat.-Sun. 11-3. Grounds no charge. Closed New Year's Day; Thanksgiving; Christmas.
Attendance: 15,000 (estimated)

Wailuku

HAWAII NATURE CENTER, MAUI, 875 Iao Valley Rd., Wailuku, HI 96793-3009. Tel.: 808-244-6525.
E-mail: bookmaui@hawaiinaturecenter.org
Web Site: www.hawaiinaturecenter.org
Key Personnel: Exec. Dir., Jeeyun Lee.
Institution Type/Description: Nature Center.
Hours & Admission Prices: Daily 10-4. Adults $6; members no charge.

MAUI HISTORICAL SOCIETY - HALE HO'IKE'IKE AT THE BAILEY HOUSE, 2375A Main St., Wailuku, HI 96793-1661. Tel.: 808-244-3326.
E-mail: info@mauimuseum.org
Web Site: www.mauimuseum.org
Formerly: Hale Hoikeike
Key Personnel: Exec. Dir., Naomi Lake-Farm; Mgr. Operations, Viola Yee; Archivist, Marianne Klaus; Volunteer Coord., Kimo Guequierre; Museum Shop Mgr., Brendi Simpson.
Institution Type/Description: Historic House: housed on an ancient Hawaiian site.
Hours & Admission Prices: Mon.-Sat. 10-4. Adults $7, seniors $5, children 6-12 $2; discounts to seniors 60 & over; active military, members & travel professionals no charge. Closed holidays.
Attendance: 11,000 (estimated)

MAUI OCEAN CENTER, 192 Maalaea Rd., Wailuku, HI 96793-5931. Tel.: 808-270-7000. Fax: 808-270-7070. Facebook: Maui Ocean Center.
E-mail: info@mauioceancenter.com
Web Site: www.mauioceancenter.com
Key Personnel: Gen. Mgr., Tapani Vuori; Controller, Alexander Arndt; Dir. Education, Colleen Foster; Dir. Sales, Sue Stisher; Dir. Mktg., Elyse Ditzel; Cur., John Gorman.
Institution Type/Description: Aquarium.
Hours & Admission Prices: July-Aug. daily 9-6; Sept.-May daily 9-5. Adults $27.95, senior citizens 65 & over $24.95, children 3-12 $19.95; discounts to groups; members no charge. &
Attendance: 330,000 (estimated)

MAUI OKINAWA CULTURAL CENTER, 688 Nukuwai Place, Wailuku, HI 96793-1340. Mailing Address: P.O. Box 1884, Wailuku, HI 96793-6884. Tel.: 808-242-1560. Fax: 808-242-5952.
Institution Type/Description: Art Museum.
Hours & Admission Prices: Mon.-Fri. 8:30-11:30; other times by appointment. No charge; donations accepted.

Waimanalo

SEA LIFE PARK HAWAII, 41-202 Kalanianaole Hwy., Ste. 7, Waimanalo, HI 96795-1897. Tel.: 866-393-5158 (Toll Free).
Web Site: www.sealifeparkhawaii.com
Institution Type/Description: Nature Center.
Hours & Admission Prices: Daily 10:30-5. Adult $29.99, children 3-11 $19.

Waimea

FAYE MUSEUM, 9400 Kaumualii Hwy., Waimea, HI 96796. Mailing Address: c/o Waimea Plantation Cottages, P.O. Box 367, Waimea, HI 96796. Tel.: 808-338-1625.
E-mail: waimeasugar@hawaiilink.net
Key Personnel: Cur., Chris Faye.
Institution Type/Description: History Museum: a pioneer sugar planter in West Kauai, H.P. Faye helped form Kekaha Sugar, incorporated in 1898.
Hours & Admission Prices: Open Year Round: Mon.-Fri. 9-5. No charge.

GALLERY WEST, 9400 Kaumualii Hwy., Waimea, HI 96796. Mailing Address: c/o Waimea Plantation Cottages, P.O. Box 367, Waimea, HI 96796. Tel.: 808-338-1625 & 2340.
Key Personnel: Mgr., Kathleen Miguel.
Institution Type/Description: Art Gallery.
Hours & Admission Prices: Call for hours.

WAIMEA SUGAR MILL CAMP MUSEUM, 9400 Kaumualii Hwy., Waimea, HI 96796. Mailing Address: c/o Waimea

Plantation Cottages, P.O. Box 367, Waimea, HI 96796. Tel.: 808-335-2824. Fax: 808-337-9449.
Institution Type/Description: History Museum.
Hours & Admission Prices: Tues., Thurs. & Sat. 9am by appointment. Tour: $10.

WEST KAUAI TECHNOLOGY & VISITOR CENTER, 9565 Kaumualii Hwy., Waimea, HI 96796. Mailing Address: c/o West Kauai Business & Professional Association, P.O. Box 903, Waimea, HI 96796. Tel.: 808-338-1332.
E-mail: visitorcenter@KEDB.com
Institution Type/Description: History Museum.
Hours & Admission Prices: Mon.-Fri. 9:30-5.

Waipahu

HAWAII OKINAWA CENTER, 94-587 Ukee St., Waipahu, HI 96797-4214. Tel.: 808-676-5400. Fax: 808-676-7811.
E-mail: info@huoa.org
Institution Type/Description: Cultural Center.
Hours & Admission Prices: Mon.-Fri. 8:30-5. Closed New Year's Day; Presidents' Day; Memorial Day; Independence Day; Labor Day; Thanksgiving; Christmas.

HAWAII'S PLANTATION VILLAGE, 94-695 Waipahu St., Waipahu, HI 96797-2601. Tel.: 808-677-0110. Fax: 808-676-6727. Facebook.
E-mail: hpv.waipahu@hawaiiantel.net
Web Site: www.hawaiiplantationvillage.org
Key Personnel: Acting Exec. Dir., Deanna Espinas.
Institution Type/Description: General Museum.
Hours & Admission Prices: Office: Mon.-Sat. 8-4:30. Guided Tours: Mon.-Sat. 10-2. Adults $15, seniors 62 & over $12, Kama'aina & military $8, youth 4-11 $6; children 3 & under no charge. Closed New Year's Day; Good Friday; Memorial Day; Independence Day; Labor Day; Thanksgiving; Christmas. &
Attendance: 60,000 (estimated)

IDAHO

(125 listings)

Almo

CITY OF ROCKS NATIONAL RESERVE, 3035 Elba Almo Rd., Almo, ID 83312. Mailing Address: P.O. Box 169, Almo, ID 83312-0169. Tel.: 208-824-5901.
E-mail: wallace_keck@partner.nps.gov
Web Site: www.nps.gov/ciro/index.htm
Key Personnel: Park Superintendent, Wallace Keck.
Institution Type/Description: Park Museum.
Hours & Admission Prices: Park: daily. Visitor Center: April 17-Oct. 23 daily 8-4:30; Oct. 24-April 11 Mon.-Fri. 8-4:30. No charge; donations accepted. &

American Falls

MASSACRE ROCKS STATE PARK, 3592 Park Lane, American Falls, ID 83211-5556. Tel.: 208-548-2672. Fax: 208-548-2671.
E-mail: mas@idpr.idaho.gov
Web Site: parksandrecreation.idaho.gov/parks/massacre-rocks
Key Personnel: Park Mgr., L. Max Newlin.
Institution Type/Description: Park Museum.
Hours & Admission Prices: Visitor Center: May 15-Sept. 15 daily 7:30am-9pm. Park: Summer: daily 8:30-8:30; Sept.-June daily 7-3:30. $4 per vehicle. &
Attendance: 50,000

Arco

CRATERS OF THE MOON NATIONAL MONUMENT AND PRESERVE, 1266 Craters Loop Rd, Arco, ID 83213. Mailing Address: P.O. Box 29, Arco, ID 83213-0029. Tel.: 208-527-1300. Fax: 208-527-3073.
E-mail: crmo_information@nps.gov
Web Site: www.nps.gov/crmo
Formerly: Craters of the Moon National Monument
Key Personnel: Supt., Dan Buckley.
Institution Type/Description: Natural History Museum.
Hours & Admission Prices: Memorial Day-Labor Day daily 8-6; Sept.-May daily 8-4:30. Visitor Center: no charge; donations accepted. Park: $8 per vehicle. Closed winter holidays. &
Attendance: 217,000 (actual)

Athol

FARRAGUT STATE PARK, 13550 E. Hwy. 54, Athol, ID 83801. Tel.: 208-683-2425.
E-mail: far@idpr.idaho.gov
Web Site: www.parksandrecreation.idaho.gov
Institution Type/Description: State Park.
Hours & Admission Prices: Daily.

Atlanta

ATLANTA HISTORICAL SOCIETY, Middle Fork Rd., Atlanta, ID 83601. Mailing Address: P.O. Box 53, Atlanta, ID 83601.
Institution Type/Description: Historical Society Museum.
Hours & Admission Prices: Summer: daily 10-9; other times by appointment. No charge.

Blackfoot

BLACKFOOT COMMUNITY CENTER'S CHILDREN'S MUSEUM OF IDAHO, 157 W. Sexton, Blackfoot, ID 83221. Mailing Address: 257 S. Broadway, Blackfoot, ID 83221. Tel.: 208-785-8022.
E-mail: thecenter@cableone.net
Web Site: blackfootcommunitycenter.blogspot.com
Key Personnel: Dir., Ashlee Howell.
Institution Type/Description: Children's Museum.
Hours & Admission Prices: Mon. & Fri.-Sat. 10-2, Tues.-Thurs. 12-2. Admission $3.

IDAHO POTATO MUSEUM, 130 N.W. Main St., Blackfoot, ID 83221-0801. Mailing Address: P.O. Box 801, Blackfoot, ID 83221-0801. Tel.: 208-785-2517.
E-mail: info@idahopotatomuseum.com
Web Site: idahopotatomuseum.com
Key Personnel: Exec. Dir., Tish Dahmen; Pres. (V), Shirley Brumfield.
Institution Type/Description: Agriculture Museum.
Hours & Admission Prices: June-Aug. daily 9:30-7; Sept.-May Mon.-Sat. 9:30-5. Adults $6, seniors 60 & over $5.50, children 5-12 $3; discounts to groups, military & AAA members; children 4 & under no charge.
Attendance: 25,000 (estimated)

Boise

AQUARIUM OF BOISE, 64 N. Cole Rd., Boise, ID 83704. Tel.: 208-375-1932. Facebook: @AquariumBoise; Instagram & Twitter: @aquariumofboise.
E-mail: frontdesk@aquariumboise.net
Web Site: www.aquariumboise.net
Formerly: Idaho Aquarium
Key Personnel: Exec. Dir., Joni Sullivan; Office Mgr., Lyla Workman.
Institution Type/Description: Aquarium.
Hours & Admission Prices: Mon.-Sat. 10-5, Sun. 12-5. See website for admission prices.

BASQUE MUSEUM & CULTURAL CENTER, 611 Grove St., Boise, ID 83702-5971. Tel.: 208-343-2671. Fax: 208-336-4801.
E-mail: info@basquemuseum.com
Web Site: www.basquemuseum.com
Key Personnel: Dir., Annie Gavica.
Institution Type/Description: Culture & History Museum.
Hours & Admission Prices: Tues.-Fri. 10-5, Sat. 11-4. Adults $5, students & seniors $4, children 6-12 $3; children 5 & under and members no charge. Closed holidays.

BOISE ART MUSEUM, 670 Julia Davis Dr., Boise, ID 83702-7646. Tel.: 208-345-8330, ext. 10. Fax: 208-345-2247. Facebook: Boise Art Museum.
E-mail: info@boiseartmuseum.org
Web Site: www.boiseartmuseum.org
Key Personnel: Exec. Dir. & C.E.O., Melanie Fales; Museum Store Mgr., Nora Sweeney.
Institution Type/Description: General Art Museum.
Hours & Admission Prices: Tues.-Sat. 10-5, Sun. 12-5. Adults $6, seniors 62 & over and military $4, students with ID & children grades 1-12 $3; discounts to AAM members & 1st Thurs. of month; members & children under 6 no charge. Closed New Year's Day; Easter; Thanksgiving & day after; Christmas. &
Attendance: 50,303 (actual)

THE DISCOVERY CENTER OF IDAHO, 131 Myrtle St., Boise, ID 83702-7652. Tel.: 208-343-9895. Fax: 208-343-0105.
E-mail: webmail@dcidaho.org
Web Site: www.dcidaho.org
Institution Type/Description: Science Museum.
Hours & Admission Prices: Tues.-Sat. 10-4:30, Sun. 12-4:30. Adults 13 & over $18, senior citizens 60 & over $17, children 2-17 $16; discounts to groups & ASTC affiliate members; members & children under 2 no charge. Closed New Year's Day; Easter; Thanksgiving; Christmas. &
Attendance: 98,700 (actual)

IDAHO BLACK HISTORY MUSEUM, 508 Julia Davis Dr., Boise, ID 83702-7694. Tel.: 208-789-2164.
E-mail: request.information@ibhm.org
Web Site: www.ibhm.org
Key Personnel: Pres., Phillip Thompson.
Institution Type/Description: History Museum.
Hours & Admission Prices: Sat.-Sun. 11-4; groups by appointment. No charge; donations accepted. &

IDAHO BOTANICAL GARDEN, 2355 Old Penitentiary Rd., Boise, ID 83712. Tel.: 208-343-8649. Fax: 208-343-3601.
E-mail: info@idahobotanicalgarden.org
Web Site: www.idahobotanicalgarden.org
Key Personnel: Exec. Dir., Erin Anderson; Education Dir., Elizabeth Dickey; Dir. Horticulture, Michele Leisca.
Institution Type/Description: Botanical Garden.
Hours & Admission Prices: Daily 9-5. Adults $8, seniors $6, children 4-12 $5; discounts to groups of 10 or more AAA members & military; members no charge. &
Attendance: 120,000 (actual)

IDAHO MILITARY HISTORY MUSEUM, 4692 W. Harvard St., Boise, ID 83705. Mailing Address: 4040 W. Guard St., Boise, ID 83705-5004. Tel.: 208-272-4841. Facebook: Idaho Military History Museum.
E-mail: galvarez@imd.idaho.gov
Web Site: museum.mil.idaho.gov
Key Personnel: Dir. & Chief Cur., Jeff Packer.
Institution Type/Description: Military History Museum.
Hours & Admission Prices: Tues.-Sat. 12-4; other times by appointment. No charge; donations accepted. Closed New Year's Day; Easter; Thanksgiving; Christmas. &
Attendance: 4,500 (estimated)

IDAHO MUSEUM OF MINING AND GEOLOGY, 2455 Old Penitentiary Rd., Boise, ID 83712-8254. Tel.: 208-368-9876.
E-mail: contact.us@idahomuseum.org
Web Site: www.idahomuseum.org
Key Personnel: Pres., Steve Cox.
Institution Type/Description: Mining & Geology Museum.
Hours & Admission Prices: April-Oct. Wed.-Sun. 12-5. No charge; donations accepted. &
Attendance: 10,000 (estimated)

IDAHO STATE CAPITOL, 700 W. Jefferson, Boise, ID 83720-0002. Mailing Address: P.O. Box 83720, Boise, ID 83720. Tel.: 208-332-1012.
E-mail: ConstituentServices@house.idaho.gov
Web Site: legislature.idaho.gov/capitol
Institution Type/Description: Historic Building: built in 1886.
Hours & Admission Prices: Mon.-Fri. 9-5.

IDAHO STATE HISTORICAL MUSEUM, 610 N. Julia Davis Dr., Boise, ID 83702-7646. Mailing Address: 214 Broadway Ave., Boise, ID 83702. Tel.: 208-334-2120. Fax: 208-334-4059.
E-mail: jody.ochoa@ishs.idaho.gov
Web Site: history.idaho.gov/idaho-state-museum
Key Personnel: Exec. Dir., Janet Gallimore.
Institution Type/Description: History Museum.
Hours & Admission Prices: Museum: Mon.-Sat. 10-5, Sun. 12-5. Pioneer Village: Memorial Day to Labor Day Fri.-Sat. 11:30-2:30, Sun. 12-3. Adults $10, seniors, college students & military $8, children 6-17 $5; members and children 5 & under no charge. &
Attendance: 190,000 (actual)

MORRISON KNUDSEN NATURE CENTER, IDAHO DEPARTMENT OF FISH & GAME, 600 S. Walnut St., Boise, ID 83712-7729. Tel.: 208-334-2225. Fax: 208-287-2905.

E-mail: david.cannamela@idfg.idaho.gov
Web Site: http://fishandgame.idaho.gov/public/education/?getpage=234
Key Personnel: Supt., David Cannamela.
Institution Type/Description: Nature Center.
Hours & Admission Prices: Park: daily sunrise to sunset. Visitors Center: Tues.-Sun. 10-3. No charge; donations accepted. &
Attendance: 150,000 (estimated)

OLD IDAHO PENITENTIARY STATE HISTORIC SITE, 2445 Old Penitentiary Rd., Boise, ID 83712-8254. Tel.: 208-334-2844. Fax: 208-334-3225.
E-mail: amber.beierle@ishs.idaho.gov
Web Site: history.idaho.gov/oldpen
Key Personnel: Historic Sites Admin., Amber Beierle.
Institution Type/Description: Historic Building Museum: built in 1870, the penitentiary received over 13,000 convicts while in operation for more than a century. Listed on the National Register of Historic Places.
Hours & Admission Prices: Memorial Day to Labor Day daily 10-5; Sept.-May daily 12-5. Adults $6, seniors $4, children 6-12 $3; discounts for groups of 10 or more; children 5 & under no charge. Closed state holidays.
Attendance: 23,539 (actual)

WORLD CENTER FOR BIRDS OF PREY, 5668 W. Flying Hawk Lane, Boise, ID 83709-7289. Tel.: 208-362-8687. Fax: 208-362-2376.
E-mail: tpf@peregrinefund.org
Web Site: www.peregrinefund.org
Formerly: Velma Morrison Interpretive Center
Key Personnel: Dir., Tate Mason.
Institution Type/Description: Nature Center.
Hours & Admission Prices: March-Oct. daily 9-5; Nov.-Feb. Tues.-Sun. 10-4. Adults $10, seniors 62 & over $8, children 4-16 $5; members & children under 4 no charge. &
Attendance: 35,000 (actual)

ZOO BOISE, 355 Julia Davis Dr., Boise, ID 83702-7670. Tel.: 208-608-7760. Fax: 208-384-4059. TDD: 208-384-4240. Facebook: Zoo Boise.
E-mail: zooboise@cityofboise.org
Web Site: www.zooboise.org
Key Personnel: Dir., Steve Burns.
Institution Type/Description: Zoo.
Hours & Admission Prices: Daily 10-5. Seasonal admission prices. Closed New Year's Day; Thanksgiving; Christmas. &
Attendance: 329,084 (actual)

Bonners Ferry

BOUNDARY COUNTY HISTORICAL SOCIETY AND MUSEUM, 7229 Main St., Bonners Ferry, ID 83805. Mailing Address: P.O. Box 808, Bonners Ferry, ID 83805-0808. Tel.: 208-267-7720. Facebook: Boundary County Historical Society & Museum.
E-mail: bcmuseum@meadowcrk.com
Web Site: bonnersferrymuseum.org
Key Personnel: Pres., Cal Russell; Sec., Dottie Gray; Cur. & Collections Mgr., Sue Kemmis.
Institution Type/Description: History Museum.
Hours & Admission Prices: May-Sept. Mon.-Sat. 10-4; Oct.-April Fri.-Sat. 10-4. Admission $2, family $5; members and children 14 & under no charge. &
Attendance: 3,000 (estimated)

KOOTENAI NATIONAL WILDLIFE REFUGE, 287 Westside Rd., Bonners Ferry, ID 83805-5172. Tel.: 208-267-3888. Fax: 208-267-5570.
E-mail: fw1KootenaiNWR@fws.gov
Web Site: www.fws.gov
Key Personnel: Mgr., Dianna Ellis.
Institution Type/Description: Wildlife Refuge.
Hours & Admission Prices: Refuge: daily dawn to dusk. Office: Mon.-Fri. 7:30-4.
Attendance: 20,000

Burley

CASSIA COUNTY MUSEUM, E. Main & Hiland Ave., Burley, ID 83318. Mailing Address: P.O. Box 331, Burley, ID 83318-0331. Tel.: 208-678-7172.
E-mail: cassiamuseum@cassiacounty.org
Key Personnel: Pres., Rod Smith; Financial Dir. & Treas., Joel Robins; Cur., Valerie Bowen.

Institution Type/Description: History Museum.
Hours & Admission Prices: April 15-Oct. 15 Tues.-Sat. 10-5. No charge; donations accepted. Closed Independence Day. ♿
Attendance: 1,750 (estimated)

Caldwell

AEROPLANES OVER IDAHO MUSEUM, 5017A Aviation Way, Caldwell, ID 83605. Tel.: 208-455-1708.
E-mail: info@aeroplanesoveridaho.org
Web Site: www.aeroplanesoveridaho.org
Institution Type/Description: Aviation History Museum.
Hours & Admission Prices: Daily. No charge; donations accepted.

CITY OF CALDWELL VAN SLYKE MUSEUM, 621 Harrison St., Caldwell, ID 83605. Mailing Address: 411 Blaine St., Caldwell, ID 83605-3619. Tel.: 208-455-3011. Fax: 208-455-3003.
E-mail: smiller@cityofcaldwell.org
Web Site: www.cityofcaldwell.org
Formerly: Kiwanis Van Slyke Museum Foundation Inc.
Key Personnel: Dir. & Chm. City Hall, Susan Miller.
Institution Type/Description: Park Museum & Visitors Center.
Hours & Admission Prices: By appointment only. Donations accepted.
Attendance: 350 (estimated)

ORMA J. SMITH MUSEUM OF NATURAL HISTORY, The College of Idaho, 2112 Cleveland Blvd., Caldwell, ID 83605-4432. Tel.: 208-459-5507.
E-mail: bclark@collegeofidaho.edu
Web Site: www.collegeofidaho.edu/about/campus-facilities/natural-history-museum
Key Personnel: Dir., Adjunct Prof. of Biology, Cur. Invertebrates, & Bd. Member, William H. Clark; Research Assoc., Dr. Paul Blom; Cur. Lepidoptera, Dr. Paul Castrovillo; Archaeologist, Cur. Ethnology, Janet L. Summers Duffy; Cur. Paleontology, Howard Emry; Research Assoc., Mammalogy & Bd. Member, Dr. Sean Farley; Cur. Entomology, Dr. Alan R. Gillogly; Cur. Ethnography, Bill Nance; Cur. Entomology, Dr. James K. Ryan; Cur. Entomology, Dr. Craig R. Baird; Cur. Fossil Fishes, Dr. Gerald R. Smith; Gen. Entomology, Dr. David Ward; Research Assoc., Librarian & Cur. Invertebrates, Wayne Lewis; Prof. Biology, Cur. Mammals, Biology Dept. Coord. of Museum Affairs & Bd. Member, Dr. Eric Yensen; Cur. Fishes, Dr. Donald W. Zaroban; Bd. Member & Research Assoc. Entomology, Dr. Ron Bitner.
Institution Type/Description: Natural History Museum.
Hours & Admission Prices: Mon.-Fri. 1-5. No charge. ♿
Attendance: 3,000 (actual)

OUR MEMORIES INDIAN CREEK MUSEUM, 1122 Main St., Caldwell, ID 83605. Mailing Address: c/o Canyon County Historical Society, P.O. Box 595, Nampa, ID 83651. Tel.: 208-467-7611.
E-mail: info@canyoncountyhistory.com
Web Site: www.canyoncountyhistory.com/ourmemories
Institution Type/Description: History Museum.
Hours & Admission Prices: Tues. & Fri. 11-4; other times by appointment. Adults $3; members no charge.
Attendance: 1,000 (estimated)

ROSENTHAL GALLERY OF ART, The College of Idaho, 2112 Cleveland Blvd., Caldwell, ID 83605-4432. Tel.: 208-459-5321 & 5209 & 5011. Fax: 208-459-5885.
E-mail: gclaassen@collegeofidaho.edu
Web Site: www.collegeofidaho.edu
Key Personnel: Dir., Garth Claassen.
Institution Type/Description: Art Exhibition Gallery.
Hours & Admission Prices: Mon.-Fri. 10-5; Sat.-Sun. by appointment. No charge; donations accepted. Closed academic holidays & breaks. ♿
Attendance: 1,500

WHITTENBERGER PLANETARIUM, Boone Science Hall, The College of Idaho, 2112 Cleveland Blvd., Caldwell, ID 83605. Tel.: 208-459-5211. Fax: 208-459-5414.
E-mail: atruksa@collegeofidaho.edu
Web Site: www.collegeofidaho.edu/planetarium
Key Personnel: Dir. & Museum Shop Mgr., Amy Truksa; Administrative Asst., Kinga Britschgi.
Institution Type/Description: Planetarium.
Hours & Admission Prices: Call for hours. Adults $4, students $2; discount to groups.
Attendance: 3,000 (estimated)

Cambridge

CAMBRIDGE MUSEUM, 15 N. Superior, Cambridge, ID 83610. Mailing Address: P.O. Box 35, Cambridge, ID 83610-0035. Tel.: 208-257-3485.
E-mail: shansen@ctcweb.net
Key Personnel: Dir., Sandra Hansen; Museum Shop Mgr., Bo Thorsen.
Institution Type/Description: History Museum.
Hours & Admission Prices: June-Aug. Wed.-Sat. 10-2; call to confirm. Library: by appointment. No charge; donations accepted. ♿
Attendance: 850 (actual)

Cataldo

COEUR D'ALENES OLD MISSION STATE PARK, 31732 S. Mission Rd., Cataldo, ID 83810. Mailing Address: P.O. Box 30, Cataldo, ID 83810-0030. Tel.: 208-682-3814. Fax: 208-682-4032.
E-mail: old@idpr.idaho.gov
Web Site: www.parksandrecreation.idaho.gov
Key Personnel: Park Mgr., Kathleen Durfee.
Institution Type/Description: Historic Building: built by the Coeur d'Alene Tribe & Jesuit missionaries in 1850.
Hours & Admission Prices: April-Sept. 9-5, Oct.-March 10-3. Family $10, single admission $5. Closed New Year's Day; Thanksgiving; Christmas. ♿
Attendance: 90,000 (estimated)

Challis

NORTH CUSTER MUSEUM, 1201 E. Main Ave., Challis, ID 83226. Mailing Address: P.O. Box 776, Challis, ID 83226-0776. Tel.: 208-879-2846.
E-mail: pegperks@custertel.net
Key Personnel: Chair (V), Carolyn Naillon; Treas., Margaret Parks; Museum Shop Mgr., Grace Barry.
Institution Type/Description: History Museum.
Hours & Admission Prices: Memorial Day to Labor Day Sat.-Sun. 10-4. No charge; donations accepted. ♿
Attendance: 525 (estimated)

Coeur d'Alene

THE ART SPIRIT GALLERY, 415 Sherman Ave., Coeur d'Alene, ID 83814-2728. Tel.: 208-765-6006.
E-mail: steve@theartspiritgallery.com
Web Site: www.theartspiritgallery.com
Key Personnel: Dir., Steven J. Gibbs.
Institution Type/Description: Art Gallery.
Hours & Admission Prices: May-Aug. daily 11-6; Sept.-April Tues.-Sat. 11-6. No charge. ♿

MUSEUM OF NORTH IDAHO, 115 N.W. Blvd., Coeur d'Alene, ID 83814-2798. Mailing Address: P.O. Box 812, Coeur d'Alene, ID 83816-0812. Tel.: 208-664-3448. Facebook.
E-mail: dd@museumni.org
Web Site: www.museumni.org
Key Personnel: Dir., Dorothy Dahlgren.
Institution Type/Description: Local History Museum.
Hours & Admission Prices: Museum: April-Oct. Tues.-Sat. 11-5. Library: by appointment. Family $10, adults $4, children 6-16 $1; discounts to AAM, ICOM & AASLH members; members no charge. Closed Independence Day. ♿
Attendance: 5,500 (actual)

Coolin

PRIEST LAKE STATE PARK, 314 Indian Creek Park Rd., Coolin, ID 83821-9769. Tel.: 208-443-2200. Fax: 208-443-3893.
E-mail: pri@idrp.idaho.gov
Web Site: parksandrecreation.idaho.gov
Institution Type/Description: State Park.
Hours & Admission Prices: Daily.

Cottonwood

HISTORICAL MUSEUM AT ST. GERTRUDE, 465 Keuterville Rd., Cottonwood, ID 83522-5183. Tel.: 208-962-2054.
E-mail: dgraham@stgertrudes.org
Web Site: www.historicalmuseumatstgertrude.org
Formerly: St. Gertrude's Museum
Key Personnel: C.E.O., Mary Schmidt; Museum Technician, Shirley Gehring.
Institution Type/Description: History Museum.

Hours & Admission Prices: Mon.-Sat. 9:30-4:30. Adults $6, student 7-17 $3; discounts to AAM members; members and children 6 & under no charge. &
Attendance: 7,000 (estimated)

Council

COUNCIL VALLEY MUSEUM, 100 S. Galena St., Council, ID 83612. Mailing Address: 2202 Ridge Rd., Council, ID 83612. Tel.: 208-253-4582.
E-mail: dafisk@ctcweb.net
Web Site: www.councilmuseum.com
Institution Type/Description: History Museum.
Hours & Admission Prices: Memorial Day to Labor Day Tues.-Sat. 10-4, Sun. 1-4. &
Attendance: 1,000 (estimated)

Donnelly

VALLEY COUNTY MUSEUM, 13131 Farm to Market Rd., Donnelly, ID 83615. Mailing Address: P.O. Box 444, Donnelly, ID 83615-0444. Tel.: 208-325-8628. Facebook: Historic Roseberry.
E-mail: info@historicroseberry.com
Web Site: www.historicroseberry.com
Formerly: Long Valley Museum
Key Personnel: Acting Pres. (V), Barbara Kwader; Museum Shop Mgr., Ann McQuade; Volunteer Coord., Katie Morgan; Groundskeeper, Thomas Schmidt.
Institution Type/Description: Historical Museum.
Hours & Admission Prices: May & Oct. Sun. 1-5; June-Sept. Sat.-Sun. 1-5; other times by appointment. No charge; donations accepted. &
Attendance: 10,500 (estimated)

Dubois

HERITAGE HALL MUSEUM, 110 S. Reynolds, Dubois, ID 83423. Mailing Address: P.O. Box 253, Dubois, ID 83423-0253.
E-mail: heritagehall@mudlake.net
Key Personnel: Chm. (V), Conni Owen; Pres. (V), Barbara Kidd.
Institution Type/Description: Historical Society Museum.
Hours & Admission Prices: Memorial Day to Labor Day Fri.-Sat. 2-6; other times by appointment. No charge; donations accepted.
Attendance: 300 (estimated)

Elk River

ELK RIVER HISTORICAL MUSEUM, City Hall of Elk River, 112 S. Second St. (Basement), Elk River, ID 83827. Mailing Address: P.O. Box 63, Elk River, ID 83827-0063. Tel.: 208-790-8939.
Key Personnel: Dir., Chm. (V) & Pres. (V), Deanna L. Kreisher; Sec., Randy Johnson; Treas., Judy Miller.
Institution Type/Description: History Museum.
Hours & Admission Prices: Summer: Sat. 10 to noon; other times by appointment. Adults $5; discounts to members. &
Attendance: 129 (actual)

Emmett

GEM COUNTY HISTORICAL VILLAGE MUSEUM, 501 E. First St., Emmett, ID 83617-3005. Tel.: 208-365-9530 & 4340.
E-mail: gemcountymuseum@gmail.com
Web Site: www.gemcountymuseum.org
Formerly: Gem County Historical Society and Museum
Key Personnel: Pres. Bd. (V), Kathleen Derig; Dir. Museum Shop Mgr., Meg Davis.
Institution Type/Description: Historical Society Museum.
Hours & Admission Prices: Wed.-Sat. 1-5; tours & other times by appointment. No charge; donations accepted. &
Attendance: 1,000 (actual)

Filer

TWIN FALLS COUNTY HISTORICAL MUSEUM, 21337A Hwy. 30, Filer, ID 83328-5513. Tel.: 208-736-4675. Fax: 208-736-4675. Facebook: Twin Falls County Historical Museum.
E-mail: info@twinfallsmuseum.org
Web Site: www.twinfallsmuseum.org
Key Personnel: Pres., Steve Westphal; Vice Pres., Alex Kunkel; Dir., Laurie Warren.
Institution Type/Description: History Museum & Visitor Center: housed in the former Union School built in 1914.

Hours & Admission Prices: March-Nov. Tues.-Sat. 12-5; Winter: by appointment. No charge; donations accepted. Closed holidays. &
Attendance: 1,600 (actual)

Fort Hall

SHOSHONE-BANNOCK TRIBAL MUSEUM, Simplot Rd., Fort Hall, ID 83203. Mailing Address: Box 306, Fort Hall, ID 83203-0306. Tel.: 208-237-9791. Fax: 208-237-0797.
E-mail: publicaffairs@sbtribes.com
Web Site: www.sbtribes.com
Key Personnel: Mgr., Coord. & Museum Shop Mgr., Rosemary Devinney.
Institution Type/Description: Tribal Museum.
Hours & Admission Prices: June-Aug. daily 9:30-5; Sept.-May Mon.-Fri. 9:30-5. Adults $3.50, youth 6-17 $2; Native American Indians with Tribal ID no charge. Closed Federal & Tribal holidays.
Attendance: 3,000 (estimated)

Glenns Ferry

GLENNS FERRY HISTORICAL MUSEUM, 152 W. Cleveland Ave., Glenns Ferry, ID 83623. Mailing Address: 161 W. Cleveland Ave., Glenns Ferry, ID 83623. Tel.: 208-366-2320.
E-mail: glennsferryhistoricalmuseum@gmail.com
Web Site: glennsferryidaho.org/visitors/museums
Institution Type/Description: Historic Building: housed in a former school; built in 1909. Listed on the National Register of Historic Places.
Hours & Admission Prices: Memorial Day to Sept. Sat.-Sun. 12-5; other times by appointment. No charge; donations accepted.

Gooding

GOODING COUNTY HISTORICAL SOCIETY MUSEUM, 273 Euskadi Lane, Gooding, ID 83330. Mailing Address: P.O. Box 89, Gooding, ID 83330-0089. Tel.: 208-934-5318.
E-mail: gchstoponis@yahoo.com
Web Site: goodingcountyhistoricalsociety.shutterfly.com
Key Personnel: Pres. (V), Jay Thueber; Dir., Dr. Sharon Cheney; Cur., Joani Pauls.
Institution Type/Description: Historical Society Museum.
Hours & Admission Prices: By appointment. No charge; donations accepted. &
Attendance: 700 (actual)

Grangeville

BICENTENNIAL HISTORICAL MUSEUM, 305 N. College, Grangeville, ID 83530. Mailing Address: P.O. Box 212, Grangeville, ID 83530-0212. Tel.: 208-983-2104 & 2277.
E-mail: info@bicentennialmuseum.com
Institution Type/Description: History Museum.
Hours & Admission Prices: June-Sept. Wed. & Fri. 1-5; other times by appointment. No charge; donations accepted.

Hagerman

HAGERMAN FOSSIL BEDS NATIONAL MONUMENT, 221 N. State St., Hagerman, ID 83332. Mailing Address: P.O. Box 570, Hagerman, ID 83332-0570. Tel.: 208-837-4793 & 208-933-4100. Fax: 208-837-4857.
E-mail: hafo_information@nps.gov
Web Site: www.nps.gov
Institution Type/Description: History Museum.
Hours & Admission Prices: mid-June to Labor Day daily 9-5; Sept. to mid-June Thurs.-Mon. 9-5. Closed New Year's Day; Thanksgiving; Christmas.

HAGERMAN VALLEY HISTORICAL SOCIETY, Hagerman State Ave., 100 S. State St., Hagerman, ID 83332. Mailing Address: P.O. Box 86, Hagerman, ID 83332-0086. Tel.: 208-837-6288.
E-mail: hagermanhistory@gmail.com
Web Site: www.hagermanmuseum.com
Key Personnel: Pres. (V), Mike Owsley; Chm. (V), Leroy Jazwick.
Institution Type/Description: Historical Society Museum.
Hours & Admission Prices: April-Oct. Wed.-Sun. 1-4. No charge; donations accepted.
Attendance: 500 (estimated)

Hailey

BLAINE COUNTY HISTORICAL MUSEUM, 218 N. Main St., Hailey, ID 83333. Mailing Address: P.O. Box 124, Hailey, ID 83333. Tel.: 208-788-1801 & 4210. Fax: 208-788-1801.
E-mail: info@bchistoricalmuseum.org
Web Site: bchistoricalmuseum.org
Key Personnel: Dir. & Museum Shop Mgr., Teddie Daley; Pres. (V), Robert MacLeod.
Institution Type/Description: History Museum: housed in an 1880 old armory & social center & Friedman warehouse.
Hours & Admission Prices: Memorial Day weekend to Oct. daily 11-5. No charge; donations accepted. &
Attendance: 1,500 (actual)

Harrison

CRANE HISTORICAL SOCIETY MUSEUM, 201 Coeur d'Alene Ave., Harrison, ID 83833. Mailing Address: P.O. Box 152, Harrison, ID 83833-0152. Tel.: 208-689-3111.
E-mail: cranehistsoc@gmail.com
Web Site: www.cranehistoricalsociety.org
Key Personnel: Pres. (V), Berti Arnzen.
Institution Type/Description: Historical Society Museum.
Hours & Admission Prices: Memorial Day to Labor Day Sat.-Sun. & holidays 12-4; other times by appointment. No charge; donations accepted.
Attendance: 800 (estimated)

Idaho City

BOISE BASIN MUSEUM, 503 Montgomery St., Idaho City, ID 83631. Mailing Address: P.O. Box 358, Idaho City, ID 83631-0358. Tel.: 208-392-9551. Fax: 208-392-9905. Facebook: Idaho City Historical Foundation.
E-mail: secretarylg@idahocityhf.org
Web Site: www.idahocityhf.org
Key Personnel: Pres. (V), Loveta Geesey; Museum Shop Mgr., Joyce Obland.
Institution Type/Description: History Museum.
Hours & Admission Prices: May & Sept. Sat. & Sun. 11-4; Memorial Day to Labor Day daily 11-4; tours by appointment. No charge; donations accepted.
Attendance: 5,000 (estimated)

IDAHO CITY VISITOR CENTER, 100 Main St., Ste. A, Idaho City, ID 83631. Mailing Address: P.O. Box 350, Idaho City, ID 83631-0350. Tel.: 208-392-6040. Fax: 208-392-9512.
Institution Type/Description: Visitor Center.
Hours & Admission Prices: Summer: daily 9-5; Winter: call for hours.

Idaho Falls

THE ART MUSEUM OF EASTERN IDAHO, 300 S. Capital Ave., Idaho Falls, ID 83402-3952. Tel.: 208-524-7777. Fax: 208-529-6666.
E-mail: jmartin@theartmuseum.org
Web Site: www.theartmuseum.org
Formerly: Eagle Rock Art Museum and Education Center
Key Personnel: Exec. Dir., Miyai Abe Griggs; Business Mgr., Jessica Hull Livesay; Dir. Education, Alexa Stanger; Museum Coord., Jesse Martin.
Institution Type/Description: Art Museum.
Hours & Admission Prices: Tues.-Wed. & Fri.-Sat. 11-5, Thurs. 11-8. Adults $4; youth 6-18 $2; children under 6 no charge. North American reciprocal museums. &
Attendance: 30,000 (estimated)

COLLECTORS' CORNER MUSEUM, 900 John Adams Pkwy., Idaho Falls, ID 83401-4049. Tel.: 208-528-9900. Facebook.
E-mail: collectors_corner@hotmail.com
Web Site: tripadvisor.com
Key Personnel: Co Dir., Museum Shop Mgr. & Chm. (V), Nida Gyorfy; Co Dir., Jim Gyorfy.
Institution Type/Description: Collectors Museum.
Hours & Admission Prices: Tues.-Sat. 10-5. Adults $5, senior citizens 50 & up and students $4; children under 3 no charge. Closed holidays. &
Attendance: 5,000 (actual)

LDS TEMPLE VISITOR CENTER, 1000 Memorial Dr., Idaho Falls, ID 83402. Tel.: 208-523-4504.
E-mail: vcidaho@ldschurch.org
Web Site: www.lds.org
Key Personnel: Dir., Gary J. Higley.

Institution Type/Description: Religious Museum.
Hours & Admission Prices: Center: daily 9-9. Temple Grounds: Summer daily. Temple interior closed to public. No charge. &
Attendance: 50,000 (estimated)

MUSEUM OF IDAHO, 200 N. Eastern Ave., Idaho Falls, ID 83402-4029. Tel.: 208-522-1400. Fax: 208-524-5060. Facebook: Museum of Idaho.
E-mail: marketinq@museumofidaho.org
Web Site: www.museumofidaho.org
Key Personnel: Exec. Dir., David Pennock, Ph.D.; Dir. Devel., Nick Gailey; Dir. Education, Sunny Katseangs; Dir. Business Affairs, Allison Ball; Dir. Exhibitions, Rod Hansen; Dir. Mktg., Laura Cooley; Business Asst., Susan Van Orden; Devel. Asst., Nicki McDaniel; Cur., Claire Smith; Mgr. Facilities, Greg Stoddard.
Institution Type/Description: History Museum.
Hours & Admission Prices: Mon.-Tues. 9-8, Wed.-Sat. 9-5. Adults $8, senior citizens 62 & over $7, youth 4-17 $6, family $25; discounts to groups, AAM members & military; members & children under 4 no charge. &
Attendance: 100,000 (actual)

TAUTPHAUS PARK ZOO, 2725 Carnival Way, Idaho Falls, ID 83402. Mailing Address: P.O. Box 50220, Idaho Falls, ID 83405-0220. Tel.: 208-612-8552. Fax: 208-528-6256.
E-mail: ifzoo@idahofallszoo.org
Web Site: www.idahofallszoo.org
Key Personnel: Supt., Linda Beard.
Institution Type/Description: Zoo.
Hours & Admission Prices: mid-April to Sept. daily 9-4; Memorial Day to Labor Day daily 9-5. Adults 13 & over $7, seniors 62 & over $5.50, children 4-12 $4; children 3 & under no charge. &
Attendance: 125,000 (estimated)

WILLARD ARTS CENTER, CARR AND HALL GALLERIES, 498 A St., Idaho Falls, ID 83402-3617. Tel.: 208-522-0471. Facebook: Idaho Falls Arts Council.
E-mail: info@idahofallsarts.org
Web Site: www.idahofallsarts.org
Key Personnel: Exec. Dir., Brandi Newton; Dir. Visual Arts, Georgina Goodlander; Technical Dir., Brad Higbee; Devel. Coord., Kate Salomon; Mgr. Mktg., Amy Carr.
Institution Type/Description: Art Gallery.
Hours & Admission Prices: Willard Arts Center: Mon.-Fri. 9-5, Sat. 10-4. No charge; donations accepted.

Island Park

JOHNNY SACK'S CABIN, Big Springs, Hwy. 20, Island Park, ID 83429. Mailing Address: Ashton/Island Park Ranger District, Box 858, Ashton, ID 83420. Tel.: 208-652-7442.
Institution Type/Description: Historic House: housed in the hand-built former home of German immigrant, Johnny Sack; built in 1939. Listed on the National Register of Historic Places.
Hours & Admission Prices: mid-June to Labor Day daily 10-4. No charge; donations accepted.

Jerome

JEROME COUNTY HISTORICAL SOCIETY, INC. AND IDAHO FARM & RANCH MUSEUM, 212 1st Ave. E., Jerome, ID 83338-2325. Mailing Address: P.O. Box 50, Jerome, ID 83338-0050. Tel.: 208-324-5641. Fax: 208-324-7694. Facebook: Jerome County Idaho Historical Society.
E-mail: info@historicaljeromecounty.com
Web Site: www.historicaljeromecounty.com
Key Personnel: C.E.O., Dale Ross; Treas., Shonna Fraser; Cur., Marguerite Roberson.
Institution Type/Description: General Museum.
Hours & Admission Prices: Museum: Jan.-March Thurs.-Sat. 1-4; April-Dec. Tues.-Sat. 1-5. No charge; donations accepted. Idaho Farm & Ranch Museum by appointment. IFARM: adults $5, seniors & youth 7-18 $2, children under 7 no charge. Live History Day in Sept.: adults $5, children under 12 no charge. Closed legal holidays. &
Attendance: 750 (estimated)

LAND OF THE YANKEE FORK HISTORIC ASSOCIATION MUSEUM, 249 N. 250 W., Jerome, ID 83338. Mailing Address: c/o Land of the Yankee Fork Historical Assn., P.O. Box 57, Stanley, ID 83278. Tel.: 208-410-5168.

E-mail: musicratdog@gmail.com
Formerly: Custer Museum
Key Personnel: District Forest Ranger, Russ Camper.
Institution Type/Description: History Museum: located on site of Custer Gold Mining Town.
Hours & Admission Prices: Memorial Day weekend to Labor Day daily 10-5. No charge; donations accepted. &
Attendance: 10,000 (estimated)

Kellogg

CRYSTAL GOLD MINE MUSEUM, 51931 Silver Valley Rd., Kellogg, ID 83837. Tel.: 208-783-4653. Fax: 208-783-4653.
E-mail: crystalgoldmine1881@gmail.com
Web Site: www.goldmine-idaho.com
Institution Type/Description: Natural History Museum: housed in an 1880s underground gold mine.
Hours & Admission Prices: May-Sept. daily 9-6; Oct.-April daily 10-4. Adults $14, senior citizens $12, children 4-16 $8.50; children under 4 no charge.

SHOSHONE COUNTY MINING AND SMELTING MUSEUM DBA THE STAFF HOUSE MUSEUM, 820 McKinley Ave., Kellogg, ID 83837-2525. Mailing Address: P.O. Box 783, Kellogg, ID 83837-0783. Tel.: 208-786-4141.
E-mail: admin@staffhousemuseum.com
Web Site: www.staffhousemuseum.com
Key Personnel: Pres. (V), Oradell Triplett.
Institution Type/Description: Mining & Smelting Museum: housed in the historic home of Stanley A. Easton, manager of Bunker Hill & Sullivan Mining & Concentrating Company; later converted to a residence for single Bunker Hill staff members.
Hours & Admission Prices: May-Sept. daily 10-6; other times by appointment. Suggested: adults $4, seniors 55 & over $3, children 6-18 $1; discounts to groups; members & children under 6 no charge.
Attendance: 2,600 (actual)

Ketchum

GAIL SEVERN GALLERY, 400 First Ave. N., Ketchum, ID 83340. Mailing Address: P.O. Box 1679, Ketchum, ID 83340. Tel.: 208-726-5079. Fax: 208-726-5092.
E-mail: info@gailseverngallery.com
Web Site: www.gailseverngallery.com
Institution Type/Description: Art Gallery.
Hours & Admission Prices: Mon.-Sat. 9-6, Sun. 12-6.

KETCHUM/SUN VALLEY HISTORICAL SOCIETY, 180 1st Ave. E., Ketchum, ID 83340. Mailing Address: P.O. Box 1641, Ketchum, ID 83353-1641. Tel.: 208-726-8118.
Institution Type/Description: Historical Society Museum.
Hours & Admission Prices: Mon.-Fri. 12-4, Sat. 1-4. Adults $5; children under 18 & members no charge; donations accepted.
Attendance: 750 (estimated)

SUN VALLEY CENTER FOR THE ARTS, 191 5th St. E., Ketchum, ID 83340. Mailing Address: P.O. Box 656, Sun Valley, ID 83353-0656. Tel.: 208-726-9491. Fax: 208-726-2344.
E-mail: information@sunvalleycenter.org
Web Site: www.sunvalleycenter.org
Key Personnel: Exec. Dir., Sally Boettger; Pres. (V), Tod Hamachek; Vice Pres., Shelley Williams; Artistic Dir., Kristin Poole.
Institution Type/Description: Art Museum.
Hours & Admission Prices: Summer: Mon.-Fri. 9-5, Sat. 11-5; Winter: Mon.-Fri. 9-5. No charge. &

Kooskia

LOCHSA HISTORICAL RANGER STATION, US Hwy. 12 Mile Marker 121.5, Kooskia, ID 83539. Mailing Address: 502 Lowry St., Kooskia, ID 83539. Tel.: 208-926-4274. Fax: 208-926-6450.
E-mail: cschacher@fs.fed.us
Web Site: www.fs.usda.gov
Formerly: Lochsa Ranger Station
Key Personnel: Central Zone Archaeologist, Cindy Schacher.
Institution Type/Description: Historic Building: housed in a former forest service ranger station used during the 1920s & 1930s.
Hours & Admission Prices: Memorial Day to Labor Day daily 9-5. No charge; donations accepted.
Attendance: 6,000 (estimated)

Lava Hot Springs

SOUTH BANNOCK COUNTY HISTORICAL CENTER, 110 E. Main St., Lava Hot Springs, ID 83246. Mailing Address: P.O. Box 387, Lava Hot Springs, ID 83246-0387. Tel.: 208-776-5254.
E-mail: sobanco83246@gmail.com
Web Site: lavahistoricmuseum.weebly.com
Institution Type/Description: Historical Society.
Hours & Admission Prices: Daily 12-5; other times by appointment. Admission $2. &
Attendance: 16,123 (actual)

Lewiston

LEWIS-CLARK STATE COLLEGE CENTER FOR ARTS & HISTORY, 500 8th Ave., Lewiston, ID 83501-2698. Mailing Address: 415 Main St., Lewiston, ID 83501-1821. Tel.: 208-792-2243. Fax: 208-792-2850.
E-mail: admissions@lcsc.edu
Web Site: www.lcsc.edu
Institution Type/Description: Art & History Museum: housed in the former Vollmer Great Bargain Store designed by architect, Kirtland Cutter; built in 1884. Listed on the National Register of Historic Places.
Hours & Admission Prices: Tues.-Sat. 11-4.

NEZ PERCE COUNTY HISTORICAL SOCIETY AND MUSEUM, 0306 Third St., Lewiston, ID 83501-1860. Tel.: 208-743-2535. Facebook: NPC Historical Society.
E-mail: npcmuseum@gmail.com
Web Site: www.nezpercecountymuseum.com
Formerly: Luna House Museum
Key Personnel: Exec. Dir., Leah Boots; Pres., Dr. Dan Miller, M.D.; Cur., Mary E. White Romero; Office Asst., Corina Larsen.
Institution Type/Description: History Museum.
Hours & Admission Prices: Jan. to mid-Dec. Tues.-Sat. 10-4. Adults $4, children 11-17 $2; children 10 & under and members no charge. Closed major federal holidays. &
Attendance: 3,472 (actual)

Mackay

LOST RIVER MUSEUM, 109 S. Main, Mackay, ID 83251. Mailing Address: P.O. Box 572, Mackay, ID 83251. Tel.: 208-588-3148.
E-mail: earlandcora@atcnet.net
Formerly: Lost River Museum
Key Personnel: Dir., Earl Lockie; Pres. (V), Lana Pehrson.
Institution Type/Description: History Museum: housed in a remodeled old Western store.
Hours & Admission Prices: Memorial Day through Sept. Fri.-Sat 1-5; other times by appointment. No charge. &
Attendance: 500 (estimated)

Malad

ONEIDA COUNTY PIONEER MUSEUM, 27 Bannock St., Malad, ID 83252-1240. Mailing Address: P.O. Box 79, Malad City, ID 83252-0079. Tel.: 208-766-4847.
E-mail: maladcity@hotmail.com
Web Site: www.maladidaho.org/museum/museum.htm
Institution Type/Description: History Museum: built in 1914.
Hours & Admission Prices: Tues.-Sat. 1-5; other times by appointment. No charge; donations accepted.

McCall

CENTRAL IDAHO HISTORICAL MUSEUM, 1001 State St., McCall, ID 83638-3705. Tel.: 208-634-4497.
E-mail: cihmuseum@gmail.com
Web Site: centralidahohistoricalmuseum.com
Formerly: Central Idaho Cultural Center
Key Personnel: Pres. (V), Marlee Wilcomb.
Institution Type/Description: Historic Site: built in 1937 by the Civilian Conservation Corps. Listed on the National Register of Historic Places.
Hours & Admission Prices: Memorial Day to Sept. 15 Wed.-Sat. 12-3:30; Winter: by appointment. House Tours: adults $3. &
Attendance: 1,250 (estimated)

Melba

CELEBRATION PARK, 6530 Hot Spot Ln., Melba, ID 83641-5275. Tel.: 208-495-2745.
E-mail: tbicak@canyonco.org
Key Personnel: Dir., Tom Bicak; Museum Shop Manager, Laura Barbour.
Institution Type/Description: Park Museum.
Hours & Admission Prices: Celebration Park: daily. Parking $2, overnight parking $5; Visitor Center & Tours: April-Oct. daily 9-4. No charge for tours. Closed major holidays.

Montpelier

NATIONAL OREGON/CALIFORNIA TRAIL CENTER, 320 N. 4th St., Montpelier, ID 83254-1256. Mailing Address: P.O. Box 323, Montpelier, ID 83254-0323. Tel.: 208-847-3800, 866-847-3800 (toll free). Fax: 208-847-1863.
E-mail: info@oregontrailcenter.org
Web Site: www.oregontrailcenter.org
Key Personnel: Dir., Becky Smith; Pres. (V), Al Harrison; Vice Pres., Steve Allred; Sec. & Treas., Jene Parker; Museum Shop Mgr., Cindy Raymond.
Institution Type/Description: History Museum.
Hours & Admission Prices: May-Sept. Sun.-Thurs. 9-5, Fri.-Sat. 9-6; Oct. Tues.-Sat. 10-3; Nov.-April Mon.-Thurs. 10-3 by reservation. Tours every 1/2 hour. Discounts to AAM & ICOM members. &
Attendance: 48,000 (actual)

Moscow

THE APPALOOSA MUSEUM AND HERITAGE CENTER, 2720 W. Pullman Rd., Moscow, ID 83843-4024. Tel.: 208-882-5578, ext. 279. Fax: 208-882-8150.
E-mail: museum@appaloosa.com
Web Site: www.appaloosamuseum.com
Key Personnel: Pres. (V), King Rockhill.
Institution Type/Description: History Museum.
Hours & Admission Prices: Mon.-Fri. 10-5, Sat. 10-4. Suggested Donation: adults $2. Closed legal holidays. &
Attendance: 5,000 (estimated)

IDAHO FOREST FIRE MUSEUM, 310 N. Main St., Moscow, ID 83843-2629. Tel.: 208-882-4767.
Institution Type/Description: Firefighting History Museum.
Hours & Admission Prices: Jan.-May Mon.-Fri. 9-4; June-Dec. Mon.-Fri. 9-5, Sat. 9-4. No charge.

MCCONNELL MANSION, 110 S. Adams, Moscow, ID 83843-2829. Mailing Address: 327 E. Second St., Moscow, ID 83843-2819. Tel.: 208-882-1004.
E-mail: lchslibrary@latah.id.us
Web Site: www.latahcountyhistoricalsociety.org
Key Personnel: Exec. Dir., Dulce Kersting-Lark; Cur., Zachary Wnek.
Institution Type/Description: Local History Museum: housed in 1886 Governor McConnell Mansion.
Hours & Admission Prices: Tues.-Fri. 1-4, Sat. call for hours. Suggested Donation: family $5, adults $2.
Attendance: 3,500 (estimated)

UNIVERSITY OF IDAHO PRICHARD ART GALLERY, 414 S. Main St., Moscow, ID 83843-2916. Tel.: 208-885-3586. Fax: 208-885-3622. Facebook: Prichard Art Gallery.
E-mail: rrowley@uidaho.edu
Web Site: www.uidaho.edu/caa/galleries-centers-and-labs/prichard
Key Personnel: Dir., Roger Rowley.
Institution Type/Description: Art Gallery.
Hours & Admission Prices: Winter: Tues.-Sat. 10-8, Sun. 10-6; Summer: Tues.-Fri. 1-7, Sat. 9-4. No charge. &
Attendance: 17,000 (actual)

Mountain Home

BRUNEAU DUNES OBSERVATORY, 27608 Sand Dunes Rd., Mountain Home, ID 83647. Tel.: 208-366-7919. Fax: 208-366-2844.
E-mail: bru@idpr.idaho.gov
Web Site: parksandrecreation.idaho.gov/parks/bruneau-dunes
Institution Type/Description: Observatory & Visitor Center.
Hours & Admission Prices: Observatory: April to mid-Oct. Fri.-Sat. one hour before sundown to midnight. Park: $5 per vehicle. Observatory: $3 per person; children 5 & under no charge. &

MOUNTAIN HOME HISTORICAL MUSEUM, 180 S. 3rd E., Mountain Home, ID 83647-3019. Tel.: 208-587-6847. Facebook: Mountain Home Historical Society.
E-mail: director@mountainhomemuseum.com
Web Site: www.mountainhomemuseum.com
Key Personnel: Dir., Debbie Shoemaker; Pres. (V), Marilyn Landers.
Institution Type/Description: Historic Building: housed in the former Carnegie Public Library; built in 1908. Listed on the National Register of Historic Places.
Hours & Admission Prices: Tues.-Fri. 10-4. No charge; donations accepted. Closed New Year's Day; Martin Luther King Jr. Day; Presidents' Day; Memorial Day; Independence Day; Labor Day; Columbus Day; Veterans Day; Thanksgiving; Christmas.

Mullan

CAPTAIN JOHN MULLAN MUSEUM, 229 Earle St., Mullan, ID 83846. Mailing Address: P.O. Box 675, Mullan, ID 83846-0675. Tel.: 208-744-1155 (June-Aug.) & 1557 (Sept.-May).
Web Site: www.mullanmuseum.org
Key Personnel: Pres. (V), Butch Jacobson.
Institution Type/Description: History Museum: housed in the old Liberty Theater.
Hours & Admission Prices: June-Aug. 10-4; other times by appointment. No charge; donations accepted. Closed holidays.
Attendance: 850 (estimated)

Murphy

OWYHEE COUNTY HISTORICAL MUSEUM, 17085 Basey St., Murphy, ID 83650. Tel.: 208-495-2319. Fax: 208-495-9824.
E-mail: administration@owyheemuseum.org
Web Site: www.owyheemuseum.org
Key Personnel: Exec. Dir., Amy Johnson; Pres. (V), Mary O'Malley; Office Mgr., Vivian Good; Librarian/Archivist, Julie Hyslop; Museum Shop Mgr., Betsy Kendrick.
Institution Type/Description: Historical Society Museum.
Hours & Admission Prices: Tues.-Sat. 10-4. Adults $2; discounts to AAM & ICOM members & Owyhee County Residence; members no charge. Closed holidays. &
Attendance: 14,321 (estimated)

Nampa

CANYON COUNTY HISTORICAL SOCIETY & MUSEUM, 1200 Front St., Nampa, ID 83651-3931. Mailing Address: P.O. Box 595, Nampa, ID 83653-0595. Tel.: 208-467-7611.
E-mail: info@canyoncountyhistory.com
Web Site: www.canyoncountyhistory.com
Institution Type/Description: Historical Society Museum.
Hours & Admission Prices: Depot: May-Oct. Thurs.-Fri. 11-4, Sat. 10-2; Nov.-April Thurs.-Fri. 11-4, Sat. 11-2. Our Memories Indian Creek Museum: Tues. & Fri. 11-4; other times by appointment. Adults $3, youth 13-18 $2, seniors & children 6-12 $1; members no charge.
Attendance: 5,000 (estimated)

DEER FLAT NATIONAL WILDLIFE REFUGE, 13751 Upper Embankment Rd., Nampa, ID 83686-8046. Tel.: 208-467-9278. Fax: 208-467-1019. Facebook: Deer Flat NWR.
E-mail: deerflat@fws.gov
Web Site: www.fws.gov/deerflat
Key Personnel: Refuge Mgr., Annette de Knijf.
Institution Type/Description: Wildlife Refuge.
Hours & Admission Prices: Park: daily daylight hours. Visitor Center: Mon.-Fri. 8-4, Sat. 10-4. No charge. Closed Federal holidays. &
Attendance: 170,000 (estimated)

WARHAWK AIR MUSEUM, 201 Municipal Dr., Nampa, ID 83687-8582. Tel.: 208-465-6446. Fax: 208-465-6232.
E-mail: admin@warhawkairmuseum.org
Web Site: warhawkairmuseum.org
Key Personnel: Exec. Dir., Sue Paul; Pres. (V), John Paul; Museum Shop Mgr., Tammy John; Administrative Asst., Heather Mullins.
Institution Type/Description: Military Museum.
Hours & Admission Prices: Tues.-Sat. 10-5, Sun. 11-4. Adults $10, senior citizens & military with ID $8, children 5-12 $4; discount to AAA members; members no charge. &
Attendance: 23,500 (estimated)

Oakley

OAKLEY VALLEY HISTORICAL MUSEUM, 140 W. Main St., Oakley, ID 83346. Mailing Address: P.O. Box 239, Oakley, ID 83346-0239. Tel.: 208-431-9202.
E-mail: oakleymuseum@hotmail.com
Key Personnel: Pres., Robert Fehlman.
Institution Type/Description: History Museum: listed on the National Register of Historic Places.
Hours & Admission Prices: Summer: Fri.-Sat. 1-4; other times by appointment. No charge; donations accepted.
Attendance: 1,000 (estimated)

Orofino

CLEARWATER HISTORICAL MUSEUM, 433 Bartlett St., Orofino, ID 83544-1454. Mailing Address: P.O. Box 1454, Orofino, ID 83544-1454. Tel.: 208-476-5033.
E-mail: chmuseum@frontier.com
Web Site: www.clearwatermuseum.org
Key Personnel: Pres., Mike Goodwin; Vice Pres., Rodger Colgan.
Institution Type/Description: History Museum.
Hours & Admission Prices: mid-May to Sept. Tues.-Sat. 12:30-5:30; Oct. to early May Tues.-Sat. 1:30-4:30. No charge; donations accepted. Closed holidays.
Attendance: 1,500 (estimated)

Paris

PARIS TABERNACLE HISTORICAL SITE, 109 S. Main St., Paris, ID 83261. Mailing Address: c/o Bear Lake Valley Convention & Visitors Bureau, P.O. Box 471, Garden City, UT 84028. Tel.: 208-945-2686, 800-448-2327.
E-mail: visitors@bearlake.org
Web Site: www.bearlake.org/recreation/history-activities
Institution Type/Description: Historic Building: housed in the Church of Jesus Christ of Latter Day Saints; built by Mormon pioneers in 1889. Listed on the National Register of Historic Places.
Hours & Admission Prices: Guided Tours: Memorial Day to Labor Day daily 9:30-5:30. No charge.
Attendance: 9,000 (actual)

Parma

OLD FORT BOISE REPLICA AND MUSEUM, 20847 Old Fort Boise Rd., Parma, ID 83660. Mailing Address: P.O. Box 942, Parma, ID 83660-0942. Tel.: 208-722-5138.
Institution Type/Description: History Museum.
Hours & Admission Prices: June-Aug. Fri.-Sun. 1-3; other times by appointment. No charge; donations accepted.
Attendance: 620 (estimated)

Payette

PAYETTE COUNTY MUSEUM, 90 S. 9th St., Payette, ID 83661. Mailing Address: P.O. Box 696, Payette, ID 83661-0696. Tel.: 208-642-4883.
E-mail: payettemuseum@qwestoffice.net
Institution Type/Description: History Museum: housed in a former church.
Hours & Admission Prices: Wed.-Sat. 12-4; other times by appointment. No charge; donations accepted.

Pierce

J. HOWARD BRADBURY MEMORIAL LOGGING MUSEUM, 101 S. Main St., Pierce, ID 83546. Mailing Address: P.O. Box 378, Weippe, ID 83553-0378. Tel.: 208-464-2531 & 435-4670.
E-mail: jhbloggingmuseum@gmail.com
Institution Type/Description: Logging History Museum.
Hours & Admission Prices: mid-June to mid-Oct. Fri.-Sat. 12-4; other times by appointment.

Pocatello

BANNOCK COUNTY HISTORICAL SOCIETY MUSEUM, 3000 Ave. of the Chiefs, Pocatello, ID 83204. Mailing Address: P. O. Box 253, Pocatello, ID 83204-0253. Tel.: 208-233-0434; Fax: 208-234-3773.
E-mail: bancohismus@gmail.com
Web Site: www.bchm-id.org

Key Personnel: Society Pres., Richard Hansen; Dir. & Cur., Lynn Murdoch.
Institution Type/Description: History Museum.
Hours & Admission Prices: Memorial Day to Labor Day Mon.-Sat. 10-6, Sun. 1-5; Labor Day to Memorial Day Tues.-Sat. 10-4. Summer fees: adults $6, seniors & military $5; youth 6-17 $3; Winter fees: adults $5, seniors $4, youth 6-17 $3; members no charge.
Attendance: 6,000 (actual)

FORT HALL REPLICA, 3000 Ave of the Chiefs, Upper Level Ross Park, Pocatello, ID 83204. Mailing Address: Pocatello Parks & Recreation, 144 Wilson Ave., Pocatello, ID 83201. Tel.: 208-234-1795; 208-233-0434. Fax: 208-234-6578. Facebook: Fort Hall Replica.
E-mail: bchm.director@gmail.com
Web Site: www.forthall.net
Key Personnel: Dir. & Cur., Lynn Murdoch; Asst. Dir.. Collections Mgr. & Registrar, Deb Mullins.
Institution Type/Description: History Museum: housed in a replica of the historic facility that served pioneers along the Oregon Trail.
Hours & Admission Prices: Memorial Day to Labor Day Mon.-Sat. 10-6, Sun. 1-5. Adults $4, seniors $3, youth 3-17 $2; discounts to school & large groups; Bannock County Historical Society members no charge.
Attendance: 2,500 (estimated)

IDAHO MUSEUM OF NATURAL HISTORY, 5th & Dillon, Pocatello, ID 83209. Mailing Address: 921 S. 8th Ave., Stop 8096, Pocatello, ID 83201. Tel.: 208-282-3168. Fax: 208-282-5893. Facebook: Idaho Museum of Natural History.
E-mail: imnh@isu.edu
Web Site: imnh.isu.edu
Key Personnel: Dir. & Cur. Anthropology, Dr. Herbert Maschner; Store Mgr., Bill Angle; Earth Sciences Cur., Dr. Leif Tapanila; Education Resource Coord. & Education Cur., Kelly Pokorny; Life Sciences Cur., Dr. Rick Williams; Southeast Idaho Repository Mgr., Amy Commendador; Registrar, Curt Schmitz; Office Admin., Mary Moses; Office Admin., Faith Tan.
Institution Type/Description: Natural History Museum.
Hours & Admission Prices: Tues.-Sat. 11-5. Adults $5, college students with valid ID $2, children K-12 $1. Closed holidays.
Attendance: 9,147 (actual)

MIND'S EYE GALLERY - IDAHO STATE UNIVERSITY, Rendezvous Complex, 921 S. 8th Ave., Pocatello, ID 83209. Tel.: 208-282-3451.
E-mail: info@isu.edu
Institution Type/Description: Art Gallery.
Hours & Admission Prices: Mon.-Fri. 8-5.

THE MUSEUM OF CLEAN, 711 S. Second Ave., Pocatello, ID 83201-6520. Tel.: 208-236-6906. Facebook: Don Aslett's Museum of Clean.
E-mail: contact@museumofclean.com
Web Site: museumofclean.com
Formerly: Don Aslett's Cleaning Museum
Key Personnel: C.E.O., Don Aslett; Dir., Brad Kisling.
Institution Type/Description: History Museum.
Hours & Admission Prices: Tues.-Sat. 10-5. Family (2 adults, 3 children) $20, adults $6, children 3-15 $5, children under 3 free; discounts for AAA members.
Attendance: 9,200 (actual)

POCATELLO ART CENTER, GALLERY AND SCHOOL, 444 N. Main, Pocatello, ID 83204-5071. Tel.: 208-232-0970.
E-mail: pocartctr@ida.net
Web Site: www.pocatelloartctr.org
Key Personnel: Pres. (V), Carolyn Purnell.
Institution Type/Description: Art Gallery.
Hours & Admission Prices: Mon.-Fri. No charge; donations accepted. Closed Federal holidays.

POCATELLO ZOO, 3101 Ave. of the Chiefs, Pocatello, ID 83201. Tel.: 208-234-6264.
E-mail: yourzoo@pocatello.us
Web Site: www.pocatellozoo.org
Key Personnel: Zoo Dir., Scott Ransom; Cur. Education, Bonnie Jakubos.
Institution Type/Description: Zoo.
Hours & Admission Prices: April & Sept.-Oct. Sat.-Sun. 10-4; May to Labor Day daily 10-5. Adults $5.75, seniors 60 & over $4.50, children 3-11 $3.75; children 2 & under no charge.

THE TRANSITION GALLERY - IDAHO STATE UNIVERSITY, Earl R. Pond Student Union, 921 S. 8th Ave., Pocatello, ID 83209. Tel.: 208-282-3451.
E-mail: babcrya9@isu.edu
Web Site: www.isu.edu/union/student-life/art-gallery
Institution Type/Description: Art Gallery.
Hours & Admission Prices: Mon.-Fri. 10-8.

Priest Lake

PRIEST LAKE MUSEUM ASSOCIATION, 38 W. Lakeshore Dr., Priest Lake, ID 83856. Mailing Address: P.O. Box 44, Coolin, ID 83821-0044. Tel.: 208-443-2676.
E-mail: priestlakemuseum@gmail.com
Web Site: www.plmuseum.org
Formerly: Priest Lake Museum
Key Personnel: Pres. (V), Mike Rydbom; Museum Shop Mgr., Kay Coykendall.
Institution Type/Description: Historic Building Museum: housed in a former forest ranger cabin; c.1930s.
Hours & Admission Prices: Memorial Day to Labor Day Tues.-Sun. 10-4. No charge; donations accepted. &
Attendance: 3,500 (actual)

Priest River

KEYSER HOUSE TIMBER MUSEUM, 390 Montgomery St., Priest River, ID 83856. Mailing Address: Priest River Museum & Timber Education Ctr. Inc., P.O. Box 1204, Priest River, ID 83856.
Key Personnel: Pres. (V), Peggylee A. Smith.
Institution Type/Description: Historic House Museum: housed in the former home of Henry and Elizabeth Keyser; built in 1895.
Hours & Admission Prices: Summer: Mon.-Fri. 8-4; call for additional hours. No charge; donations accepted.
Attendance: 300 (estimated)

Rexburg

LEGACY FLIGHT MUSEUM, Rexburg Airport, 435 Kelly Johnson Way, Rexburg, ID 83440. Mailing Address: P.O. Box 122, Rexburg, ID 83440-0122. Tel.: 208-359-5905. Fax: 208-356-7989.
E-mail: legacyflightmuseum@yahoo.com
Web Site: www.legacyflightmuseum.com
Key Personnel: Dir. & Pres. (V), John Bagley; Chm. (V), Glenn Embree; Museum Shop Mgr., Noelle Walker.
Institution Type/Description: Military History Museum.
Hours & Admission Prices: Memorial Day to Labor Day Mon.-Sat. 9-5; Sept.-May Sat. 9-5. Adults $6; discounts to veterans & BYU-Idaho students.
Attendance: 1,000 (estimated)

MUSEUM OF REXBURG: HOME OF THE TETON FLOOD EXHIBIT, 51 N. Center St., Rexburg, ID 83440-1539. Tel.: 208-359-3063. Fax: 208-359-3063.
E-mail: museum@rexburg.org
Web Site: museum.rexburg.org
Institution Type/Description: History Museum: the disaster of the Teton Dam collapse on June 5, 1976.
Hours & Admission Prices: Mon. & Thurs.-Sat. 10-2. Adults $2; youth 4-18 $1; discounts to groups of 10 or more; children 3 & under no charge. &
Attendance: 5,000 (estimated)

UPPER SNAKE RIVER VALLEY HISTORICAL SOCIETY, 51 N. Center St., Rexburg, ID 83440-1539. Mailing Address: P.O. Box 244, Rexburg, ID 83440-0244. Tel.: 208-356-9100. Facebook; Twitter.
E-mail: usrvhistsoc@hotmail.com
Web Site: rexburghistoricalsociety.com
Institution Type/Description: Local Historic Museum.
Hours & Admission Prices: Memorial Day to Labor Day Mon. 10-7, Tues.-Sat. 10-5; Winter: Mon. 11-7, Tues.-Fri. 11-5. Adults $2, children 12-18 $1; children under 12 no charge. Closed national holidays. &
Attendance: 10,129 (actual)

Rigby

JEFFERSON COUNTY HISTORICAL SOCIETY AND FARNSWORTH TV PIONEER MUSEUM, 118 West 1st South, Rigby, ID 83442-1303. Mailing Address: P.O. Box 284, Rigby, ID 83442-0284. Tel.: 208-745-8423.
E-mail: farnsworthtvmuseum@outlook.com

Key Personnel: Pres. (V), Gary Spaulding; Sec., Kathryn McLain; Treas., Linda Kite; Cur., Cleave Reddick.
Institution Type/Description: History Museum.
Hours & Admission Prices: Tues.-Sat. 1-5. Requested Donations: adults $2, children 6-17 $1; discounts to veterans & school groups; children under 6 no charge. Tax-exempt. &
Attendance: 1,500 (estimated)

Rupert

MINIDOKA COUNTY HISTORICAL MUSEUM, 99 E. Baseline Rd., Rupert, ID 83350. Mailing Address: Box 21, Rupert, ID 83350-0021. Tel.: 208-436-0336. Facebook: Minidoka Museum.
E-mail: mchs@pmt.org
Web Site: minidokamuseum.weebly.com
Key Personnel: Pres., Gus Bryngelson; Museum Shop Mgr., Ginger Cooper.
Institution Type/Description: History Museum.
Hours & Admission Prices: Mon.-Sat. 10-3. No charge; donations accepted. Closed New Year's Day; Memorial Day; Independence Day; Labor Day; Thanksgiving Weekend; Christmas Day. &
Attendance: 1,100 (actual)

MINIDOKA NATIONAL WILDLIFE REFUGE, Rte. 4, 961 E. Minidoka Dam, Rupert, ID 83350-9414. Tel.: 208-436-3589.
E-mail: jeffrey_krueger@fws.gov
Web Site: www.fws.gov/refuge/minidoka
Institution Type/Description: Wildlife Refuge.
Hours & Admission Prices: Call for hours.

Saint Maries

HISTORICAL HUGHES HOUSE, 538 Main Ave., Saint Maries, ID 83861.
Key Personnel: Pres. (V), Priscilla Derry.
Institution Type/Description: Historic House Museum: housed in a former men's club and later a doctor's office; built in 1902.
Hours & Admission Prices: mid-May to Sept. Wed.-Sun. 12-4; call to confirm. No charge; donations accepted.
Attendance: 300 (estimated)

Salmon

LEMHI COUNTY HISTORICAL MUSEUM, 210 Main, Salmon, ID 83467-4111. Tel.: 208-756-3342. Facebook: Lemhi County Historical Museum.
E-mail: llemhi@centurytel.net
Web Site: www.lemhicountymuseum.org
Key Personnel: Pres. (V), Bob Russell; Vice Pres., John Logan; Sec., Fredde Haworth; Cur., Clair Wiley.
Institution Type/Description: History Museum.
Hours & Admission Prices: May 15 to mid-Oct. Mon.-Fri. 10-4, Sat. 11-3. Admission 12 & over $2; members & children under 12 no charge. &
Attendance: 5,500 (estimated)

SACAJAWEA INTERPRETIVE, CULTURAL & EDUCATIONAL CENTER, 110 Lewis and Clark, Salmon, ID 83467-5340. Mailing Address: 200 Main St., Salmon, ID 83467-4111. Tel.: 208-756-1188.
E-mail: jlb.sac@gmail.com
Web Site: www.sacajaweacenter.org
Key Personnel: Dir., Judy Barkley.
Institution Type/Description: History Museum.
Hours & Admission Prices: Park: daily. Visitor Center: May-Oct. Family $12, adult $5. &

Sandpoint

BIRD AVIATION MUSEUM & INVENTION CENTER, Bird Ranch Rd., Sandpoint, ID 83864. Mailing Address: P.O. Box 817, Sandpoint, ID 83864. Tel.: 208-255-4321. Fax: 208-255-7630.
E-mail: rachel@birdaviationmuseum.com
Web Site: www.birdaviationmuseum.com
Key Personnel: Dir., Rachel Riddle Schwam.
Institution Type/Description: Aviation History Museum.
Hours & Admission Prices: May 17 to Oct. 8 Mon.-Sat. 8-4; other times by appointment. No charge.

BONNER COUNTY HISTORICAL MUSEUM, 611 S. Ella Ave., Sandpoint, ID 83864-1100. Tel.: 208-263-2344.

E-mail: bchs@frontier.com
Web Site: www.bonnercountyhistory.org
Key Personnel: Exec. Dir., Olivia Luther; Cur., Heather Upton.
Institution Type/Description: Local History Museum.
Hours & Admission Prices: Tues.-Fri. 10-4, 1st Sat. each month 10-2. Adults $4, students $3, children 6-18 $1. discounts to AAM members; members, children under 6 & Sat. no charge. &
Attendance: 5,000 (estimated)

Shoshone

SHOSHONE INDIAN ICE CAVES, 1561 N. Hwy. 75, Shoshone, ID 83352-5246. Tel.: 208-886-2058.
E-mail: coastlover22@live.com
Web Site: shoshoneicecaves.com
Institution Type/Description: History Museum.
Hours & Admission Prices: May-Sept. daily 8am-7:15pm. Adults $10, seniors $8, children 4-12 $6; discounts to groups; children 3 & under no charge.

Spalding

NEZ PERCE NATIONAL HISTORICAL PARK, 39063 U.S. Hwy. 95, Spalding, ID 83540-9715. Mailing Address: P.O. Box 237, Wisdom, MT 59761-0237. Tel.: 208-843-7009. Fax: 208-843-7003.
E-mail: bob_chenoweth@nps.gov
Web Site: www.nps.gov/nepe
Key Personnel: Supt., Steve Black; Cur., Bob Chenoweth; Museum Shop Mgr., Mary Lou Tiede; Archivist & Library Technician, Robert Applegate; Museum Technician, Linda J. Paisano.
Institution Type/Description: Park Museum: located on a site of prehistoric occupation & early mission.
Hours & Admission Prices: Winter: daily 8-4:30; Summer: daily 8-5:30. No charge. Closed New Year's Day; Thanksgiving; Christmas. &
Attendance: 152,393 (actual)

Twin Falls

HERRETT CENTER FOR ARTS & SCIENCE, FAULKNER PLANETARIUM AND CENTENNIAL OBSERVATORY, 315 Falls Ave., College of Southern Idaho, Twin Falls, ID 83301-3367. Mailing Address: P.O. Box 1238, Twin Falls, ID 83303-1238. Tel.: 208-732-6655. Fax: 208-736-4712.
E-mail: herrett@csi.edu
Web Site: herrett.csi.edu
Key Personnel: Dir., Dr. Teri Fattig; Art Gallery Mgr., Milica Popovic; Planetarium Mgr., Rick Greenawald; Observatory Mgr., Chris Anderson; Herrett Center Coord. & Gift Shop Mgr., Carolyn Browning; Exhibits & Collections Mgr., Joey Heck; Mktg. Coord., Doug Maughan; Education Coord., Laura Browarny; Events & Academic Coord., Kindy Combe; Facility, Display & Planetarium Technician, Robert (Nick) Peterson.
Institution Type/Description: Arts & Science Museum, Planetarium & Observatory.
Hours & Admission Prices: Tues. & Fri. 9:30-9, Wed.-Thurs. 9:30-4:30, Sat. 1-9. Planetarium: call for show times. Planetarium: adults $6, senior $5, students & children 2-18 $4; discounts to AAM members; children under 2 no charge. Museum: no charge. Observatory: call for hours. Closed holidays. &
Attendance: 60,000 (estimated)

Wallace

NORTHERN PACIFIC DEPOT RAILROAD MUSEUM, 219 6th St., Wallace, ID 83873-2283. Mailing Address: P.O. Box 469, Wallace, ID 83873-0469. Tel.: 208-752-0111. Fax: 208-753-9361.
E-mail: npdepot@gmail.com
Web Site: www.npdepot.org
Key Personnel: Museum Shop Mgr., Shauna Hillman.
Institution Type/Description: Railroad Museum: listed on the National Register of Historical Places.
Hours & Admission Prices: April 15-Oct. 15 daily 9-5. Bus Groups $30, family $8, adults $3.50; discounts to AAM, ICOM & museum members.
Attendance: 8,500 (estimated)

OASIS BORDELLO MUSEUM, 605 Cedar St., Wallace, ID 83873. Mailing Address: P.O. Box 928, Osburn, ID 83849. Tel.: 208-753-0801. Facebook: @oasisbordellomuseum.
Key Personnel: Mgr., Eva Truean.
Institution Type/Description: History Museum: housed in a former brothel.
Hours & Admission Prices: May-Oct. Mon.-Sat. 10-5, Sun. 11-3. Adults $5.

SIERRA SILVER MINE TOUR, 420 5th St., Wallace, ID 83873-2212. Tel.: 208-752-5151. Facebook: Sierra Silver Mine.
E-mail: info@silverminetour.org
Web Site: www.silverminetour.org
Institution Type/Description: Geology Museum.
Hours & Admission Prices: May & Sept. daily 10-2; June-Aug. daily 10-4. Adults $15, seniors 60 & over $13, children 4-16 $8.50; discounts to groups; children under 4 no charge.
Attendance: 10,000 (actual)

WALLACE DISTRICT MINING MUSEUM, 509 Bank St., Wallace, ID 83873-2224. Mailing Address: P.O. Box 469, Wallace, ID 83873-0469. Tel.: 208-556-1592. Fax: 208-556-1592.
E-mail: director@wallaceminingmuseum.com
Web Site: www.wallaceminingmuseum.com
Key Personnel: Exec. Dir., Jim McReynolds; Museum Shop Mgr., Peggy McReynolds.
Institution Type/Description: Mining Museum.
Hours & Admission Prices: Wed.-Mon. 9-3. &
Attendance: 49,000 (estimated)

Weippe

WEIPPE DISCOVERY CENTER, 204 Wood St., Weippe, ID 83553. Mailing Address: P.O. Box 435, Weippe, ID 83553-0435. Tel.: 208-435-4058. Fax: 208-435-4374.
E-mail: discovery@weippe.com
Web Site: www.weippediscoverycenter.com
Key Personnel: Dir., Terri Summerfield.
Institution Type/Description: History Museum.
Hours & Admission Prices: Mon. & Thurs.-Fri. 10-5, Tues.-Wed. 10-7, Sat. 10-1. No charge; donations accepted. &
Attendance: 600

WEIPPE HILLTOP HERITAGE MUSEUM, 105 N. 1st St. E., Weippe, ID 83553. Mailing Address: P.O. Box 279, Weippe, ID 83553-0279. Tel.: 208-435-4200.
E-mail: salmar930@yahoo.com
Key Personnel: Pres. (V), Sally Marks; Chm. (V), Dawn Cloin.
Institution Type/Description: History Museum.
Hours & Admission Prices: May-Oct. Wed. & Fri.-Sat. 12-4; other times by appointment. No charge; donations accepted. &
Attendance: 1,200 (actual)

Weiser

SNAKE RIVER HERITAGE CENTER, 2295 Paddock Ave., Weiser, ID 83672-1195. Mailing Address: P.O. Box 307, Weiser, ID 83672-0307. Tel.: 208-549-0205. Facebook: Weiser Museum.
E-mail: info@weisermuseum.com
Web Site: www.weisermuseum.com
Key Personnel: Pres. Bd. (V), Wes Higgins.
Institution Type/Description: Cultural Center & Museum: housed in 1899-1933 preparatory school.
Hours & Admission Prices: Memorial Day-Labor Day Fri.-Sat. 10-1; tours by appointment. No charge; donations accepted.
Attendance: 1,000 (estimated)

Winchester

WOLF EDUCATION & RESEARCH CENTER, 1721 Forest Rd, Winchester, ID 83555. Mailing Address: P.O. Box 217, Winchester, ID 83555. Tel.: 888-422-1110, ext. 1.
E-mail: chris.anderson@wolfcenter.org
Web Site: wolfcenter.org
Key Personnel: Dir., Chris Anderson.
Institution Type/Description: Nature Center.
Hours & Admission Prices: May & Sept. Self-Guided Tours: Sat.-Sun. 9-4; Guided Tours: call for appointment. Memorial Day to Labor Day Self-Guided Tours: daily 9-5; Guided Tours: daily 7:30-7; other times by appointment.
Attendance: 3,400 (estimated)

ILLINOIS
(485 listings)

Aledo

ESSLEY-NOBLE MUSEUM: MERCER COUNTY HISTORICAL SOCIETY, 1406 S.E. 2nd Ave., Aledo, IL 61231-2504. Mailing Address: P.O. Box 269, Aledo, IL 61231-0269. Tel.: 309-582-2280.
E-mail: mcmuseum@frontier.com
Web Site: www.mchsil.org
Key Personnel: Pres., Ronn Dillavou.
Institution Type/Description: Historical & Preservation Society: housed in the Essley-Noble Memorial Building.
Hours & Admission Prices: April-Oct. Thurs.-Sat. 1-5; Nov.-March Sat. 12-4; groups by appointment. No charge; donations accepted.
Attendance: 1,200 (estimated)

Alton

ALTON MUSEUM OF HISTORY AND ART, INC., 2809 College Ave., Alton, IL 62002-4743. Tel.: 618-462-2763. Facebook: Alton Museum of History and Art Inc.
E-mail: altonmuseum@gmail.com
Web Site: altonmuseum.com
Key Personnel: Founder, Charlene Gill; Chm. (V), Charlene Johnson; Pres., Brian Combs; 1st Vice Pres., Patti Culp; Immediate Past Pres. & Office Mgr., Dr. Norman Showers; Museum Shop Mgr., Lois Lobbig.
Institution Type/Description: History & Art Museum: c.1832 educational building & museum.
Hours & Admission Prices: Wed.-Sat. 10-4, Sun. 1-4. Adults $5, children $1; discounts to seniors on Wed., veterans, and AAM & ICOM members; members & current SIU dental students no charge. Closed New Year's Day; Easter; Independence Day; Thanksgiving; Christmas.
Attendance: 11,000 (actual)

Amboy

AMBOY DEPOT MUSEUM, 50 S. East Ave., Amboy, IL 61310. Mailing Address: P.O. Box 108, Amboy, IL 61310. Tel.: 815-857-4700.
E-mail: information@amboydepotmuseum.org
Web Site: www.amboydepotmuseum.org
Key Personnel: Chm. (V), Jack Dempsey.
Institution Type/Description: Historic Building Museum: housed in a former depot and division headquarters of the Illinois Central Railroad. Listed on the National Register of Historic Places.
Hours & Admission Prices: Sun. & Thurs. 1-4, Fri.-Sat. 10-4. No charge; donations accepted.
Attendance: 2,436 (actual)

Antioch

LAKES REGION HISTORICAL SOCIETY ARCHIVE CENTER, 965 Main St., Antioch, IL 60002. Tel.: 847-395-4912.
E-mail: info@lakesregionhistory.org
Web Site: lakesregionhistory.org
Institution Type/Description: Historical Society Museum.
Hours & Admission Prices: 1st Sat. each month; other times by appointment.

LAKES REGION HISTORICAL SOCIETY MUSEUM, 817 Main St., Antioch, IL 60002. Mailing Address: c/o Lakes Region Historical Society, 965 Main St., Antioch, IL 60002. Tel.: 847-395-4912.
E-mail: info@lakesregionhistory.org
Web Site: lakesregionhistory.org
Institution Type/Description: Historical Society Museum: housed in a former school house; built in 1892.
Hours & Admission Prices: March-Dec. Sat. 11-3. No charge; donations accepted.

LAKES REGIONAL HISTORICAL SOCIETY MEETING HOUSE, 977 Main St., Antioch, IL 60002. Tel.: 847-395-4912.
E-mail: info@lakesregionhistory.org
Web Site: lakesregionhistory.org
Institution Type/Description: Historical Society Museum: housed in a former church; built in 1863.
Hours & Admission Prices: 1st Sat. each month; other times by appointment. No charge; donations accepted.

Arlington Heights

ARLINGTON HEIGHTS HISTORICAL MUSEUM, 110 W. Fremont St., Arlington Heights, IL 60004-5912. Tel.: 847-255-1225. Fax: 847-255-1570.
Web Site: www.ahmuseum.org
Key Personnel: Pres., Warren Wahl; Devel. Coord., Carol Frieburg; Cur., Mickey Horndasch.
Institution Type/Description: History Museum.
Hours & Admission Prices: Tours: Sat.-Sun. 2:30; other times & groups by appointment. Adults $4, children $2; discount to AAM members; members no charge. Heritage Gallery (current exhibit): Fri.-Sun. 1:30-4:30. No charge; donations accepted. Closed national holidays.
Attendance: 14,000 (estimated)

Athens

ABRAHAM LINCOLN LONG NINE MUSEUM, 200 S. Main St., Athens, IL 62613. Tel.: 217-636-8755.
Web Site: www.abrahamlincolnlongninemuseum.com
Key Personnel: Dir., John R. Eden.
Institution Type/Description: History Museum: built by Colonel Matthew Rogers in 1832. Listed on the National Register of Historic Places.
Hours & Admission Prices: June-Sept. 1 Tues.-Sat. 1-5. No charge; donations accepted.
Attendance: 800 (estimated)

Atlanta

ATLANTA LIBRARY & MUSEUM, 112 S.W. Arch St., Atlanta, IL 61723-7526. Mailing Address: 100 Race St., P.O. Box 568, Atlanta, IL 61723. Tel.: 217-648-2003 & 2112.
E-mail: atlanta.library@frontier.com
Institution Type/Description: Historic Building: built in 1908. Listed on the National Register of Historic Places.
Hours & Admission Prices: Library: Mon. 10am-12:30, Tues. & Thurs. 10:30-7, Wed. & Fri. 10:30-4:30, Sat. 9-3. Museum: April-Oct. Mon.-Thurs. 9-4, Fri. 9am to noon.

Aurora

AURORA HISTORICAL SOCIETY, 305 Cedar St., Aurora, IL 60507. Mailing Address: P.O. Box 905, Aurora, IL 60507. Tel.: 630-897-9029.
E-mail: ahs@aurorahistory.net
Web Site: aurorahistory.net
Key Personnel: Dir., John Jaros.
Institution Type/Description: History Museum.
Hours & Admission Prices: Tues. & Thurs. by appointment. Adults $5; members no charge.

AURORA REGIONAL FIRE MUSEUM, 53 N. Broadway, Aurora, IL 60505. Mailing Address: P.O. Box 1782, Aurora, IL 60507-1782. Tel.: 630-256-4140.
E-mail: info@auroraregionalfireman.org
Web Site: www.auroraregionalfiremuseum.org
Key Personnel: Mgr., Deborah Davis; Cur., David Lewis.
Institution Type/Description: Firefighting Museum: housed in the 1894 Old Central Fire Station.
Hours & Admission Prices: Thurs.-Fri. 12-4, Sat. 10-4; groups by appointment. Adults $5, children 12 & under $3; discounts to AAM members. Closed all major holidays. &
Attendance: 5,500 (estimated)

BLACKBERRY FARM PIONEER VILLAGE, 100 S. Barnes Rd., Aurora, IL 60506-8118. Tel.: 630-892-1550. Fax: 630-892-1597.
E-mail: ssmith@fvpd.net
Web Site: www.foxvalleyparkdistrict.org
Key Personnel: Mgr., Sandy Smith; Supvr., Laureen Baumgartner.
Institution Type/Description: Village Museum.
Hours & Admission Prices: May Mon.-Fri. 9:30-2, Sat. 9:30-5, Sun. 11-5; June-Aug. Mon.-Fri. 9:30-3:30, Sat. 9:30-5, Sun. 11-5; Sept. Fri. 9:30-3:30, Sat. 9:30-5, Sun. 11-5; Oct. Sat.-Sun. & Columbus Day 11-4. Admission 2 & over $9; discounts to residents; children under 2 no charge. Special Events: $7. &
Attendance: 72,500 (actual)

DAVID L. PIERCE ART & HISTORY CENTER, 20 E. Downer Place, Aurora, IL 60505-3302. Mailing Address: 44 E. Downer Place, Aurora, IL 60505-3302. Tel.: 630-906-0654 & 0650. Fax: 630-906-0657.

E-mail: rchurch@aurora-il.org
Web Site: www.aurora-il.org
Key Personnel: Chm., Chris Hoban; Dir. & Cur., Rena J. Church.
Institution Type/Description: Art Commission: located in Stolp Island Historic District.
Hours & Admission Prices: Wed.-Fri. 12-4. No charge. &
Attendance: 9,000 (actual)

THE SCHINGOETHE CENTER OF AURORA UNIVERSITY,

1315 Prairie St., Aurora, IL 60506-4892. Mailing Address: c/o Aurora University, 347 S. Gladstone Ave., Aurora, IL 60506-4892. Tel.: 630-844-7843. Fax: 630-844-6529.
E-mail: museum@aurora.edu
Web Site: www.aurora.edu/museum
Formerly: Schingoethe Center for Native American Cultures
Key Personnel: Exec. Dir. & Chief Cur., Meg Bero; Aurora Univ. Pres., Rebecca Sherrick; Finance Dir., Dr. Sharon Maxwell.
Institution Type/Description: Art Museum.
Hours & Admission Prices: Academic Year: Tues. 10-7, Wed.-Fri. 10-4. Suggested Donation: adults $3, students & seniors $2, children under 12 $1; discounts to AAM & ICOM members; members no charge. Closed university holidays. &
Attendance: 9,912 (estimated)

THE SCIENCE AND TECHNOLOGY INTERACTIVE CENTER,

18 W. Benton, Aurora, IL 60506-6013. Tel.: 630-859-3434, ext. 217. Fax: 630-859-8692.
E-mail: director@scitechmuseum.org
Web Site: www.scitechmuseum.org
Formerly: SciTech Hands On Museum
Key Personnel: Exec. Dir., Arlene S. Hawks; Operations Dir., Camille Coller.
Institution Type/Description: Science & Technology Museum: housed in historic former Aurora Post Office Building.
Hours & Admission Prices: Tues.-Sat. 10-3. Adults & children 4-17 $8, seniors 60 & over and active military $6; discount to ASTC members; children 3 & under no charge. Closed New Year's Eve; Memorial Day; Independence Day; Thanksgiving; Christmas. &
Attendance: 75,000 (actual)

THE WILLIAM TANNER HOUSE MUSEUM - AURORA HISTORICAL SOCIETY,

305 Cedar St., Aurora, IL 60506. Mailing Address: P.O. Box 905, Aurora, IL 60507-0905. Tel.: 630-906-0650. Fax: 630-906-0657.
E-mail: ahs@aurorahistory.net
Web Site: www.aurorahistoricalsociety.org
Key Personnel: Exec. Dir., John R. Jaros.
Institution Type/Description: Local History Museum: housed in 1857 mansion. Listed on the National Register of Historic Places.
Hours & Admission Prices: Tanner House Tours: early April to Sept. Wed. & Sun. 1, 2, & 3. Art & History Center: Wed.-Sat. 12-4. No charge. Archives: by appointment.
Attendance: 10,000 (actual)

Barrington

BARRINGTON HISTORY MUSEUM,

212 W. Main St., Barrington, IL 60010-3011. Tel.: 847-381-1730. Fax: 847-381-1766.
Web Site: barringtonhistorymuseum.org
Key Personnel: C.E.O. & Pres., Michael J. Harkins.
Institution Type/Description: History Museum: housed in two Folk Victorian Houses.
Hours & Admission Prices: Tues.-Fri. 10-4, Sat. 10-1. Tours by appointment. Blacksmith Shop: Sat. 12-4. &

CRABTREE NATURE CENTER,

3 Stover Rd., Barrington, IL 60010-5342. Tel.: 847-381-6592.
E-mail: crabtree.naturecenter@cookcountyil.gov
Web Site: fpdcc.com
Institution Type/Description: Nature Center.
Hours & Admission Prices: March to late Oct. Sat.-Thurs. 9-4:30; late Oct. to Feb. Sat.-Thurs. 9-3:30. No charge; donations accepted. Closed New Year's Day; Thanksgiving; Christmas. &

Bartlett

BARTLETT DEPOT MUSEUM,

100 W. Railroad Ave., Bartlett, IL 60103. Mailing Address: 2228 Main St., Bartlett, IL 60103. Tel.: 630-837-0800.
E-mail: prohleder@vbartlett.org
Web Site: www.villageofbartlettmuseums.org

Institution Type/Description: Railroad History Museum: housed in a former railroad depot; built in 1873.
Hours & Admission Prices: Tues. 12-7, Thurs. 12-6, 1st Sat. each month 9am to noon. No charge. &

VILLAGE OF BARTLETT MUSEUMS,

228 S. Main St., Bartlett, IL 60103. Tel.: 630-837-0800.
E-mail: prohleder@vbartlett.org
Web Site: www.villageofbartlettmuseums.org
Key Personnel: Dir., Pam Rohleder.
Institution Type/Description: History Museum.
Hours & Admission Prices: Bartlett History Museum: Mon.-Fri. 8:30-4:30, Sat. 9-12; Bartlett Depot Museum: Tues. 12-5, 1st & 3rd Sat. 9 to noon. No charge. &

Batavia

BATAVIA DEPOT MUSEUM,

155 Houston St., Batavia, IL 60510-1924. Mailing Address: P.O. Box 14, Batavia, IL 60510. Tel.: 630-406-5274. Fax: 630-593-5202.
E-mail: jenniferp@bataviaparks.org
Web Site: bataviahistoricalsociety.org
Key Personnel: Dir., Jennifer Putzier; Cur., Chris Winter.
Institution Type/Description: Historical Society Museum: housed in 1854 Batavia Depot, one of the oldest railroad station on the Chicago, Burlington & Quincy Line.
Hours & Admission Prices: March-May & Sept. to Thanksgiving Wed. & Fri.-Mon. 2-4; June-Aug. Wed. & Fri.-Mon. 12-4 other times by appointment. No charge; donations accepted. &

LEDERMAN SCIENCE EDUCATION CENTER AT FERMILAB,

Fermilab, Kirk Rd. & Pine St., Batavia, IL 60510. Mailing Address: Fermilab MS 777, Box 500, Batavia, IL 60510. Tel.: 630-840-8258. Fax: 630-840-2500.
E-mail: edreg@fnal.gov
Web Site: ed.fnal.gov/office/index.shtml
Key Personnel: Education & Public Outreach Mgr., Spencer Pasero; Coord. Teacher Resource Center, Susan Dahl; Exhibit Specialist, Ketevan Akhobadze.
Institution Type/Description: Science Center.
Hours & Admission Prices: Mon.-Fri. 8:30-4:30, Sat. 9-3; groups by appointment.

RED OAK NATURE CENTER,

2343 S. River St., Batavia, IL 60510-9664. Tel.: 630-897-1808. Fax: 630-264-0056.
E-mail: redoak@fvpd.net
Web Site: www.foxvalleyparkdistrict.org
Institution Type/Description: Nature Center.
Hours & Admission Prices: Mon.-Fri. 9-4:30, Sat.-Sun. 10-3. No charge; donations accepted.
Attendance: 23,000 (estimated)

Belleville

LABOR AND INDUSTRY MUSEUM,

123 N. Church St., Belleville, IL 62220-1418. Tel.: 618-222-9430.
E-mail: laborandindustry@yahoo.com
Web Site: www.laborandindustrymuseum.org
Key Personnel: Chm. (V), Pat Schmeder; Coord. Collections, Judy Belleville.
Institution Type/Description: History Museum.
Hours & Admission Prices: Sat. 10-2; other times by appointment.

ST. CLAIR COUNTY HISTORICAL SOCIETY,

701 E. Washington St., Belleville, IL 62220-3846. Tel.: 618-234-0600. Fax: 618-234-3060. Facebook.
E-mail: stcchs.curator@gmail.com
Web Site: www.stcchs.org
Key Personnel: Pres. (V), Ken Lickenbrock; Cur., William Shannon, IV.
Institution Type/Description: Historical Museum: housed in 1866 Victorian home.
Hours & Admission Prices: Mon.-Fri. 10-2; other times by appointment. Adults $2, children $1; discounts to AAA members; members no charge. Closed national holidays.
Attendance: 1,500 (estimated)

WILLIAM & FLORENCE SCHMIDT ART CENTER,

2500 Carlyle Ave., Belleville, IL 62221-5859. Tel.: 618-222-5278, 800-222-5131, ext. 5278.
E-mail: nicole.dutton@swic.edu
Web Site: www.swic.edu/theschmidt/about
Key Personnel: Exec. Dir., Libby Reuter; Asst. Cur. & Registrar, Christina Cosio; Cur. & Facility Coord., Nicole Dutton; Asst. Cur., Jessica Mannisi.
Institution Type/Description: Art Center.

Hours & Admission Prices: Academic Year: Mon.-Wed. 9-5, Thurs. 9-8, Fri. 10-5, Sat. 11-5; Summer: call for hours. No charge.

Bellflower

BELLFLOWER HISTORICAL AND GENEALOGICAL SOCIETY, 210 N. Latcha St., Bellflower, IL 61724.
Key Personnel: Pres. (V), Phyllis Kumler.
Institution Type/Description: Historic Building: early 1900 Illinois Central Railroad Depot.
Hours & Admission Prices: By appointment. No charge; donations accepted.
Attendance: 128 (actual)

Belvidere

BOONE COUNTY HISTORICAL MUSEUM, 314 S. State, Belvidere, IL 61008-3609. Tel.: 815-544-8391. Fax: 815-547-1691.
E-mail: info@bchmuseum.org
Web Site: bchmuseum.org
Key Personnel: Dir., Anna Pivoras; Research, Lonna Bentley.
Institution Type/Description: Historical Society Museum.
Hours & Admission Prices: Museum: Tues.-Fri. 9-5, Sat. 9-3; other times by appointment. Library: Tues.-Fri. 9-3. No charge; donations accepted. &
Attendance: 4,000 (estimated)

Bement

BRYANT COTTAGE, 146 E. Wilson Ave., Bement, IL 61813-1250. Mailing Address: P.O. Box 41, Bement, IL 61813-0041. Tel.: 217-678-8184. Facebook.
E-mail: hpa.bryantcottage@illinois.gov
Web Site: www.bement.com/about-bement/parks-recreation-and-historical-tours/bryant-cottage-state historicsite
Key Personnel: Site Mgr., Benjamin Pollard.
Institution Type/Description: Historic House Museum: 1856 Bryant Cottage where the Lincoln-Douglas Debates were verbally agreed to as part of the 1858 Senate campaigns.
Hours & Admission Prices: Call for hours. Donations accepted. Closed some holidays. &

Berwyn

BERWYN ROUTE 66 MUSEUM, 7003 W. Ogden Ave., Berwyn, IL 60402. Tel.: 708-484-9349. Fax: 708-484-1015.
E-mail: info@berwynrt66museum.org
Web Site: www.berwynrt66museum.org
Key Personnel: Dir., Jon Fey; Museum Shop Mgr., Myles Slaughter.
Institution Type/Description: History Museum.
Hours & Admission Prices: Mon., Wed. & Fri. 1-4.
Attendance: 3,550 (estimated)

Bishop Hill

BISHOP HILL HERITAGE MUSEUM, Steeple Building, 103 N. Bishop Hill St., Bishop Hill, IL 61419. Mailing Address: P.O. Box 92, Bishop Hill, IL 61419-0092. Tel.: 309-927-3899. Fax: 309-927-3010.
E-mail: bhha@mymctc.net
Web Site: www.bishophillheritage.org
Key Personnel: Dir., Todd L. DeDecher; Museum Shop Mgr., Glenda Wallace.
Institution Type/Description: History Museum: housed in 1854 Steeple Building, located in Bishop Hill, a Swedish communal settlement founded in 1846 by religious dissenters.
Hours & Admission Prices: Jan.-March daily 10-4; April-Oct. Mon.-Fri. 10-5, Sat. 11-4, Sun. 12-4. No charge; donations accepted. &
Attendance: 90,000 (estimated)

BISHOP HILL STATE HISTORIC SITE, 304 S. Bishop Hill St., Bishop Hill, IL 61419-0104. Mailing Address: P.O. Box 104, Bishop Hill, IL 61419-0104. Tel.: 309-927-3345. Fax: 309-927-3343.
E-mail: bishophill@mymctc.net
Web Site: www.bishophill.com
Key Personnel: Site Mgr., Martha Downey.
Institution Type/Description: History Museum: complex consists of 1848 Colony Church, located on the site of a Swedish communal settlement, 1850s Bjorklund Hotel and 1988 Bishop Hill Museum.
Hours & Admission Prices: March-Oct. Wed.-Sun. 9-5, Nov.-Feb. Wed.-Sun. 9-4. Suggested Donation: family $10, adults $4, children 17 & under $2. Closed New

Year's Day; Martin Luther King Jr. Day; Presidents' Day; Columbus Day; Veterans Day; Thanksgiving; Christmas. &
Attendance: 67,093 (actual)

Blandinsville

BLANDIN HOUSE MUSEUM, 215 S. Chestnut St., Blandinsville, IL 61420. Mailing Address: P.O. Box 21, Blandinsville, IL 61420-9169. Tel.: 309-652-3673.
Key Personnel: Pres. (V), Karen Moore.
Institution Type/Description: History Museum.
Hours & Admission Prices: Mon.-Fri. call for hours. No charge; donations accepted.

Bloomington

THE DAVID DAVIS MANSION, 1000 Monroe Dr., Bloomington, IL 61701-3333. Tel.: 309-828-1084. Fax: 309-828-3493. Facebook: David Davis Mansion.
E-mail: davismansion@yahoo.com
Web Site: www.davismansion.org
Key Personnel: Site Mgr., Marcia Young; Asst. Mgr., Jeannie Riordan; Cur., Jeff Saulsbery; Museum Shop Mgr., Bekah Litchfield.
Institution Type/Description: Historic House: 1872 David Davis' Second Empire Italianate brick mansion. David Davis was the campaign manager for Abraham Lincoln who appointed him as a judge of the U.S. Supreme Court.
Hours & Admission Prices: Wed.-Sun. 9-4. No charge; donations accepted. Closed New Year's Day; Thanksgiving; Christmas; state holidays. &
Attendance: 60,000 (estimated)

MCLEAN COUNTY ARTS CENTER, 601 N. East St., Bloomington, IL 61701-3094. Tel.: 309-829-0011. Fax: 309-829-4928. Facebook: McLean Arts Center.
E-mail: info@mcac.org
Web Site: www.mcac.org
Key Personnel: C.E.O. & Exec. Dir., Douglas Johnson; Cur., Claire Hedden; Education Coord., Sarah Sciba.
Institution Type/Description: Arts Center.
Hours & Admission Prices: Tues. 10-7, Wed.-Fri. 10-5, Sat. 12-4. No charge; donations accepted. Closed national holidays. &
Attendance: 12,548 (actual)

MCLEAN COUNTY MUSEUM OF HISTORY, 200 N. Main, Bloomington, IL 61701-3912. Tel.: 309-827-0428. Fax: 309-827-0100.
E-mail: mcmh@mchistory.org
Web Site: www.mchistory.org
Key Personnel: Exec. Dir., Adam Lovell; Pres., Bob Watkins; Treas., John Killian; Dir. Devel., Divah Griffin; Cur., Susan Hartzold; Librarian & Archivist, Bill Kemp; Dir. Mktg., Jeff Woodard; Dir. Education, Candace Summers; Registrar, Emma Meyer; Coord. Education Programs, Hannah Johnson; Dir. Volunteers & Interns, Rachael Masa; Devel. Asst., Brandy Maloney; Archivist, George Perkins; Educator Outreach Coordr., Anthony Bowman; Asst. Volunteer Coordr., Betty Turchirollo; Cur. Digital Humanities, Torii More.
Institution Type/Description: Historic Building: 1904 courthouse.
Hours & Admission Prices: May-Sept. Mon. & Wed.-Sat. 9-5, Tues. 9-9, Sun. 10-3; Oct.-April Mon. & Wed.-Sat. 9-5, Tues. 9-9. Adults $5, senior citizens $4; discounts to Time Travelers and AAM & ICOM members; students, children and society members no charge. Closed New Year's Eve & Day; Memorial Day; Independence Day, Labor Day; Thanksgiving; Christmas Eve & Day. &
Attendance: 27,257 (actual)

MILLER PARK ZOO, 1020 S. Morris Ave., Bloomington, IL 61701-6307. Tel.: 309-434-2250. Fax: 309-434-2823. Facebook: Miller Park Zoo.
E-mail: jtetzloff@cityblm.org
Web Site: www.millerparkzoo.org
Key Personnel: Supt., Jay Tetzloff; Cur., Peter Burvenich; Business Mgr., Anthony Nelson; Education Instructor, Shannon Reedy; Museum Shop Mgr., Jennifer Rogers.
Institution Type/Description: Zoo.
Hours & Admission Prices: Zoo: daily 9:30-4:30. Adults 13-59 $6.25, senior citizens 60 & over and children 3-12 $4.25; members & children under 3 no charge. Closed Thanksgiving; Christmas. &
Attendance: 114,311 (actual)

PRAIRIE AVIATION MUSEUM, 2929 E. Empire St., Bloomington, IL 61704-5452. Tel.: 309-663-7632. Fax: 309-663-8411. Facebook.
E-mail: info@prairieaviationmuseum.org

Web Site: www.prairieaviationmuseum.org
Key Personnel: Pres. (V), Steven Schmidt.
Institution Type/Description: Aviation History Museum.
Hours & Admission Prices: Thurs.-Sat. 11-4, Sun. 12-4. Adults $5, children 6-11 $3; children 5 & under and members no charge. Closed New Year's Day; Thanksgiving; Christmas.
Attendance: 3,000 (estimated)

Bolingbrook

ILLINOIS AVIATION MUSEUM, 130 S. Clow International Pkwy., Bolingbrook, IL 60440. Tel.: 630-771-1937. Fax: 630-771-9063.
E-mail: info@illinoisaviationmuseum.org
Web Site: www.illinoisaviationmuseum.org
Institution Type/Description: Aviation History Museum.
Hours & Admission Prices: Sat. 10-2; other times by appointment.

Bourbonnais

EXPLORATION STATION(R)....A CHILDREN'S MUSEUM, 1095 W. Perry St., Bourbonnais, IL 60914-1970. Tel.: 815-933-9905. Fax: 815-933-5468. Facebook.
E-mail: brittaneyb@btpd.org
Web Site: www.btpd.org
Key Personnel: Dir., Hollice Clark, III; Gen. Mgr., Brittaney Beck; Group & Reservation Coord., Tammy Anderson; Museum Asst. Gen. Mgr., Brittaney Beck; Education & Community Rels. Coord., Kristi Schu.
Institution Type/Description: Children's Museum.
Hours & Admission Prices: June-Aug. Mon.-Sat. 10-5, Sun. 1-5; Sept.-May Tues.-Sat. 10-5, Sun. 1-5. Adults & children $7; children one & under no charge. &
Attendance: 39,000 (actual)

Brookfield

BROOKFIELD HISTORICAL SOCIETY, 8820-1/2 Brookfield Ave., Brookfield, IL 60513-1670. Tel.: 708-485-3420.
Institution Type/Description: Historic Building: housed in the former Grossdale Railroad Station; built in 1889.
Hours & Admission Prices: 2nd & 4th Sun. of the month 1-4.

CHICAGO ZOOLOGICAL SOCIETY'S BROOKFIELD ZOO, 3300 Golf Rd., Brookfield, IL 60513-1060. Tel.: 708-688-8000. Fax: 708-485-3532. TDD: 708-485-0360; Facebook Brookfield Zoo.
E-mail: webmaster@czs.org
Web Site: www.czs.org
Key Personnel: Chm. (V), William C. Kunkler, III; Women's Bd. Pres., Mrs. James M. Guyette; C.E.O. & Pres., Stuart D. Strahl, Ph.D.; Vice Pres. Mktg., Joseph A. Couceiro; Vice Pres. HR, Sandra Dornhecker; Sr. Vice Pres. Opers., Richard G. Gamble; Sr. Vice Pres. Conservation, Education & Training, Alejandro Grajal; Sr. Vice Pres. Finance & Admin., Ken Kaduk; Sr. Vice Pres. Institutional Planning & Inclusion, Jo-Elle Mogerman; Chief Advancement Officer, Cindy Zeigler; Sr. Vice Pres. Animal Programs, William Zeigler; Sr. Vice Pres. Devel., Chris Jabin; Vice Pres. Plant & Facilities, John Kramer; Vice Pres. Guest Services, Jerry Johnston.
Institution Type/Description: Zoo.
Hours & Admission Prices: Mon.-Fri. 10-5, Sat. & Sun. 10-6. Adults $16.95, senior citizens 65 & over and children 3-11 $11.95; active, reserve & retired military personnel, Oct.-Dec. Tues. & Thurs. & members no charge. Parking: buses $15, cars $10. Additional fees for shows & special areas. &
Attendance: 2,180,000 (estimated)

Buffalo Grove

RAUPP MEMORIAL MUSEUM, 901 Dunham Lane, Buffalo Grove, IL 60089. Tel.: 847-459-2318. Fax: 847-459-3148.
E-mail: museum@bgparks.org
Web Site: bgparks.org/facilities/museum.aspx
Institution Type/Description: History Museum.
Hours & Admission Prices: Sun. 1-4, Mon.-Thurs. 11-4:30.

Byron

BYRON MUSEUM OF HISTORY, 110 N. Union St., Byron, IL 61010. Mailing Address: P.O. Box 186, Byron, IL 61010. Tel.: 815-234-5031. Fax: 815-234-4447.
E-mail: info@byronmuseum.org
Web Site: byronmuseum.org
Key Personnel: Dir., Kira Halvey.

Institution Type/Description: History Museum.
Hours & Admission Prices: Wed.-Sat. 10-3; other times by appointment. No charge; donations accepted. Closed New Year's Day; Thanksgiving & day after; Christmas Eve & Day.

Cahokia

CAHOKIA COURTHOUSE STATE HISTORIC SITE, 107 Elm St., Cahokia, IL 62206-1014. Tel.: 618-332-1782. Fax: 618-332-1737.
Institution Type/Description: History Museum: housed in 1737 residence.
Hours & Admission Prices: Tues.-Sat. 9-5. No charge. Jarrot Mansion, Martin-Boismenue, Holy Family Church: by appointment. Closed major holidays. &
Attendance: 25,600 (estimated)

GREATER ST. LOUIS AIR & SPACE MUSEUM, 2300 Vector Dr., Cahokia, IL 62206. Tel.: 618-332-3664.
E-mail: info@airandspacemuseum.org
Web Site: www.airandspacemuseum.org
Institution Type/Description: Aviation History Museum.
Hours & Admission Prices: Call for hours. No charge; donations accepted.

Cairo

CAIRO CUSTOMS HOUSE MUSEUM, 1400 Washington Ave., Cairo, IL 62914-1870. Tel.: 618-734-9632.
E-mail: cplibrary@lazernetwireless.net
Institution Type/Description: Historic Building: housed in the former United States Custom House; built from 1867-1872.
Hours & Admission Prices: Tues.-Fri. 10-12 & 1-3. Adults $2, Students $1.

MAGNOLIA MANOR, 2700 Washington Ave., Cairo, IL 62914-1458. Mailing Address: P.O. Box 286, Cairo, IL 62914-0286. Tel.: 618-734-0201. Fax: 618-734-0201. Facebook: magnoliamanor-cairo.
E-mail: ilovecarstoo@yahoo.com
Web Site: www.visitmagnoliamanor.com
Key Personnel: C.E.O. & Pres., Charles McGinness; Vice Pres., Susan Holland; Cur. & Museum Shop Mgr., Tim Slapinski.
Institution Type/Description: Historic House Museum; 1869 Magnolia Manor.
Hours & Admission Prices: Summer: Mon., Tues., Thurs.-Sat. 9-4:30, Sun. 1-4:30. Adults $8, children $2. Closed Wednesdays; New Year's Eve & Day; Easter; Independence Day; Thanksgiving; Christmas Eve, Day & week.
Attendance: 2,500 (estimated)

Carbondale

THE SCIENCE CENTER, University Mall, 1237 E. Main Space 1048, Carbondale, IL 62901-5830. Tel.: 618-529-5431. Fax: 618-457-2195. Facebook.
E-mail: si.sciencecenter@gmail.com
Web Site: yoursciencecenter.org
Key Personnel: Exec. Dir., Chris Walls; Pres., Peter Gregory.
Institution Type/Description: Children's Science Museum.
Hours & Admission Prices: Tues.-Thurs. 11-5, Fri.-Sat. 11-6, Sun. 12-5. Adults $5; discount to ASTC members; children 2 & under and ASTC & museum members no charge. Closed Easter; Thanksgiving; Christmas. &
Attendance: 64,000 (estimated)

UNIVERSITY MUSEUM, Southern Illinois University Carbondale, 1000 Faner Dr., MC 4508, Carbondale, IL 62901-4328. Tel.: 618-453-5388. Fax: 618-453-7409.
E-mail: museum@siu.edu
Web Site: www.museum.siu.edu
Key Personnel: Cur. Anthropology, Susannah Munson; Cur. Exhibits, Alison Erazmus.
Institution Type/Description: General Museum.
Hours & Admission Prices: Tues.-Fri. 10-4, Sat. 1-4; pre-arranged group tours available. No charge; donations accepted. Closed university & national holidays. &
Attendance: 15,000 (estimated)

Carlinville

MACOUPIN COUNTY HISTORICAL SOCIETY - ANDERSON MANSION, 920 Breckenridge St., Carlinville, IL 62626. Mailing Address: P.O. Box 432, Carlinville, IL 62626. Tel.: 217-854-2141.
E-mail: info@carlinvillechamber.com
Web Site: www.macsociety.org

Institution Type/Description: Historical Society Museum: housed in the former home of John Anderson; built in 1883.
Hours & Admission Prices: April-Nov. Wed. 10-2. No charge; donations accepted.

Carmi

WHITE COUNTY HISTORICAL SOCIETY, 203 N. Church St., Carmi, IL 62821. Mailing Address: P.O. Box 121, Carmi, IL 62821-0121. Tel.: 618-382-8425.
E-mail: w.c.h.s-genealogy@hotmail.com
Web Site: www.rootsweb.com/~ilwcohs
Institution Type/Description: History Museum.
Hours & Admission Prices: Ratcliff Inn; Robinson-Stewart House; L. Haas Store Museum; Matsel Cabin; Mary Smith Fay Genealogy Library: Tues.-Fri. 11:30-4:30; other times by appointment, contact Mary Smith Fay Library 618-382-8425. No charge; donation accepted. Closed national holidays.
Attendance: 1,500 (estimated)

Carterville

JOHN A. LOGAN COLLEGE MUSEUM, 700 Logan College Rd., Carterville, IL 62918-2501. Tel.: 618-985-2828, ext. 8287. Fax: 618-985-2248. TDD: 618-985-2752.
E-mail: museum@jalc.edu
Web Site: www.jalc.edu/museum/index.html
Key Personnel: Dir., Adrienne Barkley Giffin.
Institution Type/Description: College Museum.
Hours & Admission Prices: During regular college hours: Mon.-Fri. 8-9, Sat. 9-5. No charge. &
Attendance: 40,000 (estimated)

Carthage

HANCOCK COUNTY HISTORICAL SOCIETY, 306 Walnut, Carthage, IL 62321.
E-mail: hancockhistory@yahoo.com
Key Personnel: Pres., Keith Bruns; Vice Pres., Ned Casady; Sec., Janet Holtman; Treas., Susan Cheney; Office Mgr., Frank Burkett.
Institution Type/Description: Historical Society: housed in Kibbe Museum at Carthage site.
Hours & Admission Prices: Mon.-Fri. 9-3. No charge; donations accepted. Closed holidays. &
Attendance: 1,000 (estimated)

Champaign

CHAMPAIGN COUNTY HISTORICAL MUSEUM, 102 E. University Ave., Champaign, IL 61820-4111. Tel.: 217-356-1010. Fax: 217-356-1478.
E-mail: president@champaigncountyhistory.org
Web Site: www.champaigncountyhistory.org
Key Personnel: Pres. & Exhibits Committee Chair, T.J. Blakeman.
Institution Type/Description: County History Museum: housed in the Cattle Bank; built in 1857. Listed on the National Register of Historic Places.
Hours & Admission Prices: Wed.-Fri. & Sun. 1-5, Sat. 10-5; other times by appointment; groups by appointment. Suggested Donation: $3 per person.
Attendance: 2,400 (estimated)

GIERTZ GALLERY AT PARKLAND COLLEGE, 2400 W. Bradley Ave., Champaign, IL 61821-1899. Tel.: 217-351-2485 & 2200. Fax: 217-373-3899.
E-mail: lcostello@parkland.edu
Web Site: www.parkland.edu/gallery
Formerly: Parkland College Art Gallery
Key Personnel: Dir., Lisa Costello; Chm. (V), Prof. Chris Berti; Coord. Exhibits Coord., Anna Peters; Coord. Collections, Laura O'Donnell.
Institution Type/Description: Art Gallery.
Hours & Admission Prices: Academic Year: Mon.-Thurs. 10-7, Sat. 12-2. Summer: Mon.-Thurs. 10-7. No charge; donations accepted. Closed college & major holidays. &
Attendance: 10,000 (estimated)

KRANNERT ART MUSEUM AND KINKEAD PAVILION, 500 E. Peabody Dr., University of Illinois, Champaign, IL 61820-6913. Tel.: 217-333-1861. Fax: 217-333-0883. Facebook: @krannertmuseum; Twitter: @KAMillinois.
E-mail: kam@illinois.edu
Web Site: kam.illinois.edu
Key Personnel: Assoc. Dir., Claudia Corlett-Stahl; Mktg. & Communications, Julia Nucci Kelly; Office Admin., Chris Schaede; Registrar & Exhibit Coord.,

Christine Saniat; Collections Mgr., Kimberly Sissons; Exhibition Designer, Eric Lemme; Exhibition Designer, Walter Wilson; Sr. Cur., Allyson Purpura; Cur. Modern & Contemporary Art, Amy L. Powell; Cur. European & American Art, Maureen Warren; Dir. Education, Anne Sautman; Dir. Devel., Brenda Nardi; Security Chief, David Holzner.
Institution Type/Description: Art Museum.
Hours & Admission Prices: Academic Year: Mon.-Wed. & Fri.-Sat. 9-5, Thurs. 9-9; Summer: Mon.-Sat. 9-5. Suggested Donation: $3. Closed national holidays. &
Attendance: 138,000 (actual)

ORPHEUM CHILDREN'S SCIENCE MUSEUM CLOSED, 346 N. Neil St., Champaign, IL 61820-3614. Tel.: 217-352-5895. Fax: 217-352-8160. Facebook.
E-mail: orpheumkids@gmail.com
Web Site: www.orpheumkids.com
Key Personnel: Pres., Angela Urban; Exec. Dir., Rene A. Dunn.
Institution Type/Description: Children's Museum.
Hours & Admission Prices: Mon.-Fri. 10-4, Sat.-Sun. 1-5; other times by appointment. Adults & children $5, seniors $4; discounts to ACM & ASTC members; members no charge. Closed New Year's Day; Easter; Christmas. &
Attendance: 13,658 (actual)

SOUSA ARCHIVES AND CENTER FOR AMERICAN MUSIC, Harding Band Bldg., Second Fl., 1103 S. Sixth St., Univ. of Illinois at Urbana-Champaign, Champaign, IL 61820. Tel.: 217-244-9309. Fax: 217-333-2868.
E-mail: sousa@library.illinois.edu
Web Site: sousaarchives.org
Formerly: Sousa Archives for Band Research
Key Personnel: Archivist Music & Fine Arts, Scott Schwartz.
Institution Type/Description: American Music Museum.
Hours & Admission Prices: Mon.-Fri. 8:30-12 & 1-5. No charge; donations accepted. &
Attendance: 2,606 (actual)

WILLIAM M. STAERKEL PLANETARIUM, Parkland College, 2400 W. Bradley Ave., Champaign, IL 61821-1806. Tel.: 217-351-2568. Fax: 217-373-3809.
E-mail: planetarium@parkland.edu
Web Site: www.parkland.edu/planetarium
Key Personnel: Dir., David C. Leake.
Institution Type/Description: Planetarium.
Hours & Admission Prices: Aug.-May call for hours. Adults $5, children, seniors, & students $4; members no charge. &
Attendance: 30,000 (estimated)

Charleston

TARBLE ARTS CENTER, EASTERN ILLINOIS UNIVERSITY, 2010 9th St., Charleston, IL 61920. Mailing Address: 600 Lincoln Ave., Charleston, IL 61920-3011. Tel.: 217-581-ARTS (2787). Fax: 217-581-7138. Facebook, Instagram; Twitter.
E-mail: tarble@eiu.edu
Web Site: www.eiu.edu/tarble
Key Personnel: Dir. & Chief Cur., Rehema C. Barber; Chm. (V), Dorothy Bennett; Asst. Dir., Michael Schuetz; Dean, Anita Shelton.
Institution Type/Description: University Art Museum.
Hours & Admission Prices: Tues.-Fri. 10-5, Sat.-Sun. 1-4. No charge; donations accepted. Closed major holidays & during installations period. &
Attendance: 16,000 (estimated)

Chatham

CHATHAM RAILROAD MUSEUM, 100 N. State St., Chatham, IL 62629-1350. Tel.: 217-483-7792.
Key Personnel: Pres. (V), William Shannon.
Institution Type/Description: Railroad Museum: housed in 1902 era depot.
Hours & Admission Prices: 2nd & 4th Sun. 2-4. No charge; donations accepted. Closed holidays.

Chester

RANDOLPH COUNTY ARCHIVES AND MUSEUM, 1 Taylor St., Chester, IL 62233-1970. Tel.: 618-826-2667. Fax: 618-826-3363.
E-mail: elyons@powrup.net
Key Personnel: Dir., Emily Lyons.
Institution Type/Description: History Museum.

Hours & Admission Prices: Mon.-Fri. 9-4; other times by appointment. No charge; donations accepted. Closed holidays.
Attendance: 800 (actual)

Chicago

A. PHILIP RANDOLPH PULLMAN PORTER MUSEUM, 10406 S. Maryland Ave., Chicago, IL 60628-3090. Mailing Address: P.O. Box 6276, Chicago, IL 60680-6276. Tel.: 773-850-8580.
E-mail: talktous@aprpullmanportermuseum.org
Web Site: www.aphiliprandolphmuseum.com
Key Personnel: Exec. Dir., David A. Peterson, Jr.; Cur. Collections. Dr. Lyn Hughes.
Institution Type/Description: Black Labor History Museum & Cultural Institution.
Hours & Admission Prices: April-Dec. 1 Thurs.-Sat. 11-4; groups by appointment. General admission $5. &

ADLER PLANETARIUM & ASTRONOMY MUSEUM, 1300 S. Lake Shore Dr., Chicago, IL 60605-2489. Tel.: 312-922-7827. Fax: 312-322-9909.
E-mail: guestservices@adlerplanetarium.org
Web Site: www.adlerplanetarium.org
Key Personnel: Pres. & C.E.O., Michelle B. Larson, Ph.D.
Institution Type/Description: Planetarium, History & Science Museum.
Hours & Admission Prices: Daily 9:30-4. Museum: adults $12, students & seniors over 65 $10, children 3-11 $8; discounts to Chicago residents, AAM & ICOM members; members no charge. Basic Pass: adults $24.95, children $19.95. Closed Thanksgiving; Christmas. &
Attendance: 550,000 (estimated)

AMERICAN WRITERS MUSEUM, 180 N. Michigan Ave., 2nd Fl., Chicago, IL 60601. Tel.: 312-374-8790.
Web Site: americanwritersmuseum.org
Key Personnel: Pres., Carey Cranston; Dir. Operations, Christopher Burrow; Dir. Devel., Linda Dunlavy; Dir. Mktg., Karie McGahan; Dir. Programs, Allison Sansone; Dir. Devel. & Membership, Nikki Geslani.
Institution Type/Description: Communications Museum
Hours & Admission Prices: July-Aug. Thurs. 10-6, Fri.-Wed. 10-5. Sept.-June Tues.-Wed. & Fri.-Sun. 10-5, Thurs. 10-6. Adults $12, seniors 65 & over and students $8; discounts to groups; children 12 & under no charge. Closed Thanksgiving; Christmas. &

ARC GALLERY (ARTISTS, RESIDENTS OF CHICAGO), 2156 N. Damen Ave., Chicago, IL 60647-6482. Tel.: 773-252-2232.
E-mail: info@arcgallery.org
Web Site: www.arcgallery.org
Key Personnel: Pres., Carolyne King.
Institution Type/Description: Art Gallery.
Hours & Admission Prices: Wed.-Sat. 12-6, Sun. 12-4. No charge; donations requested. Closed all major holidays. &
Attendance: 6,200 (estimated)

THE ART INSTITUTE OF CHICAGO, 111 S. Michigan Ave., Chicago, IL 60603-6492. Tel.: 312-443-3600. Fax: 312-443-0849.
Web Site: www.artic.edu
Key Personnel: Chm. (V), Robert M. Levy; Pres. & Eloise W. Martin Dir., James Rondeau; Pres. School of the Art Inst., Elissa Tenny; Exec. Vice Pres. & C.F.O., Alison Sowden; Exec. Vice Pres., Gen. Counsel & Sec., Julia E. Getzels; Deputy Dir., Chair & Cur. Modern & Contemporary Art, Ann Goldstein; C.O.O., David Thurm; Grainger Exec. Dir. Conservation & Sr. Painting Conservator, Frank Zuccari; Exec. Dir. Libraries, Mary Woolever; Exec. Dir. Museum Registration, Jennifer Draffen; Vice Pres. Devel., Evelyn Jeffers; Dir. Dept. Protection Services Opers., Thomas Henkey; Dir. Design & Construction, Sara Urizar; Dir. Visitor Services & Museum Shop, Marianne Rathslag; Deputy Dir. Education, Judith Kirshner.
Institution Type/Description: Art Museum.
Hours & Admission Prices: Thurs. 10:30-8, Fri.-Wed. 10:30-5. Adults $25, teens 14-17, students & senior citizens 65 & over $19; children under 14, Illinois residents on Thurs. and members no charge. Closed Thanksgiving; Christmas. &
Attendance: 1,550,000 (estimated)

AVERILL AND BERNARD LEVITON A + D GALLERY, 619 S. Wabash Ave., Chicago, IL 60605. Tel.: 312-369-8687. Fax: 312-369-8009.
E-mail: adgallery@colum.edu
Web Site: www.colum.edu/adgallery
Key Personnel: Gallery Dir., Meg Duguid; Asst. Dir., Julianna Cuevas.
Institution Type/Description: Art Gallery.
Hours & Admission Prices: Tues.-Wed. & Fri.-Sat. 12-5, Thurs. 12-7. No charge. &
Attendance: 5,500 (estimated)

BALZEKAS MUSEUM OF LITHUANIAN CULTURE, 6500 S. Pulaski Rd., Chicago, IL 60629-5136. Tel.: 773-582-6500. Fax: 773-582-5133.
E-mail: info@balzekasmuseum.org
Web Site: www.balzekasmuseum.org
Key Personnel: Chm. & Pres. (V), Stanley Balzekas, Jr.; Exec. Dir., Rita Janz; Genealogist & Editor, Karile Vaitkute; Head Library, Robert Balzekas; Mgr. Membership & Collections, Regina Vasiliauskiene; Office Mgr., Barbara Howley.
Institution Type/Description: Lithuanian Culture Museum.
Hours & Admission Prices: Daily 10-4. Adults $9, senior citizens & students $7, children 12 & under $3; discounts to AAM & ICOM members; members no charge. Closed New Year's Day; Easter; Christmas. &
Attendance: 44,000 (estimated)

BRONZEVILLE CHILDREN'S MUSEUM, 9301 S. Stony Island Ave., Chicago, IL 60617-3644. Tel.: 773-721-9301. Fax: 773-721-9303.
E-mail: bronzvlle@aol.com
Web Site: www.bronzevillechildrensmuseum.com
Key Personnel: Pres., Peggy A. Montes.
Institution Type/Description: Children's Museum.
Hours & Admission Prices: Tues.-Sat. 10-2. Admission $5; members no charge.

BUSY BEAVER BUTTON MUSEUM, 3407 W. Armitage Ave., Chicago, IL 60647. Tel.: 773-645-3359.
E-mail: museum@busybeaver.net
Web Site: www.buttonmuseum.org
Key Personnel: Dir., Joel Carter; Dir., Christen Carter.
Institution Type/Description: Button History Museum.
Hours & Admission Prices: Mon.-Fri. 10-4; other times by appointment. No charge; donations accepted. &

CAMBODIAN AMERICAN HERITAGE MUSEUM AND KILLING FIELDS MEMORIAL, 2831 W. Lawrence Ave., Chicago, IL 60625-3619. Tel.: 773-878-7090. Fax: 773-878-5299.
E-mail: info@cai-nationalmuseum.org
Web Site: www.cai-nationalmuseum.org
Key Personnel: Pres., Mr. Sophorn Jeff Loeung.
Institution Type/Description: Cambodian Heritage Museum.
Hours & Admission Prices: Museum & Memorial: Tues.-Fri. 10-4, Sat.-Sun. by appointment. Community Center: Mon.-Fri. 9-5. Adults $6, students & seniors $4; children 12 & under no charge.

CHARNLEY-PERSKY HOUSE MUSEUM, 1365 N. Astor St., Chicago, IL 60610-2144. Tel.: 312-915-0105 & 573-1365. Fax: 312-573-1141.
E-mail: psaliga@sah.org
Web Site: www.sah.org
Key Personnel: Exec. Dir., Pauline Saliga; Pres. (V), Ken Tadashi Oshima.
Institution Type/Description: Historic House Museum: 1891-92 Charnley-Persky house designed by Louis Sullivan & Frank Lloyd Wright.
Hours & Admission Prices: Tour of House: Wed. 12-1, Sat. 10-1; groups by appointment. Adults $10, seniors $8, children 5-12 $5; IL teachers, members & Wed. no charge.
Attendance: 1,354 (actual)

THE CHICAGO ACADEMY OF SCIENCES/PEGGY NOTEBAERT NATURE MUSEUM, 2430 N. Cannon Dr., Chicago, IL 60614-2874. Tel.: 773-755-5100. Fax: 773-549-0344.
E-mail: info@naturemuseum.org
Web Site: naturemuseum.org
Key Personnel: Pres. & C.E.O., Deborah Lahey; Chm. (V), James C. Murray; Sr. Dir. Public Engagement, Jill Doub; Vice Pres., Chief Devel. & Mktg. Officer, Marc Miller; Vice Pres. Education, Michelle Rabkin; Chief Cur., Peggy Notebaert Nature Museum & Vice Pres. Museum Experience, Alvaro Ramos; Chief Cur., Chicago Academy of Sciences, Doug Taron, Ph.D.; Vice Pres., Dir. Finance & Administration & C.F.O., Sharon Walton.
Institution Type/Description: Natural Science Museum.
Hours & Admission Prices: Mon.-Fri. 9-5, Sat.-Sun. 10-5; call to confirm. Adults $9, seniors & students $7, children 3-12 $6; discounts to groups and AAM, ICOM & ASTC members; suggested donation days for Illinois residents on Thurs. Closed 1st Fri. in May; Thanksgiving; Christmas. &
Attendance: 308,000 (actual)

CHICAGO ARCHITECTURE FOUNDATION, 224 S. Michigan Ave., Chicago, IL 60604. Tel.: 312-922-3432, ext. 245. Fax: 312-922-2607.
E-mail: info@architecture.org
Web Site: www.architecture.org

Key Personnel: Pres. & C.E.O., Lynn Osmond; C.F.O., Matthew Biecker; Vice Pres. Education & Experiences, Gabrielle Lyon; Vice Pres. Operations & Business Strategy, Michael Malak.
Institution Type/Description: Architecture Museum & Center.
Hours & Admission Prices: Mon.-Sat. 9-7, Sun. 9-6. Bus Tours: $40. River Cruise: $39.74. Walking Tour: $20. Closed New Year's Day; Thanksgiving; Christmas. &
Attendance: 582,900 (estimated)

CHICAGO CHILDREN'S MUSEUM, Navy Pier, 700 E. Grand Ave., Suite 127, Chicago, IL 60611-3428. Tel.: 312-527-1000. Fax: 312-527-9082.
Web Site: www.chicagochildrensmuseum.org
Key Personnel: Chm. Bd., Jeffery S. Perry; Pres. & C.E.O., Jennifer Farrington; Vice Pres. Experience Devel. & Educational Programming, Natalie Bortoli; Vice Pres. Human Resources, Catherine Patyk; Vice Pres. Exhibit & Bldg. Operations, Peter Williams.
Institution Type/Description: Children's Museum.
Hours & Admission Prices: Thurs. 10-8, Fri.-Wed. 10-5. Adults & children $14, seniors $13; children under one, Thurs. 5pm-8pm & members no charge. Closed Thanksgiving; Christmas. &
Attendance: 400,000 (actual)

CHICAGO CULTURAL CENTER, 78 E. Washington St., Chicago, IL 60602-4801. Tel.: 312-744-6630. Fax: 312-744-2089. TDD: 312-744-2947.
E-mail: dcase@cityofchicago.org
Web Site: www.chicagoculturalcenter.org
Key Personnel: Commissioner, Chicago Dept. Cultural Affairs, Mark Kelly; Deputy Commissioner Visual Arts, Gregory Knight; Cur. Exhibitions, Lanny Silverman; Exhibitions Designer & Preparator, Greg Lunceford.
Institution Type/Description: Art Museum & Cultural Center.
Hours & Admission Prices: Cultural Center: Mon.-Thurs. 9-7, Fri.-Sat. 9-6, Sun. 10-6. No charge. Closed holidays. &
Attendance: 875,000 (estimated)

CHICAGO DESIGN MUSEUM, 108 N. State St., 3rd Fl., Chicago, IL 60602. Tel.: 312-894-6263. Facebook, Twitter.
E-mail: info@chidm.com
Web Site: chid.com
Institution Type/Description: Design Museum
Hours & Admission Prices: Tues.-Sat. 12-7. No charge.

CHICAGO HISTORY MUSEUM, 1601 N. Clark St., Chicago, IL 60614-6038. Tel.: 312-642-4600. Fax: 312-266-2077. TDD: 800-526-0857.
E-mail: lewis@chicagohistory.org
Web Site: www.chicagohistory.org
Formerly: Chicago Historical Society
Key Personnel: Dir., C.E.O. & Pres., Gary T. Johnson; Chm. (V), James L. Alexander; Exec. Vice Pres. & Chief Historian, Russell Lewis; Vice Pres. Finance & C.F.O., Cheryl Obermeyer; Vice Pres. External Rels., David Deyhle; Vice Pres. Interpretation & Education, John Russick; Sr. Cur., Olivia Mahoney; Dir. Corporate Events, Jessica Trent; Dir. Research & Access, Ellen Keith; Dir. Institutional Advancement, Randy Adamsick; Dir. Exhibitions, Tamara Biggs; Dir. Properties, John Yelen; Dir. Accounting, Leigh Stevenson; Dir. Technology, Reyes Garcia; Dir. Human Resources, Diane Ohi; Dir. Print & Multimedia Publications, Rosemary Adams; Dir. Visitors & Member Svcs., Virginia Fitzgerald; Dir. Curatorial Affairs, Joy Bivins; Andrew W. Mellon Dir. Collections, Alison Eisendrath; Historian & Dir. Studs Terkel Ctr. for Oral History, Peter Alter; Elizabeth F. Cheney Dir. Education, Nancy Villafranca; Dir. Chicago Metro/History Fair, Frank Valadez; Cur. Costumes, Petra Slinkard.
Institution Type/Description: History Museum.
Hours & Admission Prices: Museum: Mon.-Sat. 9:30-4:30, Sun. 12-5. Research Center: Sept.-Nov. Tues.-Fri. 1-4:30, Sat. 10-4:30. Audio Tours: adults $16, senior citizens 65 & over and students 13-22 $14; discounts for groups of 10 or more, AAM & ICOM members; DuSable Museum, National Museum of Mexican Art, and National Museum of Puerto Rican Arts & Culture members, and children 12 & under no charge. Research Center: daily $10; members no charge. Closed New Year's Eve & Day; day before Thanksgiving, Thanksgiving & day after Thanksgiving; Christmas Eve, Day & week. &
Attendance: 270,919 (actual)

CHICAGO MARITIME MUSEUM, 1200 W. 35th St., Ste. 0E-5010-River Level, Chicago, IL 60609-1305. Tel.: 773-376-1982. Fax: 773-696-9037.
E-mail: info@chicagomaritimemuseum.org
Web Site: chicagomaritimemuseum.org
Formerly: Chicago Maritime Society
Key Personnel: Pres. (V), Gerald H. Thomas; Museum Shop Mgr., Don Glasell.
Institution Type/Description: Maritime Museum.

Hours & Admission Prices: Call for hours. Adults $10, students $5; members no charge. &
Attendance: 1,000 (estimated)

CHICAGO PUBLIC LIBRARY, 400 S. State St., Harold Washington Library Center, Chicago, IL 60605-1216. Tel.: 312-747-4300.
E-mail: hwlc@chipublib.org
Web Site: www.chipublib.org
Key Personnel: Commissioner & C.E.O., Brian Bannon; First Deputy Commr., Andrea Saenz; Deputy Commr. Administration & Finance, Baronica Roberson; Dir. Learning & Economic Advancement, Mark Andersen; Asst. Commr. Ctrl. Library Services, Rodney Freeman; Dir. Fin., Teri Campbell; Dir. Cultural & Civic Engagement, Craig Davis; Dir. Teen Services, Jeremy Dunn; Chief Technology, Content & Innovation, Michelle Frisque; Dir. Procurement, Maria Kellner-Ligammari; Dir. Mktg., Mary Beth Mulholland; Dir. Engagement & Special Projects, Diane Marshbank-Murphy; Dir. Children's Services, Elizabeth McChesney; Asst. Chief Technology, Content & Innovation, Andrew Medlar; Dir. Govt. & Public Affairs, Patrick Molloy; Dir. Human Resources, Jennifer Ross; Asst. Commr. Neighborhood Svcs., Andrea Telli.
Institution Type/Description: History Museum: general exhibition site housed in the Chicago Public Library, Harold Washington Library Center.
Hours & Admission Prices: Library: Mon.-Thurs. 9-9, Fri.-Sat. 9-5, Sun. 1-5. Special Collections: Mon.-Tues. 12-6, Fri.-Sat. 12-4. No charge. &
Attendance: 182,489 (estimated)

CHICAGO STATE UNIVERSITY, PRESIDENT'S GALLERY, 9501 S. Martin Luther King Dr., Cook Admin. Bldg., 3rd Fl., Chicago, IL 60628-1598. Tel.: 773-995-3984.
E-mail: jander20@csu.edu
Web Site: www.csu.edu
Key Personnel: Cur., Joyce Owens Anderson.
Institution Type/Description: Art Gallery.
Hours & Admission Prices: Mon.-Fri. 8:30-6. No charge.

CHINESE-AMERICAN MUSEUM OF CHICAGO, 238 W. 23rd St., Chicago, IL 60616-1904. Tel.: 312-949-1000. Fax: 312-949-1001.
E-mail: office@ccamuseum.org
Web Site: www.ccamuseum.org
Institution Type/Description: Chinese-American Museum.
Hours & Admission Prices: Tues.-Wed. 9:30-2:30, Thurs.-Fri. 9:30-1:30, Sat.-Sun. 10-4. Suggested Donation: adults $5, seniors & students $3; members no charge.

CITY GALLERY AT THE HISTORIC WATER TOWER, 806 N. Michigan Ave., Chicago, IL 60611-2103. Mailing Address: Department of Cultural Affairs, 78 E. Washington St., 4th Fl., Chicago, IL 60602-4801. Tel.: 312-744-2400 & 742-0808.
E-mail: dcase@cityofchicago.org
Web Site: www.cityofchicago.org
Institution Type/Description: Photography Gallery: housed in the historic Chicago Water Tower; built in 1869. Listed on the National Register of Historic Places.
Hours & Admission Prices: Building: daily 10-6:30. No charge.

CLARKE HOUSE MUSEUM, 1827 S. Indiana Ave., Chicago, IL 60616-1308. Mailing Address: Glessner House Museum, 1800 S. Prairie Ave., Chicago, IL 60616-1320. Tel.: 312-745-0040. Fax: 312-745-0077.
E-mail: info@clarkehousemuseum.org
Web Site: www.clarkehousemuseum.org
Key Personnel: Cur., Rebecca LaBarre.
Institution Type/Description: Historic House Museum: 1836 Greek Revival building.
Hours & Admission Prices: Guided Tours: Wed. & Fri.-Sat. 1 & 3. No charge. Closed New Year's Day; Easter; Memorial Day; Independence Day; Labor Day; Thanksgiving; Christmas Eve & Day. &
Attendance: 6,000 (estimated)

COLUMBIA COLLEGE CHICAGO CENTER FOR THE BOOK & PAPER ARTS, 1104 S. Wabash, 2nd Fl., Chicago, IL 60605-2334. Tel.: 312-369-6630. Fax: 312-369-8082.
E-mail: bookandpaper@colum.edu
Web Site: www.bookandpaper.org
Key Personnel: Dir., Dr. Steve Woodall.
Institution Type/Description: Art Gallery.
Hours & Admission Prices: Gallery: Tues.-Wed. & Fri.-Sat. 12-5, Thurs. 12-7. Office: Mon.-Fri. 9:30-5. No charge.

DEPAUL ART MUSEUM, 935 W. Fullerton Ave., Chicago, IL 60614. Tel.: 773-325-7506 & 7593. Fax: 773-325-4506.
E-mail: artmuseum@depaul.edu
Web Site: depaul.edu/museum
Formerly: DePaul University Art Museum
Key Personnel: Dir. & Chief Cur., Julie Rodrigues Widholm; Collection & Exhibition Mgr., Laura-Caroline Johnson; Asst. Cur., Mia Lopez; Administrative Asst., Kaylee Wyant.
Institution Type/Description: University Art Museum.
Hours & Admission Prices: Wed.-Thurs. 11-7, Fri. 11-5, Sat.-Sun. 12-5. No charge; donations accepted. Closed university holidays. &
Attendance: 18,500 (actual)

DRIEHAUS MUSEUM, 40 E. Erie St., Chicago, IL 60611. Tel.: 312-482-8933, ext. 21.
E-mail: info@driehausmuseum.org
Web Site: www.driehausmuseum.org
Institution Type/Description: Historic House Museum: housed in the Samuel M. Nickerson Mansion.
Hours & Admission Prices: Tues.-Sun. 10-5. Adults $20, seniors 65 & over $15, students $10, active military, members and children 12 & under no charge. Closed New Year's Day; Independence Day; Thanksgiving; Christmas. &

DUSABLE MUSEUM OF AFRICAN-AMERICAN HISTORY, INC., 740 E. 56th Place, Chicago, IL 60637-1495. Tel.: 773-947-0600, ext. 246. Fax: 773-947-0677.
E-mail: cbethea@dusablemuseum.org
Web Site: www.dusablemuseum.org
Key Personnel: C.E.O. & Pres., Perri L. Irmer; C.O.O., Troy Ratliff; C.F.O., Alan Brazil; Education Svcs. Mgr., Amani Conley; Chief Cur., Leslie Guy; Dir. Special Events, Tracey Williams; Mgr. Visitor Svcs., Whitney Hamilton.
Institution Type/Description: History Museum.
Hours & Admission Prices: Tues.-Sat. 10-5, Sun. 12-5; groups by appointment. Adults $10, students & senior citizens $7, children 6-11 $3; discounts to AAM & ICOM members, Chicago residents & police, military; children under 5, members, Museums in the Park staff & Sun. no charge. Closed New Year's Day; Easter; Independence Day; Labor Day; Thanksgiving; Christmas. &
Attendance: 100,000 (actual)

EDGEWATER HISTORICAL SOCIETY, 5358 N. Ashland Ave., Chicago, IL 60640. Tel.: 773-506-4849.
E-mail: edgewaterhistoricalsociety@yahoo.com
Web Site: www.edgewaterhistory.org
Institution Type/Description: History Museum.
Hours & Admission Prices: Sat.-Sun. 1-4. No charge; donations accepted. Closed New Year's Eve & Day; Christmas Eve & Day. &

FASHION STUDY COLLECTION, Columbia College Chicago, 618 S. Michigan Ave., 8th Fl., Chicago, IL 60605-1901. Mailing Address: 600 S. Michigan Ave., Chicago, IL 60605. Tel.: 312-369-6283. Fax: 312-369-8422. Facebook.
E-mail: jwayneguite@colum.edu
Web Site: www.colum.edu/FashionCollection
Formerly: Fashion Columbia Study Collection
Key Personnel: Collections Mgr., Jacqueline WayneGuite.
Institution Type/Description: Fashion Collection.
Hours & Admission Prices: Research Center: Mon.-Thurs. 10-5. Garment Collection: Mon.-Thurs. 9-5, Fri. 9-3, by appointment only. No charge; donations accepted. &

FIELD MUSEUM, 1400 S. Lake Shore Dr., Chicago, IL 60605-2496. Tel.: 312-922-9410 & 665-7669. Fax: 312-922-0741. TDD: 312-341-9299.
E-mail: rlariviere@fieldmuseum.org
Web Site: www.fieldmuseum.org
Key Personnel: Pres. & C.E.O., Richard W. Lariviere, PhD; Bd. Chm. (V), Connie Keller; C.F.O., LeMont G. Booker, Sr.; Vice Pres. Institutional Advancement, Charles Katzenmeyer; Chief Human Resources Officer, Shawn VanDerziel; Vice Pres. Science & Education, Debra Moskovits; Chief Mktg. Officer, Ray DeThorne; Gen. Counsel, Lori Breslaur; Chief Tech. Oficer, Rob Zschernitz.
Institution Type/Description: Natural History Museum.
Hours & Admission Prices: Daily 9-5. Adults $24, senior citizens 65 & over and students with ID $21, children 3-11 $17; discounts to members, Chicago residents, AAM & ICOM members, military personnel, individual teachers, children under 3 & groups of 10 or more with appointment. All Access Pass: adults $38, student & senior $33, children 3-11 $27. Closed Christmas. &
Attendance: 1,390,000 (estimated)

FIRE MUSEUM OF GREATER CHICAGO, 5218 S. Western, Chicago, IL 60609. Mailing Address: 517 Senon Dr., Lemont, IL 60439-4093. Tel.: 877-225-7491.
Web Site: www.firemuseumofgreaterchicago.org
Institution Type/Description: Fire History Museum.
Hours & Admission Prices: Open House: Jan.-Nov. 4th Sat. each month, call for hours; groups by appointment. No charge; donations accepted. &

FREDERICK C. ROBIE HOUSE, 5757 S. Woodlawn Ave., Chicago, IL 60637-1698. Mailing Address: 209 S. LaSalle St., Ste. 118, Chicago, IL 60604. Tel.: 312-994-4000. Fax: 773-324-6099.
E-mail: info@flwright.org
Web Site: flwright.org
Key Personnel: C.E.O. & Pres., Celeste Adams; Chm. Bd., John Rafkin.
Institution Type/Description: Historic House Museum: 3-story residence designed by Frank Lloyd Wright, c.1908.
Hours & Admission Prices: Tours: Thurs.-Mon. 11-3; groups by appointment. Book Shop: Thurs.-Mon. 9:30-4:30. Adults $17, students, military and seniors 65 & over $14; members & children under 3 no charge. Closed New Year's Day; Thanksgiving; Christmas Eve & Day.
Attendance: 36,800 (actual)

GALLERY 400 - UNIVERSITY OF ILLINOIS AT CHICAGO, Art and Exhibition Hall, 400 S. Peoria St. (MC 034), Chicago, IL 60607. Tel.: 312-996-6114. Fax: 312-355-3444.
E-mail: gallery400@uic.edu
Web Site: gallery400.uic.edu
Key Personnel: Dir., Lorelei Stewart; Asst. Dir., Erin Nixon.
Institution Type/Description: Art Gallery.
Hours & Admission Prices: Tues.-Fri. 10-6, Sat. 12-6; other times by appointment. No charge. &
Attendance: 6,702 (actual)

GARFIELD PARK CONSERVATORY, 300 N. Central Park Ave., Chicago, IL 60624-1945. Tel.: 312-746-5100. Fax: 773-638-1777.
E-mail: donorservices@garfieldpark.org
Web Site: www.garfieldconservatory.org
Key Personnel: Dir. Conservatories, Mary Eysenbach; Deputy Dir., Matthew Barrett; Foreman, Thomas Costanza.
Institution Type/Description: Horticultural Conservatory.
Hours & Admission Prices: Wed. 9-8, Thurs.-Tues. 9-5. No charge; donations accepted. &
Attendance: 160,000 (actual)

THE GLASS GALLERY, 410 S. Michigan Ave., Ste. 207, Chicago, IL 60605. Tel.: 312-583-1177. Fax: 312-583-1177. Facebook: @lhselmanltd.
E-mail: info@selman.com
Web Site: www.theglassgallery.com
Key Personnel: Owner, Ben Clark; Gallery Rels. Mgr., Penelope Turgeon.
Institution Type/Description: Paperweight Museum.
Hours & Admission Prices: Showroom: Mon.-Fri. 9-5, Sat. & Sun. 10-4.

GLESSNER HOUSE MUSEUM, 1800 S. Prairie Ave., Chicago, IL 60616-1320. Tel.: 312-326-1480. Facebook: Glessner House Museum.
E-mail: info@glessnerhouse.org
Web Site: www.glessnerhouse.org
Key Personnel: Exec. Dir., William Tyre; Pres., Barbara Gordon; Tour Coord., Gwen Carrion.
Institution Type/Description: Historic House: 1887 home designed by H.H. Richardson.
Hours & Admission Prices: Visitors Center: Wed.-Sun. 11-4. Guided Tours: 11:30, 1 & 2:30. Adults $15, senior citizens & students $12, children 5-12 $8; discounts to AAM, AAA, National Trust & Public Broadcasting members; children under 5, members & Wed. no charge. Closed New Year's Day; Easter; Memorial Day; Independence Day; Labor Day; Thanksgiving; Christmas Eve & Day.
Attendance: 10,000 (estimated)

HISTORIC PULLMAN FOUNDATION, Visitor Center & Museum, 11141 S. Cottage Grove Ave., Chicago, IL 60628-4614. Mailing Address: 614 E. 113th St., Chicago, IL 60628-5100. Tel.: 773-785-8181, 3828 (Tours) & 8901 (Visitor Center). Fax: 773-785-8182. Facebook: Historic Pullman Foundation.
E-mail: foundation@pullmanil.org
Web Site: www.pullmanil.org
Institution Type/Description: Historic District: 1880-84 built by Pullman's Palace Car Co.; first planned model industrial community.

Hours & Admission Prices: Visitor Center: Tues.-Sun. 11-3. No charge; donations accepted. Tours: May-Oct. first Sun. each month 1:30; groups of 20 or more by appointment. Adults $10, seniors & students $7. Closed national holidays. &
Attendance: 475,000 (estimated)

HYDE PARK ART CENTER, 5020 S. Cornell Ave., Chicago, IL 60615-3016. Tel.: 773-324-5520. Fax: 773-324-6641.
E-mail: generalinfo@hydeparkart.org
Web Site: hydeparkart.org
Key Personnel: Exec. Dir., Kate Lorenz; Chm. (V), Richard Wright.
Institution Type/Description: Art Gallery & School.
Hours & Admission Prices: Mon.-Thurs. 9-8, Fri.-Sat. 9-5, Sun. 12-5. No charge; donations accepted. &
Attendance: 45,000 (estimated)

ILLINOIS STATE MUSEUM, CHICAGO GALLERY, 100 W. Randolph, Ste. 2-100, Chicago, IL 60601-3921. Tel.: 312-814-5322. Fax: 312-814-3471.
E-mail: dstapleton@museum.state.il.us
Web Site: www.museum.state.il.us/ismsites/chicago/
Formerly: State of Illinois Art Gallery
Key Personnel: Assoc. Cur. & Gallery Mgr., Jane Stevens; Assoc. Cur. Art, Douglas Stapleton.
Institution Type/Description: Art Gallery.
Hours & Admission Prices: Mon.-Fri. 9-5; call to confirm. No charge. Closed national holidays. &
Attendance: 41,762 (actual)

INDO-AMERICAN HERITAGE MUSEUM, 6328 N. California Ave., Chicago, IL 60659. Tel.: 708-658-4246. Facebook.
E-mail: info@iahmuseum.org
Web Site: www.iahmuseum.org
Key Personnel: Pres., Padma Rangaswamy.
Institution Type/Description: Heritage Museum.
Hours & Admission Prices: Mon.-Sat. 10-5 by appointment. No charge; donations accepted.
Attendance: 3,569

INTERNATIONAL MUSEUM OF SURGICAL SCIENCE, 1524 N. Lake Shore Dr., Chicago, IL 60610-1651. Tel.: 312-642-6502.
E-mail: info@imss.org
Web Site: www.imss.org
Institution Type/Description: Medical Museum: housed in 1917 Howard Van Doren Shaw Mansion.
Hours & Admission Prices: Mon.-Fri 10-4, Sat.-Sun. 10-5. Adults $17, senior citizens 65 & over, students, educators, and military $13, children 4-17 $9; children 3 & under and Illinois residents on Tues. no charge. Closed New Year's Eve & Day; Easter; Memorial Day; Independence Day; Labor Day; Thanksgiving; Christmas Eve & Day. &
Attendance: 15,000 (actual)

INTUIT: THE CENTER FOR INTUITIVE AND OUTSIDER ART, 756 N. Milwaukee Ave., Chicago, IL 60642-5939. Tel.: 312-243-9088. Fax: 312-243-9089.
E-mail: intuit@art.org
Web Site: www.art.org
Key Personnel: Exec. Dir., Debra Kerr; Education Mgr., Joel Javier; Cur. & Collections Mgr., Alison Amick; Mgr. Learning & Engagement, Melissa Smith; Interim Mktg. Mgr., Maureen M. Jasculca.
Institution Type/Description: Art Museum.
Hours & Admission Prices: Tues.-Wed. & Fri.-Sat. 11-6, Thurs. 11-7:30. Suggested Donation: adults $5; discounts for AAM & ICOM members; members & children under 12 no charge. Closed New Year's Day; Thanksgiving; Christmas Eve & Day. &
Attendance: 10,000 (estimated)

IRISH AMERICAN HERITAGE CENTER, 4626 N. Knox Ave., Chicago, IL 60630-4035. Tel.: 773-282-7035. Fax: 773-282-0380.
E-mail: info@irishahc.org
Web Site: irish-american.org
Key Personnel: Pres. (V), Gene Cooney.
Institution Type/Description: Heritage Center.
Hours & Admission Prices: Office: Mon.-Fri. 8:30-5:30, Sat. 9-1. Museum: by appointment. No charge; donations accepted. &
Attendance: 9,000,000 (estimated)

JAMES P. FITZGIBBONS HISTORICAL MUSEUM, 9801 Ave. G, Calumet Park Fieldhouse, Chicago, IL 60617. Tel.: 312-721-7948.
E-mail: karenbrozynski@sbcglobal.net

Key Personnel: Pres. (V), Karen Brozynski.
Institution Type/Description: Historical Society Museum.
Hours & Admission Prices: Thurs. 1-4. No charge; donations accepted.

JANE ADDAMS HULL-HOUSE MUSEUM, UNIVERSITY OF ILLINOIS CHICAGO, 800 S. Halsted, (M/C 051), Chicago, IL 60607-7017. Tel.: 312-413-5353. Fax: 312-413-2092. Facebook; Twitter; Instagram.
E-mail: jahh@uic.edu
Web Site: www.hullhousemuseum.org
Key Personnel: Dir., Jennifer A. Scott.
Institution Type/Description: Historic House Site: 1856 Hull Mansion occupied by Jane Addams in 1889; serving as the first settlement building of Hull House complex; 1907 Resident's Dining Hall.
Hours & Admission Prices: Tues.-Fri. 10-4, Sun. 12-4. Suggested Donation: $5. Closed major holidays.
Attendance: 13,000 (actual)

JOHN DAVID MOONEY FOUNDATION, 114 W. Kinzie St., Chicago, IL 60654. Tel.: 312-822-0483. Fax: 312-222-4119.
E-mail: info@jdmf.org
Web Site: mooneyfoundation.org
Key Personnel: John David Mooney.
Institution Type/Description: Art Gallery.
Hours & Admission Prices: Call for hours.

JOHN G. SHEDD AQUARIUM, 1200 S. Lake Shore Dr., Chicago, IL 60605-2490. Tel.: 312-939-2438. Fax: 312-939-8069.
E-mail: contactus@sheddaquarium.org
Web Site: www.sheddaquarium.org
Key Personnel: Pres. & C.E.O., Bridget Coughlin; Exec. Vice Pres. & C.O.O., Michael Delfini; Sr. Vice Pres. External & Regulatory Affairs, Jim Robinett; Sr. Vice Pres. Corp. Partnerships & Programs, Sandy Marek; Sr. Vice Pres. Conservation Partnerships & Programs, Cheryl Mell; Sr. Vice Pres. Human Resources, Nancy Anschel; Exec. Vice Pres. & C.F.O., Joyce Simon; Sr. Vice Pres. Mktg., Guest Experiences & Sales, Meghan Curran; Exec. Vice Pres. Animals, Tim Binder.
Institution Type/Description: Aquarium.
Hours & Admission Prices: June 10-Aug. 20 daily 9-6; Aug. 21-June 9 Mon.-Fri. 9-5, Sat.-Sun. 9-6. Total Experience Pass (Waters of the World, Amazon Rising, Wild Reef, Abbott Oceanarium, Polar Play Zone, one 4-D Experience & ticket to Shedd Aquatic Show): adults $39.95, youth $30.95. Shedd Pass (Waters of the World, Amazon Rising, Wild Reef, Oceanarium, & Polar Play Zone): adults $30.95, youth $21.95. Abbott Aquarium only: adults $8, youth $6; members no charge. Closed Christmas. &
Attendance: 2,000,000 (estimated)

LATVIAN FOLK ART MUSEUM, 4146 N. Elston Ave., Chicago, IL 60618-1828. Tel.: 773-588-2085. Facebook: Latvian Folk Art Museum.
E-mail: latvianfolkart@gmail.com
Key Personnel: Pres. (V), Dace Kezbers; Dir. & Treas., Marite Plume.
Institution Type/Description: Folk Art Museum.
Hours & Admission Prices: By appointment. No charge; donations accepted. Closed holidays.
Attendance: 100 (estimated)

LINCOLN PARK CONSERVATORY, 2391 N. Stockton Dr., Chicago, IL 60614-3419. Tel.: 312-742-7736 & 746-5995. Fax: 312-742-5619.
E-mail: mary@cpd.com
Web Site: www.chicagoparkdistrict.com
Key Personnel: Facility Supvr., Mary Eysenbach.
Institution Type/Description: Horticultural Conservatory: housed in 1892 Lincoln Park Conservatory.
Hours & Admission Prices: Daily 9-5; guided tours by appointment. No charge; donations accepted. &
Attendance: 460,000 (estimated)

LINCOLN PARK ZOOLOGICAL GARDENS, 2001 N. Clark St., Chicago, IL 60614-4757. Mailing Address: P.O. Box 14903, Chicago, IL 60614-0903. Tel.: 312-742-2000. Fax: 312-742-2137. Facebook & Twitter: @lincolnparkzoo.
Web Site: www.lpzoo.org
Key Personnel: Zoo Dir., Pres. & C.E.O., Kevin J. Bell; Bd. Chair, John Ettelson; Vice Pres. Conservation & Science, Lisa Faust; Exec. Vice Pres., Megan Reinertsen Ross, Ph.D.; Sr. Vice Pres. Capital & Programmatic Planning, Steven Thompson, Ph.D.; Dr. Lester E. Fisher Dir. Veterinary Sciences, Kathryn Gamble, D.V.M.; Animal Records & Permits Mgr., Adrienne Horrigan; Dir.

Urban Wildlife Inst., Seth Magle, Ph.D.; Conservation & Science Coord., Julie Somor; Veterinary Technician, Lauren Granger.
Institution Type/Description: Zoo.
Hours & Admission Prices: Winter: daily 9-5; Summer: Mon.-Fri. 9-6, Sat.-Sun. & holidays 9-7. No charge. ♿
Attendance: 3,600,000 (estimated)

THE LITHUANIAN MUSEUM, 5600 S. Claremont Ave., Chicago, IL 60636-1039. Tel.: 773-434-4545. Fax: 773-434-9363. Facebook: Lithuanian Research and Studies Center.
E-mail: info@lithuanianresearch.org
Web Site: www.lithuanianresearch.org
Key Personnel: Pres., Dr. Augustine Idzelis, Ph.D., J.D.; Exec. Vice Pres., Kristina Lapienyte; Chm. (V), Dr. Robert Vitas, Ph.D.; Vice Pres. Communications, Loreta Timukiene.
Institution Type/Description: Lithuanian History Museum.
Hours & Admission Prices: Wed.-Fri. 9-3; other times by appointment. No charge; donations accepted. ♿
Attendance: 6,000 (estimated)

LOYOLA UNIVERSITY MUSEUM OF ART, 820 N. Michigan Ave., Chicago, IL 60611-2147. Tel.: 312-915-7600. Fax: 312-915-6388. Facebook: LUMA Chicago.
E-mail: luma@luc.edu
Web Site: www.luc.edu/luma
Key Personnel: Cur., Natasha Ritsma; Head Preparator, Tim Duncan; Administrative & Museum Shop Mgr., Guadalupe Pastenes; Registrar, Mary Albert; Information Asst., Julie Kuzera.
Institution Type/Description: Art Museum.
Hours & Admission Prices: Tues. 11-8, Wed.-Sat. 11-6. Adults $8, senior citizens $6, students under 25 with ID $2; discounts to groups, AAM, AAMUG, NARM, MSA, ROAM & ICOM members; military families, children under 18, members of the clergy, museum professionals, LUC Staff, faculty, students & Tues. no charge. Closed New Year's Eve & Day; Good Friday; Easter; Independence Day; Thanksgiving; Christmas Eve & Day. ♿
Attendance: 15,000 (estimated)

MAYA POLSKY GALLERY, 980 N. Michigan Ave., #1448, Chicago, IL 60654. Tel.: 312-440-0055. Facebook: @mayapolskagallery.
E-mail: info@mayapolskagallery.com
Key Personnel: Owner, Maya Polsky.
Institution Type/Description: Art Gallery.
Hours & Admission Prices: Tues.-Fri. 10-5, Sat. 11-5.

MUSEUM OF BROADCAST COMMUNICATIONS, 360 N. State St., Chicago, IL 60654-5411. Tel.: 312-245-8200. Fax: 312-245-8207.
E-mail: sjajkowski@museum.tv
Web Site: www.museum.tv
Key Personnel: Founder, Pres. & C.E.O., Bruce DuMont.
Institution Type/Description: Broadcast History Museum.
Hours & Admission Prices: Tues.-Sat. 10-5. Adults $12, seniors 65 & over $10, children 4-12 $6; children under 4 & members no charge. Closed federal holidays.

MUSEUM OF CONTEMPORARY ART CHICAGO, 220 E. Chicago Ave., Chicago, IL 60611-2644. Tel.: 312-280-2660. Fax: 312-799-3510.
E-mail: info@mcachicago.org
Web Site: www.mcachicago.org
Key Personnel: Pritzker Dir., Madeleine Grynsztejn; Chm., Anne Kaplan; James W. Alsdorf Chief Cur., Michael Darling; Chief Content Officer, Susan Chun.
Institution Type/Description: Art Museum & Center.
Hours & Admission Prices: Tues. 10-8, Wed.-Sun. 10-5. Adults $12, students with ID & seniors $7; discounts to AAM & ICOM members; members, military, children 12 & under & IL residents on Tues. no charge. Closed New Year's Day; Thanksgiving; Christmas. ♿
Attendance: 249,000 (estimated)

MUSEUM OF CONTEMPORARY PHOTOGRAPHY, COLUMBIA COLLEGE CHICAGO, 600 S. Michigan Ave., Chicago, IL 60605-1900. Tel.: 312-663-5554. Fax: 312-369-8067.
E-mail: mocp@colum.edu
Web Site: www.mocp.org
Key Personnel: Exec. Dir., Natasha Egan; Deputy Dir. & Chief Cur., Karen Irvine; Head Operations, Stephanie Conaway.
Institution Type/Description: Photography Museum.
Hours & Admission Prices: Academic Year: Mon.-Wed. & Fri.-Sat. 10-5, Thurs. 10-8, Sun. 12-5; see website to confirm. No charge; donations accepted. Closed

New Year's Eve & Day; Martin Luther King Jr. Day; Memorial Day; Independence Day; Labor Day; Thanksgiving weekend; Christmas Eve, Day & week. ♿
Attendance: 50,000 (estimated)

MUSEUM OF SCIENCE AND INDUSTRY, 5700 S. Lake Shore Dr., Chicago, IL 60637-2003. Tel.: 773-684-1414. Fax: 773-684-7141. Facebook, Instagram & Twitter.
E-mail: contact@msichicago.org
Web Site: www.msichicago.org
Key Personnel: Pres. & C.E.O., David R. Mosena; Vice Pres. Ops. & Chief of Staff, Mary Krinock; Vice Pres. External Affairs, Sheila M. Cawley; Vice Pres. Finance & Admin. & C.F.O., Rose B. Fealy; Chief of People and Culture, Yolanda Stephens; Vice Pres. Mktg. & Communications & Chief Mktg. Officer, Matthew C. Simpson.
Institution Type/Description: Science & Technology Museum: housed in classic Greek structure constructed as the Palace of Fine Arts for the World's Fair Columbian Exposition of 1893 in Chicago, located on the site of the Exposition in Jackson Park.
Hours & Admission Prices: Daily 9:30-4. Call for seasonal hours. Adults $21.95, children 3-11 $12.95; members & children under 3 no charge. Closed Thanksgiving; Christmas. ♿
Attendance: 1,400,000 (estimated)

NATIONAL HELLENIC MUSEUM, 333 S. Halsted St., Chicago, IL 60661-5415. Tel.: 312-655-1234. Fax: 312-655-1221.
E-mail: info@hellenicmuseum.org
Web Site: www.nationalhellenicmuseum.org
Formerly: Hellenic Museum & Cultural Center
Key Personnel: Interim Pres., Laura Calamos Nasir; Collections Mgr., Margaret Fraser; Devel. Coord., Francesca Peppiatt; Finance & Operations Mgr., Kelly Mikronis-Obrzut; Guest Svcs. Mgr., Ingrid Koepcke.
Institution Type/Description: Greek History, Culture & Art Museum.
Hours & Admission Prices: Tues.-Wed. & Fri. 11-5, Thurs. 11-8, Sat.-Sun. 11-5. Adults $10, seniors & students $8, children 3-12 $7; children under 3 & members no charge. Closed New Year's Day; Thanksgiving; Christmas. ♿
Attendance: 10,000 (estimated)

NATIONAL ITALIAN AMERICAN SPORTS HALL OF FAME, 1431 W. Taylor St., Chicago, IL 60607-4625. Tel.: 312-226-5566. Fax: 312-226-5678.
E-mail: info@niashf.org
Web Site: www.niashf.org
Key Personnel: Founder & Chm., George Randazzo.
Institution Type/Description: Sports Museum.
Hours & Admission Prices: Mon.-Sat. 12-4. Adults $5, seniors $4, children $3. ♿

NATIONAL MUSEUM OF MEXICAN ART, 1852 W. 19th St., Chicago, IL 60608-2706. Tel.: 312-738-1503. Fax: 312-738-9740.
E-mail: info@nationalmuseumofmexicanart.org
Web Site: www.nationalmuseumofmexicanart.org
Formerly: Mexican Fine Arts Center Museum
Key Personnel: C.E.O., Pres. & Founder, Carlos Tortolero; Chief Cur. & Dir. Visual Arts, Cesareo Moreno.
Institution Type/Description: Art Museum.
Hours & Admission Prices: Tues.-Sun. 10-5. No charge; donations accepted. Closed major holidays. ♿
Attendance: 168,000 (actual)

THE NATIONAL MUSEUM OF PUERTO RICAN ARTS & CULTURE, 3015 W. Division St., Chicago, IL 60622. Tel.: 773-486-8345. Fax: 773-486-8806.
E-mail: info@nmprac.org
Web Site: nmprac.org
Formerly: Institute of Puerto Rican Arts & Culture
Key Personnel: Dir., Billy Ocasio.
Institution Type/Description: Art Gallery.
Hours & Admission Prices: Tues.-Fri. 10-4, Sat. 10-1. No charge; donations accepted.
Attendance: 25,000 (estimated)

NATIONAL PUBLIC HOUSING MUSEUM, 625 N. Kingsbury St., Chicago, IL 60654. Tel.: 773-245-1621. Fax: 312-996-0708.
E-mail: info@nphm.org
Web Site: www.nphm.org
Key Personnel: Dir. Public Programs & Engagement, Shirley Alfaro; Assoc. Dir., Robert J. Smith, III.
Institution Type/Description: History Museum.
Hours & Admission Prices: Mon-Fri. 10-5. No charge; donations accepted.

NATIONAL VETERANS ART MUSEUM, 4041 N. Milwaukee Ave., 2nd Fl., Chicago, IL 60641-1834. Tel.: 312-326-0270. Facebook: @NationalVeteransArtMuseum.
E-mail: info@nvam.org
Web Site: www.nvam.org
Formerly: National Vietnam Veterans Art Museum
Key Personnel: Exec. Dir., Brendan Foster; Chm. (V), Lionel Rabb; Gallery Coord., Destinee Oitzinger; Asst. Education Coord., Monica Tantoco; Programming Asst., Monserrat Wisdom.
Institution Type/Description: Veteran Art Museum.
Hours & Admission Prices: Tues.-Sat. 10-5. No charge; donations accepted. &
Attendance: 8,112 (estimated)

ORIENTAL INSTITUTE MUSEUM, UNIVERSITY OF CHICAGO, 1155 E. 58th St., Chicago, IL 60637-1569. Tel.: 773-702-9520. Fax: 773-702-9853.
E-mail: oi-museum@uchicago.edu
Web Site: oi.uchicago.edu
Key Personnel: Dir., Christopher Woods; Conservator, Laura D'Alessandro; Registrar, Helen McDonald; Gift Shop Mgr., Denise Browning; Conservator, Alison Whyte.
Institution Type/Description: Archaeology, Ancient History & Art Museum.
Hours & Admission Prices: Tues. & Thurs.-Sun. 10-5, Wed. 10-8. Suggested Donation: adults $10, seniors $7, children under 12 $5. Closed New Year's Day; Independence Day; Thanksgiving; Christmas. &
Attendance: 60,113 (actual)

PACKER SCHOPF GALLERY, 7445 N. Campbell, Chicago, IL 60645. Tel.: 773-458-3150. Facebook, Instagram & Twitter: @packergallery.
E-mail: packer@packergallery.com
Web Site: www.packergallery.com
Key Personnel: Owner, Aron Packer.
Institution Type/Description: Virtual Art Gallery.
Hours & Admission Prices: Visit www.packergallery.com for online exhibits.

THE PALETTE & CHISEL, 1012 N. Dearborn, Chicago, IL 60610-2804. Tel.: 312-642-4400. Fax: 312-642-4317.
E-mail: fineart1012@sbcglobal.net
Web Site: www.paletteandchisel.org
Key Personnel: Exec. Dir., William Ewers; Pres. (V), Val Yachik; Vice Pres., Jack Beckstrom; Treas., Sharon Williams.
Institution Type/Description: Art Academy: housed in c.1875 double bay Italianate mansion.
Hours & Admission Prices: Mon.-Fri. 10:30-6:30; other times by appointment. No charge for exhibitions; fees for classes; workshops & lectures; discounts for members. Office closed New Year's Day; Memorial Day; Independence Day; Labor Day; Thanksgiving; Christmas Eve & Day.
Attendance: 750 (estimated)

PERIMETER GALLERY, 210 W. Superior St., Chicago, IL 60654. Tel.: 312-266-9473. Fax: 312-266-7984.
E-mail: perimeterchicago@perimetergallery.com
Web Site: perimetergallery.com
Key Personnel: Dir., Frank Paluch; Assoc. Dir., Scott Ashley; Registrar, Joanna Foley.
Institution Type/Description: Art Gallery.
Hours & Admission Prices: Tues.-Sat. 10:30-5:30. No charge.

THE POLISH MUSEUM OF AMERICA, 984 N. Milwaukee Ave., Chicago, IL 60642-4101. Tel.: 773-384-3352. Facebook.
E-mail: pma@polishmuseumofamerica.org
Web Site: www.polishmuseumofamerica.org
Key Personnel: Managing Dir., Malgorata Kot; Pres., Richard Owsiany; Archivist, Halina Misterka; Museum Shop Mgr., Mary Jane Robles.
Institution Type/Description: Ethnic Museum.
Hours & Admission Prices: Museum: Wed. 11-7, Fri.-Tues. 11-4. Library: Mon.-Tues. & Fri. 10-4, Wed. 1-7. Adults $7, students & senior citizens $6, members $5. &
Attendance: 10,000 (estimated)

THE PRITZKER MILITARY MUSEUM & LIBRARY, 104 S. Michigan Ave., Chicago, IL 60603. Tel.: 312-374-9333. Fax: 312-374-9314. Facebook.
E-mail: info@pritzkermilitary.org
Web Site: www.pritzkermilitary.org
Key Personnel: Pres. & C.E.O., Kenneth Clarke; Chm. (V), Col. J.N. Pritzker, IL ARNG (Ret.); Chief Librarian, Theresa A.R. Embrey, MLIS.
Institution Type/Description: Library & Gallery.

Hours & Admission Prices: Mon. & Fri.-Sat. 10-4, Tues.-Thurs. 10-6, Sun. 12-4. Adults $5; members & active duty military with ID no charge. Closed New Year's Day; Thanksgiving & day after; Christmas & 2 days after. &
Attendance: 18,129 (actual)

THE RENAISSANCE SOCIETY AT THE UNIVERSITY OF CHICAGO, 5811 S. Ellis Ave., Cobb Hall, 4th Fl., Chicago, IL 60637-1404. Tel.: 773-702-8670. Fax: 773-702-9669.
E-mail: info@renaissancesociety.org
Web Site: www.renaissancesociety.org
Key Personnel: Exec. Dir., Solvelg Ovstebo; Devel. Assoc., Julia DeRose; Registrar & Dir. Publications, Karen Reimer; Chief Preparator, Pierre Sondeijker.
Institution Type/Description: Contemporary Art Museum.
Hours & Admission Prices: Academic Year: Tues.-Fri. 10-5, Sat.-Sun. 12-5. No charge. Closed national holidays. &
Attendance: 20,000 (estimated)

RIDGE HISTORICAL SOCIETY - GRAVER-DRISCOLL HOUSE, 10621 S. Seeley Ave., Chicago, IL 60643-2618. Tel.: 773-881-1675. Facebook.
E-mail: ridgehistory@hotmail.com
Web Site: www.ridgehistoricalsociety.org
Institution Type/Description: Historical Society Museum: housed in the former home of the Herbert Spencer Graver family; built in 1922.
Hours & Admission Prices: By appointment. No charge; donations accepted. &

SACKRIDER MUSEUM OF HANDBAGS, Mailing Address: 2452 N. Richmond St., Chicago, IL 60647-2618. Tel.: 312-330-7601.
E-mail: info@thesack.org
Web Site: thesack.org
Key Personnel: Founding Dir. & Pres., Jill Brady.
Institution Type/Description: Virtual Handbag Museum.
Hours & Admission Prices: Visit thesack.org for online exhibts.

SCHNEIDER GALLERY, 770 N. LaSalle Dr. #401, Chicago, IL 60654. Tel.: 312-988-4033.
E-mail: schneidergalleryinfo@gmail.com
Web Site: schneidergallerychicago.com
Key Personnel: Dir., Martha Schneider.
Institution Type/Description: Art Gallery.
Hours & Admission Prices: Tues.-Sat. 11-5. No charge. &
Attendance: 2,400 (estimated)

SCHOOL OF THE ART INSTITUTE OF CHICAGO, BETTY RYMER GALLERY, Physical/Mailing Address: 111 S. Michigan Ave., Chicago, IL 60603-6404. Tel.: 312-629-6635. Fax: 312-443-1493.
E-mail: exhibitions-saic@saic.edu
Web Site: www.artic.edu/exhibitions
Institution Type/Description: Art Gallery.
Hours & Admission Prices: Tues.-Sat. 11-6.

SCHOOL OF THE ART INSTITUTE OF CHICAGO, SULLIVAN GALLERIES, 33 S. State St., 7th Fl., Chicago, IL 60603-2809. Mailing Address: 37 S. Wabash - Sharp Bldg., Ste. 821, Chicago, IL 60603. Tel.: 312-629-6635. Fax: 312-629-6636.
E-mail: exhibitions-saic@saic.edu
Web Site: www.saic.edu/sullivangalleries
Formerly: School of the Art Institute of Chicago, Gallery 2
Key Personnel: Exec. Dir., Mary Jane Jacob.
Institution Type/Description: College Art Gallery.
Hours & Admission Prices: Tues.-Sat. 11-6. No charge. Closed holidays. &
Attendance: 97,098 (actual)

SMART MUSEUM OF ART, University of Chicago, 5550 S. Greenwood Ave., Chicago, IL 60637-1506. Tel.: 773-702-0200. Fax: 773-702-3121.
E-mail: smart-museum@uchicago.edu
Web Site: smartmuseum.uchicago.edu
Key Personnel: Dana Feitler Dir., Alison Gass; Cur., Global Comtemp. Art, Orianna Cacchione; Assoc. Cur., Modern & Contemp. Art, Jennifer Carty; Deputy Dir. & Cur. Pub. Practice, Michael Christiano; Head Registrar, Sara Hindmarch; Deputy Dir. Academic & Curatorial Affairs and Dir. Feitler Center for Academic Inquiry, Issa Lampe; Assoc. Dir. Communications, C.J. Lind; Dir. Develop., Molly McKenzie; Adjunct Cur., Christine Mehring; Asst. Cur. Academic Initiatives, Berit Ness; Deputy Dir. Museum Affairs & Strategic Impact, Jill Sterrett; Cur. Public Art, Laura Steward; Curatorial Fellow for Diversity in the Arts, Leslie Wilson; Adjunct Cur., Wu Hung.
Institution Type/Description: University Art Museum.

Hours & Admission Prices: Tues.-Wed. & Fri.-Sun. 10-5, Thurs. 10-8. No charge; donations accepted. Closed holidays. ♿
Attendance: 56,990 (actual)

SPERTUS INSTITUTE, 610 S. Michigan Ave., Chicago, IL 60605-1901. Tel.: 312-322-1747 & 1700. Fax: 312-922-3934.
E-mail: info@spertus.edu
Web Site: www.spertus.edu
Key Personnel: Pres. & C.E.O., Dr. Hal M. Lewis; Cur. Collections & Exhibitions, Ionit Behar.
Institution Type/Description: Cultural, Art & Children's Museum.
Hours & Admission Prices: Sun.-Wed. 10-5, Thurs. 10-6, Fri. 10-3. Closed Jewish & national holidays. ♿
Attendance: 50,000 (actual)

STEPHEN A. DOUGLAS TOMB, 636 E. 35th St., Chicago, IL 60616-4196. Mailing Address: Illinois Historic Preservation Agency, 1 N. Old State Capitol Plz., Springfield, IL 62701-1507. Tel.: 312-225-2620. Fax: 312-225-7855.
E-mail: hpa.info@illinois.gov
Web Site: www.state.il.us/hpa/hs/douglas_tomb.htm
Institution Type/Description: Historic Site: 1866-1881 Stephen A. Douglas Tomb designed by Leonard W. Volk. Listed on the National Register of Historic Places.
Hours & Admission Prices: Wed.-Sun. 9-5. No charge. Closed New Year's Day; Thanksgiving; Christmas. ♿
Attendance: 15,000 (estimated)

SWEDISH AMERICAN HISTORICAL SOCIETY, 3225 W. Foster Ave., Chicago, IL 60625-4823. Mailing Address: 3225 W. Foster Ave., Box 48, Chicago, IL 60625-4823. Tel.: 773-538-5722.
E-mail: info@swedishamericanhist.org
Web Site: www.swedishamericanhist.org
Institution Type/Description: Historical Society Archives.
Hours & Admission Prices: Mon.-Fri. by appointment. No charge. Closed legal holidays. ♿

SWEDISH AMERICAN MUSEUM, 5211 N. Clark St., Chicago, IL 60640-2101. Tel.: 773-728-8111. Fax: 773-728-8870.
E-mail: museum@samac.org
Web Site: www.swedishamericanmuseum.org
Key Personnel: Exec. Dir., Karin Moen Abercrombie; Chair, Janet Nelson.
Institution Type/Description: Swedish History & Immigration Museum.
Hours & Admission Prices: Mon.-Fri. 10-4, Sat.-Sun. 11-4. Family $10, adults $4, seniors, students & children $3; members no charge. Children's Museum of Immigration: Mon.-Thurs. 1-4, Fri. 10-4, Sat.-Sun. 11-4. ♿
Attendance: 45,000 (estimated)

UKRAINIAN INSTITUTE OF MODERN ART, 2320 W. Chicago Ave., Chicago, IL 60622-4722. Tel.: 773-227-5522.
E-mail: info@uima-chicago.org
Web Site: www.uima-chicago.org
Key Personnel: Chm., Dr. Paul Nadzikewycz; Vice Chm., Orysia Cardoso; Cur., Adrienne Kochman.
Institution Type/Description: Art Museum.
Hours & Admission Prices: Wed.-Sun. 12-4. No charge; donations accepted. ♿
Attendance: 5,500 (actual)

UKRAINIAN NATIONAL MUSEUM, INC., 2249 W. Superior St., Chicago, IL 60612-1327. Tel.: 312-421-8020. Fax: 773-772-2883.
E-mail: info@ukrainiannationalmuseum.org
Web Site: www.ukrainiannationalmuseum.org
Key Personnel: Cur., Maria Klimchak.
Institution Type/Description: Folk Art Museum.
Hours & Admission Prices: Thurs.-Sun. 11-4, other times by appointment only. Adults $5, students & children $2; tours require advanced notice. Closed New Year's Day; Easter; Independence Day; Labor Day; Thanksgiving; Christmas. ♿
Attendance: 5,623 (actual)

UNITED STATES PIZZA MUSEUM, 1146 S. Delano Ct. W., Chicago, IL 60647. Facebook.
E-mail: tickets@uspizzamuseum.com
Web Site: uspizzamuseum.com
Key Personnel: Founder & Dir., Kendall Bruns.
Institution Type/Description: Pizza Museum.
Hours & Admission Prices: By appointment: Fri. 1-8, Sat.-Sun. 11-6. No charge. Closed Easter.

WESTERN EXHIBITIONS, 1709 W. Chicago Ave., Chicago, IL 60622. Tel.: 312-480-8390.
E-mail: scott@westernexhibitions.com
Web Site: www.westernexhibitions.com
Key Personnel: Dir., Scott Speh.
Institution Type/Description: Art Gallery.
Hours & Admission Prices: Wed.-Sat. 11-6; call for additional hours. No charge. ♿

WOMAN MADE GALLERY, 685 N. Milwaukee Ave., Chicago, IL 60642-8021. Tel.: 312-738-0400. Fax: 312-738-0404.
E-mail: general@womanmade.org
Web Site: www.womanmade.org
Key Personnel: Exec. Dir., Deb Flagel; Coord. Exhibitions, Vivian Le.
Institution Type/Description: Art Gallery.
Hours & Admission Prices: Wed.-Fri. 12-6, Sat.-Sun. 12-4. No charge; donations accepted.
Attendance: 6,000 (estimated)

Chicago Heights

UNION STREET GALLERY, 1527 Otto Blvd., Chicago Heights, IL 60411-3442. Tel.: 708-754-2601. Facebook: Union Street Gallery.
E-mail: unionstreetart@gmail.com
Web Site: www.unionstreetgallery.org
Key Personnel: Gallery Dir., Samantha Goss; Pres. (V), Michael Petrouski; Asst. to Dir., Madeline Henry.
Institution Type/Description: Art Gallery.
Hours & Admission Prices: Wed. & Fri. 12-4, Thurs. 12-7, Sat. 11-4. No charge; donations accepted. Closed New Year's Day; Easter; Thanksgiving; Christmas. ♿
Attendance: 3,000 (estimated)

Chillicothe

CHILLICOTHE AREA HISTORY MUSEUM, 723 N. Fourth St., Chillicothe, IL 61523. Mailing Address: P.O. Box 181, Chillicothe, IL 61523-0181. Tel.: 309-274-9076.
E-mail: chillicothehistorical@gmail.com
Web Site: chillicothehistorical.org/
Key Personnel: Pres. (V), Dianne M. Colwell.
Institution Type/Description: History Museum.
Hours & Admission Prices: Wed. & 1st Sun. each month 1-4. Suggested Donation: adults 12-59 $4, seniors 60 & over and children $3; discounts to groups. Prices include admission to all 3 locations if visited on the same day.
Attendance: 1,100 (estimated)

ROCK ISLAND DEPOT MUSEUM, Cedar St. & 3rd St., Chillicothe, IL 61523. Mailing Address: P.O. Box 181, Chillicothe, IL 61523-0181. Tel.: 309-274-9076.
E-mail: rockislanddepotmuseum@gmail.com
Web Site: www.chillicothehistorical.org
Key Personnel: Pres. (V), Gill Colwell, Sr.
Institution Type/Description: Historic Depot Museum: built in 1889.
Hours & Admission Prices: Wed. & 1st Sun. each month 1-4. Adults $3, children 6-12 $2; prices include admission to all 3 locations if visited on the same day.
Attendance: 1,100 (estimated)

Cicero

HAWTHORNE WORKS MUSEUM, Morton College, 3801 S. Central Ave., Cicero, IL 60804-4300. Tel.: 708-656-8000, ext. 2322. Fax: 708-656-3297.
E-mail: jennifer.butler@morton.edu
Web Site: www.morton.edu/museum/index.html
Key Personnel: Pres., Dr. Stanley Fields; Dir., Jennifer Butler.
Institution Type/Description: Local Industrial History Museum.
Hours & Admission Prices: Call for hours. No charge. Closed Martin Luther King Jr. Day; Presidents' Day; Pulaski's Birthday; spring & winter break; Memorial Day; Columbus Day; Thanksgiving & weekend after. ♿
Attendance: 1,000 (estimated)

Clinton

C.H. MOORE HOMESTEAD - DEWITT COUNTY MUSEUM, 219 E. Woodlawn St., Clinton, IL 61727-1052. Tel.: 217-935-6066. Fax: 217-935-0553. Facebook: dewittcountymuseum.
E-mail: chmoore123@yahoo.com
Web Site: chmoorehomestead.org

Key Personnel: Dir., Joey Woolridge; Pres. (V), Katherine Ferguson; Co-Treas., Jane Tedrick; Co-Treas., Susan Golden.

Institution Type/Description: General Museum: housed in c.1867 C.H. Moore home, remodeled & expanded in 1876 & 1887.

Hours & Admission Prices: April-Dec. Tues.-Sat. 10-5, Sun. 1-5. Adults $5, children 12-18 $2; members & children under 12 no charge.

Attendance: 5,000 (estimated)

Coal Valley

NIABI ZOO, 12908 Niabi Zoo Rd., Coal Valley, IL 61240-9467. Tel.: 309-799-3482 & 5107. Fax: 309-799-5761.

E-mail: ask@niabizoo.com

Web Site: www.niabizoo.com

Key Personnel: Dir., Lee Jackson; Asst. Dir. & Dir. Education, Sharon Freedman; Asst. Registrar, LeaAnn Bishop; Museum Shop Mgr., Scarlett Behrens.

Institution Type/Description: Zoo.

Hours & Admission Prices: Spring & Summer: Mon.-Sat. 10-5, Sun. 11-5; Fall: Tues.-Sat. 10-4, Sun. 11-4. Adults $8.25, senior citizens $7.25, children $6.25; members & children under 2 no charge. &

Attendance: 250,000 (estimated)

Cobden

UNION COUNTY, IL HISTORICAL AND GENEALOGICAL SOCIETY, 117 S. Appleknocker Dr., Cobden, IL 62920. Mailing Address: P.O. Box 93, Cobden, IL 62920. Tel.: 618-893-2865.

E-mail: uchgsillinois@gmail.com

Web Site: www.unioncountyilmuseum.com

Key Personnel: Pres. (V), Patrick Brumleve; Museum Shop Mgr., Judy Travelstead.

Institution Type/Description: Historical Society Museum.

Hours & Admission Prices: Sat.-Sun. 1-5; other times by appointment. No charge; donations accepted. Closed mid-Dec. to March & Easter Sunday.

Attendance: 500 (estimated)

Collinsville

CAHOKIA MOUNDS STATE HISTORIC SITE, 30 Ramey St., Collinsville, IL 62234-7617. Tel.: 618-346-5160. Fax: 618-346-5162. Facebook.

E-mail: cahokia.mounds@sbcglobal.net

Web Site: www.cahokiamounds.org

Key Personnel: C.E.O. Cahokia Mounds Museum Society, Lori Belknap; Pres. (V) Cahokia Mounds Museum Society, Dale Yonker; Asst. Site Mgr., Matt Migalla; Asst. Site Mgr. & Dir. Public Rels., William Iseminger; Site Interpreter, Linda Sinco; Museum Shop Mgr. Cahokia Mounds Museum Society, Linda Krieg; Site Technician, Kevin Fernandez; Site Technician, Joseph Seago; Site Technician, Kevin Schwaegel.

Institution Type/Description: Archaeology Museum & Site: 800-1500 A.D., site of largest prehistoric Indian city in North America.

Hours & Admission Prices: Wed.-Sun. 9-5. Suggested Donations: families $15, adults $7, seniors $5, students $2. Closed holidays except Memorial Day, Independence Day & Labor Day. &

Attendance: 330,000 (estimated)

Crystal Lake

COLONEL PALMER HOUSE, 660 E. Terra Cotta Ave., Crystal Lake, IL 60014. Mailing Address: One E. Crystal Lake Ave., Crystal Lake, IL 60014. Tel.: 815-477-5873.

E-mail: palmerhouse@crystallakeparks.org

Web Site: www.crystallakeparks.org

Key Personnel: Facility Mgr., Mary Ott.

Institution Type/Description: Historic House Museum: built in 1858.

Hours & Admission Prices: Winter/Spring: Tues., Thurs.-Fri. 11-4, 1st Sat. of month; Fall/Summer: Tues. 3-7, Thurs.-Fri. 11-4. No charge; donations accepted.

Cypress

ILLINOIS DEPARTMENT OF NATURAL RESOURCES, CACHE RIVER STATE NATURAL AREA, BARKHAUSEN CACHE RIVER WETLANDS CENTER, 8885 State Rte. 37 S., Cypress, IL 62923-2323. Mailing Address: 930 Sunflower Lane, Belknap, IL 62908. Tel.: 618-657-2064. Fax: 618-657-2065.

E-mail: molie.oliver@illinois.gov

Web Site: www.dnr.illinois.gov

Institution Type/Description: Wetlands Center.

Hours & Admission Prices: Wed.-Sun. 9-4. No charge. Closed New Year's Day; Lincoln's Birthday; Veterans Day; Thanksgiving & day after; Christmas. &

Attendance: 15,000 (estimated)

Danville

VERMILION COUNTY MUSEUM SOCIETY, 116 N. Gilbert St., Danville, IL 61832-8506. Tel.: 217-442-2922. Fax: 217-442-2001.

E-mail: vermilioncounty@att.net

Web Site: www.vermilioncountymuseum.org

Key Personnel: Pres. (V), Donald Richter; Dir. & Museum Shop Mgr., Susan Richter.

Institution Type/Description: History Museum: housed in 1855 Dr. Fithian Home, doctor's residence, often visited by Abraham Lincoln.

Hours & Admission Prices: Tues.-Sat. 10-5. Adults: $3 one site, $5 two sites, children 13-17 $1; discounts to AAA members & Time Travelers; members & children under 13 no charge. Closed Independence Day; Thanksgiving; Christmas.

Attendance: 5,354 (actual)

VERMILION COUNTY WAR MUSEUM, 307 N. Vermilion, Danville, IL 61832-4769. Tel.: 217-431-0034. Facebook.

E-mail: vcwm@comcast.net

Web Site: vcwm.org

Key Personnel: Dir., A. Dudich; Pres. (V), J. Kouzmanoff.

Institution Type/Description: Military History Museum.

Hours & Admission Prices: Tues.-Fri. 12-4, Sat. 10-4. Adults $5; discounts to Blue Star Museum members; active military & family and members no charge. &

Attendance: 10,000 (estimated)

DeKalb

THE ANTHROPOLOGY MUSEUM, Northern Illinois University, Department of Anthropology, DeKalb, IL 60115. Tel.: 815-753-2520. Fax: 815-753-7027. Facebook.

E-mail: jkirker@niu.edu

Web Site: www.niu.edu/anthro_museum

Key Personnel: Cur., Rachelle Wilson-Loring; Exhibition Research, Shelby Holtz.

Institution Type/Description: Anthropology & Archaeology Museum.

Hours & Admission Prices: Tues.-Thurs. 10-4, Fri. 10-2, Sat. by appointment. Suggested Donation: $5 per person. Closed school holidays. &

Attendance: 2,000 (estimated)

BARB CITY MOTORCYCLE MUSEUM, Pierce Harley-Davidson, 969 Peace Rd., DeKalb, IL 60115. Tel.: 815-756-4558.

Institution Type/Description: Motorcycle Museum.

Hours & Admission Prices: Mon.-Tues. & Thurs. 9-6, Wed. 9-5, Fri. 9-7, Sat. 9-3, Sun. 10-2.

ELLWOOD HOUSE MUSEUM, 509 N. First St., DeKalb, IL 60115-3232. Tel.: 815-756-4609. Fax: 815-756-4645.

E-mail: info@ellwoodhouse.org

Web Site: www.ellwoodhouse.org

Key Personnel: Pres. (V), Kelli Bender; Exec. Dir., Brian Reis; Asst. Dir., Scott Tews; Dir. Visitor Svcs., Donna Gable.

Institution Type/Description: Historic House Museum: housed in 1879 Victorian mansion Ellwood House.

Hours & Admission Prices: Museum Tours: March to mid-Nov. Tues.-Sat. 1 & 3, Sun. 1, 2 & 3. Highlight Tours: March to mid-Nov. Fri.-Sat. 2 pm. Visitors Center: Tues.-Sun. 12:30-4:30. Adults $10, youth 6-17 $5; discounts to AAM members; members & children under 6 no charge. Closed New Year's Eve & Day; Easter; Mother's Day; Independence Day; Thanksgiving; Christmas Eve & Day. &

Attendance: 8,000 (estimated)

JACK OLSON GALLERY - NORTHERN ILLINOIS UNIVERSITY, School of Art & Design, 200 Visual Arts Bldg., DeKalb, IL 60115. Tel.: 815-753-4521. Fax: 815-753-7701.

E-mail: pvanael@niu.edu

Web Site: www.olsongallery.niu.edu

Key Personnel: Gallery Coord., Peter Van Ael.

Institution Type/Description: Art Gallery.

Hours & Admission Prices: Sept. to early May Mon.-Thurs. 10-4, Fri. 10am to noon. No charge; donations accepted. &

NIU ART MUSEUM, Northern Illinois University, Altgeld Hall, DeKalb, IL 60115-2825. Mailing Address: NIU Art Museum, 1425 W. Lincoln Hwy., DeKalb, IL 60115. Tel.: 815-753-1936. Fax: 815-753-7897.

E-mail: jburke2@niu.edu

Web Site: www.niu.edu/artmuseum

Key Personnel: Dir., Jo Burke; Asst. Dir., Peter Olson.

Institution Type/Description: University Art Museum.

Hours & Admission Prices: Sept.-May Tues.-Fri. 10-5, Sat. 12-4; group tours by appointment. No charge; donations accepted.
Attendance: 9,000 (estimated)

Decatur

CHILDREN'S MUSEUM OF ILLINOIS, 55 S. Country Club Rd., Decatur, IL 62521-4470. Tel.: 217-423-5437. Fax: 217-423-5455. Facebook, Instagram.
Web Site: www.cmofil.org
Key Personnel: Exec. Dir., Amber Kaylor.
Institution Type/Description: Children's Museum.
Hours & Admission Prices: May-Aug. Mon.-Fri. 9:30-4:30, Sat. 10-5, Sun. 1-5; Sept.-April Tues.-Fri. 9:30-4:30, Sat. 10-5, Sun. 1-5. Admission $5, seniors, military, families with EBT/Link Card $3; members no charge. Reciprocal benefits for Association of Children's Museum & Association of Science-Technology Centers members. Closed major holidays.
Attendance: 64,000 (actual)

GALLERY 510 ARTS GUILD, 160 E. Main St., Ste. 100, Decatur, IL 62523-1283. Tel.: 217-422-1509. Fax: 217-475-1509.
E-mail: info@gallery510.org
Web Site: gallery510.org
Key Personnel: Exec. Dir., Barbara J. Dove.
Institution Type/Description: Art Gallery.
Hours & Admission Prices: Tues.-Fri. 11-5, Sat. 11-3.

HIERONYMUS MUELLER MUSEUM, 420 W. Eldorado St., Decatur, IL 62522-2189. Tel.: 217-423-6161.
E-mail: muellermuseum@aol.com
Key Personnel: Mgr., Mike Deatherage.
Institution Type/Description: History Museum.
Hours & Admission Prices: Thurs.-Sat. 1-4. Adults $2, children under 17 $1.50.

KIRKLAND FINE ARTS CENTER, 1184 W. Main St., Decatur, IL 62522-2039. Tel.: 217-424-6318. Fax: 217-424-3993.
E-mail: kfac@Millikin.edu
Web Site: www.millikin.edu/kirkland
Formerly: Perkinson Gallery
Key Personnel: Dir., Jan Saddoris-Traughber.
Institution Type/Description: Art Museum.
Hours & Admission Prices: Mon.-Fri. during the school year 8-5. Closed university holidays.
Attendance: 20,000

MACON COUNTY HISTORY MUSEUM, 5580 N. Fork Rd., Decatur, IL 62521-1859. Tel.: 217-422-4919. Fax: 217-422-4773.
E-mail: info@mchsdecatur.org
Web Site: www.mchsdecatur.org
Key Personnel: Exec. Dir., Nathan Pierce; Pres. (V), Karen Anderson.
Institution Type/Description: Historical Society Museum.
Hours & Admission Prices: Tues.-Sat. 1-4. Adults $2, children 12 & under $1.
Attendance: 5,000 (estimated)

SCOVILL ZOO, 71 S. Country Club Rd., Decatur, IL 62521-4470. Tel.: 217-421-7435. Fax: 217-422-7330. Facebook: Scovill Zoo.
E-mail: bill@decparks.com
Web Site: www.decatur-parks.org/scovill-zoo/
Key Personnel: Dir., Dave Webster; Asst. Dir., Ken Frye.
Institution Type/Description: Zoo.
Hours & Admission Prices: Spring: Mon.-Fri. 10-5, Sat.-Sun. 10-7; Summer: daily 10-7. Adults $5.50, seniors 65 & over $4.50, children 2-12 $3.50; children under 2 no charge. Z.O. & O Express Train: adults $2.50, seniors 65 & over and children 2-12 $2.50; children under 2 no charge. Carousel Ride: $2.
Attendance: 98,000 (actual)

Des Plaines

DES PLAINES HISTORY CENTER, 781 Pearson St., Des Plaines, IL 60016-4506. Tel.: 847-391-5399. Fax: 847-297-4741. Facebook: Des Plains History; Twitter: @desplaineshist.
E-mail: contact@desplaineshistory.org
Web Site: desplaineshistory.org; desplainestour.toursphere.com
Formerly: Des Plaines Historical Museum
Key Personnel: Exec. Dir., Shari Caine; Pres., Tom Christiansen; Cur., Philip Mohr; Publicity Coord., Sue Fox McGovern.
Institution Type/Description: Local History Museum.

Hours & Admission Prices: Tues.-Fri. 10-5, Sun. 1-4; see website to confirm; other times by appointment. No charge; donations accepted; see website for group tour admission fees.
Attendance: 2,000 (estimated)

KOEHNLINE MUSEUM OF ART, Oakton Community College, 1600 E. Golf Rd., Des Plaines, IL 60016-1234. Tel.: 847-635-2633. Fax: 847-635-1764.
E-mail: nharpaz@oakton.edu
Web Site: www.oakton.edu/museum
Key Personnel: Mgr. & Cur., Nathan Harpaz.
Institution Type/Description: Art Museum.
Hours & Admission Prices: June-Aug. Mon.-Thurs. 10-7; Sept.-May Mon.-Fri. 10-6, Sat. 11-4.

Dixon

JOHN DEERE HISTORIC SITE, 8334 S. Clinton St., Grand Detour, Dixon, IL 61021-9499. Tel.: 815-652-4551. Fax: 815-652-3835.
E-mail: holstbrian@johndeere.com
Web Site: johndeereattractions.com
Key Personnel: Dir. & Pres., Mara Sovey; Site Mgr., Kristen Veto.
Institution Type/Description: Historic Site: 1836 Deere House.
Hours & Admission Prices: May-Oct. Wed.-Sun. 9-5; Winter: tours by appointment only. Adults $5; children under 12 no charge.
Attendance: 22,000 (estimated)

RONALD REAGAN BOYHOOD HOME PRESERVATION FOUNDATION, 810 & 816 S. Hennepin Ave., Dixon, IL 61021-3646. Mailing Address: 810 S. Hennepin Ave., Dixon, IL 61021. Tel.: 815-288-5176.
E-mail: director@reaganhome.org
Web Site: www.reaganhome.org
Key Personnel: Exec. Dir., Patrick Gorman; Bd. Pres., Jeff Reene.
Institution Type/Description: Historic House: boyhood home of 40th U.S. President Ronald Reagan.
Hours & Admission Prices: April-Oct. Mon.-Sat. 10-5, Sun. 1-5. Adults 12 & over $8, children under 12 & veterans $5; active military, police, firefighter, first responders & members no charge. Closed Easter.
Attendance: 5,000 (actual)

Downers Grove

DOWNERS GROVE MUSEUM, 831 Maple Ave., Downers Grove, IL 60515-4904. Tel.: 630-963-1309. Fax: 630-963-0496. Facebook; Twitter.
E-mail: cchristensen@dgparks.org
Web Site: www.dgparks.org (click museum)
Key Personnel: Exec. Dir., William McAdam; Dir. Recreation, Dave Haring.
Institution Type/Description: Local History.
Hours & Admission Prices: June-Aug. Mon.-Fri. 12-4, Sat. 10-4; Sept.-May Tues.-Fri. 12-4, Sat. 10-4. No charge; donations accepted. Closed holidays. Closed holidays.
Attendance: 2,800 (estimated)

Dundee

DUNDEE TOWNSHIP HISTORICAL SOCIETY, INC., 426 Highland Ave., Dundee, IL 60118-1225. Mailing Address: 437 Highland Ave., Dundee, IL 60118-1277. Tel.: 847-428-6996.
E-mail: dths@sbcglobal.net
Web Site: www.northstarnet.org/dukhome/DTHS
Key Personnel: Pres. (V), Marge Edwards; Museum Co-Chm., Nancy Wendt; Museum Co-Chm., Jack Wendt; Programs Chm. & Library Volunteer, Marge Edwards; Library Volunteer, Mary Lamp; Library Volunteer, Lana Graf; Library Volunteer, Connie Kashub.
Institution Type/Description: Historical Society.
Hours & Admission Prices: Wed. & Sun. 2-4; other times by appointment. Adults $1; members donations accepted.
Attendance: 1,000 (estimated)

Dunlap

WHEELS O' TIME MUSEUM, 1710 W. Woodside Dr., Dunlap, IL 61525. Mailing Address: P.O. Box 9636, Peoria, IL 61612-9636. Tel.: 309-243-9020. Facebook.
E-mail: wotmuseum@aol.com
Web Site: wheelsotime.org

Key Personnel: Pres., Gary O. Bragg; Treas., Fred Roland; Public Rels., Bobbie Rice; Museum Shop Mgr., Janice M. Bragg.
Institution Type/Description: Transportation & Mechanical Museum.
Hours & Admission Prices: May-Oct. Wed.-Sun. 12-5; other times by appointment. Adults $7; discounts to AAA members, groups over 20 & handicapped. &
Attendance: 7,000 (estimated)

East Alton

U.S. ARMY CORPS OF ENGINEERS - NATIONAL GREAT RIVERS MUSEUM, #2 Lock & Dam Way, East Alton, IL 62024. Tel.: 618-462-6979. Fax: 618-462-7650. Facebook.
E-mail: riversproject@usace.army.mil
Web Site: www.mvs.usace.army.mil/Missions/Recreation/RiversProjectOffice/NGRM.aspx
Key Personnel: Dir., Angela N. Smith.
Institution Type/Description: Science & History Museum.
Hours & Admission Prices: Daily 9-5; groups of 10 or more by appointment. No charge; donations accepted. Closed New Year's Eve & Day; Thanksgiving; Christmas Eve & Day. &
Attendance: 90,000 (actual)

East Saint Louis

KATHERINE DUNHAM DYNAMIC MUSEUM, 1005 Pennsylvania Ave., East Saint Louis, IL 62201-1407. Mailing Address: P.O. Box 6, East Saint Louis, IL 62202-0006. Tel.: 618-874-8560. Fax: 618-874-8562.
E-mail: lbackstrom1947@yahoo.com
Web Site: www.kdcah.org
Key Personnel: Pres. (V), Leverne E. Backstrom; Museum Shop Mgr., Gloria Atkins.
Institution Type/Description: General Museum.
Hours & Admission Prices: By appointment. Private Tours: adults $10, students $8; discounts to groups.
Attendance: 500 (estimated)

Edwardsville

1820 COL. BENJAMIN STEPHENSON HOUSE, 409 S. Buchanan, Edwardsville, IL 62025. Mailing Address: P.O. Box 754, Edwardsville, IL 62025-0754. Tel.: 618-692-1818. Fax: 618-692-6418. Facebook: 1820 Col. Benjamin Stephenson House.
E-mail: stephensonhouse@sbcglobal.net
Web Site: www.stephensonhouse.org
Key Personnel: Dir., RoxAnn Raisner.
Institution Type/Description: Historic House Museum: built in 1820.
Hours & Admission Prices: Jan.-Feb. Sat. 10-4, Sun. 12-4; March-Dec. Thurs.-Sat. 10-4, Sun. 12-4. Adults $6, children 6-12 $3; children under 5 no charge. &

MADISON COUNTY HISTORICAL MUSEUM & ARCHIVAL LIBRARY, 715 N. Main St., Edwardsville, IL 62025-1111. Tel.: 618-656-7562 (museum) & 7569 (library). Fax: 618-659-3457.
E-mail: info@madcohistory.org
Web Site: madcohistory.org
Key Personnel: MCHS Bd. Pres (V), Gary Denue; MCHS Bd. Vice Pres., Russell Marti; Dir. Museum & Library, Suzanne Dietrich; Cur. Objects & Textiles, Jennifer Walta; Research Mgr., Mary Westerhold; Research Asst., LaVerne Bloemker; Research Asst., Carol Frisse.
Institution Type/Description: Historical Society Museum: housed in 1836 John H. Weir home. Listed on the National Register of Historic Places.
Hours & Admission Prices: Museum closed for repairs. Archival library open. &
Attendance: 1,500 (actual)

THE UNIVERSITY MUSEUM, Southern Illinois University at Edwardsville, Edwardsville, IL 62026. Mailing Address: Box 1150, Southern Illinois University at Edwardsville, Edwardsville, IL 62026. Tel.: 618-650-2996.
E-mail: evignea@siue.edu
Key Personnel: Collections Mgr., Erin Vigneau Dimick; Preparator, Mike Whisenhunt.
Institution Type/Description: General Museum.
Hours & Admission Prices: Mon.-Fri. 9-4:30. No charge; donations accepted. &
Attendance: 30,000 (estimated)

Elburn

TOWN AND COUNTRY PUBLIC LIBRARY, 320 E. North St., Elburn, IL 60119. Tel.: 630-365-2244. Fax: 630-365-2358.
E-mail: library@elburn.lib.il.us

Web Site: www.elburn.lib.il.us
Key Personnel: Dir., Glenn Kahmann.
Institution Type/Description: Library.
Hours & Admission Prices: Mon.-Thurs. 9-9, Fri.-Sat. 9-5, Sun. 1-5. No charge.

Elgin

ELGIN FIRE BARN NO. 5 MUSEUM, 533 St. Charles St., Elgin, IL 60120. Tel.: 847-697-6242. Facebook.
E-mail: efb5m@outlook.com
Web Site: elginfiremuseum.weebly.com
Key Personnel: Pres. (V), James Carrigan; Vice Pres., Cathy Hemmings; Museum Shop Mgr., Dale Betts.
Institution Type/Description: Firefighting History Museum: housed in the city's former fire barn; built in 1903.
Hours & Admission Prices: March 19-Dec. 24 call for hours. Suggested Donation: adults $2, children 5 & over $1; members no charge.

ELGIN HISTORY MUSEUM, 360 Park St., Elgin, IL 60120-4455. Tel.: 847-742-4248. Fax: 847-931-6199.
E-mail: museum@elginhistory.org
Web Site: www.elginhistory.org
Formerly: Elgin Area Historical Society
Key Personnel: Dir., Elizabeth Marston; Pres. (V), Bill Briska; Museum Shop Mgr., Sandi McClure; Registrar, Beth Nawara; Researcher, David Siegenthaler; Educator, Sara Russell.
Institution Type/Description: History Museum: housed in c.1856 Greek Revival landmark building.
Hours & Admission Prices: Wed.-Sat. 11-4. Adults $3, students $1; discounts to AAM, ICOM, AASLH & AMM members; children 6 & under & members no charge. Closed New Year's Day; Independence Day; Thanksgiving; Christmas Eve & Day. &
Attendance: 5,000 (estimated)

ELGIN PUBLIC MUSEUM, 225 Grand Blvd., Elgin, IL 60120-4278. Tel.: 847-741-6655. Fax: 847-931-6787. Facebook.
E-mail: epm@cityofelgin.org
Web Site: www.elginpublicmuseum.org
Key Personnel: Exec. Dir., Margaret (Peggie) Stromberg; Pres. (V), Marty Kellams; Education Coord., Sara Russell.
Institution Type/Description: Natural History Museum: housed in 1907, Neo-Classical building with 30 ft. sky-lighted ceiling.
Hours & Admission Prices: June-Sept. 1 Tues.-Sat. 12-4; Sept. 2-May Sat.-Sun. 12-4; school programs by reservation. No charge; donations accepted. Closed most major holidays. &
Attendance: 20,000 (estimated)

Elk Grove Village

ELK GROVE HISTORICAL MUSEUM, 399 Biesterfield Rd., Elk Grove Village, IL 60007-3381. Tel.: 847-439-3994 & 690-1440.
E-mail: ako@elkgroveparks.org
Web Site: www.elkgroveparks.org
Formerly: The Schuette Biermann Farmhouse Museum
Key Personnel: Museum Coord., Audrey Ko; Chm., Cliff Schultz.
Institution Type/Description: Farmhouse Museum.
Hours & Admission Prices: June-Aug. Wed.-Fri. 12-5, Sat. 11-2; Sept.-May Wed. & Fri. 2:30-5:30, Sat. 11-2; other times by appointment. Adults $1; members no charge. Closed major holidays.
Attendance: 4,500 (estimated)

Ellis Grove

PIERRE MENARD HOME STATE HISTORIC SITE, 4230 Kaskaskia St., Ellis Grove, IL 62241-1718. Tel.: 618-859-3031 & 284-7230. Fax: 618-859-3031.
Web Site: www.illinois.gov/dnrhistoric/experience/sites/southwest/pages/pierre-menard.aspx
Institution Type/Description: Historic House Museum: c.1815-1820 home of Pierre Menard, the first Lt. Governor of Illinois and U.S. Agent of Indian Affairs.
Hours & Admission Prices: May-Oct. Wed.-Sun. 9-5; other times by appointment. No charge; donations requested. Closed New Year's Day; Martin Luther King Jr. Day; Thanksgiving; Christmas. &
Attendance: 6,000 (actual)

Elmhurst

ELMHURST ART MUSEUM, 150 S. Cottage Hill Ave., Elmhurst, IL 60126-3329. Tel.: 630-834-0202. Fax: 630-834-0234.
E-mail: info@elmhurstartmuseum.org
Web Site: www.elmhurstartmuseum.org

Key Personnel: Dir., John McKinnon; Dir. Education, Admin., Advancement, Joseph Hladik; Mgr. Exhibitions, Lal Bahcecioglu; Membership & Visitor Experience Mgr., Luisa Castellanos.
Institution Type/Description: Art Museum.
Hours & Admission Prices: Tues.-Thurs. & Sat.-Sun. 11-5, Fri. 11-7. Adults $9, seniors $8; 1st Fri. of month, children 18 & under and students no charge. Closed national holidays. &
Attendance: 35,000 (actual)

ELMHURST HISTORY MUSEUM, 120 E. Park Ave., Elmhurst, IL 60126-3420. Tel.: 630-833-1457. Fax: 630-833-1326. Facebook: @elmhursthistorymuseum.
E-mail: ehm@elmhurst.org
Web Site: www.elmhursthistory.org
Key Personnel: Dir., Brian F. Bergheger; Pres. Foundation, Michael LoCicero; Cur. Collections, Nancy Wilson; Cur. Exhibits, Lance Tawzer.
Institution Type/Description: History Museum: housed in 1892 Glos Mansion.
Hours & Admission Prices: Tues.-Sun. 1-5. No charge; donations accepted. &
Attendance: 15,000 (actual)

LIZZADRO MUSEUM OF LAPIDARY ART, 220 Cottage Hill Ave., Elmhurst, IL 60126-3351. Tel.: 630-833-1616.
E-mail: info@lizzadromuseum.org
Web Site: www.lizzadromuseum.org
Key Personnel: Exec. Dir., John S. Lizzadro; Dir., Dorothy J. Asher; Museum Shop Mgr., Laura McCall.
Institution Type/Description: Lapidary Arts Museum.
Hours & Admission Prices: Tues.-Sat. 10-5, Sun. 1-5. Adults $5, senior citizens $4, students $3, children 7-12 $2; children under 7, museum members, active members of the armed forces & Fridays no charge. Closed New Year's Day; Easter; Independence Day; Thanksgiving; Christmas. &
Attendance: 37,985 (actual)

Elsah

VILLAGE OF ELSAH MUSEUM, 26 Lasalle St., Elsah, IL 62028. Mailing Address: P.O. Box 117, Elsah, IL 62028-0028. Tel.: 618-374-1059. Fax: 618-374-2625.
E-mail: historicelsah@gmail.com
Web Site: www.elsah.org
Institution Type/Description: History Museum: housed in 1887 village hall.
Hours & Admission Prices: April-Oct. Sat.-Sun. 1-4. No charge; donations accepted. &
Attendance: 1,200 (actual)

Eureka

BURGESS HALL ART GALLERY - EUREKA COLLEGE, 300 E. College Ave., Burgess Hall, 3rd Fl., Eureka, IL 61530-1500. Tel.: 309-467-6866.
E-mail: redge@eureka.edu
Web Site: www.eureka.edu/arts/visual/exhibitions
Key Personnel: Dir., Prof. Rhea Edge.
Institution Type/Description: Art Gallery.
Hours & Admission Prices: Mon.-Fri. 8-5; other times by appointment. No charge. &
Attendance: 600 (estimated)

THE RONALD W. REAGAN SOCIETY OF EUREKA COLLEGE, 300 E. College Ave., Eureka, IL 61530. Tel.: 309-467-6477.
E-mail: reagan@eureka.edu
Key Personnel: Cur., Dr. Brian Sajko.
Institution Type/Description: History Museum.
Hours & Admission Prices: late Aug. to May Mon.-Fri. 8-8, Sat. 10-6, Sun. 12-8; Summer: Mon.-Fri. 8-4, Sat. 10-2. No charge; donations accepted. Closed holidays.

Evanston

DITTMAR MEMORIAL GALLERY - NORTHWESTERN UNIVERSITY, Norris University Center, 1999 S. Campus Dr., Evanston, IL 60208. Tel.: 847-491-2348. Fax: 847-491-4333.
E-mail: dittmargallery@northwestern.edu
Institution Type/Description: Art Gallery.
Hours & Admission Prices: Daily 10-10.

EVANSTON ART CENTER, 1717 Central St., Evanston, IL 60201. Tel.: 847-475-5300. Fax: 847-475-5330.

Web Site: www.evanstonartcenter.org
Key Personnel: Pres. & C.E.O., Paula Danoff; Dir. IT & Admin., Larry Boswell; Dir. Educ., Christena Gunther; Dir. Design, Alyssa Brubaker.
Institution Type/Description: Contemporary Art Center.
Hours & Admission Prices: Mon.-Thurs. 9am-10pm, Fri. 9-5, Sat.-Sun. 9-4. No charge. Closed Memorial Day; Independence Day; Labor Day; Thanksgiving; Christmas to New Year's Day. &
Attendance: 25,000 (estimated)

EVANSTON ENVIRONMENTAL ASSOCIATION/EVANSTON ECOLOGY CENTER, 2024 McCormick Blvd., Evanston, IL 60201-3055. Tel.: 847-448-8256. Fax: 847-448-8805.
E-mail: ecologycenter@cityofevanston.org
Web Site: www.laddarboretum.org
Institution Type/Description: Environmental Education Center & Arboretum.
Hours & Admission Prices: Mon.-Fri. 8:30-5. No charge. Closed national holidays; Memorial Day; Independence Day weekend; Labor Day weekend. &
Attendance: 8,000 (estimated)

EVANSTON HISTORICAL CENTER AND CHARLES GATES DAWES HOUSE, 225 Greenwood St., Evanston, IL 60201-4713. Tel.: 847-475-3410. Fax: 847-475-3599.
E-mail: evanstonhs@northwestern.edu
Web Site: www.evanstonhistorycenter.org
Key Personnel: Exec. Dir., Eden Juron Pearlman.
Institution Type/Description: Historic House Museum: restored 1894 home of former Vice Pres. & Nobel laureate Dawes: 28-room mansion. National Historic Landmark.
Hours & Admission Prices: Call for hours. &
Attendance: 6,000 (actual)

FRANCES WILLARD HOUSE MUSEUM, 1730 Chicago Ave., Evanston, IL 60201-4502. Tel.: 847-328-7500.
E-mail: info@franceswillardhouse.org
Web Site: franceswillardhouse.org
Formerly: The Willard House (WCTU Museum)
Key Personnel: Nat. Pres., Woman's Christian Temperance Union, Rita Kaye Wert.
Institution Type/Description: Historic House: home of Frances E. Willard (1865-1898).
Hours & Admission Prices: 1st & 3rd Sun. of each month 1-4; other times by appointment only. Adults $10, children 12 & under $5; discounts to AAM & ICOM members; Woman's Christian Temperance Union & Frances Willard Historical Association members no charge.
Attendance: 400 (estimated)

GROSSE POINT LIGHTHOUSE, 2601 Sheridan Rd., Evanston, IL 60201-1752. Tel.: 847-328-6961.
E-mail: lpdnhl@grossepointlighthouse.net
Web Site: www.nps.gov
Institution Type/Description: Lighthouse: built in 1873. Listed on the National Register of Historic Places.
Hours & Admission Prices: Tours: June-Sept. Sat.-Sun. 2, 3, 4. Adults $6, children 8-12 $3. Children under 8 not admitted on light tower tour. Closed Independence Day; Labor Day.

LEVERE MEMORIAL TEMPLE, 1856 Sheridan Rd., Evanston, IL 60201-3837. Mailing Address: P.O. Box 1856, Evanston, IL 60204-9918. Tel.: 847-475-1856, 800-233-1856. Fax: 847-475-2250. Facebook: Levere Memorial Temple.
E-mail: foundation@sae.net
Web Site: www.sae.net
Key Personnel: Dir., Blaine Ayers; Pres. (V), Ed Fuller, Jr.
Institution Type/Description: Preservation Society.
Hours & Admission Prices: Memorial Day to Labor Day Mon.-Thurs. 9-4:30, Fri. 9 to noon, Sat.-Sun. by appointment; Sept.-May Mon.-Fri. 9-4:30, Sat.-Sun. by appointment only. No charge; donations accepted. Closed New Year's Eve & Day; Presidents' Day; Easter; Memorial Day; Independence Day; Labor Day; Thanksgiving & day after; Christmas Day & week. &
Attendance: 3,000 (estimated)

MARY AND LEIGH BLOCK MUSEUM OF ART, NORTHWESTERN UNIVERSITY, 40 Arts Circle Dr., Evanston, IL 60208-2410. Tel.: 847-491-4001. Fax: 847-491-2261.
E-mail: block-museum@northwestern.edu
Web Site: www.blockmuseum.northwestern.edu
Key Personnel: Dir., Lisa G. Corrin; Chm., Christine O. Robb; Business Admin., Rita Shorts; Grants Mgr., Kate Hadley Toftness; Communications Coord., Caroline Claflin; Collections & Exhibitions Coord., Joseph Scott; Cur. Academic Programs, Corinne Granof; Sr. Registrar, Kristina Bottomley; Assoc.

Dir. Collections & Exhibitions Mgmt., Dan Silverstein; Mgr. Security Svcs., James Foster; Asst. Mgr. Visitor Svcs., Aaron Chatman.
Institution Type/Description: University Art Museum.
Hours & Admission Prices: Tues. & Sat.-Sun. 10-5, Wed.-Fri. 10-8. No charge; donations accepted. ㅎ
Attendance: 39,000 (actual)

MITCHELL MUSEUM OF THE AMERICAN INDIAN, 3001 Central St., Evanston, IL 60201-1102. Tel.: 847-475-1030.
E-mail: kmcdonald@mitchellmuseum.org
Web Site: www.mitchellmuseum.org
Key Personnel: Exec. Dir., Kathleen McDonald; Cur. Exhibitions & Collections, Melissa Halverson.
Institution Type/Description: Native American Museum.
Hours & Admission Prices: Tues.-Wed. & Fri.-Sat. 10-5, Thurs. 10-8, Sun. 12-4. Adults $5, students, children & senior citizens $3; discounts to AAM, ICOM, AAA & AASLH members; tribal citizens no charge. Closed New Year's Eve & Day; Independence Day; Thanksgiving; Christmas Eve & Day. ㅎ
Attendance: 10,000 (estimated)

NOYES CULTURAL ARTS CENTER, 927 Noyes St., Ste. 100, Evanston, IL 60201-6205. Tel.: 847-448-8260.
E-mail: info@artencounter.org
Web Site: www.cityofevanston.org/government/departments/parks-recreation-community-services/facilities/noyes-cultural-arts-center
Institution Type/Description: Art Gallery.
Hours & Admission Prices: Mon.-Sat. 10-7, Sun. 10-6. No charge. ㅎ

THE PREHISTORIC LIFE MUSEUM, 711 Main St., Evanston, IL 60202-1702. Tel.: 847-866-7374. Fax: 847-866-6854.
E-mail: rockshop1@att.net
Web Site: www.davesrockshop.com
Institution Type/Description: Paleontology Museum.
Hours & Admission Prices: Mon.-Tues. & Thurs.-Fri. 10:30-5:30, Sat. 10-5. No charge.
Attendance: 6,000 (estimated)

SHOREFRONT LEGACY CENTER, 2214 Ridge Ave., Evanston, IL 60201. Mailing Address: P.O. Box 1894, Evanston, IL 60204. Tel.: 847-864-7467. Facebook: Shorefront.
E-mail: shorefront@me.com
Web Site: www.shorefrontlegacy.org
Key Personnel: Exec. Dir., Dino Robinson; Pres. (V), Chip Ratliff.
Institution Type/Description: History Museum.
Hours & Admission Prices: Sat. 9-2; other times by appointment. No charge; donations accepted. Closed major holidays. ㅎ
Attendance: 300 (estimated)

Fairbury

FAIRBURY ECHOES MUSEUM, 126 W. Locust, Fairbury, IL 61739-1549. Tel.: 815-692-2191. Facebook: Fairbury Echoes Museum.
E-mail: museum1976@yahoo.com
Web Site: historicfairbury.com
Key Personnel: Pres. (V), Mary Catherine Carter.
Institution Type/Description: History Museum.
Hours & Admission Prices: Thurs.-Fri. 1-4:30, Sat. 9-11:30. No charge; donations accepted.

Fairfield

WAYNE COUNTY HISTORICAL SOCIETY'S HANNA HOUSE MUSEUM, 101 E. Center, Fairfield, IL 62837-2101. Mailing Address: 300 S.E. 2nd St., Fairfield, IL 62837-2127.
E-mail: wayneillinoishistory@gmail.com
Web Site: www.wayneillinoishistory.com
Formerly: Hanna House Museum
Key Personnel: Pres. (V), Judith Puckett; Museum Mgr., Jami Roethe; Museum Mgr., Niki Roethe.
Institution Type/Description: Local History Museum.
Hours & Admission Prices: April-Oct. Sat. 10-2. No charge; donations accepted. Closed holidays.
Attendance: 500 (estimated)

Farmer City

FARMER CITY GENEALOGICAL AND HISTORICAL SOCIETY MUSEUM, 224 S. Main St., Farmer City, IL 61842. Tel.: 309-928-9411.

E-mail: admin@fcghsociety.org
Institution Type/Description: Historical Society Museum.
Hours & Admission Prices: Mon., Wed. & Fri. 9-12.

Frankfort

FRANKFORT FIRE DEPARTMENT MUSEUM, 333 W. Nebraska St., Frankfort, IL 60423. Tel.: 815-469-1700.
E-mail: michelle@frankfortfire.org
Institution Type/Description: Firefighting History Museum.
Hours & Admission Prices: Call for hours.

KIDSWORK CHILDREN'S MUSEUM, 11 S. White St., Frankfort, IL 60423. Tel.: 815-469-1199.
E-mail: info@kidsworkchildrensmuseum.org
Key Personnel: Pres. (V), Deborah Powers; Museum Shop Mgr., Angela Spiro.
Institution Type/Description: Children's Museum.
Hours & Admission Prices: Tues.-Fri. 9-3, Sat. 9-4, Sun. 11-4. Admission $7, seniors $6; children 1 & under no charge.

Freeport

FREEPORT ART MUSEUM, 121 N. Harlem Ave., Freeport, IL 61032-3845. Tel.: 815-235-9755. Fax: 815-235-6015. Facebook: Freeport Art Museum.
E-mail: director@freeportartmuseum.org
Web Site: www.freeportartmuseum.org
Key Personnel: C.E.O. & Dir., Jessica J. Modica; Pres. (V), Adam Schulz; Dir. Education, Barry Treu; Collections & Exhibitions Mgr., Carrie Baxter.
Institution Type/Description: Art Museum.
Hours & Admission Prices: Tues.-Fri. 10-5, Sat. 12-5. No charge; $3 suggested donation. Closed holidays. ㅎ
Attendance: 11,000 (actual)

HIGHLAND COMMUNITY COLLEGE ARBORETUM, 2998 Pearl City Rd., Freeport, IL 61032-9341. Tel.: 815-235-6121. Fax: 815-235-6130. TDD: 815-235-9584.
E-mail: pete.willging@highland.edu
Institution Type/Description: Arboretum.
Hours & Admission Prices: Daily 7-7. No charge; donations accepted. Closed legal holidays. ㅎ
Attendance: 5,000 (estimated)

SILVERCREEK MUSEUM, 2954 S. Walnut Rd., Freeport, IL 61032-9528. Tel.: 815-235-7329 & 2198.
E-mail: jkayklever@frontier.com
Web Site: www.thefreeportshow.com
Key Personnel: Pres. (V), Larry Buttel; Vice Pres., Mary Seefeldt-Swanson; Sec., Siri McMahon; Treas., Kris McNames; Dir., Jerry Klever; Dir., Ida DeBoer; Dir., Ed Keech.
Institution Type/Description: General Museum: housed in 1906 county poor farm.
Hours & Admission Prices: Memorial Day to mid-Oct. 11-4. Adults $4; discounts to AAM members. ㅎ
Attendance: 5,000 (estimated)

STEPHENSON COUNTY HISTORICAL SOCIETY, 1440 S. Carroll Ave., Freeport, IL 61032-6530. Tel.: 815-232-8419. Fax: 815-297-0313. Facebook: Stephenson County Historical Society.
E-mail: director@stephcohs.org
Web Site: stephcohs.org
Key Personnel: C.E.O., Edward F. Finch; Pres. (V), Connie Sorn; Museum Shop Mgr., Brigitte Rayhorn.
Institution Type/Description: History Museum: housed in 1857 house built by Oscar & Malvina Taylor, listed on National Register of Historic Sites.
Hours & Admission Prices: Wed.-Sun. 12-4; groups of 10 or more by appointment. Adults $8, children 6-12 $4; members no charge. ㅎ
Attendance: 7,800 (actual)

Galena

GALENA-JO DAVIESS COUNTY HISTORICAL SOCIETY & MUSEUM, 211 S. Bench St., Galena, IL 61036-2203. Tel.: 815-777-9129.
E-mail: info@galenahistorymuseum.org
Web Site: www.galenahistory.org
Key Personnel: Pres. (V), Christine Harris; Exec. Dir., Nancy Breed.
Institution Type/Description: Historical Society Museum: housed in 1858 Daniel A. Barrows house.

Hours & Admission Prices: Daily 9-4:30. Family $22; adults $10, seniors 65 & over $9, youth 10-18 $8; children under 10 & members no charge. Closed New Year's Eve & Day; Easter; Thanksgiving; Christmas Eve & Day.
Attendance: 13,945 (actual)

OLD MARKET HOUSE STATE HISTORIC SITE, Market Square, Galena, IL 61036. Mailing Address: 307 Decatur St., P.O. Box 333, Galena, IL 61036-0333. Tel.: 815-777-3310. Fax: 815-777-3310.
E-mail: granthome@granthome.com
Key Personnel: Site Mgr., Terry J. Miller.
Institution Type/Description: Historic House Museum: c.1845 Greek Revival-style Market House.
Hours & Admission Prices: Wed.-Sun. 9-12 & 1-5; Winter: 10-12 & 1-4. Donations suggested.
Attendance: 32,395 (actual)

US GRANT'S HOME STATE HISTORIC SITE, 500 Bouthillier St., Galena, IL 61036-2704. Mailing Address: 307 Decatur St., P. O. Box 333, Galena, IL 61036-0333. Tel.: 815-777-3310. Fax: 815-777-3310.
E-mail: granthome@granthome.com
Web Site: www.granthome.com
Key Personnel: Site Mgr., Terry J. Miller.
Institution Type/Description: Historic House Museum: 1860 Italianate bracketed style house presented to Gen. Grant in 1865.
Hours & Admission Prices: March-Oct. Wed.-Sun. 9-4:45; Nov.-Feb. Wed.-Sun. 9-4. Suggested Donation: adults $4, children under 18 $2. Closed New Year's Day; Martin Luther King Jr. Day; Presidents' Day; Election Day; Veterans Day; Thanksgiving; Christmas. &
Attendance: 84,770 (actual)

Galesburg

CARL SANDBURG STATE HISTORIC SITE, 313 E. 3rd St., Galesburg, IL 61401-6021. Mailing Address: P.O. Box 104, Bishop Hill, IL 61419. Tel.: 309-342-2361. Fax: 309-342-2141.
E-mail: carl@sandburg.org
Web Site: www.sandburg.org
Key Personnel: Site Supt., Martha Downey.
Institution Type/Description: Historic Home Museum: c.1870 immigrant railroad worker's cottage.
Hours & Admission Prices: May-Oct. Thurs.-Sun. 9-5. Suggested Donations: family $10, adults $4, children 17 & under $2. &
Attendance: 1,000 (estimated)

DISCOVERY DEPOT CHILDREN'S MUSEUM, 128 S. Chambers St., Galesburg, IL 61401-4966. Tel.: 309-344-8876.
E-mail: discoverydepot@grics.net
Web Site: www.discoverydepot.org
Institution Type/Description: Children's Museum.
Hours & Admission Prices: July-Aug. Mon.-Sat. 10-5, 3rd Fri. of month 10-7, Sun. 1-5; Sept.-June Tues.-Sat. 10-5, 3rd Fri. of month 10-7, Sun. 1-5. Admission $3.50.

GALESBURG CIVIC ART CENTER, 114 E. Main St., Galesburg, IL 61401-4601. Tel.: 309-342-7415.
E-mail: info@galesburgarts.org
Web Site: www.galesburgarts.org
Key Personnel: Exec. Dir., Tuesday Cetin; Bd. Pres., Jim Straub; Office Mgr., Lynn Miller.
Institution Type/Description: Art Gallery & Civic Center: housed in c.1897 building.
Hours & Admission Prices: Tues.-Fri. 10:30-4:30, Sat. 10:30-3; tours by appointment. No charge; donations accepted. Closed all holidays. &
Attendance: 8,000 (estimated)

GALESBURG RAILROAD MUSEUM, 211 S. Seminary St., Galesburg, IL 61401-4955. Tel.: 309-342-9400.
E-mail: grrm211@gmail.com
Web Site: www.galesburgrailroadmuseum.org
Key Personnel: Pres., Jim Clayton; Museum Shop Mgr., Annette Godsil.
Institution Type/Description: History Museum.
Hours & Admission Prices: April-Sept. Tues.-Sat. 10-4, Sun. 12-4. Adults $5, children 8-16 $3; children 7 & under and members no charge. Closed holidays. &
Attendance: 16,000 (estimated)

ILLINOIS CITIZEN SOLDIER MUSEUM, 1001 Michigan Ave., Galesburg, IL 61401-6481. Tel.: 309-342-1181.

E-mail: vfwpost2257@centurylink.net
Key Personnel: Bldg. Mgr. & Museum Shop Mgr., Bill Knott; Pres. (V) & Treas., Dan Jacobs.
Institution Type/Description: Military Museum: housed in Admiral James Stockdale building, home of Veterans of Foreign Wars Post 2257.
Hours & Admission Prices: Mon.-Fri. 9-1:30, Sat. 9-4. No charge; donations accepted. Closed New Year's Day; Christmas; federal holidays. &
Attendance: 1,500 (estimated)

NATIONAL RAILROAD HALL OF FAME, 311 E. Main St., Ste. 512, Galesburg, IL 61401-4838. Tel.: 309-345-4634.
E-mail: info@nrrhof.org
Web Site: www.nrrhof.org
Key Personnel: Exec. Dir., Julie King.
Institution Type/Description: Railroad Museum.
Hours & Admission Prices: By appointment. No charge.

Geneva

FABYAN VILLA MUSEUM & JAPANESE GARDEN, 1511 S. Batavia Ave., Geneva, IL 60134. Mailing Address: P.O. Box 903, Saint Charles, IL 60174-0903. Tel.: 630-377-6424. Fax: 630-377-6424.
E-mail: fabyanvilla@ppfv.org
Web Site: www.ppfv.org/fabyan.htm
Formerly: Fabyan Villa Museum, Dutch Windmill & Japanese Gardens
Key Personnel: Dir., Lynn Dransoff; Museum Asst., Hannah Walters.
Institution Type/Description: Historic House & Gardens: c.1907 home of Col. George Fabyan, re-designed by Frank Lloyd Wright, located in forest preserve, land formerly the estate of Col. Fabyan.
Hours & Admission Prices: Museum: May & Sept. to mid-Oct. Wed. & Sat.-Sun. 1-4:30; June-Aug. Wed.-Thurs. 1-4, Sat.-Sun. 1-4:30. Japanese Gardens: mid-May to mid-Oct. Sun. & Wed. 1-4. Adults $2, seniors & children $1.
Attendance: 6,075 (actual)

GENEVA HISTORY MUSEUM, 113 S. Third St., Geneva, IL 60134. Tel.: 630-232-4951.
E-mail: info@genevahistorymuseum.org
Web Site: www.genevahistorymuseum.org
Institution Type/Description: History Museum.
Hours & Admission Prices: Tues.-Sat. 11-4.

Glen Ellyn

STACY'S TAVERN MUSEUM AND GLEN ELLYN HISTORICAL SOCIETY, 800 N. Main St., Glen Ellyn, IL 60137. Tel.: 630-469-1867, ext. 101.
E-mail: director@gehs.org
Web Site: www.gehs.org
Key Personnel: Museum Shop Mgr., Jennifer Porter.
Institution Type/Description: Historic House: 1846 Moses Stacy House & Inn; local Glen Ellyn Historical Collection & Archives.
Hours & Admission Prices: Spring, Summer & Fall: Wed. & Sat. 1:30-4:30; tours & other times by appointment. Gift Shop: Tues.-Sat. 10-5. Recommended Donations: adults $5, students $2.50. Closed New Year's Eve & Day; Easter; Mother's Day; Independence Day; Thanksgiving; Christmas. &
Attendance: 3,500 (actual)

Glencoe

CHICAGO BOTANIC GARDEN, 1000 Lake Cook Rd., Glencoe, IL 60022-1168. Tel.: 847-835-5440. Fax: 847-835-4484.
Web Site: www.chicagobotanic.org
Key Personnel: Chm. (V), Robert F. Finke; Pres. & C.E.O., Jean M. Franczyk; Exec. Vice Pres. & Dir., Fred Spicer; Exec. Vice Pres. & C.F.O., Thomas J. Nissly; Exec. Vice Pres. External Affairs, James F. Boudreau; Vice Pres. Human Resources, Aida Giglio; Chief Scientist & Negaunee Foundation Vice Pres. Science, Dr. Gregory Mueller; Vice Pres. Visitor Experience & Business Devel., Harriet Resnick; Vice Pres. Education & Community Programs, Jennifer Schwarz Ballard.
Institution Type/Description: Botanic Garden.
Hours & Admission Prices: Daily 8-8. No admission charge; fee for parking except for garden members & U.S. military personnel & their families. &
Attendance: 955,000 (actual)

Glenview

GLENVIEW HISTORY CENTER, 1121 Waukegan Rd., Glenview, IL 60025-3036. Tel.: 847-724-2235. Fax: 847-724-2235.
E-mail: berdaw@juno.com

Web Site: www.glenviewhistory.org
Formerly: Glenview Area Historical Society
Key Personnel: Pres., Mary A. Long; Librarian, Beverly Dawson.
Institution Type/Description: Historical Society Museum: housed in original 1864 farm house.
Hours & Admission Prices: Museum: Sun. 1-4; other times by appointment. Library: Tues. 1-4. No charge; donations accepted. Closed holidays.
Attendance: 750 (estimated)

THE GROVE, 1421 Milwaukee Ave., Glenview, IL 60025-1436. Tel.: 847-299-6096. Fax: 847-299-0571.
E-mail: lorin.ottlinger@glenviewparks.org
Web Site: www.thegroveglenview.org
Key Personnel: Dir., Stephan Swanson; Museum Shop Mgr., Kris VanVoorhis.
Institution Type/Description: Natural History Museum: housed in 1856 Kennicott House, site of original grounds.
Hours & Admission Prices: Mon.-Fri. 8-4:30, Sat.-Sun. 9-5. No charge; donations accepted. Closed New Year's Day; Independence Day; Christmas. ♿
Attendance: 125,000 (estimated)

HANGAR ONE NAVAL AIR STATION GLENVIEW MUSEUM, 2040 Lehigh Ave., Glenview, IL 60026-1619. Tel.: 847-657-0000. Facebook: Naval Air Station Glenview Museum.
E-mail: wam51@comcast.net
Web Site: www.thehangarone.org
Key Personnel: Pres., Bill Marquardt.
Institution Type/Description: Naval Air Museum.
Hours & Admission Prices: Sat. 10-5, Sun. 12-5; other times by appointment. Closed major holidays.

ILLINOIS PGA GOLF HALL OF FAME MUSEUM, 2901 W. Lake Ave., Glenview, IL 60025. Tel.: 847-729-5700, ext. 100.
E-mail: lmoy@pgahq.com
Web Site: www.illinoisgolfhof.org
Institution Type/Description: Golf History Museum.
Hours & Admission Prices: Daily. No charge.

KOHL CHILDREN'S MUSEUM OF GREATER CHICAGO, 2100 Patriot Blvd., Glenview, IL 60026-8018. Tel.: 847-832-6600. Fax: 847-724-6469. Facebook.
E-mail: info@kohlchildrensmuseum.org
Web Site: www.kcmgc.org
Key Personnel: C.E.O. & Pres., Mike Delfini; Vice Pres. Business Affairs, Bill Sanders; Vice Pres. Programs, Stephanie Bynum; Sr. Dir. Public Rels. & Mktg., Dave Judy.
Institution Type/Description: Children's Museum.
Hours & Admission Prices: Wed.-Sun. 9-5. Adults & children $14; discounts ACM reciprocal program members & EBT card holders; children under one no charge. Closed New Year's Day; Independence Day; Labor Day; Thanksgiving; Christmas Eve & Day. ♿
Attendance: 312,311 (actual)

Granite City

OLD SIX MILE HISTORICAL SOCIETY AND OLD SIX MILE MUSEUM, 3279 Maryville Rd., Granite City, IL 62040. Mailing Address: P.O. Box 483, Granite City, IL 62040. Tel.: 618-731-3101.
E-mail: sixmilehistorical@gmail.com
Web Site: oldsixmile.wordpress.com
Institution Type/Description: Historical Society Museum.
Hours & Admission Prices: May-Oct. Sun. 1-4; groups by appointment. No charge.

Grayslake

ROBERT T. WRIGHT COMMUNITY GALLERY OF ART, Library, College of Lake County, 19351 W. Washington St., Grayslake, IL 60030-1148. Tel.: 847-543-2240.
E-mail: sjones@clcillinois.edu
Web Site: gallery.clcillinois.edu/
Key Personnel: Dir., Steven Jones; Museum Shop Mgr., Rachel Wolfe.
Institution Type/Description: Art Gallery.
Hours & Admission Prices: Mon.-Thurs. 8am-9pm, Fri. 8-4:30, Sat. 9-4:30, Sun. 1-5. No charge; donations accepted. ♿
Attendance: 8,000 (estimated)

Great Lakes

NATIONAL MUSEUM OF THE AMERICAN SAILOR, Bldg. 42, 610 Farragut Ave., Great Lakes, IL 60088-3607. Tel.: 847-688-3154. Fax: 847-688-3169. Facebook.
E-mail: nmasifct@navy.mil
Web Site: www.history.navy.mil/nmas
Formerly: Great Lakes Naval Museum
Key Personnel: Dir., Jennifer Searcy.
Institution Type/Description: Military Museum.
Hours & Admission Prices: Mon.-Sat. 9-5. No charge. ♿
Attendance: 50,000 (actual)

Greenup

CUMBERLAND COUNTY HISTORIC AND GENEALOGICAL SOCIETY, 216 Cumberland St., Greenup, IL 62428. Mailing Address: P.O. Box 582, Greenup, IL 62428-0582. Tel.: 217-923-9306.
E-mail: historic@rr1.net
Institution Type/Description: Historical Society Museum: housed in the Johnson Building. Listed on the National Register of Historic Places.
Hours & Admission Prices: Mon.-Sat. 10-4, Sun. 12-4. No charge; donations accepted. Closed Easter; Thanksgiving; Christmas.

Greenville

HOILES-DAVIS MUSEUM, 318 W. Winter St., Greenville, IL 62246-1722. Mailing Address: P.O. Box 376, Greenville, IL 62246-0376. Tel.: 618-664-1590.
E-mail: president@bondcountyhistorical.org
Key Personnel: Pres., Lester Harnetiaux; Vice Pres. & Historian, Kevin Kaegy; Treas., John S. Coleman; Sec., Jane Hopkins.
Institution Type/Description: Historical Society Museum.
Hours & Admission Prices: Sat. 1-3, Sun. 2-4. No charge; donations accepted. ♿
Attendance: 700 (estimated)

Gridley

TELEPHONE MUSEUM OF GRIDLEY, 318 N. Center St., Gridley, IL 61744. Mailing Address: P.O. Box 370, Gridley, IL 61744. Tel.: 309-747-2284 (Tours).
E-mail: gpld@gridcom.net
Web Site: www.telephonemuseumofgridley.com
Key Personnel: Library Dir., Linda Zimmerman.
Institution Type/Description: Telephone Museum.
Hours & Admission Prices: Tues.-Fri. 1:30-3:30, Sat. by appointment. No charge; donations accepted. ♿

Gurnee

MOTHER RUDD HOME MUSEUM, 4690 Old Grand Ave., Gurnee, IL 60031. Mailing Address: P.O. Box 84, Gurnee, IL 60031-0084. Tel.: 847-263-9540.
E-mail: info@motherrudd.org
Web Site: motherrudd.org
Institution Type/Description: Historical Society Museum: housed in a former inn; built in 1841.
Hours & Admission Prices: By appointment. No charge; donations accepted.

Hanna City

WILDLIFE PRAIRIE PARK, 3826 N. Taylor Rd., Hanna City, IL 61536-9467. Tel.: 309-676-0998. Fax: 309-676-7783. Facebook: Wildlife Prairie Park.
E-mail: irequest@wildlifeprairie.org
Web Site: wildlifeprairiepark.org
Key Personnel: Exec. Dir., Doug Dillow; Operations Mgr., Jim Wetherington; Cur. Animals, Adrienne Bauer; Mktg. Coord., Eva Kirschbaum; Volunteer Coord., Lindsay Seiberlich; Security, Alan Burgett.
Institution Type/Description: Wildlife Park.
Hours & Admission Prices: Summer: mid-March through Oct. 9-6:30; Winter: Nov. to mid-March 9-4:30. Adults $9, seniors $7, children 3-12 $6; discounts to groups; $1 off admissions during winter season; members and children 2 & under no charge. Closed Christmas Day & New Year's Day. ♿
Attendance: 150,000 (actual)

Harrisburg

SALINE CREEK PIONEER VILLAGE & POOR HOUSE MUSEUM, 1600 S. Feazel St., Harrisburg, IL 62946. Tel.: 618-253-7342.
Key Personnel: Pres. (V), Mary E. Shackleford.
Institution Type/Description: Historic Village.
Hours & Admission Prices: Tours: Tues.-Sat. 2pm; other times by appointment. Adults $5.
Attendance: 200 (estimated)

Harvard

GREATER HARVARD AREA HISTORICAL SOCIETY, 308 N. Hart Blvd., Harvard, IL 60033-3018. Mailing Address: P.O. Box 505, Harvard, IL 60033-0505. Tel.: 815-943-6141.
E-mail: harvardhistoricalsociety@gmail.com
Key Personnel: C.E.O., Chm. (V) & Pres., Brian Schultz; Vice Pres., Alice Hayden; Sec., Elzora Stoxen; Treas., Jim Finke.
Institution Type/Description: History Museum & Historic Building.
Hours & Admission Prices: May-Oct. Wed. 10-12, Sun. 1:30-4; other times by appointment, call 815-943-5720. No charge; donations accepted.
Attendance: 200 (estimated)

Heyworth

SIMPKINS MILITARY HISTORY MUSEUM, 605 E. Cole St., Heyworth, IL 61745. Mailing Address: P. O. Box 336, Heyworth, IL 61745-0336. Tel.: 309-473-3989.
E-mail: simpkinsmuseum@gmail.com
Web Site: www.simpkinsmuseum.com
Formerly: Simpkins War Museum
Key Personnel: Dir., Gary A. Simpkins; Chm. (V), Carol J. Simpkins.
Institution Type/Description: Military Museum.
Hours & Admission Prices: Feb.-Nov. Tues., Thurs. & Sat. 1-5. No charge; donations accepted. Closed legal holidays except Veterans Day.
Attendance: 1,250 (estimated)

Highland Park

THE ART CENTER - HIGHLAND PARK (TAC), 1957 Sheridan Rd., Highland Park, IL 60035-2540. Tel.: 847-432-1888. Fax: 847-432-9106. Facebook: The Art Center HP.
E-mail: info@theartcenterhp.org
Web Site: www.theartcenterhp.org
Key Personnel: Exe. Dir., James M. Lynch; Pres. Bd. Dir., Gwen Heyman; Cur., Caren Helene Rudman; Exec. Asst., Jessica Williams.
Institution Type/Description: Art Gallery & Art School.
Hours & Admission Prices: Mon.-Thurs. 9-5, Fri. 9-4:30, Sat. 9-3:30, Sun. by appointment. No charge; donations accepted.
Attendance: 30,000 (actual)

HIGHLAND PARK HISTORICAL SOCIETY, 494 Laurel Ave., Highland Park, IL 60035-2623. Tel.: 847-432-7090.
E-mail: hphistorical@sbcglobal.net
Web Site: www.highlandparkhistory.com
Key Personnel: Pres. (V), V. Robert Rotering; Archivist, Nancy Webster.
Institution Type/Description: Local History Museum: housed in 1871 brick Victorian House.
Hours & Admission Prices: Feb. 15-Dec. 15 Wed.-Fri. 1-4, Sun. 2-4. Cabin: spring & summer only. Occasional special exhibit fee charged. Closed holidays.
Attendance: 2,300 (estimated)

WALTER E. HELLER NATURE CENTER, 2821 Ridge Rd., Highland Park, IL 60035-1533. Mailing Address: 636 Ridge Rd., Highland Park, IL 60035-4361. Tel.: 847-433-6901 & 831-3810. Fax: 847-433-8856.
E-mail: heller@pdhp.org
Web Site: www.hellernaturecenter.org
Key Personnel: Site Mgr., Jeff Smith; Naturalist, Leah Holloway; Naturalist, Jessica Reyes.
Institution Type/Description: Nature Center & Preserve.
Hours & Admission Prices: Mon.-Fri. 8:30-5, Sat.-Sun. 9-3. No charge; donations accepted. Closed national holidays.
Attendance: 17,000 (estimated)

Hinsdale

HINSDALE HISTORICAL SOCIETY, 15 S. Clay St., Hinsdale, IL 60521-3244. Mailing Address: P.O. Box 336, Hinsdale, IL 60522-0336. Tel.: 630-789-2600.
E-mail: info@hinsdalehistory.org
Web Site: www.hinsdalehistory.org
Key Personnel: Exec. Dir., Lynne Mickle Smaczny; Pres., Jayne Coyne; First Vice Pres., Champ Davis, III.
Institution Type/Description: Historical Society Museum: housed in a restored 1874 middle class residence.
Hours & Admission Prices: History Museum: Fri.-Sat. noon-4; other times by appointment. Immanuel Hall: Tues.-Wed. 10-2; other time by appointment. No charge; donations accepted.
Attendance: 600 (estimated)

ROBERT CROWN CENTER FOR HEALTH EDUCATION, 21 Salt Creek Lane, Hinsdale, IL 60521-2902. Tel.: 630-325-1900. Fax: 630-325-3970.
E-mail: rcche@robertcrown.org
Web Site: www.robertcrown.org
Key Personnel: Chm. (V), Mick Kane; Dir., Caryn Glover.
Institution Type/Description: Health Education Center.
Hours & Admission Prices: School Groups: mid-Sept. to mid-June Mon.-Fri. 9-2:30 by appointment. Admission $5; teachers no charge. Outreach: $7 per person. Closed national holidays.
Attendance: 120,000 (actual)

Ingleside

FOX LAKE-GRANT TOWNSHIP AREA HISTORICAL SOCIETY, 411 Washington St., Ingleside, IL 60041. Mailing Address: P.O. Box 224, Ingleside, IL 60041. Tel.: 847-587-0544.
E-mail: flgranthall@yahoo.com
Key Personnel: Pres. (V), Nancy Kubalanza.
Institution Type/Description: Historical Society Museum.
Hours & Admission Prices: Feb.-Dec. 1st & 3rd Sun. of the month 1-4. No charge; donations accepted.
Attendance: 800 (estimated)

Jacksonville

DAVID STRAWN ART GALLERY, 331 W. College Ave., Jacksonville, IL 62650-2474. Mailing Address: P.O. Box 1213, Jacksonville, IL 62651-1213. Tel.: 217-243-9390. Facebook: David Strawn Art Gallery.
E-mail: strawnartgallery@frontier.com
Web Site: www.strawnartgallery.org
Key Personnel: Pres., Amy Jackson; Dir., Kelly M. Gross.
Institution Type/Description: Art Gallery: housed in 1915 former home of Dr. David Strawn.
Hours & Admission Prices: Sept.-May Tues.-Sat. 4-6, Sun. 1-3. No charge. Closed holidays.
Attendance: 5,974 (estimated)

Joliet

JOLIET AREA HISTORICAL MUSEUM, 204 N. Ottawa St., Joliet, IL 60432-4007. Tel.: 815-723-5201. Fax: 815-723-9039.
E-mail: t.contos@jolietmuseum.org
Web Site: www.jolietmuseum.org
Formerly: Joliet Area Historical Society
Key Personnel: Exec. Dir., Anthony B. Contos; Museum Shop Mgr., Elaine Stonich.
Institution Type/Description: Local History Museum.
Hours & Admission Prices: Tues.-Sat. 10-5, Sun. 12-5. Adults $6, senior citizens 60 & over $5; youth 4-17 $3; discounts to AAM members; members no charge. Closed New Year's Eve & Day; Good Friday; Easter; Memorial Day; Independence Day; Labor Day; Thanksgiving; Christmas Eve & Day.
Attendance: 25,000 (actual)

LAURA A. SPRAGUE ART GALLERY, Joliet Junior College Main Campus, 1215 Houbolt Rd., Spicer-Brown Hall, Joliet, IL 60431-8938. Tel.: 815-280-2423 & 2223.
E-mail: joemilosevich@gmail.com
Web Site: www.jjc.edu/info/fine-arts-events
Key Personnel: Gallery Dir., Joe Milosevich.
Institution Type/Description: Art Gallery.
Hours & Admission Prices: Fall & Spring Semesters Mon.-Fri. 8-8; Summer Semester Mon.-Thurs. 8-8. No charge.

RIALTO SQUARE THEATRE, 15 E. Van Buren St., Joliet, IL 60432-4211. Tel.: 815-726-7171.
E-mail: jsungaila@rialtosquare.com
Institution Type/Description: Historic Building Museum: housed in a former movie theatre; built in 1926.
Hours & Admission Prices: Tours: Tues. 1:30; other times by appointment. $5 per person.

SLOVENIAN WOMEN'S UNION HERITAGE MUSEUM, 431 N. Chicago St., Joliet, IL 60432-1785. Tel.: 815-727-1926. Fax: 815-723-0670.
E-mail: swvhome@svva.org
Web Site: www.swua.org
Institution Type/Description: Heritage Museum.
Hours & Admission Prices: Mon.-Fri. 10-2. No charge; donations accepted.

Kampsville

CENTER FOR AMERICAN ARCHEOLOGY, Hwy. 100, Kampsville, IL 62053. Mailing Address: P.O. Box 366, Kampsville, IL 62053-0366. Tel.: 618-653-4316. Fax: 618-653-4232.
E-mail: caa@caa-archeology.org
Web Site: www.caa-archeology.org
Formerly: Kampsville Archeological Museum
Key Personnel: Pres. (V), Jane E. Buikstra, Ph.D.; Museum Shop Mgr., Jason King.
Institution Type/Description: Archaeology Museum.
Hours & Admission Prices: May-Oct. Tues.-Fri. 10-5, Sat. 10-4, Sun. 12-4. No charge; donations accepted. Fee for tours.
Attendance: 3,000 (estimated)

Kankakee

KANKAKEE COUNTY MUSEUM, 801 S. 8th Ave., Kankakee, IL 60901-4744. Tel.: 815-932-5279. Fax: 815-932-5204.
E-mail: kankakeecountymuseum@gmail.com
Web Site: www.kankakeecountymuseum.org
Formerly: Kankakee County Historical Society Museum
Institution Type/Description: County Historical Museum.
Hours & Admission Prices: Tues.-Thurs. 10-4, Sat. 1-4. Adults $3, seniors & students $2, children 15 & under $1; members & Tues. no charge. Closed holidays.
Attendance: 25,000 (estimated)

WILLOWHAVEN INTERPRETIVE CENTER, 1451 N. 4000 E Rd., Kankakee, IL 60901. Mailing Address: Bourbonnais Township Park District, 456 N. Kennedy Dr., Bourbonnais, IL 60914. Tel.: 815-933-9905, ext. 472.
E-mail: nicole@btpd.org
Key Personnel: Facility Mgr., Nicole Jenkins.
Institution Type/Description: Natural History Museum & Aquarium.
Hours & Admission Prices: Call for hours.

Kenilworth

THE KENILWORTH HISTORICAL SOCIETY, 415 Kenilworth Ave., Kenilworth, IL 60043-1134. Tel.: 847-251-2565. Facebook: Kenilworth History.
E-mail: kenilworthhistory@sbcglobal.net
Web Site: www.kenilworthhistory.org
Key Personnel: Dir., Virginia Anderson; Pres., Steve Crawford; Sec., Laurel Flentye; Cur., Melinda F. Kwedar; Cur., Kyle Mathers.
Institution Type/Description: Historical Society Museum.
Hours & Admission Prices: Mon. 9-4:30, Thurs. 9-12; other times by appointment. No charge; donations accepted.
Attendance: 750 (estimated)

Knoxville

KNOX COUNTY MUSEUM, 33 Public Square, Knoxville, IL 61448-1378. Tel.: 309-289-2088.
Web Site: www.kville.org
Key Personnel: C.E.O. & Pres. (V), Peg Bivens; Cur., Joan Johnson.
Institution Type/Description: Historical Society Museum.
Hours & Admission Prices: May-Sept. Tues.-Sat. 10-2, Sun. 2-4; Oct.-April Tues.-Sat. 10-2; tours by appointment. No charge, donations accepted.
Attendance: 1,000 (estimated)

La Grange

LA GRANGE AREA HISTORICAL SOCIETY, 444 S. LaGrange Rd., La Grange, IL 60525-2448. Tel.: 708-482-4248. Fax: 708-482-4248. Facebook.
E-mail: lagrangehistory@sbcglobal.net
Web Site: lagrangehistory.org
Key Personnel: Pres. (V), Karen Lynch.
Institution Type/Description: Historical Society Museum: housed in the Vial House, built in 1874.
Hours & Admission Prices: Open House: last Sun. each month 1-4. Research: Wed. 9:30-12:30; other times by appointment. No charge; donations accepted.

LaFox

GARFIELD FARM MUSEUM, 3N016 Garfield Rd., LaFox, IL 60147-0403. Mailing Address: P.O. Box 403, LaFox, IL 60147-0403. Tel.: 630-584-8485. Fax: 630-584-8522.
E-mail: info@garfieldfarm.org
Web Site: garfieldfarm.org
Key Personnel: Dir., Jerome Martin Johnson; Dir. Museum Operations, William Wolcott; Asst. Site Mgr., Joseph Coleman; Pres. C.H.A.L. Inc., Helen Bauer; Pres. G.H.S. Inc., Susan Lloyd; Treas. G.H.S. Inc., Marty Germann.
Institution Type/Description: Living Historic Farm & Inn Museum.
Hours & Admission Prices: June-Sept. Wed. & Sun. 1-4; other times by appointment only. Adults $3, youth groups under 13 $2; members no charge. Closed Thanksgiving; Christmas.
Attendance: 10,000 (estimated)

LaSalle

HEGELER CARUS MANSION, 1307 7th St., LaSalle, IL 61301. Tel.: 815-224-6543. Fax: 815-224-5801. Facebook: Hegeler Carus Mansion.
E-mail: execdirector@hegelercarus.org
Web Site: www.hegelercarus.org
Institution Type/Description: Historic Home Museum: built in 1874.
Hours & Admission Prices: Wed.-Sun. 12, 1, 2, & 3; groups by appointment. Suggested Donation: adults $10, students K-12 $5; discounts to groups of 20 or more. Closed New Year's Eve & Day; Easter; Memorial Day; Independence Day; Labor Day; Thanksgiving; Christmas Eve & Day.

Lake Forest

LAKE FOREST-LAKE BLUFF HISTORICAL SOCIETY, 509 E. Deerpath, Lake Forest, IL 60045-2255. Tel.: 847-234-5253.
E-mail: info@lflbhistory.org
Web Site: www.lflbhistory.org
Key Personnel: Exec. Dir., Janice Hack; Cur., Laurie Stein.
Institution Type/Description: Historical Society Museum.
Hours & Admission Prices: Tues.-Thurs. 10-4, Fri. by appointment, Sun. 1-4. No charge. Closed major holidays.
Attendance: 1,500 (estimated)

Lerna

LINCOLN LOG CABIN STATE HISTORIC SITE, 402 S. Lincoln Hwy. Rd, Lerna, IL 62440. Tel.: 217-345-1845. Fax: 217-345-6472. Facebook: Lincoln Log Cabin.
E-mail: hpa.lincolnlog@illinois.gov
Web Site: www.lincolnlogcabin.org
Key Personnel: Site Mgr., Matthew Mittelstaedt; Museum Shop Mgr., Susan Colgrove.
Institution Type/Description: Historic Houses & Site: reconstructed cabin and farm of Thomas and Sara Lincoln on original site.
Hours & Admission Prices: Wed.-Sun. 9-5. No charge; donations accepted. Closed New Year's Day; Veterans Day; Thanksgiving; Christmas.
Attendance: 126,000 (actual)

REUBEN MOORE HOME STATE HISTORIC SITE, 400 S. Lincoln Hwy. Rd., Lerna, IL 62440-2840. Mailing Address: 400 S. Lincoln Hwy. Rd., P.O. Box 100, Lerna, IL 62440-0100. Tel.: 217-345-1845. Fax: 217-345-6472. Facebook: Lincoln Log Cabin.
E-mail: hpa.lincolnlog@illinois.gov
Web Site: www.lincolnlogcabin.org
Key Personnel: Site Supt., Matthew Mittelstaedt.
Institution Type/Description: Historic House Museum: mid-19th century home of Matilda Moore, stepsister of Abraham Lincoln; site of Lincoln's last visit with his stepmother & family before leaving to assume the presidency in 1861.

Hours & Admission Prices: June-Aug. Wed.-Sun.; Sept.-May by appointment only. No charge. Closed New Year's Day; Thanksgiving; Christmas. &
Attendance: 4,326 (actual)

Lewistown

DICKSON MOUNDS MUSEUM, 10956 N. Dickson Mounds Rd., Lewistown, IL 61542-9112. Tel.: 309-547-3721. Fax: 309-547-3189. TDD: 217-782-9175.
E-mail: wiant@museum.state.il.us
Web Site: www.museum.state.il.us/ismsites/dickson/
Key Personnel: Dir. Dickson Mounds Museum, Dr. Michael D. Wiant; Assoc. Cur., Dr. Michael Conner; Asst. Cur., Christa Foster; Asst. Cur., Kelvin Sampson; Office Mgr., Kim Dunnigan.
Institution Type/Description: Anthropology Museum & Site.
Hours & Admission Prices: Daily 8:30-5. No charge; donations accepted. Closed New Year's Day; Thanksgiving; Christmas. &
Attendance: 40,103 (actual)

Libertyville

LIBERTYVILLE-MUNDELEIN HISTORICAL SOCIETY, INC., 413 N. Milwaukee Ave., Libertyville, IL 60048-2247. Tel.: 847-362-2330. Facebook: Libertyville-Mundelein Historical Society, Inc..
E-mail: info@lmhistory.org
Web Site: www.lmhistory.org
Key Personnel: House Mgr., Mary Tompson; Pres. (V), Jenny Barry.
Institution Type/Description: History Museum: housed in 1878 Ansel B. Cook home. Listed on The National Register of Historic Places.
Hours & Admission Prices: Summer: Sun. 2-4; first 2 weekends in Dec.; private tours by appointment. Adults $2, students & seniors $1.
Attendance: 1,100 (estimated)

Lincoln

HERITAGE IN FLIGHT MUSEUM, Logan County Airport, 1351 Airport Rd., Lincoln, IL 62656-5444. Tel.: 217-732-3333.
Institution Type/Description: History Museum: housed in a former WWII barracks from Camp Ellis.
Hours & Admission Prices: Sat. 9-12 by appointment.

LINCOLN HERITAGE MUSEUM, 1115 Nicholson Rd., Lincoln, IL 62656-1699. Mailing Address: 300 Keokuk St., Lincoln, IL 62656-1699. Tel.: 217-735-7399. Fax: 217-732-2815.
E-mail: tmclaughlin@lincolncollege.edu
Web Site: museum.lincolncollege.edu
Formerly: Lincoln College Museum
Key Personnel: Dir., Tom McLaughlin; Asst. Dir. & Cur., Anne Moseley.
Institution Type/Description: History Museum.
Hours & Admission Prices: Mon.-Fri. 9-4, Sat. 1-4. Suggested Donations: adults $7, youth 6-17 $4; children under 6 no charge. Closed Federal holidays except Lincoln's Birthday. &
Attendance: 6,000 (estimated)

LOGAN COUNTY GENEALOGICAL & HISTORICAL SOCIETY, 114 N. Chicago St., Lincoln, IL 62656. Tel.: 217-732-3200. www.rootsweb.ancestry.com/~illcghs/.
E-mail: lcghs1@hotmail.com
Web Site: www.logancoil-genhist.org
Key Personnel: Pres. (V), Marla Blair.
Institution Type/Description: Historical Society Museum.
Hours & Admission Prices: Tues.-Fri. 11-4, 2nd & 4th Sat. 10-1; call to confirm hours. No charge; donations accepted.
Attendance: 1,500 (actual)

POSTVILLE COURTHOUSE STATE HISTORIC SITE, 914 Fifth St., Lincoln, IL 62656-2308. Mailing Address: P.O. Box 355, Lincoln, IL 62656-0355. Tel.: 217-732-8930 & 8687.
E-mail: hpa.info@illinois.gov
Institution Type/Description: History Site/Museum.
Hours & Admission Prices: Tues.-Sat. 12-4; other times by appointment. No charge; donations accepted. Closed New Year's Day; Lincoln's Birthday; Veterans Day; Independence Day; Thanksgiving; Christmas.
Attendance: 2,600 (actual)

Lisle

JURICA-SUCHY NATURE MUSEUM, Benedictine University, 5700 College Rd., Lisle, IL 60532-2851. Tel.: 630-829-6569. Fax: 630-829-6547.
E-mail: ktumminello@ben.edu
Web Site: ben.edu/museum
Formerly: Jurica Nature Museum
Key Personnel: Dir. & Cur., Karly Tumminello.
Institution Type/Description: Natural History Museum.
Hours & Admission Prices: June-July Tues.-Thurs. 1-4; Sept.-april Mon.-Thurs. 1-5, Fri.-Sun. 2-4; groups by advance arrangement. No charge; donations accepted. Closed school vacations. &
Attendance: 6,000 (actual)

THE MORTON ARBORETUM, 4100 Illinois Rte. 53, Lisle, IL 60532-1293. Tel.: 630-968-0074. Fax: 630-719-2433.
E-mail: trees@mortonarb.org
Web Site: www.mortonarb.org
Key Personnel: Pres. & C.E.O., Dr. Gerard T. Donnelly; Volunteer Coord., Kristin Sabatino; Museum Shop Mgr., Jacqueline Fucilla.
Institution Type/Description: Arboretum.
Hours & Admission Prices: Grounds: daily 7am to sunset. Buildings: call for hours. Adults $14, seniors $12, children 2-17 $9; discounts on Wed., active military & during winter; children under 2 & members no charge. &
Attendance: 1,056,000 (actual)

THE MUSEUMS AT LISLE STATION PARK, 921 School St., Lisle, IL 60532-1951. Tel.: 630-968-0499. Facebook: Museums at Lisle Station Park.
E-mail: museum@lisleparkdistrict.org
Web Site: www.lisleparkdistrict.org/museumsatlislestationpark
Key Personnel: Museum Cur., Concetta Gibson.
Institution Type/Description: History Museum.
Hours & Admission Prices: Feb.-May & Sept.-Dec. Tues. & Sat. 10-1; June-Sept. Tues. & Sat. 10-4, Thurs. 1-4. No charge; donations accepted. &
Attendance: 8,800 (actual)

Lockport

THE GAYLORD BUILDING - NATIONAL TRUST HISTORIC SITE, 200 W. 8th St., Lockport, IL 60441-2878. Tel.: 815-838-9400. Fax: 815-838-9449.
E-mail: info@gaylordbuilding.org
Web Site: www.gaylordbuilding.org
Key Personnel: Dir., Mark S. Harmon, M.A.
Institution Type/Description: Historic Building: housed in the former building that stored construction materials for the Illinois & Michigan Canal; built in 1838. A Historic Site.
Hours & Admission Prices: Mon.-Sat. 10-5, Sun. 11-5. No charge; donations accepted; Closed major holidays. &
Attendance: 87,000 (estimated)

ILLINOIS STATE MUSEUM/LOCKPORT GALLERY, 201 W. 10th St., Lockport, IL 60441-4039. Tel.: 815-838-7400. Facebook; Twitter.
Web Site: www.museum.state.il.us/ismsites/lockport/
Key Personnel: Gallery Mgr., John Lustig.
Institution Type/Description: Art Museum.
Hours & Admission Prices: Wed.-Fri. 10-5, Sat.-Sun. 11-5. No charge; donations accepted. Closed state holidays. &
Attendance: 16,500 (estimated)

WILL COUNTY HISTORICAL MUSEUM & RESEARCH CENTER, 803 S. State St., Lockport, IL 60441-3433. Tel.: 815-838-5080. Fax: 815-838-4547. Facebook.
E-mail: info@willhistory.org
Web Site: www.willhistory.org
Formerly: Illinois and Michigan Canal Commissioners Office Museum
Key Personnel: Exec. Pres. (V), Sandy Vasko.
Institution Type/Description: History Museum.
Hours & Admission Prices: mid-Feb. to late Nov. Wed.-Sun. 12-4. No charge; donations accepted. Closed major holidays.
Attendance: 4,500 (estimated)

Lombard

LILACIA PARK-LOMBARD PARK DISTRICT, 227 W. Parkside Ave., Lombard, IL 60148-2592. Tel.: 630-627-1281. Fax: 630-627-1286.

E-mail: info@lombardparks.com
Web Site: www.lombardparks.com
Key Personnel: Museum Shop Mgr., Jackie Brzezinski.
Institution Type/Description: Horticultural Park.
Hours & Admission Prices: Daily 9-6. No charge; donations accepted. &
Attendance: 10,500 (estimated)

LOMBARD HISTORICAL SOCIETY - VICTORIAN COTTAGE MUSEUM, 23 W. Maple, Lombard, IL 60148-2512. Tel.: 630-629-1885. Facebook: Lombard History.
E-mail: info@lombardhistory.net
Web Site: lombardhistory.org
Key Personnel: Dir., Sarah Richardt; Pres. (V), Jennifer Henaghan.
Institution Type/Description: Local History Museum: housed in a historic home; features lifestyle of a middle class family in Lombard during the 1870s.
Hours & Admission Prices: Feb.-Dec. Wed. & Fri. 1-4, Sat. 1-4; other times by appointment. No charge; donations accepted. &
Attendance: 6,000 (actual)

SHELDON PECK HOMESTEAD, 355 E. Parkside, Lombard, IL 60148-2776. Mailing Address: Lombard Historical Society, 23 W. Maple, Lombard, IL 60148. Tel.: 630-629-1885. Facebook: Lombard History.
E-mail: info@lombardhistory.net
Web Site: lombardhistory.org
Key Personnel: Dir., Sarah Richardt; Pres., Jennifer Henaghan.
Institution Type/Description: Historic House Museum: housed in an 1840s restored farmhouse; National Park Service Network to Freedom, Underground Railroad site.
Hours & Admission Prices: Feb.-Nov. Tues. & Thurs. 1-4, Sat. 10-2. No charge; donations accepted. Closed holidays. &
Attendance: 4,500 (actual)

Macomb

WESTERN ILLINOIS UNIVERSITY ART GALLERY, 1 University Circle, Macomb, IL 61455-1390. Tel.: 309-298-1587.
E-mail: AM-Hayes-Hawkinson@wiu.edu
Web Site: www.wiu.edu/artgallery
Key Personnel: Dir., Ann Marie Hayes-Hawkinson.
Institution Type/Description: Art Museum.
Hours & Admission Prices: School Year Tues.-Fri. 9-4, Sat. 1-4. No charge. Closed university vacations. &
Attendance: 4,900 (actual)

Mahomet

MABERY GELVIN BOTANICAL GARDEN, 109 S. Lake of the Woods Rd., Mahomet, IL 61853. Mailing Address: P.O. Box 1040, Mahomet, IL 61853. Tel.: 217-586-4389 & 4630. Fax: 217-586-6852.
E-mail: hq@ccfpd.org
Institution Type/Description: Botanical Garden.
Hours & Admission Prices: Daily 7 am to sundown. No charge.

MUSEUM OF THE GRAND PRAIRIE, 600 N. Lombard, Mahomet, IL 61853. Mailing Address: P.O. Box 1040, Mahomet, IL 61853-1040. Tel.: 217-586-2612. Fax: 217-586-3491.
E-mail: hq@ccfpd.org
Web Site: www.ccfpd.org
Formerly: Early American Museum
Key Personnel: Dir., Cheryl Kennedy; Asst. Dir., Barbara Oehlschlaeger-Garvey.
Institution Type/Description: History Museum.
Hours & Admission Prices: March-May & Sept.-Dec. daily 1-5; June-Aug. Mon.-Sat. 10-5, Sun. 1-5. Fee for special programs only. Closed Easter; Christmas Eve & Day. &
Attendance: 14,000 (estimated)

Makanda

GIANT CITY STATE PARK, 235 Giant City Rd., Makanda, IL 62958-3207. Tel.: 618-457-4836.
E-mail: DNR.TeachKids@illinois.gov
Web Site: www.dnr.illinois.gov
Institution Type/Description: Park Museum.
Hours & Admission Prices: Call for hours. No charge.
Attendance: 14,715 (actual)

Marion

CRAB ORCHARD NATIONAL WILDLIFE REFUGE, 8588 Rte. 148, Marion, IL 62959-5822. Tel.: 618-997-3344.
E-mail: craborchard@fws.gov
Web Site: www.fws.gov/refuge/Crab_Orchard
Institution Type/Description: Wildlife Refuge.
Hours & Admission Prices: Visitor Center: daily 8-4:30. Admission: Daily: $2 per vehicle; Weekly: $5 per vehicle.

WILLIAMSON COUNTY HISTORICAL SOCIETY, 105 S. Van Buren, Marion, IL 62959-2509. Tel.: 618-997-5863 (Mon.-Sat. 9:30-3). Facebook: Williamson County Illinois Historical Society.
E-mail: wchsmail@yahoo.com
Web Site: www.wcihs.org
Key Personnel: Pres. (V), Sam Lattuca; Cur., Sharon Vansaghi; Membership Chm., Dolores Thetford.
Institution Type/Description: County Historical Society Museum: housed in 1913 former county jail & sheriff's home.
Hours & Admission Prices: March to late Nov. Thurs. & Sat. 9:30-3; other times by appointment. Research Library: March-Nov. Requested Tour Donation: adults $2, children under 12 $1; discounts to students; members no charge. Closed Thanksgiving & day after.
Attendance: 2,000 (estimated)

Marshall

CLARK COUNTY MUSEUM, 502 S. Fourth St., Marshall, IL 62441. Mailing Address: P.O. Box 207, Marshall, IL 62441-0207.
E-mail: publishdc@gmail.com
Key Personnel: Dir. & Pres. (V), Dwight Connelly.
Institution Type/Description: Local History Museum.
Hours & Admission Prices: May-Oct. Sun. 2-4; other times by appointment. No charge; donations accepted.
Attendance: 269 (actual)

Maywood

WEST TOWN MUSEUM OF CULTURAL HISTORY, 104 S. 5th Ave., Maywood, IL 60153-1308. Tel.: 708-516-0628. Fax: 708-345-5887. Facebook: West Town Museum of Cultural History.
E-mail: operationupliftinc@gmail.com
Web Site: www.operationuplift.westtownmuseum.org
Key Personnel: Pres., Northica H. Stone; Chm. (V), M.E. Millon; Cur., L. Jeri Stenson.
Institution Type/Description: Cultural History Museum.
Hours & Admission Prices: Wed. 9:30-3; other times by appointment. Adults $5, children under 13 $3; discounts to members.
Attendance: 700 (estimated)

Mendota

BREAKING THE PRAIRIE MUSEUM, 684 8th St., Mendota, IL 61342-0433. Mailing Address: P.O. Box 433, Mendota, IL 61342-0433. Tel.: 815-539-3373.
E-mail: mmhsmuseum@yahoo.com
Web Site: www.mendotamuseums.org
Key Personnel: Dir., Dar Wujek; Chm. (V), Mark Heiman.
Institution Type/Description: History Museum.
Hours & Admission Prices: Daily call for hours. No charge; donations accepted. &
Attendance: 225 (estimated)

HUME-CARNEGIE MUSEUM, 901 Washington St., Mendota, IL 61342. Mailing Address: P.O. Box 433, Mendota, IL 61342. Tel.: 815-539-3373.
E-mail: mmhsmuseum@yahoo.com
Web Site: www.mendotamuseums.org
Key Personnel: Dir., Dar Wujek; C.E.O., Bill Greenwood; Admin. Asst., Julie Kobold.
Institution Type/Description: History Museum: housed in the Andrew Carnegie Library; c.1904.
Hours & Admission Prices: March-Nov. Sat.-Sun. 1-4. Suggested Donation: adults $2, student $1. &
Attendance: 660 (estimated)

UNION DEPOT RAILROAD MUSEUM, 783 Main St., Mendota, IL 61342. Mailing Address: P.O. Box 433, Mendota, IL 61342-0433. Tel.: 815-539-3373.
E-mail: mmhsmuseum@yahoo.com
Web Site: www.mendotamuseums.org/udrr.htm

Key Personnel: Chm. (V), Alan Russell; Museum Shop Mgr., Janis Shirey.
Institution Type/Description: Railroad Museum.
Hours & Admission Prices: Sat.-Sun. 12-4. Adults $3, students $1. &
Attendance: 700 (estimated)

Metamora

METAMORA COURTHOUSE HISTORIC SITE, 113 E. Partridge, Metamora, IL 61548-7021. Mailing Address: P.O. Box 628, Metamora, IL 61548. Tel.: 309-367-4470. Facebook: Metamora Courthouse Historic Site.
E-mail: metcourt@mtco.com
Web Site: www.villageofmetamora.com/?hiscourt
Key Personnel: Cur., Jean Myers.
Institution Type/Description: History Museum: housed in a restored 1845 Greek Revival courthouse located in the 8th Judicial Circuit that Abraham Lincoln traveled as a circuit lawyer.
Hours & Admission Prices: March-Oct. Tues.-Sat. 1-5; Nov.-Feb. Tues.-Sat. 12-4; groups by appointment. No charge; donations accepted. Closed New Year's Day; Martin Luther King Jr. Day; Presidents' Day; Veterans Day; Election Day; Thanksgiving; Christmas. &
Attendance: 6,869 (actual)

Metropolis

THE ALLARD HOUSE AND MORRIS TOY MUSEUM, 21 Henry Rd., Metropolis, IL 62960-2939. Tel.: 270-988-3591.
Institution Type/Description: Historic House & Toy Museum.
Hours & Admission Prices: Call for hours. Admission: $2 per person.

FORT MASSAC STATE PARK AND HISTORIC SITE, 1308 E. 5th St., Metropolis, IL 62960-2380. Tel.: 618-524-9321 & 4712. Fax: 618-524-9321.
E-mail: dnr.r5parks@illinois.gov
Key Personnel: Site Supt., Terry Johnson.
Institution Type/Description: History Museum: located on the site of 1756-1814, Military Post.
Hours & Admission Prices: Daily. No charge. Closed Thanksgiving; Christmas. &
Attendance: 1,604,115 (actual)

Moline

JOHN DEERE PAVILION, 1400 River Dr., Moline, IL 61265. Tel.: 309-765-1000.
Web Site: www.deere.com/en/connect-with-john-deere/visit-john-deere/pavilion/
Institution Type/Description: Agricultural History Museum.
Hours & Admission Prices: Mon.-Fri. 9-5, Sat. 10-5, Sun. 12-4. No charge. Closed Good Friday; Memorial Day; Independence Day; Labor Day.

ROCK ISLAND COUNTY HISTORICAL SOCIETY, 822 11th Ave., Moline, IL 61265-1221. Tel.: 309-764-8590. Fax: 309-764-4748. Facebook: @RICHS1905.
E-mail: richs@richs.cc
Web Site: www.richs.cc
Key Personnel: Pres., Merredith Peterson; Admin., Ronna Stickrod; Cur. Museum, Anne Robinson.
Institution Type/Description: Historical Society Museum: housed in c.1877 Victorian three story house.
Hours & Admission Prices: House Museum & Carriage House: by appointment. Library: Wed.-Sat. 9-4. Adults $5; discounts to AAM & ICOM members; members no charge. &
Attendance: 5,000 (estimated)

Monmouth

BUCHANAN CENTER FOR THE ARTS, 64 Public Square, Monmouth, IL 61462-1756. Tel.: 309-734-3033. Facebook: Buchanan Center for the Arts - BCA.
E-mail: buchanancenter@mtcnow.net
Web Site: bcaarts.org
Key Personnel: Dir., Kristyne Gilbert-Bradford; Office Mgr., Lynn Miller; Pres. (V), Victoria Hennenfent.
Institution Type/Description: Art Museum & Arts Agency.
Hours & Admission Prices: Tues.-Fri. 10-5, Sat. 10-2. No charge; donations accepted. Closed major holidays. &
Attendance: 13,000 (estimated)

WYATT EARP BIRTHPLACE HOME, 406 S. 3rd St., Monmouth, IL 61462. Mailing Address: 300 2nd St. NE, Apt. 306, Mason City, IA 50401-3497. Tel.: 309-734-6771.
E-mail: wyattearpbirthp@aol.com
Web Site: www.earpmorgan.com/wyattearpbirthplacewebsite.html
Key Personnel: Pres. (V), Cindy Reidhead; Chm. (V) & Museum Shop Mgr., Jane Lee.
Institution Type/Description: Historic House: built c.1841. Listed on the National Register of Historic Places.
Hours & Admission Prices: Open daily or by appointment. No charge; donations accepted. &
Attendance: 500 (actual)

Monticello

ALLERTON PARK AND RETREAT CENTER, 515 Old Timber Rd., Monticello, IL 61856-8279. Tel.: 217-333-3287 & 762-7011. Fax: 217-762-3742.
E-mail: depetrsn@illinois.edu
Web Site: allerton.illinois.edu/contact-us
Institution Type/Description: Historic House & Park.
Hours & Admission Prices: Visitor Center: Staffed: April-Nov. Sat.-Sun. 9-5; Unstaffed: Dec.-March daily 9-5. Closed New Year's Day; Thanksgiving; Christmas.

MONTICELLO RAILWAY MUSEUM, 992 Iron Horse Pl., Monticello, IL 61856. Mailing Address: P.O. Box 401, Monticello, IL 61856-0401. Tel.: 217-762-9011, 877-762-9011. Facebook: Monticello Railway Museum.
E-mail: info@mrym.org
Web Site: www.mrym.org
Key Personnel: Supt. Locomotives, Kent McClure; Chm. (V), Brian Downing; Pres. (V), John Sciutto; Vice Pres., Travis Atchison; Sec., Donna McClure; Gen. & Museum Shop Mgr., Sylvester Keller; Treas., Doug Butzow.
Institution Type/Description: Railway Museum.
Hours & Admission Prices: May-Oct. Sat.-Sun. Museum: no charge. Diesel Train Rides (Steam Weekends): adults $12, senior citizens $10, youth 2-12 $8; discount to Illinois Central Railroad employees, AAA members & groups of 20 or more; children under 2 & members no charge. Write for schedule of events. Fares may differ for special events. &
Attendance: 22,000 (actual)

PIATT COUNTY MUSEUM, 1 Heritage Ln., Monticello, IL 61856. Tel.: 217-762-4731.
E-mail: piattcountymuseum@gmail.com
Web Site: www.piattmuseum.org
Key Personnel: Pres. (V), T.J. Shambaugh, IV; Trustee, Lorin I. Nevling, Ph.D.; Dir. Devel., Peg Bargon.
Institution Type/Description: General Museum.
Hours & Admission Prices: Call for hours.
Attendance: 600 (estimated)

Morris

GRUNDY COUNTY HISTORICAL SOCIETY AND MUSEUM, 510 W. Illinois Ave., Morris, IL 60450. Tel.: 815-942-4880. Facebook.
E-mail: grundyhistory@sbcglobal.net
Key Personnel: Pres. (V), D.G. Sroczynski; Museum Shop Mgr., Dorothy Cunnea.
Institution Type/Description: Historical Society Museum.
Hours & Admission Prices: Thurs.-Sat. 10-3; groups by appointment. No charge. &
Attendance: 1,600 (actual)

Morrison

MORRISON'S HERITAGE MUSEUM, 202 E. Lincoln Way, Morrison, IL 61270-2825. Mailing Address: P.O. Box 1, Morrison, IL 61270. Tel.: 815-772-8889 & 3084.
E-mail: mhmmemories@frontier.com
Key Personnel: Pres., Harvey Zuidema.
Institution Type/Description: History Museum.
Hours & Admission Prices: April-Nov. Fri.-Sun. 1-4; other times by appointment. No charge; donations accepted. &
Attendance: 1,200 (estimated)

Morton Grove

MORTON GROVE HISTORICAL MUSEUM/HAUPT-YEHL HOUSE, 6240 Dempster St., Morton Grove, IL 60053. Mailing Address: 6834 N. Dempster, Morton Grove, IL 60053-2631. Tel.: 847-965-0203. Fax: 847-965-7484.
E-mail: gomgpd@mortongroveparks.com
Web Site: www.mortongroveparks.com
Key Personnel: Pres. Morton Grove Historical Society, Donna Hedrick; Cur., Mary Busch.
Institution Type/Description: Historical Society Museum: housed in c.1888 farm home.
Hours & Admission Prices: Sun. 2-4, Wed. 1-3; other times tours of 10 persons or more by appointment. No charge; donations accepted. Closed national holidays.
Attendance: 2,234 (actual)

Mount Carmel

WABASH COUNTY MUSEUM, 320 N. Market St., Mount Carmel, IL 62863. Mailing Address: P.O. Box 512, Mount Carmel, IL 62863-0512. Tel.: 618-262-8774.
E-mail: ctdant@frontier.com
Web Site: www.museum.wabash.il.us
Key Personnel: Pres. (V), Claudia Dant.
Institution Type/Description: History Museum.
Hours & Admission Prices: Tues., Thurs. & Sun. 2-5. Winter hours: Nov. - Feb. Tues. Thurs. Sun. 2-4. No charge; donations accepted. Closed Easter; Thanksgiving; Christmas. &
Attendance: 2,000 (estimated)

Mount Prospect

MOUNT PROSPECT HISTORICAL SOCIETY MUSEUMS, 101 S. Maple, Mount Prospect, IL 60056-3229. Tel.: 847-392-9006. Fax: 847-577-9660. Facebook: Mount Prospect Historical Society.
E-mail: info@mtphistory.org
Web Site: www.yourcentralschool.org
Key Personnel: Pres. (V), Frank Corry; Exec. Dir., Lindsay Rice; Financial Dir., Chad Busse; Administrative Asst., Cindy Brok.
Institution Type/Description: Local History Museum: housed in a c.1906 home.
Hours & Admission Prices: Tues.-Thurs. 10-3:30 by appointment. No charge; donations accepted. Closed New Year's Day; Independence Day; Thanksgiving; Christmas. &
Attendance: 5,000 (estimated)

Mount Pulaski

MOUNT PULASKI COURTHOUSE STATE HISTORIC SITE, 113 S. Washington St., Mount Pulaski, IL 62548. Mailing Address: 113 S. Washington St., P.O. Box 171, Mount Pulaski, IL 62548-0171. Tel.: 217-792-3919.
E-mail: doulos@frontiernet.net
Institution Type/Description: Historic Building: 1848 Greek Revival County Court House; part of Illinois 8th Judicial Circuit where Abraham Lincoln practiced law.
Hours & Admission Prices: Tues.-Sat. 12-4. No charge; donations accepted. Closed most holidays.
Attendance: 1,919 (actual)

MOUNT PULASKI HISTORICAL SOCIETY MUSEUM, 104 E. Cooke St., Mount Pulaski, IL 62548. Mailing Address: 102-104 E. Cooke St., Mount Pulaski, IL 62548-0181. Tel.: 217-792-5430.
E-mail: sueeddie@frontier.com
Key Personnel: Pres. (V), Sue Schaffenacker.
Institution Type/Description: Historical Society Museum.
Hours & Admission Prices: April-Nov. Wed.-Fri. 12-4, Sat. by appointment. No charge; donations accepted. Closed New Year's Day; Martin Luther King's Birthday; Presidents' Day; Veterans Day; General Election Day; Thanksgiving; Christmas. &
Attendance: 300 (actual)

Mount Vernon

CEDARHURST CENTER FOR THE ARTS, 2600 Richview Rd., Mount Vernon, IL 62864. Mailing Address: P.O. Box 923, Mount Vernon, IL 62864-0019. Tel.: 618-242-1236. Fax: 618-242-9530.
E-mail: mitchellmuseum@cedarhurst.org
Web Site: cedarhurst.org
Formerly: Mitchell Museum at Cedarhurst

Key Personnel: Exec. Dir., Sharon Bradham; Craft Fair Coord., Linda Wheeler; Dir. Visual Arts, Rusty Freeman; C.F.O., Heather Owens; Dir. Communications, Sarah Sledge; Dir. Devel., Hillary Esser; Dir. Education, Jennifer Sarver; Dir. Operations, Greg Hilliard; Museum Shop Mgr. & Historian, Sarah Lou Bicknell.
Institution Type/Description: Art Museum & Sculpture Park.
Hours & Admission Prices: Tues.-Sat. 10-5, Sun. 1-5. Exhibits: members no charge. Closed national holidays. &
Attendance: 50,000 (estimated)

SHRODE ART CENTER, 2600 Richview Rd., Mount Vernon, IL 68264. Mailing Address: P.O. Box 923, Mount Vernon, IL 68264. Tel.: 618-242-1236, ext. 249.
E-mail: carrie@cedarhurst.org
Web Site: www.cedarhurst.org
Key Personnel: Dir., Carrie Gibbs.
Institution Type/Description: Art Gallery.
Hours & Admission Prices: Tues.-Sat. 10-5, Sun. 1-5. Closed national holidays.

Murphysboro

GENERAL JOHN A. LOGAN MUSEUM, 1613 Edith St., Murphysboro, IL 62966-2542. Mailing Address: P.O. Box 563, Murphysboro, IL 62966-0563. Tel.: 618-684-3455. Fax: 618-684-3569. Facebook: General John A. Logan Museum.
E-mail: director@loganmuseum.org
Web Site: www.loganmuseum.org
Key Personnel: Dir., P. Michael Jones; Pres., Harvey Welch; Cur., Laura Varner.
Institution Type/Description: Military History Museum.
Hours & Admission Prices: June-Aug. Tues.-Sat. 10-4, Sun. 1-4; Sept.-May Tues.-Sun. 1-4; groups by appointment. Suggested Donation: adults $2, children $1. Closed New Year's Eve & Day; Christmas Eve & Day. &
Attendance: 3,500 (actual)

JACKSON COUNTY HISTORICAL SOCIETY, 1616 Edith St., Murphysboro, IL 62966. Tel.: 618-684-6989.
E-mail: jchsil@yahoo.com
Key Personnel: Pres. (V), Laura Cates Duncan.
Institution Type/Description: Historical Society Museum.
Hours & Admission Prices: Wed. & Fri. 12-3, Thurs. 12-3 & 6:30-9. No charge; donations accepted.

Naperville

DUPAGE CHILDREN'S MUSEUM, 301 N. Washington St., Naperville, IL 60540-4537. Tel.: 630-637-8000. Fax: 630-637-1276.
E-mail: admin@dupagechildrensmuseum.org
Web Site: dupagechildrens.org
Institution Type/Description: Children's Museum.
Hours & Admission Prices: Sept.-May Mon.-Thurs. 9-4, Third Thurs. of month & Fri. 9-8, Sat. 9-5, Sun. 12-5; June-Aug. Mon.-Fri. 9-4, Third Thurs. of month 9-8, Sat. 9-5, Sun. 12-5. Adults & children $12, seniors $10, discounts to ACM members; children under one no charge. Closed New Year's Eve & Day; Easter; Memorial Day; Independence Day; Labor Day; Thanksgiving; Christmas Eve & Day. (Rates & hours subject to change, check website). &
Attendance: 325,144 (actual)

NAPER SETTLEMENT MUSEUM, 523 S. Webster St., Naperville, IL 60540-6517. Tel.: 630-420-6010. Fax: 630-305-4044.
E-mail: towncrier@naperville.il.us
Web Site: www.napersettlement.org
Key Personnel: Pres. & C.E.O., Macarena Tamayo-Calabrese; Vice Pres. & Chief Prog. Officer, Donna Sack; C.O.O., Harriet Pistorio; Dir., Learning Experiences & Historical Resources, Jeanne Schultz Angel; Dir. Finance, Alex Atkinson; Dir. Mktg., Brittany Tepper; Dir. Oper., Daniel Rogers; Dir. Devel., Julie Nelligan.
Institution Type/Description: Historic Museum.
Hours & Admission Prices: April-Oct. Tues.-Sat. 10-4, Sun. 1-4. Adults $12, senior citizens 62 & over $10, youth 4-12 $8; members & Naperville residents no charge. Nov.-March Tues.-Fri. 10-4. Adults $6, senior citizens 62 & over $5, youth 4-12 $4; members & Naperville residents no charge. Self-guided mobile tours included in admission. Discounts to Blue Star Museums and Museums for All. Closed New Year's Day; Memorial Day; Thanksgiving & day after; Christmas Eve & Day. &
Attendance: 272,000 (estimated)

Nauvoo

JOSEPH SMITH HISTORIC SITE, 865 Water St., Nauvoo, IL 62354. Mailing Address: P.O. Box 338, Nauvoo, IL 62354-0338. Tel.: 217-453-2246. Fax: 217-453-6416.
E-mail: jshs@frontiernet.net
Web Site: cofchrist.org/js/
Key Personnel: C.E.O., Joyce A. Shireman, Ph.D.
Institution Type/Description: Historic Sites & Buildings: 1803 & 1840 Joseph Smith Homestead; 1842 Joseph Smith Red Brick Store; 1843 Joseph Smith Mansion House.
Hours & Admission Prices: May-Oct. Mon.-Sat. 9-5, Sun. 1-5; Nov.-Dec. Tues.-Sat. 10-4. Summer Kitchen: Memorial Day to mid-Aug. daily 10-4. Guided Tour: $2 per person. &
Attendance: 90,000 (estimated)

NAUVOO HISTORICAL SOCIETY MUSEUM, 980 S. Bluff St., Nauvoo, IL 62354. Mailing Address: P.O. Box 426, Nauvoo, IL 62354-0426. Tel.: 217-453-2512. Fax: 217-453-2512.
Key Personnel: Chm. & Pres. (V), Mary Reed; Site Supt., Regan Ramsey; Maintenance Supvr., Michael Locke; Site Tech, Mike Middendorf.
Institution Type/Description: Historical Society Museum.
Hours & Admission Prices: mid-May to mid-Oct. daily 1-5. No charge; donations accepted. &
Attendance: 5,000 (estimated)

Newton

NEWTON PUBLIC LIBRARY AND MUSEUM, 100 S. Van Buren, Newton, IL 62448-1559. Tel.: 618-783-8141. Fax: 618-783-8149. Facebook: Newton Public Library and Museum.
E-mail: newtonp2016@outlook.com
Web Site: www.newton.lib.il.us
Key Personnel: Dir., Connie Davidson.
Institution Type/Description: Local History Museum.
Hours & Admission Prices: Mon., Wed. & Fri. 10-5, Tues. & Thurs. 10-7, Sat. 10-1. No charge. Closed national holidays. &
Attendance: 23,000 (estimated)

Nokomis

BOTTOMLEY-RUFFING-SCHALK BASEBALL MUSEUM, 121 W. State St., Nokomis, IL 62075-1658. Mailing Address: P.O. Box 75, Nokomis, IL 62075-0075. Tel.: 217-563-8807. Fax: 217-324-6616.
E-mail: info@brsmuseum.org
Web Site: brsmuseum.org
Key Personnel: Treas., Steve Johnson.
Institution Type/Description: Sports Museum.
Hours & Admission Prices: Sat. 9-12, Sun 1-4; other times by appointment. No charge; donations accepted. &
Attendance: 700 (estimated)

Normal

CHILDREN'S DISCOVERY MUSEUM, 101 E. Beaufort, Normal, IL 61761-3026. Tel.: 309-433-3444. Fax: 309-451-3614.
E-mail: museum@normal.org
Web Site: childrensdiscoverymuseum.net
Key Personnel: Museum Mgr., Sheila Riley; Chm. (V), Mark Jontry; Education Coord., Bethany Thomas; Volunteer & Membership Coord., Shelly Hanover.
Institution Type/Description: Children's Museum.
Hours & Admission Prices: June-Aug. Mon.-Wed. & Fri.-Sat. 9-5, Thurs. 9-8, Sun. 1-5; Sept.-May Tues.-Wed. & Fri. 9-5, Thurs. 9-8, Sun. 1-5; Admission $7, field trips $4; ASTC, ACM, members & children under 2 no charge. Closed New Year's Day; Easter; Labor Day; Thanksgiving; Christmas. &
Attendance: 143,027 (actual)

NORMAL EDITIONS WORKSHOP - ILLINOIS STATE UNIVERSITY, 5620 School of Art, Normal, IL 61790-5620. Tel.: 309-438-7530. Fax: 309-438-2215.
E-mail: normaleditionsworkshop@ilstu.edu
Web Site: normaleditions.illinoisstate.edu
Key Personnel: Dir., Veda M. Rives.
Institution Type/Description: Printmaking.
Hours & Admission Prices: Mon.-Thurs. 9-5; other times by appointment. No charge. &

UNIVERSITY GALLERIES OF ILLINOIS STATE UNIVERSITY, 110 Center for Visual Arts, Normal, IL 61790. Mailing Address: P.O. Box 5600, Normal, IL 61790-5600. Tel.: 309-438-5487. Facebook: University Galleries of Illinois State University.
E-mail: gallery@ilstu.edu
Web Site: www.cfa.ilstu.edu/galleries
Key Personnel: Dir., Barry Blinderman; Cur. Exhibitions, Kendra Paitz; Cur. & Interpretive Programs Coord., Tony Preston-Schreck; Registrar, Gabriel Johnson.
Institution Type/Description: Art Gallery.
Hours & Admission Prices: Academic Year: Tues. 9:30-7, Wed.-Fri. 9:30-4:30, Sat.-Mon. 12-4; Summer: Mon. & Wed.-Sat. 12-4, Tues. 12-7. &

North Chicago

FEET FIRST: THE SCHOLL STORY, ROSALIND FRANKLIN UNIVERSITY OF MEDICINE AND SCIENCE, 3333 Green Bay Rd., North Chicago, IL 60064-3037. Tel.: 847-578-8417. Fax: 847-578-8643.
E-mail: kelly.reiss@rosalindfranklin.edu
Web Site: www.rosalindfranklin.edu
Key Personnel: C.E.O., K. Michael Welch; Chm., Gail Warden.
Institution Type/Description: Podiatry Museum: housed in the Dr. William M. Scholl College of Podiatric Medicine.
Hours & Admission Prices: Daily 9-4. No charge; donations accepted. &
Attendance: 5,000 (estimated)

O'Fallon

O'FALLON HISTORICAL SOCIETY, 101 W. State St., O'Fallon, IL 62269-0344. Mailing Address: P.O. Box 344, O'Fallon, IL 62269-0344. Tel.: 618-624-8409.
E-mail: info@ofallonhistory.net
Web Site: ofallonhistory.net
Institution Type/Description: Historical Society Museum: housed in the former First National Bank; built in 1904.
Hours & Admission Prices: Wed. & Fri.-Sat. 1-4; other times by appointment.

Oak Brook

GRAUE MILL AND MUSEUM, 3800 York Rd., Oak Brook, IL 60523-2738. Tel.: 630-655-2090 & 920-9720. Fax: 630-920-9721. Facebook: Grave Mill & Museum.
E-mail: info@grauemill.org
Web Site: www.grauemill.org
Key Personnel: Exec. Dir., Connie Buczkowski; Pres. (V), Bonnie Sartore; Dir. Operations, Cathy Kolessar.
Institution Type/Description: History Museum: housed in 1852 restored waterwheel gristmill.
Hours & Admission Prices: mid-April to mid-Nov. Tues.-Sun. 10-4:30. Adults $4.50, senior citizens $4, children 3-12 $2; discounts to groups of 20 or more; members, military & children under 3 no charge. &
Attendance: 15,000 (estimated)

MAYSLAKE PEABODY ESTATE, 1717 W. 31st St., Oak Brook, IL 60523-1701. Tel.: 630-206-9588. Fax: 630-850-2362. Facebook: Mayslake Peabody Estate.
E-mail: jfowers@dupageforest.org
Web Site: www.mayslakepeabody.com
Institution Type/Description: Historic House Museum: housed in the former home of Francis Stuyvesant Peabody, a coal baron & national figure in Democratic politics; built in 1921.
Hours & Admission Prices: Guided Tours: mid-Jan. to mid-Dec. Wed. 11 & 12:30, Sat. 9:30, 10, 11, & 11:30; other times by appointment. $5 per person.
Attendance: 120,000 (estimated)

Oak Lawn

CHILDREN'S MUSEUM IN OAK LAWN, 5100 Museum Dr., Oak Lawn, IL 60453-7005. Tel.: 708-423-6709. Fax: 708-423-6723.
E-mail: general.information@cmoaklawn.org
Web Site: www.cmoaklawn.org
Key Personnel: Exec. Dir., Adam Woodworth; Visitor Svcs. Mgr., Angelia Martin; Program Coord., Barb McMillin; Store Mgr., Theresa Tarver.
Institution Type/Description: Children's Museum.
Hours & Admission Prices: Nov.-March Tues.-Sat. 9:30-5, Sun. 10-5. Oct.-April Tues.-Thurs. & Sat. 9:30-5, Fri. 9:30-8, Sun. 10-5. Adults & children 1-16 $8,

seniors 55 & over $6, teachers & active military & up to 6 family members $4; children under 1 no charge. Closed Christmas. &

Attendance: 20,000

Oak Park

FRANK LLOYD WRIGHT HOME AND STUDIO, 951 Chicago Ave., Oak Park, IL 60302-2007. Mailing Address: 209 S. LaSalle St., Ste. 118, Chicago, IL 60604. Tel.: 312-994-4000.

E-mail: info@flwright.org
Web Site: flwright.org
Key Personnel: C.E.O. & Pres., Celeste Adams; Chm. Bd., John Rafkin.
Institution Type/Description: Historic House Museum: 1889-1909 residence & office of Frank Lloyd Wright; birthplace of Prairie-style architecture.
Hours & Admission Prices: Tours: daily 10-4; groups by appointment, call 312-994-4040. Shop: daily 9-5. Adults $18, students, military and seniors 65 & over $15; members & children 3 & under no charge. Closed New Year's Day; Thanksgiving; Christmas Eve & Day.
Attendance: 88,500 (actual)

THE HEMINGWAY MUSEUM AND THE ERNEST HEMINGWAY BIRTHPLACE CLOSED, 200 N. Oak Park Ave., Oak Park, IL 60302-2128. Mailing Address: P.O. Box 2222, Oak Park, IL 60303-2222. Tel.: 708-848-2222. Fax: 708-386-2952.

E-mail: ehfop@sbcglobal.net
Web Site: www.ehfop.org
Key Personnel: Chm. (V), Allan Baldwin; Vice Chm., Virginia R. Cassin; Archivist, Barbara Ballinger; Museum Shop Mgr., Conni Irwin.
Institution Type/Description: History Museum: housed in the birthplace of Ernest Hemingway.
Hours & Admission Prices: Sun.-Fri. 1-5, Sat. 10-5. Adults $10, senior citizens & students $8; discounts to AAA members & tour groups of 10 or more; members & children 5 & under no charge. Closed New Year's Day; Martin Luther King Jr. Day; Easter; Memorial Day; Independence Day; Labor Day; Thanksgiving; Christmas. &
Attendance: 6,976 (estimated)

HISTORICAL SOCIETY OF OAK PARK & RIVER FOREST, 217 Home Ave., Oak Park, IL 60302-3101. Mailing Address: P.O. Box 771, Oak Park, IL 60303-0771. Tel.: 708-848-6755. Fax: 708-848-0246.

E-mail: oprfhistorian@sbcglobal.net
Web Site: oprfhistory.org
Key Personnel: Exec. Dir., Frank Lipo; Pres. (V), Jan Novak Dressel; Pres. (V), Mary Ann Porucznik; Treas., Jim Taglia; Public Rels., Jean Guarino.
Institution Type/Description: Historical Society Museum: housed in 1897 Prairie style mansion.
Hours & Admission Prices: Museum: Thurs.-Sun. 12:30-3:30; group tours by appointment. Office: Tues. & Thurs. 1-5. Adults $10, children 18 & under $3; Fri. & members no charge. Closed New Year's Day; Easter; Christmas.
Attendance: 5,000 (actual)

THE OAK PARK CONSERVATORY, 615 Garfield St., Oak Park, IL 60304-2001. Tel.: 708-725-2400.

E-mail: patti.staley@pdop.org
Web Site: www.oakparkparks.com
Key Personnel: Mgr., Patti Staley.
Institution Type/Description: Conservatory.
Hours & Admission Prices: Suggested Donations $5. &
Attendance: 34,105 (actual)

THE SUBURBAN, 125 N. Harvey Ave., Oak Park, IL 60302. Tel.: 708-305-2657.

E-mail: bkmgcar@comcast.net
Web Site: www.thesuburban.org
Institution Type/Description: Art Gallery.
Hours & Admission Prices: Call for hours.

WONDER WORKS CHILDREN'S MUSEUM, 6445 W. North Ave., Oak Park, IL 60302-1009. Tel.: 708-383-4815. Facebook: @wonderworkschildrensmuseum.

E-mail: info@wonder-works.org
Web Site: www.wonder-works.org
Key Personnel: C.E.O., Rachel Rettberg; Dir. Volunteer Svcs., Jessica Taylor; Dir. Operations, David Hoambrecker.
Institution Type/Description: Children's Museum.
Hours & Admission Prices: Mon. & Wed.-Sat. 10-5, Sun. 12-5. Admission $7; teachers, military & seniors $3; discounts to Museums for All-linked card hold-

ers; children under one & members no charge. Closed New Year's Day; Memorial Day; Independence Day; Labor Day; Thanksgiving; Christmas.

Attendance: 60,000

Oakbrook Terrace

LAKE VIEW NATURE CENTER, 17W063 Hodges Rd., Oakbrook Terrace, IL 60181-4505. Tel.: 630-941-8747. Fax: 630-941-3558.

E-mail: lvnc@obtpd.org
Web Site: www.obtpd.org
Key Personnel: Dir., Liane Knight.
Institution Type/Description: Nature Center.
Hours & Admission Prices: Mon.-Fri. 9-4, Sat.-Sun. 12-4. No charge; donations accepted. Closed 1st Mon. each month; New Year's Eve & Day; Good Friday; Easter weekend; Memorial Day; Independence Day; Labor Day; Thanksgiving & day after; Christmas Eve & Day. &
Attendance: 20,000 (actual)

Oglesby

STARVED ROCK STATE PARK, 2678 E. 873rd Rd., Oglesby, IL 61348. Mailing Address: P.O. Box 509, Utica, IL 61373-0509. Tel.: 815-667-4906 & 5356. Fax: 815-667-5354. Facebook: Starved Rock Visitor's Center.

E-mail: starvedrockv@ivnet.com
Web Site: dnr.state.il.us
Key Personnel: Site Supt., Mark McConnaughhay; Site Interpreter, Jolyn Wise.
Institution Type/Description: Historic Park & Museum: located on the sites of former Indian village of Illinois Indians; 1673-1760 French occupation and 1683 French Fort St. Louis.
Hours & Admission Prices: Park: daily 5am-9pm. Interpretive Center: daily 9-4. No charge; donations accepted. Closed Thanksgiving; Christmas. &
Attendance: 216,869 (actual)

Ottawa

OTTAWA HISTORICAL AND SCOUTING HERITAGE MUSEUM, 1100 Canal St., Ottawa, IL 61350-4940. Mailing Address: P.O. Box 2241, Ottawa, IL 61350-6841. Tel.: 815-431-9353.

E-mail: scouter07@hotmail.com
Web Site: www.ottawascoutingmuseum.org
Key Personnel: C.E.O., Cur. & Public Rels., Mollie Perrot; Pres. & Museum Shop Mgr., Christine Hasty; Financial Dir., Kathy Hite; Archivist, Bruno Polli; Security, Steve Perrot.
Institution Type/Description: Local History & Scouting Heritage Museum.
Hours & Admission Prices: Thurs.-Mon. 10-4. Adults $3, students & children $2; discount to groups of 10 or more; members no charge. Closed New Year's Eve & Day; Easter; Independence Day; Labor Day; Thanksgiving; Christmas Eve & Day. &
Attendance: 3,000 (actual)

REDDICK MANSION AND GARDENS, 100 W. Lafayette St., Ottawa, IL 61350. Tel.: 815-433-6100. Facebook.

E-mail: contact@reddickmansion.org
Web Site: reddickmansion.org
Key Personnel: Pres. (V), Diane Sanders; Museum Shop Mgr., Larry Swanson.
Institution Type/Description: Historic House Museum: housed in the former home of businessman & politician, William Reddick; built in 1856 across from site of 1st Lincoln-Douglas debate.
Hours & Admission Prices: Mansion Tours: Mon. & Wed.-Sat. 11-3, last tour at 2pm. Sun. 11-2. Adults $8; discounts to AAM members; members no charge. Closed holidays.
Attendance: 5,000 (actual)

Paris

BICENTENNIAL ART CENTER & MUSEUM, 132 S. Central Ave., Paris, IL 61944-1729. Tel.: 217-466-8130. Fax: 217-466-8130.

E-mail: parisartcenter@frontier.com
Web Site: www.parisartcenter.com
Key Personnel: Dir., Susan Stafford.
Institution Type/Description: Art Museum.
Hours & Admission Prices: Tues.-Fri. 10-4. No charge. Closed New Year's Eve & Day; Easter; Independence Day; Thanksgiving & day after; Christmas Eve & Day. &
Attendance: 5,456 (actual)

EDGAR COUNTY HISTORICAL MUSEUM, 408 N. Main, Paris, IL 61944-1549. Tel.: 217-463-5305.
E-mail: echs1900@gmail.com
Web Site: echistoricalsociety.com
Key Personnel: Pres. (V), Kay Wolfe.
Institution Type/Description: Historical Society Museum: housed in 1876 Arthur House. Listed on the National Register of Historic Places.
Hours & Admission Prices: Wed.-Fri. 9-4. No charge. ⑃
Attendance: 1,200 (estimated)

Park Forest

TALL GRASS ARTS ASSOCIATION, 367 Artist Walk, Park Forest, IL 60466-2059. Tel.: 708-748-3377. Fax: 708-748-9132.
E-mail: tallgrass367@sbcglobal.net
Web Site: www.tallgrassarts.org
Key Personnel: Exec. Dir., Cody Ziebell; Chm. (V), Janet Muchnik; Museum Shop Mgr., Gisele Perrault.
Institution Type/Description: Art Gallery.
Hours & Admission Prices: Tues.-Sat. 11-4. No charge; donations accepted. ⑃
Attendance: 10,000 (estimated)

Park Ridge

BRICKTON ART CENTER, 306 Busse Hwy., Park Ridge, IL 60068-3251. Tel.: 847-823-6611. Fax: 847-823-6622. Facebook: Brickton Art Center.
E-mail: bricktondirector@gmail.com
Web Site: www.bricktonartcenter.org
Key Personnel: Pres. (V), Anna Maria Hallagan.
Institution Type/Description: Art Gallery.
Hours & Admission Prices: Mon.-Thurs. 10-5, Fri.-Sat. 10-4. No charge; donations accepted.

Paxton

FORD COUNTY HISTORICAL SOCIETY, 145 S. Market St., Paxton, IL 60957-1284. Mailing Address: P.O. Box 115, Paxton, IL 60957-0115. Tel.: 217-379-3723. Facebook: The Ford County, Illinois Heritage.
E-mail: ilfchs@gmail.com
Web Site: sites.google.com/site/fordcountyhistoricalsociety/
Key Personnel: Cur., Cynthia Swanson; Pres. (V), Judith Jepsen-Popel.
Institution Type/Description: Historical Museum: housed in historic water tower.
Hours & Admission Prices: April-Nov. Sat. 11-2; Dec.-March 1st Sat. of month only 11-2; tours anytime by appointment. No charge; donations accepted. Closed national holidays.
Attendance: 3,000 (estimated)

Pekin

TAZEWELL COUNTY GENEALOGICAL & HISTORICAL SOCIETY LIBRARY, Ehrlicher Research Center, 719 N. Eleventh St., Pekin, IL 61555. Mailing Address: P.O. Box 312, Pekin, IL 61555-0312. Tel.: 309-477-3044. Facebook: Tazewell County Genealogical & Historical Society Library.
E-mail: tcghs@tcghs.org
Web Site: www.tcghs.org
Key Personnel: Pres. (V), John W. Durdle.
Institution Type/Description: Historical Society Museum.
Hours & Admission Prices: Library: Mon. & Thurs.-Fri. 9-1, Tues. 9-1 & 7-9, Wed. 9-4:30, Sun. 2-4:30; call to confirm. No charge; donations accepted. Closed holidays and holiday weekends. ⑃
Attendance: 2,000 (estimated)

TAZEWELL COUNTY MUSEUM, 15 S. Capitol St., Ste. 101, Pekin, IL 61554-4175. Tel.: 309-347-8375 & 346-1889.
E-mail: dagit1413@comcast.net
Web Site: www.tazewellcountymuseum.com
Institution Type/Description: History Museum.
Hours & Admission Prices: Mon. & Wed. 10-2, Sat. 10-12.

Peoria

CATERPILLAR VISITORS CENTER, 110 S.W. Washington St., Peoria, IL 61602. Tel.: 309-675-0606. Facebook: Caterpillar Visitors Center.
E-mail: caterpillarvisitorscenter@cat.com
Web Site: visitcaterpillar.com

Institution Type/Description: Company History Museum.
Hours & Admission Prices: Mon.-Sat. 10-5 (last ticket entry at 3:30). Adults $7, seniors 55 & over, veterans and active military $6, military 55 & over $5; discounts to groups; children 12 & under no charge. Closed holidays. ⑃
Attendance: 100,000 (actual)

CONTEMPORARY ART CENTER, 305 S.W. Water St., Peoria, IL 61602-1425. Tel.: 309-674-6822.
E-mail: artcentr@mtco.com
Web Site: www.peoriacac.org
Institution Type/Description: Art Gallery.
Hours & Admission Prices: Tues.-Sat. 11-5, Fri. 11-8. No charge. ⑃

LUTHY BOTANICAL GARDEN, 2520 N. Prospect Rd., Peoria, IL 61603-2126. Tel.: 309-686-3362.
E-mail: bstreitmatter@peoriaparks.org
Web Site: peoriaparks.org
Formerly: George L. Luthy Memorial Botanical Garden
Key Personnel: Dir., Emily Cahill; Business Officer, Jan Budzynski; Mgr., Bob Streitmatter; Museum Shop Mgr., Mary Mulay.
Institution Type/Description: Botanical Garden.
Hours & Admission Prices: Daily 10-5. No charge; donations accepted. Closed New Year's Day; Thanksgiving; Christmas. ⑃
Attendance: 135,000 (estimated)

THE PEORIA ART GUILD, 203 Harrison St., Peoria, IL 61602-1536. Tel.: 309-637-2787, ext. 2.
E-mail: events@peoriaartguild.org
Web Site: www.peoriaartguild.org
Key Personnel: Dir., Beth Reusch.
Institution Type/Description: Contemporary Art Museum.
Hours & Admission Prices: Mon.-Thurs. 10-6, Fri.-Sat. 10-5.
Attendance: 20,000 (estimated)

PEORIA HISTORICAL SOCIETY, 611 S.W. Washington St., Ste. A, Peoria, IL 61602-5105. Tel.: 309-674-1921. Fax: 309-674-1882. Facebook: Peoria Historical Society.
E-mail: adminphs@peoriahistoricalsociety.org
Web Site: www.peoriahistoricalsociety.org
Key Personnel: Pres., Mark Johnson; Vice Pres., Deborah Dougherty; Exec. Dir., Walter C. Ruppman; Dir. Collections, Robert Killion; Museum Shop Mgr., Kathy Dallinger.
Institution Type/Description: Historical Society: housed in c.1837 Flanagan House & 1868 Pettengill-Morron House.
Hours & Admission Prices: Open House: 1st Sun each month 1-4; other times by appointment. Adults $7, children 12 & under $3; members no charge. Closed holidays.
Attendance: 1,700 (estimated)

PEORIA RIVERFRONT MUSEUM, 222 S.W. Washington St., Peoria, IL 61602. Tel.: 309-686-7000.
E-mail: info@peoriariverfrontmuseum.org
Web Site: www.peoriariverfrontmuseum.org
Institution Type/Description: History Museum & Planetarium.
Hours & Admission Prices: Mon.-Thurs. & Sat. 10-5, Fri. 10-8, Sun. 12-5, Galleries & Planetarium: adults $11, seniors 60 & over $10, youth 3-17 $9. Movies: additional fee. Combo tickets available. Closed New Year's Day; Easter; Thanksgiving; Christmas.

PEORIA ZOO, 2320 N. Prospect Rd., Peoria, IL 61603-2126. Tel.: 309-686-3365. Fax: 309-685-6240.
E-mail: info@peoriazoo.org
Web Site: www.peoriazoo.org
Formerly: Glen Oak Zoo
Key Personnel: Dir., Yvonne Strode; Exec. Dir. Parks, Emily Cahill; Museum Shop Mgr., Mary Mulay.
Institution Type/Description: Zoo.
Hours & Admission Prices: Daily 10-5. Adults $9, seniors $8, children 2-12 $6; PZS, AZA, other zoo members and children 1 & under no charge. Closed New Year's Eve & Day; Thanksgiving; Christmas Eve & Day. ⑃
Attendance: 138,656 (actual)

Petersburg

LINCOLN'S NEW SALEM STATE HISTORIC SITE, 15588 History Lane, Petersburg, IL 62675-6010. Tel.: 217-632-4000. Fax: 217-632-4010.
E-mail: tim.guinan@illinois.gov
Web Site: www.lincolnsnewsalem.com

Key Personnel: Site Supt., Tim Guinan; Pres., Al Grosboll; Account Clerk, Glen Baum; Museum Shop Mgr., Donna Hitchcock.
Institution Type/Description: Village Museum: site of New Salem Village, in the 1830s where Lincoln lived as a young man. Structures are reconstructed.
Hours & Admission Prices: March-April 15 & Sept.-Oct. Wed.-Sun. 9-5; April 16 to Labor Day daily 9-5; Nov.-Feb. Wed.-Sun. 8-4. No charge; donations accepted. Closed New Year's Day; Thanksgiving; Christmas. &
Attendance: 400,000 (estimated)

STARHILL FOREST ARBORETUM, 12000 Boy Scout Tr., Petersburg, IL 62675-6034. Tel.: 217-632-3685. Fax: 217-632-3685.
E-mail: guy@starhillforest.com
Web Site: www.starhillforest.com
Key Personnel: Owner, Guy Sternberg; Owner, Edie Sternberg.
Institution Type/Description: Arboretum & Botanical Gardens.
Hours & Admission Prices: By appointment only. No charge; donations accepted. &
Attendance: 200 (estimated)

Pontiac

CATHERINE V. YOST MUSEUM & ARTS CENTER, 298 W. Water, Pontiac, IL 61764-1757. Mailing Address: 115 W. Howard, Pontiac, IL 61764-1819. Tel.: 815-844-6574 & 5847 (Pontiac tourism).
E-mail: tourism@pontiac.org
Key Personnel: Cur., Carol Gardner.
Institution Type/Description: Historic House Museum: housed in Queen Anne-style home.
Hours & Admission Prices: May-Dec. by appointment. Donations accepted.

THE INTERNATIONAL WALLDOG MURAL & SIGN ART MUSEUM, 217 N. Mill St., Pontiac, IL 61764. Tel.: 815-842-1848.
E-mail: kristen@muralmuseum.com
Institution Type/Description: Art Museum.
Hours & Admission Prices: April-May & Aug.-Oct. Mon.-Fri. 9-5, Sat.-Sun. 10-4; June-July Mon.-Thurs. 9-5, Fri. 9-9, Sat.-Sun. 10-4; Nov.-March daily 10-4. No charge; donations accepted.

THE JONES HOUSE, 314 E. Madison St., Pontiac, IL 61764. Mailing Address: 115 W. Howard St., Pontiac, IL 61764. Tel.: 815-844-5847, 800-835-2055.
Institution Type/Description: Historic House Museum: housed in the former home of Henry C. Jones; built in 1857. Listed on the National Register of Historic Places.
Hours & Admission Prices: By appointment.

LIVINGSTON COUNTY WAR MUSEUM & DAL ESTES EDUCATION CENTER, 321 N. Main St., Pontiac, IL 61764-1929. Tel.: 815-842-0301.
E-mail: eclong@meaircombb.net
Web Site: www.warmuseum.us
Key Personnel: Pres., Ed Long.
Institution Type/Description: Military History Museum.
Hours & Admission Prices: Tues.-Sat. 10-4, Sun. 12-4; other times by appointment. No charge; donations accepted. &
Attendance: 10,000

PONTIAC OAKLAND AUTOMOBILE MUSEUM, 205 N. Mill St., Pontiac, IL 61764. Tel.: 815-842-2345. Facebook: Pontiac Oakland Automobile Museum.
E-mail: info@pontiacoaklandmuseum.org
Web Site: www.pontiacoaklandmuseum.org
Key Personnel: Dir., Tim Dye.
Institution Type/Description: Automobile Museum.
Hours & Admission Prices: April-Oct. daily 9-5; Nov.-March daily 10-4. No charge; donations accepted. Closed New Year's Day; Easter; Thanksgiving; Christmas. &
Attendance: 20,000 (actual)

ROUTE 66 ASSOCIATION HALL OF FAME & MUSEUM, 110 W. Howard St., Pontiac, IL 61764-1820.
Institution Type/Description: History Museum.
Hours & Admission Prices: Summer: Mon.-Fri. 9-5, Sat.-Sun. 10-4; Winter: Mon.-Fri. 11-3, Sat.-Sun. 10-4.

Poplar Grove

POPLAR GROVE VINTAGE WINGS & WHEELS MUSEUM, 5151 Orth Rd., Ste. A-1, Poplar Grove, IL 61065. Tel.: 815-547-3115. Fax: 815-544-1666. Facebook.
E-mail: vintagemuseum@gmail.com
Web Site: poplargrovewingsandwheels.com
Formerly: Vintage Wings and Wheels
Institution Type/Description: Transportation Museum.
Hours & Admission Prices: May-Sept. Mon.-Fri. 11-3, 1st Sat. each month 10-2, 2nd Sun. each month 9-1.
Attendance: 3,000 (estimated)

Prairie du Rocher

FORT DE CHARTRES STATE HISTORIC SITE, 1350 State Rt. 155, Prairie du Rocher, IL 62277. Tel.: 618-284-7230. Fax: 618-284-7230.
E-mail: ftdchart@htc.net
Web Site: fortdechartres.us
Key Personnel: Site Svcs. Specialist I, David Schultz.
Institution Type/Description: State Historic Site & Museum: located on the original site of the French Fort de Chartres; built in 1753.
Hours & Admission Prices: Thurs.-Sun. 9-5. Suggested Donation: families $10, adults $4, children $2. Closed New Year's Day; Thanksgiving; Christmas. &
Attendance: 45,000 (estimated)

Princeton

BUREAU COUNTY HISTORICAL SOCIETY MUSEUM, 109 Park Ave., W., Princeton, IL 61356-1927. Tel.: 815-875-2184.
E-mail: director@bureaucountyhistoricalsociety.com
Web Site: bureaucountyhistoricalsociety.com
Key Personnel: Pres., Michael Smith; Dir., Jean Babcock.
Institution Type/Description: Historical Society Museum.
Hours & Admission Prices: March-Dec. Tues.-Sat. 12-4; group tours by advance reservation. Requested Donation: adults $5, children $3. Closed Easter; Mother's Day; Independence Day; Labor Day; Thanksgiving.
Attendance: 1,500 (actual)

Quincy

ALL WARS MUSEUM, Illinois Veterans Home, 1707 N. 12th St., Quincy, IL 62301-1355. Tel.: 217-222-8641, ext. 380. Fax: 217-222-9621.
E-mail: rick.gengenbacher@illinois.gov
Key Personnel: Dir., Rick Gengenbacher; Cur., Bob Craig.
Institution Type/Description: Military History Museum.
Hours & Admission Prices: March-Dec. 7 Tues.-Sat. 9-12 & 1-4, Sun. 1-4. No charge; donations accepted.

HISTORICAL SOCIETY OF QUINCY AND ADAMS COUNTY, 332 Maine St., Quincy, IL 62301. Tel.: 217-214-1888.
E-mail: info@hsqac.org
Web Site: www.hsqac.org
Key Personnel: Exec. Officer, Robert Mellon; Pres. (V), Todd Shackelford; Treas., Joseph Ott.
Institution Type/Description: History Museum: former Gardner Museum.
Hours & Admission Prices: Tours & Gov. John Wood Mansion/Office: Tues.-Sat. 10-4. Adults $8, children $4. Time Traveler program. History Museum: Tues.-Sat. 10-4; no charge. Closed holidays.
Attendance: 5,500 (estimated)

QUINCY ART CENTER, 1515 Jersey St., Quincy, IL 62301-4250. Tel.: 217-223-5900. Fax: 217-223-6950. Facebook: Quincy Art Center.
E-mail: jnelson@quincyartcenter.org
Web Site: quincyartcenter.org
Key Personnel: Exec. Dir. & Cur., Julie D. Nelson; Pres. (V), Bruce Broemmel; Chm. (V), Dan Selby.
Institution Type/Description: Art Museum: housed in 1887 carriage house designed by Joseph Lyman Silsbee, mentor of Frank Lloyd Wright.
Hours & Admission Prices: Mon.-Fri. 9-4, Sat.-Sun. 1-4. No charge; donations accepted. &
Attendance: 21,900 (estimated)

THE QUINCY MUSEUM, 1601 Maine St., Quincy, IL 62301-4264. Tel.: 217-224-7669.
E-mail: quinmu1@adams.net
Web Site: thequincymuseum.com

Key Personnel: Exec. Dir., Barbara Wilkinson; Pres., Richard Hopkins; 1st Vice Pres., Joseph Mays; Volunteer Coord., Sandra Huddleston; Collections, Jane Huelsmeyer.
Institution Type/Description: Natural History Museum.
Hours & Admission Prices: Tues.-Sun. 1-5. Adults $4, children 5-18 & college students $2; discounts to AAM members; members & children under 5 no charge. ♿
Attendance: 8,500 (actual)

WORLD AEROSPACE MUSEUM, 1645 Hwy. 104, Quincy, IL 62305. Tel.: 217-885-3143.
Institution Type/Description: Aerospace History Museum.
Hours & Admission Prices: Mon.-Fri. 10-4 by appointment.

River Grove

CERNAN EARTH & SPACE CENTER, Triton College, 2000 N. 5th Ave., River Grove, IL 60171-1907. Tel.: 708-456-0300, ext. 3372. Fax: 708-583-3153. Facebook: cernancenter.
E-mail: cernan@triton.edu
Web Site: www.triton.edu/cernan
Key Personnel: Dir., Kris McCall; Program Producer, Neil Wickman; Reservations & Accounting, Joyce Edwards-Robertson; Technician, Joe Schultz.
Institution Type/Description: Planetarium.
Hours & Admission Prices: Mon.-Thurs. 9-5, Fri. 9-1, Sat. 6pm-9:30pm, Sun. 1:30-4:30. Fulldome Features: adults $8, children & senior citizens $4. Cosmic Light Shows: adults $10, children & senior citizens $5. Closed major holidays.
Attendance: 11,000 (actual)

Riverside

RIVERSIDE HISTORICAL MUSEUM, 10 Pine Ave., Riverside, IL 60546-2264. Mailing Address: 27 Riverside Rd., Riverside, IL 60546-2264. Tel.: 708-447-2542.
E-mail: history@riverside.il.us
Web Site: www.riversidemuseum.net
Key Personnel: Chm., Judith Cizek.
Institution Type/Description: History Museum.
Hours & Admission Prices: Sat. 10-2; other times by appointment. No charge; donations accepted. ♿
Attendance: 5,000

Rochelle

FLAGG TOWNSHIP MUSEUM, 518 Fourth Ave., Rochelle, IL 61068. Tel.: 815-562-3040. Facebook: Flagg Township Museum.
E-mail: mail@flaggtownshipmuseum.org
Web Site: www.flaggtownshipmuseum.org
Institution Type/Description: History Museum: housed in the former City and Town Hall building; built in 1884.
Hours & Admission Prices: Thurs.-Sun. 11-4. Family $7, adults $3, children $2; Thurs. and children 6 & under no charge. Closed New Year's Day; Easter; Thanksgiving; Christmas.

ROCHELLE FIRE DEPARTMENT MUSEUM, 401 5th Ave., Rochelle, IL 61068. Tel.: 815-562-2122.
Institution Type/Description: Firefighting History Museum.
Hours & Admission Prices: Call for hours.

Rock Island

AUGUSTANA COLLEGE ART MUSEUM, 7th Ave. & 38th St., Art & Art History Dept., Rock Island, IL 61201-2296. Mailing Address: 639 38th St., Rock Island, IL 61201-2273. Tel.: 309-794-7231. Fax: 309-794-7678.
E-mail: sherrymaurer@augustana.edu
Web Site: www.augustana.edu/arts/artmuseum
Key Personnel: C.E.O., Steven Bahls; Dir., Sherry C. Maurer; Devel. & Membership, Lynn Jackson; Preparator & Registrar, Dana Densberger; Public Rels., Scott Cason.
Institution Type/Description: Art Museum.
Hours & Admission Prices: Sept.-May Tues.-Sat. 12-4. No charge; donations accepted. Closed college holidays. ♿
Attendance: 43,708 (actual)

BLACK HAWK STATE HISTORIC SITE: HAUBERG INDIAN MUSEUM, 1510 46th Ave., Rock Island, IL 61201-6853. Tel.: 309-788-9536. Fax: 309-788-9865.
E-mail: haubergmuseum@aol.com
Web Site: www.blackhawkpark.org/
Key Personnel: Site Supt., Scott Roman; Museum Dir., Elizabeth Carvey-Stewart.
Institution Type/Description: State Historic Site Museum: 1740-1831 site of the main villages of the Sauk & Fox Nations.
Hours & Admission Prices: March-Oct. daily 9-12 & 1-5; Nov.-Feb. daily 9-12 & 1-4. No charge; donations accepted. Closed New Year's Day; Thanksgiving; Christmas. ♿
Attendance: 32,344 (actual)

COLONEL DAVENPORT HISTORICAL FOUNDATION, Hillman St. and Mississippi River, Rock Island Arsenal, Rock Island, IL 61201. Mailing Address: P.O. Box 4603, Rock Island, IL 61204-4603. Tel.: 309-786-7336.
E-mail: coloneldavenport1833@hotmail.com
Web Site: www.davenporthouse.org
Key Personnel: Pres. (V), Judy Tumbleson; Membership, Bill Hamps; Museum Shop Mgr., Ginny Bauersfeld.
Institution Type/Description: Historical House Museum: George Davenport Home.
Hours & Admission Prices: May-Oct. Thurs.-Sun. 12-4; Nov.-April by appointment. Adults $6, seniors 65 and over $4, children 12 and under & active Military no charge; discounts to YPN Hot Spot, AAA, CDHF & WQPT members. ♿
Attendance: 1,500 (estimated)

FRYXELL GEOLOGY MUSEUM, Swenson Hall of Geosciences, Augustana College, 38th St., Rock Island, IL 61201-2296. Tel.: 309-794-7318. Fax: 309-794-7564. Facebook: fryxellgeologymuseum.
E-mail: susanwolf@augustana.edu
Web Site: http://www.augustana.edu/fryxellmuseum
Key Personnel: Dir., Michael B. Wolf.
Institution Type/Description: Geology Museum.
Hours & Admission Prices: Sept.-May Mon.-Fri. 8-4:30, Sat.-Sun. 1-4. No charge. Closed holidays. ♿
Attendance: 8,000 (estimated)

JOHN DEERE PLANETARIUM, Augustana College, 820 38th St., Rock Island, IL 61201-2210. Tel.: 309-794-7327, 7000 & 7318. Fax: 309-794-7564.
E-mail: leecarkner@augustana.edu
Web Site: helios.augustana.edu/astronomy
Key Personnel: Dir., Lee Carkner.
Institution Type/Description: Planetarium.
Hours & Admission Prices: Gallery: Sept.-May Mon.-Fri. 8-4. Planetarium: by reservation only. No charge. ♿
Attendance: 6,000 (estimated)

QUAD CITY ARTS, 1715 2nd Ave., Rock Island, IL 61201. Tel.: 309-793-1213. Fax: 309-793-1265.
E-mail: info@quadcityarts.com
Web Site: www.quadcityarts.com
Key Personnel: Exec. Dir., Carmen Darland.
Institution Type/Description: Art Gallery.
Hours & Admission Prices: Gallery: Tues.-Fri. 10-5, Sat. 11-5; other times by appointment. Office: Mon.-Fri. 9-5. Closed New Year's Day; Martin Luther King Jr. Day; Good Friday; Memorial Day; Independence Day; Labor Day; Thanksgiving & day after; Christmas Eve.

QUAD CITY BOTANICAL CENTER, 2525 Fourth Ave., Rock Island, IL 61201. Tel.: 309-794-0991. Fax: 309-794-1572. Facebook: QC Gardens.
E-mail: jenkins@qcgardens.com
Web Site: www.qcgardens.com
Key Personnel: Exec. Dir., Ami Jenkins; Chm. (V), Bill Nelson; Education & Program Mgr., Greg Wolf; Dir. Mktg. & Guest Svcs., Ryan Wille; Museum Shop Mgr., Kari Campbell.
Institution Type/Description: Botanical Garden.
Hours & Admission Prices: April-Oct. Mon. & Wed.-Sat. 10-5, Tues. 10-7, Sun. 11-4; Nov.-March Mon., Wed.-Sat. 10-4, Tues. 10-7, Sun. 11-4. Adults $6, seniors & military $5, children 6-15 $4, children 2-5 $2; members & children under 2 no charge. Closed New Year's Day, Thanksgiving & Christmas. ♿

ROCK ISLAND ARSENAL MUSEUM, Bldg. 60, Rock Island Arsenal, Rock Island, IL 61299-5000. Mailing Address: 3500 North Ave., Bldg. 60, Rock Island Arsenal, Rock Island, IL 61299-5000. Tel.: 309-782-5021. Fax: 309-782-3598.
E-mail: kris.g.leinicke.civ@mail.mil
Web Site: www.arsenalhistoricalsociety.org
Formerly: John M. Browning Memorial Museum
Key Personnel: Dir., Kris G. Leinicke.
Institution Type/Description: Military Museum.

Hours & Admission Prices: Tues.-Sat. noon-4. No charge; donations accepted. Closed major holidays. ᵴ
Attendance: 14,993 (actual)

Rockford

ANDERSON JAPANESE GARDENS, 318 Spring Creek Rd., Rockford, IL 61107-1035. Tel.: 815-229-9390. Facebook: Anderson Japanese Gardens.
E-mail: info@andersongardens.org
Web Site: www.andersongardens.org
Institution Type/Description: Japanese Gardens.
Hours & Admission Prices: May-Oct. Mon.-Fri. 9-6, Sat.-Sun. 9-5. Adults $9.50, seniors 62 & over $8.50, students $7.50; discounts to American Horticulture Society members; children 5 & under no charge.
Attendance: 40,000 (estimated)

BURPEE MUSEUM OF NATURAL HISTORY, 737 N. Main St., Rockford, IL 61103-6966. Tel.: 815-965-3433. Fax: 815-986-0023. Facebook.
E-mail: anne.weerda@burpee.org
Web Site: www.burpee.org
Key Personnel: Pres. Bd., Dennis Harezlak; Exec. Dir., Anne Weerda; Dir. Education, Alexandra Benson; Dir. Paleontology, Joshua Mathews; Dir. Operations & Events Coord., Joseph Gackstetter; Mgr. Visitor Svcs. & Coord. Membership, Lynn Hart.
Institution Type/Description: Natural History Museum.
Hours & Admission Prices: Tues.-Sun. 10-5. Adults $8, children 3-12 $7; ASTC & museum members and children under 3 no charge. Closed New Year's Day; Easter; Thanksgiving; Christmas Eve & Day. ᵴ
Attendance: 42,297 (actual)

DISCOVERY CENTER MUSEUM, 711 N. Main St., Rockford, IL 61103-7204. Tel.: 815-963-6769.
E-mail: sarahw@discoverycentermuseum.org
Web Site: www.discoverycentermuseum.org
Key Personnel: Pres. Bd., Joel Huotari; Exec. Dir., Sarah Wolf; Exhibits Coord., Bruce Quast; Mktg. Mgr., Ann Marie Walker; Dir. Education & Programs, Corinne Sosso; Education Specialist, Jessica Williams; Assoc. Dir., Mike Rathbun; Dir. Devel., Sara McKevitt; Museum Shop Mgr., Joyce Mazzola.
Institution Type/Description: Children's Science Museum.
Hours & Admission Prices: Daily 10-5. Admission $8; discount to ASTC & ACM member; members no charge. Closed Easter; Thanksgiving; Christmas. ᵴ
Attendance: 150,000 (estimated)

THE ERLANDER HOME MUSEUM, 404 S. 3rd St., Rockford, IL 61104-2013. Mailing Address: c/o Swedish Historical Society, 404 S. 3rd St., Rockford, IL 61104-2013. Tel.: 815-963-5559. Facebook: Swedish Historical Society.
E-mail: museum@swedishhistorical.org
Web Site: www.swedishhistorical.org
Key Personnel: Pres., Mike Lunde; Administrative Dir., Alix Fox.
Institution Type/Description: Historic House Museum.
Hours & Admission Prices: March-Dec. Sun. 1-3; tours by appointment only with one week advanced notice. Adults $7; members no charge. Closed major holidays.
Attendance: 5,000 (estimated)

ETHNIC HERITAGE MUSEUM, 1129 S. Main St., Rockford, IL 61101. Mailing Address: P.O. Box 382, Rockford, IL 61105-0382. Tel.: 815-962-7402 & 877-2287.
E-mail: ehm1129@comcast.net
Web Site: www.ethnicheritagemuseum.org
Key Personnel: Pres., Sue Lewandowski; Education & Vice Pres. Devel., Lynell Cannell; Treas., Joanne Baylis; Sec., Erica Toledo.
Institution Type/Description: History Museum.
Hours & Admission Prices: Feb.-Dec. Sun. 2-4; other times by appointment. Special Events: family $10, individual $5; discounts to AAM, ICOM & Time Traveler members; members no charge. Closed New Year's Day & day after; Mother's Day; Memorial Day; Father's Day; Independence Day; Labor Day; Christmas Day & day after. ᵴ
Attendance: 1,900 (estimated)

KLEHM ARBORETUM & BOTANIC GARDEN, 2715 S. Main St., Rockford, IL 61102-3925. Tel.: 815-965-8146. Fax: 815-965-5914.
E-mail: info@klehm.org
Web Site: www.klehm.org
Formerly: Northern Illinois Botanical Society
Key Personnel: Dir., Daniel Riggs; Pres. (V), Alise Howlett.

Institution Type/Description: Arboretum & Botanical Garden.
Hours & Admission Prices: April-May & Sept.-Oct. daily 9-4; June-Aug. Fri. 9-8, Sat.-Thurs. 9-4; Nov.-March Tues.-Sat. 9-4. Adults $6, seniors 65 & over, children and students under 18 $3; members no charge. Closed New Year's Eve & Day; Thanksgiving; Christmas Eve & Day. ᵴ
Attendance: 35,622 (actual)

LAURENT HOUSE MUSEUM, 4646 Spring Brook Rd., Rockford, IL 61114-6362. Tel.: 815-877-2952.
E-mail: info@laurenthouse.com
Web Site: www.laurenthouse.com
Institution Type/Description: Historic House Museum: designed by Frank Lloyd Wright; built in 1949.
Hours & Admission Prices: By appointment. Adults $20, seniors 65 & over, military and students $15; discounts to groups. ᵴ

MIDWAY VILLAGE MUSEUM, 6799 Guilford Rd., Rockford, IL 61107-2613. Tel.: 815-397-9112. Fax: 815-397-9156. Facebook: Midway Village Museum.
E-mail: admin@midwayvillage.com
Web Site: www.midwayvillage.com
Key Personnel: Chm., Constance Keyes; Pres., David Byrnes; Operations, Shawn Baxter; Dir. Mktg. & Social Media, Lonna Converso; Customer Svc. Mgr. & Rentals, Mary Friel; Cur., Laura Furman; Special Events Coord., Kristin Hoeker; Educator, Caitlyn Treece; Volunteer Coord., Cherie Bertsch; Dir. Devel., Deb Nau; Garden Historian, Tari Rowland; Visitor Services Coord., Jay Sklar; Business Mgr., Ken Thomson.
Institution Type/Description: History Village Museum: 26 historic turn-of-the-century buildings located on 137 acres.
Hours & Admission Prices: Museum Center, Mill House & Old Dolls' House Museum: May-Aug. Tues.-Fri. 10-4, Sat.-Sun. 10:30-4; Sept.-April Tues.-Fri. 10-4, Sat. 10:30-4. Village: May Thurs.-Sun. 11-4; June-Aug. Tues.-Sun. 11-4; Sept.-April by appointment. Office: Mon.-Fri. 8:30-5. Adults $7, children 3-17 $5; discounts to senior citizens & AAM members; members no charge. Admission varies for special events. Closed major holidays. ᵴ
Attendance: 70,000 (actual)

ROCKFORD ART MUSEUM, 711 N. Main St., Rockford, IL 61103. Tel.: 815-968-2787. Fax: 815-316-2179.
Web Site: www.rockfordartmuseum.org
Key Personnel: Exec. Dir., Linda Dennis; Cur., Carrie Johnson; Office Mgr., Nancy E. Sauer.
Institution Type/Description: Art Museum.
Hours & Admission Prices: Daily 10-5. Adults $7, seniors & students $3; children under 12 & members no charge. ᵴ
Attendance: 42,380 (actual)

ROCKFORD COLLEGE ART GALLERY/CLARK ARTS CENTER, 5050 E. State St., Rockford, IL 61108-2393. Tel.: 815-226-4105. Fax: 815-394-5167.
E-mail: DBarton@Rockford.edu
Key Personnel: Dir., Danielle Barton.
Institution Type/Description: College Art Gallery.
Hours & Admission Prices: Sept.-May Tues.-Thurs. 3-6, Fri. 12-3; other times by appointment. No charge; donations accepted. ᵴ

TINKER SWISS COTTAGE MUSEUM, 411 Kent St., Rockford, IL 61102-2915. Tel.: 815-964-2424. TDD: 815-963-3323; Facebook: Tinker Swiss Cottage Museum.
E-mail: info@tinkercottage.com
Web Site: www.tinkercottage.com
Key Personnel: Dir., Steve Litteral.
Institution Type/Description: Historic House Museum: 1865 Swiss-style home built by Robert H. Tinker.
Hours & Admission Prices: Guided tours: Tues.-Sun. 1 & 3; closed major holidays. Adults $8, senior citizens 65 & up $7, students $5; discounts to Time Traveler, AASLH & AAA, members; members & children 5 & under no charge. ᵴ
Attendance: 12,000 (estimated)

Rockton

MACKTOWN, A LIVING HISTORY EDUCATION CENTER, 2221 Freeport Rd., Rockton, IL 61072-1817. Mailing Address: P. O. Box 566, Rockton, IL 61072-0566. Tel.: 815-624-4200. Facebook.
E-mail: macktownlivinghistory@gmail.com
Web Site: www.macktownlivinghistory.com
Institution Type/Description: Historic Houses: 1839 Stephen Mack House, two-story farm house, home to one of the first white settlers in Winnebago County; 1846 Whitman Trading Post, limestone building.

Hours & Admission Prices: Fri. 10-2, Sun. 12-4 (seasonally); groups by appointment. No charge; donations accepted. &
Attendance: 6,500 (estimated)

Romeoville

ISLE A LA CACHE MUSEUM, 501 E. Romeo Rd., Romeoville, IL 60446-1538. Tel.: 815-886-1467.
E-mail: ccain@fpdwc.org
Web Site: www.fpdwc.org/isle.cfm
Institution Type/Description: History Museum.
Hours & Admission Prices: Tues.-Sat. 10-4, Sun. 12-4. &

Roscoe

HISTORIC AUTO ATTRACTIONS, 13825 Metric Dr., Roscoe, IL 61073-7607. Tel.: 815-389-9999. Fax: 800-779-6461.
E-mail: museum@historicautoattractions.com
Web Site: www.historicautoattractions.com
Key Personnel: Dir., Wayne Lensing; Treas., Cathy Ellis.
Institution Type/Description: History Museum.
Hours & Admission Prices: Memorial Day to Labor Day Tues.-Sat. 10-5, Sun. 11-4; Sept.-Nov. Sat. 10-5, Sun. 11-4. Adults $12, senior citizens $10, students 6-15 $7; children under 6 no charge. Season Pass: $35. &
Attendance: 10,000 (estimated)

Roselle

ROSELLE HISTORY MUSEUM, 102 S. Prospect St., Roselle, IL 60172. Mailing Address: 39 E. Elm St., Roselle, IL 60172. Tel.: 630-351-5300.
E-mail: rosellehistory@sbcglobal.net
Web Site: www.rosellehistory.com
Formerly: Roselle Historical Society
Key Personnel: Raymond Hitzemann.
Institution Type/Description: History Museum.
Hours & Admission Prices: Sun. 2-4; other times by appointment. No charge; donations accepted.
Attendance: 500 (estimated)

Rosemont

DONALD E. STEPHENS MUSEUM OF HUMMELS, 9511 Higgins Rd., Rosemont, IL 60018. Tel.: 847-692-4000.
E-mail: stephensmuseum@rosemont.com
Web Site: www.stephenshummelmuseum.com
Institution Type/Description: General Museum.
Hours & Admission Prices: Mon.-Fri. 10-4, Sat. 9-3; groups by appointment. No charge.

Rosiclare

THE AMERICAN FLUORITE MUSEUM, Main St., Rosiclare, IL 62982. Mailing Address: P.O. Box 755, Rosiclare, IL 62982. Tel.: 618-285-3513.
E-mail: spar@shawneelink.net
Key Personnel: Pres. (V), Eric Livingston.
Institution Type/Description: Mineral Museum.
Hours & Admission Prices: March-Dec. Thurs.-Fri. & Sun. 1-4, Sat. 10-4; tours by appointment. Adults $4.50, children 6-12 $3.
Attendance: 300 (estimated)

Roxana

WOOD RIVER REFINERY HISTORY MUSEUM, 900 S. Central, Roxana, IL 62084. Mailing Address: P.O. Box 76, Roxana, IL 62084-0076. Tel.: 618-255-3718. Fax: 618-255-2552.
E-mail: wrrmu@p66.com
Web Site: www.wrrhm.org
Key Personnel: Pres. (V), David Lewis.
Institution Type/Description: History Museum.
Hours & Admission Prices: Wed.-Thurs. 10-4. No charge; donations accepted.
Attendance: 650 (estimated)

Rushville

SCHUYLER JAIL MUSEUM, 200 S. Congress St., Rushville, IL 62681-1410. Tel.: 217-322-6975.
E-mail: Schuylerjailmuseum@frontier.com
Key Personnel: Pres., Lillian Hoover; Cur., Maryjane Busby.

Institution Type/Description: Historical Society Museum: housed in 1857-58 Schuyler Jail.
Hours & Admission Prices: April-Oct. daily 1-4; Nov.-March Sat.-Sun. 1-4. No charge; donations accepted. Closed all holidays. &
Attendance: 300 (estimated)

Saint Charles

BEITH HOUSE MUSEUM, 8 W. Indiana St., Saint Charles, IL 60174-2829. Mailing Address: c/o PPFV, P.O. Box 903, Saint Charles, IL 60174-0903. Tel.: 630-377-6424. Fax: 630-377-6424.
E-mail: info@ppfv.org
Web Site: www.ppfv.org/beith.htm
Key Personnel: Dir., Elizabeth Safanda.
Institution Type/Description: Historic House Museum: housed in the home of Kane County stone mason, William Beith, built in 1850.
Hours & Admission Prices: May-Oct. Tues. 1-4; other times by appointment. Suggested Donations: family $3, individual $1.

DURANT HOUSE MUSEUM, 37W370 Dean St., Saint Charles, IL 60175. Mailing Address: P.O. Box 903, Saint Charles, IL 60174-0903. Tel.: 630-377-6424. Fax: 630-377-6424.
E-mail: info@ppfv.org
Web Site: www.ppfv.org/durant.htm
Institution Type/Description: Historic House Museum: farmstead built in 1843.
Hours & Admission Prices: June-Aug. Thurs. & Sun. 1-4; Sept.-Oct. Sun. 1-4. Suggested Donation: adults $2, children $1.

ST. CHARLES HERITAGE CENTER, 215 E. Main St., Saint Charles, IL 60174-2040. Tel.: 630-584-6967. Fax: 630-584-6077.
E-mail: info@stcmuseum.org
Web Site: www.stcmuseum.org
Key Personnel: Pres., Laura Haule; Registrar, Julie Bunke.
Institution Type/Description: Historical Museum: housed in 1920s era gas station & a c.1840 historic house.
Hours & Admission Prices: Tues.-Sat. 10-4. No charge; donations accepted. Closed most holidays. &
Attendance: 6,000 (estimated)

Sandwich

SANDWICH HISTORICAL SOCIETY/STONE MILL MUSEUM, 315 E. Railroad, Sandwich, IL 60548-2241. Mailing Address: P.O. Box 82, Sandwich, IL 60548-0082. Tel.: 815-786-2513.
Key Personnel: Pres. (V), Pat Clapper.
Institution Type/Description: Historical Society Museum: housed in an 1856 mill.
Hours & Admission Prices: April-Oct. Sun. 1-4; other times by appointment. No charge; donations accepted. Closed holidays.
Attendance: 1,500 (estimated)

Schaumburg

SPRING VALLEY NATURE CENTER & HERITAGE FARM, 1111 E. Schaumburg Rd., Schaumburg, IL 60194-3648. Tel.: 847-985-2100. Fax: 847-985-9692.
E-mail: info@parkfun.com
Web Site: www.parkfun.com
Formerly: Spring Valley Nature Sanctuary & Volkening Heritage Farm
Key Personnel: Mgr., Dave Brooks; Coord. Programs, Mary Rice; Conservation Svcs. Mgr., Matt McBrien.
Institution Type/Description: Natural History Museum & Sanctuary; Living History Farm.
Hours & Admission Prices: Grounds: April-Oct. daily 8-8; Nov.-March daily 8-5. Visitors Center: daily 9-5. Farm Site: April-Oct. Tues.-Fri. 9-2, Sat.-Sun. 10-4; special events & groups by appointment. No charge; donations accepted. Closed New Year's Day; Thanksgiving; Christmas. &
Attendance: 85,000 (estimated)

WOOD LIBRARY-MUSEUM OF ANESTHESIOLOGY, 1061 American Ln., Schaumburg, IL 60173-4973. Tel.: 847-825-5586. Fax: 847-825-2085.
E-mail: wlm@asahq.org
Web Site: www.woodlibrarymuseum.org
Key Personnel: Pres., Mark E. Schroeder, M.D.; Librarian & Dir., Karen Bieterman, MLIS; Librarian, Jim Fontsas, MLIS; Cur., Hon. George S. Bause, M.D.; Museum Registrar, Judith Robins, M.A.
Institution Type/Description: Medical Museum.
Hours & Admission Prices: By appointment only. No charge. Closed holidays. &
Attendance: 200 (estimated)

Shabbona

SHABBONA-LEE-ROLLO HISTORICAL MUSEUM, 119 W. Comanche, Shabbona, IL 60550-0334. Mailing Address: P.O. Box 334, Shabbona, IL 60550-0334. Tel.: 815-824-2597.
E-mail: slrmuseum@gmail.com
Web Site: slrmuseum.com
Key Personnel: Cur., Ada Gallagher.
Institution Type/Description: History Museum.
Hours & Admission Prices: Tues. & Thurs. 9-11:30am & 12:30-3, Sat. 9-11am. No charge; donations accepted. ௧

Shelbyville

PAM AND BOB BOARMAN CHEVY BEL AIR MUSEUM, 224 W. Main St., Shelbyville, IL 62565-1614. Tel.: 217-774-4919.
E-mail: info@robinhoodwoods.com
Institution Type/Description: Car Museum.
Hours & Admission Prices: Mon.-Fri. 8-7, Sat. 8-6.

Skokie

ILLINOIS HOLOCAUST MUSEUM AND EDUCATION CENTER, 9603 Woods Dr., Skokie, IL 60077. Tel.: 847-967-4800. Fax: 847-967-4801.
E-mail: info@ilhmec.org
Web Site: www.ilholocaustmuseum.org
Formerly: Holocaust Memorial Foundation of Illinois, Inc.
Key Personnel: Exec. Dir., Richard S. Hirschhaut; Deputy Dir., Evette L. Simon; Dir. Finance & Accounting, Eric Schwager; Dir. Devel., Ken Cooper; Dir. Mktg. & Communications, Karen Goodman Minter; Dir. Training & Public Programs, Noreen Brand; Dir. Educational Outreach & Genocide Initiatives, Kelley H. Szany; Chief Cur. Collections & Exhibitions, Arielle Weininger.
Institution Type/Description: History Museum.
Hours & Admission Prices: Mon.-Wed. & Fri. 10-5, Thurs. 10-8, Sat.-Sun. 11-4. Adults $12, seniors 65 & over and students 12-22 $8, children 5-11 $6; discounts to military members; member no charge.
Attendance: 75,180 (actual)

SKOKIE ART MUSEUM, 5452 Greenleaf St., Skokie, IL 60077-2045.
Key Personnel: Dir., Janine Henning.
Institution Type/Description: Art Museum.
Hours & Admission Prices: By appointment.

SKOKIE HERITAGE MUSEUM & LOG CABIN, 8031 Floral Ave., Skokie, IL 60077-3605. Tel.: 847-674-1500, ext. 3000; 677-6672.
E-mail: ajhanson@skokieparks.org
Web Site: www.skokieparks.org
Key Personnel: Facility Mgr., Amanda Hanson.
Institution Type/Description: History Museum.
Hours & Admission Prices: Museum: Thurs.-Fri. 12-4, Sat.-Sun. 10-2. Log Cabin: by appointment. No charge; donations accepted. ௧
Attendance: 4,000 (estimated)

South Elgin

FOX RIVER TROLLEY MUSEUM/FOX RIVER TROLLEY ASSOCIATION, 361 S. La Fox (IL Rte. 31), South Elgin, IL 60177. Mailing Address: P.O. Box 315, South Elgin, IL 60177-0315. Tel.: 847-697-4676.
E-mail: info@foxtrolley.org
Web Site: www.foxtrolley.org
Key Personnel: Pres. (V), Edward J. Konecki; Public Rels., Doug Rundell; Museum Shop Mgr., Laura Taylor.
Institution Type/Description: Trolley Museum.
Hours & Admission Prices: mid-May to July 3 & Sept. to early Nov. Sun. 11-5; July 4 to Labor Day Sat.-Sun. 11-5; call for additional holiday hours. One Ride: adult $5, senior 65 & up $3, child 3-11 $2. Two Rides: adult $6, senior 65 & over $4, children $3. All day ticket: $8 per person; discount to groups of 20 or more.
Attendance: 10,500 (actual)

South Holland

SOUTH HOLLAND HISTORICAL SOCIETY, 16250 Wausau Ave., South Holland, IL 60473-2199. Mailing Address: Box 48, South Holland, IL 60473-0048. Tel.: 708-596-2722.
E-mail: shhistoricalsoc@yahoo.com

Key Personnel: Pres. (V), Robin Scheldberg; Vice Pres., Bill Paarlberg; Sec., Barbara O'Donnell; Treas., Joyce Becker; Acting Cur., Edward Smith.
Institution Type/Description: Historical Society Museum: housed in Village Library.
Hours & Admission Prices: Sat. 1-4. No charge; donations accepted. ௧
Attendance: 300 (estimated)

Springfield

ABRAHAM LINCOLN PRESIDENTIAL LIBRARY & MUSEUM, 212 N. 6th St., Springfield, IL 62701-1004. Tel.: 217-558-8844. TDD: 217-524-7128.
Web Site: www.illinois.gov/alplm
Key Personnel: Exec. Dir., Alan Lowe; Mktg. Dir. & Guest Experience Dir., Patty Knepper; Communications Dir., Chris Wills; Education Dir., Michelle Poe; Exhibits Mgr., Dave Bourland; C.F.O., Ed Harmeyer; Finance Dir., Theresa Cherrier; Theater Dir., Phil Funkenbusch; Systems Tech Dir., Sam Cooper.
Institution Type/Description: Historical Library & Museum.
Hours & Admission Prices: Library: Mon.-Fri. 9-5. No charge. Museum: daily 9-5. Adults $15, students & seniors 62 & over $12, military $10, children 5-15 $6; discounts to groups & AAA members; children under 5 no charge. Research: call for appointment. Closed New Year's Day; Thanksgiving; Christmas. ௧
Attendance: 350,000 (actual)

AIR COMBAT MUSEUM, 835 S. Airport Rd., Springfield, IL 62707. Tel.: 217-522-2181.
E-mail: contact@aircombatmuseum.org
Web Site: www.aircombatmuseum.org
Institution Type/Description: Military Museum.
Hours & Admission Prices: Mon.-Fri. 9-12 & 1-4; guided tours by appointment. Closed national holidays.

THE DANA-THOMAS HOUSE STATE HISTORIC SITE, 301 E. Lawrence Ave., Springfield, IL 62703-2232. Tel.: 217-782-6776 & 6773. Fax: 217-788-9450.
E-mail: dthf@sbcglabal.net
Web Site: dana-thomas.org
Institution Type/Description: Historic House Museum: 1902 Frank Lloyd Wright prairie period house.
Hours & Admission Prices: Thurs.-Sun. 9-4. Suggested Donation: families $15, adults $10, children $5. Closed some holidays.
Attendance: 40,000 (actual)

DAUGHTERS OF UNION VETERANS OF THE CIVIL WAR MUSEUM, 503 S. Walnut, Springfield, IL 62704-1932. Mailing Address: P.O. Box 211, Springfield, IL 62705-0211. Tel.: 217-544-0616.
Institution Type/Description: History Museum.
Hours & Admission Prices: Mon.-Fri. 9-12 & 1-4; other times by appointment.

GRAND ARMY OF THE REPUBLIC MEMORIAL MUSEUM, 629 S. 7th St., Springfield, IL 62703-1636. Tel.: 217-522-4373.
E-mail: WRCmembership@gmail.com
Web Site: www.suvcw/WRC/garmuseum
Key Personnel: Museum Bd. Chm. (V), Lois Didier.
Institution Type/Description: History Museum.
Hours & Admission Prices: April to mid-Dec. Thurs.-Sat. 10-4; other times by appointment. No charge; donations accepted. Closed national holidays.

HENSON ROBINSON ZOO, 1100 E. Lake Dr., Springfield, IL 62712-5536. Tel.: 217-585-1821.
E-mail: emcevoy@hensonrobinsonzoo.org
Web Site: www.hensonrobinsonzoo.org
Key Personnel: Dir., John Wright; Cur. Education, Emily McEvoy.
Institution Type/Description: Zoo.
Hours & Admission Prices: Jan.-Feb. Sat.-Sun. 10-4; April-Oct. Mon.-Fri. 10-5, Sat.-Sun. 10-6; March & Nov.-Dec. daily 10-4. Adults $5.25, seniors over 62 $3.75, children 3-12 $3.50; members and children 2 & under no charge. ௧
Attendance: 103,546 (actual)

ILLINOIS EXECUTIVE MANSION, 410 E. Jackson St., Springfield, IL 62701. Tel.: 217-782-6450.
E-mail: mansionassociation@gmail.com
Institution Type/Description: Historic Building: housed in the home of the Illinois Governor; built in 1855. Listed on the National Register of Historic Places.
Hours & Admission Prices: Tours: Tues. & Thurs. 9:30-11:30 & 2-3:15, Sat. 9:30-11.

ILLINOIS FIRE MUSEUM, State Fairgrounds, Main & Central Aves., Springfield, IL 62794. Mailing Address: P.O. Box 19427, Springfield, IL 62794-9427. Tel.: 217-785-1030.
Institution Type/Description: Fire-Fighting Museum: housed in the former fire house; built in 1857.
Hours & Admission Prices: By appointment.

ILLINOIS STATE MILITARY MUSEUM, Dept. of Military Affairs, 1301 N. MacArthur, Springfield, IL 62702-2317. Tel.: 217-761-3910. Fax: 217-761-3709.
E-mail: ng.il.ilarng.list.staff-pao@mail.mil
Web Site: www.il.ngb.army.mil/heritage/museum.aspx
Key Personnel: Dir., Paul Fanning; Cur., William Lear.
Institution Type/Description: Military History Museum.
Hours & Admission Prices: Tues.-Sat. 1-4:30; other times by appointment. No charge; donations accepted. &
Attendance: 14,000 (actual)

ILLINOIS STATE MUSEUM, 502 S. Spring St., Springfield, IL 62706-5000. Tel.: 217-782-7386; 217-782-9175 (TTY). Fax: 217-782-1254.
E-mail: info@museum.state.il.us
Web Site: www.museum.state.il.us
Key Personnel: Interim Museum Dir., Robert Sill; Bd. Chm. Illinois State Museum Board, Dr. Lorin Nevling; Assoc. Cur. Exhibits, Education & Outreach, Erich Schroeder; Exhibits Preparator, Kelvin Sampson; Exhibits Production Chief, Paul Countryman; Interim Dir. Visitor Svcs., Karen Everingham; Mng. Editor, Andy Hanson; Art Preparator, Phil Kennedy; Membership Coord., Marilyn Sabo; Interim Dir. Art & History, Robert Sill; Fiscal & HR Liaison, Tammy Wheeler.
Institution Type/Description: Natural History, Anthropology, History & Art Museum.
Hours & Admission Prices: Mon.-Sat. 9-4:30, Sun. 12-4:30. No charge; donations accepted. Closed New Year's Day; Thanksgiving; Christmas. &
Attendance: 323,650 (actual)

ILLINOIS STATE POLICE HERITAGE FOUNDATION MUSEUM, 4000 N. Peoria Rd., Springfield, IL 62702-1033. Mailing Address: PO Box 8168, Springfield, IL 62791-8168. Tel.: 217-525-1922.
E-mail: isphf123@gmail.com
Web Site: www.isphf.org
Key Personnel: Pres. (V), Ron Cooley.
Institution Type/Description: Police History Museum.
Hours & Admission Prices: Thurs. & Sat. 10-2. Suggested Donation: $1. Closed holidays. &
Attendance: 475 (estimated)

LINCOLN DEPOT, 930 E. Monroe St., Springfield, IL 62701-1612. Tel.: 217-544-8695. Fax: 217-544-8775.
E-mail: pinky@noll-law.com
Web Site: www.lincolndepot.org
Institution Type/Description: Historic Building: housed in the former depot from which Lincoln left Springfield to start his inaugural journey to Washington DC. on Feb. 11, 1861.
Hours & Admission Prices: Mon.-Fri. 10-4. No charge. Closed holidays. &

LINCOLN HERNDON LAW OFFICES STATE HISTORIC SITE, 112 N. Sixth St., Springfield, IL 62701. Mailing Address: c/o Historic Sites, DNR-One Natural Resources Way, Springfield, IL 62702-1271. Tel.: 217-785-7289. Fax: 217-557-0282.
Web Site: www.dnr.illinois.gov
Key Personnel: Site Mgr., Justin Blanford.
Institution Type/Description: State Historic Site: located in 1840-1841 three-story commercial Greek Revival building built by Springfield merchant Seth M. Tinsley across from the 1839 Illinois Statehouse, now the Old State Capital Historic Site.
Hours & Admission Prices: Call for hours. Requested Donations: adults $2, children $1. Closed New Year's Eve & Day; Martin Luther King Jr. Day; Presidents' Day; Veterans Day; General Election Day; Thanksgiving; Christmas. &
Attendance: 30,000 (actual)

LINCOLN HOME NATIONAL HISTORIC SITE, 413 S. 8th St., Springfield, IL 62701-1905. Tel.: 217-492-4241. Fax: 217-492-4673. Facebook: Lincoln Home National Historic Site; TDD: 217-492-4244.
Web Site: www.nps.gov/liho
Key Personnel: Cur., Susan M. Haake; Historian, Timothy P. Townsend; Chief Interpretation, Laura Gundrum.

Institution Type/Description: Historic District & Historic House Museum: Home of Abraham Lincoln, 16th President of the United States.
Hours & Admission Prices: Daily 8:30-5. tickets to entrance available on first-come, first serve basis at Visitor's Center. No charge; donations accepted. Closed New Year's Day; Thanksgiving; Christmas. &
Attendance: 239,718 (actual)

LINCOLN MEMORIAL GARDEN AND NATURE CENTER, 2301 E. Lake Shore Dr., Springfield, IL 62712-8908. Tel.: 217-529-1111. Fax: 217-529-0134.
E-mail: joel@lincolnmemorialgarden.org
Web Site: www.lincolnmemorialgarden.org
Key Personnel: Exec. Dir., Joel Horwedel; Pres., Tom Wilkin; Environmental Educator, Audra Walters.
Institution Type/Description: Arboretum & Nature Center.
Hours & Admission Prices: Tues.-Sat. 10-4, Sun. 1-4. No charge; donations accepted. Center closed Easter; Independence Day; Thanksgiving; Christmas week. &
Attendance: 50,000 (estimated)

LINCOLN TOMB STATE HISTORIC SITE, Oak Ridge Cemetery, 1441 Monument Ave., Springfield, IL 62702. Mailing Address: 1500 Monument Ave., Springfield, IL 62702-2500. Tel.: 217-782-2717. Fax: 217-524-3738.
E-mail: lincoln.monument.association@gmail.com
Institution Type/Description: Historic Site: 1874, the tomb of Abraham Lincoln.
Hours & Admission Prices: March-April & Sept.-Oct. Tues.-Sat. 9-5; May to Labor Day daily 9-5; Nov.-Feb. Tues.-Sat. 9-4. No charge; donations accepted. Closed New Year's Day; Martin Luther King Jr. Day; Presidents' Day; Veterans Day; General Election Day; Thanksgiving; Christmas. &
Attendance: 345,000 (actual)

OLD STATE CAPITOL, Old State Capitol Plaza, 6th & Adams Sts., Springfield, IL 62701. Mailing Address: 1 Old State Capitol Plaza, Lev 3, Springfield, IL 62701-1323. Tel.: 217-785-7960. Fax: 217-557-0282. TDD: 217-524-7128.
Web Site: www.illinois.gov/ihpa/
Key Personnel: Site Interpreter, Pat Baska.
Institution Type/Description: Historic Building: 1839-1876, Illinois's fifth Statehouse.
Hours & Admission Prices: Wed.-Sun. 9-5. No charge; donations requested. Closed New Year's Day; Martin Luther King Jr. Day; Presidents Day; Labor Day; Veterans Day; Thanksgiving; Christmas. &
Attendance: 108,000 (actual)

THE PEARSON MUSEUM, 801 N. Rutledge, Springfield, IL 62702-4910. Mailing Address: S.I.U. School Medicine, P.O. Box 19635, Springfield, IL 62794-9635. Tel.: 217-545-8017 & 4261. Fax: 217-545-7903.
E-mail: jhouston@siumed.edu
Web Site: www.siumed.edu/medhum/pearson
Key Personnel: Dir. & Devel. Dir., Phillip V. Davis, Ph.D.; Registrar, Karla Henebry; Business & Admin. Assoc., Joseph Houston.
Institution Type/Description: University Medical Science Museum.
Hours & Admission Prices: Tues. 8:30-4:30; group tours by appointment. No charge; donations accepted. &
Attendance: 6,000 (estimated)

SPRINGFIELD ART ASSOCIATION, 700 N. Fourth St., Springfield, IL 62702-5232. Tel.: 217-523-2631. Fax: 217-523-3866.
E-mail: office@springfieldart.org
Web Site: www.springfieldart.org
Key Personnel: Exec. Dir., Betsy Dollar; Pres. (V), Diane McEvoy; Cur. Collections, Erika Holst; Dir. Library, Jan Arnold; Coord. Education, Erin Svendsen; Office Mgr., Charlotte Kane; Devel. Coord., Mary Beth Burke.
Institution Type/Description: Historic Home: c.1833.
Hours & Admission Prices: House Tours: Tues.-Fri. 1, 2, & 3, Sat. 12, 1 & 2. Library: Mon.-Fri. 9-5, Sat. 10-3. Gallery: Mon.-Fri. 10-5, Sat. 10-3. Adults $5; children under 10 & members no charge. Closed New Year's Day; Presidents' Day; Columbus Day; Labor Day; Thanksgiving & day after; Christmas Eve, Day & week. &
Attendance: 5,000 (estimated)

STATE OF ILLINOIS-HISTORIC PRESERVATION AGENCY, HISTORIC SITES DIVISION, 313 S. 6th St., Springfield, IL 62701-1805. Tel.: 217-785-7930. Fax: 217-785-8117.
E-mail: hpa.info@illinois.gov
Web Site: www.illinoishistory.gov

Key Personnel: Dir., Heidi Brown-McCreery.
Institution Type/Description: State Agency.
Hours & Admission Prices: Call for hours & admission information. No charge; donations accepted. ♿
Attendance: 2,400,000 (actual)

TRUTTER MUSEUM, 5250 Shepherd Rd., Springfield, IL 62794. Tel.: 217-786-2217.
Institution Type/Description: History Museum.
Hours & Admission Prices: mid-Aug. to mid-May Tues.-Thurs. 10-3; other times by appointment.

VACHEL LINDSAY HOME STATE HISTORIC SITE, 603 S. Fifth St., Springfield, IL 62703-1604. Tel.: 217-524-0901. Fax: 217-557-0282.
E-mail: vachellindsay@gmail.com
Web Site: www.illinois-history.gov & www.vachellindsay.org
Key Personnel: Mgr. Old State Capitol Complex, Justin Blandford; Admin., Jennie Battles.
Institution Type/Description: Historic House: 1846 home of Vachel Lindsay.
Hours & Admission Prices: Tours: Tues.-Sat. 10-4; groups of 10 or more by appointment. Suggested Donations: adults $4, students $2.
Attendance: 4,978 (estimated)

WASHINGTON PARK BOTANICAL GARDEN, 1740 W. Fayette, Springfield, IL 62704-2356. Tel.: 217-546-4116. Fax: 217-546-0257.
E-mail: chad@springfieldparks.org
Web Site: www.springfieldparks.org
Key Personnel: Exec. Dir., Springfield Park Dist., Derek Harms; Supv. Horticulture, Chad Scaife; Park Bd. Pres., Leslie Sgro.
Institution Type/Description: Botanical Garden.
Hours & Admission Prices: Mon.-Fri. 12-4, Sat.-Sun. 12-5; tours by appointment. No charge; donations accepted. Call for state holiday closures. ♿
Attendance: 80,000 (estimated)

Sterling

STERLING-ROCK FALLS HISTORICAL SOCIETY MUSEUM, 1005 E. 3rd. St., Sterling, IL 61081-0065. Tel.: 815-622-6215.
E-mail: srfhs@comcast.net
Web Site: www.srfhs.com
Key Personnel: Dir. & Cur., Terence Buckaloo; Pres. (V), David B. Lowe.
Institution Type/Description: Historical Society Museum.
Hours & Admission Prices: Tues., Thurs. & Sat. 10-12 & 1-4, Fri. 2-6, Sun. 1-5. No charge; donations accepted. ♿
Attendance: 2,700 (actual)

Stockton

STOCKTON HERITAGE MUSEUM, 107 W. Front Ave., Stockton, IL 61085-1317. Mailing Address: P.O. Box 93, Stockton, IL 61085-0093. Tel.: 815-947-9144. Facebook: Stockton Heritage Museum.
E-mail: stocktonmuseum@yahoo.com
Key Personnel: Dir. & Cur., Bobbi Reagan; Pres. (V), Melody Heidenreich.
Institution Type/Description: History Museum.
Hours & Admission Prices: May-Dec. Sat. 9-1. No charge; donations accepted. ♿
Attendance: 450 (estimated)

Stone Park

ITALIAN CULTURAL CENTER OF CASA ITALIA, 1621 N. 39th Ave., Stone Park, IL 60165-1186. Tel.: 708-345-3842. Fax: 708-345-3891.
E-mail: dominic.cardeloro@gmail.com
Web Site: www.casaitaliachicago.net
Key Personnel: Chm., Leonardo S. DeFranco; Dir. Exhibits, Josetta Mentesana Weber.
Institution Type/Description: Italian Heritage Museum.
Hours & Admission Prices: Mon.-Fri. 9-4 by appointment. No charge; donations accepted.

Sugar Grove

AIR CLASSIC INC. MUSEUM OF AVIATION, 43W624 U.S. 30, Sugar Grove, IL 60554. Tel.: 630-466-0888.
E-mail: webmaster@airclassicsmuseum.org

Web Site: www.airclassicsmuseum.org
Key Personnel: Pres., Mike Luman; Vice Pres., Lawrence Matt.
Institution Type/Description: Aviation & Military Museum.
Hours & Admission Prices: early April to late Nov. Sat.-Sun. 10-3. Group Tours: Tues.-Fri. Adults $8, seniors & children 5-16 $5; children under 5 no charge.
Attendance: 3,000 (estimated)

Sullivan

MOULTRIE COUNTY HISTORICAL & GENEALOGICAL SOCIETY, 117 E. Harrison St., Sullivan, IL 61951. Mailing Address: P.O. Box 588, Sullivan, IL 61951-0588. Tel.: 217-728-4085. Fax: 217-728-7230. Facebook: @MCHGS.
E-mail: mocohgs@gmail.com
Formerly: Moultrie County Heritage Center
Institution Type/Description: History Museum.
Hours & Admission Prices: Mon. & Sat. 12-3; other times by appointment. No charge; donations accepted. ♿

Sycamore

DEKALB COUNTY HISTORY CENTER, 1730 N. Main St., Sycamore, IL 60178. Mailing Address: P.O. Box 502, Sycamore, IL 60178-0502. Tel.: 815-895-5762.
E-mail: info@sycamorehistory.org
Web Site: sycamorehistory.org
Formerly: Sycamore History Museum
Key Personnel: Dir., Michelle Donahoe; Pres., Jim Lyon.
Institution Type/Description: History Museum.
Hours & Admission Prices: Tues.-Sat. 10-3 by appointment. Adults $5; members & children under 14 no charge. ♿
Attendance: 5,000 (estimated)

MIDWEST MUSEUM OF NATURAL HISTORY, 425 W. State St., Sycamore, IL 60178-1410. Tel.: 815-895-9777. Fax: 815-899-2552. Facebook: Midwest Museum of Natural History.
E-mail: director@mmnh.org
Web Site: www.mmnh.org
Key Personnel: Exec. Dir., Cindy Khatri.
Institution Type/Description: Natural History Museum.
Hours & Admission Prices: Tues.-Sat. 10-5. Adults $8, seniors & children $5; discounts to groups of 20 or more, Time Travelers Club & ROAM; members & children under 2 no charge. ♿
Attendance: 10,000 (estimated)

Tampico

RONALD REAGAN BIRTHPLACE & MUSEUM, 111 S. Main St., Tampico, IL 61283. Mailing Address: P.O. Box 344, Tampico, IL 61283. Tel.: 815-438-2130. Facebook.
E-mail: reaganbirthplace@thewisp.net
Web Site: www.tampicohistoricalsociety.com
Key Personnel: Dir. (V), Joan Johnson.
Institution Type/Description: Historic Building: housed in the birthplace of Ronald Reagan; born Feb. 6, 1911.
Hours & Admission Prices: April-Oct. Mon.-Sat. 10-4, Sun. 1-4; other times by appointment. No charge; donations accepted. Closed Easter; Mother's Day.
Attendance: 2,500 (estimated)

TAMPICO AREA HISTORICAL SOCIETY, 119 S. Main St., Tampico, IL 61283. Mailing Address: P.O. Box 154, Tampico, IL 61283. Tel.: 815-438-7581. Facebook.
E-mail: tampicohistoricalsociety@gmail.com
Web Site: www.tampicohistoricalsociety.com
Key Personnel: Pres. (V), Joan Johnson.
Institution Type/Description: Historical Society Museum.
Hours & Admission Prices: Open by appointment. No charge; donations accepted. ♿
Attendance: 500 (estimated)

Teutopolis

TEUTOPOLIS MONASTERY MUSEUM, Rte. 40, & S. Garrott St., Teutopolis, IL 62467-1161. Tel.: 217-857-3586.
E-mail: monasterymuseum_st.francis@yahoo.com
Key Personnel: Pres. (V), Ray Vahling; Vice Pres., Carol Hoelscher; Treas., Henry Hawickhorst; Sec. & Helping Tour Chm., Joyce Vahling; Helping Tour Chm., Eleanor Gebben.
Institution Type/Description: Local History Museum: housed in 1862 Franciscan Novitiate.

Hours & Admission Prices: April-Nov. first Sun. each month 12:30-4; tours by appointment. Adults $5, children $1. Closed Easter; Independence Day. &
Attendance: 500 (estimated)

Tinley Park

TINLEY PARK HISTORICAL SOCIETY, 6727 W. 174th St., Tinley Park, IL 60477-3529. Mailing Address: P.O. Box 325, Tinley Park, IL 60477-0325. Tel.: 708-429-4210. Fax: 708-444-5099. TDD: 708-444-5000.
E-mail: bbettenh@tinleypark.org
Key Personnel: Chm. (V), Ed Siemsen; Treas., Brad Bettenhausen.
Institution Type/Description: Historical Society Museum: housed in an 1884 frame church in Prairie Gothic style.
Hours & Admission Prices: Wed. 10-2; other times by appointment. No charge; donations accepted. Closed federal & state holidays. &

Toulon

STARK COUNTY HISTORICAL SOCIETY, 318 W. Jefferson St., Toulon, IL 61483. Tel.: 309-286-3104.
Institution Type/Description: Historical Society Museum.
Hours & Admission Prices: By appointment.

Tremont

TREMONT MUSEUM & HISTORICAL SOCIETY, Corner of Sampson & Madison Sts., Tremont, IL 61568. Mailing Address: P. O. Box 738, Tremont, IL 61568. Tel.: 309-231-1123.
E-mail: richsauder@gmail.com
Web Site: www.tremontil.com
Key Personnel: Pres. (V), Richard Sauder.
Institution Type/Description: History Museum.
Hours & Admission Prices: 2nd Sun. each month 2-4; other times by appointment. Adults $5, children $3; members no charge. &
Attendance: 300 (estimated)

Union

DONLEY'S WILD WEST TOWN MUSEUM, 8512 S. Union Rd., Union, IL 60180-9661. Tel.: 815-923-9000. Fax: 815-923-2253.
E-mail: info@wildwesttown.com
Web Site: www.wildwesttown.com
Institution Type/Description: History Museum.
Hours & Admission Prices: April-May 24 & Sept. 5-Oct. Sat.-Sun. 10-6; May 25-Sept. 4 daily 10-6. Adults $15; children 2 & under no charge. (museum included in Wild West Town admission).

ILLINOIS RAILWAY MUSEUM, 7000 Olson Rd., Union, IL 60180. Mailing Address: P.O. Box 427, Union, IL 60180-0427. Tel.: 815-923-4391, ext. 404. Fax: 815-923-2006.
E-mail: nkallas@irm.org
Web Site: www.irm.org
Key Personnel: Exec. Dir., Nick Kallas; Pres. (V), Joe Stupar; Museum Shop Mgr., Tom Blodgett.
Institution Type/Description: Railway Museum: housed in c.1851 Marengo, Illinois rail depot.
Hours & Admission Prices: Memorial Day-Labor Day daily 10-4; Spring & Fall Sat.-Sun. 10-5. Admission & rides: adults $14, children $10; discounts to AAM members & groups; members no charge.
Attendance: 65,214 (actual)

MCHENRY COUNTY HISTORICAL SOCIETY AND MUSEUM, 6422 Main St., Union, IL 60180. Mailing Address: P. O. Box 434, Union, IL 60180-0434. Tel.: 815-923-2267. Fax: 815-923-2271.
E-mail: info@mchenrycountyhistory.org
Web Site: www.mchenrycountyhistory.org
Key Personnel: Admin., Kurt Begalka; Pres. (V), Mary Ott; Vice Pres. (V), Bob Frenz; Office Mgr., Nancy Roozee; Coord. Exhibits & Collection, Kira Halvey; Coord. Membership & Volunteers, Kim Ortega.
Institution Type/Description: Historical Society Museum.
Hours & Admission Prices: May to early Oct. Tues.-Fri. Adults $5, children & senior citizens 60 and over $3; members no charge. Blue Star program. Closed holidays. &
Attendance: 5,500 (estimated)

University Park

NATHAN MANILOW SCULPTURE PARK, GOVERNORS STATE UNIVERSITY, 1 University Pkwy., University Park, IL 60484-3165. Tel.: 708-534-4021.
E-mail: jstevenson@govst.edu
Web Site: www.govst.edu/sculpture
Key Personnel: Dir. & Cur., Jeff Stevenson; Bd. Pres., Lee Kelley.
Institution Type/Description: Sculpture Park.
Hours & Admission Prices: Dawn to dusk. No charge; donations accepted. Guided Tours: $10 per person; discounts to students & seniors.
Attendance: 15,000 (estimated)

Urbana

SPURLOCK MUSEUM, UNIVERSITY OF ILLINOIS AT URBANA-CHAMPAIGN, 600 S. Gregory St., Urbana, IL 61801-3759. Tel.: 217-333-2360. Fax: 217-244-9419. Facebook: Spurlock Museum.
E-mail: spurlock-museum@illinois.edu
Web Site: www.spurlock.illinois.edu
Key Personnel: Dir., Elizabeth Sutton; Bd. Pres., Lisa Wilson; Collections Mgr., Christa Deacy-Quinn; Asst. Collections Mgr., John Holton; Coord. Collections, Melissa Sotelo; Registrar, Jennifer White; Asst. Registrar, Amy Heggemeyer; Dir. Education, Elisabeth Stone; Asst. Dir. Education, Kim Sheahan; Coord. Education, Beth Watkins; Information Technology, Jack Thomas; Business Mgr., Karen Flesher; Coord. Special Events, Brian Cudiamat; Cur. Asia, Chiou-Peng TzeHuey; Cur. Africa, Mahir Saul; Cur. East Asia, Kai Wing Chow; Cur. Oceania, Janet Keller; Cur. South America, Norman Whitten; Cur. East Asia, Yu Wang; Security Supvr., Cipriano Martinez; Lead Guard, Thomas Yu.
Institution Type/Description: World Cultures Museum.
Hours & Admission Prices: Tues. 12-5, Wed.-Fri. 9-5, Sat. 10-4, Sun. 12-4. No charge; donations accepted. Closed university holidays. &
Attendance: 19,000 (estimated)

WANDELL SCULPTURE GARDEN, Meadowbrook Park, Vine St., Urbana, IL 61801. Mailing Address: Urbana Park District, 303 W. University Ave., Urbana, IL 61801. Tel.: 217-367-1536. Fax: 217-367-1391.
E-mail: robinhall@mcleodusa.net
Institution Type/Description: Sculpture Garden.
Hours & Admission Prices: Daily dawn to dusk.

Utica

LASALLE COUNTY HISTORICAL SOCIETY MUSEUM, 101 E. Canal, Utica, IL 61373. Mailing Address: P.O. Box 278, Utica, IL 61373-0278. Tel.: 815-667-4861. Fax: 815-310-7613. Facebook: LaSalle County Historical Society Museum.
E-mail: lchsmuseum@gmail.com
Web Site: lasallecountymuseum.org
Key Personnel: Pres. (V), Doug Holland.
Institution Type/Description: History Museum: housed in 1848 pre-Civil War stone warehouse along the Illinois Michigan canal.
Hours & Admission Prices: Wed.-Fri. 10-4, Sat.-Sun. 12-4; other times by appointment. No charge; donations accepted. Closed major holidays. &
Attendance: 12,000 (estimated)

Vandalia

THE LITTLE BRICK HOUSE, 621 Saint Clair St., Vandalia, IL 62471. Mailing Address: Vandalia Historical Society, Inc., 105 S. 4th, Vandalia, IL 62471-2809. Tel.: 618-283-4866.
Key Personnel: Dir., Dale Timmermann.
Institution Type/Description: Historic House Museum: 1840-1860 James W. Berry property.
Hours & Admission Prices: By appointment only. Suggested Donations: adults $3, children 12 & under $1.
Attendance: 150 (estimated)

VANDALIA STATEHOUSE STATE HISTORIC SITE, 315 W. Gallatin St., Vandalia, IL 62471-2820. Tel.: 618-283-1161.
E-mail: hpa.vandalia@illinois.gov
Key Personnel: Dir. IHPA, Jan Grimes; Site Supt., Mary Cole.
Institution Type/Description: Historic Site: 1836 Vandalia Statehouse is the oldest Capitol building in the state of Illinois.
Hours & Admission Prices: March-Oct. Tues.-Sat. 9-5; Nov.-Feb. Tues.-Sat. 9-4. Suggested Donations: adults $4, children $2. Closed New Year's Day; Thanksgiving; Christmas. &
Attendance: 35,000 (actual)

Vernon Hills

LOYOLA AT CUNEO MANSION & GARDENS, 1350 N. Milwaukee, Vernon Hills, IL 60061-1540. Tel.: 847-362-3042. Fax: 847-362-4130.
E-mail: mdavi13@luc.edu
Web Site: www.luc.edu/cuneo
Formerly: Cuneo Mansion & Gardens
Key Personnel: Pres., Dr. JoAnn Rooney; Dir., Dr. Lisa Cushing Davis.
Institution Type/Description: Historic House & Garden: 1914 Cuneo Mansion.
Hours & Admission Prices: Feb.-Dec. Fri.-Sun. 11-4. Adults $10, seniors & students with ID $9; members no charge. Closed major holidays. &
Attendance: 30,000 (estimated)

Versailles

VERSAILLES AREA GENEALOGICAL & HISTORICAL SOCIETY, 113 W. First St., Versailles, IL 62378. Mailing Address: P.O. Box 92, Versailles, IL 62337. Tel.: 217-225-3401.
E-mail: vaghs83@yahoo.com
Web Site: vaghs.tripod.com
Institution Type/Description: Historical Society Museum.
Hours & Admission Prices: April-Oct. Mon., Wed. & Fri. 1:30-5; Nov.-March Wed. & Fri. 1:30-5; other times by appointment. No charge; donations accepted.
Attendance: 200 (estimated)

Villa Park

VILLA PARK HISTORICAL MUSEUM, 220 S. Villa Ave., Villa Park, IL 60181. Tel.: 630-941-0223. Facebook: Villa Park Historical Museum.
E-mail: info@vphistoricalsociety.com
Web Site: www.vphistorical society.com
Key Personnel: Pres. (V), Carol Marcus.
Institution Type/Description: Historical Museum: housed in a former train station. Listed on the National Register of Historic Places.
Hours & Admission Prices: Tues.-Fri. 1-5, Sat.-Sun. 10-4. No charge; donations accepted.
Attendance: 5,089 (actual)

Volo

VOLO AUTO MUSEUM, 27582 W. Volo Village Rd., Volo, IL 60073-9613. Tel.: 815-385-3644. Fax: 815-385-0703. Facebook.
E-mail: brian@volocars.com
Web Site: www.volocars.com
Formerly: Volo Antique Auto Museum and Village
Key Personnel: C.E.O. & Owner, Greg Grams; Dir., Brien Grams; Devel. & Museum Shop Mgr., Myra Grams.
Institution Type/Description: Automobile Museum.
Hours & Admission Prices: Daily 10-5. Adults $14.95, senior citizens $12.95, children 5-12 $8.95; discounts to military; members no charge. Closed Easter; Thanksgiving; Christmas. &
Attendance: 500,000 (estimated)

Washington

WASHINGTON HISTORICAL SOCIETY, 105 Zinser Place, Washington, IL 61571. Mailing Address: P.O. Box 54, Washington, IL 61571. Tel.: 309-444-4793. Facebook: Washington Historical Society.
E-mail: leri.slonneger2@gmail.com
Web Site: www.washington-historical-society.org
Key Personnel: Pres., Leri Slonneger; Vice Pres., Peg Gregory.
Institution Type/Description: Historical Society Museum: housed in the c.1916 former medical office of Dr. Harley Zinser & c.1858 doctor's house.
Hours & Admission Prices: March-Nov. Thurs.-Sat. 11-2; other times by appointment. No charge; donations accepted.
Attendance: 150 (estimated)

Watseka

IROQUOIS COUNTY HISTORICAL SOCIETY, 103 W. Cherry St., Watseka, IL 60970-1524. Tel.: 815-432-2215. Fax: 815-432-2215.
E-mail: ichs2215@mchsi.com
Web Site: www.iroquoiscountyhistoricalsociety.com
Key Personnel: Pres., Rolland Light; Vice Pres., Jean Hiles; Sec., Marilyn Wilken; Treas., Diane Gagnon; Office Mgr., Judy Ficke.

Institution Type/Description: General Museum: housed in 1866 Old Iroquois County Courthouse.
Hours & Admission Prices: Mon.-Fri. 10-4, Sun. call for hours; other times by appointment. Suggested Donations: adults $2, children $.50; members no charge. Closed major holidays. &
Attendance: 5,000 (estimated)

Wauconda

LAKE COUNTY DISCOVERY MUSEUM, 27277 N. Forest Preserve Dr., Wauconda, IL 60084. Tel.: 847-968-3400. Fax: 847-526-0024.
E-mail: lcmuseum@lcfpd.org
Web Site: www.lcfpd.org/museum
Key Personnel: Dir., Katherine Hamilton-Smith.
Institution Type/Description: General Museum.
Hours & Admission Prices: Mon.-Sat. 10-4:30, Sun. 1-4:30. Adults $6, seniors & students $3, children 4-17 $2.50; discounts to AAM members; children 3 & under and members no charge. Closed New Year's Day; Thanksgiving; Christmas Eve & Day. &
Attendance: 70,000 (actual)

WAUCONDA TOWNSHIP HISTORICAL SOCIETY, 711 Main St., Wauconda, IL 60084. Mailing Address: Wauconda Township Historical Society, 505 W. Bonner Rd., Wauconda, IL 60084. Tel.: 847-526-9303.
E-mail: wths@wauconda-history.org
Web Site: www.wauconda-history.org
Key Personnel: Pres. (V), Pat Oaks; Vice Pres. (V), Chuck Black; Sec., Cindy Graff; Treas., Roberta Francisco.
Institution Type/Description: Historical Society Museum: housed in c.1840 brick farm home of Andrew C. Cook.
Hours & Admission Prices: May-Sept. Sun. 1-4; other times by appointment. No charge; donations accepted. &
Attendance: 150 (estimated)

Waukegan

WARBIRD HERITAGE FOUNDATION & MUSEUM, 3000 Corporate Dr., Waukegan, IL 60087. Tel.: 847-244-8701. Fax: 847-244-8703.
E-mail: info@warbirdheritagefoundation.org
Web Site: www.warbirdheritagefoundation.org
Institution Type/Description: Military Aircraft Museum.
Hours & Admission Prices: By appointment.

WAUKEGAN HISTORY MUSEUM, WAUKEGAN HISTORICAL SOCIETY, WAUKEGAN PARK DISTRICT, 1917 N. Sheridan Rd., Bowen Park, Waukegan, IL 60087-5131. Tel.: 847-336-1859 & 360-4749. Fax: 847-662-6190. Facebook: Waukegan history Museum.
E-mail: museum@waukeganhistorical.org
Web Site: www.waukeganhistorical.org
Formerly: Waukegan History Museum, Waukegan Historical Society
Key Personnel: Pres. (V), Harry Came; Supvr., Ty Rohrer; Specialist, Bryan Escobar; Librarian, Beverly Millard.
Institution Type/Description: Local History Museum.
Hours & Admission Prices: Tues. & Thurs. 10-4, Sat. 1-4; other times by appointment. No Charge; donations accepted. Closed all major holidays. &
Attendance: 1,500 (estimated)

West Chicago

KLINE CREEK FARM, 1N600 County Farm Rd., West Chicago, IL 60185. Mailing Address: P.O. Box 5000, Wheaton, IL 60189-5000. Tel.: 630-876-5900. Fax: 630-293-9421. Facebook: Kline Creek Farm.
E-mail: kcf@dupageforest.com
Web Site: www.dupageforest.com
Key Personnel: Pres., Joe Cantore; Supvr., Keith R. McClow; Coord. Collection, Carol Nardbrook; Staff Asst., Sue Clark; Heritage Interpreter, Kate Garret; Heritage Interpreter, Dennis Buck; Heritage Interpreter, Wayne Hill; Heritage Interpreter, Carmen Guerrero.
Institution Type/Description: Living History Museum: re-creation of a turn-of-the-century farm in northeast Illinois.
Hours & Admission Prices: Thurs.-Mon. 9-5. No charge; donations accepted. Closed New Year's Eve & Day; Independence Day; Thanksgiving; Christmas Eve & Day. &
Attendance: 74,000 (estimated)

KRUSE HOUSE MUSEUM, 527 Main St., West Chicago, IL 60185-2842. Mailing Address: P.O. Box 246, West Chicago, IL 60186-0246. Tel.: 630-231-0564 & 2329.
E-mail: krusehouse@comcast.net
Web Site: www.krusehousemuseum.org
Key Personnel: Pres. (V), Lance Conkright; Dir., Jim Beifuss; Museum Shop Mgr., Donna Orlandini.
Institution Type/Description: Historical Society Museum; housed in 1917 Kruse House.
Hours & Admission Prices: May-Sept. Sat. 11-3; tours by appointment. No charge; donations accepted.
Attendance: 520 (estimated)

WEST CHICAGO CITY MUSEUM, 132 Main St., West Chicago, IL 60185-2835. Tel.: 630-231-3376 & 293-2266. Fax: 630-293-2943.
E-mail: museum@westchicago.org
Web Site: www.westchicago.org
Key Personnel: Dir., Curator, Sara Phalen; Archivist, Sally DeFauw.
Institution Type/Description: History Museum; housed in the former Town Hall & Fire Station; Chicago, Burlington & Quincy Station; c.1860. Listed on the National Register of Historic Places.
Hours & Admission Prices: Jan.-March Wed.-Fri. 12-4; April-Dec. Wed.-Sat. 12-4; other times by appointment. Research: by appointment. No charge; donations accepted. &
Attendance: 3,000 (estimated)

West Frankfort

FRANKFORT AREA HISTORICAL MUSEUM, 2000 E. St. Louis St., West Frankfort, IL 62896-1647. Tel.: 618-932-6159.
Key Personnel: Pres., Mary Ellen Maragni; Vice Pres. & Museum Shop Mgr., Winona Harris; Sec., Sylvia Tharp; Treas., Ervin Thomas; Asst. Dir. & Cur. Veteran's Museum, James Harriss; Asst. Dir., Daryl McCoy; Librarian, Barbara Cariel.
Institution Type/Description: Historical Building: housed in a former school building; built c.1916.
Hours & Admission Prices: Wed.-Thurs. 9-3. No charge; donations accepted. Closed New Year's Day; Easter; Independence Day; Thanksgiving; Christmas. &
Attendance: 9,000 (estimated)

VETERANS DEPOT MUSEUM, 101 W. Main St., West Frankfort, IL 62896-2317. Mailing Address: 2000 E. St. Louis, West Frankfort, IL 62896-1647.
Key Personnel: Dir., James Harriss; Chm. (V), Daryl McCoy.
Institution Type/Description: Military Museum.
Hours & Admission Prices: March-Nov. Sun. 1-4; Dec.-Feb. by appointment. No charge; donations accepted. Closed national holidays.
Attendance: 400 (estimated)

Western Springs

WESTERN SPRINGS HISTORICAL SOCIETY, 4211 Grand Ave., Western Springs, IL 60558-1435. Mailing Address: P.O. Box 139, Western Springs, IL 60558-0139. Tel.: 708-246-9230.
E-mail: info@westernspringshistory.org
Web Site: www.westernspringshistory.org
Key Personnel: Pres., Vicki Lezon; Vice Pres., Susan Wyckoff; Cur. Res. & Artifacts, Anne Kozak.
Institution Type/Description: General Museum; housed in 1892 Old Water Tower.
Hours & Admission Prices: Call for hours. No charge; donations accepted.
Attendance: 1,000 (estimated)

Wheaton

BILLY GRAHAM CENTER MUSEUM, 500 E. College Ave., Wheaton, IL 60187-5534. Tel.: 630-752-5909, ext. 0. Fax: 630-752-5916.
E-mail: BGCMus@wheaton.edu
Web Site: www.billygrahamcenter.org/museum
Key Personnel: Museum Coord., Christian Sawyer; Dir. Resources, Paul Ericksen.
Institution Type/Description: Religious Museum.
Hours & Admission Prices: Mon.-Sat. 9:30-5:30, Sun. 1-5. Suggested Donations: adults $7, seniors & students $4, children 12 & under $2. Closed New Year's Eve & Day; Christmas Eve, Day & week. &

CENTER FOR HISTORY, 315 W. Front St., 2nd Fl., Wheaton, IL 60187-5015. Mailing Address: P.O. Box 373, Wheaton, IL 60187-0373. Tel.: 630-871-6601.

E-mail: info@wheatonhistory.com
Web Site: www.wheatonhistory.org
Formerly: Wheaton History Center
Key Personnel: Pres. & C.E.O., Alberta Adamson, CFRE; Chm., Ed Ewoldt.
Institution Type/Description: History Museum.
Hours & Admission Prices: Mon.-Sat. 10-5; tours, programs & research by appointment. Admission $5; discounts to AAM members; members and children 8 & under no charge. Closed New Year's Day; Easter; Memorial Day; Labor Day; Thanksgiving; Christmas. &
Attendance: 9,000 (estimated)

COSLEY ZOO, 1356 N. Gary Ave., Wheaton, IL 60187. Tel.: 630-665-5534. Fax: 630-260-6408. Facebook: Cosley Zoo.
E-mail: cosleyzoo@wheatonparks.org
Web Site: cosleyzoo.org
Key Personnel: Dir., Susan Wahlgren; Pres. (V), Arthur Pape.
Institution Type/Description: Zoo.
Hours & Admission Prices: Jan.-March & Nov. daily 9-4; April-Oct. daily 9-5; late Nov.-Dec. daily 9-9; groups by appointment. Adults $5, seniors 55 & over $4; discounts to AZA members; members, youth 17 & under, and Wheaton Park District residents no charge. Closed New Year's Day; Thanksgiving; Christmas. &
Attendance: 150,000 (actual)

DUPAGE COUNTY HISTORICAL MUSEUM, 102 E. Wesley St., Wheaton, IL 60187-5321. Tel.: 630-510-4941. Fax: 630-665-5880.
E-mail: mpodkowa@wheatonparks.org
Web Site: www.dupagemuseum.com
Key Personnel: Mgr., Michelle Podkowa.
Institution Type/Description: History Museum.
Hours & Admission Prices: Mon.-Fri. 9:30-4, Sat.-Sun. 12-4. No charge; donations accepted. Closed New Year's Eve & Day; Memorial Day; Independence Day; Labor Day; Thanksgiving; Christmas Eve & Day. &
Attendance: 8,669 (actual)

THE FIRST DIVISION MUSEUM AT CANTIGNY, 1s151 Winfield Rd., Wheaton, IL 60189-3353. Tel.: 630-260-8185. Fax: 630-260-9298.
E-mail: info@firstdivisionmuseum.org
Web Site: www.firstdivisionmuseum.org
Key Personnel: Exec. Dir., Paul H. Herbert, Ph.D.; Dir. Research Center, Eric Gillespie; Dir. Media, Gayln Piper; Cur. Collections, Bill Brewster; Asst. Cur. Collections, Chris Zielinski; Museum Public Programs Mgr., JD Kammes; Museum Educator, Melissa Tyler; Collections Mgr., Shane Keil; Reference Librarian, Mary Manning; Research Historian, Andrew Woods; Graphic Designer, Dave Blake; Registrar, John Maniatis; Archivist, Kate Kleiderman.
Institution Type/Description: Military Museum; located on the grounds of Cantigny Park.
Hours & Admission Prices: Closed 11/12/16-8/17 for renovations. Feb. Fri.-Sun. 10-4; March-April & Nov.-Dec. Tues.-Sun. 10-4; May-Oct. Tues.-Sun. 10-5. No charge. Parking $5. Closed Thanksgiving Day & day after; Christmas Eve & Day; New Year's Eve. &
Attendance: 145,000 (actual)

ROBERT R. McCORMICK MUSEUM AT CANTIGNY, 1 S. 151 Winfield Rd., Wheaton, IL 60189-3353. Tel.: 630-260-8163. Fax: 630-260-8160. Facebook: Robert R. McCormick Museum.
E-mail: mccormickmuseum@cantigny.org
Web Site: www.cantigny.org
Key Personnel: C.E.O., David Hiller; Dir., William Buhlig; Exec. Dir. Cantigny Foundation, Matt Lafond; Tour Coord., Jeff Anderson; Museum Shop Mgr., Alicia Anderson; Educator, Stephanie Moyer.
Institution Type/Description: Historic House: 1896, country home of Joseph Medill, editor of the Chicago Tribune built by architect C.A. Coolidge; house enlarged, 1936 for Col. Robert R. McCormick (grandson of Medill) editor & publisher of the Chicago Tribune.
Hours & Admission Prices: Museum: Feb. Fri.-Sun. 10-4; March, April, Nov. & Dec. Tues.-Sun. 10-4; May-Oct. Tues.-Sun. 10-5. No charge. Parking: $5. Closed New Year's Eve & Day; Thanksgiving & day after; Christmas Eve & Day. &
Attendance: 55,342 (actual)

Whittington

SOUTHERN ILLINOIS ART & ARTISANS CENTER, 14967 Gun Creek Trail, Whittington, IL 62897-1000. Tel.: 618-629-2220. Fax: 618-629-2704.
E-mail: mgalloway@museum.state.il.us
Web Site: www.museum.state.il.us
Key Personnel: Dir., Mary Lou Galloway; Cur., Debra Tayes; Museum Shop Mgr., Romaula Coleman.

Institution Type/Description: Art & Artisans Center.
Hours & Admission Prices: Daily 9-5. No charge. Closed New Year's Day; Easter; Thanksgiving; Christmas. &
Attendance: 39,741

Wilmette

WILMETTE HISTORICAL MUSEUM, 609 Ridge Rd., Wilmette, IL 60091-2441. Tel.: 847-853-7666. Fax: 847-853-7706.
E-mail: museum@wilmette.com
Web Site: www.wilmettehistory.org
Key Personnel: Dir., Kathy Hussey-Arntson.
Institution Type/Description: Local History Museum.
Hours & Admission Prices: Sun.-Thurs. 1-4:30. No charge. Closed national holidays. &
Attendance: 6,000 (estimated)

Winnetka

WINNETKA HISTORICAL SOCIETY, Museum & Research Center, 411 Linden, Winnetka, IL 60093. Mailing Address: P.O. Box 365, Winnetka, IL 60093-0365. Tel.: 847-446-0001. Fax: 847-501-3221.
E-mail: winnetka411@comcast.net
Web Site: www.winnetkahistory.org
Key Personnel: Pres., Charlie Shapica; Exec. Dir., Patti Van Cleave; Cur., Siera Erazo; Cur. Costume, Elizabeth Carlson.
Institution Type/Description: Local History Museum and Archives.
Hours & Admission Prices: Call for hours. Museum & participants of Time Travelers: no charge. Log House: call for admission prices. &
Attendance: 1,200 (estimated)

Zion

PLATEN PRESS PRINTING MUSEUM, 3051 Sheridan Rd., Zion, IL 60099-3243. Tel.: 847-746-8170.
E-mail: platenpress@sbcglobal.net
Web Site: platenpressmuseum.com
Institution Type/Description: Printing Museum.
Hours & Admission Prices: By appointment.

RUSSELL MILITARY MUSEUM, 43363 Old Hwy. 41, Zion, IL 60099. Tel.: 847-395-7020. Fax: 847-395-7025. Facebook: Russell Military Museum.
E-mail: ksonday@db3mail.com
Web Site: www.russellmilitarymuseum.com
Formerly: Kenosha Military Museum
Key Personnel: Dir., Mark Sonday; Museum Shop Mgr., Joyce Sonday.
Institution Type/Description: Military Museum.
Hours & Admission Prices: See website for hours. Adults 13 & over $10, children & seniors $5; children 2 & under no charge. &
Attendance: 20,000 (estimated)

ZION HISTORICAL SOCIETY, 1300 Shiloh Blvd., Zion, IL 60099-2622. Tel.: 847-746-2427 & 872-4566.
E-mail: tr91752@sbcglobal.net
Web Site: www.zionhs.com
Key Personnel: Pres., Carol Ruesch; Vice Pres., Lorna Yates.
Institution Type/Description: Historic House Museum: 1902 Shiloh House, the residence of the founder of the city of Zion.
Hours & Admission Prices: Memorial Day to Labor Day Sun. 2-5; other times by appointment. Adults $5, children $2.
Attendance: 150 (estimated)

INDIANA

(318 listings)

Albion

OLD JAIL MUSEUM, 215 W. Main St., Albion, IN 46701-1115. Mailing Address: P.O. Box 152, Albion, IN 46701-0152. Tel.: 260-740-8932.
E-mail: kirsch@ligtel.com
Web Site: www.rootsweb.ancestry.com/~innchs/index.html
Key Personnel: Vice Pres., Bill Landon; Dir., Carol Kirsch; Pres., Bill Shultz; Bd. Directors, Mary Stolte; Treas., Judy Richter; Dir. & Museum Shop Mgr., Margaret Ott; Bd. Directors, Sondra Luke; Sec., Sarah Knopp.
Institution Type/Description: Historic Building: 1876 Noble County Old Jail & sheriff's residence.

Hours & Admission Prices: Memorial Day to 3rd week in Sept. Sat. 1:30-4:30; group tours by appointment. Adults $3, school children $1; members no charge.
Attendance: 422 (actual)

Alexandria

ALEXANDRIA MONROE TOWNSHIP HISTORICAL SOCIETY, 313 N. Harrison St., Alexandria, IN 46001. Tel.: 765-724-2993.
E-mail: lmaple@att.net
Web Site: alexandriahistoricalsociety.com
Institution Type/Description: Historical Society Museum.
Hours & Admission Prices: Call for hours.

Anderson

THE ANDERSON CENTER FOR THE ARTS, 32 W. Tenth St., Anderson, IN 46016-1409. Mailing Address: P.O. Box 1218, Anderson, IN 46015-1218. Tel.: 765-649-1248. Fax: 765-649-0199.
E-mail: info.taca@sbcglobal.net
Web Site: www.andersonart.org
Formerly: Anderson Fine Arts Center
Key Personnel: Dir., Deborah McBratney-Stapleton; Bd. Pres. (V), Andrew Hopper; Administrative Asst., Cheryl Mitchell.
Institution Type/Description: Fine Arts Center.
Hours & Admission Prices: Tues.-Fri. 12-5, Sat. 10-5, Sun. 2-5. Families $5, adults $2, seniors $1.50, children & students $1; discounts to AAM & ICOM members; Tues., 1st. Sun. of each month, members & children under 4 no charge. Closed national holidays. &
Attendance: 35,000 (estimated)

GRUENEWALD HISTORIC HOUSE, 626 Main St., Anderson, IN 46016-1514. Tel.: 765-648-6875.
E-mail: ghh1873@sbcglobal.net
Web Site: www.gruenewaldhouse.com
Key Personnel: Dir., Jean Whitsell-Sherman; Pres. Bd. (V), David Cagley.
Institution Type/Description: Historic House Museum.
Hours & Admission Prices: By appointment. Adults $5; discounts to AAA members; students & members no charge. Closed Thanksgiving; Christmas. &
Attendance: 750 (estimated)

GUSTAV JEENINGA MUSEUM OF BIBLE AND NEAR EASTERN STUDIES, Theology Bldg., 1123 Anderson University Blvd., Anderson, IN 46012-3495. Mailing Address: 1100 E. 5th St., Anderson, IN 46012-3462. Tel.: 765-641-4445.
E-mail: dtmurphy@anderson.edu
Web Site: www.anderson.edu/jeeninga-museum
Key Personnel: Dir., Dr. David Murphy.
Institution Type/Description: Archaeological Museum.
Hours & Admission Prices: Mon.-Fri. 9-5. No charge; donations accepted. &
Attendance: 500 (estimated)

JESSIE C. WILSON ART GALLERIES, Anderson University, Krannert Fine Arts Center, 1100 E. 5th St., Anderson, IN 46012-3462. Tel.: 765-641-4322. Facebook.
E-mail: talipan@anderson.edu
Web Site: anderson.edu/academics/art-and-design/wilson
Key Personnel: Dir., Tai Lipan; Office Mgr., Robyn Davis.
Institution Type/Description: Art Gallery.
Hours & Admission Prices: Mon.-Fri. 9-4. No charge.

Angola

TRINE UNIVERSITY, GENERAL LEWIS B. HERSHEY MUSEUM, 1 University Ave., Angola, IN 46703-1764. Tel.: 260-665-4162 & 4100. Fax: 260-665-4283.
E-mail: library@trine.edu
Web Site: www.trine.edu
Key Personnel: C.E.O. & Cur., Dr. Earl D. Brooks, II.
Institution Type/Description: Military Museum.
Hours & Admission Prices: Mon.-Fri. 8-4:30; other times upon request. No charge; donations accepted. Closed national holidays. &

Auburn

AUBURN AUTOMOTIVE HERITAGE, INC. DBA AUBURN CORD DUESENBERG AUTOMOBILE MUSEUM, 1600 S. Wayne St., Auburn, IN 46706-3509. Mailing Address: P.O. Box 271, Auburn, IN 46706-0271. Tel.: 260-925-1444. Fax: 260-925-6266.
E-mail: info@automobilemuseum.org
Web Site: automobilemuseum.org
Key Personnel: Exec. Dir., Laura Brinkman; Cur., Jon Bill; Museum Store Mgr., Kelby Park.
Institution Type/Description: Transportation Museum: located in original 1930 Administration Building of the Auburn Automobile Co. A National Historic Landmark.
Hours & Admission Prices: Daily 9-5. Adults $12.50, students $7.50; discounts to groups, AAM, ICOM & AAA members or any member of a recognized car club; children under 6 & members no charge. Closed New Year's Day; Thanksgiving; Christmas. &
Attendance: 44,384 (actual)

HOOSIER AIR MUSEUM, 2822 Cty. Rd. 62, Auburn, IN 46706. Mailing Address: P.O. Box 87, Auburn, IN 46706. Tel.: 260-927-0443.
E-mail: info@hoosierairmuseum.org
Web Site: www.hoosierairmuseum.org
Institution Type/Description: Military History Museum.
Hours & Admission Prices: mid-March to early Dec. Fri.-Sun. 10-4; groups by appointment. Adults $5, students 12-18 $4; students, active military and children 11 & under no charge. Closed Good Friday; Easter; Thanksgiving.
Attendance: 4,400 (estimated)

KRUSE MUSEUMS, 5634 County Road 11A, Auburn, IN 46706. Mailing Address: P.O. Box 1, Auburn, IN 46706-0001. Tel.: 260-927-9144. Fax: 260-927-8043. Facebook.
E-mail: info@dvkfoundation.org
Formerly: Kruse Automotive & Carriage Museum
Key Personnel: Opers. Mgr., Terri Hug.
Institution Type/Description: History Museums.
Hours & Admission Prices: Daily 9-5. Adults $15, seniors 55 & over $10, children 7-12 & retired military $5, active military $4; discounts to groups; WWII veterans & children under 7 no charge. Closed Thanksgiving; Christmas.

NATIONAL AUTOMOTIVE & TRUCK MUSEUM OF THE UNITED STATES, INC. (NATMUS), 1000 Gordon M. Buehrig Place, Auburn, IN 46706-3525. Tel.: 260-925-9100. Fax: 260-925-8695.
E-mail: info@natmus.com
Web Site: www.natmus.org
Key Personnel: Pres. (V), John Pontius; Museum Shop Mgr., John Webb.
Institution Type/Description: Automotive & Truck Museum: housed in c.1923 former Service Building & 1928 former L29 Cord/Experimental Building of the Auburn Automobile Company.
Hours & Admission Prices: Daily 9-5. Adults $8, children 6-12 $4; discount to AAA members; children 5 & under and NATMUS members no charge. Closed New Year's Day; Thanksgiving; Christmas. &
Attendance: 11,347 (actual)

NATIONAL MILITARY HISTORY CENTER, 5634 County Rd. 11A, Auburn, IN 46706. Mailing Address: P.O. Box 1, Auburn, IN 46706. Tel.: 260-927-9144. Fax: 260-927-8043. Facebook.
E-mail: info@dvkfoundation.org
Web Site: www.militaryhistorycenter.org
Formerly: World War II Victory Museum
Key Personnel: Pres. (V), Dean V. Kruse; Mgr. Operations, Judy Burrell; Property Mgr., Eric Seifert.
Institution Type/Description: Military Museum.
Hours & Admission Prices: Daily 9-5. No charge; donations accepted. Closed Thanksgiving; Christmas. &
Attendance: 10,000 (estimated)

Aurora

HILLFOREST HOUSE MUSEUM, 213 Fifth St., Aurora, IN 47001-1211. Mailing Address: P.O. Box 127, Aurora, IN 47001-0127. Tel.: 812-926-0087. Fax: 812-926-1075.
E-mail: hillforest@embarqmail.com
Web Site: www.hillforest.org
Key Personnel: Pres. (V), Judy Ullrich; Dir., Cindy Schuette; Volunteer Coord., Suzanne Ullrich.

Institution Type/Description: Victorian House Museum: 1855-91 Hillforest, Victorian Ohio River Valley mansion.
Hours & Admission Prices: April-Dec. Tues.-Sun. 1-5; groups by appointment. Adults 14 & over $10, students 7-13 $4; discounts to groups & AAA members; children 6 & under and members no charge. Closed major holidays. &
Attendance: 3,000 (actual)

Batesville

BATESVILLE AREA HISTORICAL SOCIETY MUSEUM, 15 W. George St., Batesville, IN 47006. Tel.: 812-932-0999. Facebook: Batesville Area Historical Society.
E-mail: bahs@etczone.com
Web Site: batesvilleareahistoricalsociety.org
Key Personnel: Pres. (V), Jean Struewing.
Institution Type/Description: Historical Society Museum.
Hours & Admission Prices: March-Dec. Thurs.-Fri. 10-2, Sat. 9 to noon. No charge; donations accepted &
Attendance: 1,200 (estimated)

Battle Ground

HISTORIC PROPHETSTOWN, 3534 Prophetstown Rd., Battle Ground, IN 47920-7018. Mailing Address: P.O. Box 331, Battle Ground, IN 47920-0331. Tel.: 765-567-4700. Fax: 765-567-4736.
E-mail: reservations@prophetstown.org
Web Site: www.prophetstown.org
Formerly: The Museums At Prophetstown
Key Personnel: C.O.O., Dris Abraham.
Institution Type/Description: Agriculture Museum.
Hours & Admission Prices: April-Oct. daily 8-5; Nov.-March Mon.-Fri. 9-4. State Park entry fee: cars $6; members no charge. &
Attendance: 35,000 (estimated)

TIPPECANOE BATTLEFIELD MUSEUM & HISTORY STORE, 200 Battle Ground Ave., Battle Ground, IN 47920-7026. Mailing Address: c/o Tippecanoe County Hist. Assoc., 1001 South St., Lafayette, IN 47901. Tel.: 765-567-2147. Fax: 765-567-2149.
E-mail: info@tippecanoehistory.org
Web Site: www.tippecanoehistory.org
Formerly: Tippecanoe Battlefield Museum and Park
Key Personnel: Dir., Kathy Atwell; Museum Shop Mgr., Rick Conwell.
Institution Type/Description: Park Museum & Visitor Center, site of Nov. 7, 1811 Battle of Tippecanoe. National Historic Site.
Hours & Admission Prices: Thurs.-Tues. 10-5, call for winter hours. Adults $5, seniors, AAM & AAA members $4, children & students $2; members no charge. Closed New Year's Day; Easter; Thanksgiving; Christmas. &
Attendance: 35,000 (actual)

Bedford

LAWRENCE COUNTY HISTORICAL AND GENEALOGICAL SOCIETY, 929 15th St., Bedford, IN 47421-3813. Tel.: 812-278-8575. Fax: 812-278-8583.
E-mail: lchgs@hpcisp.com
Web Site: www.lawrencecountyhistory.org
Key Personnel: Pres., Rowena Cross-Najafi; Dir. Library, Joyce Shepherd; Collection Mgr., Glenda Reynolds.
Institution Type/Description: General Museum.
Hours & Admission Prices: Tues.-Fri. 9-4, Sat. 9-3. No charge; donations accepted. &
Attendance: 3,500 (actual)

Berne

SWISS HERITAGE VILLAGE & MUSEUM, 1200 Swiss Way, Berne, IN 46711. Mailing Address: P.O. Box 88, Berne, IN 46711-0088. Tel.: 260-589-8007. Facebook.
E-mail: debbyn@swissheritage.org
Web Site: www.swissheritage.org
Key Personnel: Exec. Dir., Debby Neuenschwander.
Institution Type/Description: Historic Buildings: late 1800s & early 1900s village.
Hours & Admission Prices: Call for hours. Adults $6, seniors 55 & over $5, children 6-12 $3; discounts to groups; children under 6 no charge.

Beverly Shores

BEVERLY SHORES HISTORY MUSEUM & ART GALLERY, INC., 525 Broadway, Beverly Shores, IN 46301. Mailing Address:

P.O. Box 305, Beverly Shores, IN 46301-0305. Tel.: 219-250-2290.
E-mail: lisa.sarsany@gmail.com
Web Site: thedepotmag.org
Key Personnel: Pres. (V), Nancy Nichols.
Institution Type/Description: History Museum.
Hours & Admission Prices: May-Oct. Fri.-Sun. 11-3. No charge; donations accepted. &

Attendance: 1,000 (estimated)

Bloomington

GRUNWALD GALLERY OF ART, INDIANA UNIVERSITY, 1201 E. 7th St., Bloomington, IN 47405-5501. Tel.: 812-855-8490. Fax: 812-855-7498.
E-mail: grunwald@indiana.edu
Web Site: www.indiana.edu/~grunwald
Formerly: School of Fine Arts Gallery, Indiana University
Key Personnel: Dir., Betsy Stirratt.
Institution Type/Description: Art Gallery.
Hours & Admission Prices: Tues.-Sat. 12-4. No charge; donations accepted. Closed spring break; Thanksgiving; Christmas. &

Attendance: 20,000 (estimated)

INDIANA UNIVERSITY ART MUSEUM, 1133 E. Seventh St., Bloomington, IN 47405-7509. Tel.: 812-855-5445. Fax: 812-855-1023.
E-mail: iuam@indiana.edu
Web Site: www.artmuseum.iu.edu
Key Personnel: Dir., David Brenneman; Dir. Devel., Patricia Winterton; Dir. Administration, Carol Dell; Dir. Creative Svcs., Mariah Keller; Lucienne M. Glaubinger Dir. Education, Heidi Davis-Soylu; Registrar, Anita Bracalente.
Institution Type/Description: Art Museum.
Hours & Admission Prices: Gallery houres: Tues.-Fri. 10-5, Sat. 10-7, Sun. noon-5. No charge. &

Attendance: 40,883 (actual)

THE KINSEY INSTITUTE GALLERY, Morrison Hall, 4th Fl., 1165 E. Third St., Bloomington, IN 47405. Tel.: 812-855-7686. Fax: 812-855-8277.
E-mail: libknsy@indiana.edu
Web Site: www.kinseyinstitute.org
Key Personnel: Dir., Liana Zhou.
Institution Type/Description: Health Museum.
Hours & Admission Prices: Mon.-Fri. 1;30-5; other times by appointment. Children under 18 not admitted without parent. No charge. Closed major holidays. &

Attendance: 4,000 (estimated)

MATHERS MUSEUM OF WORLD CULTURES, 416 N. Indiana Ave., Bloomington, IN 47408-3742. Tel.: 812-855-6873. Fax: 812-855-0205.
E-mail: mathers@indiana.edu
Web Site: www.mathers.indiana.edu
Formerly: William Hammond Mathers Museum
Key Personnel: Dir., Jason Baird Jackson; Asst. Dir., Judith Kirk; Registrar, Theresa Harley-Wilson; Cur. Collections, Ellen Sieber; Head Programs & Education, Sarah Hatcher; Facilities Mgr., Kelly Wherley; Mgr. Exhibitions, Matthew Sieber.
Institution Type/Description: General Museum.
Hours & Admission Prices: Tues.-Fri. 9-4:30, Sat.-Sun. 1-4:30. No charge; donations accepted. Closed national holidays. &

Attendance: 35,000 (estimated)

MONROE COUNTY HISTORY CENTER, 202 E. Sixth St., Bloomington, IN 47408-3518. Tel.: 812-332-2517. Fax: 812-355-5593. Facebook: Monroe County History Center.
E-mail: director@monroehistory.org
Web Site: www.monroehistory.org
Key Personnel: Dir., Susan Dyar; Bd. Pres. (V), Linda Williamson; Exhibit Mgr., A.J. Gianopoulos; Collections Mgr., Hilary Fleck; Office Mgr., Rose Merrick; Education Mgr., Dana Duffy; Museum Shop Mgr., Mary Lee Deckard.
Institution Type/Description: History Museum: housed in the former Bloomington Carnegie Library Building.
Hours & Admission Prices: Tues.-Sat. 10-4. Adults $2, children 6-18 $1; discounts to AAM, AAA, AASLH, NARM & Time Traveler members; members no charge. Closed major holidays. &

Attendance: 12,000 (actual)

THE SAGE COLLECTION, 2805 E. 10th St., Ste. 140, Bloomington, IN 47405. Tel.: 812-855-4627. Fax: 812-855-4627.

E-mail: ksrichar@indiana.edu
Formerly: Elizabeth Sage Historic Costume Collection
Key Personnel: Dir., Heather Akou; Cur., Kelly Richardson.
Institution Type/Description: Textile & Costume Museum.
Hours & Admission Prices: By appointment only. No charge; donations accepted.

WONDERLAB MUSEUM OF SCIENCE, HEALTH AND TECHNOLOGY, 308 W. Fourth St., Bloomington, IN 47404-5120. Tel.: 812-337-1337. Fax: 812-330-1337. Facebook.
E-mail: writeus@wonderlab.org
Web Site: www.wonderlab.org/
Key Personnel: Dir., Karen Jepson-Innes; Volunteer Dir., Jeanne Gunning; Museum Shop Mgr., Colleen Couper.
Institution Type/Description: Children's Museum.
Hours & Admission Prices: Tues.-Sat. 9:30-5, Sun. 1-5, 1st Fri. of month 9:30-8. General admission $8; discounts to groups of 10 or more with reservation; children under one, members & ASTC Passport members no charge. &

Attendance: 83,000 (actual)

WYLIE HOUSE MUSEUM, 307 E. 2nd St., Bloomington, IN 47401-4701. Mailing Address: 317 E. 2nd St., Bloomington, IN 47401-4701. Tel.: 812-855-6224.
E-mail: libwylie@indiana.edu
Web Site: libraries.indiana.edu/wylie-house-museum
Key Personnel: Dir., Carey Beam.
Institution Type/Description: Historic House Museum: housed in 1835 home of Indiana University's first president.
Hours & Admission Prices: March-Nov. Tues.-Sat. 10-2. No charge; donations accepted. Closed major holidays.

Attendance: 2,000 (actual)

Bluffton

WELLS COUNTY HISTORICAL MUSEUM, 420 W. Market St., Bluffton, IN 46714. Mailing Address: P.O. Box 143, Bluffton, IN 46714-0143. Tel.: 260-824-9956.
E-mail: jcsturgeon@adamswells.com
Web Site: www.wchs-museum.org
Key Personnel: Pres., James Sturgeon; Vice Pres., Connie Brubaker; Sec., Marcia Hotopp; Treas., Lynn Elliott.
Institution Type/Description: Local History Museum.
Hours & Admission Prices: Sun. & Tues.-Wed. 1-4. No charge; donations accepted.

Attendance: 610 (estimated)

Boonville

WARRICK COUNTY MUSEUM, INC., 217 S. First St., Boonville, IN 47601-1701. Tel.: 812-897-3100. Fax: 812-897-6104.
E-mail: wcmuseum@aol.com
Web Site: www.warrickcountymuseum.org
Key Personnel: Pres., Connie Barnhill.
Institution Type/Description: History Museum: located in 1901 Ella Williams School, in historic district.
Hours & Admission Prices: Tues.-Wed. 1-4, 1st & 3rd Sat each month 11-2; tours by appointment. Adults $2. Closed holidays. &

Attendance: 1,250 (actual)

Bristol

BONNEYVILLE MILL, 53373 County Rd. 131, Bristol, IN 46507. Mailing Address: 211 W. Lincoln Ave., Goshen, IN 46526-3218. Tel.: 574-825-9324. Facebook.
E-mail: info@elkhartcountyparks.org
Web Site: www.elkhartcountyparks.org/properties_locations/ bonneyville_mill.htm
Institution Type/Description: History Museum: housed in mid-1830s mill.
Hours & Admission Prices: May-Oct: Wed.-Sun. 10-5; guided tours by appointment. No charge; donations accepted.

Attendance: 10,000 (actual)

ELKHART COUNTY HISTORICAL MUSEUM, 304 W. Vistula St. (St. Rd. 120), Bristol, IN 46507. Mailing Address: P.O. Box 434, Bristol, IN 46507. Tel.: 574-848-4322. Fax: 574-848-5703. TDD: 574-535-6420.
E-mail: museum@elkhartcountyparks.org
Web Site: elkhartcountyhistory.org
Key Personnel: Mgr., Kelby Rose.
Institution Type/Description: History Museum: housed in the 1st consolidated school in Elkhart County. Listed on the National Register of Historic Places.

Hours & Admission Prices: Tues.-Sat. 9-5. No charge; donations accepted. Closed federal holidays. &
Attendance: 5,500 (estimated)

Brook

GEORGE ADE MEMORIAL ASSOCIATION INC., Hwy. #16, Brook, IN 47922. Mailing Address: P.O. Box 221, Brook, IN 47922-0221. Tel.: 219-275-0895.
Institution Type/Description: Historic House Museum: home of George Ade, humorist, author & playwright.
Hours & Admission Prices: Call for hours. No charge; donations accepted. &

Brookville

FRANKLIN COUNTY SEMINARY AND MUSEUM, 412 5th St., Brookville, IN 47012. Mailing Address: P.O. Box 342, Brookville, IN 47012-0342. Tel.: 765-647-5182.
E-mail: beneker@verizon.net
Key Personnel: Pres., Franklin County Historical Society, Pamela Beneker; Museum Shop Mgr., Martha Shea.
Institution Type/Description: Local History Museum: housed in c.1828-30 original Franklin County Seminary building.
Hours & Admission Prices: By appointment only. No charge; donations accepted.
Attendance: 250 (estimated)

Buckskin

HENAGER "MEMORIES AND NOSTALGIA" MUSEUM AND NATIONAL VETERANS MEMORIAL, Hwy. 57, Buckskin, IN 47613. Mailing Address: 8837 S. State Rd. 57, Elberfeld, IN 47613-8445. Tel.: 812-795-2230 & 2237. Facebook: Henager Museum; National Veterans Memorial; Hollywood Support Group.
E-mail: nationalveteransmemorial@gmail.com
Web Site: www.henagermuseum.com; www.nationalveteransmemorial.org
Key Personnel: Chm. (V), James G. Henager.
Institution Type/Description: History & Military Museum: the National Veterans Memorial headquarters.
Hours & Admission Prices: June-Aug. Mon.-Thurs. 8-7, Fri. 8-5, Sat. 8-4; Sept.-May Mon.-Fri. 8-5, Sat. 8-4. Adults $6, children $3; discounts to members, OLSR members & AAA members.

Cambridge City

HUDDLESTON FARMHOUSE MUSEUM, 838 National Rd., Mt. Auburn, Cambridge City, IN 47327. Mailing Address: P.O. Box 284, Cambridge City, IN 47327-0284. Tel.: 765-478-3172. Fax: 765-478-3410.
E-mail: east@indianalandmarks.org
Web Site: www.historiclandmarks.org
Key Personnel: Museum Dir., Karen Trent; Pres., Marsh Davis.
Institution Type/Description: Historic Building: c.1840 federal style brick, 3-story farmhouse.
Hours & Admission Prices: By appointment. &
Attendance: 3,633 (actual)

MUSEUM OF OVERBECK ART POTTERY, Cambridge City Public Library, 600 W. Main St., Cambridge City, IN 47327-1117. Tel.: 765-478-3335. Fax: 765-478-6144.
E-mail: ccitypl@yahoo.com
Web Site: www.cclib.lib.in.us
Key Personnel: Dir. (V), Jill King; Dir. Library, Vicki Melek.
Institution Type/Description: Art Museum.
Hours & Admission Prices: Mon.-Wed. & Fri.-Sat. 10-12 & 2-5, Thurs. 2-5. No charge; donations accepted. &
Attendance: 100 (estimated)

Carmel

CARMEL CLAY HISTORICAL SOCIETY - THE MONON DEPOT MUSEUM, 211 First St., S.W., Carmel, IN 46032. Tel.: 317-846-7117.
E-mail: carmelclayhistory@yahoo.com
Web Site: www.carmelclayhistory.org
Key Personnel: Dir., Emily Ehrgott; Pres. (V), Dan McFeeley; Museum Shop Mgr., Susan Bock.
Institution Type/Description: Historical Society Museum: depot built in 1883.

Hours & Admission Prices: Museum: April-Oct. Fri.-Sat. 1-4, Sun. 2-4. Archives: Tues.-Wed. 8:30-3. No charge; donations accepted. &
Attendance: 10,000 (estimated)

EVAN LURIE FINE ART GALLERY, 30 W. Main St., Carmel, IN 46032. Tel.: 317-844-8400. Fax: 317-844-8460. Facebook.
E-mail: info@evanluriegallery.com
Web Site: www.evanluriegallery.com
Key Personnel: Dir., Evan Lurie.
Institution Type/Description: Art Gallery.
Hours & Admission Prices: Tues.-Sat. 11-7. No charge. &

THE MUSEUM OF MINIATURE HOUSES AND OTHER COLLECTIONS, INC., 111 E. Main St., Carmel, IN 46032-1823. Tel.: 317-575-9466. Fax: 317-575-0240. Facebook; Pinterest; Instagram.
E-mail: info@museumofminiatures.org
Web Site: www.museumofminiatures.org
Key Personnel: Dir., Suzanne Moffett; Exec. Dir., Elaine Mancini; Collections Mgr., Caitlin Rogers; Museum Shop Mgr., Kathy Birk.
Institution Type/Description: Decorative Arts Museum.
Hours & Admission Prices: Wed.-Sat. 11-4, Sun. 1-4. Admission $10, military and Seniors 65 & over $8, children 3-9 $5; members no charge. Closed New Year's Day; Easter; Memorial Day; Independence Day; Labor Day; Thanksgiving; Christmas Eve & Day. &
Attendance: 6,500 (estimated)

NATIONAL ASSOCIATION OF MINIATURE ENTHUSIASTS, 130 N. Rangeline Rd., Carmel, IN 46032-1743. Mailing Address: P.O. Box 69, Carmel, IN 46082-0069. Tel.: 317-571-8094. Fax: 317-571-8105.
E-mail: name@miniatures.org
Web Site: www.miniatures.org
Key Personnel: Program Coord., Toni Cochran.
Institution Type/Description: Arts & Crafts/Hobby Museum.
Hours & Admission Prices: Mon.-Fri. 9-4, Sat.-Sun. by appointment only. No charge; donations accepted. Closed New Year's Eve & Day; Labor Day; Thanksgiving & day after; Christmas Eve, Day & week. &
Attendance: 500 (estimated)

Cedar Lake

LAKE OF THE RED CEDARS MUSEUM, 7408 Constitution Ave., Cedar Lake, IN 46303-9186. Mailing Address: P.O. Box 421, Cedar Lake, IN 46303-0421. Tel.: 219-374-6157. Fax: 219-374-6157.
E-mail: jimlaud55@gmail.com
Web Site: cedarlakehistory.org
Key Personnel: C.E.O. & Pres. (V), James Laud; Dir., Anne Zimmerman.
Institution Type/Description: Local History Museum: housed in 1920s 60-room hotel.
Hours & Admission Prices: May-Sept. Fri.-Sun. 1-4; other times by special arrangement for groups. Adults $2, children $1. &
Attendance: 1,000 (estimated)

Charlestown

THOMAS DOWNS HOUSE, 1045 Main St., Charlestown, IN 47111-1223. Mailing Address: 8524 State Rd. 403, Charlestown, IN 47111. Tel.: 812-256-5777. Facebook.
E-mail: hart2827@sbcglobal.net
Key Personnel: Dir., Chm. (V) & Museum Shop Mgr., Sue Koetter.
Institution Type/Description: History Museum.
Hours & Admission Prices: Call for hours. No charge; donations accepted.

Chesterton

CHESTERTON ART CENTER, 115 S. 4th St., Chesterton, IN 46304-2344. Tel.: 219-926-4711.
E-mail: gallery@chestertonart.com
Web Site: www.chestertonart.com
Key Personnel: Dir., Judy Gregurich.
Institution Type/Description: Art Gallery.
Hours & Admission Prices: Mon.-Fri. 11-4, Sat. 10-2. No charge; donations accepted. &
Attendance: 3,000 (estimated)

WESTCHESTER TOWNSHIP HISTORY MUSEUM, 700 W. Porter Ave., Chesterton, IN 46304-2205. Tel.: 219-983-9715. Fax: 219-926-6424.
E-mail: museum@wpl.lib.in.us
Web Site: www.wpl.lib.in.us/museum
Key Personnel: Cur., Serena Sutliff.
Institution Type/Description: History Museum.
Hours & Admission Prices: Wed.-Sun. 1-5; other times by appointment. No charge.
Attendance: 4,650 (actual)

Clarksville

FALLS OF THE OHIO STATE PARK, 201 W. Riverside Dr., Clarksville, IN 47129-3148. Tel.: 812-280-9970, ext. 400. Fax: 812-280-7110. Facebook: Falls of the Ohio.
E-mail: park@fallsoftheohio.org
Web Site: www.fallsoftheohio.org
Key Personnel: Park Mgr., Lucas Green; Registrar & Interpretive Naturalist, Alan Goldstein; Interpretive Naturalist, Jeremy Beavin.
Institution Type/Description: Historic Site: State Park includes the George Rogers Clark homesite.
Hours & Admission Prices: Mon.-Sat. 9-5, Sun. 1-5. Admission: 12 & over $9, children 5-11 $7; children under 5 no charge. Closed Thanksgiving; Christmas Eve & Day. &

Columbia City

WHITLEY COUNTY HISTORICAL MUSEUM, 108 W. Jefferson St., Columbia City, IN 46725-1744. Tel.: 260-244-6372. Facebook.
E-mail: wcmuseum@whitleymuseum.com
Web Site: www.whitleymuseum.com
Key Personnel: Dir., Dani Tippmann; Cur., Susan Richey.
Institution Type/Description: Historic Home & History Museum: housed in c.1875-1908 Vice Pres. Thomas R. Marshall home.
Hours & Admission Prices: Tues.-Thurs. 9-5, Fri. 9-12; other times by appointment. No charge; donations accepted. &
Attendance: 9,400 (estimated)

Columbus

ATTERBURY-BAKALAR AIR MUSEUM, 4742 Ray Boll Blvd., Columbus, IN 47203. Tel.: 812-372-4356.
E-mail: 434abmuseum@gmail.com
Web Site: atterburybakalarairmuseum.org
Institution Type/Description: Military History Museum.
Hours & Admission Prices: By appointment. No charge; donations accepted. &

BARTHOLOMEW COUNTY HISTORICAL SOCIETY, 524 Third St., Columbus, IN 47201-6724. Tel.: 812-372-3541. Fax: 812-372-3113.
E-mail: info@bartholomewhistory.org
Web Site: www.bartholomewhistory.org
Key Personnel: Exec. Dir., Julie Hughes; Pres. (V), Amy Kaiser.
Institution Type/Description: Local History Museum.
Hours & Admission Prices: Tues.-Fri. 9-4; other times by appointment. No charge; donations accepted.
Attendance: 4,000 (estimated)

KIDSCOMMONS, COLUMBUS' COMMUNITY CHILDREN'S MUSEUM, 309 Washington St., Columbus, IN 47201. Tel.: 812-378-3046. Fax: 812-373-9085.
E-mail: duane.robbins@kidscommons.org
Web Site: www.kidscommons.org
Key Personnel: Exec. Dir., Ben Wagner.
Institution Type/Description: Children's Museum.
Hours & Admission Prices: Tues.-Sat. 10-5, Sun. 1-5. Admission $7; discounts to groups, military & seniors. &
Attendance: 44,000

ZAHARAKOS MUSEUM, 329 Washington St., Columbus, IN 47201. Tel.: 812-378-1900.
E-mail: info@zaharakos.com
Web Site: zaharakos.com
Institution Type/Description: History Museum.
Hours & Admission Prices: Daily 11-8. Closed New Year's Day; Thanksgiving; Christmas.

Connersville

FAYETTE COUNTY HISTORICAL MUSEUM, 103 S. Vine St., Connersville, IN 47331-2649. Mailing Address: P.O. Box 197, Connersville, IN 47331. Tel.: 765-825-5325.
E-mail: glass1@ydial.net
Key Personnel: Pres. (V) & Museum Shop Mgr., Paulette Hayes.
Institution Type/Description: History Museum.
Hours & Admission Prices: March-Dec. Thurs. & Sun. 1-4; other times by appointment. No charge. &
Attendance: 400

WHITEWATER VALLEY RAILROAD MUSEUM, 455 Market St., Connersville, IN 47331-2073. Mailing Address: P.O. Box 406, Connersville, IN 47331-0406. Tel.: 765-825-2054. Fax: 765-825-4550.
E-mail: officemanager@whitewatervalleyrr.org
Web Site: www.whitewatervalleyrr.org
Key Personnel: Chm. (V), Ryan Scott; Pres. (V) & Museum Shop Mgr., John R. Hillman.
Institution Type/Description: Railroad Museum.
Hours & Admission Prices: May-Oct. daily 9-5. Train Rides (round trip): adults $24, children 2-12 $15.
Attendance: 40,000 (estimated)

Corydon

CORYDON CAPITOL STATE HISTORIC SITE, 202 E. Walnut St, Corydon, IN 47112-1516. Tel.: 812-738-4890. Fax: 812-738-4904.
E-mail: corydoncapitolshs@indianamuseum.org
Web Site: www.indianamuseum.org
Key Personnel: Site Mgr., Bec Riley; Program Developer, Laura Van Fossen.
Institution Type/Description: Historic Site: 1816, first State Capitol Building; Gov. William Hendricks headquarters 1822-1825.
Hours & Admission Prices: Tues.-Sun. 10-5. Adults $6, seniors $5, children $3; discounts to groups; Indiana State Museum members & children under 3 no charge. Closed New Year's Day; Easter; Veterans Day; Columbus Day; Election Day; Thanksgiving; Christmas.
Attendance: 87,800 (estimated)

Crawfordsville

CARNEGIE MUSEUM OF MONTGOMERY COUNTY, 222 S. Washington St., Crawfordsville, IN 47933-2444. Mailing Address: 205 S. Washington St., Crawfordsville, IN 47933. Tel.: 765-362-4618 & 4622. Facebook.
E-mail: carnegie@cdpl.lib.in.us
Web Site: www.cdpl.lib.in.us/carnegie
Institution Type/Description: Interdisciplinary Museum: housed in the former Crawfordsville Public Library; built in 1902.
Hours & Admission Prices: Wed.-Sat. 10-5; other times by appointment. No charge; donations accepted. &
Attendance: 4,850 (actual)

GENERAL LEW WALLACE STUDY & MUSEUM, 200 Wallace Ave., Crawfordsville, IN 47933-2546. Mailing Address: P.O. Box 662, Crawfordsville, IN 47933-0662. Tel.: 765-362-5769. Fax: 765-362-5769. Facebook, Twitter.
E-mail: study@ben-hur.com
Web Site: www.ben-hur.com
Formerly: Ben-Hur Museum (Gen. Lew Wallace Study)
Key Personnel: Dir., Larry Paarlberg; Grounds Mgr., Deb King.
Institution Type/Description: History Museum.
Hours & Admission Prices: early Feb. to early March Tues.-Fri. 10-5; early March to early Dec. Tues.-Sat. 10-5; other times by appointment. Adults $5, students $1; discounts to AAM, AAA & AASLH members; LWS Preservation Society members and children 6 & under no charge. Closed holidays. &
Attendance: 7,000 (actual)

MONTGOMERY COUNTY HISTORICAL SOCIETY AT LANE PLACE, 212 S. Water St., Crawfordsville, IN 47933-2535. Mailing Address: P.O. Box 127, 212 S. Water St., Crawfordsville, IN 47933-0127. Tel.: 765-362-3416. Facebook: Montgomery County Historical Society.
E-mail: info@lane-mchs.org
Web Site: www.lane-mchs.org
Key Personnel: Asst. Dir., Ann Harvey; Cur., Jennifer Rigsby.

Institution Type/Description: Historic House: c.1845 home of Henry S. Lane, governor & senator of Indiana.
Hours & Admission Prices: March to mid-Dec. Tues. 1-4:30, Wed.-Sun. 10-4:30. Adults $5, children under 12 $3; members no charge. Closed all holidays.
Attendance: 2,000 (estimated)

THE ROTARY JAIL MUSEUM, 225 N. Washington, Crawfordsville, IN 47933-1737. Mailing Address: Montgomery County Cultural Foundation, Inc., P.O. Box 771, Crawfordsville, IN 47933-0771. Tel.: 765-362-5222. Fax: 765-362-5222. Facebook: Rotary Jail Museum.
E-mail: contactus@rotaryjailmuseum.org
Web Site: www.rotaryjailmuseum.org
Formerly: The Old Jail Museum
Key Personnel: Dir., Matt Salzman; Pres. (V), Amber DuBois.
Institution Type/Description: Historic Building: housed in an 1882 jail, a rotating circular prison still in working condition and the former living quarters of the sheriff.
Hours & Admission Prices: March-May & Sept. to mid-Dec. Wed.-Sat. 10-3; Memorial Day to Labor Day Wed.-Sat. 10-5. Adults $5, children 5-12 $1; members no charge. Closed holidays. &
Attendance: 5,000 (estimated)

Crown Point

LAKE COUNTY HISTORICAL MUSEUM, Old Lake Courthouse, Courthouse Sq., Ste. 205, Crown Point, IN 46307. Mailing Address: P.O. Box 556, Crown Point, IN 46308. Tel.: 219-662-3975.
Key Personnel: Dir., Bruce L. Woods.
Institution Type/Description: History Museum.
Hours & Admission Prices: May-Oct. Thurs.-Sat. 1-4. Adults $1, children $.50.

Dale

DR. TED'S MUSICAL MARVELS, 11896 S. U.S. 231, Dale, IN 47523. Mailing Address: 911 Hickory Dr., Huntingburg, IN 47542. Tel.: 812-937-4250. Fax: 812-937-4250.
E-mail: mmarvels@psci.net
Web Site: drteds.com
Formerly: House of Mechanical Music Machines
Key Personnel: Dir., Theodore Waflart, M.D.; Pres. (V), Mary Kay Waflart; Museum Shop Mgr., Mary K. Waflart.
Institution Type/Description: Musical Instrument Museum.
Hours & Admission Prices: By appointment for groups of 15 or more. &
Attendance: 1,000 (estimated)

Dana

ERNIE PYLE WORLD WAR II MUSEUM, 120 W. Briarwood Ave., Dana, IN 47847-0338. Mailing Address: Friends of Ernie Pyle, P.O. Box 345, Dana, IN 47847. Tel.: 765-665-3633.
E-mail: president@erniepyle.org
Web Site: www.erniepyle.org
Key Personnel: Pres. (V), Steve Key; Vice Pres. (V), Joanie Rumple; Treas., Roxanne Scott; Sec., Scott Craig.
Institution Type/Description: Visitor Center & Historic House.
Hours & Admission Prices: May-Veterans Day Fri. & Sat. 10-5, Sun. 1-5; other times by appointment. Adults $5, seniors $4, Children 4-12 $3.
Attendance: 8,000 (estimated)

Danville

FRIENDS OF THE HENDRICKS COUNTY HISTORICAL MUSEUM, INC., 170 S. Washington St., Danville, IN 46122. Mailing Address: P.O. Box 226, Danville, IN 46122. Tel.: 317-718-6158.
E-mail: museum@co.hendricks.in.us
Web Site: hendrickscountyhistoricalmuseum.org
Formerly: Hendricks County Historical Museum
Key Personnel: Dir. & Museum Shop Mgr., Gail Tharp; Pres. (V) & Chm. (V), Deanna Hindsley.
Institution Type/Description: History Museum.
Hours & Admission Prices: Fri.-Sat. 11-3; other times by appointment. No charge; donations accepted.
Attendance: 1,800 (estimated)

Decatur

ADAMS COUNTY HISTORICAL MUSEUM, 420 W. Monroe St., Decatur, IN 46733-1622. Mailing Address: P.O. Box 262, Decatur, IN 46733-0262. Tel.: 260-724-3493.
Web Site: adamscountyinhistoricalmuseum.com
Key Personnel: Pres., Max Miller.
Institution Type/Description: Historical Society Museum: housed in c.1903 Charles Dugan Home.
Hours & Admission Prices: June-Aug. Sat.-Sun. 1-4; other times by appointment only. Adults $5; members and children 12 & under no charge.
Attendance: 3,000 (estimated)

Delphi

CARROLL COUNTY HISTORICAL SOCIETY MUSEUM, 101 W. Main St., Ground Fl., Court House, Delphi, IN 46923-1574. Mailing Address: P.O. Box 277, Delphi, IN 46923-0277. Tel.: 765-564-3152. Fax: 765-564-6161.
E-mail: carrollcountycchs@gmail.com
Web Site: www.carrollcountymuseum.org
Key Personnel: Dir., Mark Smith; Pres., Randy Myers.
Institution Type/Description: History Museum & Genealogy Library.
Hours & Admission Prices: Tues. & Thurs.-Fri. 9-4; other times by appointment. No charge; donations accepted. Closed holidays. &
Attendance: 6,500 (estimated)

Dugger

DUGGER COAL MUSEUM, 1080 S. Section St., Dugger, IN 47848. Mailing Address: P.O. Box 501, Dugger, IN 47848-0501.
Key Personnel: Pres., Terry Smith; Dir., James Marlow; Dir., Peggy Marlow; Dir., Joe Smith; Cur., Martha Marlow.
Institution Type/Description: Coal Mine Museum.
Hours & Admission Prices: Coal Festival: Sept. daily 9-9; other times by appointment. No charge; donations accepted. &
Attendance: 500 (estimated)

Dunkirk

THE GLASS MUSEUM, 309 S. Franklin, Dunkirk, IN 47336-1209. Tel.: 765-768-6872. Fax: 765-768-6894.
E-mail: glassmuseumdunkirk@gmail.com
Web Site: www.dunkirkpubliclibrary.com
Key Personnel: Cur., Bob Rawlings.
Institution Type/Description: Glass Museum: housed next to the Dunkirk library.
Hours & Admission Prices: May-Oct. Tues.-Fri. 10-4, Sat. 10-2; Sun. by appointment only. Adults $2; discounts to AAA members & Enjoy Indiana cardholders; children 12 & under no charge. Closed Memorial Day; Independence Day; Labor Day. &
Attendance: 1,200 (actual)

Edinburgh

CAMP ATTERBURY MUSEUM, Welcome Ctr., Hospital Rd., Edinburgh, IN 46124-5000. Mailing Address: P.O. Box 5000, Camp Atterbury, Edinburgh, IN 46124-5000. Tel.: 812-526-1744.
E-mail: int-cajmtcpao@ng.army.mil
Web Site: www.campatterbury.in.ng.mil
Key Personnel: Artifact Responsible Officer, Cpt. Jessica Cates.
Institution Type/Description: Military Museum.
Hours & Admission Prices: Mon.-Fri. 9-4, Sat. 10-2. No charge; donations accepted. Closed federal holidays. &
Attendance: 1,500 (estimated)

Elkhart

MIDWEST MUSEUM OF AMERICAN ART, 429 S. Main St., Elkhart, IN 46516-3210. Tel.: 574-293-6660. Fax: 574-293-6660 (call first). Facebook: Midwest Museum of American Art.
E-mail: info@midwestmuseum.us
Web Site: www.midwestmuseum.us
Key Personnel: Chm. Trustee, Jennifer Abrell; Dir. & Cur., Brian Byrn; Asst. Cur., Randall Roberts.
Institution Type/Description: Art Museum.
Hours & Admission Prices: Tues.-Fri. 10-4, Sat.-Sun. 1-4. Adults $10, students $8; discounts to AAM, AAA & Mobile Guide members; members no charge. Closed New Year's Day; Memorial Day; Independence Day; Labor Day; Thanksgiving; Christmas. &
Attendance: 20,000 (actual)

NATIONAL NEW YORK CENTRAL RAILROAD MUSEUM, 721 S. Main St., Elkhart, IN 46516-3112. Mailing Address: 229 S. Second St., Elkhart, IN 46516. Tel.: 574-294-3001. Fax: 574-295-9434.
E-mail: info@nycrrmuseum.org
Web Site: www.nycrrmuseum.org
Key Personnel: Exec. Dir., Robin Hume.
Institution Type/Description: Transportation Museum: housed in c.1885-1906 New York Central Freighthouse complex.
Hours & Admission Prices: Tues.-Sat. 10-5, Sun. 12-4. Adults $6, senior citizens 61 & over and children 4-12 $5; children 3 & under no charge. Closed major holidays. &
Attendance: 10,000 (estimated)

RV/MH HALL OF FAME & MUSEUM, 21565 Executive Pkwy., Elkhart, IN 46514-9693. Tel.: 574-293-2344, 800-378-8694. Fax: 574-293-3466.
E-mail: rvmhhall@aol.com
Web Site: rvmhhalloffame.org
Key Personnel: Dir., Jeff White; Pres. (V), Darryl Searer; Museum Shop Mgr., Ralph Wilkens.
Institution Type/Description: Industry & Transportation Museum.
Hours & Admission Prices: Winter: Mon.-Sat. 10-4; Summer: Mon.-Sat. 9-5, Sun. 10-3. Adults $10, seniors $8, youth 6-18 $7; discounts to groups; children under 6 no charge. &
Attendance: 30,000 (estimated)

RUTHMERE MUSEUMS CAMPUS, 302 E. Beardsley Ave., Elkhart, IN 46514-2719. Tel.: 574-264-0330, 888-287-7696. Fax: 574-266-0474.
E-mail: info@ruthmere.org
Web Site: www.ruthmere.org
Key Personnel: Exec. Dir., Bill Firstenberger; Collections Mgr., Joy Olsen; Cur., Jennifer Johns; Communications Coord., Carolyn Bonanno; Campus Coord., Carla Riley; Outreach Cur., Victoria Johnston; Membership Coord., Mark Doddington; Grants & Site Mgr., Callista Wert.
Institution Type/Description: Historic House Museum: c.1910 & 1848/1874.
Hours & Admission Prices: Ruthmere Tours: April-Dec. Tues.-Sat. 10-4, Sun. 1-4; tours on the hour; last tour at 3pm. Adults $10, students $4; discounts to AAM & Blue Start Museum members & groups; members no charge. Havilah Beardsley House & Historic District Tour: Tues.-Sat. 10-4, Sun. 1-4. Adults $5, students $2; discounts to AAM & Blue Start Museum members; members no charge. Campus Day Pass: adults $13, students $5, family $40 (5 visitors); children under 5 no charge.
Attendance: 242,070 (estimated)

Evansville

ANGEL MOUNDS STATE HISTORIC SITE, 8215 Pollack Ave., Evansville, IN 47715-6231. Tel.: 812-853-3956. Fax: 812-858-7686.
E-mail: angelmoundsshs@indianamuseum.org
Web Site: www.angelmounds.org
Key Personnel: C.E.O., Historic Site Cur. & Site Mgr., Mike Linderman; Sectional Archaeology Program Developer, Haley Tallman; Museum Shop Mgr., Patrick Thomas.
Institution Type/Description: Archaeology Museum and Pre-Historic Site: Middle Mississippian Indian Site & WPA facility.
Hours & Admission Prices: Tues.-Sun. 10-5. Adults $7, senior citizens $6, children 3-12 $4; members and children 2 & under no charge. &
Attendance: 49,000 (estimated)

EVANSVILLE AFRICAN AMERICAN MUSEUM, 579 S. Garvin, Evansville, IN 47713. Mailing Address: P.O. Box 3124, Evansville, IN 47731-3124. Tel.: 812-423-5188. Fax: 812-426-1885.
E-mail: nmcclure@evansvilleaamuseum.org
Web Site: www.evansvilleaamuseum.com
Key Personnel: Exec. Dir., Lu Porter; Pres. (V), Harold W. Calloway; Museum Shop Mgr., Nancy McClure.
Institution Type/Description: History Museum: housed in one of the nation's first housing projects, Lincoln Gardens; built in 1938.
Hours & Admission Prices: Tues.-Sat. 10-5. Adults $5, children $3; members no charge. Closed New Year's Day; Martin Luther King, Jr. Day; Memorial Day; Independence Day; Labor Day; Thanksgiving; Christmas. &
Attendance: 4,018 (estimated)

EVANSVILLE MUSEUM OF ARTS, HISTORY & SCIENCE, 411 S.E. Riverside Dr., Evansville, IN 47713-1098. Mailing Address: P.O. Box 3435, Evansville, IN 47733. Tel.: 812-425-2406. Fax: 812-421-7509. Facebook: Evansville Museum.
E-mail: info@emuseum.org
Web Site: www.evansvillemuseum.org
Key Personnel: John W. Streetman Exec. Dir., Bryan W. Knicely; Pres., William Bartelt; Dorothy & George Eykamp Dir. Science Experiences, Mitchell Luman; Dir. Begley Art Source, Chris Jackson; Dir. Devel. & Communications, Pat Barmer; Chief Cur. & Virginia G. Schroeder Cur. Collections, Mary Bower; Cur. History, Thomas R. Lonnberg; Ruby C. Strickland Cur. Education, Karen Malone; Registrar, Liz Fuhrman Bragg.
Institution Type/Description: Arts, History & Science Museum.
Hours & Admission Prices: Tues., Wed., Fri. & Sat. 11-5, Thurs. 11-8, Sun. 12-5. Adults $7, youth 4-17 $5; discounts to AAM members; ASTC & museum members no charge. Call for theater prices. Closed New Year's Day; Easter; Independence Day; Thanksgiving; Christmas Eve & Day. &
Attendance: 72,500 (actual)

KOCH FAMILY CHILDREN'S MUSEUM OF EVANSVILLE, 22 S.E. 5th St., Evansville, IN 47708-1604. Mailing Address: P.O. Box 122, Evansville, IN 47701-0122. Tel.: 812-464-2663. Fax: 812-477-4339.
E-mail: info@cmoekids.org
Web Site: www.cmoekids.org
Formerly: Hands On Discovery
Key Personnel: Exec. Dir., Stephanie Terry; Pres., Brian Hicks.
Institution Type/Description: Children's Museum.
Hours & Admission Prices: Tues.-Thurs. 9-4, Fri.-Sat. 9-5, Sun. 12-5. Admission 18 months & over $8; discount to ACM Reciprocal members; members no charge.
Attendance: 51,839 (actual)

MESKER PARK ZOO & BOTANIC GARDEN, 1545 Mesker Park Dr., Evansville, IN 47720-8206. Tel.: 812-435-6143. Fax: 812-435-6140.
E-mail: info@meskerparkzoo.com
Web Site: www.meskerparkzoo.com
Key Personnel: Dir., Erik Beck; Visitor Svcs. Cur., Stephanie Sanderson; Education Cur., Diana Barber; Animal Cur., Susan Lindsey, Ph.D.; Botanic Cur., Paul Bouseman.
Institution Type/Description: Zoo.
Hours & Admission Prices: Daily 9-5. March-Oct. Adults $9.50, children 3-12 $8.50; discounts to AAZPA & other zoo society members; members and children 2 & under no charge. Nov.-Feb. adults $7.50, children 3-12 $6.50; children 2 & under no charge. &
Attendance: 140,019 (actual)

REITZ HOME MUSEUM, 112 Chestnut St., Evansville, IN 47713-1024. Mailing Address: P.O. Box 1322, Evansville, IN 47706-1322. Tel.: 812-426-1871. Fax: 812-426-2179. Facebook.
E-mail: information@reitzhome.com
Web Site: www.reitzhome.com
Key Personnel: Dir., Matt Rowe; Cur., Pam Guthrie.
Institution Type/Description: Victorian Historic House: located in the Riverside Historic District, the 1871 house was built by hardwood lumber magnate John Augustus Reitz.
Hours & Admission Prices: Tues.-Sat. 11-3:30, Sun. 1-3:30; last tour begins at 2:30. Adults $7.50, students $2.50, children 12 & under $1.50; discounts to groups & schools; Reitz Home members no charge. &
Attendance: 12,000 (actual)

WESSELMAN WOODS NATURE PRESERVE, 551 N. Boeke Rd., Evansville, IN 47711-5923. Tel.: 812-479-0771. Fax: 812-479-7573.
E-mail: info@wesselmannaturesociety.org
Web Site: www.wesselmannaturesociety.org
Formerly: Wesselman Park Nature Center
Key Personnel: Exec. Dir., Levy Schroeder; Pres. (V), Joe Theby, IV.
Institution Type/Description: Nature Center.
Hours & Admission Prices: Feb.-Oct. Tues.-Sat. 9-5, Sun. 12-5; Nov.-Jan. Tues.-Sat. 9-4, Sun. 12-4. Adults $5, children 3-12 $3; discounts to groups. &
Attendance: 40,000 (estimated)

Fairmount

FAIRMOUNT HISTORICAL MUSEUM & GIFT SHOP, 203 E. Washington St., Fairmount, IN 46928-1700. Mailing Address: P.O. Box 92, Fairmount, IN 46928-0092. Tel.: 765-948-4555. Fax: 765-948-4259.
E-mail: fhmuseum@live.com
Web Site: www.jamesdeanartifacts.com/index.php

Key Personnel: Fairmount Historian, Ann Warr; Vice Pres., Gale Hikade; Chm. (V), Robert McManaman.
Institution Type/Description: History Museum.
Hours & Admission Prices: March-Nov. Mon.-Sat. 10-5, Sun. 12-5; other times by appointment. No charge; donations accepted. Closed Easter; Thanksgiving. &
Attendance: 7,000 (actual)

Fishers

CONNER PRAIRIE INTERACTIVE HISTORY PARK, 13400 Allisonville Rd., Fishers, IN 46038-4499. Tel.: 317-776-6000, 800-966-1836. Fax: 317-776-6014.
E-mail: info@connerprairie.org
Web Site: www.connerprairie.org
Institution Type/Description: Interactive History Park & Museum.
Hours & Admission Prices: Call for hours & admission prices. Closed Easter; Thanksgiving; Christmas Eve & Day. &
Attendance: 315,455 (actual)

Fort Wayne

ARTLINK, 300 E. Main St., Fort Wayne, IN 46802. Tel.: 260-424-7195. Fax: 260-424-8453.
E-mail: amber@artlinkfw.com
Web Site: www.artlinkfw.com
Key Personnel: Exec. Dir., Amber Recker; Education, Rebecca Stockert.
Institution Type/Description: Art Gallery.
Hours & Admission Prices: Tues.-Fri. 10-5, Sat. 12-6, Sun. 12-5. No charge; donations accepted. Closed New Year's Day; Memorial Day; Independence Day; Labor Day; Thanksgiving; Christmas Eve & Day. &
Attendance: 16,278 (estimated)

CATHEDRAL MUSEUM, Archbishop Noll Catholic Center, 915 S. Clinton St., Fort Wayne, IN 46801. Mailing Address: P.O. Box 390, Fort Wayne, IN 46801. Tel.: 260-422-4611, ext. 3337. Fax: 260-426-2029.
E-mail: jan.stmarys@verizon.net
Web Site: www.diocesefwsb.org
Key Personnel: Dir., Rev. Phillip A. Widmann; Chm. (V), Margaret Venderley.
Institution Type/Description: Catholic Church Museum.
Hours & Admission Prices: Tues.-Fri. 10-2; other times by appointment. No charge; donations accepted. Parking: no charge. &
Attendance: 6,121 (actual)

FOELLINGER-FREIMANN BOTANICAL CONSERVATORY, 1100 S. Calhoun St., Fort Wayne, IN 46802-3007. Tel.: 260-427-6440. Fax: 260-427-6450.
E-mail: mitch.sheppard@ci.ft-wayne.in.us
Web Site: www.botanicalconservatory.org
Key Personnel: Dir., Mitch Sheppard; Museum Shop Mgr., Jane Ford; Business Devel., Linda Miller.
Institution Type/Description: Botanical Garden.
Hours & Admission Prices: Tues.-Wed. & Fri.-Sat. 10-5, Thurs. 10-8, Sun. 12-4. Adults $5, children 3-17 $3; discount to AAA members & AHS reciprocal program members; members and children 2 & under no charge. Closed New Year's Day; Christmas. &
Attendance: 70,000 (actual)

FORT WAYNE CHILDREN'S ZOO, 3411 Sherman Blvd., Fort Wayne, IN 46808-1594. Tel.: 260-427-6800. Fax: 260-427-6820. Facebook.
E-mail: zoo@kidszoo.org
Web Site: www.kidszoo.org
Key Personnel: Dir., Jim Anderson; Dir. Animal Programs, Dr. Joe Smith; Communs., Bridget Pearson; Devel., Amy Lazoff; Operations, John Mikolajczyk; Finance, Ann Barker.
Institution Type/Description: Zoo.
Hours & Admission Prices: late April to mid-Oct. daily 9-5. Adults $14, seniors 60 & over $10.50, children 2-18 $9; discounts to AZA members & reciprocal zoos; children under 2 no charge. &
Attendance: 600,000 (actual)

FORT WAYNE FIREFIGHTERS MUSEUM, 226 W. Washington Blvd., Fort Wayne, IN 46802-3021. Tel.: 260-426-0051. Facebook.
E-mail: fwfmuseum@netscape.net
Web Site: www.fortwaynefiremuseum.com
Key Personnel: Pres. (V), Joel Degitz.
Institution Type/Description: Fire-Fighting Museum: housed in an 1893 structure.
Hours & Admission Prices: Mon.-Tues. & Thurs.-Fri. 10-4, Sat. 10-3. Adults $4, senior citizens & students $3; discounts to groups with reservations; members

and children 5 & under no charge. Closed New Year's Day; Memorial Day; Independence Day; Labor Day; Thanksgiving; Christmas.
Attendance: 3,113 (actual)

FORT WAYNE MUSEUM OF ART, 311 E. Main St., Fort Wayne, IN 46802-1997. Tel.: 260-422-6467. Fax: 260-422-1374.
E-mail: mail@fwmoa.org
Web Site: www.fwmoa.org
Key Personnel: Pres. & C.E.O., Charles A. Shepard, III; Chair, Catherine Hill; Vice Pres. & C.F.O., Lon R. Braun; Vice Pres. & C.O.O., Amanda Shepard; Dir. Children's Education, Alyssa Dumire; Exhibitions Content Mgr., Elizabeth Goings; Registrar, Leah Reeder.
Institution Type/Description: Art Museum.
Hours & Admission Prices: Tues.-Wed. & Fri.-Sat. 10-6, Thurs. 10-8, Sun. 12-5. Families $20, adults $8, seniors 65 & over and students PreK to college $6; discounts to AAM members & last Sat. each month; members & Thurs. 5-8 no charge. Closed New Year's Day; Easter; Memorial Day; Independence Day; Labor Day; Thanksgiving; Christmas. &
Attendance: 100,000 (estimated)

GREATER FORT WAYNE AVIATION MUSEUM, Fort Wayne International Airport, Lt. Paul Baer Terminal, 3801 W. Ferguson Rd., Fort Wayne, IN 46809-3142. Mailing Address: P.O. Box 9573, Fort Wayne, IN 46899. Tel.: 260-478-7146.
E-mail: rogerfortwayne@aol.com
Web Site: www.fwairport.com/air-museum.aspx
Key Personnel: Pres. (V), Barbara Kraegel; Cur., Roger Myers.
Institution Type/Description: Aviation Museum.
Hours & Admission Prices: Mon. & Wed.-Fri. 10-4, Tues. & Sat. 10-2, Sun. 12-5. No charge; donations accepted. &
Attendance: 3,000 (estimated)

THE HISTORY CENTER, 302 E. Berry St., Fort Wayne, IN 46802-2708. Tel.: 260-426-2882. Fax: 260-424-4419. Facebook.
E-mail: histsociety@fwhistorycenter.com
Web Site: www.fwhistorycenter.com
Formerly: Allen County-Fort Wayne Historical Society Museum
Key Personnel: Exec. Dir., Todd Maxwell Pelfrey; Administration Mgr., Kathy Baker.
Institution Type/Description: History Museum: housed in Fort Wayne City Hall; c.1893.
Hours & Admission Prices: Mon.-Fri. 10-5, Sat. & 1st Sun. of month 12-5. Adults $6, seniors & children 3-17 $4; members and children 2 & under no charge. Chief Richardville House: May-Nov. 1st Sat. of month 1-4. Adults $7, senior citizens & students $5; members no charge. New Year's Day; Memorial Day; Independence Day; Labor Day; Thanksgiving; Christmas. &
Attendance: 41,167 (estimated)

MACEDONIAN MUSEUM, 124 W. Wayne St., Ste. 204, Fort Wayne, IN 46802-2505. Tel.: 260-422-5900. Fax: 260-422-1348.
E-mail: mtfw@macedonian.org
Web Site: www.macedonian.org
Key Personnel: Pres. (V), Jordan Lebamoff; Museum Shop Mgr., Lois Levihn.
Institution Type/Description: History Museum.
Hours & Admission Prices: Mon.-Fri. 10-12 & 1:30-4; other times by appointment. Adults $3, youth 13-19 $2; members and children 12 & under no charge. Closed Federal holidays; Christmas week; day after Thanksgiving; snow emergencies.
Attendance: 150 (estimated)

SCIENCE CENTRAL, 1950 N. Clinton St., Fort Wayne, IN 46805-4049. Tel.: 260-424-2400. Fax: 260-422-2899.
E-mail: martin@sciencecentral.org
Web Site: www.sciencecentral.org
Key Personnel: Exec. Dir., Martin S. Fisher.
Institution Type/Description: Science Center.
Hours & Admission Prices: School Year: Wed.-Fri. 10-4, Sat. 10-5, Sun. 12-5; Summer: Tues.-Sat. 10-5, Sun. 12-5. Admission $9, seniors $8; discounts to military & AAA members; members, ASTC members and children 2 & under no charge. Closed New Year's Day; Easter; Memorial Day; Independence Day; Labor Day; Thanksgiving; Christmas Eve & Day. &
Attendance: 93,053 (actual)

SWINNEY HOMESTEAD, 1424 W. Jefferson Blvd., Fort Wayne, IN 46802-4111. Tel.: 260-424-7212.
E-mail: ahuge77@frontier.com
Web Site: www.settlersinc.org
Key Personnel: Pres. (V), Linda H. Huge; Museum Shop Mgr., Kristine Conner.
Institution Type/Description: Historic House Museum: housed in the former home of Thomas & Lucy Swinney, built in 1844. Listed on the National Register of Historic Places.

Hours & Admission Prices: Groups by appointment. Homestead: no charge; donations accepted. Hands Art Series: $60 for 6 sessions; School Living History Program: Adults $5, students $1. &

Attendance: 2,032 (estimated)

Fountain City

LEVI & CATHARINE COFFIN STATE HISTORICAL SITE, Mailing Address: 201 U.S. 27 N., P.O. Box 26, Fountain City, IN 47341. Tel.: 765-847-1691.

E-mail: levicoffincenter@indianamuseum.org
Web Site: www.indianamuseum.org/levi-and-catharine-coffin-state-historic-site
Key Personnel: Site Mgr., Joanna Hahn; Tour Guide, Robyn Zitnick.
Institution Type/Description: Historic House: 1839 Levi Coffin House.
Hours & Admission Prices: Tues.-Sat. 10-5, Sun. 1-5. Adults $10, seniors $8, child $5; discounts to groups of 15 or more and school groups booked in advance.
Attendance: 12,000 (estimated)

Frankfort

CLINTON COUNTY MUSEUM, 301 E. Clinton St., Frankfort, IN 46041-1908. Tel.: 765-659-2030 & 4079. Fax: 765-654-7773.

E-mail: cchsm@geetel.net
Web Site: www.cchsm.org; www.oldstoney.org
Key Personnel: Dir., Nancy Hart; Clinton County Historian, James Miller.
Institution Type/Description: Local History Museum: housed in c.1892 Old Stoney, former Frankfort High School building.
Hours & Admission Prices: Tues.-Fri. 10:30-4. No charge; donations accepted. Closed holidays. &
Attendance: 1,563 (actual)

Franklin

JOHNSON COUNTY MUSEUM OF HISTORY, 135 N. Main St., Franklin, IN 46131-1720. Tel.: 317-346-4500. Fax: 317-736-5451.

E-mail: bcundiff@co.johnson.in.us
Web Site: www.johnsoncountymuseum.org
Key Personnel: Dir., David Pfeiffer; Cur., Emily Spuhler; Librarian, Linda Talley.
Institution Type/Description: History Museum.
Hours & Admission Prices: Tues.-Fri. 9-4, Sat. 10-3. No charge. &
Attendance: 10,000 (actual)

French Lick

BODY REFLECTIONS SALON & HAIR MUSEUM, 448 S. Maple St., French Lick, IN 47432-1083. Tel.: 812-936-7008.

Web Site: www.bodyreflectionsfrenchlick.com/
Key Personnel: Dir., Tony Kendall.
Institution Type/Description: Hair Museum.
Hours & Admission Prices: Tues.-Fri. 9-7, Sat. 9-2. No charge.

FRENCH LICK WEST BADEN MUSEUM, 469 S. Maple St., Ste. 103, French Lick, IN 47432. Mailing Address: P.O. Box 250, French Lick, IN 47432. Tel.: 812-936-3592.

E-mail: flwbmuseum@gmail.com
Web Site: www.flwbmuseum.com
Key Personnel: Dir., Patty Drabing.
Institution Type/Description: History Museum.
Hours & Admission Prices: Mon.-Sat. 10-4. Adults $8, seniors & students $7, children 6-12 $2; members and children 5 & under no charge. &

INDIANA RAILWAY MUSEUM, 8594 W. State Rd. 56, French Lick, IN 47432. Mailing Address: P.O. Box 150, French Lick, IN 47432-0150. Tel.: 800-748-7246. Fax: 812-936-2904.

E-mail: infoirm@indianarailwaymuseum.org
Web Site: www.indianarailwaymuseum.org
Institution Type/Description: Railway Museum.
Hours & Admission Prices: Trains: March-Dec. see website for schedule. Adults $16, children 2-11 $8; children under 2 no charge. &
Attendance: 47,668 (actual)

Garrett

GARRETT HISTORICAL MUSEUM, Heritage Park, 300 N. Randolph St., Garrett, IN 46738. Mailing Address: P.O. Box 225, Garrett, IN 46738-0225. Tel.: 260-357-5575 & 4812.

E-mail: jmohre@mchsi.com
Web Site: garretthistoricalsociety.org
Key Personnel: Pres. & C.E.O., John Mohre.
Institution Type/Description: History Museum.

Hours & Admission Prices: Memorial Day to Oct. Sat.-Sun. 1-4; Winter: by appointment. No charge; donations accepted. &
Attendance: 4,400 (estimated)

Geneva

LIMBERLOST STATE HISTORIC SITE, 202 E. 6th St., Geneva, IN 46740-1004. Mailing Address: P.O. Box 356, Geneva, IN 46740-0356. Tel.: 260-368-7428. Fax: 260-368-7007. Facebook.

E-mail: limberlostshs@indianamuseum.org
Web Site: www.indianamuseum.org/limberlost
Key Personnel: Cur. & Site Mgr. & Museum Shop Mgr., Randy Lehman.
Institution Type/Description: Historic House: Home of Gene Stratton-Porter 1895-1913, author & naturalist.
Hours & Admission Prices: Tues.-Sun. 10-5; other times by appointment. Adults $6, seniors $5, children $3; members of other Indiana State Historic Sites, children under 3 & state museum members no charge. Closed national holidays. &
Attendance: 6,000 (actual)

Greencastle

PUTNAM COUNTY MUSEUM, 1105 N. Jackson St., Greencastle, IN 46135-1072. Tel.: 765-653-8419. Facebook.

E-mail: info@putnamcountymuseum.org
Web Site: putnamcountymuseum.org
Key Personnel: Exec. Dir., Lisa Mock; Pres. Bd., Warren Macy.
Institution Type/Description: History Museum.
Hours & Admission Prices: Tues.-Fri. 1-4, Sat. 10-2; other times by appointment. No charge; donations accepted. Closed Memorial Day; Independence Day; Labor Day; Thanksgiving; Christmas. &
Attendance: 3,000 (actual)

RICHARD E. PEELER ART CENTER, 10 W. Hanna St., Greencastle, IN 46135-1911. Mailing Address: DePauw University, 10 W. Hanna St., Greencastle, IN 46135. Tel.: 765-658-4336. Fax: 765-658-6552.

E-mail: craighadley@depauw.edu
Web Site: www.depauw.edu/arts/galleries
Key Personnel: Dir. & Cur. University Galleries, Museums & Collections, Kaytie Johnson; Registrar Univ. Exhibitions & Collections, Christie Anderson.
Institution Type/Description: Art Museum.
Hours & Admission Prices: Tues.-Fri. 10-4, Sat. 11-5, Sun. 1-5. No charge. Closed university holidays & breaks. &
Attendance: 5,000 (estimated)

Greenfield

JAMES WHITCOMB RILEY BIRTHPLACE & MUSEUM, Riley Home, 250 W. Main St., Greenfield, IN 46140. Mailing Address: Greenfield Parks and Recreation, 280 N. Apple St., Greenfield, IN 46140-2656. Tel.: 317-462-8539 & 477-4340 (Park Office). Fax: 317-477-4341.

E-mail: parks_rec@greenfieldin.org
Web Site: www.greenfieldin.org
Institution Type/Description: Historic House & Museum: housed in 1849 birthplace of James Whitcomb Riley.
Hours & Admission Prices: April-Oct. Tues.-Sat. 11-4; Nov.-March Mon.-Thurs. 10-4. House: adults $4, seniors $3.50, children 6-17 $1.50, school groups $1; children under 5 no charge. &
Attendance: 4,118 (actual)

OLD LOG JAIL AND CHAPEL MUSEUMS, Rte. 40 & Apple St., Greenfield, IN 46140. Mailing Address: P.O. Box 375, Greenfield, IN 46140-0375. Tel.: 317-462-7780 & 0631.

E-mail: hancockhistory@live.com
Key Personnel: C.E.O. & Pres. (V), Greg Roland; Cur. & Museum Shop Mgr., Jim Arthur.
Institution Type/Description: Historical Society Museum.
Hours & Admission Prices: April-Oct. Sat.-Sun. 1-5; other times by appointment. Adults $2, children $1.
Attendance: 800

Greensburg

DECATUR COUNTY HISTORICAL SOCIETY, 222 N. Franklin St., Greensburg, IN 47240. Mailing Address: P.O. Box 163, Greensburg, IN 47240. Tel.: 812-663-2764. Facebook: Historic Society of Decatur County Greensburg.

E-mail: dechissoc@etczone.com

Web Site: www.decaturcountyhistory.org
Key Personnel: Dir., Lynne Saylor; Pres. (V), Chris Harping.
Institution Type/Description: Historical Society Museum.
Hours & Admission Prices: Jan.-March Tues. & Thurs. 10-2; April-Dec. Tues., Thurs. & Sat. 10-2, Fri. 1-4.

Greentown

GREENTOWN GLASS MUSEUM, INC., 112 N. Meridian, Greentown, IN 46936-0161. Mailing Address: P.O. Box 161, Greentown, IN 46936-0161. Tel.: 765-628-6206.
E-mail: greentownglass@yahoo.com
Web Site: www.greentownglass.org
Key Personnel: Pres. (V), Merrill Swisher; Vice Pres., Jeffrey Martin; Sec., Sally Mower; Head Cur., Norma Jean David; Treas., Sharon Oldaker.
Institution Type/Description: Glass Museum.
Hours & Admission Prices: March-May 14 & Nov. Sat.-Sun. 1-4; May 15-Oct. Wed.-Fri. 10-12 & 1-4, Sat.-Sun. 1-4. No charge; donations accepted. Closed Easter. &
Attendance: 2,000 (estimated)

Hagerstown

HAGERSTOWN MUSEUM AND ARTS PLACE, 96 1/2 E. Main, Hagerstown, IN 47346-1213. Mailing Address: P.O. Box 126, Hagerstown, IN 47346-0126. Tel.: 765-489-4005. Fax: 765-489-4005.
E-mail: tom@hagerstownmuseum.comcastbiz.net
Formerly: Nettle Creek Cultural Center
Key Personnel: Dir., Tom Butters.
Institution Type/Description: Historic Building: built in 1880.
Hours & Admission Prices: Feb.-Dec. Fri.-Sun. 1-6; groups & other times by appointment. No charge; donations accepted. Closed major holidays.

WILBUR WRIGHT BIRTHPLACE & MUSEUM, 1525 N. Co. Rd. 750 E., Hagerstown, IN 47346. Tel.: 765-332-2495. Facebook: Wilbur Wright Birthplace & Museum.
E-mail: wilbur@nltc.net
Web Site: www.wwbirthplace.com
Key Personnel: Chm. (V), Charles Fields; Vice Chm., Herbert Weller; Treas., Sara Denny; Museum Shop Mgr., Thornton McKay.
Institution Type/Description: Historic House: c.1867 re-created birthplace of Wilbur Wright.
Hours & Admission Prices: House & Museum: April-Oct. Tues.-Sat. 10-5, Sun. 1-5. Family $10, adults $4, seniors $3, students $2; members no charge. &
Attendance: 10,000 (estimated)

Hammond

SUZANNE G. LONG LOCAL HISTORY ROOM, 564 State St., Hammond, IN 46320-1532. Tel.: 219-931-5100, ext. 306. Fax: 219-931-3474. TDD: 219-852-2232.
E-mail: localhistory@hammond.lib.in.us
Web Site: www.hammond.lib.in.us
Formerly: Hammond Historical Society
Key Personnel: Dir., Rene Greenleaf; Librarian, Amanda Aguilera; Public Information Coord., Linda Swisher.
Institution Type/Description: Local History Repository.
Hours & Admission Prices: Tues. & Thurs.-Fri. 1-5, Wed. 1-9, Sat. by appointment. No charge. &
Attendance: 1,500 (actual)

Hartford City

BLACKFORD COUNTY HISTORICAL SOCIETY, 321 N. High St., Hartford City, IN 47348. Mailing Address: P.O. Box 264, Hartford City, IN 47348-0264.
E-mail: sinuardcastelo3@gmail.com
Web Site: www.bchs.org
Key Personnel: Dir. & Pres. (V), Sinuard Castelo.
Institution Type/Description: Historical Society Museum.
Hours & Admission Prices: April-Nov. Sun. 1-4. No charge; donations accepted. Closed Memorial Day; Independence Day & Labor Day. &
Attendance: 200 (estimated)

Hebron

RAILROAD DEPOT MUSEUM, 125 N. Main St., Hebron, IN 46341. Mailing Address: P.O. Box 679, Hebron, IN 46341. Tel.: 219-996-3192.

E-mail: info@visithebron.org
Web Site: hebronindiana.org/historic-society
Institution Type/Description: History Museum: housed in a former depot; built in 1868.
Hours & Admission Prices: By appointment. No charge; donations accepted. &

Hobart

HOBART HISTORICAL SOCIETY MUSEUM, 706 E. Fourth St., Hobart, IN 46342-4411. Mailing Address: P.O. Box 24, Hobart, IN 46342-0024. Tel.: 219-942-0970.
Institution Type/Description: Historical Society Museum: housed in c.1914-1915 Carnegie Library Building. Listed on the National Register of Historic Places.
Hours & Admission Prices: Sat. 10-12; other times by appointment. No charge; donations accepted.
Attendance: 1,500 (actual)

WOOD'S HISTORIC GRIST MILL, 9410 Old Lincoln Hwy., Hobart, IN 46342-7049. Mailing Address: Lake County Parks & Recreation Dept., 8411 E. Lincoln Hwy., Crown Point, IN 46307. Tel.: 219-947-1958. Fax: 219-945-0452.
E-mail: info@lakecountyparks.com
Web Site: www.lakecountyparks.com
Key Personnel: C.E.O., Jim Basala; Supt. Recreation & Special Facilities, Sasha Mateer; Historic Bldgs. Programmer, Dyan Wheeler-Quilter.
Institution Type/Description: Historic Building: grist mill built late 1800s.
Hours & Admission Prices: May-Oct. Mon.-Thurs. 10-4, Sat. 10-5, Sun. 12-5. No charge; donations accepted. Closed Memorial Day, Independence Day; Labor Day; Columbus Day. &

Huntingburg

HUNTINGBURG MUSEUM, 508 E. 4th St., Huntingburg, IN 47542. Mailing Address: P.O. Box 10, Huntingburg, IN 47542. Tel.: 812-683-2211. Fax: 812-683-5561.
E-mail: webmaster@huntingburg-in.gov
Web Site: www.huntingburg-in.gov
Institution Type/Description: History Museum.
Hours & Admission Prices: Mon.-Fri. 8-5; other times by appointment.

Huntington

HUNTINGTON COUNTY HISTORICAL SOCIETY MUSEUM, 315 Court St., Huntington, IN 46750-2862. Tel.: 260-356-7264.
E-mail: huntingtonhistoricalmuseum@gmail.com
Web Site: www.huntingtonhistoricalmuseum.com
Key Personnel: Dir., Mark Stouder; Pres., Michael Howell.
Institution Type/Description: Historical Society Museum.
Hours & Admission Prices: Wed.-Fri. 10-4, Sat. 1-4. Adults $2; members no charge. Closed Independence Day; Thanksgiving; Christmas. &
Attendance: 3,500 (estimated)

ROBERT E. WILSON GALLERY, Huntington University, 2303 College Ave., Huntington, IN 46750-1237. Tel.: 260-356-6000.
E-mail: mduffer@huntington.edu
Web Site: www.huntington.edu/Wilson-Gallery/
Key Personnel: Dir., Melissa Duffer.
Institution Type/Description: Art Museum.
Hours & Admission Prices: Mon.-Fri. 9-5 and before & after all Merillat Centre for the Arts performances; other times by appointment. No charge. &
Attendance: 3,000

SHEETS WILDLIFE MUSEUM, 200 Safari Trail, Huntington, IN 46750-8049. Tel.: 260-356-9453.
E-mail: sheetswildlife@gmail.com
Web Site: sheetswildlifemuseum.com
Key Personnel: Exec. Dir., Chelsea Heiney; Pres. (V), Bob Zahm.
Institution Type/Description: Wildlife Museum.
Hours & Admission Prices: Wed.-Sat. 10-4. Adults $4, seniors & children $2; discounts to groups; children under 4 no charge. Closed all major holidays. &
Attendance: 791 (actual)

U.S. VICE PRESIDENTIAL MUSEUM AT THE DAN QUAYLE CENTER, 815 Warren St., Huntington, IN 46750-2151. Mailing Address: P.O. Box 856, Huntington, IN 46750-0856. Tel.: 260-356-6356. Fax: 260-356-1455.
E-mail: info@quaylemuseum.org
Web Site: www.quaylemuseum.org
Formerly: The Dan Quayle Center & Museum

Key Personnel: Exec. Dir., Daniel Johns.
Institution Type/Description: History Center: housed in 1919 former Christian Scientist Church; focus on the Vice Presidency & its challenges.
Hours & Admission Prices: Mon.-Fri. 9:30-4:30. Adults $3, children 7-17 $1; children under 6 & members no charge. Closed major holidays. &
Attendance: 6,000 (actual)

Indianapolis

BENJAMIN HARRISON PRESIDENTIAL SITE, 1230 N. Delaware St., Indianapolis, IN 46202-2531. Tel.: 317-631-1888. Fax: 317-632-5488.
E-mail: harrison@bhpsite.org
Web Site: www.bhpsite.org
Formerly: President Benjamin Harrison Home
Key Personnel: Pres. & C.E.O., Charles A. Hyde; Dir. Opers., Margaret Sallee; Vice Pres. Devel., Bethany Gosewehr; Vice Pres. Curation & Exhibition, Jennifer Capps; Vice Pres. Education, Roger Hardig; Dir. Learning Resources, David Pleiss; Vol. Experience Mgr., Lukas Ramey; Special Events & Mktg. Mgr., Delia Robertson.
Institution Type/Description: Historic House Museum: c.1874-75 Benjamin Harrison Presidential Site.
Hours & Admission Prices: Late Jan. to May. & Aug.-Dec. Mon.-Sat. 10-3:30; June-July Mon.-Sat. 10-3:30, Sun. 12-3:30. Adults $10, seniors $9, children 5-12 $5; members no charge. Closed Memorial Day weekend; Labor Day; Thanksgiving; Christmas Eve & Day. &
Attendance: 26,000 (actual)

THE CHILDREN'S MUSEUM OF INDIANAPOLIS, 3000 N. Meridian St., Indianapolis, IN 46208-4716. Tel.: 317-334-4000, 800-820-6214. Fax: 317-921-4019.
E-mail: customerservice@childrensmuseum.org
Web Site: www.childrensmuseum.org
Institution Type/Description: Children's Museum.
Hours & Admission Prices: March to mid-Sept. daily 10-5; mid-Sept. to Feb. Tues.-Sun. 10-5. Adults $23.50, seniors 60 & over $22.50, youth 2-17 $19; discounts to members. Closed Easter; Thanksgiving; Christmas. &
Attendance: 1,200,000 (actual)

CRISPUS ATTUCKS CENTER MUSEUM, 1140 Dr. Martin Luther King Jr. St., Indianapolis, IN 46202-2221. Tel.: 317-226-2432.
E-mail: museumca@ips.k12.us
Web Site: www.crispusattucksmuseum.org
Key Personnel: Dir., Pat Payne.
Institution Type/Description: History Museum.
Hours & Admission Prices: Call for hours & admissions.
Attendance: 5,000 (estimated)

EITELJORG MUSEUM OF AMERICAN INDIANS AND WESTERN ART, 500 W. Washington St., Indianapolis, IN 46204-2775. Tel.: 317-636-9378. Fax: 317-264-1724.
E-mail: msass@eiteljorg.com
Web Site: www.eiteljorg.org
Key Personnel: Pres. & C.E.O., John Vanausdall; Vice Pres. Advancement, Nataly Lowder; Vice Pres. Administration & C.F.O., Susan Lewis, CPA; Vice Pres. Public Programs & Dir. Education, Martha Hill; Vice Pres. Opers, LaMarr Easter; Cur. Contemporary Art, Jennifer Complo McNutt; Dir. Collections, Amy McKune; Vice Pres., Chief Cur. Officer & Gund Cur. Western Art, James Nottage; Hoback Cur. Native American Art, History & Culture, Scott Shoemaker; Assoc. Cur. Western Art, Johanna Blume; Mgr. Membership, Sheila Jackson; Dir. Mktg. & Communs., Bert Beiswanger; Dir. Earned Revenue, Robert Tate.
Institution Type/Description: Art, History & Culture Museum.
Hours & Admission Prices: Mon.-Sat. 10-5, Sun. 12-5; groups by appointment. Adults $13, senior citizens 65 & over $11, children 5-17 & full-time students $7; discount to AAM members, military & groups; members, IUPUI students, and children 4 & under no charge. Closed New Year's Day; Thanksgiving; Christmas Day. &
Attendance: 145,000

EMIL A. BLACKMORE MUSEUM OF THE AMERICAN LEGION, 700 N. Pennsylvania St., Indianapolis, IN 46204-1129. Mailing Address: P.O. Box 1055, Indianapolis, IN 46206-1055. Tel.: 317-630-1200.
E-mail: library@legion.org
Web Site: legion.org/library/museum
Key Personnel: Dir. Library & Museum, Howard Trace.
Institution Type/Description: Military History Museum.
Hours & Admission Prices: Mon.-Fri. 8:30-4. No charge. Closed New Year's Eve & Day; Martin Luther King Jr. Day; Presidents' Day; Good Friday; Memorial Day; Independence Day; Labor Day; Veterans Day; Thanksgiving & day after; Christmas Eve & Day. &

FRANKLIN TOWNSHIP HISTORICAL SOCIETY, 6510 S. Franklin Rd., Indianapolis, IN 46239. Mailing Address: P.O. Box 39015, Indianapolis, IN 46239.
E-mail: franklintownshiphistory@gmail.com
Web Site: fths.org
Institution Type/Description: Historical Society Museum: housed in a former church; built in 1871. Listed on the National Register of Historic Buildings.
Hours & Admission Prices: March-Oct. 1st Sat. & 3rd Sun. 1-4. No charge; donations accepted. &
Attendance: 300 (estimated)

FREETOWN VILLAGE LIVING HISTORY MUSEUM, 625 Indiana Ave., Ste. 200, Indianapolis, IN 46202-3133. Mailing Address: P.O. Box 1041, Indianapolis, IN 46206-1041. Tel.: 317-631-1870. Fax: 317-631-0224.
E-mail: freetown@freetownvillage.org
Web Site: www.freetownvillage.org
Key Personnel: Dir., Ophelia Wellington; Program Dir., Marriam Umar.
Institution Type/Description: Living History Museum.
Hours & Admission Prices: Mon.-Fri. 10-5. Prices vary with program. Closed major holidays. &
Attendance: 17,500 (estimated)

HERRON GALLERIES, 735 W. New York St., Indianapolis, IN 46202. Tel.: 317-278-9419. Fax: 317-278-9435. Facebook: Herron Galleries.
E-mail: mlweintr@iu.edu
Web Site: herron.iupui.edu
Key Personnel: Dir., Max Weintraub.
Institution Type/Description: Art Gallery.
Hours & Admission Prices: Mon.-Tues. & Thurs.-Sat. 10-5, Wed. 10-8. No charge; donations accepted. &
Attendance: 25,000 (estimated)

HOOK'S HISTORICAL DRUG STORE AND PHARMACY MUSEUM, Indiana State Fairgrounds, 1202 E. 38th St., Indianapolis, IN 46205-2807. Tel.: 317-924-1503.
E-mail: info@hooksmuseum.org
Web Site: www.hooksmuseum.org
Institution Type/Description: History Museum: built in 1849.
Hours & Admission Prices: By appointment. No charge; donations accepted.
Attendance: 50,000 (estimated)

HOOSIER SALON PATRONS ASSOCIATION GALLERIES, 711 E. 65th St., #202, Indianapolis, IN 46220-1609. Tel.: 317-669-6051.
E-mail: jmay@hoosiersalon.org
Web Site: hoosiersalon.org
Key Personnel: Exec. Dir., Jim May.
Institution Type/Description: Art Gallery.
Hours & Admission Prices: Call for appointment.

IUPUI CULTURAL ARTS GALLERY, 420 University Blvd., Ste. 148, Indianapolis, IN 46202-5147. Tel.: 317-274-7514. Fax: 317-278-0828. Facebook.
E-mail: cagcc@iupui.edu
Web Site: www.iupui.edu/~cagcc/
Institution Type/Description: Art Museum.
Hours & Admission Prices: Mon.-Sat. 10-7, Sun. 11-7. No charge. &
Attendance: 18,000 (estimated)

IMA - INDIANAPOLIS MUSEUM OF ART, 4000 Michigan Rd., Indianapolis, IN 46208-3326. Tel.: 317-923-1331. Fax: 317-931-1978. Facebook.
E-mail: info@imamuseum.org
Web Site: www.imamuseum.org
Key Personnel: Melvin & Bren Simon Dir. & C.E.O., Dr. Charles L. Venable.
Institution Type/Description: Art Museum & Historic Site: Lilly House - former home of J.K. Lilly, Jr., the late Indianapolis businessman, collector & philanthropist. National Historic Landmark.
Hours & Admission Prices: Gardens & Grounds: daily dawn to dusk. Museum & Gardens: Tues.-Wed. & Fri.-Sat. 11-5, Thurs. 11-9, Sun. 12-5. Adults $18, youth 6-17 $10; 1st Thurs. of month 4-9, members & children 5 & under no charge. Closed New Year's Day; Thanksgiving; Christmas. &
Attendance: 258,000 (estimated)

INDIANA HISTORICAL SOCIETY, Eugene and Marilyn Glick Indiana History Center, 450 W. Ohio St., Indianapolis, IN 46202-3269. Tel.: 317-232-1882; 233-6615 (TDD). Fax: 317-234-0079. Facebook, Instagram, Twitter.
E-mail: welcome@indianahistory.org
Web Site: www.indianahistory.org
Key Personnel: C.E.O. & Pres., Jody Blankenship; Chm. (V), David S. Evans; Vice Pres. Library & Archives, Suzanne Hahn; VPres Business & Opers., Jeffery Matsuoka; Vice Pres. Devel. & Membership, Andrew Halter; Dir. Education & Engagement, Bethany Hrachovec; Dir. External Engagement & Special Initiatives, Marianne Sheline; VPres. Mktg. & Publications, Amy Lamb.
Institution Type/Description: Historical Society & Archives.
Hours & Admission Prices: Tues.-Sat. 10-5. Adults $9, seniors $8, youth 5-17 $5; discount to AAM & ICOM members; members and active military & their families, children under 5 no charge. Library: no charge. Closed New Year's Day; Thanksgiving; Christmas. &
Attendance: 101,100 (estimated)

INDIANA LANDMARKS, 1201 Central Ave., Indianapolis, IN 46202-2656. Mailing Address: 1201 Central Ave., Indianapolis, IN 46202-2656. Tel.: 317-639-4534. Fax: 317-639-6734.
E-mail: info@indianalandmarks.org
Web Site: www.indianalandmarks.org
Formerly: Historic Landmarks Foundation of Indiana
Key Personnel: Pres., Marsh Davis; Exec. Vice Pres., Tina Connor; Honorary Chm., Randall T. Shepard; Chm., James P. Fadely; Vice Pres. Devel., Sharon Gamble; Vice Pres. Preservation Svcs., Mark Dollase; Dir. Southern Rgnl. Office, Greg Sekula; Vice Pres. & CFO, Mary F. Burger; Dir. Northern Rgnl. Office, Todd Zieger; Dir. Eastern Rgnl. Office, J.P. Hall; Dir. Western Rgnl. Office, Tommy Kleckner; Dir. Indianapolis Volunteers & Heritage Experiences, Gwendolen Raley; Dir. Heritage Education & Information, Suzanne Stanis.
Institution Type/Description: Historic Houses.
Hours & Admission Prices: Office: Mon.-Fri. 8:30-5. No charge; donations accepted. Closed legal holidays. &

INDIANA MEDICAL HISTORY MUSEUM, 3045 W. Vermont St., Indianapolis, IN 46222-4943. Tel.: 317-635-7329. Fax: 317-635-7349.
E-mail: edenharter@imhm.org
Web Site: www.imhm.org
Key Personnel: Exec. Dir., Sarah M. Halter.
Institution Type/Description: Medical Museum: housed in c.1896 pathology laboratory.
Hours & Admission Prices: Guided Tours: Thurs.-Sat. 10-4, on the hour, last tour at 3. Adults $7, university students $5, students 18 & under $3; discounts to AAM members; members & children under 6 no charge. Closed New Year's Day; Independence Day; Thanksgiving weekend; Christmas. &
Attendance: 8,000 (estimated)

INDIANA STATE MUSEUM & HISTORIC SITES CORPORATION, 650 W. Washington St., Indianapolis, IN 46204-2185. Tel.: 317-232-1637; 317-234-2447 (TDD). Fax: 317-232-7090. Facebook, Instagram, Twitter.
E-mail: museumcommunication@indianamuseum.org
Web Site: www.indianamuseum.org
Key Personnel: C.E.O. & Pres., Charlie Shock; Chm. Bd., William A. Browne, Jr.; Sr. Research Cur., Paleobiology, Ron Richards; Cur. Geology & Registrar, Peggy Fisherkeller; Chief Cur. Science & Technology, Damon Lowe; Chief Cur. Fine Arts, Mark Ruschman; Cur. Social History, Mary Jane Teeters-Eichacker; Chief Cur. & Research Officer, Susannah Koerber; Cur. Agriculture, Industry & Technology, Todd Stockwell; Mgr. New Media, Leslie Lorance; Dir. Facility Mgmt. & Security, Ron Tolan; Vice Pres. State Historic Sites, Bruce Beesley; Retail Opers. Mgr., Virginia Whitaker; Chief Officer of Engagement, Beth Van Why.
Institution Type/Description: General Museum.
Hours & Admission Prices: Tues.-Sun. 10-5. Adults $14.95; seniors $13.95, college students $12.95, children $9.95; members no charge. Closed Thanksgiving; Christmas. &
Attendance: 325,000 (actual)

INDIANA STATE POLICE MUSEUM, 8660 E. 21st St., Indianapolis, IN 46219-2562. Tel.: 317-899-8293. Facebook.
E-mail: ispmuseum@isp.in.gov
Web Site: www.in.gov/isp/museum.htm
Formerly: Indiana State Police Museum and Education Center
Key Personnel: Cur., Lauren Baker.
Institution Type/Description: History Museum.
Hours & Admission Prices: Tours: Mon.-Fri. 9-3, third Sat. of month 12-4. No charge; donations accepted. Closed state holidays. &
Attendance: 35,000 (estimated)

INDIANA STATEHOUSE, 200 W. Washington St., Indianapolis, IN 46204. Mailing Address: c/o State Capitol Tour Office, 200 W. Washington St., Rm. 220, Indianapolis, IN 46204. Tel.: 317-233-5293.
E-mail: captours@idoa.in.gov
Web Site: www.in.gov/idoa/2371.htm
Key Personnel: Coord., Jennifer Hodge.
Institution Type/Description: Historic Buildings: built 1888.
Hours & Admission Prices: Building: Mon.-Fri. 7:30-5. Tours: Mon.-Fri. 9-3, Sat. 10:15am, 11am, 12pm, & 1pm. No charge.

INDIANA WAR MEMORIALS, 431 N. Meridian St., Indianapolis, IN 46204-1711. Tel.: 317-232-7615. Fax: 317-233-4285.
E-mail: events@iwm.in.us
Web Site: www.in.gov/iwm/
Key Personnel: Pres. Commission, Carol Mutter; Exec. Dir., J. Stewart Goodwin; Administrative Dir., Jessica Sears; Museum Dir., Ethan Wright; Museum Specialist Database, Chase Brazel; Physical Plant Dir., Steve Stiegelmeyer.
Institution Type/Description: Historic Commission & Military Museum: housed in 1927 Indiana War Memorial.
Hours & Admission Prices: Indiana War Memorial Shrine Room & Military Museum: Wed.-Sun. 9-5. Soldiers & Sailors Monument, Colonel Eli Lilly Civil War Museum, Observation Deck & Gift Shop: May-Oct. Wed.-Sun. 10:30-5:30; Nov.-April Fri.-Sun. 10:30-5:30. Colonel Eli Lilly Civil War Museum: no charge; donations accepted. &
Attendance: 250,000 (actual)

INDIANAPOLIS ART CENTER, 820 E. 67th St., Indianapolis, IN 46220-1199. Tel.: 317-255-2464.
E-mail: info@indplsartcenter.org
Web Site: www.indplsartcenter.org
Key Personnel: Pres. & Exec. Dir., Patrick Flaherty; Dir. Education & Outreach, Michelle Winkelman; Dir. Exhibitions & Events, Kyle Herrington; Dir. Devel., Emily Hunter; Dir. Mktg. & Communs., Shannon Bennett; Dir. Finance, Susan Meyer.
Institution Type/Description: Studio Art Teaching Center & Exhibitions.
Hours & Admission Prices: Mon.-Fri. 9am-10pm, Sat. 9-6, Sun. 12-6; hours may vary when classes are not in session. No charge; donations accepted. Closed New Year's Day; Memorial Day; Independence Day; Labor Day; Thanksgiving; Christmas. &
Attendance: 324,451 (estimated)

INDIANAPOLIS FIREFIGHTERS MUSEUM & HISTORICAL SOCIETY, 748 Massachusetts Ave., Indianapolis, IN 46204-1609. Tel.: 317-262-5161.
Web Site: www.indy.gov/eGov/City/DPS/IFD/History/Pages/museum.aspx
Institution Type/Description: Fire-Fighting Museum.
Hours & Admission Prices: Call for hours. No charge; donations accepted. Closed holidays. &
Attendance: 5,000 (estimated)

INDIANAPOLIS MOTOR SPEEDWAY HALL OF FAME MUSEUM, 4790 W. 16th St., Indianapolis, IN 46222-2573. Mailing Address: P.O. Box 24518, Speedway, IN 46224-0152. Tel.: 317-492-8500.
E-mail: imspr@brickyard.com
Web Site: www.indianapolismotorspeedway.com
Key Personnel: Exec. Dir., Elizabeth Smith.
Institution Type/Description: Transportation Museum.
Hours & Admission Prices: March-Oct. daily 9-5; Nov.-Feb. daily 10-4. Museum: adults $10, youth 6-15 $5; children 5 & under no charge. Bus ride around track when not in use: adults $8, youth 6-15 $5; children 5 & under no charge. Closed Thanksgiving; Christmas. &
Attendance: 350,000 (estimated)

INDIANAPOLIS MUSEUM OF CONTEMPORARY ART CLOSED, 216 E. South St., Indianapolis, IN 46204. Tel.: 317-790-5757. Facebook.
E-mail: info@indymoca.org
Web Site: www.indymoca.org
Key Personnel: Exec. Dir., Paula Katz; Dir. Exhibitions, Mike Barclay; Pres., Scott Travis; Sec., Pamela Perry; Treas., Mike Halstead.
Institution Type/Description: Art Museum.
Hours & Admission Prices: Daily 9-7. No charge; donations accepted. Closed holidays. &
Attendance: 25,000 (actual)

INDIANAPOLIS ZOO, 1200 W. Washington St., Indianapolis, IN 46222-0309. Tel.: 317-630-2001. Fax: 317-630-5153. Facebook.
E-mail: info@indyzoo.com

Web Site: www.indianapoliszoo.com
Formerly: Indianapolis Zoological Society
Key Personnel: C.E.O. & Pres., Michael I. Crowther; Deputy Dir. & Sr. Vice Pres. Conservation & Science, Paul Grayson.
Institution Type/Description: Zoo, Aquarium, & Botanical Garden.
Hours & Admission Prices: Prices and hours vary, see website. ৬
Attendance: 1,249,840 (actual)

J.I. HOLCOMB OBSERVATORY AND PLANETARIUM, 4600 Sunset Ave., Indianapolis, IN 46208-3443. Tel.: 317-940-8333.
E-mail: holcombobservatory@butler.edu
Web Site: www.butler.edu/holcomb-observatory/public-tours
Key Personnel: Dir., Dr. Brian Murphy; Assoc. Dir., Richard Brown.
Institution Type/Description: Planetarium & Observatory.
Hours & Admission Prices: See website for hours. Adults $5, children & students under 18 $3.

JAMES WHITCOMB RILEY MUSEUM HOME, 528 Lockerbie St., Indianapolis, IN 46202-3617. Tel.: 317-631-5885.
E-mail: rileyhome@rileykids.org
Key Personnel: Dir., Jim Obergfell; C.E.O., Kevin O'Keefe.
Institution Type/Description: Historic House Museum: 1872 home of James Witcomb Riley; Visitor Center.
Hours & Admission Prices: Tues.-Sat. 10-3:30. Adults $4, students $1; children under 7 no charge. Closed major holidays.
Attendance: 8,000 (actual)

NATIONAL ART MUSEUM OF SPORT, INC., P.O. Box 441155, Indianapolis, IN 46244. Tel.: 317-931-8600. Facebook.
E-mail: info@nationalartmuseumofsport.org
Web Site: www.nationalartmuseumofsport.org
Institution Type/Description: Sports Art Museum.
Hours & Admission Prices: Temporarily closed. ৬

NCAA HALL OF CHAMPIONS, One NCAA Plaza, 700 W. Washington, Indianapolis, IN 46204-2710. Tel.: 317-916-4255.
E-mail: hocmail@ncaa.org
Web Site: ncaahallofchampions.org
Key Personnel: Dir., Mike King; Asst. Dir., Kelly Dodds; Assoc. Dir. External Affairs, Gail Dent.
Institution Type/Description: Sports Museum.
Hours & Admission Prices: March-Dec. Tues.-Sat. 10-5, Sun. 12-5. Jan.-Feb. Wed.-Sat. 10-5, Sun. 12-5. Adults $5, senior citizens 65 & over and youth 6-18 $3; children under 6 no charge. ৬
Attendance: 53,556 (actual)

RHYTHM! DISCOVERY CENTER, 110 W. Washington St., Ste. A, Indianapolis, IN 46204-3423. Tel.: 317-275-9030. Fax: 317-974-4499. Facebook: Rhythm! Discovery Center.
E-mail: rhythm@pas.org
Web Site: www.rhythmdiscoverycenter.org
Formerly: Percussive Arts Society Museum
Key Personnel: Dir., Joshua Simonds; Pres. (V), Dr. Brian Zator.
Institution Type/Description: Musical Instruments Museum.
Hours & Admission Prices: May-Aug. Mon. & Thurs.-Sat. 10-5, Wed. 12-7, Sun. 12-5; Sept.-April Mon. & Wed. Sat. 10-5, Sun. 12-5. Adults $12, students $9, seniors $8, children 6-16 $6; children 5 & under and members no charge. Closed New Year's Day; Easter; Thanksgiving; Christmas. ৬
Attendance: 18,000 (estimated)

Jamestown

JACKSON TOWNSHIP HISTORICAL SOCIETY, 41 W. Main St., Jamestown, IN 46147. Mailing Address: P.O. Box 297, Jamestown, IN 46147-0297. Tel.: 765-676-5891.
Institution Type/Description: Historical Society Museum.
Hours & Admission Prices: Call for hours. No charge; donations accepted. ৬
Attendance: 100 (estimated)

Jasper

DUBOIS COUNTY MUSEUM, 2704 N. Newton St., Jasper, IN 47546. Tel.: 812-634-7733.
E-mail: mhayes@duboiscountymuseum.org
Web Site: duboiscountymuseum.org
Key Personnel: Pres., Mary Ann Hayes.
Institution Type/Description: History Museum.

Hours & Admission Prices: Tues.-Fri. 10-2, Sat. 10-4, Sun. 1-4. Adults $5, high school students $3, elementary & middle school students $2; children under 4 no charge. ৬
Attendance: 12,000 (estimated)

INDIANA BASEBALL HALL OF FAME, Vincennes Univ. - Jasper Ruxer Student Ctr., 851 College Ave., Jasper, IN 47546. Mailing Address: 1436 Leopold St., Jasper, IN 47546-2117. Tel.: 812-482-2262. Fax: 812-482-1982.
E-mail: rajahoward@psci.net
Web Site: indbaseballhalloffame.org
Institution Type/Description: Hall of Fame.
Hours & Admission Prices: mid-May to mid-Aug. daily 11-3; mid-Aug. to mid-May Thurs.-Sun. 11-3. Adults 13 & over $4, children 5-12 $3, senior citizens 60 & over $2; children 4 & under no charge. ৬

KREMPP GALLERY, 951 College Ave., Jasper, IN 47546-9382. Tel.: 812-482-3070. Fax: 812-634-6997.
E-mail: jasperarts@jasperindiana.gov
Web Site: www.jasperarts.org
Key Personnel: Dir., Kyle Rupert.
Institution Type/Description: Art Center.
Hours & Admission Prices: Mon.-Wed. & Fri. 8:30-5, Thurs. 8:30-7. No charge; donations accepted. ৬
Attendance: 40,000 (estimated)

Jeffersonville

HOWARD STEAMBOAT MUSEUM AND MANSION, 1101 E. Market St., Jeffersonville, IN 47130-4333. Mailing Address: P.O. Box 606, Jeffersonville, IN 47131-0606. Tel.: 812-283-3728.
E-mail: hsmsteam@aol.com
Web Site: www.howardsteamboatmuseum.org
Formerly: Howard Steamboat Museum, Inc.
Key Personnel: Dir., Keith Norrington; Pres. (V), Roger Fisher; Admin. & Museum Shop Mgr., Travis Vasconcelos.
Institution Type/Description: Historic House Museum: 1894 home of Edmonds J. Howard, son of James E. Howard, founder of the Howard Shipyards 1834.
Hours & Admission Prices: Tues.-Sat. 10-4, Sun. 1-4; last tour at 3pm. Adults $7; discounts to groups, students, seniors, military, AARP& AAA members; under 6 & members no charge. Closed most holidays.
Attendance: 10,000 (estimated)

SCHIMPFF'S CONFECTIONERY MUSEUM, 347 Spring St., Jeffersonville, IN 47130. Tel.: 812-283-8367. Fax: 812-288-2229.
E-mail: info@schimpffs.com
Web Site: schimpff.com
Key Personnel: Owner, Jill Schimpff.
Institution Type/Description: Candy Museum.
Hours & Admission Prices: Mon.-Sat. 10-5; groups tours by appointment. Closed New Year's Eve & Day; Memorial Day, Independence Day; Labor Day; Thanksgiving; Christmas Day & week.

Kendallyille

MID-AMERICA WINDMILL MUSEUM, 732 S. Allen Chapel Rd., Kendallville, IN 46755-3220. Mailing Address: P.O. Box 5048, Kendallville, IN 46755-5048. Tel.: 260-347-2334.
E-mail: choward4912@gmail.com
Web Site: www.midamericawindmillmuseum.org
Key Personnel: Dir. & Chm. (V), Mike Harkey; Pres. (V), Christine Howard; Museum Shop Mgr., JoAnn Burke.
Institution Type/Description: Technology Museum.
Hours & Admission Prices: April-Nov. Tues.-Fri. 10-4, Sat. 10-5, Sun. 1-4. Adults $5, senior citizens $4, students $3z; children under 6 no charge. ৬
Attendance: 1,350 (estimated)

Knox

STARKE COUNTY HISTORICAL SOCIETY, 401 S. Main St., Knox, IN 46534. Tel.: 574-772-5393.
E-mail: vendlr@yahoo.com
Web Site: www.starkehistory.com
Key Personnel: Pres., Ron Vendl; Vice Pres., Jim Shilling.
Institution Type/Description: Historical Society Museum.
Hours & Admission Prices: Tues.-Fri. 12-4. No charge; donations accepted.
Attendance: 900 (estimated)

Kokomo

AUTOMOTIVE HERITAGE MUSEUM, 1500 N. Reed Rd., U.S. 31 N., Kokomo, IN 46901-2592. Tel.: 765-454-9999. Fax: 765-454-9956.
E-mail: jsgkphone@yahoo.com
Web Site: www.kokomoautomotivemuseum.org
Key Personnel: Gen. Mgr., James Parsons.
Institution Type/Description: Automobile Museum.
Hours & Admission Prices: Tues.-Sun. 10-4; groups by appointment. Adults $5, seniors $4, children 7-14 $2.

ELWOOD HAYNES MUSEUM, 1915 S. Webster St., Kokomo, IN 46902-2040. Tel.: 765-456-7500. Fax: 765-456-7577.
E-mail: kfrazer@cityofkokomo.org
Key Personnel: Cur., Pete Kelley.
Institution Type/Description: Industrial Museum; housed in 1915 home of Elwood Haynes.
Hours & Admission Prices: Tues.-Sat. 11-4, Sun. 1-4. No charge; donations accepted. Closed most holidays. &
Attendance: 4,000 (estimated)

HOWARD COUNTY HISTORICAL MUSEUM, 1200 W. Sycamore St., Kokomo, IN 46901-4386. Tel.: 765-452-4314. Fax: 765-452-4581.
E-mail: info@howardcountymuseum.org
Web Site: howardcountymuseum.org
Key Personnel: Exec. Dir., Dave Broman.
Institution Type/Description: History Museum & Historic House.
Hours & Admission Prices: Museum: Feb.-Dec. Tues.-Sun. 1-4. Adults $10, students 18 & under $5; discounts to senior tour groups; members no charge. Closed national holidays. &
Attendance: 10,000 (estimated)

INDIANA UNIVERSITY KOKOMO ART GALLERY, 2300 S. Washington St., Kokomo, IN 46902-3557. Tel.: 765-455-9523.
E-mail: gallery2@iuk.edu
Web Site: www.iuk.edu/admin-services/gallery/
Key Personnel: Gallery Dir., Tara Scott.
Institution Type/Description: Art Gallery.
Hours & Admission Prices: Mon. 10-2, Tues. & Thurs. 10-4, Wed. 9-6, Sat. 12-4. No charge.

KAA ART CENTER, 525 W. Ricketts St., Kokomo, IN 46902-2029. Tel.: 765-457-9480.
E-mail: bwanke1@juno.com
Web Site: www.kaaonline.org
Formerly: Kokomo Art Center
Key Personnel: Dir., Chm. (V) & Volunteer Coord., Elaine Wanke; Volunteer Coord., Leslie Wysong; Pres. (V), Cheryl Sullivan; Bd. Member, Colette Inderhees.
Institution Type/Description: Art Center.
Hours & Admission Prices: House Tours: Feb.-Nov. Tues.-Sat. 1-4. No charge; donations accepted. Closed Labor Day; Memorial Day; Independence Day; Good Friday; Easter weekend; Thanksgiving. &
Attendance: 450 (estimated)

La Porte

HESSTON STEAM MUSEUM, 1201 E. 1000 N., La Porte, IN 46350-8642. Tel.: 219-778-2783.
E-mail: ted.rita@hesston.org
Web Site: www.hesston.org
Institution Type/Description: History Museum.
Hours & Admission Prices: Museum: Sat.-Sun. & holidays 11:30-5. No charge. Train Rides: Memorial Day to Labor Day Sat.-Sun. & holidays 12-5. Adults $5, children over 3 $3; children under 3 no charge.

LA PORTE COUNTY HISTORICAL SOCIETY MUSEUM, 2405 Indiana Ave., Ste. 1, La Porte, IN 46350-6063. Tel.: 219-324-6767. Fax: 219-324-9029. Facebook: La Porte County Historical Society Museum.
E-mail: info@laportecountyhistory.org
Web Site: www.laportecountyhistory.org
Key Personnel: Pres., Bruce R. Johnson; Cur., Susie Richter; Museum Shop Mgr. & Asst. Cur., Janet Sikorski.
Institution Type/Description: History Museum.
Hours & Admission Prices: Tues.-Sat. 10-4:30. Adults $5, seniors $4; members, children under 18 & Time Travelers no charge. Closed national holidays. &
Attendance: 7,634 (actual)

LaGrange

LAGRANGE COUNTY HISTORICAL SOCIETY, INC., 109 S. High St., LaGrange, IN 46761. Mailing Address: P.O. Box 134, LaGrange, IN 46761-0134. Tel.: 260-463-3763; 350-8561 (cell).
E-mail: blmccoy2@yahoo.com
Institution Type/Description: Historical Society Museum.
Hours & Admission Prices: By appointment only. No charge; donations accepted.
Attendance: 500 (estimated)

Lafayette

ART MUSEUM OF GREATER LAFAYETTE, 102 S. 10th St., Lafayette, IN 47905-1173. Tel.: 765-742-1128. Fax: 765-742-1120.
E-mail: ksmith@artlafayette.org
Web Site: www.artlafayette.org
Formerly: Greater Lafayette Museum
Key Personnel: Exec. Dir., Kendall Smith, II; Cur. Collections & Exhibitions, Michael Crowthers; Museum Admin., Glenda McClatchey.
Institution Type/Description: Art Museum.
Hours & Admission Prices: Daily 11-4. No charge; donation accepted. Closed New Year's Day; Memorial Day; Independence Day; Labor Day; Thanksgiving; Christmas Eve & Day. &
Attendance: 16,500 (actual)

COLUMBIAN PARK ZOO, 1915 Scott St., Lafayette, IN 47904-2929. Tel.: 765-807-1540. Fax: 765-807-1547.
E-mail: claufman@city.lafayette.in.us
Web Site: www.lafayette.in.gov/zoo
Key Personnel: Zoo Dir., Dana Rhodes; Asst. Zoo Dir., Noah Shields.
Institution Type/Description: Zoo.
Hours & Admission Prices: mid-April to late May & mid-Aug. to mid-Oct. daily 10-4:30; late May to mid-Aug. daily 10-7. No charge. &
Attendance: 75,000 (estimated)

IMAGINATION STATION, 600 N. 4th St., Lafayette, IN 47901. Tel.: 765-420-7780. Fax: 765-420-8260.
E-mail: info@imagination-station.org
Web Site: www.imagination-station.org
Institution Type/Description: Children's Museum.
Hours & Admission Prices: Tues.-Fri. 10-2, Sat. 10-3, Sun. 2-5. Admission $5; members & children under 2 no charge.

Lawrenceburg

DEARBORN COUNTY HISTORICAL SOCIETY, 508 W. High St., Lawrenceburg, IN 47025-1916. Tel.: 812-537-4075.
E-mail: deahistory@embarqmail.com
Web Site: www.rootsweb.ancestry.com~indbchs
Key Personnel: Pres. (V), Charles A. Whiting, Jr.
Institution Type/Description: Historical Society Museum.
Hours & Admission Prices: Mon.-Fri. 1-4; other times by appointment. No charge; donations accepted. Closed holidays.
Attendance: 900 (estimated)

Lebanon

CRAGUN HOUSE, 404 W. Main St., Lebanon, IN 46052. Mailing Address: P.O. Box 141, Lebanon, IN 46052-0140. Tel.: 765-483-9414.
E-mail: cragunhouse@mymetronet.net
Web Site: www.boonecountyhistorical.org/the-cragun-house.html
Institution Type/Description: Historic House: built in 1893.
Hours & Admission Prices: Call for hours.

Liberty

UNION COUNTY HISTORICAL MUSEUM, One Railroad St. N., Liberty, IN 47353. Mailing Address: P.O. Box 143, Liberty, IN 47353-0143. Tel.: 765-458-8928.
E-mail: jk2083@frontier.com
Key Personnel: Vice Pres., Jon Walton.
Institution Type/Description: History Museum.
Hours & Admission Prices: Call for hours. No charge; donations accepted. &
Attendance: 200 (estimated)

Ligonier

LIGONIER HISTORICAL MUSEUM, 503 S. Main St., Ligonier, IN 46767. Mailing Address: 300 S. Main St., Ligonier, IN 46767. Tel.: 260-894-7580 & 4511. Facebook.
Web Site: www.ligoniertemple.blogspot.com
Institution Type/Description: History Museum.
Hours & Admission Prices: May-Nov. Tues. & Sat.-Sun. 1-4; other times by appointment. No charge.

STONE'S TRACE HISTORICAL SOCIETY, State Rd. 5 & U.S. 33, Ligonier, IN 46767-9603. Mailing Address: 1588 N. 650 W., Kimmell, IN 46760. Tel.: 574-529-3693. Fax: 260-635-1313.
E-mail: rogertransport@hotmail.com
Web Site: www.stonestrace.com
Key Personnel: Pres., Jim Hossler.
Institution Type/Description: Historic Building Museum: 1839 Stone's Tavern.
Hours & Admission Prices: June-Sept. Sat. 9-5; Sun. 10-4; other times by appointment. Adults $7, Children 11 & under free; donations accepted. Sept. Crafts Festival Sat.-Sun. after Labor Day 10-5. Adults $5, children under 12 no charge.
Attendance: 5,000 (estimated)

Lincoln City

LINCOLN BOYHOOD NATIONAL MEMORIAL, 3027 E. South St., Lincoln City, IN 47552. Mailing Address: P.O. Box 1816, Lincoln City, IN 47552-1816. Tel.: 812-937-4541. Fax: 812-937-9929. TDD: 812-937-4541.
E-mail: libo_superintendent@nps.gov
Web Site: www.nps.gov/libo
Key Personnel: Supt., Kendell Thompson; Chief of Interpretation & Resource Management, Mike Capps.
Institution Type/Description: Park History Museum.
Hours & Admission Prices: Daily 8-5. Family $5, adults $3. Closed New Year's Day; Thanksgiving; Christmas. ♿

Attendance: 150,000 (actual)

LINCOLN STATE PARK & COLONEL JONES HOME, Hwy. 162, Lincoln City, IN 47552. Mailing Address: Lincoln State Park, P.O. Box 216, Lincoln City, IN 47552-0216. Tel.: 812-937-4710 & 2802. Fax: 812-937-4833.
E-mail: mcrews@dnr.in.gov
Web Site: www.in.gov/dnr/parklake/parks/lincoln.html
Formerly: Colonel William Jones State Historic Site/Lincoln State Park & Colonel Jones Home
Key Personnel: Site Mgr., Michael Crews.
Institution Type/Description: Historic House: c.1834 Colonel William Jones House & property.
Hours & Admission Prices: May 10-Oct. Sat.-Sun. 11-4; other times by appointment. Suggested Donation: adults $2.
Attendance: 2,000 (actual)

Linden

LINDEN DEPOT MUSEUM, 520 N. Main St., Linden, IN 47955-0061. Mailing Address: P.O. Box 154, Linden, IN 47955-0154. Tel.: 765-339-7245.
E-mail: lindendepotmuseum@gmail.com
Web Site: lindendepotmuseum.org
Key Personnel: Pres., Gary Vierk; Vice Pres., Elizabeth Hendrickson; Sec., Troy Deckard.
Institution Type/Description: Historic railroad depot museum.
Hours & Admission Prices: April-Oct. Fri.-Sun. noon-5. Adults $5, children 12 & under $1, members no charge. Christmas Open House: Thanksgiving to New Year's Day. Sat.-Sun. 12-5.
Attendance: 2,000 (estimated)

Logansport

CASS COUNTY HISTORICAL SOCIETY, 1004 E. Market St., Logansport, IN 46947-3560. Tel.: 574-753-3866. Fax: 574-722-9267.
E-mail: cchistoricalsoc@frontier.com
Web Site: www.casshistory.org
Key Personnel: Pres., Jeanie Jones; Exec. Dir., Thelma Conrad; Vice Pres., Jeff Stuart; Sec., Barbara Stein; Treas., Mike Stajduhar.
Institution Type/Description: Historical Society: housed in 1853 Jerolaman-Long House.

Hours & Admission Prices: Feb.-Dec. Tues.-Sat. 1-5; other times by appointment. No charge; donations accepted. Closed legal holidays.
Attendance: 2,500 (estimated)

COLE CLOTHING MUSEUM, 900 E. Broadway, Logansport, IN 46947-3162. Tel.: 574-753-4058.
Institution Type/Description: Clothing Museum.
Hours & Admission Prices: April-Dec. Tues.-Fri. 1-4; other times by appointment. Adults $3, children $1.50.

INDIANA TRANSPORTATION MUSEUM, Ivy Tech Campus, 1 Don Heckard Way, Logansport, IN 46947. Tel.: 317-773-6000 & 776-7887. Fax: 317-770-1902.
E-mail: info@itm.org
Web Site: www.itm.org
Key Personnel: Dir. Rail Operations, Paul Meister; Chm., John McNichol.
Institution Type/Description: Rail Transportation and Technology Museum: office housed in 1930 railroad station from Hobbs, IN.
Hours & Admission Prices: April-Oct. Sat.-Sun. 11-4. Adults $3, children 3-12 $2; children 2 & under and members no charge. Excursion fares: call for information.
Attendance: 40,000 (estimated)

Madison

HISTORIC ELEUTHERIAN COLLEGE - HOYT HOUSE, 6927 W. State Rd. 250, Madison, IN 47250. Mailing Address: P.O. Box 705, Madison, IN 47250-0705. Tel.: 812-866-7129.
E-mail: eleutheriancollege2012@hotmail.com
Institution Type/Description: Historic House Museum: built in 1848.
Hours & Admission Prices: By appointment. Admission $3.

HISTORIC MADISON, INC., 500 West St., Madison, IN 47250-3399. Tel.: 812-265-2967.
E-mail: hmi@historicmadisoninc.com
Web Site: www.historicmadisoninc.com
Key Personnel: Exec. Dir. & Pres., John M. Staicer.
Institution Type/Description: Preservation Project and Historic House Museum.
Hours & Admission Prices: Sullivan House & Dr. Wm. Hutchings Office: May-Oct. Sun. & Tues.-Thurs. 1-4:30, Mon. & Sat. 10-4:30. Francis Costigan House: May-Oct. Mon. 10-4:30, Sat.-Sun. 1-4:30. Schroeder Saddletree Factory Museum: May-Oct. Mon. 10-4:30, Sat.-Sun. 1-4:30. Adults $3; students & members no charge.

JEFFERSON COUNTY HISTORICAL SOCIETY, INC., 615 W. First St., Madison, IN 47250-3731. Tel.: 812-265-2335. Fax: 812-273-5023.
E-mail: info@jchshc.org
Web Site: www.jchshc.org
Key Personnel: Dir., John Nyberg; Museum Shop Mgr., Diana Hand.
Institution Type/Description: County History Museum & Madison Railroad Station: built in 1895.
Hours & Admission Prices: mid-March to mid-Dec. Tues.-Sat. 10-4:30. Adults $6; discounts to military & seniors. ♿
Attendance: 18,000 (actual)

LANIER MANSION STATE HISTORIC SITE, 601 W. First St., Madison, IN 47250-3731. Tel.: 812-625-3526. Fax: 812-265-3501.
E-mail: laniermansionshs@indianamuseum.org
Web Site: www.indianamuseum.org/explore/lanier-mansion
Formerly: Lanier State Historic Site
Institution Type/Description: Historic House and Site: 1844 Greek revival home of J.F.D. Lanier.
Hours & Admission Prices: Tues.-Sun. 10-5. Adults $10, seniors 60 & over $8, children 3-12 $5; discount to school groups; members & children under 3 no charge. Closed most state holidays.
Attendance: 10,162 (actual)

SCHOFIELD HOUSE, 217 W. Second St., Madison, IN 47250-3722. Mailing Address: P.O. Box 44210, 525 N. Illinois St., Indianapolis, IN 42244-0210. Tel.: 812-265-4759.
E-mail: ginglespgc@comcast.net
Institution Type/Description: Historic Tavern House: c.1816.
Hours & Admission Prices: Mon.-Sat. 9:30-4, Sun. 12:30-4. No charge.

SHREWSBURY-WINDLE HOUSE, 301 W. First St., Madison, IN 47250-3705. Mailing Address: Historic Madison Inc., 500 West St., Madison, IN 47250. Tel.: 812-265-2967.
Web Site: historicmadisoninc.com

Key Personnel: Exec. Dir., John M. Staicer.
Institution Type/Description: Historic House: housed in the former home of riverboat captain & merchant Charles Shrewsbury; built in 1848. Listed on the National Register of Historic Places.
Hours & Admission Prices: By appointment. Adults $3; children no charge.

Marengo

MARENGO CAVE, 400 E. State Rd. 64, Marengo, IN 47140. Mailing Address: P.O. Box 217, Marengo, IN 47140-0217. Tel.: 888-702-2837, 812-365-2705.
Web Site: www.marengocave.com
Institution Type/Description: Natural History Museum.
Hours & Admission Prices: Memorial Day to Labor Day Mon.-Fri. 9-6, Sat.-Sun. 9-6:30; Sept.-May daily 9-5. Tours prices vary. Closed Thanksgiving; Christmas.

Marion

MARION PUBLIC LIBRARY & MUSEUM, Carnegie Bldg., 600 S. Washington St., Marion, IN 46953-1963. Tel.: 765-668-2900, ext. 150. Fax: 765-668-2911. TDD: 765-668-2907.
E-mail: jfelton@marion.lib.in.us
Web Site: www.marion.lib.in.us
Key Personnel: Dir., Mary Eckerle; Head of Indiana History & Genealogy Svcs., Rhonda Stoffer; Cur., June Felton.
Institution Type/Description: General Museum & History Museum: housed in renovated 1902 Carnegie library building.
Hours & Admission Prices: Summer: Mon., Wed. & Fri. 9-5:30, Tues. & Thurs. 9-8, Sat. 9-5; Sept.-May Mon., Wed. & Fri. 9-5:30, Tues. & Thurs. 9-8, Sat. 9-5, Sun. 1-4. No charge; donations accepted. Closed New Year's Eve & Day; Presidents' Day; Good Friday; Easter; Memorial Day; Independence Day; Labor Day; Thanksgiving; Christmas Eve & Day. &
Attendance: 8,000 (estimated)

THE QUILTERS HALL OF FAME, INC., 926 S. Washington St., Marion, IN 46953-1969. Mailing Address: P.O. Box 681, Marion, IN 46952-0681. Tel.: 765-664-9333. Fax: 765-664-9333. Facebook: The Quilters Hall of Fame.
E-mail: quiltershalloffame@sbcglobal.net
Web Site: quiltershalloffame.net
Key Personnel: Bd. Pres. & Public Rels., Deborah Divine; Treas., Arlan Christ; Museum Mgr., Deb Geyer; Collections, Dale Drake.
Institution Type/Description: History Museum: housed in the former home of Marie D. Webster, a nationally known quilt designer of the early 20th century.
Hours & Admission Prices: April-Dec. Thurs.-Sat. 10-3. Adults $4, seniors & Students $3; members no charge. Closed major holidays.
Attendance: 500 (actual)

Mentone

LAWRENCE D. BELL AIRCRAFT MUSEUM INC., 210 S. Oak St., Mentone, IN 46539. Mailing Address: P.O. Box 411, Mentone, IN 46539-0411. Tel.: 574-353-7318.
E-mail: bilinda2@frontier.com
Key Personnel: Dir., Chm. (V) & Pres. (V), Tim Croy; Treas. & Museum Shop Mgr., Mary Boggs.
Institution Type/Description: Aviation History Museum.
Hours & Admission Prices: Summer: Sun. 1-5; other times by appointment. No charge; donations accepted. &
Attendance: 1,500 (estimated)

Merrillville

MERRILLVILLE COMMUNITY PLANETARIUM, Clifford Pierce Middle School, 199 E. 70th Ave., Merrillville, IN 46410-3679. Tel.: 219-650-5486. Fax: 219-650-5470.
E-mail: info@mcpstars.org
Web Site: www.mcpstars.org
Key Personnel: Planetarium Dir., Gregg Williams; Show Presenter, Linda Charnetzky; Show Presenter, Pam Gower; Show Presenter, Marjorie Ellis; Show Presenter, Ruth Drapeau; Gift Shop Mgr., Pam Powell.
Institution Type/Description: Planetarium.
Hours & Admission Prices: By appointment. Adults $4, children $2. &
Attendance: 29,000 (actual)

Metamora

WHITEWATER CANAL STATE HISTORIC SITE, 19083 Clayborn St., Metamora, IN 47030. Tel.: 765-647-6512. Fax: 765-647-2734.

E-mail: wwcshs@indianamuseum.org
Web Site: www.indianastatemuseum.org/whitewater
Key Personnel: Site Mgr., Jay Dishman.
Institution Type/Description: Historic Site & Buildings.
Hours & Admission Prices: Grist Mill: April-Nov. Wed.-Sun. 10-5. No charge; donations accepted. Ben Franklin III Canal Boat: May-Oct. Wed.-Sun. 12, 1, 2, 3, & 4. Adults $6, seniors 60 & over $5, children 3-12 $3; discounts to school groups; children under 3 no charge. Closed New Year's Day; Easter; Thanksgiving; Christmas. &
Attendance: 131,896 (actual)

Michigan City

BARKER MANSION, 631 Washington St., Michigan City, IN 46360-3419. Tel.: 219-873-1520. Facebook: Barker Mansion.
E-mail: jrosier@emichigancity.com
Web Site: www.barkermansion.com
Key Personnel: Dir., Jessica Rosier.
Institution Type/Description: Historic House Museum: housed in the former home of John H. Barker owner of Haskell & Barker Railroad Car Company, later known as Pullman-Standard.
Hours & Admission Prices: Hours vary seasonally; call (219)873-1520 for tour times & fees. &
Attendance: 10,000 (actual)

GREAT LAKES MUSEUM OF MILITARY HISTORY, 360 Dunes Plaza, W., U.S. Hwy. 20, Michigan City, IN 46360-7342. Mailing Address: 350 Menke Rd., Trail Creek, IN 46360-6521. Tel.: 219-872-2702, 800-726-5912.
E-mail: info@militaryhistorymuseum.org
Web Site: www.militaryhistorymuseum.org/
Institution Type/Description: Military Museum.
Hours & Admission Prices: Memorial Day to Labor Day Tues.-Fri. 9-4, Sat. 10-4, Sun. 12-4; Sept.-May Tues.-Fri. 9-4, Sat. 10-4. Adults $3, seniors & veterans $2, children 8-18 $1; discounts to AIM members; children under 8 & active military no charge. Closed New Year's Eve & Day; Thanksgiving; Christmas Eve & Day. &
Attendance: 2,500 (estimated)

LUBEZNIK CENTER FOR THE ARTS, 101 W. 2nd St., Michigan City, IN 46360-3228. Tel.: 219-874-4900. Facebook.
E-mail: artinfo@lubeznikcenter.org
Web Site: www.lubeznikcenter.org
Formerly: John G. Blank Center for the Arts
Key Personnel: Exec. Dir., Janet Bloch; Pres. (V), Nick Bridge; Cur. Exhibitions, Carol Ann Brown; Mktg. Dir., Amy Davis.
Institution Type/Description: Art Museum.
Hours & Admission Prices: Mon.-Fri. 10-5, Sat. & Sun. 11-4. Suggested Donation: $3 per person; discounts to groups & NARM; members no charge. Closed New Year's Eve & Day; Martin Luther King Jr. Day; Independence Day; Memorial Day; Labor Day; Thanksgiving; Christmas. &
Attendance: 25,000 (estimated)

OLD LIGHTHOUSE MUSEUM, 100 Heisman Harbor Rd., Washington Park, Michigan City, IN 46360. Mailing Address: P.O. Box 512, Michigan City, IN 46361-0512. Tel.: 219-872-6133.
E-mail: mchistorical@att.net
Web Site: www.oldlighthousemuseum.org
Key Personnel: Dir. & Museum Shop Mgr., Laura Shields.
Institution Type/Description: Maritime & History Museum: housed in 1858 keepers dwelling.
Hours & Admission Prices: April-Oct. Tues.-Sun. 1-4; other times by appointment. Adults and children 14 & over $5, children under 14 $2; members no charge. Closed New Year's Day; Good Friday; Easter; Memorial Day; Independence Day; Thanksgiving; Christmas.
Attendance: 5,000 (estimated)

WASHINGTON PARK ZOO, 115 Lakeshore Dr., Michigan City, IN 46360-3256. Tel.: 219-873-1510. Fax: 219-873-1540. Facebook.
E-mail: jhuss@emichigancity.com
Web Site: www.washingtonparkzoo.com
Formerly: Washington Park Zoological Gardens
Key Personnel: Zoo Dir., Jamie Huss; Asst. Dir., Elizabeth Emerick.
Institution Type/Description: Zoological Gardens & Nature Center.
Hours & Admission Prices: April-May & Sept.-Oct. daily 10-4; Memorial Day to Labor Day daily 10-5. Adults $7, seniors 62 & over and children 3-11 $6; discounts reciprocal with member zoos; children 2 & under no charge. &
Attendance: 82,000 (actual)

Middletown

VERA'S LITTLE RED DOLLHOUSE MUSEUM, 4385 W. County Rd. 850, N., Middletown, IN 47356-9462. Tel.: 765-533-3453.
Institution Type/Description: Doll Museum.
Hours & Admission Prices: Call for hours. No charge; donations accepted. &

Mishawaka

HANNAH LINDAHL CHILDREN'S MUSEUM, 1402 S. Main St., Mishawaka, IN 46544-5241. Tel.: 574-254-4540. Fax: 574-254-4585.
E-mail: director@hlcm.org
Web Site: www.hlcm.org
Key Personnel: Pres. (V), Dave Eisen; Dir. & Cur., Lexie Schroeder Kobb.
Institution Type/Description: Local History & Children's Museum.
Hours & Admission Prices: June Tues.-Thurs. 10-2; Sept.-May Tues.-Fri. 9-4. Adults $3, senior citizens 60 & over, students 5-17 $2, children 2-4 $1; discounts to AAM, WNIT & ACM reciprocal members; members no charge. Closed school holidays. &
Attendance: 5,500 (estimated)

MISHAWAKA SPORTS MUSEUM, 109 Lincoln Way E., Mishawaka, IN 46544-2016. Tel.: 574-257-0039. Facebook.
Web Site: www.sportsmuseum.8m.com
Key Personnel: Cur., Lawrence La Cluyse.
Institution Type/Description: Sports Museum.
Hours & Admission Prices: Tues.-Fri. 9-4. No charge; donations accepted. Closed holidays.

OTIS BOWEN MUSEUM & ARCHIVES, 1001 Bethel Cir., Mishawaka, IN 46545-2232. Tel.: 574-807-7219 & 257-3329. Fax: 574-257-3499.
E-mail: roots@bethelcollege.edu
Web Site: www.bethelcollege.edu/library/archives
Key Personnel: Dir., Dr. Clyde Root.
Institution Type/Description: History Museum.
Hours & Admission Prices: By appointment. No charge; donations accepted. &
Attendance: 50 (estimated)

Mitchell

PIONEER VILLAGE & VIRGIL GRISSOM MEMORIAL AT SPRING MILL STATE PARK, 3333 State Rd. 60 E., Mitchell, IN 47446. Mailing Address: P.O. Box 376, Mitchell, IN 47446-0376. Tel.: 812-849-3534. Fax: 812-849-5249.
E-mail: springmillstatepark@dnr.in.gov
Web Site: www.in.gov/dnr/parklake/2968.htm
Formerly: Spring Mill State Park Pioneer Village & Grissom Memorial
Institution Type/Description: Village Museum: housed in 1817 Grist Mill, & other restored buildings, located on the site of a flourishing pioneer village in the 1800s.
Hours & Admission Prices: Call for hours. Out-of-State Residents $7-9 per vehicle; Indiana Residents $5-7 per vehicle. Closed New Year's Day; Thanksgiving; Christmas. &
Attendance: 670,000 (estimated)

Monticello

WHITE COUNTY HISTORICAL SOCIETY MUSEUM, 101 S. Bluff St., Monticello, IN 47960-2308. Tel.: 574-583-3998.
E-mail: museum@lightstreamin.com
Web Site: www.white-county-history.org
Key Personnel: Dir. & Museum Shop Mgr., Judith Baker; Pres., Kean MacOwan; Vice Pres., Rod Pool.
Institution Type/Description: Historical Society Museum.
Hours & Admission Prices: Wed.-Fri. 10-4; other times by appointment. No charge; donations accepted. Closed Christmas Eve & Day; national holidays.
Attendance: 1,000 (estimated)

Mooresville

ACADEMY OF HOOSIER HERITAGE, 250 N. Monroe St., Fl. 2, Mooresville, IN 46158-1551. Tel.: 317-474-8866.
E-mail: jrkylelee@comcast.net
Web Site: www.academymuseum.org
Formerly: Academy Building Museum
Key Personnel: Dir., Julie Kyle-Lee.

Institution Type/Description: Local History Museum: housed in a former school built in 1861. Listed on the National Register of Historic Places.
Hours & Admission Prices: Wed. 2-7, 2nd Sat. each month 11-3; other times by appointment. No charge; donations accepted.

Muncie

ACADEMY OF MODEL AERONAUTICS/NATIONAL MODEL AVIATION MUSEUM, 5151 E. Memorial Dr., Muncie, IN 47302-9252. Tel.: 765-287-1256. Fax: 765-281-7904. Facebook: Academy of Model Aeronautics/National Model Aviation Museum.
E-mail: museum@modelaircraft.org
Web Site: www.modelaircraft.org/museum/museuminfo.aspx
Key Personnel: Pres. (V), Dave Mathewson; Archivist, Jackie Shalberg; Collections Mgr., Maria VanVreede; Museum Dir., Michael Smith; Education Specialist, Emily Loy; Museum Shop Mgr., Wendy Neal.
Institution Type/Description: Aeronautics Museum.
Hours & Admission Prices: April 1-Sept. 30 Mon.-Fri. 8-4:30; Oct. 1- March 31 Tues.-Sat. 10-4; call for holiday hours; Adults $3, children 6-17 $1.50; discounts to group of 10 or more; members no charge. &
Attendance: 5,709 (actual)

DAVID OWSLEY MUSEUM OF ART BALL STATE UNIVERSITY, 2021 W. Riverside Ave., Muncie, IN 47306-0420. Tel.: 765-285-5242 & 5270. Fax: 765-285-4003. Facebook: Ball State Art Museum.
E-mail: artmuseum@bsu.edu
Web Site: www.bsu.edu/artmuseum
Formerly: Ball State University Museum of Art
Key Personnel: Dir., Robert G. La France; Asst. Dir., Rachel Buckmaster; Dir. Education, Tania Said; Preparator & Exhibition Designer, Randy Salway; Registrar, Rebecca Vaughn; Admin., Shannon Bryan.
Institution Type/Description: Art Museum.
Hours & Admission Prices: Mon.-Fri. 9-4:30, Sat.-Sun. 1:30-4:30. No charge; donations accepted. Closed holidays. &
Attendance: 26,719 (actual)

MINNETRISTA, 1200 N. Minnetrista Pkwy., Muncie, IN 47303-2925. Tel.: 765-282-4848. Fax: 765-741-5110. Facebook: Minnetrista.
E-mail: info@minnetrista.net
Web Site: www.minnetrista.net
Formerly: Minnetrista Cultural Center
Key Personnel: Pres. & C.E.O., Betty Brewer; Chm. (V), Kathy White; Vice Pres. Visitor Experience, Rebecca Gilliam; Vice Pres. Finance & Operations, Phillip Dunn; Dir. Collections, Karen Vincent; Dir. Education & Experience, George Buss; Retail Mgr., Molly Harty.
Institution Type/Description: General Museum.
Hours & Admission Prices: Mon.-Sat. 9-5:30, Sun. 11-5:30. Adults $5; discounts to groups, APGA, AAA, ASTC, ICOM & AAM members; members no charge. Gift Shop: The Orchard Shop at Minnetrista: Mon.-Sat. 9-5:30, Sun. 11-5:30. Closed New Year's Day; Easter; Thanksgiving; Christmas Eve & Day. &
Attendance: 104,278 (estimated)

THE MOORE-YOUSE HOME MUSEUM, 122 E. Washington St., Muncie, IN 47305-1734. Mailing Address: 120 E. Washington St., Muncie, IN 47303-1734. Tel.: 765-282-1550.
E-mail: museum@the-dchs.org
Web Site: www.the-dchs.org/moore-youse_home_museum.htm
Key Personnel: Dir., Mary Maxon; C.E.O., Jack Maxon.
Institution Type/Description: Historic House Museum.
Hours & Admission Prices: March-Nov. 1st Sun. of month 1-4; other times by appointment. Adults $3; members no charge.

MUNCIE CHILDREN'S MUSEUM, 515 S. High St., Muncie, IN 47305-2376. Mailing Address: P.O. Box 544, Muncie, IN 47308-0544. Tel.: 765-286-1660. Fax: 765-286-1662.
E-mail: museum@munciemuseum.com
Web Site: www.munciechildrensmuseum.com
Key Personnel: Mng. Dir., Kynda Rinker.
Institution Type/Description: Children's Museum.
Hours & Admission Prices: Wed.-Sat. 10-12:30 & 2-5. Adults $6; discounts to ASTC members. Closed major holidays. &
Attendance: 37,850 (actual)

Munster

MUNSTER HISTORY MUSEUM - KASKE HOUSE, 1154 Ridge Rd., Munster, IN 46321. Mailing Address: Munster Historical Society, Museum Committee, 1005 Ridge Rd., Munster, IN 46321. Tel.: 219-836-6530. Fax: 219-838-3296.
E-mail: curator@munsterhistory.org
Web Site: munsterhistory.org
Institution Type/Description: History Museum.
Hours & Admission Prices: Closed for renovation.

SOUTH SHORE ARTS, 1040 Ridge Rd., Munster, IN 46321-1876. Tel.: 219-836-1839, ext. 100. Fax: 219-836-1863.
E-mail: kelly@southshoreartsonline.org
Web Site: www.southshoreartsonline.org
Formerly: Northern Indiana Arts Association
Key Personnel: Exec. Dir., John Cain; Gallery Mgr., Bridget Covert; Education, Kelly Freeman; Dir. Finance & Administration, George Matusik; Dir. Mktg. & Devel., Tricia Hernandez; Special Projects Dir., Donna Catalano; Museum Shop Mgr., Jackie Wickland.
Institution Type/Description: Art Association Museum.
Hours & Admission Prices: Mon.-Fri. 10-5, Sat. 10-4, Sun. 12-4. Adults $3, students $2; members no charge. &

Nappanee

AMISH ACRES, 1600 W. Market St., Nappanee, IN 46550. Tel.: 800-800-4942 & 574-773-4188. Fax: 574-773-4180.
E-mail: amishacres@amishacres.com
Web Site: www.amishacres.com
Institution Type/Description: Historic Farm Museum.
Hours & Admission Prices: May-Oct. Tues.-Sat. 10-7, Sun. 10-5. &

Nashville

BROWN COUNTY ART GALLERY AND MUSEUM, #1 Artist Dr., Nashville, IN 47448-8101. Mailing Address: P.O. Box 443, Nashville, IN 47448-0443. Tel.: 812-988-4609.
E-mail: brncagal@att.net
Web Site: www.browncountyartgallery.org
Key Personnel: Pres., Lyn Letsinger-Miller; Vice Pres., Cheryl Eyed.
Institution Type/Description: Art Association Gallery.
Hours & Admission Prices: Mon.-Sat. 10-5, Sun. 12-5. No charge; donations accepted. Closed New Year's Eve & Day; Thanksgiving; Christmas Eve & Day. &
Attendance: 7,500 (estimated)

BROWN COUNTY HISTORY CENTER, 46 E. Gould St., Nashville, IN 47448. Mailing Address: Box 668, Nashville, IN 47448-0668. Tel.: 812-988-2899.
E-mail: director@browncountyhistorycenter.org
Web Site: browncountyhistorycenter.org
Formerly: Brown County Historical Society Pioneer Village
Key Personnel: Museum Mgr., Kathy Sparks; Cur., Barbara Livesey; Pres. (V), Robert Shook; Archives, Rhonda A. Dunn.
Institution Type/Description: Historical Society Museum Village.
Hours & Admission Prices: Pioneer Village: May-Oct. Sat.-Sun. 1-4:30; History Center: Thurs.-Sun. 11-4. No charge; donations accepted. &
Attendance: 6,000 (estimated)

T.C. STEELE STATE HISTORIC SITE, 4220 T.C. Steele Rd., Nashville, IN 47448-9586. Tel.: 812-988-2785. Fax: 812-988-8457. Facebook: T.C. Steele State Historic Site.
E-mail: tcsteeleshs@indianamuseum.org
Web Site: www.tcsteele.org
Key Personnel: Historic Site Mgr., Andrea Smith DeTarnowsky.
Institution Type/Description: Historic Site.
Hours & Admission Prices: Tues.-Sat. 9-5, Sun. 1-5. Adults $7, seniors 60 & over $6, children 17 & under $4; discounts to groups & National Trust for Historic Preservation members; children 3 & under, Friends Group & Indiana State Museum Society members no charge. Tours on the quarter hour beginning 9:15, last tour 4:15. Closed most holidays. &
Attendance: 10,340 (actual)

New Albany

CARNEGIE CENTER FOR ART & HISTORY, 201 E. Spring St., New Albany, IN 47150-3422. Tel.: 812-944-7336. Fax: 812-981-3544. Facebook.
E-mail: snewkirk@carnegiecenter.org
Web Site: carnegiecenter.org
Key Personnel: Dir., Eileen Yanoviak; Cur., Daniel Pfaczgraf; Coord. Public Programs & Engagements, Al Gorman; Public Rels. Assoc., Delesha Thomas.
Institution Type/Description: History Museum & Art Gallery; housed in 1904 Carnegie Library.
Hours & Admission Prices: Tues.-Sat. 10-5:30. No charge. Closed major holidays. &
Attendance: 24,000 (actual)

CULBERTSON MANSION STATE HISTORIC SITE, 914 E. Main St., New Albany, IN 47150-5841. Tel.: 812-944-9600. Fax: 812-949-6134.
E-mail: culbertsonmansionshs@indianamuseum.org
Web Site: www.indianamuseum.org/explore/culbertson
Key Personnel: Site Mgr., Jessica Stavros.
Institution Type/Description: Historic House: 1867 W.S. Culbertson Home, a 25-room Victorian mansion.
Hours & Admission Prices: Tues.-Sun. 10-5; other times by appointment. Adults $10, seniors $8, children $5; discounts to groups with appointment; children under 3 no charge. Closed state holidays. &
Attendance: 20,000 (actual)

New Carlisle

HISTORIC NEW CARLISLE, INC. LOCAL HISTORY MUSEUM, 304 E. Michigan St., New Carlisle, IN 46552. Mailing Address: P.O. Box 107, New Carlisle, IN 46552-0107. Tel.: 574-654-3897.
E-mail: historicnc@townofnewcarlisle.com
Web Site: www.historicnewcarlisle.org
Key Personnel: Exec. Dir., Dana Groves; Pres. (V), Rich Kopkowski.
Institution Type/Description: History Museum.
Hours & Admission Prices: Mon.-Fri. 8-4 or by appointment. No charge, donations accepted. &

New Castle

ART ASSOCIATION OF HENRY COUNTY, INC., 218 S. 15th St., New Castle, IN 47362-3201. Mailing Address: P.O. Box 842, New Castle, IN 47362-0842. Tel.: 765-529-2634. Facebook: Art Association of Henry County.
E-mail: henrycountyarts@gmail.com
Web Site: henrycountyarts.org
Key Personnel: Pres., Steve Weidert; Dir., Manny Mena.
Institution Type/Description: Art Association & Gallery.
Hours & Admission Prices: Tues.-Fri. 9-4, Sat. 1-4. No charge; donations accepted. &
Attendance: 2,000 (estimated)

HENRY COUNTY HISTORICAL SOCIETY, 606 S. 14th St., New Castle, IN 47362-3339. Tel.: 765-529-4028.
E-mail: henrycountyhistoricalsociety@gmail.com
Web Site: www.henrycountyhs.org
Key Personnel: Pres., Gene Ingram; Exec. Dir., A. Kaye Ford.
Institution Type/Description: Historic House: 1870 home of Civil War General William Grose. Listed on the National Register of Historic Places.
Hours & Admission Prices: March-Dec. Wed.-Fri. 1-4:30, Sat. 10-1. Adults $3, students $2; children under 6 & members no charge. Closed holidays.
Attendance: 1,200 (estimated)

INDIANA BASKETBALL HALL OF FAME, 408 Trojan Lane, New Castle, IN 47362. Mailing Address: One Hall of Fame Ct., New Castle, IN 47362-2941. Tel.: 765-529-1891. Fax: 765-529-0273.
E-mail: info@hoopshall.com
Web Site: www.hoopshall.com
Key Personnel: Exec. Dir., Chris May.
Institution Type/Description: Sports Museum.
Hours & Admission Prices: Mon.-Sat. 10-5, Sun. 1-5. Adults $5, children 5-12 $3; discounts to AAM members; members & children under 5 no charge. Closed major holidays. &
Attendance: 10,000 (actual)

New Harmony

HISTORIC NEW HARMONY, 603 West St., New Harmony, IN 47631. Mailing Address: P.O. Box 579, New Harmony, IN 47631-0579. Tel.: 812-682-4488. Fax: 812-682-4313.
E-mail: harmony@usi.edu
Web Site: www.usi.edu/hnh

Key Personnel: Dir. Historic New Harmony, Connie Weinzapfel; Collections Mgr., Amanda Bryden; Community Engagement Mgr., Erin McCracken Merris; Administrative Asst., Christine Crews; Collections Asst., Robin Bischof; Museum Shop Buyer, Allison Brown; Visitor Svcs. Coord., Melissa Williams.
Institution Type/Description: History Museum & Preservation Project: located on the site of two early utopian experiments-George Rapp's 1814-1825 Harmony Society & Welsh-born social reformer & industrialist Robert Owen's New Harmony; it is also the site of the early headquarters of the U.S. Geological Survey; it provided many of the earliest collections of the Smithsonian Institution.
Hours & Admission Prices: March 15-Dec. 30 daily 9:30-5; Dec. 30-March 14 groups by appointment. Family $30, adults $18, senior citizens $15, children $5; discounts to groups, AAM, ICOM & AAA members. &
Attendance: 21,183 (actual)

NEW HARMONY GALLERY OF CONTEMPORARY ART, 506 Main St., New Harmony, IN 47631. Mailing Address: P.O. Box 627, New Harmony, IN 47631-0627. Tel.: 812-682-3156. Fax: 812-682-3870.
E-mail: skrhoades@usi.edu
Web Site: www.nhgallery.com
Key Personnel: Dir., Garry Holstein.
Institution Type/Description: Contemporary Art Gallery.
Hours & Admission Prices: Jan.-March Tues.-Sat. 10-5; April-Dec. Tues.-Sat. 10-5, Sun. 12-4. No charge. &
Attendance: 40,000 (estimated)

WORKING MEN'S INSTITUTE, 407 W. Tavern St., New Harmony, IN 47631. Mailing Address: P.O. Box 368, New Harmony, IN 47631-0368. Tel.: 812-682-4806.
E-mail: cochran.stephen@gmail.com
Web Site: www.workingmensinstitute.org
Formerly: New Harmony Working Men's Institute
Key Personnel: Dir., Stephen Cochran.
Institution Type/Description: 19th Century Museum & Library.
Hours & Admission Prices: Tues.-Sat. 10-4. No charge; donations accepted. Closed New Year's Eve & Day; Easter; Independence Day; Thanksgiving; Christmas Eve & Day. &
Attendance: 8,500 (actual)

Noblesville

HAMILTON COUNTY MUSEUM OF HISTORY, 810 Conner St., Noblesville, IN 46060. Mailing Address: P.O. Box 397, Noblesville, IN 46061. Tel.: 317-770-0775. Fax: 317-770-0775.
E-mail: hamiltoncomuseum@att.net
Web Site: hamiltoncoinhs.org
Key Personnel: Dir., Diane Nevitt.
Institution Type/Description: History Museum: housed in the Old Hamilton County Sheriff's Residence and Jail; built in 1875.
Hours & Admission Prices: Thurs.-Sat. 10-4; other times by appointment. No charge; donations accepted. &
Attendance: 2,550 (actual)

North Judson

HOOSIER VALLEY RAILROAD MUSEUM, 507 Mulberry St., North Judson, IN 46366-0075. Mailing Address: P.O. Box 75, North Judson, IN 46366-0075. Tel.: 574-896-3950. Facebook.
E-mail: questions@hoosiervalley.org
Web Site: www.hoosiervalley.org
Institution Type/Description: Railroad Museum.
Hours & Admission Prices: Museum: Sat. 9-4. No charge.

North Manchester

MANCHESTER UNIVERSITY ART COLLECTION, Funderburg Library, 604 E. College Ave., North Manchester, IN 46962. Tel.: 260-982-5000.
E-mail: tsrohrer@manchester.edu
Institution Type/Description: Art Gallery.
Hours & Admission Prices: Call for hours.

NORTH MANCHESTER CENTER FOR HISTORY, 122 E. Main St., North Manchester, IN 46962. Mailing Address: P.O. Box 361, North Manchester, IN 46962. Tel.: 260-982-0672. Facebook: North Manchester Historical Society.
E-mail: nmhistory@cinergymetro.net
Web Site: www.nmanchesterhistory.org
Formerly: North Manchester Historical Society

Key Personnel: Pres. (V), Mary L. Chrastil.
Institution Type/Description: Historical Society Museum: housed in the former Oppenheim's Department Store and the Thomas Marshall House.
Hours & Admission Prices: Call for hours. No charge. &
Attendance: 5,000 (estimated)

North Vernon

HAYDEN HISTORICAL MUSEUM, 6715 W. County Rd. 20 S., North Vernon, IN 47265. Mailing Address: P.O. Box 58, Hayden, IN 47245. Tel.: 812-346-8212.
E-mail: haydenmuseum@gmail.com
Institution Type/Description: History Museum: housed in a former chicken house; built in 1949.
Hours & Admission Prices: Memorial Day to Labor Day Sun. 1-4; Wed. 4-8; Sept.-May Mon. 4-5:30, Wed. 4-8; other times by appointment.

Notre Dame

MUSEUM OF BIODIVERSITY AND GREENE-NIEUWLAND HERBARIUM, Dept. of Biological Sciences, Univ. of Notre Dame, Notre Dame, IN 46556-0369. Tel.: 574-631-6684. Fax: 574-631-7413.
E-mail: Barbara.J.Hellenthal.2@nd.edu
Web Site: biodiversity.nd.edu
Key Personnel: Dir. Museum of Biodiversity, Ronald A. Hellenthal; Cur., Barbara J. Hellenthal.
Institution Type/Description: Herbarium Museum.
Hours & Admission Prices: By appointment only. No charge. &
Attendance: 2,000 (actual)

THE SNITE MUSEUM OF ART, UNIVERSITY OF NOTRE DAME, University of Notre Dame, 100 Moose Krause Cir., Notre Dame, IN 46556-0368. Mailing Address: P.O. Box 368, Notre Dame, IN 46556-0368. Tel.: 574-631-5466. Fax: 574-631-8501.
E-mail: sniteart@nd.edu
Web Site: snitemuseum.nd.edu
Key Personnel: Assoc. Dir., Ann M. Knoll; Cur. European Art, Cheryl K. Snay, Ph. D.; Cur. Photographs, David Acton, Ph.D.; Cur. Education, Public Programs, Sarah Martin; Cur. Education & Academic Programs, Bridget Hoyt; Mktg. & Public Affairs Specialist, Gina Costa; Registrar, Victoria Perdomo; Exhibit Coord., Ramiro Rodriguez; Coord. Friends of the Snite Museum, Mary Rattenburg.
Institution Type/Description: University Art Museum.
Hours & Admission Prices: Tues.-Fri. 10-5, Sat. 12-5, Thurs. open until 7:30. No charge; donations accepted. Closed major holidays. &
Attendance: 43,557 (actual)

Ogden Dunes

HISTORICAL SOCIETY OF OGDEN DUNES, The Hour Glass Museum, 8 Lupine Ln., Ogden Dunes, IN 46368. Mailing Address: 115 Hillcrest Rd. #101, Ogden Dunes, IN 46368.
E-mail: rmeister@depaul.edu
Web Site: odhistory.org
Institution Type/Description: Historical Society Museum.
Hours & Admission Prices: 3rd Sun. of month 4-5:30; other times by appointment. No charge.

Peru

CIRCUS CITY FESTIVAL MUSEUM, 154 N. Broadway, Peru, IN 46970-2234. Tel.: 765-472-3918. Fax: 765-472-2826.
E-mail: info@perucircus.com
Web Site: www.perucircus.com
Key Personnel: Pres., Curt Powell; Exec. Vice Pres., Bill Anderson; Vice Pres. Museum & Exhibits, Timothy Bessignano; Vice Pres. Festival, Kevin Gallahan.
Institution Type/Description: Circus Museum.
Hours & Admission Prices: Sept.-Feb. Mon.-Thurs. 9-12; Feb.-Aug Mon.-Fri. 9-12 & 2-4. No charge; donations accepted. Closed holidays. &
Attendance: 13,000 (estimated)

GRISSOM AIR MUSEUM, 1000 W. Hoosier Blvd., Peru, IN 46970-3723. Tel.: 765-689-8011, 574-398-1451. Facebook.
E-mail: director@grissomairmuseum.com
Web Site: www.grissomairmuseum.com
Key Personnel: Dir. & Museum Shop Mgr., Jim Price.
Institution Type/Description: Military & Aviation Museum: located adjacent to Grissom Air Reserve Base.

Hours & Admission Prices: See website for hours. Adults $6, seniors 61 & over and military $5; children 5 & under no charge. &
Attendance: 15,000 (estimated)

INTERNATIONAL CIRCUS HALL OF FAME & MUSEUM, 3076 E. Circus Lane, Peru, IN 46970-7133. Tel.: 800-771-0241.
E-mail: circushalloffame@gmail.com
Institution Type/Description: Circus History Museum.
Hours & Admission Prices: May-June & Aug. Mon.-Fri. 10-4; other times by appointment; July Mon.-Sat. 10-4, Sun. 12-4.

MIAMI COUNTY MUSEUM, 51 N. Broadway, Peru, IN 46970-2237. Tel.: 765-473-9183. Facebook.
E-mail: admin@mcmuseum.org
Web Site: www.miamicountyhistory.org
Key Personnel: Dir. & Cur., Anna Pohlman; Collections Mgr. & Registrar, Shirley Griffin; Archivist, Beverly Parker.
Institution Type/Description: General Museum.
Hours & Admission Prices: Tues.-Sat. 9-5. Suggested donation: $3. Closed holidays. &
Attendance: 7,000 (estimated)

Plymouth

MARSHALL COUNTY HISTORICAL MUSEUM, 123 N. Michigan St., Plymouth, IN 46563-2132. Tel.: 574-936-2306. Fax: 574-936-9306. Facebook.
E-mail: mchistory@mchistoricalsociety.org
Web Site: www.mchistoricalsociety.org
Key Personnel: Exec. Dir., Linda Rippy.
Institution Type/Description: History Museum.
Hours & Admission Prices: Tues.-Sat. 10-4. No charge; donations accepted. Closed county holidays. &
Attendance: 8,370 (actual)

Portage

PORTAGE COMMUNITY HISTORICAL SOCIETY - AL GOIN HISTORICAL MUSEUM, 5250 U.S. Hwy. 6, Portage, IN 46368. Mailing Address: P.O. Box 305, Portage, IN 46368-0305. Tel.: 219-762-8349. Facebook: Portage Community Historical Society (Indiana).
E-mail: pchs.1@frontier.com
Web Site: www.inpchs.com
Key Personnel: Pres. (V), Valeria Roach; Vice Pres., Anne Koehler; Sec., Donna Smith; Treas., Barbara Borg-Jenkins; Newsletter, Kathy Heckman; Bd. Member, Patricia Coppess; Bd. Member, Susan Cowsert; Bd. Member, Jim Franzen; Bd. Member, Lois Mollick; Bd. Member, Wanda Samuelson; Bd. Member, Richard Turnak; Bd. Member, Evan Dick.
Institution Type/Description: Local History.
Hours & Admission Prices: April to early Dec. Sat.-Sun. 1-4; call to confirm. No charge; donations accepted. Closed Independence Day. &
Attendance: 2,500 (estimated)

Porter

INDIANA DUNES NATIONAL LAKESHORE, 1215 N. State Rd. 49, Porter, IN 46304. Mailing Address: 1100 N. Mineral Springs Rd., Porter, IN 46304-1225. Tel.: 219-395-1882. Fax: 219-395-1767.
Web Site: www.nps.gov/indu
Key Personnel: Supt., Paul Labovitz.
Institution Type/Description: Park Visitor Center.
Hours & Admission Prices: Park: daily. Parking Fee: $4 at West Beach. Visitor Center: Summer daily 8-6; Winter daily 8:30-4:30. No charge; donations accepted. &
Attendance: 1,834,435 (estimated)

Portland

JAY COUNTY HISTORICAL SOCIETY MUSEUM AND GENEALOGY LIBRARY, 903 E. Main St., Portland, IN 47371. Tel.: 260-726-7168. Fax: 260-726-7178.
E-mail: research@jaycountyhistory.org
Web Site: www.jaycountyhistory.org
Institution Type/Description: History Museum & Library.
Hours & Admission Prices: Tues.-Fri. 10-4. No charge; donations accepted. Closed major holidays. &

MUSEUM OF THE SOLDIER, 510 E. Arch St., Portland, IN 47371-1525. Mailing Address: P.O. Box 518, Portland, IN 47371-0518. Tel.: 260-726-2967. Facebook.
E-mail: museum@bright.net
Web Site: www.museumofthesoldier.com/
Key Personnel: Bd. Mem., Matt Simmons; Bd. Mem., Jim Waechter.
Institution Type/Description: Military Museum.
Hours & Admission Prices: April to Veterans Day 1st & 3rd Sat.-Sun. 12-5; other times by appointment. No charge.

Rensselaer

JASPER COUNTY HISTORICAL SOCIETY MUSEUM, 479 N. Van Rensselaer St., Rensselaer, IN 47978. Tel.: 219-866-7825 & 863-6860.
E-mail: jchsmuseum@gmail.com
Key Personnel: Cur., Judy Kanne.
Institution Type/Description: History Museum.
Hours & Admission Prices: 1st & 3rd Sat. each month; other times by appointment. No charge.

LILIAN FENDIG ART GALLERY, 301 N. Van Rensselaer St., Rensselaer, IN 47978-2630. Tel.: 219-866-5278. Fax: 219-866-5278.
E-mail: pacrensselaer@gmail.com
Institution Type/Description: Art Gallery.
Hours & Admission Prices: Tues. & Thurs. 12-4. No charge; donations accepted. &
Attendance: 12,000 (estimated)

Richmond

AGNES AND ABRAM GAAR FOUNDATION - GAAR HOUSE MUSEUM, 2593 Pleasant View Rd., Richmond, IN 47374-2050. Mailing Address: 1623 N. St. Rd. 227, Richmond, IN 47374. Tel.: 765-966-1262.
E-mail: sarahsambradley@aol.com
Web Site: www.thegaarhouse.com
Formerly: Gaar Mansion and Farm Museum
Key Personnel: Dir., Sarah Bradley.
Institution Type/Description: Historic Building: housed in the home of Abram Gaar & his wife Agnes; built in 1876. Listed on the National Register of Historic Places.
Hours & Admission Prices: June-Aug. 1st & 3rd Sun. 1-4; Dec. 1st 3 Sun. 1-4; tours by appointment. Adults $5, children 18 & under $2.

HAYES ARBORETUM, 801 Elks Rd., Richmond, IN 47374-2526. Tel.: 765-962-3745. Fax: 765-966-1931.
E-mail: stephenhayes13@yahoo.com
Web Site: www.hayesarboretum.org
Key Personnel: Pres., Stephen H. Hayes, Sr.; Exec. Dir., Stephen H. Hayes, Jr., LEED, AP.
Institution Type/Description: Arboretum & Nature Center.
Hours & Admission Prices: Tues.-Sat. 9-5. No charge; donations accepted. closed New Year's Day; Thanksgiving; Christmas. &
Attendance: 10,000 (estimated)

INDIANA FOOTBALL HALL OF FAME, 815 N. A St., Richmond, IN 47374-3119. Mailing Address: P.O. Box 40, Richmond, IN 47375-0040. Tel.: 765-966-2235. Fax: 765-966-5700.
E-mail: contact@indiana-football.org
Web Site: www.indiana-football.org
Key Personnel: Dir., Lou Ann Moore, Ph.D.
Institution Type/Description: Sports Museum.
Hours & Admission Prices: mid-Jan. to Dec. Tues.-Sat. 11-5; other times by appointment. No charge; donations appreciated. Closed major National holidays.

JOSEPH MOORE MUSEUM, Earlham College, 801 National Rd. W., Richmond, IN 47374. Tel.: 765-983-1303. Fax: 765-983-1497. Facebook.
E-mail: lernere@earlham.edu
Web Site: www.earlham.edu/joseph-moore-museum
Key Personnel: Dir., Dr. Heather R.L. Lerner; Coord. Educational Outreach, Carol Stocksdale; Mgr. Collections, Dr. Ann-Eliza Lewis.
Institution Type/Description: Natural History Museum.
Hours & Admission Prices: Wed. & Fri.-Mon. 1-5; tours by appointment only. No charge; donations accepted. Closed New Year's Day; Independence Day; Christmas Eve & Day. &
Attendance: 4,500 (estimated)

LEEDS GALLERY - EARLHAM COLLEGE, 801 National Rd. W., Richmond, IN 47374-4095. Tel.: 765-983-1410.
Institution Type/Description: Art Gallery.
Hours & Admission Prices: Mon.-Fri. 9-8, Sat.-Sun. 1-8.

MODEL T MUSEUM, 309 N. 8th St., Richmond, IN 47374. Mailing Address: P.O. Box 996, Richmond, IN 47375-0996. Tel.: 765-488-0026. Fax: 765-855-3428. Facebook: Model T Museum.
E-mail: admin@mtfca.com
Web Site: www.mtfca.com
Key Personnel: Exec. Dir. & Museum Shop Mgr., Susan Yaeger.
Institution Type/Description: Automobile Museum.
Hours & Admission Prices: Tues.-Sun. 10-5. Adults $3; members & veterans no charge. Closed New Year's Day; Easter; Independence Day; Thanksgiving; Christmas. &
Attendance: 10,000 (estimated)

RICHMOND ART MUSEUM, 350 Hub Etchison Pkwy., Richmond, IN 47374-5339. Mailing Address: P.O. Box 816, Richmond, IN 47375. Tel.: 765-966-0256. Fax: 765-973-3738.
E-mail: shaun@richmondartmuseum.org
Web Site: www.richmondartmuseum.org
Formerly: Art Association of Richmond
Key Personnel: Exec. Dir., Shaun Dingwerth; Pres., Barry Jonston.
Institution Type/Description: Art Museum.
Hours & Admission Prices: Tues.-Fri. 10-4, Sun. 1-4. No charge; donations accepted. Closed national & school holidays. &
Attendance: 20,000 (estimated)

RONALD GALLERY - EARLHAM COLLEGE, 801 National Rd. W., Richmond, IN 47374-4095. Tel.: 765-983-1410.
E-mail: koehnly@earlham.edu
Key Personnel: Cur., Julia May.
Institution Type/Description: Art Gallery.
Hours & Admission Prices: Mon.-Thurs. 8am to midnight, Fri. 8am-10pm, Sat. 10-10, Sun. noon to midnight.

WAYNE COUNTY HISTORICAL MUSEUM, 1150 N. A St., Richmond, IN 47374-3298. Tel.: 765-962-5756. Fax: 765-939-0909. Facebook: Wayne County Historical Museum.
E-mail: director@wchmuseum.org
Web Site: www.waynecountyhistoricalmuseum.org
Key Personnel: C.E.O. , Dir. & Museum Shop Mgr., James D. Harlan; Pres. (V), Dick Smith.
Institution Type/Description: General Museum: housed in 1864 Hicksite Friends Meeting House.
Hours & Admission Prices: Jan.-Feb. Mon.-Fri. 9-4, Sat. 1-4; March-Dec. Mon.-Fri. 9-4, Sat.1-4. Adults $7, students 6-18 $4; discounts to groups; children under 6 & members no charge. Closed national holidays. &
Attendance: 12,000 (estimated)

Rising Sun

OHIO COUNTY HISTORICAL SOCIETY, INC. & MUSEUM, 212 S. Walnut, Rising Sun, IN 47040. Tel.: 812-438-4915. Facebook.
Web Site: www.ohiocountymuseum.org
Key Personnel: Dir. & Museum Shop Mgr., Clifford Wm. Thies.
Institution Type/Description: Historical Society Museum.
Hours & Admission Prices: Call for hours. No charge; donations accepted. &
Attendance: 1,500 (estimated)

Rochester

FULTON COUNTY HISTORICAL SOCIETY MUSEUM, 37 E. 375 N., Rochester, IN 46975-9718. Tel.: 574-223-4436. Fax: 574-224-4436. Facebook.
E-mail: fchs@rtcol.com
Web Site: www.fultoncountyhistory.org
Key Personnel: Dir., Melinda Clinger; Pres., Fred Oden, Jr.; Treas., Lola Riddle.
Institution Type/Description: Living History Village & History Museum: 35-acre village including 14 buildings.
Hours & Admission Prices: Mon.-Sat. 9-5. No charge; donations accepted. Closed holidays. &
Attendance: 45,000 (estimated)

Rockport

LINCOLN PIONEER VILLAGE & MUSEUM, 928 Fairground Dr., Rockport, IN 47635. Tel.: 812-649-9147.
Institution Type/Description: History Museum.
Hours & Admission Prices: Seasonal hours.

Rockville

BILLIE CREEK VILLAGE, INC., 65 S. Billie Creek Rd., Rockville, IN 47872. Mailing Address: P.O. Box 357, Rockville, IN 47872-0357. Tel.: 765-569-0252. Fax: 765-569-3582.
E-mail: billiecreekvillage@billiecreekvillage.org
Web Site: www.billiecreekvillage.org
Key Personnel: Dir. & C.E.O., Charles Cooper; Museum Shop Mgr., Sue Cooper.
Institution Type/Description: History Museum.
Hours & Admission Prices: Village: Wed.-Sat. 10-4, Sun. 12-4. General Store: Mon.-Sat. 10-4, Sun. 12-4. Admission $5; children under 6 no charge. Special Events: $7.

PARKE COUNTY HISTORICAL MUSEUM, 503 W. Ohio St., Rockville, IN 47872. Mailing Address: P.O. Box 332, Rockville, IN 47872. Tel.: 765-569-2223.
E-mail: info@parkecountyhs.ord
Web Site: www.parkecountyhistoricalsociety.org
Institution Type/Description: History Museum: housed in a former seminary; later used as an armory during the Civil War; built in 1839.
Hours & Admission Prices: April-Oct. Wed.-Sat. 1-5, Sun. by appointment.

Rome City

GENE STRATTON-PORTER STATE HISTORIC SITE, 1205 Pleasant Point, Rome City, IN 46784-9644. Tel.: 260-854-3790. Fax: 260-854-9102. Facebook.
E-mail: genestrattonportershs@indianamuseum.org
Web Site: indianamuseum.org
Institution Type/Description: Historic House: c.1920 home of Gene Stratton Porter.
Hours & Admission Prices: Carriage House Visitor Center: April-Dec. 1 Tues.-Sun. 10-5. No charge. Cabin Tours: Tues.-Sat. 10-4, Sun. 1-4. Adults $7, seniors 60 & over $6, children 3-17 $4; discounts to groups. Closed New Year's Day; Memorial Day; Independence Day; Labor Day; Thanksgiving; Christmas. &
Attendance: 60,000 (estimated)

Rushville

RUSH COUNTY HISTORICAL SOCIETY MUSEUM, 619 N. Perkins St., Rushville, IN 46173. Mailing Address: P.O. Box 302, Rushville, IN 46173. Tel.: 765-932-2492.
E-mail: rchs1@frontier.com
Web Site: rushcountyhistory.org
Institution Type/Description: Historical Society Museum.
Hours & Admission Prices: March-Nov. Mon. & Thurs. 9am-11am. No charge.

Salem

JOHN HAY CENTER, 307 E. Market St., Salem, IN 47167-2119. Tel.: 812-883-6495. Facebook.
E-mail: info@johnhaycenter.org
Web Site: www.johnhaycenter.org
Formerly: Stevens Museum
Key Personnel: Pres. Bd., Danny Newby.
Institution Type/Description: Local History, 1824 John Hay birthplace, Pioneer Village & Depot Museum.
Hours & Admission Prices: Tues.-Sat. 9-5. Genealogy research: Tues.-Sat. 9-5. Museum: adults $3; members & children under 6 no charge. Library: $3. Closed New Year's Day; Easter; Memorial Day; Independence Day; Labor Day; Thanksgiving; Christmas. &
Attendance: 30,000 (estimated)

Santa Claus

SANTA CLAUS MUSEUM AND VILLAGE, 69 N. State Rd. 245, Santa Claus, IN 47579. Mailing Address: P.O. Box 1, Santa Claus, IN 47579. Tel.: 812-544-2434.
E-mail: elf@santaclausmuseum.org
Web Site: www.santaclausmuseum.org
Key Personnel: Dir., Emily Thompson.
Institution Type/Description: History Museum.

Hours & Admission Prices: Call for hours. Requested Donation: $5 per family, $2 per person.
Attendance: 10,000 (actual)

Scottsburg

SCOTT COUNTY HERITAGE CENTER AND MUSEUM, 1050 S. Main St., Scottsburg, IN 47170-6663. Mailing Address: P.O. Box 122, Scottsburg, IN 47170-0122. Tel.: 812-752-1050.
E-mail: contact@schcam.org
Web Site: scottcountyheritagemuseum.org
Key Personnel: Dir. & Museum Shop Mgr., Jeanne Abbott; Pres. (V), Marty Randall.
Institution Type/Description: History Museum.
Hours & Admission Prices: Mon.-Fri. 9-5, Sat. 9-1. No charge. &
Attendance: 3,000 (actual)

Seymour

FREEMAN ARMY AIRFIELD MUSEUM, 1035 A Ave., Seymour, IN 47274. Mailing Address: P.O. Box 714, Seymour, IN 47274. Tel.: 812-271-1821. Facebook.
E-mail: faafmuseum@gmail.com
Web Site: www.freemanarmyairfieldmuseum.org
Key Personnel: Cur., Larry Bothe; Chm. (V), Joseph Clegg.
Institution Type/Description: Military Museum.
Hours & Admission Prices: Sat. 10-1; other times by appointment. No charge; donations accepted. &
Attendance: 3,000 (estimated)

Shelbyville

LOUIS H. & LENA FIRN GROVER MUSEUM, 52 W. Broadway, Shelbyville, IN 46176-1256. Tel.: 317-392-4634.
E-mail: director@grovermuseum.org
Web Site: www.grovermuseum.org
Key Personnel: Dir., Alex Krach.
Institution Type/Description: Historical Society Museum.
Hours & Admission Prices: Tues.-Sat. 10-5. No charge; donations accepted. Closed holidays. &
Attendance: 7,800 (actual)

Sheridan

SHERIDAN HISTORICAL SOCIETY MUSEUM, 308 S. Main St., Sheridan, IN 46069. Tel.: 317-758-5054.
E-mail: sheridanhistorical@sbcglobal.net
Web Site: www.sheridanhistoricalsociety.com
Key Personnel: Exec. Dir., Jim Pickett.
Institution Type/Description: Historical Society Museum.
Hours & Admission Prices: Tues. & Fri. 1-4. No charge; donations accepted.
Attendance: 400 (estimated)

Shoals

MARTIN COUNTY HISTORICAL SOCIETY COUNTY MUSEUM, 220 Capitol, Shoals, IN 47581-0564. Mailing Address: P.O. Box 564, Shoals, IN 47581-0564. Tel.: 812-247-1133. Facebook: Martin County Historical Society Indiana.
E-mail: historical@frontier.com
Key Personnel: Pres. (V), Bill Greene; Museum Shop Mgr., Rick Bowling.
Institution Type/Description: History Museum.
Hours & Admission Prices: May-Oct. Mon., Wed. & Fri. 10-4. No charge; donations accepted. &
Attendance: 500 (estimated)

South Bend

COPSHAHOLM - THE OLIVER MANSION, Center for History, 808 W. Washington, South Bend, IN 46601-1439. Tel.: 574-235-9664. Fax: 574-235-9059.
E-mail: director@centerforhistory.org
Web Site: www.centerforhistory.org
Formerly: Copshaholm House Museum & Historic Oliver Gardens
Key Personnel: C.E.O. & Dir., Randy W. Ray; Pres. (V), Mark Noeldner; Cur., Kristie Erickson; Dir. Mktg., Marilyn Thompson; Dir. Facilities & Grounds, Tom Rapach; Registrar, Kristi Dunn; Dir. Education, Travis Childs; Visitor Svcs. Dir., Ken Cencelewski; Dir. Devel., Amanda Miller; Finance Mgr., Marilyn Jurgonski.

Institution Type/Description: Historic House; 1895-1896 38-room Oliver Family mansion.
Hours & Admission Prices: Mon.-Sat. 10-5, Sun. 12-5; last tour leaves at 2. Adults $8, seniors $6.50, children $5; children under 5, staff of other museums, AAM, & NIHS members no charge. Closed major holidays.
Attendance: 25,000 (actual)

HEALTHWORKS! KIDS' MUSEUM, Memorial Leighton Healthplex, 111 W. Jefferson St., Ste. 200, South Bend, IN 46601-1993. Tel.: 574-647-5437. Fax: 574-239-6459.
E-mail: jsimmons@memorialsb.org
Web Site: www.healthworkskids.org
Institution Type/Description: Children's Health Museum.
Hours & Admission Prices: Tues.-Fri. 9-4, Sat.-Sun. 12-4. Admission $5; members, ACM & children under 2 no charge. Closed New Year's Day; Memorial Day; Independence Day; Labor Day; Thanksgiving; Christmas Eve & Day. &
Attendance: 70,000 (estimated)

THE HISTORY MUSEUM, 808 W. Washington, South Bend, IN 46601-1439. Tel.: 574-235-9664. Fax: 574-235-9059.
E-mail: director@historymuseumsb.org
Web Site: www.historymuseumsb.org
Formerly: Center for History
Key Personnel: C.E.O. & Exec. Dir., Randy W. Ray; Deputy Exec. Dir., Brandon J. Anderson; Pres. (V), Kevin Murphy; Dir. Visitor Svcs., Ken Cencelewski; Dir. Education, Travis Childs; Dir. Devel., Hannah Couch; Dir. Mktg., Marilyn Thompson; Dir. Facilities & Grounds, Tom Rapach; Registrar, Kristi Dunn; Finance Mgr., Marilyn Jurgonski; Cur. Copshaholm, Kristie Erickson; Archivist, Kristen Madden.
Institution Type/Description: History Museum & Children's Interactive Museum; historic house museum.
Hours & Admission Prices: Mon.-Sat. 10-5, Sun. 12-5. Adults $8, seniors $6.50, children $5; discounts to staff of other museums & AAM members; members & children under 6 no charge. &
Attendance: 49,250 (actual)

POTAWATOMI ZOO, 500 S. Greenlawn Ave., South Bend, IN 46615-1341. Mailing Address: P.O. Box 1764, South Bend, IN 46634. Tel.: 574-235-9800. Fax: 574-235-9080.
E-mail: info@potawatomizoo.org
Web Site: potawatomizoo.org
Key Personnel: Exec. Dir., Mary Dean; Dir. Animal Care & Education, Josh Sisk; Veterinarian, Dr. Ronan Eustace.
Institution Type/Description: Zoo.
Hours & Admission Prices: April to late Nov. daily 10-5. Admission 15 & over $10, children 3-14 and seniors 62 & over $8; discount to school groups; members and children 2 & under, no charge. Closed Thanksgiving. &
Attendance: 205,000 (actual)

SOUTH BEND MUSEUM OF ART, 120 S. St. Joseph St., South Bend, IN 46601-1902. Tel.: 574-235-9102. Fax: 574-235-5782.
E-mail: info@southbendart.com
Web Site: southbendart.org
Formerly: South Bend Regional Museum of Art
Key Personnel: Exec. Dir., Susan R. Visser; Cur., Mark Rospenda; Cur. Education, Christyn Overstake; Dir. Mktg., Cathy Dietz; Devel. Mgr., Claudia Maskowski.
Institution Type/Description: Art Museum.
Hours & Admission Prices: Office: Mon.-Fri. 9-5. Galleries & Retail: Wed.-Sun. 12-5. Suggested Donation: adults $5; members no charge. Closed major holidays. &
Attendance: 60,000 (estimated)

STUDEBAKER NATIONAL MUSEUM, INC., 201 S. Chapin St., South Bend, IN 46601-2521. Tel.: 574-235-9714, 888-391-5600. Fax: 574-235-5522.
E-mail: info@studebakermuseum.org
Web Site: www.studebakermuseum.org
Key Personnel: Exec. Dir., Patrick Slebonick; Archivist, Andrew Beckman; Asst. Dir., Jo McCoy; Cur., Aaron Warkentin; Museum Shop Mgr., Susan Boocher; Facility Mgr., John Dawson.
Institution Type/Description: Automobile Museum.
Hours & Admission Prices: Mon.-Sat. 10-5, Sun. 12-5. Archives: Mon.-Thurs. 10-4; other times by appointment. Museum: adults $10, senior citizens over 60 & student over 18 $8.50, children 6-17 $6; discounts to groups and AAM & AAA members; members and children 5 & under no charge. Museum: closed New Year's Day; Easter; Thanksgiving; Christmas Eve & Day. &
Attendance: 39,000 (actual)

Syracuse

SYRACUSE-WAWASEE HISTORICAL MUSEUM, 1013 N. Long Dr., Syracuse, IN 46567-1060. Tel.: 574-457-3599. Facebook: Syracuse-Wawasee Historical Museum.
E-mail: director@syracusemuseum.org
Web Site: www.syracusemuseum.org
Key Personnel: Dir., Jamie Clemons; Pres. (V) Peggy Genshaw.
Institution Type/Description: History Museum.
Hours & Admission Prices: Tues.-Sat. 10-2; other times by appointment. No charge; donations accepted. Closed major holidays. &
Attendance: 4,000 (estimated)

Terre Haute

CANDLES HOLOCAUST MUSEUM AND EDUCATION CENTER, 1532 S. Third St., Terre Haute, IN 47802-1012. Tel.: 812-234-7881. Fax: 812-478-2824.
E-mail: info@candlesholocaustmuseum.org
Web Site: www.candlesholocaustmuseum.org
Key Personnel: Dir., Dorothy Chambers; Chm. (V), Gianfranco Grande; Deputy Dir., Leah Simpson; Communications Coord., Jessica McDonald; Office Mgr., Catie Charlton; Program Coord., Amy Guess; Project & Facilities Mgr., Trent Andrews.
Institution Type/Description: Holocaust Museum.
Hours & Admission Prices: Tues.-Sat. 10-4. Admission $5; children 5 & under no charge &
Attendance: 10,000 (estimated)

CLABBER GIRL MUSEUM, 900 Wabash Ave., Terre Haute, IN 47807-3208. Mailing Address: P.O. Box 150, Terre Haute, IN 47808-0150. Tel.: 812-232-9446. Fax: 812-478-7181.
E-mail: mmorgan@clabbergirl.com
Web Site: www.clabbergirl.com
Key Personnel: Cur., Meegan Morgan; Museum Shop Mgr., Lisa Yowell.
Institution Type/Description: Historic Building: housed in the former home of Herman Hulman & his sons; built by them in 1892 and where they founded their family wholesale grocery business.
Hours & Admission Prices: Mon.-Fri. 10-6, Sat. 9-3; guided tours by appointment. No charge. Closed holidays. &

EUGENE V. DEBS HOME, 451 N. Eighth St., Terre Haute, IN 47807-3006. Mailing Address: P.O. Box 9454, Terre Haute, IN 47808-9454. Tel.: 812-232-2163 & 237-3443.
E-mail: info@debsfoundation.org
Web Site: debsfoundation.org
Key Personnel: Pres., Noel Beasley; Treas., Benjamin Kite; Sec., Michelle Killion Morahn.
Institution Type/Description: Historic House: c.1894 home of Eugene V. Debs.
Hours & Admission Prices: Tues. & Thurs. 3-7, Wed. & Fri.-Sat. 10-2. No charge; donations accepted. Closed national holidays; New Year's Eve & Day; Christmas Eve, Day & week.
Attendance: 1,230 (actual)

NATIVE AMERICAN MUSEUM, 5170 E. Poplar St., Dobbs Park, Terre Haute, IN 47803-9313. Tel.: 812-877-6007.
E-mail: jane.creedon@terrehaute.in.gov
Web Site: www.terrehaute.in.gov
Key Personnel: Cur., Jane Creedon.
Institution Type/Description: Museum of Native American Cultures.
Hours & Admission Prices: Tues.-Sat. 9-5, Sun. 12-5. No charge; donations accepted. Closed all legal holidays. &
Attendance: 13,000 (estimated)

PAUL DRESSER MEMORIAL BIRTHPLACE, First & Farrington Sts., Terre Haute, IN 47802. Mailing Address: 1411 S. 6th St., Terre Haute, IN 47802. Tel.: 812-235-9717. Fax: 812-235-9717.
E-mail: vchs@joink.com
Web Site: www.vchsmuseum.org
Key Personnel: Exec. Dir., Marylee Hagan.
Institution Type/Description: Historic House Museum: c.1850 Paul Dresser Birthplace.
Hours & Admission Prices: May-Sept. Sun. 1-4. Museum: Tues.-Sun. 1-4; other times by appointment, weather permitting. No charge; donations accepted. Closed holidays.
Attendance: 15,000 (estimated)

SWOPE ART MUSEUM, 25 S. 7th St., Terre Haute, IN 47807-3692. Tel.: 812-238-1676. Fax: 812-238-1677.

E-mail: info@swope.org
Web Site: www.swope.org
Key Personnel: Exec. Dir., Susan Baley; Mgr. Communications, Kristi Finley; Cur., Edward Trover.
Institution Type/Description: Art Museum: housed in 1901 Renaissance Revival building.
Hours & Admission Prices: Tues.-Thurs. & Sat.-Sun. 12-5, Fri. 12-8; call for additional hours. No charge; donations accepted. Closed national holidays. &
Attendance: 13,000 (actual)

TERRE HAUTE CHILDREN'S MUSEUM, 727 Wabash Ave., Terre Haute, IN 47807-3203. Tel.: 812-235-5548.
E-mail: info@terrehautechildrensmuseum.com
Web Site: www.terrehautechildrensmuseum.com
Institution Type/Description: Children's Museum.
Hours & Admission Prices: Tues.-Thurs. 10-6, Fri. 10-8, Sat. 10-5, Sun. 12-5. Admission $7; children under 2 no charge. &

UNIVERSITY ART GALLERY, INDIANA STATE UNIVERSITY, Center for Performing & Fine Arts, N. 7th & Chestnut St., Terre Haute, IN 47809. Mailing Address: Dept. of Art, FA 108, Terre Haute, IN 47809. Tel.: 812-237-3720. Fax: 812-237-4359.
E-mail: jason.saavedra@indstate.edu
Web Site: www.indstate.edu/artgallery
Institution Type/Description: Art Gallery.
Hours & Admission Prices: Mon.-Wed. & Sat. 11-4, Thurs. 11-7. No charge. Closed holidays. &
Attendance: 18,000 (estimated)

VIGO COUNTY HISTORICAL MUSEUM, 929 Wabash Ave., Terre Haute, IN 47807. Tel.: 812-235-9717.
E-mail: info@vchsmuseum.org
Web Site: www.vchsmuseum.org
Key Personnel: Exec. Dir., Susan Tingley; Cur., Tanis Nicklasch.
Institution Type/Description: History Center: housed in historic Ehrmann manufacturing bldg.
Hours & Admission Prices: Tues.-Sat. 10-5, Sun. 12-5. Adults $7, seniors $6, children $4. Closed national holidays.
Attendance: 15,000 (estimated)

WABASH VALLEY RAILROADERS MUSEUM, 1316 Plum St., Terre Haute, IN 47801. Mailing Address: The Haley Tower Historical & Technical Society, P.O. Box 10291, Terre Haute, IN 47801. Tel.: 812-238-9958.
E-mail: wvrrminfo@gmail.com
Institution Type/Description: History Museum.
Hours & Admission Prices: May-Oct. Sat.-Sun. 11-4; other times by appointment.

Thorntown

THORNTOWN HERITAGE MUSEUM, 124 W. Main St., Thorntown, IN 46071-1128. Mailing Address: 124 N. Market St., Thorntown, IN 46071-1144. Tel.: 765-436-7348. Fax: 765-436-7011.
E-mail: pmyers@thorntown.lib.in.us
Key Personnel: Pres. (V), John Gillan.
Institution Type/Description: History Museum.
Hours & Admission Prices: May-Sept. Sat. 1-5; other times by appointment. No charge; donations accepted. &
Attendance: 450 (estimated)

Tipton

TIPTON COUNTY HERITAGE CENTER, 323 W. South St., Tipton, IN 46072-2068. Tel.: 765-675-5828.
E-mail: tchs@tds.net
Web Site: www.tiptonhistorical.com
Key Personnel: Dir., Jill Curnutt-Howerton; Pres. (V), Donald Manlove.
Institution Type/Description: History Museum.
Hours & Admission Prices: Tues.-Sat. 1-5. No charge.
Attendance: 400 (estimated)

Union City

ART ASSOCIATION OF RANDOLPH COUNTY, INC., 115 N. Howard, Union City, IN 47390-1435. Tel.: 765-964-7227. Fax: 765-964-4569. Facebook: Arts Depot.
E-mail: info@artsdepot.org

Web Site: www.artsdepot.org
Key Personnel: Exec. Dir., Vicki Vardaman.
Institution Type/Description: Art Museum.
Hours & Admission Prices: Tues.-Fri. 10-4; other times by appointment. Museum: no charge; donations accepted. Special events may require an admission donation. Closed major holidays. &
Attendance: 5,000 (estimated)

Valparaiso

BRAUER MUSEUM OF ART, Mailing Address: Valparaiso University Center for the Arts, 1709 Chapel Dr., Valparaiso, IN 46383-4519. Tel.: 219-464-5365. Fax: 219-464-5244.
E-mail: gregg.hertzlieb@valpo.edu
Web Site: www.valpo.edu/brauer-museum-of-art
Key Personnel: Dir. & Cur., Gregg Hertzlieb; Assoc. Cur. & Registrar, Gloria Ruff.
Institution Type/Description: Art Museum.
Hours & Admission Prices: Academic year: Tues. & Thurs.-Fri. 10-5, Wed. 10-8:30, Sat.-Sun. 12-5. Academic recess & summer: Tues.-Sun. 12-5. No charge; donations accepted. Closed New Year's Eve & Day, Good Friday; Easter; Independence Day; Thanksgiving; Christmas Eve & Day. &
Attendance: 10,000 (estimated)

THE MEMORIAL OPERA HOUSE, 104 E. Indiana Ave., Valparaiso, IN 46383-5603. Tel.: 219-548-9137. Fax: 219-462-2640.
Key Personnel: Exec. Dir., Scot MacDonald.
Institution Type/Description: Historic Building: built in 1893. Listed on the National Register of Historic Places.
Hours & Admission Prices: Call for hours.

PORTER COUNTY MUSEUM/POCO MUSE, 153 S. Franklin St., Valparaiso, IN 46383-5631. Tel.: 219-465-3595. Facebook: PoCo Muse.
E-mail: info@pocomuse.org
Web Site: pocomuse.org
Formerly: Old Jail Museum
Key Personnel: Chm., Joanne Urschel; Exec. Dir., Kevin Matthew Pazour.
Institution Type/Description: Local History Museum.
Hours & Admission Prices: Wed.-Sat. 9-5. No charge: donations accepted. Closed some national holidays.
Attendance: 8,000 (estimated)

Veedersburg

FOUNTAIN COUNTY WAR MUSEUM, INC., 116 E. First St., Veedersburg, IN 47987-1402. Tel.: 765-376-6474.
E-mail: auters69@yahoo.com
Key Personnel: Dir. & Pres. (V), Archie Campbell.
Institution Type/Description: War Museum.
Hours & Admission Prices: Mon.-Fri. 10-2, Sat. 10-4; other times by appointment. No charge; donations accepted. &
Attendance: 500 (estimated)

Vernon

JENNINGS COUNTY HISTORICAL SOCIETY, 134 E. Brown St., Vernon, IN 47282. Mailing Address: P.O. Box 335, Vernon, IN 47282. Tel.: 812-346-8989.
E-mail: hector1838@frontier.com
Web Site: jenningscounty.org
Key Personnel: Pres., Brad Bender; Vice Pres., Pat Rice; Museum Shop Mgr., Helen Amburgey.
Institution Type/Description: Historical Society Museum: housed in the North American House; built in 1838.
Hours & Admission Prices: Wed.-Fri. 11-4 and during festivals. No charge; donations accepted. &
Attendance: 15,000 (estimated)

Versailles

RIPLEY COUNTY, INDIANA, HISTORICAL SOCIETY MUSEUM, Water & Main Sts., Versailles, IN 47042. Mailing Address: Box 525, Versailles, IN 47042-0525.
E-mail: staff@rchslib.org
Key Personnel: Dir. & Treas., Owen Menchhofer; Pres. & Acting Cur., Cheryl Welch.
Institution Type/Description: Historical Society Museum.

Hours & Admission Prices: Museum: Memorial Day to Labor Day Mon.-Tues. & Thurs.-Fri. 10-4. Library: Mon.-Fri. 1-4. No charge; donations accepted. Library Research: Adults $5; members no charge. &
Attendance: 1,000 (estimated)

Vevay

LIFE ON THE OHIO RIVER HISTORY MUSEUM, 208 E. Market St., Vevay, IN 47043-1233.
E-mail: swcomuseums@embarqmail.com
Key Personnel: Dir. & Coord. Collections, Martha Bladen; Pres. (V), Sundra Whitham; Treas., Anita Danner; Sec., Joyce Benbow.
Institution Type/Description: History Museum.
Hours & Admission Prices: April-Oct. daily 10-4; Nov.-March daily 12-4. No charge. Closed Christmas Eve & Day. &
Attendance: 4,200 (actual)

SWITZERLAND COUNTY HISTORICAL MUSEUM, 210 E. Main, Vevay, IN 47043. Mailing Address: 208 E. Market St., Vevay, IN 47043-1233. Tel.: 812-427-3560.
E-mail: swcomuseums@embarqmail.com
Web Site: www.switzcomuseums.org
Key Personnel: Dir., Martha Bladen; Pres. (V), Sundra Whitham; Recording Sec., Joyce Benbow.
Institution Type/Description: County History Museum.
Hours & Admission Prices: Daily 12-4. No charge. Closed Easter; Thanksgiving; Christmas. &
Attendance: 4,200 (actual)

Vincennes

GEORGE ROGERS CLARK NATIONAL HISTORICAL PARK, 401 S. Second St., Vincennes, IN 47591-1001. Tel.: 812-882-1776, ext. 110. Fax: 812-882-7270.
E-mail: gero_ranger_activities@nps.gov
Web Site: www.nps.gov/gero
Key Personnel: Supt., Frank Doughman.
Institution Type/Description: Park Museum.
Hours & Admission Prices: Daily 9-5. Adults 17 & over $3. Closed New Year's Day; Thanksgiving; Christmas. &
Attendance: 129,950 (actual)

INDIANA MILITARY MUSEUM INC., 715 S. 6th St., Vincennes, IN 47591-8922. Mailing Address: P.O. Box 977, Vincennes, IN 47591-8922. Tel.: 812-882-1941.
Web Site: www.indianamilitarymuseum.org
Key Personnel: Dir. & Pres. (V), Jim R. Osborne; Volunteer Coord., Kassie Roush.
Institution Type/Description: Military Museum.
Hours & Admission Prices: Daily 10-4. Adults $5, children $3; discounts to groups, seniors & veterans; museum members no charge. Closed New Year's Day; Thanksgiving; Christmas. &
Attendance: 5,000 (actual)

MICHEL BROUILLET HOUSE & MUSEUM, 509 N. 1st St., Vincennes, IN 47591-1401. Mailing Address: P.O. Box 1979, Vincennes, IN 47591. Tel.: 812-882-7422. Fax: 812-882-0928.
Key Personnel: Cur., Richard Day.
Institution Type/Description: History Museum: housed in 1806 restored French pioneer home.
Hours & Admission Prices: By appointment. Adults $2, children $1.

OLD CATHEDRAL LIBRARY & MUSEUM, 205 Church St., Vincennes, IN 47591-1133. Tel.: 812-882-5638.
Key Personnel: Dir., John Schipp.
Institution Type/Description: Religious Museum.
Hours & Admission Prices: Memorial Day to Labor Day Mon.-Fri. 12:30-4; other times by appointment. Adults $1, children 12 & under $.50.

OLD FRENCH HOUSE & INDIAN MUSEUM, 1st & Seminary St., Vincennes, IN 47591. Mailing Address: The Old Northwest Corp., P.O. Box 1979, Vincennes, IN 47591. Tel.: 812-882-7742, 800-886-6443.
E-mail: vincennesshs@indianamuseum.org
Key Personnel: Mgr., David Weaver.
Institution Type/Description: History Museum: housed in the former home of Michael Brouillet; c.1806.
Hours & Admission Prices: Tours: Mon.-Sat. 2:30 pm; other times by appointment. Adults $2, students $1.

RED SKELTON MUSEUM AND EDUCATION CENTER, 20 Red Skelton Blvd., Vincennes, IN 47591. Mailing Address: Vincennes University, 1002 N. 1st St., DC-38, Vincennes, IN 47591. Tel.: 812-888-4184.
E-mail: redskelton@vinu.edu
Web Site: www.redskeltonmuseum.org
Institution Type/Description: History Museum.
Hours & Admission Prices: Tues.-Sat. 10-5, Sun. 12-5. Adults $8, seniors 60 & over $7, students $5; discounts to groups; children under 5 no charge.

VINCENNES STATE HISTORIC SITE, INDIANA TERRITORY, First & Harrison Sts., Vincennes, IN 47591. Mailing Address: P.O. Box 81, Vincennes, IN 47591-0081. Tel.: 812-882-7422. Fax: 812-882-0928.
E-mail: museumcommunication@indianamuseum.org
Web Site: www.state.in.us/ism/sites/vincennes/
Key Personnel: Cur., Bruce A. Beesley; Asst. Cur., Richard Day.
Institution Type/Description: Historic Site: c.1805 Territory Capitol Building.
Hours & Admission Prices: Mon.-Sat. 9-5. Adults $3.50, seniors $3, children $2. Closed state holidays. &
Attendance: 33,000 (actual)

VINCENNES STATE HISTORIC SITE: VINCENNES BRANCH OF STATE BANK OF INDIANA, 1 W. Harrison St., Vincennes, IN 47591. Mailing Address: P.O. Box 81, Vincennes, IN 47591-0081. Tel.: 812-882-7422. Fax: 812-882-0928.
E-mail: vincennesshs@indianamuseum.org
Web Site: www.state.in.us/ism/sites/vincennes/
Key Personnel: Historic Site Cur., Bruce Beesley.
Institution Type/Description: History Museum: housed in the former state bank building; built in 1838.
Hours & Admission Prices: Tues.-Sun. 10-5. Adults $6, seniors $5, children $3; discounts to groups of 15 or more; children under 3 no charge. &
Attendance: 5,000 (estimated)

WILLIAM HENRY HARRISON MANSION, GROUSELAND, 3 W. Scott St., Vincennes, IN 47591-1433. Tel.: 812-882-2096. Fax: 812-882-7626. Facebook: Grouseland Foundation.
E-mail: grouseland@sbcglobal.net
Web Site: grouselandfoundation.org
Key Personnel: Exec. Dir., Lisa Ice-Jones; Cur., Dennis Latta.
Institution Type/Description: History Museum: Presidential Home. A National Historic Landmark.
Hours & Admission Prices: Jan.-Feb. Tues.-Sun. 11-4; March-Dec. daily 10-5 Adults $7, seniors $6, students & children $5, discounts to groups of 10 & more. Closed New Year's Day; Easter; Thanksgiving; Christmas Eve & Day.
Attendance: 10,500 (actual)

Wabash

CHARLEY CREEK GARDENS, 551 N. Miami St., Wabash, IN 46992. Mailing Address: P.O. Box 454, Wabash, IN 46992-0454. Tel.: 260-563-1020.
E-mail: KSMITH@HONEYWELLFOUNDATION.ORG
Web Site: www.charleycreekgardens.org/about-us
Key Personnel: Dir., Kelly Smith.
Institution Type/Description: Gardens.
Hours & Admission Prices: Gardens: daily dawn to dusk. Center: by appointment.

DR. JAMES FORD HISTORIC HOME, 177 W. Hill St., Wabash, IN 46992-3049. Mailing Address: P.O. Box 454, Wabash, IN 46992-0454. Tel.: 260-563-8686.
E-mail: director@jamesfordmuseum.org
Web Site: jamesfordmuseum.org
Key Personnel: Dir., Michele Hughes.
Institution Type/Description: Historic House Museum: housed in a 19th century physician's home; built 1841.
Hours & Admission Prices: Fri.-Sat. 11-4; other times by appointment. Adults $4; discounts to groups; children 12 & under and members no charge. Call for seasonal hours & holiday closings. &
Attendance: 1,500 (estimated)

HONEYWELL CENTER, 275 W. Market St., Wabash, IN 46992-3057. Tel.: 260-563-1102. Fax: 260-563-0873.
Web Site: www.honeywellcenter.org
Key Personnel: Pres. & C.E.O., Tod Minnich; Exec. Asst., Kara Fulmer.
Institution Type/Description: Art Gallery.
Hours & Admission Prices: Daily 9am-10pm. No charge.

WABASH COUNTY HISTORICAL MUSEUM, 36 E. Market St., Wabash, IN 46992-3124. Tel.: 260-563-9070. Fax: 260-569-9070. Facebook: Wabash County Historical Museum.
E-mail: director@wabashmuseum.org
Web Site: www.wabashmuseum.org
Key Personnel: Exec. Dir., Mitch Figert; Chm. (V), Sam Frazier; Mgr. Communications, Brooke Duecker; Dir. Operations, Brian Haupert; Assoc. Dir., Shelby McLaughlin.
Institution Type/Description: History Museum.
Hours & Admission Prices: Tues.-Fri. 10-5, Sat. 10-4. Adults $5, children 6-12 & seniors $3; members and children 5 & under no charge. Closed major holidays.
Attendance: 14,000 (estimated)

Wakarusa

BIRD'S EYE VIEW MUSEUM OF MINIATURES, 325 S. Elkhart St., Wakarusa, IN 46573-9727. Mailing Address: c/o Wakarusa Historical Society, P.O. Box 2, Wakarusa, IN 46573. Tel.: 574-862-2367.
Institution Type/Description: History Museum.
Hours & Admission Prices: Mon.-Fri. 8-5. No charge; donations accepted.

Warsaw

KOSCIUSKO COUNTY HISTORICAL SOCIETY, 121 N. Indiana St., Warsaw, IN 46581. Mailing Address: P.O. Box 1071, Warsaw, IN 46581-1071. Tel.: 574-269-1078.
E-mail: director@kosciuskohistory.com
Web Site: www.kosciuskohistory.com
Key Personnel: Pres., Jerry Frush; Museum Dir., Sally Hogan.
Institution Type/Description: Historical Society Museum.
Hours & Admission Prices: Wed.-Sat. 10-4, Sat. 10-4. No charge; donations accepted. Closed major holidays. &
Attendance: 3,500 (estimated)

Washington

DAVIESS COUNTY HISTORICAL SOCIETY MUSEUM, 212 1/2 E. Main St., Washington, IN 47501. Mailing Address: P.O. Box 2341, Washington, IN 47501-0981. Tel.: 812-257-0301. Fax: 812-257-0301.
E-mail: dchistory@sbcglobal.net
Web Site: www.daviesscountyhistory.com
Formerly: Daviess County Museum
Institution Type/Description: History Museum.
Hours & Admission Prices: Mon.-Fri. 10-4, Sat. 9-12. Adults $2; members no charge. &
Attendance: 1,500 (estimated)

West Lafayette

THE ARTHUR & KRIEBEL HERBARIA, PURDUE UNIVERSITY, 915 W. State St., Dept. of Botany & Plant Pathology, West Lafayette, IN 47907-2054. Tel.: 765-494-4623. Fax: 765-494-0363.
E-mail: herbaria@purdue.edu
Web Site: ag.purdue.edu/btny/herbaria/pages/default.aspx
Key Personnel: Dir., M. Catherine Aime.
Institution Type/Description: Herbarium.
Hours & Admission Prices: Mon.-Fri. 9:30-4:30. No charge. Closed state & national holidays. &
Attendance: 150 (estimated)

PURDUE UNIVERSITY GALLERIES, Yue-Kong Pao Hall, 552 W. Wood St., West Lafayette, IN 47907-2002. Tel.: 765-494-3061. Fax: 765-496-2817.
E-mail: galleries@purdue.edu
Web Site: www.purdue.edu/galleries
Key Personnel: Interim Dir., Michal Hathaway.
Institution Type/Description: University Art Gallery.
Hours & Admission Prices: Mon.-Wed. & Fri.-Sat. 10-5, Thurs. 10-8, Sun. 1-5. No charge. Closed university holidays. &
Attendance: 24,797 (actual)

Westfield

WESTFIELD WASHINGTON HISTORICAL SOCIETY & MUSEUM, 130 Penn St., Westfield, IN 46074. Tel.: 317-804-5365.
E-mail: communications@wwhs.us
Web Site: www.wwhs.us
Key Personnel: Dir., Jim Peyton; Vice Pres., Steve Osborne; Sec., Diana Peyton; Treas., Terry Carrithers; Communs. & Newsletter, Teri Dervenis; Prog. Dir., Bruce Hansen; Archives & Collection Mgr., Michael Kobrowski; Mem. Dir., Rachel Merrill; Mem. Clerk, Paula Monroe; Special Projects, Curt Epp; Recorder, Tom Roberts.
Institution Type/Description: Historical Society Museum.
Hours & Admission Prices: Sat. 11-3, call to confirm. No charge.

Whiting

MASCOT HALL OF FAME, 1851 Front St., Whiting, IN 46394. Tel.: 219-354-8814. Facebook.
E-mail: info@mascothalloffame.com
Web Site: mascothalloffame.com
Institution Type/Description: Sports Mascot Museum.
Hours & Admission Prices: Mon.-Wed. & Fri.-Sat. 10-6, Thurs. 10-8, Sun. 10-5. Admission $12, teachers & seniors over 65 $10; active military & children under 2 no charge. Closed New Year's Day; Easter; Thanksgiving; Christmas. &

WHITING-ROBERTSDALE HISTORICAL MUSEUM, 1610 119th St., Whiting, IN 46394-1702. Tel.: 219-659-1432.
E-mail: puccini99@aol.com
Institution Type/Description: History Museum.
Hours & Admission Prices: Call for hours.

Winchester

RANDOLPH COUNTY HISTORICAL MUSEUM, 416 S. Meridian St., Winchester, IN 47394-2028. Tel.: 317-584-1334.
E-mail: rchsin2@comcast.net
Web Site: www.randolphcountyindianahistoricalsociety.org
Key Personnel: Pres. (V), Ted Martin; Cur., Monisa Wisener.
Institution Type/Description: Genealogy & History Museum: housed in 1858 brick home built by Carey Goodrich.
Hours & Admission Prices: Mon.-Fri. 1:30-6; other times by appointment. No charge; donations accepted. &
Attendance: 750 (estimated)

Wingate

MIDTOWN MUSEUM OF NATIVE CULTURES, Mailing Address: 208 S. Vine St., Wingate, IN 47994. Tel.: 765-376-7128. Facebook.
E-mail: midtownmuseum@yahoo.com
Web Site: www.midtowninwaynetown.com
Formerly: Mid'Town Museum
Key Personnel: Owner, Joyce Jones.
Institution Type/Description: History Museum.
Hours & Admission Prices: Tues.-Fri. 9-4:30, Sat. 9-2. Adults $2, seniors $1.50, children $1; discounts to groups.

Winona Lake

THE WINONA HISTORY CENTER AND BILLY SUNDAY HISTORIC HOME, Westminster Hall, Grace College, 105 9th St., Winona Lake, IN 46590-1062. Mailing Address: Westminster Hall, Grace College, 200 Seminary Dr., Winona Lake, IN 46590. Tel.: 574-372-5193 & 527-9573. Facebook.
E-mail: winonamuseum@grace.edu
Web Site: winonahistorycenter.com
Formerly: Reneker Museum of Winona History
Key Personnel: Dir., Jared S. Burkholder.
Institution Type/Description: Historic Site: housed in former home of professional baseball player turned evangelist, Billy Sunday.
Hours & Admission Prices: Tues.-Sat. 2-5. Visitors Center: donations accepted. Museum & Archives: $2. Sunday Home Tour: $4; discounts to groups with appointment; children 12 & under no charge. Closed New Year's Day; Good Friday; Thanksgiving; Christmas. &
Attendance: 1,000 (actual)

Wolcott

HISTORIC WOLCOTT HOUSE, 502 N. Range St., Wolcott, IN 47995-8276. Mailing Address: Anson Wolcott Historical Society, P.O. Box 242, Wolcott, IN 47995. Tel.: 219-279-2951.
Key Personnel: Pres., Ann Cain.
Institution Type/Description: Historic House Museum.
Hours & Admission Prices: Tues. & Thurs. 10-2. No charge; donations accepted.

Wolf Lake

LUCKEY HOSPITAL MUSEUM, 1346 Market St., Wolf Lake, IN 46796. Mailing Address: 5635 W. 100 S., Kimmell, IN 46760. Tel.: 260-610-3314.
E-mail: shile112635@gmail.com
Web Site: www.luckeyhospitalmuseum.org
Key Personnel: Chm. (V), Shirley A. Hile; Pres. (V), Sue Johnson.
Institution Type/Description: History Museum: housed in the 1920s former hospital founded by 3 family physicians, Dr. James Luckey, Dr. Robert Luckey, & Dr. Harold Luckey. Listed on the National Register of Historic Places.
Hours & Admission Prices: Memorial Day to Labor Day Wed. & Sat. 10-2; groups & other times by appointment. Adults $5, K-12 yrs. $3; members & pre-school students no charge.
Attendance: 500 (actual)

Zionsville

ANTIQUE FAN MUSEUM, 10983 Bennett Pkwy., Zionsville, IN 46077. Tel.: 888-567-2055 (Toll Free), 317-733-4113. Fax: 317-733-4162.
Institution Type/Description: History Museum.
Hours & Admission Prices: Mon.-Fri. 10-4.

P.H. SULLIVAN MUSEUM AND GENEALOGY LIBRARY, 225 W. Hawthorne St., Zionsville, IN 46077-1620. Tel.: 317-873-4900.
E-mail: info@sullivanmunce.org
Web Site: www.sullivanmunce.org
Key Personnel: Pres. Bd. Dir. (V), Kelly Masoncup; Exec. Dir., Cynthia Young; Pres. Museum Women's Guild (V), Judi Potts.
Institution Type/Description: Local History Museum.
Hours & Admission Prices: Tues.-Sat. 10-4. No charge; donations accepted. Closed New Year's Day; Thanksgiving; Christmas. &
Attendance: 7,000 (estimated)

SULLIVANMUNCE CULTURAL CENTER, 205-225 W. Hawthorne St., Zionsville, IN 46077-1620. Tel.: 317-873-4900.
E-mail: info@sullivanmunce.org
Web Site: www.sullivanmunce.org
Formerly: Munce Art Center
Key Personnel: Exec. Dir., Cynthia Young; Pres., Kelly Masoncup.
Institution Type/Description: History and The Arts.
Hours & Admission Prices: Tues.-Sat. 10-4. No charge; donations accepted. Closed holidays. &
Attendance: 11,000 (estimated)

IOWA
(369 listings)

Ackley

ACKLEY HERITAGE CENTER, 120 State St., Ackley, IA 50601-1545. Tel.: 641-847-2201. Facebook.
E-mail: ackleyhc@mchsi.com
Web Site: www.ackleyheritagecenter.com
Key Personnel: Dir., Larry Wright.
Institution Type/Description: History Museum.
Hours & Admission Prices: Tues. & Thurs.-Fri. 1:30-4:30; other times by appointment. No charge; donations accepted. &
Attendance: 850 (estimated)

Adel

ADEL HISTORICAL MUSEUM, 1129 Main St., Adel, IA 50003-1424. Mailing Address: 1204 Locust St., Adel, IA 50003. Tel.: 515-993-1032. Fax: 515-993-3384.
E-mail: donprice555@msn.com
Web Site: www.adeliowa.org
Key Personnel: Dir., Chm. (V) & Museum Shop Mgr., Jan Price.

Institution Type/Description: History Museum: housed in a former schoolhouse; built in 1857.
Hours & Admission Prices: May-Sept. Sat. 10-4; other times by appointment. No charge; donations accepted. &
Attendance: 400 (estimated)

Albert City

ALBERT CITY HISTORICAL MUSEUM, 212 2nd St., N., Albert City, IA 50510-1210. Mailing Address: Box 431, Albert City, IA 50510. Tel.: 712-843-5684.
Key Personnel: Pres. (V), Dick Aronson.
Institution Type/Description: History Museum.
Hours & Admission Prices: Memorial Day to Labor Day Sun. 2-5; other times by appointment. Adults $5; members no charge.
Attendance: 200 (estimated)

Algona

CAMP ALGONA POW MUSEUM, 114 S. Thorington St., Algona, IA 50511-2616. Mailing Address: P.O Box 174, Algona, IA 50511-0174. Tel.: 515-395-2267 & 295-3719.
E-mail: yocumcampalgona@netamumail.com
Web Site: www.pwcamp.algona.org
Key Personnel: Pres. & Chm. (V), Richard Schiek; Vice Pres., Jerry Yocum; Sec. & Treas., Don Hansen.
Institution Type/Description: History Museum: former camp for German POW's from 1944-1946.
Hours & Admission Prices: April-Dec. Sat.-Sun. 1-4; other times by appointment. Adults $3. &
Attendance: 2,500 (actual)

THORESON MUSEUM OF PHARMACY, 808 Hwy. 18 W., Algona, IA 50511. Tel.: 800-247-5930.
E-mail: info@phmic.com
Web Site: www.phmic.com
Institution Type/Description: History Museum.
Hours & Admission Prices: Mon.-Fri. 8-5. &

Allison

BUTLER COUNTY HISTORICAL SOCIETY, 219 1/2 S. Main St., Allison, IA 50602-9507. Mailing Address: 714 Elm St., Allison, IA 50602-9727. Tel.: 319-267-2255.
E-mail: djpoppen@netins.net
Formerly: Butler County Historical Museum-Little Yellow Schoolhouse
Key Personnel: Pres., Andrew Menchyk, Jr.; Vice Pres., Debi Kruger; Sec., Brian Abels; Treas., Kenny Bonus.
Institution Type/Description: Historical Society Museum: residing on the Butler County Fairgrounds.
Hours & Admission Prices: June-Sept. by appointment. No charge; donations accepted. &
Attendance: 850 (estimated)

Amana

AMANA HERITAGE MUSEUM, 705 44th Ave., Amana, IA 52203-0081. Mailing Address: P.O. Box 81, Amana, IA 52203-0081. Tel.: 319-622-3567. Fax: 319-622-6481.
E-mail: amanaheritage@southslope.net
Web Site: www.amanaheritage.org
Formerly: Museum of Amana History
Key Personnel: Dir., Jon Childers; Cur., Rebecca Dickman.
Institution Type/Description: Historical Society Museum: housed in 1865 & 1870 buildings.
Hours & Admission Prices: April-Oct. 30 Mon.-Sat. 10-5, Sun. 12-5. Adults $8, children 5-17 $4; discounts to groups; children under 5, students & members no charge. &
Attendance: 25,000 (actual)

Ames

BRUNNIER ART MUSEUM, University Museums, Iowa State University, 2nd Fl. Scheman Bldg., 1805 Center Dr., Ames, IA 50011. Tel.: 515-294-3342. Fax: 515-294-3342.
Web Site: www.museums.iastate.edu
Key Personnel: Dir. & Chief Cur., Lynette L. Pohlman; Collections Mgr., Allison Sheridan; Interpretive Specialist, Brooke Rogers; Devel. Sec., Sue Olson; Educator, Visual Literacy & Learning, Lilah Anderson; Administrative Specialist, Susan Larson.

Institution Type/Description: Decorative & Fine Arts Museum.
Hours & Admission Prices: Mon.-Fri. 10-4, Sat.-Sun.1-4. Suggested Donation: $3. Closed Memorial Day; Independence Day; Labor Day; Thanksgiving; Christmas; university holidays. &
Attendance: 15,000 (estimated)

CHRISTIAN PETERSEN ART MUSEUM, Morrill Hall, Iowa State University, Ames, IA 50011. Mailing Address: University Museums, Iowa State University, 290 Scheman Bldg., Ames, IA 50011. Tel.: 515-294-9500.
E-mail: lpohlman@iastate.edu
Web Site: www.museums.iastate.edu
Key Personnel: Dir. & Chief Cur., Lynette Pohlman; Asst. Cur. Collections & Education, Adrienne Gennett; Collections Mgmt. & Communications Coord., Allison Sheridan; Interpretive Specialist, David Faux; Campus Outreach Coord., Kate Greder; Devel. Sec., Sue Olson; Educator, Visual Literacy & Learning, Nancy Girard; Administrative Specialist, Susan Larson.
Institution Type/Description: Art Museum.
Hours & Admission Prices: Mon.-Fri. 11-4. No charge; donations accepted. Closed major holidays; semester breaks. &
Attendance: 15,000 (estimated)

FARM HOUSE MUSEUM, Farm House Ln., Iowa State University, Ames, IA 50011. Mailing Address: University Museums, Iowa State University, 290 Scheman Bldg., Ames, IA 50011. Tel.: 515-294-7426. Fax: 515-294-3342.
Web Site: www.museums.iastate.edu
Key Personnel: Dir. & Chief Cur., Lynette Pohlman; Collections Mgmt. & Communications Coord., Allison Juull; Devel Sec., Sue Olson; Educator, Visual Literacy & Learning, Nancy Gebhart.
Institution Type/Description: Historic Site: c.1860-1864 The Farm House.
Hours & Admission Prices: Mon.-Fri. 12-4 by appointment only. No charge; donations accepted. Closed university holidays; semester breaks. &
Attendance: 6,000 (estimated)

OCTAGON CENTER FOR THE ARTS, 427 Douglas Ave., Ames, IA 50010-6281. Tel.: 515-232-5331. Fax: 515-232-5088. Instagram: @octagon_arts.
E-mail: info@octagonarts.org
Web Site: www.octagonarts.org
Key Personnel: Acting Exec. Dir. & Cur., Heather Johnson; Pres., Lee Anne Wilson; Vice Pres., Linda Lewis Lieberman; Octagon Shop Mgr., Ruth Wiedemeier; Educ. Dir., Beth Weninger.
Institution Type/Description: Art Center.
Hours & Admission Prices: Gallery: Mon.-Fri. 10-5, Sat. 1-5. Office: Mon.-Fri. 8-5. Shop: Mon.-Wed., Fri. & Sat. 10-5, Thurs. 10-7. Gallery: no charge; donation suggested. Fees for classes & special events. Closed major holidays. &
Attendance: 30,000 (estimated)

REIMAN GARDENS - IOWA STATE UNIVERSITY, 1407 University Blvd., Ames, IA 50011. Tel.: 515-294-2710. Fax: 515-294-4817.
E-mail: reimangardens@iastate.edu
Web Site: www.reimangardens.com
Key Personnel: Cur., Nathan Brockman.
Institution Type/Description: Garden.
Hours & Admission Prices: Gardens: June-Sept. 6 daily 9-6; Sept. 7-May daily 9-4:30. Butterfly Wing: daily 9-4:30. Adults 18-64 $8, seniors 65 & over $7, youth 4-17 $4; children 3 & under, members & ISU students no charge. Closed New Year's Day; Thanksgiving; Christmas.

STORY COUNTY CONSERVATION CENTER, McFarland Park, 56461 180th St., Ames, IA 50010-9451. Tel.: 515-232-2516. Fax: 515-232-6989.
E-mail: conservation@storycountyiowa.gov
Web Site: www.storycountyconservation.org
Institution Type/Description: Conservation Center.
Hours & Admission Prices: Mon.-Fri. 8:30-4:30.

Anamosa

ANAMOSA STATE PENITENTIARY MUSEUM, 406 N. High St., Anamosa, IA 52205-1199. Mailing Address: P.O. Box 144, Anamosa, IA 52205-0144. Tel.: 319-462-2386.
E-mail: aspmuseum@mchsi.com
Web Site: www.asphistory.com/museum
Key Personnel: Chm. (V), Don Folkerts; Museum Shop Mgr., Jan Pearson.
Institution Type/Description: Penitentiary Museum.

Hours & Admission Prices: Memorial Day to Oct. Fri.-Mon. 12-4; other times by appointment. Adults $3; children, students & members no charge. &
Attendance: 1,700 (actual)

GRANT WOOD ART GALLERY, 124 E. Main St., Anamosa, IA 52205-1879. Tel.: 319-462-4267.
E-mail: grantwoodartgallery@grantwoodgallery.org
Web Site: www.grantwoodartgallery.org
Key Personnel: Chm. (V) & Museum Shop Mgr., Jon D. Hatcher.
Institution Type/Description: Art Gallery.
Hours & Admission Prices: Jan.-March Sun. 1-4; April-Dec. Mon.-Sat. 10-4, Sun. 1-4. No charge. &

NATIONAL MOTORCYCLE MUSEUM, 102 Chamber Dr., Anamosa, IA 52205-1806. Mailing Address: P.O. Box 405, Anamosa, IA 52205-0405. Tel.: 319-462-3925. Fax: 319-462-3982.
E-mail: museum@nationalmcmuseum.org
Web Site: www.nationalmcmuseum.org
Institution Type/Description: Motorcycle Museum.
Hours & Admission Prices: April-Oct. daily 9-5; Nov.-March Mon.-Sat. 9-5, Sun. 10-4. Adults $8, seniors $7; children 12 & under no charge. &
Attendance: 18,000 (actual)

Ankeny

ANKENY AREA HISTORICAL SOCIETY MUSEUM, 301 S.W. Third St., Ankeny, IA 50023. Mailing Address: P.O. Box 1111, Ankeny, IA 50021-0973. Tel.: 515-965-5795.
E-mail: history@ankenyhistorical.org
Web Site: ankenyhistorical.org
Key Personnel: Dir., Rosemary Hutton Taylor; Pres. (V), Ron Sampson.
Institution Type/Description: Historical Society Museum.
Hours & Admission Prices: April-Nov. 1st Sun. of month 2-4; other times by appointment. No charge; donations accepted. &
Attendance: 1,200 (estimated)

ANKENY ART CENTER, 1520 S.W. Ordnance Rd., Ankeny, IA 50023-2510. Tel.: 515-965-0940. Fax: 515-963-1009.
E-mail: ankenyarts@ankenyartcenter.com
Web Site: www.ankenyartcenter.com
Key Personnel: Dir., Barb Vaske.
Institution Type/Description: Art Center.
Hours & Admission Prices: Tues.-Wed. & Fri. 9-1, Thurs. 4-7, Sat. 9-12. No charge.
Attendance: 5,000 (estimated)

IOWA AVIATION HERITAGE MUSEUM, 3704 S.E. Convenience Blvd., Ankeny, IA 50021. Tel.: 515-964-4515.
E-mail: mlcallison@myway.com
Web Site: iowaaviationheritagemuseum.webs.com
Key Personnel: Chm. (V), Roger L. Pointer; Pres. (V), Mike Callison; Museum Shop Mgr., Mickey McGilvra.
Institution Type/Description: Aviation History Museum.
Hours & Admission Prices: April-Oct. Tues., Thurs. & Sat. 10-3; other times by appointment. No charge; donations accepted. &
Attendance: 3,000 (actual)

Armstrong

ARMSTRONG HERITAGE MUSEUM, 425 Sixth St., Armstrong, IA 50514. Mailing Address: 401 C Ave., Armstrong, IA 50514. Tel.: 712-868-3593.
E-mail: cggc@ringtelco.com
Web Site: www.armstrongiowa.net/libmus.php
Key Personnel: Dir., Paula Dyer.
Institution Type/Description: History Museum.
Hours & Admission Prices: By appointment. No charge; donations accepted.
Attendance: 350 (estimated)

Arnolds Park

ABBIE GARDNER STATE SITE, 34 Monument Dr., Arnolds Park, IA 51331. Mailing Address: P.O. Box 74, Arnolds Park, IA 51331-0074. Tel.: 712-332-7248. Fax: 515-282-0502.
Key Personnel: Dir., Mike Koppert.
Institution Type/Description: Historic House Museum: housed in log cabin built in 1856; located on the site of the Spirit Lake Massacre in 1857. Listed on the National Register of Historic Places.

Hours & Admission Prices: Memorial Day to Labor Day daily 12-4; Sept. Sat. 12-4. No charge; donations accepted. &
Attendance: 15,000

IOWA GREAT LAKES MARITIME MUSEUM, 243 W. Broadway, Arnolds Park, IA 51331-7779. Mailing Address: P.O. Box 726, Arnolds Park, IA 51331-0726. Tel.: 712-332-5264.
E-mail: marykennedy@mchsi.com
Web Site: www.arnoldspark.com
Key Personnel: C.E.O., Charley Wittenberg; Cur., Mary Kennedy.
Institution Type/Description: Maritime Museum.
Hours & Admission Prices: Daily 10am, closing time varies. No charge; donations accepted. Closed Easter; Thanksgiving; Christmas. &
Attendance: 75,000 (estimated)

IOWA ROCK 'N ROLL MUSIC ASSOCIATION MUSEUM, 91 Lake St., Arnolds Park, IA 51331. Mailing Address: P.O. Box 557, Arnolds Park, IA 51331-0557. Tel.: 712-332-6540 & 330-0889 (office).
E-mail: info@iowarocknroll.com
Web Site: iowarocknroll.com
Institution Type/Description: Music Museum; housed on the site of the Roof Garden Ballroom.
Hours & Admission Prices: mid-May to mid-Sept. daily 11-7; mid-Sept. to mid-May Thurs.-Sat. 11-3. Adults 13 & over $1; IRRMA members and children 12 & under no charge. Closed New Year's Day; Veterans Day; Thanksgiving; Christmas. &
Attendance: 6,000 (estimated)

Ashton

DEBOER GROCERY MUSEUM AND LITTLE HOUSE MUSEUM, 320 Third St., Ashton, IA 51232. Tel.: 712-724-6239.
E-mail: chonkomp@hotmail.com
Institution Type/Description: History Museum.
Hours & Admission Prices: Memorial Day-Labor Day 1st & 3rd Sun. 10-2; other times by appointment. No charge; donations accepted.
Attendance: 200 (estimated)

Aurora

RICHARDSON-JAKWAY HISTORIC SITE, 2791 136th St., Aurora, IA 50607. Mailing Address: 1883 125th St., Hazleton, IA 50641-9695. Tel.: 319-636-2617. Fax: 319-636-2624.
E-mail: bccbdan@iowatelecom.net
Web Site: www.buchanancountyparks.com
Formerly: Fontana Interpretive Nature Center
Key Personnel: Dir., Dan Cohen.
Institution Type/Description: Historic House Museum.
Hours & Admission Prices: By appointment. No charge; donations accepted.

Avoca

FARMALL-LAND USA MUSEUM CLOSED, 2101 N. LaVista Heights Rd., Avoca, IA 51521. Mailing Address: 1523 N. Willow, Avoca, IA 51521. Tel.: 712-307-6806 & 712-343-6354.
E-mail: jwmez@walnutel.net
Web Site: www.farmall-land-usa.com
Institution Type/Description: History & Farming Museum.
Hours & Admission Prices: April-Oct. Tues.-Sat. 10-5, Sun. 12-5; other times by appointment. Adults $8, students $5, children 5-12 $3; children under 5 no charge.
Attendance: 5,500 (estimated)

SWEET VALE OF AVOCA MUSEUM, 504 N. Elm St., Avoca, IA 51521-3521. Tel.: 712-343-2477.
Institution Type/Description: History Museum.
Hours & Admission Prices: Memorial Day to Labor Day daily 1-4.

Beaman

BEAMAN HERITAGE CENTER, 223 Main St., Beaman, IA 50609. Mailing Address: P.O. Box 135, Beaman, IA 50609-0135. Tel.: 641-366-2912. Fax: 641-366-3141.
E-mail: bcmlib@heartofiowa.net
Web Site: library.beaman.lib.ia.us
Key Personnel: Dir., LaVonne Sternhagen.
Institution Type/Description: History Museum.

Hours & Admission Prices: Mon.-Fri. 2-6, Sat. 10 to noon; other times by appointment. No charge; donations accepted. &
Attendance: 145 (estimated)

Bedford

TAYLOR COUNTY HISTORICAL MUSEUM AND ROUND BARN, 1001 Pollock Blvd., Bedford, IA 50833. Tel.: 712-523-2041.
E-mail: taylorcomuseum@frontiernet.net
Institution Type/Description: History Museum.
Hours & Admission Prices: Call for hours. &

Belmond

JENISON-MEACHAM MEMORIAL ART CENTER AND MUSEUM, 1179 Taylor Ave., Belmond, IA 50421-7568. Tel.: 641-444-3557 & 4635.
Institution Type/Description: Art & History Museum.
Hours & Admission Prices: May-Nov. Sat.-Sun. 1:30-4:30. No charge. &

Bettendorf

FAMILY MUSEUM, 2900 Learning Campus Dr., Bettendorf, IA 52722-7710. Tel.: 563-344-4106. Fax: 563-344-4164. Facebook: Family Museum.
E-mail: familymuseum@bettendorf.org
Web Site: www.familymuseum.org
Key Personnel: Dir., Kim Kidwell; Business & Community Rels. Mgr., Amy Cannady; Exhibits Mgr., Tom Stanger; Coord. Group Svcs., Julie Klein; Coord. Events, Becky Ortner; Coord. Mktg, Elly Gerdts; Volunteer Coord., Steph DeLacy; Dance Coord., Jessica Halfhill; Museum Shop Mgr., Caroline O'Sullivan-Jens.
Institution Type/Description: Children's Museum.
Hours & Admission Prices: Memorial Day-Labor Day: Mon.-Sat. 9-5, Sun. 12-5; Sept.-May: Mon.-Thurs. 9-8, Fri.-Sat. 9-5, Sun. 12-5. Admission 2-59 $8, seniors 60 & over $4, children $4; discounts to military & ASTC members; children under one & members no charge. Closed major holidays. &
Attendance: 96,000 (estimated)

Bloomfield

FINDLEY HOUSE - DAVIS COUNTY HISTORICAL SOCIETY COMPLEX, 205 S. Dodge St., Bloomfield, IA 52537. Tel.: 641-664-1855 & 799-7463.
E-mail: hairynation104@netins.net
Key Personnel: Dir., Nancy Clancy; Vice Pres. (V), Cherri Casteell.
Institution Type/Description: Historical Society Museum: housed in the former home of Civil War physician, Dr. William Findley; built in 1867.
Hours & Admission Prices: Sat. 1-4; other times by appointment. No charge; donations accepted.
Attendance: 200 (estimated)

Boone

BOONE COUNTY HISTORICAL CENTER, 602 Story St., Boone, IA 50036-2832. Tel.: 515-432-1907.
E-mail: director@boonecountyhistory.org
Web Site: www.boonecountyhistory.org
Key Personnel: Dir., Pamela Schwartz; Chm., Lee McNair; Sec., Janet Tait; Treas., Judy Russell.
Institution Type/Description: Cultural Center & Museum: housed in 1907 Masonic Temple.
Hours & Admission Prices: Mon.-Fri. 1-4; other times by appointment. Adults $3; children & members no charge. Closed New Year's Day; Easter; Thanksgiving; Christmas. &
Attendance: 5,150 (actual)

IOWA RAILROAD HISTORICAL SOCIETY, 225 10th St., Boone, IA 50036-0603. Mailing Address: P.O. Box 603, Boone, IA 50036-0603. Tel.: 515-432-4249, ext. 14, 800-626-0319. Fax: 515-432-4253.
E-mail: info@bsvrr.com
Web Site: www.bsvrr.com
Key Personnel: C.E.O., Fenner Stevenson; Pres. (V), Alan Schroeder; Museum Dir., Mike Wendel; Financial Dir., Philip Deats; Museum Shop Mgr., Mechell Sikes.
Institution Type/Description: Historical Railroad Museum.
Hours & Admission Prices: Memorial Day to Oct. Mon.-Fri. 8:30-4:30, Sat.-Sun. 10-6; Nov.-May Mon.-Fri. 8:30-4:30. Historical Society & Museum: adults $20,

children $7; Museum: adults $8, children $3. Closed New Year's Day; Thanksgiving; Christmas. &
Attendance: 56,025 (actual)

KATE SHELLEY RAILROAD MUSEUM, 1198 - 232nd St., Boone, IA 50036-7118. Mailing Address: 602 Story St., Boone, IA 50036-2832. Tel.: 515-432-1907.
E-mail: director@boonecountyhistory.org
Web Site: www.boonecountyhistory.org
Key Personnel: Dir., Pamela Schwartz.
Institution Type/Description: Historic Site & Railroad Depot.
Hours & Admission Prices: Museum: by appointment. Grounds & Trails: daily dawn to dusk. No charge for general admission; bus tours: $1 per person.
Attendance: 2,000 (actual)

MAMIE DOUD EISENHOWER BIRTHPLACE, 709 Carroll St., Boone, IA 50036. Mailing Address: 602 Story St., Boone, IA 50036-2832. Tel.: 515-432-1907.
E-mail: director@boonecountyhistory.org
Web Site: www.boonecountyhistory.org
Key Personnel: Exec. Dir., Pamela Schwartz; Pres. (V), Lee McNair.
Institution Type/Description: Historic House: c.1890 Mamie Doud Eisenhower birthplace.
Hours & Admission Prices: Mon.-Sat. 10-5, Sun. 1:30-5. Adults $5; children 17 & under no charge.
Attendance: 6,000 (estimated)

Britt

HANCOCK COUNTY AGRICULTURAL MUSEUM, 2210 Jewel Ave., Britt, IA 50423-8584. Mailing Address: 2090 James Ave., Britt, IA 50423-8549. Tel.: 641-843-4362.
E-mail: judar59@msn.com
Key Personnel: Pres. (V) & Museum Shop Mgr., Darrell C. Schaper.
Institution Type/Description: Agriculture Museum.
Hours & Admission Prices: By appointment. No charge; donations accepted. &
Attendance: 1,273 (actual)

HOBO MUSEUM, 51 Main Ave. S., Britt, IA 50423-1664. Mailing Address: 21 N. Main, Britt, IA 50423. Tel.: 641-843-9104. Facebook: Hobo Museum.
E-mail: rdsykora@comcast.net
Web Site: hobo.com
Key Personnel: Pres. Hobo Foundation & Admin. Dir., Rod Sykora.
Institution Type/Description: History Museum.
Hours & Admission Prices: June-Aug. 15 Mon.-Fri. 10-5; other times by appointment. Admission $3. &
Attendance: 1,200 (estimated)

Burlington

ART GUILD OF BURLINGTON, INC. DBA ART CENTER OF BURLINGTON, 301 Jefferson St., Burlington, IA 52601-5333. Tel.: 319-754-8069. Fax: 319-754-4731. Facebook: Burlington Art Center.
E-mail: artsforliving@artcenterofburlington.com
Web Site: artcenterofburlington.com
Key Personnel: Exec. Dir., Tammy McCoy; Dir. Communications, Hillaurie Fritz-Bonar; Program Coord., Nicole Kamrath; Mgr. Artists Market, Magon VanZee.
Institution Type/Description: Art Gallery.
Hours & Admission Prices: No charge; donations accepted. &
Attendance: 10,000 (estimated)

HAWKEYE LOG CABIN, c/o Des Moines County Historical Society, 501 N. Fourth St., Burlington, IA 52601. Tel.: 319-752-7449.
E-mail: info@dmchs.org
Web Site: www.dmchs.org
Key Personnel: Dir., Angela Beenken; Chm. (V), Randy Bloomberg; Pres., Lyle Magneson; Treas., Terri Dowell.
Institution Type/Description: History Museum; Historic House: 1909 log cabin.
Hours & Admission Prices: May-Sept. Sat.-Sun. 1:30-4:30. No charge; donations accepted. &
Attendance: 1,654 (actual)

PHELPS HOUSE, 521 Columbia, Burlington, IA 52601-5117. Tel.: 319-753-5880.
E-mail: dmchs.jhunt@yahoo.com

Key Personnel: Pres. (V), Lyle Magneson; Vice Pres., Randy Bloom Berg; Treas., Terri Dowell; Dir., Angela Beeken; Publications & Public Rels. Dir., Debra Olson.
Institution Type/Description: Historical Preservation of Historic House: 1851 Victorian Mansion.
Hours & Admission Prices: May-Oct. Sat.-Sun. 1:30-4:30; group tours by appointment. Adults $3; members and children 12 & under no charge.
Attendance: 1,300 (actual)

Burr Oak

LAURA INGALLS WILDER PARK & MUSEUM, INC., 3603 236th Ave., Burr Oak, IA 52101-7889. Tel.: 563-735-5916. Fax: 563-735-5464.
E-mail: museum@lauraingallswilder.us
Web Site: www.lauraingallswilder.us
Key Personnel: Dir. & Museum Shop Mgr., Barb Olson; Pres. Bd., Dawn Maroushek; Vice Pres., Paul Hexom; Treas., Tammy Bjork.
Institution Type/Description: Park & Museum.
Hours & Admission Prices: Open May 1-Memorial Day Mon.-Sat. 10-4, Sun. 12-4; Memorial Day to Labor Day Mon.-Sat. 10-5, Sun. 12-4; Sept.-Oct. Thurs.-Sat. 10-4. Adult $8, children 6-17 $6; members no charge. Closed Sun.-Wed. in Sept. & Oct. and from Oct. 15-April 30. &
Attendance: 6,400 (actual)

Carroll

SWAN LAKE FARMSTEAD MUSEUM, 22676 Swan Lake Dr., Carroll, IA 51401-9153. Tel.: 712-792-4614. Fax: 712-792-8078. Facebook: Swan Lake Farmstead Museum.
E-mail: jason@carrollcountyiowa.org
Web Site: www.mycounmtyparks.com/county/carroll.aspx
Key Personnel: Dir., Jason Lambertz.
Institution Type/Description: Farm Museum.
Hours & Admission Prices: May-Oct. daily 5 am-10:30 pm. No charge.

Cascade

TRI-COUNTY HISTORICAL SOCIETY MUSEUM, 608 2nd Ave., S.W., Cascade, IA 52033. Mailing Address: P.O. Box 234, Cascade, IA 52033. Tel.: 563-852-3371. Facebook.
E-mail: cascadehistory@netins.net
Web Site: www.tricountyhistoricalsociety.com
Institution Type/Description: Historical Society Museum.
Hours & Admission Prices: May-Oct. 1st Sun. 1-4; other times by appointment. No charge.
Attendance: 700 (estimated)

Cedar Falls

CEDAR FALLS HISTORICAL SOCIETY, 308 W. 3rd St., Cedar Falls, IA 50613-2745. Tel.: 319-266-5149. Fax: 319-268-1812.
E-mail: cfhistory@cfu.net
Web Site: www.cfhistory.org
Key Personnel: Dir., Karen Smith.
Institution Type/Description: Local History Museums.
Hours & Admission Prices: Victorian Home: Tues.-Sat. 10-4, Sun. 1-4. Ice House Museum: May-Oct. Sat. 10-4, Sun. 1-4. Adults $5; children 12 & under no charge. Little Red Schoolhouse: May: Sat.-Sun. 1-4; June-Aug.: Wed. & Sat.-Sun. 1-4; Sept.: Sat.-Sun. 1-4. &

HARTMAN RESERVE NATURE CENTER, 657 Reserve Dr., Cedar Falls, IA 50613-4723. Tel.: 319-277-2187. Fax: 319-277-4420.
E-mail: hartmanreserve@co.black-hawk.ia.us
Web Site: www.hartmanreserve.org
Key Personnel: Dir., Ed Gruenwald; Program Coord., Chris Anderson; Devel. Coord., Connie Svoboda.
Institution Type/Description: Nature Center.
Hours & Admission Prices: March-May & Sept.-Oct. Mon.-Fri. 8-4:30, Sun. 1-5; June-Aug. & Nov.-Feb. Mon.-Fri. 8-4:30. No charge; donations accepted. Fees charged for specific programs. &
Attendance: 51,000 (estimated)

ICE HOUSE MUSEUM, Franklin St., (at W. 1st St.), Cedar Falls, IA 50613. Mailing Address: Cedar Falls Historical Society, 308 W. 3rd St., Cedar Falls, IA 50613-2745. Tel.: 319-266-5149.
E-mail: cfhistory@cfu.net
Web Site: www.cfhistory.org
Key Personnel: Dir., Karen Smith.

Institution Type/Description: History Museum: listed on the National Register of Historic Places.
Hours & Admission Prices: May-Oct. Wed. & Sat. 10-4, Sun. 1-4. Adults $5; children 12 & under no charge. &

JAMES & MERYL HEARST CENTER FOR THE ARTS AND HEARST SCULPTURE GARDEN, 304 W. Seerley Blvd., Cedar Falls, IA 50613-4050. Tel.: 319-273-8641. Fax: 319-273-8659. Facebook: Hearst Center.
E-mail: heather.skeens@cedarfalls.com
Web Site: www.thehearst.org
Key Personnel: Pres. Bd., James Kerns; Dir., Heather Skeens; Cur., Emily Drennan; Svcs. Coord., Lea Stewart; Education Coord., Angie Hickok; Museum Shop Mgr., Abby Haigh.
Institution Type/Description: Art Museum. Sculpture Garden & Community Public Art Collections.
Hours & Admission Prices: Tues. & Thurs. 9-9, Wed. & Fri. 9-5, Sat.-Sun. 1-4. No charge; donations accepted. Closed New Year's Day; Good Friday; Easter weekend; Memorial Day weekend; Independence Day; Labor Day weekend; Thanksgiving weekend; Christmas. &
Attendance: 56,200 (estimated)

LITTLE RED SCHOOL HOUSE MUSEUM, 1 W. 1st St., Cedar Falls, IA 50613. Mailing Address: Cedar Falls Historical Society, 308 W. 3rd St., Cedar Falls, IA 50613. Tel.: 319-266-5149.
E-mail: cfhistory@cfu.net
Web Site: www.cfhistory.org
Formerly: R Little Red School House Museum
Institution Type/Description: Historic Building Museum; built in 1909.
Hours & Admission Prices: May: Sat.-Sun. 1-4; June-Aug.: Wed., Sat. & Sun. 1-4; Sept.: Sat.-Sun. 1-4.

UNI GALLERY OF ART, UNIVERSITY OF NORTHERN IOWA, 1601 W. 27th St., 104 Kamerick Art Bldg., Cedar Falls, IA 50614-0362. Tel.: 319-273-3095. Fax: 319-273-7333.
E-mail: galleryofart@uni.edu
Web Site: www.uni.edu/art/gallery.html
Key Personnel: Head Dept. Art, Jeffery Byrd; Dir. Gallery, Darrell Taylor.
Institution Type/Description: Art Gallery.
Hours & Admission Prices: Mon.-Thurs. 10-7, Fri.-Sat. 12-5 & by appointment. No charge. Closed holidays; when classes are not in session. &
Attendance: 12,000 (actual)

UNIVERSITY OF NORTHERN IOWA MUSEUM & CENTER FOR THE HISTORY OF RURAL IOWA EDUCATION AND CULTURE, 1227 W. 27th St., Cedar Falls, IA 50614. Tel.: 319-273-2188. Facebook: @unimuseums.
E-mail: nathan.arndt@uni.edu
Web Site: museum.library.uni.edu
Formerly: University of Northern Iowa Museums & Collections - Marshall Center One-Room School
Key Personnel: Asst. & Cur., Nathan Arndt.
Institution Type/Description: College University Museum.
Hours & Admission Prices: Visit museum.library.uni.edu/about-us. No charge. Closed holidays. &

UNIVERSITY OF NORTHERN IOWA MUSEUMS & COLLECTIONS - UNIVERSITY MUSEUM, 3219 Hudson Rd., Cedar Falls, IA 50614-0199. Tel.: 319-273-2188. Fax: 319-273-6924.
E-mail: katherine.martin@uni.edu
Web Site: www.uni.edu/museum
Key Personnel: Dir., Katherine Martin; Cur., Nathan Arndt; Exhibit Preparator, Jessica Cruz.
Institution Type/Description: Natural & Human History Museum.
Hours & Admission Prices: University Museum & Marshall Center School: by appointment. No charge. Closed holidays. &
Attendance: 500 (estimated)

Cedar Rapids

AFRICAN AMERICAN HISTORICAL MUSEUM & CULTURAL CENTER OF IOWA, 55 12th Ave., S.E., Cedar Rapids, IA 52401-2202. Mailing Address: P.O. Box 1626, Cedar Rapids, IA 52406-1626. Tel.: 319-862-2101. Fax: 319-862-2105.
E-mail: information@blackiowa.org
Web Site: blackiowa.org
Key Personnel: Exec. Dir., Thomas Moore.
Institution Type/Description: History Museum.

Hours & Admission Prices: Mon.-Sat. 10-4. Adults $5, seniors $4, children $2.50; discounts to groups; members no charge. Closed New Year's Day; Martin Luther King Jr. Day; Memorial Day; Independence Day; Labor Day; Thanksgiving; Christmas. &
Attendance: 10,772 (actual)

BRUCEMORE, 2160 Linden Dr., S.E., Cedar Rapids, IA 52403-1748. Tel.: 319-362-7375. Fax: 319-362-9481.
E-mail: mail@brucemore.org
Web Site: www.brucemore.org
Key Personnel: Exec. Dir., David Janssen; Pres., Echo Batson; Deputy Dir., Brett Lobello; Mgr. Interpretations & Collections, Jessica Peel-Austin; Dir. Community Engagement, Tara Richards; Bldg. & Grounds Supt., Roger Johnson; Museum Shop Mgr., Kaycie Schatz; Accountant, Kelly Costello; Constituent Mgr., Katie Benedix; Head Gardener, David Morton; Buildings & Grounds Specialist, Taylor Manley; Maintenance Technician, Mike Schrvandt.
Institution Type/Description: Historic Site & Community Cultural Center.
Hours & Admission Prices: Tours: March-Dec. Wed.-Sat. 10-3, Sun. 1-3; other times by appointment. Adults $7, students $3; Brucemore, National Trust & museum members no charge. &
Attendance: 43,000 (estimated)

CEDAR RAPIDS MUSEUM OF ART, 410 Third Ave., S.E., Cedar Rapids, IA 52401-1620. Tel.: 319-366-7503. Fax: 319-366-4111.
E-mail: info@crma.org
Web Site: www.crma.org
Key Personnel: Exec. Dir., Sean Ulmer; Devel., Joanne Wzontek; Dir. Operations, Deanna Clemens Pedersen; Assoc. Cur., Kate Kunau; Preparator, Judy Frauenholtz; Dir. Education, Erin Thomas; Registrar, Jaci Falco; Communs. Coord., Lori Tofanelli; Bldg. Supvr., Carlis Faurot; Retail & Visitor Svcs. Mgr., Lou Wendel.
Institution Type/Description: Art Museum.
Hours & Admission Prices: Tues.-Wed., Fri. & Sun. 12-4, Thurs. 12-8, Sat. 10-4. Adults $7, students & senior citizens $6, children 6-18 $3; AAM, CRMA, NARM individual members and children 5 & under no charge. Closed national holidays. &
Attendance: 38,000 (estimated)

COE COLLEGE ART GALLERIES, 1220 1st Ave., N.E., Cedar Rapids, IA 52402-5092. Tel.: 319-399-8647. Fax: 319-399-8557.
E-mail: rlueth@coe.edu
Institution Type/Description: Art Gallery.
Hours & Admission Prices: Daily 3-5. No charge.

THE HISTORY CENTER, 716 Oakland Rd., N.E., Cedar Rapids, IA 52402-4668. Tel.: 319-362-1501.
E-mail: history@historycenter.org
Web Site: historycenter.org
Formerly: Linn County Historical Society The Carl & Mary Koehler History Center
Key Personnel: Exec. Dir., Jason S. Wright; Pres. (V), Dr. Adam Ebert.
Institution Type/Description: History Museum.
Hours & Admission Prices: Call for hours. &
Attendance: 8,000 (actual)

IOWA MASONIC LIBRARY AND MUSEUM, 813 1st Ave., S.E., Cedar Rapids, IA 52402-5001. Mailing Address: P.O. Box 279, Cedar Rapids, IA 52406-0279. Tel.: 319-365-1438. Fax: 319-365-1439.
E-mail: librarian@gl-iowa.org
Web Site: grandlodgeofiowa.org
Key Personnel: Grand Sec. & Librarian, Craig Davis; Asst. Librarian, William R. Kreuger.
Institution Type/Description: Library & History Museum.
Hours & Admission Prices: Mon.-Fri. 8-12 & 1-5. No charge; donations accepted. Closed national holidays. &
Attendance: 1,300 (actual)

NATIONAL CZECH & SLOVAK MUSEUM & LIBRARY, 1400 Inspiration Place S.W., Cedar Rapids, IA 52404. Tel.: 319-362-8500. Fax: 319-363-2209.
E-mail: gnaughton@ncsml.org
Web Site: www.ncsml.org
Key Personnel: C.E.O. & Pres., Gail Naughton; Chm., George Drost; Cur., Stefanie Kohn; Librarian, David Muhlena; Dir. Learning & Civic Engagement, Nicholas Hartmann; Dir. Devel., Emily Weber; Dir. Operations, Brittany Scanlon.
Institution Type/Description: Ethnic Museum; Czech and Slovak history and culture. Historic Building: 1880, restored Czech immigrant home.
Hours & Admission Prices: Mon.-Sat. 9:30-4, Sun. 12-4. Adults $10, seniors $9, active military $5, students 14 & up $5, youth 6-13 $3, children 5 & under &

members no charge. Closed New Year's Day; Easter; Thanksgiving; Christmas. &
Attendance: 45,000 (actual)

ROCKWELL COLLINS MUSEUM, 400 Collins Rd., N.E., Bldg. 120 South Door, Cedar Rapids, IA 52498.
E-mail: tours@rockwellcollinsmuseum.org
Web Site: rockwellcollinsmuseum.org
Institution Type/Description: Company Museum.
Hours & Admission Prices: Wed. 11:30-1 by appointment.

Centerville

APPANOOSE COUNTY HISTORICAL & COAL MINING MUSEUM, 100 W. Maple St., Centerville, IA 52544-2211. Tel.: 641-856-8040. Facebook: Appanoose County Historical & Coal Mining Museum.
E-mail: appanoosehistory@yahoo.com
Web Site: www.appunoosehistory.com
Institution Type/Description: History Museum: housed in the former Centerville Post Office; built 1903.
Hours & Admission Prices: April & Sept.-Oct. Mon.-Fri. 1-5; Memorial Day to Labor Day Mon.-Fri. 1-5, Sat. 10-2; Nov.-March Wed.-Fri. 1-4. Adults $4, students $1; members no charge. Closed New Year's Eve & Day; Memorial Day; Independence Day; Labor Day; Thanksgiving.

Chariton

LUCAS COUNTY HISTORICAL SOCIETY MUSEUM, 123 N. 17th St., Chariton, IA 50049-1618. Mailing Address: P.O. Box 807, Chariton, IA 50049. Tel.: 641-774-4464. Facebook: Lucas County Museum.
E-mail: lchs@iowatelecom.net
Web Site: www.lucascountyhistoricalsociety.blogspot.com/
Key Personnel: Pres. (V), Frank Myers.
Institution Type/Description: History Museum.
Hours & Admission Prices: Memorial Day to Oct. 1 Tues.-Sat. 1-4; other times by appointment. No charge.
Attendance: 1,000 (estimated)

Charles City

CARRIE CHAPMAN CATT GIRLHOOD HOME AND MUSEUM, 2379 Timber Ave., Charles City, IA 50616-8979. Mailing Address: P.O. Box 33, Charles City, IA 50616. Tel.: 641-228-3336.
E-mail: visit@catt.org
Web Site: catt.org
Key Personnel: Pres. (V), Susan McDonnell.
Institution Type/Description: Historic House: housed in the childhood home of Carrie Chapman Catt, coordinator of the woman suffrage movement & political strategist. Listed on the National Register of Historic Places.
Hours & Admission Prices: Memorial Day to Labor Day Mon.-Sat. 10-4, Sun. 12-4; other times by appointment. No charge; donations accepted.
Attendance: 700 (estimated)

CHARLES CITY ARTS CENTER, 301 N. Jackson St., Charles City, IA 50616-2006. Tel.: 641-228-6284. Facebook: Charles City Arts Center.
E-mail: charlescityarts@gmail.com
Web Site: www.charlescityarts.org
Institution Type/Description: Art Center.
Hours & Admission Prices: Wed.-Thurs. 1-9, Fri.-Sat. 1-5. No charge; donations accepted. &

FLOYD COUNTY HISTORICAL MUSEUM, 500 Gilbert St., Charles City, IA 50616-2738. Tel.: 641-228-1099.
E-mail: fchs@fiai.net
Web Site: www.floydcountymuseum.org
Key Personnel: Co-Pres. (V), Jody Flint; Co-Pres. (V), Tony Lessin; Dir., Mary Ann Townsend; Office Asst. & Receptionist, Elaine Mead.
Institution Type/Description: History Museum.
Hours & Admission Prices: June-Aug. Mon.-Fri. 9-4:30, Sat.-Sun. 1-4; Sept.-May Mon.-Fri. 9-4:30. Adults 13 & over $5, children 6-12 $3; members & children under 10 no charge. Closed New Year's Day; Thanksgiving; Christmas. &
Attendance: 5,500 (actual)

MOONEY ART COLLECTION - CHARLES CITY LIBRARY, 106 Milwaukee Mall, Charles City, IA 50616. Tel.: 641-257-6319. Fax: 641-257-6325.
E-mail: director@charles-city.lib.ia.us
Web Site: www.charles-city.lib.ia.us/artgal
Institution Type/Description: Library & Art Gallery.
Hours & Admission Prices: May-Sept. Mon.-Thurs. 10-8, Fri. 10-5, Sat. 1-5; Labor Day to Memorial Day Mon.-Thurs. 10-8, Fri. 10-5, Sat.-Sun. 1-5. No charge. &

Cherokee

SANFORD MUSEUM AND PLANETARIUM, 117 E. Willow St., Cherokee, IA 51012-1854. Tel.: 712-225-3922. Facebook.
E-mail: sanfordmuseum@sanfordmuseum.org
Web Site: sanfordmuseum.org
Key Personnel: Dir., Linda Burkhart; Asst. Dir., Michele Deiber Kumm; Educator & Museum Shop Manager, Kerisa Pingel; Cur. Archaeology, Megan Stroh Messerole.
Institution Type/Description: General Museum.
Hours & Admission Prices: Museum: Mon.-Fri. 9-5, Sat.-Sun. 12-5. No charge. Planetariums: Wed. & Sun. 4 pm. &
Attendance: 30,000 (estimated)

Clarinda

GLENN MILLER BIRTHPLACE HOME, 601 S. Glenn Miller Ave., Clarinda, IA 51632-2657. Mailing Address: P.O. Box 61, Clarinda, IA 51632. Tel.: 712-542-2461. Fax: 712-542-2461.
E-mail: gmbs@glennmiller.org
Web Site: www.glennmiller.org
Key Personnel: Exec. Dir., Shari Greenwood.
Institution Type/Description: Historic House Museum: housed in the birthplace of band leader, Glenn Miller.
Hours & Admission Prices: Tues.-Sun. 1-5. Adults 18-61 $6, seniors 62 & over $5, students & members $4; children 5 & under no charge. Closed holidays.

GLENN MILLER BIRTHPLACE MUSEUM, 122 W. Clark St., Clarinda, IA 51632. Mailing Address: P.O. Box 61, Clarinda, IA 51632. Tel.: 712-542-2461. Facebook.
E-mail: gmbs@glennmiller.org
Web Site: www.glennmiller.org
Key Personnel: Dir., Shari Greenwood; C.E.O., Marvin Negley.
Institution Type/Description: History Museum.
Hours & Admission Prices: Tues.-Sun. 1-5; other times by appointment. Adults $6, seniors 62 & over $5; children 12 & under no charge. Closed holidays. &
Attendance: 1,000 (estimated)

NODAWAY VALLEY HISTORICAL MUSEUM, 1600 S. 16th St., Clarinda, IA 51632. Mailing Address: P.O. Box 393, Clarinda, IA 51632-0393. Tel.: 712-542-3073.
E-mail: nvm@iowatelecom.net
Web Site: nodawayvalleymuseum.org
Institution Type/Description: History Museum.
Hours & Admission Prices: Tues. 9-4, Wed.-Sun. 1-4; groups by appointment.

Clarion

4-H SCHOOLHOUSE MUSEUM, 1st Ave. & Central Ave. W., Clarion, IA 50525. Mailing Address: 302 S. Main St., Clarion, IA 50525. Tel.: 515-532-3453.
Web Site: clarioniowa.com/pages/Museums
Key Personnel: Chm. (V), Yvonne Stevens.
Institution Type/Description: History Museum: birthplace of the 4-H emblem.
Hours & Admission Prices: Memorial Day to Labor Day Sat. 9-12; other times by appointment. No charge; donations accepted.
Attendance: 1,200 (actual)

HEARTLAND MUSEUM, Hwy. 3 W. & 9th St., S.W., Clarion, IA 50525. Mailing Address: P.O. Box 652, Clarion, IA 50525-0652. Tel.: 515-602-6000.
E-mail: hmfclarionia@hotmail.com
Web Site: www.heartlandmuseum.org
Key Personnel: Pres. (V) & Dir., Mary Tesdahl; Chm. (V) & Museum Shop Mgr., Normajene Collier; Museum Shop Mgr., Peggy O'Neil.
Institution Type/Description: History Museum.
Hours & Admission Prices: Memorial Day to Labor Day Mon.-Sat. 10-3; other times by appointment. Adults $12, children 5-11 $6; children 4 & under no charge. &
Attendance: 4,100 (estimated)

Clear Lake

CLEAR LAKE ARTS CENTER, 17 S. 4th St., Clear Lake, IA 50428-1816. Tel.: 641-357-1998.
E-mail: clac@cltel.net
Web Site: clartscenter.com/cgi-bin/index.pl
Key Personnel: Exec. Dir., Paula Chenchar Hanus.
Institution Type/Description: Art Gallery.
Hours & Admission Prices: Tues.-Sat. 10-5. No charge.

CLEAR LAKE FIRE MUSEUM, 112 N. 6th St., Clear Lake, IA 50428. Mailing Address: c/o Clear Lake Fire Dept., 711 2nd Ave. N., Claer Lake, IA 50428. Tel.: 641-357-2613.
Institution Type/Description: Firefighting History Museum.
Hours & Admission Prices: Memorial Day to Labor Day Sat.-Sun. 1-4. No charge; donations accepted.

PIONEER MUSEUM & HISTORICAL SOCIETY OF NORTH IOWA, 9184 G 265th St., Clear Lake, IA 50428-8507. Mailing Address: P.O. Box 421, Mason City, IA 50402-0421. Tel.: 641-423-1258.
E-mail: kinneypioneermuseum@yahoo.com
Key Personnel: Pres., Richard Peterson; Dir., Kay Ingersoll; Sec., Becky Lisor; Treas., Paul Pirkl.
Institution Type/Description: Historical Society Museum.
Hours & Admission Prices: May-Sept. Tues.-Sun. 1-5. Adults $3, children $1; members no charge. Season Pass: family $20, adult $10. &
Attendance: 3,000 (estimated)

Clermont

MONTAUK, 26223 Harding Rd., Clermont, IA 52135-8600. Mailing Address: P.O. Box 372, Clermont, IA 52135-0372. Tel.: 563-423-7173. Fax: 563-423-7378.
E-mail: montauk@acegroup.cc
Web Site: www.iowahistory.org/historic-sites/montauk/index.html
Key Personnel: Acting Mgr., Wade Schott.
Institution Type/Description: Historic House: 1874 home of William Larrabee, Iowa's 12th Governor.
Hours & Admission Prices: Memorial Day to Labor Day daily 12-4; Sept.-Oct. Fri.-Sun. 12-4. No charge; donations accepted. &
Attendance: 4,500 (actual)

Clinton

BICKELHAUPT ARBORETUM, 340 S. 14th St., Clinton, IA 52732-5432. Tel.: 563-242-4771.
E-mail: mahansen@eicc.edu
Web Site: www.bickelhaupt.org
Key Personnel: Dir. Programs, Margo Hansen.
Institution Type/Description: Arboretum.
Hours & Admission Prices: Daily dawn-dusk. No charge; donations accepted. &
Attendance: 31,000 (estimated)

CLINTON COUNTY HISTORICAL SOCIETY, 601 S. 1st St., Clinton, IA 52732-4118. Mailing Address: P.O. Box 2435, Clinton, IA 52733-2435. Tel.: 563-242-1201.
E-mail: info@clintonpahistory.org
Key Personnel: Pres., Don Dethmann; Treas., Janice Hansen.
Institution Type/Description: Historical Society Museum.
Hours & Admission Prices: Sun. 1-4; other times by appointment. No charge; donations accepted. &
Attendance: 2,000 (estimated)

FELIX ADLER CHILDREN'S DISCOVERY CENTER, 332 8th Ave. S, Clinton, IA 52732-5666. Tel.: 563-243-3600. Fax: 563-243-3600.
E-mail: info@adlerdiscoverycenter.org
Web Site: adlerdiscoverycenter.org
Key Personnel: Exec. Dir., Sarah Lind; Pres., Shawn Judd; Education & Prog. Coord., Roberta Schwartz.
Institution Type/Description: Children's Museum.
Hours & Admission Prices: Wed.-Sat. 9:30-4:30, Sun. 12:30-4:30. Adults $4, senior citizens 65 & over $3; members, children with disabilities & children under 2 no charge. &
Attendance: 250 (estimated)

Colfax

TRAINLAND U.S.A., 3135 Hwy. 117 N., Colfax, IA 50054-7534. Tel.: 515-674-3813. Fax: 515-674-3813.
E-mail: red@trainlandusa.com
Web Site: www.trainlandusa.com
Key Personnel: Pres. (V), Leland Atwood; Museum Shop Mgr., Judy Smith-Atwood.
Institution Type/Description: Toy Museum.
Hours & Admission Prices: Memorial Day-Labor Day daily 10-6. Adults $7.50, senior citizens over 55 $7, children 2-12 $5; discounts to groups of 15 or more; children under 2 no charge. (prices subject to change) ⬥
Attendance: 15,000 (estimated)

Coralville

ANTIQUE CAR MUSEUM OF IOWA, 860 Quarry Rd., Coralville, IA 52241-2226. Tel.: 319-354-3310. Fax: 319-354-3310.
E-mail: info@acmoi.com
Web Site: www.acmoi.com
Key Personnel: Pres., Dean Oakes.
Institution Type/Description: Car Museum.
Hours & Admission Prices: Tues.-Sat. 10-5, Sun. 12-5. Adults $5. ⬥
Attendance: 6,300 (estimated)

THE IOWA CHILDREN'S MUSEUM, 1451 Coral Ridge Ave., Ste. 502A, Coralville, IA 52241-2804. Tel.: 319-625-6255.
E-mail: ask@theicm.org
Web Site: www.theicm.org/
Key Personnel: Exec. Dir., Deb Dunkhase; Dir. Devel. & Mktg., Fran Jensen; Dir. Visitor Experience, Jordan Hougham; Coord. Special Programs, Julie Thomas; Exhibit Fabricator, Leonid Stepanov.
Institution Type/Description: Children's Museum.
Hours & Admission Prices: June to mid-Sept. Mon.-Thurs. & Sat. 10-6, Fri. 10-8, Sun. 11-6; Sept.-May Tues.-Thurs. & Sat. 10-6, Fri. 10-8, Sun. 11-6. Admission $6, seniors 60 & over $5; discounts to groups of 10 or more; children under 1 & members no charge. Closed major holidays.
Attendance: 90,000 (actual)

JOHNSON COUNTY HISTORICAL SOCIETY, 860 Quarry, Coralville, IA 52241-2226. Mailing Address: P.O. Box 5081, Coralville, IA 52241-5081. Tel.: 319-351-5738. Fax: 319-351-5310.
E-mail: questions@johnsoncountyhistory.org
Web Site: www.johnsoncountyhistory.org
Formerly: Johnson County Heritage Museum
Key Personnel: Pres. (V), Elaine Haddy; Chm. (V), Steve Weeber.
Institution Type/Description: Historical Society Museum: located in 1876 two-story school.
Hours & Admission Prices: Tues.-Sat. 10-5, Sun. 12-5. Adults $5; members no charge. Bus tours welcome. Closed major holidays.
Attendance: 6,200 (estimated)

Corning

AMERICA'S FRENCH ICARIAN VILLAGE, 710 Davis Ave., Ste. 1, Corning, IA 50841. Tel.: 641-322-4717.
E-mail: lcaria@frontiernet.net
Web Site: www.icaria.net
Formerly: Icaria Museum and Research Library
Institution Type/Description: History Museum.
Hours & Admission Prices: Tues.-Fri. 10-3; other times by appointment. Donation requested.

CORNING CENTER FOR THE FINE ARTS, 706 Davis Ave., Corning, IA 50841-1451. Tel.: 641-322-4549.
Institution Type/Description: Art Gallery.
Hours & Admission Prices: Wed.-Fri. 10-5, Sat. 10-4. No charge.

JOHNNY CARSON BIRTHPLACE HOME MUSEUM, 500 13th St., Corning, IA 50841-1106. Mailing Address: 701 Davis Ave., Corning, IA 50841-1418. Tel.: 641-322-3212.
E-mail: johnnycarsonbirthplace@gmail.com
Institution Type/Description: Historic House Museum: housed in the birthplace of Johnny Carson, born Oct. 23, 1925.
Hours & Admission Prices: By appointment.

Correctionville

CORRECTIONVILLE MUSEUM, Fifth and Driftwood Sts., Correctionville, IA 51016-7732. Mailing Address: Rural Woodbury County Historical Society, P.O. Box 255, Correctionville, IA 51016-0255. Tel.: 712-372-4791.
E-mail: cville@ruralwaves.us
Key Personnel: Pres. (V), Marjorie E. Hoppe; Treas., Sonya Kostan.
Institution Type/Description: History Museum: housed in old Merchants State Bank.
Hours & Admission Prices: Memorial Day-Labor Day Sat. 10-1, Sun. 2-4. No charge; donations accepted.
Attendance: 130 (estimated)

Corydon

PRAIRIE TRAILS MUSEUM OF WAYNE COUNTY, Hwy. 2 E., Corydon, IA 50060. Mailing Address: P.O. Box 104, Corydon, IA 50060-0104. Tel.: 641-872-2211. Fax: 641-872-2211. Facebook: Prairie Trails Museum.
E-mail: ptmuseum@grm.net
Web Site: www.prairietrailsmuseum.org
Key Personnel: Pres., Warren Lunsford; Dir., Brenda DeVore.
Institution Type/Description: History Museum.
Hours & Admission Prices: April-May & Sept.-Oct. Mon.-Sat. 1-5; June-Aug. Mon.-Fri. 10-5, Sat. 1-5; call for additional hours. Family $15, adults $5, college $3, students 7th-12th grade $2, children K-6th grade $1; members with card no charge. Group Tours of 20 or more: $4. ⬥
Attendance: 2,500 (actual)

Council Bluffs

GREAT PLAINS WING MUSEUM, 16803 McCandless Rd., Council Bluffs, IA 51503. Tel.: 712-322-2435.
E-mail: nlswede@netins.net
Web Site: www.greatplainswing.org
Institution Type/Description: Military History Museum.
Hours & Admission Prices: Wed. 6pm-9pm, Sat. 9-4, Sun. 12-4. No charge. ⬥
Attendance: 2,500 (estimated)

HISTORIC GENERAL DODGE HOUSE, 605 3rd St., Council Bluffs, IA 51503-6614. Mailing Address: 621 3rd St., Council Bluffs, IA 51503-6614. Tel.: 712-322-2406 & 3504. Fax: 712-322-3504.
E-mail: gmdodge@dodgehouse.org
Web Site: www.dodgehouse.org
Key Personnel: Exec. Dir., Kori L. Nelson; Pres., Todd Lehan; Museum Shop Mgr., Cathy Born.
Institution Type/Description: Historic House: 1869 Victorian 14-room home of General Grenville M. Dodge. Victorian Arts, RR history, Civil War history.
Hours & Admission Prices: Feb.-Dec. Tues.-Sat. 10-5, Sun. 1-5. Adults $7, seniors 62 & over $5, children 6-16 $3; discounts to groups of 20 or more & AAA members; children under 6 & members no charge. Closed some holidays.
Attendance: 11,000 (actual)

HISTORIC SQUIRREL CAGE JAIL MUSEUM, 226 Pearl St., Council Bluffs, IA 51503. Mailing Address: P.O. Box 2, Council Bluffs, IA 51502-0002. Tel.: 712-323-2509. Facebook: Squirrel Cage.
E-mail: info@thehistoricalsociety.org
Web Site: thehistoricalsociety.org
Key Personnel: Dir. & Mgr., Kat Slaughter; Asst. Mgr., Brad Dinovo.
Institution Type/Description: Historic Building Museum: housed in the former county jail; built in 1885. Listed on the National Register of Historic Places.
Hours & Admission Prices: April-Oct. Thurs.-Sat. 11-4. Adults $7, seniors 60 & over $6, children 6-12 $5; discounts to AAM & AAA members & groups; children 5 & under and members no charge. Closed Jan. & major holidays.
Attendance: 15,000 (estimated)

IOWA SCHOOL FOR THE DEAF MUSEUM, 3501 Harry Langdon Blvd., Council Bluffs, IA 51503. Tel.: 712-366-0571; 712-366-0571 (TTY). Fax: 712-366-3218.
E-mail: cangeroth@iowaschoolforthedeaf.org
Web Site: www.iowaschoolforthedeaf.org/lmc-and-museum
Institution Type/Description: History Museum.
Hours & Admission Prices: By appointment.

RAILS WEST RAILROAD MUSEUM, 16th Ave. & S. Main St., Council Bluffs, IA 51503. Mailing Address: P.O. Box 2, Council Bluffs, IA 51502-0002. Tel.: 712-323-5182. Facebook: Council Bluffs, IA Railroads.
E-mail: info@thehistoricalsociety.org
Web Site: thehistoricalsociety.org
Key Personnel: Dir. & Mgr., Kat Slaughter; Asst. Museum Shop Mgr., Brad Dinovo.
Institution Type/Description: Historic Building Museum: housed in the former Chicago Rock Island and Pacific Railroad Passenger Depot; built in 1899.
Hours & Admission Prices: April-Oct. Thurs.-Sat. 11-4; other times by appointment. Adults $7, seniors 60 & over $6, children 6-16 $5; discounts to AAA members & groups of 15 or more; members and children 5 & under no charge. Closed Jan. & major holidays.
Attendance: 15,000 (estimated)

UNION PACIFIC RAILROAD MUSEUM, 200 Pearl St., Council Bluffs, IA 51503-0825. Tel.: 712-329-8307. Fax: 712-323-4973. Facebook: Union Pacific Railroad Museum.
E-mail: palabount@up.com
Web Site: www.uprrmuseum.org
Key Personnel: Mgr. Museum & Collections, Patricia LaBounty; Collections & Devel. Coord., Abby Cape; Volunteer & Outreach Coord., Beth Maynes; Facility & Operations Coord., Bruce Bianchetta; Communications Specialist, Alison Freemyer.
Institution Type/Description: History Museum.
Hours & Admission Prices: Tues.-Sat. 10-4. No charge; donations accepted. Closed New Years Eve & Day; Presidents Day; Memorial Day; Independence Day; Labor Day; Thanksgiving; Christmas Eve & Day. &
Attendance: 26,000 (actual)

WESTERN HISTORIC TRAILS CENTER, 3434 Richard Downing Ave., Council Bluffs, IA 51501-7962. Tel.: 712-366-4900. Fax: 712-366-5080.
E-mail: teressa.swand@iowa.gov
Web Site: www.iowahistory.org/historic-sites
Institution Type/Description: History Center.
Hours & Admission Prices: April-Oct. daily 9-5; Nov.-March Tues.-Sun. 9-5. No charge.

Creston

UNION COUNTY HISTORICAL VILLAGE, 601 McKinley St., Creston, IA 50801. Mailing Address: P.O. Box 693, Creston, IA 50801. Tel.: 641-782-8220.
E-mail: tourism@crestoniowachamber.com
Web Site: unioncountyiowatourism.com/sites.html
Formerly: Union County Historical Complex
Key Personnel: Dir., Mark Huff; Chm. (V), Richard Anderson.
Institution Type/Description: Village Museum.
Hours & Admission Prices: June to Labor Day Fri.-Sun. 1-4:30. No charge; donations accepted. &
Attendance: 1,000 (estimated)

Dakota City

HUMBOLDT COUNTY HISTORICAL ASSOCIATION MUSEUM, 905 1st Ave., N., Dakota City, IA 50529-5134. Mailing Address: P.O. Box 162, Humbolt, IA 50548-0162. Tel.: 515-332-5280.
E-mail: hcha@goldfieldaccess.net
Key Personnel: Museum Dir., Sandra Back; Pres. (V), Gregg Stobbe.
Institution Type/Description: County Historical Museum.
Hours & Admission Prices: June-Sept. Mon.-Tues. & Thurs.-Sat. 10-4, Sun. 1:30-4:30; special tours by appointment. Adults $5, children 6-21 $1; youth under 18 accompanied by an adult no charge. &
Attendance: 2,000 (estimated)

Dallas Center

THE BRENTON ARBORETUM, 25141 260th St., Dallas Center, IA 50063-8336. Tel.: 515-992-4211. Fax: 515-992-3303. Facebook: The Brenton Arboretum.
E-mail: mail@thebrentonarboretum.org
Web Site: thebrentonarboretum.org
Key Personnel: Gen. Mgr. & Dir. Horticulture, Andy Schmitz; Exec. Dir., Melissa Burdick.
Institution Type/Description: Arboretum.

Hours & Admission Prices: Daily 9am to sunset; groups by appointment. No charge, donations accepted. AHS reciprocal admission program participant. &
Attendance: 20,000 (estimated)

Davenport

FIGGE ART MUSEUM, 225 W. 2nd St., Davenport, IA 52801-1804. Tel.: 563-326-7804. Fax: 563-326-7876.
E-mail: info@figgeartmuseum.org
Web Site: figgeartmuseum.org
Formerly: Davenport Museum of Art
Key Personnel: Exec. Dir., Michelle Hargrave.
Institution Type/Description: Art Museum.
Hours & Admission Prices: Tues.-Wed. & Fri.-Sat. 10-5, Thurs. 10-8, Sun. 12-5. Adults $10, seniors 60 & over and students $6, children 4-12 $4, discount to North American Reciprocal Member Veterans; members, children 4 & under, Thurs. after 5 no charge. &
Attendance: 60,000 (estimated)

GERMAN AMERICAN HERITAGE CENTER, 712 W. Second St., Davenport, IA 52802-1410. Tel.: 563-322-8844. Fax: 563-322-2687. Facebook: German American Heritage Center.
E-mail: admin@gahc.org
Web Site: www.gahc.org
Key Personnel: Dir., Janet Brown-Lowe; Asst. Dir., Kelly Lao; Chm. (V), Cal Werner; Museum Shop Mgr., Joan Finkenhoefer.
Institution Type/Description: Cultural Heritage Museum.
Hours & Admission Prices: Tues.-Sat. 10-4, Sun. 12-4; other times by appointment. Group tours $25 min. hostess fee, adults $5, senior citizens $4, children 5-17 $3; children under 5 & members no charge. &
Attendance: 8,000 (estimated)

PALMER FAMILY AND CHIROPRACTIC HISTORY MUSEUM, 115 W. 7th St., Davenport, IA 52803. Tel.: 563-884-5245.
E-mail: pfch@palmer.edu
Web Site: www.palmer.edu/about-us/history/palmer-family-chiropractic-museum
Key Personnel: Dir., Dr. Roger Hynes; Museum Coord., Julie Knaak.
Institution Type/Description: Chiropractic History Museum.
Hours & Admission Prices: Mon.-Fri. 8:30-4:30. No charge.
Attendance: 400 (estimated)

PUTNAM MUSEUM OF HISTORY & NATURAL SCIENCE, 1717 W. 12th St., Davenport, IA 52804-3597. Tel.: 563-324-1933. Fax: 563-324-6638.
E-mail: museum@putnam.org
Web Site: www.putnam.org
Key Personnel: C.E.O. & Pres., Kim Findlay; Chm., Perry Hansen; C.F.O., Lisa Crews; Cur. History & Anthropology, Christina Kastell; Cur. Natural History, Christine Chandler; Vice Pres. Education, Octavia Houtekier-Boyd; Education Specialist, Maureen Mincks; Exhibits Mgr., Shaun Graves; Facilities Mgr., Darren Chandler.
Institution Type/Description: History, Natural Science & Anthropology Museum.
Hours & Admission Prices: Mon.-Sat. 10-5, Sun. 12-5. Adults 8, seniors over 60, youth 3-16, college students, & military with ID $7, members no charge. Closed New Year's Day; Easter; Thanksgiving; Thurs. Dec. 17 2-5; Fri. Dec. 18 all day; Sat. Dec. 19 4-5; Christmas Eve afternoon & Christmas Day. &
Attendance: 160,000 (estimated)

VANDER VEER BOTANICAL PARK, 215 W. Central Park Ave., (Btw. Brady & Harrison Sts.), Davenport, IA 52803. Mailing Address: 214 W. Central Park Ave., Davenport, IA 52803-1503. Tel.: 563-326-7818.
Web Site: www.cityofdavenportiowa.com
Institution Type/Description: Botanical Garden.
Hours & Admission Prices: Park: daily sunrise to sunset. The Conservatory and Park Store: Tues.-Sun. 10-4. Adults $1, children 15 & under no charge.
Attendance: 60,000 (estimated)

DeWitt

CENTRAL COMMUNITY HISTORICAL SOCIETY MUSEUM, 628 6th Ave., DeWitt, IA 52742. Tel.: 563-659-3686. Facebook: Central Community Historical Society Museum.
E-mail: ahsoenk@gmail.com
Web Site: centralcommunityhistoricalsociety.webs.com
Key Personnel: Dir. & Pres. (V), Ann Soenksen.
Institution Type/Description: Historical Society Museum.

Hours & Admission Prices: Mon. 8:30 am-11:30 am, Thurs. 8:30 am-11 am, Sun. 1 pm-4 pm. No charge; donations accepted. Closed holidays. &
Attendance: 800 (estimated)

Decorah

FINE ARTS COLLECTION, LUTHER COLLEGE, 700 College Dr., Luther College Library, Decorah, IA 52101-1041. Tel.: 563-387-1328 & 1300. Fax: 563-387-1132.
E-mail: elli03@luther.edu
Web Site: finearts.luther.edu
Key Personnel: Cur., Kate Elliott; Gallery Coord., David Kamm.
Institution Type/Description: Art Museum.
Hours & Admission Prices: Sept.-June Mon.-Fri. 8-10, Sat. 9-5, Sun. 12-10. No charge. Closed college holidays. &
Attendance: 10,000

GEOLOGY COLLECTION, LUTHER COLLEGE, 700 College Dr., Anthropology Lab, Decorah, IA 52101-1045. Tel.: 563-387-1508.
E-mail: laura.peterson@luther.edu
Web Site: geology.luther.edu
Key Personnel: Cur., Dr. Laura Peterson.
Institution Type/Description: Geology Museum.
Hours & Admission Prices: By appointment. No charge.

LUTHER COLLEGE ETHNOGRAPHIC AND ARCHAEOLOGICAL COLLECTIONS, 700 College Dr., Anthropology Lab, Decorah, IA 52101-1041. Tel.: 563-387-2156.
E-mail: cridde01@luther.edu
Web Site: www.luther.edu/collections/archeology
Key Personnel: Lab & Collections Mgr., Dr. Destiny Crider.
Institution Type/Description: History Museum.
Hours & Admission Prices: Call for hours.

THE PORTER HOUSE MUSEUM, 401 W. Broadway St., Decorah, IA 52101. Mailing Address: P.O. Box 115, Decorah, IA 52101-0115. Tel.: 563-382-8465. Facebook.
E-mail: porterhousemuseum@gmail.com
Web Site: porterhousemuseum.org
Key Personnel: Chm. (V), David Wright, Jr.; Dir., Emily Mineart.
Institution Type/Description: Historic House Museum; built in 1867.
Hours & Admission Prices: June-Aug. Mon.-Sat. 10-4, Sun. 1-4, Sept.-Oct. Fri.-Sun. 1-4; off-season and school & bus groups by appointment. Adults $7, seniors over 65 $5, children 6-17 $4; children under 6, school groups & members no charge.

VESTERHEIM NORWEGIAN-AMERICAN MUSEUM, 523 W. Water St., Decorah, IA 52101-1733. Mailing Address: P.O. Box 379, Decorah, IA 52101-0379. Tel.: 563-382-9681. Fax: 563-382-8828. Facebook: Vesterheim Norwegian-American Museum.
E-mail: info@vesterheim.org
Web Site: www.vesterheim.org
Key Personnel: Chm., Lorie Reins Schween; Pres. & C.E.O., Chris Johnson; Dir. Admin., Marcia McKelvey; Coord. Tours to Norway, Katherine Johnson; Volunteer Coord., Martha Griesheimer; Membership Mgr., Peggy Sersland; Chief Cur., Laurann Gilbertson; Exhibit Mgr., Zach Row-Heyveld; Registrar & Archivist, Jennifer Johnston Kovarik; Communs. & Mktg. Mgr., Charlie Langton; Communs. & Mktg. Mgr., Becky Idstrom; Office Asst., Jocelyn Bruening; Museum Shop Mgr., Ken Koop; Educ. Specialist, Darlene Fossum-Martin.
Institution Type/Description: Immigrant History & Art Museum.
Hours & Admission Prices: May-Oct. daily 9-5; Nov.-April daily 10-4. Adults $10, seniors $8, children 6-18 $5; discounts for families & groups; first Thurs. of month, children 6 & under and members no charge. Closed New Year's Day; Easter; Thanksgiving; Christmas. &
Attendance: 15,727 (actual)

Denison

DONNA REED HERITAGE MUSEUM, 1305 Broadway, Denison, IA 51442-1923. Tel.: 712-263-3334. Fax: 712-263-8026.
E-mail: info@donnareed.org
Web Site: www.donnareed.org
Institution Type/Description: History Museum; housed in a former German opera house; built in 1914.
Hours & Admission Prices: Mon.-Fri. 10-2; other times by appointment. No charge; donations accepted.

W.A. MCHENRY HOUSE, 1428 First Ave. N., Denison, IA 51442-1402. Mailing Address: P.O. Box 741, Denison, IA 51442. Tel.: 712-674-3750. Facebook: Crawford County Historical Society.
Key Personnel: Pres. (V), Teresa Keairnes; Museum Tours, Nancy Bliesman.
Institution Type/Description: Historic House Museum.
Hours & Admission Prices: Feb.-July & Sept.-Dec. 1st & 3rd Sat.-Sun. No charge; donations accepted.
Attendance: 500 (estimated)

Des Moines

ANDERSON GALLERY - DRAKE UNIVERSITY, Harmon Fine Arts Center, 2505 Carpenter Ave., Des Moines, IA 50311. Tel.: 515-271-1994. Fax: 515-271-2558.
E-mail: joshua.cox@drake.edu
Web Site: www.drake.edu/andersongallery
Key Personnel: Dir., Joshua Cox.
Institution Type/Description: Art Gallery.
Hours & Admission Prices: Tues.-Wed. & Fri.-Sun. 12-4, Thurs. 12-8. No charge.

BLANK PARK ZOO, 7401 S.W. 9th St., Des Moines, IA 50315-6667. Tel.: 515-285-4722. Fax: 515-974-2590. Facebook; Twitter; Instagram; YouTube.
E-mail: info@blankparkzoo.com
Web Site: www.blankparkzoo.com
Key Personnel: Pres. & C.E.O., Mark Vukovich; Dir. Mktg., Ryan Bickel; Dir. Animal Care & Conservation, Kevin Drees; Dir. Devel., Angela Hilbert; Dir. Accounting, Gwen Parks; Dir. Guest Opers. & Education., Anne Shimerdla.
Institution Type/Description: Zoo.
Hours & Admission Prices: May-Sept. daily 9-5; Oct.-April daily 10-4. Adults $14, seniors 65 & over $11, children 3-12 $8; children 2 & under no charge. &
Attendance: 459,096 (actual)

DES MOINES ART CENTER, 4700 Grand Ave., Des Moines, IA 50312-2099. Tel.: 515-277-4405. Fax: 515-271-0350.
E-mail: info@desmoinesartcenter.org
Web Site: www.desmoinesartcenter.org
Key Personnel: Pres. Bd., James Wallace; Dir., Jeff Fleming; Dir. Studio Programs, Tracy Duran; Dir. Finance, Cheryl Tuttle; Retail Operations Dir., Sarah Jane Shimasaki.
Institution Type/Description: Art Museum.
Hours & Admission Prices: Tues.-Wed. & Fri.-Sat. 10-4, Thurs. 11-9, Sun. 12-4. No charge; donations accepted. Closed New Year's Eve & Day; Independence Day; Thanksgiving; Christmas. &
Attendance: 377,062 (actual)

FORT DES MOINES MUSEUM AND EDUCATION CENTER, 75 E. Army Post Rd., Des Moines, IA 50315-5866. Tel.: 888-828-FORT, 515-282-8060.
Institution Type/Description: History Museum.
Hours & Admission Prices: Mon.-Sat. 10-4. Adults $2; members no charge. &
Attendance: 10,000 (actual)

GREATER DES MOINES BOTANICAL GARDEN, 909 Robert D. Ray Dr., Des Moines, IA 50309-2897. Tel.: 515-323-6290. Fax: 515-243-2631. Facebook: dmbotanicalgarden; Twitter: dm_garden.
E-mail: info@dmbotanicalgarden.com
Web Site: www.dmbotanicalgarden.com
Formerly: Des Moines Botanical Center
Key Personnel: Pres. & C.E.O., Stephanie Jutila; Dir. Horticulture, Kelly D. Norris; Dir. Facility & Grounds Svcs., Sandy Stundins; Asst. Dir. Retail & Guest Experience, David Regan.
Institution Type/Description: Botanical Garden.
Hours & Admission Prices: Daily 10-5. April-Oct. adults $8, seniors & military $7, youth 4-17 $6; children under 3 and members no charge; Nov.-March adults $6, senior citizens & military $5, youth 4-17 $4; American Horticultural Society's Reciprocal Admissions Program participant; children under 3 & members no charge. Closed New Year's Day; Memorial Day, Independence Day, Labor Day, Thanksgiving; Christmas. &
Attendance: 134,823 (actual)

HOYT SHERMAN PLACE, 1501 Woodland Ave., Des Moines, IA 50309-3283. Tel.: 515-244-0507. Fax: 515-237-3582.
E-mail: roberts@hoytsherman.org
Web Site: www.hoytsherman.org
Key Personnel: Exec. Dir., Robert Warren; Pres. Bd., Teri Wood TeBockhorst; Business Mgr., Jeremy Purdy.
Institution Type/Description: Art Museum Complex: comprised of 1877 House; 1907 Art Museum; 1923 Theater.

Hours & Admission Prices: Mon.-Fri. 9-4. No charge; donations accepted. Guided Tours: $5 per person. &

Attendance: 90,000 (estimated)

IOWA DEPARTMENT OF NATURAL RESOURCES, 502 E. 9th St., 4th Floor, Des Moines, IA 50319-0034. Tel.: 515-725-8200.

Web Site: www.iowadnr.gov

Key Personnel: Dir., Chuck Gipp.

Institution Type/Description: State Park Museum.

Hours & Admission Prices: See website for hours & admissions. &

Attendance: 35,000

IOWA HALL OF PRIDE, 330 Park St., Des Moines, IA 50309-1701. Tel.: 515-280-8969. Fax: 515-280-3211.

Web Site: www.iowahallofpride.com

Key Personnel: Dir., Taylor Anderson.

Institution Type/Description: History Museum.

Hours & Admission Prices: Mon.-Fri. 9-4, Sat. by appointment. Adults $10, seniors 65 & over $7; Iowa children K-12 no charge. Closed major holidays. &

IOWA STATE CAPITOL, 1007 E. Grand Ave., Des Moines, IA 50319. Mailing Address: c/o Legislative Information Office, 1007 E. Grand Ave., Des Moines, IA 50319. Tel.: 515-281-5591.

Web Site: www.legis.iowa.gov

Institution Type/Description: Historic Building: built in 1886.

Hours & Admission Prices: Tours: Mon.-Sat. by appointment.

POLK COUNTY HERITAGE GALLERY, Polk County Office Bldg., 111 Court Ave., Des Moines, IA 50309-2218. Tel.: 515-286-2242.

Web Site: polkcountyheritagegallery.org

Institution Type/Description: Art Gallery: housed in 1908 post office. Listed on the National Register of Historic Places.

Hours & Admission Prices: Mon.-Fri. 11-4:30. No charge; donations accepted. Closed legal holidays. &

Attendance: 4,000 (actual)

SALISBURY HOUSE & GARDENS, 4025 Tonawanda Dr., Des Moines, IA 50312-2909. Tel.: 515-274-1777.

E-mail: contactus@salisburyhouse.org

Web Site: www.salisburyhouse.org

Key Personnel: Exec. Dir., Kit Curran; Dir. Sales & Private Events, Bonnie Bronson; Dir. Bldgs. & Grounds, Kerry Johnson; Dir. Public Events, Beth Johnson; Cur. & Historian, Megan Stout Sibbert, Ph.D.; Guest Experience Assoc., Dawn Parizek; Grants & Community Engagement Mgr., Geena Torti; Mktg. & Guest Experience Mgr., Emily Kist.

Institution Type/Description: Historic House Museum & Gardens: built 1923-28.

Hours & Admission Prices: Guided Tours: Tues.-Sat. 11 & 1:30, Sun. 1:30; reduced hours in Jan. & Feb. Adults $12, seniors $11, youth 6-12 $3; children 5 & under with a paying adult no charge. Self-Guided Tours: Tues.-Sat. 10-5, Sun. 12-5. Adults $8, seniors $7, youth 6-12 $2; members & children 5 & under with a paying adult no charge. Closed most holidays. &

Attendance: 13,000 (actual)

SCIENCE CENTER OF IOWA & BLANK IMAX DOME THEATER, 401 W. Martin Luther King Jr. Pkwy., Des Moines, IA 50309-4776. Tel.: 515-274-6868, ext. 222. Fax: 515-274-3404. Facebook.

Web Site: www.sciowa.org

Key Personnel: Pres. & C.E.O., Curt Simmons; Dir. Sales & Retail Operations, Kent Maahs.

Institution Type/Description: Science & Technology Museum.

Hours & Admission Prices: Memorial Day to Labor Day Mon.-Sat. 9-5, Sun. 12-5, Sun. 12-5; Sept.-May Tues.-Sat. 10-5, Sun. 12-5. Science Center: adults $12, senior citizens & children 2-12 $8; members no charge. IMAX: adults $9, senior citizens & children $7, members $5. Closed Easter; Thanksgiving; Christmas. &

Attendance: 350,000 (actual)

STATE HISTORICAL MUSEUM OF IOWA, 600 E. Locust St., Des Moines, IA 50319-1006. Tel.: 515-281-5111. Facebook.

E-mail: susan.kloewer@iowa.gov

Web Site: iowaculture.gov/history/museum

Formerly: State Historical Society of Iowa

Key Personnel: Museum Dir., Susan Kloewer; Registrar, Jodi Evans; Exhibits Mgr., Andrew Harrington; State Cur., Leo Landis; Collections Coord., Kay Coats.

Institution Type/Description: History Museum.

Hours & Admission Prices: Mon.-Sat. 9-4:30. No charge; donations accepted. Closed state holidays. &

Attendance: 90,000 (estimated)

TERRACE HILL HISTORIC SITE AND GOVERNOR'S MANSION, 2300 Grand Ave., Des Moines, IA 50312-5308. Tel.: 515-281-7205. Facebook: terracehilliowa.

E-mail: diane.becker@iowa.gov

Web Site: www.terracehill.iowa.gov

Key Personnel: Admin., Diane Becker; Communications & Events Coord., Nicole Phend; Maintenance, Michael Miner.

Institution Type/Description: Historic Site: restored to the opulent Victorian lifestyle of the late 1880s-early 1900s, a mansion, carriage house & gardens are situated on 9 acres.

Hours & Admission Prices: March-Dec. Tues.-Sat. 10-1:30. Tours at 10:30, 11:30, 12:30 & 1:30. Adults $5, children 6-12 $2. Closed state holidays; New Year's Eve; Christmas Eve. &

Attendance: 10,000 (actual)

THE WALLACE CENTERS OF IOWA - WALLACE HOUSE FOUNDATION, 756 16th St., Des Moines, IA 50314-1601. Tel.: 515-243-7063.

E-mail: info@wallace.org

Web Site: www.wallace.org

Institution Type/Description: Historic House Museum: built in 1883.

Hours & Admission Prices: Tues.-Fri. 9-2; other times by appointment. No charge; donations accepted.

Attendance: 1,000 (estimated)

WELLS FARGO HISTORY MUSEUM CLOSED, 666 Walnut St., Des Moines, IA 50309. Mailing Address: Wells Fargo Historical Services, 420 Montgomery St., San Francisco, CA 94163. Tel.: 515-245-8400. Fax: 877-399-2170. Facebook.

E-mail: wfmuseum.dsm@wellsfargo.com

Web Site: www.wellsfargohistory.com

Institution Type/Description: Company History Museum.

Hours & Admission Prices: Mon.-Fri. 8:30-5. No charge. Closed bank holidays; New Year's Day; Martin Luther King Jr. Day; Memorial Day; Independence Day; Labor Day; Veterans Day; Thanksgiving; Christmas.

Diagonal

DIAGONAL PRINTING MUSEUM, 1391 County Hwy. P27, Diagonal, IA 50845. Tel.: 641-344-0677.

E-mail: ringgoldtourism@gmail.com

Key Personnel: Pres. (V), Jan Johnston.

Institution Type/Description: History Museum.

Hours & Admission Prices: Memorial Day to Labor Day call for hours. No charge; donations accepted. &

Attendance: 185 (estimated)

Dow City

DOW HOUSE HISTORIC SITE, 513 S. Prince St., Dow City, IA 51528. Mailing Address: Crawford County Conservation Board, 2237 Yellow Smoke Rd., Denison, IA 51442. Tel.: 712-263-2748. Fax: 712-263-3352.

E-mail: crawfco@crawfordcounty.org

Web Site: www.crawfordcountyconservationboard.com/historic.html

Key Personnel: Dir., Chris Gosch; Chm. (V), Jodi Head; Pres. (V), Neal Moeller.

Institution Type/Description: Historic House: housed in the home of businessman, Simeon E. Dow; built in 1872. Listed on the National Register of Historic Places.

Hours & Admission Prices: Memorial Day to Labor Day Sat.-Sun. 12-4: Adults $2, children 14 & under $1.

Attendance: 500 (estimated)

Dows

DOWS DEPOT WELCOME CENTER, 1896 Railroad St., Dows, IA 50071. Mailing Address: P.O. Box 287, Dows, IA 50071-0287. Tel.: 515-852-3595.

E-mail: cyriaunderwood@yahoo.com

Institution Type/Description: Railroad Museum: Wright County's first depot built in 1896. Listed on the National Register of Historical Places.

Hours & Admission Prices: Mon.-Fri. 9:30-4:30, Sun. 1-4. No Charge. Closed New Year's Day; Easter; Thanksgiving; Christmas. &

Attendance: 4,000 (estimated)

1880 ONE-ROOM SCHOOLHOUSE, 201 E. Ellsworth, Dows, IA 50071. Mailing Address: Dows Welcome Center, Ellsworth & Garfield, Dows, IA 50071. Tel.: 515-852-3595.

E-mail: dowsdepot@fbx.com

Web Site: dowsiowa.com
Institution Type/Description: Historic Building & Museum.
Hours & Admission Prices: Call for hours.

EVANS LITTLE PRAIRIE HOUSE, 201 W. Railroad St., Dows, IA 50071. Tel.: 515-852-3595. Fax: 515-852-4326.
Web Site: www.dowsiowa.com
Institution Type/Description: Historic House Museum: built late 1800s.
Hours & Admission Prices: Mon.-Sat. 9-5, Sun. 12-5. No charge; donations accepted. &

QUASDORF BLACKSMITH AND WAGON MUSEUM, Railroad St., Dows, IA 50071. Mailing Address: P.O. Box 312, Dows, IA 50071. Tel.: 515-852-3595. Fax: 515-852-4326.
Institution Type/Description: Historic House Museum: built in 1899. Listed on the National Register of Historic Places.
Hours & Admission Prices: Mon.-Sat. 9-5, Sun. 12-5. Call for hours. No charge.

Dubuque

DUBUQUE ARBORETUM & BOTANICAL GARDENS, 3800 Arboretum Dr., Dubuque, IA 52001-1040. Tel.: 563-556-2100. Facebook.
Web Site: www.dubuquearboretum.net
Key Personnel: Exec. Dir., Sandi Helgerson; Vol. Coord., Sue Lemon.
Institution Type/Description: Arboretum & Botanical Garden.
Hours & Admission Prices: Grounds: daily dawn to dusk. Gift Shop & Library: April-Sept. daily 9-7; Oct. daily 9-5. No charge; donations accepted. &
Attendance: 100,000 (estimated)

DUBUQUE MUSEUM OF ART, 701 Locust St., Dubuque, IA 52001-6817. Tel.: 563-557-1851.
E-mail: info@dbqart.com
Web Site: www.dbqart.com
Key Personnel: Exec. Dir., David Schmitz; Membership & Visitor Svcs. Assoc., Amethyst Barron; Dir. Education, Margaret Buhr; Bus. & Finance Mgr., Jean Hoeger; Mktg. & Events Coord., Katherine Schroeder; Assoc. Cur. & Registrar, Stacy Peterson.
Institution Type/Description: Art Museum
Hours & Admission Prices: Tues-Fri. 10-5, Sat.-Sun. 1-4. Adults $6, senior citizens 65 & over $5, college students with ID $3; children 18 & under and members no charge. &
Attendance: 8,740 (actual)

MATHIAS HAM HOUSE HISTORIC SITE, 2241 Lincoln Ave., Dubuque, IA 52001-1424. Tel.: 563-557-9545.
Web Site: www.rivermuseum.com
Key Personnel: Pres. & C.E.O., Kurt Strand.
Institution Type/Description: Historical Society Museum.
Hours & Admission Prices: Memorial Day to Labor Day Wed.-Sun. 11-4. Adults $5, youth 3-17 $3.50; DCHS members & children 2 & under no charge.
Attendance: 1,250 (estimated)

NATIONAL MISSISSIPPI RIVER MUSEUM & AQUARIUM, 350 E. 3rd St., Dubuque, IA 52001-2302. Tel.: 800-226-3369, 563-557-9545. Facebook.
E-mail: info@rivermuseum.com
Web Site: www.rivermuseum.com
Key Personnel: Pres. & C.E.O., Dr. Kurt Strand; Dir. Curatorial Svcs., Cristin Waterbury; Dir. Living Collections, Andy Allison; Dir. Mktg. & Communications, Wendy Scardino; Vice Pres. Devel., Erin Dragotto; Dir. Education, Mark Wagner.
Institution Type/Description: Marine Museum & Aquarium.
Hours & Admission Prices: Summer daily 9-6; fall daily 9-5; winter Tues.-Sun. 10-5; spring daily 10-5. Adults $15, seniors 65 & over $13, youth 3-17 $10; members & children under 3 no charge. &
Attendance: 180,000 (estimated)

Dunlap

MCLEAN MUSEUM AND DOUGAL HOUSE, 1211 Iowa Ave., Dunlap, IA 51529-1538. Mailing Address: c/o Dunlap Historical Society, 716 Iowa Ave., Dunlap, IA 51529. Tel.: 712-643-5721 & 5908.
E-mail: dunlapia@loganet.net
Institution Type/Description: History Museum.
Hours & Admission Prices: Summer: Sat.-Sun. call for hours; other times by appointment.

Dyersville

DYER-BOTSFORD VICTORIAN HOUSE AND DOLL MUSEUM, 331 1st Ave., Dyersville, IA 52040. Tel.: 563-875-2414.
E-mail: dyersvillehs@iowatelecom.net
Web Site: dyersvillehistory.com
Institution Type/Description: Historic House & Doll Museum: housed in an 1850 Victorian home.
Hours & Admission Prices: May to early Nov. Mon.-Fri. 10-4, Sat.-Sun. 1-4.

FIELD OF DREAMS MOVIE SITE, 28995 Lansing Rd., Dyersville, IA 52040-8005. Mailing Address: P.O. Box 300, Dyersville, IA 52040-0300. Tel.: 888-875-8404. Fax: 563-875-7253.
E-mail: fodbetty@aol.com
Web Site: www.fodmoviessite.com
Institution Type/Description: Movie Site: Iowa farm used for the filming of Field of Dreams.
Hours & Admission Prices: April-Nov. daily 9-6. No charge; donations accepted. &
Attendance: 60,000 (estimated)

NATIONAL FARM TOY MUSEUM, 1110 16th Ave. Ct., S.E., Dyersville, IA 52040-2374. Tel.: 563-875-2727. Fax: 563-875-8467. Facebook: National Farm Toy Museum.
E-mail: farmtoys@dyersville.com
Web Site: www.nationalfarmtoymuseum.com
Key Personnel: Exec. Dir., Jacque Rahe; Chm. (V), Dave Bell; Museum Mgr. & Membership Coord., Amanda Schwartz.
Institution Type/Description: Farm Toy.
Hours & Admission Prices: Mon.-Sat. 9-6, Sun. 10-4. Adults $ 7, seniors $6, juniors 6-17 $5; youth 5 & under and active duty military & their families no charge. Closed New Year's Day; Easter; Thanksgiving; Christmas. &
Attendance: 15,000 (estimated)

Eldon

AMERICAN GOTHIC HOUSE CENTER, 300 American Gothic St., Eldon, IA 52554-9654. Tel.: 641-652-3352. Fax: 641-652-3352. Facebook: American Gothic House.
E-mail: theamericangothichouse@gmail.com
Web Site: www.americangothichouse.net
Key Personnel: Pres. (V), Steve Siegel; Admin., Holly Berg.
Institution Type/Description: Historic House: housed next to the home used as the backdrop of Grant Wood's 1930 painting; built in 1882. Listed on the National Register of Historic Places.
Hours & Admission Prices: May-Sept. Sun.-Mon. 1-4, Tues.-Sat. 10-5; Oct.-April Tues.-Fri. 10-4, Sat.-Mon. 1-4. No charge; donations accepted. Closed New Year's Day; Martin Luther King Jr. Day; Presidents' Day; Veterans Day; Thanksgiving & day after; Christmas Eve & Day. &
Attendance: 16,550 (actual)

Eldora

ELDORA WELCOME CENTER AND RAILROAD MUSEUM, 1215 Park St., Eldora, IA 50627. Mailing Address: 1442 Washington, Eldora, IA 50627-1633. Tel.: 641-939-3241. Fax: 641-939-7555.
E-mail: eldoraecondeu@heartofiowa.net
Web Site: www.eldoraiowa.com
Institution Type/Description: Visitors Center & History Museum.
Hours & Admission Prices: Memorial Day to Oct. 1 Sat. 12-4, Sun. 1-5; other times by appointment. No charge.

HARDIN COUNTY FARM MUSEUM, 203 Washington St., Eldora, IA 50627. Mailing Address: P.O. Box 41, Eldora, IA 50627-0041. Tel.: 641-939-7107. Facebook: Hardin County Farm Museum.
E-mail: hardincountyfarmmuseum@heartofiowa.net
Web Site: eldoraiowa.com/pages/farm-museum
Key Personnel: Pres. (V), Jason Reinertson.
Institution Type/Description: Farm Museum.
Hours & Admission Prices: By appointment. No charge; donations accepted.
Attendance: 1,505 (actual)

HARDIN COUNTY HISTORICAL SOCIETY, 1603 Washington St., Eldora, IA 50627. Mailing Address: P.O. Box 187, Eldora, IA 50627-0187. Tel.: 641-939-5137.
E-mail: dlbabcock@heartofiowa.net

Web Site: historicalsocietyhardincountyiowa.org
Key Personnel: Treasurer & Researcher, Leola Babcock; Pres. (V), Callie Wiesner.
Institution Type/Description: Historical Society Museum.
Hours & Admission Prices: May-Oct. 3rd Sun. of the month 2-4; other times by appointment. No charge; donations accepted. ♿
Attendance: 1,000 (estimated)

Elgin

GILBERTSON NATURE CENTER, 22580 A Ave., Elgin, IA 52141-9567. Tel.: 563-426-5740.
E-mail: gncfccb@alpinecom.net
Institution Type/Description: Nature Center.
Hours & Admission Prices: Center: Memorial Day to Labor Day Wed.-Sun. 11-7; other times by appointment. Petting Zoo: May by appointment.

MAVIS & CONNER DUMMERMUTH HISTORICAL BUILDING AND HART DUMMERMUTH HISTORICAL HOUSE, 22580 A Ave., Elgin, IA 52141. Tel.: 563-426-5740.
E-mail: gncfccb@alpinecom.net
Web Site: www.elginiowa.org/GILBERTSON.html
Institution Type/Description: Historic Buildings.
Hours & Admission Prices: mid-May to Labor Day call for hours. ♿

Elk Horn

BEDSTEMOR'S HOUSE, 2105 College St., Elk Horn, IA 51531-8005. Mailing Address: 2212 Washington St., Elk Horn, IA 51531. Tel.: 800-759-9192. Fax: 712-764-7002.
E-mail: registrar@danishmuseum.org
Web Site: www.danishmuseum.org
Institution Type/Description: Historic House Museum: built in 1908.
Hours & Admission Prices: May 15-Sept. 15 daily 1-4. Adults $5; discounts to AAM members; members no charge.
Attendance: 700 (actual)

MUSEUM OF DANISH AMERICA, 2212 Washington St., Elk Horn, IA 51531-2116. Tel.: 712-764-7001. Fax: 712-764-7002.
E-mail: info@danishmuseum.org
Web Site: www.danishmuseum.org
Formerly: The Danish Immigrant Museum
Institution Type/Description: Ethnic History Museum.
Hours & Admission Prices: Museum: Mon.-Fri. 9-5, Sat. 10-5, Sun. 12-5. Bedstemor's House: May 15-Sept. 15 daily 1-4. Genealogy Center: May-Oct. Tues.-Wed. & Sat. 9-5; Nov.-April Tues.-Wed. & Fri. 10-4. Adults $5, children 8-17 $2; discounts to AAM members; members no charge. Closed New Year's Day; Easter; Thanksgiving; Christmas. ♿
Attendance: 8,000 (estimated)

Elkader

CARTER HOUSE MUSEUM, 101 S.E. High St., Elkader, IA 52043-0444. Mailing Address: c/o Elkader Historical Society, 101 Main, S.E., Elkader, IA 52043-0444. Tel.: 563-245-1573.
E-mail: carterhousemuseum@alpinecom.net
Web Site: www.carterhousemuseum.com
Key Personnel: Dir. & Pres. (V), Betty Buchholz.
Institution Type/Description: Historic House Museum: built in 1855.
Hours & Admission Prices: Memorial Day to Labor Day Sat.-Sun. 12-4; groups by appointment. Adults $5, senior citizens $3. ♿
Attendance: 900 (actual)

OSBORNE VISITOR, WELCOME AND NATURE CENTER, 29862 Osborne Rd., Elkader, IA 52043. Tel.: 563-245-1516. Fax: 563-245-2222.
E-mail: cccb@claytoncountyia.gov
Web Site: claytoncountyconservation.org
Institution Type/Description: Visitor Center & Nature Center.
Hours & Admission Prices: mid-April to mid-Oct. Mon.-Sat. 8-4, Sun. 12-4; mid-Oct. to mid-April Mon.-Sat. 8-4. No charge; donations accepted.
Attendance: 8,063 (actual)

Emmetsburg

VICTORIAN ON MAIN, 1703 Main St., Emmetsburg, IA 50536-1653. Tel.: 712-852-3781.
E-mail: mayoung@mchsi.com
Institution Type/Description: Historic House: built in 1883.
Hours & Admission Prices: Sun. 1-4; other times by appointment.

Estherville

H.G. ALBEE MEMORIAL MUSEUM, 1720 Third Ave., S., Estherville, IA 51334. Mailing Address: P.O. Box 101, Estherville, IA 51334-0101. Tel.: 712-362-2750.
E-mail: mbryan@yourstarnet.net
Key Personnel: Pres., Mildred Bryan; Sec., Mary Gray; Treas., Mike Maloney.
Institution Type/Description: Historical Society Museum.
Hours & Admission Prices: June-Aug. daily 2-5; other times by appointment. No charge; donations accepted. ♿
Attendance: 1,200 (actual)

Exira

AUDUBON COUNTY HISTORICAL SOCIETY, Courthouse Museum, Washington St., Exira, IA 50076. Mailing Address: 1745 160th St., Audubon, IA 50025-7483. Tel.: 712-563-3984.
E-mail: webmaster@auduboncounty.net
Key Personnel: Pres., Carma Hutchins; Vice Chm. (V), William Roth.
Institution Type/Description: History Museum.
Hours & Admission Prices: Memorial Day-Labor Day Sun. 1:30-4:30. Adults $3; discounts to members; members & students no charge. ♿
Attendance: 1,500 (estimated)

Fairfield

CARNEGIE HISTORICAL MUSEUM, 112 S. Court, Fairfield, IA 52556. Mailing Address: P.O. Box 502, Fairfield, IA 52556-0009. Tel.: 641-472-6343.
E-mail: carnegie@lisco.com
Web Site: www.fairfieldmuseum.com
Key Personnel: Pres., Gene Luedtke; Bd. Member, Jaimie Johnston; Bd. Member, Mandy Mellum; Dir., Mark Shafer; Treas., Keith Dimmitt.
Institution Type/Description: General Museum: housed in Carnegie library building.
Hours & Admission Prices: Tues., Thurs. & Sat. 1-4; other times by appointment. First Friday Art Walk: 6pm-9pm. No charge; donations accepted. ♿

FAIRFIELD ART ASSOCIATION, 200 N. Main St., Fairfield, IA 52556-2835. Tel.: 641-472-2000. Fax: 641-472-7890.
E-mail: info@fairfieldacc.com
Web Site: www.fairfieldacc.com/artgallery.html
Institution Type/Description: Arts & Convention Center.
Hours & Admission Prices: Call for hours. ♿
Attendance: 1,000 (estimated)

Forest City

HERITAGE PARK OF NORTH IOWA - WINNEBAGO HISTORICAL SOCIETY, 1225 Hwy. 69 S., Forest City, IA 50436. Mailing Address: 225 N. Golf Course Rd., Forest City, IA 50436. Tel.: 641-590-2009.
E-mail: rholland@wctatel.net
Web Site: heritageparkofnorthiowa.com
Key Personnel: Chm. (V), Ron Holland; Chm. (V), Loren Ehrich; Pres. (V), Riley Lewis.
Institution Type/Description: Regional History Museum.
Hours & Admission Prices: May-Oct.; other times by appointment. Events: $2-$6.
Attendance: 20,000 (estimated)

MANSION MUSEUM - WINNEBAGO HISTORICAL SOCIETY, 336 Clark St. N., Forest City, IA 50436. Mailing Address: P.O. Box 27, Forest City, IA 50436. Tel.: 641-581-3283. Facebook: Winnebago Historical Society.
E-mail: lewisrk@wctatel.net
Web Site: winnebagohistoricalsocietyiowa.org
Key Personnel: Chm. (V) & Pres. (V), Riley Lewis.
Institution Type/Description: Historical Society Museum: built c.1900.
Hours & Admission Prices: May-Oct. Sun. 1-4; other times by appointment. Adults $5; members no charge.
Attendance: 500 (estimated)

WINNEBAGO INDUSTRIES FACTORY TOUR, 1045 S. 4th St., Forest City, IA 50436. Tel.: 641-585-6936 & 800-643-4892.
Web Site: winnebagoind.com
Institution Type/Description: Motorhome Factory Tour & Visitors Center.
Hours & Admission Prices: Factory Tours: Forest City - April-Oct Mon.-Thurs. 9 &1. Lake Mills - April-Oct. Mon.-Thurs. 9:30, Fri. 9:30 & 1. Closed holidays.

Fort Dodge

BLANDEN MEMORIAL ART MUSEUM, 920 Third Ave., S., Fort Dodge, IA 50501-4723. Tel.: 515-573-2316. Fax: 515-573-2317.
E-mail: pkay@blanden.org
Web Site: www.blanden.org
Key Personnel: Dir., Margaret A. Skove; Pres., Dr. Kenneth Adams; Business Office, Pam Kay; Educator, Linda Flaherty; Maintenance & Security, Mark Jessen.
Institution Type/Description: Art Museum.
Hours & Admission Prices: Tues.-Sat. 11-5. No charge; donations accepted. Closed holidays. &
Attendance: 13,421 (actual)

FORT MUSEUM, 1 Museum Rd., Fort Dodge, IA 50501. Tel.: 515-573-4231.
E-mail: thefort@frontiernet.net
Web Site: www.fortmuseum.com
Institution Type/Description: History Museum.
Hours & Admission Prices: mid-April to mid-Oct. Mon.-Sat. 9-5, Sun. 11-5. Adults $6, students 6-18 $3; children 5 & under no charge.

Fort Madison

NORTH LEE COUNTY HISTORICAL SOCIETY AND SANTA FE DEPOT MUSEUM COMPLEX, 814 10th St. & Ave. H, Fort Madison, IA 52627-0285. Mailing Address: Box 285, Fort Madison, IA 52627-0285. Tel.: 319-372-7661. Facebook: North Lee County Historical Society.
E-mail: nlchs@iowatelecom.net
Key Personnel: Pres., Andy Andrews; Museum Shop Mgr., Linda Smith.
Institution Type/Description: Historic Center: located in 1910 Santa Fe Railroad depot (National Register of Historic Buildings in historic district); 1870s country school; Brush College; 1993 Flood museum; Louis Koch Gallery of Historic Paintings; 1898 Chicago Burlington & Quincy Railroad Depot.
Hours & Admission Prices: Mon.-Sat. 10-4, Sun. 12-4. No charge; donations accepted. &
Attendance: 4,000 (actual)

SHEAFFER PEN MUSEUM, 627 Ave. G, Fort Madison, IA 52627. Tel.: 319-372-1674.
E-mail: sheafferpenmuseum@gmail.com
Institution Type/Description: History Museum.
Hours & Admission Prices: Mon. & Fri.-Sat. 10-2.

Garnavillo

GARNAVILLO HISTORICAL MUSEUM, 203 N. Washington St., Garnavillo, IA 52049-7220. Mailing Address: P.O. Box 371, Garnavillo, IA 52049-0371. Tel.: 563-880-5078.
E-mail: garnavillohistoricalsociety@gmail.com
Web Site: www.garnavillohistoricalsociety.org
Key Personnel: Pres., Lanny Kuehl.
Institution Type/Description: General Local History Museum: housed in brick 1866 church.
Hours & Admission Prices: June-Sept. Sat.-Sun. & Independence Day 1-4. No charge; donations accepted.
Attendance: 250 (estimated)

George

GEORGE BICENTENNIAL MUSEUM, 204 E. Michigan Ave., George, IA 51237. Mailing Address: 210 N. Washington St., George, IA 51237. Tel.: 712-475-3612 (Office) & 2581 (Chm.).
Key Personnel: Chm. (V), Helen Fiihr.
Institution Type/Description: History Museum.
Hours & Admission Prices: June-Aug. Sun. 2-4; July 4th 9-4; other times by appointment. No charge; donations accepted.
Attendance: 100 (estimated)

Gladbrook

MATCHSTICK MARVELS TOURIST CENTER & MUSEUM, 319 Second St., Gladbrook, IA 50635-7718. Tel.: 641-473-2410.
E-mail: glbktheater@iowatelecom.net
Web Site: www.matchstickmarvels.com
Institution Type/Description: General Museum.
Hours & Admission Prices: April-Nov. daily 1-5; groups by appointment. Adults $3, children 5-12 $1; children under 5 no charge.

Glenwood

MILLS COUNTY HISTORICAL SOCIETY AND MUSEUM, 2 Lake Dr., Glenwood, IA 51534. Mailing Address: P.O. Box 255, Glenwood, IA 51534-0255. Tel.: 712-527-5038.
E-mail: millscountymuseum@qwestoffice.net
Key Personnel: Dir., Steve Hunt; Pres. (V), Ted Mintle.
Institution Type/Description: Local History Museum.
Hours & Admission Prices: May-Sept. Sat.-Sun. 1-4; other times by appointment. No charge; donations accepted. &
Attendance: 2,015 (estimated)

Grafton

GRAFTON HERITAGE DEPOT MUSEUM, County Rds A39 & S62, Grafton, IA 50440. Mailing Address: Worth County Historical Society, 917 Central Ave., Northwood, IA 50459-1525. Tel.: 641-748-2337. Facebook: Worth County Historical Society, Iowa.
E-mail: president@worthhistory.org
Web Site: www.worthhistory.org
Institution Type/Description: Historic Building: built in 1878. Listed on the National Register of Historic Places.
Hours & Admission Prices: Groups by appointment.

Greenfield

ADAIR COUNTY HERITAGE MUSEUM, 2393 S. Lakeview Dr., Hwy. 92 W., Greenfield, IA 50849. Mailing Address: P.O. Box 214, Greenfield, IA 50849-0214. Tel.: 641-743-2232.
Web Site: www.adaircountymuseum.com
Key Personnel: Pres. (V), Earl Carroll.
Institution Type/Description: History Museum.
Hours & Admission Prices: May-Oct. 1 daily 1-4; other times by appointment. Adults $3, children 5-12 $1.50; children under 5 no charge. &
Attendance: 200

IOWA AVIATION MUSEUM, Greenfield Municipal Airport, 2251 Airport Rd., Greenfield, IA 50849. Mailing Address: P.O. Box 31, Greenfield, IA 50849-0031. Tel.: 641-343-7184. Fax: 641-343-7184. Facebook: Iowa Aviation Museum.
E-mail: aviation@iowatelecom.net
Web Site: www.flyingmuseum.com
Formerly: Iowa Aviation Preservation Center
Key Personnel: Pres., Greg Schildberg; Vice Pres. & Treas., Dick Westbrook.
Institution Type/Description: Aviation Museum.
Hours & Admission Prices: May-Sept. Mon.-Sat. 10-5, Sun. 1-5; Oct.-April Mon.-Fri. 10-5, Sat.-Sun. 1-5. Adults $10, seniors $9, children K-12 $5; discounts to groups of 20 or more; members and children 4 & under no charge. Closed New Year's Day; Easter; Thanksgiving; Christmas Eve & Day. &
Attendance: 3,000 (estimated)

Grinnell

FAULCONER GALLERY AT GRINNELL COLLEGE, 1108 Park St., Grinnell, IA 50112-1643. Tel.: 641-269-4660. Fax: 641-269-4626.
E-mail: Strongdj@Grinnell.edu
Web Site: www.grinnell.edu/faulconergallery
Key Personnel: Dir., Lesley Wright; Assoc. Dir. & Cur. Exhibitions, Daniel Strong; Cur. Collections, Kay Wilson; Cur. Academic & Community Outreach, Tilly Woodward; Exhibition Designer, Milton Severe; Admin. Support Asst., Constance Gause.
Institution Type/Description: College Art Museum.
Hours & Admission Prices: Daily 11-5. No charge; donations accepted. Closed holidays. &
Attendance: 15,000 (estimated)

GRINNELL HISTORICAL MUSEUM, 1125 Broad St., Grinnell, IA 50112. Mailing Address: P.O. Box 254, Grinnell, IA 50112-0254. Tel.: 641-236-7827. Facebook.
E-mail: grinnellhistoricalmuseum@gmail.com
Web Site: www.grinnellhistoricalmuseum.org
Key Personnel: Pres., Cheryl Neubert; Sec., Dan Kaiser; Treas., Vera Cousins.
Institution Type/Description: History Museum: housed in an 1895-1896 home.
Hours & Admission Prices: April-May & Sept.-Dec. Sat.-Sun. 2-4; June-Aug. Thurs.-Sun. 2-4; groups by appointment. No charge; donations accepted. Closed New Year's Day; Independence Day; Christmas.
Attendance: 200 (estimated)

SPAULDING CENTER FOR TRANSPORTATION - HOME OF THE IOWA TRANSPORTATION MUSEUM, 829 Spring St., Grinnell, IA 50112-2043. Mailing Address: 927 4th Ave., Grinnell, IA 50112. Tel.: 641-236-9860. Fax: 641-236-2626.
E-mail: contact@iowatransportationmuseum.org
Web Site: www.iowatransportationmuseum.com
Key Personnel: Exec. Dir., Charles Brooke.
Institution Type/Description: Transportation Museum.
Hours & Admission Prices: Call for hours. No charge; donations accepted. &

Griswold

CASS COUNTY HISTORICAL SOCIETY MUSEUM, 412 Main St., Griswold, IA 51535-5800. Mailing Address: P.O. Box 254, Griswald, IA 51535. Tel.: 712-778-5040 & 2191.
Web Site: www.casscountymuseumiowa.com
Institution Type/Description: Historic Building: Listed on the National Register of Historic Places.
Hours & Admission Prices: May-Dec. Wed.-Sun. 1-4; other times by appointment. No charge; donations accepted. Closed holidays. &

Grundy Center

HERBERT QUICK SCHOOLHOUSE, Hwy. 175 E., Grundy Center, IA 50638. Mailing Address: 703 F Ave., Ste. 2, Grundy Center, IA 50638. Tel.: 319-825-6118. Fax: 319-825-6471.
E-mail: cityclerk@gcmuni.net
Web Site: www.grundycenter.com
Institution Type/Description: Historic Building: housed in the former school of author Herbert Quick.
Hours & Admission Prices: By appointment. No charge.
Attendance: 500 (estimated)

Guttenberg

LOCKMASTER'S HOUSE HERITAGE MUSEUM, Lock & Dam Lane, Guttenberg, IA 52052. Mailing Address: Guttenberg Heritage Society, P.O. Box 701, Guttenberg, IA 52052-0701. Tel.: 319-252-1531.
Web Site: www.visitiowa.org/business/lockmasters-heritage-house-museum.html
Institution Type/Description: Historic Building: housed in the former lockmaster's house. Listed on the National Register of Historic Places.
Hours & Admission Prices: Memorial Day to mid-Oct. Tues.-Sun. 12-4.

Hampton

REA POWER PLANT MUSEUM, 1450 110th St., Hampton, IA 50441. Mailing Address: P.O. Box 114, Hampton, IA 50441-0442. Tel.: 641-456-5777.
E-mail: visit@silosandsmokestacks.org
Web Site: www.silosandsmokestacks.org/attraction/rea-power-plant
Institution Type/Description: History Museum.
Hours & Admission Prices: By appointment. No charge.

Harlan

SHELBY COUNTY HISTORICAL MUSEUM, 1805 Morse Ave., Harlan, IA 51537-2042. Tel.: 712-755-2437. Facebook: Shelby County Historical Museum.
E-mail: shelbyco.museum@gmail.com
Web Site: www.shelbycoiamuseum.org
Key Personnel: Dir., Nathan Buman.
Institution Type/Description: History Museum.
Hours & Admission Prices: Mon.-Fri. 8-4; other times by appointment. No charge; donations accepted. &
Attendance: 3,500 (estimated)

Haverhill

MATTHEW EDEL BLACKSMITH SHOP, 214 1st St., Haverhill, IA 50120. Mailing Address: c/o Historical Society of Marshall County, 202 E. Church St., Marshalltown, IA 50158. Tel.: 641-752-6664.
E-mail: marshallhistory@live.com
Institution Type/Description: History Museum: housed in the former blacksmith shop & 1st home of Matthew Edel which he purchased in 1883. Listed on the National Register of Historic Places.
Hours & Admission Prices: Memorial Day to Labor Day daily 12-4; groups by appointment. No charge.

Hawarden

CALLIOPE VILLAGE, 19th St. & Ave. E, Hawarden, IA 51023. Mailing Address: City of Hawarden, 1150 Central Ave., Hawarden, IA 51023-1815. Tel.: 712-551-2403.
E-mail: happ@cityofhawarden.com
Institution Type/Description: Village History Museum.
Hours & Admission Prices: Memorial Day to Labor Day Sun. 1-4. No charge; donations accepted.

Homestead

HOMESTEAD STORE MUSEUM, 4430 V St., Homestead, IA 52236. Mailing Address: Amana Heritage Society, P.O. Box 81, Amana, IA 52203. Tel.: 319-622-3567.
E-mail: amanaheritage@southslope.net
Web Site: www.amanaheritage.org
Key Personnel: Museum Dir., Lanny Haldy.
Institution Type/Description: Historic Building Museum: housed in a former general store.
Hours & Admission Prices: By appointment only.

Honey Creek

HITCHCOCK NATURE CENTER, 27792 Ski Hill Loop, Honey Creek, IA 51542-4398. Tel.: 712-545-3283.
E-mail: mark.shoemaker@pottcounty.com
Key Personnel: C.E.O., Mark Shoemaker; Program Mgr., Tina Popson.
Institution Type/Description: Nature Center.
Hours & Admission Prices: Gallery: March-Nov. Tues.-Sat. 9-5, Sun. 1-5; Dec.-Feb. Fri.-Sat. 9-5. Park: daily 6 am-10 pm. Park: $2 per vehicle. &
Attendance: 36,000 (estimated)

Hopkinton

DELAWARE COUNTY HISTORICAL MUSEUM COMPLEX, College Square Hwy. 38, Hopkinton, IA 52237. Tel.: 563-926-2639.
E-mail: cityhopk@iowatelecom.net
Web Site: www.hopkintoniowa.org
Institution Type/Description: Historic Buildings: listed on the National Register of Historic Places.
Hours & Admission Prices: June-Sept. Tues.-Sun. 1-4. Adults $3.

Independence

WAPSIPINICON MILL MUSEUM, 100 1st St. W., Independence, IA 50644-2601. Mailing Address: P.O. Box 321, Independence, IA 50644-0321. Tel.: 319-334-4616. Facebook: Wapsi Mill.
E-mail: leannekay@indytel.com
Web Site: www.buchanancountyhistory.com
Institution Type/Description: Historic Building: housed in an 1870s grain mill. Listed on the National Register of Historic Places.
Hours & Admission Prices: mid-May to mid-Sept. Tues.-Sun. 12-4; other times by appointment. No charge; donations accepted. Group Tours: $3 per person. &
Attendance: 3,000 (estimated)

Indianola

NATIONAL BALLOON MUSEUM AND US BALLOONING HALL OF FAME, 1601 N. Jefferson Way, Indianola, IA 50125-1484. Mailing Address: P.O. Box 149, Indianola, IA 50125-0149. Tel.: 515-961-3714. Facebook: National Balloon Museum and US Ballooning Hall of Fame.
E-mail: museum@nationalballoonmuseum.com
Web Site: www.nationalballoonmuseum.com
Formerly: National Balloon Museum and Hall of Fame
Key Personnel: Pres. (V), Bev Wilson; Cur., Becky Wigeland; Museum Shop Mgr., Marlene Wall.
Institution Type/Description: Balloon Museum & Hall of Fame: aviation research library.
Hours & Admission Prices: Open Mar.-Dec. Wed.-Sun. 1-4; tours & other times by appointment. Adults $5; members no charge. Tours: adults $7; members no charge. Closed Closed Jan.-Feb.; national holidays. &
Attendance: 4,700 (estimated)

SIMPSON COLLEGE/FARNHAM GALLERIES, 701 N. C St., Mary Berry Hall, 3rd Fl., Indianola, IA 50125-1202. Tel.: 515-961-1761, 800-362-2454. Fax: 515-961-1498.

E-mail: jnostra@simpson.edu
Web Site: www.simpson.edu/art/gallery
Key Personnel: Dir. & Chair, Art Dept., Justin Nostrala; Vice Pres. Business & Finance, Ken Birkenholtz.
Institution Type/Description: Art Gallery.
Hours & Admission Prices: Mon.-Fri. 8:30-4:30; other times by appointment. No charge; donations accepted. &
Attendance: 300 (estimated)

WARREN COUNTY HISTORICAL SOCIETY MUSEUM, 1400 W. 2nd Ave., Indianola, IA 50125. Mailing Address: P.O. Box 256, Indianola, IA 50125-0256. Tel.: 515-961-8085.
E-mail: contact@warrencountyhistory.org
Institution Type/Description: Historical Society Museum.
Hours & Admission Prices: Thurs. 9-4, Sat. 9am-12pm; other times by appointment.

Iowa City

OLD CAPITOL MUSEUM, The University of Iowa, 21 Old Capitol, Iowa City, IA 52242. Tel.: 319-335-0548. Fax: 319-353-2982.
E-mail: shalla-wilson@uiowa.edu
Web Site: www.uiowa.edu/~oldcap/
Key Personnel: Dir., Pamela Trimpe; Cur., Shalla Wilson.
Institution Type/Description: Historic Building: Old Capitol, Iowa's last territorial capitol from 1842-46; first state capitol with the admission of Iowa to the Union in 1846.
Hours & Admission Prices: mid-Jan. to late Dec. Tues.-Wed. & Fri.-Sat. 10-5, Thurs. 10-8, Sun. 1-5. No charge; donations accepted. Closed national holidays; Christmas Eve, Day & week. &
Attendance: 30,000 (actual)

PLUM GROVE HISTORIC HOME, 1030 Carroll St., Iowa City, IA 52240-4601. Mailing Address: Johnson County Historical Society Museum, 860 Quarry Rd., Coralville, IA 52241-2421. Tel.: 319-337-6846 & 351-5738. Fax: 319-351-5310.
E-mail: questions@johnsoncountyhistory.org
Web Site: www.johnsoncountyhistory.org
Key Personnel: C.E.O., Alexandra Drehman; Chm. (V), Steve Weeber.
Institution Type/Description: Historic Building: 1844 home of Robert Lucas, first governor of Territory of Iowa.
Hours & Admission Prices: Memorial Day to Labor Day Wed.-Sun. 1-5; Sept.-Oct. Sat.-Sun. 1-5. No charge; donations accepted. Closed Independence Day. &
Attendance: 2,000 (actual)

PROJECT ART-UNIVERSITY OF IOWA AND CLINICS, 200 Hawkins Dr., Iowa City, IA 52242-1009. Tel.: 319-353-6417. Fax: 319-384-8141.
E-mail: adrienne-drapkin@uiowa.edu
Web Site: uihealthcare.com/projectart
Key Personnel: Dir., Adrienne Drapkin.
Institution Type/Description: Art Museum.
Hours & Admission Prices: Mon.-Fri. 8-5; permanent collection is on view 24 hours a day in the public corridors, lobbies & waiting rooms. No charge. &
Attendance: 40,000 (estimated)

STANLEY MUSEUM OF ART, Iowa Memorial Union, 3rd Fl., 125 N. Madison St., Iowa City, IA 52242. Tel.: 319-335-1727. Fax: 319-335-3677.
E-mail: uima@uiowa.edu
Web Site: stanleymuseum.uiowa.edu
Key Personnel: Dir., Lauren Lessing; Chief Cur., Joyce Tsai; Cur. Learning & Education, Kimberly Datchuk; Mng. Communications, Mktg., & Membership, Elizabeth Menninger Wallace; Mng. Exhibitions & Collections, Katherine Wilson; Mng. Design, Preparation & Installation, Steve Erickson; Cur. Arts of Africa, Oceania, & the Americas, Cory Gundlach.
Institution Type/Description: Art Museum.
Hours & Admission Prices: Stanley visual classroom: Tues.-Wed. & Fri. 10-5, Thurs. 10-9, Sat.-Sun.12-5; Figge art museum: Tues.-Wed. & Fri.-Sat. 10-5, Thurs. 10-9, Sun. 12-5. No charge; donations accepted. &
Attendance: 137,000 (estimated)

UNIVERSITY OF IOWA ATHLETICS HALL OF FAME AND MUSEUM, 2425 Prairie Meadow Dr., Iowa City, IA 52242. Tel.: 319-384-1031.
E-mail: halloffame@hawkeyesports.com
Key Personnel: Dir., Dale Arens.
Institution Type/Description: Sports Museum.

Hours & Admission Prices: Mon.-Thurs. 8-5, Fri. 8-6, Sat. 10-6, Sun 12-5. No charge. Closed Thanksgiving, Christmas & New Year. &

UNIVERSITY OF IOWA HOSPITALS & CLINICS MEDICAL MUSEUM, 200 Hawkins Dr. 8014 RCP, Iowa City, IA 52242-1009. Mailing Address: UIHC Medical Museum, Iowa City, IA 52242. Tel.: 319-353-6417; 356-7106. Fax: 319-384-8141.
E-mail: adrienne-drapkin@uiowa.edu
Web Site: uihealthcare.com/medmuseum
Key Personnel: Dir., Adrienne Drapkin.
Institution Type/Description: Medical Museum.
Hours & Admission Prices: Mon.-Fri. 8-5, Sat.-Sun. 1-4. No charge. Closed New Year's Day; Thanksgiving; Christmas. &
Attendance: 50,000 (estimated)

UNIVERSITY OF IOWA MUSEUM OF NATURAL HISTORY, 11 Macbride Hall, Iowa City, IA 52242-1322. Tel.: 319-335-0606. Fax: 319-335-3677. Facebook: Iowa Natural History.
E-mail: uimnh@uiowa.edu
Web Site: www.uiowa.edu/mnh
Key Personnel: Dir., John Logsdon; Assoc. Dir., Trina Roberts; Education & Outreach Coord. & Museum Shop Mgr., Sarah Horgen; Collections Mgr., Cindy Opitz; Exhibits Mgr., Byron Preston.
Institution Type/Description: Natural History Museum.
Hours & Admission Prices: Tues.-Wed. & Fri.-Sat. 10-5, Thurs. 10-8, Sun. 1-5. No charge; donations accepted. Closed national holidays. &
Attendance: 30,000 (estimated)

Iowa Falls

CALKINS NATURE AREA/FIELD MUSEUM, 18335 135th St., Iowa Falls, IA 50126-8512. Tel.: 641-648-9878. Fax: 641-648-9878.
E-mail: calkinsnatureareahccb@gmail.com
Key Personnel: Exec. Dir., Wes Wiese; Chm. (V), William H. Schmidt.
Institution Type/Description: Natural Science & History Museum.
Hours & Admission Prices: Interpretive Center: Mon.-Fri. 8-4. No charge; donations accepted. &
Attendance: 4,700

DOW HOUSE - IOWA FALLS HISTORICAL SOCIETY, 519 Stevens St., Iowa Falls, IA 50126. Mailing Address: P.O. Box 364, Iowa Falls, IA 50126. Tel.: 641-648-4017 & 3606.
E-mail: chamber@iowafallschamber.com
Institution Type/Description: Historic House Museum: built in 1909.
Hours & Admission Prices: Summer: Tues.-Thurs. 1-4; other times by appointment.

ILLINOIS CENTRAL DEPOT MUSEUM, Rocksylvania Ave., Iowa Falls, IA 50126. Mailing Address: P.O. Box 364, Iowa Falls, IA 50126. Tel.: 641-648-5900 & 2849.
Institution Type/Description: Historic Building: depot built in 1904.
Hours & Admission Prices: By appointment.

IOWA FALLS HISTORICAL MUSEUM, 520 Rocksylvania Ave., Carnegie Ellsworth Library Bldg., Iowa Falls, IA 50126. Mailing Address: P.O. Box 364, Iowa Falls, IA 50126. Tel.: 641-648-4017.
E-mail: chamber@iowafallschamber.com
Institution Type/Description: History Museum.
Hours & Admission Prices: June-Sept. Thurs. 1-3; Oct.-May 1st Sun. each month 1-3. &

PAT CLARK ART COLLECTION GALLERY, 520 Rocksylvania Ave., Iowa Falls, IA 50126. Tel.: 641-648-8576.
E-mail: kristie.nevenhoven@iavalley.edu
Web Site: www.patclarkart.org
Institution Type/Description: Art Gallery.
Hours & Admission Prices: Mon.-Fri. 9-12 & 1-4; guided tours by appointment. No charge.

Jefferson

GREENE COUNTY HISTORICAL SOCIETY MUSEUM, 219 E. Lincolnway, Jefferson, IA 50129-2205. Tel.: 515-386-8544.
Institution Type/Description: Historical Society Museum.
Hours & Admission Prices: May-Sept. Wed. 1-5, Sat. 9 to noon; other times by appointment. No charge. &

JEFFERSON TELEPHONE MUSEUM, 105 W. Harrison, Jefferson, IA 50129-2105. Mailing Address: P.O. Box 269, Jefferson, IA 50129-0269. Tel.: 515-386-4141. Fax: 515-386-2600.
E-mail: jtcobob@netius.net
Web Site: www.jeffersontelecom.com
Key Personnel: Gen. Mgr., James Daubendiek.
Institution Type/Description: Technology Museum.
Hours & Admission Prices: Mon.-Fri. 9-4. No charge. Closed major holidays.
Attendance: 100 (estimated)

Johnston

IOWA GOLD STAR MILITARY MUSEUM, 7105 N.W. 70th Ave., Johnston, IA 50131-1824. Tel.: 515-252-4531. Fax: 515-727-3107.
E-mail: goldstarmuseum@iowa.gov
Web Site: www.goldstarmuseum.iowa.gov
Key Personnel: Dir., Sherrie Cobert; Chm. (V), Bob Holliday.
Institution Type/Description: Military Museum.
Hours & Admission Prices: Mon.-Fri. 8:30-4:30, Sat. 10-4. Closed holidays. No charge; donations accepted. &
Attendance: 24,510 (actual)

Kalona

KALONA HISTORICAL VILLAGE, 715 D Ave., Kalona, IA 52247. Mailing Address: P.O. Box 292, Kalona, IA 52247. Tel.: 319-656-3232. Facebook: Kalona Historical Village.
E-mail: kalonatours@kctc.net
Web Site: www.kalonaiowa.org
Key Personnel: Mng. Dir., Nancy Roth.
Institution Type/Description: Historic Buildings: 1800s village including 13 historic buildings.
Hours & Admission Prices: April-Oct. Mon.-Sat. 10-5; Nov.-March Mon.-Sat. 11-3. Admission $8. Closed Easter; Thanksgiving; Christmas Eve & Day; New Year's Eve & Day. &

Kellogg

KELLOGG HISTORICAL SOCIETY, 218 High St., Kellogg, IA 50135. Mailing Address: P.O. Box 295, Kellogg, IA 50135-0295. Tel.: 641-526-3430.
E-mail: khs@partnercom.net
Key Personnel: Pres. (V), David Faircloth; Financial Dir., Jenna Shine.
Institution Type/Description: Historical Society Museum.
Hours & Admission Prices: Memorial Day weekend to Sept. 1 Mon.-Fri. 9-4, Sun. 1:30-5, Sat. by appointment. No charge; donations requested. Closed all holidays. &
Attendance: 1,000 (estimated)

Kensett

KENSETT COMMUNITY CHURCH MUSEUM, Second St., Kensett, IA 50448. Mailing Address: Worth County Historical Society, 917 Central Ave., Northwood, IA 50459-1525. Tel.: 641-324-1180. Facebook.
E-mail: president@worthhistory.org
Web Site: www.worthhistory.org
Institution Type/Description: Historic Building: built in 1899. Listed on the National Register of Historic Places.
Hours & Admission Prices: June-Aug. Sun. 2-4; call for additional hours. No charge; donations accepted.
Attendance: 200 (estimated)

Keokuk

KEOKUK RIVER MUSEUM, 101 Mississippi Dr., Keokuk, IA 52632. Mailing Address: P.O. Box 400, Keokuk, IA 52632-0400. Tel.: 319-524-4765. Fax: 319-524-2642. geomverity.org.
E-mail: chuckpietscher@cityofkeokuk.org
Web Site: keokukiowatourism.org
Key Personnel: Chm. (V), Charles R. Pietscher.
Institution Type/Description: Maritime Museum: housed in 1927 George M. Verity Mississippi River Steamboat.
Hours & Admission Prices: April-Oct. Mon. & Thurs.-Fri. 9-12 & 4-6, Sat.-Sun. 9-6. Adults $4, children $1.50; special group rates for 12 or more.
Attendance: 4,000 (actual)

SAMUEL F. MILLER HOUSE & MUSEUM, 318 N. 5th St., Keokuk, IA 52632. Tel.: 319-524-7283.
Institution Type/Description: Historic House Museum: built in 1859.
Hours & Admission Prices: Memorial Day to Labor Day Fri.-Sun. 1-4.

Keosauqua

VAN BUREN COUNTY HISTORICAL SOCIETY, 1st St., Keosauqua, IA 52565. Mailing Address: P.O. Box 423, Keosauqua, IA 52565-0423. Tel.: 319-293-3494.
E-mail: vanburenhistory@netins.net
Web Site: iavanburen.org/historical_society.htm
Key Personnel: Pres., Marvin Danneil; Sec., Doris Secor; Treas., Joe Stump.
Institution Type/Description: Historical House Museum.
Hours & Admission Prices: Society: June to mid-Oct. Sun. & holidays 1-4; other times by appointment. No charge; donations accepted. Pearson House Memorial Day to Labor Day Sun. 1-4; other times by appointment. Suggested Donation: adults $2; students $1. Closed holidays.
Attendance: 325 (actual)

Knoxville

NATIONAL SPRINT CAR HALL OF FAME & MUSEUM, One Sprint Capital Pl., Knoxville, IA 50138. Mailing Address: P.O. Box 542, Knoxville, IA 50138-0542. Tel.: 641-842-6176. Fax: 641-842-6177.
E-mail: bbaker@sprintcarhof.com
Web Site: www.sprintcarhof.com
Key Personnel: Exec. Dir., Bob Baker; Pres. (V), Jeff Savage; Cur., Tom Schmeh; Devel., Doug Lockin; Coord. Special Events, Mike Noftsger; Education, Lori Demoss; Coord. Museum Store., Laci White; Security, Gary Van Waardhuizen.
Institution Type/Description: Sports Museum.
Hours & Admission Prices: Mon.-Fri. 8-5, Sat.-Sun. 12-5. Adults $4; discounts to AAA & ISHA members; members no charge. Closed New Year's Day; Easter; Thanksgiving; Christmas. &
Attendance: 10,722 (actual)

Lake City

CENTRAL SCHOOL PRESERVATION, INC. - HISTORIC CENTRAL SCHOOL, 211 S. Center St., Lake City, IA 51449-2003. Tel.: 712-464-8639.
E-mail: centralschool@windstream.net
Web Site: historiccentralschool.com
Key Personnel: Pres. (V), Jim Bruce.
Institution Type/Description: History Museum: housed in a restored 1884 school-house. Listed on the National Historic Register.
Hours & Admission Prices: Daily 9:30am-11:30am; other times by appointment. No charge; donations accepted.
Attendance: 900 (estimated)

Lake Mills

BURNAP COUNTRY SCHOOL MUSEUM, 308 N. Mill St., Lake Mills, IA 50450-1221. Mailing Address: c/o Lake Mills Area Historical Society, 308 S. Lincoln St., Lake Mills, IA 50450. Tel.: 641-592-5253. Fax: 641-592-5252.
E-mail: lmcdc@wctatel.net
Web Site: www.lakemillsiowa.com
Institution Type/Description: Historic Buildings: housed in a former rural country school used from 1936-1954.
Hours & Admission Prices: Memorial Day to Labor Day Sun. 2-4; other times by appointment. No charge.

Lamoni

LIBERTY HALL HISTORIC CENTER - HOME OF JOSEPH SMITH III, 1138 W. Main St., Lamoni, IA 50140-1273. Tel.: 641-784-6133.
E-mail: libhall@grm.net
Web Site: www.libhall.net
Key Personnel: C.E.O., Lach Mackay; Pres., Jeff Naylor; Museum Site Dir., Steve Smith.
Institution Type/Description: Historic House: 1881 building; 1876 schoolhouse.
Hours & Admission Prices: March-Dec. 20 Tues.-Sat. 10-4, Sun. 1:30-4. No charge, donations accepted; group tours by appointment, call 641-784-6133.
Attendance: 2,500 (estimated)

Lansing

RIVER HISTORY MUSEUM, 60 S. Front St., Lansing, IA 52151. Mailing Address: 621 S. Second St., Lansing, IA 52151. Tel.: 563-538-4641.
Key Personnel: Dir., Karen Galena.
Institution Type/Description: History Museum.
Hours & Admission Prices: Summer: Sat. 1-4; other times by appointment. No charge; donations accepted.
Attendance: 800 (estimated)

Latimer

LATIMER HISTORICAL MUSEUM, 108 S. Akir St., Latimer, IA 50452-7593. Tel.: 641-579-6452. Fax: 641-579-6508.
E-mail: latimer@iowaconnect.com
Web Site: www.latimeriowa.net
Institution Type/Description: History Museum.
Hours & Admission Prices: Mon.-Fri. 8-3, Sat. by appointment. No charge.

Laurens

POCAHONTAS COUNTY IOWA HISTORICAL SOCIETY MUSEUM, 271 N. 3rd St., Laurens, IA 50554-1274. Mailing Address: 272 N. 3rd St., Laurens, IA 50554-0148. Tel.: 712-841-2577.
E-mail: marcialeu@yahoo.com
Key Personnel: C.E.O., Ann Beneke; Chm. (V) & Pres. (V), Marcia Leu; Financial Dir., Kristy Mather; Cur., Dorothy Lamberti; Archivist, Jane Kirchner.
Institution Type/Description: Historical Society Museum: housed in Carnegie library.
Hours & Admission Prices: Memorial Day-Oct. every other Sun. 2-5, call for reservations. No charge; donations accepted. &
Attendance: 650 (estimated)

Le Claire

BUFFALO BILL MUSEUM OF LE CLAIRE, IOWA, INC., 199 N. Front St., Le Claire, IA 52753-7713. Tel.: 563-289-5580.
E-mail: contact@buffalobillmuseumleclaire.com
Web Site: www.buffalobillmuseumleclaire.com
Key Personnel: Pres., Ron Leiby; Exec. Dir., Robert Schiffke; Vice Pres., Packy Huettman; Sec., Debbie Smith; Treas., Dorothy Sebastian.
Institution Type/Description: Preservation Project.
Hours & Admission Prices: Mon.-Sat. 9-5, Sun. 12-5; Winter: Mon.-Sat. 9-4, Sun. 12-4. Adults $5, students & children 5-15 $1; discounts to tour groups of 10 or more, seniors 65 & over, military and AAM members; scout groups, school groups & members no charge. Closed New Year's Day; Thanksgiving; Christmas. &
Attendance: 20,000 (actual)

Le Mars

BLUE BUNNY ICE CREAM PARLOR & MUSEUM, Wells Dairy, Inc., 115 Central Ave. N.W., Le Mars, IA 51031. Tel.: 712-546-4522.
E-mail: dlsusemihl@bluebunny.com
Web Site: www.bluebunny.com/parlor
Formerly: Ice Cream Capital of the World Visitor Center
Institution Type/Description: General Museum: home of Blue Bunny Ice Cream.
Hours & Admission Prices: April-Sept. Mon.-Sat. 9-10, Sun. 12-10; Oct. March Mon.-Sat. 10-9, Sun. 12-9. No charge. &

PLYMOUTH COUNTY HISTORICAL MUSEUM, 335 1st Ave., S.W., Le Mars, IA 51031-2000. Tel.: 712-546-7002.
E-mail: pchmuseum@gmail.com
Web Site: plymouthcountymuseum.homestead.com/museum.html
Key Personnel: Admin., Judy Bowman; Registrar & Exhibit Mgr., Mary Holub.
Institution Type/Description: History Museum. Listed on the National Register of Historic Places.
Hours & Admission Prices: Tues.-Sun. 1-5. No charge; donations accepted. &

Leon

DECATUR COUNTY MUSEUM, 401 S.E. 3rd St., Leon, IA 50144. Mailing Address: 105 N. Main St., Leon, IA 50144. Tel.: 641-446-3297. Facebook.
E-mail: redmanch@grm.net
Key Personnel: Pres. (V), Corey Lindsey.
Institution Type/Description: History Museum.

Hours & Admission Prices: Memorial Day to Labor Day Tues. & Fri. call for hours.

Lewis

HITCHCOCK HOUSE, 63788 567th Lane, Lewis, IA 51544-5137. Mailing Address: 1609 Lomas Circle, Atlantic, IA 50022-2734. Tel.: 712-769-2323.
Web Site: www.hitchcockhouse.org
Key Personnel: Chm., Dana Kunze; Museum Shop Mgr., Sandy Fairbairn.
Institution Type/Description: Historic House Museum: housed in the former home of Rev. George Hitchcock; built in 1856. A National Historic Landmark.
Hours & Admission Prices: May-Sept. Tues.-Sun. 1-4:30. High School & up $5; bus tour facilitators & bus drivers no charge.
Attendance: 2,252,800 (actual)

Lockridge

JOHNNY CLOCK MUSEUM, 711 W. Main St., Lockridge, IA 52635. Tel.: 319-696-3711.
Key Personnel: Owner, John McLain; Owner, Pat McLain.
Institution Type/Description: Clock Museum.
Hours & Admission Prices: May-Sept.1st daily 9-5; other times by appointment. Adults $5, children $3; children under 5 no charge.

Logan

MUSEUM OF RELIGIOUS ARTS, 2697 Niagara Trail, Logan, IA 51546-0122. Mailing Address: P.O. Box 122, Logan, IA 51546-0122. Tel.: 712-644-3888. Facebook: Museum of Religious Arts.
E-mail: museum@loganet.net
Web Site: www.mrarts.org
Key Personnel: Pres. (V), Kris Haase; Dir., Rhonda McHugh.
Institution Type/Description: Religious Museum.
Hours & Admission Prices: Summer: Tues.-Sat. 10-4, Sun. 12-4; Winter: Thurs.-Sat. 10-4, Sun. 12-4; other times by appointment. Adults $5; discounts to children groups and AAA & AAM members. Closed New Year's Day, Easter, Memorial Day, Independence Day, Labor Day, Thanksgiving & Christmas. &
Attendance: 6,000 (estimated)

Lone Tree

LONE TREE HISTORICAL MUSEUM, 203 S. Devoe, Lone Tree, IA 52755. Tel.: 319-338-0104.
E-mail: daleandardath@mchsi.com
Institution Type/Description: History Museum.
Hours & Admission Prices: May to mid-Oct. call for hours. &

Long Grove

DAN NAGLE WALNUT GROVE PIONEER VILLAGE, 18817 290th St., Long Grove, IA 52756-9615. Tel.: 563-328-3283.
E-mail: conservation@scottcountyiowa.com
Web Site: www.scottcountyiowa.com/conservation
Key Personnel: Dir., Chm. & Pres., Deborah Leistikow.
Institution Type/Description: Historic Buildings.
Hours & Admission Prices: April-Oct. daily 9-6. No charge; donations accepted.
Attendance: 10,000 (estimated)

Lucas

JOHN L. LEWIS MINING & LABOR MUSEUM, 102 Division St., Lucas, IA 50151-0003. Mailing Address: P.O. Box 3, Lucas, IA 50151-0003. Tel.: 641-766-6831. Fax: 641-766-6831.
E-mail: jllmuseum@iowatelecom.net
Web Site: www.coalmininglabormuseum.com
Key Personnel: Pres. (V), Earl Seymour.
Institution Type/Description: Mining & Labor Museum.
Hours & Admission Prices: April 15-Oct. 15 Mon.-Sat. 9-3; groups by appointment. Adults $2, students 11 & over $1; children under 10 no charge. Closed holidays. &
Attendance: 1,000 (estimated)

Lynnville

LYNNVILLE HISTORICAL SOCIETY WAGAMAN MILL MUSEUM, 200 East St., Lynnville, IA 50153. Mailing Address: P. O. Box 113, Lynnville, IA 50153. Tel.: 641-527-2080. Fax: 641-791-9976.
E-mail: conservation@co.jasper.ia.us

Web Site: www.co.jasper.ia.us/conservation
Key Personnel: Treas., Garnet Gertsma; Walt Van Maanen.
Institution Type/Description: Historic Building: built in 1846. Listed on the National Register of Historic Places.
Hours & Admission Prices: Memorial Day Sun. to Sept. Sun. 1-4; other times by appointment. No charge; donations accepted. Groups: $1 per person. &
Attendance: 477 (actual)

Macedonia

STEMPEL BIRD COLLECTION, 311 Main St., Macedonia, IA 51549-3002. Tel.: 712-486-2323.
Institution Type/Description: General Museum.
Hours & Admission Prices: April-Nov. 1 Mon.-Fri. 9-3; other times by appointment. No charge. Closed holidays. &

Madrid

MADRID HISTORICAL MUSEUM, 109 W. Second St., Madrid, IA 50156-1339. Mailing Address: P.O. Box 105, Madrid, IA 50156. Tel.: 515-795-3249.
E-mail: madridmuseum@windstream.net
Web Site: www.madridiamuseum.com
Formerly: Clay Castle Museum & Madrid Historical Museum
Key Personnel: Pres., Ray Ortmann; Pres. (V), Roger Peterson.
Institution Type/Description: Historical Society Museum.
Hours & Admission Prices: Call for hours. No charge; donations accepted. &
Attendance: 500 (estimated)

Manning

MANNING HAUSBARN HERITAGE PARK, 130 Heritage Dr., Manning, IA 51455. Tel.: 712-655-3131. Fax: 712-655-2941.
E-mail: heritag@mmctsu.com
Web Site: www.germanhausbarn.com
Key Personnel: Dir., Freda Dammann; Chm. (V), Warren Puck.
Institution Type/Description: Historic Building: housed in a dwelling that consists of family living quarters & areas for livestock and farm equipment; built in 1660 in Schleswig-Holstein Germany, dismantled and reconstructed here in 1999.
Hours & Admission Prices: May-Oct. Mon.-Sat. 10-4, Sun. 1-4. Adults $6.
Attendance: 5,000 (estimated)

Maquoketa

CLINTON ENGINES MUSEUM, 605 E. Maple St., Maquoketa, IA 52060. Mailing Address: P.O. Box 1245, Maquoketa, IA 52060-1245. Tel.: 563-652-1803. Fax: 563-652-1803. Facebook.
E-mail: museum@jciahs.com
Web Site: www.jciahs.com
Key Personnel: C.E.O. & Chm., David Stockham; Dir., Bonnie W. Mitchell; Museum Shop Mgr., Marcella Heneke.
Institution Type/Description: History Museum.
Hours & Admission Prices: Tues.-Fri. 10-4, Sat.-Sun. 12-4. Adults $5; discounts to Time Travelers; members no charge. Closed major holidays. &
Attendance: 1,550 (estimated)

JACKSON COUNTY HISTORY MUSEUM & MACHINE SHED, 1212 E. Quarry, Fairgrounds, Maquoketa, IA 52060. Mailing Address: P.O. Box 1245, Maquoketa, IA 52060-1245. Tel.: 563-652-5020. Fax: 563-652-5020. Facebook: jacksoniowa-historicalsociety.
E-mail: museum@jciahs.com
Web Site: www.jciahs.com
Formerly: Jackson County Historical Museum & Research Library
Key Personnel: Pres., Jack Willey; Dir., Bonnie W. Mitchell; Museum Shop Mgr., Marcella Heneke.
Institution Type/Description: History Museum.
Hours & Admission Prices: Tues.-Fri. 10-4, Sat.-Sun. 12-4. Adults $5; discount to Time Travelers; members no charge. Closed major holidays. &
Attendance: 6,000 (estimated)

OLD CITY HALL ART GALLERY, 121 S. Olive, Maquoketa, IA 52060. Tel.: 563-652-3405.
E-mail: wefrantzen@yahoo.com
Web Site: oldcityhallgallery.com
Institution Type/Description: Art Gallery: housed in the former town's fire station; built in 1901.
Hours & Admission Prices: Daily 11-7; call to confirm.

Marion

THE GRANGER HOUSE VICTORIAN MUSEUM, 970 10th St., Marion, IA 52302-3572. Tel.: 319-377-6672. Facebook; Twitter.
E-mail: info@grangerhouse.org
Web Site: grangerhousemuseum.org
Key Personnel: Pres. (V), Adam Hyatt.
Institution Type/Description: Historic House & Site.
Hours & Admission Prices: Sat. & Sun. 1-4; other times by appointment. Adults $10; children $5; members no charge. Closed New Year's Eve & Day; Easter; Mother's Day; Memorial Day; Father's Day; Independence Day; Labor Day; Thanksgiving; Christmas Eve & Day.
Attendance: 1,200 (estimated)

MARION HERITAGE CENTER, 590 Tenth St., Marion, IA 52302-4409. Mailing Address: P.O. Box 753, Marion, IA 52302-0753. Tel.: 319-477-6376. Facebook: @marionheritagecenter.
E-mail: marionheritage@marionhistoricalsociety.org
Web Site: marionheritagecenter.org
Key Personnel: Dir., Lynette Brenzel; Marion Historical Society Pres., Vic Klopfenstein.
Institution Type/Description: History Museum; changing exhibits 2 times per year, 3 months art & 6 months local historical topic.
Hours & Admission Prices: Wed.-Sun. 1-4. Adults $5, children $2; members & Blue Star military no charge. &
Attendance: 2,000 (estimated)

Marshalltown

CENTRAL IOWA ART ASSOCIATION, Fisher Community Center, Marshalltown, IA 50158. Mailing Address: 709 S. Center St., Ste. #1, Marshalltown, IA 50158-2876. Tel.: 641-753-9013.
E-mail: ciaa@iowatelecom.net
Web Site: www.centraliowaartassociation.org
Key Personnel: Pres. (V), William Flowers; Museum Shop Mgr., Jeanne Newton-Schoborg.
Institution Type/Description: Impressionist & Ceramics Museum.
Hours & Admission Prices: Mon.-Fri. 11-5. No charge; donations accepted. Closed holidays. &
Attendance: 4,000 (estimated)

FISHER ART GALLERY, 709 S. Center St., Marshalltown, IA 50158-2876. Tel.: 515-753-9013.
E-mail: ciaa@iowatelecom.net
Institution Type/Description: Art Gallery.
Hours & Admission Prices: mid-April to mid-Oct. daily 11-5; mid-Oct. to mid-April Mon.-Fri. 11-5. No charge; donations accepted. &
Attendance: 500 (estimated)

HISTORICAL SOCIETY OF MARSHALL COUNTY, 202 E. Church St., Marshalltown, IA 50158-2943. Tel.: 641-752-6664. Facebook: Historical Society of Marshall County.
E-mail: marshallhistory@live.com
Formerly: Marshall County Historical Museum
Institution Type/Description: History Museum.
Hours & Admission Prices: Mon.-Fri. 9-3. No charge; donations accepted.
Attendance: 2,000 (estimated)

Mason City

CHARLES H. MACNIDER MUSEUM, 303 2nd St., S.E., Mason City, IA 50401-3988. Tel.: 641-421-3666. Fax: 641-422-9612.
E-mail: eblanchard@masoncity.net
Web Site: www.macniderart.org
Key Personnel: Dir., Edith M. Blanchard; Pres., Jay Hansen; Coord. Education, Linda Willeke; Registrar & Curatorial Asst., Mara Linskey; Museum Shop Mgr., Jennifer Klein.
Institution Type/Description: American Art Museum.
Hours & Admission Prices: Tues.-Wed. & Fri.-Sat. 9-5, Thurs. 9-9. No charge; donations accepted. Closed national holidays. &
Attendance: 20,043 (actual)

FRANK LLOYD WRIGHT STOCKMAN HOUSE AND ARCHITECTURAL INTERPRETIVE CENTER, 530 First St., N.E., Mason City, IA 50401-3534. Mailing Address: P.O. Box 565, Mason City, IA 50402. Tel.: 641-423-1923.
E-mail: info@stockmanhouse.org
Web Site: www.stockmanhouse.org
Institution Type/Description: Historic House Museum: housed in Frank Lloyd Wright's Stockman House.

Hours & Admission Prices: See website for hours & admission prices. &
Attendance: 2,500 (estimated)

KINNEY PIONEER MUSEUM, Municipal Airport, Hwy. 122 W., Mason City, IA 50401. Mailing Address: P.O. Box 421, Mason City, IA 50402. Tel.: 641-423-1258.
Key Personnel: Dir., Kay Ingersoll; Pres. (V), Richard Peterson.
Institution Type/Description: History Museum.
Hours & Admission Prices: May-Sept. Tues.-Sun. 1-5; groups & other times by appointment. Adults $3, children under 12 $1; discounts to groups. &
Attendance: 1,900 (estimated)

LIME CREEK NATURE CENTER, 3501 Lime Creek Rd., Mason City, IA 50401-9256. Tel.: 515-423-5309. Fax: 641-423-1566.
E-mail: tvonehw@co.cerro-gordo.ia.us
Web Site: www.co.cerro-gordo.ia.us
Key Personnel: Dir., Mike Webb; Chm. (V), Bruce McKee.
Institution Type/Description: Nature Center.
Hours & Admission Prices: Summer: Mon.-Fri. 7:30-4, Sat. 9-5, Sun. 1-5; Winter: Mon.-Fri. 7:30-4, Sat. 9-4, Sun. 1-4. No charge; donations accepted. &
Attendance: 35,000 (estimated)

MEREDITH WILLSON BOYHOOD HOME, 314 S. Pennsylvania Ave., Mason City, IA 50401-3913. Tel.: 641-424-2852, 866-228-6262 (Toll Free).
E-mail: mmsquare@mach3ww.com
Web Site: www.themusicmansquare.org
Institution Type/Description: Historic House Museum: housed in the birthplace & boyhood home of Meredith Willson, songwriter & playwright of The Music Man.
Hours & Admission Prices: Tues.-Sun. 1-5; other times by appointment. Adults $6, students $3. Closed holidays.

Maxwell

THE COMMUNITY HISTORICAL SOCIETY, Main St., Maxwell, IA 50161. Tel.: 515-382-4085.
E-mail: bamddswans@gmail.com
Key Personnel: Pres. (V), Robert Swanson; Vice Pres., Jerry White; Historian, Mrs. Mildred McIntosh.
Institution Type/Description: General Museum.
Hours & Admission Prices: April-Sept. Sun., holidays & by appointment. No charge; donations accepted. &
Attendance: 1,350 (actual)

Melcher

MELCHER-DALLAS COAL MINING AND HERITAGE MUSEUM, 101 N.E. Center, Melcher, IA 50163. Mailing Address: P.O. Box 412, Melcher, IA 50163-0412. Tel.: 641-947-5651 & 891-7438.
E-mail: gramspop_1@iowatelecom.net
Key Personnel: Dir., Sandra Haug.
Institution Type/Description: Mining Museum.
Hours & Admission Prices: Memorial Day to Labor Day Sat.-Sun. 1-4. No charge. &
Attendance: 225 (estimated)

Middle Amana

COMMUNAL KITCHEN AND COOPER SHOP MUSEUM, 1003 26th Ave., Middle Amana, IA 52203. Mailing Address: Amana Heritage Society, P.O. Box 81, Amana, IA 52203-0081. Tel.: 319-622-3567.
E-mail: amanaheritage@southslope.net
Web Site: www.amanaheritage.org
Institution Type/Description: History Museum.
Hours & Admission Prices: March & Nov. Dec. Mon.-Sat. 10-5, Sun. 12-4; April-Oct. Mon.-Fri. 10-5, Sun. 12-4. Adults $4; children 17 & under no charge.

Milford

CLARK MUSEUM OF OKOBOJI AREA AND IOWA HISTORY, 2151 213th Ave., Milford, IA 51351-7200. Tel.: 712-338-2147.
E-mail: ijclark1@msm.com
Web Site: clarkmuseum.com
Institution Type/Description: History Museum.

Hours & Admission Prices: April-Oct. Tues.-Sat. 10-6, Sun. 11-6. No charge; donations accepted.

Minburn

THE VOAS NATURE AREA/VOAS MUSEUM, 1930 Lexington Rd., Minburn, IA 50167-8148. Mailing Address: 14581 K Avenue, Perry, IA 50220-6379. Tel.: 515-465-3577. Fax: 515-465-3579.
E-mail: pete.malmberg@dallascountyiowa.gov
Web Site: www.dallascounty.gov/conservation
Key Personnel: C.E.O., Mike Wallace; Cur., Archivist & Education, Pete Malmberg.
Institution Type/Description: Geological Museum.
Hours & Admission Prices: May-Oct. Sat.-Sun. 1-4 when volunteers are available; other times by appointment; Nov.-April by appointment only. No charge; donations accepted.
Attendance: 1,000 (estimated)

Missouri Valley

DESOTO NATIONAL WILDLIFE REFUGE, 1434 316th Lane, Missouri Valley, IA 51555-7033. Tel.: 712-642-4121.
E-mail: desoto@fws.gov
Web Site: midwest.fws.gov/desoto
Institution Type/Description: Wildlife Refuge.
Hours & Admission Prices: Refuge: sunrise to sunset, Visitor Center: daily 9-4:30. Buses & Vans: $20-$30; Cars: $3. Closed federal holidays.

HARRISON COUNTY HISTORICAL VILLAGE, 2931 Monroe Ave., Missouri Valley, IA 51555. Tel.: 712-642-2114. Fax: 712-642-2114.
E-mail: welcome@harrisoncountyparks.org
Institution Type/Description: History Museum & Welcome Center.
Hours & Admission Prices: Village: mid-April to Nov. daily. Welcome Center: Mon.-Sat. 9-5, Sun. 12-5. No charge; donations accepted. Closed New Year's Day; Easter; Thanksgiving; Christmas.

STEAMBOAT BERTRAND COLLECTION, DeSoto National Wildlife Refuge, 1434 316th Lane, Missouri Valley, IA 51555-7033. Tel.: 712-388-4800, 402-359-1299. Fax: 712-388-4872. Facebook: Desoto Boyer Chute.
E-mail: dean_knudsen@fws.gov
Web Site: refuges.fws.gov/refuge/Desoto/
Key Personnel: Refuge Mgr., Tom Cox; Cur., Dean Knudsen.
Institution Type/Description: Park Museum Center & Historic Site: excavation of the 1865 steamboat Bertrand.
Hours & Admission Prices: Daily 9-4:30. $3 per vehicle. Bus: 20 people or less $20; over 20 people $30. Federal Golden Age Passport, Federal Golden Access Passport, Federal Golden Eagle Passport, Federal Duck Stamp no charge. Closed federal holidays except Memorial Day, Independence Day & Labor Day. &
Attendance: 60,000 (actual)

WISECUP FARM MUSEUM, 1200 W. Canal St., Missouri Valley, IA 51555. Mailing Address: 1772 305th St., Missouri Valley, IA 51555. Tel.: 402-689-4002 & 1984. Fax: 712-642-4232.
E-mail: cjwcup@live.com
Web Site: wisecupfarmmuseum.com
Key Personnel: Dir., Bd. Member & Museum Shop Mgr., Charles Wisecup; Bd. Member, Melba Struble; Bd. Member, Paul Lane; Bd. Member, Dennis Smith; Bd. Member, Julie Wisecup; Bd. Member, Mary Hansen; Bd. Member, Sherman Struble.
Institution Type/Description: Farm History Museum.
Hours & Admission Prices: April 2-Sept. Tues. & Sun. 1-5, Sat. 9-5. No charge; donations accepted. &
Attendance: 800 (estimated)

Montezuma

POWESHIEK COUNTY HISTORICAL & GENEALOGICAL SOCIETY, 200 S. 3rd St., Montezuma, IA 50171. Mailing Address: P.O. Box 280, Montezuma, IA 50171. Tel.: 641-623-3322. Facebook.
E-mail: gcres@zumatel.net
Web Site: poweshiekcountyhistory.org
Key Personnel: Pres. (V), Sue Eichhorn; Dir., Joan Ehrig; Dir., Carol Klein; Dir., Sandy Cooper; Dir., Bev Creps; Dir., Pat Smith.
Institution Type/Description: History Museum.
Hours & Admission Prices: Mon. & Thurs. 9-4, Sat. 9-2. No charge; donations accepted. Closed holidays. &
Attendance: 675 (estimated)

Moravia

MORAVIA WABASH DEPOT MUSEUM COMPLEX, 800 W. North St., Moravia, IA 52571. Mailing Address: P.O. Box 216, Moravia, IA 52571. Tel.: 641-724-3736.
E-mail: judy@iowatelecom.net
Institution Type/Description: History Museum: depot built by the Wabash Railroad in the early 1900s. Listed on the National Register of Historic Places.
Hours & Admission Prices: May-Oct. 1st weekend each month. No charge; donations accepted. &
Attendance: 500 (estimated)

Morrison

GRUNDY COUNTY HERITAGE MUSEUM, 204 Fourth St., Morrison, IA 50657. Tel.: 319-345-2688. Fax: 319-345-2688.
E-mail: gccb@gccourthouse.org
Web Site: www.grundycounty.org
Key Personnel: Dir., Kevin Williams; Museum Shop Mgr., Sue Eckhoff.
Institution Type/Description: History Museum.
Hours & Admission Prices: Tues.-Thurs. 8-4:30. No charge; donations accepted. &
Attendance: 3,000 (estimated)

Moulton

MOULTON HISTORICAL SOCIETY MUSEUM, 712 N. Main St., Moulton, IA 52572. Mailing Address: 14763 331st Ave., Unionville, IA 52594-8052. Tel.: 641-642-3684.
Institution Type/Description: Historical Society Museum.
Hours & Admission Prices: Memorial Day to Labor Day Sun. 1-4; tours by appointment.

Mount Pleasant

HARLAN-LINCOLN HOUSE, 101 W. Broad St., Mount Pleasant, IA 52641-1337. Mailing Address: Iowa Wesleyan College, 601 N. Main St., Mount Pleasant, IA 52641. Tel.: 319-385-6215. Fax: 319-385-6324.
E-mail: iwcarch@iwc.edu
Web Site: iwc.edu
Key Personnel: C.E.O., Lynn Ellsworth; Chm. (V), Elizabeth Garrels.
Institution Type/Description: Historic House: housed in retirement home of U.S. Senator James Harlan (1876-1899); the summer home of the Robert Todd Lincoln Family (1876-1907).
Hours & Admission Prices: By appointment only. Adults $3; members no charge. &
Attendance: 1,000 (actual)

MIDWEST OLD SETTLERS & THRESHERS ASSOCIATION, INC., 405 E. Threshers Rd., Mount Pleasant, IA 52641-2584. Tel.: 319-385-8937. Fax: 319-385-0563.
E-mail: info@oldthreshers.org
Web Site: www.oldthreshers.com
Key Personnel: C.E.O., Terry McWilliams; Chm. (V), Bob Welander; Pres. (V), Bob Gerdes; Museum Shop Mgr., Julie Scott.
Institution Type/Description: Agricultural History Museum.
Hours & Admission Prices: Office: Mon.-Fri. 8-5. Museum: call for hours. Adults $5; children 10 & under no charge. Theatre: $3 per person. &
Attendance: 5,127 (estimated)

Mount Vernon

PETER PAUL LUCE GALLERY, MCWETHY HALL, CORNELL COLLEGE, 600 1st St., S.W., Mount Vernon, IA 52314-1098. Tel.: 319-895-4491. Fax: 319-895-4519. Facebook: Cornell College Department of Art & Art History.
E-mail: scoleman@cornellcollege.edu
Web Site: www.cornellcollege.edu
Formerly: Armstrong Gallery, Cornell College
Key Personnel: Pres., Jonathan Brand; Dept. Chm., Susannah Biondo-Gemmell; Dean, Joseph Dieker; Business Officer, Anissa Wolfe; Coord. Exhibitions, Susan Coleman; Dir. Public Information, DeeAnn Rexroat.
Institution Type/Description: College Art Gallery.
Hours & Admission Prices: Academic Year: Mon.-Fri. 9-4, Sun. 2-4; Summer: by appointment only. No charge. Closed school holidays. &
Attendance: 5,000 (estimated)

Muscatine

MUSCATINE ART CENTER, 1314 Mulberry Ave., Muscatine, IA 52761-3429. Tel.: 563-263-8282. Fax: 563-263-4702. Facebook, Instagram, Pinterest, Flickr & Tumblr: Muscatine Art Center.
E-mail: art@muscatineiowa.gov
Web Site: www.muscatineartcenter.org
Formerly: Laura Musser Museum and Stanley Gallery
Key Personnel: Dir., Melanie K. Alexander; Registrar, Virginia Cooper; Office Coord., Lynn Bartenhagen.
Institution Type/Description: Art Center: housed in 1908 Edwardian style Musser Mansion & 1976 Stanley Gallery.
Hours & Admission Prices: Tues.-Wed. & Fri. 10-5, Thurs. 10-7, Sat.-Sun. 1-5. No charge; donations accepted. Closed national holidays. &
Attendance: 32,000 (actual)

MUSCATINE HISTORY & INDUSTRY CENTER, 117 W. Second St., Muscatine, IA 52761-3714. Tel.: 563-263-1052. Facebook: Muscatine History and Industry Center.
E-mail: muscatinehistory@machlink.com
Web Site: www.muscatinehistory.org
Key Personnel: Exec. Dir., Mary Wildermuth; Pres., Steve Forbes.
Institution Type/Description: History Museum.
Hours & Admission Prices: Tues.-Sat. 10-4. Suggested Donation: adults $5, students $1. &
Attendance: 10,000 (actual)

PINE CREEK GRIST MILL, Wildcat Den State Park, 1884 Wildcat Den Rd., Muscatine, IA 52761-9479. Tel.: 319-263-4337. Fax: 319-264-8329.
E-mail: tomhanifan@yahoo.com
Web Site: www.pinecreekgristmill.com
Institution Type/Description: Historic Building: built in 1848 by Benjamin Nye. Listed on the National Register of Historic Places.
Hours & Admission Prices: May & Sept.-Oct. 4 Sat.-Sun. 12:30-4:30; June-Aug. Wed.-Sun. 12:30-4:30.

Nashua

CHICKASAW COUNTY HISTORICAL SOCIETY BRADFORD PIONEER VILLAGE MUSEUM, 2729 Cheyenne Ave., Nashua, IA 50658-9611. Tel.: 641-435-2567. Facebook: Chickasaw County Historical Society.
E-mail: chickasawhist@gmail.com
Key Personnel: Pres., Ruth Rosauer; Vice Pres., Ann Fails; Sec. & Treas., Barb Cairns; Museum Shop Mgr., Leatha Springer.
Institution Type/Description: General Museum: located on site of 1859 original Bradford village.
Hours & Admission Prices: May-Oct. Mon.-Sat. 9-5, Sun. 12-5; groups by appointment only. Adults $5, children K-12 $3; members no charge. &
Attendance: 3,000 (estimated)

New London

DOVER HISTORICAL MUSEUM, 213 W. Main St., New London, IA 52645-1337. Tel.: 877-468-7700.
E-mail: dovermus@iowatelecom.net
Web Site: www.dovermuseum.org
Key Personnel: Pres., Gale Riley.
Institution Type/Description: Historic Building: property includes former glove factory on the National Register of Historic Places; c.1890s railroad depot; rural chapel.
Hours & Admission Prices: Nov.-May Sat.-Sun. 1-4. No charge; donations accepted. &
Attendance: 1,700 (estimated)

Newton

JASPER COUNTY MUSEUM, 1700 S. 15th Ave. W., Newton, IA 50208-4321. Tel.: 641-792-9118.
E-mail: director@jaspercountymuseum.com
Web Site: www.jaspercountymuseum.net
Key Personnel: Dir., Audrey C. Rex; Pres. (V), Linda K. Wormley.
Institution Type/Description: History Museum.
Hours & Admission Prices: May-Sept. daily 1-4. Adults $5, students $3. Closed holidays. &
Attendance: 600 (estimated)

NEWTON ARBORETUM AND BOTANICAL GARDEN, 3000 N. 4th Ave. E, Newton, IA 50208-8745. Tel.: 641-791-3021.

E-mail: newtonarboretum@gmail.com
Web Site: www.newtonarboretum.com
Institution Type/Description: Arboretum & Botanical Garden.
Hours & Admission Prices: Daily daylight hours. Learning Center: Mon.-Fri. 8-4.
&

Northwood

GLADYS PIXLEY MEMORIAL LOG HOUSE, Central Ave. &
4th St., Northwood, IA 50459. Mailing Address: Worth County
Historical Society, 917 Central Ave., Northwood, IA 50459-1525.
Tel.: 641-324-1180. Facebook: Worth County Historical Society,
Iowa.
E-mail: president@worthhistory.org
Web Site: www.worthhistory.org
Institution Type/Description: Historic Building: housed in the former home of
James Randall; built in 1858.
Hours & Admission Prices: Memorial Day to Labor Day Sun. 2-4. No charge; dona-
tions accepted.

MACHINERY MUSEUM, Central Ave. & 4th St., Northwood, IA
50459. Mailing Address: Worth County Historical Society, 917
Central Ave., Northwood, IA 50459-1525. Tel.: 641-324-1180.
Facebook: Worth County Historical Society, Iowa.
E-mail: president@worthhistory.org
Web Site: www.worthhistory.org
Institution Type/Description: Historic Building: housed on the former site of the
Charles Wordall Saw Mill, the A.J. Dwelle Grist Mill, and the Ice House.
Hours & Admission Prices: Memorial Day to Labor Day Sun. 2-4. No charge; dona-
tions accepted.

**MAIN MUSEUM - WORTH COUNTY HISTORICAL
SOCIETY,** 917 Central Ave., Northwood, IA 50459-1525. Tel.:
641-324-1180. Facebook.
E-mail: president@worthhistory.org
Web Site: www.worthhistory.org
Institution Type/Description: Historical Society Museum: housed in the former
Worth County Courthouse; built in 1879.
Hours & Admission Prices: Memorial Day to Labor Day Sun. 2-4. No charge; dona-
tions accepted. &

OLD CREAMERY MUSEUM, Central Ave. & 4th St., Northwood,
IA 50459. Mailing Address: Worth County Historical Society, 917
Central Ave., Northwood, IA 50459-1525. Tel.: 641-324-1180.
Facebook: Worth County Historical Society, Iowa.
E-mail: president@worthhistory.org
Web Site: www.worthhistory.org
Institution Type/Description: Historic Building: built in 1892.
Hours & Admission Prices: Memorial Day to Labor Day Sun. 2-4. No charge; dona-
tions accepted.

SWENSRUD SCHOOL MUSEUM, Central Ave. & 10th St.,
Northwood, IA 50459. Mailing Address: Worth County Historical
Society, 917 Central Ave., Northwood, IA 50459-1525. Tel.: 641-
324-1180. Facebook: Worth County Historical Society, Iowa.
E-mail: president@worthhistory.org
Web Site: www.worthhistory.org
Institution Type/Description: Historic Building: housed in a former school built by
William G. Stott in 1874.
Hours & Admission Prices: Memorial Day to Labor Day Sun. 2-4. No charge; dona-
tions accepted.

Norway

IOWA BASEBALL MUSEUM OF NORWAY, 112 E. Railroad St.,
Norway, IA 52318. Mailing Address: P.O. Box 151, Norway,
52318. Tel.: 319-721-6288. Fax: 319-227-2044. Facebook:
Norway Baseball Museum.
E-mail: frese1@southslope.net
Web Site: www.norwaybaseball.org
Key Personnel: Dir. & Museum Shop Mgr., Shona Frese; C.E.O. & Pres. (V), Gary
Frame.
Institution Type/Description: Sports Museum.
Hours & Admission Prices: Tues., Thurs. & Sat. 1-4. No charge; donations
accepted.
Attendance: 1,200 (actual)

Oakland

NISHNA HERITAGE MUSEUM, 117 N. Main St., Oakland, IA
51560. Tel.: 712-482-6802.
E-mail: oaklandclerk@frontiernet.net
Web Site: www.nishnaheritagemuseum.com
Key Personnel: Pres., Cyndy Haines; Finance Dir., Wilson Pechacek; Trustee, Jo
Kates.
Institution Type/Description: Heritage Museum.
Hours & Admission Prices: Mon.-Thurs. 8-3. Adults $5. &
Attendance: 500 (estimated)

Odebolt

ODEBOLT HISTORICAL MUSEUM, 2nd & Maple Sts., Odebolt,
IA 51458. Mailing Address: 137 W. Second St., Odebolt, IA
51458-0196. Tel.: 712-668-2766.
E-mail: dweeze1817@hotmail.com
Web Site: www.odebolt.net/museum.html
Key Personnel: Pres. & Cur., Kathy Larson; Vice Pres., Alice Hemphill; Sec., Mary
Schroeder; Treas., Renae Babcock.
Institution Type/Description: History Museum.
Hours & Admission Prices: Memorial Day & Odebolt Creek Days in June; other
times by appointment. No charge; donations accepted.
Attendance: 360 (actual)

Oelwein

OELWEIN AREA HISTORICAL SOCIETY MUSEUM, 900 2nd
Ave., S.E., Oelwein, IA 50662-3055. Mailing Address: P.O. Box
445, Oelwein, IA 50662-0445. Tel.: 319-283-4203.
E-mail: oelwein_area_historical_society@earthlink.net
Institution Type/Description: Historical Society Museum.
Hours & Admission Prices: June-Sept. Sun. 1-4; Oct.-May by appointment. Adults
$2, students $1; discounts to groups; children under 12 & members no charge. &
Attendance: 750 (estimated)

Ogden

HICKORY GROVE RURAL SCHOOL MUSEUM, Baltin Chapel
Complex, Junction of E 41 & J Ave., Ogden, IA 50212. Mailing
Address: 602 Story St., Boone, IA 50036-2832. Tel.: 515-432-
1907.
E-mail: director@boonecountyhistory.org
Web Site: www.boonecountyhistory.org
Key Personnel: Exec. Dir., Pamela Schwartz; Pres. (V), Lee McNair; Sec., Janet
Tait; Treas., Judy Russell.
Institution Type/Description: Historic House & Museum: housed in an 1889
restored rural school.
Hours & Admission Prices: By appointment. Adults $1, children 17 & under no
charge.
Attendance: 400 (estimated)

Okoboji

THE HIGGINS MUSEUM, 1507 Sanborn Ave., Okoboji, IA 51355.
Mailing Address: P.O. Box 258, Okoboji, IA 51355-0258. Tel.:
712-332-5859. Fax: 712-332-5859.
E-mail: ladams@thehigginsmuseum.org
Web Site: www.thehigginsmuseum.org
Key Personnel: Bd. Pres. & Chm. (V), Dean Oakes; Cur., Larry Adams.
Institution Type/Description: History & Numismatics Museum.
Hours & Admission Prices: Memorial Day Weekend to Labor Day Tues.-Sun. 11-
5:30. No charge; donations accepted. &
Attendance: 950 (estimated)

PEARSON LAKES ART CENTER, 2201 Hwy. 71, Okoboji, IA
51355-0255. Mailing Address: P.O. Box 255, Okoboji, IA 51355-
0255. Tel.: 712-332-7013. Fax: 712-332-7014. Facebook: Pearson
Lakes Art; Instagram: @pearsonlakesartcenter.
E-mail: info@lakesart.org
Web Site: www.lakesart.org
Key Personnel: Exec. Dir., Bob Kirschbaum; Office Mgr., Amber Jonas;
Accountant, Juli Johnson; Dir. Visual Arts, Danielle Clouse Gast; Dir.
Education, Holly Zinn.
Institution Type/Description: Art Center.
Hours & Admission Prices: June-Aug. Mon.-Wed. & Fri.-Sat. 10-4, Thurs. 10-9,
Sun. 12-3; Sept.-May Tues.-Wed. & Fri.-Sat. 10-4, Thurs. 10-9. No charge; don-
ations accepted. &
Attendance: 40,000 (actual)

Onawa

MONONA COUNTY HISTORICAL MUSEUM, 47 12th St., Onawa, IA 51040. Mailing Address: Box 382, Onawa, IA 51040-0382. Tel.: 712-423-3452.
E-mail: jrobbins@longlines.com
Key Personnel: Pres., Jim Robbins.
Institution Type/Description: History Museum: birthplace of the Eskimo Pie.
Hours & Admission Prices: Memorial Day to Labor Day Sat.-Sun. 1-4:30; other times by appointment. No charge; donations accepted. &
Attendance: 1,000 (estimated)

MONONA COUNTY VETERAN'S MEMORIAL MUSEUM, 203 13th St., Onawa, IA 51040. Mailing Address: P.O. Box 418, Onawa, IA 51040-0418. Tel.: 712-423-2411. Facebook: Monona County Veteran's Memorial Museum.
E-mail: democrat@longlines.com
Key Personnel: Dir. & Cur., William Wonder.
Institution Type/Description: Military Museum.
Hours & Admission Prices: May-Sept. Sat.-Sun. 1-4; other times by appointment. No charge; donations accepted. Bus Tours: $3 per person. &
Attendance: 2,750 (actual)

Orient

HENRY A. WALLACE COUNTRY LIFE CENTER, 2773 290th St., Orient, IA 50858. Mailing Address: P.O. Box 363, Greenfield, IA 50849-0363. Tel.: 641-337-5019.
E-mail: haw@mddc.com
Web Site: www.henryawallacecenter.com
Key Personnel: Dir., Diane Weiland.
Institution Type/Description: History Museum: housed on the birthplace farmstead of Henry A. Wallace, born Oct. 7, 1888.
Hours & Admission Prices: Self-Guided Tours: daily. Guided Tours: Summer daily 10-5. Donations requested.

Osage

CEDAR VALLEY MEMORIES, 1 1/2 Mile W. Hwy. 9, Osage, IA 50461. Mailing Address: Cedar Valley Memories c/o Mitchell County Historical Society, P.O. Box 51, Osage, IA 50461-0051. Tel.: 641-732-1269.
E-mail: mchsosage@gmail.com
Web Site: www.mitchellcountyhistoricalsociety.org/home
Institution Type/Description: History Museum.
Hours & Admission Prices: Memorial Day to Labor Day Sat.-Sun. 1-4; other times by appointment. No charge.

MILTON R. OWEN NATURE CENTER, 18793 Hwy. 9, Osage, IA 50461. Tel.: 641-732-5204. Fax: 641-732-1138. Facebook: Mitchell County Conservation Board.
E-mail: mccb@osage.net
Web Site: www.mitchellcountyconservation.com
Formerly: Mitchell County Nature Center.
Institution Type/Description: Nature Center.
Hours & Admission Prices: Tues.-Fri. 9-4, Sun. 1-4. No charge. &

MITCHELL COUNTY HISTORICAL MUSEUM, 809 Sawyer Dr., Ste. 2, Osage, IA 50461. Tel.: 641-832-2574. Facebook.
E-mail: mchsosage@gmail.com
Web Site: www.mitchellcountyhistoricalsociety.org
Key Personnel: Cur., Starla Cassman; Pres., Bob Wetherell.
Institution Type/Description: History Museum: housed on 7 sites in Mitchell County.
Hours & Admission Prices: Wed.-Sun. 1-5; other times by appointment. No charge; donations accepted. Closed holidays. &
Attendance: 10,000 (actual)

Osceola

CLARKE COUNTY HISTORICAL SOCIETY & MUSEUM, 1030 S. Main, Osceola, IA 50213. Mailing Address: c/o Osceola Public Library, 300 S Fillmore, Osceola, IA 50213. Tel.: 641-342-4838.
E-mail: clarke.coordinator@gmail.com
Web Site: iagenweb.org/clarke/
Institution Type/Description: History Museum.
Hours & Admission Prices: May-Sept. call for hours. No charge. &

Oskaloosa

NELSON PIONEER FARM AND MUSEUM, 2211 Nelson Lane, Oskaloosa, IA 52577-9609. Mailing Address: Mahaska County Historical Society, P.O. Box 578, Oskaloosa, IA 52577-0578. Tel.: 641-672-2989. Facebook: Nelson Pioneer Farm - Mahaska County Historical Society.
E-mail: curator@nelsonpioneer.org
Web Site: www.nelsonpioneer.org
Key Personnel: Dir., Kelley Halbert; Pres., Jay Fox.
Institution Type/Description: General Museum: housed on an 1844 homestead.
Hours & Admission Prices: mid-May to mid-Oct. Tues.-Sat. 10-4; bus tours by special arrangement. Adults $7, students 5-16 $2; children under 5 & society members no charge. &
Attendance: 3,537 (actual)

Ottumwa

AIRPOWER MUSEUM INC., 22001 Bluegrass Rd., Ottumwa, IA 52501-8569. Tel.: 641-938-2773. Fax: 641-938-2093.
E-mail: antiqueairfield@sirisonline.com
Web Site: www.antiqueairfield.com
Institution Type/Description: Aeronautics Museum.
Hours & Admission Prices: Mon.-Fri. 9-5, Sat. 10-5, Sun. 1-5. No charge; donations accepted. Closed New Year's Day; Independence Day; Labor Day; Thanksgiving; Christmas. &
Attendance: 6,500 (estimated)

WAPELLO COUNTY HISTORICAL MUSEUM, 210 W. Main, Ottumwa, IA 52501-2500. Tel.: 641-682-8676. Fax: 641-682-8676.
E-mail: wchs@pcsia.net
Web Site: www.wapellocountymuseum.com
Key Personnel: Pres. (V), Mary Ellen Schmitz; Vice Pres., John Cobler.
Institution Type/Description: History Museum.
Hours & Admission Prices: Tues.-Fri. 10-4, Sat. 12-4. Adults $5, children under 12 $3; scheduled student tours & members no charge. &
Attendance: 1,423 (actual)

Panora

GUTHRIE COUNTY HISTORICAL VILLAGE, 206 W. South St., Panora, IA 50216-1015. Tel.: 641-755-2989. Fax: 641-755-4066. Facebook: Guthrie County Historical Village.
E-mail: gchv@netins.net
Web Site: www.panora.org/museum
Key Personnel: Dir., Kristine Jorgensen.
Institution Type/Description: Historical Village.
Hours & Admission Prices: Tues.-Fri. 10-4:30, Sat. 1-4:30; other times by appointment. Adults $2, children 6-17 $1; children 5 & under no charge. &
Attendance: 2,500 (estimated)

Parkersburg

PARKERSBURG HISTORICAL HOME, 401 5th St., Parkersburg, IA 50665. Mailing Address: P.O. Box 142, Parkersburg, IA 50665. Tel.: 319-346-1461. Fax: 319-231-0079. Facebook.
E-mail: gersey6@msn.com
Key Personnel: Pres. (V), Rick Gersema.
Institution Type/Description: Historic House Museum: built in 1895. Listed on the National Register of Historic Places.
Hours & Admission Prices: Memorial Day to Labor Day Sun. 1-3. No charge; donations accepted.
Attendance: 300 (estimated)

Pella

PELLA HISTORICAL VILLAGE, 507 Franklin St., Pella, IA 50219-1671. Mailing Address: P.O. Box 145, Pella, IA 50219-0145. Tel.: 641-628-4311. Fax: 515-628-9192.
E-mail: pellatuliptime@iowatelecom.net
Web Site: www.pellatuliptime.com
Key Personnel: Pres. (V), Mike Morgan.
Institution Type/Description: Ethnic (Dutch) Museum Complex: located in 20 historic buildings.
Hours & Admission Prices: March-Dec. Mon.-Sat. 9-4. Adults $8, K-12 $2; members no charge. Closed national holidays. &
Attendance: 20,000 (estimated)

SCHOLTE HOUSE MUSEUM, 728 Washington, Pella, IA 50219-1523. Mailing Address: 909 W. 1st St., Apt. 4, Pella, IA 50219-1441. Tel.: 641-628-3684.
E-mail: scholtehouse@windstream.net
Web Site: scholtehouse.com
Key Personnel: Dir., Beverly J. Graves.
Institution Type/Description: Historic House Museum: home of the founding father of the town of Pella, Dominie Hendrik Pieter Scholte c.1847.
Hours & Admission Prices: March-Dec. Mon.-Sat. 1-4; other times by appointment. Adults $5, students & children $2; Pella district & Central College students, members no charge. Windmill Historical Village & Scholte House: adults $13. Closed New Year's Day; Easter; Memorial Day; Independence Day; Labor Day; Thanksgiving; Christmas Eve & Day.
Attendance: 3,000 (estimated)

VERMEER MUSEUM & GLOBAL PAVILION, 2110 Vermeer Rd. E., Pella, IA 50219. Tel.: 641-621-7017.
E-mail: pavilion@vermeer.com
Institution Type/Description: History Museum.
Hours & Admission Prices: Call for hours.

Perry

CARNEGIE LIBRARY MUSEUM, 1123 Willis Ave., Perry, IA 50220. Mailing Address: c/o City of Perry, Iowa, P.O. Box 545, Perry, IA 50220. Tel.: 515-465-2518. Fax: 515-465-4844.
E-mail: corey.eastman@perryia.org
Web Site: www.perryia.org
Key Personnel: City Admin., Sven Peterson.
Institution Type/Description: Library Museum: built in 1904. Listed on the National Register of Historic Places.
Hours & Admission Prices: Tours: Thurs.-Sat. by appointment. No charge; donations accepted.
Attendance: 750 (estimated)

FOREST PARK MUSEUM AND ARBORETUM, 14581 K Ave., Perry, IA 50220-6379. Tel.: 515-465-3577. Fax: 515-465-3579.
E-mail: pete.malmberg@dallascountyiowa.gov
Web Site: www.dallascountyiowa.gov/conservation
Key Personnel: C.E.O., Mike Wallace; Cur., Archivist & Education, Pete Malmberg.
Institution Type/Description: History Museum.
Hours & Admission Prices: May-Oct. Mon.-Fri. 9-4:30, Sat.-Sun. 1-4:30; Nov.-April by appointment only. No charge.
Attendance: 3,700 (estimated)

Peterson

PRAIRIE HERITAGE CENTER, 4931 Yellow Ave., Peterson, IA 51047-7528. Tel.: 712-295-7200.
E-mail: occb@iowatelecom.net
Web Site: prairieheritagecenter.org
Institution Type/Description: History Museum.
Hours & Admission Prices: Wed.-Fri. 9-4, Sat.-Sun. 1-4.

Pocahontas

THE KALEIDOSCOPE FACTORY, 214 N. Main St., Pocahontas, IA 50574. Tel.: 712-468-2420.
E-mail: kaleidoscopeguy@hotmail.com
Web Site: www.kaleidoscopefactory.com
Key Personnel: Head Kaleidoscope Maker, Leonard Olson.
Institution Type/Description: History Museum.
Hours & Admission Prices: Tours: Tues. & Thurs. 1-9, Sat. 10-5; other times by appointment. No charge.

Polk City

BIG CREEK HISTORICAL MUSEUM, 112 Third St., Polk City, IA 50226. Mailing Address: P.O. Box 201, Polk City, IA 50226.
E-mail: bchs1863@gmail.com
Institution Type/Description: History Museum: housed in the city hall building; built in 1863. Listed on the National Register of Historic Places.
Hours & Admission Prices: Open House: May-Oct. 2nd Sun. each month 1-3; other times by appointment. No charge.

Pomeroy

POMEROY TORNADO MUSEUM, 114 S. Ontario St., Pomeroy, IA 50575. Tel.: 515-574-1615.

Institution Type/Description: Science Museum.
Hours & Admission Prices: Call for hours.

Prairie City

NEIL SMITH NATIONAL WILDLIFE REFUGE PRAIRIE LEARNING CENTER, 9981 Pacific St., Prairie City, IA 50228-7820. Mailing Address: P.O. Box 399, Prairie City, IA 50228-3400. Tel.: 515-994-3400.
E-mail: buffalo@tallgrass.org
Web Site: www.tallgrass.org
Key Personnel: Pres. Friends of Prairie Learning Center, Mark Lyle; Park Ranger, Al Murray; Park Ranger, Hallie Runeussen.
Institution Type/Description: Wildlife Refuge.
Hours & Admission Prices: Refuge: dawn to dusk. Learning Center: Jan.-March Mon.-Sat. 9-4; April-Dec. Mon.-Sat. 9-4, Sun. 12-5. No charge. Closed New Year's Day; Thanksgiving; Christmas.

Prescott

KLINE MUSEUM, 112 6th Ave., Prescott, IA 50859. Mailing Address: 605 5th Ave., Prescott, IA 50859. Tel.: 641-335-2445.
Key Personnel: Dir. & Pres. (V), Randy Cooper.
Institution Type/Description: History Museum.
Hours & Admission Prices: Memorial Day to Labor Day Sun. 1-4; other times by appointment. Adults $3.
Attendance: 25 (estimated)

Princeton

BUFFALO BILL CODY HOMESTEAD, 28050 230th Ave., Princeton, IA 52768-9713. Mailing Address: 14910 110th Ave., Davenport, IA 52804-9020. Tel.: 563-225-2981. Fax: 563-381-2805. Facebook: Scott County Conservation.
E-mail: conservation@scottcountyiowa.com
Web Site: www.scottcountyiowa.com
Key Personnel: C.E.O., Roger Kean; Museum Shop Mgr., Marilyn McCool.
Institution Type/Description: Historic House: 1847 boyhood home of Buffalo Bill Cody.
Hours & Admission Prices: April-Oct. daily 9-5. Adults $2; children 16 & under no charge.
Attendance: 7,000 (estimated)

Quimby

GRAND MEADOW HERITAGE CENTER AND MUSEUM, 767 610th St., Quimby, IA 51049-7053. Tel.: 712-447-6201.
Institution Type/Description: History Museum.
Hours & Admission Prices: June-Sept. Sun. 1-5; other times by appointment. No charge, donations accepted.

Red Oak

MONTGOMERY COUNTY HISTORY CENTER, 2700 N. 4th St., Red Oak, IA 51566-1369. Tel.: 712-623-2289.
E-mail: mchsociet@qwestoffice.net
Key Personnel: Dir., David McFarland.
Institution Type/Description: History Museum.
Hours & Admission Prices: Tues.-Sun. 12-4; other times by appointment. Adults $3, children $2; members no charge.

RESTORED BURLINGTON NORTHERN DEPOT & WWII MEMORIAL MUSEUM, 305 S. 2nd St., Red Oak, IA 51566-2655. Tel.: 712-623-6048.
E-mail: museum@depothill.net
Web Site: depothill.net
Key Personnel: C.E.O., Steve Adams; Chm., Pat Maher; Museum Shop Mgr., Lynn Adams.
Institution Type/Description: History Museum: housed in the Burlington Northern Depot; built in 1903.
Hours & Admission Prices: March-Dec. Mon.-Fri. 10 to noon; other times by appointment. No charge; donations accepted.
Attendance: 2,000 (estimated)

Rock Rapids

LYON COUNTY HISTORICAL SOCIETY MUSEUM COMPLEX, 110 1/2 N. Story St., Rock Rapids, IA 51246.

Mailing Address: P.O. Box 322, Rock Rapids, IA 51246. Tel.: 712-472-2016.
E-mail: lycomu@osprey.net
Key Personnel: Pres. (V), Jon Kruse.
Institution Type/Description: History Museum: housed in the former Rock Island Depot.
Hours & Admission Prices: Summer: Heritage Days Sun. 2-5; other times by appointment. Adults $1. Closed holidays.
Attendance: 125 (estimated)

Rockwell City

CALHOUN COUNTY MUSEUM, 150 High St., Rockwell City, IA 50579. Mailing Address: P.O. Box 368, Jolley, IA 50551-0368. Tel.: 712-297-5081 & 8139 (summer). Fax: 712-297-5216.
E-mail: jmjolley@iowatelecom.net
Key Personnel: Pres., Marlene Johnson; 1st Vice Pres., Iola Zimbeck; Sec., Bonnie Debolt; Treas., Toni Kerns; Museum Shop Mgr., JoAnn Maguire.
Institution Type/Description: General Museum.
Hours & Admission Prices: May-Oct. Sat.-Sun. 1-4. No charge; donations accepted.
Attendance: 2,500 (estimated)

Sac City

SAC CITY MUSEUM, 1301 W. Main St., Sac City, IA 50583. Mailing Address: 111 N. 7th, Sac City, IA 50583. Tel.: 712-662-7376.
E-mail: kaychris@mchsi.com
Web Site: saccountyiowa.com
Institution Type/Description: History Museum.
Hours & Admission Prices: Memorial Day-Labor Day Sat.-Sun. 2-4. No charge; donations accepted.
Attendance: 2,500 (actual)

Saint Ansgar

ST. ANSGAR HERITAGE MUSEUM, 126 W. Fourth St., Saint Ansgar, IA 50472. Mailing Address: P.O. Box 214, Saint Ansgar, IA 50472. Tel.: 641-713-2776.
Web Site: www.stansgarheritage.org
Institution Type/Description: History Museum.
Hours & Admission Prices: April-Sept. Wed.-Fri. 10-4. No charge.
Attendance: 500 (estimated)

Scotch Grove

EDINBURGH PIONEER VILLAGE, 13838 Edinburgh Rd., Scotch Grove, IA 52310. Tel.: 563-487-3711.
E-mail: iajchs@aol.com
Institution Type/Description: History Museum.
Hours & Admission Prices: May-Sept. call for hours.

Shelby

CARSTENS 1880 MEMORIAL FARMSTEAD, 32409 - 380th St., Shelby, IA 51570. Mailing Address: P.O. Box 302, Shelby, IA 51570-0302. Tel.: 712-554-2638 & 2341.
E-mail: info@carstensfarm.com
Web Site: www.carstensfarm.com
Institution Type/Description: Farming History Museum.
Hours & Admission Prices: By appointment. Adults $5, students & seniors $2.

Sheldon

SHELDON PRAIRIE MUSEUM, 319 10th St., Box 35, Sheldon, IA 51201. Mailing Address: 2406 E. 3rd St, Sheldon, IA 51201. Tel.: 712-324-5108.
E-mail: carnegiemuseum33@gmail.com
Web Site: Facebook: Sheldon Prairie Museum
Formerly: Prairie Queen Museum
Key Personnel: Historian, Millie Voss.
Institution Type/Description: History Museum: housed in the former Carnegie Library building; built in 1908.
Hours & Admission Prices: Mon. 6pm-8pm, Thurs. 1pm-4pm, Sat. 1pm-3pm; other times by appointment. No charge; donations accepted.

WANSINK ART GALLERY, PRAIRIE SCHOOLHOUSE & PIONEER HOME, Hwy. 18, E., Sheldon, IA 51201. Mailing Address: P.O. Box 61, Sheldon, IA 51201-0061. Tel.: 712-324-4190.
E-mail: hptuttle@nethtc.net
Key Personnel: Dir., Hal Tuttle.
Institution Type/Description: Historic Buildings & Art Gallery.
Hours & Admission Prices: Call for hours.

Shell Rock

SHELL ROCK COMMUNITY HISTORICAL MUSEUM, 127 E. Adair St., Shell Rock, IA 50670-9713. Mailing Address: P.O. Box 57, Shell Rock, IA 50670-0057. Tel.: 319-885-4478 & 6687. Facebook: Shell Rock Historical Society.
E-mail: shellrockhistory@yahoo.com
Key Personnel: Chm. (V), Sherri Willey; Museum Shop Mgr., Linda McCann.
Institution Type/Description: Historic House Museum: housed in a 1920s craftsman-style home.
Hours & Admission Prices: May-Oct. Sat.10-2; other times by appointment. No charge; donations accepted.
Attendance: 200 (actual)

Shenandoah

GREATER SHENANDOAH HISTORICAL SOCIETY, 800 W. Sheridan Ave., Shenandoah, IA 51601-1645. Mailing Address: P. O. Box 182, Shenandoah, IA 51601. Tel.: 712-246-1669.
E-mail: gshmuseum@hotmail.com
Web Site: www.greatershenandoahhs.org
Key Personnel: Dir., Sallie Brownlee; Pres. (V), Ron Qestmann.
Institution Type/Description: History Museum.
Hours & Admission Prices: March-Dec. Tues.-Fri. 1-4; other times by appointment. No charge; donations accepted.
Attendance: 650 (estimated)

Sibley

MCCALLUM MUSEUM & BRUNSON HERITAGE HOME, 5th St. & 8th Ave., Sibley, IA 51249. Mailing Address: 724 3rd Ave, Sibley, IA 51249-1606. Tel.: 712-754-3710.
E-mail: jstoff1@hotmail.com
Web Site: www.osceolacountyia.com/info/museums.htm
Key Personnel: Dir., Jan Stofferan; Pres. (V), Shirley Swenson.
Institution Type/Description: History Museum.
Hours & Admission Prices: May-Sept. Tues. 20-4 & Sun. 1:30-4:30; April & Oct. Tues. 2-4; other times by appointment. No charge; donations accepted. Closed holidays.
Attendance: 1,000 (estimated)

Sigourney

DUMONT MUSEUM, 20545 255th St., Sigourney, IA 52591-8352. Tel.: 641-622-2592 & 9937.
E-mail: oliver@lisco.com
Web Site: www.dumontmuseum.com
Institution Type/Description: History Museum.
Hours & Admission Prices: May-Oct. Sat.-Sun. 10-5; other times by appointment. Adults $8.

Sioux City

DOROTHY PECAUT NATURE CENTER, 4500 Sioux River Rd., Sioux City, IA 51109-1657. Tel.: 712-258-0838. Fax: 712-258-1261. Facebook: Dorothy Pecaut Nature Center.
E-mail: dsnyder@sioux-city.org
Web Site: www.woodburyparks.com
Institution Type/Description: Nature Center.
Hours & Admission Prices: Tues.-Sat. 9-5, Sun. 1-5. No charge; donations accepted. Closed New Year's Day; Thanksgiving; Christmas Eve & Day.
Attendance: 47,276 (estimated)

LOREN D. CALLENDAR GALLERY, City Hall, Clocktower Rm., 1st Fl., 405 6th St., Sioux City, IA 51101-1255. Tel.: 712-279-6174. Fax: 712-252-5615.
E-mail: scpm@sioux-city.org
Web Site: www.siouxcitymuseum.org
Institution Type/Description: Art Gallery.
Hours & Admission Prices: Mon.-Fri. 8-4:30. No charge. Closed holidays.

MID AMERICA MUSEUM OF AVIATION AND TRANSPORTATION, 2600 Expedition Ct., Sioux City, IA 51111. Mailing Address: P.O. Box 3525, Sioux City, IA 51102-3525. Tel.: 712-252-5300. Fax: 712-222-1688.
E-mail: airmuseum@longlines.com
Web Site: midamericaairmuseum.org
Key Personnel: Dir., Larry L. Finley; Chm. (V), Pamela Mickelson.
Institution Type/Description: Aviation & Transportation Museum.
Hours & Admission Prices: April-Sept. Thurs.-Tues. 10-4; Oct.-March Mon. & Thurs.-Sat. 10-4. Adults $6, seniors 55 & over and active military $5, children 5-14 $3; children under 5 no charge. Closed New Year's Day; Easter; Memorial Day; Independence Day; Thanksgiving; Christmas. ♿
Attendance: 10,000 (actual)

SERGEANT FLOYD RIVER MUSEUM & WELCOME CENTER, 1000 Larsen Park Rd., Sioux City, IA 51103-4914. Tel.: 712-279-0198. Fax: 712-279-6934.
E-mail: scpm@sioux-city.org
Web Site: www.siouxcitymuseum.org
Key Personnel: Museum Shop Mgr., Christine Dekker.
Institution Type/Description: Maritime History Museum.
Hours & Admission Prices: Daily 10-4. No charge; donations accepted. ♿
Attendance: 26,583 (actual)

SIOUX CITY ART CENTER, 225 Nebraska St., Sioux City, IA 51101-1712. Tel.: 712-279-6272, ext. 208. Fax: 712-255-2921. Facebook: Sioux City Art Center.
E-mail: kwelch@sioux-city.org
Web Site: www.siouxcityartcenter.org
Key Personnel: Dir., Al Harris-Fernandez; Pres. (V), Richard Roth; Chm. (V), Gregory Jones; Exhibitions & Collections Coord., Shannon Sargent; Sec., Kjersten Welch.
Institution Type/Description: Art Museum.
Hours & Admission Prices: Tues.-Wed. & Fri.-Sat. 10-4, Thurs. 10-9, Sun. 1-4. No charge; donations accepted. Closed holidays. ♿
Attendance: 44,053 (actual)

THE SIOUX CITY LEWIS & CLARK INTERPRETIVE CENTER, 900 Larsen Park Rd., Sioux City, IA 51103-4916. Tel.: 712-224-5242. Fax: 712-224-5244.
E-mail: mpoole@siouxcitylcic.com
Web Site: www.siouxcitylcic.com
Key Personnel: Exec. Dir., Marcia Poole; Business Mgr., Russell Movall.
Institution Type/Description: History Museum.
Hours & Admission Prices: Tues.-Wed. & Fri. 9-5, Thurs. 9-8, Sat.-Sun. 12-5. No charge. Closed New Year's Day; Easter; Thanksgiving; Christmas.

SIOUX CITY PUBLIC MUSEUM, 607 4th St., Sioux City, IA 51101-1634. Tel.: 712-279-6174. Fax: 712-252-5615.
E-mail: scpm@sioux-city.org
Web Site: www.siouxcitymuseum.org
Key Personnel: Dir., Steven D. Hansen; Chm. (V), Miles Patton, Jr.; Cur. History, Grace Linden; Cur. Education, Theresa Weaver-Basye; Exhibits Designer, Matt Anderson; Devel. Coord., Mary Green-Warnstadt; Welcome Center Supvr., Kathy Meisner; Administrative Asst., Deanna Mayo.
Institution Type/Description: General Museum: Sergeant Floyd River Museum & Welcome Center; Loren D. Callendar Gallery.
Hours & Admission Prices: Museum: Tues.-Sat. 9-5, Sun. 1-5. Sergeant Floyd River Museum & Welcome Center daily 10-4. No charge; donations accepted. Closed holidays. ♿
Attendance: 50,741 (actual)

South Amana

COMMUNAL AGRICULTURE MUSEUM, 505 P St., South Amana, IA 52334. Mailing Address: Amana Heritage Society, P.O. Box 81, Amana, IA 52203-0081. Tel.: 319-622-3567.
Web Site: www.cr.nps.gov/nr/travel/amana/agr.htm
Key Personnel: Dir., Lanny Haldy; Cur., Kelly Duffy.
Institution Type/Description: Agriculture Museum.
Hours & Admission Prices: May-Sept. Mon.-Sat. 10-5, Sun. 12-5. Call for admission prices.

Spencer

CLAY COUNTY HERITAGE, 7 Grand Ave., Spencer, IA 51301. Tel.: 712-262-3304.
E-mail: parkermuseum@smunet.net
Web Site: www.parkermuseum.org
Institution Type/Description: History Museum.

Hours & Admission Prices: Tues.-Fri. 11:30-3:30; other times by appointment. No charge; donations accepted.

PARKER HISTORICAL SOCIETY OF CLAY COUNTY, 7 Grand Ave., Spencer, IA 51301. Mailing Address: P.O. Box 91, Spencer, IA 51301-0091. Tel.: 712-262-3304. Fax: 712-262-3304. Facebook: Parker Historical Society of Clay County.
E-mail: parkermuseum@smunet.net
Web Site: parkermuseum.org
Key Personnel: Dir., Cindy McGranahan.
Institution Type/Description: Local History Museum: housed in an historic house, built in 1916.
Hours & Admission Prices: Tues.-Wed. & Fri. 10-4, Thurs. 10-6, Sat. 10-3; other times by appointment. Adults $5, children 5-12 $3; members & preschool no charge. ♿

Spillville

BILY CLOCK MUSEUM/ANTONIN DVORAK EXHIBIT, 323 S. Main, Spillville, IA 52168. Mailing Address: P.O. Box 258, Spillville, IA 52168-0258. Tel.: 563-562-3569.
E-mail: bilyclocks@mchsi.com
Web Site: www.bilyclocks.com
Key Personnel: Dir. & Museum Shop Mgr., Shirley Francis.
Institution Type/Description: Clock Museum.
Hours & Admission Prices: May-Oct. Mon.-Sat. 9-5, Sun. 12-4; Nov.-April open by appointment. Adults $8, seniors $7, children $4; special group rates; discounts to AAA members.
Attendance: 9,000 (estimated)

Stanton

SWEDISH HERITAGE & CULTURAL CENTER, 410 Hilltop Ave., Stanton, IA 51573. Mailing Address: P.O. Box 231, Stanton, IA 51573-0231. Tel.: 712-829-2840. Fax: 712-829-2393.
E-mail: shcc@myfmtc.com
Web Site: www.stantoniowa.com
Key Personnel: Dir. & Pres. (V), Carroll Peterson.
Institution Type/Description: Swedish Heritage Center.
Hours & Admission Prices: April-Nov. Wed.-Sat. 1-4; other times by appointment. Adults $5. ♿
Attendance: 500

State Center

WATSON'S GROCERY STORE MUSEUM, 106 W. Main St., State Center, IA 50247. Mailing Address: P.O. Box 156, State Center, IA 50247. Tel.: 641-483-3002.
E-mail: scda@partnercom.net
Key Personnel: Dir., Everett Halsted; Pres. (V), Mike Riemenschneider.
Institution Type/Description: Grocery Store Museum: housed in a c.1895 historic building.
Hours & Admission Prices: Memorial Day to Labor Day Sat.-Sun. 1-4; other times by appointment. No charge; donations accepted.
Attendance: 2,000 (estimated)

Storm Lake

BUENA VISTA HISTORICAL SOCIETY, 214 W. 5th St., Storm Lake, IA 50588-2346. Tel.: 712-732-4955.
E-mail: granny@nwiowa.com
Key Personnel: Pres. (V), James R. Kennedy; Office Mgr., Gwen Henrich.
Institution Type/Description: Historical Society Museum.
Hours & Admission Prices: Mon.-Fri. 12-4; other times by appointment. Adults $2, children 12 & under $1. ♿
Attendance: 1,999 (actual)

HARKER HOUSE, 328 Lake Ave., Storm Lake, IA 50588-2435. Mailing Address: P.O. Box 368, Aurelia, IA 51005. Tel.: 712-732-3267.
E-mail: info@harkerhouse.com
Web Site: www.harkerhouse.com
Key Personnel: Pres. (V), Roger Redig.
Institution Type/Description: Historic House: built in 1875.
Hours & Admission Prices: June-Aug. Sat.-Sun. 2-4; special tours available upon request for groups over 10. Adults $5; youth under 18 no charge.
Attendance: 263 (actual)

LIVING HERITAGE TREE MUSEUM, W. Lakeshore Dr., Sunset Park, Storm Lake, IA 50588. Tel.: 712-732-3780, 888-752-4692.
E-mail: info@stormlakeunited.com
Web Site: visitstormlake.com
Institution Type/Description: Tree Museum.
Hours & Admission Prices: Daily dawn to dusk.

WITTER GALLERY, 609 Cayuga St., Storm Lake, IA 50588-2239. Tel.: 712-732-3400.
E-mail: wittergallery@yahoo.com
Web Site: thewittergallery.org
Key Personnel: Gallery Dir., Ron Stevenson.
Institution Type/Description: Art Gallery.
Hours & Admission Prices: Summer: Tues.-Wed. & Fri. 1-5, Thurs. 1-6, Sat. 10-2; Winter: Tues.-Wed. & Fri. 1-5, Thurs. 1-6, Sat. 10-2. No charge, donations accepted. Closed national holidays. &
Attendance: 11,000 (actual)

Story City

MUSEUMS OF STORY CITY, 619 Grand Ave., Story City, IA 50248-1412. Mailing Address: P.O. Box 104, Story City, IA 50248-0104. Tel.: 515-460-1749. Facebook.
E-mail: storycityhistory@gmail.com
Web Site: www.storycityhistory.org
Formerly: Bartlett Museum and Carriage House
Key Personnel: Dir., Kate Feil; Pres. (V) Dwayne Fiihr.
Institution Type/Description: Historic House Museum: built in 1903. Listed on the National Register of Historic Places.
Hours & Admission Prices: Wed.-Fri. 12-5. No charge; donations accepted.

Strawberry Point

WILDER MEMORIAL MUSEUM, 123 W. Mission, Strawberry Point, IA 52076. Mailing Address: Box 206, Strawberry Point, IA 52076-0206. Tel.: 563-933-4615.
E-mail: director@wildermuseum.org
Web Site: www.wildermuseum.org
Key Personnel: Pres., Dean Knight; Dir., Angela Beenken.
Institution Type/Description: Historical Museum.
Hours & Admission Prices: May & Sept.-Oct. Sat. 10-4, Sun. 1-4; Memorial Day-Labor Day Sun.-Thurs. 1-4, Fri.-Sat. 10-4; other times by appointment. Family $10, adults $4, students $2; discounts for senior citizens on Wed., AAA members & adult groups of 10 or more; pre-school & members no charge. Participating Blue Star Museum. &
Attendance: 675 (estimated)

Swedesburg

SWEDISH AMERICAN MUSEUM, 107 James Ave., Swedesburg, IA 52652. Tel.: 319-254-2317. Facebook: Swedish American Museum and Historical Society.
E-mail: swedish@iowatelecom.net
Key Personnel: Pres. (V) Betty Molander; Vice Pres. (V) Trish Woepking; Dir., Louise Unkrich; Museum Shop Mgr., Norma Lindeen.
Institution Type/Description: Swedish American Museum.
Hours & Admission Prices: Jan.-March Thurs.-Sat. 9-4; April-Dec. Mon.-Tues. & Thurs.-Sat. 9-4. No charge; donations accepted. Closed New Year's Day; Thanksgiving; Christmas. &
Attendance: 3,360 (actual)

Tipton

CEDAR COUNTY HISTORICAL SOCIETY & MUSEUM, 1094 Hwy. 38, Tipton, IA 52772. Mailing Address: P.O. Box 254, Tipton, IA 52772. Tel.: 563-886-2899.
E-mail: cchsmus@iowatelecom.net
Institution Type/Description: Historical Society Museum.
Hours & Admission Prices: Tues. & Thurs. 10-4, Sat. 10-2.

OLD CEDAR COUNTY JAIL, 118 W. 4th St., Tipton, IA 52772. Mailing Address: 707 King Ave., Stanwood, IA 52337-9619. Tel.: 563-886-2131.
E-mail: kwhitll601@gmail.com
Web Site: www.oldcedarcountyjail.com
Institution Type/Description: Historic Building: housed in the former county jail & sheriff's residence. Listed on the National Register of Historic Places.
Hours & Admission Prices: 1st Sat. each month 10-2.

Toledo

TAMA COUNTY HISTORICAL MUSEUM, 200 N. Broadway, Toledo, IA 52342-1308. Tel.: 641-484-6767.
E-mail: tracers@pcpartner.net
Web Site: www.tamacountyhistory.org
Key Personnel: Chm. (V) & Pres. (V) Joyce Wiese; Treas., Gail Kilstofte; Exec. Sec., Bonnie Grimmius.
Institution Type/Description: Local History Museum: housed in 1869 former Tama County Jail.
Hours & Admission Prices: March to mid-Dec. Tues.-Sat. 1-4:30; other times by appointment. Bus tours available. No charge; donations accepted. Closed holidays. &
Attendance: 1,750 (estimated)

Traer

TRAER HISTORICAL MUSEUM, 514 2nd St., Traer, IA 50675-1139. Tel.: 319-478-2346. Facebook.
E-mail: traermuseum@gmail.com
Institution Type/Description: History Museum: highlights the life of "Tama Jim" Wilson, U.S. Secretary of Agriculture.
Hours & Admission Prices: By appointment. No charge; donations accepted. &

TRAER SALT & PEPPER SHAKER GALLERY, 411 Second St., Traer, IA 50675. Tel.: 319-231-7654.
E-mail: saltandpepper@traer.net
Web Site: www.traer.com
Institution Type/Description: Shaker Gallery.
Hours & Admission Prices: March-Nov. Tues.-Sat. 1-5; groups & other times by appointment. Adults $3, children 5-12 $1; children under 5 no charge. Closed major holidays.

Urbandale

LIVING HISTORY FARMS, 11121 Hickman Rd., Urbandale, IA 50322. Tel.: 515-278-5286. Fax: 515-278-9808.
E-mail: info@lhf.org
Web Site: www.livinghistoryfarms.org
Key Personnel: C.E.O. & Pres., Ruth Haus; Vice Pres. Finance & Retail Opers., Jen Albers; Vice Pres. Devel., Jim Dietz-Kilen; Dir. Events & Sales, Judy Downs; Dir. Interpretation, Janet Clair Dennis; Vice Pres. Mktg. & Communications, Jennie Deerr; Dir. Facilities & Maintenance, Dean Irving.
Institution Type/Description: Living History Museum.
Hours & Admission Prices: May-Oct. call for hours. Adults $15, children 2-12 $9, discounts to senior citizens, military & AAA members, children one & under and members no charge. &
Attendance: 130,000 (actual)

Van Meter

BOB FELLER MUSEUM, 310 Mill St., Van Meter, IA 50261. Mailing Address: P.O. Box 160, Van Meter, IA 50261-0160. Tel.: 515-996-2806, 866-996-2806. Fax: 515-996-2952.
E-mail: info@bobfellermuseum.org
Web Site: www.bobfellermuseum.org/
Key Personnel: Mgr., Scott Havick.
Institution Type/Description: Sports Museum: housed in the hometown of Cleveland Indians pitcher, Bob Feller, 1936-1956; member of the Baseball Hall of Fame.
Hours & Admission Prices: Oct.-March Tues.-Sat. 10-3, Sun. 12-4; April-Sept. Tues.-Sat. 10-5, Sun. 12-4. Adults $5, seniors & school-aged children $3; discounts to groups with appointment.

Vinton

FRANK G. RAY HOUSE, 912 First Ave., Vinton, IA 52349-1712.
Key Personnel: Pres., Larry W. Petcovic.
Institution Type/Description: Historic House Museum: built in 1893. Listed in the National Register of Historical Places.
Hours & Admission Prices: June-Aug. Sat.-Sun. 1-4. No charge, donations requested.

HORRIDGE HOUSE, 612 First Ave., Vinton, IA 52349-1705. Mailing Address: PO Box 22, Vinton, IA 52349-0022. Tel.: 319-472-4465.
E-mail: bentoncohistorical@gmail.com
Web Site: www.bchsiowa.com
Key Personnel: Benton County Historical Soc. Pres., Sharon Happel.
Institution Type/Description: Historic House Museum: c.1860.
Hours & Admission Prices: By appointment only

Walcott

IOWA 80 TRUCKING MUSEUM, I-80 Exit 284, Walcott, IA 52773. Mailing Address: 505 Sterling Dr., Walcott, IA 52773. Tel.: 563-468-5500. Fax: 563-468-5506.
E-mail: joni.waller@iowa80group.com
Web Site: www.iowa80truckingmuseum.com
Institution Type/Description: Trucking Museum.
Hours & Admission Prices: Memorial Day to Labor Day Mon.-Sat. 9-5, Sun. 12-5; Sept.-May Wed.-Sat. 9-5, Sun. 12-5. No charge; donations requested. &
Attendance: 12,400 (estimated)

Wall Lake

ANDY WILLIAMS BIRTHPLACE, 102 E. First St., Wall Lake, IA 51466-7707. Mailing Address: P.O. Box 566, Wall Lake, IA 51466-0566. Tel.: 712-664-2119.
Institution Type/Description: Historic House Museum: housed in the birthplace of Andy Williams.
Hours & Admission Prices: Memorial Day to Labor Day Sat.-Sun. 2-4; other times by appointment.

Walnut

WALNUT CREEK HISTORICAL MUSEUM, 304 Antique City Dr., Walnut, IA 51577. Mailing Address: P.O. Box 737, Walnut, IA 51577. Tel.: 712-784-2100 & 2244.
E-mail: wcshadelands@sbcglobal.net
Web Site: walnutcreekhistory.info/wchs/museum
Institution Type/Description: History Museum.
Hours & Admission Prices: Memorial Day to Labor Day Sat.-Sun. 1-4; other times by appointment. No charge; donations accepted.
Attendance: 500 (estimated)

WALNUT CREEK HISTORICAL SOCIETY MUSEUM AND MONROE #8 ONE-ROOM COUNTRY SCHOOLHOUSE, 304 Antique City D. & 610 Highland St., Walnut, IA 51577. Mailing Address: c/o Walnut Historical Society, 210 Redwood Rd., Walnut, IA 51577. Tel.: 712-784-2100 & 2244.
Key Personnel: Pres. (V), Neal Smith; Museum Shop Mgr., Ardythe Smith.
Institution Type/Description: Historic Buildings: c.1911 lodge building & c.1920 schoolhouse.
Hours & Admission Prices: Memorial Day to Labor Day Sat.-Sun. 1-4; other times by appointment.
Attendance: 250 (estimated)

Wapello

LOUISA COUNTY HERITAGE CENTER, 609 N. James L. Hodges Ave., Wapello, IA 52653. Tel.: 319-527-5247. Facebook: Louisa County Iowa Historical Society.
E-mail: lchs@louisacomm.net
Key Personnel: Pres. (V), Norma McCormac.
Institution Type/Description: History Museum.
Hours & Admission Prices: March-Nov. Thurs., Fri. & Sun. 1-4. No charge; donations accepted. Closed all major holidays. &
Attendance: 400 (estimated)

Waterloo

GROUT MUSEUM DISTRICT, 503 South St., Waterloo, IA 50701-1517. Tel.: 319-234-6357. Fax: 319-236-0500.
E-mail: info@gmdistrict.org
Web Site: www.groutmuseumdistrict.org
Key Personnel: Exec. Dir., Billie K. Bailey; Chm. & Pres. (V), Barbara Corson; Cur. Exhibits, Robin Venter; Dir. Devel. & Mktg., Cyd McHone; Mktg. Coord. & Graphic Designer, Shelby Sitzmann; Mgr. Collections, Lorraine Ihnen; Devel. & Visitor Service Asst., Nancy Kinter; Mgr. Russell House, Annette Freeseman; Imaginarium Mgr., Alan Sweeney; Mgr. Operations, Diane Popelka; Archivist, Catreva Manning; Coord. Veterans Project, Bob Neymeyer; Education Asst., Jane Ryan; Exhibit Technician, William Bisbee; Outreach Coord., Jason Dornbush; Museum Shop Mgr., Judith Slaikeu.
Institution Type/Description: General Museum.
Hours & Admission Prices: Tues.-Sat. 9-5. Sullivan Brothers Iowa Veterans Museum & Grout Museum of History & Science: adults 14 & over $10, children 4-13, active military & veterans $5; children 3 & under no charge. Bluedorn Science Imaginarium & Rensselaer Russell House Museum: adults & children 4 & over $5 (per site); children 3 & under no charge. &
Attendance: 33,630 (actual)

JOHN DEERE TRACTOR & ENGINE MUSEUM, 500 Westfield Ave., Waterloo, IA 50701. Tel.: 319-292-6126.
E-mail: johnDeereTractor_EngineMuseum@JohnDeere.com
Web Site: deere.com
Institution Type/Description: Tractor Museum.
Hours & Admission Prices: Mon.-Sat. 9-5, Sun. 12-4. No charge. Closed New Year's Eve & Day; Easter; Thanksgiving; Christmas Eve & Day.

NATIONAL WRESTLING HALL OF FAME DAN GABLE MUSEUM, 303 Jefferson St., Waterloo, IA 50701. Tel.: 319-233-0745. Fax: 319-233-3477. Facebook: NWHOFDGM.
E-mail: dgmstaff@nwhof.org
Web Site: www.nwhof.org
Institution Type/Description: Sports Museum.
Hours & Admission Prices: Mon.-Fri. 9-5; other times by appointment. Adults $6, students 17 & under $3; children 6 & under no charge.

PHELPS YOUTH PAVILION, Waterloo Center for the Arts, 225 Commercial St., Waterloo, IA 50701-1313. Tel.: 319-291-4490. Fax: 319-291-4270.
E-mail: museum@waterloo-ia.org
Web Site: www.phelpsyouthpavilion.org
Key Personnel: Dir., Carolyn Carpenter; Museum Shop Mgr., Maureen Newbill.
Institution Type/Description: Children's Museum.
Hours & Admission Prices: Tues.-Sat. 10-5, Sun. 1-5. Admissions $5 per person; active military, members, children under one & Association of Children's Museums Reciprocal Program no charge. &
Attendance: 25,000 (estimated)

WATERLOO CENTER FOR THE ARTS, 225 Commercial St., Waterloo, IA 50701-1313. Tel.: 319-291-4490. Fax: 319-291-4270.
E-mail: museum@waterloo-ia.org
Web Site: www.waterloocenterforthearts.org
Formerly: Waterloo Museum of Art
Key Personnel: Exec. Dir., Kent Shankle; Registrar, Elizabeth Andrews; Cur., Chawne Paige.
Institution Type/Description: Art Museum.
Hours & Admission Prices: Tues.-Sat. 10-4, Sun. 1-5. No charge; donations accepted. Closed New Year's Day; Memorial Day; Independence Day; Labor Day; Veterans Day; Thanksgiving & day after; Christmas Day & day after. &
Attendance: 100,000 (estimated)

Waukee

IOWA JEWISH HISTORICAL SOCIETY, 33158 Ute Ave., Waukee, IA 50263. Tel.: 515-987-0899 ext. 116.
E-mail: ijhs@dmjfed.org
Web Site: www.jewishdesmoines.org
Key Personnel: Dir., Sandi Yoder.
Institution Type/Description: Jewish History Museum.
Hours & Admission Prices: Call for hours. No charge; donations accepted. &

Wayland

WAYLAND MUSEUM, 217 W. Main St., Wayland, IA 52654. Mailing Address: P.O. Box 144, Wayland, IA 52654. Tel.: 319-256-3276.
E-mail: bconrad@waylandiowa.com
Web Site: www.waylandiowa.com
Institution Type/Description: History Museum.
Hours & Admission Prices: Tues. & Thurs. mornings; other times by appointment. No charge; donations appreciated.

West Bend

GROTTO OF THE REDEMPTION, 300 N. Broadway, West Bend, IA 50597. Mailing Address: P.O. Box 376, West Bend, IA 50597-0376. Tel.: 515-887-2371. Fax: 515-887-2372. Facebook: Grotto of the Redemption.
E-mail: info@westbendgrotto.com
Web Site: westbendgrotto.com
Institution Type/Description: Religious History Museum.
Hours & Admission Prices: Shrine: daily. Office: Mon.-Fri. 9-5. Gift Shop: daily 10-5; other times by appointment. No charge; donations accepted. Closed New Year's Eve & Day; Easter; Thanksgiving; Christmas Eve, Day & week. &
Attendance: 25,000 (estimated)

WEST BEND HISTORICAL SOCIETY & MUSEUM, 7 3rd St., S.E., West Bend, IA 50597. Mailing Address: P.O. Box 23, West Bend, IA 50597. Tel.: 515-200-9234.
E-mail: dbanwart@ncn.net
Key Personnel: Chm. (V) & Pres. (V), Pat Lauck.
Institution Type/Description: Historical Society Museum.
Hours & Admission Prices: Memorial Day to Labor Day Sat.-Sun. 1:30-3:30; other times by appointment. Adults $4, students $2. &
Attendance: 1,000 (estimated)

West Branch

HERBERT HOOVER NATIONAL HISTORIC SITE, 110 Parkside Dr., West Branch, IA 52358. Mailing Address: P.O. Box 607, West Branch, IA 52358-0607. Tel.: 319-643-2541. Fax: 319-643-7864.
E-mail: heho_information@nps.gov
Web Site: www.nps.gov/heho
Key Personnel: Museum Shop Mgr., Adam Prato.
Institution Type/Description: Historic Site: birthplace of Herbert Hoover and graves of President & Mrs. Hoover.
Hours & Admission Prices: Daily 9-5. No charge; donations accepted. Closed New Year's Day; Thanksgiving; Christmas. &
Attendance: 153,000 (actual)

HERBERT HOOVER PRESIDENTIAL LIBRARY-MUSEUM, 210 Parkside Dr., West Branch, IA 52358-9685. Mailing Address: P.O. Box 488, West Branch, IA 52358-0488. Tel.: 319-643-5301. Fax: 319-643-6045.
E-mail: hoover.library@nara.gov
Web Site: www.hoover.archives.gov
Key Personnel: Dir., Thomas Schwartz; Cur., Marcus Eckhardt; Registrar, Karen Maxville; Photo Archivist, Lynn Smith; Outreach Archivist, Matthew Schaefer; Internet Archivist, Craig Wright; Museum Shop Mgr., Pamela Hinkhouse.
Institution Type/Description: Presidential Library.
Hours & Admission Prices: Daily 9-5. Adults $10, senior citizens $5, children 6-15 $3; members and children 5 & under no charge. Closed New Year's Day; Thanksgiving; Christmas. &
Attendance: 50,000 (estimated)

West Des Moines

THE BENNETT SCHOOL, 4001 Fuller Rd., West Des Moines, IA 50061. Mailing Address: West Des Moines Historical Society, 2001 Fuller Rd., West Des Moines, IA 50265-5528. Tel.: 515-225-1286.
E-mail: info@wdmhs.org
Web Site: wdmhs.org/the-bennett-school
Institution Type/Description: Historical Society Museum: housed in c.1926 one room school.
Hours & Admission Prices: By appointment. Tours: adults $5, students $3; children 5 & under no charge.

THE JORDAN HOUSE, 2001 Fuller Rd., West Des Moines, IA 50265-5528. Mailing Address: P.O. Box 65563, West Des Moines, IA 50265. Tel.: 515-225-1286.
E-mail: info@wdmhs.org
Web Site: thejordanhouse.org
Institution Type/Description: Historic House Museum: housed in the former home of James Jordan, the founder of Valley Junction (later renamed West Des Moines); the home served as a station on the Underground Railroad. National Register of Historic Places.
Hours & Admission Prices: Guided Tours: Memorial Day to Labor Day Fri.-Sun. 11 am & 1 pm. Sept.-May Fri. & Sun. 11 am & 1 pm. Adults $5, students $3; children 5 & under no charge.

West Union

FAYETTE COUNTY HISTORICAL & GENEALOGICAL SOCIETY, 100 N. Walnut St., West Union, IA 52175-1347. Tel.: 563-422-5797.
E-mail: fayettehistorical@gmail.com
Formerly: Fayette County Helpers Club & Historical Society
Key Personnel: Pres., Frances Bowden; Admin., Phyllis Holmstrom.
Institution Type/Description: Historical & Preservation Society.
Hours & Admission Prices: Jan. to mid-Dec. Mon.-Fri. 10-3; other times by appointment. No charge; donations accepted. Closed national holidays. &
Attendance: 1,500 (estimated)

Williams

THE HEMKEN COLLECTION, 202 Main St., Williams, IA 50271. Tel.: 515-854-2749.
Web Site: www.the-hemken-collection.org
Institution Type/Description: Automobile Museum.
Hours & Admission Prices: May-Oct. Wed. & Fri. 1-5; other times by appointment.

Winfield

WINFIELD HISTORICAL SOCIETY AND MUSEUM, 114 S. Locust St., Winfield, IA 52659-9586. Mailing Address: P.O. Box 184, Winfield, IA 52659-0184. Tel.: 319-257-6974.
Web Site: www.winfieldhistoricalsociety.com
Key Personnel: Dir., Judy Rawson.
Institution Type/Description: Historical Society Museum.
Hours & Admission Prices: Mon. 10-12; other times by appointment. No charge; donations accepted.
Attendance: 400 (estimated)

Winterset

JOHN WAYNE BIRTHPLACE & MUSEUM, 205 S. John Wayne Dr., Winterset, IA 50273-1910. Tel.: 515-462-1044. Fax: 515-462-3289.
E-mail: director@johnwaynebirthplace.museum
Web Site: www.johnwaynebirthplace.museum
Formerly: John Wayne Birthplace
Key Personnel: Pres., Joe Zuckschwerdt; Exec. Dir., Brian Downes; Dir. & Museum Shop Mgr., Carolyn Farr; Treas., Rebecca Kile; Sec., Wayne Davis.
Institution Type/Description: Historic House & Preservation Project: c.1907 frame house, birthplace of film star John Wayne.
Hours & Admission Prices: Daily 10-5. Adults $15, seniors $14, children 8 & over $8; children 7 & under no charge. &
Attendance: 40,000 (estimated)

MADISON COUNTY HISTORICAL SOCIETY, 815 S. 2nd Ave., Winterset, IA 50273-2108. Mailing Address: P.O. Box 15, Winterset, IA 50273-0015. Tel.: 515-462-2134.
E-mail: mchistory@historyonthehill.com
Web Site: www.historyonthehill.com
Key Personnel: Pres. (V), Robert Young; Cur., Jared McDonald; Vice Pres., Sally Oldham; Treas., Tim Waddingham.
Institution Type/Description: Historic Society Museum Complex.
Hours & Admission Prices: May-Oct. Mon.-Sat. 11-4, Sun. 1-5. Museum or House: adults $3; members no charge. Combination Ticket: $5; group rate $4; members & children under 12 no charge. &
Attendance: 10,000 (estimated)

WINTERSET ART CENTER, 224 S. John Wayne Dr., Winterset, IA 50273. Mailing Address: P.O. Box 325, Winterset, IA 50273-0325. Tel.: 515-210-3286.
E-mail: wacjnarland@aol.com
Web Site: www.wintersetartcenter.org
Key Personnel: Chm., Jerrold Narland; Sec., Ethel Lee Osborne; Public Rels., Joe Held.
Institution Type/Description: Art Museum: housed in c.1854 building used as an Underground Railway stop during the Civil War.
Hours & Admission Prices: Mon.-Sat. 10-4 & by appointment. No charge; donations accepted.
Attendance: 3,000 (estimated)

KANSAS

(346 listings)

Abilene

DICKINSON COUNTY HERITAGE CENTER, 412 S. Campbell St., Abilene, KS 67410-2905. Tel.: 785-263-2681. Fax: 785-263-0380.
E-mail: heritagecenterdk@sbcglobal.net
Web Site: heritagecenterdk.com
Key Personnel: Dir. & C.E.O., Jeff Sheets; Pres. (V), Thelma Lexow; Museum Shop Mgr., Twila Jackson.
Institution Type/Description: History Museum.
Hours & Admission Prices: Winter: Mon.-Fri. 9-3, Sat. 10-5, Sun. 1-5; Summer: Mon.-Fri. 9-4, Sat. 10-8, Sun. 1-5. Adults $4, seniors 62 & over $3, children 2-

14 $2; discounts to groups & AAM members & telephone pioneers. Carousel Rides $2. Closed New Year's Day; Thanksgiving; Christmas. &
Attendance: 14,000 (actual)

EISENHOWER PRESIDENTIAL LIBRARY, MUSEUM AND BOYHOOD HOME, 200 S.E. 4th St., Abilene, KS 67410-2900. Tel.: 785-263-6700. Fax: 785-263-6718. Facebook: Ike Library.
E-mail: eisenhower.library@nara.gov
Web Site: www.eisenhower.archives.gov
Key Personnel: Dir., Karl Weissenbach; Cur., William D. Snyder; Museum Shop Mgr., Tim Sheehan.
Institution Type/Description: Presidential Library & Museum.
Hours & Admission Prices: June-July daily 8-5:45; Aug.-May daily 9-4:45. Museum: adults $10, seniors $9, children 6-15 $2; children 5 & under no charge. Closed New Year's Day; Thanksgiving; Christmas. &
Attendance: 189,697 (actual)

GREYHOUND HALL OF FAME, 407 S. Buckeye, Abilene, KS 67410-2925. Tel.: 785-263-3000. Fax: 785-263-2604.
E-mail: info@greyhoundhalloffame.com
Web Site: greyhoundhalloffame.com
Key Personnel: Mgr., Kathryn Lounsbury; Bd. Pres., Tom Taplin.
Institution Type/Description: Sports Museum.
Hours & Admission Prices: Daily 9-4:45. No charge; donations accepted. Closed New Year's Day; Thanksgiving; Christmas. &
Attendance: 50,000 (estimated)

MUSEUM OF INDEPENDENT TELEPHONY, 412 S. Campbell, Abilene, KS 67410-2905. Tel.: 785-263-2681. Fax: 785-263-0380.
E-mail: heritagecenterdk@sbcglobal.net
Web Site: www.heritagecenterdk.com
Key Personnel: C.E.O. & Dir., Jeff Sheets.
Institution Type/Description: Telephonic History Museum.
Hours & Admission Prices: Memorial Day-Labor Day Mon.-Fri. 9-4, Sat. 9-8; Winter: Mon.-Fri. 9-3, Sat. 10-5. Adults 16 & over $4, seniors 62 & over $3, children 2-15 $2; discounts to groups, AAA & AAM members. Closed New Year's Day; Thanksgiving; Christmas. &
Attendance: 10,904 (estimated)

THE SEELYE MANSION & PATENT MEDICINE MUSEUM, 1105 N. Buckeye Ave., Abilene, KS 67410-1942. Mailing Address: P.O. Box 337, Abilene, KS 67410-0337. Tel.: 785-263-1084.
E-mail: terryt@access-one.com
Web Site: www.seeleymansion.org
Institution Type/Description: Historic House: former home of Dr. and Mrs. A.B. Seelye; built in 1905.
Hours & Admission Prices: Mon.-Sat. 10-6, Sun. 1-5. Adults $10, children 6-12 $5. Closed Christmas.

Alma

WABAUNSEE COUNTY HISTORICAL MUSEUM, 227 Missouri, Alma, KS 66401. Mailing Address: P.O. Box 387, Alma, KS 66401-0387. Tel.: 785-765-2200.
E-mail: wabcomuseum@embarqmail.com
Web Site: www.wabaunsee.org
Key Personnel: Pres. (V), John Hund; Cur., Alan Winkler; Asst. Cur., Linda Maas.
Institution Type/Description: Historical Society Museum: housed in 100-year old native stone building.
Hours & Admission Prices: March-Nov. Tues.-Sat. 10-12 & 1-4; Dec.-Feb. Tues.-Wed. 10-12 & 1-4. Suggested Donations: adults 22-64 $2; seniors & students no charge. Closed major holidays. &
Attendance: 1,650 (actual)

Anthony

HISTORICAL MUSEUM OF ANTHONY INC., 526 W. Main St., Anthony, KS 67003. Mailing Address: P.O. Box 185, Anthony, KS 67003. Tel.: 620-842-3852.
Key Personnel: Pres. (V), Kathy Francis; Dir., Connie L. Robinson.
Institution Type/Description: History Museum: housed in the former Santa Fe Railroad Depot; built in 1928.
Hours & Admission Prices: Thurs.-Sat. 10-12 & 1-4; other times by appointment. No charge, donations accepted. &
Attendance: 500 (estimated)

Argonia

SALTER MUSEUM, 220 W. Garfield, Argonia, KS 67004. Mailing Address: P.O. Box 126, Argonia, KS 67004-0126. Tel.: 620-435-6376.
E-mail: argonia@sutv.com
Key Personnel: Pres. Argonia & Western Sumner Historical Society, Troy Bookless; Docent, Carol Pearce; Chief Cur., Mary Beth Bookless.
Institution Type/Description: Historic House Museum: 1884 home of America's first woman mayor, Mrs. Susanna M. Salter.
Hours & Admission Prices: By appointment. No charge; donations accepted. &

Arkansas City

CHEROKEE STRIP LAND RUSH MUSEUM, 31639 US 77, Arkansas City, KS 67005. Tel.: 620-442-6750. Fax: 620-441-4332.
E-mail: srandel@arkansascityks.gov
Web Site: arkcity.org/index.aspx?ID=216
Key Personnel: City Mgr., Nick Hernandez; Chm., Jerry Hooley; Dir., Heather Ferguson.
Institution Type/Description: History Museum.
Hours & Admission Prices: Wed.-Sat. 10-5; Sun. 1-4. Adults $4.50, senior citizens $3.50, children 6-10 $2; children under 6 no charge. Closed major holidays. &
Attendance: 10,428 (actual)

Ashland

PIONEER-KRIER MUSEUM, 430 W. 4th, Ashland, KS 67831. Tel.: 620-635-2227. Fax: 620-635-2227 (call first).
E-mail: pioneer@ucom.net
Web Site: www.pioneer-krier.com
Key Personnel: Pres., Denny Denton; Vice Pres., Gary Whit; Dir., Tony Maphet; Chm. (V), Jeff Krier.
Institution Type/Description: Pioneer & Aerobatic Museum.
Hours & Admission Prices: Tues.-Fri. 10-12 & 1-4. No charge; donations accepted. Closed New Year's Day; Thanksgiving; Christmas. &
Attendance: 2,000 (actual)

Atchison

AMELIA EARHART BIRTHPLACE MUSEUM, 223 North Ter., Atchison, KS 66002-2525. Mailing Address: 609 Meridian Rd., Chester, NE 68327-7004. Tel.: 913-367-4217.
E-mail: aemuseum@att.com
Web Site: ameliaearhartmuseum.org
Key Personnel: Chm. (V), Carole Sutton; Museum Shop Mgr., Jan Coyle.
Institution Type/Description: Historic House: 1861 Gothic Revival cottage, birthplace of Amelia Earhart.
Hours & Admission Prices: Feb. 16-Dec. 14 Mon.-Fri. 9-4, Sat. 10-4, Sun. 1-4; Dec. 15-Feb. 15 Wed.-Sat. 10-4, Sun. 1-4. No charge; donations accepted. Closed New Year's Day; Christmas. &
Attendance: 12,000 (estimated)

ATCHISON COUNTY HISTORICAL SOCIETY, 200 S. 10th St., Atchison, KS 66002-2772. Mailing Address: P.O. Box 201, Atchison, KS 66002-0201. Tel.: 913-367-6238. Facebook.
E-mail: gowest@atchisonhistory.org
Web Site: www.atchisonhistory.org
Key Personnel: Dir. & C.E.O., Chris W. Taylor.
Institution Type/Description: Historic Building: housed in c.1880 Santa Fe Freight Depot.
Hours & Admission Prices: Mon.-Fri. 8-5, Sat. 9-5, Sun. 12-5. Entry by donation. &
Attendance: 24,000 (estimated)

EVAH C. CRAY HISTORICAL HOME MUSEUM, 805 N. 5th St., Atchison, KS 66002-1807. Tel.: 913-367-3046. Facebook.
E-mail: crayhome@att.net
Institution Type/Description: Historic House: housed in a 25-room Victorian era mansion; built in 1882.
Hours & Admission Prices: April & Oct. Thurs.-Sat. 10-4, Sun. 1-4; May-Sept. Mon. & Wed.-Sat. 10-4, Sun. 1-4; last tour starts at 3pm. Special tours available by appointment. Adults $5, seniors 65 & over $4, students $3; children 5 & under no charge. &
Attendance: 500 (estimated)

THE MUCHNIC GALLERY, 704 N. 4th St., Atchison, KS 66002-1924. Tel.: 913-367-4278. Fax: 913-367-2939.
E-mail: atchisonart@gmail.com
Web Site: www.atchisonart.org
Key Personnel: Dir. & Cur., Deborah Geiger; Pres. (V), Patty Boldridge.

Institution Type/Description: Art Gallery: housed in 1885 Victorian brick residence.
Hours & Admission Prices: Gallery: Wed. 1-5, Sat.-Sun. 1-5, Special Exhibits: Sat.-Sun. 1-5; special tours available. No charge, donations accepted.
Attendance: 2,500 (actual)

Atwood

RAWLINS COUNTY MUSEUM, 308 State, Atwood, KS 67730. Tel.: 785-626-3885.
E-mail: rchsmuseum@atwoodtv.net
Key Personnel: Dir., Ashley Braley.
Institution Type/Description: History Museum.
Hours & Admission Prices: Tues.-Fri. 10-12 & 1-5, Sat. 1-4. No charge; donations accepted.

Augusta

AUGUSTA HISTORICAL MUSEUM, 303 State, Augusta, KS 67010-1103. Tel.: 316-775-5655.
E-mail: brenda@augustahistoricalsociety.com
Web Site: www.augustahistoricalsociety.net
Key Personnel: Pres., Jane Mathias; Dir., Brenda Barber.
Institution Type/Description: General Museum.
Hours & Admission Prices: Mon.-Fri. 11-3, Sat.-Sun. 1-4. No charge; donations accepted. Closed holidays.
Attendance: 8,500 (actual)

KANSAS MUSEUM OF MILITARY HISTORY, 135 S. Hwy. 77, Augusta, KS 67010-7681. Tel.: 316-775-1425.
E-mail: info@kmmh.org
Web Site: www.kmmh.org
Key Personnel: Museum Dir. & Pres., John Lara.
Institution Type/Description: Military Museum.
Hours & Admission Prices: April-Sept. daily 1-5; Oct.-March Sat.-Sun. 1-5.

Baldwin City

OLD CASTLE MUSEUM, 511 Fifth St., Baldwin City, KS 66006. Mailing Address: Baker University, P.O. Box 65, Baldwin City, KS 66006-0065. Tel.: 785-594-8380. Fax: 785-594-2522.
E-mail: sara.decaro@bakeru.edu
Key Personnel: Dir. Archives & Museum, Sara DeCaro.
Institution Type/Description: Historic Buildings Complex.
Hours & Admission Prices: Temporarily closed. No charge; donations accepted.
Attendance: 5,436 (actual)

QUAYLE BIBLE COLLECTION, Collins Library-Spencer Quayle Wing, 518 8th St., Baldwin City, KS 66006-0065. Mailing Address: Collins Library, P.O. Box 65, Baldwin City, KS 66006-0065. Tel.: 785-594-8393. Fax: 785-594-6721.
E-mail: quayle@bakeru.edu
Web Site: www.bakeru.edu/quayle
Key Personnel: Dir., Nate Poell.
Institution Type/Description: Rare Bible Museum.
Hours & Admission Prices: Sat.-Sun. 1-4; other times by appointment. No charge; donations accepted. Closed university holidays. ♿
Attendance: 400 (estimated)

Barnes

BARNES STATE BANK MUSEUM, 107 W. Railroad Ave., Barnes, KS 66933. Mailing Address: P.O. Box 94, Barnes, KS 66933. Tel.: 785-763-4569.
E-mail: historictrust@barnesks.net
Web Site: www.barnesks.net
Key Personnel: Dir., Cindy Hiesterman; Chm. (V) & Museum Shop Mgr., Gloria Moore; Pres. (V), Todd Frye.
Institution Type/Description: Historic Building: built in 1911. Listed on the National Register of Historic Places.
Hours & Admission Prices: Mon.-Sat. 12-4. No charge; donations accepted.
Attendance: 540 (actual)

Baxter Springs

BAXTER SPRINGS HERITAGE CENTER AND MUSEUM, 740 East Ave., Baxter Springs, KS 66713. Mailing Address: P.O. Box 514, Baxter Springs, KS 66713-0514. Tel.: 620-856-2385.
E-mail: heritagectr@embarqmail.com
Web Site: www.baxterspringsmuseum.org

Key Personnel: Dir., Mary Billington.
Institution Type/Description: History Museum.
Hours & Admission Prices: Tues.-Sat. 10-4:30, Sun. 1-4; other times by appointment. No charge; donations accepted. ♿
Attendance: 6,500 (estimated)

Belleville

BOYER MUSEUM OF ANIMATED CARVINGS, 1205 M St., Belleville, KS 66935-3069. Tel.: 785-527-5884.
E-mail: boyermuseum@sbcglobal.net
Web Site: www.kansastravel.org/boyergallery.htm
Formerly: Boyer Gallery
Key Personnel: Owner, Paul Boyer; Museum Shop Mgr., Ann Lewellyn.
Institution Type/Description: Mechanical Sculpture Museum.
Hours & Admission Prices: May-Sept. Wed.-Sat. 1-5; other times by appointment (weather permitting); call to confirm hours. Adults $5, children 6-12 $2.
Attendance: 2,000 (estimated)

HIGHBANKS HALL OF FAME & NATIONAL MIDGET AUTO RACING MUSEUM, 1204 H St., Belleville, KS 66935. Mailing Address: P.O. Box 264, Belleville, KS 66935-0264. Tel.: 785-527-2526.
E-mail: highbanksmuseum@nckcn.com
Web Site: www.highbanks-museum.org
Key Personnel: C.E.O., Dir. & Cur., Don McChesney; Pres. (V) & Chm. (V), Ken Effenbeck.
Institution Type/Description: Hall of Fame & Racing Museum.
Hours & Admission Prices: May-Sept. Tues.-Sun. 10-5; Oct.-April Wed.-Sun. & holidays 11-4; other times by appointment. No charge; donations accepted. ♿
Attendance: 2,400 (actual)

REPUBLIC COUNTY HISTORICAL SOCIETY MUSEUM, 615 28th St., Belleville, KS 66935-2469. Tel.: 785-527-5971.
E-mail: repcomuse@nckcn.com
Web Site: www.nckcn.com/homepage/repcomuse/home.htm
Key Personnel: C.E.O., Cur. & Archivist, Sherrie Larson; Pres. (V), Nancy Holt; Treas., David Bowersox.
Institution Type/Description: Historical Society Museum.
Hours & Admission Prices: April-Nov. Mon.-Fri. 1-5, Sun. 1:30-4:30; Dec.-March Mon.-Fri. 1-5. Adults $3; members & children under 10 no charge. Closed major holidays. ♿
Attendance: 2,420 (estimated)

Beloit

MITCHELL COUNTY HISTORICAL SOCIETY MUSEUM, 402 W. 8th, Beloit, KS 67420. Tel.: 785-738-5355. Facebook: Mitchell County Historical Society.
E-mail: mchistorical@yahoo.com
Institution Type/Description: Historical Society Museum.
Hours & Admission Prices: Sun. 1-5, Mon.-Tues. & Thurs. 10-4; other times by appointment. No charge; donations accepted.

Blue Rapids

BLUE RAPIDS HISTORICAL SOCIETY AND MUSEUM, #36 Public Square, Round Town Square, Blue Rapids, KS 66411. Tel.: 785-363-7949.
E-mail: brhissoc@yahoo.com
Key Personnel: Cur., Patricia Osborne; Pres. (V), Nolan Sump.
Institution Type/Description: Historical Society Museum.
Hours & Admission Prices: Sat. 9-12; other times by appointment. No charge; donations accepted. ♿
Attendance: 1,000 (estimated)

Bonner Springs

THE NATIONAL AGRICULTURAL CENTER & HALL OF FAME, 630 N. 126th St., Bonner Springs, KS 66012-9045. Tel.: 913-721-1075. Fax: 913-721-1202.
E-mail: info@aghalloffame.com
Web Site: www.aghalloffame.com
Key Personnel: Exec. Dir., Dawn Gabel; Dir. Education, Lee Sigley.
Institution Type/Description: Agriculture Museum.
Hours & Admission Prices: April 23-Nov. 10 Wed.-Sat. 10-4, Sun. 1-4; other times by appointment. No charge; donations accepted. ♿
Attendance: 100,000 (estimated)

WYANDOTTE COUNTY MUSEUM, 631 N. 126th St., Bonner Springs, KS 66012-9046. Tel.: 913-573-5002.
E-mail: pschurkamp@wycokck.org
Web Site: www.wycomuseum.org
Formerly: Wyandotte County Historical Society and Museum
Key Personnel: C.E.O. & Dir., Trish Schurkamp; Cur., Jennifer Laughlin.
Institution Type/Description: History Museum.
Hours & Admission Prices: Mon.-Fri. 9-4, Sat. 9-12. No charge; donations accepted. Closed holidays. &

Attendance: 300 (actual)

Burlingame

BURLINGAME SCHUYLER MUSEUM, 117 S. Dacotah, Burlingame, KS 66413-1225. Mailing Address: P.O. Box 74, Burlingame, KS 66413-0074. Tel.: 785-654-3170.
E-mail: museum@burlingamemuseum.com
Web Site: www.burlingamemuseum.com
Key Personnel: Chm. (V), Pres. (V) & Dir., Carolyn Strohm.
Institution Type/Description: History Museum: former home of The Schuyler Grade School, built in 1902.
Hours & Admission Prices: Wed., Fri. & Sun. 1-4, Sat. 10-4. No charge; donations accepted. Closed New Year's Day; Easter; Mother's Day; Father's Day; Independence Day; Christmas. &

Attendance: 1,500 (estimated)

Burlington

THE COFFEY COUNTY HISTORICAL MUSEUM, 1101 Neosho St., Burlington, KS 66839-1656. Tel.: 620-364-2653. Fax: 620-364-8933. Facebook: Coffey Museum.
E-mail: visit.us@coffeymuseum.org
Web Site: www.coffeymuseum.org
Key Personnel: Dir., Shirley Gorge; Administrative Asst., Erin Burdick.
Institution Type/Description: Historical Society Museum.
Hours & Admission Prices: Summer: Mon.-Fri. 10-5, Sat.-Sun. 1-4; Winter: Mon.-Fri. 10-5. No charge; donations accepted. Closed national & state holidays.

Attendance: 3,500 (estimated)

Bushton

BUSHTON MUSEUM, 218 S. Main St., Bushton, KS 67427. Tel.: 620-562-3411.
Institution Type/Description: History Museum.
Hours & Admission Prices: Call for hours.

Caney

CANEY VALLEY HISTORICAL SOCIETY, 310 W. 4th St., Caney, KS 67333. Mailing Address: P.O. Box 354, Caney, KS 67333-0354. Tel.: 620-879-2233. Fax: 620-879-2233. Facebook: Caney Valley Historical Society.
E-mail: cvhistsoc@terraworld.net
Key Personnel: Pres., Leslie Baker.
Institution Type/Description: General Museum.
Hours & Admission Prices: Tues.-Thurs. 9-12 & 12:30-3. No charge; donations accepted. Closed Mon. & Fri., New Year's Eve & Day; Memorial Day; Independence Day; Christmas Eve & Day. &

Attendance: 550 (estimated)

SAFARI ZOOLOGICAL PARK, CR 1425, Caney, KS 67333. Mailing Address: 1751a CR 1425, Caney, KS 67333. Tel.: 620-879-2885.
E-mail: safaripark@terraworld.net
Web Site: www.safaripark.org
Key Personnel: Dir., Tom Harvey; Chm. (V), Randy Smith.
Institution Type/Description: Zoo.
Hours & Admission Prices: Summer; daily call for hours. Adults $10, children 2-12 and seniors 60 & over $8.

Chanute

MARTIN AND OSA JOHNSON SAFARI MUSEUM, 111 N. Lincoln Ave., Chanute, KS 66720-1819. Tel.: 620-431-2730. Fax: 620-431-2730. Facebook: Martin and Osa Johnson Safari Museum.
E-mail: osajohns@safarimuseum.com
Web Site: www.safarimuseum.org
Key Personnel: Pres. Bd. Trustees, Jay Witt; Dir., Conrad G. Froehlich; Cur., Jacquelyn Borgeson Zimmer; Store & Office Mgr., Shirley Rogers-Naff.

Institution Type/Description: Biographical Museum: located in historic Santa Fe Train Depot.
Hours & Admission Prices: Tues.-Sat. 10-5, Sun. 1-5. Adults $6, senior citizens & students over 12 $4, children 6-12 $3; discounts to prearranged bus tours, KMA, ICOM, AASLH, AAM, ICOM, MPMA and AAA members; children under 6 no charge. Closed New Year's Day; Easter; Independence Day; Thanksgiving; Christmas. &

Attendance: 6,000 (actual)

Chapman

KANSAS AUTO RACING MUSEUM, 1205 Manor Rd., Chapman, KS 67431. Mailing Address: P.O. Box 549, Chapman, KS 67431. Tel.: 785-922-6644. Fax: 785-922-6684.
E-mail: karm@eaglecom.net
Web Site: kansasautoracingmuseum.com
Key Personnel: Dir., Doug Thompson.
Institution Type/Description: Auto Racing Museum.
Hours & Admission Prices: Mon.-Sat. 9-5, Sun. by appointment. Adults $5. Closed New Year's Day; Easter; Thanksgiving; Christmas. &

Attendance: 4,000 (actual)

Cheney

EAGLE VALLEY RAPTOR CENTER, 927 N. 343rd St., W., Cheney, KS 67025. Tel.: 316-393-0710.
E-mail: raptorcare@aol.com
Web Site: www.eaglevalleyraptorcenter.org
Key Personnel: Dir. Programs, Ken Lockwood.
Institution Type/Description: Wildlife Center.
Hours & Admission Prices: Call for hours. Donation: $5 per person.

Cherryvale

CHERRYVALE MUSEUM, 215 E. 4th St., Cherryvale, KS 67335-2102. Mailing Address: 19037 Anderson Rd., Cherryvale, KS 67335-8551. Tel.: 620-336-3350.
Institution Type/Description: History Museum.
Hours & Admission Prices: April-Oct. Sun. 2-4; other times by appointment. No charge; donations accepted. &

Chetopa

CHETOPA HISTORICAL MUSEUM, 406 Locust, Chetopa, KS 67336. Mailing Address: P.O. Box 648, Chetopa, KS 67336-0648. Tel.: 620-236-7121.
E-mail: chmuseum406locust@gmail.com
Institution Type/Description: History Museum.
Hours & Admission Prices: April-Oct. Tues.-Wed. & Fri. 1-4. No charge; donations accepted. &

Attendance: 450 (estimated)

Clay Center

CLAY COUNTY HISTORICAL MUSEUM, 518 Lincoln Ave., Clay Center, KS 67432-2902. Tel.: 785-632-3786.
E-mail: ccmuseum@twinvalley.net
Web Site: www.claycomuseum.com
Key Personnel: Dir., Jeff Gaiser; Cur. Artifacts, Diana Shaner; Cur. Documents, Angelic Nelson.
Institution Type/Description: County History Museum.
Hours & Admission Prices: Tues.-Fri. 12-7, Sat. 10-5, Sun. 1-5. No charge; donations accepted. Closed New Year's Day; Independence Day; Thanksgiving; Christmas. &

Attendance: 1,500 (actual)

Clearwater

CLEARWATER HISTORICAL SOCIETY, 149 N. 4th, Clearwater, KS 67026. Tel.: 620-584-2444.
E-mail: museum@sktc.net
Web Site: www.clearwaterhistoricalsociety.com
Institution Type/Description: History Museum.
Hours & Admission Prices: Sun. 1-4. No charge; donations accepted. &

Clifton

CLIFTON COMMUNITY HISTORICAL SOCIETY, 105 Clifton St., Clifton, KS 66937-9780. Mailing Address: P.O. Box 5, Clifton, KS 66937-0005.

Key Personnel: Pres. (V), Mary Veesart; Treas., Erma Bouley.
Institution Type/Description: General Museum: housed in Old Missouri Pacific Depot & Caboose.
Hours & Admission Prices: By appointment only. No charge; donations accepted. Closed New Year's Day; Easter; Independence Day; Thanksgiving; Christmas. ⟨⟩
Attendance: 62 (estimated)

Coffeyville

BROWN MANSION, 2019 S. Walnut, Coffeyville, KS 67337-6819. Mailing Address: P.O. Box 843, Coffeyville, KS 67337-0843. Tel.: 620-251-0431. Fax: 620-251-5448.
E-mail: kcrane5@cox.net
Web Site: www.brownmansion.com
Key Personnel: Pres., Kris Crane; Vice Pres., Darla Thornburg; Mgr. & Cur., Rob Burrows.
Institution Type/Description: Historic House.
Hours & Admission Prices: Tours: Mon., Thurs.-Fri. 10, 12, 2, Sat.-Sun. 11, 1, 3, 5. Adults $6.50, children 7-17 $4.50; children 6 & under no charge. Closed Easter; Thanksgiving; Christmas; during special events.
Attendance: 7,500 (estimated)

COFFEYVILLE AVIATION HERITAGE MUSEUM, 2002 N. Buckeye St., Coffeyville, KS 67337. Mailing Address: P.O. Box 774, Coffeyville, KS 67337-0774. Tel.: 620-251-0494.
Institution Type/Description: Aviation History Museum.
Hours & Admission Prices: Sat. 10-4, Sun. 1-4; other times by appointment. No charge; donations accepted.

DALTON DEFENDERS MUSEUM, 113 E. 8th, Coffeyville, KS 67337-5803. Mailing Address: P.O. Box 843, Coffeyville, KS 67337-0843. Tel.: 620-251-5944.
E-mail: chamber@coffeyville.com
Web Site: www.daltondefendersmuseum.com
Key Personnel: Pres., Kris Crane; Vice Pres., Darla Thornburg; Museum Mgr., John Alvey; Museum Mgr., Wendy Alvey.
Institution Type/Description: History Museum.
Hours & Admission Prices: Daily 10-4; other times by appointment. Adults $6.50, children $4.50; discounts to AAA members; children 7 & under no charge. Closed Easter; Thanksgiving; Christmas.
Attendance: 9,000 (estimated)

Colby

THE PRAIRIE MUSEUM OF ART & HISTORY, 1905 S. Franklin, Colby, KS 67701-3710. Tel.: 785-460-4590. Fax: 785-460-4592. Facebook: Prairie Museum of Art & History.
E-mail: prairiem@st-tel.net
Web Site: www.prairiemuseum.org
Key Personnel: Dir., Chris Griffin; Museum Shop Mgr., Kelsi Lewis.
Institution Type/Description: Historical Society Museum.
Hours & Admission Prices: April-Oct. Mon.-Fri. 9-5, Sat.-Sun. 1-5; Nov.-March Tues.-Fri. 9-5, Sat.-Sun. 1-5. Adults $8, senior citizens $6, children 6-16 $2; military during the summer & members no charge. Closed New Year's Day; Easter; Thanksgiving; Christmas. ⟨⟩
Attendance: 15,000 (actual)

Coldwater

COMANCHE COUNTY HISTORICAL MUSEUM, 105 W. Main St., Coldwater, KS 67029. Tel.: 620-582-2108.
Institution Type/Description: History Museum.
Hours & Admission Prices: Call for hours.

Concordia

BROWN GRAND THEATRE, 310 W. 6th St., Concordia, KS 66901. Mailing Address: P.O. Box 347, Concordia, KS 66901. Tel.: 785-243-2553.
E-mail: director@browngrand.org
Web Site: browngrandtheatre.org
Key Personnel: Dir., Amber Rogers.
Institution Type/Description: Historic Building: built in 1907. Listed on the National Register of Historic Places.
Hours & Admission Prices: Tues.-Fri. 10-4; other times by appointment. Self-Guided Tours: $2. Guided Tours: adults $5, children under 12 $3; discounts to groups of 10 or more. ⟨⟩
Attendance: 10,000 (estimated)

CLOUD COUNTY HISTORICAL SOCIETY MUSEUM, 635 Broadway, Concordia, KS 66901-2914. Tel.: 785-243-2866.
E-mail: museum@cloudcountyks.org
Web Site: www.cloudcountyks.org
Key Personnel: Pres., Dana Brewer; Sec., Aline Luecke; Treas., Betty Losh.
Institution Type/Description: Historical Society Museum: housed in 1908 Andrew Carnegie Library.
Hours & Admission Prices: Tues.-Fri. 1-5, Sat. 10-5; call to confirm; other times by appointment. No charge; donations accepted. ⟨⟩
Attendance: 6,000 (actual)

NATIONAL ORPHAN TRAIN MUSEUM, 300 Washington St., Concordia, KS 66901. Mailing Address: P.O. Box 322, Concordia, KS 66901. Tel.: 785-243-4471. Facebook.
E-mail: orphantraindepot@gmail.com
Web Site: www.orphantraindepot.com
Formerly: Orphan Train Heritage Society of America
Key Personnel: Cur., Shaley K. George; Museum Shop Mgr., Lori Halfhide.
Institution Type/Description: History Museum.
Hours & Admission Prices: Tues.-Fri. 10-12 & 1-4, Sat. 10-4. Adults $6, military $5 children $3; discounts to groups of 10 or more. ⟨⟩
Attendance: 4,000 (actual)

Cottonwood Falls

CHASE COUNTY HISTORICAL SOCIETY AND MUSEUM, 301-303 Broadway, Cottonwood Falls, KS 66845. Mailing Address: Box 375, Cottonwood Falls, KS 66845-0375. Tel.: 620-273-8500.
E-mail: cscohist@sbcglobal.net
Web Site: chasecountychamber.org
Key Personnel: Pres., Mike Schmidt; Dir. & Cur., Dawn Sisson.
Institution Type/Description: Historical Museum.
Hours & Admission Prices: Tues.-Sat. 10-3. Admission 10 & over $3; children under 10 & local school children no charge. Closed New Year's Eve & Day; Memorial Day; Independence Day; Thanksgiving; 1st two weeks of January.
Attendance: 2,000 (estimated)

FLINT HILLS GALLERY, 321 Broadway St., Cottonwood Falls, KS 66845-2884. Tel.: 620-273-6454. Facebook: Judith A Mackey.
E-mail: judithamackey@gmail.com
Web Site: www.flinthillsgallery.com
Institution Type/Description: Art Gallery.
Hours & Admission Prices: Mon.-Sat. 10-4; other times by appointment. No charge.

RONIGER MEMORIAL MUSEUM, 315 Union St., Cottonwood Falls, KS 66845. Mailing Address: P.O. Box 70, Cottonwood Falls, KS 66845-0070. Tel.: 620-273-6310 & 6412. Fax: 620-273-6335.
E-mail: deroy10@sbcglobal.net
Key Personnel: Pres. & Cur., David E. Croy; Sec. & Treas., John Roniger.
Institution Type/Description: History Museum: located on lawn of 100-year old courthouse.
Hours & Admission Prices: Tues.-Wed. & Fri.-Sun. 1-5; other times by appointment. No charge; donations accepted. ⟨⟩
Attendance: 2,000

Council Grove

KAW MISSION STATE HISTORIC SITE, 500 N. Mission, Council Grove, KS 66846-1433. Tel.: 620-767-5410. Fax: 620-767-5816.
E-mail: kawmission@kshs.org
Web Site: www.kawmission.org
Key Personnel: Historic Site Admin., Mary Honeyman; Pres. (V), Jeremiah Hershberger.
Institution Type/Description: Historical Society Museum: 1850-1851, 2-story building.
Hours & Admission Prices: Wed.-Sat. 9-5. Adults $2, students $1; children under 5 & members no charge. Closed state holidays. ⟨⟩
Attendance: 1,170 (actual)

Cunningham

CUNNINGHAM HISTORICAL MUSEUM, 100 N. Main, Cunningham, KS 67035.
Key Personnel: Chm. (V), Todd Shelman; Pres. (V), Dave Steffen; Museum Shop Mgr. & Sec., Donna Glenn.
Institution Type/Description: History Museum.

Hours & Admission Prices: Fri. 9:30-4:30. No charge; donations accepted. &
Attendance: 500 (estimated)

Delphos

DELPHOS MUSEUM, 101 N. Washington St., Delphos, KS 67436. Mailing Address: P.O. Box 338, Delphos, KS 67436. Tel.: 785-523-4540.
Key Personnel: Dir., Mary Ballou; Pres. (V), C.J. Ballou.
Institution Type/Description: History Museum: housed in the former Brock Auto repair building.
Hours & Admission Prices: Mon. & Fri. 9-12, Tues. 12-4, Sat. 9-12 & 1-4; other times by appointment. No charge; donations accepted.

Derby

DERBY HISTORICAL SOCIETY, 208 N. Westview, Derby, KS 67037. Mailing Address: P.O. Box 1054, Derby, KS 67037-1054. Tel.: 316-788-7740.
E-mail: info@derbyhistorical.org
Web Site: derbyhistorical.org/
Key Personnel: Pres. (V), Jason Crippen; Treas., Darrell Butterfield.
Institution Type/Description: History Museum.
Hours & Admission Prices: mid-April to Oct. Sat. 10-2. No charge; donations accepted.
Attendance: 1,500 (estimated)

Dighton

LANE COUNTY HISTORICAL MUSEUM, 333 N. Main St., Dighton, KS 67839. Mailing Address: P.O. Box 821, Dighton, KS 67839-0821. Tel.: 620-397-5652. Fax: 620-397-5652. Facebook: Lane County Historical Society.
E-mail: lchm@st-tel.net
Web Site: www.lanecountymuseum.org
Key Personnel: Pres., Joel Herndon; Dir., Curator, Museum Shop Mgr., Sonya Thomas.
Institution Type/Description: History Museum.
Hours & Admission Prices: Memorial Day to Labor Day Tues.-Sat. 1-5, Sun. 2-5; Sept.-May Tues.-Sat. 1-5. No charge; donations accepted. Closed legal holidays. &
Attendance: 1,200 (estimated)

Dodge City

BOOT HILL MUSEUM, INC., 500 Wyatt Earp Blvd., Dodge City, KS 67801. Tel.: 620-227-8188. Fax: 620-227-7673.
E-mail: info@boothill.org
Web Site: boothill.org
Key Personnel: Exec. Dir., Lara Brehm; Chm. Bd., Kerri Baker; Cur. Exhibits & Interpretation, Karen Pankratz; Cur. Collections & Education, Kathie Bell; Retail Operations Mgr., Sharlene Roesener.
Institution Type/Description: Western History Museum: located on Boot Hill.
Hours & Admission Prices: Off-Season: Mon.-Sat. 9-5, Sun. 1-5; Memorial Day to Labor Day daily 8-8. Summer: adults $10; children 4 & under no charge. Off-Season: adults $9; children 4 & under and members no charge. Closed New Year's Day; Thanksgiving; Christmas. &
Attendance: 81,311 (actual)

HOME OF STONE (THE MUELLER-SCHMIDT HOUSE 1881), A FORD COUNTY MUSEUM, CURATED BY FORD COUNTY HISTORIC SOCIETY, Ave. A & Vine St., Dodge City, KS 67801. Mailing Address: P.O. Box 131, Dodge City, KS 67801-0131. Tel.: 620-227-6791.
E-mail: glaughead@sbcglobal.net
Web Site: www.kansashistory.us/fordco
Key Personnel: Pres. (V), Kent Stehlik, Jr.; Financial Dir., Sonja Hughes; Archivist, Ann Warner; Museum Shop Mgr., Janice Klein.
Institution Type/Description: Historic House.
Hours & Admission Prices: Memorial Day to Labor Day Mon.-Sat. 9-5, Sun. 2-4. Adults $3.
Attendance: 4,000 (actual)

THE KANSAS TEACHERS' HALL OF FAME, 603 5th St., Dodge City, KS 67801-1674. Mailing Address: P.O. Box 1674, Dodge City, KS 67801-1674. Tel.: 620-225-7311.
E-mail: ksteachers@thof.kscoxmail.com
Web Site: www.teachershallfamedodgecityks.org
Key Personnel: Volunteer Dir., Kathy Frederking.
Institution Type/Description: Outstanding Teachers Museum.

Hours & Admission Prices: April-May & Sept.-Oct. Thurs.-Sat. 1-5; Memorial Day-Labor Day Mon.-Sat. 10-5, Sun. 1-5. Adults $8. &
Attendance: 2,500 (estimated)

Douglass

DOUGLASS HISTORICAL MUSEUM, 318 S. Forest, Douglass, KS 67039. Mailing Address: P.O. Box 95, Douglass, KS 67039-0095. Tel.: 316-746-2319 & 747-2166.
E-mail: knethercot@cityofdouglassks.com
Web Site: www.cityofdouglassks.com/douglass-historical-museum.htm
Key Personnel: Dir. & Cur., Frances Renfro.
Institution Type/Description: Pioneer Museum.
Hours & Admission Prices: Mon., Wed. & Fri. 9-11 & 1-3; other times by appointment. No charge; donations accepted. Closed New Year's Eve & Day; Christmas Eve, Day & week. &
Attendance: 750 (estimated)

Edgerton

LANESFIELD HISTORIC SITE - JOHNSON COUNTY MUSEUM, 18745 Dillie Rd., Edgerton, KS 66021. Tel.: 913-893-6645. Fax: 913-882-9730.
Institution Type/Description: History Museum: housed in a former one-room school house; built in 1869.
Hours & Admission Prices: Tues.-Sun. 1-5. No charge.

Edna

EDNA HISTORICAL MUSEUM, 100 S. Delaware, Edna, KS 67342. Mailing Address: P.O. Box 368, Edna, KS 67342-0368.
Key Personnel: Pres. (V), Kenneth E. Cary; Treas., Hazel Stone; Cur., Ronald Neidigh.
Institution Type/Description: History Museum: housed in the old First National Bank building.
Hours & Admission Prices: May-Oct. Fri. 1-4, Sat. 9-12; other times by appointment. No charge; donations accepted. Closed all holidays.
Attendance: 100 (estimated)

El Dorado

COUTTS MUSEUM OF ART, 110 N. Main St., El Dorado, KS 67042-2016. Mailing Address: P.O. Box 1, El Dorado, KS 67042. Tel.: 316-321-1212. Fax: 316-321-1215. Facebook: Coutts Museum.
Web Site: couttsmuseum.org
Key Personnel: Pres. Bd., Steve Funk; Exec. Dir, Rod Seel; Vice Pres., Jackie Clark.
Institution Type/Description: Fine Art Museum: housed in 1917 bank building.
Hours & Admission Prices: Tues.-Fri. 9-5, Sat. 12-4; groups of 12 or more by appointment. No charge; donations accepted. Closed federal & state holidays. &
Attendance: 7,800 (actual)

THE ERMAN B. WHITE GALLERY, 901 S. Haverhill Rd., El Dorado, KS 67042. Tel.: 316-321-2222, 800-794-0188.
E-mail: joehm@butlercc.edu
Institution Type/Description: Art Gallery.
Hours & Admission Prices: Sept.-May call for hours.

KANSAS OIL MUSEUM, 383 E. Central Ave., El Dorado, KS 67042-2133. Tel.: 316-321-9333. Fax: 316-321-3619.
E-mail: history@kansasoilmuseum.org
Web Site: www.kansasoilmuseum.org
Formerly: Butler County History Center & Kansas Oil Museum
Key Personnel: Bd. Pres., Tim Connell; Exec. Dir., Anna Bassford-Woods; Museum Educator, Ardath Lawson; Museum Shop Mgr., Cynthia Clugston.
Institution Type/Description: History Museum.
Hours & Admission Prices: May-Sept. Mon.-Sat. 10-4; Oct.-April Tues.-Fri. 10-4, Sat. 12-5. Adults $4; discounts to Blue Star Museums members; members no charge. Closed major holidays. &
Attendance: 9,500 (actual)

Elkhart

MORTON COUNTY HISTORICAL SOCIETY MUSEUM, 370 E. Hwy. U.S. 56, Elkhart, KS 67950. Mailing Address: P.O. Box 1248, Elkhart, KS 67950-1248. Tel.: 620-697-2833. Fax: 620-697-4390.
E-mail: mtcomuseum@elkhart.com

Web Site: www.mtcoks.com/museum
Key Personnel: Dir., Myrna K. Barnes; Museum Shop Mgr., Becky Ellis.
Institution Type/Description: Historical Society Museum.
Hours & Admission Prices: Tues.-Fri. 1-5; other times by appointment. No charge; donations accepted. &
Attendance: 3,368 (actual)

Ellis

ELLIS RAILROAD MUSEUM, 911 Washington, Ellis, KS 67637. Mailing Address: P.O. Box 82, Ellis, KS 67637. Tel.: 785-726-4493. Fax: 785-726-3294.
E-mail: allaboard@ellisrailroadmuseum.com
Web Site: www.ellisrailroadmuseum.com
Institution Type/Description: Railroad Museum.
Hours & Admission Prices: Museum: April-Oct. Tues.-Sat. 10-4; Nov.-March Tues.-Sat. 11-4. Adults 12 & over $2, children 5-12 $1; discounts to groups of 8 or more; children under 5 no charge. Miniature Train Rides: Memorial Day to Labor Day Mon.-Sat. 11am, 1pm, 3pm, & 5pm, Sun. 1pm, 3pm, 5pm. Adults 12 & over $2, children 5-12 $1; children under 5 no charge.

WALTER P. CHRYSLER BOYHOOD HOME AND MUSEUM, 102 W. 10th, Ellis, KS 67637. Tel.: 785-726-3636. Fax: 785-726-3653.
E-mail: chrysler55@eaglecom.net
Web Site: www.chryslerboyhoodhome.com
Key Personnel: Dir., Dena Patee; Pres. (V), Chad Pritchett; Treas., Swede Swenson.
Institution Type/Description: History Museum.
Hours & Admission Prices: March-Oct. Mon.-Sat. 9-4, Sun. 1-4; Nov.-Feb. Mon.-Sat. 11-3, Sun. 1-4. Adults $4, seniors $3, children 6-11 $2; children 5 & under no charge. Closed New Year's Day; Easter; Thanksgiving; Christmas.
Attendance: 1,200 (estimated)

Ellsworth

HODGDEN HOUSE MUSEUM COMPLEX, 104 W. South Main, Ellsworth, KS 67439-3232. Mailing Address: P.O. Box 144, Ellsworth, KS 67439-0144. Tel.: 785-472-3059.
E-mail: echs@eaglecom.net
Formerly: Ellsworth County Museum Complex
Key Personnel: C.E.O., Phyllis Dolenzal.
Institution Type/Description: Museum Complex.
Hours & Admission Prices: Tues.-Sat. 9-5, Sun. 1-5. Adults $3 (includes entrance to Fort Harker Museum Complex). Closed New Year's Day; Easter; Thanksgiving; Christmas. &
Attendance: 3,000 (estimated)

ROGERS HOUSE MUSEUM GALLERY, 102 E. Main St., Ellsworth, KS 67439. Tel.: 785-472-5674.
Key Personnel: Dir., Robert Rogers.
Institution Type/Description: Art Museum: housed in 1870, American House, cowboy hotel.
Hours & Admission Prices: Open by appointment; call for information. No charge; donations accepted. &

Emporia

DAVID TRAYLOR ZOO OF EMPORIA, 75 Soden Rd., Emporia, KS 66801-8702. Mailing Address: P.O. Box 928, Emporia, KS 66801-0928. Tel.: 620-341-4365. Fax: 620-341-4367. Facebook: Emporia Zoo.
E-mail: emporiazoo@emporia-kansas.gov
Web Site: www.emporiazoo.org
Key Personnel: Dir., Lisa Keith; Pres., Janel Wiederholt; Museum Shop Mgr., Lori Heavener.
Institution Type/Description: Zoo: located in Soden's Grove Park, one of Emporia's earliest parks.
Hours & Admission Prices: Winter: daily 10-4:30; Summer: Mon.-Tues. & Thurs.-Sat. 10-4:30, Wed. & Sun. 10-8. No charge; donations accepted. Closed Thanksgiving, Christmas, New Year's Day. &
Attendance: 93,765 (actual)

EMPORIA STATE UNIVERSITY - JOHNSTON GEOLOGY MUSEUM, 1200 Commercial St., Emporia, KS 66801-5087. Mailing Address: ESU Cram Science Hall, 14th and Merchant St., Emporia, KS 66801. Tel.: 620-341-5330. Fax: 620-341-6055.
E-mail: moralesm@emporia.edu
Web Site: www.emporia.edu/earthsci/museum/museum.htm
Key Personnel: Dir., Michael Morales.
Institution Type/Description: Geology Museum.

Hours & Admission Prices: Academic Year: Mon.-Fri. 8am-10pm, Sat. 8am to noon. No charge; donations accepted. Closed holidays.
Attendance: 750 (estimated)

LYON COUNTY HISTORICAL SOCIETY AND MUSEUM, 118 E. 6th Ave., Emporia, KS 66801-3922. Tel.: 620-340-6310.
E-mail: lycomu@osprey.net
Key Personnel: Exec. Dir., J. Greg Jordon; Pres. (V), Lisa Goldstein; Chm. (V), Annette Rice; Education Coord., Laura Dodge; Registrar, Jake Dalton; Asst. Registrar, Clerk & Museum Store Mgr., Carolyn Eckstrom.
Institution Type/Description: County General History Museum: housed in 1904 Carnegie Library.
Hours & Admission Prices: June-Aug. Tues.-Fri. 10-5, Sat. 1-5; Sept.-May Tues.-Sat. 1-5; other times by appointment. No charge; donations accepted. Closed major holidays. &
Attendance: 10,000 (estimated)

THE NATIONAL TEACHERS HALL OF FAME, 1 Kellogg Cir. #4017, Emporia, KS 66801. Tel.: 620-341-5660, 800-96-TEACH. Fax: 620-341-5912. Facebook: The National Teachers Hall of Fame.
E-mail: hallfame@emporia.edu
Web Site: www.nthf.org
Key Personnel: Dir., Carol Strickland; Chm. (V), Lindy Whetzel; Museum Shop Mgr., Jennifer Baldwin.
Institution Type/Description: Hall of Fame & Teaching History Museum.
Hours & Admission Prices: Call for hours. No charge; donations accepted. &
Attendance: 3,557 (estimated)

NORMAN R. EPPINK ART GALLERY, EMPORIA STATE UNIVERSITY, 1 Kellogg Cir., Emporia, KS 66801-5057. Tel.: 620-341-5246. Fax: 316-341-6246. Facebook: Eppink Art Gallery.
E-mail: reichenb@emporia.edu
Web Site: www.emporia.edu/m/www/art/eppink.htm
Key Personnel: C.E.O., Michael Shomrock; Dir., Roberta Eichenberg.
Institution Type/Description: University Art Gallery.
Hours & Admission Prices: Mon.-Fri. 9-4. No charge; donations accepted. Closed university holidays. &
Attendance: 11,000 (estimated)

RED ROCKS HISTORIC SITE, 927 Exchange St., Emporia, KS 66801-3040. Tel.: 620-342-2800. Fax: 620-342-2800. Facebook: Red Rocks State Historic Site.
E-mail: redrocks@kshs.org
Web Site: kshs.org/red_rocks
Formerly: William Allen White State Historic Site
Key Personnel: Site Admin., Ken Wick; Chm. (V), Beverly Bueller.
Institution Type/Description: Historic House: housed in the former home of William Allen White, nationally known newspaperman & author.
Hours & Admission Prices: April-Oct. Thurs.-Sat. 10-5. Adults $5, college students & children 6-18 $3; discounts to groups; members, active military & children 5 and under no charge.
Attendance: 854 (actual)

RICHARD H. SCHMIDT MUSEUM OF NATURAL HISTORY, 1200 Commercial St., Emporia State Univ., Emporia, KS 66801-5057. Mailing Address: Dept. of Biological Sciences, Box 4050, Emporia State Univ., Emporia, KS 66801. Tel.: 620-341-5311. Fax: 620-341-5607.
E-mail: wjensen1@emporia.edu
Web Site: www.emporia.edu/smnh/
Key Personnel: Dir., Dr. William Jensen.
Institution Type/Description: Natural History Museum.
Hours & Admission Prices: Mon.-Fri. 8-5. No charge. Closed school holidays. &

TOAD HOLLOW DAYLILY FARM, 1534 Rd. 170, Emporia, KS 66801-8125. Tel.: 620-343-8655.
Institution Type/Description: Botanical Garden.
Hours & Admission Prices: May-July Tues.-Sun. 10-7; other times by appointment. No charge; donations accepted.
Attendance: 550 (estimated)

Erie

MEM-ERIE HISTORICAL MUSEUM, 403 S. Main St., Erie, KS 66733. Mailing Address: 508 N. Main, Erie, KS 66733. Tel.: 620-605-8058.
E-mail: lobenhaus@cox.net
Key Personnel: Pres., Kindra Holland; Sec., Lois Carlson; Treas., Leon Obenhaus.

Institution Type/Description: Historical Society Museum.
Hours & Admission Prices: May-Sept. Wed. & Fri. 1-3; Oct.-April Fri.-Sat. 10-4; other times by appointment. No charge; donations accepted. &
Attendance: 1,880 (actual)

Eureka

GREENWOOD COUNTY HISTORICAL SOCIETY & MUSEUM, 120 W. 4th St., Eureka, KS 67045-1445. Mailing Address: P.O. Box 86, Eureka, KS 67045-0086. Tel.: 620-583-6682.
E-mail: gwhistory@sbcglobal.net
Web Site: gwhistory.com
Key Personnel: Pres., Mike Pitko; Vice Pres., Mike French; Sec., Hazel Russell; Treas., Sue Williams; Historian, Faith Butler.
Institution Type/Description: Historical Society Museum.
Hours & Admission Prices: Mon.-Fri. 10-12 & 1-4, Sat. by appointment only. No charge; donations accepted. Closed national holidays. &
Attendance: 1,100 (estimated)

Florence

HARVEY HOUSE MUSEUM, 221 Marion, Florence, KS 66851-1263. Mailing Address: P.O. Box 143, Florence, KS 66851-0143. Tel.: 620-878-4296.
E-mail: info@florenceks.com
Web Site: www.florenceks.com
Key Personnel: Pres., Bob Harris; Vice Pres., Shirley Grinstead; Treas., Edna M. Robinson; Sec., Marjorie Jackson.
Institution Type/Description: Historic Building: 1878 first Fred Harvey Restaurant-Hotel.
Hours & Admission Prices: By appointment. No charge; donations accepted. Closed New Year's Day; Easter; Thanksgiving; Christmas. &
Attendance: 700 (estimated)

Fort Dodge

FORT DODGE MUSEUM - KANSAS SOLDIERS HOME, 714 Sheridan - Unit 128, Fort Dodge, KS 67843. Tel.: 620-227-2121.
E-mail: info@forttours.org
Key Personnel: Supt., David E. Smith.
Institution Type/Description: History Museum.
Hours & Admission Prices: Museum: daily 1-4. Grounds: daily dawn to dusk.

Fort Leavenworth

FORT LEAVENWORTH HISTORICAL SOCIETY, Gift Shop-Post Museum, 100 Reynolds Ave., Fort Leavenworth, KS 66027. Mailing Address: P.O. Box 3356, Fort Leavenworth, KS 66027-0356. Tel.: 913-651-7440. Facebook: Fort Leavenworth Historical Society.
E-mail: flhsgs@kc.rr.com
Web Site: www.ftlvnhistsoc.org
Institution Type/Description: Historical Society.
Hours & Admission Prices: Mon.-Fri. 9-4, Sat. 11-4. No charge; donations accepted. &
Attendance: 50,000 (actual)

FRONTIER ARMY MUSEUM, 100 Reynolds Ave., Fort Leavenworth, KS 66027-2334. Tel.: 913-684-3767.
E-mail: usarmy.leavenworth.tradoc.mbx.csi-frontier-army-museum@mail.mil
Web Site: www.armyupress.army.mil/Educational-Services/Frontier-Army-Museum/
Key Personnel: Dir., George Moore; Pres., Connie Croft.
Institution Type/Description: Military Museum: located at Fort Leavenworth.
Hours & Admission Prices: Tues.-Fri. 9-4, Sat. 10-4. No charge; donations accepted. Closed federal holidays. &
Attendance: 25,000 (estimated)

Fort Riley

FIRST TERRITORIAL CAPITOL OF KANSAS, Bldg. 693, Huebner Rd., K-18, Fort Riley, KS 66442. Mailing Address: P.O. Box 381, Junction City, KS 66441-0381. Tel.: 785-784-5535 & 238-1666.
E-mail: information@kshs.org
Web Site: www.kshs.org
Key Personnel: Cur., Ron Tedder.
Institution Type/Description: Historic House Museum: 1855 two-story stone structure that served as the first territorial capitol of Kansas.

Hours & Admission Prices: March-Oct. Fri.-Sun. 1-5; Winter: call for hours. No charge; donations accepted. Closed major holidays. &
Attendance: 493 (actual)

U.S. CAVALRY MUSEUM, Bldg. 205, Fort Riley, KS 66442. Mailing Address: Bldg. 500 Huebner Rd., Fort Riley, KS 66442. Tel.: 785-239-2737. Fax: 785-239-6243.
E-mail: robert.j.smith906.civ@mail.mil
Key Personnel: C.E.O., Robert J. Smith, Ph.D.; Exhibit Specialist, Ron Doyle.
Institution Type/Description: Military Museum: housed in 1855 building used as a hospital, 1855-1890 & as post headquarters 1890-1948.
Hours & Admission Prices: Mon.-Sat. 9-4:30, Sun. 12-4:30. No charge; donations accepted. Closed New Year's Day; Easter; Thanksgiving; Christmas. &
Attendance: 49,176 (actual)

Fort Scott

FORT SCOTT NATIONAL HISTORIC SITE, Old Fort Blvd., Fort Scott, KS 66701. Mailing Address: P.O. Box 918, Fort Scott, KS 66701-0918. Tel.: 620-223-0310. Fax: 620-223-0188.
E-mail: fosc_superintendent@nps.gov
Web Site: www.nps.gov/fosc
Key Personnel: Supt., Betty Boyko; Chief Interpretation & Resource Management, Holly Baker; Program Coord., Bill Fischer; Cooperating Assoc. Coord., Barak Geertsen.
Institution Type/Description: Historic Site: 1842 restored & reconstructed Fort Scott.
Hours & Admission Prices: April-Nov. daily 8-5; Dec.-March daily 8:30-4:30. No charge; donations accepted. Closed New Year's Day; Thanksgiving; Christmas. &
Attendance: 26,650 (actual)

Fredonia

STONE HOUSE GALLERY, 320 N. 7th St., Fredonia, KS 66736-1337. Mailing Address: P.O. Box 355, Fredonia, KS 66736-0355. Tel.: 620-378-2052. Facebook: Fredonia Arts Council.
E-mail: stonehouse320@embarqmail.com
Key Personnel: Dir., Joan Bayles; Pres. (V), Gail Harshaw; Vice Pres., Angela Traylor.
Institution Type/Description: Art Museum: housed in 1872 Stone House.
Hours & Admission Prices: Mon.-Fri. 10-2; other times by appointment. No charge; donations accepted. Closed Federal holidays. &
Attendance: 1,000 (estimated)

WILSON COUNTY HISTORICAL SOCIETY MUSEUM, 420 N. 7th, Fredonia, KS 66736-1315. Tel.: 620-378-3965.
E-mail: wilcohisoc@twinmounds.com
Key Personnel: C.E.O. & Pres. (V), Emma Crites; Vice Pres., Christina Valentin; Sec., Mary Jean Browne; Finance Officer, Joe Bambick; Museum Shop Mgr., E. Nadine Dishman.
Institution Type/Description: General Museum: located in old county jail.
Hours & Admission Prices: Mon.-Fri. 12-4:30. No charge; donations accepted. Closed national holidays.
Attendance: 550 (actual)

Galena

GALENA MINING & HISTORICAL MUSEUM, 319 W. Seventh St., Galena, KS 66739-1211. Tel.: 620-783-2192. Fax: 620-783-1974.
Key Personnel: Pres. (V), Gene Russell; Treas., Don Noe.
Institution Type/Description: Mining Museum: housed in the old Katy Train Depot.
Hours & Admission Prices: Mon.-Sat. 9-11:30 & 1-3:30; Winter: reduced hours in the afternoon. No charge; donations accepted. Closed New Year's Day; Memorial Day; Independence Day; Labor Day; Thanksgiving; Christmas.
Attendance: 1,200 (estimated)

Galva

GALVA HISTORICAL MUSEUM, 204 S. Main, Galva, KS 67443. Mailing Address: P.O. Box 505, Galva, KS 67443. Tel.: 620-654-3343.
Key Personnel: Chm. (V), Naomi Ford.
Institution Type/Description: History Museum.
Hours & Admission Prices: 1st Sun. each month 2-4, 3rd Thurs. each month 7 pm-9 pm, 2nd Sat. each month 10 am to noon; other times by appointment. No charge; donations accepted. &
Attendance: 250 (estimated)

Garden City

FINNEY COUNTY KANSAS HISTORICAL MUSEUM, 403 S. 4th, Garden City, KS 67846. Mailing Address: P.O. Box 796, Garden City, KS 67846-0796. Tel.: 620-272-3664. Fax: 620-272-3662. Facebook: Finney County Museum.
E-mail: fico.historical@gcnet.com
Web Site: www.finneycounty.org/history
Key Personnel: Dir. & C.E.O., Steve Quakenbush; Pres., Carla Algrim; Asst. Dir., Laurie Oshel; Registrar, Yadira Hernandez; Mgr. Collections, Todd Roberts; Education & Museum Shop Mgr., Johnetta Hebrlee.
Institution Type/Description: History Museum.
Hours & Admission Prices: Winter: daily 1-5; Summer: Mon.-Sat. 10-5, Sun. 1-5. No charge; donations accepted.
Attendance: 22,000 (actual)

LEE RICHARDSON ZOO IN FINNUP PARK, 312 E. Finnup Dr., Garden City, KS 67846-6561. Tel.: 620-276-1250. Fax: 620-276-1259.
E-mail: zoo.department@gardencityks.us
Web Site: www.leerichardsonzoo.org
Key Personnel: Dir., Kristi Newland; Society Dir., Jessica Norton.
Institution Type/Description: Zoo, Arboretum & Nature Center.
Hours & Admission Prices: April to Labor Day daily 8-7; Sept.-March daily 8-5. Vehicles $10; members & pedestrians no charge. AZA reciprocal. Closed New Year's Day; Thanksgiving; Christmas.
Attendance: 232,496 (estimated)

Gardner

GARDNER HISTORICAL MUSEUM, 204 W. Main St., Gardner, KS 66030. Mailing Address: P.O. Box 442, Gardner, KS 66030. Tel.: 913-856-4447.
E-mail: gardnerhistoricalmuseum@centurylink.net
Web Site: www.gardnerhistoricalmuseum.com
Institution Type/Description: History Museum: housed in the Herman B. Foster house; built in 1893. Listed on the National Register of Historic Places.
Hours & Admission Prices: Gardner: Fri. 4-7, Sat.-Tues. 1-4; tours by appointment. Bray House: Tues.-Wed. & Sat. 1-4. No charge; donations accepted.

Garnett

ANDERSON COUNTY HISTORICAL MUSEUM, 406 W. 4th Ave., Garnett, KS 66032. Mailing Address: P.O. Box 183, Garnett, KS 66032. Tel.: 785-304-2810 & 448-5740.
E-mail: contact_us@historyandersoncoks.org
Web Site: www.historyandersoncoks.org
Key Personnel: Chm. & Pres. (V), Kristie Kinney.
Institution Type/Description: Local History Museum: 1886 home & carriage house of Dr. Harris; Longfellow school building.
Hours & Admission Prices: Oct.-May Tues.-Sat. 1-4. No charge; donations accepted.
Attendance: 1,800 (actual)

THE WALKER ART COLLECTION OF THE GARNETT PUBLIC LIBRARY, 125 W. 4th Ave., Garnett, KS 66032-1313. Tel.: 785-448-5496. Fax: 913-448-3936 & 5555.
E-mail: joyce@garnettks.net
Web Site: www.garnettks.net
Key Personnel: Chm. (V), Barbara Foltz; Dir., Robert Cugno.
Institution Type/Description: Art Gallery.
Hours & Admission Prices: Mon.-Tues. & Thurs. 10-8, Wed. & Fri. 10-5:30, Sat. 10-4. No charge; donations accepted. Closed New Year's Day; Presidents' Day; Memorial Day; Independence Day; Labor Day; Veterans Day; Thanksgiving; Christmas.
Attendance: 10,000 (estimated)

Girard

GIRARD HISTORY MUSEUM, Summit St. and Buffalo St., Girard, KS 66743-1543. Mailing Address: P.O. Box 132, Girard, KS 66743. Tel.: 620-724-4570. Facebook.
Formerly: Historical Museum of Crawford County
Institution Type/Description: History Museum: housed in the former St. John's Episcopal Church. Listed on the National Historic Register.
Hours & Admission Prices: Temporarily closed for renovations.

Glasco

OSBORNE COUNTY HISTORICAL MUSEUM, 929 N. 2nd St., Glasco, KS 67445. Mailing Address: P.O. Box 572, Glasco, KS 67445-0572. Tel.: 785-346-2881 & 2798.
Institution Type/Description: History Museum.
Hours & Admission Prices: Memorial Day to Labor Day Mon.-Thurs. 2-4; other times by appointment.

Goddard

LAKE AFTON PUBLIC OBSERVATORY, 25,000 W. 39th St., S., (Mac Arthur Rd.), Goddard, KS 67052. Mailing Address: 1845 Fairmont, Wichita, KS 67260-0032. Tel.: 316-978-3191. Fax: 316-978-3350.
E-mail: observatory@wichita.edu
Web Site: webs.wichita.edu/lapo
Key Personnel: Dir., Greg Novacek; Program Mgr., Robert Henry.
Institution Type/Description: Astronomy Museum.
Hours & Admission Prices: March-Sept. Fri.-Sat. call for hours; Oct.-Feb. Fri.-Sat. 7:30 pm-10 pm. Adults 13 & over $6, children 6-12 $4; children under 6 & members no charge. Closed New Year's Eve & Day; Christmas Eve, Day & week.
Attendance: 4,000 (estimated)

TANGANYIKA WILDLIFE PARK, 1000 S. Hawkins Lane, Goddard, KS 67052. Tel.: 316-794-8954. Fax: 316-794-2153.
E-mail: twp@twpark.com
Web Site: www.twpark.com
Key Personnel: Dir., Jim Fouts; Asst. Dir., Matt Fouts.
Institution Type/Description: Zoo.
Hours & Admission Prices: April & Oct. Fri.-Sun. 10:30-5; May-Sept. daily 9-5. Adults $13.95, seniors 60-89 $10.95, children 3-12 $8.95; seniors 90 & over and children under 3 no charge.

Goessel

MENNONITE HERITAGE & AGRICULTURAL MUSEUM, 200 N. Poplar St., Goessel, KS 67053. Mailing Address: P.O. Box 231, Goessel, KS 67053-0231. Tel.: 620-367-8200.
E-mail: mhmuseum@mtelco.net
Web Site: www.goesselmuseum.com
Formerly: Mennonite Heritage Museum
Key Personnel: Pres. & Chm. (V), Steven Banman; Dir., Cur. & Museum Shop Mgr., Marjorie J. Shoemaker; Treas., Aileen Esau.
Institution Type/Description: History Museum.
Hours & Admission Prices: March-April & Oct.-Nov. Tues.-Sat. 12-4; May-Sept. Tues.-Sat. 10-5; groups of 10 or more by appointment. Adults $4, children 7-12 $2; discounts to seniors and AAA & AAM members; members no charge. Closed major holidays.
Attendance: 1,100 (estimated)

Goodland

CARNEGIE ARTS CENTER, 120 W. 12th, Goodland, KS 67735. Mailing Address: P.O. Box 526, Goodland, KS 67735. Tel.: 785-890-6442. Facebook: Goodland Carnegie Arts Center.
E-mail: gldarts@st-tel.net
Web Site: goodlandarts.org
Key Personnel: Interim Dir., Sherry Brandvit.
Institution Type/Description: Art Gallery.
Hours & Admission Prices: Tues.-Thurs. 12-4, Sat. 10-4. No charge; donations accepted.

HIGH PLAINS MUSEUM, 1717 Cherry, Goodland, KS 67735-3200. Tel.: 785-890-4595. Fax: 785-890-4532.
E-mail: museum@cityofgoodland.org
Web Site: www.highplainsmuseum.org
Key Personnel: Dir., Samantha Philbrick.
Institution Type/Description: History Museum.
Hours & Admission Prices: June-Aug. Sun. 1-5, Mon. & Wed.-Sat. 9-5, Sept.-May Mon. & Wed.-Sat. 9-5. No charge; donations accepted. Closed major holidays.
Attendance: 3,000 (actual)

SHERMAN COUNTY HISTORICAL SOCIETY - THE ENNIS-HANDY HOUSE, 202 W. 13th St., Goodland, KS 67735-2806. Tel.: 785-899-6773.
Institution Type/Description: Historic House Museum: built in 1907.

Hours & Admission Prices: Wed.-Mon. 1-5. Suggested Donations: adults $5, senior citizens $4, children 3-11 $3; discounts to school groups. Closed Thanksgiving; Christmas.
Attendance: 350 (actual)

Great Bend

BARTON COUNTY HISTORICAL MUSEUM & VILLAGE, 85 S. Hwy. 281, Great Bend, KS 67530. Mailing Address: P.O. Box 1091, Great Bend, KS 67530-1091. Tel.: 620-793-5125. Fax: 620-793-5125 (call first). Facebook: Barton County Historical Society Museum and Village.
E-mail: bchsdirector@gmail.com
Web Site: www.bartoncountymuseum.org
Formerly: Barton County Historical Society Village & Museum
Key Personnel: C.E.O. & Chm., Beverly Komarek; Pres. (V), Rose Kelly; Registrar, Leslie Helsec.
Institution Type/Description: Historic Village.
Hours & Admission Prices: Tues.-Fri. 10-5, Sat.-Sun. 1-5. Adults $4; members no charge. Blue Star Museum. Closed most major holidays. ♿
Attendance: 5,000 (estimated)

GREAT BEND-BRIT SPAUGH ZOO & GREAT BEND RAPTOR CENTER, 2123 N. Main St., Great Bend, KS 67530. Mailing Address: P.O. Box 215, Great Bend, KS 67530. Tel.: 620-793-4226. Fax: 620-791-5001.
E-mail: scott@greatbendzoo.com
Web Site: greatbendzoo.com
Key Personnel: Dir., Scott Gregory.
Institution Type/Description: Zoo.
Hours & Admission Prices: Mon.-Thurs. 9-4:30, Fri.-Sun. 10-7. No charge; donations accepted. ♿
Attendance: 55,000 (estimated)

SHAFER GALLERY - BARTON COMMUNITY COLLEGE, 245 N.E. 30 Rd., Great Bend, KS 67530-9107. Tel.: 800-722-6842, 620-792-9342. Facebook: Shafer Gallery - Barton Community College.
E-mail: barnesd@bartonccc.edu
Web Site: www.bartonccc.edu/community/artsentertainment/shafergallery
Key Personnel: Dir., David E. Barnes.
Institution Type/Description: Art Gallery.
Hours & Admission Prices: Mon.-Fri. 10-5, Sun. 1-4; groups by appointment. No charge; donations accepted. Closed college-related holidays. ♿
Attendance: 7,000 (estimated)

Greensburg

BIG WELL, 315 S. Sycamore, Greensburg, KS 67054-1758.
Key Personnel: Museum Shop Mgr., Rich Stephenson.
Institution Type/Description: General Museum.
Hours & Admission Prices: Memorial Day to Labor Day 8-8; Winter: Mon.-Sat. 9-5, Sun. 1-5. Adults $2, children $1.50. Closed Thanksgiving; Christmas.
Attendance: 42,672 (actual)

Grenola

GRENOLA HISTORICAL SOCIETY - GRENOLA ELEVATOR MUSEUM, 313 N. Main St., Grenola, KS 67346. Mailing Address: P.O. Box 111, Grenola, KS 67346. Tel.: 620-358-3241.
E-mail: dorothykeplinger@yahoo.com
Key Personnel: Chm. (V), Dorothy Keplinger.
Institution Type/Description: Historical Society Museum: housed in the former Grenola Mill and Elevator.
Hours & Admission Prices: Sat. 1-5, Sun. 2-5, open anytime by appointment. No charge, donations accepted. Closed Dec.-April. ♿
Attendance: 200 (estimated)

Halstead

HALSTEAD HERITAGE MUSEUM & DEPOT, 116 E. First, Halstead, KS 67056-1713. Mailing Address: P.O. Box 88, Halstead, KS 67056-0088. Tel.: 316-835-2267.
E-mail: historicalsociety@halsteadkansas.com
Web Site: historicalsociety.halsteadkansas.com
Key Personnel: Pres. (V), Helen Collins; Sec., Carolyn Williams.
Institution Type/Description: History Museum. housed in the former Halstead Railway Station; built in 1917.

Hours & Admission Prices: Sat.-Sun. 2-5; other times by appointment. No charge; donations accepted. ♿
Attendance: 400 (estimated)

KANSAS LEARNING CENTER FOR HEALTH, 505 Main St., Halstead, KS 67056-2233. Mailing Address: P.O. Box 288, Halstead, KS 67056-0288. Tel.: 316-835-2662. Fax: 316-835-2755. Facebook: Kansas Learning Center for Health.
E-mail: brendas@leaningcenter.org
Web Site: www.learningcenter.org
Key Personnel: C.E.O. & Dir., Carrie M. Herman; Pres. (V), Jack Bender.
Institution Type/Description: Health Museum.
Hours & Admission Prices: Mon.-Fri. 9-4. Full Day Program: $13; Half Day Program: $9; Self-Guided Tour: $6. Closed New Year's Day; Easter; Memorial Day; Independence Day; Labor Day; Thanksgiving; Christmas. ♿
Attendance: 10,000 (estimated)

Hanover

HOLLENBERG PONY EXPRESS STATION STATE HISTORIC SITE, 2889 23rd Rd., Hanover, KS 66945-8901. Tel.: 785-337-2635. Fax: 785-337-2635. Facebook: Hollenberg Pony Express Station State Historic Site.
E-mail: hollenberg@kshs.org
Web Site: www.kshs.org/hollenberg
Formerly: Hollenberg Station State Historic Site
Key Personnel: Site Admin., Jarrett M. Willet; Pres. Friends Group, Gary Minge.
Institution Type/Description: Historic Site: 1857 Pony Express station.
Hours & Admission Prices: May-Oct. Wed.-Sat. 10-5. Adults $3, students $1; discounts to groups; children under 5 & KSHS members no charge. Closed holidays. ♿
Attendance: 567 (actual)

Harper

HARPER CITY HISTORICAL SOCIETY, 804 E. 12th St., Harper, KS 67058-1804. Mailing Address: 708 W. 14th, Harper, KS 67058-1528. Tel.: 620-896-7877.
E-mail: gbellar@att.net
Key Personnel: Pres., Mary Helen Baker; Sec., Gail Bellar; Treas., Mary Helen Baker.
Institution Type/Description: Historical Society Museum: housed in a former German Apostolic Church; built in 1887.
Hours & Admission Prices: By appointment. No charge; donations accepted.
Attendance: 300 (estimated)

Hays

BERENS' ANTIQUE FARM MACHINERY, 1915 Holmes Rd., Hays, KS 67601-2520. Tel.: 785-735-9364.
Institution Type/Description: Farm Machinery Museum.
Hours & Admission Prices: By appointment. No charge.

ELLIS COUNTY HISTORICAL SOCIETY, 100 W. 7th St., Hays, KS 67601-4429. Tel.: 785-628-2624. Fax: 785-628-0386.
E-mail: office@elliscountyhistoricalsociety.org
Web Site: www.elliscountyhistoricalmuseum.org
Key Personnel: Pres., Tom Drees; Treas., Brad Boyer; Cur., Elisha Beck; Archivist & Dir., Janet Johannes; Dir. & Museum Shop Mgr., Sharon Behrman.
Institution Type/Description: History Museum.
Hours & Admission Prices: June-Aug. Tues.-Fri. 10-5, Sat. 1-5; Sept.-May Tues.-Fri. 10-5. Adults $4; members no charge.
Attendance: 3,000 (actual)

FORT HAYS STATE HISTORIC SITE, 1472 Hwy. 183 Alt., Hays, KS 67601-9212. Tel.: 785-625-6812. Fax: 785-625-6812. Facebook: Fort Hays State Historic Site.
E-mail: thefort@kshs.org
Web Site: www.kshs.org/fort_hays
Key Personnel: Exec. Dir. KSHS, Jennie Chinn.
Institution Type/Description: Military Museum; Visitors & Tourist Information Center.
Hours & Admission Prices: Tues.-Sat. 9-5. Adults $5, students $1; KHS, Friends and children 5 & under no charge. Closed legal holidays. ♿
Attendance: 3,142 (actual)

HAYS ARTS CENTER GALLERY, 112 E. 11th St., Hays, KS 67601. Tel.: 785-625-7522.
E-mail: bmeder1038@aol.com

Key Personnel: Exec. Dir., Brenda K. Meder.
Institution Type/Description: Art Gallery.
Hours & Admission Prices: Mon.-Fri. 10-4, Sat. 10-1.

KANSAS MERCI BOXCAR MUSEUM, E. 13th St. & Canterbury Dr., Hays, KS 67601. Tel.: 785-625-3813.
Institution Type/Description: History Museum.
Hours & Admission Prices: By appointment.

STERNBERG MUSEUM OF NATURAL HISTORY, Fort Hays State University, 3000 Sternberg Dr., Hays, KS 67601-2006. Tel.: 785-628-5516. Fax: 785-628-4518.
E-mail: rebarrick@fhsu.edu
Web Site: sternberg.fhsu.edu
Key Personnel: C.E.O. & Cur. Paleontology, Reese Barrick; Cur. Mammals & Adjunct Cur. Birds & Mammals, E. Finck; Cur. Plants, J.R. Thomasson; Asst. Cur. Birds, G. Farley; Asst. Cur. Insects, R. Packauskas; Museum Educator, David Levering; Chief Cur. & Cur. Vertebrate Paleontology, Laura Wilson; Collection Mgr., Curtis Schmidt; Exhibits Dir., G. Walters; Office Mgr., A. Klein; Operations Mgr., James Helget; Education Asst., Thea Haugen; Mgr. Visitor Svcs., Brad Penka; Research Assoc. Herptiles, T. Taggart; Adjunct Cur. Vertebrate Paleontology, Mike Everhart; Adjunct Cur. Vert Paleontology, K. Shimada; Adjunct Cur. Vert Paleontology, B. Schumacher; Asst. Cur. Fishes, W. Stark; Building Maintenance, G. Beilman.
Institution Type/Description: Natural History Museum.
Hours & Admission Prices: April-Sept. Mon.-Sat. 9-6, Sun. 1-6; Oct.-March Tues.-Sat. 9-6, Sun. 1-6. Adults $9, seniors $7, children $6; ASTC members no charge. &
Attendance: 39,273 (actual)

Herington

HERINGTON HISTORICAL SOCIETY & MUSEUM, INC. - SE DICKINSON COUNTY, 800 S. Broadway, Herington, KS 67449-3060. Tel.: 785-258-2842.
E-mail: heringtonmuseum@att.net
Formerly: Tri-County Historical Society & Museum, Inc.
Key Personnel: Dir., Museum Shop Mgr. & Membership Chm., Jolene Bradford; Pres., Verl Schlesener; Sec., Paula Strickland; Treas., Helen Mitchell.
Institution Type/Description: General & Rock Island Railroad History Museum.
Hours & Admission Prices: Tues.-Fri. 1-5. No charge; donations accepted. Closed New Years Eve & Day; Thanksgiving; Christmas Eve, Day & week. &
Attendance: 500 (estimated)

Hiawatha

AG MUSEUM & WINDMILL LANE, 301 E. Iowa St., Hiawatha, KS 66434-9826. Tel.: 785-742-3702. Fax: 785-742-3330.
E-mail: bchsdirector@yahoo.com
Web Site: www.bckshistory.com
Key Personnel: Dir. & Cur., Eric Oldham; Pres. (V), Jere Bruning.
Institution Type/Description: Historical Society Museum.
Hours & Admission Prices: Tues.-Fri. 10-4, Sat. 10-2. Adults $5.
Attendance: 500 (estimated)

MEMORIAL AUDITORIUM AND MUSEUM, 611 Utah St., Hiawatha, KS 66434-2319. Tel.: 785-742-3330. Fax: 785-742-3330.
E-mail: bchsdirector@yahoo.com
Web Site: www.bckshistory.com
Key Personnel: Dir., Eric Oldham; Pres. (V), Jere Bruning.
Institution Type/Description: Historical Society Museum.
Hours & Admission Prices: May 2-Oct. Mon.-Fri. 10-12 & 1-3, Sat. 10-2. Adults $5. &
Attendance: 500

Highland

YOST ART GALLERY, Highland Community College, 101 N. Elmira, Highland, KS 66035. Tel.: 785-442-6000.
E-mail: jtyler@highlandcc.edu
Key Personnel: Dir., Janet Tyler.
Institution Type/Description: Art Gallery.
Hours & Admission Prices: Mon.-Fri. 8:30-4.

Hill City

GRAHAM COUNTY HISTORICAL SOCIETY, 103 E. Cherry, Hill City, KS 67642. Tel.: 785-421-2543.
E-mail: queenb@ruraltel.net

Web Site: www.grahamhistorical.ruraltel.net
Institution Type/Description: Historical Society Museum.
Hours & Admission Prices: Fri.-Sat. 1-4.

Hillsboro

HILLSBORO MUSEUMS, 501 S. Ash St., Hillsboro, KS 67063-1531. Mailing Address: P.O. Box 125, Hillsboro, KS 67063-0125. Tel.: 620-947-3775.
E-mail: hillsboro_museums@yahoo.com
Web Site: www.hillsboro-museums.com
Formerly: Hillsboro Historical Society & Museum
Key Personnel: C.E.O., Stan R. Harder.
Institution Type/Description: History Museum.
Hours & Admission Prices: March-Dec. Tues.-Fri. 10-12 & 1:30-4, Sat.-Sun. 2-4. Adults $3, students $1; discounts to AAM members. Closed holidays. &
Attendance: 3,000 (estimated)

Hoisington

HOISINGTON HISTORICAL SOCIETY MUSEUM, 120 E. 2nd St., Hoisington, KS 67544. Mailing Address: Hoisington Historical Society, 358 West 8th St., Hoisington, KS 67544. Tel.: 620-653-4320, 2857 & 4683.
E-mail: customerservice@hoisingtonhistoricalsociety.org
Web Site: www.hoisingtonhistoricalsociety.org
Key Personnel: Pres. (V), Lon Palmer.
Institution Type/Description: Historical Society Museum; building built in 1905.
Hours & Admission Prices: 1st & 3rd Sat. each month 1-3. No charge; donations accepted.
Attendance: 300 (estimated)

Holton

JACKSON COUNTY HISTORICAL SOCIETY, 216 New York Ave., Holton, KS 66436-1738. Tel.: 785-364-4991. Facebook: Jackson County Historical Society.
E-mail: jacohistsoc@gmail.com
Key Personnel: Chm. (V), Anna Wilhelm; Pres. (V), Suzette McCord-Rogers.
Institution Type/Description: Historical Society Museum.
Hours & Admission Prices: May-Oct. Fri. 10-4; other times by appointment. No charge; donations accepted. &
Attendance: 500 (actual)

Howard

BENSON HISTORICAL MUSEUM, 145 S. Wabash, Howard, KS 67349.
Key Personnel: Chm. (V), Gleneva Winn.
Institution Type/Description: History Museum.
Hours & Admission Prices: By appointment. No charge.

Hugoton

STEVENS COUNTY GAS AND HISTORICAL MUSEUM, 905 S. Adams, Hugoton, KS 67951-2817. Mailing Address: P.O. Box 87, Hugoton, KS 67951-0087. Tel.: 620-544-8751. Fax: 620-428-6553.
Key Personnel: Pres., Jim Bell; Cur. & Museum Shop Mgr., Stanley McGill.
Institution Type/Description: History Museum Complex.
Hours & Admission Prices: June-Sept. Mon.-Fri. 10-12 & 1-5, Sat. 1-4, Sun. by appointment; Sept.-June Mon.-Fri. 1-5, Sat. 1-4, Sun. by appointment. No charge; donations accepted. Closed Easter; Memorial Day; Labor Day; Columbus Day; Veterans Day; Thanksgiving; Christmas. &
Attendance: 1,217 (actual)

Humboldt

HUMBOLDT HISTORICAL MUSEUM, 416 N. Second, Humboldt, KS 66748-1402. Mailing Address: P.O. Box 63, Humboldt, KS 66748-0063. Tel.: 620-473-5055.
E-mail: rrthompson504@yahoo.com
Web Site: www.humboldtksmuseum.com
Key Personnel: Dir., Roland E. Thompson; Sec., Michelle McDown; Treas., Ellen Lee.
Institution Type/Description: History Museum.
Hours & Admission Prices: Open year round by appointment. No charge. &
Attendance: 1,525 (actual)

Hutchinson

COSMOSPHERE, 1100 N. Plum, Hutchinson, KS 67501-1418. Tel.: 620-662-2305. Fax: 620-662-3693.
E-mail: info@cosmo.org
Web Site: www.cosmo.org
Formerly: Kansas Cosmosphere and Space Center
Key Personnel: C.E.O., Richard Hollowell; Pres. & C.O.O., Jim Remar; CFO, Steven Birdsall; Vice Pres. Devel. & Mktg., Mimi Meredith; Retail Mgr., Steve Barnum.
Institution Type/Description: Space Museum.
Hours & Admission Prices: Summer & Christmas Breaks: Mon.-Sat. 9-7, Sun. 12-7; Fall, Spring & Winter: Mon.-Thurs. 9-5, Fri.-Sat. 9-7, Sun. 12-5. All Day Mission Pass: adults $26, senior citizens 60 & over $23, children 4-12 $17; children 2 & under no charge. Single Venue: adults $8, senior citizens 60 & over $7, children 3-12 $6.50. Closed Easter; Thanksgiving; Christmas. &
Attendance: 120,000 (actual)

HUTCHINSON ART CENTER, 405 N. Washington, Hutchinson, KS 67501-4852. Tel.: 620-663-1081. Fax: 620-663-6367.
E-mail: hutchart2@hac.kscoxmail.com; hrah@hrah.kscoxmail.com
Web Site: hutchinsonartcenter.net
Key Personnel: Dir., Mark L. Rassette; Pres. (V), Jane Dronberger; Museum Shop Mgr., Beth Kammerer.
Institution Type/Description: Art Museum.
Hours & Admission Prices: Tues.-Fri. 9-5, Sat.-Sun. 1-5. No charge. &
Attendance: 5,000 (actual)

HUTCHINSON ZOO, 6 Emerson Loop E., Hutchinson, KS 67501-7500. Mailing Address: P.O. Box 1567, Hutchinson, KS 67504. Tel.: 620-694-2693. Fax: 620-694-2654. Facebook: Hutchinson Friends of the Zoo.
E-mail: janad@hutchgov.com
Web Site: www.hutchgov.com/zoo
Key Personnel: Dir., Jana Durham; Cur., Kiley Buggeln; Gift Shop Mgr., Nelda Petering.
Institution Type/Description: Zoo.
Hours & Admission Prices: Daily call for hours. No charge; donations accepted. Closed New Year's Day; Thanksgiving; Christmas.
Attendance: 48,851

RENO COUNTY MUSEUM, 100 S. Walnut, Hutchinson, KS 67501-7406. Mailing Address: P.O. Box 664, Hutchinson, KS 67504-0664. Tel.: 620-662-1184. Fax: 620-662-0236.
E-mail: marygrace@renocomuseum.org
Web Site: renocomuseum.org
Key Personnel: Exec. Dir., Linda Schmitt; Chief Cur., Jamin Landavazo.
Institution Type/Description: County History Museum.
Hours & Admission Prices: Museum: Tues.-Fri. 9-5, Sat. 11-5. Office: Mon.-Fri. 8-5. No charge; donations accepted. &
Attendance: 22,129 (actual)

STRATACA, 3650 E. Ave. G, Hutchinson, KS 67501-8200. Tel.: 620-662-1425, 866-755-3450. Fax: 620-259-6134. Facebook: Strataca.
Web Site: www.underkansas.org
Formerly: Kansas Underground Salt Museum
Key Personnel: Volunteer Coord., Tonya Gehring; Maintenance, Dave Unruh; Customer Svc., Sarah Voran.
Institution Type/Description: Mining Museum: housed in a salt mine.
Hours & Admission Prices: Tues.-Sat. 9-6, Sun. 1-6. Adults $14.35, seniors 60 & over, active military & AAA members $12.75; Reno County residents & children 4-12 $9.05.

Independence

INDEPENDENCE HISTORICAL MUSEUM & ART CENTER, 123 N. 8th, Independence, KS 67301-3501. Mailing Address: P.O. Box 294, Independence, KS 67301-0294. Tel.: 620-331-3515.
E-mail: museum123@cableone.net
Web Site: independencehistoricalmuseum.org
Formerly: Independence Museum
Key Personnel: Pres., Ray Rothgeb; Dir., Sylvia Augustine; Museum Shop Mgr., Ellie Culp.
Institution Type/Description: History & Art Museum.
Hours & Admission Prices: Tues.-Sat. 10-4; call for special tours. Adults $3; discounts to NARM members; members no charge. Closed national holidays. &
Attendance: 2,500 (actual)

INDEPENDENCE SCIENCE AND TECHNOLOGY CENTER, 125 S. Pennsylvania, Independence, KS 67301-3525. Tel.: 620-331-1999. Facebook.
E-mail: indyscitech@valnet.net
Web Site: www.indyscitech.org
Key Personnel: Dir., Amy Finney; Chm. (V), Ned Stichman; Pres. (V), Lloyd Harding.
Institution Type/Description: Science Center.
Hours & Admission Prices: Mon.-Sat. 1-5. Admission $3; members & children under 3 no charge.
Attendance: 1,050 (estimated)

LITTLE HOUSE ON THE PRAIRIE MUSEUM, 2507 CR 3000, Independence, KS 67301-7265. Tel.: 620-289-4238. Facebook; Little House on the Prairie Museum.
E-mail: lhopmuseumks@gmail.com
Web Site: www.littlehouseontheprairiemuseum.com
Formerly: Little House on the Prairie Historic Site
Key Personnel: Dir, Jean Kurtis Schodorf.
Institution Type/Description: Historic House: official site of Little House on the Prairie from Laura Ingalls Wilder's books.
Hours & Admission Prices: April -Oct. Mon.-Sat. 10-5, Sun. 1-5. No charge; donations accepted.
Attendance: 20,000 (estimated)

RALPH MITCHELL ZOO, Riverside Park, Oak & Park St., Independence, KS 67301. Mailing Address: P.O. Box 9, Independence, KS 67301-0009. Tel.: 620-332-2513.
Institution Type/Description: Zoo.
Hours & Admission Prices: Call for hours.

Ingalls

SANTA FE TRAIL MUSEUM OF GRAY CO., INC., 204 S. Main St., Ingalls, KS 67853. Mailing Address: P.O. Box 74, Ingalls, KS 67853-0074. Tel.: 620-335-5220.
E-mail: dlmkwend@ucom.net
Key Personnel: Chm. (V) & Pres. (V), Dan Thomas; Sec. & Treas., Linda Hirschler; Dir. Museum Shop Mgr., Debbie Milne.
Institution Type/Description: Historical Site & Local History Museum: housed in two Santa Fe railroad depot buildings.
Hours & Admission Prices: May-Oct. Mon.-Sat. 9-11 & 1-4; other times by appointment; Nov.-April by appointment only. No charge; donations accepted. &
Attendance: 256 (actual)

Iola

ALLEN COUNTY HISTORICAL SOCIETY, 20 S. Washington Ave., Iola, KS 66749-3204. Tel.: 620-365-3051.
E-mail: info@allencountyhistory.org
Web Site: www.allencountyhistory.org
Key Personnel: Exec. Dir. & Cur., Elyssa Jackson; Pres. (V), Leon Smith.
Institution Type/Description: Local History Museum.
Hours & Admission Prices: May-Oct. Tues.-Sat. 12:30-4; Nov.-April Tues.-Sat. 2-4. No charge; donations accepted. &
Attendance: 1,888 (actual)

ALLEN COUNTY JAIL MUSEUM, 203 N. Jefferson Ave., Iola, KS 66749. Mailing Address: 20 S. Washington, Iola, KS 66749. Tel.: 620-365-3051. Facebook; Allen County Jail Museum.
E-mail: info@.allencountyhistory.org
Web Site: www.allencountyhistory.org
Formerly: Old Jail Museum
Key Personnel: Dir., Elyssa Jackson; Pres. (V), Leon Smith.
Institution Type/Description: Historic Building: housed in the former Allen County Jail; built in 1869. Listed on the National Register of Historic Places.
Hours & Admission Prices: Tours: May-Sept. Tues.-Sat. 1:30; other times by appointment. No charge; donations accepted.
Attendance: 325 (actual)

THE MAJOR GENERAL FREDERICK FUNSTON BOYHOOD HOME AND MUSEUM, 14 S. Washington Ave., Iola, KS 66749-3204. Tel.: 620-365-3051. Facebook; The Major General Frederick.
E-mail: info@allencountyhistory.org
Web Site: www.allencountyhistory.org
Key Personnel: Exec. Dir. & Cur., Elyssa Jackson; Pres. (V), Leon Smith.

Institution Type/Description: History Museum: housed in the c.1860 Frederick Funston childhood residence, originally located on a homestead approximately five miles north of Iola.
Hours & Admission Prices: May-Oct. Tues.-Sat. 12:30-4; Nov.-April Tues.-Sat. 2-4; other times by appointment. No charge; donations accepted. &
Attendance: 460 (actual)

Jennings

CZECH MEMORIAL MUSEUM, 114 S. Kansas Ave., Jennings, KS 67643.
E-mail: swilliby@oberlinkansas.gov
Key Personnel: Chm. (V), Mary Wahlmeier.
Institution Type/Description: History Museum: housed in a former United Methodist Church Royal Neighbor Lodge Bldg.
Hours & Admission Prices: By appointment. No charge; donations accepted. &
Attendance: 1,400 (estimated)

Jetmore

HAUN MUSEUM, Rte. 2, Jetmore, KS 67854. Tel.: 620-357-8794.
Institution Type/Description: History Museum.
Hours & Admission Prices: Memorial Day to Labor Day Sat. 9-12 & 1-5, Sun. 1-5; other times by appointment.

Jewell

PALMER MUSEUM, 108 S. Washington, Jewell, KS 66949. Mailing Address: P.O. Box 282, Jewell, KS 66949. Tel.: 785-428-3466 & 3335.
E-mail: jlc5075@psu.edu
Web Site: palmermuseum.psu.edu
Key Personnel: Chm. (V), Roberta Holbren.
Institution Type/Description: General Museum.
Hours & Admission Prices: By appointment. No charge; donations accepted.
Attendance: 480 (estimated)

Johnson

STANTON COUNTY MUSEUM, 104 E. Highland, Johnson, KS 67855. Mailing Address: P.O. Box 806, Johnson, KS 67855. Tel.: 620-492-1526. Fax: 620-492-1785.
E-mail: scmuse@pld.com
Web Site: stantoncountymuseum.org
Institution Type/Description: History Museum.
Hours & Admission Prices: Memorial Day to Labor Day & Dec. Mon.-Fri. 10:30-12 & 1-5, Sun. 1-4; other times by appointment.

Junction City

GEARY COUNTY HISTORICAL SOCIETY & MUSEUM, 530 N. Adams St., Junction City, KS 66441. Mailing Address: P.O. Box 1161, Junction City, KS 66441. Tel.: 785-238-1666. Fax: 785-238-1666 (call first). Facebook: Geary History.
E-mail: gearyhistory@gmail.com
Web Site: gchsweb.org
Key Personnel: Dir., Jamie Clark; Pres. (V), Florence Whitebread; Museum Shop Mgr., Sue Steinfort.
Institution Type/Description: Historical Society Museum.
Hours & Admission Prices: Tues.-Sun. 1-4. No charge; donations accepted. &
Attendance: 10,000 (estimated)

JUNCTION CITY ARTS COUNCIL GALLERY, 107 W. Seventh St., Junction City, KS 66441. Mailing Address: P.O. Box 403, Junction City, KS 66441-0403. Tel.: 785-762-2581.
E-mail: jcartscouncil@yahoo.com
Institution Type/Description: Art Gallery.
Hours & Admission Prices: Tues.-Fri. 9-5, Sat. 12-4.

MILFORD NATURE CENTER, 3415 Hatchery Dr., Junction City, KS 66441-8651. Tel.: 785-238-5323. Fax: 785-238-5775.
E-mail: pat.silovsky@ksoutdoors.com
Web Site: www.kdwp.state.ks.us
Key Personnel: Dir., Pat Silovsky.
Institution Type/Description: Nature Center.
Hours & Admission Prices: April-Sept. Mon.-Fri. 9-4:30, Sat.-Sun. 1-5; Oct.-March Mon.-Fri. 9-4:30. No charge; donations accepted. &
Attendance: 19,347 (estimated)

SPRING VALLEY HISTORIC SITE, K-18 & Spring Valley Rd., Junction City, KS 66441. Mailing Address: P.O. Box 1161, Junction City, KS 66441. Tel.: 785-238-1666.
E-mail: gearyhistory@gmail.com
Web Site: www.gchsweb.org
Key Personnel: Dir., Jamie Clark.
Institution Type/Description: Historic Site.
Hours & Admission Prices: Call for hours. No charge, donations accepted.
Attendance: 200 (estimated)

STARCKE HOUSE, 306 W. 5th, Junction City, KS 66441. Mailing Address: P.O. Box 1161, Junction City, KS 66441. Tel.: 785-238-1666.
E-mail: gearyhistory@gmail.com
Web Site: www.gchsweb.org
Key Personnel: Dir., Jamie Clark.
Institution Type/Description: Historic House Museum: housed in the former home of pioneer jeweler & watch-maker Andrew Vogler; built in 1880s.
Hours & Admission Prices: Open by request, Tues.-Sun. 1-4; no charge, donations accepted.

Kanopolis

FORT HARKER MUSEUM COMPLEX, 309 W. Ohio St., Kanopolis, KS 67454. Mailing Address: P.O. Box 144, Ellsworth, KS 67439-0144. Tel.: 785-472-3059.
E-mail: echs@eaglecom.net
Key Personnel: Chm. (V) & Pres. (V), Phyllis Dolezal.
Institution Type/Description: Military Museum.
Hours & Admission Prices: April & Oct. Tues.-Fri. & Sun. 1-5, Sat. 10-5; May-Sept. Tues.-Sat. 10-5, Sun. 1-5; Nov.-March Sat. 10-5, Sun. 1-5. Adults $3 (includes entrance to Hodgdon House Museum complex); discounts to groups; members no charge. Closed New Year's Day; Easter; Memorial Day; Independence Day; Labor Day; Thanksgiving; Christmas. &
Attendance: 3,000 (estimated)

Kansas City

GRINTER PLACE STATE HISTORIC SITE, 1420 S. 78th St., Kansas City, KS 66111-3208. Tel.: 913-299-0373. Fax: 913-788-8046. Facebook: Grinter Place.
E-mail: grinter@kshs.org
Web Site: www.kshs.org/grinter_place
Formerly: Grinter Place Museum.
Key Personnel: Site Admin., Joe Brentano.
Institution Type/Description: Historic House: built by Moses Grinter.
Hours & Admission Prices: Thurs.-Sat. 9:30-5. Adults $3, students $1; members, and children 5 & under no charge. Closed state holidays. &
Attendance: 521 (actual)

STRAWBERRY HILL ETHNIC MUSEUM & CULTURAL CENTER, 720 N. 4th St., Kansas City, KS 66101-2908. Tel.: 913-371-3264.
E-mail: shecs@strawberryhillmuseum.org
Web Site: strawberryhillmuseum.org
Institution Type/Description: History Museum.
Hours & Admission Prices: Sat.-Sun. 12-5; other times by appointment. Adults $7, children 6-12 $3; children under 6 no charge. Closed New Year's Day; Easter; Mother's Day; Father's Day; Christmas. &
Attendance: 4,000

UNIVERSITY OF KANSAS MEDICAL CENTER, CLENDENING HISTORY OF MEDICINE LIBRARY AND MUSEUM, 3901 Rainbow Blvd., Kansas City, KS 66160. Tel.: 913-588-7098. Fax: 913-588-7060.
E-mail: ccrenner@kumc.edu
Web Site: clendening.kumc.edu
Key Personnel: Dir., Christopher Crenner; Rare Book Librarian, Dawn McInnis.
Institution Type/Description: Medical Museum.
Hours & Admission Prices: Museum: daily 8-4:30. Library: Mon. & Wed. 9-1, Tues. & Thurs. 12-4; other times by appointment. No charge. Closed New Year's Day; Martin Luther King Jr. Day; Easter; Memorial Day; Independence Day; Labor Day; Thanksgiving & day after; Christmas. &
Attendance: 1,000

Kingman

KINGMAN COUNTY HISTORICAL MUSEUM, 400 N. Main, Kingman, KS 67068-1304. Mailing Address: P.O. Box 281, Kingman, KS 67068-0281. Tel.: 620-532-5274.
E-mail: kcomuseum@gmail.com
Key Personnel: Pres., Sharon Kostner.
Institution Type/Description: History Museum: housed in 1888 City Hall.
Hours & Admission Prices: Fri. 9-3, Sat. 9-12; other times by appointment. No charge; donations accepted. Closed Christmas. &
Attendance: 2,500 (estimated)

Kinsley

EDWARDS COUNTY HISTORICAL MUSEUM, Hwy. 50 & 56, #183, Kinsley, KS 67547-0064. Mailing Address: P.O. Box 64, Kinsley, KS 67547-0064. Tel.: 620-233-0247.
E-mail: librarian281942@yahoo.com
Web Site: edwardscountymuseum.info
Key Personnel: Pres., Robert Cross; Cur., Julie Miller.
Institution Type/Description: History Museum.
Hours & Admission Prices: May-Sept. Mon.-Sat. 9-5, Sun. 1-5; other times by appointment. No charge; donations accepted. &
Attendance: 2,695 (estimated)

La Crosse

BARBED WIRE MUSEUM, W. 1st St., La Crosse, KS 67548. Mailing Address: P.O. Box 578, La Crosse, KS 67548-0578. Tel.: 785-222-9900.
E-mail: barbedwire@rushcounty.org
Web Site: www.rushcounty.org/barbedwiremuseum
Key Personnel: C.E.O. & Pres. (V), Bradley R. Penka.
Institution Type/Description: Barbed Wire Museum.
Hours & Admission Prices: May-Sept. Mon.-Sat. 10-4:30, Sun. 1-4:30. No charge; donations accepted. &
Attendance: 2,000 (actual)

RUSH COUNTY HISTORICAL SOCIETY, INC., 202 W. 1st St., La Crosse, KS 67548. Mailing Address: P.O. Box 473, La Crosse, KS 67548-0473. Tel.: 785-222-2719 & 3403. Facebook: Rush County Historical Society.
E-mail: historical@rushcounty.org
Web Site: rushcounty.org/rchs
Formerly: Post Rock Museum
Key Personnel: Pres. (V), Lawrence Erbes; Vice Pres., Cur. & Museum Shop Mgr., Judith Reynolds; Treas., Ron Sandstrom.
Institution Type/Description: History Museum.
Hours & Admission Prices: May to Labor Day Mon.-Sat. 10-4:30, Sun. 1-4:30; other times by appointment. No charge; donations accepted. &
Attendance: 1,500 (estimated)

La Cygne

LA CYGNE HISTORICAL SOCIETY MUSEUM, 300 N. Broadway, La Cygne, KS 66040. Mailing Address: P.O. Box 98, La Cygne, KS 66040. Tel.: 913-757-2101.
E-mail: lchs@peoplestelecom.net
Web Site: sites.google.com/site/lacygnehs
Institution Type/Description: Historical Society Museum.
Hours & Admission Prices: Sat.-Sun. 1-4.

Lakin

KEARNY COUNTY HISTORICAL MUSEUM, 111 S. Buffalo, Lakin, KS 67860. Mailing Address: P.O. Box 329, Lakin, KS 67860-0329. Tel.: 620-335-7448. Facebook: Kearny County Historical Museum.
E-mail: kchs@pld.com
Web Site: www.kearnycountymuseum.org
Key Personnel: Exec. Dir., Julie Grubbs McCombs.
Institution Type/Description: History Museum.
Hours & Admission Prices: Tues.-Fri. 9-4, No charge; donations accepted. &

Lansing

LANSING HISTORICAL MUSEUM, 115 E. Kansas Ave., Lansing, KS 66043-1667. Tel.: 913-250-0203. Facebook: Lansing Historical Museum.

E-mail: jmyer@lansing.ks.us
Web Site: www.lansinghistoricalsociety.com
Key Personnel: Site Supvr., Jennifer Myer.
Institution Type/Description: Historic Building: housed in the restored Atchison, Topeka & Santa Fe depot built in 1887.
Hours & Admission Prices: Tues.-Fri. 10-2, Sat. 10 to noon. No charge; donations accepted. Closed federal holidays. &
Attendance: 1,200 (estimated)

Larned

CENTRAL STATES SCOUT MUSEUM, Larned, KS 67550-2525. Mailing Address: P.O. Box 392, Larned, KS 67550-0392. Tel.: 620-285-6427 & 6431.
Key Personnel: Dir., C.E.O. & Chm. (V), Charles Sherman; Pres. (V), Jack Dipman.
Institution Type/Description: Scouting Museum.
Hours & Admission Prices: Closed for relocation. Daily 12-5. Adults $3, youth $2. &
Attendance: 484 (actual)

FORT LARNED NATIONAL HISTORIC SITE, 1767 KS Hwy. 156, Larned, KS 67550. Tel.: 620-285-6911. Fax: 620-285-3571. Facebook.
E-mail: george_elmore@nps.gov
Web Site: www.nps.gov/fols
Key Personnel: Supt., Betty Boyko; Cur., George Elmore; Museum Shop Mgr., Celeste Dixon.
Institution Type/Description: Historic Site: historic fort on Santa Fe Trail.
Hours & Admission Prices: Daily 8:30-4:30. No charge; donations accepted. Closed New Year's Day; Thanksgiving; Christmas. &
Attendance: 32,000 (actual)

SANTA FE TRAIL CENTER MUSEUM & RESEARCH LIBRARY, 1349 K-156 Hwy., Larned, KS 67550-5347. Tel.: 620-285-2054. Fax: 620-285-7491.
E-mail: museum@santafetrailcenter.org
Web Site: www.santafetrailcenter.org
Key Personnel: Pres. (V), Tom Seltmann; Dir., Rebecca Hiller; Collections Asst., Ron Laveau; Office Mgr., Linda Revello; Supt. Bldgs. & Grounds, Mark Brownlee.
Institution Type/Description: History Museum.
Hours & Admission Prices: Tues.-Sat. 9-5, Mon. by appointment. Adults $6, student 12-18 $3, children 6-11 $2; discounts to organized school groups; members no charge. Closed New Year's Day; Thanksgiving; Christmas. &
Attendance: 5,770 (actual)

Lawrence

KU BIODIVERSITY INSTITUTE - KU NATURAL HISTORY MUSEUM, The University of Kansas, 1345 Jayhawk Blvd., Dyche Hall, Lawrence, KS 66045-7505. Tel.: 785-864-4540. Fax: 785-864-5335.
E-mail: naturalhistory@ku.edu
Web Site: naturalhistory.ku.edu
Key Personnel: Dir., Dr. Leonard Krishtalka.
Institution Type/Description: Natural History Museum: housed in c.1901 Romanesque Revival building, listed on National Register of Historic Places.
Hours & Admission Prices: Tues.-Sat. 9-5, Sun. 12-4. Suggested Donations: adults $5, children 6-18 & seniors $3; museum members, KU students, staff & faculty and children under 6 no charge. Closed major holidays. &
Attendance: 46,000 (estimated)

MUSEUM OF ODD, 1012 New York St., Lawrence, KS 66044. Tel.: 785-843-8750.
Key Personnel: Owner, Randy Walker.
Institution Type/Description: General Museum.
Hours & Admission Prices: By appointment.

PRAIRIE PARK NATURE CENTER, 2730 S.W. Harper, Lawrence, KS 66046. Tel.: 785-832-7980.
E-mail: mbirrell@lawrenceks.org
Institution Type/Description: Nature Center.
Hours & Admission Prices: Tues.-Sat. 9-5, Sun. 1-4. No charge.

THE ROBERT J. DOLE INSTITUTE OF POLITICS, 2350 Petefish Dr., Lawrence, KS 66045-7555. Tel.: 785-684-4900. Fax: 785-684-1414.
E-mail: doleinstitute@ku.edu

Web Site: www.doleinstitute.org/vistors.html
Key Personnel: Dir., William B. "Bill" Lacy; Assoc. Dir. Programming, Jonathan Earle; Assoc. Dir. Outreach, Barbara Ballard; Senior Archivist, Dole Archive, Morgan Davis; Dir. Facilities & Events, Lawrence D. Bush; Media & Exhibits Archivist, Judy Sweets; Communications & Events Coord., Cori Ast; Asst. to Dir., Maggie Mahoney; Friends of Dole Institute, Lori Hutfles; Asst. Archivist, Catherine "Cat" C. Riggs; Asst. Archivist, Robert Lay; Mktg., Alison Heath Carther; Dir. Devel., Shawn McDaniel.
Institution Type/Description: History Museum.
Hours & Admission Prices: Mon.-Sat. 9-5, Sun. 12-5. No charge; donations accepted. Closed New Year's Day; Thanksgiving; Christmas.

SPENCER MUSEUM OF ART, THE UNIVERSITY OF KANSAS, 1301 Mississippi St., Lawrence, KS 66045-7500. Tel.: 785-864-4710. Fax: 785-864-3112. TDD: 800-776-3777 (Kansas Relay).
E-mail: spencerart@ku.edu
Web Site: www.spencerart.ku.edu
Key Personnel: Dir., Saralyn Reece Hardy; Deputy Dir. Opers. & Innovation, Jennifer Talbott; Cur. European & American Arts, Susan Earle; Cur. Global Contemporary & Asian Art, Kris Ercums; Cur. Global Indigenous Art, Cassandra Mesick Braun; Curator Works on Paper, Kate Meyer; Dir. External Affairs, Elizabeth Kanost; Dir. Creative Svcs., Ryan Waggoner; Assoc. Dir. & Sr. Cur. Emeritus, Stephen Goddard; Dir. Advancement & Planning, Alexis Fekete-Shukla; Exhibition Mng., Richard Klocke; Database Mgr. & Archivist, Robert Hickerson; Head of Collection Mgmt., Sofia Galarza Liu; Dir. Education, Kristina Walker.
Institution Type/Description: Art Museum.
Hours & Admission Prices: Gallery hours: Tues., Fri. & Sat. 10-4; Wed. & Thurs. 10-8; Sun. 12-4. No charge; donations accepted. Closed holidays. &
Attendance: 142,000 (estimated)

WATKINS MUSEUM OF HISTORY, 1047 Massachusetts St., Lawrence, KS 66044-2961. Tel.: 785-841-4109. Fax: 785-841-9547.
E-mail: info@watkinsmuseum.org
Web Site: www.watkinsmuseum.org
Formerly: Watkins Community Museum of History
Key Personnel: Dir., Steven J. Nowak; Cur. Collections Mgr., Brittany Keegan; Coord. Education Programs, Abby Magariel; Business Mgr., John Jewell; Asst. Coord. Programs, Will Hickox.
Institution Type/Description: Local History Museum: housed in 1888 Richardsonian Romanesque building built by J.B. Watkins.
Hours & Admission Prices: Museum: Tues.-Wed. & Fri.-Sat. 10-4, Thurs. 10-8. Research Room: by appointment. No charge; donations accepted. Closed holidays. &
Attendance: 15,390 (actual)

Leavenworth

C.W. PARKER CAROUSEL MUSEUM, 320 S. Esplanade, Leavenworth, KS 66048-1585. Tel.: 913-682-1331.
E-mail: j-m-reinhardt@sbcglobal.net
Web Site: www.cwparkercarouselmuseum.org
Key Personnel: Dir., Jerry Reinhardt.
Institution Type/Description: History Museum.
Hours & Admission Prices: Feb.-Dec. Thurs.-Sat. 11-5, Sun. 1-5. Tours: adults $6, children $3; discounts to groups of 20 or more; members no charge. Carousel Ride: $1.25. Closed New Year's Eve & Day; Easter; Independence Day; Thanksgiving; Christmas Eve & Day. &
Attendance: 23,000 (estimated)

CARROLL MANSION MUSEUM HOME OF LEAVENWORTH COUNTY HISTORICAL SOCIETY, 1128 5th Ave., Leavenworth, KS 66048-3213. Tel.: 913-682-7759. Fax: 913-682-7759. Facebook: Leavenworth Historical Society.
E-mail: leavenworthhistory@kc.twcbc.com
Web Site: www.leavenworthhistory.org
Key Personnel: Pres., Mike Stephenson; Interim Dir., Beverly Lynch; Museum Shop Mgr., Hazel May Fackler.
Institution Type/Description: History Museum: housed in 1867 Carroll Mansion.
Hours & Admission Prices: Tues.-Sat. 10:30-4:30. Admission $6 per person; children under 5 no charge. Closed holidays & inclement weather.
Attendance: 3,000 (estimated)

FIRST CITY MUSEUM, 743 Delaware St., Leavenworth, KS 66048-2472. Tel.: 913-682-1866. Fax: 913-682-1866.
E-mail: first_city_museum@yahoo.com
Web Site: www.firstcitymuseums.org
Key Personnel: Pres., John Sanders; Dir., Jerry Reinhardt; Treas., Audrey Sanders; Museum Shop Mgr., Nancy Klemp.

Institution Type/Description: History Museum.
Hours & Admission Prices: Thurs. 1-5 & by appointment. No charge; donations accepted. &
Attendance: 335 (estimated)

NATIONAL FRED HARVEY MUSEUM, 624 Olive St., Leavenworth, KS 66048-2653. Mailing Address: Leavenworth Historical Museum Assn., 743 Delaware St., Leavenworth, KS 66048. Tel.: 913-682-1866.
E-mail: fredharveymuseum@lvnworth.com
Web Site: www.firstcitymuseums.org/fredharvey_main.html
Institution Type/Description: Historic House Museum.
Hours & Admission Prices: Tours by appointment.

Lecompton

CONSTITUTION HALL, 319 Elmore, Lecompton, KS 66050. Mailing Address: P.O. Box 198, Lecompton, KS 66050-0198. Tel.: 785-887-6520. Fax: 785-887-6520.
E-mail: consthall@kshs.org
Web Site: www.lecomptonkansas.com
Institution Type/Description: History Museum.
Hours & Admission Prices: Wed.-Sat. 9-5, Sun. 1-5; other times by appointment. Adults $3, students $1; members, active military and children 5 & under no charge. Closed state holidays. &
Attendance: 3,684 (actual)

TERRITORIAL CAPITAL-LANE MUSEUM, 640 E. Woodson, Lecompton, KS 66050. Tel.: 785-887-6148 & 6285. Fax: 785-887-6148.
E-mail: lanemuseum@aol.com
Web Site: www.lecomptonkansas.com
Key Personnel: C.E.O. & Pres., Paul M. Bahnmaier; Chm. (V) & Education, Charlene Winter; Dir., Rich McConnell; Treas. & Gift Shop Mgr., Ron Thacker; Cur., Elsie Middleton; Archivist & Registrar, Lynn Ward; Membership, Iona Spencer; Public Rels., Opal Goodrick; Security, Bob Weeks.
Institution Type/Description: History Museum: located on foundation of proposed capitol building of Kansas.
Hours & Admission Prices: Wed.-Sat. 10-4, Sun. 1-5; tours by appointment; call 913-887-6285 for more information. No charge; donations accepted. &
Attendance: 6,500 (estimated)

Lenexa

LEGLER BARN MUSEUM, 14907 W. 87th St., Lenexa, KS 66215-4135. Tel.: 913-492-0038.
E-mail: info@leglerbarn.org
Web Site: www.leglerbarn.org
Key Personnel: Pres. (V), Todd Crow.
Institution Type/Description: Historic Building: housed in stone barn built by Adam Legler in 1864.
Hours & Admission Prices: Wed. & Sat. 10-4. No charge; donations accepted. Closed holidays.
Attendance: 3,000 (estimated)

Leoti

WICHITA COUNTY HISTORICAL SOCIETY AND THE MUSEUM OF THE GREAT PLAINS, 201 N. 4th St., Leoti, KS 67861. Mailing Address: P.O. Box 1561, Leoti, KS 67861-1561. Tel.: 620-375-2316.
E-mail: museum@wichitacountymuseum.org
Web Site: www.wichitacountymuseum.org
Key Personnel: Dir., Curtis Walk.
Institution Type/Description: History Museum.
Hours & Admission Prices: Tues.-Fri. 1-5, Sat.-Sun. 2-5; other times by appointment. No charge; donations accepted. &
Attendance: 1,200 (estimated)

Liberal

BAKER ARTS CENTER, 624 N. Pershing Ave., Liberal, KS 67901-3115. Tel.: 620-624-2810. Fax: 620-624-7726. Facebook: Baker Arts Center.
E-mail: tonismith@bakerartscenter.org
Web Site: www.bakerartscenter.org
Institution Type/Description: Art Gallery.
Hours & Admission Prices: Tues.-Fri. 9-12 & 1-5, Sat. 2-5. No charge.

MID-AMERICA AIR MUSEUM, 2000 W. 2nd St., Liberal, KS 67901. Mailing Address: P.O. Box 2199, Liberal, KS 67905-2199. Tel.: 620-624-5263. Fax: 620-624-5454.
E-mail: harriett.gick@liberalofcity.org
Web Site: www.liberalairmuseum.com
Formerly: Liberal Air Museum
Key Personnel: Chm. (V), Steven Graham.
Institution Type/Description: Aviation Museum.
Hours & Admission Prices: Mon.-Fri. 8-5, Sat. 10-5, Sun. 1-5. Adults $7, senior citizens $5, children 6-18 $3; discounts for groups of 10 or more; children 5 & under and members no charge. Closed New Year's Day; Thanksgiving; Christmas. &
Attendance: 12,000 (actual)

SEWARD COUNTY HISTORICAL MUSEUM, 567 E. Cedar, Liberal, KS 67901-3865. Tel.: 620-624-7624.
E-mail: information@kshs.org
Key Personnel: Exec. Dir., JoAnne Mansell.
Institution Type/Description: History Museum.
Hours & Admission Prices: Memorial Day to Labor Day Mon.-Sat. 9-6, Sun. 1-6; Sept.-May Tues.-Sat. 9-5, Sun. 1-5. Dorothy's House & Land of Oz: adults $5, senior citizens & children 6-18 $3.50; children 5 & under no charge.

Lincoln

CRISPIN'S DRUG STORE MUSEUM, 161 E. Lincoln Ave., Lincoln, KS 67455. Tel.: 785-524-5383.
E-mail: rxmuseumist@yahoo.com
Web Site: crispinsdrugstoremuseum.com
Key Personnel: Dir., Jack D. Crispin, Jr.
Institution Type/Description: History Museum.
Hours & Admission Prices: By appointment. No charge; donations accepted.
Attendance: 300 (estimated)

KYNE HOUSE MUSEUM, 216 W. Lincoln Ave., Lincoln, KS 67455. Mailing Address: P.O. Box 85, Lincoln, KS 67455-0085. Tel.: 785-524-9997.
E-mail: lchs10@att.net
Web Site: www.lincolncohistmuseum.com
Key Personnel: Pres. (V), Kathie Crispin; Dir., Bud DeArvil.
Institution Type/Description: Historic House Museum: built in 1885.
Hours & Admission Prices: Kyne House: Oct.-April Wed. 1-4, Thurs. 4-7, Sat. 10-2; April-Sept. Wed. & Fri. 1-4, Thurs. 4-7, Sat. 10-2. Entry by donation. Marshall-Yohe House: by appointment. Adults $5, groups $4. &
Attendance: 600 (estimated)

LINCOLN COUNTY HISTORICAL SOCIETY, 216 W. Lincoln Ave., Lincoln, KS 67455. Mailing Address: P.O. Box 85, Lincoln, KS 67455-0085. Tel.: 785-524-9997. Facebook: facebook.com/lchistoricalmuseum.
E-mail: lchs10@att.net
Web Site: www.lincolncohistmuseum.com
Key Personnel: Pres., Kathie Crispin; Treas., Brenda Peterson; Dir., Bud DeArvil.
Institution Type/Description: General Museum.
Hours & Admission Prices: Kyne House Museum: Oct.-April Wed. 1-4, Thurs. 4-7, Sat. 10-2; April-Sept. Wed. & Fri. 1-4, Thurs. 4-7, Sat. 10-4. Entry by donation. Marshall-Yohe House: by appointment. Adults $5, groups $4. &
Attendance: 600 (estimated)

POST ROCK SCOUT MUSEUM, 161 E. Lincoln Ave., Lincoln, KS 67455-2050. Tel.: 785-524-5383. Facebook: Post Rock Scout Museum.
E-mail: postrockscoutmuseum@yahoo.com
Web Site: www.postrockscoutmuseum.com
Key Personnel: Owner, Kathie Crispin.
Institution Type/Description: Scout Museum.
Hours & Admission Prices: By appointment. No charge; donations accepted.
Attendance: 350 (estimated)

Lindsborg

BIRGER SANDZEN MEMORIAL GALLERY, 401 N. 1st St., Lindsborg, KS 67456-1813. Mailing Address: P.O. Box 348, Lindsborg, KS 67456-0348. Tel.: 785-227-2220. Fax: 785-227-4170. Facebook: Birger Sandzen Memorial Gallery.
E-mail: fineart@sandzen.org
Web Site: www.sandzen.org
Key Personnel: Sandzen Foundation Pres. & C.E.O., Bryce Loder; Dir., Ron Michael; Cur., Cori North; Sec., Muriel Gentine.

Institution Type/Description: Art Museum. Built in memory of Swedish-American painter and printmaker Birger Sandzen.
Hours & Admission Prices: Tues.-Sat. 10-5, Sun. 1-5. No charge; donations accepted. Closed New Year's Eve & Day; Memorial Day; Independence Day; Thanksgiving; Christmas Eve & Day. &
Attendance: 11,000 (estimated)

MCPHERSON COUNTY OLD MILL MUSEUM AND PARK, 120 Mill St., Lindsborg, KS 67456-2815. Mailing Address: P.O. Box 94, Lindsborg, KS 67456-0094. Tel.: 785-227-3595. Fax: 785-227-2810.
E-mail: oldmillmuseum@hotmail.com
Web Site: www.oldmillmuseum.org
Key Personnel: C.E.O. & Dir., Lorna Nelson; Museum Shop Mgr., Lenora Lynam.
Institution Type/Description: History Museum & Historic Site.
Hours & Admission Prices: Mon.-Sat. 9-5. Adults $2, children 6-12 $1; discounts to school & group tours; children under 6 no charge. Closed New Year's Day; Thanksgiving; Christmas. &
Attendance: 10,000 (estimated)

RED BARN STUDIO MUSEUM, 212 S. Main, Lindsborg, KS 67456-2614. Tel.: 785-227-2217. Facebook.
E-mail: raymer@redbarnstudio.org
Web Site: www.redbarnstudio.org/
Key Personnel: Dir., Marsha Howe; Pres. (V), Todd Ray.
Institution Type/Description: Art Museum.
Hours & Admission Prices: Tues.-Fri. 10-5, Sat.-Sun. 1-5; other times by appointment. No charge; donations accepted.
Attendance: 3,000 (estimated)

Logan

DANE G. HANSEN MEMORIAL MUSEUM, 110 W. Main St., Logan, KS 67646. Mailing Address: P.O. Box 187, Logan, KS 67646-0187. Tel.: 785-689-4846. Fax: 785-689-4892.
E-mail: hansenmuseum@ruraltel.net
Web Site: www.hansenmuseum.org
Key Personnel: Dir., Nova Bates; Pres. Museum Bd., Carol Bales.
Institution Type/Description: Art Museum.
Hours & Admission Prices: Mon.-Fri. 9-12 & 1-4, Sat. 9-12 & 1-5, Sun. & holidays 1-5. No charge. Closed New Year's Day; Thanksgiving; Christmas. &
Attendance: 8,000 (estimated)

Louisburg

CEDAR COVE FELINE SANCTUARY & EDUCATION CENTER, 3783 Hwy. K68, Louisburg, KS 66053. Tel.: 913-837-5515, 816-739-0363.
E-mail: info@saveoursiberians.org
Web Site: www.saveoursiberians.org
Key Personnel: Acting Dir. & Pres., Steve Klein.
Institution Type/Description: Wildlife Refuge & Education Center.
Hours & Admission Prices: April-Oct. Sat.-Sun. 10-3; Nov.-March Sat.-Sun. 11-3. Admission 3 & over $5. &

Lucas

GARDEN OF EDEN AND CABIN HOME, 305 E Second St., Lucas, KS 67648. Mailing Address: P.O. Box 57, Lucas, KS 67648. Tel.: 785-525-6395.
E-mail: info@garden-of-eden-lucas-kansas.com
Web Site: www.garden-of-eden-lucas-kansas.com
Key Personnel: Pres., John Hachmeister; Vice Pres., Doug Hickman; Mgr., Lynn Schneider.
Institution Type/Description: Historic House Museum: housed in the former home of S.P. Dinsmoor. Listed on the National Register of Historic Places.
Hours & Admission Prices: March-April daily 1-4; May-Oct. daily 10-5; Nov.-Feb. Sat.-Sun. 1-4. Adults $7, children 6-12 $2; discounts to groups; children 5 & under no charge. Closed major holidays.
Attendance: 10,000 (estimated)

GRASSROOTS ART CENTER, 213 S. Main St., Lucas, KS 67648. Mailing Address: P.O. Box 304, Lucas, KS 67648-0304. Tel.: 785-525-6118. Facebook: Grassroots Art Center.
E-mail: grassroots@wtciweb.com
Web Site: www.grassrootart.com
Key Personnel: Dir., Rosslyn Schultz; Pres. (V), Janice Zamecnik; Museum Shop Mgr., Peg Gilbert.
Institution Type/Description: Art Museum.

Hours & Admission Prices: April & Oct. Thurs.-Mon. 1-4; May-Sept. Mon.-Sat. 10-5, Sun. 1-5; Nov.-March Thurs.-Sat. 1-4. Adults $7, children 6-12 $3; discounts to groups of 10 or more; members no charge. Closed winter holidays. &
Attendance: 5,800 (actual)

Lyndon

OSAGE COUNTY HISTORICAL SOCIETY RESEARCH CENTER, 631 Topeka Ave., Lyndon, KS 66451. Mailing Address: P.O. Box 361, Lyndon, KS 66451-0361. Tel.: 785-828-3477. Facebook: Osage County Kansas Historical Society.
E-mail: researchosagechs@embarqmail.com
Web Site: www.osagechs.org
Key Personnel: C.E.O. & Pres. (V), Eileen Matzek Davis; Vice Pres., Marilyn Sanders; Sec. & Treas., Ann Rogers.
Institution Type/Description: History Museum & Genealogy Library.
Hours & Admission Prices: Lyndon Museum & Research Center: April-Oct. Wed.-Sat. 1-5; other times by appointment. No charge; donations accepted. Closed holidays. &
Attendance: 850 (estimated)

Lyons

RICE COUNTY HISTORICAL SOCIETY CORONADO QUIVIRA MUSEUM, 105 W. Lyon, Lyons, KS 67554-2703. Tel.: 620-257-3941.
E-mail: director@cqmuseum.org
Web Site: www.cqmuseum.org
Key Personnel: Dir., Charlene Akers; Pres. (V), Shirley Fair.
Institution Type/Description: General Museum: housed in 1910-1911 Carnegie library building.
Hours & Admission Prices: Tues.-Sat. 9-5. Out of county visitors: ages 13 & over $3, children 6-12 $2; discounts to AAM members; children under 5 no charge. Closed major holidays. &
Attendance: 3,500 (estimated)

Manhattan

FLINT HILLS DISCOVERY CENTER, 315 S. Third St., Manhattan, KS 66502-6205. Tel.: 785-587-2726. Fax: 785-587-2784.
E-mail: adams@cityofmhk.com
Web Site: www.flinthillsdiscovery.org
Key Personnel: Dir., Susan Adams; Asst. Dir. Devel., Katharine Hensler; Exhibits & Oper. Supvr., Roy Garrett; Guest Svcs. & Membership Mgr., Mary Hildreth; Events Supvr., Jonathan Mertz; Education Cur., Stephen Bridenstine; Gift Store Coord., Penny Cullers.
Institution Type/Description: History Museum.
Hours & Admission Prices: Mon.-Wed. & Fri.-Sat. 10-5, Thurs. 10-8, Sun. 12-5; Adults $9, military, students and seniors 65 & over $7, children $4; children under 2 no charge. Closed Christmas; Thanksgiving. &

GOODNOW HOUSE STATE HISTORIC SITE, 2301 Claflin Rd., Manhattan, KS 66502. Mailing Address: 2309 Claflin Rd., Manhattan, KS 66502-3421. Tel.: 785-565-6490. Fax: 785-565-6491.
E-mail: ccollins@rileycountyks.gov
Web Site: www.kshs.org
Key Personnel: Contact, D. Cheryl Collins.
Institution Type/Description: Historic House: home of pioneer Kansas educator, Isaac Tichenor Goodnow and his wife, Ellen Denison Goodnow.
Hours & Admission Prices: Tues.-Fri. 9-5 as staff is available, Sat.-Sun. 2-5. No charge; donations accepted. Closed national holidays.
Attendance: 2,458 (actual)

HAROLD M. FREUND AMERICAN MUSEUM OF BAKING, 1213 Bakers Way, Manhattan, KS 66502-4555. Mailing Address: P.O. Box 3999, Manhattan, KS 66505-3999. Tel.: 785-537-4750. Fax: 785-537-1493.
E-mail: information@aibonline.org
Web Site: www.aibonline.org
Key Personnel: Librarian, Tammy L. Popejoy.
Institution Type/Description: Baking Museum.
Hours & Admission Prices: Mon.-Fri. 8-5. No charge. Closed major holidays.
Attendance: 900 (estimated)

HARTFORD HOUSE MUSEUM, 2309 Claflin Rd., Manhattan, KS 66502-3421. Tel.: 785-565-6490.
E-mail: ccollins@rileycountyks.gov
Web Site: www.rileycountyks.gov/museum

Key Personnel: Dir., D. Cheryl Collins; Pres. (V), John White.
Institution Type/Description: Historic House: restored 1855 pre-fabricated house shipped on the Hartford Steamboat to Manhattan, KS.
Hours & Admission Prices: Tues.-Fri. 8:30-5 subject to availability of staff, Sat.-Sun. 2-5. No charge; donations accepted. Closed national holidays.
Attendance: 1,500 (estimated)

KANSAS STATE UNIVERSITY HERBARIUM, Div. of Biology, Ackert Hall, Manhattan, KS 66506-4901. Tel.: 785-532-6619. Fax: 785-532-6653.
E-mail: herbarium@ksu.edu
Web Site: www.ksu.edu/herbarium
Key Personnel: Dir., Carolyn Ferguson, Ph.D.
Institution Type/Description: Herbarium.
Hours & Admission Prices: Mon.-Fri. 8-5. No charge. Closed national holidays. &

THE KANSAS STATE UNIVERSITY INSECT ZOO, 1500 Denison Ave., Manhattan, KS 66506. Tel.: 785-532-2847.
E-mail: insect@ksu.edu
Web Site: www.k-state.edu/butterfly/index.htm
Institution Type/Description: Insect Museum.
Hours & Admission Prices: Tues.-Sat. 12-6; other times by appointment. Adults $2, senior citizens $1.50.

MANHATTAN ARTS CENTER, 1520 Poyntz Ave., Manhattan, KS 66502-4147. Tel.: 785-537-4420. Facebook.
E-mail: director@manhattanarts.org
Web Site: www.manhattanarts.org
Key Personnel: Exec. Dir., Penny Senften; Devel. Dir., Anat Eshar; Education & Mktg. Dir., Michele Ward.
Institution Type/Description: Art Museum.
Hours & Admission Prices: Mon.-Fri. 12-5, Sat. 1-4. No charge; donations accepted. Closed Christmas. &
Attendance: 5,000 (estimated)

MARIANNA KISTLER BEACH MUSEUM OF ART AT KANSAS STATE UNIVERSITY, 701 Beach Lane, Manhattan, KS 66506-0601. Tel.: 785-532-7718. Fax: 785-532-7498.
E-mail: beachart@ksu.edu
Web Site: beach.k-state.edu
Key Personnel: Dir., Linda Duke; Pres. (V), Jackie Hartman; Operations & Finance Mgr., Robin Lonborg; Cur., Liz Seaton; Registrar & Collections Mgr., Sarah Price; Exhibitions Designer, Lindsay Smith; Exhibition & Design Coord., Luke Dempsey; Sr. Educator, Kathrine Walker Schlageck; Coord. Operations, Kelsey Longpine; Assoc. Cur., Aileen June Wang; Asst. Cur., April Bojorquez; Asst. Registrar, Theresa Ketterer; Public Rels. Coord., Martha Scott.
Institution Type/Description: Art Museum.
Hours & Admission Prices: Tues., Wed. & Fri. 10-5, Thurs. 10-8, Sat. 11-4. No charge; donations accepted. Closed major holidays. &
Attendance: 32,273 (actual)

PIONEER LOG CABIN, City Park, 11th & Poyntz, Manhattan, KS 66502. Mailing Address: 2309 Claflin, Manhattan, KS 66502-3421. Tel.: 785-565-6490. Fax: 785-565-6491.
E-mail: rcmuseum@rileycountyks.gov
Web Site: www.rileycountyks.gov/museum
Key Personnel: Pres. (V), Margaret Pendleton; Dir., D. Cheryl Collins.
Institution Type/Description: History Museum: housed in log cabin.
Hours & Admission Prices: April-Oct. Sun. 2-5; other times by appointment. No charge; donations accepted. &
Attendance: 2,917 (estimated)

RILEY COUNTY HISTORICAL MUSEUM, 2309 Claflin Rd., Manhattan, KS 66502-3421. Tel.: 785-565-6490. Fax: 785-565-6491.
E-mail: ccollins@rileycountyks.gov
Web Site: www.rileycountyks.gov/museum
Key Personnel: Dir., D. Cheryl Collins; Chm. (V), Janet Duncan.
Institution Type/Description: History Museum.
Hours & Admission Prices: Museum: Tues.-Fri. 8:30-5, Sat.-Sun. 2-5. Library: by appointment. No charge; donations accepted. Closed national holidays. &
Attendance: 13,423 (actual)

STRECKER-NELSON GALLERY, 406 1/2 Poyntz Ave., Manhattan, KS 66502. Tel.: 785-537-2099. Fax: 785-539-2139.
E-mail: gallery@kansas.net
Web Site: www.strecker-nelsongallery.com
Institution Type/Description: Art Gallery.
Hours & Admission Prices: Mon.-Sat. 10-6.

SUNSET ZOOLOGICAL PARK, 2333 Oak St., Manhattan, KS
66502-3824. Tel.: 785-587-2737. Fax: 785-587-2730.
E-mail: shoemaker@cityofmhk.com
Web Site: www.sunsetzoo.com
Key Personnel: C.E.O., Scott Shoemaker.
Institution Type/Description: Zoo.
Hours & Admission Prices: April-Oct. daily 9:30-5; Nov.-March daily 12-5. Adults,
   senior citizens & students $4, children 3-12 $2; discounts to groups; members no
   charge. &
Attendance: 79,800 (actual)

WOLF HOUSE MUSEUM, 630 Fremont, Manhattan, KS 66502-
5820. Mailing Address: Riley County Historical Society, 2309
Claflin Rd., Manhattan, KS 66502. Tel.: 785-565-6490. Fax: 785-
565-6491.
E-mail: ccollins@rileycountyks.gov
Web Site: www.rileychs.com
Key Personnel: Pres. (V), Margaret Pendleton; Dir., D. Cheryl Collins.
Institution Type/Description: Historic House: 1868 boarding house.
Hours & Admission Prices: Sat.-Sun. 2-5. No charge; donations accepted.
Attendance: 1,731 (actual)

WONDER WORKSHOP CHILDREN'S MUSEUM, 506 S. 4th
St., Manhattan, KS 66502. Tel.: 785-776-1234.
E-mail: wonder@kansas.net
Web Site: www.wonderworkshop.org
Key Personnel: Exec. Dir., Richard Pitts.
Institution Type/Description: Children's Museum.
Hours & Admission Prices: Sat. 10-1, Sun. 1-3; groups by appointment. Adults $4,
   children 2 & over $3; children one & under no charge. &
Attendance: 2,000 (estimated)

Mankato

JEWELL COUNTY HISTORICAL SOCIETY MUSEUM, 118 N.
Commercial St., Mankato, KS 66956-2207. Tel.: 785-545-7658.
Facebook.
E-mail: jwchsmuseum@gmail.com
Web Site: www.jewellcountyhistory.com
Key Personnel: Pres., Leon Boden; Cur. & Museum Shop Mgr., Jane Pahls.
Institution Type/Description: Local History & Agricultural Museum.
Hours & Admission Prices: Wed.-Fri. 10-2; other times by appointment. No charge;
   donations accepted. Closed holidays. &
Attendance: 300 (estimated)

Marion

MARION CITY MUSEUM, 623 E. Main St., Marion, KS 66861-
1800. Tel.: 620-382-9134 & 3703.
E-mail: chinga@eaglecom.net
Institution Type/Description: History Museum: housed in the former Baptist church
   building; built in 1887.
Hours & Admission Prices: May to mid-Oct. Tues.-Sat. 10-2, Sun. 12-2; other times
   by appointment. No charge; donations accepted.
Attendance: 1,500 (estimated)

Marquette

KANSAS MOTORCYCLE MUSEUM, 120 N. Washington,
Marquette, KS 67464. Tel.: 785-546-2449.
Key Personnel: Cur., LaVona Engdahl.
Institution Type/Description: Motorcycle Museum.
Hours & Admission Prices: Mon.-Sat. 10-5, Sun. 11-5; groups by appointment. No
   charge; donations accepted.

MARQUETTE MUSEUM, 202 N. Washington, Marquette, KS
67464. Mailing Address: City Hall, 113 N. Washington St.,
Marquette, KS 67464. Tel.: 785-546-2205.
Institution Type/Description: Historical Society Museum: building built in 1910.
Hours & Admission Prices: May-Sept. Sun. 2-5. &
Attendance: 1,200

RANGE SCHOOL MUSEUM, 206 N. Washington St., Marquette,
KS 67464. Mailing Address: City Hall, 113 N. Washington St.,
Marquette, KS 67464. Tel.: 785-546-2205.
Institution Type/Description: History Museum: housed in a former country school;
   built in 1906.
Hours & Admission Prices: April-Oct. Sun. 1-4 or by appointment. No charge.
Attendance: 1,000 (estimated)

Marysville

DOLL HOUSE MUSEUM, 912 Broadway, Marysville, KS 66508-
1805. Mailing Address: 1107 Pony Express Hwy., Marysville, KS
66508. Tel.: 785-562-3029. Fax: 785-562-2990.
E-mail: candcdoll@yahoo.com
Key Personnel: Dir., Lois Cohorst; Pres. (V), Deb Krashaar.
Institution Type/Description: Doll, Toy, & Indian Artifacts Museum.
Hours & Admission Prices: By appointment. Suggested Donation: $5 per person. &
Attendance: 650 (estimated)

KOESTER HOUSE MUSEUM, 919 Broadway, Marysville, KS
66508-1637. Tel.: 785-562-2417.
Web Site: www.marysvillemuseumsks.org
Institution Type/Description: Historic House Museum: housed in the former home
   of banker, Charles F. Koester; c.1876.
Hours & Admission Prices: Mon.-Sat. 10-4:30, Sun. 1-4.

MARSHALL COUNTY HISTORICAL SOCIETY, 1207
Broadway, Marysville, KS 66508-1845. Tel.: 785-562-5012.
Facebook.
E-mail: mchs@bluevalley.net
Web Site: www.marysvillemuseumsks.org
Institution Type/Description: Historic Building: housed in the county courthouse;
   built in 1891.
Hours & Admission Prices: Museum: Memorial Day to Sept. 15 daily 10-4; Winter:
   Mon.-Fri. 10-4. Library: Mon.-Fri. 10-4. No charge; donations accepted.
Attendance: 700 (estimated)

PONY EXPRESS ORIGINAL HOME - STATION #1, 106 S. 8th
St., Marysville, KS 66508-1832. Tel.: 785-562-3825.
Institution Type/Description: Historic Building: built in 1859 by Joseph Cottrell;
   original home station along the Pony Express route.
Hours & Admission Prices: April-Oct. Mon.-Sat. 9-4, Sun. 12-4.
Attendance: 2,132 (actual)

McCracken

MCCRACKEN HISTORICAL MUSEUM, 200 Main St.,
McCracken, KS 67556. Mailing Address: P.O. Box 342,
McCracken, KS 67556-0342. Tel.: 785-394-2540 & 2446.
Institution Type/Description: History Museum: housed in the former city jail; built
   in 1901.
Hours & Admission Prices: By appointment.

McPherson

MCPHERSON MUSEUM & ARTS FOUNDATION, 1111 E.
Kansas Ave., McPherson, KS 67460. Tel.: 620-241-8464. Fax:
620-241-2676. Facebook; Instagram; Twitter.
E-mail: director@mcphersonmuseum.com
Web Site: mcphersonmuseum.com
Key Personnel: Exec. Dir., Anna A. Ruxlow; Pres., Gary Casebeer.
Institution Type/Description: General Museum.
Hours & Admission Prices: May to Sept. Mon.-Fri. 8-5, Sat.-Sun. 1-5. Sept.-May
   Mon.-Fri. 8-5, Sat. 1-5. Adults $5, seniors 65 & up and students $3; children
   under 4 & members no charge. &
Attendance: 4,500 (estimated)

Meade

DALTON GANG HIDEOUT, 502 S. Pearlette St., Meade, KS
67864. Mailing Address: P.O. Box 515, Meade, KS 67864-0515.
Tel.: 620-873-2731, 800-354-2743.
E-mail: daltonhideout@yahoo.com
Web Site: oldmeadecounty.com
Key Personnel: Mgr., Marc S. Ferguson.
Institution Type/Description: Historic House Museum: housed in the former home
   of Eva Dalton, sister of the Dalton Gang.
Hours & Admission Prices: Mon.-Sat. 9-5, Sun. 1-5. Admission $5.
Attendance: 9,000 (actual)

MEADE COUNTY HISTORICAL SOCIETY MUSEUM, 200 E.
Carthage, Meade, KS 67864-0893. Mailing Address: P.O. Box 893,
Meade, KS 67864-0893. Tel.: 620-873-2359. Fax: 620-873-2359.
Facebook: Meade County Historical Museum.
E-mail: meademuseums@yahoo.com
Web Site: www.meadecountymuseum.com

Key Personnel: C.E.O., Norman Dye; Vice Chm., Glen Lauppe; Administration, Nancy Ohnick.
Institution Type/Description: General Museum.
Hours & Admission Prices: Tues.-Sat. 10-5, Sun. 1-5. No charge; donations accepted. Closed major holidays. &
Attendance: 5,000 (estimated)

Medicine Lodge

CARRY A. NATION HOME AND STOCKADE MUSEUM, 209-211 W. Fowler, Hwy. 160, Medicine Lodge, KS 67104. Mailing Address: P.O. Box 132, Medicine Lodge, KS 67104. Tel.: 620-886-3553. Facebook: Medicine Lodge Stockade.
Web Site: www.medicinelodgestockade.org
Key Personnel: Pres. (V), John Nixon; Museum Shop Mgr., Mariann Jarboe; Museum Shop Mgr., Kathy DeGeer.
Institution Type/Description: Historic House Museum: 1880-1903 home of Carry A. Nation.
Hours & Admission Prices: Summer: 10:30-5; Winter: 1-4. Adults $5, senior citizens $4, children 6-17 $3; children under 5 no charge.
Attendance: 500 (estimated)

Minneapolis

OTTAWA COUNTY HISTORICAL MUSEUM, 110 S. Concord St., Minneapolis, KS 67467-2322. Tel.: 785-392-3621.
E-mail: otcomu@networksplus.net
Key Personnel: Dir., Mr. Jettie Condray.
Institution Type/Description: County History Museum.
Hours & Admission Prices: Tues.-Sat. 10-12 & 1-5. No charge; donations accepted. &
Attendance: 3,000 (estimated)

Montezuma

STAUTH MEMORIAL MUSEUM, 111 N. Aztec St., Montezuma, KS 67867-0396. Mailing Address: P.O. Box 396, Montezuma, KS 67867-0396. Tel.: 620-846-2527. Fax: 620-846-2810.
E-mail: stauthm@ucom.net
Web Site: stauthmemorialmuseum.org
Key Personnel: Dir., Financial Dir. & Public Rels., Kim Legleiter.
Institution Type/Description: Decorative Arts Museum.
Hours & Admission Prices: Tues.-Sat. 9-12 & 1-4:30; Sun. 1:30-4:30. No charge; donations accepted. Closed New Year's Day; Easter; Independence Day; Thanksgiving; Christmas. &
Attendance: 2,286 (actual)

Mulvane

MULVANE HISTORICAL MUSEUM, 300 W. Main, Mulvane, KS 67110-1779. Mailing Address: P.O. Box 17, Mulvane, KS 67110-1779. Tel.: 316-777-0506.
E-mail: cwalker@mulvanekansas.com
Web Site: mulvanedepot.com
Institution Type/Description: History Museum.
Hours & Admission Prices: Tues.-Sat. 10-4. No charge; donations accepted. Closed holidays.
Attendance: 1,300 (estimated)

Neodesha

NORMAN #1 OIL WELL MUSEUM, 106 S. First St., Neodesha, KS 66757-1802. Mailing Address: P.O. Box 336, Neodesha, KS 66757-0336. Tel.: 620-325-5316. Fax: 316-325-5316.
E-mail: norman1@terraworld.net
Key Personnel: Pres., Dan Railsback; Dir., Jackie Clark.
Institution Type/Description: Historical & Oil Museum: first commercial oil well in the mid-continent oil fields.
Hours & Admission Prices: Tues.-Sat. 10-5. No charge; donations accepted. Closed Independence Day; holidays. &
Attendance: 1,000 (estimated)

Ness City

NESS COUNTY HISTORICAL MUSEUM, 123 S. Pennsylvania, Ness City, KS 67560-1907. Mailing Address: P.O. Box 512, Ness City, KS 67560-0512. Tel.: 785-798-3298.
E-mail: ncmuseum@gbta.net
Institution Type/Description: History Museum.

Hours & Admission Prices: Tues.-Fri. 1-5; other times by appointment. Closed holidays.

New Century

CAF HEART OF AMERICA WING EDUCATION CENTER, 6 Aero Plaza, New Century, KS 66031. Tel.: 913-907-7902.
E-mail: hoacafinfo@yahoo.com
Web Site: www.kcghostsquadron.org
Institution Type/Description: Military Aviation History Museum.
Hours & Admission Prices: By appointment. &

Newton

HARVEY COUNTY HISTORICAL SOCIETY, 203 N. Main, Newton, KS 67114-3442. Mailing Address: P.O. Box 4, Newton, KS 67114-0004. Tel.: 316-283-2221. Facebook: Harvey County Historical Society.
E-mail: info@hchm.org
Web Site: www.hchm.org
Key Personnel: Dir., Debra Hiebert; Chm. (V), Carol Kirk; Archivist, Jane Jones; Cur., Kris Schmucker; Photo Registrar, John Whitlock; Office Mgr., Gaylord Sanneman.
Institution Type/Description: Historical Society Museum: housed in 1903 Carnegie Library Building.
Hours & Admission Prices: Tues.-Fri. and 1st & 3rd Sat. 10-4. General Admission: no charge; donations accepted. Programs: fees vary. Closed most major holidays.
Attendance: 1,200 (estimated)

Nickerson

HEDRICK'S EXOTIC ANIMAL FARM, 7910 N. Roy L. Smith Rd., Nickerson, KS 67561-9049. Tel.: 620-422-3296, 800-618-9577.
Institution Type/Description: Animal Farm.
Hours & Admission Prices: By appointment.

North Newton

KAUFFMAN MUSEUM, Bethel College, 2801 N. Main, North Newton, KS 67117-1700. Mailing Address: Bethel College, 300 E. 27th St., North Newton, KS 67117-8061. Tel.: 316-283-1612.
E-mail: kauffman@bethelks.edu
Web Site: www.bethelks.edu/kauffman
Key Personnel: Dir., Annette LeZotte; Pres., Richard Walker; Cur. Education, Andrea Schmidt Andres; Cur. Exhibits, Charles Regier; Museum Technician, David Kreider.
Institution Type/Description: Cultural & Natural History Museum.
Hours & Admission Prices: Tues.-Fri. 9:30-4:30, Sat.-Sun. 1:30-4:30. Adults $4, children 6-16 $2; discounts to AAM & ICOM; members no charge. &
Attendance: 7,000 (estimated)

MENNONITE LIBRARY AND ARCHIVES, Bethel College, 300 E. 27th St., North Newton, KS 67117-0531. Tel.: 316-284-5304, 800-522-1887 ext. 304. Fax: 316-284-5843.
E-mail: mla@bethelks.edu
Web Site: www.bethelks.edu/mla
Key Personnel: Archivist, John D. Thiesen; Librarian, Barbara A. Thiesen.
Institution Type/Description: Religious Museum.
Hours & Admission Prices: Mon.-Thurs. 10-12 & 1-5, first & third Thurs. evenings of the month 6:30-9:30. No charge; donations accepted. Closed national holidays. &
Attendance: 927 (estimated)

Norton

NORTON COUNTY HISTORICAL SOCIETY & MUSEUM, 105 E. Lincoln, Norton, KS 67654. Mailing Address: P.O. Box 303, Norton, KS 67654-0303. Tel.: 785-877-5107.
Institution Type/Description: Historical Society Museum.
Hours & Admission Prices: May-Sept. Wed. & Sat. 2-4; other times by appointment.

STATION 15, Water Tower Park, W. Hwy. 36, Norton, KS 67654-0097. Mailing Address: Norton Area Chamber of Commerce, 104 S. State, 205 S. State, Norton, KS 67654-0097. Tel.: 785-877-2501. Fax: 785-877-3300.
E-mail: nortoncc@ruraltel.net

Web Site: discovernorton.com
Key Personnel: Exec. Dir., Tara Vance; Chm. (V), Jim Ray.
Institution Type/Description: Historic Site.
Hours & Admission Prices: Daily 24 hours. No charge. ♿
Attendance: 1,000 (estimated)

Oakley

FICK FOSSIL & HISTORY MUSEUM, 700 W. 3rd St., Oakley, KS 67748-1256. Tel.: 785-671-4839.
E-mail: fickmuseum@st-tel.net
Web Site: www.DiscoverOakley.com
Key Personnel: Dir., Kelsey Shellito; Registrar, Ruth Clark; Tour Guide, Nadine Kuasnicka.
Institution Type/Description: Geology, Paleontology & History Museum.
Hours & Admission Prices: Call for hours. No charge; donations accepted. Closed holidays. ♿
Attendance: 10,000

Oberlin

DECATUR COUNTY LAST INDIAN RAID MUSEUM, 258 S. Penn Ave., Oberlin, KS 67749-2245. Tel.: 785-475-2712.
E-mail: lirm@sbcglobal.net
Web Site: skyways.lib.ks.us/museums/lirm
Key Personnel: Pres., Dana Marintzer; Vice Pres., Chris Koerperich; Cur., Sharleen Wurm; Sec. & Treas., Barbara Dehlinger.
Institution Type/Description: History Museum: located near the site of 1878 last Indian raid on Kansas soil.
Hours & Admission Prices: Museum: April-Nov. Tues.-Sat. 10 to noon & 1-4. Office: Dec.-March Tues.-Thurs. 9:30-12 & 1-4:30. Adults $5, children 6-12 $3; children 6 & under and members no charge. Closed holidays. ♿
Attendance: (actual)

Olathe

ENSOR PARK AND MUSEUM, 18995 W. 183rd St., Olathe, KS 66062-9278. Tel.: 913-592-4141.
E-mail: larryw0hxs@yahoo.com
Web Site: www.ensorparkandmuseum.org
Formerly: Ensor Farmsite and Museum
Key Personnel: Mgr., Larry Woodworth.
Institution Type/Description: Historic Buildings.
Hours & Admission Prices: May-June & Sept.-Oct. Sat.-Sun. 1-5; other times by appointment. Donation: $2.
Attendance: 1,000 (estimated)

ERNIE MILLER NATURE CENTER, 909 N. Hwy. 7, Olathe, KS 66061-4040. Tel.: 913-764-7759. Fax: 913-764-0109.
E-mail: bill.mcgowan@jocogov.org
Web Site: www.erniemiller.com
Key Personnel: Dir., Bill McGowan.
Institution Type/Description: Nature Center.
Hours & Admission Prices: Center: April-May & Sept.-Oct. Mon.-Sat. 9-12 & 1-5, Sun. 1-5; June-Aug. Mon.-Sat. 9-12 & 1-5; Nov.-Feb. Mon.-Sat. 9-12 & 1-4:30, Sun. 12:30-4:30. Trails: daily dawn to dusk. No charge; donations accepted. ♿
Attendance: 35,000 (actual)

MAHAFFIE STAGECOACH STOP AND FARM HISTORIC SITE, 1200 E. Kansas City Rd., Olathe, KS 66061-3002. Tel.: 913-971-5111. Fax: 913-971-5114.
E-mail: mahaffie@olatheks.org
Web Site: www.mahaffie.org
Key Personnel: Site Mgr., Tim Talbott.
Institution Type/Description: Historic Site & House: 1865 Mahaffie house and stagecoach stop on Santa Fe Trail.
Hours & Admission Prices: April-May & Nov.-Dec. Wed.-Sat. 10-4, Sun. 12-4; June-Oct. Thurs.-Sat. 10-4; other times by appointment. Call for admission prices. ♿
Attendance: 38,000 (estimated)

MUSEUM OF DEAF HISTORY, ARTS & CULTURE, 455 E. Park St., Olathe, KS 66061-5436. Tel.: 913-324-5348. Facebook: Museum of Deaf History Arts & Culture.
E-mail: deafcc.director@gmail.com
Web Site: www.museumofdeaf.org
Formerly: Deaf Cultural Center
Key Personnel: Bd. Dirs. Pres., Chriz Dally; Bd. Dirs., Vice Pres. External Affairs, Kim Anderson.
Institution Type/Description: History Museum.

Hours & Admission Prices: Wed.-Sat. 10-4, 2nd Sun. 12-4. No charge; donations accepted. Closed New Year's Day; Independence Day; Thanksgiving; Christmas. ♿
Attendance: 2,500 (estimated)

Osawatomie

JOHN BROWN MUSEUM STATE HISTORIC SITE, 10th & Main Sts., Osawatomie, KS 66064. Mailing Address: P.O. Box 37, Osawatomie, KS 66064-0037. Tel.: 913-755-4384. Fax: 913-755-4164.
E-mail: adaircabin@kshs.org
Web Site: www.kshs.org/john_brown
Formerly: John Brown State Historic Site
Key Personnel: Site Admin., Grady Atwater.
Institution Type/Description: Historic House & Site: 1854 Adair Cabin, used as headquarters by John Brown 1855-58; 1856 Battle of Osawatomie; Underground Railroad stop.
Hours & Admission Prices: Tues.-Sat. 10-5, Sun. 1-5. Adults $3; students $1. Closed national holidays. ♿
Attendance: 1,952 (actual)

Oskaloosa

OLD JEFFERSON TOWN - JEFFERSON COUNTY HISTORICAL SOCIETY, 703 Walnut, Hwy. 59, Oskaloosa, KS 66066. Mailing Address: P.O. Box 146, Oskaloosa, KS 66066-0146. Tel.: 785-863-2070. Facebook.
E-mail: washerman89@yahoo.com
Key Personnel: Pres. (V), Leann Chapman; Cur., Marilyn Sharkey.
Institution Type/Description: Preservation Society: housed in nine c.1880 buildings, relocated to Old Jefferson Town.
Hours & Admission Prices: Museum: May-Sept. Sat. 1-5, Sun. 1:30-5. Library: mid-May to Sept. Sat. 1-5, Sun. 1:30-5; Oct. to mid-May Sat. 1-5. Tours by appointment. No charge; donations accepted. ♿
Attendance: 400 (estimated)

Oswego

OSWEGO HISTORICAL SOCIETY, INC., 410 Commercial St., Oswego, KS 67356-2018. Tel.: 620-795-4500. Facebook: Oswego Historical Museum, Inc..
E-mail: historyatoswego@embarqmail.com
Web Site: www.oswegohistory.org
Formerly: Oswego Historical Museum, Inc.
Key Personnel: Pres. (V) & Dir. (V), Richard W. Farris; Vice Pres. (V) & Dir. (V), Philip Blair; Treas. & Dir. (V), Jolene Gaier; Dir. (V), John Davis; Dir. (V), Marna Taylor; Dir. (V), Janet King.
Institution Type/Description: History Museum.
Hours & Admission Prices: June-Oct. Mon.-Fri. 1-5, Nov.-May Wed. 1-5. No charge; donations accepted. ♿
Attendance: 300 (estimated)

Ottawa

OLD DEPOT MUSEUM, 135 W. Tecumseh, Ottawa, KS 66067. Mailing Address: P.O. Box 145, Ottawa, KS 66067-0145. Tel.: 785-242-1250. Fax: 785-242-1267.
E-mail: info@olddepotmuseum.org
Web Site: www.olddepotmuseum.org
Key Personnel: C.E.O. & Dir., Deborah Barker; Chm. (V), Kevin Blackwell; Treas., Robert T. Burkhart; Archivist, Susan Geiss; Registrar, Gloria Kruse; Museum Asst., Ashley Brannan; Museum Shop Mgr., Diana Staresinic-Deane.
Institution Type/Description: Historical Society Museum.
Hours & Admission Prices: Tues.-Sat. 10-4, Sun. 1-4. Adults $3, students $1; discounts to groups; members & preschoolers no charge. Closed New Year's Day; Easter; Thanksgiving; Christmas. ♿
Attendance: 3,150 (actual)

Overland Park

DEANNA ROSE CHILDREN'S FARMSTEAD, 13800 Switzer Rd., Overland Park, KS 66221-7803. Tel.: 913-897-2360.
E-mail: farmsteadquestservices@opkansas.org
Web Site: www.opkansas.org
Key Personnel: Dir., Virgil Miles; Museum Shop Mgr., Stephanie Jones.
Institution Type/Description: Farmstead.
Hours & Admission Prices: April-May & Sept.-Oct. daily 9-5; June-Aug. Tues. & Thurs. 9-8, Wed. & Fri.-Mon. daily 9-5. Fri.-Sun. 2 & over $2; members & Mon.-Thurs. no charge.
Attendance: 400,000 (actual)

KANSAS CITY JEWISH MUSEUM OF CONTEMPORARY ART - EPSTEN GALLERY, 5500 W. 123rd St., Overland Park, KS 66209. Tel.: 913-266-8414.
E-mail: egarry@kcjmca.org
Key Personnel: Exec. Dir., Eileen Garry; Cur., Marcus Cain; Prog. & Devel. Asst., Abby Rufkahr.
Institution Type/Description: Art Gallery.
Hours & Admission Prices: Tues.-Fri. 11-4, Sat.-Sun. 1-4. No charge; donations accepted.

NERMAN MUSEUM OF CONTEMPORARY ART, 12345 College Blvd., Overland Park, KS 66210-1283. Tel.: 913-469-3000. Fax: 913-469-2348. Facebook: Nerman Museum of Contemporary Art.
E-mail: info@nermanmuseum.org
Web Site: www.nermanmuseum.org
Formerly: Johnson County Community College, Gallery of Art
Key Personnel: Exec. Dir. & Chief Cur., Bruce Hartman; Chm., Greg Musil; Registrar, Whitney Williamson; Cur. Art Education, Karen Gerety Folk; Exhibition Preparator, Art Miller; Education Coord., Katherine Morse.
Institution Type/Description: Contemporary Art Museum.
Hours & Admission Prices: Tues., Fri. & Sat. 10-5, Wed. & Thurs. 10-8, Sun. 12-5. No charge. Closed major holidays. &
Attendance: 80,000 (actual)

Paola

MIAMI COUNTY HISTORICAL MUSEUM, 12 E. Peoria, Paola, KS 66071-1707. Tel.: 913-294-4940.
E-mail: info@thinkmiamicountyhistory.com
Web Site: www.thinkmiamicountyhistory.com
Formerly: Swan River Museum
Institution Type/Description: History Museum.
Hours & Admission Prices: Mon.-Fri. 10-4. No charge; donations accepted. Closed holidays. &
Attendance: 2,000 (estimated)

Parker

PARKER HISTORICAL MUSEUM, 207 W. Main, Parker, KS 66072. Mailing Address: Parker Community Historical Society, P. O. Box 173, Parker, KS 66072-0173.
E-mail: parkerkansashistorical@gmail.com
Web Site: www.parkergen-historical.org
Key Personnel: Pres., Louise Stites; Janice Stahl; Sec. & Treas., Marilyn Rhoads.
Institution Type/Description: Historic Buildings.
Hours & Admission Prices: By appointment.

Parsons

PARSONS HISTORICAL COMMISSION MUSEUM, 401 S. 18th St., Parsons, KS 67357-4220. Mailing Address: P.O. Box 540, Parsons, KS 67357-0540. Tel.: 620-421-7000 & 3694.
E-mail: parsonshistory@gmail.com
Formerly: Parsons Historical Society Museum
Key Personnel: Chm. (V), Lewis Hevel; Financial Dir., Betty Olmsted.
Institution Type/Description: Historical Society Museum.
Hours & Admission Prices: May-Oct. Fri.-Sun. 1-4. No charge; donations accepted. &
Attendance: 1,200 (estimated)

Peabody

PEABODY HISTORICAL MUSEUM, 106 E. Division, Peabody, KS 66866. Mailing Address: 1556 E. 59, Peabody, KS 66866-9485. Tel.: 620-983-2174.
E-mail: info@peabodyhistorical.org
Web Site: www.peabodyhistorical.org/
Key Personnel: Hostess, Gwen Gaines; Pres. (V), Marilyn Jones.
Institution Type/Description: History Museum.
Hours & Admission Prices: Call for hours. No charge; donations accepted. &
Attendance: 498 (actual)

Phillipsburg

FORT BISSELL MUSEUM, 501 Fort Bissell Ave., Phillipsburg, KS 67661-7116. Mailing Address: P.O. Box 53, Phillipsburg, KS 67661-0053. Tel.: 785-543-6212.
E-mail: ftbissell@live.com

Web Site: www.phillipsburgks.us
Formerly: Old Fort Bissell
Key Personnel: Chm. (V) & Sec., Shelly Lare; Vice Pres., Connie Cox; Treas., Kathy Beard.
Institution Type/Description: Historical Society Museum.
Hours & Admission Prices: Memorial Day to Labor Day Tues-Fri. 9-4, Sat. 9-2; tours by appointment. No charge; donations accepted. Closed Independence Day. &
Attendance: 1,500 (estimated)

Pittsburg

CRAWFORD COUNTY HISTORICAL MUSEUM, 651 S. Hwy. 69, Pittsburg, KS 66762-8600. Tel.: 620-231-1440 & 3794.
E-mail: crcomuseum@gmail.com
Web Site: www.crawfordcountymuseum.com
Key Personnel: C.E.O., Alan Ross.
Institution Type/Description: General Museum.
Hours & Admission Prices: Thurs.-Sun. 12-4 or by appointment. No charge; donations accepted. &
Attendance: 2,895 (actual)

Pleasanton

LINN COUNTY MUSEUM/GENEALOGY LIBRARY, 307 E. Park (Dunlap Park), Pleasanton, KS 66075. Mailing Address: P.O. Box 137, Pleasanton, KS 66075-0137. Tel.: 913-352-8739. Fax: 913-352-8739.
Formerly: Linn County Museum
Key Personnel: Pres. (V) & Museum Shop Mgr., Ola May Earnest.
Institution Type/Description: History Museum.
Hours & Admission Prices: Tues. & Thurs. 9-4, Sat.-Sun. 1-5 & by appointment. No charge; donations accepted. &
Attendance: 3,000 (estimated)

MINE CREEK BATTLEFIELD STATE HISTORIC PARK, 20485 Kansas Hwy. 52, Pleasanton, KS 66075-9549. Tel.: 913-352-8890. Facebook.
E-mail: minecreek@kshs.org
Web Site: www.kshs.org/p/mine-creek-civil-war-battlefield/19567
Institution Type/Description: Historic Site: location of the Civil War battle fought on Oct. 25, 1864.
Hours & Admission Prices: May to Oct. Wed.-Sat. 10-5. Adults $5, students $1; members and children 5 & under no charge. Closed state holidays. &
Attendance: 584 (actual)

Pratt

KANSAS DEPARTMENT OF WILDLIFE, PARKS & TOURISM, 512 S.E. 25th Ave., Pratt, KS 67124-8174. Tel.: 620-672-5911, ext. 108 & 0708. Fax: 620-672-6020.
E-mail: mike.rader@ksoutdoors.com
Web Site: www.kdwpt.state.ks.us
Key Personnel: C.E.O., Mike Rader; Caretaker, Chris Shrack.
Institution Type/Description: Nature Center.
Hours & Admission Prices: Mon.-Fri. 8-5. No charge; donations accepted. &
Attendance: 4,300 (estimated)

PRATT COUNTY HISTORICAL SOCIETY MUSEUM, 208 S. Ninnescah St., Pratt, KS 67124-2715. Tel.: 620-672-7874. Facebook: Pratt Historical Museum.
E-mail: pchsmuseum@sctelcom.net
Web Site: prattcountymuseum.org/
Key Personnel: Pres. (V), Tim Kuhn; Vice Pres., Kent Goyen; Treas., Thad Henry; Bd. Sec., Debbie Boley; Cur., Charmaine Swanepoel.
Institution Type/Description: General Museums.
Hours & Admission Prices: Mon.-Fri. 1-4, Sat.-Sun. 1-3; other times by appointment. No charge; donations accepted. Closed New Year's Day; Easter; Memorial Day; Independence Day; Labor Day; Thanksgiving; Christmas. &
Attendance: 3,000 (estimated)

Republic

PAWNEE INDIAN VILLAGE STATE HISTORIC SITE, 480 Pawnee Trail, Republic, KS 66964-8057. Tel.: 785-361-2255. Fax: 785-361-2255.
E-mail: piv@kshs.org
Web Site: www.kshs.org
Key Personnel: Historic Property Cur., Richard Gould; Chm. (V), Narveen Brzon; Pres. (V), Beth Carlgren.

Institution Type/Description: Archaeology Museum: located on the preserved Pawnee Site.
Hours & Admission Prices: Wed.-Sat. 9-5; other times by appointment. Adults $3, seniors & students $2; members, military, and children 5 & under no charge. Closed major holidays. ♿
Attendance: 1,683 (actual)

Russell

DEINES CULTURAL CENTER, 820 N. Main St., Russell, KS 67665-1932. Tel.: 785-483-3742. Fax: 785-483-4397.
E-mail: deinescenter@russellcity.org
Web Site: deinesculturalcenter.org
Key Personnel: Dir., Shannon Trevethan; Marvel Castor.
Institution Type/Description: Art Center.
Hours & Admission Prices: Tues.-Fri. 12-5, Sat.-Sun. 1-5. No charge; donations accepted. ♿
Attendance: 2,500 (estimated)

GERNON HOUSE & BLACKSMITH SITE, 818 N. Kansas St., Russell, KS 67665. Mailing Address: P. O. Box 245, Russell, KS 67665. Tel.: 785-483-3637.
E-mail: rchs@ruraltel.net
Web Site: www.russellkshistory.com
Institution Type/Description: Historic House Museum: built in 1872.
Hours & Admission Prices: Memorial Day to Labor Day Sat. 11-4, Sun. 1-4; other times by appointment. Donations accepted.

HEYM-OLIVER HOUSE - RUSSELL COUNTY HISTORICAL SOCIETY, 503 N. Kansas St., Russell, KS 67665. Tel.: 785-483-3637.
E-mail: rchs@russellks.net
Web Site: www.russellkshistory.com
Institution Type/Description: Historic House Museum: housed in the former home of Nicholas Heym; built in 1878.
Hours & Admission Prices: Summer: Sat.-Sun. 1-4. Adults $2.

OIL PATCH MUSEUM, 100 Edwards Ave., Russell, KS 67665. Tel.: 785-483-6640.
E-mail: rchs@rural.net
Web Site: www.russellkshistory.com
Key Personnel: Dir., Kay Homewood.
Institution Type/Description: Oil History Museum.
Hours & Admission Prices: June-Aug. daily 4-8; Winter: by appointment. Donation Requested.
Attendance: 250 (estimated)

RUSSELL COUNTY HISTORICAL SOCIETY/FOSSIL STATION MUSEUM, 331 Kansas St., Russell, KS 67665-2019. Mailing Address: P.O. Box 245, Russell, KS 67665-0245. Tel.: 785-483-3637.
E-mail: rchs@russellks.net
Web Site: www.russellkshistory.com
Key Personnel: Pres., Kay Homewood; Sec. & Treas., Aldean Banker.
Institution Type/Description: County History Museum & Preservation.
Hours & Admission Prices: Memorial Day to Labor Day Sun. 1-4, Mon.-Sat. 11-4; other times by appointment. No charge; donations accepted.
Attendance: 503 (actual)

Russell Springs

BUTTERFIELD TRAIL HISTORICAL MUSEUM, 515 Hilts, Russell Springs, KS 67764. Tel.: 785-751-4242. Facebook: Butterfield Trail Historical Museum.
E-mail: btassn@st-tel.net
Web Site: www.butterfieldtrailmuseum.org
Key Personnel: Pres., Jarett Haremza; Museum Shop Mgr., Debbie Mather.
Institution Type/Description: History Museum: housed in 1887 Logan County Courthouse & Jail.
Hours & Admission Prices: May to Labor Day Tues.-Sat. 9-12 & 1-5, Sun. 1-5. No charge; donations accepted.
Attendance: 1,000 (actual)

Sabetha

ALBANY HISTORICAL SOCIETY, INC., 415 Grant, Sabetha, KS 66534-2317. Tel.: 785-284-3446 & 3529.
Web Site: www.albanydays.org
Key Personnel: Pres., Alex Dawdy; Vice Pres., Jason Lang; Sec., Travis McCoy.

Institution Type/Description: General Museum: housed in 1867 two-story stone schoolhouse.
Hours & Admission Prices: Memorial Day-Labor Day Sat.-Sun. 2-5; other times by appointment. No charge; donations accepted. ♿
Attendance: 3,000 (estimated)

Saint Francis

CHEYENNE COUNTY MUSEUM, U.S. Hwy. 36 W., Saint Francis, KS 67756. Mailing Address: P.O. Box 611, Saint Francis, KS 67756-0611. Tel.: 785-332-2504.
Institution Type/Description: History Museum.
Hours & Admission Prices: May-Sept. Thurs.-Fri. 9:30-12:30 and by appointment; Oct.-April by appointment only. No charge; donations accepted. ♿

Saint John

ST. JOHN SCIENCE MUSEUM, 312 N. Main St., Saint John, KS 67576-1733. Tel.: 620-549-3818.
E-mail: webmaster@stjohnsciencemuseum.org
Institution Type/Description: Science Museum.
Hours & Admission Prices: Call for hours; groups by appointment. No charge; donations accepted.

Saint Marys

INDIAN PAY STATION MUSEUM, 111 E. Mission, Saint Marys, KS 66536-1526. Mailing Address: c/o City of Saint Marys, P.O. Box 130, Saint Marys, KS 66536. Tel.: 785-437-6600.
E-mail: smccityclerk@gmail.com
Web Site: www.smks.info/museum.html
Institution Type/Description: Historic Building Museum: built in 1857 as an Indian Agency for the Pottawatomie; later used to receive payments for lands taken from them. Listed on the National Register of Historic Places.
Hours & Admission Prices: Daily 1-4; other times by appointment.

Saint Paul

OSAGE MISSION - NEOSHO COUNTY MUSEUM, 203 Washington St., Saint Paul, KS 66771. Tel.: 620-449-2320.
E-mail: museum@osagemission.org
Web Site: osagemission.org
Institution Type/Description: History Museum.
Hours & Admission Prices: Tues.-Sat. 9-2; other times by appointment.

Salina

ROLLING HILLS ZOO, 625 N. Hedville Rd., Salina, KS 67401-9764. Tel.: 785-827-9488.
E-mail: bobj@rollinghillszoo.org
Web Site: www.rollinghillszoo.org
Formerly: Rolling Hills Wildlife Adventure
Key Personnel: Dir., Robert Jenkins; Chm. (V) & Pres. (V), Sandy Walker; Cur., Peter Burvenich; Dir. Operations, Jeff Parker; Dir. Education, Amy Barnhill; Exec. Asst., Debra Preston; Group Sales Mgr. & Special Events, Tracy Green.
Institution Type/Description: Zoo, Natural History Museum & Art Gallery.
Hours & Admission Prices: Summer: daily 8-5; winter: daily 9-5. Zoo: adults $10.95, senior citizens 65 & over $9.95, children 3-12 $5.95; members & children under 3 no charge. Museum: adults $9.95, senior citizens 65 & over $8.95, children 3-12 $4.95; members & children under 3 no charge. Combo: adults $13.95, senior citizens 65 & over $12.95, children 3-12 $7.95; members & children under 3 no charge. Closed New Year's Day; Christmas Eve & Day. ♿
Attendance: 119,016 (actual)

SALINA ART CENTER, 242 S. Santa Fe, Salina, KS 67402-0743. Mailing Address: P.O. Box 743, Salina, KS 67402-0743. Tel.: 785-827-1431. Fax: 785-827-0686. Facebook: Salina Art Center.
E-mail: info@salinaartcenter.org
Web Site: www.salinaartcenter.org
Key Personnel: Pres., Karen Black; Exec. Dir. & Cur., Bill North; Cinema, Heather Greene.
Institution Type/Description: Art Center.
Hours & Admission Prices: Wed.-Sat. 12-5, Sun. 1-5. No charge; donations accepted. Closed major holidays. ♿
Attendance: 18,600 (actual)

SMOKY HILL MUSEUM, 211 W. Iron Ave., Salina, KS 67401-2613. Mailing Address: P.O. Box 101, Salina, KS 67402-0101. Tel.: 785-309-5776. Fax: 785-826-7414.
E-mail: museum@salina.org

Web Site: www.smokyhillmuseum.org
Key Personnel: C.E.O., Brad Anderson; Dir., Susan Hawksworth; Cur. Collections/ Research, Jennifer Toelle; Administrative Asst., Rosa De la Cruz; Cur. Exhibits, Joshua Morris; Cur. Education, Nona Miller; Devel. Coord., Kay Quinn; Museum Shop Mgr., Judy Kuasnicka.
Institution Type/Description: History Museum: housed in 1937 federal building.
Hours & Admission Prices: Tues.-Fri. 12-5, Sat. 10-5. Closed all major holidays. No charge. &
Attendance: 32,256 (actual)

YESTERYEAR MUSEUM, 1100 W. Diamond Dr., Salina, KS 67401-9542. Tel.: 785-825-8473.
E-mail: ckf@yesteryearmuseum.org
Institution Type/Description: History Museum.
Hours & Admission Prices: Call for hours.

Scandia

SCANDIA MUSEUM, 409 4th St., Scandia, KS 66966. Tel.: 785-335-2620.
Key Personnel: Pres. (V), Jim Erickson.
Institution Type/Description: History Museum.
Hours & Admission Prices: Memorial Day to Labor Day Mon.-Sat. 1-4; other times by appointment. No charge. &
Attendance: 500 (estimated)

Scott City

EL QUARTELEJO MUSEUM, 902 W. 5th St., Scott City, KS 67871. Tel.: 602-872-5912.
Institution Type/Description: History Museum.
Hours & Admission Prices: Mon.-Fri. 1-5; other times by appointment. No charge.

KEYSTONE GALLERY, 401 U.S. Hwy. 83, Scott City, KS 67871-8013. Tel.: 620-872-2762. Facebook: Keystone Gallery.
E-mail: keystone@keystonegallery.com
Web Site: www.keystonegallery.com
Key Personnel: Dir., Barbara Shelton.
Institution Type/Description: Fossils & Art Gallery.
Hours & Admission Prices: Call for hours. No charge; donations accepted. Closed Thanksgiving; Christmas.
Attendance: 5,000 (estimated)

Sedan

EMMETT KELLY HISTORICAL MUSEUM, 202 E. Main, Sedan, KS 67361-1629. Tel.: 620-725-3470.
E-mail: ekm@emmettkellymuseum.com
Web Site: www.emmettkellymuseum.com
Key Personnel: Chm. (V), Roger Floyd; Museum Shop Mgr., Ed Henderson.
Institution Type/Description: Clown & Historical Museum: housed in the Sedan Opera House. Listed on the National Register of Historic Places.
Hours & Admission Prices: June-Aug. 15: Tues.-Fri. 10-12 & 1-5, Sat. 10-5. No charge; donations accepted. &
Attendance: 1,500 (actual)

Seneca

NEMAHA COUNTY HISTORICAL SOCIETY, 113 N. 6th St., Seneca, KS 66538-1748. Mailing Address: P.O. Box 41, Seneca, KS 66538-1748. Tel.: 785-336-6366.
E-mail: nchs@rainbowtel.net
Web Site: nemahacountyhistoricalsociety.com
Key Personnel: Dir., Diane Rottinghaus; Pres., Anita Heiman; Researcher, Karen Holthaus.
Institution Type/Description: Historical Society Museum: housed in the former Nemaha County Jail and Sheriff's home; built in 1879.
Hours & Admission Prices: Memorial Day to Labor Day Wed.-Sat.
Attendance: 500

Shawnee

JOHNSON COUNTY MUSEUM, 6305 Lackman Rd., Shawnee, KS 66217-9740. Tel.: 913-715-2550. Fax: 913-715-2565. TDD: 913-782-7188.
E-mail: jcmuseum@jocogov.org
Web Site: www.jocomuseum.org
Key Personnel: Dir., Mindi C. Love; Cur. Collections, Anne Jones; Cur. Education, Jennifer Crane; Cur. Interpretation, Matt Gilligan; Collections Mgr., Russ Czaplewski.

Institution Type/Description: History Museum.
Hours & Admission Prices: Museum: Mon.-Sat. 10-4:30. No charge. 1950s All-Electric House: Mon.-Sat. 1-4, Adults $2, children 12 & under $1. Lanesfield Historic Site: Fri.-Sat. 1-5 & by appointment. No charge. Closed legal holidays.
Attendance: 54,904 (actual)

SHAWNEE TOWN 1929, 11501 W. 57th St., Shawnee, KS 66203-2225. Tel.: 913-248-2360. Fax: 913-248-2363. Facebook: Shawnee Town 1929.
E-mail: cpautler@cityofshawnee.org
Web Site: www.shawneetown.com
Key Personnel: Dir., Charles Pautler; Cur. Collections, Shannon Hsu; Cur. Education, Sharron Uhler.
Institution Type/Description: History Museum.
Hours & Admission Prices: March-Oct. Tues.-Sat. 10-4:30. Self-Guided Tours: adults $3, students 5-17 $1; discounts to AAM members & Time Travelers; members & children under 6 no charge. Closed Memorial Day; Independence Day; Labor Day. &
Attendance: 120,000 (estimated)

WONDERSCOPE CHILDREN'S MUSEUM OF KANSAS CITY, 5700 King, Shawnee, KS 66203-2708. Tel.: 913-287-8888. Fax: 913-268-4608.
E-mail: info@wonderscope.org
Web Site: www.wonderscope.org
Key Personnel: Dir. & C.E.O., Roxane Hill; Chm. (V), Jill Jolicoeur.
Institution Type/Description: Children's Museum.
Hours & Admission Prices: Tues.-Fri. 9-4:30, Sat. 9-5, Sun. 12-5. Admission 3-63 $7, senior citizens 64 & over $6, children 1-2 $4; discounts to ACM members; children under 1 & members no charge. Closed major holidays. &
Attendance: 60,000 (actual)

Stafford

QUIVIRA NATIONAL WILDLIFE REFUGE AND VISITOR CENTER, 1434 N.E. 80th St., Stafford, KS 67578. Tel.: 620-486-2393.
E-mail: quivira@fws.gov
Institution Type/Description: Wildlife Refuge.
Hours & Admission Prices: Visitors Center: Mon.-Fri. 7:30-4. Refuge: daily sunrise to sunset. No charge. &

STAFFORD COUNTY HISTORICAL SOCIETY MUSEUM, 100 N. Main, Stafford, KS 67578-1343. Tel.: 620-234-5664. Facebook: Stafford County Museum.
E-mail: schgs1976@gmail.com
Web Site: staffordcountymuseum.weebley.com
Key Personnel: Pres. (V), Marion Hearn.
Institution Type/Description: Historical Society Museum & Library.
Hours & Admission Prices: Mon.-Fri. 9-3:30; weekends & special tours by appointment. No charge; donations accepted.
Attendance: 1,000 (estimated)

Stockton

FRANK WALKER MUSEUM, 921 S. Cedar, Stockton, KS 67669. Tel.: 785-425-7217.
Institution Type/Description: History Museum.
Hours & Admission Prices: Tues., Thurs. & Sat. 10-4; other times by appointment. No charge; donations accepted.

WALLER-COOLBAUGH 20TH-CENTURY HOUSE, 421 N. Walnut, Stockton, KS 67669. Mailing Address: 319 Gracie St., Stockton, KS 67669. Tel.: 785-425-7227.
Institution Type/Description: Historic House Museum: built in 1905.
Hours & Admission Prices: Call for hours.

Strong City

TALLGRASS PRAIRIE NATIONAL PRESERVE, 2480 KS Hwy. 177, Strong City, KS 66869. Tel.: 620-273-8494 & 6034. Fax: 620-273-8066. Facebook: Tallgrass Prairie National Preserve.
E-mail: tapr-interpretation@nps.gov
Web Site: www.nps.gov/tapr
Institution Type/Description: Nature Preserve with Historic Buildings.
Hours & Admission Prices: Preserve & Trails: daily 24 hours. Buildings: daily 8:30-4:30. No charge; donations accepted. Closed some holidays.
Attendance: 18,500 (actual)

Studley

COTTONWOOD RANCH, 14432 E. US Hwy. 24, Studley, KS 67740-4135. Mailing Address: 746 S. Rd. 148 E., Hoxie, KS 67740-4130. Tel.: 785-627-5866.
E-mail: cottonwoodranchks@gmail.com
Institution Type/Description: Historic Site: built by John Fenton Pratt from 1885-1896.
Hours & Admission Prices: Jan. 5-Feb. Fri.-Sat. 10-4, Sun. 1-4; March-Nov. Wed.-Sat. 9-5, Sun. 1-5. Adults $2, seniors & students $1; active military & children under 5 no charge. Closed state holidays. ᴅ
Attendance: 499 (actual)

Sublette

HASKELL COUNTY HISTORICAL SOCIETY, North Fairground Rd., Sublette, KS 67877. Mailing Address: P.O. Box 101, Sublette, KS 67877-0101. Tel.: 620-675-8344.
E-mail: jimgroth@pld.com
Formerly: The Haskell County Historical Museum
Key Personnel: Pres. (V), James Groth; Dir., Darlene Groth.
Institution Type/Description: General Museum.
Hours & Admission Prices: Tues.-Sat. 1-5. No charge; donations accepted. Closed major holidays ᴅ
Attendance: 650 (actual)

Sylvan Grove

YESTERDAY HOUSE MUSEUM, 118 S. Main St., Sylvan Grove, KS 67481. Mailing Address: P.O. Box 68, Sylvan Grove, KS 67481. Tel.: 785-526-7270.
Institution Type/Description: History Museum.
Hours & Admission Prices: May-Oct. Sat.-Sun. 1-5; other times by appointment.

Syracuse

HAMILTON COUNTY MUSEUM, Hwy. 50 & Gates St., Syracuse, KS 67878. Mailing Address: 102 N. Gates, P.O. Box 923, Syracuse, KS 67878-0923. Tel.: 620-384-7496. Facebook.
E-mail: historic@pld.com
Web Site: www.hamiltoncountymuseum.org
Key Personnel: Mgr., Joanice Jantz; Pres. Bd. (V), Jason R. Ochs; Vice Pres., Rusty Wharton; Sec., Marcia Ashmore; Treas., Jo Dean Hawkins; Member, Marcus Ashlock.
Institution Type/Description: History Museum.
Hours & Admission Prices: Tues.-Sat. 9-12 & 1-4. No charge; donations accepted. Closed New Year's Day; Labor Day; Thanksgiving; Christmas.
Attendance: 1,900 (estimated)

Tonganoxie

TONGANOXIE COMMUNITY HISTORICAL SOCIETY, 201 W. Washington St., Tonganoxie, KS 66086. Mailing Address: P.O. Box 785, Tonganoxie, KS 66086-0785. Tel.: 913-845-2960. Facebook.
E-mail: tchs2002@att.net
Web Site: www.tonganoxiehistoricalsociety.org
Key Personnel: Dir., Laurie Walters; Chm. (V), Ray Stockman; Pres. (V), Kris Roberts.
Institution Type/Description: Local History Museum.
Hours & Admission Prices: Tues. 9-4, Wed. 9 am to noon, Sun. 1-4. No charge; donations accepted. ᴅ
Attendance: 3,680 (estimated)

Topeka

ALICE C. SABATINI GALLERY-TOPEKA AND SHAWNEE COUNTY PUBLIC LIBRARY, 1515 W. 10th, Topeka, KS 66604-1304. Tel.: 785-580-4515 & 4400. Fax: 785-580-4496.
E-mail: gallery@tscpl.org
Web Site: www.tscpl.org/gallery
Key Personnel: C.E.O., Gina Millsap; Deputy Dir., Robert Banks; Coord., Kari Zimmerman; Exhibit Cur., Zan Popp; Cur. Art Collection, Sherry Best; Museum Shop Mgr., Laura Schmidt.
Institution Type/Description: Fine Arts Gallery.
Hours & Admission Prices: Mon.-Fri. 9-9, Sat. 9-6, Sun. 12-9. No charge. Closed New Year's Day; Martin Luther King Jr. Day; Washington's Birthday; Memorial Day; Independence Day; Labor Day; Veterans Day; Thanksgiving; Christmas. ᴅ
Attendance: 22,000 (estimated)

BROWN V. BOARD OF EDUCATION NATIONAL HISTORIC SITE, 1515 S.E. Monroe St., Topeka, KS 66612-1143. Tel.: 785-354-4273. Fax: 785-354-7213.
E-mail: brvb_superintendent@nps.gov
Web Site: www.nps.gov/brvb
Key Personnel: Superintendent, Sherda Williams; Chief of Interpretation, Education, & Cultural Resources, Enimini Ekong.
Institution Type/Description: Historic Site.
Hours & Admission Prices: Daily 9-5. No charge; donations accepted. Closed New Year's Day; Thanksgiving; Christmas.

CHARLES CURTIS HOUSE MUSEUM, 1101 S.W. Topeka Blvd., Topeka, KS 66612-1602. Tel.: 785-597-5380 & 357-1371.
E-mail: curtishousemuseum@embargmail.com
Web Site: www.charlescurtismuseum.com
Institution Type/Description: Historic House: former home of Senator Charles Curtis; built in 1879.
Hours & Admission Prices: By appointment. Adults $5.

COMBAT AIR MUSEUM, INC., 7016 S.E. Forbes Ave., Topeka, KS 66619-1444. Tel.: 785-862-3303. Fax: 785-862-3304. Facebook: Combat Air Museum.
E-mail: combatairmuseum@aol.com
Web Site: www.combatairmuseum.org
Key Personnel: Chm. & Pres., Gene Howerter.
Institution Type/Description: Military Aviation Museum: 1942 Topeka Army Air Field-later Forbes AFB, now Forbes Field.
Hours & Admission Prices: Jan.-Feb. daily 12-4:30; March-Dec. Mon.-Sat. 9-4:30, Sun. 12-4:30; last admission 3:30. Adults $6, active military & children 5-17 $4; discounts to AAA members; children under 5 & members no charge. Closed New Year's Day; Easter; Thanksgiving; Christmas. ᴅ
Attendance: 10,000 (actual)

THE GREAT OVERLAND STATION, 701 N. Kansas Ave., Topeka, KS 66608-1260. Mailing Address: P.O. Box 8792, Topeka, KS 66608-0792. Tel.: 785-232-5533. Fax: 785-232-6259.
E-mail: info@greatoverlandstation.com
Web Site: greatoverlandstation.com
Key Personnel: Pres. & C.O.O., Bette Allen; Chm., Robert St. John; Dir. Capital Campaign, Beth Fager; Business Mgr., Jeannie Rose; Events Mgr., Algen Sigare.
Institution Type/Description: Railroad Heritage Museum: housed in the historic Union Pacific Depot.
Hours & Admission Prices: Tues.-Sat. 10-4, last admission 3:15. Adults $5, seniors & military $4, children $2; members no charge. Closed national holidays. ᴅ
Attendance: 23,000 (estimated)

HOLLEY MUSEUM OF MILITARY HISTORY, Mailing Address: Ramada Hotel & Convention Center, 420 S.E. 6th St., Topeka, KS 66606. Tel.: 785-272-6204. Fax: 785-224-5034.
Key Personnel: Cur., Vernon Fisher.
Institution Type/Description: Military History Museum.
Hours & Admission Prices: Daily 10-8. No charge; donations accepted.

KANSAS CHILDREN'S DISCOVERY CENTER, Gage Park, 4400 S.W. 10th Ave., Topeka, KS 66604. Tel.: 785-783-8300. Fax: 785-783-7662.
E-mail: jmorrell@kansasdicovery.org
Web Site: www.kansasdiscovery.org
Key Personnel: Exec. Dir., Joanne Morrell; Dir. Operations, Carolyn Chinn Lewis; Dir. Education & Programs, Margaret Hennessey Springe; Visitor Svcs. & Membership, Maureen Washatka; Mktg., Andrea Etzel.
Institution Type/Description: Children's Museum.
Hours & Admission Prices: Tues.-Sat. 10-5, Sun. 1-5. Admission $7.25, seniors 65 & over $6.25; discounts to ACM members; children under one and members no charge.

KANSAS MUSEUM OF HISTORY, 6425 S.W. Sixth Ave., Topeka, KS 66615-1099. Tel.: 785-272-8681, ext. 417. Fax: 785-272-8682.
E-mail: kshs.kansasmuseum@ks.gov
Web Site: www.kshs.org
Key Personnel: Exec. Dir. Kansas State Historical Foundation, Vicky Henley; Exec. Dir. Kansas Historical Society, Jennie Chinn; Chm. & Pres. (V), Paul Stuewe; Division Dir. Admin., Matthew Chappell; Dir. Communications, Bobbie Athon; Division Dir. Education & Museum, Mary Madden; Exhibit Dir., Nate Forsberg; Museum Cur., Blair D. Tarr; Museum Cur., Matt Renick; Registrar, Nikaela Zimmerman.
Institution Type/Description: History Museum.

Hours & Admission Prices: Museum: Tues.-Sat. 9-5, Sun. 1-5. Historic Sites; Tues.-Sat. 10-5, Sun. 1-5. Adults $8, senior citizens 65 & up and military $7, students $5; members no charge. Closed New Year's Day; Thanksgiving; Christmas; state holidays. &
Attendance: 31,359 (actual)

KANSAS STATE ARCHIVES, Center for Historical Research, Reference Dept., 6425 S.W. Sixth Ave., Topeka, KS 66615-1099. Tel.: 785-272-8681, ext. 117.
E-mail: pmichaelis@kshs.org
Key Personnel: Dir. State Archives Div., Patricia Michaelis; Exec. Dir. Kansas Historical Society, Jennie Chinn.
Institution Type/Description: Archives.
Hours & Admission Prices: Call for hours. &
Attendance: 3,677 (actual)

KANSAS STATE CAPITOL, 10th & Jackson, Topeka, KS 66612. Mailing Address: 6425 S.W. 6th Ave., Topeka, KS 66615. Tel.: 785-296-3966.
E-mail: capitol@kshs.org
Key Personnel: Museum & Education, Andrea Burton.
Institution Type/Description: Historic Building: built in 1903.
Hours & Admission Prices: Self-Guided Tours: Mon.-Fri. 8-5, Sat. 8-1. Guided Tours: Jan.-May Mon.-Fri. 9am, 10am, 11am, 1pm, 2pm, & 3pm; June-Dec. Mon.-Fri. 9am, 11am, 1pm & 3pm. No charge. &
Attendance: 71,400 (actual)

MULVANE ART MUSEUM, 17th & Jewell Sts., Topeka, KS 66621-1150. Mailing Address: 1700 S.W. College Ave., Topeka, KS 66621. Tel.: 785-670-1124. Fax: 785-670-1329.
E-mail: mulvane.info@washburn.edu
Web Site: www.washburn.edu/mulvane
Key Personnel: Dir., Connie Gibbons; Cur. Education, Kandis Barker; Asst. Cur. Education, Jane Hanni; Preparator, Michael Allen; Office Asst., Delene VanSickel.
Institution Type/Description: Art Museum.
Hours & Admission Prices: Tues. 10-7, Wed.-Fri. 10-5, Sat. 1-4. No charge; donations accepted. Closed major holidays. &
Attendance: 60,000 (actual)

MUSEUM OF THE KANSAS NATIONAL GUARD, 125 S.E. Airport Dr., Topeka, KS 66619. Tel.: 785-862-7203.
E-mail: office@kngmuseum.org
Web Site: www.kansasguardmuseum.org
Key Personnel: Pres. (V), BG Ed Gerhardt, (Ret.); Dir., MSG Jeremy Byers; C.E.O., Ed Gerhardt; Museum Shop Mgr., Mrs. Karen Morrow.
Institution Type/Description: Army and Air National Guard Museum.
Hours & Admission Prices: Mon.-Sat. 10-4. No charge, but donations accepted. &
Attendance: 12,000 (actual)

OLD PRAIRIE TOWN AT WARD-MEADE HISTORIC SITE, 124 N.W. Fillmore, Topeka, KS 66606-1171. Tel.: 785-251-2989. Fax: 785-368-3890. Facebook: Old Prairie Town.
E-mail: john.bell@snco.us
Web Site: parks.snco.us
Formerly: Historic Ward-Meade Park
Key Personnel: Dir., John Bell.
Institution Type/Description: History Museum.
Hours & Admission Prices: Park: daily 8am to dusk. General Store & Drugstore: Mon.-Sat. 10-4, Sun. 12-4. Guided Tours: Mon.-Fri. 10, 12 & 2, Sat.-Sun. 12 & 2. Tours: adults $4.50, senior citizens $4, children 6-12 $2; discounts to school groups; children under 5 & botanical garden no charge. Stores closed federal holidays. &
Attendance: 70,000 (estimated)

TOPEKA ZOOLOGICAL PARK, 635 S.W. Gage Blvd., Topeka, KS 66606-2066. Tel.: 785-368-9180. Fax: 785-368-9152.
E-mail: zoo@topeka.org
Web Site: www.topeka.org/zoo
Key Personnel: Dir. Zoo, Brendan Wiley; Mgr. Zoo Operations, Fawn Moser; Education Cur., Dennis Dinwiddie; Zoo Veterinarian, Dr. Shirley Llizo; Animal Care Supvr., Shanna Simpson.
Institution Type/Description: Zoo.
Hours & Admission Prices: Daily 9-5. Adults $5.75, senior citizens 65 & up $4.75, children 3-12 $4.25; discounts to AZA members; members and children 2 & under no charge. Closed New Year's Day; Christmas. &
Attendance: 180,000 (actual)

Towanda

PARADISE DOLL MUSEUM & HOSPITAL, 119 S. Sixth St., Towanda, KS 67144-9040. Tel.: 316-536-2710. Fax: 316-536-2780.
E-mail: fbrush@cox.net
Key Personnel: Pres. (V) & Museum Shop Mgr., Barbara Brush.
Institution Type/Description: Doll Museum.
Hours & Admission Prices: Tues.-Sat. 1-5. No charge; donations accepted. &
Attendance: 2,000 (estimated)

Tribune

HORACE GREELEY MUSEUM, 214 E. Harper, P.O. Box 231, Tribune, KS 67879. Tel.: 620-376-4996.
E-mail: museum1@fairpoint.com
Institution Type/Description: History Museum: housed in the former county courthouse.
Hours & Admission Prices: Thurs. 9-4; other times by appointment. No charge; donations accepted.
Attendance: 900 (estimated)

Ulysses

GRANT COUNTY MUSEUM AKA HISTORIC ADOBE MUSEUM, 300 E. Oklahoma, Ulysses, KS 67880-2542. Mailing Address: P.O. Box 906, Ulysses, KS 67880-0906. Tel.: 620-356-3009. Fax: 620-356-5082.
E-mail: ulyksmus@pld.com
Web Site: www.historicadobemuseum.org
Key Personnel: Dir. & Chm. (V), Ginger Anthony; Pres. (V), Pam Meile; Treas., Jim Hickok.
Institution Type/Description: General Museum.
Hours & Admission Prices: Mon.-Fri. 10-5, Sat. 1-5. No charge; donations accepted. Closed holidays. &
Attendance: 9,000 (estimated)

Valley Center

VALLEY CENTER HISTORICAL MUSEUM, 112 N. Meridian, Valley Center, KS 67147. Tel.: 316-755-0783.
Web Site: www.vchistory.org
Institution Type/Description: History Museum.
Hours & Admission Prices: Call for hours. No charge; donations accepted.

WaKeeney

TREGO COUNTY HISTORICAL SOCIETY MUSEUM, Fairgrounds, 128 N. 13th/Hwy. 283, WaKeeney, KS 67672. Mailing Address: P.O. Box 132, WaKeeney, KS 67672-0132. Tel.: 785-743-2964. Facebook: Trego County Historical Society.
E-mail: tregohistorical@ruraltel.net
Web Site: tregohistorical.org
Key Personnel: Dir., Marjean Deines; Pres. (V), Evea Rumpel.
Institution Type/Description: Historical Society Museum.
Hours & Admission Prices: Tues. & Fri. 10-12 & 1-5, Wed.-Thurs. 1-5, Sat. 10-12 & 1-4, Sun. 1-4. No charge; donations accepted. &
Attendance: 700 (estimated)

Wakefield

WAKEFIELD MUSEUM ASSOCIATION, 604 6th St., Wakefield, KS 67487. Mailing Address: P.O. Box 193, Wakefield, KS 67487. Tel.: 785-461-5516. Facebook: Wakefield Museum Association.
E-mail: wakefieldmuseum@eaglecom.net
Web Site: www.wakefieldmuseum.com
Key Personnel: Dir. & Pres. (V), Joy Shandy; Treas., Sharon Babst; Museum Shop Mgr., Christy Hayes.
Institution Type/Description: General Museum.
Hours & Admission Prices: Jan. 7-March Sat.-Sun. 1-4; April-Dec. 18 Wed.-Sun. 1-4. No charge; donations accepted. Closed Easter; Independence Day; Thanksgiving. &
Attendance: 1,010 (actual)

Wallace

FORT WALLACE MUSEUM, 2655 Hwy. 40, Wallace, KS 67761. Tel.: 785-891-3564. Facebook: Fort Wallace Museum.
E-mail: museum@ftwallace.com
Web Site: www.ftwallace.org

Key Personnel: Pres. (V), Jayne Humphrey Pearce.
Institution Type/Description: History Museum.
Hours & Admission Prices: Mon.-Sat. 9-5, Sun. 1-5. No charge; donations accepted. &
Attendance: 3,000 (estimated)

Wamego

OZ MUSEUM, 511 Lincoln, Wamego, KS 66547-1633. Tel.: 866-458-TOTO (toll free). Fax: 785-456-9498.
E-mail: shop@ozmuseum.com
Web Site: www.ozmuseum.com
Key Personnel: Exec. Dir., Clint Stueve; Museum Shop Mgr., Kimberly Shepherd.
Institution Type/Description: Movie Museum.
Hours & Admission Prices: Memorial Day-Labor Day Mon.-Fri. 10-6, Sun. 12-6. Adults 13 & over $8, children 4-8 $8; discounts to groups & military; children 3 & under no charge. &
Attendance: 36,000 (actual)

OZ MUESUM/COLUMBIAN THEATRE FOUNDATION, INC., 521 Lincoln Ave., Wamego, KS 66547-1633. Tel.: 785-456-2029. Fax: 785-456-9498.
E-mail: boxoffice@columbiantheatre.com
Web Site: columbiantheatre.com; ozmuseum.com
Formerly: The Columbian Theatre, Museum & Art Center
Key Personnel: Exec. Dir., Clint Stueve; Pres., Jon Pachta; Gift Shop Operations Mgr., Kimberly Shepherd; Event Coordr., Tara Jackson; Mktg. Asst., Alyssa Smith; Production Mgr., Libby Stratton; Box Office Coord., Rhonda Jacques.
Institution Type/Description: Decorative Arts Museum: housed in 1895 building to display the 1893 Chicago World's Fair paintings bought by J.C. Rogers; a museum that celebrates the cultural legacy of The Wizard of Oz.
Hours & Admission Prices: The Columbian Theatre & Museum: Tues.-Fri. 1-5, Sat. 10-3. Suggested Donation: $5. The OZ Museum: March-Sept. Mon.-Sat. 10-5, Sun. 12-5; Oct.-Feb. Mon.-Sat. 10-3, Sun. 12-3. Adults $7, children $4. Closed New Year's Day; Easter; Thanksgiving; Christmas. &
Attendance: 60,000 (estimated)

WAMEGO HISTORICAL SOCIETY & MUSEUM, E. 4th St., City Park, Wamego, KS 66547. Mailing Address: P.O. Box 84, Wamego, KS 66547-0084. Tel.: 785-456-2040.
E-mail: wamegomuseum@wamego.net
Web Site: wamegohistoricalmuseum.org
Institution Type/Description: Historical Society Museum: housed in a KS Pacific Railroad mechanics rock building; built in 1862.
Hours & Admission Prices: April-Oct. Mon.-Sat. 10-12 & 1-4, Sun. 1-4; Nov.-March Tues.-Sun. 1-4; groups by appointment. Adults $4; discounts to seniors, military, groups, students & AAA members; members no charge. &
Attendance: 3,243 (actual)

Washington

WASHINGTON COUNTY HISTORICAL SOCIETY, 216 Ballard, Washington, KS 66968-1901. Tel.: 785-325-2198.
E-mail: wchgs31@hotmail.com
Key Personnel: Pres. (V), Duane Klozenbucher; Editor of Genealogy, Jo Rippe; Treas., Arlene Dague; Archivist & Genealogy, Mary Alice Pacey.
Institution Type/Description: Historical Society Museum.
Hours & Admission Prices: Tues.-Fri. 9-4. $3, donations accepted. Closed New Year's Day; Thanksgiving; Christmas. &
Attendance: 2,500 (actual)

Wellington

CHISHOLM TRAIL MUSEUM, 502 N. Washington, Wellington, KS 67152-4061. Tel.: 620-326-3820 & 7466.
E-mail: ctmuseum@live.com
Key Personnel: Pres. (V), Richard M. Gilfillan; Sec., Nancy McNett; Treas., Cur. Archives & Librarian, Doris Dwyer.
Institution Type/Description: History Museum: housed in first hospital in Wellington.
Hours & Admission Prices: mid-April to Memorial Day Sat.-Sun. 1-4; June-Oct. daily 1-4, Nov. Sat.-Sun. 1-4. No charge; donations accepted.
Attendance: 2,000 (estimated)

PANHANDLE RAILROAD MUSEUM, 425 E. Harvey, Wellington, KS 67152-3065. Tel.: 620-399-8611.
E-mail: phwiley@sutv.com
Key Personnel: Dir. & Museum Shop Mgr., Perry H. Wiley; Chm. (V), Sherry Wiley.
Institution Type/Description: Railroad Museum.

Hours & Admission Prices: By appointment. No charge; donations accepted. &
Attendance: 325 (estimated)

Westmoreland

ROCK CREEK VALLEY HISTORICAL SOCIETY, 507 Burkman St., Westmoreland, KS 66549. Mailing Address: P.O. Box 13, Westmoreland, KS 66549-0013. Tel.: 785-457-0100.
E-mail: museum@westmorelandkshistory.org
Web Site: www.westmorelandkshistory.org
Key Personnel: Pres. (V), Judy Hinrichsen.
Institution Type/Description: Historical Society Museum.
Hours & Admission Prices: April-Nov. Tues.-Sun. 1-4; other times by appointment. No charge; donations accepted. Closed holidays.
Attendance: 754 (actual)

Wichita

BOTANICA, THE WICHITA GARDENS, 701 Amidon, Wichita, KS 67203-3199. Tel.: 316-264-0448. Fax: 316-264-0587. Facebook: Botanica Wichita.
E-mail: mmiller@botanica.org
Web Site: www.botanica.org
Key Personnel: C.E.O., Marty Miller; Pres. (V), Justus Fugate; Cur., Pat McKernan; Public Rels., Kristin Marlett; Volunteer Coord., Jodi McArthur; Facilities Coord., Linda Keller; Memberships, Kathy Osler; Dir. Finance, Kathy Oster.
Institution Type/Description: Botanical Gardens.
Hours & Admission Prices: April-Oct. Mon.-Sat. 9-5, Sun. 1-5; Nov.-March Mon.-Sat. 9-5. Adults $7, seniors $6, children 3-12 $5; discounts to active military & American Public Garden Assoc. members; children under 2 no charge. American Horticultural Society reciprocal program. Closed Martin Luther King Jr. Day; Presidents' Day; Veterans Day; Thanksgiving; Christmas Eve & Day. &
Attendance: 175,000 (estimated)

COLEMAN FACTORY OUTLET AND MUSEUM, 235 N. St. Francis, Wichita, KS 67202. Tel.: 316-264-0836.
Institution Type/Description: History Museum.
Hours & Admission Prices: Mon.-Fri. 9-6, Sat. 9-1. No charge.

EXPLORATION PLACE, INC., 300 N. McLean Blvd., Wichita, KS 67203-5901. Tel.: 316-660-0600. Fax: 316-660-0670. Facebook: Exploration Place, Inc..
E-mail: christina.bluml@exploration.org
Web Site: www.exploration.org
Formerly: Exploration Place, Inc. dba the Children's Museum of Wichita
Key Personnel: Pres., Jan. B. Luth; Chm., Jason Cox; Dir. Mktg., Christina Bluml; Dir. Devel., Diana Gordon; Dir. Exhibits, Lynn Corona; Museum Shop Mgr., Lucia Fierro.
Institution Type/Description: Science Museum.
Hours & Admission Prices: Jan.-March 9 & Sept. 17 to mid-March Tues.-Sat. 10-5, Sun. 12-5; March 16-Sept. 7 Mon.-Sat. 10-5, Sun. 12-5. Adults $9.50, senior citizens 65 & over $8, youth 3-11 $6; discounts to Reciprocal Program, ACM & ASTC members; children 2 & under & members no charge. Dome Theater & Planetarium: adults $5, senior citizens 65 & over $4, youth 3-11 $3. Closed Thanksgiving; Christmas. &
Attendance: 168,628 (actual)

FISCH HAUS GALLERY, 524 S. Commerce, Wichita, KS 67202-4610. Tel.: 316-263-6770.
E-mail: info@fischhaus.com
Web Site: www.fischhaus.com
Institution Type/Description: Art Gallery.
Hours & Admission Prices: Sept.-June last Fri. each month 7pm-10pm; other times by appointment.

GREAT PLAINS NATURE CENTER, 6232 E. 29th St. N., Wichita, KS 67220-2200. Tel.: 316-683-5499. Fax: 316-688-9555.
E-mail: jim@gpnc.org
Web Site: www.gpnc.org
Key Personnel: Dir., Jim Mason; Volunteer Coord., Heidi Bowen; Museum Shop Mgr., Charlene Van Walleghen.
Institution Type/Description: Nature Center.
Hours & Admission Prices: Mon.-Sat. 9-5. No charge; donations accepted. Closed holidays. &
Attendance: 160,702 (actual)

GREAT PLAINS TRANSPORTATION MUSEUM, 700 E. Douglas, Wichita, KS 67202-3506. Tel.: 316-263-0944.
E-mail: info@gptm.us

Web Site: www.gptm.us
Key Personnel: Vice Pres., Steve Corp; Pres. (V), John Gries; Financial Dir., Gale Meek; Public Rels., Affairs & Devel., J. Harvey Koehn; Membership, Fred Tefft; Security, Norman Walters; Museum Shop Mgr., David Meek.
Institution Type/Description: Transportation Museum.
Hours & Admission Prices: April-Oct. Sat. 9-4, Sun. 1-4; Nov.-March Sat. 9-4. Adults $5, children 3-12 $3; children under 3 no charge. Closed Christmas.
Attendance: 2,979 (actual)

THE KANSAS AFRICAN AMERICAN MUSEUM, 601 N. Water St., Wichita, KS 67203-3833. Tel.: 316-262-7651. Fax: 316-265-6953.

E-mail: info@tkaamueum.org
Web Site: tkaamuseum.org
Key Personnel: Exec. Dir., Mark E. McCormick; Pres. (V), Lee Williams.
Institution Type/Description: Art & Culture Museum.
Hours & Admission Prices: Tues.-Fri. 10-5, Sat. 12-4. Adults $5.50, students & seniors $4.50, children 5-17 $2.50; members and children 5 & under no charge. Closed major holidays. &
Attendance: 3,081 (actual)

KANSAS AVIATION MUSEUM, 3350 George Washington Blvd., Wichita, KS 67210-2194. Tel.: 316-683-9242, 877-683-9242. Fax: 316-683-0573.

E-mail: info@kansasaviationmuseum.org
Web Site: www.kansasaviationmuseum.org
Key Personnel: Exec. Dir., Dana Steffee; Pres. (V), Ron Williams.
Institution Type/Description: Aviation Museum: housed in c.1935 art deco municipal air terminal administration building.
Hours & Admission Prices: Tues.-Fri. 9-3, Sat.-Sun. 9-5. Adults $9.50, seniors 65 & over $8.50, children 4-12 $7.50; discounts to military & AAA members; children under 3 no charge. Closed New Year's Day; Easter; Thanksgiving; Christmas. &
Attendance: 20,000 (actual)

KANSAS FIREFIGHTERS MUSEUM, 1300 S. Broadway, Wichita, KS 67211. Tel.: 316-264-3616.

E-mail: kansasfirefightersmuseum@gmail.com
Web Site: www.kansasfirefightersmuseum.com
Key Personnel: Pres. (V), Nick Mendoza; Museum Shop Mgr., Ruth Cox.
Institution Type/Description: Firefighting History Museum: housed in Engine House No. 6; built in 1910. Listed on the National Register of Historic Places.
Hours & Admission Prices: Call for hours. Adults $3, seniors $2.50; members no charge.
Attendance: 450 (estimated)

KANSAS SPORTS HALL OF FAME AT THE WICHITA BOATHOUSE, 515 S. Wichita St., Wichita, KS 67202-3633. Tel.: 316-262-2038. Fax: 316-263-2539.

E-mail: info@kshof.org
Web Site: www.kshof.org
Key Personnel: Dir., KSHOF, Jordan Poland; Dir. Wichita Boathouse, Laura Hartley.
Institution Type/Description: Sports Museum.
Hours & Admission Prices: Mon.-Fri. 10-4. No charge; donations accepted. Closed New Year's Day; Easter; Thanksgiving; Christmas. &
Attendance: 10,000 (actual)

LOWELL D. HOLMES MUSEUM OF ANTHROPOLOGY, Wichita State Univ., Neff Hall, 1845 Fairmount Box 52, Wichita, KS 67260. Tel.: 316-978-7068. Fax: 316-978-3351.

E-mail: rachelle.meinecke@wichita.edu
Key Personnel: Dir., Jerry Martin.
Institution Type/Description: Anthropology Museum.
Hours & Admission Prices: Sept.-May Mon.-Fri. 1-5. No charge; donations accepted.

MID-AMERICA ALL INDIAN CENTER, 650 N. Seneca, Wichita, KS 67203-3204. Tel.: 316-350-3340. Fax: 316-262-4216.

E-mail: ascott@wichita.gov
Web Site: www.theindiancenter.org
Key Personnel: Exec. Dir., April Scott; Museum Dir., Deborah Roseke; Education Dir., Crystal Flannery-Bachicha.
Institution Type/Description: Native American Museum: located on the site of old Indian council grounds.
Hours & Admission Prices: Tues.-Sat. 10-4. Adults $7, military, student 13 & up w/ ID and seniors 55 & over $5, children 6-12 $3, children under 6 no charge. Closed New Year's Eve & Day; Easter; Thanksgiving; Christmas. &
Attendance: 60,000 (estimated)

MIDWEST HISTORICAL AND GENEALOGICAL LIBRARY, 1203 N. Main, Wichita, KS 67203-3614. Mailing Address: P.O. Box 1121, Wichita, KS 67201-1121. Tel.: 316-264-3611.

Institution Type/Description: Library.
Hours & Admission Prices: Tues. & Sat. 9-4, call to confirm.

MUSEUM OF WORLD TREASURES, 835 E. First St. N., Wichita, KS 67202-2700. Tel.: 316-263-1311. Facebook: Museum of World Treasures.

E-mail: marketing@worldtreasures.org
Web Site: www.worldtreasures.org
Key Personnel: Founder, Dr. Jon Kardatzke; Pres. & C.E.O., Mike Noller; Chm. (V), Bernard Hentzen; Operations Dir., Tracy Dickson; Dir. Education, Kristin Martin; Cur. Collections, Steven King; Cur. Exhibits., Timothy Howard.
Institution Type/Description: General Museum.
Hours & Admission Prices: Mon.-Sat. 10-5, Sun. 12-5. Adults 13-59 $8.95, seniors 60 & over $7.95, children 4-12 $6.95; members & children under 4 no charge. Closed Easter; Thanksgiving; Christmas. &
Attendance: 36,748 (actual)

OLD COWTOWN MUSEUM, 1865 W. Museum Blvd., Wichita, KS 67203-3295. Tel.: 316-350-3323. Fax: 316-858-7968.

E-mail: dflask@wichita.gov
Web Site: www.oldcowtown.org
Key Personnel: Exec. Dir., Jacky Goerzen; Cur., James Vannurden; Business Affairs, Yvonne Kirker; Mktg. Dir., Angela Cato; Education & Interpretation Coord., J. Anthony Horsch; Volunteer Coord., Jacky Goerzen; Gift Store Mgr. & Rentals Coord., David Abbott.
Institution Type/Description: History Museum: 1865-1880 era of Wichita & Sedgwick County Kansas.
Hours & Admission Prices: Tues.-Sat. 10-5. Adults $7.75, senior citizens $6.50, youth 12-17 $6, children 4-11 $5.50; discounts to AAM & ICOM members & groups of 15 or more; children under 4 & member adults no charge. Closed New Year's Day; Thanksgiving; Christmas. &
Attendance: 51,890 (actual)

PIZZA HUT MUSEUM, Marcus Welcome Center, Wichita, KS 67260. Mailing Address: 1845 Fairmount St., Wichita, KS 67260.

Web Site: www.wichita.edu/museums/pizzahutmuseum
Institution Type/Description: History Museum: housed on the site of the original Pizza Hut restaurant which opened in 1958.
Hours & Admission Prices: Mon.-Fri. 8-5. No charge.

SEDGWICK COUNTY ZOO, 5555 Zoo Blvd., Wichita, KS 67212-1643. Tel.: 316-660-9453. Fax: 316-942-3781.

E-mail: ask@scz.org
Web Site: www.scz.org
Key Personnel: Exec. Dir., Jeff Ettling; Pres. (V), Scott Ochs; C.F.O., Vickie Moore; Dir. Guest Svcs., Steve Fairchild.
Institution Type/Description: Zoo.
Hours & Admission Prices: Winter: daily 10-5; Summer: daily 8:30-5. Adults $13.95, seniors 62 & up $11.95, children 3-11 $8.95; discounts to school groups & AZA members; children 2 & under & members no charge. &
Attendance: 548,919 (actual)

ULRICH MUSEUM OF ART, Wichita State University, 1845 Fairmount St., Wichita, KS 67260-0046. Tel.: 316-978-3664. Fax: 316-978-3898. Facebook: Ulrich Museum.

E-mail: ulrich@wichita.edu
Web Site: www.ulrich.wichita.edu
Formerly: Edwin A. Ulrich Museum of Art
Key Personnel: Dir., Bob Workman; Chm. (V), Nancy Martin; Finance & Opers. Mgr., Linda Doll; Public Rels & Mktg. Mgr., Jennifer Lane; Designer & Preparator, James Porter; Coord. Special Projects, Carolyn Copple; Museum Educator, Jana Durfee.
Institution Type/Description: University Art Museum.
Hours & Admission Prices: Tues.-Fri. 11-5, Sat.-Sun. 1-5. No charge; donations accepted. Closed major & university holidays. &
Attendance: 21,005 (actual)

WICHITA ART MUSEUM, 1400 W. Museum Blvd., Wichita, KS 67203-3296. Tel.: 316-268-4921 & 4976. Fax: 316-268-4980.

E-mail: info@wichitaartmuseum.org
Web Site: www.wichitaartmuseum.org
Key Personnel: Chm., Sondra Langel; Dir., Patricia McDonnell; Dir. Education, Courtney Spousta; Registrar, Leslie Servantez; Museum Shop Mgr., Melanie Zuercher.
Institution Type/Description: Art Museum.
Hours & Admission Prices: Sun. 12-5, Tues.-Sat. 10-5; guided tours by appointment. Adults $7, seniors 60 & over $5, students & youth 5-17 $3; discount to

AAM members; children under 5, Sat. & members no charge. Closed national holidays. &
Attendance: 62,028 (actual)

WICHITA CENTER FOR THE ARTS, 9112 E. Central, Wichita, KS 67206-2506. Tel.: 316-634-2787. Fax: 316-634-0593.
E-mail: arts@wcfta.com
Web Site: www.wcfta.com
Key Personnel: Exec. Dir., Katy Dorrah; Gallery Dir., Amy Reep; Dir. Education, Lauren Baldwin; Pres. (V), Karla Fazio.
Institution Type/Description: Art Center.
Hours & Admission Prices: Tues.-Sun. 1-5. No charge; donations accepted. Closed national holidays. &
Attendance: 22,250 (actual)

WICHITA-SEDGWICK COUNTY HISTORICAL MUSEUM ASSOCIATION, 204 S. Main, Wichita, KS 67202-3796. Tel.: 316-265-9314. Fax: 316-265-9319.
E-mail: wschm@wichitahistory.org
Web Site: wichitahistory.org
Key Personnel: Dir., Eric M. Cale; Pres., Janet Meyer; Museum Shop Mgr., Nancy Shawver.
Institution Type/Description: History Museum: housed in 1892 old City Hall.
Hours & Admission Prices: Tues.-Fri. 11-4, Sat.-Sun. 1-5. Adults $5, children $2; members no charge. Closed national holidays. &
Attendance: 8,900 (actual)

Wilson

WILSON CZECH OPERA HOUSE CORPORATION, FOUNDATION, INC. & HOUSE OF MEMORIES MUSEUM, 415 27th St., Old Hwy. #40, Wilson, KS 67490-0271. Mailing Address: P.O. Box 271, Wilson, KS 67490-0271. Tel.: 785-658-3505 & 3343.
Key Personnel: C.E.O., Pres. & Chm., Libbie Sebesta; Vice. Pres., Laverne Libal; Dir. House of Memories Museum, Pres. (V), & Museum Shop Mgr., Jean T. Kingston; Treas., Ida Mae Goodman; Sec. & City Delegate, Joe E. Vocasek; Security, Bill Seifers; Security, Tim Heard; Asst. & Tour Guide Museum Shop Mgr., Una Joyce Podlena.
Institution Type/Description: History Museum.
Hours & Admission Prices: Mon.-Sat. 10-12 & 1-4, Sun. 1-4. No charge; donations accepted. &
Attendance: 575 (estimated)

Winfield

THE COWLEY COUNTY HISTORICAL SOCIETY, 1011 Mansfield St., Winfield, KS 67156-3557. Tel.: 620-221-4811.
E-mail: cchsm@kans.com
Web Site: www.cchsm.com
Key Personnel: Pres. (V), Jerry Aistrup; Museum Shop Mgr., Jane Reeves.
Institution Type/Description: General Museum.
Hours & Admission Prices: Tues.-Sun. 1-4. No charge; donations accepted. Closed New Year's Day; Easter; Memorial Day; Labor Day; Thanksgiving; Christmas. &
Attendance: 8,000 (actual)

Yates Center

WOODSON COUNTY HISTORICAL SOCIETY, 208 W. Mary, Yates Center, KS 66783-1728. Mailing Address: P.O. Box 105, Yates Center, KS 66783-0105. Tel.: 620-625-2626.
E-mail: rcall1@cox.net
Key Personnel: Pres. (V), Ron Shaffer; Vice Pres., Susanne Shaffer; Dir. & Treas., Linda Call; Cur., Geri Town.
Institution Type/Description: Historical Society Museum.
Hours & Admission Prices: June-Sept. Mon.-Wed. & Fri.-Sat. 10-4. No charge; donations accepted. &
Attendance: 360 (actual)

KENTUCKY

(241 listings)

Alexandria

CAMPBELL COUNTY LOG CABIN HISTORY AND FARM HERITAGE MUSEUM, 890 Clayridge Rd., Alexandria, KY 41001. Tel.: 859-466-0638.
E-mail: kennethareis@yahoo.com

Key Personnel: Owner, Dir. & Museum Shop Mgr., Kenneth A. Reis.
Institution Type/Description: Local History & Agriculture Museum.
Hours & Admission Prices: Daily 9-5. No charge; donations accepted. &
Attendance: 700 (estimated)

Ashland

HIGHLANDS MUSEUM & DISCOVERY CENTER, 1620 Winchester Ave., Ashland, KY 41101. Tel.: 606-329-8888. Fax: 606-324-3218. Facebook: Highlands Museum & Discovery Center.
E-mail: info@highlandsmuseum.com
Web Site: www.highlandsmuseum.com
Key Personnel: Exec. Dir., Carol Rice Allen; Dir. Education & Mktg., Emily Roush; Cur., Heather Akers; Military Cur., Matt Potter; Clothing Cur., Carolyn Warnock; Facility Dir., Matt Potter; Museum Shop Mgr., Sheila Rice; Office Mgr., Collin Hite; Housekeeping Supvr., Leesa Reeves.
Institution Type/Description: Children's & History Museum.
Hours & Admission Prices: Wed. & Fri. 10-4, Thurs. 10-8, Sat. 10-6. Adults $6.50, senior citizens & children $5; discounts to AAM members, ASTC reciprocal & groups; children under 2 & members no charge. Closed New Year's Day; Memorial Day; Independence Day; Labor Day; Thanksgiving; Christmas. &
Attendance: 22,000 (actual)

Auburn

THE AUBURN MUSEUM, 433 W. Main St., Auburn, KY 42206. Tel.: 270-542-4677.
Web Site: www.auburnhistoricalsociety.com
Key Personnel: Pres. (V), Eloise W. Hadden.
Institution Type/Description: Historical Society Museum.
Hours & Admission Prices: Mon.-Fri. 1-4; other times by appointment. Adults $5, children $2; children 6 & under and members no charge.
Attendance: 100 (estimated)

Augusta

THE ROSEMARY CLOONEY HOUSE, 106 E. Riverside Dr., Augusta, KY 41002. Mailing Address: P.O. Box 197, Augusta, KY 41002. Tel.: 866-898-8091.
E-mail: info@rosemaryclooney.org
Web Site: www.rosemaryclooney.org
Institution Type/Description: History Museum: housed in the former home of singer & actress, Rosemary Clooney.
Hours & Admission Prices: Tues.-Fri. 11-3, Sat. 11-5, sun. 1-5; other times by appointment. Adults $5, members $4; discounts to AAM members. &
Attendance: 97,000 (estimated)

Barbourville

APPALACHIAN FOOTHILLS FIRE HISTORICAL SOCIETY, 227 S. Main St., Barbourville, KY 40906. Mailing Address: 208 Sycamore Dr., Barbourville, KY 40906. Tel.: 606-627-8385.
E-mail: affhs@yahoo.com
Web Site: www.affhs.com
Institution Type/Description: Historical Society Museum.
Hours & Admission Prices: Call for hours.

DR. THOMAS WALKER STATE HISTORIC SITE, 4929 KY 459, Barbourville, KY 40906-7232. Tel.: 606-546-4400. Fax: 606-546-4400.
E-mail: andy.teasley@ky.gov
Web Site: parks.ky.gov
Key Personnel: Park Mgr., Andy Teasley.
Institution Type/Description: Historic Site.
Hours & Admission Prices: March-Nov. 1 open daily. Gift shop closed Nov.-Mar. 1. No charge. &
Attendance: 15,000 (estimated)

KNOX HISTORICAL MUSEUM - HISTORY & GENEALOGY CENTER, 196 Daniel Boone Dr., Barbourville, KY 40906-1164. Mailing Address: P.O. Box 1446, Barbourville, KY 40906-5446. Tel.: 606-546-7581. Facebook.
E-mail: khm1446@gmail.com
Web Site: knoxhistoricalmuseum.org
Key Personnel: Pres. (V), Michael C. Mills.
Institution Type/Description: History & Genealogy Museum.
Hours & Admission Prices: Wed. 10-4. No charge; donations accepted. &

Bardstown

HEAVEN HILL DISTILLERIES BOURBON HERITAGE CENTER, 1311 Gilkey Run Rd., Bardstown, KY 40004. Tel.: 502-337-1000.
Web Site: www.bourbonheritagecenter.com
Institution Type/Description: History Museum.
Hours & Admission Prices: March-Dec. Mon.-Sat. 10-5, Sun. 12-4. Tours: call for pricing. Closed New Year's Eve & Day; Easter; Election Day; Thanksgiving; Christmas.

MY OLD KENTUCKY HOME STATE PARK, 501 E. Stephen Foster Ave., Bardstown, KY 40004-2205. Mailing Address: P.O. Box 323, Bardstown, KY 40004-0323. Tel.: 502-348-3502, 800-323-7803. Fax: 502-349-0054. TDD: 502-348-3502.
E-mail: gail.downs@ky.gov
Web Site: www.kystateparks.com
Key Personnel: Park Supt., Alice Heaton; Pres. (V), Dr. Harry Spalding; Museum Shop Mgr., Gail Downs.
Institution Type/Description: Historic House: 1818 home of Judge John Rowan, where Stephen Foster wrote My Old Kentucky Home.
Hours & Admission Prices: Daily 9-5. Adults $7, children 6-12 $3.50. Closed New Year's Day; Thanksgiving; Christmas week.
Attendance: 100,000 (estimated)

OLD BARDSTOWN VILLAGE - CIVIL WAR MUSEUM OF THE WESTERN THEATER, 310 E. Broadway, Bardstown, KY 40004. Tel.: 502-349-0291. Fax: 502-331-4939. Facebook: Old Bardstown Village.
E-mail: museum@bardstowncabb.net
Web Site: www.civil-war-museum.org
Key Personnel: Dir. & Treas., Kathleen Llewellen; Museum Shop Mgr., Kenny Johnson.
Institution Type/Description: History Museum.
Hours & Admission Prices: March-Oct. daily 10-5; Nov. Fri.-Sun. 10-5. Adults $10, children 6-15 $5; children 5 & under no charge. Closed Thanksgiving; Christmas.
Attendance: 10,000 (actual)

OSCAR GETZ MUSEUM OF WHISKEY HISTORY AND THE BARDSTOWN HISTORICAL MUSEUM, 114 N. Fifth St., Bardstown, KY 40004-1449. Tel.: 502-348-2999.
E-mail: whiskeymuseum@bardstowncable.net
Web Site: www.whiskeymuseum.com
Key Personnel: Cur., Mary Ellyn Hamilton.
Institution Type/Description: Local History Museum: housed in the former St. Joseph College and Seminary; built c.1819.
Hours & Admission Prices: May-Oct. Mon.-Fri. 10-5, Sat. 10-4, Sun. 12-4; Nov.-April Tues.-Sat. 10-4, Sun. 12-4. No charge; donations accepted. Guided Group Tours: $3 per person. Call for holiday closings.
Attendance: 10,040 (actual)

Barlow

BARLOW HOUSE MUSEUM, 509 Broadway St., Barlow, KY 42024. Mailing Address: P.O. Box 400-509 Broadway, Barlow, KY 42024. Tel.: 270-334-3691 & 3010.
Web Site: bhm@brtc.net
Institution Type/Description: Historic House Museum.
Hours & Admission Prices: Mon., Fri., and 2nd & 4th Sun. 1-4; other times by appointment. Adults 13 & over $3; children under 12 no charge.

Barstown

NATIVE AMERICAN MUSEUM, 310 E. Broadway, Barstown, KY 40004-1566. Tel.: 502-349-0291.
E-mail: museumrow@barstowncable.net
Formerly: Neal Spalding Native American Museum
Key Personnel: Pres. (V), Michael A. Thomas.
Institution Type/Description: History Museum.
Hours & Admission Prices: March-Oct. daily 10-5, Nov.- Dec. 15 Fri.-Sun. 10-5. Tour groups year-round by appointment only.

Benham

KENTUCKY COAL MUSEUM, 231 Main St., Benham, KY 40807. Mailing Address: P.O. Box A, Benham, KY 40807. Tel.: 606-848-1530. Fax: 606-848-1546.
E-mail: psizemore0005@kctcs.edu

Web Site: kycoalmuseum.com
Formerly: Kentucky Coal Mining Museum
Key Personnel: Pres., Dr. Lynn Moore; Cur. & Museum Shop Mgr., Phyllis Sizemore.
Institution Type/Description: Coal Mining Museum.
Hours & Admission Prices: Adults $8, senior citizens 62 & over $6, high school & college students $5, elementary school children $4; children 2 & under no charge.
Attendance: 12,000 (estimated)

Berea

BEREA COLLEGE BURROUGHS GEOLOGICAL MUSEUM, Main St., Berea, KY 40404. Mailing Address: CPO 2191, Berea, KY 40404. Tel.: 859-985-3351 & 3893. Fax: 859-985-3303.
E-mail: larry_lipchinsky@berea.edu
Web Site: www.berea.edu
Key Personnel: Dir., Chm. (V) & Cur., Prof. Zelek L. Lipchinsky.
Institution Type/Description: Science Museum.
Hours & Admission Prices: Mon.-Fri. 9-5. No charge; donations accepted.
Attendance: 2,000 (estimated)

BEREA COLLEGE, DORIS ULMANN GALLERIES, Corner of Chestnut & Ellipse St., Berea, KY 40404. Mailing Address: CPO 2162, Berea, KY 40404. Tel.: 859-985-3530. Facebook: Doris Ulmann Galleries.
E-mail: meghan_doherty@berea.edu
Web Site: dulmanngalleries.berea.edu
Key Personnel: Dir., Meghan C. Doherty, Ph.D.
Institution Type/Description: College Art Galleries.
Hours & Admission Prices: Academic Year: Mon.-Thurs. 8-6, Fri. 8-5, Sun. 1-5; No charge. Closed college holidays.
Attendance: 3,000 (estimated)

BEREA COLLEGE WEATHERFORD PLANETARIUM, Science Bldg., Rm. 108, Berea, KY 40404. Mailing Address: C.P.O. Box 2191, Berea, KY 40404. Tel.: 859-985-3277. Fax: 859-985-3303.
E-mail: hookera@berea.edu
Web Site: www.physics.berea.edu/planetarium.php
Key Personnel: Chm., Amer S. Lahamer.
Institution Type/Description: Planetarium.
Hours & Admission Prices: Sept.-May Sun. 4 pm; other times by appointment. Adults $1, $10 per group (seats 50).
Attendance: 1,000 (actual)

Bowling Green

HARDIN PLANETARIUM, Western Kentucky University, Dept. of Physics & Astronomy, 1906 College Heights Blvd., #11077, Bowling Green, KY 42101-1077. Tel.: 270-745-4044. Fax: 270-745-2014.
E-mail: ronn.kistler@wku.edu
Web Site: physics.wku.edu/planetarium.html
Key Personnel: Dir., Dr. Richard Gelderman; Coord., Ronn Kistler.
Institution Type/Description: Planetarium, Observatory & Astronomy Museum.
Hours & Admission Prices: Mon.-Fri. 8-4:30. No charge. Public Shows: Tues. & Thurs. 7pm, Sun. 2pm. No charge. Closed major holidays.
Attendance: 11,000 (estimated)

HISTORIC RAILPARK TRAIN MUSEUM - L&N DEPOT, 401 Kentucky St., Bowling Green, KY 42101-1260. Tel.: 270-745-7317. Fax: 270-782-3398. Facebook: Historic Railpark and Train Museum-Bowling Green.
E-mail: info@historirailpark.com
Web Site: www.historicalrailpark.com
Key Personnel: Pres. (V), Mike Davenport; Dir., Jaime Johnson; Museum Shop Mgr., Summer Bibb.
Institution Type/Description: Railroad Museum.
Hours & Admission Prices: April-Oct. Mon.-Sat. 9-5, Sun. 1-4, Nov.-March Tues.-Sat. 9-5, Sun. 1-4. Adults $12, seniors 65 & over $10, children 5-12 $6; children under 4 no charge.
Attendance: 14,000 (actual)

THE KENTUCKY MUSEUM, 1906 College Heights Blvd. #11092, Bowling Green, KY 42101-1092. Tel.: 270-745-2592. Fax: 270-745-6264.
E-mail: brent.bjorkman@wku.edu
Web Site: www.wku.edu/kentuckymuseum

Formerly: The Kentucky Museum
Key Personnel: Dir., Brent Bjorkman; Chm. (V), Dan Murph; Business Mgr., Fran Matheis; Cur. Exhibits, Donna Parker; Registrar & Cur. Collections, Sandra Staebell; Education Cur., Christy Spurlock; Exhibits Technician, Tony Thurman; Artist-in-Residence, Lynne Ferguson; Devel. Officer, John Perkins; Museum Asst., Lynn Claycomb; Attendant, Deborah Cole; Attendant, Mike Dowell.
Institution Type/Description: General Museum & Historic House.
Hours & Admission Prices: Mon.-Sat. 9-4, Sun. 1-4; groups by appointment. Adults $10, seniors & children 6-16 $5; discounts to AAM, AASLH & KAM members; children 5 & under and members no charge. Closed major holidays. &
Attendance: 84,000 (actual)

NATIONAL CORVETTE MUSEUM, 350 Corvette Dr., Bowling Green, KY 42101-9134. Tel.: 270-781-7973. Fax: 270-781-5286.
E-mail: strode@corvettemuseum.org
Web Site: www.corvettemuseum.org
Key Personnel: Dir., Wendell Strode.
Institution Type/Description: Automobile Museum.
Hours & Admission Prices: Daily 8-5. Museum: adults $10, seniors $8; children 6-16 $5; discounts AAA members & GM employees; members and children under 6 no charge. Closed New Year's Day; Easter; Thanksgiving; Christmas Eve & Day. &
Attendance: 130,000

RIVERVIEW AT HOBSON GROVE, 1100 W. Main Ave., Bowling Green, KY 42101-4894. Tel.: 270-843-5565. Fax: 270-843-5557.
E-mail: riverview.at.hg@att.net
Web Site: www.bgky.org/riverview/
Key Personnel: Dir., Brooke Westcott Peterson; Chm., Lynda Neale; Pres., Jennifer Steen.
Institution Type/Description: Historic House Museum: housed in a c.1872 Italianate architecture home which was used to store Confederate munitions during the Civil War.
Hours & Admission Prices: March-Dec. Tues.-Sat. 10-4, Sun. 1-4. Adults $8, Children $4; discount to groups, veterans & members; children under 6 no charge. Closed holidays.
Attendance: 3,600 (actual)

WESTERN KENTUCKY UNIVERSITY GALLERY, Rm. 441 Ivan Wilson Center for Fine Arts, Bowling Green, KY 42101-1000. Mailing Address: 1906 College Heights Blvd., Art Dept., Bowling Green, KY 42101-1000. Tel.: 270-745-3944. Fax: 270-745-5932.
E-mail: brent.oglesbee@wku.edu
Web Site: www.wku.edu/art/
Key Personnel: Dept. Head, Brent Oglesbee; Dir., Kristina Arnold.
Institution Type/Description: Art Gallery.
Hours & Admission Prices: Mon.-Fri. 8-4:30. No charge. Closed between exhibitions. &
Attendance: 3,500 (estimated)

Burlington

DINSMORE HOMESTEAD FOUNDATION, 5656 Burlington Pike, Burlington, KY 41005-8668. Mailing Address: P.O. Box 453, Burlington, KY 41005-0453. Tel.: 859-586-6117. Fax: 859-334-3690.
Web Site: www.dinsmorefarm.org
Key Personnel: Chm., Dr. Barbara Bardes; Education Coord., Cathy Collopy; Program & Events Asst., Elizabeth Tankersley.
Institution Type/Description: History Museum: housed in c.1842 Federal farmhouse.
Hours & Admission Prices: April-Dec. 15 Wed. & Sat.-Sun. 1-5; other times by appointment. Adults $5, senior citizens $3, students 5-17 $2; members no charge.
Attendance: 3,500

Cadiz

JANICE MASON ART MUSEUM, 71 Main St., Cadiz, KY 42211-9101. Mailing Address: P.O. Box 303, Cadiz, KY 42211-0303. Tel.: 270-522-9056. Facebook: Janice Mason Art Museum.
E-mail: jmam@bellsouth.net
Web Site: www.jmam.org
Institution Type/Description: Art Museum.
Hours & Admission Prices: Tues.-Sat. 10-4, Sun. 1-4. No charge; donations accepted. Closed holidays. &
Attendance: 5,000 (actual)

Campbellsville

THE FRIENDSHIP SCHOOL HOUSE, 300 Ingram Ave., Campbellsville, KY 42718-1625. Tel.: 270-465-5410, 5106, 2055.
Web Site: campbellsvilleky.com/what-to-see/historical/
Institution Type/Description: History Museum.
Hours & Admission Prices: 1st Sun. of the month 1-4 or by appointment.

GREEN RIVER LAKE VISITOR'S CENTER, 544 Lake Rd., Campbellsville, KY 42718. Tel.: 270-465-4463. Facebook.
E-mail: andrea.m.obryan@usace.army.mil
Key Personnel: Chair (V), Andrea O'Bryan.
Institution Type/Description: Visitor's Center.
Hours & Admission Prices: Daily 7:30-5, call to verify. No charge; donations accepted. &
Attendance: 12,800 (estimated)

JACOB HIESTAND HOUSE-TAYLOR COUNTY MUSEUM, 1075 Campbellsville Bypass, Campbellsville, KY 42718-8835. Tel.: 270-789-4343. Facebook.
E-mail: smithgorin@windstream.net
Web Site: taylorcounty.us/history
Key Personnel: Dir., Betty Gorin; C.E.O., Jeremy Wood; Volunteer Sec., Debbie Gilpin.
Institution Type/Description: Historic House Museum: built in 1823.
Hours & Admission Prices: Tues.-Sat. 10-3. Tours: $3; discounts to groups; children under 12 no charge. Closed New Year's Day; Memorial Day; Independence Day; Labor Day; Christmas. &
Attendance: 1,000 (estimated)

Carlisle

BLUE LICKS PIONEER MUSEUM, 10299 Maysville Rd., Carlisle, KY 40311. Mailing Address: Blue Licks Battlefield State Resort Park, P.O. Box 66, Mount Olivet, KY 41064. Tel.: 800-443-7008. Fax: 859-289-5409.
E-mail: bluelicks@ky.gov
Web Site: www.parks.ky.gov
Key Personnel: Resort Park Mgr., Michael Schwendau; Business Mgr., Erik Unthank; Park Naturalist, Cur. & Museum Shop Mgr., Paul Tierney; Museum Shop Mgr., Jean Dillon.
Institution Type/Description: History Museum.
Hours & Admission Prices: March 15-Nov. 15 Mon.-Sat. 9-5, Sun. 1-5. Admission $2; children under 6 no charge. &
Attendance: 10,000 (estimated)

KENTUCKY DOLL & TOY MUSEUM, 106 W. Main St., Carlisle, KY 40311. Tel.: 859-289-3344. Facebook: Kentucky Doll & Toy Museum.
E-mail: dollymama45@att.net
Web Site: kydollandtoymuseum.com
Key Personnel: Cur. & Dir., Jan Taylor.
Institution Type/Description: Toy & Doll Museum.
Hours & Admission Prices: April-Dec. Wed.-Fri. 11-4. Adults $2; members & children under 12 no charge. &

NICHOLAS COUNTY HISTORY MUSEUM & L&N PASSENGER DEPOT, 101 E. Market St., Carlisle, KY 40311. Mailing Address: P.O. Box 222, Carlisle, KY 40311. Tel.: 859-289-4200.
Institution Type/Description: Historic Building: housed in a former depot built in 1910.
Hours & Admission Prices: Call for hours.

Carrollton

BUTLER-TURPIN STATE HISTORIC HOUSE, General Butler State Resort Park, 1608 Hwy. 227, Carrollton, KY 41008-8051. Mailing Address: P.O. Box 325, Carrollton, KY 41008. Tel.: 502-732-4384, 866-462-8853.
E-mail: generalbutler@ky.gov
Web Site: www.generalbutler.com
Key Personnel: Park Mgr., Eddie Moore.
Institution Type/Description: Historic House: former home of the Butler family, built in 1859.
Hours & Admission Prices: May-Sept. daily by appointment. Adults $10.
Attendance: 2,000 (estimated)

Cave City

DINOSAUR WORLD, 711 Mammoth Cave Rd., Cave City, KY 42127-8437. Tel.: 270-773-4345. Fax: 270-773-5303.
E-mail: dinosaurworlds@gmail.com
Web Site: www.dinosaurworld.com
Institution Type/Description: Natural History Museum.
Hours & Admission Prices: Daily 8:30-4:30. Adults $12.75, seniors over 60 $10.75, children 3-12 $9.75. Closed Thanksgiving; Christmas.
Attendance: 80,000 (estimated)

FLOYD COLLINS MUSEUM, 1240 Old Mammoth Cave Rd., Cave City, KY 42127. Tel.: 270-773-3366.
Institution Type/Description: History Museum.
Hours & Admission Prices: Call for hours.

MAMMOTH CAVE WILDLIFE MUSEUM, 409 E. Happy Valley St., Hwy. 90, Cave City, KY 42127. Mailing Address: P.O. Box 236, Cave City, KY 42127. Tel.: 270-773-2255.
E-mail: ham@scrtc.com
Web Site: www.mammothcave.com/guntown/wildlife.htm
Institution Type/Description: Wildlife Museum.
Hours & Admission Prices: Call for hours.

Clay City

RED RIVER HISTORICAL SOCIETY MUSEUM, 4541 Main Street, Clay City, KY 40312. Mailing Address: P.O. Box 195, Clay City, KY 40312-0195. Tel.: 606-663-9930 & 4000.
E-mail: theredrivermuseum@yahoo.com
Key Personnel: Dir., Ovie Hollon.
Institution Type/Description: General Museum: located in 1889 National Bank.
Hours & Admission Prices: May-Oct. Sat.-Sun. & holidays 12-5; other times by appointment. No charge; donations accepted.
Attendance: 5,500

Clermont

BERNHEIM ARBORETUM AND RESEARCH FOREST, Hwy. 245, Clermont, KY 40110. Mailing Address: P.O. Box 130, Clermont, KY 40110-0130. Tel.: 502-955-8512. Fax: 502-955-4039. Facebook; Twitter; Instagram.
E-mail: alandon@bernheim.org
Web Site: www.bernheim.org
Key Personnel: Exec. Dir., Mark Wourms, Ph.D.; C.O.O., Scott Turner; Pres. Bd. Trustees, Ann Price Davis; Dir. Education, Whitney Wurzel; Dir. Mktg., Amy Joseph Landon; Dir. Operations, Harold Hendricks; Museum Shop Mgr., Deborah P'Pool Midgett.
Institution Type/Description: Nature Museum & Arboretum.
Hours & Admission Prices: Daily. Admission: Sat.-Sun. & holidays $5 per vehicle; discounts to APGA & AHS members under reciprocal visitation agreement; Mon.-Fri. & members no charge. Closed New Year's Day; Thanksgiving; Christmas.
Attendance: 270,000 (actual)

Clinton

HICKMAN COUNTY MUSEUM, 221 E. Clay St., Clinton, KY 42031-1224. Mailing Address: P.O. Box 284, Clinton, KY 42031. Tel.: 270-994-5530.
E-mail: hickmancountymuseum@yahoo.com
Web Site: kygreatriverroad.org/HickmanCountyMuseum
Institution Type/Description: Historic House Museum: housed in the former home of Captain Henry C. Watson of the Confederate 7th Kentucky Infantry Regiment; c.1870.
Hours & Admission Prices: Wed.-Sat. 1-4; other times by appointment. No charge; donations accepted.

Cloverport

CLOVERPORT DEPOT MUSEUM, 415 E. Houston St., Cloverport, KY 40111. Mailing Address: c/o City of Cloverport, 212 W. Main St, Cloverport, KY 40111.
Web Site: www.cloverport.com/history/historic-sites/
Formerly: Cloverport Community Museum
Institution Type/Description: History Museum.
Hours & Admission Prices: Sun. 12:30-3. No charge.

Columbia

TRABUE RUSSELL HOUSE, 201 Jamestown St., Columbia, KY 42728. Mailing Address: 116 Campbellsville St., Columbia, KY 42728. Tel.: 270-384-2501.
E-mail: mayor@cityofcolumbiaky.com
Institution Type/Description: Historic House Museum: built in 1821 by Daniel Trabue.
Hours & Admission Prices: By appointment.

Columbus

COLUMBUS-BELMONT CIVIL WAR MUSEUM, Columbus-Belmont State Park, 350 Park Rd., Columbus, KY 42032. Mailing Address: P.O. Box 9, Columbus, KY 42032-0009. Tel.: 270-677-2327. Fax: 270-677-4013. TDD: 270-677-2327.
E-mail: cindy.lynch@ky.gov
Web Site: www.kystateparks.com/agencies/parks/columbus.htm
Key Personnel: Park Mgr., Cindy Lynch.
Institution Type/Description: History Museum.
Hours & Admission Prices: May-Labor Day daily; Labor Day-Oct. weekends; other times by appointment. Adults $4, children $3; discount to senior citizens & groups.
Attendance: 6,000 (actual)

Corbin

HARLAND SANDERS MUSEUM & CAFE, 688 US Hwy. 25W., Corbin, KY 40701. Tel.: 606-528-2163. Fax: 931-490-4802.
E-mail: frankie.bostick@jrninc.com
Institution Type/Description: General Museum: housed in the original restaurant of Kentucky Fried Chicken; built in 1937. Listed on the National Register of Historic Places.
Hours & Admission Prices: Daily 10-10. No charge.

KENTUCKY NATIVE AMERICAN HERITAGE MUSEUM, 4116 Cumberland Falls Hwy., Corbin, KY 40701. Tel.: 606-526-5635. Facebook: Sioux 80.
E-mail: sioux80@msn.com
Web Site: www.knahm.org
Key Personnel: C.E.O. & Pres. (V), Ken Phillips; Chm. (V), Michael Davis.
Institution Type/Description: History Museum.
Hours & Admission Prices: Call for hours. No charge.
Attendance: 10,000 (actual)

Covington

BEHRINGER-CRAWFORD MUSEUM, 1600 Montague Rd., Devou Park, Covington, KY 41011-5648. Tel.: 859-491-4003. Facebook: Behringer-Crawford Museum.
E-mail: info@bcmuseum.org
Web Site: www.bcmuseum.org
Key Personnel: Exec. Dir., Laurie Risch; Pres., Pam Spoor; Education Dir., Kim Gehring-Cook; Community Engagement Coodr., Regina Siegrist; Visitor Svcs. Coord., Linda Schneider; Communications Mgr., Sharen Kardon; Communications & Social Media, Alex Whitehead.
Institution Type/Description: History & Culture Museum.
Hours & Admission Prices: Tues.-Sat. 10-5, Sun. 1-5. Adults $9, seniors 60 & up $8, children $5; discount to AAM, SEMC & Kentucky Heritage Alliance members; members no charge. Closed national holidays.
Attendance: 33,000 (estimated)

JAMES A. RAMAGE CIVIL WAR MUSEUM, 1402 Highland Ave., Covington, KY 41011-3743. Tel.: 859-344-1145.
E-mail: ramagecivilwarmuseum@gmail.com
Institution Type/Description: Civil War Museum.
Hours & Admission Prices: Fri.-Sat. 10-5, Sun. 12-5. Closed holidays.

Crestwood

YEW DELL BOTANICAL GARDENS, 6220 Old LaGrange Rd., Crestwood, KY 40014. Tel.: 502-241-4788. Fax: 502-241-8338. Facebook: Yew Dell Gardens.
E-mail: grow@yewdellgardens.org
Web Site: www.yewdellgardens.org
Key Personnel: Exec. Dir., Paul E. Cappiello, Ph.D.
Institution Type/Description: Botanical Gardens: listed on the National Register of Historic Places.

Hours & Admission Prices: May to mid-Dec. Tues.-Wed. & Fri.-Sat. 10-4, Thurs. 10-8, Sun. 12-4; mid-Dec. to March Mon.-Fri. 10-4. Adults $7, seniors over 55 $5; members, active military & children under 12 no charge.

Cynthiana

CYNTHIANA - HARRISON COUNTY MUSEUM, 124 S. Walnut St., Cynthiana, KY 41031-1592. Mailing Address: P.O. Box 411, Cynthiana, KY 41031-0411. Tel.: 859-234-7179.
E-mail: harricynmuseum@gmail.com
Web Site: www.harricynmuseum.org
Institution Type/Description: History Museum.
Hours & Admission Prices: Fri.-Sat. 10-5; other times by appointment. No charge.

Danville

CONSTITUTION SQUARE STATE HISTORIC SITE, 134 S. Second St., Danville, KY 40422-1802. Mailing Address: c/o Kentucky Department of Parks, 500 Metro St., Ste. 1107, Frankfort, KY 40601-1957. Tel.: 859-239-7089. Fax: 859-239-7894.
Web Site: www.ky.parks.ky.gov
Key Personnel: Park Mgr., Jack Bailey.
Institution Type/Description: Historic Site.
Hours & Admission Prices: March-Dec. Thurs.-Sat. 10-4. Call for admission prices & tours. &
Attendance: 60,000 (estimated)

THE GREAT AMERICAN DOLLHOUSE MUSEUM, 344 Swope Ave., Danville, KY 40422. Tel.: 859-236-1883.
E-mail: lori@thedollhousemuseum.com
Web Site: www.thedollhousemuseum.com
Key Personnel: Cur., Lori Kagan-Moore; Sculptor & Dollmaker, Nicola Cooper; Diversity Advisor, J.H. Atkins; Web Designer, Jon Sachs; Consultant Asian Design & History, Akiki Otake; Set Designer, Ruth Neeman.
Institution Type/Description: Dollhouse & Miniatures Museum.
Hours & Admission Prices: Tues.-Sat. 11-5. Adults $7.50, seniors $6.60, children $5. &

MCDOWELL HOUSE MUSEUM, 125 S. 2nd St., Danville, KY 40422-1801. Tel.: 859-236-2804.
E-mail: mcdowellhouse1@att.net
Web Site: www.mcdowellhouse.com
Formerly: McDowell House and Apothecary Shop
Key Personnel: Chm., Dr. Barry Spoonamore; Dir., Carol J. Senn; Asst. Dir., Lauren E. Clontz; Administrative Asst., Linda Thygesen.
Institution Type/Description: Historic Building: housed in the former home & shop of pioneer surgeon, Ephraim McDowell; built from 1792-1820.
Hours & Admission Prices: March-Oct. Mon.-Sat. 10-12 & 1-4, Sun. 2-4; Nov.-Feb. Tues.-Sat. 10-12 & 1-4, Sun. 2-4. Adults $7, senior citizens 62 & over $5, students 13-18 $3, children 5-12 $2; discounts to prearranged groups of 10 or more & AAA members; children under 5 & members no charge. Closed New Year's Day; Easter; Thanksgiving; Christmas Eve & Day. Last tour begins at 3:30.
Attendance: 1,500 (estimated)

Dawson Springs

DAWSON SPRINGS MUSEUM AND ART CENTER, INC., 127 S. Main St., Dawson Springs, KY 42408-1713. Mailing Address: P. O. Box 107, Dawson Springs, KY 42408-0107. Tel.: 270-797-3503.
Key Personnel: C.E.O., Kathy Beshears; Exec. Dir., Sylvia Lynn Thomas; Pres., Kathy Lyon; Chm. (V), Shirley Menser.
Institution Type/Description: Art & History Museum: housed in the 1907 Romanesque style Commercial Bank.
Hours & Admission Prices: Feb.-Dec. Tues.-Fri. 1-4. No charge; donations accepted. Closed major holidays. &
Attendance: 2,200 (estimated)

Eddyville

ROSE HILL - LYON COUNTY MUSEUM, Water St., Eddyville, KY 42038. Mailing Address: P.O. Box 811, Eddyville, KY 42038. Tel.: 270-388-2924.
Institution Type/Description: Historic House Museum: built c.1834.
Hours & Admission Prices: mid-May to mid-Oct. Thurs.-Sun. 1-4. Adults $5; children no charge. &

Elizabethtown

BLACK HISTORY GALLERY, 602 Gallery Place, Elizabethtown, KY 42701. Mailing Address: Elizabethtown Tourism & Convention Bureau, 1030 N. Mulberry St., Elizabethtown, KY 42701. Tel.: 270-765-2175.
Institution Type/Description: History Museum.
Hours & Admission Prices: Temporarily closed.

BROWN-PUSEY HOUSE, 128 N. Main St., Elizabethtown, KY 42701-1415. Tel.: 270-765-2515.
E-mail: brownpuseyhouse@windstream.net
Web Site: brownpuseyhouse.org
Key Personnel: Dir., Twylane Van Lahr; Chm. (V), Morris Miller.
Institution Type/Description: Historic House Museum: built in 1825.
Hours & Admission Prices: Tues.-Sat. 10-4; groups by appointment. No charge; donations accepted. Closed most major holidays.
Attendance: 16,000 (estimated)

HARDIN COUNTY HISTORY MUSEUM, 201 W. Dixie Ave., Elizabethtown, KY 42701-1533. Tel.: 270-763-8339.
E-mail: info@hardinkyhistory.org
Web Site: www.hardinkyhistory.org
Institution Type/Description: History Museum.
Hours & Admission Prices: By appointment.

LINCOLN HERITAGE HOUSE, 212 Freeman Lake Park Rd., Elizabethtown, KY 42701-2702. Tel.: 270-769-3916, 800-437-0092.
Institution Type/Description: Historic House Museum: housed in the home of Hardin Thomas; the first section was built in 1789 & the second part in 1805 with the help of President Abraham Lincoln's father, Thomas Lincoln.
Hours & Admission Prices: June-Oct. 1 Tues.-Sun. 10-5.

ONE ROOM SCHOOL HOUSE MUSEUM, Freeman Lake Park, Blue Heron Way, Elizabethtown, KY 42701. Mailing Address: c/o Elizabethtown Tourism & Convention Bureau, 1030 N. Mulberry St., Elizabethtown, KY 42701. Tel.: 800-437-0092.
Institution Type/Description: Historic House Museum: built in 1892.
Hours & Admission Prices: Call for hours.

SWOPE'S CARS OF YESTERYEAR, 1100 N. Dixie Ave., Elizabethtown, KY 42701-2534. Tel.: 270-765-2181. Fax: 270-763-6187.
E-mail: fwswope@swope.com
Web Site: www.swopemuseum.com
Key Personnel: Dir. & Chm. (V), Bill Swope; Pres. (V), Carl Swope; Cur., Sue Marski; Hostess, Shannon Avila; Host, Morris Judd.
Institution Type/Description: Auto Museum.
Hours & Admission Prices: Mon.-Sat. 10-5. No charge. Closed holidays. &
Attendance: 9,000 (estimated)

Elkhorn City

ELKHORN CITY RAILROAD MUSEUM, 100 Pine St., Elkhorn City, KY 41522. Tel.: 606-754-8300.
E-mail: elkhorncityrailroadmuseum@yahoo.com
Web Site: elkhorncityrrm.tripod.com
Institution Type/Description: Railroad Museum.
Hours & Admission Prices: March-Nov. Tues.-Sat. 10-4, Sun. 12-4.

Fairview

JEFFERSON DAVIS STATE HISTORIC SITE, 258 Pembroke-Fairview Rd., Fairview, KY 42221. Mailing Address: Box 157, Fairview, KY 42221-0157. Tel.: 270-889-6100. Fax: 270-889-6102.
E-mail: ron.sydnor@ky.gov
Key Personnel: Site Supt., Ron Sydnor.
Institution Type/Description: State Park Monument.
Hours & Admission Prices: April to Nov. 15 Tours: 9-5. Adults $8, senior citizens, students & military $7, children 5-12 $6, groups of 10 $4; children 4 & under no charge. &
Attendance: 25,000 (estimated)

Flemingsburg

FLEMING COUNTY COVERED BRIDGE MUSEUM, 119 E. Water St., Flemingsburg, KY 41041. Mailing Address: P.O. Box 12, Flemingsburg, KY 41041. Tel.: 606-845-1223.
Institution Type/Description: History Museum.
Hours & Admission Prices: March-Dec. Wed. 10-4, Sat. 12-4; other times by appointment. No charge; donations accepted.

Fordsville

FORDSVILLE L&N DEPOT COMMUNITY MUSEUM, 32 Ridge Rd., Fordsville, KY 42343. Mailing Address: P.O. Box 18, Fordsville, KY 42343. Tel.: 270-292-5792. Facebook: Fordsville Depot.
E-mail: fordsvilleweb@hughes.net
Web Site: fordsvilledepot.com
Key Personnel: Dir. & Museum Shop Mgr., Don Locke; Chm. (V), Charley Mattingly.
Institution Type/Description: Railroad Depot Museum.
Hours & Admission Prices: Thurs.-Sat. 11-5, Sun. 1-5. No charge; donations accepted. &
Attendance: 450 (estimated)

Fort Campbell

DON F. PRATT MEMORIAL MUSEUM, 5702 Tennessee Ave., Fort Campbell, KY 42223-5919. Mailing Address: P.O. Box 2133, Fort Campbell, KY 42223-2133. Tel.: 270-798-3215.
E-mail: foundation@fortcampbell.com
Web Site: www.fortcampbell.com/pratt.php
Key Personnel: Museum Dir., Daniel Peterson; Historian, John O'Brien, III; Museum Technician, John Foley; Exhibits Specialist, Jim Spencer.
Institution Type/Description: Airborne Military Museum.
Hours & Admission Prices: Mon.-Sat. 9:30-4:30; guided tours of 10 or more by appointment. No charge; donations accepted. Closed New Year's Day; Christmas. &
Attendance: 55,000 (actual)

Fort Knox

GENERAL GEORGE PATTON MUSEUM AND CENTER OF LEADERSHIP, 356 Fayette Ave., Bldg. 4554, Fort Knox, KY 40121. Mailing Address: P.O. Box 25, Fort Knox, KY 40121-0025. Tel.: 502-624-3729. Fax: 502-624-4333.
E-mail: education@generalpatton.org
Web Site: www.generalpatton.org
Formerly: Patton Museum of Cavalry and Armor
Key Personnel: C.E.O., Robert Keats; Cur., Nathan C. Jones; Mgr. Collections, Amber Hills; Mgr. Collections, O.B. Edens.
Institution Type/Description: Military Museum.
Hours & Admission Prices: Mon.-Fri. 9-4:30, Sat.-Sun. & holidays 10-4:30. No charge; donations accepted. Closed New Year's Eve & Day; Easter; Thanksgiving; Christmas Eve & Day. &
Attendance: 150,000 (actual)

Fort Mitchell

VENT HAVEN MUSEUM, 33 W. Maple Ave., Fort Mitchell, KY 41011-2616. Tel.: 859-341-0461.
E-mail: venthaven@insightbb.com
Web Site: www.venthavenmuseum.net
Key Personnel: Cur., Jen Dawson.
Institution Type/Description: Theater Museum.
Hours & Admission Prices: May-Sept. by appointment only. Admission Donation: $5.
Attendance: 1,000

Fort Thomas

FORT THOMAS MILITARY AND COMMUNITY MUSEUM, 940 Cochran Ave., Fort Thomas, KY 41075. Tel.: 859-572-1225 & 815-8481.
Web Site: www.ftthomas.org
Institution Type/Description: Military History Museum.
Hours & Admission Prices: Wed.-Sun. 12-4; other times by appointment.

Frankfort

CAPITAL CITY MUSEUM, 325 Ann St., Frankfort, KY 40601-2803. Tel.: 502-696-0607.
E-mail: frankforthistory@gmail.com
Web Site: www.capitalcitymuseum.com
Key Personnel: Collection Mgr., John Patrick Downs; Asst. Cur., Russ Hatter.
Institution Type/Description: History Museum: housed in the former Gayle Drug Store.
Hours & Admission Prices: Mon.-Sat. 10-4. No charge. &
Attendance: 16,000 (actual)

CENTRAL KENTUCKY AUDUBON SOCIETY, 1305 Germany Rd., Frankfort, KY 40601-8257. Tel.: 859-873-5711. Fax: 859-873-5711.
E-mail: info@lifeadventurecenter.org
Web Site: www.centralkentuckyaudubon.org/
Formerly: Clyde E. Buckley Wildlife Sanctuary
Institution Type/Description: Wildlife Sanctuary & Nature Center.
Hours & Admission Prices: Call for hours. &
Attendance: 10,000

THE GOVERNOR'S MANSION, 704 Capitol Ave., Frankfort, KY 40601-3448. Tel.: 502-564-8004. Fax: 502-564-5022.
E-mail: ann.evans@ky.gov
Web Site: www.governorsmansion.ky.gov
Formerly: The Executive Mansion
Key Personnel: Exec. Dir., Ann Evans.
Institution Type/Description: Historic House: c.1914 Beaux-Arts style 25-room residence of 23 of Kentucky's governors.
Hours & Admission Prices: Tues. & Thurs. 9-11. No charge; donations accepted. Closed legal holidays. &

KENTUCKY DEPARTMENT OF FISH & WILDLIFE RESOURCES-SALATO WILDLIFE EDUCATION CENTER, 1 Sportsman Ln, Frankfort, KY 40601-3951. Tel.: 502-564-7863, ext. 4407, 800-858-1549. Fax: 502-564-2179.
E-mail: salato@ky.gov
Web Site: fw.ky.gov
Key Personnel: Commissioner, Dr. Greg Johnson.
Institution Type/Description: Wildlife Museum.
Hours & Admission Prices: March 3-Nov. 28 Tues.-Fri. 9-5, Sat. 10-5, Adult $4, youth 5-18 $2, children under 5 no charge. Closed state holidays. &
Attendance: 100,000 (actual)

KENTUCKY HISTORICAL SOCIETY, 100 W. Broadway, Frankfort, KY 40601-1931. Tel.: 502-564-1792. Fax: 502-564-4701.
E-mail: KHS@ky.gov
Web Site: www.history.ky.gov
Key Personnel: Exec. Dir., Scott Alvey.
Institution Type/Description: History Museum.
Hours & Admission Prices: Museum: Tues.-Sat. 10-5. Library: Wed.-Sat. 10-5. Adults $8, youth 6-18 & veterans $6; children 5 & under and members no charge. &
Attendance: 70,000 (actual)

KENTUCKY MILITARY HISTORY MUSEUM, 128 E. Main St., Frankfort, KY 40601. Mailing Address: 100 W. Broadway, Frankfort, KY 40601-1931. Tel.: 502-564-3265. Fax: 502-564-4054.
Web Site: history.ky.gov
Key Personnel: Cur., Bill Bright.
Institution Type/Description: Military Museum: housed in 1850 State Arsenal, built for Kentucky Militia.
Hours & Admission Prices: Tues.-Sat. 10-5; call to confirm. Adults $4; members no charge. Closed New Year's Eve & Day; Easter; Thanksgiving; Christmas Eve & Day. &
Attendance: 15,000 (actual)

KENTUCKY STATE CAPITOL, 700 Capital Ave., Frankfort, KY 40601. Mailing Address: Historic Properties, Berry Hill Mansion, 700 Louisville Rd., Frankfort, KY 40601-3304. Tel.: 502-564-3000 & (Tour Information) 564-3449. Fax: 502-564-6505.
E-mail: david.buchta@ky.gov
Web Site: www.historicproperties.ky.gov
Institution Type/Description: Historic Building; c.1910 Kentucky's fourth Statehouse.

Hours & Admission Prices: April-Oct. Mon.-Fri. 8-4:30, Sat. 10-2; Nov.-March Mon.-Fri. 8-4:30. No charge. Closed New Year's Day; Easter; Thanksgiving; Christmas Eve & Day. &
Attendance: 100,000 (estimated)

KENTUCKY STATE POLICE MUSEUM, 633 Chamberlin Ave., Frankfort, KY 40601. Tel.: 502-875-1625.
E-mail: quartermaster@ksppa.com
Web Site: www.ksppa.com
Institution Type/Description: Police Museum.
Hours & Admission Prices: Mon.-Thurs. 8-4, Fri. 8-3.

LIBERTY HALL HISTORIC SITE, 202 Wilkinson St., Frankfort, KY 40601-1826. Tel.: 502-227-2560, 888-516-5101. Fax: 502-227-3348.
E-mail: libhall@dcr.net
Web Site: www.libertyhall.org
Key Personnel: Coord. Education, Jennifer Koach; Cur., Kate Hesseldenz; Museum Shop Mgr., Becky Shipp.
Institution Type/Description: Historic Site: housed on the site of Senator John Brown's home, Kentucky's first US senator.
Hours & Admission Prices: Tours: March to mid-Dec. Tues.-Sat. 10:30, 12, 1:30 & 3, Sun. 1:30 & 3. Adults $4, seniors 60 & over $3, children 5-18 $1; members and children 4 & under no charge. Closed New Year's Day; Thanksgiving; Christmas.
Attendance: 4,276 (actual)

THE OLD GOVERNOR'S MANSION, 420 High St., Frankfort, KY 40601-2175. Mailing Address: 700 Capitol Ave., Frankfort, KY 40601-3410. Tel.: 502-564-3449. Fax: 502-564-4099.
E-mail: Erin.Warford@ky.gov
Key Personnel: Dir., David Buchta.
Institution Type/Description: Historic Building: 1798 transitional Federal-Georgian style Old Governor's Mansion.
Hours & Admission Prices: Mon.-Tues. & Thurs. 1:30-3:30. No charge. &
Attendance: 6,000 (estimated)

VEST-LINDSEY HOUSE, 401 Wapping St., Frankfort, KY 40601-2607. Tel.: 502-564-3000 & 6980. Fax: 502-564-6505.
E-mail: Dalaina.Bean@ky.gov
Key Personnel: Dir. & Cur., David Buchta.
Institution Type/Description: Historic House: c.1820 12-room home located in a four-block area of 28 historic homes & churches; official state meeting house.
Hours & Admission Prices: By appointment. No charge. Closed state & national holidays. &

Franklin

AFRICAN AMERICAN HERITAGE CENTER, 500 Jefferson St., Franklin, KY 42134-1728. Mailing Address: P.O. Box 369, Ansted, WV 25812. Tel.: 270-598-9986. Fax: 270-586-5719.
E-mail: africanamericanh@bellsouth.net
Web Site: www.aahconline.org
Institution Type/Description: History Museum: listed on the National Register of Historic Places.
Hours & Admission Prices: Mon.-Fri. 9-12 & 1-4:30, Sat. 9-11. Closed holidays.

OCTAGON HALL MUSEUM, 6040 Bowling Green Rd., Franklin, KY 42134. Tel.: 270-791-0071.
E-mail: kycsa@accessky.net
Web Site: www.octagonhall.com
Institution Type/Description: Historic House Museum: housed in an eight-sided home used during the Civil War by Confederate and Federal troops; it also served as a Civil War hospital.
Hours & Admission Prices: Wed.-Sat. 9-11 & 1-3:30. Adults $5, children 6-12 $1. Closed major holidays.

SIMPSON COUNTY ARCHIVES & MUSEUM, 206 N. College St., Franklin, KY 42134-1826. Tel.: 270-586-4228. Fax: 270-586-4429. Facebook: www.facebook.com/simpson-county-historical-society-inc-131416273588210/.
E-mail: oldjail@comcast.net
Web Site: www.simpsoncountykyarchives.com
Institution Type/Description: History Museum: housed in the old jail and jailer's residence. Maintained by the Simpson County Historical Society, Inc.
Hours & Admission Prices: Mon. 9-7, Tues.-Fri. 9-4, Sat. 10-2; other times by appointment. No charge, but donations accepted. Closed federal holidays.
Attendance: 1,500 (estimated)

Georgetown

CARDOME CENTER - MUSEUM OF THE WRITTEN WORD, 800 Cincinnati Rd., Ste. 3, Georgetown, KY 40324. Tel.: 502-863-1575.
Web Site: www.cardomecenter.com
Institution Type/Description: Communications Museum.
Hours & Admission Prices: Call for hours.

GEORGETOWN COLLEGE FINE ARTS GALLERIES, 400 E. College St., Georgetown, KY 40324-1628. Tel.: 502-863-8399. Facebook.
E-mail: samantha_simpson@georgetowncollege.edu
Web Site: www.georgetowncollege.edu/galleries
Key Personnel: Dir. & Cur. Collections, Samantha Simpson; Chm., Daniel Graham.
Institution Type/Description: Art Gallery.
Hours & Admission Prices: Mon.-Fri. 12-4:30; other times by appointment. No charge. &
Attendance: 2,500 (estimated)

GEORGETOWN-SCOTT COUNTY MUSEUM, 229 E. Main St., Georgetown, KY 40324-1759. Tel.: 502-863-6201.
E-mail: museum.scottco@yahoo.com
Institution Type/Description: History Museum.
Hours & Admission Prices: Wed.-Sat. 10-4; other times by appointment. No charge; donations accepted. &

SCOTT COUNTY ARTS & CULTURAL CENTER & VISITOR'S WELCOME CENTER, 117 N. Water St., Georgetown, KY 40324. Mailing Address: Scott County Arts Consortium, Inc., P.O. Box 1126, Georgetown, KY 40324. Tel.: 502-570-8366.
E-mail: artscenter@bellsouth.net
Web Site: www.scottcountyartworks.org
Institution Type/Description: Art Museum: housed in an historic house built in 1870s.
Hours & Admission Prices: Tues.-Sat. 12-4; other times by appointment.

WARD HALL, 1782 Frankfort Rd., Georgetown, KY 40324. Mailing Address: P.O. Box 1957, Georgetown, KY 40324-6957. Tel.: 859-879-9393 & 396-4257.
E-mail: wardhall@wardhall.net
Web Site: www.wardhall.net
Institution Type/Description: Historic House: 1853 Classical Greek Revival House.
Hours & Admission Prices: Call for hours. Adults $5.

Glasgow

SOUTH CENTRAL KENTUCKY CULTURAL CENTER, 200 W. Water St., Glasgow, KY 42142-1714. Mailing Address: P.O. Box 1714, Glasgow, KY 42142. Tel.: 270-651-9792. Fax: 270-651-2806. Facebook.
E-mail: sckculturalcenter@glasgow-ky.com
Web Site: www.kyculturalcenter.org
Key Personnel: Dir., Sherry Wesley; Chm., Debbie Livingston.
Institution Type/Description: History Museum housed in the old Kentucky Pants factory.
Hours & Admission Prices: Mon.-Fri. 9-4, Sat. 9-2. No charge; donations accepted. Closed Presidents Day; Memorial Day; Independence Day; Labor Day; Thanksgiving & day after; Christmas; New Year's Eve & Day. &
Attendance: 6,000 (actual)

Golden Pond

U.S.D.A. FOREST SERVICE - LAND BETWEEN THE LAKES, 100 Van Morgan Dr., Golden Pond, KY 42211-9001. Tel.: 270-924-2000. Fax: 270-924-2060.
E-mail: lblinfo@fs.fed.us
Web Site: www.lbl.org
Key Personnel: Gen. Mgr., Bill Lisowsky.
Institution Type/Description: Historic Building & Site, Park & Nature Center, Planetarium & Natural History Museum.
Hours & Admission Prices: The Homeplace-1850: March & Nov. Wed.-Sat. 9-5, Sun. 10-5; April-Oct. Mon.-Sat. 9-5, Sun. 10-5. Adults $4, children 5-12 $2; discounts to groups of 100 or more by appointment; children 4 & under no charge. &
Attendance: 1,300,000 (estimated)

Gravel Switch

FORKLAND COMMUNITY CENTER - LINCOLN MUSEUM, 16479 Forkland Rd., Gravel Switch, KY 40328. Tel.: 859-936-7489 & 2061.
E-mail: info@forklandcomctr.org
Web Site: www.forklandcomctr.org
Key Personnel: Chm. (V), Wayne Thurman.
Institution Type/Description: History Museum.
Hours & Admission Prices: May-Oct. Sat. 12-4; other times by appointment. No charge; donations accepted.
Attendance: 2,000 (estimated)

Greenville

DUNCAN CENTER MUSEUM & ART GALLERY, 122 S. Cherry St., Greenville, KY 42345-1234. Mailing Address: P.O. Box 289, Greenville, KY 42345-0289. Tel.: 270-338-2605. Facebook: Duncan Center Museum & Art Gallery.
E-mail: duncan.museum@gmail.com
Web Site: www.duncancentermuseum.com
Formerly: Duncan Cultural Center Museum and Art Gallery
Key Personnel: Dir., Shara Sumner; Chm. (V), Wesley Harris.
Institution Type/Description: History Museum & Art Gallery.
Hours & Admission Prices: Mon.-Fri. 11-4. No charge; donations encouraged.
Attendance: 3,000 (estimated)

Guthrie

ROBERT PENN WARREN BIRTHPLACE, Third & Cherry Sts., Guthrie, KY 42234. Mailing Address: P.O. Box 296, Guthrie, KY 42234. Tel.: 270-483-2683.
E-mail: burt@brandeis.edu
Web Site: www.robertpennwarren.com
Key Personnel: Dir., Jeane Moore; Museum Shop Mgr., Amye Posey.
Institution Type/Description: Historic House Museum: housed in the birthplace of Robert Penn Warren.
Hours & Admission Prices: Tues.-Sat. 11:30-3:30; other times by appointment. No charge.
Attendance: 3,250 (estimated)

Hardinsburg

BRECKINRIDGE COUNTY HISTORICAL SOCIETY MUSEUM, 204 E. 3rd St., Hardinsburg, KY 40143. Mailing Address: P.O. Box 498, Hardinsburg, KY 40143. Tel.: 270-756-5216.
E-mail: breakcohistoricalsocietyky@gmail.com
Key Personnel: Dir. & Pres., Melissa Kampars.
Institution Type/Description: Historical Society Museum: housed in a 1920s home.
Hours & Admission Prices: Wed. 10-2, Sat. 1-4. No charge; donations accepted.
Attendance: 200 (estimated)

Harrodsburg

MORGAN ROW MUSEUM AND HARRODSBURG-MERCER COUNTY RESEARCH LIBRARY, 220 S. Chiles St., Harrodsburg, KY 40330-1631. Mailing Address: P.O. Box 316, Harrodsburg, KY 40330-0316. Tel.: 859-734-5985.
E-mail: bauerhaus@roadrunner.com
Formerly: Morgan Row Museum and Research Center
Key Personnel: Pres. (V), Richard Bauer.
Institution Type/Description: Historic House: 1800s Row House built by Joseph Morgan.
Hours & Admission Prices: Tues. 10-4, Wed.-Fri. & 1st & 3rd Sat. 1-4. Museum: no charge; donations accepted. Library: $5.
Attendance: 900 (estimated)

OLD FORT HARROD STATE PARK MANSION MUSEUM, 100 S. College St., Harrodsburg, KY 40330-1508. Mailing Address: P.O. Box 156, Harrodsburg, KY 40330-0156. Tel.: 859-734-3314. Fax: 859-734-0794.
E-mail: fortharrod@ky.gov
Web Site: www.parks.ky.gov/findparks/recparks/fh
Key Personnel: Park Mgr., David Coleman.
Institution Type/Description: Museum & Historic House: 1813 Greek revival mansion; replica of original fort built by James Harrod.
Hours & Admission Prices: Museum: April-Oct. Wed.-Sat. 10-5, Sun. 12-5. Fort: March-Nov. Wed.-Sat. 9-5; Dec.-Feb. Mon.-Fri. 8-4:30. April-Oct.: adults $7,

seniors $6, children $4; Nov.-March adults $3, children $2. Park: closed New Year's Eve & Day; Thanksgiving; Christmas Eve, Day & week.
Attendance: 30,000 (actual)

SHAKER VILLAGE OF PLEASANT HILL, 3501 Lexington Rd., Harrodsburg, KY 40330-8846. Tel.: 859-734-1549. Fax: 859-734-7278.
E-mail: lcurry@shakervillageky.org
Web Site: www.shakervillageky.org
Key Personnel: C.E.O. & Pres., Madge B. Adams; Vice Pres. & Cur., Larrie Spier Curry; Chm. Bd. (V), James G. Kenan; Dir. Human Resources, Candace Parker; Mgr. Interpretation & Education, Susan Lyons Hughes; Mgr. Historic Farm, Ralph E. Ward; Mgr. Craft Store, Lorrin Ingerson; Mgr. Preservation, Mike McGinnis.
Institution Type/Description: Historic Village Museum: over 3,000 acres former Shaker farmland includes 34 original 19th century buildings.
Hours & Admission Prices: April-Oct. daily 10-5. Village Tour: adults 13 & over $15, youth 6-12 $5. Riverboat Excursions: children 13 & over $10, youth 6-12 $5; discounts to groups; children under 6 accompanied by a parent & members no charge. Nov.-March tour hours & prices reduced.
Attendance: 51,700 (actual)

Hartford

THE BLUEGRASS MOTORCYCLE MUSEUM, 5608 US Hwy. 231 N., Hartford, KY 42347-9583. Tel.: 270-298-7764.
Key Personnel: Owner, Jack Embry; Owner, Nancy Embry.
Institution Type/Description: Motorcycle Museum.
Hours & Admission Prices: Tues.-Fri. 10-5, Sat. 10-3; other times by appointment.

OHIO COUNTY MUSEUM & OHIO COUNTY VETERANS MUSEUM, 415 Mulberry St., Hartford, KY 42347. Mailing Address: P.O. Box 44, Hartford, KY 42347. Ohio County Historical Society.
E-mail: helen@mckeown.com
Web Site: www.ochistoricalsociety.org
Key Personnel: Pres. (V), Robert Clements.
Institution Type/Description: History Museum.
Hours & Admission Prices: County Museum: May-Oct. Mon., Wed., Thurs.-Fri. 11-4. Veterans Museum: Mon., Wed., Thurs.-Fri. 11-4, Sat. 9-3; other times by appointment. Adults $2.
Attendance: 50 (estimated)

Hawesville

HANCOCK COUNTY MUSEUM, INC., 110 River St., Hawesville, KY 42348. Mailing Address: P.O. Box 605, Hawesville, KY 42348. Tel.: 270-927-8721.
E-mail: ssisser@hancockhistoricalmuseum.org
Web Site: hancockhistoricalmuseum.org
Key Personnel: Dir., James H. Fallin.
Institution Type/Description: History Museum: housed in the former railroad station; built in 1902.
Hours & Admission Prices: April-Oct. Sun. 2-4; other times by appointment. No charge; donations accepted. Closed Easter; Mother's Day; Memorial Day & weekend; Father's Day; Independence Day & weekend; Labor Day & weekend.
Attendance: 200 (estimated)

Hazard

BOBBY DAVIS MUSEUM AND PARK, 234 Walnut St., Hazard, KY 41701-1852. Tel.: 606-439-4325. Facebook: Bobby Davis Museum and Park.
E-mail: bdwalnutforest@msn.com
Formerly: Perry County Museum
Key Personnel: Dir., Martha Quigley; Pres. (V), Anne Gilbert; Museum Shop Mgr., Sydney Francis.
Institution Type/Description: History Museum.
Hours & Admission Prices: Mon.-Fri. 8-4. No charge; donations accepted.
Attendance: 1,500 (estimated)

Henderson

JOHN JAMES AUDUBON MUSEUM, 3100 U.S. Hwy. 41 N., Henderson, KY 42420-2055. Mailing Address: P.O. Box 576, Henderson, KY 42419-0576. Tel.: 270-827-1893. Fax: 270-826-2286. TDD: 270-826-2247.
E-mail: audubon@ky.gov
Web Site: parks.ky.gov/findparks/recparks/au/

Key Personnel: Dir., Mark Kellen; Cur., Jennifer Spence; Museum Shop Mgr., Raini Hall.
Institution Type/Description: State Park Museum: located on migratory bird route.
Hours & Admission Prices: Jan.-Feb. Thurs.-Sun. 10-5; March-Nov. daily 10-5. Family $12, adults $5, seniors 62 & over $4, children 6-12 $3; discounts to groups; members, Friends of Audubon members & children under 6 no charge. Closed New Year's Eve & Day; Thanksgiving & day after; Christmas week. &
Attendance: 18,000 (estimated)

Hickman

CARNEGIE LIBRARY MUSEUM AND VISITOR CENTER, 808 Moscow Ave., Hickman, KY 42050. Tel.: 270-236-2902.
Institution Type/Description: Historic Building Museum: built in 1906. Listed on the National Register of Historic Places.
Hours & Admission Prices: Daily 9-4.

Highland Heights

MUSEUM OF ANTHROPOLOGY, University Drive, Northern Kentucky Univ., 216 Landrum Academic Center, Highland Heights, KY 41099. Tel.: 859-572-1569. Fax: 859-572-6086.
E-mail: voelkerj1@nku.edu
Web Site: anthropologymuseum.nku.edu
Key Personnel: Dir., Dr. Judy Voelker.
Institution Type/Description: Anthropology Museum.
Hours & Admission Prices: By appointment only. No charge. Closed university holidays; Christmas. &
Attendance: 800 (estimated)

NORTHERN KENTUCKY UNIVERSITY ART GALLERIES, Nunn Dr., Highland Heights, KY 41099. Tel.: 859-572-5148 & 5421. Fax: 859-572-6501.
E-mail: knight@nku.edu
Web Site: www.nku.edu/~art/galleries.html
Key Personnel: Dir., David J. Knight.
Institution Type/Description: Art Museum.
Hours & Admission Prices: mid-Jan. to mid-Dec. Mon.-Fri. 9-9, other hours by appointment. No charge; donations accepted. Closed legal holidays; spring break. &
Attendance: 18,000 (estimated)

Hodgenville

ABRAHAM LINCOLN BIRTHPLACE NATIONAL HISTORICAL PARK, 2995 Lincoln Farm Rd., Hodgenville, KY 42748-9707. Tel.: 270-358-3137. Fax: 270-358-3874. Facebook: Lincoln Birthplace NPS.
E-mail: abli_superintendent@nps.gov
Web Site: www.nps.gov/abli
Institution Type/Description: Historic Site: birthplace of Abraham Lincoln.
Hours & Admission Prices: Daily 9-5. No charge. Closed New Year's Day; Thanksgiving; Christmas. &
Attendance: 200,000 (estimated)

THE LINCOLN MUSEUM, 66 Lincoln Sq., Hodgenville, KY 42748-1551. Tel.: 270-358-3163.
E-mail: abe@lincolnmuseum-ky.org
Web Site: www.lincolnmuseum-ky.org
Key Personnel: Dir., Iris LaRue; Museum Shop Mgr., Rob Thurman.
Institution Type/Description: History Museum.
Hours & Admission Prices: Mon.-Sat. 8:30-4:30, Sun. 12:30-4:30. Adults $3; discounts to AAA members; members no charge. &
Attendance: 30,000 (actual)

Hopkinsville

CHEROKEE TRAIL OF TEARS COMMEMORATIVE PARK & HERITAGE CENTER, 100 Trail of Tears Dr., Hopkinsville, KY 42240. Tel.: 270-886-7503.
E-mail: ccook@visithopkinsville.com
Institution Type/Description: Cherokee Indian History Museum.
Hours & Admission Prices: Center: Tues.-Sat. 10-3.

PENNYROYAL AREA MUSEUM, 217 E. Ninth St., Hopkinsville, KY 42240-3448. Mailing Address: P.O. Box 1093, Hopkinsville, KY 42241-1093. Tel.: 270-887-4270. Fax: 270-887-4271.
E-mail: pennyroyal.museum@gmail.com
Key Personnel: Dir., Donna K. Stone; Education & Program Dir., Janet Bravard.

Institution Type/Description: History Museum.
Hours & Admission Prices: Tues.-Fri. 9-5, Sat. 10-3. Adults $2, senior citizens & children $1; discounts for prearranged group tours & AAM members; members & prearranged museum professionals no charge. Closed New Year's Day; Memorial Day; Independence Day; Labor Day; Thanksgiving; Christmas. &
Attendance: 17,000 (actual)

Horse Cave

AMERICAN CAVE MUSEUM & HIDDEN RIVER CAVE, 119 E. Main St., Horse Cave, KY 42749-1112. Mailing Address: P.O. Box 409, Horse Cave, KY 42749-0409. Tel.: 270-786-1466. Fax: 270-786-1467.
E-mail: acca@cavern.org
Web Site: cavern.org
Institution Type/Description: Natural Science Museum.
Hours & Admission Prices: Tours: Memorial Day-Labor Day daily 9:30-6; Sept.-May daily 9:30-4. Cave Tour: adults 16 & over $15, youth 6-15 $10; children 5 & under no charge. Closed New Year's Eve & Day; Thanksgiving; Christmas Eve & Day. &

KENTUCKY DOWN UNDER, 3700 L & N. Tpke. Rd., Horse Cave, KY 42749. Mailing Address: P.O. Box 189, Horse Cave, KY 42749-0189. Tel.: 800-762-2869, 270-786-2634.
E-mail: info@kdu.com
Web Site: www.kdu.com
Key Personnel: Dir., Judy Austin; Dir. Mktg., Melissa McGuire; Animal Crew Mgr., April Hatcher; Bookkeeping, Vicki Fancher; Gift Shop Mgr., Courtney Eaton.
Institution Type/Description: Animal Park.
Hours & Admission Prices: Kentucky Caverns: April-May 26 daily 8-5; May 27-Aug. 11 daily 8-6; Aug. 12-March daily 9-4. Animal Areas: March 12-March 31 & Aug. 12-Oct. daily 9-4; April-May 26 daily 8-5; May 27-Aug. 11 daily 8-6. Adults $22, seniors 62 & over $19.30, children 5-14 $13; discounts to AAA members; children 4 & under and active military with ID no charge.

Irvington

IRVINGTON DEPOT AND MUSEUM, 243 N. First St., Irvington, KY 40146. Tel.: 270-547-3835.
E-mail: mayor@Irvingtonky.org
Institution Type/Description: Historic Building: built c.1920.
Hours & Admission Prices: Call for hours.

Jackson

BREATHITT COUNTY MUSEUM, INC., 329 Broadway St., Jackson, KY 41339-1040. Tel.: 606-666-4159. Facebook: Breathitt County Museum.
E-mail: breathittmuseum@bellsouth.net
Key Personnel: Dir., Janie Griffith; Chm. & Pres. (V), Grace Warrix.
Institution Type/Description: Appalachian History Museum.
Hours & Admission Prices: Mon., Wed. & Fri. 9-3:30. &

Jeffersontown

JEFFERSONTOWN HISTORICAL MUSEUM, 10635 Watterson Tr., Jeffersontown, KY 40299-3850. Tel.: 502-261-8290.
E-mail: bwilder@jeffersontownky.com
Web Site: www.jeffersontownky.gov
Key Personnel: Dir., Beth Wilder; Arts Program Mgr., Rhonda Rowland.
Institution Type/Description: History Museum.
Hours & Admission Prices: Mon.-Fri. 10-5. No charge. Closed holidays. &
Attendance: 5,000 (actual)

Knifley

THE GILES SOCIETY, 6112 Elkhorn Rd., Knifley, KY 42753. Mailing Address: 380 Spout Springs Rd., Knifley, KY 42753. Tel.: 270-849-8803. Fax: 270-849-0547.
E-mail: keysha.tucker@yahoo.com
Web Site: www.gilessociety.org
Key Personnel: Pres. (V), Keysha Tucker; Treas., Gayla Baker.
Institution Type/Description: Historical Society Museum: housed in the former home of author Janice Holt Giles and her husband Henry Giles. Listed on the National Register of Historic Homes.
Hours & Admission Prices: June-Sept. Sat.-Sun. 1-5. No charge; donations accepted.
Attendance: 700 (estimated)

La Grange

OLDHAM COUNTY HISTORY CENTER, 106 N. Second Ave., La Grange, KY 40031-1102. Tel.: 502-222-0826. Fax: 502-222-7115.
Web Site: www.oldhamcountyhistoricalsociety.org
Key Personnel: Exec. Dir., Nancy Theiss; Pres., Robert Martin.
Institution Type/Description: History Museum & Center.
Hours & Admission Prices: Tues.-Sat. 10-4. No charge; donations accepted. Closed legal holidays. &
Attendance: 22,000 (actual)

Lancaster

GARRARD COUNTY JAIL MUSEUM, 103 Stanford St., Lancaster, KY 40444. Tel.: 859-792-9452.
E-mail: garrardjail@yahoo.com
Web Site: www.garrardcounty.ky.gov
Institution Type/Description: Historic Building: county jail built in 1873. Listed on the National Register of Historic Places.
Hours & Admission Prices: Call for hours.

GOVERNOR WILLIAM OWSLEY HOUSE - "PLEASANT RETREAT", Gov. William Owsley House Foundation, Inc., 656 Stanford Rd., Lancaster, KY 40444-9543. Tel.: 859-792-2500.
E-mail: director@owsleyhouse.org
Web Site: owsleyhouse.org/public/Welcome.html
Institution Type/Description: Historic House Museum: housed in the home of Kentucky's 16th Governor.
Hours & Admission Prices: April-Nov. by appointment. Adults $9, children 6-18 $4; children 5 & under no charge.

Leitchfield

GRAYSON COUNTY HISTORICAL SOCIETY, 122 E. Main St., Leitchfield, KY 42754. Mailing Address: P.O. Box 84, Leitchfield, KY 42755. Tel.: 270-230-8989. Facebook: Grayson Co Historical Society.
E-mail: graysoncokyhistsoc@windstream.net
Web Site: www.graysoncokyhistsoc.org
Key Personnel: Pres. (V), William Carter; Museum Shop Mgr., Phyllis Webb.
Institution Type/Description: Historical Society Museum: housed in the Jack Thomas House.
Hours & Admission Prices: Mon.-Fri. 10-4. No charge; donations accepted. &
Attendance: 1,100 (estimated)

Lexington

AMERICAN SADDLEBRED MUSEUM, 4083 Iron Works Pkwy., Lexington, KY 40511-8401. Tel.: 859-259-2746. Fax: 859-255-4909. Facebook: @americansaddlebredmuseum; Instagram & Twitter: @asbmuseum.
E-mail: museum@asbmuseum.org
Web Site: www.asbmuseum.org
Key Personnel: Exec. Dir., Jennifer K. Foster; Pres. Bd. Trustees, Keith Kurz; Cur., Librarian & Membership, Kim Skipton; Gift Shop Consultant, Eeta Sachon.
Institution Type/Description: History Museum and Art Gallery.
Hours & Admission Prices: Memorial Day-Labor Day daily 9-6; Sept.-Oct. & mid-March to Memorial Day daily 9-5; Nov. to mid-March Wed.-Sun. 9-5. Adults $20 (includes Kentucky Horse Park); discounts to groups, Kroger Plus, military, AAM, AAA & AARP members; children under 6 & members no charge. &
Attendance: 30,000 (actual)

ASHLAND, THE HENRY CLAY ESTATE, 120 Sycamore Rd., Lexington, KY 40502-1842. Tel.: 859-266-8581. Fax: 859-268-7266. Facebook: Ashland, The Henry Clay Estate.
E-mail: jclark@henryclay.org
Web Site: www.henryclay.org
Key Personnel: Exec. Dir., James Clark; Pres. (V), Brenda Barrett; Chm. (V), A.J. Singleton; Cur., Eric Brooks.
Institution Type/Description: Historic House: c.1806 estate of Henry Clay; c.1856 house of James Clay.
Hours & Admission Prices: Feb. by appointment; March-Dec. Tues.-Sat. 10-4, Sun. 1-4. Adults $12, children $6; discounts to AAA members & groups; members no charge. Closed major holidays. &
Attendance: 12,402 (actual)

AVIATION MUSEUM OF KENTUCKY INC., 4029 Airport Rd., Blue Grass Airport, Lexington, KY 40510-9682. Tel.: 859-231-1219. Fax: 859-381-8739.
E-mail: jrm@aviationky.org
Web Site: aviationky.org
Formerly: Kentucky Aviation History Round Table
Institution Type/Description: Aviation Museum.
Hours & Admission Prices: April-Dec. Tues.-Sat. 10-5, Sun. 1-5. Adults $8, senior citizens $6, children 6-16 $5; discounts to AAM members & groups; members and children 5 & under no charge. &
Attendance: 45,000 (estimated)

BODLEY-BULLOCK HOUSE, 200 Market St., Lexington, KY 40507-1030. Tel.: 859-259-1266.
Institution Type/Description: History Museum: built c.1814 for Lexington Mayor Thomas Pindell, shortly after sold to General Thomas Bodley, a veteran of the War of 1812. Served as headquarters for both Union and Confederate forces during the Civil War.
Hours & Admission Prices: By appointment. Closed holidays.

EXPLORIUM OF LEXINGTON, 440 W. Short St., Lexington, KY 40507-1206. Tel.: 859-258-3253. Fax: 859-258-3255.
E-mail: explore@explorium.com
Web Site: www.explorium.com
Formerly: Lexington Children's Museum
Key Personnel: Exec. Dir., Lee Ellen Martin; Programming Coord. & Cur., Catie Richwine; Education Coord., Kalli Turner; Visitor Svcs. Mgr., Rachel Chandler.
Institution Type/Description: Children's Museum: located in Victorian Square.
Hours & Admission Prices: Tues.-Sat. 10-5, Sun. 1-5. Admission $8; discounts to senior citizens and active duty military; members & children under one no charge. Closed Easter; Labor Day week; Thanksgiving; Christmas Eve & Day. &
Attendance: 51,000 (actual)

HEADLEY-WHITNEY MUSEUM OF ART, 4435 Old Frankfort Pike, Lexington, KY 40510-9657. Tel.: 859-255-6653. Fax: 859-255-8375.
E-mail: hwmuseum@headley-whitney.org
Web Site: www.headley-whitney.org
Key Personnel: Dir. & Cur., Amy Gundrum Greene.
Institution Type/Description: Decorative Arts Museum.
Hours & Admission Prices: March-Dec. Wed.-Fri. 10-5, Sat.-Sun. 12-5. Adults $10, seniors & students $8; discounts for AAA members; members & children 10 & under no charge. Blue Star Program. Closed federal holidays. &
Attendance: 10,000 (estimated)

HUNT-MORGAN HOUSE, 201 N. Mill St., Lexington, KY 40507-1034. Mailing Address: 253 Market St., Lexington, KY 40507-1031. Tel.: 859-253-0362. Fax: 859-259-9210.
E-mail: info@bluegrasstrust.org
Web Site: bluegrasstrust.org
Key Personnel: Dir., Sheila Omer Ferrell.
Institution Type/Description: Historic House: housed in a c.1814 Federal-style home located in Gratz Park historic district.
Hours & Admission Prices: March to mid-Dec. Wed.-Fri. & Sun. 1-5, Sat. 10-4. Adults $7, students & children 3 & up $4; members no charge. Closed major holidays.
Attendance: 5,000 (estimated)

INTERNATIONAL MUSEUM OF THE HORSE, 4089 Iron Works Pkwy., Lexington, KY 40511-8483. Tel.: 859-259-4232. Fax: 859-225-4613. TDD: 859-233-4303.
E-mail: info@kyhorsepark.com
Web Site: www.imh.org
Key Personnel: Dir., Bill Cooke; Graphic Designer, Jim Shambhu; Cur. Collections, Amy Beisel; Asst. Dir., Travis Robinson.
Institution Type/Description: Equine Museum.
Hours & Admission Prices: March 15-Oct. daily 9-5; Nov.-March 14 Wed.-Sun. 9-5. Adults $12, children 6-12 $6; discounts to AAM, SEMC, AASLH & KMHA members; children 5 & under no charge. &
Attendance: 200,000 (estimated)

KENTUCKY PRO FOOTBALL HALL OF FAME, 3364 Leestown Rd., Lexington, KY 40511. Tel.: 859-276-3488.
E-mail: info@kyprofootballhof.com
Web Site: www. kyprofootballhof.org
Key Personnel: Contact, Tammy Fagley.
Institution Type/Description: Sports Museum.
Hours & Admission Prices: Mon.-Fri. 9-4. No charge.

THE LEXINGTON CEMETERY, 833 W. Main St., Lexington, KY 40508-2094. Tel.: 859-255-5522. Fax: 859-258-2774.
E-mail: info@lexcem.org
Web Site: www.lexcem.org
Key Personnel: Gen. Mgr., Mark Durbin.
Institution Type/Description: Union & Confederate Civil War Cemetery.
Hours & Admission Prices: Cemetery: daily 8-5. Office: Mon.-Fri. 8-1, Sat. 8am-12pm. No charge. &

LEXINGTON CENTER MUSEUM & GALLERY, 430 W. Vine St., Lexington, KY 40507. Tel.: 859-233-4567.
Institution Type/Description: General Museum.
Hours & Admission Prices: Call for hours.

LEXINGTON HISTORY MUSEUM, 401 W. Main St., Ste. 312, Lexington, KY 40507. Mailing Address: P.O. Box 748, Lexington, KY 40588-0748. Tel.: 859-254-0530.
E-mail: info@lexhistory.org
Web Site: www.lexhistory.org
Key Personnel: Pres. & Chief Historian, Foster Ockerman, Jr.; Chm. (V), Jim Dickinson; Treas., William Ambrose.
Institution Type/Description: History Museum.
Hours & Admission Prices: Temporarily closed. &

THE LIVING ARTS AND SCIENCE CENTER, INC., 362 N. Martin Luther King Blvd., Lexington, KY 40508-1889. Tel.: 859-252-5222 & 255-2284. Fax: 859-255-7448. Facebook: Living Arts and Science Center Lexington.
E-mail: info@lasclex.org
Web Site: www.lasclex.org
Key Personnel: Pres. (V), Emmy Hartley; Exec. Dir., Heather Lyons; Discovery Education Dir., Katherine Bullock; Gallery Dir., Jeffrey Nichols; Art Education Coord., Mollie Rabiner; Office Mgr., LeAnn Jenkins.
Institution Type/Description: Children's Art and Science Center.
Hours & Admission Prices: Academic Year: Mon.-Fri. 8:30-5, Sat. 10-2; Summer: Mon.-Fri. 8-5. No charge; donations accepted. Closed New Year's Day; Independence Day; Thanksgiving; Christmas. &
Attendance: 25,000 (estimated)

MARY TODD LINCOLN HOUSE, 578 W. Main, Lexington, KY 40507-1642. Mailing Address: P.O. Box 132, Lexington, KY 40588-0132. Tel.: 859-233-9999. Fax: 859-252-2269.
E-mail: mtlhouse@windstream.net
Web Site: www.mtlhouse.org
Key Personnel: Dir., Gwen Thompson; Store Mgr. & Admin. Asst., Linda Scott.
Institution Type/Description: Historical & Preservation Society Museum: housed in 1803-1806 Inn occupied by Todd family from 1832-1849.
Hours & Admission Prices: March 15-Nov. Mon.-Sat. 10-4; last tour at 3pm. Adults $10, children 6-12 $5; discounts to groups of 15 or more and AAA & KMPF members. Closed holidays. &
Attendance: 11,000 (estimated)

MONROE MOOSNICK MEDICAL & SCIENCE MUSEUM, 300 N. Broadway, Lexington, KY 40508-1797. Tel.: 859-233-8411.
E-mail: jday@transy.edu
Web Site: libguides.transy.edu/SpecialCollections/Moosnick
Key Personnel: Dir., Dr. James Day.
Institution Type/Description: Science Museum: housed in 1833 Greek Revival University Bldg.
Hours & Admission Prices: Mon.-Fri. 1-4, by appointment. No charge. Closed national holidays. &
Attendance: 150

PHOTOGRAPHIC ARCHIVES, University of Kentucky, Special Collections & Archives, M.I. King Library, 104 A King Bldg., Lexington, KY 40506. Tel.: 859-257-2654. Fax: 859-257-6311.
E-mail: jasonf@uky.edu
Key Personnel: Dir., Ruth Bryan; Photographic Archivist, Jason Flahardy.
Institution Type/Description: Library of Photographic Material.
Hours & Admission Prices: Mon.-Fri. 9:30-5. No charge. Closed legal & academic holidays. &
Attendance: 2,000

21C MUSEUM HOTEL LEXINGTON, 167 W. Main St., Lexington, KY 40507. Tel.: 859-899-6800.
E-mail: abrooks@21cMuseum.org
Web Site: www.21cmuseumhotels.com/lexington/
Key Personnel: Museum Mgr., Alex Brooks.
Institution Type/Description: Contemporary Art Gallery.

Hours & Admission Prices: See website for hours. No charge.

UNIVERSITY OF KENTUCKY ART MUSEUM, 405 Rose St., Lexington, KY 40506-0241. Tel.: 859-257-5716. Fax: 859-323-1994. Facebook; Twitter; Instagram; Pinterest; Blogger; Youtube.
E-mail: artmuseum@uky.edu
Web Site: finearts.uky.edu/art-museum
Key Personnel: Dir., Stuart Horodner; Registrar, Barbara Lovejoy; Preparator, Alan Rideout; Cur., Janie Welker; Coord. Membership, Lyndi Van Deursen; Publications & Public Rels., Dorothy Freeman; Visitor Svcs. Mgr. & Museum Shop Mgr., Michaela Miles.
Institution Type/Description: Art Center.
Hours & Admission Prices: Tues.-Thurs. 10-5, Fri. 10-8, Sat.-Sun. 12-5. No charge; donations accepted. Closed university holidays. &
Attendance: 27,300 (estimated)

WAVELAND STATE HISTORIC SITE, 225 Waveland Museum Lane, Lexington, KY 40514-1618. Tel.: 859-272-3611. Fax: 859-272-4834.
E-mail: charla.reed@ky.gov
Web Site: www.parks.ky.gov
Key Personnel: Park Mgr., Charla Reed.
Institution Type/Description: Historic Site & House: 1847 Greek Revival Mansion.
Hours & Admission Prices: Mon.-Sat. 10-5, Sun. 1-5. Adults $7, seniors $6, students $4; discount to groups; children under 6 no charge.
Attendance: 44,366 (actual)

WHEELER MUSEUM, Kentucky Horse Park, 3870 Cigar Lane, Lexington, KY 40511. Tel.: 859-225-6704. Fax: 859-258-9033.
Web Site: www.ushja.org
Institution Type/Description: Equestrian History Museum.
Hours & Admission Prices: Call for hours. No charge; donations accepted.
Attendance: 550 (estimated)

London

MOUNTAIN LIFE MUSEUM, Levi Jackson Park, 998 Levi Jackson Mill Rd., London, KY 40744-8325. Tel.: 606-330-2130. Fax: 606-330-2123. TDD: 606-330-2130.
E-mail: ben.sizemore@ky.gov
Web Site: parks.ky.gov/parks/recreationparks/levi-jackson
Key Personnel: Dir., Recreational Parks, Museums and Shrines & Park Supt., Ben Sizemore; Museum Supt., Ella Goodin.
Institution Type/Description: History Museum.
Hours & Admission Prices: April-Oct. call for hours. Adults $3.50, children $2.50; discounts to groups; children 2 & under no charge.
Attendance: 10,967 (actual)

Louisa

FRED M. VINSON MUSEUM AND WELCOME CENTER, 315 E. Madison St., S.E., Corner Court House Sq., Louisa, KY 41230. Tel.: 606-638-0078.
Institution Type/Description: Historic House Museum: housed in the former home of Frederick Moore Vinson, 13th Chief Justice of the U.S. Supreme Court.
Hours & Admission Prices: Call for hours.

Louisville

ALLEN R. HITE ART INSTITUTE, Univ. of Louisville, Belknap Campus, Schneider Hall, Louisville, KY 40292. Tel.: 502-852-4483. Fax: 502-852-6791.
E-mail: john.begley@louisville.edu
Web Site: louisville.edu/art
Key Personnel: Professor, Dir. & Chm., James Grubola; Professor Emeritus, William Morgan; Professor Emeritus, Donald R. Anderson; Professor Emeritus, Henry J. Chodkowski; Professor Emeritus, Suzanne Mitchell; Professor Emeritus, Stephanie J. Maloney; Professor, John Whitesell; Asst. Professor, Che Rhodes; Assoc. Professor, Jay M. Kloner; Assoc. Professor, Linda Gigante; Professor, Lida Gordon; Assoc. Professor, Barbara Hanger; Professor, Steven Skaggs; Professor, Ying Kit Chan; Dir. Speed Art Museum, Peter Morrin; Assoc. Professor, Mark Priest; Asst. Professor, Mary Carothers; Asst. Professor, Mitch Eckert; Assoc. Professor, Stow Chapman; Assoc. Professor, Moon-He Baik; Gallery Dir. & Adjunct Professor, John Begley; Asst. Professor, Benjamin Hufbauer; Asst. Professor, Christopher Fulton; Art Librarian, Gail Gilbert; Professor Emeritus, Dario A. Covi; Assoc. Professor Emerita, Nancy L. Pearcy; Asst. Professor, Todd Burns; Asst. Professor, Scott Massey; Unit Business Mgr., Linda Rowley; Facilities Coord., Wesley Kent; Designer-in-Residence, Leslie Friesen; Asst. Professor, Susan Jarosi; Asst. Professor, Delin Lai.
Institution Type/Description: Art Institute.

Hours & Admission Prices: Mon.-Fri. 9-4:30, Sat. 10-2, Sun. 1-6. No charge; donations accepted. Closed national holidays. &
Attendance: 48,000 (estimated)

THE BRENNAN HOUSE HISTORIC HOME AND GARDENS,
631 S. Fifth St., Louisville, KY 40202. Tel.: 502-540-5145.
E-mail: director@thebrennanhouse.org
Web Site: thebrennanhouse.org
Institution Type/Description: Historic House Museum: housed in the former home of inventor Thomas Brennan and his wife, Anna Bruce; built in 1868. Listed on the National Register of Historic Places.
Hours & Admission Prices: Call for hours.

CONRAD-CALDWELL HOUSE MUSEUM, 1402 St. James Ct.,
Louisville, KY 40208-2127. Tel.: 502-636-5023.
E-mail: conradcaldwellhouse@gmail.com
Web Site: conrad-caldwell.org
Key Personnel: Exec. Dir., Kate Meador; Pres., Keith Kleehammer.
Institution Type/Description: Historic House Museum.
Hours & Admission Prices: Sun. & Wed.-Fri. 12-4, Sat. 10-4; other times by appointment. Adults $10, senior citizens $6, students $4. &
Attendance: 5,000 (actual)

FARMINGTON HISTORIC PLANTATION, 3033 Bardstown Rd.,
Louisville, KY 40205-3019. Tel.: 502-452-9920.
E-mail: farmington@historichomes.org
Web Site: www.farmingtonhistoricplanning.org
Key Personnel: Dir. Farmington Historic Plantation, Kathy L. Nichols; Dir. Whitehall House & Gardens, Kristen Lutes; Bookkeeper, Terry Malcom.
Institution Type/Description: Historic Site: Kentucky hemp plantation, house built in 1816.
Hours & Admission Prices: Farmington: Tues.-Fri. 10-4, Sat. 10-2; Sun. by appointment. Adults $9, seniors over 60 $8, students $4; children under 5 no charge. Whitehall: Mon.-Fri. 10-2. Adults $5, students $3; children under 5 no charge.
Attendance: 140,000 (estimated)

THE FILSON HISTORICAL SOCIETY, INC., 1310 S. Third St.,
Louisville, KY 40208-5506. Tel.: 502-635-5083. Fax: 502-635-5086.
E-mail: marian@filsonhistorical.org
Web Site: www.filsonhistorical.org
Formerly: Filson Club Historical Society, Inc.
Key Personnel: C.E.O. & Dir., Craig Buthod; Pres. (V), J. McCauley Brown.
Institution Type/Description: History Museum.
Hours & Admission Prices: House & Museum: Mon.-Fri. 9-5. No charge. Library: Mon.-Fri. 9-5, 1st Sat. of month 9-4. Adults $10; discount to members. Special Collections: Mon.-Fri. 9-5, 1st Sat. of month 9-4. Adults $10; discount to members. Closed national holidays. &
Attendance: 28,000 (estimated)

FRAZIER HISTORY MUSEUM, 829 W. Main St., Louisville, KY
40202-2619. Tel.: 502-753-5663, 866-886-7103. Fax: 502-412-8148.
E-mail: info@fraziermuseum.org
Web Site: www.fraziermuseum.org
Formerly: Frazier International History Museum
Key Personnel: Dir. Mktg., Andy Treinen; Mktg. & Public Rels., Susan McNeese Lynch; Dir. Public Programs, Jodi Lewis; Chief Cur., Brigid Muldoon.
Institution Type/Description: History Museum.
Hours & Admission Prices: Mon.-Sat. 9-5, Sun. 12-5. Adults $12, seniors & military $10, children 5-17 & college students $8; discounts to AAM members; children 4 & under, teachers and members no charge. Closed Thanksgiving; Christmas Eve & Day. &
Attendance: 100,000 (estimated)

GHEENS SCIENCE HALL AND RAUCH PLANETARIUM,
Univ. of Louisville, Belknap Campus, 106 W. Brandeis Ave., Louisville, KY 40292. Mailing Address: Rauch Planetarium, University of Louisville, Louisville, KY 40292. Tel.: 502-852-6664 & 7597. Fax: 502-852-0831.
E-mail: planet@louisville.edu
Web Site: www.louisville.edu/planetarium
Key Personnel: Dir., Rachel Connolly; Technical Coord., Drew Foster; Mktg., Dorothy J. Vittitow; Devel., Paula Campbell; Operations Mgr., Paula McGuffey.
Institution Type/Description: Planetarium.
Hours & Admission Prices: Call for hours. Adults $8, children 12 & under, seniors & Metroversity students $6. &
Attendance: 91,000 (actual)

HISTORIC HOMES FOUNDATION, INC., 3110 Lexington Rd.,
Louisville, KY 40206-3002. Tel.: 502-899-5079.
E-mail: farmingtondirector@historichomes.org
Web Site: www.historichomes.org
Key Personnel: Pres. HHF, Dean Wilkinson; Dir. Farmington Historic Plantation, Diane Carman-Young; Dir. Whitehall House & Gardens, Merrill Simmons; Bookkeeper, Terry Malcolm.
Institution Type/Description: Historic Houses.
Hours & Admission Prices: Farmington: Tues.-Sat. 10-4:30, Sun. 1:30-4:30; last tour 3:45. Adults $9, senior citizens $8, students $4; children 5 & under no charge. Whitehall Mon.-Fri. 10-2. Adults $5, senior citizens $4, students $3; children 5 & under no charge. Thomas Edison House: Tues.-Sat. 10-2 or by appointment. Adults $5, senior citizens $3; children under 5 no charge. Group Tours: minimum 25. $3 per person. Closed New Year's Day; Easter; Derby Day; Thanksgiving; Christmas Eve & Day. &
Attendance: 29,000 (estimated)

KENTUCKY DERBY MUSEUM, 704 Central Ave., Gate 1,
Churchill Downs, Louisville, KY 40208-1212. Tel.: 502-637-1111. Fax: 502-636-5855. Facebook: Kentucky Derby Museum; Twitter & Instagram: @derbymuseum.
E-mail: info@derbymuseum.org
Web Site: www.derbymuseum.org
Key Personnel: Pres. & C.E.O., Patrick Armstrong; Vice Pres. & C.F.O., Jane Driskell; Chief Devel. Officer, Erik Brown; Dir. Retail, Katie Stephenson; Dir. Facilities, David Sweazy; Museum Educator, Ronnie Dreistadt; Communications Mgr., Lindsay English; Mgr. Membership, Carla Grego; Mktg. & Museum Shop Mgr., Brittany Gorter.
Institution Type/Description: Thoroughbred Racing & Equine Art, History & Science: located at Gate 1 of Churchill Downs, a National Historic Landmark.
Hours & Admission Prices: March 15- Nov. Mon.-Sat. 8-5, Sun. 11-5; Dec.-March 14 Mon.-Sat. 9-5, Sun. 11-5. Adults $15, senior citizens 60 & over $14, children 5-14 $7; discounts to AAA members & military; children under 5 no charge. Behind the Scenes Tour: $11. Backside Track Tours: $11. Closed Oaks Day; Derby Day; Thanksgiving; Christmas Eve & Day. &
Attendance: 220,000 (actual)

KENTUCKY MUSEUM OF ART AND CRAFT, 715 West Main,
Louisville, KY 40202-2633. Tel.: 502-589-0102. Fax: 502-589-0154.
E-mail: admin@kentuckyarts.org
Web Site: www.kmacmuseum.org
Formerly: Kentucky Museum of Arts & Design
Key Personnel: Bd. Pres., John Schriber; Exec. Dir., Aldy Milliken; Assoc. Cur., Joey Yates; Dir. Devel., Michelle Stuggs Doninger.
Institution Type/Description: Art & Craft Museum.
Hours & Admission Prices: Tues.-Sat. 10-5, Sun. 11-5. Adults $8, seniors & military $5, students $4; members & children under 12 no charge. Closed Derby Day; most public holidays. &
Attendance: 63,000 (estimated)

KENTUCKY SCIENCE CENTER, 727 W. Main St., Louisville,
KY 40202-2681. Tel.: 502-561-6100.
E-mail: kyscience@louisvilleky.gov
Web Site: kysciencecenter.org
Formerly: Louisville Science Center
Key Personnel: C.E.O. & Dir., JoAnna Haas; Chm. (V), Tim Condon; Mng. Dir. Visitor Experiences, Kim Hunter; Museum Shop Mgr., Toph Bryant.
Institution Type/Description: Science & Technology Center: housed in 1878 five-building structure.
Hours & Admission Prices: Mon.-Thurs. & Sun. 9:30-5, Fri.-Sat. 9:30-9. See website for admission prices. Closed Derby Day; Thanksgiving; Christmas Eve & Day. &
Attendance: 500,000 (estimated)

LASER TAG MUSEUM, 4121 Shelbyville Rd., Louisville, KY
40207. Tel.: 317-965-9482.
E-mail: erik@lasertagmuseum.com
Web Site: www.lasertagmuseum.com
Institution Type/Description: History Museum.
Hours & Admission Prices: Call for hours. No charge.

LOCUST GROVE, 561 Blankenbaker Lane, Louisville, KY 40207-
7100. Tel.: 502-897-9845. Fax: 502-897-0103. Facebook: Historic Locust Grove; Twitter: @locustgrove.
E-mail: lghh@locustgrove.org
Web Site: www.locustgrove.org
Key Personnel: Dir., Carol Ely; Pres., Christopher Green; Treas., James Statler; Programs, Mary Beth Williams; Museum Shop Mgr., Jennifer Jansen.
Institution Type/Description: Historic Site: housed in the former home of the Croghan family & General George Rogers Clark; built 1790s.

Hours & Admission Prices: Mon.-Sat. 10-4:30, Sun. 1-4:30. Adults $9, seniors $8, children $4; discounts to National Trust, AAA, AASLH, ICOM & AAM members; members & children under 6 no charge. Closed January; Easter; Derby Day; Thanksgiving; Christmas Eve & Day & New Year's Eve & Day. ♿
Attendance: 28,483 (actual)

LOUISVILLE FIRE DEPARTMENT LEARNING CENTER & MUSEUM, 3228 River Park Dr., Louisville, KY 40210. Tel.: 502-574-3731.
Institution Type/Description: Fire Fighting History Museum.
Hours & Admission Prices: By appointment.

LOUISVILLE SLUGGER MUSEUM & FACTORY, 800 W. Main St., Louisville, KY 40202-2637. Tel.: 877-775-8443. Fax: 502-585-1179.
E-mail: museum@slugger.com
Web Site: www.sluggermuseum.com
Key Personnel: Exec. Dir., Anne Jewell; Museum Shop Mgr. & Retail Dir., Whitney Pfister; Dir. Operations, Deana Lockman.
Institution Type/Description: Baseball Museum and Bat Factory.
Hours & Admission Prices: Mon.-Sat. 9-5, Sun. 12-5. Adults $10, senior citizens $9, children $5; discounts to groups & AAM members. Closed New Year's Day; Thanksgiving; Christmas Day. ♿
Attendance: 220,000 (actual)

LOUISVILLE STONEWARE COMPANY MUSEUM, 731 Brent St., Louisville, KY 40204. Tel.: 502-582-1900.
E-mail: retail@louisvillestoneware.com
Web Site: www.louisvillestoneware.com
Institution Type/Description: Company History Museum.
Hours & Admission Prices: Factory Tours: Mon.-Fri. 10:30-1:30; groups of 8 or more by appointment. Tours: adults $7, seniors 65 & over $6, students & children 6-12 $5; children 5 & under no charge. Tour & Paint Your Own Pottery: adults $30, seniors 65 & over $24, students & children 6-12 $23; children 5 & under no charge.

LOUISVILLE VISUAL ART ASSOCIATION, 609 W. Main St., 2nd Floor, Louisville, KY 40202. Mailing Address: 1538 Lytle St., Louisville, KY 40202. Tel.: 502-584-8166. Fax: 502-896-2148.
E-mail: shannon@louisvillevisualart.org
Web Site: www.louisvillevisualart.org
Key Personnel: Exec. Dir., Shannon Westerman; Pres. (V), Robert Hallenberg; Vice Pres., Anne O'Daniel; Treas., John Lewis; Education Coord., Jackie Pallesen; Sec., Rick Sneed.
Institution Type/Description: Art Gallery: 1860 neo-classical building once housed public water systems first pumping station.
Hours & Admission Prices: Mon.-Fri. 9-5, Sun. 12-4. Adults $3, seniors & students $2; members & children under 12 no charge. Closed New Year's Day; Easter; Independence Day; Thanksgiving; Christmas Eve & Day. ♿
Attendance: 150,000 (actual)

LOUISVILLE ZOOLOGICAL GARDEN, 1100 Trevilian Way, Louisville, KY 40213-1559. Mailing Address: P.O. Box 37250, Louisville, KY 40233-7250. Tel.: 502-459-2181. Fax: 502-459-2196.
Web Site: www.louisvillezoo.org
Key Personnel: Exec. Dir., John Walczak; Senior Veterinarian, Zoli Gyimesi, D.V.M.; Asst. Dir., Stephanie Moore; Dir. Communications, Robert Kemnitz; Dir. Mktg. & Public Rels., Maureen Horrigan; Dir. Devel., Kelly Grether; Education Cur., Kim Allgeier; Museum Shop Mgr., Kathy Kline.
Institution Type/Description: Zoo & Botanical Gardens.
Hours & Admission Prices: mid-March to late Sept. daily 10-6; late Sept. to mid-March daily 10-5; call for additional Halloween Party hours. March-Oct. adults $16.25, senior citizens 60 & over and children 3-11 $11.75; Nov.-Feb. adults $9.95, senior citizens 60 & over and children 3-11 $6.95; discounts to groups of 15 or more, military, AZA, reciprocal Zoos & Aquaria members; children under 3 & members no charge. Closed New Year's Day; Thanksgiving; Christmas. ♿
Attendance: 810,546 (actual)

MUHAMMAD ALI CENTER, 144 N. Sixth St., Louisville, KY 40202-2939. Tel.: 502-584-9254. Fax: 502-589-4905. Facebook.
E-mail: info@alicenter.org
Web Site: www.alicenter.org
Key Personnel: Pres. & C.E.O., Donald Lassere; Sr. Dir. Public Rels. & External Affairs, Jeanie Kahnke.
Institution Type/Description: History Museum.
Hours & Admission Prices: Tues.-Sat. 9:30-5, Sun. 12-5. Adults $9, seniors 65 & over $8, military & students $5, children 6-12 $4; discounts to groups; members & children 5 & under no charge. Closed New Year's Eve & Day; Easter;

Memorial Day; Independence Day; Columbus Day; Thanksgiving; Christmas Eve & Day. ♿
Attendance: 135,000 (actual)

MUSEUM OF THE AMERICAN PRINTING HOUSE FOR THE BLIND, 1839 Frankfort Ave., Louisville, KY 40206-3148. Tel.: 502-895-2405, ext. 365, 800-223-1839, ext. 365. Fax: 502-899-2363.
E-mail: museum@aph.org
Web Site: www.aph.org
Formerly: Callahan Museum
Key Personnel: Dir., Michael A. Hudson; Mgr. Collections, Anne Rich.
Institution Type/Description: History Museum.
Hours & Admission Prices: Mon.-Fri. 8:30-4:30, Sat. 10-3. Plant Tours: Mon.-Thurs. 10 & 2. No charge; donations accepted. Closed New Year's Day; Derby Day; Memorial Day; Independence Day; Labor Day; Thanksgiving; Christmas. ♿
Attendance: 5,000 (actual)

NATIONAL SOCIETY OF THE SONS OF THE AMERICAN REVOLUTION, 809 W. Main St., Louisville, KY 40202-2619. Tel.: 502-589-1776. Fax: 502-589-1671.
E-mail: nssar@sar.org
Web Site: www.sar.org
Key Personnel: Exec. Dir., Donald Shaw.
Institution Type/Description: National Historical Society.
Hours & Admission Prices: Museum & Library: Mon.-Fri. 9:30-4:30. Museum: No charge. Library Research: $5 per day; SAR & DAR members no charge. Closed New Year's Eve & Day; Independence Day; Thanksgiving; Christmas Eve & Day; national holidays. ♿
Attendance: 5,000 (estimated)

THE NICOL & EISENBERG ARCHAEOLOGICAL COLLECTION, Southern Baptist Theological Seminary, 2825 Lexington Rd., Louisville, KY 40280. Tel.: 502-897-4039. Fax: 502-897-4036.
E-mail: campinfo@sbts.edu
Web Site: www.sbts.edu
Formerly: The Joseph A. Callaway Archaeological Museum
Key Personnel: Librarian, Bruce Keisling.
Institution Type/Description: Biblical Archaeology Museum.
Hours & Admission Prices: Closed indefinitely. ♿

PORTLAND MUSEUM, 2308 Portland Ave., Louisville, KY 40212-1036. Tel.: 502-776-7678. Fax: 502-776-9874.
E-mail: pmuse@iglou.com
Web Site: www.goportland.org
Key Personnel: Exec. Dir., Nathalie Taft Andrews; Pres., Christian Trabue; Chm. (V), Sally Craven; Asst. to Dir & Museum Shop Mgr., Jessica Dawkins.
Institution Type/Description: General Museum: housed in 1850 Beach Grove residence of William Skene.
Hours & Admission Prices: Tues.-Fri. 10-4:30. Adults $7, senior citizens $6, students 6 & over $5; discounts to AAA & AAM members; children 5 & under no charge. ♿
Attendance: 5,000 (estimated)

RIVERSIDE, THE FARNSLEY-MOREMEN LANDING, 7410 Moorman Rd., Louisville, KY 40272-4572. Tel.: 502-935-6809. Fax: 502-935-6821.
E-mail: info@riverside-landing.org
Web Site: www.riverside-landing.org
Institution Type/Description: Historic House Museum.
Hours & Admission Prices: Visitor Center: Tues.-Sat. 9-5. House: March-Nov. Tues.-Sat. 10-4:30, Sun. 1-4:30; Dec.-Feb. Tues.-Sat. 10-4:30. Family $15, adults $6, senior citizens $5, children 6-12 $3; members no charge. Closed major holidays. ♿
Attendance: 25,000 (estimated)

THE SPEED ART MUSEUM, 2035 S. Third St., Louisville, KY 40208-1812. Tel.: 502-634-2700. Fax: 502-636-2899. Twitter: @speedartmuseum.
E-mail: info@speedmuseum.org
Web Site: www.speedmuseum.org
Key Personnel: Interim Dir., Stephen Reily; C.O.O., Paul Esselman; Dir. Devel., Jennifer Humphries; Dir. Mktg. & Communications, Steven Bowling.
Institution Type/Description: Art Museum.
Hours & Admission Prices: Tues.-Sat. 10-5, Sun. noon-5. Adults $12, children 4-17, military personnel & seniors $8; children 3 & under & members no charge. ♿
Attendance: 74,452 (actual)

THOMAS EDISON HOUSE, 729-731 E. Washington St., Louisville, KY 40202-1050. Mailing Address: 3110 Lexington Rd., Louisville, KY 40206. Tel.: 502-585-5247. Fax: 502-585-5231.
E-mail: edisonhouse@historichomes.org
Web Site: www.historichomes.org
Key Personnel: Exec. Dir., Kristen Lutes.
Institution Type/Description: Historic House.
Hours & Admission Prices: Tues.-Sat. 10-2; other times by appointment. Adults $5, senior citizens $4, students $3; discounts to AAA members; children under 5, Historic Homes Foundation & members no charge (not including special events). Closed New Year's Day; Thanksgiving; Christmas Eve & Day. &
Attendance: 5,500 (estimated)

21C MUSEUM HOTEL LOUISVILLE, 700 W. Main St., Louisville, KY 40202-2634. Tel.: 502-217-6300. Fax: 502-217-6347.
E-mail: agraystites@21cmuseum.org
Web Site: www.21cmuseum.org
Key Personnel: Dir., Alice Gray Stites.
Institution Type/Description: Art Gallery.
Hours & Admission Prices: Call for hours. No charge. &

Madisonville

HISTORICAL SOCIETY OF HOPKINS COUNTY, 107 Union St., Madisonville, KY 42431-2529. Tel.: 270-821-3986.
Institution Type/Description: Historical Society Museum.
Hours & Admission Prices: Mon.-Fri. 1-5.

Mammoth Cave

MAMMOTH CAVE NATIONAL PARK, Maintenance Rd., SRM Division, Mammoth Cave, KY 42259. Mailing Address: P.O. Box 7, Mammoth Cave, KY 42259-0007. Tel.: 270-758-2153. Fax: 270-758-2663.
E-mail: terry_langford@contractor.nps.gov
Web Site: www.nps.gov/maca/home.htm
Key Personnel: Supt., Sarah Craighead; Chm. (V), Eddie Wells; Education Coord., Cheryl Messenger.
Institution Type/Description: National Park: 52,000+ acre park with over 390 miles of underground passageways, some exposed for public viewing.
Hours & Admission Prices: mid-March to mid-June & Sept.-Oct. daily 8-6; mid-June to mid-Aug. daily 8-7; Nov. to mid-March 8:45-5. Seasonal Tours: 1 to 6 hours, call or see website for information and reservations. Closed Christmas.
Attendance: 1,800,000 (estimated)

Marion

BEN E. CLEMENT MINERAL MUSEUM, 205 N. Walker St., Marion, KY 42064. Mailing Address: P.O. Box 391, Marion, KY 42064-0391. Tel.: 270-965-4263. Facebook: Clement Mineral Museum.
E-mail: beclement@att.net
Web Site: www.clementmineralmuseum.org
Key Personnel: Dir. & Museum Shop Mgr., Tina Walker; Chm. (V), Bill Frazer.
Institution Type/Description: Mineral Museum.
Hours & Admission Prices: May-Sept. Mon.-Sat. 10-3; Oct.-March Wed.-Sat. 10-3; other times by appointment. Adults $8; members no charge. Closed major holidays. &
Attendance: 4,000 (estimated)

CRITTENDEN COUNTY HISTORICAL MUSEUM, 124 E. Bellville St., Marion, KY 42064-1410. Mailing Address: 124 E. Bellville St., P.O. Box 25, Marion, KY 42064. Tel.: 270-965-9257.
Key Personnel: Chm. (V), Brenda Underdown.
Institution Type/Description: Historic Building: housed in the first church in Marion, built in 1881.
Hours & Admission Prices: April-Oct. Wed.-Sat. 10-3; other times by appointment. No charge; donations accepted.
Attendance: 500 (actual)

Mayfield

ICEHOUSE GALLERY, 120 N. 8th St., Mayfield, KY 42066. Tel.: 270-247-6971.
E-mail: icehousearts@gmail.com
Web Site: www.icehousearts.org
Formerly: Ice House Gallery
Key Personnel: Dir., Nanc Gunn.

Institution Type/Description: Art Gallery.
Hours & Admission Prices: Tues.-Fri. 10-5, Sat. 10-1. No charge. &
Attendance: 3,000 (estimated)

Maysville

ALBERT SIDNEY JOHNSTON HOUSE, 503 S. Court St., Maysville, KY 41056. Mailing Address: c/o Maysville-Mason County CVB, 2 East Third St., Maysville, KY 41056. Tel.: 606-759-7411.
E-mail: suziepratt@maysvilleky.net
Institution Type/Description: Historic House Museum: housed in the birthplace of Confederate General Johnston.
Hours & Admission Prices: Guided Tours: April-Nov. by appointment.

HARRIET BEECHER STOWE SLAVERY TO FREEDOM MUSEUM, 2124 Old Main St., Maysville, KY 41096. Mailing Address: The Cox Building, 2 E. Third St., Maysville, KY 41056. Tel.: 606-759-7411.
E-mail: info@maysvilleky.net
Web Site: www.cityofmaysville.com/listings/museums/
Key Personnel: Dir., Suzie Pratt.
Institution Type/Description: History Museum.
Hours & Admission Prices: Sat. 10-4, Sun. 12-4.

KENTUCKY GATEWAY MUSEUM CENTER, 215 Sutton St., Maysville, KY 41056-1109. Tel.: 606-564-5865. Fax: 606-564-4372.
E-mail: businessoffice@kygmc.org
Web Site: www.kentuckygatewaymuseumcenter.org
Formerly: Mason County Museum & Museum Center
Key Personnel: Registrar, Pat King; Dir., Dewey Applegate; Cur. Books, Art & Artifacts, Sue Ellen Grannis; Business Mgr., Gayle McKay; Mktg. & Sales Coord, & Museum Shop Mgr., Paula Ruble; Researcher, Caye Chamness; Researcher, Myra Hardy; Accounting, Joyce Weigott; Cur. Education, James Shires, Ph.D.; Reference Registrar, Anne Pollitt.
Institution Type/Description: Art Gallery, Genealogical & Historical Library & Museum: housed in 1881, restored library building.
Hours & Admission Prices: Tues.-Sat. 10-4. Museum: adults $10, students $2; discounts to AAA members; AASLH members no charge. Library: adults $5. Closed New Year's Day; Easter; Mother's Day; Father's Day; Independence Day; Thanksgiving; Christmas. &
Attendance: 5,000 (estimated)

NATIONAL UNDERGROUND RAILROAD MUSEUM, 38 W. 4th St., Maysville, KY 41056. Mailing Address: P.O. Box 421, Maysville, KY 41056. Tel.: 606-564-3200 & 4413.
Web Site: llbierbower.org
Institution Type/Description: History Museum.
Hours & Admission Prices: Wed. & Fri.-Sat. 10-3; other times by appointment.

OLD CHURCH MUSEUM, 2028 Old Main St., Maysville, KY 41056. Mailing Address: Maysville-Mason Co CVB, The Cox Building, 2 E. Third St., Maysville, KY 41056. Tel.: 606-759-7411 & 564-9419. Fax: 606-564-9416.
E-mail: info@maysvilleky.net
Web Site: www.cityofmaysville.com
Institution Type/Description: History Museum: housed in a former Methodist Episcopal Church - South; built in 1848.
Hours & Admission Prices: Call for hours.

Middlesboro

ALEXANDER ARTHUR MUSEUM, 2215 Cumberland Ave., Middlesboro, KY 40965. Tel.: 606-248-2482.
Institution Type/Description: History Museum.
Hours & Admission Prices: Call for hours.

BELL COUNTY HISTORICAL SOCIETY, 207 N. 20th St., Middlesboro, KY 40965. Mailing Address: P.O. Box 1344, Middlesboro, KY 40965-3144. Tel.: 606-242-0005.
Institution Type/Description: Historical Society Museum.
Hours & Admission Prices: Tues.-Sat. 10-3.

CUMBERLAND GAP NATIONAL HISTORICAL PARK, 91 Bartlett Park Rd., Middlesboro, KY 40965. Tel.: 606-248-2817. Fax: 606-248-7276.
E-mail: cuga_superintendent@nps.gov

Web Site: www.nps.gov/cuga
Institution Type/Description: History Museum.
Hours & Admission Prices: Visitor Center and Pinnacle: daily 8-5. Park Gates: April-May & Sept.-Oct. 8-7; June-Aug. 8 am-9 pm; Nov.-March 8-5. Park: no charge. Wilderness Road Campground: user fee charged. Visitor Center closed: New Year's Day; Christmas. &
Attendance: 85,000 (estimated)

Monticello

WILLIAM CRENSHAW KENNEDY, JR. MEMORIAL MUSEUM, 75 N. Main St., Monticello, KY 42633-1439. Mailing Address: P.O. Box 67, Monticello, KY 42633-0067. Tel.: 606-340-2300.
E-mail: museum123@windstream.net
Web Site: waynecountykymuseum.com
Key Personnel: Dir. & Cur., Harlan Ogle.
Institution Type/Description: History Museum.
Hours & Admission Prices: Tues.-Sat. 10-4; other times by appointment. No charge; donations accepted. &
Attendance: 4,000 (actual)

Morehead

CLAYPOOL-YOUNG ART GALLERY - MOREHEAD STATE UNIVERSITY, Claypool Young Bldg., Morehead, KY 40351. Tel.: 606-783-5446. Facebook: Claypool-Young Art Gallery.
E-mail: j.reis@moreheadstate.edu
Key Personnel: Dir., Jennifer Reis.
Institution Type/Description: Art Gallery.
Hours & Admission Prices: Mon.-Fri. 8-4. No charge.

THE KENTUCKY FOLK ART CENTER, 102 W. First St., Morehead, KY 40351-1723. Tel.: 606-783-2204. Fax: 606-783-5034.
E-mail: t.stone@moreheadstate.edu
Web Site: www.kyfolkart.org
Key Personnel: Dir., Matt Collingsworth.
Institution Type/Description: Folk Art Museum.
Hours & Admission Prices: Mon.-Sat. 9-5. Adults 12 & over $3, seniors & children under 12 $2; members no charge. &
Attendance: 8,000 (estimated)

Morganfield

CAMP BRECKINRIDGE MUSEUM & ARTS CENTER, 1116 N. Village Rd., Morganfield, KY 42437. Mailing Address: P.O. Box 60, Morganfield, KY 42437-0060. Tel.: 270-389-4420. Fax: 270-389-3546.
E-mail: campbreckinridge@bellsouth.net
Web Site: www.breckinridge-arts.org
Key Personnel: Dir., Vicki Ricketts.
Institution Type/Description: History Museum.
Hours & Admission Prices: Tues.-Fri. 10-3, Sat. 10-4, Sun. 1-4. &

Mount Sterling

MONTGOMERY COUNTY HISTORY MUSEUM, 36 Broadway St., Mount Sterling, KY 40353. Tel.: 859-498-4669.
E-mail: mchmky@gmail.com
Institution Type/Description: History Museum.
Hours & Admission Prices: Fri.-Sat. 10-2.

Munfordville

HART COUNTY HISTORICAL MUSEUM, 109 Main St., Munfordville, KY 42765. Mailing Address: P.O. Box 606, Munfordville, KY 42765-0606. Tel.: 270-524-0101.
E-mail: hartmuseum@scrtc.com
Web Site: www.hartcountymuseum.org
Key Personnel: Pres. (V), Nathaniel Crenshaw; Museum Shop Mgr., Carolyn Short.
Institution Type/Description: History Museum; housed in the historic 1893 Chapline Building.
Hours & Admission Prices: Mon.-Fri. 9-4, Sat. 8-4. No charge; donations accepted. Closed major holidays. &
Attendance: 3,000 (estimated)

Murray

UNIVERSITY ART GALLERIES, MURRAY STATE UNIVERSITY, Price Doyle Fine Arts Center, 15th & Olive Sts., 6th Fl., Murray, KY 42071. Mailing Address: 604 Fine Arts Center, Murray, KY 42071-3342. Tel.: 270-809-3052 & 6734.
E-mail: msu.eaglegallery@murraystate.edu
Web Site: www.murraystate.edu/artgallery
Institution Type/Description: University Art Gallery.
Hours & Admission Prices: Summer: Mon.-Fri. 9-4; Sept.-May Mon.-Fri. 8-5, Sat.-Sun. 1-4. No charge. Closed university holidays. &
Attendance: 12,000 (actual)

WRATHER WEST KENTUCKY MUSEUM, Murray State University, 100 Wrather Museum, Murray, KY 42071-3315. Tel.: 270-809-4771. Fax: 270-809-4485.
E-mail: msu.wrather@murraystate.edu
Web Site: www.murraystate.edu/info/wrather/wrather.htm
Key Personnel: C.E.O., Kate A. Reeves.
Institution Type/Description: History Museum.
Hours & Admission Prices: Mon.-Fri. 8:30-4, Sat. 10-1. No charge; donations accepted. Closed university holidays. &
Attendance: 20,200 (actual)

Nancy

MILL SPRINGS BATTLEFIELD VISITOR CENTER AND MUSEUM, 9020 W. Hwy. 80, Nancy, KY 42544. Mailing Address: Mill Springs Battlefield Association, P.O. Box 282, Nancy, KY 42544-0282. Tel.: 606-636-4045. Fax: 606-636-4050.
E-mail: info@millsprings.net
Web Site: www.millsprings.net
Key Personnel: Dir., Monica De Carlo; Pres. (V), Bruce Burkett, D.V.M.
Institution Type/Description: History Museum.
Hours & Admission Prices: See website for hours. Adults $5, seniors & military $3, students $2; members no charge. &
Attendance: 10,000 (estimated)

New Haven

KENTUCKY RAILWAY MUSEUM, INC., 136 S. Main St., New Haven, KY 40051-6355. Mailing Address: P.O. Box 240, New Haven, KY 40051-0240. Tel.: 800-272-0152, 502-549-5470. Fax: 502-549-5472.
E-mail: kyrail@bardstown.com
Web Site: kyrail.org
Key Personnel: Exec. Dir. & Pres., Greg Mathews; Chm. Bd. (V), Charlie Buccola; Office Mgr., Kim Maupin; Marketing & Public Rels., Lynn Dawson; Maintenance, William Ward; Museum Store Mgr., Christopher Cecil.
Institution Type/Description: Railroad Transportation Museum.
Hours & Admission Prices: Train Rides: March-May & Aug.-Dec. Sat. 11-2, Sun. 2; June-July Tues. & Fri. 1. Museum: adults $5, children 2-12 $2. Train Tickets: adults $17.50, children $12.50; discounts to AAA members; museum members no charge. Package rates available. &
Attendance: 40,000 (actual)

Newport

NEWPORT AQUARIUM, One Aquarium Way, Newport, KY 41071-1679. Tel.: 859-261-7444. Fax: 859-261-5888.
Web Site: www.newportaquarium.com
Institution Type/Description: Aquarium.
Hours & Admission Prices: June-Aug. daily 9-7; Sept.-May daily 10-6. Adults $23, children 2-12 $15; children under 2 no charge.

Nicholasville

NATIONAL SOFTBALL SPORTS HALL OF FAME MUSEUM, 101 NSA Way, Nicholasville, KY 40340. Mailing Address: P.O. Box 7, Nicholasville, KY 40340. Tel.: 859-887-4114. Fax: 859-887-4874.
E-mail: nsahdqtrs@playnsa.com
Web Site: www.playnsa.com
Key Personnel: C.E.O., Hugh Cantrell; Chm. (V), Tommy Zehmer; Pres. (V), Eddie R. Cantrell; Museum Shop Mgr., Faye Cantrell.
Institution Type/Description: History Museum.
Hours & Admission Prices: Call for hours. No charge.
Attendance: 200 (estimated)

OLD JESSAMINE COUNTY JAIL, 200 S. Main St., Nicholasville, KY 40356. Tel.: 859-885-4500.
E-mail: tshewmaker@jessamineco.com
Web Site: www.jessamineco.com
Institution Type/Description: Historic Building: 1870 jail.
Hours & Admission Prices: Call for hours.

Olive Hill

NORTHEASTERN KENTUCKY MUSEUM, 1385 Carter Caves Rd., Olive Hill, KY 41164-8295. Tel.: 606-286-6012.
E-mail: jimplummer47@gmail.com
Web Site: www.kymuseum.org
Institution Type/Description: History Museum.
Hours & Admission Prices: Spring to Summer daily 9-5, Winter by appointment. No charge.

Owensboro

INTERNATIONAL BLUEGRASS MUSIC MUSEUM, 117 Daviess St., Owensboro, KY 42303-4201. Mailing Address: 207 E. 2nd St., Owensboro, KY 42303-4201. Tel.: 270-926-7891. Fax: 270-689-9440. Facebook: Rompfest.
E-mail: chrisjoslin@bluegrassmuseum.org
Web Site: www.bluegrassmuseum.org
Key Personnel: Exec. Dir., Chris Joslin; Chm., Terry Woodward.
Institution Type/Description: Music Museum: housed in renovated c.1895 three-story brick Victorian storefront building attached to River Park Performing Arts Center.
Hours & Admission Prices: Tues.-Sat. 10-5, Sun. 1-4; other times by appointment. Adult $5, students with ID $2; discounts to groups; members and children 6 & under no charge. Closed Easter; Memorial Day; Independence Day; Labor Day; Christmas; New Year's Eve & Day. &
Attendance: 48,000 (estimated).

OWENSBORO MUSEUM OF FINE ART, INC., 901 Frederica St., Owensboro, KY 42301-3052. Tel.: 270-685-3181. Fax: 270-685-3181.
E-mail: mail@omfa.us
Web Site: www.omfa.us
Key Personnel: C.E.O. & Dir., Mary Bryan Hood; Chm., B. Dean Stanley; Dir. Devel. & Mktg., Jason Hayden; Business Mgr., Horace Hardison.
Institution Type/Description: Art Museum.
Hours & Admission Prices: Tues.-Thurs. 10-4, Fri. 10-7, Sat.-Sun. 1-4. Suggested Donations: adult $2, children $1; discounts to AAM members. Closed New Year's Day; Memorial Day; Independence Day; Labor Day; Christmas. &
Attendance: 72,000 (estimated)

OWENSBORO MUSEUM OF SCIENCE AND HISTORY, 122 E. 2nd St., Owensboro, KY 42303-4108. Tel.: 270-687-2732. Fax: 270-687-2738.
E-mail: information@owensboromuseum.com
Web Site: www.owensboromuseum.com
Key Personnel: Exec. Dir., Kathy Olson; Cur. Exhibits, Chris Norton; Dir. Publicity & Patron Devel., Debbie Stites; Guest Services Mgr., Peggy Welsh.
Institution Type/Description: General Museum.
Hours & Admission Prices: Tues.-Sat. 10-5, Sun. 1-5. Admission $3; discounts to ASTC, AAM, SEMC & KAM members; members and children 2 & under no charge. Closed major holidays. &
Attendance: 70,000 (estimated)

Paducah

LLOYD TILGHMAN HOUSE & CIVIL WAR MUSEUM, 631 Kentucky Ave., Paducah, KY 42003. Tel.: 270-575-5477.
E-mail: bpcbaxter@comcast.net
Formerly: Tilghman Heritage Foundation
Key Personnel: Dir., Chm. (V) & Museum Shop Mgr., Bill Baxter.
Institution Type/Description: Historic House Museum: housed in the former home of General Lloyd Tilghman; built in 1852.
Hours & Admission Prices: April-Nov. Tues.-Sat. 12-4; other times by appointment. Adults $5; discounts to groups. &
Attendance: 1,150 (estimated)

NATIONAL QUILT MUSEUM, 215 Jefferson St., Paducah, KY 42001-0714. Mailing Address: P.O. Box 1540, Paducah, KY 42002-1540. Tel.: 270-442-8856. Fax: 270-442-5448.
E-mail: info@quiltmuseum.org
Web Site: www.quiltmuseum.org
Formerly: Museum of the American Quilter's Society

Key Personnel: C.E.O., Frank Bennett; Pres. (V), Donna Wilder; Vice Pres., Fowler Black; Registrar & Cur. Collections, Judith Schwender; Museum Shop Mgr., Pam Hill.
Institution Type/Description: Arts & Quilt Museum.
Hours & Admission Prices: March-Nov. Mon.-Sat. 10-5, Sun. 1-5; Dec.-Feb. Mon.-Sat. 10-5. Adults $11, seniors $10, youth 13 & over $5; discounts to groups; members no charge. Closed New Year's Day; Easter; Thanksgiving; Christmas Eve & Day. &
Attendance: 39,000 (actual)

PADUCAH RAILROAD MUSEUM, 200 Washington St., Paducah, KY 42003-1557. Tel.: 270-908-6451.
Institution Type/Description: Railroad Museum.
Hours & Admission Prices: Wed.-Fri. 12-4, Sat. 10-4; other times by appointment. Adults $5, children $2.

RIVER DISCOVERY CENTER, 117 S. Water St., Paducah, KY 42001-0787. Tel.: 270-575-9958. Fax: 270-444-9944.
E-mail: jharris@riverdiscoverycenter.org
Web Site: www.riverdiscoverycenter.org
Formerly: River Heritage Museum
Key Personnel: Exec. Dir., Julie Harris; Chm., Alex Edwards; Education, E.J. Abell.
Institution Type/Description: General Museum.
Hours & Admission Prices: April-Nov. Mon.-Sat. 9:30-5, Sun. 1-5. Adults $7, senior citizens $6.50, children $5; discounts to groups; members no charge. Closed Thanksgiving; Christmas Eve & Day. &
Attendance: 15,000 (actual)

WHITEHAVEN TOURIST WELCOME CENTER, 1845 Lone Oak Rd., Paducah, KY 42001-7903. Tel.: 270-554-2077.
E-mail: whitehaven.wc@ky.gov
Key Personnel: Supvr., Regina Topp.
Institution Type/Description: Historic House: c.1860 Classical Revival Mansion.
Hours & Admission Prices: Daily 8-4:30; tours every half hour 1-4. No charge. Closed New Year's Eve & Day; Thanksgiving & day after; Christmas Day & day after. &
Attendance: 23,000 (actual)

WILLIAM CLARK MARKET HOUSE MUSEUM, 121 S. 2nd St., Market House Sq., Paducah, KY 42001-0789. Tel.: 270-443-7759.
E-mail: info@markethousemuseum.com
Web Site: www.markethousemuseum.com
Key Personnel: Exec. Dir., Penny Fields.
Institution Type/Description: History Museum: built in 1905 the Market House was used as a farmer's market.
Hours & Admission Prices: March to mid-Dec. Tues.-Sat. 10-4. Adults $4, children 6-11 $1; children under 6 no charge. Closed major holidays. &
Attendance: 10,000 (estimated)

YEISER ART CENTER, 200 Broadway, Paducah, KY 42001-0732. Tel.: 270-442-2453.
E-mail: jewhite@theyeiser.org
Web Site: www.theyeiser.org
Key Personnel: Exec. Dir., Joshua E. White; Pres. Bd. (V), Jane Gamble; Administrative Asst., John Paul Henry.
Institution Type/Description: Art Museum: housed in 1905 Market House.
Hours & Admission Prices: Tues.-Sat. 10-4. No charge; donations accepted. Closed major holidays. &
Attendance: 10,000 (estimated)

Paris

DUNCAN TAVERN HISTORIC CENTER, 323 High St., Paris, KY 40361-2002. Tel.: 859-987-1788.
E-mail: DUNCANSHRINE@BELLSOUTH.NET
Web Site: www.duncantavern.com
Institution Type/Description: History Museum: built in 1788.
Hours & Admission Prices: Tours: April to mid-Dec. Wed.-Sat. 1:30; other times by appointment. Adults $8, senior citizens $6, children 6-12 $2; children under 6 no charge.

HOPEWELL MUSEUM, 800 Pleasant St., Paris, KY 40361-1734. Tel.: 859-987-7274. Fax: 859-987-7274.
E-mail: hopewellmuseum@yahoo.com
Web Site: www.hopewellmuseum.org
Key Personnel: Dir., Leah Craig.
Institution Type/Description: History & Art Museum: housed in a 1909 Beaux-Arts style post office building.

Hours & Admission Prices: Wed.-Sat. 12-5, Sun. 2-4. Adults $3; students, children & members no charge. &
Attendance: 5,487 (actual)

Perryville

PERRYVILLE BATTLEFIELD STATE HISTORIC SITE, 1825 Battlefield Rd., Perryville, KY 40468-0296. Mailing Address: P.O. Box 296, Perryville, KY 40468-0296. Tel.: 859-332-8631. Fax: 859-332-2440. TDD: 859-332-8631.
E-mail: joan.house@ky.gov
Web Site: www.perryvillebattlefield.org
Formerly: Perryville Battlefield Museum
Key Personnel: Park Supt., Kurt Holman; Program Coord., Joan House.
Institution Type/Description: Civil War Museum.
Hours & Admission Prices: Grounds: March-Dec. daily. Museum: daily 9-5. Adults $4, children under 7-12 $3; discount to groups of 10 or more; children 6 & under no charge.
Attendance: 50,000 (estimated)

Petersburg

CREATION MUSEUM, 2800 Bullittsburg Church Rd., Petersburg, KY 41080-9364. Mailing Address: P.O. Box 510, Hebron, KY 41048-0510. Tel.: 888-582-4253.
E-mail: dmangus@creationmuseum.org
Web Site: creationmuseum.org
Key Personnel: Dir., Dan Mangus.
Institution Type/Description: Natural History Museum.
Hours & Admission Prices: Mon.-Fri. 10-6, Sat. 9-6, Sun. 12-6. Adults $29.95, senior citizens 60 & over $23.95, children 5-12 $15.95; children under 5 no charge.
Attendance: 300,000 (actual)

Pikeville

BIG SANDY HERITAGE CENTER, 773 Hambley Blvd., Pikeville, KY 41501-9078. Mailing Address: 172 Division St., Pikeville, KY 41501. Tel.: 606-218-6050.
E-mail: director@tourpikecounty.com
Web Site: www.tourpikecounty.com/big-sandy-heritage-center/
Key Personnel: Cur., Everett Johnson.
Institution Type/Description: History Museum.
Hours & Admission Prices: Mon.-Fri. 10-5, Sat.-Sun. evenings by appointment. Adults $3, seniors & children $2.

Prestonburg

EAST KENTUCKY SCIENCE CENTER, 7 Bert Combs Dr., Prestonburg, KY 471653. Tel.: 606-889-8260.
Institution Type/Description: Science Center.
Hours & Admission Prices: Center: Tues.-Fri. 1-4. Planetarium Show: Tues.-Fri. 2pm, Sat. 12:30 & 2pm. Laser Show: Tues.-Fri. 3:15, Sat. 12-4. Adults $6, students & seniors $4; children under 4 no charge.

Princeton

ADSMORE MUSEUM, 304 N. Jefferson St., Princeton, KY 42445-1551. Tel.: 270-365-3114. Fax: 270-365-3310. Facebook: Adsmore House & Gardens.
E-mail: adsmoremuseum@gmail.com
Web Site: www.adsmore.org
Key Personnel: Cur., Rebecca Pool.
Institution Type/Description: Living History Museum.
Hours & Admission Prices: Mar.-Dec. Tues.-Sat. 11-4. Adults $7, senior citizens 65 & over $6, children 6-12 $2; discounts to groups, AAA members & active duty military and their families. Closed Jan. 1-Feb. 29; New Year's Day; Martin Luther King Jr. Day; Presidents' Day; Easter; Independence Day; Thanksgiving; Christmas Eve & Day. &
Attendance: 2,500 (estimated)

Providence

PARKER WARNER HISTORIC MUSEUM, 500 S. Broadway, Providence, KY 42450-1638. Mailing Address: 48 Park St., Clay, KY 42404.
E-mail: pecowan@bellsouth.net
Key Personnel: Dir., Paul Cowan; Dir., David Fraser; Dir., Lowell Childress.
Institution Type/Description: History Museum: built in 1885.

Hours & Admission Prices: April-Nov. Thurs.-Sat. 1-4. No charge; donations accepted. Closed holidays.
Attendance: 55 (estimated)

Renfro Valley

KENTUCKY MUSIC HALL OF FAME AND MUSEUM, 2590 Richmond Rd., Renfro Valley, KY 40473. Mailing Address: P.O. Box 85, Renfro Valley, KY 40473-0085. Tel.: 606-256-1000. Fax: 606-256-2989.
E-mail: info@kentuckymusicmuseum.com
Web Site: kentuckymusicmuseum.com
Key Personnel: Chm. Bd., Roy Martin; Exec. Dir., Robert Lawson.
Institution Type/Description: Music Museum.
Hours & Admission Prices: Mon.-Sat. 10-6, Sun. 9-3. Adults $7.50, seniors $7, children 6-12 $4.50; discounts to groups; children under 6 & teachers no charge. &

Richmond

FORT BOONESBOROUGH MUSEUM, 4375 Boonesboro Rd., Richmond, KY 40475-9333. Tel.: 859-527-3131. Fax: 859-527-3328. TDD: 859-527-3131.
E-mail: phil.gray@ky.gov
Web Site: parks.ky.gov/findparks/recparks/fb
Key Personnel: Dir. Living History & Museum Shop Dir., Bill Farmer; Parks Mgr., Phil Gray; Cur., Jerry Raisor.
Institution Type/Description: History Museum.
Hours & Admission Prices: April-Oct. daily 9-5. Adults $7, children $5; discount to groups. &
Attendance: 60,000

IRVINTON HOUSE MUSEUM, 345 Lancaster Ave., Richmond, KY 40475. Tel.: 859-626-1422.
Institution Type/Description: History Museum.
Hours & Admission Prices: Call for hours.

WHITE HALL STATE HISTORIC SITE, 500 White Hall Shrine Rd., Richmond, KY 40475-9159. Mailing Address: Capital Plaza Tower, 10th Fl., 500 Mero St., Frankfort, KY 40601. Tel.: 859-623-9178. Fax: 859-626-8489.
E-mail: whitehall@ky.gov
Web Site: parks.ky.gov/findparks/histparks/wh
Key Personnel: Dir., Kathleen White; Cur., Lashe Mullins.
Institution Type/Description: Historic House: 1798 Georgian style building, added to in 1861 in the Italianate style, with 44 rooms & eight levels. Home of Cassius M. Clay, Ambassador to Russia during the 1860's under Abraham Lincoln.
Hours & Admission Prices: April-Oct. Wed.-Sun. 9-4; Nov.-March by appointment. Adults $7, children 6-12 $4; discounts to Kentucky Junior Historical Society, groups of 10 or more, AAA members & military with ID.
Attendance: 5,000 (estimated)

Rosine

BILL MONROE HOMEPLACE, 6210 Hwy. 62 E., Rosine, KY 42370. Mailing Address: P.O. Box 22, Hartford, KY 42347. Tel.: 270-298-0036. Facebook.
E-mail: ohiocountytour@gmail.com
Web Site: visitohiocountyky.com
Key Personnel: Dir., Jody Flener.
Institution Type/Description: Historic House Museum: housed in the birthplace & childhood home of the Father of Bluegrass Music, Bill Monroe.
Hours & Admission Prices: Mon.-Sat. 9-4, Sun. 1-4. No charge; donations accepted. &
Attendance: 3,000 (estimated)

Russellville

1817 SADDLE FACTORY MUSEUM, 280 E. 4th St., Russellville, KY 42276-1822. Mailing Address: c/o Logan County Tourism Commission, P.O. Box 1678, Russellville, KY 42276. Tel.: 270-726-4181.
Web Site: www.historicrussellville.com
Institution Type/Description: History Museum: housed in a former saddle factory built in 1817 by the Caldwell brothers.
Hours & Admission Prices: Call for hours.

Salyersville

MAGOFFIN COUNTY PIONEER VILLAGE AND MUSEUM, 239 S. Church St., Salyersville, KY 41465. Mailing Address: P.O. Box 222, Salyersville, KY 41465. Tel.: 606-349-1607.
E-mail: magoffin@foothills.net
Institution Type/Description: History Museum.
Hours & Admission Prices: Call for hours.

Sandy Hook

LAUREL GORGE CULTURAL HERITAGE CENTER, Old Rte. 7 & 32, Old Laurel Curves Rd., Sandy Hook, KY 41171. Mailing Address: P.O. Box 653, Sandy Hook, KY 41171. Tel.: 606-738-5543.
E-mail: info@laurelgorge.com
Web Site: www.laurelgorge.com
Institution Type/Description: History Museum.
Hours & Admission Prices: Call for hours.

Scottsville

ALLEN COUNTY HISTORICAL SOCIETY MUSEUM, 301 N. Fourth St., Scottsville, KY 42164. Mailing Address: P.O. Box 393, Scottsville, KY 42164. Tel.: 270-237-3026.
E-mail: chamber@scottsvilleky.info
Institution Type/Description: Historical Society Museum.
Hours & Admission Prices: Mon.-Thurs. 11-3:30; other times by appointment.

Shepherdsville

BULLITT COUNTY HISTORY MUSEUM, 300 S. Buckman St., Shepherdsville, KY 40165. Mailing Address: P.O. Box 206, Shepherdsville, KY 40165. Tel.: 502-921-0161.
E-mail: will.burden@bullitthistory.org
Key Personnel: Dir., Will Burden.
Institution Type/Description: History Museum.
Hours & Admission Prices: Mon.-Fri. 8-4. No charge.
Attendance: 5,000 (estimated)

Slade

KENTUCKY REPTILE ZOO, 200 L&E Railroad, Slade, KY 40376. Tel.: 606-663-9160. Fax: 606-663-6917.
E-mail: reptilezoo@bellsouth.net
Web Site: www.kyreptilezoo.org
Institution Type/Description: Reptile Museum.
Hours & Admission Prices: March to mid-May & Labor Day-Oct. Fri.-Sun. 11-6; Memorial Day-Sept. daily 11-6. Adults $6, children 3-15 $4; discounts to AAA members, seniors & groups of 10 or more; children under 3 no charge.

South Union

SOUTH UNION SHAKER VILLAGE, 850 Shaker Museum Rd., South Union, KY 42283. Mailing Address: P.O. Box 177, Auburn, KY 42206-0177. Tel.: 502-542-4167 & 7734. Fax: 502-542-7558.
E-mail: shakmus@logantele.com
Web Site: www.shakermuseum.com
Formerly: Shaker Museum at South Union
Key Personnel: Pres., Arthur Cleavinger; Dir. & Cur., Tommy Hines; Museum Shop Mgr., Bonnie Eilers.
Institution Type/Description: Historic Site: located on the site of 1807 South Union Shaker Village.
Hours & Admission Prices: March-Nov. Sun. 1-5, Tues.-Sat. 9-5; Dec.-Feb. Tues.-Sat. 10-4. Adults $8, children 6-12 $4; discounts to AAA members; members & children under 6 no charge. Closed New Year's Eve & Day; Thanksgiving; Christmas Eve & Day.
Attendance: 10,000 (actual)

Springfield

LINCOLN HOMESTEAD STATE PARK, 5079 Lincoln Park Rd., Springfield, KY 40069-9504. Tel.: 859-336-7461. Fax: 859-336-0659. TDD: 606-336-7461.
E-mail: lincolnhomestead@ky.gov
Web Site: www.state.ky.us/agencies/parks/linchome.htm
Key Personnel: Park Mgr., Robert Bartholomai.
Institution Type/Description: Park Museum.

Hours & Admission Prices: May-Sept. Thurs.-Sun. 10-5:30; Oct. Sat.-Sun. 10-5:30. Adults $2, children $1.50; discounts to groups of 10 or more.
Attendance: 4,000 (estimated)

Staffordsville

MOUNTAIN HOMEPLACE, 745 Ky. Route 2275, Staffordsville, KY 41256. Mailing Address: P.O. Box 809, Paintsville, KY 41240. Tel.: 606-297-1850.
E-mail: mountainhomeplacefarm@gmail.com
Institution Type/Description: History Museum.
Hours & Admission Prices: April-Dec. Tues.-Sat. 9-5. Adults $6, seniors $5, children $4.

U.S. 23 COUNTRY MUSIC HIGHWAY MUSEUM, 100 Stave Branch, Staffordsville, KY 41256-9001. Mailing Address: P.O. Box 809, Paintsville, KY 41240. Tel.: 606-297-1469.
E-mail: info@us23countrymusichwymuseum.com
Web Site: www.us23countrymusichwymuseum.com
Institution Type/Description: Country Music History Museum.
Hours & Admission Prices: Call for hours.

Stanford

WILLIAM WHITLEY HOUSE STATE HISTORIC SITE, 625 William Whitley Rd., Stanford, KY 40484-9770. Tel.: 606-355-2881. Fax: 606-355-2778.
E-mail: Carol.Kirby@ky.gov
Web Site: parks.ky.gov/statehistoricsites/ww/index.htm
Key Personnel: Acting Park Mgr., Stacy Thomason.
Institution Type/Description: Historic House: c.1792 William Whitley House, one of the first brick homes west of the Alleghenies.
Hours & Admission Prices: May-Oct. Wed.-Sat. 9-5, Sun. 11-5; other times by appointment. Adults $5, seniors $4, children $3. Closed Thanksgiving; Christmas.
Attendance: 5,000 (estimated)

Stanton

GLADIE CULTURAL ENVIRONMENTAL LEARNING CENTER, 3451 Sky Bridge Rd., Stanton, KY 40380. Tel.: 606-663-8100.
Institution Type/Description: History Museum.
Hours & Admission Prices: March to mid-Nov. daily 9-5:30; mid-Nov. to March call for reduced hours.

Stearns

MCCREARY COUNTY MUSEUM, 1Henderson St., Stearns, KY 42647. Mailing Address: P.O. Box 452, 1 Henderson St., Stearns, KY 42647-0452. Tel.: 606-376-5730. Fax: 606-376-5332. Facebook: McCreary County Museum.
E-mail: s.gilreath@mccrearymuseum.com
Web Site: www.mccrearycountymuseum.com
Formerly: Stearns Museum
Key Personnel: Volunteer Coord., Shane Gilreath; C.E.O., Rebecca Egnew; Museum Shop Mgr., Barbara Edwards.
Institution Type/Description: History Museum: housed in the old Stearns Coal and Lumber Company Corporate Headquarters, built in 1907.
Hours & Admission Prices: April & Nov. Thurs.-Sat. 9-4; May-Oct. Wed.-Sat. 9-4, Sun. 11-4. Adults 12-59 $5, seniors 60 & over $4, children 6-12 $3; discounts to KY Museum & Heritage Alliance members, local residents, military & school groups; members and children 5 & under no charge. Closed Thanksgiving.
Attendance: 12,000 (estimated)

Tompkinsville

OLD MULKEY MEETINGHOUSE STATE HISTORIC SITE, 38 Old Mulkey Park Rd., Tompkinsville, KY 42167-6781. Tel.: 270-487-8481. Fax: 270-487-8481. Facebook.
E-mail: sheila.rush@ky.gov
Web Site: www.parks.ky.gov
Key Personnel: Park Mgr., Sheila Rush.
Institution Type/Description: Historic Building: housed in a former log church; built in 1804.
Hours & Admission Prices: April-Nov. 15 daily 9-5. No charge.
Attendance: 20,000 (estimated)

Union

BIG BONE LICK STATE HISTORIC SITE, 3380 Beaver Rd., Union, KY 41091. Tel.: 859-384-3522. Fax: 859-384-4775.
E-mail: dean.henson@ky.gov
Web Site: www.parks.ky.gov
Key Personnel: Park Mgr., Dean Henson.
Institution Type/Description: Historic Site.
Hours & Admission Prices: Park: sunrise to sunset. Museum: April-Oct. Mon.-Thurs. 8-4:30, Fri.-Sun. 9-5. Park: no charge.
Attendance: 50,000 (estimated)

Van Lear

COAL MINERS' MUSEUM/VAN LEAR HISTORICAL SOCIETY, INC., 78 Miller's Creek Rd., Van Lear, KY 41265. Mailing Address: P.O. Box 369, Van Lear, KY 41265-0369. Tel.: 606-789-8540.
E-mail: vanleartourism@yahoo.com
Web Site: www.vanlearkentucky.com
Key Personnel: Pres., Debra B. Music; Dir. & Vice Pres., Tina S. Webb.
Institution Type/Description: Historical Society Museum: housed in the former office building of The Consolidation Coal Company.
Hours & Admission Prices: Nov.-Sept. by appointment. Adults $5, senior citizens $4; members and children 5 & under no charge. &
Attendance: 500 (estimated)

Vanceburg

VANCEBURG RAILROAD DEPOT MUSEUM, 218 Main St., Vanceburg, KY 41179. Mailing Address: c/o Lewis County Historical Society, P.O. Box 362, Vanceburg, KY 41179. Tel.: 606-796-0238.
Institution Type/Description: Historic Building: housed in a former railroad depot; built in 1910.
Hours & Admission Prices: Call for hours.

Versailles

BLUEGRASS RAILROAD MUSEUM, 175 Beasley Rd., Versailles, KY 40383-8992. Mailing Address: P.O. Box 27, Versailles, KY 40383-0027. Tel.: 859-873-2476, 800-755-2476 (outside KY). Fax: 859-873-0408.
E-mail: bluegrassrailroad@yahoo.com
Web Site: www.bgrm.org
Key Personnel: Exec. Dir. & Pres., John Penfield.
Institution Type/Description: Railroad Museum.
Hours & Admission Prices: Call for hours. Train rides: adults $11.50, senior citizens $10.50, children 2-12 $9.50; members & children under 2 no charge. &
Attendance: 7,500 (estimated)

JACK JOUETT HOUSE, 255 Craig's Creek Rd., Versailles, KY 40383-9649. Tel.: 859-873-7902.
E-mail: info@jouetthouse.org
Web Site: www.jouetthouse.org
Key Personnel: Exec. Dir., Michael Lynch.
Institution Type/Description: Historic House Museum: housed in a Federal-style house, built in 1797.
Hours & Admission Prices: April-Oct. Mon. 10-12, Fri. 12-5, Sat. 10-5, Sun. 1-5; other times by appointment. No charge; donations accepted.

NOSTALGIA STATION TOY AND TRAIN MUSEUM, 279 Depot St., Versailles, KY 40383. Tel.: 859-873-2497.
Web Site: www.bluegrassrailroad.com
Institution Type/Description: Toy Museum: housed in a restored 1911 railroad station.
Hours & Admission Prices: Wed.-Sat. 10-5, Sun. 1-5. Adults $3.50, seniors 62 & over $3, children $1; children 3 & under no charge. Closed major holidays.

WOODFORD COUNTY HISTORICAL SOCIETY MUSEUM, 121 Rose Hill Ave., Versailles, KY 40383-1221. Tel.: 859-873-6786.
E-mail: woodford@qx.net
Web Site: www.woodfordkyhistory.org
Institution Type/Description: History Museum.
Hours & Admission Prices: Tues.-Sat. 10-4. No charge.

West Liberty

MEMORY HILL FOUNDATION MUSEUM, 89 Memory Hill Lane, West Liberty, KY 41001. Tel.: 859-743-4482.
Institution Type/Description: History Museum.
Hours & Admission Prices: Call for hours.

Wickliffe

WICKLIFFE MOUNDS STATE HISTORIC SITE, 94 Green St., Wickliffe, KY 42087. Mailing Address: P.O. Box 155, Wickliffe, KY 42087-0155. Tel.: 270-335-3681. Facebook: @WickliffeMounds.
E-mail: carla.hildebrand@ky.gov
Web Site: www.parks.ky.gov
Key Personnel: Park Mgr., Carla Hildebrand.
Institution Type/Description: Archaeology Museum.
Hours & Admission Prices: April-Oct. Wed.-Sun. 9-5. Adults $5, children 6-12 $4, discount to groups, active duty military, and AAM & AAA members. &
Attendance: 6,800 (actual)

Williamsburg

CUMBERLAND INN & MUSEUM, 649 S. 10th St., Williamsburg, KY 40769-1647. Tel.: 800-315-0286, 606-539-4100.
E-mail: customerservice@cumberlandinn.com
Web Site: cumberlandinn.com
Key Personnel: Gen. Mgr., Priscilla Martin.
Institution Type/Description: History Museum.
Hours & Admission Prices: Call for hours. Adults $4, seniors over 65 $3, children 6-12 $2, children 5-1 $1. No charge; donations accepted. &

WHITLEY COUNTY HISTORICAL & GENEALOGICAL SOCIETY, 529 Main St., Williamsburg, KY 40769. Mailing Address: P.O. Box 536, Williamsburg, KY 40769-9634. Tel.: 606-549-7089.
E-mail: whitleycountyhis@bellsouth.net
Web Site: www.wchgs.org
Key Personnel: Pres. (V), Pat Jones; Museum Shop Mgr., Mary Alice Siler.
Institution Type/Description: Historical Society Museum: housed in the Old Williamsburg Depot.
Hours & Admission Prices: Wed. 10-1, 1st & last Sat. each month 10-12; other times by appointment. No charge; donations accepted.
Attendance: 509 (estimated)

Winchester

BLUEGRASS HERITAGE MUSEUM, 217 S. Main St., Winchester, KY 40391-2455. Tel.: 859-745-1358.
E-mail: bgheritage@bellsouth.net
Web Site: www.bgheritage.com
Key Personnel: Dir., Sandy Stults; Pres., Gardner Wagers.
Institution Type/Description: History Museum.
Hours & Admission Prices: Mon.-Sat. 12-4.

LOUISIANA

(236 listings)

Abbeville

ALLIANCE CENTER MUSEUM AND ART GALLERY, 200 N. Magdalen Square, Abbeville, LA 70510-4645. Mailing Address: P.O. Box 935, Abbeville, LA 70511. Tel.: 337-898-4114.
E-mail: info@abbevillemuseum.org
Web Site: www.abbevillemuseum.org
Key Personnel: Pres., Lloyd Dore, III.
Institution Type/Description: General Museum.
Hours & Admission Prices: Tues. & Sat. 10-3, Wed.-Fri. 10-5.

DEPOT AT MAGDALEN PLACE, 201 W. Lafayette St., Abbeville, LA 70510. Tel.: 337-740-2112. Fax: 337-893-5983.
Web Site: www.magdalenplace.com
Institution Type/Description: Historic Building: housed in a former train depot; built in 1894.
Hours & Admission Prices: Mon.-Sat. 10-5. &

SAM GUARINO AND SON BLACKSMITH SHOP MUSEUM, 304 S. State St., Abbeville, LA 70510. Tel.: 337-893-8550.

Institution Type/Description: History Museum: housed in a former blacksmith shop; built in 1913.
Hours & Admission Prices: By appointment.

Alexandria

ALEXANDRIA MUSEUM OF ART, 933 Second St., Alexandria, LA 71301-8322. Mailing Address: P.O. Box 1028, Alexandria, LA 71309-1028. Tel.: 318-443-3458. Fax: 318-443-0545. Facebook: AMOA Downtown.
E-mail: catherine@themuseum.org
Web Site: www.themuseum.org
Key Personnel: Exec. Dir., Catherine M. Pears; Pres. (V), Robert Radcliffe, Sr.; Devel. & Community Rels. Officer, Sarah Cortell Vandersypen; Education & Outreach, Anne Reid; Education & Outreach, Cindy Blair; Facilities & Communications, Natalie Walker; Visitor Svcs., Jenny Gallent.
Institution Type/Description: Art Museum: housed in c.1900 Bank Building.
Hours & Admission Prices: Tues.-Fri. 10-5, Sat. 10-4. Adults $5, seniors, students & military $4, children under 12 $3; discounts to groups, NARM, SEMC & LAM members; members no charge. Closed legal holidays. &
Attendance: 8,803 (actual)

ALEXANDRIA ZOOLOGICAL PARK, 3016 Masonic Dr., Alexandria, LA 71301-4240. Mailing Address: P.O. Box 6015, Alexandria, LA 71307-6015. Tel.: 318-473-1143, ext. 0. Fax: 318-473-1149.
E-mail: info@thealexandriazoo.com
Web Site: www.thealexandriazoo.com
Key Personnel: Gen. Cur., Carla Oncay.
Institution Type/Description: Zoo.
Hours & Admission Prices: Daily 9-5. Adults 13 & over $7.50, children 4-12 $5.50, seniors 65 & over $4.50; discounts to groups of 15 or more; children 3 & under and FOTAZ members no charge. Train Rides: $1.50; children under 1 no charge. Closed New Year's Day; Thanksgiving; Christmas.

ARNA BONTEMPS AFRICAN AMERICAN MUSEUM, 1327 Third St., Alexandria, LA 71301-8248. Tel.: 318-473-4692. Fax: 318-473-4675.
E-mail: admin@arnabontempsmuseum.com
Web Site: www.arnabontempsmuseum.com
Institution Type/Description: Historic House Museum: housed in the boyhood home of poet, author, anthologist & librarian, Arna Bontemps. Listed on the National Register of Historic Places.
Hours & Admission Prices: Tues.-Fri. 10-4, Sat. 10-2. No charge; donations accepted.

KENT PLANTATION HOUSE, 3601 Bayou Rapides Rd., Alexandria, LA 71303-3629. Tel.: 318-487-5998. Fax: 318-442-4154.
E-mail: admin@kenthouse.org
Web Site: kenthouse.org
Key Personnel: Dir., Alice V. Scarborough; Pres. (V), Carolyn Pate.
Institution Type/Description: Historic House Museum: built c.1796. Listed on the National Register of Historic Places.
Hours & Admission Prices: Mon.-Sat. 9-5. Adults $10, military, AAA members and seniors 65 & over $8, children 6-12 $3; discounts to groups; children 5 & under no charge.
Attendance: 20,000 (estimated)

LOUISIANA STATE UNIVERSITY AT ALEXANDRIA ART GALLERY, 8100 Hwy. 71 S., Alexandria, LA 71302. Tel.: 318-473-6449.
E-mail: rdeville@lsua.edu
Key Personnel: Dir., Roy V. de Ville.
Institution Type/Description: Art Gallery.
Hours & Admission Prices: Mon.-Fri. 8-12. No charge. &

T.R.E.E. HOUSE - THE RAPIDES EXPLORATORY EDUCATION HOUSE, DBA T.R.E.E. HOUSE CHILDREN'S MUSEUM, 1403 Third St., Alexandria, LA 71301-8250. Tel.: 318-619-9394. Fax: 318-619-9395.
E-mail: kidstreehouse@bellsouth.net
Web Site: www.kidtreehouse.org
Key Personnel: Dir., Kara Edwards; Pres. (V), Richard Hare.
Institution Type/Description: Children's Museum.
Hours & Admission Prices: Tues.-Fri. 9-3, Sat. 9-4. Admission $4; discounts to military; members & children under 2 no charge. Closed major holidays. &
Attendance: 14,000 (estimated)

Angola

LOUISIANA STATE PENITENTIARY MUSEUM, Hwy. 66, Angola, LA 70712. Mailing Address: General Delivery, Angola, LA 70712-9999. Tel.: 225-655-2592. Fax: 225-655-2842.
E-mail: lspmuseu@bellsouth.net
Web Site: angolamuseum.org
Key Personnel: Dir., Marsha Lindsey.
Institution Type/Description: Penitentiary Museum.
Hours & Admission Prices: Mon.-Fri. 8-4:30, Sat. 9-5, Sun. 10-5. No charge; donations accepted. Closed New Year's Day; Easter; Independence Day; Thanksgiving; Christmas; major holidays. &
Attendance: 14,400 (estimated)

Avery Island

JUNGLE GARDENS, Hwy. 329, Avery Island, LA 70513. Mailing Address: P.O. Box 126, Avery Island, LA 70513. Tel.: 337-369-6243. Fax: 337-369-6245.
E-mail: junglegardens@bellsouth.net
Web Site: www.junglegardens.org
Institution Type/Description: Garden & Bird Sanctuary.
Hours & Admission Prices: Daily 9-5. Adults $8, children $5; discounts to groups; children under 6 no charge. Island Toll: $1.

MCILHENNY COMPANY & VISITOR CENTER, Hwy. 329, Avery Island, LA 70513. Tel.: 800-634-9599, 337-365-8173.
E-mail: linda.clause@tabasco.com
Web Site: www.tabasco.com
Institution Type/Description: Company Museum.
Hours & Admission Prices: Daily 9-4. Island Toll: $1. Visitor Center: no charge. Closed major holidays. &
Attendance: 100,000 (estimated)

TABASCO(R) MUSEUM AND FACTORY TOUR, 32 Wisteria Rd., Avery Island, LA 70513. Tel.: 337-373-6139.
Web Site: tabasco.com/visit-avery-island
Institution Type/Description: Company Museum.
Hours & Admission Prices: Daily 9-4. Admission 5 & over $5.50, senior citizens 55 & over and veterans $4.95; children under 4 no charge.

Baker

HERITAGE MUSEUM & CULTURAL CENTER, 1606 Main St., Hwy. 19, Baker, LA 70714. Mailing Address: P.O. Box 707, 1606 Main St., Baker, LA 70704-0707. Tel.: 225-774-1776. Fax: 225-775-5635.
E-mail: bakermuseum@bellsouth.net
Web Site: www.bakerheritagemuseum.org
Institution Type/Description: History Museum.
Hours & Admission Prices: Mon.-Fri. 9-4. No charge; donations accepted.

Barksdale AFB

BARKSDALE GLOBAL POWER MUSEUM, 88 Shreveport Rd., Barksdale AFB, LA 71110. Tel.: 318-456-5553. Facebook; Twitter; Instagram.
E-mail: bgpma@outlook.com
Web Site: barksdaleglobalpowermuseum.com
Formerly: 8th Air Force Museum
Key Personnel: Dir., Amy Russell.
Institution Type/Description: Military Museum.
Hours & Admission Prices: Daily 9:30-4. No charge; donations accepted. Closed New Year's Day; Thanksgiving; Christmas. &
Attendance: 30,000

Bastrop

SNYDER MUSEUM & CREATIVE ARTS CENTER, 1620 E. Madison Ave., Bastrop, LA 71220-4062. Tel.: 318-281-8760.
E-mail: snydermuseum@gmail.com
Web Site: snydermuseum.com
Key Personnel: Exec. Dir., Emily Graves; Pres. (V), Melissa Smith.
Institution Type/Description: Local History Museum & Art Center.
Hours & Admission Prices: Jan. to mid-Dec. Tues.-Fri. 9-4. No charge; donations accepted. Closed New Year's Day; Independence Day; Thanksgiving week. &
Attendance: 1,000 (estimated)

Baton Rouge

ALFRED C. GLASSELL JR. EXHIBITION GALLERY, LSU School of Art, Shaw Center for the Arts, 100 Lafayette St., Baton Rouge, LA 70801. Tel.: 225-389-7180.
E-mail: artgallery@lsu.edu
Web Site: www.glassellgallery.org
Key Personnel: Dir., K. Malia Krolak.
Institution Type/Description: Art Gallery.
Hours & Admission Prices: Tues.-Fri. 10-5, Sat.-Sun. 12-5. No charge; donations accepted. ⅃
Attendance: 5,000 (estimated)

BATON ROUGE GALLERY CENTER FOR CONTEMPORARY ART, City Park Pavilion, 1515 Dalrymple Dr., Baton Rouge, LA 70808-1037. Tel.: 225-383-1470. Fax: 225-336-0943. Facebook, Instagram & Twitter: @BRGallery.
E-mail: info@batonrougegallery.org
Web Site: www.batonrougegallery.org
Key Personnel: Exec. Dir., Jason Andreasen; Special Facility Mgr., Jenny Poulter; Devel. Dir., Jennifer Dewey.
Institution Type/Description: Art Gallery.
Hours & Admission Prices: Tues.-Sun. 12-6. No charge. ⅃
Attendance: 15,000 (estimated)

BATON ROUGE ZOO, 3601 Thomas Rd., Baton Rouge, LA 70807. Tel.: 225-775-3877. Fax: 225-775-3931. Facebook: @brecsbrzoo.
E-mail: info@brzoo.org
Web Site: www.brzoo.org
Formerly: BREC's Baton Rouge Zoo
Key Personnel: Dir., Phillip L. Frost; Asst. Dir. & Gen. Cur., Sam Winslow; Cur. Education, Jennifer Shields; Cur. Birds, Lee Schoen; Cur. Hoofstock, John Marshall; Cur. Carnivores & Primates, Erin Dauenhauer-Decota; Cur. Aquarium & Kids Zoo, Nicole Strauss; Administrative Svcs. Supervisor, Lois Cook; Vet. Tech., Holly Taylor; Commissarian, Melissa Prisk; Zoo Veterinarian, Dr. Gordon Pirie; Souvenir Shop Mgr., Carroll Shirey; Guest Svcs. Mgr., Vicki Jones; Concessions Mgr., Gilda Conrad; Membership & Events Coord., Kelsey Megilligan; Admin. Asst., Kim Lodrigue.
Institution Type/Description: Zoological Park.
Hours & Admission Prices: Daily 9:30-5. Adults & teens $8.25, senior citizen 65 & over $7.25, children 2-12 $5.25; children one & under, AZA members & Friends of the Zoo no charge. Closed New Year's Day; Thanksgiving; Christmas Eve & Day. ⅃
Attendance: 266,260 (actual)

BRECS BLUEBONNET SWAMP NATURE CENTER, 10503 N. Oak Hills Pkwy., Baton Rouge, LA 70810. Tel.: 225-757-8905.
E-mail: Ccoco@brec.org
Web Site: www.brec.org/index.cfm/park/BluebonnetSwamp
Institution Type/Description: Nature Center.
Hours & Admission Prices: Tues.-Sat. 9-5, Sun. 12-5; group tours by appointment. Adults $3, seniors 65 & over and college students $2.50; children 2 & under no charge.

BREC'S MAGNOLIA MOUND PLANTATION, 2161 Nicholson Dr., Baton Rouge, LA 70802-8105. Tel.: 225-343-4955. Fax: 225-343-6739.
E-mail: lwebb@brec.org
Web Site: www.brec.org/magnoliamound
Formerly: Magnolia Mound Plantation
Key Personnel: Dir., John Sykes; Education Cur., Patricia McCarthy; Volunteer Coord., Mary Kathryn Merchant; Guest Svcs. Coord., Pauline Poole; Admin. Asst., Laura Webb.
Institution Type/Description: Historic Houses: 1791-1830 plantation house & outbuildings.
Hours & Admission Prices: Mon.-Sat. 10-4, Sun. 1-4; tours on the hour; last tour at 3pm. Adults $10, senior citizens 65 & over $8, children 3-17 $4; discounts to groups, LAM, BREC, military, teachers, AAA & AAM members; children under 3 no charge. Closed New Year's Day; Mardi Gras Day; Easter; Independence Day; Thanksgiving; Christmas.
Attendance: 21,656 (actual)

CAPITOL PARK MUSEUM, 660 N. 4th St., Baton Rouge, LA 70802. Tel.: 225-342-5428. Fax: 225-219-0728. Facebook: @LaStateMuseum.
E-mail: capitolparkmuseum@crt.la.gov
Web Site: louisianastatemuseum.org/museums/capitol-park-museum
Key Personnel: Dir., Bill Stark.
Institution Type/Description: History Museum.

Hours & Admission Prices: Tues.-Sat. 9-4:30. Adults $6, students, seniors & active military $5; discounts to AAA members; children 12 & under and school groups no charge.
Attendance: 63,941 (actual)

LAURENS HENRY COHN, SR. MEMORIAL PLANT ARBORETUM, 12206 Foster Rd., Baton Rouge, LA 70811-1231. Tel.: 225-775-1006. Fax: 225-775-1006.
E-mail: info@brec.org
Web Site: www.brec.org/cohn
Key Personnel: Mgr. Horticulture, K. Ed Norred.
Institution Type/Description: Arboretum & Botanical Garden.
Hours & Admission Prices: Daily 8-5. No charge. ⅃
Attendance: 2,500 (actual)

LOUISIANA ART & SCIENCE MUSEUM - IRENE W. PENNINGTON PLANETARIUM, 100 River Rd. S., Baton Rouge, LA 70802-5730. Tel.: 225-344-5272 & 9478. Fax: 225-344-9477.
E-mail: lasm@lasm.org
Web Site: www.lasm.org
Key Personnel: Pres. & Exec. Dir., Carol S. Gikas; Asst. Dir., Sam Losavio; Editor & Comm. Coord., Sheri Gibson; Planetarium Mgr., Sheree Westerhaus; Dir. Devel. & Comm., Keith Dixon; Dir. Interpretation for Art & Museum Cur., Elizabeth Weinstein; Interpreter for Science, Nita Mitchell; Collections Mgr., Lexi Guillory; Events Coord., Leslie Charleville; Visitor Svcs. & Store Mgr., Paula Taylor; Receptionist & Membership Coord., Barbara Miller; Bldg., Facilities & Systems Mgr., David Kors; Planetarium Interpreter, Chandra Weathers; Planetarium Mgr., Sheree Westerhaus; Bldg. Supvr., Michael Cavalier.
Institution Type/Description: Art & Science Museum: housed in renovated & expanded former Illinois Central Railroad Station; space theater.
Hours & Admission Prices: Tues.-Fri. 10-3, Sat. 10-5, Sun. 1-4. Planetarium: Tues.-Fri. 10-3, Sat. 10-8, Sun. 1-4. Galleries: adults $7.25; discounts to seniors, children, AAA & ASTC members; members no charge. Galleries Plus Theater: adults $9; discounts to members, seniors, children, AAA & ASTC members. Closed major holidays. ⅃
Attendance: 198,807 (actual)

LOUISIANA MUD PAINTINGS, 16950 Strain Rd., Baton Rouge, LA 70816-1823. Tel.: 225-275-5126.
Web Site: www.mudpainting.com
Institution Type/Description: Art Gallery.
Hours & Admission Prices: Tues.-Sat. 10-5.

LOUISIANA STATE UNIVERSITY MUSEUM OF ART, Shaw Center for the Arts, 100 Lafayette St., Baton Rouge, LA 70801-1201. Tel.: 225-389-7200. Fax: 225-389-7219.
E-mail: radam14@lsu.edu
Web Site: www.lsu.edu/lsumoa
Key Personnel: Exec. Dir., Daniel Stetson; Chm. (V), Brian Schneider; Asst. Dir. Collections Mgmt., Fran Huber; Dir. Devel., Heather Nelson; Cur., Courtney Taylor; Events & Mktg. Facility Rentals Coord., Renee Bourgeois; Business Mgr., Becky Abadie; Museum Store Mgr. & Membership Coord., LeAnn Russo.
Institution Type/Description: Art Museum.
Hours & Admission Prices: Tues.-Wed. & Fri.-Sat. 10-5, Thurs. 10-8, Sun. 1-5. Adults $5; discounts to AAM & NARM members; members no charge. Closed New Year's Day; Mardi Gras; Easter; Thanksgiving; Christmas Eve & Day. ⅃
Attendance: 32,500 (estimated)

LOUISIANA'S OLD STATE CAPITOL, 100 North Blvd., Baton Rouge, LA 70801-1502. Mailing Address: State of Louisiana, Secretary of State, P.O. Box 94125, Baton Rouge, LA 70804-9125. Tel.: 225-342-0500, 800-488-2968. Fax: 225-342-0316.
Web Site: www.louisianaoldstatecapitol.org
Key Personnel: Dir. Events, Suzette Crocker; Cur., Lauren Davis.
Institution Type/Description: Political History Museum.
Hours & Admission Prices: Tues.-Sat. 9-4. No charge. Closed most state holidays. ⅃
Attendance: 26,500 (actual)

LSU STUDENT UNION ART GALLERY, 310 LSU Student Union, Louisiana State University, Baton Rouge, LA 70803. Mailing Address: LSU Student Union Art Gallery, LSU Box 25123, Baton Rouge, LA 70803. Tel.: 225-578-5162. Fax: 225-578-4329.
E-mail: unionartgallery@lsu.edu
Web Site: as.lsu.edu/union-art-gallery
Key Personnel: Dir., Judi Stahl.

Institution Type/Description: Art Gallery.
Hours & Admission Prices: Mon.-Fri. 10-6, Sun. 1-5. No charge. Closed major holidays.

MUSEUM OF AFRICAN AMERICAN HISTORY, 538 S. Boulevard, Baton Rouge, LA 70802-6442. Tel.: 225-343-4431.
E-mail: oswafricanamericanmuseum@gmail.com
Key Personnel: Founder & Cur., Sadie Roberts-Joseph.
Institution Type/Description: History Museum.
Hours & Admission Prices: Wed.-Sat. 10-5; other times by appointment. Adults $4; discounts to AAM & ICOM members. Closed major holidays. &
Attendance: 1,500

MUSEUM OF NATURAL SCIENCE, 119 Foster Hall, LSU, Baton Rouge, LA 70803. Tel.: 225-578-2855. Fax: 225-578-3075.
E-mail: museum@lsu.edu
Web Site: appl003.lsu.edu/natsci/lmnh.nsf/index
Key Personnel: Dir. & Cur. Genetic Resources, Dr. Robb Brumfield; Cur. Ichthyology, Dr. Prosanta Chakrabarty; Cur. Ornithology, Dr. Van Remsen; Cur. Paleontology (Emeritus), Dr. Judith A. Schiebout; Cur. Anthropology, Dr. Rebecca A. Saunders; Cur. Herpetology, Dr. Christopher C. Austin; Dir. Education, Dr. Sophie Warny; Cur. Mammalogy (Emeritus), Dr. Mark Hafner.
Institution Type/Description: Natural History Museum.
Hours & Admission Prices: Mon.-Fri. 8-4. No charge. Closed university holidays. &
Attendance: 32,000

OLD ARSENAL MUSEUM, 900 Capitol Lake Dr., Baton Rouge, LA 70802. Mailing Address: P.O. Box 94125, Baton Rouge, LA 70804-9125. Tel.: 225-342-0401. Fax: 225-342-5577.
E-mail: arsenal@sos.louisiana.gov
Web Site: www.sos.louisiana.gov/oam
Formerly: Old Arsenal Powder Magazine Museum
Key Personnel: Dir., Gregory Leggio.
Institution Type/Description: History Museum: built in 1838; used by the US military during the Mexican & Civil Wars. Listed on the National Register of Historic Places.
Hours & Admission Prices: Tues.-Sat. 9-4. No charge. Closed most state holidays. &
Attendance: 3,107 (actual)

OLD GOVERNOR'S MANSION, 502 North Blvd., Baton Rouge, LA 70802. Mailing Address: P.O. Box 908, Baton Rouge, LA 70821. Tel.: 225-387-2464. Fax: 225-343-3989. Facebook: Old Governor's Mansion.
E-mail: info@preserve-louisiana.org
Web Site: preserve-louisiana.org
Formerly: Old Louisiana Governor's Mansion
Key Personnel: Dir., Farleigh Jackson; Chm. (V), Doug Cochran; Front Desk Mgr. & Membership Coord., Selena Grant; Dir. Education & Cur., Natalie Mault Mead.
Institution Type/Description: Historic Mansion: built in 1930. Listed on the National Register of Historic Places.
Hours & Admission Prices: Tours: Tues.-Fri. 10-4. Adults $7; discounts to AAM & ICOM members; members no charge. &
Attendance: 5,000 (estimated)

ROBERT A. BOGAN FIRE MUSEUM, 427 Laurel St., Baton Rouge, LA 70801-1810. Tel.: 225-892-6891. Fax: 225-344-7777.
E-mail: rchatelain@artsbr.org
Web Site: www.artsbr.org
Formerly: Old Bogan Firefighters Museum
Key Personnel: Deputy Dir., Katherine Scherer.
Institution Type/Description: Fire-Fighting Museum.
Hours & Admission Prices: By appointment. No charge; donations accepted. &
Attendance: 3,000 (estimated)

RURAL LIFE MUSEUM & WINDRUSH GARDENS, 4560 Essen Lane, Baton Rouge, LA 70809-3424. Mailing Address: P.O. Box 80498, Baton Rouge, LA 70898-0498. Tel.: 225-765-2437. Fax: 225-765-2639.
E-mail: rurallife@lsu.edu
Web Site: rurallife.lsu.edu
Key Personnel: Exec. Dir., David Floyd; Interpretive Program Specialist, Steven Ramke; Registrar & Conservator, David Nicolosi; Dir. Mktg., Elizabeth McInnis; Devel. Dir., Molly Sanchez.
Institution Type/Description: History Museum.

Hours & Admission Prices: Daily 8:30-5. Adults & children 12-61 $7, seniors 62 & over $6, children 5-11 $5; children under 5 no charge. Closed New Year's Day; Easter; Thanksgiving; Christmas Eve & Day. &
Attendance: 15,000 (actual)

SHIRLEY C. TUCKER HERBARIUM - LOUISIANA STATE UNIVERSITY, A257 Life Sciences Annex, LSU, Baton Rouge, LA 70803-1715. Mailing Address: 130 Life Sciences Bldg., Department of Biological Sciences, Baton Rouge, LA 70803-1715. Tel.: 225-578-8564. Fax: 225-578-2597.
E-mail: llagomarsino1@lsu.edu
Web Site: www.herbarium.lsu.edu
Key Personnel: Dir., Laura Lagomarsino; Collections Mgr., Jennifer Kluse.
Institution Type/Description: Herbarium.
Hours & Admission Prices: Mon.-Fri. 8:30-4:30. No charge; donations accepted.
Attendance: 150 (estimated)

USS KIDD VETERANS MEMORIAL, 305 S. River Rd., Baton Rouge, LA 70802-6220. Tel.: 225-342-1942. Fax: 225-342-2039.
E-mail: info@usskidd.com
Web Site: www.usskidd.com
Institution Type/Description: Maritime Museum & Historic Ship.
Hours & Admission Prices: Daily 9-5. Ship & Museum: adults $8, senior citizens 60 & over $7, active military with ID $6, children 5-12 $5; discounts for groups of 20 or more; members & children 4 and under no charge. Museum only: adults $5, children 5-12 $4; children 4 & under no charge. Closed New Year's Eve & Day; Thanksgiving; Christmas Eve & Day. &
Attendance: 80,000 (actual)

Belle Chasse

THE TULANE UNIVERSITY MUSEUM OF NATURAL HISTORY, 3705 Main St., Bldg. A-3, Belle Chasse, LA 70037-3001. Tel.: 504-394-1711. Fax: 504-394-5045.
E-mail: hank@museum.tulane.edu
Web Site: www.museum.tulane.edu
Key Personnel: Cur. Fish, Dr. Henry L. Bart; Collections Mgr., Nelson Rios; Adjunct Cur. Mammals, Dr. Craig Hood.
Institution Type/Description: Natural History Museum.
Hours & Admission Prices: Mon.-Fri. 8:30-5 by appointment.

Bernice

BERNICE DEPOT MUSEUM, Fourth and Louisiana St., Bernice, LA 71222. Mailing Address: P.O. Box 633, Bernice, LA 71222-0633. Tel.: 318-285-2433.
Key Personnel: Museum Shop Mgr., Gladys Harkins.
Institution Type/Description: Historic Building: built in 1899.
Hours & Admission Prices: Mon.-Fri. 10-12 & 1-3. No charge; donations accepted.

Bossier City

ARK-LA-TEX MARDI GRAS MUSEUM, 2101 E. Texas St., Bossier City, LA 71111. Mailing Address: P.O. Box 6432, Bossier City, LA 71171-6432. Tel.: 318-218-2865.
Institution Type/Description: Mardi Gras History Museum.
Hours & Admission Prices: By appointment.

Broussard

ZOO OF ACADIANA, 5601 Hwy. 90 E., Broussard, LA 70518. Mailing Address: 116 Lakeview Dr., Broussard, LA 70518-8004. Tel.: 337-837-4325. Fax: 337-837-4253.
E-mail: wild@zooofacadiana.org
Key Personnel: Co-Owner, George Oldenburg; Co-Owner, Marleen Oldenburg.
Institution Type/Description: Zoo.
Hours & Admission Prices: Jan.-Nov. daily 9-5; Dec. daily 9-4. Safari of Lights: Dec. 5pm-9pm. Adults 13-54 $11.25, seniors 55 & over $10.25, children 3-12 $7.50; children 2 & under no charge. Closed New Year's Day; Easter; Thanksgiving; Christmas.

Carville

NATIONAL HANSEN'S DISEASE MUSEUM, Bldg. 12, Carville Historic District, 5445 Point Clair Rd., Carville, LA 70721-2119. Mailing Address: 1770 Physicians Dr., Baton Rouge, LA 70816. Tel.: 225-642-1950. Fax: 225-642-1949.
E-mail: NHDPmuseum@hrsa.gov
Web Site: www.hrsa.gov/hansens/museum/default.htm

Key Personnel: Dir., Elizabeth Schexnyder; C.E.O., Dr. James Krahenbuhl; Interim Cur., Vicki Joseph.
Institution Type/Description: History & Medical Museum.
Hours & Admission Prices: Tues.-Sat. 10-4. No charge; donations accepted. Closed federal holidays. ♿
Attendance: 2,000 (actual)

Charenton

CHITIMACHA MUSEUM, 3289 Chitimacha Trail, Charenton, LA 70523. Mailing Address: P.O. Box 661, Charenton, LA 70523-0661. Tel.: 337-923-4830.
E-mail: info@chitimacha.gov
Web Site: www.chitimacha.org
Institution Type/Description: Native American Museum.
Hours & Admission Prices: Tues.-Sat. 9-4:30. No charge. ♿

Columbia

THE SCHEPIS, LOUISIANA ARTISTS MUSEUM, 106 Main St., Columbia, LA 71418. Mailing Address: P.O. Box 743, Columbia, LA 71418-0743. Tel.: 318-649-9931.
Key Personnel: Cur., Jane Meredith.
Institution Type/Description: Art Museum: built by John Schepis c.1916. Listed on the National Register of Historic Places.
Hours & Admission Prices: Call for hours. No charge; donations accepted.

Cottonport

COTTONPORT MUSEUM, 220 Cottonport Ave., Cottonport, LA 71327. Mailing Address: P.O. Box 1161, Cottonport, LA 71327. Tel.: 318-876-3517. Fax: 318-876-3517.
E-mail: cottonportmuseum@gmail.com
Institution Type/Description: History Museum.
Hours & Admission Prices: Call for hours.

Covington

INSTA-GATOR RANCH & HATCHERY, 23440 Lowe Davis Rd., Covington, LA 70435-6512. Tel.: 985-892-3669, 888-448-1560.
E-mail: Info@Insta-gatorRanch.com
Web Site: www.insta-gatorranch.com
Institution Type/Description: Alligator Farm.
Hours & Admission Prices: Daily call for hours. Adults $18, seniors & military $15, children 12 & under $12; discounts to groups; infants no charge.

Crowley

CROWLEY ART ASSOCIATION & GALLERY, 220 N. Parkerson, Crowley, LA 70526-5003. Tel.: 337-783-3747. Fax: 337-783-3747.
E-mail: gallerythe@bellsouth.net
Web Site: www.crowleyartgallery.com
Key Personnel: C.E.O., Hurley Gautreaux; Vice Pres., Virgie LeBlue; Museum Shop Mgr., Becky Faulk.
Institution Type/Description: Art Association & Gallery.
Hours & Admission Prices: Mon.-Fri. 10-4. No charge. Closed New Year's Day; Independence Day; Thanksgiving; Christmas week. ♿

CRYSTAL RICE HERITAGE FARM, 6428 Airport Rd, Crowley, LA 70526-1604. Mailing Address: P.O. Box 1425, Crowley, LA 70527-1425. Tel.: 337-783-6417. Fax: 337-788-0123.
E-mail: dwrighth@cs.com
Web Site: www.crystalrice.com
Formerly: Crystal Rice Plantation
Key Personnel: C.E.O., Diane Hoffpauer; Treas., Elaine Wright; Dir. & Museum Shop Mgr., Redell Miller.
Institution Type/Description: Classic Car Museum & Historical Society: c.1848 plantation home.
Hours & Admission Prices: Mon.-Fri. 9-3 by appointment. Adults $10, senior citizens $6, students $4.50; discounts to AAA members; members no charge. Closed all holidays.
Attendance: 1,000 (actual)

RICE INTERPRETIVE CENTER, J.D. MILLER MUSIC RECORDING STUDIO MUSEUM AND FORD AUTOMOTIVE MUSEUM, 425 N. Parkerson Ave., Crowley, LA 70526. Mailing Address: P.O. Box 1463, Crowley, LA 70527-1463. Tel.: 337-783-0824. Fax: 337-783-4331.

E-mail: charlotte.jeffers@crowley-la.com
Web Site: www.crowley-la.com
Key Personnel: Tourism Coord., Charlotte R. Jeffers; Chm., Mayor Greg Jones.
Institution Type/Description: History Museum.
Hours & Admission Prices: Mon.-Fri. 8-4; other times by appointment. No charge. ♿
Attendance: 5,000 (estimated)

Darrow

HOUMAS HOUSE PLANTATION AND GARDENS, 40136 Hwy. 942, Darrow, LA 70725-2302. Tel.: 225-473-9380 & 7841. Fax: 225-473-7891.
E-mail: kk@houmashouse.com
Web Site: houmashouse.com
Key Personnel: Owner, Kevin Kelly; Historian, Jim Blanchard.
Institution Type/Description: Historic House.
Hours & Admission Prices: Mon.-Tues. 9-5, Wed.-Sun. 9-7. Tours: Mansion & Gardens $24. Gardens & Grounds: $10. Closed New Year's Day; Christmas.

DeQuincy

DEQUINCY RAILROAD MUSEUM, 400 Lake Charles Ave., DeQuincy, LA 70633. Tel.: 337-786-2823. Facebook: DeQuincy Railroad Museum.
E-mail: dequincyrailroadmuseum@centurylink.net
Web Site: www.dequincyrailroadmuseum.com
Key Personnel: Pres. (V), Gary Cooper; Museum Shop Mgr., Evalin Hester.
Institution Type/Description: Railroad Museum.
Hours & Admission Prices: Tues.-Sat. 10-5. No charge; donations accepted. Closed city holidays.
Attendance: 8,332 (actual)

DeRidder

THE LOIS LOFTIN DOLL MUSEUM, 120 S. Washington Ave., DeRidder, LA 70634-4062. Tel.: 337-463-6217.
E-mail: wlbg@beau.org
Web Site: www.library.beau.org
Institution Type/Description: Doll Museum.
Hours & Admission Prices: Tues.-Sat. 10-4.

Destrehan

DESTREHAN PLANTATION, 13034 River Rd., Destrehan, LA 70047-5202. Tel.: 985-764-9315, 877-453-2095. Fax: 985-725-1929.
E-mail: info@destrehanplantation.org
Web Site: www.destrehanplantation.org
Key Personnel: Site Mgr., Nancy Robert.
Institution Type/Description: Plantation: a National Historic Landmark, established in 1787.
Hours & Admission Prices: Daily 9-4. Adults $18, children 6-16 $7; discounts to groups. Closed major holidays.

Donaldsonville

RIVER ROAD AFRICAN AMERICAN MUSEUM, 406 Charles St., Donaldsonville, LA 70346-3312. Mailing Address: P.O. Box 266, Donaldsonville, LA 70346-0266. Tel.: 225-474-5553.
E-mail: kathe@africanamericanmuseum.org
Web Site: www.africanamericanmuseum.org
Key Personnel: Dir., Kathe Hambrick.
Institution Type/Description: History Museum.
Hours & Admission Prices: Wed.-Sat. 10-5, Sun. 1-5; groups of 10 or more by appointment. Museum or School & Church Tour: adults $4. Heritage Tour: adults $25.

Edgard

EVERGREEN PLANTATION, 4677 Hwy. 18, Edgard, LA 70049. Tel.: 985-497-3837.
E-mail: evergreenplantation@gmail.com
Web Site: evergreenplantation.org
Institution Type/Description: Historic Plantation: listed on the National Register of Historic Places.
Hours & Admission Prices: Guided Tours: Mon.-Sat. 9:30, 11:30, & 2. Adults $20, children 5-18 $6; discounts to students; military, seniors & groups of 10 or more; children under 5 no charge. Closed New Year's Eve & Day; Thanksgiving & day after; Christmas Eve & Day.

Erath

THE ACADIAN MUSEUM, 203 S. Broadway, Erath, LA 70533-4003. Tel.: 337-233-5832. Fax: 337-235-4382.
E-mail: info@acadianmuseum.com
Web Site: www.acadianmuseum.com
Key Personnel: Dir., Warren A. Perrin.
Institution Type/Description: History Museum.
Hours & Admission Prices: Mon.-Fri. 1-4; other times by appointment. No charge.

Eunice

EUNICE DEPOT MUSEUM, 220 S. C.C. Duson Dr., Eunice, LA 70535-7808. Mailing Address: P.O. Box 508, Eunice, LA 70535. Tel.: 337-457-6540 & 2565.
Institution Type/Description: Historic Site: housed in the building where C.C. Duson sold the first land sites & named the town after his wife Eunice; 1893-1894. Listed on the National Register of Historic Places.
Hours & Admission Prices: Tues.-Sat. 8-12 & 1-5. No charge.

PRAIRIE ACADIAN CULTURAL CENTER, 250 W. Park Ave., Eunice, LA 70535-4628. Tel.: 337-457-8499.
Web Site: www.nps.gov/jela/prairie-acadian-cultural-center-eunice.htm
Key Personnel: Park Ranger, Jeremy Wirtz.
Institution Type/Description: History Museum.
Hours & Admission Prices: Tues.-Fri. 8-5, Sat. 8-6. Closed Christmas. &

Ferriday

DELTA MUSIC MUSEUM, 218 Louisiana Ave., Ferriday, LA 71334-2828. Mailing Address: State of Louisiana, Secretary of State, P.O. Box 94125, Baton Rouge, LA 70804-9125. Tel.: 318-757-9999. Fax: 318-757-1973.
E-mail: deltamusic@sos.louisiana.gov
Web Site: www.sos.louisiana.gov/dmm
Key Personnel: Dir., Judith Bingham.
Institution Type/Description: Music Museum.
Hours & Admission Prices: Mon.-Fri. 9-4; student groups by appointment. No charge. Closed most state holidays. &
Attendance: 4,067 (actual)

Folsom

GLOBAL WILDLIFE CENTER, 26389 Hwy. 40, Folsom, LA 70437. Tel.: 985-796-3585. Fax: 985-796-9487.
E-mail: reservations@globalwildlife.com
Web Site: www.globalwildlife.com
Key Personnel: Museum Shop Mgr., Brittany Ricks.
Institution Type/Description: Wildlife Center.
Hours & Admission Prices: Daily call for hours. Suggested Donations: adults $19, seniors $15, children $13; discounts to AAA members; children under one no charge. &
Attendance: 350,000

Fort Polk

FORT POLK MILITARY MUSEUM, 7881 Mississippi Ave., Fort Polk, LA 71459. Tel.: 337-531-7905 & 4840.
Key Personnel: Dir., Fred Adolphus.
Institution Type/Description: Military History Museum.
Hours & Admission Prices: Tues.-Sat. 9-4. No charge. Closed federal holidays.

FORT POLK MUSEUM ACTIVITY, Bldg. 917 S. Carolina Ave., Fort Polk, LA 71459. Mailing Address: 6661 Warrior Tr., Fort Polk, LA 71459-5366. Tel.: 337-531-7905 & 4840. Fax: 337-531-4202.
E-mail: binghamd@polk.army.mil
Formerly: Fort Polk Historical Holding Area
Key Personnel: Historian & Cur., David S. Bingham.
Institution Type/Description: Military Museum.
Hours & Admission Prices: Wed.-Fri. 10-2, Sat.-Sun. 9-4. No charge. Closed major holidays. &
Attendance: 15,000 (estimated)

Franklin

GREVEMBERG HOUSE MUSEUM, 407 Sterling Rd., Hwy. 322, Franklin, LA 70538-0400. Mailing Address: P.O. Box 400, Franklin, LA 70538-0400. Tel.: 337-828-2092. Fax: 337-828-2028.

E-mail: info@grevemberghouse.com
Web Site: www.grevemberghouse.com
Key Personnel: Pres., Katie Seim; Treas., Margaret Todd; Archivist, Margie Luke; Lead Interpreter, Craig Landry.
Institution Type/Description: Historical Society Museum: housed in c.1851 Greek-revival townhouse. Listed on National Register of Historic Places.
Hours & Admission Prices: Daily 10-4. Adults $10, senior citizens & students 12-18 $8, children under 12 $5; discounts to groups of 20 or more; members no charge. Closed New Year's Day; Good Friday; Easter; Thanksgiving; Christmas Eve & Day. &
Attendance: 262 (actual)

OAKLAWN MANOR, 3296 E. Oaklawn Dr., Franklin, LA 70538-3218. Tel.: 337-828-0434. Fax: 337-828-1937.
E-mail: oaklawnmanor@yahoo.com
Web Site: oaklawnmanor.com
Key Personnel: C.E.O., Murphy J. Foster, Jr.
Institution Type/Description: Historic House Museum.
Hours & Admission Prices: Daily 10-4. Adults $15, students $10; discounts to groups of 10 or more.
Attendance: 500 (estimated)

YOUNG SANDERS CENTER, 104 Commercial St., Franklin, LA 70538-5427. Mailing Address: P.O. Box 545, Franklin, LA 70538-0545.
E-mail: ysc1861@aol.com
Web Site: www.youngsanders.org
Institution Type/Description: History Museum.
Hours & Admission Prices: Mon.-Fri. 9-5. No charge. &

Franklinton

WASHINGTON AREA MUSEUM FOUNDATION/VARNADO STORE MUSEUM, 936 Pearl St., Franklinton, LA 70438-1736. Mailing Address: P.O. Box 184, Franklinton, LA 70438-0184. Tel.: 985-795-0680. Fax: 985-795-0680. Facebook: The Varnado Store Museum.
E-mail: varnadostoremuseum@yahoo.com
Web Site: www.davaranadostoremuseum.com
Key Personnel: Pres., Mary Jo Poole; Dir., Terry Seal.
Institution Type/Description: History Museum.
Hours & Admission Prices: Fri. by appointment, Sat. 10-4, Sun. 1-4. No charge; donations accepted. &
Attendance: 1,500 (estimated)

Frierson

YOGIE AND FRIENDS EXOTIC CAT SANCTUARY, 128 Fob Lane, Frierson, LA 71027-2065. Tel.: 318-795-0455.
E-mail: Paige@PaigeBass.com
Key Personnel: Exec. Dir., Jenny Senier.
Institution Type/Description: Wildlife Sanctuary.
Hours & Admission Prices: Sat. 12-5.

Frogmore

FROGMORE COTTON PLANTATION & GINS - COTTON THEN & NOW, 11656 Hwy. 84, Frogmore, LA 71334-4655. Mailing Address: 11054 Hwy. 84, Frogmore, LA 71334. Tel.: 318-757-2453 & 3333. Fax: 318-757-6535.
E-mail: frogmore@bayou.com
Web Site: www.frogmoreplantation.com
Institution Type/Description: History Museum.
Hours & Admission Prices: Call or see website for hours. Historical Tour: adults 19 & over $12, students $5; children 5 & under no charge. Modern Tour: adults 19 & over and students $5; children 5 & under no charge. Complete Tour: adults 19 & over $15, students $5; children 5 & under no charge. &
Attendance: 15,000 (estimated)

Garyville

SAN FRANCISCO PLANTATION, 2646 Hwy. 44 (River Rd.), Garyville, LA 70051. Mailing Address: P.O. Box 950, Garyville, LA 70051-0950. Tel.: 888-322-1756, 985-535-2341. Fax: 985-535-5450.
E-mail: sanfran@rtconline.com
Web Site: www.sanfranciscoplantation.org
Institution Type/Description: History Museum: plantation built in 1856.
Hours & Admission Prices: April-Oct. daily 9:30-5; Nov.-March daily 9:40-4:40. Adults $15, students 17 & under $10; discounts to military & AAA members;

children 5 & under no charge. Closed New Year's Day; Mardi Gras Day; Thanksgiving; Christmas.

Gibsland

BONNIE AND CLYDE AMBUSH MUSEUM, 2419 Main St., Gibsland, LA 71028. Mailing Address: P.O. Box 34, Gibsland, LA 71028. Tel.: 318-843-1934.
E-mail: perrycarver61@gmail.com
Web Site: www.bonnieandclydemuseum.com
Key Personnel: Owner & Museum Shop Mgr., Perry Carver; Owner, Ken M. Holmes, Jr.
Institution Type/Description: History Museum: housed in the former Ma Canfield's Cafe, the last place Bonnie Parker & Clyde Barrow visited before they were killed.
Hours & Admission Prices: Daily 10-6. Adults $7, seniors, active duty military & children 12 and under $5.
Attendance: 20 (estimated)

Gonzales

TEE JOE GONZALES MUSEUM, 217 W. Main St., Gonzales, LA 70737-2811. Mailing Address: 120 S. Irma Blvd., Gonzales, LA 70737-3604. Tel.: 225-647-9549. Fax: 225-647-9557.
E-mail: lisa@gonzalesla.com
Institution Type/Description: History Museum.
Hours & Admission Prices: By appointment only. No charge; donations accepted. Closed major holidays.

Greenwood

GATORS & FRIENDS - ALLIGATOR PARK AND EXOTIC ZOO, 11441 US Hwy. 80, Greenwood, LA 71033-2106. Tel.: 318-938-1199.
Institution Type/Description: Zoo.
Hours & Admission Prices: May-Aug. daily 10-6; Sept.-April Wed.-Sun. 10-6. Adults 13 & over $7.95, children 3-12 $5.95; children 2 & under no charge. Animal Feed: $2.

Gretna

GRETNA HISTORICAL SOCIETY MUSEUM, 209 Lafayette St., Gretna, LA 70053. Mailing Address: P.O. Box, Gretna, LA 70054. Tel.: 504-362-3854. Fax: 504-368-8236.
Key Personnel: Pres. (V), Paul Coles; Museum Shop Mgr., Ken Hunter.
Institution Type/Description: Historical Society Museum: housed in the former home of Claudius Strehle and Catherine Nousz; built in 1840.
Hours & Admission Prices: Call for hours.

Hammond

LOUISIANA CHILDREN'S DISCOVERY CENTER, 113 N. Cypress, Hammond, LA 70401. Mailing Address: P.O. Box 1765, Hammond, LA 70404-1765. Tel.: 985-340-9150. Fax: 985-340-9156. Facebook.
E-mail: info@lcdcofhammond.org
Web Site: www.lcdcofhammond.org
Key Personnel: Dir. Operations, Leon Philpot; Pres. (V), Alexis Ducorbier; Museum Shop Mgr., Cheryl Landry.
Institution Type/Description: Children's Museum.
Hours & Admission Prices: Tues.-Fri. 10-4, Sat. 10-5, Sun. 1-5. Admission $8 per person, seniors 60 & over $7; discounts to ACM members; members, military with ID and children 24 months and under no charge. &
Attendance: 42,000 (actual)

SOUTHEASTERN LOUISIANA UNIVERSITY CONTEMPORARY ART GALLERY, 100 E. Stadium, Hammond, LA 70402. Tel.: 985-549-5080.
E-mail: dnewkirk@southeastern.edu
Web Site: www.southeastern.edu/acad_research/depts/vis_art/gallery/
Institution Type/Description: Art Gallery.
Hours & Admission Prices: Mon.-Tues. & Thurs.-Fri. 8-4:30, Wed. 8-8, Sat. 10-2.

Haughton

TOUCHSTONE WILDLIFE AND ART MUSEUM, 3386 Hwy. 80 E., Haughton, LA 71037. Tel.: 318-949-2323.
Web Site: touchstonemuseum.com
Institution Type/Description: Wildlife & Art Museum.

Hours & Admission Prices: Feb.-Aug. Tues.-Sat. 10-4:30; Sept.-Jan. Thurs.-Sat. 10-4:30. Adults $5; children 3 & under no charge. &

Homer

THE HERBERT S. FORD MEMORIAL MUSEUM, 519 S. Main St., Homer, LA 71040-3955. Mailing Address: P.O. Box 157, Homer, LA 71040-0157. Tel.: 318-927-9190. Facebook.
E-mail: fordmuseum@bellsouth.net
Web Site: www.hfordmuseum.com
Key Personnel: Pres. (V), Terry Clason; Project Dir., Linda Volentine.
Institution Type/Description: History Museum.
Hours & Admission Prices: Mon., Wed. & Fri. 9-4; other times by appointment. Families $5, adults $3, children $1.
Attendance: 1,350 (estimated)

Houma

BAYOU TERREBONNE WATERLIFE MUSEUM, 7910 Park Ave., Houma, LA 70364-3285. Tel.: 985-580-7200.
E-mail: apicou@tpcg.org
Web Site: www.tpcg.org/waterlife
Key Personnel: Dir., Ann Picon.
Institution Type/Description: History Museum.
Hours & Admission Prices: Tues.-Fri. 10-5, Sat. noon-4. Adults $3, seniors $2.50, children 2-12 $2.

REGIONAL MILITARY MUSEUM, 1154 Barrow St., Houma, LA 70360-5608. Mailing Address: P.O. Box 10247, Station 1, Houma, LA 70363-0247. Tel.: 985-873-8200. Fax: 985-873-0035. Facebook.
E-mail: rmmuseum@gmail.com
Web Site: regionalmilitarymuseum.com
Key Personnel: Pres. & Chm. Bd., C.J. Christ; Vice Pres. & Treas., Will Theriot; Exec. Asst., Dexter Babin, II; Sec. Bd., Mart Black.
Institution Type/Description: Military Museum.
Hours & Admission Prices: Mon.-Fri. 10-4, Sat. 10-2. Adults $5, seniors $3, college & high school students $2, elementary school students $1; members & active military no charge. Closed New Year's Day; Thanksgiving; Christmas. &
Attendance: 25,000 (estimated)

SOUTHDOWN PLANTATION HOUSE/THE TERREBONNE MUSEUM, 1208 Museum Dr., Houma, LA 70360-6072. Mailing Address: P.O. Box 2095, Houma, LA 70361-2095. Tel.: 985-851-0154.
E-mail: info@southdownmuseum.org
Web Site: www.southdownmuseum.org
Formerly: Terrebonne Historical and Cultural Society
Key Personnel: Pres., David Ellender; Vice Pres., Liz Bass; Sec., Angel Luke; Treas., Dawn Pierron; Exec. Dir., Nicole Chiasson.
Institution Type/Description: General Museum: housed in the Southdown Plantation House.
Hours & Admission Prices: Tues.-Sat. 10-3, Sun. by appointment. Adults $17, active military $ 16, senior citizens & students $15, children $14-17 $10, children 5-13 $8; discounts to AAM members & groups of 20 and above (reservations required); children under 5 & members no charge. Closed New Year's Eve & Day; Mardi Gras; Good Friday; Easter; Independence Day weekend; Thanksgiving; Christmas Eve & Day. &
Attendance: 26,000 (actual)

Jackson

PORT HUDSON STATE HISTORIC SITE, 236 Hwy. 61, Jackson, LA 70748-4217. Tel.: 225-654-3775, 888-677-3400 (Toll Free). Fax: 225-654-4413.
E-mail: porthudson@crt.la.gov
Institution Type/Description: Historic Site: a National Historic Landmark.
Hours & Admission Prices: Tues.-Sat. 9-5; groups by appointment. Adults $4; seniors 62 & over and children 12 & under no charge. Closed New Year's Day; Thanksgiving; Christmas. &
Attendance: 25,000 (estimated)

Jeanerette

JEANERETTE BICENTENNIAL PARK AND MUSEUM, 500 E. Main St., Jeanerette, LA 70544-3712. Mailing Address: P.O. Box 1011, Jeanerette, LA 70544. Tel.: 337-276-4408. Fax: 337-276-9557.
E-mail: jeanerettemuseum@gmail.com
Web Site: www.jeanerettemuseum.com

Key Personnel: Bd. Pres., Gail Garcia.
Institution Type/Description: History Museum.
Hours & Admission Prices: Call for hours. Adults $3, children under 12 $1. &
Attendance: 1,938 (actual)

Jennings

W.H. TUPPER GENERAL MERCHANDISE MUSEUM, 311 N. Main St., Jennings, LA 70546-5341. Tel.: 337-821-5532.
E-mail: tuppermuseum@bellsouth.net
Web Site: www.tuppermuseum.com
Key Personnel: Dir., Polly Henry.
Institution Type/Description: History Museum.
Hours & Admission Prices: Mon.-Fri. 9-5. Adults $3, students $1. Closed major holidays. &
Attendance: 2,000 (estimated)

ZAM - ZIGLER ART MUSEUM, 154 N. Main St., Jennings, LA 70546-5235. Tel.: 337-824-0114. Fax: 337-824-0120.
E-mail: museum@ziglerart.org
Web Site: www.ziglerart.org
Key Personnel: Dir., Celia Joe Black.
Institution Type/Description: European & American Art.
Hours & Admission Prices: Mon.-Sat. 10-4. Adults $5, seniors $4, children 6 & over $2; discounts to tour groups and ICOM & AAM members; members no charge. Closed major holidays. &
Attendance: 4,385 (estimated)

Kaplan

LE MUSEE DE KAPLAN, 405 N. Cushing Ave., Kaplan, LA 70548. Tel.: 337-643-1528.
E-mail: info@kaplanla.com
Web Site: www.kaplanla.com
Institution Type/Description: History Museum.
Hours & Admission Prices: Wed.-Sat. 9-1.

Lafayette

ACADIAN CULTURAL CENTER - LAFAYETTE, 501 Fisher Rd., Lafayette, LA 70508-2033. Tel.: 337-232-0789.
Institution Type/Description: History Museum.
Hours & Admission Prices: Daily 8-5. No charge. Closed Mardi Gras; Christmas.

ALEXANDRE MOUTON HOUSE/LAFAYETTE MUSEUM, 1122 Lafayette St., Lafayette, LA 70501-6838. Tel.: 337-234-2208. Fax: 337-234-2208.
E-mail: lafayettemuseum@gmail.com
Web Site: www.lafayettemuseum.com
Key Personnel: Docent, Priscilla DeVille; Docent, Jody Smyth; Quartre Bd. Mem., Les Vingt.
Institution Type/Description: House Museum on National Register of Historic Places.
Hours & Admission Prices: Tues.-Sat. 10-4, Sun. 1-4. Adults $5, senior citizens $3, students $2; discounts to groups; school tours no charge. Closed New Year's Day; Mardi Gras; Independence Day; Thanksgiving; Christmas. &

CATHEDRAL OF ST. JOHN THE EVANGELIST MUSEUM, 914 St. John St., Lafayette, LA 70501. Mailing Address: 515 Cathedral St., Lafayette, LA 70501-6701. Tel.: 337-232-1322 & 1325. Fax: 337-232-1379.
E-mail: info@saintjohncathedral.org
Web Site: www.saintjohncathedral.org
Key Personnel: Dir., Chm. (V) & Museum Shop Mgr., Janice McNeil; Asst., Cheryl Luke; Museum Shop Mgr., Becky Peyton.
Institution Type/Description: Religious Museum.
Hours & Admission Prices: By appointment. Tours: Mon.-Thurs. 9-12 & 1-4, Fri. 9-12. Adults $3, senior citizens $2, children 12 & under $1; discounts to groups of 20 or more. &
Attendance: 2,178 (actual)

CHILDREN'S MUSEUM OF ACADIANA, 201 E. Congress St., Lafayette, LA 70501-6919. Tel.: 337-232-8500. Fax: 337-232-8167. Facebook: Children's Museum of Acadiana.
E-mail: info@cmalaf.org
Web Site: www.childrensmuseumofacadiana.org
Institution Type/Description: Children's Museum.
Hours & Admission Prices: Tues.-Sat. 10-5. Admission $7; children one & under no charge. &
Attendance: 44,500 (actual)

LARC'S ACADIAN VILLAGE, 200 Greenleaf Dr., Lafayette, LA 70506-7400. Tel.: 337-981-2364, 800-962-9133. Fax: 337-988-4554. Facebook: LARC's Acadian Village.
E-mail: thomas@acadianvillage.org
Web Site: www.acadianvillage.org
Institution Type/Description: Folk Life and History Museum.
Hours & Admission Prices: Jan.-Oct. Tues.-Sat. 10-4. Adults $8, students $6; discounts to groups; military no charge. Closed major holidays. &

LAFAYETTE SCIENCE MUSEUM, 433 Jefferson St., Lafayette, LA 70501-7013. Tel.: 337-291-5544. Fax: 337-291-5464.
Web Site: www.lafayettesciencemuseum.org
Formerly: Lafayette Natural History Museum and Planetarium
Key Personnel: Dir., Kevin Krantz; Cur. Planetarium, David Hostetter; Cur. Collections, Dr. Deborah J. Clifton; Cur. Exhibits, Blake Lagneaux; Museum & Planetarium Technician, Paul McCasland; Asst. Cur. Planetarium, Charlotte Guillot.
Institution Type/Description: Science Museum & Planetarium.
Hours & Admission Prices: Tues.-Fri. 9-5, Sat. 10-6, Sun. 1-6. Adults $5, seniors $3, children 4-17 & chaperones $2, school groups outside of Lafayette Parish $1 per student; discounts to AAM members; members & children under 4 no charge. Closed Mardi Gras; Easter; Thanksgiving; Christmas. &
Attendance: 45,000 (estimated)

PAUL AND LULU HILLIARD UNIVERSITY ART MUSEUM, UNIVERSITY OF LOUISIANA AT LAFAYETTE, 710 E. St. Mary Blvd., Lafayette, LA 70503-2332. Mailing Address: P.O. Drawer 42571, Lafayette, LA 70504-2571. Tel.: 337-482-2278. Fax: 337-262-1268. Twitter.
E-mail: artmuseum@louisiana.edu
Web Site: hillardmuseum.org
Formerly: University Art Museum University of Southwestern Louisiana Campus; University Art Museum, University of Louisiana at Lafayette
Key Personnel: Dir., Louanne Greenwald; Registrar, Misty Taylor; Cur., Laura Blereau; Mktg., Jolie Johnson; Security, Jacob Spaetgens; Store Mgr., Kristin Straub; Lauren Pitts; Educator, Olivia Morgan; Asst. to Dir., Cami Joseph.
Institution Type/Description: Art Museum.
Hours & Admission Prices: Tues. & Thurs.-Fri. 9-5, Wed. 9-8, Sat. 10-5. Adults $5, senior citizens $4, students 5-17 $3; discounts to NARM, AAM & ICOM members & groups of 20 or more; tours at 2 on Fri. & Sat. & members no charge. Closed major holidays. &
Attendance: 30,000 (actual)

VERMILIONVILLE, 300 Fisher Rd., Lafayette, LA 70508-2028. Tel.: 337-233-4077, 866-992-2968. Fax: 337-233-1694. Facebook, Instagram.
E-mail: curator@bayouvermiliondistrict.org
Web Site: www.vermilionville.org
Key Personnel: Dir. & C.E.O., David Cheramie; Museum Shop Mgr., Chris Benoit.
Institution Type/Description: Folklife Park.
Hours & Admission Prices: Tues.-Sun. 10-4. Adults $10, seniors 65 & over $8, students 5-18 $6; discounts to AAA members, active-duty military & dependents, seniors/retirees, Le Guide Routard, University of Louisiana-Lafayette alumni, Louisiana Public Broadcasting members, National Preservation for Historic Trust members; members & children under 5 no charge. Closed New Year's Eve & Day; Martin Luther King Day; Mardi Gras Day; Memorial Day; Labor Day; Thanksgiving; Christmas Eve & Day. &
Attendance: 50,000 (estimated)

Lafitte

LAFITTE BARATARIA MUSEUM, Leo E. Kerner Multi-Purpose Center, 4917 City Park Dr., Lafitte, LA 70067. Tel.: 504-689-7888.
E-mail: jeanlafittetownhall@yahoo.com
Formerly: Louisiana Marine Fisheries Museum
Institution Type/Description: Cultural Heritage Museum.
Hours & Admission Prices: Call for hours.

Lake Charles

ABERCROMBIE GALLERY & GRAND GALLERY, McNeese State University, Ryan & Sale Sts., Lake Charles, LA 70609. Mailing Address: MSU Dept. of Visual Arts, P. O. Box 92295, Lake Charles, LA 70609. Tel.: 337-475-5060. Fax: 337-475-5927.
E-mail: hkelley@mcneese.edu
Web Site: www.mcneeseartonline.org
Formerly: Abercrombie Gallery
Key Personnel: Dir., Heather Ryan Kelley; Chm., Lynn Reynolds.
Institution Type/Description: Art Gallery.
Hours & Admission Prices: Mon.-Fri. 9-4:30. No charge. Closed school holidays. &

CHILDREN'S MUSEUM OF LAKE CHARLES, INC., 327 Broad St., Lake Charles, LA 70601-4223. Tel.: 318-433-9420. Fax: 318-433-0144.
E-mail: dan@child-museum.org
Web Site: www.child-museum.org
Key Personnel: Exec. Dir., Dan Ellender; Asst. Dir., Allyson Blackwell; Education & Program Dir., Erin Bentley.
Institution Type/Description: Children's Museum.
Hours & Admission Prices: Mon.-Sat. 10-5. Admission 2 & over $7.50, active military $6.75, senior citizens 55 & over $5.75; discounts to groups of 10 or more with a reservation; children under 2 & members no charge. Closed major holidays. &
Attendance: 24,000 (actual)

IMPERIAL CALCASIEU MUSEUM, INC., 204 W. Sallier St., Lake Charles, LA 70601-5844. Tel.: 337-439-3797. Fax: 337-439-6040.
E-mail: impmuseum@bellsouth.net
Web Site: www.imperialcalcasieumuseum.org
Key Personnel: Exec. Dir., Susan H. Reed.
Institution Type/Description: Local History Museum.
Hours & Admission Prices: Tues.-Sat. 10-5. Adults $2, children $1; members no charge. Closed major holidays. &
Attendance: 6,800 (estimated)

USS RADFORD NATIONAL NAVAL MUSEUM, 604 N. Enterprise Blvd., Lake Charles, LA 70606. Mailing Address: 482 Windyville Rd., Spencer, WV 25276. Tel.: 304-927-0094.
E-mail: ussradford@gmail.com
Web Site: www.ussradford446.org
Key Personnel: Pres. (V), Chuck Parsons.
Institution Type/Description: Naval Military Museum.
Hours & Admission Prices: Mon.-Fri. 10-3, Sat.-Sun. 10-4; bus & family tours by appointment. &
Attendance: 18,000 (estimated)

Lake Providence

LOUISIANA STATE COTTON MUSEUM, 7162 Hwy. 65 N., Lake Providence, LA 71254-5226. Mailing Address: State of Louisiana, Secretary of State, P.O. Box 94125, Baton Rouge, LA 70804-9125. Tel.: 318-559-2041. Fax: 318-559-2217.
E-mail: cotton@sos.louisiana.gov
Web Site: www.sos.louisiana.gov/lscm
Key Personnel: Dir., Harriet Bridges.
Institution Type/Description: Cotton Museum.
Hours & Admission Prices: Tues.-Sat. 10-4. No charge. Closed most state holidays. &
Attendance: 4,573 (actual)

Leesville

MUSEUM OF WEST LOUISIANA, 803 S. Third St., Leesville, LA 71446-4703. Tel.: 337-239-0927.
E-mail: museumofwestla@gmail.com
Web Site: museumofwestlouisiana.org
Key Personnel: Dir., Fleeta Penton; Museum Shop Mgr., Mary Cleveland.
Institution Type/Description: History Museum.
Hours & Admission Prices: Tues.-Sun. 1-5; other times by appointment. No charge; donations accepted. Closed major holidays. &
Attendance: 8,000 (actual)

Lockport

BAYOU LAFOURCHE FOLKLIFE & HERITAGE MUSEUM, 110 Main St., Lockport, LA 70374. Mailing Address: P.O. Box 416, Lockport, LA 70374. Tel.: 985-532-5909. Fax: 985-532-1108.
E-mail: bayoulafourchefo@bellsouth.net
Web Site: www.bayoumuseum.org
Institution Type/Description: History Museum.
Hours & Admission Prices: Tues. & Thurs. 10-4; other times by appointment.

Long Leaf

SOUTHERN FOREST HERITAGE MUSEUM, 77 Longleaf Rd., Long Leaf, LA 71448. Mailing Address: P.O. Box 101, Long Leaf, LA 71448-0101. Tel.: 318-748-8404. Fax: 318-748-8410. Facebook: Southern Forest Heritage Museum.
E-mail: longleaf@centurytel.net

Web Site: www.forestheritagemuseum.org
Key Personnel: Dir., Claudia Troll, M.Ed.; Pres., Everett Lueck; Public Rels., Buck Vandersteen; Treas., Jim Barnett; Security, Charles Hudson.
Institution Type/Description: History Museum.
Hours & Admission Prices: Tues.-Sat. 9-4, Sun. 1-4, Mon. by appointment. $10; discounts to groups; members no charge. See website for holiday closings. &
Attendance: 13,000 (estimated)

Madisonville

LAKE PONTCHARTRAIN BASIN MARITIME MUSEUM, 133 Mabel Dr., Madisonville, LA 70447-9301. Tel.: 985-845-9200. Fax: 985-845-9201.
E-mail: info@lpbmm.org
Web Site: www.lpbmm.org
Key Personnel: Dir., Don Lynch; Educator, Stephanie Imel; Administrative Asst., Melanie Waddell; Museum Shop Mgr., Sharon Street.
Institution Type/Description: Maritime Museum.
Hours & Admission Prices: Tues.-Sat. 10-4, Sun. 12-4. Adults $5, seniors & children 6-12 $3; discount to groups; members and children under 6 & uniformed military no charge. Closed New Year's Day; Mardi Gras; Thanksgiving; Christmas. &
Attendance: 30,000 (estimated)

MADISONVILLE MUSEUM, 201 Cedar St., Madisonville, LA 70477. Mailing Address: P.O. Box 160, Madisonville, LA 70447-0160. Tel.: 985-845-2100.
Key Personnel: Dir. & Museum Shop Mgr., Ginger Stanga.
Institution Type/Description: History Museum.
Hours & Admission Prices: Sat.-Sun. 12-4. No charge; donations accepted.
Attendance: 600 (estimated)

OTIS HOUSE - FAIRVIEW-RIVERSIDE SATE PARK, 119 Fairview Dr., Madisonville, LA 70447. Tel.: 985-845-3318, 888-677-3247.
E-mail: fairview@crt.la.gov
Institution Type/Description: Park & Historic House: built in the 1880s. Listed on the National Register of Historic Places.
Hours & Admission Prices: Wed.-Sun. 9-5. Adults $4; children 12 & under and seniors 62 & over no charge. Closed New Year's Day; Thanksgiving; Christmas.

Mansfield

MANSFIELD FEMALE COLLEGE MUSEUM, 101 Monroe St., Mansfield, LA 71052. Mailing Address: State of Louisiana, Secretary of State, P.O. Box 94125, Baton Rouge, LA 70804-9125. Tel.: 318-871-9978. Fax: 318-871-9978.
E-mail: barbara.valentine@sos.la.gov
Web Site: www.sos.louisiana.gov/mfcm
Key Personnel: Dir., Barbara Valentine.
Institution Type/Description: History Museum.
Hours & Admission Prices: Tues.-Fri. 8-4:30. No charge. Closed most state holidays. &
Attendance: 1,414 (actual)

MANSFIELD STATE HISTORIC SITE - CIVIL WAR BATTLEFIELD, 15149 Hwy. 175, Mansfield, LA 71052-4774. Tel.: 318-872-1474, 888-677-6267. Fax: 318-871-4345. Facebook: @mansfieldshs.
E-mail: mansfield@crt.la.gov
Web Site: www.crt.state.la.us
Formerly: Mansfield State Commemorative Area
Key Personnel: Park Mgr., Scott Dearman.
Institution Type/Description: Civil War Battlefield
Hours & Admission Prices: Wed.-Sun. 9-5. Adults 4-61 $4, children 3 & under and senior citizens 62 & over no charge. Closed New Year's Day; Thanksgiving; Christmas. &
Attendance: 11,850 (actual)

Mansura

LA COMMISSION DES AVOYELLES, INC. - DR. JULES CHARLES DESFOSSE HOUSE, 1832 L'Eglise St., Mansura, LA 71350. Mailing Address: P.O. Box 26, Hamburg, LA 71339. Tel.: 318-964-2152.
Key Personnel: Pres. (V), Carlos Mayeux.
Institution Type/Description: Historic House: housed in a French Colonial home containing mud walls; built c.1790. Listed on the National Register of Historic Places.

Hours & Admission Prices: Wed.-Thurs. 8-3, Fri. 8-2. Adults $2, children $1. Closed major holidays.
Attendance: 2,500 (estimated)

LOUISIANA 4-H MUSEUM, 8592 Hwy. 1, Ste. 2, Mansura, LA 71350. Tel.: 318-964-2245. Fax: 318-964-2259.
E-mail: web@agcenter.lsu.edu
Institution Type/Description: History Museum.
Hours & Admission Prices: Mon.-Fri. 8:30-4; other times by appointment. Admission $3; discounts to groups; children under 3 no charge.

Many

FORT JESUP STATE HISTORIC SITE, 32 Geoghagan Rd., Many, LA 71449. Tel.: 318-256-4117, 888-677-5378.
E-mail: fortjesup@crt.state.la.us
Institution Type/Description: Historic Site: housed on the grounds of Fort Jesup; built in 1822. A National Historic Landmark.
Hours & Admission Prices: Daily 9-5. Adults $2; seniors 62 & over and children 12 & under no charge. Closed New Year's Day; Thanksgiving; Christmas.

Marksville

HYPOLITE BORDELON HOME, 242 Tunica Dr. W., Marksville, LA 71351. Mailing Address: P.O. Box 585, Marksville, LA 71351-0767. Tel.: 318-253-0284.
E-mail: info@travelavoyelles.com
Key Personnel: Chm. (V), Clyde M. Neck.
Institution Type/Description: Historic House Museum: built in 1820. Listed on the National Register of Historic Places.
Hours & Admission Prices: Tues.-Sat. 9-5. Adults $2, children $1.
Attendance: 900 (estimated)

MARKSVILLE STATE HISTORIC SITE, 837 Martin Luther King Dr., Marksville, LA 71351-2478. Tel.: 225-342-8111. Facebook: Marksville State Historic Site.
E-mail: marksville@crt.la.gov
Web Site: www.crt.state.la.us/louisiana-state-parks/historic-sites/marksville-state-historic-site
Institution Type/Description: Historic Site. Designated as a National Historic Landmark.
Hours & Admission Prices: Fri. 9-5; other times by appointment. Groups up to 10 $46, $4 per person after 10. No charge on Fri. Closed New Year's Day; Thanksgiving; Christmas.

TUNICA-BILOXI CULTURAL & EDUCATIONAL RESOURCES CENTER, 150 Melancon Rd., Marksville, LA 71351. Mailing Address: P.O. Box 1589, Marksville, LA 71351-1589. Tel.: 318-240-6451. Fax: 318-253-7711.
E-mail: earlii@tunica.org
Web Site: www.tunica.org
Formerly: Tunica-Biloxi Native American Museum
Key Personnel: CERC Dir., Earl J. Barbry, Jr.; C.F.O., Doug Burke; Security, Police Chief Harold Pierite, Sr.; Museum Shop Mgr., Melissa Barbin.
Institution Type/Description: History Museum.
Hours & Admission Prices: Call for hours. Adults $5, children $3; discounts to groups, seniors & veterans. &
Attendance: 2,400 (estimated)

Marrero

BARATARIA PRESERVE, JEAN LAFITTE NATIONAL HISTORICAL PARK AND PRESERVE, 6588 Barataria Blvd., Marrero, LA 70072-7526. Tel.: 504-689-3690. Fax: 504-689-7897. Facebook: Barataria Preserve, Jean Lafitte National Historical Park and Preserve.
E-mail: kristy_wallisch@nps.gov
Web Site: www.nps.gov/jela/
Key Personnel: Supervisory Park Ranger, Alentia Scott; Education Coord., Stacy Lafayette; Volunteer Coord., Stephanie Click; Publications Coord., Kristy Wallisch; Bookstore Mgr., Julie Castille.
Institution Type/Description: Park Visitor Center, Folkway & Natural History Museum.
Hours & Admission Prices: Daily 9-5. No charge; donations accepted. Closed Christmas; Mardi Gras. &
Attendance: 35,000

Marthaville

REBEL STATE HISTORIC SITE & LOUISIANA COUNTRY MUSIC MUSEUM, 1260 Hwy. 1221, Marthaville, LA 71450-3459. Tel.: 318-472-6255, 888-677-3600. Fax: 318-472-9315.
E-mail: rebel@crt.state.la.us
Web Site: www.crt.state.la.us
Formerly: Rebel State Commemorative Area Louisiana Country Music Museum
Institution Type/Description: Louisiana Country Music Museum: housed in a treble clef shaped building; Rebel State Historic Site; resting place of the Unknown Confederate Soldier.
Hours & Admission Prices: Daily 9-5. Adults $4; seniors 62 & over, children 12 & under and school groups no charge. Closed New Year's Day; Thanksgiving; Christmas. &
Attendance: 7,710 (actual)

Melrose

MELROSE PLANTATION, Melrose General Delivery, 3533 Hwy. 119, Melrose, LA 71452. Mailing Address: Box 2248, Natchitoches, LA 71457-2248. Tel.: 318-379-0055. Facebook; Twitter; Instagram.
E-mail: info@melroseplantation.org
Web Site: www.melroseplantation.org
Key Personnel: Facilities Mgr., Molly Dickerson; Pres. (V), Vicki Parrish; Museum Shop Mgr., Betty Metoyer.
Institution Type/Description: Historic House: 1833 early Louisiana type plantation home of Marie Therese Coin; her children freed slaves.
Hours & Admission Prices: Tues.-Sun. 10-5; other times by appointment. Adults $10, children $5; discounts to AAM members & groups of 15 or more by appointment; members no charge. Closed Easter; Independence Day; Thanksgiving; Christmas.
Attendance: 13,347 (actual)

Merryville

THE MERRYVILLE MUSEUM, 628 N. Railroad St., Merryville, LA 70653. Mailing Address: P.O. Box 637, Merryville, LA 70653. Tel.: 337-825-0101.
Web Site: www.merryvilleheritagefestival.com
Institution Type/Description: History Museum.
Hours & Admission Prices: Sat.-Sun. 2-4; other times by appointment.

Minden

DORCHEAT HISTORICAL MUSEUM, 116 Pearl St., Minden, LA 71055. Tel.: 318-377-3002.
E-mail: dorcheatmuseum@yahoo.com
Web Site: museuminminden.blogspot.com
Key Personnel: Dir., Schelley Brown Francis.
Institution Type/Description: History Museum.
Hours & Admission Prices: Tues.-Fri. 10-1 & 2-4; other times by appointment. No charge.

GERMANTOWN COLONY AND MUSEUM, 200 Museum Rd., Minden, LA 71055-7331. Mailing Address: P.O. Box 178, Minden, LA 71058. Tel.: 318-377-6061. Fax: 318-377-6061.
E-mail: jean.daerge@sos.la.gov
Institution Type/Description: History Museum.
Hours & Admission Prices: March-Dec. Wed.-Sat. 10-3; other times by appointment. No charge; donations accepted.

Monroe

BIEDENHARN MUSEUM & GARDENS, 2000 Riverside Dr., Monroe, LA 71201-4268. Tel.: 318-387-5281, 800-362-0983. Fax: 318-387-8253. Facebook: Biedenharn Museum & Gardens.
E-mail: director@bmuseum.org
Web Site: www.bmuseum.org
Key Personnel: Pres., Henry Biedenharn, III; Exec. Dir., Ralph Calhoun; Museum Shop Mgr., Mona Orloski.
Institution Type/Description: Historic House, Garden & Museum Complex: Bible Museum: c.1914 Southern house, home of Joseph A. Biedenharn, first bottler of Coca-Cola; 1946 formal Elsong Gardens; 1971 Biblical Museum; Coca-Cola Museum.
Hours & Admission Prices: Tues.-Sat. 10-5; groups of 10 or more by appointment. Adults $6, children $4. Closed New Year's Day; Easter; Independence Day; Thanksgiving; Christmas Eve & Day. &
Attendance: 30,000 (actual)

CHENNAULT AVIATION AND MILITARY MUSEUM, 701 Kansas Lane, Monroe, LA 71203-4775. Mailing Address: State of Louisiana Secretary of State, P.O. Box 94125, Baton Rouge, LA 70804-9125. Tel.: 318-362-5540. Fax: 318-362-5545.
E-mail: nell.calloway@sos.la.gov
Web Site: www.sos.louisiana.gov/camm
Formerly: Aviation and Military Museum of Louisiana
Key Personnel: Dir., Nell Calloway.
Institution Type/Description: Military Museum.
Hours & Admission Prices: Tues.-Sat. 9-4. No charge. Closed most state holidays. ♿
Attendance: 27,763 (actual)

LOUISIANA PURCHASE GARDENS AND ZOO, 1405 Bernstein Park Rd., Monroe, LA 71202-5545. Mailing Address: P.O. Box 123, Monroe, LA 71210. Tel.: 318-329-2400.
E-mail: kim.dooley@ci.monroe.la.us
Web Site: www.monroezoo.org
Key Personnel: Cur. Education, Kimberly Dooley.
Institution Type/Description: Gardens & Zoo.
Hours & Admission Prices: Daily 10-5. Adults 13-64 $4.50, seniors 65 & over and children 3-12 $3; discounts to groups of 10 or more; children 2 & under no charge. Boat Rides: March 2-Oct. 10-4:30. Admission $2. Closed New Year's Day; Thanksgiving; Christmas.

MASUR MUSEUM OF ART, 1400 S. Grand St., Monroe, LA 71202-2012. Tel.: 318-329-2237. Fax: 318-329-2847.
E-mail: info@masurmuseum.org
Web Site: www.masurmuseum.org
Key Personnel: Dir., Evelyn P. Stewart; Chief Cur., Benjamin Hickey; Cur. Education, Jenny Burnham; Office Asst., Kaitlin Sanson; Bookkeeper, Christal Winfield.
Institution Type/Description: Art Museum.
Hours & Admission Prices: Tues.-Fri. 9-5, Sat. 12-5. No charge. Closed national holidays.
Attendance: 20,000 (estimated)

NORTHEAST LOUISIANA CHILDREN'S MUSEUM, 323 Walnut St., Monroe, LA 71201-6711. Tel.: 318-361-9611. Fax: 318-361-9613.
E-mail: nelcm@nelcm.org
Web Site: www.nelcm.org
Key Personnel: Exec. Dir., Melissa Saye; Chm. (V), Leigh Ann Goff; Pres. (V), Rhonda Neal; Museum Shop Mgr., Sarah Maimon.
Institution Type/Description: Children's Museum.
Hours & Admission Prices: Tues.-Fri. 9-2, Sat. 10-5. Admission 1 & over $6; discounts to groups of 15 or more; members no charge. ♿
Attendance: 35,000 (estimated)

NORTHEAST LOUISIANA DELTA AFRICAN AMERICAN HERITAGE MUSEUM, 1051 Chennault Park Dr., Monroe, LA 71203. Tel.: 318-323-3745.
Web Site: www.nldaahm.com
Key Personnel: Exec. Dir., Lorraine Slacks; Sec., Patricia Hudson.
Institution Type/Description: History Museum.
Hours & Admission Prices: Tues.-Sat. 10-4. Adults $2. ♿
Attendance: 10,000 (estimated)

Moreauville

ADAM PONTHIEU GROCERY STORE AND BIG BEND POST OFFICE MUSEUM, 8554 Louisiana Hwy. 451, Moreauville, LA 71355. Tel.: 318-997-2465.
E-mail: bigbendmuseum@gmail.com
Institution Type/Description: History Museum.
Hours & Admission Prices: Tues. & Thurs.-Fri. 7:30-3:30, Sun. 12-4:30; other times by appointment. Adults $2, children K-12 $1.

Morgan City

INTERNATIONAL PETROLEUM MUSEUM AND EXPOSITION - RIG MUSEUM, 111 First St., Morgan City, LA 70380. Mailing Address: P.O Box 1988, Morgan City, LA 70381. Tel.: 985-384-3744.
E-mail: rigmuseum@rigmuseum.com
Web Site: rigmuseum.com
Institution Type/Description: Petroleum Industry Museum.

Hours & Admission Prices: Guided tours: Mon.-Sat. 10 & 2, weather permitting; groups by appointment. Adults $8, seniors $7, students $5; discounts to groups; children under 5 no charge.

Mound

SOUTHERN HERITAGE AIR FOUNDATION MUSEUM, Vicksburg-Tallulah Rgnl. Airport, Mound, LA 71282. Mailing Address: 179 VTR Airport Rd., Tallulah, LA 71282. Tel.: 601-415-1902. Facebook: Southern Heritage Air Foundation.
E-mail: info@southernheritageair.org
Web Site: www.southernheritageair.org
Institution Type/Description: Aviation History Museum.
Hours & Admission Prices: Tues.-Sat. Adults $8, seniors and children 18 & under $5. Closed major holidays. ♿
Attendance: 10,000 (estimated)

Natchitoches

FORT ST. JEAN BAPTISTE STATE HISTORIC SITE, 155 Jefferson, Natchitoches, LA 71457-4350. Tel.: 318-357-3101. Fax: 318-357-7055.
E-mail: fortstjean@crt.state.la.us
Web Site: www.crt.state.la.us
Formerly: Fort St. Jean Baptiste State Commemorative Area
Key Personnel: Cur., James Prud'Homme; Mgr., Justin French; Interpretive Ranger, Tommy Adkins; Interpretive Ranger, Rhonda Gauthier.
Institution Type/Description: Historical Fort: reconstruction of 1732 fort & related buildings.
Hours & Admission Prices: Daily 9-5. Adults $4; children under 12 & senior citizens 62 & over no charge. Closed New Year's Day; Thanksgiving; Christmas. ♿
Attendance: 14,283 (actual)

THE LEMEE HOUSE, APHN Headquarters, 310 Jefferson St., Natchitoches, LA 71457-4355. Mailing Address: P.O. Box 2248, Natchitoches, LA 71457-2248. Tel.: 318-581-8042.
E-mail: info@melroseplantation.org
Web Site: www.melroseplantation.org
Key Personnel: Facilities Mgr., Molly Dickerson; Pres (V), Vicki Parrish; Museum Shop Mgr., Betty Metoyer.
Institution Type/Description: Historic House: c.1833 house bought by Alexis Lemee in 1849 to serve as his home & the Union Bank of New Orleans.
Hours & Admission Prices: Oct. call for hours. ♿
Attendance: 2,400 (estimated)

LOUISIANA SPORTS HALL OF FAME AND NORTHWEST LOUISIANA HISTORY MUSEUM, 800 Front St., Natchitoches, LA 71457. Tel.: 318-357-2492. Fax: 318-357-2495.
E-mail: jbiddiscombe@crt.la.gov
Web Site: louisianastatemuseum.org/museums/louisiana-sports-hall-of-fame-northwest-louisiana-history-museum
Key Personnel: Dir., Jennae Biddiscomb.
Institution Type/Description: Sports History Museum.
Hours & Admission Prices: Tues.-Sat. 10-4:30, Sun. 1-5; groups by appointment. Adults $5, students, senior citizens & active military $4; children 12 & under no charge. Closed state holidays.

MINOR BASILICA OF THE IMMACULATE CONCEPTION, 605 Second St., Natchitoches, LA 71457-4624. Tel.: 318-352-3422. Fax: 318-352-3822.
E-mail: church4321@catholic.org
Formerly: Immaculate Conception Catholic Church
Key Personnel: Sec., Susan Chesal.
Institution Type/Description: Historic Building & Museum: c.1856 Immaculate Conception Church and 1885 Rectory.
Hours & Admission Prices: Church: daily 9-4. Bishop Martin Museum: call 318-352-3422 for appointment. No charge; donations accepted.
Attendance: 500 (estimated)

NATCHITOCHES NATIONAL FISH HATCHERY, 615 South Dr., Natchitoches, LA 71457-3056. Tel.: 318-352-5324. Fax: 318-352-8082.
E-mail: jan_dean@fws.gov
Key Personnel: Deputy Project Leader, Dr. Jan Dean; Biologist, Tony Brady; Maintenance Mechanic, Dennis W. Scarbrough, Jr.; Office Asst., Lana J. Litton.
Institution Type/Description: Aquarium & Fish Hatchery.
Hours & Admission Prices: Daily 8-3, group tours: call for appointment. No charge. Closed all federal holidays. ♿
Attendance: 10,000 (estimated)

New Iberia

BAYOU TECHE MUSEUM, 131 E. Main St., New Iberia, LA 70560. Mailing Address: P.O. Box 14151, New Iberia, LA 70562-4151. Tel.: 337-606-5977. Fax: 337-369-2346. Facebook: Bayou Teche Museum.
E-mail: bayoutechemuseum@gmail.com
Web Site: bayoutechemuseum.org
Key Personnel: Dir. & Public Rels., Marcia Patout; Chm. (V), Chris Wiseman; Pres. (V), Larry Hensgens; Treas., Art Mixon.
Institution Type/Description: History Museum.
Hours & Admission Prices: Thurs.-Sat. 10-4; other times by appointment. Adults $5, senior citizens $3, children $2. Closed major holidays. &
Attendance: 5,000 (estimated)

CONRAD RICE MILL, 307 Ann St., New Iberia, LA 70560. Mailing Address: P.O. Box 10640, New Iberia, LA 70562. Tel.: 800-551-3245.
E-mail: info@conradricemill.com
Web Site: www.conradricemill.com
Institution Type/Description: Historic Building.
Hours & Admission Prices: Mon.-Sat. 9-5; groups by appointment. Adults $4, seniors $3.50, children 3-11 $2.25.

RIP VAN WINKLE GARDENS ON JEFFERSON ISLAND, 5505 Rip Van Winkle Rd., New Iberia, LA 70560-8167. Tel.: 337-359-8525. Fax: 337-359-8526.
E-mail: jislgdns@earthlink.net
Web Site: www.ripvanwinklegardens.com
Key Personnel: Mgr., Michelle Richard.
Institution Type/Description: Botanical Garden & Historic Houses: c.1870 house built by actor Joseph Jefferson; semi-tropical 25 acre landscape garden.
Hours & Admission Prices: Tours: daily 9-4. Adults $10, children & senior citizens $8; discounts to groups; children under 8 & members no charge. Closed New Year's Day; Thanksgiving, Christmas Eve & Day. &
Attendance: 40,000 (actual)

THE SHADOWS-ON-THE-TECHE, 317 E. Main St., New Iberia, LA 70560-3728. Tel.: 337-369-6446. Fax: 337-365-5213.
E-mail: shadows@shadowsontheteche.org
Web Site: www.shadowsontheteche.org
Key Personnel: Chm. Property Council, Taylor Barras; Dir., Patricia Kahle; Cur. Education, Catherine T. Schramm; Curatorial Technician, Yvonne Leblanc.
Institution Type/Description: Historic House Museum: 1834 plantation home & restored landscape.
Hours & Admission Prices: Mon.-Sat. 9-4:30. Adults $10, senior citizens 65 & over $8, students 6-17 $6.50; discount to groups; National Trust for Historic Preservation members, Friends of the Shadows & children under 6 no charge. Closed major holidays. &
Attendance: 18,591 (actual)

New Orleans

AFRICAN AMERICAN MUSEUM, 1418 Gov. Nicholls St., New Orleans, LA 70116-2344. Tel.: 504-566-1136. Facebook.
E-mail: noaam1418@gmail.com
Web Site: noaam.org
Key Personnel: Interim Exec. Dir., Mora Beauchamp-Byrd, Ph.D.
Institution Type/Description: Art and History Museum: housed in the Treme Villa, built in 1828-29.
Hours & Admission Prices: Closed for renovations. &

AMERICAN ITALIAN CULTURAL CENTER, 537 S. Peters St., New Orleans, LA 70130-1628. Tel.: 504-522-7294. Fax: 504-522-1657.
E-mail: questions@americanitalianculturalcenter.com
Web Site: www.americanitalianculturalcenter.com
Formerly: American Italian Renaissance Foundation
Key Personnel: Dir., Community Outreach, Stephanie Rios; Dir., Programs, Alessandro Steinhaus; Cur., American Italian Research Library, Sal Serio.
Institution Type/Description: History Museum.
Hours & Admission Prices: Tues.-Fri. 10-4. Adults $8, seniors & students $5; children under 12 & members no charge. Closed holidays. &
Attendance: 1,000 (estimated)

AMISTAD RESEARCH CENTER, INC., Tilton Hall-Tulane University, 6823 St. Charles Ave., New Orleans, LA 70118-5665. Tel.: 504-862-3222. Fax: 504-862-8961. Facebook.
E-mail: info@amistadresearchcenter.org
Web Site: www.amistadresearchcenter.org

Key Personnel: Exec. Dir., Kara Tucina Olidge, Ph.D.; Dir. Reference & Library Svcs., Christopher Harter; Dir. Processing, Laura J. Thomson; Audiovisual Archivist, Brenda Flora; Reference Archivist, Chianta Dorsey; Archivist, Jasmaine Talley.
Institution Type/Description: History Museum.
Hours & Admission Prices: Mon.-Fri. 8:30-4:30, Sat. 9-1. No charge; donations accepted. Closed Martin Luther King Jr. Day; Lundi Gras; Mardi Gras; Good Friday; Memorial Day; Independence Day; Labor Day; Thanksgiving; Dec. 23-Jan. 1. &
Attendance: 1,771 (actual)

ANSEL M. SHROUD JR. MILITARY HISTORY & WEAPONS MUSEUM, 6400 St. Claude Ave., New Orleans, LA 70117-1456. Tel.: 504-278-8664. Facebook.
E-mail: heather.s.englehart.mil@mail.mil
Web Site: www.geauxguardmuseums.com
Formerly: The Jackson Barracks Military Museum
Key Personnel: Dir., Heather Englehart.
Institution Type/Description: Military Museum.
Hours & Admission Prices: Mon.-Sat. 10-4. No charge; donations accepted. Closed New Year's Day; Independence Day; Thanksgiving; Christmas. &

AUDUBON AQUARIUM OF THE AMERICAS, 1 Canal St., New Orleans, LA 70130-1175. Mailing Address: c/o Audubon Nature Institute, 6500 Magazine St., New Orleans, LA 70118. Tel.: 504-565-3033.
E-mail: air@auduboninstitute.org
Web Site: www.auduboninstitute.org
Key Personnel: Pres. & C.E.O., L. Ronald Forman; Sr. Vice Pres. & Chief of Staff, Bill Kurtz; Exec. Vice Pres. & Chief Admin. Officer, Laurie Conkerton; Vice Pres. Sales & Events, Richard Buchsbaum; Vice Pres. Mktg., Chimene Grant; Vice Pres. & Gen. Cur., Joel Hamilton; Vice Pres. Retail Operations, Debra McGuire; Sr. Vice Pres., Chief Svc. Officer, Toni Mobley; Vice Pres. Education and Mng. Dir. Audubon Louisiana Nature Center, David Niebuhr; Mng. Dir. Westbank Facilities, Jason Recher; Dir. Finance, Caroline Tierney; Vice Pres. & Mng. Dir. Downtown Facilities, Rich Toth; Vice Pres. Construction, Ashley McClaran.
Institution Type/Description: Aquarium.
Hours & Admission Prices: Tues.-Sun. 10-5. Aquarium: adults $29.95, senior citizens 65 & up $24.95, children 2-12 $21.95; discounts to groups; members no charge. Closed Mardi Gras; Christmas Eve & Day. &
Attendance: 990,000 (estimated)

AUDUBON INSECTARIUM, 423 Canal St., New Orleans, LA 70130. Tel.: 800-774-7394, 504-861-2537.
Web Site: audubonnatureinstitute.org/insectarium
Key Personnel: Pres. & C.E.O., L. Ronald Forman; Exec. Vice Pres. & Chief of Staff, Bill Kurtz; Exec. Vice Pres. & C.A.O., Laurie Conkerton.
Institution Type/Description: Nature Center.
Hours & Admission Prices: Tues.-Sun. 10-5. Adults 13-64 $22.95, seniors 65 & over $19.95, children 2-12 $17.95; discounts to groups.

AUDUBON ZOO, 6500 Magazine St., New Orleans, LA 70118-4848. Tel.: 504-861-2537. Facebook.
E-mail: air@auduboninstitute.org
Web Site: www.auduboninstitute.org
Formerly: Audubon Park and Zoological Garden
Key Personnel: Pres. & C.E.O., L. Ronald Forman; Vice Pres. Mktg., Chimene Grant.
Institution Type/Description: Zoo and Park.
Hours & Admission Prices: Tues.-Fri. 10-4, Sat.-Sun. 10-5. Adults $22.95, senior citizens 65 & up $19.95, children 2-12 $17.95; members no charge. Closed Mardi Gras; Thanksgiving; Christmas. &
Attendance: 717,000 (estimated)

BACKSTREET CULTURAL MUSEUM, Mailing Address: 1116 Henriette Delille St., New Orleans, LA 70116. Tel.: 504-606-4809.
E-mail: info@backstreetmuseum.org
Web Site: www.backstreetmuseum.org
Key Personnel: Exec. Dir., Sylvester Francis.
Institution Type/Description: Folk-Life and History Museum.
Hours & Admission Prices: Tues.-Sat. 10-4. Admission $10.

BEAUREGARD-KEYES HOUSE, 1113 Chartres St., New Orleans, LA 70116-2504. Tel.: 504-523-7257. Fax: 504-523-7257. Facebook: @BeauregardKeyesHouse.
E-mail: bkeyeshouse@gmail.com
Web Site: www.bkhouse.org
Key Personnel: Exec. Dir., Annie Irvin; Pres. Keyes Foundation, Ann Masson.

Institution Type/Description: Historic House Museum: c.1826 home of wealthy auctioneer Joseph LeCarpentier, famed New Orleans author, Francis Parkinson Keyes & confectioner General P.G.T. Beauregard.
Hours & Admission Prices: Mon.-Sat. 10-3. Adults $10, students & senior citizens $9, children 6-12 $4; discounts to AAM members; children under 6 no charge. Closed major holidays; Mardi Gras.
Attendance: 7,500

BLAINE KERN'S MARDI GRAS WORLD, 1380 Port of New Orleans Pl., New Orleans, LA 70130-1805. Tel.: 504-475-2317.
E-mail: brookep@mardigrasworld.com
Web Site: mardigrasworld.com
Institution Type/Description: General Museum.
Hours & Admission Prices: Daily 10-5:30. Adults $19.95, seniors 65 & over & college students with ID $15.95, children 2-11 $12.95. Closed Mardi Gras; Easter; Thanksgiving; Christmas. &

CATHOLIC CULTURAL HERITAGE CENTER/OLD URSULINE CONVENT/ST. LOUIS CATHEDRAL, 1100 Chartres St., New Orleans, LA 70116-2505. Mailing Address: 615 Pere Antoine Alley, New Orleans, LA 70116. Tel.: 504-525-9585. Fax: 504-525-9583.
E-mail: cathedral@arch-no.org
Web Site: stlouiscathedral.org
Key Personnel: Dir., Very Rev. Philip G. Landry; Chm. (V), Barbara Windhorst; Museum Shop Mgr., Jolie Sekinger.
Institution Type/Description: Religious Museum: built in 1752.
Hours & Admission Prices: Tours: Mon.-Sat. 10-4. Adults $10, seniors $9, students $5; discounts to groups of 20 or more; members no charge. &
Attendance: 56,000 (actual)

COLLINS C. DIBOLL ART GALLERY, 4th Fl. Monroe Library, 6363 St. Charles Ave., New Orleans, LA 70118-6143. Tel.: 504-861-5456.
E-mail: gallery@loyno.edu
Web Site: www.loyno.edu/dibollgallery
Key Personnel: Gallery Dir., Karoline Schleh.
Institution Type/Description: Art Gallery.
Hours & Admission Prices: Mon.-Sat. 10-6, Sun. 12-6. No charge.

CONFEDERATE MEMORIAL HALL MUSEUM, 929 Camp St., New Orleans, LA 70130-3907. Tel.: 504-523-4522.
E-mail: memhall@confederatemuseum.com
Web Site: www.confederatemuseum.com
Key Personnel: Dir. & Cur., Patricia Ricci.
Institution Type/Description: Military Museum: housed in 1890 Memorial Hall.
Hours & Admission Prices: Tues.-Sat. 10-4. Adults $10, children under 14 $5; discounts to groups.
Attendance: 15,000

CONTEMPORARY ARTS CENTER, 900 Camp St., New Orleans, LA 70130-3908. Tel.: 504-528-3805. Fax: 504-528-3828.
E-mail: nbarclay@cacno.org
Web Site: www.cacno.org
Key Personnel: Dir. & C.E.O., Neil A. Barclay; The Helis Foundation Chief Cur. Visual Arts, Andrea Andersson.
Institution Type/Description: Arts Center.
Hours & Admission Prices: Wed.-Mon. 11-5. Adults $10, senior citizens & students $8; members, LA residents on Sun. and children & students grade 12 & under no charge. Performance & special events prices may vary. Closed most major holidays. &
Attendance: 125,000 (estimated)

DEGAS HOUSE, 2306 Esplanade Ave., New Orleans, LA 70119-2502. Tel.: 504-821-5009. Fax: 504-821-0870.
E-mail: info@degashouse.com
Web Site: www.degashouse.com
Institution Type/Description: Historic House: former home of the French Impressionist painter Edgar Degas.
Hours & Admission Prices: Guided tours by appointment only.

FORT PIKE STATE HISTORIC SITE, 27100 Chef Menteur Hwy., New Orleans, LA 70129-3106. Mailing Address: P.O. Box 44426, Baton Rouge, LA 70804-4426. Tel.: 504-255-9171, 888-662-5703. Fax: 504-662-0147.
E-mail: fortpike_mgr@crt.state.la.us
Web Site: www.crt.state.la.us
Formerly: Fort Pike State Commemorative Area

Institution Type/Description: Military Museum: housed in 1818-1827 fort built by U.S. government.
Hours & Admission Prices: Fri. 9-5; other times by appointment. Admission: groups of 10 or less $$46; Fri. no charge. Closed New Year's Day; Thanksgiving; Christmas.
Attendance: 13,500 (estimated)

GALLIER HOUSE, 1132 Royal St., New Orleans, LA 70116. Mailing Address: P.O. Box 56836, New Orleans, LA 70156-6836. Tel.: 504-274-0748. Fax: 504-568-9735.
E-mail: info@hgghh.org
Web Site: www.hgghh.org
Key Personnel: Interim Exec. Dir., Steve Smith; Bd. Pres. (V), Mary Johnson; Vice Pres., Elizabeth Adler; Chief Devel. Officer, Lisa Samuels; Communications Officer, Nadine Segari; Education Coord., Jenny Dyer; Devel. Assoc., Claire Leftwich.
Institution Type/Description: Historic House: housed in the former home of architect, James Gallier, Jr.; built in 1857.
Hours & Admission Prices: Tours: Mon., Tues., Thurs. & Fri. 10, 11, noon, 1 & 2, Sat. noon, 1, 2 & 3; other times by appointment. Adults $15, students & senior citizens $12; discounts to AAM, LAM, National Trust & SEMC members; members & children under 8 no charge. Closed major holidays.
Attendance: 4,281 (actual)

HERMANN-GRIMA HISTORIC HOUSE, 820 St. Louis St., New Orleans, LA 70112-3416. Mailing Address: P.O. Box 56836, New Orleans, LA 70156-6836. Tel.: 504-274-0746. Fax: 504-568-9735.
E-mail: info@hgghh.org
Web Site: www.hgghh.org
Key Personnel: Interim Exec. Dir., Steve Smith; Bd. Pres. (V), Mary Johnson; Vice Pres. (V), Elizabeth Adler; Devel. Assoc., Claire Leftwich; Education Coord., Jenny Dyer; Dir. Communications, Nadine Segari.
Institution Type/Description: Historic House: built in 1831
Hours & Admission Prices: Tours: Mon.-Tues. & Thurs.-Fri. 10, 11, 12, 1 & 2, Sat. 12, 1, 2 & 3; other times by appointment. Adults $15, students, senior citizens & children 8-18 $10; discounts to AAM, LAM, National Trust & SEMC members; members & children under 8 no charge. Closed major holidays.
Attendance: 12,462 (actual)

THE HISTORIC NEW ORLEANS COLLECTION, 533 Royal St., New Orleans, LA 70130-2113. Tel.: 504-523-4662. Fax: 504-598-7108. Facebook; Instagram; Twitter.
E-mail: wrc@hnoc.org
Web Site: www.hnoc.org
Key Personnel: Exec. Dir., Priscilla O'Reilly-Lawrence; C.F.O., Michael Cohn; Dir. Museum Programs, John H. Lawrence; Deputy Dir., Daniel Hammer; Manager Admin. Svcs., Kathy Slimp; Dir. Technology, Carol Bartels; Mktg. Mgr., Teresa Devlin; Exhibitions Coord., Warren J. Woods; Dir. Williams Research Center, Alfred E. Lemmon; Dir. Publications & Student Education, Jessica Dorman; Head Registrar, Jennifer Rebuck Ghabrial; Mgr. Retail Operations, Michelle Gaynor.
Institution Type/Description: History Museum & Research Center.
Hours & Admission Prices: Tues.-Sat. 9:30-4:30, Sun. 10:30-4:30. Tours: Tues.-Sat.: 10, 11, 2, 3, Sun. 11, 2, 3. Tour: $5; discounts to AAM members; members, changing exhibitions & research areas no charge. Closed major holidays. &
Attendance: 77,041 (estimated)

HOUSE OF BROEL'S VICTORIAN MANSION AND DOLLHOUSE MUSEUM, 2220 St. Charles Ave., New Orleans, LA 70130. Tel.: 504-522-2220 & 494-2220.
E-mail: info@houseofbroel.com
Web Site: www.houseofbroel.com
Institution Type/Description: Historic Mansion: built c.1850.
Hours & Admission Prices: Mon. & Wed.-Fri. 11-3. Adults $15, children $10; tours by appointment.

JEAN LAFITTE NATIONAL HISTORICAL PARK & PRESERVE, 419 Decatur St., New Orleans, LA 70130-1035. Tel.: 504-589-3882. Fax: 504-589-3851.
E-mail: courtney_amabile@nps.gov
Web Site: www.nps.gov/jela
Key Personnel: Supt., Lance Hatten.
Institution Type/Description: History Museum.
Hours & Admission Prices: Tues.-Sat. 9:30-4:30. No charge. Closed New Year's Day; Mardi Gras; Christmas. &
Attendance: 391,019 (estimated)

LONGUE VUE HOUSE & GARDENS, 7 Bamboo Rd., New Orleans, LA 70124-1007. Tel.: 504-488-5488. Fax: 504-486-7015.
E-mail: info@longuevue.com

Web Site: www.longuevue.com
Key Personnel: Interim Exec. Dir. & Administrative Dir., Ribby Ferguson; Cur., Lenora Costa; Dir. Finance, Patrick Nedd; Education Dir., Edna Lanieri; Facilities Dir., Tim Evans; Horticulture Dir., Amy Graham; Mktg. & Communcations, Marguerite Andrews.
Institution Type/Description: Historic House & Gardens: 1939-42, Palladian style, Longue Vue, home of cotton broker Edgar Bloom Stern & Edith Rosenwald Stern, daughter of Sears Roebuck financier & philanthropist, Julius Rosenwald.
Hours & Admission Prices: Mon.-Sat. 10-5, Sun. 1-5. Adults $12, seniors $10, students 11 & over with ID $8, children 3-10 $5; children under 3, AAM & AHS members with card, active military & veterans on Veterans Day no charge. Closed New Year's Day; Martin Luther King Jr. Day; Mardi Gras; Easter; Independence Day; Labor Day; Thanksgiving; Christmas Eve & Day. &
Attendance: 45,000 (actual)

LOUISIANA CHILDREN'S MUSEUM, 420 Julia St., New Orleans, LA 70130-3606. Tel.: 504-523-1357. Fax: 504-529-3666.
E-mail: info@lcm.org
Web Site: www.lcm.org
Key Personnel: C.E.O., Julia W. Bland; Communications & PR, Leslie Doles.
Institution Type/Description: Children's Museum.
Hours & Admission Prices: Winter: Tues.-Sat. 9:30-4:30, Sun. 12-4:30; Summer: Mon.-Sat. 9:30-5, Sun. 12-5. Admission $8.50; children under one no charge. Closed New Year's Day; Mardi Gras; Easter; Independence Day; Thanksgiving; Christmas. &
Attendance: 140,000 (estimated)

LOUISIANA STATE MUSEUM, 701 Chartres St., New Orleans, LA 70116-3205. Mailing Address: P.O. Box 2448, New Orleans, LA 70176-2448. Tel.: 800-568-6968. Fax: 504-568-4995. Facebook.
E-mail: lgueringer@crt.la.gov
Web Site: louisianastatemuseum.org
Key Personnel: Interim Dir., Steven Maklansky; Deputy Dir., Bridgette Thibodeaux; Curatorial Svcs. Dir., Polly Rolman-Smith; Museum Division Dir., Rodneyna Hart.
Institution Type/Description: Historical Museum Complex: five National Historic Landmark buildings located in the New Orleans' French Quarter; six additional museums in Baton Rouge, Patterson, Thibodaux & Natchitoches.
Hours & Admission Prices: The Louisiana State Museum-Baton Rouge: Tues.-Sat. 9-4:30. The Cabildo: Tues.-Sun. 10-4:30 Presbytere: Tues.-Sun. 10-4:30. Old U. S. Mint, 1850 House: call for hours. The Cabildo: adults $6, students, seniors & active military $5; discounts to groups, & AAA members; children 6 & under and members no charge. Presbytere: adults $12, students, seniors & active military $10; discounts to Louisiana Assoc. of Museums, Louisiana Museum Foundation, Friends of the Cabildo and AAM & ICOM members; children 6 & under, school groups & members no charge. Madame John's Legacy, Louisiana State Museum-Baton Rouge and Louisiana State Museum-Patterson: no charge. Combination tickets to all LSM properties available. Closed legal & state holidays. &
Attendance: 420,682 (actual)

MUSEUM OF DEATH, 227 Dauphine St., New Orleans, LA 70112. Tel.: 504-593-3968.
Institution Type/Description: General Museum.
Hours & Admission Prices: Daily 10-7. Adults $15.

NATIONAL SHRINE OF BLESSED FRANCIS XAVIER SEELOS, 919 Josephine St., New Orleans, LA 70130. Tel.: 504-525-2495. Fax: 504-581-9181.
E-mail: hgrile@seelos.org
Web Site: www.seelos.org
Key Personnel: Dir., Rev. Harry Grile, C.Ss.R.; Museum Shop Mgr. & Admin., Bro. Leo Paten.
Institution Type/Description: Religious Museum.
Hours & Admission Prices: Shrine: Mon.-Fri. 9-3, Sat. 10:30-3:30, Sun. between masses. Shop: Mon.-Fri. 9-3, Sat. 10:30-3:30. Shrine: no charge; donations accepted. &
Attendance: 50,000 (estimated)

THE NATIONAL WWII MUSEUM, 945 Magazine St., New Orleans, LA 70130-3813. Tel.: 504-528-1944. Fax: 504-527-6088.
E-mail: info@nationalww2museum.org
Web Site: www.nationalww2museum.org
Formerly: The National D-Day Museum
Key Personnel: C.E.O. & Pres., Stephen Watson; Chm. (V), C. Paul Hilliard; Sr. Vice Pres. & C.O.O., Becky Mackie; Sr. Vice Pres. Capital Projects, Bob Farnsworth; Vice Pres. Education & Access, Peter Crean; Vice Pres. & C.F.O., Cathy Green; Vice Pres. & C.M.O., Jonah Langenbeck; Vice Pres. Sales, James B. Williams.

Institution Type/Description: History Museum.
Hours & Admission Prices: Daily 9-5. Museum: adults $28, seniors 65 & over $24, students & military $18; members & WWII veterans no charge. Combination tickets available. Closed Mardi Gras; Thanksgiving; Christmas Eve & Day. &
Attendance: 650,000 (actual)

NEW ORLEANS BOTANICAL GARDEN, 1 Palm Dr., New Orleans, LA 70124. Tel.: 504-483-9488. Fax: 504-483-9485.
E-mail: garden@nocp.org
Web Site: garden.neworleanscitypark.com
Key Personnel: Dir., Paul M. Soniat; Gift Shop Mgr., Jessica Matthews.
Institution Type/Description: Botanical Garden.
Hours & Admission Prices: Daily 10-5. Admission $12, children 3-12 $4; children under 3, members & LA residents on Wed. no charge. &

NEW ORLEANS FIRE DEPT. MUSEUM & EDUCATIONAL CENTER, 1135 Washington Ave., New Orleans, LA 70130-5632. Tel.: 504-658-4713.
Web Site: www.nola.gov/nofd
Institution Type/Description: Fire-Fighting Museum: c.1852 firehouse.
Hours & Admission Prices: By appointment. No charge; donations accepted. Closed New Year's Eve & Day; Martin Luther King Jr. Day; Mardi Gras; Good Friday; Memorial Day; Independence Day; Thanksgiving; Christmas Eve & Day.
Attendance: 5,200 (actual)

NEW ORLEANS HISTORIC VOODOO MUSEUM, 724 Dumaine St., New Orleans, LA 70116. Tel.: 504-680-0128.
E-mail: voodoo@voodoomuseum.com
Web Site: voodoomuseum.com
Institution Type/Description: History Museum.
Hours & Admission Prices: Daily 10-6. Adults $7, seniors & college students $5.50, high school students $4.50, children under 12 $3.50.

NEW ORLEANS MUSEUM OF ART, One Collins Diboll Cir., New Orleans, LA 70124-4605. Tel.: 504-658-4100. Fax: 504-658-4199.
E-mail: gasprodites@noma.org
Web Site: www.noma.org
Key Personnel: The Montine MdDaniel Freeman Dir., Susan M. Taylor; Deputy Dir. Admin. & Fin., Gail Asprodites; Deputy Dir., Anne Banos; IT Mgr., Karl Oelkers; Sculpture Garden Mgr., Pamela Buckman; Deputy Dir. Curatorial Affairs & Cur. Asian Art, Lisa Rotondo McCord; Deputy Dir. Interpretation & Audience Engagement, Allison Reid; Freeman Family Cur. Photography, Prints & Drawings, Russell Lord; Head Registrar, Jennifer Ickles; Cur. Decorative Arts & Designs, Mel Buchanan; Cur. Education, Tracy Kennan; Cur. Modern & Contemp. Arts, Katie Pfohl; Dir. Devel., Jenni Daniel; Mgr. Creative Design, Mary Degnan; Mgr. Communications & Mktg., Margaux Krane; Editor Museum Publications, David Johnson; Museum Shop Mgr., Christina Lossi; Librarian, Shelia Cork.
Institution Type/Description: Art Museum.
Hours & Admission Prices: Tues.-Thurs. 10-6, Fri. 10-9, Sat. 10-5, Sun. 11-5. Adults $10, senior citizens 65 & over and university students $8, children 7-17 $6; discounts to AAM & ICOM members; children 6 & under no charge. Sculpture Garden: Mon.-Fri. 10-6, Sat.-Sun. 10-5. Closed Thanksgiving; Christmas. &
Attendance: 234,471 (actual)

NEW ORLEANS PHARMACY MUSEUM, 514 Chartres St., New Orleans, LA 70130-2110. Tel.: 504-565-8027. Fax: 504-565-8028. Facebook: New Orleans Pharmacy Museum.
E-mail: nopharmsm@att.net
Web Site: www.pharmacymuseum.org
Key Personnel: Chm., Anthony D'Angelo; Dir., Elizabeth Sherman; Events Mgr., Stephanie Mackin.
Institution Type/Description: Pharmacy & Medicine Museum: housed in 1823 building constructed for Louis Joseph Dufilho, Jr., first licensed pharmacist in the U.S.
Hours & Admission Prices: Call for hours. Adults $5, senior citizens & students $4; discounts to AAM & AAA members; children under 6 & members no charge. Closed New Year's Day; Mardi Gras; Easter; Independence Day; Labor Day; Thanksgiving; Christmas.
Attendance: 20,000 (estimated)

NEWCOMB ART MUSEUM, Woldenberg Art Center, Tulane University, Bldg. 81, Corner of Newcomb Pl. & Drill Rd., New Orleans, LA 70118-5698. Mailing Address: Woldenberg Art Center #202, 6823 St. Charles Avenue, New Orleans, LA 70118. Tel.: 504-865-5328. Fax: 504-865-5329.
E-mail: museum@tulane.edu

Web Site: newcombartmuseum.tulane.edu
Formerly: Newcomb Art Gallery
Key Personnel: Dir., Monica Ramirez-Montagut; External Affairs Mgr., Miriam Taylor; Collections Mgr. & Exhibitions Registrar, Sierra Polisar; Coord. Interpretation & Public Engagement, Tom Friel; Financial Svcs. Assoc., Corie Talano.
Institution Type/Description: Art Museum.
Hours & Admission Prices: Tues.-Fri. 10-5, Sat. 11-4. No charge. Closed New Year's Eve & Day; Mardi Gras; Thanksgiving; Christmas Eve & Day. &
Attendance: 10,000 (estimated)

THE OGDEN MUSEUM OF SOUTHERN ART, 925 Camp St., New Orleans, LA 70130-3907. Tel.: 504-539-9650. Facebook.
E-mail: info@ogdenmuseum.org
Web Site: www.ogdenmuseum.org
Key Personnel: Exec. Dir., William Pittman Andrews; Chm. (V), Allison Kendrick; Treas., Bryan Fitzpatrick.
Institution Type/Description: Art Museum.
Hours & Admission Prices: Wed. & Fri.-Mon. 10-5, Thurs. 10-5 & 6-8. Adults $13.50, senior citizens 65 & over, students & teachers $11, children 5-17 & under $6.75; UNO students, faculty & staff with ID, NARM, art institution employees with ID, children under 5, members & Louisiana residents Thurs. 10-5 no charge. Closed New Year's Day; Mardi Gras; Memorial Day; Independence Day; Thanksgiving; Christmas. &
Attendance: 75,000 (estimated)

PITOT HOUSE MUSEUM, 1440 Moss St., New Orleans, LA 70119-2904. Tel.: 504-482-0312. Facebook.
E-mail: info@louisianalandmarks.org
Web Site: www.louisianalandmarks.org
Key Personnel: Pres., Sandra L. Stokes; Dir., Carol Gniady.
Institution Type/Description: Historic House: 1799 French West Indies Country house.
Hours & Admission Prices: Wed.-Sat. 10-3. Adults $10, senior citizens & children $7; discounts to groups & National Trust members; members no charge. Closed major holidays.
Attendance: 1,000 (estimated)

PRESERVATION RESOURCE CENTER OF NEW ORLEANS, 923 Tchoupitoulas St., New Orleans, LA 70130-3819. Tel.: 504-581-7032. Fax: 504-636-3073.
E-mail: prc@prcno.org
Web Site: www.prcno.org
Key Personnel: Interim Dir., Jack Davis; Chief Admin. Officer, Leah S. Tubbs; Chief Financial Officer, Anh Nga Geauthreaux.
Institution Type/Description: Historical & Preservation Society: housed in 1853 Gothic Revival style building designed by James H. Dakin.
Hours & Admission Prices: Mon.-Fri. 9-5. No charge; donations accepted. &
Attendance: 2,500 (estimated)

SAINTS HALL OF FAME MUSEUM, 1500 Poydras St., Mercedes-Benz Superdome Gate B, Plaza Level, New Orleans, LA 70112. Mailing Address: 5800 Airline Dr., Metairie, LA 7003. Tel.: 504-471-2192.
E-mail: saintshalloffame@aol.com
Web Site: saintshalloffame.com
Key Personnel: Gen. Mgr. & Chm. Bd., Ken Trahan; Exec. Vice Pres. & Gen. Mgr., Mickey Loomis; SHOF Pres., Joe Impastato; Vice Pres. Exhibits, Michael C. Hebert; Vice Pres. Exhibits, Chris Bennett.
Institution Type/Description: Sports Museum.
Hours & Admission Prices: NFL Game Days: 3 hours before the game & 45 minutes after the game; Mon.-Fri. 9-3 by appointment. Adult $7, seniors 55 & over and children 12 & under $5; discounts to groups of 10 or more. &

SOUTHERN FOOD AND BEVERAGE MUSEUM AND THE MUSEUM OF THE AMERICAN COCKTAIL, 1504 Oretha C. Haley Blvd., New Orleans, LA 70113. Tel.: 504-569-0405.
E-mail: info@southernfood.org
Web Site: www.southernfood.org
Key Personnel: Dir., Elizabeth Williams; Chm. Bd., Butler Burdine; Dir. Operations, Kelsey Parris; Dir. Education, Jennie Merrill; Dir. Culinary Programming, Jyl Benson; Dir. Outreach & Adventures, Holly Barrett.
Institution Type/Description: Cultural History Museum.
Hours & Admission Prices: Wed.-Mon. 11-5:30. Adults $10.50, students, seniors & military $5.25; members no charge. &
Attendance: 35,000 (estimated)

New Roads

THE JULIEN POYDRAS MUSEUM & ARTS CENTER, 500 W. Main St., New Roads, LA 70760. Mailing Address: P.O. Box 462, New Roads, LA 70760. Tel.: 225-638-6575. Fax: 225-638-6578. Facebook: Julien Poydras Center.
E-mail: pointecoupeehistoricalsociety@gmail.com
Web Site: pointecoupeehistoricalsociety.org
Key Personnel: Exec. Dir., Rene Major.
Institution Type/Description: Art Museum: housed in the former Poydras High School building; built in 1924.
Hours & Admission Prices: Wed.-Fri. 1-5, Sat. 10-3.

POINTE COUPEE MUSEUM, 8348 False River Rd., New Roads, LA 70760. Mailing Address: P.O. Box 462, New Roads, LA 70760. Tel.: 225-638-7788.
E-mail: e.angelique.bergeron@gmail.com
Key Personnel: Pres. (V), Angelique Bergeron, Ph.D.; Museum Shop Mgr., Winona Sicard.
Institution Type/Description: Historic Building.
Hours & Admission Prices: Daily 10-3; other times by appointment. No charge; donations accepted.
Attendance: 1,000 (estimated)

Newellton

WINTER QUARTERS STATE HISTORIC SITE, 4929 Hwy. 608, Newellton, LA 71357-6314. Tel.: 888-677-2784, 318-766-3530.
E-mail: winterquarters@crt.la.gov
Institution Type/Description: Historic Site: built in 1805.
Hours & Admission Prices: By appointment. Adults $2; seniors 62 & over and children 12 & under no charge. Closed New Year's Day; Thanksgiving; Christmas.

Oil City

LOUISIANA STATE OIL & GAS MUSEUM, 200 S. Land Ave., Oil City, LA 71061. Mailing Address: State of Louisiana, Secretary of State, P.O. Box 94125, Baton Rouge, LA 70804-9125. Tel.: 318-995-6845. Fax: 318-995-6848.
E-mail: oil@sos.louisiana.gov
Web Site: www.sos.louisiana.gov/lsoagm
Formerly: Caddo-Pine Island Oil & Historical Society Museum
Key Personnel: Dir., Coe McKenzie.
Institution Type/Description: Oil and Gas Museum.
Hours & Admission Prices: Wed.-Fri. 10-4. No charge. Closed major federal & state holidays.
Attendance: 1,415 (actual)

Olla

CENTENNIAL CULTURAL CENTER, 2962 Front St., Olla, LA 71465. Mailing Address: P.O. Box 896, Olla, LA 71465-0896. Tel.: 318-495-7988. Fax: 318-495-7988.
E-mail: cultural@centurytel.net
Web Site: www.culturalcenter.us
Key Personnel: Dir., Donna Lindsey.
Institution Type/Description: History Museum.
Hours & Admission Prices: Mon.-Fri. 9-1. No charge.

Opelousas

LOUISIANA ORPHAN TRAIN SOCIETY, INC., 610 Garland Ave., Opelousas, LA 70570. Tel.: 337-945-4691.
E-mail: hdupre2433@aol.com
Web Site: laorphantrain.com
Key Personnel: Dir., Pres. (V) & Devel., Harold Dupre; Treas. & Archivist, Florella Inhern.
Institution Type/Description: History Museum.
Hours & Admission Prices: Tues.-Fri. 10-3, Sat. 10-2. Adults $5, senior citizens, students & children $3. Closed New Year's Eve, Day & week; Christmas Day & week. &
Attendance: 500

OPELOUSAS FIRE MUSEUM, 109 N. Union St., Opelousas, LA 70570. Mailing Address: c/o City of Opelousas Fire Dept., 1334 South Union, Opelousas, LA 70570. Tel.: 337-948-2543.
E-mail: info@firemuseumnetwork.org
Institution Type/Description: Firefighting History Museum: housed in the former headquarters of the Hope Hook & Ladder Company.

Hours & Admission Prices: Call for hours.

OPELOUSAS MUSEUM AND INTERPRETIVE CENTER, 315 N. Main St., Opelousas, LA 70570-6201. Tel.: 337-948-2589. Fax: 337-948-2592.
E-mail: museum@cityofopelousas.com
Web Site: www.cityofopelousas.com
Institution Type/Description: History Museum.
Hours & Admission Prices: Mon.-Fri. 8-4:30, Sat. 10-3. Tour Buses: $3 per person; discounts to AAM & ICOM members. Closed Easter; Thanksgiving; Christmas. &
Attendance: 6,000 (estimated)

Patterson

WEDELL-WILLIAMS AVIATION AND CYPRESS SAWMILL MUSEUM, 118 Cotten Rd., Patterson, LA 70392. Mailing Address: P.O. Box 38, Patterson, LA 70392-0038. Tel.: 985-399-1268. Fax: 985-399-9910.
E-mail: glacoste@crt.state.la.us
Web Site: louisianastatemuseum.org
Formerly: Louisiana State Museum-Patterson
Key Personnel: Museum Div. Dir., William Stark; Administrative Program Specialist, Gloria LaCoste.
Institution Type/Description: Aviation and Cypress Museum.
Hours & Admission Prices: Tues.-Sat. 9:30-4. No charge; donations accepted. Closed select holidays. &
Attendance: 12,000 (actual)

Pioneer

POVERTY POINT STATE HISTORIC SITE, 6859 Hwy. 577, Pioneer, LA 71266. Tel.: 318-926-5492, 888-926-5492.
E-mail: povertypoint@crt.la.gov
Institution Type/Description: Historic Site: archaeological site dated from 1700 & 1100 B.C. A National Historic Landmark.
Hours & Admission Prices: Daily 9-5; groups by appointment. Adults $4; seniors 62 & over and children 12 & over no charge. Closed New Year's Day; Thanksgiving; Christmas.

Plaquemine

IBERVILLE MUSEUM, 57735 Main St., Plaquemine, LA 70764-2564. Mailing Address: P.O. Box 701, Plaquemine, LA 70765-0701. Tel.: 225-687-7197. Fax: 225-687-3060. Facebook; Instagram.
E-mail: contact@ibervillemuseum.org
Web Site: ibervillemuseum.org
Key Personnel: Dir. & Cur., Meghan Sylvester.
Institution Type/Description: History Museum: housed in old Parish Court House.
Hours & Admission Prices: Tues.-Sat. 10-4. Adults 13 & over $2, children 6-12 $1; school groups no charge. Closed major holidays. &

PLAQUEMINE LOCK STATE HISTORIC SITE, 57730 Main St., Plaquemine, LA 70764-2530. Tel.: 225-687-7158, 877-987-7158.
E-mail: plaqlock@crt.state.la.gov
Web Site: www.lastateparks.com
Institution Type/Description: Historic Site. Listed on the National Register of Historic Places.
Hours & Admission Prices: Tues.-Sat. 9-5. Adults $4; seniors 62 & over and children 12 & under no charge. Closed New Year's Day; Thanksgiving; Christmas.
Attendance: 5,000 (estimated)

Port Allen

WEST BATON ROUGE MUSEUM, 845 N. Jefferson Ave., Port Allen, LA 70767-2417. Tel.: 225-336-2422. Fax: 225-336-2448. Facebook: West Baton Rouge Museum.
E-mail: contact_us@wbrmuseum.org
Web Site: westbatonrougemuseum.com
Key Personnel: Dir., Julia Rose; Chm. (V), Ellis Gauthier; Vice Chm., Sue Blanchard; Cur., Lauren Davis; Education Cur., Jeannie Luckett; Museum Shop Mgr., Tommy McMorris.
Institution Type/Description: Regional History Museum.
Hours & Admission Prices: Tues.-Sat. 10-4:30, Sun. 2-5. Adults $4, students, military & seniors $2; discounts offered to AAM, AAA, LAM members & other tourism coupon holders; WBR Historical Assoc. members, citizens of WBR par-

ish & members no charge. Closed major holidays. Business Office: Mon.-Fri. 9-4:30. &
Attendance: 20,000 (actual)

Rivertown

RIVERTOWN MUSEUMS, 2020 Fourth St., Rivertown, LA 70062. Tel.: 504-468-7231.
E-mail: hglorioso@kenner.la.us
Institution Type/Description: Science Museum & Planetarium.
Hours & Admission Prices: Groups: Tues.-Fri. by appointment. General Public: Sat. 11-4. Space Station & Science Complex: adults $5, seniors $4, children $3. Planetarium & Megadome: adults $6, seniors & children $5. Combination tickets available.

Robeline

ADAI INDIAN NATION CULTURAL CENTER, 4460 Hwy. 485, Robeline, LA 71469-4946. Tel.: 877-472-1007, 318-472-1007.
Institution Type/Description: Historic Site.
Hours & Admission Prices: Daily 9-5. Adults $6.50, children 3-12 $4.75; children under 3 no charge. Closed New Year's Day; Easter; Thanksgiving; Christmas.

LOS ADAES STATE HISTORIC SITE, 6354 Hwy. 485, Robeline, LA 71469. Tel.: 318-472-9449, 888-677-5378.
E-mail: fortjesup@crt.la.gov
Institution Type/Description: Historic Site: a National Historic Landmark.
Hours & Admission Prices: Temporarily closed.

Ruston

LINCOLN PARISH MUSEUM & HISTORICAL SOCIETY, 609 N. Vienna St., Ruston, LA 71270-3842. Tel.: 318-251-0018. Fax: 318-251-0018. Facebook.
E-mail: lpmuseum@bellsouth.net
Web Site: www.lincolnparishmuseum.org
Key Personnel: C.E.O., Chm. (V) & Pres. (V), William Davis Green; Dir., Margaret Anne Emory; Treas., Jimmy Moore; Sec., Linda Graham.
Institution Type/Description: Historical Society Museum: housed in 1886 Victorian home.
Hours & Admission Prices: Tues.-Fri. 10-4. No charge; donations accepted. Closed New Year's Eve & Day; Independence Day; Thanksgiving; Christmas Eve, Day & week. &
Attendance: 3,000 (actual)

LOUISIANA MILITARY MUSEUM, 201 Memorial Dr., Ruston, LA 71270-3955. Mailing Address: State of Louisiana, Secretary of State, P.O. Box 94125, Baton Rouge, LA 70804-9125. Tel.: 318-251-5099. Fax: 318-251-5088.
E-mail: military@sos.louisiana.gov
Web Site: www.sos.louisiana.gov/lmm
Key Personnel: Dir., Ernest Stevens.
Institution Type/Description: Military Museum.
Hours & Admission Prices: Tues.-Sat. 10-4. No charge. Closed most state holidays.
Attendance: 6,318 (actual)

LOUISIANA TECH MUSEUM, Louisiana Tech University, Ruston, LA 71272. Tel.: 318-257-2935 & 3660. Fax: 318-257-2579.
E-mail: pcarter@latech.edu
Key Personnel: Devel., Jonathan Donehoo; Education, Joan Marie Edinger; Public Rels., Sally R. Hollis; Archivist, Peggy Carter.
Institution Type/Description: University Museum.
Hours & Admission Prices: Mon.-Fri. 9-4. No charge; donations accepted. Closed New Year's Day; Thanksgiving; Christmas; university holidays. &
Attendance: 400 (estimated)

Saint Bernard

ISLENO MUSEUM COMPLEX - LOS ISLENOS HERITAGE & CULTURAL SOCIETY, 1357 Bayou Rd., Saint Bernard, LA 70085. Tel.: 504-676-3098. Fax: 504-676-3491.
E-mail: islenoshis@gmail.com
Web Site: www.losislenos.org
Key Personnel: Dir., William Hyland; Pres. (V), Dorothy L. Benge; Museum Shop Mgr., Celie Robin.
Institution Type/Description: History Museum.
Hours & Admission Prices: Call for hours. &
Attendance: 35,000 (estimated)

Saint Francisville

AUDUBON STATE HISTORIC SITE, 11788 Hwy. 965, Saint Francisville, LA 70775. Mailing Address: P.O. Box 546, Saint Francisville, LA 70775-0546. Tel.: 225-635-3739, 888-677-2838. Fax: 225-784-0578.
E-mail: audubon@crt.state.la.us
Web Site: www.crt.state.la.us
Formerly: Audubon State Commemorative Area
Key Personnel: Historic Site Mgr., John House.
Institution Type/Description: State Park Museum: housed in 1806 Oakley House.
Hours & Admission Prices: Oakley House & Grounds: Tues.-Sat. 9-5. Adults $8; senior citizens 62 & over $6, children 6-17 $4; children 5 & under no charge. Closed New Year's Day; Thanksgiving; Christmas.
Attendance: 30,000 (actual)

ROSEDOWN PLANTATION, 12501 Hwy. 10, Saint Francisville, LA 70775. Tel.: 888-376-1867, 225-635-3332.
E-mail: rosedown@crt.la.gov
Institution Type/Description: Historic House.
Hours & Admission Prices: Daily 9-5. Adults $10, senior citizens 62 & over $8, students 6-17 $4; children 5 & under no charge. Closed New Year's Day; Thanksgiving; Christmas.

Saint Martinville

AFRICAN AMERICAN MUSEUM, 125 S. New Market St., Saint Martinville, LA 70582. Mailing Address: P.O. Box 379, Saint Martinville, LA 70582-0379. Tel.: 337-394-2230. Fax: 337-394-2244.
Key Personnel: Dir., Danielle Fontenette.
Institution Type/Description: History Museum.
Hours & Admission Prices: Daily 10-4:30. Adults $3; children 12 & under no charge.
Attendance: 10,000 (actual)

LONGFELLOW EVANGELINE STATE HISTORIC SITE, 1200 N. Main St., Saint Martinville, LA 70582-3516. Tel.: 888-677-2900, 337-394-3754. Fax: 337-394-3553. Facebook: Longfellow Evangeline State Historic Site.
E-mail: longfellow@crt.state.la.us
Web Site: www.crt.state.la.us/Parks/ilongfell.aspx
Formerly: Oliver House & Interpretive Center
Institution Type/Description: History Museum.
Hours & Admission Prices: Tues.-Sat. 9-5. Adult $4; senior citizens over 62, children 12 & under no charge. Closed New Year's Day; Thanksgiving; Christmas.
Attendance: 27,000 (actual)

MUSEUM OF THE ACADIAN MEMORIAL, 121 S. New Market St., Saint Martinville, LA 70582. Mailing Address: P.O. Box 379, Saint Martinville, LA 70582-0379. Tel.: 337-394-2258. Fax: 337-394-2260. Facebook.
E-mail: info@acadianmemorial.org
Web Site: www.acadianmemorial.org
Key Personnel: Bd. Mem., Michelle Verret Johnson; Dir., Elaine Clement; Pres. (V), Patty Gutekunst; Museum Shop Mgr., Jane G. Bulliard.
Institution Type/Description: History Museum.
Hours & Admission Prices: Daily 10-4:30. Adults $3; members no charge.
Attendance: 12,000 (estimated)

Scott

FLOYD SONNIER'S BEAU CAJUN ART GALLERY, 1010 St. Mary St., Scott, LA 70583. Mailing Address: P.O. Box 397, Scott, LA 70583. Tel.: 337-237-7104.
Institution Type/Description: Art Gallery: built in 1918.
Hours & Admission Prices: Wed.-Fri. 10-5, Sat. 10-2; other times by appointment.

Shreveport

ARK-LA-TEX SPORTS MUSEUM OF CHAMPIONS, 400 Caddo St., Shreveport, LA 71101. Tel.: 318-221-8445. Fax: 318-227-2442.
Institution Type/Description: Sports Museum.
Hours & Admission Prices: Sat.-Sun. during events at the convention center.

GARDENS OF THE AMERICAN ROSE CENTER, 8877 Jefferson Paige Rd., Shreveport, LA 71119-5402. Tel.: 318-938-5534.
E-mail: carol@ars-hg.org
Web Site: www.ars.org
Institution Type/Description: Garden.
Hours & Admission Prices: Mon.-Sat. 9-5, Sun. 1-5. Adults $5.50, seniors 65 & over $4.50, children 5-12 $3.50; discounts to groups of 10 or more; children under 5 no charge.

LOUISIANA STATE EXHIBIT MUSEUM, 3015 Greenwood Rd., Shreveport, LA 71109-4640. Mailing Address: State of Louisiana, Secretary of State, P.O. Box 94125, Baton Rouge, LA 70804-9125. Tel.: 318-632-2020. Fax: 318-632-2056.
E-mail: lsem@sos.louisiana.gov
Web Site: www.sos.louisiana.gov/lsem
Key Personnel: Dir., Wayne Waddell; Education, Cynthia Grogan; Cur., Nita Cole.
Institution Type/Description: History & Art Museum.
Hours & Admission Prices: Mon.-Fri. 9-4. No charge. Closed most state holidays.
&
Attendance: 13,723 (actual)

MEADOWS MUSEUM OF ART AT CENTENARY COLLEGE OF LOUISIANA, 2911 Centenary Blvd., Shreveport, LA 71104-3335. Tel.: 318-869-5040. Fax: 318-869-5730. Facebook.
E-mail: meadows@centenary.edu
Web Site: www.centenary.edu/meadows
Key Personnel: Dir., Sean Fitzgibbons.
Institution Type/Description: Art Museum.
Hours & Admission Prices: Academic Year: Sept.-April Mon.-Fri. 10-5. No charge. Closed New Year's Day; Easter; Memorial Day; Labor Day; Thanksgiving; Christmas. &
Attendance: 2,500 (actual)

THE MULTICULTURAL CENTER OF THE SOUTH, 520 Spring St., Shreveport, LA 71101. Mailing Address: P.O. Box 305, Shreveport, LA 71101-0305. Tel.: 318-424-1380. Fax: 318-424-1384.
E-mail: jgatlin-mccs@comcast.net
Web Site: mecsouth.org
Key Personnel: Dir. Programs, Janice Gatlin.
Institution Type/Description: Multicultural Center.
Hours & Admission Prices: Gallery: Tues.-Fri. 10-4. Guided Tours: Sat. by appointment. Adults $3, seniors & students $2. Closed holidays.

THE MUSEUM OF AMERICAN FENCING, 1413 Fairfield Ave., Shreveport, LA 71101. Tel.: 318-227-7575.
E-mail: andy@museumofamericanfencing.com
Web Site: museumofamericanfencing.com
Institution Type/Description: Fencing Museum.
Hours & Admission Prices: Mon.-Thurs. 3-8, Sat. 9am to noon.

PIONEER HERITAGE CENTER, LSU-SHREVEPORT, One University Pl., Shreveport, LA 71115-2301. Tel.: 318-797-5339. Fax: 318-797-5110.
E-mail: pioneer@lsus.edu
Web Site: www.lsus.edu/pioneer
Key Personnel: Dir., Marvin R. Young, II; Pres. (V), Dr. Vincent J. Marsala; Treas., Michael Ferrell.
Institution Type/Description: History Museum Complex.
Hours & Admission Prices: Tues.-Fri. 9-12; other times by appointment. Closed major holidays; Dec. 15-Feb. 1.
Attendance: 5,000 (actual)

THE R.W. NORTON ART GALLERY, 4747 Creswell Ave., Shreveport, LA 71106-1899. Tel.: 318-865-4201. Fax: 318-869-0435.
E-mail: gallery@rwnaf.org
Web Site: www.rwnaf.org
Key Personnel: C.E.O. & Pres. Bd. Control, M. Lewis Norton; Dir. Public Rels., Sec. & Treas., Jerry M. Bloomer; Bldg. & Grounds Supt., Gerry Ward.
Institution Type/Description: Art Museum & Gallery.
Hours & Admission Prices: Tues.-Fri. 10-5, Sat.-Sun. 1-5. Library: by appointment. No charge; donations accepted. Closed national holidays. &
Attendance: 26,609 (actual)

SCI-PORT: LOUISIANA'S SCIENCE CENTER, 820 Clyde Fant Pkwy., Shreveport, LA 71101-3667. Tel.: 318-424-3466. Fax: 318-222-5592. Facebook: Sci-Port.
E-mail: jmcmen@sciport.org
Web Site: www.sciport.org
Formerly: Sci-Port Discovery Center
Key Personnel: Pres. & C.E.O., Ann Fumarolo; Dir. Devel. & Mktg., Jennifer McMenamin; Museum Shop Mgr., Jessica Turner.
Institution Type/Description: Science Museum.
Hours & Admission Prices: March-May Tues.-Sat. 9-5, Sun. 12-5; June-Aug. Mon.-Sat. 9-5, Sun. 12-5; Sept.-Feb. Wed.-Sat. 9-5, Sun. 12-5. Sci-Port: adults $13, children 3-12, seniors & military $10; discounts to groups or more; members no charge. IMAX: adults $9.50, children 3-12, seniors & military $8.50; discounts to members & groups of 15 or more. Center & IMAX: adults $23, seniors & military $19, children 3-12 $18; discounts to groups of 15 or more. Closed Easter; Thanksgiving; Christmas. &
Attendance: 170,000 (estimated)

SHREVEPORT WATER WORKS MUSEUM, 142 N. Common St., Shreveport, LA 71101-2614. Mailing Address: State of Louisiana, Secretary of State, P.O. Box 94125, Baton Rouge, LA 70804-9125. Tel.: 318-221-3388.
E-mail: mcneill1887@gmail.com
Web Site: www.shreveportwaterworks.org
Formerly: McNeill Street Pumping Station Museum
Key Personnel: Chm. (V), Dale Ward.
Institution Type/Description: Water Works Museum.
Hours & Admission Prices: Tues.-Sat. 10-4, Sun. 12-4. No charge. Closed most state holidays.
Attendance: 5,000 (actual)

SOUTHERN UNIVERSITY MUSEUM OF ART IN SHREVEPORT, 3050 Martin Luther King, Jr. Dr., Shreveport, LA 71107. Tel.: 318-670-6000.
E-mail: afeaster@susla.edu
Institution Type/Description: Art Museum.
Hours & Admission Prices: Tues.-Fri. 10-5, Sat. 10-4; groups by appointment. No charge.

SPRING STREET HISTORICAL MUSEUM, 525 Spring St., Shreveport, LA 71101-3231. Mailing Address: State of Louisiana, Secretary of State, P.O. Box 94125, Baton Rouge, LA 70804-9125. Tel.: 318-424-0964. Fax: 318-424-0964.
E-mail: mloschen@sos.la.gov
Web Site: www.sos.louisiana.gov/sshm
Key Personnel: Dir., Marty Loschen.
Institution Type/Description: History Museum.
Hours & Admission Prices: Wed.-Fri. 10-4; group tours by appointment. No charge. Closed most state holidays. &
Attendance: 1,356 (actual)

STAGE OF STARS MUSEUM, 705 Elvis Presley Ave., Shreveport, LA 71101. Mailing Address: 9068 Melody Ln., Shreveport, LA 71118. Tel.: 318-222-9391, 800-551-8682.
Institution Type/Description: History Museum.
Hours & Admission Prices: Call for hours.

STEPHENS AFRICAN-AMERICAN MUSEUM, 2810 Lindholm, Shreveport, LA 71108-2610. Tel.: 318-635-2147. Fax: 318-635-2147.
Key Personnel: C.E.O., Chm. (V) & Pres. (V), Spencer Stephens; Museum Shop Mgr., Gwendolyn Frazier.
Institution Type/Description: Art Museum.
Hours & Admission Prices: Tues.-Sat. 12-4. Adults $2, senior citizens $1.75, students & children $1; discounts to AAM & ICOM members; members no charge. Closed Independence Day; Easter; Christmas. &
Attendance: 15,000 (estimated)

WALTER B. JACOBS MEMORIAL NATURE PARK, 8012 Blanchard Furrh Rd., Shreveport, LA 71107-8310. Tel.: 318-929-2806. Fax: 318-929-3718.
E-mail: rscarborough@caddo.org
Web Site: www.caddoparks.com/memorial.cfm
Key Personnel: Dir., Larry R. Raymond; Sr. Park Naturalist, Rusty Scarborough; Park Naturalist, Rachel Demascal; Park Naturalist, Kimberly Warren; Park Naturalist, Stacy Gray; Park Naturalist, Halya Onel.
Institution Type/Description: Nature Park & Interpretive Center.

Hours & Admission Prices: Wed.-Sat. 8-5, Sun. 1-5. No charge. Closed New Year's Day; Easter; Thanksgiving; Christmas. &
Attendance: 13,063 (actual)

Slidell

SLIDELL CULTURAL CENTER, 2055 Second St., Slidell, LA 70458-3430. Mailing Address: P.O. Box 828, Slidell, LA 70459-0828. Tel.: 985-646-4375. Fax: 985-646-4231.
E-mail: kbergeron@cityofslidell.org
Web Site: slidell.la.us
Institution Type/Description: Art Center.
Hours & Admission Prices: Call for hours. No charge; donations accepted. Closed New Year's Day; Martin Luther King Jr. Day; Mardi Gras; Good Friday; Memorial Day; Independence Day; Labor Day; Thanksgiving; Christmas Eve & Day. &
Attendance: 7,000 (estimated)

SLIDELL MUSEUM, 2020 First St., Slidell, LA 70458-3402. Mailing Address: P.O. Box 828, Slidell, LA 70459-0828. Tel.: 985-646-4380. Fax: 985-646-6107.
E-mail: cityslidell@charter.net
Web Site: www.slidell.la.us
Key Personnel: Financial Dir., Sharon Howes; Cur., Reinhard Dearing.
Institution Type/Description: History Museum: housed in the city's original town hall & jail built in 1907.
Hours & Admission Prices: Tues.-Sat. 9-4. No charge; donations accepted. Closed city holidays.
Attendance: 1,500 (actual)

Sorrento

LOUISIANA POTTERY MUSEUM, 6470 Hwy. 22, Cajun Village, Sorrento, LA 70778. Tel.: 225-675-5572.
E-mail: lapottery@cox.net
Web Site: www.louisianapottery.com
Key Personnel: Dir., Judy L. Starrett.
Institution Type/Description: General Museum: housed in an Acadian style home; c.1830.
Hours & Admission Prices: Tues.-Sun. 10-5. No charge. &

Sulphur

BRIMSTONE MUSEUM, 900 S. Huntington St., Sulphur, LA 70663-4420. Tel.: 337-527-0357. Fax: 337-527-0359.
E-mail: trahan@brimstonemuseum.org
Web Site: www.brimstonemuseum.org
Key Personnel: Pres., Randall Broussard; Dir., Thomas Trahan.
Institution Type/Description: History Museum: housed in 1915 railroad station.
Hours & Admission Prices: By appointment. No charge; donations accepted. Closed New Year's Eve & Day; Good Friday; Memorial Day; Independence Day; Labor Day; Thanksgiving weekend; Christmas Eve & Day. &
Attendance: 7,600 (actual)

HENNING CULTURAL CENTER, 923 S. Ruth St., Sulphur, LA 70663. Tel.: 337-527-0537.
E-mail: manuel@brimstonemuseum.org
Institution Type/Description: Art Center.
Hours & Admission Prices: Mon.-Fri. 10-12 & 1-5, Sat. 10-2.

Tallulah

HERMIONE MUSEUM, 315 N. Mulberry, Tallulah, LA 71282-3828. Mailing Address: P.O. Box 268, Tallulah, LA 71284-0268. Tel.: 318-574-0082. Fax: 318-574-0082.
E-mail: hermionemuseum@bayou.com
Key Personnel: Dir. & Museum Shop Mgr., John Earl Martin; Cur., Geneva Williams; Pres. (V), Charles M. Finlayson.
Institution Type/Description: Historic House Museum.
Hours & Admission Prices: Tues.-Fri. 10-4. No charge; donations accepted. &
Attendance: 1,000 (estimated)

Tangipahoa

CAMP MOORE CONFEDERATE CEMETERY AND MUSEUM, 70640 Camp Moore Rd., Tangipahoa, LA 70465. Mailing Address: P.O. Box 25, Tangipahoa, LA 70465-0025. Tel.: 985-229-2438.
E-mail: manager@campmoorela.com

Web Site: www.campmoorela.com
Key Personnel: Dir., Kevin J. Miller.
Institution Type/Description: History Museum.
Hours & Admission Prices: Wed.-Sat. 10-3. Adults $5, students $3; discounts to F.O.C.M. members; children under 6 no charge. Closed all major holidays.
Attendance: 1,500 (estimated)

Thibodaux

E. D. WHITE HISTORIC SITE, 2295 LA Hwy. 1, Thibodaux, LA 70301. Tel.: 985-447-0915. Fax: 985-447-4249.
Institution Type/Description: Historic House: housed in the former home of Gov. Edward Douglas White, and his son, Chief Justice Edward Douglass White. A National Historic Landmark.
Hours & Admission Prices: Tues.-Sat. 10-4:30. No charge; donations accepted. Closed major holidays.
Attendance: 3,513 (actual)

Vacherie

LAURA: A CREOLE PLANTATION, 2247 Hwy. 18, River Rd., Vacherie, LA 70090. Tel.: 888-799-7690, 225-265-7690. Fax: 225-265-7960.
E-mail: info@lauraplantation.com
Web Site: www.lauraplantation.com
Institution Type/Description: Historic House: built in 1840.
Hours & Admission Prices: Guided Tours: daily by appointment. Adults $20, students 6-17 $6; discounts to AAA, military & National Trust members; children 5 & under no charge. Closed New Year's Day; Mardi Gras Day; Easter; Thanksgiving; Christmas.

OAK ALLEY PLANTATION, 3645 Hwy. 18, Vacherie, LA 70090. Tel.: 225-265-2151. Fax: 225-265-7035.
E-mail: contactus@oakalleyplantation.com
Web Site: www.oakalleyplantation.org
Key Personnel: Dir., Zeb Mayhew, Jr.; Chm. (V), Shelby Saer.
Institution Type/Description: Historic Mansion.
Hours & Admission Prices: Mon.-Fri. 10-4, Sat.-Sun. 10-5. Adults 19 & over $20, students 13-18 $7.50, children 6-12 $4.50; members & their guest no charge. Closed New Year's Day; Mardi Gras Day; Thanksgiving; Christmas. ⅃
Attendance: 226,809 (actual)

ST. JOSEPH PLANTATION, 3535 Hwy. 18, Vacherie, LA 70090. Tel.: 225-265-4078. Fax: 225-265-4843. Facebook: St. Joseph Plantation.
E-mail: stjoe@stjosephplantation.com
Web Site: www.stjosephplantation.com
Institution Type/Description: Historic House: built c.1830.
Hours & Admission Prices: Mon.-Sat. 9:30-5. Adults $15, youth 13-18 $7, children 6-12 $5; children under 6 no charge. Closed New Year's Day; Easter; Independence Day; Labor Day; Thanksgiving; Christmas Eve & Day.

Ville Platte

LOUISIANA ARBORETUM, STATE PRESERVATION AREA, 1300 Sudie Lawton Lane, Ville Platte, LA 70586-7527. Tel.: 337-363-6289 & 888-677-6100. Fax: 337-363-5616.
E-mail: arboretum@crt.la.us
Web Site: www.louisianaarboretum.wordpress.com
Key Personnel: Interpretive Naturalist, Eric Bush; Cur., Kim Hollier; Horticulturist, Emma Debenport.
Institution Type/Description: Arboretum.
Hours & Admission Prices: Daily 9-5. No charge. Closed New Year's Day; Thanksgiving; Christmas. ⅃
Attendance: 7,500 (actual)

LOUISIANA SWAMP POP MUSEUM, 205 N.W. Railroad Ave., Ville Platte, LA 70586. Mailing Address: P.O. Box 390, Ville Platte, LA 70586. Tel.: 337-363-0900. Facebook: Louisiana Swamp Pop Museum.
E-mail: laswamppop@gmail.com
Key Personnel: Dir., Janie Knighten.
Institution Type/Description: Music History Museum.
Hours & Admission Prices: Fri.-Sat. 10-3. Adults $3, seniors 60 & over $2. ⅃
Attendance: 350 (estimated)

Wallace

WHITNEY PLANTATION MUSEUM, 5099 Hwy. 18, Wallace, LA 70049. Tel.: 504-586-0003, 617-406-9225.
E-mail: jim@ornana.com
Web Site: whitneyplantation.com
Key Personnel: Owner & Cur., John Cummings.
Institution Type/Description: Historic Plantation: 1790 home.
Hours & Admission Prices: By appointment.

Washington

WASHINGTON MUSEUM & TOURIST CENTER, 404 N. Main St., Washington, LA 70589. Mailing Address: P.O. Box 597, Washington, LA 70589-0597. Tel.: 337-826-3627. Fax: 337-826-3601. Facebook: Washington Museum.
E-mail: towtourism@bellsouth.net
Web Site: washington-la.org
Key Personnel: Dir. Tourism, Danielle Kazemi; Cur., Deborah Joubert; Cur., Lienola Chelette.
Institution Type/Description: History Museum.
Hours & Admission Prices: Daily 8-12 & 1-4. No charge.
Attendance: 1,000 (estimated)

West Monroe

OUACHITA RIVER ART GALLERY, 308 Trenton St., West Monroe, LA 71291. Tel.: 318-322-2380.
E-mail: wharolds@whidbey.com
Institution Type/Description: Art Gallery.
Hours & Admission Prices: Tues.-Sat. 10-5.

Westwego

WESTWEGO HISTORICAL MUSEUM, 275 Sala Ave., Westwego, LA 70094-3650. Tel.: 504-341-3161. Fax: 504-341-2570.
E-mail: info@cityofwestwego.com
Key Personnel: Museum Coord., Lori Guin.
Institution Type/Description: History Museum.
Hours & Admission Prices: Mon.-Tues. & Thurs.-Fri. 8-4, Wed. & Sat. 10-4; groups by appointment. Adults $3, seniors & children under 12 $2; discounts to groups of 10 or more; society members no charge.

White Castle

NOTTOWAY PLANTATION AND RESORT, 31025 Louisiana Hwy. 1, White Castle, LA 70788. Tel.: 866-527-6884, 225-545-2730. Fax: 225-545-8632. Facebook: Nottoway Plantation.
E-mail: info@nottoway.com
Web Site: www.nottoway.com
Key Personnel: Gen. Mgr., Neil Castaldi; Mansion Cur. & Historian, Marie Stagg; Dir. Sales, Susan Ringwald.
Institution Type/Description: Historic House: built in 1859. Listed on the National Register of Historic Places.
Hours & Admission Prices: Guided Tours: daily 9-4. Adults $20, children under 12 $6; discounts to seniors, military & AAA members. Grounds: adults $8; children under 12 no charge. ⅃

Winnfield

LOUISIANA POLITICAL MUSEUM AND HALL OF FAME, 499 E. Main St., Winnfield, LA 71483-3224. Tel.: 318-628-5928. Fax: 318-628-2551. Facebook: Friends of the Louisiana Political Museum.
E-mail: lapolmus@bellsouth.net
Web Site: www.lapoliticalmuseum.com
Key Personnel: Dir., Carolyn Phillips.
Institution Type/Description: Political History Museum.
Hours & Admission Prices: Mon.-Fri. 9-5, Sat. by appointment. No charge; donations accepted. ⅃
Attendance: 7,500 (estimated)

Winnsboro

THE OLD POST OFFICE MUSEUM, 513 Prairie St., Winnsboro, LA 71295. Tel.: 318-435-3781.
E-mail: contact@oldpostofficemuseum.com
Institution Type/Description: Historic Building: built in 1936.
Hours & Admission Prices: Mon.-Fri; other times by appointment. 9-5. No charge.

Zachary

ZACHARY HISTORIC VILLAGE, 4524 Virginia St., Zachary, LA 70791. Mailing Address: P.O. Box 1144, Zachary, LA 70791. Tel.: 225-654-1912.
Web Site: zachary.la.www.net/historical
Key Personnel: Dir., Lois Hastings.
Institution Type/Description: Historic Village.
Hours & Admission Prices: Mon.-Fri. 9-4; groups by appointment. Suggested Donation: $2 per person.

MAINE
(238 listings)

Allagash

ALLAGASH HISTORICAL SOCIETY MUSEUM, 456 Dickey Rd., Allagash, ME 04774-4113. Tel.: 207-398-3148 & 3278. Fax: 207-398-3148.
E-mail: marilyn.mcbreairty@yahoo.com
Key Personnel: Dir., Linda McBreairty; Pres. (V), Marilyn McBreairty.
Institution Type/Description: History Museum.
Hours & Admission Prices: Memorial Day to Labor Day Fri.-Sun. 1-5; other times by appointment. No charge; donations accepted. ⑃
Attendance: 25 (estimated)

Alna

WISCASSET, WATERVILLE & FARMINGTON RAILWAY MUSEUM, 97 Cross Rd., Alna, ME 04535. Mailing Address: P.O. Box 242, Alna, ME 04535-0242. Tel.: 207-563-2516.
E-mail: info@wwfry.org
Web Site: www.wwfry.org
Key Personnel: Pres., Stephen T. Zuppa; Membership, Michael Fox; Treas., James Patten; Archivist & Museum Shop Mgr., Linda Zollers.
Institution Type/Description: Operating Narrow Gauge Railroad Museum.
Hours & Admission Prices: Memorial Day to Columbus Day Sat.-Sun. 9-5; Oct.-May Sat. 9-5. Museum: no charge. Steam Train Rides (May-Oct. only): adults $7, seniors $6, children $4; children 3 & under no charge. ⑃
Attendance: 4,900 (actual)

Ashland

ASHLAND LOGGING MUSEUM, INC., 267 Garfield Rd., Ashland, ME 04732-5105. Mailing Address: P.O. Box 631, Ashland, ME 04732-0866. Tel.: 207-435-6679. Fax: 207-435-6579.
Web Site: www.townofashland.com/Ashland_Logging_Museum.htm
Key Personnel: Pres. (V), Robert Sawyer, V; Vice Pres., Robert Sawyer, IV; Cur., Ed Chase.
Institution Type/Description: Logging Museum: housed in a reproduction of an early logging camp.
Hours & Admission Prices: Fri. 1-4; other times by appointment. No charge; donations accepted.
Attendance: 500

Athens

ATHENS HISTORICAL SOCIETY MUSEUM, Chapman Ridge Rd., Athens, ME 04912. Mailing Address: P.O. Box 230, Athens, ME 04912-0230. Tel.: 207-654-2393.
Institution Type/Description: Historical Society Museum: housed in the former Somerset Academy building. Listed on the National Register of Historic Places.
Hours & Admission Prices: Call for hours.

Auburn

ANDROSCOGGIN HISTORICAL SOCIETY, 2 Turner St. Unit 8, Auburn, ME 04210-5978. Tel.: 207-784-0586.
E-mail: info@androhist.org
Web Site: www.androhist.org
Key Personnel: Pres., Douglas Hodgkin; Treas., David Chittim.
Institution Type/Description: Historical Society Museum.
Hours & Admission Prices: Wed.-Thurs. 1-4:30, Fri. 1-4. No charge. Library research fee for non-members; society members no charge. Closed national holidays. ⑃
Attendance: 200 (actual)

Augusta

BLAINE HOUSE, 192 State St., Augusta, ME 04330-6406. Tel.: 207-624-7500.
E-mail: info@blainehouse.org
Key Personnel: Dir., Paula Benoit.
Institution Type/Description: Historic House: 1830-1833 Blaine House, governor's mansion of Maine.
Hours & Admission Prices: Tues.-Thurs. 2-4; tours on the half-hour. No charge. Closed national holidays. ⑃
Attendance: 10,500 (actual)

CHILDREN'S DISCOVERY MUSEUM, 171 Capitol St., Ste. 2, Augusta, ME 04330-4615. Tel.: 207-622-2209.
E-mail: info@childrensdiscoverymuseum.org
Web Site: www.childrensdiscoverymuseum.org
Key Personnel: Dir. & Museum Shop Mgr., Carne Arsenault; Chm. (V) & Pres. (V), Melissa Merfeld.
Institution Type/Description: Children's Museum.
Hours & Admission Prices: Tues.-Thurs. 10-4, Fri.-Sat. 10-5, Sun. 11-4. Children $5.50, adults $4.50; infants under 12 months no charge. ⑃
Attendance: 25,000 (estimated)

KENNEBEC HISTORICAL SOCIETY, 107 Winthrop St., Augusta, ME 04332. Mailing Address: P.O. Box 5582, Augusta, ME 04332-5582. Tel.: 207-622-7718. Fax: 207-622-7718.
E-mail: mail@kennebechistorical.org
Web Site: www.kennebechistorical.org
Institution Type/Description: Historical Society Museum.
Hours & Admission Prices: Wed.-Fri. 10-2.

MAINE STATE MUSEUM, State House Complex, 230 State St., Augusta, ME 04333-0083. Mailing Address: 83 State House Station, Augusta, ME 04333-0083. Tel.: 207-287-2301. Fax: 207-287-6633.
E-mail: maine.museum@maine.gov
Web Site: www.mainestatemuseum.org
Key Personnel: Dir., Bernard Fishman; Deputy Dir., Sheila McDonald; Chief Scientist, David Work; Acting Cur. Photography, Ben Stickney; Chief Cur. History & Decorative Arts, Laurie LaBar; Cur. Historical Collections, Angela Goebel-Bain; Cur. Natural History Archaeology, Paula Work; Chief Educator, Joanna Torow; Museum Store Mgr., Colleen Freise.
Institution Type/Description: General Museum.
Hours & Admission Prices: Tues.-Fri. 9-5, Sat. 10-4. Adults $3, seniors & children 6-18 $2; discounts to AAM members; members & children under 6 no charge. Closed state holidays. ⑃
Attendance: 49,023 (actual)

OLD FORT WESTERN, 16 Cony St., Augusta, ME 04330-5200. Tel.: 207-626-2385. Fax: 207-620-8150.
E-mail: oldfort@oldfortwestern.org
Web Site: www.oldfortwestern.org
Key Personnel: Dir. & Cur. Collections, Linda J. Novak; Chair, Tom Doore.
Institution Type/Description: Living History Museum & National Landmark.
Hours & Admission Prices: June Fri.-Mon. 10-4; July-Aug. daily 10-4; Sept.-Oct. Fri.-Mon. 10-4. Family $25, adults $10, seniors & veterans $8, children 6-14 $6; discounts to AAA members; active military, children under 6 & members no charge. ⑃
Attendance: 4,000

Bangor

BANGOR MUSEUM AND HISTORY CENTER, 159 Union St., Bangor, ME 04401-6147. Tel.: 207-942-1900. Fax: 207-942-1910.
E-mail: info@bangormuseum.org
Web Site: www.bangormuseum.org
Formerly: Thomas A. Hill Historical House and Civil War Museum
Key Personnel: Exec. Dir., Jennifer Pictou; Pres. (V), Michael Aube; Dir. Museum Operations, Dana Lippitt.
Institution Type/Description: History Museum.
Hours & Admission Prices: June-Sept. Tues.-Fri. 10-4; other times by appointment. Adults $5, senior citizens $4; discounts to students, AAA, AAM & NEMA members; children & members no charge. Closed national holidays.
Attendance: 2,800 (actual)

BANGOR POLICE MUSEUM, 240 Main, Bangor, ME 04401. Mailing Address: P.O. Box 4, Dixmont, ME 04932-0004. Tel.: 207-947-7384.
E-mail: bangor.police@bangormaine.gov
Institution Type/Description: Police History Museum.

Hours & Admission Prices: Mon.-Fri. 8-5.
Attendance: 2,000 (estimated)

COLE LAND TRANSPORTATION MUSEUM, 405 Perry Rd., Bangor, ME 04401-6725. Mailing Address: 359 Perry Rd., Bangor, ME 04401-6723. Tel.: 207-990-3600. Fax: 207-990-2653. Facebook: Cole Land Transportation Museum.
E-mail: mail@colemuseum.com
Web Site: www.colemuseum.org
Key Personnel: Chm. (V) & Pres. (V), Garret E. Cole; Projects Mgr., Christopher Thorne; Museum Shop Mgr., Pat Trice.
Institution Type/Description: Transportation Museum & the WWII, Korean & Vietnam Veterans Memorial.
Hours & Admission Prices: May-Nov. 11 daily 9-5. Adults $7, senior citizens $5; discounts to AAA members; students & children under 19 no charge. &
Attendance: 17,410 (actual)

HOSE 5 FIRE MUSEUM, 247 State St., Bangor, ME 04401-5418. Mailing Address: P.O. Box 25, Bangor, ME 04401. Tel.: 207-945-3229.
Web Site: www.bangormaine.gov/cs_ps_hose5museum.php
Institution Type/Description: Fire Museum.
Hours & Admission Prices: Call for hours; tours by appointment. No charge; donations accepted.

MAINE AVIATION HISTORICAL SOCIETY - MAINE AIR MUSEUM, 98 Maine Ave., Bangor, ME 04401. Mailing Address: P.O. Box 2641, Bangor, ME 04401. Tel.: 207-941-6757.
E-mail: mam@maineairmuseum.com
Web Site: www.maineairmuseum.com/page/955-722/contact-maine-air-museum
Key Personnel: Pres. (V) & Museum Shop Mgr., Charles W. Byrum.
Institution Type/Description: History Museum.
Hours & Admission Prices: Memorial Day to Sept. Sat. 10-4, Sun. 12-4; call for additional hours. Families $10, adults $6, children under 12 $1; discounts for members; active duty military no charge. &
Attendance: 300 (estimated)

MAINE DISCOVERY MUSEUM, 74 Main St., Bangor, ME 04401-6304. Tel.: 207-262-7200.
E-mail: nparker@mainediscoverymuseum.org
Web Site: www.mainediscoverymuseum.org
Key Personnel: Exec. Dir., Niles Parker.
Institution Type/Description: Children's Museum.
Hours & Admission Prices: Winter: Tues.-Sat. 10-5:30, Sun. 12-5; Summer: call for extended hours; groups by appointment. Adults $7.50; discounts to groups; members and children one & under no charge. ACM reciprocal program & ASTC Passport program. &
Attendance: 65,000 (estimated)

UNIVERSITY OF MAINE MUSEUM OF ART, 40 Harlow St., Bangor, ME 04401-5102. Tel.: 207-561-3350. Fax: 207-561-3351. Facebook: University of Maine Museum of Art.
E-mail: george.kinghorn@umit.maine.edu
Web Site: www.umma.umaine.edu
Key Personnel: Museum Dir., George Kinghorn; Asst. Museum Coord. & Membership Mgr., Kathryn Jovanelli; Exhibits Preparator, Sharon LeFevre; Education Coord., Kat Johnson; Museum Technician, Aaron Pyle.
Institution Type/Description: Art Museum: housed in downtown Bangor's historic Norumbega Hall.
Hours & Admission Prices: Mon.-Sat. 10-5. No charge; donations accepted. Closed major holidays. &
Attendance: 14,000 (actual)

Bar Harbor

ABBE MUSEUM, 26 Mount Desert St. & Sieur de Monts Spring, Acadia National Park, Bar Harbor, ME 04609. Mailing Address: P.O. Box 286, Bar Harbor, ME 04609-0286. Tel.: 207-288-3519. Fax: 207-288-8979.
E-mail: info@abbemuseum.org
Web Site: www.abbemuseum.org
Key Personnel: C.E.O., Cinnamon Catlin-Legutko; Pres. Bd., Sandy Wilcox, Ph.D.; Vice Pres., Ann Cox-Halkett; Museum Shop Mgr., Allison Shank; Business Mgr., John Brown; Collections Mgr., Julia Gray; Public Affairs, Heather Anderson.
Institution Type/Description: Archaeology, Anthropology & Ethnology Museum: located on site at Sieur de Monts Spring, within Acadia National Park and downtown Bar Harbor at 26 Mount Desert Street.

Hours & Admission Prices: Sieur de Monts: May-Oct. daily 10-5. Mount Desert St.: May-Oct. daily 10-5; Nov.-April Thurs.-Sat. 10-4. Adults $8, children $4; AAM & museum members no charge. &
Attendance: 30,000 (actual)

BAR HARBOR HISTORICAL SOCIETY, 33 Ledgelawn Ave., Bar Harbor, ME 04609-1303. Tel.: 207-288-0000 & 3807. Facebook: Bar Harbor Historical Society.
E-mail: bhhistorical@gwi.net
Web Site: barharborhistorical.org
Key Personnel: Pres. (V), Sherwood Carr; Cur., Debbie Dyer.
Institution Type/Description: Local History Museum.
Hours & Admission Prices: mid-June to mid-Oct. Mon.-Fri. 1-4. No charge; donations accepted. Closed holidays.
Attendance: 1,500 (actual)

BAR HARBOR WHALE MUSEUM, 52 West St., Bar Harbor, ME 04609-1858. Mailing Address: c/o Allied Whale, College of the Atlantic, 105 Eden St., Bar Harbor, ME 04609-1136. Tel.: 207-288-0288. Fax: 207-288-3218.
E-mail: whalemuseum@coa.edu
Web Site: barharborwhalemuseum.org
Key Personnel: Dir. & Cur., Toby Stephenson; Museum Shop Mgr., Mindy Viechnicki.
Institution Type/Description: Natural History Museum.
Hours & Admission Prices: June & Sept.-Oct. daily 10-8; July-Aug. daily 9-9. No charge; donations accepted. &
Attendance: 70,000 (actual)

GEORGE B. DORR MUSEUM OF NATURAL HISTORY, 105 Eden St., College of the Atlantic, Bar Harbor, ME 04609-1136. Tel.: 207-288-5395. Fax: 207-288-2917.
E-mail: museum@coa.edu
Web Site: www.coa.edu/dorr-museum-microsite.htm
Formerly: The Natural History Museum
Key Personnel: College Pres., Darron Collins; Dir., Dr. Stephen Ressel; Program Dir., Dianne Clendaniel.
Institution Type/Description: Natural History Museum.
Hours & Admission Prices: Tues.-Sat. 10-5. No charge; donations accepted. &
Attendance: 10,000 (estimated)

MOUNT DESERT OCEANARIUM, 1351 State Rte. 3, Bar Harbor, ME 04609. Mailing Address: P.O. Box 696, Southwest Harbor, ME 04679. Tel.: 207-288-5005.
E-mail: theoceanarium@earthlink.com
Web Site: theoceanarium.com
Key Personnel: C.E.O. & Co Dir., David K. Mills; Co Dir. & Museum Shop Mgr., Audrey S. Mills.
Institution Type/Description: Oceanarium.
Hours & Admission Prices: Call for hours & admission prices. &

SIEUR DE MONTS SPRINGS NATURE CENTER, Acadia National Park, Rte. 233, Eagle Lake Rd., Bar Harbor, ME 04609. Mailing Address: P.O. Box 177, Bar Harbor, ME 04609-0177. Tel.: 207-288-3338. Fax: 207-288-8813.
E-mail: acadia_information@nps.gov
Institution Type/Description: Nature Center & Botanical Gardens.
Hours & Admission Prices: May call for hours; June-Aug. 9-5; Sept. to early Oct. 9-4. No charge. &
Attendance: 65,500 (estimated)

WILLIAM OTIS SAWTELLE COLLECTIONS AND RESEARCH CENTER, Acadia National Park, 20 McFarlund Hill Dr., Bar Harbor, ME 04609. Mailing Address: Acadia National Park, P.O. Box 177, Bar Harbor, ME 04609-0177. Tel.: 207-288-8729. Fax: 207-288-8709.
E-mail: rebecca_cole-will@nps.gov
Web Site: www.nps.gov/acad/historyculture/collections.htm
Key Personnel: Supt., Sheridan Steele.
Institution Type/Description: Research Center.
Hours & Admission Prices: Tues.-Fri. 8:30-3:30 by appointment only. No charge. &
Attendance: 70 (actual)

Bath

MAINE MARITIME MUSEUM, 243 Washington St., Bath, ME 04530-1638. Tel.: 207-443-1316. Fax: 207-443-1665.

E-mail: reservations@maritimeme.org
Web Site: mainemaritimemuseum.org
Key Personnel: Exec. Dir., Amy Lent; Dir. Finance, Jackie Berry; Cur., Dir. Library & Archivist, Nathan Lipfert; Cur. Exhibits, Chris Hall; Dir. Public Programs, Jason Morin; Volunteer Coord., Ann Harrison; Education Coord., James Nelson.
Institution Type/Description: Maritime Museum & Historic Shipyard.
Hours & Admission Prices: Daily 9:30-5. Adults $12, seniors $11, children 4-17 $9; discounts to groups, AAM, ICOM & CAMM members; children under 4, museum members & staff no charge. Closed New Year's Day; Thanksgiving & Christmas. &
Attendance: 40,000 (actual)

Belfast

BELFAST HISTORICAL SOCIETY AND MUSEUM, 10 Market St., Belfast, ME 04915-6555. Tel.: 207-338-9229.
E-mail: info@belfastmuseum.org
Web Site: belfastmuseum.org
Institution Type/Description: Historical Society Museum.
Hours & Admission Prices: late June to Labor Day Tues.-Sat. 11-4. No charge; donations accepted.
Attendance: 1,000 (actual)

Belmont

GREENE PLANTATION HISTORICAL SOCIETY, 169 Howard Rd., Belmont, ME 04952. Tel.: 207-342-5208.
E-mail: mareshme@fairpoint.net
Key Personnel: Dir. & Archivist, Isabel Morse Maresh; Pres., Eugene Newton, Jr.
Institution Type/Description: Historical Society Museum: housed in a former one-room schoolhouse; built in 1908. Listed on the National Register of Historic Places.
Hours & Admission Prices: By appointment. No charge; donations accepted.
Attendance: 75 (estimated)

Bethel

BETHEL HISTORICAL SOCIETY, 10 Broad St., Bethel, ME 04217-0012. Mailing Address: P.O. Box 12, Bethel, ME 04217-0012. Tel.: 207-824-2908, 800-824-2910. Fax: 207-824-0882.
E-mail: info@bethelhistorical.org
Web Site: www.bethelhistorical.org
Formerly: Bethel Historical Society Regional History Center
Key Personnel: Exec. Dir., Randall H. Bennett; Pres. (V), Tineke Ouwinga; Librarian & Archivist, William F. Chapman; Administrative Asst. & Museum Shop Mgr., Danna B. Nickerson.
Institution Type/Description: Local Regional History Center: housed in Robinson House; built in 1821.
Hours & Admission Prices: Jan.-June, Sept., Oct. & Dec. Tues.-Fri. 10-4; July & Aug. Sat. 1-4. Period House: adults $3; discounts to AAM members; members no charge; Robinson House: no charge. &
Attendance: 5,000 (estimated)

DR. MOSES MASON HOUSE, 14 Broad St., Bethel, ME 04217. Mailing Address: P.O. Box 12, Bethel, ME 04217. Tel.: 207-824-2908, 800-824-2910.
Institution Type/Description: Historical Society Museum: housed in the former home of Dr. Moses Mason; built in 1813.
Hours & Admission Prices: July-Aug. Tues.-Sun. 1-4; Sept.-June by appointment. Adults $3, children 6-12 $1.50; member no charge.

MAINE MINERAL AND GEM MUSEUM, 99 Main St., Bethel, ME 04217. Mailing Address: P.O. Box 500, Bethel, ME 04217. Tel.: 207-824-3036.
E-mail: info@mainemineralmuseum.org
Web Site: mainemineralmuseum.com
Institution Type/Description: Mineral & Gem Museum.
Hours & Admission Prices: Call for hours.

Biddeford

BIDDEFORD HISTORICAL SOCIETY, McArthur Library, 270 Main St., Biddeford, ME 04005. Mailing Address: P.O. Box 200, Biddeford, ME 04005-0200.
E-mail: info@biddefordhistoricalsociety.org
Web Site: www.biddefordhistoricalsociety.org
Institution Type/Description: Historical Society Museum.
Hours & Admission Prices: Call for hours.

HEARTWOOD COLLEGE OF ART MAIN GALLERY, 2 Main St., Bldg. 18, Ste. 230, North Dam Mill, Biddeford, ME 04005. Tel.: 207-307-2171.
Web Site: www.heartwoodcollegeofart.org
Key Personnel: Pres., Berri Kramer.
Institution Type/Description: Art Gallery.
Hours & Admission Prices: Mon.-Fri. 9-4.

Bingham

OLD CANADA ROAD HISTORICAL SOCIETY, 16 Sidney St., Bingham, ME 04920. Mailing Address: P.O. Box 742, Bingham, ME 04920. Tel.: 207-672-3440.
E-mail: ocrhs@oldcanadaroad.org
Web Site: www.oldcanadaroad.org
Institution Type/Description: Historical Society Museum.
Hours & Admission Prices: Fri. 1-5, Sat. 11-4. No charge; donations accepted.

Blue Hill

BLUE HILL HISTORICAL SOCIETY, Water St., Blue Hill, ME 04614. Mailing Address: P.O. Box 710, Blue Hill, ME 04614-0710.
E-mail: info@bluehistory.org
Web Site: www.bluehillhistory.org
Institution Type/Description: Historical Society Museum: housed in Holt House, built in 1815.
Hours & Admission Prices: Summer: Tues. & Fri. 1-4, Sat. 11-2. No charge; donations accepted.
Attendance: 300 (estimated)

THE JONATHAN FISHER MEMORIAL, INC., 44 Mines Rd., Blue Hill, ME 04614. Mailing Address: P.O. Box 537, Blue Hill, ME 04614-0537. Tel.: 207-374-2459. Fax: 207-374-5082.
E-mail: info@jonathanfisherhouse.org
Web Site: www.jonathanfisherhouse.org
Formerly: Parson Fisher House
Key Personnel: Pres. (V), Brad Emerson.
Institution Type/Description: Historic House: 1814 Jonathan Fisher House.
Hours & Admission Prices: July 5-Sept. 7 Wed.-Sat. 1-4; Sept. 13-Oct. 19 Fri.-Sat. 1-4; other times by appointment. No charge; donations accepted. &
Attendance: 350 (estimated)

Boothbay

BOOTHBAY RAILWAY VILLAGE, 586 Wiscasset Rd., Boothbay, ME 04537. Mailing Address: P.O. Box 123, Boothbay, ME 04537-0123. Tel.: 207-633-4727. Fax: 207-633-4733 (call first).
E-mail: staff@railwayvillage.org
Web Site: www.railwayvillage.org
Key Personnel: Dir., Robert Ryan; Sec. & Museum Shop Mgr., Maureen H. Stormont.
Institution Type/Description: Transportation Museum.
Hours & Admission Prices: Memorial Day to mid-June Sat.-Sun. 9:30-5; mid-June to mid-Oct. daily 9:30-5. Adults $10, children $5; members no charge. &
Attendance: 25,000 (actual)

Boothbay Harbor

BOOTHBAY REGION ART FOUNDATION, INC., One Townsend Ave., Boothbay Harbor, ME 04538-1765. Mailing Address: P.O. Box 124, Boothbay Harbor, ME 04538-0124. Tel.: 207-633-2703.
E-mail: braf@boothbayartists.org
Web Site: www.boothbayartists.org
Key Personnel: Pres. of Trustees, Sally Giddings Smith.
Institution Type/Description: Art Gallery.
Hours & Admission Prices: Mon.-Sat. 10-5, Sun. 1-5. No charge; donations suggested.
Attendance: 10,000 (estimated)

BOOTHBAY REGION HISTORICAL SOCIETY, 72 Oak St., Boothbay Harbor, ME 04538. Mailing Address: P.O. Box 272, Boothbay Harbor, ME 04538-0272. Tel.: 207-633-0820.
E-mail: brhs@gwi.net
Web Site: www.boothbayhistorical.org
Key Personnel: Dir., Barbara Rumsey.
Institution Type/Description: Historical Society Museum: house built in 1874.

Hours & Admission Prices: Thurs.-Sat. 10-2. No charge; donations accepted.
Attendance: 1,500 (estimated)

Bradley

MAINE FOREST AND LOGGING MUSEUM, 686 Government Rd., Bradley, ME 04411. Mailing Address: P.O. Box 104, Bradley, ME 04411-0104. Tel.: 207-974-6278. Facebook: Maine Forest and Logging Museum.
E-mail: info@maineforestandloggingmuseum.org
Web Site: www.maineforestandloggingmuseum.org
Key Personnel: Dir., Sherry Davis; Bd. Pres., Melissa Doane.
Institution Type/Description: Forestry Museum.
Hours & Admission Prices: Ground: daily during daylight hours; tours by appointment. See website for events & demonstrations.

Brewer

BREWER HISTORICAL SOCIETY'S CLEWLEY MUSEUM, 199 Wilson St., Brewer, ME 04412-2029. Tel.: 207-989-6165.
E-mail: brewerhistoricalsociety@gmail.com
Web Site: brewerhistoricalsociety.org
Key Personnel: Pres. (V), Charlotte Thompson.
Institution Type/Description: History Museum.
Hours & Admission Prices: Museum: by appointment. No charge; donations accepted.

Bridgton

BRIDGTON HISTORICAL SOCIETY, 5 Gibbs Ave., Bridgton, ME 04009. Mailing Address: P.O. Box 44, Bridgton, ME 04009-0044. Tel.: 207-647-3699 (Gibbs Ave. museum) & 9954 (Narramissic).
E-mail: info@bridgtonhistory.org
Web Site: www.bridgtonhistory.org
Key Personnel: Pres. (V), Ned Allen.
Institution Type/Description: Historical Society Museum & Historic House Museum: housed in 1902 former firehouse.
Hours & Admission Prices: Call for hours & admission prices. &

THE RUFUS PORTER MUSEUM AND CULTURAL HERITAGE CENTER, 121 Main St., Bridgton, ME 04009-1111. Mailing Address: P.O. Box 544, Bridgton, ME 04009-0544. Tel.: 207-647-2828. Facebook.
E-mail: rufusportermuseum@myfairpoint.net
Web Site: www.rufusportermuseum.org
Key Personnel: Co-Pres., Beth Cossey; Co-Pres., Margaret Lindsey Sanborn; Dir. & Cur., Martha Cummings; Museum Shop Mgr., Virginia Eilertson.
Institution Type/Description: History Museum.
Hours & Admission Prices: June-Oct. Thurs. 12-4, Fri.-Sat. 10-4; other times by appointment. Adults $8, seniors & students $7; discounts to groups and AAM & ICOM members; children 12 & under no charge. &
Attendance: 350 (estimated)

Brunswick

BOWDOIN COLLEGE MUSEUM OF ART, Walker Art Bldg., Brunswick, ME 04011. Mailing Address: 9400 College Station, Brunswick, ME 04011-8494. Tel.: 207-725-3275. Fax: 207-725-3762.
E-mail: artmuseum@bowdoin.edu
Web Site: www.bowdoin.edu/art-museum
Key Personnel: Co Dir., Anne Collins Goodyear; Co Dir., Frank Goodyear; Asst. Dir. Operations, Rebekah Beaulieu; Asst. Dir. Communications, Suzanne Bergeron; Cur., Joachim Homann; Museum Shop Mgr., Liza Nelson.
Institution Type/Description: Art Museum: housed in 1894, Walker Art Building, designed by Charles Follen McKim, located on the campus of Bowdoin College.
Hours & Admission Prices: Tues.-Wed. & Fri.-Sat. 10-5, Thurs. 10-8:30, Sun. 1-5. No charge; donations accepted. Closed national holidays. &
Attendance: 45,000 (actual)

ICON CONTEMPORARY ART, 19 Mason St., Brunswick, ME 04011. Tel.: 207-725-8157.
Institution Type/Description: Art Gallery.
Hours & Admission Prices: Mon.-Fri. 1-5, Sat. 1-4. No charge.

THE PEARY-MACMILLAN ARCTIC MUSEUM, Bowdoin College, 9500 College Station, Brunswick, ME 04011-8495. Tel.:

207-725-3416 & 3062. Fax: 207-725-3499. Facebook: Arctic Museum.
E-mail: skaplan@bowdoin.edu
Web Site: www.bowdoin.edu/arctic-museum
Key Personnel: Dir., Dr. Susan A. Kaplan; Technician & Designer, David R. Maschino; Museum Outreach & Svcs. Coord., James Tanzer; Cur., Dr. Genevieve LeMoine; Asst. to the Dir., Julie Santorella; Asst. Cur., Michael Quigley; Exhibit Tech., Steve Bunn.
Institution Type/Description: College Museum.
Hours & Admission Prices: Tues.-Sat. 10-5, Sun. 2-5. No charge; donations accepted. Closed national holidays.
Attendance: 14,709 (actual)

PEJEPSCOT HISTORICAL SOCIETY, 159 Park Row, Brunswick, ME 04011-2005. Tel.: 207-729-6606.
E-mail: info@pejepscothistorical.org
Web Site: www.pejepscothistorical.org
Institution Type/Description: Historical Society Museums.
Hours & Admission Prices: Skolfield-Whittier House: Memorial Day to Columbus Day Wed.-Sat. Tours 10 & 4. Adults $12, children $6; discounts to seniors 65 & over, active military & AAA members. Chamberlain House: Memorial Day to Columbus Day Tues.-Sat. 10-4, Sun. 1-4; Oct. to Veterans Day Fri.-Sat. 10-4, Sun. 1-4. Adults $12, children $6; discounts to seniors 65 & over, active military & AAA members. Combination tickets to both houses available. Pejepscot Museum: Memorial Day to Columbus Day Tues.-Sat. 10-4; Oct.-May Wed.-Fri. 10-4. No charge; donations accepted. Closed holidays. &
Attendance: 5,000 (actual)

Bryant Pond

WOODSTOCK HISTORICAL SOCIETY, 21 N. Main St., Bryant Pond, ME 04219-6424. Mailing Address: P.O. Box 317, Bryant Pond, ME 04219-0317.
E-mail: woodstockhistoricalsociety.me89@yahoo.com
Key Personnel: Pres. (V), Olive Risko; Treas., Paul Billings; Cur., Larry Billings.
Institution Type/Description: Historical Society Museum.
Hours & Admission Prices: June-Aug. Sat. 2-5; Other times by appointment by calling Woodstock Town Office; No charge; donations accepted.
Attendance: 250 (estimated)

Bucksport

BUCKSPORT HISTORICAL SOCIETY, INC., 379 Main St., Bucksport, ME 04416. Mailing Address: P.O. Box 206, Bucksport, ME 04416. Tel.: 207-469-0924.
E-mail: info@mainehistory.org
Institution Type/Description: General Museum: housed in 1874 Old Maine Central Railroad Station.
Hours & Admission Prices: July-Aug. Wed.-Fri. 1-4; other times by appointment. Admission $1; members no charge. &
Attendance: 350 (actual)

NORTHEAST HISTORIC FILM, 85 Main St., Bucksport, ME 04416. Mailing Address: P.O. Box 900, Bucksport, ME 04416-0900. Tel.: 207-469-0924.
E-mail: nhf@oldfilm.org
Web Site: www.oldfilm.org
Key Personnel: Exec. Dir., Brook Minner.
Institution Type/Description: Historic Building: housed in a 1916 cinema, The Alamo Theatre.
Hours & Admission Prices: Mon.-Fri. 9-4; call for additional hours. No charge; donations accepted. &
Attendance: 15,000 (estimated)

Burlington

STEWART M. LORD MEMORIAL HISTORICAL SOCIETY, INC., Rte. 188, Burlington, ME 04417. Mailing Address: P.O. Box 367, Howland, ME 04448-0367. Tel.: 207-732-3129.
E-mail: info@smlmhs.org
Web Site: www.smlmhs.org
Key Personnel: Cur., Fern P. Cummings.
Institution Type/Description: History Museum.
Hours & Admission Prices: July-Labor Day Sun. 2-4; other times by appointment. No charge; donations accepted. &
Attendance: 145 (estimated)

Calais

DR. JOB HOLMES COTTAGE AND MUSEUM - ST. CROIX HISTORICAL SOCIETY, 527 Main St., Calais, ME 04619. Tel.: 207-454-3061.
E-mail: schs@stcroixhistorical.com
Web Site: stcroixhistorical.com/holmescottage
Institution Type/Description: Historic House Museum; housed in the former home & office of Dr. Job Holmes from 1846-1864; built c.1790s.
Hours & Admission Prices: July-Aug. call for hours. No charge; donations accepted.

Cape Elizabeth

PORTLAND HEAD LIGHT MUSEUM, 1000 Shore Rd., Cape Elizabeth, ME 04107. Mailing Address: P.O. Box 6260, Cape Elizabeth, ME 04107. Tel.: 207-799-2661. Fax: 207-799-2800.
E-mail: cephl@aol.com
Web Site: www.portlandheadlight.com
Institution Type/Description: Historic Building: c.1790 lighthouse.
Hours & Admission Prices: late April to May & Nov. to early Dec. Sat.-Sun. 10-4; Memorial Day to Oct. daily 10-4. Adults $2, children 6-18 $1; children under 6 no charge.

Caribou

THE NYLANDER MUSEUM OF NATURAL HISTORY, 657 Main St., Caribou, ME 04736. Tel.: 207-493-5923.
E-mail: nylandermuseum@gmail.com
Web Site: nylander.mainememory.net
Key Personnel: Exec. Dir., Jeanie McGowan.
Institution Type/Description: Natural History Museum.
Hours & Admission Prices: Sat.-Sun. 1-3; other times by appointment. No charge; donations accepted.
Attendance: 701 (actual)

THOMAS HERITAGE HOUSE, 444 Main St., Caribou, ME 04736. Mailing Address: P.O. Box 446, Caribou, ME 04736. Tel.: 207-496-3011. Fax: 207-493-3188.
Institution Type/Description: Historic House Museum.
Hours & Admission Prices: By appointment.

Casco

RAYMOND-CASCO HISTORICAL SOCIETY MUSEUM, Shadow Lane, Rte. 302, Casco, ME 04015. Mailing Address: P.O. Box 1055, Raymond, ME 04071. Tel.: 207-655-7672.
E-mail: pamelawgrant@msn.com
Web Site: raymondcascohistory.org
Key Personnel: RCHS Pres., Pamela Grants.
Institution Type/Description: Historical Society Museum.
Hours & Admission Prices: Wed., Sat.-Sun. 1-3. No charge; donations accepted.
Attendance: 800 (estimated)

Castine

CASTINE SCIENTIFIC SOCIETY AKA WILSON MUSEUM, 120 Perkins St., Castine, ME 04421. Mailing Address: P.O. Box 196, Castine, ME 04421-0196. Tel.: 207-326-9247. Fax: 207-326-9237.
E-mail: info@wilsonmuseum.org
Web Site: www.wilsonmuseum.org
Key Personnel: Dir., Patricia Hutchins; Administrative Asst., Debra Morehouse.
Institution Type/Description: History Museum.
Hours & Admission Prices: Perkins House & Blacksmith Shop: July-Aug. Wed. & Sun. 2-5. Perkins House: $5 per person; discounts to National Trust, NEMA Institutional staff, AAM & AAA members. Blacksmith Shop: no charge. Wilson Museum: May 27 to Sept. Mon.-Fri. 10-5, Sat.-Sun. 2-5. No charge; donations accepted.
Attendance: 4,000 (estimated)

Chebeague Island

MUSEUM OF CHEBEAGUE HISTORY, 137 South Rd., Chebeague Island, ME 04017-3100. Tel.: 207-846-5237.
E-mail: history@chebeague.net
Institution Type/Description: History Museum: built in 1871.
Hours & Admission Prices: Tues.-Sun. 1-6. No charge; donations accepted.
Attendance: 1,200 (actual)

Cherryfield

CHERRYFIELD NARRAGUAGUS HISTORICAL SOCIETY, 88 River Rd., Cherryfield, ME 04622. Mailing Address: P.O. Box 122, Cherryfield, ME 04622-0122. Tel.: 207-546-2076.
E-mail: info@cherryfieldhistorical.com
Web Site: www.cherryfieldhistorical.com
Institution Type/Description: Historical Society Museum.
Hours & Admission Prices: Call for hours.

Columbia Falls

RUGGLES HOUSE SOCIETY, 1/4 mile off U.S. Rte. 1, 146 Main St., Columbia Falls, ME 04623. Mailing Address: 298 Tenan Lane, Cherryfield, ME 04622-4334. Tel.: 207-483-4637 & 546-7903. Facebook: The Ruggles House.
E-mail: etenan@ruggleshouse.org
Web Site: www.ruggleshouse.org
Key Personnel: Pres. (V), Larry D. Smith, Sr.; Sec., Ellen Tenan.
Institution Type/Description: Historic House Museum: housed in the former home of Judge Thomas Ruggles; built in 1818.
Hours & Admission Prices: June to mid-Oct. Mon.-Sat. 10-4, Sun. 12-4. Adults $5, children $2. Closed Independence Day; Labor Day.
Attendance: 1,800 (estimated)

Corinth

CORINTH HISTORICAL SOCIETY, Old Grange Hall, 306 Main St., Corinth, ME 04427. Mailing Address: P.O. Box 541, Corinth, ME 04427-0541. Facebook: Corinth Historical Society.
E-mail: pilgrimpt@zoho.com
Web Site: www.facebook.com/corinth-historical-society-180191645371371/.
Key Personnel: Pres. & Cur., Betty LaForge.
Institution Type/Description: Historical Society Museum: built in 1907.
Hours & Admission Prices: June 6 to Sept. 5 Wed. 2-7; other times by appointment. No charge; donations accepted.
Attendance: 200 (estimated)

Deer Isle

DEER ISLE-STONINGTON HISTORICAL SOCIETY, 416 Sunset Rd., Deer Isle, ME 04627. Mailing Address: P.O. Box 652, Deer Isle, ME 04627-0652. Tel.: 207-348-6400.
E-mail: dishs.info@gmail.com
Web Site: www.dis-historicalsociety.org
Key Personnel: Pres. (V), Susan A. Greenlaw.
Institution Type/Description: History Museum.
Hours & Admission Prices: mid-June to mid-Sept. Wed.-Fri. 1-4; Oct.-May Wed. & Fri. 1-4 for research only. No charge; donations accepted.
Attendance: 400 (estimated)

Dennysville

ACADEMY/VESTRY MUSEUM - DENNYS RIVER HISTORICAL SOCIETY, 115 Main St., Dennysville, ME 04628. Mailing Address: P.O. Box 11, Dennysville, ME 04628-0011. Tel.: 207-726-3905 & 5258. Facebook.
E-mail: arhs@myfairpoint.net
Key Personnel: Pres., Ronald A. Windhorst; Treas., Barbara J. Ward; Dir. Programs & Devel., Colin J.C. Windhorst; Cur. & Sec., Melinda Jaques.
Institution Type/Description: History Museum.
Hours & Admission Prices: Lincoln Memorial Library: Tues.-Fri. 1-4. Academy/ Vestry Museum: Memorial Day to Columbus Day Sat. 1-4; other times by appointment. No charge; donations accepted. Closed national & state holidays.
Attendance: 276 (actual)

Dexter

DEXTER HISTORICAL SOCIETY CAMPUS, 3 Water St., Dexter, ME 04930. Mailing Address: P.O. Box 481, Dexter, ME 04930-0481. Tel.: 207-924-5721.
E-mail: info@dexterhistoricalsociety.com
Web Site: dexterhistoricalsociety.com
Formerly: Dexter Historical Society Museum
Key Personnel: Dir. & Cur., Richard Whitney.
Institution Type/Description: General Museum: housed in 1854 Grist Mill, located on the site 1818 canal.
Hours & Admission Prices: mid-June to Labor Day Mon.-Fri. 10-4, Sat. 1-4, Sun. & holidays by appointment. Abbott Museum: Memorial Day to Columbus Day

Mon.-Sat. 10-4; Oct.-May Wed.-Fri. 1-4. Sat. 10-4. No charge; donations accepted. Closed Independence Day. &
Attendance: 2,000 (estimated)

Dover-Foxcroft

BLACKSMITH SHOP MUSEUM, 107 Dawes Rd., Dover-Foxcroft, ME 04426-3732. Tel.: 207-564-8618.
E-mail: dlockwood3@myfairpoint.net
Web Site: doverfoxcrofthistoricalsociety.org
Key Personnel: Pres. (V), Mary Annis; Cur., Dave Lockwood; Treas., James Annis; Sec., Priscilla Higgins.
Institution Type/Description: Historic Building: 1863 Blacksmith Shop.
Hours & Admission Prices: May-Oct. daily 8am-7pm. No charge; donations accepted.
Attendance: 250 (estimated)

OBSERVER BUILDING MUSEUM - DOVER-FOXCROFT HISTORICAL SOCIETY, Union Square, Dover-Foxcroft, ME 04426. Mailing Address: 28 Orchard Rd., Dove-Foxcroft, ME 04426. Tel.: 207-564-0820. Facebook.
E-mail: mannis@myfairpoint.net
Web Site: dover-foxcrofthistoricalsociety.org
Key Personnel: C.E.O., Chm. (V) & Pres (V), Mary Annis; Cur., Dennis Lyford; Cur., Dave Lockwood.
Institution Type/Description: Historical Society Museum: housed in the former county newspaper company building; built in 1854. Listed on the National Register of Historic Places.
Hours & Admission Prices: Summer: Thurs. 11-2; other times by appointment. No charge; donations accepted.
Attendance: 400 (estimated)

Dresden

1761 POWNALBOROUGH COURTHOUSE, 23 Courthouse Rd., Rte. 128, Dresden, ME 04342. Mailing Address: P.O. Box 61, Wiscasset, ME 04578-0061. Tel.: 207-737-2504 & 882-6817.
E-mail: lcha@wiscasset.net
Web Site: www.lincolncountyhistory.org
Key Personnel: Court House Chm., Steve Eagles; Pres. (V), John Rienhardt.
Institution Type/Description: Historic Building: 1761 Pownalborough Court House.
Hours & Admission Prices: Memorial Day to June & Sept.-Columbus Day Sat. 10-4, Sun. 12-4; July-Aug. Tues.-Fri. 10-4. Adults $4; members no charge.
Attendance: 1,000 (estimated)

East Vassalboro

VASSALBORO HISTORICAL SOCIETY MUSEUM, Rte. 32, East Vassalboro, ME 04935. Mailing Address: P.O. Box 43, East Vassalboro, ME 04935. Tel.: 207-923-3533 & 3505.
Key Personnel: Cur., Julie Lyon.
Institution Type/Description: Historical Society Museum.
Hours & Admission Prices: May-Nov. 2nd & 4th Sun. of the month 1-4; other times by appointment. &

Easton

FRANCIS MALCOLM SCIENCE CENTER, 776 Houlton Rd., Easton, ME 04740. Mailing Address: P.O. Box 186, Easton, ME 04740. Tel.: 207-488-5451. Fax: 207-488-2951.
E-mail: info@francismalcolmsciencecenter.com
Web Site: www.francismalcolmsciencecenter.com
Institution Type/Description: Science Center.
Hours & Admission Prices: late Aug. to mid-June Tues.-Fri. 9-3 by appointment.

Eastport

BORDER HISTORICAL SOCIETY, 14 Key St., Eastport, ME 04631. Mailing Address: P.O. Box 95, Eastport, ME 04631-0095. Tel.: 207-853-2963.
E-mail: borderhistoricalsociety@yahoo.com
Web Site: borderhistoricalsociety.com
Key Personnel: Pres., Phyllis Siebert; Museum Mgr., Eleanor Norton; Museum, Cory Critchley.
Institution Type/Description: Historical Society Museum.
Hours & Admission Prices: Call for hours. No charge; donations accepted.

RAYE'S MUSTARD MILL MUSEUM, 83 Washington St., Eastport, ME 04631. Mailing Address: P.O. Box 2, Eastport, ME 04631. Tel.: 207-853-4451, 800-853-1903.
E-mail: mustards@rayesmustard.com
Web Site: rayesmustard.com/pages/mustard-mill-museum
Institution Type/Description: Historic Building: housed in a working stone ground mustard mill.
Hours & Admission Prices: Tours: Mon.-Fri. 10-3 by appointment.

TIDES INSTITUTE & MUSEUM OF ART, 43 Water St., Eastport, ME 04631. Mailing Address: P.O. Box 161, Eastport, ME 04631. Tel.: 207-853-4047.
E-mail: tides@tidesinstitute.org
Web Site: www.tidesinstitute.org
Key Personnel: Dir., Hugh French; Dir. Programs, Jude Valentine; Exhibitions, Kristin McKinlay.
Institution Type/Description: Historic Building: housed in a former bank building; built in 1887.
Hours & Admission Prices: Tues.-Sun. 10-4.

Ellsworth

STANWOOD WILDLIFE SANCTUARY, Rte. 3 289 High St., Ellsworth, ME 04605. Mailing Address: P.O. Box 485, Ellsworth, ME 04605-0485. Tel.: 207-667-8460.
E-mail: birdsacre@hotmail.com
Web Site: www.birdsacre.com
Key Personnel: Pres. (V) & Museum Shop Mgr., Grayson Richmond; Chm. (V), Donald Knowles.
Institution Type/Description: Homestead Museum & Nature Center: home of Cordelia Stanwood, pioneer naturalist, photographer & conservationist.
Hours & Admission Prices: Sanctuary: daily dawn-dark. Homestead Museum & Nature Center: June to mid-Oct. daily 10-4. No charge; donations accepted. Closed Independence Day; Labor Day. &
Attendance: 10,000 (estimated)

THE TELEPHONE MUSEUM, 166 Winkumpaugh Rd., Ellsworth, ME 04605-3035. Mailing Address: P.O. Box 1377, Ellsworth, ME 04605-1377. Tel.: 207-667-9491.
E-mail: switchboard@nemot.net
Web Site: www.thetelephonemuseum.org
Key Personnel: Dir. & Pres. (V), Sandra Galley; Treas., Bryan McLellan.
Institution Type/Description: Communications Museum.
Hours & Admission Prices: June & Oct. by appointment only; July-Sept. Sat. 1-4 or by appointment. Adults $10, children $5. &
Attendance: 350 (estimated)

WOODLAWN: MUSEUM GARDENS & PARK, 19 Black House Dr., Ellsworth, ME 04605-2320. Mailing Address: P.O. Box 1478, Ellsworth, ME 04605-1478. Tel.: 207-667-8671. Fax: 207-667-7950.
E-mail: director@woodlawnmuseum.org
Web Site: www.woodlawnmuseum.org
Formerly: Woodlawn Museum/The Black House
Key Personnel: Exec. Dir., Joshua C. Torrance; Chm. (V), Terry Carlisle.
Institution Type/Description: Historic House: 1827 Black Family House.
Hours & Admission Prices: May & Oct. Tues.-Sun. 1-4; June-Sept. Tues.-Sat. 10-5, Sun. 1-4. Tours every hour. Adults $10, children $3; discount to AAA & AAM members; members & public park no charge. Closed Independence Day.
Attendance: 10,000 (estimated)

Fairfield

FAIRFIELD HISTORY HOUSE - THE COTTON-SMITH HOUSE, 42 High St., Fairfield, ME 04937. Tel.: 207-453-2998.
E-mail: fhs2@myfairpoint.net
Web Site: www.fairfieldmehistoricalsociety.net
Key Personnel: Pres. (V), Douglas Cutchin.
Institution Type/Description: Historic House: built c.1890.
Hours & Admission Prices: March-Nov. Tues. & 2nd Sat.10-3; other times by appointment. No charge; donations accepted.
Attendance: 480 (estimated)

Falmouth

THE FALMOUTH HISTORICAL SOCIETY, 60 Woods Rd., Falmouth, ME 04102. Mailing Address: 190 U.S. Rte. 1, Unit 3, Falmouth, ME 04105-1313. Tel.: 207-781-4727.
E-mail: falmouthhistorical@myfairpoint.net

Web Site: www.falmouthmehistory.org
Key Personnel: Pres., Scott McLeod; Vice Pres., Janice Delima.
Institution Type/Description: Historical Society Museum.
Hours & Admission Prices: Call for hours.

Farmington

NORDICA HOMESTEAD, 116 Nordica Lane, Farmington, ME
  04938. Mailing Address: c/o Franklin County Savings Bank, P.O.
  Box 825, Farmington, ME 04938-0825. Tel.: 207-778-2042.
E-mail: lilliannordica@gmail.com
Web Site: www.lilliannordica.com
Key Personnel: C.E.O. & Pres. (V), Tom Sawyer; Vice Pres. & Publicity Dir.,
  Marion Smith; Treas., Cindy Wright.
Institution Type/Description: Historical Society Museum: housed in c.1840 Nordica
  Homestead.
Hours & Admission Prices: June-Sept. 15 Tues.-Sat. 10-12 & 1-5, Sun. 1-5;
  Sept.16-Oct. 15 by appointment only. Adults $2, children $1; discounts to AAA
  members & school children groups; children under 6 no charge. &
Attendance: 700 (estimated)

Franklin

FRANKLIN HISTORICAL SOCIETY, Rte. 200, Sullivan Rd.,
  Franklin, ME 04634. Mailing Address: P.O. Box 317, Franklin,
  ME 04634-0317. Tel.: 207-565-3635. Fax: 207-565-3323.
Institution Type/Description: Historical Society Museum: housed in Old East
  Franklin Church.
Hours & Admission Prices: late June to Labor Day Sat. 2-4; other times by appoint-
  ment. No charge; donations accepted. &
Attendance: 90

Freeport

DESERT OF MAINE & BARN MUSEUM, 95 Desert Rd.,
  Freeport, ME 04032. Tel.: 207-865-6962.
E-mail: info@desertofmaine.com
Web Site: www.desertofmaine.com
Institution Type/Description: History Museum.
Hours & Admission Prices: May to mid-Oct. daily 9-5:30. Adults $10.50, teens 13-
  16 $7.75, children 4-12 $6.75.

FREEPORT HISTORICAL SOCIETY, 45 Main St., Freeport, ME
  04032-1212. Tel.: 207-865-3170. Facebook: Freeport Historical
  Society.
E-mail: info@freeporthistoricalsociety.org
Web Site: www.freeporthistoricalsociety.org
Key Personnel: Pres. (V), Andrea Martin; Exec. Dir., Jim Cram.
Institution Type/Description: Historical Society Museum.
Hours & Admission Prices: Office: Mon.-Fri. 8:30-5. Archives: Winter: Wed.-Fri.
  9-5; Summer: Mon.-Fri. 9-5; other times by appointment. Suggested Donation:
  $5 per person. Closed all major federal & state holidays.
Attendance: 2,000 (estimated)

Frenchboro

**FRENCHBORO LIBRARY AND THE FRENCHBORO
  HISTORICAL SOCIETY,** Schoolhouse Hill, Frenchboro, ME
  04635. Tel.: 207-334-2924.
Web Site: www.frenchboro.lib.me.us
Key Personnel: Pres. (V), Sandra Lunt; Museum Shop Mgr., Donna Hasal.
Institution Type/Description: History Museum & Library.
Hours & Admission Prices: Library: daily. Society: mid-June to Sept. Mon.-Fri. 1-
  5. No charge; donations accepted.

Friendship

FRIENDSHIP MUSEUM INC., 1 Martin Point Rd., Friendship, ME
  04547. Mailing Address: P.O. Box 226, Friendship, ME 04547.
E-mail: info@friendshipmuseum.org
Web Site: www.friendshipmuseum.org
Key Personnel: Pres. (v), Margaret W. Gagnon.
Institution Type/Description: History Museum: housed in a former one-room
  schoolhouse, 1851-1923.
Hours & Admission Prices: late June to Labor Day Mon.-Sat. 1-4, Sun. 2-4; Sept. to
  Columbus Day Sat. 1-4, Sun. 2-4. No charge; donations accepted.
Attendance: 451 (estimated)

Fryeburg

FRYEBURG FAIR FARM MUSEUM, 113 N. Fryeburg Rd.,
  Fryeburg, ME 04037. Tel.: 207-935-3268. Fax: 207-935-3662.
E-mail: info@fryeburgfair.org
Web Site: www.fryeburgfair.org
Key Personnel: Cur., Edward W. Jones; Asst. Cur., Diane L. Jones.
Institution Type/Description: Agricultural Museum: housed in 1832 barn & carriage
  house.
Hours & Admission Prices: Daily 9-9; school tours by appointment. Adults $10;
  children under 12 no charge. &
Attendance: 50,000

FRYEBURG HISTORICAL SOCIETY, 83 Portland St., Fryeburg,
  ME 04037. Tel.: 207-256-3001.
E-mail: fryeburg_historical_society@netwcbc.com
Web Site: www.fryeburghistorical.org
Key Personnel: Pres. (V), Nancy D. Ray; Vice Pres. (V), Sally Whitaker; Sec.,
  Lonni Lewis; Treas., Judith DeMille; Bd. Member, Diane Jones; Bd. Member,
  Edward Jones; Bd. Member, June O'Donal; Bd. Member, Linda Drew.
Institution Type/Description: Historical Society Museum.
Hours & Admission Prices: Library: Tues. 10-2, Wed. 9-1, Thurs. 1-4; Museum:
  Tues. & Sat. 10-2; other times by appointment. No charge; donations accepted.

**THE PALMINA F. & STEPHEN S. PACE GALLERIES OF
  ART,** Leura Hill Eastman Performing Arts Center, 18 Bradley St.,
  Fryeburg, ME 04037. Mailing Address: Fryeburg Academy, 745
  Main St., Fryeburg, ME 04037. Tel.: 207-935-9232.
E-mail: jday@fryeburgacademy.org
Key Personnel: Dir., John M. Day.
Institution Type/Description: Art Gallery.
Hours & Admission Prices: Mon.-Fri. 9-1; other times by appointment. No charge.
  &
Attendance: 5,000 (estimated)

Gorham

BAXTER HOUSE MUSEUM, 67 South St., Gorham, ME 04038.
  Tel.: 207-839-3878. Fax: 207-839-7749.
E-mail: jrathbun@msln.net
Web Site: www.baxter-memorial.lib.me.us
Key Personnel: Guide, Chm. (V) & Pres. Bd. Library Trustees (V), Linda M.
  Frinsko.
Institution Type/Description: Historic House: c.1797 Baxter House.
Hours & Admission Prices: June-Aug. Tues. & Thurs. 10-1; other times by appoint-
  ment. No charge; donations accepted. &
Attendance: 300 (estimated)

GORHAM HISTORICAL SOCIETY, 28 School St., Gorham, ME
  04038. Mailing Address: P.O. Box 141, Gorham, ME 04038.
E-mail: society@gorhamhistorical.com
Web Site: gorhamhistorical.com
Institution Type/Description: Historical Society Museum.
Hours & Admission Prices: April-Oct. Thurs. 10-2; other times by appointment.

USM ART GALLERY, 37 College Ave., Gorham Campus, Gorham,
  ME 04038-1032. Tel.: 207-780-5460 & 5008. Fax: 207-780-5759.
  TDD: 207-780-5646.
E-mail: ceyler@maine.edu
Web Site: www.usm.maine.edu/~gallery
Key Personnel: Dir. Exhibits & Programs, Carolyn Eyler.
Institution Type/Description: Art Museum.
Hours & Admission Prices: Academic Year: Tues.-Sun. 12-4. No charge; donations
  accepted. &

Gouldsboro

GOULDSBORO HISTORICAL SOCIETY, 452 U.S. Rte. 1,
  Gouldsboro, ME 04607. Mailing Address: P.O. Box 94,
  Gouldsboro, ME 04607. Tel.: 207-963-7155.
E-mail: c.hodge@myfairpoint.net
Key Personnel: Pres. (V) & Chm. (V), Charles E. Hodge.
Institution Type/Description: Historical Society Museum: housed in the former
  Gouldsboro town hall; built in 1884.
Hours & Admission Prices: July-Aug. Sat. 2-4. No charge; donations accepted. &
Attendance: 400 (actual)

Gray

GRAY HISTORICAL SOCIETY, 1 Main St., Gray, ME 04039. Mailing Address: P.O. Box 544, Gray, ME 04039-0544. Tel.: 207-657-4783.
E-mail: pkttaylor@aol.com
Institution Type/Description: Historical Society Museum: housed in the Old Fire Barn.
Hours & Admission Prices: By appointment.

Greenville

MOOSEHEAD HISTORICAL SOCIETY AND MUSEUM, 444 Pritham Ave., Greenville, ME 04441-1116. Mailing Address: P.O. Box 1116, Greenville, ME 04441-1116. Tel.: 207-695-2909.
E-mail: mooseheadhistory@myfairpoint.net
Web Site: mooseheadhistory.org
Key Personnel: Exec. Dir., Suzanne M. AuClair.
Institution Type/Description: Historical Society & Museums.
Hours & Admission Prices: Eveleth-Crafts-Sheridan House & Lumberman's Museum: June-Sept. Wed.-Fri. 1-4. Adults $5; The Center for Moosehead History & Moosehead Aviation Museum: June-Oct. Thurs.-Sun. No charge; donations accepted.
Attendance: 2,000 (estimated)

MOOSEHEAD MARINE MUSEUM, 12 Lily Bay Rd., Greenville, ME 04441. Mailing Address: P.O. Box 1151, Greenville, ME 04441-1151. Tel.: 207-695-2716. Facebook.
E-mail: info@katahdincruises.com
Web Site: katahdincruises.com
Key Personnel: Dir., Pres. (V) & Museum Shop Mgr., Liz McKeil.
Institution Type/Description: Marine Museum.
Hours & Admission Prices: Hours & cruise rates available at website. ♿
Attendance: 7,500 (actual)

Hallowell

HARLOW GALLERY, KENNEBEC VALLEY ART ASSOCIATION, 160 Water St., Hallowell, ME 04347-1315. Tel.: 207-622-3813. Facebook & Twitter: @harlowgallery.
E-mail: kvaa@harlowgallery.org
Web Site: harlowgallery.org
Key Personnel: C.E.O., Deborah Fahy; Pres. (V), Susan MacPherson; Vice Pres. (V), Helene Farrar; Sec. (V), Anne Young; Co-Treas. (V), Diana Scully; Gallery Mgr., Cassie Bouton; Public Rels. & Documentation Specialist, Allison McKeen.
Institution Type/Description: Art Gallery.
Hours & Admission Prices: Wed.-Sat. 12-6. No charge; donations accepted. Closed most holidays.
Attendance: 6,500 (estimated)

Hampden

HAMPDEN HISTORICAL SOCIETY - KINSLEY HOUSE, 83 Main Rd. S., Hampden, ME 04444. Mailing Address: P.O. Box 456, Hampden, ME 04444. Tel.: 207-862-2027. Facebook.
E-mail: hampdenhistorical@gmail.com
Key Personnel: Pres., Mary Poulin.
Institution Type/Description: Historical Society Museum: housed in the former home of Martin Kinsley; built in 1794.
Hours & Admission Prices: April-Oct. Tues. 10-4; other times by appointment. No charge; donations accepted. ♿
Attendance: 135 (estimated)

Harpswell

HARPSWELL HISTORICAL SOCIETY MUSEUM, 929 Harpswell Neck Rd., Harpswell, ME 04079. Mailing Address: 852 Harpswell Neck Rd., Harpswell, ME 04079. Tel.: 207-833-6322.
E-mail: harpshistory@gmail.com
Institution Type/Description: History Museum.
Hours & Admission Prices: Memorial Day to Columbus Day Sun. 2-4.

Harrison

SCRIBNER'S SAW MILL & HOMESTEAD MUSEUM, 244 Scribner's Mill Rd., Harrison, ME 04040. Mailing Address: P.O. Box 323, Harrison, ME 04040. Tel.: 207-583-6455.
E-mail: hatchscribml@gwi.net

Web Site: www.scribnersmill.org
Key Personnel: Pres. (V), Rick Johnson; Dir., Marilyn Hatch.
Institution Type/Description: Historic Buildings: mill & homestead; built in 1847.
Hours & Admission Prices: Memorial Day to Labor Day 1st & 3rd Sat. of month 1-4. Donations: adults $5 minimum. ♿
Attendance: 1,000 (estimated)

Hinckley

L.C. BATES MUSEUM, Good Will-Hinckley Home For Boys & Girls, Rte. 201, 14 Easler Rd., Hinckley, ME 04944-0159. Mailing Address: 14 Easler Rd., P.O. Box 159, Hinckley, ME 04944-0159. Tel.: 207-238-4250. Fax: 207-238-4007.
E-mail: lcbates@gwh.org
Web Site: www.gwh.org/html/lcbatesmuseum.htm
Key Personnel: Exec. Dir., Cur. & Museum Shop Mgr., Deborah Staber; Chm. (V), John Willey; Museum Educator, Serena Sandborn.
Institution Type/Description: Historic Building: built in 1903.
Hours & Admission Prices: April-Nov. Wed.-Sat. 10-4:30, Sun. 1-4:30; Dec.-March Wed.-Sat. 10-4:30; other times by appointment. Adults $3, youth under 18 $1; discounts to AAM & AAA members, MEMA & group tours; members no charge.
Attendance: 24,100 (actual)

Houlton

AROOSTOOK COUNTY HISTORICAL & ART MUSEUM, 109 Main St., Houlton, ME 04730-2123. Tel.: 207-532-2519.
E-mail: info@mainehistory.org
Institution Type/Description: Art & History Museum: housed in a Colonial Revival building; built in 1903. Listed on the National Register of Historic Places.
Hours & Admission Prices: Call for hours.

Indian Island

PENOBSCOT NATION MUSEUM, 12 Wabanaki Way, Indian Island, ME 04468. Tel.: 207-827-4153.
E-mail: museum@penobscotnation.org
Institution Type/Description: Native American Museum.
Hours & Admission Prices: Mon.-Thurs. 9-2, Sat. 10-3.

Island Falls

ISLAND FALLS HISTORICAL SOCIETY, 16 Nina Sawyer Ln., Island Falls, ME 04747. Mailing Address: P.O. Box 204, Island Falls, ME 04747. Tel.: 207-463-2264. Facebook.
E-mail: rdrew@katahdin.lib.me.us
Key Personnel: Pres., Gregory Ryan.
Institution Type/Description: Historical Society Museum.
Hours & Admission Prices: June to Labor Day Wed. 1-3; school groups & other times by appointment. No charge; donations accepted.
Attendance: 300 (estimated)

Islesboro

ISLESBORO HISTORICAL SOCIETY AND MUSEUM, 388 Main Rd., Islesboro, ME 04848. Mailing Address: P.O. Box 301, Islesboro, ME 04848-0301. Tel.: 207-734-6733.
E-mail: info@islesborohistorical.org
Web Site: www.islesborohistorical.org
Key Personnel: Pres. (V), Patrick O'Bannon.
Institution Type/Description: Historical & Preservation Society Museum: housed in 1894 Town Hall.
Hours & Admission Prices: Society: by appointment. Museum: July-Aug. Sat.-Wed. 12:30-4:30. No charge; donations accepted.
Attendance: 650 (actual)

SAILOR'S MEMORIAL MUSEUM, Grindle Point, Islesboro, ME 04848. Mailing Address: P.O. Box 76, Islesboro, ME 04848-0076. Tel.: 207-734-2253. Fax: 207-734-8394.
Institution Type/Description: Maritime Museum: housed in 1850 Lighthouse.
Hours & Admission Prices: mid-June to Labor Day Tues. 12-4:30, Wed.-Sun. 9:30-12 & 1-4:30. No charge; donations accepted. ♿
Attendance: 1,500 (estimated)

Islesford

ISLESFORD HISTORICAL MUSEUM, Little Cranberry Island, Islesford, ME 04646. Mailing Address: Acadia National Park, P.O. Box 177, Bar Harbor, ME 04609-0177. Tel.: 207-288-8729. Fax: 207-288-8709.
E-mail: marie_yarborough@nps.gov
Web Site: www.nps.gov/acad & www.islesfordhistoricalmuseum.info
Key Personnel: Supt., Sheridan Steele.
Institution Type/Description: History Museum.
Hours & Admission Prices: mid-June to Sept. Mon.-Sat. 9-12 & 12:30-3:30, Sun. 10:45-12 & 12:30-3:30. No charge; donations accepted.
Attendance: 14,935 (actual)

Jackman

JACKMAN - MOOSE RIVER VALLEY HISTORICAL SOCIETY, 574 Main St., Jackman, ME 04945. Mailing Address: P.O. Box 875, Jackman, ME 04945.
Key Personnel: Dir. & Pres. (V), Sheryl Harth.
Institution Type/Description: Historical Society Museum.
Hours & Admission Prices: mid-May to mid-Oct. No charge; donations accepted.
Attendance: 401 (actual)

Jay

JAY HISTORICAL SOCIETY, 14 Main St., Jay, ME 04239. Mailing Address: 287 Main St., Jay, ME 04239. Tel.: 207-897-4876. Fax: 207-897-9420.
E-mail: joffice@jay-maine.org
Web Site: www.jay-maine.org
Key Personnel: Pres. (V), Dorothy White.
Institution Type/Description: Historical Society Museum: housed in a Federal style home built in the 1820s.
Hours & Admission Prices: By appointment. No charge.
Attendance: 110 (estimated)

Jonesport

MAINE COAST SARDINE HISTORY MUSEUM, 34 Mason Bay Rd., Jonesport, ME 04649. Tel.: 207-497-2961.
E-mail: ronniep6@myfairpoint.net
Web Site: www.mainesardinemuseum.org
Key Personnel: Dir. & Chm. (V), Ronnie Peabody; Dir., Mary Peabody; Dir., Gary Ray.
Institution Type/Description: History Museum.
Hours & Admission Prices: Memorial Day to mid-Oct. Tues., Thurs. & Sun. 10-4; other times by appointment. Adults $4; discount to groups.
Attendance: 264 (actual)

Kennebunk

BRICK STORE MUSEUM, 117 Main St., Kennebunk, ME 04043-7088. Tel.: 207-985-4802. Facebook: Brick Store Museum.
E-mail: info@brickstoremuseum.org
Web Site: www.brickstoremuseum.org
Key Personnel: Exec. Dir., Cynthia Walker; Pres. Bd. Trustees, David Moravick; Archivist, Rosalind Magnuson; Registrar, Kathryn Hussey; Collections Mgr., Leanne Hayden; Devel. Coord., Deborah Williams.
Institution Type/Description: Local History Museum Complex: housed in 1825 William Lord's Brick Store building & three adjacent restored 19th-century buildings.
Hours & Admission Prices: Tues.-Fri. 10-4:30, Sat. 10-1. Adults $7.50, seniors $6, families $20; discounts to AAM, ICOM, NEMA & AAA members; members no charge. Closed holidays.
Attendance: 5,036 (actual)

Kennebunkport

KENNEBUNKPORT HISTORICAL SOCIETY, 125 North St., Kennebunkport, ME 04046. Mailing Address: P.O. Box 1173, Kennebunkport, ME 04046-1173. Tel.: 207-967-2751.
E-mail: kporths@roadrunner.com
Web Site: www.kporthistory.org
Key Personnel: Pres., David Micca; Treas., Diana Dakers; Exec. Admin., Kirsten Camp.
Institution Type/Description: Historic House & History Museum; housed in 1853 Greek Revival Nott House; c.1900 District 5 Schoolhouse.
Hours & Admission Prices: Town House School: Research Wed. & Fri. 10-1. Pasco Exhibit Center: July-Sept. Tues.-Fri. 9-3, Sat. 10-1; Oct.-June Tues.-Fri. 9-3.

Nott House: Memorial Day to Columbus Day Mon.-Sat. 10-4. Admission $10; members no charge. Closed holidays.
Attendance: 2,000 (estimated)

SEASHORE TROLLEY MUSEUM, 195 Log Cabin Rd., Kennebunkport, ME 04046-1690. Mailing Address: P.O. Box A, Kennebunkport, ME 04046-1690. Tel.: 207-967-2712. Fax: 207-967-0867.
E-mail: busi.ofc@neerhs.org
Web Site: www.trolleymuseum.org
Key Personnel: Chm. (V), James D. Schantz; Exec. Dir., Sally Bates; Treas. & Comptroller, Jeffrey N. Sisson; Museum Shop Mgr., Gayle Dion; Museum Shop Mgr., Birnie Bisnette.
Institution Type/Description: Electric Railway History & Technology Museum.
Hours & Admission Prices: May & Oct. Sat.-Sun. 10-5; Memorial Day to Columbus Day daily 10-5. Adults $10, seniors over 60 $8, children 6-16 $7.50; discounts to groups and AAM & ARM members; members and children 5 & under no charge.
Attendance: 19,000 (estimated)

Kingfield

THE SKI MUSEUM OF MAINE, 256 Main St., Kingfield, ME 04947. Mailing Address: P.O. Box 359, Kingfield, ME 04947. Tel.: 207-265-2023.
E-mail: info@skimuseumofmaine.org
Web Site: www.skimuseumofmaine.org
Key Personnel: Exec. Dir., Theresa Shanahan.
Institution Type/Description: Ski Museum.
Hours & Admission Prices: Call for hours.

STANLEY MUSEUM, INC., 40 School St., Kingfield, ME 04947. Mailing Address: P.O. Box 77, Kingfield, ME 04947-0077. Tel.: 207-265-2729. Fax: 207-265-4700.
E-mail: maine@stanleymuseum.org
Web Site: www.stanleymuseum.org
Key Personnel: Exec. Dir., Debbie Smith; Vice Chm., John Linderman; Archivist, Jim Merrick; Museum Shop Mgr., Kim Richmond White.
Institution Type/Description: History & Transportation Museum: housed in 1903 school designed by F.E. Stanley, inventor of the steam car.
Hours & Admission Prices: March-May & Nov. Tues.-Fri. 1-4; June-Oct. Tues.-Sun. 11-4; other times by appointment. Adults $4, seniors $3, children $2; discounts to AAM, AAA, & ICOM members; members no charge.
Attendance: 45,000 (actual)

Kittery

KITTERY HISTORICAL & NAVAL MUSEUM, 200 Rogers Rd. Ext., Kittery, ME 03904-1458. Mailing Address: P.O. Box 453, Kittery, ME 03904. Tel.: 207-439-3080. Facebook.
E-mail: kitterymuseum@netzero.net
Web Site: kitterymuseum.com
Key Personnel: Dir., Kim Sanborn.
Institution Type/Description: Naval & History Museum.
Hours & Admission Prices: June to Columbus Day Wed.-Sat. 10-4, Sun. 1-4; Nov.-May Wed. & Sat. 10-4 or by appointment. Family 2 adults with children under 15 $10, adults $5, children 7-15 $3; discounts to groups, seniors, military & AAA members; members no charge.
Attendance: 1,200 (actual)

Lewiston

BATES COLLEGE MUSEUM OF ART, 75 Russell St., Lewiston, ME 04240-6044. Tel.: 207-786-6158. Fax: 207-786-8335.
E-mail: museum@bates.edu
Web Site: www.bates.edu/museum.xml
Key Personnel: Dir., Dan Mills; Cur., William Low; Cur. Education, Anthony Shostak; Collections Mgr., Corie Audette.
Institution Type/Description: Art Museum.
Hours & Admission Prices: Mon.-Sat. 10-5. No charge. Closed major holidays.
Attendance: 19,700 (actual)

MUSEUM L-A, 35 Canal St., Lewiston, ME 04240-7775. Mailing Address: P.O. Box A7, Lewiston, ME 04240. Tel.: 207-333-3881. Fax: 207-376-3353.
E-mail: info@museumla.org
Web Site: museumla.org
Key Personnel: Exec. Dir., Rachel Desgrosseilliers.
Institution Type/Description: History Museum.

Hours & Admission Prices: Tues.-Fri. 10-4, Sat. 12-4; groups by appointment. Adults $5, seniors 62 & over $4, students $3; discounts to groups of 10 or more. Closed New Year's Day; Thanksgiving; Christmas Eve & Day. &

UNIVERSITY OF SOUTHERN MAINE - FRANCO-AMERICAN, 51 Westminster St., Rm. 153, Lewiston, ME 04240. Tel.: 207-753-6545.
E-mail: franco@usm.maine.edu
Web Site: usm.maine.edu/franco
Institution Type/Description: History Museum.
Hours & Admission Prices: Mon.-Thurs. 9-4.

Liberty

THE DAVISTOWN MUSEUM, 58 Main St., #4, Liberty, ME 04949. Mailing Address: Hulls Cove Office, P.O. Box 144, Hulls Cove, ME 04644-0144. Tel.: 207-288-5126. Fax: 207-288-2725.
E-mail: curator@davistownmuseum.org
Web Site: www.davistownmuseum.org
Key Personnel: C.E.O., Harold G. Brack.
Institution Type/Description: History & Art Museum.
Hours & Admission Prices: Summer: Wed.-Fri. & Sun. 11-5, Sat. 10-5; call for additional seasonal hours. No charge; donations accepted.
Attendance: 1,000 (estimated)

Limestone

AROOSTOOK NATIONAL WILDLIFE REFUGE, 97 Refuge Rd., Limestone, ME 04750. Tel.: 207-328-4634.
Web Site: www.fws.gov/refuge/aroostook
Institution Type/Description: Wildlife Refuge.
Hours & Admission Prices: Call for hours.

Lincolnville

SCHOOL HOUSE MUSEUM LINCOLNVILLE HISTORICAL SOCIETY, 33 Beach Rd. (Rte. 173), Lincolnville, ME 04849. Mailing Address: P.O. Box 204, Lincolnville, ME 04849-0204. Tel.: 207-789-5445.
E-mail: history@sent.com
Web Site: www.lincolnvillehistory.org/
Institution Type/Description: Historical Society Museum: housed in a one room school built in 1892.
Hours & Admission Prices: June to early Oct. Mon., Wed. & Fri. 1-4. No charge.

Littleton

SOUTHERN AROOSTOOK AGRICULTURAL MUSEUM, 1664 U.S. Rte. 1, Littleton, ME 04730. Mailing Address: 304 Campbell Rd., Littleton, ME 04730. Tel.: 207-538-9300. Facebook: Southern Aroostook Agricultural Museum.
E-mail: countymuseum@hotmail.com
Web Site: www.oldplow.net
Key Personnel: Pres., Francis Fitzpatrick.
Institution Type/Description: Agriculture Museum.
Hours & Admission Prices: By appointment. Adults $5; members no charge. &
Attendance: 2,000 (estimated)

Livermore

WASHBURN-NORLANDS LIVING HISTORY CENTER, 290 Norlands Rd., Livermore, ME 04253-3807. Tel.: 207-897-4366. Fax: 207-897-4963. Facebook.
E-mail: norlands@norlands.org
Web Site: www.norlands.org
Key Personnel: Dir., Sheri Leahan.
Institution Type/Description: Living History Museum.
Hours & Admission Prices: Summer Drop-in Living History Tours: July-Aug. Tues., Thurs. & Sat. Tours & Programs: by appointment. Adults $10.
Attendance: 3,500 (estimated)

Lovell

LOVELL HISTORICAL SOCIETY - KIMBALL-STANFORD HOUSE, 551 Main St., (Rte. 5), Lovell, ME 04051. Mailing Address: P.O. Box 166, Lovell, ME 04051. Tel.: 207-925-3234.
E-mail: lovellhistoricalsociety@gmail.com
Web Site: lovellhistoricalsociety.org
Key Personnel: Pres., Catherine Stone.

Institution Type/Description: Historical Society Museum: house built in 1839.
Hours & Admission Prices: Tues.-Wed. 9-4, Sat. 9-12; other times by appointment. No charge.
Attendance: 700 (estimated)

Lubec

LUBEC HISTORICAL SOCIETY & MUSEUM, 135 Main St., Lubec, ME 04652. Mailing Address: 155 Main St., Lubec, ME 04652. Tel.: 207-733-2994. Facebook.
E-mail: lubechistoricalsociety@yahoo.com
Web Site: www.lubechistoricalsociety.com
Key Personnel: Chm. (V) & Pres. (V), Barbara Sellitto; Museum Shop Mgr., Cecil Moores.
Institution Type/Description: Historical Society Museum.
Hours & Admission Prices: June 10-Oct. 15 Mon.-Wed. & Fri. 9-3. No charge; donations accepted. &
Attendance: 1,110 (actual)

QUODDY HEAD STATE PARK, 973 S. Lubec Rd., Lubec, ME 04652. Tel.: 207-733-0911 (Park season) & 941-4014 (Off season).
E-mail: DACF@Maine.gov
Web Site: www.maine.gov/cgi-bin/online/doc/parksearch/index.pl
Institution Type/Description: State Park Museum: located on the easternmost point of land in the U.S.
Hours & Admission Prices: May 15 to Oct. 15.

Machias

BURNHAM TAVERN MUSEUM, 14 Colonial Way, Machias, ME 04654. Mailing Address: 1027 N. Lubec Rd., Lubec, ME 04652. Tel.: 207-255-6930.
E-mail: info@burnhamtavern.com
Web Site: www.burnhamtavern.com
Key Personnel: Sec., Ruth H. Ahrens, Ed.D.
Institution Type/Description: Historic Building: c.1770 Burnham Tavern.
Hours & Admission Prices: mid-June through Sept. Mon.-Fri. 10-3. Adults $5; discounts to MPBN members. Closed Independence Day; Labor Day.
Attendance: 1,000 (estimated)

Machiasport

GATES HOUSE, MACHIASPORT HISTORICAL SOCIETY, 344 Port Rd., Machiasport, ME 04655. Mailing Address: P.O. Box 301, Machiasport, ME 04655-0301. Tel.: 207-255-8461.
E-mail: folknoter@maineline.net
Web Site: www.gateshouse.org
Key Personnel: C.E.O. & Pres. (V), Al Sousa; Recording Sec., Celeste Sherman; Treas., Barbara Maloy.
Institution Type/Description: Historic House: c.1810 Gates House.
Hours & Admission Prices: July-Aug. Tues.-Fri. 12:30-4:30; Sept. Sat. 12:30-4:30; other times by appointment. No charge; donations accepted.
Attendance: 500 (estimated)

Madawaska

MARTIN ACADIAN HOMESTEAD, 137 Saint Catherine St., Madawaska, ME 04756-1423. Tel.: 207-728-6412. Fax: 207-728-6412. Facebook.
E-mail: martinacadianhomestead@yahoo.com
Web Site: visitaroostook.com
Formerly: Violette House - Acadian Crafters
Key Personnel: Pres. & Chm. (V), Lois Muller; Treas. & Museum Shop Mgr., Lisa Schroeder; Dir., Paul Muller.
Institution Type/Description: Historic House Museum: built 1823-1860. Listed on the National Register of Historic Places.
Hours & Admission Prices: Daily 10-4 by appointment. No charge; donations accepted. Closed Easter; Thanksgiving; Christmas. &
Attendance: 300 (estimated)

TANTE BLANCHE MUSEUM, U.S. #1, Madawaska, ME 04756-1165. Mailing Address: Madawaska Public Library, 393 Main St., Madawaska, ME 04756-1165. Tel.: 207-728-6412. Fax: 207-728-6412. Facebook: Madawaska Historical Society.
E-mail: ljmuller@ymail.com
Web Site: madawaskahistorical.org
Formerly: Madawaska Historical Society
Key Personnel: Pres. (V), Lois Muller; Chm. (V), Paul Muller; Treas., Cecile Lausier.
Institution Type/Description: History Museum.

Hours & Admission Prices: June-Sept. Wed.-Sun. 12-4. No charge; donations accepted.

Attendance: 3,000 (estimated)

Milbridge

MILBRIDGE HISTORICAL SOCIETY AND MUSEUM, Main St., Milbridge, ME 04658. Mailing Address: P.O. Box 194, Milbridge, ME 04658-0194. Tel.: 207-546-4471.
E-mail: info@milbridgehistoricalsociety.org
Web Site: milbridgehistoricalsociety.org
Key Personnel: Museum Shop Mgr., Ellen Strout.
Institution Type/Description: Local History Museum.
Hours & Admission Prices: June to early Sept. Tues. & Sat.-Sun. 1-4. No charge; donations accepted. &
Attendance: 400 (actual)

Millinocket

NORTH LIGHT GALLERY, 256 Penobscot St., Millinocket, ME 04462-1510. Tel.: 207-723-4414. Facebook.
E-mail: artnorthlight@gmail.com
Web Site: www.artnorthlight.com
Key Personnel: Founder, Dir. & C.E.O., Marsha Donahue.
Institution Type/Description: Art Gallery.
Hours & Admission Prices: Mon.-Sat. 10-6; other times by appointment. No charge.

Milo

MILO HISTORICAL SOCIETY, 23 Park St., Milo, ME 04463-1315. Tel.: 207-943-2268. Facebook: Milo Historical Society.
E-mail: amonroeart@gmail.com
Web Site: www.milohistorical.org
Key Personnel: Dir., Gwen Bradeen; Cur., Virgil Valente.
Institution Type/Description: Historical Society Museum.
Hours & Admission Prices: June-Aug. Tues.-Fri. 1-3; other times by appointment. No charge; donations accepted.
Attendance: 100 (estimated)

Monhegan

THE MONHEGAN MUSEUM, 1 Lighthouse Hill, Monhegan, ME 04852. Tel.: 207-596-7003.
E-mail: museum@monheganmuseum.org
Web Site: www.monheganmuseum.org
Key Personnel: Dir. & Pres., Edward Deci; Cur., Jennifer Pye; Cur., Emily Grey.
Institution Type/Description: Art & History Museum: housed in 19th-century lighthouse & outbuildings.
Hours & Admission Prices: June 24-June 30 & Sept. daily 1:30-3:30; July-Aug. daily 11:30-3:30. Adults $5; members no charge. &
Attendance: 6,000 (estimated)

Mount Desert

MOUNT DESERT ISLAND HISTORICAL SOCIETY, 373 Sound Dr., Mount Desert, ME 04660. Mailing Address: P.O. Box 653, Mount Desert, ME 04660-0653. Tel.: 207-276-9323.
E-mail: tim.garrity@mdihistory.org
Web Site: www.mdihistory.org
Key Personnel: Pres. (V), William Horner, M.D.; Exec. Dir., Tim Garrity.
Institution Type/Description: Local History Museum.
Hours & Admission Prices: Somesville Museum: late June to Sept. daily 10-4. Sound School House: Mon.-Fri. 10-4. Suggested donation $5. &
Attendance: 3,000 (estimated)

Naples

NAPLES HISTORICAL SOCIETY, 19 Village Green Ln., Lambs Mill Rd./Rte. 302, Naples, ME 04055. Mailing Address: 19 Village Green Ln., Naples, ME 04055. Tel.: 207-693-3500.
E-mail: nhs@fairpoint.net, napleshs@fairpoint.net
Web Site: www.napleshs.org, www.townofnaples.org
Key Personnel: Dir. & Pres. (V), Meryl J. Watson; Cur., Merry Watson; Cur. Dillingham Collection, Richard Doyle.
Institution Type/Description: Naples History Museum.
Hours & Admission Prices: June-Labor Day Thurs.-Sat. 10-4, Labor Day-June Fri. 10-2. No charge; donations accepted. &
Attendance: 100 (estimated)

New Gloucester

SHAKER MUSEUM, 707 Shaker Rd., New Gloucester, ME 04260-2652. Tel.: 207-926-4597.
E-mail: info@maineshakers.com
Web Site: www.maineshakers.com
Key Personnel: C.E.O., Bro. Arnold Hadd; Dir., Michael S. Graham; Librarian, Charles E. Rand; Office Mgr., Jamie Ribisi-Braley.
Institution Type/Description: History Museum & Library: located at an active Shaker religious community, comprising of 18 buildings on 1,900 acres dating from the 1760s to 1960s.
Hours & Admission Prices: Memorial Day to Columbus Day Mon.-Sat. 10-4:30. Tours: adults $10, children $3. &
Attendance: 15,000 (actual)

New Harbor

COLONIAL PEMAQUID, 2 Colonial Pemaquid Dr., New Harbor, ME 04554. Mailing Address: P.O. Box 117, New Harbor, ME 04554-0117. Tel.: 207-677-2423 (April-Oct), 207-624-6075 (Off-Season).
E-mail: DACF@Maine.gov
Web Site: www.friendsofcolonialpemaquid.org
Key Personnel: Pres. (V), Bob Howell; Museum Shop Mgr., Carol Ring.
Institution Type/Description: Archaeological Dig Site.
Hours & Admission Prices: Memorial Day to Labor Day daily 9-6. Adults $2; children under 12 & seniors over 65 no charge. &
Attendance: 100,000 (estimated)

THE FISHERMEN'S MUSEUM, Lighthouse Park, End of Rte. 130, New Harbor, ME 04554. Mailing Address: P.O. Box 263, New Harbor, ME 04554-0263. Tel.: 207-677-2726.
E-mail: johnallan@roadrunner.com
Web Site: www.thefishermensmuseum.org
Key Personnel: Dir., John Allan; Pres., Robert Cushing; Chm. (V), Barbara Marshall.
Institution Type/Description: Historical & Preservation Society: housed in old 1827 lighthouse keeper's house.
Hours & Admission Prices: June to mid-Oct. Mon.-Sat. 10-5, Sun. 11-5. No charge; donations accepted. &
Attendance: 46,479 (actual)

New Portland

NOWETAH'S INDIAN MUSEUM & STORE, 2 Colegrove Rd., New Portland, ME 04961-3821. Tel.: 207-628-4981. Facebook: Nowetah's Indian Store and Museum.
E-mail: info@mainemuseums.org
Web Site: www.mainemuseums.org
Key Personnel: Owner & Cur., Mrs. Nowetah Cyr; Tour Guide & Visitor Speaker, Thomas Cyr.
Institution Type/Description: Native American Museum.
Hours & Admission Prices: Daily 10-5. No charge; donations accepted. Closed Thanksgiving; Christmas. &
Attendance: 1,548 (actual)

New Sweden

LARS NOAK BLACKSMITH SHOP, LARSSON/OSTLUND LOG HOME & ONE-ROOM CAPITOL SCHOOL, Station Rd., New Sweden, ME 04762. Tel.: 207-896-5728. Fax: 207-896-3199.
E-mail: info@maineswedishcolony.info
Web Site: www.maineswedishcolony.info
Institution Type/Description: Historic Village.
Hours & Admission Prices: By appointment. &
Attendance: 4,500 (estimated)

NEW SWEDEN HISTORICAL SOCIETY, 116 Station Rd., New Sweden, ME 04762-3523. Mailing Address: P.O. Box 33, New Sweden, ME 04762. Tel.: 207-896-5200.
E-mail: bill@williamlduncan.com
Web Site: www.maineswedishcolony.info
Key Personnel: Pres., Gary Dickinson; Sec., Janice McDougal; Treas., Pat Williams; Museum Shop Mgr., Gloria Ringdahl.
Institution Type/Description: Historical Society Museum: replica of original colony capital which burned in 1971.
Hours & Admission Prices: Memorial Day to Labor Day Mon.-Fri. 12-4, Sat.-Sun. 1-4; Sept.-May by appointment. No charge; donations accepted. &
Attendance: 500 (estimated)

Newcastle

NEWCASTLE HISTORICAL SOCIETY - TANISCOT ENGINE HOUSE, Main St., Newcastle, ME 04553. Mailing Address: P.O. Box 482, Newcastle, ME 04553. Tel.: 207-563-3347.
E-mail: newcastlehistoricalsociety@hotmail.com
Web Site: newcastlemainehistoricalsociety.org
Institution Type/Description: Historical Society Museum.
Hours & Admission Prices: By appointment.

Newfield

19TH CENTURY WILLOWBROOK VILLAGE, 70 Elm St., Newfield, ME 04056. Mailing Address: P.O. Box 28, Elm St., Newfield, ME 04056-0028. Tel.: 207-793-2784. Facebook: 19th Century Willowbrook Village.
E-mail: director@willowbrookmuseum.org
Web Site: www.willowbrookmuseum.org
Key Personnel: C.E.O. & Museum Shop Mgr., Robert Schmick, Ph.D.; Chm. & Pres. (V), Doug King.
Institution Type/Description: History Museum.
Hours & Admission Prices: Memorial Day to Columbus Day Thurs.-Mon. 10-5. Adults $15, seniors $12, students 7-18 $7; discounts to groups over 8, AAM, AAA, Time Traveler & local historical society members; children 6 & under, members and active military & their family no charge. &
Attendance: 7,582 (actual)

Nobleboro

NOBLEBORO HISTORICAL SOCIETY, 198 Center St., Nobleboro, ME 04555. Mailing Address: P.O. Box 122, Nobleboro, ME 04555-0122. Tel.: 207-563-5376.
E-mail: sheldon@tidewater.com
Web Site: www.nobleborohistoricalsociety.org
Key Personnel: Pres. & Cur., Mary K. Sheldon; Treas., Britt Hatch; Pres. (V), Mary K. Sheldon.
Institution Type/Description: Historical Society Museum: housed in an 1818 schoolhouse.
Hours & Admission Prices: July-Aug. Sat. 1:30-4:30 & for special exhibits; also by appointment. No charge; donations accepted.
Attendance: 450 (estimated)

Norridgewock

NORRIDGEWOCK HISTORICAL SOCIETY, 11 Mercer Rd., Norridgewock, ME 04957. Mailing Address: P.O. Box 903, Norridgewock, ME 04957. Tel.: 207-634-5032 & 5064.
E-mail: norridgewockhistsoc@gmail.com
Web Site: www.norridgewockmuseum.com
Institution Type/Description: Historical Society Museum: housed in a former school for women; built in 1832.
Hours & Admission Prices: Memorial Day to Labor Day Sat. 11-1.

North Amity

A.E. HOWELL WILDLIFE CONSERVATION CENTER & SPRUCE ACRES REFUGE, 101 Lycette Rd., North Amity, ME 04471-5114. Tel.: 207-532-6880. Fax: 207-532-6880 (call first).
E-mail: eagleman1008@earthlink.net
Web Site: www.spruceacresrefuge.org
Key Personnel: Vice Pres., Janet M. Easter; Dir., Kim Keehn.
Institution Type/Description: Wildlife Refuge.
Hours & Admission Prices: mid-May to Oct. 15 Tues.-Sat. 10-4 by appointment. Adults $10; children under 16 no charge.

Northeast Harbor

GREAT HARBOR MARITIME MUSEUM, 124 Main St., Northeast Harbor, ME 04662. Mailing Address: P.O. Box 145, Northeast Harbor, ME 04662-0145. Tel.: 207-276-5262 & 5650 (Off Season).
E-mail: sydr@me.com
Web Site: www.greatharbormaritimemuseum.org
Formerly: Great Harbor Collection
Key Personnel: Chm. (V), Sydney Roberts Rockefeller.
Institution Type/Description: Maritime Museum.
Hours & Admission Prices: Mon.-Sat. 10-5. Suggested Donation: $3. &
Attendance: 5,000 (estimated)

Norway

NORWAY HISTORICAL SOCIETY MUSEUM, 471 Main St., Norway, ME 04268. Tel.: 207-743-7377.
E-mail: NorwayMeHistory@gmail.com
Key Personnel: Cur., Charles Longley.
Institution Type/Description: Historical Society Museum.
Hours & Admission Prices: June-Aug. Tues. & Sat. 9 to noon; Sept.-May Sat. 9 to noon; other times by appointment.

Oakfield

OAKFIELD RAILROAD MUSEUM, Station St., #40, Oakfield, ME 04763. Mailing Address: Oakfield Historical Society, P.O. Box 176, Oakfield, ME 04763-0176. Tel.: 207-267-1647. Facebook.
E-mail: gacrac@hotmail.com
Web Site: www.oakfieldmuseum.org
Key Personnel: Chm. (V), Pres. (V), & Museum Shop Mgr., Alberta McDonald.
Institution Type/Description: Railroad Museum.
Hours & Admission Prices: late May to Labor Day Sat.-Sun. 1-4. No charge; donations accepted.
Attendance: 250 (estimated)

Oakland

MACARTNEY HOUSE MUSEUM, 25 Main St., Oakland, ME 04963. Mailing Address: P.O. Box 59, Oakland, ME 04963-0059. Tel.: 207-649-4942.
Web Site: www.rootsweb.ancestry.com/~me@oakla/
Key Personnel: Pres. (V), Alberta Porter; Treas., Richard Lord.
Institution Type/Description: History Museum; housed in the former home of mill owner, Leonard Cornforth, built 1815.
Hours & Admission Prices: Summer: Wed. 1:30-4:30; other times by appointment. No charge; donations accepted.

Ogunquit

BARN GALLERY, Shore Rd. & Bourne Lane, Ogunquit, ME 03907. Mailing Address: P.O. Box 794, Ogunquit, ME 03907-0794. Tel.: 207-646-8400.
E-mail: stonoverfarm@aol.com
Institution Type/Description: Art Gallery.
Hours & Admission Prices: Call for hours.

OGUNQUIT HERITAGE MUSEUM, 86 Obeds Lane, Ogunquit, ME 03907. Mailing Address: P.O. Box 875, Ogunquit, ME 03907. Tel.: 207-646-0296.
E-mail: info@ogunquitheritagemuseum.org
Web Site: ogunquitheritagemuseum.org
Institution Type/Description: History Museum: housed in the former home of Captain James Winn; c.1780.
Hours & Admission Prices: June-Oct. Tues.-Sat. 1-5. No charge. &
Attendance: 1,000 (actual)

OGUNQUIT MUSEUM OF AMERICAN ART, 543 Shore Rd., Ogunquit, ME 03907-0815. Mailing Address: P.O. Box 815, Ogunquit, ME 03907-0815. Tel.: 207-646-4909. Fax: 207-646-6903.
E-mail: averzosa@ogunquitmuseum.org
Web Site: ogunquitmuseum.org
Key Personnel: Interim Dir., Andres A. Verzosa; Pres. (V), David J. Mallen; Museum Shop Mgr., Patricia Toro; Business Mgr., Kimberly Plaisted.
Institution Type/Description: Art Museum.
Hours & Admission Prices: May-Oct. daily 10-5. Adults $10, seniors & students $9; children under 12 & members no charge. Closed Labor Day. &
Attendance: 16,000 (actual)

Old Orchard Beach

OLD ORCHARD BEACH HISTORICAL SOCIETY INC., 4 Portland Ave., Old Orchard Beach, ME 04064. Mailing Address: P.O. Box 464, Old Orchard Beach, ME 04064. Tel.: 207-934-9319.
E-mail: oobhistsoc@maine.rr.com
Web Site: www.harmonmuseum.org
Key Personnel: Museum Trustee, Daniel Blaney; Pres., Arthur Guerin; Vice Pres., Charles Davis; Sec., Arlene Hanson; Treas., Stanley Quinlan; Cur., Jeanne Guerin; Projects Mgr. & Researcher, Janet Hamilton.
Institution Type/Description: Historical Society Museum.

Hours & Admission Prices: June 24 to Labor Day Tues.-Fri. 10-4, Sat. 10-2; other times by appointment. No charge; donations accepted.
Attendance: 450 (estimated)

Old Town

OLD TOWN MUSEUM, 353 Main St., Old Town, ME 04468-1536. Mailing Address: P.O. Box 375, Old Town, ME 04468-0375. Tel.: 207-827-7256.
E-mail: bparadis@belfastlibrary.org
Web Site: oldtownmuseum.com
Key Personnel: Pres. (V), Betsy Paradis; Vice Pres. (V), Carol May; Museum Shop Mgr., Peggy Manzer.
Institution Type/Description: History Museum: housed in c.1928 former Church.
Hours & Admission Prices: May-Oct. Fri.-Sun. 1-5. No charge; donations accepted. &
Attendance: 750 (actual)

Orland

ORLAND HISTORICAL SOCIETY, 23 Schoolhouse Rd., Orland, ME 04472. Mailing Address: P.O. Box 242, Orland, ME 04472. Tel.: 207-469-3354.
E-mail: rwood80519@aol.com
Web Site: www.orlandmainehistoricalsociety.com
Key Personnel: Pres. (V), Roger Wood; Treas., JoAnn Carlson.
Institution Type/Description: General Museum: housed in late 1800s Old Orland Town Hall.
Hours & Admission Prices: July-Sept. 1st & 3rd Fri. 1-3; other times by appointment. No charge, donations accepted. &
Attendance: 100 (estimated)

Orono

THE FAY HYLAND BOTANICAL PLANTATION, 5751 Murray Hall, Univ. of Maine, Orono, ME 04469. Tel.: 207-581-2540. Fax: 207-581-2537.
Key Personnel: Chm., Dr. Christopher S. Campbell.
Institution Type/Description: Arboretum.
Hours & Admission Prices: Daily dawn-dusk. No charge.

HUDSON MUSEUM, THE UNIVERSITY OF MAINE, 5746 Collins Center for the Arts, Orono, ME 04469. Tel.: 207-581-1904. Fax: 207-581-1950.
E-mail: hudsonmuseum@umit.maine.edu
Web Site: umaine.edu/hudsonmuseum/
Key Personnel: Dir., Gretchen Faulkner; Chief Cooperating Cur., Dan Sandweiss.
Institution Type/Description: Anthropology Museum.
Hours & Admission Prices: Mon.-Fri. 9-4, Sat. 11-4. No charge; donations accepted. Closed federal & state holidays. &
Attendance: 67,427 (estimated)

PAGE FARM & HOME MUSEUM - THE UNIVERSITY OF MAINE, 5787 Museum Barn, Portage Rd., Orono, ME 04469-5787. Tel.: 207-581-4100.
E-mail: pagefarm@umit.maine.edu
Web Site: www.umaine.edu/pagefarm/
Key Personnel: Dir., Patricia Hemer.
Institution Type/Description: History Museum.
Hours & Admission Prices: Tues.-Sat. 9-4. Closed holidays.

Orrington

CURRAN HOMESTEAD LIVING HISTORY FARM & MUSEUM, 372 Fields Pond Rd., Orrington, ME 04474. Mailing Address: P.O. Box 107, Orrington, ME 04474-0107. Tel.: 207-945-9311. Fax: 207-942-9914.
E-mail: irv@bangorlettershop.com
Web Site: curranhomestead.org
Key Personnel: Pres. (V), Karen L. Marsters; Vice Chair, Ron Sucy; Sec., Richard A. Stockford.
Institution Type/Description: Living History Farm & Museum.
Hours & Admission Prices: Call or see website for hours or to arrange tours.
Attendance: 1,500 (estimated)

Owls Head

OWLS HEAD TRANSPORTATION MUSEUM, 117 Museum St., Rte. 73, Owls Head, ME 04854. Mailing Address: P.O. Box 277, Owls Head, ME 04854-0277. Tel.: 207-594-4418. Fax: 207-594-4410.
E-mail: info@ohtm.org
Web Site: www.ohtm.org
Key Personnel: Dir., Charles Chiarchiaro; Cur. & Dir. Education, Ethan Yankura; Chm., James S. Rockefeller, Jr.
Institution Type/Description: Transportation Museum.
Hours & Admission Prices: Daily 10-5. Adults $10, seniors 65 & over $8; children under 18 & members no charge. Closed New Year's Day; Thanksgiving; Christmas. &
Attendance: 96,377 (actual)

Patten

PATTEN LUMBERMEN'S MUSEUM, INC., 61 Shin Pond Rd., Patten, ME 04765. Mailing Address: P.O. Box 300, Patten, ME 04765-0300. Tel.: 207-528-2650. Fax: 207-528-2650. Facebook: Patten Lumbermen's Museum.
E-mail: curator@lumbermensmuseum.org
Web Site: www.lumbermensmuseum.org
Key Personnel: Dir. & Cur., Rhonda R. Brophy; Pres., Frank Rogers; Vice Pres., Stephen Giles.
Institution Type/Description: Logging & Lumbering History Museum.
Hours & Admission Prices: Memorial Day to June Fri.-Sun. 10-4; July to Columbus Day Tues.-Sun. 10-4, Mon. holidays 10-4. Adults $8, seniors $7, children 7-12 $3; discounts to groups, AAM & AAA members; members & children under 6 no charge. &
Attendance: 3,800 (estimated)

Peaks Island

FIFTH MAINE REGIMENT MUSEUM, 45 Seashore Ave., Peaks Island, ME 04108-1311. Mailing Address: P.O. Box 41, Peaks Island, ME 04108-0041. Tel.: 207-766-3330. Fax: 207-766-5514.
E-mail: Curator@fifthmainemuseum.org
Web Site: www.fifthmainemuseum.org
Key Personnel: Pres. Bd., Bill Hall.
Institution Type/Description: Military Museum: housed in the Fifth Maine Regiment Memorial Hall, built in 1888 as a Civil War Memorial & Reunion Hall; listed in the National Register of Historic Places.
Hours & Admission Prices: Mon.-Fri. 12-4, Sat.-Sun. 11-4. Suggested Donation: adults $5; discounts to AAM, MAM, & NEMA, AASLH and Civil War Preservation Trust members. &
Attendance: 6,000 (actual)

THE UMBRELLA COVER MUSEUM, 62-B Island Ave., Peaks Island, ME 04108-1225. Tel.: 207-939-0301. Facebook: Umbrella Cover Museum.
E-mail: info@umbrellacovermuseum.org
Web Site: www.umbrellacovermuseum.org
Key Personnel: Dir. & Cur., Nancy 3. Hoffman.
Institution Type/Description: Umbrella Cover Museum.
Hours & Admission Prices: Summer: Tues.-Sat. 10-1 & 2-5, Sun. 10-12:30. No charge; donations requested. Peaks Island is a 20 minute ferry ride from Portland.
Attendance: 4,500 (actual)

Pemaquid

HARRINGTON MEETING HOUSE MUSEUM, 278 Harrington Rd., Pemaquid, ME 04558. Mailing Address: 239 Harrington Rd., Pemaquid, ME 04558. Tel.: 207-677-2193.
Institution Type/Description: Historic House Museum: built in 1772.
Hours & Admission Prices: July-Aug. Mon., Wed. & Fri. 2-4:30. No charge; donations accepted.

Phillips

PHILLIPS HISTORICAL SOCIETY, 8 Pleasant St., Phillips, ME 04966. Mailing Address: P.O. Box 216, Phillips, ME 04966-0216. Tel.: 207-639-3111 & 2888 (Tours).
E-mail: nlvhg@tdstelme.net
Key Personnel: Pres., Dennis Atkinson.
Institution Type/Description: General Museum: housed in 1832 house owned by important local families connected with town's history.

Hours & Admission Prices: June-Aug. first & third Sun. 1-3; other times by appointment. Railroad: June-Sept. 1st & 3rd Sun. No charge; donations accepted. &
Attendance: 1,000 (estimated)

Phippsburg

PHIPPSBURG HISTORICAL SOCIETY, Parker Head Rd., Phippsburg, ME 04562. Mailing Address: P.O. Box 21, Phippsburg, ME 04562-0021. Tel.: 207-389-2393.
E-mail: jsutfin@rsu1.org
Web Site: www.phippsburghistorical.com
Key Personnel: Pres., Jessie Sutfin.
Institution Type/Description: Historical Society Museum.
Hours & Admission Prices: Summer: Mon.-Fri. 2-4.

Pittsfield

THE DEPOT HOUSE MUSEUM, 114 Central St., Pittsfield, ME 04967. Mailing Address: Pittsfield Historical Society, P.O. Box 181, Pittsfield, ME 04967-0181. Tel.: 207-487-4926.
Institution Type/Description: Historic Building: built in 1886.
Hours & Admission Prices: April-Oct. Tues.-Sat. 10-1; Nov.-March by appointment.

Pittston

MAJOR REUBEN COLBURN HOUSE, 33 Arnold Rd., Pittston, ME 04345-5145. Mailing Address: Bureau of Parks & Lands, 22 State House Station, Augusta, ME 04333.
E-mail: sclark60@live.com
Institution Type/Description: Historic House: built in 1765. Listed on the National Register of Historic Places.
Hours & Admission Prices: Summer: Sat.-Sun. call for hours.

Poland

POLAND HISTORICAL SOCIETY MUSEUM, 1231 Maine St., Poland, ME 04274. Tel.: 207-998-4601. Fax: 207-998-2002.
Institution Type/Description: Historical Society Museum: housed in a former schoolhouse.
Hours & Admission Prices: July-Aug. call for hours.

Poland Spring

POLAND SPRING PRESERVATION SOCIETY, 37 Preservation Way, Poland Spring, ME 04274. Mailing Address: P.O. Box 444, Poland Spring, ME 04274. Tel.: 207-998-4142. Facebook, Twitter.
E-mail: polandspringpreservation@gmail.com
Web Site: www.polandspringps.org
Formerly: Maine State Building
Institution Type/Description: Historic Building: built in 1893 for the Chicago World's Fair with materials sent from Maine to Chicago. The structure was later dismantled and moved back to Maine by train in 1895.
Hours & Admission Prices: Memorial Day to Columbus Day Wed.-Sat. 9-4, Sun. 9-1. Adults $5; discounts to resort guests; members no charge. &

Port Clyde

MARSHALL POINT LIGHTHOUSE MUSEUM, 179 Marshall Point Rd., Port Clyde, ME 04855. Mailing Address: P.O. Box 247, Port Clyde, ME 04855-0247. Tel.: 207-372-6450.
Web Site: www.marshallpoint.org
Key Personnel: Chm., Diana Bolton; Cur., Nat Lyon.
Institution Type/Description: History Museum.
Hours & Admission Prices: May Sat.-Sun. 1-5; Memorial Day to Columbus Day Sun.-Fri. 1-5, Sat. 10-5. No charge; donations accepted.
Attendance: 13,152 (actual)

Porter

PARSONSFIELD-PORTER HISTORICAL SOCIETY, 92 Main St., Porter, ME 04068. Mailing Address: P.O. Box 250, Parsonsfield, ME 04047-0250. Tel.: 207-625-7019. localhistory-matters.blogspot.com.
E-mail: pphs@parsonsfieldporterhistorical.org
Web Site: www.parsonsfieldporterhistorical.org
Key Personnel: Pres., Lynda Sudlow; Vice Pres., Martha Richmond; Sec., Janice M. Iler; Treas., Sylvia Wilson.

Institution Type/Description: Historic House Museum: Parsonsfield-Porter History House.
Hours & Admission Prices: April-Nov. by appointment. No charge; donations accepted. Closed holidays. &
Attendance: 350 (estimated)

Portland

CHILDREN'S MUSEUM & THEATRE OF MAINE, 142 Free St., Portland, ME 04101-3961. Mailing Address: P.O. Box 4041, Portland, ME 04101-0241. Tel.: 207-828-1234. Fax: 207-828-5726. Facebook.
E-mail: info@kitetails.org
Web Site: www.kitetails.org
Key Personnel: Exec. Dir., Julie Butcher Pezzino; Deputy Dir., Lucia Stancioff; Dir. Theatre & Education, Reba Askari.
Institution Type/Description: Children's Museum: housed in modified four-story historic business building.
Hours & Admission Prices: Memorial Day-Labor Day & school vacation weeks daily 10-5; Sept.-May Tues.-Sun. 10-5. Adults $10; discounts to groups and AAA & ACM reciprocal members; 1st Fri. each month 5pm-8pm, children under 18 months & members no charge. Closed New Year's Day; Easter; Independence Day; Thanksgiving; Christmas Eve & Day. &
Attendance: 115,000 (actual)

INSTITUTE OF CONTEMPORARY ART AT MAINE COLLEGE OF ART (ICA AT MECA), 522 Congress St., Portland, ME 04101-3378. Tel.: 207-699-5025.
E-mail: ica@meca.edu
Web Site: www.meca.edu/ica
Key Personnel: Dir. Exhibitions & Special Projects, Erin Hutton; Exhibitions Coord., Nikki Rayburn.
Institution Type/Description: Art Museum: housed in 1904 Beaux Art design Porteous Building.
Hours & Admission Prices: Wed. & Fri.-Sun. 11-5, Thurs. 11-7. No charge; donations accepted. Closed legal holidays. &
Attendance: 20,000 (actual)

INTERNATIONAL CRYPTOZOOLOGY MUSEUM, 4 Thompson's Point Rd., Ste. 106, Portland, ME 04102.
E-mail: executives@cryptozoologymuseum.com
Web Site: cryptozoologymuseum.com
Key Personnel: Dir. & Founder, Loren Coleman; Asst. Dir., Jeff Meuse.
Institution Type/Description: Cryptozoology Museum.
Hours & Admission Prices: Sun.-Mon. &Wed.-Thurs. 11-4, Fri.-Sat. 11-6. Adults $10, seniors 65 & over $8, children 12 & under $5; infants no charge. Closed New Year's Day; Thanksgiving & day before; Christmas.

MAINE HISTORICAL SOCIETY, 489 Congress St., Portland, ME 04101-3414. Tel.: 207-774-1822. Fax: 207-775-4301.
E-mail: info@mainehistory.org
Web Site: www.mainehistory.com
Key Personnel: Exec. Dir., Stephen Bromage; Dir. Finance, Karen Pelletier; Dir. Institutional Advancement, Christina Traister; Dir. Collections & Research, Jamie Kingman Rice; Curator, Tilly Laskey.
Institution Type/Description: History Museum.
Hours & Admission Prices: Library: May-Oct. Tues.-Sat. 10-4; Nov.-April Wed.-Sat. 10-4. Maine Historical Society Museum: May-Oct. Mon.-Sat. 10-5, Sun. 12-5; Nov.-April Tues.-Sat. 10-5; Dec. 1-23 Tues.-Wed. 10-5, Thurs.-Sat. 10-7. Wadsworth-Longfellow House Tours: May daily 12-5; June-Oct. Mon.-Sat. 10-5, Sun. 12-5. Museum: adults $8, seniors over 65, students & AAA members $7, children 6-17 $2; discounts to National Trust Members; children 5 & under and members no charge. Library $10; members no charge. Closed state & federal holidays. &
Attendance: 17,500 (actual)

MAINE NARROW GAUGE RAILROAD CO. & MUSEUM, 58 Fore St., Portland, ME 04101-4842. Tel.: 207-828-0814. Fax: 207-879-6132. Facebook; Twitter; Instagram.
E-mail: info@mainenarrowgauge.org
Web Site: www.mainenarrowgauge.org
Key Personnel: Exec. Dir., Donnell Carroll; Pres. (V), John Marr; Mgr. Visitor Svcs., Christina Napoli.
Institution Type/Description: Railroad Museum.
Hours & Admission Prices: May-Oct. daily 9:30-4; call for additional open hours during school vacation weeks. Museum: adults 13 & over $5, seniors $4, children 3-12 $3, children 2 & under no charge. Museum & Train Rides: adults $10, senior citizens $9, children 3-12 $6; children under 2 no charge. &
Attendance: 40,000 (estimated)

PORTLAND FIRE MUSEUM, 157 Spring St., Portland, ME 04104. Mailing Address: P.O. Box 1743, Portland, ME 04104-1743. Tel.: 207-772-2040.
E-mail: history@portlandfiremuseum.com
Web Site: www.portlandfiremuseum.com
Institution Type/Description: Fire-Fighting Museum.
Hours & Admission Prices: 1st Fri. each month 6pm.

PORTLAND MUSEUM OF ART, Seven Congress Square, Portland, ME 04101-1119. Tel.: 207-775-6148. Fax: 207-773-7324. Facebook.
E-mail: info@portlandmuseum.org
Web Site: www.portlandmuseum.org
Key Personnel: Judy & Leonard Lauder Dir., Mark Bessire; Dir. Leadership Circles, Abigail Baguio; Deputy Dir. & C.F.O., Elena Henry; Deputy Dir. & Chief Cur., Jessica May; Dir. Communications, Graeme Kennedy; Dir. Registration & Collections, Lauren Silverson; Peggy L. Osher Dir. Learning & Interpretation, Jennifer DePrizio; Visitor Experience & PMA Store Mgr., Danielle Farr; Dep. Dir. & Dir. External Affairs, Elizabeth Jones; Dir. Philanthropy, Christi Lumiere; Dir. Protection Svcs., Faiz Mohammad.
Institution Type/Description: Art Museum.
Hours & Admission Prices: Memorial Day to Columbus Day Fri. 10-9, Sat.-Thurs. 10-5; Winter Wed. & Sat.-Sun. 10-6, Thurs.-Fri. 10-8. Adults $15, senior citizens 65 & over and students with ID $13, students with valid ID $10; children 14 & under, Portland high school students with ID, members & Fri. 4-8 no charge. ⑆
Attendance: 177,824 (actual)

PORTLAND OBSERVATORY MUSEUM, 138 Congress St., Portland, ME 04101. Mailing Address: Greater Portland Landmarks, 93 High St., Portland, ME 04101. Tel.: 207-774-5561. Facebook.
E-mail: education@portlandlandmarks.org
Web Site: www.portlandlandmarks.org
Key Personnel: Dir., Hilary Bassett; Pres. (V), Jane Batzell; Mgr. Education Prog., Alessa Wylie.
Institution Type/Description: Portland Observatory: built in 1807. A National Historic Landmark.
Hours & Admission Prices: Self-Guided & Guided Tours: Memorial Day to Columbus Day daily 10-4:30. Family $30, adults $10, seniors & students $8, children 6-16 $5; discounts to Portland residents & AAA members; members & children under 6 no charge.
Attendance: 12,000 (actual)

SOUTHWORTH PLANETARIUM, 70 Falmouth St., Portland, ME 04103-4864. Tel.: 207-780-4249.
E-mail: edward.gleason@maine.edu
Web Site: usm.maine.edu/planet
Formerly: Portland Planetarium
Key Personnel: Mgr., Edward Gleason; Dir., Jerry LaSala.
Institution Type/Description: Planetarium.
Hours & Admission Prices: See website for hours and admission prices.

TATE HOUSE MUSEUM, 1267 Westbrook St., Portland, ME 04102-1934. Tel.: 207-774-6177. Fax: 207-774-6198. Facebook: Tate House Museum.
E-mail: info@tatehouse.org
Web Site: www.tatehouse.org
Key Personnel: Bd. Pres., Ralph C. Carmona, Ph.D.; Dir. Operations, Betty Janus; Sec., Joan Hatch.
Institution Type/Description: Historic House: 1755 George Tate House.
Hours & Admission Prices: June-Oct. Wed.-Sat. 10-4, Sun. 1-4. Adults $12, seniors $10, children & students $5; discount to members. Closed Independence Day; Labor Day.
Attendance: 2,000 (estimated)

UNIVERSITY OF NEW ENGLAND ART GALLERY, 716 Stevens Ave., University of New England, Portland, ME 04103-2693. Tel.: 207-221-4499.
E-mail: azill@une.edu
Web Site: www.une.edu/artgallery
Formerly: Payson Gallery
Key Personnel: Dir., Anne B. Zill.
Institution Type/Description: Fine Art Gallery.
Hours & Admission Prices: Wed. & Fri.-Sun. 12-5, Thurs. 12-7 & by appointment. No charge; donations accepted.
Attendance: 10,000 (estimated)

VICTORIA MANSION, 109 Danforth St., Portland, ME 04101-4504. Tel.: 207-772-4841. Fax: 207-772-6290.
Web Site: victoriamansion.org
Key Personnel: Dir., Thomas B. Johnson; Cur., Arlene Palmer Schwind; Asst. Dir., Timothy Brosnihan; Dir. Devel., Samuel Heck; Dir. Education & Visitor Svcs., Lucinda Hannington; Devel. & Communs Coord. & Events Coord., Victoria Levesque; Museum Shop & Site Mgr., Patti Chase.
Institution Type/Description: Historic House Museum: National Historic Landmark.
Hours & Admission Prices: May-Oct. Mon.-Sat. 10-3:45, Sun. 1-4:45, group tours by appointment. Families $35, adults $15, seniors 62 & over & AAA members $13.50, college students with valid ID $7, students 6-17 $5; children under 6, members & active military with valid ID no charge. ⑆
Attendance: 17,759 (actual)

Presque Isle

THE NORTHERN MAINE MUSEUM OF SCIENCE, UNIVERSITY OF MAINE, Folsom Hall, 181 Main St., Presque Isle, ME 04769-2844. Tel.: 207-768-9482. Fax: 207-768-9553.
E-mail: mcgowanj@polaris.umpi.maine.edu
Web Site: www.umpi.maine.edu/info/nmms/about.htm
Key Personnel: Dir., Dr. Kevin McCartney; Cur. Chemistry, Michael Knopp, Ph.D.; Cur. Herbarium, Robert J. Pinette, Ph.D.; Cur. Mathematics, Richard Kimball; Cur. Collections, Jeanie McGowan.
Institution Type/Description: Science Museum.
Hours & Admission Prices: Daily 7am-10pm. No charge. Closed university holidays & breaks.

PRESQUE ISLE AIR MUSEUM, Northern Maine Regional Airport, 650 Airport Dr., Ste. 4, Presque Isle, ME 04769. Tel.: 207-764-2542. Fax: 207-764-2544.
E-mail: piairmuseum@fcmail.com
Key Personnel: Pres. (V), Nate Grass.
Institution Type/Description: History & Pictorial Museum.
Hours & Admission Prices: Call for hours. No charge. ⑆
Attendance: 10,000 (estimated)

Prospect

FORT KNOX STATE HISTORIC SITE AND PENOBSCOT NARROWS OBSERVATORY, 711 Fort Knox Rd., Prospect, ME 04981-3125. Mailing Address: P.O. Box 456, Bucksport, ME 04416-0456. Tel.: 207-469-6553. Fax: 207-469-6906.
E-mail: info@fortknoxmaine.com
Web Site: www.fortknoxmaine.com
Key Personnel: Exec. Dir. & Mgr., Dean L. Martin; Pres. (V), Carol Weston.
Institution Type/Description: Historic Site: 1844 Fort Knox.
Hours & Admission Prices: May-Oct. call for hours & admission prices.
Attendance: 105,000 (estimated)

Rangeley

MAINE FORESTRY MUSEUM, 221 Stratton Rd., Rangeley, ME 04970. Mailing Address: P.O. Box 154, Rangeley, ME 04970-0154. Tel.: 207-864-3939. Facebook: @maineforestrymuseumMFM
E-mail: maineforestry@gmail.com
Web Site: www.maineforestrymuseum.org
Formerly: Rangeley Lakes Region Logging Museum
Key Personnel: Pres., Mark Beauregard; Vice Pres. (V), Tom McAllister; Cur., Kenneth White; Treas., Barb Eller; Docent & Sec., Eleanor Doyle.
Institution Type/Description: Forestry Museum.
Hours & Admission Prices: See website for hours. No charge; donations accepted. ⑆
Attendance: 1,400 (estimated)

RANGELEY LAKES HISTORICAL SOCIETY, Main St., Rangeley, ME 04970. Mailing Address: P.O. Box 521, Rangeley, ME 04970. Tel.: 207-864-5571.
E-mail: palmer@rangeley.org
Institution Type/Description: Historical Society Museum: housed in a Classical Revival style building; built c.1905. Listed on the National Register of Historic Places.
Hours & Admission Prices: July-Sept. Mon.-Sat. 10-2.

RANGELEY PUBLIC LIBRARY, 7 Lake St., Rangeley, ME 04970. Mailing Address: P.O. Box 1150, Rangeley, ME 04970-1150. Tel.: 207-864-5529. Fax: 207-864-2523.
E-mail: info@rangeleylibrary.com
Web Site: www.rangeleylibrary.com
Institution Type/Description: Library: housed in a Romanesque Revival style building; c.1909. Listed on the National Register of Historic Places.

Hours & Admission Prices: Tues. 10-7, Wed.-Fri. 10-4:30, Sat. 10-2.

WILHELM REICH MUSEUM - ORGONON, Dodge Pond Rd., Rangeley, ME 04970. Mailing Address: P.O. Box 687, Rangeley, ME 04970-0687. Tel.: 207-864-3443. Fax: 207-864-5156.
E-mail: wreich@rangeley.org
Web Site: www.wilhelmreichtrust.org
Institution Type/Description: Historic House Museum: housed in the home, laboratory & research center of physician & scientist, Wilhelm Reich, M.D.
Hours & Admission Prices: Conference Center: Mon.-Fri. 9-2. Observatory: July-Aug. Wed.-Sun. 1-5; Sept. Sat. 1-5; other times by appointment. Adults $6; discounts to AAM & ICOM members; children 12 & under no charge.
Attendance: 3,000 (estimated)

Readfield

READFIELD HISTORICAL SOCIETY AND MUSEUM, 759 Main St., Readfield Depot, Readfield, ME 04355. Mailing Address: P.O. Box 354, Readfield, ME 04355. Tel.: 207-377-2299. Facebook.
E-mail: readfieldhistorical@gmail.com
Web Site: www.readfieldhistorical.org
Key Personnel: Dir. & Pres. (V), Robert Harris.
Institution Type/Description: History Museum.
Hours & Admission Prices: June to mid-Sept. Thurs. & Sat. 10-2. No charge; donations accepted. &
Attendance: 200 (estimated)

Rockland

COASTAL CHILDREN'S MUSEUM, 75 Mechanic St., Rockland, ME 04841. Tel.: 207-596-0300.
E-mail: info@coastalchildrensmuseum.org
Web Site: www.coastalchildrensmuseum.org
Key Personnel: Chm. (V) & Pres. (V), Elaine Wilson; Chm. (V), Felicity Bowelitch.
Institution Type/Description: Children's Museum.
Hours & Admission Prices: Wed.-Sat. 10-4, Sun. 1-4. Discounts to ACM members. Closed New Year's Day; Easter; Independence Day; Labor Day; Thanksgiving; Christmas Eve & Day. &

MAINE LIGHTHOUSE MUSEUM, One Park Dr., Rockland, ME 04841. Mailing Address: P.O. Box 1116, Rockland, ME 04841-1116. Tel.: 207-594-3301. Fax: 207-596-6549.
E-mail: dot@mainelighthousemuseum.org
Web Site: www.mainelighthousemuseum.org
Formerly: Shore Village Museum
Key Personnel: Dir., Dorothy Black; Chm. (V), Paul Dilger; Museum Shop Mgr., Sue Luok.
Institution Type/Description: Maritime Museum.
Hours & Admission Prices: June-Oct. Mon.-Fri. 10-5, Sat.-Sun. 10-4; Nov.-Dec. & March-May Thurs.-Fri. 10-5, Sat. 10-4. Adults $8, seniors $6; members, Coast Guard & children under 12 no charge. &
Attendance: 12,000 (estimated)

WILLIAM A. FARNSWORTH LIBRARY AND ART MUSEUM, INC. DBA FARNSWORTH ART MUSEUM, 16 Museum St., Rockland, ME 04841-2867. Tel.: 207-596-6457. Fax: 207-596-0509.
E-mail: writeus@farnsworthmuseum.org
Web Site: www.farnsworthmuseum.org
Key Personnel: Dir., Christopher J. Brownawell; Pres., Susan Deutsch; Chief Cur, Michael Komanecky; Registrar, Angela Waldron; Museum Shop Mgr., Wendy Kirklian.
Institution Type/Description: Art Museum.
Hours & Admission Prices: Jan.-March Wed.-Sun. 10-5; April-May Tues.-Sun. 10-5; June-Oct. Wed. 10-8, Thurs.-Tues. 10-5; Nov.-Dec. Tues.-Sun. 10-5. Adults $12, senior citizens & students $10; discounts to AAM & ICOM members; members & New England Consortium of Museums members no charge. Closed New Year's Day; Easter; Thanksgiving; Christmas.
Attendance: 66,281 (actual)

Rockport

CENTER FOR MAINE CONTEMPORARY ART, 21 Winter St., Rockland, ME 04841. Mailing Address: P.O. Box 1767, Rockland, ME 04841-1767. Tel.: 207-701-5005. Facebook & Instagram: @cmcanow.
E-mail: info@cmcanow.org
Web Site: www.cmcanow.org
Key Personnel: Dir., Suzette McAvoy; Mgr. Operations & Communications, Jean Thompson; Creative Dir., Jonathan Laurence; Chm. (V) Bd. Trustees, Charlotte Dixon; Museum Shop Mgr., Tara Gardner.
Institution Type/Description: Contemporary Art.
Hours & Admission Prices: Galleries: May-Dec. Tues.-Sat. 10-6, Sun. 1-6. Offices: Mon.-Fri. 9-5. Admission $6; discounts to AAM members; members no charge. &
Attendance: 35,000 (estimated)

CONWAY HOMESTEAD & CRAMER MUSEUM, 223 Union St. #747, Rockport, ME 04856. Mailing Address: P.O. Box 747, Rockport, ME 04856-0747. Tel.: 207-236-2257.
E-mail: crhs@midcoast.com
Web Site: www.conwayhouse.org
Key Personnel: Pres., Frank Carr.
Institution Type/Description: History Museum: listed on the National Register of Historic Places.
Hours & Admission Prices: Call for hours. Adults $5; discounts to AAA members & other local historical societies; members no charge. &
Attendance: 1,254 (estimated)

Rumford

GREATER RUMFORD HISTORICAL SOCIETY, 145 Congress St., Rumford, ME 04276. Tel.: 207-364-2540.
E-mail: rhs@gwi.net
Key Personnel: Pres. (V), Jane W. Peterson; Museum Cur. & Museum Shop Mgr., David Gawtry; Archives, Dru Breton.
Institution Type/Description: Historical Society Museum & Archives.
Hours & Admission Prices: June-Aug. Sat. 9-3. No charge; donations accepted.
Attendance: 35 (actual)

Saco

SACO MUSEUM, 371 Main St., Saco, ME 04072-1520. Tel.: 207-283-3861. Fax: 207-283-0754.
E-mail: traiselis@sacomuseum.org
Web Site: www.sacomuseum.org
Formerly: York Institute Museum
Key Personnel: Dir., Tara Vose Raiselis; Exec. Dir., Leslie Rounds; Collections Mgr., Carolyn Parsons Roy; Program & Education Mgr., Zoe B. Thomas.
Institution Type/Description: History & Art Museum: housed in an historic building built in 1926 by John Calvin Stevens.
Hours & Admission Prices: June-Dec. Tues.-Thurs. & Sun. 12-4. Fri. 12-8, Sat. 10-4; Jan.-May. Tues.-Thurs. 12-4. Fri. 12-8, Sat. 10-4. Adults $5, seniors $3, students & children $2; discounts to NEMA, AAA & AAM members; members & Fri. 4-8 no charge. Closed legal holidays. &
Attendance: 10,305 (actual)

Saint Francis

ST. FRANCIS HISTORICAL SOCIETY, 1074 Main St., Saint Francis, ME 04774. Tel.: 207-398-3387.
E-mail: geneperreault@hotmail.com
Institution Type/Description: Historical Society Museum.
Hours & Admission Prices: Sun.-Mon. & Wed. 12:30-3:30. No Charge. &
Attendance: 175 (estimated)

Scarborough

SCARBOROUGH HISTORICAL MUSEUM, 647 U.S. Rte. 1 Dunstan, Scarborough, ME 04074. Mailing Address: P.O. Box 156, Scarborough, ME 04070-0156. Tel.: 207-885-9997.
E-mail: scarboroughhist@maine.rr.com
Key Personnel: Pres. (V), Rodney Laughton.
Institution Type/Description: History Museum.
Hours & Admission Prices: Tues. 9-12, 2nd Sat. each month 9-12. No charge; donations accepted. &
Attendance: 225 (estimated)

Seal Cove

THE SEAL COVE AUTO MUSEUM, 1414 Tremont Rd., Seal Cove, ME 04674. Mailing Address: P.O. Box 106, Seal Cove, ME 04674. Tel.: 207-244-9242. Fax: 207-244-9772. Facebook.
E-mail: info@sealcoveautomuseum.org
Web Site: www.sealcoveautomuseum.org
Key Personnel: Exec. Dir., Raney Bench; Pres. (V), Elizabeth McMullen; Museum Shop Mgr., Eric Novella.
Institution Type/Description: Transportation Museum.

Hours & Admission Prices: May-Oct. daily 10-5. Adults $6, senior citizens $5, teens 13-17 $4, children 5-12 $2; discounts to AAM, ICOM & AAA members; members & children under 5 no charge. &
Attendance: 14,000 (actual)

Searsport

PENOBSCOT MARINE MUSEUM, 5 Church St., Searsport, ME 04974-3351. Mailing Address: P.O. Box 498, Searsport, ME 04974-0498. Tel.: 207-548-2529. Fax: 207-548-2520. Facebook: Penobscot.
E-mail: museumoffices@pmm-maine.org
Web Site: www.penobscotmarinemuseum.org
Key Personnel: Exec. Dir., Liz Lodge; Cur., Benjamin A.G. Fuller; External Rels. Dir., Kathy Goldner; Finance & Operations Dir., Catherine Moore; Museum Shop Mgr., Sabrina Kettell.
Institution Type/Description: Maritime Museum: housed in 10 buildings including 8 buildings listed on the National Register of Historic Places.
Hours & Admission Prices: Mon.-Sat. 10-5, Sun. 12-5. Family $30, adults $12, seniors (65+) $10, children 7-15 $8, discounts to local guests of Inns, groups, AAM & CAMM members; children under 6, members & residents no charge. &
Attendance: 18,000 (actual)

Sedgwick

SEDGWICK-BROOKLIN HISTORICAL SOCIETY, 575 N. Sedgwick Rd., Sedgwick, ME 04676. Mailing Address: P.O. Box 171, Sedgwick, ME 04676-0063. Tel.: 207-359-8086.
E-mail: eggemoggin@gmail.com
Key Personnel: Pres. (V), Anne P. Dentino.
Institution Type/Description: History Museum: housed in 1795 Rev. Daniel Merrill house.
Hours & Admission Prices: July-Aug. Sun. 2-4; other times by appointment. No charge; donations accepted.
Attendance: 100 (estimated)

Skowhegan

MARGARET CHASE SMITH LIBRARY, 56 Norridgewock Ave., Skowhegan, ME 04976-1204. Tel.: 207-474-7133. Facebook.
E-mail: mcsl@mcslibrary.org
Web Site: www.mcslibrary.org
Key Personnel: Dir., David Richards.
Institution Type/Description: Library & Archives.
Hours & Admission Prices: Mon.-Fri. 10-4. No charge; donations accepted.
Attendance: 2,500 (estimated)

SKOWHEGAN HISTORY HOUSE MUSEUM & RESEARCH CENTER, 66 Elm St., Skowhegan, ME 04976-0832. Mailing Address: P.O. Box 832, Showhegan, ME 04976-0832. Tel.: 207-474-6632.
E-mail: melvinburnham@skowheganhistoryhouse.org
Web Site: skowheganhistoryhouse.org
Key Personnel: Dir. & Pres., Melvin Burnham; Sec., Bonnie Chamberlain; Treas., Patricia Horine; Cur., Lee Granville.
Institution Type/Description: Local History Museum: built in 1839.
Hours & Admission Prices: June to mid-Oct. Tues.-Sat. 10-4; other times by appointment. No charge; donations accepted. Closed holidays.
Attendance: 511 (actual)

South Berwick

COUNTING HOUSE MUSEUM, Main & Liberty Sts., South Berwick, ME 03908. Mailing Address: P.O. Box 296, South Berwick, ME 03908-0296. Tel.: 207-384-0000.
E-mail: info@oldberwick.org
Web Site: www.oldberwick.org
Key Personnel: Pres., Wendy Pirsig; Vice Pres., Nicole St. Pierre; Museum Shop Mgr., Norma Keim.
Institution Type/Description: Historic House Museum.
Hours & Admission Prices: June-Oct. Sat.-Sun. 1-4; other times by appointment. No charge; donations accepted. &
Attendance: 500 (estimated)

HAMILTON HOUSE, 40 Vaughan's Lane, South Berwick, ME 03908-1711. Mailing Address: 141 Cambridge St., Boston, MA 02114-2702. Tel.: 207-384-2454, 617-227-3956 (Historic New England).
E-mail: news@historicnewengland.org
Web Site: www.historicnewengland.org

Key Personnel: Pres. & C.E.O., Carl R. Nold.
Institution Type/Description: National Historic House/Landmark: c.1785 Hamilton House, Georgian estate overlooking the Salmon Falls River.
Hours & Admission Prices: June-Oct. 15 Wed.-Sun. 11-5, last tour at 4pm. Adults $10; discounts to seniors, AAM, ICOM, AAA, WGBH members; members no charge.
Attendance: 7,379 (actual)

SARAH ORNE JEWETT HOUSE, 5 Portland St., South Berwick, ME 03908. Mailing Address: 141 Cambridge St., Boston, MA 02114-2702. Tel.: 207-384-2454, 617-227-3956 (Historic New England). Facebook: Sarah Orne Jewett House.
E-mail: jewetthouse@historicnewengland.org
Web Site: www.historicnewengland.org
Key Personnel: Pres. & C.E.O., Carl R. Nold.
Institution Type/Description: Natuibak Historic House/Landmark: 1774 Georgian residence of the celebrated regional author Sarah Orne Jewett.
Hours & Admission Prices: June-Oct. 15 Fri.-Sun. 11-5, (last tour at 4); Nov.-May first & third Sat. 11-5. Adults $8; discounts to seniors, AAM, ICOM, AAA, WGBH members; members no charge.
Attendance: 2,933 (actual)

South Bristol

SOUTH BRISTOL HISTORICAL SOCIETY, 2124 State Rte. 129, South Bristol, ME 04568. Mailing Address: P.O. Box 229, South Bristol, ME 04568. Tel.: 207-315-0558.
E-mail: sbhistorical@gmail.com
Web Site: southbristolhistoricalsociety.org
Institution Type/Description: Historical Society Museum.
Hours & Admission Prices: Jan.-May Thurs. 1-3; June-Aug. Fri. 1-4; other times by appointment. No charge; donations accepted.

South Paris

HAMLIN MEMORIAL LIBRARY & MUSEUM, 16 Hannibal Hamlin Dr., South Paris, ME 04281. Mailing Address: P.O. Box 43, Paris, ME 04271-0043. Tel.: 207-743-2980. Facebook: Hamlin Library.
E-mail: hamlinstaff@hamlin.lib.me.us
Web Site: www.hamlin.lib.me.us
Key Personnel: Museum Cur., Alana DePerte.
Institution Type/Description: Historic Building: built in 1822.
Hours & Admission Prices: Year-round. Tues. 11-5, Thurs. 1-6, Sat. 10-2. No charge; donations accepted.
Attendance: 2,000 (actual)

Southport

HENDRICKS HILL MUSEUM, 417 Hendricks Hill Rd., Rte. 27, Southport, ME 04576. Mailing Address: P.O. Box 3, Southport, ME 04576-0003. Tel.: 207-633-1102.
Institution Type/Description: History Museum: housed in 1810 farmhouse.
Hours & Admission Prices: July to Labor Day Tues., Thurs. & Sat. 11-3; Sept. by appointment. No charge; donations accepted. &
Attendance: 382 (actual)

Southwest Harbor

WENDELL GILLEY MUSEUM, 4 Herrick Rd., Southwest Harbor, ME 04679-4431. Mailing Address: P.O. Box 254, Southwest Harbor, ME 04679-0254. Tel.: 207-244-7555. Fax: 207-244-5134. Facebook: Wendell Gilley Museum.
E-mail: info@wendellgilleymuseum.org
Web Site: www.wendellgilleymuseum.org
Key Personnel: C.E.O. & Dir., Nina Z. Gormley; Pres., Tad Templeton; Vice Pres., Michael Musetti; Carver-in-Residence, Steven L. Valleau.
Institution Type/Description: Folk Art & Woodcarving Museum.
Hours & Admission Prices: Call or see website for hours. Adults $5; discounts to AAM & NEMA members; members no charge. &
Attendance: 25,000 (estimated)

Standish

MARRETT HOUSE, 40 Ossipee Trail E., Rte. 25, Standish, ME 04084-0003. Mailing Address: P.O. Box 3, Rte. 25, Standish, ME 04084-0003. Tel.: 207-882-7169. Fax: 207-882-7169.
E-mail: marretthouse@historicnewengland.org
Web Site: www.historicnewengland.org

Key Personnel: Pres., Carl Nold; Regl. Mgr., Peggy Konitzky.
Institution Type/Description: Historic House: 1789 late Georgian house externally remodeled in the later Greek Revival & 19th century styles.
Hours & Admission Prices: June-Oct. 15 1st & 3rd Sat. of month 11-4. Adults $5; discounts to seniors, children, AAM, ICOM, AAA & WGBH members; Historic New England members no charge.
Attendance: 1,210 (actual)

Stockholm

STOCKHOLM HISTORICAL SOCIETY MUSEUM, P.O. Box 1, Stockholm, ME 04783. Tel.: 207-896-5812.
E-mail: jhede@mfx.net
Web Site: aroostook.me.us
Key Personnel: Pres. (V), Sandra Hara; Vice Pres., Albertine Dufour; Sec., Rosemary Hede; Treas., Membership and Librarian, Collection & Display, Linda Callison.
Institution Type/Description: Historical Society Museum: housed in 1900 store & post office.
Hours & Admission Prices: July to early Sept. Sat. 1-4; other times by appointment. No charge; donations accepted.
Attendance: 200 (estimated)

Thomaston

THE GENERAL HENRY KNOX MUSEUM DBA KNOX MUSEUM, 30 High St., Thomaston, ME 04861. Mailing Address: P.O. Box 326, Thomaston, ME 04861-0326. Tel.: 207-354-8062. Fax: 207-354-0886.
E-mail: info@knoxmuseum.org
Web Site: www.knoxmuseum.org
Key Personnel: Chm., Anne E. Perkins.
Institution Type/Description: Historic House: 1795 Montpelier home of Major General Henry Knox.
Hours & Admission Prices: Tours: Memorial Day to Labor Day Wed.-Fri. 10-4, Sat. 10-1; Sept. to Columbus Day Thurs.-Fri. 10-4; groups & other times by appointment. Family $20; adults $10, seniors $8, children 5-13 $4; discounts to AAA members; children under 5 & members no charge.
Attendance: 5,100 (actual)

THOMASTON HISTORICAL SOCIETY, 80 Knox St., Thomaston, ME 04861-3714. Mailing Address: P.O. Box 384, Thomaston, ME 04861-0384. Tel.: 207-354-2295.
E-mail: info@thomastonhistoricalsociety.com
Web Site: www.thomastonhistoricalsociety.com
Key Personnel: Pres. (V) & Cur., Susan Devlin; Treas., Ron Gamage; Sec. & Museum Shop Mgr., Aleta Kilborn; Finance, Brooks Stevens; Historian, Margaret McCrea.
Institution Type/Description: Historic House Museum: housed in Henry Knox farmhouse; built in 1797.
Hours & Admission Prices: June-Aug. Tues.-Thurs. 2-4; Winter: Tues. 2-4 other tours by appointment. No charge; donations accepted.
Attendance: 380 (estimated)

Thorndike

BRYANT STOVE & MUSIC MUSEUM, 27 Stovepipe Alley, Thorndike, ME 04986. Tel.: 207-568-3665. Fax: 207-568-3666.
E-mail: sales@bryantstove.com
Web Site: bryantstove.com
Key Personnel: Owner, Joe Bryant.
Institution Type/Description: History Museum.
Hours & Admission Prices: Daily; groups by appointment. No charge; donations accepted.
Attendance: 600 (estimated)

Union

MATTHEWS MUSEUM OF MAINE HERITAGE, Union Fairgrounds, Union, ME 04862. Mailing Address: P.O. Box 582, Union, ME 04862-0582. Tel.: 207-785-4330. Fax: 207-785-5145.
E-mail: mmomh@matthewsmuseum.org
Web Site: matthewsmuseum.org
Key Personnel: Chm. & Pres. (V), George R. Gross; Cur., Irene Hawes; Museum Shop Mgr., Clark Hooper.
Institution Type/Description: Heritage Museum: one-room Hodge Schoolhouse (1864-1954).
Hours & Admission Prices: July-Aug. Wed.-Sat. 12-4. Adults $5, senior citizens and children 12 & over $3; discounts to groups; members & children under 12 no charge. Closed Independence Day & Aug. 6.
Attendance: 4,000 (actual)

UNION HISTORICAL SOCIETY - ROBBINS HOUSE & OLD TOWN HOUSE, 343 Common Rd., Union, ME 04862. Mailing Address: P.O. Box 154, Union, ME 04862. Tel.: 207-785-5444.
E-mail: info@unionhistoricalsociety.org
Web Site: www.unionhistoricalsociety.org
Key Personnel: Pres. (V), Dan Day.
Institution Type/Description: Historical Society Museum: housed in a Greek Revival home; built in 1847.
Hours & Admission Prices: Tues.-Wed. & Sat. 9-12; call to confirm; other times by appointment. No charge; donations accepted.
Attendance: 700 (estimated)

Van Buren

ACADIAN VILLAGE, 120 St. Mary's Brook Rd., Van Buren, ME 04785-1610. Tel.: 207-868-5042.
E-mail: mack53197@yahoo.com
Key Personnel: Dir., Pres. (V) & Museum Shop Mgr., Anne L. Roy.
Institution Type/Description: Historic Village: listed on the National Registry for the Preservation of Historical Landmarks.
Hours & Admission Prices: June 14-Sept. 15 daily 12-5. Adults $6, children $3; discount to AAA members.
Attendance: 700 (estimated)

Vinalhaven

THE VINALHAVEN HISTORICAL SOCIETY MUSEUM, 41 High St., Vinalhaven, ME 04863. Mailing Address: P.O. Box 339, Vinalhaven, ME 04863-0339. Tel.: 207-863-4410.
E-mail: vhhissoc@myfairpoint.net
Web Site: www.vinalhavenhistoricalsociety.org
Key Personnel: Pres., William Chilles; Dir., Susan Rodley; Vice Pres., Wyman Philbrook; Treas., Jacob Thompson.
Institution Type/Description: History Museum: housed in 1838 church built in Rockland, moved to Vinalhaven Island in 1875.
Hours & Admission Prices: June & Sept. Mon.-Sat. 11-4; July-Aug. Mon.-Sat. 11-4, Sun. 12-3; other times by appointment. No charge; donations accepted.
Attendance: 1,600 (estimated)

Waldoboro

WALDOBOROUGH HISTORICAL SOCIETY MUSEUM, 1164 Main St., Waldoboro, ME 04572. Mailing Address: P.O. Box 110, Waldoboro, ME 04572.
E-mail: info@waldoborohistory.us
Web Site: waldoborohistory.us/
Institution Type/Description: Historical Society Museum.
Hours & Admission Prices: June-Sept. Wed.-Mon. 12-3. No charge; donations accepted.

Warren

WARREN HISTORICAL SOCIETY, 225 Main St., Warren, ME 04864. Mailing Address: P.O. Box 11, Warren, ME 04864-0011. Tel.: 207-273-2726.
E-mail: warrenhs@midcoast.com
Web Site: warrenhistoricalsociety.org
Institution Type/Description: Regional History Museum.
Hours & Admission Prices: Call for appointment. No charge; donations accepted.
Attendance: 300

Waterville

COLBY COLLEGE MUSEUM OF ART, 5600 Mayflower Hill, Waterville, ME 04901-8856. Tel.: 207-859-5600. Fax: 207-859-5606.
E-mail: museum@colby.edu
Web Site: www.colby.edu/museum
Key Personnel: Carolyn Muzzy Dir. & Chief Cur., Sharon Corwin; Chm. (V), Karen Packman; Asst. Dir. Operations, Gregory J. Williams; Assoc. Dir., Patricia King; Mirken Cur. Education, Lauren Lessing; Lunder Cur. American Art, Elizabeth Finch; Administrative Sec., Karen Wickman; Mirken Coord. Education & Public Programs, Matthew Timme; Cur., Diana Tuite Katz; Curatorial Fellow, Ramey Mize; Lunder Consortium for Whistler Studies Fellow, Justin McCann; Senior Preparator, Stew Henderson; Registrar, Lorraine Delancey; Curricular Registrar, Paige Doore; Cur. Academic Programs, Shalini Le Gall; Mirken Family Postbaccalaureate Fellow & Museum Practice, Francisca Moraga.
Institution Type/Description: Art Museum.

Hours & Admission Prices: Tues.-Sat. 10-5, Sun. 12-5; tours by appointment. No charge. Closed major holidays. &
Attendance: 50,000 (actual)

REDINGTON MUSEUM, 62 Silver St., Unit B, Waterville, ME 04901-6524. Tel.: 207-872-9439. Facebook: The Redington Museum.
E-mail: info@redingtonmuseum.org
Web Site: www.redingtonmuseum.org
Key Personnel: Pres. Historical Society (V), Frederic P. Johnson; Cur., Sarah Sudgren.
Institution Type/Description: Historical Society Museum: housed in 1814 residence of Asa Redington.
Hours & Admission Prices: Memorial Day-Labor Day Tues.-Sat. Tours: 10, 11, 1 & 2. Adults $5; members & children under 18 when accompanied by an adult no charge. Closed holidays.
Attendance: 500 (estimated)

Wells

HISTORICAL SOCIETY OF WELLS AND OGUNQUIT, Rte. 1, 938 Post Rd., Wells, ME 04090. Mailing Address: P.O. Box 801, Wells, ME 04090-0801. Tel.: 207-646-4775. Fax: 207-646-0832.
E-mail: wohistory@gwi.net
Web Site: www.historicalsocietyofwellsandogunquit.org
Key Personnel: Chm. (V), Lee Richheimer.
Institution Type/Description: Historic Structure: 1862 Meeting House in Wells.
Hours & Admission Prices: Memorial Day to Columbus Day Tues.-Thurs. 10-4; Oct.-May Wed.-Thurs. 10-4; other times by appointment. Requested Donation: $5; discounts to AAM members. &
Attendance: 600 (estimated)

Windham

WINDHAM HISTORICAL SOCIETY, 234 Windham Center Rd., Windham, ME 04062. Mailing Address: P.O. Box 1475, Windham, ME 04062. Tel.: 207-892-1433.
E-mail: info@windhamhistorical.org
Web Site: windhamhistorical.org
Institution Type/Description: Historical Society Museum.
Hours & Admission Prices: May-Nov. call for hours. No charge; donations accepted.
Attendance: 500 (estimated)

Winterport

WINTERPORT HISTORICAL SOCIETY, 183 Main St., Winterport, ME 04496. Mailing Address: P.O. Box 342, Winterport, ME 04496. Tel.: 207-223-5556.
Key Personnel: Archivist, Theodora Weston.
Institution Type/Description: Historical Society Museum.
Hours & Admission Prices: July-Aug. Tues. 2-4; other times by appointment.

Wiscasset

CASTLE TUCKER, 2 Lee St., Wiscasset, ME 04578-4121. Mailing Address: Historic New England, 141 Cambridge St., Boston, MA 02114-2702. Tel.: 207-882-7169, 617-227-3956 (Historic New England). Facebook: Castle Tucker.
E-mail: news@historicnewengland.org
Web Site: www.historicnewengland.org
Key Personnel: Pres. & C.E.O., Carl R. Nold; Site Mgr., Peggy Konitzky.
Institution Type/Description: Historic House: 1807 mansion overlooking Wiscasset Harbor.
Hours & Admission Prices: June-Oct. 15 Wed.-Sun. 11-5; last tour at 4pm. Adults $8; discounts for seniors, AAA, AAM, WBGH & ICOM members; members no charge.
Attendance: 4,034 (actual)

THE 1811 LINCOLN COUNTY MUSEUM & OLD JAIL, 133 Federal St., Wiscasset, ME 04578. Mailing Address: P.O. Box 61, Wiscasset, ME 04578-0061. Tel.: 207-882-6817.
E-mail: lcha@wiscasset.net
Web Site: www.lincolncountyhistory.org
Key Personnel: Pres. (V), John Rienhardt.
Institution Type/Description: Regional History Museum.
Hours & Admission Prices: Memorial Day to June & Sept. to Columbus Day Sat. 10-4, Sun. 12-4; July-Aug. Tues.-Fri. 10-4; other times by appointment. Adults $4; members no charge.
Attendance: 2,000 (estimated)

MAINE ART GALLERY, 15 Warren St., Wiscasset, ME 04578-4032. Tel.: 207-882-7511.
E-mail: info@maineartgallery.org
Web Site: www.maineartgallery.org
Key Personnel: Gallery Mgr., Michele Roberge.
Institution Type/Description: Art Gallery.
Hours & Admission Prices: Tues.-Sat. 10-4, Sun. 11-4. No charge; donations accepted.
Attendance: 1,600 (actual)

NICKELS-SORTWELL HOUSE, 121 Main St., Rte. 1, Wiscasset, ME 04578. Mailing Address: 141 Cambridge St., Boston, MA 02114-2702. Tel.: 207-882-7169, 617-227-3956 (Historic New England).
E-mail: news@historicnewengland.org
Web Site: www.historicnewengland.org
Key Personnel: Pres. & C.E.O., Carl R. Nold; Site Mgr., Peggy Konitzky.
Institution Type/Description: National Historic House/Landmark: 1807 mansion designed with an elliptical stairway, lit by a skylight; Colonial Revival furnishings.
Hours & Admission Prices: June-Oct. 15 Fri.-Sun. 11-5, (last tour at 4). Adults $8; discounts to seniors, AAM, ICOM & AAA members; Historic New England members no charge.
Attendance: 2,116 (actual)

Woodland

LAGERSTROM HOUSE MUSEUM, Beckstrom Rd., Woodland, ME 04736. Mailing Address: Woodland Historical Society, 1149 New Sweden Rd., Woodland, ME 04736. Tel.: 207-493-4478 & 3081.
Institution Type/Description: Historic House: built in 1896.
Hours & Admission Prices: July-Aug. Sun. 1-4; other times by appointment.

SNOWMAN SCHOOL HOUSE, Woodland Center Rd., Woodland, ME 04736. Mailing Address: Woodland Historical Society, 1149 New Sweden Rd., Woodland, ME 04736-5703. Tel.: 207-498-8430 & 3081.
Institution Type/Description: Historic Building: housed in a former school built in 1895 by carpenter & school teacher David Snowman.
Hours & Admission Prices: Memorial Day to June Sun. 1-4; other times by appointment.

Woolwich

WOOLWICH HISTORICAL SOCIETY MUSEUM, Nequasset Rd., Woolwich, ME 04579. Mailing Address: P.O. Box 98, Woolwich, ME 04579. Tel.: 207-443-4833 & 5684.
E-mail: whs@gwi.net
Web Site: woolwichhistoricalsociety.org
Key Personnel: Pres. (V), Debbie Locke.
Institution Type/Description: Historical Society Museum.
Hours & Admission Prices: Call for hours.

Yarmouth

YARMOUTH HISTORY CENTER, 118 E. Elm St., Yarmouth, ME 04096. Mailing Address: P.O. Box 107, Yarmouth, ME 04096-0107. Tel.: 207-846-6259.
E-mail: info@yarmouthmehistory.org
Web Site: www.yarmouthmehistory.org
Formerly: Museum of Yarmouth History
Key Personnel: Exec. Dir., Amy Aldredge; Chm. (V), William Harwood.
Institution Type/Description: Local History Museum.
Hours & Admission Prices: Tues.-Sat. 10-5. No charge; donations accepted. Closed holiday weekends. &
Attendance: 3,000 (estimated)

York

MUSEUMS OF OLD YORK, 3 Lindsay Rd., York, ME 03909-1044. Mailing Address: P.O. Box 312, York, ME 03909-0312. Tel.: 207-363-4974. Fax: 207-363-4021.
E-mail: oyhs@oldyork.org
Web Site: www.oldyork.org
Formerly: Old York Historical Society
Key Personnel: Pres., Georgia Bennett; Dir., Joel Lefever; Dir. Devel., Laura Dehler; Dir. Education, Zoe Keefer-Norris; Registrar, Cynthia Young-Gomes;

Program Specialist, Eileen Sewell; Office & Database Mgr., Katy Kreiger; Supvr. Bldgs. & Grounds, Jon Powers; Librarian, Virginia Spiller.
Institution Type/Description: Historic Building Complex.
Hours & Admission Prices: Exhibits: June-Oct. Mon.-Sat. 9:30-4. Office: Mon.-Fri. 8:30-4:30. Family $25, adults $12, senior citizens $10, children 6-16 $5; discounts to AAA & AAM members and groups; members & children under 6 no charge. Library: Thurs.-Fri. 9-12 & 1-5. Adults $5; members no charge. ♿
Attendance: 30,000 (estimated)

York Harbor

SAYWARD-WHEELER HOUSE, Nine Barrell Lane Extension, York Harbor, ME 03911. Mailing Address: 141 Cambridge St., Boston, MA 02114-2702. Tel.: 207-384-2454, 617-227-3956.
E-mail: news@historicnewengland.org
Web Site: www.historicnewengland.org
Key Personnel: Pres. & C.E.O., Carl R. Nold.
Institution Type/Description: Historic House: c.1718 house built on a slope overlooking the York River.
Hours & Admission Prices: Tours: June-Oct. 15 2nd & 4th Sat. each month 11-5, (last tour at 4). Adults $5; discounts to groups & seniors, ICOM, AAM & AAA members; Historic New England members no charge.
Attendance: 1,342 (actual)

MARYLAND

(340 listings)

Aberdeen

ABERDEEN ROOM ARCHIVES & MUSEUM, 18 N. Howard St., Aberdeen, MD 21001. Tel.: 410-273-6325.
E-mail: sayhello@aberdeenroom.org
Web Site: www.aberdeenroom.org
Key Personnel: Museum Dir., Paul Ciesla.
Institution Type/Description: History Museum.
Hours & Admission Prices: Tues.-Thurs. 10-1; other times by appointment. No charge; donations accepted. Closed national holidays. ♿
Attendance: 2,000 (estimated)

Accident

DRANE HOUSE, Old Cemetery Rd., Accident, MD 21520. Mailing Address: P.O. Box 190, Accident, MD 21520. Tel.: 301-746-6346. Fax: 301-746-7376.
E-mail: accidenttownhall@verizon.net
Web Site: accidentmd.org
Institution Type/Description: Historic House: frontier plantation house; built 1798.
Hours & Admission Prices: By appointment. No charge; donations accepted.

Accokeek

THE ACCOKEEK FOUNDATION AT PISCATAWAY PARK, 3400 Bryan Point Rd., Accokeek, MD 20607-9676. Tel.: 301-283-2113. Facebook: Accokeek Foundation.
E-mail: info@accokeek.org
Web Site: www.accokeek.org
Key Personnel: Pres. & C.E.O., Dr. Lisa Hayes; Chm. (V), Virginia Busby; Dir. Mktg., Anjela Barnes; Dir. Programs & Visitor Engagement, Andrea Jones; Museum Shop Mgr., Jessica Burton.
Institution Type/Description: Agriculture Museum.
Hours & Admission Prices: Park: open every day dawn to dusk. Colonial Farm: March-Dec. daily 10-4. Guided Tours: available by appointment only. No charge; donations accepted. Closed New Year's Day; Christmas. ♿
Attendance: 30,000 (estimated)

Annapolis

ANNAPOLIS MARITIME MUSEUM, 723 Second St., Annapolis, MD 21403-3323. Mailing Address: P.O. Box 3088, Annapolis, MD 21403-0088. Tel.: 410-295-0104. Fax: 410-295-2962. Facebook, Instagram, Twitter.
E-mail: office@maritime.org
Web Site: www.amaritime.org
Key Personnel: Dir., Alice Estrada; Devel. Dir., M.K. Richardson; Admin. Mgr., Mary Ostrye; Cur., Caitlin Swaim; Venue Mgr., Paige Skrikus; Communications Coord., Sydney Boom.
Institution Type/Description: Maritime Museum.
Hours & Admission Prices: Museum: Tues.-Sun. 11-3. Lighthouse Tours: call for hours. No charge; donations accepted. Boat Ride: adults 12 & over $70; children under 12 not admitted. ♿

BANNEKER-DOUGLASS MUSEUM, 84 Franklin St., Annapolis, MD 21401-2738. Tel.: 410-216-6180. Fax: 410-974-2553.
E-mail: bannekerdouglassmuseum@gmail.com
Web Site: bdmuseum.maryland.gov
Key Personnel: Exec. Dir., Chanel Compton; Programs Dir., Sabriyah Hassan; Outreach Coord., LeRonn Herbert; Dir. Mktg. & Communications, Robert James; Cur. Collections, Schillica Howard.
Institution Type/Description: African American Heritage Museum.
Hours & Admission Prices: Tues.-Sat. 10-4. No charge. ♿

CHARLES CARROLL HOUSE, 107 Duke of Gloucester St., Annapolis, MD 21401. Tel.: 410-269-1737. Facebook.
E-mail: info@charlescarrollhouse.com
Web Site: www.charlescarrollhouse.com
Institution Type/Description: Historic House Museum: housed in the home of Charles Carroll, a signer of the Declaration of Independence in 1776.
Hours & Admission Prices: June-Oct.: Sat. & Sun. 12-4.. No charge; donations accepted. Closed Easter; Thanksgiving; Christmas Eve & Day.

CHASE-LLOYD HOUSE, 22 Maryland Ave., Annapolis, MD 21401-8006. Tel.: 410-263-2723.
E-mail: chasehomeinc@gmail.com
Web Site: www.chaselloydhouse.com
Key Personnel: Dir., Carol Kelly.
Institution Type/Description: Historic House Museum.
Hours & Admission Prices: March-Dec. Mon.-Sat. 2-4. Adults $5. Closed holidays.
Attendance: 600 (estimated)

THE CHESAPEAKE CHILDREN'S MUSEUM, 25 Silopanna Rd., Annapolis, MD 21403-1117. Tel.: 410-990-1993. Fax: 410-990-1007. Facebook: The Chesapeake Children's Museum.
E-mail: info@theccm.org
Web Site: www.theccm.org/
Key Personnel: Exec. Dir., Deborah Wood, Ph.D.
Institution Type/Description: Children's Museum.
Hours & Admission Prices: School year: 10-4. Summer: 10-5; groups of 10 to 110 by appointment. Admission one & over $5; discounts to ACM reciprocal members. Ask for group workshop fees. ♿
Attendance: 10,041 (estimated)

ELIZABETH MYERS MITCHELL ART GALLERY, ST. JOHN'S COLLEGE, 60 College Ave., Annapolis, MD 21401-1687. Tel.: 410-626-2556. Facebook & Instagram.
E-mail: social.media@sjc.edu
Web Site: www.sjc.edu
Key Personnel: Dir., Hydee Schaller; Art Educator, Lucinda Edinberg; Membership Coord., Alexandra Fotos; Chm. Bd., Casey Pingle.
Institution Type/Description: College Art Gallery.
Hours & Admission Prices: Tues.-Thur. & Sat.-Sun. 12-5, call for details. No charge; donations accepted. ♿
Attendance: 11,000 (actual)

HAMMOND-HARWOOD HOUSE ASSOCIATION, 19 Maryland Ave., Annapolis, MD 21401-1626. Tel.: 410-263-4683.
E-mail: hhhcurator@gmail.com
Web Site: www.hammondharwoodhouse.org
Key Personnel: Exec. Dir., Barbara Goyette; Cur. & Asst. Dir., Rachel Lovett; Office Mgr. & Events Coord., Eleni Bozori; Pres., Rick Struse; Vice Pres., Jim Dolezal.
Institution Type/Description: Historic House: 1774 Hammond-Harwood House.
Hours & Admission Prices: April-Dec. Mon. & Wed.-Sun. 12-5; Jan.-March by appointment. Adults $10, students & senior citizens $8, children $5; discounts to groups, AAM & AAA members; children under 6 & members no charge. Closed Easter; Thanksgiving; Christmas.
Attendance: 13,004 (estimated)

HISTORIC ANNAPOLIS FOUNDATION, 99 Main St., Annapolis, MD 21401. Mailing Address: 42 East St., Annapolis, MD 21401-1731. Tel.: 410-267-7619 & 267-6656.
E-mail: carrie.kiewitt@annapolis.org
Web Site: www.annapolis.org
Key Personnel: Pres., Robert C. Clark; Chm., William Kardash; Exec. Vice Pres. Operations, Ariane Hofstedt; Sr. Vice Pres. Preservation, Karen Theimer Brown; Sr. Vice Pres. Membership, Comm., & Engagement, Carrie Kiewitt; Vice Pres. Finance, Lucy Mikhailova; Retail Mgr., Lisa Wilson; Cur. Collections, Robin Matty.

Institution Type/Description: Preservation & Education Organization: housed in 11 historic sites.
Hours & Admission Prices: Mon.-Thur. 10-5, Fri.-Sat. 10-8, Sun. 11-5. Admission no charge. Closed New Year's Day; Thanksgiving; Christmas. &
Attendance: 120,000 (estimated)

HOGSHEAD, 43 Pinkney St., Annapolis, MD 21401-1717. Tel.: 410-267-7619.
E-mail: Robert.clark@annapolis.org
Web Site: www.annapolis.org
Key Personnel: Pres. & C.E.O., Robert Clark.
Institution Type/Description: Historic Building Museum: housed in the former home of soldiers during the American Revolution.
Hours & Admission Prices: Late March-Early Dec.: Sat.-Sun. 12-4. No charge, donations accepted.

MARYLAND STATE ARCHIVES, 350 Rowe Blvd., Annapolis, MD 21401-1686. Tel.: 410-260-6400. Fax: 410-974-3895. TDD: 800-735-2258.
E-mail: archives@mdsa.net
Web Site: www.msa.md.gov
Key Personnel: State Archivist, Edward C. Papenfuse; Dept. Archivist, Timothy Baker; Dir. Artistic Property, Elaine Rice Bachmann; Dir. Reference Svcs., Mike McCormick; Dir. Acquisition & Preservation, Kevin J. Swanson; Dir. Government Information Svc., Diane P. Evartt; Personnel, Richard Richardson; Dir. Special Collections, Rob Schoeberlein; Dir. Information Svcs., Wei Yang; Cur. Artistic Property, Alexander "Sasha" Lourie; Librarian, Christine Alvey; Registrar, Christopher Kintzel.
Institution Type/Description: State Archival Institution.
Hours & Admission Prices: Tues.-Sat. 8:30-4:30. No charge; donations accepted. Closed state holidays; holiday weekends; first Sat. each month. &

MARYLAND STATE HOUSE, 100 State Cir., Annapolis, MD 21401. Tel.: 410-974-3400.
E-mail: elaineb@masa.net
Institution Type/Description: Historic Building.
Hours & Admission Prices: Mon.-Fri. 9-5, Sat.-Sun. 10-9. Tours: 11 & 3. No charge. Closed New Year's Day; Thanksgiving; Christmas. &

UNITED STATES NAVAL ACADEMY MUSEUM, 118 Maryland Ave., Annapolis, MD 21402-1321. Tel.: 410-293-2108. Fax: 410-293-5220.
E-mail: museumdirector@usna.edu
Web Site: www.usna.edu/Museum
Key Personnel: Dir., Claude Berube; Senior Cur., James W. Cheevers; Mng. Dir., Charles Swift; Cur. Rogers Ship Model Collection, Donald R. Preul.
Institution Type/Description: Naval Museum: located at the U.S. Naval Academy.
Hours & Admission Prices: Mon.-Sat. 9-5, Sun. 11-5. No charge; donations accepted. Closed New Year's Day; Thanksgiving; Christmas. &
Attendance: 170,000 (actual)

Annapolis Junction

NATIONAL CRYPTOLOGIC MUSEUM, 8290 Colony Seven Rd., Annapolis Junction, MD 20701. Mailing Address: P.O. Box 1682, Fort George G. Meade, MD 20755-9998. Tel.: 301-688-5849. Fax: 301-688-5847.
E-mail: crypto_museum@nsa.gov
Web Site: www.nsa.gov/about/cryptologic_heritage/museum/
Key Personnel: Cur., Patrick Weadon.
Institution Type/Description: Cryptologic Museum.
Hours & Admission Prices: Mon.-Fri. 9-4, 1st & 3rd Sat. of month 10-2. No charge. Closed federal holidays. &
Attendance: 50,000 (estimated)

Arnold

HERBARIUM AT ANNE ARUNDEL COMMUNITY COLLEGE, 101 College Pkwy., Arnold, MD 21012-1895. Tel.: 410-541-2260.
E-mail: info@cylburnassociation.org
Key Personnel: Prof., David H. Williams.
Institution Type/Description: Herbarium.
Hours & Admission Prices: Mon.-Fri. by appointment.

Baltimore

THE ALBIN O. KUHN LIBRARY & GALLERY, UNIVERSITY OF MARYLAND-BALTIMORE COUNTY, 1000 Hilltop Cir., Baltimore, MD 21250. Tel.: 410-455-2353. Fax: 410-455-1567.
E-mail: beck@umbc.edu
Web Site: www.umbc.edu/library
Key Personnel: Acting Dir. and Cur., Archivist, Lindsey Loeper; Cur. Exhibitions, Emily Hauver; Special Collections Librarian, Susan Graham.
Institution Type/Description: University Museum.
Hours & Admission Prices: Gallery: Fall & Spring Semesters: Mon.-Wed. & Fri. 10-4:30, Thurs. 10-8, Sat.-Sun. 12-5. Library: Mon.-Thurs. 8-12, Fri. 8-6, Sat. 10-6, Sun. 12-12. No charge; donations accepted. Closed university & major holidays. &
Attendance: 12,000 (estimated)

AMERICAN VISIONARY ART MUSEUM, 800 Key Hwy., Baltimore, MD 21230-3940. Tel.: 410-244-1900. Fax: 410-244-5858.
E-mail: info@avam.org
Web Site: www.avam.org
Key Personnel: Founder & Dir., Rebecca Alban Hoffberger; C.O.O. & C.F.O., Donna Katrinic; Human Resources & Admin., Lisa Nowell; Dir. K-12 Education, Beka Plum; Dir. Mktg. & Comm., Helen Yuen; Dir Design, Theresa Segreti; Dir. Exhibitions, George Geary; Facility Rental, Michele Coziahr; Group Visits & Volunteer Coord., Sara Pike; Membership, Melissa Mauro; Registrar, Diana Van Wagner; Museum Security, Will Wells.
Institution Type/Description: Art Museum: located on 1.1 acre campus at Baltimore's Inner Harbor.
Hours & Admission Prices: Tues.-Sun. 10-6. Adults $10, senior citizens 60 & over $8, students $6; discounts to groups & museum employees; members, children 6 & under and Martin Luther King Jr. Day no charge. Closed Thanksgiving; Christmas. &
Attendance: 121,362 (actual)

THE BABE RUTH BIRTHPLACE AND SPORTS LEGENDS MUSEUM AT CAMDEN YARDS, 216 Emory St., Baltimore, MD 21230-2235. Tel.: 410-727-1539. Fax: 410-727-1652. Facebook; Twitter.
E-mail: info@baberuthmuseum.org
Web Site: www.baberuthmuseum.org
Key Personnel: Exec. Dir., Michael L. Gibbons; Deputy Dir., Shawn Herne.
Institution Type/Description: Sports Museum.
Hours & Admission Prices: April-Oct. daily 10-5 (10-7 when Orioles play at home); Nov.-March Tues.-Sun. 10-5. Museum: Adults $6, senior citizens $4, children 3-12 $3; discounts to military, AAA & AAM members. Sports Legends at Camden Yards: adults $8, senior citizens $6, children 3-12 $5. Closed New Year's Day; Thanksgiving; Christmas. &
Attendance: 70,000 (actual)

BALTIMORE AMERICAN INDIAN CENTER, 113 S. Broadway, Baltimore, MD 21231-1727. Mailing Address: Heritage Museum, P.O. Box 6050, Baltimore, MD 21231. Tel.: 410-675-3535.
E-mail: contact@baicmuseum.org
Web Site: www.baicmuseum.org/
Key Personnel: Chair, Dr. Dennis E. Seymour, Ph. D.
Institution Type/Description: History Museum.
Hours & Admission Prices: mid-April to mid-Nov. Wed.-Sat. 11-5; mid-Nov. to mid-April Sat. 11-4; groups by appointment. Suggested Donation: adults $5; children under 12 no charge.

BALTIMORE & OHIO RAILROAD MUSEUM, 901 W. Pratt St., Baltimore, MD 21223-2644. Tel.: 410-752-2490. Facebook, Twitter.
E-mail: info@borail.org
Web Site: www.borail.org
Formerly: The B&O Railroad Museum
Key Personnel: Chm. Bd., Francis X. Smyth; Exec. Dir., Kris Hoellen; Vice Pres., Charles J. Nahit; Vice Pres., Gerard M. Hiller; Vice Pres., James E. Ross.
Institution Type/Description: Transportation Museum: located on site of the historic Baltimore & Ohio Railroad's Mt. Clare Shops, site of the birthplace of American railroading.
Hours & Admission Prices: Mon.-Sat. 10-4, Sun. 11-4. Adults $20, senior citizens $17, children 2-12 $12; discount to groups of 20 or more with reservations and AAM & AAA members; members & children under 2 no charge. Closed New Year's Day; Easter; Memorial Day; Independence Day; Labor Day; Thanksgiving; Christmas Eve & Day. &
Attendance: 200,000 (estimated)

BALTIMORE CITY ARCHIVES, 2615 Mathews St., Baltimore, MD 21218-4705. Tel.: 410-396-3884.
E-mail: baltimorecityarchives@gmail.com
Web Site: baltimorecityhistory.net
Key Personnel: Archivist, Dr. Robert Schoeberlein.
Institution Type/Description: History Museum.
Hours & Admission Prices: By appointment.

BALTIMORE CITY FIRE MUSEUM, Old Town Mall, 414 N. Gay St., Baltimore, MD 21202-4134. Tel.: 410-727-2414.
Institution Type/Description: History Museum.
Hours & Admission Prices: Thurs. 9:30am-12pm, Fri. 6:30pm-9:30pm, Sun. 1-4; other times by appointment.

BALTIMORE CIVIL WAR MUSEUM, 601 President St., Baltimore, MD 21202-4472. Tel.: 443-220-0290.
E-mail: info@baltimorecivilwarmuseum.com
Web Site: www.mdhs.org
Key Personnel: Dir., Ralph Vincent.
Institution Type/Description: History Museum: located in the c.1850 President Street Station.
Hours & Admission Prices: Fri.-Mon. 10-4. Adults $3, students (13-19) $2, children (12 and under) no charge. &
Attendance: 14,129 (actual)

BALTIMORE LITHUANIAN MUSEUM, 851-3 Hollins St., Baltimore, MD 21201-1003. Tel.: 301-774-3445.
E-mail: lituva@verizon.net
Formerly: Lithuanian Hall Museum
Key Personnel: Dir. & Cur., Henry Gaidis.
Institution Type/Description: Lithuanian Heritage Museum.
Hours & Admission Prices: By appointment. No charge; donations accepted.
Attendance: 750 (estimated)

THE BALTIMORE MUSEUM OF ART, 10 Art Museum Dr., Baltimore, MD 21218-3827. Tel.: 443-573-1700. Fax: 443-573-1582. TDD: 410-396-4930.
E-mail: abrown@artbma.org
Web Site: www.artbma.org
Key Personnel: Dir., Christopher Bedford; Chair (V), Clair Zamoiski Segal; Chief Advancement Officer, Judith Gibbs; C.O.O., Christine Dietz; Dir. Matisse Studies, Jay Fisher; Senior Cur. European Painting & Sculpture, Katherine Rothkopf; Sr. Cur. Contemporary Art, Kristen Hileman; Sr. Cur. Prints, Drawings & Photographs, Rena Hoisington; Cur. Textiles, Anita Jones; Librarian, Emily Rafferty; Dir. Communications, Anne Brown; Dir. Retail Operations, Greg Ferrara; Dir. Security, Timothy Hurlbut.
Institution Type/Description: Art Museum: housed in 1929 building designed by John Russell Pope with later additions & adjoining sculpture gardens.
Hours & Admission Prices: Wed.-Sun. 10-5. No charge; donations accepted. Fee charged for special exhibitions. Closed New Year's Day; Independence Day; Thanksgiving; Christmas. &
Attendance: 208,976 (actual)

BALTIMORE MUSEUM OF INDUSTRY, 1415 Key Hwy., Inner Harbor South, Baltimore, MD 21230-5100. Tel.: 410-727-4808. Facebook, Instagram, Twitter.
E-mail: info@thebmi.org
Web Site: www.thebmi.org
Key Personnel: Exec. Dir., Anita Kassof; Asst. Dir., Margaret De Arcangelis; Finance Mgr., Paula Hankins.
Institution Type/Description: History & Industry Museum: housed in 1865 waterfront oyster cannery.
Hours & Admission Prices: Tues.-Sun. 10-4. Adults $12, seniors $9, children 7-18 & students with ID $7; discounts to AAM & ICOM members; children 6 & under and members no charge. Closed Thanksgiving; Christmas Eve & Day. &
Attendance: 160,000 (estimated)

BALTIMORE STREETCAR MUSEUM, INC., 1901 Falls Rd., Baltimore, MD 21211. Mailing Address: P.O. Box 4881, Baltimore, MD 21211-0881. Tel.: 410-547-0264. Fax: 410-547-0264. Facebook.
E-mail: cmcnally7407@gmail.com
Web Site: www.baltimorestreetcar.org/
Key Personnel: Exec. Vice Pres., Christopher M. McNally.
Institution Type/Description: Transportation Museum: located on site of the Maryland & Pennsylvania RR Terminal in Baltimore.
Hours & Admission Prices: April-May & Nov.-Dec. Sun. 12-5; June-Oct. Sat.-Sun. 12-5. Adults $10, children 4-11 $8. &
Attendance: 15,000 (estimated)

BALTIMORE TATTOO MUSEUM, 1534 Eastern Ave., Baltimore, MD 21231-2330. Tel.: 410-522-5800. Facebook, Instagram.
E-mail: bmoremuseum@gmail.com
Web Site: www.baltimoretattoomuseum.com
Institution Type/Description: Tattoo Art Museum.
Hours & Admission Prices: Mon.-Sat. 10-9, Sun. 11-7. No charge.

BALTIMORE'S BLACK AMERICAN MUSEUM, 1767 Carswell St., Baltimore, MD 21218-4908. Tel.: 410-243-9600.
Institution Type/Description: History Museum.
Hours & Admission Prices: Wed.-Fri. 11-5, Sat.-Sun. 11-6 other times by appointment.

THE CARROLL MANSION, 800 E. Lombard St., Baltimore, MD 21202. Tel.: 410-605-2964. Fax: 410-528-1196.
E-mail: info@carrollmuseums.org
Web Site: www.carrollmuseums.org
Key Personnel: Exec. Dir., Paula Hankins.
Institution Type/Description: Historic House Museum: housed in the winter home of Charles Carroll, signer of the Declaration of Independence; built in 1828.
Hours & Admission Prices: Guided Tours: Sat.-Sun. 12-4. Adults $5, children 6-18, seniors 65 & over, students and military $4; children under 6 no charge.

CENTER FOR ART DESIGN AND VISUAL CULTURE, 1000 Hilltop Circle, Fine Arts Bldg., 105, Baltimore, MD 21250. Tel.: 410-455-3188.
E-mail: cadvc@umbc.edu
Key Personnel: Exec. Dir., Symmes Gardner; Research Prof. & Chief Cur., Maurice Berger, Ph.D.; Cur. of Collections & Outreach, Sandra Abbott; Business Mgr., Janet Magruder.
Institution Type/Description: Fine Arts Gallery.
Hours & Admission Prices: Tues.-Sat. 10-5. Closed UMBC holidays; New Year's Eve & Day; Christmas Eve, Day & week.

CYLBURN ARBORETUM, Cylburn Mansion, 4915 Greenspring Ave., Baltimore, MD 21209-4642. Tel.: 410-367-2217.
E-mail: info@cylburn.org
Web Site: www.cylburn.org
Key Personnel: Pres., Rebecca Henry; Exec. Dir., Patricia Foster; Asst. Dir., Megan Young; Devel. Dir., Christine Kouwenhoven; Accounting, John Handley; Head Gardener, Patricia Sherman; Asst. Gardener, Jackson Lehman; Asst. Gardener, Mitchel Matthews.
Institution Type/Description: Natural History Museum: housed in a Victorian mansion of Renaissance revival style, built of stone from a nearby chromite mine & 207 acre arboretum.
Hours & Admission Prices: Grounds & Gardens: Tues.-Sun. 8-8. Vollmer Visitor Center: Tues.-Sun. 10-4. Mansion: Tues.-Fri. 8-3. No charge. &
Attendance: 15,000 (estimated)

DR. SAMUEL D. HARRIS NATIONAL MUSEUM OF DENTISTRY, 31 S. Greene St., Baltimore, MD 21201-1504. Tel.: 410-706-0600. Fax: 410-706-8313.
E-mail: pcutter@umaryland.edu
Web Site: www.dentalmuseum.org
Key Personnel: Exec. Dir., Dr. Richard Manski; Cur., Dr. Scott D. Swank; Research Assoc., Patrick Cutter.
Institution Type/Description: Dentistry Museum.
Hours & Admission Prices: Mon.-Fri. 9-4. Adults $7, seniors & students $6, children (3-12) $5, special group rates. Closed New Year's Day, Martin Luther King Jr. Day, Memorial Day, Independence Day & Labor Day. &
Attendance: 10,000 (estimated)

EDGAR ALLAN POE HOUSE AND MUSEUM, 203 N. Amity St., Baltimore, MD 21223-2501. Mailing Address: P.O. Box 23773, Baltimore, MD 21203. Tel.: 410-462-1763. Facebook, Instagram, & Twitter.
E-mail: poebaltimore@gmail.com
Key Personnel: Dir., Enrica Jang.
Institution Type/Description: Historic House: 1830 home of Edgar Allan Poe.
Hours & Admission Prices: Thur.-Sun. 11-4. General Admission $8, Military & Students $6, Children (under 12) no charge. Closed national holidays.
Attendance: 6,000 (estimated)

EUBIE BLAKE NATIONAL JAZZ INSTITUTE AND CULTURAL CENTER, 847 N. Howard St., Baltimore, MD 21201-4605. Tel.: 410-916-8509.
E-mail: eventsebcc@yahoo.com
Web Site: www.eubieblake.org

Key Personnel: Exec. Dir., Troy Burton.
Institution Type/Description: History Museum.
Hours & Admission Prices: Wed.-Fri. 1-6, Sat. 11-3, Tues. & Sun. by appointment. Closed federal holidays. &
Attendance: 10,000 (estimated)

EVERGREEN MUSEUM & LIBRARY, JOHNS HOPKINS UNIVERSITY MUSEUMS, 4545 N. Charles St., Baltimore, MD 21210-2693. Tel.: 410-516-0341. Facebook.
E-mail: evergreenmuseum@jhu.edu
Web Site: www.museums.jhu.edu
Key Personnel: Interim Dir. & Cur., Sylvia Eggleston Wehr; Registrar, Natalie Shores; Facilities & Opers. Coord., Ben Renwick; Visitor Svcs. Coord., Nancy Powers; Groundskeeper, Blair Scarbath.
Institution Type/Description: Historic House: housed in an 1850s Italianate mansion formerly owned by philanthropic Garrett family.
Hours & Admission Prices: Tues.-Fri. 11-4, Sat.-Sun. 12-4. Adults $8, senior citizens $7, students with ID, youth 6-17 & Johns Hopkins alumni & retirees $5; discounts to groups, AAM & ICOM members, JHU faculty & staff; members, children 5 & under & JHU faculty, staff & students no charge. Closed holidays. &
Attendance: 11,600 (actual)

FELLS POINT MARITIME MUSEUM, 1724 Thames St., Baltimore, MD 21231. Tel.: 410-675-6750.
E-mail: preservationsocietyfellspt@gmail.com
Web Site: www.preservationsociety.com/about-us/visitor-center.html
Key Personnel: Pres., David Gleason; Vice Pres., Jeffrey Dewberry; Treas., John Highby; Sec., Emily Ward.
Institution Type/Description: Maritime Museum.
Hours & Admission Prices: April 1-May 10: Fri.-Sun. 11-3; May 11-Sept. 5: Wed.-Sun. 10-4; Labor Day-Nov. 20: Fri.-Sun. 11-3. No charge, donations excepted.

FORT MCHENRY NATIONAL MONUMENT AND HISTORIC SHRINE, 2400 E. Fort Ave., Baltimore, MD 21230-5393. Tel.: 410-962-4290. Fax: 410-962-2500.
E-mail: fomc_superintendent@nps.gov
Web Site: www.nps.gov/fomc
Key Personnel: Supt., Tina Cappetta; Cur., Gregory Weidman.
Institution Type/Description: Historic Site: War of 1812 fort, site of the bombardment that inspired Francis Scott Key to write "The Star-Spangled Banner", the National Anthem; fort also served during the American Civil War (1861-65) as a Union prison camp for Confederate soldiers and sympathizers, and as a hospital in WWI (1917-1925).
Hours & Admission Prices: Memorial Day-Labor Day daily 9-6, rest of year daily 9-5. Adults 16 & over $15; senior citizens 62 & over with Golden Age Passport/Senior Pass and children 15 & under no charge. Research: by appointment. Closed New Year's Day; Thanksgiving; Christmas. &
Attendance: 600,000 (estimated)

FREDERICK DOUGLASS-ISAAC MYERS MARITIME PARK, 1417 Thames St., Baltimore, MD 21231. Tel.: 410-685-0295. Fax: 410-276-6347.
E-mail: mjews@douglassmyers.org
Web Site: www.douglassmyers.org
Institution Type/Description: History Museum & Park.
Hours & Admission Prices: Mon.-Fri. 10-4. Adults $5, seniors 60 & over $4, students 6-17 $2; discounts to groups; children 5 & under no charge. &

GLENN L. MARTIN MARYLAND AVIATION MUSEUM, 701 Wilson Point Rd., Hangar 5, Ste. 531, Baltimore, MD 21220-4238. Mailing Address: P.O. Box 5024, Baltimore, MD 21220-0024. Tel.: 410-682-6122. Facebook: @glm.marylandaviationmuseum.
E-mail: martinmuseum@gmail.com
Web Site: www.mdairmuseum.org
Key Personnel: Dir., Ted Cooper; Chm., Robert Byrnes.
Institution Type/Description: Aviation Museum.
Hours & Admission Prices: Wed.-Sat. 11-3. Adults $5, children under 12 $3; members no charge; increased fees for special events. &
Attendance: 7,000 (actual)

GOLDSMITH MUSEUM OF CHIZUK AMUNO CONGREGATION, 8100 Stevenson Rd., Baltimore, MD 21208-1899. Tel.: 410-486-6400. Facebook.
E-mail: geaston@chizukamuno.org
Web Site: www.chizukamuno.org
Key Personnel: Exec. Dir., Glenn S. Easton; Chm. (V), Linda Katz.
Institution Type/Description: Jewish Heritage Museum.
Hours & Admission Prices: Call for hours. No charge; donations accepted.

THE HERITAGE MUSEUM, Hamlet Court, 4509 Prospect Circle, Baltimore, MD 21216-1615. Mailing Address: Hamlet Court, PO Box 18666, Baltimore, MD 21216-1615. Tel.: 410-664-6711. Fax: 410-664-6711.
E-mail: heritagemuseum@usa.com
Institution Type/Description: Cultural, Historical & Environmental Museum.
Hours & Admission Prices: By appointment. No charge.

HISTORIC SHIPS IN BALTIMORE, Pier 1, 301 E. Pratt St., Baltimore, MD 21202-3134. Tel.: 410-539-1797. Fax: 410-539-6238. Facebook.
E-mail: administration@historicships.org
Web Site: historicships.org
Formerly: USS Constellation Museum & Baltimore Maritime Museum
Key Personnel: Exec. Dir., Christopher Rowsom; Membership Coord., Dayna Aldridge; Mktg. Dir., Lisa Hansen; Operations Dir., Brian Auer; Cur., Paul Cora.
Institution Type/Description: Maritime Museum: homeport to USS Constellation, USS Torsk, USCGC Taney, Lightship Chesapeake & the seven foot Knoll Lighthouse.
Hours & Admission Prices: Jan.-Mar. & Nov.-Dec. daily 10-4:30; April-Memorial Day, 10-5; Memorial Day-August Sun.-Thur. 10-5, Fri.-Sat. 10-6; Sept. & Oct. 10-5. Adults $15-$18, senior citizens & students $13-$16, children 6-14 $7-$9; discount to groups, AAM members; children 5 & under and members no charge. Closed Thanksgiving; Christmas Eve & Day. &
Attendance: 100,000 (estimated)

HOMEWOOD MUSEUM, The Johns Hopkins Univ., 3400 N. Charles St., Baltimore, MD 21218-2608. Tel.: 410-516-5589. Fax: 410-516-7859.
E-mail: homewoodmuseum@jhu.edu
Web Site: www.museums.jhu.edu
Key Personnel: Interim Dir., Heather Stalfort.
Institution Type/Description: Historic House Museum: 1801 Federal period home.
Hours & Admission Prices: Tues.-Fri. 11-4, Sat.-Sun. 12-4; last tour at 3:30. Adults $8, senior citizens $7, students with ID $5; discounts to AAM & ICOM members and JHU faculty & staff; members, children 5 & under and JHU students no charge. Closed holidays.
Attendance: 5,000 (actual)

IRISH RAILROAD WORKERS MUSEUM AND SHRINE, 920 Lemmon St., Baltimore, MD 21202. Mailing Address: P.O. Box 20627, Baltimore, MD 21223. Tel.: 410-347-4747. Facebook.
E-mail: info@irishshrine.org
Web Site: www.irishshrine.org
Key Personnel: Pres., Michael Mellett.
Institution Type/Description: Historic Building Museum: built in 1848.
Hours & Admission Prices: Fri. 11-3, Sat. 11-4. No charge; donations accepted.

JAMES E. LEWIS MUSEUM OF ART, MORGAN STATE UNIVERSITY, 2201 Argonne Dr., Baltimore, MD 21251. Tel.: 443-885-3030. Facebook & Twitter.
E-mail: jelmamuseum@morgan.edu
Web Site: www.jelmamuseum.org
Key Personnel: Dir., Gabriel S. Tenabe; Assoc. Dir. Center of Museums, Robin Howard.
Institution Type/Description: University Museum.
Hours & Admission Prices: Tues.-Fri. 10-4, Sat.-Sun. 12-4. No charge; donations accepted. Closed New Year's Eve & Day; Martin Luther King Jr. Day; Easter; Memorial Day; Independence Day; Thanksgiving; Christmas break. &
Attendance: 40,000 (actual)

JEWISH MUSEUM OF MARYLAND, 15 Lloyd St., Baltimore, MD 21202-4606. Tel.: 410-732-6400. Fax: 410-732-6451. Facebook: Jewish Museum of Maryland.
E-mail: info@jewishmuseummd.org
Web Site: www.jewishmuseummd.org
Formerly: Jewish Historical Society of Maryland
Key Personnel: Exec. Dir., Marvin Pinkert; Mgr. Devel. & Mktg. Mgr., Rachel Kassman; Deputy Dir. Programs & Devel., Deborah Cardin; Cur., Karen Falk; Collections Mgr., Joanne Church; Dir. Education, Ilene Dackman-Alon; Museum Shop Mgr., Esther Weiner.
Institution Type/Description: History Museum: housed in a 3-building complex, including history museum & the Lloyd St. Synagogue, built in 1845 and the B'nai Israel Synagogue built in 1876.
Hours & Admission Prices: Museum: Sun.-Thurs. 10-5. Library & Archives by appointment. Adults $10, seniors $8, students $6, children 4-12 $4; discounts to groups, AAM, & GBHA members; members & children under 4 no charge.

Closed major Jewish holidays; New Year's Day; Labor Day; Thanksgiving & day after. &
Attendance: 8,977 (actual)

THE JOHNS HOPKINS UNIVERSITY ARCHAEOLOGICAL COLLECTION, 150 Gilman Hall, 3400 N. Charles St., Baltimore, MD 21218-2608. Tel.: 410-516-0383. Fax: 410-516-5218.
E-mail: archmuseum@jhu.edu
Web Site: archaeologicalmuseum.jhu.edu/
Key Personnel: Dir. Museum, Dr. Betsy Bryan; Mgr. Collection, Kate Gallagher; Cur., Sanchita Balachandran.
Institution Type/Description: Art & Archaeology Museum.
Hours & Admission Prices: Academic Year: Mon.-Fri. 10:30-1:30. &
Attendance: 700

MARSHY POINT NATURE CENTER, 7130 Marshy Point Rd., Baltimore, MD 21220. Tel.: 410-887-2817. Fax: 410-335-8995. TDD: 410-887-5319.
Web Site: www.marshypoint.org/about/
Key Personnel: Dir. & Senior Naturalist, Ben Porter.
Institution Type/Description: Nature Center.
Hours & Admission Prices: Nature Center: daily 9-5. Closed holidays.

MARYLAND ART PLACE, 218 W. Saratoga St., Baltimore, MD 21201. Tel.: 410-962-8565. Fax: 410-244-8017. TDD: 1-800-735-2258.
E-mail: map@mdartplace.org
Web Site: www.mdartplace.org
Key Personnel: Exec. Dir., Amy Cavanaugh Royce; Program Mgr., Naomi Davidoff.
Institution Type/Description: Art Museum.
Hours & Admission Prices: Office: Tues.-Sat. 9-5. Gallery: Tues.-Sat. 12-4. No charge; donations accepted. Closed federal holidays. &
Attendance: 50,000 (estimated)

MARYLAND HISTORICAL SOCIETY, 201 W. Monument St., Baltimore, MD 21201-4674. Tel.: 410-685-3750. Fax: 410-962-7058.
E-mail: info@mdhs.org
Web Site: www.mdhs.org
Key Personnel: Pres. & C.E.O., Mark Letzer; Vice Pres. Finance & Administration, Dennis Elder; Vice Pres. Collections & Interpretations, Alexandra Deutsch; Vice Pres. Advancement, Clay Braswell; Vice Pres. Education Initiatives, Katie Caljean.
Institution Type/Description: History Museum
Hours & Admission Prices: Museum: Wed.-Sat. 10-5, Sun. 12-5. Library: Wed.-Sat. 10-4:30. Museum: adults $9, senior citizens 60 & over $7, students & children 3-18 $6; members & children under 3 no charge. Closed New Year's Eve & Day; Labor Day; Columbus Day; Independence Day; Thanksgiving; Christmas. &
Attendance: 18,000 (actual)

THE MARYLAND INSTITUTE, COLLEGE OF ART: DECKER GALLERY, 1303 W. Mt. Royal Ave., Baltimore, MD 21217-4191. Tel.: 410-669-9200 & 225-2280. Fax: 410-225-2396.
E-mail: refer@mica.edu
Web Site: www.mica.edu
Institution Type/Description: Art Gallery
Hours & Admission Prices: Call for hours. No charge. &

MARYLAND SCIENCE CENTER, 601 Light St., Baltimore, MD 21230-3803. Tel.: 410-685-5225 & 2370. Fax: 410-545-5973. TDD: 410-962-0223.
E-mail: kszondy@marylandsciencecenter.org
Web Site: www.marylandsciencecenter.org
Formerly: Maryland Academy of Sciences
Key Personnel: C.E.O., Van R. Reiner; Chm. (V), Mark P. Huston; Dir. Education, Pete Yancone; Senior Scientist, Jim O'Leary; Senior Dir. Mktg., Christopher Cropper; C.O.O., Richard Hesse; Senior Dir. Guest Svcs., Lori Blau; Dir. Facilities, Bill Bernard; Museum Shop Mgr., Donna Plitt.
Institution Type/Description: Science & Technology Museum.
Hours & Admission Prices: Tues.-Fri. 10-5, Sat. 10-6, Sun. 11-5. Adults $24.95-$28.95, senior citizens 62 & over $23.95-$27.95, children 3-12 $18.95-$22.95; members & children under 3 no charge for Exhibit Halls, Planetarium, & Demo Stage. Closed Thanksgiving; Christmas. &
Attendance: 700,000 (estimated)

THE MARYLAND ZOO IN BALTIMORE, 1876 Mansion House Dr., Druid Hill Park, Baltimore, MD 21217. Tel.: 410-396-7102.
E-mail: info@marylandzoo.org
Web Site: www.marylandzoo.org
Formerly: The Baltimore Zoo
Institution Type/Description: Zoo.
Hours & Admission Prices: Jan.-Feb. Fri.-Mon. 10-4; March-Dec. daily 10-4. Adults 12-64 $18, seniors 65 & over $15, children 2-11 $14, discounts to AZA members & winter Jan.-Feb.; members & children under 2 no charge. Reciprocal discounts with other participating zoos & organizations. Closed Thanksgiving; Christmas. &
Attendance: 409,843 (actual)

MOTHER SETON HOUSE, 600 N. Paca St., Baltimore, MD 21201-1995. Tel.: 410-523-3443.
E-mail: smscbalto@verizon.net
Institution Type/Description: Religious Museum: housed in the home of Saint Elizabeth Ann Seton, the first American native-born canonized Saint of the Roman Catholic Church. Founder of Sisters of Charity of St. Joseph which later became the Daughters and Sisters of Charity in the US & Canada.
Hours & Admission Prices: By appointment. No charge. Closed New Year's Eve & Day; Martin Luther King Jr. Day; Presidents' Day; Holy Week; Memorial Day; Independence Day; Labor Day; Columbus Day; Thanksgiving week; Christmas Eve, Day & week.

MOUNT CLARE MUSEUM HOUSE, 1500 Washington Blvd., Carroll Park, Baltimore, MD 21230. Tel.: 410-837-3262. Fax: 410-837-0251.
E-mail: info@mountclare.org
Web Site: www.mountclare.org
Key Personnel: Site Mgr., Rose Gallenberger; Museum Shop Mgr., Marguerite Ayers.
Institution Type/Description: Historic House: built in 1760.
Hours & Admission Prices: Tours: May-Dec. Thurs.-Sat. 11-4 on the hour. Adults $8, seniors $7, children 2-12 $6; discounts to groups, tour operators, AAA & AAM members; members & children under 2 no charge. Closed major holidays.
Attendance: 5,700 (estimated)

MUSEUM OF BALTIMORE LEGAL HISTORY, Clarence M. Mitchell Jr. Courthouse, 100 N. Calvert St., Rm. 243, Baltimore, MD 21202. Mailing Address: 101 W. Lombard St., Rm. 9442, Baltimore, MD 21201-2605. Tel.: 410-962-2820.
E-mail: william.dunn@mdcourts.gov
Key Personnel: Dir., Judge James F. Schneider.
Institution Type/Description: Legal History Museum.
Hours & Admission Prices: Mon.-Fri. 12-1 by appointment. Closed holidays. &
Attendance: 5,000

NATIONAL AQUARIUM, 501 E. Pratt St., Baltimore, MD 21202-3103. Tel.: 410-576-3800. Fax: 410-576-8238. TDD: 410-727-3022.
Web Site: www.aqua.org
Key Personnel: Pres. & C.E.O., John C. Racanelli; Chm., Thomas E. Robinson; Exec. Vice Pres. & C.O.O., Dale Schmidt; Sr. Vice Pres. & Chief Mktg. Officer, Margot Amelia; Sr. Vice Pres. & C.F.O., Bruce Hoffberger; Sr. Vice Pres. & Chief of Staff, Candace Osunsade; Sr. Vice Pres. External Affairs, Kathy A. Sher; Acting Sr. Vice Pres. & Chief Conservation Officer, Brent Whitaker; Sr. Vice Pres. & Chief Philanthropy Officer, Marisa Wigglesworth.
Institution Type/Description: Aquarium.
Hours & Admission Prices: Call for hours & admission prices. &
Attendance: 1,431,077 (actual)

THE NATIONAL GREAT BLACKS IN WAX MUSEUM, INC., 1601-03 E. North Ave., Baltimore, MD 21213-1409. Tel.: 410-563-3404, ext. 17 & ext. 16. Fax: 410-675-5040 & 563-7806 (Exec. Office). Facebook: Great Blacks in Wax.
E-mail: jmartin@greatblacksinwax.org
Web Site: www.greatblacksinwax.org
Key Personnel: C.E.O., Dr. Joanne M. Martin; Deputy Dir., Jon Wilson; Devel. Dir., Karaleigh Henson; Museum Educator, Reba Bullock; Public & Media Rels., Ginger Williams; Gift Shop Mgr., Eric Cherry.
Institution Type/Description: History & Wax Museum.
Hours & Admission Prices: Tues.-Sat. 9-5, Sun. 12-6. Adults $12, senior citizens 55 & up, college students & children 12-17 $11, children 3-11 $10; discount to military, teachers, educators, government employees, AARP, AAM, ICOM, AAA members & groups of 10 or more; children under 3 & members no charge. Closed New Year's Day; Thanksgiving; Christmas. &
Attendance: 200,000 (estimated)

NATIONAL MUSEUM OF CERAMIC ART AND GLASS, 2406 Shelleydale Dr., Baltimore, MD 21209-3242. Tel.: 410-764-1042. Fax: 410-764-1042.
Key Personnel: Dir., Chm. (V) & Education, Shirley B. Brown; Pres. (V), Richard Taylor; Vice Pres. & Membership, Paulyn Hyman; Financial Dir., Robert B. Brown; Devel., Bruce T. Taylor, M.D.
Institution Type/Description: Ceramic Art Museum.
Hours & Admission Prices: Please call for hours. No charge; donations accepted. &
Attendance: 11,500 (estimated)

NORMAN AND SARAH BROWN ART GALLERY, Jewish Community Center, 5700 Park Heights Ave., Baltimore, MD 21215-3930. Tel.: 410-542-4900, ext. 239.
Institution Type/Description: Art Gallery.
Hours & Admission Prices: Mon.-Tues. 11-5, Wed.-Thurs. 3-5, Fri. 12-2:30, Sun. 12-5.

OLD ST. PAUL'S CEMETERY, 737 W. Redwood St., Baltimore, MD 21201-1011. Mailing Address: Old St. Paul's Parish Office, 309 Cathedral St., Baltimore, MD 21201-4410. Tel.: 410-685-3404. Fax: 410-385-0186.
E-mail: gordon@osp1692.org
Institution Type/Description: Cemetery.
Hours & Admission Prices: Cemetery: by appointment. Office: Mon.-Fri. 11:30-1:30.

PORT DISCOVERY CHILDREN'S MUSEUM, 35 Market Pl., Baltimore, MD 21202-4002. Tel.: 410-727-8120 & 864-2700. Fax: 410-727-3042. TDD: 410-823-2551.
E-mail: info@portdiscovery.org
Web Site: www.portdiscovery.org
Key Personnel: C.E.O. & Pres., Bryn Parchman; Dir. Exhibits, David Berman.
Institution Type/Description: Children's Museum.
Hours & Admission Prices: Call for hours. Admission 2 & over $17.95; discounts for ACM reciprocal members; passholders & children under one no charge. Closed Thanksgiving; Christmas Eve & Day. &
Attendance: 265,000 (estimated)

REGINALD F. LEWIS MUSEUM OF MARYLAND AFRICAN AMERICAN HISTORY AND CULTURE, 830 E. Pratt St., Baltimore, MD 21202-4403. Tel.: 443-263-1800. Fax: 410-333-1138.
E-mail: info.services@lewismuseum.org
Web Site: www.africanamericanculture.org
Key Personnel: Exec. Dir., Wanda Draper; Dir. Collections, Charles Bethea; Registrar, Deborah Nobles-McDaniel.
Institution Type/Description: History Museum.
Hours & Admission Prices: Wed.-Sat. 10-5, 3rd Thurs. each month 10-8, Sun. 12-5. Cafe 10-4. Adults $8, senior citizens & youth 7-17 & students with ID $6, discount to groups; children under 6 & members no charge. Closed New Year's Day; Easter; Thanksgiving; Christmas Eve & Day. &

RIPLEY'S BELIEVE IT OR NOT! MUSEUM, 301 Light St., Light Street Pavilion, Baltimore, MD 21202. Tel.: 443-615-7878.
E-mail: baltimore@ripleys.com
Web Site: www.ripleys.com/baltimore
Institution Type/Description: General Museum.
Hours & Admission Prices: Mon.-Sat. 10-9, Sun. 10-6.

SCHOOL 33 ART CENTER, 1427 Light St., Baltimore, MD 21230. Tel.: 443-263-4350. Fax: 410-837-6947.
E-mail: school33@promotionandarts.org
Web Site: www.school33.org
Key Personnel: Dir., Randi Vega.
Institution Type/Description: Art Gallery.
Hours & Admission Prices: Gallery: Wed.-Sat. 11-4. No charge; donations accepted. &
Attendance: 6,500 (estimated)

SILBER ART GALLERY, GOUCHER COLLEGE, 1021 Dulaney Valley Rd., Baltimore, MD 21204-2780. Tel.: 410-337-6477. Fax: 410-337-6405. TDD: Maryland Relay System.
E-mail: laura.amussen@goucher.edu
Web Site: www.goucher.edu/rosenberg
Formerly: Rosenberg Gallery, Goucher College
Key Personnel: Dir. Exhibitions & Cur., Laura Amussen.
Institution Type/Description: Art Gallery.
Hours & Admission Prices: Tues.-Sun. 11-4. No charge. &
Attendance: 175,000 (estimated)

THE STAR-SPANGLED BANNER FLAG HOUSE, 844 E. Pratt St., Baltimore, MD 21202-4495. Tel.: 410-837-1793. Fax: 410-837-1812.
E-mail: info@flaghouse.org
Web Site: www.flaghouse.org
Key Personnel: Exec. Dir., Amanda S. Davis.
Institution Type/Description: History Museum: The Flag House, a National Historic Landmark, home of Mary Pickersgill, who sewed the Star-Spangled Banner which inspired Francis Scott Key to write the poem that became the National Anthem.
Hours & Admission Prices: Tues.-Sat. 10-4. Adults $9, senior citizens 55 & up & military $8, students K-12 $6; discount to AAM members & groups; members & children under 6 no charge. Closed major holidays. &
Attendance: 13,127 (actual)

UNITED METHODIST HISTORICAL SOCIETY OF BALTIMORE WASHINGTON CONFERENCE, 2200 St. Paul St., Baltimore, MD 21218-5805. Tel.: 410-889-4458.
E-mail: rshindle@bwcumc.org
Web Site: www.lovelylanemuseum.com
Key Personnel: Dir., Robert W. Shindle; Pres., Emora T. Brannan.
Institution Type/Description: Historical & Preservation Societies.
Hours & Admission Prices: Thurs.-Fri. 10-4; other times by appointment. No charge; donations accepted. &
Attendance: 3,500 (estimated)

UNIVERSITY OF MARYLAND SCHOOL OF NURSING MUSEUM, 655 W. Lombard St., Rm. 727, Baltimore, MD 21201-1512. Tel.: 410-706-2822.
E-mail: sikorski@son.umaryland.edu
Web Site: nursing.umaryland.edu/museum
Formerly: University of Maryland School of Nursing Living History Museum
Key Personnel: Dir. & Cur., Daniel Caughey.
Institution Type/Description: Nursing History Museum.
Hours & Admission Prices: Academic Year: Tues.-We. 10-2; other times by appointment. No charge. &
Attendance: 1,000 (estimated)

WALTERS ART MUSEUM, 600 N. Charles St., Baltimore, MD 21201-5185. Tel.: 410-547-9000.
E-mail: info@thewalters.org
Web Site: www.thewalters.org
Key Personnel: Exec. Dir., Dr. Julia Marciari-Alexander; Dir. Mktg. & Communication, Becca Seitz; Museum Shop Mgr., Alice McAuliffe.
Institution Type/Description: Art Museum.
Hours & Admission Prices: Wed. & Fri.-Sun. 10-5, Thurs. 10-9. Fees for some special exhibitions. Closed Martin Luther King Jr. Day; Thanksgiving; Christmas Eve & Day. &
Attendance: 156,051 (actual)

Bel Air

HAYS HOUSE MUSEUM, 324 Kenmore Ave., Bel Air, MD 21014. Tel.: 410-838-7691.
E-mail: info@harfordhistory.org
Key Personnel: Dir. of Properties, Jonathan Poston.
Institution Type/Description: Historic House Museum: built in 1788.
Hours & Admission Prices: March-Dec. 2nd & 4th Sun. 1-4; May-Aug. 1st Fri. 5-8; other times by appointment. Adults $3, students & seniors $2; children under 4 & members no charge. Closed major holidays.

Beltsville

ABRAHAM HALL, 7612 Old Muirkirk Rd., Beltsville, MD 20705-1341. Tel.: 240-264-3415.
E-mail: blackhistory@pgparks.com
Web Site: history.pgparks.com
Institution Type/Description: Historic House Museum: built in 1889.
Hours & Admission Prices: Daily 9-5, except major holidays & by appointment.

UNITED STATES NATIONAL AGRICULTURAL LIBRARY, 10301 Baltimore Ave., Beltsville, MD 20705-2326. Tel.: 301-504-5755.
E-mail: Paul.Wester@ARS.USDA.GOV
Web Site: www.nal.usda.gov
Institution Type/Description: Library.
Hours & Admission Prices: Mon.-Fri. 8:30-4:30. Special Collections: Mon.-Fri. 8:30-12 & 1-4 by appointment.

Berlin

CALVIN B. TAYLOR HOUSE MUSEUM, 208 N. Main St., Berlin, MD 21811. Mailing Address: Berlin Heritage Foundation, Inc., P.O Box 351, Berlin, MD 21811-0351. Tel.: 410-641-1019. Facebook & Twitter.
E-mail: taylorhousemuseum@verizon.net
Web Site: www.taylorhousemuseum.org
Key Personnel: Pres. (V), Jan Quick; Cur., Susan Taylor.
Institution Type/Description: Historic House Museum.
Hours & Admission Prices: Memorial Day to Oct. Mon., Wed. & Fri.-Sat. 11-3; other times by appointment. Adults $5.
Attendance: 3,500 (estimated)

Bethesda

DENNIS & PHILLIP RATNER MUSEUM, 10001 Old Georgetown Rd., Bethesda, MD 20814. Tel.: 301-897-1518.
E-mail: info@ratnermuseum.org
Web Site: www.ratnermuseum.org
Key Personnel: C.E.O. & Co-Founder, Dennis Ratner; Co-Founder, Phillip Ratner.
Institution Type/Description: Art Museum.
Hours & Admission Prices: Mon.-Thur. 12-4, Sun. 10-4:30. No charge.

OFFICE OF NIH HISTORY AND STETTEN MUSEUM, 1 Cloister Ct., Bldg. 60, Rm. 236, Office of Intramural Research, Bethesda, MD 20814. Tel.: 301-496-6610 & 7695. Fax: 301-402-1434. Facebook.
E-mail: history@nih.gov
Web Site: www.pinterest.com/nihhistory; www.historyatnih.tumblr.com
Formerly: DeWitt Stetten, Jr., Museum of Medical Research
Key Personnel: Dir., Chris Wanjek, Ph.D.; Archivist, Barbara Harkins, M.L.S.; Cur., Michele Lyons, M.A.; Program Asst., Dee Andrews; Exhibits & Education, Henry Grasso, M.A.
Institution Type/Description: Medical Museum.
Hours & Admission Prices: Clinical Center: daily 24 hours. Exhibits: daily 9-9. Campus access through security entrance. No charge. ₺
Attendance: 20,000 (estimated)

UNITED STATES NATIONAL LIBRARY OF MEDICINE, 8600 Rockville Pike, Bethesda, MD 20894. Mailing Address: 8600 Rockville Pike, Mail Stop 3809, Bethesda, MD 20814. Tel.: 301-496-6308.
E-mail: custserv@nlm.nih.gov
Web Site: www.nlm.nih.gov
Key Personnel: Acting Dir., Betsy L. Humphreys.
Institution Type/Description: Biomedical Library.
Hours & Admission Prices: Main Reading Room: Mon.-Fri. 8:30-5, Sat. 8:30-2, History of Medicine Reading Room: Mon.-Fri. 8:30-5. Tours: Mon.-Fri. 1:30.

Big Pool

FORT FREDERICK STATE PARK, 11115 Fort Frederick Rd., Big Pool, MD 21711-1313. Tel.: 301-842-2155. Fax: 301-842-0028.
E-mail: info@friendsoffortfrederick.info
Web Site: www.dnr.state.md.us
Key Personnel: Park Mgr., Angie Hummer; Asst. Park Mgr., Ben Sanderson; Administrative Specialist, Sherian Hose; Park Sec., Betsy Mellott; Ranger, Steve Robertson; Maintenance Chief, Kevin Zeigler; Ranger, Andy Simmons; Maintenance Tech, Dean Smook.
Institution Type/Description: Historic Building & Site.
Hours & Admission Prices: April-May & Sept.-Oct. Sat.-Sun. 10-5; Memorial Day-Labor Day daily 10-5. Adults $3 per car MD residents, $5 per car non-residents. ₺
Attendance: 197,000 (actual)

Boonsboro

BOONSBOROUGH MUSEUM OF HISTORY, 113 N. Main St., Boonsboro, MD 21713-1007. Tel.: 301-432-6969. Fax: 301-432-4050. Facebook.
Key Personnel: Dir. & Owner, Douglas G. Bast.
Institution Type/Description: History Museum.
Hours & Admission Prices: May-Sept. Sun. 1-5; tours by appointment. Donations Requested: adults $4, tours & groups $3, children $1.50; discounts to AAM & ICOM members; local school groups no charge.
Attendance: 600 (estimated)

WASHINGTON COUNTY RURAL HERITAGE MUSEUM, 7313 Sharpsburg Pike (Rte. 65), Boonsboro, MD 21713-2431. Tel.: 240-420-1714.
E-mail: eoverdorff@washco-md.net
Web Site: www.ruralheritagemuseum.org
Key Personnel: Pres., Marge Peters.
Institution Type/Description: History & Rural Heritage Museum and Village.
Hours & Admission Prices: Sat.-Sun. 1-4; other times by appointment. No charge; donations accepted. ₺
Attendance: 2,500 (estimated)

Bowie

BELAIR MANSION, 12207 Tulip Grove Dr., Bowie, MD 20715-2340. Tel.: 301-809-3089. Fax: 301-809-2308.
E-mail: museums@cityofbowie.org
Web Site: www.cityofbowie.org/museum
Key Personnel: Dir., Pamela Williams.
Institution Type/Description: Historic House Museum: housed in c.1745 Georgian plantation of Governor Samuel Ogle, and later country estate of William Woodward.
Hours & Admission Prices: Tues.-Sun. 12-4. No charge; donations accepted. Closed major holidays. ₺
Attendance: 5,400 (actual)

BELAIR STABLE MUSEUM, 2835 Belair Dr., Bowie, MD 20715. Tel.: 301-809-3089.
E-mail: museums@cityofbowie.org
Web Site: www.cityofbowie.org/museum
Key Personnel: Dir., Pamela Williams.
Institution Type/Description: History Museum.
Hours & Admission Prices: Tues.-Sun. 12-4. No charge; donations accepted. Closed major holidays. ₺
Attendance: 3,700 (actual)

BOWIE HERITAGE WELCOME CENTER, 8606 Chestnut Ave., Bowie, MD 20715. Tel.: 240-544-5677.
E-mail: pwilliams@cityofbowie.org
Web Site: www.cityofbowie.org/museum
Key Personnel: Dir., Pamela Williams.
Institution Type/Description: Children's Museum.
Hours & Admission Prices: Tues.-Sun. 10-4. No charge; donations accepted. ₺
Attendance: 5,000 (estimated)

BOWIE RAILROAD STATION MUSEUM, 8614 Chestnut Ave., Bowie, MD 20715-3732. Tel.: 301-809-3089.
E-mail: museums@cityofbowie.org
Web Site: www.cityofbowie.org/museum
Key Personnel: Dir., Pamela Williams.
Institution Type/Description: History Museum.
Hours & Admission Prices: Tues.-Sun. 10-4. No charge; donations accepted. Closed major holidays. ₺
Attendance: 3,000 (actual)

CITY OF BOWIE MUSEUMS, 12207 Tulip Grove Dr., Bowie, MD 20715-2340. Tel.: 301-809-3089. Fax: 301-809-2308.
E-mail: museums@cityofbowie.org
Web Site: www.cityofbowie.org/museum
Key Personnel: Dir., Pamela L. Williams.
Institution Type/Description: History Museums.
Hours & Admission Prices: Mansion & Stable: Tues.-Sun. 12-4. Railroad & Welcome Center: Tues.-Sun. 10-4. Office: Mon.-Fri. 9-5. No charge; donations accepted. ₺
Attendance: 11,000 (actual)

NATIONAL CAPITAL RADIO & TELEVISION MUSEUM, 2608 Mitchellville Rd., Bowie, MD 20716-1392. Mailing Address: P.O. Box 1809, Bowie, MD 20717. Tel.: 301-390-1020. Fax: 301-809-2308. Facebook, Twitter.
E-mail: info@ncrtv.org
Web Site: www.ncrtv.org
Key Personnel: Exec. Dir., Karen Whitehair; Pres., David Wolf; Cur., Brian Belanger.
Institution Type/Description: History Museum.
Hours & Admission Prices: Fri. 10-4, Sat.-Sun. 1-4. No charge; donations accepted. Closed major holidays.
Attendance: 2,100 (actual)

NORTHAMPTON SLAVE QUARTERS AND ARCHAEOLOGICAL PARK, 10915 Water Port Ct., Bowie, MD 20721. Mailing Address: c/o Prince George's Co. Dept. Parks & Recreation, 6600 Kenilworth Ave., Riverdale, MD 20737. Tel.: 301-627-1286 & 454-1780. TDD: 301-699-2544 & 454-1472.
Web Site: history.pgparks.com
Institution Type/Description: History Museum.
Hours & Admission Prices: Call for hours. No charge.

PRINCE GEORGE'S COUNTY GENEALOGICAL SOCIETY LIBRARY, 12219 Tulip Grove Dr., Bowie, MD 20715. Mailing Address: P.O. Box 819, Bowie, MD 20718-0819. Tel.: 301-262-2063. Facebook: www.facebook.com/pgcgenealogy?fref=af.
E-mail: library@pgcgs.org
Web Site: www.pgcgs.org
Key Personnel: Registrar, Carol Borchardt.
Institution Type/Description: History Museum.
Hours & Admission Prices: 1st Wed. of month 10-1; Wed. 10-5; other times by appointment. No charge. &
Attendance: 500 (estimated)

Boyds

BOYDS NEGRO SCHOOL MUSEUM, 19510 White Ground Rd., Boyds, MD 20841. Mailing Address: P.O. Box 161, Boyds, MD 20841. Facebook, Instagram, Twitter.
E-mail: info@boydshistory.org
Web Site: www.boydshistory.org
Key Personnel: Pres., Miriam Schoenbaum; Vice Pres., Maggie Bartlett; Treas., Steve Gibson; Sec., Charlotte Sanford.
Institution Type/Description: Historic Building Museum: housed in a former public school for African American students from 1895-1936.
Hours & Admission Prices: By appointment & April-Nov. last Sun. of every month 2-4. No charge; donations accepted. &
Attendance: 144 (actual)

KING BARN DAIRY MOOSEUM, S. Germantown Recreational Park, 18028 Central Park Cir., Boyds, MD 20841. Mailing Address: P.O. Box 76, Boyds, MD 20841-0076. Tel.: 301-528-6530.
E-mail: info@mooseum.com
Web Site: www.mooseum.com
Institution Type/Description: Dairy Heritage Museum.
Hours & Admission Prices: May-Oct. Sat. 10-3, 4th Sun. each month 1-4. No charge; donations accepted.
Attendance: 3,000 (actual)

Brunswick

BRUNSWICK RAILROAD MUSEUM AND C&O CANAL VISITORS CENTER, 40 W. Potomac St., Brunswick, MD 21716-1111. Tel.: 301-834-7100. Fax: 301-745-5805. Facebook & Twitter.
E-mail: contact@brrm.net
Key Personnel: Cur., Rebecca O'Leary.
Institution Type/Description: Transportation & Social History Museum.
Hours & Admission Prices: Thur.-Fri. 10-2, Sat. 10-4, Sun. 1-4, hours change seasonally, call ahead. No charge. &
Attendance: 8,000 (estimated)

Cambridge

BRANNOCK EDUCATION & RESEARCH CENTER, 100 Maryland Ave., Cambridge, MD 21613. Mailing Address: James B. Richardson Foundation, Inc., P.O. Box 1198, Cambridge, MD 21613. Tel.: 410-221-1871. Fax: 410-228-5471.
E-mail: info@richardsonmuseum.org
Web Site: www.richardsonmuseum.org
Key Personnel: Exec. Dir., Jane Devlin; Exec. Asst., Melissa Thomas.
Institution Type/Description: Science Museum.
Hours & Admission Prices: Call for hours.

HARRIET TUBMAN MUSEUM, 424 Race St., Cambridge, MD 21613. Tel.: 410-228-0401. Facebook & Twitter.
E-mail: wajjrchoptank@comcast.net
Web Site: htorganization.blogspot.com
Key Personnel: Tour Dir., Royce L. Sampson.
Institution Type/Description: History Museum.

Hours & Admission Prices: Tues.-Fri. 12-3, Sat. 12-4.

HERITAGE MUSEUMS & GARDENS OF DORCHESTER, 1003 Greenway Dr., Cambridge, MD 21613-2009. Tel.: 410-228-7953. Facebook, Instagram, & Twitter.
E-mail: dchs@verizon.net
Web Site: dorchesterhistory.org
Formerly: Dorchester County Historical Society
Key Personnel: Exec. Dir., Ann W. Phillips; Collections Mgr., George Mitch Anderson; Pres., Lynne Mills; Vice Pres., Herschel Johnson; Treas., Bernard "Nick" Roetzel; Sec., Nancy Malwitz.
Institution Type/Description: Historical Society Museum.
Hours & Admission Prices: Thur.-Fri. 10-4; Sat. 10-2. Admission $5; discounts to bus tours; NARM & museum members no charge. Closed major holidays. &
Attendance: 3,000 (estimated)

RICHARDSON MARITIME MUSEUM, 401 High St., Cambridge, MD 21613-1804. Mailing Address: P.O. Box 1198, Cambridge, MD 21613-5198. Tel.: 410-221-1871. Fax: 410-228-5471.
E-mail: info@richardsonmuseum.org
Web Site: www.richardsonmuseum.org/
Key Personnel: Exec. Dir., Jane Devlin; Operating Mgr. Ruark Boatworks, Dan Cada; Cur., Melvin Hickman.
Institution Type/Description: Maritime Museum.
Hours & Admission Prices: Wed. & Sun. 1-4, Sat. 10-4 or by appointment. Suggested Donation: $3. Closed New Year's Day; Easter; Independence Day; Thanksgiving; Christmas. &

Catonsville

BENJAMIN BANNEKER HISTORICAL PARK & MUSEUM, 300 Oella Ave., Catonsville, MD 21228. Tel.: 410-887-1081. Facebook.
E-mail: bannekermuseum@baltimorecountymd.gov
Web Site: friendsofbenjaminbanneker.com
Key Personnel: Pres., Cynthia Dejesus; Site Supvr., Justine Schaeffer.
Institution Type/Description: Historical Park & Museum.
Hours & Admission Prices: Museum: Tues.-Sat. 10-4. No charge; donations accepted. Charge for events & programs. Closed holidays. &
Attendance: 40,000 (estimated)

CATONSVILLE HISTORICAL SOCIETY, 1824 Frederick Rd., Catonsville, MD 21228. Mailing Address: P.O. Box 9311, Catonsville, MD 21228-0311. Tel.: 410-744-3034.
E-mail: info@catonsvillehistory.org
Web Site: www.catonsvillehistory.org
Key Personnel: Pres. (V), Polly Gardenghi.
Institution Type/Description: History Museum.
Hours & Admission Prices: Temporarily closed for repairs. &
Attendance: 350 (estimated)

SPRING GROVE HOSPITAL CENTER, ALUMNI MUSEUM, 55 Wade Ave., Garrett Bldg., Catonsville, MD 21228-4663. Tel.: 410-402-7786 & 6000. Fax: 410-402-7050.
Web Site: www.springgrove.com/history.html
Key Personnel: Chm. (V), Joseph Sanphilipo; Treas., Diane Johns; Sec., Ella Nora Hoerl.
Institution Type/Description: History Museum.
Hours & Admission Prices: Thurs. 9am to noon; other times by appointment. No charge; donations accepted. Closed holidays.
Attendance: 132 (estimated)

Centerville

HISTORIC SITES CONSORTIUM OF QUEEN ANNE'S COUNTY, 124 S. Commerce St., Centerville, MD 21617. Mailing Address: P.O. Box 655, Centreville, MD 21617-0062. Tel.: 410-758-2502.
E-mail: info@qachistory.org
Web Site: www.qachistory.org
Key Personnel: Dir., Rebecca Marquardt.
Institution Type/Description: Historic Sites Preservation Consortium.
Hours & Admission Prices: Office: Wed. 10-1. Historic Sites: call for hours. No charge; donations accepted.
Attendance: 3,239 (actual)

Centreville

QUEEN ANNE'S MUSEUM OF EASTERN SHORE LIFE, 126 Dulin Clark Rd., Centreville, MD 21617. Mailing Address: P.O. Box 525, Centreville, MD 21617. Tel.: 410-758-8641. Facebook: Queen Anne's Museum of Eastern Shore Life.
E-mail: mesl@myshorelink.com
Web Site: www.historicqac.org/sites/mesl.htm
Institution Type/Description: History Museum.
Hours & Admission Prices: April-Oct. Sat.-Sun. 1-4; other times by appointment.

TUCKER HOUSE - QUEEN ANNE'S COUNTY HISTORICAL SOCIETY, 124 S. Commerce St., Centreville, MD 21617. Mailing Address: P.O. Box 62, Centreville, MD 21617. Tel.: 410-758-3010.
E-mail: info@qachistory.org
Web Site: www.qachistory.org
Key Personnel: Pres. (V), Rebecca Marquardt.
Institution Type/Description: Historical Society Museum.
Hours & Admission Prices: May-Oct. 1st Sat. each month 10-2; other times by appointment. No charge; donations accepted.
Attendance: 520 (estimated)

WRIGHT'S CHANCE HOUSE MUSEUM - QUEEN ANNE'S COUNTY HISTORICAL SOCIETY & TUCKER HOUSE, 124 S. Commerce St., Centreville, MD 21617. Mailing Address: P.O. Box 62, Centreville, MD 21617. Tel.: 410-758-3010.
E-mail: info@qachistory.org
Web Site: qachistory.org
Formerly: Wrights Chance House Museum Queen Annex County Historical Society
Key Personnel: Pres. (V), Rebecca Marquardt.
Institution Type/Description: Historic House Museum: built c.1744.
Hours & Admission Prices: May-Oct. 1st Sat. each month 10-2 by appointment. No charge; donations accepted.

Charlestown

TORY HOUSE/107 HOUSE, 343 Market St., Charlestown, MD 21914. Mailing Address: P.O. Box 52, Charlestown, MD 21914. Tel.: 410-287-8262.
Key Personnel: Pres. (V), Rebecca C. Phillips.
Institution Type/Description: Historic House Museum: built c.1810.
Hours & Admission Prices: May-Sept. 3rd Sun. each month 2-4; other times by appointment. No charge; donations accepted.
Attendance: 100 (estimated)

Chesapeake Beach

THE CHESAPEAKE BEACH RAILWAY MUSEUM, 4155 Mears Ave., Chesapeake Beach, MD 20732. Mailing Address: P.O. Box 1227, Chesapeake Beach, MD 20732-1227. Tel.: 410-257-3892.
E-mail: cbrailway@co.cal.md.us
Web Site: www.cbrm.org
Key Personnel: Chief Cur., Harriet M. Stout; Administrative Asst., Correine E. Moore.
Institution Type/Description: History Museum: housed in 1898-1899 Chesapeake Beach Railway Station.
Hours & Admission Prices: mid-March to March 31 & Nov. Sat.-Sun. 1-4; April-May & Sept.-Oct. daily 1-4; June-Aug. Mon.-Fri. 1-4, Sat.-Sun. 11-5; other times by appointment; call for groups & tours. No charge; donations accepted. Closed New Year's Day; Christmas. &
Attendance: 12,000 (actual)

Chester

KENT ISLAND HERITAGE SOCIETY - KIRWAN STORE AND HOUSE, Rte. 552 - 641 Dominion Rd., Chester, MD 21619. Mailing Address: P.O. Box 321, Stevensville, MD 21666. Tel.: 410-758-2502.
E-mail: sally.lewis@live.com
Web Site: www.kentislandheritagesociety.org
Institution Type/Description: Historic House & Country Store: built in 1879.
Hours & Admission Prices: May-Oct. 1st Sat. each month 12-4; other times by appointment. No charge; donations accepted.
Attendance: 650 (actual)

Chestertown

CHESAPEAKE FARMS, 7319 Remington Dr., Chestertown, MD 21620. Mailing Address: P.O. Box 80705, CRP 705/L1S11, Wilmington, DE 19880-0705. Tel.: 410-778-8400. Fax: 410-778-8405.
E-mail: ag.info@usa.dupont.com
Web Site: www.dupont.com
Institution Type/Description: Agricultural Research & Demonstration Area.
Hours & Admission Prices: Call for hours.

CLIFFS SCHOOLHOUSE, Rte. 289, Quaker Neck Rd., Chestertown, MD 21620. Tel.: 410-778-2529.
Web Site: www.kentcounty.com/attractions/museums/cliffs-schoolhouse
Key Personnel: Chm. (V), Carol Cordes.
Institution Type/Description: Historic Building: housed in a former one-room schoolhouse; built in 1878.
Hours & Admission Prices: May-Oct. 3rd Sat. each month 1-4. No charge; donations accepted.
Attendance: 250 (estimated)

HISTORICAL SOCIETY OF KENT COUNTY, INC. AND BORDLEY HISTORY CENTER, 301 High St., Chestertown, MD 21620-1505. Mailing Address: P.O. Box 665, Chestertown, MD 21620-0665. Tel.: 410-778-3499.
E-mail: director@kentcountyhistory.org
Web Site: www.kentcountyhistory.org
Key Personnel: Cur., Amanda Tuttle-Smith; Librarian, Joan Andersen; Admin. Asst., Carol Roe Combs.
Institution Type/Description: History Museum.
Hours & Admission Prices: Tues.-Fri. 12-5, Sat. 10-3. No charge. &
Attendance: 4,000 (estimated)

KOHL GALLERY - WASHINGTON COLLEGE, Gibson Center for the Arts, 300 Washington Ave., Chestertown, MD 21620. Tel.: 410-778-2800, 800-422-1782.
E-mail: kohl_gallery@washcoll.edu
Web Site: www.washcoll.edu/about/campus/kohl-gallery
Key Personnel: Cur., Donald McColl.
Institution Type/Description: Art Gallery.
Hours & Admission Prices: Tues. 2-8, Wed.-Fri. 2-5, Sat. 11-4; groups of 10 or more by appointment.

Chevy Chase

AUDUBON NATURALIST SOCIETY, 8940 Jones Mill Rd., Chevy Chase, MD 20815-4799. Tel.: 301-652-9188. Facebook, Twitter.
E-mail: Contact@anshome.org
Web Site: www.anshome.org
Key Personnel: Exec. Dir., Lisa Alexander.
Institution Type/Description: Nature Center & Conservation Area: headquarters housed in c.1927 Georgian Revival brick and stone house, located on 40-acre Woodend Sanctuary.
Hours & Admission Prices: Offices: Mon.-Fri. 9-5. Grounds: daily dawn-dusk. No charge; donations accepted. Closed federal holidays. &

Clinton

POPLAR HILL HISTORIC HOUSE MUSEUM, 7606 Woodyard Rd., Clinton, MD 20735. Tel.: 301-856-0358.
E-mail: info@poplarhillonhlk.com
Web Site: www.poplarhillonhlk.com
Institution Type/Description: Historic House Museum.
Hours & Admission Prices: Thurs.-Fri. 10-4, Sun. 12-4; other times by appointment.

SURRATT HOUSE MUSEUM, 9118 Brandywine Rd., Clinton, MD 20735-2501. Tel.: 301-868-1121. Fax: 301-868-8177. TDD: 301-699-2544.
E-mail: laurie.verge@pgparks.com
Web Site: www.surrattmuseum.org
Key Personnel: C.E.O., Dir. & Staff Historian, Laurie Verge; Museum Shop Mgr., Joan Chaconas; Pres. (V), Kevin Kelly.
Institution Type/Description: Historic House Museum.
Hours & Admission Prices: Wed.-Fri. 11-3, Sat.-Sun. 12-4. Adults $5, senior citizens $4, students 5-18 $2; discounts to groups, Civil War Trust, National Historical Trust, military, AAA & AAM members; children under 5 & members

no charge. Closed Easter; Independence Day; Labor Day; Veteran's Day; Thanksgiving; Christmas. ♿
Attendance: 8,084 (actual)

Cockeysville

HISTORICAL SOCIETY OF BALTIMORE COUNTY, 9811 Van Buren Ln., Cockeysville, MD 21030-5022. Tel.: 410-666-1878.
E-mail: info@hsobc.org
Web Site: www.hsobc.org
Institution Type/Description: Historical Society Museum.
Hours & Admission Prices: Fri. 12-4, Sat. 10-2. Adults $5; members no charge. ♿
Attendance: 979 (actual)

OREGON RIDGE NATURE CENTER AND PARK, 13555 Beaver Dam Rd., Cockeysville, MD 21030. Tel.: 410-887-1815. TDD: 410-887-5319; Facebook: Oregon Ridge Nature Center.
E-mail: info@oregonridgenaturecenter.org
Web Site: www.oregonridgenaturecenter.org
Institution Type/Description: Nature Center & Park.
Hours & Admission Prices: Tues.-Sun. 9-5. No charge; donations accepted.

College Park

COLLEGE PARK AVIATION MUSEUM, 1985 Cpl. Frank Scott Dr., College Park, MD 20740-2000. Tel.: 301-864-6029. Fax: 301-927-6472. Facebook & Twitter.
E-mail: aviationmuseum@pgparks.com
Web Site: www.collegeparkaviationmuseum.com
Key Personnel: Dir., Andrea Cochrane Tracey.
Institution Type/Description: Aviation Museum: located on the grounds of College Park Airport.
Hours & Admission Prices: Daily 10-5. Adults $5, seniors $4, children under 2-18 $2; members & children under 2 no charge. Closed major holidays. ♿
Attendance: 50,000 (actual)

THE DAVID C. DRISKELL CENTER, 1214 Cole Student Activities Bldg., University of Maryland, College Park, MD 20742. Tel.: 301-314-2615. Fax: 301-314-0679.
E-mail: driskellcenter@umd.edu
Web Site: www.driskellcenter.umd.edu
Key Personnel: Exec. Dir., Dr. Robert E. Steele; Deputy Dir., Dorit Yaron; Office Mgr., Veronica McDougal; Archivist, Jennifer Eidson.
Institution Type/Description: Art Gallery.
Hours & Admission Prices: Gallery: Mon.-Tues. & Thurs.-Fri. 11-4, Wed. 11-6. Office: Mon.-Fri. 8:30-4:30. Closed holidays.

GEORGE MEANY MEMORIAL ARCHIVES, 4130 Campus Dr., College Park, MD 20740. Tel.: 301-405-9212.
E-mail: askhornbake@umd.edu
Web Site: www.lib.umd.edu/special/about/home
Key Personnel: Head of Donations, Doug McElrath; Dir. Tours., Laura Cleary; Head Student Employment, Amber Kohl.
Institution Type/Description: History Museum: labor organizations.
Hours & Admission Prices: Research by appointment: Mon.-Tues. & Fri. 8:30-5, Wed.-Thurs. 7:30-6. No charge. Closed federal holidays. ♿
Attendance: 3,000 (estimated)

NATIONAL ARCHIVES AT COLLEGE PARK, 8601 Adelphi Rd., College Park, MD 20740-6002. Tel.: 301-837-2000, 866-272-6272.
E-mail: Archives2reference@nara.gov
Web Site: www.archives.gov/index.html
Institution Type/Description: Archives.
Hours & Admission Prices: Research: Mon.-Tues. & Sat. 9-5, Wed.-Fri. 9-9. Closed Thanksgiving; Christmas.

UNION GALLERY, 1220 Stamp Student Union, Adele Stamp Memorial Union, The University of Maryland, College Park, MD 20742. Tel.: 301-314-8492.
E-mail: jmilad@umd.edu
Web Site: www.union.umd.edu/gallery
Key Personnel: Program Coord., Jackie Milad.
Institution Type/Description: Art Gallery.
Hours & Admission Prices: Fall & Spring Mon.-Thurs. 10-8, Fri. 10-6, Sat. 11-4; Summer Mon.-Thurs. 10-6, Fri.-Sat. 11-4.

UNIVERSITY OF MARYLAND ART GALLERY, 2202 Art-Sociology Building, University of Maryland, College Park, MD 20742. Mailing Address: 1202 Art-Sociology Building, University of Maryland, College Park, MD 20742. Tel.: 301-405-2763. Fax: 301-314-7774. Facebook & Twitter: UMD Art Gallery.
E-mail: tmatla@umd.edu
Web Site: www.artgallery.umd.edu
Formerly: The Art Gallery at the University of Maryland, College Park
Key Personnel: Acting Dir., Taras W. Matla.
Institution Type/Description: Art Gallery.
Hours & Admission Prices: Aug.-May Mon.-Fri. & select Saturdays 11-4. No charge; donations accepted. Closed national & university holidays. ♿
Attendance: 8,000 (actual)

Colton's Point

ST. CLEMENTS ISLAND AND PINEY POINT MUSEUMS, 38370 Point Breeze Rd., Colton's Point, MD 20626-2011. Tel.: 301-769-2222. Fax: 301-769-2225.
Web Site: www.stmarysmd.com/recreate/museums
Key Personnel: Dir., Debra L. Pence; Chm. (V), Barbara McWilliams; Site Supvr. SCI, Christina Barbour; Site Supvr. PPLM, April Havens; Mktg. & Programs, Kimberly Cullins; Exhibits Fabricator & Museum Tech, Tom Emery; Museum Shop Mgr., Carol Cribbs.
Institution Type/Description: Archaeology & History Museum: located on 1634 landing site of Maryland colonists; site of first Roman Catholic mass in English colonies.
Hours & Admission Prices: See website for hours. Adults $3, students 6-18 $1; discounts to AAM members; members & children under 6 no charge. Water Taxi Service: $5 per person. ♿
Attendance: 54,437 (actual)

Columbia

HOWARD COUNTY CENTER OF AFRICAN AMERICAN CULTURE, 5434 Vantage Point Rd., Columbia, MD 21044-2644. Tel.: 410-715-1921. Fax: 410-715-8755. Facebook.
E-mail: hccaacmd@juno.com
Web Site: www.hccaac.org
Key Personnel: Admin., Barbara J. Patterson; Research Librarian, Edna Baker.
Institution Type/Description: History Museum.
Hours & Admission Prices: Temporarily Closed
Attendance: 5,000 (estimated)

THE ROUSE COMPANY FOUNDATION GALLERY - HOWARD COMMUNITY COLLEGE, Peter and Elizabeth Horowitz Visual and Performing Arts Center, 10901 Little Patuxent Pkwy., Columbia, MD 21044. Tel.: 443-518-1200.
Key Personnel: Art Dir., Rebecca Bafford; Asst. To Dir., Chaya Shapiro.
Institution Type/Description: Art Gallery.
Hours & Admission Prices: Mon.-Fri. 10-8, Sat.-Sun. 12-5. Closed university holidays.

Crisfield

J. MILLARD TAWES MUSEUM, 3 Ninth St., Crisfield, MD 21817. Mailing Address: P.O. Box 253, Crisfield, MD 21817-0253. Tel.: 410-968-2501.
E-mail: thoward@crisfieldheritagefoundation.org
Web Site: www.crisfieldheritagefoundation.org
Key Personnel: Claire Otterbein; Asst. to Exec. Dir., Casey Goldsborough.
Institution Type/Description: Maritime History Museum.
Hours & Admission Prices: Tues.-Sat. 10-4, Sun. 10-2. Adults $3; discounts to groups; members no charge. ♿
Attendance: 5,000 (actual)

Crownsville

RISING SUN INN, 1090 Generals Hwy., Crownsville, MD 21032-1417. Tel.: 410-268-9249. Fax: 410-268-1994.
E-mail: ellanwt@aol.com
Web Site: marylanddar.org.annarundel/patriots.html
Key Personnel: Pres. (V), Ellan Thorson.
Institution Type/Description: Historic House Museum: housed in the former home of the Ann Arundel Chapter of the Daughters of the American Revolution; built c.1753. Listed on the National Register of Historic Places.
Hours & Admission Prices: 2nd Sun. of month 1-4; other times by appointment. Donation: adults $5; members no charge.
Attendance: 400 (estimated)

Cumberland

THE ALLEGANY COUNTY HISTORICAL SOCIETY, INC., 218 Washington St., Cumberland, MD 21502-2827. Tel.: 301-777-8678. Fax: 301-777-8678. Facebook: The Allegany County Historical Society.
E-mail: info@gordon-robertshouse.com
Web Site: www.gordon-robertshouse.com
Key Personnel: Exec. Dir., Evan Sloanker; Pres., Nancy Cotton; Asst., Lindsay Droll.
Institution Type/Description: Historic House Museum: housed in a Second Empire-style home built by Josiah Hance Gordon; 1867.
Hours & Admission Prices: Wed.-Sat. 10-4; bus tours available. Adults $7, seniors 60 & over $ 6, children 12 & under $5; veterans & members no charge. Closed major holidays.
Attendance: 4,000 (actual)

ALLEGANY MUSEUM, 3 Pershing St., Cumberland, MD 21502-3042. Tel.: 301-777-7200.
E-mail: info@alleganymuseum.org
Web Site: www.alleganymuseum.org
Formerly: Allegany County Museum
Key Personnel: Pres. (V) & Dir., Gary Bartik; Vice Pres. (V), Joseph H. Weaver; Museum Mgr., Courtney McKay; Museum Devel. Dir., Daryl Smith; Cur. Assoc., Suzanne Trussell.
Institution Type/Description: History Museum.
Hours & Admission Prices: March 17-Dec. Tues.-Sat. 10-4, Sun. 1-4. No charge; donations accepted. ❧
Attendance: 16,100 (estimated)

C. WILLIAM GILCHRIST MUSEUM OF THE ARTS, 104 Washington St., Cumberland, MD 21502. Tel.: 301-724-5800.
E-mail: info@gilchristgallery.com
Web Site: www.gilchristgallery.com
Key Personnel: Pres., Christina Collins-Smith; Vice Pres., Cristina Freas.
Institution Type/Description: Art Gallery.
Hours & Admission Prices: April-Dec. Fri.-Sun. 1-4.

F. BROOKE WHITING HOUSE MUSEUM, 632 Washington St., Cumberland, MD 21502-2827. Tel.: 301-777-8678. Facebook.
E-mail: achs218@gmail.com
Web Site: www.thewhitinghouse.org
Institution Type/Description: Historic House: housed in the home of F. Brook Whiting I; built in 1911.
Hours & Admission Prices: Tours by appointment. No charge; donations accepted.
Attendance: 350 (estimated)

GEORGE WASHINGTON'S HEADQUARTERS, 38 Greene St., Cumberland, MD 21502. Mailing Address: Parks/Recreation City Hall, 57 N. Liberty St., Cumberland, MD 21502. Tel.: 301-777-5132. Fax: 301-759-3223.
E-mail: djohnson@ci.cumberland.md.us
Key Personnel: Dir. Parks & Recreation, Diane Johnson; Dir., Cathy McKenny.
Institution Type/Description: Historic Building: 1755 log cabin built during the French & Indian War.
Hours & Admission Prices: By appointment only. No charge.

THE SAVILLE GALLERY, 9 N. Centre St., Cumberland, MD 21502. Tel.: 301-777-2787.
E-mail: arts@allconet.org
Web Site: www.alleganyartscouncil.org
Institution Type/Description: Art Gallery.
Hours & Admission Prices: mid-May to mid-Nov. Mon.-Fri. 9-5, Sat.-Sun. 11-4; mid-Nov. to mid-May Mon.-Fri. 9-5, Sat. 11-4. No charge. ❧

Denton

MUSEUM OF RURAL LIFE, 16 N. 2nd St., Denton, MD 21629-1004. Mailing Address: P.O. Box 514, Denton, MD 21629-0514. Tel.: 410-479-2730.
E-mail: info@carolinehistory.org
Web Site: www.carolinehistory.org
Key Personnel: Pres. Historical Society, J.O.K. Walsh; Dir., Cur. & Museum Shop Mgr., Carol D. Stockley; Treas., Carolyn D. Spicher.
Institution Type/Description: History Museum.
Hours & Admission Prices: Fri.-Sat. 10-3, Sun. 12-4; Linchester Mill: May-Oct. 2nd & 4th Fri. & Sat. of the month 10-4. No charge; donations accepted. ❧
Attendance: 1,700 (actual)

Drayden

DRAYDEN AFRICAN-AMERICAN SCHOOLHOUSE, 18287 Cherryfield Rd., Drayden, MD 20630. Mailing Address: c/o St. Clement's Island Museum, 38370 Point Breeze Rd., Colton's Point, MD 20626. Tel.: 301-994-1471. Fax: 301-769-2225.
E-mail: april.havens@stmarysmd.com
Web Site: www.stmarysmd.com/recreate/Draydenschool
Key Personnel: Museum Division Mgr., Debra Pence.
Institution Type/Description: Historic Schoolhouse: built c.1890.
Hours & Admission Prices: By appointment.

Earleville

MOUNT HARMON PLANTATION, 600 Mount Harmon Rd., Earleville, MD 21919. Mailing Address: P.O. Box 65, Earleville, MD 21919. Tel.: 410-275-8819.
E-mail: info@mountharmon.org
Web Site: www.mountharmon.org
Key Personnel: Exec. Dir., Paige Howard.
Institution Type/Description: Historic Plantation: housed in an 18th century manor home on a former tobacco plantation.
Hours & Admission Prices: May-Oct. Thurs.-Sun. 10-3; other times by appointment.

Easton

ACADEMY ART MUSEUM, 106 South St., Easton, MD 21601. Tel.: 410-822-2787. Fax: 410-822-5997.
E-mail: info@academyartmuseum.org
Web Site: www.academyartmuseum.org
Key Personnel: Dir., Ben Simons; Dir. Fin., Patrick Murphy; Chief Cur., Anke Van Wagenberg, Ph. D.; Dir. Devel., Damika Baker.
Institution Type/Description: Art Museum.
Hours & Admission Prices: Mon.-Thurs. 10-8, Fri.-Sun. 10-4. Non-members $3; Wednesday, children under 12, AAM & museum members no charge. Closed New Year's Day; Easter; Memorial Day; Independence Day; Labor Day; Thanksgiving; Christmas. ❧
Attendance: 71,230 (actual)

PICKERING CREEK AUDUBON CENTER, 11450 Audubon Lane, Easton, MD 21601. Tel.: 410-822-4903. Fax: 410-822-5041.
E-mail: sscallion@audubon.org
Web Site: pickeringcreek.audubon.org/
Key Personnel: Dir., Mark Scallion.
Institution Type/Description: Audubon Center.
Hours & Admission Prices: Trails: daily dawn to dusk. Office: Mon.-Fri. 9-5. No charge.

TALBOT HISTORICAL SOCIETY, 30 S. Washington St., Easton, MD 21601. Tel.: 410-822-0773. Fax: 410-822-7911.
E-mail: director@hstc.org
Web Site: www.hstc.org
Formerly: Historical Society of Talbot County
Key Personnel: Pres. (V), Carla Howell; Cur., Beth Hansen; Office Mgr., Karen Clements.
Institution Type/Description: Historical Society Museum.
Hours & Admission Prices: Wed.-Sat. 10-4; call to confirm. Tours: adults $5, children 6-12 $2; discounts to groups of 20 or more; members and children 6 & under no charge. Closed major holidays. ❧
Attendance: 7,382 (actual)

Edgewater

HISTORIC LONDON TOWN AND GARDENS, 839 Londontown Rd., Edgewater, MD 21037-2120. Tel.: 410-222-1919.
E-mail: londontown@historiclondontown.org
Web Site: historiclondontown.org
Key Personnel: Exec. Dir., Rod Cofield; Dir. Public Programs, Kristen Butler; Public Programs Admin., Kyle Dalton; Dir. of Horitculture, Meenal Harankhedkar; Cur., Vicki Lerch; Dir. Events & Sales, Keara Mahan; Maintenance & Facilities, DeVon Brown; Office Mgr., Karen Olsen; Visitor Svcs. Coord., Rachel Rabinowitz; Deputy Dir., Lauren Silberman.
Institution Type/Description: Historic Building & Botanical Gardens: c.1760 Georgian mansion & 8-acre botanical garden; significant archaeological site.
Hours & Admission Prices: Wed.-Sun. 10-4:30. Adults $12, senior citizens $10, children 7-17 $7; children 4-6 $3; discounts to AAM members; members & children 3 and under no charge. Additional fee for special events. Closed major holidays.
Attendance: 17,883 (actual)

Elkton

HISTORICAL SOCIETY OF CECIL COUNTY, 135 E. Main St., Elkton, MD 21921-5955. Tel.: 410-398-1790. Facebook & Instagram.
E-mail: questions@cecilhistory.org
Web Site: www.cecilhistory.org
Key Personnel: Pres. (V), Paula Newton.
Institution Type/Description: History Museum.
Hours & Admission Prices: Mon. & Thurs. 10-4, 1st Sat. each month 10-2. Adults $5; members no charge. &
Attendance: 2,000 (actual)

Ellicott City

B&O RAILROAD MUSEUM: ELLICOTT CITY STATION, 3711 Maryland Ave., Ellicott City, MD 21043. Tel.: 410-461-1945.
E-mail: jfeirson@howardcountymd.gov
Web Site: www.ecborail.org
Key Personnel: Exec. Dir., John R. Byrd; Site Mgr., Jake Feirson; Asst. & Program Mgr., Aaron Lippincott.
Institution Type/Description: Transportation Museum: housed in 1831 B&O Railroad Station, first terminus in the United States; terminus is located at the end of the first 13 miles of track laid in the U.S.
Hours & Admission Prices: Wed.-Thur. 10-2; Fri.-Sat. 10-7; Sun. 12-5. No charge. Closed major holidays. &
Attendance: 25,000 (actual)

ELLICOTT CITY COLORED SCHOOL, RESTORED, 8683 Frederick Rd., Ellicott City, MD 21043-4310. Tel.: 410-313-0420 & 1423 & 1428.
E-mail: cchamberlain@howardcountymd.gov
Web Site: howardcountymd.gov/historicsites
Institution Type/Description: Historic Building: housed in a one-room schoolhouse, the first public school for black children in Howard County; built in 1880.
Hours & Admission Prices: Tours: May-Dec. Sat. & Sun. 1-4; other times by appointment.
Attendance: 7,000 (estimated)

THE FIREHOUSE MUSEUM, 3829 Church Rd., Ellicott City, MD 21043. Mailing Address: Howard County Recreation & Parks, 7120 Oakland Hills Rd., Columbia, MD 21046-1621. Tel.: 410-313-0420.
E-mail: info@firemuseummd.org
Web Site: www.howardcountymd.gov
Institution Type/Description: Firefighting Museum: 1889 Ellicott City fire station.
Hours & Admission Prices: April-Dec. Sat.-Sun. 1-4; other times by appointment. No charge; donations accepted. &
Attendance: 2,000 (estimated)

HOWARD COUNTY HISTORICAL SOCIETY, 8328 Court Ave., Ellicott City, MD 21043. Mailing Address: 9421 Frederick Rd., Ellicott City, MD 21042-3801. Tel.: 410-480-3250. Facebook & Twitter.
E-mail: info@hchsmd.org
Web Site: www.hchsmd.org
Key Personnel: Pres., Steve Castro; Exec. Dir., Shawn Gladden; Deputy Dir., Paulette Lutz; Museum Mgr., Mary Sanphilipo.
Institution Type/Description: County History, Archives & Library.
Hours & Admission Prices: Museum: Fri.-Sun. 1-5. Archives: Mon.-Tues. 1-8, Wed.-Sat. 1-5. No charge; donations accepted. Closed New Year's Day; Independence Day; Thanksgiving; Christmas.
Attendance: 10,000 (actual)

HOWARD DISTRICT ORIGINAL COURT HOUSE, 8334 Main St., Ellicott City, MD 21043-4604. Mailing Address: 9944 Clarksville Pike, Ellicott City, MD 21042. Tel.: 410-313-0420.
E-mail: cchamberlain@howardcountymd.gov
Web Site: www.howardcountymd.gov
Formerly: Heritage Orientation Center
Key Personnel: Heritage Program Mgr., Caitlin Chamberlain; Heritage Opers. Supvr., Tim Nedzel.
Institution Type/Description: History Museum.
Hours & Admission Prices: Daily 11-4.
Attendance: 10,000 (estimated)

MT. IDA VISITOR CENTER, 3691 Sarah's Lane, Ellicott City, MD 21041. Mailing Address: P.O. Box 293, Ellicott City, MD 21041. Tel.: 410-465-8500.
E-mail: fpfi@prodigy.net
Key Personnel: Pres. (V), Marydele Donnelly.
Institution Type/Description: History Museum; house built in 1828.
Hours & Admission Prices: Call for hours. No charge, donations accepted.
Attendance: 1,000

PATAPSCO VALLEY STATE PARK - THE AVALON VISITOR CENTER, 8020 Baltimore National Pike, Ellicott City, MD 21043. Tel.: 410-461-5005, 888-432-2267.
Institution Type/Description: Park & Visitor Center: housed in a 19th century stone dwelling.
Hours & Admission Prices: Call for hours.

THOMAS ISAAC LOG CABIN, 8394 Main St., Ellicott City, MD 21043-4604. Mailing Address: c/o Historic Ellicott City, Inc., P.O. Box 244, Ellicott City, MD 21041. Tel.: 410-313-1413.
Institution Type/Description: Historic Building: built c.1780.
Hours & Admission Prices: Sat.-Sun. 1-4.

Emmitsburg

FREDERICK COUNTY VOLUNTEER FIRE & RESCUE MUSEUM AND PRESERVATION SOCIETY, Physical/ Mailing Address: 300B South Seton, Emmitsburg, MD 21727. Tel.: 301-600-6736.
E-mail: museum@frederickmdfiremuseum.org
Web Site: www.frederickmdfiremuseum.org
Key Personnel: Contact Person, James Deater, Sr.
Institution Type/Description: Fire-Fighting Museum.
Hours & Admission Prices: April 14-Oct. 14: Sat. & Sun. 12-4, other times by appointment. No charge.

MILLER FAMILY VISITORS CENTER, 16300 Old Emmitsburg Rd., Emmitsburg, MD 21727. Tel.: 301-447-6122.
E-mail: grotto@msmary.edu
Institution Type/Description: Visitors Center: housed on the campus of Mount St. Mary's University, National Shrine Grotto of Our Lady of Lourdes.
Hours & Admission Prices: Call for hours.

SETON HERITAGE MUSEUM & THEATER AT THE NATIONAL SHRINE OF SAINT ELIZABETH ANN SETON, 339 S. Seton Ave., Emmitsburg, MD 21727-9297. Tel.: 301-447-6606. Fax: 301-447-6061. Facebook.
E-mail: office@setonshrine.org
Web Site: www.setonshrine.org
Institution Type/Description: History Museum.
Hours & Admission Prices: Daily 10-4:30; see website to confirm. No charge; donations accepted. Closed major holidays. &

Ewell

SMITH ISLAND CENTER, 20846 Caleb Jones Rd., Ewell, MD 21824. Tel.: 410-425-3351, 800-521-9189. Facebook.
E-mail: smithisland@verizon.net
Web Site: www.smithisland.org
Institution Type/Description: History Museum.
Hours & Admission Prices: May-Oct. daily 12-4. Accessible by boat from Crisfield and Solomons. Adults $3; members no charge. &

Fort Meade

FORT GEORGE G. MEADE MUSEUM, 4674 Griffin Ave., Fort Meade, MD 20755-7047. Mailing Address: Attn: IMNE-MEA-M, Fort George G. Meade, MD 20755-5094. Tel.: 301-677-6966 & 7054. Fax: 301-677-2953.
E-mail: robert.s.johnson212.civ@mail.mil
Web Site: www.ftmeade.army.mil/museum/index.htm
Key Personnel: Cur., Robert S. Johnson; Pres. (V), David L. Burget; Exhibits Specialist, Barbara Taylor; Museum Specialist, David Manning.
Institution Type/Description: Military Museum.
Hours & Admission Prices: Wed.-Sat. 11-4, Sun. 1-4; other times by appointment. No charge. Closed national holidays. &
Attendance: 23,741 (actual)

Fort Washington

FORT WASHINGTON PARK, 13551 Fort Washington Rd., Fort Washington, MD 20744-7044. Tel.: 301-763-4600. Fax: 301-763-1389. Facebook.
E-mail: nace_fort_washington_park@nps.gov
Web Site: www.nps.gov/fowa
Key Personnel: Supt., Christine Smith; Supervisory Ranger, Adam Gresek.
Institution Type/Description: Military Museum: housed in 1824 Fort Washington; 1817 Commandant's house.
Hours & Admission Prices: Park: daily 7-sunset; visitor center daily 9-4:30. Annual Pass $30; $10 per vehicle, buses & walk-in $3 per person. Closed New Year's Day; Thanksgiving; Christmas. ♿
Attendance: 297,000 (actual)

Frederick

BARBARA FRITCHIE HOUSE, 154 W. Patrick St., Frederick, MD 21701. Tel.: 301-600-4047.
Institution Type/Description: Historic House: housed in the former home of Barbara Fritchie, heroine of John Greenleaf Whittier's poem from the Civil War.
Hours & Admission Prices: Call for hours.

BJORLEE MUSEUM, 101 Clarke Pl., Frederick, MD 21701. Tel.: 240-575-2959.
Institution Type/Description: History Museum.
Hours & Admission Prices: Weekdays 9-2, weekends by appointment.

CATOCTIN CENTER FOR REGIONAL STUDIES, 7932 Opossumtown Pike, Frederick, MD 21702. Tel.: 301-624-2773.
E-mail: catoctincenter@frederick.edu
Web Site: catoctincenter.frederick.edu
Institution Type/Description: History Museum.
Hours & Admission Prices: By appointment.

THE CHILDREN'S MUSEUM OF ROSE HILL MANOR PARK AKA ROSE HILL MANOR PARK & MUSEUM, 1611 N. Market St., Frederick, MD 21701-4304. Tel.: 301-600-1646 (reservations) & 2743 (office). Fax: 301-600-2749. TDD: 301-600-2936.
E-mail: ksaavedra@frederickcountymd.gov
Web Site: rosehillmuseum.com
Key Personnel: Pres. Museum Council (V), Joann Ramsburg; Museum Mgr., Kari Saavadra; Museum Shop Mgr., Shirley Swaim.
Institution Type/Description: Children's Museum.
Hours & Admission Prices: April-Sept. Mon.-Sat. 11-4, Sun. 1-4; Oct.-Nov. Sat. 11-4, Sun. 1-4; other times by appointment. Adults $5, senior citizens 55 & over & children 2-18 $4; discounts to AAM & AAA members; museum employees & volunteers no charge.
Attendance: 13,449 (estimated)

DELAPLAINE VISUAL ARTS EDUCATION CENTER, 40 S. Carroll St., Frederick, MD 21701. Tel.: 301-698-0656. Facebook, Instagram, & Twitter.
E-mail: info@delaplaine.org
Web Site: delaplaine.org
Key Personnel: CEO, Catherine Moreland.
Institution Type/Description: Art Gallery.
Hours & Admission Prices: Mon.-Sat. 9-5, Sun. 11-5. Closed New Year's Day; Easter; Memorial Day; Independence Day; Labor Day; Thanksgiving; Christmas.

HERITAGE FREDERICK, 24 E. Church St., Frederick, MD 21701-5402. Tel.: 301-663-1188.
E-mail: mboswell@frederickhistory.org
Web Site: www.frederickhistory.org
Formerly: Historical Society of Frederick County, Inc.
Key Personnel: Pres. (V), Yvonne Reinsch; Exec. Dir., C.E.O. & Cur., Mary Rose Boswell; Treas., Charles G. Mann; Programs & Education Mgr., Jennifer Winter; Registrar, Anastasia Suryaputri Diggs; Program Coord., Melissa Henemyer; Education Coord. & Library Asst., Kaitlyn Shorter, kshorter@frederickhistory.org.
Institution Type/Description: History Museum.
Hours & Admission Prices: Wed.-Sat. 10-4, Sun. 1-4. Roger Brooke Taney House: by appointment. Adults $8, senior $7, youth 6-16 $6; discounts to AAM, AAA & Maryland Passport members; members, children under 5 & museum no charge. Closed Independence Day; Thanksgiving; Christmas. ♿
Attendance: 11,200 (estimated)

MONOCACY NATIONAL BATTLEFIELD, 5201 Urbana Pike, Frederick, MD 21704-7303. Mailing Address: 4632 Araby Church Rd., Frederick, MD 21704. Tel.: 301-662-3515. Fax: 301-668-7437. Facebook: Monocacy National Battlefield.
E-mail: tracy_evans@nps.gov
Web Site: www.nps.gov/mono
Key Personnel: Acting Supt., Andrew Banasick; Acting Facility Mgr., Phil Grewe; Administrative Officer, Cory Wolfensberger; Park Ranger & Collateral Curator, Tracy L. Evans; Museum Shop Mgr., Meaghan Barry.
Institution Type/Description: Historic Site & Monument: dedicated to soldiers who fought in the Battle of Monocacy, July 9, 1864.
Hours & Admission Prices: Daily 9-5. No charge; donations accepted. Closed New Year's Day; Thanksgiving; Christmas. ♿
Attendance: 50,000 (estimated)

NATIONAL MUSEUM OF CIVIL WAR MEDICINE, 48 E. Patrick St., Frederick, MD 21701-5628. Mailing Address: P.O. Box 470, Frederick, MD 21705-0470. Tel.: 301-695-1864. Fax: 301-695-6823.
E-mail: joanna.jennings@civilwarmed.org
Web Site: www.CivilWarMed.org
Key Personnel: Interim Exec. Dir. & C.O.O., David Price; Chm. (V), Gordon E. Dammann, D.D.S.; Pres. (V), Betsy Estilow; Treas., Meredith Harshman; Museum Shop Mgr., Emily Dean.
Institution Type/Description: History Museum: housed in Carty Building, former 1832 furniture store & funeral home.
Hours & Admission Prices: Natl. Museum of Civil War Medicine: Mon.-Sat. 10-5, Sun. 11-5. Adults $9.50, seniors 60 & over, military & students $8.50, children 10-16 $7; discounts to AAM members; members & children under 9 no charge. Pry House Field Hospital Museum: June-Oct. Fri.-Sun. 11-5; May & Nov. Sat.-Sun. 11-4. Suggested donation $5. ♿
Attendance: 35,000 (actual)

SCHIFFERSTADT ARCHITECTURAL MUSEUM, 1110 Rosemont Ave., Frederick, MD 21701-4127. Tel.: 301-668-6088.
E-mail: fredcolandmarks@aol.com
Web Site: frederickcountylandmarksfoundation.org
Key Personnel: Pres., Alan Imhoff; Vice Pres., Joe Sweeney.
Institution Type/Description: Architecture Museum: housed in c.1758 German sandstone farmhouse; wattle & daub construction; hand-hewn oak beams pinned with wooden pegs.
Hours & Admission Prices: April to mid-Dec. Sat.-Sun. 1-4; other times by appointment. Adults $5; discounts to members, AAA, seniors & students; children under 12 no charge.
Attendance: 20,000 (estimated)

Freeland

MERRY MEADOWS HISTORICAL MUSEUM, 1523 Freeland Rd., Freeland, MD 21053. Tel.: 410-357-4088.
E-mail: mmrf@comcast.net
Web Site: www.merrymeadows.com
Institution Type/Description: History Museum.
Hours & Admission Prices: By appointment. ♿

Frostburg

FROSTBURG MUSEUM, 50 E. Main St., Frostburg, MD 21532. Mailing Address: P.O. Box 92, Frostburg, MD 21532. Tel.: 301-689-1195. Facebook.
E-mail: frostburgmuseum@verizon.net
Web Site: frostburgmuseum.org
Key Personnel: Museum Pres., Elizabeth Eshleman; Museum Vice Pres., Joe Williams.
Institution Type/Description: Historic Building: housed in the former Hill Street School; built in 1899.
Hours & Admission Prices: Tues.-Sat. 12-5. No charge; donations accepted.
Attendance: 800 (estimated)

FROSTBURG SCIENCE DISCOVERY CENTER, Compton Science Center, 1st Fl., 101 Braddock Rd., Frostburg, MD 21532. Tel.: 301-687-4723.
E-mail: srsnow@frostburg.edu
Web Site: www.frostburg.edu/FSDC
Formerly: Frostburg State University Planetarium
Key Personnel: Contact Person, Susan Snow.
Institution Type/Description: Science Center.
Hours & Admission Prices: Call for hours. No charge; donations accepted. ♿
Attendance: 5,000 (actual)

THRASHER CARRIAGE MUSEUM, 19 Depot St., Frostburg, MD 21532-1309. Mailing Address: c/o Allegany County Historical Society, 218 Washington St., Cumberland, MD 21502. Tel.: 301-689-3380. Fax: 301-689-3380.
E-mail: info@thethrashercarriagemuseum.com
Web Site: www.thethrashercarriagemuseum.com
Key Personnel: Exec. Dir., Jeff Nealis.
Institution Type/Description: Transportation Museum: housed in a renovated 1800s era warehouse.
Hours & Admission Prices: Jan.-April by appointment; May 2-Oct. Thurs.-Sun. 12-2; Nov. to mid-Dec. Sat.-Sun. 12-2. Adults $4, students $2; discount to groups; children under 6 no charge. Closed New Year's Day; Martin Luther King Jr. Day; Presidents' Day; Thanksgiving; Christmas. &
Attendance: 18,000 (actual)

Fulton

AFRICAN ART MUSEUM OF MARYLAND, 11711 E. Market Pl., Fulton, MD 20759-2596. Tel.: 301-490-6070. Fax: 301-490-6070. Facebook.
E-mail: africanartmuseumofmd@verizon.net
Web Site: www.africanartmuseum.org
Formerly: Maryland Museum of African Art
Key Personnel: Founder & Dir., Doris H. Ligon.
Institution Type/Description: Art Museum.
Hours & Admission Prices: Wed.-Sat 10-3; other times by appointment for groups. Museum: no charge; donations accepted. Special Events: admission charged; discounts to AAM, AAA & ICOM members. &
Attendance: 45,000 (estimated)

Gaithersburg

GAITHERSBURG COMMUNITY MUSEUM, 9 S. Summit Ave., Gaithersburg, MD 20877. Tel.: 301-258-6160. Fax: 301-258-6329. Facebook.
E-mail: museum@gaithersburgmd.gov
Web Site: www.gaithersburgmd.gov
Key Personnel: Dir., Nansie Wilde.
Institution Type/Description: History Museum: housed in the former B&O train station freight house; built in 1884. Listed on the National Register of Historic Places.
Hours & Admission Prices: Tues.-Sat. 10-3; other times by appointment. No charge; donations accepted. &
Attendance: 4,500 (actual)

GAITHERSBURG - WASHINGTON GROVE V.F.D. FIRE MUSEUM, 13 E. Diamond Ave., Gaithersburg, MD 20877. Mailing Address: P.O. Box 2748, Gaithersburg, MD 20886. Tel.: 301-646-1222. Facebook & Twitter.
E-mail: firemansfund@gwgvfd.org
Web Site: www.gwgvfd.org
Key Personnel: Pres., Steve Hayes; Vice Pres., Angela Blom.
Institution Type/Description: Fire Museum.
Hours & Admission Prices: Sat. 10-2. No charge; donations accepted. &
Attendance: 500 (estimated)

Galesville

GALESVILLE HERITAGE MUSEUM - CARRIE WEEDON HOUSE, 988 Main St., Galesville, MD 20765-0373. Mailing Address: P.O. Box 373, Galesville, MD 20765-0373. Tel.: 410-867-9499.
E-mail: galesvillemuseum@gmail.com
Web Site: www.galesvilleheritagesociety.com
Key Personnel: Pres., Mark Steinlein; Vice Pres., Jim Chandler; Treas., Adrianne Day; Correspondance Sec., Cathy Oliver; Records Sec., Betsy Derrick.
Institution Type/Description: History Museum.
Hours & Admission Prices: April-Nov. Sun. 1-4; other times by appointment. No charge, donation accepted.

Germantown

BLACKROCK CENTER FOR THE ARTS, 12901 Town Commons Dr., Germantown, MD 20874. Tel.: 301-528-2260. Fax: 301-528-2266.
E-mail: info@blackrockcenter.org
Web Site: blackrockcenter.org
Key Personnel: Exec. Dir., Alyona Aleksandra Ushe.
Institution Type/Description: Art Gallery.
Hours & Admission Prices: Mon.-Sat. 10-6; call for additional hours.

BUTTON FARM LIVING HISTORY CENTER, 16820 Black Rock Rd., Germantown, MD 20874. Tel.: 202-903-4140.
E-mail: menarefoundation@aol.com
Key Personnel: Pres., Anthony Cohen; Farm Mgr., Steven Gillick.
Institution Type/Description: History Center.
Hours & Admission Prices: Public hours: Sat. 12-4; Weekday hours: Mon., Wed., Fri. by appointment only. No charge.

WATERS HOUSE HISTORY CENTER, 12535 Milestone Manor Ln., Germantown, MD 20876. Tel.: 301-515-2887.
E-mail: germantownmdhistory@gmail.com
Institution Type/Description: Historic House Museum: built c.1790.
Hours & Admission Prices: Wed. & Sat. 10-4; other times by appointment. No charge.

Girdletree

GIRDLETREE BARNES BANK, Snow Hill Rd., Girdletree, MD 21829. Mailing Address: c/o Girldtree Historical Foundation Inc., P.O. Box 4, Girdletree, MD 21829.
E-mail: info@worcestermuseums.org
Web Site: www.worcestermuseums.org
Institution Type/Description: Historic Building: built in 1901.
Hours & Admission Prices: May-Sept. Tues. 1-4 & by appointment.

Glen Echo

CLARA BARTON NATIONAL HISTORIC SITE, 5801 Oxford Rd., Glen Echo, MD 20812-1201. Mailing Address: 700 George Washington Memorial Pkwy., McLean, VA 22101. Tel.: 301-320-1410. Fax: 301-320-1415.
E-mail: gwmp_clara_barton_nhs@nps.gov
Web Site: www.nps.gov/clba
Key Personnel: Museum Cur., Kimberly Robinson.
Institution Type/Description: Historic House Museum: 1897-1912 home of Clara Barton, founder of the American Red Cross.
Hours & Admission Prices: Temporarily closed.
Attendance: 17,000 (actual)

Glenn Dale

DORSEY CHAPEL, 10704 Brookland Rd., Glenn Dale, MD 20769. Mailing Address: 6611 Kenilworth Ave, Riverdale, MD 20737. Tel.: 240-264-3415 & 352-5544.
E-mail: blackhistory@pgparks.com
Institution Type/Description: Historic Building: housed in a former African-American church; built in 1900.
Hours & Admission Prices: By appointment. Adults $3, seniors $2, children 5-18 $1; children 4 & under no charge.

MARIETTA HOUSE MUSEUM, 5626 Bell Station Rd., Glenn Dale, MD 20769-9120. Tel.: 301-464-5291. Fax: 301-464-5654. TDD: 301-699-2544.
E-mail: mary.amen@pgparks.com
Web Site: www.pgparks.com
Key Personnel: Natural & Historical Div. Chief, Gregory Kernan; Facility Mgr., Mary Amen; Chm. (V), Stacey Hawkins.
Institution Type/Description: Historic House: c.1815 Federal style brick home.
Hours & Admission Prices: Open by appointment only, please call ahead. Adults $3, senior citizens $2, students $1; discounts to groups; Metropolitan Washington Historic Houses Consortium & Prince George County History Consortium no charge. Closed major holidays. &
Attendance: 5,000 (actual)

Grantsville

NEW GERMANY STATE PARK NATURE CENTER, 349 Headquarters Lane, Grantsville, MD 21536. Tel.: 301-895-5453.
E-mail: newgermanyfriends@yahoo.com
Institution Type/Description: Nature Center.
Hours & Admission Prices: Call for hours.

SPRUCE FOREST ARTISAN VILLAGE, 177 Casselman Rd., Grantsville, MD 21536. Tel.: 301-895-3332.
E-mail: artisans@spruceforest.org
Web Site: www.spruceforest.org
Key Personnel: Acting Dir., Lynn Lois; Chm. (V), Reita Marks.
Institution Type/Description: History & Art Museum.

Hours & Admission Prices: May-Dec. call for hours. No charge; donations accepted. &

Attendance: 15,000 (estimated)

Grasonville

CHESAPEAKE BAY ENVIRONMENTAL CENTER, 600 Discovery Lane, Grasonville, MD 21638. Tel.: 410-827-6694. Facebook.

E-mail: jwink@bayrestoration.org

Key Personnel: Exec. Dir., Judy Wink; Asst. Dir., Vicki Paulas; Dir. Comm. & Strategic Initiatives, Courtney Leigh; Education Coord., Katey Nelson; Early Childhood Education Coord., Karen Bogue; Business Coord., Alissa Quinton; Membership Coord., Bobbie Hunt; Volunteer Coord., Anne Brunson; Volunteer Coord., Dave Brunson.

Institution Type/Description: Environmental Education Center.

Hours & Admission Prices: Mon.-Sun. daily 9-5. Closed new Year's Day, Thanksgiving & Christmas.

Greenbelt

GREENBELT MUSEUM, 15 Crescent Rd., Rm. 110, Greenbelt, MD 20770-0805. Mailing Address: P.O. Box 1025, Greenbelt, MD 20768. Tel.: 301-507-6582.

E-mail: info@greenbeltmuseum.org

Web Site: www.greenbeltmuseum.org

Key Personnel: Dir., Megan Searing Young; Education & Volunteer Coord., Sheila Maffay-Tuthill; Office Mgr., Lawana Holland-Moore.

Institution Type/Description: History Museum.

Hours & Admission Prices: Sun. 1-5; other times by appointment. Exhibition Gallery: Mon.-Sat. 9-10, Sun. 10-7. Admission $5. &

Attendance: 2,500 (estimated)

NASA GODDARD SPACE FLIGHT CENTER, 8800 Greenbelt Rd., Greenbelt, MD 20771-2400. Mailing Address: Goddard Visitors Center, 8800 Greenbelt Road - Code 130, Greenbelt, MD 20771. Tel.: 301-286-2000 & 3978.

E-mail: gsfc-pao@listserv.gsfc.nasa.gov

Web Site: www.gsfc.nasa.gov/vc/index.html

Institution Type/Description: Space Science Museum.

Hours & Admission Prices: Flight Center: tours available to school, community & cultural groups by appointment. Visitor Center: by appointment. No charge.

Attendance: 39,000 (actual)

Hagerstown

CHESAPEAKE AND OHIO CANAL NATIONAL HISTORICAL PARK, 1850 Dual Hwy., Ste. 100, Hagerstown, MD 21740-6622. Tel.: 301-739-4200. Fax: 301-739-5275. Facebook, Twitter, & Instagram.

E-mail: choh_information@nps.gov

Web Site: www.nps.gov/choh

Formerly: Chesapeake & Ohio Canal Tavern Museum

Key Personnel: Chief Park Ranger, Edward R. Wenschhof, Jr.; Acting Supt., John A. Noel.

Institution Type/Description: Historic Canal between Georgetown, District of Columbia to Cumberland, Maryland.

Hours & Admission Prices: Park: daylight hours. Great Falls: cars 3 day pass $10, buses $25-$100. National Parks Passes honored. Visitor Center: closed major Federal holidays. &

Attendance: 5,100,000 (estimated)

CONTEMPORARY SCHOOL OF THE ARTS AND GALLERY, 4 W. Franklin St., Hagerstown, MD 21740. Tel.: 301-791-6191. Facebook.

E-mail: ronlytle3@netzzero.net

Key Personnel: Exec. Dir. & Pres., Ron Lytle.

Institution Type/Description: Art Gallery.

Hours & Admission Prices: Mon.-Thur. 11-7, Fri.-Sat. 11-5, Sun. 1-5.

DISCOVERY STATION AT HAGERSTOWN, 101 W. Washington St., Hagerstown, MD 21740-4709. Tel.: 301-790-0076. Facebook, Instagram, & Twitter.

E-mail: info@discoverystation.com

Web Site: www.discoverystation.org

Key Personnel: Bd. Pres., Phil Kelly; Dir. Opers., Brittany Wedd.

Institution Type/Description: History & Science Museum.

Hours & Admission Prices: Open Tues.-Sat. 10-4; Adults $7, children 4-17 $6, seniors 55 & over $5; discounts to Travel Passport Program & ASTC members;

members, children under 4. Military families no charge. Closed New Year's Eve & Day; Independence Day; Thanksgiving; Christmas Eve, Day. &

Attendance: 14,016 (actual)

HAGERSTOWN AVIATION MUSEUM, 14235 Oak Springs Rd., Hagerstown, MD 21742. Tel.: 301-733-8717. Facebook & Twitter.

E-mail: info@hagerstownaviationmuseum.org

Web Site: www.hagerstownaviationmuseum.org

Key Personnel: Pres. (V), John P. Seburn.

Institution Type/Description: Aviation Museum.

Hours & Admission Prices: Call for hours. No charge; donations accepted.

HAGERSTOWN ROUNDHOUSE MUSEUM, 296 S. Burhans Blvd., Hagerstown, MD 21740-5339. Mailing Address: P.O. Box 2858, Hagerstown, MD 21741-2858. Tel.: 301-739-4665.

E-mail: info@roundhouse.org

Web Site: www.roundhouse.org

Key Personnel: Chm. (V), Gerry Smith; Pres. (V), Walter Jackson; Vice Pres. (V), Matt Mattingly.

Institution Type/Description: Railroading History.

Hours & Admission Prices: Fri.-Sun. 1-5. Adults $6; Children (4-15) $1; discounts to groups of 20 or more; members no charge. Closed New Year's Eve & Day; Easter; Independence Day; Christmas Eve & Day.

Attendance: 10,000 (actual)

JONATHAN HAGER HOUSE & MUSEUM, 351 N. Cleveland Ave., Hagerstown, MD 21740-4155. Tel.: 301-739-8393.

E-mail: hagerhouse@hagerstownmd.org

Web Site: www.hagerhouse.org

Key Personnel: Cur., John Bryan.

Institution Type/Description: Historic House: housed in 1739 Hager House constructed as a private frontier fort.

Hours & Admission Prices: April-Dec. Thurs.-Sat. 10-4; other times by appointment. Adults $3, senior citizens & groups of 20 or more $2, children 6-12 $1; children under 6 no charge. Closed New Year's Day, Easter, Thanksgiving week; Christmas.

Attendance: 13,000 (estimated)

MANSION HOUSE ART CENTER, 501 Highland Way, Hagerstown, MD 21740. Tel.: 301-797-6813.

Institution Type/Description: Art Gallery.

Hours & Admission Prices: Fri.-Sat. 11-4, Sun. 1-5. No charge; donations accepted.

Attendance: 1,500 (estimated)

THE TRAIN ROOM AND MUSEUM, 360 S. Burhans Blvd., Hagerstown, MD 21740-5339. Tel.: 301-745-6681. Fax: 301-766-4697.

E-mail: trainroom@verizon.net

Web Site: www.the-train-room.com

Key Personnel: Museum Shop Mgr., Charles Lee Mozingo.

Institution Type/Description: Lionel Train & Toy Museum.

Hours & Admission Prices: Summer: Mon.-Sat. 9-5; Winter: Sun. 12pm-5pm, Mon. & Fri. 9-6, Tues.-Thurs. & Sat. 9-5. Adults $5, children 3-12 $1.

Attendance: 5,000 (estimated)

WASHINGTON COUNTY ARTS COUNCIL, 34 S. Potomac St., Hagerstown, MD 21740-5513. Tel.: 301-791-3132. Facebook: Washington County Arts Council Inc.

E-mail: maryanneb@washingtoncountyarts.com

Web Site: www.washingtoncountyarts.com

Key Personnel: Dir., Mary Anne Burke; Pres., James Pierne; Gallery Mgr., Chris Brewer.

Institution Type/Description: Art Gallery.

Hours & Admission Prices: Tues.-Fri. 11-5, Sat. 10-4; other times by appointment. No charge; donations accepted. &

Attendance: 4,789 (estimated)

WASHINGTON COUNTY HISTORICAL SOCIETY AND MILLER HOUSE MUSEUM, 135 W. Washington St., Hagerstown, MD 21740-4709. Tel.: 301-797-8782. Fax: 240-625-9498. Facebook.

E-mail: info@washcomdhistoricalsociety.org

Web Site: www.washcomdhistoricalsociety.org

Key Personnel: Exec. Dir., Stefanie Basalik; Cur., Anna Cueto.

Institution Type/Description: Antique Museum: housed in Miller House, an 1825 Federal style townhouse.

Hours & Admission Prices: Library: Tues.-Sat. 9-4:30. Beaver Creek: by appointment. No charge, donations accepted. Miller House: Tues.-Sat. 9-4. Adults $7, students 13-17 $5, children 7-12 $3; members and children 6 & under no charge.

Guided Tours: adults $15, members $5; discounts to groups of 10 or more. Closed major holidays.
Attendance: 2,500 (estimated)

WASHINGTON COUNTY MUSEUM OF FINE ARTS, City Park, 401 Museum Dr., Hagerstown, MD 21740-6271. Mailing Address: P.O. Box 423, Hagerstown, MD 21741. Tel.: 301-739-5727. Fax: 301-745-3741.
E-mail: info@wcmfa.org
Web Site: www.wcmfa.org
Key Personnel: Dir., Rebecca Massie Lane; Pres., Mary Helen Strauch; Vice Pres., Howard Kaylor; Vice Pres., John Schnebly; Sec., John League; Treas. Bd., Alfred Martin; Collections & Exhibition Mgr., Jennifer Smith; Educator & Museum Shop Mgr., Amy Hunt; Registrar, Linda Dodson; Head Security, Ed Lewis.
Institution Type/Description: Art Museum.
Hours & Admission Prices: Tues.-Fri. 9-5, Sat. 9-4, Sun. 1-5. No charge; donations accepted. Closed New Year's Eve & Day; Good Friday; Independence Day; Thanksgiving & day after; Christmas Eve & Day. &
Attendance: 50,000 (actual)

WILLIAM M. BRISH PLANETARIUM, 820 Commonwealth Ave., Hagerstown, MD 21740-6836. Mailing Address: 10435 Downsville Pike, Hagerstown, MD 21740. Tel.: 301-766-2898.
E-mail: kopcochr@wcps.k12.md.us
Web Site: www.wbplanetarium.weebly.com
Key Personnel: Dir., Christopher Kopco.
Institution Type/Description: Planetarium.
Hours & Admission Prices: Sept.-May 1st & 4th Tues. of month unless otherwise noted 5:30pm-6:15pm & 7pm-8pm. Adults $3, children & students $2; senior citizens no charge. &

Havre de Grace

HAVRE DE GRACE DECOY MUSEUM, 215 Giles St., Havre de Grace, MD 21078-3661. Tel.: 410-939-3739. Facebook & Twitter.
E-mail: information@decoymuseum.com
Web Site: www.decoymuseum.com
Key Personnel: Pres., Patrick Vincenti; Exec. Dir., Kerri S. Kneisley.
Institution Type/Description: Folk Art Museum.
Hours & Admission Prices: Mon.-Sat. 10:30-4:30, Sun. 12-4. Adults $6, senior citizens $5, children 9-18 $2; members & children 8 and under no charge. Closed New Year's Day; Easter; Independence Day; Thanksgiving; Christmas. &
Attendance: 10,811 (actual)

HAVRE DE GRACE MARITIME MUSEUM, 100 Lafayette St., Havre de Grace, MD 21078-3542. Tel.: 410-939-4800.
E-mail: hdgmaritimemuseum@verizon.net
Web Site: www.hdgmaritimemuseum.org
Key Personnel: Exec. Dir., Mary Leavens; Environmental Center Project Coord., Logan Poore; Environmental Center Educator, Sarah Shpak; Admin. Asst., Juliette Moore; Receptionist/Customer Svc., Laura Chouinard.
Institution Type/Description: History Museum.
Hours & Admission Prices: Wed.-Sat. 10-5, Sun. 1-5. No charge; donations accepted. Closed major holidays. &
Attendance: 11,000 (estimated)

STEPPINGSTONE FARM MUSEUM, 461 Quaker Bottom Rd., Havre de Grace, MD 21078-1329. Tel.: 410-939-2299 & 2321.
E-mail: director@steppingstonemuseum.org
Web Site: www.steppingstonemuseum.org
Key Personnel: Exec. Dir., Lara Murphy; Cur., Abigail Harting; Coord. (V), Meghann Mahoney.
Institution Type/Description: 23-Acre Farm Museum.
Hours & Admission Prices: April-Oct. Sat.-Sun. 1-5. Special Events: Adults $10; children 12 & under no charge. &
Attendance: 40,000 (estimated)

SUSQUEHANNA MUSEUM OF HAVRE DE GRACE INC. AT THE LOCK HOUSE, 817 Conesteo St., Havre de Grace, MD 21078. Mailing Address: P.O. Box 253, Harve de Grace, MD 21078-0253. Tel.: 410-939-5780. Facebook: The Susquehanna Museum of Havre de Grace.
E-mail: lockhousemuseum@gmail.com
Web Site: www.thelockhousemuseum.org
Key Personnel: Exec. Dir., Ciera Fisher; Pres., Carol McGowan; Vice Pres., Ann Marie Serwa.
Institution Type/Description: History Museum.

Hours & Admission Prices: mid-April to Oct. Fri.-Sun. 1-5; group tours by appointment. No charge; donations accepted. Charge for group tours. &
Attendance: 2,500 (actual)

Highland Beach

FREDERICK DOUGLASS MUSEUM AND CULTURAL CENTER, 3200 Wayman Ave., Highland Beach, MD 21403. Tel.: 410-267-6960 & 410-268-2956. Fax: 410-267-0091.
E-mail: jeanw57@aol.com
Web Site: highlandbeachmd.org
Key Personnel: Dir., Jean Langston.
Institution Type/Description: History Museum.
Hours & Admission Prices: By appointment. No charge; donations accepted.
Attendance: 2,500 (estimated)

Hollywood

SOTTERLEY PLANTATION, 44300 Sotterley Lane, Hollywood, MD 20636. Mailing Address: Historic Sotterley, Inc., P.O. Box 67, Hollywood, MD 20636-0067. Tel.: 301-373-2280, 800-681-0850. Fax: 301-373-8474.
E-mail: officemanager@sotterley.org
Web Site: www.sotterley.org
Key Personnel: Exec. Dir., Nancy L. Easterling; Chm. Bd. Trustees & Pres. (V), Janice Briscoe; Education Dir., Jeanne Pirtle; Office Mgr., Kim Husick; Museum Shop Mgr., Ginger Newman-Askew.
Institution Type/Description: Historic House Museum: 1703 mansion & outbuildings illustrating Tidewater Plantation culture.
Hours & Admission Prices: Guided Plantation House Tours: May 1-Oct. 31 Tues.-Sat. 10-4, Sun. 12-4. Adults $10, seniors $8, children 6-12 $5; discount to National Trust for Historic Preservation members, military & AAA members; children 5 & under no charge. Self-guided grounds tour $3; Sotterley members with unlimited touring no charge. Please visit website for additional information. &
Attendance: 26,000 (actual)

Jefferson

GATHLAND STATE PARK, 900 Arnoldstown Rd., Jefferson, MD 21755. Mailing Address: c/o Greenbrier State Park, 21843 National Pike, Boonsboro, MD 21713-9535. Tel.: 301-791-4767.
Web Site: www.dnr.state.md.us/publiclands/western/gathland.html
Key Personnel: Park Manager, Mary Ironside.
Institution Type/Description: Park Museum: located on the estate of George Alfred Townsend.
Hours & Admission Prices: Park: daily 8-sunset. Museums: April & Oct. Sat.-Sun.; May-Sept. daily. No charge. Closed Christmas. &
Attendance: 78,000 (estimated)

Kennedyville

KENT COUNTY FARM MUSEUM, 13689 Turner's Creek Rd., Kennedyville, MD 21645. Mailing Address: P.O. Box 43, Kennedyville, MD 21645-0043. Tel.: 410-348-5543.
E-mail: kentmuseuminc@yahoo.com
Web Site: www.kentcounty.com/farmmuseum
Institution Type/Description: Farm Museum.
Hours & Admission Prices: May-Oct. 1st & 3rd Sat. 10-4; other times by appointment. No charge; donations accepted.

Kensington

WASHINGTON D.C. TEMPLE VISITORS' CENTER, 9900 Stoneybrook Dr., Kensington, MD 20895. Tel.: 301-587-0144.
E-mail: vcwashington@ldschurch.org
Institution Type/Description: Religious Museum.
Hours & Admission Prices: Daily 10-9. No charge.

Kingsville

JERUSALEM MILL VILLAGE MUSEUM AND VISITOR CENTER, 2813 Jerusalem Rd., Kingsville, MD 21087. Mailing Address: P.O. Box 237, Kingsville, MD 21087. Tel.: 410-877-3560.
E-mail: jerusalemmill@yahoo.com
Web Site: www.jerusalemmill.org
Key Personnel: Pres. (V), Rick Decker; Historian, Chris Scovill; Cur., Rich Albright.
Institution Type/Description: History Museum and Visitor Center.

Hours & Admission Prices: Fri. 1-4, Sat.-Mon. 10-4. No charge; donations accepted. ঙ
Attendance: 37,604 (actual)

La Plata

AFRICAN AMERICAN HERITAGE SOCIETY OF CHARLES COUNTY, INC., 7485 Crain Hwy., La Plata, MD 20646-4935. Tel.: 301-843-2150.
E-mail: dorothea.smith42@gmail.com
Key Personnel: Trustee, Dorothea Holt Smith.
Institution Type/Description: History Museum.
Hours & Admission Prices: By appointment.

FRIENDSHIP HOUSE, 8730 Mitchell Rd., La Plata, MD 20646-2867. Mailing Address: Historical Society of Charles County, Inc., P.O. Box 2806, La Plata, MD 20646. Tel.: 301-934-2564.
E-mail: info@charlescountyhistorical.org
Web Site: www.charlescountyhistorical.org
Formerly: La Plata Train Station Museum
Key Personnel: Pres. (V), Ronald G. Brown.
Institution Type/Description: History Museum: housed in 18th century historic structure.
Hours & Admission Prices: Call for hours. No charge.
Attendance: 120

LaVale

LAVALE TOLL GATE HOUSE, 14302 National Hwy., LaVale, MD 21502. Mailing Address: c/o Maryland National Road Assn., 12985 Frederick Rd., West Friendship, MD 21794. Tel.: 410-489-9100.
E-mail: info@marylandnationalroad.org
Web Site: marylandnationalroad.org
Institution Type/Description: Historic Building: housed in a seven-sided Toll Gate House; built in 1811. Listed on the National Register of Historic Places.
Hours & Admission Prices: May-Oct. Sat.-Sun. 1:30-4:30; other times by appointment.

Lanham

HOWARD B. OWENS SCIENCE CENTER AND CHALLENGER LEARNING CENTER, 9601 Greenbelt Rd., Lanham, MD 20706-3397. Tel.: 301-918-8750. Fax: 301-918-8753.
E-mail: howardb.owens@pgcps.org
Web Site: www1.pgcps.org/howardbowens
Key Personnel: Program Admin., Traketa K. Wray; Planetarium Dir., Patty Seaton.
Institution Type/Description: Science Museum & Planetarium.
Hours & Admission Prices: Center: call for hours. Planetarium Shows: Sept.-May 2nd Fri. each month 7:30pm; groups of 16 or more by appointment. Adults $5, students, teachers, senior citizens & military $3. ঙ
Attendance: 30,000 (estimated)

SEABROOK SCHOOLHOUSE, 6116 Seabrook Rd., Lanham, MD 20706. Mailing Address: c/o Marietta House Museum, 5626 Bell Station Rd., Glenn Dale, MD 20769. Tel.: 301-464-5291; 301-446-3302 (TTY).
E-mail: public.affairs@pgparks.com
Institution Type/Description: Historic Building Museum: housed in Seabrook's former one-room school, grades 1-7 until early 1950s.
Hours & Admission Prices: By appointment.

Laurel

DINOSAUR PARK, 13100 Mid-Atlantic Blvd., Laurel, MD 20708. Tel.: 301-627-7755 & 1286.
Web Site: www.pgparks.com/3003/Dinosaur-Park
Institution Type/Description: Park Museum.
Hours & Admission Prices: Garden & play area: open daily sunrise-sunset; Interpretive Programs: 1st & 3rd Sat. 12-4.

THE LAUREL MUSEUM, 817 Main St., Laurel, MD 20707-3429. Tel.: 301-725-7975. Fax: 301-725-2675.
E-mail: info@laurelhistoricalsociety.org
Web Site: www.laurelhistoricalsociety.org
Key Personnel: Exec. Dir., Lindsey Baker.
Institution Type/Description: History Museum: housed in an 1840 millworkers house.

Hours & Admission Prices: Wed. & Fri. 10-2, Sun. 1-4; groups & other times by appointment. No charge. ঙ
Attendance: 3,000 (estimated)

MONTPELIER ARTS CENTER, 9652 Muirkirk Rd., Laurel, MD 20708. Tel.: 301-377-7800, 410-792-0664. Fax: 301-377-7801.
E-mail: montpelier.arts@pgparks.com
Web Site: arts.pgparks.com
Institution Type/Description: Art Center.
Hours & Admission Prices: Daily 10-5. No charge. Closed major holidays.

MONTPELIER MANSION, 9650 Muirkirk Rd., Laurel, MD 20708-2605. Tel.: 301-377-7817; 301-699-2544 (TTY). Fax: 301-377-7818.
E-mail: mary.jurkiewicz@pgparks.com
Web Site: www.pgparks.com
Key Personnel: Pres. Volunteer Group, Friends of Montpelier, Helen Hass; Dir. & Museum Shop Mgr., Mary Jurkiewicz; Chief, Natural & Historical Resources Div., Kyle Lowe.
Institution Type/Description: Historic House: 18th-century Georgian mansion.
Hours & Admission Prices: Self-Guided Tours: Thurs.-Tues. 11-3. Guided Tours: group tours by appointment. Adults $5, seniors over 60 & groups of 10 or more $4, children 5-18 $2; discounts to members of Consortium of Historic House Museums of Metropolitan Washington, DC & members of Friends of Montpelier; active military & members no charge. Closed major holidays.
Attendance: 7,350 (actual)

NATIONAL WILDLIFE VISITOR CENTER, PATUXENT RESEARCH REFUGE, 10901 Scarlet Tanager Loop, Laurel, MD 20708-4011. Tel.: 301-497-5763. Fax: 301-497-5765.
E-mail: patuxent@fws.gov
Web Site: www.fws.gov/northeast/patuxent
Key Personnel: Refuge Mgr., Brad Knudsen; Chm. Friends of Patuxent (V), Jeanne Latham; Treas., Bob Schroeder; Public Rels. & Education, Amy Shoop; Museum Shop Mgr. & Bookstore Mgr., Linda Shive.
Institution Type/Description: Science & Environmental Education Center.
Hours & Admission Prices: Visitor Center: Fri.-Wed. 9-4:30. Tram Tours: mid-March to late June & late Aug. to mid-Nov. Sat.-Sun. 11:30am & 1pm; late June to late Aug. Mon.-Fri. 11:30am & 1pm Sat.-Sun. 11:30am & 1pm. Grounds open sunrise to sunset. No charge. Closed federal holidays. ঙ
Attendance: 100,000 (estimated)

SNOW HILL MANOR, 13301 Laurel-Bowie Rd., Laurel, MD 20708-1509. Tel.: 301-725-6037; 301-446-3302 (TTY). Fax: 301-498-2053.
E-mail: snowhill.manor@pgparks.com
Web Site: www.pgelegantsettings.com/Our_Sites/Snow_Hill_Manor.htm
Institution Type/Description: Historic House Museum: housed in a home formerly owned by the Snowden family; built in 1764. Listed on the National Register of Historic Places.
Hours & Admission Prices: By appointment.

Leonardtown

NORTH END GALLERY, 41652 Fenwick St., Leonardtown, MD 20650. Mailing Address: P.O. Box 1238, Leonardtown, MD 20650. Tel.: 301-475-3130.
E-mail: lindaepstein1@mac.com
Web Site: www.northendgallery.org
Institution Type/Description: Art Gallery.
Hours & Admission Prices: Tues.-Sat. 11-6, Sun. 12-4.

OLD JAIL MUSEUM - ST. MARY'S COUNTY HISTORICAL SOCIETY, 4625 Courthouse Dr., Leonardtown, MD 20650. Mailing Address: P.O. Box 212, Leonardtown, MD 20650. Tel.: 301-475-2467.
E-mail: director@stmaryschs.org
Institution Type/Description: Historic Building: built in 1858.
Hours & Admission Prices: By appointment. No charge.
Attendance: 4,800 (estimated)

ST. MARY'S COUNTY HISTORICAL SOCIETY, 41680 Tudor Pl., Leonardtown, MD 20650. Mailing Address: P.O. Box 212, Leonardtown, MD 20650. Tel.: 301-475-2467 & 9455.
E-mail: director@stmaryschs.org
Key Personnel: Exec. Dir., Susan J. Wolfe.
Institution Type/Description: Historical Society Museum.
Hours & Admission Prices: By appointment. No charge; donations accepted. ঙ
Attendance: 2,400 (estimated)

Lexington Park

PATUXENT RIVER NAVAL AIR MUSEUM, 22156 Three Notch
Rd., Lexington Park, MD 20653-2008. Tel.: 301-863-1900.
E-mail: association@paxmuseum.com
Web Site: www.paxmuseum.com
Key Personnel: Bd. Pres., Mr. George Hill; Office Mgr., Amy Davis; Museum Shop
Mgr., Brandi Blake.
Institution Type/Description: Naval Air Museum.
Hours & Admission Prices: Tues.-Sun. 10-5. Adults $5; active duty military, seniors
& children $3; members no charge. &

Linthicum

**BENSON HAMMOND HOUSE - ANN ARRUNDELL COUNTY
HISTORICAL SOCIETY, INC.,** 7101 Aviation Blvd.,
Linthicum, MD 21090. Mailing Address: P.O. Box 385,
Linthicum, MD 21090-0385. Tel.: 410-760-9679. Facebook,
Twitter.
E-mail: info@aachs.org
Web Site: www.aachs.org
Key Personnel: Pres., Steve Hammond; 1st Vice Pres., John Kille.
Institution Type/Description: Historical Society Museum: listed on the National
Register of Historic Places.
Hours & Admission Prices: March-Dec. open second Sat. each mont 11-3. No
charge, $5 donation requested.
Attendance: 300 (estimated)

NATIONAL ELECTRONICS MUSEUM, 1745 W. Nursery Rd.,
Linthicum, MD 21090-2906. Mailing Address: P.O. Box 1693,
MS4015, Baltimore, MD 21203-1693. Tel.: 410-765-0230. Fax:
410-765-0240. Facebook: National Electronics Museum.
E-mail: nemuseum@gmail.com
Web Site: nationalelectronicsmuseum.org
Formerly: Historical Electronics Museum
Key Personnel: Pres., Roland Anders; Dir., Michael Aurele Simons; Asst. Dir.,
Alice Donahue; Financial Dir., Larraine Clark.
Institution Type/Description: History & Technology Museum.
Hours & Admission Prices: Mon.-Fri. 9-4, Sat. 10-2. Adults $5, seniors, students &
active military $3; members no charge. Closed major holidays. &
Attendance: 28,000 (actual)

Lutherville

FIRE MUSEUM OF MARYLAND, INC., 1301 York Rd.,
Lutherville, MD 21093-6023. Tel.: 410-321-7500. Facebook,
Instagram, & Twitter.
E-mail: info@firemuseummd.org
Web Site: www.firemuseummd.org
Key Personnel: Dir. & Cur., Steve Heaver; Cur., Eric Kelso; Registrar & Museum
Shop Mgr., Melissa M. Heaver.
Institution Type/Description: Fire Museum.
Hours & Admission Prices: Museum hours: June, July, August Wed.-Sat. 10-4; rest
of year Sat. 10-4; Office hours: Mon.-Fri. 9-5. Adults $15, seniors & firefighters
$13, children 2-18 $7, children under 2 & members no charge. &
Attendance: 11,975 (actual)

**LUTHERVILLE   HISTORICAL   COLORED   SCHOOL
NUMBER 24 MUSEUM,** 1426 School Lane, Lutherville, MD
21093. Tel.: 410-825-6114.
Web Site: www.luthervillecoloredschool.webs.com
Institution Type/Description: Historic Building Museum: housed in a former
schoolhouse; built c.1900.
Hours & Admission Prices: By appointment.

Marbury

MATTAWOMAN CREEK ART CENTER, Smallwood State Park,
Marbury, MD 20658. Mailing Address: P.O. Box 258, Marbury,
MD 20658-0258. Tel.: 301-743-5159.
E-mail: mattawomanart@aol.com
Web Site: www.mattawomanart.org
Institution Type/Description: Art Gallery.
Hours & Admission Prices: Gallery: Fri.-Sun. 11-4. Office: Mon. & Wed.-Thurs. 9-
1. No charge; donations accepted. Closed Memorial Day; Thanksgiving. &
Attendance: 3,500 (estimated)

SMALLWOOD STATE PARK, 2750 Sweden Point Rd., Marbury,
MD 20658-2102. Tel.: 301-743-7613, 888-432-2267; 866-804-
7864 (TTY). Fax: 301-743-9405.
E-mail: smallwood.statepark@maryland.gov
Web Site: dnr.maryland.gov
Key Personnel: Asst. Park Mgr., Robert Cantin; Park Ranger, Nakia Johnson; Park
Ranger, Elena Gilroy.
Institution Type/Description: State Park Museum & Historic House: Gen.
Smallwood's retreat.
Hours & Admission Prices: May-Sept. Sun. 1-5; groups by appointment. Park
Service Charge: April-Oct. Sat.-Sun. & holidays $3 per person. &
Attendance: 10,000 (estimated)

Marion

ACCOHANNOCK INDIAN TRIBAL MUSEUM, 28325 Farm
Market Rd., Marion, MD 21838. Mailing Address: P.O. Box 404,
Marion, MD 21838-0404. Tel.: 410-623-2660. Fax: 410-623-2079.
E-mail: accohannock@verizon.net
Institution Type/Description: Native American Indian Cultural Museum.
Hours & Admission Prices: Closed for relocation.

Massey

MASSEY AIR MUSEUM, INC., 33541 Maryland Line Rd.,
Massey, MD 21650. Tel.: 410-928-5270.
E-mail: masseyaero@dmv.com
Web Site: www.masseyaero.org
Institution Type/Description: Air Museum.
Hours & Admission Prices: Daily 10-4; other times by appointment. Suggested
Donation: $5 per person; members no charge. Closed Christmas. &

Middletown

MIDDLETOWN VALLEY HISTORICAL SOCIETY, 305 W.
Main St., Middletown, MD 21769-7928. Mailing Address: P.O.
Box 294, Middletown, MD 21769-0294. Tel.: 301-371-7582.
E-mail: j.dwighthut@juno.com
Web Site: mvhistoricalsociety.weebly.com
Key Personnel: Pres. (V), Mrs. Devra Boesch; Museum Shop Mgr., Edna Alice
Hoffman.
Institution Type/Description: Historical Society: housed in 1840 stone house.
Hours & Admission Prices: May-Oct. Sun. 2-4; Nov.-April for special events only.
No charge; donations accepted.
Attendance: 100 (estimated)

Mitchellville

NEWTON WHITE MANSION, 2708 Enterprise Rd., Mitchellville,
MD 20721-2544. Tel.: 301-249-2004; 301-454-1472 (TTY). Fax:
301-446-3302.
E-mail: nwmansion@pgparks.com
Web Site: www.pgparks.com
Institution Type/Description: Historic Mansion: housed in the former home of U.S.
Navy Captain Newton H. White; built in 1938.
Hours & Admission Prices: By appointment.

Monkton

LADEW TOPIARY GARDENS, 3535 Jarrettsville Pike, Monkton,
MD 21111-1910. Tel.: 410-557-9570 (office) & 9466 (informa-
tion). Fax: 410-557-7763. Facebook: Ladew Topiary Gardens.
E-mail: information@ladewgardens.com
Web Site: www.ladewgardens.com
Key Personnel: Exec. Dir., Emily W. Emerick; Assoc. Dir. Finance, Vicki Farlow;
Assoc. Dir. Mktg. & Devel., Heather Wilhelm; Educ. Dir., Sheryl Pedrick.
Institution Type/Description: Topiary Gardens & Manor House Museum.
Hours & Admission Prices: Gardens: April-Oct. daily 10-5. Gardens, House &
Nature Walk: adults $18, students and senior citizens 62 & over $15, children 2-
12 $9; members & children under 2 no charge. Gardens & Nature Walk: adults
$13, students & seniors $10, children 2-12 $4; members & children under 2 no
charge. &
Attendance: 47,000 (actual)

Mount Airy

SWETCHARNIK ART STUDIO, 7044 Woodville Rd., Mount
Airy, MD 21771-7934. Tel.: 301-829-0137.
E-mail: sara@swetcharnik.com
Web Site: www.swetcharnik.com

Key Personnel: Dir. & Artist, William Swetcharnik; Project Coord. & Artist, Sara Morris Swetcharnik.
Institution Type/Description: Art Museum.
Hours & Admission Prices: Visits by appointment only. No charge; donations accepted.

Mount Savage

EVERGREEN HERITAGE CENTER, 15603 Trimble Rd., N.W., Mount Savage, MD 21545. Tel.: 301-687-0664. Facebook, Instagram, & Twitter.
E-mail: foundation@evergreenheritagecenter.org
Web Site: www.evergreenheritagecenter.org
Key Personnel: Dir., Janice Keene; Grounds Mgr., Matt Diehl; Mgr. Agriculture, Allison Boyd; Dir. of Arts, Maggie Pratt; Mgr. Science Education, Heather Katz; Agroecologist, Ian Cheek.
Institution Type/Description: Heritage Center.
Hours & Admission Prices: Tours: April-Oct. by appointment; Field Trips: April-Nov. daily by appointment. &
Attendance: 2,500 (estimated)

MOUNT SAVAGE MUSEUM BANK JAIL AND MINING BUILDING, Main St., Mount Savage, MD 21545. Mailing Address: Mount Savage Historical Society, P.O. Box 401, Mount Savage, MD 21545. Tel.: 301-876-7847.
E-mail: denlashley@hotmail.com
Web Site: www.mountsavagehistoricalsociety.org
Institution Type/Description: History Museum.
Hours & Admission Prices: By appointment.

National Harbor

NATIONAL CHILDREN'S MUSEUM, 145 Fleet St., Ste. 202, National Harbor, MD 20745. Tel.: 301-392-2400.
E-mail: ncm.contactus@gmail.com
Web Site: www.ccm.org
Formerly: Capital Children's Museum
Key Personnel: Exec. Dir., Wendy Camilla Blackwell; Chm. (V), S. Ross Hechinger.
Institution Type/Description: Children's Museum.
Hours & Admission Prices: Sun. 12-4, Tues.-Sat. 10-4. Admission $10; members and children one & under no charge. Closed New Year's Day; Thanksgiving; Christmas. &

New Windsor

STRAWBRIDGE SHRINE, 2650 Strawbridge Lane, New Windsor, MD 21776. Mailing Address: P.O. Box 388, New Windsor, MD 21776-0388. Tel.: 410-635-2600.
E-mail: tours@strawbridgeshrine.org
Web Site: strawbridgeshrine.org
Institution Type/Description: History Museum: housed in a replica of a 1760 Methodist meeting house.
Hours & Admission Prices: By appointment. &

Newark

QUEPONCO RAILWAY STATION MUSEUM, 8378 Patey Woods Rd., Newark, MD 21841. Mailing Address: P.O. Box 146, Newark, MD 21841-0146. Tel.: 410-632-0950 & 641-0067.
Web Site: www.octhebeach.com/museum/Queponco.html
Key Personnel: Pres. (V), Ralph L. Mason, Jr.
Institution Type/Description: Railway Station Museum: housed in a 1910 depot.
Hours & Admission Prices: May-Oct. 1st & 3rd Sat. 1-4; other times by appointment. No charge. &
Attendance: 200 (estimated)

North Beach

BAYSIDE HISTORY MUSEUM, 4025 4th St., North Beach, MD 20714. Mailing Address: P.O. Box 348, North Beach, MD 20714. Tel.: 410-610-5970.
E-mail: president@baysidehistorymuseum.org
Key Personnel: Founder, Grace Mary Brady.
Institution Type/Description: History Museum.
Hours & Admission Prices: May 1-Oct. 31: Wed.-Sun. 1-4; Nov. 1-April 30: Sat.-Sun. 1-4.

North Bethesda

THE MANSION AT STRATHMORE, 10701 Rockville Pike, North Bethesda, MD 20852-3224. Tel.: 301-581-5109.
E-mail: info@strathmore.org
Web Site: www.strathmore.org/mansion
Institution Type/Description: Art Museum.
Hours & Admission Prices: Call for hours.

North Brentwood

PRINCE GEORGE'S AFRICAN AMERICAN MUSEUM & CULTURAL CENTER (PGAAMCC), 4519 Rhode Island Ave., North Brentwood, MD 20722. Tel.: 301-809-0440. Fax: 301-403-1382. Facebook: Prince Georges African American Museum.
E-mail: programs@pgaamcc.org
Web Site: www.pgaamcc.org
Key Personnel: Dir., Dr. Jacqueline F. Brown; Dir. Government & Corp. Rels., Tracey Tolbert Jones; Chief Cur. & Operations Officer, Jon West-Bey.
Institution Type/Description: African American History Museum.
Hours & Admission Prices: Tues.-Sat. 10-5; other times by appointment. Museum: no charge; donations accepted. Public Programs: $10 per person. Tours: fees vary.
Attendance: 4,000 (estimated)

North East

UPPER BAY MUSEUM, 219 W. Walnut St., North East Community Park, North East, MD 21901. Mailing Address: P.O. Box 275, North East, MD 21901-0275.
E-mail: info@upperbaymuseum.org
Web Site: www.upperbaymuseum.org
Institution Type/Description: History Museum.
Hours & Admission Prices: Memorial Day to mid-Oct. Sat. 10-4, Sun. 12-4; other times by appointment. No charge; donations accepted. &

Oakland

GARRETT COUNTY HISTORICAL MUSEUM, 107 S. Second St., Oakland, MD 21550-1519. Tel.: 301-334-3226.
E-mail: info@garrettcountymuseums.com
Web Site: www.garrettcountymuseums.com/historicalmuseum
Key Personnel: Pres., Robert Boal.
Institution Type/Description: Historical Society Museum.
Hours & Admission Prices: Summer hours: Mon.-Sat. 10-3; Winter hours: Thur., Fri. & Sat. 10-3. Closed major holidays. &
Attendance: 6,000 (estimated)

OAKLAND B&O MUSEUM, 117 E. Liberty St., Oakland, MD 21550-1201. Mailing Address: 15 S. 3rd St., Oakland, MD 21550. Tel.: 301-334-3204. Fax: 301-334-4401. Facebook: Oakland B&O Museum.
E-mail: townofoak@gmail.com
Web Site: www.oaklandbandomuseum.org
Formerly: Oakland B&O Train Station
Key Personnel: Chm. (V), Terry Helbig; Museum Shop Mgr., Kathy Biltz.
Institution Type/Description: Historic Train Station: built in 1884.
Hours & Admission Prices: Spring, Summer & Fall: Wed.-Sat. 10-3, Sun. 12-3. No charge; donations accepted. &
Attendance: 41,465 (estimated)

Ocean City

OCEAN CITY LIFE-SAVING STATION MUSEUM, 813 S. Atlantic Ave., Ocean City, MD 21842. Mailing Address: P.O. Box 603, Ocean City, MD 21843-0603. Tel.: 410-289-4991.
E-mail: sandy@ocmuseum.org
Web Site: www.ocmuseum.org
Institution Type/Description: History Museum.
Hours & Admission Prices: May-Oct. daily 10-4; Nov.-April Sat.-Sun. 10-4 other times by appointment. Adults $5, seniors 62 & over, active military, youth 12-18 $3; children 11 & under and members no charge.
Attendance: 18,454 (actual)

Oldtown

IRVIN ALLEN/MICHAEL CRESAP MUSEUM, 19015 Opessa St., S.E., Oldtown, MD 21555-9702. Tel.: 301-478-5848.
E-mail: NFO@MICHAELCRESAPMUSEUM.ORG
Web Site: www.michaelcresapmuseum.org

Key Personnel: Pres., Jilla Diane Smith; Sec. & Treas., Judy Allen O'Hara.
Institution Type/Description: Historic House Museum: built in 1764.
Hours & Admission Prices: May-Sept. by appointment.

Owings Mills

SOLDIERS DELIGHT NATURAL ENVIRONMENT AREA, 5100 Deer Park Rd., Owings Mills, MD 21117. Tel.: 410-461-5005.
E-mail: customerservice.dnr@maryland.gov
Institution Type/Description: Environment Area & Visitor Center.
Hours & Admission Prices: Visitor Center: Sat. 11-3; other times by appointment.

Oxford

OXFORD MUSEUM, INC., Morris and Market Sts., Oxford, MD 21654. Mailing Address: P.O. Box 131, Oxford, MD 21654-0131. Tel.: 410-226-0191.
E-mail: oxford_museum@verizon.net
Web Site: www.oxfordmuseum.org
Key Personnel: Pres. Bd. (V), Pat Jessup; Dir., Ellen Anderson.
Institution Type/Description: Local History Museum.
Hours & Admission Prices: late April to May & Oct. to mid-Nov. Mon. & Fri.-Sat. 10-4, Sun. 1-4; May-Oct. Tues. 10-4; June-Sept. Mon., Wed. & Fri.-Sat. 10-4, Sun. 1-4. No charge; donations suggested. &
Attendance: 4,000 (estimated)

Oxon Hill

OXON COVE PARK, 6411 Oxon Hill Rd., Oxon Hill, MD 20745-1100. Mailing Address: 1900 Anacostia Dr., S.E., Washington, DC 20020-6722. Tel.: 301-839-1176. Fax: 301-763-1066. TDD: 301-839-1783.
E-mail: vanessa-molineaux@nps.gov
Web Site: www.nps.gov/oxhi
Key Personnel: Dir., Lisa Mendelson-Lelmini; Park Mgr., Sharon Vanessa Molineaux.
Institution Type/Description: Agriculture Museum: housed in c.1900 farm & farm outbuildings.
Hours & Admission Prices: Daily 8-4:30. No charge; donations accepted. Closed New Year's Day; Thanksgiving; Christmas. &
Attendance: 100,000 (estimated)

OXON HILL MANOR, 6901 Oxon Hill Rd., Oxon Hill, MD 20745. Tel.: 301-839-7782; 301-446-6802 (TTY). Fax: 301-839-4867.
E-mail: ohmanor@pgparks.com
Institution Type/Description: Historic House Museum: housed in the former home of nephews of George Washington, & the nephew of John Hanson, the first president elected by the Continental Congress under the Articles of Confederation; c.1928.
Hours & Admission Prices: Mon. 1-4, Tues.-Fri. 9-4 by appointment.

Pasadena

HANCOCK'S RESOLUTION FARM, 2795 Bayside Beach Rd., Pasadena, MD 21056. Mailing Address: P.O. Box 233, Gibson Island, MD 21056. Tel.: 410-255-4048.
E-mail: info@historichancocksresolution.org
Web Site: www.historichancocksresolution.org
Key Personnel: Pres., Jim Morrison.
Institution Type/Description: Historic Farm.
Hours & Admission Prices: April-Oct. Sun. 1-4. No charge; donations accepted. Closed Easter.

Perryville

RODGERS TAVERN, 259 Broad St., Perryville, MD 21903-0322. Mailing Address: P.O. Box 322, Perryville, MD 21903-0322. Tel.: 410-642-6066. Fax: 410-642-6391.
E-mail: townhall@perryvillemd.org
Web Site: www.Perryvillemd.org
Key Personnel: Chm. (V), Barbara Brown.
Institution Type/Description: Historic House: pre-1743 building, operated by Rodgers family.
Hours & Admission Prices: By appointment. No charge; donations accepted.
Attendance: 6,000 (estimated)

Pikesville

MARYLAND STATE POLICE MUSEUM, 1201 Reisterstown Rd., Pikesville, MD 21208-3898. Tel.: 410-653-4278. Fax: 410-653-4341.
E-mail: mringley@mdsp.org
Web Site: www.mdsp.org
Key Personnel: Coord., Margaret Ringley.
Institution Type/Description: Police History Museum.
Hours & Admission Prices: Mon.-Fri.

Piney Point

PINEY POINT LIGHTHOUSE MUSEUM AND HISTORIC PARK, 44720 Lighthouse Rd., Piney Point, MD 20674. Tel.: 301-994-1471.
E-mail: april.havens@stmarysmd.com
Institution Type/Description: History Museum.
Hours & Admission Prices: April-Sept. daily 10-5; Oct.-Jan. 1 Fri.-Mon. 12-4; call for special Christmas hours. Adults $7, seniors, military & children $3.50. Closed Easter; Thanksgiving; Christmas. &

Pocomoke City

COSTEN HOUSE & HALL-WALTON MEMORIAL GARDEN, 206 Market St., Pocomoke City, MD 21851. Tel.: 410-957-3110. Facebook.
E-mail: ritarae1@comcast.net
Institution Type/Description: History Museum: housed in the home of the first mayor of Pocomoke.
Hours & Admission Prices: Memorial Day-Labor Day: Wed. & Sat. 1-4; After Labor Day by appointment only. Adults $3. &
Attendance: 1,000 (estimated)

DELMARVA DISCOVERY CENTER & MUSEUM, 2 Market St., Pocomoke City, MD 21851. Tel.: 410-957-9933. Facebook.
E-mail: contact@delmarvadiscoverycenter.org
Web Site: delmarvadiscoverycenter.org
Key Personnel: Pres. & C.E.O., Stacey Weisner; Chm. (V), Susan B. Pusey.
Institution Type/Description: Cultural & Natural Heritage Center.
Hours & Admission Prices: Mon.-Sat 10-4, Sun. 12-4. Adult $10, Senior (60 & over) & Student $8, Military & Youth (4-17) $5, children (3 and under) & members no charge. Closed New Year's Day, Easter, Thanksgiving, & Christmas. &
Attendance: 14,000 (actual)

STURGIS ONE-ROOM SCHOOL MUSEUM, 209 Willow St., Pocomoke City, MD 21851. Mailing Address: P.O. Box 697, Pocomoke City, MD 21851-0697. Tel.: 410-957-1913.
E-mail: gatling144@verizon.net
Web Site: www.sturgismuseum.org
Key Personnel: Pres., James Gatling; Cur., Sudie Gatling.
Institution Type/Description: History Museum: housed in a one-room African American school house used for first through seventh grades until 1937.
Hours & Admission Prices: May-Oct. Tues.-Sat. 1-4; other times by appointment. Adults $3, children $1.

Poolesville

JOHN POOLE HOUSE, 19923 Fisher Ave., Poolesville, MD 20837. Mailing Address: P.O. Box 232, Poolesville, MD 20837. Tel.: 301-972-8588.
E-mail: info@historicmedley.org
Web Site: www.historicmedley.org
Institution Type/Description: Historic House Museum: housed in a former trading post built by John Poole, Jr.; built in 1793.
Hours & Admission Prices: By appointment. No charge; donations accepted.

SENECA SCHOOLHOUSE MUSEUM, 16800 River Rd., Poolesville, MD 20837-0232. Mailing Address: Historic Medley District, Inc., P.O. Box 232, Poolesville, MD 20837-0232. Tel.: 301-972-8588.
E-mail: info@historicmedley.org
Web Site: www.historicmedley.org
Key Personnel: Dir., Patty Cooper.
Institution Type/Description: Historic Building Museum.
Hours & Admission Prices: By appointment. No charge; donations accepted.

Port Deposit

PAW PAW MUSEUM, 98 N. Main St., Port Deposit, MD 21904-1210. Tel.: 410-378-4480.
E-mail: pawpawmuseum@gmail.com
Institution Type/Description: Historic Building: housed in a former Methodist Church; built in 1821.
Hours & Admission Prices: May-Oct. 2nd & 4th Sun. of month 1-5.

Port Tobacco

PORT TOBACCO COURTHOUSE, Chapel Point Rd., Port Tobacco, MD 20677. Mailing Address: P.O. Box 302, Port Tobacco, MD 20677. Tel.: 301-934-4313.
Web Site: www.somd.com
Institution Type/Description: Historic Building Museum: housed in a former courthouse built in 1819. Listed on the National Register of Historic Places.
Hours & Admission Prices: Call for hours.

PORT TOBACCO ONE ROOM SCHOOL, 7215 Chapel Point Rd., Port Tobacco, MD 20677. Mailing Address: c/o Society for the Restoration of Port Tobacco, P.O. Box 302, Port Tobacco, MD 20677-0302. Tel.: 301-934-9483.
E-mail: idcornette@gmail.com
Key Personnel: Dir. & Chm. (V), Dale Cornette.
Institution Type/Description: History Museum: built in 1871.
Hours & Admission Prices: By appointment. No charge; donations accepted. &
Attendance: 1,000 (estimated)

THOMAS STONE NATIONAL HISTORIC SITE, 6655 Rose Hill, Port Tobacco, MD 20677. Tel.: 301-392-1776. Fax: 301-934-8793.
Web Site: www.nps.gov
Institution Type/Description: Historic Site: housed in a 1770s Georgian mansion, former home of Thomas Stone, a Maryland signer of the Declaration of Independence.
Hours & Admission Prices: Call for hours. &

Potomac

GLENSTONE, 12100 Glen Rd., Potomac, MD 20854. Tel.: 301-983-5001. Facebook, Twitter, Instagram.
E-mail: info@glenstone.org
Web Site: glenstone.org
Key Personnel: Co-Founder & Dir., Emily Wei Rales; Co-Founder, Mitchell Rales.
Institution Type/Description: Modern & Contemporary Art Museum.
Hours & Admission Prices: Thurs.-Sun. 10-5 by appointment; visitors must be 12 & over. No charge.

GREAT FALLS TAVERN MUSEUM AND VISITOR CENTER, 11710 MacArthur Blvd., Potomac, MD 20854. Tel.: 301-767-3714.
E-mail: choh_information@nps.gov
Institution Type/Description: Historic Building: built in 1831.
Hours & Admission Prices: Daily 9-4:30. Closed New Year's Day; Thanksgiving; Christmas.

Preston

LINCHESTER MILL, 3390 Linchester Mill Rd., Preston, MD 21655. Mailing Address: c/o Caroline Historical Society, 16 N. Second St., Denton, MD 21629. Tel.: 410-310-9202.
E-mail: info@carolinehistory.org
Web Site: www.carolinehistory.org
Institution Type/Description: Historic Mill: housed in the former mill that sold grain to George Washington's army during the Revolutionary War; c.1840. Listed on the National Register of Historic Places.
Hours & Admission Prices: Call for hours.

Prince Frederick

BATTLE CREEK CYPRESS SWAMP SANCTUARY, 2880 Gray's Rd., Prince Frederick, MD 20678. Mailing Address: c/o Calvert Nature Society, P.O. Box 122, Port Republic, MD 20676. Tel.: 410-535-5327.
E-mail: CypressSwamp@co.cal.md.us
Web Site: calvertparks.org/bccss.html
Key Personnel: Exec. Dir., Anne Sundermann.
Institution Type/Description: Nature Sanctuary.

Hours & Admission Prices: Memorial Day-Labor Day: Mon.-Fri 9-4:30, Sat. 10-6, Sun. 1-6; Labor Day-Memorial Day: Mon.-Fri. 9-4:30, Sat. 10-4:30, Sun. 1-4:30. No charge. Closed most county holidays.

CALVERT COUNTY HISTORICAL SOCIETY, 70 Church St., Prince Frederick, MD 20678. Mailing Address: P.O. Box 358, Prince Frederick, MD 20678. Tel.: 410-535-2452. Fax: 410-535-4660.
E-mail: cchsadmin@calverthistory.org
Web Site: www.calverthistory.org
Key Personnel: Dir. & Research Historian, Leila Boyer.
Institution Type/Description: Historical Society.
Hours & Admission Prices: Tues.-Thurs. 10-3; other times by appointment.

THE SPACEFLIGHT AMERICA MUSEUM AND SCIENCE CENTER AT ARTHUR STORER PLANETARIUM, 520 Fox Run Blvd., Prince Frederick, MD 20678. Mailing Address: 10383 Southern Maryland Blvd., P.O. Box 81, Dunkirk, MD 20754-0081. Tel.: 301-812-6480.
E-mail: sa-museum@wsi-edu.org
Web Site: wsi-edu.info/spaceflightamericamuseum
Institution Type/Description: Science Center & Planetarium.
Hours & Admission Prices: Call for hours.

Princess Anne

THE SOMERSET COUNTY HISTORICAL SOCIETY, INC. - TEACKLE MANSION, 11736 Mansion St., Princess Anne, MD 21853. Mailing Address: P.O. Box 181, Princess Anne, MD 21853-0181. Tel.: 410-651-2238.
E-mail: moreinfo@teacklemansion.org
Web Site: www.teacklemansion.org
Formerly: Olde Princess Anne Days, Inc.
Key Personnel: Pres., Rich Ziolkowski; Vice Pres., Jill Hall; Museum Shop Mgr., Sharon Upton.
Institution Type/Description: General Museum: housed in 1801 Teackle Mansion, early 19th-century federal period building.
Hours & Admission Prices: April to mid-Dec. Thurs. & Sat.-Sun. 1-3; tours by appointment. Adults $5, students $2; discounts to members; children under 12 accompanied by adult no charge.
Attendance: 778 (estimated)

Queenstown

QUEENSTOWN COLONIAL COURTHOUSE, 100 Del Rhodes Ave., Queenstown, MD 21658. Mailing Address: P.O. Box 4, Queenstown, MD 21658. Tel.: 410-827-7646 & 0177. Fax: 410-827-7661.
E-mail: townoffice@queenstown-md.com
Web Site: www.queenstown-md.com
Institution Type/Description: History Museum.
Hours & Admission Prices: May-Oct. Mon.-Fri. 8:30-4, 1st Sat. each month 10-2; Nov.-April Mon.-Fri. 8:30-4. No charge.
Attendance: 120 (estimated)

Ridgely

ADKINS ARBORETUM, 12610 Eveland Rd., Ridgely, MD 21660. Tel.: 410-634-2847. Fax: 410-634-2878.
E-mail: info@adkinsarboretum.org
Web Site: www.adkinsarboretum.org
Key Personnel: Exec. Dir., Ginna Tiernan; Asst. Dir., Jenny Houghton.
Institution Type/Description: Arboretum.
Hours & Admission Prices: Tues.-Sat. 10-4, Sun. 12-4. Adults $5, students 6-18 $2; members and children 5 & under no charge. Closed major holidays. &
Attendance: 20,000 (actual)

Riverdale Park

RIVERSDALE HOUSE MUSEUM, 4811 Riverdale Rd., Riverdale Park, MD 20737-1911. Mailing Address: 6005 48th Ave., Riverdale Park, MD 20737-2015. Tel.: 301-864-0420. Fax: 301-927-3498. TDD: 301-699-2544.
E-mail: riversdale@pgparks.com
Web Site: history.pgparks.com/sites_and_museums/riversdale_house_museum.htm
Key Personnel: Acting Dir., Ann Wass; Pres. (V), Patrick Gossett; Museum Shop Mgr., Michelle Krestch.
Institution Type/Description: National Historic Landmark. Historic House: 1803 five-part stucco covered brick manor, blending Belgian & American architec-

tural styles built by Henri Stier & occupied by his daughter, Rosalie & her husband George Calvert and inherited by their son Charles Benedict. Later, residents included Senator Hiram Johnson (CA) & Senators Thaddeus & Hattie Caraway (AR).
Hours & Admission Prices: Sun. & Fri. 12:15-3:15; other times by appointment. Adults $5, senior citizens 60 & over $4, children $2; discounts to groups & members. Closed New Year's Day; Independence Day; Christmas. &
Attendance: 11,500 (estimated)

Rock Hall

ROCK HALL MUSEUM, Municipal Bldg., S. Main St., Rock Hall, MD 21661. Mailing Address: P.O. Box 367, Rock Hall, MD 21661. Tel.: 410-639-7611. Fax: 410-639-7298.
E-mail: dougfrancis50@hotmail.com
Web Site: www.rockhallmd.com/museum/index/php
Key Personnel: Chm., Doug Francis.
Institution Type/Description: History Museum.
Hours & Admission Prices: Sat.-Sun. 11-3; other times by appointment. No charge; donations accepted.
Attendance: 500 (estimated)

WATERMAN'S MUSEUM, 20880 Rock Hall Ave., Rock Hall, MD 21661-1407. Tel.: 410-778-6697. Fax: 410-639-2971.
E-mail: email@havenharbour.com
Web Site: www.havenharbour.com/hhwatmus.htm
Key Personnel: Mgr., Woodrow Loller.
Institution Type/Description: History Museum.
Hours & Admission Prices: Daily 8-5. No charge; donations accepted.
Attendance: 200 (estimated)

Rockville

LATVIAN MUSEUM, 400 Hurley Ave., Rockville, MD 20850-3121. Tel.: 301-340-1914. Fax: 301-340-8732.
E-mail: lbergs1027@gmail.com
Web Site: www.alausa.org
Key Personnel: Dir. & Cur., Lilita Bergs.
Institution Type/Description: Ethnic Museum: Latvian historic & cultural development from Ice Age to 20th Century.
Hours & Admission Prices: By appointment. No charge; donations accepted. &
Attendance: 2,000 (estimated)

THE MONTGOMERY COUNTY HISTORICAL SOCIETY, INC., 103 W. Montgomery Ave., Rockville, MD 20850-4212. Mailing Address: 111 W. Montgomery Ave., Rockville, MD 20850-4212. Tel.: 301-340-2825 & 762-1492. Fax: 301-340-2871. Facebook: The Montgomery County Historical Society.
E-mail: info@montgomeryhistory.org
Web Site: www.montgomeryhistory.org
Key Personnel: Pres. (V), Jack Devine; Exec. Dir., Matthew Logan; Librarian, Patricia Andersen; Coord. Education, April Bryan; Office Mgr., Kathy Wilson.
Institution Type/Description: Historic House: 1815 Beall-Dawson House; 1852 Stonestreet Medical Museum.
Hours & Admission Prices: Museum: Wed.-Sun. 12-4. Library: Wed.-Fri. 10-4, Sat. 12-4. Adults $5; members no charge.
Attendance: 6,000 (estimated)

PEERLESS ROCKVILLE HISTORIC PRESERVATION, LTD., 29 Courthouse Sq., Rm. 110, Rockville, MD 20850. Mailing Address: P.O. Box 4262, Rockville, MD 20849. Tel.: 301-762-0096.
E-mail: info@peerlessrockville.org
Web Site: www.peerlessrockville.org
Formerly: Peerless Rockville Collection & Research Library
Key Personnel: Dir., Mary A. van Balgooy; Pres., Erick Ledbetter.
Institution Type/Description: History Museum: housed in the Red Brick Courthouse.
Hours & Admission Prices: Center & Library: Mon.-Fri. 10-1; other times by appointment. Office: Mon.-Fri. 9-3. No charge. &
Attendance: 12,000 (estimated)

Saint Leonard

JEFFERSON PATTERSON PARK & MUSEUM, 10515 Mackall Rd., Saint Leonard, MD 20685-2433. Tel.: 410-586-8501. Fax: 410-586-0080. TDD: 800-735-2258 (Maryland Relay).
E-mail: jef.pat@maryland.gov
Web Site: www.jefpat.org

Key Personnel: Dir., Mark Thompson; Pres. (V), Pat Furey; Chief Conservator, Betty Seifert; Fiscal Officer, Denise America; Dir. Education, Rachelle M. Green; Admin. Research, Edward E. Chaney; Collections, Rebecca Morehouse; Museum Shop Mgr., Michele Parlett; Dir. Maryland Archaeological Conservation Laboratory, Patricia Samford; Education Coord., Julie Hall; Education & Archaeology Specialist, Kate Dinnel; Head Conservation, Nichole Doub; Conservation Tech, Gareth McNair-Lewis; Admin. & Mktg. & Events Coord., Sherwana Knox; Sec., Sharon Raftery; Federal Cur., Sara Rivers-Cofield; Maintenance Supvr., Dimitrios Papadakis; Maintenance Chief, Jim House; Maintenance Mechanic, Stephen Embrey; Maintenance Asst., William Wyatt.
Institution Type/Description: Park & Museum.
Hours & Admission Prices: April 15-Oct. 15 Wed.-Sun. 10-5. No charge; donations accepted. &
Attendance: 59,000 (actual)

Saint Mary's City

THE DWIGHT FREDERIC BOYDEN GALLERY, St. Mary's College of Maryland, 18952 E. Fisher Rd., Saint Mary's City, MD 20686-3002. Tel.: 240-895-4246. Fax: 240-895-4958.
E-mail: lnscheer@smcm.edu
Web Site: www.smcm.edu/boydengallery
Institution Type/Description: Art Gallery.
Hours & Admission Prices: Sept.-May Mon.-Fri. 11-5; Summer: call for hours. No charge; donations accepted. &
Attendance: 4,000 (estimated)

HISTORIC ST. MARY'S CITY, 18751 Hogaboom Ln., Saint Mary's City, MD 20686. Mailing Address: P.O. Box 39, Saint Mary's City, MD 20686-0039. Tel.: 240-895-4990. Fax: 240-895-4968.
E-mail: Info@HSMCdigsHistory.org
Web Site: www.hsmcdigshistory.org
Key Personnel: Exec. Dir., Regina Faden.
Institution Type/Description: Outdoor Living History Museum.
Hours & Admission Prices: March 13-June 30; Tues.-Sat. 10-5; July 4-Sept. 2: Wed.-Sun. 10-5; Sept. 4-Nov. 24: Tues.-Sat. 10-5. Adults $10, senior citizens $9, youth 6-18 $6; members and children 5 & under no charge. &
Attendance: 45,000 (estimated)

Saint Michaels

CHESAPEAKE BAY MARITIME MUSEUM, 213 N. Talbot St., Saint Michaels, MD 21663-0636. Tel.: 410-745-2916. Fax: 410-745-6088. Facebook.
E-mail: havefun@cbmm.org
Web Site: cbmm.org
Key Personnel: Pres., Kristen L. Greenaway; Chm., Diane J. Staley; Chief Cur., Pete Lesher; Vice Pres. Finance, Branden Meredith; Vice Pres. Operations, Steven Byrnes; Vice Pres. Communications, Tracey Johns.
Institution Type/Description: Regional Maritime History Museum.
Hours & Admission Prices: May-Oct. daily 9-5; Nov.-April. daily 10-4. Adults $15, seniors, college students & retired military $12, children 6-17 $6; discounts to groups; active military, children 5 & under & members no charge. Closed New Year's Day; Thanksgiving; Christmas. &
Attendance: 63,000 (actual)

ST. MICHAELS MUSEUM, E. Chestnut St. & St. Mary's Sq., Saint Michaels, MD 21663. Mailing Address: P.O. Box 714, Saint Michaels, MD 21663. Tel.: 410-745-9561.
E-mail: stmichaelsmuseum@atlanticbb.net
Web Site: www.stmichaelsmuseum.org
Key Personnel: Pres. (V), Jeff Fones; Cur., Kate Fones.
Institution Type/Description: History Museum.
Hours & Admission Prices: May-Oct. Fri. & Sun. 1-4, Sat. 10-4; other times by appointment. Adults $3, youth 6-17 $1.

Salisbury

ART INSTITUTE & GALLERY, 212 W. Main St., Ste. 101, Salisbury, MD 21801. Tel.: 410-546-4748. Facebook, Instagram & Twitter.
E-mail: alison@aiandg.org
Web Site: www.salisburyartspace.org
Key Personnel: Dir., Alison Grice; Shop Mgr., Barb Atkins; Volunteer Coord., Deb Dickerson.
Institution Type/Description: Art Gallery.
Hours & Admission Prices: Wed.-Sat. 12-5 & 3rd Fri. of month 12-8. No charge; donations are accepted. &

CHARLES H. CHIPMAN CULTURAL CENTER, 325 Broad St., Salisbury, MD 21801. Mailing Address: P.O. Box 4374, Salisbury, MD 21803. Tel.: 410-860-9290. Facebook & Instagram.
E-mail: chipmancenter@comcast.net
Web Site: www.chipmancenter.org
Key Personnel: Pres., Shanie Shields; Vice Pres., Dr. Bessie Green; Treas., Herb Fletcher; Asst. Treas., Wirt Wolfe; Sec., Dr. R. Neil Carey.
Institution Type/Description: History Museum: housed in a former African American church; built in 1837.
Hours & Admission Prices: Call for hours.

EDWARD H. NABB RESEARCH CENTER FOR DELMARVA HISTORY & CULTURE AT SALISBURY UNIVERSITY, Salisbury University, Guerrieri Academic Commons #430, Salisbury, MD 21801. Mailing Address: 1101 Camden Ave., Salisbury, MD 21801. Tel.: 410-543-6312. Fax: 410-543-6203.
E-mail: nabbcenter@salisbury.edu
Web Site: salisbury.edu/nabb
Key Personnel: Exhibits & Artifacts Cur., Janie Kreines; Chm. (V), Michael Hitch.
Institution Type/Description: History Museum.
Hours & Admission Prices: Mon. 10-6, Tues.-Fri. 10-4:30, Sat. 10-2. Adults $5; members, faculty, students & staff no charge. Closed holidays.
Attendance: 5,000 (estimated)

HERITAGE CENTRE AND PEMBERTON HALL, Pemberton Historical Park, Pemberton Dr., Salisbury, MD 21804. Tel.: 410-860-0447. Fax: 410-860-1441. Facebook, Instagram, & Twitter.
Web Site: www.americanheritage.com/about/company
Key Personnel: Pres., Edwin S. Grosvenor.
Institution Type/Description: History Museum.
Hours & Admission Prices: Thurs.-Sun. 12-4. Heritage Center: adults $2, children under 12 $1.

POPLAR HILL MANSION, 117 Elizabeth St., Salisbury, MD 21801. Tel.: 410-749-1776. Facebook: Poplar Hill Mansion.
E-mail: curator@poplarhillmansion.org
Web Site: www.poplarhillmansion.org
Key Personnel: Dir., Sarah Meyers; Chm. (V), Aleta Davis.
Institution Type/Description: Historic House Museum.
Hours & Admission Prices: Feb.-Dec. 1st & 3rd Sun. each month 1-4; other times by appointment. No charge. Private Tours at other times: adults $5; discounts to school groups. Closed city holidays.
Attendance: 1,500 (actual)

SALISBURY STATE UNIVERSITY GALLERIES, 1101 Camden Ave., Salisbury, MD 21801-6837. Tel.: 410-548-2547 & 6000. Fax: 410-548-3002.
E-mail: galleries@salisbury.edu
Web Site: salisbury.edu
Key Personnel: Cur., Linda Shipp; Dir. Cultural Affairs, June Krell-Salgado.
Institution Type/Description: University Art Gallery.
Hours & Admission Prices: Fulton Hall Gallery: Sept.-May Tues.-Fri. 10-4. Atrium Gallery: Sept.-May Mon.-Wed. 10-4. No charge; donations accepted. Closed major holidays.
Attendance: 20,000 (actual)

THE SALISBURY ZOOLOGICAL PARK, 755 S. Park Dr., Salisbury, MD 21804-5600. Mailing Address: P.O. Box 2979, Salisbury, MD 21802-2979. Tel.: 410-548-3188. Fax: 410-860-0919.
E-mail: salisburyzooed@gmail.com
Web Site: www.salisburyzoo.org
Key Personnel: Dir., Ralph Piland; Chm. (V), Ronald G. Alessi, Sr.
Institution Type/Description: Zoo.
Hours & Admission Prices: Daily 9-4:30. No charge; donations accepted. Closed Thanksgiving; Christmas.
Attendance: 192,000 (estimated)

THE WARD MUSEUM OF WILDFOWL ART, SALISBURY UNIVERSITY, 909 S. Schumaker Dr., Salisbury, MD 21804-8722. Tel.: 410-742-4988. Fax: 410-742-3107.
E-mail: wardinfo@salisbury.edu
Web Site: www.wardmuseum.org
Key Personnel: Exec. Dir., Lora Bottinelli; Dir. Education, Mark McMullen-Bushman; Dir. Outreach, Rose Taylor.
Institution Type/Description: Art Museum.
Hours & Admission Prices: Mon.-Sat. 10-5, Sun. 12-5. Families $17 on Sun., adults $7, seniors $5, children under 18 $3; discounts to AAM members; members, pre-

schoolers, military/veterans; Salisbury Univ. staff, students & faculty no charge. Closed New Year's Day; Thanksgiving; Christmas.
Attendance: 50,000 (estimated)

Sandy Spring

SANDY SPRING MUSEUM, 17901 Bentley Rd., Sandy Spring, MD 20860-1001. Tel.: 301-774-0022. Fax: 301-774-8149.
E-mail: info@sandyspringmuseum.org
Web Site: www.sandyspringmuseum.org
Key Personnel: Exec. Dir., Allison Weiss; Pres., Marcia Ferranto.
Institution Type/Description: History Museum.
Hours & Admission Prices: Mon. & Wed.-Thurs. 9-4, Sat.-Sun. 12-4. Adults $5; members & children no charge. Closed New Year's Eve & Day; Labor Day; Christmas Eve, Day & week.
Attendance: 10,000 (estimated)

SANDY SPRING SLAVE MUSEUM & AFRICAN ART GALLERY, INC., 18524 Brooke Rd., Sandy Spring, MD 20860-1407. Tel.: 301-774-4066.
Institution Type/Description: Art & History Museum
Hours & Admission Prices: Adults $5. No charge; donations accepted. Closed national holidays.

Scotland

POINT LOOKOUT STATE PARK & MUSEUM, 11175 Point Lookout Rd., Scotland, MD 20687. Tel.: 301-872-5688.
E-mail: customerservice.dnr@maryland.gov
Institution Type/Description: Park & History Museum.
Hours & Admission Prices: Daily 6am to sunset.

Shady Side

CAPTAIN AVERY MUSEUM, INC., 1418 E.W. Shadyside Rd., Shady Side, MD 20764-9713. Mailing Address: P.O. Box 89, Shady Side, MD 20764-0089. Tel.: 410-867-4486.
E-mail: info@captainaverymuseum.org
Web Site: captainaverymuseum.org
Formerly: Shady Side Rural Heritage Society, Inc.
Key Personnel: Exec. Dir., Deborah Gangloff; Cur., Candi Claggett; Program Coord., Donna Anderson; Operations Mgr., Pat Youngmann.
Institution Type/Description: Historic House: 1860 waterman's house & 1920s fishing club.
Hours & Admission Prices: Museum: April-Nov. Sun. 1-4. Library: Mon. 12-3. Grounds & Outdoor Exhibits: daily dawn to dusk. No charge; donations accepted.
Attendance: 4,000 (actual)

Sharpsburg

ANTIETAM NATIONAL BATTLEFIELD-VISITOR CENTER, 5831 Dunker Church Rd., Sharpsburg, MD 21782. Mailing Address: P.O. Box 158, Sharpsburg, MD 21782-0158. Tel.: 301-432-5124. Facebook, Instagram, Twitter.
Web Site: www.nps.gov/anti
Institution Type/Description: Historic Site: site of 1862 Civil War Maryland Campaign & battle of Antietam or Sharpsburg.
Hours & Admission Prices: Visitor Center: daily 9-5. Day Pass: family $6, adults $4. Closed New Year's Day; Thanksgiving; Christmas.
Attendance: 313,201 (actual)

BARRON'S C&O CANAL MUSEUM, Physical/Mailing Address: 5632 Mose Cir., Sharpsburg, MD 21782. Tel.: 410-583-5299.
E-mail: tylerscanoe@verizon.net
Key Personnel: Co Owner, John Tyler; Co Owner, Renay Tylers.
Institution Type/Description: History Museum: housed in a country store.
Hours & Admission Prices: Sat.-Sun. 9-6.

KENNEDY FARM HOUSE MUSEUM, 2406 Chestnut Grove Rd., Sharpsburg, MD 21782. Tel.: 202-537-8900.
Web Site: johnbrown.org
Institution Type/Description: Historic House Museum: housed in the farmhouse that served as a staging area for John Brown and his army as they prepared for the Harpers Ferry raid in the summer of 1859. A National Historic Landmark.
Hours & Admission Prices: May-Oct. by appointment.

Silver Spring

NATIONAL CAPITAL TROLLEY MUSEUM, 1313 Bonifant Rd., Silver Spring, MD 20905-5955. Tel.: 301-384-6352. Fax: 301-384-2865.
Web Site: www.dctrolley.org
Key Personnel: C.E.O., Pres. (V) & Museum Shop Mgr., Ken Rucker; Treas., Charles Tirschman; Dir. Devel., Wesley Paulson.
Institution Type/Description: Transportation Museum.
Hours & Admission Prices: Call for hours. Adults $7.
Attendance: 15,155 (actual)

NATIONAL MUSEUM OF HEALTH AND MEDICINE, 2500 Linden Ln., Silver Spring, MD 20910. Mailing Address: 2460 Linden Ln., Bldg. 2500, Silver Spring, MD 20910. Tel.: 301-319-3300 & 3349. Facebook.
E-mail: usarmy.detrick.medcon-usamrmc.list.medical-museum@mail.mil
Web Site: www.medicalmuseum.mil
Formerly: Army Medical Museum
Key Personnel: Dir., Adrianne Noe, Ph.D.; Admin., Kevin Monahan; Public Programs Mgr., Andrea Schierkolk; Public Affairs Officer, Tim Clarke, Jr.
Institution Type/Description: Medical History Museum.
Hours & Admission Prices: Daily 10-5:30. No charge. Closed Christmas. &
Attendance: 50,000 (estimated)

PYRAMID ATLANTIC ART CENTER, 8230 Georgia Ave., Silver Spring, MD 20910. Mailing Address: 4318 Gallatin St., Hyattsville, MD 20781. Tel.: 301-608-9101. Fax: 301-608-9102.
E-mail: hello@pyramid-atlantic.org
Web Site: www.pyramidatlanticartcenter.org
Key Personnel: Dir., Jose Dominguez.
Institution Type/Description: Art Gallery.
Hours & Admission Prices: Tues.-Sat. 10-6, Sun. 12-5; other times by appointment. No charge.

SEVENTH-DAY ADVENTIST CHURCH, 12501 Old Columbia Pike, Silver Spring, MD 20904. Tel.: 301-680-6310.
E-mail: info@contact.adventist.org
Web Site: www.adventist.org/en/utility/contact/
Institution Type/Description: Religious Museum.
Hours & Admission Prices: Church Tours: Mon.-Thurs. 9am; groups by appointment. No charge. Ellen White Estate: Mon.-Thurs.

Snow Hill

FURNACE TOWN LIVING HERITAGE VILLAGE, 3816 Old Furnace Rd., Snow Hill, MD 21863-3420. Mailing Address: P.O. Box 207, Snow Hill, MD 21863-0207. Tel.: 410-632-2032. Fax: 410-632-1735. Facebook & Twitter.
E-mail: info@furnacetown.org
Web Site: www.furnacetown.org
Key Personnel: Bd. Pres. (V), Ron Geesey; Treas., Eric Tobiassen; Exec. Dir., Patrick Rofe.
Institution Type/Description: Living Heritage Museum.
Hours & Admission Prices: April-Oct. daily 10-5. Adults $7, senior citizens & military $6, children 4-16 $4; discount to AAA members; members no charge. Closed Memorial Day, Independence Day, Labor Day. &
Attendance: 10,077 (actual)

JULIA A. PURNELL MUSEUM, 208 W. Market St., Snow Hill, MD 21863-1059. Tel.: 410-632-0515. Fax: 410-632-0515. Facebook: Julia Purnell Museum.
E-mail: mail@purnellmuseum.com
Web Site: www.purnellmuseum.com
Key Personnel: Dir., Claire Otterbein; Bd. Pres. (V), Meme Suznavick.
Institution Type/Description: History Museum: housed in 1891 former Catholic Church.
Hours & Admission Prices: April-Oct. Tues.-Sat. 10-4, Sun. 1-4; Nov.-March by appointment. Adults $2, children $.50; discounts to AAM & ICOM members; members no charge. Package tours available for surrounding museums. Closed major holidays. &
Attendance: 4,000 (estimated)

Solomons

ANNMARIE SCULPTURE GARDEN & ART CENTER, 13470 Dowell Rd., Solomons, MD 20629. Mailing Address: P.O. Box 99, Dowell, MD 20629-0099. Tel.: 410-326-4640. Fax: 410-326-4887. Facebook: Annmarie Arts.

E-mail: info@annmariegarden.org
Web Site: www.annmariegarden.org
Key Personnel: Dir., Stacey Hann-Ruff; Deputy Dir./Cur. Public Programs, Jamie Jeffrey.
Institution Type/Description: Sculpture Park & Arts Center.
Hours & Admission Prices: Park: daily 9-5. artLAB: daily 10-4:30. Murray Arts Building: daily 10-5. Adults $5, military & senior citizens 65 & older $4, children 6-17 $3; children under 5 & AMG members no charge. Check website for closures. &
Attendance: 50,000 (estimated)

CALVERT MARINE MUSEUM, 14200 Solomons Island Rd., Solomons, MD 20688. Mailing Address: P.O. Box 97, Solomons, MD 20688-0097. Tel.: 410-326-2042. Fax: 410-326-6691. Facebook & Twitter.
E-mail: information@calvertmarinemuseum.com
Web Site: www.calvertmarinemuseum.com
Key Personnel: Dir., Sherrod Sturrock; Accountant, Dawn Wood; Business Mgr., Roxie Welch.
Institution Type/Description: Marine Museum.
Hours & Admission Prices: Daily 10-5. Adults $9, seniors & military $7, children (5-12) $4; discount to AAM & CAMM members; members & children (under 5) no charge. Closed New Year's Day; Thanksgiving; Christmas. &
Attendance: 84,800 (actual)

CHESAPEAKE BIOLOGICAL LABORATORY VISITORS CENTER, 200 Farren Ave., Solomons, MD 20688. Mailing Address: P.O. Box 775, Cambridge, MD 21613. Tel.: 410-326-7443. Twitter.
E-mail: shutchinson@umces.edu
Web Site: www.umces.edu/cbl
Key Personnel: Outreach Coordinator, Sarah Brzezinski.
Institution Type/Description: Environmental Heritage Museum.
Hours & Admission Prices: May-Memorial Day: Fri.-Sun. 9:30-4:30; Memorial Day-Sept.: Wed.-Sun. 9:30-4:30; Sept.-Nov.: Fri.-Sun. 9:30-4:30. No charge; donations accepted.

Sparks

THE LACROSSE MUSEUM & NATIONAL HALL OF FAME/ US LACROSSE, 2 Loveton Cir., Sparks, MD 21152-9202. Tel.: 410-235-6882, ext. 100. Fax: 410-366-6735.
E-mail: bfairson@uslacrosse.org
Web Site: www.uslacrosse.org
Institution Type/Description: National Lacrosse Hall of Fame.
Hours & Admission Prices: Call or see website for information. &

Stevenson

STEVENSON UNIVERSITY ART GALLERY, 1525 Greenspring Valley Rd., Stevenson, MD 21153. Tel.: 443-352-4491. Facebook: SU Art Effects.
E-mail: exhibitions@stevenson.edu
Web Site: stevenson.edu/arts
Institution Type/Description: Art Gallery.
Hours & Admission Prices: Mon.-Wed. & Fri. 11-5, Thurs. 11-8, Sat. 1-4. No charge; donations accepted. &

Stevensville

HISTORIC CHRIST CHURCH, 121 E. Main St., Stevensville, MD 21617. Mailing Address: 312 Safety Dr., Centreville, MD 21617-2172. Tel.: 410-758-2502.
Institution Type/Description: Historic Building: built in 1880.
Hours & Admission Prices: By appointment. No charge; donations accepted.
Attendance: 800 (actual)

KENT ISLAND HERITAGE SOCIETY - CRAY HOUSE, Cockey's Ln., Stevensville, MD 21666. Mailing Address: P.O. Box 321, Stevensville, MD 21666. Tel.: 410-758-2502.
E-mail: sally.lewis@live.com
Institution Type/Description: Historic House Museum: housed in the former home of Nora Cray; built c.1809. Listed on the National Register of Historic Places.
Hours & Admission Prices: April-Nov. 1st Sat. each month 12-4 by appointment. No charge; donations accepted.
Attendance: 675 (actual)

KENT ISLAND HERITAGE SOCIETY - HISTORIC STEVENSVILLE BANK, 409 Love Point Rd., Stevensville, MD 21666. Mailing Address: P.O. Box 321, Stevensville, MD 21666. Tel.: 410-758-2502.
E-mail: rclowesr@atlanticbb.net
Formerly: Old Stevensville Post Office - Kent Island Heritage Society
Institution Type/Description: HistoricBuilding: built 1903.
Hours & Admission Prices: May-Nov. 1st Sat. each month 12-4 by appointment. No charge; donations accepted.
Attendance: 600 (actual)

KENT ISLAND HERITAGE SOCIETY, INC. - STEVENSVILLE TRAIN DEPOT, Cockey's Ln., Stevensville, MD 21666. Mailing Address: P.O. Box 321, Stevensville, MD 21666. Tel.: 410-758-2502.
Institution Type/Description: Historic Building: built in 1902.
Hours & Admission Prices: April-Nov. 1st Sat. each month 12-4 by appointment. No charge; donations accepted. ♿
Attendance: 650 (actual)

Sudlersville

SUDLERSVILLE TRAIN STATION MUSEUM, 101 Linden St., Sudlersville, MD 21668. Mailing Address: P.O. Box 2, Sudlersville, MD 21668. Tel.: 410-438-3501.
E-mail: sudlersvillemuseum@gmail.com
Web Site: www.sudlersvillemuseum.org
Key Personnel: Chmn. (V), Mary Godfrey.
Institution Type/Description: Historic Building: built in 1885.
Hours & Admission Prices: 1st Sat. each month 10-2. No charge; donations accepted.
Attendance: 500 (estimated)

Suitland

AIRMEN MEMORIAL MUSEUM, 5211 Auth Rd., Suitland, MD 20746-4339. Tel.: 301-899-3500.
E-mail: kreed@hqafsa.org
Web Site: www.afsahq.org
Key Personnel: Dir. & Sec., Keith A. Reed.
Institution Type/Description: Military Museum.
Hours & Admission Prices: Mon.-Fri. 8-5. No charge; donations accepted. Closed federal holidays. ♿

Sykesville

GATE HOUSE MUSEUM OF HISTORY, 7283 Cooper Dr., Sykesville, MD 21784. Tel.: 410-549-5150. Facebook.
E-mail: gatehouse@sykesville.net
Web Site: www.townofsykesville.org
Key Personnel: Cur., Jack White.
Institution Type/Description: History Museum.
Hours & Admission Prices: Fri. & Sun. 1-5. No charge; donations accepted.
Attendance: 2,346 (estimated)

Thurmont

CATOCTIN IRON FURNACE & MANOR HOUSE RUINS, 14039 Catoctin Hollow Rd., Thurmont, MD 21788. Tel.: 301-271-7574.
E-mail: ecomer@catoctinfurnace.org
Institution Type/Description: History Museum.
Hours & Admission Prices: April-Oct. daily 8am to sunset; Nov.-March daily 10am to sunset.

CATOCTIN WILDLIFE PRESERVE & ZOO, 13019 Catoctin Furnace Rd., Thurmont, MD 21788-2134. Tel.: 301-271-4922 & 3180. Fax: 301-271-2673. Facebook & Twitter.
E-mail: info@catoctinwildlifepreserve.com
Web Site: www.cwpzoo.com
Key Personnel: Dir., Chuck Eicholz; Preserve Cur., Laurie Hahn.
Institution Type/Description: Zoological Park.
Hours & Admission Prices: March 10: 10-4, April 1: 10-5, May 26-Sept. 3: 9-6, Sept. 4-Sept 28: 9-5, Sept. 29-Nov. 4: 10-5, Nov weekends (weather permitting): 10-4. Adults (13 and over) $19.75, children (3-12) $14.75, senior (60 and over) $17.75. ♿
Attendance: 80,000 (estimated)

Towson

ASIAN ARTS & CULTURE CENTER, TOWSON UNIVERSITY, Asian Arts & Culture Center, Towson University, 8000 York Rd., Towson, MD 21252. Tel.: 410-704-2000. Fax: 410-704-4032. Facebook, Instagram, Twitter.
E-mail: asianarts@towson.edu
Web Site: www.towson.edu/asianarts
Key Personnel: Dir., Joanna Pecore; Pres. (V), Yoshinobu Shiota.
Institution Type/Description: University Arts Center.
Hours & Admission Prices: Academic Year: Mon.-Sat. 11-4; call to confirm hours. Exhibits: no charge. Special Events: adults $10-$20; discounts to senior citizens, students, AAM members & museum members. Closed Easter; Christmas; national holidays. ♿
Attendance: 10,000 (estimated)

HAMPTON NATIONAL HISTORIC SITE, 535 Hampton Lane, Towson, MD 21286-1397. Tel.: 410-823-1309. Fax: 410-823-8394.
Web Site: www.nps.gov/hamp
Key Personnel: Cur. & Principal Author, Gregory R. Weidman; Registrar, Debbie Patterson; Supervisory Park Ranger, Laurie Coughlan.
Institution Type/Description: Historic House & Site: c.1783-1790 late Georgian Mansion including slave quarters located on agricultural-industrial complex.
Hours & Admission Prices: Mansion: Thur.-Sun. 9-4. Grounds: daily 8:30-4. Tours: Thur.-Sun. 10-3; groups of 10 or more by appointment. No charge; donations accepted. Closed New Year's Day; Martin Luther King Jr. Day; President's Day; Thanksgiving; Christmas. ♿
Attendance: 30,000 (estimated)

Union Bridge

WESTERN MARYLAND RAILWAY HISTORICAL SOCIETY, 41 N. Main St., Union Bridge, MD 21791-9100. Mailing Address: P.O. Box 395, Union Bridge, MD 21791-0395. Tel.: 410-775-0150.
E-mail: wmrhs1118@comcast.net
Web Site: www.westernmarylandrhs.com
Key Personnel: Chm. (V), Stan Johnson; Pres. (V), Dennis Wertz; Museum Shop Mgr., Dick Liebno.
Institution Type/Description: Historical Society Museum.
Hours & Admission Prices: Sun. 1-4, Wed. 9-12 & 1-3; other times by appointment. No charge; donations accepted. Closed New Year's Day; Easter; Christmas.
Attendance: 1,000 (estimated)

Upper Marlboro

BILLINGSLEY HOUSE MUSEUM, 6900 Green Landing Rd., Upper Marlboro, MD 20772-7618. Tel.: 301-627-0730. Fax: 301-627-7085.
E-mail: billingsley@pgparks.com
Web Site: www.pgparks.com/3024/Billingsley-House
Institution Type/Description: Historic House Museum: built c.1740.
Hours & Admission Prices: Tours: Tues. & Fri. 9-3; call for additional hours.

DARNALL'S CHANCE HOUSE MUSEUM, M-NCPPC, 14800 Gov. Oden Bowie Dr., Upper Marlboro, MD 20772-3073. Tel.: 301-952-8010.
E-mail: darnallschance@pgparks.com
Key Personnel: Museum Mgr., Mary Haley Amen.
Institution Type/Description: Historic House: 1742, 18th century home of James and Lettice Lee Wardrop.
Hours & Admission Prices: Tues.-Thurs. tours by appointment, Fri. & Sun. 12-4. Adults $5, seniors & groups $4, Children (5-18) $2, children (4 and under) no charge. Closed major holidays. ♿
Attendance: 7,500 (actual)

MERKLE WILDLIFE SANCTUARY & VISITOR CENTER, 11704 Fenno Rd., Upper Marlboro, MD 20772-8179. Tel.: 301-888-1377.
E-mail: customerservice.dnr@maryland.gov
Web Site: www.dnr.state.md.us/publiclands/merkletrails.html
Institution Type/Description: Wildlife Sanctuary.
Hours & Admission Prices: Grounds: daily 7-sunset. Visitor Center: Sat.-Sun. 10-4.

MOUNT CALVERT HISTORICAL AND ARCHAEOLOGICAL PARK, 16801 Mt. Calvert Rd., Upper Marlboro, MD 20772. Tel.: 301-627-1286; 301-699-2544 (TTY).
E-mail: help4smartlink@pgparks.com

Institution Type/Description: History Museum.
Hours & Admission Prices: April-Oct. Sat. 8:30-5, Sun. 12-4; other times by appointment.

THE PATUXENT RURAL LIFE MUSEUMS, Patuxent River Park, 16000 Croom Airport Rd., Upper Marlboro, MD 20772-8395. Mailing Address: 6706 Green Landing Rd., Upper Marlboro, MD 20772-7618. Tel.: 301-627-6074. Fax: 301-627-7085. TDD: 301-699-2544.
E-mail: mary.haley-amen@pgparks.com
Web Site: www.pgparks.com/places/eleganthistoric/patuxent_intro.html
Formerly: W. Henry Duvall Tool Museum
Key Personnel: Dir., Mary Haley-Amen.
Institution Type/Description: Tool Museum.
Hours & Admission Prices: April-Oct. Sat.-Sun. 1-4; other times by appointment. Guided Tours: by appointment. Sat.-Sun. no charge. &
Attendance: 2,158 (actual)

Waldorf

DR. SAMUEL A. MUDD HOUSE, 3725 Dr. Samuel Mudd Rd., Waldorf, MD 20601. Tel.: 301-274-9358 & 645-6870.
E-mail: muddnews@gmail.com
Key Personnel: Head Docent, Donna Peterson; Membership Chm., Henry Mudd.
Institution Type/Description: Historic House Museum: housed on site of Booth escape route.
Hours & Admission Prices: Late March to mid Nov., Wed. & Sat. 11-4, Sun. 12-4. Adults $7, children 6-12 $2; children 5 and under & members no charge. Closed Easter. &
Attendance: 5,000 (estimated)

PISCATAWAY INDIAN MUSEUM, 16816 Country Ln., Waldorf, MD 20601. Tel.: 240-432-7878.
E-mail: info@piscatawayindians.org
Web Site: www.piscatawayindians.org
Institution Type/Description: Native American History Museum.
Hours & Admission Prices: Sun. 1-4; other times by appointment.

Walkersville

FOUNTAIN ROCK NATURE CENTER, 8511 Nature Center Place, Walkersville, MD 21793-8325. Tel.: 301-600-4460. Facebook, Instagram & Twitter.
E-mail: kketzenberger@frederickcountymd.gov
Web Site: www.recreater.com
Key Personnel: Park Naturalist, Kelly Ketzenberger.
Institution Type/Description: Nature Center.
Hours & Admission Prices: 8am to sunset; groups by appointment. No charge. Nature Programs: adults $5, children $4. Closed holidays. &
Attendance: 10,000 (estimated)

WALKERSVILLE SOUTHERN RAILROAD MUSEUM, 34 W. Pennsylvania Ave., Walkersville, MD 21793-8505. Mailing Address: P.O. Box 651, Walkersville, MD 21793-0651. Tel.: 301-898-0899, 877-363-WSRR (toll free).
E-mail: musdir@wsrr.org
Web Site: www.wsrr.org/museum.htm
Key Personnel: Dir., John Meise.
Institution Type/Description: Railroad History Museum.
Hours & Admission Prices: Museum: call for hours. Train: May-June & Sept. Sat.-Sun. 11am & 2pm; Oct. Sat.-Sun. 11am, 1pm & 3pm; July-Aug. Sat. 11am & 2pm; additional special event hours. Adults $9, seniors over 55 $8, children $5; members and children under 3 no charge. &
Attendance: 12,000 (actual)

Warwick

OLD BOHEMIA HISTORICAL SOCIETY, Bohemia Church Rd., Warwick, MD 21912. Mailing Address: P.O. Box 61, Warwick, MD 21912. Tel.: 302-328-4803.
Key Personnel: Pres. & Museum Shop Mgr., Margaret Matyniak; Pastor, Rev. Steven B. Giuliano.
Institution Type/Description: Historical Society Museum: 1704 Jesuit mission site, 1797 church, rectory with museum of religious artifacts (liturgical vessels, vestments, prayer books, devotional articles), barn with farm conveyances & tools, historic cemetery.
Hours & Admission Prices: Call for hours. No charge; donations accepted.
Attendance: 700 (estimated)

Westernport

WESTERNPORT HERITAGE SOCIETY, 136 Main St., Westernport, MD 21562-1401. Tel.: 301-359-0388.
Web Site: pages.prodigy.net/jimertz
Key Personnel: Pres. (V), Allan T. LaRue; Museum Shop Mgr., Mary Ann Imhoff.
Institution Type/Description: Heritage Society Museum.
Hours & Admission Prices: 2nd & 4th Sat.-Sun. 1-4. No charge; donations accepted. &
Attendance: 315 (estimated)

Westminster

CARROLL COUNTY ARTS COUNCIL TEVIS AND COMMUNITY GALLERIES, 91 W. Main St., Westminster, MD 21157. Tel.: 410-848-7272. Fax: 410-848-8962.
E-mail: info@carrollcountyartscouncil.org
Web Site: www.carrollcountyartscouncil.org
Key Personnel: Exec. Dir., Judy Morley, PhD; Asst. Dir. Programs, Andrew Woodard; Asst. Dir. Operations, Will Abbott; Visual Arts Coord., Susan Williamson; Theatre Coord., Lindsay Sier; Financial Coord., Claudia Rogers; Communications Coord., JoAnna Crone; Box Office & Special Events Asst., Donna Biemiller.
Institution Type/Description: Art Gallery.
Hours & Admission Prices: Mon.-Wed. & Fri.-Sat. 10-4, Thurs. 10-7. No charge.

CARROLL COUNTY FARM MUSEUM, 500 S. Center St., Ste. 1, Westminster, MD 21157-5664. Tel.: 410-386-3880 & 800-654-4645. Fax: 410-876-8544. Facebook.
E-mail: ccfarm@ccg.carr.org
Web Site: www.carrollcountyfarmmuseum.org
Key Personnel: Park Supt., Joanne Weant.
Institution Type/Description: Agricultural & Historical Museum: housed in c.1852 historic building on 142 acres.
Hours & Admission Prices: Winter hours: Mon.-Fri. 9-4, Sat. & Sun. 12-4; Farm Museum Hours: Mon.-Sat. 9-4, Sun. 12-4. Winter admission: no charge; regular admission: families $10, adults $5, seniors (60 and over) $4. &
Attendance: 100,000 (actual)

HISTORICAL SOCIETY OF CARROLL COUNTY, 210 E. Main St., Westminster, MD 21157-5225. Tel.: 410-848-6494. Fax: 410-848-3596.
E-mail: info@hsccmd.org
Web Site: www.hsccmd.org
Key Personnel: Exec. Dir., Gainor B. Davis, Ph.D.; Chm. (V), Frank J. Batavick; Treas., Art Palaia; Cur., Catherine E. Baty; Special Even/ Media Asst., Gianna Baccala; Administrative Asst., Marty Mathis; Museum Shop Mgr., Debbie Leister; Bookkeeper, Krista Seifert.
Institution Type/Description: Historical Society Museum.
Hours & Admission Prices: Office: Mon.-Fri. 8:30-5. Research Library: Wed.-Fri. 12-4, 2nd & 4th Sat. 9-12. Gift Shop: Wed.-Sat. 10-4. House Tours: by appointment. Shipley Garden: open all day. No charge; donations accepted. Sherman-Fisher Shellman House Museum Guided Tours: adults $5; members no charge. Research Library: adults $5. Student Tours: $5 per person. Closed New Year's Day; Martin Luther King Jr. Day; Presidents' Day; Good Friday; Memorial Day; Independence Day; Labor Day; Thanksgiving Day & day after; Christmas week. &
Attendance: 3,000 (estimated)

UNION MILLS HOMESTEAD & GRIST MILL, 3311 Littlestown Pike, Westminster, MD 21158-2137. Tel.: 410-848-2288.
E-mail: ejss61@aol.com
Web Site: www.unionmills.org
Key Personnel: Exec. Dir. & Museum Shop Mgr., Jane S. Sewell; Pres. Bd., Dr. Dawn Thomas.
Institution Type/Description: Historic House Museum: 1797 Shriver Homestead and Mill.
Hours & Admission Prices: May & Sept. Sat.-Sun. 12-4; June-Sept. 1 Tues.-Fri. 10-4, Sat.-Sun. 12-4; bus tours by appointment. Adults $5, children 6-12 $3; discounts to groups & senior citizens; members no charge. Combination ticket for house & mill: adults $5, children 6-12 $3. Closed Independence Day.
Attendance: 10,000 (estimated)

Wheaton

BROOKSIDE GARDENS, 1800 Glenallan Ave., Wheaton, MD 20902-1369. Tel.: 301-962-1400. Facebook.
E-mail: Info@MontgomeryParks.org
Web Site: www.brooksidegardens.org
Key Personnel: Visitor Svcs. Supvr., Ellen Hartranft; Mktg. & Public Affairs Mgr., Susan Stafford.

Institution Type/Description: Botanical Garden.
Hours & Admission Prices: Visitor Center: daily 9-5. Conservatories: daily 10-5. Gardens: sunrise-sunset. No charge; donations accepted. Closed Christmas. ♿
Attendance: 320,000 (estimated)

Williamsport

MCMAHON'S MILL CIVIL WAR MILITARY & AMERICAN HERITAGE MUSEUM, 7900 Avis Mill Rd., Williamsport, MD 21795-2006. Tel.: 301-223-8778 & 9314.
Key Personnel: Dir., William B. McMahon.
Institution Type/Description: History Museum.
Hours & Admission Prices: Temporarily closed.

Wye Mills

WYE GRIST MILL, 900 Wye Mills Rd., Wye Mills, MD 21679. Mailing Address: P.O. Box 277, Wye Mills, MD 21679-0277. Tel.: 410-827-3850.
E-mail: oldwyemill@atlanticbbn.net
Web Site: oldwyemill.org
Institution Type/Description: History Museum.
Hours & Admission Prices: mid-April to mid-Nov. Mon.-Sat. 10-4, Sun. 1-4. Tours: by appointment. Suggested Donation: $2.

MASSACHUSETTS

(450 listings)

Abington

DYER MEMORIAL LIBRARY, 28 Centre Ave., Abington, MA 02351-2228. Mailing Address: P.O. Box 2245, Abington, MA 02351-0745. Tel.: 781-878-8480.
E-mail: info@dyerlibrary.org
Web Site: www.dyerlibrary.org
Key Personnel: Dir., Joice Himawan; Librarian, Merlyn Liberty.
Institution Type/Description: General Museum.
Hours & Admission Prices: Tues.-Fri. 1-5, 2nd & 4th Sat. 12-4; other times by appointment. No charge; donations accepted. Closed holidays.
Attendance: 900 (estimated)

Acton

THE DISCOVERY MUSEUMS, 177 Main St., Acton, MA 01720-3647. Tel.: 978-264-4200. Fax: 978-264-0210.
E-mail: fun@discoverymuseum.org
Web Site: www.discoverymuseums.org
Key Personnel: C.E.O., Neil H. Gordon; Mktg. Specialist & Museum Store Mgr., Jill Jacques.
Institution Type/Description: Children's Museums: consisting of The Children's Discovery Museum, housed in a 10-room Victorian house, and The Science Discovery Museum.
Hours & Admission Prices: Children's Discovery Museum: Tues.-Sun. 9-4:30. Science Discovery Museum: Tues.-Fri. 1-4:30, Sat.-Sun. 10-4:30. Adults & children $11.50, seniors 60 & over $10.50; members, teachers, & children under one no charge. Closed Independence Day; Labor Day; Thanksgiving Eve & Day; Christmas Eve & Day. ♿
Attendance: 140,000 (estimated)

Adams

SUSAN B. ANTHONY BIRTHPLACE MUSEUM, 67 E. Rd., Adams, MA 01220. Mailing Address: P.O. Box 244, Adams, MA 01220. Tel.: 413-743-7121. Fax: 413-895-0472.
E-mail: cpeltier@susanbanthonybirthplace.org
Web Site: www.susanbanthonybirthplace.org
Key Personnel: Pres. (V), Carol Crossed; Exec. Dir., Cassandra Peltier; Museum Shop Mgr., Kristen Demeo.
Institution Type/Description: History Museum: housed in the birthplace of suffragist Susan B. Anthony, born in 1820; house built in 1817. Listed on the National Register of Historic Places.
Hours & Admission Prices: Memorial Day to Columbus Day Thurs.-Mon. 10-4; Columbus Day to Memorial Day Mon., Fri. & Sat. 10-4, Sun. 11:30-4. Adults $6, seniors $4, students $3; discounts to AAM members; NARM, NEMA, ROAM, & museum members and children 5 & under no charge. Blue Star Museum. ♿
Attendance: 2,000 (estimated)

Agawam

AGAWAM HISTORICAL & FIRE HOUSE MUSEUM, 35 Elm St., Agawam, MA 01001-2407. Mailing Address: P.O. Box 552, Agawam, MA 01001-0552. Tel.: 413-786-4631.
Institution Type/Description: Fire-Fighting Museum.
Hours & Admission Prices: May-Dec. 2nd Sun. each month 1-4.

Amesbury

THE BARTLETT MUSEUM, 270 Main St., Amesbury, MA 01913. Mailing Address: P.O. Box 692, Amesbury, MA 01913-0016. Tel.: 978-388-4528.
E-mail: museum@bartlettmuseum.org
Web Site: bartlettmuseum.org
Key Personnel: Dir., Hazele Kray.
Institution Type/Description: History Museum: housed in 1870 Old Victorian School House.
Hours & Admission Prices: Memorial Day weekend to Labor Day Fri.-Sun. 1-4, other times by appointment. Adults $3, children & senior citizens $1; AAM & museum members no charge.
Attendance: 1,000 (estimated)

JOHN GREENLEAF WHITTIER HOME, 86 Friend St., Amesbury, MA 01913-2746. Mailing Address: P.O. Box 632, 86 Friend St., Amesbury, MA 01913-0014. Tel.: 978-388-1337. Fax: 978-388-1337.
E-mail: whittierhome@verizon.net
Web Site: www.whittierhome.org
Key Personnel: Pres. (V), Cynthia C. Costello; Museum Shop Mgr., Dianne Cole.
Institution Type/Description: Historic House: 1836 home of poet & abolitionist John Greenleaf Whittier.
Hours & Admission Prices: May-Oct. Sat. 10-4, last tour 3:30; other times by appointment. Adults $6, seniors & students $5, children 7-17 $3; discounts to AAM members & groups; members & children under 7 no charge. Closed Thanksgiving; Christmas.
Attendance: 600 (actual)

LOWELL'S BOAT SHOP, 459 Main St., Amesbury, MA 01913-4207. Tel.: 978-834-0050.
E-mail: info@lowellsboatshop.com
Web Site: www.lowellsboatshop.com
Key Personnel: Exec. Dir., Graham McKay; Chm. Bd., Bob Barton; Chm., Steven Batchelder; Pres., Sally McKay.
Institution Type/Description: Historic Buildings: housed in working 19th century boat building shop.
Hours & Admission Prices: May-Oct. Tues.-Sat. 11-4; Nov.-April Tues.-Fri. 11-4. Office: Mon.-Fri. 10-5. Guided tours: $8, seniors & students $6; self-guided tours: $5, seniors & students $4; members no charge. ♿
Attendance: 3,500 (estimated)

Amherst

AMHERST COLLEGE MUSEUM OF NATURAL HISTORY, Amherst College, 11 Barrett Hill Rd., Amherst, MA 01002-5000. Tel.: 413-542-2165. Fax: 413-542-2713.
E-mail: kwellspring@amherst.edu
Web Site: www.amherst.edu/museums/naturalhistory
Formerly: Pratt Museum of Natural History
Key Personnel: Dir., Peter Crowley; Mgr. Collections, Kate Wellspring.
Institution Type/Description: Natural History Museum.
Hours & Admission Prices: Tues.-Wed. & Fri.-Sun. 11-4, Thurs. 11-4 & 6-10. No charge. Closed holidays. ♿
Attendance: 25,000 (actual)

AMHERST HISTORY MUSEUM AT THE SIMEON STRONG HOUSE - AMHERST HISTORICAL SOCIETY, 67 Amity St., Amherst, MA 01002-2214. Tel.: 413-256-0678.
E-mail: info@amhersthistory.org
Web Site: www.amhersthistory.org
Key Personnel: Pres. (V), Philip A. Shaver.
Institution Type/Description: History Museum/History Site: housed in c.1750 Strong house. Listed on the National Register of Historic Places.
Hours & Admission Prices: May-Nov. Fri.-Sun. 12-4. Suggested Donation: adults $5, seniors, students & children $3; children 6 & under and Amherst Historical Society members no charge.
Attendance: 2,400 (estimated)

EMILY DICKINSON MUSEUM: THE HOMESTEAD AND THE EVERGREENS, 280 Main St., Amherst, MA 01002-2349. Tel.: 413-542-8161.
E-mail: info@emilydickinsonmuseum.org
Web Site: www.emilydickinsonmuseum.org
Formerly: Dickinson Homestead
Key Personnel: Exec. Dir., Jane H. Wald; Chm. (V), John Beeson; Dir. Programming, Brooke Steinhauser.
Institution Type/Description: Historic Houses: The Dickinson Homestead c.1813, birthplace & home of poet Emily Dickinson; The Evergreens 1856, home of the poet's brother Austin & sister-in-law Susan.
Hours & Admission Prices: March-May & Sept.-Dec. Wed.-Sun. 11-4; June-Aug. Wed.-Sun. 10-5. Guided Tours: adults $10-$12; members no charge. Closed major holidays. ♿
Attendance: 14,000 (actual)

THE ERIC CARLE MUSEUM OF PICTURE BOOK ART, 125 W. Bay Rd., Amherst, MA 01002-3357. Tel.: 413-559-6300. Fax: 413-256-8390. Facebook.
E-mail: info@carlemuseum.org
Web Site: www.carlemuseum.org
Key Personnel: Exec. Dir., Alexandra Kennedy; Chm. (V), Chris Milne; Chief Cur., Ellen Keiter; Dir. Devel., Rebecca Miller Goggins; Cur. Education, Courtney Waring; Dir. Finance & Administration, Andrea Powers; Registrar, Erica Jacobs; Mgr. Facilities, John Stark; Mgr. Mktg., Sandy Soderberg; Museum Shop Mgr., Eliza Brown.
Institution Type/Description: Art Museum.
Hours & Admission Prices: July-Aug. & MA School Vacation Weeks Mon.-Fri. 10-4, Sat. 10-5, Sun. 12-5; Sept.-June Tues.-Fri. 10-4, Sat. 10-5, Sun. 12-5. Adults $9, senior citizens & children $6; discount to groups & AAM members; members no charge. Closed New Year's Day; Independence Day; Thanksgiving; Christmas Eve & Day. ♿
Attendance: 49,820 (actual)

HERTER ART GALLERY, 125a Herter Hall, University of Massachusetts Amherst, Amherst, MA 01003. Tel.: 413-545-0976.
Institution Type/Description: Art Gallery.
Hours & Admission Prices: Mon.-Fri. 11-4, Sun. 1-4. No charge.

MEAD ART MUSEUM, Amherst College, 41 Quadrangle Dr., Amherst, MA 01002. Mailing Address: Amherst College, P.O. Box 5000, Amherst, MA 01002-5000. Tel.: 413-542-2335. Fax: 413-542-2117. Facebook.
E-mail: mead@amherst.edu
Web Site: www.amherst.edu/mead
Key Personnel: Dir. & Chief Cur., David E. Little; Public Programs & Mktg. Coord., Danielle Amodeo; Mgr. Collections, Stephen Fisher; Preparator, Timothy Gilfillan; Security Supvr., Nicholas Taupier.
Institution Type/Description: Art Museum.
Hours & Admission Prices: Academic Season: Tues.-Thurs. & Sun. 9-midnight, Fri. 9-8, Sat. 9-5. Academic Recess: Tues.-Thurs. & Sat.-Sun. 9-5, Fri. 9-8. No charge; donations accepted. ♿
Attendance: 36,000 (estimated)

NATURAL HISTORY COLLECTIONS, Univ. of Massachusetts, Rm. 146 Morrill 2, 622 N. Pleasant St., Amherst, MA 01002-1526. Mailing Address: 611 N. Pleasant St., Amherst, MA 01003. Tel.: 413-577-2303. Fax: 413-545-3243.
E-mail: bdumont@bio.umass.edu
Web Site: bcrc.bio.umass.edu/ummnh
Formerly: Museum of Zoology
Key Personnel: Dir., Benjamin Normark; Cur. Mammals, Elizabeth Dumont.
Institution Type/Description: Zoology Museum.
Hours & Admission Prices: Call for appointment. No charge. Closed state & national holidays. Exhibits not open to public. ♿

UNIVERSITY GALLERY, UNIVERSITY OF MASSACHUSETTS AT AMHERST, University Gallery, Fine Arts Center, University of Massachusetts, 151 Presidents Drive, Office 2, Amherst, MA 01003-9331. Tel.: 413-545-3670. Fax: 413-545-2018.
E-mail: ugallery@acad.umass.edu
Web Site: www.umass.edu/fac/universitygallery
Key Personnel: Dir., Loretta Yarlow; Communications, Thonsey Keopanya; Education Cur., Eva Fierst; Gallery Mgr., Craig Allaben; Collections Registrar & Preparator, Justin Griswold.
Institution Type/Description: University Art Gallery.
Hours & Admission Prices: Academic Year Tues.-Fri. 11-4:30, Sat.-Sun. 2-5. No charge. ♿
Attendance: 12,600 (estimated)

YIDDISH BOOK CENTER, Harry & Jeanette Weinberg Bldg., 1021 West St., Amherst, MA 01002-3375. Tel.: 413-256-4900. Facebook; Twitter..
E-mail: yiddish@yiddishbookcenter.org
Web Site: www.yiddishbookcenter.org
Key Personnel: Founder & Pres., Aaron Lansky; Exec. Dir., Susan Bronson.
Institution Type/Description: Jewish Cultural Organization.
Hours & Admission Prices: See website for hours and admissions. Closed Jewish & legal holidays. ♿
Attendance: 11,000 (actual)

Andover

ADDISON GALLERY OF AMERICAN ART, Phillips Academy, Andover, MA 01810-4161. Mailing Address: 180 Main St., Andover, MA 01810-4166. Tel.: 978-749-4015. Fax: 978-749-4025.
E-mail: addison@andover.edu
Web Site: www.addisongallery.org
Key Personnel: Dir., Judith Dolkart; Assoc. Dir. & Cur., Susan Faxon; Cur., Allison Kemmerer; Dir. Education, Rebecca Hayes; Museum Shop Mgr., Anna Gesing.
Institution Type/Description: Art Museum.
Hours & Admission Prices: Tues.-Sat. 10-5, Sun. 1-5. No charge; donations accepted. ♿.
Attendance: 30,000 (estimated)

ANDOVER HISTORICAL SOCIETY, 97 Main St., Andover, MA 01810-3803. Tel.: 978-475-2236.
E-mail: info@andoverhistorical.org
Web Site: www.andoverhistorical.org
Key Personnel: Exec. Dir., Elaine Clements; Pres. (V), Susan McKelliget; Dir. Devel. & Collections, Marilyn Helmers; Dir. Programs & Social Media, Lauren Kosky-Stamm.
Institution Type/Description: Local History Museum: c.1818-19 house & barn.
Hours & Admission Prices: Museum, Library & Archives: Tues.-Sat. 10-4. Office: Tues.-Fri. 10-4. No charge; donations accepted. Closed national holidays.
Attendance: 10,000 (estimated)

ROBERT S. PEABODY MUSEUM OF ARCHAEOLOGY, 180 Main St., Andover, MA 01810. Tel.: 978-749-4490. Fax: 978-749-4495. Facebook; Twitter.
E-mail: rspeabody@andover.edu
Web Site: www.andover.edu/rspeabody/
Key Personnel: Dir., Ryan J. Wheeler; Educator, Donald Slater; Cur. Education & Outreach, Lindsay Randall; Cur. Collection, Marla Taylor.
Institution Type/Description: Archaeology Museum.
Hours & Admission Prices: by appointment only. No charge; donations accepted. Closed New Year's Day; Memorial Day; Independence Day; Labor Day; Thanksgiving; Christmas. ♿
Attendance: 6,800 (estimated)

Arlington

ARLINGTON CENTER FOR THE ARTS, Gibbs Center, 41 Foster St., Arlington, MA 02474-6813. Tel.: 781-648-6220.
E-mail: info@acarts.org
Institution Type/Description: Art Gallery.
Hours & Admission Prices: Mon.-Fri. 9-5; other times by appointment.

THE ARLINGTON HISTORICAL SOCIETY, 7 Jason St., Arlington, MA 02476-6410. Tel.: 781-648-4300.
E-mail: contact@arlingtonhistorical.org
Web Site: www.arlingtonhistorical.org
Key Personnel: Pres., Pamela Meister; Museum Admin., Doreen Stevens.
Institution Type/Description: Historic Building & Site.
Hours & Admission Prices: April-Oct. Sat.-Sun. 1-4; other times by appointment. Adults $5, children under 12 $2; discounts to AAM, members of Lexington Historical Society & Massachusetts Teacher's Association; society members no charge.
Attendance: 700 (estimated)

CYRUS E. DALLIN ART MUSEUM, INC., 1 Whittemore Park, Arlington, MA 02474-1105. Tel.: 781-641-0747.
E-mail: radioroly@aol.com
Web Site: www.dallin.org
Key Personnel: Co Chm., Roland Chaput; Co Chm., Heather Leavell.
Institution Type/Description: Art Museum.
Hours & Admission Prices: Wed.-Sun. 12-4. No charge; donations accepted. ♿

THE OLD SCHWAMB MILL, 17 Mill Lane, Arlington, MA 02476-4189. Tel.: 781-643-0554. Fax: 781-643-0640.
E-mail: info@oldschwambmill.org
Web Site: www.oldschwambmill.org
Key Personnel: Site Admin., Ed Gordon.
Institution Type/Description: Industrial History Museum: housed in 1860 The Old Schwamb Mill, a water-powered mill.
Hours & Admission Prices: Tues. & Sat. 11-3. No charge; donations accepted. Tour groups (6-10 people) $35; members no charge. Closed legal holidays.
Attendance: 1,000 (estimated)

Ashfield

ASHFIELD HISTORICAL SOCIETY, 457 Main St., Ashfield, MA 01330. Mailing Address: P.O. Box 277, Ashfield, MA 01330-0277. Tel.: 413-428-4541.
E-mail: grace240@verizon.net
Web Site: www.ashfieldhistorical.org
Key Personnel: Pres. (V), Alden Gray; Cur., Grace Lesure; Museum Shop Mgr., Suzi Day.
Institution Type/Description: Historic Building: built in 1830.
Hours & Admission Prices: June-1st weekend in Oct. Sat.-Sun. 11-1; other times by appointment.

Ashland

ASHLAND HISTORICAL SOCIETY, INC., 2 Myrtle St., Ashland, MA 01721-1106. Mailing Address: P.O. Box 145, Ashland, MA 01721-0145. Tel.: 508-881-8183.
E-mail: ashlandhistsoc@msn.com
Web Site: ashlandhistsociety.com
Key Personnel: Pres. (V), Clifford Wilson.
Institution Type/Description: History Museum.
Hours & Admission Prices: Wed. 7-9 by appointment. No charge. &
Attendance: 450 (estimated)

Ashley Falls

THE ASHLEY HOUSE, Cooper Hill Rd., Ashley Falls, MA 01222. Mailing Address: P.O. Box 792, Stockbridge, MA 01262-0792. Tel.: 413-298-3239, ext. 3013. Fax: 413-298-5239.
E-mail: naumkeag@ttor.org
Web Site: www.thetrustees.org
Key Personnel: Cultural Site Mgr., Colleen Henry.
Institution Type/Description: Historic House: 1735 oldest house in Berkshire County.
Hours & Admission Prices: July-Aug. Sat.-Sun. 1-3; other times by appointment. Adults $5; discounts to AAM, ICOM members; children 12 & under and members no charge.
Attendance: 800 (actual)

Attleboro

ATTLEBORO AREA INDUSTRIAL MUSEUM, INC., 42 Union St., Ste. 2, Attleboro, MA 02703-2948. Tel.: 508-222-3918. Fax: 508-222-1498.
E-mail: info@industrialmuseum.com
Web Site: www.industrialmuseum.com
Key Personnel: Exec. Dir., Carleton Legg.
Institution Type/Description: Industrial Museum.
Hours & Admission Prices: Museum: Thurs.-Fri. 10-4, Sat. 10-3; Research Library & groups by appointment only. No charge; Guided Tours: adults $4, children $3. Closed Independence Day & week. &
Attendance: 3,000 (estimated)

ATTLEBORO ARTS MUSEUM, 86 Park St., Attleboro, MA 02703-2335. Tel.: 508-222-2644. Fax: 508-226-4401.
E-mail: office@attleboroartsmuseum.org
Web Site: www.attleboroartsmuseum.org
Formerly: Attleboro Museum, Center for the Arts
Key Personnel: Pres. Bd. of Trustees, Nancy Aleo; Exec. Dir., Mim Fawcett; Museum Shop Mgr., Marion Volterra; Coord. Programs, Abby Roualdi; Office Mgr., Kerry St. Pierre; Tech Admin., Patrick Garriepy.
Institution Type/Description: Art Museum & Cultural Center.
Hours & Admission Prices: Summer: June-Aug. Tues.-Sat. 10-4; Sept.-May Tues.-Sat. 10-5. No charge; donations accepted. Closed national holidays & holiday weekends. &
Attendance: 10,000 (estimated)

CAPRON PARK ZOO, 201 County St., Attleboro, MA 02703-3510. Tel.: 774-203-1840. Fax: 508-223-2208.
E-mail: jean.benchimol@capronparkzoo.com
Web Site: www.capronparkzoo.com
Key Personnel: Dir., Jean Benchimol; Asst. Zoo Dir., Brenda Young; Cur. Education, Melanie Fernandes.
Institution Type/Description: Zoo.
Hours & Admission Prices: April-Oct. daily 10-5, last admission at 4. Nov.-March call for hours. Non-Residents: adults $7, youth 3-12 $5.50, seniors 65 & over $4.75. Residents: adults $5.50, youth 3-12 $4.50, seniors 65 & over $3.75; children under 3 no charge. &

WOMEN AT WORK MUSEUM, Rte. 123, Attleboro, MA 02703. Mailing Address: P.O. Box 355, 35 County St., Attleboro, MA 02703-0006. Tel.: 508-222-4430.
E-mail: info@womenatworkmuseum.org
Web Site: www.womenatworkmuseum.org
Key Personnel: Pres., Nancy Young; Treas., Kelly Fox.
Institution Type/Description: History Museum.
Hours & Admission Prices: Sat. 11-4. No charge; donations accepted. &
Attendance: 1,000 (estimated)

Barnstable

BARNSTABLE HISTORICAL SOCIETY - PHINNEY/JONES HOUSE, 3087 Main St., Barnstable, MA 02630. Mailing Address: P.O. Box 829, Barnstable, MA 02630. Tel.: 508-362-2982.
E-mail: barnstablehistoricalsociety@gmail.com
Web Site: www.barnstablehistoricalsociety.org
Key Personnel: House Admin., Betsy Wheeler.
Institution Type/Description: Historical Society Museum: housed in the former home of Sylvanus B. Phinney, publisher & founder of The Barnstable Pilot, a local newspaper.
Hours & Admission Prices: mid-June to mid-Oct. Wed.-Sat. 1-4, Tues. by appointment. No charge; donations accepted.
Attendance: 2,015 (actual)

OLDE COLONIAL COURTHOUSE, TALES OF CAPE COD, INC., Olde Colonial Courthouse, Rondezvous Lane & Rt. 6A, Barnstable, MA 02630. Mailing Address: P.O. Box 41, Barnstable, MA 02630-0041. Tel.: 508-362-8927. Fax: 508-362-9056.
E-mail: tales@talesofcapecod.org
Web Site: talesofcapecod.org
Key Personnel: Pres., Joe Berlandi; Vice Pres., Judith Arsenault; Treas., Ken Robinson.
Institution Type/Description: Historic Site Museum & Olde Colonial Courthouse: Sachem Iyanough's gravesite dedicated to early Indians who befriended Pilgrims.
Hours & Admission Prices: By appointment only. Donations accepted. Lecture Series: July-Aug. Tues. 7:30pm.
Attendance: 1,250 (estimated)

STURGIS LIBRARY, 3090 Main St., Barnstable, MA 02630. Mailing Address: Box 606, Barnstable, MA 02630-0606. Tel.: 508-362-6636. Fax: 508-362-5467.
E-mail: sturgislibrary@comcast.net
Web Site: www.sturgislibrary.org
Key Personnel: Dir., Lucy Loomis; Pres. Bd. Trustees, Ellie Claus.
Institution Type/Description: Historic Building: housed in 1644 Rev. Lothrop House.
Hours & Admission Prices: Mon. & Wed.-Fri. 10-5, Tues. 1-8, Sat. 10-4. No charge; donations accepted. Closed holidays. &
Attendance: 45,000 (actual)

TRAYSER MUSEUM GROUP DBA COAST GUARD HERITAGE MUSEUM, 3353 Main St., Barnstable, MA 02630. Mailing Address: P.O. Box 161, Barnstable, MA 02630-0161. Tel.: 508-362-8521.
E-mail: cgheritage@comcast.net
Web Site: coastguardheritagemuseum.org
Formerly: Donald G. Trayser Memorial Museum/Barnstable County Customs House
Key Personnel: Pres., William Collette.
Institution Type/Description: History Museum: housed in 1856 Old Customs House.
Hours & Admission Prices: May-Oct. Tues.-Sat. 10-3. Adults $5; members, active Coast Guard and children 10 & under no charge. &
Attendance: 4,000 (estimated)

Barre

BARRE HISTORICAL SOCIETY, INC., 18 Common St., Barre, MA 01005. Mailing Address: P.O. Box 755, Barre, MA 01005-0755. Tel.: 978-355-4978.
E-mail: lesterpaquin@verizon.net
Key Personnel: Pres., W. Robert Bentley; Cur., Margaret Marshall; Treas., Margaret Frost; Asst. Treas., George Marshall; Sec., Lester W. Paquin.
Institution Type/Description: Local History Museum: housed in 1839 home of Spencer Field; built by Elias Carter, architect.
Hours & Admission Prices: Thurs. 10-12; other times by appointment. No charge; donations accepted. &
Attendance: 300 (estimated)

Becket

BECKET LAND TRUST HISTORIC QUARRY & FOREST, Quarry Rd., Becket, MA 01223. Mailing Address: P.O. Box 44, Becket, MA 01223-0044. Tel.: 413-623-2100. Facebook: Becket Land Trust Historic Quarry and Forest.
E-mail: landtrust@becketlandtrust.org
Web Site: www.becketlandtrust.org
Key Personnel: Dir., Dorothy Napp Schindel.
Institution Type/Description: History Museum.
Hours & Admission Prices: Dawn-dusk. No charge.

Belchertown

THE STONE HOUSE MUSEUM, 20 Maple St., Belchertown, MA 01007-9416. Mailing Address: P.O. Box 1211, Belchertown, MA 01007-1211. Tel.: 413-323-6573.
E-mail: ttstockton@earthlink.net
Web Site: www.stonehousemuseum.org
Key Personnel: Pres. (V), Tom Stockton; Asst. Cur., Shirley Bock; Archivist, Cliff McCarthy.
Institution Type/Description: Historic House Museum: 1827 stone house.
Hours & Admission Prices: mid-May to mid-Oct. Sat. 2-5 & by appointment. Adults $5, seniors $4, children $2; discounts to AAM, ICOM & MTA members; members no charge.
Attendance: 2,000 (estimated)

Berlin

BERLIN ART AND HISTORICAL SOCIETY, 4 Woodward Ave., Berlin, MA 01503. Mailing Address: P.O. Box 35, Berlin, MA 01503. Tel.: 978-838-2502.
Web Site: www.townofberlin.com/historical
Key Personnel: Pres. (V), June Miller.
Institution Type/Description: General Museum.
Hours & Admission Prices: By appointment. No charge.

Beverly

BEVERLY HISTORICAL SOCIETY AND MUSEUM, 117 Cabot St., Beverly, MA 01915-5196. Tel.: 978-922-1186. Fax: 978-922-7387.
E-mail: info@beverlyhistory.org
Web Site: www.beverlyhistory.org
Key Personnel: Dir., Susan Goganian; Pres. (V), Dan Lohnes; Mgr. Collections, Darren Brown.
Institution Type/Description: Historical Society Museum: housed in 1781 John Cabot Mansion.
Hours & Admission Prices: Museum: Tues. & Thurs.-Sat. 9:30-4, Wed. 1-9. Research-Galloupe Library: Tues. & Wed. Museum: adults $5, students & seniors $4; discounts to AAM & NEMA members; active duty military, members & children under 16 no charge. Library: adults $5 per hour; members no charge.
Attendance: 2,487 (estimated)

Billerica

BILLERICA HISTORICAL SOCIETY - CLARA SEXTON HOUSE, 36 Concord Rd., Billerica, MA 01821. Mailing Address: P.O. Box 381, Billerica, MA 01821-0381. Tel.: 978-667-7020. Facebook.
E-mail: billericahistorical@verizon.net
Web Site: billericahistory.org
Key Personnel: Pres. (V), Maria Seminatore; Museum Shop Mgr., Ann Stadtman.
Institution Type/Description: Historical Society: built in c.1723.

Hours & Admission Prices: May-Oct. 1st Sun. each month 1-3. No charge; donations accepted.
Attendance: 600 (estimated)

Bolton

BOLTON HISTORICAL SOCIETY, INC., Sawyer House, 676 Main St., Bolton, MA 01740. Mailing Address: P.O. Box 211, Bolton, MA 01740-0211. Tel.: 978-779-6392.
E-mail: mary@boltonhistoricalsociety.org
Web Site: www.boltonhistoricalsociety.org
Institution Type/Description: General Museum: housed in c.1810 Sawyer House & farm/barn blacksmith shop.
Hours & Admission Prices: Thurs. 1:30-3:30; tours by appointment. No charge; donations accepted.
Attendance: 300 (estimated)

Boston

ANCIENT AND HONORABLE ARTILLERY COMPANY OF MASSACHUSETTS, 1 Faneuil Hall, Armory, 4th Fl., Boston, MA 02109-1604. Tel.: 617-227-1638. Fax: 617-227-7221.
E-mail: ahac.curator@verizon.net
Web Site: www.ahac.us.com
Formerly: The Military Company of the Massachusetts
Key Personnel: Cur., Lt. Charles Fazio.
Institution Type/Description: Military Museum.
Hours & Admission Prices: Call for information. No charge, donations accepted. &
Attendance: 40,000 (estimated)

ARNOLD ARBORETUM OF HARVARD UNIVERSITY, 125 Arborway, Boston, MA 02130-3500. Tel.: 617-524-1718. Fax: 617-524-1418.
E-mail: arbweb@arnarb.harvard.edu
Web Site: www.arboretum.harvard.edu
Institution Type/Description: Arboretum.
Hours & Admission Prices: Visitor Center: Thurs.-Tues. 10-5. Library: Mon.-Fri. 10-4. Closed holidays. Grounds: daily sunrise-sunset. No charge; donations accepted. &
Attendance: 250,000 (estimated)

BARBARA AND STEVEN GROSSMAN GALLERY, School of the Museum of Fine Arts, Boston, 230 The Fenway, Boston, MA 02115. Tel.: 617-627-0075.
E-mail: exhibitions@smfa.edu
Institution Type/Description: Art Gallery.
Hours & Admission Prices: Mon.-Wed. & Fri.-Sat. 10-5, Thurs. 10-8. No charge. Closed holidays.

THE BOSTON ATHENAEUM, 10 1/2 Beacon St., Boston, MA 02108-3777. Tel.: 617-227-0270. Fax: 617-227-5266.
E-mail: cure@bostonathenaeum.org
Web Site: www.bostonathenaeum.org
Formerly: Boston Athenaeum Library
Key Personnel: Pres., John S. Reed; Dir., Dr. Elizabeth Barker; Dir. Opers., Bob West; Cur. Prints & Photographs, Catharina Slautterback; Cur. Art, David Dearinger; Cur. Rare Books, Stanley E. Cushing; Assoc. Cur. Paintings & Sculpture, Casey Riley; Conservator, Dawn Walus; Acquisition Librarian, Anthea Harrison Reilly.
Institution Type/Description: Library with Art Collection: housed in 1847-49 library building.
Hours & Admission Prices: Mon.-Thurs. 9-8, Fri. 9-5:30, Sat. 9-4, Sun. noon-4. No charge. Closed major holidays. &

BOSTON CHILDREN'S MUSEUM, 308 Congress St., Boston, MA 02210-1034. Tel.: 617-426-6500. Fax: 617-426-1944.
E-mail: info@BostonChildrensMuseum.org
Web Site: www.BostonChildrensMuseum.org
Formerly: The Children's Museum, Inc.
Key Personnel: Chm. Bd., Nirav Dagli, M.D.; Pres. & C.E.O., Carole Charnow; Sr. Vice Pres. Research & Program Planning, Leslie Swartz; Vice Pres. Family Learning & Early Childhood Programs, Jeri Robinson; Vice Pres. Mktg. & Communications, Peter Broderick.
Institution Type/Description: Children's Museum.
Hours & Admission Prices: See website for hours. Admission $18; AAM members, other museum staff with ID, children under 12 months, & members no charge. Closed Thanksgiving; Christmas. &
Attendance: 589,000 (estimated)

BOSTON FIRE MUSEUM, 344 Congress St., Boston, MA 02210-1204. Tel.: 617-338-9700. Facebook: Boston Fire Museum.
E-mail: info@bostonfiremuseum.com
Web Site: bostonfiremuseum.com
Key Personnel: Chm. (V), Daniel O'Neill; Pres. (V), Paul Boudreau; Museum Shop Mgr., James Daly.
Institution Type/Description: Fire-Fighting History and Education Museum: housed in 1891 Congress Street Fire Station, a National Historic Landmark Building.
Hours & Admission Prices: Sat. 11-5; other times by appointment. No charge; donations accepted. &
Attendance: 3,500 (actual)

BOSTON NATIONAL HISTORICAL PARK, Charlestown Navy Yard, 21 Second Ave., Boston, MA 02129. Tel.: 617-242-5601. Fax: 617-241-8650.
E-mail: david_vecchioli@nps.gov
Web Site: www.nps.gov/bost/
Key Personnel: Supt., Cassius Cash; Museum Specialist, Brandon Sexton.
Institution Type/Description: Historic Houses & Sites.
Hours & Admission Prices: Daily 9-5. No charge. &
Attendance: 2,700,000 (actual)

BOSTON PUBLIC LIBRARY, 700 Boylston St., Boston, MA 02116-2813. Tel.: 617-536-5400 & 859-2328. TDD: 617-536-7055.
E-mail: fineartsref@bpl.org
Web Site: www.bpl.org
Key Personnel: Dir., Jen Inglis; Cur. Fine Arts, Eve Griffin; Head Special Collections, Beth Prindle.
Institution Type/Description: Public Library with Art Collections.
Hours & Admission Prices: Mon.-Thurs. 9-9, Fri.-Sat. 9-5; Sun. 1-5. No charge. Closed national holidays. &
Attendance: 2,000,000

BOSTON SCULPTORS GALLERY, 486 Harrison Ave., Boston, MA 02118. Tel.: 617-482-7781.
E-mail: bostonsculptors@yahoo.com
Web Site: www.bostonsculptors.com
Key Personnel: Dir., Almitra Stanley.
Institution Type/Description: Art Gallery.
Hours & Admission Prices: Wed.-Sun. 12-6. No charge. Closed New Year's Day; Thanksgiving; Christmas. &

BOSTON UNIVERSITY ART GALLERY, 855 Commonwealth Ave., Boston, MA 02215-1303. Tel.: 617-353-3329. Fax: 617-353-4509.
E-mail: gallery@bu.edu
Web Site: www.bu.edu/ART
Key Personnel: Dir., Josh Buckno.
Institution Type/Description: Art Gallery.
Hours & Admission Prices: Academic Year: Tues.-Wed. & Fri.-Sun. 12-5, Thurs. 12-8. No charge. Closed university & major holidays. &
Attendance: 7,450 (actual)

BROMFIELD GALLERY, 450 Harrison Ave., Boston, MA 02118-2400. Tel.: 617-451-3605.
E-mail: info@bromfieldgallery.com
Web Site: www.bromfieldgallery.com
Key Personnel: Gallery Mgr., Gary Duehr.
Institution Type/Description: Cooperative Art Gallery.
Hours & Admission Prices: Wed.-Sun. 12-5. No charge; donations accepted. Closed major holidays. &
Attendance: 3,000 (estimated)

CHASE YOUNG GALLERY, 450 Harrison Ave., No. 57, Boston, MA 02118. Tel.: 617-859-7222.
E-mail: mail@chaseyounggallery.com
Web Site: www.chaseyounggallery.com
Key Personnel: Dir. & Owner, Jane Young.
Institution Type/Description: Art Gallery.
Hours & Admission Prices: Tues.-Wed. & Fri.-Sat. 11:30-5, Thurs. 11:30-4; other times by appointment.

THE COMMONWEALTH MUSEUM, 220 Morrissey Blvd., Boston, MA 02125-3314. Tel.: 617-727-9268. Fax: 617-825-3613.
E-mail: commonwealthmuseum@sec.state.ma.us
Web Site: www.sec.state.ma.us/mus/index.html
Key Personnel: Dir., Stephen Kenney, Ph.D.
Institution Type/Description: State History Museum.

Hours & Admission Prices: Memorial Day to Labor Day Mon.-Fri. 9-5, Sat.-Sun. 9-3; Sept.-May Mon.-Fri. 9-5. No charge. Closed major holidays. &
Attendance: 10,000 (estimated)

COPLEY SOCIETY OF ART, 158 Newbury St., Boston, MA 02116. Tel.: 617-536-5049. Fax: 617-267-9396.
E-mail: info@copleysociety.org
Key Personnel: Exec. Dir., Suzan W. Redgate; Gallery Coord., Aly Schuman.
Institution Type/Description: Art Gallery.
Hours & Admission Prices: Tues.-Sat. 11-6, Sun. 12-5; other times by appointment.

THE GIBSON SOCIETY, INC. DBA GIBSON HOUSE MUSEUM, 137 Beacon St., Boston, MA 02116-1504. Tel.: 617-267-6338. Fax: 617-267-6338. Facebook.
E-mail: info@thegibsonhouse.org
Web Site: thegibsonhouse.org
Key Personnel: Museum Administrator, Michelle Coughlin; Pres., Samuel H. Duncan; Treas., Lorraine Hanley; Cur., Wendy Swanton.
Institution Type/Description: Historic House Museum: 1859 Gibson House.
Hours & Admission Prices: Tours: Wed.-Sun. 1, 2 & 3. Adults $9, senior citizens & students $6, children under 12 $3; discount to Victorian Society (New England) & AAA members; members no charge. Closed national holidays.
Attendance: 3,500 (actual)

HISTORIC NEW ENGLAND, 141 Cambridge St., Boston, MA 02114-2799. Tel.: 617-227-3956. Facebook: Historic New England.
E-mail: news@historicnewengland.org
Web Site: www.historicnewengland.org
Key Personnel: Pres., Carl R. Nold.
Institution Type/Description: History Museum: housed in Otis house; designed by Charles Bulfinch; built in 1796.
Hours & Admission Prices: Offices: Mon.-Fri. 9-5. Archives: by appointment. Otis House Tours: April-Nov. Wed.-Sun. 11-4:30; Dec.-Feb. Fri.-Sun. 11-4:30. Adults $10, seniors $9, students $5; discounts to ICOM, AAA & AAM members; members & Boston residents no charge.
Attendance: 208,368 (actual)

THE INSTITUTE OF CONTEMPORARY ART/BOSTON, 25 Harbor Shore Dr., Boston, MA 02210-2172. Tel.: 617-478-3100. TDD: 617-927-6622.
E-mail: info@icaboston.org
Web Site: www.icaboston.org
Key Personnel: Dir., Jill Medvedow; Dir., Ellen Matilda Poss.
Institution Type/Description: Art Museum.
Hours & Admission Prices: Tues.-Wed. & Sat.-Sun. 10-5, Thurs.-Fri. 10-9. Adults $15, senior citizens $13, students $10; discounts to AAM members; children under 17, families on last Sat. of month, Thurs. after 5 & members no charge. Closed New Year's Day; Martin Luther King, Jr. Day; Presidents' Day; Memorial Day; Independence Day; Labor Day; Columbus Day; Thanksgiving; Christmas. &
Attendance: 200,000 (actual)

ISABELLA STEWART GARDNER MUSEUM, 25 Evans Way, Boston, MA 02115-5538. Tel.: 617-566-1401 & 278-5156. Fax: 617-264-6096.
E-mail: information@isgm.org
Web Site: www.gardnermuseum.org
Key Personnel: Dir., Peggy Fogelman; Cur. Education, Margaret Burchenal; Dir. Mktg., Kathy Sharpless; Cur. Music, Scott Nickrenz; Cur. Contemporary Art, Pieranna Cavalchini; Cur. Collection, Christina Nielsen; Consulting Cur. Landscape, Charles Waldheim; Museum Shop Mgr., Victor Oliveira.
Institution Type/Description: Art Museum: housed in 15th-century Venetian style palace.
Hours & Admission Prices: Wed. & Fri.-Mon. 11-5, Thurs. 11-9; Adults $15, senior citizens 65 & over $12, college students with current ID $5; discounts to AAM & ICOM members; children under 18, members, anyone named Isabella, & on your birthday no charge. Closed New Year's Day; Patriot's Day; Independence Day; Thanksgiving; Christmas Day. &
Attendance: 220,000 (estimated)

JOHN F. KENNEDY PRESIDENTIAL LIBRARY & MUSEUM, Columbia Point, Boston, MA 02125. Tel.: 617-514-1600. Fax: 617-514-1652. TDD: 617-514-1573.
E-mail: kennedy.library@nara.gov
Web Site: www.jfklibrary.org
Key Personnel: Deputy Dir., James Roth; Treas., Marie Carbone; Cur., Stacey Bredhoff; Education, Nancy McCoy; Registrar, Kathryn Dodge; Archivist, Karen Adler Abramson; Museum Shop Mgr., Alene Bowns; Security, Norm Beland.

Institution Type/Description: History & Presidential Library.
Hours & Admission Prices: Daily 9-5; groups by appointment. Adults $12, senior citizens & college students with ID $10, children 13-17 $9; discounts to groups, museums of Boston, NEMA & AAM members; members & children under 12 no charge. Closed New Year's Day; Thanksgiving; Christmas. &
Attendance: 220,000 (actual)

KINGSTON GALLERY, 450 Harrison Ave., #43, Boston, MA 02118. Tel.: 617-423-4113.
E-mail: info@kingstongallery.com
Web Site: www.kingstongallery.com/contact/index.php
Institution Type/Description: Art Gallery.
Hours & Admission Prices: Wed.-Sun. 12-5; other times by appointment.

THE MARY BAKER EDDY LIBRARY, 200 Massachusetts Ave., Boston, MA 02115-3017. Tel.: 617-450-7000. Fax: 617-450-7048. Facebook.
E-mail: librarymail@mbelibrary.org
Web Site: www.mbelibrary.org
Key Personnel: Exec. Dir., Michael W. Hamilton; Programs Mgr., Jonathon Eder; Communications & Content Mgr., Stephen Graham; Sr. Research Archivist, Judith Huenneke; Records Management Mgr., Allyson Lazar; Cur., Pamela Winstead.
Institution Type/Description: History Museum.
Hours & Admission Prices: Tues.-Sun. 10-4. Adults $6, seniors, students, military & children 6-17 $4; MTA, AAM & NEMA members, children 5 & under and donors no charge. Closed New Year's Day; Martin Luther King Jr. Day; Presidents' Day; Patriots' Day; Memorial Day; Independence Day; Labor Day; Thanksgiving; Christmas Eve & Day. &
Attendance: 60,000 (estimated)

MASSACHUSETTS COLLEGE OF ART + DESIGN - BAKALAR & PAINE GALLERIES, 621 Huntington Ave., Boston, MA 02115-5801. Tel.: 617-879-7337. Fax: 617-879-7340.
E-mail: galleryinfo@massart.edu
Web Site: www.massart.edu/galleries
Key Personnel: Dir., Lisa Tung.
Institution Type/Description: Art Gallery.
Hours & Admission Prices: Mon.-Tues. & Thurs.-Sat. 12-6, Wed. 12-8.

MASSACHUSETTS HISTORICAL SOCIETY, 1154 Boylston St., Boston, MA 02215-3695. Tel.: 617-536-1608. Fax: 617-859-0074.
E-mail: library@masshist.org
Web Site: www.masshist.org
Key Personnel: Pres., Catherine Allgor, Ph.D.; Librarian, Peter Drummey; Editor in Chief, Sara Martin.
Institution Type/Description: Library.
Hours & Admission Prices: Library: Mon.-Fri. 9-4:45, Sat. 9-4. Exhibitions: Mon.-Sat. 10-4. No charge. Closed national holidays. &
Attendance: 8,750 (estimated)

MASSACHUSETTS STATE HOUSE, 24 Beacon St., Boston, MA 02108. Mailing Address: State House Tours, Rm. 194, Boston, MA 02133. Tel.: 617-727-3676. Fax: 617-973-4858.
E-mail: mastatehousetours@sec.state.ma.us
Web Site: www.sec.state.ma.us/trs/trsgen/genidx.htm
Institution Type/Description: Historic Building: built in 1798.
Hours & Admission Prices: Guided Tours: Mon.-Fri. 10-3:30 by appointment. No charge. &

MCMULLEN MUSEUM OF ART, BOSTON COLLEGE, Devlin Hall, 2101 Commonwealth Ave., Boston, MA 02135-3101. Mailing Address: 140 Commonwealth Ave., Chestnut Hill, MA 02467-3800. Tel.: 617-552-8587. Fax: 617-552-8577.
E-mail: artmusm@bc.edu
Web Site: bc.edu/artmuseum
Key Personnel: Dir., Dr. Nancy Netzer; Chm. (V), C. Michael Daley; Devel., Ginger Saariaho; Asst. Dir., Exhibition Design & Collections Mgmt., Diana Larsen; Asst. Dir., Multimedia & Design Svcs., John McCoy; Mgr. Publications & Exhibitions, Kate Shugert; Education & Outreach Specialist, Rachel Chamberlain.
Institution Type/Description: Art Museum.
Hours & Admission Prices: Mon.-Tues. & Fri. 10-5, Wed.-Thurs. 10-8, Sat.-Sun. 12-5. No charge; donations accepted. Closed New Year's Day; Martin Luther King Jr. Day; Washington's Birthday; Good Friday; Easter; Memorial Day; Labor Day; Columbus Day; Christmas. &
Attendance: 75,000 (actual)

MILLS GALLERY - BOSTON CENTER FOR THE ARTS, 551 Tremont St., Boston, MA 02116-6338. Tel.: 617-426-8835.
E-mail: rhopkins@bcaonline.org
Institution Type/Description: Art Gallery.
Hours & Admission Prices: Wed. & Sun. 12-5, Thurs.-Sat. 12-9. No charge.

MUSEUM OF AFRICAN AMERICAN HISTORY, 46 Joy St., Boston, MA 02114-4005. Mailing Address: 14 Beacon St., Ste. 401, Boston, MA 02108-3742. Tel.: 617-725-0022. Fax: 617-720-5225.
E-mail: history@maah.org
Web Site: www.maah.org
Key Personnel: Exec. Dir., Marita Rivero; Chm., Cathleen Douglas Stone; Museum Shop Mgr., Diana Parcon.
Institution Type/Description: History Museum.
Hours & Admission Prices: Boston: Mon.-Sat. 10-4. Nantucket: Summer: Mon.-Sat. 10-4, Sun. 12-4; Fall: Tues.-Sun. 11-4; Winter: Sat-Sun. 11-4; other times by appointment. No charge; donations requested. Closed major holidays. &
Attendance: 230,000 (estimated)

MUSEUM OF FINE ARTS, 465 Huntington Ave., Boston, MA 02115-5597. Tel.: 617-267-9300. Fax: 617-369-3064. Facebook, Instagram, Twitter.
E-mail: tickets@mfa.org
Web Site: www.mfa.org
Key Personnel: Dir., Matthew Teitelbaum; Chief Brand Officer & Deputy Dir., Katherine Getchell; Chief, External Rels. & Deputy Dir., Maria Muller; C.F.O. & Deputy Dir., Mark Kerwin; Sr. Dir. Communications, Dawn Griffin; Chm. Prints, Drawings & Photographs, Anne Havinga; Chm. Art of Asia, Oceania & Africa, Chris Newth; Chm. Art of the Americas, Elliot Davis; Chm. Art of the Ancient World, Rita Freed; Chm. Conservation & Collections Management, Matthew Siegal; Chief, Director's Office, Kristin Ferguson; Chief, Exhibitions, Strategy & Gallery Displays, Edward Saywell; Dir. Libraries & Archives and Museum Historian, Maureen Melton; Dir. Exhibitions, Patrick McMahon; Chm. Contemporary Art & MFA Programs, Jen Mergel; Dir. Human Resources, Jane O'Reilly; Chm. Textiles & Fashion Arts, Pamela A. Parmal; Cur. Education, Barbara Martin; Cur. Musical Instruments, Darcy Kuronen; Dir. MFA Publications, Emiko Usui; Dir. Intellectual Property, Debra LaKind; Dir. Collections, Ben Weiss; Dir. Curatorial Admin., Chris Newth; Museum Shop Mgr., Ellen Bragalone; Chm. (V), Lis Tarlow; Pres. (V), David Croll.
Institution Type/Description: Art Museum & School.
Hours & Admission Prices: Museum: Wed.-Fri. 10-10, Sat.-Tues. 10-5. Adults $25, senior citizens and students 18 & over $23; discounts to AAM & ICOM members; youth 17 & under outside BPS hours & members no charge. Closed New Year's Day; Patriot's Day; Independence Day; Thanksgiving; Christmas. &
Attendance: 1,181,000 (actual)

MUSEUM OF SCIENCE, 1 Science Park, Boston, MA 02114-1099. Tel.: 617-723-2500; 617-589-0417 (TTY).
E-mail: information@mos.org
Web Site: www.mos.org
Key Personnel: Dir. & Pres., Dr. Ioannis Miaoulis; Chm. (V) Bd. Trustees, Gwill York; C.O.O., Wayne Bouchard; C.F.O., John Slakey; Sr. Vice Pres. Strategic Initiatives, Larry Bell; Sr. Vice Pres. Mktg., Strategy & Communications, Todd Sperry; Sr. Vice Pres. Advancement, Ellie Starr; Pres. Volunteer Service League, Bobbie Ewels; Vice Pres. Exhibit Devel. & Conservation, Christine Reich; Vice Pres. Visitor Svcs. & Operations, Jonathan Burke; Vice Pres. Human Resources, Britton O'Brien; Vice Pres. Elementary Curriculum Devel., Christine Cunningham; Vice Pres. Education & Enrichment Programs, Annette Sawyer; Dir. Hayden Planetarium & Adult Program, David Rabkin.
Institution Type/Description: Science & Technology Museum.
Hours & Admission Prices: July 5 to Labor Day Fri. 9-9, Sat.-Thurs. 9-7; Sept. to Independence Day Fri. 9-9, Sat.-Thurs. 9-5. Omni Theater, Planetarium, Laser Shows: call for hours. Exhibit Halls: adults $25, seniors $21, children 3-11 $20; members no charge. Omni Theater or Planetarium: adults $10, seniors 60 & over $9, children 3-11 $8. 4D Theater or Butterfly Garden $6; discounts to members. Call 617-723-2500 or visit website for special holiday & vacation hours. Closed Thanksgiving; Christmas. &
Attendance: 1,536,000 (actual)

MUSEUM OF THE NATIONAL CENTER OF AFRO-AMERICAN ARTISTS, 300 Walnut Ave., Boston, MA 02119-1369. Tel.: 617-442-8614. Fax: 617-445-5525.
E-mail: bgaither@mfa.org
Web Site: www.ncaaa.org
Key Personnel: Dir. & Cur., Edmund Barry Gaither.
Institution Type/Description: Art Museum.
Hours & Admission Prices: Tues.-Sun. 1-5. Adults $5, students & senior citizens $4; members no charge.
Attendance: 10,000 (estimated)

NEW ENGLAND AQUARIUM CORPORATION, 1 Central Wharf, Boston, MA 02110-3399. Tel.: 617-973-5200, ext. 0. Fax: 617-720-5098. TDD: 617-973-0223.
E-mail: kids.ed@neaq.org
Web Site: www.neaq.org
Key Personnel: Pres. & C.E.O., Maliz Beams; Chief Operating & Financial Officer, P. Eric Krauss; Vice Pres. Programs, Exhibits & Planning, William Spitzer; Dir. Visitor Experience, Deb Bobek; Vice Pres. Devel., David Whalen; Vice Pres. Research, Scott Kraus; Vice Pres. Mktg. & Communications, Jane Wolfson; Dir. Design, Jim Duffey; Dir. Education, John Anderson; Dir. Foundation, Rebecca Thibault; Dir. Media Rels., Tony Lacasse.
Institution Type/Description: Aquarium.
Hours & Admission Prices: July to Labor Day Sun.-Thurs. 9-6, Fri.-Sat. 9-7; Fall: Mon.-Fri. 9-5, Sat.-Sun. 9-6. Adults $26.95, senior citizens $24.95, children 3-11 $18.95; discounts to groups; children under 3 & members no charge. Closed Thanksgiving; Christmas. &
Attendance: 1,300,000 (actual)

NICHOLS HOUSE MUSEUM, 55 Mount Vernon St., Boston, MA 02108-1330. Tel.: 617-227-6993. Fax: 617-723-8026.
E-mail: info@nicholshousemuseum.org
Web Site: www.nicholshousemuseum.org
Key Personnel: Exec. Dir., Linda Marshall; Pres., Kate Euroth.
Institution Type/Description: Historic House Museum: housed in former Beacon Hill home of Rose Standish Nichols.
Hours & Admission Prices: April-Oct. Tues.-Sat. 11-4; Nov.-March Thurs.-Sat. 11-4. Adults $10, seniors $8, students $5; discounts to MA Teachers Assoc., AAA, AAM, WGBH & ICOM members; children under 12 & members no charge. Closed holidays.
Attendance: 4,500 (actual)

OLD SOUTH MEETING HOUSE, 310 Washington St., Boston, MA 02108-4616. Tel.: 617-482-6439. Fax: 617-482-9621.
E-mail: info@osmh.org
Web Site: www.oldsouthmeetinghouse.org
Key Personnel: Exec. Dir., Emily Curran; Pres., Carl Sciortino.
Institution Type/Description: Historic Site: 1729 Old South Meeting House.
Hours & Admission Prices: April-Oct. daily 9:30-5; Nov.-March daily 10-4. Adults $6, senior citizens 62 & over and students 18 & over w/I.D. $5, children 5-17 $1; members & children under 5 no charge. Closed New Year's Day; Thanksgiving; Christmas Eve & Day. &
Attendance: 78,000 (actual)

OLD STATE HOUSE-THE BOSTONIAN SOCIETY, 206 Washington St., Boston, MA 02109-1773. Tel.: 617-720-1713. Fax: 617-720-3289.
E-mail: amyn@bostonhistory.org
Web Site: www.bostonhistory.org
Key Personnel: Exec. Dir., Nathaniel Sheidley; Bd. Chm. (V), Martha McNamara; Mgr. Old State Visitor Svcs. & Museum Shop Mgr., Alex Stiles Greenlaw; Dir. Finance & Admin., Lisa Goldstein; Finance & Administrative Asst., Aaron Krol; Mgr. Collections, Sira Dooley Fairchild; Dir. Devel., Jeff Kubiatowicz; Devel. Assoc., Heather Rockwood; Mgr. Library & Archives, Elizabeth Roscio; Dir. Education & Exhibitions, Kathy Mulvaney; Dir. Facilities, Matthew Ottinger; Dir. Mktg., Chuck Gordon; Mgr. Distribution, Jim Fitzgerald.
Institution Type/Description: History Museum: built in 1713 to house government offices.
Hours & Admission Prices: Labor Day to Memorial Day daily 9-5; Sept.-May daily 9-5. Adults $10, senior citizens & students $8.50; discount to AAM members; children 6-18, members, veterans & active military no charge. Closed New Year's Day; Thanksgiving; Christmas.
Attendance: 105,538 (actual)

PAUL REVERE HOUSE/PAUL REVERE MEMORIAL ASSOCIATION, 19 North Sq., Boston, MA 02113-2405. Tel.: 617-523-2338. Fax: 617-523-1775.
E-mail: staff@paulreverehouse.org
Web Site: www.paulreverehouse.org
Key Personnel: Exec. Dir., Nina Zannieri; Pres. (V), Paul Revere, Jr.; Cur., Edith Steblecki; Dir. Education, Emily Holmes; Dir. Research, Robert Shimp; Interpretations & Visitor Svcs. Dir., Kristin Peszka.
Institution Type/Description: History Museum & Historic Houses: c.1680 Paul Revere House, Boston's oldest house; c.1711 Pierce-Hichborn House.
Hours & Admission Prices: Jan.-March Sun. & Tues.-Fri. 9:30-4:15; early April & Nov.-Dec. daily 9:30-4:15; mid-April to Oct. daily 9:30-5:15. Adults $5, college students & senior citizens $4.50, children $1; discounts to active military, museum professionals, AAM, NEMA, AASLH & ICOM members; members no charge. Closed New Year's Day; Thanksgiving; Christmas. &
Attendance: 323,301 (actual)

PAUL S. RUSSELL MUSEUM OF MEDICAL HISTORY AND INNOVATION, 2 N. Grove St., Boston, MA 02114. Tel.: 617-724-8009.
E-mail: mghhistory@partners.org
Web Site: www.massgeneral.org/museum
Institution Type/Description: Medical Museum.
Hours & Admission Prices: April 16-Oct. 15 Mon.-Fri. 9-5, Sat. 11-5; Oct. 16-April 15 Mon.-Fri. 9-5. No charge. Closed New Year's Day; Martin Luther King, Jr. Day; Presidents' Day; Memorial Day; Independence Day; Labor Day; Columbus Day; Thanksgiving; Christmas. &

PHOTOGRAPHIC RESOURCE CENTER AT BOSTON UNIVERSITY, 832 Commonwealth Ave., Boston, MA 02215-1205. Tel.: 617-975-0600. Fax: 617-975-0606.
E-mail: info@prcboston.org
Web Site: www.prcboston.org
Key Personnel: Exec. Dir., Glenn Ruga.
Institution Type/Description: Photography Museum.
Hours & Admission Prices: Wed. 1-5, Thurs. 11-8, Fri.-Sat. 11-4. Suggested Donation $5. Closed major holidays. &
Attendance: 10,000 (estimated)

ROBERT KLEIN GALLERY, 38 Newbury St., 4th Fl., Boston, MA 02116. Tel.: 617-267-7997. Fax: 617-267-5567.
E-mail: inquiry@robertkleingallery.com
Key Personnel: Owner, Robert Klein; Dir., Hank Hauptmann.
Institution Type/Description: Art Gallery.
Hours & Admission Prices: Tues.-Fri. 10-5:30, Sat. 11-5; other times by appointment.

RUBIN-FRANKEL GALLERY AT HILLEL HOUSE - BOSTON UNIVERSITY, 213 Bay State Rd., Boston, MA 02215-1499. Tel.: 617-353-7200. Fax: 617-353-7660.
E-mail: hillel@bu.edu
Web Site: www.bu.edu/hillel
Key Personnel: Exec. Dir., Reb Jevin Eagle; Dir. Operations, Brian Agnew.
Institution Type/Description: Art Gallery.
Hours & Admission Prices: Mon.-Thurs. & Sat. 9am-9pm, Fri. 9am-11pm.

SHIRLEY-EUSTIS HOUSE, 33 Shirley St., Boston, MA 02119-2725. Tel.: 617-442-2275. Fax: 617-442-2270.
E-mail: governorshirley@gmail.com
Web Site: www.shirleyeustishouse.org
Key Personnel: Exec. Dir., Una McMahon.
Institution Type/Description: Historic House: 1747 Georgian country house designed by Peter Harrison, built by Royal Governor William Shirley; restored to Federal appearance, 1800; furnished according to Gov. William Eustis inventory, 1825; 1806 Gardner Carriage House.
Hours & Admission Prices: June-Sept. Thurs.-Sun. 1-4; other times by appointment. Adults $7, students & senior citizens $5; discounts to groups, NEMA, AAA, Blue Star & AAM members. Closed New Year's Day; Independence Day; Thanksgiving; Christmas.
Attendance: 2,000 (estimated)

SKYWALK OBSERVATORY - DREAMS OF FREEDOM IMMIGRATION MUSEUM, The Prudential Center, 800 Boyleston St., Boston, MA 02199-8001. Tel.: 617-859-0648. Facebook: Skywalk Observatory.
E-mail: skywalk@topofthehub.net
Web Site: skywalkboston.com
Key Personnel: Skywalk Mgr., Po Yan Yeung.
Institution Type/Description: History Museum.
Hours & Admission Prices: April-Nov. daily 10-10; Nov.-March daily 10-8. Adults $16, seniors 62 & over and university students with ID $13; children 12 & under $11; US military & Massachusetts Teachers Assoc. no charge. Closed Christmas.
Attendance: 250,000 (estimated)

THE SOCIETY OF ARTS & CRAFTS, 100 Pier 4 Blvd., Boston, MA 02110-1974. Tel.: 617-266-1810. Fax: 617-266-5654.
E-mail: businessmanager@societyofcrafts.org
Web Site: www.societyofcrafts.org
Key Personnel: Exec. Dir., Fabio J. Fernandez; Museum Shop Mgr., George Summers, Jr.
Institution Type/Description: Art Gallery.
Hours & Admission Prices: Tues.-Wed. & Fri.-Sat. 10-6, Thurs. 10-9; other times by appointment. No charge; donations accepted.
Attendance: 25,800 (estimated)

SOUTH END HISTORICAL SOCIETY - FRANCIS DANE HOUSE, 532 Massachusetts Ave., Boston, MA 02118. Tel.: 617-536-4445.
E-mail: admin@southendhistoricalsociety.org
Web Site: www.southendhistoricalsociety.org
Institution Type/Description: Historical Society Museum: housed in the former home of prominent businessman & shoe manufacturer, Francis Dane & his wife Zervia.
Hours & Admission Prices: By appointment.

THE SPORTS MUSEUM, TD Garden, 100 Legends Way, Boston, MA 02114-1300. Tel.: 617-624-1235. Fax: 617-624-1238. Facebook: The Sports Museum.
E-mail: bcodagnone@sportsmuseum.org
Web Site: www.sportsmuseum.org
Formerly: The Sports Museum of New England
Key Personnel: Exec. Dir., Rusty Sullivan; Cur., Richard Johnson; Assoc. Cur., Brian Codagnone; Dir. Education & Public Program, Michelle Gormley; Devel. Mgr., Ashley Walenta.
Institution Type/Description: Sports Museum.
Hours & Admission Prices: Mon.-Fri. 10-4, Sat.-Sun. 11-4. Adults $12, students 10-18 & seniors 65 & over $6; discounts to groups; active duty military with valid ID, participating library members & children under 10 no charge. Closed during TD Garden events & major holidays.
Attendance: 111,000 (estimated)

USS CONSTITUTION MUSEUM, Boston National Historical Park, Charlestown Navy Yard, Bldg. 22, Boston, MA 02129. Mailing Address: P.O. Box 291812, Boston, MA 02129-0215. Tel.: 617-426-1812. Fax: 617-242-0496. Facebook.
E-mail: getinvolved@ussconstitutionmuseum.org
Web Site: www.ussconstitutionmuseum.org
Key Personnel: Dir. Exhibits, Robert Kiihne; Dir. Collections & Learning, Sarah Watkins; Dir. Devel., Laura O'Neill.
Institution Type/Description: History Museum.
Hours & Admission Prices: April-Oct. daily 9-6; Nov.-March daily 10-5; groups by appointment. No charge; donations accepted. Closed New Year's Day; Thanksgiving; Christmas.
Attendance: 331,677 (actual)

VILLA VICTORIA CENTER FOR THE ARTS, 85 W. Newton St., Boston, MA 02118-1523. Tel.: 617-927-1742. Fax: 617-236-7375.
E-mail: info@worldmusic.org
Web Site: www.ibaboston.org
Key Personnel: Dir., Elsa Mosquera Sterenberg.
Institution Type/Description: Art Gallery.
Hours & Admission Prices: Thurs.-Fri. 4-7, Sat. 1-4.

VILNA SHUL BOSTON'S CENTER FOR JEWISH CULTURE, 18 Phillips St., Boston, MA 02114-3711. Tel.: 617-523-2324. Fax: 781-459-2660.
E-mail: info@vilnashul.org
Web Site: www.vilnashul.org
Formerly: Boston Center for Jewish Heritage
Key Personnel: Exec. Dir., Barnet Kessel; Pres. (V), Debbie Kurnisky.
Institution Type/Description: Cultural Heritage Museum.
Hours & Admission Prices: March-Nov. Wed.-Fri. 11-5, Sun. 1-5. Adults $5; members no charge. Closed Jewish holidays.
Attendance: 8,000 (actual)

ZOO NEW ENGLAND, One Franklin Park Rd., Boston, MA 02121-3255. Tel.: 617-541-5466. Fax: 617-989-2025. Facebook: Franklin Park Zoo; Facebook: Stone Zoo.
E-mail: info@zoonewengland.com
Web Site: www.zoonewengland.com
Formerly: Franklin Park Zoo & Stone Zoo
Key Personnel: C.E.O. & Pres., John Linehan; Chm. Commonwealth Zoological Corp., David C. Porter.
Institution Type/Description: Zoo.
Hours & Admission Prices: April-Sept. Mon.-Fri. 10-5, Sat.-Sun. 10-6; Oct.-March daily 10-4. Franklin Park Zoo: adults $19.95, seniors 62 & over $16.95, children 2-12 $12.95; Stone Zoo: adults $15.95, seniors 62 & over $13.95, children 2-12 $11.95; members & children under 2 no charge.
Attendance: 537,660 (actual)

Bourne

APTUCXET TRADING POST MUSEUM, 24 Aptucxet Rd., Bourne, MA 02532-5434. Mailing Address: P.O. Box 3095, Bourne, MA 02532-0795. Tel.: 508-759-8167.
E-mail: bournehistoricalsociety@comcast.net
Web Site: www.bournehistoricalsociety.org
Key Personnel: C.E.O., Judith McAlister; Pres., Galon Barlow, Jr.; Site Mgr., Carol Wynne; Museum Shop Mgr., Mary Reid.
Institution Type/Description: Historic Building: trading post reconstructed on original 1627 site.
Hours & Admission Prices: Memorial Day to Columbus Day Tues.-Sat. 11-4; other times by appointment. Adults $5, seniors $4, children 6-18 $2; discounts to groups, AAM and AAA & their guests; members no charge.
Attendance: 6,000 (estimated)

Boylston

BOYLSTON HISTORICAL SOCIETY AND MUSEUM, 7 Central St., Boylston, MA 01505. Mailing Address: P.O. Box 459, Boylston, MA 01505. Tel.: 508-869-2720.
E-mail: info@boylstonhistory.org
Web Site: boylstonhistory.org
Key Personnel: Cur., Fred Brown.
Institution Type/Description: Historical Society Museum: housed in the former Old Town Hall; built in 1830.
Hours & Admission Prices: Sat. 9am to noon, Sun. 2-4; other times by appointment. No charge; donations accepted.
Attendance: 450 (estimated)

WORCESTER COUNTY HORTICULTURAL SOCIETY/ TOWER HILL BOTANIC GARDEN, 11 French Dr., Boylston, MA 01505-1008. Mailing Address: P.O. Box 598, Boylston, MA 01505-0598. Tel.: 508-869-6111 (hold or dial 10). Fax: 508-869-0314. Facebook, Instagram & Twitter: @TowerHillBG.
E-mail: thbg@towerhillbg.org
Web Site: www.towerhillbg.org
Key Personnel: Exec. Dir., Kathy Abbott.
Institution Type/Description: Arboretum & Botanical Garden.
Hours & Admission Prices: Mon. holidays & Tues.-Sun. 9-5. Adults $12, seniors $9, children 6-18 $7; discounts to members of AAM, AHS (American Horticultural Society) reciprocal admissions, AABGA, MA Horticultural Society, WICN & groups; members & children under 6 no charge. Closed New Year's Day; Thanksgiving; Christmas Eve & Day.
Attendance: 60,000 (actual)

Braintree

BRAINTREE HISTORICAL SOCIETY, INC. AND GILBERT BEAN MUSEUM, 31 Tenney Rd., Braintree, MA 02184-6512. Tel.: 781-848-1640. Fax: 781-380-0731.
E-mail: bhsinc@braintreehistorical.org
Web Site: www.braintreehistorical.org
Key Personnel: Pres., Tom Fiorelli; Treas., Blaine Banker; Vice Pres., Military Archivist & Cur., James Fahey; Librarian & Archivist, Marjorie P. Maxham; Dir. Membership, Alan Weinberg; School Program, Gail Burns; Museum Shop Mgr., Ruth Powell.
Institution Type/Description: Historical Society Museum.
Hours & Admission Prices: Gilbert Bean Museum & Research Library: Thurs.-Sat. 10-4. Thayer Birthplace: April-Nov. Wed.-Fri. 1-3; Dec.-March by appointment only. Adults $3, children $2; discounts to AAA & AAM members; members no charge. Closed major holidays.
Attendance: 7,000 (actual)

Brewster

CAPE COD MUSEUM OF NATURAL HISTORY, INC., 869 Rte. 6A, Brewster, MA 02631-1056. Tel.: 508-896-3867. Fax: 508-896-8844.
E-mail: rdwyer@ccmnh.org
Web Site: www.ccmnh.org
Key Personnel: Chm. Bd. Trustees, John McNair; Exec. Dir., Robert F. Dwyer; Museum Shop Mgr., Donna Durkee.
Institution Type/Description: Natural History Museum.
Hours & Admission Prices: Jan. open for special programs only; Feb.-March Thurs.-Sun. 11-3; April-May & Oct.-Dec. Wed.-Sun. 11-3; June-Sept. daily 9:30-4. Additional hours during school vacation weeks. Adults $8, seniors 65 & over $7, children 3-12 $3.50; members & children under 3 no charge. Closed Federal holidays; Christmas Eve.
Attendance: 31,000 (estimated)

Brockton

BROCKTON FIRE MUSEUM, 216 N. Pearl St., Brockton, MA 02301-1712. Tel.: 508-580-0039.
E-mail: mhreed7@comcast.net
Web Site: www.firemuseums.com
Institution Type/Description: Fire-Fighting Museum.
Hours & Admission Prices: By appointment.

FULLER CRAFT MUSEUM, 455 Oak St., Brockton, MA 02301-1340. Tel.: 508-588-6000. Fax: 508-587-6191. Facebook: Fuller Craft Museum.
E-mail: communications@fullercraft.org
Web Site: www.fullercraft.org
Formerly: Fuller Museum of Art
Key Personnel: Dir., Jonathan Fairbanks; Cur. Exhibitions & Collections, Beth McLaughlin; Mgr. Operations, Denise Lebica; Dir. Communications, Titilayo Ngwenya; Facilities Mgr., John Hastie; Mgr. Registrar & Collections, Cassandra Ortiz; Assoc. Cur., Michael McMillan; Devel. Assoc., Maria Francisco; Museum Shop Mgr., Denise Karas.
Institution Type/Description: Craft Museum.
Hours & Admission Prices: Tues.-Wed. & Fri.-Sun. 10-5, Thurs. 10-9. Adults $10, senior citizens $8, students $5; discounts to AAM members; members, children under 12 & Thurs. 5-9 no charge. Closed New Year's Day; Christmas. &
Attendance: 18,000 (estimated)

Brookline

BROOKLINE HISTORICAL SOCIETY, 347 Harvard St., Brookline, MA 02446-2907. Tel.: 617-566-5747.
E-mail: brooklinehistory@gmail.com
Web Site: www.brooklinehistoricalsociety.org
Key Personnel: Pres., Ken Liss.
Institution Type/Description: Historical Society Museum: housed in c.1740 Edward Devotion House.
Hours & Admission Prices: Call for hours. No charge; donations accepted.
Attendance: 500 (estimated)

FREDERICK LAW OLMSTED NATIONAL HISTORIC SITE, 99 Warren St., Brookline, MA 02445-5930. Tel.: 617-566-1689. Fax: 617-232-4073.
E-mail: alan_banks@nps.gov
Web Site: www.nps.gov/frla
Key Personnel: Supt., Myra Harrison; Supervisory Park Ranger, Alan Banks; Site Mgr., Lee Farrow Cook.
Institution Type/Description: Historic Site: 1810 home & office of Frederick Law Olmsted.
Hours & Admission Prices: Grounds: daily dawn to dusk. &
Attendance: 4,500 (actual)

GATEWAY ARTS GALLERIES, 62 Harvard St., Brookline, MA 02445. Tel.: 617-734-1577. Fax: 617-734-3199.
E-mail: gatewayarts@vinfen.org
Web Site: www.gatewayarts.org
Institution Type/Description: Art Gallery.
Hours & Admission Prices: Call for hours.

JOHN FITZGERALD KENNEDY NATIONAL HISTORIC SITE, 83 Beals St., Brookline, MA 02446-6010. Tel.: 617-566-7937. Fax: 617-730-9884. Facebook: JF Kennedy NHS.
E-mail: frla_kennedy_nhs@nps.gov
Web Site: www.nps.gov/jofi
Key Personnel: Supt., Myra Harrison; Site Mgr., Lee Farrow Cook; Supervisory Park Ranger, Volunteer Coord. & Museum Shop Mgr., Jim Roberts; Museum Shop Mgr., Lois Brown.
Institution Type/Description: Historic House Museum: housed in c.1917 home of Joe & Rose Kennedy, birthplace of our 35th president, John F. Kennedy.
Hours & Admission Prices: late May to Oct. Wed.-Sun. 9:30-5, house tours every half hour; groups by appointment. No charge; donations accepted.
Attendance: 33,000 (actual)

LARZ ANDERSON AUTO MUSEUM, 15 Newton St., Brookline, MA 02445-7406. Tel.: 617-522-6547. Fax: 617-524-0170.
E-mail: help@larzanderson.org
Web Site: www.larzanderson.org
Formerly: Museum of Transportation
Key Personnel: Exec. Dir. & Cur., Sheldon Steele; Pres. (V), Michael Iandoli.
Institution Type/Description: Transportation Museum.
Hours & Admission Prices: Tues.-Sun. 10-4. Adults $10, children, seniors, students, & military $5; discounts to groups, AAA, AARP, WGBH, AAM, ICOM &

MTA members; children under 6 & members no charge. Closed New Year's Day; Easter; Patriot's Day; Independence Day; Labor Day; Thanksgiving; Christmas. &
Attendance: 34,000 (estimated)

Burlington

BURLINGTON HISTORICAL MUSEUM, 13 Bedford St., Burlington, MA 01803. Mailing Address: Town Hall, 29 Center St., Burlington, MA 01803-3058. Tel.: 781-272-1049 & 270-1600.
E-mail: archives@burlmass.org
Web Site: www.burlington.org
Key Personnel: C.E.O., Museum Guide & Museum Moderator, Joyce Fay; Co Chm. (V) Burlington Historical Commission, Mike Tredeau; Co Chm. & Museum Guide, Toni Faria; Archivist, Daniel McCormack.
Institution Type/Description: History Museum.
Hours & Admission Prices: Summer: Tues. & Sat. 10-2. Archives: 8-12 & 1-4:30. No charge; donations accepted.
Attendance: 600 (estimated)

Buzzards Bay

ABS INFORMATION COMMONS, Massachusetts Maritime Academy, 101 Academy Dr., Buzzards Bay, MA 02532-3405. Tel.: 508-830-5034. Fax: 508-830-5074.
E-mail: library@maritime.edu
Web Site: www.maritime.edu; library.maritime.edu
Formerly: Captain Charles H. Hurley Library
Key Personnel: Dir., Susan S. Berteaux; Pres., Richard G. Gurnon.
Institution Type/Description: Maritime Naval Museum & Library.
Hours & Admission Prices: Academic Year: Sun. 2-10, Mon.-Thurs. 7:30am-10pm, Fri. 7:30-4; extended hours during exams. No charge. Closed state & federal holidays. &
Attendance: 83,900 (actual)

NATIONAL MARINE LIFE CENTER, 120 Main St., Buzzards Bay, MA 02532-3221. Mailing Address: P.O. Box 269, Buzzards Bay, MA 02532-0269. Tel.: 508-743-9888. Fax: 508-759-5477. Facebook: National Marine Life Center.
E-mail: nmlc@nmlc.org
Web Site: www.nmlc.org
Formerly: The National Marine Life Center's Marine Animal Discovery Center
Key Personnel: Pres. & Exec. Dir., Kathy Zagzebski, M.E.M.; Chm. (V), Brian Moore; Opers. & Fundraising Admin. & Museum Shop Mgr., Casey Shetterly; Dir. Marine Animal Rehabilitation, Kate Shaffer; Science Dir. & Assoc. Veterinarian, Sea Rogers Williams, V.M.D.; Animal Care & Volunteer Coordr., Margot Madden.
Institution Type/Description: Marine Museum.
Hours & Admission Prices: Memorial Day-Labor Day daily 10-5; call for additional hours. No charge; donations accepted. &
Attendance: 9,000 (actual)

Cambridge

THE ART INSTITUTE OF BOSTON MAIN GALLERY, 29 Everett St., Cambridge, MA 02138-2702. Tel.: 617-585-6656. Fax: 617-437-1226.
Web Site: www.lesley.edu
Key Personnel: C.E.O., Bonnell Robinson.
Institution Type/Description: Art Gallery.
Hours & Admission Prices: Jan. 4-Dec. 23 Tues.-Fri. 12-6, Sat.-Sun. 12-5. No charge. Closed major holidays. &
Attendance: 8,200 (estimated)

CAMBRIDGE HISTORICAL SOCIETY, 159 Brattle St., Cambridge, MA 02138-3300. Tel.: 617-547-4252.
E-mail: info@cambridgehistory.org
Web Site: www.cambridgehistory.org
Key Personnel: Exec. Dir., Marieke Vam Damme; Pres. (V), Richard Beatty; Treas., Anand Master; Bookkeeper, Marianne Hicks; Archivist, Maggie Hoffman; Devel. & Admin. Assoc., Rosemary Previte; Programs Cons., Lynn Waskelis.
Institution Type/Description: Historical Society Museum: 1685 building remodeled in early Georgian period.
Hours & Admission Prices: Mon.-Fri. by appointment. Adults $5, senior citizens & children $3; discounts to AAM & ICOM members; members no charge. Closed major holidays.
Attendance: 2,000 (estimated)

COLLECTION OF HISTORICAL SCIENTIFIC INSTRUMENTS - HARVARD UNIVERSITY, Science Ctr., 1 Oxford St., Cambridge, MA 02138. Mailing Address: Dept. of the History of Science, Science Ctr. 371, 1 Oxford St., Cambridge, MA 02138. Tel.: 617-495-2779. Facebook & Twitter: @harvardchsi.
E-mail: chsi@fas.harvard.edu
Web Site: chsi.harvard.edu/chsi
Key Personnel: Dir., Peter L. Galison; Dir. Administration, Dr. Jean-Francois Gauvin; Collections, Dr. Sara Schechner; Mgr. Collections, Sara Frankel.
Institution Type/Description: Science Museum.
Hours & Admission Prices: By appointment. No charge; donations accepted. ♿
Attendance: 10,000 (estimated)

HARVARD ART MUSEUMS, 32 Quincy St., Cambridge, MA 02138-3845. Tel.: 617-495-9400, ext. 0.
E-mail: jennifer_aubin@harvard.edu
Web Site: www.harvardartmuseums.org
Key Personnel: Elizabeth & John Moors Cabot Dir., Martha Tedeschi; Deputy Dir., Maureen Donovan; Chief Cur., Soyoung Lee; Head, Div. Asian & Mediterranean Art and Cur. Ancient Art, Susanne Ebbinghaus; Cur. Ancient Coins, Carmen Arnold-Biucchi; Cur. Islamic & Later Indian Art, Mary McWilliams; Assoc. Cur. Asian Art, Rachel Saunders; Head, Div. European & American Art and Cur. American Art, Ethan Lasser; Cur. European Art, A. Cassandra , Albinson; Assoc. Cur. Prints, Elizabeth Rudy; Head Div. Modern & Contemporary Art and Cur. Busch-Reisinger Museum, Lynette Roth; Cur. Photography, Makeda Best; Assoc. Cur. Modern & Contemporary Art, Mary Schneider Enriquez; Admin. Archaeological Exploration of Sardis, Bahadir Yildirim; Mgr. Harvard Art Museums Archives, Megan Schwenke; Dir. Straus Center for Conservation & Technical Studies, Narayan Khandekar; Dir. Collections Management, Jennifer Allen; Dir. Communications, Daron Manoogian; Dir. Academic & Pub. Programs, Jessica Levin Martinez; Dir. Facilities Planning & Management, Peter Atkinson; Dir. Finance, Juliana Wong; Dir. Digital Infrastructure & Emerging Technology, Jeff Steward; Dir. Major Gifts & Strategic Initiatives, Elizabeth Cartland; Dir. Security, Nilton Barbosa; Dir. Visitor Svcs., Sanja Cvjeticanin.
Institution Type/Description: University Art Museums.
Hours & Admission Prices: Daily 10am-5pm. Adults $15, seniors $13; students, Harvard ID holders plus one guest, museum members, youth under 18, Cambridge residents, MA Teachers Association Members, MA residents Sat. 10 am to noon, active military plus five family members, SNAP & EBT card holders plus five family members no charge. Closed major holidays. ♿
Attendance: 150,000 (estimated)

HARVARD MUSEUM OF NATURAL HISTORY, 26 Oxford St., Cambridge, MA 02138-2932. Tel.: 617-495-3045. Fax: 617-496-8206. Facebook.
E-mail: hmnh@hmsc.harvard.edu
Web Site: www.hmnh.harvard.edu
Key Personnel: Exec. Dir., Jane Pickering; Dir. Education, Wendy Derjue-Holzer; Dir. Public Programs, Diana Xochitl Munn; Dir. Exhibitions, Janis Sacco; Volunteer Coord., Carol Carlson; Dir. Communications, Timothy Letteney; Dir. Institutional Advancement, Susan Thompson; Dir. Operations, Kevin Ebert.
Institution Type/Description: Natural History Museum.
Hours & Admission Prices: Daily 9-5. Adults $15, senior citizens 65 & over $13, non-Harvard students & children 3-18 $10; discounts to AAM, ASTC & NEMA members; Harvard students with ID, members & children under 3 no charge. Closed New Year's Day; Thanksgiving; Christmas Eve & Day. ♿
Attendance: 237,000 (actual)

HARVARD SEMITIC MUSEUM, 6 Divinity Ave., Cambridge, MA 02138-2020. Tel.: 617-495-4631. Fax: 617-496-8904. Facebook.
E-mail: semiticm@fas.harvard.edu
Web Site: www.semiticmuseum.fas.harvard.edu
Key Personnel: Dir. & Cur., Dr. Peter Der Manuelian; Cur. Cuneiform Collections, Prof. Dr. Piotr Steinkeller; Deputy Dir., Dr. Joseph A. Greene; Asst. Cur. Collections, Dr. Adam J. Aja; Dir. Publication, Dr. M.D. Coogan.
Institution Type/Description: Archaeological Museum: specializing in ancient Near East archaeology.
Hours & Admission Prices: Sun.-Fri. 11-4. No charge. Closed holidays.
Attendance: 5,000 (estimated)

THE HARVARD UNIVERSITY HERBARIA, 22 Divinity Ave., Cambridge, MA 02138-2020. Tel.: 617-495-2365. Fax: 617-495-9484.
E-mail: huh-requests@oeb.harvard.edu
Web Site: www.huh.harvard.edu
Key Personnel: Dir. Herbaria, Charles Davis; Dir. Botany Libraries, Judith A. Warnement.
Institution Type/Description: Herbarium.

Hours & Admission Prices: Mon.-Fri. 9-5. Closed university holidays. ♿

LONGFELLOW HOUSE-WASHINGTON'S HEADQUARTERS NATIONAL HISTORIC SITE, 105 Brattle St., Cambridge, MA 02138-3499. Tel.: 617-876-4491. Fax: 617-497-8718.
Web Site: www.nps.gov/long
Key Personnel: Site Mgr., Beth Law; Supt., Myra Harrison; Archives Specialist, Christine Wirth; Collections Mgr., David Daly.
Institution Type/Description: Historic House & Site Museum: 1759 house, headquarters of George Washington, 1775-1776; later home of Henry Wadsworth Longfellow.
Hours & Admission Prices: May-Oct. Wed.-Sun. 10-4:30. No charge. National park passes honored. ♿
Attendance: 50,000 (actual)

MIT MUSEUM, 265 Massachusetts Ave., Cambridge, MA 02139-4307. Mailing Address: Bldg. N51, 265 Massachusetts Ave., Cambridge, MA 02139-4307. Tel.: 617-253-5927. Fax: 617-253-8994. Facebook: MIT Museum.
E-mail: museum@mit.edu
Web Site: mitmuseum.mit.edu
Key Personnel: Dir., John Durant; Chm. (V), Prof. Phillip Sharp; Assoc. Dir., Mary Leen; Mgr. Exhibitions, Emma Westling; Dir. Cambridge Science Festival, P.A. d'Arboloff; Dir. Programs, Brindha Muniappan; Dir. Galleries & Exhibitions, Ann Neumann; Visitor Svcs. Mgr., Patricia Lane; Cur. Hart Nautical Collections, Kurt Hasselbalch; Cur. Science & Technology Collections, Deborah Douglas, Ph.D.; Collections Mgr. & Registrar, Joan Parks-Whitlow; Cur. Architecture & Design, Gary van Zante.
Institution Type/Description: Science & Technology Museum.
Hours & Admission Prices: Main facility at 265 Massachusetts Ave.: daily 10-5. Adults $10, youth under 18, students & seniors $5; discounts to AAM, NEMA, MTA members, WGBH Ed. Org., Blue Star Museums Program, Bank of America Museums on U.S. Program; MIT Community members, children under 5, last Sun. Sept.-June, & evening programs with museum admission no charge. Hart Nautical Galleries: daily 10-5. No charge. Compton Gallery: daily 10-5. No charge. Closed holidays. ♿
Attendance: 150,000 (actual)

MOUNT AUBURN CEMETERY, 580 Mount Auburn St., Cambridge, MA 02138-5517. Tel.: 617-547-7105.
E-mail: info@mountauburn.org
Web Site: www.mountauburn.org
Institution Type/Description: Historic Site: founded in 1831. A National Historic Landmark.
Hours & Admission Prices: Cemetery: May-Sept. daily 8-7; Oct.-April daily 8-5; groups by appointment. Office: Mon.-Fri. 8:30-4:30, Sat. 8:30-4. No charge. ♿
Attendance: 200,000 (estimated)

MUSEUM OF COMPARATIVE ZOOLOGY, 26 Oxford St., Cambridge, MA 02138-2902. Tel.: 617-495-2460. Fax: 617-496-8308. Facebook: @MuseumofComparativeZoology.
E-mail: maja@oeb.harvard.edu
Web Site: www.mcz.harvard.edu
Key Personnel: Dir., James Hanken.
Institution Type/Description: Zoological Museum.
Hours & Admission Prices: see Harvard Museum of Natural History for hours & admission. ♿

PEABODY MUSEUM OF ARCHAEOLOGY & ETHNOLOGY, 11 Divinity Ave., Cambridge, MA 02138-2096. Tel.: 617-496-1027. Fax: 617-495-7535.
E-mail: pmae-ed@fas.harvard.edu
Web Site: www.peabody.harvard.edu
Key Personnel: Dir., Dr. Jeffrey Quilter; Deputy Dir. Administration, Catherine Cezeaux; Dir. Collections, Kara Schneiderman; Dir. Research & Collections Devel., Dr. Pamela Gerardi; Registrar, Dr. Viva Fisher; Cur. North American Ethnography, Dr. Irene Castle McLaughlin; Dir. Academic Partnerships & Museum Cur., Dr. Diana Loren; Cur. Osteology, Dr. Michele Morgan; Dir. Repatriation & Museum Cur., Dr. Patricia Capone; Head Conservator, T. Rose Holdcraft; Senior Collections Mgr., David DeBono Schafer; Bldg. Mgr., Eugene Ayres.
Institution Type/Description: Anthropology Museum.
Hours & Admission Prices: Daily 9-5. Adults $12, senior citizens 65 & over and college students $10, children 3-18 $8; children under 3, current Harvard students, Harvard Museums of Science & Culture members, and Harvard Art Museums members, AAM & ICOM members, MA residents on Sun. 9-12 & Sept.-May Wed. 3-5 no charge. Closed New Year's Day; Thanksgiving; Christmas Eve & Day. ♿
Attendance: 155,000 (estimated)

Canton

CANTON HISTORICAL SOCIETY, 1400 Washington St., Canton, MA 02021-2240. Tel.: 781-828-6957. Fax: 781-821-5780.
E-mail: historical@canton.org
Web Site: canton.org
Key Personnel: Pres., Wallis Gibbs.
Institution Type/Description: History Museum.
Hours & Admission Prices: Open select holidays & by request. No charge; donations accepted.
Attendance: 50

MILTON ART MUSEUM, 900 Randolph St., Canton, MA 02021-1355. Tel.: 508-588-9100, ext. 2124. Fax: 781-575-9428.
E-mail: info@miltonartmuseum.org
Web Site: www.miltonartmuseum.org
Key Personnel: Chm. (V), Ellyn Moller.
Institution Type/Description: Art Museum.
Hours & Admission Prices: Mon.-Thurs. 8-6:30, Fri. 8-4:30, Sat. 9-1. No charge; donations accepted. ♿
Attendance: 10,000 (estimated)

MUSEUM OF AMERICAN BIRD ART AT MASS AUDUBON, 963 Washington St., Canton, MA 02021-2117. Tel.: 781-821-8853.
E-mail: maba@massaudubon.org
Web Site: www.massaudubon.org/maba
Formerly: Mass Audubon Visual Arts Center
Key Personnel: Dir., Amy Montague.
Institution Type/Description: Art Museum & Nature Center
Hours & Admission Prices: Gallery: Tues.-Sun. 1-5. Trail: Tues.-Sun. 9-5. Adults $4, children & seniors $3; Mass Audubon members no charge.

Centerville

CENTERVILLE HISTORICAL MUSEUM, 513 Main St., Centerville, MA 02632-2913. Tel.: 508-775-0331. Fax: 508-862-9211.
E-mail: chsm@centervillehistoricalmuseum.org
Web Site: www.centervillehistoricalmuseum.org
Key Personnel: C.E.O., Cur. & Devel., Randall Hoel; Pres., Barbara Fahrenholz; Treas., Robyn Simmons.
Institution Type/Description: 19th century Cape Cod History Museum.
Hours & Admission Prices: Feb. 15-Dec. 15 Tues.-Sat. 12-4; other times by appointment. Adults $8, senior citizens & students $7; discounts to MTA members; members & children under 8 no charge. ♿
Attendance: 2,137 (actual)

Charlestown

BUNKER HILL MUSEUM, 43 Monument Sq., Charlestown, MA 02129-3430. Mailing Address: Boston National Historic Park, Charlestown Navy Yard, Charlestown, MA 02129-4543. Tel.: 617-242-7275.
E-mail: bost_rangers@nps.gov
Web Site: www.nps.gov/bost/historyculture/bhmuseum.htm
Key Personnel: Pres. & C.E.O. (V), Arthur L. Hurley; Chm. (V) & Museum Shop Mgr., Terry Savage.
Institution Type/Description: History Museum: located across from the Bunker Hill Monument grounds.
Hours & Admission Prices: Daily 9-5. No charge; donations accepted. Closed New Year's Day; Thanksgiving; Christmas.
Attendance: (estimated)

Chatham

ATWOOD HOUSE MUSEUM, HOME OF THE CHATHAM HISTORICAL SOCIETY, 347 Stage Harbor Rd., Chatham, MA 02633-2229. Mailing Address: P.O. Box 709, Chatham, MA 02633-0709. Tel.: 508-945-2493. Fax: 508-945-1205.
E-mail: info@chathamhistorical.org
Web Site: www.chathamhistoricalsociety.org
Key Personnel: Chm. (V), Steve Burlingame; Exec. Dir., Danielle Jeanloz; Museum Shop Mgr., Margaret Martin.
Institution Type/Description: Historical Museum: housed in 1752 Atwood House and additions.
Hours & Admission Prices: June-Sept. call for hours. Oct. Fri.-Sat. 1-4; open for special events throughout the year. Adults $10, students $5; discount to AAM members; members & children 6 & under no charge. Closed Independence Day; Labor Day. ♿
Attendance: 3,700 (actual)

Chester

CHESTER HISTORICAL SOCIETY, 15 Middlefield St., Chester, MA 01011.
E-mail: HistoricalSociety@chestermass.com
Institution Type/Description: Historical Society Museum: housed in the former jail; built in 1840.
Hours & Admission Prices: By appointment.

Chestnut Hill

LONGYEAR MUSEUM, 1125 Boylston St., Chestnut Hill, MA 02467-1811. Tel.: 617-278-9000. Fax: 617-278-9003.
E-mail: letters@longyear.org
Web Site: www.longyear.org
Key Personnel: Exec. Dir., Sandra J. Houston; Pres. (V), Ellen Williams; Dir. Collections, Cheryl Moneyhun.
Institution Type/Description: Historical Museum.
Hours & Admission Prices: Museum: Mon. & Thurs.-Sat. 10-4, Sun. 1-4. Historic Houses: call for hours. No charge; donations accepted. Closed holidays. ♿
Attendance: 6,000 (actual)

Clinton

MUSEUM OF RUSSIAN ICONS, 203 Union St., Clinton, MA 01510-2903. Tel.: 978-598-5000. Fax: 978-598-5009.
E-mail: info@museumofrussianicons.org
Web Site: www.museumofrussianicons.org
Key Personnel: Dir. & Chm. (V), Gordon B. Lankton; C.E.O., Kent Russell; Registrar, Laura Garrity-Arquitt; Museum Shop Mgr., Jocelyn Willis.
Institution Type/Description: Art Museum.
Hours & Admission Prices: Tues.-Sat. 11-4; groups by appointment. Adults $10; discounts to groups, veterans and NEMA & AAM members; members, students & children no charge. Closed New Year's Day; Independence Day; Thanksgiving; Christmas. ♿
Attendance: 16,000 (estimated)

Cohasset

CAPTAIN JOHN WILSON HOUSE, 4 Elm St., Cohasset, MA 02025-1829. Mailing Address: 106 S. Main St., P.O. Box 627, Cohasset, MA 02025-0627. Tel.: 781-383-1434.
E-mail: cohassethistory@yahoo.com
Web Site: www.cohassethistoricalsociety.org
Key Personnel: Pres., Kathleen O'Malley; Exec. Dir., Lynne DeGiacomo; Historian, Rebecca Bates-McArthur.
Institution Type/Description: Historic House Museum.
Hours & Admission Prices: June-Labor Day Wed.-Fri. 1-4, Sat. 10-2. No charge; donations accepted.
Attendance: 800 (estimated)

MARITIME MUSEUM - COHASSET HISTORICAL SOCIETY, 6 Elm St., Cohasset, MA 02025. Mailing Address: P.O. Box 627, Cohasset, MA 02025-0627. Tel.: 781-383-1434.
E-mail: cohassethistory@yahoo.com
Key Personnel: Pres., Kathleen O'Malley; Exec. Dir., Lynne DeGiacomo; Historian, Rebecca Bates-McArthur.
Institution Type/Description: Maritime Museum.
Hours & Admission Prices: Mid-June to Aug. Wed.-Fri. 1-4, Sat. 10-2. No charge; donations accepted.
Attendance: 800 (estimated)

OUR WORLD CHILDREN'S GLOBAL DISCOVERY MUSEUM, 100 Sohier St., Cohasset, MA 02025. Mailing Address: 20 Hobart Ln., Cohasset, MA 02025-1424. Tel.: 781-383-3198.
Institution Type/Description: Children's Museum.
Hours & Admission Prices: Tues.-Fri. 10-5, Sat. 10am-12pm. Admission $7. ♿

PRATT BUILDING - COHASSET HISTORICAL SOCIETY, 106 S. Main St., Cohasset, MA 02025-2097. Mailing Address: P.O. Box 627, Cohasset, MA 02025-0627. Tel.: 781-383-1434.
E-mail: cohassethistory@yahoo.com
Web Site: cohassethistoricalsociety.org
Key Personnel: Pres., Kathleen O'Malley; Exec. Dir., Lynne DeGiacomo; Historian, Rebecca Bates-McArthur.
Institution Type/Description: History Museum.
Hours & Admission Prices: Mon.-Fri. 10-4. No charge; donations accepted. ♿
Attendance: 1,500 (estimated)

SOUTH SHORE ART CENTER, 119 Ripley Rd., Cohasset, MA 02025-1744. Tel.: 781-383-2787. Fax: 781-383-2964.
E-mail: info@ssac.org
Web Site: www.ssac.org
Key Personnel: Dir., Sarah Hannan.
Institution Type/Description: Art Gallery.
Hours & Admission Prices: Mon.-Sat. 10-4, Sun. 12-4. No charge; donations accepted. &
Attendance: 12,000 (estimated)

Concord

CONCORD ART ASSOCIATION, 37 Lexington Rd., Concord, MA 01742-2570. Tel.: 978-369-2578. Fax: 978-371-2496. Facebook: Concord Art Association.
E-mail: katejames@concordart.org
Web Site: www.concordart.org
Key Personnel: Dir., Kate James; Chm. (V), Nancy Huggins.
Institution Type/Description: Art Gallery & Sculpture Garden: building built in 1760.
Hours & Admission Prices: Tues.-Sat. 10-4:30, Sun. 12-4. No charge; donations accepted. Closed holidays. &
Attendance: 8,500 (estimated)

CONCORD MUSEUM, Cambridge Turnpike, at Lexington Rd., Concord, MA 01742-3711. Mailing Address: P.O. Box 146, Concord, MA 01742-0146. Tel.: 978-369-9763. Fax: 978-369-9660. Facebook: Concord Museum.
E-mail: cm1@concordmuseum.org
Web Site: www.concordmuseum.org
Key Personnel: Pres. (V), Churchill Franklin; Dir., Margaret Burke; Cur., David Wood; Dir. Devel., Sue Gladstone; Public Rels., Emer McCourt; Museum Shop Mgr., Judy Flam.
Institution Type/Description: History & Decorative Arts Museum.
Hours & Admission Prices: Jan.-March Mon.-Sat. 11-4, Sun. 1-4; April-May & Sept.-Dec. Mon.-Sat. 9-5, Sun. 12-5; June-Aug. daily 9-5. Adults $10, senior citizens & students $8, children $5; discounts to AAM, AAA & MTA members; members no charge. &
Attendance: 40,000 (estimated)

LOUISA MAY ALCOTT'S ORCHARD HOUSE, 399 Lexington Rd., Concord, MA 01742-3712. Mailing Address: P.O. Box 343, Concord, MA 01742-0343. Tel.: 978-369-4118. Fax: 978-369-1367.
E-mail: info@louisamayalcott.org
Web Site: www.louisamayalcott.org
Key Personnel: Exec. Dir., Jan Turnquist; Pres. (V), Beth Neeley Kubacki; Museum Shop Mgr., Sally Cody; Exec. Asst., Maria Powers; Education Dir., Lis Adams; Bldg. & Grounds Supt., Jay Powers.
Institution Type/Description: History Museum: house where Louisa May Alcott wrote Little Women, and also the site of Bronson Alcott's School of Philosophy.
Hours & Admission Prices: April-Oct. Mon.-Sat. 10-4:30, Sun. 1-4:30; Nov.-March Mon.-Fri. 11-3, Sat. 10-4:30, Sun. 1-4:30. Adults $9, senior citizens 62 and over & college students with ID $8, youth 6-17 $5; discounts to families, military, teachers, AAM & MTA members; members & children under 6 no charge. Closed Easter; Thanksgiving; Christmas.
Attendance: 48,910 (actual)

MINUTE MAN NATIONAL HISTORICAL PARK, 174 Liberty St., Concord, MA 01742-1705. Tel.: 978-369-6993. Fax: 978-318-7800.
E-mail: mima_info@nps.gov
Web Site: www.nps.gov/mima
Key Personnel: Supt., BJ Dunn; Museum Tech., Steve Noth; Museum Shop Mgr., Elaine Lally.
Institution Type/Description: National Park & Historic Houses: located along 1775 Battle Road Trail; 19th-century Wayside, Nathaniel Hawthorne & Alcott & Lothrop family home.
Hours & Admission Prices: Park: daily sunrise to sunset. No charge; donations accepted. Wayside Historic Houses: late-June to Oct. call for hours. Admission $7. Closed New Year's Day; Thanksgiving; Christmas. &
Attendance: 1,000,000 (estimated)

THE OLD MANSE, 269 Monument St., Concord, MA 01742-1837. Mailing Address: P.O. Box 572, Concord, MA 01742-0572. Tel.: 978-369-3909. Fax: 978-287-6154.
E-mail: oldmanse@ttor.org
Web Site: www.thetrustees.org/places-to-visit/greater-boston/old-manse.html
Key Personnel: Historic Site Mgr., Tom Beardsley; Dir. Historic Resources, Susan C.S Edwards.

Institution Type/Description: Historic House & Site: built in 1770 for Rev. William Emerson, town minister & patriot; located next to the North Bridge, site of the 1st major skirmish of the Revolutionary War, April 19, 1775. Later home to Emerson's grandson, Ralph Waldo, who drafted his first published work, Nature, here; home of Nathaniel & Sophia Hawthorne 1842-45.
Hours & Admission Prices: mid-March to May & Nov.-Dec. Sat.-Sun. 12-5; Memorial Day to Oct. Tues.-Sun. 12-5; other times by appointment. Adults $8, senior citizens & students $7, children 6-12 $5; discounts for groups of 10 or more & for AAA, MTA & WGBH members; Trustees members & children under 6 no charge. &
Attendance: 11,400 (actual)

RALPH WALDO EMERSON HOUSE, 28 Cambridge Tpke., Concord, MA 01742-3700. Tel.: 978-369-2236.
E-mail: ss@jmforbes.org
Key Personnel: Pres., Mrs. Nicholas Bancroft; Dir., Marie A. Gordinier.
Institution Type/Description: Memorial Museum: housed in 1835 Ralph Waldo Emerson House. Ralph Waldo Emerson's home for the greater part of his life 1835 to his death in 1882.
Hours & Admission Prices: mid-April to Oct. Thurs.-Sat. 10-4:30, Sun. 1-4:30; group tours by appointment. Adults $9, seniors & students $7; discounts to groups & AAM members; children under 6 no charge.
Attendance: 3,454 (actual)

Cotuit

CAHOON MUSEUM OF AMERICAN ART, 4676 Falmouth Rd., Cotuit, MA 02635. Mailing Address: P.O. Box 1853, Cotuit, MA 02635-1853. Tel.: 508-428-7581. Fax: 508-420-3709.
E-mail: rwaterhouse@cahoonmuseum.org
Web Site: www.cahoonmuseum.org
Key Personnel: Pres., Carol Wilgus; Museum Shop Coord., Gwen Manloss.
Institution Type/Description: Art Museum: housed in 1775 Cape Cod Colonial tavern used for overnight stops on Hyannis-Sandwich Stagecoach line.
Hours & Admission Prices: Feb.-Dec. Tues.-Sat. 10-4, Sun. 1-4. Adults $8, seniors & students $6; discounts to teachers; members & children under 12 no charge. Closed major holidays. &
Attendance: 2,500 (actual)

COTUIT CENTER FOR THE ARTS, 4404 Falmouth Rd. (Rte. 28), Cotuit, MA 02635. Mailing Address: P.O. Box 2042, Cotuit, MA 02635. Tel.: 508-428-0669.
E-mail: info@cotuitcenterforthearts.org
Web Site: www.artsonthecape.org
Key Personnel: Dir., David Kuehn.
Institution Type/Description: Art Gallery.
Hours & Admission Prices: Memorial Day to Columbus Day Mon.-Sun. 10-4; Oct.-May Mon.-Sat. 10-4. Gallery: no charge; donations accepted. Special Events: call for admission prices. Closed major holidays. &
Attendance: 30,000 (estimated)

HISTORICAL SOCIETY OF SANTUIT AND COTUIT, 1148 Main St., Cotuit, MA 02635. Mailing Address: P.O. Box 1484, Cotuit, MA 02635-1484. Tel.: 508-428-0461. Facebook: Historical Society of Santuit and Cotuit.
E-mail: info@cotuithistoricalsociety.org
Web Site: www.cotuithistoricalsociety.org
Key Personnel: Pres., Victoria Vieira; Vice Pres., Beth Johnson; Treas., Cindy Capaccioli; Sec., Lorri Devlin; Admin., T.C. Carter; Museum Shop Mgr., Melanie Curtis.
Institution Type/Description: Historic House: 1800-1850 restored home of village carpenter, Dotridge Homestead; Cotuit Museum; William Morse Fire Museum; Rothwell Ice House.
Hours & Admission Prices: Memorial Day to Christmas Fri.-Sun. 1-5. No charge; donations accepted.
Attendance: 5,000 (estimated)

Cummington

KINGMAN TAVERN HISTORICAL MUSEUM, 41 Main St., Cummington, MA 01026-9742. Mailing Address: P.O. Box 10, Cummington, MA 01026-0010. Tel.: 413-634-5527 & 8828 (administrative).
E-mail: cummington1779@gmail.com
Web Site: hiddenhills.com/kingmantavern/
Key Personnel: Chm. (V), Carla Ness; Historic Commission, Stephanie Pasternak; Historic Commission, Stephen Howes; Historic Commission, Matthew Grallert; Historic Commission, Karen Westergaard.
Institution Type/Description: Historical Museum: housed in 1800 frame building used as a post office, Masonic Lodge meeting hall & tavern.

Hours & Admission Prices: Aug. Sat. 2-5; other times by appointment. No charge; donations accepted. &
Attendance: 150 (estimated)

WILLIAM CULLEN BRYANT HOMESTEAD, 205 Bryant Rd., Cummington, MA 01026-9639. Tel.: 413-532-1631, ext. 3110.
E-mail: bryanthomestead@thetrustees.org
Web Site: www.thetrustees.org
Key Personnel: Supt., Jim Caffrey.
Institution Type/Description: Historic House: 1789 boyhood home & adult summer residence of famed poet William Cullen Bryant.
Hours & Admission Prices: Tours: Spring to Fall by appointment. See website for information. Member discounts. &
Attendance: 800 (estimated)

Dalton

CRANE MUSEUM OF PAPERMAKING, Housatonic St. off Rte. 8 & 9, Dalton, MA 01226. Mailing Address: c/o Crane & Co., Inc., 30 South St., Dalton, MA 01226-1751. Tel.: 413-684-6481. Fax: 413-684-0817.
E-mail: mediarelations@crane.com
Web Site: www.crane.com
Institution Type/Description: Historic Building: housed in the former papermaking business of Crane and Co.'s Old Stone Mill, built in 1844. Crane produces the rag paper that US currency is printed on.
Hours & Admission Prices: May to mid-Oct. Mon.-Fri. 1-5; mid-Oct. to April Tues.-Thurs. 1-5. No charge.
Attendance: 1,000 (estimated)

Danvers

DANVERS ARCHIVAL CENTER, 15 Sylvan St., Danvers, MA 01923-2735. Tel.: 978-774-0554. Fax: 978-762-0251.
E-mail: trask@noblenet.org
Web Site: www.danverslibrary.org/archive
Key Personnel: Town Archivist, Richard B. Trask.
Institution Type/Description: Town Archives: housed in 1892, Peabody Institute Library.
Hours & Admission Prices: Mon. 1-7:30, Wed.-Thurs. & 1st. Sat. of month 9-12 & 1-5; 2nd & 4th Fri. of month 1-5. No charge. Closed state & national holidays. &
Attendance: 1,200 (estimated)

DANVERS HISTORICAL SOCIETY, 11 Page St., Danvers, MA 01923-2813. Mailing Address: Box 381, Danvers, MA 01923-0681. Tel.: 978-777-1666. Fax: 978-777-5028.
E-mail: dhs@danvershistory.org
Web Site: www.danvershistory.org
Key Personnel: Dir. Operations, Catherine Gareri; Devel. Coord., Laura Cilley.
Institution Type/Description: Historical Society Museum.
Hours & Admission Prices: Society: Mon.-Fri. 9-1; other times by appointment. Donations accepted. Glen Magna & McIntyre Tea House: June-Labor Day Tues. & Thurs. 10-4; other times by appointment. Adults $5. &
Attendance: 11,500 (estimated)

REBECCA NURSE HOMESTEAD, 149 Pine St., Danvers, MA 01923-2693. Mailing Address: P.O. Box 456, Hathorne, MA 01937-0456. Tel.: 978-774-8799.
E-mail: president@rebeccanurse.org
Web Site: www.rebeccanurse.org
Key Personnel: Pres. & Bd. Chm., Marta Driscoll; Vice Pres., Jackson Tingle; Treas., William Quilnan; Clerk, Niamh Dolan; Bldg. Chm., Henry W. Rutkowski; Cur., Kathryn P. Rutkowski; Museum Shop Mgr., Candice Clemenzi.
Institution Type/Description: Historic House: 1678 home of Rebecca Nurse, hanged as a witch in 1692.
Hours & Admission Prices: June 15 to Labor Day Fri.-Sun. 10-4; Sept.-Oct. Sat.-Sun. 10-4; other times by appointment. Adults $6.50, seniors $5, children under 16 $4.50; discount to school groups; members no charge.
Attendance: 4,000 (estimated)

Dartmouth

LLOYD CENTER FOR THE ENVIRONMENT, 430 Potomska Rd., Dartmouth, MA 02748. Tel.: 508-990-0505. Fax: 508-993-7868. Facebook: Lloyd Center for the Environment.
E-mail: fcallen@lloydcenter.org
Web Site: www.lloydcenter.org
Key Personnel: Exec. Dir., Rachel L. Stronach.

Institution Type/Description: Nature Center.
Hours & Admission Prices: June-Sept. Tues.-Sun. 10-4; Oct.-May Tues.-Sat. 10-4. No charge; donations accepted.
Attendance: 30,000 (estimated)

Dedham

DEDHAM HISTORICAL SOCIETY MUSEUM, 612 High St., Dedham, MA 02026-1833. Mailing Address: P.O. Box 215, Dedham, MA 02027-0215. Tel.: 781-326-1385.
E-mail: society@dedhamhistorical.org
Web Site: dedhamhistorical.org
Key Personnel: Exec. Dir., Vicky L. Kruckeberg.
Institution Type/Description: History Museum & Genealogy Library.
Hours & Admission Prices: Office: Tues.-Fri. 9-4. Museum: Tues.-Fri. 12-4, even dated Sat. 1-4. Museum: adults $2; DHS, NEMA, ICOM & AAM members no charge. Library: Tues. & Thurs. by appointment 9-4, even dated Sat. 1-4 by appointment. Library: call for fees. Closed state & national holidays; Thanksgiving & day after; Christmas week.
Attendance: 2,000 (estimated)

FAIRBANKS HOUSE, 511 East St., Dedham, MA 02026-3060. Tel.: 781-326-1170. Fax: 781-326-2147. Facebook: The Fairbanks House; Twitter @fairbanks_house.
E-mail: homestead@fairbankshouse.org
Web Site: www.fairbankshouse.org
Key Personnel: Pres., Tina Blood; Treas., Lynn Fairbank; Business Mgr., Leslie Griesmer; Cur., Daniel Neff.
Institution Type/Description: Historic House: c.1637-1641 home built for Jonathan & Grace Fairbanks and their family.
Hours & Admission Prices: May-Oct. Wed.-Sun. 10-5. Tours begin on the hour 10-4. Family $35, adults $12, seniors $10, children 6-12 $6; discounts to AAM, AAA, MTA & NEMA members; members no charge.
Attendance: 3,000 (actual)

Deerfield

HISTORIC DEERFIELD, INC., 84B Old Main St., Deerfield, MA 01342. Mailing Address: P.O. Box 321, Deerfield, MA 01342-0321. Tel.: 413-774-5581. Fax: 413-775-7220.
E-mail: tours@historic-deerfield.org
Web Site: www.historic-deerfield.org
Key Personnel: Pres., Philip Zea; Chm. (V), Anne K. Groves; Vice Pres. Museum Affairs, Anne Digan Lanning; Chm. Curatorial Dept., Amanda E. Lange; Public Historian, Barbara Mathews; Vice Pres. Business Affairs, Susan Martinelli; Dir. Museum Education & Interpretation, Amanda Rivera Lopez; Librarian, David C. Bosse; Museum Shop Mgr., Tina Harding; Supt. Properties Maintenance, George Holmes.
Institution Type/Description: Outdoor History Museum Village: consisting of 14 18th & 19th-century structures.
Hours & Admission Prices: April 17-Nov. 28 daily 9:30-4:30. Flynt Center of Early New England Life: Jan.-March Sat.-Sun. Adults $12, children $5; discounts to groups of 20 or more with reservations & AAM members; members no charge. Closed Thanksgiving; Christmas Eve & Day. &
Attendance: 30,000 (estimated)

MEMORIAL HALL MUSEUM, POCUMTUCK VALLEY MEMORIAL ASSOC., 8 Memorial St., Deerfield, MA 01342. Mailing Address: Box 428, Deerfield, MA 01342-0428. Tel.: 413-774-7476, ext. 10. Fax: 413-774-5400.
E-mail: tneumann@deerfield.history.museum
Web Site: www.deerfield-ma.org
Key Personnel: Dir. & C.E.O., Timothy C. Neumann; Dir. Youth Programs, Lynne Manring; Pres. (V), Carol Letson; Cur., Suzanne Flynt; Librarian, David Bosse; Museum Shop Mgr., Tom Mershon.
Institution Type/Description: History & Decorative Arts Museum: housed in 1798 Deerfield Academy Building.
Hours & Admission Prices: May Sat.-Sun. 10:30-4:30; June-Oct. Tues.-Sun. 11-4:30. Adults $6, children & students 6-21 $3; discounts to museum employees, MA Teachers, NEMA & AAM members; members no charge. Library: call for hours. &
Attendance: 52,292 (actual)

Dennis

CAPE COD MUSEUM OF ART, 60 Hope Ln., off Rte. 6A, Dennis, MA 02638. Mailing Address: P.O. Box 2034, Dennis, MA 02638-5034. Tel.: 508-385-4477. Fax: 508-385-7933.
E-mail: info@ccmoa.org
Web Site: www.ccmoa.org
Formerly: Cape Museum of Fine Arts, Inc.

Key Personnel: Dir., Edith A. Tonelli,
Institution Type/Description: Art Museum & Center.
Hours & Admission Prices: Memorial Day to Columbus Day Mon.-Wed. & Fri.-Sat. 10-5, Thurs. 10-8, Sun. 12-5; Oct.-May Tues.-Wed. & Fri.-Sat. 10-5, Thurs. 10-8, Sun. 12-5. Adults $8; discounts to groups & AAM, ICOM, MASS. Teacher's Assoc., New England Consortium of Art Museums, & WGBH members; children & members no charge. Thurs. by donation. Closed New Year's Day; Thanksgiving; Christmas. &
Attendance: 29,961 (actual)

DENNIS HISTORICAL SOCIETY - 1736 JOSIAH DENNIS MANSE MUSEUM, 77 Nobscusset Rd., Dennis, MA 02638. Mailing Address: P.O. Box 705, Dennis, MA 02638. Tel.: 508-385-2232.

E-mail: info@dennishistoricalsociety.org
Web Site: www.dennishistoricalsociety.org
Key Personnel: Chm. (V), Nancy Howes.
Institution Type/Description: Historical Society Museum: housed in the former home of Rev. Josiah Dennis, for whom the town was named; built in 1736. Listed on the National Register of Historic Places.
Hours & Admission Prices: Call for hours. No charge; donations accepted. &
Attendance: 1,900 (actual)

Dover

CARYL HOUSE AND FISHER BARN, 107 Dedham St., Dover, MA 02030-2223. Mailing Address: P.O. Box 534, Dover, MA 02030-0534. Tel.: 508-785-1832. Fax: 508-785-0789.

E-mail: info@doverhistoricalsociety.org
Web Site: www.doverhistoricalsociety.org
Key Personnel: Dir., Elisha F. Lee, Jr.; Vice Pres., Jack Hoehlein.
Institution Type/Description: Historic House: built c.1777.
Hours & Admission Prices: April-June & Sept.-Nov. Sat. 1-4; other times by appointment. No charge; donations accepted. Closed Sat. holidays.
Attendance: 500 (estimated)

DOVER HISTORICAL SOCIETY - SAWIN MUSEUM, 80 Dedham St., Dover, MA 02030. Mailing Address: P.O. Box 534, Dover, MA 02030-0534. Tel.: 508-785-1832.

E-mail: janetcomiskey@comcast.net
Web Site: doverhistoricalsociety.org
Key Personnel: Pres., Elisha Lee; Vice Pres., Jack Hoehlein; Cur. Sawin, Fay Bacher; Cur. Caryl, Janet Comiskey; Cur. Barn, Richard White.
Institution Type/Description: Historical Society Museum.
Hours & Admission Prices: April-June & Sept.-Nov. Sat. 1-4 & by appointment. No charge; donations accepted. Closed Sat. holidays.
Attendance: 200 (estimated)

Duxbury

ALDEN HOUSE HISTORIC SITE, 105 Alden St., Duxbury, MA 02332. Mailing Address: P.O. Box 2754, Duxbury, MA 02331-2754. Tel.: 781-934-9092. Fax: 781-934-9149. Facebook: Alden House Historic Site.

E-mail: dmobed@alden.org
Web Site: www.alden.org
Formerly: Alden House Museum
Key Personnel: Dir., Desiree Mobed; Pres. (V), Pauline Kezer.
Institution Type/Description: Historic House Museum: homestead of Pilgrims John Alden and Priscilla Mullins.
Hours & Admission Prices: June to mid-Oct. Wed.-Sat. 12-4; other times by appointment. Adults $8, children 3-17 $5; members no charge. &
Attendance: 1,506 (actual)

THE ART COMPLEX MUSEUM, 189 Alden St., Duxbury, MA 02332-3801. Mailing Address: P.O. Box 2814, Duxbury, MA 02331-2814. Tel.: 781-934-6634. Fax: 781-934-5117. Facebook.

E-mail: info@artcomplex.org
Web Site: www.artcomplex.org
Key Personnel: Dir. & C.E.O., Charles A. Weyerhaeuser; Collections Mgr., Maureen Wengler; Education Coord., Sally Dean Mello; Communications Coord., Laura Doherty; Community Coord., Doris Collins; Grounds & Maintenance, William Thomas; Preparator, Sue Aygarn-Kowalski; Contemporary Cur., Craig Bloodgood; Asian Cons., Alice Hyland; Asst. Collections Mgr., Kyle Turner; Librarian, Cheryl O'Neill; Mgr. Operations, Mary Curran.
Institution Type/Description: Art Museum.
Hours & Admission Prices: Wed.-Sun. 1-4. No charge; donations accepted. Closed legal holidays. &
Attendance: 10,000 (estimated)

DUXBURY RURAL AND HISTORICAL SOCIETY, INC., 479 Washington St., Duxbury, MA 02331. Mailing Address: P.O. Box 2865, Duxbury, MA 02331-2865. Tel.: 781-934-6106. Fax: 781-934-5730. Facebook: Duxbury Rural and Historical Society.

E-mail: colson@duxburyhistory.org
Web Site: www.duxburyhistory.org
Key Personnel: Pres. (V) Bd., Christopher Sherman; Exec. Dir., Erin McGough.
Institution Type/Description: Historical Society Museum: housed in the Nathaniel Winsor, Jr. House; built in 1807.
Hours & Admission Prices: Winsor House & Office: Mon.-Fri. 9-4; call to confirm. No charge. King Caesar House & Bradford Houses: summer & by appointment. Adults $5, seniors & students $3; children under 6, AAM, NEMA, & museum members no charge. Drew Library: Mon.-Fri. 9-1. Closed holidays.
Attendance: 15,000 (estimated)

East Sandwich

THORNTON W. BURGESS SOCIETY GREEN BRIAR NATURE CENTER AND JAM KITCHEN, 6 Discovery Hill Rd., East Sandwich, MA 02537. Tel.: 508-888-6870. Fax: 508-888-1919.

E-mail: info@thorntonburgess.org
Web Site: www.thorntonburgess.org
Formerly: Thornton W. Burgess Museum
Key Personnel: Exec. Dir., Gene A. Schott; Pres. (V), Wendy Maggio.
Institution Type/Description: History Museum, Nature Center & Jam Kitchen: housed in 1780 Nye House.
Hours & Admission Prices: Jan.-April Tues.-Sat. 10-4; May-Dec. Mon.-Sat. 10-4, Sun. 12-4. No charge; donations accepted. &
Attendance: 40,000 (estimated)

East Taunton

BEER CAN MUSEUM & BEER CAN HALL OF FAME, East Taunton, MA Facebook; Twitter; Instagram.

E-mail: beercanmuseum@gmail.com
Web Site: www.beercanmuseum.org
Key Personnel: Owner & Cur., Kevin Logan.
Institution Type/Description: Beer Can Museum
Hours & Admission Prices: By appointment.

Easthampton

MASSACHUSETTS AUDUBON AT CONNECTICUT RIVER VALLEY SANCTUARIES, 127 Combs Rd., Easthampton, MA 01027-9704. Tel.: 413-584-3009, ext. 12. Fax: 413-584-0250.

E-mail: mshanley@massaudubon.org
Web Site: www.massaudubon.org
Formerly: Massachusetts Audubon at Hampshire Sanctuaries
Key Personnel: Dir., Jonah Keane; Chm., Janet Bissel.
Institution Type/Description: Nature Center & Wildlife Sanctuary.
Hours & Admission Prices: Office: Mon.-Fri. 8:30-12:30. Grounds: Tues.-Sun. dawn-dusk. Adults $4, children 3-15 & senior citizens $3; members & children under 3 no charge. &
Attendance: 20,000 (estimated)

Edgartown

FELIX NECK WILDLIFE SANCTUARY, 100 Felix Neck Dr., Edgartown, MA 02539. Mailing Address: P.O. Box 494, Vineyard Haven, MA 02568-0494. Tel.: 508-627-4850.

E-mail: felixneck@massaudubon.org
Web Site: www.massaudubon.org
Institution Type/Description: Wildlife Sanctuary.
Hours & Admission Prices: Nature Center: Mon.-Sat. 9-4, Sun. 10-3; call for off-season hours. Trails: daily dawn to dusk. Adults $4, seniors & children 2-12 $3.

GUS BEN DAVID'S WORLD OF REPTILES AND BIRDS PARK, Batchedler Rd., Edgartown, MA 02539. Mailing Address: P.O. Box 1055, Oak Bluffs, MA 02557. Tel.: 508-627-5634.

Key Personnel: Dir., Gus Ben David.
Institution Type/Description: Nature Park.
Hours & Admission Prices: Tues.-Sun. 10-3. Admission: $5 per person.

MARTHA'S VINEYARD MUSEUM, 59 School St., Edgartown, MA 02539. Mailing Address: P.O. Box 1310, Edgartown, MA 02539-1310. Tel.: 508-627-4441. Fax: 508-627-4436.

E-mail: frontdesk@mvmuseum.org
Web Site: www.mvmuseum.org

Formerly: Martha's Vineyard Historical Society
Key Personnel: C.E.O. & Dir., David Nathans; Chm. (V) & Pres. (V), Sheldon Hackney; Chief Cur., Bonnie Stacy; Asst. Cur., Anna Carringer; Genealogist, Catherine M. Mayhew; Dir. Devel., Noelle Colome; Education Dir., Nancy Cole; Asst. Mgr. Devel. & Membership Svcs., Jessica Barken; Dir. Finance & Museum Shop Mgr., Betsey Mayhew; Administrative Coord., Chris Bahara; Cur. Oral History, Linsey Lee.
Institution Type/Description: History Museum.
Hours & Admission Prices: Fall & Spring: Mon.-Sat. 10-4; Summer: Mon.-Sat. 10-5. Winter: adults $6, seniors $5, children 6-15 $4; discounts to Blue Star Museum & AAM members; children under 6 & members no charge. Summer: adults $7, seniors $6, children 6-15 $4; children under 6 & members no charge. Closed major holidays. &
Attendance: 5,000 (estimated)

Essex

COGSWELL'S GRANT, 60 Spring St., Essex, MA 01929-1308. Mailing Address: Historic New England, 141 Cambridge St., Boston, MA 02130. Tel.: 978-768-3632. Facebook: Cogswells Grant.
E-mail: cogswellsgrant@historicnewengland.org
Web Site: www.historicnewengland.org
Key Personnel: Pres. & C.E.O., Carl R. Nold; Site Mgr., Kristen Weiss.
Institution Type/Description: Historic House Museum: housed in an 18th century farmhouse used by American folk art collectors Bertram and Nina Fletcher Little as their summer home.
Hours & Admission Prices: June to Oct. 15 Wed.-Sun. 11-4. Adults $10; discounts to ICOM, AAA, AAM & WGBH members; members no charge.
Attendance: 6,418 (actual)

ESSEX SHIPBUILDING MUSEUM, 66 Main St., Essex, MA 01929-1343. Mailing Address: P.O. Box 277, Essex, MA 01929-0005. Tel.: 978-768-7541. Facebook: Essex Shipbuilding Museum.
E-mail: info@essexshipbuildingmuseum.org
Web Site: www.essexshipbuildingmuseum.org
Key Personnel: Pres., Lee Spence; Treas., Sarah Willwerth-Dyer; Coord. Education, Nancy Dudley.
Institution Type/Description: Shipbuilding Museum: housed in 1835 schoolhouse, 1840's hearse house & Maritime History Museum; Historic Site: 1680-1860 burying ground; old Story Yard site where A.D. Story launched 397 fishing schooners.
Hours & Admission Prices: Call for hours. Adults $7, senior citizens $6, children $5; children under 6 & members no charge. &
Attendance: 7,000 (estimated)

Fall River

FALL RIVER HISTORICAL SOCIETY AND BORDEN MURDER MYSTERY MUSEUM, 451 Rock St., Fall River, MA 02720-3398. Tel.: 508-679-1071. Fax: 508-675-5754.
E-mail: curator@lizzieborden.org
Web Site: www.lizzieborden.org
Key Personnel: Cur., Michael Martins; Pres. (V), Jay Lambert; Asst. Cur., Dennis Binette.
Institution Type/Description: Historical Society Museum: housed in 1843 Granite House, used as underground railroad station c.1843-1860s.
Hours & Admission Prices: May & Oct. Tues.-Fri. 9-4; June-Sept. Tues.-Fri. 9-4, Sat.-Sun. 1-4:30. Adults $8, children 6-14 $6; discount to groups; children under 6 & members no charge. Closed holidays.
Attendance: 14,520 (actual)

GRIMSHAW-GUDEWICZ ART GALLERY, Jackson Art Center, Bristol Community College, 777 Elsbree St., Fall River, MA 02720-7307. Tel.: 508-678-2811, ext. 2439. Fax: 508-730-3285.
E-mail: kathleen.hancock@bristolcc.edu
Web Site: www.bristol.mass.edu/gallery
Key Personnel: Dir., Kathleen Hancock.
Institution Type/Description: Art Gallery.
Hours & Admission Prices: Mon., Wed. & Sat. 1-4, Tues. & Thurs.-Fri. 10-1. No charge.

MARINE MUSEUM AT FALL RIVER, 70 Water St., Fall River, MA 02721-1598. Tel.: 508-674-3533. Fax: 508-674-3534.
E-mail: director@marinemuseumfr.org
Web Site: marinemuseumfr.org
Key Personnel: Chm. Bd., Dr. Robert Lawrence; Dir., Maria Vann; Vice Chm., Stewart Kusinitz; Treas., Pamela W. Prescott.
Institution Type/Description: Marine Museum: housed in restored textile mill machine shop.

Hours & Admission Prices: Wed.-Sat. 10-3. Adults $8, senior citizens, children 6-12 & groups $6, family $25; discounts to groups or 20 or more; members no charge. Closed New Year's Day; Martin Luther King Jr. Day; Presidents' Day; Memorial Day; Independence Day; Labor Day; Columbus Day; Veterans Day; Thanksgiving; Christmas. &
Attendance: 7,000 (estimated)

OLD COLONY & FALL RIVER RAILROAD MUSEUM, 2 Water St. at Battleship Cove, Fall River, MA 02720. Mailing Address: P.O. Box 3455, Fall River, MA 02722-3455. Tel.: 508-674-9340. Fax: 508-678-1220. Facebook: Old Colony and FR Railroad Museum.
E-mail: railroadjc@aol.com
Web Site: www.ocandfrrailroadmuseum.com
Key Personnel: Pres. (V), Jay Chatterton.
Institution Type/Description: Railroad Museum.
Hours & Admission Prices: May to Sept. 13 Sat.-Sun. 12-4. Adults $3, senior citizens 65 & over $2.50, children 5-12 $1.50; members & children under 5 no charge.
Attendance: 450 (actual)

USS MASSACHUSETTS MEMORIAL COMMITTEE, INC., Battleship Cove, 5 Water St., Fall River, MA 02721-1540. Mailing Address: Battleship Cove, 5 Water St., P.O. Box 111, Fall River, MA 02722-0111. Tel.: 508-678-1100 & 1905, 800-533-3194. Fax: 508-674-5597.
E-mail: battleship@battleshipcove.org
Web Site: battleshipcove.org
Formerly: Battleship Massachusetts
Key Personnel: Exec. Dir., Bradley M. King; Pres. (V), Carl F. Sawejko; Dir. Finance, David W. Keyes; Cur., Christopher J. Nardi; Museum Shop Mgr., Sharon Michaud.
Institution Type/Description: Historic Ships Museum.
Hours & Admission Prices: April-Oct. daily 9-5; Nov.-March Fri.-Sun. 9-4. Adults $25, senior citizens & military veterans w/ID $23, children 4-12 $15; active duty military w/ID & children 3 & under no charge. Closed New Year's Day; Thanksgiving; Christmas.
Attendance: 78,259 (actual)

Falmouth

FALMOUTH MUSEUMS ON THE GREEN, 55-65 Palmer Ave., Falmouth, MA 02540. Mailing Address: P.O. Box 174, Falmouth, MA 02541-0174. Tel.: 508-548-4857. Facebook, Twitter, Instagram: Falmouth Museums on the Green.
E-mail: mark@museumsonthegreen.org
Web Site: museumsonthegreen.org
Formerly: Falmouth Historical Society
Key Personnel: Exec. Dir., Mark A. Schmidt; Pres., Rocco Maffei; Mgr. Mktg., Sarah Murphy; Mgr. Events, Carolyn Tarr; Mgr. Research, Meg Costello; Mgr. Collections, Jennifer Krumfolz.
Institution Type/Description: Historical Society Museum.
Hours & Admission Prices: Memorial Day to Columbus Day Tues.-Fri. 11-4, Sat. 11-2; other times by appointment. Adults $5; discounts to AAM, MTA & NEMA members; children 13 & under, members & Falmouth residents on Fri. no charge. &
Attendance: 12,500 (estimated)

Fitchburg

FITCHBURG ART MUSEUM, 185 Elm St., Fitchburg, MA 01420. Tel.: 978-345-4207. Fax: 978-345-2319. Facebook: Fitchburg Art Museum.
E-mail: info@fitchburgartmuseum.org
Web Site: www.fitchburgartmuseum.org
Key Personnel: Dir., Nick Capasso; Pres. Bd., Annelisa Addante; Dir. Corp. Member Svcs., Jane Keough; Devel. Assoc., Jessie Olson; Dir. Education, Laura Howick; Dir. Mktg. & Community Rels., Kledia Spiro; Dir. Docents, Ann Descoteaux; Cur., Mary Tinti; Business Mgr., Sheryl Demers.
Institution Type/Description: Art Museum.
Hours & Admission Prices: Wed.-Fri. 12-4, Sat.-Sun. 11-5. Adults $9, senior citizens & students $5; discount to AAA & AAM members; active military & their families and members no charge. Closed major holidays. &
Attendance: 15,000 (estimated)

FITCHBURG HISTORICAL SOCIETY, 781 Main St., Fitchburg, MA 01420-3116. Mailing Address: P.O. Box 953, Fitchburg, MA 01420-0009. Tel.: 978-345-1157.
E-mail: fitchburghistoricalsociety@fitchburghistoricalsociety.com
Web Site: www.fitchburghistoricalsociety.org

Key Personnel: Dir., Susan Navarre; Chm. & Pres. (V), Jay Bry; Museum Shop Mgr., Daniel Fish.
Institution Type/Description: Local History Museum.
Hours & Admission Prices: Mon.-Tues. 10-4, Wed. 10-6. Historical Society: no charge; donations accepted. Research Library: $10; students & members no charge. Closed holidays. &
Attendance: 12,000 (estimated)

TOP FUN AVIATION TOY MUSEUM, 21 Pritchard St., Fitchburg, MA 02140. Mailing Address: P.O. Box 700, Dracut, MA 01826. Tel.: 978-342-2809.
E-mail: topfunaviation@verizon.net
Web Site: www.topfunaviation.com
Institution Type/Description: Children's Museum.
Hours & Admission Prices: Sat. 10:30-4:30, Sun. 1:30-4:30. Adults $5, youth 14-18 $4, children 3-14 $3; discounts to groups; children under 3 no charge.

Framingham

DANFORTH MUSEUM OF ART, 123 Union Ave., Framingham, MA 01702-8291. Tel.: 508-620-0050. Fax: 508-872-5542.
E-mail: dhagan@danforthmuseum.org
Web Site: www.danforthmuseum.org
Key Personnel: Pres. Bd. (V), Robert Martin; Dir., Katherine French; Dir. Finance & Operations, Mary Kiely; Museum School Mgr., Ashley Ocching; Museum School Registrar, Catherine Sullivan; Dir. Education, Pat Walker; Membership & Mktg. Asst., Chelsea Long; Mktg. & Communications Dir., Debbie Hagan.
Institution Type/Description: Art Museum & School.
Hours & Admission Prices: Wed.-Thurs. & Sun. 12-5, Fri.-Sat. 10-5. Adults $11, seniors $9, students $8; discounts to AAM, ICOM & NEMA members; children under 17 & members no charge. &
Attendance: 30,000 (estimated)

FRAMINGHAM HISTORY CENTER, 16 Vernon St., Framingham, MA 01701-4783. Mailing Address: P.O. Box 2032, Framingham, MA 01703-2032. Tel.: 508-872-3780. Fax: 508-872-3780.
E-mail: info@framinghamhistory.org
Web Site: www.framinghamhistory.org
Formerly: Framingham Historical Society & Museum
Key Personnel: Exec. Dir., Anne Murphy; Pres. (V), Kevin Swope; Cur., Dana Dauterman Ricciardi, Ph.D.; Program & Devel. Coord., Jennifer Toth; Museum Asst., Jane Whiting.
Institution Type/Description: American History Museum.
Hours & Admission Prices: Academy: by appointment. Edgell Memorial Library: Wed.-Sat. 1-4. No charge; donations accepted.
Attendance: 6,140 (actual)

GARDEN IN THE WOODS OF THE NEW ENGLAND WILD FLOWER SOCIETY, 180 Hemenway Rd., Framingham, MA 01701-2699. Tel.: 508-877-7630, ext. 0; 508-877-6553 (TTY). Fax: 508-877-3658.
E-mail: information@newenglandwild.org
Web Site: www.newenglandwild.org
Key Personnel: Exec. Dir., Debbi Edelstein; Chm. (V), Deirdre C. Menoyo; Dir. Education, Bonnie Drexler; Dir. Horticulture, Mark Richardson; Dir. Conservation, William Brumback; Dir. Philanthropy, Tracey Willmott; Retail Mgr., Noni Macon.
Institution Type/Description: Botanical Garden.
Hours & Admission Prices: April 15-July 3 Tues.-Wed., Sat.-Sun. & holiday Mon. 9-5, Thurs. 8-8; July 4-Oct. Tues.-Sun. & holiday Mon. 9-5. Guided Walking Tours: Tues.-Fri. 10 am, Sat.-Sun. 2 pm; tours by appointment. Adults $10, senior citizens 65 & over $7, youth 3-17 $5; members & children under 3 no charge. &
Attendance: 20,000 (estimated)

Gardner

THE GARDNER MUSEUM, INC., 28 Pearl St., Gardner, MA 01440-2308. Tel.: 978-632-3277. Facebook: The Gardner Museum.
E-mail: info@gardnermuseuminc.com
Web Site: www.gardnermuseuminc.com
Key Personnel: Pres., Scott Huntoon; Pres. Elect, Michael Gerry; Coord., Marion Knoll; Treas., Robert Venning; Asst. Treas., Thomas Mailloux; Historian, Robert Treptow; Recording Sec., Janet Stankaitis; Corresponding Sec., Jan Korhonen.
Institution Type/Description: Local History Museum: housed in 1886 Richardson Romanesque brick building.

Hours & Admission Prices: March-Dec. Wed.-Sun. 1-4. Adults $3; AASLH, GAAMHA & museum members no charge. Closed occasional holidays. &
Attendance: 3,000 (estimated)

Georgetown

BROCKLEBANK MUSEUM, 108 E. Main St., Georgetown, MA 01833-2104. Mailing Address: Georgetown Historical Society, P. O. Box 376, Georgetown, MA 01833.
E-mail: info@georgetownhistoricalsociety.com
Web Site: www.georgetownhistoricalsociety.com
Key Personnel: Pres., Christine Comiskey; Cur., Karen Brockelbank.
Institution Type/Description: Historic House: built in the late 1600s.
Hours & Admission Prices: late June to Columbus Day Sun. 2-5; other times by appointment. Adults $5, seniors 65 & over and students $3.

Gloucester

BEAUPORT, SLEEPER-MCCANN HOUSE, 75 Eastern Point Blvd., Gloucester, MA 01930-4433. Mailing Address: 141 Cambridge St., Boston, MA 02114-2702. Tel.: 978-283-0800, 617-227-3956 (Historic New England). Facebook.
E-mail: beauport@historicnewengland.org
Web Site: www.historicnewengland.org
Key Personnel: Pres. & C.E.O., Carl R. Nold; Site Mgr., Martha Van Koevering.
Institution Type/Description: National Historic House/Landmark: housed in the former summer home of interior designer, Henry Davis Sleeper; built in 1907.
Hours & Admission Prices: Tours: June-Oct. 15 Tues.-Sat. 10-5, (last tour at 4). Adults $15; discounts to seniors, groups, AAM, ICOM, AAA, WGBH members.
Attendance: 6,574 (actual)

CAPE ANN MUSEUM, 27 Pleasant St., Gloucester, MA 01930-5909. Tel.: 978-283-0455. Fax: 978-283-4141.
E-mail: rondafaloon@capeannmuseum.org
Web Site: www.capeannmuseum.org
Key Personnel: Dir., Ronda Faloon; Pres. (V), John Cunningham; Museum Shop Mgr., Cara White.
Institution Type/Description: History, Art & Maritime Museum: c.1710 First Period House.
Hours & Admission Prices: Jan. - Dec. Tues.-Sat. 10-5, Sun. 1-4; group tours by appointment only. Adults $10, senior citizens, students, & Cape Ann residents $8; members & children under 18 no charge. Closed major holidays. &
Attendance: 25,000 (actual)

HAMMOND CASTLE MUSEUM, 80 Hesperus Ave., Gloucester, MA 01930-5299. Tel.: 978-283-2080. Fax: 978-283-1643.
Web Site: www.hammondcastle.org
Key Personnel: Acting Dir. & Cur. Education, John W. Pettibone; Pres. (V), Craig Lentz.
Institution Type/Description: Historic Building & Museum: castle built in 1928 by inventor John Hays Hammond, Jr., in the style of a combination of Roman, Medieval & Renaissance periods.
Hours & Admission Prices: May-Oct. Sat.-Sun. 10-4, last ticket sold at 3:30; groups by appointment. Adults $10, seniors 65 & over $9, children 6-12 $8. Closed Memorial Day; Independence Day; Labor Day; Columbus Day.
Attendance: 69,000

MARITIME GLOUCESTER, 23 Harbor Loop, Gloucester, MA 01930-5004. Tel.: 978-281-0470. Fax: 978-281-0327.
E-mail: info@maritimegloucester.org
Web Site: www.maritimegloucester.org
Formerly: Gloucester Maritime Heritage Center
Key Personnel: Interim Dir., Lee Cunningham.
Institution Type/Description: Maritime Museum.
Hours & Admission Prices: Memorial Day weekend to Oct. daily 10-5. Adults $9, seniors & children $7; discounts to families; members & children under 1 no charge.

NORTH SHORE ARTS ASSOCIATION, 11 Pirate's Lane, Gloucester, MA 01930-3810. Tel.: 978-283-1857.
E-mail: arts@nsarts.org
Web Site: www.nsarts.org
Key Personnel: Pres. (V), George Martin; Dir., Suzanne Gilbert.
Institution Type/Description: Art Gallery: housed in c.1870 barn.
Hours & Admission Prices: May-Oct. Mon.-Sat. 10-5, Sun. 12-5. No charge; donations accepted. &
Attendance: 12,000 (estimated)

THE SARGENT HOUSE MUSEUM, 49 Middle St., Gloucester, MA 01930-5736. Tel.: 978-281-2432. Fax: 978-281-2432.

E-mail: sargenthouse@verizon.net
Web Site: sargenthouse.org
Key Personnel: Exec. Dir., Ronda Faloon; Cur., Martha Oaks.
Institution Type/Description: Historic House: 1782 Georgian style house built for early American philosopher, writer & activist Judith Sargent Murray (1751-1820).
Hours & Admission Prices: Memorial Day to Labor Day Fri.-Sun. 12-4. Adults $12, students over 5 $5; members no charge.
Attendance: 2,500 (actual)

Grafton

WILLARD HOUSE AND CLOCK MUSEUM, INC., 11 Willard St., Grafton, MA 01536-2011. Tel.: 508-839-3500. Fax: 508-839-3599.
E-mail: patrick@willardhouse.org
Web Site: www.willardhouse.org
Key Personnel: Dir., Patrick Keenan; Pres., Richard Currier.
Institution Type/Description: Horological Museum: housed in 1718 Willard Homestead and 1766 Clock Shop.
Hours & Admission Prices: Jan.-March Fri.-Sat. 10-4, Sun. 1-4; April-Dec. Wed.-Sat. 10-4, Sun. 1-4. Adults $10, senior citizens $9, children $6; discounts to AAM & AAA members; Willard House members no charge. Closed all major holidays.
Attendance: 2,595 (actual)

Granville

NOBLE & COOLEY CENTER FOR HISTORIC PRESERVATION, 42 Water St., Granville, MA 01034. Mailing Address: P.O. Box 325, Granville, MA 01034-0325. Tel.: 413-357-8814. Fax: 413-357-6314.
E-mail: ncchp.org@gmail.com
Web Site: ncchp.org
Key Personnel: Dir., Liz Smith; Pres. (V), Matt Jones; Museum Shop Mgr., Carol Jones.
Institution Type/Description: Preservation Society: housed in the Noble & Cooley drum factory.
Hours & Admission Prices: See website for hours. Adults $5; discounts to AAM members; members no charge.

Greenfield

THE ASSOCIATION FOR GRAVESTONE STUDIES, Greenfield Corporate Center, 101 Munson St., Ste. 108, Greenfield, MA 01301-9675. Tel.: 413-772-0836. Fax: 413-772-0836 (call first).
E-mail: info@gravestonestudies.org
Web Site: www.gravestonestudies.org
Key Personnel: Pres., Ian Brown; Admin., Andrea Carlin.
Institution Type/Description: Preservation Society.
Hours & Admission Prices: Office: Tues.-Thurs. 9-3. No charge. Closed holidays. &

HISTORICAL SOCIETY OF GREENFIELD, 43 Church St., Greenfield, MA 01302. Mailing Address: P.O. Box 415, Greenfield, MA 01302-0415. Tel.: 413-774-3663 & 5363.
E-mail: hsg1907@yahoo.com
Key Personnel: Pres. (V), Tim Blagg.
Institution Type/Description: General Museum: housed in 1852 Museum Building.
Hours & Admission Prices: Open year-round by appointment; special events & open houses scheduled throughout the year; call for information. No charge.
Attendance: 600 (estimated)

Groton

GROTON HISTORICAL SOCIETY, 172 Main St., Groton, MA 01450-1238. Mailing Address: P.O. Box 202, Groton, MA 01450-0202. Tel.: 978-448-0092.
E-mail: info@grotonhistoricalsociety.org
Web Site: www.grotonhistoricalsociety.org
Key Personnel: Pres. (V), John H. Ott; Cur., Bobbie Spigelman.
Institution Type/Description: Historic House: housed in the Governor Boutwell House; built in 1851.
Hours & Admission Prices: Mon. & Wed. 10-2. No charge; donations accepted. &
Attendance: 400 (estimated)

Hadley

HADLEY FARM MUSEUM, 224 River Dr., Hadley, MA 01035-9641. Tel.: 413-584-7459.
E-mail: admin@hadleyfarmmuseum.org
Key Personnel: Pres., Thomas West; Sec., Mrs. Glenn Clark.
Institution Type/Description: Farm Museum: housed in 1782 barn.
Hours & Admission Prices: May-Oct. Sat.-Sun. 2-4; other times by appointment. Adults $5.
Attendance: 1,000 (estimated)

PORTER-PHELPS-HUNTINGTON FOUNDATION, INC., 130 River Dr., Hadley, MA 01035-9782. Tel.: 413-584-4699.
E-mail: pphmuseumassistant@gmail.com
Web Site: www.pphmuseum.org
Key Personnel: Dir. & C.E.O., Susan J. Lisk; Pres., Tom Harris; Vice Pres. Bd., Dan Huntington Fenn, Jr.; Treas., Sidney Poritz; Clerk, Craig Malone.
Institution Type/Description: Historic House: 1752 Georgian home & grounds.
Hours & Admission Prices: mid-Oct. to mid-May Sat.-Wed. 1-4:30. Adults $5, children $1.
Attendance: 2,200 (estimated)

Hardwick

HARDWICK HISTORICAL SOCIETY, 40 Common St., Hardwick, MA 01037. Mailing Address: P.O. Box 492, Hardwick, MA 01037-0492. Tel.: 413-967-4002. Facebook: Hardwick, MA Memories.
E-mail: hardwickhistoricalsociety@yahoo.com
Web Site: townofhardwick.org
Key Personnel: Pres., Randall Noble; Cur., Emily Bancroft; Sec., Anne Barnes.
Institution Type/Description: Local History Museum: housed in 1840 Old Brick School House.
Hours & Admission Prices: By appointment. No charge; donations accepted.
Attendance: 320 (estimated)

Harvard

FRUITLANDS MUSEUMS, 102 Prospect Hill Rd., Harvard, MA 01451. Tel.: 978-456-3924. Fax: 978-456-8078.
E-mail: ghermann@thetrustees.org
Web Site: www.fruitlands.org
Key Personnel: Dir, Wyona Lynch-McWhite; Pres., Marie LeBlanc.
Institution Type/Description: History Museum.
Hours & Admission Prices: Museums: May 14-Oct. Mon.-Fri. 11-4, Sat.-Sun. & holidays 11-5. Tours: by reservation. Grounds: daily 10-5. Library: by appointment only. Adults $10, seniors 60 and over & students with college ID $8, children 5-17 $4; discounts to AAM, NEMA & AAA members; members no charge. &
Attendance: 30,000 (actual)

Harwich

BROOKS ACADEMY MUSEUM, 80 Parallel St., Harwich, MA 02645-2716. Tel.: 508-432-8089.
E-mail: harwichhistoricalsociety@verizon.net
Web Site: www.harwichhistoricalsociety.org
Key Personnel: Dir., Janet Cassidy; Pres., Taffy Aldrovandi; Treas., Brian Michaelan; Recording Sec., Sally Cormier; Museum Shop Mgr., Jane Chase.
Institution Type/Description: Historical Society Museum: housed in c.1844 building that served as a private secondary school.
Hours & Admission Prices: late June to mid-Oct. Thurs.-Sat. 1-4. Adults $5; members no charge. Closed Independence Day. &
Attendance: 2,000 (actual)

BROOKS FREE LIBRARY, 739 Main St., Harwich, MA 02645-2752. Tel.: 508-430-7562. Fax: 508-430-7564.
E-mail: bfl_mail@clamsnet.org
Web Site: www.brooksfreelibrary.org
Key Personnel: Dir., Virginia A. Hewitt; Reference Librarian, Jennifer Pickett; Public Svcs. Librarian, Suzanne Martell; Youth Svcs. Librarian, Ann Carpenter; Principal Clerk, Mary Jo Metzger; Sr. Library Technician, Phil Inman; Sr. Library Technician, Pam Paine; Sr. Library Technician, Joanne Clingan.
Institution Type/Description: Library.
Hours & Admission Prices: Tues.-Thurs. 10-7, Fri.-Sat. 10-4. Local History Room: call for hours. No charge. Closed national & state holidays. &
Attendance: 82,569 (actual)

Haverhill

HAVERHILL HISTORICAL SOCIETY, 240 Water St., Haverhill, MA 01830-6433. Tel.: 978-374-4626. Fax: 978-521-9176.
E-mail: Haverhill.Historical.Society@gmail.com
Web Site: haverhillhistory.org
Key Personnel: Pres. (V), Jay Cleary; Cur., Jan Williams; Program Coord., Stacey Fraser-deHaan; Weekend Supvr., Thomas Spitalere; Bookkeeper, Lisa O'Hearn.
Institution Type/Description: History Museum.
Hours & Admission Prices: Summer: Tues.-Sun. 10-5; Winter: Tues.-Sat. 10-5. Adults $5, children $4; discounts to AAM members; members no charge. Closed major holidays. &
Attendance: 3,849 (actual)

Hingham

BARE COVE FIRE MUSEUM, 45 Bare Cove Park Dr., Hingham, MA 02043. Tel.: 781-749-0028.
E-mail: bcfm.hingham@gmail.com
Web Site: barecovefiremuseum.org
Key Personnel: Pres. & Chief, David Clark; Vice Pres. & Treas., Jack Crandall; Dir., Don Lincoln; Dir., Jaclyn Howard; Dir., Russell Clark; Dir., Ben Wentworth; Clerk & Archivist, Geri Duff.
Institution Type/Description: Fire-Fighting Museum.
Hours & Admission Prices: Wed. 7:30-9:30; other times by appointment. No charge; donations accepted. Closed Christmas Eve & Day. &
Attendance: 300 (estimated)

HINGHAM HISTORICAL SOCIETY, 34 Main St., Hingham, MA 02043-2523. Mailing Address: P.O. Box 434, Hingham, MA 02043-0434. Tel.: 781-749-7721. Fax: 781-749-0091.
E-mail: director@hinghamhistorical.org
Web Site: www.hinghamhistorical.org
Formerly: Old Ordinary House Museum
Key Personnel: Dir., Suzanne Buchanan; Pres., Virginia Tay; Museum Shop Mgr., Susan Achille.
Institution Type/Description: Historical Society.
Hours & Admission Prices: mid-June to early Sept. Tues.-Sat. 1:30-4:30; other times by appointment. Tours: 1:30, 2:30 & 3:30. Adults $5, children under 12 $3; members no charge.
Attendance: 6,000 (estimated)

Holyoke

CHILDREN'S MUSEUM AT HOLYOKE, INC., 444 Dwight St., Holyoke, MA 01040-5842. Tel.: 413-536-7048. Fax: 413-533-2999.
E-mail: skelley@childrensmuseumholyoke.org
Web Site: www.childrensmuseumholyoke.org/
Key Personnel: C.E.O. & Pres. (V), Barry Waite; Exec. Dir., Susan Kelley; Visitor & Family Svcs. Coord., Diane West; Museum Shop Mgr., Margaret Boulais; Bookkeeper, Kathleen McCreary.
Institution Type/Description: Children's Museum.
Hours & Admission Prices: Wed.-Sat. 10-4, Sun. 12-4. Adults & children $6, senior citizens $3; discounts to AYM members & groups; children under one & members no charge. Closed New Year's Day; Easter; Memorial Day; Independence Day; Labor Day; Thanksgiving; Christmas. &
Attendance: 40,000 (actual)

HOLYOKE HERITAGE STATE PARK, 221 Appleton St., Holyoke, MA 01040-5714. Tel.: 413-534-1723.
E-mail: mass.parks@state.ma.us
Web Site: www.mass.gov/dcr/parks/central/hhsp.htm
Key Personnel: Supvr., Charlie Lotspeich.
Institution Type/Description: Park Museum.
Hours & Admission Prices: Visitor's Center: Tues.-Sun. 10-4, No charge.

VOLLEYBALL HALL OF FAME, 444 Dwight St., Holyoke, MA 01040-5842. Tel.: 413-536-0926. Fax: 413-539-6673.
E-mail: info@volleyhall.org
Web Site: www.volleyhall.org
Key Personnel: Pres. (V), David C. Casey.
Institution Type/Description: Sports Museum.
Hours & Admission Prices: Tues.-Sun. 12-4:30.

WISTARIAHURST MUSEUM, 238 Cabot St., Holyoke, MA 01040-3904. Tel.: 413-322-5660. Fax: 413-534-2344. Facebook: Wistariahurst Museum.
E-mail: preisslerk@holyoke.org
Web Site: www.wistariahurst.org

Key Personnel: Dir., Kate Preissler; Cur., Penni Martorell.
Institution Type/Description: Historic House: built in c.1868 26-room mansion & carriage house; former home of local silk manufacturer William Skinner with two additions made in 1914 & 1927.
Hours & Admission Prices: Museum: see website for hours & admissions. Grounds & Gardens: dawn to dusk. Group tours by appointment. &
Attendance: 14,000 (estimated)

Hull

HULL LIFESAVING MUSEUM INC., THE MUSEUM OF BOSTON HARBOR HERITAGE, 1117 Nantasket Ave., Hull, MA 02045-1310. Mailing Address: P.O. Box 221, Hull, MA 02045-0221. Tel.: 781-925-5433. Fax: 781-925-0992. Facebook: Hull Lifesaving Museum.
E-mail: info@hulllifesavingmuseum.org
Web Site: www.hulllifesavingmuseum.org
Key Personnel: Exec. Dir., Peter Wild; Dir. Maritime & New Program Devel., Edward P. McCabe; Dir. Advancement & Communications, Corinne Leung; Pres., Robert MacIntyre; Treas., Paul Carlson.
Institution Type/Description: Maritime Museum: headquarters housed in restored c.1889 Point Allerton United States Life Saving Service Station.
Hours & Admission Prices: Point Allerton Life-Saving Station: Jan.-April Mon.-Thurs. 10-4; May-June & Sept.-Dec. Mon.-Thurs. & Sat. 10-4; July-Aug. Sat.-Thurs 10-4; guided tours & other times by appointment. Adults $5, senior citizens $3; discounts to AAM members; NEMA & CAMM members no charge. Closed National holidays. &
Attendance: 12,000 (estimated)

Hyannis

THE CAPE COD MARITIME MUSEUM, 135 South St., Hyannis, MA 02601-4014. Mailing Address: P.O. Box 443, Hyannis, MA 02601-0443. Tel.: 508-775-1723. Fax: 508-775-1706. Facebook: Cape Cod Maritime Museum.
E-mail: info@capecodmaritimemuseum.org
Web Site: www.capecodmaritimemuseum.org
Key Personnel: Dir., Chris Galazzi; Pres. (V), Craig Ashworth; Admin., Erin Trainor.
Institution Type/Description: Maritime Museum.
Hours & Admission Prices: March-Dec. Tues.-Sat. 10-4, Sun. 12-4. Adults $5, senior citizens & students $4; discounts to AAM, ICOM, MTA & NEMA members; members & children under 6 no charge. Closed most holidays. &
Attendance: 5,000 (estimated)

JOHN F. KENNEDY HYANNIS MUSEUM, 397 Main St., Hyannis, MA 02601-3914. Mailing Address: P.O. Box 2488, Hyannis, MA 02601. Tel.: 508-790-3077. Fax: 508-827-7369.
E-mail: jennifer@jfkhyannismuseum.org
Web Site: www.jfkhyannismuseum.org
Key Personnel: C.E.O., Jessica Tinti; Dir., John L. Allen; Museum Shop Mgr., Jennifer Pappalardo.
Institution Type/Description: History Museum.
Hours & Admission Prices: mid-Feb. to mid-April & Nov.-Dec. Thurs.-Sat. 10-4, Sun. 12-4; April-Memorial Day & day after Columbus Day to Oct. 31 Mon.-Sat. 10-4, Sun. 12-4; May to Columbus Day Mon.-Sat. 9-5, Sun. 12-5. Adults $9, seniors 62 & over $6, children 8-17 & student w/ID $5; children under 8 no charge. &
Attendance: 64,000 (estimated)

ZION UNION HERITAGE MUSEUM, INC., 276 North St., Hyannis, MA 02601-3826. Mailing Address: P.O. Box 2591, Hyannis, MA 02601-7591. Tel.: 508-790-9466.
E-mail: zuhmi@comcast.net
Web Site: zionunionheritagemuseum.org
Key Personnel: Dir., John L. Reed.
Institution Type/Description: History Museum.
Hours & Admission Prices: Feb.-April Thurs.-Sat. 11-5, May-Oct. Tues.-Sat. 11-5, Nov.-Dec. Thurs.-Sat. 10-4. Adults 18 & over $5, seniors $4, children 10-17 $3; members & children under 10 no charge. &
Attendance: 2,100 (actual)

Indian Orchard

THE TITANIC MUSEUM, 208 Main St., Indian Orchard, MA 01151-1132. Mailing Address: P.O. Box 51053, Indian Orchard, MA 01151-5053. Tel.: 413-543-4770. Fax: 413-583-3633.
E-mail: titanicinfo@titanichistoricalsociety.org
Web Site: www.titanic1.org/museum
Institution Type/Description: History Museum.

Hours & Admission Prices: Mon.-Fri. 10-4, Sat. 10-3. Adults $4, children 6-11 $2; discounts to AAM & ICOM members; Titanic Historical Society members & children 5 and under no charge.

Ipswich

GREAT HOUSE AT CASTLE HILL ON THE CRANE ESTATE, 290 Argilla Rd., Ipswich, MA 01938. Mailing Address: 290 Argilla Rd., Ipswich, MA 01938. Tel.: 978-356-4351, ext. 4049.
E-mail: lmarshall@ttor.org
Key Personnel: Cultural Site Admin., Linda Marshall; Cultural Resources Mgr., Susan Hill-Dolan.
Institution Type/Description: Historic House Museum.
Hours & Admission Prices: May-Oct. call for hours. Grounds: daily 8am to sunset. Adults $10; discounts to groups of 15 or more; members no charge. &
Attendance: 6,000 (estimated)

IPSWICH MUSEUM, 54 S. Main St., (Rte. 1A), Ipswich, MA 01938-2322. Tel.: 978-356-2811.
E-mail: admin@ipswichmuseum.org
Web Site: www.ipswichmuseum.org
Formerly: Ipswich Historical Society
Key Personnel: Dir., Terri Stephens; Pres., Stephanie Haskins; Treas., Larry Pszenny.
Institution Type/Description: History Museum.
Hours & Admission Prices: Feb.-April Sun. 2-4; May-Oct. Wed.-Sun. 12-4; Nov.-Dec. call for hours. One House: adults $10; children 6-12 $5; children under 6 & members no charge. Three Houses: adults $15, children 6-12 $5; children under 6 & members no charge.
Attendance: 2,000 (actual)

THE PAINE HOUSE AT GREENWOOD FARM, A PROPERTY OF THE TRUSTEES OF RESERVATIONS, 47 Jeffrey's Neck Rd., Ipswich, MA 01938. Mailing Address: 290 Argilla Rd., Ipswich, MA 01938. Tel.: 978-356-4351, ext. 4049.
E-mail: lmarshall@ttor.org
Web Site: www.ttor.org
Key Personnel: Cultural Site Admin., Linda Marshall; Cultural Resources Mgr., Susan Hill-Dolan.
Institution Type/Description: Historic House: housed in the former Paine family farmhouse; built in 1694.
Hours & Admission Prices: June-Oct. 1st Sat. each month; other times by appointment.
Attendance: 200 (estimated)

Kingston

MAJOR JOHN BRADFORD HOUSE, 50 Landing Rd., Kingston, MA 02364. Mailing Address: P.O. Box 22, Kingston, MA 02364-0022. Tel.: 781-585-6300.
E-mail: colleen@jrvhs.org
Web Site: www.jrvhs.org
Key Personnel: Pres. (V), Norman P. Tucker.
Institution Type/Description: Historic House: 1714 Major John Bradford home.
Hours & Admission Prices: Summer: Sun. 9-11:30, tours by appointment. No charge; donations accepted.
Attendance: 2,500 (estimated)

Lancaster

FIRST CHURCH OF CHRIST UNITARIAN, 725 Main St., P.O. Box 66, Lancaster, MA 01523. Mailing Address: P.O. Box 66, Lancaster, MA 01523-0066. Tel.: 978-365-2427.
E-mail: office@firstchurchlancasterma.org
Web Site: firstchurchlancasterma.org
Formerly: Fifth Meeting House
Key Personnel: Minister, Rev. Dr. Paul Hull; Church Admin., Karen Plaskon.
Institution Type/Description: Religious Museum: housed in 1816 The First Church of Christ.
Hours & Admission Prices: Sun. 10; other times by appointment. No charge. &

Lawrence

ESSEX ART CENTER, 56 Island St., Lawrence, MA 01840-1889. Tel.: 978-685-2343. Fax: 978-688-0276. Facebook: Essex Art Center.
E-mail: info@essexartcenter.com
Web Site: essexartcenter.com
Key Personnel: Exec. Dir., John Budzyna.

Institution Type/Description: Art Gallery.
Hours & Admission Prices: Mon.-Thurs. 10-6. No charge; donations accepted.
Attendance: 7,000 (actual)

LAWRENCE HERITAGE STATE PARK, 1 Jackson St., Lawrence, MA 01840-1613. Tel.: 978-794-1655. Fax: 978-794-9241. TDD: 978-794-1655.
E-mail: lawrence.heritage@state.ma.us
Web Site: www.mass.gov/eea/agencies/dcr/massparks/region-north/lawrence-heritage-state-park.html
Key Personnel: Park Supvr., Michael Mitchell; Chm. (V), Joe Bella; Visitor Svcs. Supvr. & Museum Shop Mgr., Jim Beauchesne; Maintenance, Tom Ceder; Maintenance, Will McDowell.
Institution Type/Description: State Park Visitor's Center: housed in a former mill boardinghouse; built c.1847.
Hours & Admission Prices: Daily 9-4. No charge. Closed New Year's Day; Thanksgiving; Christmas. &
Attendance: 100,000 (estimated)

LAWRENCE HISTORY CENTER: IMMIGRANT CITY ARCHIVES, 6 Essex St., Lawrence, MA 01840-1710. Tel.: 978-686-9230.
E-mail: director@lawrencehistory.org
Web Site: www.lawrencehistory.org
Formerly: Immigrant City Archives, Historical Society of Lawrence and Its People
Key Personnel: Exec. Dir., Barbara Brown; Pres. (V), Pamela Yameen; Asst. to Dir., Amita Kiley.
Institution Type/Description: Historical Society Museum: housed in 1883 buildings.
Hours & Admission Prices: Winter: Tues.-Fri. 9-4, Sat. 9-1 by appointment. Summer: Tues.-Fri. 9-4. Research: members no charge. Closed Independence Day & week; Christmas week. &
Attendance: 3,000 (estimated)

Lenox

BERKSHIRE SCENIC RAILWAY MUSEUM, 10 Willow Creek Rd., Lenox, MA 01240. Mailing Address: P.O. Box 2195, Lenox, MA 01240-5195. Tel.: 413-637-2210. Fax: 413-637-4965.
E-mail: marketing@berkshirescenicrailroad.org
Web Site: www.berkshirescenicrailroad.org
Key Personnel: Pres. (V). Jay Green; Cur., John Trowill; Mktg., Pieter Lips; Public Rels., Pamela Green; Museum Shop Mgr., Cathleen Chittenden.
Institution Type/Description: Train Museum: housed in the restored 1903 Lenox station.
Hours & Admission Prices: Memorial Day-Oct. Sat.-Sun. & holidays 9-4. Train: Adults $15, seniors $14, children 4-14 $8; children under 4 & members no charge. Museum & Exhibits: no charge. &
Attendance: 8,500 (actual)

THE MOUNT: EDITH WHARTON'S HOME, 2 Plunkett St., Lenox, MA 01240-2704. Mailing Address: P.O. Box 974, Lenox, MA 01240-0974. Tel.: 413-551-5111. Fax: 413-637-0619.
E-mail: info@edithwharton.org
Web Site: edithwharton.org
Key Personnel: Exec. Dir., Susan Wissler; Dir. Facilities, Ross Jolly; Finance Dir., Tammy Walger.
Institution Type/Description: Historic House: home designed by Pulitzer-Prize winning author Edith Wharton. A National Historic Landmark.
Hours & Admission Prices: May-Oct. daily. Winter: Sat.-Sun. Guided Tour: adults $18, seniors $17; children 18 & under no charge. &
Attendance: 52,000 (estimated)

VENTFORT HALL MANSION AND GILDED AGE MUSEUM, 104 Walker St., Lenox, MA 01240. Mailing Address: P.O. Box 2424, Lenox, MA 01240. Tel.: 413-637-3206. Fax: 413-637-8805.
E-mail: info@gildedage.org
Web Site: gildedage.org
Key Personnel: Pres. (V), Lorraine Becker; Museum Shop Mgr., Beverly Rainey.
Institution Type/Description: Historic House: former home of Sarah Morgan, sister of J.P. Morgan, built in 1893. Listed on the National Register of Historic Places.
Hours & Admission Prices: Mon.-Fri. 10-5, Sat.-Sun. 10-3. Adults $18, seniors 65 & over and students 18-23 with ID $17, children 5-17 $7; members on the 1st floor no charge. Closed New Year's Day; Easter; Thanksgiving; Christmas. &
Attendance: 10,000 (estimated)

Leominster

NATIONAL PLASTICS CENTER AND MUSEUM, 90 Main St., Leominster, MA 01453-5521. Tel.: 978-537-9529.
Key Personnel: Cur., Marianne Zephir.

Institution Type/Description: Industrial Museum: housed in a school building built in 1888.
Hours & Admission Prices: Call for hours. Adults $5, children 4-11 & senior 65 & over $3; ASTC members & members no charge. ⑅
Attendance: 12,000 (actual)

Leverett

LEVERETT HISTORICAL SOCIETY, N. Leverett Rd., Leverett, MA 01054. Mailing Address: P.O. Box 57, Leverett, MA 01054-0057. Tel.: 413-548-9452.
E-mail: jshively@leverettnet.net
Key Personnel: Dir., Edith Field.
Institution Type/Description: Historic House: 1820s schoolhouse.
Hours & Admission Prices: Schoolhouse: Summer: Sun. 1-3; other times by appointment. Leverett Family Museum: Sat. 10-12; other times by appointment. No charge; donations accepted.
Attendance: 100 (estimated)

Lexington

LEXINGTON HISTORICAL SOCIETY, 13 Depot Sq., Lexington, MA 02420. Mailing Address: P.O. Box 514, Lexington, MA 02420-0005. Tel.: 781-862-1703.
E-mail: info@lexingtonhistory.org
Web Site: www.lexingtonhistory.org
Key Personnel: C.E.O., Susan Bennett; Pres. (V), William Mix; Museum Shop Mgr., Carla Fortmann.
Institution Type/Description: Historical Society Museum.
Hours & Admission Prices: April-Oct. daily. One House: adults $7, children $5. Three Houses: adults $12, children 6-16 $8; members & children under 6 no charge.
Attendance: 30,000 (actual)

MUNROE CENTER FOR THE ARTS, 1403 Massachusetts Ave., Lexington, MA 02420-3828. Tel.: 781-862-6040. Fax: 781-674-2787.
E-mail: RENESE@MUNROECENTER.ORG
Web Site: www.munroecenter.org/contact-us-find-us.html
Key Personnel: Admin., Nancy Sofen.
Institution Type/Description: Art Gallery.
Hours & Admission Prices: Call for hours.

SCOTTISH RITE MASONIC MUSEUM & LIBRARY, 33 Marrett Rd., Lexington, MA 02421-5703. Tel.: 781-861-6559; 781-274-8539 (TTY). Fax: 781-861-9846.
E-mail: info@monh.org
Web Site: www.nationalheritagemuseum.org
Formerly: National Heritage Museum.
Key Personnel: Pres., John William McNaughton; Exec. Dir., Richard V. Travis; Dir. Exhibitions & Audience Devel., Hilary Anderson Stelling; Dir. Collections, Aimee Newell; Museum Designer, Michael Rizzo; Archivist, Catherine Swanson; Public Rels., Linda Patch; Collections Mgr. & Registrar, Maureen Harper; Mgr. Library & Archives, Jeff Croteau.
Institution Type/Description: History Museum.
Hours & Admission Prices: Wed.-Sat. 10-4:30. No charge; donations accepted. Closed New Year's Day; Easter; Thanksgiving; Christmas. ⑅
Attendance: 39,174 (actual)

Lincoln

CODMAN ESTATE, 34 Codman Rd., Lincoln, MA 01773. Mailing Address: 141 Cambridge St., Boston, MA 02114-2702. Tel.: 617-994-6690.
E-mail: codmanestate@historicnewengland.org
Web Site: www.historicnewengland.org
Key Personnel: Pres. & C.E.O., Carl R. Nold; Site Mgr., Wendy Hubbard.
Institution Type/Description: Historic House: c.1740 Georgian mansion expanded in 1790s to resemble an English country seat. Home of Codman family through 1968.
Hours & Admission Prices: House: June-Oct. 15 2nd & 4th Sat. each month 10-2. Grounds: dawn to dusk. Adults $10; discounts to seniors, AAM, ICOM, AAA & WGBH members; Historic New England members no charge.
Attendance: 11,882 (actual)

DECORDOVA SCULPTURE PARK AND MUSEUM, 51 Sandy Pond Rd., Lincoln, MA 01773-2699. Tel.: 781-259-8355. Fax: 781-259-3650. Facebook, Instagram, Twitter.
E-mail: marketing@decordova.org
Web Site: www.decordova.org

Key Personnel: Bd. Pres., Linda G. Hammett Ory; Exec. Dir., John B. Ravenal; Deputy Dir. Learning & Engagement, Julie Bernson; Deputy Dir. External Affairs, Bruce Smith; Assoc. Cur., Sarah Montross; Dir. Bldgs. & Grounds, Douglas Holston; Deputy Dir. Operations, David Duddy; Retail Mgr., Samantha Linnane.
Institution Type/Description: Contemporary Art Museum & Sculpture Park.
Hours & Admission Prices: Summer: daily 10-5; Winter: Wed.-Fri. 10-4, Sat. & Sun. 10-5. Adults $14, seniors $12, students $10; discounts to Zipcar, WGBH, WBUR & AAM members; deCordova members, bicyclists, active duty military & their families, Lincoln residents and children 12 & under no charge. ⑅
Attendance: 80,000 (estimated)

DRUMLIN FARM EDUCATION CENTER, 208 S. Great Rd., Lincoln, MA 01773-4800. Tel.: 781-259-2200 & 2203. Fax: 781-259-7917.
E-mail: drumlinfarm@massaudubon.org
Web Site: www.massaudubon.org
Key Personnel: Dir., Christy Foote-Smith; Dir. Education, Kris Scopinich.
Institution Type/Description: Living Farm Museum.
Hours & Admission Prices: Tues.-Sun. 9-5; school tours by reservation only. Adults $6, senior citizens & children 2-12 $4; Lincoln residents & children under 2 no charge. Closed New Year's Eve & Day; Thanksgiving; Christmas. ⑅
Attendance: 150,000 (estimated)

GROPIUS HOUSE, 68 Baker Bridge Rd., Lincoln, MA 01773-3105. Tel.: 781-259-8098. Fax: 781-259-9722.
E-mail: gropiushouse@historicnewengland.org
Web Site: www.historicnewengland.org
Key Personnel: Pres., Carl Nold; Museum Site Mgr., Wendy L. Hubbard.
Institution Type/Description: Historic House: c.1937-38 Walter Gropius, one of the innovators of modern architecture, designed his family residence by combining Bauhaus principles with New England building materials.
Hours & Admission Prices: Tours: June-Oct. 15 Wed.-Sun. 11-4 on the hour; Oct. 16-May Sat.-Sun. 11-5 on the hour. Adults $15, seniors $12, children & students $8; discounts to groups and AAM, AAA & WGBH members; members, Historic New England members & Lincoln residents no charge.
Attendance: 6,429 (actual)

THE THOREAU INSTITUTE AT WALDEN WOODS, 44 Baker Farm, Lincoln, MA 01773-3004. Tel.: 781-259-4700. Fax: 781-259-4710.
E-mail: Jeff.Cramer@walden.org
Web Site: www.walden.org/institute
Key Personnel: Exec. Dir., Kathi Anderson; Cur. Collections, Jeffrey S. Cramer.
Institution Type/Description: Historical Society Museum.
Hours & Admission Prices: By appointment only. No charge; donations accepted. ⑅

Longmeadow

RICHARD SALTER STORRS HOUSE, 697 Longmeadow St., Longmeadow, MA 01106-2215. Tel.: 413-567-3600.
E-mail: LCAsearch@aol.com
Key Personnel: C.E.O. & Pres. (V), Michael Gelinas; Cur. & Genealogist, Linda C. Abrams.
Institution Type/Description: Historical Society Museum: housed in 1786 Storrs House.
Hours & Admission Prices: By appointment. Adults $3; discounts to senior citizens, family reunion groups, children 12-18, AAM & ICOM members; members & children under 12 no charge.
Attendance: 800 (estimated)

Lowell

THE LOADING DOCK GALLERY, 122 Western Ave., Lowell, MA 01851.
E-mail: info@theloadingdockgallery.com
Web Site: www.theloadingdockgallery.com
Institution Type/Description: Art Gallery.
Hours & Admission Prices: Wed.-Sun. 11-4:30.

LOWELL NATIONAL HISTORICAL PARK, 246 Market St., Lowell, MA 01852-1029. Mailing Address: 67 Kirk St., Lowell, MA 01852-1029. Tel.: 978-970-5000. Fax: 978-275-1762. TDD: 978-970-5002.
E-mail: lowe_reservations@nps.gov
Web Site: www.nps.gov/lowe
Key Personnel: Supt., Celeste Bernardo; Education & Dir. Tsongas Industrial History Center, Sheila Kirschbaum; Cur., David Blackburn; Public Information, Sue Andrews; Librarian, Jack Herlihy; Museum Shop Mgr., Joan Gagnon.

Institution Type/Description: History Museum District.

Hours & Admission Prices: Visitor Center: Winter: daily 9-4:30; Summer: daily 9-5. Boott Cotton Mills Museum: Winter: daily 9:30-4:30; Summer: daily 9:30-5. Mill Girls & Immigrants Exhibit: call for hours. Adults $6, seniors $4, students & youth 6-16 $3; children 5 & under no charge. Closed New Year's Day; Thanksgiving; Christmas. ♿

Attendance: 550,000 (estimated)

MIDDLESEX CANAL COLLECTION, Center for Lowell History, 40 French St., Lowell, MA 01852-1113. Tel.: 978-934-4998. Fax: 978-934-4995.

E-mail: martha_mayo@uml.edu

Web Site: library.uml.edu/clh

Key Personnel: Dir., Martha Mayo.

Institution Type/Description: History Museum/Center.

Hours & Admission Prices: Mon.-Fri. 9-6, Sat. 10-3. No charge. ♿

Attendance: 15,000 (estimated)

NEW ENGLAND QUILT MUSEUM, 18 Shattuck St., Lowell, MA 01852-1820. Tel.: 978-452-4207. Fax: 978-452-5405.

E-mail: director@nequiltmuseum.org

Web Site: www.nequiltmuseum.org

Key Personnel: Exec. Dir., Nora Burchfield; Museum Shop Mgr., Debbie Janes.

Institution Type/Description: Quilt Museum: housed in landmark savings bank building.

Hours & Admission Prices: May-Oct. Tues.-Sat. 10-4, Sun. 12-4; Nov.-April Tues.-Sat. 10-4. Adults $8; discounts to MTA & AAA members; members no charge. Closed major holidays. ♿

Attendance: 8,000 (estimated)

WHISTLER HOUSE MUSEUM OF ART, 243 Worthen St., Lowell, MA 01852-1874. Tel.: 978-452-7641. Fax: 978-454-2421.

E-mail: mlally@whistlerhouse.org

Web Site: www.whistlerhouse.org

Key Personnel: Chm. (V), Nancy Donahue; Chm. (V), Richard Donahue; Pres., Sara Bogosian; Exhibits & Gallery Mgr., James Dyment.

Institution Type/Description: Art Gallery: housed in 1823 Whistler House, birthplace of James A. M. Whistler.

Hours & Admission Prices: Wed.-Sat. 11-4. Adults $5, senior citizens & students 6-21 $4; discounts to groups, AAA, AAM & NEMA members; children under 6, museum professionals & members no charge. Closed major holidays. ♿

Attendance: 7,000 (estimated)

Lynn

GRAND ARMY OF THE REPUBLIC HALL MUSEUM, 58 Andrew St., Lynn, MA 01901-1102. Mailing Address: c/o Lynn City Hall, 3 City Hall Sq., Lynn, MA 01901. Tel.: 781-477-7085.

E-mail: mlynngar@aol.com

Web Site: www.ci.lynn.ma.us/attractions_gar.shtml

Institution Type/Description: Historic Building: built in 1885 as a meeting place for General Frederick W. Lander Post No. 5. Listed on the National Register of Historic Places.

Hours & Admission Prices: By appointment.

LYNN MUSEUM & HISTORICAL SOCIETY, 590 Washington St., Lynn, MA 01901-1406. Tel.: 781-581-6200. Fax: 781-581-6202.

E-mail: office@lynnmuseum.org

Web Site: www.lynnmuseum.org

Formerly: Lynn Historical Society

Key Personnel: Dir. & Cur., Kate Luchini; Pres., Joseph Scanlon; Asst. Dir., Abby Battis; Public Rels. & Administrative Support, JoAnn Baker.

Institution Type/Description: Local History Museum: housed in old shoe factory building; Lynn Heritage State Park Visitor Center.

Hours & Admission Prices: Museum: Tues.-Wed. & Fri.-Sat. 12-4, Thurs. 12-8. Research & tours by appointment. Adults $5, children $2; discounts to AAA, AAM & ICOM members; members & Lynn School children 18 & under no charge. Closed state & national holidays. ♿

Attendance: 12,000 (estimated)

LYNNARTS, INC., 25 Exchange St., Lynn, MA 01901-1423. Tel.: 781-598-5244. Fax: 781-599-8926. Facebook: LynnArts, Inc..

E-mail: jenashworth@lynnarts.org

Web Site: www.lynnarts.org

Key Personnel: Coord. Operations, Jennifer Ashworth.

Institution Type/Description: Art Gallery.

Hours & Admission Prices: Mon.-Mon. & Fri. 10-4, Thurs. 11-7, Sat. 11-4. No charge, donations accepted. Closed New Year's Eve & Day; Thanksgiving; Dec. 23-Jan. 1 for Christmas.

Malden

MALDEN PUBLIC LIBRARY, 36 Salem St., Malden, MA 02148-5291. Tel.: 781-324-0218 & 388-0800. Fax: 781-324-4467.

E-mail: dmalgeri@maldenpubliclibrary.org

Web Site: www.maldenpubliclibrary.org

Key Personnel: Librarian, Dina G. Malgeri.

Institution Type/Description: Public Library with Special Art Collection.

Hours & Admission Prices: June-Aug. Mon.-Wed. 9-9, Thurs. 9-1 & 2-6, Fri. 9-6; Sept.-May Mon.-Wed. 9-9, Thurs. 9-1 & 2-9, Fri.-Sat. 9-6. No charge; donations accepted. Closed national holidays. ♿

Attendance: 100,000 (estimated)

Manchester

MANCHESTER HISTORICAL MUSEUM, 10 Union St., Manchester, MA 01944-1553. Tel.: 978-526-7230. Fax: 978-526-0060. Facebook: Manchester Historical Museum.

E-mail: info@manchesterhistoricalmuseum.org

Web Site: manchesterbytheseahistorical.org

Key Personnel: Dir., Beth Welin; Pres. (V), John Huss; Vice Pres. (V), Fafa Diedrich; Archivist, Christine Virden.

Institution Type/Description: Decorative Arts Museum.

Hours & Admission Prices: Tues.-Fri. 10-3; other times by appointment. Tours: adults $5; members no charge. ♿

Attendance: (estimated)

Marblehead

MARBLEHEAD ARTS ASSOCIATION - KING HOOPER MANSION, 8 Hooper St., Marblehead, MA 01945-3213. Tel.: 781-631-2608. Facebook: Marblehead Arts Association - King Hooper Mansion.

E-mail: info@marbleheadarts.org

Web Site: marbleheadarts.org

Key Personnel: Dir., M. Kristine Fisher; Asst. Dir., Betsy Hoffman Hundahl; Pres., Robin Taliesin.

Institution Type/Description: Art Association: housed in c.1728 colonial style mansion of Greenfield Hooper.

Hours & Admission Prices: Tues.-Sat. 10-5, Sun. 12-5. No charge; donations accepted. Large Tours: $3 per person. Closed week before Christmas; New Year's Day; Easter; Thanksgiving; Christmas.

Attendance: 5,000 (actual)

MARBLEHEAD MUSEUM, 170 Washington St., Marblehead, MA 01945-3340. Tel.: 781-631-1768. Fax: 781-631-0917. Facebook: Marblehead Museum & Historical Society.

E-mail: info@marbleheadmuseum.org

Web Site: www.marbleheadmuseum.org

Formerly: Marblehead Museum & Historical Society

Key Personnel: Dir., Pam Peterson; Pres., Jack Altridge; Treas., Mike Meehan; Cur. Museum & Jeremiah Lee Mansion, Karen MacInnis; Registrar, Jean Fallon.

Institution Type/Description: History & Folk Art Museum.

Hours & Admission Prices: Museum: Tues.-Sat. 10-4. Lee Mansion: June-Oct. Tues.-Sat. 10-4. Mansion: adults $10. Frost Gallery & Civil War Museum: no charge; donations accepted. Closed major holidays.

Attendance: 5,500 (estimated)

1768 JEREMIAH LEE MANSION, 161 Washington St., Marblehead, MA 01945-3303. Mailing Address: Marblehead Museum, 170 Washington St., Marblehead, MA 01945. Tel.: 781-631-1768. Fax: 781-631-0917.

E-mail: info@marbleheadmuseum.org

Web Site: www.marbleheadmuseum.org

Key Personnel: Dir., Pam Peterson; Cur. Collections, Emilia Boehm Emig.

Institution Type/Description: Decorative Arts & History Museum.

Hours & Admission Prices: Mansion: June-Oct. Tues.-Sat. 10-4. Adults $10, senior citizens $4.50; discounts to Massachusetts Teachers Assoc.; children under 12, students, & members no charge.

Attendance: 3,000 (estimated)

Marion

THE MARION ART CENTER GALLERY, 80 Pleasant St., Marion, MA 02738. Tel.: 508-748-1266. Fax: 508-748-2759.

E-mail: marionartcenter@verizon.net

Institution Type/Description: Art Gallery.

Hours & Admission Prices: Tues.-Fri. 1-5, Sat. 10-2. No charge.

MARION NATURAL HISTORY MUSEUM, 8 Spring St., Marion, MA 02738-1519. Mailing Address: P.O. Box 644, Marion, MA 02738-0011. Tel.: 508-748-2098.
E-mail: lizleid@msn.com
Web Site: www.marionmuseum.org
Key Personnel: Dir., Elizabeth Leidhold.
Institution Type/Description: Natural History Museum.
Hours & Admission Prices: Call for hours.

Marlboro

PETER RICE HOMESTEAD, HOME OF THE MARLBOROUGH HISTORICAL SOCIETY, INC., 377 Elm St., Marlboro, MA 01752-4518. Mailing Address: P.O. Box 513, Marlboro, MA 01752-0513. Tel.: 508-485-4763 & 251-1057.
E-mail: info@historicmarlborough.org
Web Site: www.historicmarlborough.org
Key Personnel: Pres., Janet Licht; Vice Pres., Peggy Ayres.
Institution Type/Description: Historic Museum: housed in 1688 Peter Rice homestead.
Hours & Admission Prices: By appointment and for special events & programs. No charge.
Attendance: 1,200 (estimated)

Marshfield

HISTORIC 1699 WINSLOW HOUSE, 634 Careswell St., Marshfield, MA 02050-5623. Mailing Address: P.O. Box 531, Marshfield, MA 02050-0531. Tel.: 781-837-5753.
E-mail: info@winslowhouse.org
Web Site: www.winslowhouse.org
Formerly: Isaac Winslow House
Key Personnel: Exec. Dir., Mark A. Schmidt; Pres. (V), Cynthia Hagar Krusell; Cur., Karin J. Goldstein.
Institution Type/Description: Historic House Museum: housed in the former home of Hon. Isaac Winslow, Marshfield's founding family; built in 1699.
Hours & Admission Prices: Wed.-Sun. 11-5. Adults $3, children $1; discounts for MA Teachers Association, WGBH, AAM & AAA members; members no charge. Closed Memorial Day; Independence Day; Labor Day.

Mashpee

CAPE COD CHILDREN'S MUSEUM, 577 Great Neck Rd. S., Mashpee, MA 02649-3708. Tel.: 508-539-8788. Fax: 508-539-3285.
E-mail: info@capecodchildrensmuseum.org
Web Site: www.capecodchildrensmuseum.org
Key Personnel: Exec. Dir., Barbara Cotton; Pres., Beth Russell; Dir. Exhibits & Operations and Museum Shop Mgr., Holly M. Dayton; Controller, Carol Pardee; Dir. Mktg. & Administration, Lisa Sheehy.
Institution Type/Description: Children's Museum.
Hours & Admission Prices: Summer: Mon.-Sat. 10-5, Sun. 12-5; Winter (after Labor Day): Mon.-Fri. 10-3, Sat. 10-5, Sun. 12-5. Adults & children $8, senior citizens 60 & over $7; discounts to groups, military & ACM; members & children under one no charge. Closed New Year's Day; Easter; Independence Day; Labor Day; Thanksgiving; Christmas Eve & Day.
Attendance: 50,000 (estimated)

MASHPEE HISTORICAL COMMISSION, 13 Great Neck Rd., N., Mashpee, MA 02649-2521. Mailing Address: 16 Great Neck Rd., N., Mashpee, MA 02649-2528. Tel.: 508-539-1400, ext. 8550.
E-mail: historic@ci.mashpee.ma.us
Web Site: www.ci.mashpee.ma.us
Key Personnel: Chm. (V), Lee Gurney; Historian, Rosemary Burns.
Institution Type/Description: History Museum.
Hours & Admission Prices: Mon. & Thurs. 10-2 & by appointment

MASHPEE WAMPANOAG INDIAN MUSEUM, 414 Main St., Mashpee, MA 02649-3707. Mailing Address: 483 Great Neck Rd. S., Mashpee, MA 02649. Tel.: 508-477-9339 & 0208, ext. 101. Fax: 508-477-1218.
E-mail: rpeters@mwtribe.com
Web Site: mashpeewampanoagtribe.com
Key Personnel: Dir. Tribal Historic Preservation, Ramona Peters; Museum Cultural Programs Devel., Gertrude (Kitty) Hendricks.
Institution Type/Description: History Museum: housed in the Bourne-Avant house; built in 1793. Listed on the National Register of Historic Places.
Hours & Admission Prices: Call for hours. No charge; donations accepted. &
Attendance: 4,300 (estimated)

Mattapoisett

MATTAPOISETT HISTORICAL SOCIETY MUSEUM, 5 Church St., Mattapoisett, MA 02739-2618. Mailing Address: P.O. Box 535, Mattapoisett, MA 02739-0535. Tel.: 508-758-2844. Facebook: Mattapoisett Historical Society.
E-mail: mattapoisett.museum@verizon.net
Web Site: www.mattapoisetthistoricalsociety.org
Key Personnel: Pres., Jennifer McIntire; Cur., Elizabeth Hutchison.
Institution Type/Description: History Museum: housed in the former Mattapoisett Christian Meeting House; built in 1821.
Hours & Admission Prices: July-Aug. Wed.-Sat. 1-4; Sept.-June by appointment only. Adults $5, children 6 & over $2; discounts to groups; members no charge. &
Attendance: 1,250 (estimated)

Medford

ROYALL HOUSE ASSOCIATION, 15 George St., Medford, MA 02155-4513. Tel.: 781-396-9032.
E-mail: royallhouseevent@aol.com
Web Site: www.royallhouse.org
Key Personnel: Exec. Dir., Tom Lincoln; Vice Pres., John Woods.
Institution Type/Description: Colonial History Museum.
Hours & Admission Prices: Tours: May 17-Oct. 26 Sat.-Sun. 1, 2, & 3. Families $16, adults $7, senior citizens & students $5; discounts to groups; children 17 & under & members no charge.
Attendance: 1,837 (actual)

TUFTS UNIVERSITY ART GALLERIES, Aidekman Arts Center, 40 Talbot Ave., Medford, MA 02155. Tel.: 617-627-3518. Fax: 617-627-3121.
E-mail: artgallery@tufts.edu
Web Site: artgallery.tufts.edu
Key Personnel: Chm. (V), Mara Williams; Chm. (V), Kenneth Aidekman; Dir. Galleries & Collections, Amy Ingrid Schlegel, Ph.D.; Sr. Exhibits Designer & AA Preparator, Doug Bell; Exhibitions Coord., Lissa Cramer.
Institution Type/Description: University Art Museum.
Hours & Admission Prices: Tues.-Wed. & Fri.-Sun. 11-5, Thurs. 11-8. Suggested Donation: adults $3; discounts to AAM & ICOM members. Closed major & university holidays. &
Attendance: 9,000 (actual)

Mendon

SOUTHWICK'S ZOO, 2 Southwick St., Mendon, MA 01756-1234. Tel.: 800-258-9182. Fax: 508-883-0242.
E-mail: betsey@southwickszoo.com
Web Site: southwickszoo.com
Institution Type/Description: Zoo.
Hours & Admission Prices: April 16-Oct. 16 daily 10-5. Adults 13 & over $20, senior citizens 62 & over and children 3-12 $15; discounts to AAM & AAA members; children 2 & under no charge. Combo Tickets: adults $28, children $25.
Attendance: 230,000 (estimated)

Middleborough

MIDDLEBOROUGH HISTORICAL ASSOCIATION, INC., 18 Jackson St., Middleborough, MA 02346-2469. Mailing Address: P. O. Box 304, Middleborough, MA 02346-0304. Tel.: 508-947-1969.
E-mail: middleboroughhistory@yahoo.com
Web Site: middleboroughhistoricalassociation.org/
Key Personnel: Pres., Doug Vantran.
Institution Type/Description: History Museum.
Hours & Admission Prices: May 30-Oct. Wed. & Sat. 12-3; other times by appointment. Adults $5, senior citizens $4, students $2; discounts to groups of 10 or more; MHA members & children under 6 no charge. Closed holidays.
Attendance: 400 (estimated)

ROBBINS MUSEUM OF ARCHAEOLOGY, 17 Jackson St., Middleborough, MA 02346-2413. Mailing Address: P.O. Box 700, Middleborough, MA 02346-0700. Tel.: 508-947-9005. Fax: 508-947-9005.
E-mail: info@massarchaeology.org
Web Site: www.massarchaeology.org/museum
Key Personnel: Pres., Philip Graham; Vice Pres., Frederick Robinson; Museum Coord., David DeMello; Financial Officer, Daniel Lorraine.
Institution Type/Description: Archaeology Museum: housed in c.1920 factory building.

Hours & Admission Prices: Wed. 10-4, Thurs. 10-2. Adults $5, children $2. &
Attendance: 1,100 (estimated)

Middleton

MIDDLETON HISTORICAL SOCIETY - LURA WOODSIDE WATKINS MUSEUM, 9 Pleasant St., Middleton, MA 01949. Mailing Address: P.O. Box 98, Middleton, MA 01949-8132. Tel.: 978-774-9301.
Key Personnel: Pres., Henry Tragert.
Institution Type/Description: Historical Society Museum.
Hours & Admission Prices: Sept.-May by appointment only, meetings 3rd Mon. each month. No charge; donations accepted.
Attendance: 500 (estimated)

Milton

BLUE HILLS TRAILSIDE MUSEUM, 1904 Canton Ave., Milton, MA 02186-2335. Tel.: 617-333-0690, ext. 0. Fax: 617-333-0814.
E-mail: bluehills@massaudubon.org
Web Site: www.massaudubon.org
Key Personnel: Dir., Norman Smith; Museum Shop Mgr., Liz Bastable.
Institution Type/Description: Natural History Museum & Environmental Education Center.
Hours & Admission Prices: April-Nov. Tues.-Sun. 10-5; Dec.-March Thurs.-Sun. 10-5. Adults $5, senior citizens 65 & over $4, children 2-12 $3; MAS members no charge. Closed New Year's Day; Thanksgiving; Christmas. &
Attendance: 125,000 (estimated)

FORBES HOUSE MUSEUM, 215 Adams St., Milton, MA 02186-4215. Tel.: 617-696-1815. Fax: 617-696-1907.
E-mail: info@forbeshousemuseum.org
Web Site: forbeshousemuseum.org
Key Personnel: Exec. Dir., Robin M Tagliaferri; Chm. Bd. Trustees, Mary Wendell.
Institution Type/Description: Historic House: restored to 1870s-1880s.
Hours & Admission Prices: Tours: Wed. & Sat.-Sun. 1 & 3. Adults $8, senior citizens & students $5; discounts to AAM members; children under 5 no charge. Closed major holidays & during large events; call for details.
Attendance: 4,000 (estimated)

SUFFOLK RESOLVES HOUSE, 1370 Canton Ave., Milton, MA 02186. Tel.: 617-333-9700.
E-mail: askmhs@miltonhistoricalsociety.org
Web Site: www.miltonhistoricalsociety.org
Institution Type/Description: Historic Society Museum: c.1774.
Hours & Admission Prices: By appointment, seasonal open houses. No charge; donations accepted. &

Monterey

THE BIDWELL HOUSE MUSEUM, 100 Art School Rd., Monterey, MA 01245. Mailing Address: P.O. Box 537, Monterey, MA 01245-0537. Tel.: 413-528-6888.
E-mail: bidwellhouse@gmail.com
Web Site: www.bidwellhousemuseum.org
Key Personnel: Pres., Robert Hoogs; Exec. Dir., Heather Kowalski.
Institution Type/Description: Historic House Museum: c.1760.
Hours & Admission Prices: Grounds: daily. No charge. Museum Guided Tours: Memorial Day to Columbus Day Thurs.-Mon. 11-4. Adults $10, seniors $8, students $5; discounts to AAM, MTA & AAA members; children under 6 & members no charge.
Attendance: 1,185 (actual)

Nantucket

ARTISTS ASSOCIATION OF NANTUCKET, 19 Washington St., Nantucket, MA 02554-3848. Mailing Address: P.O. Box 1104, Nantucket, MA 02554-1104. Tel.: 508-228-0722 (office) & 0294 (gallery). Fax: 508-228-9700.
E-mail: cecil@nantucketarts.org
Web Site: www.nantucketarts.org
Key Personnel: Mng. Dir., Cecil Barron Jensen; Gallery Dir., Robert Frazier; Gallery Asst., Susan Duane; Special Events & Membership Coord., Alison Cooley; Arts Program, Elizabeth Hunt O'Brien; Office Admin., Lucy Cobb.
Institution Type/Description: Art Gallery.
Hours & Admission Prices: Mon.-Fri. 10-3; call for seasonal hours. &
Attendance: 5,000

EGAN MARITIME INSTITUTE, 5 Bayberry Ct., Nantucket, MA 02554. Mailing Address: P.O. Box 2923, Nantucket, MA 02584. Tel.: 508-228-2505. Fax: 508-228-7069.
E-mail: egan@eganmaritime.org
Web Site: www.eganmaritime.org
Formerly: Egan Maritime Foundation
Key Personnel: Exec. Dir., Pauline Proch; Pres., Peter E. Hoey.
Institution Type/Description: Maritime, Art & History Museum.
Hours & Admission Prices: May-Oct. daily 10-4. Adults $10, seniors & students 6-17 $5; discounts to AAM & ICOM members; members, children under 6 & military no charge. &
Attendance: 5,000 (estimated)

MARIA MITCHELL ASSOCIATION NATURAL HISTORY MUSEUM, 7 Milk St., Nantucket, MA 02554-2635. Mailing Address: 4 Vestal St., Nantucket, MA 02554-2609. Tel.: 508-228-0898.
E-mail: info@mmo.org
Formerly: Hinchman House Natural History Museum
Key Personnel: Exec. Dir., Janet Shulte; Chm. (V), Malcolm MacNab, M.D.; Museum Shop Mgr., Cheryl Beaton.
Institution Type/Description: Natural History Museum.
Hours & Admission Prices: mid-June to early Sept. Mon.-Sat. 10-4; Oct. Fri.-Sat. 10-4. Adults $5, children $4; members no charge. &
Attendance: 2,000 (estimated)

NANTUCKET HISTORICAL ASSOCIATION, 15 Broad St., Nantucket, MA 02554-3502. Mailing Address: Box 1016, Nantucket, MA 02554-1016. Tel.: 508-228-1894, ext. 0. Fax: 508-228-5618.
E-mail: ask@nha.org
Web Site: www.nha.org
Key Personnel: Exec. Dir., Dr. William Tramposch; Pres., Janet L. Sherlund; 1st Vice Pres., Kenneth L. Beaugrand; Treas., William J. Boardman; Curatorial & Library Assoc., Sarah Helm; Chief Cur., Ben Simons; Dir. Visitor Experience, Marjan Shirzad; Museum Shop Mgr., Georgina Winton.
Institution Type/Description: History Museum.
Hours & Admission Prices: Museum: Feb. 2-April 14 & Nov. 2-Nov. 24 Sat.-Sun. 11-4; April 15-May 24 & Nov. 25-Dec. 1 daily 11-4; May 25-Nov. 1 & Dec.30-Dec. 31 daily 10-5; Dec. 6-Dec. 29 Fri.-Sun. 10-5. Museum & Historic Sites: adults $20, seniors & students with ID $18, youth 6-17 $5. Sites: adults $6, youth 6-17 $3. Closed New Year's Day; Thanksgiving. &
Attendance: 61,000 (actual)

NANTUCKET LIGHTSHIP BASKET MUSEUM, 49 Union St., Nantucket, MA 02554-3869. Mailing Address: P.O. Box 2517, Nantucket, MA 02584-2517. Tel.: 508-228-1177. Fax: 508-228-7092.
E-mail: adminoffice@nantucketlightshipbasketmuseum.org
Web Site: www.nantucketlightshipbasketmuseum.org
Key Personnel: Pres., Daryl Westbrook; Exec. Dir., Maryann Wasik; Dir., Mary Bergman.
Institution Type/Description: History Museum: housed in c.1821 home.
Hours & Admission Prices: May 21 to Oct. 10 Tues.-Sat. 10-4:30. Adults $5; discounts to senior & children; members no charge. Closed Independence Day. &
Attendance: 3,000 (actual)

NANTUCKET MARIA MITCHELL ASSOCIATION, 4 Vestal St., Nantucket, MA 02554-2609. Tel.: 508-228-9198. Fax: 508-228-1031.
E-mail: info@mmo.org
Web Site: www.mmo.org
Key Personnel: Pres. (V), Malcolm MacNab; Exec. Dir., Janet Schulte, Ph.D.; Dir. Education & Dir. Dept. Natural Science, Andrew McKenna-Foster; Dir. Astronomy, Vladimir Strelnitski, Ph.D.; Cur. Mitchell House, Jascin Leonardo-Finger; Museum Shop Mgr., Cheryl Comeau Beaton.
Institution Type/Description: Observatories, Natural Science & Historic House Museum.
Hours & Admission Prices: Historic House & Natural Science Museum: mid-June to Labor Day Mon.-Sat. 10-4. Adults $10, children under 14 $8; library & members no charge. &
Attendance: 15,000 (estimated)

NANTUCKET SHIPWRECK & LIFESAVING MUSEUM, 158 Polpis Rd., Nantucket, MA 02554-2320. Mailing Address: 4 Winter St., Nantucket, MA 02554-3638. Tel.: 508-228-1885.
E-mail: info@nantucketshipwreck.org
Web Site: www.nantucketshipwreck.org
Key Personnel: Exec. Dir. Egan Maritime Institute, Jean Grimmer; Pres. Bd., Allen Reinhard; Cur., Lisa McCandless.

Institution Type/Description: History Museum.
Hours & Admission Prices: Memorial Day to Columbus Day daily 10-4; other times by appointment. Adults $5, students & children $3; discounts to groups and AAM & ICOM members; members, active USCG, CAMM & museum professionals no charge. &
Attendance: 9,000 (actual)

Natick

MUSEUM OF WORLD WAR II, 8 Mercer Rd., Natick, MA 01760. Mailing Address: 46 Eliot St., Natick, MA 01760-6042. Tel.: 508-651-1944. Fax: 508-655-1944.
E-mail: museumofworldwarii@yahoo.com
Web Site: www.museumofworldwarii.com
Key Personnel: Dir. & Pres., Kenneth W. Rendell; Visitation & Veteran Affairs, Jeff Farrell.
Institution Type/Description: Military Museum.
Hours & Admission Prices: Tues.-Sat. by appointment. No charge; donations accepted. &
Attendance: 10,500 (actual)

NATICK HISTORICAL SOCIETY, 58 Eliot St., Natick, MA 01760-5542. Tel.: 508-647-4841.
E-mail: info@natickhistoricalsociety.org
Web Site: www.natickhistoricalsociety.org
Formerly: Historical Natural History & Library Society of Natick dba Natick Historical Society
Key Personnel: Exec. Dir., Jane Hennedy; Pres. (V), Margarita Balcom; Cur., Benjamin Federlin.
Institution Type/Description: Historical Society Museum.
Hours & Admission Prices: Tues. 2-8, Wed. 10-2, Sat. 10-1. No charge; donations accepted. Research $10; special events $5; discounts to AAM & ICOM members, members no charge. &
Attendance: 1,300 (estimated)

New Bedford

ARTWORKS!, 608 Pleasant St., New Bedford, MA 02740. Tel.: 508-984-1588.
E-mail: info@artworksforyou.org
Web Site: artworksforyou.org
Institution Type/Description: Art Gallery.
Hours & Admission Prices: Tues.-Sat. 12-5. No charge.

BUTTONWOOD PARK ZOO, 425 Hawthorn St., New Bedford, MA 02740-1418. Tel.: 508-991-6178. Fax: 508-979-1508.
E-mail: info@bpzoo.org
Web Site: bpzoo.org
Key Personnel: Dir., Keith Lovett.
Institution Type/Description: Zoo.
Hours & Admission Prices: Daily 10-5. Adults New Bedford resident $6, non-resident $8; seniors & students New Bedford resident $4.50, non-resident $6; children 3-12 New Bedford resident $3, non-resident $4; children under 3 no charge. Closed New Year's; Thanksgiving; Christmas. &
Attendance: 210,000 (estimated)

MUSEUM OF MADEIRAN HERITAGE, 1 Funchal Pl., New Bedford, MA 02746. Mailing Address: 50 Madeira Ave., New Bedford, MA 02746-2343. Tel.: 508-994-2573. Fax: 508-992-5382.
E-mail: mmh1999@comcast.net
Web Site: www.museumofmadeiranheritage.com
Key Personnel: Chm. (V), Joseph V. Sousa.
Institution Type/Description: History Museum: dedicated to preserving the art and artifacts of the Portuguese island of Madeira.
Hours & Admission Prices: May-Oct. Sun. 1-4. No charge; donations accepted. &
Attendance: 200 (estimated)

NEW BEDFORD ART MUSEUM, 608 Pleasant St., New Bedford, MA 02740-6204. Tel.: 508-961-3072.
E-mail: info@newbedfordartmuseum.org
Web Site: www.newbedfordartmuseum.org
Key Personnel: Interim Dir., Kathryn Dinneen; Pres., Marilyn Whalley; Treas., Kevin Baptista; Museum Shop Mgr., Nooshin Navidi.
Institution Type/Description: Art Museum.
Hours & Admission Prices: Wed.-Sun. 12-5. Adults $5, seniors & students $3; 2nd Tues. of month & members no charge. Closed holidays. &
Attendance: 5,000 (estimated)

NEW BEDFORD FIRE MUSEUM, Old Station No. 4, 51 Bedford St., New Bedford, MA 02740-4815. Tel.: 508-992-2162.
Key Personnel: Dir., Larry Roy.
Institution Type/Description: Fire Museum: housed in 1867 fire station.
Hours & Admission Prices: July-Aug. Mon.-Sat. 12-4. Adults $3, seniors $2, children 6 & over $1; children under 6 no charge.

NEW BEDFORD WHALING MUSEUM, 18 Johnny Cake Hill, New Bedford, MA 02740-6398. Tel.: 508-997-0046. Fax: 508-997-0018.
E-mail: frontdesk@whalingmuseum.org
Web Site: www.whalingmuseum.org
Key Personnel: Chm. Bd., Armand Fernandes; Pres. & CEO, James Russell; Vice Pres. Opers. & C.F.O., Michelle Taylor.
Institution Type/Description: Whaling & Maritime Museum.
Hours & Admission Prices: April-Oct. daily 9-5; Nov.-March Tues.-Sat. 9-4, Sun.11-4. Adults $14, seniors 65 & over $12, students $9, children $6; children 5 & under no charge. Closed New Year's Day; Thanksgiving; Christmas. &
Attendance: 110,000 (actual)

THE ROTCH-JONES-DUFF HOUSE & GARDEN MUSEUM, INC., 396 County St., New Bedford, MA 02740-4934. Tel.: 508-997-1401. Fax: 508-997-6846.
E-mail: info@rjdmuseum.org
Web Site: www.rjdmuseum.org
Key Personnel: Exec. Dir., Kate Corkum; Pres. (V), Stewart Young; Treas., Nathanel R. Brayton.
Institution Type/Description: Historic House & Garden: c.1834, Greek Revival house & formal gardens.
Hours & Admission Prices: Mon.-Sat. 10-4, Sun. 12-4. Adults $6, senior citizens and AAM & AAA members $5, children under 12 $2; members no charge. Closed major holidays. &
Attendance: 10,603 (actual)

UNIVERSITY ART GALLERY, UNIVERSITY OF MASSACHUSETTS DARTMOUTH, College of Visual and Performing Arts, 715 Purchase St., New Bedford, MA 02740-6341. Tel.: 508-999-8555. Fax: 508-999-8912.
E-mail: vlevitt@umassd.edu
Web Site: www.umassd.edu/universityartgallery
Key Personnel: Dir., Viera Levitt.
Institution Type/Description: Art Gallery.
Hours & Admission Prices: June-Aug. Mon.-Sat. 9-6, Sun. 12-5; Sept.-May daily 9-6. No charge. &
Attendance: 10,000 (estimated)

New Braintree

NEW BRAINTREE HISTORICAL SOCIETY, 10 Utley Rd., New Braintree, MA 01531-9800. Mailing Address: P.O. Box 112, New Braintree, MA 01531-0112. Tel.: 508-867-8608.
E-mail: NBHS@newbraintreehistoricalsociety.org
Web Site: www.newbraintreehistoricalsociety.org
Key Personnel: Pres., Tom Fiorelli.
Institution Type/Description: Historical Society.
Hours & Admission Prices: By appointment only.

Newbury

COFFIN HOUSE, 14 High Rd., Newbury, MA 01951. Mailing Address: 141 Cambridge St., Boston, MA 02114-2702. Tel.: 978-462-2634.
E-mail: coffinhouse@historicnewengland.org
Web Site: www.historicnewengland.org
Key Personnel: Pres. & C.E.O., Carl R. Nold; Site Mgr., Bethany Groff.
Institution Type/Description: Historic House: 1678 Coffin House.
Hours & Admission Prices: June-Oct. 15 1st & 3rd Sat. each month 11-5; last tour at 4pm. Adults $8; discounts to seniors, AAM, ICOM, AAA, WGBH members; Historic New England members no charge.
Attendance: 1,242 (actual)

SPENCER-PEIRCE-LITTLE FARM, 5 Little's Lane, Newbury, MA 01951-1802. Mailing Address: 141 Cambridge St., Boston, MA 02114-2702. Tel.: 978-462-2634. Facebook: Spencer-Peirce-Little Farm.
E-mail: Info@HistoricNewEngland.org
Web Site: www.historicnewengland.org
Key Personnel: Pres. & C.E.O., Carl R. Nold; Site Mgr., Bethany Groff.

Institution Type/Description: National Historic House/Landmark: c.1690 rare stone & brick cruciform-plan house.
Hours & Admission Prices: June-Oct. 15 Thurs.-Sun. 11-5, grounds open sunrise to sunset. Adults $8, children $4; discounts to seniors, AAM, ICOM & AAA members; Historic New England members no charge. Call for more information.
Attendance: 32,336 (actual)

Newburyport

THE CUSTOM HOUSE MARITIME MUSEUM, 25 Water St., Newburyport, MA 01950-2754. Mailing Address: Newburyport Maritime Society, Inc., 25 Water St., Newburyport, MA 01950. Tel.: 978-462-8681. Fax: 978-462-8740. Facebook: The CHMM.
E-mail: info@thechmm.org
Web Site: www.thechmm.org
Key Personnel: Chm., Michael Mroz.
Institution Type/Description: Maritime Museum: housed in 1835 Greek Revival style Custom House.
Hours & Admission Prices: Jan.-April Sun. & holiday Mon. 12-4, Sat. 10-4; May-Dec. Sun. & holiday Mon. 12-4, Tues.-Sat. 10-4. Adults $7, senior citizens $5, children 6-18 $3.50; active military, members & children under 6 no charge.
Attendance: 22,853 (actual)

MUSEUM OF OLD NEWBURY, 98 High St., Newburyport, MA 01950-3053. Tel.: 978-462-2681. Facebook; Historical Society of Old Newbury, Cushing House Museum.
E-mail: info@newburyhist.org
Web Site: www.newburyhist.org
Formerly: Historical Society of Old Newbury, Cushing House Museum
Key Personnel: Exec. Dir., Susan Edwards; Co-Pres., Christopher Armstrong; Co-Pres., David Mack.
Institution Type/Description: History Museum: housed in 1808 Cushing House, a Federal mansion, home of Caleb Cushing, first envoy to China.
Hours & Admission Prices: Museum: May-Oct. Tues.-Fri. 10-4, Sat.-Sun. 12-4. Library by appointment only. Adults $8, senior citizens $7, students & children under 12 $2; discounts to AAM members, groups; members no charge. Closed holidays.
Attendance: 2,000 (estimated)

Newton

HISTORIC NEWTON, JACKSON HOMESTEAD AND MUSEUM, DURANT-KENRICK HOUSE & GROUNDS, 527 Washington St., Newton, MA 02458-1433. Tel.: 617-796-1450. Fax: 617-552-7228. Facebook: Historic Newton.
E-mail: cstone@newtonma.gov
Web Site: historicnewton.org
Formerly: The Newton History Museum at The Jackson Homestead
Key Personnel: Dir. & C.E.O., Cynthia Stone; Pres. Newton Historical Soc. (V), Carl M. Cohen; Cur., Sara Goldberg; Cur. Education, Melissa Westlake.
Institution Type/Description: History Museum.
Hours & Admission Prices: Tues.-Fri. 11-5, Sat.-Sun. 12-5; research by appointment. Adults $5, senior citizens & children 6-17 $3; discounts to Newton residents and AAA, NARM, AAM, ICOM & NEMA members; members no charge. &
Attendance: 17,000 (actual)

MAYYIM HAYYIM ART GALLERY, 1838 Washington St., Newton, MA 02466. Tel.: 617-244-1836, ext. 211. Fax: 617-244-1830.
E-mail: info@mayyimhayyim.org
Web Site: www.mayyimhayyim.org
Key Personnel: Exec. Dir., Carrie Bornstein; Mgr. Devel., DeDe Jacobs-Komisar.
Institution Type/Description: Art Gallery.
Hours & Admission Prices: Call for hours. No charge; donations accepted. &

Newtonville

NEW ART CENTER, 61 Washington Park, Newtonville, MA 02460-1915. Tel.: 617-964-3424. Fax: 617-630-0081.
E-mail: info@newartcenter.org
Web Site: www.newartcenter.org
Formerly: Newton Art Center
Institution Type/Description: Art Gallery.
Hours & Admission Prices: Mon.-Fri. 9-5, Sat.-Sun. 1-5. No charge; donations accepted.

North Adams

MASS MOCA, 87 Marshall St., North Adams, MA 01247-2402. Mailing Address: 1040 Mass MoCA Way, North Adams, MA 01247-2499. Tel.: 413-664-4481. Fax: 413-663-8548.
E-mail: info@massmoca.org
Web Site: www.massmoca.org
Key Personnel: Dir., Joseph Thompson; Chm. (V), Hans Morris; Financial Dir., Andrea Hockridge; Cur., Susan Cross; Cur., Denise Markonish; Mktg. & Public Rels., Jodi Joseph; Museum Shop Mgr., Phyllis Criddle.
Institution Type/Description: Art Museum.
Hours & Admission Prices: July-Aug. daily 10-6; Sept.-June Wed.-Mon. 11-5. Adults $18, seniors & veterans $16; students $12, children 6-16 $8; discount to groups; kidspace, children 5 & under and members no charge. Closed Thanksgiving; Christmas. &
Attendance: 165,000 (estimated)

NORTH ADAMS MUSEUM OF HISTORY AND SCIENCE, Western Gateway Heritage State Park, Bldg. 5A, 9 Furnace St. Bypass, North Adams, MA 01247-3820. Tel.: 413-664-4700. Facebook: North Adams History.
E-mail: nahs@bcn.net
Web Site: northadamshistory.org
Institution Type/Description: Historical Society Museum.
Hours & Admission Prices: May-Oct. Thurs.-Sat. 10-4, Sun. 1-4; Nov.-April Sat. 10-4, Sun. 1-4. No charge; donations accepted. Closed holidays.
Attendance: 2,127 (actual)

North Andover

MUSEUM OF PRINTING, 800 Massachusetts Ave., North Andover, MA 01845-4544. Mailing Address: P.O. Box 5580, Beverly, MA 01915. Tel.: 978-686-0450.
E-mail: info@museumofprinting.org
Web Site: www.museumofprinting.org
Key Personnel: Exec. Dir., Ted Leigh; Pres. (V), Kim Pickard.
Institution Type/Description: Printing History Museum.
Hours & Admission Prices: Fri.-Sat. 10-4; other times by appointment. Adults $5, students & seniors $3; members & children under 6 no charge. Closed national holidays. &
Attendance: 2,211 (actual)

NORTH ANDOVER HISTORICAL SOCIETY, 153 Academy Rd., North Andover, MA 01845-4037. Tel.: 978-686-4035. Fax: 978-686-6616. Facebook; North Andover Historical Society.
E-mail: director.nahistory@gmail.com
Web Site: www.northandoverhistoricalsociety.org
Key Personnel: Dir. & C.E.O., Carol Majahad; Pres. (V), Stanley Limpert.
Institution Type/Description: Historical Society: housed in the Samuel Dale Stevens Memorial Building.
Hours & Admission Prices: Johnson Cottage: Tues.-Fri. 10-3; other times by appointment. Adults $7, senior citizens 65 & over, students and children $5; discounts to AAM, NEMA, & MTA members; members no charge. Parson Barnard House: June-Oct. 1st Sat. each month 11-3. Admission by donation. Research Library: $15 1st hour, $10 each additional hour; discounts to students; NEMA & AAM members no charge. Closed holidays except Veterans Day.
Attendance: 3,000 (estimated)

THE STEVENS-COOLIDGE PLACE, A PROPERTY OF THE TRUSTEES, 137 Andover St., North Andover, MA 01845. Mailing Address: 113 Andover St., North Andover, MA 01845. Tel.: 978-689-9105. Facebook: @stevenscoolidgeplace.
E-mail: kblock@thetrustees.org
Web Site: www.thetrustees.org
Key Personnel: Supt., Kevin Block; Pres. & C.E.O., Barbara Erickson; Cultural Resources Program Dir., Cindy Brockway; Engagement Site Mgr., Kate Bibeau.
Institution Type/Description: Historic House: early 19th century restored Colonial Revival style house with period gardens.
Hours & Admission Prices: Gardens: daily 8am to sunset. House: by appointment only. No charge; donations accepted.
Attendance: 10,000 (estimated)

North Easton

THE CHILDREN'S MUSEUM IN EASTON, 9 Sullivan Ave., North Easton, MA 02356-1419. Mailing Address: P.O. Box 417, North Easton, MA 02356-0417. Tel.: 508-230-3789. Fax: 508-230-7130.
E-mail: paula@childrensmuseumeaston.org
Web Site: childrensmuseumineaston.org

Key Personnel: C.E.O., Paula J. Peterson; Chm., Karen Rodgers; Museum Shop Mgr., Karen Frick.

Institution Type/Description: Children's Museum: located in fire station in town's historical district.

Hours & Admission Prices: Tues.-Fri. 9-5, Sat.-Sun. 12-5; call for holiday & summer hours. Admission $9; discounts to ACM reciprocal members. Closed major holidays.

Attendance: 55,000 (estimated)

North Oxford

CLARA BARTON BIRTHPLACE MUSEUM, 66 Clara Barton Rd., North Oxford, MA 01537-1301. Mailing Address: P.O. Box 356, North Oxford, MA 01537-0356. Tel.: 508-987-2056, ext. 2006. Fax: 508-987-2002.

E-mail: clarabartonbirthplace@bartoncenter.org

Web Site: www.clarabartonbirthplace.org

Key Personnel: Mgr., Donna Joly.

Institution Type/Description: Historic House Museum: c.1818-20 Clara Barton Birthplace.

Hours & Admission Prices: June-Aug. Fri.-Sun. 10-4; Sept. Sat. 10-4; other times by appointment. Adults $6, children 6-12 $3; discounts to groups, Mass. Teachers Assn., & Red Cross volunteers; members no charge.

Attendance: 1,200 (estimated)

North Woburn

RUMFORD HISTORICAL ASSOCIATION, 90 Elm St., North Woburn, MA 01801. Mailing Address: # 11 Lowell St., Woburn, MA 01801.

Key Personnel: Pres. (V), Leonard Harmon.

Institution Type/Description: Historic House: 1714 Count Rumford's birthplace.

Hours & Admission Prices: Sat.-Sun. 1-4:30. No charge; donations accepted. Closed New Year's Day; Christmas.

Attendance: 500 (estimated)

Northampton

THE BOTANIC GARDEN OF SMITH COLLEGE, Lyman Plant House & Conservatory, 16 College Lane, Northampton, MA 01063-6352. Tel.: 413-585-2740 & 2742. Fax: 413-585-2744.

E-mail: garden@smith.edu

Web Site: www.smith.edu/garden

Key Personnel: Dir., Tim Johnson.

Institution Type/Description: Botanical Garden: housed in 1890s greenhouses built by Lord & Burnham, on site of Smith College campus, a 125 acre arboretum.

Hours & Admission Prices: Daily 8:30-4. Suggested Donation: $2. Closed New Year's Day; Thanksgiving; Christmas Eve, Day & week. &

Attendance: 100,000

CALVIN COOLIDGE PRESIDENTIAL LIBRARY & MUSEUM, 20 West St., Northampton, MA 01060-3713. Tel.: 413-587-1014, 1012 or 1011. Fax: 413-587-1015.

E-mail: coolidge@forbeslibrary.org

Web Site: www.forbeslibrary.org

Formerly: Calvin Coolidge Memorial Room, Forbes Library

Key Personnel: Archivist, Julie Bartlett.

Institution Type/Description: Presidential Museum.

Hours & Admission Prices: Mon. & Wed. 3-9, Tues. & Thurs. 1-5, Sat. by appointment. No charge. Closed major holidays. &

HISTORIC NORTHAMPTON, 46 Bridge St., Northampton, MA 01060-2428. Tel.: 413-584-6011. Fax: 413-584-7956.

E-mail: mailbox@historic-northampton.org

Web Site: www.historic-northampton.org

Key Personnel: Dir., Kerry W. Buckley; Pres., Ronald Story; Museum Asst., Marie Panik.

Institution Type/Description: History Museum.

Hours & Admission Prices: Museum: Tues.-Sat. 10-5, Sun. 12-5. Adults $3; members no charge. Research: by appointment. No charge. &

Attendance: 2,728 (actual)

NORTHAMPTON CENTER FOR THE ARTS, 5 Strong Ave., Ste. 202, Northampton, MA 01060-4075. Mailing Address: P.O. Box 366, Northampton, MA 01061-0366. Tel.: 413-584-7327. Fax: 413-582-9014.

E-mail: ncfa@nohoarts.org

Web Site: nohoarts.org

Institution Type/Description: Art Gallery.

Hours & Admission Prices: Closed for relocation.

SMITH COLLEGE MUSEUM OF ART, 20 Elm St. at Bedford Ter., Northampton, MA 01063. Tel.: 413-585-2760. Fax: 413-585-2782.

E-mail: artmuseum@smith.edu

Web Site: www.smith.edu/artmuseum

Key Personnel: Dir., Jessica F. Nicoll; Assoc. Dir., Lily Foster; Cur. Prints, Drawings, & Photographs, Aprile Gallant; Collections Mgr. & Registrar, Deborah Diemente; Cur. Education, Maggie Lind Newey; Dir. Membership & Mktg., Margi Caplan.

Institution Type/Description: Art Museum.

Hours & Admission Prices: Tues.-Sat. 10-4, Thurs. 10-8, Sun. 12-4, 2nd Fri. of month 10-8. Adults $5, seniors 65 & over $4; 2nd Fri. of month 4-8 & members no charge. Closed major holidays. &

Attendance: 37,960 (actual)

Northborough

NORTHBOROUGH HISTORICAL SOCIETY, INC., 50 Main St., Northborough, MA 01532. Mailing Address: P.O. Box 661, Northborough, MA 01532-0661. Tel.: 508-393-6298 & 2343.

E-mail: nhs1906@verizon.net

Web Site: www.northboroughhistsoc.org

Key Personnel: Pres., Kevin Carroll; Cur., Ellen Racine; Historian, Bob Ellis.

Institution Type/Description: General Museum: housed in 1860 Baptist Church.

Hours & Admission Prices: May-June & Sept.-Oct. Sun. 2-4; others times by appointment. No charge; donations accepted.

Attendance: 871 (actual)

Norton

BEARD & WEIL GALLERIES, 26 E. Main St., Norton, MA 02766-2311. Tel.: 508-286-3574. Fax: 508-286-3565.

E-mail: lheureux_michele@wheatoncollege.edu

Web Site: wheatoncollege.edu/gallery

Formerly: Watson Gallery, Wheaton College

Key Personnel: Cur. Collections & Registrar, Leah Niederstadt.

Institution Type/Description: College Art Gallery: located within the Norton, MA historic district.

Hours & Admission Prices: Mon.-Sat. 12:30-4:30. No charge. Closed during college vacations. &

Attendance: 2,000 (estimated)

MASSACHUSETTS GOLF MUSEUM, 300 Arnold Palmer Blvd., Norton, MA 02766-1365. Tel.: 774-430-9100. Fax: 774-430-9101.

E-mail: info@mgalinks.org

Web Site: www.mgalinks.org/about-us/history_golfmuseum.html

Key Personnel: Exec. Dir., Jesse Menachem.

Institution Type/Description: Golf Museum.

Hours & Admission Prices: Mon.-Fri. 9-4. No charge. &

Norwell

SOUTH SHORE NATURAL SCIENCE CENTER, INC., 48 Jacobs Lane, Norwell, MA 02061-1149. Tel.: 781-659-2559. Fax: 781-659-5924.

E-mail: ssnsc@comcast.net

Web Site: www.ssnsc.org

Key Personnel: Exec. Dir., Pam Musk; Chm. Bd. (V), Andrew Sullivan; Business Mgr., Tracey Cooke; Museum Shop Mgr., Wendy Blomberg.

Institution Type/Description: Nature Center/Conservation Area.

Hours & Admission Prices: Mon.-Sat. 9-5, Sun. 11-4. Adults $7, seniors $5, children 3-15 $3; members no charge. Closed New Year's Day; Easter; Memorial Day; Independence Day; Labor Day; Thanksgiving; Christmas. &

Attendance: 48,000 (estimated)

Norwood

THE F. HOLLAND DAY HOUSE & NORWOOD HISTORY MUSEUM, 93 Day St., Norwood, MA 02062-2118. Tel.: 781-762-9197.

E-mail: info@norwoodhistoricalsociety.org

Web Site: www.norwoodhistoricalsociety.org

Institution Type/Description: Historic House: former home of Fred Holland Day. Listed on the National Register of Historic Places.

Hours & Admission Prices: Tours: June-Aug. Sun. 1-4; group tours & other times by appointment. Adults $5; Norwood Historical Society members no charge.

Oak Bluffs

COTTAGE MUSEUM - MARTHA'S VINEYARD CAMP MEETING ASSOCIATION, 1 Trinity Park, Oak Bluffs, MA 02557. Mailing Address: P.O. Box 1176, 80 Trinity Park, Oak Bluffs, MA 02557-1176. Tel.: 508-693-0525. Fax: 508-696-8661.
E-mail: office@mvcma.org
Web Site: www.mvcma.org/museum.htm
Key Personnel: Gen. Mgr. & Exec. Dir., Bob Clermont; Museum Shop Mgr., Earl Jecoy.
Institution Type/Description: Historic House: 1800s campground cottage. Listed on the National Register of Historic Places. A Historical Landmark.
Hours & Admission Prices: Summer: Mon.-Sat. 10-4, Sun. 1-4. Adults $2, children 3-12 $.50; children under 3 no charge.
Attendance: 15,000 (estimated)

Orleans

FRENCH CABLE STATION MUSEUM IN ORLEANS, 41 S. Orleans Rd., Orleans, MA 02653. Mailing Address: Box 85, Orleans, MA 02653-0085. Tel.: 508-240-1735.
E-mail: info@frenchcablestationmuseum.org
Web Site: www.frenchcablestationmuseum.org
Key Personnel: Pres. (V) & Dir., Joseph Manas.
Institution Type/Description: Atlantic Cable Terminal; Communications Museum: housed in 1891 building, built to house cable laid from France to Orleans.
Hours & Admission Prices: June-Sept. Fri.-Sun. 1-4. No charge; donations accepted.
Attendance: 1,050 (actual)

Osterville

OSTERVILLE HISTORICAL MUSEUM, 155 W. Bay Rd., Osterville, MA 02655-2427. Mailing Address: P.O. Box 3, Osterville, MA 02655-0003. Tel.: 508-428-5861.
E-mail: ohs@ostervillemuseum.org
Web Site: www.ostervillemuseum.org
Key Personnel: Exec. Dir., Jennifer Williams; Pres. (V), Kathleen Capo.
Institution Type/Description: Historical Society Museum: housed in late 18th-century Jonathan Parker House; 18th-century Cammett House; Wooden Boat Museum; Colonial Garden.
Hours & Admission Prices: June-Sept. Thurs.-Sat. 10-2; other times by appointment. No charge; donations accepted.
Attendance: 6,370 (actual)

Oxford

OXFORD LIBRARY MUSEUM, 339 Main St., Oxford, MA 01540-1729. Tel.: 508-987-6003. Fax: 508-987-3896.
E-mail: oplreference@town.oxford.ma.us
Web Site: oxfordmapubliclibrary.com
Key Personnel: Dir. Library, Brittany McDougal.
Institution Type/Description: Local History Museum.
Hours & Admission Prices: By appointment only, preferably at least a week's notice. No charge; donations accepted. ♿
Attendance: 20 (estimated)

Paxton

FINE ARTS CENTER AT MIRIAM HALL, ANNA MARIA COLLEGE, 50 Sunset Ln., Paxton, MA 01612-1106. Tel.: 508-849-3450. Fax: 508-849-3408.
Web Site: www.annamaria.edu
Formerly: Moll Art Center, Anna Maria College
Institution Type/Description: Art Gallery.
Hours & Admission Prices: Mon.-Fri. 10-1. No charge; donations accepted. Closed major holidays. ♿
Attendance: 600 (estimated)

Peabody

FELTON-SMITH HISTORIC SITE - PEABODY HISTORICAL FIRE MUSEUM, 38 Rear Felton St., Peabody, MA 01960. Mailing Address: Peabody Historical Society, 33 Washington St., Peabody, MA 01960. Tel.: 978-531-0805. Fax: 978-531-7292.
E-mail: info@peabodyhistorical.org
Web Site: www.peabodyhistorical.org
Key Personnel: Exec. Dir., William Power.
Institution Type/Description: Historic Buildings.
Hours & Admission Prices: Fire Museum & Senior House: April-Nov. 1 Mon. & Fri. 10-3. Junior House: April-Nov. 1 Mon. & Fri. 11-3.

GEORGE PEABODY HOUSE MUSEUM & PEABODY LEATHERWORKERS MUSEUM, 205 Washington St., Peabody, MA 01960. Tel.: 978-531-0355.
Web Site: www.peabodymuseums.org
Institution Type/Description: Historic House Museum: housed in the birthplace of George Peabody, an international merchant & financier.
Hours & Admission Prices: House: Mon.-Wed. & Fri.-Sat. 10-3, Thurs. 10-7, Sun. 12-4. Museum: Tues.-Thurs. & Sat. 11-3. No charge. Closed New Year's Eve & Day; Independence Day; Labor Day; Columbus Day; Veterans Day; Thanksgiving; Christmas.

OSBORNE-SALATA HOUSE, RUTH HILL LIBRARY & ARCHIVES, 33 Washington St., Peabody, MA 01960. Mailing Address: 35 Washington St., Peabody, MA 01960. Tel.: 978-531-0805. Fax: 978-531-7292.
E-mail: info@peabodyhistorical.org
Web Site: www.peabodyhistorical.org
Institution Type/Description: Historic House Museum: c.1860.
Hours & Admission Prices: Wed. 1-4; other times by appointment. No charge; donations accepted.

PEABODY HISTORICAL SOCIETY, 35 Washington St., Peabody, MA 01960-5520. Tel.: 978-531-0805. Fax: 978-531-7292.
E-mail: phs_m@juno.com
Web Site: www.peabodyhistorical.org
Key Personnel: Pres., William Power; Vice Pres., Andrew Metropolis; Treas., Thomas Zellen; Cur., Heather Leavell.
Institution Type/Description: Historical Society Museum: housed in the former home of General Gideon Foster from 1818-1831.
Hours & Admission Prices: Tues.-Fri. 10-3, 1st & 3rd Sun. each month; other times by appointment. No charge.

Pembroke

PEMBROKE HISTORICAL SOCIETY, INC., 116 Center St., Pembroke, MA 02359. Mailing Address: P.O. Box 122, Pembroke, MA 02359-0239. Tel.: 781-293-9083. Facebook: Pembroke Historical Society.
E-mail: info@pembrokehistorical/society.ort@aol.org
Web Site: www.townofpembrokemass.org/historicalsociety
Key Personnel: Pres. (V), Beth Dwyer; Treas., Suzanne Scroggins; Sec., Lauren Richmond; Cur., Jaclyn Robinson; Research Dir., Karen Proctor.
Institution Type/Description: Historical Society Museums.
Hours & Admission Prices: By appointment only. No charge; donations accepted.
Attendance: 200 (estimated)

Petersham

FISHER MUSEUM OF FORESTRY, 324 N. Main St., Petersham, MA 01366-9504. Tel.: 978-724-3302. Fax: 978-724-3595.
E-mail: hf-edu@fas.harvard.edu
Web Site: harvardforest.fas.harvard.edu/fisher-museum
Key Personnel: Dir. Harvard Forest, David R. Foster.
Institution Type/Description: Forestry Museum.
Hours & Admission Prices: May-Oct. Mon.-Fri. 9-4, Sat.-Sun. 12-4; Nov.-April Mon.-Fri. 9-4. No charge; donations accepted. Closed holidays. ♿
Attendance: 5,000 (estimated)

PETERSHAM HISTORICAL SOCIETY, INC., 10 N. Main St., Petersham, MA 01366. Mailing Address: P.O. Box 364, Petersham, MA 01366-0364.
E-mail: info@historicalsocietyofphillipston.org
Key Personnel: Pres. (V), Henry Woolsey; Cur., Christine Mandel.
Institution Type/Description: History Society Museum.
Hours & Admission Prices: May-Oct. Sat. 12-4; other times by appointment. No charge.
Attendance: 400 (estimated)

Pittsfield

BERKSHIRE COUNTY HISTORICAL SOCIETY, INC. - ARROWHEAD, 780 Holmes Road, Pittsfield, MA 01201-7199. Tel.: 413-442-1793. Fax: 413-443-1449. Facebook: Herman Melville's Arrowhead.
E-mail: melville@berkshire.net

Web Site: www.mobydick.org
Key Personnel: Exec. Dir. & Cur., Will Garrison.
Institution Type/Description: History House Museum: Arrowhead, home of Herman Melville, 1850-1863. A National Historic Landmark.
Hours & Admission Prices: Society: Mon.-Fri. 9:30-4. Library & Archives: by appointment. Arrowhead: Memorial Day-Oct. Fri.-Wed. 10:30-4; other times by appointment. Adults $12, children 6-18 $8; discount to members; AASLH, NEMA, & BSHL members and children under 5 no charge. Closed New Year's Day; Easter; Thanksgiving; Christmas. &
Attendance: 4,500 (actual)

BERKSHIRE MUSEUM, 39 South St. (Route 7), Pittsfield, MA 01201-6169. Tel.: 413-443-7171. Fax: 413-443-2135.
E-mail: info@berkshiremuseum.org
Web Site: berkshiremuseum.org
Key Personnel: Exec. Dir., Van Shields; Pres. (V), William M. Hines, Jr.; Dir. Finance & Administration, Jon C. Provost; Dir. Communications, Lesley Ann Beck; Dir. Devel., Nina Garlington; Dir. Education & Public Programs, Craig Langlois; Dir. Advancement, Laurie Werner; Dir. Curatorial Affairs & Collections, Maria Mingalone; Museum Shop Mgr., Tracey Rock.
Institution Type/Description: General Museum.
Hours & Admission Prices: Mon.-Sat. 10-5, Sun. 12-5; docent tours by appointment. Adults $13, children under 18 $6; discounts to AAM, ICOM & CNECM members; ASTC members, members & children 3 & under no charge. Closed New Year's Day; Memorial Day; Independence Day; Labor Day; Thanksgiving; Christmas. &
Attendance: 85,000 (actual)

HANCOCK SHAKER VILLAGE, INC., 1843 W. Housatonic St., Pittsfield, MA 01201. Mailing Address: P.O. Box 927, Pittsfield, MA 01202-0927. Tel.: 413-443-0188. Fax: 413-447-9357.
E-mail: info@hancockshakervillage.org
Web Site: www.hancockshakervillage.org
Key Personnel: Chm. (V), Richard Seltzer; C.E.O., Jennifer Trainer; Bd. Trustees Chm., Mary Rentz; Cur. Collections, Lesley Herzberg; Dir. Education, Cindy Dickerson; Shaker Mercantile Buyer, Nadia Dole.
Institution Type/Description: Historic Village Museum: 20 buildings with constructions dating back to 1790.
Hours & Admission Prices: Village & Galleries: April-Nov. Adults $20, youth 13-17 $8; discounts to AAM & AAA members; members and children 12 & under no charge. Closed New Year's Day; Thanksgiving; Christmas. &
Attendance: 60,000 (actual)

LICHTENSTEIN CENTER FOR THE ARTS, 28 Renne Ave., Pittsfield, MA 01201-4720. Tel.: 413-499-9348. Fax: 413-448-9811.
E-mail: berkart@taconic.net
Web Site: www.pittfield-ma.org
Key Personnel: Dir. Cultural Devel., Megan Whilden.
Institution Type/Description: Art Gallery: housed in the former factory building of William Stanley, inventor of alternating current and the birthplace of General Electric.
Hours & Admission Prices: Wed.-Sat. 12-5. No charge; donations accepted. Closed legal holidays. &
Attendance: 50,000

Plymouth

JABEZ HOWLAND HOUSE, 33 Sandwich St., Plymouth, MA 02360-3353. Tel.: 508-746-9590.
E-mail: elgay@verizon.net
Web Site: www.pilgrimjohnhowlandsociety.org
Key Personnel: Pres., Ashley E. Smith; Museum Shop Mgr., Gail Dobbins; Historian, Eldon Gay.
Institution Type/Description: Historic House Museum: 1667 Howland House.
Hours & Admission Prices: Summer: daily 10-4:30. Tours 10-4. Adults $5, students & seniors $4, children $1; discounts to AAA, AAM & ICOM members; members & children under 6 no charge.
Attendance: 2,898 (actual)

JENNEY MUSEUM, 48 Summer St., Plymouth, MA 02360-3400. Tel.: 508-747-4544. Fax: 508-747-4544.
E-mail: info@jenneymuseum.org
Web Site: www.jenneymuseum.org
Formerly: The Jenney Grist Mill
Key Personnel: Mgr., Nancy Martin; Volunteer, Leo Martin.
Institution Type/Description: Historic Site: established in 1636 by Pilgrim, John Jenney.
Hours & Admission Prices: April-Nov. Mon.-Sat. 9-5. Adults $8, members no charge. Walking tours of historic district: adult $12, children 5-17 $8; National

Monument to the Fore Fathers tour; adults 10, children $8. Closed Easter; Thanksgiving.
Attendance: 10,000 (estimated)

MAYFLOWER SOCIETY MUSEUM, 4 Winslow St., Plymouth, MA 02360-3313. Mailing Address: 67 Bay Shore Dr., Plymouth, MA 02360-2085. Tel.: 508-746-2590.
E-mail: gsmd.libr@verizon.net
Key Personnel: Cur., Judith A. MacDonald.
Institution Type/Description: Historic House: 1754 Mayflower Museum.
Hours & Admission Prices: June & Sept. to mid-Oct. Fri.-Sun. 11-4; July-Aug. daily 11-4. Library: Mon.-Fri. 10-3:30. Museum: adults $7, senior citizens $5, children 12-18 $5; discounts for veterans & AAA members; Plymouth residents, children under 12, & members no charge. Library: non-members $7 per day; members no charge. Closed Columbus Day; Memorial Day; Independence Day; Labor Day.
Attendance: 2,000 (estimated)

PILGRIM HALL MUSEUM, 75 Court St., Plymouth, MA 02360-3891. Tel.: 508-746-1620. Fax: 508-746-3396.
E-mail: donna.curtin@pilgrimhall.org
Web Site: www.pilgrimhallmuseum.org
Key Personnel: C.E.O., Donna D. Curtin; Pres. (V), Sue Giovanetti; Archivist, Rebecca Piccirillo; Dir. Devel., Robin Nutter; Museum Shop Mgr., Carol Reynolds.
Institution Type/Description: Historical Society & Museum.
Hours & Admission Prices: Feb.-Dec. 30 daily 9:30-4:30. Adults $10, senior citizens $8, children $6; discounts to AAA members; members no charge. Closed Christmas. &
Attendance: 25,000 (actual)

PLIMOTH PLANTATION INC., 137 Warren Ave., Plymouth, MA 02360-2436. Mailing Address: Box 1620, Plymouth, MA 02362-1620. Tel.: 508-746-1622, ext. 8601. Fax: 508-746-3407.
E-mail: info@plimoth.org
Web Site: www.plimoth.org
Key Personnel: Exec. Dir., John McDonagh.
Institution Type/Description: Outdoor Living History Museum.
Hours & Admission Prices: Mayflower II: April-Nov. daily 9-5. July-Aug. extended hours 9-7. Adults $10, seniors $9, children 5-12 $7. Plimoth Plantation: daily 9-5. Adults $25.95, Seniors $23.95, children 5-12 $15. Other sites: April-Nov. daily 9-5. Combination admission (ship & other sites): adults $29.95, seniors 62 & over $26.95; children 5-12 $19; discount to groups; members, AAM members, Massachusetts Teacher's Association & children under 5 no charge.
Attendance: 350,000 (estimated)

PLYMOUTH ANTIQUARIAN SOCIETY, 126 Water St., Plymouth, MA 02360. Mailing Address: Box 3773, Plymouth, MA 02361-3773. Tel.: 508-746-0012.
E-mail: pasm@verizon.net
Web Site: www.plymouthantiquariansociety.org
Key Personnel: Exec. Dir., Donna D. Curtin; Pres., Rose Stearns.
Institution Type/Description: Historical Society Museum.
Hours & Admission Prices: Hedge House: Wed.-Sun. 2-6. Spooner House: Thurs. & Sun. 2-6. Harlow House: Tues. 11-3; tour groups by appointment. Adults $6, children $3; discounts to AAA, AAM, & NEMA members; members & Plymouth residents no charge. Closed Independence Day.
Attendance: 3,000 (estimated)

RICHARD SPARROW HOUSE INC., 42 Summer St., Plymouth, MA 02360-3456. Tel.: 508-747-1240. Fax: 508-746-9521.
E-mail: director@sparrowhouse.com
Web Site: www.sparrowhouse.com
Key Personnel: Dir. & Museum Shop Mgr., Lois Atherton.
Institution Type/Description: Historic House Museum: 1640 Richard Sparrow House; a half house with cross-summer beam construction, the house is the oldest in Plymouth. The adjoining 1720 half house, houses a craft shop, supporting local crafts.
Hours & Admission Prices: Mon.-Tues, Thurs.-Sun. 10-6. No charge, donations accepted.
Attendance: 4,000 (estimated)

Provincetown

HUDSON D. WALKER GALLERY AT THE FINE ARTS WORK CENTER, 24 Pearl St., Provincetown, MA 02657. Tel.: 508-487-9960. Fax: 508-487-8873. Facebook: Fine Arts Work Center.
E-mail: general@fawc.org
Web Site: www.fawc.org

Key Personnel: Exec. Dir., Margaret Murphy.
Institution Type/Description: Art Gallery.
Hours & Admission Prices: Mon.-Fri. 9-5. No charge; donations accepted. Closed holidays.

PILGRIM MONUMENT AND PROVINCETOWN MUSEUM, One High Pole Hill Rd., Provincetown, MA 02657. Mailing Address: P.O. Box 1125, Provincetown, MA 02657-1125. Tel.: 508-487-1310. Fax: 508-487-4702.
E-mail: info@pilgrim-monument.org
Web Site: www.pilgrim-monument.org
Formerly: Cape Cod Pilgrim Memorial Association
Key Personnel: Pres., Christopher J. Snow; Exec. Dir., John McDonagh; Museum Shop Mgr., Bobo Hino.
Institution Type/Description: History Museum: located on the site of the 1907-10, Pilgrim Monument.
Hours & Admission Prices: April-May & mid-Sept. to Nov. daily 9-5; June-Sept. 15 daily 9-7. Adults $12, senior citizens 65 & over $9, students with ID $7, children 4-12 $4; discounts to MTA members & groups; children 3 & under no charge. &
Attendance: 94,000 (actual)

PROVINCETOWN ART ASSOCIATION AND MUSEUM, 460 Commercial St., Provincetown, MA 02657-2415. Tel.: 508-487-1750. Fax: 508-487-4372.
E-mail: info@paam.org
Web Site: www.paam.org
Key Personnel: C.E.O., Christine McCarthy; Pres. (V), James Bakker; Archivist, James Zimmerman; Education Coord., Lynn Stanley; Bookkeeper, Steven Roderick; Bldg. & Grounds, William Rigby.
Institution Type/Description: Art Museum.
Hours & Admission Prices: Memorial Day to Sept. Mon.-Thurs. 11-8, Fri. 11-10, Sat.-Sun. 11-5; Oct.-April Thurs.-Sun. 12-5. Adults $10; discounts to AAA, ICOM & AAM members; members & children under 12 no charge. &
Attendance: 52,000 (estimated)

THE SCHOOLHOUSE GALLERY, 494 Commercial St., Provincetown, MA 02657-2414. Tel.: 508-487-4800.
E-mail: mike@schoolhouseprovincetown.com
Web Site: schoolhouseprovincetown.com
Key Personnel: Dir., Mike Carroll.
Institution Type/Description: Art Gallery.
Hours & Admission Prices: Daily by appointment.

Quincy

ADAMS NATIONAL HISTORICAL PARK, 135 Adams St., Quincy, MA 02169-1749. Tel.: 617-773-1177. Fax: 617-847-3015.
E-mail: kelly_cobble@nps.gov
Web Site: www.nps.gov/adam
Key Personnel: Supt., Marianne Peak; Cur., Kelly Cobble.
Institution Type/Description: History Museum: housed in 1731 Adams family home.
Hours & Admission Prices: April 19-Nov. 10 daily 9-5. Adults $10; children under 16 no charge. Golden Eagle, Golden Access & Golden Age passports honored. Tours begin at Visitor Center. &
Attendance: 130,000 (actual)

ADAMS NATIONAL HISTORICAL PARK-JOHN ADAMS AND JOHN QUINCY ADAMS BIRTHPLACES, 133-141 Franklin St., Quincy, MA 02269. Mailing Address: 135 Adams St., Quincy, MA 02169-1749. Tel.: 617-773-1177 & 770-1175. Fax: 617-847-3015.
E-mail: adam_visitor_center@nps.gov
Web Site: www.nps.gov/adam
Key Personnel: Supt., Marianne Peak; Cur., Kelly Cobble.
Institution Type/Description: History Museum: housed in early 18th-century New England saltbox houses.
Hours & Admission Prices: April 19-Nov. 10 daily 9-5. Adults $5; Golden Eagle, Golden Age, Golden Access & children under 16 no charge. &
Attendance: 150,000 (estimated)

QUINCY HISTORICAL SOCIETY, Adams Academy Bldg., 8 Adams St., Quincy, MA 02169-2002. Tel.: 617-773-1144. Fax: 617-773-1872.
E-mail: info@quincyhistory.org
Web Site: quincyhistory.org
Key Personnel: Pres. (V), James P. Edwards; Exec. Dir., Edward Fitzgerald, Ph.D.
Institution Type/Description: Historical Museum: housed in 1872 Adams Academy building.

Hours & Admission Prices: Summer: Mon.-Fri. 9-4, Sat. 10-2; Winter: call for hours. Adults $3, seniors $1.50; members & children under 14 no charge. &

QUINCY HOUSE, 20 Muirhead St., Quincy, MA 02170. Mailing Address: 141 Cambridge St., Boston, MA 02114. Tel.: 617-994-5930.
E-mail: news@historicnewengland.org
Web Site: www.historicnewengland.org
Key Personnel: Pres. & C.E.O., Carl R. Nold; Site Mgr., Melinda Huff.
Institution Type/Description: Historic House: built in 1770 by Revolutionary War Colonel Josiah Quincy. The family produced three mayors of Boston & president of Harvard University.
Hours & Admission Prices: June-Oct. 15 1st & 3rd Sat. each month 11-4; tours on the hour. Adults $5; members no charge.
Attendance: 1,177 (actual)

UNITED STATES NAVAL SHIPBUILDING MUSEUM, 739 Washington St., Quincy, MA 02169-7330. Tel.: 617-479-7900. Fax: 617-479-8792.
E-mail: webteam@uss-salem.org
Web Site: www.uss-salem.org
Institution Type/Description: Naval Museum: housed aboard the USS Salem which served a 10 year career as flagship of the U.S. Sixth Fleet in the Mediterranean and the Second Fleet in the Atlantic.
Hours & Admission Prices: Temporarily closed. Adults $8, seniors & children 4-12 $6; children 3 & under no charge.

Reading

PARKER TAVERN, 103 Washington St., Reading, MA 01867-3523. Mailing Address: Reading Antiquarian Soc., P.O. Box 842, Reading, MA 01867. Tel.: 781-944-5056.
E-mail: ras@friendsofparkertavern.org
Web Site: parkertavern.org
Key Personnel: Pres. (V), Alan Ulrich.
Institution Type/Description: History Museum: housed in 1694 Parker Tavern, saltbox style house. Headquarters for Scotch Highlanders prisoners of war during the American Revolution.
Hours & Admission Prices: May-Oct. Sun. 2-5. No charge; donations accepted.
Attendance: 700 (estimated)

Rehoboth

CARPENTER MUSEUM, 4 Locust Ave., Rehoboth, MA 02769-2321. Mailing Address: P.O. Box 2, Rehoboth, MA 02769-0002. Tel.: 508-252-3031. Facebook: Carpenter Museum.
E-mail: carpentermuseum@gmail.com
Web Site: www.carpentermuseum.org
Key Personnel: Dir., Barbara Spencer; Cur., Laura Napolitano.
Institution Type/Description: History Museum.
Hours & Admission Prices: March-Nov. Sun. 2-4, Tues. & Thurs. 1-4; other times by appointment. Suggested Donation: $3. Closed holidays. &

Rockport

THE PAPER HOUSE, 52 Pigeon Hill St., Rockport, MA 01966.
E-mail: paperhouse52@hotmail.com
Web Site: paperhouserockport.com
Key Personnel: Owner, Edna Beaudoin.
Institution Type/Description: Historic House: housed in the home of Elis F. Stenman, a mechanical engineer who designed the machines that make paper clips; built of newspaper, glue, & varnish in 1922.
Hours & Admission Prices: Spring to Fall: daily 10-5. Adults $2, children 6-14 $1.

ROCKPORT ART ASSOCIATION, 12 Main St., Rockport, MA 01966-1594. Tel.: 978-546-6604. Fax: 978-546-9767. Facebook. com/Rockportartassn.
E-mail: rockportart@verizon.net
Web Site: www.rockportartassn.org
Key Personnel: Exec. Dir., Abby Battis; Pres. (V), David Curtis.
Institution Type/Description: Arts Center.
Hours & Admission Prices: Feb.-April Wed.-Fri. 10-4, Sat. 10-5, Sun. 12-5; May Tues.-Fri. 10-4, Sat. 10-5, Sun. 12-5; June to Columbus Day Mon.-Sat. 10-5, Sun. 12-5; Oct.-Dec. Tues.-Sat. 10-4, Sun. 12-5. No charge; donations accepted. Closed New Year's Day; Veterans Day; Thanksgiving; Christmas. &
Attendance: 50,000 (estimated)

SANDY BAY HISTORICAL SOCIETY & MUSEUMS, INC., 40 King St., Rockport, MA 01966-1460. Mailing Address: P.O. Box 63, Rockport, MA 01966-0063. Tel.: 978-546-9533.
E-mail: info@sandybayhistorical.org
Web Site: www.sandybayhistorical.org
Key Personnel: Pres., Debra Legg.
Institution Type/Description: History Museum.
Hours & Admission Prices: Museum: mid-June to mid-Sept. Tues.& Fri.-Sat. 2-5; other times by appointment. Admission $5; members no charge. Research: Mon. 9-1.
Attendance: 800

THACHER ISLAND MUSEUM AND CAPE ANN LIGHT STATION, Mailing Address: P.O. Box 73, Rockport, MA 01966. Tel.: 508-284-0144.
E-mail: info@thacherisland.org
Web Site: thacherisland.org
Institution Type/Description: History Museum & Historic Building: built 1861. A National Historic Landmark.
Hours & Admission Prices: Call for information.

Rowe

THE KEMP-MCCARTHY MEMORIAL MUSEUM OF THE ROWE HISTORICAL SOCIETY, INC., 282 Zoar Rd., Rowe, MA 01367-9774. Mailing Address: P.O. Box 455, Rowe, MA 01367. Tel.: 413-339-4238 & 775-3109 (cell).
E-mail: rowehistoricalsociety@gmail.com
Web Site: www.rowehistoricalsociety.org
Key Personnel: Pres. (V), Wayne A. Zavotka; Vice Pres., John Magnago; Sec., Joanne Semanie; Treas., Ellen Miller.
Institution Type/Description: Historical Society Museum.
Hours & Admission Prices: July 2 to Oct. 8 Sat. 10-2; other times by appointment. No charge; donations accepted. &
Attendance: 600 (estimated)

Rowley

ROWLEY HISTORICAL SOCIETY, 233 Main St., Rowley, MA 01969-1503. Mailing Address: P.O. Box 41, Rowley, MA 01969-0041. Tel.: 978-948-7483.
E-mail: info@rowleyhistory.org
Web Site: www.rowleyhistory.org
Key Personnel: Pres., Susan G. Hazen; Vice Pres., G. Robert Merry; Sec., Kathleen Cousins; Treas., Elizabeth Hicken; Museum Shop Mgr., Shirley G. Todd.
Institution Type/Description: Historical Building/Site Society Museum.
Hours & Admission Prices: By appointment only, call 978-948-2858. Donation $4; children under 12 & members no charge.

Roxbury

ROXBURY HERITAGE STATE PARK, 183 Roxbury St., John Eliot Sq., Roxbury, MA 02119-1525. Mailing Address: 251 Causeway St., Boston, MA 02114. Tel.: 617-445-3399. Fax: 617-445-5883.
E-mail: antonio.menefee@state.ma.us
Web Site: www.mass.gov/dcr/parks/metroboston/rxhp.htm
Institution Type/Description: History Museum: housed in 1750 Dillaway-Thomas House.
Hours & Admission Prices: Pulpit Rock by reservation only. No charge. Dillaway-Thomas House: Tues. & Sat. 10-5; other times by appointment. No charge. Guided walking tours of Roxbury by appointment only. &
Attendance: 20,000 (estimated)

Salem

THE HOUSE OF THE SEVEN GABLES, 115 Derby St., Salem, MA 01970-5640. Tel.: 978-744-0991; 978-745-5391 (TTY). Fax: 978-741-4350.
E-mail: kmclaughlin@7gables.org
Web Site: www.7gables.org
Key Personnel: Exec. Dir., Kara McLaughlin; Pres. (V), George Irving; Museum Shop Mgr., Everett Phillbrook.
Institution Type/Description: Historic Museum Site: located on Salem Harbor, this 2.5 acre area includes five original historic structures representing 17th-, 18th- and 19th-century architecture, Nathaniel Hawthorne and the lives of the people who lived on site.
Hours & Admission Prices: mid-Jan. to June & Nov.-Dec. daily 10-5; July-Oct. daily 10-7. Adults $12.50, children 5-12 $7.50; discounts to seniors & AAM

members; reciprocal museums, military, first responders, teachers, museums staff & members no charge. Closed New Year's Day; Thanksgiving; Christmas.
Attendance: 100,000 (estimated)

NEW ENGLAND PIRATE MUSEUM, 274 Derby St., Salem, MA 01970-3635. Tel.: 978-741-2800. Fax: 978-741-2902.
E-mail: salemwitchpirate@aol.com
Web Site: www.piratemuseum.com
Institution Type/Description: History Museum.
Hours & Admission Prices: April & Nov. Sat.-Sun. 10-5; May-Oct. daily 10-5. Haunted Happenings: extended hours. Adults $8, senior citizens 65 & over $7, children 4-13 $6; discount to groups. &

PEABODY ESSEX MUSEUM, E. India Sq., Salem, MA 01970-3783. Mailing Address: 161 Essex St., Salem, MA 01970-3783. Tel.: 978-745-1876 & 9500.
E-mail: pem@pem.org
Web Site: pem.org
Key Personnel: Exec. Dir. & C.E.O., Dan L. Monroe.
Institution Type/Description: General Museum.
Hours & Admission Prices: Tues.-Sun. 10-5, third Thurs. of month 10-9. Historic House Tours (Ward, Crowninshield-Bentley, Gardner-Pingree) daily. Adults $18, seniors $15, students with ID $10; discounts to AAM, ICOM & NEMA members; members, youth 16 & under and Salem residents no charge. Chinese House: adults $5. Closed New Year's Day; Thanksgiving; Christmas. &
Attendance: 200,000 (estimated)

PHILLIPS HOUSE, 34 Chestnut St., Salem, MA 01970-3129. Mailing Address: 141 Cambridge St., Boston, MA 02114-2702. Tel.: 978-744-0440. Facebook.
E-mail: info@phillipsmuseum.org
Web Site: www.historicnewengland.org
Key Personnel: Pres. & C.E.O., Carl R. Nold.
Institution Type/Description: Historic House Museum: housed in a 1821 Federal style mansion.
Hours & Admission Prices: June-Oct. Tues.-Sun. 11-5; Nov.-May Sat.-Sun. 11-5; last tour at 4pm. Adults $8; discounts to AAM & ICOM members; members no charge.
Attendance: 7,836 (actual)

SALEM MARITIME NATIONAL HISTORIC SITE, 160 Derby St., Salem, MA 01970-5643. Tel.: 978-740-1680. Fax: 978-740-1685.
E-mail: sama_orientation_center@nps.gov
Web Site: www.nps.gov/sama
Key Personnel: Supt., Paul DePrey.
Institution Type/Description: Maritime, Commerce & World Trade Site: located on 9 acres on Salem Harbor.
Hours & Admission Prices: Park: daily; Visitor Center: Wed.-Sun 10-5; Friendship of Salem: by scheduled tour only; No charge; donations accepted. Special Events: adults $5, children $3. Closed New Year's Day; Thanksgiving; Christmas. &
Attendance: 652,000 (estimated)

SALEM WITCH MUSEUM, 19 1/2 Washington Sq. N., Salem, MA 01970-4096. Tel.: 978-744-1692. Fax: 978-745-4414. Facebook: Salem Witch Museum.
E-mail: faq@salemwitchmuseum.com
Web Site: www.salemwitchmuseum.com
Key Personnel: C.E.O. & Public Rels., Bruce P. Michaud; Dir., Tina Jordan; Dir. Communications, Stacy Tilney; Dir. Sales., Merry Ward.
Institution Type/Description: History Museum.
Hours & Admission Prices: July-Aug. daily 10-7; Sept.-June daily 10-5. Adults $12, senior citizens $10.50, children 6-14 $9; discounts to AAM members & groups. Closed New Year's Day; Thanksgiving; Christmas. &
Attendance: 367,000 (estimated)

WITCH DUNGEON MUSEUM, 16 Lynde St., Salem, MA 01970. Tel.: 978-741-3570.
E-mail: salemwitchpirate@aol.com
Web Site: witchdungeon.com
Institution Type/Description: History Museum.
Hours & Admission Prices: April-Nov. daily 10-6. Adults $8, seniors 65 & over $7, children 4-13 $6; discounts to groups.

WITCH HISTORY MUSEUM, 197-201 Essex St., Salem, MA 01970. Tel.: 978-741-7770. Fax: 978-741-1139.
E-mail: salemwitchpirate@aol.com
Web Site: witchhistorymuseum.com
Institution Type/Description: History Museum.

Hours & Admission Prices: April-Nov. daily 10-6. Adults $8, seniors 65 & over $7, children 4-13 $6; discounts to groups.

THE WITCH HOUSE AKA THE JONATHAN CORWIN HOUSE, 310 1/2 Essex St., Salem, MA 01970. Tel.: 978-744-8815. Fax: 978-741-0578.
E-mail: info@witchhouse.info
Web Site: www.salemweb.com/witchhouse
Institution Type/Description: Historic House Museum: housed in the home of Judge Jonathan Corwin who served on the court for the Witchcraft Trials in 1692.
Hours & Admission Prices: May to early Nov. daily 10-5. Guided Tours: adults $10.25, seniors $8.25, children 7-14 $6.25. Self-Guided Tours: adults $8.25, seniors $6.25, children 6-14 $4.25; children under 6 no charge.

Sandwich

HERITAGE MUSEUMS & GARDENS, 67 Grove St., Sandwich, MA 02563-2110. Tel.: 508-888-3300. Fax: 508-888-9535. Facebook: Heritage Museums and Gardens.
E-mail: info@heritagemuseums.org
Web Site: www.heritagemuseum.org
Formerly: Heritage Plantation of Sandwich
Key Personnel: Chm. (V) Bd. Trustees, Louis M. Ricciardi; Dir. & C.E.O., Ellen Spear; Dir. Visitor Engagement, Heather Mead; Dir. Collections, Jennifer Madden; Dir. Horticulture, Les Lutz; Dir. Mktg., Andrea Early.
Institution Type/Description: General Museum.
Hours & Admission Prices: April-Oct. see website for hours. Adults $18, children $8; discounts to groups, school groups, active military, MA teachers, AAM, ICOM, NEMA, MTA & AAA members; members no charge. &
Attendance: 103,000 (actual)

THE OLD HOXIE HOUSE, Rte. 130, Water St., Sandwich, MA 02563-2280. Mailing Address: Sandwich Recreation Dept., P.O. Box 1336, Forestdale, MA 02644. Tel.: 508-888-4361. Fax: 508-888-5884.
E-mail: recreation@townofsandwich.net
Web Site: sandwichrec.com
Key Personnel: Dir., Guy J. Boucher.
Institution Type/Description: Historic House: c.1675 Hoxie House.
Hours & Admission Prices: mid-June to Columbus Day Mon.-Sat. 11-4:30, Sun. 1-4:30. Call for admission prices; discounts to bus tours.
Attendance: 5,000 (actual)

SANDWICH GLASS MUSEUM, 129 Main St., Sandwich, MA 02563. Mailing Address: P.O. Box 103, Sandwich, MA 02563-0103. Tel.: 508-888-0251. Fax: 508-888-4941. Facebook: Sandwich Glass Museum.
E-mail: katie.campbell@sandwichglassmuseum.org
Web Site: www.sandwichglassmuseum.org
Key Personnel: Exec. Dir., Katharine H. Campbell; Pres. (V), David Leary; Cur., Dorothy Schofield; Museum Shop Mgr., Robert Ward.
Institution Type/Description: Glass Museum.
Hours & Admission Prices: Feb.-March Wed.-Sun. 9:30-4; April-Dec. daily 9:30-5. Library by appointment only. Adults $9, children 6-14 $2; discounts to groups; members no charge. Closed New Year's Day; Easter; Thanksgiving; Christmas Eve & Day. &
Attendance: 70,000 (estimated)

Saugus

SAUGUS IRON WORKS NATIONAL HISTORIC SITE, 244 Central St., Saugus, MA 01906-2188. Tel.: 781-233-0050.
Web Site: www.nps.gov/sair
Institution Type/Description: Historic Site: 17th century Iron Works House; reconstructed blast furnace, forge & slitting mill.
Hours & Admission Prices: May-Oct. daily 9-5. No charge.
Attendance: 23,000 (estimated)

Scituate

SCITUATE HISTORICAL SOCIETY, Laidlaw Historical Center, 43 Cudworth Rd., Scituate, MA 02066. Mailing Address: P.O. Box 276, Scituate, MA 02066-0276. Tel.: 781-545-1083 & 0942. Fax: 781-544-1249.
E-mail: director@scituatehistoricalsociety.org
Web Site: scituatehistoricalsociety.org
Key Personnel: Pres. (V), David Ball; Treas., Denise Castro.
Institution Type/Description: Historic Building.
Hours & Admission Prices: Cudworth House, Mann Farmhouse; Grist Mill, Old Oaken Bucket Homestead, Lawson Tower & Lighthouse: Summer: call for

hours; organizations by appointment. Adults $2; children & New England Museum Assoc. no charge. Little Red Schoolhouse: daily 10-4; organizations by appointment.
Attendance: 7,500 (estimated)

SCITUATE MARITIME AND IRISH MOSSING MUSEUM, 301 The Driftway, Scituate, MA 02066-1904. Mailing Address: P.O. Box 276, Scituate, MA 02066-0276. Tel.: 781-545-1083. Fax: 781-544-1249.
E-mail: director@scituatehistoricalsociety.org
Web Site: www.scituatehistoricalsociety.org
Key Personnel: Chm. (V), Elizabeth Miessner; Pres. (V), David Ball.
Institution Type/Description: General Museum.
Hours & Admission Prices: June by appointment; July-Aug. Sat.-Sun. 1-4; Sept.-May Sun. 1-4; call for updated schedule. Adults $4, senior citizens $3; NEMA members, members, children 12 and under no charge.
Attendance: 5,000 (estimated)

Sheffield

THE SHEFFIELD HISTORICAL SOCIETY, 159-161 Main St., Sheffield, MA 01257. Mailing Address: P.O. Box 747, Sheffield, MA 01257. Tel.: 413-229-2694. Facebook: Sheffield Historical Society.
E-mail: shs@sheffieldhistory.org
Web Site: sheffieldhistory.org
Institution Type/Description: Historical Society Museum: housed in the Dan Raymond House; built in 1774.
Hours & Admission Prices: Memorial Day to Columbus Day Tues.-Thurs. 11-4 by appointment.

Shelburne Falls

SHELBURNE FALLS TROLLEY MUSEUM, 14 Depot St., Shelburne Falls, MA 01370. Mailing Address: P.O. Box 272, Shelburne Falls, MA 01370. Tel.: 413-625-9443.
E-mail: trolley@sftm.org
Web Site: www.sftm.org
Institution Type/Description: History Museum.
Hours & Admission Prices: Call for hours. Adults $3. &
Attendance: 3,150 (actual)

Somerville

MUSEUM OF BAD ART, Somerville Theatre Basement, 55 Davis Sq., Somerville, MA 02144. Mailing Address: 46 Dale St., Needham, MA 02494. Tel.: 781-444-6757. Facebook; YouTube.
E-mail: moba@museumofbadart.org
Web Site: www.museumofbadart.org
Key Personnel: Exec. Dir., Louise Reilly Sacco; Cur.-in-Chief, Mike Frank.
Institution Type/Description: Art Museum.
Hours & Admission Prices: Open during theater hours, typically Mon.-Fri. 4-9, Sat.-Sun. 2-9. No charge with movie ticket purchase or send email (info@museumofbadart.org) for free pass. &
Attendance: 7,500 (estimated)

THE SOMERVILLE MUSEUM, One Westwood Rd., Somerville, MA 02143-1517. Tel.: 617-666-9810.
E-mail: somemuseum@gmail.com
Web Site: somervillemuseum.org
Key Personnel: Pres. Bd., Barbara Mangum; Dir., Evelyn M. Battinelli.
Institution Type/Description: General Museum: housed in c.1925 three-story, red brick neo-Federal style building.
Hours & Admission Prices: Sept.-June Thurs. 2-7, Fri. 2-5, Sat. 12-5. No charge; donations accepted. Closed national holidays.

South Chelmsford

THE CHELMSFORD HISTORICAL SOCIETY, INC., 40 Byam Rd., South Chelmsford, MA 01824-3827. Tel.: 978-256-2311.
E-mail: chelmhist@comcast.net
Web Site: www.chelmhist.org
Key Personnel: Pres. (V), Carol Merriam; Cur., Judy Fichtenbaum; Museum Dir., Donald Patterschal.
Institution Type/Description: History Museum: housed in c.1663 Barrett-Byam homestead.
Hours & Admission Prices: By appointment & during special events. No charge; donations accepted. Closed New Year's Day; Memorial Day; Labor Day; Thanksgiving; Christmas. &
Attendance: 250 (estimated)

South Deerfield

MAGIC WINGS BUTTERFLY CONSERVATORY & GARDENS, 281 Greenfield Rd., South Deerfield, MA 01373-9790. Tel.: 413-665-2805. Fax: 413-665-4062.
E-mail: info@magicwings.net
Web Site: www.magicwings.com
Institution Type/Description: Conservatory & Garden.
Hours & Admission Prices: Memorial Day-Labor Day daily 9-6; Sept.-May daily 9-5. Adults $14, senior citizens 62 & over $12, children 3-17 $10; children under 3 no charge.

South Hadley

MOUNT HOLYOKE COLLEGE ART MUSEUM, Lower Lake Rd., South Hadley, MA 01075-1499. Tel.: 413-538-2245. Fax: 413-538-2144.
E-mail: artmuseum@mtholyoke.edu
Web Site: www.mtholyoke.edu/artmuseum
Key Personnel: Dir. Florence Finch Abbott, Tricia Y. Paik; Chm. (V), Susan Noonan; Assoc. Cur., Hannah Blunt; Assoc. Cur. Visual & Material Culture, Aaron Miller; Asst. Cur. Education, Kendra Weisbin; Financial Coord., John Burt; Weatherbie Cur. Education & Academic Programs, Ellen Alvord; Curricular Preparator, Sam Lopes; Website Mgr., Hilary Caws-Elwitt; Mgr. Collections, Linda Delone Best; Preparator, Jackie Finnegan; Digital Assets Coord. & Museum Photographer, Laura Shea; Art Advisory Bd. Fellow, Katie Allen; Sr. Administrative Asst., Glenys Rignall; Museum Guard, Sue Sormanti; Museum Guard, Dennis Campbell.
Institution Type/Description: Art Museum.
Hours & Admission Prices: Tues.-Fri. 11-5, Sat.-Sun. 1-5. No charge; donations accepted.
Attendance: 11,050 (estimated)

THE OLD FIREHOUSE MUSEUM, 4 N. Main St., South Hadley, MA 01075. Mailing Address: P.O. Box 387, South Hadley, MA 01075-0387. Tel.: 413-536-4970.
Institution Type/Description: Fire-Fighting Museum.
Hours & Admission Prices: May-June & Sept. Sun. 1:30-4; July-Aug. Wed. & Sun. 1:30-4. No charge; donations accepted.
Attendance: 100 (estimated)

THE SKINNER MUSEUM OF MOUNT HOLYOKE COLLEGE, 33 Woodbridge St., South Hadley, MA 01075-1138. Mailing Address: c/o Mount Holyoke College Art Museum, Lower Lake Rd., South Hadley, MA 01075. Tel.: 413-538-2245. Fax: 413-538-2144.
E-mail: artmuseum@mtholyoke.edu
Web Site: www.mtholyoke.edu/artmuseum
Key Personnel: Dir., John Stomberg; Cur., Wendy Watson; Asst. Cur. Visual & Material Culture, Aaron Miller.
Institution Type/Description: History Museum.
Hours & Admission Prices: May-Oct. Wed. & Sun. 2-5. No charge; donations accepted.
Attendance: 350 (estimated)

South Weymouth

SHEA FIELD NAVAL AVIATION HISTORICAL MUSEUM, 495 Shea Memorial Dr., South Weymouth, MA 02190-4009. Tel.: 781-534-1043.
E-mail: inquires@anapatriotsquadron.org
Web Site: ww.anapatriotsquadron.org
Institution Type/Description: Naval Aviation Museum.
Hours & Admission Prices: last Sat. each month 9am-11am. No charge; donations accepted.

WEYMOUTH HISTORICAL SOCIETY - JASON HOLBROOK HOMESTEAD, 238 Park Ave., South Weymouth, MA 02190-2512. Tel.: 781-340-1022.
Institution Type/Description: Historical Society Museum: housed in the former home of actor, Jason Holbrook; c.1763.
Hours & Admission Prices: Wed. 9-1; other times by appointment. No charge; donations accepted.

Springfield

NAISMITH MEMORIAL BASKETBALL HALL OF FAME, 1000 Hall of Fame Ave., Springfield, MA 01105. Tel.: 413-781-6500. Fax: 413-781-1939.
E-mail: mediarelations@positionsports.com
Web Site: www.hoophall.com
Key Personnel: Pres. & C.E.O., John Doleva; Vice Pres. Finance & Operations, Don Senecal; Vice Pres. Enshrinement Svcs., Paul Lambert.
Institution Type/Description: Sports Museum.
Hours & Admission Prices: Sun.-Fri. 10-4, Sat. 10-5. Adults $22, seniors 65 & over $17, youth 5-15 $16; discounts to groups; children 4 & under no charge. Closed New Year's Day; Thanksgiving; Christmas. &
Attendance: 300,000 (estimated)

PAN AFRICAN HISTORICAL MUSEUM USA, Tower Square, Mezzanine Level, 1500 Main St., #2, Springfield, MA 01115-1004. Tel.: 413-733-4823. Facebook: The Pan African Historical Museum USA.
E-mail: pahmusa1@juno.com
Web Site: www.pahmusa.mysite.com
Key Personnel: Exec. Dir., LuJuana Hood; Art Dir., Carl Edward Yates.
Institution Type/Description: History Museum.
Hours & Admission Prices: By appointment.

SPRINGFIELD ARMORY NATIONAL HISTORIC SITE, One Armory Sq., Ste. 2, Springfield, MA 01105-1299. Tel.: 413-734-8551, ext. 235. Fax: 413-747-8062.
E-mail: joannem_gangi@nps.gov
Web Site: www.nps.gov/spar/
Key Personnel: Supt., James Woolsey; Cur., Alex MacKenzie; Visitor Svcs., Joanne M. Gangi-Wellman; Historian, Richard Colton; Conservator, Alex Mackenzie.
Institution Type/Description: National Historic Site Museum: the main museum is housed in 1850 Arsenal.
Hours & Admission Prices: Nov. to Memorial Day Wed.-Sun.; Memorial Day to Oct. daily. No charge; donations accepted. Closed New Year's Day; Thanksgiving; Christmas. &
Attendance: 20,000 (estimated)

SPRINGFIELD MUSEUMS - GEORGE WALTER VINCENT SMITH ART MUSEUM, 21 Edwards St., Springfield, MA 01103-1548. Tel.: 413-263-6800, ext. 302. Fax: 413-263-6897.
E-mail: info@springfieldmuseums.org
Web Site: www.springfieldmuseums.org
Key Personnel: Pres., Kathleen Simpson; Chm. (V), Sam Hanmer; Dir., Heather Haskell; Cur., Julia Courtney; Dir. Public Rels. & Mktg., Matt Longhi.
Institution Type/Description: Decorative Arts Museum: housed in 1895 building designed by Renwick, Aspinwall & Renwick.
Hours & Admission Prices: Tues.-Sat. 10-5, Sun. 11-5. Adults $18, seniors & college students $12, children 3-17 $9.50, discounts to AAM members; children 2 & under & members no charge. Closed New Year's Day; Easter; Independence Day; Thanksgiving; Christmas. &
Attendance: 76,000 (estimated)

SPRINGFIELD MUSEUMS - LYMAN & MERRIE WOOD MUSEUM OF SPRINGFIELD HISTORY, 21 Edwards St., Springfield, MA 01103-1548. Tel.: 413-263-6800, ext. 304. Fax: 413-263-6898.
E-mail: info@springfieldmuseums.org
Web Site: www.springfieldmuseums.org
Key Personnel: Pres., Kathleen Simpson; Chm. (V), Sam Hanmer; Dir., Heather Haskell; Cur., Julia Courtney; Dir. Public Rels. & Mktg., Matt Longhi.
Institution Type/Description: History Museum.
Hours & Admission Prices: Tues.-Sat. 10-5, Sun. 11-5. Adults $18, seniors & college students $12, children 3-17 $9.50; discounts to AAM members; children 2 & under & members no charge. Closed New Year's Day; Easter; Independence Day; Thanksgiving; Christmas. &
Attendance: 65,000 (estimated)

SPRINGFIELD MUSEUMS - MICHELE & DONALD D'AMOUR MUSEUM OF FINE ARTS, 21 Edwards St., Springfield, MA 01103-1548. Tel.: 413-263-6800, ext. 302. Fax: 413-263-6889.
E-mail: info@springfieldmuseums.org
Web Site: www.springfieldmuseums.org
Key Personnel: Pres., Kathleen Simpson; Chm. (V), Sam Hanmer; Dir., Heather Haskell; Cur., Julia Courtney.
Institution Type/Description: Art Museum.
Hours & Admission Prices: Tues.-Sat. 10-5, Sun. 11-5. Adults $15, includes entry to 5 museums; discounts to AAM members; members no charge. Closed New Year's Day; Easter; Independence Day; Thanksgiving; Christmas. &
Attendance: 86,000 (estimated)

SPRINGFIELD MUSEUMS - SPRINGFIELD SCIENCE MUSEUM, 21 Edwards St., Springfield, MA 01103-1548. Tel.: 413-263-6800, ext. 325. Fax: 413-263-6884.
E-mail: info@springfieldmuseums.org
Web Site: www.springfieldmuseums.org
Key Personnel: Pres., Kathleen Simpson; Chm., Sam Hamner; Dir., Heather Haskell; Cur., Julia Courtney.
Institution Type/Description: Science Museum.
Hours & Admission Prices: Tues.-Sat. 10-5, Sun. 11-5. Planetarium: hours vary; guided tours available; special events. Museum (includes entry to 5 museums at Quadrangle location). Adults $18; seniors $12, children 3-17 $9.50, discounts to AAM members; children 2 & under & members no charge. Planetarium: adults $3, children $2. Closed New Year's Day; Easter; Independence Day; Thanksgiving; Christmas. &
Attendance: 228,000 (estimated)

THE ZOO IN FOREST PARK AND EDUCATION CENTER, 302 Sumner Ave., Springfield, MA 01108. Mailing Address: P.O. Box 80295, Springfield, MA 01138-0295. Tel.: 413-733-2251. Fax: 413-733-2330. Facebook: The Zoo in Forest Park and Education Center.
E-mail: john@forestparkzoo.com
Web Site: forestparkzoo.org
Formerly: The Zoo in Forest Park
Key Personnel: Dir., John R. Lewis; Dir. Education, Alison Summers; Business Mgr., Darlene Blaney.
Institution Type/Description: Zoo.
Hours & Admission Prices: April to Columbus Day daily weather permitting; Oct. weekends 10-3 weather permitting. Prices & hours subject to change. &
Attendance: 93,000 (estimated)

Still River

HARVARD HISTORICAL SOCIETY, Still River Baptist Church, 215 Still River Rd., Still River, MA 01467. Mailing Address: P.O. Box 542, Harvard, MA 01451-0542. Tel.: 978-456-8285.
E-mail: curator@harvardhistory.org
Web Site: www.harvardhistory.org
Key Personnel: Cur., Karen Zaikis.
Institution Type/Description: History Museum.
Hours & Admission Prices: Mon.-Tues. 1-5 by appointment. No charge; donations accepted. &
Attendance: 1,000 (estimated)

Stockbridge

BERKSHIRE BOTANICAL GARDEN, Rte. 102 & Rte. 183, Stockbridge, MA 01262. Mailing Address: Box 826, Stockbridge, MA 01262-0826. Tel.: 413-298-3926. Fax: 413-298-4897. Facebook: Berkshire Botanical Garden.
E-mail: mbeck@berkshirebotanical.org
Web Site: www.berkshirebotanical.org
Key Personnel: Exec. Dir., Michael Beck; Chm., Matthew Larkin; Education Coord., Elisabeth Cary.
Institution Type/Description: Botanic Garden.
Hours & Admission Prices: May to mid-Oct. daily 9-5. Adults $15, senior citizens & students $12; discounts to American Horticultural Society Reciprocal Admission Program; NARM & ROAM; children 12 & under and members no charge. &
Attendance: 24,000 (estimated)

CHESTERWOOD, 4 Williamsville Rd., off Rte. 183, Glendale Sect., Stockbridge, MA 01262-0827. Mailing Address: P.O. Box 827, Stockbridge, MA 01262-0827. Tel.: 413-298-3579. Fax: 413-298-1065. Facebook: Chesterwood.
E-mail: chesterwood@savingplaces.org
Web Site: www.chesterwood.org
Key Personnel: Dir., Donna Hassler; Chm. Advisory Council, Carol Bosco Baumann; Office Mgr., Lisa Reynolds; Bldgs. & Grounds Supt., Gerard Blache; Curatorial Asst., Anne Cathcart; Bldgs. & Grounds Coord., Brian McElhiney.
Institution Type/Description: Historic Site: housed in the summer estate of Daniel Chester French (1850-1931).
Hours & Admission Prices: May-Oct. daily. Adults $16; members no charge. &
Attendance: 12,500 (estimated)

MERWIN HOUSE, TRANQUILITY, 14 Main St., Stockbridge, MA 01262. Mailing Address: P.O. Box 1543, Stockbridge, MA 01262-9701. Tel.: 617-994-6662. Fax: 413-298-0121.
E-mail: MERWINHOUSE@HISTORICNEWENGLAND.ORG
Web Site: www.historicnewengland.org

Key Personnel: Site Mgr., Lisa Centola; Pres., Carl Nold.
Institution Type/Description: Historic House: c.1825 late Federal style period house.
Hours & Admission Prices: Jan. 5, Oct. 2 & Dec. 4 11-4. Tours on the hours. Adults $5; members no charge.
Attendance: 569 (actual)

THE MISSION HOUSE, 19 Main St., Stockbridge, MA 01262-9800. Mailing Address: P.O. Box 792, Stockbridge, MA 01262-0792. Tel.: 413-298-3239, ext. 3013. Fax: 413-298-5239.
E-mail: naumkeag@ttor.org
Web Site: www.thetrustees.org
Key Personnel: Cultural Site Mgr., Colleen Henry.
Institution Type/Description: Historic House: housed in the former home of Rev. John Sergeant, first missionary to the Stockbridge Mohicans; built in 1743.
Hours & Admission Prices: July-Aug. Sat.-Sun. 10-3. House: guided tours. Gardens: self-guided tours. Adults $6; discounts to AAM, ICOM members; children 12 & under and members no charge.
Attendance: 3,000 (actual)

NAUMKEAG, 5 Prospect Hill Rd., Stockbridge, MA 01262. Mailing Address: P.O. Box 792, Stockbridge, MA 01262-0792. Tel.: 413-298-3239, ext. 3013. Fax: 413-298-5239.
E-mail: naumkeag@ttor.org
Web Site: www.thetrustees.org
Key Personnel: Cultural Site Mgr., Colleen Henry.
Institution Type/Description: Historic House: 1886 shingle style house, designed by architect McKim, Mead, & White, the summer home of Joseph Hodges Choate, U.S. Ambassador to the Court of St. James. Original gardens designed by Fletcher Steele.
Hours & Admission Prices: May 15 to Oct. daily 10-5. House & Garden: adults $15; discounts to AAM & ICOM members; children 12 & under and members no charge.
Attendance: 10,000 (actual)

NORMAN ROCKWELL MUSEUM, 9 Glendale Rd., Rte. 183, Stockbridge, MA 01262. Mailing Address: P.O. Box 308, Stockbridge, MA 01262-0308. Tel.: 413-298-4100, ext. 221. Fax: 413-298-4142. Facebook.
E-mail: inforequest@nrm.org
Web Site: www.nrm.org
Key Personnel: C.E.O. & Dir., Laurie Norton Moffatt; Chm. Bd., Robert Horvath; Pres. Bd., Alice Carter; C.O.O., Jill Gellert; Deputy Dir. & Chief Cur., Stephanie Haboush Plunkett; Chief Advancement Officer, Michelle Clarkin; Dir. Human Resources, Holly Coleman; Mgr. Media Svcs., Jeremy Clowe; Dir. Visitor Experience, Laura Berliner; Mgr. Facilities, David Slick; Dir. Collections & Registration, Martin Mahoney; Registrar & Image Svcs., Thomas Mesquita; Mgr. Information Technology, Frank Kennedy; Dir. Digital Learning & Engagement, Rich Bradway; Mgr. Traveling Exhibitions, Mary Melius; Deputy Dir. Audience & Business Devel., Margit Hotchkiss; Cur. Education, Thomas Daly; Museum Shop Mgr., Mike Duffy; Mgr. Visitor Svcs., Carolyn Grogan; Education & Outreach Mgr., Patrick O'Donnell; Sales & Mktg. Coord., Ellen Swan Mazzer.
Institution Type/Description: Art Museum: dedicated to education & art appreciation inspired by Norman Rockwell and the art of other illustrators.
Hours & Admission Prices: May-Oct. daily 10-5; Nov.-April Mon.-Fri. 10-4, Sat.-Sun. 10-5. May-Oct. admission includes studio tour: adults $20, college students $10; discounts to NEMA, AAM, & ICOM members & bus tour groups; members and children 18 & under no charge. Closed New Year's Day; Thanksgiving; Christmas. &
Attendance: 125,000 (estimated)

STOCKBRIDGE LIBRARY, MUSEUM & ARCHIVES, Mailing Address: 46 Main St., P.O. Box 119, Stockbridge, MA 01262-0119. Tel.: 413-298-5501.
E-mail: ballen@cwmars.org
Web Site: www.stockbridgelibrary.org
Key Personnel: Cur., Barbara Allen; C.E.O., Katherine O'Neil; Pres. (V), John Gillespie; Cur. Asst., Joshua Hall.
Institution Type/Description: History Museum.
Hours & Admission Prices: Tues., Wed., Fri. 9-5, Thurs. 9-1, Sat. 9-2. No charge; donations accepted. Closed national holidays. &
Attendance: 2,500 (estimated)

Stoneham

STONE ZOO, 149 Pond St., Stoneham, MA 02180. Tel.: 781-438-5100.
E-mail: development@zoonewengland.com
Web Site: www.zoonewengland.org/stone-zoo
Institution Type/Description: Zoo.

Hours & Admission Prices: Daily 10-4. Adults $13, seniors $11, children 2-12 $9; children under 2 no charge. &

Stoughton

STOUGHTON HISTORICAL SOCIETY, 324 S. Page St., Stoughton, MA 53589. Mailing Address: Box 542, Stoughton, MA 02072-0542. Tel.: 608-873-4797.
E-mail: stoughtonhistoricalsociety@verizon.net
Web Site: www.stoughtonhistoricalsociety.org
Key Personnel: Pres., David Kalland.
Institution Type/Description: History Museum: housed in Lucius Clapp Memorial.
Hours & Admission Prices: Mid-May-Sept. Sun. 1-4, other times by appointment. No charge; donations accepted.
Attendance: 500 (estimated)

Stow

RANDALL LIBRARY, 19 Crescent St., Stow, MA 01775-1188. Tel.: 978-897-8572. Fax: 978-897-7379.
E-mail: stow@minlib.net
Key Personnel: Dir., Melissa Fournier; Chm. (V), Tim Reed.
Institution Type/Description: Historical Society Museum.
Hours & Admission Prices: July-Aug. Tues.-Thurs. 10-8, Fri. 10-2; Sept.-June Tues.-Thurs. 10-8, Fri. 10-2, Sat. 10-5. No charge; donations accepted. Closed legal holidays. &
Attendance: 7,200 (estimated)

STOW WEST SCHOOL MUSEUM, Harvard Rd., Stow, MA 01775. Mailing Address: 380 Great Rd., Stow, MA 01775-2127. Tel.: 978-562-6843.
E-mail: kcthreads@earthlink.net
Key Personnel: Chm. (V), Karen C. Gray.
Institution Type/Description: Historic House Museum: housed in an 1825 one-room schoolhouse.
Hours & Admission Prices: July & Sept.-Oct. call for hours. No charge; donations accepted.
Attendance: 150 (estimated)

Sturbridge

OLD STURBRIDGE VILLAGE, 1 Old Sturbridge Village Rd., Sturbridge, MA 01566-1198. Tel.: 508-347-3362. Fax: 508-347-0377. TDD: 508-347-5383.
E-mail: osv@osv.org
Web Site: www.osv.org
Key Personnel: Pres. & C.E.O., Jim Donahue; Chief of Staff & Asst. to Pres., Renee Chambers; Chm (V), Robert W. Reeder, III; Vice Pres. Finance, Tina Krasnecky; Sr. Vice Pres. Museum Opers., Brad King; Vice Pres. Visitor Svcs., Alexis Conte; Dir. Interpretation, Rhys Simmons; Curatorial Dir., Caitlin Emery; Vice Pres. Operations, Brad King; Dir. Education, Emily Dunnack; Dir Devel., Anne McBride; Dir. Mktg. & Communs., Michael Arnum; Museum Shop Mgr., Joh Rios.
Institution Type/Description: History Museum.
Hours & Admission Prices: Call for hours. Adults $28, senior citizens 65 & over $26, youth 3-17 $14; children under 3 & members no charge. &
Attendance: 250,000 (estimated)

Sudbury

LONGFELLOW'S WAYSIDE INN, 72 Wayside Inn Rd., Sudbury, MA 01776-3224. Tel.: 978-443-1776. Fax: 978-443-8041. Facebook: Longfellows Wayside Inn.
E-mail: history@wayside.org
Web Site: www.wayside.org
Formerly: Howe's Tavern
Key Personnel: Pres. (V), Lily Gordon; Innkeeper, Steve Pickford.
Institution Type/Description: History Museum.
Hours & Admission Prices: School & Grist Mill: April-Nov. Wed.-Sun. 9-5. No charge, donations accepted. Closed Independence Day; Christmas.
Attendance: 15,000 (estimated)

SUDBURY HISTORICAL SOCIETY, 322 Concord Rd., Sudbury, MA 01776. Tel.: 978-443-3747. Fax: 978-443-3747.
E-mail: sudburyhist01776@verizon.net
Web Site: www.sudbury01776.org
Institution Type/Description: Historical Society Museum.
Hours & Admission Prices: Mon.-Fri. 1-5 by appointment. No charge; donations accepted. Closed holidays.

Sutton

SUTTON HISTORICAL SOCIETY MUSEUM & RUFUS PUTNAM MUSEUM, 4 Uxbridge Rd., Sutton, MA 01590. Tel.: 508-865-8722.
Institution Type/Description: Historical Society Museum.
Hours & Admission Prices: Tues. 7pm-9pm.

Swampscott

ATLANTIC NO. 1 VETERANS FIREMEN'S ASSOCIATION, INC., 76 Burrill St., Swampscott, MA 01907-1915. Mailing Address: 41 Lynn Shore Dr., Lynn, MA 01902-4927. Tel.: 781-595-4050.
Key Personnel: Pres., Rowe Austin; Dir., J. Richard Maitland; Sec., Edna Maitland; Treas., Douglas B. Maitland.
Institution Type/Description: Fire-Fighting Museum.
Hours & Admission Prices: Call for appointment. No charge.
Attendance: 100 (estimated)

SWAMPSCOTT HISTORICAL SOCIETY (SIR JOHN HUMPHREY HOUSE), 99 Paradise Rd., Swampscott, MA 01907-1955. Tel.: 781-599-1297.
Key Personnel: C.E.O., Annie C. Harris; C.O.O., Bill Steelman.
Institution Type/Description: Historic House Museum: 1637 Sir John Humphrey House.
Hours & Admission Prices: By appointment. No charge; donations accepted.
Attendance: 500 (estimated)

Taunton

OLD COLONY HISTORY MUSEUM, 66 Church Green, Taunton, MA 02780-3445. Tel.: 508-822-1622. Fax: 508-880-6317.
E-mail: info@oldcolonyhistorymuseum.org
Web Site: www.oldcolonyhistorymuseum.org
Key Personnel: Dir., Katherine M. MacDonald; Pres. (V), William F. Hanna, III; Cur. Collections, Bronson Michaud; Community Program Coord., Saria E. Sweeney; Asst. to Dir., Elizabeth Bernier.
Institution Type/Description: Historical Society & Museum: housed in 1852 Bristol Academy Building designed by Richard Upjohn.
Hours & Admission Prices: Tues.-Sat. 10-4. Adults $4, seniors & children 12-18 $2; NEMA members no charge. Genealogical Research Admission: $7. Closed Saturdays preceding Monday holidays.
Attendance: 5,025 (actual)

Templeton

NARRAGANSETT HISTORICAL SOCIETY, INC., 1 Boynton Rd., Templeton, MA 01468. Mailing Address: P.O. Box 354, Templeton, MA 01468-0354. Tel.: 978-939-2303. Facebook: Narragansett Historical.
E-mail: narragansetthistoricalsociety@yahoo.com
Web Site: www.narragansetthistoricalsociety.org
Key Personnel: Pres., Brian P. Tanguay; Historian, Harry Aldrich; Treas., Debra Caisse.
Institution Type/Description: Historical Society: housed in 1810 two-story brick house.
Hours & Admission Prices: April & Dec. Tues. 6pm-8pm; July-Aug. Tues. 6pm-8pm, Sat. 2-5. No charge; donations accepted.
Attendance: 2,500 (estimated)

Topsfield

IPSWICH RIVER WILDLIFE SANCTUARY (MASSACHUSETTS AUDUBON SOCIETY), 87 Perkins Row, Topsfield, MA 01983-1922. Tel.: 978-887-9264. Fax: 978-887-0875.
E-mail: ipswichriver@massaudubon.org
Web Site: www.massaudubon.org
Key Personnel: Dir., Carol J. Decker; Adult Program Coord. & Volunteer Coord., Susan Baeslack; Property Mgr., Richard Wolniewicz; Sec., Janet Barnes; Office Mgr., Christina MacDougall; Master Naturalist, Bob Speare; Caretaker & Property Worker, Fred Goodwin; Education Coord., Lois Bairstow; Teacher & Naturalist, Scott Santino; Education Coord., Sally Willard.
Institution Type/Description: Wildlife Refuge and Bird Sanctuary.
Hours & Admission Prices: Sanctuary: May-Oct. Tues.-Fri. 9-4; Nov.-April Tues.-Sun. & Mon. holidays 9-4. Trails: Tues.-Sun. & Mon. holidays dawn-dusk. Adults $4, senior citizens 65 & over and children 2-12 $3; members of MA Audubon no charge.
Attendance: 30,000

TOPSFIELD HISTORICAL SOCIETY, One Howlett St., Topsfield, MA 01983-1409. Mailing Address: P.O. Box 323, Topsfield, MA 01983-0523. Tel.: 978-887-9724.
E-mail: membership@topsfieldhistory.org
Web Site: www.topsfieldhistory.org
Formerly: Parson Capen House and Gould Barn
Key Personnel: Pres. (V) & Museum Shop Mgr., Norman J. Isler; Vice Pres., Anne Barrett; Treas., Larry Lindquist.
Institution Type/Description: Historic Houses: 1683 Parson Capen House & 1710 Gould Barn.
Hours & Admission Prices: mid-June to early Sept. Wed., Fri. & Sun. 1-4. No Charge, Suggested Donation $3; discounts to Essex National Heritage volunteers.
Attendance: 3,500 (estimated)

Truro

TRURO CENTER FOR THE ARTS AT CASTLE HILL, 10 Meetinghouse Rd., Truro, MA 02666. Mailing Address: P.O. Box 756, Truro, MA 02666-0756. Tel.: 508-349-7511. Fax: 508-349-7513.
E-mail: info@castlehill.org
Web Site: www.castlehill.org
Key Personnel: Exec. Dir., Cherie Mittenthal.
Institution Type/Description: Art Gallery.
Hours & Admission Prices: Call for hours.

Turners Falls

GREAT FALLS DISCOVERY CENTER, 2 Avenue A, Turners Falls, MA 01376-1101. Tel.: 413-863-3221.
Web Site: www.greatfallsdiscoverycenter.org
Key Personnel: Pres. (V), Don Clegg; Museum Shop Mgr., Karen Latka.
Institution Type/Description: Natural History Museum.
Hours & Admission Prices: May-Sept. daily 10-6; Oct.-April Fri.-Sat. 10-4; other times by appointment. No charge; donations accepted. Closed New Year's Day; Thanksgiving; Christmas.

Wakefield

WAKEFIELD HISTORICAL SOCIETY, 39 Prospect St., Wakefield, MA 01880. Mailing Address: P.O. Box 1902, Wakefield, MA 01880-5902. Tel.: 781-246-3070.
E-mail: wakefieldhistory@gmail.com
Web Site: www.wakefieldma.org
Key Personnel: Pres. (V), Nancy Bertrand; Treas., David Gooch.
Institution Type/Description: Local History Museum.
Hours & Admission Prices: Sept.-May second Tues. of month; other times by appointment. No charge.

Waltham

CHARLES RIVER MUSEUM OF INDUSTRY & INNOVATION, 154 Moody St., Waltham, MA 02453-5302. Tel.: 781-893-5410. Fax: 781-891-4536.
E-mail: elln@ormi.org
Web Site: www.crmi.org
Key Personnel: Dir. & Exec. Dir., Elln Hagney; Pres. (V), Arthur Nelson; Treas., Kim Washisuo; Asst. Dir., Kim Kalen.
Institution Type/Description: Textile and Industrial Museum: museum of innovation.
Hours & Admission Prices: Thurs.-Sat. 10-5. Adults $5, seniors & students $3; discounts to WGBH, AAM, AAA & NAWCC members; children under 6 & members no charge.
Attendance: 13,000 (estimated)

GORE PLACE, 52 Gore St., Waltham, MA 02453-6866. Tel.: 781-894-2798. Fax: 781-894-5745.
E-mail: goreplace@goreplace.org
Web Site: goreplace.org
Key Personnel: Pres. (V), James F. Hunnewell, Jr.; Exec. Dir., Susan Robertson; Collections Mgr., Lana Lewis; Devel., Matthew Dickey; Supt. Grounds, Scott Clarke.
Institution Type/Description: Historic House & Farm: 1806 22-room Gore Mansion.
Hours & Admission Prices: Estate & Farm: daily. Mansion Tours: Mon.-Thurs. 10-3, Fri. 10-3 & 7-9, Sat. 12-4. Adults $12, children under 12 $6; discounts to AAM members & New England Museum Association members; members no charge. Closed Federal holidays.
Attendance: 30,000 (estimated)

LYMAN ESTATE AND GREENHOUSES, 185 Lyman St., Waltham, MA 02452-5645. Mailing Address: 141 Cambridge St., Boston, MA 02114-2702. Tel.: 617-994-5912 (Estate) & 5913 (Greenhouse). Facebook.
E-mail: Info@HistoricNewEngland.org
Web Site: www.historicnewengland.org
Key Personnel: Pres. & C.E.O., Carl R. Nold; Site Manager, Rebecca Clower; Mgr. Greenhouses, Lynn Ackerman.
Institution Type/Description: National Historic House/Landmark: housed in the country estate of Boston merchant Theodore Lyman; built in 1793; greenhouses among the oldest in the country.
Hours & Admission Prices: Mansion: 3rd Sat. each month 10-1, last tour 12pm. Greenhouse: July 16-Dec. 14 Tues.-Sat. 9:30-4; Dec. 15-July 15 Tues.-Sun. 9:30-4. Grounds: sunrise to sunset. House tours $8; discount to AAM members; Historic New England members no charge.
Attendance: 24,257 (actual)

THE ROSE ART MUSEUM OF BRANDEIS UNIVERSITY, 415 South St., MS069, Brandeis Univ., Waltham, MA 02453-2728. Tel.: 781-736-2028 & 3432. Fax: 781-736-3439.
E-mail: roseartmuseum@brandeis.edu
Web Site: www.brandeis.edu/rose
Formerly: The Rose Art Museum
Key Personnel: Henry & Lois Foster Dir., Christopher Bedford; Deputy Dir., Kristin Parker; Dir. Devel., Nancy Gunn; Registrar & Collections Mgr., Joseph Leduc.
Institution Type/Description: Art Museum.
Hours & Admission Prices: Academic Year: Wed.-Sun. 11-5. No charge; donations accepted. Closed major holidays.
Attendance: 11,737 (actual)

WALTHAM HISTORICAL SOCIETY, 190 Moody St., Waltham, MA 02453-5384. Tel.: 781-891-5815.
E-mail: waynemccarthy@comcast.net
Web Site: www.walthamhistoricalsociety.org
Key Personnel: Co-Pres. & Communications, Wayne McCarthy; Co-Pres., Sheila E. FitzPatrick; Treas., Mary Selig; Recording Sec., Leona Lindsay; Corresponding Sec., Joseph Vizard; Cur., Michelle Morello; Asst. Cur., Winifred W. Kneisel.
Institution Type/Description: Local History Museum.
Hours & Admission Prices: By appointment only. Annex: Sat. 9-1. No charge; donations accepted. Closed holidays.
Attendance: 400

THE WALTHAM MUSEUM, 25 Lexington St., Waltham, MA 02452-4415. Tel.: 781-893-9020.
E-mail: thewalthammuseum@verizon.net
Web Site: walthammuseum.com
Key Personnel: Dir., Albert A. Arena, Sr.; Museum Shop Mgr., Louise Butler.
Institution Type/Description: Local History Museum.
Hours & Admission Prices: Tues.-Sat. 1-4:30; other times by appointment. Adults $4, seniors & children $2; discount to local non profits; members no charge. Closed holidays.
Attendance: 1,000 (estimated)

Watertown

ARMENIAN MUSEUM OF AMERICA, 65 Main St., Watertown, MA 02472-4400. Tel.: 617-926-2562. Fax: 617-926-0175.
E-mail: info@almainc.org
Web Site: www.armenianmuseum.org
Formerly: Armenian Library and Museum of America (ALMA)
Key Personnel: Chm. (V), Haig Der Manuelian; Exec. Dir., Berj Chekijian; Asst. Dir., Howayda Abu Affan; Treas. (V), Jae Erdekian; Cur., Susan Lind-Sinanian; Cur. & Program Mgr., Gary Lind-Sinanian.
Institution Type/Description: Cultural Museum.
Hours & Admission Prices: Thurs.-Sun. 12-6, Wed. by appointment. Adults $7, seniors & students $3; ALMA members & children under 12 no charge. Closed New Year's Day; Easter; Thanksgiving; Christmas.
Attendance: 7,000 (estimated)

BROWNE HOUSE, 562 Main St., Watertown, MA 02472. Mailing Address: Historic New England, 141 Cambridge St., Boston, MA 02114-2702. Tel.: 617-994-6660.
E-mail: news@historicnewengland.org
Web Site: www.historicnewengland.com
Institution Type/Description: Historic House: built c.1698.
Hours & Admission Prices: Call for hours. Adults $5, seniors $4, students $2.50; Historic New England members & Watertown residents no charge.
Attendance: 162

PERKINS HISTORY MUSEUM, PERKINS SCHOOL FOR THE BLIND, 175 North Beacon St., Watertown, MA 02472-2790. Tel.: 617-924-3434. Fax: 617-972-7271. Facebook; Twitter; Flickr.
E-mail: historymuseum@perkins.org
Web Site: www.perkins.org/history; www.perkinsarchives.org
Formerly: Museum on the History of Blindness, Perkins School for the Blind
Key Personnel: Cur., Jennifer Hale.
Institution Type/Description: History Museum.
Hours & Admission Prices: Tues. & Thurs. 2-4; tours & other times by appointment. No charge. &
Attendance: 2,930 (estimated)

THE PLUMBING MUSEUM CLOSED, 80 Rosedale Rd., Watertown, MA 02471. Tel.: 617-926-2111.
E-mail: info@theplumbingmuseum.org
Web Site: www.theplumbingmuseum.org
Institution Type/Description: History Museum: housed in a former ice house; c.1860.
Hours & Admission Prices: Mon.-Thurs. by appointment. Closed holidays.

Wayland

WAYLAND HISTORICAL SOCIETY, 12 Cochituate Rd., Wayland, MA 01778. Mailing Address: P.O. Box 56, Wayland, MA 01778-0056. Tel.: 508-358-7959.
E-mail: wayhistsoc@comcast.net
Web Site: www.waylandhistoricalsociety.org
Key Personnel: Pres., Jane Dunn; Cur., Lois Davis.
Institution Type/Description: General Museum.
Hours & Admission Prices: Tues. & Fri. 9:30 to noon. No charge; donations accepted. &
Attendance: 2,000 (estimated)

Wellesley

WELLESLEY HISTORICAL SOCIETY, INC., 229 Washington St., Wellesley, MA 02481-3105. Tel.: 781-235-6690. Fax: 781-239-0660.
E-mail: info@wellesleyhistoricalsociety.org
Web Site: www.wellesleyhistoricalsociety.org
Key Personnel: Exec. Dir., Robert Damon; Pres., John Celi.
Institution Type/Description: Local History Museum: housed in 1824 Dadmun-McNamara house.
Hours & Admission Prices: Tues.-Thurs. 10-3. No charge; donations accepted. Research by appointment. Research: non-members $10. Closed holidays. &
Attendance: 2,000 (estimated)

Wellfleet

CAPE COD NATIONAL SEASHORE, 99 Marconi Site Rd., Wellfleet, MA 02667. Tel.: 508-255-3421. Fax: 508-349-9052.
E-mail: hope_morrill@nps.gov
Web Site: www.nps.gov/caco
Key Personnel: Superintendent, Brian Carlstrom; Deputy Superintendent, Kathy Tevyaw.
Institution Type/Description: Park Museum & Visitor Center.
Hours & Admission Prices: Headquarters: Mon.-Fri. 8-4:30. Salt Pond Museum: mid-June to Labor Day daily 9-5; Sept.-May 9-4:30. Salt Pond Visitor Center: daily 9-4:30 (extended summer hours); Province Lands Visitor Center: mid-May to Oct. daily 9-5; No charge; donations accepted. Beaches: season pass $45, vehicles $15, pedestrians & bicycles $3. &
Attendance: 500,000

WELLFLEET HISTORICAL SOCIETY MUSEUM, 266 Main St., Wellfleet, MA 02667. Mailing Address: P.O. Box 58, Wellfleet, MA 02667. Tel.: 508-349-9157 & 2247 (Cur.).
E-mail: wellfleethistoricalsociety@gmail.com
Web Site: www.wellfleethistoricalsociety.com
Key Personnel: Staff, David Wright; Staff, Barbara Kennedy.
Institution Type/Description: Historic Building: c.1800 two-story Victorian building.
Hours & Admission Prices: June 24-Sept. 6 Tues. & Fri. 10-4, Wed.-Thurs. & Sat. 1-4. No charge; donations accepted.
Attendance: 400 (estimated)

Wenham

WENHAM MUSEUM, 132 Main St., Wenham, MA 01984-1520. Tel.: 978-468-2377. Fax: 978-468-1763.
E-mail: info@wenhammuseum.org

Web Site: www.wenhammuseum.org
Key Personnel: Exec. Dir., Kristin Noon; Museum Shop Mgr., Cynthia Novotny.
Institution Type/Description: History Museum: housed in late 17th-century Claflin-Richards House & modern exhibition building.
Hours & Admission Prices: mid-May to mid-Sept. Tues.-Wed. & Fri.-Sat. 10-4, Thurs. 10-6; mid-Sept. to mid-May Tues.-Wed. & Fri.-Sun. 10-4. Adults $10, children 1-16 $6; discounts to groups and New England Museum Association, Massachusetts Teachers Assoc. & AAA members; members & children under no charge. Closed Martin Luther King Jr. Day; Presidents' Day; Veterans Day. &
Attendance: 35,000 (actual)

West Barnstable

HIGGINS ART GALLERY - CAPE COD COMMUNITY COLLEGE, 2240 Iyannough Rd., West Barnstable, MA 02668-1599. Tel.: 508-362-2131, ext. 4844. Fax: 508-375-4020.
E-mail: higginsartgalley@capecod.edu
Web Site: www.capecod.mass.edu
Key Personnel: Dir., Betty Carroll Fuller; Pres., Kathleen Schatzberg.
Institution Type/Description: Art Museum.
Hours & Admission Prices: Sept.-May Mon.-Thurs. 11-2; also open prior to events in adjacent college auditorium. No charge. Closed all official national & MA holidays. &
Attendance: 2,000 (estimated)

WILLIAM BREWSTER NICKERSON CAPE COD HISTORY ARCHIVES, Cape Cod Community College, 2240 Iyannough Rd., West Barnstable, MA 02668-1532. Tel.: 508-362-2131, ext. 4445. Fax: 508-375-4020.
E-mail: mlabombard@capecod.edu
Web Site: www.capecod.edu/web/nickerson/home
Key Personnel: Archivist, Mary LaBombard.
Institution Type/Description: Archives.
Hours & Admission Prices: Mon.-Wed. 9-3:30; other times by appointment. No charge. Closed MA state & federal holidays. &
Attendance: 500 (actual)

West Springfield

RAMAPOGUE HISTORICAL SOCIETY, 70 Park St., West Springfield, MA 01089-3318. Mailing Address: P.O. Box 826, West Springfield, MA 01090-0826. Tel.: 413-734-8322 & 732-6187.
Key Personnel: Cur., Raymond Wellspeake.
Institution Type/Description: Historic House: 1754 Josiah Day House, original all brick salt box style house.
Hours & Admission Prices: May-Oct. by appointment.
Attendance: 534 (actual)

STORROWTON VILLAGE MUSEUM, 1305 Memorial Ave., Eastern States Exposition Grounds, West Springfield, MA 01089-3578. Tel.: 413-205-5051 & 737-2443. Fax: 413-205-5054.
E-mail: storrow@thebige.com
Web Site: thebige.com
Key Personnel: Dir., Dennis Picard.
Institution Type/Description: Historic Village.
Hours & Admission Prices: Museum: Feb. to 3rd week in June & Sept.-Dec. by appointment only; 3rd week in June to Labor Day Tues.-Sat. 11-3. Admission $5; discounts to NEMA members; AAM members & children under 6 no charge. Administration building, restaurant & gift shops open year round. Closed holidays. &
Attendance: 500,000 (estimated)

West Tisbury

POLLY HILL ARBORETUM, 795 State Rd., West Tisbury, MA 02575. Mailing Address: P.O. Box 561, West Tisbury, MA 02575. Tel.: 508-693-9426. Fax: 508-693-5772.
E-mail: info@pollyhillarboretum.org
Web Site: www.pollyhillarboretum.org
Institution Type/Description: Botanical Garden.
Hours & Admission Prices: Grounds: daily sunrise to sunset. Visitor Center: Memorial Day to Columbus Day daily 9:30-4. Guided Tours: daily 2pm; groups by appointment. Suggested Donation: adults $5; children 12 & under no charge.

Westfield

AMELIA PARK CHILDREN'S MUSEUM, 29 S. Broad St., Westfield, MA 01086. Mailing Address: P.O. Box 931, Westfield, MA 01086-0931. Tel.: 413-572-4014. Fax: 413-572-1206.
E-mail: fun@ameliaparkmuseum.org
Web Site: www.ameliaparkmuseum.org
Institution Type/Description: Children's Museum.
Hours & Admission Prices: Wed.-Mon. 10-4. Adults & children $7, seniors $3.50; children under one no charge.

JASPER RAND ART MUSEUM, AT WESTFIELD ATHENAEUM, 6 Elm St., Westfield, MA 01085-2904. Tel.: 413-568-7833. Fax: 413-568-0988.
E-mail: dpaquette@westath.org
Web Site: www.westath.org
Key Personnel: Dir., Daniel Paquette; Pres., Bob Brown.
Institution Type/Description: Art Gallery.
Hours & Admission Prices: July-Aug. Mon.-Thurs. 8:30-8, Fri. 8:30-5; Sept.-June Mon.-Thurs. 8:30-8, Fri.-Sat. 8:30-5. No charge. Closed holidays. &

Westford

THE BUTTERFLY PLACE, 120 Tyngsboro Rd., Westford, MA 01886. Mailing Address: P.O. Box 1541, Westford, MA 01886. Tel.: 978-392-0955. Fax: 978-256-1080.
E-mail: butterflyplace@comcast.net
Web Site: www.butterflyplace-ma.com
Key Personnel: Dir., C.E.O. & Museum Shop Mgr., Sylvia L. Weslie.
Institution Type/Description: Butterfly Garden.
Hours & Admission Prices: See website for hours & admission prices. &
Attendance: 42,000 (estimated)

THE WESTFORD MUSEUM & HISTORICAL SOCIETY, 4 Boston Rd., Westford, MA 01886. Mailing Address: P.O. Box 411, Westford, MA 01886-0411. Tel.: 978-692-5550.
E-mail: museum@museum.westford.org
Web Site: www.museum.westford.org
Key Personnel: Dir., Penny Lacroix.
Institution Type/Description: History Museum: housed in the Westford Academy school house, built in 1794.
Hours & Admission Prices: Mon. & Wed.-Fri. 9-1; other times by appointment. No charge; donations accepted. Closed holidays. &
Attendance: 1,437 (actual)

Weston

GOLDEN BALL TAVERN MUSEUM, 662 Boston Post Rd., Weston, MA 02493-1511. Mailing Address: P.O. Box 223, Weston, MA 02493. Tel.: 781-894-1751. Fax: 781-861-6218.
E-mail: joanb5@aol.com
Web Site: www.goldenballtavern.org
Key Personnel: Dir., Dr. Joan P. Bines; Chm. (V), William W. Gallagher, III; Pres. (V), William Wiseman.
Institution Type/Description: Historic House: 1768 Georgian house.
Hours & Admission Prices: Tours: by appointment. Adults $5, senior citizens & students $2; members no charge.
Attendance: 1,350 (estimated)

SPELLMAN MUSEUM OF STAMPS AND POSTAL HISTORY, 235 Wellesley St., Regis College, Weston, MA 02493-1545. Tel.: 781-768-7331. Fax: 781-768-7332.
E-mail: info@spellman.org
Web Site: www.spellman.org
Key Personnel: Chm. (V) & Pres. (V), Mark W. Gallagher; Education & Community Outreach, Henry Lukas; Cur. Philatelic Collections, George Norton; Museum Shop Mgr., Anne O'Keefe.
Institution Type/Description: Philatelic Museum.
Hours & Admission Prices: July-Aug. Thurs.-Sat. 12-5; Sept.-June Thurs.-Sun. 12-5. Adults $8, seniors & students $5, children 5-16 $3; discounts to AAM, ICOM, AAA & NEMA members; children 4 & under and members no charge. Closed New Year's Day, Easter; Memorial Day weekend; Labor Day weekend; Thanksgiving & day after; Christmas. &
Attendance: 6,395 (actual)

WESTON HISTORICAL SOCIETY, INC., 358 Boston Post Rd., Weston, MA 02493. Mailing Address: P.O. Box 343, Weston, MA 02493-0002.
E-mail: info@westonhistoricalsociety.org

Web Site: www.westonhistoricalsociety.org
Key Personnel: Pres. (V), Pamela W. Fox.
Institution Type/Description: History Museum.
Hours & Admission Prices: By appointment. No charge.

Williamstown

CHAPIN LIBRARY OF RARE BOOKS, 26 Hopkins Hall Dr., Williams Libraries, Williamstown, MA 01267-2526. Tel.: 413-597-4200.
E-mail: specialcollections@williams.edu
Web Site: specialcollections.williams.edu
Key Personnel: Chapin Librarian, Wayne G. Hammond.
Institution Type/Description: Library.
Hours & Admission Prices: Mon.-Fri. 10-5. No charge. Closed national holidays except Independence Day. &
Attendance: 10,000 (estimated)

STERLING AND FRANCINE CLARK ART INSTITUTE, 225 South St., Williamstown, MA 01267-2891. Mailing Address: P.O. Box 8, Williamstown, MA 01267-0008. Tel.: 413-458-2303. Fax: 413-458-2324. Facebook: Clark Art Institute.
E-mail: info@clarkart.edu
Web Site: www.clarkart.edu
Key Personnel: Dir., Olivier Meslay; Deputy Dir., Anthony G. King; Sr. Cur., Kathleen Morris; Center for Education in the Visual Arts, Michael Cassin; Registrar, Mattie Kelley; Preparator, Paul Dion; Librarian, Susan Roeper; Dir. Communications, Vicki Saltzman; Museum Shop Mgr., Rachelle Jones; Public Rels. Mgr., Sally Majewski.
Institution Type/Description: Art Museum.
Hours & Admission Prices: July-Aug. daily 10-5; Sept.-June Tues.-Sun. & Mon. holidays 10-5. June-Oct. Adults $21.50; discounts to AAM & ICOM members, children under 18 & students; members no charge. Closed New Year's Day; Thanksgiving; Christmas. &
Attendance: 200,000 (actual)

WILLIAMS COLLEGE MUSEUM OF ART, 15 Lawrence Hall Dr., Ste. 2, Williamstown, MA 01267-3248. Tel.: 413-597-2429. Fax: 413-597-5000.
E-mail: WCMA@williams.edu
Web Site: artmuseum.williams.edu
Key Personnel: Dir. Exhibitions & Collection Mgmt., Noah Smalls; Deputy Dir. Curatorial Affiars, Lisa Dorin; Deputy Dir. Engagement & Curator of Education, Christina Yang; Asst. to Dir., Amy Tatro; Dir. Communications, Joellen Adae; Dir. Museum Fin. & Opers., Barbara Palmer; Dir. Development, Alex Groff; Sr. Cur. American Art, Kevin Murphy; Asst. Cur., Horace Ballard; Coord. Mellon Academic Programs, Elizabeth Gallerani; Asst. Cur. Public Programs, Nina Pelaez; Sr. Museum Registrar, Diane Hart; Asst. Registrar, Rachel Tassone.
Institution Type/Description: Art Museum.
Hours & Admission Prices: June-Aug. Thurs. 10-8, Fri.-Wed. 10-5; Sept. to late Dec. & late March to May Thurs. 10-8, Fri.-Tues. 10-5; Winter: . No charge; donations accepted. Closed New Year's Eve & Day; Christmas Eve & Day. &
Attendance: 53,452 (actual)

Wilmington

WILMINGTON TOWN MUSEUM, 430 Salem St., Wilmington, MA 01887-1211. Tel.: 978-658-5475.
E-mail: htavern@town.wilmington.ma.us
Web Site: www.town.wilmington.ma.us/tavern1.html
Key Personnel: Cur., Theresa McDermott.
Institution Type/Description: History Museum: housed in the Col. Joshua Harnden Tavern.
Hours & Admission Prices: July-Aug. Thurs.-Fri. 10-2; Sept.-June. Tues. & Thurs. 10-2; other times by appointment.

Winchendon

WINCHENDON HISTORICAL SOCIETY, INC., 151 Front St., Winchendon, MA 01475-1521. Mailing Address: P.O. Box 279, Winchendon, MA 01475-0279. Tel.: 978-297-2142.
E-mail: info@winchendonhistoricalsociety.org
Web Site: www.winchendonhistoricalsociety.org
Key Personnel: Pres. (V), Don O'Neil; Cur., Mary Bulger.
Institution Type/Description: History Museum.
Hours & Admission Prices: June 2-Oct. Tues. & Thurs. 11-4, Wed. 10-4, Sun.1-4; other times by appointment. Tours: 1 & 2:30. Adults $5; members no charge. &
Attendance: 300 (estimated)

Winchester

GRIFFIN MUSEUM OF PHOTOGRAPHY, 67 Shore Rd., Winchester, MA 01890-2821. Tel.: 781-729-1158. Fax: 781-721-2765.
E-mail: photos@griffinmuseum.org
Web Site: www.griffinmuseum.org
Formerly: Arthur Griffin Center For Photographic Art
Key Personnel: Pres. (V), Peter Griffin; Exec. Dir., Paula Tognarelli; Vice Pres., John McConnell; Treas., Doug Marmon; Assoc. Dir., Frances Jakubek; Gallery Monitor, Martha Stone.
Institution Type/Description: Photography Museum.
Hours & Admission Prices: Tues.-Thurs. 11-5, Fri. 11-4, Sat.-Sun. 12-4. Adults $5, seniors $2; members, children, students & Thurs. no charge. Closed major holidays. ♿
Attendance: 7,000 (estimated)

Woods Hole

WOODS HOLE HISTORICAL MUSEUM, 579 Woods Hole Rd., Woods Hole, MA 02543. Mailing Address: P.O. Box 185, Woods Hole, MA 02543. Tel.: 508-548-7270.
E-mail: woods_hole_historical@hotmail.com
Web Site: www.woodsholemuseum.org
Institution Type/Description: History Museum.
Hours & Admission Prices: Call for hours. No charge; donations accepted.

WOODS HOLE OCEANOGRAPHIC INSTITUTION, OCEAN SCIENCE EXHIBIT CENTER, 15 School St., Woods Hole, MA 02543-1126. Mailing Address: Mail Stop 45, Woods Hole, MA 02543. Tel.: 508-289-2663. Fax: 508-457-2147.
E-mail: information@whoi.edu
Web Site: www.whoi.edu
Key Personnel: Dir., Susan Avery; Museum Shop Mgr., Kathy Patterson.
Institution Type/Description: Oceanographic Research Institution.
Hours & Admission Prices: mid-April to Oct. Mon.-Fri. 11-4; Nov.-Dec. Tues.-Fri. 11-4. Suggested Donation $3. Closed Easter; Independence Day; Thanksgiving; Christmas. ♿
Attendance: 30,000

WOODS HOLE SCIENCE AQUARIUM, 166 Water St., Woods Hole, MA 02543-1097. Tel.: 508-495-2001. Fax: 508-495-2382.
E-mail: george.liles@noaa.gov
Web Site: aquarium.nefsc.noaa.gov
Formerly: Aquarium of the National Marine Fisheries Service
Key Personnel: Cur., George Liles; Dir. Science & Research, William Karp.
Institution Type/Description: Aquarium.
Hours & Admission Prices: Tues.-Sat. 11-4; groups by appointment during school year. No charge; donations accepted. Closed federal holidays. ♿
Attendance: 80,000 (actual)

Worcester

AMERICAN ANTIQUARIAN SOCIETY, 185 Salisbury St., Worcester, MA 01609-1634. Tel.: 508-755-5221. Fax: 508-753-3311.
E-mail: library@mwa.org
Web Site: www.americanantiquarian.org
Key Personnel: Pres., Ellen S. Dunlap; Andrew W. Mellon Cur. Graphic Arts, Lauren Hewes; Marcus A. McLorison Librarian & Cur. Manuscripts, Thomas Knoles; Dir. Outreach, James David Moran.
Institution Type/Description: Research Library.
Hours & Admission Prices: Mon.-Tues. & Thurs.-Fri. 9-5, Wed. 10-8. No charge; donations accepted. Closed national holidays; New Year's Eve; Thanksgiving weekend; Christmas Eve. ♿
Attendance: 5,975 (actual)

BROAD MEADOW BROOK CONSERVATION CENTER AND WILDLIFE SANCTUARY, 414 Massasoit Rd., Worcester, MA 01604-3546. Tel.: 508-753-6087.
E-mail: bmbrook@massaudubon.org
Institution Type/Description: Wildlife Sanctuary & Nature Center.
Hours & Admission Prices: Nature Center: Tues.-Sat. 9-4, Sun. 12:30-4. Trails: daily dawn to dusk. Adults $4, seniors & children 2-12 $3; members no charge.

ECOTARIUM, 222 Harrington Way, Worcester, MA 01604-1899. Tel.: 508-929-2700. Fax: 508-929-2701. Facebook: EcoTarium.
E-mail: info@ecotarium.org
Web Site: www.ecotarium.org
Formerly: Worcester Natural History Society

Key Personnel: Dir. Institutional Advancement, Kerry Castorano; Dir. Exhibits, Betsy Loring; Deputy Dir., Patricia Crawford.
Institution Type/Description: Science & Nature Museum.
Hours & Admission Prices: Tues.-Sat. 10-5, Sun. 12-5. Adults $18, children 2-18, senior citizens, college students with ID $14; discounts to groups, AAM, ASTC, ACM, AAA, MTA, & NEMA members, and staff members of other museums; members & children under 2 no charge. ASTC Passport Program. Planetarium: $5. Train (seasonal): $3. Closed New Year's Day; Easter; Thanksgiving; Christmas Eve & Day. ♿
Attendance: 175,000 (actual)

IRIS & B. GERALD CANTOR ART GALLERY-COLLEGE OF THE HOLY CROSS, One College St., Worcester, MA 01610-2322. Tel.: 508-793-3356. Fax: 508-793-3030. Facebook: Cantor Art Gallery-College of the Holy Cross.
E-mail: rhankins@holycross.edu
Web Site: www.holycross.edu/cantorartgallery
Key Personnel: Dir., Roger Hankins.
Institution Type/Description: Art Gallery.
Hours & Admission Prices: Mon.-Fri. 10-5, Sat. noon-5. No charge. Closed school holidays. ♿
Attendance: 3,000 (estimated)

WORCESTER ART MUSEUM, 55 Salisbury St., Worcester, MA 01609-3123. Tel.: 508-799-4406. Fax: 508-798-5646. Facebook.
E-mail: information@worcesterart.org
Web Site: www.worcesterart.org
Key Personnel: The C. Jean & Myles McDonough Dir., Matthias Waschek; Deputy Exec. Dir., Heather L. Davis; Pres., Joseph L. Bafaro, Jr.; Dir. Philanthropy, Nora Maroulis; Dir. Curatorial Affairs & Cur. European Art, Jon L. Seydl; Cur. Arms & Armor and Medieval Art, Jeffrey L. Forgeng; Chief Preparator & Exhibition Designer, Patrick Brown; Asst. Cur. Prints, Drawings & Photographs, Nancy K. Burns; Cur. Education, Marcia Lagerwey; Librarian, Deborah Aframe; Dir. Operations, Francis Pedone; Museum Shop Mgr., Susan Giordano; Cafe Mgr., Laurie Krohn.
Institution Type/Description: Art Museum.
Hours & Admission Prices: Wed.-Sun. 10-4, third Thurs. each month 10-8. Adults $16, senior citizens 65 & over, children 4-17 and college students with ID $14; members & children under 4 no charge. Parking: no charge. Closed holidays. ♿
Attendance: 92,559 (actual)

WORCESTER CENTER FOR CRAFTS, 25 Sagamore Rd., Worcester, MA 01605-3914. Tel.: 508-753-8183. Fax: 508-797-5626.
E-mail: wcc@worcestercraftcenter.org
Web Site: www.worcestercraftcenter.org
Key Personnel: Exec. Dir., Carol Donnelly; Dir. Finance & Administration, Tammy Nigosian; Head Ceramics Dept., Tom O'Malley; Head Glass Dept., Jacob Vincent; Head Metals Dept., Lauren Beaudoin; Head Fiber Arts, Patti Sims; Head Wood Dept., Tony Gardner; Gallery Dir. & Gallery Shop Mgr., Candace Casey; Mgr. Organization Advancement, Caitlin Barkoskic; Registrar, Bettie Carlson.
Institution Type/Description: Arts & Crafts Center.
Hours & Admission Prices: Mon., Wed. & Fri. 10-5:30, Tues. & Thurs. 10-7:30. No charge; donations accepted. Closed national holidays.
Attendance: 25,000 (estimated)

WORCESTER HISTORICAL MUSEUM, 30 Elm St., Worcester, MA 01609-2570. Tel.: 508-753-8278. Fax: 508-753-9070.
E-mail: info@worcesterhistory.net
Web Site: www.worcesterhistory.org
Key Personnel: Pres., Mark L. Shelton; Exec. Dir., William Wallace.
Institution Type/Description: History Museum.
Hours & Admission Prices: Tues.-Sat. 10-4, 4th Thurs. of month 10-8:30. Adults $5, seniors 62 & over and college students with ID $4; discounts to AAM members; children under 18 & members no charge. Closed major holidays. ♿
Attendance: 22,000 (actual)

Yarmouth Port

EDWARD GOREY HOUSE, 8 Strawberry Lane, Yarmouth Port, MA 02675. Tel.: 508-362-3909. Facebook: Edward Gorey House.
E-mail: info@edwardgoreyhouse.org
Web Site: www.edwardgoreyhouse.org
Key Personnel: Dir., Rick Jones.
Institution Type/Description: Historic House Museum: housed in the former home of artist & writer Edward Gorey.
Hours & Admission Prices: April 18-June 30 Thurs.-Sat. 11-4, Sun. 12-4; July 4-Oct. 13 Wed.-Sat. 11-4, Sun. 12-4; Oct. 18-Dec. 29 Fri.-Sat. 11-4, Sun. 12-4.

Adults $8, students & seniors $5, children 6-12 $2; children under 6 & members no charge. &
Attendance: 9,000 (actual)

HISTORICAL SOCIETY OF OLD YARMOUTH, 11 Strawberry Lane, Yarmouth Port, MA 02675-1726. Mailing Address: P.O. Box 11, Yarmouth Port, MA 02675-0011. Tel.: 508-362-3021.
E-mail: info@hsoy.org
Web Site: www.hsoy.org
Key Personnel: Pres., Judith LeGrand.
Institution Type/Description: Historical & Preservation Society: housed in 1840, Capt. Bangs Hallet House.
Hours & Admission Prices: House Tours: mid-June to mid-Oct. Thurs.-Sun. 1-4; other times by appointment. Admission $5; members & Yarmouth residents no charge. Archives: Tues. & Thurs. 10-3:30; other times by appointment. Closed holidays.
Attendance: 2,100 (estimated)

WINSLOW CROCKER HOUSE, (Old King's Hwy.) 250 Rte. 6A, Yarmouth Port, MA 02675. Mailing Address: c/o Historic New England, 141 Cambridge St., Boston, MA 02114. Tel.: 617-994-6661.
E-mail: winslowcrocker@historicnewengland.org
Web Site: www.historicnewengland.org
Key Personnel: Pres., Carl R. Nold; Site Mgr., Melinda Huff.
Institution Type/Description: Historic House: c.1780 Georgian house.
Hours & Admission Prices: June-Oct. 15 2nd & 4th Sat. of month 11-4. Adults $5; discounts to seniors, AAM, ICOM & AAA members; Historic New England members no charge.
Attendance: 456 (actual)

MICHIGAN

(347 listings)

Ada

AVERILL HISTORICAL MUSEUM OF ADA, 7144 Headley St., Ada, MI 49301. Mailing Address: P.O. Box 741, Ada, MI 49301. Tel.: 616-676-9346.
Institution Type/Description: History Museum.
Hours & Admission Prices: March-Dec. Fri.-Sat. 1-4; other times by appointment. No charge; donations accepted.

Adrian

KLEMM GALLERY, Siena Heights University, 1247 E. Siena Heights Dr., Adrian, MI 49221-1755. Tel.: 517-264-7860 & 7864. Fax: 517-264-7738.
E-mail: ddaniels@sienaheights.edu
Web Site: www.studioangelico.com
Key Personnel: Chm. Art Dept., Peter Barr, Ph.D.; Dir. Gallery, Deborah Danielson.
Institution Type/Description: Arts Center and Institute.
Hours & Admission Prices: Sept.-May Tues.-Fri. 9-4, Sun. 12-4. No charge. Closed Easter; Christmas; semester breaks. &
Attendance: 1,000 (estimated)

Albion

ALBION COLLEGE DEPARTMENT OF ART AND ART HISTORY, 805 E. Cass St., Albion, MI 49224-1831. Mailing Address: Bobbitt Visual Arts Center, 611 E. Porter St., Albion, MI 49224-1887. Tel.: 517-629-0246 & 0000. Fax: 517-629-0752.
E-mail: jmerrild@albion.edu
Web Site: www.albion.edu
Formerly: Albion College Department of Visual Arts
Key Personnel: Prof., Lynne Chytilo; Prof., Bille Wickre; Prof., Anne McCauley; Assoc. Prof. & Dept. Chair, Michael Dixon; Asst. Prof., Ashley Feagin.
Institution Type/Description: Art Museum.
Hours & Admission Prices: Sept.-May Mon.-Thurs. 9-9, Fri. 9-5, Sat. 10-2. No charge. Closed school holidays & vacations. &
Attendance: 2,000 (estimated)

GARDNER HOUSE MUSEUM, 509 S. Superior St., Albion, MI 49224-2137. Tel.: 517-629-5100.
E-mail: info@albionhistoricalsociety.org
Web Site: www.albionhistoricalsociety.org
Key Personnel: Chm. & Pres. (V), Celeste Connamacher.

Institution Type/Description: Local History Museum: housed in c.1875 A.P. Gardner House.
Hours & Admission Prices: May-Sept. Sat.-Sun. 2-4. No charge; donations accepted. &
Attendance: 600 (estimated)

KIDS 'N' STUFF CHILDREN'S MUSEUM, 301 S. Superior St., Albion, MI 49224-1752. Mailing Address: P.O. Box 718, Albion, MI 49224-0718. Tel.: 517-629-8023.
E-mail: operations@kidsnstuff.org
Web Site: www.kidsnstuff.org
Key Personnel: Dir., Audrey Dean.
Institution Type/Description: Children's Museum.
Hours & Admission Prices: Tues.-Sat. 10-4, Sun. noon to 4. Admission $6.50; discounts to ACM members; children one & under and members no charge. &
Attendance: 18,000 (actual)

WHITEHOUSE NATURE CENTER - ALBION COLLEGE, Farley Dr., Albion, MI 49224-1887. Tel.: 517-629-0582. Fax: 517-629-0509.
E-mail: naturecenter@albion.edu
Web Site: www.albion.edu/naturecenter
Key Personnel: Dir., David Green.
Institution Type/Description: Nature Center & Arboretum.
Hours & Admission Prices: Mon.-Fri. 9-5, Sat.-Sun. 12-4; call to confirm. No charge; donations accepted. Closed national holidays & some Albion College holidays.
Attendance: 12,500 (estimated)

Algonac

ALGONAC-CLAY HISTORICAL SOCIETY, 1240 St. Clair River Dr., Algonac, MI 48001-1472. Mailing Address: P.O. Box 228, Algonac, MI 48001-0228. Tel.: 810-794-9015.
E-mail: achs@algonac-clay-history.com
Web Site: www.algonac-clay-history.com
Institution Type/Description: Historical Society Museum.
Hours & Admission Prices: late April-Nov. Sat.-Sun. 1-4; other times by appointment. No charge; donations accepted.

ALGONAC-CLAY TOWNSHIP HISTORICAL SOCIETY MARITIME MUSEUM, 1117 St. Clair River Dr., Algonac, MI 48001. Mailing Address: P.O. Box 228, Algonac, MI 48001. Tel.: 810-794-9015 & 671-7968.
E-mail: achs@algonac-clay-history.com
Web Site: www.achistory.com
Institution Type/Description: Maritime Museum.
Hours & Admission Prices: late April to Nov. Sat.-Sun. 1-4; other times by appointment. No charge; donations accepted. Closed Easter. &
Attendance: 1,600 (estimated)

Allegan

ALLEGAN COUNTY HISTORICAL SOCIETY AND OLD JAIL MUSEUM, 113 Walnut St., Allegan, MI 49010-1249. Tel.: 269-673-8292.
E-mail: oldjailmuseum06@yahoo.com
Web Site: www.alleganoldjail.com
Key Personnel: Pres., Scott Kuykendall; Vice Pres., Mark Lovett; Treas., Allen Philley.
Institution Type/Description: Regional History Museum: housed in 1906 former county jail & sheriff's home.
Hours & Admission Prices: May-Aug. Fri. & Sat. 10-4; Sept.-April Sat. 10-4. No charge; donations accepted. Closed New Year's Day; Christmas.
Attendance: 2,800 (estimated)

Allendale

ENGINE HOUSE NO. 5 MUSEUM, 6610 Lake Michigan Dr., P.O. Box 188, Allendale, MI 49401-0188. Tel.: 616-895-8121.
E-mail: information@enginehouse5.com
Web Site: www.enginehouse5.com
Key Personnel: Dir. & Museum Shop Mgr., Kimberly Blum; Pres. (V), Jeffrey Blum; Chm. (V), Jeffrey Dupilka.
Institution Type/Description: Fire Fighting History Museum.
Hours & Admission Prices: Wed.-Fri. 11-6, Sat. 11-3, or by appointment. Adults $4, children $1.
Attendance: 3,500 (estimated)

GRAND VALLEY STATE UNIVERSITY ART GALLERY, 1121
Performing Arts Center, Allendale, MI 49401-9403. Tel.: 616-331-
2563. Fax: 616-331-8565.
E-mail: bazuinc@gvsu.edu
Web Site: www.gvsu.edu/artgallery
Key Personnel: Dir., Henry Matthews; Cur. Collections, Nathan Kemler.
Institution Type/Description: Art Museum.
Hours & Admission Prices: Winter: Mon.-Wed. & Fri. 10-5, Thurs. 10-7; Summer:
Mon.-Fri. 10-4. No charge. Closed holidays.

Alpena

BESSER MUSEUM FOR NORTHEAST MICHIGAN, 491
Johnson St., Alpena, MI 49707-1496. Tel.: 989-356-2202. Fax:
989-356-3133.
E-mail: cwitulski@bessermuseum.org
Web Site: www.bessermuseum.org
Key Personnel: Dir., Christine Witulski; Pres. (V), Steve Lappan; Cur., Danyeal
Dorr; Facilities & Exhibits Mgr., Matt Klimczak; Exec. Asst., Kat
Tomaszewski.
Institution Type/Description: General Museum.
Hours & Admission Prices: Mon.-Sat. 10-5, Sun. 12-4. Adults $5, children, students
& senior citizens $3; discounts to active military, AAM & AAA members; mem-
bers, children under 5, persons with disabilities & Wed. 3-5 no charge.
Planetarium Programs: Sat. 2pm. Adults $3, seniors & children $2. Closed major
holidays.
Attendance: 23,000 (estimated)

GREAT LAKES MARITIME HERITAGE CENTER, 500 W.
Fletcher St., Alpena, MI 49707. Tel.: 989-356-8805. Fax: 989-354-
0144.
E-mail: thunderbay@noaa.gov
Web Site: thunderbay.noaa.gov
Key Personnel: Supt., Jeff Gray; Deputy Supt. Research Coord., Russ Green.
Institution Type/Description: Maritime History Museum.
Hours & Admission Prices: Winter: Mon.-Sat. 10-5, Sun. noon-5; Summer: daily 9-
5. No charge; donations accepted. Closed New Year's Day; Thanksgiving;
Christmas.
Attendance: 80,000 (estimated)

Alto

BOWNE TOWNSHIP HISTORICAL COMMISSION, 8240
Alden Nash, S.E., Alto, MI 49302. Mailing Address: P.O. Box 35,
Alto, MI 49302.
E-mail: srjohnson4@charter.net
Web Site: www.bownetwp.org/museum.html
Formerly: Bowne Township Historical Museum
Key Personnel: Pres. (V), Richard W. Johnson.
Institution Type/Description: History Museum: Historic buildings; one room school
house; carriage shed.
Hours & Admission Prices: June-Aug. 1st Sun. each month 2-4; other times by
appointment. No charge; donations accepted.
Attendance: 300 (estimated)

Ann Arbor

ANN ARBOR ART CENTER, 117 W. Liberty St., Ann Arbor, MI
48104-1380. Tel.: 734-994-8004. Fax: 734-994-3610.
E-mail: mklopf@annarborartcenter.org
Web Site: annarborartcenter.org
Key Personnel: C.E.O. & Pres. (V), Marie Klopf; Mktg. Dir., Nicholas Farrell;
Gallery Shop Dir., Amy Cameron; Dir. Programs, Erika Villarreal Bunce;
Exhibitions Mgr., Nathan Rice; Financial Controller, Eric Wolff.
Institution Type/Description: Art Center.
Hours & Admission Prices: Mon.-Fri. 10-7, Sat. 10-6, Sun. 12-5. No charge. Closed
legal holidays.
Attendance: 100,000

ANN ARBOR HANDS-ON MUSEUM, 220 E. Ann St., Ann Arbor,
MI 48104-1445. Tel.: 734-995-5439. Fax: 734-995-1188.
Facebook: Ann Arbor Hands-On Museum.
E-mail: info@aahom.org
Web Site: www.aahom.org
Key Personnel: Dir., Mel Drumm; Shop Mgr., Alice Klute.
Institution Type/Description: Science Museum.
Hours & Admission Prices: Mon.-Sat. 10-5, Sun. 12-5. Admission 2 & over $12;
discounts to ASTC members & groups of 20 or more; members & children under

2 no charge. Closed Memorial Day; Independence Day; Labor Day;
Thanksgiving; Christmas.
Attendance: 201,000 (estimated)

ARGUS IMRA PLANETARIUM, Seventh St., Ann Arbor, MI
48103-5812. Mailing Address: 601 W. Stadium Blvd., Ann Arbor,
MI 48103. Tel.: 734-994-1771. Fax: 734-994-1724.
E-mail: robinson@aaps.k12.mi.us
Web Site: argusplanetarium.weebly.com
Key Personnel: Dir., Ron Robinson.
Institution Type/Description: Planetarium.
Hours & Admission Prices: By appointment. School groups outside of district $5
per student, $75 min.
Attendance: 6,000

COBBLESTONE FARM MUSEUM, 2781 Packard Rd., Ann
Arbor, MI 48108. Tel.: 734-794-7120. Facebook: Cobblestone
Farm Museum.
E-mail: coblestonefarm@provide.net
Web Site: www.cobblestonefarm.org
Institution Type/Description: Historic Farmstead: built in 1845.
Hours & Admission Prices: Thurs. 11-2; other times by appointment. Family $5,
adults $2, children & seniors $1; members no charge.
Attendance: 2,200 (estimated)

GERALD R. FORD PRESIDENTIAL LIBRARY, 1000 Beal Ave.,
Ann Arbor, MI 48109-2114. Tel.: 734-205-0555. Fax: 734-205-
0571.
E-mail: ford.library@nara.gov
Web Site: www.fordlibrarymuseum.gov
Key Personnel: Dir., Elaine K. Didier; Supervisory Archivist, Geir Gundersen.
Institution Type/Description: Presidential Library.
Hours & Admission Prices: Mon.-Fri. 8:45-4:45. No charge. Closed New Year's
Day; Martin Luther King Jr. Day; Presidents' Day; Memorial Day; Independence
Day; Labor Day; Columbus Day; Veterans Day; Thanksgiving; Christmas.
Attendance: 15,000 (estimated)

HERBARIUM OF THE UNIVERSITY OF MICHIGAN, 3600
Varsity Dr., Ann Arbor, MI 48108-2228. Tel.: 734-615-6200. Fax:
734-998-0038.
E-mail: cwdick@umich.edu
Web Site: herbarium.lsa.umich.edu
Key Personnel: Dir., Christopher Dick; Cur., Paul E. Berry; Cur. Emeritus, Michael
Wynne; Cur., A.A. Reznicek; Cur., Timothy James; Research Scientist, Florence
S. Wagner; Research Scientist, Christiane Anderson; Asst. Research Scientist,
Richard K. Rabeler.
Institution Type/Description: Herbarium.
Hours & Admission Prices: Mon.-Fri. 8:30-4. No charge; donations accepted.
Attendance: 12 (estimated)

**THE INTERNATIONAL MUSEUM OF DINNERWARE
DESIGN,** Office: 520 N. Main St., Ann Arbor, MI 48104. Tel.:
607-382-1415. Facebook.
E-mail: director@dinnerwaremuseum.org
Web Site: dinnerwaremuseum.org
Key Personnel: Dir., Dr. Margaret Carney.
Institution Type/Description: Dinnerware Museum.
Hours & Admission Prices: By appointment only. No charge.

KELSEY MUSEUM OF ARCHAEOLOGY, 434 S. State St., Ann
Arbor, MI 48109-1390. Tel.: 734-764-9304. Fax: 734-763-8976.
E-mail: sherbert@umich.edu
Web Site: www.lsa.umich.edu/kelsey/
Key Personnel: Pres., Mary Sue Coleman; Provost & Exec. Vice Pres. Academic
Affairs, Teresa A. Sullivan; Dir. & Cur., Sharon Herbert; Assoc. Dir. & Cur.
Academic Outreach, Lauren Talalay; Cur. Conservation, Suzanne Davis;
Conservator, Claudia Chemello; Cur. Greece & Near East, Margaret Root; Cur.
Hellenistic & Roman Empire, Elaine Gazda; Cur. Dynastic Egypt, Janet
Richards; Cur. Graeco-Roman Egypt, Terry Wilfong; Coord. Museums
Collections, Michelle Fontenot; Coord. Museum Exhibitions, Scott Meier;
Coord. Museum Collections, Sebastian Encina; Editor, Peg Lourie; Coord.
Museum Visitor Programs& Museum Shop Mgr., Todd E. Gerring; Gift Mgmt.
& Graphic Artist, Lorene Stervier.
Institution Type/Description: Archaeology Museum.
Hours & Admission Prices: Jan. 2-Dec. 24 Tues.-Fri. 9-4, Sat.-Sun. 1-4. No charge;
donations accepted. Closed major holidays.
Attendance: 21,490 (actual)

KEMPF HOUSE MUSEUM, 312 S. Division St., Ann Arbor, MI 48104. Tel.: 734-994-4898.
E-mail: kempfhousemuseum@gmail.com
Web Site: kempfhousemuseum.org
Institution Type/Description: Historic House Museum: housed in the former home of Reuben & Pauline Kempf; built 1853. Listed on the National Register of Historic Places.
Hours & Admission Prices: mid-Feb. to June & Sept.-Dec. Sun. 1-4; other times by appointment. No charge; donations accepted.

MATTHAEI BOTANICAL GARDENS AND NICHOLS ARBORETUM, 1800 N. Dixboro Rd., Ann Arbor, MI 48105-9741. Tel.: 734-647-7600. Fax: 734-998-6205.
E-mail: matthaeinichols@umich.edu
Web Site: mbgna.umich.edu
Key Personnel: Dir., Robert E. Grese; Chief Administrative Officer, David Betz.
Institution Type/Description: Botanical Garden-Arboretum.
Hours & Admission Prices: Grounds: daily sunrise to sunset. Conservatory: Wed. 10-8, Thurs.-Tues. 10-4:30. No charge. Parking: $1.70 per hour. American Horticultural Society reciprocity to botanical garden/arboretum members.
Attendance: 465,000 (estimated)

SINDECUSE MUSEUM OF DENTISTRY, University of Michigan, 1011 N. University - G565 Dental Bldg., Ann Arbor, MI 48109-1078. Tel.: 734-763-0767. Fax: 734-615-1429. Facebook.
E-mail: dentalmuseum@umich.edu
Web Site: www.dent.umich.edu/sindecuse
Key Personnel: Cur., Shannon O'Dell; Coord. Collections, Adam Johnson.
Institution Type/Description: Dental Museum.
Hours & Admission Prices: Mon.-Fri. 8-6. No charge. Closed New Year's Day; Memorial Day; Independence Day; Labor Day; Thanksgiving & day after; Christmas Day & week.
Attendance: 7,000 (estimated)

STEARNS COLLECTION OF MUSICAL INSTRUMENTS, University of Michigan School of Music, 1100 Baits Dr., Ann Arbor, MI 48109-2085. Mailing Address: University of Michigan School of Music, 3084 Fleming, Ann Arbor, MI 48109-2085. Tel.: 734-936-2891. Fax: 734-647-1897.
E-mail: stearnsoutreach@umich.edu
Web Site: www.music.umich.edu/research/stearns_collection/index.htm
Key Personnel: Dir., Lester Monts.
Institution Type/Description: Musical Instrument Museum.
Hours & Admission Prices: Mon.-Fri. 9-5; groups by appointment. No charge; donations accepted. Group Tour: $1 per person.
Attendance: 660

UNIVERSITY OF MICHIGAN MUSEUM OF ANTHROPOLOGICAL ARCHAEOLOGY, 4013 Ruthven Museums Bldg., 1109 Geddes, Ann Arbor, MI 48109-1079. Tel.: 734-764-0485. Fax: 734-763-7783.
E-mail: anthro-museum@umich.edu
Web Site: www.lsa.umich.edu/umma/
Key Personnel: Dir., Cur. Latin American Archaeology & Ethnohistory, Joyce Marcus; Cur. Mediterranean Archaeology, Robert Whallon; Cur. Asian Archaeology, Carla Sinopoli; Cur. of Human Ecology, Kent V. Flannery; Cur. Great Lakes Archaeology, John O'Shea; Cur. Near East Archaeology, Henry T. Wright; Cur. North American Archaeology, Robin Beck; Cur. Circumpolar Archaeology, Raven Garvey; Cur. African Archaeology, Brian A. Stewart.
Institution Type/Description: Anthropology Museum.
Hours & Admission Prices: By appointment only. No charge.

UNIVERSITY OF MICHIGAN MUSEUM OF ART, 525 S. State St., Ann Arbor, MI 48109-1354. Tel.: 734-764-0395. Fax: 734-764-3731. Facebook.
E-mail: umma.info@umich.edu
Web Site: umma.umich.edu
Key Personnel: Dir., Christina Olsen ; Deputy Dir. Education, Ruth Slavin; Deputy Dir. & Chief Administrative Officer, Kathryn Huss; Assoc. Curator of African Art, Laura De Becker; Assoc. Cur. Asian Art, Natsu Oyobe; Asst. Cur. Photography, Jennifer Friess; Chief Registrar Collections & Exhibitions, Roberta Frey Gilboe.
Hours & Admission Prices: Tues.-Sat. 11-5, Sun. 12-5. Suggested Donation: $10. Closed New Year's Day; Memorial Day; Independence Day; Labor Day; Thanksgiving; Christmas.
Attendance: 225,000 (estimated)

UNIVERSITY OF MICHIGAN MUSEUM OF NATURAL HISTORY, 1109 Geddes Ave., Ann Arbor, MI 48109-1079. Tel.: 734-764-0480. Fax: 734-647-2767.
E-mail: ummnh.info@umich.edu
Web Site: www.ummnh.org
Key Personnel: Dir., Amy S. Harris; Asst. Dir. Exhibits, Eugene Dillenberg; Exhibit Designer, John B. Klausmeyer; Asst. Dir. Devel., Nora Webber; Communications Coord., Shannon Davis; Mgr. Planetarium, Matthew P. Linke; Asst. Dir. Education, Kira Berman; Finance & Museum Shop Mgr., Kelly Sullivan; Office Mgr., Anna Volante; Program Mgr., Brittany Chunn.
Institution Type/Description: University Natural History Museum.
Hours & Admission Prices: Mon.-Sat. 9-5, Sun. 12-5. Museum: no charge; donations accepted. $75 nonrefundable deposit for groups of 10 or more. Planetarium Shows: $5 per person. Closed major holidays.
Attendance: 100,000 (estimated)

WASHTENAW COUNTY HISTORICAL SOCIETY, 500 N. Main St., Ann Arbor, MI 48104-1027. Mailing Address: P.O. Box 3336, Ann Arbor, MI 48106-3336. Tel.: 734-662-9092.
E-mail: wchs-500@ameritech.net
Web Site: www.washtenawhistory.org
Institution Type/Description: Historical Society Museum.
Hours & Admission Prices: Wed. & Sat.-Sun. 12-4; other times by appointment. No charge; donations accepted.

Arcadia

ARCADIA AREA HISTORICAL MUSEUM, 3340 Lake St., Arcadia, MI 49613-5157. Mailing Address: P.O. Box 67, Arcadia, MI 49613-0067. Tel.: 231-889-3389. Facebook: Arcadia Area Historical Museum.
E-mail: lmatt613@msn.com
Web Site: www.arcadiami.com
Formerly: Arcadia Township Historical Commission
Key Personnel: Chm., Edward Howard; Dir. & Pres. (V), Lyle Matteson; Chm. (V), Ray Knudsen; Museum Shop Mgr., Keith McArthur.
Institution Type/Description: Historical Society & Furniture Museum.
Hours & Admission Prices: June 25 to Labor Day Thurs.-Sat. 1-4, Sun. 1-3; other times by appointment. No charge; donations accepted.
Attendance: 800 (estimated)

Auburn Hills

WALTER P. CHRYSLER MUSEUM, One Chrysler Dr., CIMS 488.00.00, Auburn Hills, MI 48326-2766. Tel.: 888-456-1924 (U. S.), 248-944-0001. Fax: 248-944-0460.
Web Site: www.wpchryslermuseum.org
Key Personnel: Pres. & C.E.O., Lori Pinter; Exec. Dir. & C.O.O., Jim Worton; Cur., Brandt Rosenbusch; Dir. Museum Operations, Doreen Wright.
Institution Type/Description: Automotive Museum.
Hours & Admission Prices: Tues.-Sat. 10-5, Sun. 12-5. Adults $8, senior citizens 62 & over $7, juniors 6-12 & groups of 15 and over $4; children 5 & under no charge. Closed New Year's Eve & Day; Easter; Independence Day; Thanksgiving; Christmas Eve & Day.
Attendance: 30,000 (actual)

Augusta

W.K. KELLOGG BIRD SANCTUARY OF MICHIGAN STATE UNIVERSITY, 12685 East C Ave., Augusta, MI 49012-9707. Tel.: 269-671-2510. Fax: 269-671-2474.
E-mail: scarroll@kbs.msu.edu
Web Site: kbs.msu.edu/birdsanctuary
Key Personnel: Facilities Mgr., Karen Charleston; Environmental Education Coord., Tracey Kast; Office Mgr., Sarah Carroll.
Institution Type/Description: Bird Sanctuary.
Hours & Admission Prices: Grounds: May-Oct. daily 9-7; Nov.-April daily 9-5. Adults $5, senior citizens 62 & over and college students $4, children 2-17 $3; children under 2 no charge.
Attendance: 12,000 (actual)

Bad Axe

ALLEN HOUSE MUSEUM, 303 N. Port Crescent Ave., Bad Axe, MI 48413. Mailing Address: P.O. Box 62, Bad Axe, MI 48413. Tel.: 989-712-0050.
E-mail: huroncountyhistoricalsociety@yahoo.com
Institution Type/Description: History Museum: housed in the former home of Wallace E. Allen; built in 1902.
Hours & Admission Prices: Temporarily closed. June-July Sun. 2-5. No charge.

BAD AXE HISTORICAL SOCIETY MUSEUM, Old City Hall, 110 S. Hanselman St., Bad Axe, MI 48413. Tel.: 989-712-0050.
E-mail: badaxehistorical@yahoo.com
Institution Type/Description: Historical Society Museum.
Hours & Admission Prices: Jan.-April 3rd Sun. each month 2-5.

Baraga

BARAGA COUNTY HISTORICAL MUSEUM, 863 US 41 South, Baraga, MI 49908. Mailing Address: P.O. Box 567, Baraga, MI 49908-0567. Tel.: 906-353-8444. Fax: 906-353-8444.
E-mail: baragacountyhistory@gmail.com
Web Site: baragacountyhistoricalmuseum.com
Key Personnel: Pres. (V), Lowell Harshaw.
Institution Type/Description: History Museum.
Hours & Admission Prices: May-Sept. Thurs. & Fri. 11-3. Other times by appointment. Adults $2; teens $1; children under 12 no charge.
Attendance: 400 (actual)

Battle Creek

ART CENTER OF BATTLE CREEK, 265 E. Emmett St., Battle Creek, MI 49017-4601. Tel.: 269-962-9511. Fax: 616-969-3838.
E-mail: artcenterofbc@yahoo.com
Web Site: www.artcenterofbattlecreek.com
Key Personnel: Exec. Dir., Linda Holderbaum.
Institution Type/Description: Art Gallery.
Hours & Admission Prices: Tues.-Fri. 10-5, Sat. 11-3. Adults $3; seniors & students $2; discounts to AAM & ICOM members; Thurs. & members no charge. Closed national holidays.
Attendance: 35,241 (actual)

BINDER PARK ZOO, 7400 Division Dr., Battle Creek, MI 49014-9500. Tel.: 269-979-1351. Fax: 269-979-8834. Facebook; Instagram.
E-mail: info@binderparkzoo.org
Web Site: www.binderparkzoo.org
Institution Type/Description: Zoological Park.
Hours & Admission Prices: April-Oct. Mon.-Fri. 9-4, Sat. 9-6, Sun. 11-6. Adults $13.50, senior citizens 65 & over $12.50, children 2-10 $11.50; discounts to groups by appointment & AAA members; children under 2, AZA, zoo members & reciprocal zoo members no charge.
Attendance: 320,000 (estimated)

KIMBALL HOUSE MUSEUM, 196 Capital Ave., N.E., Battle Creek, MI 49017-3925. Mailing Address: 165 N. Washington, Battle Creek, MI 49037-2929. Tel.: 269-965-2613. Fax: 269-660-9072.
E-mail: info@heritagebattlecreek.org
Web Site: www.heritagebattlecreek.org
Key Personnel: Pres., Charles Rose; Dir. Research, Mary Butler.
Institution Type/Description: Historic House: 1886 Victorian home.
Hours & Admission Prices: April-Dec. Sun. 1-4; tours by appointment. Adults $3, children 12 & under $2; members no charge.
Attendance: 20,000 (estimated)

KINGMAN MUSEUM, 175 Limit St., Battle Creek, MI 49037-2176. Tel.: 269-965-5117. Fax: 269-965-3330.
E-mail: droberts@kingmanmuseum.org
Web Site: www.kingmanmuseum.org
Key Personnel: Dir. Operations, Donna C. Roberts; Pres. (V), Corey LaGro; Collections, Museum Shop Mgr., Jamie Schiltz; Education, Katy Avery.
Institution Type/Description: Natural History Museum.
Hours & Admission Prices: Sat. 1-5. Families $20, adults $7, senior citizens, veterans & active duty military $6, student $5; ASTC members and children under 3 no charge; groups of 10 or more by appointment only; discounts to groups 10 or more; additional charge for Planetarium shows, programs or tours.
Attendance: 14,912 (actual)

WOLVERINE FIRE COMPANY MUSEUM, 13280 Verona Rd., Battle Creek, MI 49014. Tel.: 616-968-2998.
Institution Type/Description: Fire Fighting History Museum.
Hours & Admission Prices: By appointment.

Bay City

ANTIQUE TOY AND FIRE TRUCK MUSEUM, 3456 Patterson Rd., Bay City, MI 48706. Mailing Address: P.O. Box 188,

Kawkawlin, MI 48631-0188. Tel.: 888-888-1270. Fax: 989-667-4772.
E-mail: info@toyandfiretruckmuseum.org
Web Site: toyandfiretruckmuseum.org
Key Personnel: Founder & C.E.O., James E. Dobson.
Institution Type/Description: Toy & Firefighting Museum.
Hours & Admission Prices: May-Oct. Sat.-Sun. 12-3; other times by appointment. Family $15, adults $10, seniors $7, children 5-17 $5; discounts to groups, veterans and AAM & ICOM members.
Attendance: 5,500 (estimated)

HISTORICAL MUSEUM OF BAY COUNTY, 321 Washington Ave., Bay City, MI 48708-5837. Tel.: 989-893-5733. Fax: 989-893-5741. Facebook: The Bay County Historical Society / The Historical Museum of Bay County.
E-mail: info@bchsmuseum.org
Web Site: www.bchsmuseum.org
Key Personnel: Dir. Opers. & Chief Historian, Ron Bloomfield; Pres. Bd., Judy Jeffers; Vice Pres. Bd., Stephen Kent; Cur. Exhibits & Education, Corrine Bloomfield.
Institution Type/Description: County History Museum: housed in 1910 National Guard Armory.
Hours & Admission Prices: Mon.-Fri. 10-5, Sat. 12-4. Research Library: Tues.-Thurs. 1-5 (librarian on duty). No charge; donations accepted. Closed major holidays.
Attendance: 61,000 (estimated)

Bay View

BAY VIEW HISTORICAL MUSEUM, Bay View Association Encampment 1715, Bay View, MI 49770. Mailing Address: P.O. Box 583, Petoskey, MI 49770-0583. Tel.: 231-347-6225. Fax: 231-347-4330.
E-mail: contact@bayviewassociation.org
Web Site: bayviewassoc.org
Key Personnel: Pres., Lawrence R. Ternan; Exec. Dir., Rodney J. Slocum; Cur. & Archivist, Anne Lewis; Cur. & Archivist, Sophia McGee.
Institution Type/Description: Historic Site: a National Historic Landmark consisting of 12 buildings & 430 summer homes.
Hours & Admission Prices: July-Aug. Sun. after church until 1 pm, Wed. 2:30-4:30; Sept.-June after church until 1pm. No charge; donations accepted.
Attendance: 1,000 (estimated)

Beaver Island

BEAVER ISLAND HISTORICAL SOCIETY OF MICHIGAN, 26275 Main St., Beaver Island, MI 49782-5101. Mailing Address: P.O. Box 263, Beaver Island, MI 49782. Tel.: 231-448-2254. Facebook.
E-mail: beaverislandhistory@gmail.com
Web Site: beaverislandhistory.org
Key Personnel: Dir., Lori Taylor-Blitz; Pres., Doug Hartle; Vice Pres., Mike Weede; Treas., Sandy Birdsall; Sec., Linda Wearn.
Institution Type/Description: Local History Museum.
Hours & Admission Prices: Father's Day to Labor Day Mon.-Sat. 11-5, Sun. 12-3. No charge; donations accepted.
Attendance: 4,187 (actual)

Belding

BELDING MUSEUM AND THE BEL (BELDING EXPLORATION LAB), 108 Hanover St., Belding, MI 48809-1726. Mailing Address: P.O. Box 45, Belding, MI 48809-0045. Tel.: 616-794-1900 ext. 425. Facebook: Belding Museum at the Historic Belrockton.
E-mail: beldingmuseum@gmail.com
Key Personnel: Dir., Barb Fagerlin; Treas., Jill Mason; Sec., Jane Forth.
Institution Type/Description: History & Children's Museum.
Hours & Admission Prices: 1st Sun. of month 1-4. No charge. Closed New Year's Day; Easter; Independence Day; Thanksgiving; Christmas.
Attendance: 1,500 (estimated)

Belleville

BELLEVILLE AREA MUSEUM, 405 Main St., Belleville, MI 48111-2617. Tel.: 734-697-1944. Facebook; Twitter.
E-mail: kdallos@provide.net
Web Site: belleville.mi.us/belleville-area-museum/
Key Personnel: Dir., Katie Dallos.
Institution Type/Description: Local History Museum.

Hours & Admission Prices: Tues.-Sat. 1-5. &
Attendance: 3,081 (actual)

OAKWOODS METROPARK NATURE CENTER, 17845 Savage Rd., Belleville, MI 48111-9668. Tel.: 800-477-3182, 734-697-9181. Fax: 734-782-3956.
E-mail: kevin.arnold@metroparks.com
Web Site: metroparks.com
Key Personnel: Dir., Dave Moilanen; Chief Interpretive Svcs., C. Michael George; Supervising Interpreter, Kevin J. Arnold; Interpreter, Roni Hutchinson.
Institution Type/Description: Nature Center: located on 1818-1842 Wyandot Indian Reservation.
Hours & Admission Prices: June-Aug. Tues.-Sun. 10-5; Sept.-May Tues.-Fri. 1-5, Sat.-Sun. 10-5. No charge. Motor vehicle permit required: annual $25, senior citizens $15, daily $5. Closed New Year's Day; Thanksgiving; Christmas. &
Attendance: 100,000 (estimated)

YANKEE AIR FORCE, INC. - D/B/A YANKEE AIR MUSEUM, 47884 D St., Belleville, MI 48111. Mailing Address: P.O. Box 590, Belleville, MI 48112-0590. Tel.: 734-483-4030. Fax: 734-483-5076. Facebook: Yankee Air Force, Inc. - d/b/a Yankee Air Museum.
E-mail: supportyankee@yankeeairmuseum.org
Web Site: www.yankeeairmuseum.org
Formerly: Yankee Air Force, Inc. (Yankee Air Museum)
Key Personnel: Exec. Dir., Kevin Walsh; Sec., Speed Gant; Aircraft Appearance Coord., Norman Ellickson; Curatorial Dir., Julie Osborne; Membership, Ashley Turner; Public Rels., Dave Callanan; Security, William Tonak; Museum Shop Mgr., Steve Hopper.
Institution Type/Description: Aeronautics Museum.
Hours & Admission Prices: Museum: Tues.-Sat. 10-4, Sun. 12-5. Flight Experience Rides: May-Oct. Museum: Tues.-Sat. 10-4. Adults $8, children, seniors 65 & over and military with ID $5; members with ID and children 2 & under no charge. Closed major holidays. &
Attendance: 28,000 (estimated)

Belmont

HYSER RIVERS MUSEUM, 6440 W. River Rd., N.E., Belmont, MI 49306. Mailing Address: c/o Plainfield Charter Township, 6161 Belmont Ave., N.E., Belmont, MI 49306-9609. Tel.: 616-364-8466 & 1182 (museum). Fax: 616-364-6537.
E-mail: suzannec@iserv.net
Web Site: www.commoncorners.com
Key Personnel: Pres. (V), Sue Carpenter.
Institution Type/Description: Historic House Museum: housed in former home of pioneer surgeon & Civil War Captain William Hyser, built in 1852.
Hours & Admission Prices: April-Dec. first Sun. of month 2-4:30; other times by appointment. No charge; donations accepted.

Benton Harbor

MORTON HOUSE MUSEUM, 501 Territorial, Benton Harbor, MI 49022-3238. Mailing Address: P.O. Box 173, Benton Harbor, MI 49023-0173. Tel.: 269-925-7011.
E-mail: mortonhousemuseum@yahoo.com
Web Site: www.mortonhousemuseum.com
Key Personnel: House Chm. & Pres., Denise Reeves; Vice Pres. & Trustee, Miriam Pede; Sec. & Treas., Cherie Messinger; Trustee, Deb Geib; Trustee, Stuart Boekeloo; Trustee, Gineen Wiley; Trustee, Marcia Smith; Trustee, Denise Tackett; Trustee, Peg Williamson; Trustee, Brenda Layne.
Institution Type/Description: Historic House Museum.
Hours & Admission Prices: mid-April to Oct. Sun. 1-4. Adults $5; members no charge.
Attendance: 500 (estimated)

SARETT NATURE CENTER, 2300 Benton Center Rd., Benton Harbor, MI 49022-9704. Tel.: 269-927-4832. Fax: 616-927-2742.
E-mail: sarett@sarett.com
Web Site: www.sarett.com
Key Personnel: Dir., Dianne Braybrook; Pres. (V), Walter Schmuhl; Museum Shop Mgr., Mindy Walker.
Institution Type/Description: Nature Center & Wildlife Sanctuary.
Hours & Admission Prices: Tues.-Fri. 9-5, Sat. 10-5, Sun. 1-5. Adults $3; members & children under 12 no charge. Closed New Year's Day; Easter; Independence Day; Thanksgiving; Christmas. &
Attendance: 35,000 (actual)

Benzonia

BENZIE AREA HISTORICAL MUSEUM, 6941 Traverse Ave., Benzonia, MI 49616. Mailing Address: P.O. Box 185, Benzonia, MI 49616-0185. Tel.: 231-882-5539. Fax: 231-882-4435.
E-mail: info@benziemuseum.org
Web Site: www.benziemuseum.org
Key Personnel: Pres. Bd. Dir. (V), David Reid; Museum Mgr., Dr. Misty Sheehan.
Institution Type/Description: Historical Museum: housed in 1884-1887 church building.
Hours & Admission Prices: May-Nov. Tues.-Sun. 11-5, Nov.-May Tues.-Sat. 11-5. No charge; donations accepted. Closed major holidays. &
Attendance: 4,277 (estimated)

Berrien Springs

BERRIEN COUNTY HISTORICAL ASSOCIATION, History Center at Courthouse Sq., 313 N. Cass St., Berrien Springs, MI 49103. Mailing Address: P.O. Box 261, Berrien Springs, MI 49103-0261. Tel.: 269-471-1202. Fax: 269-471-7412.
E-mail: kcyr@berrienhistory.org
Web Site: www.berrienhistory.org
Key Personnel: Pres. (V), Gary Campbell; Dir., Kathy A. Cyr; Cur., Robert Myers; Museum Svcs. Coord., Madge Bibler.
Institution Type/Description: Historic Building Museum Complex.
Hours & Admission Prices: Jan.-March Mon.-Fri. 10-5; April-Dec. Mon.-Sat. 10-5. No charge, donations accepted. Closed holidays. &
Attendance: 18,000 (actual)

SIEGFRIED H. HORN ARCHAEOLOGICAL MUSEUM, Andrews University, Institute of Archaeology, Berrien Springs, MI 49104-0990. Tel.: 269-471-3273. Fax: 269-471-3619.
E-mail: hornmuseum@andrews.edu
Web Site: www.andrews.edu/archaeology
Key Personnel: Cur., Constance Gane; Asst. to Cur., L.S. Baker, Jr.
Institution Type/Description: Archaeological Museum.
Hours & Admission Prices: Academic Year: Sat. 3-5; other times by appointment. No charge; donations accepted. Closed holidays. &
Attendance: 1,100 (estimated)

Big Rapids

JIM CROW MUSEUM - FERRIS STATE UNIVERSITY, 1010 Campus Dr., Big Rapids, MI 49307. Tel.: 231-591-5873. Fax: 231-591-2541.
E-mail: jimcrowmuseum@ferris.edu
Web Site: www.ferris.edu/jimcrow
Key Personnel: Dir., J. Andy Karafa, Ph.D.; Cur., David Pilgrim, Ph.D.
Institution Type/Description: History Museum.
Hours & Admission Prices: Mon.-Fri. 8-5 by appointment. No charge; donations accepted. Closed national holidays. &
Attendance: 1,500 (estimated)

MECOSTA COUNTY HISTORICAL MUSEUM, 129 S. Stewart Ave., Big Rapids, MI 49307-1968. Tel.: 231-592-5091 & 796-0368.
E-mail: atornblom25@yahoo.com
Key Personnel: Pres. (V), Fredda Hankes; Museum Co-Dir., Agnes Tornblom; Museum Co-Dir., Barb Johnson.
Institution Type/Description: General Museum: housed in two-story frame Victorian house.
Hours & Admission Prices: May-Oct. Sat. 2-4; other times by appointment. No charge; donations accepted.
Attendance: 1,200 (estimated)

Birmingham

BIRMINGHAM BLOOMFIELD ART CENTER, 1516 S. Cranbrook Rd., Birmingham, MI 48009-1855. Tel.: 248-644-0866. Fax: 248-644-7904.
E-mail: annievangelderen@bbartcenter.org
Web Site: www.bbartcenter.org
Key Personnel: Pres. & C.E.O., Annie Van Gelderen; Chm. Bd., Maria Marcotte; Vice Pres. Programs, Cynthia Mills; Vice Pres. Finance, Gwenn Rosseau.
Institution Type/Description: Community Art Center.
Hours & Admission Prices: Mon.-Thurs. 9-6, Fri.-Sat. 9-5. No charge. Closed major holidays. &
Attendance: 20,000 (estimated)

BIRMINGHAM HISTORICAL MUSEUM & PARK, 556 W. Maple, Birmingham, MI 48009-3360. Tel.: 248-530-1928. Facebook; Birmingham Historical Museum & Park.
E-mail: museum@bhamgov.org/museum
Web Site: bhamgov.org/museum
Key Personnel: Dir., Leslie Pielack; Pres. (V), Catherine Tuczek; Chm. (V), Russell Dixon.
Institution Type/Description: Historical Society Museum.
Hours & Admission Prices: Wed.-Sat. 1-4; other times by appointment. Adults $5, seniors & students $3; children 5 & under & members no charge. Closed city holidays. ♿
Attendance: 5,000 (estimated)

Bloomfield Hills

CRANBROOK ART MUSEUM, 39221 Woodward Ave., Bloomfield Hills, MI 48304-5162. Mailing Address: P.O. Box 801, Bloomfield Hills, MI 48303-0801. Tel.: 248-645-3319. Fax: 248-645-3323. Facebook: Cranbrook Art Museum.
E-mail: artmuseum@cranbrook.edu
Web Site: www.cranbrook.edu
Key Personnel: Dir., Andrew Blauvelt; Administrative Asst., Kim Larsen; Preparator, Mark Baker; Collections Fellow, Steffi Duarte.
Institution Type/Description: Art Museum.
Hours & Admission Prices: Museum: Academic Year: Tues.-Fri. 10-5, Sat.-Sun. 11-5; Summer: Wed.-Sun. 11-5. Adults $10, senior citizens 65 & over $8, students with ID $6; discounts to AAM members; children under 12 & members no charge. Saarinen House Tours: May-Oct. 2pm. Adults $15. Closed New Year's Eve & Day; Easter; Memorial Day; Independence Day; Labor Day; Thanksgiving; Christmas Eve & Day. ♿
Attendance: 37,000 (estimated)

CRANBROOK HOUSE AND GARDENS AUXILIARY, 380 Lone Pine Rd., Bloomfield Hills, MI 48303-0801. Mailing Address: P.O. Box 801, Bloomfield Hills, MI 48303-0801. Tel.: 248-645-3149. Fax: 248-645-3151. Facebook: Cranbrook House and Gardens.
E-mail: csmith@cranbrook.edu
Web Site: www.cranbrook.edu
Key Personnel: Chm. House & Garden, Virginia Latimer.
Institution Type/Description: Historic House: 1908 home of George Gough & Ellen Scripps Booth.
Hours & Admission Prices: Gardens: May to Labor Day Mon.-Sat. 10-5, Sun. 11-5; Sept. daily 11-3; Oct. Thurs.-Sun. 11-3. House Tours: June-Aug. Thurs. & Fri. 11am & 1pm, Sun. 1pm & 3pm; Sept.-Oct. Thurs. 11am & 1pm, Fri. 1pm, Sun. 1pm; group tours at other times by prior arrangement. Gardens: $6 per person; American Horticultural Society's Reciprocal Admissions Program members no charge. House Tour & Gardens: $10 per person; discounts to senior citizens; members no charge.
Attendance: 8,000 (estimated)

CRANBROOK INSTITUTE OF SCIENCE, 39221 Woodward Ave., Bloomfield Hills, MI 48304-5162. Mailing Address: P.O. Box 801, Bloomfield Hills, MI 48303-0801. Tel.: 248-645-3200. Fax: 248-645-3050.
E-mail: mstafford@cranbrook.edu
Web Site: science.cranbrook.edu
Key Personnel: Chm. Bd. Governors, Richard E. Warren; Dir., Dr. Michael D. Stafford; Cur. Collections, Cameron Wood; Head Mktg., Stephen Pagnani.
Institution Type/Description: Science Museum.
Hours & Admission Prices: Tues.-Thurs. 10-5, Fri-Sat. 10-10, Sun. 12-4. Adults $13, senior citizens & children 2-12 $9.50; discounts to AAM members, groups and Fri. & Sat. evenings; children under 2, ASTC members & members no charge. Additional fee for Planetarium & Laser programs. Closed New Year's Eve & Day; Easter; Memorial Day; Independence Day; Labor Day; Thanksgiving; Christmas Eve & Day. ♿
Attendance: 176,000 (actual)

Byron Center

VAN SINGEL ART GALLERY, 8500 Burlingame, S.W., Byron Center, MI 49315. Tel.: 616-878-6801. Fax: 616-878-6820.
E-mail: cindifordll@gmail.com
Web Site: vsfac.com
Formerly: Gainey Gallery - Van Singel Fine Arts Center
Key Personnel: Cur., Cindi Ford.
Institution Type/Description: Art Gallery.
Hours & Admission Prices: June-Aug. Mon.-Thurs. 12-5; Sept.-May Mon.-Fri. 12-5.

Cadillac

WEXFORD COUNTY HISTORICAL SOCIETY & MUSEUM, 127 Beech St., Cadillac, MI 49601-1901. Mailing Address: P.O. Box 124, Cadillac, MI 49601-0124. Tel.: 231-775-1717.
E-mail: info@wexfordcountyhistory.org
Web Site: wexfordcountyhistory.org
Key Personnel: Pres. (V), Pam Welliver; Pres., Kristine Anderson; Museum Shop Mgr., Richard Kraemer.
Institution Type/Description: County Historical Society Museum: housed in former Carnegie Library of Cadillac.
Hours & Admission Prices: May-Aug. Thurs.-Sat. 12-4; Sept.-Dec. Sat. 12-4. Adults $5, family $10; children under 16 & members no charge. Closed Jan.-April.
Attendance: 3,200 (estimated)

Calumet

COPPER COUNTRY FIREFIGHTERS HISTORY MUSEUM, 327 Sixth St., Calumet, MI 49913. Mailing Address: P.O. Box 503, Calumet, MI 49913. Tel.: 906-337-4579. Facebook.
E-mail: jshs907@yahoo.com
Web Site: coppercountryfirefightershistorymuseum.com
Formerly: Upper Peninsula Firefighters Memorial Museum
Key Personnel: Chm. (V) & Pres. (V), William Schniederhan; Dir., John A. Sullivan.
Institution Type/Description: Firefighting History Museum: housed in the former Red Jacket Fire Station; built in 1898.
Hours & Admission Prices: mid-June to Labor Day Mon.-Sat. 1-4:30. Adults $3; children under 12 no charge.
Attendance: 1,080 (estimated)

COPPERTOWN U.S.A., 25815 Red Jacket Rd., Calumet, MI 49913-2904. Mailing Address: 56638 Calumet Ave., Calumet, MI 49913-1965. Tel.: 906-337-4354.
Web Site: www.uppermichigan.com/coppertown
Key Personnel: Pres. (V), Richard Dana.
Institution Type/Description: Restored Mining Co. Complex: situated on the site of the former Calumet & Hecla Mining Co. headquarters complex.
Hours & Admission Prices: June to mid-Oct. Mon.-Sat. 11-5. Adults $4, Golden Age Pass $3, children 6-15 $2; children under 6 no charge. ♿
Attendance: 3,000 (estimated)

Caspian

IRON COUNTY HISTORICAL & MUSEUM SOCIETY, 100 Brady Ave., Caspian, MI 49915. Tel.: 906-265-2617. Facebook: Iron County Historical & Museum Society; TDD: 906-265-2617.
E-mail: info@ironcountyhistoricalmuseum.org
Web Site: www.ironcountyhistoricalmuseum.org
Formerly: Bernadette Coates
Key Personnel: Pres., Maggie Scheffer; Museum Dir., Bernadette Coates; Founder, Harold Bernhardt.
Institution Type/Description: History Museum.
Hours & Admission Prices: June-Sept. 1 Mon.-Sat. 10-4; Sept.-April by appointment. Family $25, adults $10, youth 5-18 & groups of 10 or more $5; children under 5 no charge. ♿
Attendance: 5,000 (estimated)

Centreville

NOTTAWA STONE SCHOOL, 204 E. Burr Oak St., Centreville, MI 49032-9620. Tel.: 616-467-5400 & 6155.
Key Personnel: Pres., Richard A. Cripe.
Institution Type/Description: Historic Building: 1870 Stone School.
Hours & Admission Prices: Sept.-June Mon.-Fri. No charge.

Charlotte

COURTHOUSE SQUARE ASSOCIATION, 100 W. Lawrence Ave., Charlotte, MI 48813-1494. Mailing Address: P.O. Box 411, Charlotte, MI 48813-0411. Tel.: 517-543-6999. Fax: 517-543-6999. Facebook: Eaton County's Museum at Courthouse Square.
E-mail: preserve@ia4u.net
Web Site: csamuseum.net
Key Personnel: Mgr., Julia Kimmer; Pres. (V), Christi Dutcher.
Institution Type/Description: Historic Area: listed on the National Register of Historic Sites.

Hours & Admission Prices: Sept.-June Mon.-Thurs. 9-4; July-August Mon.-Wed. 9-4, Thurs. 9-4 & 6-8; other times by appointment. Adults $1; discounts to groups & families; children 12 & under and members no charge. Closed major holidays.
Attendance: 2,000 (actual)

Chassell

CHASSELL HISTORICAL ORGANIZATION, 42373 N. Hancock St., Chassell, MI 49916. Mailing Address: P.O. Box 331, Chassell, MI 49916-0331. Tel.: 906-523-1155. Facebook: @ChasselHeritageCenter.
E-mail: info@ChassellHistory.org
Web Site: www.chassellhistory.org
Key Personnel: Pres., Corinne Hauring.
Institution Type/Description: Heritage Center.
Hours & Admission Prices: July-Aug. Tues. & Sat. 1-4, Thurs. 4-7. No charge; donations accepted.
Attendance: 1,000 (estimated)

Cheboygan

THE HISTORY CENTER OF CHEBOYGAN COUNTY, INC., 427 Court Street, Cheboygan, MI 49721-1908. Mailing Address: P.O. Box 5005, Cheboygan, MI 49721-5005. Tel.: 231-627-9597. Fax: 231-268-3555.
E-mail: museum@cheboyganhistory.org
Web Site: www.cheboyganhistory.org
Formerly: The Cheboygan County History Center
Key Personnel: Exec. Dir., Lewis D. Crusoe; Membership, Kay Forster; Registrar, Sharon Ecker.
Institution Type/Description: History Museum.
Hours & Admission Prices: mid-June to Sept. Tues.-Sat. 1-4. Adults $5; discounts to groups; children, Cheboygan County permanent residents, Time Traveler Program & museum members no charge.
Attendance: 1,029 (actual)

Chelsea

GERALD E. EDDY DISCOVERY CENTER, 17030 Bush Rd., Chelsea, MI 48118-9747. Mailing Address: Waterloo Recreation Area, 16345 McClure Rd., Chelsea, MI 48118. Tel.: 734-475-3170. Fax: 734-475-6421.
E-mail: mcglashenk@michigan.gov
Web Site: www.michigan.gov/dnr
Key Personnel: Dir., Keith Creagh; Katie McGlashen.
Institution Type/Description: Natural history: located on glacial moraine overlooking a kettle lake.
Hours & Admission Prices: April-Sept. Mon.-Sat. 10-5; Sun. 12-5. No charge. Parking: $11, Closed state holidays. &
Attendance: 30,859 (actual)

Chesaning

CHESANING HISTORICAL SOCIETY & MUSEUM, 602 W. Broad St., Chesaning, MI 48616. Mailing Address: P.O. Box 52, Chesaning, MI 48616. Tel.: 989-845-3155.
E-mail: oahs@centurytel.net
Web Site: cahs.chesaning.com
Institution Type/Description: Historical Society Museum.
Hours & Admission Prices: Jan.-April & Dec. Mon.-Wed. 10 to noon; May-Nov. Mon.-Wed. 10 to noon, 1st Sat. each month 1-4; other times by appointment.

Clarkston

CLARKSTON HERITAGE MUSEUM, 6495 Clarkston Rd., Clarkston, MI 48346-1501. Tel.: 248-922-0270. Facebook: Clarkston Community Historical Society and Heritage Museum.
E-mail: info@clarkstonhistorical.org
Web Site: www.clarkstonhistorical.org/museum.htm
Key Personnel: Dir., Toni Smith; Pres. (V), Bart Clark.
Institution Type/Description: Historical Society Museum.
Hours & Admission Prices: Mon.-Thurs. 10-9, Fri.-Sat. 10-6, Sun 1-5. Closed Sun. in summertime. No charge; donations accepted. &
Attendance: 5,000 (estimated)

Clawson

CLAWSON HISTORICAL MUSEUM, 41 Fisher Ct., Clawson, MI 48017. Mailing Address: 425 N. Main, Clawson, MI 48017-1500. Tel.: 248-588-9169.
E-mail: historicalmuseum@cityofclawson.com
Web Site: www.cityofclawson.com/your_government/historical_museum
Key Personnel: Cur., Melodie Nichols.
Institution Type/Description: History Museum.
Hours & Admission Prices: Wed. & Sun. 1-4. No charge; donations accepted. Closed holidays.

Clinton Township

CLINTON TOWNSHIP HISTORICAL VILLAGE MUSEUM, 40700 Romeo Plank Rd., Clinton Township, MI 48038-2942. Tel.: 586-286-9173.
E-mail: gcthsnewsletter@yahoo.com
Institution Type/Description: Historical Society Museum.
Hours & Admission Prices: Call for hours.

Coldwater

WING HOUSE MUSEUM, 27 S. Jefferson St., Coldwater, MI 49036. Tel.: 517-278-2871. Facebook.
E-mail: info@branchcountyhistoricalsociety.org
Web Site: www.branchcountyhistoricalsociety.org
Key Personnel: Pres. (V), David McDonald.
Institution Type/Description: History Museum: housed in the former home of Jay and Frances Chandler; built in 1875.
Hours & Admission Prices: By appointment. No charge; donations requested.

Coloma

NORTH BERRIEN HISTORICAL MUSEUM, 300 Coloma Ave., Coloma, MI 49038-9724. Mailing Address: P.O. Box 207, Coloma, MI 49038-0207. Tel.: 269-468-3330. Facebook.
E-mail: info@northberrienhistory.org
Web Site: www.northberrienhistory.org
Key Personnel: Exec. Dir., Jack Greve; Pres. (V), Scott Young.
Institution Type/Description: History Museum.
Hours & Admission Prices: May-Sept. Tues.-Sat. 10-4; Oct.-April Tues.-Fri. 10-4; other times by appointment. No charge; donations accepted. Closed holidays. &
Attendance: 5,300 (actual)

Concord

HISTORIC MANN HOUSE, 205 Hanover St., Concord, MI 49237. Mailing Address: Michigan Historical Museum, 702 W. Kalamazoo, P.O. Box 30740, Lansing, MI 48909-8240. Tel.: 517-373-1359.
E-mail: perkinsl1@michigan.gov
Web Site: www.michigan.gov/museum
Institution Type/Description: Historic House: 1880 Mann House.
Hours & Admission Prices: Memorial Day-Labor Day Tues.-Sat. 10-4. No charge.
Attendance: 1,000 (estimated)

Constantine

JOHN S. BARRY HISTORICAL SOCIETY, 300 N. Washington St., Constantine, MI 49042. Mailing Address: 485 Centerville Rd., Constantine, MI 49042-0068. Tel.: 269-506-1575.
E-mail: kevinm1963@comcast.net
Key Personnel: Pres. (V), Kevin Mallo; Vice Pres., Brian Myers; Sec., Angie Birdsall.
Institution Type/Description: Historical Society Museum: housed in 1835-1847 Governor Barry House, home of Michigan's third elected governor.
Hours & Admission Prices: By appointment only. No charge; donations accepted.
Attendance: 550

Coopersville

THE COOPERSVILLE AREA HISTORICAL SOCIETY MUSEUM, 363 Main St., Coopersville, MI 49404-1234. Tel.: 616-997-6978.
E-mail: budphoto@j2k.com
Web Site: www.coopersville.com/museum
Key Personnel: Dir., Lillian Budzynski; Cur., Jim Budzynski.
Institution Type/Description: Historical Society Museum.

Hours & Admission Prices: Aug. to mid-Dec. Tues. 3-8, Wed. 10-1, Sat. 10-4, Sun. 1-4; mid-Dec. to July Tues. 3-8, Wed. 10-1, Sat. 10-4; other times by appointment. Suggested Donation: adults $1. ⅋
Attendance: 5,000 (estimated)

Copper Harbor

FORT WILKINS HISTORIC COMPLEX, 15223 US 41, Fort Wilkins State Park, Copper Harbor, MI 49918. Mailing Address: P. O. Box 71, Copper Harbor, MI 49918-0071. Tel.: 906-289-4215. Fax: 906-289-4939.
E-mail: burnettw@michigan.gov
Web Site: www.michigan.gov/historicfortwilkins
Key Personnel: Museum Shop Mgr., Barb Wachowski.
Institution Type/Description: General Museum & Outdoor Museum Complex: including restored Fort Wilkins, the Pittsburgh & Boston Company mine site, Copper Harbor lighthouse.
Hours & Admission Prices: mid-May to mid-Oct. daily 8am to dusk. Recreation Passport: $11 annual fee for Michigan residents. Nonresident Passport: $9 daily, $34 annual. ⅋
Attendance: 150,000 (estimated)

Crystal Falls

CRYSTAL FALLS MUSEUM SOCIETY - HARBOUR HOUSE, 17 N. 4th St., Crystal Falls, MI 49920-1205. Mailing Address: P.O. Box 65, Crystal Falls, MI 49920-0065. Tel.: 906-875-4341. Facebook: Harbour House Museum.
E-mail: info@harbourhousemuseum.org
Web Site: www.harbourhousemuseum.org
Formerly: Harbour House Museum
Key Personnel: Pres. (V), Pat Olson; Cur., Gloria Frederickson.
Institution Type/Description: History Museum.
Hours & Admission Prices: June-Aug. Thurs-Sat. 10-2 (or by appointment). Family $5, adults $2. Closed Independence Day. ⅋
Attendance: 350 (estimated)

Davison

THE ART CAFE', 217 Shoppers Alley, Davison, MI 48423-1424. Mailing Address: 7700 Dilley Rd., Davisburg, MI 48350-2639. Tel.: 248-210-0862.
E-mail: staff@artcafeonline.org
Web Site: www.artcafeonline.org
Key Personnel: C.E.O., Cora Smilkovich.
Institution Type/Description: Art Gallery.
Hours & Admission Prices: Check website for hours. No charge; donations accepted. ⅋

Dearborn

ARAB AMERICAN NATIONAL MUSEUM, 13624 Michigan Ave., Dearborn, MI 48126-3519. Tel.: 313-582-2266. Fax: 313-582-1086.
E-mail: aanm@accesscommunity.org
Web Site: www.arabamericanmuseum.org
Key Personnel: Dir., Devon Akmon; Deputy Dir., Jumana Salamey.
Institution Type/Description: History Museum.
Hours & Admission Prices: Wed.-Sat. 10-6, Sun. 12-5. Adults $8, students, seniors 62 & over and children 6-12 $4; discounts to AAM members; children 5 & under no charge. Closed New Year's Day; Thanksgiving; Christmas. ⅋
Attendance: 50,000

AUTOMOTIVE HALL OF FAME, INC., 21400 Oakwood Blvd., Dearborn, MI 48124-4078. Tel.: 313-240-4000. Fax: 313-240-8641.
E-mail: kathy@thedrivingspirit.org
Web Site: www.automotivehalloffame.org
Key Personnel: Pres., Jeffrey K. Leestma; Chm., Jason Vines; Sec., Neil DeKoker; Treas., Ronald J. Martoia.
Institution Type/Description: Automotive Museum & Library.
Hours & Admission Prices: Wed.-Sun. 9-5. Adults $6, seniors $5, children 5-18 $3. Closed national holidays. ⅋
Attendance: 30,000 (actual)

DEARBORN HISTORICAL MUSEUM, 915 S. Brady Rd., Dearborn, MI 48124-2322. Tel.: 313-565-3000. Fax: 313-565-4848. Facebook: @dearbornhistoricalmuseum.
E-mail: museum@ci.dearborn.mi.us
Web Site: thedhm.com

Key Personnel: Chm. (V), L. Glenn O'Kray; Chief Cur., Jack Tate; Registrar, Matthew Graff; Asst. Chief Cur., Andrew Kercher; Archivisit, Mason Christensen; Exhibit Coord., Jaime Croskey.
Institution Type/Description: Local History Museum: housed in 1839 Powder Magazine, now McFadden-Ross House; 1833 Commandant's Quarters; 1831 Gardner House.
Hours & Admission Prices: Commandant's Quarters: Tues. & Thurs. 10-3. McFadden-Ross House: Mon.-Fri. 9-5 Archives: Tues. & Thurs. 9-4 and by appointment. No charge; donations accepted. Closed holidays.
Attendance: 10,000 (estimated)

THE HENRY FORD, 20900 Oakwood Blvd., Dearborn, MI 48124-4088. Tel.: 313-982-6100. Fax: 313-982-6250. TDD: 313-271-2455.
E-mail: elainem@thehenryford.org
Web Site: www.thehenryford.org
Formerly: Henry Ford Museum & Greenfield Village
Key Personnel: Pres., Patricia E. Mooradian; Chm. (V), S. Evan Weiner; Exec. Vice Pres., Christian Overland; Vice Pres. Institutional Advancement, J. Spencer Medford; Vice President Venues, John Neilson; Vice Pres. Business Devel., Communications & Strategy, Carol Kendra; Vice Pres. Business Svcs. & C.F.O., Brett Ott; Sr. Dir. Guest Operations, Amy Louise Liedel; Sr. Dir. External Rels., George Moroz; Chief Cur. & Sr. Dir. Historical Resources, Marc Greuther; Sr. Dir. Business Devel. & Licensing, Terri Anderson; Sr. Dir. Human Resources, Anne Marie DeGrazia; Sr. Dir. Facilities Mgmt., Robert Hanna; Dir. Workforce Devel., James Van Bochove; Dir., Media & Film Rels., Wendy Metros; Dir. Security & Safety, Christian Cullen.
Institution Type/Description: History Museum.
Hours & Admission Prices: Henry Ford Museum: daily 9:30-5. Greenfield Village: April 14-Oct. 28 daily 9:30-5; Oct. 29-Nov. 25 Fri.-Sun. 9:30-5; Nov. 26-Dec. call for hours. Henry Ford Museum: adults $25, senior citizens 62 & over $22.50, children 5-11 $18.75; members and children under 5 no charge. Greenfield Village: adults $28, senior citizens 62 & over $25.25; children 5-11 $21; children under 5 no charge. Closed Thanksgiving; Christmas. ⅋
Attendance: 1,710,754 (actual)

PADZIESKI ART GALLERY, 15801 Michigan Ave., Dearborn, MI 48126-2904. Tel.: 313-943-3095.
Institution Type/Description: Art Gallery.
Hours & Admission Prices: Tues.-Fri. 12-6, Sat. 12-5:30. No charge.

Decatur

HISTORIC NEWTON HOME, 20689 Marcellus Hwy., Decatur, MI 49045-9455. Mailing Address: 14916 Dutch Settlement, Marcellus, MI 49067. Tel.: 269-782-2008.
Key Personnel: Chm. Cass County Historical Commission, Abigail Schten; Sec., Marjorie Federowski.
Institution Type/Description: Historic House Museum: 1867 Newton Home.
Hours & Admission Prices: Home: mid-March to mid-Nov. Sun. 1-4:30; tours by appointment all year. School: by appointment. No charge; donations accepted.
Attendance: 110 (estimated)

Deckerville

DECKERVILLE HISTORICAL MUSEUM, 2485 Black River St., Deckerville, MI 48427-9355. Mailing Address: 4028 N. Ruth Rd., Deckerville, MI 48427-9355. Tel.: 810-376-6695.
Key Personnel: Dir. & Museum Shop Mgr., Rev. Joyce Reid; Chm. (V), Carol Walton; Pres. (V), Elaine Phillips.
Institution Type/Description: History Museum.
Hours & Admission Prices: June-Sept. Sat. 10-2 by appointment. Adults $3, children 6-12 $1; members & children under 5 no charge.
Attendance: 300 (estimated)

Delton

BERNARD HISTORICAL SOCIETY AND MUSEUM, 7135 Delton Rd., Delton, MI 49046. Mailing Address: P.O. Box 307, Delton, MI 49046-0307. Tel.: 269-623-3565.
E-mail: museumbernard@gmail.com
Web Site: www. bernardmuseum.org
Key Personnel: Pres., Janet Dimond.
Institution Type/Description: Local History Museum.
Hours & Admission Prices: June & Sept. Sun. 1-5; July & Aug. Sat.-Sun. 1-5; other times by appointment. No charge; donations accepted. ⅋
Attendance: 2,000 (estimated)

Detroit

ANNA SCRIPPS WHITCOMB CONSERVATORY, Belle Isle Park, 900 Inselruhe Ave., Detroit, MI 48207-4345. Mailing Address: 300 River Pl. Dr., Ste. 2800, Detroit, MI 48207. Tel.: 313-822-2867. Fax: 313-821-5793.
E-mail: info@belleisleconservancy.org
Web Site: belleisleconservancy.org
Key Personnel: Pres. Belle Isle Conservancy, Michele Hodges.
Institution Type/Description: Botanical Garden & Conservatory.
Hours & Admission Prices: Wed.-Sun. 10-5. No charge; donations accepted. &
Attendance: 68,700 (estimated)

CENTER GALLERIES, COLLEGE FOR CREATIVE STUDIES, 301 Frederick Douglas Ave., Detroit, MI 48202-4024. Tel.: 313-664-7800. Fax: 313-664-7880.
E-mail: mperron@collegeforcreativestudies.edu
Web Site: www.collegeforcreativestudies.edu/center_galleries
Key Personnel: Dir., Michelle M. Perron.
Institution Type/Description: Art Gallery.
Hours & Admission Prices: Sept.-July Tues.-Sat. 10-5; other times by appointment. No charge. Closed Independence Day; Thanksgiving; Christmas. &
Attendance: 12,000 (actual)

CHARLES H. WRIGHT MUSEUM OF AFRICAN AMERICAN HISTORY, 315 E. Warren Ave., Detroit, MI 48201-1443. Tel.: 313-494-5800. Fax: 313-494-5855.
E-mail: info@thewright.org
Web Site: www.chwmuseum.org
Key Personnel: Pres. & C.E.O., Juanita Moore; Chm. (V), Eric Peterson; Treas., Darrell Burks; C.F.O., Sharron Rose; Sr. Vice Pres. Education & Exhibitions, LaNesha DeBardelaben.
Institution Type/Description: History Museum.
Hours & Admission Prices: Feb. Mon.-Sat. 9-5, Sun. 1-5; March-Jan. Tues.-Sat. 9-5, Sun. 1-5. Adults $8, seniors 62 7 over and children 3-12 $5; discounts to AAM & ICOM members; members & children under 3 no charge. Closed major holidays. &
Attendance: 150,000 (estimated)

DETROIT ARTISTS MARKET, 4719 Woodward Ave., Detroit, MI 48201-1307. Tel.: 313-832-8540. Facebook: Detroit Artists Market.
E-mail: info@detroitartistsmarket.org
Web Site: www.detroitartistsmarket.org
Key Personnel: Chm. Bd. Directors, Darcel Deneau; Exec. Dir., Matt Fry; Mgr. Programs, Dalia Reyes.
Institution Type/Description: Contemporary Art Gallery.
Hours & Admission Prices: Tues.-Sat. 11-6. No charge; donations accepted. &
Attendance: 21,000 (estimated)

DETROIT CHILDREN'S MUSEUM, 6134 Second Ave., Detroit, MI 48202-3404. Tel.: 313-873-8100.
E-mail: julie.johnsondcm@gmail.com
Web Site: detroitk12.org/childrens_museum
Formerly: Children's Museum/Detroit Public Schools
Key Personnel: Mgr. Collections, Don Bogart; Lead Educator, David Lehner; Education, Steve Mackenzie.
Institution Type/Description: Children's Museum.
Hours & Admission Prices: Oct.-June Mon.-Fri. 9-4. Closed national holidays. &
Attendance: 43,000 (actual)

DETROIT HISTORICAL SOCIETY, 5401 Woodward Ave., Detroit, MI 48202-4097. Tel.: 313-833-1805. Fax: 313-833-5342.
E-mail: bobsadler@detroithistorical.org
Web Site: detroithistorical.org
Key Personnel: Exec. Dir. & C.E.O., Robert Bury; Chief Community & Operations Officer, Kate Baker; Mgr. Mktg. & Public Rels., Sarah Murphy.
Institution Type/Description: History Museum.
Hours & Admission Prices: Detroit Historical Museum: Tues.-Fri. 9:30-4, Sat.-Sun. 10-5. No charge; donations accepted. Dossin Great Lakes Museum: Sat.-Sun. 11-4. No charge; donations accepted. Closed national holidays. &
Attendance: 194,388 (actual)

DETROIT INSTITUTE OF ARTS, 5200 Woodward Ave., Detroit, MI 48202-4094. Tel.: 313-833-7900. Fax: 313-833-2357 & 3756. TDD: 313-833-1454.
Web Site: www.dia.org
Key Personnel: Dir., Salvador Salort-Pons.
Institution Type/Description: Art Museum.

Hours & Admission Prices: Tues.-Thurs. 9-4, Fri. 9-10, Sat.-Sun. 10-5; see website for extended hours. Suggested Donation: adults $14, seniors $9, college students with valid ID $8, youth 6-17 $6; discounts to AAM members; children 5 & under, residents of Wayne, Oakland & Macomb counties & members no charge. Closed holidays. &
Attendance: 598,000 (estimated)

DETROIT REPERTORY THEATRE GALLERY, 13103 Woodrow Wilson, Detroit, MI 48238. Tel.: 313-868-1347. Fax: 313-259-8242.
E-mail: gsnow19543@aol.com
Web Site: www.detroitreptheatre.com
Institution Type/Description: Art Gallery.
Hours & Admission Prices: Thurs.-Sat. 8:30pm-11:30pm, Sun. 2-4 & 7:30pm-10:30.

DOSSIN GREAT LAKES MUSEUM, 100 Strand Dr., Belle Isle, Detroit, MI 48207-4372. Mailing Address: c/o Detroit Historical Society, 5401 Woodward, Detroit, MI 48202. Tel.: 313-833-5538. Fax: 313-833-5342.
E-mail: sarahm@detroithistorical.org
Web Site: detroithistorical.org
Key Personnel: Exec. Dir. & C.E.O., Robert Bury; Mng. Dir., Kate Baker.
Institution Type/Description: Great Lakes History Museum.
Hours & Admission Prices: Fri.-Sun. 10-4. Belle Isle Park Recreation Passport needed to enter the island: Michigan residents $11, Out of State $9 per day, Commercial Vehicles $16. Museum: no charge. Closed major holidays.
Attendance: 70,000

ELAINE L. JACOB GALLERY - WAYNE STATE UNIVERSITY, 480 W. Hancock St., Detroit, MI 48202. Tel.: 313-993-7813.
Web Site: art.wayne.edu/jacob-gallery/index.php
Institution Type/Description: Art Gallery.
Hours & Admission Prices: May-Aug. Tues.-Fri. 12-5; Sept.-April Tues.-Thurs. 10-6, Fri. 10-7.

FIRST UNDERGROUND RAILROAD MUSEUM, 33 E. Forest Ave., Detroit, MI 48201-1813. Tel.: 313-831-4080.
Institution Type/Description: Historic Building: housed in the First Congregational Church of Detroit, used to hide slaves en route to freedom.
Hours & Admission Prices: Tues.-Sat. 11-3. Adults $14, seniors & children $12; discounts to groups.

HELLENIC MUSEUM OF MICHIGAN, 67 E. Kirby St., Detroit, MI 48202. Tel.: 313-871-4100.
E-mail: hellenicmi@gmail.com
Web Site: www.hellenicmi.org
Institution Type/Description: Greek History Museum.
Hours & Admission Prices: Sun. 1-5.

INTERNATIONAL GOSPEL MUSIC HALL OF FAME & MUSEUM, Detroit, MI 48219-4112. Mailing Address: P.O. Box 19009, Detroit, MI 48219-0009. Tel.: 313-444-8352.
E-mail: igmhfm@cs.com
Web Site: www.igmhf.org
Formerly: Gospel Music Hall of Fame & Museum
Key Personnel: C.E.O., Chm. & Pres., David Gough; Archivist & Chief Cur., Sherry Dupree; Program Mgr., Jean Anderson.
Institution Type/Description: Gospel Music Museum.
Hours & Admission Prices: Call for information.
Attendance: 250 (estimated)

MOTOWN HISTORICAL MUSEUM, 2648 W. Grand Blvd., Detroit, MI 48208-1237. Tel.: 313-875-2264. Fax: 313-875-2267.
E-mail: rterry@motownmuseum.org
Web Site: motownmuseum.org
Key Personnel: Founder, Esther Gordy Edwards; C.E.O. & Chairwoman, Robin Terry.
Institution Type/Description: History Museum.
Hours & Admission Prices: Tues.-Sat. 10-6. Adults $15, seniors 62 & up and youth 5-17 $10; children 4 & under and members no charge. Closed New Year's Day; Easter; Memorial Day; Independence Day; Labor Day; Thanksgiving; Christmas Eve & Day. &
Attendance: 50,000 (actual)

MUSEUM OF CONTEMPORARY ART DETROIT, 4454 Woodward Ave., Detroit, MI 48201-1822. Tel.: 313-832-6622. Facebook: MOCA Detroit.

E-mail: info@mocadetroit.org
Web Site: mocadetroit.org
Key Personnel: Exec. Dir., Elysia Borowy-Reeder; Bd. Chair (V), Julie Reyes Taubman; Bd. Pres. (V), Marsha Miro; Dir. Operations, Marie Patton; Dir. Philanthropy, Emily Remington; Exhibition Mgr., Zeb Smith; Store Mgr., Miah Davis; Mktg. & Sales Mgr., Leto Rankine; Foundation Rels. & Grants Mgr., Kimberly Kleinhaus; Cur. Public Programs, Monty Luke; Cur. Education & Public Engagements, Amy Corle; Facilities Assoc., Chris Riddell; Education Assoc., Augusta Morrison; Graphic Designer, Dan DeMaggio; Exhibitions Asst., Ayaka Hibino; Operations & Support Asst., Lizzy Courtois; Admin. Asst., Mark Sleeman.
Institution Type/Description: Contemporary Art Museum.
Hours & Admission Prices: Wed. & Sat.-Sun. 11-5, Thurs.-Fri. 11-8. Suggested Donation: $5. Cafe: Tues.-Thurs. 8-8, Fri. 8-10, Sat. 10-10, Sun. 11-5. Closed New Year's Eve & Day; Martin Luther King Jr. Day; Memorial Day; Independence Day; Labor Day; Thanksgiving; Christmas Eve & Day. &
Attendance: 200,000 (estimated)

THE N'NAMDI CENTER FOR CONTEMPORARY ART, 52 E.
Forest Ave., Detroit, MI 48201. Tel.: 313-831-8700.
E-mail: nnamdicenter@gmail.com
Web Site: nnamdicontemporary.com/
Key Personnel: Owner, George N'Namdi; Dir., Jumaane N'Namdi.
Institution Type/Description: Art Gallery.
Hours & Admission Prices: Tues.-Sat. 11-6.

NATIONAL MUSEUM OF THE TUSKEGEE AIRMEN, Historic
Fort Wayne, 6325 W. Jefferson Ave., Detroit, MI 48209. Mailing Address: P.O. Box 32549, Detroit, MI 48232-0549. Tel.: 313-843-8849. Fax: 313-843-1540.
E-mail: info@tuskegeemuseum.org
Web Site: tuskegeeairmenmuseum.com
Institution Type/Description: Military Museum.
Hours & Admission Prices: Daily 10-4 by appointment. No charge; donations accepted.

PEWABIC POTTERY, 10125 E. Jefferson, Detroit, MI 48214-
3138. Tel.: 313-626-2000. Fax: 313-626-2100.
E-mail: info@pewabic.org
Web Site: www.pewabic.org
Key Personnel: Sr. Dir. Product Devel., Christina Devlin; C.O.O., Heather Simmet.
Institution Type/Description: Arts & Crafts Museum & Pottery Factory: housed in 1907 William Buck Stratton-designed English style structure; built 1906-1907. Pottery founded in 1903 by Mary Chase Perry & Horace J. Caulkins. National Historic Landmark.
Hours & Admission Prices: Mon.-Sat. 10-6, Sun. 12-4. Museum: no charge; donations accepted. Guided Tours by appointment. $5 per person. Tile Workshops: adults $20, students $17. Closed New Year's Day; Martin Luther King Jr. Day; Easter; Memorial Day; Independence Day; Labor Day; Thanksgiving; Christmas.
Attendance: 40,000 (estimated)

SWORDS INTO PLOWSHARES GALLERY AND PEACE
CENTER, 33 E. Adams St., Detroit, MI 48226. Tel.: 313-963-7575.
E-mail: swordsintoplowshares313@gmail.com
Web Site: www.swordsintoplowsharesdetroit.org
Institution Type/Description: Art Gallery.
Hours & Admission Prices: Thurs.-Sat. 12-6; call to confirm.

WAYNE STATE UNIVERSITY ART GALLERIES, 150 Art
Bldg., Dept. of Art, Detroit, MI 48202-3917. Tel.: 313-993-7813. Fax: 313-577-3491.
E-mail: art@wayne.edu
Web Site: www.art.wayne.edu
Key Personnel: Art Collection Coord., Sandra Schemske.
Institution Type/Description: Art Gallery.
Hours & Admission Prices: Academic Year: Tues.-Thurs. 10-6, Fri. 10-7; Summer: Tues.-Fri. 12-5. No charge. &
Attendance: 15,000 (estimated)

WAYNE STATE UNIVERSITY MUSEUM OF
ANTHROPOLOGY, 4841 Cass Ave., Detroit, MI 48201-1203. Mailing Address: Dept. of Anthropology, Wayne State University, 3054 Faculty Administration Bldg., 656 W. Kirby, Detroit, MI 48202. Tel.: 313-577-2598. Fax: 313-577-5958.
E-mail: dy6390@wayne.edu
Web Site: www.clas.wayne.edu/anthromuseum
Key Personnel: Dir., Tamara Bray, Ph.D.
Institution Type/Description: Anthropology Museum.

Hours & Admission Prices: Sept.-May Mon.-Thurs. 10-4. No charge; donations accepted. &
Attendance: 1,200 (actual)

Dexter

DEXTER AREA HISTORICAL SOCIETY & MUSEUM, 3443
Inverness, Dexter, MI 48130-1409. Tel.: 734-426-2519.
E-mail: dexmuseum@aol.com
Web Site: www.dexterhistory.org
Formerly: Dexter Area Museum
Key Personnel: Pres. Historical Society, Beverly Hill; Museum Dir., Nina Rackham; Genealogist, Nancy Van Blaricum; Museum Shop Mgr., Rhea Berry.
Institution Type/Description: Historical Museum: housed in 1883 German Lutheran Church.
Hours & Admission Prices: May-Dec. Fri.-Sat. 1-3. No charge; donations accepted.
Attendance: 2,500 (estimated)

Dowagiac

HEDDON MUSEUM, 414 West St., Dowagiac, MI 49047-1045.
Mailing Address: 204 W. Telegraph St., Dowagiac, MI 49047-1241. Tel.: 269-782-5698.
E-mail: heddonmuseum@lyonsindustries.com
Web Site: heddonmuseum.org
Formerly: National Heddon Museum
Key Personnel: Dir. & Museum Shop Mgr., Joan Lyons; Dir., Don Lyons.
Institution Type/Description: History Museum: housed in James Heddon's Sons Fishing Tackle Co.
Hours & Admission Prices: Tues. 6:30 p.m.-8:30 p.m., last Sun. of month 1:30-4; other times by appointment. No charge; donations accepted. Closed New Year's Eve; Thanksgiving Day; Christmas Eve & Day. &
Attendance: 600 (estimated)

MUSEUM AT SOUTHWESTERN MICHIGAN COLLEGE,
58900 Cherry Grove Rd., Dowagiac, MI 49047-9726. Tel.: 269-782-1374 & 1000. Fax: 269-782-1460.
E-mail: museum@swmich.edu
Web Site: www.swmich.edu/museum
Formerly: Southwestern Michigan College Museum
Key Personnel: Dir., Steve Arseneau; Chm. (V), Chuck Timmons; Exhibit Designer, Tom J. Caskey; Educator, Jennifer Quail; Volunteer Coord., Jo Silvia.
Institution Type/Description: History Museum & Science Center.
Hours & Admission Prices: Tues.-Fri. 10-5, Sat. 11-3. No charge. Closed college & major holidays. &
Attendance: 7,000 (actual)

Drummond Island

DRUMMOND ISLAND HISTORICAL MUSEUM, 33492 S.
Water St., Drummond Island, MI 49726. Mailing Address: Box 293, Drummond Island, MI 49726-0293. Tel.: 906-493-5245.
E-mail: drhistmuseum@alphacomm.net
Key Personnel: Pres., Robert Newell; Township Supvr., Frank Sasso; Treas., K. C. Lowe; Sec., Martha Carlin; Dir., Harry Ropp; Dir., Gerry Bailey; Dir., Betty Bailey; Dir., Shelby Gibbons; Dir., Joan Riordan; Dir., Ann Statler; Dir., Clayton Ledy; Cur., Audrey Moser.
Institution Type/Description: Local History Museum.
Hours & Admission Prices: Memorial Day to mid-Oct. daily 1-5. No charge; donations accepted. &
Attendance: 3,000

Dryden

DRYDEN HISTORICAL SOCIETY MUSEUM, 5488 Dryden Rd.,
Dryden, MI 48428. Mailing Address: P.O. Box 93, Dryden, MI 48428.
E-mail: drydenhistoricalsociety@gmail.com
Web Site: drydenhistoricalsociety.webs.com
Key Personnel: Chm. (V), Jeanine Risch; Pres. (V), Karen Broecker.
Institution Type/Description: Historical Society Museum.
Hours & Admission Prices: Mon. 5:30pm-7pm. No charge; donations accepted.
Attendance: 300 (estimated)

Dundee

OLD MILL MUSEUM, 242 Toledo St., Dundee, MI 48131-1246.
Tel.: 734-529-8596.
E-mail: museum@dundeeoldmill.com
Web Site: www.dundeeoldmill.com

Key Personnel: Pres., Sara Alexin; Vice Pres., Mary Schultz; Sec., Meg Heinlen; Treas., Shirley Massingill; Archivist, Randi Kominek; Gift Shop Mgr. & Newsletter Editor, Grace Hudson.
Institution Type/Description: History Museum.
Hours & Admission Prices: Fri.-Mon. 12-4. No charge; donations accepted. Closed major holidays. &
Attendance: 2,000 (estimated)

East Jordan

EAST JORDAN PORTSIDE ART & HISTORICAL MUSEUM, 01656 South M-66 Hwy., East Jordan, MI 49727. Mailing Address: P.O. Box 1355, East Jordan, MI 49727-1355.
E-mail: kprebble@ejps.org
Web Site: www.portsideartsfair.org/histsoc.htm
Key Personnel: Dir., Kim Prebble.
Institution Type/Description: Historical Society Museum.
Hours & Admission Prices: June-Sept. Sat.-Sun. 1:30-4:30 & by appointment. No charge; donations accepted. &
Attendance: 3,000 (estimated)

East Lansing

ABRAMS PLANETARIUM, MICHIGAN STATE UNIVERSITY, 755 Science Rd., East Lansing, MI 48824. Tel.: 517-355-4676. Fax: 517-432-3838.
E-mail: abrams@pa.msu.edu
Web Site: www.pa.msu.edu/abrams/
Key Personnel: Interim Dir., John French; Planetarium Education Coord., Shane Horvatin.
Institution Type/Description: Planetarium.
Hours & Admission Prices: Display Hall: Mon.-Fri. 9-12 & 1-4:30. No charge. Programs: Fri.-Sat. 8pm, Sun. 2:30 & 4pm. Adults $3, students & senior citizens $2.50, children 12 & under $2. For public show information call 517-355-4672. Closed national holidays. &
Attendance: 32,000 (estimated)

ELI AND EDYTHE BROAD ART MUSEUM, 556 E. Circle Dr., 344 Student Svcs., East Lansing, MI 48824. Mailing Address: 556 E. Circle Dr., Rm. 344, East Lansing, MI 48824. Tel.: 517-884-3900. Fax: 517-884-3901. Facebook, Instagram & Twitter: @broadmsu.
E-mail: eebam@msu.edu
Web Site: broadmuseum.msu.edu
Key Personnel: Dir., Marc-Olivier Wahler; HR & Finance Coodr., Shelly Harbenski; Museum Shop Mgr., Stephanie Kribs.
Institution Type/Description: Art Museum.
Hours & Admission Prices: Tues.-Thurs. & Sat.-Sun. 10-5, Fri. 12-9. No charge; donations accepted.
Attendance: 73,000 (estimated)

KRESGE ART MUSEUM, Michigan State University, East Lansing, MI 48824-1119. Tel.: 517-353-9834. Fax: 517-355-6577.
E-mail: kamuseum@msu.edu
Web Site: www.artmuseum.msu.edu
Key Personnel: Cur., April Kingsley; Communications, Christine Nichols; Registrar, Rachel Vargas; Educator, Cari Wolfe; Devel., Bridget Paff; Preparator, Norbert J. Freese; Museum Shop Mgr., Angelica Santos.
Institution Type/Description: Art Museum.
Hours & Admission Prices: June-July Tues.-Fri. 11-5, Sat.-Sun. 12-5; Sept.-May Mon.-Wed. & Fri. 10-5, Thurs. 10-8, Sat.-Sun. 12-5. No charge; donations accepted. Closed holiday weekends. &
Attendance: 25,000 (estimated)

MICHIGAN STATE UNIVERSITY HERBARIUM, Plant Biology Laboratories, 612 Wilson Rd., Rm. 166, East Lansing, MI 48824-1312. Tel.: 517-355-4696. Fax: 517-353-1926.
E-mail: alan@msu.edu
Web Site: herbarium.msu.edu
Key Personnel: Dir. & Cur., Alan Prather; Asst. Cur., Alan Fryday; Sec., Kim Ferguson.
Institution Type/Description: Herbarium.
Hours & Admission Prices: Mon.-Fri. 8-5. No charge. Closed national holidays.

THE MICHIGAN STATE UNIVERSITY MUSEUM, 409 W. Circle Dr., East Lansing, MI 48824-1045. Tel.: 517-355-2370. Fax: 517-432-2846.
E-mail: jilda@msu.edu
Web Site: museum.msu.edu

Key Personnel: Acting Dir., Lora Helou; Exhibitions Mgr., Teresa Goforth; Cur. Folklife & Cultural Heritage, Kurt Dewhurst; Cur. Vertebrate, Michael Goffried; Cur. Anthropology, Willim Lovis.
Institution Type/Description: Science & Cultural History Museum.
Hours & Admission Prices: Mon.-Fri. 9-5, Sat. 10-5, Sun. 1-5. No charge, suggested donation $5. Closed New Year's Day; Easter; Memorial Day; Independence Day; Labor Day; Thanksgiving; Christmas. &
Attendance: 410,000 (estimated)

W.J. BEAL BOTANICAL GARDEN, 408 W. Circle Dr., Rm. 412, Michigan State University, East Lansing, MI 48824-1047. Tel.: 517-884-0764. Fax: 517-432-1090.
E-mail: telewski@msu.edu
Web Site: www.cpa.msu.edu/beal/index.htm
Key Personnel: Cur., Dr. Frank W. Telewski; Botanical Garden Technician, Peter Murray; Botanical Garden Technician, Katie McPeek.
Institution Type/Description: Botanical Garden.
Hours & Admission Prices: Daily sunrise-sunset. No charge. &
Attendance: 20,000 (estimated)

East Tawas

IOSCO COUNTY HISTORICAL MUSEUM, 405 W. Bay St., East Tawas, MI 48730-1103. Tel.: 989-362-8911.
E-mail: iosco.history@gmail.com
Web Site: ioscomuseum.org
Key Personnel: Pres., Leonard Wilkuski; Vice Pres., Regina Kelley; Recording Sec., Judy Clark; Treas., Lisa Ernst.
Institution Type/Description: Historical Building: built by J.D. Hawks, 1st president of the Detroit & Mackinaw Railway; built in 1903.
Hours & Admission Prices: Jan.-March Sat. 1-4; April-June 15 & Sept. 4-Dec. Thurs.-Sat. 1-4; June 16-Sept. 3 Tues.-Sat. 10-4. Suggested Donation: $2. &
Attendance: 1,894 (actual)

Edwardsburg

LAW ENFORCEMENT MEMORIAL ASSOCIATION, INC., Edwardsburg, MI 49112-0293. Tel.: 847-409-8691.
E-mail: forgottenheroes@aol.com
Web Site: forgottenheroes-lema.org
Institution Type/Description: Law Enforcement Museum.
Hours & Admission Prices: Museum under construction; call for information.

Elk Rapids

ELK RAPIDS AREA HISTORICAL SOCIETY, 301 Traverse St., Elk Rapids, MI 49629. Mailing Address: P.O. Box 2, Elk Rapids, MI 49629-0002. Tel.: 231-264-5692.
E-mail: president@elkrapidshistory.org
Web Site: www.elkrapidshistory.org
Key Personnel: Pres. (V), Dan LeBlond; Museum Shop Mgr., Marcia Graham.
Institution Type/Description: Historical Society Museum.
Hours & Admission Prices: Memorial Day to Labor Day Wed. & Sat. 1-4; Sept.-May Wed. 1-4. Suggested Donation: adults $5; member no charge. Closed major holidays. &
Attendance: 1,100 (estimated)

Empire

EMPIRE AREA HERITAGE GROUP, 11544 S. La Core, Empire, MI 49630-9401. Mailing Address: Box 192, Empire, MI 49630-0192. Tel.: 231-326-5568.
E-mail: empiremuseum@centurytel.net
Web Site: www.empiremimuseum.org
Key Personnel: Pres. (V), David Taghon; Vice Pres., Leigh Payment; Sec., Anne Krawczak.
Institution Type/Description: History Museum.
Hours & Admission Prices: Memorial Day to June & Labor Day to mid-Oct. Sat.-Sun. 1-4; July-Aug. Thurs.-Tues. 1-4. Suggested Donation: family $5, adults $2. &
Attendance: 5,000 (estimated)

SLEEPING BEAR DUNES NATIONAL LAKESHORE, 9922 Front St., (Hwy. M-72), Empire, MI 49630-9797. Tel.: 231-326-4700. Fax: 231-326-4719. Facebook: SBDNL; Twitter: SleepingBearNPS.
E-mail: slbe_interpretation@nps.gov
Web Site: www.nps.gov/slbe
Key Personnel: Supt., Dusty Shultz.
Institution Type/Description: Park Museum.

Hours & Admission Prices: Philip A. Hart Visitor Center: Memorial Day-Labor Day daily 8-6; Sept.-May daily 8:15-4. Cannery Boat Museum: Memorial Day to Labor Day daily 11-5; call for additional hours. Sleeping Bear Point Maritime Museum: Memorial Day to Labor Day daily 11-5. Annual Pass $20; Golden Age Pass (senior citizens) $10; Weekly Pass $10. &
Attendance: 1,300,000

Escanaba

DELTA COUNTY HISTORICAL SOCIETY MUSEUM, 16 Waterplant Rd., Escanaba, MI 49829-4052. Tel.: 906-789-6790.
E-mail: deltacountyhistsoc@sbcglobal.net
Web Site: www.deltahistorical.org
Key Personnel: Chm., Charles Lindquist; Archives, Karen Lindquist.
Institution Type/Description: Historical Society Museum & Archives.
Hours & Admission Prices: Archives: Memorial Day to Labor Day Mon.-Fri. 1-4; Labor Day to Memorial Day Mon. 1-4. Museum: Memorial Day to Labor Day open daily 11-4. Labor Day to Memorial Day by appointment. Museum & Lighthouse: family $5, adults $3, children under 12 no charge. Bus $75. Archives: no charge. Members no charge. &
Attendance: 7,400 (estimated)

SANDPOINT LIGHTHOUSE, 16 Water Plant Rd., Sandpoint, Ludington Park, Escanaba, MI 49829. Mailing Address: Delta County Historical Society, 16 Water Plant Rd., Escanaba, MI 49829-4052. Tel.: 906-789-6790.
E-mail: deltacountyhistsoc@sbcglobal.net
Web Site: www.deltahistorical.org
Institution Type/Description: Historical Society Museum: housed in turn-of-the-century lighthouse.
Hours & Admission Prices: Memorial Day to Labor Day daily 9-5, Sept. daily 1-4. Adults $1, students under 18 $.50; members & school groups no charge.
Attendance: 8,000 (estimated)

WILLIAM BONIFAS FINE ARTS CENTER, 700 1st Ave. S., Escanaba, MI 49829-3703. Tel.: 906-786-3833, ext. 16. Fax: 906-786-3840.
E-mail: events@bonifasarts.org
Web Site: www.bonifasarts.org
Key Personnel: Exec. & Gallery Dir., Pasqua Warstler; Business Mgr., Melissa Ekberg; Events & Mktg. Coord., Jon Becker; Bookkeeper, Helen Sherman; Custodian, Rick Kenyon; Communications & Programming, J.J. Spaulding.
Institution Type/Description: Arts Center.
Hours & Admission Prices: Tues.-Fri. 10-5:30, Sat. 10-3. Center: no charge. Classes: discounts to members. Closed major holidays. &
Attendance: 4,568 (estimated)

Farmington

GOVERNOR WARNER MANSION, 33805 Grand River Ave., Farmington, MI 48335-3431. Mailing Address: City of Farmington, 23600 Liberty St., Farmington, MI 48335. Tel.: 248-474-5500 ext. 2225 & ext. 2218. Fax: 248-473-7278. Facebook: Governor Mansion.
E-mail: warner_mansion@tds.net
Web Site: ci.farmington.mi.us
Key Personnel: Volunteer Coord., Jean Schornick; Volunteer Coord., Sharon Bernath; City Clerk, Susan Halberstadt; Dep. Clerk, Susan Wendel.
Institution Type/Description: Historic House Museum: built in 1867.
Hours & Admission Prices: April-Dec. Wed. & 1st Sun. of month 1-5. Tours: adults $3, children $1; military & military families no charge.
Attendance: 2,400 (estimated)

Farmington Hills

HOLOCAUST MEMORIAL CENTER, 28123 Orchard Lake Rd., Farmington Hills, MI 48334-3738. Tel.: 248-553-2400. Fax: 248-553-2433.
E-mail: info@holocaustcenter.org
Web Site: www.holocaustcenter.org
Key Personnel: CEO, Rabbi Eli Mayerfeld; Exec. Dir., Stephen M. Goldman; Chm. (V), Dr. Steven Grant, M.D.; Pres. (V), Gary Karp; Dir. Devel., Cheryl Guyer; Dir. Education, Robin Axelrod; Events Mgr., Sarah Saltzman; Dir. Annual Giving, Beth Snider; Librarian Archivist, Feiga Weiss.
Institution Type/Description: History Museum.
Hours & Admission Prices: Sun & Tues.-Thurs. 9-3:30, Mon. 9-7:30. Adults $8, senior citizens & college students $6, middle & high students $5; discounts to AAM members; uniform services & members no charge. Closed Jewish holidays; most legal holidays. &
Attendance: 65,000 (estimated)

MARVIN'S MARVELOUS MECHANICAL MUSEUM, 31005 Orchard Lake Rd., Farmington Hills, MI 48334-1384. Tel.: 248-626-5020. Fax: 248-626-7945.
E-mail: marvin@marvin3m.com
Web Site: www.marvin3m.com/
Key Personnel: Owner, Marvin Yagoda.
Institution Type/Description: Mechanical Machine Museum.
Hours & Admission Prices: Mon.-Thurs. 10-9, Fri.-Sat. 10am-11pm, Sun. 12-9. No charge. &

Fenton

FENTON HISTORICAL SOCIETY, 310 S. Leroy St., Fenton, MI 48430. Mailing Address: 310 S. Leroy St., Fenton, MI 48430. Tel.: 810-629-2570.
E-mail: information@fentonhistorycenter.org
Web Site: www.fentonhistorycenter.org
Institution Type/Description: Historical Society Museum: housed in the former office of A.J. Phillips; built in 1900.
Hours & Admission Prices: Sun. 1-4; other times by appointment.

THE PIONEER MEMORIAL ASSOCIATION OF FENTON AND MUNDY TOWNSHIPS, 2436 N. Long Lake Rd., Fenton, MI 48430. Mailing Address: P.O. Box 154, Fenton, MI 48430-0154. Tel.: 810-955-3336. Facebook: The Pioneer Memorial Association of Fenton and Mundy Townships.
E-mail: podunkpioneers@aol.com
Web Site: www.addorio.com/podunk
Key Personnel: Pres., Mary J. Pinkston; Vice Pres., Bill Pinkston; Treas., Hewitt R. Judson; Sec., Phyllis Heusted.
Institution Type/Description: Historic Society: housed in an 1836 pioneer farm home; now called Podunk House.
Hours & Admission Prices: June-Aug. by appointment only; call Phyllis Yancy, 810-629-8747. Pioneer Day: adults $1, children $.50.
Attendance: 250 (estimated)

Ferndale

FERNDALE HISTORICAL SOCIETY, 1651 Livernois, Ferndale, MI 48220. Tel.: 248-545-7606.
E-mail: info@ferndalehistoricalsociety.org
Web Site: www.ferndalehistoricalsociety.org
Key Personnel: Pres. (V), Garry Taylor.
Institution Type/Description: Historical Society Museum.
Hours & Admission Prices: Mon.-Wed. 10-1, Sat. 1-4. No charge; donations accepted.
Attendance: 400 (actual)

LAWRENCE STREET GALLERY, 22620 Woodward Ave., Ste. A, Ferndale, MI 48220. Tel.: 248-544-0394. Facebook.
E-mail: lawrencestgallery@gmail.com
Web Site: www.lawrencestreetgallery.com
Key Personnel: Pres. (V), Cindy Parsons.
Institution Type/Description: Art Gallery.
Hours & Admission Prices: Wed. & Sat. 12-5, Thurs.-Fri. 12-9. No charge.
Attendance: 1,000 (estimated)

PAUL KOTULA PROJECTS, 23255 Woodward Ave., Ferndale, MI 48220-1361. Tel.: 248-544-3020.
E-mail: info@paulkotula.com
Web Site: www.paulkotula.com
Institution Type/Description: Art Gallery.
Hours & Admission Prices: Thurs.-Sat. 11-5 during exhibitions; other times by appointment.

Flat Rock

FLAT ROCK HISTORICAL SOCIETY - MUNGER GENERAL STORE MUSEUM, 25200 Gibraltar Rd., Flat Rock, MI 48134. Mailing Address: P.O. Box 337, Flat Rock, MI 48134. Tel.: 734-782-5220.
E-mail: archives@frdigitalhistory.org
Web Site: flatrockhistory.org
Institution Type/Description: History Museum: housed in a former general store, 1875-1937.
Hours & Admission Prices: 2nd Sun. each month 1-4.

Flint

FLINT CHILDREN'S MUSEUM, 1602 W. University Ave., Flint, MI 48504. Tel.: 810-767-5437. Fax: 810-767-4936. Facebook: @FlintChildrensMuseum; Twitter: @flintchildrensm.
E-mail: discovery@flintchildrensmuseum.org
Web Site: thefcm.org
Key Personnel: Exec. Dir., Kimberly Roddy; Pres. Bd. Dirs., Delores Sharpe; Museum Shop Mgr., Diana Osman.
Institution Type/Description: Children's Museum.
Hours & Admission Prices: Tues.-Sat. 10-5, Sun. 12-4; other times by appointment. Admission $6; discounts to ASTC members and families receiving food/cash/EBT/BridgeCard assistance; children under one no charge. ♿
Attendance: 56,000 (estimated)

FLINT INSTITUTE OF ARTS, 1120 E. Kearsley St., Flint, MI 48503-1915. Tel.: 810-234-1695. Fax: 810-234-1692.
E-mail: info@flintarts.org
Web Site: www.flintarts.org
Key Personnel: Exec. Dir., John B. Henry; Pres., Dean Yeotis; Pres. (V), Thomas Mitchell; Dir. Finance & Administration, Michael Melenbrink; Dir. Art School, Donovan Entrekin; Membership Coord., Valarie Allen; Facilities Mgr., Bryan Christie; Cur. Collections & Exhibitions, Tracee Glab; Cur. Education, Monique Desormeau; Registrar, Pete Ott; Museum Shop Mgr., Cory Potter; Dir. Devel., Kathryn Sharbaugh.
Institution Type/Description: Art Museum & School.
Hours & Admission Prices: Mon.-Wed. & Fri. 12-5, Thurs. 12-9, Sat. 10-5, Sun. 1-5. Collections: no charge. Temporary Exhibits: adult $7, seniors & students 13-17 $5; discounts to AAM & ICOM members; Sat., children 12 & under, college students with ID & members no charge. Closed national holidays. ♿
Attendance: 150,614 (actual)

MOTT COMMUNITY COLLEGE FINE ARTS GALLERY, Visual Arts & Design Bldg., 1401 E. Court St., Flint, MI 48503-2089. Tel.: 810-762-0443. Fax: 810-232-3452.
E-mail: Debbie.Killian@mcc.edu
Web Site: www.mcc.edu
Institution Type/Description: Art Gallery.
Hours & Admission Prices: Mon.-Fri. 8-5.

ROBERT T. LONGWAY PLANETARIUM, 1310 E. Kearsley St., Flint, MI 48503-1987. Tel.: 810-237-3400. Fax: 810-237-3417.
E-mail: tshickles@sloanlongway.org
Web Site: www.sloanlongway.org
Key Personnel: Dir., Tim Shickles; Office Mgr., Pam Atwell; Lecturer & Instructor, Richard A. Walker; Science Program Presenter, Loe'l Murphy; Cur. Programs, Laurie Bone; Museum Shop Mgr., Judith Latreille; Receptionist, Cindy Goodall.
Institution Type/Description: Planetarium.
Hours & Admission Prices: Call for hours. Adults $6, seniors & children 2-11 $4; members and children one & under no charge. ♿
Attendance: 62,000 (estimated)

SLOAN MUSEUM, 1221 E. Kearsley St., Flint, MI 48503-1988. Tel.: 810-237-3450. Fax: 810-237-3451.
E-mail: sloan@sloanlongway.org
Web Site: www.sloanlongway.org
Key Personnel: Dir., Todd Slisher.
Institution Type/Description: Regional History & Science Museum and Planetarium.
Hours & Admission Prices: Mon.-Fri. 10-5, Sat.-Sun. 12-5. Adults $9, senior citizens $8, children 2-11 $6; discounts to groups & AAM members; members & children 1 & under no charge. Closed New Year's Day; Easter; Memorial Day; Independence Day; Labor Day; Thanksgiving; Christmas. ♿
Attendance: 117,646 (actual)

WHALEY HISTORIC HOUSE MUSEUM, 624 E. Kearsley St., Flint, MI 48503-1909. Tel.: 810-471-4714. Facebook: Whaley Historic House Museum.
E-mail: 1885@whaleyhouse.com
Web Site: www.whaleyhouse.com
Formerly: Whaley House Museum
Key Personnel: Dir., Samantha Engel.
Institution Type/Description: Historic House: former home of Robert and Mary McFarlan Whaley.
Hours & Admission Prices: 1st & 3rd Sat. of month 10-1, Mon.-Fri. by appointment. Adults $5, children 12 & under & students $3; members receive complimentary tours.

Flushing

FLUSHING AREA HISTORICAL SOCIETY, 431 W. Main St., Flushing, MI 48433. Tel.: 810-487-0814.
E-mail: fahs@att.net
Web Site: flushinghistorical.org
Institution Type/Description: Historical Society Museum: housed in a former depot; built in 1888.
Hours & Admission Prices: Jan.-April Tues. 10-1; May-Dec. Tues. 10-1, Sun. 1-4; other times by appointment. No charge; donations accepted. Closed holidays. ♿

Frankenmuth

FRANKENMUTH HISTORICAL MUSEUM, 613 S. Main, Frankenmuth, MI 48734-1689. Tel.: 989-652-9701.
E-mail: fhadirector1963@gmail.com
Web Site: www.frankenmuthmuseum.org
Key Personnel: Dir., Alyssa Black; Pres., Adele Martin, Jr.; Asst. Dir. Programs, Heidi Champman; Registrar & Collection Mgr., Mary Nuechterlein; Museum Shop Mgr., Lorraine Eckert.
Institution Type/Description: Regional History Museum.
Hours & Admission Prices: Jan.-March Mon. & Thurs. 10-5, Fri. & Sat. 10-7, Sun. noon-6; April-Dec. Mon.-Thurs. 10-5, Fri. & Sat. 10-8, Sun. noon-6. Self Guided Tours: family $5, adults $2, children $1. Guided Tours: call for reservations. Closed New Year's Day; Easter; Thanksgiving; Christmas. ♿
Attendance: 20,000 (actual)

LAGER MILL BEER STORE & BREWING MUSEUM, 701 Mill St., Frankenmuth, MI 48734. Mailing Address: 613 S. Main St., Frankenmuth, 48734. Tel.: 989-652-9701. Facebook.
E-mail: fhadirector@airadv.net
Formerly: Lager Mill History of Brewing Museum
Key Personnel: Dir., Jonathan Webb; Museum Shop Mgr., Tom Taylor.
Institution Type/Description: History Museum.
Hours & Admission Prices: Mon.-Thurs. 11-7, Fri.-Sat. 11-8, Sun. 12-5. Family $5, adults $2, students $1; members no charge. ♿
Attendance: 7,000 (actual)

Franklin

FRANKLIN HISTORICAL MUSEUM, 26165 13 Mile Rd., Franklin, MI 48025. Mailing Address: P.O. Box 7, Franklin, MI 48025. Tel.: 248-538-0273.
E-mail: info@kregerhouse.org
Web Site: www.franklin-history.org
Institution Type/Description: History Museum.
Hours & Admission Prices: 1st Sat. each month 1-3 by appointment.

Garden

FAYETTE HISTORIC STATE PARK, 4785 II Rd., Garden, MI 49835-9411. Tel.: 906-644-2603. Fax: 906-644-2666.
E-mail: brownr1@michigan.gov
Web Site: www.michigan.gov/fayettetownsite; www.michigan.gov/fayette
Key Personnel: Unit Supvr., Dept. Natural Resources, Randall W. Brown; Site Historian, Dr. Troy Henderson.
Institution Type/Description: Historic Town Museum: site of iron smelting town 1867-1891, owned & operated by Jackson Iron Co. includes nineteen structures.
Hours & Admission Prices: mid-May to mid-June & Sept. to mid-Oct. daily 9-5; mid-June to Aug. daily 8-9. Motor vehicle passport required. Michigan resident car $11; non-Michigan car: annual $31, daily $9. ♿
Attendance: 62,500 (actual)

Gaylord

CALL OF THE WILD MUSEUM, 850 S. Wisconsin Ave., Gaylord, MI 49735-1747. Tel.: 989-732-4336. Fax: 989-732-3749.
E-mail: callofthewildgaylord@live.com
Web Site: www.callofthewildgaylord.com
Key Personnel: Bd. Directors, William C. Johnson; Bd. Directors, Judy Fleet; Pres., Janis Vollmer.
Institution Type/Description: Natural History Museum.
Hours & Admission Prices: mid-June to Labor Day daily 9-9; Sept. to mid-June Mon.-Sat. 9:30-6, Sun. 11-5. Adults $7, seniors 62 & up $6.50, children 5-13 $4.50; discount to AAM members. Closed New Year's Day; Thanksgiving; Christmas. ♿
Attendance: 20,000 (estimated)

Gibraltar

GIBRALTAR HISTORICAL MUSEUM, 29450 Munro St., Gibraltar, MI 48173. Tel.: 734-676-3900.
E-mail: gibraltarhm@yahoo.com
Institution Type/Description: Historical Society Museum.
Hours & Admission Prices: 1st Sun. each month 2-4.

Grand Haven

TRI-CITIES HISTORICAL MUSEUM, 200 Washington Ave., Grand Haven, MI 49417-1357. Tel.: 616-842-0700. Fax: 616-842-3698. Facebook.
E-mail: jbunke@tri-citiesmuseum.org
Web Site: www.tri-citiesmuseum.org
Key Personnel: Bd. Pres., Ann White; Museum Shop Mgr., Abbei Monroe.
Institution Type/Description: Historical Museum: housed in 1871 Akeley building.
Hours & Admission Prices: Tues.-Fri. 10-5, Sat.-Sun. noon-5. No charge; donations accepted. &
Attendance: 60,286 (actual)

Grand Ledge

GRAND LEDGE AREA HISTORICAL SOCIETY MUSEUM, 118 W. Lincoln, Grand Ledge, MI 48837. Mailing Address: P.O. Box 203, Grand Ledge, MI 48837. Tel.: 517-627-4889. Facebook: Grand Ledge Area Historical Society Museum.
E-mail: langenbergd@aol.com
Web Site: gdledgehistsoc.org
Key Personnel: Museum Chair (V), Cindy Langenberg; Pres. (V) Historical Society, Ann Lawrence; Archives, Cindy Langenberg.
Institution Type/Description: Historical Society Museum: housed in the former home of local minister, Byron S. Pratt; built in 1880.
Hours & Admission Prices: March-Dec. Sun. 2-4. Festival Days: 12-4; other times by appointment. No charge; donations accepted. Closed national holidays. &
Attendance: 1,000 (estimated)

Grand Marais

PICKLE BARREL HOUSE MUSEUM, 21795 Randolph, Grand Marais, MI 49839. Mailing Address: P.O. Box 179, Grand Marais, MI 49839. Tel.: 906-494-2404.
Institution Type/Description: History Museum: housed in the former summer home of cartoonist, William Donahey; built in 1926. Listed on the National Register of Historic Places.
Hours & Admission Prices: June & Sept. Sat.-Sun. 1-4; July-Aug. daily 1-4.

Grand Rapids

CALVIN COLLEGE CENTER ART GALLERY, Covenant Fine Arts Center, 1795 Knollcrest Cir., S.E., Grand Rapids, MI 49546. Tel.: 616-526-6271. Fax: 616-526-8551.
E-mail: jhz2@calvin.edu
Web Site: www.calvin.edu/centerartgallery
Key Personnel: Dir., Joel Zwart.
Institution Type/Description: Art Gallery.
Hours & Admission Prices: Winter: Mon.-Tues. 9-5, Wed.-Fri. 9-9, Sat. 10-4. No charge. Closed during school vacations except for special exhibitions. &
Attendance: 12,000 (actual)

COMMUNITY ARCHIVES AND RESEARCH CENTER, 223 Washington St., S.E., Grand Rapids, MI 49503-4314. Tel.: 616-456-4127. Fax: 616-456-4411.
E-mail: awright@grcity.us
Web Site: grcity.us/city-clerk/pages/city-archives-and-research-center.aspx
Key Personnel: City Archives Officer, Tony Wright; Archives Asst., Matthew Ellis.
Institution Type/Description: Archives.
Hours & Admission Prices: By appointment.

FREDERIK MEIJER GARDENS & SCULPTURE PARK, 1000 E. Beltline Ave., N.E., Grand Rapids, MI 49525-5804. Tel.: 888-957-1580 (Toll Free), 616-957-1580. Facebook: Meijer Gardens.
E-mail: info@meijergardens.org
Web Site: www.meijergardens.org
Key Personnel: Pres. & C.E.O., David S. Hooker; Chief Cur., Joseph Becherer.
Institution Type/Description: Botanical Garden & Sculpture Park.
Hours & Admission Prices: Mon.-Sat. 9-5, Sun. 11-5. Adults $12, seniors 65 & over & students with ID $9, children 5-13 $6, children 3-4 $4, children 2 &

under & members no charge. Closed New Year's Day; Thanksgiving; Christmas. &
Attendance: 650,000 (estimated)

GERALD R. FORD PRESIDENTIAL MUSEUM, 303 Pearl St., N. W., Grand Rapids, MI 49504-5353. Tel.: 616-254-0400 & 0367. Fax: 616-254-0386. Facebook; Twitter; Tumblr; YouTube.
E-mail: ford.museum@nara.gov
Web Site: www.fordlibrarymuseum.gov
Key Personnel: Dir., Dr. Elaine Didier; Cur., Donald Holloway; Exhibits Specialist, Bettina Cousineau; Registrar, James Draper; Education, Barbara McGregor; Public Rels., Kristin Mooney; Museum Shop Mgr., Janice Berling.
Institution Type/Description: Presidential History Museum.
Hours & Admission Prices: Mon.-Sat. 9-5, Sun. 12-5. Adults $8, senior citizens & military $7, college students $6, children 6-18 $4; discounts to groups; members and children 5 & under no charge. Closed New Year's Day; Thanksgiving; Christmas. &
Attendance: 311,122 (actual)

GRAND RAPIDS ART MUSEUM, 101 Monroe Center, N.W., Grand Rapids, MI 49503-2801. Tel.: 616-831-1000. Fax: 616-831-1001.
E-mail: pr@artmuseumgr.org
Web Site: www.artmuseumgr.org
Key Personnel: C.E.O. & Dir., Dana Friis-Hansen; C.O.O., Neil Bremer; Cur., Ron Platt.
Institution Type/Description: Art Museum.
Hours & Admission Prices: Tues.-Wed. & Fri.-Sat. 10-5, Thurs. 10-9, Sun. 12-5. Adults $8, senior citizens 62 $7, youth 6-17 $5; discounts to AAM members; members & children under 6 no charge. Closed major holidays. &
Attendance: 319,459 (actual)

GRAND RAPIDS CHILDREN'S MUSEUM, 11 Sheldon Ave., N. E., Grand Rapids, MI 49503-3218. Tel.: 616-235-4726, ext. 100. Fax: 616-235-4728. Facebook; Twitter.
E-mail: mlancaster@grcm.org
Web Site: www.grcm.org
Key Personnel: Exec. Dir., Maggie Lancaster; Dir. Devel., Leslie Griswold; Mktg. & Membership Mgr., Adrienne Brown; Exhibits & Community Rels. Mgr., Jan Stone; Exhibits Mgr., Jake Bouck.
Institution Type/Description: Children's Museum.
Hours & Admission Prices: Tues.-Wed. & Fri.-Sat. 9:30-5, Thurs. 9:30-8, Sun. 12-5. Adults $8.50; reciprocal membership & members no charge. &
Attendance: 184,000 (estimated)

GRAND RAPIDS PUBLIC MUSEUM, 272 Pearl St., N.W., Grand Rapids, MI 49504-5371. Mailing Address: Van Andel Museum Center, 272 Pearl St., N.W., Grand Rapids, MI 49504-5371. Tel.: 616-929-1700. Fax: 616-929-1780.
E-mail: info@grpm.org
Web Site: www.grpm.org
Formerly: Public Museum of West Michigan
Key Personnel: Pres. & C.E.O., Dale A. Robertson; Foundation Chm. (V), Jim Williams; Foundation Vice Chm., Carol Van Andel; C.F.O. & Vice Pres. Admin., Karen Wilburn; Vice Pres. Education, Mike Posthumus; Vice Pres. Mktg. & Public Rels., Kate Moore; Vice Pres. Devel., Gina Schulz; Asst. to Pres./C.E.O., Leslie Milstead.
Institution Type/Description: General Museum.
Hours & Admission Prices: Museum: Tues. 9-8, Mon. & Wed.-Sat. 9-5, Sun. 12-5. Adults $8, senior citizens $7, college students with ID & children 3-17 $3; discount to Kent County residents, military, GR Conventioneers, Teacher Club members, Culture Pass, AAA & AAM members; museum members, ASTC & children 2 & under no charge. Planetarium: $5, $4 with general admission; members no charge. Closed New Year's Day; Easter; Memorial Day; Labor Day; Thanksgiving; Christmas. &
Attendance: 247,371 (actual)

JOHN BALL ZOO, 1300 W. Fulton St., Grand Rapids, MI 49504-6100. Tel.: 616-336-4301. Fax: 616-336-3907.
E-mail: info@jbzoo.org
Web Site: www.jbzoo.org
Key Personnel: C.E.O., Peter D'Arienzo; Museum Shop Mgr., Theresa Danneffel.
Institution Type/Description: Zoological Gardens.
Hours & Admission Prices: Call for hours. Adults $10, senior citizens 62 & over $9, children 2-12 $8; members no charge. &
Attendance: 523,000 (actual)

KENDALL GALLERIES - KENDALL COLLEGE OF ART AND DESIGN, Ferris State University, 17 Fountain St., N.W.,

Grand Rapids, MI 49503. Tel.: 800-676-2787. Facebook: Kendall Galleries.
E-mail: kcadgallery@ferris.edu
Web Site: www.kcad.edu
Key Personnel: Dir. Exhibitions, Sarah Joseph; Cur. Exhibitions, Michele Bosak; Lead Preparator, Tanya Bakija; Gallery Mgr., Sara Idziak; Asst. Preparator, Steven Vinson; Exhibitions Asst., Mike Wolf.
Institution Type/Description: Art Galleries.
Hours & Admission Prices: Call for hours. No charge; donations accepted. &
Attendance: 46,400 (actual)

URBAN INSTITUTE FOR CONTEMPORARY ARTS, 2 W. Fulton, Grand Rapids, MI 49503. Tel.: 616-454-7000, ext. 11. Fax: 616-459-9395.
E-mail: info@uica.org
Web Site: www.uica.org
Key Personnel: Exec. Dir., Miranda Krajniak; Assoc. Dir., Megan Bylsma; Film Coord., Nick Hartman; Devel. Officer, Kristan Taylor.
Institution Type/Description: Civic Art, Cultural Center.
Hours & Admission Prices: Tues.-Sat. noon-10, Sun. noon-7. Adults $8; members no charge. &
Attendance: 120,000 (actual)

Grass Lake

WATERLOO AREA HISTORICAL SOCIETY, 13493 Waterloo-Munith Rd., Grass Lake, MI 49240. Mailing Address: P.O. Box 37, Stockbridge, MI 49285-0037. Tel.: 517-596-2254.
E-mail: info@waterloofarmmuseum.org
Web Site: waterloofarmmuseum.org
Key Personnel: Pres., Henry Crawford; Treas., John Z. Ocwieja; Museum Shop Mgr., Nancy Wisman.
Institution Type/Description: History Museum.
Hours & Admission Prices: June-Aug. 1-5. Adults $5, senior citizens 60 & over $4, children under 12 $2. discounts to AAA, AAM & Michigan Historical Society members; members & children under 5 no charge.
Attendance: 8,000 (estimated)

Grayling

HARTWICK PINES LOGGING MUSEUM, 4216 Ranger Rd., Grayling, MI 49738. Tel.: 989-348-2537. Fax: 989-344-6803.
E-mail: pineh@michigan.gov
Key Personnel: Site Historian, Hillary Pine; Park Interpreter, Craig Kasmer.
Institution Type/Description: Logging History Museum.
Hours & Admission Prices: Call for hours. State of Michigan Recreation Passport required for entry. &

Greenville

THE FIGHTING FALCON MILITARY MUSEUM, 516 W. Cass St., Greenville, MI 48838. Tel.: 616-225-1940.
E-mail: bachristensen@charter.net
Web Site: www.thefightingfalcon.com
Key Personnel: Pres. (V), Bill Garlick.
Institution Type/Description: Military History Museum.
Hours & Admission Prices: Call for hours. No charge; donations accepted. &

Grosse Ile

GROSSE ILE HISTORICAL SOCIETY, 25020 E. River Rd., Grosse Ile, MI 48138. Mailing Address: P.O. Box 131, Grosse Ile, MI 48138-0131. Tel.: 734-675-1250. Facebook: Grosse Ile Historical Society.
E-mail: gihistsoc@hotmail.com
Web Site: www.gihistsoc.org
Key Personnel: Pres., Tony Krukowski; Vice Pres., Sue Zink.
Institution Type/Description: Historical Society Museum.
Hours & Admission Prices: March-Dec. Thurs. 10-12, Sun. 1-4. No charge; donations accepted. Closed holidays.
Attendance: 1,500 (estimated)

Grosse Pointe

GROSSE POINTE ART CENTER, 32 Lake Shore Rd., Grosse Pointe, MI 48236-3726. Tel.: 313-881-3454.
E-mail: gpaa@grossepointeartcenter.org
Web Site: www.grossepointeartcenter.org
Institution Type/Description: Art Gallery.
Hours & Admission Prices: Tues.-Sat. 12-6. No charge.

Grosse Pointe Shores

EDSEL & ELEANOR FORD HOUSE, 1100 Lake Shore Rd., Grosse Pointe Shores, MI 48236-4106. Tel.: 313-884-4222. Fax: 313-884-5977.
E-mail: info@fordhouse.org
Web Site: www.fordhouse.org
Key Personnel: Pres., Kathleen Stiso Mullins; Chm. (V), Edsel B. Ford, II; Vice Pres., Communications, Ann Fitzpatrick; Dir. Education, Christopher Shires; Dir. Devel., Bernadette Banke; Cur., Josephine Shea; Vice Pres., Finance & Admin., Robert Seestadt; Dir. Group Tours Sales, Donna Buchanan; Gallery Shop Mgr., Matthew Peplinski.
Institution Type/Description: Historic Building & Site: Family home of Edsel & Eleanor Ford, designed by architect Albert Kahn & built in 1926-29 with interiors from historic English homes & four rooms designed in the modern style by Walter Dorwin Teague. Gardens & grounds designed by Jens Jensen.
Hours & Admission Prices: Jan.-March Tues.-Sun. 12-4; April-Dec. Tues.-Sat. 10-4, Sun. 12-4. Adults $12, senior citizens $11, children 6-12 $8; discounts to AAM members; children 5 & under no charge. Grounds $5. Closed New Year's Day; Thanksgiving; Christmas. &
Attendance: 40,000 (estimated)

HENRY FORD ESTATE-FAIR LANE, 1100 Lake Shore Rd., Grosse Pointe Shores, MI 48236. Tel.: 313-884-4222.
E-mail: info@fordhouse.org
Web Site: www.henryfordestate.org
Key Personnel: Pres. & C.E.O., Kathleen S. Mullins.
Institution Type/Description: Nature Center & Historic House: former home of Henry Ford.
Hours & Admission Prices: Historic buildings currently closed for restoration. Grounds remain open year round. &
Attendance: 150,000 (estimated)

Hamtramck

UKRAINIAN-AMERICAN ARCHIVES & MUSEUM, 11756 Charest St., Hamtramck, MI 48212. Tel.: 313-366-9764.
E-mail: ukrainianmuseum@sbcglobal.net
Web Site: www.ukrainianmuseumdetroit.org
Key Personnel: Exec. Dir., Chrystyna Nykorak.
Institution Type/Description: History Museum & Archives.
Hours & Admission Prices: Tues.-Fri. 9-5; other times by appointment. Adults $3, students $1; discounts to veterans. Blue Star Museum. Closed holidays.
Attendance: 500 (estimated)

Hanover

HANOVER-HORTON AREA HISTORICAL SOCIETY, 105 Fairview, Hanover, MI 49241-0256. Mailing Address: P.O. Box 256, Hanover, MI 49241-0256. Tel.: 517-563-8927. Fax: 517-563-8927.
E-mail: hhahs@frontier.com
Web Site: www.conklinreedorganmuseum.org
Formerly: Conklin Reed Organ & History Museum
Key Personnel: Pres. (V), Betty Jo DeForest; Treas., Richard Tallis; Museum Gift Mgr., Jenny Crews.
Institution Type/Description: Historical Society & Antique Reed Organ Museum: housed in 1911 Hanover High School.
Hours & Admission Prices: May-Oct. Sun. 1-5; call for additional hours. No charge; donations accepted. Closed Easter. &
Attendance: 3,359 (actual)

Harbor Beach

FRANK MURPHY MEMORIAL MUSEUM, 142 S. Huron Ave., Harbor Beach, MI 48441. Mailing Address: P.O. Box 113, Harbor Beach, MI 48441-0113. Tel.: 989-479-6477.
Key Personnel: Cur., Barb McGowan.
Institution Type/Description: Historic House Museum: housed in the home of statesman, Frank Murphy.
Hours & Admission Prices: Memorial Day-Labor Day Tues.-Fri. 12-4, Sat.-Sun. 10-4 & by appointment. Adults $2, children $1.

THE GRICE HOUSE MUSEUM, 865 N. Huron Ave., Harbor Beach, MI 48441. Mailing Address: Harbor Beach Chamber of Commerce, P.O. Box 113, Harbor Beach, MI 48441-0113. Tel.: 989-479-6477.
E-mail: info@gricehouse.com
Web Site: harborbeachchamber.com/grice.html

Institution Type/Description: Historic House: former home of the Grice family, built in 1875.
Hours & Admission Prices: Memorial Day-Labor Day Tues.-Sun. 1-5.

Harbor Springs

ANDREW J. BLACKBIRD MUSEUM, 368 E. Main St., Harbor Springs, MI 49740-1514. Mailing Address: P.O. Box 678, Harbor Springs, MI 49740-0678. Tel.: 231-526-0612 (museum); 2104 (City of Harbor Springs). Fax: 231-526-6865.
E-mail: mary@harborspringshistory.org
Web Site: www.cityofharborsprings.com/museums-48/
Key Personnel: Mgr., Joyce Shagonaby; Pres. (V), Robert Shagonaby.
Institution Type/Description: Indian Museum: housed in c. 1855 home of Andrew J. Blackbird.
Hours & Admission Prices: Mon.-Fri. 10-4. No charge; donations accepted. &
Attendance: 600 (estimated)

Hartland

FLORENCE B. DEARING MUSEUM - HARTLAND HISTORICAL SOCIETY, 3503 Avon St., Hartland, MI 48353. Mailing Address: P.O. Box 49, Hartland, MI 48353. Tel.: 810-299-7621.
E-mail: hrfoley@earthlink.net
Web Site: www.hartlandareahistory.org
Key Personnel: Pres., Hildy R. Foley; Cur., Michael Forster.
Institution Type/Description: History Museum: housed in the former Hartland's town hall; built in 1891 also used as fire hall from 1891-1970.
Hours & Admission Prices: Sun. 2-4; groups by appointment. Adults in group tours $1; individual adults no charge; donations accepted.
Attendance: 750 (estimated)

Hastings

HISTORIC CHARLTON PARK VILLAGE, MUSEUM AND RECREATION AREA, 2545 S. Charlton Park Rd., Hastings, MI 49058-8102. Tel.: 269-945-3775. Fax: 269-945-0390.
E-mail: info@charltonpark.org
Web Site: www.charltonpark.org
Key Personnel: Dir., Dan Patton.
Institution Type/Description: History Museum.
Hours & Admission Prices: Park: Memorial Day to Labor Day daily 8am to dusk. Museum & Village: Memorial Day-Labor Day daily 9-4; other times by appointment. Office: Mon.-Fri. 8-5. Special Events & Activities: adults $6, children 5-12 $4; children under 4 no charge. &
Attendance: 41,000 (estimated)

Hickory Corners

GILMORE CAR MUSEUM, 6865 W. Hickory Rd., Hickory Corners, MI 49060-9788. Tel.: 269-671-5089. Fax: 269-671-5843. Facebook: Gilmore Car Museum.
E-mail: info@gilmorecarmuseum.org
Web Site: www.gilmorecarmuseum.org
Key Personnel: Dir., Michael J. Spezia; Museum Shop Mgr., Jane Vander Slik.
Institution Type/Description: Transportation Museum.
Hours & Admission Prices: Museum: Mon.-Fri. 9-5, Sat.-Sun. 9-6. Blue Moon Diner: daily 11-4. Historic Campus: April-Nov. call for hours. Adults $13, youth $10; children 6 & under no charge. Car Shows: $12 per person. Closed New Year's Day; Easter; Thanksgiving; Christmas. &
Attendance: 72,250 (actual)

Holland

CAPPON & SETTLERS HOUSE MUSEUMS, 228 W. 9th St., Holland, MI 49423-3116. Mailing Address: 31 W. 10th St., Holland, MI 49423-3101. Tel.: 616-796-3329. Fax: 616-394-4756.
E-mail: hollandmuseum@hollandmuseum.org
Web Site: www.hollandmuseum.org
Key Personnel: Chm., Andrew Baldus; Exec. Dir., Christopher Shires.
Institution Type/Description: Historic Houses: 1874 Italianate Style home of Holland's first mayor; 1867 cottage of a Great Lakes Ship's Carpenter.
Hours & Admission Prices: May-Sept. Fri.-Sat. 12-4; special hours during Tulip Time. Adults $5; discounts to AAM members; members & children under 6 no charge. &
Attendance: 1,794 (actual)

DE GRAAF NATURE CENTER, 600 Graafschap Rd., Holland, MI 49423-4549. Tel.: 616-355-1057. Fax: 616-355-1069.

E-mail: degraafnaturecenter@cityofholland.com
Web Site: www.degraaf.org
Key Personnel: Dir., Robert Venner; Naturalist, Mike Graves; Naturalist, Lisa McKellips; Naturalist, Erin Wildt.
Institution Type/Description: Nature Center.
Hours & Admission Prices: Brower Interpretive Center: Tues.-Fri. 9-5, Sat. 10-5. No charge. Trails: dawn-dusk. School Programs: students $2.25. Closed holidays. &
Attendance: 13,000

DEPREE ART CENTER & GALLERY, 275 Columbia Ave., Holland, MI 49423. Mailing Address: P.O. Box 9000, Holland, MI 49422-9000. Tel.: 616-395-7500. Fax: 616-395-7499.
E-mail: art@hope.edu
Web Site: hope.edu/academic/art
Key Personnel: Dir., Dr. Heidi Kraus.
Institution Type/Description: Academic Art Center & Gallery.
Hours & Admission Prices: May-Aug. Mon.-Fri. 10-5; Sept.-April Mon.-Sat. 10-5, Sun. 1-5; summer hours apply during college breaks. No charge. Closed New Year's Day; Memorial Day; Thanksgiving; Christmas. &
Attendance: 20,500 (estimated)

HOLLAND AREA ARTS COUNCIL, 150 E. 8th St., Holland, MI 49423-3504. Tel.: 616-396-3278. Fax: 616-396-6298. Facebook: Holland Area Arts Council.
E-mail: margaret@hollandarts.edu
Web Site: www.hollandarts.org
Key Personnel: Exec. Dir., Lorma Williams Freestone; Pres. Bd., Patricia Flynn; Mgr. Communications & Exhibitions, Margaret Foreman; Program Dir., Mary Sundstrom; Artistic Dir., Derek Johnson; Asst. to Dir., Tennina Miozza; Visitor Svcs., Kailey Schroeder.
Institution Type/Description: Arts Council.
Hours & Admission Prices: Mon.-Thurs. 10-8, Sat. 10-3. No charge; donations accepted. Closed New Year's Day; Memorial Day; Independence Day; Labor Day; Thanksgiving; Christmas. &
Attendance: 50,000

THE HOLLAND MUSEUM, 31 W. 10th St., Holland, MI 49423-3101. Tel.: 616-796-3329. Fax: 616-394-4756.
E-mail: hollandmuseum@hollandmuseum.org
Web Site: www.hollandmuseum.org
Key Personnel: Chm., Andrew Baldus; Exec. Dir., Ricki L. Levine; Operations Mgr., Paula Dunlap; Museum Shop Mgr., Paula Dunlap.
Institution Type/Description: History Museum: housed in 1914 restored Federal Post Office building.
Hours & Admission Prices: May-Sept. Wed.-Sat. 11-4, Sun. 12-4; Oct.-April Wed.-Sat. 11-4; call for additional hours. Adults $7, seniors $6, students $4; discounts to AAM & AAA members; members & children under 6 no charge. Closed major holidays. &
Attendance: 20,983 (actual)

WINDMILL ISLAND GARDENS, 1 Lincoln Ave., Holland, MI 49423. Tel.: 616-355-1030, 888-535-5792. Fax: 616-355-1035. Facebook: Windmill Island.
E-mail: windmill@cityofholland.com
Web Site: www.windmillisland.org
Formerly: Windmill Island Municipal Park
Institution Type/Description: Park Museum.
Hours & Admission Prices: late April to early Oct. daily 9:30-6; last ticket sold 5pm. Tulip Time: daily 9-6. Adults $9, children 3-15 $5; discounts to American Horticulture Society Reciprocal Program & groups of 20 or more; children 2 & under no charge. &
Attendance: 90,000 (actual)

Houghton

A. E. SEAMAN MINERAL MUSEUM, 1404 E. Sharon Ave., Michigan Technological University, Houghton, MI 49931-1295. Tel.: 906-487-2572. Fax: 906-487-3027.
E-mail: tjb@mtu.edu
Web Site: www.museum.mtu.edu
Key Personnel: Exec. Dir. & Prof., Dr. Theodore J. Bornhorst; Assoc. Cur., Dr. Chris Stefano; Museum Asst., Monica Rovano.
Institution Type/Description: Mineral Museum.
Hours & Admission Prices: May-Oct. Mon.-Sat. 9-5; Nov.-April Tues.-Sat. 9-4:30. Adults $6, seniors 65 & over $5, college students with ID $3, junior 9-17 $2; discounts to groups and AAM & ICOM members; children 8 & under no charge. Closed New Year's Eve, Day & first two weeks of Jan.; Independence Day; Memorial Day; Labor Day; Thanksgiving & two days after; Christmas Eve, Day & week. &
Attendance: 12,700 (actual)

ISLE ROYALE NATIONAL PARK, 800 E. Lakeshore Dr., Houghton, MI 49931-1869. Tel.: 906-482-0984. Fax: 906-482-8753.
E-mail: liz_valencia@nps.gov
Web Site: www.nps.gov/isro
Institution Type/Description: National Park & Historic Site: 1890 Edisen Commercial Fishery complex. Historic Structure: 1855 Rock Harbor Lighthouse. Park Museum: located in Houghton, MI.
Hours & Admission Prices: Rock Harbor Visitor Center: May-June & Sept. call for hours; July-Aug. daily 8-6. Windigo Visitor Center May-June & Sept. call for hours; July-Aug. daily 8-4:30. Houghton Visitor Center: call for hours. Museum: by appointment. No charge; donations accepted.
Attendance: 2,000 (estimated)

Imlay City

IMLAY CITY HISTORICAL COMMISSION, INC., 77 Main St., Imlay City, MI 48444-1313. Tel.: 810-724-1111.
E-mail: bswihart1904@charter.net
Key Personnel: Pres. (V), Carla Jepsen; Museum Shop Mgr., Marilyn Swichart.
Institution Type/Description: History Museum: housed in the Grand Truck Depot.
Hours & Admission Prices: April-Dec. Wed. 9 to noon, Sat. 1-4. No charge; donations accepted. ♿
Attendance: 1,000 (actual)

Ironwood

IRONWOOD AREA HISTORICAL MUSEUM, 150 N. Lowell St., Ironwood, MI 49938-2032. Mailing Address: P.O. Box 553, Ironwood, MI 49938-0553. Tel.: 906-932-0287.
E-mail: ironwoodhistoricalsociety@gmail.com
Key Personnel: Dir., Gary Harrington.
Institution Type/Description: History Museum: housed in former Chicago & Northwestern Depot.
Hours & Admission Prices: Memorial Day to Labor Day Mon.-Sat. 12-4; Sept.-May by appointment. No charge; donations accepted. Closed Independence Day. ♿
Attendance: 2,000 (estimated)

Ishpeming

U.S. SKI & SNOWBOARD HALL OF FAME, 610 Palms, Ishpeming, MI 49849-1035. Mailing Address: P.O. Box 191, Ishpeming, MI 49849-0191. Tel.: 906-485-6323. Fax: 906-486-4570.
E-mail: twest@skihall.com
Web Site: www.skihall.org
Formerly: U.S. National Ski and Snowboard Hall of Fame & Museum
Key Personnel: C.E.O., J. Thomas West; Chm. (V), Tom Kelly; Admin., Ann Schroeder; Chm., Bernie Weichsel; Museum Shop Mgr., Bob Hendrickson.
Institution Type/Description: Sports Museum.
Hours & Admission Prices: Mon.-Sat. 10-5. No charge; donations accepted. Closed New Year's Day; Independence Day; Thanksgiving; Christmas. ♿
Attendance: 10,000 (estimated)

Ithaca

GRATIOT COUNTY GENEALOGICAL LIBRARY, 228 W. Center St., Ithaca, MI 48847. Mailing Address: Gratiot County Historical & Genealogical Society, P.O. Box 73, Ithaca, MI 48847. Tel.: 989-875-6232.
E-mail: carol@gchgs.org
Institution Type/Description: Genealogical Library: housed in the Peet/Miller house.
Hours & Admission Prices: May-Sept. Tues. 1-5, last Tues. each month 1-8; Oct.-April Tues. 1-5. Closed New Year's Day; Christmas.

GRATIOT COUNTY HISTORICAL MUSEUM, 129 W. Center St., Ithaca, MI 48847. Mailing Address: Gratiot County Historical & Genealogical Society, P.O. Box 73, Ithaca, MI 48847. Tel.: 989-463-5896.
E-mail: johnkemler@gmail.com
Web Site: gchgs.org
Key Personnel: Dir., John Kemler; Dir., Linda Weburg.
Institution Type/Description: Historical Society Museum: housed in a Victorian-style house; built in 1881. Listed on the National Register of Historic Places.
Hours & Admission Prices: mid-May to Oct. Wed. 1-4. No charge; donations accepted. ♿
Attendance: 300 (estimated)

Jackson

ELLA SHARP MUSEUM, 3225 Fourth St, Jackson, MI 49203-5094. Tel.: 517-787-2320. Fax: 517-787-2933. Facebook: Ella Sharp Museum.
E-mail: info@ellasharp.org
Web Site: www.ellasharp.org
Key Personnel: Exec. Dir., Amy Reimann; Dir. Collections, Judy Horn; Museum Shop Mgr., Florence Csage.
Institution Type/Description: Art & History Museum.
Hours & Admission Prices: Tues.-Wed. & Fri.-Sat. 10-5, Thurs. 10-7. Galleries: Adults $5, children 5-12 $3; Galleries & tour Adults $7, children 5-12 $5; discounts to AAA, NARM & Public Broadcasting members; members & military no charge. Closed major holidays. ♿
Attendance: 20,000 (estimated)

K.I. Sawyer AFB

K.I. SAWYER HERITAGE AIR MUSEUM, 402 3rd St., K.I. Sawyer AFB, MI 49841. Tel.: 906-362-3531. Facebook: KI Sawyer Heritage Air Museum.
E-mail: bvick37@gmail.com
Web Site: www.kishamuseum.org
Key Personnel: Pres., C.E.O. & Museum Shop Mgr., Robert H. Vick.
Institution Type/Description: Military History Museum.
Hours & Admission Prices: Museum & Community Center Wed.-Sun. 1-5 year round. No charge.
Attendance: 500 (estimated)

Kalamazoo

AIR ZOO, 6151 Portage Rd., Kalamazoo, MI 49002-3003. Tel.: 269-382-6555, 866-524-7966 (Toll Free). Fax: 269-382-1044.
E-mail: airzoo@airzoo.org
Web Site: www.airzoo.org
Formerly: Kalamazoo Aviation History Museum
Key Personnel: Pres. & C.E.O., Troy A. Thrash; Chm. Bd., Donald Parfet; Cur. & Registrar, Laurie Burkhardt; Dir. Operations, Kim Robinson; Dir. Mktg., Patrick Brent; Volunteer & Membership Mgr., Tamra Stafford; Librarian, Carol Smith; Museum Store Mgr., Meredith Martin; Sr. Cur. Aircraft, Greg Ward.
Institution Type/Description: Aviation Museum.
Hours & Admission Prices: Mon.-Sat. 9-5, Sun. 12-5. Adults $13.50, youth $12.50, seniors $10.50, additional fees for rides & attractions; discounts to veterans, groups & AZ members. Closed Thanksgiving; Christmas Eve & Day. ♿
Attendance: 136,300 (actual)

ALAMO TOWNSHIP MUSEUM-JOHN E. GRAY MEMORIAL MUSEUM, 8119 N. 6th St., Kalamazoo, MI 49009-8808. Mailing Address: 7180 N. 2nd St., Kalamazoo, MI 49009-8814. Tel.: 269-344-2107.
E-mail: williamsmichigan@earthlink.net
Web Site: home.earthlink.net/~tommaas/Alamo_Township_museum.htm
Key Personnel: Cur., Brian Smith.
Institution Type/Description: Historic House: built in 1865 as a Presbyterian Church.
Hours & Admission Prices: May-Oct. Tues. 1-3, Sat.-Sun. 2-4; groups by appointment. No charge; donations accepted. ♿
Attendance: 5,000 (estimated)

KALAMAZOO INSTITUTE OF ARTS, 314 S. Park St., Kalamazoo, MI 49007-5102. Tel.: 269-349-7775, ext. 3001. Fax: 269-349-9313.
E-mail: museum@kiarts.org
Web Site: www.kiarts.org
Key Personnel: Exec. Dir., Belinda Tate; Dir. Finance & Personnel, George Baltmanis; Dir. Devel., Joe Bower; Dir. Museum Education, Susan Eckhardt; Dir. Advancement, Cindy Kole; Registrar, Corey Gross; Museum Shop Mgr., Karyn Juergens.
Institution Type/Description: Art Museum/Center & School. Focus: American Art.
Hours & Admission Prices: Tues.-Wed. & Sat. 11-5, Thurs. & Fri.11-8, Sun. 12-5. Adults $5, students $2; members, youth 12 & under, school groups & military no charge. Closed major holidays. ♿
Attendance: 109,000 (actual)

KALAMAZOO NATURE CENTER, INC., 7000 N. Westnedge Ave., Kalamazoo, MI 49009-6309. Tel.: 269-381-1574. Fax: 269-381-2557.
E-mail: lpanich@naturecenter.org
Web Site: www.naturecenter.org

Key Personnel: C.E.O. & Pres., Willard M. Rose, Ph.D.; COO, Jenn Wright; Dir. Finance, Tina Adams; Dir. Camps, Lauren Lott; Dir. Exhibits & Public Programs, Emma Vasicek; Dir. School Programs, Jay Tatara; Vice Pres. Devel., Rayline Manni; Dir. Communications, Lisa Panich; Events Mgr., Rose Norwood.
Institution Type/Description: Nature Center.
Hours & Admission Prices: Mon.-Sat. 9-5, Sun. 1-5. Adults $7, senior citizens $6, children 4-17 $4; discounts to AAM members; members & children 3 & under no charge. Closed New Year's Day; Independence Day; Thanksgiving; Christmas Eve & Day. &
Attendance: 265,995 (actual)

KALAMAZOO VALLEY MUSEUM, 230 N. Rose St., Kalamazoo, MI 49007-5803. Mailing Address: P.O. Box 4070, Kalamazoo, MI 49003-4070. Tel.: 269-373-7990, 800-772-3370. Fax: 269-373-7997.
E-mail: museumstaff@kvcc.edu
Web Site: www.kalamazoomuseum.org
Key Personnel: Dir., Bill McElhone; Asst. Dir., Education, Lexie Schroeder Kobb; Asst. Dir. Material Culture, Tammy Barnes; Exhibits Tech., Zak Hemsteger; Exhibits Tech., Tom Howes; Coord. Programs, Annette Hoppenworth; Museum Support Specialist, Elizabeth Barker; Coord. Science/STEM/Education, Kathy Godin; Admin. Asst., Lindsay Baker; Design Asst., Alecia Cross; Coord. Interpretation, Megan O'Kon; Weekend Supvr. & Prog. Asst., Anna Koenig.
Institution Type/Description: Participatory Museum: history, science & technology.
Hours & Admission Prices: Mon.-Sat. 9-5, Sun. & holidays 1-5. General Admission: no charge. Closed Easter; Thanksgiving; Christmas Eve & Day. &
Attendance: 122,000 (actual)

WESTERN MICHIGAN UNIVERSITY RICHMOND CENTER FOR VISUAL ARTS - GWEN FROSTIC SCHOOL OF ART, 1903 W. Michigan Ave., Kalamazoo, MI 49008-5213. Tel.: 269-387-2455. Fax: 269-387-2477.
E-mail: donald.desmett@wmich.edu
Key Personnel: C.E.O. College of Fine Arts, Dean Dan Guyette; Dir. School of Art, Tricia Hennessy; Dir. Exhibitions, Don Desmett; Cur. University Art Collection, Milinda Bagnall.
Institution Type/Description: Art Galleries.
Hours & Admission Prices: May-July Mon.-Fri. 10-5; Sept.-April Mon.-Thurs. 10-6, Fri. 10-9, Sat. 12-6. No charge; donations accepted. &
Attendance: 8,000 (actual)

Kaleva

BOTTLE HOUSE MUSEUM, 14551 Wuoksi Ave., Kaleva, MI 49645-9341. Mailing Address: P.O. Box 252, Kaleva, MI 49645-0252. Tel.: 231-362-2080. allartsmanistee.com.
E-mail: caasiala@jackpine.com
Web Site: kalevami.com
Key Personnel: Chm. & Pres. (V), Cynthia Asiala.
Institution Type/Description: Historic House: housed in a home built in 1941 with over 60,000 soft drink bottles.
Hours & Admission Prices: Memorial Day to Labor Day Sat.-Sun. 12-4; Sept.-Oct. Sat. 12-4. Suggested Donation: adults $3.
Attendance: 1,500 (estimated)

KALEVA DEPOT RAILROAD MUSEUM, 14420 Walta St., Kaleva, MI 49645. Mailing Address: P.O. Box 252, Kaleva, MI 49645. Tel.: 231-362-3480, 2080 & 3481 (summer).
E-mail: caasiala@jackpine.com
Web Site: kalevami.com
Formerly: Kaleva Train Depot Museum
Key Personnel: Chm. (V), Cynthia Asiala.
Institution Type/Description: Historic Building: housed in a former railroad depot; built in 1908.
Hours & Admission Prices: Memorial Day to Labor Day Sat. 12-4. No charge; donations accepted. &
Attendance: 200 (estimated)

Lake Linden

HOUGHTON COUNTY HISTORICAL MUSEUM SOCIETY, 53102 Hwy. M-26, Lake Linden, MI 49945. Mailing Address: P.O. Box 127, Lake Linden, MI 49945-0127. Tel.: 906-296-4121. Fax: 906-296-8006.
E-mail: president@houghtonhistory.org
Web Site: www.houghtonhistory.org
Institution Type/Description: History Museum: located on Calumet & Hecla Millsite.

Hours & Admission Prices: Office: Mon.-Fri. 10-12. Museum: call for hours. Adults $5, seniors & students 6-16 $3; members no charge. Train Rides: adults $5, students 6-16 & seniors $3. &
Attendance: 10,000 (estimated)

Lansing

CARL G. FENNER NATURE CENTER, 2020 E. Mt. Hope Rd., Lansing, MI 48910-1905. Tel.: 517-483-4224. Fax: 517-377-0012. TDD: 517-483-4479.
E-mail: info@mynaturecenter.org
Web Site: www.mynaturecenter.org
Key Personnel: Exec. Dir., Jason Meyer; Program Mgr., Katie Woodhams; Naturalist, Andrea Lazzari; Volunteer Coord., Dani Torcolacci.
Institution Type/Description: Natural History Museum.
Hours & Admission Prices: Grounds: daily 8am-dark. Visitor Center: Wed.-Fri. 10-4, Sat.-Sun. 12-4. No charge. Closed holidays. &
Attendance: 40,000 (estimated)

IMPRESSION 5 SCIENCE CENTER, 200 Museum Dr., Lansing, MI 48933-1914. Tel.: 517-485-8116, ext. 132. Facebook.
E-mail: zeller@impression5.org
Web Site: www.impression5.org
Key Personnel: Exec. Dir., Erik D. Larson; Dir. Innovation & Learning, Micaela Balzer; Dir. Communications, Laura Zeller; Exhibit Futurist, Cyrus Miller.
Institution Type/Description: Interactive Hands-On Learning Center.
Hours & Admission Prices: Tues.-Sat. 10-5, Sun. 12-5. Adults & children 2 & over $8.50; seniors & military families $7; discounts to groups with advance reservation; children under 2, ASTC & museum members no charge. Closed New Year's Day; Easter; Memorial Day; Independence Day; Thanksgiving; Christmas Eve & Day. &
Attendance: 161,207 (actual)

LANSING ART GALLERY & EDUCATION CENTER, 119 N. Washington Sq., Lansing, MI 48933. Tel.: 517-374-6400. Fax: 517-374-6385. Facebook: @LansingArtGallery; Twitter: @LansingArtGall.
E-mail: barb@lansingartgallery.org
Web Site: lansingartgallery.org
Key Personnel: Exec. Dir., Barb Whitney; Gallery Coord., Sara Pulver; Education Coord., Sydney Richards.
Institution Type/Description: Art Gallery.
Hours & Admission Prices: Tues.-Fri. 11-6, Sat. & 1st Sun. of month 11-3. No charge; donations accepted. Closed holiday weekends. &
Attendance: 25,000 (estimated)

MICHIGAN HISTORICAL MUSEUM, MICHIGAN HISTORICAL CENTER, 702 W. Kalamazoo, Lansing, MI 48909-8240. Mailing Address: P.O. Box 30740, Lansing, MI 48909-8240. Tel.: 517-373-3559. Fax: 517-241-4738. TDD: 1-800-827-7007.
E-mail: archives@michigan.gov
Web Site: www.michigan.gov/museum
Key Personnel: C.E.O., Sandra S. Clark.
Institution Type/Description: History Museum.
Hours & Admission Prices: Mon.-Fri. 9-4:30, Sat. 10-4, Sun. 1-5. Adults $6, seniors $4, youth 6-17 $2; children 5 & under no charge. Field Museums & Historic Sites: call for information. Closed New Year's Day; Christmas; state holidays. &
Attendance: 87,574 (actual)

MICHIGAN STATE CAPITOL, 100 N. Capitol Ave., Lansing, MI 48933. Mailing Address: Michigan Capitol Facilities, P.O. Box 30014, Lansing, MI 48909. Tel.: 517-373-2348 & 2353. Fax: 517-373-7599. Facebook: @MIStateCapitol.
E-mail: capitolfacilities@legislature.mi.gov
Web Site: capitol.michigan.gov
Key Personnel: Dir. Capitol Operations, Robert Blackshaw; Capitol Historian, Valerie Marvin; Dir. Capitol Tour & Information, Matt VanAcker.
Institution Type/Description: Historic Building: built in 1879. A National Historic Landmark.
Hours & Admission Prices: Self-Guided Tours: Mon.-Fri. 8-5. Guided Tours: Mon.-Fri. 9-4; groups of 10 or more by appointment. No charge. &
Attendance: 125,000 (actual)

MICHIGAN WOMEN'S HISTORICAL CENTER & HALL OF FAME, 213 W. Malcolm X St., Lansing, MI 48933-2315. Tel.: 517-484-1880. Fax: 517-372-0170. Facebook: Michigan Women's Hall of Fame.
E-mail: info@michiganwomen.org

Web Site: www.michiganwomenshalloffame.org
Key Personnel: Exec. Dir., Dr Caitlyn Perry Dial.
Institution Type/Description: Women's History Museum & Hall of Fame.
Hours & Admission Prices: Wed.-Sat. 12-4, 1st Sun. each month 2-4; groups by appointment. Adults $3; students 6-18 $2; discounts to AAM & ICOM members; members & children under 5 no charge. Closed major holidays. &
Attendance: 2,500 (estimated)

POTTER PARK ZOO, 1301 S. Pennsylvania Ave., Lansing, MI 48912-1646. Tel.: 517-483-4222. Fax: 517-483-3894.
E-mail: zoocontact@ingham.org
Web Site: www.potterparkzoo.org
Key Personnel: Cur., Cynthia Wagner.
Institution Type/Description: Zoo.
Hours & Admission Prices: April to Labor Day daily 9-6; Sept.-Oct. Mon.-Fri. 9-4, Sat.-Sun. 9-6; Nov.-March daily 10-4. Residents: adults $4, senior citizens 60 & over $3, children 3-12 $2; Non-Resident: adults $10, senior citizens 60 & up $8, children 3-16 $2; members & children under 3 no charge. &
Attendance: 380,000

R.E. OLDS TRANSPORTATION MUSEUM, 240 Museum Dr., Lansing, MI 48933-1905. Tel.: 517-372-0529. Fax: 517-372-2901. Facebook: R.E. Olds Transportation Museum.
E-mail: autos@reoldsmuseum.org
Web Site: reoldsmuseum.org
Key Personnel: Dir., William Adcock; Pres. (V), J.T. March; Mgr., Kristi Schwartzly.
Institution Type/Description: Transportation Museum.
Hours & Admission Prices: April-Oct. Tues.-Sat. 10-5, Sun. 12-5; Nov.-March Tues.-Sat. 10-5. Family of 5 children under 18 $15, adults $7, senior citizens, veterans & students $5; discounts for groups; members no charge. Closed major holidays. &
Attendance: 15,000 (estimated)

WOLDUMAR NATURE CENTER, 5739 Old Lansing Rd., Lansing, MI 48917-8503. Tel.: 517-322-0030. Fax: 517-322-9394. Facebook: Woldumar.
E-mail: lori@woldumar.org
Web Site: www.woldumar.org
Key Personnel: Exec. Dir., Lori McSweeney.
Institution Type/Description: Nature Center Conservation Area & Historic Building.
Hours & Admission Prices: Visitors Center: Tues.-Sat. 10-5 & Sun. 12-4. Office: Mon.-Fri. 9-5. Trails: dawn-dark. Donation: $1 per person; discounts to ANCA members & groups; members no charge. Closed New Year's Day; Easter weekend; Memorial Day weekend; Labor Day weekend; Thanksgiving; Christmas. &
Attendance: 40,000 (estimated)

Leland

LEELANAU HISTORICAL MUSEUM, 203 E. Cedar St., Leland, MI 49654-5015. Mailing Address: P.O. Box 246, Leland, MI 49654-0246. Tel.: 231-256-7475. Facebook: Leelanau Historical Museum.
E-mail: info@leelanauhistory.org
Web Site: www.leelanauhistory.org
Key Personnel: Dir., Francie Gits; Pres. (V), Tom Reahard; Pres. (V), Cathy Reahard.
Institution Type/Description: Local History Museum.
Hours & Admission Prices: May 15-Oct. 15; Wed.-Fri. 10-4, Sat. 10-3. Adult $2. &
Attendance: 5,000 (estimated)

Lincoln Park

LINCOLN PARK HISTORICAL MUSEUM, 1335 Southfield Rd., Lincoln Park, MI 48146-2370. Tel.: 313-386-3137.
E-mail: curator@lphistorical.org
Web Site: www.lphistorical.org
Key Personnel: Dir., Muriel Lobb; Pres., Jim Nelson; Cur., Jeff Day; Museum Shop Mgr., Lucille Stroh.
Institution Type/Description: Local & Regional History Museum: housed in former U.S. Post Office building; built in 1938.
Hours & Admission Prices: Wed.-Thurs. & Sat. 1-5; other times by appointment. No charge; donations accepted. Closed New Year's Day; Martin Luther King Jr. Day; Easter; Memorial Day; Independence Day; Thanksgiving; Christmas. &
Attendance: 6,500 (estimated)

Lowell

JAMES C. VEEN OBSERVATORY OF THE GRAND RAPIDS AMATEUR ASTRONOMICAL ASSOCIATION, 3308 Kissing Rock Ave., S.E., Lowell, MI 49331-8918. Tel.: 616-897-7065.
E-mail: graaa@graaa.org
Web Site: www.graaa.org
Key Personnel: Dir., David L. DeBruyn.
Institution Type/Description: Observatory.
Hours & Admission Prices: April-Oct. call for hours. Adults $3; discounts to Grand Rapids Public Museum Friend members.
Attendance: 1,500 (estimated)

LOWELL AREA HISTORICAL MUSEUM, 325 W. Main St., Lowell, MI 49331-1609. Mailing Address: P.O. Box 81, Lowell, MI 49331-0081. Tel.: 616-897-7688. Fax: 616-897-7688. Facebook: Lowell Area Historical Museum.
E-mail: history@lowellmuseum.org
Web Site: lowellmuseum.org
Key Personnel: C.E.O. & Dir., Lisa Plank; Pres., James M. Doyle; Education, Luanne Kaeb; Treas., Cathy Haefner.
Institution Type/Description: History Museum: listed on the National Register of Historic Places.
Hours & Admission Prices: Tues. & Sat.-Sun. 1-4, Thurs. 1-8. Adults $3, students & children $1.50; discounts to groups; members no charge. Closed holidays. &
Attendance: 20,000 (estimated)

Ludington

MASON COUNTY HISTORICAL SOCIETY/HISTORIC WHITE PINE VILLAGE, 1687 S. Lakeshore Dr., Ludington, MI 49431-8316. Tel.: 231-843-4808. Fax: 231-843-7089.
E-mail: info@historicwhitepinevillage.org
Web Site: www.historicwhitepinevillage.org
Key Personnel: Exec. Dir., Kate J. Arbogast; Pres. Bd. (V), Dr. William Anderson; Asst. to Exec. Dir., Carmen Tiffany.
Institution Type/Description: Local History Museum & Reconstructed Historical Village.
Hours & Admission Prices: mid-April to May & Sept. to mid-Oct. Tues.-Sat. 10-5; Memorial Day to Labor Day Tues.-Sat. 10-5, Sun. 1-5. Families $25, adults $9, children 6-17 $6; discounts to AAA members, seniors & Great Lakes Energy Co-op cardholders; children 5 & under and MCHS members no charge. Additional charge for special events & food events. &
Attendance: 18,000 (actual)

Mackinac Island

MACKINAC STATE HISTORIC PARKS-FORT MACKINAC & MACKINAC ISLAND STATE PARK, 7029 Huron Rd., Mackinac Island, MI 49757. Mailing Address: P.O. Box 873, Mackinaw City, MI 49701-0873. Tel.: 906-847-3328 (Summer), 231-436-4100 (Winter). Fax: 231-436-4210. Facebook.
E-mail: mackinacparks@michigan.gov
Web Site: www.mackinacparks.com
Key Personnel: Dir., Phil Porter; Chm. (V), Chuck Yob; Park Mgr., Sue Topham; Deputy Dir., Steven C. Brisson; Cur. Archaeology, Lynn Evans; Cur. Natural History, Jeffrey A. Dykehouse; Cur. Education, Katherine Mallory; Public Rels. & Mktg. Officer, Kelsey Schnell; Registrar, Brian Jaeschke; Grant Writer & Membership, Diane A. Dombroski; Group Sales Coord., Dominick Miller; Chief Finance & Accounting, Nancy A. Stempky; Exhibit Designer, Keeney Swearer; Museum Shop Mgr., Suzette Schmalzried; Human Resources Coord., Kenneth Fegan.
Institution Type/Description: Historic Site: 1780-1895 Fort Mackinac.
Hours & Admission Prices: Mackinac Island State Park: daily. No charge. Fort Mackinac: May-Oct. daily 9:30-6; Spring & Fall call for reduced hours. Adults $12, children 6-17 $7; discounts to AAM & ICOM members; members & children 5 & under no charge. &
Attendance: 207,000 (actual)

MACKINAC STATE HISTORIC PARKS - RICHARD & JANE MANOOGIAN MACKINAC ART MUSEUM, Huron Rd., Mackinac Island, MI 49757. Mailing Address: P.O. Box 873, Mackinaw City, MI 49701-0873. Tel.: 906-847-3328 (summer), 231-436-4100. Fax: 231-436-4210. Facebook.
E-mail: mackinacparks@michigan.gov
Web Site: www.mackinacparks.com
Key Personnel: Dir., Phil Porter; Chm. (V), Chuck Yob; Deputy Dir., Steven C. Brisson; Park Mgr., Sue Topham; Registrar, Brian Jaeschke; Cur. Education, Katherine Mallory; Exhibit Designer, Keeney Swearer; Museum Historian,

Craig Wilson; Cur. Archaeology, Lynn Evans; Museum Shop Mgr., Suzette Schmalzried; Grant Writer & Membership, Diane A. Dombroski.

Institution Type/Description: Art Museum: housed in a former Federal Indian Dormitory; built in 1838.

Hours & Admission Prices: early May to early Oct. daily 10-5:30; Spring & Fall: call for hours. Adults $5.50, children 6-17 $4; members and children 5 & under no charge. Fort Mackinac tickets accepted. &

Attendance: 16,466 (actual)

STUART HOUSE CITY MUSEUM, 7342 Market St., Mackinac Island, MI 49757-0906. Tel.: 906-847-8181.

Web Site: www.mightymac.org/stuarthousecitymuseum.htm

Key Personnel: Dir., Armand Horn.

Institution Type/Description: Historic House Museum: c.1817 home of American Fur Company resident Mgr. Robert Stuart.

Hours & Admission Prices: Early May to mid-Oct. 10-4. No charge; donations accepted.

Mackinaw City

MACKINAC ISLAND STATE PARK COMMISSION-MACKINAC STATE HISTORIC PARKS, 207 W. Sinclair Ave., Mackinaw City, MI 49701-9635. Mailing Address: P.O. Box 873, Mackinaw City, MI 49701-0873. Tel.: 231-436-4100, 906-847-3328. Fax: 231-436-4210, 906-847-3815. Facebook.

E-mail: mackinacparks@michigan.gov

Web Site: www.mackinacparks.com

Key Personnel: Dir., Phil Porter; Commission Chm. (V), Chuck Yob; Deputy Dir., Steven Brisson; Cur. Education, Katherine Mallory; Cur. Archaeology, Lynn Evans; Registrar, Brian Jaeschke; Museum Historian, Craig Wilson; Cur. Natural History, Jeffrey A. Dykehouse; Public Rels. & Mktg. Officer, Kelsey Schnell; Group Sales Coord., Dominick Miller; Chief Finance & Accounting, Nancy Stempky; Museum Shop Mgr., Suzette Schmalzried; Grant Writer & Membership, Diane A. Dombroski; Exhibit Designer, Keeney Swearer; Human Resources Coord., Kenneth Fegan.

Institution Type/Description: Regional History Museum.

Hours & Admission Prices: Mackinac Island State Park: daily. Historic Sites: early May to mid-Oct. daily. Park: no charge. Historic Sites: adults $6-$12. &

Attendance: 375,239 (actual)

MACKINAC STATE HISTORIC PARKS-COLONIAL MICHILIMACKINAC & OLD MACKINAC POINT LIGHTHOUSE, 102 W. Straits Ave., Mackinaw City, MI 49701. Mailing Address: Box 873, Mackinaw City, MI 49701-0873. Tel.: 231-436-4100. Fax: 231-436-4210. Facebook.

E-mail: mackinacparks@michigan.gov

Web Site: www.mackinacparks.com

Key Personnel: Dir., Phil Porter; Park Supvr., Michael Sutton; Commission Chm. (V), Chuck Yob; Deputy Dir., Steven C. Brisson; Cur. Education, Katherine Mallory; Registrar, Brian Jaeschke; Museum Historian, Craig Wilson; Public Rels. & Mktg. Officer, Kelsey Schnell; Cur. Archaeology, Lynn Evans; Cur. Natural History, Jeffrey A. Dykehouse; Groups Sales Coord., Dominick Miller; Chief Finance & Accounting, Nancy A. Stempky; Grant Writer & Membership, Diane A. Dombroski; Exhibit Designer, Keeney Swearer; Museum Shop Mgr., Suzette Schmalzried; Human Resources Coord., Kenneth Fegan.

Institution Type/Description: History Museum: housed in reconstructed French & British military outpost & fur-trading village founded in 1715.

Hours & Admission Prices: May-Oct. daily 9-6; Fall & Spring: call for reduced hours. Colonial Michilimackinac: adult $11, children 6-17 $6.50; discount to AAM & ICOM members; members & children under 5 no charge. Lighthouse: adult $6, children $4. &

Attendance: 110,771 (actual)

MACKINAC STATE HISTORIC PARKS-HISTORIC MILL CREEK DISCOVERY PARK, 9001 U.S. 23 S., Mackinaw City, MI 49701. Mailing Address: Box 873, Mackinaw City, MI 49701-0873. Tel.: 231-436-4100. Fax: 231-436-4210. Facebook.

E-mail: mackinacparks@michigan.gov

Web Site: www.mackinacparks.com

Key Personnel: Commission Chm., Chuck Yob; Dir., Phil Porter; Deputy Dir., Steven C. Brisson; Cur. Education, Katherine Mallory; Registrar, Brian Jaeschke; Cur. Natural History, Jeffrey A. Dykehouse; Cur. Archaeology, Lynn Evans; Public Rels. & Mktg. Officer, Kelsey Schnell; Group Sales Coord., Dominick Miller; Chief Finance & Accounting, Lana L. Cotton; Museum Shop Mgr., Suzette Schmalzried; Park Supvr., Michael Sutton; Human Resources Coord., Kenneth Fegan; Exhibit Designer, Keeney Swearer.

Institution Type/Description: History Site Museum: reconstructed 18th-century water-powered sawmill and support buildings.

Hours & Admission Prices: May to mid-Oct. daily 9-5; Spring & fall: call for hours. Adults $8, children 6-17 $4.75; members & children under 6 no charge. &

Attendance: 38,865 (actual)

Manistee

MANISTEE COUNTY HISTORICAL MUSEUM, 425 River St., Manistee, MI 49660-1522. Tel.: 231-723-5531.

E-mail: manisteemuseum@yahoo.com

Web Site: www.manisteemuseum.org

Key Personnel: Dir., Mark Fedder.

Institution Type/Description: History Museum: housed in 1883 A.H. Lyman Drug Company.

Hours & Admission Prices: Jan.-April Thurs.-Sat. 10-5; May & Oct.-Dec. Tues.-Sat. 10-5; June-Sept. Mon.-Sat. 10-5. Families $7, adults $3, students $1. Closed national holidays except Independence Day.

Attendance: 7,000 (estimated)

Manistique

SCHOOLCRAFT COUNTY HISTORICAL SOCIETY, Deer St., Pioneer Park, Manistique, MI 49854. Mailing Address: P.O. Box 284, Manistique, MI 49854-0284. Tel.: 906-341-5045.

E-mail: m085@centurytel.net

Formerly: Imogene-Herbert Historical Museum

Key Personnel: Pres. (V), M. Vonciel Le Duc; Vice Pres., Paul Walker; Treas., Darlene Furmanek.

Institution Type/Description: Local History Museum.

Hours & Admission Prices: June-Sept. Wed.-Sat. 1-4. Adults $1, children $.50; members no charge.

Attendance: 500 (estimated)

Marine City

COMMUNITY PRIDE & HERITAGE MUSEUM, 405 S. Main St., Marine City, MI 48039-1634. Mailing Address: P.O. Box 184, Marine City, MI 48039-0184. Tel.: 810-765-5446.

E-mail: marinecitymuseum@hotmail.com

Web Site: www.marinecitymuseum.org

Formerly: Marine City Pride & Heritage Museum

Key Personnel: Dir. (V), John Foley; Pres. (V), Gary Beals.

Institution Type/Description: History Museum.

Hours & Admission Prices: June-Oct. Sat.-Sun. 1-4; tours by appointment. No charge; donations accepted. &

Attendance: 300 (estimated)

THE LESTER HOUSE, 406 S. Main St., Marine City, MI 48039-1628. Mailing Address: 325 E. St. Clair St., Marine City, MI 48039. Tel.: 810-765-5912. Fax: 810-765-5916.

E-mail: contact@visitlesterhouse.com

Web Site: www.visitlesterhouse.com

Institution Type/Description: Historic House: former home of Captain David Lester.

Hours & Admission Prices: Tours: May-Sept. by appointment. Tour: adults $5.

Attendance: 250 (estimated)

Marquette

THE DEVOS ART MUSEUM AT NORTHERN MICHIGAN UNIVERSITY, 1401 Presque Isle Ave., Marquette, MI 49855-5305. Tel.: 906-227-1481. Fax: 906-227-2276.

E-mail: mmatusca@nmu.edu

Web Site: art.nmu.edu/devosartmuseum

Key Personnel: Dir. & Cur., Melissa Matuscak.

Institution Type/Description: University Art Museum.

Hours & Admission Prices: Mon.-Wed. & Fri. 10-5, Thurs. 12-8, Sat.-Sun. 1-4. No charge; donations accepted. Closed New Year's Eve & Day; Independence Day; Memorial Day; Christmas Eve, Day & week. &

Attendance: 10,000 (actual)

MARQUETTE REGIONAL HISTORY CENTER, 145 W. Spring St., Marquette, MI 49855-4220. Tel.: 906-226-3571. Fax: 906-226-0919. Facebook: Marquette Regional History Center.

E-mail: mrhc@marquettehistory.org

Web Site: marquettehistory.org

Formerly: Marquette County History Museum

Key Personnel: Bd. Pres., James Paquette; Exec. Dir. & Dir. Devel., Cris Osier; Business Mgr., Jennifer Naze; Research Librarian, Rosemary Michelin; Cur., Jo Wittler.

Institution Type/Description: History Museum.

Hours & Admission Prices: Mon.-Tues. & Thurs.-Fri. 10-5, Wed. 10-8, Sat. 10-3. Adults $7, seniors $6, students 12 & over $3, children $2; members no charge. Closed legal holidays. &

Attendance: 9,100 (actual)

UPPER PENINSULA CHILDREN'S MUSEUM, 123 W. Baraga Ave., Marquette, MI 49855-4744. Tel.: 906-226-3911. Fax: 906-226-7065.
E-mail: nittner@chartermi.net
Web Site: www.upcmkids.org
Key Personnel: Dir., Nheena Weyer Ittner; Dir. 8-18 Media, Dennis Whitley; Explainers Dir. & Gen. Programming Mgr., Jim Edwards; Mgr. Facilities & Exhibits, Aaron Sault.
Institution Type/Description: Children's Museum.
Hours & Admission Prices: Mon.-Wed. & Sat. 10-6, Thurs. 10-7:30, Fri. 10-8, Sun. 12-5. Adults & children $5; discounts to Art Serve Michigan, MEA & AAA members. &
Attendance: 51,000

Marshall

THE AMERICAN MUSEUM OF MAGIC, INC., 107 E. Michigan, Marshall, MI 49068-1543. Mailing Address: P.O. Box 5, Marshall, MI 49068-0005. Tel.: 269-781-7570. Facebook: @AmericanMuseumOfMagic; Twitter: @ammusofmagic.
E-mail: ammuseumofmagic@yahoo.com
Web Site: americanmuseumofmagic.org
Formerly: American Museum of Magic & Lund Memorial Library, Inc.
Key Personnel: Pres. Bd. (V), Susan Collins; Dir., Keli Spears Hindenach.
Institution Type/Description: Magic Museum: housed in 1869 building.
Hours & Admission Prices: April-May Thurs.-Sat. 10-4, Sun. 2-4; June-Aug. Tues.-Sat. 10-4, Sun. 2-4; Sept.-Oct. Thurs.-Sat. 10-4, Sun. 2-4; other times by appointment. Adults $5, children 5-12 $3.50. Closed major holidays.
Attendance: 2,000 (actual)

GRAND ARMY OF THE REPUBLIC HALL MUSEUM, 402 E. Michigan Ave., Marshall, MI 49068. Mailing Address: 107 N. Kalamazoo Ave., Marshall, MI 49068. Tel.: 269-781-8544.
E-mail: info@marshallhistoricalsociety.org
Web Site: marshallhistoricalsociety.org
Institution Type/Description: Historic Building: housed in the meeting place for Marshall Civil War veterans; built in 1902.
Hours & Admission Prices: Call for hours.
Attendance: 100 (estimated)

HONOLULU HOUSE MUSEUM, 107 N. Kalamazoo Ave., Marshall, MI 49068-1526. Tel.: 269-781-8544.
E-mail: info@marshallhistoricalsociety.org
Web Site: www.marshallhistoricalsociety.org
Key Personnel: Pres. (V), Ann Rhodes.
Institution Type/Description: History Museum: c.1860 Honolulu House.
Hours & Admission Prices: May-Oct. daily 11-4:30. Admission $5; discounts may apply. &
Attendance: 3,600 (estimated)

Marysville

MARYSVILLE HISTORICAL MUSEUM, 887 E. Huron Blvd., Marysville, MI 48040-1573. Mailing Address: 111 Delaware Ave., Marysville, MI 48040. Tel.: 810-364-6613.
E-mail: rfernandez@cityofmarysvillemi.com
Web Site: www.cityofmarysvillemi.com/museum/index.htm
Key Personnel: Pres. (V), Kim Coggins.
Institution Type/Description: History Museum.
Hours & Admission Prices: June-Aug. Sun. 1:30-4. Suggested Donation: $1.
Attendance: 200 (estimated)

THE WILLS STE. CLAIRE AUTO MUSEUM, 2408 Wills St., Marysville, MI 48040-1978. Tel.: 810-987-2854.
E-mail: willsmuseum@sbcglobal.net
Web Site: www.willsautomuseum.org
Key Personnel: Dir., Terry Ernest; Sec., Pete Canjemi; Treas., Laurie Baker.
Institution Type/Description: Automobile Museum: former Dow Chemical munitions factory built during WWII.
Hours & Admission Prices: June-Aug. 2nd & 4th Sun. 1-5; Sept.-May 2nd Sun. 1-5. Adults $5. &

Mayville

MAYVILLE AREA MUSEUM OF HISTORY AND GENEALOGY, 2124 Ohmer Rd., Mayville, MI 48744. Mailing Address: P.O. Box 242, Mayville, MI 48744-0242. Tel.: 989-843-7185. Facebook: Mayville Museum.
E-mail: mayvillemuseum@hotmail.com

Key Personnel: Dir., Pres. & Cur., Frank E. Franzel, Sr.; Vice Pres., Ron Johnson; Sec. & Treas., Fran Campbell.
Institution Type/Description: History & Genealogy Museum.
Hours & Admission Prices: May to Labor Day Fri.-Sat. 10-4; other times by appointment. No charge; donations accepted. &
Attendance: 800 (estimated)

Menominee

MENOMINEE COUNTY HERITAGE MUSEUM, 904 11 Ave., Menominee, MI 49858-3044. Mailing Address: P.O. Box 151, Menominee, MI 49858-0151. Tel.: 906-863-9000.
E-mail: ambera@new.rr.com
Key Personnel: Dir., Michael Kaufman; Pres., Lou Ann Borski; Librarian, Amber Allard; Cur., Jeanette Stegeman.
Institution Type/Description: General Museum.
Hours & Admission Prices: Memorial Day-Sept. Mon.-Sat. 10-4. No charge; donations accepted.
Attendance: 2,000 (estimated)

Middleville

HISTORIC BOWENS MILLS & PIONEER PARK, 55 Briggs Rd., Middleville, MI 49333-9194. Tel.: 269-795-7530. Fax: 269-795-7530.
E-mail: carleen@bowensmills.com
Web Site: www.bowensmills.com
Key Personnel: Dir. Operations, Carleen Sabin; Dir. Operations, Owen Sabin.
Institution Type/Description: State Historic Site: 1864 water-powered grist & cider mill.
Hours & Admission Prices: May-Dec. by appointment. Mill or Festivals: $5. Horse-drawn rides with admission to Festivals.
Attendance: 30,000 (estimated)

Midland

ALDEN B. DOW HOME & STUDIO, 315 Post St., Midland, MI 48640-4099. Tel.: 989-839-2744, 866-315-7678 (Toll Free). Fax: 989-839-2611.
E-mail: info@abdow.org
Web Site: www.abdow.org
Key Personnel: House Mgr., Mary Lou Timmons.
Institution Type/Description: Historic House Museum: housed in the former home & architectural studio of 20th century architect Alden B. Dow. A National Historic Landmark.
Hours & Admission Prices: Mon.-Sat. 8-5. Tours: Mon.-Sat. 2pm, Fri.-Sat. 10am. Adults $10, students $5. Children under 8 not admitted. Closed major holidays.

ALDEN B. DOW MUSEUM OF SCIENCE AND ART OF THE MIDLAND CENTER FOR THE ARTS, 1801 W. St. Andrews Rd., Midland, MI 48640-2656. Tel.: 989-631-5930. Fax: 989-631-7890.
E-mail: info@mcfta.org
Web Site: www.mcfta.org
Formerly: Arts Midland: Galleries and School
Key Personnel: C.E.O. & Pres., Terri Trotter; Chm. (V), Al Blinke; Dir., Bruce Winslow; Exec. Asst. & Special Events Mgr., Eminor Mills; Museum School Education Mgr. & Artist-in-Residence, Armin Mersmann; Mgr. Educational Programming, Debbie Anderson; Education Asst., Sarah Brandt.
Institution Type/Description: Science & Art Museum and School.
Hours & Admission Prices: Tues.-Sat. 10-5, Sun. 1-5. Adults $9, children 4-14 $5; discounts to AAM members; members & children under 3 no charge. ASTC reciprocal. Closed major holidays. &
Attendance: 60,000

CHIPPEWA NATURE CENTER, 400 S. Badour Rd., Midland, MI 48640-8661. Tel.: 989-631-0830. Fax: 989-631-7070.
E-mail: dtouvell@chippewanaturecenter.org
Web Site: www.chippewanaturecenter.org
Key Personnel: Exec. Dir., Dick Touvell; Dir. Education, Rachel Latimore.
Institution Type/Description: Nature & Historical Center.
Hours & Admission Prices: Mon.-Sat 8-5, Sun. & holidays 12-5. No charge; donations accepted. Closed Thanksgiving; Christmas Eve afternoon & Christmas Day. &
Attendance: 50,000 (actual)

DOW GARDENS, 1809 Eastman Ave., Midland, MI 48640. Mailing Address: 1018 W. Main St., Midland, MI 48640-4292. Tel.: 989-631-2677, 800-362-4874. Fax: 989-631-0675.
E-mail: info@dowgardens.org

Web Site: www.dowgardens.org
Key Personnel: Mng. Dir., Ed Haycock; Dir. Visitors Center, Michelle Holmes.
Institution Type/Description: Botanical Garden: located on the Herbert H. Dow Estate.
Hours & Admission Prices: April 15-Labor Day: 9-8:30; Whiting Forest: 10-6; Sept. 4-Oct. 9-6:30; Whiting Forest: 10-5; Nov.-Jan.-April 14 9-4:15; Whiting Forest: 10-4. Adult $5, students 6-17 with college ID $1, children 5 & under no charge. Closed New Year's Eve & Day; Thanksgiving; Christmas Eve & Day. ර
Attendance: 260,500 (actual)

MIDLAND COUNTY HISTORICAL SOCIETY, 3417 W. Main St., Midland, MI 48640. Tel.: 989-631-5930, ext. 1300. Fax: 989-835-9120.
E-mail: skory@mcfta.org
Web Site: www.mcfta.org
Key Personnel: Chm., Bill Collins; Dir., Gary F. Skory; Special Events & Museum Asst., Stephanie Lewandowski.
Institution Type/Description: History Museum.
Hours & Admission Prices: History Center: Mon.-Fri. 8:30-5; Research Library: Tues.-Thurs. 1-4. No charge. Closed New Year's Day; Good Friday; Memorial Day; Thanksgiving; Christmas. ර
Attendance: 75,000 (estimated)

Milan

THE HACK HOUSE MUSEUM, 775 County St., Milan, MI 48160-9701. Mailing Address: Milan Area Historical Society, P.O. Box 245, Milan, MI 48160-0245. Tel.: 734-439-1664.
Web Site: www.historicmilan.com
Institution Type/Description: Historic House.
Hours & Admission Prices: May-Nov. Fri. 1-4. No charge; donations accepted.
Attendance: 600 (estimated)

Milford

KENSINGTON METROPARK NATURE CENTER, 2240 W. Buno Rd., Milford, MI 48380-4410. Tel.: 248-685-0603. Fax: 248-684-5836, 810-227-8917.
E-mail: jennifer.hollenbeck@metroparks.com
Web Site: www.metroparks.com
Key Personnel: Supervising Interpreter, Jennifer Hollenbeck; Park Interpreter, Michael Tucker; Park Interpreter, Michael Broughton; Interpreter, Laura Rogers; Interpreter, Andy Swift; Interpreter, Lynette Score.
Institution Type/Description: Nature Center.
Hours & Admission Prices: Mon. 1-5, Tues.-Sun. 10-5. Park: $30 annual; $7 daily. Closed Thanksgiving; Christmas. ර
Attendance: 337,497 (estimated)

MILFORD HISTORICAL MUSEUM, 124 E. Commerce St., Milford, MI 48381-5300. Tel.: 248-685-7308.
E-mail: milfordhistory@hotmail.com
Web Site: www.milfordhistory.org
Key Personnel: Dir., Elaine Hunter.
Institution Type/Description: Historical Society Museum: housed in 1853 Greek Revival House.
Hours & Admission Prices: May to mid-Dec. Wed. & Sat.-Sun. 1-4. No charge; donations accepted.
Attendance: 450 (estimated)

Mohawk

KEWEENAW COUNTY HISTORICAL SOCIETY, 670 Lighthouse Rd., Mohawk, MI 49950. Tel.: 906-289-4990 & 337-2244.
E-mail: aboggio@pasty.net
Web Site: www.keweenawhistory.org
Key Personnel: Pres. (V), Virginia Petermann Jamison.
Institution Type/Description: History Museum.
Hours & Admission Prices: mid-June to mid-Oct. daily 10-5. Adults $5; members and children 13 & under no charge. Group rates available.
Attendance: 10,119 (actual)

Monroe

MONROE COUNTY HISTORICAL MUSEUM, 126 S. Monroe St., Monroe, MI 48161-2275. Tel.: 734-240-7780. Fax: 734-240-7788.
E-mail: andy_clark@monroemi.org
Web Site: www.co.monroe.mi.us/museum

Key Personnel: Education Coord., Lynn Reaume; Archivist, Christine L. Kull; Dir., H. Andrew Clark.
Institution Type/Description: History Museum: housed on the site of Gen. George A. Custer home.
Hours & Admission Prices: Jan.-April Wed.-Sat. 10-5; May-Dec. Wed.-Sun. noon-5 (may be seasonal). Suggested donation: adult $4, child $2. Closed New Year's Day; Easter; Thanksgiving; Christmas; county holidays. ර
Attendance: 20,000 (actual)

MONROE COUNTY LABOR HISTORY MUSEUM, 41 W. Front St., Monroe, MI 48161. Tel.: 734-693-0446.
E-mail: lwconnerjr@mail.com
Web Site: www.monroelabor.org
Key Personnel: Pres., Bill Conner.
Institution Type/Description: Labor History Museum.
Hours & Admission Prices: Mon.-Fri. 9-5; other times by appointment. No charge.

VIETNAM VETERANS HISTORICAL MUSEUM, 1095 N. Dixie Hwy., Norman Heck Park, Monroe, MI 48162. Mailing Address: c/o Monroe County Historical Museum, 126 S. Monroe St., Monroe, MI 48161. Tel.: 734-240-7780.
E-mail: gpodhola0282@comcast.net
Web Site: historicmonroe.org/war-memorials/viet.htm
Key Personnel: Chm. (V) & Museum Shop Mgr., Glenn R. Podhola.
Institution Type/Description: Military History Museum.
Hours & Admission Prices: May 15-Sept. Wed. & Sat. 12-4; other times by appointment. No charge; donations accepted. ර
Attendance: 600 (actual)

Montague

MONTAGUE MUSEUM & HISTORICAL ASSOCIATION, 8778 Ferry St., Montague, MI 49437. Tel.: 231-894-8249. Fax: 231-894-9955. Facebook; Twitter.
E-mail: michiganoh@aol.com
Web Site: www.montaguemuseum.org
Key Personnel: Pres. (V), Sally Mclouth; Cur. & Museum Shop Manager, James Haley.
Institution Type/Description: General Museum: housed in a former United Methodist Church.
Hours & Admission Prices: Summer: Sat.-Sun. 1-5; private tours for groups available. No charge; donations accepted.
Attendance: 700 (estimated)

Montrose

MONTROSE HISTORICAL & TELEPHONE PIONEER MUSEUM, 144 E. Hickory St., Montrose, MI 48457-9464. Mailing Address: P.O. Box 577, Montrose, MI 48457-0577. Tel.: 810-639-6644. Fax: 810-639-6644.
E-mail: staff@montrosemuseum.com
Web Site: www.montrosemuseum.com
Key Personnel: Pres. (V), Joe Follett.
Institution Type/Description: History (local) & Telephone Museum.
Hours & Admission Prices: Museum: Sun. 1-5. Museum & Office: Mon.-Tues. 9:30-3:30. Genealogy & Personal Tours: anytime call for appointment. No charge; donations accepted. Closed major holidays. ර
Attendance: 3,035 (actual)

Mount Clemens

ANTON ART CENTER, 125 Macomb Place, Mount Clemens, MI 48043-5650. Tel.: 586-469-8666. Fax: 586-469-4529.
E-mail: information@theartcenter.org
Web Site: www.theartcenter.org
Formerly: The Art Center
Key Personnel: Exec. Dir., Philip Gilchrist; Pres. (V), Don Morandini.
Institution Type/Description: Art Gallery.
Hours & Admission Prices: Tues.-Sat. 10-5. No charge; donations accepted. ර
Attendance: 20,000 (estimated)

CROCKER HOUSE MUSEUM & MACOMB COUNTY HISTORICAL SOCIETY, 15 Union St., Mount Clemens, MI 48043-5502. Tel.: 586-465-2488. Fax: 586-465-2932.
E-mail: crockerhousemuseum@sbcglobal.net
Web Site: www.crockerhousemuseum.com
Key Personnel: Pres., Ross Champion; Dir., Kimberly Parr; Office Mgr., Marcia Swiderski; Museum Shop Mgr., Gladys Stevenson.
Institution Type/Description: Historical Society Museum: residence built 1869 Crocker House, a Victorian Italianate style house.

Hours & Admission Prices: March-Dec. Tues.-Thurs. 10-4, 1st Sun. of month 1-4. Suggested Donations & Special Events: adults $3, children $1; discounts to members.
Attendance: 2,500 (estimated)

MICHIGAN TRANSIT MUSEUM, INC., 200 Grand Ave., Mount Clemens, MI 48043-5412. Mailing Address: P.O. Box 12, Mount Clemens, MI 48046-0012. Tel.: 586-463-1863.
E-mail: information@michigantransitmuseum.org
Web Site: www.michigantransitmuseum.org
Key Personnel: Chm. (V) & Pres. (V), Billie H. Henning; Treas., Gary J. Michaels.
Institution Type/Description: Transportation Museum: equipment housed at Selfridge Air National Guard Base & 1859, Grand Trunk Depot Railroad Museum, national historic site.
Hours & Admission Prices: Depot Museum: Sat.-Sun. 1-4. No charge; donations accepted. Train rides: adults $7, children 4-12 $4. &
Attendance: 3,500 (estimated)

Mount Pleasant

MUSEUM OF CULTURAL & NATURAL HISTORY, 103 Rowe Hall, Corner of Bellows & East Campus Dr., Mount Pleasant, MI 48859. Tel.: 989-774-3829. Fax: 989-774-2612. Facebook: CMUMuseum.
E-mail: cmuseum@cmich.edu
Web Site: www.museum.cmich.edu/
Key Personnel: Dir., Dr. Jay C. Martin; Cur. Natural History, Dr. Kirsten Nicholson; Educator, Caity Burnell; Collections Mgr., Ron Bloomfield; Exec. Sec., Sarah Avery.
Institution Type/Description: University Museum.
Hours & Admission Prices: Mon.-Fri. 8-5, Sat. 1-5. No charge; donations accepted. Closed national & university holidays. &
Attendance: 30,000 (estimated)

UNIVERSITY ART GALLERY - CENTRAL MICHIGAN UNIVERSITY, 251 E. Preston St., Mount Pleasant, MI 48859. Mailing Address: Wightman 132, Mount Pleasant, MI 48859. Tel.: 989-774-3800.
E-mail: goche1as@cmich.edu
Web Site: www.uag.cmich.edu
Key Personnel: Dir., Anne Gochenour.
Institution Type/Description: Art Gallery.
Hours & Admission Prices: Sept.-May Tues.-Fri. 11-6, Sat. 11-3; Summer: call for hours. No charge; donations accepted. &
Attendance: 9,727 (actual)

ZIIBIWING CENTER OF ANISHINABE CULTURE & LIFEWAYS, 6650 E. Broadway, Mount Pleasant, MI 48858-8950. Tel.: 989-775-4750. Fax: 989-775-4770.
E-mail: smartin@sagchip.org
Web Site: www.sagchip.org/ziibiwing
Key Personnel: Dir., Shannon Martin; Asst. Dir., Judy Pamp; Cur., William Johnson.
Institution Type/Description: General Museum.
Hours & Admission Prices: Mon.-Sat. 10-6. Adults $6.50, college students $4.50, senior citizens 60 & over, children 5-17 and active military $3.75; children under 4, members & teachers no charge. Closed New Year's Eve & Day; Thanksgiving; Christmas Eve & Day. &

Munising

ALGER COUNTY HISTORICAL SOCIETY, 1496 Washington St., Munising, MI 49862-1492. Tel.: 906-387-4308. Fax: 906-387-4188.
E-mail: algerchs@jamadots.com
Key Personnel: Pres. (V), Mary Jo Cook.
Institution Type/Description: Historical Society Museum.
Hours & Admission Prices: Tues.-Sat. 11-4. No charge; donations accepted. &
Attendance: 4,000 (actual)

Muskegon

GREAT LAKES NAVAL MEMORIAL AND MUSEUM - USS SILVERSIDES SUBMARINE MUSEUM, 1346 Bluff St., Muskegon, MI 49441-1089. Mailing Address: P.O. Box 1692, Muskegon, MI 49443-1692. Tel.: 231-755-1230. Fax: 231-755-5883.
E-mail: contactus@silversidesmuseum.org
Web Site: www.silversidesmuseum.org

Key Personnel: Dir., Denise Herzhaft.
Institution Type/Description: Historic Ship: World War II navy sub U.S.S. Silversides, served with the Pacific Fleet in waters controlled by the Japanese Empire: East China Sea & through key enemy shipping routes; USCGC McLane (WMEC 146).
Hours & Admission Prices: Summer: daily 10-5:30; Winter Sun.-Thurs. 10-4, Fri.-Sat. 10-5:30. Museum: adults $15, veterans and seniors $12.50, children 5-18 $10.50; children 4 & under no charge. Overnight Program Camping: reservations required. &
Attendance: 35,000 (estimated)

HACKLEY & HUME HISTORIC SITE, W. Webster Ave. & Sixth St., Muskegon, MI 49440. Mailing Address: 430 W. Clay Ave., Muskegon, MI 49440-1002. Tel.: 231-722-7578. Fax: 231-728-4119.
E-mail: dawn@lakeshoremuseum.org
Web Site: www.lakeshoremuseum.org
Key Personnel: Exec. Dir., John H. McGarry, III; Site Mgr., Dawn Willi; Pres. (V), Eric Gielow; Museum Shop Mgr., Peggy Jobe.
Institution Type/Description: Historic Houses: homes of C.H. Hackley & Thomas Hume.
Hours & Admission Prices: May-Oct. Wed.-Sun. 12-4; group tours by appointment; special holiday hours between Thanksgiving & Christmas. Adults $3; children 12 & under no charge. Closed major holidays.
Attendance: 7,095 (actual)

LAKESHORE MUSEUM CENTER, 430 W. Clay, Muskegon, MI 49440-1002. Tel.: 231-722-0278. Fax: 231-728-4119. Facebook: Lakeshore Museum Center.
E-mail: info@lakeshoremuseum.org
Web Site: www.lakeshoremuseum.org
Formerly: Muskegon County Museum
Key Personnel: Dir. & CEO, Annoesjka Soler; Pres. (V), Greg Scott; C.F.O., Cheryl Graves; Historic Sites Mgr. & Cur. and Volunteer Coord., Erin Schnutz; Cur. Exhibits, Krista Menacher; Dir. Visitor Services, Melissa Horton; Program Mgr., Jackie Huss; Asst. Program Mgr., Patrick Horn; Archivist, Jeff Bessenger; Maintenance Dir., Ryan Videtich; Dir. Communications, Joni Dorsett; Cur. Collections, Sharon McCullar; Museum Shop Mgr., Holly Priest.
Institution Type/Description: Historic Site/Building; Historic Museum; Children's Science Museum.
Hours & Admission Prices: Mon.-Fri. 9:30-4:30, Sat.-Sun. 12-4. No charge; donations accepted. Closed major holidays. &
Attendance: 46,555 (actual)

MUSKEGON HERITAGE MUSEUM, 561 W. Western Ave., Muskegon, MI 49440-1042. Tel.: 231-722-1363.
E-mail: info@muskegonheritage.org
Web Site: www.muskegonheritage.org
Key Personnel: Dir., Allan Dake; Pres. (V), Jim Funnell.
Institution Type/Description: History Museum: housed in the former Hathaway Building; built in 1910.
Hours & Admission Prices: mid-May to mid-Oct. Thurs.-Sat. 11-4; other times by appointment. Adults $5, students $2; discounts to active military; members & Muskegon County school groups no charge. &
Attendance: 3,000 (actual)

MUSKEGON MUSEUM OF ART, 296 W. Webster, Muskegon, MI 49440-1282. Tel.: 231-720-2570 & 2571. Fax: 231-720-2585.
Web Site: www.muskegonartmuseum.org
Key Personnel: Exec. Dir., Judith Hayner; Senior Cur., Dir. Collections & Exhibitions, Arthur Martin; Public Rels., Marguerite Curran; Pres., Charles Johnson, III; Cur. Education, Catherine Mott; Preparator, Lee Brown; Museum Store Mgr., Shawnee Larabee.
Institution Type/Description: Art Museum.
Hours & Admission Prices: Tues.-Wed. & Fri.-Sat. 11-5, Thurs. 11-8, Sun. 12-5. Adults $8, college students $5; members no charge. Reciprocal with North American Program. Closed major holidays. &
Attendance: 29,165 (actual)

Muskegon Heights

MUSKEGON COUNTY MUSEUM OF AFRICAN AMERICAN HISTORY, 7 E. Center St., Muskegon Heights, MI 49444. Mailing Address: 610 W. Western Ave., Muskegon, MI 49440. Tel.: 231-739-9500.
Institution Type/Description: History Museum.
Hours & Admission Prices: Mon.-Sat. 2-5:30. No charge; donations accepted.

Newaygo

NEWAYGO COUNTY MUSEUM AND HERITAGE CENTER, 12 Quarterline St., Newaygo, MI 49337. Mailing Address: P.O. Box 361, Newaygo, MI 49337-0361. Tel.: 231-652-5003. Fax: 231-518-4816. Facebook: Newaygo County Museum.
E-mail: museum@newaygocountyhistory.org
Web Site: newaygocountyhistory.org
Formerly: Newaygo County Society of History and Genealogy
Key Personnel: Dir., Roxanne Bassett; Pres. (V), James Rynberg.
Institution Type/Description: Regional Museum.
Hours & Admission Prices: April 1-Oct. 31 call for hours. No charge; donations accepted.
Attendance: 5,000 (actual)

Niles

FERNWOOD BOTANICAL GARDEN & NATURE PRESERVE, 13988 Range Line Rd., Niles, MI 49120-9042. Tel.: 269-695-6491. Fax: 269-695-6688.
E-mail: info@fernwoodbotanical.org
Web Site: www.fernwoodbotanical.org
Key Personnel: Exec. Dir., Carol Line; Lead Horticulturist, Steve Bornell; Gallery Cur., Kathee Kiesselbach; Museum Shop Mgr., Kathy Lawrence.
Institution Type/Description: Garden & Nature Preserve.
Hours & Admission Prices: May-Oct: Tues.-Sat. 10-6, Sun. 12-6; Nov.-April: Tues.-Sat. 10-5, Sun. 12-5. Adults $8, seniors $6, youth 13-18 $4, children 6-12 $3; children 5 & under & members no charge. Closed New Year's Eve & Day; Easter; Thanksgiving weekend; Christmas Eve, Day & week. &
Attendance: 30,000

NILES HISTORY CENTER, 508 E. Main St., Niles, MI 49120-2618. Tel.: 269-683-4700. Fax: 269-684-3930.
E-mail: hcdirector@nilesmi.org
Web Site: nileshistorycenter.org
Formerly: Fort St. Joseph Museum
Institution Type/Description: History Museum; housed in 1882 Henry A. Chapin Carriage House & Historic Chapin Mansion
Hours & Admission Prices: History Center: Wed.-Fri. 10-4, Sat. 10-3; group tours by appointment. No charge; donations accepted. Chapin Mansion Tours: April-Dec. Fri. & Sat. 11:30 & 1:30. Admission $5; under 10 no charge. Closed holidays.
Attendance: 4,493 (actual)

Northport

WRIGHT GALLERY, 210 Mill St., Northport, MI 49670. Mailing Address: P.O. Box 910, Northport, MI 49670. Tel.: 231-386-5594.
E-mail: info@wrightartgallery.com
Web Site: wrightartgallery.com
Institution Type/Description: Art Gallery.
Hours & Admission Prices: Thurs.-Sat. 10-5.

Northville

MILL RACE HISTORICAL VILLAGE, 215 Griswold Ave., Northville, MI 48167-1664. Tel.: 248-348-1845. Fax: 248-348-0056.
E-mail: mrv1845@yahoo.com
Web Site: www.millracenorthville.org
Key Personnel: Pres., Ed Gabrys; Vice Pres., Leanie Bayly; Office Mgr., Jennifer Luikart; Archivist, Carri Lee.
Institution Type/Description: Restored Village Museum.
Hours & Admission Prices: Grounds: dawn-dusk; Buildings: June to Oct. Sun. 1-4; other times by appointment. Office: Mon.-Fri. 9-1. No charge. Closed New Year's Day; Thanksgiving; Christmas. &
Attendance: 2,500 (estimated)

Ontonagon

ONTONAGON COUNTY HISTORICAL SOCIETY MUSEUM, 422 River St., Ontonagon, MI 49953-1614. Tel.: 906-884-6165. Fax: 906-884-6165.
E-mail: ochs@jamadots.com
Web Site: www.ontonagonmuseum.org
Key Personnel: Chm. & Pres. (V), Bruce H. Johanson; Museum Shop Mgr., Corriane Panegon.
Institution Type/Description: History Museum.
Hours & Admission Prices: Mon.-Fri. 10-5, Sat. 10-4, call for additional hours & to confirm winter hours. Adults $3 (first visit of season, thereafter no charge); dis-

counts for AAM & ICOM members and large groups; children 15 & under no charge. &
Attendance: 6,759 (actual)

Orchard Lake

GALERIA, 3535 Indian Trail, Orchard Lake, MI 48324-1623. Tel.: 248-683-0412.
E-mail: contact@polishmission.com
Web Site: www.polishmission.com/galeria-at-orchard-lake/
Key Personnel: Dir. Polish Mission, Marcin Chumiecki; Polonica Americana Research Institute Dir., Cecile Wendt Jensen; Polonica Americana Research Institute Co-Dir., Dr. Hal Learman.
Institution Type/Description: Art Gallery; housed in former Michigan Military Academy.
Hours & Admission Prices: Galeria: Mon., Wed. & Fri. 8:30-4. Museums, Archives & Rare Book Room by appointment. No charge; donations accepted. Closed Easter; Thanksgiving; Christmas. &
Attendance: 1,250 (estimated)

Oscoda

AUSABLE-OSCODA HISTORICAL SOCIETY & MUSEUM, 114 E. River Rd., Oscoda, MI 48750. Mailing Address: P.O. Box 679, Oscoda, MI 48750. Tel.: 989-739-2782.
E-mail: director@oscodachamber.com
Institution Type/Description: Historical Society Museum.
Hours & Admission Prices: April-May & Sept.-Oct. Sat. 11-4, Sun. 12-4; Memorial Day to Labor Day Thurs.-Sat. 10-5, Sun. 11-4; other times by appointment.

WURTSMITH AIR MUSEUM, 4071 E. Van Ettan St., Oscoda, MI 48750. Mailing Address: P.O. Box 664, Oscoda, MI 48750. Tel.: 989-739-7555. Facebook.
E-mail: visit@wurtsmithairmuseum.org
Web Site: www.wurtsmithairmuseum.org/index.html
Formerly: Yankee Air Museum, Wurtsmith Div.
Key Personnel: Chm. (V), Don Gauvreau; Museum Shop Mgr. (V), Judy Shuler.
Institution Type/Description: Military History Museum.
Hours & Admission Prices: May-Sept. Fri.-Sun. 11-3. Adults $5; members no charge.
Attendance: 2,500 (actual)

Ossineke

DINOSAUR GARDENS, LLC, 11160 U.S. 23 S., Ossineke, MI 49766. Mailing Address: 3010 E. Nicholson Hill Rd., Ossineke, MI 49766-9601. Tel.: 989-471-5477. Fax: 989-732-6951.
E-mail: garyjstephan@gmail.com
Web Site: dinosaurgardensllc.com
Key Personnel: Owner, Gary Stephan.
Institution Type/Description: Paleontology Museum.
Hours & Admission Prices: Memorial Day-Labor Day daily 10-5; Sept. Sat.-Sun. 10-4. Adults $8, children 3-15 $6, children 2 & under no charge. &
Attendance: 10,000 (estimated)

Owosso

CURWOOD CASTLE, 224 Curwood Castle Dr., Owosso, MI 48867-2723. Mailing Address: 301 W. Main St., Owosso, MI 48867-2915. Tel.: 989-725-0597.
E-mail: robert.doran@ci.owosso.mi.us
Web Site: www.ci.owosso.mi.us/government/historical-commission
Key Personnel: Chm. (V), Michael Erfourth.
Institution Type/Description: Historic Building; 1922 Norman castle, studio of novelist James Oliver Curwood.
Hours & Admission Prices: Feb.-Dec. Tues.-Sun. 1-5, tour groups on off hours by appointment only. Adults $2, children $1. Closed holidays.
Attendance: 4,000

SHIAWASSEE ARTS CENTER, 206 Curwood Castle Dr., Owosso, MI 48867-2723. Tel.: 989-723-8354. Fax: 989-729-9134.
E-mail: sac@shiawasseearts.org
Web Site: www.shiawasseearts.org
Institution Type/Description: Art Gallery.
Hours & Admission Prices: Tues.-Sun. 1-5. No charge.

STEAM RAILROADING INSTITUTE, 405 S. Washington St., Owosso, MI 48867-3523. Mailing Address: P.O. Box 665, Owosso, MI 48867-0665. Tel.: 989-725-9464. Fax: 989-723-1225.

E-mail: dlshorter@mstrp.com
Web Site: www.michigansteamtrain.com
Formerly: Michigan State Trust for Railway Preservation, Inc./ MSU Railroad Club
Key Personnel: Exec. Dir. & C.E.O., David Shorter; Pres., Aarne Frobom; Chm. (V), Jay Fulkerson; Vice Pres., Rich Greter; Treas., Chris Kurzweil; Chief Mechanical Officer, Kevin Mayer; Museum Shop Mgr., Carole Stevens.
Institution Type/Description: Railroad History Museum: housed in the former Ann Arbor Railroad machine shop; built in 1887.
Hours & Admission Prices: Memorial Day to Labor Day Wed.-Sun. 10-5; Winter: Sat.-Sun. 10-5. Adults $5; discounts to AAM & museum members. Closed major holidays. &
Attendance: 20,000 (estimated)

Oxford

NORTHEAST OAKLAND HISTORICAL MUSEUM, One N. Washington St., Oxford, MI 48371-4673. Mailing Address: P.O. Box 617, Oxford, MI 48371-0617. Tel.: 248-628-8413 & 391-1367.
E-mail: neohs@charterinternet.com
Web Site: www.orion.lib.mi.us/nohm
Key Personnel: Pres., Gerald Griffin; Vice Pres., Ron Brock; Cur., Marie English; Treas., Darryl Lambertson.
Institution Type/Description: History Museum.
Hours & Admission Prices: June-Aug. Wed. & Sat. 1-4; Sept.-May Sat. 1-4. No charge; donations accepted.
Attendance: 1,000 (estimated)

Paradise

GREAT LAKES SHIPWRECK MUSEUM, 18335 N. Whitefish Point Rd., Paradise, MI 49768-9618. Mailing Address: 400 W. Portage Ave., Sault Ste. Marie, MI 49783-1993. Tel.: 906-492-3747. Fax: 906-492-3383. Facebook: Great Lakes Shipwreck Museum.
E-mail: glshs@shipwreckmuseum.com
Web Site: www.shipwreckmuseum.com
Key Personnel: Exec. Dir., Bruce Lynn; Devel. Officer, Sean Ley; Operations Mgr., Sarah Wilde.
Institution Type/Description: Maritime Museum.
Hours & Admission Prices: May-Oct. daily 10-6. Adults $13, children 6-17 $9; children 5 & under no charge.
Attendance: 75,000 (estimated)

Peshawbestown

EYAAWING MUSEUM AND CULTURAL CENTER, 2304 N. West Bayshore Dr., Peshawbestown, MI 49682-9365. Tel.: 231-534-7764 & 7768.
E-mail: museum@gtbindians.com
Web Site: www.gtbindians.org
Institution Type/Description: Native American History Museum.
Hours & Admission Prices: mid-June to Labor Day Wed.-Sat. 10-4; Sept. to mid-June call for hours.

Petoskey

CROOKED TREE ARTS CENTER, 461 E. Mitchell St., Petoskey, MI 49770-2623. Tel.: 616-347-4337. Fax: 616-347-5414.
E-mail: liz@crookedtree.org
Web Site: www.crookedtree.org
Key Personnel: Exec. Dir., Liz Ahrens; Pres. (V), Kurt Wietzke; Cur., Membership & Museum Shop Mgr., Gail Hosner; Business Mgr., Donna McDougall; Cultural Coord., Mary Wiklanski.
Institution Type/Description: Arts Center: housed in 1890 Methodist Church.
Hours & Admission Prices: Mon.-Tues. & Fri. 9-5, Wed. 10-5, Sat. 10-4. Fee charged for concerts & special events. Closed legal holidays. &
Attendance: 55,000 (estimated)

LITTLE TRAVERSE HISTORICAL SOCIETY AND MUSEUM, 100 Depot St., Petoskey, MI 49770-2476. Mailing Address: P.O. Box 2418, Petoskey, MI 49770. Tel.: 231-347-2620. Facebook: @LittleTraverseHistoryMuseum; Twitter @petoskeymuseum; Instagram: @petosky_museum.
E-mail: info@petoskeymuseum.org
Web Site: www.petoskeymuseum.org
Key Personnel: Dir., Jane Garver; Exec. Dir., Dylan Taylor; Pres., Richard Clark.
Institution Type/Description: Historical Society Museum.

Hours & Admission Prices: Mon.-Sat. 10-4, Sat. 1-4. Adults $3; members & children no charge.
Attendance: 5,000 (estimated)

Plymouth

PLYMOUTH HISTORICAL MUSEUM, 155 S. Main St., Plymouth, MI 48170-1635. Tel.: 734-455-8940. Fax: 734-455-7797. Facebook: Plymouth Historical Museum.
E-mail: director@plymouthhistory.org
Web Site: www.plymouthhistory.org
Key Personnel: Exec. Dir., Elizabeth K. Kerstens; Pres., Margaret Harris; Museum Shop Mgr., Paula Holmes.
Institution Type/Description: History Museum.
Hours & Admission Prices: Wed. & Fri.-Sun. 1-4. Adults $5, students 6-17 $2; discounts to AAA members; members no charge. Closed holidays. &
Attendance: 15,000 (estimated)

Pontiac

OAKLAND COUNTY PIONEER AND HISTORICAL SOCIETY, 405 Cesar E. Chavez Ave., Pontiac, MI 48342-1068. Tel.: 248-338-6732. Fax: 248-338-6731. Facebook: Oakland County Pioneer and Historical Society.
E-mail: office@ocphs.org
Web Site: www.ocphs.org
Key Personnel: Pres. (V), Fred Liimatta; Museum Shop Mgr., Judy Hudalla.
Institution Type/Description: Historic House Museum: c.1845 Pine Grove, the Governor Moses Wisner Historic House.
Hours & Admission Prices: Jan. to mid-Dec. office & library Tues.-Thurs. 11-4; other times by appointment. Museum: tours by appointment. Admission $5; discounts to military. Closed Thanksgiving week & Christmas week. &
Attendance: 1,500 (estimated)

PONTIAC CREATIVE ARTS CENTER, 47 Williams St., Pontiac, MI 48341-1759. Tel.: 248-333-7849. Facebook.
E-mail: pcacdirector@gmail.com
Web Site: pontiacarts.org
Key Personnel: Exec. Dir., William E. Dwyer; Pres. (V), Laurie Slade.
Institution Type/Description: Civic Art & Cultural Center: housed in 1898 Public Library of Oakland County.
Hours & Admission Prices: Wed.-Fri. 10-4; Sat. 11-1. No charge; donations accepted. Closed holidays. &
Attendance: 12,000 (estimated)

Port Austin

HURON CITY MUSEUMS, 7995 Pioneer Rd., Port Austin, MI 48467-9400. Mailing Address: c/o William Lloyd Phelps Foundation, 3169 Robina, Berkley, MI 48072-3816. Tel.: 989-428-4123, 313-640-0123. Fax: 989-428-4473.
E-mail: info@huroncitymuseums.org
Web Site: www.huroncitymuseums.org
Key Personnel: Pres. (V), Kathryn H. Parcells.
Institution Type/Description: General Museum.
Hours & Admission Prices: July-Aug. Fri.-Sat. 10-4; groups by appointment. Seven Gables or Village Museum: adults $6, senior citizens $5, youths 10-15 $3. Both Tours: adults $10, senior citizens $8, youths 10-15 $5; discounts to AAM & AAA members; children accompanied by an adult no charge. &
Attendance: 1,500 (estimated)

Port Hope

POINTE AUX BARQUES LIGHTHOUSE AND MUSEUM, 7320 Lighthouse Rd., Port Hope, MI 48468-9759. Mailing Address: P.O. Box 97, Port Hope, MI 48468. Tel.: 989-428-3035. Fax: 989-856-4505.
E-mail: president@pointeauxbarqueslighthouse.org
Key Personnel: Pres. (V), Upton D. Bonner; Museum Shop Mgr., Carolyn Curtis.
Institution Type/Description: History Museum.
Hours & Admission Prices: Call for hours. No charge; donations accepted. &
Attendance: 10,000 (actual)

Port Huron

FORT GRATIOT LIGHT, 2802 Omar St., Port Huron, MI 48060. Tel.: 810-216-6923.
Web Site: phmuseum.org
Institution Type/Description: Lighthouse: built in 1829.

Hours & Admission Prices: Park: daily 7 am - 10 pm. Station & Tower Tours: May 5-June 10 & Nov.-Dec. Sat.-Sun. 10-5; June 11-Sept. 3 daily 10-5; Sept. 4-Oct. Fri.-Sun. 10-5. Family $25, adults $10, seniors & students $8, additional child $3; discounts to groups of 20 or more; children 4 & under no charge.

THE KNOWLTON'S ICE MUSEUM, 317 Grand River Ave., Port Huron, MI 48060-3814. Tel.: 810-987-5441. Facebook: Knowlton's Ice Museum.
E-mail: knowltonsicemuseum@yahoo.com
Web Site: www.knowltonsicemuseum.org
Institution Type/Description: History Museum.
Hours & Admission Prices: June-Sept. Thurs.-Sat. 11-5; Oct.-May Sat. 11-5; groups of 12 or more by appointment. Adults $5, seniors $4, children 6-10 $2; children 5 & under no charge. Closed major holidays. &
Attendance: 4,000 (estimated)

PORT HURON MUSEUM, 1115 Sixth St., Port Huron, MI 48060-5346. Tel.: 810-982-0891. Fax: 810-982-0053. Facebook: Port Huron Museum.
E-mail: info@phmuseum.org
Web Site: www.phmuseum.org
Key Personnel: Dir. Collections & Exhibits, Veronica Campbell; Port Huron Museum Educational Coord., Caitlyn Wallace; Thomas Edison Depot Site Mgr., Dave Dazer; Fort Gratiot Light Station General Mgr., Lauren Nelson; Fort Gratiot Light Station Site Mgr., Jerry Rome.
Institution Type/Description: General Museum: housed in 1904 Carnegie Library Building. HURON Lightship: National Landmark. Edison Depot: Historic Train Depot; Fort Gratiot Light Station.
Hours & Admission Prices: See website for hours. Family (2 adults & 2 children) $25, adults $10, seniors & students $8. Passport (single visit to 4 sites each): Family $70, adults $35, seniors & students $28. &
Attendance: 37,120 (actual)

Port Sanilac

SANILAC COUNTY HISTORICAL VILLAGE AND MUSEUM, 228 S. Ridge St., Port Sanilac, MI 48469-9704. Mailing Address: P.O. Box 158, Port Sanilac, MI 48469-0158. Tel.: 810-622-9946.
E-mail: sanilacmuseum@gmail.com
Web Site: www.sanilaccountymuseum.org
Key Personnel: Pres. (V), Thomas Fisher.
Institution Type/Description: Historic Village: housed on the former estate of Dr. Joseph Loop; built in 1853.
Hours & Admission Prices: Museum: May-Sept. Wed.-Sun. 11-4. Office: May-Sept. Wed.-Sun. 11-4; Oct.-April Mon., Wed. & Fri. 10-2; other times by appointment. Archives & Genealogy Rooms: Wed. 10-2. Admission varies by event; discount to military. &
Attendance: 3,300 (actual)

Rochester

MEADOW BROOK HALL, 350 Estate Dr., Rochester, MI 48309. Tel.: 248-364-6200. Fax: 248-364-6201. Facebook: @meadow-brookhall; Instagram: @meadowbrookhallandgardens.
E-mail: stobersk@oakland.edu
Web Site: www.meadowbrookhall.org
Key Personnel: Exec. Dir., Geoff Upward; Dir. Mktg. & Community Relations, Shannon O'Berski; Dir. Curatorial Svcs., Madelyn Rzadkowolski.
Institution Type/Description: Historic House Museum: housed in the Tudor-revival style mansion of Matilda Dodge Wilson, widow of automobile pioneer John Dodge & her second husband, Alfred Wilson, a Wisconsin lumber broker.
Hours & Admission Prices: Guided Tours: Mon.-Fri. 1:30, Sat.-Sun. 11:30, 12:30, 1:30, 2:30. Adults $15, senior citizens, OU/Cooley, Staff & Alumni with ID $10; children 12 & under & members no charge. Closed New Year's Eve & Day Easter; Memorial Day; Independence Day; Labor Day; Thanksgiving; Christmas Eve, Day & week. &
Attendance: 111,000 (actual)

OAKLAND UNIVERSITY ART GALLERY, 2200 N. Squirrel Rd., 208 Wilson Hall, Rochester, MI 48309-4401. Tel.: 248-370-3005. Fax: 248-370-4368.
E-mail: goody@oakland.edu
Web Site: www.ouartgallery.org
Formerly: Meadow Brook Art Gallery
Key Personnel: Dir., Dick Goody; C.E.O., Kevin J. Corcoran; Asst. to Dir., Jacky Leow.
Institution Type/Description: Art Gallery.
Hours & Admission Prices: Tues.-Sun. 12-5. Special Events & Meadow Brook Theatre performances: Wed.-Fri. 7pm through 1st intermission, Sat.-Sun. 5pm through 1st intermission. No charge; donations accepted. &
Attendance: 16,000 (estimated)

PAINT CREEK CENTER FOR THE ARTS, 407 Pine St., Rochester, MI 48307-1933. Tel.: 248-651-4110. Fax: 248-651-4110.
E-mail: comments@pccart.org
Web Site: www.pccart.org
Key Personnel: Dir. Exhibitions, Rana Edgar.
Institution Type/Description: Art Gallery.
Hours & Admission Prices: Mon.-Thurs. 9-7, Fri. 9-5, Sat. 9-4. No charge; donations accepted. Closed major holidays.

Rochester Hills

ROCHESTER HILLS MUSEUM AT VAN HOOSEN FARM, 1005 Van Hoosen Rd., Rochester Hills, MI 48306-4555. Tel.: 248-656-4663. Facebook: Rochester Hills Museum.
E-mail: rhmuseum@rochesterhills.org
Web Site: www.rochesterhills.org
Key Personnel: Mayor, Bryan Barnett; Museum Mgr., Patrick J. McKay.
Institution Type/Description: History Museum.
Hours & Admission Prices: Fri.-Sat. 1-4. Adults $5, senior citizen & students $3; members no charge. Closed major holidays. &
Attendance: 50,000 (estimated)

Rogers City

PRESQUE ISLE COUNTY HISTORICAL MUSEUM, 176 W. Michigan Ave., Rogers City, MI 49779-1638. Mailing Address: P. O. Box 175, Rogers City, MI 49779-0175. Tel.: 989-734-4121. Fax: 989-734-4121.
E-mail: bradleymuseum@yahoo.com
Web Site: www.thebradleyhouse.org
Key Personnel: Pres., David Nadolsky; Cur. & Museum Shop Mgr., Rose Buck; Cur., Mark Thompson.
Institution Type/Description: General Museum: housed in 1914 home of Carl D. Bradley, owner of Bradley Transportation Line.
Hours & Admission Prices: May-Sept. Tues.-Sat. 12-4. No charge; donations accepted.
Attendance: 2,500 (actual)

Royal Oak

DETROIT ZOOLOGICAL SOCIETY, 8450 W. 10 Mile Rd., Royal Oak, MI 48067-3001. Tel.: 248-541-5717. Fax: 248-398-0504.
E-mail: rlkagan@dzs.org
Web Site: www.detroitzoo.org
Key Personnel: Exec. Dir. & C.E.O., Ron L. Kagan; Chm. (V), Lloyd Semple.
Institution Type/Description: Zoo.
Hours & Admission Prices: April-June daily 9-5; July to Labor Day Wed. 9-8, Thurs.-Tues. 9-5; Sept. daily 10-5; Oct.-March daily 10-4. Adults $14, senior citizens 62 & over and active military, and children 2-14 $10; discounts to groups; members & children under 2 no charge. Closed New Year's Day; Thanksgiving; Christmas. &
Attendance: 1,475,000 (actual)

Saginaw

CASTLE MUSEUM OF SAGINAW COUNTY HISTORY, 500 Federal Ave., Saginaw, MI 48607-1253. Tel.: 989-752-2861, ext. 301. Fax: 517-752-1533.
E-mail: info@castlemuseum.org
Web Site: www.castlemuseum.org
Key Personnel: Dir., Ken Santa; Dir., Irene Hensinger; Museum Shop Mgr., Sherri D. Greene.
Institution Type/Description: History Museum: housed in an 1898 Federal post office building in the style of a French Chateau.
Hours & Admission Prices: Tues.-Sat. 10-4:30, Sun. 1-4:30. Adults $1, children $.50; members no charge. Closed major holidays. &
Attendance: 24,000 (actual)

CHILDREN'S ZOO AT CELEBRATION SQUARE, 1730 S. Washington Ave., Saginaw, MI 48601-2876. Tel.: 989-759-1408. Fax: 989-759-1328.
E-mail: info@saginawzoo.com
Web Site: saginawzoo.com
Formerly: Saginaw Valley Zoological Society
Key Personnel: Exec. Dir., Nancy Parker; Mgr. Animal Collection, Megan Olmstead.
Institution Type/Description: Children's Zoo.

Hours & Admission Prices: April-Sept. daily 10-5; Oct. 1st three weekends Sat.-Sun. 10-5; Nov.-Feb. call for hours. Zoo: admission $5, senior citizens 65 & over on 1st Wed. of month, members & children under one no charge. Carousel or Train Rides: $1. &

Attendance: 95,000 (actual)

MID-MICHIGAN CHILDREN'S MUSEUM, 315 W. Genesee, Saginaw, MI 48602. Mailing Address: P.O. Box 2283, Saginaw, MI 48605-2283. Tel.: 989-399-6626. Fax: 989-399-0431.
E-mail: eyeager@michildrensmuseum.com
Web Site: www.michildrensmuseum.com
Key Personnel: Pres. & C.E.O., Emily Yeager.
Institution Type/Description: Children's Museum.
Hours & Admission Prices: June-Sept. Tues.-Sat. 9:30-5; Oct.-May Tues.-Sat. 9:30-5, Sun. 12-5. Admission $7.50, seniors 60 & over $6.50; children under 2 no charge. &
Attendance: 40,000

SAGINAW ART MUSEUM, 1126 N. Michigan Ave., Saginaw, MI 48602-4795. Tel.: 989-754-2491, ext. 106. Fax: 989-754-9387. Facebook: Saginaw Art Museum.
E-mail: staff@saginawartmuseum.org
Web Site: www.saginawartmuseum.org
Key Personnel: Dir., Stacey Gannon; Registrar & Asst. Colls. Coord., Loissa Harrison-Parks; Mktg. Coord., Thor Rasmussen; Chm. (V), Paul Furlo; Pres. (V), Stacie Rose; Mus. Svcs. Coord., Ashley Stoddard.
Institution Type/Description: Art Museum: housed in former residence of Clark L. Ring family, building designed in 1904 by Charles Adams Platt.
Hours & Admission Prices: Tues.-Sat. 10-5. Adults $5, senior citizens 65 & over and students $3; discounts to AAM & ICOM members; members & youth under 15 no charge. Michigan Art Museums, NARM & American Horticultural Society reciprocal memberships. Closed national holidays. &
Attendance: 5,156 (actual)

Saint Clair Shores

SELINSKY-GREEN FARMHOUSE MUSEUM, 22500 Eleven Mile Rd., Saint Clair Shores, MI 48081-1312. Tel.: 586-771-9020. Fax: 586-771-8935.
E-mail: stachowm@libcoop.net
Institution Type/Description: Historic House.
Hours & Admission Prices: June-Aug. Wed. 1-4; Sept.-May Wed. & Sat. 1-4.

Saint Ignace

FATHER MARQUETTE NATIONAL MEMORIAL, 720 Church St., Saint Ignace, MI 49781-1729. Tel.: 906-643-8620. Fax: 906-643-9329. TDD: 800-827-7007.
Web Site: www.michigan.gov
Key Personnel: Park Mgr., Wayne Burnett.
Institution Type/Description: National Memorial.
Hours & Admission Prices: Memorial Day to Labor Day daily 10-8. No charge. &
Attendance: 14,810 (actual)

Saint Johns

CLINTON COUNTY HISTORICAL SOCIETY PAINE-GILLAM-SCOTT MUSEUM, 106 Maple Ave., Saint Johns, MI 48879-1838. Mailing Address: P.O. Box 174, Saint Johns, MI 48879-0174. Tel.: 989-224-2894. Facebook: Paine Gillam Scott Museum.
E-mail: pgsmuseum@hotmail.com
Web Site: pgsmuseum.com
Institution Type/Description: Historic House: Oldest Brick House in St. Johns.
Hours & Admission Prices: April-Dec. Wed. 2-6, Sun. 1-4; other times by appointment. Suggested Donations: family $5, adults $2, children $1; discounts to military members. Blue Start Museum. Closed legal holidays.
Attendance: 200 (actual)

CLINTON NORTHERN RAILWAY MUSEUM, 107 E. Railroad St., Saint Johns, MI 48879-1525. Mailing Address: 411 S. Clinton Ave., Saint Johns, MI 48879. Tel.: 989-224-6134. Facebook.
E-mail: mccampbell60@gmail.com
Web Site: clintonnorthernrailway.org
Formerly: Depot Center for the Arts
Key Personnel: Co Mgr. & Chm. (V), Gary McCampbell; Co Mgr. & Museum Shop Mgr., Jenny McCampbell.
Institution Type/Description: Railroad Museum: housed in the historic Grand Trunk Railroad Depot.

Hours & Admission Prices: May-Oct. Sun. 1-3. No charge; donations accepted. &
Attendance: 500 (estimated)

Saint Joseph

CURIOUS KIDS' MUSEUM AND DISCOVERY ZONE, 415 Lake Blvd., Saint Joseph, MI 49085-1231. Tel.: 269-983-2543. Fax: 269-983-3317.
E-mail: ckm@curiouskidsmuseum.org
Web Site: www.curiouskidsmuseum.org
Key Personnel: Exec. Dir., Lori Marciniak.
Institution Type/Description: Children's Museum: located in the former Memorial Hall.
Hours & Admission Prices: June to Labor Day Mon.-Sat. 10-5, Sun. 12-5; Sept.-May Wed.-Sat. 10-5, Sun. 10-4. Joint admission to both locations $10, one location $6. Closed New Year's Day; Easter; Memorial Day; Independence Day; Labor Day; Thanksgiving; Christmas Eve & Day. &
Attendance: 130,000 (actual)

THE HERITAGE MUSEUM AND CULTURAL CENTER, 601 Main St., Saint Joseph, MI 49085-3354. Tel.: 269-983-1191. Facebook: The Heritage Museum and Cultural Center.
E-mail: info@theheritagemcc.org
Web Site: www.theheritagemcc.org
Formerly: Fort Miami Heritage Society
Key Personnel: Dir., Christina H. Arseneau; Dir., Amy Zapal.
Institution Type/Description: History Museum.
Hours & Admission Prices: Tues., Wed., Fri. & Sat. 10-4, Thurs. 10-8. No charge. &

KRASL ART CENTER, 707 Lake Blvd., Saint Joseph, MI 49085-1313. Tel.: 269-983-0271. Fax: 269-983-0275.
E-mail: info1@krasl.org
Web Site: krasl.org
Key Personnel: Exec. Dir., Julia Gourley; Pres., Rick Dyer; Vice Pres., Marjorie Zibbel; Dir. Administration, Patrice Rose; Dir. Exhibitions & Collections, Tami Miller; Dir. Art Affairs, Sara Shambarger; Dir. Community Rels, Colleen Villa; Volunteer Coord., Cathie Pflaumer; Office Asst., Caryl Meister; Museum Shop Mgr., Brittany Stecker.
Institution Type/Description: Art Center.
Hours & Admission Prices: Mon.-Wed. & Fri.-Sat. 10-4, Thurs. 10-9, Sun. 1-4. No charge; donations accepted. Closed holidays. &
Attendance: 30,000 (estimated)

Sault Sainte Marie

KEMP MINERAL RESOURCES MUSEUM, Lake Superior State University, 650 W. Easterday Ave., Sault Sainte Marie, MI 49783-1656. Tel.: 906-632-6841, ext. 2267.
E-mail: kmrm@lssu.edu
Web Site: www.lssu.edu
Key Personnel: Cur., Dr. David M. Knowles.
Institution Type/Description: Mineral Resources Museum.
Hours & Admission Prices: Call for hours.

LE SAULT DE SAINTE MARIE HISTORICAL SITES, INC., 501 E. Water St., Sault Sainte Marie, MI 49783-2038. Tel.: 906-632-3658. Fax: 906-632-9344.
E-mail: admin@saulthistorics.com
Web Site: www.saulthistoricsites.com
Key Personnel: Dir., Rich Brawley; Pres. (V), John P. Wellington; Bookkeeper, Charlotte Hendrickson.
Institution Type/Description: Maritime Museum.
Hours & Admission Prices: mid-May to June & Sept. to mid-Oct. Mon.-Sat. 10-4, Sun. 11-4; July to Aug. Mon.-Sat. 10-5, Sun. 11-5 Call for admission prices. &
Attendance: 28,100 (actual)

RIVER HISTORY MUSEUM, 531 Ashmun St., Sault Sainte Marie, MI 49783. Mailing Address: P.O. Box 627, Sault Sainte Marie, MI 49783. Tel.: 906-632-1999. Facebook.
E-mail: robinsonbirchpoint@jamadots.com
Web Site: www.riverofhistory.com
Key Personnel: Chm. (V), Thomas G. Robinson; Pres. (V), Cathy Tibbett; Museum Shop Mgr., Carol Askwith.
Institution Type/Description: History Museum.
Hours & Admission Prices: mid-May to Oct. Mon.-Sat. 11-5. Adults $7, children $3.50. &
Attendance: 2,500 (actual)

Sebewaing

LUCKHARD MUSEUM - THE INDIAN MISSION, 612 E. Bay
St., Sebewaing, MI 48759-1644. Tel.: 989-883-2539 & 3730.
E-mail: info@michigandistrict.org
Key Personnel: Dir., Jim Bunke.
Institution Type/Description: Historic House: 1849 mission home.
Hours & Admission Prices: June-Sept. 1st Sun. of month 2-4. Sebewaing Sugar
   Festival: call for hours. No charge; donations accepted.
Attendance: 40 (estimated)

Selfridge ANG Base

SELFRIDGE MILITARY AIR MUSEUM, 27333 C St., Bldg.
1011, Selfridge ANG Base, MI 48045-4901. Tel.: 586-239-5035.
Fax: 586-239-6646.
E-mail: info@selfridgeairmuseum.org
Web Site: www.selfridgeairmuseum.org
Key Personnel: Exec. Dir., Louis J. Nigro.
Institution Type/Description: History Museum.
Hours & Admission Prices: April-Oct. Sat.-Sun., Memorial Day, Independence Day
   12-4:30; other times by appointment. Adults $4, children 4-12 $3.

Seney

SENEY NATIONAL WILDLIFE REFUGE VISITOR CENTER,
   1674 Refuge Entrance Rd., Seney, MI 49883-9509. Tel.: 906-586-
   9851, ext. 15. Fax: 906-586-3800.
E-mail: jennifer_mcdonough@fws.gov
Web Site: www.fws.gov/midwest/seney
Key Personnel: Pres. Seney Natural History Assoc., Dee Phinney; Museum Shop
   Mgr., Claudia Slater.
Institution Type/Description: Nature Center.
Hours & Admission Prices: May 15-Oct. 15 daily 9-5. No charge; donations
   accepted. &
Attendance: 60,000 (estimated)

South Haven

LIBERTY HYDE BAILEY MUSEUM, 903 S. Bailey Ave., South
Haven, MI 49090. Mailing Address: P.O. Box 626, South Haven,
MI 49090-0626. Tel.: 269-637-3251. Facebook.
E-mail: info@libertyhydebailey.org
Web Site: libertyhydebailey.org
Key Personnel: Dir., Michael J. Fiedorowicz; Chm. (V), Anne Long; Master
   Gardener, Dr. David Fenske.
Institution Type/Description: Historic House Museum: housed in the former home
   of Liberty Hyde Bailey; built in 1857.
Hours & Admission Prices: May 17-Sept. 23 Wed.-Sat. 9-4. No charge. &
Attendance: 6,600 (actual)

MICHIGAN MARITIME MUSEUM, 260 Dyckman Ave., South
Haven, MI 49090-1065. Tel.: 269-637-8078, 800-747-3810.
Facebook, Instagram, Twitter.
E-mail: patti@mimaritime.org
Web Site: michiganmaritimemuseum.org
Key Personnel: Exec. Dir., Patti Montgomery-Reinert; Pres. Bd. of Trustees (V),
   Joan Bauer; Dir. Education & Admin., Ashley Deming; Collections & Office
   Mgr., Emily Stap; Friends Good Will Captain, Zach McGee.
Institution Type/Description: Maritime History Museum.
Hours & Admission Prices: Call or see website for seasonal hours. Adults $8, senior
   citizens $7, children 5-17 $5; discounts to educators, veterans, USCG & USCG
   Auxiliary; members no charge. Closed New Year's Day; Christmas. &
Attendance: 35,000 (estimated)

South Range

COPPER RANGE HISTORICAL MUSEUM, Champion &
   Trimountain, South Range, MI 49963. Mailing Address: P.O. Box
   148, South Range, MI 49963-0148. Tel.: 906-482-6125.
E-mail: johnandjeanp@chartermi.net
Web Site: www.pasty.com/crhm
Key Personnel: Pres. (V), Jean Pemberton.
Institution Type/Description: History Museum.
Hours & Admission Prices: June & Sept. Tues.-Fri. 12-3; July-Aug. Mon.-Fri. 12-3,
   Sat. by appointment. Adults $1; members no charge.
Attendance: 810 (actual)

Tecumseh

TECUMSEH AREA HISTORICAL MUSEUM, 302 E. Chicago
Blvd., Tecumseh, MI 49286-1551. Mailing Address: P.O. Box 26,
Tecumseh, MI 49286-0026. Tel.: 517-423-2374. Facebook.
E-mail: historictecumseh@gmail.com
Web Site: www.historictecumseh.org
Key Personnel: Pres. (V), Gary Naugle; Treas., Cynthia Given.
Institution Type/Description: Historical Society Museum: housed in a gothic stone
   church c.1913.
Hours & Admission Prices: April-Dec. Sat. 10:30-3:30; other times by appointment.
   No charge; donations accepted.
Attendance: 700 (estimated)

Three Oaks

**DEWEY CANNON TRADING COMPANY & BICYCLE
MUSEUM,** 3 Dewey Cannon Ave., P.O. Box 366, Three Oaks, MI
49128. Tel.: 269-756-3361. Fax: 269-756-9124.
Institution Type/Description: Bicycle Museum.
Hours & Admission Prices: Call for hours.

THE REGION OF THREE OAKS MUSEUM, 5 Featherbone
Ave., P.O. Box 121, Three Oaks, MI 49128.
E-mail: trotommuseum@gmail.com
Web Site: regionofthreeoaksmuseum.com
Institution Type/Description: History Museum.
Hours & Admission Prices: May Sat.-Sun. 12-5; June-Aug. Thurs.-Sun. 12-5; call
   for additional hours.

Tipton

**HIDDEN LAKE GARDENS OF MICHIGAN STATE
UNIVERSITY,** 6214 Monroe Rd., (M-50), Tipton, MI 49287-
9766. Tel.: 517-431-2060. Fax: 517-431-9148.
E-mail: pfeife21@msu.edu
Web Site: www.hiddenlakegardens.msu.edu
Key Personnel: Mgr., Paul Pfeifer; Sec. & Gift Shop Mgr., Cheryl Roe.
Institution Type/Description: Arboretum.
Hours & Admission Prices: April-Oct. daily 9-7; Nov.-March daily 9-4. Admission
   $3; members no charge.
Attendance: 48,000 (actual)

Traverse City

ARTCENTER TRAVERSE CITY, 322 Sixth St., Traverse City, MI
49684-2414. Tel.: 231-941-9488, 866-242-0120 (Toll Free). Fax:
231-941-0886.
E-mail: patt@artcentertraversecity.com
Web Site: artcentertraversecity.com
Institution Type/Description: Art Gallery.
Hours & Admission Prices: Call for hours.

**DENNOS MUSEUM CENTER OF NORTHWESTERN
MICHIGAN COLLEGE,** 1410 College Dr., Traverse City, MI
49686. Mailing Address: 1701 E. Front St., Traverse City, MI
49686-1055. Tel.: 231-955-1055. Fax: 231-995-1597.
E-mail: dmc@nmc.edu
Web Site: www.dennosmuseum.org
Key Personnel: Dir., Eugene A. Jenneman; Registrar, Kim Hanninen; Museum
   Shop Mgr., Terry Tarnow; Cur. Education, Jason Dake; Opers. Mgr., Megan
   Heator.
Institution Type/Description: College Art Museum.
Hours & Admission Prices: Mon.-Wed. & Fri.-Sat. 10-5, Thurs. 10-8, Sun. 1-5.
   Adults $6, students & children $4; discounts to groups, AAM & ICOM mem-
   bers; members no charge. Closed New Year's Day; Easter; Memorial Day;
   Independence Day; Labor Day; Thanksgiving; Christmas. &
Attendance: 60,000 (actual)

GREAT LAKES CHILDREN'S MUSEUM, 13240 S. West Bay
   Shore Dr., Traverse City, MI 49684. Tel.: 231-932-4526.
Web Site: www.greatlakeskids.org
Key Personnel: Pres., Dan Smith; Exec. Dir., Michael Long; Museum Educator,
   Anne Drake; Events & Fundraising Mgr., Lisa Pointe.
Institution Type/Description: Children's Museum.
Hours & Admission Prices: Tues.-Sat. 10-5, Sun. 1-5. Admission 1 & over $7; dis-
   counts to active duty military & their families with ID; children under one &
   members no charge. Closed New Year's Day; Thanksgiving; Christmas Eve &
   Day. &
Attendance: 30,000 (actual)

Trenton

TRENTON HISTORICAL MUSEUM, 306 St. Joseph, Trenton, MI 48183-2823. Mailing Address: 2800 Third St., Trenton, MI 48183-2918. Tel.: 734-675-2130.
E-mail: liglehart@trenton-mi.com
Web Site: www.trentonhistoricalcommission.org
Formerly: The Moore House
Key Personnel: Dir., Linda Murdock; Vice Chm. (V), Nada Frost.
Institution Type/Description: Historic House Museum: c.1881 Italianate construction.
Hours & Admission Prices: Under renovation.
Attendance: 300 (estimated)

Troy

TROY HISTORIC VILLAGE, 60 W. Wattles Rd., Troy, MI 48098-4699. Tel.: 248-524-3570. Fax: 248-524-3572. Facebook: Troy Historic Village.
E-mail: info@thvmail.org
Web Site: www.troyhistoricvillage.org
Key Personnel: Dir., Loraine Campbell; Pres. Historical Society, Judy Iceman; Adult Program Dir., Stephanie Suszek; Village Store Mgr., Sue Broihan.
Institution Type/Description: History Museum.
Hours & Admission Prices: Tues.-Thurs. 10-3. Adults $5, children & seniors $3; discounts to AAM members; members, active military & veterans no charge. Closed New Year's Eve & Day; Memorial Day; weekend; Independence Day; Labor Day weekend; Thanksgiving weekend; Christmas Eve & Day. &
Attendance: 25,000 (estimated)

University Center

MARSHALL M. FREDERICKS SCULPTURE MUSEUM, Arbury Fine Arts Center, Saginaw Valley State University, 7400 Bay Rd., University Center, MI 48710. Tel.: 989-964-7125. Fax: 989-964-7221.
E-mail: mfsm@svsu.edu
Web Site: www.marshallfredericks.org
Key Personnel: Chm. (V), Sue Vititoe; Dir., Marilyn L. Wheaton; Cur. Education, Andrea Ondish; Sr. Sec., Laurie Allison; Archivist, Melissa Ford; Collection Mgr., Geoffe Haney.
Institution Type/Description: Sculpture Museum.
Hours & Admission Prices: Mon.-Fri. 11-5, Sat. noon-5. No charge; donations accepted. Closed national & university holidays. &
Attendance: 17,500 (actual)

Vicksburg

VICKSBURG DEPOT MUSEUM, 300 N. Richardson St., Vicksburg, MI 49097. Mailing Address: P.O. Box 103, Vicksburg, MI 49097. Tel.: 269-649-1733.
E-mail: vixmus1@yahoo.com
Institution Type/Description: History Museum: housed in a former railroad depot; built in 1908.
Hours & Admission Prices: May-Dec.

Vulcan

IRON MOUNTAIN IRON MINE, W. 4852 Hwy. U.S. 2, Vulcan, MI 49892. Mailing Address: P.O. Box 216, Iron Mountain, MI 49801. Tel.: 906-563-8077. Facebook, Twitter, Google+ & TripAdvisor: Iron Mountain Iron Mine.
E-mail: ironmine@uplogon.com
Web Site: www.ironmountainironmine.com
Key Personnel: Dir., Eugene R. Carollo; Dir. Public Rels., Karen Secinaro.
Institution Type/Description: Mining Museum: located on Menominee Iron Range.
Hours & Admission Prices: Fri. of Memorial Day Weekend to Oct. 15 daily 9-5. Adults $14, children 6-12 $10; discount to members, AAM, ICOM, AARP, AAA & school groups; military and children 5 & under no charge. &
Attendance: 16,000 (estimated)

Wayne

CITY OF WAYNE HISTORICAL MUSEUM, 1 Town Square, Wayne, MI 48184-1637. Tel.: 734-722-0113. Facebook: @wayne-historicalsociety.
Web Site: waynehistoricalmuseum.wordpress.com
Formerly: Wayne Village Hall
Key Personnel: Dir., Lindsey Wooten.
Institution Type/Description: Local History Museum: housed in 1878 Village Hall.

Hours & Admission Prices: Wed. noon-3, Thurs. 4-7; groups by appointment. No charge; donations accepted. &
Attendance: 1,200 (actual)

West Bloomfield

CHALDEAN CULTURAL CENTER, 5600 Walnut Lake Rd., West Bloomfield, MI 48323-2370. Tel.: 248-681-5050. Fax: 248-681-9191.
E-mail: info@chaldeanculturalcenter.org
Web Site: www.chaldeanculturalcenter.org
Formerly: Chaldean Community Cultural Center
Key Personnel: Dir., Mary Romaya.
Institution Type/Description: Cultural Art Center.
Hours & Admission Prices: Call for hours. No charge. &

ORCHARD LAKE MUSEUM, 3951 Orchard Lake Rd., West Bloomfield, MI 48325. Tel.: 248-757-2451. Facebook: Greater West Bloomfield.
E-mail: contact@gwbhs.com
Web Site: www.gwbhs.org
Institution Type/Description: History Museum.
Hours & Admission Prices: 2nd Sun. each month 1-4; other times by appointment. No charge; donations accepted.

SHALOM STREET, 6600 W. Maple Rd., West Bloomfield, MI 48322-3003. Tel.: 248-432-5451.
E-mail: rmorais@jccdet.org
Web Site: www.shalomstreet.org
Key Personnel: Dir., Rabbi S. Robert Morais; Asst. Dir., Andrea Liberman.
Institution Type/Description: Children's Museum.
Hours & Admission Prices: Sept.-June Mon. & Wed.-Thurs. 10-7, Tues. 10-5, Sat. 10-3; Summer: see website for hours. No charge. &

Whitehall

ARTS COUNCIL OF WHITE LAKE, 106 E. Colby St., Whitehall, MI 49461-1009. Tel.: 231-894-2787.
E-mail: info@artscouncilofwhitelake.org
Web Site: www.artscouncilofwhitelake.org
Formerly: Nuveen Community Center for the Arts
Institution Type/Description: Art Gallery.
Hours & Admission Prices: Tues.-Fri. 12-5, Sat. 10-2.

Williamsburg

MUSIC HOUSE MUSEUM, 7377 U.S. 31 N., Williamsburg, MI 49690. Mailing Address: P.O. Box 297, Acme, MI 49610-0297. Tel.: 231-938-9300. Fax: 231-938-3650.
E-mail: info@musichouse.org
Web Site: www.musichouse.org
Key Personnel: Pres. (V), Dorothy Clore; Museum Shop Mgr., Patte Richards.
Institution Type/Description: Music/Musical Instrument Museum.
Hours & Admission Prices: May-Oct. Mon.-Sat. 10-4, Sun. 12-4; Nov.-Dec. Sat. 10-4, Sun. 12-4; call for additional holiday hours Adults $12, children 6-15 $5; discounts to AAA & AAM members and groups; children under 6 no charge. &
Attendance: 12,000 (estimated)

Wyandotte

WYANDOTTE MUSEUM, 2610 Biddle Ave., Wyandotte, MI 48192-5208. Tel.: 734-324-7284. Fax: 734-324-7283.
E-mail: museum@wyan.org
Web Site: www.wyandotte.net
Key Personnel: Dir. Museums, Jody Chansuolme; Pres. (V), Ken Navarre; Museum Shop Mgr., Sandra Noble.
Institution Type/Description: History Museum: housed in 1896 Ford-MacNichol period home.
Hours & Admission Prices: Tours: Mon.-Fri. 9-5. Adults $2, students $.50; children under 13 & members no charge. Closed Easter; Labor Day; Thanksgiving; Christmas. &
Attendance: 999

Ypsilanti

FORD GALLERY - EASTERN MICHIGAN UNIVERSITY, Ford Hall, Ypsilanti, MI 48197. Tel.: 734-487-0465.
E-mail: gtom@emich.edu
Web Site: emich.edu/fordgallery
Key Personnel: Dir., Greg Tom.

Institution Type/Description: Art Gallery.
Hours & Admission Prices: Mon. & Thurs. 10-5, Tues.-Wed. 10-7, Fri.-Sat. 10-2.

MICHIGAN FIREHOUSE MUSEUM AND EDUCATION CENTER, 110 W. Cross St., Ypsilanti, MI 48197-2445. Tel.: 734-547-0663. Fax: 734-547-0669.
E-mail: firemuseum@msn.com
Web Site: www.michiganfirehousemuseum.org
Key Personnel: Mgr., Steve Wilson; Cur., Maura Overland.
Institution Type/Description: Fire-Fighting Museum.
Hours & Admission Prices: Tues.-Sat. 10-4, Sun. 12-4, Adults $5, children 2-16 $3; children under 2 no charge. &
Attendance: 6,400 (actual)

YPSILANTI HISTORICAL MUSEUM, 220 N. Huron St., Ypsilanti, MI 48197-2516. Tel.: 734-482-4990. Facebook: Ypsilanti Historical Society.
E-mail: yhs.museum@gmail.com
Web Site: www.ypsilantihistoricalsociety.org
Key Personnel: Pres. (V), Alvin Rudisill.
Institution Type/Description: Local History Museum.
Hours & Admission Prices: Museum: Tues.-Sun. 2-5. No charge; donations accepted. &
Attendance: 3,000 (estimated)

YPSILANTI'S AUTOMOTIVE HERITAGE MUSEUM, 100 E. Cross, Ypsilanti, MI 48198-2936. Tel.: 734-482-5200. Fax: 734-480-2784. Facebook.
E-mail: info@ypsiautoheritage.org
Web Site: www.ypsiautoheritage.org
Formerly: Ypsilanti's Automotive Heritage Museum & Miller Motors Hudson
Key Personnel: Pres. (V), Ron Bluhm.
Institution Type/Description: Automobile Museum.
Hours & Admission Prices: Tues.-Sun. 1-4; Adults $5; children 13 & under no charge. Closed New Year's Day; Easter; Mother's Day; Memorial Day; Independence Day; Labor Day; Thanksgiving; Christmas. &
Attendance: 3,000 (estimated)

Zeeland

THE DEKKER HUIS/ZEELAND HISTORICAL MUSEUM, 37 E. Main St., Zeeland, MI 49464. Mailing Address: P.O. Box 165, Zeeland, MI 49464-0165. Tel.: 616-772-4079. Facebook: Zeeland Historical Society.
E-mail: zeelandmuseum@charter.net
Web Site: www.zeelandhistory.org
Key Personnel: Pres., Sara Donkersloot; Cur., Suzy Frederick.
Institution Type/Description: Historic House Museum: housed in former home of Dirk Dekker and his wife, built in 1876.
Hours & Admission Prices: Call for hours. No charge; donations accepted.
Attendance: 2,500 (actual)

MINNESOTA

(264 listings)

Aitkin

AITKIN COUNTY HISTORICAL SOCIETY, 20 Pacific St., Aitkin, MN 56431-1628. Mailing Address: P.O. Box 215, Aitkin, MN 56431-0215. Tel.: 218-927-3348.
E-mail: achs3348@embarqmail.com
Web Site: www.aitkincohs.org
Key Personnel: Admin., Mathew Nix; Pres. (V), Cheryl Meld; Vice Pres. (V), Jennie Hakes.
Institution Type/Description: Historical Society Museum: housed in the Northern Pacific Depot, built 1916. Listed on the National Register of Historic Places.
Hours & Admission Prices: June-Aug. Wed.-Sat. 10-4; Sept.-May Wed. & Fri.-Sat. 10-4. Adults $2; members no charge. &
Attendance: 5,000 (actual)

THE JAQUES ART CENTER, 121 Second St., N.W., Aitkin, MN 56431. Tel.: 218-927-2363.
E-mail: info@jaquesart.com
Institution Type/Description: Art Center.
Hours & Admission Prices: Tues.-Sat. 11-4. No charge.

Albert Lea

FREEBORN COUNTY HISTORICAL MUSEUM, LIBRARY & VILLAGE, 1031 Bridge Ave., Albert Lea, MN 56007-2205. Tel.: 507-373-8003. Fax: 507-552-1269.
E-mail: executivedirector@fchm.us
Web Site: www.fchm.us
Formerly: Freeborn County Historical Society
Key Personnel: Exec. Dir., Kim Nelson; Chm. (V), Abbie Lotts; Pres. (V), Brad Kirchner; Vice Pres., Dean Johnson; Vice Pres. (V), Mark Light.
Institution Type/Description: History Museum & Historical Village.
Hours & Admission Prices: Museum & Library: Wed.-Sat. 10-4. Village: May-Sept. Wed.-Sat. 10-4. Adults $7.50, students 12-18 $2; discounts to AAA members; FCHM members, children 11 & under & members no charge. Closed New Year's Day, Thanksgiving, Christmas Day. Hours subject to change. &
Attendance: 11,942 (actual)

Alexandria

DOUGLAS COUNTY HISTORICAL SOCIETY, 1219 Nokomis St., Alexandria, MN 56308-3712. Tel.: 320-762-0382. Facebook.
E-mail: historic@dchsmn.org
Web Site: dchsmn.org
Key Personnel: Exec. Dir., Kim Dillon; Pres. (V), Gary Lund; Vice Pres., Lloyd Flaaten.
Institution Type/Description: Historical Society Museum: housed in the former home of Senator Knute Nelson. Listed on the National Register of Historic Places.
Hours & Admission Prices: Tours: Mon.-Fri. 9-3. Adults $5, children 11 & under $3. Research: Mon.-Fri. 9-4. &
Attendance: 766 (estimated)

MINNESOTA LAKES MARITIME MUSEUM, 205 3rd Ave., W., Alexandria, MN 56308-1364. Mailing Address: P.O. Box 1216, Alexandria, MN 56308-3216. Tel.: 320-759-1114. Fax: 320-759-1101.
E-mail: boat@mnlakesmaritime.org
Web Site: mnlakesmaritime.org
Key Personnel: Dir., Bruce T. Olson; Pres. (V), Kevin Kopischke.
Institution Type/Description: Maritime Museum.
Hours & Admission Prices: May 15-Oct. Mon.-Sat. 10-5, Sun. 12-4; other times by appointment. Family $18, adults $8, seniors $7, students 5-17 $5; members no charge. &
Attendance: 4,000 (estimated)

RUNESTONE MUSEUM, 206 Broadway St., Alexandria, MN 56308-1417. Tel.: 320-763-3160. Facebook, Twitter.
E-mail: bigole@rea-alp.com
Web Site: www.runestonemuseum.org
Key Personnel: Exec. Dir., Amanda Seim; Admin. Asst., Amber Hieb; Museum Staff, Lucillia DiCenso.
Institution Type/Description: History, Heritage, and Natural Science Museum.
Hours & Admission Prices: April-Oct.: Mon.-Sat. 9-5, Sun. 11-4; Nov.-March Mon.-Sat. 10-4. April-Oct.: Family $20, adult $8, senior $7, children $5; members no charge. Nov.-March: Family $15, adults $7, senior citizens $6, students 5-17 $3; members no charge. &
Attendance: 13,000 (actual)

Annandale

MINNESOTA PIONEER PARK MUSEUM, 725 Pioneer Park Trail, Annandale, MN 55302-3128. Tel.: 320-274-8489.
E-mail: pioneerp@lakedalelink.net
Web Site: pioneerpark.org
Key Personnel: Pres., Pete Axford.
Institution Type/Description: Historic Site.
Hours & Admission Prices: Memorial Day to mid-Oct. Mon.-Fri. 10-4, Sat.-Sun. 12-4. Adults $5, senior citizens $4, children 6-16 $3; members and children 5 & under no charge.
Attendance: 8,000 (estimated)

Anoka

ANOKA COUNTY HISTORICAL SOCIETY, 2135 Third Ave. N., Anoka, MN 55303-2258. Tel.: 763-421-0600. Fax: 763-323-0218.
E-mail: achs@ac-hs.org
Web Site: www.ac-hs.org
Key Personnel: Pres. (V), Paul Pierce, III; Exec. Dir., Todd Mahon.
Institution Type/Description: County History Museum.

Hours & Admission Prices: Tues. 10-8, Wed.-Fri. 10-5, Sat. 10-4. Adults $3; discounts to groups of 15 or more; members no charge. Library: no charge. &
Attendance: 15,000 (actual)

Apple Valley

MINNESOTA ZOO, 13000 Zoo Blvd., Apple Valley, MN 55124-4621. Tel.: 952-431-9200. Fax: 952-431-9336.
E-mail: INFO@MNZOO.ORG
Web Site: www.mnzoo.org
Key Personnel: Interim Pres. & Dir., Kevin Willis; Gift Shop Mgr., Laurel Wright.
Institution Type/Description: Zoo.
Hours & Admission Prices: May & Sept. Mon.-Fri. 9-4, Sat.-Sun. 9-6; Memorial Day-Labor Day daily 9-6; Oct.-April daily 9-4. Adults 13-64 $18, senior citizens 65 & over and children 3-12 $12; discounts to AZA members; members and children 2 & under no charge. Parking: cars $7, buses $10, motor coaches $15; members no charge. Closed Thanksgiving; Christmas. &
Attendance: 1,338,581 (actual)

Austin

MOWER COUNTY HISTORICAL SOCIETY, Mower County Fairgrounds, 1303 6th Ave., S.W., Austin, MN 55912-2472. Tel.: 507-437-6082. Fax: 507-437-6082. Facebook: Mower County Historical Society.
E-mail: info@mowercountyhistory.org
Web Site: www.mowercountyhistory.org
Key Personnel: Dir., Dustin Heckman; Pres. (V), Garry Ellingson.
Institution Type/Description: Historical Society Museum.
Hours & Admission Prices: Tues.-Fri. 10-4. Adults $5; children under 12 no charge.
Attendance: 30,000 (estimated)

THE SPAM MUSEUM, 101 3rd Ave., N.E., Austin, MN 55912-3690. Mailing Address: Hormel Food Corp., Consumer Response, 1 Hormel Pl., Austin, MN 55912. Tel.: 507-437-5100. Fax: 800-LUV-SPAM.
E-mail: spam_museum@hormel.com
Web Site: www.spam.com
Key Personnel: Dir., Savile Lord.
Institution Type/Description: General Museum.
Hours & Admission Prices: April-Oct. Mon.-Sat. 10-6, Sun. 12-5, 1st Thurs. each month 10-8; Nov.-March Tues.-Sun. 12-5. Closed New Year's Day; Easter; Thanksgiving; Christmas Eve & Day. &
Attendance: 125,000 (estimated)

Baudette

LAKE OF THE WOODS COUNTY MUSEUM, 119 8th Ave., S. E., Baudette, MN 56623. Mailing Address: 206 8th Ave., S.E., Ste. 150, Baudette, MN 56623-2867. Tel.: 218-634-1200.
E-mail: lowhsociety@mncable.net
Web Site: www.lakeofthewoodshistoricalsociety.com
Key Personnel: C.E.O. & Cur., Marlys Hirst; Chm. (V), Dan Crompton.
Institution Type/Description: County History Museum.
Hours & Admission Prices: mid-May to Sept. Tues.-Fri. 10-4, Sat. 10-2; other times by appointment. No charge; donations accepted. Closed Labor Day. &
Attendance: 3,000 (estimated)

Becker

SHERBURNE HISTORY CENTER, 10775 27th Ave. S.E., Becker, MN 55308-4656. Tel.: 763-261-4433. Fax: 763-261-4437.
E-mail: mbrubaker@sherburnehistorycenter.org
Web Site: www.sherburnehistorycenter.org
Formerly: Sherburne County Historical Society
Key Personnel: Exec. Dir., Mike Brubaker; Pres., Teresa Warner; Pres. (V), Jean Johnson.
Institution Type/Description: Historical Society Museum.
Hours & Admission Prices: Tues.-Fri. 10-5, Sat. 10-4. No charge; donations accepted. Closed major holidays. &
Attendance: 4,000 (actual)

Bemidji

BELTRAMI COUNTY HISTORY CENTER, 130 Minnesota Ave., S.W., Bemidji, MN 56601-4009. Tel.: 218-444-3376. Fax: 218-444-3377. Facebook, Twitter, Instagram.
E-mail: depot@beltramihistory.org
Web Site: www.beltramihistory.org
Formerly: Beltrami County Historical Society

Key Personnel: Dir., Dan Karalus; Pres., Sharon Geisen; Vice Pres., Linda L. Lemmer.
Institution Type/Description: History Museum.
Hours & Admission Prices: History Center: Wed.-Sat. 12-4 or by appointment. Adults $5, seniors & students $4, children 6-12 $1, discounts to Time Travelers network; members & children 5 & under no charge. Assisted Research Fee: $15 per hour; members & self-search no charge. Closed Memorial Day; Labor Day; Thanksgiving; Christmas Eve & Day. &
Attendance: 4,500 (estimated)

HEADWATERS SCIENCE CENTER, 413 Beltrami Ave., Bemidji, MN 56601-3106. Mailing Address: P.O. Box 1176, Bemidji, MN 56619-1176. Tel.: 218-444-4472. Fax: 218-444-4473.
E-mail: contact@hscbemidji.org
Web Site: www.hscbemidji.org/index.htm
Institution Type/Description: Science Center.
Hours & Admission Prices: Mon. & Wed.-Sat. 9:30-5, Sun. 1-5. Adults 12 & over $7, seniors 65 & over and military $6, children 2-11 $5; children under 2 no charge. Closed New Year's Day; Easter; Thanksgiving; Christmas.

Benson

SWIFT COUNTY HISTORICAL SOCIETY, 2135 Minnesota Ave., Bldg. 2, Benson, MN 56215-2101. Tel.: 320-843-4467. Facebook: Swift County Historical Society.
E-mail: swiftmuseum@embarqmail.com
Key Personnel: Exec. Dir., Marie Tucker.
Institution Type/Description: History Museum.
Hours & Admission Prices: Tues.-Fri. 10-4:30. No charge; donations accepted. &
Attendance: 1,500 (estimated)

Blaine

AMERICAN WINGS AIR MUSEUM, Anoka County Airport, Colorado Ln., Blaine, MN 55449-0322. Mailing Address: P.O. Box 490322, Blaine, MN 55449-0322. Tel.: 763-786-4146.
E-mail: lburgers@pro-ns.net
Web Site: www.americanwings.org/museum.htm
Institution Type/Description: Military History Museum.
Hours & Admission Prices: Tues. 4-8, Sat. 10-5; other times by appointment.

Bloomington

ARTISTRY, 1800 W. Old Shakopee Rd., Bloomington, MN 55431-3071. Tel.: 952-563-8575. Fax: 952-563-8576. TDD: 952-563-8740.
E-mail: info@artistrymn.org
Web Site: www.artistrymn.org
Formerly: Bloomington Theatre and Art Center
Key Personnel: Pres. (V), Brian Prentice; Exec. Dir., Andrea Specht; Treas., Amy Lueders; Vice Pres., Paul Zech; Sec., Paul Seminari; Dir. Visual Arts, Rachel Daly; Dir. Publicity, Nancy Lamberger.
Institution Type/Description: Art Center.
Hours & Admission Prices: Mon.-Fri. 8am-10pm, Sat. 9-5, Sun.1-10. No charge. Closed holidays. &
Attendance: 69,000 (estimated)

BLOOMINGTON HISTORICAL SOCIETY - OLD TOWN HALL HISTORY MUSEUM, 10200 Penn Ave. S., Bloomington, MN 55431. Mailing Address: 1800 W. Old Shakopee Rd., Bloomington, MN 55431. Tel.: 952-881-4114 & 4327.
E-mail: vonda.kelly@gmail.com
Web Site: www.bloomingtonhistoricalsociety.org
Key Personnel: Pres. (V), Dir. & Museum Shop Mgr., Vonda Kelly; Museum Shop Mgr., Don Stiles.
Institution Type/Description: Regional History Museum: housed in 1892 Old Town Hall.
Hours & Admission Prices: Tues.-Thurs. & Sat. 12-4, Sun. 1-5. No charge; donations accepted. &
Attendance: 2,500 (estimated)

UNDERWATER ADVENTURES AQUARIUM, Mall of America, 120 E. Broadway, Bloomington, MN 55425-5511. Tel.: 852-883-0202, 888-348-3824. Fax: 952-883-0303.
E-mail: sales@sealifeus.com
Web Site: www.visitsealife.com/minnesota
Institution Type/Description: Aquarium.
Hours & Admission Prices: Mon.-Thurs. 10-7:30, Fri. 10-8, Sat. 9:30-8, Sun. 10-7. Adults 13 & over $24.25, children 3-12 $17.25; children under 3 no charge.

THE WORKS MUSEUM, 9740 Grand Ave. S., Bloomington, MN 55420. Tel.: 952-888-4262. Facebook; Twitter.
E-mail: info@theworks.org
Web Site: www.theworks.org
Institution Type/Description: Hands-On Children's Engineering Museum.
Hours & Admission Prices: Mon. & Thurs.-Fri. 9-3, Sat. 10-5, Sun. 12-5. Admission 3 & over $8.50; children under 3 no charge.
Attendance: 78,000

Blue Earth

FARIBAULT COUNTY HISTORICAL SOCIETY, 405 E. Sixth St., Blue Earth, MN 56013-2020. Tel.: 507-526-5421.
E-mail: fchs@bevcomm.net
Institution Type/Description: Historical Society Museum.
Hours & Admission Prices: Tues.-Fri. 10-4; other times by appointment and during County Fair. Donations Accepted. Closed holidays.
Attendance: 2,000 (estimated)

Brainerd

CROW WING COUNTY HISTORICAL SOCIETY, 320 Laurel, Brainerd, MN 56401-3523. Mailing Address: P.O. Box 722, Brainerd, MN 56401-0722. Tel.: 218-829-3268. Fax: 218-828-4434.
E-mail: history@crowwing.us
Web Site: www.crowwinghistory.org/
Key Personnel: Pres. (V), Don Samuelson; Admin., Pamela Nelson.
Institution Type/Description: Local History Museum.
Hours & Admission Prices: Tues.-Sat. 10-3. Donations: adults $3; children, students & members no charge. Closed holidays. &
Attendance: 5,000 (estimated)

NORTHLAND ARBORETUM, 14250 Conservation Dr., Brainerd, MN 56401. Mailing Address: P.O. Box 375, Brainerd, MN 56401. Tel.: 218-829-8770.
E-mail: arboretum@brainerd.net
Web Site: www.northlandarb.org
Key Personnel: Dir., Dale E. Braddy.
Institution Type/Description: Arboretum.
Hours & Admission Prices: Daily dawn to dusk. Adults $3; members no charge. &
Attendance: 50,000 (estimated)

Breckenridge

WILKIN COUNTY HISTORICAL SOCIETY, 704 Nebraska Ave., Breckenridge, MN 56520-1547. Tel.: 218-643-1303.
E-mail: sylivawchs@hotmail.com
Web Site: www.co.wilkin.mn.us
Key Personnel: C.E.O. & Pres., Gordon Martinson; Treas., Ruth Poppel; Sec., Sylvia Peterson.
Institution Type/Description: Local History Museum.
Hours & Admission Prices: Tues.-Thurs. 1:30-4. No charge, donations accepted.
Attendance: 200 (estimated)

Browns Valley

SAM BROWN LOG HOUSE, 796 W. Broadway, Browns Valley, MN 56219-0013. Mailing Address: City Hall, Box 334, Browns Valley, MN 56219-0013. Tel.: 320-695-2110. Fax: 320-695-2127.
E-mail: tom.schmitz@prtel.com
Web Site: www.brownsvalleymn.com
Key Personnel: Pres. (V), Shirley Ecker; Clerk & Treas., Thomas A. Schmitz.
Institution Type/Description: Historic House: 1863 Joseph & Sam Brown log house.
Hours & Admission Prices: Memorial Day weekend to Labor Day Fri.-Sun. 1-6 & holidays; other times by appointment. No charge; donations accepted.
Attendance: 500 (actual)

Buffalo

WRIGHT COUNTY HISTORICAL SOCIETY, 2001 Hwy. 25 N., Buffalo, MN 55313. Mailing Address: P.O. Box 304, Buffalo, MN 55313-0304. Tel.: 763-682-7323. Fax: 763-682-7324.
E-mail: info@wrighthistory.org
Web Site: www.wrighthistory.org
Key Personnel: Pres., Leander Wetter; Coord. & Cur., Erin Storc; Archivist, Betty Dircks; Business Mgr., Sally Macnab.
Institution Type/Description: General Museum.

Hours & Admission Prices: Mon.-Fri. 8-4:30. No charge; donations accepted. &
Attendance: 8,000 (estimated)

Cambridge

ISANTI COUNTY HISTORICAL SOCIETY, 33525 Flanders St., N.E., Cambridge, MN 55008-4157. Tel.: 763-689-4229. Fax: 763-552-0740.
E-mail: ichsdirector@izoom.net
Web Site: www.ichs.ws
Key Personnel: C.E.O. & Dir., Kathleen J. McCully; Chm. (V) & Pres. (V), Kay Rodrigue.
Institution Type/Description: Historical Society.
Hours & Admission Prices: Heritage Center: Mon.-Tues. & Fri. 9-4:30; other times by appointment. Historic Structures: open for special events; other times by appointment. No charge; donations accepted. &
Attendance: 1,500 (estimated)

Cannon Falls

CANNON FALLS AREA HISTORICAL MUSEUM, 206 W. Mill St., Cannon Falls, MN 55009-2029. Mailing Address: P.O. Box 111, Cannon Falls, MN 55009-0111. Tel.: 507-263-4503. Fax: 507-263-4080.
E-mail: cannonfallsmuseum@gmail.com
Web Site: www.sites.google.com/site/cannonfallsmuseum
Key Personnel: Dir., Zachary Wareham; Pres. (V), Steve Dabelow; Treas., Tom Monroe; Sec., Ilene Fox.
Institution Type/Description: Historical Society Museum: housed in 1888 town fire hall.
Hours & Admission Prices: Fri. 1-5, Sat. 10-4; groups by appointment. No charge; donations accepted.
Attendance: 700 (estimated)

Chaska

MINNESOTA LANDSCAPE ARBORETUM, UNIVERSITY OF MINNESOTA, 3675 Arboretum Dr., Chaska, MN 55318-9613. Tel.: 952-443-1400. Fax: 612-301-1274. Facebook: Minnesota Arboretum.
E-mail: arbinfo@umn.edu
Web Site: www.arboretum.umn.edu
Key Personnel: Dir., Peter C. Moe; Pres. (V), Todd Wagner.
Institution Type/Description: Arboretum.
Hours & Admission Prices: April-Oct. Mon.-Sat. 8-6, Sun. 10-6; Nov.-March Mon.-Sat. 8-4:30, Sun. 10-4:30. Admission 13 & over $12; University of Minnesota students, children 12 & under, members, April-Oct. 3rd Thurs. after 4:30 and Nov.-March Thurs. no charge. Reciprocal admission. Closed Thanksgiving; Christmas. &
Attendance: 325,239 (actual)

Chisholm

MINNESOTA DISCOVERY CENTER, 1005 Discovery Dr., Chisholm, MN 55719. Tel.: 218-254-7959, 800-372-6437. Fax: 218-254-7971.
E-mail: allyse.freeman@mndiscoverycenter.com
Web Site: www.mndiscoverycenter.com
Formerly: Ironworld
Key Personnel: Exec. Dir., Lisa Vesel; Archivist, Chris Welter; Cur., Allyse Freeman; Events Mgr., Mara Brownlee.
Institution Type/Description: General Museum.
Hours & Admission Prices: Research Center: Tues.-Sat. 10-5. No charge. Park & Museum: Summer: Tues.-Wed. & Fri.-Sun. 10-7, Thurs. 10-9; Winter: Tues.-Wed. & Fri.-Sat. 10-5, Thurs. 10-9. Adults $5, students $3; members & Thurs. after 5pm no charge. Closed New Year's Day; Easter; Memorial Day; Independence Day; Labor Day; Thanksgiving; Christmas Eve & Day. &
Attendance: 31,000 (estimated)

MINNESOTA MUSEUM OF MINING, 900 W. Lake St., Chisholm, MN 55719-1736. Mailing Address: P.O. Box 271, Chisholm, MN 55719-0271. Tel.: 218-254-5543. Facebook: Minnesota Museum of Mining.
E-mail: info@mnmuseumofmining.org
Web Site: www.mnmuseumofmining.org
Key Personnel: Pres., John Nelson.
Institution Type/Description: Mining Museum.
Hours & Admission Prices: Memorial Day to Labor Day Mon.-Sat. 9-5, Sun. 1-5; groups by appointment. Adults $5, seniors $4.50, students $3; children 5 & under no charge.

Cloquet

CARLTON COUNTY HISTORICAL SOCIETY, 406 Cloquet Ave., Cloquet, MN 55720-1750. Tel.: 218-879-1938. Fax: 218-879-1938. Facebook, Twitter.
E-mail: director@carltoncountyhistory.org
Web Site: www.carltoncountyhistory.org
Key Personnel: Dir., Rachael E. Martin; Pres., James Dennie; Treas., Vivian Bergquist; Sec., Lisbeth Boutang.
Institution Type/Description: History Museum.
Hours & Admission Prices: Tues.-Sat. 9-4. Adults $2, children 5-11 $1; children under 5 & members no charge. ♿
Attendance: 1,500 (estimated)

Cokato

COKATO MUSEUM & AKERLUND PHOTOGRAPHY STUDIO, 175 W. 4th St., Cokato, MN 55321-4852. Mailing Address: P.O. Box 686, Cokato, MN 55321-0686. Tel.: 320-286-2427. Fax: 320-286-5876. Facebook: Cokato Museum & Akerlund Photography Studio.
E-mail: cokatomuseum@embarqmail.com
Web Site: www.cokatomuseum.org
Key Personnel: Dir., Mike Worcester; Pres. (V), Connie Isaacson; Financial Dir., Dorene Erickson.
Institution Type/Description: History Museum & Historic Site.
Hours & Admission Prices: Tues.-Fri. 8:30-4:30, Sat. 8:30-3. No charge; donations accepted. Guided Tours $2. Closed major holidays. ♿
Attendance: 3,989 (actual)

Comfrey

JEFFERS PETROGLYPHS, MINNESOTA HISTORICAL SOCIETY, 27160 County Rd. 2, Comfrey, MN 56019-4430. Tel.: 507-628-5591. Facebook: Jeffers Petroglyphs; Twitter: @jefferspetro.
E-mail: jefferspetroglyphs@mnhs.org
Web Site: sites.mnhs.org/historic-sites/jeffers-petroglyphs
Key Personnel: Site Consultant, Tom Sanders.
Institution Type/Description: History Museum.
Hours & Admission Prices: Memorial Day weekend to Labor Day Mon., Wed.-Sat. 10-5, Sun. noon to 5; Sept. 10-5. Adults $8, seniors, college students & children 5-17 $6; MNHS members & children 4 & under no charge.
Attendance: 8,000 (actual)

Crookston

POLK COUNTY HISTORICAL SOCIETY, 719 E. Robert St., Crookston, MN 56716-2043. Mailing Address: P.O. Box 214, Crookston, MN 56716-0214. Tel.: 218-281-1038.
E-mail: polkcounty@q.com
Web Site: www.mnhistoricnw.org/Polkchs.htm
Key Personnel: Pres. (V) & Cur., Gerald J. Amiot; Vice Pres., Jerry Wentzel; Dir. & Museum Shop Mgr., Alyson Leas.
Institution Type/Description: History Museum.
Hours & Admission Prices: 3rd week in May to mid-Sept. Tues.-Sun. 12-4. No charge; donations accepted. ♿
Attendance: 2,000 (estimated)

Crosby

CUYUNA IRON RANGE HERITAGE NETWORK, 101 First St., N.E., Crosby, MN 56441. Mailing Address: P.O. Box 272, Crosby, MN 56441-0272. Tel.: 218-546-6178 & 545-1166. Fax: 248-545-1166. Facebook: Cuyuna Iron Range Heritage Network.
E-mail: cchps@crosbyironton.net
Web Site: cuyunahistory.org
Formerly: Cuyuna Range Historical Society & Museum
Key Personnel: Pres. (V), Myrna Nelson.
Institution Type/Description: History Museum: housed in 1910 Soo Line Depot.
Hours & Admission Prices: June-Aug. Mon.-Sat. 10-4; call for additional tour hours. No charge; donations accepted. Closed holidays. ♿
Attendance: 1,250 (estimated)

Currie

END-O-LINE RAILROAD PARK & MUSEUM, 440 N. Mill St., Currie, MN 56123-1133. Mailing Address: P.O. Box 57, Slayton, MN 56172-0057. Tel.: 507-763-3708. Fax: 507-836-8904. Facebook: @endolinemuseum.
E-mail: endoline@co.murray.mn.us
Web Site: www.endoline.com
Key Personnel: Site Coord., Jakob Etrheim; Murray County Museums Coord., Janet Timmerman.
Institution Type/Description: Railroad Museum.
Hours & Admission Prices: Memorial Day-Labor Day Wed.-Sun. 10-5; bus tours & groups by appointment. Adults 18 & over $7, students 6-17 $5; children under 5 no charge. ♿
Attendance: 2,274 (actual)

Detroit Lakes

BECKER COUNTY HISTORICAL SOCIETY, 714 Summit Ave., Detroit Lakes, MN 56501-2941. Mailing Address: P.O. Box 622, Detroit Lakes, MN 56502-0622. Tel.: 218-847-2938. Fax: 218-847-5048.
E-mail: mail@beckercountyhistory.org
Web Site: www.beckercountyhistory.org
Key Personnel: Exec. Dir., Carrie Johnston.
Institution Type/Description: Local History Museum.
Hours & Admission Prices: Tues.-Sat. 10-4. No charge; donations accepted. Closed national holidays. ♿
Attendance: 7,500 (estimated)

Duluth

CAF LAKE SUPERIOR SQUADRON 101 MUSEUM, Airport Rd., Duluth International Airport, Duluth, MN 55811. Mailing Address: 4931 Airport Rd., Duluth, MN 55811. Tel.: 218-733-0639.
E-mail: info@cafduluth.com
Web Site: www.cafduluth.com
Institution Type/Description: Military History Museum.
Hours & Admission Prices: Call for hours. No charge; donations accepted. ♿

DULUTH ART INSTITUTE, 506 W. Michigan St., Duluth, MN 55802-1519. Tel.: 218-733-7560.
E-mail: info@duluthartinstitute.org
Web Site: www.duluthartinstitute.org
Key Personnel: Exec. Dir., Christina Woods; Dir. Exhibitions, Amy Varsek; Mgr. Education Prog., Michelle Misgen.
Institution Type/Description: Art Gallery.
Hours & Admission Prices: Labor Day to Memorial Day daily 9-5; May-Sept. daily 9-6. ♿
Attendance: 50,000 (estimated)

DULUTH CHILDREN'S MUSEUM CLOSED, 115 S. 29th Ave. W., Duluth, MN 55806. Tel.: 218-733-7543 & 7546. Fax: 218-733-7547.
E-mail: explore@playduluth.org
Web Site: www.duluthchildrensmuseum.org
Key Personnel: C.E.O. & Pres., Cameron Kruger.
Institution Type/Description: Children's & Youth Museum: housed in 1892 French Norman style former railway station, the St. Louis County Heritage & Arts Center including two additional museums, an art institute & five performing arts organizations.
Hours & Admission Prices: Thurs.-Sun. 10-3. Admission one & over $9; members, Association of Children's Museums, Association of Science & Technology Center reciprocal membership programs; children under 2 no charge. Closed New Year's Day; Easter; Thanksgiving; Christmas Eve & Day. ♿
Attendance: 54,321 (actual)

GLENSHEEN HISTORIC CONGDON ESTATE, 3300 London Rd., Duluth, MN 55804-2010. Tel.: 218-726-8910, 888-454-GLEN. Fax: 218-726-8911.
E-mail: info@glensheen.org
Web Site: www.glensheen.org
Key Personnel: Dir., Daniel Hartman; Mktg. Mgr., Jane Pederson.
Institution Type/Description: Historic House & Site: 1905-08 Glensheen, 6.7-acre historic estate featuring 39-room Jacobean Revival mansion, built for Chester A. Congdon, along the shore of Lake Superior. Listed on National Register of Historic Places.
Hours & Admission Prices: See website for hours & ticket prices. Closed New Year's Day; Thanksgiving; Christmas. ♿
Attendance: 60,000 (actual)

GREAT LAKES AQUARIUM, 353 Harbor Dr., #5520, Duluth, MN 55802-2639. Tel.: 218-740-3474. Fax: 218-740-2020.

E-mail: info@glaquarium.org
Web Site: www.glaquarium.org
Institution Type/Description: Aquarium.
Hours & Admission Prices: Daily 10-6. Adults $17.99, seniors 62 & over $14.99, youth 13-17 $13.99, children 3-12 $11.99; children 2 & under no charge. Closed Christmas.
Attendance: 140,000

KARPELES MANUSCRIPT LIBRARY MUSEUM, 902 E. First St., Duluth, MN 55805-2142. Tel.: 218-728-0630.
E-mail: kmuseumdut@aol.com
Web Site: www.rain.org/~karpeles/dulfrm.html
Key Personnel: Dir., Robert Wickham; Cur., Luis E. Rego.
Institution Type/Description: Manuscript Library Museum.
Hours & Admission Prices: Tues.-Sun. 10-4. No charge; donations accepted.

LAKE SUPERIOR MARITIME VISITORS CENTER, 600 Lake Ave., S., Duluth, MN 55802-2322. Mailing Address: P.O. Box 177, Duluth, MN 55801-0177. Tel.: 218-720-5260, ext. 1. Fax: 218-720-5270.
E-mail: info@LSMMA.com
Web Site: www.LSMMA.com
Key Personnel: Dir., Thomas Holden; Public Rels., Beth M. Duncan.
Institution Type/Description: Marine Museum: located at Duluth Ship Canal.
Hours & Admission Prices: Spring & Fall Sun.-Thurs. 10-4:30, Fri.-Sat. 10-6; Summer: daily 10-9; Winter: Fri.-Sun. 10-4:30. No charge; donations accepted. &
Attendance: 408,000 (actual)

LAKE SUPERIOR RAILROAD MUSEUM, 506 W. Michigan St., Ste. 19, Duluth, MN 55802-1533. Tel.: 218-727-8025. Fax: 218-733-7596.
E-mail: museum@LSRM.org
Web Site: www.lsrm.org
Key Personnel: Dir., Ken Buehler; Pres. (V), Neal Vanstrom; Opers. Mgr., Richard Bergsrud; Cur., Tim Schandel; Museum Shop Mgr., Josh Miller.
Institution Type/Description: Railroad Museum: housed in 1891-92 Duluth Union Depot Building.
Hours & Admission Prices: Memorial Day-Labor Day Mon.-Sat. 9-6; Sun. 9-5. Adults $12, children 3-13 $6; children 2 & under & members no charge. Closed New Year's Day; Easter; Thanksgiving; Christmas. &
Attendance: 100,000 (estimated)

LAKE SUPERIOR ZOO, 7210 Fremont St., Duluth, MN 55807-1854. Tel.: 218-730-4500. Fax: 218-723-3750.
E-mail: info@lszoo.org
Web Site: www.lszooduluth.org
Key Personnel: Pres. Lake Superior Zoological Society, Diana Boucher-Dodge.
Institution Type/Description: Zoo.
Hours & Admission Prices: Summer: 10-5; Winter: 10-4. Adults 13 & over $10, seniors 62 & over $9, children 3-12 $5; discount to reciprocal members; members & children under 3 no charge. &
Attendance: 87,112 (actual)

THE ST. LOUIS COUNTY HISTORICAL SOCIETY, 506 W. Michigan St., Duluth, MN 55802-1519. Tel.: 218-733-7580. Fax: 218-733-7585. Facebook: St. Louis County Historical Society.
E-mail: history@thehistorypeople.org
Web Site: www.thehistorypeople.org; www.vets-hall.org
Key Personnel: Exec. Dir., JoAnne Coombe; Chm. (V) Veterans' Memorial Hall, Dennis Hughes; Pres., Leone Graf; Collections Mgr. & Exhibits Cur., Samantha Tubbs; Administrative Svcs. Mgr., Julie Bolos.
Institution Type/Description: History Museum: housed in restored Duluth Union Depot.
Hours & Admission Prices: Summer: daily 9-6; Winter: daily 9-5. Adults $14, children 3-13 $6; discounts to AAA & AARP members; members and children 2 & under no charge. Call 218-727-8025 for holiday closures. &
Attendance: 90,000 (estimated)

TWEED MUSEUM OF ART, Univ. of Minnesota Duluth, 1201 Ordean Ct., Duluth, MN 55812-3041. Tel.: 218-726-8222 & 7823. Fax: 218-726-8503. Facebook: Tweed Museum of Art.
E-mail: tma@d.umn.edu
Web Site: www.d.umn.edu/tma
Formerly: Tweed Gallery
Key Personnel: Dir., Ken Bloom; Public Rels., Christine Strom; Registrar, Camille Doran; Preparator, Anneliese Verhoeven; Exec. Sec. & Museum Shop Mgr., Kathy Sandstedt.
Institution Type/Description: Art Museum.

Hours & Admission Prices: Tues. 9-8, Wed.-Fri. 9-4:30, Sat.-Sun. 1-5. No charge, donations accepted. Closed university holidays. &
Attendance: 35,000 (actual)

Eden Prairie

NWA HISTORY CENTRE, INC., Administration & Archives, 10100 Flying Cloud Dr., Ste. A-306, Eden Prairie, MN 55347. Tel.: 952-698-4478. Facebook: @NWA.History.Centre.
E-mail: info@nwahistory.org
Web Site: www.nwahistory.org
Key Personnel: Exec. Dir., Bruce Kitt.
Institution Type/Description: Commercial Aviation History Museum.
Hours & Admission Prices: Mon.-Fri. 11-5, Sat. 9-1. No charge; donations accepted. Closed major holidays. &
Attendance: 1,200 (estimated)

WINGS OF THE NORTH, 14801 Pioneer Tr., Ste. 200, Eden Prairie, MN 55347. Tel.: 952-746-6100.
E-mail: info@wotn.org
Institution Type/Description: Aviation History Museum.
Hours & Admission Prices: Call for hours.

Edina

EDINA HISTORICAL SOCIETY, 4711 W. 70th St., Edina, MN 55435-4059. Tel.: 612-928-4577.
E-mail: edinahistory@yahoo.com
Web Site: www.edinahistoricalsociety.org
Key Personnel: Pres., Dan Latham; Exec. Dir., Marci Matson.
Institution Type/Description: Historical Society Museum.
Hours & Admission Prices: Thurs. 9am-2pm, Sat. 10am-12pm; other times by appointment. &

MARGARET FOSS GALLERY - EDINA ART CENTER, 4701 W. 64th St., Edina, MN 55435-1501. Tel.: 952-903-5780. Fax: 952-903-5781.
E-mail: artcenter@ci.edina.mn.us
Web Site: www.edinaartcenter.com
Key Personnel: Interim Dir., Michael Frey.
Institution Type/Description: Art Gallery.
Hours & Admission Prices: Mon.-Thurs. 9-8, Fri. 9-3:30, Sat. 9-1.

Elbow Lake

GRANT COUNTY HISTORICAL SOCIETY, 115 2nd St., N.E., Hwy. 79E, Elbow Lake, MN 56531. Mailing Address: P.O. Box 1002, Elbow Lake, MN 56531-1002. Tel.: 218-685-4864.
E-mail: gcmnhist@runestone.net
Web Site: www.facebook.com/pg/grant-county-historical-society-museum
Key Personnel: Dir. & Cur., Patricia Benson; Chm. (V), Lyle Krusemark.
Institution Type/Description: Historical Society Museum.
Hours & Admission Prices: Memorial Day to Labor Day Mon.-Fri. 10-12 & 1-4, Sat. 10-3; Sept.-May Mon.-Fri. 10-12 & 1-4; other times by appointment. No charge; donations accepted. Closed New Year's Day; Easter; Memorial Day; Independence Day; Labor Day; Thanksgiving; Christmas. &
Attendance: 800 (estimated)

Elk River

OLIVER KELLEY FARM, 15788 Kelley Farm Rd., Elk River, MN 55330-6234. Tel.: 763-441-6896. Fax: 763-441-6302.
E-mail: kelleyfarm@mnhs.org
Web Site: www.mnhs.org/kelleyfarm
Key Personnel: Site Mgr., Bob M. Quist; C.E.O. & Dir. MHS, Nina M. Archabal.
Institution Type/Description: Living History Farm: 1876 home of Oliver Kelley, founder of the Grange in 1867.
Hours & Admission Prices: May & Oct. Sat. 10-5, Sun. 12-5; Memorial Day to Labor Day Tues.-Sat. 10-5, Sun. 12-5; groups of 10 or more by appointment. Adults $8, senior citizens $6, children 6-17 $5; members & children under 6 no charge. Closed New Year's Eve & Day; Christmas. &
Attendance: 30,000 (actual)

Ely

DOROTHY MOLTER MUSEUM, Hwy. 169, Ely, MN 55731. Mailing Address: P.O. Box 391, Ely, MN 55731-0391. Tel.: 218-365-4451.
E-mail: rootbeerlady@frontiernet.net
Web Site: www.rootbeerlady.com

Institution Type/Description: History Museum: former home of Dorothy Molter.
Hours & Admission Prices: Memorial Day-Labor Day Mon.-Sat. 10-5:30, Sun. 12-5:30. &

ELY-WINTON HISTORICAL SOCIETY, 1900 E. Camp St., Ely, MN 55731-1918. Tel.: 218-365-3226. Fax: 218-365-7207. Facebook: Ely Winton Historical Society.
E-mail: ewhs@vcc.edu
Formerly: Vermilion Interpretive Center
Key Personnel: Dir., Margaret Sweet; Pres. (V), Patricia Koski.
Institution Type/Description: Historical Society Museum.
Hours & Admission Prices: Tues.-Fri. 10-4. Adults $5, senior citizens $4, children 16 & under $3; discounts to groups and AAM & ICOM members; members & children under 6 no charge. Closed New Year's Day; Easter; Labor Day; Thanksgiving; Christmas. &
Attendance: 1,800 (actual)

INTERNATIONAL WOLF CENTER, 1396 Hwy. 169, Ely, MN 55731-8129. Tel.: 218-365-4695. Fax: 218-365-3318.
E-mail: kelly@wolf.org
Web Site: www.wolf.org
Key Personnel: Operations & Finance Mgr., Linda Frisell; Program Dir., Kelly Godfrey; Retail Mgr., Kristin Nephew; Wolf Cur., Lori Schmidt; Asst. Wolf Cur., Donna Prichard; Wolf Specialist, Cameron Feaster; Exec. Dir. (MN), Rob Schultz; Devel. Dir., David Kline; Dir. Finance & Operations (MN), Sharon Reed; Web Specialist (MN), Carissa Winter.
Institution Type/Description: Nature Center.
Hours & Admission Prices: mid-May to Oct. daily; Nov. to mid-May Fri.-Sun. Adults 13 & over $10.50, seniors 60 & over $9.50, children 3-12 $6.50; discounts to groups of 8 or more, veterans & active military; members & children under 3 no charge. 2nd consecutive day admission no charge. Closed major holidays. &
Attendance: 37,000 (estimated)

NORTH AMERICAN BEAR CENTER, 1926 Hwy. 169, Ely, MN 55731-8130. Mailing Address: P.O. Box 161, Ely, MN 55731-0161. Tel.: 218-365-7879, 877-365-7879.
E-mail: info@bear.org
Web Site: www.bear.org
Key Personnel: C.E.O. & Chm. Bd. (V), Dr. Lynn Rogers; Sr. Dir. Operations, Scott Edgett; Business Mgr., Heidi Schiltz; Program Dir. & Bear Cur., Sharon Herrell; Dir. Education, Judy Thon; Volunteer Coord., Terry Hagenah; Volunteer Coord., Myra Fournier; Buyer Inventory Control Specialist, Missy Hietala.
Institution Type/Description: Nature Center.
Hours & Admission Prices: Feb.-April & Oct. 19-Nov. Fri.-Sat. 10-4, May 1-May 22 daily 10-5; May 23-Sept. 14 daily 9-6; Sept. 15-Oct. 18 daily 10-4; other times by appointment. Adults $8.50, seniors 60 & over $7, children 3-12 $4.50; children under 3 & members no charge. &
Attendance: 30,492 (estimated)

Elysian

LE SUEUR COUNTY HISTORICAL MUSEUM-CHAPTER 1, 301 N. 2nd St., Elysian, MN 56028. Mailing Address: P.O. Box 240, Elysian, MN 56028-0240. Tel.: 507-267-4202.
E-mail: skrenik@frontiernet.net
Key Personnel: Pres. (V), Shirley Krenik; Financial Dir., Michael LaFrance.
Institution Type/Description: General Museum: housed in c.1895 former Elysian School.
Hours & Admission Prices: Closed for restorations. &
Attendance: 500 (estimated)

Eveleth

UNITED STATES HOCKEY HALL OF FAME MUSEUM, 801 Hat Trick Ave., Eveleth, MN 55734-8640. Mailing Address: P.O. Box 679, Eveleth, MN 55734-0679. Tel.: 218-744-5167. Fax: 218-744-2590.
E-mail: dougp@ushockeyhallmuseum.com
Web Site: www.ushockeyhallmuseum.com
Formerly: United States Hockey Hall of Fame
Key Personnel: Exec. Dir., Doug Palazzari; Chm. (V), David Tomassoni; Bd. Pres. (V), Cal Cossalter.
Institution Type/Description: Hockey Museum.
Hours & Admission Prices: Memorial Day to Labor Day Mon.-Sat. 9-5, Sun. 10-3; Sept.-May Fri. 10-5, Sat. 9-5, Sun. 10-3. Adults $8, senior citizens & children 13-17 $7, children 6-12 $6; discounts to hockey groups and AAA & museum members; children 5 & under no charge. Closed New Year's Day; Easter; Thanksgiving; Christmas. &
Attendance: 15,000 (estimated)

Excelsior

EXCELSIOR-LAKE MINNETONKA HISTORICAL SOCIETY, 305 Water St., Excelsior, MN 55331. Mailing Address: P.O. Box 305, Excelsior, MN 55331-0305. Tel.: 952-221-4766.
E-mail: info@elmhs.org
Web Site: www.elmhs.org
Key Personnel: Pres., Paul Maravelas; Vice Pres., Lisa Stevens.
Institution Type/Description: Local History Museum.
Hours & Admission Prices: May-Sept. Thurs. 3-6, Sat. 10-3. No charge.

Fairfax

FORT RIDGELY, MINNESOTA HISTORICAL SOCIETY, 72158 County Rd. 30, Fairfax, MN 55332. Tel.: 507-508-2848. Facebook: @FortRidgely.
E-mail: ftridgely@mnhs.org
Web Site: sites.mnhs.org/historic-sites/fort-ridgely
Institution Type/Description: State Park & Museum.
Hours & Admission Prices: Memorial Day weekend to Labor Day Fri.-Sun. 10-5; Labor Day to mid-Oct. Sat. & Sun. 10-5. Adults $6, seniors & college students $5, youth 5-17 $4; children under 5 no charge. A Minnesota State Park Vehicle Permit is required.

Fairmont

PIONEER MUSEUM - MARTIN COUNTY HISTORICAL SOCIETY, 304 E. Blue Earth Ave., Fairmont, MN 56031-2865. Tel.: 507-235-5178. Fax: 507-235-5179.
E-mail: mch@frontiernet.net
Web Site: www.fairmont.org/mchs/
Key Personnel: C.E.O., Jeff Hagen; Exec. Dir., Lenny Tvedten; Vice Pres., Tom Mahoney; Cur., James Marushin; Conservator, Dona Paris.
Institution Type/Description: County Historical Society Museum.
Hours & Admission Prices: Mon.-Fri. 8:30-12 & 1-4:30, Sat.-Sun. special tours & by appointment. No charge; donations accepted. &
Attendance: 2,500 (estimated)

Falcon Heights

GIBBS MUSEUM OF PIONEER AND DAKOTAH LIFE, 2097 W. Larpenteur Ave., Falcon Heights, MN 55113-5313. Mailing Address: Ramsey County Historical Society, 323 Landmark Center, 75 W. 5th St., Saint Paul, MN 55102. Tel.: 651-646-8629 & 659-0345. Fax: 651-659-0345.
E-mail: gibbs@rchs.com
Web Site: www.rchs.com
Formerly: Gibbs Farm Museum
Key Personnel: Interim Dir., John Lindley; Cur. & Archivist, Mollie Spillman.
Institution Type/Description: household artifacts housed in 1854-1974 Gibbs farmhouse.
Hours & Admission Prices: Memorial Day Weekend to Labor Day: Wed.-Sun. 12-4; Sept. & Oct. weekends: 12-4; other times by appointment. Discounts to AAA members & groups for 15 or more; members no charge. &
Attendance: 33,000 (actual)

Faribault

PARADISE CENTER FOR THE ARTS, 321 Central Ave., Faribault, MN 55021. Tel.: 507-332-7372.
E-mail: info@paradisecenterforthearts.org
Web Site: www.paradisecenterforthearts.org
Key Personnel: Exec. Dir., Ryan Heinritz.
Institution Type/Description: Art Gallery.
Hours & Admission Prices: Call for hours.

RICE COUNTY MUSEUM OF HISTORY, 1814 N.W. 2nd Ave., Faribault, MN 55021-3033. Tel.: 507-332-2121. Fax: 507-332-2121. Facebook: Rice County Museum of History.
E-mail: rchs@rchistory.org
Web Site: www.rchistory.org
Key Personnel: Exec. Dir., Susan Garwood; Pres., Peter Waldock.
Institution Type/Description: History & Agricultural Museum Complex.
Hours & Admission Prices: Museum: Mon.-Fri. 9-4, Sat. Memorial Day-Labor Day 10-2, other times by appointment. Museum: adults $3, senior citizens 55 & over and students $2, children 12 & under $1; members no charge. Faribault House: admission $2. &
Attendance: 6,000 (estimated)

Farmington

DAKOTA CITY HERITAGE VILLAGE, Dakota County Fairgrounds, 4008 220th St. W., Farmington, MN 55024. Mailing Address: P.O. Box 73, Farmington, MN 55024-0073. Tel.: 651-460-8050. Fax: 651-463-6908.
E-mail: info@dakotacity.org
Web Site: www.dakotacity.org
Institution Type/Description: Heritage Village.
Hours & Admission Prices: May-Sept. Mon.-Sat.; groups of 15 or more by appointment. Adults $5. &
Attendance: 30,000 (estimated)

Fergus Falls

OTTER TAIL COUNTY HISTORICAL SOCIETY, 1110 Lincoln Ave. W., Fergus Falls, MN 56537-1029. Tel.: 218-736-6038. Fax: 218-739-3075.
E-mail: otchs@prtel.com
Web Site: www.otchs.org/
Key Personnel: Exec. Dir., Chris Schuelke; Cur. Collections, Kathy Evavold; Education Coord., Missy Hermes; Office Mgr., LeAnn Neuleib.
Institution Type/Description: Historical Society Museum.
Hours & Admission Prices: June-Aug. Mon.-Fri. 9-5, Sat. 10-3; Sept.-May Mon.-Fri. 9-5. Research Library: Mon.-Fri. 9-5. Adults $3, children 5-11 $1; members no charge. &
Attendance: 9,000 (estimated)

Fountain

FILLMORE COUNTY HISTORY CENTER AND GENEALOGY LIBRARY, 202 County Rd. No. 8, Fountain, MN 55935-8805. Tel.: 507-268-4449.
E-mail: fche@frontier.com
Web Site: fillmorecountyhistory.wordpress.com
Key Personnel: Dir., Debra J. Richardson; Vice Pres., Flora Grabau; Pres. (V), Donald Boyum; Sec., Rita Joerg; Treas., Kathy Tesmer.
Institution Type/Description: History Museum.
Hours & Admission Prices: Tues.-Sat. 9-4. Center: no charge; donations accepted. Library: call for fees. Closed major holidays. &
Attendance: 8,500 (estimated)

Franconia

FRANCONIA SCULPTURE PARK, 29836 St. Croix Trail, Franconia, MN 55074. Tel.: 651-257-6668.
E-mail: info@franconia.org
Web Site: www.franconia.org
Key Personnel: Site Mgr., Bobby Zokaites.
Institution Type/Description: Sculpture Park.
Hours & Admission Prices: Daily dawn to dusk. No charge.

Freeport

HEMKER PARK & ZOO, County Rd. 39, Freeport, MN 56331. Mailing Address: Box 262, Freeport, MN 56331-0262. Tel.: 320-836-2426. Facebook: Hemker Zoo.
E-mail: info@hemkerzoo.com
Web Site: www.hemkerzoo.com
Key Personnel: Owner, Joan Hemker; Dir., Heidi Roering.
Institution Type/Description: Zoo.
Hours & Admission Prices: May-Oct. daily 10-6. Adults $7.25, seniors 60 & over $6.25, children 2-12 $5.25; infants under 2 no charge.

Fridley

BANFILL-LOCKE CENTER FOR THE ARTS, 6666 E. River Rd., Fridley, MN 55432-4229. Tel.: 763-574-1850.
E-mail: info@banfill-locke.org
Web Site: banfill-locke.org
Key Personnel: Exec. Dir., Jeffrey Ebeling.
Institution Type/Description: Art Gallery.
Hours & Admission Prices: Tues.-Sat. 10-4. No charge.

SPRINGBROOK NATURE CENTER, 100 85th Ave., N.W., Fridley, MN 55432. Tel.: 763-572-3588. Facebook: @SpringbrookNature.
E-mail: mike.maher@fridleymn.gov
Web Site: www.springbrooknaturecenter.org
Key Personnel: Dir., Mike Maher.
Institution Type/Description: Nature Center: a 127-acre natural urban park.
Hours & Admission Prices: Daily 9-5. No charge. &
Attendance: 50,000 (actual)

Glenwood

POPE COUNTY HISTORICAL SOCIETY, 809 S. Lakeshore Dr., Glenwood, MN 56334-9406. Tel.: 320-634-3293.
E-mail: popecountymuseum@gmail.com
Web Site: popecountymuseum.com
Key Personnel: Pres. (V), Mary Smith; Dir., Merlin Peterson; Collections Mgr., Ann Grandy; Archivist, Brent Gulsvig.
Institution Type/Description: General Museum.
Hours & Admission Prices: Tues.-Sat. 10-5. Adults $3, students 13-18 $1.50, children 6-12 $.50; summer season & members no charge; donations accepted. &
Attendance: 3,560 (actual)

Grand Marais

COOK COUNTY HISTORICAL MUSEUM, 8 S. Broadway, Grand Marais, MN 55604-1293. Mailing Address: Cook County Historical Society, Box 1293, Grand Marais, MN 55604-1293. Tel.: 218-387-2883 & 9131.
E-mail: history@boreal.org
Web Site: www.cookcountyhistory.org
Key Personnel: C.E.O., Gene Erickson; Dir. Museum, Carrie McHugh; Dir. Johnson Heritage Post, Don Darison.
Institution Type/Description: General Museum & Art Museum: housed in 1896 lighthouse keeper's residence.
Hours & Admission Prices: June-Oct. Tues.-Sat. 11-4; Nov.-May Fri. 1-4, Sat. 10-2. No charge; donations accepted. &
Attendance: 15,000 (estimated)

Grand Portage

GRAND PORTAGE NATIONAL MONUMENT, 170 Mile Creek Rd., Grand Portage, MN 55605. Mailing Address: P.O. Box 426, Grand Portage, MN 55605-0426. Tel.: 218-475-0123. Fax: 218-475-0174. Facebook: Grand Portage National Monument.
E-mail: grpo_interpretation@nps.gov
Web Site: www.nps.gov/grpo
Key Personnel: Supt., Tim Cochrane; Chief Interpretation, Pam Neil; Chief Resource Management, Bill Clayton.
Institution Type/Description: Historical Site & Park Museum: housed in 18th-century reconstructed North West Company fur trading depot on its original site.
Hours & Admission Prices: mid-May to mid-Oct. daily 8:30-5; groups by appointment. No charge. &
Attendance: 70,000 (estimated)

Grand Rapids

CHILDREN'S DISCOVERY MUSEUM, 2727 U.S. Hwy. 169 S., Grand Rapids, MN 55744. Mailing Address: P.O. Box 724, Grand Rapids, MN 55744-0724. Tel.: 218-326-1900, 866-236-5437 (Toll Free). Fax: 218-326-1934.
E-mail: office@cdmkids.org
Web Site: cdmkids.org
Key Personnel: Dir., John A. Kelsch; Pres. (V), Douglas P. Miner.
Institution Type/Description: Children's Museum.
Hours & Admission Prices: April-May Mon.-Sat. 10-5; Memorial Day to Sept. daily 10-5; Oct.-March Fri.-Sat. 10-5. Admission $8; members no charge. Closed New Year's Day; Easter; Thanksgiving; Christmas. &
Attendance: 18,951 (actual)

FOREST HISTORY CENTER, MINNESOTA HISTORICAL SOCIETY, 2609 County Rd. 76, Grand Rapids, MN 55744-8646. Tel.: 218-327-4482. Fax: 218-327-4715.
E-mail: foresthistory@mnhs.org
Web Site: sites.mnhs.org/historic-sites/forest-history-center
Key Personnel: Site Mgr., Jeff Johns.
Institution Type/Description: Historic Site, Historic Museum, Natural History Museum.
Hours & Admission Prices: Labor Day to mid-June Sat. 10-4, Sun. noon to 4; mid-June to Labor Day daily 10-5. Adults $10, senior citizens & college students $7, children 5-17 $6; MNHS members and children 4 & under no charge. &
Attendance: 20,000 (actual)

ITASCA COUNTY HISTORICAL SOCIETY, 201 N. Pokegama Ave., Grand Rapids, MN 55744. Tel.: 218-326-6431.
E-mail: ichs@paulbunyan.net

Web Site: itascahistorical.org
Institution Type/Description: Historical Society Museum.
Hours & Admission Prices: Mon.-Fri. 9-5, Sat. 10-4. No charge; donations accepted. Closed national holidays. ᕫ
Attendance: 4,000 (actual)

JUDY GARLAND MUSEUM, 2727 U.S. Hwy. 169 S., Grand Rapids, MN 55744. Mailing Address: P.O. Box 724, Grand Rapids, MN 55744-0724. Tel.: 800-664-5839.
E-mail: jgarland@uslink.net
Web Site: www.judygarlandmuseum.com/
Key Personnel: Exec. Dir., John Kelsch; Pres. (V), Douglas P. Miner.
Institution Type/Description: Historic House Museum.
Hours & Admission Prices: April-May Mon.-Sat. 10-5; Memorial Day to Sept. daily 10-5; Oct.-March Fri.-Sat. 10-5. Admission $7; members no charge. Closed New Year's Day; Easter; Thanksgiving; Christmas. ᕫ
Attendance: 18,951 (actual)

Granite Falls

YELLOW MEDICINE COUNTY HISTORICAL SOCIETY AND MUSEUM, Junction of Hwy. 67 & 23, Granite Falls, MN 56241. Mailing Address: Box 145, Granite Falls, MN 56241-0145. Tel.: 320-564-4479. Facebook: Yellow Medicine County Historical Society.
E-mail: ymchs@co.ym.mn.gov
Web Site: www.co.ym.mn.gov
Key Personnel: Chm. (V), Jane Remiger; Dir., Teather Lacy.
Institution Type/Description: History Museum.
Hours & Admission Prices: May 1 -Sept. 30 Tues.-Thurs. 2-5, Fri. & Sat. 10-5. Available for special events or by appointment. No charge; donations accepted. ᕫ
Attendance: 1,500 (estimated)

Hanley Falls

MINNESOTA'S MACHINERY MUSEUM, 100 N. 1st St., Hanley Falls, MN 56245. Mailing Address: P.O. Box 70, Hanley Falls, MN 56245-0070. Tel.: 507-768-3522. Fax: 507-768-3522. Facebook: Minnesota's Machinery Museum.
E-mail: agmuseum@frontiernet.net
Key Personnel: Dir., Laurie Johnson; Chm. (V), Tom Offedahl.
Institution Type/Description: Agriculture & Transportation Museum.
Hours & Admission Prices: May 15-Sept. 30 Mon.-Sat. 10-4, Sun. 1-4:30; other times by appointment. No charge; donations accepted. Closed holidays. ᕫ
Attendance: 1,200 (estimated)

Hastings

CARPENTER ST. CROIX VALLEY NATURE CENTER, 12805 St. Croix Trail, Hastings, MN 55033-9499. Tel.: 651-437-4359. Fax: 651-438-2908.
E-mail: jennifer@carpenternaturecenter.org
Web Site: carpenternaturecenter.org
Key Personnel: Exec. Dir., Jennifer Vieth; Pres. (V), Vickie Batroot; Museum Shop Mgr., Alan Maloney.
Institution Type/Description: Nature Center
Hours & Admission Prices: Daily 8-4:30. No charge; donations accepted. Closed New Year's Day; Thanksgiving; Christmas. ᕫ
Attendance: 25,000 (estimated)

Henderson

SIBLEY COUNTY HISTORICAL MUSEUM, 700 Main St. W., Henderson, MN 56044-7711. Mailing Address: P.O. Box 407, Henderson, MN 56044-0407. Tel.: 507-248-3434.
E-mail: schs1@frontiernet.net
Web Site: sibleycountyhistoricalmuseum.com
Key Personnel: Chm., Jerome Petersen; Cur., Sharon Haggenmiller.
Institution Type/Description: History Museum: housed in 1884 residence.
Hours & Admission Prices: June-Oct. Sun. 2-5; other times by appointment. Adults $2, children $1; members no charge. ᕫ
Attendance: 1,200 (estimated)

Hendricks

LINCOLN COUNTY PIONEER MUSEUM, 610 W. Elm, Hendricks, MN 56136. Mailing Address: P.O. Box 211, Hendricks, MN 56136. Tel.: 507-275-5247.

E-mail: Pioneermuseum@itctel.com
Key Personnel: Pres., Orlan L. Sandro; Vice Pres. & Treas., Dr. Rolland Digre; Sec., Ms. Kate Aydin.
Institution Type/Description: Historical Society Museum: housed in c.1899 train depot & Icelandic church.
Hours & Admission Prices: Wed.-Fri. 2-5 & 7-9, Sun. 2-5; other times by appointment. No charge; donations accepted. ᕫ
Attendance: 600 (estimated)

Hibbing

HIBBING HISTORICAL SOCIETY AND MUSEUM, 400 E. 23rd St., Hibbing, MN 55746-1923. Tel.: 218-263-8522. Facebook: Hibbing Historical Society.
E-mail: hibbinghistory@mchsi.com
Web Site: www.hibbinghistory.com
Key Personnel: Pres., Leonard Hirsch; Vice Pres., Mary Keyes.
Institution Type/Description: History Museum: housed in 1936 Memorial Building.
Hours & Admission Prices: Tues.-Fri. 10-2; other times by appointment. No charge; donations accepted. Closed New Year's Day; Memorial Day; Independence Day; Labor Day; Thanksgiving; Christmas. ᕫ
Attendance: 1,320 (actual)

Hinckley

HINCKLEY FIRE MUSEUM, 106 Old Hwy. 61 S., Hinckley, MN 55037. Mailing Address: P.O. Box 40, Hinckley, MN 55037-0040. Tel.: 320-384-7338.
E-mail: info@hinckleyfiremuseum.com
Web Site: www.hinckleyfiremuseum.com
Key Personnel: Dir., Pres. (V) & Museum Shop Mgr., Steve Johnson.
Institution Type/Description: History Museum: housed in 1894, St. Paul & Duluth Railroad Depot.
Hours & Admission Prices: May to mid-Oct. Tues.-Sun. 10-5; July-Aug. daily 10-5. Adults $5, senior citizens $4, students 13-18 $2, children 6-12 $1; members & children under 6 no charge.
Attendance: 7,000 (estimated)

Hopkins

HOPKINS HISTORICAL SOCIETY MUSEUM, 33 14th Ave. N., Hopkins, MN 55343. Mailing Address: 1010 First St. S., Hopkins, MN 55343. Tel.: 952-548-6480.
E-mail: info@hopkinshistory.com
Web Site: www.hopkinshistory.org
Institution Type/Description: Historical Society Museum.
Hours & Admission Prices: Tues. & Thurs. 9am to noon; other times by appointment.

Hutchinson

MCLEOD COUNTY HISTORICAL SOCIETY, 380 School Rd., N.W., Hutchinson, MN 55350-1430. Tel.: 320-587-2109.
E-mail: asa@hutchtel.net
Web Site: www.mcleodhistory.org/index.htm
Key Personnel: Exec. Dir., Lori Pickell-Stangel; Chm. (V) & Pres. (V), Stan Ehrke; Museum Asst., Peggy Paulson.
Institution Type/Description: Historical Society Museum.
Hours & Admission Prices: Mon. & Thurs.-Fri. 10-4, Sat. 1-4. Adults $3, seniors $2, students $1; members no charge. Closed major holidays. ᕫ
Attendance: 4,000 (estimated)

International Falls

KOOCHICHING COUNTY HISTORICAL MUSEUM, 214 6th Ave., International Falls, MN 56649-2336. Tel.: 218-283-4316. Fax: 218-283-2843.
E-mail: koochmuseums@gmail.com
Web Site: www.koochichingmuseums.org
Key Personnel: C.E.O., Edgar S. Oerichbauer; Pres. (V), Mike Williams.
Institution Type/Description: Historical Society Museum.
Hours & Admission Prices: Mon.-Fri. 9-5. Adults $4, student 5-17 $2; discounts to groups; children under 5 & members no charge. ᕫ
Attendance: 5,000 (estimated)

VOYAGEURS NATIONAL PARK, 360 Hwy. 11 E., International Falls, MN 56649-8802. Tel.: 218-283-6600 (Park Headquarters).
Web Site: www.nps.gov/voya
Key Personnel: Supt., Michael M. Ward.
Institution Type/Description: National Park Visitor Centers.

Hours & Admission Prices: Park: year-round dawn-dusk. Visitor Centers: call for hours. No charge.

Kellogg

LARK TOYS & CAROUSEL, 171 Lark Lane, Kellogg, MN 55945-9629. Tel.: 507-767-3387. Fax: 507-767-4565.
E-mail: lark@wabasha.net
Web Site: larktoys.com
Key Personnel: Owner, Ron Gray; Owner, Kathy Gray; Owner, Scott Gray-Burlingham; Owner, Miranda Gray-Burlingham.
Institution Type/Description: Toy Museum.
Hours & Admission Prices: Daily 9:30-5:30. Carousel Ride: $2. Closed New Year's Day; Thanksgiving; Christmas.

Kenyon

GUNDERSON HOUSE, 107 Gunderson Blvd., Kenyon, MN 55946. Tel.: 507-298-1127.
E-mail: rhanajo1124@gmail.com
Key Personnel: Pres., Robert Peterson.
Institution Type/Description: Historic House: 1895 Gunderson House. Listed on the National Register of Historic Places.
Hours & Admission Prices: June-Sept: 3rd weekend of the month. Adults $5, students $1; preschool no charge.
Attendance: 350 (estimated)

Lake Bronson

KITTSON COUNTY HISTORY CENTER MUSEUM, 332 E. Main St., Lake Bronson, MN 56734-3448. Tel.: 218-754-4100.
E-mail: history@wiktel.com
Web Site: kittsonhistorian.ning.com
Key Personnel: Dir., Cindy Adams; Pres. (V), Dan Nordine; Business Officer, LaDonna Truedson; Treas., Cecil Fossell.
Institution Type/Description: Historical Society Museum.
Hours & Admission Prices: April-May & Sept.-Nov. Mon.-Fri. 9-5; Memorial Day to Labor Day Mon.-Fri. 9-5, Sat.-Sun. & holidays 1-5; Dec.-March Tues.-Fri. 9-5. No charge; donations accepted. ♿
Attendance: 4,000 (estimated)

Lakefield

JACKSON COUNTY HISTORICAL MUSEUM, 307 N. Hwy. 86, Lakefield, MN 56150-1259. Mailing Address: P.O. Box 238, Lakefield, MN 56150-0238. Tel.: 507-662-5505. Fax: 507-662-5505.
E-mail: jchs@frontiernet.net
Key Personnel: Pres., Mark Titus; Treas., John Hay; Mgr., Mike Kirchmeier.
Institution Type/Description: Local History Museum.
Hours & Admission Prices: Mon.-Fri. 9:30-4:30, Sat. 8am to noon; other times by appointment. No charge; donations accepted. ♿
Attendance: 400 (estimated)

Lanesboro

LANESBORO ARTS, 103 Parkway Ave. N., Lanesboro, MN 55949-0152. Mailing Address: P.O. Box 152, Lanesboro, MN 55949-0152. Tel.: 507-467-2446. Facebook: Lanesboro Arts.
E-mail: info@lanesboroarts.org
Web Site: lanesboroarts.org
Formerly: Cornucopia Art Center
Key Personnel: Exec. Dir., John Davis; Gallery Dir., Robbie Brokken; Program & Mktg. Dir., Sara Baskett.
Institution Type/Description: Art Gallery.
Hours & Admission Prices: Mon.-Thurs. 10-5, Fri.-Sat. 10-7, Sun. 11-3.

Le Sueur

LE SUEUR MUSEUM, 709 N. 2nd St., Le Sueur, MN 56058-1411. Mailing Address: P.O. Box 123, Le Center, MN 56057. Tel.: 507-665-2050.
E-mail: info@lesueurcountyhistory.org
Web Site: lesueurcountyhistory.org/
Key Personnel: Pres. (V), Jean Haas.
Institution Type/Description: History Museum: housed in first school in Le Sueur.
Hours & Admission Prices: Memorial Day to Labor Day Fri.-Sat. call for hours; other times by appointment. No charge; donations accepted. Closed holidays.
Attendance: 500 (estimated)

W.W. MAYO HOUSE, MINNESOTA HISTORICAL SOCIETY, 118 N. Main St., Le Sueur, MN 56058. Tel.: 507-665-3250. Facebook: @wwmayohouse.
E-mail: mayohouse@mnhs.org
Web Site: sites.mnhs.org/historic-sites/ww-mayo-house
Key Personnel: Site Mgr., Becky Pollack.
Institution Type/Description: Historic Building: housed in the former home & 1st medical practice of Mayo Clinic founder Dr. William Worrall Mayo.
Hours & Admission Prices: May-Sept. Sat. 10-1. Adults $6, seniors & college students $5, children 5-17 $4; discounts to groups; MNHS members and children 4 & under no charge.

Lino Lakes

WARGO NATURE CENTER, 7701 Main St., Lino Lakes, MN 55038-8741. Tel.: 651-429-8007. Fax: 651-429-8167.
Web Site: www.anokacountyparks.com/qlinks/wargonc/wargonc.htm
Key Personnel: Mgr., Lisa Gilliland; Program Coord., Deb Gallop; Recreation Specialist, Todd Murawski; Scheduler & Receptionist, Rhonda Lynch.
Institution Type/Description: Nature Center.
Hours & Admission Prices: April-Oct. Tues.-Fri. 8-4:30, Sat. 9-5, Sun. 12-5; Nov.-March Tues.-Fri. 8-4:30.

Litchfield

MEEKER COUNTY HISTORICAL SOCIETY MUSEUM & G. A.R. HALL, 308 N. Marshall Ave., Litchfield, MN 55355-2112. Tel.: 320-693-8911.
E-mail: mchsgar@hutchtel.net
Web Site: www.garminnesota.org
Key Personnel: Pres., August Anderson.
Institution Type/Description: Historic Building: c.1885 G.A.R. Hall.
Hours & Admission Prices: Tues.-Sun. 12-4. Adults $2; children & members no charge. Closed holidays except Memorial Day. ♿
Attendance: 4,000

Little Falls

CHARLES A. WEYERHAEUSER MEMORIAL MUSEUM, 2151 S. Lindbergh Dr., Little Falls, MN 56345-0239. Mailing Address: P.O. Box 239, Little Falls, MN 56345-0239. Tel.: 320-632-4007.
E-mail: contactstaff@morrisoncountyhistory.org
Web Site: www.morrisoncountyhistory.org
Key Personnel: Dir., Mary Warner; Pres. (V), Stan Wielinski; Vice Pres., Camille Warzecha; Collections Mgr., Ann Marie Johnson; Treas., Lee Obermiller.
Institution Type/Description: Local History Museum.
Hours & Admission Prices: Tues.-Sat. 10-5; groups by appointment. No charge; donations accepted. Closed holidays. ♿
Attendance: 3,500 (estimated)

CHARLES LINDBERGH HOUSE AND MUSEUM, MINNESOTA HISTORICAL SOCIETY, 1620 Lindbergh Dr. S., Little Falls, MN 56345. Tel.: 320-616-5421. Fax: 320-616-5423. Facebook: @lindberghhouse.
E-mail: lindbergh@mnhs.org
Web Site: sites.mnhs.org/historic-sites/charles-lindbergh-historic-house
Key Personnel: Site Mgr., Melissa Peterson.
Institution Type/Description: Historic House Museum & Visitor Center: housed in boyhood home of Charles A. Lindbergh, 1902-1920.
Hours & Admission Prices: Memorial Day weekend to Labor Day Thurs.-Sat. 10-5, Sun. noon to 5, Sept. Sat. 10-5; other times by appointment. Adults $8, senior citizens, college students & children 5-17 $6; members and children 4 & under no charge. ♿
Attendance: 8,000 (actual)

MINNESOTA FISHING MUSEUM AND HALL OF FAME, 304 W. Broadway, Little Falls, MN 56345-1535. Tel.: 320-616-2011.
E-mail: mnfm@mnfishingmuseum.com
Web Site: www.mnfishingmuseum.com/
Formerly: Minnesota Fishing Museum and Education Center
Key Personnel: Exec. Dir., Brenda Perlowski; Pres. (V), Jeff Doty.
Institution Type/Description: Fishing Museum.
Hours & Admission Prices: April 15-Sept. Tues.-Sat. 10-5, Sun. 12-4; Winter: call for hours. Adults $5, seniors 60 & over and students 6-17 $4; discounts to groups; members & children under 6 no charge. ♿
Attendance: 5,000 (actual)

Long Lake

WESTERN HENNEPIN COUNTY PIONEERS ASSOCIATION, 1953 W. Wayzata Blvd., Long Lake, MN 55356-9362. Mailing Address: Box 332, Long Lake, MN 55356-0332. Tel.: 952-473-6557.
E-mail: pioneer_museum@hotmail.com
Web Site: www.whcpa-museum.org
Key Personnel: Pres., Nancy Ferrell Geng; Sec., Marion Merz; Treas., Dick Vlach; Cur., Russ Ferrin.
Institution Type/Description: History Museum.
Hours & Admission Prices: Museum: Sat. 10-2. Research Center: Sat. 10-1. No charge; donations accepted.
Attendance: 1,400 (estimated)

Long Prairie

THE CHRISTIE HOUSE MUSEUM, 15 1st St., S., Long Prairie, MN 56347-1348. Mailing Address: P.O. Box 25, Long Prairie, MN 56347. Tel.: 320-491-9074.
E-mail: lornah@mufonsd.org
Web Site: www.christiehome.org
Key Personnel: Pres. (V), Lorna Hunter.
Institution Type/Description: Historic House: former home of Dr. George R. Christie. Listed on the National Register of Historic Places.
Hours & Admission Prices: Memorial Day-Labor Day Wed.-Sun. 1:30-4:30. Adults $3.
Attendance: 200 (actual)

TODD COUNTY HISTORICAL MUSEUM, 333 Central Ave., Long Prairie, MN 56347-1304. Tel.: 320-732-4426.
E-mail: tchmuseum@gmail.com
Key Personnel: Dir. & Pres. (V), Shirley Lunceford; Cur., De Eberle.
Institution Type/Description: History Museum.
Hours & Admission Prices: Wed. 11:30-6, Thurs.-Fri. 11:30-4. Adults $3; members no charge. &

Madison

LAC QUI PARLE COUNTY HISTORICAL SOCIETY, 250 8th Ave., S., Madison, MN 56256-1146. Tel.: 612-598-7678.
E-mail: lqphistorycenter@lqpco.com
Key Personnel: C.E.O. & Pres. (V), Scotty Kuehl; Cur., Janet E. Liebl.
Institution Type/Description: General Museum.
Hours & Admission Prices: May-Oct. Mon.-Fri. 11-4, Sat. 11-3. Adults $3. Family History Research: $10 per hour. &
Attendance: 2,500 (estimated)

Mankato

BLUE EARTH COUNTY HISTORICAL SOCIETY, 424 Warren St., Mankato, MN 56001-3722. Tel.: 507-345-5566. Facebook: bechshistory.
E-mail: bechs@hickorytech.net
Web Site: www.blueearthcountyhistory.com
Key Personnel: C.E.O. & Exec. Dir., Jessica Potter; Pres. (V), Shirley Piepho.
Institution Type/Description: History Museum.
Hours & Admission Prices: Tues.-Fri. 9-5, Sat. 10-4. Adult $7, children over 5 $3; members no charge. Closed legal holidays. &
Attendance: 20,000 (estimated)

CHILDREN'S MUSEUM OF SOUTHERN MINNESOTA, 224 Lamm St., Mankato, MN 56001. Tel.: 507-386-0279. Facebook: Children's Museum of Southern Minnesota.
E-mail: info@cmsouthernmn.org
Web Site: www.cmsouthernmn.org
Key Personnel: Exec. Dir., Peter Olson; Mktg. & Communications Coord., Ines Wingert.
Institution Type/Description: Children's Museum.
Hours & Admission Prices: Tues.-Sat. 9-4, Sun. 12-4. Admission 1 & over $8. &
Attendance: 100,000 (estimated)

Mantorville

DODGE COUNTY HISTORICAL SOCIETY, 615 Main St., Mantorville, MN 55955-6129. Mailing Address: P.O. Box 456, Mantorville, MN 55955-0456. Tel.: 507-635-5508.
E-mail: dchs@kmtel.com
Web Site: www.dodgecountyhistorical.org

Key Personnel: Pres., Greg Nelson; Vice Pres., Coy Borgstrom; Sec., Mary Ann Bucher; Treas., Barbara Gilliland.
Institution Type/Description: Historic Buildings & Site: Museum housed in 1869 former Episcopal church.
Hours & Admission Prices: Tues.-Fri 9:30-2:30; other times by appointment. Adults 13 & over $4, children 6-12 $2, seniors $1.50; members & children 5 and no charge. Research: hourly fee.
Attendance: 2,500 (estimated)

MANTORVILLE RESTORATION, 407 Main St., Mantorville, MN 55955-6127. Mailing Address: P.O. Box 202, Mantorville, MN 55955-0311. Tel.: 507-269-8704.
Institution Type/Description: Preservation Project: 1856 Temporary Court House & Home.
Hours & Admission Prices: May-Oct. Tues.-Sun. 1-5. Requested Donation $2.
Attendance: 25,000 (estimated)

Maplewood

MAPLEWOOD NATURE CENTER, 2659 E. 7th St., Maplewood, MN 55119-3815. Tel.: 651-249-2170. Fax: 651-249-2189.
E-mail: ann.hutchinson@maplewoodmn.gov
Web Site: www.ci.maplewood.mn.us
Key Personnel: Lead Naturalist, Ann Hutchinson.
Institution Type/Description: Nature Center.
Hours & Admission Prices: Visitor Center: Tues.-Sat. 8:30-4:30. No charge.
Attendance: 9,000 (actual)

Marshall

LYON COUNTY HISTORICAL SOCIETY MUSEUM, 301 W. Lyon St., Marshall, MN 56258-1307. Tel.: 507-537-6580.
E-mail: lyoncomuseum@iw.net
Web Site: www.lyoncomuseum.org
Key Personnel: Dir., Jennifer Andries; Pres., Andrea Hess; Vice Pres., Neal Ingebrigtson; Treas., Kathy Lozinski; Sec., Nicole DeBoer.
Institution Type/Description: General Museum.
Hours & Admission Prices: Tues.-Wed. & Fri. 10-5, Thurs. 10-7, Sat. 10-4. No charge; donations accepted. Closed national holidays. &

MUSEUM OF NATURAL HISTORY, Southwest Minnesota State University, 1501 State St., Marshall, MN 56258-3306. Tel.: 507-537-6178. Fax: 507-537-6151.
E-mail: betsy.desy@smsu.edu
Web Site: www.smsu.edu/campuslife/attractions/naturalhistorymuseum/
Key Personnel: Dir., Dr. Elizabeth A. Desy.
Institution Type/Description: Natural History Museum.
Hours & Admission Prices: Academic Year: Mon.-Fri. 8-5; guided tours by appointment. No charge. Closed New Year's Day; Easter; Thanksgiving; Christmas.
Attendance: 800 (estimated)

SOUTHWEST MINNESOTA STATE UNIVERSITY ART MUSEUM, 1501 State St., Marshall, MN 56258. Tel.: 507-537-6266. Fax: 507-537-6577.
E-mail: bill.mulso@smsu.edu
Institution Type/Description: Art Museum.
Hours & Admission Prices: Mon.-Thurs. 8am-11pm, Fri. 8-5, Sun. 2-11. Closed major holidays.

Mendota

SIBLEY HISTORIC SITE, MINNESOTA HISTORICAL SOCIETY, 1357 Sibley Memorial Hwy., Mendota, MN 55150. Tel.: 651-452-1596. Facebook: @sibleyhouse.
E-mail: sibleyhistoricsite@mnhs.org
Web Site: site.mnhs.org/historic-sites/sibley-historic-site
Key Personnel: Site Mgr., Andrew Fox.
Institution Type/Description: Historic House Museum: 1836 Henry Hastings Sibley house, dwelling & trading house for the American Fur Company factor, later Minnesota's first state governor's house; 1839 residence of trader, Jean Baptiste Faribault, which was a boarding house for visitors to the Fort Snelling area.
Hours & Admission Prices: Memorial Day weekend to Labor Day Sat. & Sun. 1-4, guided tours on the hour. Adults $7, seniors & college students $6, children 5-17 $5; children 4 & under and MNHS, DCHS & Sibley Friends members no charge. &
Attendance: 5,000 (actual)

Minneapolis

AMERICAN SWEDISH INSTITUTE, 2600 Park Ave., Minneapolis, MN 55407-1090. Tel.: 612-871-4907. Fax: 612-871-8682.
E-mail: info@asimn.org
Web Site: www.asimn.org
Formerly: American Institute of Swedish Arts, Literature and Science
Key Personnel: C.E.O. & Pres., Bruce Karstadt; Chm. (V), Dean Erickson; C.O.O., Peggy Korsmo-Kennon; C.F.O., Bonnie Nelson; Mktg. & Communications Mgr., Karen R. Nelson; Dir. Devel. & Membership, Christy Stolpestad; Dir. Exhibitions, Collections & Programs, Scott Pollock; Cur. Exhibitions & Collections, Curt Pederson; Retail Mgr., Rick Sellen.
Institution Type/Description: Swedish-American Ethnic Museum.
Hours & Admission Prices: Tues., Thurs.-Fri. & Sun. 12-5, Wed. 12-8, Sat. 10-5. Adults $10, senior citizens $7, children 6-18 & full-time students w/I.D. $5; discounts to Minnesota Public Radio members; children 5 & under & members no charge. Closed national holidays. &
Attendance: 96,500 (estimated)

THE BAKKEN MUSEUM, 3537 Zenith Ave. S., Minneapolis, MN 55416-4623. Tel.: 612-926-3878. Fax: 612-927-7265. Facebook: @thebakkenmuseum; Twitter: @thebakken.
E-mail: info@thebakken.org
Web Site: www.thebakken.org
Key Personnel: Exec. Dir., Michael Sanders; Dir. Advancement, Hannah Baines; Dir. Exhibits & Collections, Juliet Burba; Dir. Education, Steven Walvig; Dir. Facilities & Operations, Chris Lundeen; Finance Mgr., Kathy Eischens; Mktg. & Communications Production Coord., Noel Clark.
Institution Type/Description: Science Museum.
Hours & Admission Prices: Tues.-Sun. 10-4. Adults $10, seniors and teens & young adults 13-24 $8; children 5-12 $5; members and children 4 & under no charge. Closed New Year's Day; Memorial Day; Independence Day; Labor Day; Thanksgiving Day; Christmas Eve & Day. &
Attendance: 37,000 (actual)

BILL AND BONNIE DANIELS FIREFIGHTERS HALL & MUSEUM, 664 22nd Ave., N.E., Minneapolis, MN 55418. Tel.: 612-623-3817. Facebook: @bbdfirehallmuseum; Twitter: @FireHallMuseum.
E-mail: info@firehallmuseum.org
Web Site: firehallmuseum.org
Key Personnel: Exec. Dir. & Treas., Joseph Waters.
Institution Type/Description: Firefighting History Museum.
Hours & Admission Prices: Sat. 9-4; other times by appointment. Adults $7, seniors 65 & over $6, children 3-12 $4. &
Attendance: 14,000 (estimated)

CIRCA GALLERY, 210 N. First St., Minneapolis, MN 55401. Tel.: 612-332-2386. Facebook: @circagallerympls; Twitter: @circagallery.
E-mail: staff@circagallery.org
Web Site: www.circagallery.org
Key Personnel: Gallery Dir., Teresa Engeltjes.
Institution Type/Description: Art Gallery.
Hours & Admission Prices: Tues.-Fri. 1-6, Sat. 11-4; other times by appointment.

ELOISE BUTLER WILDFLOWER GARDEN AND BIRD SANCTUARY, 1 Theodore Wirth Pkwy., Minneapolis, MN 55422. Mailing Address: c/o Minneapolis Park & Recreation Board, 2117 W. River Rd., Minneapolis, MN 55411. Tel.: 612-370-4903. Facebook: Eloise Butler Wildflower Garden.
E-mail: ebwg@minneapolisparks.org
Web Site: www.minneapolisparks.org
Key Personnel: Supt. of Parks, Jayne Miller; Cur. Garden, Susan Wikins.
Institution Type/Description: Wildflower & Bird Sanctuary.
Hours & Admission Prices: April to mid-Oct. daily 7:30 to one hour before sunset; mid-Oct. to Nov. weekends 7:30 to one hour before sunset. No charge; donations accepted.
Attendance: 50,000 (estimated)

FORM + CONTENT GALLERY, 210 N. 2nd St., Minneapolis, MN 55401. Tel.: 612-436-1151. Facebook: @formandcontentgallery.
E-mail: formandcontent@gmail.com
Web Site: www.formandcontent.org
Key Personnel: Artist, Jim Dryden; Artist, Jill Evans; Artist, Joyce Lyon; Artist, Howard Oransky.
Institution Type/Description: Art Gallery.
Hours & Admission Prices: Thurs.-Sat. noon to 6; other times by appointment.

HENNEPIN HISTORY MUSEUM, 2303 3rd Ave. S., Minneapolis, MN 55404-3505. Tel.: 612-870-1329. Facebook: @HennepinHistory; Twitter: @HennHistMuseum.
E-mail: history@hennepinhistory.org
Web Site: www.hennepinhistory.org
Key Personnel: Exec. Dir., Cedar Imboden Phillips; Pres. Bd. Dir. (V), Cara Lefofsky; Cur., Jack Kabrud; Archivist, Susan Larson; Visitor Svcs. Mgr. & Volunteer Coord., James Bacigalupo; Bookkeeper, Mary Kaminski; Advancement Mgr., Kristin Kaspar; Collections Mgr., Heather Hoagland.
Institution Type/Description: History Museum.
Hours & Admission Prices: Gallery: Tues. 10-2, Wed. & Fri.-Sun. 1-5, Thurs. 1-8, Sat. & Sun. 1-5; Library: Tues. 10-2, Wed.-Sat. 1-5. Adults $5, students & seniors $3; discounts to AAM & MN Assoc. of Museums' members; members and children 6 & under no charge. Closed most federal holidays.
Attendance: 2,700 (estimated)

HENNEPIN MEDICAL HISTORY CENTER, 701 Park Ave., Minneapolis, MN 55415. Tel.: 612-873-6090.
E-mail: rondine.mehling@hcmed.org
Web Site: hennepinmedicalhistory.org
Key Personnel: Museum Coord. & Cur., Katie Baker.
Institution Type/Description: History Museum.
Hours & Admission Prices: Tues. & Thurs. 10-2; other times by appointment. No charge.
Attendance: 800 (estimated)

JUXTAPOSITION ARTS, 2007 Emerson Ave. N., Minneapolis, MN 55411-2507. Tel.: 612-588-1148. Facebook, Instagram.
E-mail: melanie.stovall@juxtaposition.org
Web Site: juxtapositionarts.org
Key Personnel: C.E.O., DeAnna Cummings; Chief Cultural Producer, Roger Cummings; Outreach & Engagement, Jared Hanks; Office & Facilities, Justin Kirkeberg; Property Maintenance Mgr., Tamala Lacy; Communications Mgr., Melanie Stovall.
Institution Type/Description: Art Gallery.
Hours & Admission Prices: Call for hours.

KATHERINE E. NASH GALLERY - UNIVERSITY OF MINNESOTA, 405 21st Ave. S., Minneapolis, MN 55455-0420. Tel.: 612-624-7530; 612-625-8096. Facebook: @UMNArtDept; Instagram & Twitter: @umn_art.
E-mail: artdept@umn.edu
Web Site: cla.umn.edu/art/galleries
Key Personnel: Dir. & Cur., Howard Oransky.
Institution Type/Description: Art Gallery.
Hours & Admission Prices: Tues.-Sat. 11-7. No charge. Closed University of Minnesota holidays & semester breaks. &
Attendance: 18,000 (estimated)

MAIL ORDER AND DIRECT MARKETING MUSEUM, 2807 Polk St., N.E., Minneapolis, MN 55418-2954. Tel.: 612-788-1673.
E-mail: info@nmoa.org
Web Site: nmoa.org
Key Personnel: Chm., John Schulte.
Institution Type/Description: History Museum.
Hours & Admission Prices: Office: Mon.-Fri. 9-5.

MCAD GALLERY, 2501 Stevens Ave., Minneapolis, MN 55404-4347. Tel.: 612-874-3667. Fax: 612-874-3704. Facebook: @MCAD.Gallery; Instagram: @mcadgallery.
E-mail: gallery@mcad.edu
Web Site: mcad.edu
Formerly: Minneapolis College of Art and Design Gallery
Key Personnel: Dir. Gallery & Exhibition Programs, Kerry Morgan; Fellowship & Gallery Coord., Melanie Pankau.
Institution Type/Description: College Art Gallery.
Hours & Admission Prices: Mon.-Fri. 9-8, Sat. 9-5, Sun. noon-5. No charge. Closed holidays. &
Attendance: 6,000 (estimated)

MIDWAY CONTEMPORARY ART, 527 Second Ave., S.E., Minneapolis, MN 55414-1103. Tel.: 612-605-4504. Fax: 612-605-4538. Facebook: @midwayartlibrary.
E-mail: info@midwayart.org
Web Site: midwayart.org
Key Personnel: Exec. Dir., John Rasmussen; Assoc. Dir., Megan McCready; Librarian, Katy Vonk; Gallery Asst., Kelsey Olson.
Institution Type/Description: Art Gallery.
Hours & Admission Prices: Wed.-Sat. 11-5; groups by appointment. No charge. &
Attendance: 8,000 (estimated)

MILL CITY MUSEUM, MINNESOTA HISTORICAL SOCIETY, 704 S. 2nd St., Minneapolis, MN 55401-2163. Tel.: 612-341-7555. Facebook & Twitter: @millcitymuseum.
E-mail: mcm@mnhs.org
Web Site: www.millcitymuseum.org
Key Personnel: Dir., Laura Salveson.
Institution Type/Description: History Museum: former site of the Washburn A Mill.
Hours & Admission Prices: July-Aug. Mon.-Sat. 10-5, Sun. 12-5; Sept.-June Tues.-Sat. 10-5, Sun. 12-5. Adults $12, seniors & students w/ID $10, children 5-17 $6; MHS members and children 4 & under no charge.

MINNEAPOLIS INSTITUTE OF ART, 2400 Third Ave. S., Minneapolis, MN 55404-3506. Tel.: 612-870-3000 & 3046. Fax: 612-870-3004. TDD: 612-870-3132; Facebook & Twitter: artsmia.
E-mail: miagen@artsMIA.org
Web Site: artsmia.org
Key Personnel: Nivin & Duncan MacMillan Dir. & Pres., Katherine Luber; Chm. Bd. Trustees, Nivin MacMillan; Chief of Staff, Michele Nichols; Deputy Dir. & C.O.O., Patricia J. Grazzini; Deputy Dir. & Chief Cur., Matthew Welch; Cur. Paintings, Patrick Noon; Head Registration, Brian Kraft; Head Retail, Ryan Ross.
Institution Type/Description: Art Museum.
Hours & Admission Prices: Tues.-Wed. & Sat. 10-5, Thurs.-Fri. 10-9, Sun. 11-5. No charge; donations accepted. Fees for some special exhibitions. Closed Independence Day; Thanksgiving; Christmas Eve & Day. &
Attendance: 750,000 (estimated)

MINNESOTA CENTER FOR BOOK ARTS, 1011 Washington Ave., S., Ste. 100, Minneapolis, MN 55415. Tel.: 612-215-2520. Fax: 612-215-2545. Facebook, Instagram & Twitter: @mnbookarts.
E-mail: mcba@mnbookarts.org
Web Site: www.mnbookarts.org
Key Personnel: Interim Exec. Dir. & Development Dir., Amanda Kaler; Artist & Adult Programs Dir., Anna Bredeson; Youth & Community Programs Dir., Angela Hed Vincent; Mktg. & Communications Coord., Kyle Krym.
Institution Type/Description: Art Gallery.
Hours & Admission Prices: Mon. & Wed.-Sat. 9:30-6:30, Tues. 9:30-9, Sun. noon to 5. No charge.

MINNESOTA STREETCAR MUSEUM, 2320 W. 42nd St., Minneapolis, MN 55410. Mailing Address: P.O. Box 16509, Minneapolis, MN 55416-0509. Tel.: 952-922-1096. Facebook: @TrolleyRide; Twitter: @MNStreetcar.
E-mail: info@trolleyride.org
Web Site: www.trolleyride.org
Key Personnel: Gen. Supt., Bruce Gustafson; Bookkeeper, Tim Crain; Merchandise Mgr., Rose Arends; Gen. Cashier, Bill Arends; Volunteer Coord., Pat Cosgrove; Chief Engineer, Keith Anderson.
Institution Type/Description: Transportation Museum.
Hours & Admission Prices: Call for hours. Adults $2; members no charge.
Attendance: 35,711 (actual)

THE MUSEUM OF RUSSIAN ART, 5500 Stevens Ave. S., Minneapolis, MN 55419-1933. Tel.: 612-821-9045. Fax: 612-821-4392. Facebook: @TheMuseumofRussianArt; Twitter: @MuseumRusArt.
E-mail: info@tmora.org
Web Site: tmora.org
Key Personnel: Dir., Vladimir von Tsurikov, Ph.D.; Cur., Maria Zavialova, Ph.D.; Devel. Officer, Alex Legeros; Events Mgr., Michelle Massey; Facilities Mgr., Cory Mahaffey; Volunteer Mgr., Andrea Champaloux; Museum Store Mgr., Elena Cooperman; Cur. Music, Denis Evstuhin.
Institution Type/Description: Art Museum.
Hours & Admission Prices: Mon.-Fri. 10-5, Sat. 10-4, Sun. 1-5. Adults $10, seniors 65& up $8, children 14 & up and students w/ID $5; discount to AAM members; children 13 & under and members no charge. Closed New Year's Day; Memorial Day; Independence Day; Labor Day; Thanksgiving; Christmas Eve & Day. &
Attendance: 52,000 (actual)

SOAP FACTORY, 514 Second St., S.E., Minneapolis, MN 55414-2105. Tel.: 612-623-9176. Facebook, Instagram & Twitter: @TheSoapFactory.
E-mail: info@soapfactory.org
Web Site: www.soapfactory.org
Key Personnel: Exec. Dir., Bill Mague; Gallery Dir., Kate Arford; Gallery Mktg. & Outreach Coord., Joni Van Bockel; Bldg. Mgr., Colin Marx.
Institution Type/Description: Art Gallery.
Hours & Admission Prices: Thurs. & Fri. 2-8, Sat. & Sun. noon-5. No charge; donations accepted.

SOO VISUAL ARTS CENTER, 2909 Bryant Ave., S, Ste. 100, Minneapolis, MN 55408-4966. Tel.: 612-871-2263. Facebook: SooVac; Twitter: @soovac.
E-mail: info@soovac.org
Web Site: www.soovac.org
Key Personnel: Exec. Dir., Carolyn Payne; Assoc. Dir., Alison Hiltner.
Institution Type/Description: Art Gallery.
Hours & Admission Prices: Wed.-Fri. 11-7, Sat.-Sun. 10-6.

TRAFFIC ZONE CENTER FOR VISUAL ARTS, 250 Third Ave. N., Minneapolis, MN 55401. Tel.: 612-419-0107.
E-mail: trafficzoneart@gmail.com
Web Site: www.trafficzoneart.com
Key Personnel: Contact, Jean KRAMER-JOHNSON.
Institution Type/Description: Art Gallery.
Hours & Admission Prices: Mon.-Sat. 9-5.

TYCHMAN SHAPIRO GALLERY, Sabes Jewish Community Center, 4330 S. Cedar Lake Rd., Minneapolis, MN 55416. Tel.: 952-381-3400. Fax: 952-381-3401.
E-mail: info@sabesjcc.org
Web Site: www.sabesjcc.org
Key Personnel: C.E.O., Joshua Wert; Dir. Cultural Arts, Robyn Awend.
Institution Type/Description: Art Gallery.
Hours & Admission Prices: Mon.-Thurs. 7:30am-8:30pm, Fri. 7:30-6, Sun. 8-3. Closed holidays.

WALKER ART CENTER, 725 Vineland Pl., Minneapolis, MN 55403. Tel.: 612-375-7600. Fax: 612-375-7567. Facebook & Twitter: @walkerartcenter.
E-mail: info@walkerart.org
Web Site: www.walkerart.org
Key Personnel: Exec. Dir., Olga Viso; William & Nadine McGuire Dir. & Sr. Cur. Performing Arts, Philip Bither; Dir. & Cur. Education & Public Programs, Nisa Mackie; Design Dir., Emmet Byrne; Artistic Dir., Fionn Meade; Sr. Cur. Film & Video, Sheryl Mousley; Sr. Cur. Visual Arts, Siri Engberg; Registrar, Joe King.
Institution Type/Description: Art Museum.
Hours & Admission Prices: Tues. & Wed. 11-5, Thurs. 11-8, Fri.-Sun. 11-6. Adults $14, seniors 62 & over $12, students $9; discounts to AAM members; members, children under 18, Thurs. 5-9 & 1st Sat. of month no charge. Closed New Year's Day; Martin Luther King, Jr. Day; Presidents' Day; Memorial Day; Labor Day; Thanksgiving; Christmas Eve & Day. &
Attendance: 700,000 (estimated)

WEISMAN ART MUSEUM, 333 E. River Rd., Minneapolis, MN 55455-0367. Tel.: 612-625-9494. Fax: 612-625-9630. Facebook, Twitter.
E-mail: waminfo@umn.edu
Web Site: www.weisman.umn.edu
Formerly: University Art Museum
Key Personnel: Dir. & Chief Cur., Lyndel King; Public Art Cur., Craig Amundsen; Dir. Mktg. & Communications, Susannah Schouweiler; Devel. Dir., Patti Phillips; Sr. Cur., Diane Mullin; Sr. Registrar, Annette Van Aken; WAM Shop Mgr. & Buyer, Marissa Onheiber.
Institution Type/Description: University Art Museum: housed in a stainless steel & brick building; designed by architect Frank Gehry.
Hours & Admission Prices: Tues., Thurs. & Fri. 10-5, Wed. 10-8, Sat. & Sun. 11-5. No charge; donations accepted. Closed New Year's Day, Independence Day; Thanksgiving; Christmas Eve & Day. &
Attendance: 130,000 (estimated)

WELLS FARGO HISTORY MUSEUM CLOSED, 90 S. 7th St., Skyway Level, Minneapolis, MN 55479-1100. Mailing Address: Wells Fargo Historical Services, 420 Montgomery St., MAC-A0101-022, San Francisco, CA 94163. Tel.: 612-667-4210. Fax: 612-316-4361. Facebook: Wells Fargo.
E-mail: wfmuseum.mn@wellsfrgo.com
Web Site: www.wellsfargohistory.com
Institution Type/Description: Company History Museum: located on Skyway level of Wells Fargo Ctr.
Hours & Admission Prices: Mon.-Fri. 9-5. No charge. Closed bank holidays. &

Montevideo

CHIPPEWA COUNTY HISTORICAL SOCIETY, 151 Arnie Anderson Dr., Montevideo, MN 56265-2127. Mailing Address: P. O. Box 303, Montevideo, MN 56265-0303. Tel.: 320-269-7636.
E-mail: ChippewaHistory@outlook.com
Web Site: www.chippewacohistory.org

Key Personnel: Pres. (V), David Lieser; Museum Shop Mgr., Carol Westberg.
Institution Type/Description: Historic Village Setting Museum: 23 buildings including 1882 church; rural school; 1870 log cabin.
Hours & Admission Prices: Chippewa City: Memorial Day to Labor Day Mon.-Fri. 9-5, Sat.-Sun. 1-5; Sept. Mon.-Fri. 9-5. Swensson Farm: Memorial Day to Labor Day Sun. 1-5 & by appointment. Adults $5, youth $2; children 5 & under and members no charge. &
Attendance: 5,000 (estimated)

LAC QUI PARLE MISSION, MINNESOTA HISTORICAL SOCIETY, Junction of Chippewa Cty Hwy. 13 & Cty Rd. 32, Montevideo, MN 56265. Mailing Address: 345 W. Kellogg Blvd., Saint Paul, MN 55102. Tel.: 320-269-7636.

E-mail: lacquiparle@mnhs.org
Web Site: sites.mnhs.org/historic-sites/lac-qui-parle-mission
Institution Type/Description: Historic Site: housed on the site of a mission, established in 1835.
Hours & Admission Prices: May-Sept. daily 8-8. No charge.

Moorhead

COMSTOCK HOUSE, MINNESOTA HISTORICAL SOCIETY, 506 8th St. S., Moorhead, MN 56560-3504. Tel.: 218-291-4211. Facebook: @comstockhouse.

E-mail: comstockhouse@mnhs.org
Web Site: sites.mnhs.org/historic-sites/comstock-house
Key Personnel: Site Mgr., Matt Eidem.
Institution Type/Description: Historical Society: housed in c.1882 Comstock home.
Hours & Admission Prices: Feb. to Memorial Day & Sept.-Oct. Sat. 1-4; Memorial Day weekend to Labor Day Sat. & Sun. 1-4. Adults $6, senior citizens & college students $5, children 5-17 $4; MNHS members and children 4 & under no charge. Closed holidays.
Attendance: 600 (estimated)

CONCORDIA CYRUS M. RUNNING GALLERY - CONCORDIA COLLEGE, 901 8th St. S., Moorhead, MN 56562. Tel.: 218-299-3310.

E-mail: slee@cord.edu
Key Personnel: Dir., Susan Lee.
Institution Type/Description: Art Gallery.
Hours & Admission Prices: Mon.-Fri. 9-4:30, Sun. 1-4. Closed academic breaks.

HISTORICAL AND CULTURAL SOCIETY OF CLAY COUNTY, 202 1st Ave. N., Moorhead, MN 56560-1985. Mailing Address: P.O. Box 157, Moorhead, MN 56561-0157. Tel.: 218-299-5511. Fax: 218-299-5510.

E-mail: maureen.jonason@hcsmuseum.org
Web Site: www.hcscconline.org
Formerly: Heritage-Hjemkomst Interpretive Center
Key Personnel: Interim Exec. Dir., Maureen Kelly Jonason; Archivist, Mark Peihl; Cur., Lisa Vedaa; Coord. Events, Tim Jorgensen; Coord. Visitor Svcs., Markus Krueger; Mktg., Brianne Carlsrud.
Institution Type/Description: History and Cultural Heritage Museum.
Hours & Admission Prices: Mon. & Wed.-Sat. 9-5, Tues. 9-8, Sun. 12-5. Adults $8, seniors/students $7, youth 5-17 $6; discounts to ASTC & AAA members; members & children under 5 no charge. Closed New Year's Eve & Day; Easter; Thanksgiving; Christmas Eve & Day. &
Attendance: 30,000 (estimated)

Mora

KANABEC HISTORY CENTER, 805 W. Forest Ave., Mora, MN 55051. Tel.: 320-679-1665. Facebook: @KanabecHistoryCenter.

E-mail: center@kanabechistory.org
Web Site: www.kanabechistory.org
Key Personnel: Exec. Dir. & Museum Shop Mgr., Wendy Quinn; Pres. (V), Robert Engberg.
Institution Type/Description: Historical Society Museum.
Hours & Admission Prices: Tues.-Fri. 10-4:30, holidays 12:30-4:30. Families $10, adults $5, students K-12 $2; children under 5, KCHS members & during winter no charge. Children under 14 must be accompanied by an adult. Closed New Year's Day; Easter; Independence Day; Thanksgiving; Christmas Eve & Day. &
Attendance: 15,000 (actual)

Morris

STEVENS COUNTY HISTORICAL SOCIETY MUSEUM, 116 W. 6th St., Morris, MN 56267-1922. Tel.: 320-589-1719. Fax: 320-589-1719 call ahead.

E-mail: randee@stevenshistorymuseum.com

Web Site: www.stevenshistorymuseum.com
Key Personnel: Dir. & Museum Shop Mgr., Randee L. Hokanson; Historian Researcher, Tina Didreakson; Pres. (V) & Chm. (V), Ward B. Voorhees; Collections Registrar, Tom Vail.
Institution Type/Description: Local History Museum: housed in 1905 Carnegie Library building.
Hours & Admission Prices: Mon.-Fri. 9-5; other times by appointment; call for additional weekend hours. No charge; donations accepted. &
Attendance: 5,000 (estimated)

Morton

BIRCH COULEE BATTLEFIELD, MINNESOTA HISTORICAL SOCIETY, Lower Sioux Agency Historic Site, 32469 Redwood County Hwy. 2, Morton, MN 56270. Tel.: 507-657-3773.

E-mail: birchcoulee@mnhs.org
Web Site: sites.mnhs.org/historic-sites/birch-coulee-battlefield
Institution Type/Description: Historic Site: former site of the Battle of Birch Coulee.
Hours & Admission Prices: May-Oct. daily dawn-dusk. No charge.

Mountain Lake

HERITAGE VILLAGE, County Rd. One, Mountain Lake, MN 56159. Mailing Address: P.O. Box 152, Mountain Lake, MN 56159-0152. Tel.: 507-427-3743.

E-mail: abdick@frontiernet.net
Formerly: Heritage House
Key Personnel: Chm. Bd, Alvin Dick; Vice Chm., Harvey Buller; Treas., Betty Lou Ritzloff; Sec. & Museum Shop Mgr., Geneva Stoesz.
Institution Type/Description: Historic House & Village: 20 historic structures representing a late 1800s to early 1900s village.
Hours & Admission Prices: Memorial Day to Labor Day daily 1-5. Adults $5, children over 7 $3; members no charge.
Attendance: 2,000 (estimated)

New Brighton

UNITED THEOLOGICAL SEMINARY OF THE TWIN CITIES, 3000 5th St., N.W., New Brighton, MN 55112. Tel.: 651-633-4311. Fax: 651-633-4315.

E-mail: cbjohnson@unitedseminary.edu
Web Site: www.unitedseminary.edu
Institution Type/Description: Religious Art Museum.
Hours & Admission Prices: Mon.-Thurs. 9-9, Fri. 9-5.

New Ulm

AUGUST SCHELL BREWERY, 1860 Schell Rd., New Ulm, MN 56073-3834. Mailing Address: P.O. Box 128, New Ulm, MN 56073. Tel.: 800-770-5020, 507-354-5528. Fax: 507-359-9119.

E-mail: schells@schellsbrewery.com
Web Site: schellsbrewery.com
Key Personnel: Dir. & Pres., Ted Marti.
Institution Type/Description: Company History Museum.
Hours & Admission Prices: Museum: Memorial Day-Labor Day daily 12-5; Winter: call for hours. Tours: Memorial Day-Labor Day Mon.-Thurs. 1, 2:30 & 4, Fri. 1, 2:30 & 4, Sat. noon, 1, 2, 3 & 4, Sun. 1, 2, 3, 4; Sept.-May Fri. 3, Sat. 1, 2, 3 & 4, Sun. 4. Museum: no charge. Tours: adults $3; children 12 & under no charge. &
Attendance: 30,000 (estimated)

BROWN COUNTY HISTORICAL SOCIETY, 2 N. Broadway, New Ulm, MN 56073-1714. Tel.: 507-233-2616. Fax: 507-354-1068.

E-mail: bchs@browncountyhistorymnusa.org
Web Site: browncountyhistorymnusa.org
Key Personnel: Exec. Dir., Robert Burgess; Pres., Lisa Besemer; Cur., Marilyn Hesse; Research Librarian, Darla Gebhard; Museum Shop Mgr. & Office Mgr., Pam Kitzberger.
Institution Type/Description: History Museum.
Hours & Admission Prices: May-Oct. Mon.-Fri. 10-4, Sat. 10-3; Nov.-April Tues.-Fri. 10-4, Sat. 10-3. Adults $3; members, students & children no charge. Closed national holidays. &
Attendance: 6,894 (actual)

HARKIN STORE, MINNESOTA HISTORICAL SOCIETY, 66250 County Rd. 21, New Ulm, MN 56073. Mailing Address: P.

O. Box 112, New Ulm, MN 56073-0112. Tel.: 507-354-8666 & 934-2160. Facebook: @harkinstore.
E-mail: harkinstore@mnhs.org
Web Site: sites.mnhs.org/historic-sites/harkin-store
Key Personnel: Site Mgr., Ruth Grewe.
Institution Type/Description: Historic Site: housed in a former general store & post-office; built in 1867.
Hours & Admission Prices: May & Sept.-Oct. Sat.-Sun. 10-5; Memorial Day to Labor Day Tues.-Sun. 10-5. Adults $6, seniors & college students $5, children 5-17 $4; MNHS members and children 4 & under no charge.
Attendance: 7,000 (estimated)

North Saint Paul

NORTH STAR MUSEUM OF BOY SCOUTING AND GIRL SCOUTING, 2640 Seventh Ave. E., North Saint Paul, MN 55109-3103. Tel.: 651-748-2880. Facebook: North Star Museum of Boy Scouting and Girl Scouting.
E-mail: dfoss@nssm.org
Web Site: www.nssm.org
Formerly: North Star Scouting Memorabilia, Inc.
Key Personnel: Exec. Dir., Brenna Barrett; Bd. Co. Chm., Tom Welna; Bd. Co. Chm., Sandy Craighead.
Institution Type/Description: Boy Scout & Girl Scout Museum.
Hours & Admission Prices: Visit website for hours. Adults $6, youth $4; active duty military, seniors, members & children under 4 no charge; donations accepted. Closed New Year's Day; Memorial Day; Independence Day; Labor Day; Thanksgiving; Christmas. &
Attendance: 3,054 (actual)

Northfield

FLATEN ART MUSEUM OF ST. OLAF COLLEGE, 1520 St. Olaf Ave., Northfield, MN 55057-1099. Tel.: 507-786-3556 & 3703. Fax: 507-786-3776.
E-mail: beckerj@stolaf.edu
Web Site: www.stolaf.edu/collections/flaten
Key Personnel: Dir., Jane Becker Nelson; Collections Specialist, Mona Weselmann.
Institution Type/Description: College Art Museum.
Hours & Admission Prices: Sept. to mid-April Mon.-Wed. & Fri. 10-5, Thurs. 10-8, Sat.-Sun. 2-5. No charge. Closed during school breaks. &
Attendance: 6,000 (actual)

GOULD LIBRARY - ROBERT C. LARSON '56 ART IN THE LIBRARY PROGRAM, One N. College St., Northfield, MN 55057-4097. Tel.: 507-222-4260. Fax: 507-222-4087.
E-mail: mpezalla@carleton.edu
Web Site: apps.carleton.edu/arts/exhibitions
Key Personnel: Cur. Library Art & Exhibitions, Margaret Pezalla-Granlund.
Institution Type/Description: Library & Art Gallery.
Hours & Admission Prices: Art Program: Mon.-Thurs. 10-5 & 7-9, Fri. 10-5, Sun. 1-5 & 7-9. Library: Mon.-Fri. 8am-1am, Sat. 9am to midnight, Sun. 9am-1am.

NORTHFIELD HISTORICAL SOCIETY MUSEUM, 408 Division St., Northfield, MN 55057-2018. Tel.: 507-645-9268, 507-663-6080.
E-mail: nhsmuseum@rconnect.com
Web Site: www.northfieldhistory.org
Key Personnel: Exec. Dir., Bob Boze Bell; Cur., Cathy Osterman.
Institution Type/Description: Historical Society Museum: housed at the site of the original 1st National Bank of Northfield.
Hours & Admission Prices: Mon.-Sat. 10-5, Sun. 1-5. Guided Tours: Sat.-Sun. Adults $4, students and senior citizens 60 & over $3; discounts to AAM members; members no charge. Closed New Year's Day; Easter; Independence Day; Thanksgiving; Christmas. &
Attendance: 12,000 (actual)

NORWEGIAN-AMERICAN HISTORICAL ASSOCIATION, St. Olaf College, 1510 St. Olaf Ave., Northfield, MN 55057-1097. Tel.: 507-786-3229. Fax: 507-646-3734.
E-mail: naha@stolaf.edu
Web Site: www.naha.stolaf.edu
Key Personnel: Dir., Amy Boxrud; Archivist, Jeff Sauve.
Institution Type/Description: Archives.
Hours & Admission Prices: Archives: Mon.-Thurs. 8:30-4, Fri. by appointment. Daily Fee: $15. &
Attendance: 300 (estimated)

PERLMAN TEACHING MUSEUM - CARLETON COLLEGE, Weitz Ctr. for Creativity, 320 Third St., Northfield, MN 55057-4001. Tel.: 507-222-4469 & 4342. Fax: 507-222-7176.
E-mail: lbradley@carleton.edu
Formerly: Carleton College Art Gallery
Key Personnel: Dir. & Cur., Laurel Bradley.
Institution Type/Description: Art Museum: housed Braucher Gallery & Kaemmer Family Gallery.
Hours & Admission Prices: Academic Year: Mon.-Wed. 11-6, Thurs.-Fri. 11-9, Sat.-Sun. 12-4. No charge. Closed winter, spring & summer breaks. &
Attendance: 5,000 (estimated)

Onamia

MILLE LACS INDIAN MUSEUM & TRADING POST, MINNESOTA HISTORICAL SOCIETY, 43411 Oodena Dr., Onamia, MN 56359-2259. Tel.: 320-532-3632. Facebook: @mille-lacsindianmuseum.
E-mail: millelacs@mnhs.org
Web Site: sites.mnhs.org/historic-sites/mille-lacs-indian-museum
Key Personnel: Site Mgr., Travis Zimmerman.
Institution Type/Description: History Museum.
Hours & Admission Prices: Museum: April-May & Sept.-Oct. Wed.-Sat. 11-4; Memorial Day weekend to Labor Day Tues.-Sat. 10-5; Trading Post: Wed.-Sat. 11-4. Adults $10, seniors & college students $8, children 5-17 $6; MNHS members and children 4 & under no charge.

Owatonna

OWATONNA ARTS CENTER, 435 Garden View Lane, West Hills Complex, Owatonna, MN 55060. Mailing Address: P.O. Box 134, Owatonna, MN 55060-0134. Tel.: 507-451-0533. Fax: 507-446-0198.
E-mail: megan.proft@oacarts.org
Web Site: www.oacarts.org
Key Personnel: Artistic Dir., Silvan Durben.
Institution Type/Description: Art Center.
Hours & Admission Prices: Tues.-Sun. 1-5. No charge. Closed holidays. &
Attendance: 25,000 (estimated)

Park Rapids

NEMETH ART CENTER, 301 Court Ave., Park Rapids, MN 56470-1421. Mailing Address: P.O. Box 328, Park Rapids, MN 56470-0328. Tel.: 218-616-2064.
E-mail: info@nemethartcenter.org
Web Site: www.nemethartcenter.org
Formerly: North Country Museum of Arts
Institution Type/Description: Art Museum: housed in 1900 Hubbard County Courthouse.
Hours & Admission Prices: Call for hours. No charge; donations accepted.
Attendance: 2,000 (estimated)

Perham

ITOW VETERANS MUSEUM, 805 W. Main, Perham, MN 56573-1131. Mailing Address: 230 1st Ave. N., Perham, MN 56573-1844. Tel.: 218-346-7678.
E-mail: info@itowmuseum.org
Web Site: www.itowmuseum.org
Key Personnel: Consulting CEO, Darla Ellingson; Facilities Coord., Julie Listrom.
Institution Type/Description: History Museum.
Hours & Admission Prices: Summer: Tues.-Fri. 10-4, Sat. 10-1; Winter: Tues.-Fri. 11-3, Sat. 10-1; tours by appointment. Self-Guided Tour: no charge; donations accepted. Tours: adults $3, students $2. &
Attendance: 1,675 (estimated)

Pine City

SNAKE RIVER FUR POST, MINNESOTA HISTORICAL SOCIETY, 12551 Voyager Lane, Pine City, MN 55063. Tel.: 320-629-6356. Fax: 320-629-4667. Facebook: @northwestcompanyfurpost.
E-mail: furpost@mnhs.org
Web Site: sites.mnhs.org/historic-sites/north-west-company-fur-post
Key Personnel: Site Mgr., Patrick Schifferdecker.
Institution Type/Description: History Museum: housed in recreated fur trading post & Ojibwe encampment.
Hours & Admission Prices: Memorial Day Weekend to Labor Day Mon. & Thurs.-Sat. 10-5, Sun. noon to 5; Sept. Sat. 10-5, Sun. noon to 5. Adults $10, senior citi-

zens & college students $8, children 5-17 $6; discounts to groups; members no charge. &
Attendance: 13,778 (actual)

Pipestone

PIPESTONE COUNTY HISTORICAL MUSEUM, 113 S. Hiawatha Ave., Pipestone, MN 56164-1664. Tel.: 507-825-2563. Fax: 507-825-2563.
E-mail: pipctymu@iw.net
Web Site: www.pipestoneminnesota.com/museum
Key Personnel: Dir., Susan Hoskins; Pres., Joni Peterson.
Institution Type/Description: History Museum; housed in 1896 Old Pipestone City Hall.
Hours & Admission Prices: Mon.-Sat. 10-5. Adults $3; discounts to AAM members; children under 12 & members no charge. Tour Bus: Museum Tour or Step-On Tour $50. Closed New Year's Day; Presidents' Day; Easter; Memorial Day; Independence Day; Labor Day; Veterans Day; Thanksgiving; Christmas Eve & Day.
Attendance: 7,051 (actual)

PIPESTONE NATIONAL MONUMENT, 36 Reservation Ave., Pipestone, MN 56164-1269. Tel.: 507-825-5464. Fax: 507-825-5466.
E-mail: pipe_interpretation@nps.gov
Web Site: www.nps.gov/pipe
Key Personnel: Supt., Glen Livermont.
Institution Type/Description: History Museum & Upper Midwest Indian Cultural Center.
Hours & Admission Prices: Daily 8-5. Car: $5, Individual $3; children 15 & under & enrolled members of federally recognized American Indian tribes no charge. Closed New Year's Day; Thanksgiving; Christmas. &
Attendance: 80,000

Reads Landing

WABASHA COUNTY MUSEUM, WABASHA COUNTY HISTORICAL SOCIETY AT READS LANDING, 70537 206th Ave., Reads Landing, MN 55968. Mailing Address: P.O. Box 255, Lake City, MN 55041-0255. Facebook: Wabasha County History.
E-mail: info@wabashacountyhistory.org
Web Site: www.wabashacountyhistory.org
Key Personnel: Pres. (V), Margaret Peterson.
Institution Type/Description: History Museum.
Hours & Admission Prices: May-Oct. Sat.-Sun. 1-4; groups by appointment. Adults $5, children 6-12 $3; children 5 & under no charge. &
Attendance: 500 (estimated)

Red Wing

GOODHUE COUNTY HISTORICAL SOCIETY, 1166 Oak St., Red Wing, MN 55066-2447. Tel.: 651-388-6024. Fax: 651-388-3577. Facebook: Goodhue County Historical Society.
E-mail: info@goodhistory.org
Web Site: goodhuehistory.org
Key Personnel: Exec. Dir., Dustin Heckman; Cur. Objects & Exhibits, Casey Mathern; Archives & Library Mgr., Afton Esson; Education & Outreach Coord., James Clinton.
Institution Type/Description: Historical Museum.
Hours & Admission Prices: May-Sept. Mon.-Sat. 9-5, Sun. 12-4; Oct.-April Mon.-Fri. 9-5, Sat. 9-3. Adults $5, children 13-18 $2; discounts to AAM & AASLH members; members no charge. Closed New Year's Day; Easter; Memorial Day; Independence Day; Labor Day; Thanksgiving; Day after Thanksgiving; Christmas Eve & Day. &
Attendance: 5,255 (actual)

Redwood

REDWOOD COUNTY MUSEUM, 913 W. Bridge St., Redwood, MN 56283. Tel.: 507-641-3329.
E-mail: rchsrf@redred.com
Web Site: redwoodcountyhistoricalsociety.com/museum
Key Personnel: Pres. (V), Bill Schwandt; Cur. & Museum Shop Mgr., Patricia Lubeck.
Institution Type/Description: General Museum.
Hours & Admission Prices: May-Sept. Thurs.-Sun. 11-4. Adults $5, children $2; children under 5 no charge. &
Attendance: 1,072 (actual)

Renville

HISTORIC RENVILLE PRESERVATION COMMISSION, 202 N. Main, Renville, MN 56284. Mailing Address: Box 681, Renville, MN 56284-0681. Tel.: 612-329-3545.
E-mail: zaskewh@rswb.coop
Key Personnel: Pres. (V), Mildred Zaske.
Institution Type/Description: Historical Society Museum.
Hours & Admission Prices: June-Sept. Tues. 1-4 & special events. No charge; donations accepted. &
Attendance: 200 (estimated)

Richfield

RICHFIELD HISTORICAL SOCIETY, 6901 Lyndale Ave., S., Richfield, MN 55423-2302. Tel.: 612-798-6140.
E-mail: staff@richfieldhistory.org
Web Site: www.richfieldhistory.org
Key Personnel: Mgr., Ruthann Clay; Pres. (V), Jon Wickett.
Institution Type/Description: Historic House Museum; listed on the National Register of Historic Places.
Hours & Admission Prices: Wed. & Sat. 12-4; other times by appointment. No charge; donations accepted.
Attendance: 1,500 (estimated)

Rochester

MAYO CLINIC HERITAGE HALL, 2001 1st St., S.W., Mathews Grand Lobby, Rochester, MN 55905-0002. Tel.: 507-284-8540.
E-mail: mayoclinic.heritagehall@mayo.edu
Web Site: www.mayoclinic.org/heritage-hall
Key Personnel: Dir., Matthew Dacy.
Institution Type/Description: Medical History Museum.
Hours & Admission Prices: Mon.-Fri. 8-5. No charge.

OLMSTED COUNTY HISTORICAL SOCIETY DBA HISTORY CENTER OF OLMSTED COUNTY, 1195 W. Circle Dr., S.W., Rochester, MN 55902-6619. Tel.: 507-282-9447. Fax: 507-289-5481.
E-mail: director@olmstedhistory.com
Web Site: www.olmstedhistory.com
Key Personnel: Dir., Patricia Carlson; Pres. (V), Douglas Boese; Accountant, Kristine Malone; Collections Mgr., Ryan Harren.
Institution Type/Description: History Museum; housed on a 46.6 historic site.
Hours & Admission Prices: Museum: Tues.-Sat. 9-5. Adults $5, children under 15 $2; discounts to AAM members; members no charge. Mayowood Mansion Tours: April-Oct. Adults $17, children 12 & under $5. Holiday Mansion Tours: Nov. 11-Dec. 17 Tues.-Sun. by appointment. Adults $22, children 12 & under $5. &
Attendance: 20,000 (estimated)

ROCHESTER ART CENTER, 40 Civic Center Dr., S.E., Rochester, MN 55904-3773. Tel.: 507-282-8629. Fax: 507-282-7737.
E-mail: info@rochesterartcenter.org
Web Site: www.rochesterartcenter.org
Key Personnel: Exec. Dir., Sarah Stauder; Administrative Operations Dir., Joan Lovelace; Chief Cur., Kristopher Douglas; Facility Dir. & Head Preparator, Phillip Ahnen; Dir. Mktg. & Public Programs, Naura Anderson; Coord. Education, Jason Pearson; Dir. Devel. & Mktg, Sandy Thompson; Event Mgr., Emily Tweten; Membership & Mktg. Asst., Kayla Benson.
Institution Type/Description: Art Center.
Hours & Admission Prices: Wed. & Fri.-Sat. 10-5, Thurs. 10-9, Sun. 12-5. Adults $5, seniors $3; discounts to AAM members; Olmsted County residents, members & students no charge. Closed holidays. &
Attendance: 20,000 (estimated)

Rockford

ROCKFORD AREA HISTORICAL SOCIETY, 8131 Bridge St., Rockford, MN 55373. Mailing Address: P.O. Box 186, Rockford, MN 55373-0186. Tel.: 763-477-5383. Facebook: Ames Florida Stork House Museum.
E-mail: storkhouse@cityofrockford.org
Web Site: www.rockfordmnhistory.org
Key Personnel: Dir., Dustin Bardon; Pres., Steve Huston; Ex Officio, Adam Smith.
Institution Type/Description: Historical Society Museum.

Hours & Admission Prices: April-Sept. Wed.-Fri. 9-5; Oct.-March Wed.-Fri. 10-4; other times by appointment. Adults $5; members and children 6 & under no charge.
Attendance: 1,500 (actual)

Rogers

ELLINGSON CAR MUSEUM, 20950 Rogers Dr., Rogers, MN 55374-9191. Tel.: 763-428-7337. Fax: 763-428-4370.
E-mail: scott@ellingsonclassiccars.com
Web Site: www.ellingsonclassiccars.com
Key Personnel: Owner, Scott Ellingson.
Institution Type/Description: Car Museum; classic car dealer.
Hours & Admission Prices: Mon.-Sat. 10-5. Adults $5; children 12 & under no charge. Closed holidays. &
Attendance: 8,000 (estimated)

Roseau

POLARIS EXPERIENCE CENTER, Ste. #2, 205 5th Ave., S.W., Roseau, MN 56751. Tel.: 218-463-4999. Facebook; Twitter..
Web Site: polaris.com
Institution Type/Description: Company Museum & Tour.
Hours & Admission Prices: Center: Mon.-Thurs. 11-6, Fri. 11-7, Sat. 11-5. Tours: Mon.-Fri. 2 pm; groups of 15 or more by appointment; children under 6 not permitted.

ROSEAU COUNTY HISTORICAL MUSEUM AND INTERPRETIVE CENTER, 121 Center St. E., Ste. 101, Roseau, MN 56751-1127. Tel.: 218-463-1918. Facebook: Roseau County Historical Museum.
E-mail: rchsroseau@mncable.net
Web Site: www.roseaucohistoricalsociety.org
Key Personnel: Pres. (V), Glenn Holm; Cur. & Dir., Britt Dahl.
Institution Type/Description: Historical Society Museum & Interpretive Center.
Hours & Admission Prices: Mon.-Fri. 9:30-5. Museum: no charge. Research Center: adults $5. Closed national holidays. &
Attendance: 9,490 (actual)

Roseville

HARRIET ALEXANDER NATURE CENTER, 2520 N. Dale St., Roseville, MN 55113-3502. Tel.: 651-765-4262. Fax: 651-792-7160.
E-mail: hanc@ci.roseville.mn.us
Web Site: www.cityofroseville.com/index.aspx?nid=183
Key Personnel: Lead Naturalist & Recreation Supvr., Debbie Cash.
Institution Type/Description: Nature Center.
Hours & Admission Prices: Tues.-Sat. 10-4, Sun. 1-4. No charge.

Sacred Heart

SACRED HEART AREA HISTORICAL SOCIETY, 300 5th Ave., Sacred Heart, MN 56285-9802. Mailing Address: P.O. Box 462, Sacred Heart, MN 56285-9802. Tel.: 320-795-8868 & 765-2274.
Institution Type/Description: Historical Society Museum.
Hours & Admission Prices: Jan.-March Tues. 1:30-4:30; April-Dec. Tues. & Fri. 1:30-4:30; other times by appointment. No charge; donations accepted.

Saint Charles

WINONA COUNTY RURAL HERITAGE MUSEUM, Winona County Fairgrounds, Hwy. 14, Saint Charles, MN 55972. Mailing Address: Winona County Historical Society, 160 Johnson St., Winona, MN 55987-3434. Tel.: 507-454-2723. Fax: 507-454-0006.
E-mail: info@winonahistory.org
Web Site: winonahistory.org
Formerly: Arches Museum of Pioneer Life
Key Personnel: Exec. Dir., Mark F. Peterson; Chm. (V), Peter Wash; Cur., Jodi Brom; Asst. Dir., Jennifer Weaver.
Institution Type/Description: History Museum.
Hours & Admission Prices: Open during Winona County Fair & for special events/programs. no charge. &
Attendance: 600 (estimated)

Saint Cloud

MINNESOTA AMATEUR BASEBALL HALL OF FAME, St. Cloud Civic Center, 2nd Fl., 10 4th Ave. S., Saint Cloud, MN 56303. Mailing Address: 541 Brook Lane, Saint Cloud, MN 56301-9611. Tel.: 320-252-8227. Fax: 320-230-3277.
E-mail: mnbaseballhof@charter.net
Web Site: www.mnamateurbaseballhof.com/
Institution Type/Description: Sports Museum.
Hours & Admission Prices: Call for hours.

MUNSINGER AND CLEMENS GARDENS, 1300 Kilian Blvd., S. E., Saint Cloud, MN 56304-1647. Mailing Address: Friends of the Gardens, 101 S. 7th Ave., Ste. 100, Saint Cloud, MN 56301-4275. Tel.: 320-257-5959. Fax: 320-257-0657.
E-mail: info@co.stcloud.mn.us
Web Site: www.ci.stcloud.mn.us
Institution Type/Description: Botanical Gardens.
Hours & Admission Prices: Spring to Fall daily 7am-10pm. No charge; donations accepted.

PARAMOUNT GALLERY, 913 W. St. Germain St., Saint Cloud, MN 56301-3460. Tel.: 320-257-3120. Fax: 320-257-3111.
E-mail: info@paramountarts.org
Web Site: www.paramountarts.org
Key Personnel: Dir., Ellen Nelson.
Institution Type/Description: Art Gallery.
Hours & Admission Prices: Mon.-Fri. 11-5, Sat. 10-2.

STEARNS HISTORY MUSEUM, 235 33rd Ave., S., Saint Cloud, MN 56301-3752. Tel.: 320-253-8424, 866-253-8424 (toll free). Fax: 320-253-2172. TDD: 320-253-8424.
E-mail: info@stearns-museum.org
Web Site: www.stearns-museum.org
Key Personnel: C.E.O., Jim Davis; C.O.O., Ann Meline; Finance Coord., Rodney Range; Dir. Archives, Steve Penick; Archivist, Jessie Storlien; Archivist, John Decker; Program Cur., Julianne O'Connell; Collections Cur., Adam Smith; Facility Mgr., Glenn Liesch; Exec. Asst. & Devel. Assoc., Gena Hiemenz.
Institution Type/Description: History Museum.
Hours & Admission Prices: Mon.-Fri. 10-5, Sat. 10-4. Adults $7, children 5-17 $3; discounts to families, Sept. Days Club, groups, Time Travelers Museum Network, AAA, AAM & ICOM members; children under 5 & members no charge. Closed major holidays. &

Saint Joseph

BENEDICTA ARTS CENTER OF THE COLLEGE OF SAINT BENEDICT, 37 S. College Ave., Saint Joseph, MN 56374-2001. Tel.: 320-363-5777. Fax: 320-363-6097.
E-mail: jdubbeldeekuhn@csbsju.edu
Web Site: www.csbsju.edu/finearts
Key Personnel: Gallery Mgr., Jill Dubbeldee Kuhn; Exec. Dir. of Fine Arts, Brian Jose.
Institution Type/Description: Art Gallery.
Hours & Admission Prices: Summer: call for hours; Sept.-May 11 Mon.-Sat. 10-9, Sun. 12-9. No charge. Closed holidays; school vacations. &
Attendance: 5,000 (estimated)

Saint Louis Park

PAVEK MUSEUM OF BROADCASTING, 3517 Raleigh Ave., Saint Louis Park, MN 55416-2625. Tel.: 952-926-8198. Fax: 952-929-6105. Facebook; Twitter.
E-mail: contact@pavekmuseum.org
Web Site: www.pavckmuseum.org
Key Personnel: Dir. & Chm. (V), Jeffrey T. Bakken.
Institution Type/Description: Technology Museum.
Hours & Admission Prices: Wed.-Sat. 10-5; other times by appointment. Adults $7, students $5. Closed holidays.
Attendance: 10,053 (actual)

Saint Paul

ALEXANDER RAMSEY HOUSE, MINNESOTA HISTORICAL SOCIETY, 265 S. Exchange St., Saint Paul, MN 55102-2416. Tel.: 651-296-8760. Fax: 651-296-0100. Facebook: @alexander-ramseyhouse.
E-mail: ramseyhouse@mnhs.org
Web Site: sites.mnhs.org/historic-sites/alexander-ramsey-house

Key Personnel: Program Devel. Specialist, Jayne Becker.
Institution Type/Description: Historic House: Late 19th-century upper class Victorian mansion.
Hours & Admission Prices: Call for hours. Admission prices vary by program. &
Attendance: 13,500 (actual)

AMERICAN MUSEUM OF ASMAT ART AT THE UNIVERSITY OF ST. THOMAS, 2115 Summit Ave., Mail 44C, Saint Paul, MN 55105-1048. Tel.: 651-962-5512. Fax: 651-962-5861.
E-mail: eric.kjellgren@stthomas.edu
Web Site: art.stthomas.edu/asmat
Formerly: Crosier Asmat Museum
Key Personnel: Dir., Eric Kjellgren; Chm. Bd. of Advisors, Gerald D. Brennan.
Institution Type/Description: Art Museum.
Hours & Admission Prices: Academic Year: Mon.-Wed. 10-4, Thurs. 10-8, Fri. 10-2, Sat.-Sun. noon to 4; Summer: Mon.-Thurs. 10-4, Fri. 10-2, Sat. noon to 4. No charge; donations accepted. &
Attendance: 3,720 (actual)

ARCHDIOCESE OF ST. PAUL AND MINNEAPOLIS ARCHIVES, 777 Forest St., Saint Paul, MN 55106. Tel.: 651-291-4400. Fax: 651-290-1629.
E-mail: records@archspm.org
Web Site: www.archspm.org/departments/archives-records-management
Key Personnel: Dir. Records & Archives, Heather Lawton; Archivist, Allison Spies; Records Mgmt., Sehri Strom.
Institution Type/Description: Religious Museum.
Hours & Admission Prices: By appointment only.
Attendance: 25 (estimated)

BELL MUSEUM + PLANETARIUM, Mailing Address: 2088 Larpenteur Ave. W., Saint Paul, MN 55113. Tel.: 612-626-9660. Facebook, Instagram, Twitter.
E-mail: bellinfo@umn.edu
Web Site: www.bellmuseum.umn.edu
Key Personnel: Exec. Dir., Denise Young; C.O.O., Steven Lott; Assoc. Dir. Visitor Svcs. & Opers., Emma Allen; Special Projects, Barb Coffin; Assoc. Dir. Education & Public Programs, Shoghig Berberian; Membership & Devel. Mgr., Laura Vitko; Sr. Mktg. Communications Mgr., Andria Waclawski; Planetarium Program Mgr., Sally Brummel; Cur. Exhibits, Don Luce.
Institution Type/Description: Natural History Museum.
Hours & Admission Prices: Call for hours. Museum: Adults $12, seniors $10, youth 3-21 $9; members, children 2 & under and UMN students no charge. Planetarium: adults $8, seniors $7, youth 3-21 $6, UMN students $4; children 2 & under no charge. Combination tickets available. Closed New Year's Day; Memorial Day; Independence Day; Labor Day; Thanksgiving; Christmas. &

CATHERINE G. MURPHY GALLERY, ST. CATHERINE UNIVERSITY, Visual Arts Bldg., 2004 Randolph Ave., Saint Paul, MN 55105-1789. Tel.: 651-690-6644. Fax: 651-690-6050. Facebook & Instagram: @stkatesgallery.
E-mail: nmwatson@stkate.edu
Web Site: www.stkate.edu/gallery
Key Personnel: Dir., Nicole M. Watson.
Institution Type/Description: Art Gallery.
Hours & Admission Prices: Mon.-Fri. 8-8, Sat. & Sun. noon to 6. No charge. &
Attendance: 4,000 (actual)

COMO PARK ZOO AND CONSERVATORY, 1225 Estabrook Dr., Saint Paul, MN 55103-1022. Tel.: 651-487-8201. Fax: 651-487-8245. Facebook & Instagram: @ComoZooConservatory; Twitter: @ComoZoo.
E-mail: comomarketing@stpaul.gov
Web Site: www.comozooconservatory.org
Formerly: St. Paul's Como Zoo
Key Personnel: Dir., St. Paul Parks & Recreation, Mike Hahm; Pres., Como Friends, Dr. Jackie Sticha; Campus Mgr., Michelle Furrer; Horticulture Mgr., Tina Dombrowski; Zoo Cur., John Dee; Mktg. & Public Relations Mgr., Matt Reinartz; Visitor & Interpretive Svcs. Mgr., Laura Wake Wiesner; Education & Conservation Cur., Susie VanBlaircom.
Institution Type/Description: Zoo & Conservatory.
Hours & Admission Prices: April-Sept. daily 10-6; Oct.-March daily 10-4. Suggested Donation: adults $3, children $2. &
Attendance: 2,230,000 (estimated)

DENLER ART GALLERY AT UNIVERSITY OF NORTHWESTERN AT ST. PAUL, 3003 Snelling Ave., N.,

Saint Paul, MN 55113-1501. Tel.: 800-692-4020. Fax: 651-631-5100. Facebook: @denlergallery.
E-mail: denlergallery@unwsp.edu
Web Site: unwsp.edu/art-design/denler-gallery
Key Personnel: Design Dir., Luke Aleckson.
Institution Type/Description: Art Gallery.
Hours & Admission Prices: Call for hours.

GALLERY OF WOOD ART, AMERICAN ASSOCIATION OF WOODTURNERS, 222 Landmark Ctr., 75 5th St. W., Saint Paul, MN 55102. Tel.: 651-484-9094. Facebook: AAW Gallery of Wood Art.
E-mail: tibshaw@galleryofwoodart.org
Web Site: www.galleryofwoodart.org
Key Personnel: Exec. Dir., Phil McDonald; Program Dir., Linda Ferber; Cur., Tib Shaw; Communications & Mktg. Dir., Kim Rymer.
Institution Type/Description: Art Gallery.
Hours & Admission Prices: Tues.-Fri. 11-4, Sun. noon to 3; other times by appointment. No charge; donations accepted. Closed New Year's Eve & Day; Easter; Memorial Day; Labor Day; Thanksgiving; Christmas Eve & Day. &
Attendance: 8,500 (actual)

GOLDSTEIN MUSEUM OF DESIGN, 364 McNeal Hall, 1985 Buford Ave., Saint Paul, MN 55108-6134. Tel.: 612-624-7434. Fax: 612-625-5762.
E-mail: gmd@umn.edu
Web Site: goldstein.design.umn.edu
Key Personnel: Dir., Lin Nelson-Mayson; Pres., Kent Hensley; Asst. Cur., Jean McElvain; Registrar & Exhibitions Coord., Eunice Haucen.
Institution Type/Description: Design Museum.
Hours & Admission Prices: McNeal Hall: Tues.-Fri. 10-4. Rapson Hall: Mon.-Thurs. 9-9, Fri. 9-6, Sat.-Sun. 1-5. No charge; donations accepted. Closed major holidays & university holidays. &
Attendance: 110,000 (estimated)

HAMLINE UNIVERSITY, SOEFFKER GALLERY, Hamline University, Drew Fine Arts Center, Saint Paul, MN 55104-1284. Mailing Address: 1536 Hewitt Ave., Saint Paul, MN 55104-1284. Tel.: 651-523-2296. Fax: 651-523-3066.
E-mail: aaudeh@gw.hamline.edu
Web Site: www.hamline.edu/art/
Formerly: Hamline University Galleries, Department of Studio Arts & Art History
Key Personnel: Dir., John-Mark Schlink.
Institution Type/Description: Art Gallery.
Hours & Admission Prices: Mon.-Fri. 10-4. No charge. Closed national holidays.

HISTORIC FORT SNELLING, MINNESOTA HISTORICAL SOCIETY, 200 Tower Ave., Saint Paul, MN 55111-4037. Tel.: 612-726-1171. Fax: 612-725-2429. Facebook: @historicfortsnelling; Twitter: @Fort_Snelling.
E-mail: ftsnelling@mnhs.org
Web Site: www.mnhs.org/fortsnelling
Key Personnel: Interim Site Mgr., Nancy Cass.
Institution Type/Description: Historic Site.
Hours & Admission Prices: June 8 - Sept. 2 Tues.-Fri. 10-4, Sat.-Sun. 10-5; Sept.-Oct. Sat. 10-5. Adults $12, seniors, college students w/ID, veterans & active military w/ID$10, children 5-17, $6; discounts to school groups; children 4 & under and Minnesota Historical Society members no charge. &
Attendance: 100,000 (actual)

IFP MN CENTER FOR MEDIA ARTS, 550 Vandalia St., Ste. 120, Saint Paul, MN 55114. Tel.: 651-644-1912. Facebook: @ifp.minnesota; Instagram: @ifpminnesota; Twitter: @IFPMN.
E-mail: word@ifpmn.org
Web Site: ifpmn.org
Key Personnel: Exec. Dir., Andrew Peterson; Deputy Dir. & Education Dir., Reilly Tillman; Dir. Technical & Facilities Operations, Max Becker; Business Dir., Bethany Gladhill; McKnight Program Admin. Eric Mueller; Devel. Dir., Nancy Paul; Youth Programs Dir., Deacon Warner.
Institution Type/Description: Media Arts Gallery.
Hours & Admission Prices: Mon. & Wed.-Sat. 10-5:30, Tues. 10-9.

INTERACT CENTER, 1860 Minnehana Ave. W., Saint Paul, MN 55104-1029. Tel.: 651-209-3575. Facebook & Instagram: @interactcenter; Twitter: @interactarts.
E-mail: info@interactcenter.com
Web Site: interactcenter.com
Key Personnel: Founder, Artistic/Exec. Dir., Jeanne Calvit; Business Mgr., Glenis Zempel; Advancement Dir., Raleigh Wolpert; Dir. Operations, Kathe Bolinder;

Advancement Coord., Katherine Smith-Flores; Operations & Transportations Mgr., Jan Gillen; Artist Support Dept. Mgr., Deb Holtz; Production Stage Mgr., Dept. Mgr., Vanessa Davis Healey; Visual Artist, Dept. Mgr., Stacey Robinson.
Institution Type/Description: Art Gallery.
Hours & Admission Prices: Call for hours.

JAMES J. HILL HOUSE, MINNESOTA HISTORICAL SOCIETY, 240 Summit Ave., Saint Paul, MN 55102-2194. Tel.: 651-297-2555. Facebook: @jjhillhouse; Twitter: @JamesJHillHouse.
E-mail: hillhouse@mnhs.org
Web Site: sites.mnhs.org/historic-sites/james-j-hill-house
Key Personnel: Site Mgr., Christine Herbaly.
Institution Type/Description: Historic House: 1891 family home of James J. Hill, builder of the Great Northern Railway.
Hours & Admission Prices: Wed.-Sat. 10-4, Sun. 1-4. Adults $10, seniors & college students $8, children 5-17 $6; MNHS members and children 4 & under no charge. ♿
Attendance: 47,598 (actual)

JULIAN H. SLEEPER HOUSE, 66 S. St. Albans St., Saint Paul, MN 55105-3501. Tel.: 651-225-1505.
Web Site: julianhsleeperhouse.com
Key Personnel: C.E.O., Dr. Seth C. Hawkins.
Institution Type/Description: Historic Site: 1884 Eastlake-Vernacular House, moved to present site in 1911, furnished & decorated in period style.
Hours & Admission Prices: Private residence, open by appointment only. Adults $7; discounts to members & AAM members.
Attendance: 1,783 (actual)

LAW WARSCHAW GALLERY, MACALESTER COLLEGE, Janet Wallace Fine Arts Center, Fine Arts Commons 105, Saint Paul, MN 55105-1899. Mailing Address: 1600 Grand Ave., Saint Paul, MN 55105. Tel.: 651-696-6416. Fax: 651-696-6266.
E-mail: gallery@macalester.edu
Web Site: www.macalester.edu/gallery
Key Personnel: Dir. & Cur., Jehra Patrick.
Institution Type/Description: College Art Gallery.
Hours & Admission Prices: Mon.-Wed. & Fri. 10-4, Thurs. 10-8, Sat.-Sun. 12-4. No charge. Closed college holidays. ♿

MINNESOTA AIR NATIONAL GUARD MUSEUM, 670 General Miller Dr., Bldg. 670, Saint Paul, MN 55111-4114. Mailing Address: P.O. Box 11598, Saint Paul, MN 55111-0598. Tel.: 612-713-2523. Facebok: Minnesota Air Guard Museum.
Web Site: mnangmuseum.org
Key Personnel: Chm. (V), Brian Wyneken; Vice Chm., Karen Wolf; Exec. Dir. Operations, Jim Atwell.
Institution Type/Description: Aviation Museum: located on grounds of the 133rd Airlift Wing, Minnesota Air National Guard.
Hours & Admission Prices: By appointment.
Attendance: 3,000 (estimated)

MINNESOTA CHILDREN'S MUSEUM, 10 W. 7th St., Saint Paul, MN 55102-2453. Tel.: 651-225-6000. Fax: 651-225-6006. Facebook: @MinnesotaChildrensMuseum; Instagram & Twitter: @MNChildMuseum.
E-mail: mcm@mcm.org
Web Site: www.mcm.org
Formerly: Minnesota's Aware House
Key Personnel: Pres., Dianne Krizan; Vice Pres. External Rels., Bob Ingrassia; Vice Pres. Visitor Svcs., Joe Olson.
Institution Type/Description: Children's Participatory Museum.
Hours & Admission Prices: General admission $12.95. Members no charge. ♿
Attendance: 404,000 (estimated)

MINNESOTA HISTORICAL SOCIETY, 345 W. Kellogg Blvd., Saint Paul, MN 55102-1903. Tel.: 651-259-3000. Fax: 651-297-3343. Facebook, Instagram, Twitter.
Web Site: www.mnhs.org
Key Personnel: C.E.O. & Dir., Kent Whitworth; Pres., David Hakensen; Deputy Dir. Preservation & Outreach, Jennifer Jones; Dir. HR, Briana Joyner; Dir. Public Policy & Government Relations, David Kelliher; Interim Deputy Dir. Learning Initiatives, Kevin Maijala; Deputy Dir. Admin., Doug Marty; C.F.O., Fred Neher; Interim Deputy Dir. Advancement & Community Engagement, Brenda Raney; Dir. Inclusion & Community Engagement, Avi Viswanathan.
Institution Type/Description: History Center & Historic Sites.
Hours & Admission Prices: Museum: Tues. 10-8, Wed.-Sat. 10-5, Sun. 12-5. Adults $12, seniors & college students $10, children 5-17 $6; discounts to AAM &

ICOM members; members and children 4 & under no charge. Library: Tues. 9-8, Wed.-Sat. 9-4. Call for hours & admissions for individual museums & historic sites. ♿
Attendance: 975,939 (actual)

MINNESOTA MUSEUM OF AMERICAN ART CLOSED, The Historic Pioneer Endicott, 141 E. 4th St., Ste. 101, Saint Paul, MN 55101. Tel.: 651-797-2571.
E-mail: info@mmaa.org
Web Site: www.mmaa.org
Key Personnel: Chair Bd. (V), Jim Rustad; Exec. Dir., Kristin Makholm; Dir. Operations, Jennifer Hensley; Devel. Assoc., Genessis Lopez; Cur. Exhibitions & Public Programs, Christopher Atkins; Registrar, Mai Vang; Cur. Learning & Engagement, Courtney Gerber; Admin. Asst., Anna Lavanger.
Institution Type/Description: Art Museum.
Hours & Admission Prices: MMAA Project Space: Thurs.-Fri. 11-6 & Sat.-Sun. 10-4. No charge; donations accepted. ♿
Attendance: 35,000 (estimated)

MINNESOTA STATE CAPITOL, MINNESOTA HISTORICAL SOCIETY, 75 Rev. Dr. Martin Luther King Jr. Blvd., Saint Paul, MN 55155-1605. Tel.: 651-296-2881. Fax: 651-297-1502. Facebook: @minnesotastatecapitol; Twitter: @mncapitol.
E-mail: statecapitol@mnhs.org
Web Site: www.mnhs.org/capitol
Key Personnel: Site Mgr., Brian Pease.
Institution Type/Description: Historic Site: designed by 19th-century architect Cass Gilbert.
Hours & Admission Prices: Mon.-Fri. 8:30-5, Sat. 10-3, Sun. 1-4. No charge; $5 donation suggested for guided tours. Closed Martin Luther King, Jr. Day; Easter; Memorial Day; Labor Day; Veterans Day; Thanksgiving & day after; Christmas Eve & Day; New Year's Eve. ♿
Attendance: 217,232 (actual)

MINNESOTA TRANSPORTATION MUSEUM, INC., 193 Pennsylvania Ave. E., Saint Paul, MN 55130-4319. Tel.: 651-228-0263. Fax: 651-225-9951.
E-mail: office@trainride.org
Web Site: www.trainride.org
Key Personnel: Chm., Phil Wellman; Sec., Ryan Heath; Treas., Jon Van Niewaal; Exec. Dir., Erik Johnson.
Institution Type/Description: Operating Transportation Museum.
Hours & Admission Prices: Osceola & St. Croix Valley Railway: May to late-Oct. Sat.-Sun. 11, 1:30, & 3. Adults $20, children $10; discounts to AAM members. Jackson Street Roundhouse: Wed. & Sat. 10-4, Sun. 12-4. Adults $12, children $10; discounts to AAM members. ♿
Attendance: 25,000 (estimated)

MINNESOTA VETERINARY HISTORICAL MUSEUM, College of Veterinary Medicine, 1365 Gortner Ave., Rm. 143, Animal Science, Saint Paul, MN 55108-1010. Tel.: 612-581-8207.
E-mail: mvhm@umn.edu
Web Site: hist.cvm.umn.edu
Key Personnel: Pres. (V), Dr. Peter E. Poss; Cur., Paul Maravelas.
Institution Type/Description: Veterinary Museum.
Hours & Admission Prices: Mon.-Fri. 9-5. No charge. Closed holidays. ♿
Attendance: 850 (estimated)

RAMSEY COUNTY HISTORICAL SOCIETY, 323 Landmark Ctr., 75 W. Fifth St., Saint Paul, MN 55102. Tel.: 651-222-0701. Fax: 651-223-8539. Facebook: Ramsey County Historical Society.
E-mail: info@rchs.com
Web Site: www.rchs.com
Key Personnel: Pres., Chad Roberts; Cur. & Archivist, Mollie Spillman; Assoc. Devel. Officer, Samantha Bossman; Mktg. & Membership Coord., Robyn Beth Priestley; Research Center Assoc., Rich Apri; Accountant, Jan Odegard; Editor, John M. Lindley.
Institution Type/Description: Historical Society Museum: housed in the former Federal Courts Building. Listed on the National Register of Historic Places.
Hours & Admission Prices: Call for hours. No charge.

THE RAPTOR CENTER, UNIVERSITY OF MINNESOTA, University of Minnesota College of Veterinary Medicine, 1920 Fitch Ave., Saint Paul, MN 55108-6108. Tel.: 612-624-4745. Fax: 612-624-8740. Facebook: The Raptor Center.
E-mail: raptor@umn.edu
Web Site: www.raptor.umn.edu
Key Personnel: Exec. Dir., Dr. Julia Ponder; Education Program Mgr., Gail Buhl; Clinic Mgr., Lori Arent; Devel. Officer, Ellen Orndorf; Staff Veterinarian, Dr. Michelle Willette, D.V.M.; Volunteer Coord., Nancie Klebba.

Institution Type/Description: Conservation Center.
Hours & Admission Prices: Tues.-Fri. 10-4, Sat.-Sun. noon to 4. No charge; donations accepted. Closed university holidays.
Attendance: 12,000 (estimated)

SAINT PAUL'S WESTERN SCULPTURE PARK, 387 Marion St., Saint Paul, MN 55103. Mailing Address: c/o Public Art Saint Paul, 381 Wabasha Station, Saint Paul, MN 55102. Tel.: 651-290-0921. Fax: 651-292-0345.
E-mail: pasp@publicartstpaul.org
Web Site: www.publicartstpaul.org
Key Personnel: Dir., Colleen Sheehy.
Institution Type/Description: Sculpture Park.
Hours & Admission Prices: Daily dawn to dusk.

THE SCHUBERT CLUB MUSEUM, 302 Landmark Center, 75 W. 5th St., 2nd Fl., Saint Paul, MN 55102-1406. Tel.: 651-292-3267. Fax: 651-292-4317. Facebook, Instagram & Twitter: @schubertclub.
E-mail: schubert@schubert.org
Web Site: schubert.org
Formerly: The Schubert Club Museum of Musical Instruments
Key Personnel: Dir. Education & Museum, Kate Cooper.
Institution Type/Description: Musical Instruments Museum.
Hours & Admission Prices: Sun.-Fri. noon to 4. No charge. &
Attendance: 8,500 (actual)

THE SCIENCE MUSEUM OF MINNESOTA, 120 W. Kellogg Blvd., Saint Paul, MN 55102-1202. Tel.: 651-221-9444. Fax: 651-221-4777. Facebook: @sciencemuseum; Instagram & Twitter: @sciencemuseummn.
E-mail: info@smm.org
Web Site: www.smm.org
Key Personnel: Chair, George J. Kehl; Pres. & C.E.O., Alison Brown; Exec. Vice Pres., Mike Day; Vice Pres. Human Resources, Juliette Francis; Vice Pres. Mission Advancement, Mimi Daly Larson; Vice Pres. Finance & Admin., Duane J. Kocik.
Institution Type/Description: Science Museum.
Hours & Admission Prices: Tues., Wed. & Sun. 9:30-5; Thurs.-Sat. 9:30-9. Museum: adults $18.95, seniors 65 & up and children 4-12 $12.95; Museum & Theater: adults $24.95, senior citizens 65 & up and children 4-12 $18.95. Discounts to groups; children 3 & under and members no charge. &
Attendance: 800,000 (estimated)

TWIN CITY MODEL RAILROAD MUSEUM, 668 Transfer Rd., Ste. 8, Saint Paul, MN 55114. Tel.: 651-647-9628. Facebook & Twitter: @TCMRM.
E-mail: tcmrm@tcmrm.org
Web Site: tcmrm.org
Key Personnel: Pres. (V), Oscar Lund, Jr.; Museum Shop Mgr., Paul Gruetzman.
Institution Type/Description: Model Railroad Museum.
Hours & Admission Prices: Mon. & Tues. 10-3, Sat. 10-5, Sun. 12-5. Adults $10; discount to groups; children 4 & under and members no charge. &
Attendance: 30,000 (estimated)

UNIVERSITY OF ST. THOMAS ART HISTORY, 2115 Summit Ave., Mail 44C, Saint Paul, MN 55105-1089. Tel.: 651-962-5560. Fax: 651-962-5861.
E-mail: arthistory@stthomas.edu
Web Site: www.stthomas.edu/arthistory
Key Personnel: Dir. American Museum of Asmat Art, Eric Kjellgren; Professor & Chair Art History, Victoria Young.
Institution Type/Description: History & College Graduate Teaching Museum.
Hours & Admission Prices: Mon.-Sat. 9am-10pm, Sun. 12-10. No charge. Closed major holidays. &
Attendance: 3,500 (estimated)

Saint Peter

E. ST. JULIEN COX HOUSE, 500 N. Washington Ave. at Skaro St., Saint Peter, MN 56082-1979. Mailing Address: 1851 N. Minnesota Ave., Saint Peter, MN 56082-1727. Tel.: 507-934-2160 & 4309. Fax: 507-934-0172.
E-mail: cox@nchsmn.org
Web Site: www.nchsmn.org
Formerly: Nicollet County Historical Society: E. St. Julien Cox House
Key Personnel: Exec. Dir., Ben Leonard; Site Mgr., Richard Tostenson.
Institution Type/Description: Historic House: c.1871 Gothic/Italianate style architecture was built by E. St. Julien Cox, a prominent lawyer & judge.

Hours & Admission Prices: By appointment only. Admission $4; members no charge.
Attendance: 1,000 (actual)

HILLSTROM MUSEUM OF ART, 800 W. College Ave., Saint Peter, MN 56082-1485. Tel.: 507-933-7171. Fax: 507-933-7205.
E-mail: dmyers@gustavus.edu
Web Site: www.gustavus.edu/finearts/hillstrom
Key Personnel: Dir., Donald Myers.
Institution Type/Description: College Art Museum.
Hours & Admission Prices: Mon.-Fri. 9-4, Sat.-Sun. 1-5. No charge. Closed New Year's Day; Easter; Thanksgiving; Christmas; academic breaks.
Attendance: 5,300 (actual)

NICOLLET COUNTY HISTORICAL SOCIETY, 1851 N. Minnesota Ave., Saint Peter, MN 56082-1727. Tel.: 507-934-2160. Fax: 507-934-0172.
E-mail: museum@nchsmn.org
Web Site: www.nchsmn.org
Formerly: Treaty Site History Center
Key Personnel: C.E.O., Ben Leonard; Pres. (V), Gary Schmidt; Harkin Store Mgr., Ruth Grewe.
Institution Type/Description: History Museum.
Hours & Admission Prices: Tues.-Sat. 10-4, Sun. 1-4; other times & tours by appointment. Adults $4, children 6-18 $2; discounts to NCHS & AAM members; children 5 and under & members no charge. Combination Pass: E. Julien Cox House and Treaty Site History Center $6. &
Attendance: 5,000 (actual)

WILLIAM & JOAN SODERLUND PHARMACY MUSEUM, 201 S. Third St., Saint Peter, MN 56082-2044. Mailing Address: 1801 Old Hwy. 8 N.W., Ste. 121, New Brighton, MN 55112-2307. Tel.: 800-603-8196 (Toll Free), 507-931-4410. Fax: 507-931-5434.
E-mail: bsoderlund@hickorytech.net
Web Site: www.villagedrug.com/index.php
Institution Type/Description: Pharmacy Museum.
Hours & Admission Prices: Mon.-Fri. 8:30-7, Sat. 8:30-2.

Sauk Centre

SINCLAIR LEWIS BOYHOOD HOME, 810 Sinclair Lewis Ave., Sauk Centre, MN 56378. Mailing Address: P.O. Box 25, Sauk Centre, MN 56378-0222. Tel.: 320-352-6119.
E-mail: sinclairlewisfoundation@gmail.com
Web Site: www.sinclairlewisfoundation.com
Key Personnel: Pres. (V) & Dir., Jim Umhoefer.
Institution Type/Description: Historic House Museum: 1920 boyhood home of Sinclair Lewis.
Hours & Admission Prices: House: June to Sept. 1 Tues.-Sat. 10-4. House Tours: adults & students $5, children 6-12 $3; discounts for AAA members; children 5 & under no charge. Call to confirm. &
Attendance: 4,000 (estimated)

Saum

FIRST NEW CONSOLIDATED SCHOOL IN MINNESOTA, Saum Community Club, 41982 Pioneer Rd., N.E., Saum, MN 56650. Mailing Address: P.O. Box 189, Kelliher, MN 56650-0189. Tel.: 218-647-9839.
Key Personnel: Sec., Eva Stengel; Treas., Ione Smischney.
Institution Type/Description: History Museum.
Hours & Admission Prices: By appointment only. No charge; donations accepted. &
Attendance: 200 (estimated)

Scandia

GAMMELGARDEN MUSEUM, 20880 Olinda Tr., Scandia, MN 55073. Tel.: 651-433-5053.
E-mail: museum@gammelgardenmuseum.org
Web Site: www.gammelgardenmuseum.org
Institution Type/Description: History Museum.
Hours & Admission Prices: Guided Tours: Fri.-Sun. 1-2:30. Adults $7; children under 12 no charge.

Shafer

FRANCONIA SCULPTURE PARK, 29836 St. Croix Tr., Shafer, MN 55074. Tel.: 651-257-6668.

E-mail: info@franconia.org
Web Site: www.franconia.org
Institution Type/Description: Sculpture Park.
Hours & Admission Prices: Daily dawn to dusk. No charge.

Shakopee

THE LANDING - MINNESOTA RIVER HERITAGE PARK,
2187 E. Hwy. 101, Shakopee, MN 55379-1750. Tel.: 763-694-
7784. Fax: 952-403-9489.
E-mail: barb.fisher@threeriversparks.org
Web Site: threeriversparks.org
Formerly: Historic Murphy's Landing
Key Personnel: Site Supvr., Jefferson Spilman.
Institution Type/Description: Living History Museum.
Hours & Admission Prices: May 23-Sept. 7 Mon.-Fri. 10-4, Sat. & holidays 10-5,
Sun. 12-5. Adults 18-64 $5, seniors & children $3. Closed New Year's Day;
Easter; Thanksgiving; Christmas Eve & Day.

SCOTT COUNTY HISTORICAL SOCIETY, 235 S. Fuller St.,
Shakopee, MN 55379-1320. Tel.: 952-445-0378, 888-325-2575.
Facebook.
E-mail: info@scottcountyhistory.org
Web Site: www.scottcountyhistory.org
Institution Type/Description: Historical Society Museum.
Hours & Admission Prices: Tues.-Wed. & Fri. 9-4, Thurs. 9-8, Sat. 10-3. Adults $4,
students $2; members & children under 5 no charge. Closed major holidays.
Attendance: 6,093 (actual)

Shevlin

CLEARWATER COUNTY HISTORICAL SOCIETY, 264 1st St.
W., Shevlin, MN 56676. Mailing Address: P.O. Box 241, Bagley,
MN 56621-0241. Tel.: 218-785-2000. Facebook: Clearwater
County Historical Society.
E-mail: cchshist@gvtel.com
Web Site: mnhistoricnw.org
Key Personnel: Dir. & Museum Shop Mgr., Tamara Edevold; Pres. (V) &
Chm. (V), Ken Braaten.
Institution Type/Description: Local History Museum.
Hours & Admission Prices: May-Aug. Tues.-Fri. 10-4, Sat. 10-2; Sept.-April Tues.-
Fri. 10-4. No charge; donations accepted. Closed Christmas week.
Attendance: 1,450 (estimated)

Slayton

MURRAY COUNTY HISTORICAL MUSEUM, 2480 29th St.,
Slayton, MN 56172. Mailing Address: P.O. Box 61, Slayton, MN
56172-0061. Tel.: 507-836-6533. Facebook: Murray County
Historical Museum.
E-mail: museum@co.murray.mn.us
Web Site: murraycountyhistoricalsociety.org
Key Personnel: Murray County Museums Coord., Janet Timmerman; Site Coord.,
Gaylene Chapman.
Institution Type/Description: History Museum.
Hours & Admission Prices: Tues.-Fri. 10-5, Sat. 10-2. No charge; donations
accepted.

Sleepy Eye

SLEEPY EYE DEPOT MUSEUM, 100 Oak St., N.W., Sleepy Eye,
MN 56085. Mailing Address: P.O. Box 544, Sleepy Eye, MN
56085-0544. Tel.: 507-794-5053.
E-mail: semuseum@sleepyeyetel.net
Web Site: thedepotlady.blogspot.com
Key Personnel: Dir., Debbie Joramo.
Institution Type/Description: Railroad Depot Museum: listed on the National
Register of Historic Places.
Hours & Admission Prices: May-Nov. Wed.-Sat. 10-4; other times by appointment.
No charge; donations accepted.

Soudan

SOUDAN UNDERGROUND MINE, 1379 Stuntz Bay Rd., Soudan,
MN 55782. Mailing Address: P.O. Box 335, Soudan, MN 55782-
0335. Tel.: 218-300-7000. Fax: 218-753-2246.
E-mail: lakevermilion-soudan.statepark@state.mn.us
Web Site: mndnr.gov/vermilionsoudan
Institution Type/Description: Historic Site & Underground Mine.

Hours & Admission Prices: Underground Mine Tour: call for hours & admission
prices.
Attendance: 37,000 (estimated)

South Saint Paul

DAKOTA COUNTY HISTORICAL SOCIETY, Lawshe Memorial
Museum, 130 3rd Ave., N., South Saint Paul, MN 55075-2002.
Tel.: 651-552-7548. Fax: 651-552-7265.
E-mail: dakotahistory@co.dakota.mn.us
Web Site: www.dakotahistory.org
Key Personnel: Exec. Dir., Matthew Carter; Pres., Thomas Achartz.
Institution Type/Description: Historical Society Museum.
Hours & Admission Prices: Wed. & Fri. 9-5, Thurs. 9-8, Sat. 10-3. Lawshe: no
charge; donations accepted. LeDuc: mid-May to late Oct. Thurs.-Sun. 10-5.
Tours at 10, 11:30, 1, 2:30 & 4. Sibley: Memorial Day to Labor Day Sat.-Sun. 1-
4. LeDuc & Sibley: adults $7, seniors 60 & over and military $6, students 6-17
$5, children 5 & under & members no charge. Closed national holidays.
Attendance: 13,000 (actual)

Spring Grove

BLUFF COUNTRY ARTISTS GALLERY, 111 W. Main St.,
Spring Grove, MN 55974. Tel.: 507-498-2787.
E-mail: bcagallery@springgrove.coop
Web Site: bluffcountryartistsgallery.org
Institution Type/Description: Art Gallery.
Hours & Admission Prices: Call for hours.

Spring Valley

SPRING VALLEY COMMUNITY HISTORICAL SOCIETY,
INC., 220 W. Courtland St., Spring Valley, MN 55975-1232. Tel.:
507-346-7659.
E-mail: wilderinspringvalley@hotmail.com
Web Site: springvalleymnmuseum.org
Key Personnel: Pres. (V), Joseph Bezdicek; Vice Pres., Ken Kujath; Dir. &
Museum Shop Mgr., Julie Mlinar.
Institution Type/Description: Pioneer History Museum, A Laura Ingalls Wilder site.
Hours & Admission Prices: June-Aug. daily 10-4; Sept.-Oct. Sat.-Sun. 10-4; May-
Oct. by appointment for groups. Church: adults $5, students $2. All Buildings:
adults $7, students $3; members no charge.
Attendance: 2,000 (actual)

Stillwater

WASHINGTON COUNTY HISTORICAL SOCIETY
WARDEN'S HOUSE MUSEUM, 602 N. Main St., Stillwater,
MN 55082-4010. Mailing Address: P.O. Box 167, Stillwater, MN
55082-0167. Tel.: 651-439-5956.
E-mail: brent.peterson@wchsmn.org
Web Site: www.wchsmn.org
Key Personnel: Pres., David Lindsey; Historic Sites Supvr., Sean Pallas; Exec. Dir.,
Brent Peterson.
Institution Type/Description: History Museum: located in 1853 former State Prison
Warden's Home.
Hours & Admission Prices: May-Oct. Thurs.-Sun. 1-5; tours by appointment.
Adults $5, children 6-17 $1; discounts to AAA members; members no charge.
Attendance: 5,000 (actual)

Taylors Falls

FOLSOM HOUSE MUSEUM, MINNESOTA HISTORICAL
SOCIETY, P.O. Box 333, 272 W. Government Rd., Taylors Falls,
MN 55084. Tel.: 651-465-3125.
E-mail: folsomhouse@mnhs.org
Web Site: sites.mnhs.org/historic-sites/folsom-house
Formerly: The Historic W.H.C. Folsom House
Key Personnel: Site Mgr., Chad Thurman.
Institution Type/Description: Historic House: 1854-55 Historic Folsom House.
Hours & Admission Prices: Memorial Day weekend to mid-Oct. Fri.-Sun. tours at
1, 2, 3 & 4. Adults $6, seniors & college students $5, children 5-17 $4;
Minnesota Historical Society & Taylor Falls Historical Society members no
charge.
Attendance: 4,000 (estimated)

Tofte

NORTH SHORE COMMERCIAL FISHING MUSEUM, 7136 W. Hwy. 61, Junction of Sawbill Trail & Hwy. 61, Tofte, MN 55615. Mailing Address: P.O. Box 2312, Tofte, MN 55615-2312. Tel.: 218-663-7050.
E-mail: info@commercialfishingmuseum.org
Web Site: www.commercialfishingmuseum.org
Key Personnel: Pres. (V), Virginia Reiner.
Institution Type/Description: Fishing Museum.
Hours & Admission Prices: Fri. 12-5. Sat. 9-5. Adult $3, children 6-16 $1; discounts to groups; children under 6 no charge.
Attendance: 3,500 (estimated)

Tower

BOIS FORTE HERITAGE CENTER, 1500 Bois Fort Rd., Tower, MN 55790-7800. Tel.: 218-753-6017. Fax: 218-753-6026.
E-mail: bmiller@boisforte-nsn.gov
Web Site: boisforte.com/divisions/heritage_center.htm
Key Personnel: Exec. Dir., Bev Miller; Cur. & Historic Preservation Officer, William Latady; Mgr. Visitor Svcs., Martha Anderson.
Institution Type/Description: History Museum.
Hours & Admission Prices: Tues.-Sat. 9-5; groups by appointment. Family $20, adults $8, seniors 55 & over and children 4-12 $6; veterans $3; discounts to groups of 10 or more; members no charge.

Two Harbors

LAKE COUNTY HISTORICAL SOCIETY, 520 South Ave., Depot Bldg., Two Harbors, MN 55616. Mailing Address: P.O. Box 128, Two Harbors, MN 55616-0128. Tel.: 218-834-4898. Fax: 218-834-7198.
E-mail: lakehist@lakenet.com
Web Site: lakecountyhistoricalsociety.org
Key Personnel: Exec. Dir., Mel Sando; Pres. (V), Sam Gangi; Museum Shop Mgr., Kim Gangi.
Institution Type/Description: History Museum & Historic Site.
Hours & Admission Prices: May-Sept. daily 10-5; other times by appointment. Lighthouse 9-5 & 6-9. Admission $5; discounts to groups; children under 8 & members no charge.
Attendance: 18,000 (estimated)

SPLIT ROCK LIGHTHOUSE, MINNESOTA HISTORICAL SOCIETY, 3713 Split Rock Lighthouse Rd., Two Harbors, MN 55616-2020. Tel.: 218-226-6372. Facebook: @splitrocklighthouse.
E-mail: splitrock@mnhs.org
Web Site: sites.mnhs.org/historic-sites/split-rock-lighthouse
Key Personnel: Site Mgr., Andrew Fox.
Institution Type/Description: Historic Site: located on 25 acres, site of 1910 Split Rock Light Station.
Hours & Admission Prices: Mid-May to mid-Oct. daily 10-6; mid-Oct. to mid-May Thurs.-Mon. 11-4. Adults $10, senior citizens & college students $8, children 5-17 $6; children 4 & under and MNHS members no charge. Closed Easter; Thanksgiving; Christmas Eve & Day.
Attendance: 101,000 (actual)

TWO HARBORS LIGHT STATION, 1 Lighthouse Point, P.O. Box 128, Two Harbors, MN 55616. Tel.: 218-834-4898.
E-mail: lakehist@lakeconnections.net
Web Site: lakecountyhistoricalsociety.org
Institution Type/Description: Historic Lighthouse: built in 1892. Listed on the National Register of Historic Places.
Hours & Admission Prices: Memorial Day to Labor Day Fri.-Sun. 11-4. Admission $5.

Victoria

LOWRY NATURE CENTER, 7025 Victoria Dr., Victoria, MN 55386-9668. Mailing Address: c/o Three Rivers Park District, 3000 Xenium Lane, N., Plymouth, MN 55441. Tel.: 763-694-7650. Facebook: @LowryNatureCenter.
E-mail: lowrync@threeriversparkdistrict.org
Web Site: www.threeriversparkdistrict.org/parks/carver-park/lowry-nature-center.aspx
Key Personnel: Supvr., Allison Neaton; Interpretive Naturalist, Judy Englund.
Institution Type/Description: Nature Center.
Hours & Admission Prices: Mon.-Sat. 9-5, Sun. 12-5.

Wabasha

NATIONAL EAGLE CENTER, 50 Pembroke Ave., Wabasha, MN 55981-1241. Mailing Address: P.O. Box 242, Wabasha, MN 55981-0242. Tel.: 651-868-4989, 877-332-4537.
E-mail: rolf@nationaleaglecenter.org
Web Site: nationaleaglecenter.org
Key Personnel: Exec. Dir., Rolf Thompson; Assoc. Dir., Eileen Hanson.
Institution Type/Description: Nature Center.
Hours & Admission Prices: Daily 10-5. Adults $10, U.S. Veterans $9, youth 4-17 $7; children 3 & under and members no charge.
Attendance: 83,000 (actual)

Wabasso

COUNTY CENTER HISTORICAL SOCIETY, 564 South St., Wabasso, MN 56293. Mailing Address: 1177 Duey St., Wabasso, MN 56293. Tel.: 507-342-5367.
Formerly: Wabasso Center Historical Society
Key Personnel: Pres., Armin Dallman; Treas., Merlin J. Goudy.
Institution Type/Description: Historic Society Museum: housed in 1903 Knox Presbyterian Church.
Hours & Admission Prices: Summer Wed.-Sun. 1-5; other times & tours by appointment. No charge; donations accepted.
Attendance: 75

Waconia

CARVER COUNTY HISTORICAL SOCIETY, 555 W. 1st St., Ste. A, Waconia, MN 55387-1223. Tel.: 952-442-4234. Fax: 952-442-2435.
E-mail: historical@co.carver.mn.us
Web Site: www.carvercountyhistoricalsociety.org/index.htm
Key Personnel: Exec. Dir., Wendy Petersen Biorn.
Institution Type/Description: History Museum.
Hours & Admission Prices: Mon.-Fri. 10-4:30, Sat. 10-3; groups by appointment. No charge; donations accepted.
Attendance: 10,600 (actual)

Walker

CASS COUNTY MUSEUM & RESEARCH CENTER, 205 Minnesota Ave. S., Walker, MN 56484-2189. Mailing Address: P. O. Box 505, Walker, MN 56484-0505. Tel.: 218-547-7251.
E-mail: casscountymuseum@gmail.com
Web Site: www.casscountymuseum.org
Formerly: Cass County Museum & Pioneer School
Key Personnel: Pres., Gloria Day.
Institution Type/Description: Historical Society Museum.
Hours & Admission Prices: Memorial Day-Labor Day Tues.-Fri. 10-4. Families $9, adults $4, children $1; discounts to groups with reservations.
Attendance: 1,300 (estimated)

Walnut Grove

LAURA INGALLS WILDER MUSEUM AND TOURIST CENTER, 330 8th St., Walnut Grove, MN 56180-1114. Tel.: 507-859-2358. Fax: 507-859-2933.
E-mail: lauramuseum@walnutgrove.org
Web Site: www.walnutgrove.org
Key Personnel: Pres., James Kleven; Dir. & Museum Shop Mgr., Amy Ankrum; Treas., Lori Julinson; Collections Mgr., Nicole Elzenga.
Institution Type/Description: General Museum: housed in c.1894 railroad station.
Hours & Admission Prices: April & Oct. Mon.-Sat. 10-4, Sun. 12-4; May & Sept. Mon.-Sat. 10-5, Sun. 12-5; June-Aug. daily 10-6. Adults $6, children 6-12 $3; members & children 5 and under no charge. Closed New Year's Day; Easter; Thanksgiving; Christmas Eve & Day.
Attendance: 17,500 (actual)

Warren

MARSHALL COUNTY HISTORICAL SOCIETY MUSEUM, 808 E. Johnson Ave., Warren, MN 56762. Mailing Address: P.O. Box 103, Warren, MN 56762-0103. Tel.: 218-745-4803.
E-mail: mchs@wiktel.com
Key Personnel: C.E.O. & Pres. (V), Delvin Potucek; Dir., Michael E. Johnson.
Institution Type/Description: Historical Society Museum.
Hours & Admission Prices: May-Sept. Mon.-Fri. 9-5, Sat.-Sun. by appointment. No charge; donations accepted. Closed major holidays.
Attendance: 2,100 (estimated)

Waseca

FARMAMERICA, THE MINNESOTA AGRICULTURAL INTERPRETIVE CENTER, 7367 360th Ave., Waseca, MN 56093-4414. Tel.: 507-835-2052. Facebook.
E-mail: info@farmamerica.org
Web Site: farmamerica.org
Key Personnel: Chm. Bd. (V), Warren Formo; Exec. Dir., Jessica Rollins; Office Mgr., Crystal Paulson.
Institution Type/Description: Farm Equipment Museum.
Hours & Admission Prices: June -Sept. Tues.-Fri. 9-2. Guided Tour: $10, Self-Guided Tour: $8. &
Attendance: 15,000 (estimated)

WASECA COUNTY HISTORICAL SOCIETY, MUSEUM AND RESEARCH LIBRARY, 315 2nd Ave., N.E., Waseca, MN 56093-2936. Mailing Address: P.O. Box 314, Waseca, MN 56093-0314. Tel.: 507-835-7700. Fax: 507-835-7811.
E-mail: director@historical.waseca.mn.us
Web Site: www.historical.waseca.mn.us
Key Personnel: Co Dir. & Museum Shop Mgr., Joan Mooney; Co Dir., Sheila Morris; Pres. (V), Jim King.
Institution Type/Description: Local History Museum.
Hours & Admission Prices: Tues.-Fri. 9-5; other times by appointment. No charge; donations accepted. Research: $5 per day; members no charge. &

Wayzata

MINNETONKA CENTER FOR THE ARTS, 2240 North Shore Dr., Wayzata, MN 55391-9347. Tel.: 952-473-7361, ext. 16. Fax: 952-473-7363. Facebook: Art Centered.
E-mail: information@minnetonkaarts.org
Web Site: www.minnetonkaarts.org
Key Personnel: Dir., Roxanne Heaton; Chm. (V), Tom Hull; Museum Shop Mgr., Robert Bowman.
Institution Type/Description: Art Gallery.
Hours & Admission Prices: Summer: Mon. & Fri. 9-4, Tues.-Thurs. 9am-9:30pm, Sat. 9-1; Winter: Mon., Fri. & Sat. 9-4, Tues.-Thurs. 9-1. &
Attendance: 20,000 (estimated)

West Saint Paul

DODGE NATURE CENTER, 365 Marie Ave., W., West Saint Paul, MN 55118-3848. Tel.: 651-455-4531. Fax: 651-455-2575.
E-mail: info@dodgenaturecenter.org
Web Site: www.dodgenaturecenter.org
Key Personnel: Exec. Dir., Jason Sanders.
Institution Type/Description: Nature Center.
Hours & Admission Prices: Mon.-Fri. 8-4:30 pre-registered school & other groups only, Sat. 10-4; occasional evening. Center Entrance: no charge. Special Programs: adults & senior citizens $2-$5, students & children $2-$4. &
Attendance: 42,000 (estimated)

Wheaton

TRAVERSE COUNTY HISTORICAL SOCIETY, 1201 Broadway, Wheaton, MN 56296. Mailing Address: 601 1st Ave. S., Wheaton, MN 56296-1712. Tel.: 320-563-8520.
E-mail: cjuelich@frontiernet.net
Web Site: www.cityofwheaton.com
Key Personnel: Pres., Clarence Juelich; Sec., Julieann Fromeke.
Institution Type/Description: Historical Society Museum: housed in c.1906 railroad depot.
Hours & Admission Prices: Memorial Day-Labor Day Thurs.-Sun. 1-5. No charge. &
Attendance: 486 (estimated)

White Bear Lake

WHITE BEAR CENTER FOR THE ARTS GALLERY, 4971 Long Ave., White Bear Lake, MN 55110. Tel.: 651-407-0597. Fax: 651-429-1569.
E-mail: wbca@whitebeararts.org
Web Site: whitebeararts.org
Institution Type/Description: Art Gallery.
Hours & Admission Prices: Mon., Wed. & Fri. 9-4, Tues.-Thurs. 9-8:30, Sat. 10-3. &

White Bear Township

TAMARACK NATURE CENTER, 5287 Otter Lake Rd., White Bear Township, MN 55110-5851. Mailing Address: c/o Ramsey County Parks & Recreation, 2015 N. Van Dyke St, Maplewood, MN 55109-3796. Tel.: 651-407-5350. Fax: 651-407-5354. Facebook: Tamarack Nature Center.
E-mail: tamarack@co.ramsey.mn.us
Web Site: www.parks.co.ramsey.mn.us/tamarack/Pages/tamarack.aspx
Key Personnel: Dir., May Vidas.
Institution Type/Description: Nature Center.
Hours & Admission Prices: Trails: daily 30 minutes before sunrise to 30 minutes after sunset; Visitor Center: Mon.-Fri. 8-4:30, Sat. 9-5, Sun. 12-5; Discovery Hollow & Garden Mon.-Fri. 10-4, Sat. 10-4:30, Sun. 12-4:30. No charge; donations accepted

Willmar

KANDIYOHI COUNTY HISTORICAL SOCIETY, 610 Hwy. 71, N.E., Willmar, MN 56201-2650. Tel.: 320-235-1881. Fax: 320-235-1881. Facebook: Kandiyohi County Historical Society.
E-mail: kandhist@msn.com
Web Site: kandiyohicountyhistoricalsociety.com
Key Personnel: Exec. Dir., Jill Wohnoutka.
Institution Type/Description: History Museum.
Hours & Admission Prices: Memorial Day-Labor Day Mon.-Fri. 9-4, Sat.-Sun. 1-4; Sept.-May Mon.-Fri. 9-4. Suggested Donation $2. &
Attendance: 8,000 (estimated)

Windom

COTTONWOOD COUNTY HISTORICAL SOCIETY, 812 Fourth Ave., Windom, MN 56101-1657. Tel.: 507-831-1134. Fax: 507-831-2665. Facebook: cottonwoodcountyhs/.
E-mail: cchs@windomnet.com
Web Site: www.cchsmn1901.org
Key Personnel: Pres., Thomas Wickie; Dir., Linda Fransen; Treas., Margaret McDonald; Sec., Rosie Davis.
Institution Type/Description: History Museum.
Hours & Admission Prices: Mon.-Fri. 8-4, Sat. 10-4. No charge; donations accepted. Research Library: $2; members no charge. &
Attendance: 8,000 (estimated)

Winnebago

WINNEBAGO AREA MUSEUM, 16 Main St. S., Winnebago, MN 56098. Mailing Address: P.O. Box 595, 16 Main St. S., Winnebogo, MN 56098-0595. Tel.: 507-893-4660.
E-mail: wmuseum@bevcomm.net
Key Personnel: Chm. (V), Carol Hill; Treas., Jean Anderson; Sec., Stephanie O'Neil.
Institution Type/Description: Historical Society & Archaeology Museum.
Hours & Admission Prices: Call for hours. No charge; donations accepted. &
Attendance: 1,295 (actual)

Winona

MINNESOTA MARINE ART MUSEUM, 800 Riverview Dr., Winona, MN 55987-2272. Tel.: 866-940-6626 (Toll Free), 507-474-6626. Fax: 507-474-6625.
E-mail: amaus@mmam.org
Web Site: www.mmam.org
Key Personnel: Exec. Dir., Andrew J. Maus.
Institution Type/Description: Art Museum.
Hours & Admission Prices: Tues.-Sun. 10-5. Adults $7, students $3; members and children 4 & under no charge. Closed holidays. &
Attendance: 20,000 (estimated)

WINONA COUNTY HISTORICAL SOCIETY, 160 Johnson St., Winona, MN 55987-3461. Tel.: 507-454-2723. Fax: 507-454-0006.
E-mail: info@winonahistory.org
Web Site: www.winonahistory.org
Key Personnel: Exec. Dir., Mark F. Peterson; Asst. Dir., Jennifer Weaver; Pres. (V), Peter Walsh; Archivist, Walt Bennick; Archivist, Andy Bloedorn; Cur. Collections, Jodi Brom.
Institution Type/Description: Local History Museum.
Hours & Admission Prices: Winona County History Center: Mon.-Fri. 9-5, Sat. 10-4, Sun. 12-4. Adults $5, students $3; members no charge. Closed Thanksgiving, Christmas. &
Attendance: 25,000 (estimated)

Worthington

NOBLES COUNTY HISTORICAL SOCIETY & PIONEER VILLAGE, 407 12th St., Worthington, MN 56187-2471. Mailing Address: 407 12th St., Ste. 2, Worthington, MN 56187-2471. Tel.: 507-376-4431. Fax: 507-376-3005.
E-mail: nchs@frontiernet.net
Web Site: www.noblespioneervillage.com
Key Personnel: Pres., Jacoba Nagel; Dir. Pioneer Village, Roy Reimer; Office Mgr., Carolyn Soper.
Institution Type/Description: Historical Society Museum.
Hours & Admission Prices: Memorial Museum: Mon.-Fri. 12-4; other times by appointment. No charge; donations accepted. Nobles County Pioneer Village: May-Sept. Mon.-Sat. 10-5, Sun. 1-5. Adults $6; discounts to groups; senior citizens 90 & over, children under 6 and members no charge. &
Attendance: 9,000 (estimated)

MISSISSIPPI

(164 listings)

Amory

AMORY REGIONAL MUSEUM, 801 Third St., S., Amory, MS 38821-5233. Tel.: 662-256-2761.
E-mail: suebrown@midsouth.com
Web Site: www.amoryms.us
Key Personnel: Dir., Bo Miller; Computer Operator, Sue Brown; Tour Guides, Gertrude Sanders; Tour Guides, Bettye Benedict.
Institution Type/Description: History Museum: housed in 2-story Greek Revival brick hospital building.
Hours & Admission Prices: Tues.-Fri. 9-5, Sat. 10-4, Sun. 1-5. No charge. Closed New Year's Day; Thanksgiving; Christmas. &
Attendance: 5,000 (estimated)

Baldwyn

MISSISSIPPI'S FINAL STANDS VISITOR AND INTERPRETIVE CENTER, 607 Grisham St., Baldwyn, MS 38824-8541. Tel.: 662-365-3969. Fax: 662-365-3322.
E-mail: finalstands@att.net
Web Site: www.finalstands.com
Formerly: Brice's Crossroads
Key Personnel: Cur., Edwina Carpenter.
Institution Type/Description: History Museum.
Hours & Admission Prices: Visitor Center: Tues.-Sat. 9-5. Adults $5, children $3; discounts to groups. Closed major holidays. &
Attendance: 3,250 (estimated)

Bay Saint Louis

ALICE MOSELEY FOLK ART AND ANTIQUE MUSEUM, 1928 Depot Way, Bay Saint Louis, MS 39520. Mailing Address: P. O. Box 3002, Bay Saint Louis, MS 39521. Tel.: 228-467-9223. Facebook: Alice Moseley Folk Art and Antique Museum.
E-mail: alicemoseley@gmail.com
Web Site: www.alicemoseley.com
Institution Type/Description: Folk Art & Antique Museum.
Hours & Admission Prices: Mon.-Sat. 10-4, Sun. 12-4; other times by appointment. No charge; donations accepted. Closed Easter; Thanksgiving; Christmas. &
Attendance: 12,000 (estimated)

KATE LOBRANO HOUSE - HANCOCK COUNTY HISTORICAL SOCIETY, 108 Cue St., Bay Saint Louis, MS 39520. Mailing Address: P.O. Box 3356, Bay Saint Louis, MS 39521. Tel.: 228-467-4090.
E-mail: hancockcountyhis@bellsouth.net
Web Site: www.hancockcountyhistoricalsociety.com
Key Personnel: Dir., Charles H. Gray.
Institution Type/Description: Historical Society Museum: housed in the former home of Katherine Maynard Lobrano; built in 1896.
Hours & Admission Prices: Mon.-Fri. 10-12 & 1-3. No charge; donations accepted.

Belzoni

CATFISH MUSEUM AND VISITOR CENTER, 111 Magnolia St., Belzoni, MS 39038. Mailing Address: P.O. Box 145, Belzoni, MS 39038-0385. Tel.: 800-408-4838, 662-247-4838. Fax: 662-247-4805.
E-mail: catfish@belzonicable.com
Web Site: www.belzonims.com
Formerly: Catfish Capital Visitors Center and Museum
Key Personnel: Dir. BHDF, Mark Bellipanni.
Institution Type/Description: History Museum.
Hours & Admission Prices: Mon.-Fri. 10-2. No charge; donations accepted. &
Attendance: 3,000 (estimated)

THE ETHEL WRIGHT MOHAMED STITCHERY MUSEUM, 307 Central, Belzoni, MS 39038-3603. Mailing Address: P.O. Box 254, Belzoni, MS 39038. Tel.: 662-247-3633. Fax: 662-247-1433.
E-mail: hwilson493@aol.com
Web Site: www.mamasdreamworld.com
Key Personnel: Cur., Carol Mohamed Ivy.
Institution Type/Description: Stitchery Museum: housed in the former home of Ethel Wright Mohamed, often called Mississippi's Grandma Moses of stitchery.
Hours & Admission Prices: By appointment only. Admission $2; children under 12 no charge.

JAKE TOWN MUSEUM, 116 W. Jackson St., Belzoni, MS 39038-3514. Mailing Address: P.O. Box 145, Belzoni, MS 39038-0145. Tel.: 662-247-4838. Fax: 662-247-4805.
E-mail: catfish@belzonicable.com
Web Site: www.belzonims.com
Key Personnel: Dir., Dianne Grant.
Institution Type/Description: History Museum.
Hours & Admission Prices: Daily 10-4. No charge; donations accepted. &
Attendance: 1,500 (estimated)

Biloxi

BEAUVOIR, THE JEFFERSON DAVIS HOME AND PRESIDENTIAL LIBRARY, 2244 Beach Blvd., Biloxi, MS 39531-5002. Tel.: 228-388-4400. Fax: 228-388-7800.
E-mail: director@beauvoir.org
Web Site: www.beauvoir.org
Key Personnel: Dir., Bert Hayes-Davis; Chm. (V), Richard V. Forte, Sr.; Cur., Richard Flowers; Business Mgr., George G. (Rusty) Trowbridge; Facilities Mgr., Quentin Kersten; Museum Shop Mgr., Rosemary Potter; Security Chief, Jay Peterson.
Institution Type/Description: Historic Site: housed in the post-war home of Confederate President Jefferson Davis; built in 1853.
Hours & Admission Prices: Daylight Savings Time: daily 9-5; Standard Time: daily 9-4. Adults $9, seniors 65 & over, military & AAA members $7.50, children 6-18 $5. Closed Thanksgiving; Christmas. &
Attendance: 31,000 (estimated)

MARITIME & SEAFOOD INDUSTRY MUSEUM, 115 First St., Biloxi, MS 39530. Mailing Address: P.O. Box 1907, Biloxi, MS 39533-1907. Tel.: 228-435-6320. Fax: 228-435-6309.
E-mail: schooner@maritimemuseum.org
Web Site: www.maritimemuseum.org
Key Personnel: Exec. Dir., Robin Krohn-David; Schooner Captain, Ron Reiter; Office Mgr., Megan Seymour; Outreach Program Coord., Ashley Davis.
Institution Type/Description: Seafood Industry, maritime & history Museum.
Hours & Admission Prices: Mon.-Sat. 9-4:30, Sun. 12-4. Adult $10, senior $8, student $6; discounts to AAA & military, members no charge. &
Attendance: 150,000 (estimated)

OHR-O'KEEFE MUSEUM OF ART, 386 Beach Blvd., Biloxi, MS 39530. Mailing Address: P.O. Box 248, Biloxi, MS 39533-0248. Tel.: 228-374-5547. Fax: 228-436-3641.
E-mail: director@georgeohr.org
Web Site: www.georgeohr.org
Formerly: George E. Ohr Arts & Culture Center
Key Personnel: Pres., Cree Cantrell; Pres. (V), Jeff O'Keefe; Dir., Kevin O'Brien; Asst. Dir., Heather Rumfelt; Finance Dir., Dorine Page; Mktg. & Public Rels. Dir., Natalea Thomson; Devel. Dir., Brenda Blount; Education Dir., Pamela Cevallos Amores; Ceramics Dir., Charlie Mabry; Museum Shop Mgr., Erin Herrera.
Institution Type/Description: Art Museum.
Hours & Admission Prices: Museum: Tues.-Sat. 9-5; Office: Mon.-Fri. 9-5. Adults $10, members $8; AAM, NARM members no charge. Closed New Year's Day; Mardi Gras; Independence Day; Thanksgiving; Christmas. &
Attendance: 40,000 (actual)

WEST END HOSE CO. NO. 3 MUSEUM AND FIRE EDUCATIONAL CENTER, 1046 Howard Ave., Biloxi, MS 39530. Tel.: 228-435-6119.
E-mail: jboney@biloxi.ms.us

Web Site: biloxi.ms.us/museums/firemuseum
Key Personnel: Pres. (V), Larry Smith; Museum Shop Mgr., Joe Boney.
Institution Type/Description: Fire Museum.
Hours & Admission Prices: Sat. 9-3; other times by appointment. No charge; donations accepted. ⑆
Attendance: 1,000 (estimated)

Booneville

RAILS & TRAILS MUSEUM, 100 W. Church St., Booneville, MS 38829-3406. Tel.: 662-728-4130, 800-300-9302.
E-mail: angienels@ida.net
Web Site: www.railsandtrails.net
Institution Type/Description: Historic Building: housed in the Gulf, Mobile & Ohio Depot; built in 1913.
Hours & Admission Prices: Thurs.-Sat. 10-4; other times by appointment. No charge.

Brandon

RANKIN COUNTY HISTORICAL MUSEUM, 1471 W. Government St., Brandon, MS 39042. Mailing Address: P.O. Box 841, Brandon, MS 39043-0841. Facebook: Rankin County Historical Museum.
E-mail: news@rankinhistory.org
Web Site: rankinhistory.com
Key Personnel: Pres. (V), Paul Davis.
Institution Type/Description: History Museum.
Hours & Admission Prices: 1st Sat. each month 9-4, 1st Sun. each month 2-4. No charge; donations accepted. ⑆
Attendance: 500 (estimated)

Camp Shelby

MISSISSIPPI ARMED FORCES MUSEUM, Bldg. 850, Camp Shelby Training Site, Camp Shelby, MS 39407. Tel.: 601-558-2757 & 2347.
E-mail: chad.e.daniels.nfg@mail.mil
Web Site: www.armedforcesmuseum.us
Key Personnel: Dir., Chad E. Daniels, M.A., M.S.; Pres. (V), MG Richard S. Poole, MSARNG (Ret.); Arms & Military Vehicle Conservator, MSG (Ret.) Glenn L. Husted, III, MSARNG; Archivist, Christy A. Jones; Registrar, Lisa Foster; Administrative Asst., Brenda Crowley.
Institution Type/Description: Military Museum.
Hours & Admission Prices: Tues.-Sat. 9-4:30; groups by appointment. Photo ID required to enter post. No charge; donations accepted. Closed holidays. ⑆
Attendance: 49,734 (actual)

Canton

CANTON MOVIE MUSEUMS, 147 N. Union St., Canton, MS 39046-3740. Mailing Address: P.O. Box 53, Canton, MS 39046. Tel.: 800-844-3369, 601-859-1307. Fax: 601-859-0346.
E-mail: canton@cantontourism.com
Web Site: cantontourism.com/movie_museums.html
Key Personnel: Exec. Dir., Jo Ann Gordon.
Institution Type/Description: Movie History Museum.
Hours & Admission Prices: Welcome Center: Mon.-Fri. 10-5, Sat. 10-2. One Movie Museum: adults $4, senior citizens $3, children & students $2. Two Movie Museums: adults $6, senior citizens $5, children & students $3. Multi-Cultural Museum: adults $3, students 12 & over $2, children 5-12 $1. All Museums: adults $7, senior citizens $6, children 5-12 $4.

CANTON MULTICULTURAL CENTER & MUSEUM, 147 N. Union St., Canton, MS 39046-3740. Mailing Address: P.O. Box 53, Canton, MS 39046-0053. Tel.: 601-859-1307. Fax: 601-859-0346.
E-mail: canton@cantontourism.com
Key Personnel: Exec. Dir., Jo Ann Gordon.
Institution Type/Description: History Museum.
Hours & Admission Prices: Mon.-Fri. 10-5, Sat. 10-2. Adults $3, seniors & groups of 15 or more & students 12 & over $2, children K-12 $1.

Carrollton

MISSISSIPPI JOHN HURT HOME MUSEUM, RR 109 Box 1973, Carrollton, MS 38917. Mailing Address: 520 Milton Ln., Hoffman Estates, IL 60169. Tel.: 312-810-1954.
E-mail: mfhurt_wright74@yahoo.com
Web Site: www.mississippijohnhurtfoundation.org

Key Personnel: C.E.O., Mary Frances Hurt Wright; Dir., Floyd Bailey.
Institution Type/Description: Historic House Museum: housed in the former home of Blues Musician, Mississippi John Hurt.
Hours & Admission Prices: By appointment. Non-members $20, members $10; discounts to AAM & ICOM members; children under 12 no charge. ⑆
Attendance: 300 (estimated)

Centreville

CAMP VAN DORN WORLD WAR II MUSEUM, 138 E. Main, Centreville, MS 39631. Mailing Address: P.O. Box 1113, Centreville, MS 39631-1113. Tel.: 601-645-9000.
E-mail: info@vandorn.org
Web Site: www.vandorn.org
Key Personnel: Dir. & Pres. (V), Michael Stewart.
Institution Type/Description: Military Museum.
Hours & Admission Prices: Mon.-Fri. and 1st & 3rd Sat. of the month 10-4. No charge; donations accepted. ⑆

Choctaw

CHOCTAW IMMI CULTURAL CENTER, 101 Industrial Rd., Choctaw, MS 39350. Mailing Address: Mississippi Band of Choctaw Indians, P.O. Box 6010, Choctaw, MS 39350-6010. Tel.: 601-650-1685. Fax: 601-650-3684.
E-mail: info@choctaw.org
Web Site: www.choctaw.org
Formerly: Choctaw Museum of the Southern Indian
Key Personnel: Dir., Martha Spencer.
Institution Type/Description: Native American History Museum.
Hours & Admission Prices: Mon.-Fri. 8-4:30.

Clarksdale

DELTA BLUES MUSEUM, #1 Blues Alley, Clarksdale, MS 38614-4336. Mailing Address: P.O. Box 459, Clarksdale, MS 38614-0459. Tel.: 662-627-6820. Fax: 662-627-7263.
E-mail: shelley@deltabluesmuseum.org
Web Site: www.deltabluesmuseum.org
Key Personnel: C.E.O. & Dir., Shelley Ritter; Chm. (V), Bill Gresham; Museum Shop Mgr., Christopher Coleman.
Institution Type/Description: Music Museum: housed in renovated freight depot.
Hours & Admission Prices: March-Oct. Mon.-Sat. 9-5; Nov.-Feb. Mon.-Sat. 10-5. Adults $7, children $5; discounts to groups, AAM, ICOM, Blues Society & National Trust members; members & children under 6 no charge. Closed major holidays. ⑆
Attendance: 26,500 (estimated)

ROCK & BLUES MUSEUM, 113 E. Second St., Clarksdale, MS 38614-4205. Tel.: 901-605-8662.
Formerly: Rock 'N Roll & Blues Heritage Museum
Institution Type/Description: History Museum.
Hours & Admission Prices: April-Oct. Thurs.-Sat. 11-5; Sun. by appointment. Admission $5.

Cleveland

FIELDING L. WRIGHT ART CENTER, Delta State University, 1003 W. Sunflower Rd., Cleveland, MS 38733. Mailing Address: Box D 2, Delta State University, Cleveland, MS 38733. Tel.: 662-846-4720. Fax: 662-846-4726.
E-mail: artinfo@deltastate.edu
Web Site: www.deltastate.edu/academics/artsci/artdept.com
Key Personnel: Chm., Ron Koelher; Dir. Art Gallery, Patricia Brown.
Institution Type/Description: Art Center.
Hours & Admission Prices: Academic Year: daily 8-5. No charge. ⑆
Attendance: 10,000

GRAMMY MUSEUM MISSISSIPPI, 800 W. Sunflower Rd., Cleveland, MS 38732. Tel.: 662-441-0100.
E-mail: info@grammymuseumms.org
Web Site: www.grammymuseumms.org
Key Personnel: Exec. Dir., Emily Havens; Cur., Nwaka Onwusa; Registrar, Athena Dryden; Mgr. External Affairs, Vickie Jackson; Mgr. Education & Public Prog, Jane Marie Dawkins; Mgr. Operations, Jack McWilliams.
Institution Type/Description: Music History Museum.
Hours & Admission Prices: Mon.-Sat. 10-5:30, Sun. 12-5:30. Adults $12, seniors 65 & over and military $10, college students & youth 6-18 $6; discounts to groups of 10 or more; members and children 5 & under no charge.

Clinton

MISSISSIPPI BAPTIST HISTORICAL COMMISSION, Mississippi College Library-College St., Clinton, MS 39058. Mailing Address: P.O. Box 4024, Clinton, MS 39058. Tel.: 601-925-3434. Fax: 601-925-3435.
E-mail: mbhc@mc.edu
Web Site: mc.libguides.com/mbhc
Key Personnel: Exec. Dir., Dr. Anthony Kay; Special Collections Librarian, Heather Moore.
Institution Type/Description: Religious Museum.
Hours & Admission Prices: Summer: Mon.-Thurs. 8-4:30, Fri. 8-12. No charge. Closed some college vacations. &
Attendance: 150 (estimated)

Columbus

AMERICAN-INDIAN ARTIFACTS MUSEUM, 179 State Line Rd., Columbus, MS 39702-7134. Tel.: 662-251-1125, 800-327-2686.
E-mail: ccvb@columbus-ms.org
Institution Type/Description: Native American History Museum.
Hours & Admission Prices: Call for hours. No charge; donations accepted.

COLUMBUS WAR MUSEUM, Columbus Municipal Complex, 1501 Main St., Columbus, MS 39701. Mailing Address: 364 Country Ln., Millport, AL 35576. Tel.: 205-557-0584.
E-mail: columbuswarmuseum@live.com
Key Personnel: Dir., Wayne White; Pres. (V), Virginia White.
Institution Type/Description: Military History Museum.
Hours & Admission Prices: Mon.-Thurs. 8-5:30. No charge; donations accepted. Closed federal holidays.
Attendance: 500 (estimated)

THE FLORENCE MCLEOD HAZARD MUSEUM, 316 Seventh St. N., Columbus, MS 39701-4680. Mailing Address: P.O. Box 571, Jackson, MS 39205-0571. Tel.: 662-329-3533. Fax: 662-329-1027.
Institution Type/Description: Historical Society Museum: housed in c.1847 Blewett-Harrison-Lee Home.
Hours & Admission Prices: Fri. 10-4; other times by appointment. Adults $5; students & children no charge. Closed Thanksgiving; Christmas.

ROSEDALE PLANTATION, 1523 9th St. S., Columbus, MS 39703. Tel.: 662-329-3533, 800-920-3533. Fax: 662-329-8969.
E-mail: dhunter@historicrosedale.org
Institution Type/Description: Historic House Museum: c.1856.
Hours & Admission Prices: By appointment. Adults $7.50.

ROSEWOOD MANOR, 719 Seventh St. N., Columbus, MS 39701. Tel.: 662-328-7313 & 364-0705. Fax: 662-327-6217.
E-mail: hicks@columbursrosewood.com
Institution Type/Description: Historic House Museum: built in 1835. Listed on the National Register of Historic Places.
Hours & Admission Prices: By appointment. Adults $10; discounts to AAM & ICOM members.

STEPHEN D. LEE HOME AND MUSEUM, 316 Seventh St., N., Columbus, MS 39701-4680. Tel.: 662-327-8888 & 435-2368. Facebook: Stephen D. Lee Home and Museum.
E-mail: leehomemuseum@yahoo.com
Web Site: www.leehomemuseum.com
Institution Type/Description: Historic House Museum: housed in the former home of Confederate Gen. Stephen D. Lee; built in 1847. Listed on the National Register of Historic Places. Mississippi Landmark.
Hours & Admission Prices: Fri. 10-4; other times by appointment. Adults $10; discounts to groups.
Attendance: 8,000 (estimated)

TENNESSEE WILLIAMS BIRTHPLACE MUSEUM, 300 Main St., Columbus, MS 39701-4532. Tel.: 662-328-0222.
Institution Type/Description: Historic House Museum: housed in the home of playwright Tennessee Williams; c.1870.
Hours & Admission Prices: Mon.-Sat. 8:30-5, Sun. 12-5.

Corinth

BLACK HISTORY MUSEUM OF CORINTH, 1109 Meigg St., Corinth, MS 38835. Tel.: 662-665-8500, 866-539-8500.
Institution Type/Description: History Museum.
Hours & Admission Prices: Thurs.-Fri. 11-4; other times by appointment. No charge; donations accepted.

CORINTH CIVIL WAR INTERPRETIVE CENTER, 501 W. Linden St., Corinth, MS 38834. Tel.: 662-287-9273.
E-mail: jcampi@civilwar.org
Web Site: www.civilwar.org/visit/heritage-sites/corinth-civil-war-interpretive-center
Institution Type/Description: History Museum.
Hours & Admission Prices: Daily 8:30-4:30.

CORINTH COCA-COLA MUSEUM, 601 Washington St., Corinth, MS 38834. Tel.: 662-284-1433.
E-mail: museum@corinthcoke.com
Web Site: www.corinthcoke.com/museum/
Institution Type/Description: Company Museum.
Hours & Admission Prices: Mon.-Fri. 8:30-4:30. No charge.

CROSSROADS MUSEUM, 221 N. Fillmore St., Corinth, MS 38834-5635. Tel.: 662-287-3120. Fax: 662-287-3120.
E-mail: director@crossroadsmuseum.com
Web Site: www.crossroadsmuseum.com
Formerly: Northeast Mississippi Museum.
Key Personnel: Dir., Brandy Steen; Pres. (V), Bryan Clausel; Treas., Lila Wade.
Institution Type/Description: History Museum.
Hours & Admission Prices: Tues.-Sat. 10-4, Sun. 1-4. Adults $5; senior citizens, military, students & members $3; discounts to groups and AAM & ICOM members; children 16 & under no charge. Closed Thanksgiving; Christmas. &
Attendance: 6,500 (estimated)

JACINTO FOUNDATION, INC., Jacinto Courthouse, County Rd. 364, Corinth, MS 38382. Mailing Address: P.O. Box 1174, Corinth, MS 38835-1174. Tel.: 662-286-8662. Fax: 662-286-6500.
Key Personnel: C.E.O., Beth Whitehurst; Pres. (V), John C. Ross.
Institution Type/Description: Historic Foundation: housed in 1854 Jacinto Courthouse. Listed on the National Register of Historic Places.
Hours & Admission Prices: Tues.-Sat. 10-5, Sun. 1-5. No charge; donations accepted.

LAKE HILL MOTORS MUSEUM, 2003 Hwy. 72 E. Annex, Corinth, MS 38834. Tel.: 662-287-4451.
Web Site: www.lakehillmotors.com
Institution Type/Description: Motorcycle Museum.
Hours & Admission Prices: Mon.-Fri. 8-5, Sat. 8-3. No charge.

VERANDAH HOUSE, 705 Jackson St., Corinth, MS 38834. Mailing Address: Corinth Visitor's Bureau, 215 N. Fillmore, Corinth, MS 38834. Tel.: 662-287-8300.
E-mail: tourism@corinth.net
Institution Type/Description: Historic House Museum: housed in the headquarters for Confederate Generals Braxton Bragg, John Bell Hood, Earl Van Dorn & Union Generals Henry W. Halleck & Granville Dodge; built in 1857. A National Historic Landmark.
Hours & Admission Prices: Tours by appointment only.

Crystal Springs

ROBERT JOHNSON HERITAGE & BLUES MUSEUM, 218 E. Marion Dr., Crystal Springs, MS 39059. Tel.: 601-892-7883. Fax: 601-892-7884.
E-mail: robertjohnsonblu@bellsouth.net
Web Site: www.robertjohnsonbluesfoundation.org/museum.html
Institution Type/Description: History Museum.
Hours & Admission Prices: Mon.-Fri. 10-5, Sat. 10-2; other times by appointment. Suggested Donation: adults $2, children $1.

DeKalb

KEMPER COUNTY HISTORICAL MUSEUM, Jackson St., DeKalb, MS 39328. Mailing Address: 5217 Kipling Rd., DeKalb, MS 39328. Tel.: 601-743-5560.
Key Personnel: Pres. Kemper Historical Society, Grace Gibson; Chm. & Pres., J.L. White.
Institution Type/Description: History Museum.

Hours & Admission Prices: By appointment. No charge; donations accepted. &
Attendance: 200 (estimated)

Fayette

HARRISON HOUSE, 414 River Rd., Fayette, MS 39069. Mailing Address: P.O. Box 310, Fayette, MS 39069. Tel.: 601-493-3420.
E-mail: louisecadney@yahoo.com
Key Personnel: Dir., M. Louise Coleman.
Institution Type/Description: Historic House Museum: built in 1900.
Hours & Admission Prices: Daily by appointment. Adults $5, children under 12 $3. &
Attendance: 15 (actual)

Flora

MISSISSIPPI PETRIFIED FOREST, 124 Forest Park Rd., Flora, MS 39071. Mailing Address: P.O. Box 37, Flora, MS 39071-0037. Tel.: 601-879-8189. Fax: 601-879-8165.
E-mail: info@mspetrifiedforest.com
Web Site: www.mspetrifiedforest.com
Key Personnel: Dir. & Owner, C. J. McNamara; Museum Shop Mgr., Deborah Shoemaker; Park Mgr.-Outdoor Museum, Doug Shoemaker.
Institution Type/Description: Geology Museum.
Hours & Admission Prices: April to Labor Day daily 9-6; Sept.-May daily 9-5. Adults $7, seniors & students grades 1-12 $6; discounts to AAA members & groups of 15 or more; pre-school children no charge. Closed Thanksgiving; Christmas. &
Attendance: 15,000 (estimated)

Friars Point

NORTH DELTA MUSEUM, 748 2nd St., Friars Point, MS 38631. Mailing Address: Box 22, Friars Point, MS 38631. Tel.: 662-383-2233. Fax: 662-383-0057.
E-mail: flolarson@bellsouth.net
Key Personnel: Dir., Flo Larson.
Institution Type/Description: History Museum.
Hours & Admission Prices: Tues.-Sat. 9-3; other times by appointment. Adults $4, children under 7 $2.

Fulton

JAMIE L. WHITTEN HISTORICAL CENTER, 100 Campground Rd., Fulton, MS 38843. Tel.: 662-862-5414.
Institution Type/Description: History Museum.
Hours & Admission Prices: April-May 25 & Sept.-Nov. 1 daily 7:30-4; May 26-Aug. daily 8:30-5; Nov.-March Mon.-Fri. 7:30-4.

Greenville

GOLDSTEIN NELKEN SOLOMON CENTURY OF HISTORY MUSEUM, 504 Main St., Greenville, MS 38701. Tel.: 662-332-4153.
Institution Type/Description: History Museum: housed in a temple built in 1906.
Hours & Admission Prices: Mon.-Fri. 9-12.

GREENVILLE AIR FORCE BASE MUSEUM, 166 Fifth Ave., Mezzanine Level - 2nd Flr., Greenville, MS 38701. Tel.: 662-334-3121. Fax: 662-335-8757.
E-mail: lredmon@greenvillems.org
Institution Type/Description: Military History Museum.
Hours & Admission Prices: Daily 7-7. No charge. &
Attendance: 6,300 (estimated)

GREENVILLE HISTORY MUSEUM, 409 Washington Ave., Greenville, MS 38701-3617. Tel.: 662-335-5802.
E-mail: info@greenvillehistorymuseum.com
Web Site: greenvillehistorymuseum.com
Key Personnel: Dir., Ben Nelken.
Institution Type/Description: History Museum: housed in the restored Miller Building.
Hours & Admission Prices: Mon.-Fri. 9-5; other times by appointment. Adults $5, children $3.
Attendance: 2,000 (estimated)

OLD FIREHOUSE MUSEUM, 230 Main St., Greenville, MS 38701. Mailing Address: P.O. Box 897, Greenville, MS 38702-0897. Tel.: 662-334-2711. Fax: 662-378-1612.

Web Site: www.greenville.ms.us
Institution Type/Description: General Museum.
Hours & Admission Prices: By appointment. No charge. Closed New Year's Day; Martin Luther King Jr. Day; Memorial Day; Independence Day; Labor Day; Thanksgiving; Christmas. &
Attendance: 2,340 (actual)

WINTERVILLE MOUNDS PARK AND MUSEUM, 2415 Hwy. 1 N., Greenville, MS 38703-9476. Tel.: 662-334-4684. Fax: 662-378-5559.
E-mail: wmounds@mdah.state.ms.us
Web Site: mdah.state.ms.us/hprop/winterville.html
Key Personnel: Dir., Dr. Mark Howell.
Institution Type/Description: Historic Site.
Hours & Admission Prices: Grounds: daily dawn to dusk. Museum: Mon.-Sat. 9-5, Sun. 1:30-5. No charge; donations accepted.
Attendance: 15,000 (actual)

Greenwood

BACK IN THE DAY MUSEUM, 200 Young St., Greenwood, MS 38930-4637. Tel.: 662-392-5370.
E-mail: deltablueslegendtours@yahoo.com
Web Site: deltablueslegendtours.com
Key Personnel: Dir. & Museum Shop Mgr., Mary Ann Hoover.
Institution Type/Description: History Museum.
Hours & Admission Prices: Call for hours. No charge; donations accepted. &

MUSEUM OF THE MISSISSIPPI DELTA, 1608 Highway 82 W., Greenwood, MS 38930-2725. Tel.: 662-453-0925. Fax: 662-455-7556.
E-mail: info@museumofthemississippidelta.com
Web Site: museumofthemississippidelta.com
Formerly: Cottonlandia Museum
Key Personnel: Exec. Dir., Cheryl A. Taylor; Pres., John Pittman; Vice Pres., Jere Stansel; Prog. Coord., Kaye Schroeder; Business Mgr., David Freeman.
Institution Type/Description: General Museum.
Hours & Admission Prices: Mon.-Sat. 9-5; other times by appointment. Adults $10, seniors $7, students $5; discounts to AAM & AAA members, Mississippi Museums Association, Southeast Museums Conference, Civil War Trust; members no charge. &
Attendance: 7,000 (estimated)

Gulfport

BUSTED WRENCH GARAGE MUSEUM, 2311 29th St., Gulfport, MS 39501. Tel.: 228-617-6660.
E-mail: 228_hans@att.net
Web Site: www.bustedwrench.com
Key Personnel: C.E.O., John Hans; Museum Shop Mgr. & Museum Dir., Stacie Banes.
Institution Type/Description: Automotive Museum.
Hours & Admission Prices: Mon.-Fri. 8-5, Sat. 10-4. No charge.
Attendance: 7,200 (estimated)

CENTER FOR MARINE EDUCATION AND RESEARCH, 10801 Dolphin Ln., Gulfport, MS 39503. Mailing Address: P.O. Box 207, Gulfport, MS 39502. Tel.: 228-896-9182. Fax: 228-896-9183.
E-mail: contactus@imms.org
Web Site: www.imms.org
Key Personnel: Exec. Dir. & Pres., Moby Solangi, Ph.D.
Institution Type/Description: Marine Science Museum.
Hours & Admission Prices: By appointment. Adults $12, children under 12 $10. &
Attendance: 35,000 (estimated)

LYNN MEADOWS DISCOVERY CENTER, 246 Dolan Ave., Gulfport, MS 39507-1310. Tel.: 228-897-6039. Fax: 228-248-0071.
E-mail: lmdc@lmdc.org
Web Site: www.lmdc.org
Key Personnel: Exec. Dir., Cindy DeFrances; Dir. Devel., Penny Patterson; Dir. Mktg. & Public Rels., Sonja Gillis; Dir. Finance & Human Resources, Christine Cooper.
Institution Type/Description: Children's Museum.
Hours & Admission Prices: Memorial Day to Labor Day Mon.-Sat. 10-5, Sun. 12-5; Sept.-May Tues.-Sat. 10-5, Sun. 12-5. Admission $10, active military & seniors $8; discounts Sunday & weekdays after 3; children under one no charge. Closed New Year's Day; Easter; Thanksgiving; Christmas Eve & Day.

Harriston

THE FROG FARM SCULPTURE GARDEN, 186 Old Hwy. 61, Harriston, MS 39069. Mailing Address: P.O. Box 310, Fayette, MS 39069-0310. Tel.: 601-493-3420.
E-mail: louisecadney@yahoo.com
Web Site: www.frogfarmharristonms
Key Personnel: Dir., Louise Cadney.
Institution Type/Description: Folk Art Museum.
Hours & Admission Prices: By appointment. No charge; donations requested.
Attendance: 100 (actual)

Hattiesburg

AFRICAN AMERICAN MILITARY HISTORY MUSEUM, 305 E. Sixth St., Hattiesburg, MS 39401-2029. Tel.: 601-450-1942.
E-mail: Lnorman@hattiesburg.org
Web Site: hattiesburguso.com
Institution Type/Description: Military History Museum.
Hours & Admission Prices: Call for hours.

HATTIESBURG AREA HISTORICAL SOCIETY AND HAHS MUSEUM, 723 Main Street, Hattiesburg, MS 39401-3431. Mailing Address: P.O. Box 1573, Hattiesburg, MS 39403-1573. Tel.: 601-582-5460; 268-0234.
E-mail: hahsmuseum@megagate.com
Web Site: www.hahsmuseum.org
Key Personnel: Pres. (V), Paula Harvey; Dir., Ursula Jones.
Institution Type/Description: History Museum.
Hours & Admission Prices: Mon., Tues. & Thurs. 2-5 & by appointment. No charge; donations accepted. &
Attendance: 500 (estimated)

HATTIESBURG ARTS COUNCIL GALLERY, 723 Main St., Hattiesburg, MS 39401-3431. Mailing Address: P.O. Box 693, Hattiesburg, MS 39403-0693. Tel.: 601-583-6005.
E-mail: pattyhac@megagate.com
Key Personnel: Dir., Patty Hall; Pres. (V), Anita Price.
Institution Type/Description: Art Gallery.
Hours & Admission Prices: Mon.-Fri. 10-3. No charge. &
Attendance: 5,000

MUSEUM OF ART - THE UNIVERSITY OF SOUTHERN MISSISSIPPI, Dept. of Art and Design, 118 College Dr., #5033, Hattiesburg, MS 39406. Mailing Address: George Hurst Bldg. 106, 118 College Dr., Box 5033, Hattiesburg, MS 39406-0001. Tel.: 601-266-5200.
E-mail: artmuseum@usm.edu
Web Site: www.usm.edu/visualarts/museum.php
Key Personnel: Dir., Mark Rigsby.
Institution Type/Description: Art Museum.
Hours & Admission Prices: Academic Year: Mon.-Fri. 10-5. No charge. Closed university holidays & breaks; during exhibit installations.
Attendance: 4,313 (actual)

Hazlehurst

HAZLEHURST DEPOT MUSEUM, 138 N. Ragsdale Ave., Hazlehurst, MS 39083-3019. Mailing Address: P.O. Box 446, Hazlehurst, MS 39083-0446. Tel.: 601-894-3752. Fax: 601-894-3752.
Institution Type/Description: History Museum.
Hours & Admission Prices: Daily 8-5. No charge. &

ROBERT JOHNSON HERITAGE HOUSE, 201 Downing St., Hazlehurst, MS 39083-3003. Tel.: 601-894-5777.
E-mail: robertjohnsonblu@bellsouth.net
Web Site: www.robertjohnsonbluesfoundation.org
Key Personnel: Contact, Dr. Janet Schriver.
Institution Type/Description: Historic House Museum: housed in the home of blues guitarist & singer, Robert Johnson; c.1900.
Hours & Admission Prices: Call for hours. No charge. &

Hernando

DESOTO COUNTY MUSEUM, 111 E. Commerce St., Hernando, MS 38632-2376. Tel.: 662-429-8852. Fax: 662-429-8852.
E-mail: info@desotomuseum.org

Web Site: www.desotomuseum.org
Key Personnel: Dir., Brian Hicks; Chm., Dr. Roma Thorn.
Institution Type/Description: History Museum.
Hours & Admission Prices: Tues.-Sat. 10-5. No charge; donations accepted. Closed federal holidays. &
Attendance: 9,750 (estimated)

Holly Springs

IDA B. WELLS-BARNETT MUSEUM, 220 N. Randolph St., Holly Springs, MS 38635-2412. Tel.: 662-252-3232. Fax: 662-252-3232.
E-mail: idabwellsmuseum@gmail.com
Web Site: www.idabwells.org
Formerly: Ida B. Wells Family Art Gallery
Key Personnel: Dir. & C.E.O., Leona Harris; Pres. (V), Rev. Cornelia Booker.
Institution Type/Description: History Museum: housed in the birthplace of journalist & women's activist, Ida B. Wells.
Hours & Admission Prices: Mon.-Fri. 10-5, Sat. 12-5. Adults $8, children 12 & under $5; discounts to AAM members & members of other museums with membership card; members no charge. Closed New Year's Day; Easter; Thanksgiving; Christmas. &
Attendance: 13,500 (estimated)

MARSHALL COUNTY HISTORICAL MUSEUM, 220 E. College Ave., Holly Springs, MS 38635-3122. Mailing Address: P. O. Box 806, Holly Springs, MS 38635-0806. Tel.: 662-252-3669. Fax: 662-252-3669.
E-mail: marshallcomuseum@bellsouth.net
Key Personnel: Pres. (V) & Chm. (V), Bobby Mitchell; Dir. & Cur., Lois Swaney Shipp; Chm. (V) & Treas., Nancy Hutchins; Museum Shop Mgr., Jennifer Bone.
Institution Type/Description: Historical Society Museum: housed in 1903 former Mississippi Synodical College Building.
Hours & Admission Prices: Mon.-Fri. 10-5. Adults $5; members no charge. Closed Independence Day; Labor Day; Thanksgiving; Christmas Eve & Day. &
Attendance: 7,000 (estimated)

WALTER PLACE ESTATE, COTTAGES, AND GARDENS, 330 W. Chulahoma Ave., Holly Springs, MS 38635. Mailing Address: Holly Springs Tourism & Recreation Bur., 195 E. Van Dorn Ave., Holly Springs, MS 38635-3026. Tel.: 662-252-2515. Fax: 662-252-2696.
E-mail: info@visithollysprings.com
Web Site: www.visithollysprings.com
Institution Type/Description: Historic House Museum: housed in the former home of General and Mrs. Ulysses S. Grant in 1862, during the Civil War.
Hours & Admission Prices: Tours: Mon.-Sat. 1pm. Admission $5-$20; discounts to groups.

Indianola

B.B. KING MUSEUM AND DELTA INTERPRETIVE CENTER, 400 Second St., Indianola, MS 38751-2851. Tel.: 662-887-9539. Fax: 662-887-9478.
E-mail: info@bbkingmuseum.org
Web Site: www.bbkingmuseum.org
Key Personnel: Exec. Dir., Christopher D. Brown; Chief Administrative Officer, Malika Polk-Lee; Dir. Education, Dr. Gloria McIntosh; Dir. Entertainment, Robert Terrell; Dir. Facilities & Earned Income Operations, James McWilliams; Dir. Allstars Choir, Dr. Cheryl Weis.
Institution Type/Description: History Museum.
Hours & Admission Prices: Sun.-Mon. 12-5, Tues.-Sat. 10-5. Adults $12, seniors & students $5, school groups $3; discounts to AARP & AAA members, military & tour groups of 20 or more adults; children under 5 no charge. Closed Mon. Nov.-March. &
Attendance: 12,001 (actual)

Iuka

OLD TISHOMINGO COUNTY COURTHOUSE MUSEUM, 203 E. Quitman St., Iuka, MS 38852-1938. Mailing Address: PO Box 273, Iuka, MS 38852-0273. Tel.: 662-423-3500. Fax: 662-423-3500.
E-mail: tishomingohistory@yahoo.com
Web Site: www.tishomingohistory.com
Key Personnel: Dir. & Pres. (V), Cindy W. Nelson; Admin. Asst., Helah Wilson.
Institution Type/Description: History Museum: housed in historic courthouse; built in 1870.
Hours & Admission Prices: Tues.-Fri. 10-4. No charge; donations accepted. Closed federal holidays. &
Attendance: 4,825 (actual)

Jackson

EUDORA WELTY HOUSE AND GARDEN, 1119 Pinehurst St., Jackson, MS 39202-1812. Mailing Address: 1109 Pinehurst St., Jackson, MS 39202. Tel.: 601-353-7762. Fax: 601-354-5227. Facebook.
E-mail: tours@eudoraweltyhouse.com
Web Site: www.mdah.ms.gov/welty
Key Personnel: Dir., Bridget Edwards; Museum Shop Mgr., Maggie Stevenson.
Institution Type/Description: Historic House Museum: housed in the former home of Eudora Welty. A National Historic Landmark.
Hours & Admission Prices: Tours: Tues.-Fri. 9, 11, 1, & 3, 2nd Sat. each month 9 & 11. Adults $5, students $3; discounts to groups & National Historic Trust members; children under 6 no charge. Closed state holidays.
Attendance: 5,000 (actual)

FIRE MUSEUM & PUBLIC FIRE SAFETY EDUCATION CENTER, 355 Woodrow Wilson, Jackson, MS 39213. Tel.: 601-960-2433. Fax: 601-960-2432.
E-mail: info@visitjackson.com
Web Site: http://www.jacksonms.gov/index.aspx?nid=128
Key Personnel: Cur., Sherri Gibson.
Institution Type/Description: Fire Museum.
Hours & Admission Prices: By appointment. No charge.

INTERNATIONAL MUSEUM OF MUSLIM CULTURES, 201 E. Pascagoula St., Ste. 102, Jackson, MS 39201-4114. Tel.: 601-960-0440.
E-mail: info@muslimmuseum.org
Institution Type/Description: Islamic History & Culture Museum.
Hours & Admission Prices: Tues.-Sat. 10-5, Sun. 12-5.

JACKSON ZOOLOGICAL SOCIETY, INC., 2918 W. Capitol St., Jackson, MS 39209-4293. Tel.: 601-352-2581. Fax: 601-352-2594. Facebook: Jackson Zoo.
E-mail: info@jacksonzoo.org
Web Site: www.jacksonzoo.org
Key Personnel: Dir., Beth Poff; Mgr. Mktg. & Communications, Angela Harris; Animal Cur., David Wetzel; Museum Shop Mgr., Sheba Moses.
Institution Type/Description: Zoo.
Hours & Admission Prices: Daily 9-4. Adults $9.25, senior citizens 65 & over & military $8.25, children 12 & under $6.75, military children $5.75; members & children under 2 no charge. AZA reciprocal zoo admission. See website for seasonal admission prices.
Attendance: 127,500 (actual)

MANSHIP HOUSE MUSEUM, 420 E. Fortification St., Jackson, MS 39202-2340. Tel.: 601-961-4724. Fax: 601-576-6975.
E-mail: info@manshiphouse.com
Web Site: www.mdah.ms.gov/museum/manship
Key Personnel: C.E.O., Katie Blount; Pres. Bd. Trustees, Kane Ditto; Dir., Marilynn Jones.
Institution Type/Description: Historic House Museum: 1857 restored Gothic Revival cottage of C.H. Manship.
Hours & Admission Prices: By appointment. Closed for long-term repairs.

MEDGAR EVERS HOME MUSEUM, 2332 Margaret Walker Alexander Dr., Jackson, MS 39213-6411. Tel.: 601-977-7839.
E-mail: mwatson@tougaloo.edu
Institution Type/Description: Historic House Museum: housed in the former home of civil rights leader, Medgar Evers & the site of his assassination in 1963.
Hours & Admission Prices: Call for hours.

MISSISSIPPI AGRICULTURE & FORESTRY/NATIONAL AGRICULTURAL AVIATION MUSEUM, 1150 Lakeland Dr., Jackson, MS 39216-4728. Tel.: 601-432-4500. Fax: 601-982-4292. Facebook: Mississippi Agriculture & Forestry Museum.
E-mail: aaron@mdac.ms.gov
Web Site: msagmuseum.org
Key Personnel: Dir., Aaron Rodgers; Deputy Dir., Theresa Love.
Institution Type/Description: General Museum.
Hours & Admission Prices: Mon.-Sat. 9-5. Adults $5, senior citizens & military $4, children 3-18 $4; discounts to groups; children under 3 no charge. Additional fee for special events. Closed New Year's Day; Martin Luther King Jr. Day; Presidents' Day; Memorial Day; Independence Day; Labor Day; Veterans Day; Thanksgiving; Christmas.
Attendance: 140,000 (actual)

MISSISSIPPI CHILDREN'S MUSEUM, 2145 Museum Blvd., Jackson, MS 39202. Mailing Address: P.O. Box 55409, Jackson, MS 39296-5409. Tel.: 601-981-5469, 877-793-5437. Fax: 601-709-2603.
E-mail: info@mississippichildrensmuseum.com
Web Site: www.mississippichildrensmuseum.com
Key Personnel: Pres., Susan Garrard; Dir. Education & Programs, Jana Perry; Asst. Dir. Programs, Patti Reiss; Dir. Museum Experience, Charley Frye; Dir. Devel., Emily Hoff; Dir. Finance & Administration, Johnny Kroeze; Mgr. Cafe, Deloris Washington.
Institution Type/Description: Children's Museum.
Hours & Admission Prices: Tues.-Sat. 9-5, Sun. 1-6. Admission $10; children under one no charge.
Attendance: 250,000 (estimated)

MISSISSIPPI GOVERNOR'S MANSION, 300 E. Capitol, Jackson, MS 39201-3403. Tel.: 601-359-3175. Fax: 601-359-6473.
E-mail: mbankston@mdah.ms.gov
Web Site: www.mdah.ms.gov
Key Personnel: Dir. Dept. Archives & History, Katie Blount; Cur., Megan Bankston.
Institution Type/Description: Historic Building: 1842 Governor's Mansion, constructed 1839-1841.
Hours & Admission Prices: Tues.-Fri. 9:30-11; tours given on the half-hour. No charge; donations accepted. Closed state & federal holidays.
Attendance: 15,224 (actual)

MISSISSIPPI MUSEUM OF ART, 380 S. Lamar St., Jackson, MS 39201-4007. Tel.: 601-960-1515. Fax: 601-960-1505.
E-mail: bbradley@msmuseumart.org
Web Site: www.msmuseumart.org
Key Personnel: Dir., Betsy Bradley; Chm., Mayo Flint; Dir. Opers., Rob Peeples; Dir. Participation, Ruthie Massey; Dir. Visitor Svcs., Monique Davis; Dir. Resource Devel. & Special Events, Vince Evans; Dir. Corp. & Government Rels., Keia Johnson; Bd. Rels., Nina Moss; Office Mgr., Allison Harrison; Accountant, Sara Ragsdale; Chief Preparator, L.C. Tucker, Jr.; Asst. Preparator, Melvin Johnson; Preparator, Tom Jones; Deputy Dir. & Chief Cur., Roger Ward; Museum Store Mgr., Elizabeth Tyler; Receptionist, Annette French; Dir. Mktg., Julian Rankin; Pub. Rels. & Creative Outreach Mgr., Lauren Von Foregger; Registrar, Caitlin Podas; Curatorial Assoc., Kathleen Funches Varnell; Cur. Collection, Elizabeth Abston; Exec. Chef, Nick Wallace; Dir. Sales & Special Events, Virginia Gage; Catering Opers. Mgr., Lawrence Crockett; Chief Engagement & Learning, daniel johnson; Chief Security, James A. Steverson; Dep. Chief Security, Julia Stewart.
Institution Type/Description: Art Museum.
Hours & Admission Prices: Tues.-Sat. 10-5. Sun. noon-5. Adults $10, seniors 60 & over $8, students $5; discounts to AAM & ICOM members; members and children 5 & under no charge. Hours & admission prices may vary during special exhibitions; no charge for The Mississippi Story. Closed New Year's Day; Easter; Thanksgiving; Christmas.
Attendance: 75,000 (estimated)

MISSISSIPPI MUSEUM OF NATURAL SCIENCE, 2148 Riverside Dr., Jackson, MS 39202-1353. Tel.: 601-576-6000. Fax: 601-354-7227.
E-mail: charles.knight@mmns.state.ms.us
Web Site: www.mdwfp.com/museum
Key Personnel: Dir., Charles Knight; Asst. Dir., Angel Rohnke; Education Coord. & Project WILD Coord., Megan Fedrick; Exhibits Supvr., Rachael Smart; Exhibits Supvr., Sam Biebers; Research/Collections Coord., Matt Roberts, Ph. D.; Natural Heritage Program Coord., Nicole Hodges; Volunteer Coord., Ann Taylor.
Institution Type/Description: Natural Science Museum.
Hours & Admission Prices: Mon.-Fri. 8-5, Sat. 9-5, Sun. 1-5. Adults $6, seniors 60 & over $5, children 3-18 $4; members no charge. ASTC Passport Program participant. Closed New Year's Day; Memorial Day; Easter; Independence Day; Labor Day; Thanksgiving; Christmas Eve & Day.
Attendance: 100,000 (estimated)

MISSISSIPPI SPORTS HALL OF FAME & MUSEUM, 1152 Lakeland Dr., Jackson, MS 39216-4701. Tel.: 601-982-8264, 800-280-FAME. Fax: 601-982-4702.
E-mail: generalinfo@msfame.com
Web Site: www.msfame.com
Key Personnel: Exec. Dir., Bill Blackwell; Chm., Ron Winford; Pres., Oscar Miskelly.
Institution Type/Description: Sports Museum.
Hours & Admission Prices: Mon.-Sat. 10-4. Adults $5, seniors 60 & over and students 6-17 $3.50; discounts to active military & groups of 12 or more; members and children 5 & under no charge.
Attendance: 40,000 (estimated)

MISSISSIPPI STATE CAPITOL, 400 High St., Jackson, MS 39201. Tel.: 601-359-3114.
E-mail: tours@house.ms.gov
Web Site: mdah.state.ms.us/new/visit/mississippi-state-capitol
Institution Type/Description: Historic Building: built in 1903.
Hours & Admission Prices: Self-Guided Tours: Mon.-Fri. 8-5. Guided Tours: Mon.-Fri. 9:30am, 11am, 1pm, & 2:30pm; groups tours by appointment.

MUSEUM OF MISSISSIPPI HISTORY & MISSISSIPPI CIVIL RIGHTS MUSEUM, 222 North St., Jackson, MS 39201. Mailing Address: Box 571, Jackson, MS 39205-0571. Tel.: 601-576-6800. Fax: 601-576-6815.
E-mail: info@2mississippimuseums.com
Web Site: www.mmh.mdah.ms.gov; www.mcrm.mdah.ms.gov
Key Personnel: 2 MM Admin., Cindy Gardner; Dir. History Museum, Rachel Myers; Dir. Civil Rights Museum, Pamela Junior.
Institution Type/Description: History Museum.
Hours & Admission Prices: Tues.-Sat. 9-5, Sun. 1-5. One Museum: adults $8, seniors 60 & over $6, youth 4-18 $5; children under 3 no charge. History Museum & Civil Rights Museum: adults $12, seniors $10, youth 4-18 $7; children under 4 no charge. &
Attendance: 180,000 (estimated)

MUSEUM OF THE SOUTHERN JEWISH EXPERIENCE, 4915 I-55 N., Ste. 204B, Jackson, MS 39206. Mailing Address: P.O. Box 16528, Jackson, MS 39236-6528. Tel.: 601-362-6357. Fax: 601-366-6293.
E-mail: rmyers@isjl.org
Web Site: www.isjl.org/museum.html
Key Personnel: C.E.O. & Pres., Macy B. Hart.
Institution Type/Description: Religious History Museum.
Hours & Admission Prices: By appointment. &

MYNELLE GARDENS, 4736 Clinton Blvd., Jackson, MS 39209-2400. Tel.: 601-960-1894.
Institution Type/Description: Garden.
Hours & Admission Prices: March-Oct. Mon.-Sat. 12-5:15, Sun. 12-4:15; Nov.-Feb. daily 8-4:15. Family pass $30, student pass $5, adults $4, children 4-12 $1. Closed New Year's Day; Martin Luther King Jr. Day; Independence Day; Thanksgiving & day after; Christmas. &

THE OAKS HOUSE MUSEUM, 823 N. Jefferson St., Jackson, MS 39202-4140. Mailing Address: PO Box 4240, Jackson, MS 39296-4240. Tel.: 601-353-9339.
E-mail: oakshousemuseum@comcast.net
Web Site: theoakshousemuseum.org
Key Personnel: Dir., Beth Batton.
Institution Type/Description: Local History Museum: housed in c.1853 historic building site, The Oaks.
Hours & Admission Prices: Tues. & Fri. 10-3; other times by appointment. Adults $4.50, senior citizens 65 & over $4, children $3.50; discount to groups of 10 or more, Southeastern Reciprocal Membership Program & AAA members. Closed major holidays. &
Attendance: 575 (actual)

OLD CAPITOL MUSEUM, 100 S. State St., Jackson, MS 39201-4400. Mailing Address: P.O. Box 571, Jackson, MS 39205-0571. Tel.: 601-576-6920. Fax: 601-576-6981. Facebook: Old Capitol Museum.
E-mail: info@oldcapitolmuseum.com
Web Site: www.oldcapitolmuseum.com
Key Personnel: Dir., Lauren Miller; Education, Maura Johnson; Education, Mike Stoll.
Institution Type/Description: Historic Building: building served as Mississippi's statehouse from 1839-1903.
Hours & Admission Prices: Tues.-Sat. 9-5, Sun. 1-5. No charge; donations accepted. Closed New Year's Day; Easter; Memorial Day; Labor Day; Thanksgiving; Christmas. &
Attendance: 40,000 (actual)

RUSSELL C. DAVIS PLANETARIUM, 201 E. Pascagoula St., Jackson, MS 39201-4101. Mailing Address: P.O. Box 17, Jackson, MS 39205. Tel.: 601-960-1552. Fax: 601-960-1555.
E-mail: jfwilliams@city.jackson.ms.us
Web Site: www.thedavisplanetarium.com
Key Personnel: Mgr., Michael Williams.
Institution Type/Description: Planetarium.
Hours & Admission Prices: Call for current program, show, and ticket information. Large-format Films: adults $6.50, seniors $5.50, children $4. Sky Shows: adults

$5.50, seniors $4.50, children $3. Closed New Year's Day; Martin Luther King Jr. Day; Presidents' Day; Easter; Memorial Day; Labor Day; Independence Day; Thanksgiving; Christmas Eve & Day. &
Attendance: 45,000 (actual)

SMITH ROBERTSON MUSEUM & CULTURAL CENTER, 528 Bloom St., Jackson, MS 39202-4005. Tel.: 601-960-1457. Fax: 601-960-2070.
Key Personnel: Mgr., Charlene Thompson; Cur., Kenyatta Stewart.
Institution Type/Description: History Museum: housed in first school built with public funds for Blacks in Jackson, MS.
Hours & Admission Prices: Mon.-Fri. 9-5, Sat. 10-1. Adults $4.50, seniors $3, children under 18 $1.50. Closed New Year's Day; Martin Luther King Jr. Day; Memorial Day; Independence Day; Labor Day; Thanksgiving; Christmas. &
Attendance: 15,000 (estimated)

WAR MEMORIAL BUILDING, 120 N. State St., Jackson, MS 39201-2810. Tel.: 601-354-7207.
Institution Type/Description: Military History Museum.
Hours & Admission Prices: Daily. No charge.

WILLIAM F. WINTER ARCHIVES & HISTORY BUILDING, 200 North St., Jackson, MS 39201. Tel.: 601-576-6850.
E-mail: info@mdah.state.ms.us
Web Site: mdah.state.ms.us/new/visit/william-f-winter-building/
Institution Type/Description: Archives & History Museum.
Hours & Admission Prices: Archives: Mon. 9-5, Tues.-Fri. 8-4:30, Sat. 8am-12:30pm. Closed state holidays.

Kosciusko

KOSCIUSKO MUSEUM AND VISITORS CENTER, Natchez Trace Pkwy., Kosciusko, MS 39090. Mailing Address: 101 N. Natchez St., Kosciusko, MS 39090. Tel.: 662-289-2981. Fax: 662-289-2986.
E-mail: thenatcheztrace@gmail.com
Web Site: www.scenictrace.com
Key Personnel: Vice Pres., Tonya Threet.
Institution Type/Description: History Museum.
Hours & Admission Prices: Daily 9-4. No charge. &

Laurel

LAUREN ROGERS MUSEUM OF ART, 565 N. 5th Ave., Laurel, MS 39440. Mailing Address: P.O. Box 1108, Laurel, MS 39441-1108. Tel.: 601-649-6374. Fax: 601-649-6379.
E-mail: gbassi@LRMA.org
Web Site: www.LRMA.org
Key Personnel: Dir., George Bassi; Chm. (V), Robert Hynson; Pres. (V), Rosemary Norton; Bldg. Supt., Todd Sullivan; Dir. Mktg., Holly Green; Registrar, Tommie Rodgers; Cur., Jill Chancey, Ph.D.; Cur. Education, Mandy Buchanan; Librarian, Donna Smith; Business Mgr., JoLynn Helton; Dir. Devel., Allyn C. Boone; Visitor Svcs. Coord., Lizabeth Brumley.
Institution Type/Description: Art Museum.
Hours & Admission Prices: Tues.-Sat. 10-4:45, Sun. 1-4. No charge; donations accepted. Closed major holidays. &
Attendance: 37,000 (estimated)

VETERANS MEMORIAL MUSEUM, 920 Hillcrest Dr., Laurel, MS 39440-4726. Tel.: 601-428-4008.
E-mail: veteransmemorialmuseum@comcast.net
Key Personnel: Dir. & Pres. (V), Jimmy Bass; Chm. (V), Victor Lee.
Institution Type/Description: Military Museum.
Hours & Admission Prices: Tues.-Fri. 10-4. No charge. &
Attendance: 2,500 (estimated)

Leakesville

GREENE COUNTY MUSEUM & HISTORICAL SOCIETY, Greene County House, 400 Main St., 4th Fl., Leakesville, MS 39451. Mailing Address: P.O. Box 841, Leakesville, MS 39451-0841. Tel.: 601-394-4343.
E-mail: museum@tds.net
Web Site: greenmuseum.org
Formerly: Greene County Courthouse Jail
Institution Type/Description: Historical Society Museum.
Hours & Admission Prices: Mon.-Tues. & Thurs. 9-4, Wed., Fri. and first Sat. of each month 9-12. No charge; donations accepted. &
Attendance: 1,000 (estimated)

Leland

HIGHWAY 61 BLUES MUSEUM, 307 N. Broad St., Leland, MS 38756-2744. Mailing Address: P.O. Box 251, Leland, MS 38756. Tel.: 662-686-2063.
E-mail: info@highway61blues.com
Web Site: www.highway61blues.com
Institution Type/Description: Blues Museum.
Hours & Admission Prices: Mon.-Sat. 10-5; other times by appointment.

Louisville

THE AMERICAN HERITAGE "BIG RED" FIRE MUSEUM, 332 N. Church Ave., Louisville, MS 39339-2302. Mailing Address: 650 N. Church Ave., Louisville, MS 39339-2033. Tel.: 662-773-3421. Fax: 662-773-9183.
Web Site: www.taylorbigred.com
Key Personnel: C.E.O., W.A. "Lex" Taylor, III; Registrar, Kay Reynolds.
Institution Type/Description: Fire-Fighting Museum.
Hours & Admission Prices: Mon.-Fri. by appointment only. No charge. Closed holidays.

Macon

NOXUBEE COUNTY HISTORICAL SOCIETY MUSEUM, 411 S. Jefferson St., Macon, MS 39341. Mailing Address: Noxubee County Historical Society, P.O. Box 892, Macon, MS 39341. Tel.: 662-726-4456. Fax: 662-726-1041.
E-mail: sconner@noxubee.lib.ms.us
Institution Type/Description: Historical Society Museum.
Hours & Admission Prices: Temporarily closed for restructuring. No charge; donations accepted.

McComb

BLACK HISTORY GALLERY, 819 Wall St., McComb, MS 39648. Tel.: 601-684-1130.
Institution Type/Description: History Museum.
Hours & Admission Prices: Call for hours.

MCCOMB CITY RAILROAD DEPOT MUSEUM, 108 N. Railroad Blvd., McComb, MS 39649-7220. Mailing Address: P.O. Box 7220, McComb, MS 39649-7220. Tel.: 601-684-2291. Facebook: McComb City Railroad Depot.
E-mail: trainmaster@mcrrmuseum.com
Web Site: www.mcrrmuseum.com
Key Personnel: C.E.O. & Dir., Winnie Len Howell; Pres. (V), Jerry Stubbs; Museum Shop Mgr., Bob Bellipanni.
Institution Type/Description: Railroad Museum.
Hours & Admission Prices: Mon.-Sat. 12-4. No charge; donations accepted. Closed official holidays. &
Attendance: 4,000 (estimated)

Meridian

JIMMIE RODGERS MUSEUM, 1725 Highland Park Dr., Meridian, MS 39307. Mailing Address: P.O. Box 4555, Meridian, MS 39304-4555. Tel.: 601-485-1808.
E-mail: jimmie_rodgers@hotmail.com
Key Personnel: C.E.O., Betty Lou Jones; Chm. (V), Greg Hatcher.
Institution Type/Description: Folk Art Museum.
Hours & Admission Prices: Feb. to mid-Dec. Tues.-Sat. 10-4; other times by appointment. Adults $10; discounts for groups, school groups, military, Smithsonian & AAA members, children 8-18 and seniors 65 & over; children under 8 no charge. Closed legal holidays; Thanksgiving week. &
Attendance: 7,000 (estimated)

MERIDIAN MUSEUM OF ART, 628 25th Ave., Meridian, MS 39301. Mailing Address: P.O. Box 5773, Meridian, MS 39302-5773. Tel.: 601-693-1501. Facebook: Meridian Museum of Art.
E-mail: meridianmuseum@bellsouth.net
Web Site: meridianmuseum.org
Key Personnel: Dir., Kate Cherry; Pres., Ravene Mitchell.
Institution Type/Description: Art Museum Gallery.
Hours & Admission Prices: Tues.-Sat. 11-5. No charge; donations accepted. Closed holidays. &
Attendance: 12,000 (estimated)

MISSISSIPPI INDUSTRIAL HERITAGE MUSEUM, 1808 4th St., Meridian, MS 39301. Mailing Address: P.O. Box 5031, Meridian, MS 39302-5031. Tel.: 601-693-9905.
E-mail: soulelivesteam@comcast.net
Web Site: www.soulelivesteam.com
Key Personnel: Dir., George W. Hatcher; Pres. (V), James L. McRae.
Institution Type/Description: History Museum: housed on the site of the former Soule Steam Feed Works. Listed on the National Register of Historic Places; Mississippi landmark & official state historical industrial museum.
Hours & Admission Prices: Guided Tours: Tues.-Fri. 10-2; other times by appointment. Admission: $10 per person. Closed holidays.

Mississippi State

CHARLES H. TEMPLETON, SR. MUSIC MUSEUM, Mitchell Memorial Library, Mississippi State, MS 39762. Mailing Address: Mitchell Memorial Library, P.O. Box 5408, Mississippi State, MS 39762-5408. Tel.: 662-325-6634. Fax: 662-325-4263.
E-mail: scunetto@library.msstate.edu
Web Site: library.msstate.edu/templeton
Institution Type/Description: Music Museum.
Hours & Admission Prices: Mon.-Fri. 9-4; groups by appointment. No charge.

COBB INSTITUTE OF ARCHAEOLOGY, College of Arts & Sciences, Mississippi State, MS 39762-5542. Mailing Address: P. O. Box AR, Mississippi State, MS 39762-5542. Tel.: 662-325-3826. Fax: 662-325-8690.
E-mail: jds1@ra.msstate.edu
Web Site: www.cobb.msstate.edu
Key Personnel: Dir., Joe Seger; Administrative Sec., Kathleen Elliott; Cur. Artifacts, Keith Baca.
Institution Type/Description: Archaeology Museum.
Hours & Admission Prices: Call for hours. No charge; donations accepted. Closed school holidays. &
Attendance: 3,000 (estimated)

DUNN-SEILER MUSEUM, Dept. of Geosciences, Mississippi State, MS 39762. Mailing Address: P.O. Box 5448, Mississippi State, MS 39762-5448. Tel.: 662-325-3915. Fax: 662-325-9423.
E-mail: rclary@geosci.msstate.edu
Web Site: geosciences.msstate.edu/museum.htm
Key Personnel: Dir., Dr. Renee M. Clary; Cur. & Mgr. Collections, Amy Moe Hoffman.
Institution Type/Description: Natural History Museum.
Hours & Admission Prices: Mon.-Fri. 8-5. No charge; donations accepted. Closed school holidays & vacations. &
Attendance: 1,000 (estimated)

JOHN GRISHAM ROOM, MITCHELL MEMORIAL LIBRARY, Mississippi State University, 395 Hardy Rd., Mississippi State, MS 39762. Mailing Address: P.O. Box 5408, Mississippi State, MS 39762. Tel.: 662-325-2559.
E-mail: fcoleman@library.msstate.edu
Web Site: library.msstate.edu/grishamroom
Institution Type/Description: History Museum.
Hours & Admission Prices: Mon.-Fri. 9-4. No charge.

MISSISSIPPI ENTOMOLOGICAL MUSEUM, Dept. of Entomology and Plant Pathology, Mississippi State, MS 39762. Mailing Address: P.O. Box 9775, Mississippi State, MS 39762-9775. Tel.: 662-325-2990. Fax: 662-325-8837.
E-mail: jmacgown@entomology.msstate.edu
Web Site: www.mississippientomologicalmuseum.org.msstate.edu
Key Personnel: Professor Entomology & Dir. Museum, Dr. Richard Brown; Cur., Terence L. Schiefer; Asst. Cur. & Scientific Illustrator, Joe A. MacGown.
Institution Type/Description: Entomology Museum.
Hours & Admission Prices: Call for hours.

Natchez

GRAND VILLAGE OF THE NATCHEZ INDIANS, 400 Jefferson Davis Blvd., Natchez, MS 39120-5110. Tel.: 601-446-6502. Fax: 601-446-6503. Facebook: Grand Village of the Natchez Indians.
E-mail: gvni@mdah.state.ms.us
Web Site: natchezgrandvillage.com
Key Personnel: Dir., Lance S. Harris; C.E.O., Katie Blount; Pres. (V), Kane Ditto; Sales Shop Mgr., Janice Sago; Historian, Rebecca Anderson.
Institution Type/Description: Anthropology Museum: 1700-1730, Natchez Indian ceremonial mound center.

Hours & Admission Prices: Mon.-Sat. 9-5, Sun. 1:30-5. No charge; donations accepted. Discounts to AAM members. Closed New Year's Day; Labor Day; Thanksgiving; Christmas.
Attendance: 27,500 (actual)

HISTORIC JEFFERSON COLLEGE, 16 Old North St., Natchez, MS 39120. Mailing Address: P.O. Box 700, Washington, MS 39190-0700. Tel.: 601-442-2901. Fax: 601-442-2902. Facebook: Historic Jefferson College.
E-mail: hjc@mdah.state.ms.us
Web Site: mdah.state.ms.us
Key Personnel: C.E.O., Katie Blount; Dir., Robin Seage Person; Sec. & Sales Shop Mgr., Maxine Clay; Historian, Kay McNeil; Historian, Toni Avance.
Institution Type/Description: Historic Site: Campus chartered in 1802 by Mississippi Territorial Legislature.
Hours & Admission Prices: Mon.-Sat. 9-5, Sun. 1-5. No charge; donations accepted. Closed New Year's Day; Independence Day; Labor Day; Thanksgiving; Christmas.
Attendance: 15,000 (estimated)

MISSISSIPPI SOCIETY DAUGHTERS OF THE AMERICAN REVOLUTION ROSALIE HOUSE MUSEUM, 100 Orleans St., Natchez, MS 39120-3452. Tel.: 601-445-4555, 601-870-8840. Fax: 601-304-1376.
E-mail: rosaliemansion@yahoo.com
Web Site: www.rosaliemansion.com
Key Personnel: Chm. (V), Pamela White; Museum Shop Mgr., Theresa Hill.
Institution Type/Description: Historic Site Museum: housed in c.1820 house & gardens located on Old Fort Rosalie grounds.
Hours & Admission Prices: Daily 9-5; group tours available upon request. Adults $10, children $8; Mississippi DAR members & children under 6 no charge. Closed Easter; Thanksgiving; Christmas. &
Attendance: 25,000 (actual)

NATCHEZ COSTUME & DOLL MUSEUM, 215 S. Pearl St., Natchez, MS 39120. Tel.: 601-446-9065.
E-mail: ntzgardenclub@bellsouth.net
Web Site: www.natchezgardenclub.org
Institution Type/Description: General Museum.
Hours & Admission Prices: Thurs.-Sat. 9-2. Last tour at 2. Admission $15.

NATCHEZ MUSEUM OF AFRICAN-AMERICAN HISTORY AND CULTURE, 301 Main St., Natchez, MS 39120-3461. Mailing Address: P.O. Box 1844, Natchez, MS 39121-1844. Tel.: 601-445-0728.
E-mail: info@visitnatchez.org
Institution Type/Description: History Museum.
Hours & Admission Prices: Tues.-Sat. 1-4:30. Adults $5, children $1.

New Albany

UNION COUNTY HERITAGE MUSEUM, 114 Cleveland St., New Albany, MS 38652-4050. Tel.: 662-538-0014. Fax: 662-538-6019.
E-mail: jill@ucheritagemuseum.com
Web Site: www.ucheritagemuseum.com
Key Personnel: Dir., Jill Smith.
Institution Type/Description: History Museum.
Hours & Admission Prices: Tues.-Fri. 9-4, Sat. 10-3. No charge; donations accepted. &
Attendance: 10,000 (estimated)

Ocean Springs

THE DOLL HOUSE, 809 Washington Ave., Ocean Springs, MS 39564. Tel.: 228-872-3971.
Institution Type/Description: Doll Museum.
Hours & Admission Prices: Tues.-Sat. 1-5.

G.I. MUSEUM, 5796 Ritcher Rd., Ocean Springs, MS 39564-2291. Tel.: 228-872-1943.
E-mail: mansfieldd@bellsouth.net
Web Site: www.gimuseum.com
Key Personnel: Dir., Doug Mansfield.
Institution Type/Description: Military Museum.
Hours & Admission Prices: 1st & 3rd Sun. of month & Wed. 10-5. No charge; donations accepted. &

J.L. SCOTT MARINE EDUCATION CENTER AND AQUARIUM, GULF COAST RESEARCH LABORATORY COLLEGE OF MARINE SCIENCES, THE UNIVERSITY OF SOUTHERN MISSISSIPPI, 703 E. Beach Dr., Ocean Springs, MS 39564-5326. Tel.: 228-818-8890. Fax: 228-818-8894.
E-mail: marine.education@usm.edu
Web Site: www.aquarium.usm.edu
Key Personnel: Admin., Sharon H. Walker, Ph.D.; Coord. Education Programs, Susan Culipher-Ross; Administrative Asst., Johnette Bosarge; Aquarium Supvr. & Facilities Coord., Alex (Buck) Schesny; Museum Shop Mgr., Sylvia Covacevich.
Institution Type/Description: Aquarium, Marine Museum & Education Center.
Hours & Admission Prices: Mon.-Sat. 9-4. Adults $4, senior citizens $3.50, children 3-17 $2.50; discounts to groups & AAA members; children under 3 & members no charge. &
Attendance: 75,000 (estimated)

WALTER ANDERSON MUSEUM OF ART, 510 Washington Ave., Ocean Springs, MS 39564-4632. Tel.: 228-872-3164. Fax: 228-875-4494.
E-mail: wama@walterandersonmuseum.org
Web Site: www.walterandersonmuseum.org
Key Personnel: Exec. Dir., Rosemary Roosa; Pres. Bd., Erich Nichols; Cur., Mattie Codling; Museum Shop Mgr., Josie Gardner; Chm. (V), Allene Chatham.
Institution Type/Description: Art Museum: located in Historic District of Ocean Springs.
Hours & Admission Prices: Mon.-Sat. 9:30-4:30, Sun. 12:30-4:30. Adults $10, seniors, students 16-24 with ID, AAA members & military $8, children 5-15 $5; discounts to groups with advance reservation, AAM, AFA, SEMC & MMA members; children under 5 & members no charge. Closed New Year's Day; Easter; Thanksgiving; Christmas Eve & Day. &
Attendance: 12,000 (actual)

WILLIAM M. COLMER VISITOR CENTER, 3500 Park Rd., Davis Bayou Area, Ocean Springs, MS 39564-9709. Tel.: 228-875-9057 & 0074, ext. 100. Fax: 228-872-2954 & 875-2358.
Web Site: www.nps.gov/guis/
Key Personnel: District Interpreter, Susan Blair.
Institution Type/Description: National Park & Natural & Cultural History Museum: located on & part of Gulf Islands National Seashore.
Hours & Admission Prices: March-Oct. daily 9-5; Nov.-Feb. 8-4:30. No charge; donations accepted. &
Attendance: 50,000 (estimated)

Oxford

L.Q.C. LAMAR HOUSE MUSEUM, 616 N. 14th St., Oxford, MS 38655. Mailing Address: c/o Oxford-Lafayette County Heritage Foundation, P.O. Box 622, Oxford, MS 38655. Tel.: 662-513-6071 & 232-2477.
E-mail: darlenepcopp@gmail.com
Web Site: www.lqclamarhouse.com
Key Personnel: Project Mgr., Darlene Copp.
Institution Type/Description: Historic House Museum: housed in the former home of Lucius Lamar, a Congressman, Senator, Secretary of the Interior, and Supreme Court Justice; built in 1888. A National Historic Landmark.
Hours & Admission Prices: By appointment. Adults $5, children $1.

ROWAN OAK, HOME OF WILLIAM FAULKNER, 916 Old Taylor Ave., Oxford, MS 38655. Mailing Address: Univ. of Mississippi Museum, P.O. Box 1848, University, MS 38677-1848. Tel.: 662-234-3284. Fax: 662-915-7035.
Web Site: www.rowanoak.com
Key Personnel: Cur., William D. Griffith.
Institution Type/Description: Historic House Museum: home of William Faulkner, 1930-1962. A National Historic Landmark & National Literary Landmark.
Hours & Admission Prices: June - August 1 Mon.-Sat. 10-6, Sun. 1-6; August 2 to May Tues.-Sat. 10-4, Sun. 1-4. Adults $5; children no charge. Closed New Year's Eve & Day; Independence Day; Thanksgiving; Christmas Eve & Day. &
Attendance: 27,000 (actual)

UNIVERSITY MUSEUM & HISTORIC HOUSES, THE UNIVERSITY OF MISSISSIPPI, 5th St. & University Ave., Oxford, MS 38655. Mailing Address: P.O. Box 1848, University, MS 38677-1848. Tel.: 662-915-7073. Fax: 662-915-7035.
E-mail: esdean@olemiss.edu
Web Site: museum.olemiss.edu
Key Personnel: Dir., Robert Saarnio; Cur. Rowan Oak, William Griffith; Mgr. Collections, Melanie Antonelli; Cur. Education, Emily McCauley; Membership

& Coord. Communications, Kate Wallace; Mgr. Finance & Administrative, Michelle Perry; Security, Mike Hash.
Institution Type/Description: Art Museum.
Hours & Admission Prices: Museum: Tues.-Sat. 10-6. Rowan Oak: Winter Tues.-Sat. 10-4, Sun. 1-4; Summer: Mon.-Sat. 10-6, Sun. 1-6. Rowan Oak: adults $5; members & UM students no charge. Closed national & university holidays.
Attendance: 19,000 (actual)

Pascagoula

SCRANTON NATURE CENTER, 3928 Nathan Hale Dr., Pascagoula, MS 39581-4727. Mailing Address: P.O. Drawer 908, Pascagoula, MS 39568-0908. Tel.: 228-938-6612. Fax: 228-938-2355.
E-mail: naturecenter@cityofpascagoula.com
Web Site: cityofpascagoula.com/scranton-nature-center
Institution Type/Description: Nature Center.
Hours & Admission Prices: Tues.-Sat. 10-5. Adults $2, children 2-12 $1.

SCRANTON SHRIMP BOAT MUSEUM, River Park, 4100 Clark St., Pascagoula, MS 39568. Mailing Address: P.O. Drawer 908, Pascagoula, MS 39568-0908. Tel.: 228-938-6612. Fax: 228-938-2355.
Web Site: cityofpascagoula.com/scranton-museum
Institution Type/Description: History Museum: housed on a 70 ft. commercial shrimp boat.
Hours & Admission Prices: Tues.-Sat. 10-4, Sun. 1-4. Adults $2.

Pearlington

INFINITY SCIENCE CENTER, INC., 1 Discovery Cir., Pearlington, MS 39572. Mailing Address: P.O. Box 580, Pearlington, MS 39572. Tel.: 228-533-9025. Fax: 228-533-9232.
E-mail: guestservices@visitinfinity.com
Web Site: www.visitinfinity.com
Formerly: MAST, Inc.
Key Personnel: Dir., John Wilson; Chm. (V), Jerry Levens; Sales & Mktg. Coord., Brian Alexander; Dir. Exhibits & Education, John Dumoulin.
Institution Type/Description: Science Center.
Hours & Admission Prices: Mon.-Fri. 9-4, Sat. 10-4. Adults $10, seniors 55 & over and military $8, children 4-17 $6; discounts to groups of 20 or more; NASA/Stennis badged employees & children 3 & under no charge. NASA/Stennis Space Center & boardwalk walking tours & dome movies included with admission require photo ID for visitors 18 & over.
Attendance: 66,000 (estimated)

Philadelphia

NESHOBA COUNTY-PHILADELPHIA HISTORICAL MUSEUM, 303 Water Ave. S., Philadelphia, MS 39350-2621. Mailing Address: P.O. Box 1482, Philadelphia, MS 39350. Tel.: 601-656-1284.
E-mail: info@neshoba.org
Formerly: Philadelphia Neshoba County Museum
Key Personnel: Chm. (V), Mack Alford.
Institution Type/Description: History Museum: housed in the home of George Pegram Woodward, c.1880.
Hours & Admission Prices: Mon.-Fri. 10-3. No charge; donations accepted.
Attendance: 400 (actual)

Picayune

THE CROSBY ARBORETUM, MISSISSIPPI STATE UNIVERSITY, 370 Ridge Rd., Picayune, MS 39466-8151. Mailing Address: P.O. Box 1639, Picayune, MS 39466-1639. Tel.: 601-799-2311, ext. 21. Fax: 601-799-2372.
E-mail: drackett@ext.msstate.edu
Web Site: www.crosbyarboretum.msstate.edu
Key Personnel: Dir., Dr. Janine Conklin; Sr. Cur., Pat Drackett.
Institution Type/Description: Arboretum.
Hours & Admission Prices: Wed.-Sun. 9-5. Adults $4, senior citizens $3, children $2; discounts to AAM, ICOM members, arboretum members & American Horticultural Society Reciprocal Garden members; members no charge. Closed New Year's Eve & Day; Thanksgiving; Christmas Eve & Day.
Attendance: 5,500 (estimated)

Piney Woods

LAURENCE C. JONES MUSEUM, Piney Woods School, 5096 Hwy. 49 S., Piney Woods, MS 39148. Mailing Address: P.O. Box 99, Piney Woods, MS 39148-0037. Tel.: 601-845-2214, ext. 2700. Fax: 601-845-2604.
E-mail: vwilson@pineywoods.org
Web Site: www.pineywoods.org
Key Personnel: C.E.O., Willie L. Crossley; Chm., Gen. Wallace Arnold; Chief of Staff, Renee Tillman.
Institution Type/Description: History Museum: housed in c.1922 Community House, The Piney Woods Country Life School.
Hours & Admission Prices: Mon.-Fri. 8-5. No charge; donations accepted. Closed major holidays.
Attendance: 5,000 (estimated)

Pontotoc

TOWN SQUARE POST OFFICE & MUSEUM, 59 S. Main St., Pontotoc, MS 38863-2824. Mailing Address: P.O. Box 141, Pontotoc, MS 38863-0141. Tel.: 662-488-0388. Fax: 662-488-0388.
E-mail: marycates@mshills.org
Key Personnel: Dir., Martha Coleman; Pres. (V) Pontotoc County Historical Society, James L. Roberts, Jr.
Institution Type/Description: History Museum.
Hours & Admission Prices: Mon.-Fri. 10-4:30; other times by appointment. No charge; donations accepted.

Poplarville

PEARL RIVER COMMUNITY COLLEGE MUSEUM, 101 Hwy. 11 N., Poplarville, MS 39470-2201. Tel.: 601-403-1000, 877-772-2338 (Toll Free).
E-mail: rhague@prcc.edu
Web Site: www.prcc.edu/museum
Key Personnel: Dir., Ronn Hague.
Institution Type/Description: History Museum.
Hours & Admission Prices: Mon.-Fri. 8-11 & 1-4; other times by appointment.

Port Gibson

BERNHEIMER HOUSE, 212 Walnut St., Port Gibson, MS 39150. Tel.: 601-437-2843, 800-735-3407.
Institution Type/Description: Historic House Museum.
Hours & Admission Prices: By appointment. Adults $5.

GRAND GULF MILITARY PARK, 12006 Grand Gulf Rd., Port Gibson, MS 39150-4549. Tel.: 601-437-5911. Fax: 601-437-2929.
E-mail: grandgulfpark@aol.com
Web Site: www.grandgulfpark.state.ms.us
Key Personnel: Chm., Robert St. John; Administrative Asst., Cathi Dodgen.
Institution Type/Description: Military Museum & Historic Site.
Hours & Admission Prices: Daily 8-5. Museum & Grounds: adults $3, senior citizens $2, students K-12 $1; discount to groups with reservations; pre-schoolers no charge. Closed major holidays.
Attendance: 80,000 (estimated)

Raymond

DUPREE HOUSE AND MAMIE'S COTTAGE, 2809 Dupree Rd., Raymond, MS 39154. Tel.: 601-857-6051, 877-629-6051.
Institution Type/Description: Historic House Museum: housed in the former home of Dr. H. T. T. Dupree; c.1850. Listed on the National Register of Historic Places.
Hours & Admission Prices: By appointment.

Ridgeland

CRAFTSMEN'S GUILD OF MISSISSIPPI & MISSISSIPPI CRAFT CENTER, 950 Rice Rd., Ridgeland, MS 39157-3040. Tel.: 601-856-7546. Fax: 601-856-7531.
E-mail: info@mscrafts.org
Web Site: www.mscrafts.org
Key Personnel: Exec. Dir., Nancy Perkins; Bd. Pres., Ken McLemore; Gallery Mgr., Sheri Cox.
Institution Type/Description: Fine Crafts Gallery & Guild.
Hours & Admission Prices: Mon.-Sat. 9-5; Sun. noon-5. No charge; donations accepted. Closed New Year's Day; Easter; Thanksgiving; Christmas.
Attendance: 150,000 (estimated)

Ripley

TIPPAH COUNTY HISTORICAL MUSEUM, 106 N. Siddell St., Ripley, MS 38663-2036. Tel.: 662-512-0099. Facebook: Tippah County Historical Museum.
E-mail: tippahmuseum@dixie.net.com
Key Personnel: Cur., Anita Decker; C.E.O. & Pres. (V), Kyle Smith; Museum Shop Mgr., Paula Jordan.
Institution Type/Description: History Museum.
Hours & Admission Prices: Mon.-Sat. 9-2. No charge; donations accepted. Closed holidays. &
Attendance: 650 (estimated)

Sandy Hook

JOHN FORD HOUSE, Hwy. 35 S., Sandy Hook, MS 19478. Mailing Address: 412 Courthouse Sq., P.O. Box 272, Columbia, MS 39429. Tel.: 601-731-3999.
Institution Type/Description: Historic House: housed in the former home of Rev. John Ford, a legislator & member of the state's Constitution Writing Committee; c.1805.
Hours & Admission Prices: Sat.-Sun. 2-5 by appointment. Adults $4, children under 12 $3.
Attendance: 2,000 (estimated)

Senatobia

HERITAGE MUSEUM FOUNDATION OF TATE COUNTY, INC., 135 N. Front St., Senatobia, MS 38668-0375. Mailing Address: P.O. Box 375, Senatobia, MS 38668-0375. Tel.: 662-562-8715.
Key Personnel: Pres., Deborah Perkins; Sec., Janie Mortimer; Treas., Sara S. Henley.
Institution Type/Description: Historic Foundation Museum: housed in historic Tate County Courthouse.
Hours & Admission Prices: Mon.-Fri. 8-5, except on courthouse holidays. No charge; donations accepted. &
Attendance: 150 (estimated)

Starkville

OKTIBBEHA COUNTY HERITAGE MUSEUM, 206 Fellowship St., Starkville, MS 39759-3378. Tel.: 662-323-0211.
E-mail: bobandjoan@bellsouth.net
Web Site: www.oktibbehaheritagemuseum.com
Key Personnel: Chm. Bd. Trustees, Joan Wilson; Chm. (V), Marion Honsinger.
Institution Type/Description: History Museum: housed in 1800s The G M & O Depot.
Hours & Admission Prices: Tues.-Thurs. 1-4, Sat. call for hours. No charge; donations accepted. &
Attendance: 3,000 (actual)

Sturgis

BENCH MARK WORKS MOTORCYCLE MUSEUM, 3400 Earles Fork Rd., Sturgis, MS 39769. Tel.: 662-465-6444.
E-mail: vech@benchmarkworks.com
Web Site: www.benchmarkworks.com
Institution Type/Description: Motorcycle Museum.
Hours & Admission Prices: Mon.-Thurs. 8-5.

Taylorsville

WATKINS MUSEUM, Eureka St., Taylorsville, MS 39168. Mailing Address: P.O. Box 358, Taylorsville, MS 39168-0358. Tel.: 601-785-6531. Fax: 601-785-2200.
E-mail: rosalynglenn@taylorsvillems.com
Key Personnel: Cur., Rosalyn Glenn.
Institution Type/Description: General Museum: housed in c.1900 Taylorsville Signal & General Store.
Hours & Admission Prices: By appointment. No charge; donations accepted. &
Attendance: 100 (estimated)

Tougaloo

TOUGALOO COLLEGE, Tougaloo College Art Collection, 500 W. County Line Rd., Tougaloo, MS 39174-9998. Tel.: 601-977-7743. Fax: 601-977-7714.
E-mail: art@tougaloo.edu
Web Site: www.tougaloo.edu/artcolony

Key Personnel: Pres., Beverly Wade Hogan; Assoc. Professor Art, Bruce O'Hara; Professor & Dept. Chair Collections, Johnnie M. Maberry-Gilbert; Head Librarian, Orthello Moman; Archives Mgr., Minnie Watson.
Institution Type/Description: Historic Site/Building: located on historic Tougaloo College Campus. Housed in the Bennie Thompson Building.
Hours & Admission Prices: Call for hours. &
Attendance: 1,000 (estimated)

Tunica

TUNICA MUSEUM, One Museum Blvd., Tunica, MS 38676. Mailing Address: P.O. Box 1914, Tunica, MS 38676-1914. Tel.: 662-363-6631. Fax: 662-363-6651.
E-mail: drdick@tunicamuseum.com
Web Site: www.tunicamuseum.com
Key Personnel: Dir., Richard Taylor; Pres. (V), Bob Gann; Museum Shop Mgr., Darlene Griffith.
Institution Type/Description: History Museum.
Hours & Admission Prices: Tues.-Sat. 10-5, Sun. 1-5. No charge; donations accepted. &
Attendance: 30,000 (estimated)

Tupelo

ELVIS PRESLEY BIRTHPLACE AND MUSEUM, 306 Elvis Presley Dr., Tupelo, MS 38804-2812. Tel.: 662-841-1245. Fax: 662-690-6623.
E-mail: info@elvispresleybirthplace.com
Web Site: www.elvispresleybirthplace.com
Key Personnel: Exec. Dir., Dick Guyton.
Institution Type/Description: History Museum: housed in the birthplace of Elvis Presley, born in 1935.
Hours & Admission Prices: Mon.-Sat. 9-5, Sun. 1-5. House: adult $8, children 7-12 $5. Museum: adult $8, child $4. Combined: adult $17, seniors & youth 13-18 $14, children 7-12 $8; discounts to groups of 15 or more; children under 7 no charge. Closed Thanksgiving; Christmas.

GUMTREE MUSEUM OF ART, 211 W. Main St., Tupelo, MS 38804-3917. Mailing Address: P.O. Box 786, Tupelo, MS 38802-0786. Tel.: 662-844-2787. Fax: 662-269-3296.
E-mail: laura.gumtreemuseum@gmail.com
Web Site: www.gumtreemuseum.com
Formerly: Tupelo Artist Guild Gallery
Key Personnel: Exec. Dir., Belle Naugher; Chm. (V), Brad Gibens.
Institution Type/Description: Art Museum.
Hours & Admission Prices: Tues.-Sat. 10-4. No charge; donations accepted. Closed New Year's Day; Independence Day; Thanksgiving; Christmas. &
Attendance: 13,200 (estimated)

HEALTHWORKS!, 219 S. Industrial Rd., Tupelo, MS 38801. Tel.: 662-377-KIDS.
E-mail: healthworks@nmhs.net
Institution Type/Description: Children's Health Museum.
Hours & Admission Prices: Mon.-Fri. 8:30-4, Sat. 10-2. Admission $5; children under 2 no charge.

NATCHEZ TRACE PARKWAY, 2680 Natchez Trace Pkwy., Tupelo, MS 38804-9715. Tel.: 662-680-4025. Fax: 662-680-4036.
E-mail: christina_smith@nps.gov
Web Site: www.nps.gov/natr
Key Personnel: Supt., Cameron H. Sholly.
Institution Type/Description: Visitor Center & Archival Study Collection.
Hours & Admission Prices: Daily 8-4:30. No charge. Closed Christmas. &
Attendance: 51,991 (actual)

OREN DUNN CITY MUSEUM, 689 Rutherford Rd., Tupelo, MS 38801. Mailing Address: P.O. Box 2674, Tupelo, MS 38803-2674. Tel.: 662-841-6438. Fax: 662-841-6458. Facebook.
E-mail: rae.mathis@tupeloms.us
Web Site: www.tupeloms.gov/oren-dunn-city-museum/
Formerly: Tupelo City Museum
Key Personnel: Pres. (V), Boyd Yarbrough; Chair Friends of the Museum, Susie Dent; Cur., Rae Mathis Guess; Asst. Cur., Della Lentz; Operations Mgr., Jerry Duckett; Educator, Janice Anthony.
Institution Type/Description: History Museum.
Hours & Admission Prices: Mon.-Fri. 8-5; call for additional hours. Adults $4, seniors 60 & over $3, children 4-16 $2; Smithsonian Day no charge. Closed City of Tupelo holidays. &
Attendance: 10,000 (actual)

TUPELO AUTOMOBILE MUSEUM, 1 Otis Blvd., Tupelo, MS 38804-4015. Tel.: 662-842-4242. Fax: 662-842-3734. Facebook.
E-mail: info@tupeloauto.com
Web Site: www.tupeloauto.com
Key Personnel: Exec. Dir. & Chm. (V), Jane Spain; Dir., Phil Sullivan; Visitor Coord. & Museum Shop Mgr., Lynn Waddle.
Institution Type/Description: Automobile Museum.
Hours & Admission Prices: Mon.-Sat. 9-4:30, Sun. 12-4:30. Adult $10, seniors, military & AAA members $9, children 5-12 $5; discounts to groups of 10 or more; children 4 & under no charge. Closed New Year's Day; Easter; Thanksgiving; Christmas. &
Attendance: 25,000 (estimated)

TUPELO VETERAN'S MUSEUM, 689 Rutherford Rd., Tupelo, MS 38801. Mailing Address: P.O. Box 7212, Tupelo, MS 38801. Tel.: 662-844-1515.
Key Personnel: Cur., Tony Lute.
Institution Type/Description: Military History Museum.
Hours & Admission Prices: Call for hours.

Union

BOLER STAGECOACH INN MUSEUM, 205 E. Jackson Rd., Hwy. 492, Union, MS 39365. Mailing Address: P.O. Box 116, Decatur, MS 39327. Tel.: 601-635-3160.
E-mail: jmmoore@decatur.net
Key Personnel: Pres. (V), Nancy Moore.
Institution Type/Description: Historic Building: c. 1856.
Hours & Admission Prices: By appointment. Adults $5, children $1.
Attendance: 60 (estimated)

Vicksburg

BIEDENHARN COCA-COLA MUSEUM, 1107 Washington St., Vicksburg, MS 39183-2959. Tel.: 601-638-6514. Fax: 601-636-5010.
E-mail: vburgfoundation@aol.com
Web Site: biedenharncoca-colamuseum.com
Key Personnel: Exec. Dir., Nancy H. Bell; Chm. (V), Charlie Gholson; Treas., Denny Allman.
Institution Type/Description: History Museum: housed in the first Coca-Cola bottling company in the world, 1894.
Hours & Admission Prices: Mon.-Sat. 9-5, Sun. 1:30-4:30. Adults $3.50, students & children $2.50; discounts to groups, families, AAM & ICOM members; members no charge. Closed New Year's Day; Easter; Thanksgiving; Christmas.
Attendance: 25,000 (actual)

CEDAR GROVE MANSION INN, 2200 Oak St., Vicksburg, MS 39180-4008. Tel.: 601-636-1000. Fax: 601-634-6126.
E-mail: info@cedargroveinn.com
Web Site: cedargroveinn.com
Key Personnel: C.E.O., Owner & Innkeeper, Colleen Small.
Institution Type/Description: Historic Site & Building: 1840-1858 southern mansion located at the site of the Siege of Vicksburg.
Hours & Admission Prices: Tours daily 9:30-11 & 1-4. Adults $6, children 6-12 $4; discounts to groups; children under 6 no charge. &

CORNERS MANSION INN-A BED & BREAKFAST, 601 Klein St., Vicksburg, MS 39180. Tel.: 601-636-7421, 800-444-7421.
E-mail: cornersmansioninn@yahoo.com
Formerly: The Corners Mansion Inn
Institution Type/Description: Historic House Museum: housed in a home built by John Alexander Klein for his daughter and her husband; built in 1873.
Hours & Admission Prices: Daily 9:30-5:30 by appointment. Home Tours: $10 per person; overnight guests no charge. &

DUFF GREEN MANSION, 1114 First East St., Vicksburg, MS 39180. Tel.: 601-636-6968 & 638-6662, 800-992-0037. Fax: 601-661-0079.
E-mail: duffgreenmansion@gmail.com
Web Site: www.duffgreenmansion.com
Institution Type/Description: Historic House Museum: served as a hospital during the Civil War for Confederate and Union soldiers; c.1856. Listed on the National Register of Historic Places.
Hours & Admission Prices: Daily 12-5 by appointment. Adults $6, students & children 5-12 $4; children under 5 no charge.

THE JACQUELINE HOUSE AFRICAN AMERICAN MUSEUM, 1325 Main St., Vicksburg, MS 39183-2647. Tel.: 601-636-0941.
Web Site: jacquelinehouse.weebly.com
Institution Type/Description: History Museum.
Hours & Admission Prices: By appointment.

OLD COURT HOUSE MUSEUM-EVA WHITAKER DAVIS MEMORIAL, 1008 Cherry St., Court Square, Vicksburg, MS 39183-2540. Tel.: 601-636-0741. Fax: 601-636-1004.
E-mail: societyhistorica@bellsouth.net
Web Site: www.oldcourthouse.org
Key Personnel: Dir. & Cur., George C. Bolm; Pres., David Maggio; Vice. Pres., Stan Whitaker.
Institution Type/Description: Historic Building: housed in the 1858 Old Warren County Courthouse. A National Historic Landmark.
Hours & Admission Prices: Mon.-Sat. 8:30-5, Sun. 1:30-5. Adults $5, senior citizens $4.50, students grades 1-12 $3; discounts to groups of 10 or more. Closed New Year's Day; Thanksgiving; Christmas Eve & Day. &
Attendance: 32,763 (actual)

VICKSBURG BATTLEFIELD MUSEUM, 1010 Levee St., #A, Vicksburg, MS 39183-2569. Tel.: 601-638-6500. Fax: 601-638-8746.
E-mail: thegunboat@bellsouth.net
Web Site: vicksburgbattlefieldmuseum.net
Key Personnel: C.E.O., Lamar Roberts; Museum Shop Mgr., Sue Roberts.
Institution Type/Description: History Museum.
Hours & Admission Prices: Mon.-Sat. 9-5. Adults $5.50. Closed Easter; Thanksgiving; Christmas. &
Attendance: 19,000 (actual)

VICKSBURG NATIONAL MILITARY PARK, 3201 Clay St., Vicksburg, MS 39183-3495. Tel.: 601-636-0583. Fax: 601-636-9497.
Web Site: www.nps.gov/vick
Key Personnel: Park Supt., Bill Justice.
Institution Type/Description: History Museum & Visitors Center: located on the site of the 1863 Union siege of the city of Vicksburg, MS.
Hours & Admission Prices: Visitor Center: daily 8-5; Cairo Museum: daily 8:30-5. Closed New Year's Day; Thanksgiving; Christmas. &
Attendance: 500,000 (estimated)

YESTERDAY'S CHILDREN ANTIQUE DOLL & TOY MUSEUM, 1104 Washington St., Vicksburg, MS 39183-2960. Tel.: 601-638-0650.
E-mail: mbakarich@aol.com
Web Site: www.yesterdayschildrenmuseum.com
Key Personnel: Dir., Michael N. Bakarich.
Institution Type/Description: Toy and Doll Museum.
Hours & Admission Prices: Mon.-Sat. 10-4; other times by appointment. Adults $3, children $2; discounts to groups of 10 or more. Closed Thanksgiving; Christmas. &
Attendance: 12,000 (estimated)

Water Valley

THE WALTER VALLEY CASEY JONES RAILROAD MUSEUM, 105 Railroad Ave., Water Valley, MS 38965-3312. Tel.: 601-473-2849. Facebook: Water Valley Casey Jones Museum.
E-mail: gurnerjack@bellsouth.net
Web Site: www.caseyjonesmuseum.com
Key Personnel: Chm. (V) & Pres. (V), Jack Gurner, Jr.; Cur. & Museum Shop Mgr., J.K. Gurner, Sr.
Institution Type/Description: Railroad Museum.
Hours & Admission Prices: Thurs.-Sat. 2-4; other times by appointment. No charge; donations accepted. &
Attendance: 200 (estimated)

West Point

HOWLIN' WOLF BLUES MUSEUM, 307 Westbrook St., West Point, MS 39773. Mailing Address: P.O. Box 1334, West Point, MS 39773. Tel.: 662-295-8361. Fax: 662-495-2007.
E-mail: jeremyklutts@yahoo.com
Web Site: www.wpnet.org/howlin_wolf.htm
Key Personnel: Dir., Richard Ramsey.
Institution Type/Description: Blues Museum.

Hours & Admission Prices: Thurs.-Sat. 10-5; other times by appointment. No charge; donations accepted.
Attendance: 250 (estimated)

SAM WILHITE TRANSPORTATION MUSEUM, #5 Depot Dr., West Point, MS 39773. Mailing Address: 331 Jefferson St., West Point, MS 39773-2826. Tel.: 662-494-8910 (cell). Facebook: West Point Train Museum.
E-mail: terry_craig@bellsouth.net
Institution Type/Description: Transportation Museum.
Hours & Admission Prices: Thurs.-Sat. 10-5, or by appointment. No charge; donations accepted. &
Attendance: 400 (estimated)

Woodville

ROSEMONT PLANTATION, Rosemont Plantation, Hwy. 24 E., Woodville, MS 39669. Mailing Address: P.O. Box 814, Woodville, MS 39669-0814. Tel.: 601-888-6809. Fax: 601-888-3327.
E-mail: pbeacroft@aol.com
Web Site: www.rosemontplantation1810.com
Key Personnel: Owner, Percival T. Beacroft; Publicity & Tours, Jenny Angeline.
Institution Type/Description: Historic House Museum: 1810, originally named Poplar Grove, family home of Jefferson Davis; family cemetery located on grounds.
Hours & Admission Prices: March to mid-Dec. Tues.-Fri. 10-4; groups by appointment; additional hours during Natchez Spring & Fall Pilgrimages. Suggested Donations: adults $10, students $4.
Attendance: 500

WILKINSON COUNTY MUSEUM, 203 Boston Row, Woodville, MS 39669. Mailing Address: P.O. Box 1055, Woodville, MS 39669-1055. Tel.: 601-888-7151. Fax: 601-276-9776.
E-mail: info@historicwoodville.com
Web Site: www.historicwoodville.org
Key Personnel: C.E.O., Ernesto Caldeira; Pres. (V), David Wilkerson.
Institution Type/Description: History Museum: housed in a Greek Revival Temple style office & banking house of the West Feliciana Railroad; built in 1834.
Hours & Admission Prices: Mon.-Fri. 10-12 & 2-4, Sat. 10-12.
Attendance: 4,900 (actual)

Yazoo City

OAKES AFRICAN AMERICAN CULTURAL CENTER, 312 S. Monroe St., Yazoo City, MS 39194. Mailing Address: Yazoo County Fair & Civic League, P.O. Box 1192, Yazoo City, MS 39194. Tel.: 662-746-7984 & 5038. Fax: 662-746-6020.
E-mail: lmteam@bellsouth.net
Institution Type/Description: Cultural Center: housed in the former home of businessman & educator, A.J. Oakes. Listed on the National Register of Historic Places.
Hours & Admission Prices: Fri. 9-12 & 1-3; other times by appointment. No charge; donations accepted.
Attendance: 350 (estimated)

SAM OLDEN YAZOO HISTORICAL SOCIETY MUSEUM, 332 N. Main St., Yazoo City, MS 39194-3958. Mailing Address: P.O. Box 575, Yazoo City, MS 39194. Tel.: 662-746-1815, 800-381-0662.
E-mail: yazoo@yazoo.org
Formerly: Yazoo Historical Museum
Institution Type/Description: History Museum.
Hours & Admission Prices: Mon.-Fri. 8:30-4:30, Sat. 12-4. No charge; donations accepted.

MISSOURI

(368 listings)

Agency

AGENCY FORD MUSEUM, 11351 Rte. FF, Agency, MO 64401. Tel.: 816-253-9301.
E-mail: rampfsharon@yahoo.com
Institution Type/Description: History Museum.
Hours & Admission Prices: By appointment only. No charge; donations accepted.
Attendance: 250 (estimated)

Altenburg

LUTHERAN HERITAGE CENTER & MUSEUM OF THE PERRY COUNTY LUTHERAN HISTORICAL SOCIETY, 75 Church St., Altenburg, MO 63732. Mailing Address: P.O. Box 53, Altenburg, MO 63732-0053. Tel.: 573-824-6070.
E-mail: carlataylorjordan@msn.com
Formerly: The Perry County Lutheran Historical Society of Altenburg, Missouri, Inc.
Key Personnel: Pres. (V), Warren Schmidt; Dir., Carla L. Jordan; Museum Shop Mgr., Dolores Schmidt.
Institution Type/Description: Religious Museum: located on the site of the principal settlement of Saxon immigrants in 1839; historic roots of Lutheran Church - Missouri Synod. Site of the 1839 Log College Concordia Seminary.
Hours & Admission Prices: Daily 10-4. No charge; donations accepted. Closed New Year's Eve & Day; Easter; Christmas Eve & Day. &
Attendance: 6,000 (actual)

Arcadia

IRON COUNTY HISTORICAL SOCIETY MUSEUM, 630 Hwy. 21, Arcadia, MO 63621. Mailing Address: P.O. Box 183, Ironton, MO 63650-0183, Tel.: 573-546-3513.
E-mail: ironcohissoc@hotmail.com
Web Site: www.rootsweb.ancestry.com/~moichs
Key Personnel: Pres., John Abney.
Institution Type/Description: Historical Society Museum.
Hours & Admission Prices: April-Nov. Mon.-Sat. 10-4, Sun. 1-4; Dec.-March Fri.-Sat. 10-4, Sun. 1-4. No charge; donations accepted.

Arrow Rock

ARROW ROCK STATE HISTORIC SITE, 39521 Visitor Center Dr., Arrow Rock, MO 65320. Mailing Address: P.O. Box 1, Arrow Rock, MO 65320. Tel.: 660-837-3330.
E-mail: moparks@dnr.mo.gov
Web Site: mostateparks.com/park/arrow-rock-state-historic-site
Key Personnel: Dir., Michael Dickey.
Institution Type/Description: Village Museum Complex: c.1830-1870, town located near eastern end of Santa Fe Trail.
Hours & Admission Prices: Historic Site Grounds: daily 7 a.m. to 10 p.m. Visitor Center: March-May & Sept.-Nov. daily 10-4; June-Aug. daily 10-5; Dec.-Feb. Fri.-Sun. 10-4. No charge. &
Attendance: 156,000 (actual)

FRIENDS OF ARROW ROCK, INC., 310 Main St., Arrow Rock, MO 65320. Mailing Address: Box 124, Arrow Rock, MO 65320-0124. Tel.: 660-837-3231. Fax: 660-837-3230.
E-mail: office@friendsofarrowrock.org
Web Site: www.friendsofarrowrock.org
Key Personnel: Pres. (V), Dr. Thomas B. Hall, III; Admin., Sandy Selby.
Institution Type/Description: Historic Buildings.
Hours & Admission Prices: Tours: April-May & Sept.-Oct. Sat.-Sun. & by appointment; Memorial Day to Labor Day daily 10, 11:30, 1:30 & 3; groups by appointment. Adults $6, children $3; discounts to groups. Night Walk Tours: by appointment. $15 per person. &
Attendance: 4,000 (estimated)

Ash Grove

OZARKS AFRO-AMERICAN HERITAGE MUSEUM, 107 W. Main St., Ash Grove, MO 65604. Mailing Address: P.O. Box 265, Ash Grove, MO 65604. Tel.: 417-672-3104.
E-mail: magberry@me.com
Web Site: www.oaahm.orrg
Key Personnel: Dir., Fr. Moses Berry.
Institution Type/Description: History Museum.
Hours & Admission Prices: Tues.-Thurs. 9-1, Sat. 10-2; other times by appointment.
Attendance: 500 (estimated)

Augusta

AUGUSTA HISTORICAL MUSEUM - FRIENDS OF HISTORIC AUGUSTA, 275 Webster St., Augusta, MO 63332. Mailing Address: 498 Shell Rd., Augusta, MO 63332. Tel.: 636-482-4558; 228-4303 & 4821. Fax: 636-228-4821.
E-mail: amh@augustamuseum.org
Institution Type/Description: Historic House Museum: built in 1861. Listed on the National Register of Historic Places.

Hours & Admission Prices: May-Oct. Sun. 1-4 by appointment. No charge; donations accepted.
Attendance: 300 (estimated)

Ava

DOUGLAS COUNTY HISTORICAL & GENEALOGICAL SOCIETY, 401 E. Washington Ave., Ava, MO 65608. Mailing Address: P.O. Box 986, Ava, MO 65608-0986. Tel.: 417-683-5799 & 2536. Facebook: Douglas County Historical Society & Museum.
E-mail: eddie037@centurytel.net
Web Site: www.rootsweb.ancestry.com/~modougla/HistSoc/HISTSOC.htm
Key Personnel: Sec., Treas. & Museum Shop Mgr., Sharon Sanders; Vice Pres., Research, Pat Carmichael; Pres. (V), Sally Hicks.
Institution Type/Description: History Museum: housed in the former Henry Wilson family home.
Hours & Admission Prices: Sat. 10-2. No charge; donations accepted. &
Attendance: 800 (estimated)

Bellefontaine Neighbors

GENERAL DANIEL BISSELL HOUSE, 10225 Bellefontaine Rd., Bellefontaine Neighbors, MO 63137-2307. Mailing Address: Parks and Recreation, 41 South Central, Clayton, MO 63105. Tel.: 636-532-7298, 314-554-6224; 314-615-7840 (TTY).
E-mail: jfoley@stlouisco.com
Web Site: www.stlouisco.com/ParksandRecreation/ParkPages/BissellHouse
Key Personnel: Dir. & Site Supvr., Tom Ott.
Institution Type/Description: Historic House: Federal Style home of Gen. Daniel Bissell, Commander of the Upper Louisiana Territory, Revolutionary War soldier & general in the War of 1812.
Hours & Admission Prices: Tours: by appointment only. Park: 8 to one half hour past sunset.

Belton

BELTON GRANDVIEW AND KANSAS CITY RAILROAD CO., 502 E. Walnut St., Belton, MO 64012-2516. Tel.: 816-331-0630. Facebook: BGKCRR.
E-mail: info@beltonrailroad.org
Web Site: www.beltonrailroad.org
Institution Type/Description: Railroad Museum.
Hours & Admission Prices: Train departures: May-Dec. Sat.-Sun. at 2. Adults $9.50-$14; children 2 & under no charge.

BELTON MUSEUM OF HISTORY, 512 Main St., Belton, MO 64012-2583. Tel.: 816-331-1905 & 322-3977.
Web Site: www.beltonhistoricalsociety.org
Institution Type/Description: History Museum.
Hours & Admission Prices: March-Dec. Tues. & Thurs. 1-4, Sat. 10-1. No charge; donations accepted.

Bloomfield

STARS AND STRIPES MUSEUM/LIBRARY, 17377 Stars and Stripes Way, Bloomfield, MO 63825-8487. Mailing Address: P.O. Box 1861, Bloomfield, MO 63825-0463. Tel.: 573-568-2055.
E-mail: stripes@newwavecomm.net
Web Site: starsandstripesmuseumlibrary.org
Key Personnel: Dir., Dr. Laura Meyer.
Institution Type/Description: Military Museum.
Hours & Admission Prices: Mon. & Wed.-Fri. 10-4, Sat. 10-2, Sun. by appointment. No charge; donations accepted. Closed New Year's Day; Easter; Thanksgiving; Christmas. &

STODDARD COUNTY MUSEUM, 501 Center St., Bloomfield, MO 63825. Mailing Address: 15248 Palo Verde Lane, Dexter, MO 63841. Tel.: 573-568-2163.
Key Personnel: Pres., Anita Peters.
Institution Type/Description: History Museum.
Hours & Admission Prices: May-Oct. fourth Sun. of each month 2-4. No charge; donations accepted.

Blue Springs

THE DILLINGHAM-LEWIS MUSEUM, 101 S.W. 15th St., Blue Springs, MO 64015-3511. Mailing Address: Blue Springs Historical Society, P.O. Box 762, Blue Springs, MO 64013. Tel.: 816-224-8979.

E-mail: bluespringshistory@gmail.com
Web Site: www.bluespringshistory.org
Key Personnel: Pres., Theresa Welch.
Institution Type/Description: House Museum: house built in 1906.
Hours & Admission Prices: Sun. 1-4; other times by appointment. Adults $3, seniors 60 & over and military $2, children 5-12 $1; children 4 & under no charge. Closed holidays.
Attendance: 1,100 (estimated)

Bolivar

THE ELLA CAROTHERS DUNNEGAN GALLERY OF ART, 511 N. Pike, Bolivar, MO 65613-1568. Mailing Address: P.O. Box 468, Bolival, MO 65613-0468. Tel.: 417-326-3438.
E-mail: joroberts@windstream.net
Web Site: www.dunnegangallery.com
Key Personnel: Dir., Jo Roberts.
Institution Type/Description: Fine Arts Museum.
Hours & Admission Prices: Mon., Wed. & Fri. 1-4, Sun. call for hours. No charge; donations accepted. Closed bank holidays. &

POLK COUNTY MUSEUM, 201 W. Locust St., Bolivar, MO 65613. Mailing Address: P.O. Box 423, Bolivar, MO 65613. Tel.: 417-326-6850.
E-mail: polkcountymuseum@hotmail.com
Key Personnel: Dir., C.E.O. & Chm. (V), Margaret Vest; C.E.O., Harlene Esther; Chm. (V), Nadine Hendrickson.
Institution Type/Description: History Museum: housed in the former North Ward Elementary School building; built in 1903.
Hours & Admission Prices: mid-May to mid-Sept. Mon.-Sat. 1-4. Adults $2, children 6-12 $1; children 5 & under no charge. &
Attendance: 622 (estimated)

Bonne Terre

THE SPACE MUSEUM, 116 E. School St., Bonne Terre, MO 63628. Tel.: 573-358-1200.
E-mail: bonneterrespace@gmail.com
Web Site: www.space-mo.org
Institution Type/Description: Space Museum.
Hours & Admission Prices: Sat. 9-5, Sun. 1-5; other times by appointment. Adults $5, student & active military $3; discounts to groups.

Boonesboro

BOONE'S LICK STATE HISTORIC SITE, State Rd. 187, Boonesboro, MO 65233. Mailing Address: Arrow Rock State Historic Site, P.O. Box 1, Arrow Rock, MO 65320. Tel.: 660-837-3330. Fax: 660-837-3300.
E-mail: moparks@dnr.mo.gov
Web Site: www.mostateparks.com/booneslick.htm
Key Personnel: Dir., Michael Dickey.
Institution Type/Description: Historic Site: c.1805 early salt manufacturing site.
Hours & Admission Prices: Sunrise-sunset. Closed during periods of snow or ice. &
Attendance: 10,000 (estimated)

Branson

COOTER'S PLACE BRANSON, 1819 W. Hwy. 76, Ste. B, Branson, MO 65616-2296. Tel.: 417-336-3494.
Institution Type/Description: History Museum.
Hours & Admission Prices: Call for hours.

HOLLYWOOD WAX MUSEUM, 3030 W. Hwy. 76, Branson, MO 65616-8312. Tel.: 417-337-8277.
E-mail: chuck@hollywoodwax.com
Web Site: www.hollywoodwaxmuseum.com/branson
Key Personnel: General Mgr., Chuck O'Day.
Institution Type/Description: Wax Museum.
Hours & Admission Prices: Early Jan. to early March daily 8-8; early March to mid-May Sun.-Thurs. 8am-11pm, Fri.-Sat. 8am-12am; mid-May to early Sept. daily 8am-12am; early Sept. to early Jan. Sun.-Thurs. 8am-11pm, Fri.-Sat. 8am-12am. Adults $17.95; seniors 55+ $15.95; children 4-11 $8.95; discounts to online ticket buyers; children 4 & under no charge. &
Attendance: 100,000

TITANIC MUSEUM ATTRACTION, 3235 76 Country Blvd., (& Hwy. 165), Branson, MO 65616-3551. Mailing Address: 714 State Hwy. 248, Ste. 520, Branson, MO 65616. Tel.: 417-334-9500, 800-

381-7670 (Toll Free). Fax: 417-334-5128. Facebook; Titanic Museum Attraction.
E-mail: info@titanicbranson.com
Web Site: www.titanicbranson.com
Formerly: Titanic Museum
Key Personnel: Co-owner & Dir., Mary Kellogg-Joslyn; Owner & C.E.O., John Joslyn.
Institution Type/Description: History Museum.
Hours & Admission Prices: Year round daily 9-5. Closed Christmas. &
Attendance: 560,000 (actual)

VETERANS MEMORIAL MUSEUM, 1250 W. 76 Country Music Blvd., Branson, MO 65616-2211. Tel.: 417-336-2300. Fax: 417-336-2301.
E-mail: info@veteransmemorialbranson.com
Web Site: www.veteransmemorialbranson.com
Institution Type/Description: History Museum.
Hours & Admission Prices: Summer: daily 9-6; Winter: daily 9-5. Adults $16.99, veterans $13.95, teens13-17 $10, children 5-12 $5; children 4 & under no charge. Closed Christmas.

WORLD'S LARGEST TOY MUSEUM COMPLEX, 3609 W. Hwy. 76, Branson, MO 65616. Tel.: 417-332-1499. Fax: 417-332-0017. Facebook.
E-mail: mail@worldslargesttoymuseum.com
Web Site: www.worldslargesttoymuseum.com
Key Personnel: Dir., Tom Beck.
Institution Type/Description: Toy & Harold Bell Wright Historical Museum.
Hours & Admission Prices: Jan.-March Mon.-Sat. 9-6; April-Dec. Mon.-Sat. 9-8. Adults $14.95, children $12.95; children 6 & under no charge. Closed Christmas. &

Brentwood

BRENTWOOD HISTORICAL SOCIETY, 2348 Brentwood Blvd., Brentwood, MO 63144-2028. Tel.: 314-713-1742.
E-mail: bwdhistsoc@yahoo.com
Key Personnel: Pres. (V), Dan Fitzgerald.
Institution Type/Description: Historical Society Museum: house built in 1910.
Hours & Admission Prices: Fri. 10am-12pm. No charge. &

Bridgeton

PAYNE-GENTRY HOUSE, 4211 Fee Fee Rd., Bridgeton, MO 63044-2217. Tel.: 314-739-5599. Fax: 314-739-2484. Facebook: City of Bridgeton.
E-mail: clay@bridgetonmo.com
Web Site: bridgetonmo.com
Institution Type/Description: Historic House: former home of Elbridge and Mary Elizabeth Payne, built in 1870.
Hours & Admission Prices: April-Nov. 1st Sun. each month 1-4; other times by appointment. Adults $3, seniors $2, children $1; children under 4 no charge. Candlelight Tour: 1st Sat.-Sun. Dec. 4-8pm.

Burfordville

BOLLINGER MILL STATE HISTORIC SITE, 113 Bollinger Mill Rd., Burfordville, MO 63739-9051. Tel.: 573-243-4591. Fax: 573-243-5385.
E-mail: bollinger.mill.state.historic.site@dnr.mo.gov
Web Site: www.mostateparks.com
Key Personnel: Site Admin., Lesley McDaniel; Park Maintenance Worker, Lee Haines; Historic Site Interpreter, Holly Rohr.
Institution Type/Description: Historic Site.
Hours & Admission Prices: Grounds: sunrise to sunset. Mill: March 15-Nov. 15 Mon.-Sat. 10-4, Sun. 12-4; Nov. 16-March 14 Mon. & Thurs.-Sat. 10-4, Sun. 12-4. Closed New Year's Day; Easter; Thanksgiving; Christmas.
Attendance: 60,000 (estimated)

Butler

BATES COUNTY MUSEUM, 802 Elks Dr., Butler, MO 64730. Mailing Address: P.O. Box 164, Butler, MO 64730-0164. Tel.: 660-679-0134. Fax: 660-679-0134.
E-mail: director@batescountymuseum.org
Web Site: www.batescountymuseum.org
Institution Type/Description: History Museum.
Hours & Admission Prices: April-Oct. Tues.-Sat. 9:30-4. Adults $5; members no charge. Closed legal holidays. &

POPLAR HEIGHTS FARM, 208 N. Delaware St., Butler, MO 64730-1504. Tel.: 660-679-0764.
E-mail: info@poplarheightsfarm.org
Web Site: www.poplarheightsfarm.org
Institution Type/Description: Living History Farm.
Hours & Admission Prices: Call for hours.

Cameron

CAMERON RAILROAD DEPOT MUSEUM, 210 N. Walnut, Cameron, MO 64429. Mailing Address: 819 E. Prospect, Cameron, MO 64429. Tel.: 816-632-7414.
E-mail: camerondepot@yahoo.com
Institution Type/Description: History Museum.
Hours & Admission Prices: Call for hours.

Canton

LEWIS COUNTY HISTORICAL SOCIETY MUSEUM & GENEALOGICAL LIBRARY, 102 N. 4th St., Canton, MO 63435-1317. Tel.: 573-288-5713.
E-mail: lewiscountyhist@centurytel.net
Web Site: www.lewiscountyhist.org
Formerly: Lewis County Historical Society Museum
Key Personnel: Pres. (V), Cynthia S. Barker.
Institution Type/Description: Historical Society Museum.
Hours & Admission Prices: Tues. & Thurs. 8-3; other times by appointment. No charge; donations accepted. Closed New Year's Day; Independence Day; Thanksgiving; Christmas. &

REMEMBER WHEN TOY MUSEUM, 19481 Rte. B, Canton, MO 63435. Tel.: 573-288-3995.
E-mail: robertwyatt11@yahoo.com
Institution Type/Description: Toy Museum.
Hours & Admission Prices: By appointment. Adults $5, children $3; discount to school & church groups.
Attendance: 200 (estimated)

Cape Girardeau

CAPE RIVER HERITAGE MUSEUM, 538 Independence St., Cape Girardeau, MO 63703-6227. Tel.: 573-334-0405.
E-mail: crhm538@hotmail.com
Web Site: www.caperiverheritagemuseum.com
Key Personnel: Dir., Bonnie Stepenoff; Pres. (V), Dr. John Holcomb.
Institution Type/Description: History Museum.
Hours & Admission Prices: mid-March to mid-Dec. Thurs.-Fri. 12-4, Sat. 11-4; other times by appointment. Adults $3.
Attendance: 2,000 (actual)

GLENN HOUSE/HISTORICAL ASSOCIATION OF GREATER CAPE GIRARDEAU, 325 S. Spanish, Cape Girardeau, MO 63703-7442. Mailing Address: P.O. Box 1982, Cape Girardeau, MO 63702-1982.
Web Site: www.glennhouse.org
Key Personnel: Pres. (V), Tom Grantham.
Institution Type/Description: Historic House Museum: housed in c.1883 Victorian home.
Hours & Admission Prices: May-Oct. Sat.-Sun. 1-4; Dec. Sat.-Sun. 1-4. Adults $5, children 12 & under $2; discounts to groups; members no charge.
Attendance: 2,500 (estimated)

THE RED HOUSE INTERPRETIVE CENTER, 128 Aquamsi St., Cape Girardeau, MO 63701. Mailing Address: 410 Kiwanis Dr., Cape Girardeau, MO 63701. Tel.: 573-334-0757 & 335-1631.
E-mail: brenschloss@sbcglobal.net
Key Personnel: Dir., Brenda Schloss.
Institution Type/Description: History Museum.
Hours & Admission Prices: April-Nov. Sat. 10-4; other times by appointment. Adults $3, children $1.

ROSEMARY BERKEL AND HARRY L. CRISP II MUSEUM, 518 S. Fountain, Southeast Missouri State University, Cape Girardeau, MO 63701. Mailing Address: One University Plaza, MS 7875, Cape Girardeau, MO 63701. Tel.: 573-651-2260.
E-mail: museum@semo.edu
Web Site: www.semo.edu/museum
Formerly: Southeast Missouri Regional Museum

Key Personnel: Dir., Peter Nguyen; Cur. Collections, James Phillips; Cur. Education, Ellen Hahs; Administrative Asst., Peggy Haney; Outreach Specialist, Gary Tyler.
Institution Type/Description: University Museum.
Hours & Admission Prices: Summer: Tues.-Fri. 10-4; Winter: Tues.-Fri. 10-5, Sat.-Sun. 1-4. No charge; donations accepted. Closed holidays. &
Attendance: 10,000 (actual)

Carrollton

CARROLL COUNTY HISTORICAL SOCIETY, 510 N. Mason, Carrollton, MO 64633-2200. Tel.: 660-542-1511.
Key Personnel: Pres. (V), Lillie Audsley.
Institution Type/Description: Historical Society Museum.
Hours & Admission Prices: First weekend in May through Sept. Sat.-Sun. 1-4; other times by appointment. No charge; donations accepted. &

Carthage

CARTHAGE CIVIL WAR MUSEUM, 205 Grant St., Carthage, MO 64836. Tel.: 417-237-7060.
E-mail: m.blizzard@carthagemo.gov
Institution Type/Description: History Museum.
Hours & Admission Prices: Call for hours. No charge.

PHELPS HOUSE, 1146 Grand Ave., Carthage, MO 64836-2832. Mailing Address: P.O. Box 375, Carthage, MO 64836-0375. Tel.: 417-358-1776.
E-mail: info@carthagehistoricpreservation.org
Web Site: www.phelpshouse.org
Institution Type/Description: Historic House.
Hours & Admission Prices: Tours: April-Nov. Wed. 10-4.

POWERS MUSEUM, INC., 1617 Oak St., Carthage, MO 64836. Mailing Address: P.O. Box 593, Carthage, MO 64836-0593. Tel.: 417-237-0456. Facebook: @PowersMuseumCurator.
E-mail: powersmuseum@att.net
Web Site: www.powersmuseum.com
Key Personnel: Pres. (V), Stephen Wagner.
Institution Type/Description: History Museum.
Hours & Admission Prices: April to Dec. with seasonal changes with days/hours. No charge, donations accepted. &
Attendance: 6,000 (actual)

Cassville

BARRY COUNTY MUSEUM, 15858 State Hwy. 76, Cassville, MO 65625. Mailing Address: P.O. Box 338, Cassville, MO 65625-0338. Tel.: 417-847-1640. Fax: 417-847-1641.
E-mail: info@barrycomuseum.com
Web Site: www.barrycomuseum.org
Institution Type/Description: History Museum.
Hours & Admission Prices: Mon.-Sat. 9-5. No charge. Closed most major holidays.

Centralia

CENTRALIA HISTORICAL SOCIETY MUSEUM, 319 E. Sneed St., Centralia, MO 65240-1341. Tel.: 573-682-5711.
E-mail: cenhis@centurylink.net
Key Personnel: Dir. & Chair (V), Marjorie Motley; Pres. (V) & Chair (V), Carolyn Dawson; Chair (V), Dorothy Davidson; Chair (V), Kay Overfelt.
Institution Type/Description: Historical Society Museum: housed in the former home of pharmacist, Robert Linwood Hope and his wife Belle Downing Hope; built in 1904.
Hours & Admission Prices: Wed. & Sun. 2-4. No charge; donations accepted.
Attendance: 1,000 (estimated)

Chaffee

CHAFFEE HISTORICAL SOCIETY, 109 S. Main, Chaffee, MO 63740. Tel.: 573-887-6225.
E-mail: chaffeehistorical@gmail.com
Web Site: www.chaffeehistory.com
Institution Type/Description: Historical Society Museum.
Hours & Admission Prices: Call for hours.

Chamois

TOWNLEY HOUSE MUSEUM, Third & Market Sts., Chamois, MO 65024. Mailing Address: P.O. Box 402, Linn, MO 65051-0402. Tel.: 573-897-2932.
E-mail: historic@osageconnect.net
Institution Type/Description: Historical House Museum: built in 1856. Listed on the National Register of Historic Places.
Hours & Admission Prices: By appointment.

Charleston

MISSISSIPPI COUNTY HISTORICAL SOCIETY, 403 N. Main, Charleston, MO 63834-1028. Mailing Address: P.O. Box 312, Charleston, MO 63834-0312. Tel.: 314-683-4348.
E-mail: misscohistoricalsociety@gmail.com
Web Site: www.misscohistoricalsociety.org
Key Personnel: Pres. (V), Tom Graham.
Institution Type/Description: General Museum.
Hours & Admission Prices: Tues. 1:30-3:30; other times by appointment only. Adults $3; members no charge.
Attendance: 2,000 (estimated)

Chesterfield

FAUST PARK FOUNDATION, 15189 Olive Blvd., Chesterfield, MO 63017-1805. Tel.: 314-615-8344 & 8345. TDD: 314-615-7840.
E-mail: toconnell@stlouisco.com
Web Site: www.stlouiscarousel.com
Formerly: Faust Cultural Heritage Foundation-The St. Louis Carousel
Key Personnel: Chm. (V), Robert Hoffman; Dir., Tonya O'Connell.
Institution Type/Description: General Museum.
Hours & Admission Prices: Exhibits: Tues.-Sun. 10-4. Carousel Ride: $2; children under one & members no charge. &
Attendance: 87,168 (actual)

FAUST PARK-THORNHILL HISTORIC SITE & FAUST HISTORIC VILLAGE, 15185 Olive Blvd., Chesterfield, MO 63017-1805. Tel.: 314-615-8328. Fax: 314-615-8325. Facebook: Faust Park.
E-mail: jfrancis@stlouisco.com
Web Site: www.stlouisco.com/parksandrecreation/parkpages/faust
Institution Type/Description: Historic House & Preservation Project.
Hours & Admission Prices: Thornhill Tours: see website for hours & admission prices. Historic Village: see website for hours. No charge; donations accepted. Carousel: Tues.-Sun. 10-4. Rides: $2 per person. &
Attendance: 425,000 (actual)

SOPHIA M. SACHS BUTTERFLY HOUSE, Faust Park, 15193 Olive Blvd., Chesterfield, MO 63017. Tel.: 636-530-0076. Fax: 636-530-1516.
E-mail: plantinformation@mobot.org
Web Site: www.butterflyhouse.org
Key Personnel: Dir., Victoria Campbell; Museum Shop Mgr., Angela Reitzell.
Institution Type/Description: Conservatory.
Hours & Admission Prices: Tues.-Sun. 10-4. Adults $6, seniors 65 & over $5, children 3-12 $4; members and children 2 & under no charge. Closed New Year's Day; Martin Luther King Jr. Day; Columbus Day; Thanksgiving; Christmas Eve & Day.

Chillicothe

THE GRAND RIVER HISTORICAL SOCIETY & MUSEUM, 1401 Forest Dr., Chillicothe, MO 64601. Mailing Address: P.O. Box 154, Chillicothe, MO 64601-0154. Tel.: 660-646-3430 & 4323.
E-mail: chillicothemuseum@gmail.com
Web Site: grandriverhistoricalsociety.com
Key Personnel: Dir. & Pres. (V), Marvin Holcer; Treas., Laura O'Donnell; Cur., Pamela Clingerman; Sec., Nancy Hoyt.
Institution Type/Description: Local History Museum.
Hours & Admission Prices: April-Oct. Sat.-Sun. 1-4; other times by appointment. No charge; donations accepted. &
Attendance: 2,000 (actual)

Clayton

HISTORIC HANLEY HOUSE, 7600 Westmoreland Ave., Clayton, MO 63105-3807. Mailing Address: The Center of Clayton, Parks Dept., 50 Gay Ave., Clayton, MO 63105. Tel.: 314-226-9893. Fax: 314-226-9326.
E-mail: sumlauf@claytonmo.gov
Web Site: www.claytonmo.gov/page388.aspx
Key Personnel: Community Resource Coord., Sarah Umlauf.
Institution Type/Description: Historic House.
Hours & Admission Prices: April-Oct. Sat.-Sun. 12-4; other times by appointment. Adults $5; children 6-12 $2; children 5 and under no charge. Closed Easter; Memorial Day weekend; Independence Day weekend; Labor Day weekend.
Attendance: 1,000 (estimated)

Clinton

DORMAN HOUSE, 302 W. Franklin St., Clinton, MO 64735-2011. Mailing Address: 203 W. Franklin, Clinton, MO 64735. Tel.: 660-885-8414.
E-mail: hcmusdir@gmail.com
Web Site: henrycountymomuseum.org
Key Personnel: Dir., Brenda Dehn; Pres. (V), Adele Bernard.
Institution Type/Description: Historic House Museum: housed in the former home of Judge J.G. Dorman; built in 1852. Listed on the National Register of Historic Places.
Hours & Admission Prices: Call for hours. Adults $3; members no charge.

HENRY COUNTY MUSEUM AND CULTURAL ARTS CENTER, 203 W. Franklin St., Clinton, MO 64735-2008. Tel.: 660-885-8414.
E-mail: hcmusdir@gmail.com
Web Site: henrycountymomuseum.org
Key Personnel: Dir., Brenda Dehn; Pres., Adele Bernard; Museum Shop Mgr., Sarah Campbell; Genealogy Library, Pat Waugh.
Institution Type/Description: Historical Museum: housed in 1886 restored Anheuser-Busch building. Listed on the National Register of Historic Places.
Hours & Admission Prices: April-Dec. Mon.-Sat. & special occasions 10-4. Adults $5, children 12 & under no charge. Closed Memorial Day; Independence Day; Labor Day; Thanksgiving; Christmas. &
Attendance: 2,300 (estimated)

Cole Camp

COLE CAMP MUSEUM, 108 S. Maple St., Cole Camp, MO 65325-1120. Mailing Address: P.O. Box 22, Cole Camp, MO 65325-0022. Tel.: 660-668-3037.
E-mail: museum@colecampmo.com
Web Site: colecampmo.com
Institution Type/Description: History Museum.
Hours & Admission Prices: Call for hours.

Columbia

DAVIS ART GALLERY, 1414 E. Walnut St., Columbia, MO 65201. Mailing Address: Campus Box 2012, Stephens College, Columbia, MO 65215. Tel.: 573-876-7255. Fax: 573-876-7248.
E-mail: dscott@stephens.edu
Web Site: www.stephens.edu
Key Personnel: Cur., Dan Scott.
Institution Type/Description: Art Gallery.
Hours & Admission Prices: Mon.-Fri. 10-3; other times by appointment. No charge; donations accepted. Closed school holidays. &
Attendance: 500 (estimated)

GEORGE CALEB BINGHAM GALLERY - UNIVERSITY OF MISSOURI, A126 Fine Arts Center, Dept. of Art, Columbia, MO 65211-6090. Tel.: 573-882-3555. Fax: 573-884-6807.
E-mail: hannahrreeves@gmail.com
Web Site: binghamgallery.missouri.edu
Key Personnel: Dir., Hannah Reeves.
Institution Type/Description: Art Gallery.
Hours & Admission Prices: Academic Year: Mon.-Fri. 8-5; Summer: Mon.-Fri. 7:30-4.

MASONIC MUSEUM, 6033 Masonic Dr., Ste. A, Columbia, MO 65202-6568. Tel.: 800-434-9804, 573-814-4663. Fax: 573-814-4660.
E-mail: bramsey@mohome.org & mphillippe@mohome.org

Web Site: www.mohome.org
Formerly: Masonic Home of Missouri
Key Personnel: Exec. Dir., Barbara Ramsey.
Institution Type/Description: History Museum.
Hours & Admission Prices: Mon.-Fri. 9-4:30. No charge; donations accepted. Closed major/state holidays. &
Attendance: 375 (actual)

MISSOURI HISTORIC COSTUME AND TEXTILE COLLECTION, 129 Stanley Hall, University of Missouri, Columbia, MO 65211. Tel.: 573-882-6457.
E-mail: johnstonnr@missouri.edu
Web Site: www.tam.missouri.edu/MHCTC/contacts.html
Key Personnel: Cur., Jean Parsons, Ph.D.
Institution Type/Description: Costume & Textile Museum.
Hours & Admission Prices: Call for hours.

MSA/GPC CRAFT STUDIO, N. 12 Memorial Union, Columbia, MO 65211. Tel.: 573-882-2889.
E-mail: craftstudio@missouri.edu
Formerly: Brady Gallery University of Missouri
Institution Type/Description: Art Gallery.
Hours & Admission Prices: Call for hours.

MUSEUM OF ANTHROPOLOGY, UNIVERSITY OF MISSOURI, 115 Business Loop 70 W., University of Missouri, Columbia, MO 65211. Tel.: 573-882-3573 & 3764. Facebook: Museum of Anthropology, Mizzou.
E-mail: anthromuseum@missouri.edu
Web Site: anthromuseum.missouri.edu
Key Personnel: Dir., Alex Barker; Assoc. Cur., Candace A. Sall; Asst. Cur., Jessica Boldt; Asst. Cur., Amanda J. Staley Harrison; Mgr. Collections, Audrey Gayou; Administrative Assoc., Carol Geisler.
Institution Type/Description: Anthropology Museum.
Hours & Admission Prices: Tues.-Fri. 9-4, Sat.-Sun. noon-4. Scheduled tours available. No charge; donations accepted. Closed university holidays. &
Attendance: 6,000 (actual)

MUSEUM OF ART AND ARCHAEOLOGY, UNIVERSITY OF MISSOURI, University Ave. & Ninth St., 1 Pickard Hall, Columbia, MO 65211. Tel.: 573-882-3591. Fax: 573-884-4039.
E-mail: museumuser@missouri.edu
Web Site: maa.missouri.edu
Key Personnel: Dir., Alex W. Barker, Ph.D.; Asst. Dir., Coord. Membership, Mktg. & Museum Shop Mgr., Bruce Cox; Pres. (V), Robin LaBrunerie; Assoc. Cur. European & American Art, Mary Pixley; Assoc. Cur. Ancient Art, J. Benton Kidd; Registrar, Jeff Wilcox; Chief Preparator, Barbara Smith; Preparator, Larry Stebbing; Dir. Missouri Folk Arts Program, Lisa Higgins; Specialist, Deborah Bailey; Assoc. Educator, Cathy Callaway.
Institution Type/Description: University Art Museum.
Hours & Admission Prices: Tues.-Wed. & Fri. 9-4, Thurs. 9-8, Sat.-Sun. 12-4. No charge; donations accepted. Closed national & university holidays; New Year's Eve & Day; Christmas Eve, Day & week. &
Attendance: 33,733 (actual)

ROGERS GALLERY - UNIVERSITY OF MISSOURI, 137 Stanley Hall, Columbia, MO 65211-6090. Tel.: 573-882-7224.
E-mail: sheajm@missouri.edu
Web Site: arch.missouri.edu/resources_rogersgallery.html
Institution Type/Description: Art Gallery.
Hours & Admission Prices: Call for hours.

STATE HISTORICAL SOCIETY OF MISSOURI, Administrative Office, 1020 Lowry St., Columbia, MO 65201-7298. Tel.: 573-882-7083. Fax: 573-884-4950. Facebook.
E-mail: contact@shsmo.org
Web Site: shsmo.org
Key Personnel: Exec. Dir., Gary R. Kremer; Museum Shop Mgr., Jeneva Pace.
Institution Type/Description: Art Museum.
Hours & Admission Prices: Society & Art Gallery: Tues.-Fri. 8:30-4:30, Sat. 8:30-3. No charge; donations accepted. Closed national holidays; holiday weekends. &
Attendance: 15,075 (actual)

WALTERS-BOONE COUNTY HISTORICAL MUSEUM, 3801 Ponderosa St., Columbia, MO 65201-5460. Tel.: 573-443-8936. Facebook: Boone County Museum Galleries.
E-mail: officemanager@bookhistory.org
Web Site: boonehistory.org

Formerly: Walters-Boone County Historical Museum and Visitors Center
Key Personnel: Dir., Chris Campbell; Pres. (V), Dick Otto; Office Mgr., Mary Lee Gentry.
Institution Type/Description: History Museum & Art Gallery.
Hours & Admission Prices: Thurs.-Sun. 12-4:30. Guided tours $5, general admission $3; members no charge. &
Attendance: 11,000 (estimated)

Concordia

CONCORDIA MUSEUM, 802 S. Gordon St., Concordia, MO 64020-9363. Mailing Address: P.O. Box 847, Concordia, MO 64020-9363. Tel.: 660-463-2105.
E-mail: concordiamuseum@yahoo.com
Key Personnel: Chm. (V), Donald Dittmer; Pres. (V), Deanna Rehmsmeyer; Museum Shop Mgr., Virginia Schnakenberg.
Institution Type/Description: History Museum.
Hours & Admission Prices: Feb.-Oct. by appointment. No charge; donations accepted. &
Attendance: 180 (estimated)

Crestwood

SAPPINGTON HOUSE MUSEUM, 1015 S. Sappington Rd., Crestwood, MO 63126-1004. Tel.: 314-822-8171 (museum) & 9469 (library). Fax: 314-729-4794.
E-mail: cab9042@yahoo.com
Key Personnel: Library Chm., Carol Bell; Chm. (V), Enid Barnes; Pres. (V), Kathy Saur; Museum Shop Mgr., Marilyn Fleming.
Institution Type/Description: Historic House: Thomas Sappington House, 1808 Federal architecture.
Hours & Admission Prices: Feb.-Dec. Wed.-Fri. 11-2, Sat. by appointment; last tour at 1:45. Adults $3, children 6-12 $1; members, school groups & scouts with prior reservations no charge. Closed New Year's Eve & Day; Good Friday & day after; Memorial Day weekend; Independence Day; Labor Day weekend; Thanksgiving Eve & Day; Christmas Eve & Day; Sat. preceding holidays.
Attendance: 1,250 (estimated)

Cuba

CRAWFORD COUNTY HISTORICAL SOCIETY & MUSEUM, 308 N. Smith St., Cuba, MO 65453-1166. Tel.: 573-885-6099.
E-mail: info@crawfordmomuseum.com
Web Site: www.crawfordmomuseum.org
Institution Type/Description: Historical Society Museum.
Hours & Admission Prices: Tues.-Sat. 10-3, Sun. 12-3; tours by appointment. No charge; donations accepted.

Davisville

DILLARD MILL STATE HISTORIC SITE, 142 Dillard Mill Rd., Davisville, MO 65456-4014. Tel.: 573-244-3120.
E-mail: dillard.mill.state.historic.site@dnr.mo.gov
Web Site: www.mostateparks.com/dillardmill.htm
Institution Type/Description: Historic Site.
Hours & Admission Prices: March-Nov. Mon.-Sat. 10-4, Sun. 12-5; Dec.-Feb. Thurs.-Sat. 10-4, Sun. 12-4.
Attendance: 29,000 (actual)

Defiance

DANIEL BOONE HOME AND BOONESFIELD VILLAGE, LINDENWOOD UNIVERSITY, 1868 Highway F, Defiance, MO 63341-1908. Tel.: 636-798-2005 & 2903. Fax: 636-798-2914.
E-mail: boonehome@lindenwood.edu
Web Site: www.lindenwood.edu/boone
Key Personnel: Dir. Operations, Pam Jensen.
Institution Type/Description: Historic House: 1803-1810 designed & built by Daniel Boone and patterned after his father's home in Pennsylvania. Historic village era 1801-1850; guided tour.
Hours & Admission Prices: June-Sept. daily 8:30-6; Oct.-May daily 8:30-5. Tours: 9:30-4. Boone Home: adults $7, senior citizens 55+ $6, children 4-11 $4; children 3 & under no charge. Boone Home & Boonesfield Village: adults $12, senior citizens $10, children 4-11 $6, children 3 & under no charge. Closed New Year's Day; Easter; Thanksgiving; Christmas Eve & Day. &
Attendance: 50,000 (actual)

Diamond

GEORGE WASHINGTON CARVER NATIONAL MONUMENT, 5646 Carver Rd., Diamond, MO 64840-8314. Tel.: 417-325-4151. Fax: 417-325-4231. Facebook: George Washington Carver National Monument; Twitter: @gwcarternps.
E-mail: gwca_interpretation@nps.gov
Web Site: www.nps.gov/gwca
Key Personnel: Supt., James Heaney.
Institution Type/Description: National Monument.
Hours & Admission Prices: Daily 9-5. No charge; donations accepted. Closed New Year's Day; Thanksgiving; Christmas. &
Attendance: 30,000 (estimated)

WORLD'S LARGEST SMALL ELECTRIC APPLIANCE MUSEUM, 51 Hwy. 59, Diamond, MO 64840. Tel.: 417-793-7936.
E-mail: toastghost1@yahoo.com
Web Site: smallelectricappliancemuseum.com
Key Personnel: Dir., C.EO. & Museum Shop Mgr., Richard Larison.
Institution Type/Description: Appliance Museum.
Hours & Admission Prices: Mon.-Sat. 9-6, Sun. 11-6; other times by appointment. No charge; donations accepted. &
Attendance: 200 (estimated)

Doniphan

CURRENT RIVER HERITAGE MUSEUM, 101 Washington St., Doniphan, MO 63935. Tel.: 573-996-5298.
E-mail: lynnmaples@doniphanmissouri.org
Web Site: www.doniphanmissouri.org
Institution Type/Description: History Museum.
Hours & Admission Prices: Mon.-Fri. 9-4, Sat. 9-12. Closed holidays.

Eagle Rock

PROMISED LAND ZOO, 32297 Hwy. 86, Eagle Rock, MO 65641-7108. Tel.: 417-271-3324. Fax: 417-271-3012.
E-mail: plzoo1@yahoo.com
Web Site: www.plzoo.com
Institution Type/Description: Zoo.
Hours & Admission Prices: Daily 9-7. Adults $14.95, children 2-12 and seniors 65 & over $9.95; foster families with ID no charge. &
Attendance: 15,000 (estimated)

East Prairie

TOWOSAHGY STATE HISTORIC SITE, East Prairie, MO 63845. Mailing Address: c/o Hunter-Dawson State Historic Site, P. O. Box 308, New Madrid, MO 63869-0308. Tel.: 573-748-5340.
E-mail: moparks@dnr.mo.gov
Web Site: www.mostateparks.com/towosahgy.htm
Institution Type/Description: Archaeological Site.
Hours & Admission Prices: Call for hours. No charge.

Edina

KNOX COUNTY HISTORICAL SOCIETY MUSEUM, Court House, 107 N. 4th St., Edina, MO 63537. Mailing Address: 309 E. Marion, P.O. Box 75, Edina, MO 63537-1248. Tel.: 660-397-2349. Fax: 660-397-3331.
E-mail: zsummers@knoxr1.us
Institution Type/Description: Local History Museum.
Hours & Admission Prices: By appointment. No charge; donations accepted. Closed legal holidays. &

Excelsior Springs

EXCELSIOR SPRINGS MUSEUM & ARCHIVES, 101 E. Broadway, Excelsior Springs, MO 64024-2513. Mailing Address: P.O. Box 144, Excelsior Springs, MO 64024-0144. Tel.: 816-630-0101. Facebook.
E-mail: emuseum101@hotmail.com
Web Site: www.exsmo.com/museum
Formerly: Excelsior Springs Historical Museum
Key Personnel: Dir. Treas. & Bd. Member, Deb Foster; Pres. (V) & Cur., Dennis Heine; Dir., Kathy Duncan.
Institution Type/Description: History Museum.

Hours & Admission Prices: Tues.-Sat. 11-4; other times by appointment. Adults $3; children under 5 & members no charge. Closed New Year's Day; Memorial Day; Independence Day; Thanksgiving; Christmas. &
Attendance: 2,000 (actual)

Fayette

THE ASHBY-HODGE GALLERY OF AMERICAN ART, CENTRAL METHODIST UNIVERSITY, 411 Central Methodist Square, Fayette, MO 65248-0009. Tel.: 660-248-6324 & 6304 (office). Fax: 660-248-2622.
E-mail: dgebhard@centralmethodist.edu
Web Site: www.centralmethodist.edu
Key Personnel: Registrar, Joseph E. Geist, Ph.D.; Chief Docent, Pat Hilgedick.
Institution Type/Description: Art Museum.
Hours & Admission Prices: Tues.-Thurs. 1:30-4:30; Special Exhibits: Sun. 1:30-4:30; groups by special arrangement. No charge; donations accepted. &
Attendance: 5,000 (actual)

THE STEPHENS MUSEUM, Central Methodist University, T. Berry Smith Hall, Fayette, MO 65248. Tel.: 660-248-6678 (office) & 6334 (museum). Fax: 660-248-2622.
E-mail: dlmorris@centralmethodist.edu
Web Site: centralmethodist.edu/about/museum.php
Key Personnel: Dir., Dana L. Morris, Ph.D.
Institution Type/Description: College Museum: housed in 1896 Romanesque educational building, T. Berry Smith Hall.
Hours & Admission Prices: Academic Year: Tues.-Thurs. 1-4; other times by appointment. Closed college vacations. No charge; donations accepted.
Attendance: 1,000 (estimated)

Fenton

FENTON HISTORY MUSEUM, 1 Church St., Fenton, MO 63026. Tel.: 636-326-0808.
E-mail: fentonhistory@hotmail.com
Web Site: www.fentonhistory.com
Institution Type/Description: Historical Society Museum: housed in the former home of Frank M. Swantner; built in 1906.
Hours & Admission Prices: 2nd & last Sat. each month 12-3; other times by appointment.

Florida

MARK TWAIN BIRTHPLACE STATE HISTORIC SITE, 37352 Shrine Rd., Florida, MO 65283-2127. Tel.: 573-565-3449. Fax: 573-565-3718.
E-mail: mark.twain.birthplace.state.historic.site@dnr.mo.gov
Web Site: www.mostateparks.com
Key Personnel: Facility Mgr., Kevin Bolling.
Institution Type/Description: Historic House: 1835 Samuel L. Clemens birthplace.
Hours & Admission Prices: April-Oct. daily 10-5; Nov.-March Fri.-Sun. 10-4. No charge; donations accepted. Closed New Year's Day; Thanksgiving; Christmas. &
Attendance: 25,251 (actual)

Florissant

FLORISSANT VALLEY HISTORICAL SOCIETY, 1896 S. Florissant Rd., Florissant, MO 63031. Mailing Address: P.O. Box 298, Florissant, MO 63032-0298. Tel.: 314-524-1100, 838-4536 & 921-5563.
E-mail: fredmary2@aol.com
Key Personnel: Pres., Joseph McDavid; Sec., Mary Kay Gladbach.
Institution Type/Description: Historic House: 1790 Taille de Noyer log cabin; house enlarged to include 3 floors.
Hours & Admission Prices: March-Dec. Sun. 1-4; group tours by appointment. Adults $3, children $1. Closed New Year's Day; Thanksgiving; Christmas.
Attendance: 2,500 (estimated)

FRIENDS OF OLD ST. FERDINAND, Friends of Old St. Ferdinand, Inc., One Rue St. Francois, Florissant, MO 63031. Tel.: 314-837-2110.
E-mail: oldstferdinandshrine@gmail.com
Web Site: www.oldstferdinandshrine.com
Formerly: Old St. Ferdinand's Shrine
Key Personnel: Pres., Douglas Riser; Sec. & Membership Chm., Geri Debo.
Institution Type/Description: History Museum: housed in historic site of church complex & community center from 1789-1957.

Hours & Admission Prices: April-Nov. Sat. 9am to noon, Sun. 1-4; Dec.-March Sat. 9am to noon; other times by appointment. Tours: $3. Closed New Year's Day; Easter; Independence Day; Thanksgiving; Christmas. &
Attendance: 15,000 (estimated)

Fort Leonard Wood

U.S. ARMY CHEMICAL CORPS MUSEUM, 495 S. Dakota Ave., Bldg. 1607, Fort Leonard Wood, MO 65473-8851. Tel.: 573-596-4221.
E-mail: usarmy.leonardwood.chemical-schl.mbx.museum@mail.mil
Web Site: www.wood.army.mil/ccmuseum/ccmuseum/
Key Personnel: Museum Specialist, Cynthia L. Riley.
Institution Type/Description: Military Museum.
Hours & Admission Prices: Mon.-Fri. 8-4, Sat. 10-4. Closed Federal holidays.

U.S. ARMY ENGINEER MUSEUM, 495 S. Dakota Ave., Bldg. 1607, Fort Leonard Wood, MO 65473-5165. Tel.: 573-596-0780.
E-mail: usarmy.leonardwood.engineer-schl.mbx.hqrfi@mail.mil
Web Site: www.wood.army.mil/museum
Key Personnel: Dir., Frank McGrane; Museum Shop Mgr., Glenn A. Stines.
Institution Type/Description: Military History & Engineer Museum: including a restored WWII company compound consisting of 14 buildings on 50-acre site.
Hours & Admission Prices: Mon.-Fri. 8-4, Sat. 10-4. No charge. Closed federal holidays. &
Attendance: 150,000 (estimated)

U.S. ARMY MILITARY POLICE CORPS MUSEUM, 14296 S. Dakota Ave., Bldg. 1607, Fort Leonard Wood, MO 65473-8851. Tel.: 573-596-0604. Fax: 573-596-0603.
E-mail: leon.usampsmuseum@conus.army.mil
Web Site: www.wood.army.mil/usamps/organizations/dpo/museum.html
Formerly: Military Police Corps Regimental Museum
Key Personnel: Dir. & Cur., Jim Rogers.
Institution Type/Description: Military Museum.
Hours & Admission Prices: Mon.-Fri. 8-4, Sat. 10-4. No charge; donations accepted. Closed holidays. &
Attendance: 58,000 (actual)

Fortescue

HOLT COUNTY HISTORICAL SOCIETY, 115 Ada St., Fortescue, MO 64437. Mailing Address: P.O. Box 55, Mount City, MO 64470-0055. Tel.: 660-442-5949.
E-mail: lizb@embarqmail.com
Institution Type/Description: Historical Society Museum: housed in a former Methodist Church.
Hours & Admission Prices: Call for hours.

Fredericktown

HISTORIC MADISON COUNTY MUSEUM, 122 N. Main St., Fredericktown, MO 63645. Tel.: 573-783-4085. Facebook.
E-mail: raskaggs_2000@yahoo.com
Key Personnel: Dir., Terry Wernecker; Chm. (V), Gary Lee.
Institution Type/Description: Historical Society Museum.
Hours & Admission Prices: Tues. 1-4. No charge; donations accepted.
Attendance: 1,500 (estimated)

Fulton

AUTO WORLD MUSEUM, 200 Peacock Dr., Fulton, MO 65251. Mailing Address: P.O. Box 128, Fulton, MO 65251-0128. Tel.: 573-642-2080.
E-mail: staff@autoworldmuseum.com
Web Site: autoworldmuseum.com
Institution Type/Description: Automobile Museum.
Hours & Admission Prices: April-Dec. daily 9-5; other times by appointment. Adults $8, seniors $7, children under 13 $5.

KINGDOM OF CALLAWAY HISTORICAL SOCIETY, 513 Court St., Fulton, MO 65251-1901. Mailing Address: P.O. Box 6073, Fulton, MO 65251-6073. Tel.: 573-642-0570.
E-mail: museum@kchsoc.org
Web Site: kchsoc.org
Institution Type/Description: Historical Society Museum.
Hours & Admission Prices: Tues.-Fri. 10-4. No charge; donations accepted.

NATIONAL CHURCHILL MUSEUM, Westminster College, 501 Westminster Ave., Fulton, MO 65251-1299. Tel.: 573-592-5233. Fax: 573-592-5222.
E-mail: jim.williams@westminster-mo.edu
Web Site: www.nationalchurchillmuseum.org
Formerly: Winston Churchill Memorial and Library
Key Personnel: Exec. Dir., James H. Williams, Ph.D.; Mgr. Operations, Meda Young.
Institution Type/Description: Historic Building: relocated & reconstructed Church of St. Mary the Virgin, Aldermanbury designed by Christopher Wren (original site: London, England). Historic Site: site on which Sir Winston Churchill delivered the Sinews of Peace Speech March 5, 1946.
Hours & Admission Prices: Daily 10-4:30. Adults $7.50, senior citizens 65 & up and active military $6.50, youth 12-18 & college students $5.50, children 6-11 $4.50; discounts to AAM & AAA members; members, Westminster College Students, Calloway County Schools and children 5 & under no charge. Closed New Year's Day; Thanksgiving; Christmas. &
Attendance: 25,000

Glasgow

GLASGOW MUSEUM, 381 County Rd. 220, Glasgow, MO 65254-9755. Mailing Address: 100 Market St., City Hall, Glasgow, MO 65254. Tel.: 660-338-9949.
E-mail: clerk@glasgowmo.org
Web Site: www.glasgowmo.com/aboutus_2.html
Institution Type/Description: History Museum: housed in a Presbyterian Church.
Hours & Admission Prices: Mid-May to mid-Oct. call for hours. No charge.
Attendance: 300 (estimated)

Glencoe

WABASH FRISCO AND PACIFIC ASSOCIATION, INC. - THE UNCOMMON CARRIER/MERAMEC RIVER - PALISADES ROUTE, 199 Grand Ave., Glencoe, MO 63038. Mailing Address: 1569 Ville Angela Lane, Hazelwood, MO 63042-1630. Tel.: 636-587-3538. Facebook: WFPRR.
Web Site: www.wfprr.com
Key Personnel: Pres., Stephen F. Marx; Treas., Michael E. Lorance; Sec., Dale A. Bitsch.
Institution Type/Description: Mini-Steam Tourist Railway Museum: located on the site of the original mainline right of way of the Pacific Railroad; building began westward from St. Louis, MO in 1852.
Hours & Admission Prices: May-Oct. Sun. 11-4:15. Trains depart every 20 minutes. Admission: $4 per person; discount to groups; members & children under 3 no charge.
Attendance: 14,000 (estimated)

Goldman

SANDY CREEK COVERED BRIDGE STATE HISTORIC SITE, Old Lemay Ferry Rd., Goldman, MO 63050. Mailing Address: 1050 Charles J. Becker Dr., Imperial, MO 63052-3524. Tel.: 636-464-2976. Fax: 636-464-3768.
E-mail: moparks@dnr.mo.gov
Web Site: www.mostateparks.com
Key Personnel: DSP Dir., Bill Bryan; District Supvr., Brian Stith.
Institution Type/Description: Listed on the National of Historic Places: 1872 covered bridge.
Hours & Admission Prices: Daily 8 am to half hour past sunset. No charge. &
Attendance: 110,000 (actual)

Grandview

HARRY S TRUMAN NATIONAL HISTORIC SITE - TRUMAN FARM HOME, 12301 Blue Ridge Blvd., Grandview, MO 64030-1159. Mailing Address: 223 N. Main St., Independence, MO 64050-2804. Tel.: 816-254-2720 & 9929. Fax: 816-254-4491. Facebook: Harry S Truman National Historic Site.
E-mail: carol_dage@nps.gov
Web Site: www.nps.gov/hstr/
Key Personnel: Supt., Carol Dage; Cur., Kristen Stalling.
Institution Type/Description: Historic House Museum: 1906-1917 home of former President Harry S Truman; farm which he operated with his family.
Hours & Admission Prices: Daily, year-round for self-guided tours of grounds. &
Attendance: 4,992 (actual)

Gray Summit

SHAW NATURE RESERVE, Hwy. 100 & I-44, Gray Summit, MO 63039. Mailing Address: P.O. Box 38, Gray Summit, MO 63039. Tel.: 636-451-3512.
E-mail: plantinformation@mobot.org
Web Site: www.missouribotanicalgarden.org
Institution Type/Description: Nature Reserve.
Hours & Admission Prices: Reserve: daily 7am to sunset. Visitor Center: Mon.-Fri. 8-4:30, Sat.-Sun. 9-5. Bascom House: daily 10-4. Adults $5, students and seniors 65 & over $3; members and children 12 & under no charge. Additional charge for some events.

Greenfield

DADE COUNTY HISTORICAL SOCIETY MUSEUM, 429 W. Water St., Greenfield, MO 65661. Tel.: 417-637-0258.
Web Site: dadecountymohistoricalsociety.com
Institution Type/Description: History Museum.
Hours & Admission Prices: By appointment.

Hamilton

J.C. PENNEY MUSEUM AND BOYHOOD HOME, 312 N. Davis St., Hamilton, MO 64644-1145. Tel.: 816-583-2168. Fax: 816-583-4929.
Key Personnel: Chm. (V) & Pres. (V), Dean Hales.
Institution Type/Description: Historic House and Museum: former boyhood home of the entrepreneur J.C. Penney.
Hours & Admission Prices: Call for hours. No charge; donations accepted.
Attendance: 1,000 (estimated)

Hannibal

MARK TWAIN BOYHOOD HOME & MUSEUM, 120 N. Main St., Hannibal, MO 63401-3537. Tel.: 573-221-9010. Fax: 573-221-7975. Facebook: Mark Twain Boyhood Home & Museum.
E-mail: henry.sweets@marktwainmuseum.org
Web Site: marktwainmuseum.org
Key Personnel: Exec. Dir., Henry H. Sweets, III; Pres. (V), Mike McKay; Finance & Gift Shop Mgr., Dena Ellis; Mktg. & Rels. Mgr., Melissa Cummins.
Institution Type/Description: Historic House: 1844 Mark Twain's boyhood home.
Hours & Admission Prices: Daily 9-5. Adults $11, seniors $9, children 6-17 $6; children 5 & under, members and Hannibal residents no charge. Closed New Year's Day; Easter; Thanksgiving; Christmas Eve & Day. &
Attendance: 50,000 (actual)

MOLLY BROWN BIRTHPLACE & MUSEUM, Hannibal Convention & Visitors Center, 505 N. Third St., Hannibal, MO 63401-3303. Tel.: 573-221-2477.
E-mail: vguide@visithannibal.com
Web Site: VisitMollyBrown.com
Institution Type/Description: History Museum.
Hours & Admission Prices: May Sat.-Sun. 10-4; Memorial Day to Labor Day daily 10-4. Adults $4, children $3; discounts to groups of 10 or more.

ROCKCLIFFE MANSION, 1000 Bird St., Hannibal, MO 63401-3436. Tel.: 573-221-4140.
E-mail: info@rockcliffemansion.com
Web Site: www.rockcliffemansion.com
Institution Type/Description: Historic House.
Hours & Admission Prices: mid-March to mid-Nov. daily 10-4; first tour begins at 10am & last tour begins at 4pm. Adults $15.

Harrisonville

BURNT DISTRICT MUSEUM & ARCHIVES, 400 E. Mechanic, Ste. 203, Harrisonville, MO 64701. Tel.: 816-380-4396.
E-mail: cchsmo@gmail.com
Institution Type/Description: History Museum.
Hours & Admission Prices: Mon.-Fri. 10-3:30; other times by appointment. No charge; donations accepted.
Attendance: 1,000 (estimated)

Hermann

DEUTSCHHEIM STATE HISTORIC SITE, 109 W. Second St., Hermann, MO 65041-1045. Tel.: 573-486-2200. Fax: 573-486-2249.

E-mail: deutschheim.state.historic.site@dnr.mo.gov
Web Site: www.mostateparks.com/deutschheim.htm
Key Personnel: Dir., Site Admin. & Museum Shop Mgr., Cynthia Browne.
Institution Type/Description: German Heritage Museum.
Hours & Admission Prices: Visitor Center: April-Oct. daily 10-4; Nov.-March Thurs.-Sun. 10-4. Tours: 10, 12:30 & 2:30. Adults $4, students $2.50, children 6-12 $1.50. Closed New Year's Day; Easter; Thanksgiving; Christmas.
Attendance: 6,000 (estimated)

HISTORIC HERMANN INC. - MUSEUM AT THE GERMAN SCHOOL, 312 Schiller St., Hermann, MO 65041-1154. Mailing Address: P.O. Box 105, Hermann, MO 65041-0105. Tel.: 573-486-2017.

E-mail: joyandcarol@centurytel.net
Web Site: www.historichermann.com
Key Personnel: Pres. (V), Steve Mueller; Sec., Carol Kallmeyer; Treas., Elaine Lalk.
Institution Type/Description: Historic Museum: housed in 1871 German school building.
Hours & Admission Prices: April-Oct. Thurs.-Tues. 10-4, Sun. 12-4. Adults $5, children 6-18 $3; discount to groups; members & children under 6 no charge.
Attendance: 5,000 (actual)

WHITE HOUSE HOTEL 1868, 232 Wharf St., Hermann, MO 65041. Tel.: 573-486-3200. Facebook: White House Hotel 1868 - A Living History Museum.

E-mail: vickie@whitehousehotel1868.com
Web Site: www.whitehousehotel1868.com
Institution Type/Description: Living History Museum: housed in a former hotel; built in 1868.
Hours & Admission Prices: Call for hours. Adults $10.

Hermitage

JOHN SIDDLES WILLIAMS HOUSE - HICKORY COUNTY HISTORICAL SOCIETY, Museum St., Hermitage, MO 65668. Mailing Address: P.O. Box 248, Hermitage, MO 65668. Tel.: 417-722-4403.

E-mail: shullhe@gmail.com
Web Site: mogenweb.org/hickory/album/hchs.htm
Key Personnel: Pres. (V), Mackey E. Snyder.
Institution Type/Description: Historical Society Museum: listed on the National Register of Historic Places.
Hours & Admission Prices: By appointment. No charge; donations accepted.
Attendance: 120 (estimated)

Higginsville

CONFEDERATE MEMORIAL STATE HISTORIC SITE, 211 W. First St., Higginsville, MO 64037-8158. Tel.: 660-584-2853. Fax: 660-584-5134.

E-mail: confederate.memorial.state.historic.site@dnr.mo.gov
Web Site: www.mostateparks.com
Formerly: Confederate Home of Missouri
Key Personnel: Site Admin., Janae Fuller.
Institution Type/Description: Historic Site: Chapel, cemetery, family cottage & park are remnants of the Confederate Home of Missouri; opened in 1891.
Hours & Admission Prices: Tours: Thurs.-Sat. 9-4, Sun. 12-5. No charge; donations accepted.
Attendance: 90,000 (estimated)

HARVEY J. HIGGINS HISTORICAL SOCIETY, 2113 S. Main St., Higginsville, MO 64037. Mailing Address: 810 Lipper Ave., Higginsville, MO 64037. Tel.: 660-584-6474 & 3232. Facebook.

E-mail: tourism@ded.mo.gov
Web Site: www.visitmo.com
Key Personnel: Dir., C.E.O. & Museum Shop Mgr., Mrs. Loberta Runge; Pres. (V), Julie Martens.
Institution Type/Description: Historical Society Museum: housed the former Higginsville Depot; built in 1889. Listed on the National Register of Historic Places.
Hours & Admission Prices: May-Oct. Wed.-Fri. 9am to noon; other times by appointment. No charge; donations accepted.
Attendance: 100 (estimated)

Imperial

MASTODON STATE HISTORIC SITE, 1050 Charles J. Becker Dr., Imperial, MO 63052-3524. Tel.: 636-464-2976. Fax: 636-464-3768.

E-mail: mastodon.state.historic.site@dnr.mo.gov
Web Site: www.mostateparks.com
Key Personnel: Site Admin., Ken Smith.
Institution Type/Description: History Museum & Historic Site: listed on the National Register of Historic Places.
Hours & Admission Prices: Site: daily 8am to sunset. Museum: March 15-Nov. 14 Mon.-Sat. 9-4:30, Sun. 12-4:30; Nov. 15-March 14 Mon. & Fri.-Sat. 11-4, Sun. 12-4. Adults $4; discounts to groups of 15 or more. Closed New Year's Day; Easter; Thanksgiving; Christmas.
Attendance: 22,898 (actual)

Independence

THE BINGHAM-WAGGONER ESTATE, 313 W. Pacific, Independence, MO 64051. Mailing Address: P.O. Box 1163, Independence, MO 64051-0663. Tel.: 816-461-3491. Fax: 816-461-1540.

E-mail: bwestate@att.net
Web Site: www.bwestate.org
Key Personnel: Dir., Shireen McLaughlin; Pres. (V), Steve Schreiber; Museum Shop Mgr., Linda Parvin.
Institution Type/Description: Historic House: former home of Missouri Civil War artist George Caleb Bingham.
Hours & Admission Prices: April-Oct. Mon.-Sat. 10-4, Sun. 1-4. Adults $6, senior citizens $5, children & students $3; members no charge.
Attendance: 3,000 (estimated)

CHICAGO & ALTON RAILROAD DEPOT, 318 W. Pacific Ave., Independence, MO 64050. Tel.: 816-325-7955.

E-mail: info@chicagoalton1879depot.org
Web Site: chicagoalton1879depot.org
Key Personnel: Pres. (V), John S. Thornton.
Institution Type/Description: Historic Building: housed in a restored railroad depot; built in 1879.
Hours & Admission Prices: April-Oct. Sun. 12:30-4:30, Mon. & Thurs.-Sat. 9:30-4:30. No charge; donations accepted.
Attendance: 1,905 (actual)

CHILDREN'S PEACE PAVILION, 1001 W. Walnut, Independence, MO 64050-3562. Tel.: 816-521-3033. Facebook: Children's Peace Pavilion.

E-mail: kidpeace@kidpeace.org
Web Site: www.kidpeace.org
Key Personnel: Dir., Barbara Harmon.
Institution Type/Description: Children's Museum.
Hours & Admission Prices: Wed. & Fri.; other times by appointment. Call for seasonal hours. No charge; donations accepted. Closed holidays.
Attendance: 3,000 (estimated)

COMMUNITY OF CHRIST, The Temple, 1001 W. Walnut, Independence, MO 64050-3562. Tel.: 816-833-1000, ext. 2030. Fax: 816-521-3089.

E-mail: cloving@cofchrist.org
Web Site: www.cofchrist.org
Formerly: Reorganized Church of Jesus Christ of Latter Day Saints
Key Personnel: Admin. Asst., Joy Goodwin.
Institution Type/Description: Religious History Museum.
Hours & Admission Prices: April-Oct. Mon.-Sat. 9-12 & 1:30-4:30, Sun. 1:30-4:30; Nov.-March Mon.-Fri. 9-12 & 1:30-4:30, Sat. 10-12 & 1:30-4:30. Prayer for Peace: daily 1pm. No charge.
Attendance: 12,000 (actual)

1859 JAIL, MARSHAL'S HOME & MUSEUM, 217 N. Main St., Independence, MO 64050-2804. Mailing Address: Jackson County Historical Society, P.O. Box 4241, Independence, MO 64051-4241. Tel.: 816-252-1892.

E-mail: info@jchs.org
Web Site: www.jchs.org
Key Personnel: Exec. Dir., Steve Noll; C.E.O., Brad Pace; Pres. (V), Ben Mann.
Institution Type/Description: History Museum: adjoining 1859 restored Jackson County Jail and federal style Marshal's House & office.
Hours & Admission Prices: April-Oct. Mon.-Sat. 10-4, Sun. 1-4. Adults $6, senior citizens 55 & over $5, children 5-15 $3; children under 5 & members no charge. Closed New Year's Day; Thanksgiving; Christmas.
Attendance: 11,000 (actual)

HARRY S TRUMAN NATIONAL HISTORIC SITE - TRUMAN HOME, 223 N. Main St., Independence, MO 64050-2804. Tel.: 816-254-2720 & 9929. Fax: 816-254-4491. Facebook.

E-mail: carol_dage@nps.gov

Web Site: www.nps.gov/hstr/.
Key Personnel: Supt., Carol Dage; Cur., Kristen Stalling.
Institution Type/Description: National Historic Site & Building: former home of President Harry S Truman.
Hours & Admission Prices: Visitor Center: daily 8:30-5. Truman House Tours: Memorial Day to Oct. daily 9-4:30; Nov.-May Tues.-Sun. 9-4:30. Adults 16 & over $5; children 15 & under no charge. Closed New Year's Day; Thanksgiving; Christmas. &
Attendance: 36,953 (actual)

HARRY S. TRUMAN OFFICE & COURTROOM, 112 W. Lexington Ave., Independence, MO 64050. Mailing Address: Jackson County Historical Society, P.O. Box 4241, Independence, MO 64051-4241. Tel.: 816-252-7454.
E-mail: info@jchs.org
Web Site: jchs.org
Key Personnel: Dir. Parks & Recreation, Gary Salva; Supt. Heritage Programs & Museums, Gordon Julich.
Institution Type/Description: Historic Site Museum: Harry S. Truman's office, 1934; courtroom used by Truman during 2nd term as Presiding Judge of County Court.
Hours & Admission Prices: Tours: Mon.-Sat. 11am & 2pm. No charge. &
Attendance: 886 (actual)

HARRY S. TRUMAN PRESIDENTIAL LIBRARY & MUSEUM, 500 West U.S. Hwy. 24, Independence, MO 64050-1798. Tel.: 816-268-8200, 800-833-1225. Fax: 816-268-8295.
E-mail: truman.library@nara.gov
Web Site: www.trumanlibrary.org
Key Personnel: Dir., Kurt Graham; Deputy Dir., Amy Williams; Public Programs Officer, Jennifer Vitela.
Institution Type/Description: Presidential Library.
Hours & Admission Prices: Mon.-Sat. 9-5, Sun. 12-5. Adults $8, senior citizens 65 & up $7, children 6-15 $3; bus groups of 15 or more with reservation $5.75; discounts to active & retired military and AAM members; Honorary Fellows and children 5 & under no charge. Closed New Year's Day; Thanksgiving; Christmas. &
Attendance: 90,000 (actual)

JACKSON COUNTY HISTORICAL SOCIETY, 112 W. Lexington Ave., Independence, MO 64051-4241. Mailing Address: P.O. Box 4241, Independence, MO 64051-4241. Tel.: 816-461-1897.
E-mail: info@jchs.org
Web Site: www.jchs.org
Institution Type/Description: Historical Society Museum.
Hours & Admission Prices: Call for hours.

LEILA'S HAIR MUSEUM, 1333 S. Noland Rd., Independence, MO 64055-1303. Tel.: 816-833-2955.
E-mail: lcohoon@aol.com
Web Site: www.hairwork.com/leila
Key Personnel: Dir., C.E.O. & Museum Shop Mgr., Leila Cohoon.
Institution Type/Description: Art Museum.
Hours & Admission Prices: Tues.-Sat. 9-4. Adults $15; senior citizens over 65 & children under 12 $7.50. Closed major holidays. &
Attendance: 2,000 (estimated)

MORMON VISITORS CENTER, 937 W. Walnut St., Independence, MO 64050-3646. Tel.: 816-836-3466. Fax: 816-252-6256.
E-mail: vcindepend@ldschurch.org
Web Site: www.ldschurch.org
Formerly: Independence Visitors Center
Key Personnel: Dir., Elder John M. Toronto.
Institution Type/Description: Religious History Museum.
Hours & Admission Prices: Daily 9-9. No charge. &
Attendance: 38,000 (actual)

NATIONAL FRONTIER TRAILS MUSEUM, 318 W. Pacific, Independence, MO 64050-4372. Tel.: 816-325-7575. Fax: 816-325-7579.
E-mail: nftminfo@indepmo.org
Web Site: frontiertrailsmuseum.org
Key Personnel: Admin., David Aamodt; Museum Oper. Mgr., Debbie Stewart; Education & Events Mgr., Richard Edwards.
Institution Type/Description: History Museum: Site is the location of an 1840s grist mill and public spring. The wagon caravans leaving from Independence in the 1840s used the spring on the property for water before starting out for Oregon, California or Santa Fe. Designated a Category 1 Interpretive Site for the Lewis

and Clark National Historic Trail, Oregon National Historic Trail, California National Historic Trail, Mormon Pioneer National Historic Trail & the Santa Fe National Historic Trail.
Hours & Admission Prices: Mon.-Sat. 9-4:30, Sun. 12:30-4:30. Adults $6, senior citizens $5, youth 6-17 $3; discounts to groups & tours; Friends of the National Frontier Trails Museum, Oregon-California Trails Assoc., Santa Fe Trail Assoc. members, children under 5 & members no charge. Closed New Year's Day; Thanksgiving; Christmas. &
Attendance: 17,000 (actual)

VAILE MANSION-DEWITT MANSION, 1500 N. Liberty, Independence, MO 64050-1821. Mailing Address: 112 W. Lexington, Independence, MO 64050. Tel.: 816-325-7111.
E-mail: rsheridan@indepmo.org
Web Site: www.visitindependence.com
Key Personnel: C.E.O. & Pres. (V), Jean Kimball.
Institution Type/Description: Historic House: c.1881 30-room Victorian Mansion.
Hours & Admission Prices: April-Oct.& late Nov.-Dec. Mon.-Sat. 10-4, Sun. 1-4. April-Oct. adults $6, senior citizens 62 & over $5, children 6-16 $3; children under 6 no charge. Nov.-Dec. adults $6, youth 6-16 $3; children under 6 no charge. Closed Easter; Mother's Day; Thanksgiving; Christmas.
Attendance: 10,000 (actual)

Jackson

THE OLIVER HOUSE, 224 E. Adams St., Jackson, MO 63755. Mailing Address: P.O. Box 114, Jackson, MO 63755. Facebook: Jackson Heritage Association / Oliver House Museum.
E-mail: jacksonpast@gmail.com
Web Site: www.jacksonpast.com
Institution Type/Description: Historic House Museum: housed in the former home of Marie Watkins Oliver, co-designer of the Missouri state flag; built in 1896. Listed on the National Register of Historic Places.
Hours & Admission Prices: Tours: 1st Sunday of the month 1pm-4pm; Christmas Tours: 1st three Sundays after Thanksgiving 1pm-4pm. Adults $5, children $1.

Jefferson City

COLE COUNTY HISTORICAL MUSEUM, 109 Madison, Jefferson City, MO 65101-3015. Tel.: 573-635-1850.
E-mail: cchs@socket.net
Web Site: www.colecohistsoc.org
Institution Type/Description: Historic House Museum: housed in 1871 Federal style row house (3 units), built by Gov. B. Gratz Brown, 20th governor of Missouri.
Hours & Admission Prices: Feb. to mid-Dec. Tues.-Sat. 1-3. Adults $4, senior citizen $3, youth K-12 $2; members & children under 5 no charge. Special tours at other times if arranged in advance. Office: Tues.-Fri. 10-3. Closed national holidays except Independence Day. &
Attendance: 2,898 (actual)

JEFFERSON LANDING STATE HISTORIC SITE, 100 Jefferson St., Jefferson City, MO 65101. Tel.: 573-751-2854. Fax: 573-526-2927.
E-mail: dsp.state.museum@dnr.mo.gov
Web Site: www.missouristatemuseum.com
Key Personnel: Site Admin., Linda Endersby; Cur. Exhibits, Michele Blackmore; Tours, Jocelyn Korsch; Cur. Collections, Kate Keil.
Institution Type/Description: Historic Site: Two buildings that were part of original steamboat landing on the Missouri River.
Hours & Admission Prices: Tues.-Sat. 10-4. No charge; donations accepted. Closed New Year's Day; Easter; Thanksgiving; Christmas. &
Attendance: 14,048 (actual)

MISSOURI GOVERNOR'S MANSION, 100 Madison St., Jefferson City, MO 65101-3061. Mailing Address: P.O. Box 1133, Jefferson City, MO 65102-1133. Tel.: 573-751-2854.
Web Site: mansion.mo.gov
Institution Type/Description: Historic Building: housed in the home for 34 governors and their families; built in 1871.
Hours & Admission Prices: By appointment.

MISSOURI STATE MUSEUM, 201 W. Capitol Ave., Jefferson City, MO 65101-1556. Mailing Address: 100 Jefferson St., Jefferson City, MO 65101. Tel.: 573-751-2854. Fax: 573-526-2927. Facebook.
E-mail: dsp.state.museum@dnr.mo.gov
Web Site: www.missouristatemuseum.com
Key Personnel: Dir., Tiffany Patterson.
Institution Type/Description: General Museum.

Hours & Admission Prices: Daily 8-5. No charge; donations accepted. Closed New Year's Day; Easter; Thanksgiving; Christmas. &
Attendance: 458,746 (estimated)

MISSOURI VETERINARY MEDICAL FOUNDATION VETERINARY MUSEUM, 2500 Country Club Dr., Jefferson City, MO 65109-1190. Tel.: 573-636-8612. Fax: 573-659-7175.
E-mail: mvma@movma.org
Web Site: www.movma.org
Formerly: Missouri Veterinary Museum
Institution Type/Description: Science Museum.
Hours & Admission Prices: Mon.-Fri. 9-4, Sat. by appointment. No charge; donations accepted. Closed holidays.

Jennings

JENNINGS HISTORICAL SOCIETY, 8741 Jennings Station Rd., Jennings, MO 63136. Mailing Address: Jennings City Hall, 2120 Hord Ave., Jennings, MO 63136. Tel.: 314-381-6650. Fax: 314-381-7378.
E-mail: linda.schmerber@swbell.net
Web Site: jenningshistroy.org
Key Personnel: Pres. (V), Alan Stichnote.
Institution Type/Description: Historical Society Museum.
Hours & Admission Prices: By appointment.
Attendance: 30 (estimated)

Joplin

DOROTHEA B. HOOVER HISTORICAL MUSEUM, 504 Schifferdecker, Joplin, MO 64801-3321. Mailing Address: P.O. Box 555, Joplin, MO 64802-0555. Tel.: 417-623-1180. Fax: 417-623-2341.
E-mail: jopmusm@ipa.net
Web Site: www.joplinmuseum.org
Key Personnel: Bd. Pres., John Joines; Exec. Dir., Brad Belk; Resident Geologist, Dr. John Knapp; Administrative Asst., Dina Taylor; Cur., Christopher Wiseman.
Institution Type/Description: Local History Museum.
Hours & Admission Prices: Tues. 10-7, Wed.-Sat. 10-5, Sun. 2-5; call for holiday hours & group tour information. Families $5, adults $2; discounts to groups of 3 or more, AAM & ICOM members; Tues. & members no charge. Closed New Year's Day; Thanksgiving; Christmas.
Attendance: 15,000 (estimated)

GEORGE A. SPIVA CENTER FOR THE ARTS, 222 West 3rd St., Joplin, MO 64801-2513. Tel.: 417-623-0183. Fax: 417-623-3805. Facebook; Twitter; Instagram.
E-mail: jmai@spivaarts.org
Web Site: www.spivaarts.org
Key Personnel: Pres. (V), Lynn Hempen; Exec. Dir., Josie Mai; Museum Shop Mgr., Shaun Conroy.
Institution Type/Description: Art Museum & Center.
Hours & Admission Prices: Tues.-Sat. 10-5. No charge; donations accepted. Closed major holidays. &
Attendance: 10,000 (estimated)

TRI-STATE MINERAL MUSEUM, 400 Schifferdecker Ave., Joplin, MO 64801. Mailing Address: P.O. Box 555, Joplin, MO 64802-0555. Tel.: 417-623-1180.
Web Site: www.joplinmuseum.org
Institution Type/Description: Mineralogical Museum.
Hours & Admission Prices: Tues. 10-7, Wed.-Sat. 10-5. Adults $2; discounts to groups and AAM & ICOM members; members no charge. Closed major holidays.
Attendance: 15,000 (estimated)

Kansas City

ADVERTISING ICON MUSEUM, 4600 Madison Ave., Ste. 1500, Kansas City, MO 64112. Tel.: 816-960-5254. Fax: 816-399-6254.
E-mail: howardboasberg@bradv.com
Web Site: www.advertisingiconmuseum.com
Key Personnel: Exec. Dir., Howard Boasberg; Chm. (V), Robert Bernstein; Pres. (V), Fred Pryor.
Institution Type/Description: Advertising Icon Museum
Hours & Admission Prices: Call for hours. &

AIRLINE HISTORY MUSEUM, Kansas City Downtown Airport, Hangar 9, 201 N.W. Lou Holland Dr., Kansas City, MO 64116-4223. Tel.: 816-421-3401, 800-513-9484. Fax: 816-421-3421.
Web Site: www.airlinehistory.org
Key Personnel: Dir. Devel. & Business Mgr., Michael Dann; Exec. Asst., Gwyneth Bowen.
Institution Type/Description: Airline History Museum.
Hours & Admission Prices: Mon.-Sat. 10-4, Sun. 12-4. Adults 18-64 $10, senior citizens 65 & over and military $9, children 6-17 $6; children under 6 no charge. &
Attendance: 15,000 (estimated)

ALEXANDER MAJORS HISTORIC HOUSE & MUSEUM, 8201 State Line Rd., Kansas City, MO 64114-2002. Mailing Address: 6115 Wornall Rd., Kansas City, MO 64113. Tel.: 816-444-1858.
E-mail: director@wornallmajors.org
Web Site: www.wornallmajors.org
Key Personnel: Dir., Kerrie Nichols.
Institution Type/Description: Historic House: former home of Alexander Majors, co-founder of the Pony Express.
Hours & Admission Prices: April to Dec. Sat.-Sun. 1-4. Adults $8, seniors & students $6, children $5; discounts to groups; children under 4 no charge. &
Attendance: 3,000

AMERICAN JAZZ MUSEUM, 1616 E. 18th St., Kansas City, MO 64108-1610. Tel.: 816-474-8463, ext. 207. Fax: 816-474-0074.
E-mail: info@kcjazz.org
Web Site: www.americanjazzmuseum.org
Key Personnel: Exec. Dir., Cheptoo Kositany-Buckner; Chm. (V), Nikki Newton; Museum Shop Mgr., Barbara Thomas.
Institution Type/Description: Jazz Museum.
Hours & Admission Prices: Tues.-Sat. 9-6, Sun.12-6. AJM: Adults $8, children $3; discounts to AAM members & groups. AJM & NLBM: adults $10, children $5; discounts to groups & AAM members. &
Attendance: 300,000 (estimated)

AMERICAN ROYAL MUSEUM & VISITORS CENTER, 1701 American Royal Court, Kansas City, MO 64102-1097. Tel.: 816-221-9800. Fax: 816-221-8189. Facebook: The American Royal.
E-mail: kristiel@americanroyal.com
Web Site: www.americanroyal.com
Key Personnel: C.E.O. & Pres., Lynn Parman; Chm. (V), Mariner Kemper; Dir. Education, Kristie Larson.
Institution Type/Description: Agriculture Museum and Visitors Center.
Hours & Admission Prices: Mon.-Fri. 10-4, Sat.-Sun. call for hours. No charge; donations accepted. Closed holidays. &
Attendance: 5,025 (actual)

AMERICAN TRUCK HISTORICAL SOCIETY, 10380 N. Ambassador Dr., Kansas City, MO 64153-1378. Mailing Address: P.O. Box 901611, Kansas City, MO 64190-1611. Tel.: 816-891-9900. Fax: 816-891-9903.
E-mail: courtney@aths.org
Web Site: www.aths.org
Key Personnel: Exec. Dir., Bill Johnson; Pres., John Vannatta; Treas., Michael C. Colton.
Institution Type/Description: Truck Library.
Hours & Admission Prices: Mon.-Fri. 8-4:30. No charge. Closed national holidays. &
Attendance: 300 (estimated)

ARABIA STEAMBOAT MUSEUM, 400 Grand Blvd., Kansas City, MO 64106-1111. Tel.: 816-471-1856. Fax: 816-471-1616. Facebook: Arabia Steamboat Museum.
E-mail: steamboatmuseum@gmail.com
Web Site: www.1856.com
Key Personnel: Cur., Public Rels. & Archivist, David Hawley; Museum Shop Mgr., Florence Hawley.
Institution Type/Description: General Museum.
Hours & Admission Prices: Mon.-Sat. 10-5, tours every 30 min. with last admission at 3:30. Sun. 12-5, tours every 30 min. with last admission 3:30. Adults $14.50, senior citizens over 60 $13.50, children 4-14 $5.50; discounts to groups of 25 or more; children 3 & under no charge. Closed New Year's Day; Easter; Thanksgiving; Christmas Eve & Day. &
Attendance: 75,221 (actual)

BATTLE OF WESTPORT VISITOR CENTER AND MUSEUM, 6601 Swope Pkwy., Kansas City, MO 64132. Mailing Address: Monnett Battle of Westport Fund, Inc., 6900 College Blvd., Ste. 510, Overland Park, KS 66211. Tel.: 913-345-2000. Fax: 913-345-2081.
E-mail: battleofwestport1864@yahoo.com
Web Site: www.battleofwestport.org
Key Personnel: Chm. (V), Daniel L. Smith.
Institution Type/Description: Civil War History Museum & Visitor Center.
Hours & Admission Prices: April-Oct. Thurs.-Sat. 1-5. No charge; donations requested.
Attendance: 1,000 (estimated)

BELGER ARTS CENTER, 2100 Walnut St., Kansas City, MO 64108. Tel.: 816-474-3250. Fax: 816-221-1621.
E-mail: mdickens@belgerartscenter.org
Web Site: www.belgerartscenter.org
Key Personnel: Dir., Evelyn Craft.
Institution Type/Description: Art Gallery.
Hours & Admission Prices: Wed.-Fri. 10-4, Sat. 12-4; other times by appointment. No charge.
Attendance: 7,000 (estimated)

BRUCE R. WATKINS CULTURAL HERITAGE CENTER AND STATE MUSEUM, 3700 Blue Pkwy., Kansas City, MO 64130-2800. Tel.: 816-513-0700. Fax: 816-513-0710. Facebook: Bruce R. Watkins Cultural Heritage Center and State Museum.
E-mail: chiluba.musonda@kcmo.org
Web Site: www.kcmo.org/CKCMO/Depts/ParksandRecreation/BruceR.Watkins/
Key Personnel: Exec. Dir., Chiluba Musonda.
Institution Type/Description: History Museum.
Hours & Admission Prices: Tues.-Sat. 10-6. No charge; donations accepted.
Attendance: 9,956 (actual)

GREENLEASE ART GALLERY - ROCKHURST UNIVERSITY, 1100 Rockhurst Rd., Kansas City, MO 64110. Tel.: 816-501-4000, 800-842-6776.
E-mail: anne.pearce@rockhurst.edu
Key Personnel: Dir., Anne Pearce.
Institution Type/Description: Art Gallery.
Hours & Admission Prices: Thurs.-Sat. 12-5; other times by appointment.

HALLMARK VISITORS CENTER, 2450 Grand Blvd., Kansas City, MO 64108. Mailing Address: P.O. Box 419580, Kansas City, MO 64141-6580. Tel.: 816-274-3613. Fax: 816-274-3148.
E-mail: visitorscenter@hallmark.com
Web Site: www.hallmarkvisitorscenter.com
Key Personnel: Dir., Linda Avery; Staff Supvr., Jeanine Ellis.
Institution Type/Description: Company History Museum.
Hours & Admission Prices: Oct.-Sept. 3. Mon.-Fri. 10-4:30, Sat. 9:30-4:30; call to confirm. No charge. Closed New Year's Day; Memorial Day; Independence Day; Labor Day; Thanksgiving; Christmas Eve & Day.
Attendance: 121,500 (actual)

THE JOHN WORNALL HOUSE MUSEUM, 6115 Wornall Rd., Kansas City, MO 64113-1417. Tel.: 816-444-1858. Fax: 816-361-8165. Facebook: John Wornall House Museum.
E-mail: director@wornallmajors.org
Web Site: www.wornallmajors.org
Key Personnel: Dir., Kerrie Nichols.
Institution Type/Description: Historic House: c.1858 Greek Revival home used as a hospital during the Civil War.
Hours & Admission Prices: Tues.-Sat. 10-4, Sun. 1-4. Adult $8, seniors & students $6, children 5-12 $5; discounts to groups; children under 4 no charge. Closed holidays.
Attendance: 8,000 (estimated)

KALEIDOSCOPE, 2450 Grand, Kansas City, MO 64108. Mailing Address: P.O. Box 419580, Kansas City, MO 64141-6580. Tel.: 816-274-8301 & 8934. Fax: 816-274-3148.
E-mail: kaleidoscope@hallmark.com
Web Site: www.hallmarkkaleidoscope.com
Key Personnel: Dir., Linda Avery; Exhibit Mgr., Cheryl Williams; Volunteer Coord., Jeanine Ellis.
Institution Type/Description: Children's Participatory Art Exhibit.
Hours & Admission Prices: Call for hours. No charge. Closed New Year's Day; Memorial Day; Independence Day; Labor Day; Thanksgiving; Christmas Eve & Day.
Attendance: 190,000 (actual)

KANSAS CITY ART INSTITUTE H&R BLOCK ARTSPACE, 16 E. 43 St., Kansas City, MO 64111-1755. Mailing Address: 4415 Warwick Blvd., Kansas City, MO 64111. Tel.: 816-561-5563.
E-mail: rmsmith@kcai.edu
Web Site: www.kcai.edu/artspace
Key Personnel: Dir., Raechell Smith.
Institution Type/Description: Art Gallery & University Museum.
Hours & Admission Prices: Tues.-Sat. 12-5. No charge.
Attendance: 9,500 (actual)

KANSAS CITY FIRE MUSEUM, 30 W. Pershing Rd, Kansas City, MO 64108. Mailing Address: 15 W. Linwood Blvd., Kansas City, MO 64111-1324. Tel.: 816-885-2086.
E-mail: paulkcfd@gmail.com
Institution Type/Description: Fire Fighting History Museum.
Hours & Admission Prices: Thurs.-Sat. 9:30-5:30, Sun. 12-5:30.

KANSAS CITY MUSEUM, 3218 Gladstone Blvd., Kansas City, MO 64123-1199. Tel.: 816-483-8300. Fax: 816-483-6050.
E-mail: steff@redquill.com
Web Site: kansascitymuseum.org
Key Personnel: Dir., Anna Marie Tutera; Chm. (V), Robert Regnier.
Institution Type/Description: History Museum: housed in an urban estate built in 1910.
Hours & Admission Prices: Visitor Center: Wed.-Sat. 10-4, Sun. 12-4. StoryTarium Programs: daily 2 p.m. No charge; donations accepted.
Attendance: 25,000

KANSAS CITY ZOO, 6800 Zoo Dr., Kansas City, MO 64132-1711. Tel.: 816-595-1234. Fax: 816-513-5850.
E-mail: askthezoo@fotzkc.org
Web Site: www.kansascityzoo.org
Formerly: Kansas City Zoological Gardens
Key Personnel: Exec. Dir., Randy Wisthoff.
Institution Type/Description: Zoological Park.
Hours & Admission Prices: Mon.-Fri. 9:30-4, Sat.-Sun. 9:30-5. Adults $13.50, seniors $12.50, children 3-11 $10.50; discounts to groups & reciprocal Zoos Friends members; members & children under 3 no charge. Closed New Year's Day; Thanksgiving; Christmas.
Attendance: 713,813 (actual)

KEMPER MUSEUM OF CONTEMPORARY ART, 4420 Warwick Blvd., Kansas City, MO 64111-1821. Tel.: 816-753-5784. Fax: 816-753-5806.
E-mail: communications@kemperart.org
Web Site: www.kemperart.org
Key Personnel: Exec. Dir., Barbara O'Brien; Dir. Finance & Accounting, Kathy Surber; Dir. Devel., Don Schreiner; Cur. & Head Adult Programs, Erin Dziedzic; Museum Educator, School & Family, Devin Rumley; Dir. Mktg. & Communications, Kent Michael Smith; Facility & Operations Mgr., Paul Watts; Collections Mgr. & Registrar, Andrea Phillips.
Institution Type/Description: Contemporary Art Museum.
Hours & Admission Prices: Kemper Museum: Tues.-Thurs. 10-4, Fri.-Sat. 10-9, Sun. 11-5. No charge; donations accepted. Kemper at the Crossroads: Wed.-Thurs. 10-4, Fri. 10-9, Sat. 12-4. Kemper East: Tues.-Fri. 10-5:30, Sat. 10-2. Closed New Year's Day; Independence Day; Thanksgiving; Christmas.
Attendance: 130,000 (estimated)

LEEDY-VOULKOS ART CENTER, 2010 Baltimore Ave., Kansas City, MO 64108-1914. Tel.: 816-474-1919.
E-mail: erin@leedy-voulkos.com
Web Site: www.leedy-voulkos.com
Key Personnel: Gallery Mgr. & Dir., Erin Woodworth; Museum Shop Mgr., Courtney Wasson.
Institution Type/Description: Art Gallery.
Hours & Admission Prices: Gallery & Shop: Thurs.-Sat. 11-5. No charge.

THE MONEY MUSEUM-FEDERAL RESERVE BANK OF KANSAS CITY, 1 Memorial Dr., Kansas City, MO 64198-0002. Tel.: 816-881-2683. Fax: 816-881-2569.
E-mail: KCtours@kc.frb.org
Web Site: www.kc.frb.org/moneymuseum
Formerly: The Roger Guffey Gallery-Federal Reserve Bank of Kansas City
Key Personnel: Economic Education Analyst, Gigi Wolf.
Institution Type/Description: Money Gallery: housed in the lobby of the Federal Reserve Bank of Kansas City; focuses on how money has evolved throughout banking history to present day.
Hours & Admission Prices: Mon.-Fri. 8:30-4:30. No charge. Closed banking holidays.

THE NATIONAL MUSEUM OF TOYS AND MINIATURES, 5235 Oak St., Kansas City, MO 64112-2824. Tel.: 816-235-8000. Facebook.
E-mail: info@toyandminiaturemuseum.org
Web Site: www.toyandminiaturemuseum.org
Formerly: Toy & Miniature Museum of Kansas City
Key Personnel: Exec. Dir., Jamie A. Berry; Collections Coord., Calleen Carver; Cur. Collections, Kristie Dobbins; Visitor Svcs. Mgr., Meg Hauser; Admin. & Mktg. Asst., Tony Julo; Community Devel. Coord., Cassie Pikarsky; Cur. Interpretation, Laura S. Taylor; Asst. Museum Educator, Katherine Mercier.
Institution Type/Description: Art & History Museum: exhibiting collection of antique toys and fine-scale miniatures.
Hours & Admission Prices: Wed.-Mon. 10-4. Adults $5; AAM members & members no charge. Closed major holidays. &
Attendance: 40,108 (actual)

NATIONAL WORLD WAR I MUSEUM AND MEMORIAL, 2 Memorial Dr., Kansas City, MO 64108. Tel.: 816-888-8100. Fax: 816-888-8123. Facebook; Instagram; Twitter.
E-mail: info@theworldwar.org
Web Site: www.theworldwar.org
Formerly: National World War I Museum at Liberty Memorial
Key Personnel: Chm. Bd. Trustees, Mark Jorgenson; Pres. & C.E.O., Dr. Matthew C. Naylor; Vice Pres. Devel., Debbie Bass; Vice Pres. Finance, Mark Gunter; Vice Pres. Facilities Operations, Chris Wyche; Dir. Mktg., Communications & Guest Svcs., Mike Vietti; Senior Cur., Doran Cart; Dir. Archives, Jonathan Casey; Cur. Education, Lora Vogt; Guest Svcs. Mgr., Kristin Fitch.
Institution Type/Description: Military History Museum.
Hours & Admission Prices: Memorial Day to Labor Day Sun.-Fri. 10-5, Sat. 9-5; Sept.-May Tues.-Sun. 10-5. Adults $16, seniors 65 & up and college students $14, youth 6-17 $10; discounts to active-duty military & their families, veterans, teachers and AAM members; members & children under 6 no charge. Closed New Year's Eve & Day; Thanksgiving; Christmas Eve & Day. &
Attendance: 282,588 (actual)

NEGRO LEAGUES BASEBALL MUSEUM, 1616 E. 18th St., Kansas City, MO 64108-1610. Tel.: 816-221-1920.
E-mail: bkendrick@nlbm.com
Key Personnel: Pres., Bob Kendrick; Chm. Bd. (V), Betty Brown.
Institution Type/Description: African-American Baseball History Museum.
Hours & Admission Prices: Tues.-Sat. 9-6, Sun. 12-6. Adults $10, seniors $9, children under 12 $6; discounts to groups; children under 5 no charge. &

THE NELSON-ATKINS MUSEUM OF ART, 4525 Oak St., Kansas City, MO 64111-1873. Tel.: 816-751-1278. Fax: 816-561-4011. Facebook, Instagram, Twitter.
E-mail: ask@nelson-atkins.org
Web Site: www.nelson-atkins.org
Key Personnel: Dir. & C.E.O., Julian Zugazagoitia; Chm. Bd. Trustees, Richard C. Green; C.O.O., Karen L. Christiansen; Dir. Finance, Tammy Bluhm; Mng. Strategic Initiatives, Casey Claps; Dir. Human Resources, Kelly Summers; Dir. Education & Interpretive Programs, Anne Manning; Dir. Mktg. & Communications, Toni Wood; Vice Pres. Earned Income & Guest, Mandy Stone; Dir. Design & Experience, Steven Waterman.
Institution Type/Description: Art Museum.
Hours & Admission Prices: Wed. & Sat.-Sun. 10-5, Thurs.-Fri. 10-9. Museum: no charge; donations accepted. Ticketed Exhibitions: adults $18, seniors 55 & over $16, students w/ID $10; members and children 12 & under no charge. Parking: $10; members no charge. Closed New Year's Day; Independence Day; Thanksgiving; Christmas Eve & Day. &
Attendance: 533,000 (estimated)

PIPER MEMORIAL MEDICAL MUSEUM, 1000 Carondelet Dr., Kansas City, MO 64114-4673. Tel.: 816-943-2183. Fax: 816-943-2786.
E-mail: jmullen@carondelet.com
Key Personnel: Cur., Joan Hilger-Mullen.
Institution Type/Description: Medical Museum.
Hours & Admission Prices: Daily 8-8. No charge; donations accepted. &

SHOAL CREEK LIVING HISTORY MUSEUM, 7000 N.E. Barry Rd., Kansas City, MO 64156-1278. Tel.: 816-792-2655.
E-mail: parks@kcmo.org
Web Site: www.kcmo.org
Key Personnel: C.E.O., Pres. (V) & Museum Shop Mgr., Martha Edmunds; Chm. (V), Pam Payne.
Institution Type/Description: History Museum: comprised of 20 buildings dating from 1807-1890.

Hours & Admission Prices: March-Dec. Mon.-Sat. 9-3. Tours, school programs & reenactments by appointment. No charge; donations accepted. Fees for programs & events. Closed government holidays. &
Attendance: 10,000 (estimated)

THOMAS HART BENTON HOME AND STUDIO STATE HISTORIC SITE, 3616 Belleview, Kansas City, MO 64111-3808. Tel.: 816-931-5722. Fax: 816-931-5722.
E-mail: benton.home.state.historic.site@dnr.mo.gov
Web Site: www.mostateparks.com/benton.htm
Institution Type/Description: Historic House: home & studio of Thomas Hart Benton.
Hours & Admission Prices: Winter: Sun. 11-4, Mon. & Thurs.-Sat. 10-4; Summer: Sun. 12-5, Mon. & Thurs.-Sat. 10-4; groups of 15 or more by appointment. Adults $4, children 6-12 $2.50; discount to groups; children under 6 no charge. Closed New Year's Day; Thanksgiving; Christmas. &
Attendance: 3,904 (actual)

THORNHILL GALLERY AT AVILA UNIVERSITY, Dallavis Center, 11901 Wornall Rd., Kansas City, MO 64145-1007. Tel.: 816-501-3653.
E-mail: aylwardme@avila.edu
Web Site: www.avila.edu/viscom/gallery
Key Personnel: Dept. Chm., Susan Lawlor; Cur., Marci Aylward.
Institution Type/Description: Art Gallery.
Hours & Admission Prices: Mon.-Thurs. 10-3; other times by appointment. No charge; donations accepted. Closed New Year's Day; Easter; Memorial Day; Independence Day; Labor Day; Christmas; spring & fall breaks. &
Attendance: 2,400 (estimated)

TRAILSIDE CENTER AND THE HISTORICAL SOCIETY OF NEW SANTA FE, 9901 Holmes Rd., Kansas City, MO 64131-4205. Mailing Address: 712 W. 121st St., Kansas City, MO 64145-1009. Tel.: 816-942-3581.
E-mail: info@trailsidecenter.org
Web Site: www.trailsidecenter.org, www.newsantafe.org
Key Personnel: Dir., Charles Loomis; Pres. & C.E.O., Ann O'Hare; Chm. (V), Charles Loomis.
Institution Type/Description: History Museum.
Hours & Admission Prices: Mon.-Sat. 10-4, Sun. 12-4. No charge; donations accepted. &
Attendance: 6,000 (actual)

UNION STATION KANSAS CITY, INC., 30 W. Pershing Rd., Kansas City, MO 64108-2410. Tel.: 816-460-2020. Fax: 816-460-2260.
E-mail: info@unionstation.org
Web Site: www.unionstation.org
Formerly: Science City at Union Station/Kansas City Museum
Key Personnel: C.E.O., George Guastello; Chm. Bd., Robert D. Regnier; Exec. Vice Pres. & C.O.O., Jerry Baber; Chief Mktg. Officer, Michael Truitt; Dir. Finance & Customer Service, Nale Uhl; Dir. Technical & Building Opers., Duane Erickson; Dir. Science City Exhibits, Jeff Rosenblatt; Dir. Science City Programming, Christy Nitsche.
Institution Type/Description: Science & History Museum.
Hours & Admission Prices: Daily 6a.m.-midnight. Union Station: no charge. Science City: adults & seniors $13.50, youth 3-12 $11.50, members no charge. Theater: fees vary. Planetarium: admission $6, members no charge. City Stage: fees vary. Discounts to AAM & ASTC members and groups of 15 or more; children 3 & under no charge. Closed Thanksgiving; Christmas. &
Attendance: 2,000,000 (estimated)

UNITED FEDERATION OF DOLL CLUBS MUSEUM, 10900 N. Pomona Ave., Kansas City, MO 64153. Tel.: 816-891-7040. Fax: 816-891-8360.
E-mail: ufdcinfo@ufdc.org
Web Site: www.ufdc.org
Key Personnel: Pres., Loretta Nardone; Cur., Lisa Shockley.
Institution Type/Description: Doll Museum.
Hours & Admission Prices: Mon.-Fri. 10-4; other times by appointment. Adults $4, children 6-12 $2, student $1; members and children 5 & under no charge. Closed Christmas to New Year's Day. &
Attendance: 300 (estimated)

UNIVERSITY OF MISSOURI-KANSAS CITY GALLERY OF ART, 5015 Holmes, Fine Arts Bldg. 203, 5100 Rockhill Rd., Kansas City, MO 64110-2499. Tel.: 816-235-1502. Fax: 816-235-5507. Facebook: UMKC Gallery of Art.
E-mail: umkcgallery@umkc.edu
Web Site: info.umkc.edu/gallery

Key Personnel: Gallery Art Coord., Davin Watne.
Institution Type/Description: Art Gallery.
Hours & Admission Prices: Mon. & Wed. 9-4, Tues. 11-4, Thurs. 11-4 & 5-7, Fri. 11-2. No charge; donations accepted. Closed holidays. &

Attendance: 10,000 (estimated)

THE WESTPORT HISTORICAL SOCIETY AND THE 1855 HARRIS-KEARNEY HOUSE MUSEUM, 4000 Baltimore, Kansas City, MO 64111-7403. Tel.: 816-561-1821. Fax: 913-345-2081. Facebook.
E-mail: westporthistorical@gmail.com
Web Site: www.westporthistorical.com/index.htm
Key Personnel: Pres. (V), Alana Smith; Publicist, Alexa Smith.
Institution Type/Description: Historic House: housed in a Greek Revival mansion and former home of Col. John Harris & his wife Henrietta.
Hours & Admission Prices: March to mid-Dec. Wed.-Sat. 1-5. Adults $6, students $4; discounts to society members, active and retired military & groups; children under 6 no charge. Closed major holidays.
Attendance: 1,500 (estimated)

Kearney

HISTORIC MT. GILEAD SCHOOL, 15918 Plattsburg Rd., Kearney, MO 64060. Tel.: 816-736-8500. Fax: 816-736-8501.
E-mail: historicsites@claycountymo.gov
Web Site: www.claycountymo.gov
Institution Type/Description: Historic Building: housed in a one-room school; built in 1879.
Hours & Admission Prices: By appointment. Admission $5 per person. Off-Site: $1 per person.

JESSE JAMES BIRTHPLACE, 21216 Jesse James Farm Rd., Kearney, MO 64060-9343. Mailing Address: c/o Friends of the James Farm, P.O. Box 404, Liberty, MO 64069. Tel.: 816-736-8500. Fax: 816-736-8501.
E-mail: bbeckett@claycountymo.gov
Web Site: jessejamesmuseum.org
Key Personnel: Dir., Elizabeth Beckett.
Institution Type/Description: Historic Buildings & Site.
Hours & Admission Prices: Memorial Day-Labor Day daily 9-4; Sept.-May Mon.-Sat. 9-4, Sun. 12-4. Adults $8.50, seniors $7.50, children 8-15 $5; discounts to groups; children under 8 no charge. &
Attendance: 12,000 (estimated)

KEARNEY HISTORIC MUSEUM, 101 S. Jefferson, Kearney, MO 64060-8503. Tel.: 816-903-1856.
E-mail: gerriantiques@aol.com
Key Personnel: Dir., Gerri Spencer.
Institution Type/Description: History Museum.
Hours & Admission Prices: Fri. & Sat. 10-2; groups by appointment. No charge; donations accepted. &
Attendance: 750 (estimated)

Kennett

DUNKLIN COUNTY MUSEUM, INC., 122 College, Kennett, MO 63857-2007. Mailing Address: 604 College, Kennett, MO 63857-2015. Tel.: 573-888-6620.
E-mail: cbbrown@clgw.net
Key Personnel: Chm. Bd. Dirs., Mrs. Charles B. Brown; Chm. (V), Sandra Brown.
Institution Type/Description: History Museum: housed in 1904 City Hall & Masonic Temple.
Hours & Admission Prices: March-Dec. Wed. 12-5, Sat. by appointment; tours by appointment. No charge; donations accepted.
Attendance: 1,500 (estimated)

Keytesville

GENERAL STERLING PRICE MUSEUM, 412 Bridge St., Keytesville, MO 65261-1016. Mailing Address: P.O. Box 40, Keytesville, MO 65261-0040. Tel.: 660-288-3204.
E-mail: janet_weaver531@hotmail.com
Key Personnel: Pres., Janet Weaver; Treas., Kessie Friesz; Sec., Jan Canyon.
Institution Type/Description: General Museum.
Hours & Admission Prices: May 15-Oct. 15 Mon.-Fri. 2-5. No charge; donations accepted. Closed holidays. &
Attendance: 300 (actual)

Kimmswick

ANHEUSER ESTATE, 6000 Windsor Harbor Lane, Kimmswick, MO 63053. Mailing Address: P.O. Box 27, Kimmswick, MO 63053-0094. Tel.: 636-464-7407 & 1698. Fax: 636-464-7477. Facebook: Anheuser Museum & Estate.
E-mail: tbenack@cityofkimmswick.org
Web Site: cityofkimmswick.org
Institution Type/Description: Historic House Museum: housed in the former home of the Anheuser family; built in 1867.
Hours & Admission Prices: Thurs. 12-4. Adults $5.

KIMMSWICK HISTORICAL SOCIETY MUSEUM, 6000 3rd St., Kimmswick, MO 63053. Mailing Address: P.O. Box 41, Kimmswick, MO 63053. Tel.: 636-464-8687.
E-mail: loretta@boemler.com
Key Personnel: Dir., Loretta Boemler.
Institution Type/Description: Historical Society Museum.
Hours & Admission Prices: March-Dec. Sat.-Sun. 1-4. No charge; donations accepted. &
Attendance: 500 (estimated)

King City

TRI-COUNTY MUSEUM & HISTORICAL SOCIETY, 508 N. Grand Ave., King City, MO 64463. Tel.: 660-535-4391. Fax: 660-535-4537.
E-mail: cascadehistory@netins.net
Web Site: www.tricountyhistoricalsociety.com/the-museum
Institution Type/Description: History Museum.
Hours & Admission Prices: By appointment. No charge.

Kingsville

POWELL GARDENS, KANSAS CITY'S BOTANICAL GARDEN, 1609 N.W. U.S. Hwy. 50, Kingsville, MO 64061. Tel.: 816-697-2600. Facebook: Powell Gardens.
E-mail: info@powellgardens.org
Web Site: www.powellgardens.org
Institution Type/Description: Botanical Garden.
Hours & Admission Prices: May-Sept. daily 9-6; Oct.-April daily 9-5. Admission: April-Oct. adults $10, seniors $9, children 5-12 $4. Nov.-March adults $7, seniors $6, children 5-12 $3. Closed New Year's Day; Thanksgiving; Christmas.

Kirksville

ADAIR COUNTY HISTORICAL SOCIETY, INC., 211 S. Elson St., Kirksville, MO 63501-3466. Tel.: 660-665-6502.
E-mail: adairhistoric@att.net
Web Site: www.adairchs.org
Key Personnel: Pres., Mrs. Blytha Ellis; Vice Pres., Marty Jayne; Treas., Mrs. Denise Treasure.
Institution Type/Description: Historical Society Museum.
Hours & Admission Prices: Wed.-Fri. 1-4. No charge; donations accepted. Closed New Year's Eve & Day; Memorial Day; Independence Day; Labor Day; Thanksgiving; Christmas Eve, Day & week.
Attendance: 224 (actual)

MUSEUM OF OSTEOPATHIC MEDICINE, 800 W. Jefferson St., Kirksville, MO 63501-1443. Tel.: 660-626-2359. Fax: 660-626-2984.
E-mail: museum@atsu.edu
Web Site: www.atsu.edu/museum
Key Personnel: Dir., Jason Haxton; Cur., Debra Loguda-Summers; Registrar, Heather Rudy; Coord. Research, Anna Mullen; Exhibit Mgr., Paige White.
Institution Type/Description: Medical Museum Complex: housed in the education building on the campus of Kirksville College of Osteopathic Medicine.
Hours & Admission Prices: Mon.-Fri. 8-5, Sat. 10-4; other times by appointment. No charge; donations accepted. &
Attendance: 9,100 (actual)

TRUMAN STATE UNIVERSITY OBSERVATORY, University Farm, Boundary St., Kirksville, MO 63501. Mailing Address: Macgruder Hall 3168, Physics Dept., Kirksville, MO 63501. Tel.: 660-785-4594.
E-mail: gokhale@truman.edu
Web Site: observatory.truman.edu
Institution Type/Description: Observatory.
Hours & Admission Prices: Call for hours.

Kirkwood

KIRKWOOD HISTORICAL SOCIETY - MUDD'S GROVE, 302 W. Argonne, Kirkwood, MO 63122. Mailing Address: P.O. Box 220602, Kirkwood, MO 63122. Tel.: 314-965-5151.
E-mail: info@kirkwoodhistoricalsociety.com
Web Site: www.kirkwoodhistoricalsociety.com
Institution Type/Description: Historical Society Museum: house built in 1860.
Hours & Admission Prices: Thurs. & Sun. 1-4. Adults $4; members no charge. ♿
Attendance: 200 (estimated)

Laclede

GENERAL JOHN J. PERSHING BOYHOOD HOME STATE HISTORIC SITE, 1100 Pershing Dr., Laclede, MO 64651. Mailing Address: P.O. Box 141, Laclede, MO 64651-0141. Tel.: 660-963-2525. Fax: 660-963-2520. Facebook: Pershing Home SHS.
E-mail: moparks@dnr.mo.gov
Web Site: www.mostateparks.com/gen-john-j-pershing-boyhood-home-state-historic-site
Key Personnel: Site Admin., Denzil R. Heaney.
Institution Type/Description: State Historic Site.
Hours & Admission Prices: April-Sept. Mon.-Sat. 10-4, Sun. 12-6; Oct.-March Tues.-Sat. 10-4. Tours: adults $4, youth 6-17 $3; discount to groups; children 5 & under no charge. Closed New Year's Day; Easter; Thanksgiving; Christmas. ♿
Attendance: 8,500 (estimated)

LOCUST CREEK COVERED BRIDGE STATE HISTORIC SITE, 16957 Dart Rd., Laclede, MO 64651. Mailing Address: P.O. Box 141, Laclede, MO 64651-0141. Tel.: 660-963-2525.
E-mail: moparks@dnr.mo.gov
Web Site: mostateparks.com/locust-creek-covered-bridge-state-historic-site
Key Personnel: Site Admin., Denzil R. Heaney.
Institution Type/Description: Historic Site: 1868 151-foot covered bridge.
Hours & Admission Prices: Daily sunrise to sunset. No charge; donations accepted.
Attendance: 18,400 (actual)

Lamar

HARRY S. TRUMAN BIRTHPLACE STATE HISTORIC SITE, 1009 Truman Ave., Lamar, MO 64759. Tel.: 417-682-2279. Fax: 417-682-6304.
E-mail: moparks@dnr.mo.gov
Web Site: mostateparks.com/harry-s-truman-birthplace-state-historic-site
Key Personnel: Site Admin., Beth Bazal.
Institution Type/Description: Historic House & Museum: housed in c.1880 Harry S. Truman birthplace.
Hours & Admission Prices: Grounds: daily sunrise to sunset; Office: March-Oct. Wed.-Sat. 10-4, Sun. 12-4; Nov.-Feb. Wed.-Sat. 10-4. No charge; donations accepted. ♿
Attendance: 26,649 (actual)

Laurie

OLD ST. PATRICK'S CHURCH AND MUSEUM, 810 Rte. O, Laurie, MO 65037. Mailing Address: P.O. Box 1098, Laurie, MO 65038. Tel.: 573-374-7855. Fax: 573-374-0627.
E-mail: parishsecretary@shrineofstpatrick.com
Key Personnel: Dir., Rev. John Schmitz.
Institution Type/Description: Church Museum: founded by Irish immigrants; built in 1868. Listed on the National Register of Historic Places.
Hours & Admission Prices: Summer: Sun. 11-1. No charge; donations accepted.
Attendance: 500 (estimated)

Lawson

WATKINS WOOLEN MILL STATE HISTORIC SITE & PARK, 26600 Park Rd., N., Lawson, MO 64062-8939. Tel.: 816-580-3387 & 3782. Fax: 816-580-3784.
E-mail: watkins.woolen.mill.state.historic.site@dnr.mo.gov
Web Site: www.mostateparks.com
Key Personnel: Facility Mgr., Mike Beckett; Historic Site Admin., Matt Carletti; Park Supt., Ron Sutton; Coord. Education, Melissa Hall; Coord. Period Clothing, Terri Gardner; Volunteer Coord., Amanda Coonce; Park Maintenance II, Russell Teague; Park Maintenance II, Farriel O'Dell; Park Maintenance II, Joe Green; Park Maintenance III, Tim Clifford; Clerk Typist, Linda Zink.
Institution Type/Description: Industrial & Agricultural Museum: 1839 Bethany, 19th-century plantation.

Hours & Admission Prices: Summer: Mon.-Sat. 9:30-5, Sun. 10:30-5; Winter: Mon.-Sat. 10-4:30, Sun. 11-4:30. Adults $2.50, children 6-12 $1.50; discounts to pre-scheduled groups of 15 or more; children under 6 no charge. Closed New Year's Day; Thanksgiving; Christmas. ♿
Attendance: 15,500 (actual)

Lebanon

NATURE INTERPRETIVE CENTER, Bennett Spring State Park, Lebanon, MO 65536-6797. Mailing Address: Bennett Spring State Park, 26250 Hwy. 64A, Lebanon, MO 65536-6797. Tel.: 417-532-3925 & 4338. Fax: 417-532-7006.
E-mail: moparks@dnr.mo.gov
Web Site: www.mostateparks.com/bennett.htm
Institution Type/Description: Natural History Museum.
Hours & Admission Prices: Feb. 25-Oct. daily 10-4. No charge; donations accepted. Closed Nov.-Feb. 24. ♿
Attendance: 35,000 (estimated)

ROUTE 66 MUSEUM AND RESEARCH CENTER, Lebanon-Laclede County Library, 915 S. Jefferson Ave., Lebanon, MO 65536. Tel.: 417-532-2148.
E-mail: mspangler@lebanon-laclede.lib.mo.us
Institution Type/Description: History Museum.
Hours & Admission Prices: Mon.-Thurs. 8-8, Fri.-Sat. 8-5. No charge; donations accepted.
Attendance: 9,500 (actual)

Lecoma

MISSOURI UNIVERSITY OF SCIENCE AND TECHNOLOGY MINERALS COLLECTION, 125 McNutt Hall, Lecoma, MO 65401. Mailing Address: Geological Sciences & Engineering, 129 McNutt Hall, 1400 N. Bishop, Rolla, MO 65409-0140. Tel.: 573-341-4616. Fax: 573-341-6935.
E-mail: rocks@mst.edu
Web Site: gse.mst.edu
Formerly: University of Missouri-Rolla Minerals Museum
Key Personnel: Prof. & Head Geology & Geophysics, Dr. Francisca Oboh-Ikuenobe, Ph.D.
Institution Type/Description: Mineralogy Museum.
Hours & Admission Prices: Mon.-Fri. 8-5. No charge. Closed holidays. ♿
Attendance: 200 (estimated)

Lee's Summit

LEE'S SUMMIT HISTORICAL SOCIETY MUSEUM, 222 S.E. Main, Lee's Summit, MO 64063-2332. Mailing Address: 1923 S.E. 3rd St., Lee's Summit, MO 64063. Tel.: 816-525-9440.
E-mail: derbyshirelane@prodigy.net
Web Site: www.leessummithistory.net
Key Personnel: Dir., Kathy Smith.
Institution Type/Description: Historical Society Museum: housed in the 1905 train depot.
Hours & Admission Prices: Sat. 10-4; other times by appointment. No charge; donations accepted. ♿

MISSOURI TOWN 1855, 8010 E. Park Rd., Lee's Summit, MO 64064. Mailing Address: 8201 Jasper Bell Rd., Blue Springs, MO 64015. Tel.: 816-503-4860. Fax: 816-795-7938. TDD: 800-735-2966.
E-mail: jklusmeyer@jacksongov.org
Web Site: www.jacksongov.org
Key Personnel: Supt., Jonathan Klusmeyer; Dir. Parks & Rec., Michele Newman; Supt. Heritage Museums & Programs, Gordon Julich; Program Specialist, Cindy Henley.
Institution Type/Description: Village Museum: over 25 structures c.1821-1860 from western Missouri.
Hours & Admission Prices: March-Nov. 15 Tues.-Sun. 9-4:30; Nov. 16-Feb. Sat.-Sun. 9-4:30. Adults $7, senior citizens & youth $4; discounts to groups with advance reservation; members & children under 5 no charge. Closed New Year's Day; Veterans Day; Truman's Birthday; Thanksgiving; Christmas. ♿
Attendance: 13,900 (actual)

Lexington

BATTLE OF LEXINGTON STATE HISTORIC SITE, 1101 Delaware St., Lexington, MO 64067. Mailing Address: P.O. Box 6,

Lexington, MO 64067-0006. Tel.: 660-259-4654. Fax: 660-259-2378. Facebook: @BattleOfLexingtonSHS.
E-mail: battle.of.lexington.state.historic.site@dnr.mo.gov
Web Site: www.mostateparks.com
Key Personnel: Site Admin., Christopher Fritsche.
Institution Type/Description: Historic House & Battlefield: 1853 Col. Oliver Anderson & Tilton Davis Home, located at site of Battle of the Hemp Bales.
Hours & Admission Prices: Call for hours. Adults $5, youth 6-17 $3; children 5 & under no charge. Closed New Year's Day; Easter; Thanksgiving; Christmas. &
Attendance: 30,000 (estimated)

LEXINGTON HISTORICAL MUSEUM, 112 S. 13th St., Lexington, MO 64067-1402. Mailing Address: P.O. Box 121, Lexington, MO 64067. Tel.: 660-259-6313 & 2900.
E-mail: rslusher@yahoo.com
Web Site: www.lexingtonmuseum.org
Key Personnel: Dir., Roger Slusher; Pres. (V), Mike Kramer.
Institution Type/Description: History Museum: housed in the 1846 Cumberland Presbyterian Church.
Hours & Admission Prices: Call 660-259-2900 for hours. Adults $3, students $2; members no charge.
Attendance: 500 (estimated)

Liberty

CLAY COUNTY HISTORICAL MUSEUM, 14 N. Main St., Liberty, MO 64068-1638. Tel.: 816-792-1849.
E-mail: info@claycountymuseum.org
Web Site: www.claycountymuseum.org
Key Personnel: Pres. (V), Carolyn Hatcher; Cur., Jay Thorne; Sec., Ann Cole.
Institution Type/Description: Local History Museum: housed in early drug store building; built in 1865.
Hours & Admission Prices: Feb.-Dec. Mon.-Sat. 1-4. No charge; donations accepted. Closed national holidays.
Attendance: 4,200 (estimated)

JESSE JAMES BANK MUSEUM, 103 N. Water, Liberty, MO 64068-1736. Mailing Address: c/o Friends of the James Farm, P.O. Box 404, Liberty, MO 64069. Tel.: 816-736-8510. Fax: 816-736-8501.
E-mail: historicsites@claycountymo.gov
Web Site: www.claycountymo.gov/Historic_Sites/Jesse_James_Bank_Museum
Key Personnel: Dir. Historic Sites, Elizabeth Beckett.
Institution Type/Description: Banking Museum: housed in 1858 old Liberty Bank building, site of James Gang bank robbery, Feb. 13, 1866.
Hours & Admission Prices: March-Dec. Mon.-Sat. 10-4. Adults $6.50, senior citizens 62 & up $6, children 8-15 $4; discounts to groups; children under 8 no charge. &
Attendance: 4,000

LIBERTY JAIL HISTORIC SITE, 216 N. Main, Liberty, MO 64068-1629. Tel.: 816-781-3188. Fax: 816-781-7311.
E-mail: HSLibertyJail@ldschurch.org
Formerly: Historic Liberty Jail Visitors Center Historic Site
Key Personnel: Dir., Elder John Toronto.
Institution Type/Description: Religious History Museum.
Hours & Admission Prices: Daily 9-9. No charge. &
Attendance: 48,000 (actual)

Linn

OSAGE COUNTY CULTURAL HERITAGE CENTER - ZEWICKI HOUSE MUSEUM, CHC, 103 S. 4th St., Linn, MO 65051. 402 Main St., Linn, MO 65051. Mailing Address: P.O. Box 402, Linn, MO 65051. Tel.: 573-897-2932. Facebook.
E-mail: historic1841@yahoo.com
Web Site: osagecounty.org
Formerly: Osage County Historical Society
Key Personnel: Chm. (V), Roberta Schwinke; Pres. (V), Stanley Strope.
Institution Type/Description: Historic House Museum: former home of dentist, Dr. E. T. Zewicki and his wife Amy; built in 1895.
Hours & Admission Prices: May 2-Dec. 14 daily 9-4. Library: call for hours. No charge; donations accepted. Closed holidays. &
Attendance: 350 (estimated)

Linn Creek

CAMDEN COUNTY HISTORICAL SOCIETY & MUSEUM, 206 S. Locust St., Linn Creek, MO 65052. Mailing Address: P.O. Box 19, Linn Creek, MO 65052-0019. Tel.: 573-346-7191.

E-mail: media@camdencountymuseum.org
Web Site: camdencountymuseum.com
Key Personnel: Chm. (V), Patricia Kitterman; Pres. (V), Daphne Jeffries; Museum Shop Mgr., Shirley Childers.
Institution Type/Description: History Museum.
Hours & Admission Prices: March-Oct. 10-4; other times by appointment. No charge; donations accepted. &

Lone Jack

LONE JACK CIVIL WAR BATTLEFIELD MUSEUM & SOLDIER'S CEMETERY, 301 S. Bynum Rd., Lone Jack, MO 64070-8508. Mailing Address: c/o Lone Jack Historical Society, P. O. Box 34, Lone Jack, MO 64070. Tel.: 816-697-8833.
E-mail: president@historiclonejack.org
Web Site: www.historiclonejack.org
Key Personnel: Chm. & Pres. (V), Alinder Miller.
Institution Type/Description: Civil War Museum: housed in modern museum building on site of the Battle of Lone Jack, Aug. 16, 1862.
Hours & Admission Prices: March-Oct. Wed.-Sat. 10-4, Sun. 1-4; Nov.-Feb. Sat. 10-4, Sun. 1-4. Adult $3, children 6-12 $1; children under 6 no charge. Closed New Year's Day; Easter; Thanksgiving; Christmas. &
Attendance: 3,357 (actual)

Macon

MACON COUNTY HISTORICAL SOCIETY, 1402 S. Missouri, Macon, MO 63552-4452. Mailing Address: P.O. Box 304, Macon, MO 63552-4452. Tel.: 660-395-0266 & 346-7780.
E-mail: mchsmuse@yahoo.com
Web Site: maconcountyhistoricalsociety.com
Key Personnel: Pres. (V), Ralph Klusman; Vice Pres., Harold Burkhardt; Treas., Ruth Master; Sec., Doris Duckworth; Tour Guide & Historian, Merlyn Amedei; Tour Guide & Historian, Mardine White.
Institution Type/Description: Historical Society Museum.
Hours & Admission Prices: Mon. 6pm-8pm, Thurs.-Sat. 10-2. No charge. &
Attendance: 350

Malden

BOOTHEEL YOUTH MUSEUM, 700A N. Douglas, Malden, MO 63863-1510. Mailing Address: P.O. Box 182, Malden, MO 63863-0182. Tel.: 573-276-3600. Fax: 573-276-3600. Facebook: Bootheel Youth Museum.
E-mail: info@bootheelyouthmuseum.org
Web Site: www.bootheelyouthmuseum.org
Key Personnel: Exec. Dir., Patsy Reublin; Chm. (V), Jason Scherer; Mktg., Allison Harvel; Museum Shop Mgr., Kaite Rhinehart.
Institution Type/Description: Children's Science Center.
Hours & Admission Prices: Tues.-Sat. 10-4, Sun. 1-4, Mon. by appointment. Children 3-17 $7, adults $5; discounts to AAM & ASTC members; museum members no charge. &
Attendance: 27,531 (actual)

MAAPS MILITARY MUSEUM, Malden Industrial Park Office, 3077 Mitchell Dr., Malden, MO 63863. Mailing Address: P.O. Box 411, Malden, MO 63863. Tel.: 573-276-2279. Fax: 573-276-2296.
E-mail: info@maaps.net
Web Site: maaps.net/museum.html
Institution Type/Description: Military History Museum.
Hours & Admission Prices: Mon.-Fri. 8-12 & 1-5. No charge; donations accepted. &

MALDEN HISTORICAL MUSEUM, 201 N. Beckwith, Malden, MO 63863. Mailing Address: P.O. Box 142, Malden, MO 63863-0142. Tel.: 573-276-5008.
Institution Type/Description: History Museum.
Hours & Admission Prices: Wed.-Thurs. & Sat. 1:30-4:30; groups by appointment.

Mansfield

LAURA INGALLS WILDER-ROSE WILDER LANE HISTORIC HOME & MUSEUM, 3060 Hwy. A, Mansfield, MO 65704-8104. Tel.: 417-924-3626. Fax: 417-924-8580.
E-mail: liwhome@getgoin.net
Web Site: www.lauraingallswilderhome.com
Key Personnel: Dir., Jean C. Coday; Treas., Jane K. Coday; Director's Asst., Anna Bradley.
Institution Type/Description: History Museum: next to the home of author Laura Ingalls Wilder.

Hours & Admission Prices: Seasonally; March-Nov. 15 Mon.-Sat. 9-5, Sun. 12:30-5. Adults $14, children 6-17 $7; children under 6 no charge. Closed Easter. &
Attendance: 35,000 (estimated)

MANSFIELD HISTORICAL SOCIETY & MUSEUM, 111 W. Park Square, Mansfield, MO 65704. Mailing Address: P.O. Box 374, Mansfield, MO 65704. Tel.: 417-924-4041.
E-mail: info@mansfieldhistorical.org
Web Site: mansfieldhistorical.org
Key Personnel: Pres. (V) & Museum Shop Mgr., Linda Duquesne; Vice Pres. (V), Vicki Blankenship; Chmn. (V), Kathy Short.
Institution Type/Description: Historical Society Museum.
Hours & Admission Prices: Mon.-Fri. 10-3, Sat. 10-12; closed Oct. 15-Mar. 1; call for appointment for special tours (417-924-3396). No charge; donations accepted. &
Attendance: 1,000 (estimated)

Marble Hill

BOLLINGER COUNTY MUSEUM OF NATURAL HISTORY, 207 Mayfield Dr., Marble Hill, MO 63764. Mailing Address: P.O. Box 676, Marble Hill, MO 63764. Tel.: 573-238-1174.
E-mail: bcmnh@sbcglobal.net
Web Site: bcmnh.org
Key Personnel: Dir., Eva Dunn.
Institution Type/Description: Natural History Museum.
Hours & Admission Prices: Thurs.-Sat. 12-4:30; other times by appointment. Adults $5, children 18 & under $2; friends of museum no charge.
Attendance: 4,800 (actual)

Marceline

WALT DISNEY HOMETOWN MUSEUM, 120 E. Santa Fe Ave., Marceline, MO 64658-1144. Tel.: 660-376-3343.
E-mail: waltdisneymuseum@att.net
Web Site: www.waltdisneymuseum.org
Key Personnel: Dir., Kaye Malins; Pres. (V), Tom Thornton; Museum Shop Mgr., Inez Johnson.
Institution Type/Description: Walt Disney History & Railroad Museum.
Hours & Admission Prices: April-Oct. Tues.-Sat. 10-4, Sun. 1-4. Adults $10, children 6-10 $5; discounts to groups of 25 or more; children under 6 no charge. &
Attendance: 10,000 (estimated)

Marshall

MARTIN COMMUNITY CENTER AND NICHOLAS BEAZLEY AVIATION MUSEUM, 1985 S. Odell, Marshall, MO 65340. Tel.: 660-886-2630. Fax: 660-886-2689.
E-mail: mccnbam@mmuonline.net
Web Site: nicholasbeazley.org
Institution Type/Description: Aviation History Museum.
Hours & Admission Prices: Tues.-Sat. 10-4; other times by appointment.

SALINE COUNTY HISTORICAL SOCIETY MUSEUM, 101 N. Lafayette St., Marshall, MO 65340-1747. Tel.: 660-886-7546.
Institution Type/Description: Historical Society Museum.
Hours & Admission Prices: April-Dec. Tues.-Fri. 9:30-12 & 1-4, Sat.-Sun. by appointment.

Marshfield

WEBSTER COUNTY HISTORICAL SOCIETY, 219 S. Clay St., Marshfield, MO 65706. Mailing Address: P.O. Box 13, Marshfield, MO 65706. Tel.: 417-468-7407 & 859-2036. Facebook: Webster County Historical Society.
Key Personnel: Dir. & Museum Shop Mgr., Linda Blazer; Pres. (V), Pat Schreiner.
Institution Type/Description: Historical Society Museum: housed in the former Carnegie Library; built in 1911.
Hours & Admission Prices: Jan.-March Fri. 1-4; April-Dec. Mon.-Sat. 1-4; other times by appointment. No charge; donations accepted.
Attendance: 2,200 (actual)

Maryland Heights

HISTORIC AIRCRAFT RESTORATION MUSEUM, 3127 Creve Coeur Mill Rd., Maryland Heights, MO 63146. Tel.: 314-434-3368. Fax: 314-878-6453.
E-mail: info@creve-coeur-airport-museum.org
Institution Type/Description: Aircraft Museum.

Hours & Admission Prices: Guided Tours: Sat.-Sun. 10-4; other times by appointment. Adults $10, children 5-12 $5; discounts to groups; children under 5 no charge. Airplane Rides $80-$110 per person.

Maryville

WARREN STUCKI MUSEUM OF BROADCASTING, Northwest Missouri State University, 800 University Dr., Maryville, MO 64468-6015. Tel.: 660-562-1163.
E-mail: rharris@nwmissouri.edu
Web Site: www.nwmissouri.edu
Institution Type/Description: Broadcasting Museum.
Hours & Admission Prices: Mon.-Fri. 8-5; other times by appointment. No charge. &

Memphis

DOWNING HOUSE/BOYER HOUSE & MEMPHIS DEPOT MUSEUM COMPLEX, 311 S. Main St., Memphis, MO 63555-1427. Tel.: 660-465-2259.
E-mail: mcb@nemr.net
Web Site: www.downinghousemuseum.org
Key Personnel: Cur., Rhonda McBee; Cur., Julie Clapp.
Institution Type/Description: History Museum: 14 room brick mansion built in 1858.
Hours & Admission Prices: Tues.-Thurs. 1-4; other times by appointment. Admission $5; children under 12 no charge.
Attendance: 750 (estimated)

Mexico

AMERICAN SADDLEBRED HORSE MUSEUM, 501 S. Muldrow, Mexico, MO 65265-2082. Tel.: 573-581-3910.
E-mail: lpratt@sbcglobal.net
Web Site: www.audrain.org/museums-saddlehorse.aspx
Key Personnel: Exec. Dir., Lori Pratt; Pres. (V), Tony Robertson; Cur., Tom Usnick.
Institution Type/Description: General History Museum: located on the grounds of the Audrain Historical Museum (see separate listing).
Hours & Admission Prices: Tues.-Sat. 10-4, Sun. 1-4. Adults $5, children under 12 $3; members no charge. Closed national holidays. &
Attendance: 1,600 (actual)

AUDRAIN HISTORICAL MUSEUM, GRACELAND, 501 S. Muldrow, Mexico, MO 65265-2082. Tel.: 573-581-3910. Fax: 573-581-7155.
E-mail: lpratt@audrain.org
Web Site: www.audrain.org
Key Personnel: Exec. Dir., Lori Pratt; Pres. (V), Tony Robertson.
Institution Type/Description: History Museum: housed in 1857 John P. Clark home, later lived in by Judge James E. Ross & his descendants, restored 1958.
Hours & Admission Prices: Tues.-Sat. 10-4, Sun. 1-4. Adults $5, children 12 & under $3; members no charge. Closed holidays. &
Attendance: 1,600 (actual)

Miami

MISSOURI'S AMERICAN INDIAN CULTURAL CENTER AT VAN METER STATE PARK, 32146 N. Hwy. 122, Miami, MO 65344. Tel.: 660-886-7537. Fax: 660-886-7512.
Web Site: mostateparks.com/park/van-meter-state-park
Key Personnel: Site Admin. & Park/Historic Site Specialist III, David Savage; Interpretive Resource Technician, Eric Fuemmeler.
Institution Type/Description: Park Museum & Visitor Center: located on Missouri Indian village archaeological site.
Hours & Admission Prices: Park: daily 8-sunset. American Indian Cultural Center: May-Sept. Wed.-Sun. 10-4; Oct.-March Sat. 10-4, Sun. 1-5; April Thurs.-Sat. 10-4, Sun. 1-5. No charge; donations accepted. &
Attendance: 50,000 (actual)

Moberly

RANDOLPH COUNTY HISTORICAL SOCIETY HISTORY MUSEUM, 223 N. Clark St., Moberly, MO 65270-1540. Tel.: 660-263-9396.
E-mail: rchs@sbcglobal.net
Web Site: www.randolphhistory.com
Key Personnel: Bd. Pres., J.W. Ballinger.
Institution Type/Description: History Museum.

Hours & Admission Prices: Mon. 10-noon, Thurs. 1-3, Sat. 9-noon; other times by appointment. Railroad Museum: April-Sept. Sat. 1-3; Also open for special events & Thurs. for farmers' market. No charge; donations accepted.
Attendance: 3,000 (estimated)

Monett

MONETT HISTORICAL SOCIETY, 705 E. Broadway, Monett, MO 65708. Mailing Address: P.O. Box 128, Monett, MO 65708. Tel.: 417-235-9030.
E-mail: historical@mo-net.com
Web Site: monetthistory.com
Key Personnel: Pres. (V), Douglas Hobson.
Institution Type/Description: History Museum.
Hours & Admission Prices: Tues. 1-3, Thurs. 6:30 pm-8:30 pm, Sat. 10-3. No charge. &
Attendance: 100 (estimated)

Montgomery City

GRAHAM CAVE STATE PARK, 217 Hwy T.T., Montgomery City, MO 63361-5509. Tel.: 573-564-3476. Fax: 573-564-2534.
E-mail: moparks@dnr.mo.gov
Web Site: www.grahamcave.com
Institution Type/Description: State Park.
Hours & Admission Prices: Park: daily 7am to sunset. No charge. &
Attendance: 55,000

Nelson

SAPPINGTON CEMETERY STATE HISTORIC SITE, Route AA, Nelson, MO 65347. Mailing Address: Arrow Rock State Historic Site, P.O. Box 1, Arrow Rock, MO 65320. Tel.: 660-837-3330. Fax: 660-837-3300.
E-mail: moparks@dnr.mo.gov
Web Site: mostateparks.com/park/sappington-cemetery-state-historic-site
Key Personnel: Site Admin., Michael Dickey.
Institution Type/Description: Historic Site: resting places of prominent Missourians, including Claiborne Fox Jackson, Dr. John Sappington & Gov. M.M. Marmaduke.
Hours & Admission Prices: Daily sunrise to sunset. No charge.
Attendance: 5,000

Neosho

CROWDER COLLEGE-LONGWELL MUSEUM & CAMP CROWDER COLLECTION, 601 Laclede, Neosho, MO 64850-9165. Tel.: 417-455-5470. Fax: 417-455-5539.
Web Site: www.crowder.edu/about-crowder/longwell-museum
Institution Type/Description: Art Museum/Center & History Museum.
Hours & Admission Prices: Mon.-Fri. 9-4. No charge; donations accepted. Closed college holidays. &
Attendance: 800 (estimated)

Nevada

BUSHWHACKER MUSEUM, 212 W. Walnut St., Nevada, MO 64772-2341. Tel.: 417-667-9602.
E-mail: bushwhackerjail@sbcglobal.net
Web Site: www.bushwhacker.org
Key Personnel: C.F.O., Tom Ramsey; Pres. (V.), Jean McQueen; Dir. & Museum Shop Mgr., Will Tollerton.
Institution Type/Description: History Museum.
Hours & Admission Prices: May-Oct. Wed.-Fri. 10-4, Sat. 10-1. Adults $5, children 12-17 $2, children under 12 $1; discounts to AAA members; AASLH & members no charge. Closed Memorial Day; Independence Day; Labor Day. &
Attendance: 2,000 (actual)

New Bloomfield

NEW BLOOMFIELD AREA HISTORICAL SOCIETY, 313 Oak St., New Bloomfield, MO 65063. Mailing Address: P.O. Box 132, New Bloomfield, MO 65063-0132. Tel.: 573-491-0180.
E-mail: museum@newbloomfieldhistorical.org
Web Site: newbloomfieldhistorical.org
Key Personnel: Gracia Backer; Museum Shop Mgr., Dale Lawson.
Institution Type/Description: Historical Society Museum.
Hours & Admission Prices: Sat. 10-1; other times by appointment. No charge; donations accepted.
Attendance: 600 (estimated)

New Madrid

HUNTER-DAWSON STATE HISTORIC SITE, 312 Dawson Rd., New Madrid, MO 63869. Mailing Address: P.O. Box 308, New Madrid, MO 63869-0308. Tel.: 573-748-5340. Fax: 573-748-7228.
E-mail: moparks@dnr.mo.gov
Web Site: www.mostateparks.com
Key Personnel: Historic Site Specialist III, Michael Comer; Interpretive Resource Specialist, Vicki Jackson; Park Maintenance Worker I, Chadd Thomas.
Institution Type/Description: Historic House: c.1859 Hunter-Dawson House, a yellow cyprus frame house in the Greek Revival & Italianate style.
Hours & Admission Prices: March-Nov. Mon.-Sat. 10-4, Sun. 12-4; Dec.-Feb. Tues.-Sat. 10-4. Adults $2.50, children 6-12 $1.50; children under 6 no charge. Closed New Year's Day; Easter; Thanksgiving; Christmas Day. &
Attendance: 8,098 (actual)

NEW MADRID HISTORICAL MUSEUM, 1 Main St., New Madrid, MO 63869. Tel.: 573-748-5944.
E-mail: nmhmnm@yahoo.com
Web Site: www.newmadridmuseum.com
Key Personnel: Dir. & Museum Shop Mgr., Jeff Grunwald; Pres. (V), Jan Farrenburg.
Institution Type/Description: History Museum.
Hours & Admission Prices: Call for hours. Adults $3, seniors $2.50, children $1.50, group rates available. &
Attendance: 8,000 (estimated)

New Melle

BOONE-DUDEN ARCHIVES AND MUSEUM, 3565 Mill St., New Melle, MO 63365-0082. Mailing Address: P.O. Box 82, New Melle, MO 63365-0082. Tel.: 636-987-2136.
E-mail: ida.g@outlook.com
Key Personnel: Dir. & Museum Shop Mgr., Ida Gerdiman; Chm. (V), Ruth Busdieker.
Institution Type/Description: History Museum: house built in 1871.
Hours & Admission Prices: Sun. 12:30-4; other times by appointment. No charge; donations accepted. &
Attendance: 89 (actual)

O'Fallon

DARIUS HEALD HOUSE, Fort Zumwalt Park, O'Fallon, MO 63366. Mailing Address: City of O'Fallon, 100 N. Main, O'Fallon, MO 63366. Tel.: 636-379-5614.
E-mail: jhoisington@ofallon.mo.us
Web Site: www.ofallon.mo.us/dept_tourism_healdhome.htm
Institution Type/Description: Historic House Museum: built in the late 1800s.
Hours & Admission Prices: By appointment.

O'FALLON HISTORICAL SOCIETY'S LOG CABIN MUSEUM, Civic Park, O'Fallon, MO 63366. Mailing Address: P. O. Box 424, O'Fallon, MO 63366. Tel.: 636-980-8015.
E-mail: info@ofallonmohistory.org
Web Site: ofallonmohistory.org
Key Personnel: Pres. (V), Lewis Swinger.
Institution Type/Description: Historic Building Museum: built c.1870.
Hours & Admission Prices: Call for hours. No charge; donations accepted.

Odessa

ODESSA AREA HISTORICAL MUSEUM, 101 W. Phillips St., Odessa, MO 64076-1543. Tel.: 573-639-0762.
E-mail: ekvodmo13@yahoo.com
Institution Type/Description: History Museum.
Hours & Admission Prices: Wed. & Sun. 3-6; other times by appointment.

Osceola

ST. CLAIR COUNTY HISTORICAL SOCIETY, 660 Main, Osceola, MO 64776. Mailing Address: P.O. Box 376, Osceola, MO 64776-0376. Tel.: 417-876-3925 & 7913.
E-mail: howardjoanmcp54@gmail.com
Web Site: www.stclaircountyhistoricalsociety.org
Key Personnel: Pres. (V), Howard McPeak; Interim Cur. & Museum Shop Mgr., Linda Anderson.
Institution Type/Description: Historical Society Museum.
Hours & Admission Prices: May-Oct.: Fri. 8-noon, Sat. 10-2:30; Nov.-April Fri. 8-10; other times by appointment. No charge, donations accepted. &
Attendance: 480 (estimated)

Overland

OVERLAND HISTORICAL SOCIETY, 2404 Gass Ave., Overland, MO 63114. Tel.: 314-426-7027. Facebook: Overland Historical Society.
E-mail: overlandhistoricalsociety@gmail.com
Web Site: www.overlandhistoricalsociety.com
Key Personnel: Pres. (V), Pat Westhoff; Museum Shop Mgr., Sandy Jackson.
Institution Type/Description: Historical Society Museum.
Hours & Admission Prices: Call for hours. Adults $2.
Attendance: 400 (estimated)

Owensville

GASCONADE COUNTY HISTORICAL SOCIETY MUSEUM, 105 W. McFadden, Owensville, MO 65066. Mailing Address: P.O. Box 131, Hermann, MO 65041-0131. Tel.: 573-437-5617 (museum) 486-4028 (archives & library).
E-mail: gchsarc@centurytel.net
Key Personnel: Dir., Bonnie Brown; Cur., Shirley Lindroth.
Institution Type/Description: Historical Society Museum: housed in a former hotel; built in 1910.
Hours & Admission Prices: Mon. & Fri.-Sat. 11-3. No charge; donations accepted. &
Attendance: 700 (estimated)

Ozark

CHRISTIAN COUNTY HISTORICAL SOCIETY AND MUSEUM, 202 E. Church St., Ozark, MO 65721. Mailing Address: P.O. Box 442, Ozark, MO 65721-0442. Tel.: 417-988-7191. Facebook: Christian County Historical Society and Museum.
E-mail: christiancohistorical@gmail.com
Web Site: www.ccmohistoricalsociety.com
Key Personnel: Pres. & Webmaster, Linda Myers; Vice Pres. & Volunteer Coord., John Nixon; Sec., Shannon Mawhiney; Treas., Avaline Harris; Property Mgmt. & Cur., John Nixon.
Institution Type/Description: Historical Society Museum.
Hours & Admission Prices: April-Oct. Sun. 2-4; other times by appointment.

Paris

UNION COVERED BRIDGE STATE HISTORIC SITE, County Rd. C, Paris, MO 65275. Mailing Address: Mark Twain Birthplace, 37352 Shrine Rd., Florida, MO 65283-2127. Tel.: 573-565-3449. Fax: 573-565-3718.
E-mail: mark.twain.birthplace.state.historic.site@dnr.mo.gov
Web Site: www.mostateparks.com/unionbridge.htm
Key Personnel: Site Admin., Kevin Bolling; Museum Shop Mgr., Marianne Bodine.
Institution Type/Description: Historic Site: 1871 Union covered bridge.
Hours & Admission Prices: Daily 8-5. No charge; donations accepted.
Attendance: 24,000 (estimated)

Perry

RALLS COUNTY HISTORICAL MUSEUM AND LIBRARY, 120 E. Main St., Perry, MO 63462. Mailing Address: P.O. Box 463, Perry, MO 63462-0463. Tel.: 573-248-6147 & 565-2025.
Institution Type/Description: History Museum.
Hours & Admission Prices: Wed. & Fri.-Sun. 10-5.

Pilot Grove

COOPER COUNTY HISTORICAL SOCIETY, 111 Roe St., Pilot Grove, MO 65276. Mailing Address: P.O. Box 51, Pilot Grove, MO 65276. Tel.: 660-834-3582.
E-mail: research@shsmo.org
Institution Type/Description: Historical Society Museum.
Hours & Admission Prices: late May to late Oct. Fri.-Sun. 1-5; other times by appointment.

Pilot Knob

BATTLE OF PILOT KNOB STATE HISTORIC SITE, 118 E. Maple St., Pilot Knob, MO 63663-0509. Mailing Address: P.O. Box 509, Pilot Knob, MO 63663-0509. Tel.: 573-546-3454. Fax: 573-546-2713.
E-mail: brick.autry@dnr.mo.gov
Web Site: www.battleofpilotknob.org

Formerly: Fort Davidson State Historic Site
Key Personnel: Pres. (V), Terry Cadenbach; Rgnl. Supvr., Brian Stith; Site Admin., Walter Busch; Cur., Brick Autry.
Institution Type/Description: Historic Site: 1864 Battle of Pilot Knob; Civil War battlefield.
Hours & Admission Prices: April 16-Nov. daily 10-4; Dec.-April 15 Tues.-Sun. 10-4. No charge; donations accepted. Closed New Year's Day; Thanksgiving; Christmas. &
Attendance: 63,147 (actual)

Pineville

MCDONALD COUNTY HISTORICAL MUSEUM, 302 Harmon, Pineville, MO 64856. Mailing Address: P.O. Box 572, Pineville, MO 64856-0572.
E-mail: info@mcdonaldcohistory.org
Institution Type/Description: History Museum.
Hours & Admission Prices: Fri.-Sat. 9-1.

Platte City

BEN FERREL 1882 MINI MANSION MUSEUM, 220 Ferrel St., Platte City, MO 64079-9511. Mailing Address: Platte County Historical & Genealogical Society, P.O. Box 103, Platte City, MO 64079-0103. Tel.: 816-431-5121.
E-mail: wjsummers@fairpoint.net
Web Site: www.rootsweb.ancestry.com/~mopchgs/
Institution Type/Description: Historic House: built in 1882.
Hours & Admission Prices: April 15-Oct. 15 Thurs.-Fri. 1-4; Oct. 16-April 14 by appointment. Adults $5; members no charge.
Attendance: 1,200 (actual)

Pleasant Hill

PLEASANT HILL HISTORICAL SOCIETY, 125 Wyoming St., Pleasant Hill, MO 64080-1643. Mailing Address: P.O. Box 31, Pleasant Hill, MO 64080-0031. Tel.: 816-540-4010 & 529-6088.
E-mail: kennedy222@kcweb.net
Web Site: www.orgsites.com/mo/pleasanthillhistoricalsociety
Key Personnel: Pres. (V), Beverly Kennedy; Cur. (V), Robert E. Kennedy.
Institution Type/Description: Historical Society Museum & Family Research Library.
Hours & Admission Prices: Mon. 1:30-3:30, Wed. & Fri. 3:30-5:30, 2nd Sat. of month 10-3; other times by appointment, call 816-529-6088. No charge; donations accepted. &
Attendance: 750 (estimated)

Point Lookout

THE RALPH FOSTER MUSEUM, College of the Ozarks, One Cultural Ct., Point Lookout, MO 65726. Mailing Address: P.O. Box 17, Point Lookout, MO 65726. Tel.: 417-690-3407. Fax: 417-690-2606.
E-mail: museum@cofo.edu
Web Site: www.rfostermuseum.com
Key Personnel: Dir. & Museum Shop Mgr., Annette J. Sain; C.E.O. & Pres., Dr. Jerry Davis; Cur., Jeanelle Ash; Cur., Thomas A. Debo; Cur., Mike Combs.
Institution Type/Description: General Museum.
Hours & Admission Prices: Feb. to mid-Dec. Mon.-Sat. 9-4:30; groups by appointment. Adults $6, seniors 62 & over and groups 20 or more $5; discounts to AAM & ICOM members; students no charge. Closed Thanksgiving week &
Attendance: 60,000 (estimated)

Poplar Bluff

MARGARET HARWELL ART MUSEUM, 421 N. Main St., Poplar Bluff, MO 63901-5107. Tel.: 573-686-8002. Fax: 573-686-8017.
E-mail: ethel@mham.org
Web Site: www.mham.org
Key Personnel: Dir., Tina M. Magill; Pres. (V), Nancy Buttry; Museum Shop Mgr., Gerry Vandervort.
Institution Type/Description: Art Museum: housed in 1883 mansion.
Hours & Admission Prices: Tues.-Fri. 12-4, Sat.-Sun. 1-4. No charge; donations accepted. Closed national holidays. &
Attendance: 18,000 (estimated)

MOARK REGIONAL RAILROAD MUSEUM AKA THE POPLAR BLUFF RAILROAD MUSEUM, 303 Moran St., Poplar Bluff, MO 63901. Tel.: 573-785-4539.

E-mail: dsilverberg@darnews.com
Key Personnel: Pres. (V), David Silverberg.
Institution Type/Description: Historic Building: built in 1928. Listed on the National Register of Historic Places.
Hours & Admission Prices: Sat. 1-4; groups by appointment. No charge; donations accepted.
Attendance: 1,300 (actual)

Portage Des Sioux

CAF MISSOURI WING MUSEUM, St. Charles County Airport - Smartt Field, 6390 Grafton Ferry Rd., Portage Des Sioux, MO 63373. Mailing Address: P.O. Box 637, Saint Charles, MO 63302. Tel.: 636-250-4515. Fax: 636-250-4515.
E-mail: pkf4@earthlink.net
Web Site: www.cafmo.org
Key Personnel: Museum Shop Mgr., Jack Seeman.
Institution Type/Description: Military History Museum.
Hours & Admission Prices: Thurs. & Sat. 10-2:30; call to confirm. No charge; donations accepted. &

Princeton

CASTEEL-LINN HOUSE AND MUSEUM, 902 E. Oak St., Princeton, MO 64673-1255. Mailing Address: P.O. Box 1583, Palm Springs, CA 92263-1583. Tel.: 660-748-3905.
Key Personnel: C.E.O. & Dir. (V), N. P. Linn; Pres., Cur. & Public Rels. (V), Nancy Paige Linn; Archivist, Pamela Elizabeth Kidd; Security, Cy Linn.
Institution Type/Description: Historic House: built on a historic site where Civil War reunions were held.
Hours & Admission Prices: April-Dec. by appointment only. No charge. &
Attendance: 200 (estimated)

MERCER COUNTY GENEALOGICAL AND HISTORICAL SOCIETY, 601 Grant St., Princeton, MO 64673-1023. Mailing Address: P.O. Box 97, Princeton, MO 64673-0097. Tel.: 660-748-3725 & 4755. Fax: 660-748-3723.
E-mail: Kimmysuet@aol.com
Web Site: www.rootsweb.ancestry.com/~momercer/
Key Personnel: Mgr., Randi Ferguson.
Institution Type/Description: Local History Museum: housed in Mercer County Library.
Hours & Admission Prices: By appointment only. No charge. Closed national holidays.

Raytown

RAYTOWN HISTORICAL SOCIETY & MUSEUM, 9705 E. 63rd St., Raytown, MO 64133. Mailing Address: P.O. Box 16652, Raytown, MO 64133. Tel.: 816-353-5033.
E-mail: raytownhistorical@sbcglobal.net
Web Site: www.raytownhistoricalsociety.org
Institution Type/Description: Historical Society Museum.
Hours & Admission Prices: Wed.-Sat. 10-4; other times by appointment. Adults $2; children under 12 no charge.

Republic

WILSON'S CREEK NATIONAL BATTLEFIELD, 6424 W. Farm Rd. 182, Republic, MO 65738-9492. Tel.: 417-732-2662, ext. 352. Fax: 417-732-1167.
E-mail: gary_p_sullivan@nps.gov
Web Site: www.nps.gov/wicr; www.civilwarvirtualmuseum.org.
Key Personnel: Supt., T. John Hillmer; Chief Resource Mgmt., Gary Sullivan.
Institution Type/Description: Military Museum: located on the battlefield on which the August 10, 1861 battle of Wilson's Creek occurred.
Hours & Admission Prices: Park: seasonal hours. Museum: Nov.-March daily 9-12 & 1-4. Park & Museum: adults 16 & over $5, maximum $10 per vehicle; school groups no charge. Closed New Year's Day; Thanksgiving; Christmas. &
Attendance: 300,000 (estimated)

Richmond

RAY COUNTY MUSEUM, 901 W. Royle St., Richmond, MO 64085-1545. Tel.: 816-776-2305.
E-mail: raycohistory@aol.com
Key Personnel: Pres. (V), David Blyth; Cur., Linda Emley.
Institution Type/Description: History Museum.
Hours & Admission Prices: Wed.-Sat. 10-4.

Rolla

MISSOURI DEPARTMENT OF NATURAL RESOURCES, DIVISION OF GEOLOGY AND LAND SURVEY, 111 Fairgrounds Rd., Rolla, MO 65401-2909. Mailing Address: P.O. Box 250, Rolla, MO 65402-0250. Tel.: 573-368-2100 & 2118. Fax: 573-368-2111.
E-mail: contact@dnr.mo.gov
Web Site: www.dnr.mo.gov/geology
Formerly: Ed Clark Museum of Missouri Geology
Key Personnel: Dir. & State Geologist, Joseph A. Gillman.
Institution Type/Description: Geology Museum.
Hours & Admission Prices: Mon.-Fri. 8-5. No charge. Closed national & Missouri holidays. &
Attendance: 3,000

PHELPS COUNTY HISTORICAL SOCIETY, 302 Third St., Rolla, MO 65402. Mailing Address: P.O. Box 1861, Rolla, MO 65402-1861. Tel.: 573-364-5977. Facebook: Phelps County Historical Society.
E-mail: pchs@rollanet.org
Key Personnel: Pres. (V), Dennis Peterman.
Institution Type/Description: Historical Society Museum: housed in Dillon Log House; built in 1839.
Hours & Admission Prices: By appointment. No charge; donations accepted.
Attendance: 500 (estimated)

Saint Charles

FIRST MISSOURI STATE CAPITOL-STATE HISTORIC SITE, 200 S. Main St., Saint Charles, MO 63301-2855. Tel.: 636-940-3322. Fax: 636-940-3324.
E-mail: first.state.capitol.state.historic.site@dnr.mo.gov
Web Site: www.dnr.state.mo.us
Key Personnel: Site Admin., Victoria Love; Asst. Site Admin., Robert Adams; Interpretive Resource Tech., Sue Love.
Institution Type/Description: Historic Buildings: c.1818 first Missouri State Capitol; temporary seat of government 1821-1826.
Hours & Admission Prices: Summer: Mon.-Sat. 10-4, Sun. 12-4; Winter: call for hours; groups by appointment. Family $15, adults $4, children 6-11 $2.50; discounts to groups; children under 6 no charge. Closed New Year's Day; Easter; Thanksgiving; Christmas. &
Attendance: 52,000 (actual)

FOUNDRY ART CENTRE, 520 N. Main Center, Saint Charles, MO 63301-2182. Tel.: 636-255-0270. Fax: 636-925-0345.
E-mail: melissa@foundryartcentre.org
Web Site: foundryartcentre.org
Institution Type/Description: Art Gallery.
Hours & Admission Prices: Tues.-Thurs. 10-8, Fri.-Sat. 10-5, Sun. 12-4. No charge; donations accepted. &
Attendance: 74,000 (actual)

LEWIS & CLARK BOAT HOUSE AND NATURE CENTER, 1050 Riverside Dr., Saint Charles, MO 63301-3481. Tel.: 636-947-3199. Fax: 636-916-0240.
E-mail: lewisandclarkmuseum@yahoo.com
Web Site: www.lewisandclarkcenter.org
Key Personnel: Dir., Bob Learned; Pres., Jan Donelson; Museum Shop Mgr., Bob Learned.
Institution Type/Description: History Museum.
Hours & Admission Prices: Mon.-Sat. 10-5, Sun. 12-5. Adults $5, children under 17 $2; discounts to groups. Closed New Year's Day; Easter; Thanksgiving; Christmas. &
Attendance: 35,000 (actual)

ST. CHARLES COUNTY HISTORICAL SOCIETY, INC., 101 S. Main St., Saint Charles, MO 63301-2802. Tel.: 636-946-9828.
E-mail: info@scchs.org
Web Site: www.scchs.org
Key Personnel: Archivist, Amy G. Haake.
Institution Type/Description: Local History Museum.
Hours & Admission Prices: Library & Archives: Mon., Wed. & Fri. 10-3; 2nd & 4th Sat. 10-3. No charge. Research duplication fees. &
Attendance: 770 (actual)

Saint James

MARAMEC MUSEUM, THE JAMES FOUNDATION, Maramec Spring Park, 21880 Maramec Spring Dr., Saint James, MO 65559. Mailing Address: 320 S. Bourbeuse St., Saint James, MO 65559-1498. Tel.: 573-265-7124. Fax: 573-265-8770.
E-mail: jamesfoundation@centurytel.net
Web Site: maramecspringpark.com
Key Personnel: Rgnl. Mgr., Danny Marshall; Dir. Interpretive Svcs., Lloyd Callies.
Institution Type/Description: History Museum.
Hours & Admission Prices: April & Oct. Sat.-Sun. 12-4; May Mon.-Fri. 10-3, Sat.-Sun. 12-4; June-Aug. Mon.-Sun. 11-5; Sept. Wed.-Sun. 12-4. No charge. &
Attendance: 30,496 (actual)

VACUUM CLEANER MUSEUM, #3 Industrial Dr., Saint James, MO 65559. Tel.: 866-444-9004. Facebook.
Web Site: vacuummuseum.com
Key Personnel: Cur., Tom Gasko.
Institution Type/Description: History Museum.
Hours & Admission Prices: Museum: Mon.-Sat. 9-5. Factory Tours: Mon.-Thurs. 9-4:30. No charge. &

Saint Joseph

THE ALBRECHT-KEMPER MUSEUM OF ART, 2818 Frederick Ave., Saint Joseph, MO 64506-2903. Tel.: 816-233-7003, 888-254-2787. Fax: 816-233-3413.
E-mail: frontdesk@albrecht-kemper.org
Web Site: www.albrecht-kemper.org
Key Personnel: Dir., Mr. Terry L. Oldham; Pres. (V), John Wilson; Registrar, Megan Benitz; Catering Mgr., Robyn Enright; Coord. Membership & Museum Shop Mgr., Chelsea Howlett-Weideman.
Institution Type/Description: Art Museum.
Hours & Admission Prices: Tues.-Fri. 10-4, Sat.-Sun. 1-4. Adults $5, seniors 60 & over $2, students $1; members, AAM & ICOM members & children under 6 no charge. Closed major holidays. &
Attendance: 22,504 (actual)

HEATON-BOWMAN-SMITH FUNERAL HOME MUSEUM, 3609 Frederick Ave., Saint Joseph, MO 64506-3033. Tel.: 816-232-3355.
E-mail: staff@heatonbowmansmith.com
Web Site: www.heatonbowmansmith.com
Institution Type/Description: General Museum.
Hours & Admission Prices: Call for hours.

JESSE JAMES HOME MUSEUM, 1202 Penn St., Saint Joseph, MO 64503. Mailing Address: P.O. Box 1022, Saint Joseph, MO 64502-1022. Tel.: 816-232-8206. Fax: 816-232-3717.
E-mail: patee@ponyexpress.net
Web Site: www.ponyexpressjessejames.com
Key Personnel: Museum Dir., Gary Chilcote; Pres. (V), Thomas Duty; Cur. Collections, Doug Chilcote; Business Mgr., Lauren Green; Library & Archives, Carolyn Chilcote.
Institution Type/Description: Historic Building: 1879 house where Jesse James was killed in 1882.
Hours & Admission Prices: Daily call for hours. Adults $4, seniors $3, students $2. Closed New Year's Day; Easter; Thanksgiving; Christmas Eve & Day. &
Attendance: 17,000 (estimated)

NATIONAL MILITARY HERITAGE MUSEUM, 701 Messanie St., Saint Joseph, MO 64501-2219. Tel.: 816-233-4321. Fax: 816-279-9667.
E-mail: nmhm90@yahoo.com
Web Site: www.nationalmilitaryheritagemuseum.com
Key Personnel: Exec. Dir., Franklin A. Flesher.
Institution Type/Description: Military History Museum: housed in a former police station; built in 1890.
Hours & Admission Prices: Mon.-Fri. 9-4, Sat. 9-1. Adults $3; discounts to AAM members; students & members no charge.
Attendance: 3,000 (actual)

PATEE HOUSE MUSEUM, 1202 Penn St., Saint Joseph, MO 64503-2560. Mailing Address: P.O. Box 1022, Saint Joseph, MO 64502-1022. Tel.: 816-232-8206. Fax: 816-232-3717.
E-mail: patee@ponyexpress.net
Web Site: www.ponyexpressjessejames.com

Key Personnel: Museum Dir., Gary Chilcote; Pres., John Wolfe; Business Mgr., Lauren Green; Cur. Collections, Doug Chilcote; Library & Archives, Carolyn Chilcote.
Institution Type/Description: Western Museum: housed in 1858, Patee hotel, used as headquarters for the Pony Express in 1860 and during the Civil War. National Historic Landmark.
Hours & Admission Prices: Daily call for hours. Adults $7, seniors 60 & over $6, students 6-18 $5; discounts to KCPT & National Railway Society members; members and children 5 & under no charge. Closed New Year's Day; Easter; Thanksgiving; Christmas Eve & Day. &
Attendance: 20,000 (estimated)

PONY EXPRESS NATIONAL MUSEUM, 914 Penn St., Saint Joseph, MO 64503-2544. Tel.: 816-279-5059 & 800-530-5930. Fax: 816-233-9370.
E-mail: pxdirector@ponyexpress.net
Web Site: www.ponyexpress.org
Key Personnel: Exec. Dir., Cindy Daffron; Pres. (V), Richard N. DeShon; Visitor Rels. Mgr., Brenda Eaves; Weekend Mgr., Megan Beech.
Institution Type/Description: Historic Building Museum: 1858 original stables of the Pony Express, formally known as the Pike's Peak Stables, located on the site from which the first Pony Express rider left St. Joseph heading west to Sacramento.
Hours & Admission Prices: March 2-Nov. Mon.-Sat. 9-5, Sun. 11-4; Dec.-March 1 Mon.-Sat. 9-4. Adults $6, seniors $5, students & children 7-17 $3, children 4-6 $1; discounts to groups, veterans, AAA & AARP members; children 3 & under and members no charge. Pony School: by appointment & during special events. Closed New Year's Eve & Day; Easter; Thanksgiving; Christmas Eve & Day.. &
Attendance: 39,000 (actual)

ROBIDOUX ROW MUSEUM, 3rd & Poulin, Saint Joseph, MO 64501. Mailing Address: 217 W. Poulin St., Saint Joseph, MO 64501-1037. Tel.: 816-232-5861. Fax: 816-232-5861.
Web Site: www.robidouxrowmuseum.org
Key Personnel: Dir. & Museum Shop Mgr., Clyde Weeks; Pres. (V), Bill Leppert; Museum Shop Mgr., Clyde Weeks.
Institution Type/Description: History Museum: housed in the city founded by Joseph Robidoux in 1843. Listed on the National Register of Historic Places.
Hours & Admission Prices: Feb.-April & Oct.-Dec. Tues.-Sat. 1-4; May-Sept. Tues.-Fri. 10-4, Sat.-Sun. 1-4. Adults $2.50, seniors 62 & over $2, students 6-18 $1; discounts to active military; members and children 5 & under no charge.
Attendance: 2,794 (actual)

ST. JOSEPH MUSEUM INC., 3406 Frederick, Saint Joseph, MO 64506-2913. Mailing Address: P.O. Box 8096, Saint Joseph, MO 64508-8096. Tel.: 816-232-8471. Fax: 816-232-8482. Facebook: St. Joseph Museum.
E-mail: sjm@stjosephmuseum.org
Web Site: www.stjosephmuseum.org
Key Personnel: Exec. Dir., Sara Wilson; C.E.O., Pres. & Chm. (V), David Lewis; Cur. Collections, Sarah M. Elder; Head Security & Maintenance, Robert Culbertson; Bookkeeper & Office Mgr., Anita Sontheimer; Head of Public Rels., Kathy Reno; Vol. Coord., Gift Shop Mgr., Joy Sander.
Institution Type/Description: Ethnology, Local, Natural, Ethnic & Medical History.
Hours & Admission Prices: Mon.-Sat. 10-5, Sun. 1-5. Adults $6, seniors 62 & over $5, children 7-18 $4; discounts to Blue Star Museum members & groups; children under 6 & members no charge. Closed New Year's Eve & Day; Martin Luther King Jr. Day; President's Day; Memorial Day; Independence Day; Labor Day; Thanksgiving; Christmas Eve & Day. &
Attendance: 25,000 (estimated)

WYETH TOOTLE MANSION, 1100 Charles St., Saint Joseph, MO 64501. Mailing Address: P.O. Box 8096, Saint Joseph, MO 64508. Tel.: 800-530-8866.
E-mail: sjm@stjosephmuseum.org
Web Site: stjosephmuseum.org
Key Personnel: Exec. Dir., Sara Wilson.
Institution Type/Description: Historic House Museum: housed in the former home of William & Eliza Wyeth; built in 1879.
Hours & Admission Prices: Summer: Fri.-Sat. 10-4; other times by appointment. Adults $6, seniors 62 & over $5, students $4; members & children under 6 no charge.

Saint Louis

ANHEUSER-BUSCH BREWERY, 12th & Lynch St., Saint Louis, MO 63118. Tel.: 314-577-2626.
Web Site: www.budweisertours.com
Institution Type/Description: Company History Museum.
Hours & Admission Prices: Sept.-May Mon.-Sat. 10-5, Sun. 11-5; June-Aug. Mon.-Thurs. 9-5, Fri.-Sat. 9-7, Sun. 11-5. No charge. Closed New Year's Eve & Day;

M.L. King Day; President's Day; Easter; Thanksgiving, Christmas Eve, Day & day after. &

ARCHIVES & MUSEUM OF OPTOMETRY, 243 N. Lindbergh Blvd., Saint Louis, MO 63141-7851. Tel.: 314-983-4136. Fax: 314-991-4101.
E-mail: khebert@aoa.org
Web Site: www.aoa.org/about-the-aoa/archives-and-museum
Institution Type/Description: Optometry Association and History Museum.
Hours & Admission Prices: Call for hours. No charge; donations accepted. &

ART SAINT LOUIS, 1223 Pine St., Saint Louis, MO 63103-2527. Tel.: 314-241-4810. Facebook: Art Saint Louis; Twitter: @ArtStLouis..
E-mail: info@artstlouis.org
Web Site: www.artstlouis.org
Key Personnel: Exec. Dir., Chandler Branch; Pres. Bd. Dirs., David Stoeberl; Artistic Dir., Robin Hirsch-Steinhoff; Program Coord., Kathy Duffin.
Institution Type/Description: Art Gallery.
Hours & Admission Prices: Mon.-Fri. 8-4, Sat. 9-3, Tues.-Fri. 10-5. No charge. Closed holidays.

ATRIUM GALLERY LTD., 4814 Washington Ave., Saint Louis, MO 63108. Tel.: 314-367-1076. Fax: 314-367-7676.
E-mail: info@atriumgallery.net
Web Site: www.atriumgallery.net
Key Personnel: C.E.O. & Dir., Carolyn P. Miles; Asst., Bryan Robertson.
Institution Type/Description: Art Gallery.
Hours & Admission Prices: Thurs.-Sat. 10-5; Tues.-Wed. by appointment. No charge. Closed New Year's Day; Memorial Day; Independence Day; Labor Day; Thanksgiving; Christmas. &
Attendance: 2,300 (estimated)

BRUNO DAVID GALLERY, 7513 Forsyth Blvd., Saint Louis, MO 63105. Tel.: 314-696-2377. Facebook & Instagram: @brunodavidgallery; Twitter: @bdavidgallery.
E-mail: info@brunodavidgallery.com
Web Site: www.brunodavidgallery.com
Key Personnel: Owner & Dir., Bruno L. David; Asst. Dir., Cleo Kelly; Art Advisor, Xizi Liu.
Institution Type/Description: Art Gallery.
Hours & Admission Prices: Wed.-Sat. 10-5; other times by appointment. No charge.

CAMPBELL HOUSE MUSEUM, 1508 Locust St., Saint Louis, MO 63103-1816. Tel.: 314-421-0325. Fax: 314-421-0113. Facebook: Campbell House Museum.
E-mail: andy@campbellhousemuseum.org
Web Site: www.campbellhousemuseum.org
Key Personnel: C.E.O., Andrew Hahn; Pres., D. Scott Johnson; Museum Shop Mgr., Mrs. Earl C. Lindburg.
Institution Type/Description: Historic House: 1851 Campbell House.
Hours & Admission Prices: March-Dec. Wed.-Sat. 10-4, Sun. 12-4; other times by appointment. Adults $8; discounts to groups; children & members no charge. Closed national holidays.
Attendance: 6,000 (actual)

CARONDELET HISTORIC CENTER, 6303 Michigan Ave., Saint Louis, MO 63111-2504. Tel.: 314-481-6303. Facebook: @CarondeletHistoricalSociety.
E-mail: carondelethistoricalsociety@yahoo.com
Key Personnel: Pres., John Remelius, I; Vice Pres., David Bouchein ; Treas., Richard Fernandez; Exec. Sec., Mary Ann Simon; Asst. Exec. Sec., John Remelius, III.
Institution Type/Description: History Museum.
Hours & Admission Prices: Wed., Fri. & Sat. 10-2, Sun. 12-3. Adults $2, children 12 & under $1; school groups no charge. &

CHATILLON-DEMENIL HOUSE FOUNDATION, 3352 DeMenil Place, Saint Louis, MO 63118-3211. Tel.: 314-771-5828. Facebook, Pinterest, Flickr, Twitter.
E-mail: demenil@sbcglobal.net
Web Site: www.demenil.org
Key Personnel: Pres. (V), Ted Atwood; Dir., Andrew M. Cooperman.
Institution Type/Description: History Museum: housed in 1848 brick farm house of Henri & Odile Chatillon, 1863 Greek Revival addition by Dr. Nicolas N. DeMenil.

Hours & Admission Prices: March-Dec. Hourly Tours: Wed.-Fri. 11-2, Sat. 11-3. Adults $8, children under 12 $5; discounts to members, groups, AAA, AAM & ICOM members; history teachers with ID no charge. Closed national holidays.
Attendance: 3,000 (estimated)

CITY MUSEUM, 750 N. 16th St., Saint Louis, MO 63103. Tel.: 314-231-2489. Fax: 314-231-1009. Facebook & Twitter: @citymuseum.
E-mail: info@citymuseum.org
Web Site: www.citymuseum.org
Key Personnel: Museum Dir., Rick Erwin; Museum Shop Buyer & Mgr., Stephanie Von Drasek.
Institution Type/Description: General Museum.
Hours & Admission Prices: Wed. & Thurs. 9-5, Fri. & Sat. 9am to midnight, Sun. 11-5; Admission 3 & up $12, parking $7; discounts to groups & Fri.-Sat. after 5pm. Closed New Year's Day; Easter; Thanksgiving; Christmas. &
Attendance: 680,714 (actual)

CONCORDIA HISTORICAL INSTITUTE, 804 Seminary Pl., Saint Louis, MO 63105-3014. Tel.: 314-505-7900. Fax: 314-505-7901. Facebook: @LutheranHistory.
E-mail: chi@lutheranhistory.org
Web Site: www.concordiahistoricalinsitute.org
Key Personnel: Exec. Dir., Rev. Dr. Daniel N. Harmelink; Pres. (V), Scott Meyer; Archivist, Rev. Todd Zittlow; Business Mgr., Debbie Lower.
Institution Type/Description: Religious History Museum.
Hours & Admission Prices: Mon.-Fri. 8:30-4. No charge, $6 donation suggested. Closed national holidays. &
Attendance: 3,000 (estimated)

CONTEMPORARY ART MUSEUM ST. LOUIS, 3750 Washington Blvd., Saint Louis, MO 63108-3612. Tel.: 314-535-4660. Fax: 314-535-1226. Facebook: @contemporaryartmuseumstl; Instagram: @camstl; Twitter: @ContemporarySTL.
E-mail: info@camstl.org
Web Site: camstl.org
Formerly: Forum for Contemporary Art
Key Personnel: Exec. Dir., Lisa Melandri; Chm., Andrew Srenco; Dir. Finance & Administration, Michael Albrecht; Dir. Learning & Engagement, Alex Elmestad; Dir. Mktg. & Audience Devel., Unitey Kull; Dir. Devel., Valerie Rudy-Valli; Asst. Dir. Devel., Jessie Youngblood; Visitor Svcs. Mgr., Victoria Donaldson.
Institution Type/Description: Contemporary Art Museum.
Hours & Admission Prices: Wed., Sat. & Sun. 10-5, Thurs.-Fri. 10-8. No charge. Closed national holidays. &
Attendance: 22,400 (actual)

CRAFT ALLIANCE, Delmar Loop, 6640 Delmar Blvd., Saint Louis, MO 63130-4503. Tel.: 314-725-1177. Fax: 314-725-2068. Facebook, Instagram & Twitter: @CraftAlliance.
E-mail: gallery@craftalliance.org
Web Site: craftalliance.org
Key Personnel: Exec. Dir., Boo McLoughlin; Bd. Chairman, Vicki Sauter; Dir. Devel. & Communications, Jackie Chambers; Sr. Dir., Dir. Education Programs, Luanne Rimel; Dir. Community Programs & Grand Ctr. Opers., Lexi Glynias; Finance Mgr., Jessica Hitchcock; Dir. Exhibitions & Artists-in-Residence Programs, Stefanie Kirkland; Studios Mgr., Dan Barnett.
Institution Type/Description: Arts & Crafts Museum.
Hours & Admission Prices: Tues.-Thurs. 10-5, Fri. & Sat. 10-6, Sun. 11-5. Classes: daily. Exhibits: no charge; donations accepted. Closed national holidays. &
Attendance: 12,000 (estimated)

DES LEE GALLERY - WASHINGTON UNIVERSITY, 1627 Washington Ave., Saint Louis, MO 63103. Tel.: 314-621-8735. Facebook: @desleegallery.
E-mail: desleegallery@gmail.com
Web Site: desleegallery.com
Key Personnel: Gallery Dir., Brandon Anschultz.
Institution Type/Description: Art Gallery.
Hours & Admission Prices: Wed.-Sat. 1-6; other times by appointment.

FIELD HOUSE MUSEUM, 634 S. Broadway, Saint Louis, MO 63102-1613. Tel.: 314-421-4689. Fax: 314-588-9468. Facebook & Instagram: @FieldHouseMuseum.
E-mail: info@eugenefieldhouse.org
Web Site: fieldhousemuseum.org
Formerly: Eugene Field House & St. Louis Toy Museum
Key Personnel: Dir., Kimberly Ann Larson.
Institution Type/Description: Historic House: built 1845, birthplace of poet & toy collector, Eugene Field; home of Roswell Field, lawyer for Dred Scott & family

during 1857 U.S. Supreme Court Decision. Listed as a National Historic Landmark.
Hours & Admission Prices: Wed.-Sat. 10-4, Sun. noon to 4; other times by appointment. Adults $10, children 7-15 $5; discounts to AAA members; children under 6 no charge. Closed major holidays. &
Attendance: 7,000 (estimated)

GALLERY 210 - UNIVERSITY OF MISSOURI-ST. LOUIS, 44 East Dr., TCC, One University Blvd., Saint Louis, MO 63121. Tel.: 314-516-5976. Facebook: Gallery 210 at UMSL; Twitter: @Gallery_210.
E-mail: gallery@umsl.edu
Web Site: www.gallery210.umsl.edu
Key Personnel: Dir., Terry Suhre.
Institution Type/Description: Art Gallery.
Hours & Admission Prices: Tues.-Sat. 11-5; other times by appointment.

GRANT'S FARM, 10501 Gravois Rd., Saint Louis, MO 63123-1808. Tel.: 314-843-1700.
E-mail: budcentral@anheuser-busch.com
Institution Type/Description: Zoo.
Hours & Admission Prices: Spring: Sat. 9-3:30, Sun. 9:30-3:30; Summer: Tues.-Fri. 9-3:30, Sat. 9-4, Sun. 9:30-4; Fall: Fri. 9:30-2:30, Sat.-Sun. 9:30-3:30.

GRIOT MUSEUM OF BLACK HISTORY, 2505 St. Louis Ave., Saint Louis, MO 63106-2324. Tel.: 314-241-7057. Fax: 314-241-7058.
E-mail: thegriotmuseum@aol.com
Web Site: www.thegriotmuseum.com
Formerly: Blackworld History Museum
Key Personnel: Founder & C.E.O., Lois D. Conley; Bd. Chair, Terri E. Cobb.
Institution Type/Description: Black History Museum.
Hours & Admission Prices: Wed.-Sat. 10-5; other times by appointment. Admission $7.50, youth 5-12 $3.75; discounts to AAM & ICOM members; members no charge. &
Attendance: 7,530 (estimated)

HEALTHWORKS! KIDS' MUSEUM ST. LOUIS, 1100 Macklind Ave., Saint Louis, MO 63110-1430. Tel.: 314-241-7391.
E-mail: info@hwstl.org
Web Site: www.hwstl.org
Formerly: Dental Health Theatre
Key Personnel: Pres. & CEO, Shannon Woodcock.
Institution Type/Description: Children's Dental & Overall Health Museum.
Hours & Admission Prices: Tues.-Sat. 9:30-4. Admission 3 & up $7. &
Attendance: 10,000 (estimated)

HISTORIC SAMUEL CUPPLES HOUSE & GALLERY, 3673 W. Pine Mall, Saint Louis, MO 63108-3303. Mailing Address: 3545 Lindell Blvd., Saint Louis, MO 63103. Tel.: 314-977-3571. Fax: 314-977-3581.
E-mail: museumsandgalleries@slu.edu
Web Site: www.slu.edu/samuel-cupples-house
Key Personnel: Dir., Petruta Lipan; Registrar & Collections Mgr., Maureen E. Lanfgraf; Admin. Sec., Fallon A. Potter; Exhibition Fabricator, Stephen L. Weber.
Institution Type/Description: Art & Decorative Art Museum: housed in a Richardsonian-Romanesque style mansion; built in 1888.
Hours & Admission Prices: Tues.-Sat. 11-4. Docent-led Tours: $5. Closed national holidays.
Attendance: 5,400 (actual)

HOLOCAUST MUSEUM & LEARNING CENTER, 12 Millstone Campus Dr., Saint Louis, MO 63146-5776. Tel.: 314-442-3715.
E-mail: jfed@jfedstl.org
Web Site: hmlc.org
Key Personnel: Dir., Jean Cavender; Cur. & Dir. Education, Daniel A. Reich; Mgr. Programs & Logistics, Andrew Goldfeder.
Institution Type/Description: History Museum.
Hours & Admission Prices: Mon.-Thurs. 9:30-4:30, Fri. 9:30-4, Sun. 10-4; other times by appointment. No charge; donations accepted. &
Attendance: 30,000 (estimated)

INTERNATIONAL PHOTOGRAPHY HALL OF FAME & MUSEUM, 3415 Olive St., Saint Louis, MO 63103. Tel.: 314-535-1999.
E-mail: info@iphf.org
Web Site: www.iphf.org
Key Personnel: C.E.O. & Pres., Patty Wente.

Institution Type/Description: Photography Museum.
Hours & Admission Prices: Wed.-Sat. 11-5. Adults $5, seniors 65 & over and students $3; children under 18 & members no charge (fee charged for special exhibits). Closed Thanksgiving; Christmas Eve & Day. &

JEFFERSON BARRACKS HISTORIC SITE, 345 North Rd., Saint Louis, MO 63125-4121. Tel.: 314-615-8800. Fax: 314-638-5009. Facebook: @JeffersonBarracksHistoricSite.
E-mail: mvenso@stlouisco.com
Web Site: www.stlouisco.com/parks/jb
Key Personnel: Dir., J.D. Magurany; Dir. St. Louis County Parks Recreation, Gary Bess; Cur., Mikall Venso.
Institution Type/Description: Historic Preservation Project: military post/museum.
Hours & Admission Prices: Museums & historic buildings open Wed.-Sun. noon-4. No charge; donations accepted. Closed national holidays. &
Attendance: 250,000 (actual)

JEFFERSON NATIONAL EXPANSION MEMORIAL, 11 N. 4th St., Saint Louis, MO 63102-1810. Tel.: 314-655-1700 & 1600. Fax: 314-655-1639. TDD: 1-800-735-2466.
Web Site: www.nps.gov/jeff
Key Personnel: Supt., Mike Ward; Facility Mgr., Edwards Dodds; Pres. & C.E.O. JNPA, David Grove; Chief Museum Svcs. & Interpretation, Rhonda Schier; Cur. Cultural Resources, Kathryn Thomas.
Institution Type/Description: Historic Building: Old Courthouse.
Hours & Admission Prices: Old Courthouse: June-Aug. daily 7:30am-8pm; Sept.-May daily 8-5. Gateway Arch: June-Aug. daily 8am-10pm; Sept.-May daily 9-6. Family $6, adults $3; additional fees for films & tram ride. Closed New Year's Day; Thanksgiving; Christmas. &
Attendance: 2,500,000 (estimated)

LACLEDE'S LANDING WAX MUSEUM, 720 N. Second St., Saint Louis, MO 63102-2519. Tel.: 314-241-1155. Facebook: Laclede's Landing Wax Museum.
E-mail: stlwaxmuseum@gmail.com
Web Site: www.stlwaxmuseum.com
Key Personnel: Owner, Michael Scauzzo; Museum Mgr., Sammy Mosley.
Institution Type/Description: Wax Museum.
Hours & Admission Prices: May-Oct. Sun.-Thurs. 11-8, Fri.-Sat. 11-10; Nov.-April Thurs.-Sun. 11-6. Adults $10, juniors 12-17 $7, seniors 55 & up $5, children 3-11 $3; discounts to groups of 15 or more.

LAUMEIER SCULPTURE PARK, 12580 Rott Rd., Saint Louis, MO 63127-1212. Tel.: 314-615-5278. Facebook; Instagram; Twitter.
E-mail: info@laumeier.org
Web Site: www.laumeier.org
Key Personnel: Bd. Chair, Matt Harvey; Exec. Dir., Lauren Ross; Cur., Dana Turkovic; Preparator, Martin Linson; Dir. Devel., Stacy West; Dir. Education, Karen Mullen; Dir. Mktg. & Communications, Jamie Vishwanat.
Institution Type/Description: Art Museum & Sculpture Park.
Hours & Admission Prices: Sculpture Park: 8am to half hour past sunset. Adam Aronson Fine Arts Center: Daily 10-4. Fee charged for special events only. Closed Art Fair weekend in May; Harvest Festival Sun. in Oct.; Christmas Day. &
Attendance: 300,000 (estimated)

THE MAGIC HOUSE, ST. LOUIS CHILDREN'S MUSEUM, 516 S. Kirkwood Rd., Saint Louis, MO 63122-5926. Tel.: 314-822-8900, ext. 524. Fax: 314-822-8930. Facebook, Instagram & Twitter: @TheMagicHouse.
E-mail: info@magichouse.org
Web Site: www.magichouse.org
Key Personnel: Pres., Elizabeth Fitzgerald; C.F.O., Cheryl Darr; Grant Mgr., Hedy Ehrlich; Asst. Dir. Devel., Vicki Peckron; Dir. Human Resources, Elizabeth Hartman; C.O.O., Paula Burdge; Mktg. & Devel. Mgr., Marissa Lorance; Human Resources Mgr., Kayla Kromer; Sr. Mgr. Visitor Svcs., Sara Modray.
Institution Type/Description: Children's Museum: housed in 1901 home of George Lane Edwards.
Hours & Admission Prices: Memorial Day to Labor Day Mon.-Thurs. & Sat. 9:30-5:30, Fri. 9:30-9, Sun. 11-5:30; Labor day to memorial Day Tues.-Thurs. 12-5:30, Fri. 12-9, Sat. 9:30-5:30, Sun. 11-5:30. Admission $12; discounts to seniors, military personnel, groups & AAM members. Closed Easter; Thanksgiving; Christmas. &
Attendance: 555,550 (actual)

MERAMEC CONTEMPORARY ART GALLERY - ST. LOUIS COMMUNITY COLLEGE, St. Louis Community College-Meramec Art Dept., Humanities East Bldg., 11333 Big Bend

Blvd., Saint Louis, MO 63122-2810. Tel.: 314-984-7632. Fax: 314-984-7920. Facebook: @merameccontemporaryartgallery.
E-mail: mkeller@stlcc.edu
Web Site: www.stlcc.edu
Key Personnel: Dir., Margaret Keller.
Institution Type/Description: Art Gallery.
Hours & Admission Prices: Mon.-Thurs. 9-9, Fri. 9-4, Sat. 10-5.

MILDRED LANE KEMPER ART MUSEUM - WASHINGTON UNIVERSITY, One Brookings Dr., Saint Louis, MO 63130-4862. Mailing Address: Campus Box 1214, One Brookings Dr., Saint Louis, MO 63130-4862. Tel.: 314-935-4523. Fax: 314-935-7282. Facebook & Twitter: @kemperartmuseum.
E-mail: kemperartmuseum@wustl.edu
Web Site: www.kemperartmuseum.wustl.edu
Formerly: Washington University Gallery of Art
Key Personnel: William T. Kemper Dir. & Chief Cur., Dr. Sabine Eckmann; Asst. Dir. Collections & Exhibitions, Mark Ryan; Mgr. Mktg., Communications & Visitor Svcs., Ida McCall; Assoc. Cur., Meredith Malone, Ph.D.; Cur. Pub. Art, Leslie Markle; Head Community Engagement, Allison Taylor; Exhibition Preparator, Ron Weaver; Administrative Coord., Melissa Meinzer; Head Publications, Jane Neidhardt; Security Supvr., Michael Hesse.
Institution Type/Description: Art Museum.
Hours & Admission Prices: Wed.-Mon. 11-5, first Fri. of month 11-8. No charge; donations accepted. &
Attendance: 23,222 (actual)

MINIATURE MUSEUM OF GREATER ST. LOUIS, 4746 Gravois, Saint Louis, MO 63116-2437. Tel.: 314-832-7790.
E-mail: FZerb@aol.com
Web Site: www.miniaturemuseum.org
Key Personnel: Pres. (V) & Museum Shop Mgr., Joanne Martin; Museum Shop Mgr., Fay Zerbolio.
Institution Type/Description: Miniature Museum.
Hours & Admission Prices: Wed.-Sat. 11-4, Sun. 1-4. Adults $5, seniors & youth 13-18 $4, children 12 & under $2; discounts to members; children under 2 no charge. Closed New Year's Eve & Day; Easter; Independence Day; Thanksgiving; Christmas Eve & Day. &
Attendance: 3,750 (estimated)

MISSOURI BOTANICAL GARDEN, 4344 Shaw Blvd., Saint Louis, MO 63110-2291. Mailing Address: P.O. Box 299, Saint Louis, MO 63166-0299. Tel.: 314-577-5110. Fax: 314-577-9595. Facebook, Twitter, Instagram.
E-mail: bob.woodruff@mobot.org
Web Site: www.mobot.org
Key Personnel: Pres., Dr. Peter Wyse Jackson; Pres. Emeritus, Dr. Peter Raven; C. O.O., Robert Woodruff; Chm. Bd. Trustees, David M. Hollo; Vice Pres. Institutional Advancement, Patty Arnold; Sr. Vice Pres. Science & Conservation, James S. Miller; Vice Pres. Information Technology & Chief Information Officer, Charles K. Miller, Jr.; Sr. Vice Pres. Horticulture, Andrew Wyatt; Vice Pres. Human Resources, Teresa Clark; Sr. Vice Pres. Gen. Svcs., Paul Brockmann; Vice Pres. Center for Conservation & Sustainable Devel., Olga Martha Montiel; Dir. Shaw Nature Reserve, Quinn Long; Vice Pres. Visitor Ops., Vickie Campbell; Dir. Earthways Center, Glenda Abney; Controller, Jennifer Mulch.
Institution Type/Description: Botanical Garden: 79 acres of horticultural displays. A National Historic Landmark.
Hours & Admission Prices: Tues.-Sun. 9-5. Adult $14; children 12 & under no charge. Closed Thanksgiving; Christmas. &
Attendance: 1,048.540 (actual)

MISSOURI CIVIL WAR MUSEUM, 222 Worth Rd., Saint Louis, MO 63125. Tel.: 314-845-1861. Facebook: @missouricivilwarmuseum; Twitter: @MOCWMuseum.
E-mail: mtrout@mcwm.org
Web Site: mcwm.org
Key Personnel: Dir. & C.E.O., Mark Trout.
Institution Type/Description: Military History Museum.
Hours & Admission Prices: Daily 9-5. Adults $5-$7; members no charge. Closed New Year's Day; Thanksgiving; Christmas. &
Attendance: 50,000

MISSOURI HISTORY MUSEUM, Lindell & De Baliviere, 5700 Lindell Blvd., Saint Louis, MO 63112. Mailing Address: P.O. Box 11940, Saint Louis, MO 63112-0040. Tel.: 314-746-4599. Fax: 314-746-4548.
E-mail: info@mohistory.org
Web Site: www.mohistory.org

Key Personnel: C.E.O. & Pres., Dr. Frances Levine; Mng. Dir. Operations, Karen M. Goering; Mng. Dir. Devel., Yvette Hartsfield; Dir. Exhibitions & Research, Jody Sowell, Ph.D.; Conservator, Crista Pack; Museum Shop Mgr., Susan Ponciroli; Sr. Cur., Shannon Berry; Mng. Dir. Museum Svcs., Katie Van Allen.
Institution Type/Description: History Museum.
Hours & Admission Prices: Museum: Tues. 10-8, Wed.-Mon. 10-5. No charge. Closed Thanksgiving; Christmas. Library & Research Center: Tues.-Fri. 12-5, Sat. 10-5. No charge. Closed major holidays; Sat. holidays. &
Attendance: 475,000 (estimated)

MORTON J. MAY FOUNDATION GALLERY - MARYVILLE UNIVERSITY, 650 Maryville University Dr., Saint Louis, MO 63141-7299. Tel.: 314-529-9381. Fax: 314-529-9940.
E-mail: artgallery@maryville.edu
Web Site: www.maryville.edu/morton-j-may-foundation-gallery.htm
Key Personnel: Dir., John Baltrushunas, M.F.A.
Institution Type/Description: Art and Design Gallery.
Hours & Admission Prices: Mon.-Thurs. 7am to midnight, Fri. 7-7, Sat. 11-7, Sun. 11am to midnight. No charge. &
Attendance: 30,000 (estimated)

MUSEUM OF CONTEMPORARY RELIGIOUS ART (MOCRA)-ST. LOUIS UNIVERSITY, 3700 W. Pine Blvd., Saint Louis, MO 63108-3306. Mailing Address: 221 N. Grand Blvd., Saint Louis, MO 63103-2006. Tel.: 314-977-7170. Fax: 314-977-2999. Facebook; Twitter.
E-mail: mocra@slu.edu
Web Site: www.slu.edu/mocra
Key Personnel: C.E.O. & Cur., Rev. Terrence E. Dempsey, S.J.; Chm. (V), Wilson Yates, Ph.D.; Devel. & Education, David Brinker.
Institution Type/Description: Interfaith Religious Contemporary Art Museum: housed in former Jesuit seminarian chapel.
Hours & Admission Prices: Tues.-Sun. 11-4. No charge; donations accepted. Closed New Year's Day; Martin Luther King Jr. Day; Easter; Memorial Day; Independence Day; Labor Day; Thanksgiving; Christmas; between exhibitions. &
Attendance: 2,600 (actual)

MUSEUM OF TRANSPORTATION, 2933 Barrett Station Rd., Saint Louis, MO 63122-3398. Tel.: 314-615-8668. Fax: 314-615-8210. Facebook: Museum of Transportation; Twitter: @MuseumTransport.
E-mail: mbutterworth@stlouisco.com
Web Site: transportmuseumassociation.org/
Key Personnel: Exec. Dir., Terri McEachern; Pres. (V), Darryl Ross; Museum Shop Mgr., Sandra Williams.
Institution Type/Description: Transportation Museum.
Hours & Admission Prices: Memorial Day to Labor Day Mon.-Sat. 9-4, Sun. 11-4; Winter: Thurs.-Sat. 9-4, Sun. 11-4. Adults $8, children $5; members no charge. Closed New Year's Day; Easter; Thanksgiving; Christmas. &
Attendance: 141,284 (actual)

THE NATIONAL BLUES MUSEUM, 615 Washington Ave., Saint Louis, MO 63101. Tel.: 314-925-0016. Facebook & Instagram: @NationalBluesMuseum; Twitter: @NatBluesMuseum.
E-mail: info@nationalbluesmuseum.org
Web Site: www.nationalbluesmuseum.org
Key Personnel: Exec. Dir., Dion Brown; External Affairs Coord., Dave Beardsley; Gift Shop Manager, Jakki Brown; Dir. Internal Affairs, Jacqueline K. Dace; Opers. Mgr., Terry L. Hardin; Sales & Events Mgr., Casey Jolley; Controller, Debbie Krall; Dir. External Affairs, Sherry Nash; Asst. Interpretive Coord., Dr. Rosalind Norman.
Institution Type/Description: Blues Museum.
Hours & Admission Prices: April-Oct. Sun. & Mon. 12-5, Tues.-Sat. 10-5; Nov.-March Tues.-Sat. 10-5. Adults $15, seniors 65 & over and military $12, children 5-17 & college students w/ID $10; discounts to groups; children under 5 no charge. Closed New Year's Day; Thanksgiving Day; Christmas Day. &

OAKLAND HOUSE - AFFTON HISTORICAL SOCIETY, 7801 Genesta Ave., Saint Louis, MO 63123. Mailing Address: P.O. Box 28855, Affton, MO 63123. Tel.: 314-352-5654; 314-821-7166. Facebook: The Oakland House Museum.
E-mail: info@oaklandhousemuseum.org
Web Site: www.oaklandhousemuseum.org
Key Personnel: Pres. (V), Chas Brown; Membership, Pam Danklef; Publicity, Ingrid Schaeffer; Editor, ` Patti Behlman; Conservator, Nancy Herndon-Ulrich.
Institution Type/Description: Historical Society Museum: housed in the former home of banker, Louis A. Benoist; built in 1850s. Listed on the National Register of Historic Places.

Hours & Admission Prices: April-Oct. 3rd Sun. each month; other times by appointment. Adults $5; members no charge. &
Attendance: 16,600 (actual)

OLD CATHEDRAL MUSEUM, 209 Walnut St., Saint Louis, MO 63102-2499. Tel.: 314-231-3250.
E-mail: oldcathedral@att.net
Web Site: www.oldcathedralstl.org
Key Personnel: Pastor, Rev. Msgr. Jerome Billing; Museum Dir., Mrs. Mary Dieterman.
Institution Type/Description: Religious Museum: housed in 1834 Cathedral.
Hours & Admission Prices: Mon.-Fri. 10-2. No charge; donations accepted. Closed New Year's Day; Easter; Independence Day; Christmas. &
Attendance: 22,000 (estimated)

OLD COURTHOUSE, 11 N. 4th St., Saint Louis, MO 63102. Tel.: 314-655-1600.   Fax: 314-655-1641.   Facebook: @GatewayArchNPS.
E-mail: info@gatewayarch.com
Web Site: www.nps.gov/jeff
Key Personnel: Supt., Michael M. Ward.
Institution Type/Description: Historic Building: built 1839-1862; part of the Jefferson National Expansion Memorial.
Hours & Admission Prices: Memorial Day to Labor Day: daily 7:30-8; Labor Day to Memorial Day: daily 8-5. No charge.

PHILIP SLEIN GALLERY, 4735 McPherson Ave., Saint Louis, MO 63108. Tel.: 314-361-2617. Facebook & Instagram: @philip-sleingallery; Twitter: @PSleinGallery.
E-mail: director@philipsleingallery.com
Web Site: www.philipsleingallery.com
Key Personnel: Co-Owner, Philip Slein; Co-Owner, Tom Bussmann; Assoc., Jim Schmidt; Assoc., Kathleen Vodicka.
Institution Type/Description: Art Gallery.
Hours & Admission Prices: Tues.-Sat. 10-5; other times by appointment.

PULITZER ARTS FOUNDATION, 3716 Washington Blvd., Saint Louis, MO 63108. Tel.: 314-754-1850. Fax: 314-754-1851.
E-mail: info@pulitzerarts.org
Web Site: www.pulitzerarts.org
Formerly: Pulitzer Foundation for the Arts
Institution Type/Description: Art Gallery.
Hours & Admission Prices: Wed. 12-5, Sat. 10-5. No charge. &

SAINT LOUIS ART MUSEUM, One Fine Arts Dr., Forest Park, Saint Louis, MO 63110-1380. Tel.: 314-721-0072. Fax: 314-721-6172.   Facebook: @Saint.Louis.Art.Museum;   Twitter: STLArtMuseum.
E-mail: publicrelations@slam.org
Web Site: www.slam.org
Key Personnel: Barbara B. Taylor Dir., Brent Benjamin.
Institution Type/Description: Art Museum: housed in both a 1904 World's Fair building & a recently opened building.
Hours & Admission Prices: Tues.-Thurs. & Sat.-Sun. 10-5, Fri. 10-9. Fee charged for featured exhibitions. Closed Thanksgiving; Christmas. &
Attendance: 346,457 (actual)

ST. LOUIS ARTISTS' GUILD & GALLERIES, 12 N. Jackson Ave., Clayton, MO 63105. Tel.: 314-727-6266 (gallery); 9599 (office). Fax: 314-727-9190. Facebook: @stlouisartistsguild.
E-mail: askus@stlouisartguild.org
Web Site: www.stlouisartistsguild.org
Key Personnel: Exec. Dir., Kathryn Nahorski; Pres. (V), Randy Allen; Exhibitions & Education Asst., Amy Firestone Rosen.
Institution Type/Description: Arts Center.
Hours & Admission Prices: Tues.-Fri. 10-6, Sat. 10-4. No charge; donations accepted. Closed holidays. &
Attendance: 30,000 (estimated)

ST. LOUIS CARDINALS HALL OF FAME AND MUSEUM, 601 Clark St., Unit 102, Saint Louis, MO 63102. Mailing Address: Busch Stadium, 700 Clark St., Saint Louis, MO 63102. Tel.: 314-345-9880.
E-mail: halloffame@cardinals.com
Web Site: stlouis.cardinals.mlb.com/stl/cardinals-nation/hof.jsp
Formerly: St. Louis Cardinals Hall of Fame Museum
Key Personnel: Mgr. & Cur., Paula Homan; Asst. Cur., Amy Berra.
Institution Type/Description: Sports Museum.

Hours & Admission Prices: Daily 10-6. Adults $12, seniors & military $10, children $8; children 3 & under no charge. &
Attendance: 30,000 (estimated)

ST. LOUIS FIRE DEPARTMENT MUSEUM, 1421 N. Jefferson Ave., Saint Louis, MO 63106-2136. Tel.: 314-533-3406. Fax: 314-533-1681.
Key Personnel: Historian, Bob Pauly.
Institution Type/Description: Fire Fighting Museum.
Hours & Admission Prices: Mon.-Fri. 9-2. No charge. &

SAINT LOUIS SCIENCE CENTER, 5050 Oakland Ave., Saint Louis, MO 63110-1460. Tel.: 314-289-4400. Fax: 314-289-4420.
E-mail: webmaster@slsc.org
Web Site: www.slsc.org
Key Personnel: C.E.O. & Pres., Bert Vescolani; Chief Mktg. & Communications Officer, Ann Balsamo; C.O.O. & C.F.O., Barbara Boyle; Chief Officer Science, Education & Experience, Christian Greer; Chief Institutional Advancement Officer, G. Patrick Williams; Mng. Dir. Visitor Svcs., Jackie Mollet; Mng. Dir. Facilities, Ron Schultz; Mng. Dir. Finance & Controller, Laura Taylor; Mng. Dir. Staff Relations, Deborah Washington.
Institution Type/Description: Science/Technology Museum.
Hours & Admission Prices: Memorial Day-Labor Day Mon.-Wed., Fri. & Sat. 9:30-5:30, Thurs. 9:30-8, Sun. 11-5:30; Labor Day-Memorial Day Mon.-Sat. 9:30-4:30, Sun. 11-4:30. Museum: no charge. OMNIMAX(R) Theater: adults $10, children $9. Closed Thanksgiving; Christmas. &
Attendance: 938,368 (actual)

SAINT LOUIS SCIENCE CENTER LIBRARY, 5236A Oakland Ave., Saint Louis, MO 63110. Tel.: 314-289-4400.
E-mail: stlarchivists@gmail.com
Web Site: stlarchivists.org
Institution Type/Description: Library.
Hours & Admission Prices: Call for hours.

SAINT LOUIS UNIVERSITY MUSEUM OF ART, 3663 Lindell Blvd., Saint Louis, MO 63108. Mailing Address: 3545 Lindell Blvd., Saint Louis, MO 63103. Tel.: 314-977-6631. Facebook.
E-mail: museumsandgalleries@slu.edu
Web Site: www.slu.edu/sluma/index.php
Key Personnel: Dir., Petruta Lipan; Registrar & Collections Mgr., Kathryn Reid; Exhibition Fabricator, Stephen L. Weber.
Institution Type/Description: Art Museum.
Hours & Admission Prices: Wed.-Sun. 11-4; call to confirm. No charge, docent led tours $5. Closed New Year's Day; Easter; Thanksgiving; Christmas. &
Attendance: 8,100 (actual)

SAINT LOUIS ZOO, Forest Park, Saint Louis, MO 63110-1395. Mailing Address: 1 Government Dr., Saint Louis, MO 63110-1395. Tel.: 314-781-0900. Fax: 314-647-7969.
E-mail: bonner@stlzoo.org
Web Site: www.stlzoo.org
Key Personnel: Chm. Zoological Park Commission, Winthrop B. Reed, III; Pres. & C.E.O., Jeffrey P. Bonner, Ph.D.; Director, Michael Macek; North Campus Dir., Jo-Elle Mogerman, Ph.D.; Vice Pres. Special Projects, Steve Barth; Snr. Vice Pres. External Rels., Cynthia S. Holter, CFRE; Vice Pres. Internal Rels. & Gen. Counsel, Dustin Deschamp; Vice Pres. Architecture & Planning, David McGuire; Vice Pres. Animal Collection, Luis Padilla, DVM Dipl. ACZM; C.F.O., Cassandra J. Brown Ray; Vice Pres. Business Opers., Jim Madison.
Institution Type/Description: Zoo.
Hours & Admission Prices: Summer: Mon.-Thurs. 8-5, Fri.-Sun. & holidays 8-7; Sept.-May 9-5. No charge; donations accepted. Closed New Year's Day; Christmas. &
Attendance: 3,245,128 (actual)

SCOTT JOPLIN HOUSE STATE HISTORIC SITE, 2658 Delmar Blvd., Saint Louis, MO 63103-1404. Tel.: 314-340-5790.
E-mail: moparks@dnr.mo.gov
Web Site: www.mostateparks/park/scott-joplin-house-state-historic-site
Key Personnel: Site Admin., Almetta Jordan.
Institution Type/Description: Historic House Museum: c.1860. Listed on the National Register of Historic Places.
Hours & Admission Prices: Feb. Tues.-Sat. 10-4; March-Oct. Mon.-Sat. 10-4. Adults $2.50, children 6-12 $1.50; discounts to groups; children 5 & under no charge. Closed Nov.-Jan. &
Attendance: 12,500

SHELDON ART GALLERIES, 3648 Washington Blvd., Saint Louis, MO 63108-3610. Tel.: 314-533-9900. Fax: 314-533-2958.
E-mail: olg@thesheldon.org

Web Site: www.thesheldon.org
Key Personnel: Dir. & Cur., Olivia Lahs-Gonzales; Museum Shop Mgr., Rebecca Gunter.
Institution Type/Description: Art Gallery.
Hours & Admission Prices: Tues. 12-8, Wed.-Fri. 12-5, Sat. 10-2. No charge; donations accepted. Closed New Year's Eve & Day; Independence Day; Thanksgiving; Christmas Eve & Day. &
Attendance: 70,000 (estimated)

SOLDIERS MEMORIAL MILITARY MUSEUM, 1315 Chestnut St., Saint Louis, MO 63103-2317. Tel.: 314-622-4550. Fax: 314-622-4237. Facebook, Instagram & Twitter: @SoldiersStLouis;.
E-mail: info@mohistory.org
Web Site: mohistory.org/soldiersmemorial
Key Personnel: Supt., Lynnea Magnuson, Ph.D.; Chmn. (V), Jim Sondermann; Dir. Opers., Karen Goering.
Institution Type/Description: Military Museum.
Hours & Admission Prices: Closed for renovations until 2018. &

WHITE FLAG PROJECTS, 4568 Manchester Ave., Saint Louis, MO 63110. Tel.: 314-531-3442. Fax: 341-531-3474.
E-mail: info@whiteflagprojects.org
Web Site: whiteflagprojects.org
Key Personnel: Founder & Dir., Matthew Strauss; Asst. Dir., Marie Heilich; Installations Mgr., Emily Keefauver.
Institution Type/Description: Art Gallery.
Hours & Admission Prices: Tue.-Sat. 12-5. No charge.

WORLD CHESS HALL OF FAME, 4652 Maryland Ave., Saint Louis, MO 63108. Tel.: 314-367-9243. Fax: 314-367-7501. Facebook: World Chess Hall of Fame.
E-mail: info@worldchesshof.org
Web Site: www.worldchesshof.org
Key Personnel: Chief Cur., Shannon Bailey; General Mgr., Joy Bray; Chmn. (V), Andrew Walker; Museum Shop Mgr., Brian Flowers.
Institution Type/Description: Art Gallery.
Hours & Admission Prices: Mon.-Tues. & Sat. 10-5, Wed.-Fri. 10-9, Sun. 12-5. No charge; donations requested. &
Attendance: 10,000 (actual)

Sainte Genevieve

BOLDUC HOUSE MUSEUM, 125 S. Main St., Sainte Genevieve, MO 63670. Tel.: 573-883-3105. Fax: 573-883-3415.
E-mail: info@bolduchouse.org
Web Site: bolduchouse.org
Key Personnel: Exec. Dir., Geoffrey Giglierano; Museum Shop Mgr., Roseanne Ahne.
Institution Type/Description: Historic Houses Museum.
Hours & Admission Prices: Mon.-Thurs. 10-4, Fri. 10-7, Sat. 10-5, Sun. noon to 4. Adults $8, seniors & adult students $6, children $2; discounts to groups; pre-schoolers & members no charge. Closed New Year's Eve & Day; Easter; Thanksgiving; Christmas Eve & Day.
Attendance: 6,609 (actual)

FELIX VALLE STATE HISTORIC SITE, 198 Merchant St., Sainte Genevieve, MO 63670-1682. Mailing Address: P.O. Box 89, Ste. Genevieve, MO 63670-0089. Tel.: 573-883-7102. Fax: 573-883-9630. TDD: 800-379-2419.
E-mail: felix.valle.state.historic.site@dnr.mo.gov
Web Site: www.mostateparks.com
Key Personnel: Site Admin., Donna J. Rausch.
Institution Type/Description: History Museum.
Hours & Admission Prices: April-Oct. Mon.-Sat. 10-4, Sun. 12-5; Nov.-March Thurs.-Sat. 10-4, Sun. 12-5. Adults $4, students $2.50; discount to groups; children under 6 no charge. Closed New Year's Day; Easter; Thanksgiving; Christmas.
Attendance: 13,000 (estimated)

STE. GENEVIEVE MUSEUM, Merchant & DuBourg St., Sainte Genevieve, MO 63670. Tel.: 573-883-3461.
E-mail: scabot@stegenevieve.org
Key Personnel: Dir., Lesley Barker.
Institution Type/Description: History Museum.
Hours & Admission Prices: April-Oct. daily 9-11 & 12-4; Nov.-March daily 12-4. Adults $2, students $1; members no charge. Closed New Year's Eve & Day; Easter; Thanksgiving; Christmas Eve & Day. &
Attendance: 5,750 (estimated)

Salem

OZARK HERITAGE MUSEUM, 701 S. Main St., Salem, MO 65560. Mailing Address: c/o Dent County Historical Society, 1202 Gertrude St., Salem, MO 65560. Tel.: 573-729-5707.
E-mail: kfiebelman@embarqmail.com
Institution Type/Description: History Museum.
Hours & Admission Prices: By appointment. No charge.

OZARK NATURAL & CULTURAL RESOURCE CENTER, 202 S. Main, Salem, MO 65560. Mailing Address: P.O. Box 732, Salem, MO 65560. Tel.: 573-729-0029.
E-mail: oncrc@salemmo.com
Web Site: www.oncrc.org
Key Personnel: Dir., Jerry Craig.
Institution Type/Description: Natural History Center.
Hours & Admission Prices: Call for hours.

Salisbury

CHARITON COUNTY HISTORICAL SOCIETY & MUSEUM, 115 E. 2nd St., Salisbury, MO 65281. Tel.: 660-388-5941.
Institution Type/Description: Historical Society Museum.
Hours & Admission Prices: April-Oct. Tues.-Sat. 1-4; other times by appointment. No charge; donations accepted.

Savannah

ANDREW COUNTY MUSEUM & HISTORICAL SOCIETY, 202 E. Duncan Dr., Savannah, MO 64485-1264. Mailing Address: P.O. Box 12, Savannah, MO 64485-0012. Tel.: 816-324-4720. Fax: 816-324-5271.
E-mail: administrator@andrewcountymuseum.org
Web Site: www.andrewcountymuseum.org
Key Personnel: Pres. (V), Dr. Jon Pray; Vice Pres., Gail Frankhauser; Dir., Dr. Jan Glenn; Cur., Elenore Leonard; Genealogy, Kathy Ridge; Museum Admin., Paula Price; Office Asst., Christy Sipes.
Institution Type/Description: History Museum.
Hours & Admission Prices: Tues.-Sat. 10-4. Adults $3, students & seniors $2; Blue Star Museum members & children under 13 no charge. &
Attendance: 5,545 (actual)

Sedalia

DAUM MUSEUM OF CONTEMPORARY ART, State Fair Community College, 3201 W. 16th St., Sedalia, MO 65301-2188. Tel.: 660-530-5888. Fax: 660-530-5890. Facebook: Daum Museum.
E-mail: info@daummuseum.org
Web Site: www.daummuseum.org
Formerly: Goddard Gallery
Key Personnel: Dir., Thomas Piche, Jr.; Pres., Dr. Joanna Anderson; Cur. Education, Victoria Weaver; Office Mgr., Marcie Teter.
Institution Type/Description: Contemporary Art Museum.
Hours & Admission Prices: Tues.-Fri. 11-5, Sat.-Sun. 1-5. No charge; donations accepted. &
Attendance: 26,000 (actual)

PETTIS COUNTY HISTORICAL SOCIETY, 228 Dundee, Sedalia, MO 65301-2339.
Key Personnel: Pres., Dr. Rhonda Chalfant; Vice Pres., Ken Bird; Sec. & Treas., Clell Furnell.
Institution Type/Description: Historical Society Museum.
Hours & Admission Prices: March-Oct. Wed.-Sun. 1-4; other times by appointment. No charge; donations accepted. &
Attendance: 100 (estimated)

Sibley

FORT OSAGE NATIONAL HISTORIC LANDMARK, 107 Osage St., Sibley, MO 64088. Mailing Address: 8201 Jasper Bell Rd., Blue Springs, MO 64015. Tel.: 816-503-4860. Fax: 816-795-7938. TDD: 800-735-2966.
Web Site: www.jacksongov.org
Key Personnel: Dir. Parks & Recreation, Michele Newman; Supt., Jonathan Klusmeyer; Site Administrator, Heather Campbell; Supt. Heritage Museums & Programs, Gordon Julich; Museum Shop Mgr., Laura King.
Institution Type/Description: Historic Site: 1808-1827 Fort Osage.

Hours & Admission Prices: Tues.-Sun. 9-4:30. Adults $8, senior citizens & youth $4. Closed Martin Luther King Jr. Day; Veterans Day; Truman's Birthday; Thanksgiving; Christmas. &
Attendance: 11,500 (actual)

Sikeston

SIKESTON DEPOT MUSEUM & CULTURAL CENTER, 116 W. Malone Ave., Sikeston, MO 63801. Mailing Address: P.O. Box 182, Sikeston, MO 63801. Tel.: 573-481-9967. Fax: 573-481-9967. Facebook.
E-mail: depotmuseum@sbcglobal.net
Web Site: sikestondepotmuseum.com
Institution Type/Description: History Museum: housed in a former railroad depot; built in 1916. Listed on the National Register of Historic Places.
Hours & Admission Prices: Tues.-Sat. 10-4. No charge; donations accepted.

Springfield

AIR AND MILITARY MUSEUM OF THE OZARKS, 2305 E. Kearney, Springfield, MO 65803-4970. Tel.: 417-864-7997. Fax: 417-866-2448. Facebook: Ammo Museum.
E-mail: ammomuseum@gmail.com
Web Site: ammomuseum.com
Key Personnel: Chmn. & Pres., Raymond Hopper; Museum Dir., Ron Cutter.
Institution Type/Description: Military Museum.
Hours & Admission Prices: Tues.-Sat. 12-4; other times by appointment. Adults $5, children 6-12 $3; discounts to AAM members and retired & active military personnel; children 5 & under no charge. &
Attendance: 6,000 (actual)

DICKERSON PARK ZOO, 1401 W. Norton Rd., Springfield, MO 65803-1023. Mailing Address: 3043 N. Fort Ave., Springfield, MO 65803-1079. Tel.: 417-833-1570. Fax: 417-833-4459.
E-mail: info@dickersonparkzoo.org
Web Site: www.dickersonparkzoo.org
Key Personnel: Dir., Michael Crocker; Dir. Public Rels. & Mktg., Joey Powell; Zoological & Gen. Cur., John Collette; Museum Shop Mgr., Joni Baurichter.
Institution Type/Description: Zoological Park.
Hours & Admission Prices: April-Sept. daily 9-5; Oct.-March daily 10-4. Adults $12, children 3-12 $8; discounts to groups of 15 or more paying individuals & members of reciprocal zoos, AZA; members & children under 3 no charge. Closed New Year's Day; Thanksgiving; Christmas. &
Attendance: 218,164 (actual)

DISCOVERY CENTER OF SPRINGFIELD, 438 St. Louis St., Springfield, MO 65806-2312. Tel.: 417-862-9910. Fax: 417-862-6898. Facebook: Discovery Center Springfield.
E-mail: info@discoverycenter.org
Web Site: www.discoverycenter.org
Key Personnel: Exec. Dir., Meleah Spencer; Bd. Pres. (V), Austin O'Reilly; Museum Shop Mgr., Amelia White.
Institution Type/Description: Science Center.
Hours & Admission Prices: Tues.-Thurs. 9-5, Fri.-Sat. 9-6, Sun. 1-5. Adults $12, seniors over 60 $10, children 3-15 $8; discounts to ASTC museum member; member no charge. &
Attendance: 100,000 (estimated)

DOLING MUSEUM, 301 E. Talmage, Springfield, MO 65803-7825.
E-mail: bbelote@springfieldmo.gov
Institution Type/Description: History Museum.
Hours & Admission Prices: April-Oct. Tues. 2-6, Fri. 11-4, Sun. 1-5. No charge.

FLOWER PENTECOSTAL HERITAGE CENTER, 1445 N. Boonville Ave., Springfield, MO 65802. Tel.: 877-840-5200 (Toll Free).
E-mail: archives@ag.org
Web Site: www.ifphc.org
Formerly: Assemblies of God Archives
Key Personnel: Dir., Darrin Rodgers.
Institution Type/Description: Religious History Museum.
Hours & Admission Prices: Mon.-Fri. 9-4:30. No charge. &
Attendance: 5,000 (estimated)

HISTORY MUSEUM ON THE SQUARE, 157 Park Central Sq., Springfield, MO 65806. Mailing Address: P.O. Box 2963, Springfield, MO 65801. Tel.: 417-831-1976. Fax: 888-965-9342.
E-mail: info@historymuseumonthesquare.org
Web Site: www.historymuseumonthesquare.org

Formerly: History Museum for Springfield-Greene County
Key Personnel: Exec. Dir., John E. Sellars; Cur., Joan Hampton-Porter.
Institution Type/Description: History Museum.
Hours & Admission Prices: Museum: Mon.-Sat. 10:30-4:30. Office: Mon.-Fri. 9-4:30. Suggested Donation: adults $5, students $3; discounts to groups; members no charge. Closed major holidays. &
Attendance: 10,000 (estimated)

MISSOURI INSTITUTE OF NATURAL SCIENCE, 2327 W. Farm Rd. 190, Springfield, MO 65810. Tel.: 417-883-0594.
E-mail: info@monatsci.com
Web Site: www.monatsci.com
Formerly: Natural History Museum of the Ozarks
Key Personnel: Dir., Matt Forir; Museum Dir., Mary Rauzi.
Institution Type/Description: Science Museum.
Hours & Admission Prices: Mon.-Fri. 8:30-4:30; call for additional hours. No charge; donations accepted. &

MISSOURI SPORTS HALL OF FAME, 3861 E. Stan Musial Dr., Springfield, MO 65809. Tel.: 417-889-3100, 800-498-5678. Fax: 417-889-2761.
E-mail: kari@mosportshalloffame.com
Web Site: www.mosportshalloffame.com
Key Personnel: C.E.O. & Exec. Dir./Pres., Jerald Andrews; Vice Pres. Operations, Marty Willadsen; Dir. Sponsorship Devel., Craig Winegar; Operations & Mktg., Kari Crawford; Accounting, Dale Witte; Special Events & Admin., Sharyn Wagoner.
Institution Type/Description: Hall of Fame.
Hours & Admission Prices: Mon.-Sat. 10-4, Sun. 12-4. Adults $5, senior citizens $4, children 6-15 $3; discounts to groups of 10 or more; children 5 & under no charge. &
Attendance: 100,000 (estimated)

OZARKS GENEALOGICAL SOCIETY LIBRARY, 534 W. Catalpa, Springfield, MO 65807-1404. Mailing Address: P.O. Box 3945, Springfield, MO 65808-3945.
E-mail: ogsadmin@ozarksgs.org
Web Site: ozarksgs.org
Institution Type/Description: Historical Society Museum.
Hours & Admission Prices: mid-March to Oct. Tues. 6pm-8:30pm, Wed. 1-4, Sat. 10-4; Nov. to mid-March Wed. 1-4, Sat. 10-4. No charge. Closed holidays; holiday weekends. &

RAILROAD HISTORICAL MUSEUM, INC., Grant Beach Park, 1300 N. Grant St., Springfield, MO 65802. Mailing Address: 1651 S. Roanoke Ave, Springfield, MO 65807-2085. Tel.: 417-865-6829.
E-mail: rrhistoricalmuseum@zoomshare.com
Web Site: rrhistoricalmuseum.zoomshare.com
Formerly: Railroad Historical Museum
Institution Type/Description: Railroad History Museum.
Hours & Admission Prices: Sat. 2-4; groups by appointment. No charge; donations accepted.
Attendance: 4,038 (actual)

THE SOFTBALL MUSEUM, Killian Sports Complex, 2141 E. Pythian St., Springfield, MO 65802. Mailing Address: c/o Springfield Amateur Softball Assocation, 1923 N. Weller, Springfield, MO 65802. Tel.: 417-837-5817.
Key Personnel: Dir., Mark Nelson.
Institution Type/Description: Sports Museum.
Hours & Admission Prices: Mon.-Fri. 11-5. No charge; donations accepted.
Attendance: 500 (estimated)

SPRINGFIELD ART MUSEUM, 1111 E. Brookside Dr., Springfield, MO 65807-1899. Tel.: 417-837-5700. Fax: 417-837-5704.
E-mail: artmuseum@springfieldmo.gov
Web Site: sgfmuseum.org
Key Personnel: Dir., Nick Nelson; Chm. (V), Sally Scheid; Cur. Art, Sarah Buhr; Museum Educator, Kate Baird; Exhibit Mgr., Cindy Quayle; Exec. Sec., Tyra Knox.
Institution Type/Description: Art Museum.
Hours & Admission Prices: Tues.-Wed. & Fri.-Sat. 9-5, Thurs. 9-8, Sun. 1-5. No charge; donations accepted. Closed City of Springfield Day; national holidays. &
Attendance: 43,848 (actual)

WONDERS OF WILDLIFE NATIONAL MUSEUM & AQUARIUM, 500 W. Sunshine St., Springfield, MO 65807. Tel.: 417-890-9453. Facebook: @wondersofwildlife.
E-mail: info@wondersofwildlife.org
Web Site: www.wondersofwildlife.org
Key Personnel: Founder, Johnny Morris.
Institution Type/Description: Wildlife Museum & Aquarium.
Hours & Admission Prices: Timed entry, please see Website for daily hours of operation. Aquarium Adventure: adults $29.95, children (ages 4-11) $19.95; Wildlife Galleries: adults $14.95, children $9.95; Wonders of Wildlife (includes Aquarium Adventure & Wildlife Galleries): adults $39.95, children $23.95.

Tarkio

TARKIO COLLEGE ALUMNI MUSEUM, 314 N. Main, Tarkio, MO 64491-1543. Mailing Address: P.O. Box 111, Tarkio, MO 64491-0111. Tel.: 660-736-4208.
E-mail: tcaa@asde.net
Web Site: www.tarkioalumni.org/museum.html
Key Personnel: Pres., Farleigh Joe Farley; Vice Pres., Marla Tollett-Ross; Sec., Sheridan Mires; Treas., Mary McAdams.
Institution Type/Description: Alumni Museum.
Hours & Admission Prices: Call for hours.

Trenton

GRUNDY COUNTY MUSEUM, 1100 Mabel St., Trenton, MO 64683. Tel.: 660-359-2411.
E-mail: schlarb@cebridge.net
Web Site: www.grundycountymuseum.org
Key Personnel: Recording Sec., Phil Schlarb.
Institution Type/Description: History Museum: built in 1895 by William McVay.
Hours & Admission Prices: Memorial Day to Oct. Sat.-Sun. & holidays 2-5; other times by appointment. Suggested Donation: adults $2; Life members no charge. &
Attendance: 900 (estimated)

Tuscumbia

MILLER COUNTY HISTORICAL SOCIETY & MUSEUM, 2005 Highway 52, Tuscumbia, MO 65082. Mailing Address: P.O. Box 57, Tuscumbia, MO 65082-0057. Tel.: 573-369-3500.
E-mail: millercountymuseum@att.net
Web Site: www.millercountymuseum.org
Key Personnel: Pres., Bill Weidinger; Dir., Karen Smith.
Institution Type/Description: Historical Society Museum.
Hours & Admission Prices: mid-May to mid-Oct. Mon., Wed. & Fri.-Sat. 10-4. No charge; donations accepted. Closed holidays. &
Attendance: 3,000

Unionville

PUTNAM COUNTY MUSEUM, 201 S. 16th St., Unionville, MO 63565. Tel.: 660-947-2955.
Web Site: putnamcountyhistoricalsociety.com
Institution Type/Description: History Museum.
Hours & Admission Prices: Call for hours.

University City

MILLSTONE GALLERY AT COCA, 524 Trinity Ave., University City, MO 63130. Tel.: 314-725-6555. Fax: 314-725-6222. Facebook, Instagram & Twitter: @COCAstl.
E-mail: info@cocastl.org
Web Site: www.cocastl.org
Key Personnel: Dir., Kelly Pollock; Pres. (V), Jesse Hunter; Dir. External Affairs & Strategic Initiatives, Jennifer Stoffel; Dir. Devel., Sophia Garner; Dir. Advancement, Pam Mandelker; Dir. Mktg. & Communications, Beth McClure; Dir. Admin., Catherine Wermert; Dir. Arts Education, Shawna Flanigan.
Institution Type/Description: Art Gallery.
Hours & Admission Prices: Sept.-May: Mon.-Fri. 9-9, Sat. 9-6, Sun. 11-6; Summer: Mon.-Thurs. 7:30-9, Fri. 7:30-6, Sat. 9-5. No charge. &
Attendance: 3,850 (estimated)

Van Buren

OZARK NATIONAL SCENIC RIVERWAYS, 404 Watercress Dr., Van Buren, MO 63965-9100. Mailing Address: P.O. Box 490, Van Buren, MO 63965-0490. Tel.: 573-323-8822. Fax: 573-323-4140 & 8823. TDD: 573-323-4270.

E-mail: ozar_interpretation@nps.gov
Web Site: www.nps.gov/ozar
Key Personnel: Supt., Reed Detring.
Institution Type/Description: Park Museum.
Hours & Admission Prices: Park: daily. Visitor Contact Station & Center: call for hours & information. Demonstrations April-Oct. Sat.-Sun.; other times by appointment. No charge. &
Attendance: 22,000 (estimated)

Versailles

MORGAN COUNTY HISTORICAL SOCIETY, 120 N. Monroe St., Versailles, MO 65084. Tel.: 573-378-5530.
Web Site: morgancohistory.org
Key Personnel: Pres. (V), Barbara Barnard.
Institution Type/Description: County Historical Society: housed in the former Martin Hotel, built in 1877 & 1884.
Hours & Admission Prices: May to mid-Oct. Mon.-Fri. 10-3; other times by appointment. Adults $3; handicapped no charge.
Attendance: 1,200 (estimated)

Walker

OSAGE VILLAGE STATE HISTORIC SITE, Hwy. C, Walker, MO 64790. Mailing Address: 1009 Truman Ave, Lamar, MO 64759. Tel.: 417-682-2279. Fax: 417-682-6304.
E-mail: moparks@dnr.mo.gov
Web Site: mostateparks.com/osage-village-state-historic-site
Key Personnel: Site Admin., Beth Bazal.
Institution Type/Description: Archaeological Site.
Hours & Admission Prices: Daily sunrise to sunset. No charge; donations accepted.
Attendance: 6,000 (estimated)

Walnut Shade

BONNIEBROOK MUSEUM, GALLERY & HOME OF ARTIST ROSE O'NEILL, 485 Rose O'Neill Rd., Walnut Shade, MO 65771. Tel.: 800-539-7437, 417-561-1509.
E-mail: oneillmuseum@aol.com
Web Site: www.roseoneill.org
Formerly: Bonniebrook Historical Society
Key Personnel: Pres. (V), Susan Scott; Museum Shop Mgr., Louise Williams.
Institution Type/Description: Art Museum.
Hours & Admission Prices: April-Nov. Tues.-Sat. 9-4. Call for admission prices.
Attendance: 5,000 (estimated)

Warrensburg

ARTHUR F. MCCLURE II ARCHIVES AND UNIVERSITY MUSEUM, JCK Library 1470, 601 S. Missouri, Warrensburg, MO 64093-5040. Tel.: 660-543-4649 & 4404.
E-mail: vrichardson@ucmo.edu
Web Site: www.ucmo.edu/archmusm
Formerly: Central Missouri State University Archives and Museum
Key Personnel: Dir., Amber Clifford-Napoleon; Asst. Dir., Vivian Richardson.
Institution Type/Description: General Museum.
Hours & Admission Prices: During University Sessions: Mon.-Fri. 9-12 & 1-4; other times by appointment. No charge; donations accepted. Closed holidays. &

JOHNSON COUNTY HISTORICAL SOCIETY MUSEUM, 302 N. Main St., Warrensburg, MO 64093-1554. Tel.: 660-747-6480.
E-mail: curator@jocomohistory.org
Web Site: jocomohistory.org
Key Personnel: Cur., Lisa Irle.
Institution Type/Description: Regional History Museum: 1838 federal style courthouse; Mary Miller Smiser Heritage Library; one room schoolhouse.
Hours & Admission Prices: Mon.-Sat. 1-4; other times by appointment. Tours: adults $3; members no charge. Closed New Year's Eve & Day; Independence Day; Thanksgiving; Christmas Eve, Day & week. &
Attendance: 4,000 (estimated)

Warrenton

SCHOWENGERDT HOUSE, 308 E. Booneslick Rd., Warrenton, MO 63383-2008. Mailing Address: 102 W. Walton St., Warrenton, MO 63383-1918. Tel.: 636-456-3820.
E-mail: museum@warrencountymohistory.com
Web Site: warrencountymohistory.com
Key Personnel: Chm. (V), Janet Sutherland; Museum Shop, Larry Wise; Museum Shop, Tom Miltenberger.

Institution Type/Description: Historic House Museum: built in 1866. Listed on the National Register of Historic Places.
Hours & Admission Prices: By appointment. Admission $5; children under 12 no charge. &

WARREN COUNTY HISTORICAL SOCIETY MUSEUM & LIBRARY, 102 W. Walton St., Warrenton, MO 63383. Tel.: 636-456-3820.
E-mail: museum@warrencountymohistory.com
Web Site: warrencountymohistory.com
Key Personnel: Chm. (V), Janet Sutherland; Museum Shop Mgr., Susie Busekrus.
Institution Type/Description: Historical Society Museum.
Hours & Admission Prices: Thurs.-Fri. 10-4, Sun. 1-4. No charge; donations accepted. &
Attendance: 1,000 (estimated)

Washington

FIREHOUSE MUSEUM, 520 W. 5th St., Washington, MO 63090. Mailing Address: Washington Historical Society, P.O. Box 146, Washington, MO 63090-0146. Tel.: 636-390-0469.
E-mail: museum@washmohistorical.org
Institution Type/Description: History Museum.
Hours & Admission Prices: By appointment.

WASHINGTON HISTORICAL SOCIETY MUSEUM, Fourth & Market Sts., Washington, MO 63090. Mailing Address: P.O. Box 146, Washington, MO 63090-0146. Tel.: 636-239-0280.
E-mail: jennifer.kilmer@wshs.wa.gov
Web Site: www.washingtonhistory.org/contact
Institution Type/Description: History Museum.
Hours & Admission Prices: March-Dec. Tues.-Sat. 10-4, Sun. 12-4. No charge.

Waynesville

THE OLD STAGECOACH STOP, 106 Lynn St., Waynesville, MO 65583. Mailing Address: P.O. Box 585, Waynesville, MO 65583-0585. Tel.: 573-336-3561.
E-mail: gjporter@embarqmail.com
Web Site: www.oldstagecoachstop.org
Key Personnel: Pres. (V), Jeanie Porter; Museum Shop Mgr., Jan Primas.
Institution Type/Description: House Museum: listed on the National Register of Historic Places.
Hours & Admission Prices: April-Sept. Sat. 10-4. No charge.
Attendance: 1,800 (actual)

PULASKI COUNTY MUSEUM & HISTORICAL SOCIETY, 301 A Historic Rte. 66, Waynesville, MO 65583. Mailing Address: P.O. Box 144, Waynesville, MO 65583. Tel.: 573-774-5368.
E-mail: mscott1108@cablemo.net
Web Site: www.oldpulaskicountycourthousemuseum.webs.com
Formerly: Pulaski County Courthouse Museum
Key Personnel: Society Pres. (V), Cur., & Museum Shop Mgr., Marge Scott.
Institution Type/Description: History Museum.
Hours & Admission Prices: April-Sept. Sat. 10-4; tours by appointment. No charge; donations appreciated.
Attendance: 1,538 (estimated)

Webb City

THE CLUBHOUSE MUSEUM, 115 N. Madison St., Webb City, MO 64870. Mailing Address: Webb City Historical Society, P.O. Box 1, Webb City, MO 64870. Tel.: 417-673-5866.
Institution Type/Description: History Museum: housed in the former clubhouse for employees of the Southwest Missouri Electric Railway; built in 1910.
Hours & Admission Prices: By appointment.

Webster Groves

MAY GALLERY AT WEBSTER UNIVERSITY, 8300 Big Bend Blvd., Webster Groves, MO 63119-3114. Mailing Address: 470 E. Lockwood Ave., Saint Louis, MO 63119-3194. Tel.: 314-246-7673. Fax: 314-963-6924.
E-mail: mgallery@webster.edu
Web Site: www.webster.edu/maygallery
Key Personnel: Dir., Bill Barrett.
Institution Type/Description: Art Gallery.
Hours & Admission Prices: Mon.-Fri. 9-9, Sat.-Sun. 12-5. No charge. &
Attendance: 4,500 (estimated)

West Plains

HARLIN MUSEUM, 505 Worcester Ave., West Plains, MO 65775. Mailing Address: P.O. Box 444, West Plains, MO 65775-0444. Tel.: 417-256-7801.
E-mail: staff@harlinmuseum.com
Web Site: harlinmuseum.com
Institution Type/Description: History Museum: housed in the home of former West Plains Mayor, James P. Harlin & his wife; built in 1889.
Hours & Admission Prices: Tues.-Sat. 12-4.

Weston

HERBERT BONNELL MUSEUM, 20755 Lamar Rd., Weston, MO 64098-9173. Mailing Address: P.O. Box 238, Weston, MO 64098-0238. Tel.: 816-386-5587 & 992-0102.
E-mail: belindak@embarqmail.com
Web Site: www.westonmo.com/history/museums_hist.html
Key Personnel: Trust, Frank Green; Co Trust, Belinda Farris.
Institution Type/Description: History Museum.
Hours & Admission Prices: May-Oct. Sat.-Sun. 1-5; other times by appointment. No charge; donations accepted.

NATIONAL SILK ART MUSEUM, Museum of Fibre Arts, Inc., 423 Main St., Weston, MO 64098-1249. Tel.: 816-536-5955.
E-mail: silkartmuseum@gmail.com
Web Site: www.nationalsilkartmuseum.com
Key Personnel: Dir. & Cur., John Pottie; Pres. (V),, Adrienne Haake; Librarian, Venessa Pottie.
Institution Type/Description: Art Museum.
Hours & Admission Prices: Sat. 11-5; groups & other times by appointment. No charge; donations accepted. &
Attendance: 30,000 (actual)

WESTON HISTORICAL MUSEUM, 601 Main St., Weston, MO 64098-1207. Mailing Address: P.O. Box 266, Weston, MO 64098-0266. Tel.: 816-386-2977.
E-mail: director@westonhistoricalmuseum.org; curator@westonhistoricalmuseum.org
Web Site: www.westonhistoricalmuseum.org
Key Personnel: Dir., Barbara Fulk; Pres., Carl Felling; Museum Shop Mgr., Jeanne Braneff.
Institution Type/Description: History Museum.
Hours & Admission Prices: late March to early Dec. Tues.-Sat. 1-4, Sun. 1:30-4:30. No charge; donations accepted. Closed holidays.
Attendance: 3,000 (estimated)

Westphalia

WESTPHALIA HISTORICAL SOCIETY, 119 E. Main St., Westphalia, MO 65085. Mailing Address: P.O. Box 244, Westphalia, MO 68085-0244.
E-mail: whs65085@yahoo.com
Web Site: westphaliahistoricalsociety
Institution Type/Description: Historical Society Museum.
Hours & Admission Prices: April-Oct. Sun. 1-3.

Wildwood

HENCKEN HOUSE MUSEUM - WILDWOOD HISTORICAL SOCIETY, 18750 Hwy. 100, Wildwood, MO 63069-3000. Mailing Address: P.O. Box 125, Wildwood, MO 63040. Tel.: 314-920-2249.
E-mail: info@wildwoodhistoricalsociety.org
Web Site: wildwoodhistoricalsociety.org
Key Personnel: Museum Dir., Martha Bunch; Pres. Society, Sandy Becker-Gurnow.
Institution Type/Description: Historical Society Museum.
Hours & Admission Prices: Mon. 9am to noon; other times by appointment. No charge; donations accepted.
Attendance: 240

RIVER HILLS VISITOR CENTER, Dr. Edmund A. Babler Memorial State Park, 800 Guy Park Dr., Wildwood, MO 63005. Mailing Address: c/o Missouri State Parks, P.O. Box 176, Jefferson City, MO 65102-0176. Tel.: 636-458-3813. Fax: 636-458-9105.
E-mail: moparks@dnr.mo.gov
Web Site: mostateparks.com/location/55677/river-hills-visitor-center
Key Personnel: Park Supt., Jeff Robinson.
Institution Type/Description: Park Museum & Visitor Center.

Hours & Admission Prices: 9-4. No charge. Closed Dec.-Feb. &
Attendance: 393,000

ROCKWOODS RESERVATION, 2751 Glencoe Rd., Wildwood, MO 63038-1919. Tel.: 636-458-2236. Fax: 636-458-6726.
E-mail: rockwoods.res@mdc.mo.gov
Institution Type/Description: Conservation Education Center.
Hours & Admission Prices: Education Center Mon.-Fri. 8-5. Reservation: daily sunrise to 1/2 hour after sunset. No charge. Closed all state holidays. &
Attendance: 150,000 (estimated)

Willow Springs

FIRE MUSEUM OF MISSOURI, 908 E. Business Rte. 60-63, Willow Springs, MO 65793. Tel.: 417-469-4589.
E-mail: jlows@socket.net
Web Site: www.usfirehouse.com
Key Personnel: Owner, John Mathieu.
Institution Type/Description: Fire-Fighting Museums.
Hours & Admission Prices: Adults $5, children 10-17 $3; children under 10 no charge.

Windsor

WINDOR HISTORICAL SOCIETY, 104 S. Franklin St., Windsor, MO 65360. Mailing Address: P.O. Box 111, Windsor, MO 65360. Tel.: 660-647-2345.
E-mail: winhissoc@socket.net
Web Site: windsormo.org
Institution Type/Description: Historical Society Museum.
Hours & Admission Prices: Fri.-Sun. 1-4.

MONTANA

(154 listings)

Anaconda

COPPER VILLAGE MUSEUM - ARTS CENTER OF DEER LODGE COUNTY - MARCUS DALY HISTORICAL SOCIETY, 401 E. Commercial, Anaconda, MT 59711-2360. Tel.: 406-563-2422 & 2220. Fax: 406-563-2422.
E-mail: copper_village@hotmail.com
Web Site: www.coppervillageartcenter.com
Key Personnel: Chief Exec. Dir. & Dir. Community Affairs, Susan Lanes; Pres. (V) & Chm. (V), Brian Tesson; Co-Pres., Barbara Beardslee; Dir. Education, Mary Johnson.
Institution Type/Description: Contemporary & Historic Art Gallery and Museum.
Hours & Admission Prices: Tues.-Sat. 10-5. No charge; donations accepted. Closed legal holidays. &
Attendance: 8,000 (estimated)

Bainville

PIONEER'S PRIDE MUSEUM, 6013 Rd. 1011, Bainville, MT 59212-9625. Mailing Address: HC58 P.O. Box 63, Bainville, MT 59212. Tel.: 406-769-2064.
Institution Type/Description: History Museum.
Hours & Admission Prices: Memorial Day-Labor Day Tues.-Sun. 1:30-4:30. No charge.

Baker

O'FALLON HISTORICAL MUSEUM, 723 S. Main St., Baker, MT 59313. Mailing Address: P.O. Box 285, Baker, MT 59313-0285. Tel.: 406-778-3265. Fax: 406-778-3967.
E-mail: ofmuseum@midrivers.com
Web Site: www.falloncounty.net
Key Personnel: C.E.O., Curt Williams; Dir., Karen Banister.
Institution Type/Description: History Museum.
Hours & Admission Prices: June-Aug. daily 8-12 & 1-5; Sept.-May Mon.-Fri. 8-12 & 1-5. No charge; donations accepted. Closed legal holidays. &
Attendance: 1,300 (estimated)

Belt

BELT MUSEUM, 37 Castner St., Belt, MT 59412-8029. Mailing Address: P.O. Box 442, Belt, MT 59412-0442. Tel.: 406-277-3574.
E-mail: mkoontz@3rivers.net

Institution Type/Description: History Museum: housed in the old jail building, built in 1895.
Hours & Admission Prices: Memorial Day-Labor Day Sat.-Sun. 12-4. No charge; donations accepted.
Attendance: 400 (estimated)

Big Timber

CRAZY MOUNTAIN MUSEUM, Exit 367 Cemetery Rd., Hwy. I-90, Big Timber, MT 59011. Mailing Address: P.O. Box 83, Big Timber, MT 59011-0083. Tel.: 406-932-5126.
E-mail: cmmuseum@mtintouch.net
Key Personnel: Chm. & Pres. (V), Steve Harvey; Treas., Joan Van Daveer; Dir. & Cur., Jean Chapel; Cur., Elli Hawks; Museum Shop Mgr., Christy Mosness.
Institution Type/Description: History Museum.
Hours & Admission Prices: Memorial Day to Sept. Mon.-Sat. 10-4:30, Sun. 1-4:30. No charge; donations accepted. &
Attendance: 5,000 (estimated)

Billings

BILLINGS CURATION CENTER, 5001 Southgate Dr., Billings, MT 59101-4669. Mailing Address: P.O. Box 36800, Billings, MT 59107. Tel.: 406-896-5213. Fax: 406-896-5317.
E-mail: MT_SO_Bcc@blm.gov
Web Site: www.blm.gov
Key Personnel: BLM State Archaeologist, Gary Smith; Cur., David K. Wade.
Institution Type/Description: Federal Agency Repository & Archaeology Site.
Hours & Admission Prices: Mon.-Fri. 9-4:30. No charge. &

MOSS MANSION HISTORIC HOUSE MUSEUM, 914 Division St., Billings, MT 59101-1921. Tel.: 406-256-5100. Facebook: @mossmansion.
E-mail: tours@mossmansion.com
Web Site: www.mossmansion.com
Key Personnel: Dir., Jenna Richter; Operations Mgr., Jennette Rasch; Pres. (V), Jared Maloney; Vice Pres. & Treas., Stephanie Dwyer; Sec. & Museum Shop Mgr., Lue Ponich; Event Coord., Marlene McCave.
Institution Type/Description: Historic House Museum: housed in the Moss Mansion built in 1901-1903.
Hours & Admission Prices: Memorial Day-Labor Day: Tues.-Sat. 10-4, Sun. 1-4, last tour 3. Labor Day-Memorial Day: Tues.-Sun. 1-4, last tour 3. Adults $10, senior citizens & military $7, children 6-17 $6, children under 5 & members no charge. Closed New Year's Day; Independence Day; Thanksgiving; Christmas. &
Attendance: 18,162 (estimated)

MUSEUM OF WOMEN'S HISTORY, 2822 3rd Ave. N., Billings, MT 59101-1932. Mailing Address: 2822 3rd Ave. N., B-3, Billings, MT 59101-1934. Tel.: 406-248-2015. Facebook: Museum of Women's History.
E-mail: mowh@imt.net
Institution Type/Description: Women's History Museum.
Hours & Admission Prices: By appointment only. No charge; donations accepted. Closed legal holidays. &
Attendance: 350 (estimated)

NORTHCUTT STEELE GALLERY - MONTANA STATE UNIVERSITY, 1500 University Dr., Billings, MT 59101. Tel.: 406-657-2903, 406-657-2324. Fax: 406-657-2187. Facebook: Northcutt Steele Gallery.
E-mail: leanne.gilbertson@msubillings.edu
Web Site: msubillings.edu/gallery
Key Personnel: Dir., Dr. Leanne Gilbertson.
Institution Type/Description: Art Gallery.
Hours & Admission Prices: Sept.-May Mon.-Fri. 8-4. No charge.

RYNIKER-MORRISON GALLERY, Rocky Mountain College, 1511 Poly Dr., Billings, MT 59102-1796. Mailing Address: 122 Ave. D, Billings, MT 59101. Tel.: 906-259-6563. Facebook: Ryniker-Morrison Gallery.
E-mail: sally.mcintosh@rocky.edu
Web Site: rocky.edu
Key Personnel: Dir., Sally McIntosh.
Institution Type/Description: Art Gallery.
Hours & Admission Prices: Mon.-Fri. 9-4. No charge. &

WESTERN HERITAGE CENTER, 2822 Montana Ave., Billings, MT 59101-2305. Tel.: 406-256-6809. Fax: 406-256-6850. Facebook.
E-mail: lisa@ywhc.org
Web Site: www.ywhc.org
Key Personnel: Community Historian, Kevin Kooistra; Operations Dir., Lisa Olmsted; Community Historian, Elisabeth DeGrenier.
Institution Type/Description: Regional History Museum: housed in 1901 Parmly Billings Memorial Library Building.
Hours & Admission Prices: Tues.-Sat. 10-5. Adults $5, seniors $3, children $1; members no charge. Closed major holidays. &
Attendance: 17,800 (estimated)

YELLOWSTONE ART MUSEUM, 401 N. 27th St., Billings, MT 59101-1241. Tel.: 406-256-6804. Fax: 406-256-6817. Facebook; Yellowstone Art Museum.
E-mail: artinfo@artmuseum.org
Web Site: www.artmuseum.org
Formerly: Yellowstone Art Center
Key Personnel: Exec. Dir., Robyn G. Peterson; Pres., Kevin Stenberg; Senior Cur., Bob Durden; Dir. Devel., Ryan Cremer; Dir. Education, Mary Serbe; Admin. & Finance Dir., John Greenberger.
Institution Type/Description: Regional Art Museum
Hours & Admission Prices: Tues.-Wed. & Sat. 10-5, Thurs.-Fri. 10-8, Sun. 11-4. Adults $6; discounts to military, AAM, AARP, ICOM & AAA members; members no charge. North American Reciprocal group. Closed major holidays. &
Attendance: 40,299 (actual)

YELLOWSTONE COUNTY MUSEUM, 1950 Airport Terminal Cir., Billings, MT 59105-1988. Tel.: 406-256-6811. Fax: 406-254-6031. Facebook: Yellowstone County Museum.
E-mail: info@ycmhistory.org
Web Site: www.ycmhistory.org
Formerly: Peter Yegen Jr. Yellowstone County Museum
Key Personnel: Chm. (V), Charlie Yegen; Dir., Benjamin Nordlund; Cur., Kathy Barton.
Institution Type/Description: Montana & Western History Museum: portion of which is housed in an 1890s log structure belonging to Montana pioneer Paul McCormick.
Hours & Admission Prices: Tues.-Sat. 10:30-5:30. No charge; donations accepted. Closed Easter; Thanksgiving; Christmas.
Attendance: 20,119 (actual)

ZOOMONTANA, 2100 S. Shiloh Rd., Billings, MT 59106-3908. Tel.: 406-652-8100. Fax: 406-652-9281. Facebook: @ZooMontana.
E-mail: director@zoomontana.org
Web Site: www.zoomontana.org
Key Personnel: Dir., Jeff Ewelt; Education, Troy Paisley; Cur., Travis Goebel.
Institution Type/Description: Zoo.
Hours & Admission Prices: May-Sept. daily 10-4; Oct.-April daily 10-2. Adults $7.95, senior citizens & military $5.95, children $4.95; discounts to groups of 15 or more; members no charge. Closed Thanksgiving; Christmas. &
Attendance: 100,000 (actual)

Bozeman

AMERICAN COMPUTER MUSEUM, 2023 Stadium Dr., Ste. 1-A, Bozeman, MT 59715. Tel.: 406-582-1288. Fax: 406-587-9620.
E-mail: director@compustory.com
Web Site: www.compustory.com
Institution Type/Description: Computer Museum.
Hours & Admission Prices: June-Aug. daily 10-4; Sept.-May Tues.-Sun. 12-4. Adults $7.50, students, seniors, military & youth 10-17 $4; children 9 & under no charge. Closed holidays. &

CHILDREN'S MUSEUM OF BOZEMAN, 202 S. Willson Ave., Bozeman, MT 59715-4631. Tel.: 406-522-9087.
E-mail: info@cmbozeman.org
Web Site: www.cmbozeman.org
Key Personnel: Exec. Dir., Susan Denson-Guy; Pres. (V), Marisa Bueno.
Institution Type/Description: Children's Museum.
Hours & Admission Prices: Mon.-Thurs. & Sat. 10-5, Fri. 10-8; groups of 12 or more by appointment. Admission $5; discounts to groups & ACM members; Fri. 5-8pm no charge.
Attendance: 21,187 (actual)

GALLATIN HISTORICAL SOCIETY DBA GALLATIN HISTORY MUSEUM, 317 W. Main St., Bozeman, MT 59715-4576. Tel.: 406-522-8122. Fax: 406-522-0367.

E-mail: director@gallatinhistorymuseum.org
Web Site: www.gallatinhistorymuseum.org
Key Personnel: Bd. Pres., Cindy Shearer; Research Coord., Rachel Phillips.
Institution Type/Description: Historical Society Museum.
Hours & Admission Prices: Memorial Day to Labor Day Tues.-Sat. 10-5; Winter: Tues.-Sat. 11-4. Adults $5; school groups, children 12 & under and members no charge. &
Attendance: 5,000 (actual)

HELEN E. COPELAND GALLERY, Physical/Mailing Address: MSU School of Art Helen E. Copeland Gallery, 213 Haynes Hall, Bozeman, MT 59717. Tel.: 406-994-4501. Fax: 406-994-3680. Facebook.
E-mail: ella.watson@montana.edu
Web Site: www.hecgallery.com
Key Personnel: Gallery Dir., Ella Watson.
Institution Type/Description: Art Gallery.
Hours & Admission Prices: Mon.-Fri. 9-5. No charge; donations accepted. Closed state & federal holidays. &
Attendance: 5,000

MUSEUM OF THE ROCKIES, 600 W. Kagy Blvd., Bozeman, MT 59717-2730. Tel.: 406-994-2251. Fax: 406-994-2682. Facebook: @mormsu.
E-mail: museum@montana.edu
Web Site: museumoftherockies.org
Key Personnel: Exec. Dir., Sheldon McKamey; Cur. History, Michael Fox; Security Chief, Ronda Harrison; Dir. Philanthropy, Kathryn Hohmann; Cur. Photography/Art, Steve Jackson; Exhibits/Paleo Dir., Patrick Leiggi; Dir. Finance, Kristi Mills; Interim Store Mgr. & Buyer, John Olsen; Cur. Paleontology, John Scannella; Mktg. Dir., Alicia Thompson.
Institution Type/Description: General Regional Museum.
Hours & Admission Prices: Memorial Day-Labor Day daily 8-6; Sept.-May daily 9-5. Museum: adults $14.50, senior citizens 65 & over $13.50, youth 5-17 $9.50, MSU students with valid ID $10, children 4 & under, no charge. Closed New Year's Day; Thanksgiving; Christmas. &
Attendance: 179,000 (actual)

Broadus

POWDER RIVER HISTORICAL MUSEUM AND MAC'S MUSEUM, 102 W. Wilson, Broadus, MT 59317. Mailing Address: P.O. Box 573, Broadus, MT 59317-0573. Tel.: 406-436-2977.
Key Personnel: Pres. (V), Ron Talcott.
Institution Type/Description: Local History Museum.
Hours & Admission Prices: June-Sept. Mon.-Fri. 9-5; other times by appointment. No charge; donations accepted. &
Attendance: 250 (actual)

Browning

BLACKFEET HERITAGE CENTER & ART GALLERY, 333 Central Ave. W., Browning, MT 59417. Mailing Address: P.O. Box 1629, Browning, MT 59417. Tel.: 406-338-5661.
E-mail: sales@blackfeetnationstore.com
Web Site: www.blackfeetnationstore.com
Institution Type/Description: Native American History & Art Center.
Hours & Admission Prices: Summer: daily. No charge.

MUSEUM OF THE PLAINS INDIAN, 19 Museum Loop, Browning, MT 59417. Mailing Address: P.O. Box 410, Browning, MT 59417-0410. Tel.: 406-338-2230. Fax: 406-338-7404.
E-mail: mpi@3rivers.net
Web Site: www.iacb.doi.gov
Key Personnel: Cur., David Dragonfly.
Institution Type/Description: Indian Art Museum.
Hours & Admission Prices: June-Sept. daily 9-4:45; Oct.-May Mon.-Fri. 10-4:30. Adults $5, seniors $4, children $1; discounts to groups of 10 or more; children under 6 no charge. Closed New Year's Day; Thanksgiving; Christmas. &
Attendance: 25,000 (estimated)

Butte

BUTTE-SILVER BOW ARTS CHATEAU, 128 W. Granite St., Butte, MT 59701. Tel.: 406-723-7600.
E-mail: bsbaf@bsbarts.org
Web Site: www.artschateau.org
Key Personnel: C.E.O., Glenn Bodish; Pres., Gretchen Miller.

Institution Type/Description: Period Museum & Arts Center; housed in 1898 The Charles Clark Mansion.
Hours & Admission Prices: June-Aug. Tues.-Sun. 12-5; Sept.-May Tues.-Sat. 11-4, Sun. 12-5. Family $10, adults $3, AAA, & CAA members $2.50, senior citizens 50 & up $2, children 16 & under $1; discounts to AAM members & groups of 10 or more; members no charge. Closed major holidays.
Attendance: 4,900 (actual)

COPPER KING MANSION, 219 W. Granite St., Butte, MT 59701-9235. Tel.: 406-782-7580.
E-mail: esigl@in-tch.com
Web Site: www.thecopperkingmansion.com
Key Personnel: Gen. Mgr., John Thompson.
Institution Type/Description: Historic House: 1884-1888, mansion built by William Andrews Clark including period furnishings.
Hours & Admission Prices: May-Sept. daily 9-4; Oct.-April by appointment. Adults $7, students 6-18 $3.50; children under 6 no charge.
Attendance: 10,000 (estimated)

MAI WAH SOCIETY, 17 W. Mercury St., Butte, MT 59701-2019. Mailing Address: P.O. Box 404, Butte, MT 59703-0404. Tel.: 406-723-3231.
E-mail: info@maiwah.org
Web Site: www.maiwah.org
Institution Type/Description: Asian Heritage Museum.
Hours & Admission Prices: Late May to Sept. Tues.-Sat. 10-4. Adults $5; members no charge.
Attendance: 500 (estimated)

MINERAL MUSEUM, Montana Tech. of the University of Montana, 1300 W. Park St., Butte, MT 59701-8932. Tel.: 406-496-4414 & 4159. Fax: 406-496-4451. Facebook: Montana Bureau of Mines & Geology.
E-mail: jfoley@mtech.edu
Web Site: www.mbmg.mtech.edu/museum/museum.asp
Key Personnel: Cur., Dr. John Metesh; Asst. Cur., John Foley.
Institution Type/Description: Mineralogy Museum.
Hours & Admission Prices: June 15-Sept. 15 daily 9-5; Winter: Mon.-Fri. 9-4. No charge; donations accepted. Closed state holidays.
Attendance: 7,000 (estimated)

PICCADILLY TRANSPORTATION MEMORABILIA MUSEUM, 20 W. Broadway, Butte, MT 59701-9222. Tel.: 406-723-3034. Fax: 406-723-7425.
E-mail: info@piccadillymuseum.com
Web Site: www.piccadillymuseum.com
Institution Type/Description: Transportation & Advertising Art Museum.
Hours & Admission Prices: Memorial Day to Oct. 1 Mon.-Sat. 10-5; Fall & Winter: by appointment only. Suggested Donation: $3.

WORLD MUSEUM OF MINING, 155 Museum Way, Butte, MT 59701. Mailing Address: P.O. Box 33, Butte, MT 59703-0033. Tel.: 406-723-7211. Facebook: @worldmuseumofmining.
E-mail: info@miningmuseum.org
Web Site: www.miningmuseum.org
Key Personnel: Dir., Jeanette Kop; Pres. (V), Lofan Dudding; Sec., Sonya Rosenthal.
Institution Type/Description: Mining Museum: located on the site of the Orphan Girl Mine, an early day zinc & silver mine, once owned by Butte Copper King Marcus Daly.
Hours & Admission Prices: April-Oct. daily 9-6, last ticket sold at 5. Adults 18 & up $8.50, seniors 65 & up $7.50, youth 5-17 $5; discounts to AAM, AAA & ICOM members, military and school groups; members & children under 5 no charge. Underground Mine Tour: adults $12, seniors $10, students $8, children $5. Museum & Underground Mine Tour: adults $17, seniors $14, youth $11, members $5.
Attendance: 25,000 (actual)

Bynum

TWO MEDICINE DINOSAUR CENTER, 120 2nd Ave. S., Bynum, MT 59419. Mailing Address: P.O. Box 786, Bynum, MT 59419-0786. Tel.: 406-469-2211, 800-238-6873.
E-mail: dinoinfo@tmdinosaur.org
Web Site: www.tmdinosaur.org
Institution Type/Description: Research and Education Institution.
Hours & Admission Prices: May & mid-Sept. to Sept. 30 Wed.-Sun. 10-5; June to mid-Sept. daily 9-6.

Charlo

NINEPIPES MUSEUM OF EARLY MONTANA, 69316 Hwy. 93, Charlo, MT 59824-9789. Tel.: 406-644-3435.
E-mail: ninepipesmuseum@montana.com
Web Site: ninepipesmuseum.org
Key Personnel: Dir., Vern Cheff, Jr.; Chm. & Pres. (V), Rod Wamsley; Admin. & Museum Shop Mgr., Jo Cheff.
Institution Type/Description: History Museum: named after Chief Joseph Ninepipes, a Bitterroot Salish Chief.
Hours & Admission Prices: April-Oct. Mon.-Sat. 9-5. Adults $5, students $3, children 6-12 $2; discounts to seniors, military & groups of 20 or more; members & children under 6 no charge. Closed Easter; Thanksgiving; Christmas.
Attendance: 5,500 (estimated)

Chester

LIBERTY COUNTY MUSEUM, 230 Second St. E., Chester, MT 59522. Mailing Address: P.O. Box 417, Chester, MT 59522-0417. Tel.: 406-759-5256.
E-mail: bubbles@itstriangle.com
Key Personnel: Chm. (V), Betty L. Marshall.
Institution Type/Description: General Museum.
Hours & Admission Prices: May to Labor Day daily 1-5 & 7-9. No charge; donations accepted.
Attendance: 500 (estimated)

LIBERTY VILLAGE ARTS CENTER & GALLERY, 410 W. Main St., Chester, MT 59522-0269. Mailing Address: P.O. Box 269, Chester, MT 59522-0269. Tel.: 406-759-5652. Fax: 406-759-5652.
E-mail: lvac@mtintouch.net
Web Site: libertyvillagearts.org
Key Personnel: Treas. (V), Laurie Lyders; Museum Shop Mgr., Marla Forbes; Museum Shop Mgr., Annie Miller.
Institution Type/Description: Folk Arts Center: housed in 1910 church building.
Hours & Admission Prices: mid-Jan. to Dec. Tues.-Wed. & Fri. 12:30-4:30, Thurs. 12:30-8. No charge; donations accepted. Closed New Year's Day; Easter; Independence Day; Thanksgiving; Christmas.
Attendance: 3,500 (estimated)

Chinook

BLAINE COUNTY MUSEUM, 501 Indiana, Chinook, MT 59523. Mailing Address: P.O. Box 927, Chinook, MT 59523-0927. Tel.: 406-357-2590. Fax: 406-357-2199.
E-mail: blmuseum@mtintouch.net
Web Site: www.blainecountymuseum.com
Key Personnel: Dir. & Cur., Jude Sheppard; Chm. (V), Stuart C. MacKenzie.
Institution Type/Description: History Museum: housed in 1915 former recreation center.
Hours & Admission Prices: May & Sept. Mon.-Fri. 8-5; June-Aug. Mon.-Sat. 8-5, Sun. 12-5; Oct.-April Mon.-Fri. 1-5. No charge.
Attendance: 4,350 (actual)

Choteau

OLD TRAIL MUSEUM, 823 N. Main St., Choteau, MT 59422-9272. Tel.: 406-466-5332.
E-mail: oldtrail2@gmail.com
Web Site: oldtrailmuseum.org
Key Personnel: Chm. & Pres. (V), Dawn Pearson; Dir. & Museum Shop Mgr., Julie Ameline; Operations, Dave Wedum.
Institution Type/Description: Village Museum: housed in 1920 six building cleaning plant.
Hours & Admission Prices: Memorial Day to Labor Day daily 9-5. Admission $2; members no charge.
Attendance: 3,350 (actual)

Circle

MCCONE COUNTY MUSEUM, 1507 Ave. B, Circle, MT 59215-0127. Mailing Address: P.O. Box 127, Circle, MT 59215-0127. Tel.: 406-485-2414.
Key Personnel: Pres. & Cur., Wendell Pawlowski.
Institution Type/Description: History Museum.
Hours & Admission Prices: May-Oct. 1 Mon.-Fri. 10-5, Sat.-Sun. call for hours. Adults $2.

Clancy

JEFFERSON COUNTY MUSEUM, 9 N. Main, Clancy, MT 59634-9547. Mailing Address: P.O. Box 50, Clancy, MT 59634-0050. Tel.: 406-933-5463. Fax: 406-933-5439.
Institution Type/Description: History Museum: housed in the 1898 Clancy Schoolhouse.
Hours & Admission Prices: Fri.-Sat. 1-5; other times by appointment. No charge; donations accepted.

Colstrip

SCHOOLHOUSE HISTORY & ART CENTER, 400 Woodrose St., Colstrip, MT 59323. Mailing Address: P.O. Box 430, Colstrip, MT 59323-0430. Tel.: 406-748-4822, Facebook: Schoolhouse History and Art Center.
E-mail: shac400@gmail.com
Web Site: www.colstripshac.org
Key Personnel: Exec. Dir. & Museum Shop Mgr., Lu Shomate; Pres. (V), Patty Dunn.
Institution Type/Description: History & Art Center: housed in former schoolhouse built in 1924.
Hours & Admission Prices: Mon.-Fri. 11-5. No charge; donations accepted.
Attendance: 2,500 (estimated)

Columbus

MUSEUM OF THE BEARTOOTHS, 440 E. 5th Ave. N., Columbus, MT 59019. Mailing Address: P.O. Box 1, Columbus, MT 59019. Tel.: 406-322-4588. Fax: 406-322-4588.
E-mail: predli@museumofthebeartooths.com
Web Site: www.museumofthebeartooths.com
Key Personnel: Dir., Penny Redli; Pres. (V), Chuck Egan.
Institution Type/Description: History Museum.
Hours & Admission Prices: April-May & Sept.-Dec. Mon.-Fri. 10-5; Memorial Day to Labor Day Mon.-Fri. 10-5, Sat.-Sun. 11-3. No charge; donations accepted.
Attendance: 3,752 (actual)

Conrad

CONRAD TRANSPORTATION AND HISTORICAL MUSEUM, 402 S. Virginia St., Conrad, MT 59425-2318. Mailing Address: P.O. Box 675, Conrad, MT 59425-0675. Tel.: 406-278-0178. Facebook.
E-mail: hbolson48@icloud.com
Web Site: www.conradmuseum.org
Key Personnel: Exec. Dir. & Pres. (V), Harold Olson; Museum Shop Mgr., Kristi Calvery.
Institution Type/Description: Transportation & Historical Museum.
Hours & Admission Prices: June-Sept. Mon.-Fri. 10-4, Sat. 1-4; Nov.-April by appointment. Adults $3 senior citizens $2; discounts to groups and AAM & ICOM members, MT Association of Museums & school groups; members no charge. Closed Independence Day.
Attendance: 462 (actual)

Crow Agency

LITTLE BIGHORN BATTLEFIELD NATIONAL MONUMENT, Interstate 90 & Hwy. 212, Crow Agency, MT 59022. Mailing Address: P.O. Box 39, Crow Agency, MT 59022-0039. Tel.: 406-638-3204. Fax: 406-638-2623.
E-mail: sharon_small@nps.gov
Web Site: www.nps.gov/libi
Key Personnel: Museum Cur., Sharon A. Small; Supt., Denice Swanke; Business Mgr., Charles Carroll.
Institution Type/Description: History Museum.
Hours & Admission Prices: April-May & Sept.-Oct. daily 8-6; Memorial Day to July daily 8-9; Aug. to Labor Day daily 8-8; Nov.-March daily 8-4:30. Vehicle $10, Individual $5; discounts to Golden Age & Annual pass holders. Closed New Year's Day; Thanksgiving; Christmas.
Attendance: 350,000 (estimated)

Culbertson

CULBERTSON MUSEUM INC., 5860 Rd. 1021, Culbertson, MT 59218. Mailing Address: P.O. Box 95, Culbertson, MT 59218-0095. Tel.: 406-787-6320 & 5283. Fax: 406-787-6320.
Formerly: Culbertson Museum
Key Personnel: Dir., Suzette Houle; Pres., Bruce Waldhausen; Treas., Jill Herness; Dir. Volunteers, Bernadette Raaum.

Institution Type/Description: History Museum.
Hours & Admission Prices: May-Sept. daily 8-4. No charge; donation requested.
Attendance: 4,800 (estimated)

Cut Bank

GLACIER COUNTY HISTORICAL SOCIETY & MUSEUM, 107 Old Kevin Hwy., Cut Bank, MT 59427. Mailing Address: P.O. Box 576, Cut Bank, MT 59427-0576. Tel.: 406-873-4904.
E-mail: gcmuseum@sofast.net
Web Site: www.glaciercountymt.org/museum
Institution Type/Description: Historical Society Museum.
Hours & Admission Prices: Memorial Day to Labor Day Tues.-Sun. 10-5; other times by appointment. No charge; donations accepted.

Darby

DARBY PIONEER MEMORIAL MUSEUM, 101 E. Tanner, Darby, MT 59829. Mailing Address: P.O. Box 37, Darby, MT 59829-0037. Tel.: 406-821-3753 & 3748. Fax: 406-821-3244.
E-mail: darbymontana@usa.net
Web Site: darbymt.net
Institution Type/Description: History Museum.
Hours & Admission Prices: June-Sept. daily 12-4. No charge; donations requested.
Attendance: 556 (actual)

Deer Lodge

GRANT-KOHRS RANCH NATIONAL HISTORIC SITE, 266 Warren Lane, Deer Lodge, MT 59722-1002. Tel.: 406-846-2070, ext. 242. Fax: 406-846-3962.
E-mail: chris_ford@nps.gov
Web Site: www.nps.gov/grko/home.htm
Key Personnel: Chm. (V), Sales Shop Mgr. & Chief Interpretation, Julie Croglio; Supt., Jacqueline Lavelle; Facility Mgr., Alan Stewart; Cur., Patricia Miller; Admin. Officer, Andy Getts.
Institution Type/Description: National Historic Site: 1862-1890 23-room ranch house & 1861-1960 bunkhouse, barns & outbuildings.
Hours & Admission Prices: Memorial Day-Labor Day daily 9-5:30; Sept.-May daily 9-4:30. No charge; donations accepted.
Attendance: 22,692 (actual)

OLD MONTANA PRISON MUSEUMS - POWELL COUNTY MUSEUM, 1106 Main St., Deer Lodge, MT 59722-1426. Tel.: 406-846-3111. Fax: 406-846-3156.
E-mail: info@pcmaf.org
Web Site: pcmaf.org
Formerly: Old Montana Prison
Key Personnel: Dir., John O'Donnell; Pres., Dick Bauman; Sec., Ed Gill; Business Mgr., Julia Smith.
Institution Type/Description: Historic Monument & Complex: 1867 site, comprised of 12 structures surrounded by 1893 sandstone wall, serving as a territorial & state prison from 1871-1979.
Hours & Admission Prices: Memorial Day to Labor Day Wed.-Sun. 10-4. Adults $10, children 10-15 $6; discounts to groups, senior citizens, AAA & Good Sam members; members & children 9 & under no charge.
Attendance: 52,600 (actual)

Dillon

BANNACK STATE PARK & GHOST TOWN, 721 Bannack Rd., Dillon, MT 59725-9685. Tel.: 406-834-3413. Fax: 406-834-3548. Facebook.
E-mail: bannack@smtel.com
Web Site: bannack.org
Formerly: Bannack State Park & Town Site
Institution Type/Description: Park & History Museum.
Hours & Admission Prices: Park: May-Oct. daily 8am-9pm; Nov.-April daily 8-5. Town Site: May & Sept.-Oct. daily 8am to dusk; Memorial Day to Labor Day daily 8am-9pm; Nov.-April daily 8-5. Visitor Center: May-Aug. daily 10-6; Sept.-Oct. Sat.-Sun. 11-5. Out-of-State Residents: vehicle $5, bus & walk-ins $3; Montana residents no charge. Closed Christmas Eve & Day.
Attendance: 36,000 (estimated)

BEAVERHEAD COUNTY MUSEUM, 15 S. Montana, Dillon, MT 59725-2433. Tel.: 406-683-5027.
E-mail: bvhdmuseum@bmt.net
Key Personnel: Dir., Lynn Giles; Sec., Ruth Little; Museum Shop Mgr., Joan McDougall.

Institution Type/Description: History Museum.
Hours & Admission Prices: May 30-Sept. 5 Mon.-Fri. 8-5, Sat. 9-5; Sept. 6-May 29 Mon.-Fri. 8-5. Adults $2, senior citizens & children 13-18 $1; discounts to AAM & ICOM members; members, school tours & children 12 & under no charge. &
Attendance: 14,000 (actual)

THE UNIVERSITY OF MONTANA WESTERN ART GALLERY & MUSEUM, Main Hall, 1st Fl., S. Entrance, Dillon, MT 59725-3511. Mailing Address: 710 S. Atlantic, Dillon, MT 59725. Tel.: 406-683-7011.
E-mail: g_bodish@umwestern.edu
Web Site: www.umwestern.edu
Formerly: Western Montana College Gallery Museum
Key Personnel: Dir., Randy Horst; Campus Security, Bob Campbell.
Institution Type/Description: Art Gallery & Museum: housed in 1893 main building.
Hours & Admission Prices: Mon.-Fri. 9-4. No charge. Closed holidays. &
Attendance: 2,000 (estimated)

Drummond

OHRMANN MUSEUM AND GALLERY, 6155 Hwy. 1, Drummond, MT 59832. Tel.: 406-288-3319.
E-mail: ohrmann814@yahoo.com
Web Site: www.ohrmannmuseum.com
Key Personnel: Owner, Phyllis Ohrmann.
Institution Type/Description: Art Museum.
Hours & Admission Prices: Daily 10-5. No charge, donations accepted. &
Attendance: 1,500 (estimated)

East Glacier Park

THE CLARKE MUSEUM, 900 Montana Hwy. 49, East Glacier Park, MT 59434. Mailing Address: P.O. Box 141, East Glacier Park, MT 59434-0141. Tel.: 406-226-9238.
Web Site: www.theclarkegallery.com
Formerly: John L. Clarke Western Art Gallery & Memorial Museum
Key Personnel: Owner, Dana Turvey.
Institution Type/Description: Art Gallery and Museum.
Hours & Admission Prices: June-Sept. daily. No charge.

East Helena

KLEFFNER RANCH, 305 Hwy. 518, East Helena, MT 59635-9602. Tel.: 406-495-9090 & 227-3521.
E-mail: kleffner@mt.net
Web Site: www.kleffnerranch.com
Institution Type/Description: Historic Site: former estate of William Child, an early Montana entrepreneur. Listed on the National Historic Register.
Hours & Admission Prices: By appointment.

Ekalaka

CARTER COUNTY MUSEUM, 306 N. Main St., Ekalaka, MT 59324. Tel.: 406-775-6886.
E-mail: ccmuseum@midrivers.com
Web Site: cartercountymuseum.org
Key Personnel: Dir., Sabre Moore; Asst. Dir., Marilyn Schultz; Cur., Nathan Carroll; Receptionist, Gwen Schultz; Receptionist, Denise Elmore; Mktg. & Communications Coord., Jennifer Hall.
Institution Type/Description: Natural & Cultural History Museum.
Hours & Admission Prices: April-Nov. Mon.-Sat. 9-5, Sun. 1-5; Dec.-March Tues.-Fri. 9-5, Sat.-Sun. 1-5. No charge; donations accepted. Closed legal holidays. &
Attendance: 5,000 (actual)

Forsyth

ROSEBUD COUNTY PIONEER MUSEUM, 1335 Main St., Forsyth, MT 59327. Mailing Address: P.O. Box 88, Forsyth, MT 59327-0088. Tel.: 406-346-7547.
E-mail: jlhall@rangeweb.net
Key Personnel: Pres. (V), Cal MacConnel.
Institution Type/Description: Pioneer History Museum.
Hours & Admission Prices: May to mid-Sept. Mon.-Sat. 9-6, Sun. 1-6. No charge; donations accepted. &
Attendance: 1,400 (actual)

Fort Benton

FORT BENTON MUSEUM OF THE UPPER MISSOURI, 1810 Front St., Fort Benton, MT 59442. Mailing Address: P.O. Box 262, Fort Benton, MT 59442-0262. Tel.: 406-622-5316. Fax: 406-622-3725.
E-mail: fbmuseums@mtintouch.net
Web Site: www.fortbenton.com
Key Personnel: Chm. (V) & Pres. (V), John G. Lepley; Dir., Randal E. Morger; Museum Shop Mgr., Cindy Baack; Museum Shop Mgr., Pam Schoonover.
Institution Type/Description: History Museum: located in park near ruins of Fort Benton, fur trading post of 1846 American Fur Co.
Hours & Admission Prices: May-Sept. Mon.-Sat. 10:30-4:30, Sun. 12-4. Adults $10, children $2 (admission includes admittance to Museum of the Northern Great Plains, Museum of the Upper Missouri River, Upper Missouri River Breaks Interpretive Center & Old Fort Benton); members & children under 6 no charge. &
Attendance: 5,000 (estimated)

MUSEUM OF THE NORTHERN GREAT PLAINS, 1205 20th St., Fort Benton, MT 59442. Mailing Address: P.O. Box 262, Fort Benton, MT 59442-0262. Tel.: 406-622-5316. Fax: 406-622-3725.
E-mail: fbmuseums@mtintouch.net
Web Site: fortbentonmuseums.com
Key Personnel: Chm., John G. Lepley; Dir., Randal E. Morger; Museum Shop Mgr., Pam Schoonover; Museum Shop Mgr., Cindy Baack.
Institution Type/Description: History Museum.
Hours & Admission Prices: May-Sept. Mon.-Sat. 10:30-4:30, Sun. 12-4. Adults $10, children $2 (admission includes admittance to Museum of the Upper Missouri, Old Fort Benton, & the Upper Missouri River Breaks Interpretive Center); members & children under 6 no charge. &
Attendance: 5,000 (estimated)

Fort Peck

FORT PECK INTERPRETIVE CENTER, Yellowstone Rd., Fort Peck, MT 59223. Mailing Address: P.O. Box 208, Fort Peck, MT 59223-0208. Tel.: 406-526-3493. Fax: 406-526-3593.
E-mail: michele.l.fromdahl@usace.army.mil
Web Site: www.nwo.usace.army.mil/html/Lake_Proj/fortpeck/museum.html
Key Personnel: Park Ranger, Michele Fromdahl.
Institution Type/Description: Paleontology Museum.
Hours & Admission Prices: May-Sept. daily 9-5; Oct.-April Tues.-Fri. 10-4; groups of 10 or more by appointment. No charge; donations accepted. &
Attendance: 30,000 (actual)

Fromberg

CLARK'S FORK VALLEY MUSEUM, 101 East River St., Fromberg, MT 59029. Mailing Address: P.O. Box 103, Fromberg, MT 59029. Tel.: 406-668-7650.
Institution Type/Description: History Museum.
Hours & Admission Prices: Late June to Sept. Wed.-Sun. 11-3; groups by appointment. No charge; donations accepted. &
Attendance: 400 (estimated)

THE LITTLE COWBOY BAR & MUSEUM, 105 W. River, Fromberg, MT 59029. Mailing Address: P.O. Box 463, Fromberg, MT 59029-0463. Tel.: 406-668-9502.
Key Personnel: Dir., Shirley Smith.
Institution Type/Description: General Museum.
Hours & Admission Prices: No charge; donations accepted.
Attendance: 5,000 (estimated)

Gardiner

YELLOWSTONE NATIONAL PARK, 20 Old Yellowstone Trail, Gardiner, MT 59030. Mailing Address: P.O. Box 168, Yellowstone Park, WY 82190-0168. Tel.: 307-344-2664. Fax: 406-848-9958. TDD: 307-344-2386.
Web Site: www.nps.gov/yell/
Key Personnel: Supt., Daniel N. Wenk.
Institution Type/Description: National Park Museums & Visitor Centers.
Hours & Admission Prices: Horace M. Albright Visitor Center in Mammoth Hot Springs: early Oct. to late May daily 9-5, late May to Labor Day daily 8-7. Museum of the National Park Ranger (Norris): late May to Labor Day 9-6. Grant Village, Fishing Bridge, Canyon Visitor Centers: late May to Labor Day daily 8-7. Norris Geyser Basin Museum: late May to early Oct. 10-5. Old Faithful: late May to Labor Day 8-7, winter while road is open 9-5. Heritage & Research Center: Mon.-Fri. 8-5. Yellowstone Research Library Tues.-Fri. 9-4. Park's

Archives & Museum Collections: by appointment to researchers. Call to confirm hours & dates, 307-344-2251. Park: $30 per car. Museums no charge. Closed Christmas. &
Attendance: 4,300,000 (estimated)

Garryowen

CUSTER BATTLEFIELD MUSEUM, Town Hall, 4185 Garryowen Rd., Garryowen, MT 59031-0200. Mailing Address: P. O. Box 200, Garryowen, MT 59031-0200. Tel.: 406-638-1876. Fax: 406-638-2019.
E-mail: info@custermuseum.org
Web Site: www.custermuseum.org
Key Personnel: C.E.O. & Founding Dir., Chris Kortlander.
Institution Type/Description: Historic Site: the site of Sitting Bull's camp, where Major Reno's division of Lt. Col. George A. Custer's Seventh Cavalry attacked on June 25, 1876.
Hours & Admission Prices: Memorial Day-Labor Day daily 8-7; Sept.-May daily 9-5. Adults $7.50; discounts to AAA members. children under 12 no charge. &
Attendance: 50,000 (estimated)

Glasgow

VALLEY COUNTY PIONEER MUSEUM, Hwy. #2 W., Glasgow, MT 59230. Mailing Address: P.O. Box 44, Glasgow, MT 59230-0044. Tel.: 406-228-8692.
E-mail: vcmuseum@nemontel.net
Web Site: valleycountymuseum.com
Key Personnel: Pres. (V) & Museum Shop Mgr., Mary Helland; Chm. (V), Norm Girard.
Institution Type/Description: History Museum.
Hours & Admission Prices: May-Sept. Mon.-Sat. 8:30-5:30. Adults $3, children $2; discounts to Life members. &
Attendance: 4,000 (estimated)

Glendive

FRONTIER GATEWAY MUSEUM, 201 State St., Glendive, MT 59330. Mailing Address: P.O. Box 1181, Glendive, MT 59330-1181. Tel.: 406-377-8168 & 365-2769.
E-mail: frontiermuseum@ymail.com
Web Site: www.frontiergatewaymuseum.org
Key Personnel: Treas., Patty Atwell; Cur., Fayette Miller; Pres. (V), Mark Geiger.
Institution Type/Description: History Museum.
Hours & Admission Prices: Memorial Day to Labor Day Mon.-Sat. 9-5, Sun. & holidays 1-5. No charge; donations accepted. &
Attendance: 2,729 (actual)

GLENDIVE DINOSAUR & FOSSIL MUSEUM, 139 State St., Glendive, MT 59330. Mailing Address: P.O. Box 684, Glendive, MT 59330-0684. Tel.: 406-377-3228.
E-mail: robert@creationtruth.org
Web Site: www.creationtruth.org
Key Personnel: Pres., Robert Canen.
Institution Type/Description: History Museum.
Hours & Admission Prices: Spring & Fall: Fri.-Sat. 10-5; Summer: Tues.-Sat. 10-5. General $8, children 3-12 $6; children 3 & under no charge.
Attendance: 9,000 (actual)

MAKOSHIKA DINOSAUR MUSEUM, 101 N. Merrill Ave., Glendive, MT 59330-1632. Tel.: 406-377-1637.
Institution Type/Description: Paleontology Museum.
Hours & Admission Prices: Tues.-Sat. 10-5; other times by appointment.

MAKOSHIKA STATE PARK VISITOR CENTER, 1301 Snyder Ave., Glendive, MT 59330. Mailing Address: P.O. Box 1242, Glendive, MT 59330. Tel.: 406-377-6256.
E-mail: makoshika@mt.gov
Web Site: stateparks.mt.gov/makoshika
Institution Type/Description: Park Visitor Center.
Hours & Admission Prices: 3rd Fri. of May to 3rd Sun. of Sept. daily 10-5; 3rd Mon. of Sept. to 3rd Thurs. of May Wed.-Sun. 10-5. Park: $5 per vehicle, $1 per person.

Great Falls

C.M. RUSSELL MUSEUM, 400 13th St. N., Great Falls, MT 59401-1498. Tel.: 406-727-8787. Fax: 406-727-2402.
E-mail: tfigarelle@cmrussell.org

Web Site: www.cmrussell.org
Key Personnel: Pres. Bd. Dirs., Christina Blackwell; Dir., Thomas Figarelle; Collections & Exhibitions Mgr., Brenda Kornick; Education & Public Programs, Eileen Laskowski; Facility Mgr., Chuck Keen; Museum Store & Guest Relations Mgr., Kari Nichols.
Institution Type/Description: Art Museum: located adjacent to the Russell home & log studio.
Hours & Admission Prices: May-Sept. Tues.-Sun. 10-5; Labor Day to Memorial Day Wed.-Sat. 10-5; tours by appointment. Adults $9, senior citizens $7, students & children $5; discounts to AAM members; children under 5 & members no charge. Closed New Year's Day; Easter; Thanksgiving; Christmas. &
Attendance: 38,000 (actual)

CHILDREN'S MUSEUM OF MONTANA, 22 Railroad Sq., Great Falls, MT 59401-4003. Tel.: 406-452-6661. Fax: 406-452-4462. Facebook: Children's Museum of Montana.
E-mail: info@childrensmuseumofmontana.org
Web Site: www.childrensmuseumofmontana.org
Key Personnel: Exec. Dir., Sandie Wright.
Institution Type/Description: Children's Museum.
Hours & Admission Prices: Mon.-Sat. 9:30-5. Per person $4; discounts to groups; members no charge. Closed New Year's Day; Independence Day; Thanksgiving; Christmas.

GALERIE TRINITAS, 1301 20th St., S., Great Falls, MT 59405-4934. Tel.: 406-791-5367.
E-mail: mdriskell01@ugf.edu
Web Site: www.ugf.edu/AboutUGF/GalerieTrinitas/tabid/723/Default.aspx
Key Personnel: Chm., Marcia Driskell.
Institution Type/Description: Art Museum.
Hours & Admission Prices: Tues. & Thurs. 12-3. No charge; donations accepted.

THE HISTORY MUSEUM, 422 2nd St. S., Great Falls, MT 59405-1816. Tel.: 406-452-3462. Fax: 406-761-3805. Facebook: @thehistorymuseum.
E-mail: info@thehistorymuseum.org
Web Site: www.thehistorymuseumgreatfalls.com
Formerly: Cascade County Historical Society Museum
Key Personnel: Exec. Dir., Jim Meinert; Pres. (V), Mary Ann Kaufman; Archive Admin., Megan Sanford; Collections Admin., Ashleigh McCann; Gist Shop Mgr., Dana Beyer; Membership Coord., Terri Billeter; Bookkeeper, Sarah Schumacher.
Institution Type/Description: Historical Museum: housed in c.1929 International Harvester building.
Hours & Admission Prices: Tues.-Fri. 10-5, Sat.-Sun. tours by appointment. No charge; donations accepted. Closed New Year's Day; Easter; Memorial Day; Independence Day; Labor Day; Thanksgiving; Christmas. &
Attendance: 7,500 (actual)

LEWIS AND CLARK NATIONAL HISTORIC TRAIL INTERPRETIVE CENTER, 4201 Giant Springs Rd., Great Falls, MT 59405-0913. Tel.: 406-727-8733. Fax: 406-453-6157.
E-mail: ecasselli@fs.fed.us
Web Site: www.fs.usda.gov/main/lcnf/learning
Key Personnel: Dir., Elizabeth Casselli; Museum Shop Mgr., Sally Murphy.
Institution Type/Description: History Museum.
Hours & Admission Prices: Memorial Day to Sept. daily 9-6; Oct.-May Tues.-Sat. 9-5, Sun. 12-5; groups by appointment. Adults 16 & over $8; children 15 & under no charge. Accept America The Beautiful, Annual, Senior & Access passes. Closed New Year's Day; Thanksgiving; Christmas. &
Attendance: 60,000 (actual)

PARIS GIBSON SQUARE MUSEUM OF ART, 1400 1st Ave. N., Great Falls, MT 59401-3299. Tel.: 406-727-8255. Fax: 406-727-8256. Facebook: PGSMOA.
E-mail: info@the-square.org
Web Site: www.the-square.org
Key Personnel: Exec. Dir., Tracy Houck; Cur. Art, Kristi Scott.
Institution Type/Description: Art Museum: housed in c.1895 stone building built as the first High School in Great Falls.
Hours & Admission Prices: Mon. & Wed.-Fri. 10-5, Tues. 10-5 & 7-9, Sat. 12-5. No charge; donations accepted. Closed national holidays. &
Attendance: 24,579 (actual)

UNIVERSITY OF GREAT FALLS LIBRARY EXHIBIT SPACE, 1301 20th St. S., Great Falls, MT 59405-4996. Tel.: 406-791-5311. Fax: 406-791-5395.
Institution Type/Description: Art Gallery.
Hours & Admission Prices: Mon.-Fri. 8-5, Sat.-Sun. 2-5.

Hamilton

DALY MUSEUM - DALY MANSION PRESERVATION TRUST, 251 Eastside Hwy., Hamilton, MT 59840. Mailing Address: P.O. Box 223, Hamilton, MT 59840-0223. Tel.: 406-363-6004. Fax: 406-375-0048.
E-mail: april.johnson@dalymansion.org
Web Site: www.dalymansion.org
Key Personnel: Dir., April Johnson; Pres., Gina Wilson.
Institution Type/Description: History Museum.
Hours & Admission Prices: April-Oct. call for hours. Adults $9, seniors $8, youth 6-17 $6; discounts to AAA members; children under 6 no charge. ♿
Attendance: 10,000 (estimated)

RAVALLI COUNTY MUSEUM/BITTER ROOT VALLEY HISTORICAL SOCIETY, 205 Bedford, Hamilton, MT 59840-2853. Tel.: 406-363-3338. Fax: 406-363-6588.
E-mail: museum@ravallimuseum.org
Web Site: www.ravallimuseum.org
Key Personnel: Exec. Dir., Tamar Stanley; Pres. (V), Brett Calder; Design & Mktg., Sarah Monson; Exhibits & Collections, Noellynn Pepos; Collections, Tara Gallagher; Educator, Rachael Woods; Accounting & Devel., Paula Frickey; Archives, Bill Whitfield.
Institution Type/Description: History Museum.
Hours & Admission Prices: Tues.-Wed. & Fri. 10-4, Thurs. 10-8, Sat. 9-1. Adults $3; discounts to schools, youth groups, veterans, seniors & NARM members; Thurs., Sat. & members no charge. ♿
Attendance: 18,000 (estimated)

Hardin

BIG HORN COUNTY HISTORICAL MUSEUM, 1163 3rd St. E., Hardin, MT 59034-9720. Mailing Address: RRI Box 1206A, Hardin, MT 59034-9720. Tel.: 406-665-1671. Fax: 406-665-3068. Facebook: Big Horn County Historical Museum.
E-mail: diana@bighorncountymuseum.org
Web Site: www.bighorncountymuseum.org
Key Personnel: Dir., Diana Scheidt; Pres. (V), Beth Mehling; Treas., Merna Kincaid; Museum Asst., Bonnie Stark; Museum Shop Mgr., Joan Miller.
Institution Type/Description: History Museum.
Hours & Admission Prices: Memorial Day-Labor Day daily 8-6; Sept.-May Mon.-Fri. 9-5. Adults $6, seniors $5, students 7-12 $3; school groups, members & children under 6 no charge. Closed New Year's Day; Thanksgiving; Christmas. ♿
Attendance: 25,000 (actual)

Harlowton

UPPER MUSSELSHELL HISTORICAL SOCIETY, 11 S. Central, Harlowton, MT 59036. Mailing Address: P.O. Box 364, Harlowton, MT 59036-0364. Tel.: 406-632-5519.
E-mail: museum@mtintouch.net
Web Site: harlowtonmuseum.com
Key Personnel: Chm. (V), R.C. Brown; Treas., Don Amundson.
Institution Type/Description: General Museum.
Hours & Admission Prices: May-Aug. Tues.-Sat. 10-5, Sun. 1-5; Sept. call for hours. Adults $2. ♿
Attendance: 600 (estimated)

Havre

H. EARL CLACK MUSEUM, Holiday Village Mall, 1753 US Hwy. 2 N.W. #1, Havre, MT 59501-3464. Tel.: 406-265-4000. Fax: 406-265-4000.
E-mail: clackmuseum@co.hill.mt.us
Key Personnel: Dir. & Museum Shop Mgr., John Bruington; Chm. (V), Judi Dritshulas.
Institution Type/Description: Local History Museum.
Hours & Admission Prices: Memorial Day to Labor Day Mon.-Sat. 10-6, Sun. 12-5; Sept.-May daily 1-5. No charge; donations accepted. Closed major holidays. ♿
Attendance: 7,193 (actual)

Helena

EXPLORATION WORKS, 995 Carousel Way, Helena, MT 59601. Tel.: 406-457-1800. Fax: 406-457-5377.
E-mail: info@explorationworks.org
Web Site: www.explorationworks.org
Key Personnel: Dir., Nikki Andersen; Chm. (V), John Cummings.
Institution Type/Description: Children's Museum.

Hours & Admission Prices: Tues. 10-8, Wed.-Sat. 10-5; other times by appointment. Adults $8, seniors 65 & over and students $6.50, youth under 18 $5.50; discounts to ASTC members; members & children under 2 no charge. Closed New Year's Day; Easter; Memorial Day; Independence Day; Labor Day; Thanksgiving; Christmas. ♿
Attendance: 36,523 (actual)

HOLTER MUSEUM OF ART, 12 E. Lawrence St., Helena, MT 59601-4019. Tel.: 406-442-6400. Fax: 406-442-2404.
E-mail: info@holtermuseum.org
Web Site: www.holtermuseum.org
Key Personnel: Exec. Dir., Caleb O. Fey; Pres., Madalyn Quinlan; Cur. Education, Sondra Hines; Education Asst., Hannah Gilbert; Exhib. Asst., Ben Pepka; Cur., Yvonne Seng; Visitor Svcs., David Spencer; Museum Shop Mgr., Jenny Gehl.
Institution Type/Description: Art Museum.
Hours & Admission Prices: Tues.-Sat. 10-5:30, Sun. 12-4. No charge; donations accepted. Closed major holidays. ♿
Attendance: 32,000 (actual)

MONTANA HISTORICAL SOCIETY, 225 N. Roberts, Helena, MT 59601-4514. Mailing Address: P.O. Box 201201, Helena, MT 59620-1201. Tel.: 406-444-2694. Fax: 406-444-2696.
E-mail: mhslibrary@mt.gov
Web Site: mhs.mt.gov
Key Personnel: Dir., Bruce Whittenberg.
Institution Type/Description: Historical Society Museum.
Hours & Admission Prices: Mon.-Sat. 9-5. Family $12, adults $5, children $1; members no charge. Closed holidays. ♿
Attendance: 40,256 (actual)

MONTANA MASONIC MUSEUM, 425 N. Park Ave., Helena, MT 59601-5020. Mailing Address: P.O. Box 1158, Helena, MT 59624-1158. Tel.: 406-442-7774. Fax: 406-442-1321.
E-mail: mtglsec@grandlodgemontana.org
Web Site: www.grandlodgemontana.org
Institution Type/Description: History Museum.
Hours & Admission Prices: Mon.-Fri. 9-4. No charge; donations accepted.

MONTANA STATE CAPITOL, 1301 E. 6th Ave., Helena, MT 59620. Tel.: 406-444-2034.
E-mail: bwhittenberg@mt.gov
Web Site: mhs.mt.gov/education/capitoltours
Institution Type/Description: Historic Building: built in 1902.
Hours & Admission Prices: Guided Tours: May-Sept. Mon.-Sat. 9am, 10am, 11am, 12pm, 1pm, & 2pm; Oct.-April Sat. 9am, 10am, 11am, 12pm, 1pm, & 2pm. Self-Guided Tours: Mon.-Fri. 8-5, Sat.-Sun. & holidays 9-3; groups by appointment.

MONTANA'S ORIGINAL GOVERNOR'S MANSION, 304 N. Ewing, Helena, MT 59620. Mailing Address: P.O. Box 201201, Helena, MT 59620. Tel.: 406-444-4789 & 2694, 800-243-9900.
E-mail: bharris2@mt.gov
Web Site: www.montanahistoricalsociety.org
Institution Type/Description: Historic Mansion: built in 1888.
Hours & Admission Prices: May-Sept. Tues.-Sat. 12-4; Oct.-April Sat. 12-4. Family $8, adults $4, children $1. Closed holidays.

Huntley

HUNTLEY PROJECT MUSEUM OF IRRIGATED AGRICULTURE, 770 Railroad Hwy., Huntley, MT 59037. Mailing Address: P.O. Box 353, Huntley, MT 59037-0353. Tel.: 406-348-2533.
E-mail: curator@huntleyprojectmuseum.org
Web Site: www.huntleyprojectmuseum.org
Key Personnel: Dir., Melissa Koch; Chm. (V), James Knapp.
Institution Type/Description: Agricultural & Homesteading History Museum.
Hours & Admission Prices: Tues.-Sat. 10-4. No charge. Suggested Donations: Families $5, adults $2, children & seniors $1. ♿
Attendance: 1,000 (actual)

Hysham

TREASURE COUNTY '89ERS, INC., 325 Elliott Ave., Hysham, MT 59038. Mailing Address: P.O. Box 489, Hysham, MT 59038-0489. Tel.: 406-342-5252.
Key Personnel: Dir., Pat Miller; Pres. (V), Linda Smith.
Institution Type/Description: History Museum.

Hours & Admission Prices: Memorial Day to Labor Day Mon.-Sat. 1-5; other times by appointment. No charge; donations accepted.
Attendance: 400 (estimated)

Jefferson City

TIZER BOTANIC GARDENS AND ARBORETUM, 38 Tizer Rd., Jefferson City, MT 59638. Mailing Address: P.O. Box 129, Jefferson City, MT 59638. Tel.: 406-933-8789. Facebook: Tizer Botanic Gardens and Arboretum.
E-mail: info@tizergardens.com
Web Site: www.tizergardens.com
Key Personnel: C.E.O., Belva Lotzer.
Institution Type/Description: Arboretum.
Hours & Admission Prices: Gardens: May-Sept. daily 10-6. Nursery: April-Sept. daily 10-6. Adults $7; members and children 5 & under no charge.
Attendance: 18,000 (estimated)

Jordan

GARFIELD COUNTY MUSEUM, Montana Hwy. 200, Jordan, MT 59337. Mailing Address: P.O. Box 150, Jordan, MT 59337. Tel.: 406-939-6404.
E-mail: gailweeding@hotmail.com
Key Personnel: Chm. (V), Pres. (V) & Museum Shop Mgr., Gail Weeding.
Institution Type/Description: Dinosaur Museum.
Hours & Admission Prices: June-Aug. daily 1-5. No charge; donations accepted.
Attendance: 1,000 (estimated)

Kalispell

CONRAD MANSION NATIONAL HISTORIC SITE MUSEUM, Btwn. Third & Fourth Sts. on Woodland Ave., Kalispell, MT 59901. Mailing Address: P.O. Box 1041, Kalispell, MT 59903-1041. Tel.: 406-755-2166. Fax: 406-755-2176. Facebook: Conrad Mansion National Historic Site Museum.
E-mail: info@conradmansion.com
Web Site: www.conradmansion.com
Key Personnel: Exec. Dir., Gennifer Sauter; Pres. (V), Mark Norley; Vice Pres., Sue Corrigan; Museum Shop Mgr., Cindy Conner.
Institution Type/Description: Historic House: Conrad Mansion is a Victorian style home completed in 1895 where 90% of furnishings are original to the Conrad family.
Hours & Admission Prices: May 15-June 20 Wed.-Sun. 10-4; June 21-Oct. 15 Tues.-Sun. 10-4. Adults $12, senior citizens $11, children 12-17 $8, children 11 & under $6; discounts to groups, military, Montana PBS, AAM & AAA members; members no charge.
Attendance: 10,000 (estimated)

HOCKADAY MUSEUM OF ART, 302 Second Ave. E., Kalispell, MT 59901-4942. Tel.: 406-755-5268. Fax: 406-755-2023.
E-mail: director@hockadaymuseum.org
Web Site: www.hockadaymuseum.org
Key Personnel: Pres. (V), Harry Wilson; Exec. Dir., Tracy Johnson; Museum Shop Mgr., Sharon Staso.
Institution Type/Description: Art Museum.
Hours & Admission Prices: Tues.-Sat. 10-5. Adults $5, seniors $4, college students $2; children K-12 & members no charge. Closed major holidays.
Attendance: 20,000 (estimated)

THE MUSEUM AT CENTRAL SCHOOL, Northwest Montana Historical Society, 124 Second Ave., E., Kalispell, MT 59901. Tel.: 406-756-8381. Fax: 406-257-5719. Facebook: The Museum at Central School.
E-mail: history@yourmuseum.org
Web Site: www.yourmuseum.org
Formerly: Central School Museum
Key Personnel: Exec. Dir., Gil Jordan; Accounting, Jan Woods; Office Mgr. & Membership, Kimberly Pinter; Museum Shop Mgr., Doreen Harper.
Institution Type/Description: History Museum: housed in the historic Central School building, which opened in 1894.
Hours & Admission Prices: Mon.-Fri. 10-5. Adults $5, seniors $4; children & members no charge. Closed New Year's Day; Independence Day; Thanksgiving; Christmas.
Attendance: 20,000 (actual)

Lewistown

CENTRAL MONTANA HISTORICAL ASSOCIATION, INC. MUSEUM, 408 N.E. Main St., Lewistown, MT 59457-2019. Tel.: 406-535-3642.
E-mail: cmha@midrivers.com
Key Personnel: Pres. (V), Shirley Barrick; Vice Pres., Janet Lewellen.
Institution Type/Description: History Museum.
Hours & Admission Prices: Memorial Day to Sat. after Labor Day daily 10-4; other times by appointment. No charge; donations accepted.
Attendance: 4,000 (estimated)

LEWISTOWN ART CENTER, 323 W. Main St., Lewistown, MT 59457-2450. Mailing Address: P.O. Box 1018, Lewistown, MT 59457-1018. Tel.: 406-535-8278. Fax: 406-535-6024.
E-mail: lewistownartcenter@gmail.com
Web Site: www.lewistownartcenter.net
Key Personnel: Exec. Dir., Mary Callahan Baumstark; Chm. (V), Clint Loomis; Program Dir., Leah Grunzke.
Institution Type/Description: Art Center.
Hours & Admission Prices: Tues.-Fri. 10-5, Sat. 10-4. No charge; donations accepted.
Attendance: 5,000 (estimated)

Libby

THE HERITAGE MUSEUM, 34067 US Hwy. 2 S., Libby, MT 59923. Mailing Address: P.O. Box 628, Libby, MT 59923-0628. Tel.: 406-293-7521.
E-mail: heritagemuseum@frontier.com
Web Site: www.libbyheritagemuseum.org
Institution Type/Description: History Museum.
Hours & Admission Prices: June-Aug. Mon.-Sat. 10-5, Sun. 1-5; other times by appointment. No charge; donations accepted.

Livingston

LIVINGSTON CENTER FOR ART AND CULTURE, 119 S. Main St., Livingston, MT 59047-2668. Tel.: 406-222-5222.
E-mail: admin@livingstoncenter.org
Web Site: www.livingstoncenter.org
Key Personnel: Dir., Kathy Bekedam; Pres. (V), Bob Ebinger.
Institution Type/Description: Art Gallery.
Hours & Admission Prices: Tues.-Fri. 11-5, Sat. 11-4. No charge; donations accepted.
Attendance: 10,200 (estimated)

LIVINGSTON DEPOT CENTER, 200 W. Park St., Livingston, MT 59047-2629. Mailing Address: P.O. Box 1319, Livingston, MT 59047-1319. Tel.: 406-222-2300.
E-mail: livingstondepot@gmail.com
Web Site: www.livingstondepot.org
Key Personnel: C.E.O. & Pres. (V), John Sullivan; Dir., Diana L. Seider.
Institution Type/Description: Historic Building: 1902 Northern Pacific railroad station.
Hours & Admission Prices: May-Sept. Mon.-Sat. 10-5, Sun. 1-5; school & group tours by appointment; winter by event. Adults $5, senior citizens, students & children $4; discounts to AAM members; members no charge. Closed New Year's Day; Thanksgiving; Christmas.
Attendance: 25,000 (actual)

YELLOWSTONE GATEWAY MUSEUM OF PARK COUNTY, 118 W. Chinook, Livingston, MT 59047-2011. Tel.: 406-222-4184. Fax: 406-222-4146.
E-mail: museum@parkcounty.org
Web Site: yellowstonegatewaymuseum.org
Formerly: Park County Museum; House of Memories
Key Personnel: Dir., Paul Shea; Registrar, Karen Reinhart.
Institution Type/Description: Historical Society Museum: housed in 1906 North Side School.
Hours & Admission Prices: May-Sept. daily 10-5; Oct.-May Thurs.-Sat. 10-5. Adults $5, senior citizens $4; discounts to AAM members; members & children under 18 no charge.
Attendance: 2,800 (actual)

Lolo

HOLT HERITAGE MUSEUM, 6800 Lewis & Clark Tr., Lolo, MT 59847. Mailing Address: P.O. Box 129, Lolo, MT 59847-0129. Tel.: 406-273-6743. Fax: 406-273-6378.

E-mail: info@holtheritagemuseum.com
Web Site: www.holtheritagemuseum.com
Key Personnel: Owner, Bill Holt; Owner, Ramona Holt.
Institution Type/Description: History Museum.
Hours & Admission Prices: By appointment.

Loma

EARTH SCIENCE MUSEUM, 208 Broadway Ave., Loma, MT 59460. Mailing Address: P.O. Box 207, Loma, MT 59460-0207. Tel.: 406-739-4282.
Institution Type/Description: Science Museum.
Hours & Admission Prices: Memorial Day to Labor Day daily 10-5. &

HOUSE OF A THOUSAND DOLLS, 106 First St., Loma, MT 59460. Mailing Address: P.O. Box 136, Loma, MT 59460-0136. Tel.: 406-739-4338.
Key Personnel: C.E.O., Marion Britton.
Institution Type/Description: Toy & Doll Museum.
Hours & Admission Prices: By appointment only. Adults $1, children $.50.
Attendance: 600 (estimated)

Malmstrom AFB

MALMSTROM AFB MUSEUM, 341 Missile Wing/MU, 21 77th St. N., Ste. 144, Malmstrom AFB, MT 59402. Tel.: 406-731-2705. Fax: 406-731-2769.
E-mail: museum@malmstrom.af.mil
Web Site: www.malmstrom.af.mil/library/malmstrommuseum
Key Personnel: Dir., Curt Shannon.
Institution Type/Description: Military History Museum.
Hours & Admission Prices: Mon.-Fri. 10-4. Non-military members visiting the museum must go to the Visitor Center located at the 2nd Ave. North gate. No charge. &
Attendance: 9,500 (actual)

Malta

BOWDOIN NATIONAL WILDLIFE REFUGE, 194 Bowdoin Auto Tour Rd., Malta, MT 59538. Tel.: 406-654-2863. Fax: 406-654-2866.
E-mail: bowdoin@fws.gov
Web Site: www.fws.gov/bowdoin/wildlife.html
Institution Type/Description: Wildlife Refuge.
Hours & Admission Prices: Mon.-Fri. 7:30-4. Closed Federal holidays.

GREAT PLAINS DINOSAUR MUSEUM AND FIELD STATION, 405 N. 1st St. E., Malta, MT 59538. Mailing Address: P.O. Box 170, Malta, MT 59538. Tel.: 406-654-5300.
E-mail: dinosaur@itstriangle.com
Key Personnel: Pres. (V), Mike Morser; Museum Shop Mgr., Dixie Lee Stordahl.
Institution Type/Description: Geology, Mineralogy, Paleontology Museum.
Hours & Admission Prices: May to Labor Day: Mon.-Sat. 10-5, Sun. 12:30-5. Adults $5, children over 6 $3; discounts to school groups; members no charge. &
Attendance: 2,500 (estimated)

PHILLIPS COUNTY MUSEUM, 431 U.S. Hwy. 2 E., Malta, MT 59538. Mailing Address: P.O. Box 518, Malta, MT 59538. Tel.: 406-654-1037. Fax: 406-654-1037.
E-mail: pcm@itstriangle.com
Web Site: www.phillipscountymuseum.org
Institution Type/Description: History Museum.
Hours & Admission Prices: April-Dec. Mon.-Sat. 10-5; other times by appointment. Adults $5, children over 5 $3; discounts to groups.

Martinsdale

BAIR FAMILY MUSEUM, 2751 MT Hwy. 294, Martinsdale, MT 59053. Tel.: 406-572-3314.
E-mail: info@bairfamilymuseum.org
Web Site: www.bairfamilymuseum.org
Key Personnel: Cur., Elizabeth Guheen.
Institution Type/Description: History Museum.
Hours & Admission Prices: Memorial Day to Labor Day daily 10-5; Sept.-Oct. Wed.-Sun. 10-5. Adults $5, seniors 62 & over $3, children 6-16 $2; children 5 & under no charge.

Miles City

RANGE RIDERS MUSEUM, 435 LP Anderson Rd., Miles City, MT 59301-4753. Tel.: 406-232-6146.
E-mail: rangeridersmuseum@gmail.com
Key Personnel: C.E.O. & Dir., Bunny Miller.
Institution Type/Description: History Museum: housed on the site of the 1876 Fort Keogh cantonment.
Hours & Admission Prices: April-Oct. daily 8-5. Adults $7.50, seniors $5; members no charge. &
Attendance: 15,000 (estimated)

WATERWORKS ART MUSEUM, 85 Waterplant Rd., Miles City, MT 59301. Mailing Address: P.O. Box 1284, Miles City, MT 59301-1284. Tel.: 406-234-0635. Fax: 406-234-0637. Facebook.
E-mail: ccartc@midrivers.com
Web Site: wtrworks.org
Formerly: Custer County Art & Heritage Center
Key Personnel: Exec. Dir., Dixie Rieger; Dir. Education, Mark Sanders; Exec. Asst., Andrew Grantham.
Institution Type/Description: Visual Arts Center & Museum: housed in 1910 waterworks building.
Hours & Admission Prices: May-Sept. Tues.-Sun. 9-5; Oct.-March Tues.-Sun. 1-5. No charge; donations accepted. Closed New Year's Day; Easter; Independence Day; Thanksgiving; Christmas. &
Attendance: 10,000 (actual)

Missoula

AERIAL FIRE DEPOT AND SMOKEJUMPER VISITOR CENTER, 5765 W. Broadway St., Missoula, MT 59808. Tel.: 406-329-4934. Fax: 406-329-4955.
E-mail: smokejumpercenter@yahoo.com
Web Site: www.fs.fed.us/fire/people/smokejumpers/missoula
Institution Type/Description: Firefighting Museum.
Hours & Admission Prices: Memorial Day to Labor Day daily 8:30-5; other times by appointment. No charge; donations accepted.

ELK COUNTRY VISITOR CENTER, 5705 Grant Creek Rd., Missoula, MT 59808-9394. Tel.: 866-266-7750.
E-mail: vc@rmef.org
Web Site: www.rmef.org/ElkCountryVisitorCenter
Institution Type/Description: Visitor Center.
Hours & Admission Prices: Jan.-May Mon.-Fri. 8-5, Sat. 10-5; June-Dec. Mon.-Fri. 8-6, Sat.-Sun. 9-6. No charge.

FAMILIES FIRST CHILDREN'S MUSEUM, 225 W. Front St., Missoula, MT 59802-4301. Tel.: 406-541-7529.
E-mail: info@familiesfirstmontana.org
Web Site: www.childrensmuseummissoula.org
Formerly: Children's Museum Missoula
Key Personnel: Exec. Dir., Nick Roberts.
Institution Type/Description: Children's Museum.
Hours & Admission Prices: Tues.-Sat. 10-5, Sun. 12-5. Admission $4.25; children under one no charge. ACM members reciprocal program. &
Attendance: 29,000 (estimated)

HISTORICAL MUSEUM AT FORT MISSOULA, 3400 Captain Rawn Way, Missoula, MT 59804. Tel.: 406-728-3476. Fax: 406-543-6277.
Web Site: www.fortmissoulamuseum.org
Key Personnel: Exec. Dir., Matt Lautzenheiser; Dir. Devel., Jessie Colt Rogers; Cur. Collections, Nicole Webb; Dir. Education, Kristjana Eyjolfsson; Museum Aide, Sharon Garner; Asst. Dir., Carolyn Thompson.
Institution Type/Description: Historical Museum Complex & Site: housed in 1911 brick quartermaster's warehouse, located on 32-acres (Historic District) at the core of what was Fort Missoula (1877-1947).
Hours & Admission Prices: Memorial Day-Labor Day Mon.-Sat. 10-5, Sun. 12-5; Sept.-May Tues.-Sun. 12-5. Adults $4, seniors $3, students $2; discounts to AAA, AAM & ICOM members and museum professionals & associations; children under 6, Missoula County residents & members no charge. &
Attendance: 45,000 (estimated)

MISSOULA ART MUSEUM, 335 N. Pattee St., Missoula, MT 59802-4520. Tel.: 406-728-0447.
E-mail: museum@missoulaartmuseum.org
Web Site: www.missoulaartmuseum.org
Key Personnel: Exec. Dir., Laura J. Millin; Pres. (V), Leslie Ann Dallapiazza; Cur. Education, Renee Taaffe; Event & Public Programs, Lily Scott; Registrar,

Theodore Hughes; Asst. Cur. & Preparator, John Calsbeek; Dir. Devel., Cassie Strauss; Dir. Mktg. & Communications, Bethany O'Connell.
Institution Type/Description: Contemporary Art Museum: housed in 1903 Carnegie Library.
Hours & Admission Prices: Tues.-Thurs. 10-5, Fri.-Sun. 10-3. No charge; donations accepted. ♿
Attendance: 60,000 (actual)

MONTANA MUSEUM OF ART & CULTURE, Main Hall 006, University of Montana, 32 Campus Dr., Missoula, MT 59812. Tel.: 406-243-2019. Fax: 406-243-2797. Facebook: Montana Museum of Art & Culture.
E-mail: museum@umontana.edu
Web Site: www.umt.edu/montanamuseum
Key Personnel: Dir., Barbara Koostra; Cur. Art & Exhibitions Coord., Jeremy Canwell; Administrative Assoc. Mgr., Stephen Edwards.
Institution Type/Description: Art Museum.
Hours & Admission Prices: June-Aug. Wed.-Thurs. & Sat. 12-3, Fri. 12-6; Sept.-May Tues.-Wed. & Sat. 12-3, Thurs.-Fri. 12-6. Suggested Donations: $5. Closed Montana state holidays. ♿
Attendance: 11,000 (actual)

MONTANA NATURAL HISTORY CENTER, 120 Hickory St., Missoula, MT 59801-1820. Tel.: 406-327-0405. Fax: 406-327-0421.
E-mail: office@montananaturalist.org
Web Site: www.montananaturalist.org
Key Personnel: Exec. Dir., Thurston Elfstrom; Educational Dir., Lisa Bickell; Pres. (V), Tom Roy; Coord. Community Programs, Christine Morris; Communications Coord., Allison DeJong; Office Mgr., Holly Klier.
Institution Type/Description: Natural History Center.
Hours & Admission Prices: Tues.-Fri. 9-5, Sat. 12-4. Adults $4, children 13 & over $2, children 3-12 $1; children under 3 & MNHC members no charge. ♿
Attendance: 2,500 (estimated)

MUSEUM OF MOUNTAIN FLYING, Missoula International Airport, Missoula, MT 59808. Mailing Address: 713 S. Third St., Missoula, MT 59801-2513. Tel.: 406-721-3644. Fax: 406-728-9280.
E-mail: phpc@montana.com
Web Site: www.museumofmountainflying.org
Key Personnel: C.E.O. & Pres. (V), Stan Cohen.
Institution Type/Description: Aviation History Museum.
Hours & Admission Prices: May-Sept. 10-4. Family $10, adult $3, children, seniors & military $2; members no charge. ♿
Attendance: 3,000 (estimated)

PHILIP L. WRIGHT ZOOLOGICAL MUSEUM AND UNIVERSITY OF MONTANA HERBARIUM, Division of Biological Sciences, University of Montana, 32 Campus Dr. #4824, Missoula, MT 59812. Tel.: 406-243-4743. Fax: 406-243-4184.
E-mail: dave.dyer@mso.umt.edu
Web Site: hs.umt.edu/umzm
Key Personnel: Assoc. Dean College Arts & Sciences, Dr. Charles Janson; Cur., Libby Beckman.
Institution Type/Description: Zoological Museum & Herbarium: the herbarium is housed in the Natural Sciences Building, which is a contributive structure within the University of Montana Historical District.
Hours & Admission Prices: research & teaching collections not open to general public. ♿

ROCKY MOUNTAIN MUSEUM OF MILITARY HISTORY, Bldgs. T-310 & T-316 at Fort Missoula, Missoula, MT 59807. Mailing Address: P.O. Box 7263, Missoula, MT 59807-7263. Tel.: 406-549-5346. Facebook: Rocky Mountain Museum of Military History.
E-mail: info@fortmissoula.org
Web Site: www.fortmissoula.org
Key Personnel: Exec. Dir., Tate Jones.
Institution Type/Description: Military History Museum.
Hours & Admission Prices: June-Labor Day daily 12-5; Labor Day-June Sat.-Sun. 12-5 & by appointment.

Moccasin

UTICA MUSEUM, 5443 Indiana Rd., Moccasin, MT 59462-9533. Tel.: 406-423-5531 & 5538.
E-mail: trinagigliotti49@gmail.com

Key Personnel: Pres., George Keating; Treas., Katherine Hodge; Sec., Judy Ennis.
Institution Type/Description: Historical Society Museum.
Hours & Admission Prices: Memorial Day-Labor Day Sat.-Sun. 10-5; other times by appointment. No charge; donations accepted. ♿
Attendance: 300 (estimated)

Pablo

THE PEOPLE'S CENTER, 53253 Hwy. 93 W., Pablo, MT 59855. Mailing Address: P.O. Box 278, Pablo, MT 59855-0278. Tel.: 406-675-0160. Fax: 406-675-0160.
E-mail: peoplescenter@cskt.org
Web Site: www.peoplescenter.net
Institution Type/Description: Native American History Museum.
Hours & Admission Prices: June-Sept. Mon.-Sat. 9-5; Oct.-May Mon.-Fri. 9-5. Adults $5, seniors & students $3; discounts to groups.

Philipsburg

GRANITE COUNTY MUSEUM & CULTURAL CENTER, 135 S. Sansome, Philipsburg, MT 59858. Mailing Address: P.O. Box 502, Philipsburg, MT 59858-0502. Tel.: 406-859-3020. Facebook.
E-mail: granitecountymuseum@gmail.com
Web Site: www.granitecountymuseum.com
Key Personnel: Pres. (V), T.J. Vietor; Museum Shop Mgr., Esther McDonald.
Institution Type/Description: History Museum.
Hours & Admission Prices: May 15 to Oct. daily 12-4. Adults $5; discounts to veterans, museum & Time Travelers Network members; children under 12 no charge. ♿
Attendance: 2,500 (actual)

Plentywood

SHERIDAN COUNTY MUSEUM, 4262 Hwy. 16 S., Plentywood, MT 59254. Mailing Address: P.O. Box 191, Plentywood, MT 59254. Tel.: 406-765-2145.
Key Personnel: Dir., Pat Tange; Chm. (V), Gordon Aus.
Institution Type/Description: History Museum.
Hours & Admission Prices: Memorial Day-Labor Day daily 10-5; other times by appointment. No charge; donations accepted. ♿

Polson

MIRACLE OF AMERICA MUSEUM INC., 36094 Memory Lane, Polson, MT 59860-8446. Tel.: 406-883-6804. Facebook: Miracle of America Museum.
E-mail: info@miracleofamericamuseum.org
Web Site: miracleofamericamuseum.org
Key Personnel: Chm. Bd. Dirs., Ned Wilde; C.E.O. & Museum Mgr., W. Gilbert Mangels; Treas., Ryan Gage.
Institution Type/Description: General Museum.
Hours & Admission Prices: Mon.-Sat. 9-5, Sun. 1:30-6; other times by appointment; call to confirm holiday hours. Adults 13 & over $6, children 2-12 $3; discounts for media reciprocal; members & children under 2 no charge. Closed Christmas. ♿
Attendance: 14,000 (estimated)

POLSON-FLATHEAD HISTORICAL MUSEUM, 708 Main St., Polson, MT 59860-3225. Mailing Address: P.O. Box 206, Polson, MT 59860-0206. Tel.: 406-883-3049.
E-mail: weolson@centurytel.net
Web Site: www.polsonflatheadmuseum.org
Key Personnel: Pres. (V), Bill Olson.
Institution Type/Description: History Museum.
Hours & Admission Prices: Memorial Day to Sept. 15 Mon.-Sat. 10-5. Admission $5; members & children under 12 no charge. ♿
Attendance: 2,500 (estimated)

Poplar

POPLAR MUSEUM, 5135 US Hwy. 2 E., Poplar, MT 59255. Mailing Address: P.O. Box 157, Poplar, MT 59255-0157. Tel.: 406-768-5223.
Key Personnel: Chm. (V), Pat Beck; Pres. (V), Ida Norgaard; Museum Shop Mgr., Helen Brzozowske.
Institution Type/Description: History Museum: housed in old Tribal Jail, built around 1920.
Hours & Admission Prices: June to early Sept. Mon.-Fri. 9-5. No charge.
Attendance: 688 (actual)

Pryor

CHIEF PLENTY COUPS MUSEUM, 1 Egdar Rd., Pryor, MT 59066. Mailing Address: P.O. Box 100, Pryor, MT 59066-0100. Tel.: 406-252-1289. Fax: 406-252-6668.
E-mail: plentycoups@plentycoups.org
Web Site: www.plentycoups.org
Key Personnel: State Parks Mgr. Region 5, Doug Habermann; Chief Plenty Coups Museum Park Mgr., Susan Stewart.
Institution Type/Description: Crow Indian Museum.
Hours & Admission Prices: Park: May-Sept. daily 8-8; Oct.-April Tues.-Sat. 8-5. Museum: May-Sept. daily 10-5. Admission: $3 per person; state residents no charge. &
Attendance: 12,000 (estimated)

Red Lodge

CARBON COUNTY HISTORICAL SOCIETY AND MUSEUM, 224 N. Broadway, Red Lodge, MT 59068. Mailing Address: P.O. Box 881, Red Lodge, MT 59068. Tel.: 406-446-3667. Fax: 406-446-1920.
E-mail: info@carboncountyhistory.com
Web Site: www.carboncountyhistory.com
Key Personnel: Dir., Debbie Brown.
Institution Type/Description: History Museum.
Hours & Admission Prices: Memorial Day to Sept. Mon.-Sat. 10-5, Sun. 11-3; Sept. 30 to May Fri.-Sat. 11-3; groups by appointment. Adults $5, seniors & students $3; discounts to groups & AAA members; members & children under 5 no charge.

Richey

RICHEY HISTORICAL SOCIETY, 122 S. Main St., Richey, MT 59259. Mailing Address: Box 264, Richey, MT 59259-0264. Tel.: 406-773-5234.
Key Personnel: Pres., Tristan Veverka; Sec., Agnes Sullivan; Cur. & Treas, Wanda Zuroff.
Institution Type/Description: Historical Society Museum.
Hours & Admission Prices: Memorial Day to Labor Day Tues. & Thurs.; other times by appointment. No charge; donations accepted.
Attendance: 200 (estimated)

Ronan

GARDEN OF THE ROCKIES MUSEUM, 45356 Hwy. 93 S., Ronan, MT 59864-9649. Tel.: 406-676-3390 & 0977.
Key Personnel: Pres. (V), Andrew Holmlund.
Institution Type/Description: History Museum: housed in a church, built in the early 1900s.
Hours & Admission Prices: Memorial Day-Labor Day Mon.-Fri. 11-4. No charge; donations accepted.

Roundup

MUSSELSHELL VALLEY HISTORICAL MUSEUM, 524 First W., Roundup, MT 59072-2437. Tel.: 406-323-1403 & 1662.
E-mail: dparrott@midrivers.com
Web Site: www.mvhm.us
Key Personnel: Pres., Bonnie DeMaio; Vice Pres., Tim Stevens; Asst. Dir. & Treas., Shirley Parrott; Sec., Phyllis Adolph.
Institution Type/Description: History Museum.
Hours & Admission Prices: May-Sept. daily 1-5. No charge; donations accepted.
Attendance: 2,000 (actual)

Scobey

DANIELS COUNTY MUSEUM AND PIONEER TOWN, 7 W. County Rd., Scobey, MT 59263. Mailing Address: P.O. Box 133, Scobey, MT 59263-0133. Tel.: 406-487-5965 & 2061.
E-mail: dcmuseum@nemont.net
Web Site: scobey.org
Key Personnel: Pres., Mike Thievin; Vice Pres., Frank Edwards; Dir., Paul Nelson; Dir., Sue Hagen; Dir. & Treas., Annette Thievin; Dir., Justin Hanson; Dir., Carla Rask; Dir. & Sec., Wayne Vatnsdal.
Institution Type/Description: Village Museum & Pioneer Town.
Hours & Admission Prices: Memorial Day to Labor Day daily 12:30-4:30; Sept.-May Tues.10-2, Fri. 1-4; other times by appointment. Tours: adults $7, children 6-11 $4; discounts to AAM members; members & children under 5 no charge. &
Attendance: 1,500 (estimated)

Seeley Lake

SEELEY LAKE HISTORICAL SOCIETY INC., 2920 Mt. Hwy. 83 N., Seeley Lake, MT 59868-8605. Tel.: 406-677-2990. Facebook: Seeley Lake Historical Society.
E-mail: slhistory@blackfoot.net
Web Site: www.seeleyhistory.org
Formerly: Seeley Lake Historical Museum and Visitor Center
Institution Type/Description: History Museum.
Hours & Admission Prices: Memorial Day to Labor Day daily 10-6; Winter: closed except by appointment & special occasions. No charge; donations accepted. &
Attendance: 2,000 (estimated)

Shelby

MARIAS MUSEUM OF HISTORY AND ART, 1129 1st St. N., Shelby, MT 59474. Mailing Address: P.O. Box 895, Shelby, MT 59474-0895. Tel.: 406-424-2551. Fax: 406-424-5422.
Key Personnel: C.E.O., Chm. (V) & Pres. (V), Larry Munson; Bd. Member & Vice Pres., Tracy Dumas; Bd. Member & Treas., Carol Mundt; Bd. Member & Sec., Lance Wallewein; Bd. Member, Meredith Beckedahl; Bd. Member, Tracy Keifer; Bd. Member, Charlotte Hanson; Bd. Member, Harriet Karst; Bd. Member, Mike Gorder; Bd. Member, Marian Hinds; Bd. Member, Merle Raph.
Institution Type/Description: History Museum.
Hours & Admission Prices: June-Aug. Mon.-Fri. 1-5 & 7-9, Sat. 1-5; Sept.-May Tues. 1-4; other times by appointment. No charge; donations accepted.
Attendance: 1,327 (actual)

Sidney

MONDAK HERITAGE CENTER, 120 Third Ave., S.E., Sidney, MT 59270-4324. Tel.: 406-433-3500. Fax: 406-433-3503. Facebook: MonDak Heritage Center.
E-mail: mdhc@richland.org
Web Site: www.mondakheritagecenter.org
Key Personnel: Pres. (V), Joe Bradley; Administrative Asst., Leann K. Pelvit.
Institution Type/Description: Historical Museum & Art Gallery.
Hours & Admission Prices: Tues.-Fri. 10-4, Sat. 1-4. No charge; donations accepted. &
Attendance: 8,000 (actual)

Stanford

JUDITH BASIN COUNTY MUSEUM, 93 3rd St., S., Stanford, MT 59479. Mailing Address: P.O. Box 315, Stanford, MT 59479-0315. Tel.: 406-566-2777 ext. 130.
E-mail: gfisher@bresnan.net
Key Personnel: Pres. (V) & Dir., Jackie Urick; Dir., Sue Evans; Dir., Gene Ernst; Dir., Tess Brady; Dir., Lorraine Boeck.
Institution Type/Description: General Museum.
Hours & Admission Prices: Memorial Day to Labor Day Wed.-Sun. 10-5; other times by appointment. No charge; donations accepted. Closed major holidays.
Attendance: 500 (estimated)

Stevensville

HISTORIC ST. MARY'S MISSION, West End of 4th St., Stevensville, MT 59870. Mailing Address: P.O. Box 211, Stevensville, MT 59870-0211. Tel.: 406-777-5734. Facebook: Historic St. Mary's Mission.
E-mail: stmary@cybernet1.com
Web Site: www.saintmarysmission.org
Key Personnel: Dir., Colleen Meyer; Pres. (V), Johni Steinke.
Institution Type/Description: History Museum: founded in 1841 by Jesuit priests.
Hours & Admission Prices: April 15-Oct. 15 Tues.-Fri. 10-4, Sat. 11-3. Adults $8, seniors $7, students $6. &
Attendance: 5,200 (estimated)

STEVENSVILLE MUSEUM, 517 Main St., Stevensville, MT 59870-2838. Mailing Address: P.O. Box 750, Stevensville, MT 59870-0750. Tel.: 406-777-1007.
E-mail: stevensvillemuseum@yahoo.com
Web Site: visitmt.com/listings/general/museum/stevensville-museum.html
Institution Type/Description: History Museum.
Hours & Admission Prices: Memorial Day to Labor Day Thurs.-Sat. 11-4, Sun. 1-4; groups by appointment. No charge, donations accepted. &

Superior

MINERAL COUNTY MUSEUM & HISTORICAL SOCIETY, 2nd Ave. E., Superior, MT 59872-0301. Mailing Address: P.O. Box 533, Superior, MT 59872-0533. Tel.: 406-822-3543.
E-mail: mchs1976@blackfoot.net
Web Site: mineralmthistory.com
Key Personnel: Pres. Historical Society, Peggy Temple; Vice Pres., Sue McLees; Cur. & Sec., Cathryn Strombo.
Institution Type/Description: Mineralogy Museum: housed in old hospital building; John Mullan & Mullan Trail Information Center.
Hours & Admission Prices: By appointment. No charge; donations accepted. ও
Attendance: 1,000

Terry

PRAIRIE COUNTY MUSEUM AND EVELYN CAMERON GALLERY, 101 S. Logan, Terry, MT 59349. Mailing Address: P. O. Box 368, Terry, MT 59349-0426. Tel.: 406-635-4040.
Key Personnel: Pres., Les Thomason; Pres. (V), Glenn Heitz.
Institution Type/Description: Historic Building: housed in the 1916 State Bank of Terry.
Hours & Admission Prices: Memorial Day to Labor Day Mon. & Wed.-Fri. 9-3, Sat.-Sun. 1-4; other times by appointment. No charge; donations accepted.
Attendance: 1,000 (estimated)

Thompson Falls

OLD JAIL MUSEUM, 109 S. Madison St., Thompson Falls, MT 59783. Mailing Address: P.O. Box 774, Thompson Falls, MT 59873-0774. Tel.: 406-827-4002.
E-mail: schs.thompsonfall@gmail.com
Web Site: saleeshhouse.org
Institution Type/Description: History Museum: former jail, sheriff's office & residence.
Hours & Admission Prices: Mother's Day-Labor Day daily 12-4. Adults $2.
Attendance: 2,000 (estimated)

Three Forks

HEADWATERS HERITAGE MUSEUM, 202 S. Main, Three Forks, MT 59752. Mailing Address: P.O. Box 116, Three Forks, MT 59752-0116. Tel.: 406-285-4778. Facebook: Headwaters Heritage Museum.
E-mail: museumthreeforks@aol.com
Web Site: www.tfhistory.org
Key Personnel: Dir., Robin Cadby-Sorensen; Chm. (V), Sally Griffin; Pres. (V), Pat O'Brien Townsend; Treas., Patrick Finnegan; Cur., Cheryl Lehr; Museum Shop Mgr., Linda Wilcox.
Institution Type/Description: History Museum.
Hours & Admission Prices: June-Sept. Mon.-Sat. 9-5, Sun. 11-3; other times by appointment. No charge; donations accepted. ও
Attendance: 2,400 (estimated)

Townsend

BROADWATER COUNTY MUSEUM, 133 N. Walnut, Townsend, MT 59644-2324. Mailing Address: P.O. Box 614, Townsend, MT 59644. Tel.: 406-266-5252. Fax: 406-266-5252.
E-mail: bwcomuseum@mt.net
Web Site: www.broadwatercountymuseum.com
Key Personnel: Pres. (V), Paul Putz; Cur., Linda Huth.
Institution Type/Description: History Museum.
Hours & Admission Prices: May 15-Sept. 15 daily 1-5. No charge; donations accepted. Closed Independence Day. ও
Attendance: 600 (estimated)

Victor

VICTOR HERITAGE MUSEUM, Blake & Main St., Victor, MT 59875. Mailing Address: P.O. Box 610, Victor, MT 59875-0610. Tel.: 406-642-3997.
E-mail: victormuseum@cybernet1.com
Web Site: victorheritagemuseum.org
Key Personnel: Pres. (V), Suzanne Tout.
Institution Type/Description: History & Heritage Museum: housed in the former NP Railroad Depot Building.
Hours & Admission Prices: Memorial Day to Labor Day Tues.-Sat. 1-4. No charge; donations accepted. ও
Attendance: 500 (estimated)

Virginia City

VIRGINIA CITY MADISON COUNTY HISTORICAL MUSEUM DBA VIRGINIA CITY J. SPENCER WATKINS MEMORIAL MUSEUM, 219 W. Wallace St., Virginia City, MT 59755. Mailing Address: P.O. Box 215, Virginia City, MT 59755-0215. Tel.: 406-581-1776, 406-843-5500 (season only).
E-mail: montyt@live.com
Key Personnel: C.E.O. & Dir., Daryl L. Tichenor.
Institution Type/Description: History Museum.
Hours & Admission Prices: May 15-Sept. daily 10-5. No charge; donations accepted.
Attendance: 20,000 (estimated)

West Glacier

GLACIER NATIONAL PARK MUSEUM, Glacier National Park, West Glacier, MT 59936. Mailing Address: P.O. Box 128, West Glacier, MT 59936. Tel.: 406-888-7936. Fax: 406-888-7937.
E-mail: deirdre_shaw@nps.gov
Key Personnel: Cur., Deirdre Shaw.
Institution Type/Description: Park Museum.
Hours & Admission Prices: Visitor Centers: call for hours. Research: Mon.-Fri. 8-4:30. No charge. Closed federal holidays.

West Yellowstone

EARTHQUAKE LAKE VISITOR CENTER, U.S. Hwy. 287, West Yellowstone, MT 59758. Mailing Address: P.O. Box 520, West Yellowstone, MT 59758-0520. Tel.: 406-682-7620. Fax: 406-823-6990.
E-mail: mailroom_r1_custer_gallatin@fs.fed.us
Web Site: www.fs.fed.us/r1/gallatin
Formerly: Madison Canyon Earthquake Lake Visitor Center
Institution Type/Description: History Museum.
Hours & Admission Prices: Call for hours.
Attendance: 30,000 (estimated)

GRIZZLY & WOLF DISCOVERY CENTER, 201 S. Canyon, West Yellowstone, MT 59758. Mailing Address: P.O. Box 996, West Yellowstone, MT 59758-0996. Tel.: 800-257-2570, 406-646-7001. Fax: 406-646-7004.
E-mail: info@grizzlydiscoveryctr.com
Web Site: grizzlydiscoveryctr.org
Key Personnel: Cur. Education, AJ Chlebnik.
Institution Type/Description: Wildlife Preserve.
Hours & Admission Prices: Daily 8:30 a.m. to dusk; call to confirm. Adults 13 & over $11.50, seniors 62 & over $10.75, children 5-12 $6.50; discounts to groups; children under 5 no charge. ও
Attendance: 150,000 (estimated)

MUSEUM OF THE YELLOWSTONE, 104 Yellowstone Ave., West Yellowstone, MT 59758. Mailing Address: P.O. Box 1299, West Yellowstone, MT 59758. Tel.: 406-646-1100. Fax: 406-646-7461.
E-mail: info@yellowstonehistoriccenter.com
Web Site: www.yellowstonehistoriccenter.org
Institution Type/Description: History Museum: housed in the historic Union Pacific Depot.
Hours & Admission Prices: Mid-May to early Oct. call for hours. Adults $6, members no charge. ও
Attendance: 20,000 (estimated)

White Sulphur Springs

MEAGHER COUNTY HISTORICAL ASSOCIATION CASTLE MUSEUM, 310 1/2 2nd Ave., N.E., White Sulphur Springs, MT 59645. Mailing Address: P.O. Box 716, White Sulphur Springs, MT 59645-0389. Tel.: 406-547-2324.
E-mail: gfisher@bresnan.net
Institution Type/Description: Historical Society Museum: housed in restored Victorian Mansion; built in 1892.
Hours & Admission Prices: mid-May to mid-Sept. daily 10-6. Adults $5, children & senior citizens $2; discount to groups of 10 or more; members no charge. ও
Attendance: 4,012 (estimated)

Whitefish

STUMPTOWN HISTORICAL SOCIETY MUSEUM, 500 Depot
St., Ste. 101, Whitefish, MT 59937-2567. Tel.: 406-862-0067.
E-mail: info@stumptownhistoricalsociety.org
Web Site: www.stumptownhistoricalsociety.org
Key Personnel: Exec. Dir., Jill Evans.
Institution Type/Description: Historical Society Museum.
Hours & Admission Prices: Mon.-Sat. 10-4.

WHITEFISH GALLERY - STUMPTOWN ART STUDIO, 145
Central Ave., Whitefish, MT 59937. Tel.: 406-862-5929. Fax: 406-
862-5029.
E-mail: info@stumptownartstudio.org
Web Site: www.whitefishgallerynights.org
Institution Type/Description: Art Gallery.
Hours & Admission Prices: Call for hours.

Whitehall

JEFFERSON VALLEY MUSEUM, 303 S. Division, Whitehall,
MT 59759. Mailing Address: P.O. Box 902, Whitehall, MT 59759-
0902. Tel.: 406-287-7813. Facebook: Jefferson Valley Museum.
E-mail: jvmuseum@hotmail.com
Key Personnel: Pres. (V), Janice Carmody; Sec., Jonie Martinell.
Institution Type/Description: History Museum: housed in a restored 1914 barn.
Hours & Admission Prices: Memorial Day to Sept. 15 Tues.-Sun. 12-4; other times
by appointment. No charge; donations accepted. &
Attendance: 750 (actual)

Wibaux

PIERRE WIBAUX MUSEUM, 112 E. Orgain Ave., Wibaux, MT
59353. Mailing Address: P.O. Box 72, Wibaux, MT 59353-0072.
Tel.: 406-796-9969. Fax: 406-796-2625. Facebook: Pierre Wibaux
Museum.
E-mail: wpmuseum@midrivers.com
Key Personnel: Chm. (V) & Sec., Lyda Schneidez; Pres. (V), Donna O'Connor.
Institution Type/Description: History Museum.
Hours & Admission Prices: May-Sept. Mon.-Sat. 9-5, Sun. 1-5. No charge; dona-
tions accepted. &
Attendance: 300 (estimated)

Winifred

WINIFRED MUSEUM, 210 Main St., Winifred, MT 59489.
Mailing Address: P.O. Box 181, Winifred, MT 59489-0181. Tel.:
406-462-5425. Fax: 406-462-5425.
E-mail: winimuse@mtintouch.net
Web Site: www.onlyinwinifred.com/the_town/museum.html
Key Personnel: Cur., Helen Rich; Asst. Cur., Teresa Lee.
Institution Type/Description: History Museum.
Hours & Admission Prices: Call for hours. No charge; donations accepted. &
Attendance: 520 (estimated)

Wisdom

BIG HOLE NATIONAL BATTLEFIELD, 16425 Hwy. 43 W.,
Wisdom, MT 59761. Mailing Address: P.O. Box 237, Wisdom,
MT 59761-0237. Tel.: 406-689-3155. Fax: 406-689-3151.
E-mail: biho_visitor_information@nps.gov
Web Site: www.nps.gov/biho
Key Personnel: Supt. & Unit Mgr., Steve Black.
Institution Type/Description: Visitor Center Exhibit Hall: located on land which
includes all major sites relating to the 1877 Battle of the Big Hole between the
Nez Perce Indians & the 7th U.S. Infantry. Plus a small number of citizen volun-
teers.
Hours & Admission Prices: Winter & Spring: 10-5; Summer & Fall: 9-5. No
charge; donations accepted. Closed New Year's Day; Martin Luther King Day;
Presidents Day; Columbus Day; Veterans Day; Thanksgiving; Christmas. &
Attendance: 50,000 (actual)

Wolf Point

WOLF POINT AREA MUSEUM INC., 203 U.S. Hwy. 2, Wolf
Point, MT 59201-1507. Mailing Address: P.O. Box 1205, Wolf
Point, MT 59201-2205. Tel.: 406-653-1912 & 1958.
Formerly: Wolf Point Area Historical Society

Key Personnel: Dir., Keith Bryan; Pres. (V) & Museum Shop Mgr., Herman E.
Shumway.
Institution Type/Description: Historical Museum.
Hours & Admission Prices: Memorial Day to Labor Day Mon.-Fri. 10-5. No charge;
donations accepted. &
Attendance: 1,100 (estimated)

NEBRASKA

(242 listings)

Ainsworth

**THE COLEMAN HOUSE MUSEUM AND BROWN COUNTY
HISTORICAL SOCIETY,** 456 Old Highway #7, Ainsworth, NE
69210. Mailing Address: 43026 Finch Rd., Ainsworth, NE 69210-
1773.
E-mail: carolarson10@hotmail.com
Key Personnel: Pres., Daniel W. Steele; Sec., Carol Larson.
Institution Type/Description: History Museum: housed in 1918 home.
Hours & Admission Prices: Open by appointment year-round. &
Attendance: 259 (actual)

SELLORS BARTON MUSEUM AKA LOG CABIN MUSEUM,
4th & Main St., City Park, Ainsworth, NE 69210-1213. Mailing
Address: 43026 Finch Rd., Ainsworth, NE 69210. Tel.: 402-387-
2740 or 2061.
E-mail: carolarson10@hotmail.com
Key Personnel: Dir., Carol Larson.
Institution Type/Description: History Museum: housed in log cabin built in 1936.
Hours & Admission Prices: late May to early Sept. Mon.-Fri. 10:30-4:30, Sat.-Sun.
1:30-4:30. No charge; donations accepted. &
Attendance: 500 (estimated)

Allen

DIXON COUNTY MUSEUM & HISTORICAL SOCIETY, 225 S.
Clark St., Allen, NE 68710. Mailing Address: Box 95, Allen, NE
68710-0095. Tel.: 402-287-2885.
E-mail: gloriao@wildblue.net
Web Site: www.visitdixoncounty.org
Key Personnel: Pres. (V), Gloria Oberg.
Institution Type/Description: History Museum.
Hours & Admission Prices: June-Aug. Sun. 2-4; other times by appointment. No
charge; donations accepted. &
Attendance: 350 (actual)

Alliance

CARNEGIE ARTS CENTER, 204 W. 4th St., Alliance, NE 69301-
3332. Tel.: 308-762-4571. Fax: 308-762-4571.
E-mail: art@carnegieartscenter.com
Web Site: www.carnegieartscenter.com
Key Personnel: Dir., Rose Pancost; Sales Gallery Mgr., Jelinda Nye.
Institution Type/Description: Art Gallery/Art Center.
Hours & Admission Prices: Tues.-Sat. 10-4, Sun. 1-4. No charge. Closed major hol-
idays. &
Attendance: 3,700 (estimated)

KNIGHT MUSEUM & SANDHILLS CENTER, 908 Yellowstone
Ave., Alliance, NE 69301. Mailing Address: P.O. Box D, Alliance,
NE 69301. Tel.: 308-762-2384. Fax: 308-763-1168.
E-mail: museum@cityofalliance.net
Web Site: knightmuseum.com
Formerly: Knight Museum of High Plains Heritage
Key Personnel: Dir., Becci Thomas; Museum Shop Mgr., Alicia Templeton.
Institution Type/Description: General Museum.
Hours & Admission Prices: May-Sept. Mon.-Fri. 8-7, Sat. 10-6, Sun. 1-5; Oct.-
April Mon.-Fri. 8-5, Sat. 10-5. No charge; donations accepted. &
Attendance: 15,250 (actual)

SALLOWS MILITARY MUSEUM, 1101 Niobrara St., Alliance,
NE 69301. Mailing Address: P.O. Box D, Alliance, NE 69301-
0770. Tel.: 308-762-2385.
Key Personnel: Dir., Becci Thomas; Chm., Suzan Davis.
Institution Type/Description: Military Museum.
Hours & Admission Prices: Summer: Mon.-Fri. 1-4, Sat. 1-5, Sun. 1:30-4:30; Oct.-
April Mon., Wed., Fri. 1-4 by appointment. No charge; donations accepted. &
Attendance: 5,500 (estimated)

Arapahoe

FURNAS-GOSPER HISTORICAL SOCIETY & MUSEUM, 401 Nebraska Ave., Arapahoe, NE 68922. Mailing Address: P.O. Box 202, Arapahoe, NE 68922-0202. Tel.: 308-962-5236. Facebook.
E-mail: chamber@arapahoe-ne.com
Key Personnel: Pres., Robert Trosper; Vice Pres., Keith Willets; Treas. & Sec., Lori Moore; Dir., Cathy Weber.
Institution Type/Description: General Museum.
Hours & Admission Prices: May-Sept. Sat.-Sun. 1-4; other times by appointment. No charge; donations accepted. &
Attendance: 1,200 (estimated)

Ashland

LEE G. SIMMONS CONSERVATION PARK AND WILDLIFE SAFARI, 16406 292 St., Ashland, NE 68003. Tel.: 402-944-9453.
E-mail: info@omahazoofoundation.org
Web Site: www.wildlifesafaripark.com
Institution Type/Description: Conservation Park.
Hours & Admission Prices: April-Oct. daily 9-5. Adults 12 & over $6.50, seniors 65 & over $5.50, children 3-11 $4.50; discounts to military; children 2 & under no charge.

STRATEGIC AIR COMMAND AND AEROSPACE MUSEUM, 28210 West Park Hwy., Ashland, NE 68003-3525. Tel.: 800-358-5029, 402-944-3100, ext. 220. Fax: 402-944-3160. Facebook.
E-mail: marketing@sacmuseum.org
Web Site: www.sacmuseum.org
Formerly: Strategic Air Command Museum
Key Personnel: Exec. Dir., Michael McGinnis; Cur., Brian York; Chief Structural Specialist, Mark Hamilton; Museum Shop Mgr., J.C. Colson.
Institution Type/Description: Aviation & Space History Museum.
Hours & Admission Prices: Daily 10-5. Adults $12, children 4-12 $6; discounts to groups, AAA members, senior citizens & military; children 3 & under and members no charge. Closed New Year's Day; Easter; Thanksgiving; Christmas. &
Attendance: 117,000 (estimated)

WILLOW POINT GALLERY & MUSEUM, 1431 Silver St., Ashland, NE 68003. Tel.: 402-944-3613, 800-861-4260. Fax: 402-944-3613.
E-mail: gr35419@windstream.net
Web Site: www.generoncka.com/
Key Personnel: Dir. & C.E.O., Gene Roncka; Museum Shop Mgr., Mary Roncka.
Institution Type/Description: Art Gallery.
Hours & Admission Prices: Mon.-Sat. 10-6, Sun. 1-4. No charge. &
Attendance: 8,234 (actual)

Ashton

POLISH HERITAGE CENTER, INC., 226 Carlton Ave., Ashton, NE 68817. Mailing Address: P.O. Box 3, Ashton, NE 68817-0003. Tel.: 308-738-2249 & 2260.
E-mail: pp1335@nctc.net
Web Site: www.polishheritagecenter.com
Key Personnel: Mgr., Phyllis Piechota; Pres., Judi Welniak; Treas., Judene Jakubowski; Sec., Chris Detlotts.
Institution Type/Description: Polish Heritage Center.
Hours & Admission Prices: Sun. 2-4; other times by appointment. Admission $5; members no charge. &
Attendance: 1,000 (estimated)

Atkinson

STURDEVANT-MCKEE MUSEUM & FOUNDATION, 308 S. Main St., Atkinson, NE 68713-4982. Mailing Address: P.O. Box 225, Atkinson, NE 68713-0225. Tel.: 402-340-1352.
Key Personnel: Dir., Helen Olson; Chm. (V), Diane Alden; Pres. (V), Debra Liewer.
Institution Type/Description: History Museum.
Hours & Admission Prices: By appointment. No charge; donations accepted.
Attendance: 150 (estimated)

Auburn

NEMAHA VALLEY MUSEUM, 1423 19th St., Auburn, NE 68305-2350. Mailing Address: P.O. Box 25, Auburn, NE 68305. Tel.: 402-274-2605.
E-mail: info@nemahavalleymuseum.org
Web Site: nemahavalleymuseum.org

Institution Type/Description: History Museum.
Hours & Admission Prices: April-Dec. Wed.-Sun. 1-4:30; other times by appointment. No charge; donations accepted. Closed holidays.

Aurora

EDGERTON EXPLORIT CENTER, 208 16th St., Aurora, NE 68818-3009. Tel.: 402-694-4032. Fax: 402-694-4035. Facebook: Edgerton Explorit Center.
E-mail: mary@edgerton.org
Web Site: www.edgerton.org
Key Personnel: Exec. Dir., Mary Molliconi; Sr. Educator, Daniel Glomski; Educator, Jessica Brock.
Institution Type/Description: Science Museum.
Hours & Admission Prices: Mon.-Sat. 9-4, Sun. 1-5. &
Attendance: 16,722 (actual)

PLAINSMAN MUSEUM, 210 16th St., Aurora, NE 68818-3009. Tel.: 402-694-6531. Facebook, Twitter.
E-mail: plainsman@hamilton.net
Web Site: www.plainsmanmuseum.org
Key Personnel: Exec. Dir., Tina Larson; Bldg. Supvr., Norm Schachenmeyer; Communications, Dawn Marie Moe.
Institution Type/Description: Historical Society Museum.
Hours & Admission Prices: Tues.-Sat. 9-4. Adults $7, senior citizens over 60 $5, youth 5-16 $3; discounts to groups of 10 or more; children under 5 & members no charge. Closed New Year's Day; Easter; Thanksgiving; Christmas. &
Attendance: 4,000 (estimated)

Bancroft

JOHN G. NEIHARDT STATE HISTORIC SITE, 306 W. Elm, Bancroft, NE 68004-0344. Mailing Address: P.O. Box 344, Bancroft, NE 68004-0344. Tel.: 402-648-3388, 888-777-4667. Facebook: John G. Neihardt State Historic Site.
E-mail: neihardt@gpcom.net
Web Site: www.neihardtcenter.org
Formerly: John G. Neihardt Center
Key Personnel: Dir. & Museum Cur., Amy Kucera; Pres. (V), Dr. Jon Cerny.
Institution Type/Description: Preservation Project.
Hours & Admission Prices: Winter: Mon.-Fri. 10-5, weekends by appointment; Summer: Mon.-Sat. 10-5, Sun. by appointment. No charge; donations accepted. Closed New Year's Day; Memorial Day; Independence Day; Labor Day; Thanksgiving; Christmas. &
Attendance: 2,600 (estimated)

Bartlett

WHEELER COUNTY HISTORICAL SOCIETY AND COURTHOUSE MUSEUM, Maine St. between 2nd & 3rd Sts., Bartlett, NE 68622. Mailing Address: 83713 Derner Ranch Ave., Bartlett, NE 68622-3046. Tel.: 308-654-3424.
Institution Type/Description: History Museum.
Hours & Admission Prices: By appointment. No charge.

Bassett

ROCK COUNTY HISTORICAL SOCIETY & HISTORICAL MUSEUM, W. Hwy. 20, Bassett, NE 68714. Mailing Address: P.O. Box 32, Bassett, NE 68714. Tel.: 402-684-3327 & 3908.
Institution Type/Description: History Museum.
Hours & Admission Prices: May to Oct. 1 daily 9-5; other times by appointment. No charge. Closed major holidays.

Bayard

BAYARD DEPOT MUSEUM, 103 S. Main St., Bayard, NE 69334. Mailing Address: P.O Box 345, Bayard, NE 69334. Tel.: 308-586-1496.
Key Personnel: Chm. (V) & Pres. (V), Evelyn Rose.
Institution Type/Description: History Museum.
Hours & Admission Prices: Memorial Day-Labor Day 12:30-4. No charge; donations accepted. &
Attendance: 500 (estimated)

NEBRASKA STATE HISOTRICAL SOCIETY'S CHIMNEY ROCK NATIONAL HISTORIC SITE AND VISITORS CENTER, 9822 Rd. 75, Bayard, NE 69334. Mailing Address: P.O.

Box F, Bayard, NE 69334. Tel.: 308-586-2581. Fax: 308-586-2589.

E-mail: nshs.chimrock@nebraska.gov

Web Site: www.nebraskahistory.org

Key Personnel: C.E.O. & Dir., Trevor Jones; Site Supvr., Loren Pospisil; Assoc. Dir. Education & Interpretation, Ann Billesbach.

Institution Type/Description: Historic Site & Visitors Center.

Hours & Admission Prices: Daily 9-5. Adults $3. Closed major holidays. &

Attendance: 25,000 (actual)

Beatrice

GAGE COUNTY HISTORICAL SOCIETY AND MUSEUM, 101 N. 2nd, Beatrice, NE 68310. Mailing Address: P.O. Box 793, Beatrice, NE 68310-0793. Tel.: 402-228-1679. Facebook: Gage County Museum.

E-mail: gagecountymuseum@beatricene.com

Web Site: gagecountymuseum.info

Key Personnel: Pres. (V), Arnold Baehr; Vice Pres., Sheila Day; Dir., Lesa Arterburn; Treas., Jarrett Willet; Cur. & Museum Shop Mgr., Rita Clawson.

Institution Type/Description: County History Museum: housed in 1906 Burlington Passenger Station.

Hours & Admission Prices: Summer: Tues.-Sat. 9-12 & 1-5; Winter: Tues.-Fri. 9-12 & 1-5. No charge; donations accepted. Closed major holidays. &

Attendance: 6,000 (actual)

HOMESTEAD NATIONAL MONUMENT OF AMERICA, 8523 W. State Hwy. 4, Beatrice, NE 68310-6743. Tel.: 402-223-3514. Fax: 402-228-4231.

Web Site: www.nps.gov

Institution Type/Description: Agriculture Museum.

Hours & Admission Prices: Mon.-Fri. 8:30-5, Sat.-Sun. 9-5. No charge. Closed New Year's Day; Thanksgiving; Christmas. &

Attendance: 70,000 (actual)

YESTERDAY'S LADY, 113 N. 5th St., Beatrice, NE 68310-3902. Tel.: 402-223-5121.

E-mail: yesterdayslady@windstream.net

Web Site: www.yesterdayslady.com

Key Personnel: Owner, Sue McLain.

Institution Type/Description: Victorian Clothing Museum.

Hours & Admission Prices: By appointment.

Bellevue

FONTENELLE FOREST, 1111 N. Bellevue Blvd., Bellevue, NE 68005-4008. Tel.: 402-731-3140. Fax: 402-731-2403. Facebook: Fontenelle Forest.

E-mail: info@fontenelleforest.org

Web Site: www.fontenelleforest.org

Formerly: Fontenelle Nature Association

Key Personnel: Exec. Dir., Merica Whitehall; Dir. Opers. & Facilities, Rick Schmid; Dir. Research & Stewardship, Jeanine Lackey; Dir. Education, Elizabeth Chalen; Dir. Raptor Progs., Janet Stander.

Institution Type/Description: Fontenelle Forest Nature Center: 1,400-acre natural forest; Neale Woods Nature Center located on 550 acre wooded & prairie reserve.

Hours & Admission Prices: Daily 8-5. Adults $9.50, senior 62 & up $8.50, children 2-17 $7.50; children under 2 no charge. Closed New Year's Day; Thanksgiving; Christmas. &

Attendance: 100,000 (estimated)

SARPY COUNTY HISTORICAL MUSEUM, 2402 Clay St., Bellevue, NE 68005-3932. Tel.: 402-292-1880.

E-mail: info@sarpycountymuseum.org

Web Site: www.sarpymuseum.org

Key Personnel: Dir., Ben Justman.

Institution Type/Description: Historical Society Museum.

Hours & Admission Prices: Tues.-Sat. 10-4. No charge; donations accepted. &

Attendance: 3,400 (actual)

Benkelman

DUNDY COUNTY HISTORICAL SOCIETY, 522 Arapahoe, Benkelman, NE 69021. Mailing Address: 605 Arapahoe St., Benkelman, NE 69021-3033. Tel.: 308-423-2291.

E-mail: clerk@dundy.nacone.org

Key Personnel: Pres., Jane Monson; Vice Pres. & Sec., Gary Monson; Treas., Shirley Mullanix.

Institution Type/Description: General Museum.

Hours & Admission Prices: Memorial Day to Labor Day Tues. 5-8 p.m., Wed. 1-4 p.m.; other times by appointment. No charge; donations accepted.

Attendance: 475 (actual)

Boys Town

BOYS TOWN HALL OF HISTORY & FATHER FLANAGAN HOUSE, 14057 Flanagan Blvd., Boys Town, NE 68010. Tel.: 402-498-1187. Fax: 402-498-1159.

E-mail: benjamin.clark@boystown.org

Web Site: www.boystown.org

Key Personnel: C.E.O., Thomas J. Lynch; Mng. Cur., Benjamin L. Clark.

Institution Type/Description: History Museum: located in Boys Town.

Hours & Admission Prices: Daily 10-4:30. No charge; donations suggested. Closed New Year's Day; Easter morning; Thanksgiving; Christmas. &

Attendance: 60,000 (actual)

Bridgeport

PIONEER TRAILS MUSEUM, Hwy. 26 & 385, Bridgeport, NE 69336. Mailing Address: P.O. Box 134, Bridgeport, NE 69336-0134. Tel.: 308-262-1117.

E-mail: pioneertrailsmuseum@hotmail.com

Key Personnel: Cur., Bern Miller.

Institution Type/Description: History Museum.

Hours & Admission Prices: Memorial Day to Labor Day Mon.-Sat. 10-6, Sun. 1-6. No charge.

Broken Bow

CUSTER COUNTY HISTORICAL SOCIETY, INC., 445 S. 9th St., Broken Bow, NE 68822-2015. Mailing Address: P.O. Box 334, Broken Bow, NE 68822-0334. Tel.: 308-872-2203.

E-mail: cchs4@live.com

Web Site: custercountymuseum.org

Key Personnel: C.E.O., Dir. & Museum Shop Mgr., Carol Christen; Sec., Dee Adams.

Institution Type/Description: General Museum.

Hours & Admission Prices: Memorial Day to Labor Day Mon.-Sat. 10-5; Sept.-May Mon.-Fri. 1-5. No charge; donations accepted. Closed national holidays. &

Attendance: 3,000 (estimated)

Brownville

BROWNVILLE HISTORICAL SOCIETY MUSEUM, 213 Main St., Brownville, NE 68521. Mailing Address: Box 1, Brownville, NE 68321. Tel.: 402-825-6001.

Web Site: brownville-ne.com

Key Personnel: Pres. Brownville Historical Society, Dr. Charles Anderson.

Institution Type/Description: Railroad History Center.

Hours & Admission Prices: mid-May to mid-Oct. Fri.-Sun. 1-5. Adults $2, children $1; members no charge.

Attendance: 3,200 (estimated)

MERIWETHER LEWIS DREDGE MUSEUM, Brownville State Recreation Area, Brownville, NE 68321. Mailing Address: P.O. Box 141, Brownville, NE 68321. Tel.: 402-825-6178. Fax: 402-825-6191.

E-mail: pw14316@windstream.net

Key Personnel: Pres., Jim Gerking; Guide, Harold Davis; Maintenance, Merlin Wright; Maintenance, Jerry Paterson.

Institution Type/Description: History Museum: housed in The Captain Meriwether Lewis, a former Corps of Engineers steam powered dredge.

Hours & Admission Prices: Spring & Fall Sat.-Sun. 1-5; June to mid-Sept. daily 1-5; groups by appointment. Adults $3, children 6-12 $1; discount to members; children under 5 no charge.

Attendance: 1,000 (estimated)

Burwell

FORT HARTSUFF STATE HISTORICAL PARK, 82036 Fort Ave., Burwell, NE 68823-6122. Tel.: 308-346-4715. Fax: 308-346-4715.

E-mail: ngpc.fort.hartsuff@nebraska.gov

Web Site: www.ngpc.state.ne.us

Key Personnel: Park Supt., Jim Domeier; Museum Shop Mgr., Mary Hughes.

Institution Type/Description: Military Museum: housed in 1874-1881 Fort Hartsuff.

Hours & Admission Prices: Memorial Day-Labor Day daily 9-8; other times by appointment. Fort: adults $2, children under 12 $1. State park vehicle entry permit required: annual $25, daily $5. &
Attendance: 20,000 (estimated)

GARFIELD COUNTY HISTORICAL MUSEUM, 737 H St., Burwell, NE 68823-0545. Tel.: 308-346-4445 & 4307.
Web Site: www.visitburwell.org
Institution Type/Description: History Museum.
Hours & Admission Prices: May-Oct. Mon.-Fri. 1-5; Nov.-April Mon.-Fri. 9-11am; other times by appointment. &

Butte

BUTTE COMMUNITY HISTORICAL CENTER AND MUSEUM, 721 First St., Butte, NE 68722. Mailing Address: 39355 W. Hwy. 46, Wagner, SD 57380-7128. Tel.: 605-384-3509. Fax: 605-384-5460.
E-mail: frenchine@neb.rr.com
Key Personnel: Co Founder, Dir. & Chm. (V), Mardell E. Schroeder.
Institution Type/Description: History Museum.
Hours & Admission Prices: April-Oct. by appointment. No charge; donations accepted. &
Attendance: 7,500 (estimated)

Cambridge

CAMBRIDGE MUSEUM, 612 Penn St., Cambridge, NE 69022. Mailing Address: P.O. Box 129, Cambridge, NE 69022-0129. Tel.: 308-697-4385.
E-mail: bettyboop1-39@hotmail.com
Key Personnel: Pres. (V), Marilyn Kester; Chm., Mae Groshong; Museum Shop Mgr., Betty Kruger.
Institution Type/Description: Local History Museum.
Hours & Admission Prices: April-Sept. Tues.-Sun. 1-5; Oct.-March Sat.-Sun. 1-5. No charge; donations accepted. &
Attendance: 1,050 (estimated)

Central City

MERRICK COUNTY HISTORICAL MUSEUM, 211 E. St., Central City, NE 68826-1326. Tel.: 308-946-2867.
Institution Type/Description: History Museum.
Hours & Admission Prices: May-Oct. Sun. 2-4; other times by appointment. No charge; donations accepted.

Chadron

DAWES COUNTY HISTORICAL SOCIETY MUSEUM, 341 Country Club Rd., Chadron, NE 69337-7329. Mailing Address: P. O. Box 1319, Chadron, NE 69337-1319. Tel.: 308-432-4999, 308-638-7402.
E-mail: dawescountymuseum@gmail.com
Web Site: dawescountymuseum.org
Key Personnel: C.E.O. & Pres., Bernard Cripps; Chm. (V), Belvadine Lecher; Exec. Dir., Phyllis Carlson.
Institution Type/Description: Local History Museum.
Hours & Admission Prices: Memorial Day weekend-last Mon. of Sept. Mon.-Sat. 10-4, Sun. & holidays 1-5. No charge; donations accepted. &
Attendance: 3,500 (estimated)

ELEANOR BARBOUR COOK MUSEUM OF GEOLOGY, Math & Science Building, Chadron State College, 1000 Main St., Chadron, NE 69337-2667. Tel.: 308-432-6377. Fax: 308-432-6434.
E-mail: mleite@csc.edu
Web Site: www.csc.edu
Key Personnel: Cur. & Professor Geoscience, Michael Leite.
Institution Type/Description: Science Museum.
Hours & Admission Prices: Sept. to early May Mon.-Fri. 8-4:30; other times by appointment. No charge. Closed spring break; major holidays. &
Attendance: 400 (estimated)

HIGH PLAINS HERBARIUM, 1000 Main St., Chadron, NE 69337-2667. Tel.: 308-432-6385.
Web Site: www.csc.edu/sci/herbarium/
Key Personnel: Dir., Steve Rolfsmeier.
Institution Type/Description: Herbarium.
Hours & Admission Prices: Daily 8-5; tours by appointment. &

MARI SANDOZ HIGH PLAINS HERITAGE CENTER, 1000 Main, Chadron, NE 69337-2667. Tel.: 308-432-6401. Fax: 308-432-6464. Facebook.
E-mail: sandozcenter@csc.edu
Web Site: www.sandozcenter.com
Formerly: Mari Sandoz Room Museum
Key Personnel: Dir., Sarah Polak.
Institution Type/Description: History Museum.
Hours & Admission Prices: Mon.-Fri. 8-12 & 1-4, Sat. 9-12 & 1-4. No charge; donations accepted. Closed college holidays. &
Attendance: 8,000 (estimated)

MUSEUM OF THE FUR TRADE, 6321 E. Hwy. 20, Chadron, NE 69337-5325. Tel.: 308-432-3843. Fax: 308-432-5943.
E-mail: museum@furtrade.org
Web Site: www.furtrade.org
Key Personnel: C.E.O. & Dir., Gail DeBuse Potter; Pres., Steve Erwin; Editor, Dr. James A. Hanson.
Institution Type/Description: History Museum.
Hours & Admission Prices: May-Oct. daily 8-5; other times by appointment. Adults $5; discount to groups of 20 or more, AAA & AAM members; members, active military, & children with parents no charge. Audio tours available. &
Attendance: 59,750 (actual)

Champion

CHAMPION MILL HISTORICAL SITE, US 6 W. to Spur 15A, Champion, NE 69023-0117. Mailing Address: P.O. Box 1299, Imperial, NE 69033. Tel.: 308-882-7521 & 7520.
E-mail: nik.johanson@nebraska.gov
Web Site: outdoornebraska.org
Key Personnel: Supt., Nik Johanson.
Institution Type/Description: Historical Park: Nebraska's last functioning water-powered mill.
Hours & Admission Prices: Grounds: daily. Mill: Memorial Day-Labor Day Sat. 8-5, Sun. 1-4. Mill: no charge; donations accepted. Park permit required. Primitive camping fee $7. &
Attendance: 10,500 (estimated)

CHASE COUNTY HISTORICAL MUSEUM, 1711 Broadway, Champion, NE 69033-3032. Mailing Address: 220 2nd St., Champion, NE 69023. Tel.: 308-882-4601 & 1699.
E-mail: aghust@chase3000.com
Key Personnel: Pres., Byron Hust.
Institution Type/Description: History Museum.
Hours & Admission Prices: Mother's Day to Labor Day Sun. 1:30-4:30; groups by appointment. No charge; donations accepted. &
Attendance: 985 (actual)

Chappell

CHAPPELL MUSEUM ASSOCIATION AND SUDMAN-NEUMANN HERITAGE HOUSE, 933 2nd St., Chappell, NE 69129. Mailing Address: P.O. Box 313, Chappell, NE 69129-0313. Tel.: 308-874-2402.
E-mail: bgboling@centurylink.net
Key Personnel: Pres. (V), Sharon Beers; Vice Pres. (V), Wanda Paulsen; Sec., Pat Paulsen; Dir., Gretchen Boling; Dir., Lana Balka; Dir., Sharon Hastings; Dir., Deena Peters; Dir., Ladene Rutt.
Institution Type/Description: History Museum.
Hours & Admission Prices: Open for special events or by appointment. No charge; donations accepted.
Attendance: 265 (actual)

Clarkson

CLARKSON HISTORICAL SOCIETY, 221 Pine St., Clarkson, NE 68629. Mailing Address: P.O. Box 121, 221 Pine St., Clarkson, NE 68629. Tel.: 402-892-3863.
Web Site: www.clarksonmuseum.weebly.com
Key Personnel: Chm. (V), Nancy Doernemann; Pres. (V), Ruth D. Waters.
Institution Type/Description: General Museum.
Hours & Admission Prices: See website for hours; other times by appointment. No charge; donations accepted. &
Attendance: 1,000 (estimated)

Clay Center

CLAY COUNTY MUSEUM & HISTORICAL SOCIETY, 316 W. Glenvil St., Clay Center, NE 68933-1153. Mailing Address: P.O. Box 191, Clay Center, NE 68933-0191. Tel.: 402-762-3563.
Web Site: www.oldtrusty.org/history.html
Institution Type/Description: History Museum.
Hours & Admission Prices: Mon.-Thurs. 10-4; other times by appointment. No charge; donations accepted. &
Attendance: 10,000 (estimated)

Columbus

PLATTE COUNTY MUSEUM, 2916 16th St., Columbus, NE 68601-4200. Mailing Address: P.O. Box 31, Columbus, NE 68602-0031. Tel.: 402-564-1856. Facebook: Platte County NE Museum.
E-mail: museum@megavision.com
Web Site: www.megavision.net/museum
Key Personnel: Dir., Cheri Schrader.
Institution Type/Description: History Museum.
Hours & Admission Prices: mid-May to Labor Day Fri.-Sun. 1-4; Oct.-April 1st Sun. each month 1-4. Adults $3; members & children under 14 no charge. &
Attendance: 1,800 (actual)

Comstock

DOWSE SOD HOUSE, 80560 Oak Grove Rd., Comstock, NE 68828. Tel.: 308-628-4370 & 4231.
Institution Type/Description: Historic House Museum: built in 1900. Listed on the National Register of Historic Places.
Hours & Admission Prices: By appointment. No charge.

Cozad

THE 100TH MERIDIAN MUSEUM, 206 E. 8th, Cozad, NE 69130-1834. Mailing Address: P.O. Box 325, Cozad, NE 69130-0325. Tel.: 308-784-1100. Facebook.
E-mail: cozadcty@cozadtel.net
Key Personnel: Pres., Curtis Sargent; Vice Pres., Maurice Andres; Treas. and Recording & Corresponding Sec., Julie Linn; Chm. (V) & Museum Shop Mgr., Judy Andres.
Institution Type/Description: Historical Museum.
Hours & Admission Prices: Memorial Day to Labor Day Tues.-Fri. 10-5, Sat. 10-4; other times by appointment. No charge; donations accepted. &
Attendance: 1,500 (estimated)

ROBERT HENRI MUSEUM & HISTORICAL WALKWAY, 218 E. 8th St., Cozad, NE 69130-1834. Mailing Address: P.O. Box 355, Cozad, NE 69130-0355. Tel.: 308-784-4154.
E-mail: rhenri@cozadtel.net
Web Site: roberthenrimuseum.org
Institution Type/Description: History Museum.
Hours & Admission Prices: June-Sept. Tues.-Sat. 10-5; other times by appointment. Adults $3, children 14 & under $1.

Crawford

CRAWFORD HISTORICAL MUSEUM, 337 2nd St., Crawford, NE 69339. Mailing Address: Crawford Historical Society, P.O. Box 333, Crawford, NE 69339. Tel.: 308-665-1732.
Web Site: crawfordmuseum.org
Institution Type/Description: History Museum.
Hours & Admission Prices: Mid-May to mid-Oct. Mon.-Sat. 10-4. No charge; donations accepted.

HUDSON-MENG MUSEUM & ARCHAEOLOGY RESEARCH CENTER, 1811 Meng Dr., Crawford, NE 69339. Mailing Address: Mammoth Site of Hot Springs, P.O. Box 692, Hot Springs, SD 57747-0692. Tel.: 308-665-3900. Fax: 308-665-3908.
E-mail: news@mammothsite.org
Web Site: www.fs.usda.gov/detail/nebraska/specialplaces/?cid=fsm9_028053
Institution Type/Description: Archaeology Museum.
Hours & Admission Prices: Memorial Day weekend to Sept. daily 9-5. Adults $5, seniors 60 & over $4.50, children 5-12 $3; children 4 & under no charge.

NEBRASKA STATE HISTORICAL SOCIETY'S FORT ROBINSON MUSEUM, 3200 U.S. Hwy. 20, Crawford, NE 69339. Mailing Address: P.O. Box 304, Crawford, NE 69339-0304. Tel.: 308-665-2919. Fax: 308-665-2917.
E-mail: nshs.fortrob@nebraska.gov
Web Site: www.nebraskahistory.org
Formerly: Fort Robinson Museum
Key Personnel: C.E.O. & Exec. Dir., Trevor Jones; Assoc. Dir., Ann Billesbach; Preservationist, Jerry Taylor.
Institution Type/Description: Military Museum: Fort Robinson history.
Hours & Admission Prices: Memorial Day-Labor Day Mon.-Sat. 8-5, Sun. 9-5; Sept.-May Mon.-Fri. 8-5. Adults $2; discount to Time Travelers; members & children with adult no charge. &
Attendance: 11,000 (actual)

TRAILSIDE MUSEUM OF NATURAL HISTORY, 3200 W. U.S. Hwy. 20, Crawford, NE 69339-3112. Mailing Address: Box 462, Crawford, NE 69339. Tel.: 308-665-2929. Fax: 308-665-2928.
E-mail: pnorman2@unl.edu
Web Site: www.trailside.unl.edu
Institution Type/Description: Natural History Museum.
Hours & Admission Prices: April-May & Sept.-Oct. Thurs.-Sun. 10-5; Memorial Day to Labor Day daily 9-6; other times by appointment. Adults 19 & over $3, children 5-18 $1; children 4 & under no charge. &

Crete

CRETE HERITAGE SOCIETY AND BENNE MEMORIAL MUSEUM, 800 W. 13th St., Crete, NE 68333-2006. Mailing Address: P.O. Box 304, Crete, NE 68333. Tel.: 402-826-5270. Facebook: Crete Heritage Society.
E-mail: janet.jeffries@doane.edu
Web Site: www.creteheritage.org
Formerly: Maples Heritage Complex
Key Personnel: Janet Jeffries.
Institution Type/Description: History Museum.
Hours & Admission Prices: Sun. 1-4; other times by appointment. &
Attendance: 300 (actual)

Crofton

LEWIS AND CLARK VISITOR CENTER, 55245 N.E. Hwy. 121, Crofton, NE 68730. Mailing Address: P.O. Box 710, Yankton, SD 57078-0710. Tel.: 402-667-2546. Fax: 402-667-2547.
E-mail: gavinspoint.nwo@usace.army.mil
Web Site: www.nwo.usace.army.mil/gavinspoint
Institution Type/Description: Visitor Center.
Hours & Admission Prices: Memorial Day to Labor Day Sat.-Sun. 9-5; Offseason: Mon.-Fri. 8-4. No charge. &
Attendance: 22,012 (actual)

Curtis

HANSEN MEMORIAL MUSEUM, 502 Prentiss, Curtis, NE 69025. Mailing Address: c/o City of Curtis, 201 Garlick Ave., Curtis, NE 69025. Tel.: 308-367-4122.
Web Site: www.curtis-ne.com/hansen/
Key Personnel: Pres (V), Tom Rue.
Institution Type/Description: History Museum: housed in the former home of Anna Marie Hansen; built in 1911.
Hours & Admission Prices: Call for hours.
Attendance: 54 (actual)

Dalton

DALTON PRAIRIE SCHOONER MUSEUM, 109 U.S. Hwy. 385, Dalton, NE 69131. Tel.: 308-377-2637.
Institution Type/Description: History Museum.
Hours & Admission Prices: Memorial Day to Labor Day Sat.-Sun. 1-4; other times by appointment. No charge.

David City

BONE CREEK MUSEUM OF AGRARIAN ART, 575 "E" St., David City, NE 68632-1638. Tel.: 402-367-4488.
E-mail: artinfo@bonecreek.org
Web Site: www.bonecreek.org
Key Personnel: Pres. (V) Ron Clarke; Cur., Amanda Mobley Guenther; Treasurer, Anna Nolan; Mgr. Collections, Gabrielle Comte.

Institution Type/Description: Art Museum: located in the boyhood hometown of artist Dale Nichols.
Hours & Admission Prices: Wed. & Fri.-Sat. 10-4, Thurs. 10-8 Sun. 1-4. No charge; donations accepted. Closed major holidays. &
Attendance: 1,500 (estimated)

Dorchester

SALINE COUNTY HISTORICAL SOCIETY, INC., 1445 State Hwy. 33, Dorchester, NE 68343. Mailing Address: P.O. Box 267, Dorchester, NE 68343. Tel.: 402-946-2129 & 243-2356.
E-mail: rjrada@diodecom.net
Key Personnel: C.E.O. & Pres. (V), Judith K. Rada; Sec., Mary Ann Placek.
Institution Type/Description: Historical Museum.
Hours & Admission Prices: Sun. 2-5; other times by appointment. No charge; donations accepted. &
Attendance: 515 (actual)

Elkhorn

ELKHORN HISTORICAL SOCIETY, 20601 Glenn St., Elkhorn, NE 68022. Mailing Address: P.O. Box 187, Elkhorn, NE 68022. Tel.: 402-238-2571.
E-mail: smaltwn@yahoo.com
Web Site: www.elkhornhistory.org
Institution Type/Description: Historical Society Museum.
Hours & Admission Prices: Thurs. 1-3.

Ellsworth

CRESCENT LAKE NATIONAL WILDLIFE REFUGE, 10630 Rd. 181, Ellsworth, NE 69340. Tel.: 308-762-4893.
E-mail: crescentlake@fws.gov
Web Site: www.fws.gov/refuge/crescent_lake/
Institution Type/Description: Wildlife Refuge.
Hours & Admission Prices: Daily sunrise to sunset.

Elm Creek

CHEVYLAND U.S.A. AUTO MUSEUM, 7245 Buffalo Creek Rd., Elm Creek, NE 68836-9802. Tel.: 308-856-4208.
E-mail: chevylandusa@rcom-ne.com
Key Personnel: C.E.O., Monte Hollertz.
Institution Type/Description: Automobile Museum.
Hours & Admission Prices: May-Sept. daily 8-5; other times by appointment. Adults $6, children 10-15 $2; discounts to AAM members & tours; children under 10 no charge. &

Elmwood

BESS STREETER ALDRICH HOUSE & MUSEUM, 204 East F St., Elmwood, NE 68349. Mailing Address: P.O. Box 167, Elmwood, NE 68349-0167. Tel.: 402-994-3855. Facebook.
E-mail: aldrichfoundation@gmail.com
Web Site: www.bessstreeteraldrich.org
Key Personnel: Dir., Kurk Shrader; Pres., Robert Clements.
Institution Type/Description: Historic House Museum: housed in the former home of author, Bess Streeter Aldrich, 1881-1954.
Hours & Admission Prices: House: May-Oct. Wed.-Thurs. & Sat.-Sun. 2-5; Nov.-April Sat.-Sun. 2-5; groups by appointment. Museum: by appointment only. House: adults $5, children 6-12 $3; children under 6 no charge. Museum: no charge with paid house admission.
Attendance: 500 (estimated)

Fairbury

FAIRBURY CITY MUSEUM, 1128 Elm St., Fairbury, NE 68352-1427. Tel.: 402-671-6879.
E-mail: deltadawn63@windstream.net
Key Personnel: Pres. (V), Ben McBride; Cur., Pa'Ren Sims.
Institution Type/Description: History Museum.
Hours & Admission Prices: Sat.-Sun. 1-4; other times by appointment. No charge; donations accepted. &
Attendance: 850 (estimated)

ROCK CREEK STATION STATE HISTORICAL PARK, 57426 710th Rd., Fairbury, NE 68352. Tel.: 402-729-5777.
E-mail: ngpc.rock.creek.station@nebraska.gov
Web Site: www.outdoornebraska.org
Key Personnel: Supt., Jeffery D. Bargar.

Institution Type/Description: Historic Site: Pony Express Station, stage & freight station, road ranches along trail & toll bridge along the Oregon/California Trail.
Hours & Admission Prices: May 1 to mid-Sept. daily 10-5; mid-Sept. to last weekend in Oct. Sat.-Sun. 10-5. Museum: adults $2, children 12 & under $1; preschool students no charge. State park entry permit required; annual $25, daily $5 per vehicle. &
Attendance: 48,000 (estimated)

ROCK ISLAND DEPOT RAILROAD MUSEUM, 910 2nd St., Fairbury, NE 68352. Tel.: 402-729-5131.
E-mail: fairburyridepot@alltel.net
Institution Type/Description: Railroad Museum.
Hours & Admission Prices: Wed.-Thurs. & Sun. 1-5; tours by appointment.

Fairmont

FILLMORE COUNTY MUSEUM AND MCCLELLAN DRUG STORE, 601 Sixth Ave., Fairmont, NE 68354. Mailing Address: P.O. Box 333, Fairmont, NE 68354. Tel.: 402-759-0597.
E-mail: dr.br@galaxycable.net
Institution Type/Description: History Museum: housed in the former office of the Fairmont Creamery; built 1886; later sold to Dr. S. F. Ashby for his medical practice.
Hours & Admission Prices: By appointment. No charge; donations accepted.
Attendance: 350 (estimated)

Falls City

RICHARDSON COUNTY HISTORICAL SOCIETY, 1401 Chase St., Falls City, NE 68355-2645. Mailing Address: P.O. Box 45, Falls City, NE 68355-0045. Tel.: 402-245-3481 & 4407.
E-mail: auxie@sentco.net
Key Personnel: Pres. (V), Richard Meinzer; Cur. & Museum Shop Mgr., JoAnn Auxier.
Institution Type/Description: Historical Society Museum.
Hours & Admission Prices: Mon.-Fri. 2-4; other times by appointment. Suggested Donations: adults $5, students $.50. Closed major holidays. &
Attendance: 1,710 (actual)

RICHARDSON COUNTY MILITARY HISTORY MUSEUM, 1700 Stone St., Falls City, NE 68355. Tel.: 402-245-4288.
E-mail: john.ricks@nebraska.gov
Institution Type/Description: Military History Museum.
Hours & Admission Prices: Mon.-Fri. 8-5.

Fort Calhoun

FORT ATKINSON STATE HISTORICAL PARK, 7th & Madison, Fort Calhoun, NE 68023. Mailing Address: Box 240, Fort Calhoun, NE 68023-0240. Tel.: 402-468-5611. Fax: 402-468-5066.
E-mail: fort.atkinson@ngpc.ne.gov
Web Site: ngpc.state.ne.us
Key Personnel: Supt., John Slader; Asst. Supt., Jerry Farber.
Institution Type/Description: Historical Park: site of 1804 Lewis & Clark's Council on the Bluff & 1819-1827 U.S. Army's Ft. Atkinson.
Hours & Admission Prices: Park: Spring & Summer: daily 8-7; Fall & Winter: 8-sunset. Interpretative Center: May & Sept.-Oct. 21 Sat.-Sun. 10-5; Memorial Day to Labor Day Mon.-Fri. 10-5. Park Entry Permit: annual $14, daily $2.50. &
Attendance: 47,500 (estimated)

WASHINGTON COUNTY HISTORICAL ASSOCIATION, 102 N. 14th St., Fort Calhoun, NE 68023-3532. Mailing Address: P.O. Box 25, Fort Calhoun, NE 68023-0025. Tel.: 402-468-5740. Fax: 402-468-5741.
E-mail: info@wchamuseum.com
Web Site: www.wchamuseum.com
Key Personnel: Chm. (V), Michael O'Brien; Cur., Faith Norwood.
Institution Type/Description: General Museum.
Hours & Admission Prices: Museum: Mon.-Wed. & Fri. 9-5, Thurs. 9-8, Sun. 12-4. Frahm House: Sat. 12-4; other times by appointment. Adults $3, children $2; discounts to Blue Star Museum members. Closed holidays. &
Attendance: 3,000 (estimated)

Franklin

FRANKLIN COUNTY MUSEUM, 1309 H Rd., Franklin, NE 68939-5168. Tel.: 308-425-3030. Fax: 530-425-3033.
E-mail: welovehistory@gtmc.net

Web Site: www.rootsweb.ancestry.com/~nefrankl/museum/fcmuseum
Key Personnel: Dir., Connie Osterbuhr; Chm. & Pres. (V), Jim Gorman.
Institution Type/Description: County History.
Hours & Admission Prices: April-Dec. Sat.-Sun. 1-4; other times by appointment. No charge; donations accepted. Closed major holidays.
Attendance: 1,400 (estimated)

Fremont

GALLERY 92 WEST - FREMONT AREA ART ASSOCIATION, 92 W. Sixth St., Fremont, NE 68026-0335. Tel.: 402-721-7779.
E-mail: gallery92west@92west.org
Web Site: www.92west.org
Key Personnel: Exec. Dir., Barbara Gehringer.
Institution Type/Description: Art Gallery.
Hours & Admission Prices: Tues.-Sun. 1-4. No charge.

LOUIS E. MAY MUSEUM, 1643 N. Nye, Fremont, NE 68025-3327. Mailing Address: P.O. Box 766, Fremont, NE 68026-0766. Tel.: 402-721-4515. Fax: 402-721-8354.
E-mail: maymuseum@qwestoffice.net
Web Site: www.maymuseum.com
Key Personnel: Pres., Julie O'Hanlon; Cur. & Museum Shop Mgr., Jeff Kappeler.
Institution Type/Description: History Museum.
Hours & Admission Prices: April-Dec. Wed.-Sat. 1:30-4:30 (last tour 3:30). Adults $5, students 5-18 $1; children under 5 & members no charge. &
Attendance: 5,000 (actual)

LUENINGHOENER PLANETARIUM - MIDLAND UNIVERSITY, Swanson Hall of Science, 8th & Irving St., Fremont, NE 68025. Mailing Address: 900 N. Clarkson, Fremont, NE 68025. Tel.: 402-941-6353.
E-mail: clements@midlandu.edu
Key Personnel: Dir., Dr. Greg Clements.
Institution Type/Description: Planetarium.
Hours & Admission Prices: By appointment. &
Attendance: 1,000 (actual)

Genoa

GENOA HISTORICAL SOCIETY & MUSEUM, 402 Willard Ave., Genoa, NE 68640. Mailing Address: P.O. Box 279, Genoa, NE 68640-0279. Tel.: 402-993-2875 & 2330.
E-mail: nfcarls@megavision.com
Institution Type/Description: Historical Society Museum.
Hours & Admission Prices: Memorial Day to Labor Day Fri.-Sun. 1-5; other times by appointment. Requested Donations: adults $2, children $1.

GENOA U.S. INDIAN SCHOOL MUSEUM AND INTERPRETIVE CENTER, 209 E. Webster Ave., Genoa, NE 68640. Mailing Address: P.O. Box 382, Genoa, NE 68640. Tel.: 402-993-6636 & 6055. Facebook: Genoa U.S. Indian School.
E-mail: nfcarls@hotmail.com
Web Site: www.megavision.net/genoamuseum
Formerly: Genoa U.S. Indian School Museum
Key Personnel: Pres. (V), Philip Swantek.
Institution Type/Description: Native American History Museum: housed in a former boarding school for Native American children from 1884-1934. Listed on the National Register of Historic Places.
Hours & Admission Prices: Memorial Day to Labor Day Sat.-Sun. 1-5; other times by appointment. No charge; donations accepted. &
Attendance: 1,784 (actual)

Gering

LEGACY OF THE PLAINS MUSEUM, 2930 Old Oregon Trail, Gering, NE 69341. Tel.: 308-436-1989. Facebook: Legacy of the Plains Museum.
E-mail: lopmdirector@gmail.com
Web Site: www.legacyoftheplains.org
Formerly: Farm and Ranch Museum/North Platte Valley Museum
Key Personnel: Pres. (V), Jodi Ruzicka; Dir., Sandra Reddish; Asst. Dir., Nancy Haney; Exec. Vice Pres. (V), Jack Preston; Vice Pres. (V), George Schlothauer; Asst. Vice Pres. (V), Paul Considine; Museum Shop Mgr., Becky Simpson; Museum Shop Mgr., Donna Considine.
Institution Type/Description: History: western life migration; settlement; agriculture; ranching.

Hours & Admission Prices: May-Sept. Mon.-Sat. 9-5, Sun. 1-5; Oct.-April Mon.-Fri. 9-5, also by appointment. Non-member adults $3; closed New Year's Day, Thanksgiving, Christmas. &
Attendance: 10,000 (estimated)

OREGON TRAIL MUSEUM AND VISITOR CENTER, Scotts Bluff National Monument, 190276 Old Oregon Trail, Gering, NE 69341. Mailing Address: Scotts Bluff National Monument, P.O. Box 27, Gering, NE 69341-0027. Tel.: 308-436-9700. Fax: 308-436-7611.
Web Site: www.nps.gov/scbl
Key Personnel: Supt., Ken Maybery; Exec. Sec., Oregon Trail Museum Assn., Jolene Kaufman.
Institution Type/Description: National Monument: dominant natural feature of the North Platte Valley which has been a human migration corridor for centuries.
Hours & Admission Prices: Summer: daily 9-5; Winter: daily 9-12 & 1-5. Non-commercial Vehicles $5; Hikers, Bicyclists & Motorcycles $3. &
Attendance: 150,000 (estimated)

SCOTTS BLUFF NATIONAL MONUMENT, 190276 Old Oregon Trail, Gering, NE 69341. Mailing Address: P.O. Box 27, Gering, NE 69341-0027. Tel.: 308-436-9700. Fax: 308-436-7611.
E-mail: scbl_superintendent@nps.gov
Web Site: www.nps.gov/scbl
Key Personnel: Supt., Ken Mabery; Gift Shop Mgr., Jolene Kaufmann.
Institution Type/Description: History Museum.
Hours & Admission Prices: Winter: daily 8-5; Summer: 8-7. Seven-day Pass: $5 per vehicle; Annual Pass: $15 per vehicle; senior pass & federal recreation lands pass no charge. &
Attendance: 121,000 (actual)

WILDCAT HILLS NATURE CENTER, 210615 Hwy. 71, Gering, NE 69341. Mailing Address: P.O. Box 65, Gering, NE 69341. Tel.: 308-436-3777.
E-mail: ngpc.wildcat.hills@nebraska.gov
Web Site: outdoornebraska.gov/wildcathills
Institution Type/Description: Nature Center.
Hours & Admission Prices: Call for hours.

Gibbon

GIBBON HERITAGE CENTER, 1st & Court St., Gibbon, NE 68840. Mailing Address: c/o City of Gibbon, 715 Front St., Gibbon, NE 68840. Tel.: 308-468-6109 & 5608.
E-mail: erika.pritchard@kearneyhub.com
Web Site: www.cityofgibbon.org/community/museum
Institution Type/Description: History Museum.
Hours & Admission Prices: 1st Sun. of month 2-4; other times by appointment. No charge; donations accepted.
Attendance: 125 (estimated)

ROWE SANCTUARY AND THE IAIN NICOLSON AUDUBON CENTER, 44450 Elm Island Rd., Gibbon, NE 68840-4019. Tel.: 308-468-5282.
E-mail: rowesanctuary@audubon.org
Web Site: rowe.audubon.org
Institution Type/Description: Wildlife Sanctuary & Audubon Center.
Hours & Admission Prices: April 16-Feb. 14 Mon.-Fri. 9-5, Sun. 1-4; Feb. 15-April 15 daily 8-5:30. Closed holidays.

Goehner

SEWARD COUNTY HISTORICAL SOCIETY MUSEUM, 364th Rd., I-80 Exit 373, Goehner, NE 68364. Mailing Address: P.O. Box 188, Goehner, NE 68364-0188. Tel.: 402-523-4055. Facebook: Seward County Historical Society Museum.
E-mail: info@sewardcountymuseum.org
Web Site: sewardcountymuseum.org
Key Personnel: Pres., Jean Kolterman; Vice Pres., Larry Ray; Treas., Miniature Train Owner & Operator, Jim Culver; Sec., Joyce Peterson; Cur., Lori Sizer.
Institution Type/Description: Historical Society Museum.
Hours & Admission Prices: May-Oct. Thurs. 10-4, Sun. 1:30-5. No charge; donations accepted. &
Attendance: 1,200 (estimated)

Gordon

SCAMAHORN CHURCH MUSEUM, 200 Block of W. 5th St., Wayland Park, Gordon, NE 69360. Tel.: 308-282-0887.

E-mail: wheelfish@hotmail.com
Web Site: sheridancountyhistoricalsociety.com
Key Personnel: Pres., Harlen Wheeler.
Institution Type/Description: History Museum; housed in a former church; built in 1884.
Hours & Admission Prices: Oct.-May Thurs. & Sat. 1:30-4; other times by appointment. No charge.

THE TRI-STATE OLD TIME COWBOYS MEMORIAL MUSEUM, City Park, Gordon, NE 69343. Mailing Address: P.O. Box 202, Gordon, NE 69343-0202. Tel.: 308-282-0749.
E-mail: gcc@gordonchamber.com
Web Site: www.gordonchamber.com
Institution Type/Description: History Museum.
Hours & Admission Prices: Memorial Day to mid-Sept. daily 1-5; other times by appointment. No charge; donations accepted. &

Gothenburg

GOTHENBURG HISTORICAL MUSEUM, 1420 Ave. F., Gothenburg, NE 69138. Mailing Address: P.O. Box 204, Gothenburg, NE 69138-1947. Tel.: 308-537-4212.
E-mail: gottenburghistory@outlook.com
Web Site: www.gottenburghistory.com
Key Personnel: Pres. (V), Roger Heidebrink.
Institution Type/Description: History Museum.
Hours & Admission Prices: Call for hours. No charge; donations accepted.
Attendance: 2,346 (actual)

PONY EXPRESS STATION MUSEUM, 1500 Lake Ave., Gothenburg, NE 69138. Mailing Address: Gothenburg Pony Express Assoc., P.O. Box 222, Gothenburg, NE 69138. Tel.: 308-537-9876. Facebook: Gothenburg Pony Express Station.
E-mail: info@ponyexpressstation.org
Web Site: ponyexpressstation.org
Key Personnel: Museum Mgr., June Blauvelt.
Institution Type/Description: Historic Building; housed in the Sam Macchette station used by the Pony Express between 1860-1861.
Hours & Admission Prices: April & Oct. 9-3; May-Sept. daily 9-7. No charge; donations accepted.
Attendance: 30,000 (estimated)

SOD HOUSE MUSEUM, 300 S. Lake Ave., Gothenburg, NE 69138. Mailing Address: P.O. Box 21, Gothenburg, NE 69138-0021. Tel.: 308-537-2076.
E-mail: sodlady2001@hotmail.com
Key Personnel: Dir., Merle Block; Museum Mgr. & Museum Shop Mgr., Linda Block.
Institution Type/Description: Historic Site & Historic House; c.1800 Farmstead & Sod House.
Hours & Admission Prices: May, June-Aug. & Sept. daily 9-3. No charge; donations accepted. &
Attendance: 20,000 (estimated)

Grand Island

STUHR MUSEUM OF THE PRAIRIE PIONEER, 3133 W. Hwy. 34, Grand Island, NE 68801-7485. Tel.: 308-385-5316. Fax: 308-385-5028. Facebook: Stuhr Museum.
E-mail: info@stuhrmuseum.org
Web Site: www.stuhrmuseum.org
Key Personnel: Exec. Dir., Joe Black; Chm. (V), Jennifer Worthington; Dir. Education, Carrie Swanson; Dir. Mktg., Mike Bockoven; Finance & Human Resources Mgr., Steve Stump; Visitor Svcs. Coord. & Museum Shop Mgr., Lynda Waring-Hauser; Historian & Research Center Mgr., Kari Stofer; Historical Interpretation Mgr., Kay Cynova.
Institution Type/Description: History Museum; Stuhr Building designed by Edward Durell Stone.
Hours & Admission Prices: Jan.-March Tues.-Sat. 9-5, Sun. 12-5; April-Dec. Mon.-Sat. 9-5, Sun. 12-5. Admission: May-Sept. adults $8, senior citizens $7, youth 7-12 $6; members no charge; Oct.-April: adults $8, senior citizens $7, youth 7-12 $6; discounts to AAA and Blue Star Museum members; members no charge. Closed New Year's Day; Thanksgiving; Christmas. &
Attendance: 71,000 (actual)

Grant

PERKINS COUNTY HISTORICAL SOCIETY, Central Ave. & 6th, Grant, NE 69140. Mailing Address: P.O. Box 562, Grant, NE 69140-0562. Tel.: 308-352-4977 & 4698. Fax: 308-352-4977.

Key Personnel: Pres. (V), Brenda Styskal.
Institution Type/Description: General Museum; housed in 1905 two-story frame home with wrap around porch.
Hours & Admission Prices: Sat. 1-4 & special events. No charge; donations accepted.
Attendance: 550 (estimated)

Greeley

GREELEY COUNTY HISTORICAL SOCIETY COURTHOUSE MUSEUM, Courthouse Square, Greeley, NE 68842. Tel.: 308-428-3115.
Institution Type/Description: Historical Society Museum.
Hours & Admission Prices: Mon.-Fri. 9-4.

Greenwood

GREENWOOD HISTORICAL SOCIETY DEPOT MUSEUM, 440 Broad St., Greenwood, NE 68366. Mailing Address: P.O. Box 1, Greenwood, NE 68366-0001. Tel.: 402-430-0238. Facebook: Greenwood Depot Museum / Greenwood Historical Society.
E-mail: jarid_massa@yahoo.com
Key Personnel: Dir. & Museum Shop Mgr., Jarid Massa; Pres. & Chm. (V), Anna Jamrog.
Institution Type/Description: Railroad & History Museum.
Hours & Admission Prices: April-Oct. Mon.-Wed. 10-5; other times by appointment. No charge; donations accepted. &
Attendance: 200 (estimated)

Gretna

AK-SAR-BEN AQUARIUM OUTDOOR EDUCATION CENTER, 21502 W. Hwy. 31, Gretna, NE 68028-7264. Tel.: 402-332-3901. Fax: 402-332-5853.
E-mail: tony.korth@nebraska.gov
Web Site: outdoornebraska.gov/aksarben
Key Personnel: Dir., Tony Korth.
Institution Type/Description: Aquarium; located on site of 1882, Hatch House, first fish hatchery & public picnic area in Nebraska.
Hours & Admission Prices: Spring: April-Fri. before Memorial Day Wed.-Mon. 10-4:30; Summer: Memorial Day weekend-Labor Day Mon.-Fri. 10-4:30, Sat.-Sun. 10-5; Fall: Wed. after Labor Day-Nov. 30 Wed.-Mon. 10-4:30; Winter: Dec. 1-March 31 Wed.-Sun. 10-4:30. No charge. Closed New Year's Day; Thanksgiving; Christmas. &
Attendance: 65,000 (estimated)

Harrisburg

BANNER COUNTY HISTORICAL SOCIETY, 200 N. Pennsylvania Ave., Harrisburg, NE 69345. Mailing Address: P.O. Box 74, Harrisburg, NE 69345-0074. Tel.: 308-575-0808. Facebook.
E-mail: bannercountyhistoricalsociety@yahoo.com
Web Site: bannercountyhistoricalsociety.com
Key Personnel: C.E.O. Pres. & Cur., Vicki Greathouse-Stone; Vice Pres., Steve Brown; Treas., Reta Pahl; Sec., Winnie Smith.
Institution Type/Description: Historical Society Museum.
Hours & Admission Prices: June to mid-Sept. Sun. 1-5; other times by appointment. No charge; donations accepted. &
Attendance: 3,000 (estimated)

Harrison

AGATE FOSSIL BEDS NATIONAL MONUMENT, 301 River Rd., 22 miles south of Harrison & 3 miles east of Hwy. 29, Harrison, NE 69346-2734. Tel.: 308-668-2211. Fax: 308-668-2318.
E-mail: mark_hertig@nps.gov
Web Site: www.nps.gov/agfo/
Key Personnel: Supt., James Hill; Cur., Mark Hertig; Museum Shop Mgr., Jolene S. Kaufmann.
Institution Type/Description: Park Museum/Visitor Center; located near the site of 19-22 million year old mammal fossil remains & historic Agate Springs Ranch on the Niobrara River.
Hours & Admission Prices: May 15-Sept. 30 daily 9-5; Sept 30.-mid-May daily 8-4. No charge. Closed New Year's Day; Thanksgiving; Christmas. &
Attendance: 12,000 (estimated)

SIOUX COUNTY HISTORICAL MUSEUM, 130 Main St., Harrison, NE 69346. Tel.: 308-668-2110.

Institution Type/Description: History Museum.
Hours & Admission Prices: Memorial Day to Labor Day Mon.-Sat. 10-4, Sun. 1-4. No charge.

Hartington

CEDAR COUNTY HISTORICAL MUSEUM, 304 W. Franklin, Hartington, NE 68739. Mailing Address: P.O. Box 181, Hartington, NE 68739. Tel.: 402-254-6597.
E-mail: cchistory@hartel.net
Institution Type/Description: History Museum.
Hours & Admission Prices: May-Aug. Sun. 2-4; other times by appointment. No charge; donations accepted.

Hastings

CHILDREN'S MUSEUM OF CENTRAL NEBRASKA, Imperial Mall, 12th & Marian Rd., Hastings, NE 68901. Mailing Address: P.O. Box 1502, Hastings, NE 68902-1502. Tel.: 402-463-3300.
E-mail: director@cmocn.org
Web Site: www.cmocn.org
Key Personnel: Pres. Bd., David Bosle; Vice Pres., Patrick Cecil; Sec. & Exec. Dir., Deb Bosle; Treas., DeWayne Boesen.
Institution Type/Description: Children's Museum.
Hours & Admission Prices: Tues.-Sat. 10-5:30, Sun. 1-5. Admission $5; members & children under 1 no charge.

CLYDE SACHTLEBEN OBSERVATORY, S. Wabash Ave., Hastings, NE 68901. Mailing Address: 710 N. Turner, Hastings, NE 68901. Tel.: 402-462-7378.
E-mail: dglomski@hastings.edu
Institution Type/Description: Observatory.
Hours & Admission Prices: Call for hours. No charge.

HASTINGS MUSEUM, 1330 N. Burlington, Hastings, NE 68901-3099. Mailing Address: P.O. Box 1286, Hastings, NE 68902-1286. Tel.: 402-461-2399. Fax: 402-461-2379. Facebook: Hastings Museum.
E-mail: museum@hastingsmuseum.org
Web Site: www.hastingsmuseum.org
Key Personnel: Dir., Rebecca Matticks; Pres., Mike Howie; Dir. Mktg. & Devel., Becky Tideman; Cur. Collections, Teresa Kreutzer-Hodson; Cur. Education, Russanne Erickson; Museum Shop Mgr., Jenny Korte.
Institution Type/Description: Natural Science & History Museum.
Hours & Admission Prices: Mon.-Sat. 9-7, Sun. 1-6. Adult $8; discounts to military & Blue Star Museum; members no charge. Closed New Year's Day; Easter; Thanksgiving; Christmas.
Attendance: 55,595 (actual)

Hay Springs

HERITAGE CENTER MUSEUM, 230 N. Baker St., Hay Springs, NE 69347. Mailing Address: P.O. Box 291, Hay Springs, NE 69347-0291. Tel.: 308-638-7643.
E-mail: dsperkins@gpcom.net
Key Personnel: Dir., Chm. (V) & Museum Shop Mgr., David Perkins.
Institution Type/Description: History Museum.
Hours & Admission Prices: Memorial Day to Labor Day Mon.-Fri. 1-4; other times by appointment. No charge; donations accepted.
Attendance: 150 (estimated)

HERITAGE CENTER MUSEUM II, 133 N. Main St., Hay Springs, NE 69347. Mailing Address: P.O. Box 291, Hay Springs, NE 69347-0291. Tel.: 308-638-7643.
E-mail: dsperkins@gpcom.net
Key Personnel: Pres. (V) & Museum Shop Mgr., David Perkins.
Institution Type/Description: Historic Building: housed in the former hardware store.
Hours & Admission Prices: Memorial Day to Labor Day Mon.-Fri. 1-4; other times by appointment. No charge; donations accepted.
Attendance: 259 (actual)

Heartwell

KEARNEY COUNTY HISTORICAL MUSEUM, 2036 Q Rd., Heartwell, NE 68945. Tel.: 308-563-2330.
E-mail: heartwellquilter@gmail.com
Key Personnel: Dir. (V) & Chm. (V), Doris Thompson; Pres. (V), Jane Kuehn.

Institution Type/Description: Historical Society Museum: housed in 1881 first schoolhouse in Minden.
Hours & Admission Prices: June-Aug. daily 1-4. No charge; donations accepted.
Attendance: 358 (actual)

Hershey

STONES AND BONES GALLERY AND EMPORIUM, 105 E. 2nd St., Hershey, NE 69143. Mailing Address: P.O. Box 85, Hershey, NE 69143. Tel.: 308-368-7400.
E-mail: fossilrocks@hotmail.com
Institution Type/Description: Art Gallery.
Hours & Admission Prices: Call for hours. No charge.
Attendance: 100

Holdrege

NEBRASKA PRAIRIE MUSEUM OF THE PHELPS COUNTY HISTORICAL SOCIETY, 2701 Burlington St., Holdrege, NE 68949-1347. Mailing Address: P.O. Box 164, Holdrege, NE 68949-0164. Tel.: 308-995-5015. Fax: 308-995-2241. Facebook.
E-mail: prairie995@gmail.com
Web Site: www.nebraskaprairie.org
Formerly: Phelps County Historical Museum
Key Personnel: Dir., Dan Christensen; Vice Pres., Nancy Morse; Chm. (V), Dr. Bob Butz; Sec., Patti Simpson; Museum Shop Mgr., Jim Englund.
Institution Type/Description: General Museum.
Hours & Admission Prices: Summer: Mon.-Fri. 9-5, Sat.-Sun. 1-5; Winter: Mon.-Fri. 9-4, Sat.-Sun. 1-4. Adults $5; members and children 13 & under no charge. Closed holidays.
Attendance: 15,000 (estimated)

Homer

DAKOTA COUNTY HISTORICAL SOCIETY & O'CONNOR HOUSE, 2470 Blyburg Rd., Homer, NE 68030. Mailing Address: P.O. Box 971, Dakota City, NE 68731-0971. Tel.: 402-698-2288 & 2538.
Institution Type/Description: History Museum.
Hours & Admission Prices: Memorial Day to Labor Day Sat. 10-5, Sun. 12-5; other times by appointment. No charge; donations accepted.

Hyannis

GRANT COUNTY MUSEUM & HISTORIC SOCIETY, Grant County Courthouse, 105 E. Harrison, Hyannis, NE 69350-9706. Mailing Address: P.O. Box 82, Hyannis, NE 69350-0082. Tel.: 308-458-2371. Fax: 308-458-2485.
Key Personnel: C.E.O., Harry Merrihew.
Institution Type/Description: General Museum: housed in the Grant County Court House.
Hours & Admission Prices: Tues.-Wed. 1-4; other times by appointment. No charge; donations accepted.
Attendance: 238 (actual)

Kearney

FORT KEARNEY MUSEUM, 131 S. Central Ave., Kearney, NE 68847-7908. Tel.: 308-234-5200. Facebook: Fort Kearney Museum.
Key Personnel: Dir., Marlo L. Johnson.
Institution Type/Description: General Museum.
Hours & Admission Prices: Memorial Day-Labor Day Thurs.-Sat. 10:30-5, Sun. 1-5. Museum: Adults $4, children under 12 $1.50; discount to groups. Boat Rides: adults $4.50, children under 12 $3.50.

FORT KEARNY STATE HISTORICAL PARK, 1020 V Rd., Kearney, NE 68847-8043. Tel.: 308-865-5305. Fax: 308-865-5306.
E-mail: ngpc.fort.kearny@nebraska.gov
Web Site: www.outdoornebraska.org
Key Personnel: Supt., Eugene A. Hunt; Asst. Supt., Joe Blazek.
Institution Type/Description: Historic Building & Site.
Hours & Admission Prices: Memorial Day-Labor Day daily 9-5. Grounds: sunrise-sunset; other times by appointment; game & parks sticker required per vehicle. Adults $2, children 3-11 $1; children 2 & under no charge. Additional Park Permit required.
Attendance: 61,000 (estimated)

G.W. FRANK MUSEUM OF HISTORY & CULTURE, 2010 University Dr., Kearney, NE 68849. Tel.: 308-865-8284. Facebook: @frankmuseum.
E-mail: frankmuseum@unk.edu
Web Site: frank.unk.edu
Formerly: The Frank House at the University of Nebraska at Kearney
Key Personnel: Dir., William F. Stoutamire, Ph.D.
Institution Type/Description: Historic House Museum: housed in the former home of G.W. Frank & his family; built in 1889. Listed on the National Register of Historic Places.
Hours & Admission Prices: Tues.-Fri. 1-5; Sat. & Sun. noon to 5. No charge; donations accepted. Closed major holidays. &
Attendance: 6,000 (estimated)

KEARNEY AREA CHILDREN'S MUSEUM, 5827 4th Ave., Kearney, NE 68845-2879. Tel.: 308-698-2228. Fax: 308-698-2229.
E-mail: contact@kearneychildrensmuseum.org
Web Site: www.kearneychildrensmuseum.org
Key Personnel: Exec. Dir., Traci Winscot; Pres., Connie Larsen; Vice Pres. (V), Kristen Sedlacek; Treas., Kayla Herrick; Sec., Carol Smith.
Institution Type/Description: Children's Museum.
Hours & Admission Prices: Tues.-Wed. & Fri.-Sat. 10-5, Thurs. 10-8, Sun. 1-5. Children 1-12 $7, adults 13 & over $6, seniors 60 & over $5; discounts to Association of Children's Museums reciprocal members; KACM members & children under one no charge. Closed all major holidays. &
Attendance: 58,000 (estimated)

MUSEUM OF NEBRASKA ART, 2401 Central Ave., Kearney, NE 68847-4501. Tel.: 308-865-8559. Fax: 308-865-8104. Facebook: Museum of Nebraska Art.
E-mail: mona@unk.edu
Web Site: mona.unk.edu
Key Personnel: Dir., Audrey S. Kauders; Cur., Teliza Rodriguez; Collections Supvr., Jean Jacobson; Dir. Education, Jackie Abel; Dir. Devel., Karen Humphrey; Coord. ARTreach, Russ Erpelding; Coord. Mktg., Gina Garden; Membership Coord., Melissa Hartman; Office Supvr., Scott Heath.
Institution Type/Description: Art Museum: housed in neoclassical revival building. Listed on the National Register of Historic Places.
Hours & Admission Prices: Tues.-Sat. 10-5, Sun. 2-5. No charge; donations accepted. NARM reciprocal. Closed major holidays. &
Attendance: 20,000 (actual)

NEBRASKA FIREFIGHTERS MUSEUM & EDUCATION CENTER, 2434 E. 1st St., Kearney, NE 68847. Tel.: 308-338-3473. Facebook: Nebraska Firefighters Museum & Education Center.
E-mail: mail@neffm.org
Web Site: www.neffm.org
Key Personnel: Dir., Ali Abler; Chm. (V), Norman Hoeft.
Institution Type/Description: Fire Fighting History Museum.
Hours & Admission Prices: Mon.-Sat. 10-5, Sun 1-5. Adults $6, seniors $4, youth $3; children 5 & under and members no charge. Closed major holidays. &
Attendance: 10,000 (estimated)

TRAILS & RAILS MUSEUM, 710 W. 11th St., Kearney, NE 68845-7340. Mailing Address: BCHS, P.O. Box 523, Kearney, NE 68848. Tel.: 308-234-3041.
E-mail: bchs.us@hotmail.com
Web Site: www.bchs.us
Key Personnel: Dir., Jennifer Murrish; Pres. (V), Dan Speirs; Education Coord., Lyn Hoffman.
Institution Type/Description: History Museum.
Hours & Admission Prices: Memorial Day to Labor Day Mon.-Sat. 10-6, Sun. 1-5; Sept.-May Mon.-Fri. 1-5; groups by appointment. Adults $5, children $2; discounts to AAM members; members no charge.
Attendance: 7,589 (actual)

Lewellen

ASH HOLLOW STATE HISTORICAL PARK, 4265 Hwy. 26, Lewellen, NE 69147. Mailing Address: P.O. Box 70, Lewellen, NE 69147-0070. Tel.: 308-778-5651.
E-mail: jeff.uhrich@nebraska.gov
Web Site: outdoornebraska.ne.gov
Key Personnel: Supt., Jeffery Uhrich.
Institution Type/Description: Historic Site: camp site along the Oregon Trail.
Hours & Admission Prices: Memorial Day to Labor Day Thurs.-Sun. 9-4. Visitor Center: adults $2, children under 13 $1; children under 3 no charge. &
Attendance: 20,562 (actual)

Lexington

DAWSON COUNTY HISTORICAL SOCIETY & MUSEUM, 805 N. Taft St., Lexington, NE 68850-2029. Mailing Address: P.O. Box 369, Lexington, NE 68850-0369. Tel.: 308-324-5340. Facebook: Dawson County Historical Museum.
E-mail: dchsociety@gmail.com
Web Site: www.dchsmuseum.com
Key Personnel: Pres., Jerry Lashley; Dir., Crystal Werger; Museum Shop Mgr., Carol Nelson.
Institution Type/Description: Local History Museum.
Hours & Admission Prices: Tues.-Fri. 10-5, Sat. 10-4. No charge; donations accepted. Closed all major holidays. &
Attendance: 2,500 (actual)

HEARTLAND MUSEUM OF MILITARY VEHICLES, 606 Heartland Rd., Lexington, NE 68850-5666. Tel.: 308-324-6329. Fax: 308-324-6329.
E-mail: heartlandmuseum@cozadtel.net
Web Site: www.heartlandmuseum.com
Key Personnel: Dir., Gary Gifford.
Institution Type/Description: Military Museum.
Hours & Admission Prices: Mon.-Sat. 10-5, Sun. 1-5. No charge; donations accepted. &
Attendance: 9,000 (actual)

Lincoln

AMERICAN HISTORICAL SOCIETY OF GERMANS FROM RUSSIA, 631 D. St., Lincoln, NE 68502-1149. Tel.: 402-474-3363. Fax: 402-474-7229.
E-mail: ahsgr@ahsgr.org
Web Site: www.ahsgr.org
Institution Type/Description: Historical Society Museum.
Hours & Admission Prices: Mon.-Fri. 9-4. Sun. 1-4. Adults $5, students $3; members & children no charge. Closed major holidays; annual convention week. &
Attendance: 2,900 (estimated)

EISENTRAGER-HOWARD GALLERY - UNIVERSITY OF NEBRASKA-LINCOLN, Dept. of Art & Art History, Richards Hall 120, Stadium Dr. & T St., Lincoln, NE 68588-0114. Tel.: 402-472-5522.
E-mail: eisentragerhowardgallery@unl.edu
Web Site: arts.unl.edu/art/eisentrager-howard-gallery
Institution Type/Description: Art Gallery.
Hours & Admission Prices: Call for hours. No charge. &

ELDER ART GALLERY, NEBRASKA WESLEYAN UNIVERSITY, Rogers Center for Fine Arts, 50th St. & Huntington Ave., Lincoln, NE 68504-2230. Mailing Address: Art Depart., Nebraska Wesleyan University, 5000 St. Paul Ave., Lincoln, NE 68504-2760. Tel.: 402-466-2371 & 465-2230. Fax: 402-465-2179.
E-mail: llockman@nebrwesleyan.edu
Key Personnel: Pres., Fred Ohles; Dir., Donald Paoletta; Gallery Asst., Regina O'Rear.
Institution Type/Description: Art Museum.
Hours & Admission Prices: Tues.-Fri. 10-4, Sat.-Sun. 1-4. No charge; donations accepted. Closed school holidays & between shows. &
Attendance: 1,500 (estimated)

FAIRVIEW, THE BRYAN MUSEUM, 49th St., (and Sumner St.), Lincoln, NE 68506-1299. Tel.: 402-481-3032.
E-mail: ellen.beans@bryanhealth.org
Web Site: www.bryanhealth.org
Formerly: The Bryan Museum
Key Personnel: Dir. Volunteer Svcs., Ellen Beans.
Institution Type/Description: Historic House: former home of William Jennings Bryan.
Hours & Admission Prices: Tours: by appointment only with 48 hours advanced notice. No charge. Closed New Year's Day; Thanksgiving; Christmas.

FRANK H. WOODS TELEPHONE MUSEUM, 2047 M St., Lincoln, NE 68510-1029. Mailing Address: 6120 Inverness Rd., Lincoln, NE 68512. Tel.: 402-436-4640. Fax: 402-436-4914.
Key Personnel: Dir., Wally Tubbs.
Institution Type/Description: History Museum: named for the founder of the Lincoln Telephone Company, 1903.

Hours & Admission Prices: Sun. 1-4; other times by appointment. No charge; donations accepted. Closed major holidays.

GALLERY NINE, 124 S. 9th St., Lincoln, NE 68508-2249. Tel.: 402-477-2822.
E-mail: info@gallerynine.com
Web Site: gallerynine.wordpress.com
Key Personnel: Gallery Coord., PJ Peters.
Institution Type/Description: Art Gallery.
Hours & Admission Prices: Wed.-Sat. 10-5, Sun. 12-5.

GREAT PLAINS ART MUSEUM, University of Nebraska-Lincoln, 1155 Q St., Hewit Place, Lincoln, NE 68588-0250. Tel.: 402-472-6220. Facebook: UNL Great Plains.
E-mail: mseaton2@unl.edu
Web Site: www.unl.edu/plains/great-plains-art-museum
Formerly: Great Plains Art Collection
Key Personnel: Dir., Richard Edwards.
Institution Type/Description: Art Museum.
Hours & Admission Prices: Tues.-Sat. 10-5. No charge; donations accepted. Closed holidays; between exhibitions. ♿
Attendance: 10,000 (estimated)

INTERNATIONAL QUILT STUDY CENTER & MUSEUM - UNIVERSITY OF NEBRASKA-LINCOLN, 1523 N. 33rd St., Lincoln, NE 68583-0838. Tel.: 402-472-6549. Fax: 402-472-2008.
E-mail: llevy2@unl.edu
Web Site: www.quiltstudy.org
Key Personnel: Exec. Dir., Leslie Levy; Museum Shop Mgr., Dean Young.
Institution Type/Description: Art Museum.
Hours & Admission Prices: Feb.-Nov.: Tues.-Sat. 10-4, Sun. 1-4; Dec.-Jan.: Tues.-Sat. 10-4. Adults $8; UNL faculty, staff & students, museum & NARM members free. Closed major university and winter break. ♿
Attendance: (actual)

LARSEN TRACTOR TEST & POWER MUSEUM, University of Nebraska, 35th & Fair Sts., Lincoln, NE 68583. Mailing Address: P.O. Box 830833, Lincoln, NE 68583-0833. Tel.: 402-472-8389. Fax: 402-472-8367. Facebook.
E-mail: larsentractormuseum@unl.edu
Web Site: tractormuseum.unl.edu
Key Personnel: Dir., Dr. Mark Riley; Mgr., Julie Thomson.
Institution Type/Description: Agriculture Museum: housed in the original Nebraska Tractor Test facility built in 1919. A Historic Landmark.
Hours & Admission Prices: Tues.-Fri. 9-4, 1st Sat. of month 10-2; other times by appointment. No charge, donations accepted. ♿
Attendance: 3,000 (estimated)

LINCOLN CHILDREN'S MUSEUM, 1420 P St., Lincoln, NE 68508-1635. Tel.: 402-477-4000. Fax: 402-477-2004. Facebook: @LincolnChildrensMuseum.
E-mail: info@lincolnchildrensmuseum.org
Web Site: www.lincolnchildrensmuseum.org
Key Personnel: Exec. Dir., Tara Knuth; Dir. Operations, Ariel Smith; Dir. Devel., Marissa Gill Keyzer; Dir. Mktg., Sharice Kucera.
Institution Type/Description: Children's Museum: inviting children to create, discover & learn through the power of play.
Hours & Admission Prices: Mon.-Wed. & Fri.-Sat. 9:30-5, Thurs. 9:30-7:30, Sun. 1-5. Ages 2-61 $9.50, 62 & up $9, 1 year $6.50; children under one no charge. Closed major holidays. ♿
Attendance: 170,000 (actual)

LINCOLN CHILDREN'S ZOO, 1222 S. 27th St., Lincoln, NE 68502-1832. Tel.: 402-475-6741. Fax: 402-475-6742.
E-mail: jchapo@lincolnzoo.org
Web Site: www.lincolnzoo.org
Formerly: Folsom Children's Zoo and Botanical Garden
Key Personnel: C.E.O. & Pres., John P. Chapo; Gen. Mgr., Evan Killeen; Gen. Cur., Randy Scheer; Dir. Education, Aimee Johns.
Institution Type/Description: Children's Zoo.
Hours & Admission Prices: April 15-May & Sept.-Oct. 15 daily 10-5; June-Aug. Wed. 10-8, Thurs.-Tues. 10-5. Adults $6.50, seniors 60 & over and children 2-11 $5.50; members & children under 2 no charge. ♿
Attendance: 155,000 (actual)

LINCOLN FIRE & RESCUE DEPARTMENT MUSEUM, 1801 "Q" St., Lincoln, NE 68508-1774. Tel.: 402-441-8360.
E-mail: dripley@lincoln.ne.gov
Institution Type/Description: Fire Fighting Museum.
Hours & Admission Prices: Daily 9-8.

LUX CENTER FOR THE ARTS, 2601 N. 48th St., Lincoln, NE 68504-3632. Tel.: 402-466-8692. Fax: 402-466-3786.
E-mail: info@luxcenter.org
Web Site: www.luxcenter.org
Formerly: University Place Art Center
Key Personnel: Exec. Dir., Susan McIntosh Kriz; Chm. (V), Trent Wilcox; Assoc. Dir., Joe Shaw; Education Dir., Lindsey Clausen; Gallery Dir., Bri Murphy; Cur., Susan Soriente; Mktg. & Operations Coord., Kylie Schildt; Education & Gallery Asst., Rachel Sullivan.
Institution Type/Description: General Museum.
Hours & Admission Prices: Tues.-Fri. 11-5, Sat. 10-5. No charge; donations accepted. Closed New Year's Day; Memorial Day; Independence Day; Labor Day; Thanksgiving; Christmas. ♿
Attendance: 14,000 (estimated)

NATIONAL MUSEUM OF ROLLER SKATING, 4730 South St., Lincoln, NE 68506-1256. Tel.: 402-483-7551, ext. 16. Fax: 402-483-1465.
E-mail: directorcurator@rollerskatingmuseum.com
Web Site: www.rollerskatingmuseum.com
Key Personnel: Pres. (V), Kim Wall; Dir., Rhonda Cann.
Institution Type/Description: Sports & Technology Museum.
Hours & Admission Prices: Mon.-Fri. 9-5. No charge; donations accepted. Closed holidays. ♿
Attendance: 2,200 (estimated)

NEBRASKA CONFERENCE UNITED METHODIST HISTORICAL CENTER, Nebraska Wesleyan Univ., Cochrane-Woods Library, Lower Level, 5000 St. Paul Ave., Lincoln, NE 68504. Mailing Address: 3333 Landmark Circle, Lincoln, NE 68504-4760. Tel.: 402-465-2175. Fax: 402-464-6203.
E-mail: kdvorak@greatplainsumc.org
Web Site: www.greatplainsumc.org
Key Personnel: Dir., Karrie Dvorak.
Institution Type/Description: Religious Archives.
Hours & Admission Prices: Tues. & Thurs. 9:30-4, Wed. 10:30-4. Historic Center: no charge; donations accepted. Staff Research Fee: $20 an hour. Closed holidays. ♿
Attendance: 200 (estimated)

NEBRASKA HISTORY MUSEUM, 131 Centennial Mall N., Lincoln, NE 68508-3805. Mailing Address: P.O Box 82554, Lincoln, NE 68501-2554. Tel.: 402-471-4754. Fax: 402-471-3314.
E-mail: ann.billesbach@nebraska.gov
Web Site: history.nebraska.gov/museum
Formerly: Nebraska State Historical Society's Museum of Nebraska History
Key Personnel: C.E.O. & Exec. Dir., Trevor Jones; Deputy Dir., Lynne Ireland; Publications, David Bristow.
Institution Type/Description: History Museum.
Hours & Admission Prices: Mon.-Fri. 10-5:30, Sat. 1-5:30. No charge. Closed federal & state holidays. ♿

NEBRASKA STATE CAPITOL, 1445 K St., Lincoln, NE 68509-4696. Mailing Address: Office of the Capitol Commission, P.O. Box 94696, Lincoln, NE 68509-4696. Tel.: 402-471-6691. Fax: 402-471-6952.
E-mail: hello@capitol.org
Web Site: www.capitol.org
Key Personnel: Tourism Supvr., Roxanne Smith.
Institution Type/Description: Historic Building & Site: 1922-1932, state capitol.
Hours & Admission Prices: Mon.-Fri. 8-5, Sat. & holidays 10-5, Sun. 1-5. No charge; donations accepted. Closed New Year's Day; Thanksgiving & day after; Christmas. ♿
Attendance: 100,000 (estimated)

NEBRASKA STATE HISTORICAL SOCIETY'S THOMAS P. KENNARD HOUSE, 1627 H St., Lincoln, NE 68508. Mailing Address: Box 82554, Lincoln, NE 68501-2554. Tel.: 402-471-4764. Fax: 402-471-3314.
E-mail: ann.billesbach@nebraska.gov
Web Site: www.nebraskahistory.org
Formerly: Thomas P. Kennard House Nebraska Statehood Memorial
Key Personnel: C.E.O. & Dir., Trevor Jones; Assoc. Dir., Ann Billesbach.
Institution Type/Description: Historic House: 1869 The Kennard House.

Hours & Admission Prices: Mon.-Fri. by appointment. Adults $3; discounts to groups of 20 or more; children under 18 accompanied by adults & members no charge. Closed state holidays.
Attendance: 869 (actual)

PIONEERS PARK NATURE CENTER, 3201 S. Coddington, Lincoln, NE 68522-9212. Mailing Address: 2740 A St., Lincoln, NE 68502-3113. Tel.: 402-441-7895. Fax: 402-441-6468,
E-mail: afaas@lincoln.ne.gov
Web Site: parks.lincoln.ne.gov
Key Personnel: Coord. Recreation Ctr., Dorothy Skorupa; Coord. Nature Ctr., Andrea Faas; Naturalist, Jamie Kelley.
Institution Type/Description: Nature Center.
Hours & Admission Prices: Mon.-Sat. 8:30-5, Sun. 12-5. No charge, donations accepted. Closed New Year's Day; Thanksgiving; Christmas. &
Attendance: 76,830 (actual)

ROBERT HILLESTAD TEXTILES GALLERY - UNIVERSITY OF NEBRASKA-LINCOLN, 234 Home Economics Bldg., Lincoln, NE 68583-0802. Tel.: 402-472-2911. Fax: 402-472-0640.
E-mail: sreeder2@unl.edu
Web Site: textilegallery.unl.edu
Key Personnel: Prof. & Chair, Michael James.
Institution Type/Description: Textile Museum.
Hours & Admission Prices: Mon.-Fri. 8:30-4; other times by appointment. No charge. Closed university holidays; between shows. &
Attendance: 3,000 (estimated)

SHELDON MUSEUM OF ART AND SCULPTURE GARDEN/ UNIVERSITY OF NEBRASKA-LINCOLN, 12th and R Sts., Lincoln, NE 68588-0300. Mailing Address: P.O. Box 880300, Lincoln, NE 68588-0300. Tel.: 402-472-2461. Fax: 402-472-4258. Facebook: Sheldon Museum.
E-mail: sheldon@unl.edu
Web Site: www.sheldonartmuseum.org
Key Personnel: Dir., Wally Mason.
Institution Type/Description: American Art Museum.
Hours & Admission Prices: Tues. 10-8, Wed.-Sat. 10-5, Sun. 12-5. No charge, donations accepted. Closed major holidays. &
Attendance: 50,000 (actual)

SPEEDWAY MOTORS MUSEUM OF AMERICAN SPEED, Speedway Motors Inc. Campus, 599 Oak Creek Dr., Lincoln, NE 68528. Mailing Address: P.O. Box 81906, Lincoln, NE 68501-1906. Tel.: 402-323-3166. Fax: 402-323-3151.
E-mail: museumofamericanspeed@gmail.com
Web Site: www.museumofamericanspeed.com
Formerly: Smith Collection Museum of American Speed
Key Personnel: C.E.O., Clay Smith; Cur., John MacKichan.
Institution Type/Description: History Museum.
Hours & Admission Prices: Guided Tours: May-Sept. Mon.-Fri. 2pm; Oct.-April Fri. 2pm. Admission. $10. &
Attendance: 5,364 (actual)

UNIVERSITY OF NEBRASKA-LINCOLN BOTANICAL GARDEN & ARBORETUM, 1309 N. 17th St, Lincoln, NE 68588-0663. Tel.: 402-472-2679. Fax: 402-472-9615.
E-mail: sbudler1@unl.edu
Web Site: www.unl.edu/bga/
Institution Type/Description: Botanical Garden.
Hours & Admission Prices: Daily dusk to dawn. No charge.

UNIVERSITY OF NEBRASKA STATE MUSEUM, 307 Morrill Hall, South of 14th and Vine Sts., Lincoln, NE 68588-0338. Tel.: 402-472-3779 & 2642 (Research Collections). Fax: 402-472-8899.
E-mail: pgrewl@unl.edu
Web Site: www.museum.unl.edu
Key Personnel: Dir., Susan Weller; Assoc. Dir., Mark Harris; Public Relations Coord., Caroline Clements.
Institution Type/Description: Natural History Museum.
Hours & Admission Prices: Museum: Mon.-Wed. & Fri.-Sat. 9:30-4:30, Thurs. 9:30-8, Sun. 12:30-4:30. Planetarium: Tues.-Sat. 9:30-4:30, Sun. 1:30-4:30. Show times vary. Museum: adults $8, seniors 65 and over & military $7, children 5-18 $4. Museum & Planetarium: adults $10, children $6; discounts to AAM members; ASTC & friends members no charge. Closed New Year's Day; Easter; Independence Day; Thanksgiving; Christmas Eve & Day. &
Attendance: 100,000 (estimated)

Lodgepole

LODGEPOLE DEPOT MUSEUM, 722 McCall St., Lodgepole, NE 69149. Mailing Address: 911 Bondegard St., Lodgepole, NE 69149. Tel.: 308-483-5339.
Web Site: www.lodgepolene.com/depot-museum
Institution Type/Description: History Museum: housed in the former Union Pacific Railroad Depot.
Hours & Admission Prices: By appointment. No charge, but donations accepted. &
Attendance: 500 (estimated)

Long Pine

LONG PINE HERITAGE SOCIETY AND HERITAGE HOUSE MUSEUM, 199 W. 3rd St., Long Pine, NE 69217-0337. Mailing Address: P.O. Box 333, Long Pine, NE 69217. Tel.: 402-273-4141.
E-mail: wardene@nntc.net
Key Personnel: Pres. (V), Wardene Roark.
Institution Type/Description: History Museum.
Hours & Admission Prices: Memorial Day to Labor Day Sat. 1-4; other times by appointment. No charge; donations accepted.
Attendance: 250 (estimated)

McCook

MUSEUM OF THE HIGH PLAINS, 421 Norris Ave., McCook, NE 69001-2003. Tel.: 308-345-3661.
E-mail: museum@cityofgoodland.org
Web Site: highplainsmuseum.org
Key Personnel: Chm. Bd. & Pres. (V), Russell Dowling; Dir., Karen Anderson; Vice Pres., Del Harsh; Treas., Korey Burkert.
Institution Type/Description: History Museum.
Hours & Admission Prices: June-Aug. Mon. & Wed.-Sat. 9-5, Sun. 1-5; Sept.-May Mon. & Wed.-Sat. 9-5. No charge; donations accepted. Closed major holidays. &
Attendance: 10,000 (estimated)

NEBRASKA STATE HISTORICAL SOCIETY'S GEORGE NORRIS STATE HISTORIC SITE, 706 Norris Ave., McCook, NE 69001-3142. Tel.: 308-345-8484.
Web Site: www.nebraskahistory.org
Formerly: Senator George Norris State Historic Site
Key Personnel: C.E.O. & Exec. Dir., Trevor Jones; Assoc. Dir., Ann Billesbach; Facilities Operator, Dawn Bates.
Institution Type/Description: Historic House Museum: 1886 home of Senator George W. Norris (1899-1944).
Hours & Admission Prices: Wed.-Fri. 1-4:30, Sat. 1-3:30. Adults $3; members & children no charge. Closed state holidays.
Attendance: 474 (actual)

Minden

HAROLD WARP PIONEER VILLAGE FOUNDATION, 138 E. Hwy. 6, Minden, NE 68959-2500. Tel.: 308-832-1181, 800-445-4447. Fax: 308-832-1181. Facebook.
E-mail: manager@pioneervillage.com
Web Site: www.pioneervillage.org
Key Personnel: Pres., Harold G. Warp; Gen. Mgr., Marshall S. Nelson.
Institution Type/Description: General Museum.
Hours & Admission Prices: Memorial Day to Labor Day daily 9-6; Sept.-May daily 9-4:30. Adults $14.25, children $7.25; discount to groups, seniors, military and AAM & ICOM members; children under 6 no charge. Two day pass available. &
Attendance: 40,000 (actual)

Murdock

MURDOCK HISTORICAL SOCIETY AND MUSEUM, 9014 310th St., Murdock, NE 68407. Tel.: 402-867-3331.
E-mail: DALEVANDEFORD@ELLIPSE.NET
Web Site: www.murdockmuseum.com/
Institution Type/Description: Historical Society Museum.
Hours & Admission Prices: Sun. 1:30-5; other times by appointment.

Nebraska City

ARBOR LODGE STATE HISTORICAL PARK, 2600 Arbor Ave., Nebraska City, NE 68410-1072. Mailing Address: P.O. Box 15, Nebraska City, NE 68410-0015. Tel.: 402-873-7222. Fax: 402-874-9885. Facebook: Arbor Lodge State Park.

E-mail: ngpc.arbor.lodge@nebraska.gov
Key Personnel: Dir., Jim Douglas; Supt., Randall J. Fox; Asst. Supt., Mark Kemper; Asst. Dir., Jim Swenson.
Institution Type/Description: Historic House Museum: 1855 home of J. Sterling Morton with addition made by eldest son Joy Morton in 1903-1905.
Hours & Admission Prices: mid-April to mid-Oct. daily 11-5. Adults $5, children 3-12 $2; children under 3 no charge. Closed Thanksgiving; Christmas.
Attendance: 75,000 (estimated)

CIVIL WAR VETERANS MUSEUM, 910 First Corso, Nebraska City, NE 68410. Tel.: 402-873-4018.
E-mail: wells55@msn.com
Institution Type/Description: Military History Museum: housed in the Grand Army of the Republic Hall; built in 1894.
Hours & Admission Prices: April-Oct. Fri.-Sun. 12-4.

KIMMEL-HARDING-NELSON CENTER FOR THE ARTS, 801 Third Corso, Nebraska City, NE 68410-2819. Tel.: 402-874-9600. Facebook: KHN Center.
E-mail: info@khncenterforthearts.org
Web Site: www.khncenterforthearts.org
Key Personnel: Program Dir., Elizabeth Stehling.
Institution Type/Description: Art Gallery.
Hours & Admission Prices: Mon.-Fri. 10-5; other times by appointment. No charge. &
Attendance: 800 (estimated)

MAYHEW CABIN WITH JOHN BROWN'S CAVE, 2012 4th Corso, Nebraska City, NE 68410. Tel.: 402-873-3115.
E-mail: mayhewcabin@hotmail.com
Web Site: www.mayhewcabin.org
Key Personnel: Dir., Bill Hayes.
Institution Type/Description: History Museum.
Hours & Admission Prices: May-Oct. Thurs.-Sun. 12-5; other times by appointment. Adults $3, children $1.
Attendance: 4,000 (estimated)

MISSOURI RIVER BASIN LEWIS & CLARK INTERPRETIVE TRAIL & VISITOR CENTER, 100 Valmont Dr., Nebraska City, NE 68410. Mailing Address: P.O. Box 785, Nebraska City, NE 68410. Tel.: 402-874-9900. Fax: 402-874-9909.
E-mail: discover@mrb-lewisandclarkcenter.org
Web Site: www.mrb-lewisandclarkcenter.org
Key Personnel: Dir., Erv Friesen.
Institution Type/Description: History Museum.
Hours & Admission Prices: May-Sept. Mon.-Sat. 9-6, Sun. 9-5; Oct.-April Mon.-Sat. 10-4, Sun. 12-4. Adults $5.50; members no charge. Closed New Year's Day; Thanksgiving; Christmas. &
Attendance: 14,000 (actual)

NEBRASKA CITY MUSEUM OF FIREFIGHTING, 1320 Central Ave., Nebraska City, NE 68410. Mailing Address: P.O. Box 376, Nebraska City, NE 68410-0376. Tel.: 402-873-4403. Fax: 402-873-5191.
E-mail: admin@ncfire.net
Web Site: www.ncmuseumoffirefighting.net
Key Personnel: Pres. (V), Steven Recker.
Institution Type/Description: Firefighting History Museum.
Hours & Admission Prices: April-Oct. Wed.-Sat. 11-5, Sun. 12-4. Adults $3, children 4-12 $1; members no charge. &
Attendance: 4,000 (estimated)

OLD FREIGHTERS MUSEUM, 407 N. 14th St., Nebraska City, NE 68410-1947. Mailing Address: P.O. Box 175, Nebraska City, NE 68410-0175. Tel.: 402-873-9360.
Institution Type/Description: History Museum: former home of the Russell-Majors-Waddell Freighting Company in 1858.
Hours & Admission Prices: Arbor Day to Oct. Fri.-Sun. 12-4.

RIVER COUNTRY NATURE CENTER, 114 S. 6th St., Nebraska City, NE 68410. Mailing Address: 719 12th Corso, Nebraska City, NE 68410-3547. Tel.: 402-873-3411.
E-mail: rcnaturecenter@windstream.net
Web Site: www.rivercountrynaturecenter.org
Institution Type/Description: Nature Center.
Hours & Admission Prices: By appointment.

TAYLOR-WESSEL-BICKEL (NELSON) HOUSE, 711 3rd Corso, Nebraska City, NE 68410-2817. Mailing Address: Nelson House, 806 1st Ave., Nebraska City, NE 68410-0075. Tel.: 402-873-9360.
Institution Type/Description: Historic House: built in 1857.
Hours & Admission Prices: By appointment. Adults $3, children $1.

WILDWOOD HISTORIC CENTER, 420 S. Steinhart Park Rd., Nebraska City, NE 68410-3300. Tel.: 402-873-6340. Facebook.
E-mail: wildwoodbarn@windstream.net
Web Site: wildwoodhistoriccenter.org
Key Personnel: Acting Chm., Pat Friedle; Museum Shop Mgr., Gail Wurtele.
Institution Type/Description: Historic House Museum: c.1869 restored two-story Victorian brick home.
Hours & Admission Prices: mid-April to Oct. Mon.-Sat. 10-5, Sun. 1-5; other times by appointment. Adults $5, children 12 & under $1. Barn no charge. &
Attendance: 3,000 (estimated)

Neligh

ANTELOPE COUNTY MUSEUM, 410 L St., Neligh, NE 68756-1419. Tel.: 402-887-5010.
E-mail: stealthecourthouse@gmail.com
Web Site: antelopecountymuseum.org
Key Personnel: Pres. & Dir., Dr. Geo. Strassler; Vice Pres., Ray Ahrens; Treas., Harlen Frasier.
Institution Type/Description: Local History Museum.
Hours & Admission Prices: Memorial Day to Labor Day: Tues.-Sat. 1-5; Sept.-May Wed.-Fri. 1-5. Adults $3; children 12 & under and members no charge. &
Attendance: 600 (estimated)

NEBRASKA STATE HISTORICAL SOCIETY'S NELIGH MILL STATE HISTORIC SITE, N St. & Wylie Dr., Neligh, NE 68756. Mailing Address: P.O. Box 271, Neligh, NE 68756-0271. Tel.: 402-887-4303. Fax: 402-887-4303.
E-mail: nshs.mill@nebraska.gov
Web Site: www.nebraskahistory.org
Formerly: Neligh Mills
Key Personnel: C.E.O. & Exec. Dir., Trevor Jones; Assoc. Dir. Education & Interpretation, Ann Billesbach; Site Supvr., Don Ofe.
Institution Type/Description: Historic Building Museum: 1873 Neligh Mills.
Hours & Admission Prices: Memorial Day-Labor Day Tues.-Sat. 10-5, Sun. 1-5; Sept.-May Mon.-Fri. 10-5. Adults $3, groups of 20 $2, children $1; discount to Time Travelers; children accompanied by an adult, youth groups, Nebraska State Historical Society members & families no charge. Closed most federal holidays.
Attendance: 2,135 (actual)

PIERSON WILDLIFE MUSEUM LEARNING CENTER, 205 E. 5th St., Neligh, NE 68756-1301. Mailing Address: P.O. Box 3, Neligh, NE 68756. Tel.: 402-887-4212 & 929-0330.
E-mail: airolg508@gmail.com
Web Site: www.piersonwildlifemuseumneligh.com
Key Personnel: Chm. (V) & Museum Shop Mgr., Gloria Christiansen; Pres., Jerry Martin; Museum Shop, Bill Hubert.
Institution Type/Description: Wildlife Museum.
Hours & Admission Prices: Summer: Tues-Sun. 1-4; Fall: Sat.-Sun. 1-4 & by appointment; Winter: by appointment. Adults $5, seniors $4, students K-12 $3; students on school field trips accompanied by teacher $1; discounts to groups of 30 or more; children under school age no charge. &
Attendance: 900 (actual)

Niobrara

NIOBRARA HISTORICAL SOCIETY MUSEUM, 89054 519 Ave., Niobrara, NE 68760-6013. Tel.: 402-857-3794.
E-mail: swansonhunting@gmail.com
Key Personnel: Pres. (V), Barb Farrar.
Institution Type/Description: History Museum.
Hours & Admission Prices: Memorial Day to Labor Day Fri. 12-3, Sat. 10-3, Sun. 1-3; other times by appointment. No charge; donations accepted. &
Attendance: 1,300 (estimated)

PONCA TRIBAL MUSEUM, 2548 Park Ave., Niobrara, NE 68760. Tel.: 402-857-3519.
E-mail: info@poncatribe-ne.org
Web Site: www.poncatribe-ne.org/culture/tribal-museum/
Key Personnel: Dir. Cultural Affairs., Gloria Hamilton.
Institution Type/Description: Native American History Museum.
Hours & Admission Prices: Mon.-Sat. 8-4. No charge. &

Norfolk

ELKHORN VALLEY MUSEUM, 515 Queen City Blvd., Norfolk, NE 68701-4060. Tel.: 402-371-3886. Fax: 402-371-3886.
E-mail: info@elkhornvalleymuseum.org
Web Site: www.elkhornvalleymuseum.org
Institution Type/Description: History Museum.
Hours & Admission Prices: Tues.-Sat. 10-5. Adults $6, seniors over 60 $5, children 3-18 $3. Closed New Year's Day; Easter; Thanksgiving; Christmas. &
Attendance: 6,250 (actual)

NORFOLK ARTS CENTER, 305 N. 5th St., Norfolk, NE 68701. Tel.: 402-371-7199. Facebook.
E-mail: info@norfolkartscenter.org
Web Site: www.norfolkartscenter.org
Key Personnel: Exec. Dir., Kara Weander-Gaster; Pres. (V), Patti Gubbels.
Institution Type/Description: Art Gallery.
Hours & Admission Prices: Tues.-Fri. 10-6, Sat. 10-4. No charge; donations accepted. &
Attendance: 1,000 (estimated)

North Platte

BUFFALO BILL RANCH STATE HISTORICAL PARK, 2921 Scouts Rest Ranch Rd., North Platte, NE 69101-8444. Tel.: 308-535-8035. Fax: 308-535-8070.
E-mail: ngpc.buffalo.bill@nebraska.gov
Web Site: outdoornebraska.org
Key Personnel: Supt., Jason Tonsfeldt.
Institution Type/Description: History Museum: housed in 1886 home of William (Buffalo Bill) Cody.
Hours & Admission Prices: May & Sept.-Oct. Mon.-Fri. 10-4; Memorial Day-Labor Day daily 9-5. Adults 13 & up $2, children 3-12 $1; children 2 & under no charge. State park permit required: daily $5 per vehicle. Times & dates of operation subject to change.
Attendance: 20,030 (actual)

CODY PARK RAILROAD MUSEUM, 1400 N. Jeffers, North Platte, NE 69101. Tel.: 308-535-6700.
Institution Type/Description: Railroad Museum.
Hours & Admission Prices: May-Sept. daily 10-6. No charge.

LINCOLN COUNTY HISTORICAL MUSEUM, 2403 N. Buffalo Bill Ave., North Platte, NE 69101-9702. Tel.: 308-534-5640.
E-mail: lincomuseum@hamilton.net
Web Site: www.lincolncountymuseum.org
Key Personnel: Chm., Phyllis Slavlik; Pres. (V), Lloyd Speicher; Dir., Cur. & Museum Shop Mgr., James Griffin.
Institution Type/Description: General Museum.
Hours & Admission Prices: May-Sept. Mon.-Sat. 9-5, Sun. 1-5. Families $10, adults 13 & over $5, seniors 55 & over and military $4; discount to groups of 10 or more; children 12 & under no charge. &
Attendance: 12,500 (actual)

NORTH PLATTE AREA CHILDREN'S MUSEUM, 314 N. Jeffers St., North Platte, NE 69101. Mailing Address: P.O. Box 2088, North Platte, NE 69103. Tel.: 308-532-3512. Facebook: North Platte Area Children's Museum.
E-mail: info@npchildrensmuseum.com
Web Site: www.npchildrensmuseum.com
Key Personnel: Dir., Casey McMann.
Institution Type/Description: Children's Museum.
Hours & Admission Prices: Tues.-Sat. 9:30-5. Children $6, adults $4, seniors $3; members and children 2 & under no charge.
Attendance: 10,000 (estimated)

O'Neill

HOLT COUNTY HISTORICAL SOCIETY MUSEUM, 401 E. Douglas, O'Neill, NE 68763. Tel.: 402-336-2344.
Institution Type/Description: Historical Society Museum.
Hours & Admission Prices: By appointment. No charge; donations accepted. Closed major holidays.
Attendance: 50 (estimated)

Oakland

SWEDISH HERITAGE CENTER, 301 N. Charde Ave., Oakland, NE 68045. Mailing Address: 1200 E. 3rd, Oakland, NE 68045. Tel.: 402-685-5489.
E-mail: foodpride1@yahoo.com
Institution Type/Description: Cultural Center.
Hours & Admission Prices: May-Sept. Tues.-Sun.; Oct.-April Sat.-Sun. No charge.

Ogallala

FRONT STREET, 519 E. First, Ogallala, NE 69153-2620. Tel.: 308-284-6000. Fax: 308-284-0865.
E-mail: frontstreet@frntst.com
Web Site: www.ogallalafrontstreet.com
Key Personnel: Dir. & C.E.O., Stacey Bauer; Dir. & C.E.O., Kathleen Bauer.
Institution Type/Description: History Museum.
Hours & Admission Prices: Mon.-Sat. 11-9. No charge; donations accepted. Closed New Year's Day; Thanksgiving; Christmas. &
Attendance: 48,854 (actual)

KEITH COUNTY HISTORICAL SOCIETY - MANSION ON THE HILL MUSEUM, 1004 N. Spruce St., Ogallala, NE 69153. Mailing Address: Keith County Historical Society, P.O. Box 5, Ogallala, NE 69153. Tel.: 308-284-0821 (summer season), 308-284-4354 (off-season).
E-mail: kchsmansion@gmail.com
Web Site: ogallalamansiononhill.com
Key Personnel: Pres. (V), Kendra Caskey; Cur. & Tour Guide Mgr., Karen A. Nelson.
Institution Type/Description: Historic House: built in 1887. Listed on the National Register of Historic Places.
Hours & Admission Prices: Fri. before Memorial Day to Sun. before Labor Day Tues.-Sat. 9-4, Sun. 11-4; other times by appointment. Adults $2, children 5-12 $1; members & children under 5 no charge. &
Attendance: 2,500 (estimated)

LAKE MCCONAUGHY VISITOR/WATER INTERPRETIVE CENTER, 1475 Hwy. 61 N., Ogallala, NE 69153. Tel.: 308-284-8800.
E-mail: ngpc.lake.mcconaughy@nebraska.gov
Web Site: www.outdoornebraska.org
Institution Type/Description: History Museum.
Hours & Admission Prices: Summer: daily 8-5; Winter Mon.-Fri. 8-5.

PETRIFIED WOOD & ART GALLERY, 418 E. 1st St., Ogallala, NE 69153-2620. Tel.: 308-284-9996. Facebook: Petrified Wood & Art Gallery.
E-mail: hhkenfi@allophone.com
Web Site: www.petrifiedwoodgallery.com
Key Personnel: Dir., Kathy Zeller; Pres. (V), Doug Teaford.
Institution Type/Description: Natural History Museum.
Hours & Admission Prices: Summer: Mon.-Sat. 8-4, Sun. 1-4. No charge; donations accepted. &
Attendance: 14,000 (estimated)

Omaha

BATCHELDER FAMILY SCOUT MUSEUM, Durham Scout Center, 12401 W. Maple Rd., Omaha, NE 68164. Tel.: 402-431-9272. Fax: 402-431-0444.
E-mail: lisa.russell@scouting.org
Web Site: www.mac-bsa.org
Key Personnel: Communications Specialist, Lisa Russell.
Institution Type/Description: Scout Museum.
Hours & Admission Prices: Call for hours. No charge. &

BEMIS CENTER FOR CONTEMPORARY ARTS, 724 S. 12th St., Omaha, NE 68102. Tel.: 402-341-7130. Fax: 402-341-9791. Facebook; Twitter; Instagram.
E-mail: info@bemiscenter.org
Web Site: www.bemiscenter.org
Key Personnel: Exec. Dir., Chris Cook.
Institution Type/Description: Contemporary Art Gallery.
Hours & Admission Prices: Tues.-Sat. 11-5; tours by appointment. No charge; donations accepted. &
Attendance: 5,736

CATHEDRAL CULTURAL CENTER, 3900 Webster St., Omaha, NE 68131-1810. Tel.: 402-551-4888.
E-mail: wjwoeger@archomaha.org
Web Site: www.cathedralartsproject.org
Key Personnel: C.E.O., Bro. William Woeger, F.S.C.; Assoc. Dir., Dorothy Begley; Chm., Joni Fogarty; Treas., Charles Schultz; Public Rels., John Wees; Museum Shop Mgr., Kathy White.
Institution Type/Description: Religious Museum.
Hours & Admission Prices: Tues.-Fri. 11-4, third Sun. of each month 10:30-4:30. Suggested Donation: $2 per person. Closed religious holidays. &
Attendance: 5,000 (estimated)

DOUGLAS COUNTY HISTORICAL SOCIETY, 5730 N. 30 St., #11B, Omaha, NE 68111-1657. Tel.: 402-451-1013 & 455-9990. Fax: 402-453-9448.
E-mail: director@omahahistory.org
Web Site: www.douglascohistory.org
Key Personnel: Exec. Dir., Kathryn Aultz.
Institution Type/Description: Historical Society Museum: housed in the General Crook House; built in 1879. Listed on the National Register of Historic Places.
Hours & Admission Prices: Museum: Tues.-Fri. 10-4, Sat.-Sun. 1-4; groups by appointment. Jan. to mid-Nov. adults $5, students $4, children 6-12 $3; members no charge. Mid-Nov. to Dec. adults $6, students $4, children 6-12 $3; members no charge.

THE DURHAM MUSEUM, 801 S. 10th St., Omaha, NE 68108-3205. Tel.: 402-444-5071. Fax: 402-444-5397.
E-mail: info@durhammuseum.org
Web Site: www.durhammuseum.org
Formerly: Durham Western Heritage Museum
Key Personnel: Exec. Dir., Christi Janssen; Dir. Finance & Admin., Amy Carolus; Dir. Education, Jill Bruckner; Exhibit Mgr., Mark Howard; Cur., Carrie Wieners; Collections Mgr., Larissa Krayer.
Institution Type/Description: History Museum: housed in c.1930, former Union Pacific Railroad Station.
Hours & Admission Prices: Tues. 10-8, Wed.-Sat. 10-5, Sun. 1-5. Adults $9, senior citizens 62 & over $7, children 3-12 $6; children under 2 & under & members no charge. Closed New Year's Day, Memorial Day, Independence Day, Labor Day, Thanksgiving, Christmas. &
Attendance: 161,000 (estimated)

EL MUSEO LATINO, 4701 S. 25th St., Omaha, NE 68107-2728. Tel.: 402-731-1137. Fax: 402-733-7012.
E-mail: mgarcia@elmuseolatino.org
Web Site: elmuseolatino.org
Key Personnel: C.E.O., Founder & Exec. Dir., Magdalena A. Garcia; Pres. (V), Jim Mammel; Vice Pres., Perry Poyner; Treas., Maria Arbelaez; Sec., Rita Melgares.
Institution Type/Description: Latino Art & History Museum.
Hours & Admission Prices: Mon., Wed. & Fri. 10-5, Tues. & Thurs. 1-5, Sat. 10-2. Adults $5, college students $4, senior citizens & students K-12 $3.50; discounts to AAM & ICOM members; children under 5 & members no charge. Closed New Year's Eve & Day; Independence Day; Thanksgiving; Christmas. &
Attendance: 50,000 (actual)

FLORENCE MILL, 9102 N. 30th St., Omaha, NE 68112. Mailing Address: 606 S. 52nd St., Omaha, NE 68106. Tel.: 402-551-1233. Fax: 402-561-0024.
E-mail: theflorencemill@gmail.com
Web Site: www.theflorencemill.org
Institution Type/Description: Historic Mill: built in 1846.
Hours & Admission Prices: Memorial Day to Labor Day Tues.-Sun. 1-5; other times by appointment.

FREEDOM PARK NAVY MUSEUM, 2497 Freedom Park Rd., Omaha, NE 68110-2745. Mailing Address: 1523 S. 24th St., Omaha, NE 68108. Tel.: 402-444-5955. Fax: 402-444-6838. Facebook: Freedom Park.
Web Site: www.cityofomaha.org
Key Personnel: Dir. Parks & Recreation, Brook Bench.
Institution Type/Description: Military Museum.
Hours & Admission Prices: June-Oct. Sat. 10-3. No charge; donations accepted.
Attendance: 3,300 (actual)

GENERAL CROOK HOUSE MUSEUM AND LIBRARY/ ARCHIVES CENTER, 5730 N. 30th St., 11B, Omaha, NE 68111-1658. Tel.: 402-455-9990. Fax: 402-453-9448.
E-mail: house@omahahistory.org
Web Site: www.omahahistory.org
Key Personnel: Exec. Dir. Historical Society, Betty J. Davis; Pres. Bd. Dirs., Mary Maxwell; Cur. General Crook House, Patricia Pixley; Chm. (V) & Museum

Shop Mgr., Virgie Ward; Dir. Education & Public Programs, Liz Rea; Dir. Library Archives Center, Travis Sing; Archivist & Librarian, Don Snoddy; Research Specialist, Gary Rosenberg; Registrar, Elizabeth Krecek.
Institution Type/Description: Library & Historical House Museum: 1878 General Crook House & archives center located at Historic Fort Omaha now the campus of Metropolitan Community College.
Hours & Admission Prices: Museum: Mon.-Fri. 10-4, Sat.-Sun. 1-4; other times by appointment. Library: Tues.-Fri. 10-4. Adults $5, students $4, children 6-12 $3; members & library no charge. Closed holidays. &
Attendance: 18,000 (estimated)

GERALD R. FORD CONSERVATION CENTER, 1326 S. 32nd St., Omaha, NE 68105-2044. Tel.: 402-595-1180. Fax: 402-595-1178.
E-mail: nshs.grfcc@nebraska.gov
Institution Type/Description: Conservation Center.
Hours & Admission Prices: By appointment only. &

GREAT PLAINS BLACK HISTORY MUSEUM, 105 N. 31st Ave., Ste. 219, Omaha, NE 68131. Fax: 866-791-7024. Facebook: Great Plains Black History Museum.
E-mail: gpblackmuseum@aol.com
Web Site: www.gpblackmuseum.org
Key Personnel: Chm. (V) & Pres. (V), Rudy Smith; Vice Pres., Terri Sanders.
Institution Type/Description: History Museum.
Hours & Admission Prices: Call for hours. No charge; donations accepted. &
Attendance: 10,000 (estimated)

HOT SHOPS ART CENTER, 1301 Nichols St., Omaha, NE 68102-4212. Tel.: 402-342-6452.
E-mail: manager@hotshopsartcenter.com
Web Site: www.hotshopsartcenter.com
Institution Type/Description: Art Gallery.
Hours & Admission Prices: Daily 8-5; other times by appointment.

JOSLYN ART MUSEUM, 2200 Dodge St., Omaha, NE 68102-1292. Tel.: 402-342-3300. Fax: 402-342-2376. Facebook.
E-mail: kdurkin@joslyn.org
Web Site: www.joslyn.org
Key Personnel: Exec. Dir. & C.E.O., Jack F. Becker, Ph.D.; Chm. Bd., Paul Smith; Dir. Education & Outreach, Nancy Round; Asst. to Exec. Dir. & C.E.O., Kristy Durkin; Chief Cur. Richard & Mary Holland Cur. American Western Art, Toby Jurovics; Cur. Contemporary Art, Karin Campbell; Cur. European Art, Dana Cowen, Ph.D.; Dir. Devel., Hillary Nather-Detisch.
Institution Type/Description: Art Museum.
Hours & Admission Prices: Tues.-Wed. & Fri.-Sun. 10-4, Thurs. 10-8. General admission no charge. Major Exhibitions: adults $10; college students with ID $5; members and children 17 & under no charge. Closed major holidays. &
Attendance: 180,000 (actual)

JOSLYN CASTLE TRUST, 3902 Davenport St., Omaha, NE 68131. Tel.: 402-595-2199. Fax: 402-595-1007. Facebook: Joslyn Castle.
E-mail: info@joslyncastle.com
Web Site: www.joslyncastle.com
Key Personnel: Interim Exec. Dir., Catherine Demes Maydew; Dir. Events, Sherri Moore; Dir. Buildings & Grounds, Trevor King; Dir. Mktg. & Devel., Amy Trenolone; Facilities Asst., Martin Digiacomo.
Institution Type/Description: Historic Building: housed in the former home of George & Sarah Joslyn; built in 1903.
Hours & Admission Prices: Tours: 1st & 3rd Sun. each month 1, 2, & 3; groups by appointment. Adults $10, students, senior & military $8; children under 5 no charge.
Attendance: 18,000 (estimated)

LAURITZEN GARDENS, 100 Bancroft St., Omaha, NE 68108. Tel.: 402-346-4002. Fax: 402-346-8948. Facebook.
E-mail: a.morris@omahabotanicalgardens.org
Web Site: www.lauritzengardens.org
Key Personnel: Exec. Dir., Spencer Crews.
Institution Type/Description: Living Plant Museum.
Hours & Admission Prices: mid-May to mid-Sept. Mon.-Tues. 9-8, Wed.-Sun. 9-5; mid-Sept. to mid-May daily 9-5. Adults $10, children 6-12 $5, members & children under 6 no charge. Tram Tours: $3 per person (May-Oct.). Closed New Year's Day; Thanksgiving; Christmas. &
Attendance: 177,788 (actual)

LOVE'S JAZZ AND ARTS CENTER, 2510 N. 24th St., Omaha, NE 68111. Tel.: 402-502-5291.
Web Site: www.ljac.org

Institution Type/Description: Art Museum.
Hours & Admission Prices: Call for hours.

MORMON TRAIL CENTER AT HISTORIC WINTER QUARTERS, 3215 State St., Omaha, NE 68112. Tel.: 402-453-9372. Fax: 402-453-1538. Facebook: Mormon Trail Center at Historic Winter Quarters.
E-mail: hswinter@ldschurch.org
Institution Type/Description: Visitors Center.
Hours & Admission Prices: Daily 9-9. No charge. Closed Thanksgiving; Christmas. &
Attendance: 55,720 (actual)

NEBRASKA JEWISH HISTORICAL SOCIETY AND RIEKES MUSEUM, 333 S. 132nd St., Omaha, NE 68154-2106. Tel.: 402-334-6442. Fax: 402-334-6507. Facebook.
E-mail: njhs@jewishomaha.org
Web Site: www.nebraskajhs.com
Key Personnel: Dir., Renee Ratner Corcoran; Pres. (V), Robert Belgrade.
Institution Type/Description: History Museum.
Hours & Admission Prices: Mon.-Thurs. 10-4. Tours by appointment. No charge; donations accepted. &
Attendance: 450 (estimated)

OMAHA CHILDREN'S MUSEUM, 500 S. 20th St., Omaha, NE 68102-2505. Tel.: 402-342-6164. Fax: 402-342-6165. Facebook.
E-mail: info@ocm.org
Web Site: www.ocm.org
Key Personnel: Exec. Dir., Lindy Hoyer.
Institution Type/Description: Children's Museum.
Hours & Admission Prices: Call for hours. Admission $14, seniors $13; discounts to ASTC members; children under 2 & members no charge. Closed major holidays. &
Attendance: 302,901 (actual)

OMAHA'S HENRY DOORLY ZOO AND AQUARIUM, 3701 S. 10th St., Omaha, NE 68107-2200. Tel.: 402-733-8401. Fax: 402-733-7868.
E-mail: connect@omahazoo.com
Web Site: www.omahazoo.com
Key Personnel: Exec. Dir., Dennis E. Pate; Pres. (V), John Boyer.
Institution Type/Description: Zoo.
Hours & Admission Prices: April-Oct.: 9-5, Nov.-March: 10-4. Zoo admission Dec.-Feb: adults 12 & over $16.95, seniors 65 & over & military $15.95, children 3-11 $10.95, military child 3-11 $9.95, children 2 & under no charge. Zoo admission Mar.-April & Oct.-Nov.: adults 12 & over $20.95, seniors 65 & over & military $19.95, children 3-11 $13.95, military child 3-11 $12.95, children 2 & under no charge. Zoo admission May-Sept.: adults 12 & over $24.95, seniors 65 & over & military $23.95, children 3-11 $17.95, military child 3-11 $16.95, children 2 & under no charge. Closed Christmas. &
Attendance: 1,608,349 (actual)

SOKOL SOUTH OMAHA CZECHOSLOVAK MUSEUM, 2021 U St., Omaha, NE 68107. Mailing Address: 1335 Z St., Omaha, NE 68107-3567. Tel.: 402-291-2893.
Institution Type/Description: Czech & Slovak Cultural History.
Hours & Admission Prices: By appointment. &

WINTER QUARTERS MILL MUSEUM, 9102 N. 30th St., Omaha, NE 68112-1816. Mailing Address: 606 S. 52nd St., Omaha, NE 68106. Tel.: 402-551-1233.
Key Personnel: Dir., Pres. (V) & Museum Shop Mgr., Linda Meigs.
Institution Type/Description: History Museum: founded in 1846 as the Mormon Winter Quarters gristmill; rebuilt by a Gold-Rusher; it contains some of the original hand-hewn beams & wooden pegs cut for the gristmill. Listed on the National Register of Historic Places.
Hours & Admission Prices: May-Oct. Wed.-Sun. 1-5; other times by appointment. No charge; donations accepted.
Attendance: 9,000 (estimated)

Ord

VALLEY COUNTY MUSEUM, 117 S. 16th St., Ord, NE 68862. Mailing Address: P.O. Box 101, Ord, NE 68862. Tel.: 308-728-3044.
E-mail: kristinafoth@ordnebraska.com
Web Site: www.ordnebraska.com/play/history
Institution Type/Description: History Museum.

Hours & Admission Prices: May-Sept. Mon.-Fri. 1-4; other times by appointment. No charge.

Oshkosh

HISTORICAL SOCIETY OF GARDEN COUNTY, West 1st & Avenue E, Oshkosh, NE 69154. Mailing Address: P.O. Box 193, Oshkosh, NE 69154-0193. Tel.: 308-772-3848.
Key Personnel: Chm. (V), Betty Kechley; Pres. (V), Verna Bairn.
Institution Type/Description: General Museum: housed in 1906-1907 Silver Hill Museum.
Hours & Admission Prices: Memorial Day-Labor Day Mon.-Sat. 9-4, Sun. 2-6; call for additional hours. No charge; donations accepted. &
Attendance: 345 (actual)

Pawnee City

PAWNEE CITY HISTORICAL SOCIETY & MUSEUM, Hwy. 50/8 East, Pawnee City, NE 68420. Mailing Address: P.O. Box 33, Pawnee City, NE 68420-0033. Tel.: 402-852-3131. Facebook.
E-mail: my.blue.heaven@windstream.net
Web Site: pawneecitymuseum.com
Key Personnel: Chm., Roy Mullin; Vice Pres., Rita Shaw; Treas., Yvonne Dalluge.
Institution Type/Description: Regional History Museum: 22 historic buildings on grounds.
Hours & Admission Prices: Summer: Wed.-Fri. 10-12 & 1-4, Sat. 10-12 & 1-4; Winter: Thurs. 10-4; other times by appointment. Adults $5; members no charge. &
Attendance: 2,500 (estimated)

Pierce

PIERCE HISTORICAL SOCIETY, Gilman Park, Pierce, NE 68767. Mailing Address: Gilman Park, P.O. Box 122, Pierce, NE 68767. Tel.: 402-329-4265. Facebook: Pierce Historical Society.
E-mail: museum@ptcnet.net
Web Site: www.ptcnet.net/museum
Institution Type/Description: Historical Society Museum.
Hours & Admission Prices: Memorial Day to Labor Day Sun. 1:30-4:30; other times by appointment. No charge; donations accepted. &
Attendance: 461 (actual)

Pilger

HISTORICAL SOCIETY OF STANTON COUNTY MUSEUMS AT STANTON AND PILGER, INC., 345 N. Main St., Pilger, NE 68768. Mailing Address: P.O. Box 234, Stanton, NE 68779. Tel.: 402-396-3422.
E-mail: rjensen98@cableone.net
Web Site: www.stantoncountyhistoricalsociety.org
Key Personnel: Pres. (V), James Duncan; Vice Pres., Rebecca Frerichs; Treas., Virgine Jensen; Sec., Frances Beck.
Institution Type/Description: Historical Society Museum.
Hours & Admission Prices: Pilger Museum: Memorial Day, Pilger Days & Labor Day; other times by appointment. Stanton Heritage Museum: May-Oct. Sat. 2-4; other times by appointment. No charge; donations accepted.
Attendance: 450 (estimated)

Plainview

PLAINVIEW HISTORICAL SOCIETY, 304 S. Main St., Plainview, NE 68769. Mailing Address: P.O. Box 495, Plainview, NE 68769. Tel.: 402-582-4730.
E-mail: plainviewdepot@yahoo.com
Institution Type/Description: Historic Building: housed in a former railroad depot; built in 1880.
Hours & Admission Prices: June-Aug. Tues.-Thurs. 1-4; other times by appointment. No charge; donations accepted.
Attendance: 300 (estimated)

PLAINVIEW KLOWN DOLL MUSEUM, Hwy. 20, Plainview, NE 68769. Mailing Address: P.O. Box 813, Plainview, NE 68769-0813. Tel.: 402-582-4433.
E-mail: clowndollmuseum@yahoo.com
Web Site: www.klowndollmuseum.com
Key Personnel: Pres. (V), Corrine Janovec.
Institution Type/Description: Clown Doll Museum.
Hours & Admission Prices: Memorial Day-Labor Day Mon.-Sat. 1-5; other times by appointment. No charge. &
Attendance: 650 (estimated)

Plattsmouth

CASS COUNTY HISTORICAL SOCIETY MUSEUM, 646 Main
St., Plattsmouth, NE 68048-1852. Tel.: 402-296-4770.
E-mail: ccohsm@windstream.net
Web Site: www.casscountynemuseum.org
Key Personnel: Pres., Douglas V. Duey; Vice Pres., Susan Rice; Treas., Diane
Berlett; Sec., Pat Meisinger; Cur., Margo Prentiss.
Institution Type/Description: Historical Society Museum.
Hours & Admission Prices: April-Oct. Tues.-Sun. 12-4; Nov.-March Tues. 12-
4. Adults $2.50; AAM, ICOM, & museum members no charge. Closed holidays.
Attendance: 3,000 (estimated)

Red Cloud

WEBSTER COUNTY HISTORICAL MUSEUM, 721 W. 4th
Ave., Red Cloud, NE 68970-2221. Mailing Address: P.O. Box 464,
Red Cloud, NE 68970-0464. Tel.: 402-746-2444. Facebook.
E-mail: wchmdirector@gpcom.net
Key Personnel: Pres., Jim Fitzgibbon; Dir., Teresa Young.
Institution Type/Description: General Museum.
Hours & Admission Prices: April-Oct. Tues.-Sun. 1-5. Adults $4, high school stu-
dents $1.50, elementary school students $1; members no charge. Closed Easter;
Mother's Day; Father's Day; Independence Day.
Attendance: 1,000 (estimated)

WILLA CATHER FOUNDATION, 413 N. Webster St., Red Cloud,
NE 68970-2466. Tel.: 402-746-2653. Fax: 402-746-2652.
E-mail: info@willacather.org
Web Site: www.willacather.org
Formerly: Willa Cather Pioneer Memorial and Educational Foundation
Key Personnel: Exec. Dir. & Museum Shop Mgr., Leslie C. Levy; Chm. (V),
Thomas Gallagher.
Institution Type/Description: Art Gallery & Historic Museum.
Hours & Admission Prices: By appointment. Town & Country Tours: adults $15,
children 5-12 $6; children 4 & under no charge. Closed New Year's Day; Easter;
Independence Day; Thanksgiving; Christmas.
Attendance: 10,000 (estimated)

Republican City

LIGHTHOUSE MUSEUM, 103 Berrigan Rd., Republican City, NE
68971. Mailing Address: 202 Center Ave., Republican City, NE
68971-7110. Tel.: 308-799-2033.
Institution Type/Description: History Museum.
Hours & Admission Prices: Memorial Day to Labor Day Sat.-Sun. 10-5; other times
by appointment.

Royal

**ASHFALL FOSSIL BEDS STATE HISTORICAL PARK &
VISITOR'S CENTER,** 86930 517 Ave., Royal, NE 68773. Tel.:
402-893-2000.
E-mail: ashfall2@unl.edu
Web Site: ashfall.unl.edu
Institution Type/Description: Park Museum & Visitor's Center.
Hours & Admission Prices: May Tues.-Sat. 10-4; Memorial Day to Labor Day
Mon.-Sat. 9-5, Sun. 11-5; Sept.-Oct. 9 Tues.-Sat. 10-4, Sun. 1-4. Admission $5.

Rushville

**SHERIDAN COUNTY HISTORICAL SOCIETY - RUSHVILLE
MUSEUM/ARMSTRONG HOUSE,** 408 E. 2nd, Rushville, NE
69360-0274. Mailing Address: P.O. Box 274, Rushville, NE
69360-0274. Tel.: 308-327-2985 & 360-0299 (cell).
E-mail: nitz@gpcom.net
Formerly: Sheridan County Historical Society - Armstrong House Museum
Key Personnel: Cur., Jerry Wellnitz.
Institution Type/Description: Historical Society Museum: house built in 1890.
Hours & Admission Prices: Memorial Day to Labor Day Mon.-Fri. 9-5; other times
by appointment. No charge; donations accepted.
Attendance: 850 (actual)

Saint Paul

MUSEUM OF NEBRASKA MAJOR LEAGUE BASEBALL, 619
Howard Ave., Saint Paul, NE 68873-2022. Tel.: 308-754-5558.
Facebook: Museum of Nebraska Major League Baseball.
E-mail: stpaulcham@qwestoffice.net
Web Site: www.nebraskabaseballmuseum.com

Institution Type/Description: Baseball Museum.
Hours & Admission Prices: Memorial Day-Labor Day Mon.-Fri. 10-4, Sat. 10-2;
other times by appointment. No charge.
Attendance: 800 (actual)

Schuyler

SCHUYLER/COLFAX COUNTY MUSEUM, 309 E. 11th St.,
Schuyler, NE 68661. Tel.: 402-352-2301 & 352-3195.
E-mail: sccmuseum@gmail.com
Key Personnel: C.E.O., Nadine Beran.
Institution Type/Description: History Museum.
Hours & Admission Prices: Jan.-March Tues. forenoons; April-Dec. Sun. 2-4, Tues.
forenoons; tours by appointment. No charge; donations accepted.
Attendance: 649 (actual)

Scotia

HAPPY JACK PEAK AND CHALK MINE, 80131 Hwy. 11,
Scotia, NE 68875. Mailing Address: P.O. Box 74, Scotia, NE
68875. Tel.: 308-245-3276. Facebook: Happy Jack Chalk Mine.
E-mail: info@happyjackchalkmine.org
Web Site: www.happyjackchalkmine.org
Institution Type/Description: Mine Museum.
Hours & Admission Prices: Memorial Day to Labor Day daily 10-5; Sept. Fri.-Sun.
10-5. Tours: adults $6.50, seniors 60 & over and children 6-12 $5.25; children 5
& under no charge.

Scottsbluff

RIVERSIDE DISCOVERY CENTER, 1600 S. Beltline Hwy. West,
Scottsbluff, NE 69361-1331. Tel.: 308-630-6236. Fax: 308-632-
2953.
E-mail: anne.james@riversidediscoverycenter.org
Web Site: riversidediscoverycenter.org
Key Personnel: Exec. Dir., Anne James.
Institution Type/Description: Zoo.
Hours & Admission Prices: April-Oct. daily 9:30-4:30; Nov.-March daily 10:30-
3:30. Adults $6, senior citizens $5, children 5-12 $4; discounts to AZA members
& groups; children under 4 & members no charge.
Attendance: 34,000 (actual)

WEST NEBRASKA ARTS CENTER GALLERY, 106 E. 18th St.,
Scottsbluff, NE 69361-2423. Tel.: 308-632-2226.
E-mail: donna@thewnac.com
Institution Type/Description: Art Gallery.
Hours & Admission Prices: Tues.-Fri. 9-5, Sat.-Sun. 1-5. No charge.

Scribner

MUSBACH MUSEUM, 429 Main St., Scribner, NE 68057. Mailing
Address: P.O. Box 136, Scribner, NE 68057. Tel.: 402-664-2788.
Institution Type/Description: History Museum.
Hours & Admission Prices: By appointment.

Seward

BARTELS MUSEUM - CONCORDIA UNIVERSITY, Link
Library, 800 N. Columbia Ave., Seward, NE 68434. Tel.: 402-643-
3566; 402-643-7253. Fax: 402-643-4073.
E-mail: marvin.plamann@cune.edu
Key Personnel: Dir., Marvin Plamann.
Institution Type/Description: Geology Museum.
Hours & Admission Prices: Sept.-April Mon.-Thurs. 8am to midnight, Fri. 8-5, Sat.
12-5, Sun. 1-5; Summer: call for hours. No charge.
Attendance: 250

MARXHAUSEN ART GALLERY, Concordia University, 800 N.
Columbia Ave., Seward, NE 68434-1500. Tel.: 402-643-3651 &
7490. Fax: 402-643-4073.
E-mail: jbockelman@cune.edu
Web Site: www.cune.edu/arts/
Key Personnel: Cur., James E. Bockelman.
Institution Type/Description: Art Gallery.
Hours & Admission Prices: Sept.-May Mon.-Fri. 11-4, Sat.-Sun. 1-4. No charge;
donations accepted. Closed Easter weekend; week of Thanksgiving; weeks
before & after Christmas; school recesses including summer break.

Sidney

FORT SIDNEY MUSEUM & POST COMMANDER'S HOME,
6th Ave. & Jackson St., Sidney, NE 69162. Mailing Address: P.O.
Box 596, Sidney, NE 69162-0596. Tel.: 308-254-2150 & 2959.
E-mail: rjorg@charter.net
Key Personnel: Pres., Roger Jorgensen; Vice Pres. & Museum Shop Mgr., Duane
Nightingale; Treas., Brenda Blanke; Bd. Member, Audrey Tremain; Bd.
Member, Gary Schmidt; Bd. Member, Ron Leal; Bd. Member, Julie Gehrig; Bd.
Member, Stephanie Disney; Sec., LaDonna Jung.
Institution Type/Description: General Museum on a Historic Building & site: 1871
Commanding Officer's Quarters; 1872 Powder House or Magazine; 1884
Officers' Quarters; Carriage House.
Hours & Admission Prices: Museum: Memorial Day-Labor Day daily 9-5; Dec.
Sat.-Sun. 1-4; other times by appointment. Commander's Home: June-Aug. &
Old Fashioned Christmas. No charge; donations accepted. &
Attendance: 2,808 (actual)

Springfield

WEISS STUDIOS AND GARDENS, 13603 Pflug Rd., Springfield,
NE 68059. Tel.: 402-680-0642 & 0224.
Web Site: www.carlweissart.com
Institution Type/Description: Art Gallery.
Hours & Admission Prices: Call for hours.

Stuart

WHITE HORSE MUSEUM AND HERITAGE VILLAGE, Hwy.
20, Stuart, NE 68780-5847. Mailing Address: P.O. Box 118, Stuart,
NE 68780. Tel.: 402-924-3861.
E-mail: visitorinfo@stuartwhitehorsemuseum.com
Web Site: www.stuartwhitehorsemuseum.com
Key Personnel: Dir., Donald J. Schmaderer.
Institution Type/Description: History Museum.
Hours & Admission Prices: Memorial Day to Labor Day call for hours. Adults $3.
Attendance: 100 (estimated)

Sutton

SUTTON HISTORICAL SOCIETY, 604 S. Way Ave., Sutton, NE
68979-2142. Tel.: 402-773-0222.
E-mail: suttonnehistory@gmail.com
Web Site: suttonhistoricalsociety.blogspot.com
Institution Type/Description: Historical Society Museum: housed in the former
home of pioneers, John and Emma Gray; built in 1908.
Hours & Admission Prices: Call for hours.

Syracuse

OTOE COUNTY MUSEUM OF MEMORIES, 1621 Thorne St.,
Syracuse, NE 68446-9730. Tel.: 402-269-2355.
E-mail: pmwitte@windstream.net
Key Personnel: Pres., Phyllis Witte; Cur. & Treas., Rose Garey; Pres. (V), Phyllis
Witte.
Institution Type/Description: History Museum.
Hours & Admission Prices: May-Sept. Sun. 1:30-4. No charge; donations accepted.
&
Attendance: 1,500 (estimated)

Table Rock

TABLE ROCK HISTORICAL SOCIETY AND MUSEUMS,
62660 Rd. 718, Table Rock, NE 68447. Mailing Address: P.O. Box
66, Table Rock, NE 68447. Tel.: 402-839-3006. Fax: 402-839-
4135.
E-mail: mustanggregg@neb.rr.com
Key Personnel: Pres. (V), Gregg Clement; Sec., Ronda Freeman.
Institution Type/Description: General Museum.
Hours & Admission Prices: May-Sept. Sun. 1-4; other times by appointment. No
charge; donations accepted. &
Attendance: 800 (actual)

Tecumseh

JOHNSON COUNTY HISTORICAL SOCIETY & MUSEUM,
3rd & Lincoln Streets, Tecumseh, NE 68450-2116. Mailing
Address: 231 Lincoln St., Tecumseh, NE 68450. Tel.: 402-335-
5900.
E-mail: jc10928@windstream.net

Key Personnel: Pres. & Cur., Boyd C. Maddox.
Institution Type/Description: History Museum: housed in 1889 Christian Church
Building.
Hours & Admission Prices: May-Oct. Tues.-Fri. 1-4; other times by appointment.
No charge; donations accepted.
Attendance: 100 (estimated)

Tekamah

BURT COUNTY MUSEUM, 319 N. 13th St., Tekamah, NE 68061-
1503. Mailing Address: P.O. Box 125, Tekamah, NE 68061-0125.
Tel.: 402-374-1505.
E-mail: burtcomuseum@abbnebraska.com
Web Site: sites.google.com/site/officialburtcountymuseum
Key Personnel: Dir. & Museum Mgr., Bonnie Newell; Pres., Marlene Kaeding;
Treas., Lisa Anderson.
Institution Type/Description: General Museum: housed in c.1904 home of E.C.
Houston. Listed on National Register of Historic Places.
Hours & Admission Prices: Tues., Thurs. & Sat. 1-5. No charge; donations
accepted. Closed major holidays.
Attendance: 2,712 (actual)

Thedford

THEDFORD ART GALLERY, 509 Court St., Thedford, NE 69166.
Tel.: 308-645-2586 & 2396.
Institution Type/Description: Art Gallery.
Hours & Admission Prices: Jan.-April Tues.-Sat. 1-5; May-Dec. Tues.-Sat. 9-5;
other times by appointment. &

THOMAS COUNTY HISTORICAL SOCIETY MUSEUM,
Mailing Address: 609 Court St., P.O. Box 224, Thedford, NE
69166. Tel.: 308-645-2489.
E-mail: hwhite@neb-sandhills.net
Key Personnel: Contact Person, Helen White.
Institution Type/Description: Historical Society Museum.
Hours & Admission Prices: Memorial Day to Labor Day Mon., Wed. & Fri. 10-12
& 2-4; other times by appointment. No charge.
Attendance: 300 (estimated)

Tobias

TOBIAS COMMUNITY HISTORICAL SOCIETY, Main St.,
Tobias, NE 68453-2073. Mailing Address: 561 County Rd. 5,
Tobias, NE 68453-2073. Tel.: 402-243-2356.
E-mail: rjrada@diodecom.net
Key Personnel: Pres. (V), Judith K. Rada; Sec. & Cataloging, Mary Kronhofman.
Institution Type/Description: General Museum: housed in original bank & Tobias
Print Shop, saved in the 1891 fire which burned most of the business district.
Hours & Admission Prices: By appointment only. No charge; donations accepted.
&
Attendance: 100 (estimated)

Valentine

CHERRY COUNTY HISTORICAL SOCIETY, Main St. & Hwy.
20, Valentine, NE 69201. Mailing Address: P.O. Box 284,
Valentine, NE 69201-0284. Tel.: 402-376-2015.
Key Personnel: C.E.O. & Pres. (V), Joyce Muirhead; Cur. & Museum Shop Mgr.,
Jan Howell.
Institution Type/Description: History Museum.
Hours & Admission Prices: Memorial Day to Labor Day Thurs.-Sat. 1-4:30; other
times by appointment. Adults $1, children under 12 $.50; members no charge. &
Attendance: 450 (estimated)

FORT NIOBRARA NATIONAL WILDLIFE REFUGE, 39983
Refuge Rd., Valentine, NE 69201. Tel.: 402-376-3789. Fax: 402-
376-3217.
E-mail: fortniobrara@fws.gov
Web Site: fortniobrara.fws.gov
Key Personnel: Refuge Mgr., Steven A. Hicks.
Institution Type/Description: Wildlife Refuge.
Hours & Admission Prices: Daily sunrise-sunset. No charge. Visitor Center:
Memorial Day-Labor Day daily 8-4:30; Sept.-May Mon.-Fri. 8-4:30. No charge;
donations accepted. &
Attendance: 50,000 (estimated)

Valley

VALLEY COMMUNITY HISTORICAL SOCIETY, INC., 218 W. Alexander St., Valley, NE 68064. Mailing Address: P.O. Box 685, Valley, NE 68064-0685. Tel.: 402-359-5877, 5323 & 2339, 402-320-4879.
Web Site: www.valleyne.org
Key Personnel: Pres., Tom Batten; Vice Pres., Pat Clauson; Treas. & Sec., Julia A. Allen.
Institution Type/Description: Local History Museum: housed in 1872 schoolhouse, then served as a Baptist Church & later a Catholic Church.
Hours & Admission Prices: Call for hours. No charge; donations accepted. &
Attendance: 400 (actual)

Wahoo

SAUNDERS COUNTY HISTORICAL COMPLEX, 240 N. Walnut, Wahoo, NE 68066-1858. Tel.: 402-443-3090. Facebook.
E-mail: saunderscomuseum@hotmail.com
Web Site: www.saunderscomuseum.org
Key Personnel: Pres., Kurt Mady; Dir. & Cur., Erin Hauser; Museum Shop Mgr., Lila Zech.
Institution Type/Description: Historical Society Museum Complex.
Hours & Admission Prices: Tues.-Sat. 10-4. No charge; donations accepted. Closed major holidays. &
Attendance: 11,000 (estimated)

Walthill

SUSAN LA FLESCHE PICOTTE CENTER, 505 Matthewson St., Walthill, NE 68067. Mailing Address: 2517 H Ave., Walthill, NE 68067-5015. Tel.: 402-406-5966.
E-mail: pmchar@hotmail.com
Key Personnel: Chm. (V), Keith Mahaney.
Institution Type/Description: Historic Building: housed in the former hospital built in 1910 by Dr. Susan La Flesche Picotte, the first Native American woman physician in the U.S.
Hours & Admission Prices: By appointment. No charge. &

Weeping Water

WEEPING WATER VALLEY HISTORICAL SOCIETY, 215 W. Eldora Ave., Weeping Water, NE 68463. Mailing Address: P.O. Box 43, Weeping Water, NE 68463-0043. Tel.: 402-267-4925.
E-mail: wd85407@navix.net
Web Site: weepingwaterhistory.org
Key Personnel: Chm. & Pres. (V), Doris Duff; Treas., Dale Nielsen.
Institution Type/Description: History & Medical Museum: located on the site of the oldest First Congregational Parsonage in state.
Hours & Admission Prices: May-Sept. Sun. 1-5. Memory Lane call for hours. No charge; donations accepted. &
Attendance: 2,200 (estimated)

West Point

CUMING COUNTY HISTORICAL MUSEUM COMPLEX, 227 N. Main St., West Point, NE 68778. Mailing Address: 227 N. Main St., West Point, NE 68788. Tel.: 402-372-3401.
E-mail: kelly@cumingcountyed.com
Key Personnel: Pres. (V), Michael Westerman.
Institution Type/Description: Historical Society Museum.
Hours & Admission Prices: Aug. during the Cuming County Fair (four days only). &

Wilber

WILBER CZECH MUSEUM, 224 N. High St., Wilber, NE 68465. Tel.: 402-821-2574.
E-mail: dorisourecky@gmail.com
Key Personnel: Pres. (V), Doris Ourecky; Gift Shop Mgr., LaVern Aksamit.
Institution Type/Description: General Museum.
Hours & Admission Prices: April-Dec. daily 1-4; other times by appointment. No charge; donations accepted. Closed national holidays. &
Attendance: 3,900 (estimated)

Winnebago

ANGEL DECORA MUSEUM AND RESEARCH CENTER, 601 E. College Dr., Winnebago, NE 68071. Mailing Address: P.O. Box 687, Winnebago, NE 68071. Tel.: 402-878-2380, ext. 113.

E-mail: smith_deleon77@yahoo.com
Key Personnel: Dir., Emily Smith-deLeon; Chm. (V), David Smith.
Institution Type/Description: History Museum.
Hours & Admission Prices: Mon.-Fri. 9-12 & 1-4. No charge; donations accepted. Closed holidays. &
Attendance: 400 (estimated)

Wisner

WISNER HERITAGE MUSEUM, 920 Ave. "E", Wisner, NE 68791. Mailing Address: P.O. Box 842, Wisner, NE 68791-0842. Tel.: 402-529-3226.
E-mail: kelly@cumingcountyed.com
Key Personnel: Pres. (V), Gregg Moeller.
Institution Type/Description: History Museum.
Hours & Admission Prices: Sat.-Sun. 1-4; other times by appointment. No charge; donations accepted. &
Attendance: 200 (estimated)

York

ANNA BEMIS PALMER MUSEUM, 211 E. 7th St., York, NE 68467-3022. Tel.: 402-362-1844. Fax: 402-362-0347. Facebook: Palmer Pals.
E-mail: jeannec@cityofyork.net
Key Personnel: Dir., Kent Bedient.
Institution Type/Description: Local York County History Museum.
Hours & Admission Prices: Daily 8-5, select evenings & weekends. No charge; donations accepted. Closed national holidays. &
Attendance: 1,500 (estimated)

WESSELS LIVING HISTORY FARM, 5520 S. Lincoln Ave., York, NE 68467. Tel.: 402-710-0682. Facebook.
E-mail: wesselsfarm@gmail.com
Web Site: www.livinghistoryfarm.org
Key Personnel: Dir., Hillary Mundt; Asst. Dir., Hillary Mundt.
Institution Type/Description: Living History Farm.
Hours & Admission Prices: Tues.-Sat. 10-4, Sun. 1-4; other times by appointment. Adults $7, senior citizens $5, students $3; veterans during summer no charge. &
Attendance: 8,000 (estimated)

NEVADA

(107 listings)

Amargosa Valley

ASH MEADOWS NATIONAL WILDLIFE REFUGE, 610 Spring Meadows Rd., Amargosa Valley, NV 89020. Tel.: 775-372-5435. Fax: 775-372-5436.
E-mail: Benjamin_Jurand@fws.gov
Web Site: www.fws.gov/desertcomplex/ashmeadows
Institution Type/Description: Wildlife Refuge.
Hours & Admission Prices: Visitor Center: daily 9-4:30. Refuge: sunrise to sunset. No charge.

Austin

AUSTIN HISTORICAL SOCIETY, 180 Main St., Austin, NV 89310. Mailing Address: P.O. Box 25, Austin, NV 89310-0025. Tel.: 775-964-1202. Facebook.
E-mail: austinmuseum@hughes.net
Web Site: www.austinnevadamuseum.com
Key Personnel: Pres., Corrie Bispo.
Institution Type/Description: Historical Society Museum.
Hours & Admission Prices: Memorial Day to Labor Day Wed.-Sun. 11-3. No charge. &

BERLIN-ICHTHYOSAUR STATE PARK, HC 61, Austin, NV 89310. Mailing Address: HC 61, Box 61200, Austin, NV 89310. Tel.: 775-964-2440. Fax: 775-964-2012.
E-mail: berlinstatepark@yahoo.com
Web Site: parks.nv.gov/parks/berlin-ichthyosau
Institution Type/Description: Park Museum.
Hours & Admission Prices: Daylight hours. Park: $3 per vehicle. Fossil House Tour: $2 per person.

Baker

GREAT BASIN NATIONAL PARK, 100 Great Basin Natl. Park, Baker, NV 89311-9701. Tel.: 775-234-7331. Fax: 775-234-7269.
E-mail: andy_ferguson@nps.gov
Web Site: www.nps.gov/grba
Key Personnel: Supt., Andy Ferguson; Chief Resources, Tod Williams; Cultural Resource Mgr., Eva A. Jensen.
Institution Type/Description: Park Museum.
Hours & Admission Prices: Winter: daily 8:30-4:30; Summer: daily 7:30-6. Visitors Center: Cave Tours: 90-minute tours: Adults 12 & over $8, youth 5-11 $4; children 4 & under not allowed. 60-minute Tours: Adults $6, youth $3. 30-minute Tours: Adults $2; children 11 & under no charge. Closed New Year's Day; Thanksgiving; Christmas. &
Attendance: 86,457 (estimated)

Beatty

BEATTY MUSEUM AND HISTORICAL SOCIETY, 417 Main St., Beatty, NV 89003. Mailing Address: P.O. Box 244, Beatty, NV 89003-0244. Tel.: 775-553-2303. Facebook: Beatty Museum and Historical Society.
E-mail: beattymuseum1@sbcglobal.net
Web Site: beattymuseum.org
Key Personnel: Mgr., Amina Anderson; Pres., Vonnie Gray.
Institution Type/Description: Historical Society Museum.
Hours & Admission Prices: Daily 10-3. No charge; donations accepted. Closed holidays. &
Attendance: 5,000 (estimated)

Blue Diamond

SPRING MOUNTAIN RANCH STATE PARK, 6375 NV 159, Blue Diamond, NV 89004. Mailing Address: P.O. Box 124, Blue Diamond, NV 89004-0124. Tel.: 702-875-4141.
E-mail: smrrangers@parks.nv.gov
Web Site: www.parks.nv.gov/smr.htm
Institution Type/Description: Park Museum.
Hours & Admission Prices: Daily 10-4.

Boulder City

BOULDER CITY/HOOVER DAM MUSEUM, 1305 Arizona St., Boulder City, NV 89005-2613. Tel.: 702-294-1988.
E-mail: info@bcmha.org
Web Site: www.bcmha.org
Formerly: Boulder City Museum/Hoover Dam Museum
Key Personnel: Pres., Bret Runion; Museum Mgr., Laura Hutton; Vice Pres., Jim Breneda; Treas., Jennifer Scheldahl; Mgr. Operations, Roger Shoaff.
Institution Type/Description: History Museum.
Hours & Admission Prices: Mon.-Sat. 10-5. Adults $2, children & students $1; members no charge. Closed New Year's Day; Thanksgiving; Christmas. &
Attendance: 16,000 (actual)

LAKE MEAD NATIONAL RECREATION AREA, 601 Nevada Hwy., Boulder City, NV 89005-2426. Tel.: 702-293-8859. Fax: 702-293-8936.
E-mail: steve_daron@nps.gov
Web Site: www.nps.gov/lame/index.htm
Key Personnel: Cultural Resource Mgr., Steve Daron; Book Shop Mgr., Gabriel Zurn.
Institution Type/Description: National Park & Visitor Center.
Hours & Admission Prices: Visitor's Center: daily 9-4:30. No charge; donations accepted. Closed New Year's Day; Thanksgiving; Christmas. &
Attendance: 200,000 (estimated)

Caliente

CALIENTE RAILROAD DEPOT & BOXCAR MUSEUM, 100 Depot, Caliente, NV 89008. Mailing Address: P.O. Box 1006, Caliente, NV 89008-1006. Tel.: 775-726-3129.
Institution Type/Description: Historic Building: built in 1923.
Hours & Admission Prices: Mon.-Fri. 10-2. No charge; donations accepted.

Carson City

BREWERY ARTS CENTER, 449 W. King St., Carson City, NV 89703-4205. Tel.: 775-883-1976. Fax: 775-883-1922.
E-mail: info@breweryarts.org
Web Site: www.breweryarts.org

Key Personnel: Dir., John Procaccini.
Institution Type/Description: Arts Center.
Hours & Admission Prices: Call for hours.

CHILDREN'S MUSEUM OF NORTHERN NEVADA, 813 N. Carson St., Carson City, NV 89701-4009. Tel.: 775-884-2226. Fax: 775-884-2179.
E-mail: info@cmnn.org
Web Site: www.cmnn.org/
Key Personnel: Exec. Dir., Luana Olsen.
Institution Type/Description: Children's Museum.
Hours & Admission Prices: Daily 10-4:30. Adults $6, seniors 55 & over $5, children 2-13 $4; discount to groups, AAM & ICOM members; children one & under no charge. ACM reciprocal memberships. Closed New Year's Day; Easter; Independence Day; Thanksgiving; Christmas. &
Attendance: 40,000 (actual)

COMSTOCK GOLD MILL, F St., Carson City, NV 89440. Mailing Address: P.O. Box 1298, Carson City, NV 89702-1298. Tel.: 775-742-9694.
Institution Type/Description: Mining History Museum.
Hours & Admission Prices: April-Oct. Wed.-Mon. 10-5. Adults $8, children 5-12 $4; children 4 & under no charge. Stagecoach Rides: Wed.-Mon. 11-5. Adults $10; children 4 & under no charge.

HISTORIC BOWERS MANSION, 4005 U.S. Hwy. 396 N., Carson City, NV 89704. Tel.: 702-849-0201.
E-mail: callcarol@mris.com
Institution Type/Description: Historic House Museum.
Hours & Admission Prices: mid-May to late Sept. daily 10-3. Closed Thanksgiving; Christmas.

NEVADA STATE CAPITOL, 101 N. Carson St., Carson City, NV 89701. Tel.: 800-638-2321.
E-mail: cccvb@visitcarsoncity.com
Web Site: www.nps.gov/nr/travel/nevada/nev.htm
Institution Type/Description: Historic Building: built in 1871.
Hours & Admission Prices: Tours: Mon.-Fri. 8-5.

NEVADA STATE LIBRARY AND ARCHIVES, 100 N. Stewart St., Carson City, NV 89701-4285. Tel.: 775-684-3360. Fax: 775-684-3330.
E-mail: mbass@admin.nv.gov
Web Site: nsla.nv.gov
Institution Type/Description: Library and Archives.
Hours & Admission Prices: Mon.-Fri. 8-5. No charge.

NEVADA STATE MUSEUM, 600 N. Carson Street, Carson City, NV 89701-4004. Tel.: 775-687-4810. Fax: 775-687-4168.
E-mail: jbarmore@nevadaculture.org
Web Site: www.carsonnvmuseum.org
Key Personnel: Chm., Robert Stoldal; Dir., Myron Freedman; Exhibits Mgr., Ray Geiser; Cur. Natural History, George Baumgardner; Cur. Anthropology, Gene Hattori; Collections Mgr. Anthropology, Maggie Brown; Cur. History, Bob Nylen; Cur. Clothing & Textiles, Jan Loverin; Registrar, Sue Ann Monteleone; Cur. Education, Deborah Stevenson.
Institution Type/Description: General Museum: located at the former U.S. Mint in Carson City; 1869.
Hours & Admission Prices: Tues.-Sun. 8:30-4:30. Adults $8; discounts to AAM & ICOM members; children 17 & under and members no charge. Closed New Year's Day; Thanksgiving; Christmas. &
Attendance: 38,983 (actual)

NEVADA STATE RAILROAD MUSEUM, 2180 S. Carson St., Carson City, NV 89701-5552. Tel.: 775-687-6953. Fax: 775-687-8294. Facebook: NSRMCC.
E-mail: amichalski@nevadaculture.org
Web Site: carsonrailroadmuseum.org
Key Personnel: Museum Dir., Dan Thielen; Chm. (V), Robert Stoldal; Cur. Education, Adam Michalski; Cur. History, Wendell Huffman; Restoration Supvr., Chris DeWitt; Facility Supvr., Mort Dolan.
Institution Type/Description: Railroad Museum.
Hours & Admission Prices: Thurs.-Mon. 9-4:30. Adults $6; members and children 17 & under no charge. Closed New Year's Day; Thanksgiving; Christmas. &
Attendance: 19,778 (actual)

ROBERT'S HOUSE MUSEUM, 1207 N. Carson St., Carson City, NV 89701-1203. Mailing Address: 112 N. Curry St., Carson City, NV 89702. Tel.: 775-887-2174.

Institution Type/Description: Historic House Museum.
Hours & Admission Prices: Closed for renovations.

STEWART INDIAN SCHOOL MUSEUM AND CULTURAL CENTER, 5366 Snyder Ave., Carson City, NV 89701-6743. Tel.: 775-882-6929 & 687-7606. Fax: 775-882-1061.
E-mail: brahder@nic.nv.gov
Key Personnel: Museum Dir., Bobbi Rahder; Cur., Chris Ann Gibbons.
Institution Type/Description: History Museum.
Hours & Admission Prices: Daily 9-5.

WARREN ENGINE COMPANY #1 MUSEUM, 777 S. Stewart St., Carson City, NV 89701-5218. Tel.: 775-887-2210. Fax: 775-887-2209.
E-mail: fireinfo@carson.org
Web Site: www.carson.org
Institution Type/Description: Fire-Fighting Museum.
Hours & Admission Prices: Mon.-Fri. 8-5. No charge; donations accepted.

Dayton

HISTORICAL SOCIETY OF DAYTON VALLEY, 135 Shady Lane, at Logan Alley, Dayton, NV 89403. Mailing Address: P.O. Box 485, Dayton, NV 89403-0485. Tel.: 775-246-6316.
E-mail: L10ANT38@gmail.com
Web Site: daytonnvhistory.org
Formerly: Dayton Museum Historical Society
Key Personnel: Pres. (V), Linda Clements.
Institution Type/Description: Historical Society Museum.
Hours & Admission Prices: March-April & June-Nov. Sat. 10-4, Sun. 1-4; May Mon.-Fri. 11-3, Sat. 10-4, Sun. 1-4. No charge; donations accepted.
Attendance: 1,500 (estimated)

Elko

NORTHEASTERN NEVADA MUSEUM, 1515 Idaho St., Elko, NV 89801-4021. Tel.: 775-738-3418. Fax: 775-778-9318.
E-mail: info@museumelko.org
Web Site: www.museumelko.org
Key Personnel: C.E.O., Kim Steninger; Dir., Claudia Wines; Registrar, Stephanie Youngquist; Archivist, Toni Mendive; Exhibit Coord., Catherine Wines; Maintenance Supvr., Ty Carrillo; Museum Shop Mgr. & Bookkeeper, Tracy Beatty.
Institution Type/Description: General Museum.
Hours & Admission Prices: Tues.-Sat. 9-5, Sun. 1-5. Adults $5, senior & students $3, children 3-12 $1; discount to groups, AAM & AASLH members; members, children under 2 & the last Sunday of every month no charge. Closed New Year's Day; Thanksgiving; Christmas.
Attendance: 30,000 (estimated)

WESTERN FOLKLIFE CENTER, 501 Railroad St., Ste. 306, Elko, NV 89801-3785. Tel.: 775-738-7508. Fax: 775-738-2900.
E-mail: wfc@westernfolklife.org
Web Site: www.westernfolklife.org
Key Personnel: Exec. Dir., Charlie Seemann; Artistic Dir., Meg Glasser.
Institution Type/Description: Cultural Center.
Hours & Admission Prices: Mon.-Sat. 10-5. Adults $5, students & seniors 60 & over $3, children 6-12 $1; 1st Sat. of month, members and children 5 & under no charge.

Ely

EAST ELY RAILROAD DEPOT MUSEUM, 1100 Avenue A, Ely, NV 89301-2486. Tel.: 775-289-1663. Fax: 775-289-1664.
E-mail: esm@mwpower.net
Key Personnel: Cur., Sean Pitts; Program Asst., Keith Stone.
Institution Type/Description: Railroad Depot Museum.
Hours & Admission Prices: Daily 8-4:30. Adults $2; children under 18 no charge.
Attendance: 15,800 (actual)

NEVADA NORTHERN RAILWAY MUSEUM, 1100 Avenue A, Ely, NV 89301-2486. Mailing Address: P.O. Box 150040, Ely, NV 89315-0040. Tel.: 775-289-2085.
E-mail: info@nnry.com
Web Site: www.nnry.com
Key Personnel: Pres., Mark S. Bassett; Museum Shop Mgr., Heather Barber.
Institution Type/Description: History & Transportation Museum.

Hours & Admission Prices: June-Aug. daily 8-6; Sept.-May Wed.-Mon. 8-5. Adults $6; discounts to National Trust for Historic Preservation members; members no charge. Closed New Year's Eve & Day; Thanksgiving; Christmas Eve & Day.
Attendance: 32,000 (estimated)

WHITE PINE PUBLIC MUSEUM, 2000 Aultman St., Ely, NV 89301-1824. Tel.: 775-289-4710. Fax: 775-289-4710. Facebook.
E-mail: wpmuseumnv@gmail.com
Web Site: wpmuseum.org
Key Personnel: Chm. & C.E.O., Doris Metcalf; Museum Shop Mgr., Amy Melvin.
Institution Type/Description: General Museum.
Hours & Admission Prices: Museum: daily 10-4. Drug Store: winter by appointment. Adults $5; children under 12 no charge. Closed New Year's Day; Memorial Day; Thanksgiving; Christmas.
Attendance: 11,000 (estimated)

Eureka

EUREKA COUNTY COURTHOUSE, 10 S. Main St., Eureka, NV 89316. Mailing Address: P.O. Box 677, Eureka, NV 89316. Tel.: 775-237-5270.
E-mail: bconley@eurekacountynv.gov
Institution Type/Description: Historic Building: built in 1879.
Hours & Admission Prices: Call for hours.

EUREKA OPERA HOUSE, 31 S. Main St., Eureka, NV 89316. Mailing Address: Convention & Cultural Arts Center, P.O. Box 284, Eureka, NV 89316-0289. Tel.: 775-237-6006. Fax: 775-237-6040.
E-mail: arossman@eureka.org
Key Personnel: Dir., Andrea Rossman.
Institution Type/Description: Historic Building: built in 1880.
Hours & Admission Prices: Call for hours.

EUREKA SENTINEL MUSEUM, 10 N. Monroe St., Eureka, NV 89316. Mailing Address: P.O. Box 82, Eureka, NV 89316-0082. Tel.: 775-237-5010. Fax: 775-237-6040.
E-mail: esm@eurekanv.org
Web Site: www.co.eureka.nv.us
Key Personnel: Mgr., Ree Taylor.
Institution Type/Description: Historic Building: housed in the 1879 Eureka Sentinel Newspaper Building.
Hours & Admission Prices: Tues.-Sat. 10-6. No charge; donations accepted.
Attendance: 5,000 (estimated)

Fallon

CHURCHILL COUNTY MUSEUM AND ARCHIVES, 1050 S. Maine St., Fallon, NV 89406-8815. Tel.: 775-423-3677. Fax: 775-423-3662.
E-mail: info@ccmuseum.org
Web Site: ccmuseum.org
Key Personnel: Pres. (V), Robert Getto, Jr.; Dir., Daniel J. Ingram.
Institution Type/Description: Local History Museum.
Hours & Admission Prices: March-Nov. Mon.-Sat. 10-5, Sun. 10-3; Dec.-Feb. Mon.-Sat. 10-4, Sun. 10-3. Hidden Cave Tours: 2nd & 4th Sat. each month 9:30 a.m. weather permitting. No charge; donations accepted. Closed county holidays; Easter; Thanksgiving; Christmas.
Attendance: 12,000 (estimated)

Gardnerville

DOUGLAS COUNTY HISTORICAL SOCIETY - CARSON VALLEY MUSEUM & CULTURAL CENTER, 1477 Hwy. 395 N., Ste. B, Gardnerville, NV 89410-5214. Tel.: 775-782-2555. Fax: 775-783-8802. Facebook: Douglas Co. Historical Society.
E-mail: dchs@historicnv.org
Web Site: historicnv.org
Formerly: Carson Valley Historical Society
Key Personnel: Dir., Cindy Rogers; Pres. (V), Dennis Little; Museum Shop Mgr., Judy Conrad.
Institution Type/Description: History Museum: housed in restored 1915 high school.
Hours & Admission Prices: Mon.-Sat. 10-4. Adults $5, children over 6 $2; discounts to tour groups & AASLH members; Douglas County schools & members no charge. Closed New Year's Day; Carson Valley Day; Independence Day; Nevada Day; Thanksgiving; Christmas Eve & Day.
Attendance: 6,000 (estimated)

Genoa

DOUGLAS COUNTY HISTORICAL SOCIETY - COURTHOUSE MUSEUM GENOA, 2304 Main St., Genoa, NV 89411. Mailing Address: 1477 Hwy. 395 N, Suite B, Gardnerville, NV 89410-5570. Tel.: 775-782-4325. Fax: 775-783-8802. Facebook: Douglas County Historical Society Courthouse Museum Genoa.
E-mail: dchs@historicnv.org
Web Site: historicnv.org
Key Personnel: Dir., Cindy Rogers; Pres. (V), Dennis Little; Museum Shop Mgr., Judy Conrad.
Institution Type/Description: History Museum; housed in 19th-century courthouse.
Hours & Admission Prices: May-Oct. daily 10-4. Adults $5, children over 6 $2; discounts to groups; Douglas County schools & members no charge. &
Attendance: 4,200 (estimated)

MORMON STATION STATE HISTORIC PARK, 2295 Main St., Genoa, NV 89411. Mailing Address: P.O. Box 302, Genoa, NV 89411-0302. Tel.: 775-782-2590.
E-mail: mormonstation@parks.nv.gov
Web Site: www.parks.nv.gov/ms.htm
Key Personnel: Rgnl. Mgr., Dale Conner; Park Supvr., Jennifer Dawson; Park Interpreter, Daniel Wassmund.
Institution Type/Description: Park, Museum & Visitor Center.
Hours & Admission Prices: Museum: May to mid-Oct. daily 10-4; mid-Oct. to April Thurs.-Mon. 11-3. Admission $1; children 12 & under no charge. &
Attendance: 70,000 (estimated)

Hawthorne

MINERAL COUNTY MUSEUM, 400 Tenth St., Hawthorne, NV 89415. Mailing Address: P.O. Box 1584, Hawthorne, NV 89415-1584. Tel.: 775-945-5142.
E-mail: gm@mcmuseum.hawthorne.nv.us
Web Site: www.web0.greatbasin.net/~mcmuseum/
Institution Type/Description: History Museum.
Hours & Admission Prices: April-Oct. Tues.-Sat. 11-5; Nov.-March Tues.-Sat. 12-4; other times by appointment. No charge.

Henderson

CLARK COUNTY MUSEUM, 1830 S. Boulder Hwy., Henderson, NV 89002-8502. Tel.: 702-455-7955. Fax: 702-455-7948. Facebook: Clark County Museum.
E-mail: mhp@clarkcountynv.gov
Web Site: www.clarkcountynv.gov/depts/parks/pages/clark-county-museum.aspx
Formerly: Clark County Heritage Museum
Key Personnel: Dir., Jane Pike; Asst. Dir., Mindy Meyers; Div. Mgr., Patrick Almeido; Museum Admin., Mark Hall-Patton; Cur. Exhibits., Malcolm vuksich; Registrar, Cynthia Sanford; Museum Guild Pres. (V), Jeanne Brady; Museum Program Specialist & Museum Shop Mgr., Amber Heman.
Institution Type/Description: History Museum.
Hours & Admission Prices: Daily 9-4:30; bus tours by appointment; call for holiday tour information. Adults $2, children under 16 & senior citizens $1; members no charge. Closed New Year's Day; Thanksgiving; Christmas. &
Attendance: 38,101 (actual)

ETHEL M. CHOCOLATE FACTORY & CACTUS GARDEN, 2 Cactus Garden Dr., Henderson, NV 89014. Tel.: 702-435-2608. Facebook; Twitter..
E-mail: customerservice@ethelm.com
Web Site: ethelm.com
Institution Type/Description: Candy Company History.
Hours & Admission Prices: Daily 8-8. No charge. Chocolate Tasting Class: daily 10 am, 12 pm, 2 pm, 4 pm, & 6 pm. Adult $15, student $10; children under 13 $6. Chocolate & Wine Tasting (21 & over): daily 11 am, 1 pm, 3 pm, 5 pm, & 7 pm. Adults $25.

HENDERSON BIRD VIEWING PRESERVE, 350 E. Galleria Dr., Henderson, NV 89011. Tel.: 702-267-4180.
Institution Type/Description: Bird Preserve.
Hours & Admission Prices: Daily 6am-3pm; groups by appointment. &

Incline Village

THUNDERBIRD LODGE PRESERVATION SOCIETY, 5000 Hwy. 28, Incline Village, NV 89451. Mailing Address: P.O. Box 6812, Incline Village, NV 89450-6812. Tel.: 775-832-8750. Fax: 775-832-8798.
E-mail: askus@thunderbirdlodge.org
Web Site: www.thunderbirdlodge.org
Institution Type/Description: Preservation Society; listed on the National Register of Historic Places.
Hours & Admission Prices: By appointment.

Las Vegas

THE AUTO COLLECTIONS AT THE IMPERIAL PALACE, 3535 Las Vegas Blvd., S., Las Vegas, NV 89109-8921. Tel.: 702-794-3174. Fax: 702-794-3182.
E-mail: info@autocollections.com
Institution Type/Description: Car Museum.
Hours & Admission Prices: Mon.-Sat. 10-5. Adults $12.95, seniors $8.95, children 12 7 under $7.95; military and children 5 & under no charge.

BELLAGIO CONSERVATORY & BOTANICAL GARDENS, 3600 S. Las Vegas Blvd., Las Vegas, NV 89109-4303. Tel.: 702-693-7111.
Institution Type/Description: Botanical Gardens.
Hours & Admission Prices: Daily 24 hours. No charge.

BELLAGIO GALLERY OF FINE ART, 3600 Las Vegas Blvd. S., Las Vegas, NV 89109-4339. Tel.: 702-693-7871 & 7865. Fax: 702-693-7872.
E-mail: fineartgallery@bellagio.com
Web Site: www.bellagio.com/bgfa
Key Personnel: Dir., Carolyn Bare.
Institution Type/Description: Art Museum.
Hours & Admission Prices: Daily 10-8. Adults $17, NV residents, seniors 65 and over, students, teachers, & military $15; children 12 & under no charge. &

BLACKBIRD STUDIOS, 1551 S. Commerce St., Ste. A, Las Vegas, NV 89102. Tel.: 702-782-0319.
Institution Type/Description: Art Gallery.
Hours & Admission Prices: Call for hours

BOXING HALL OF CHAMPIONS, 8022 S. Rainbow Blvd., Las Vegas, NV 89139-6477. Tel.: 702-582-7040.
E-mail: info@bhoc.com
Institution Type/Description: Boxing History Museum.
Hours & Admission Prices: Call for hours.

BURLESQUE HALL OF FAME, 1017 S. First St., Ste. 195, Las Vegas, NV 89101. Mailing Address: P.O. Box 580, Las Vegas, NV 89125. Tel.: 888-661-6465. Facebook.
E-mail: info@burlesquehall.com
Web Site: www.burlesquehall.com
Institution Type/Description: Burlesque History Museum.
Hours & Admission Prices: Tues.-Sun. 11-6; Sun. 12-5. Suggested Donation: adults $5, students & seniors $3. Closed New Year's Eve & Day; Thanksgiving; Christmas Eve & Day.&

CENTAUR ART GALLERIES, 4345 Dean Martin Dr., Ste. 200, Las Vegas, NV 89103. Tel.: 702-737-1234.
Web Site: centaurgalleries.com
Key Personnel: C.E.O., Richard C. Perry.
Institution Type/Description: Art Gallery.
Hours & Admission Prices: Mon.-Sat. 10-9, Sun. 11-7. No charge.

CITY OF LAS VEGAS CHARLESTON HEIGHTS ART CENTER GALLERY, 800 S. Brush St., Las Vegas, NV 89107. Tel.: 702-229-6383. Fax: 702-383-1129.
Web Site: www.artslasvegas.org
Institution Type/Description: Art Gallery.
Hours & Admission Prices: Wed.-Fri. 12:30-9, Sat. 9-6.

CONTEMPORARY ARTS CENTER, 900 S. Las Vegas Blvd., #150, Las Vegas, NV 89102. Mailing Address: P.O. Box 582, Las Vegas, NV 89125. Tel.: 702-496-0569.
E-mail: info@lasvegascac.org
Web Site: www.lasvegascac.org
Institution Type/Description: Art Gallery.
Hours & Admission Prices: Thurs.-Sun. 12-6; other times by appointment. No charge; donations accepted.

DISCOVERY CHILDREN'S MUSEUM, 360 Promenade Pl., Las Vegas, NV 89106-1470. Tel.: 702-382-3445. Fax: 702-382-0592. Facebook: @DiscoveryChildrensMuseum.
E-mail: info@discoverykidslv.org
Web Site: www.discoverykidslv.org
Formerly: Lied Discovery Children's Museum
Key Personnel: C.E.O. & Pres., Tifferney White; Dir. Exhibits & Facilities, Gary Haleamau.
Institution Type/Description: Children's Museum.
Hours & Admission Prices: Memorial Day to Labor Day Mon.-Sat. 10-5, Sun. 12-5; Sept.-May Tues.-Fri. 9-4, Sat. 10-5, Sun. 12-5. Admission $14.50; children under one & members no charge.
Attendance: 360,000 (actual)

DONNA BEAM FINE ART GALLERY, UNLV, Mailing Address: 4505 S. Maryland Pkwy., Box 5002, Las Vegas, NV 89154-5002. Tel.: 702-895-3893. Fax: 702-895-3751.
E-mail: jerry.schefcik@unlv.edu
Web Site: unlv.edu/donnabeamgallery
Key Personnel: Dir., Jerry A. Schefcik.
Institution Type/Description: Art Museum & Center.
Hours & Admission Prices: Mon.-Fri. 9-5, Sat. noon-5. No charge. Closed major holidays.
Attendance: 8,000 (estimated)

HISPANIC MUSEUM OF NEVADA, 3680 S. Maryland Pkwy., Las Vegas, NV 89169. Tel.: 702-773-2203.
Institution Type/Description: Hispanic History Museum.
Hours & Admission Prices: Daily 11-6. No charge.

HOWARD W. CANNON AVIATION MUSEUM, McCarran International Airport, 5757 Wayne Newton Blvd., Las Vegas, NV 89119. Tel.: 702-455-7968. Fax: 702-455-7948.
E-mail: ccparks@clarkcountynv.gov
Web Site: www.clarkcountynv.gov/depts/parks/pages/cannon-aviation-museum.aspx
Formerly: McCarran Aviation Heritage Museum
Key Personnel: Admin., Mark P. Hall-Patton.
Institution Type/Description: Aviation Museum.
Hours & Admission Prices: Airport Exhibits: 24 hours daily. Office: Mon.-Fri. 8-5. No charge.
Attendance: 440,000 (estimated)

LAS VEGAS INTERNATIONAL SCOUTING MUSEUM, 3025 W. Sahara Ave., Ste. 200, Las Vegas, NV 89102. Tel.: 702-878-7268. Fax: 702-822-2020. Facebook: International Scouting Museum.
E-mail: ravs4fun@aol.com
Web Site: www.worldscoutingmuseum.org
Key Personnel: Exec. Dir., Robert Lynn Horne, M.D.; Cur., James Arriola.
Institution Type/Description: Scouting Museum.
Hours & Admission Prices: Tours by appointment Mon.-Fri. 9-5. Adults $10; seniors $7; youth 6-17 $5; Scouts & Scouters $3.

LAS VEGAS NATURAL HISTORY MUSEUM, 900 Las Vegas Blvd., N., Las Vegas, NV 89101-1112. Tel.: 702-384-3466. Fax: 702-384-5343. Facebook: @LasVegasNaturalHistoryMuseum.
E-mail: dino@lvnhm.org
Web Site: www.lvnhm.org
Key Personnel: Dir., Marilyn Gillespie; Chm. (V), Matt Engle; Museum Shop Mgr., Laurie Thomas.
Institution Type/Description: Natural History Museum.
Hours & Admission Prices: Daily 9-4. Adults $12, senior citizens, students & military $10, children 3-11 $6; discounts to groups, ASTC, AAA & AAM members; children 2 & under and members no charge. Closed Thanksgiving; Christmas.
Attendance: 98,163 (actual)

LAS VEGAS SPRINGS PRESERVE, 333 S. Valley View Blvd., Las Vegas, NV 89107-4372. Mailing Address: P.O. Box 98947, Las Vegas, NV 89193-8947. Tel.: 702-822-7700. Fax: 702-822-8700.
E-mail: anne.silva@springspreserve.org
Web Site: www.springspreserve.org
Key Personnel: Dir., Andrew Belanger; Mgr., Bruno Bowles; Cur. Exhibits, Aaron Micallef.
Institution Type/Description: Historical & Cultural Complex: Origen Museum & Desert Living Center.
Hours & Admission Prices: March 11-Nov. 3 daily 10-6; Nov. 4-March 10 daily 10-4. Nevada Residents: adults $9.95, children 5-17 $4.95. Non-Residents:

adults $18.95, children 5-17 $10.95. American Horticulture Society reciprocal admission program. Closed Thanksgiving; Christmas.
Attendance: 279,000 (actual)

MADAME TUSSAUD'S WAX MUSEUM, LAS VEGAS, 3377 S. Las Vegas Blvd., Ste. 2001, Las Vegas, NV 89109-8910. Tel.: 702-862-7800. Fax: 702-862-7851.
E-mail: info@madametussaudslv.com
Web Site: www.mtvegas.com
Institution Type/Description: Wax Museum.
Hours & Admission Prices: Sun.-Thurs. 10-8, Fri.-Sat. 10-9.

THE MOB MUSEUM, 300 Stewart Ave., Las Vegas, NV 89101. Tel.: 702-229-2734. Facebook.
E-mail: info@themobmuseum.org
Web Site: themobmuseum.org
Key Personnel: Pres. & C.E.O., Jonathan Ullman; C.O.O., Mark B. Achenbach; Vice Pres. Fin. & Business Analytics, Lisa Belair; Vice Pres. Mktg., Comm., & Sales, Ashely Miller; Vice Pres. Exhibits & Programs, Geoff Schumacher.
Institution Type/Description: Mob & Organized Crime History Museum: housed in a former federal courthouse & United States Post Office. Listed on the National Register of Historic Places.
Hours & Admission Prices: Daily. 9am-8pm. Adults $29.95, seniors, law enforcement & military $20.95, students & youth 11-17 $16.95; discounts to NV residents; children 10 & under no charge. Closed Thanksgiving; Christmas.

NATIONAL ATOMIC TESTING MUSEUM, 755 E. Flamingo Rd., Las Vegas, NV 89119-7363. Tel.: 702-794-5151. Fax: 702-794-5155. Facebook.
E-mail: michael.hall@natm-nv.org
Web Site: nationalatomictestingmuseum.org
Key Personnel: Exec. Dir., Michael Hall; Chm (V), Troy Wade; Museum Store Mgr., Bailey Clark.
Institution Type/Description: Science & Technology Museum.
Hours & Admission Prices: Mon.-Sat. 10-5, Sun. 12-5. Adults $18, seniors, military & students $18; members and children 6 & under no charge. Closed New Year's Day; Thanksgiving; Christmas.
Attendance: 82,000 (actual)

THE NEON MUSEUM, 770 Las Vegas Blvd., N., Las Vegas, NV 89101-2030. Tel.: 702-387-6366. Fax: 702-477-7751.
E-mail: info@neonmuseum.org
Web Site: www.neonmuseum.org
Key Personnel: Operations Mgr., Bill Lee.
Institution Type/Description: General Museum.
Hours & Admission Prices: Daily see website for hours. Day Tours: $19, seniors, students military & Nevada residents $15. Night Tours: $25, seniors, students military & Nevada residents $22; not recommended for children under 12.

NEVADA STATE MUSEUM, LAS VEGAS, 309 S. Valley View/Springs Preserve, Las Vegas, NV 89107-2104. Tel.: 702-486-5205. Fax: 702-486-5172.
E-mail: dennis.mcbride@nevadaculture.org
Web Site: nvculture.org
Formerly: Nevada State Museum & Historical Society
Key Personnel: Exec. Dir., Dennis McBride; Chm. (V), Robert Stoldal; Cur. History, Caroline Kunioka; Cur. Education, Stacy Irvin; Cur. Natural History, Sali Underwood; Dir. Exhibits, Thomas Dyer.
Institution Type/Description: General Museum.
Hours & Admission Prices: Tues.-Sun. 9-5. Adults $18.95, NV resident adult $9.95; youth 17 & under and members no charge. Closed New Year's Day; Thanksgiving; Christmas.
Attendance: 50,000 (actual)

OLD LAS VEGAS MORMON FORT STATE HISTORIC PARK, 500 E. Washington Ave., Las Vegas, NV 89101-1000. Tel.: 702-486-3511. Fax: 702-486-3734.
E-mail: oldfort@parks.nv.gov
Web Site: www.parks.nv.gov/olvmf.htm
Institution Type/Description: History Museum.
Hours & Admission Prices: Tues.-Sat. 8-4:30. Adults 13 & over $1; children 12 & under no charge.

RED ROCK CANYON VISITOR CENTER AND NATIONAL CONSERVATION AREA, 1000 Scenic Loop Dr., HCR 33, Las Vegas, NV 89124. Mailing Address: Box 5500, Las Vegas, NV 89124. Tel.: 702-515-5350.
Web Site: www.redrockcanyonlv.org
Institution Type/Description: National Park.

Hours & Admission Prices: Visitor Center: daily 8-4:30. Daily Canyon Pass: $3-$7. Closed Thanksgiving; Christmas.

SHARK REEF AQUARIUM AT MANDALAY BAY, 3950 Las Vegas Blvd. S., Las Vegas, NV 89119-1006. Tel.: 702-632-4555. Fax: 702-632-4553.
E-mail: sharkreef@mandalaybay.com
Web Site: www.sharkreef.com
Institution Type/Description: Aquarium.
Hours & Admission Prices: Sun.-Thurs. 10-8, Fri.-Sat. 10-10. Adults $20, seniors $18, children 4-12 $14; discounts to Nevada residents; children 3 & under no charge. &

SIEGFRIED & ROY'S SECRET GARDEN & DOLPHIN HABITAT, Mirage Department of Animal Care, 3400 Las Vegas Blvd. S., Las Vegas, NV 89109-8923. Tel.: 702-791-7188. Fax: 702-792-7684.
E-mail: secretgarden@mirage.com
Web Site: www.miragehabitat.com
Institution Type/Description: Animal Garden.
Hours & Admission Prices: Daily 10-5. Adults $22, children 4-12 $17; children 3 & under no charge.

SOUTHERN NEVADA MUSEUM OF FINE ART, 450 Fremont St., #270, Las Vegas, NV 89101. Tel.: 702-382-2926.
E-mail: snmoffa@gmail.com
Web Site: mglv.org
Key Personnel: Dir., Mark Rowland; Museum Shop Mgr., Lynn Jones.
Institution Type/Description: Art Gallery.
Hours & Admission Prices: Wed.-Sat. 12-5; other times by appointment. Admission $5; discounts to groups; members and children 12 & under no charge. &

UNLV MARJORIE BARRICK MUSEUM OF ART, 4505 S. Maryland Pkwy., Las Vegas, NV 89154-9900. Mailing Address: P. O. Box 454012, Las Vegas, NV 89154-4012. Tel.: 702-895-3381. Fax: 702-895-5737.
E-mail: barrick.museum@unlv.edu
Web Site: unlv.edu/barrickmuseum
Key Personnel: Interim Exec. Dir., Alisha Kerlin.
Institution Type/Description: Art Museum.
Hours & Admission Prices: May-Aug. Mon.-Fri. 9-5, Sat. 12-5; Sept.-April Mon.-Wed. & Fri. 9-5, Thurs. 9-8, Sat. 12-5. Suggested Donations: adults $5, seniors & children $2. Closed state & federal holidays. &
Attendance: 80,000 (estimated)

THE WALKER AFRICAN AMERICAN MUSEUM & RESEARCH CENTER, 705 W. Van Buren Ave., Las Vegas, NV 89106-3042. Mailing Address: 2105 Travis St., North Las Vegas, NV 89030. Tel.: 702-752-6043.
E-mail: walkeraamuseum1@yahoo.com
Web Site: www.churchesinlasvegas.com/walkermuseum
Key Personnel: Pres. (V), Dir. & Cur., Gwendolyn Walker; Education, Margaret Crawford; Public Rels., Lillian McMorris; Treas., Juanita Walker; Security, Larry Ennis; Museum Shop Mgr., Nika Sewell.
Institution Type/Description: History Museum.
Hours & Admission Prices: By appointment. Adults $2. Closed Christmas.
Attendance: 750 (estimated)

Laughlin

DON LAUGHLIN'S CLASSIC CAR COLLECTION, Riverside Resort Hotel & Casino, 1650 S. Casino Dr., Laughlin, NV 89029-1512. Tel.: 800-227-3849, 702-298-2535. Fax: 702-298-2605.
E-mail: mosborn@riversideresort.com
Key Personnel: Cur., Mark Osborn.
Institution Type/Description: Classic Car Collection.
Hours & Admission Prices: First Floor Show Room: daily 10-10. Third Floor Show Room: Sun.-Thurs. 9am-10pm, Fri.-Sat. 9am-11pm. No charge. &
Attendance: 300,000 (estimated)

Logandale

OLD LOGANDALE SCHOOL HISTORICAL AND CULTURAL SOCIETY, 3011 N. Moapa Valley Blvd., Logandale, NV 89021-0065. Mailing Address: P.O. Box 65, Logandale, NV 89021. Tel.: 702-398-7272 & 7273.
Institution Type/Description: Historic Building: housed in the former Logandale School; built in 1899.

Hours & Admission Prices: Mon.-Fri. 10-4.

Lovelock

PERSHING COUNTY COURTHOUSE, 400 Main St., Lovelock, NV 89419. Mailing Address: Pershing County Commissioners, Drawer E, Lovelock, NV 89419. Tel.: 702-273-7144. Fax: 702-273-7647.
Institution Type/Description: Historic Building: built in 1919. Listed on the National Register of Historic Places.
Hours & Admission Prices: Mon.-Fri. 10-4. No charge.

PERSHING COUNTY MARZEN HOUSE MUSEUM, 25 Marzen Lane, Lovelock, NV 89419. Mailing Address: P.O. Box 212, Lovelock, NV 89419. Tel.: 775-273-2115.
Key Personnel: Dir., Heidi Lusby.
Institution Type/Description: Historic House Museum: built in 1874.
Hours & Admission Prices: May-Oct. daily 9-4; Nov.-April Mon.-Fri. 9-1:30. No charge; donations accepted.

McGill

HISTORIC MCGILL DRUG COMPANY, U.S. 93 E., McGill, NV 89318. Mailing Address: P.O. Box 757, McGill, NV 89318-0757. Tel.: 775-235-7082. Fax: 775-235-7802.
E-mail: bhaven1@sbcglobal.net
Web Site: www.mcgilldrugstoremuseum.org
Key Personnel: Dir., Daniel Braddock.
Institution Type/Description: Historic Building: built in 1907.
Hours & Admission Prices: By appointment. No charge; donations accepted. &
Attendance: 5,800 (actual)

Mesquite

MESQUITE FINE ARTS CENTER & GALLERY, 15 W. Mesquite Blvd., Mesquite, NV 89027-4754. Tel.: 702-346-1338. Fax: 702-346-1339.
E-mail: vvarts@gmail.com
Web Site: mesquitefineartscenter.com
Key Personnel: Pres. (V), Katherine Cole.
Institution Type/Description: Art Gallery.
Hours & Admission Prices: Mon.-Sat. 10-4. No charge; donations accepted. Closed holidays. &
Attendance: 15,000 (estimated)

VIRGIN VALLEY HERITAGE MUSEUM, 35 W. Mesquite Blvd., Mesquite, NV 89027-4707. Mailing Address: 100 W. Old Mill Rd., Mesquite, NV 89027. Tel.: 702-346-5705. Facebook: Mesquite NV Museum.
E-mail: emarler@mesquitenv.gov
Web Site: www.mesquitenv.gov/parkfacility/virginvalleymuseum
Institution Type/Description: Heritage Museum.
Hours & Admission Prices: Tues.-Sat. 10-4. No charge; donations accepted. Closed most holidays. &

Minden

DANGBERG HOME RANCH HISTORIC PARK, 1450 Hwy. 88, Minden, NV 89423. Mailing Address: P.O. Box 1158, Minden, NV 89423. Tel.: 775-783-9417.
Web Site: www.dangberghomeranch.org
Key Personnel: Cur., Mark Jensen.
Institution Type/Description: Historic House Museum: built in 1857.
Hours & Admission Prices: Tours: April to mid-Dec. Wed.-Sun. 10 & 2 by appointment. Adults $3; children 12 & under no charge. Special Exhibits: call for hours. Adults $3; children 12 & under no charge. Speaker Series: no charge.
Attendance: 3,500 (actual)

Nixon

PYRAMID LAKE PAIUTE CULTURAL CENTER, 709 State St., Nixon, NV 89424. Mailing Address: P.O. Box 256, Nixon, NV 89424-0256. Tel.: 775-574-1088. Fax: 775-574-1090.
E-mail: bjguerrero@plpt.nsn.us
Key Personnel: Dir., Shannon Mandell.
Institution Type/Description: Cultural Center.
Hours & Admission Prices: June-Sept. Tues.-Sat. 10-4:30; Oct.-May Mon.-Fri. 10-4:30.

North Las Vegas

LEFT OF CENTER ART GALLERY & STUDIO, 2207 W. Gowan Rd., North Las Vegas, NV 89032-7961. Tel.: 702-647-7378. Fax: 702-647-7734.
E-mail: leftofcentergallery@gmail.com
Web Site: www.leftofcenterart.org
Key Personnel: Dir., Vicki Richardson.
Institution Type/Description: Art Gallery & Museum.
Hours & Admission Prices: Tues.-Fri. 12-5, Sat. 10-3. No charge; donations accepted.

THE PLANETARIUM - COLLEGE OF SOUTHERN NEVADA, 3200 E. Cheyenne Ave., North Las Vegas, NV 89030-4296. Mailing Address: Sort Code CYS143, 3200 E. Cheyenne Ave., North Las Vegas, NV 89030-4296. Tel.: 702-651-4759 & 4138.
E-mail: planetarium@csn.edu
Web Site: www.csn.edu/planetarium
Key Personnel: Dir., Dr. Andrew Kerr.
Institution Type/Description: Planetarium.
Hours & Admission Prices: Public Programs: Fri. 6pm, 7pm & 8pm, Sat. 3:30pm, 6pm, 7pm, 8pm. School Groups: 9:30am & 11am. &
Attendance: 17,159 (actual)

North Washoe Valley

BOWERS MANSION, 4005 Old U.S. 395, N., North Washoe Valley, NV 89704. Tel.: 775-849-0201, 775-849-0684.
E-mail: pomara@washoecounty.us
Web Site: www.washoecounty.us/parks/parkdetails~pkid=1
Key Personnel: Park Ranger, Bryan Harrower.
Institution Type/Description: Historic House: c.1864 restored & refurbished Mansion built by L.S. Bowers.
Hours & Admission Prices: Tours: May 18 to Sept. 29 Sat.-Sun. 10-3 on the hour. Adults 18-61 $8, seniors 62 & up and children 6-17 $5; children 5 & under no charge.
Attendance: 7,000 (actual)

Overton

LOST CITY MUSEUM, 721 S. Moapa Blvd., Overton, NV 89040. Mailing Address: P.O. Box 807, Overton, NV 89040-0807. Tel.: 702-397-2193. Fax: 702-397-8987.
E-mail: lostcity@nevadaculture.org
Web Site: www.nevadaculture.org
Key Personnel: Dir., Jerrie Clarke; Admin. Asst., Janie Shakespear.
Institution Type/Description: Archaeology Museum.
Hours & Admission Prices: Daily 8:30-4:30. Adults over 18 $5; members & children under 18 no charge. Closed New Year's Day; Thanksgiving; Christmas. &
Attendance: 20,933 (actual)

Pahrump

PAHRUMP VALLEY MUSEUM, 401 E. Basin Ave., Pahrump, NV 89060. Mailing Address: P.O. Box 1510, Pahrump, NV 89041-1510. Tel.: 775-751-1970. Fax: 775-751-1970. Facebook: Pahrump Valley Museum.
E-mail: pahrumpmuseum@att.net
Web Site: pahrumpvalleymuseum.org
Key Personnel: Pres. (V), Sharon Wehryl; Dir., Marilyn Davis.
Institution Type/Description: History Museum.
Hours & Admission Prices: Tues.-Sun. 9-5. No charge; donations accepted. &
Attendance: 8,266 (actual)

Pioche

LINCOLN COUNTY HISTORICAL MUSEUM, 716 Main St., Pioche, NV 89043. Mailing Address: P.O. Box 515, Pioche, NV 89043-0515. Tel.: 775-962-5207.
E-mail: robertwynn@robertwynn.com
Institution Type/Description: History Museum.
Hours & Admission Prices: Daily 10-3. No charge; donations accepted. Closed New Year's Day; Thanksgiving; Christmas.

Reno

ANIMAL ARK, 1265 Deerlodge Rd., Reno, NV 89508. Tel.: 775-970-3111.
Web Site: animalark.org

Institution Type/Description: Wildlife Sanctuary & Nature Center.
Hours & Admission Prices: March 30-Nov. 3 Tues.-Sun. 10-4:30; adults $9.50, seniors (62+) $8, children 3-12 $6,50, children 2 & under no charge.

FLEISCHMANN PLANETARIUM, 1664 N. Virginia St., Reno, NV 89503-0703. Mailing Address: Univ. of Nevada, Reno/272, Reno, NV 89557. Tel.: 775-784-4812. Fax: 775-784-4822.
E-mail: planetarium@unr.edu
Web Site: planetarium.unr.edu
Key Personnel: Dir., Dan Ruby.
Institution Type/Description: Planetarium.
Hours & Admission Prices: Daily call for hours. Exhibits no charge. Planetarium Show: adults 18 & over $7, under 18, seniors & university students $5; discount to groups. AAM, ASTC, IPS & planetarium members. Closed New Year's Day; Thanksgiving; Christmas. &
Attendance: 20,000 (actual)

NATIONAL AUTOMOBILE MUSEUM (THE HARRAH COLLECTION), 10 South Lake St., Reno, NV 89501-1558. Tel.: 775-333-9300. Fax: 775-333-9309.
E-mail: info@automuseum.org
Web Site: www.automuseum.org
Key Personnel: Pres. & Exec. Dir., Jackie L. Frady; Chm. (V), Ranson Webster; Mgr. Business & Membership, Lisa Panko; Sales & Mktg. Mgr., Becky Contos; Mgr. Sr. Support Svcs., Barbara Clark; Automotive Collections Mgr., Jay Hubbard; Retail Mgr., Barbara Bolenbaker; Events & Operations Supvr., Nic Olson.
Institution Type/Description: Automobile Museum.
Hours & Admission Prices: Mon.-Sat. 9:30-5:30, Sun. 10-4. Adults $10, senior citizens $8, students 6-18 $4; discounts to AAM & AMG members; staff, museum members & children under 5 no charge. Closed Thanksgiving; Christmas. &
Attendance: 60,000 (actual)

NEVADA HISTORICAL SOCIETY, 1650 N. Virginia St., Reno, NV 89503-1799. Tel.: 775-688-1190. Fax: 775-688-2917. Facebook.
E-mail: cmagee@nevadaculture.org
Web Site: www.nvhistoricalsociety.org
Key Personnel: Pres (V) NHS Docent Council, Carol Coleman; Dir., Catherine Magee; Manuscript Cur., Sheryln Hayes-Zorn; Cur. Artifacts, Christine K. Johnson; Librarian, Michael Maher.
Institution Type/Description: Historical Society Museum.
Hours & Admission Prices: Museum: Tues.-Sat. 10-4:30. Library: Tues.-Sat. 12-4. Adults $5; children 17 & under and members no charge. Closed state holidays; UNR home football games. &
Attendance: 40,000 (estimated)

NEVADA MUSEUM OF ART, 160 W. Liberty, Reno, NV 89501-1916. Tel.: 775-329-3333. Fax: 775-329-1541. Facebook: @NevadaMuseumofArt; Twitter, Instagram & Snapchat: @nevadaart.
E-mail: art@nevadaart.org
Web Site: www.nevadaart.org
Key Personnel: Chair, John C. Deane; Exec. Dir. & CEO, David B. Walker; Deputy Dir. & COO, Amy Oppio; Cur. & Deputy Dir., Ann Wolfe; Registrar, Brian Eyler; Dir. Education, Marisa Cooper; Dir. Communications, Amanda Horn; Curatorial Dir. & Cur. Contemporary Art, JoAnne Northrup; Dir. Retail & Reception Svcs., Jackie Clay.
Institution Type/Description: Art Museum.
Hours & Admission Prices: Wed. & Fri.-Sun. 10-6, Thurs. 10-8. Adults $10, senior citizens & students $8, children $1; discount to AAM & NARM members; museum members no charge. Closed national holidays. &
Attendance: 150,000 (actual)

SHEPPARD CONTEMPORARY AND UNIVERSITY GALLERIES, CFA 162, University of Nevada, Reno, NV 89557. Mailing Address: Department of Art, University of Nevada/0224, Reno, NV 89557-0224. Tel.: 775-784-6658. Fax: 775-784-6655.
E-mail: bakerprindle@unr.edu
Web Site: www.unr.edu/arts/visitor-info/galleries-and-venues/sheppard
Formerly: Sheppard Fine Arts Gallery
Key Personnel: Dir. University Galleries, Paul Baker Prindle; Preparator, Richard Jackson.
Institution Type/Description: Fine Arts Gallery.
Hours & Admission Prices: Tues.-Wed. 11-5; Thurs. 11-8, Fri.-Sat. 10-8, Sun. 12-3. No charge; donations accepted. Closed state holidays. &
Attendance: 30,000 (estimated)

SIERRA ARTS GALLERY, 17 S. Virginia St., Ste. 120, Reno, NV 89501-2905. Tel.: 775-329-2787. Fax: 775-329-1328.

Web Site: www.sierra-arts.org
Key Personnel: Exec. Dir., Annie Zucker.
Institution Type/Description: Art Gallery.
Hours & Admission Prices: Call for hours. &

SIERRA SAFARI ZOO, 10200 N. Virginia St., Reno, NV 89506-9203. Tel.: 775-677-1101. Fax: 775-677-7874.
Web Site: www.sierrasafarizoo.org
Key Personnel: Gen. Mgr., Lori Acordagoitia.
Institution Type/Description: Zoo.
Hours & Admission Prices: April-Oct. daily 10-5. Adults $7, children 3-12 and seniors 55 & over $6; discounts to Public Broadcasting Members; children 2 & under no charge.

STREMMEL GALLERY, 1400 S. Virginia St., Reno, NV 89502-2806. Tel.: 775-786-0558. Fax: 775-786-0311.
E-mail: info@stremmelgallery.com
Web Site: stremmelgallery.com
Key Personnel: Exective Dir., Peter Stremmel; Dir., Turkey Stremmel; Mgr., Parker Stremmel.
Institution Type/Description: Art Gallery.
Hours & Admission Prices: Mon.-Fri. 9-5:30, Sat. 10-3. Closed holidays.

TERRY LEE WELLS NEVADA DISCOVERY MUSEUM (THE DISCOVERY), 490 S. Center St., Reno, NV 89501. Tel.: 775-786-1000. Fax: 775-786-1114.
E-mail: info@nvdm.org
Web Site: www.nvdm.org
Key Personnel: Pres. & C.E.O., Mat Sinclair, M.P.A.; Exec. Asst., Terry Butler; Dir. Devel., Danielle Williams; Dir. Devel., Leigh Fitzpatrick; Dir. Devel., Kestra Bronneke; Controller, Larissa Bayuk; VP Educ. & Exhibits, Sarah Gobbs-Hill; Exhibits Devel., Nathan Tobey; VP Mktg. & Communications, Patrick Turner.
Institution Type/Description: Science Center.
Hours & Admission Prices: Call for hours. Adults $12, children $10; members no charge. &

W.M. KECK EARTH SCIENCE AND MINERAL ENGINEERING MUSEUM, Mail Stop 168, Mackay School of Mines, University of Nevada, Reno, NV 89557. Tel.: 775-784-4528. Fax: 775-784-1766. Facebook: @keckmuseum.
E-mail: juliehill@unr.edu
Web Site: www.unr.edu/keck
Formerly: MacKay Mines Museum
Key Personnel: Admin. Asst., Julie Hill.
Institution Type/Description: Geology, Paleontology & Mineralogy Museum.
Hours & Admission Prices: Mon.-Fri. 9-4. No charge; donations accepted. Closed university holidays. &

WILBUR D. MAY MUSEUM, 1595 N. Sierra St., Inside Rancho San Rafael Regional Park, Reno, NV 89503-2862. Mailing Address: c/o Washoe County Manager's Office, 1001 E. Ninth St., Reno, NV 89512. Tel.: 775-785-5961. Fax: 775-325-6891.
Web Site: www.washoecounty.us/parks/maycenterhome
Key Personnel: Cur., Kristy Lide; Asst. Cur., Samantha Szesciorka.
Institution Type/Description: General Museum.
Hours & Admission Prices: Wed.-Sat. 10-4, Sun. 12-4. Adults $5, Seniors 62 & up and children 3-17 $3.50; children 2 & under no charge. &
Attendance: 55,000 (estimated)

Searchlight

SEARCHLIGHT HISTORIC MUSEUM & MINING PARK, 200 Michael Wendell Way, Searchlight, NV 89046. Mailing Address: P.O. Box 36, Searchlight, NV 89046-0036. Tel.: 702-297-1642.
Web Site: searchlighthistoricmuseum.org
Key Personnel: Founder, Jane Bunker Overy.
Institution Type/Description: History Museum.
Hours & Admission Prices: Mon.-Fri. 9-5; Sat. 9-1. No charge; donations accepted. Closed holidays. &
Attendance: 5,000 (estimated)

Silver Springs

FORT CHURCHILL STATE HISTORIC PARK, 1000 US Hwy. 95A N., Silver Springs, NV 89429. Tel.: 775-577-2345.
E-mail: ftchurchill@hdiss.net
Web Site: parks.nv.gov/parks/fort-churchill
Institution Type/Description: Historic Site: former U.S. Army fort; built in 1861.

Hours & Admission Prices: Call for hours.

Sparks

SPARKS HERITAGE FOUNDATION & MUSEUM, 820 Victorian Ave., Sparks, NV 89431-5077. Tel.: 775-355-1144. Fax: 775-355-6788.
E-mail: info@sparksmuseum.org
Web Site: www.sparksmuseum.org
Key Personnel: Dir., Anthea Humphreys; Pres. (V), Larma Volk.
Institution Type/Description: History Museum & Cultural Center.
Hours & Admission Prices: Museum: Tues.-Fri. 11-4, Sat.-Sun. 1-4. Train: Sat.-Sun. 1-4. Adults $5; children under 12, school groups & members no charge. Closed holidays. &
Attendance: 4,800 (actual)

Tonopah

CENTRAL NEVADA MUSEUM, 1900 Logan Field Rd., Tonopah, NV 89049. Mailing Address: P.O. Box 326, Tonopah, NV 89049-0326. Tel.: 775-482-9676. Fax: 775-482-5423. Facebook: CN Museum.
E-mail: cnmuseum@citlink.net
Web Site: www.tonopahnevada.com/CentralNevadaMuseum.html
Key Personnel: Pres. (V), Allen Metscher.
Institution Type/Description: History Museum.
Hours & Admission Prices: Tues.-Sat. 9-5, Sat. 1-5pm. No charge; donations accepted. Closed state & federal holidays. &
Attendance: 4,000 (estimated)

TONOPAH HISTORIC MINING PARK, 110 N. Burro Ave., Tonopah, NV 89049. Mailing Address: P.O. Box 965, Tonopah, NV 89049-0965. Tel.: 775-482-9274. Fax: 775-482-9327.
E-mail: tonopahminingpark@gmail.com
Web Site: www.tonopahhistoricminingpark.com
Key Personnel: Acting Admin., Rebecca Braska; Chmn. (V), Ann Carpenter; Museum Shop Mgr., Christy Perry.
Institution Type/Description: Mining History Museum.
Hours & Admission Prices: Daily 9-5. Walking tour: adults $5, children $4, seniors $3; members, veterans, active military & children 6 & under no charge; discounts to overnight visitors.
Attendance: 5,000 (estimated)

Virginia City

COMSTOCK HISTORY CENTER, 20 N. E St., Virginia City, NV 89440. Mailing Address: P.O. Box 128, Virginia City, NV 89440. Tel.: 775-847-0419. Fax: 775-847-0653. Facebook.
E-mail: jeff.wood@shpo.nv.gov
Key Personnel: Mgr., Jeff Wood.
Institution Type/Description: History Museum.
Hours & Admission Prices: Thurs.-Sat. 10-4:30. No charge; donations accepted. &
Attendance: 4,700 (actual)

FOURTH WARD SCHOOL MUSEUM, 537 S. C St., Virginia City, NV 89440. Mailing Address: P.O. Box 4, Virginia City, NV 89440-0004. Tel.: 775-847-0875. Fax: 775-847-1011.
E-mail: director@fourthwardschool.org
Web Site: www.fourthwardschool.org
Key Personnel: Dir., Barbara Mackey; Pres. (V), Ron Gallagher.
Institution Type/Description: History Museum.
Hours & Admission Prices: May-Oct. daily 10-5. Adults $5, children 6-16 $3; discounts to Smithsonian Day, Blue Star Museum, AAM & National Trust members; members & children under 6 no charge. &
Attendance: 21,362 (actual)

MACKAY MANSION, 129 S. D St., Virginia City, NV 89440. Mailing Address: P.O. Box 971, Virginia City, NV 89440-0971. Tel.: 775-847-0173.
E-mail: mackaymansion291@gmail.com
Web Site: www.therealmackaymansion.com
Institution Type/Description: Historic House; built in 1859. Listed on the National Register of Historic Places.
Hours & Admission Prices: Daily 10-6.

MARSHALL MINT MUSEUM, 96 N. C St., Virginia City, NV 89440. Mailing Address: P.O. Box 447, Virginia City, NV 89440-0447. Tel.: 775-847-0777, 800-321-6374. Fax: 775-847-9543.

Institution Type/Description: Mint Museum: housed in the Assay Office building; built in 1861.
Hours & Admission Prices: Daily 10-5. Closed Thanksgiving; Christmas.

NEVADA STATE FIRE MUSEUM & COMSTOCK FIREMEN'S MUSEUM, 125 S. C St., Virginia City, NV 89440. Mailing Address: P.O. Box 466, Virginia City, NV 89440-0466. Tel.: 775-847-0717. Fax: 775-847-9010.
E-mail: comstockfiremensmuseum@yahoo.com
Web Site: comstockfiremuseum.com
Key Personnel: Chm. (V), Michael E. Nevin; Sec. & Treas., Joseph L. Curtis; Museum Shop Mgr., Eleanor Curtis.
Institution Type/Description: Fire-Fighting Museum: housed in c.1870 structure.
Hours & Admission Prices: late April & Nov.-Dec. Sat.-Sun. 10-5 weather permitting; May-Oct. daily 10-5. No charge; donations accepted. &
Attendance: 43,917 (actual)

THE WAY IT WAS MUSEUM, 113 N. C St., Virginia City, NV 89440. Mailing Address: P.O. Box 158, Virginia City, NV 89440-0158. Tel.: 775-847-0766.
Institution Type/Description: History Museum.
Hours & Admission Prices: Daily 10-6. Adults $3; children 11 & under no charge. Closed Christmas.

Winnemucca

BUCKAROO HALL OF FAME, 30 W. Winnemucca Blvd., Winnemucca, NV 89445-3129. Mailing Address: 30774 Culp Lane, Burns, OR 97720. Tel.: 775-623-2225. Fax: 800-962-2638.
E-mail: BuckarooHallofFame@yahoo.com
Web Site: www.buckaroohalloffame.com
Key Personnel: Cur., Carl Hammond.
Institution Type/Description: Art Museum.
Hours & Admission Prices: Daily 8-12 & 1-5. No charge; donations accepted.

HUMBOLDT MUSEUM, 175 Museum Ln., Winnemucca, NV 89446. Mailing Address: P.O. Box 819, Winnemucca, NV 89446-0819. Tel.: 775-623-2912. Fax: 775-623-5640.
E-mail: dana@humboldtmuseum.org
Web Site: humboldtmuseum.org
Key Personnel: Dir., Dana Toth; Pres. (V), Judy Adams.
Institution Type/Description: History Museum.
Hours & Admission Prices: Wed.-Fri. 9-4, Sat. 10-4. No charge; donations accepted. &
Attendance: 8,000 (estimated)

Yerington

LYON COUNTY MUSEUM, 215 S. Main St., Yerington, NV 89447-2536. Tel.: 775-463-6576.
E-mail: info@lyoncomus.com
Web Site: www.lyoncountymuseum.com
Key Personnel: Chm. (V), Mike Hagen; Museum Shop Mgr., Mary Page.
Institution Type/Description: History Museum.
Hours & Admission Prices: Thurs.-Sun. 1-4; other times by appointment. No charge; donations accepted. &
Attendance: 1,500 (estimated)

NEW HAMPSHIRE

(144 listings)

Allenstown

MUSEUM OF FAMILY CAMPING, Bear Brook State Park, 157 Deerfield Rd., Allenstown, NH 03275-2503. Mailing Address: 100 Athol Rd., Richmond, NH 03470-4200. Tel.: 603-239-4768.
Institution Type/Description: Camping History Museum.
Hours & Admission Prices: Memorial Day to Sept. daily 10-4. No charge; donations accepted.

THE NEW HAMPSHIRE SNOWMOBILE MUSEUM, Bear Brook State Park, Rte. 28, Allenstown, NH 03275. Mailing Address: P.O. Box 10112, Concord, NH 03301-0112. Tel.: 603-722-7069.
E-mail: info@nhsnowmobilemuseum.com
Web Site: www.nhsnowmobilemuseum.com
Key Personnel: Dir., Greg Lewis; Pres., Dan Lewis; Vice Pres., George Burdick.

Institution Type/Description: Snowmobile Museum.
Hours & Admission Prices: Jan.-March Sat. 1-3; Memorial Day to Columbus Day by appointment. No charge; donations accepted.

Alton

THE HAROLD S. GILMAN MUSEUM, Main St. & Rte. 140, Alton, NH 03809. Mailing Address: 1 Monument Square, P.O. Box 637, Alton, NH 03809-0637. Tel.: 603-875-2161. Fax: 603-875-0207.
Web Site: www.alton.nh.gov/government/gilman-museum
Institution Type/Description: History Museum.
Hours & Admission Prices: Call for hours.

Amherst

THE CHAPEL MUSEUM, 5 Middle St., Amherst, NH 03031. Mailing Address: Historical Society of Amherst, P.O. Box 717, Amherst, NH 03031-0717. Tel.: 603-672-9831. Facebook: @amhearsthistoricalsociety.
E-mail: historicalsociety@hsanh.org
Web Site: www.hsanh.org
Key Personnel: Dir. Museums & Cur., Susan Fischer; Asst. Cur., Bonnie Knott.
Institution Type/Description: History Museum: built in 1858.
Hours & Admission Prices: May-Oct. 2nd Sat. each month 1-4. No charge; donations accepted.

THE WIGWAM MUSEUM, 17 Middle St., Amherst, NH 03031. Mailing Address: Historical Society of Amherst, P.O. Box 717, Amherst, NH 03031-0717. Tel.: 603-672-9831; 8029. Facebook: @amhearsthistoricalsociety.
E-mail: historicalsocieity@hsanh.org
Web Site: www.hsanh.org
Key Personnel: Genealogy Chair, Jackie Marshall; Dir. Museums, Susan Fischer; Cur., Lisa Montesanto; Asst. Cur., Chris Marshall.
Institution Type/Description: History Museum: former Methodist chapel built in 1839.
Hours & Admission Prices: May-Oct. 2nd Sat. each month 1-4. No charge; donations accepted.

Ashland

ASHLAND RAILROAD STATION MUSEUM, 69 Depot St., Ashland, NH 03217. Mailing Address: P.O. Box 175, Ashland, NH 03217-0175. Tel.: 603-968-7716.
E-mail: davidruell@gmail.com
Key Personnel: Pres. Historical Society, David Ruell; Vice Pres., Jeanette Stewart; Treas., Robert Baker.
Institution Type/Description: Transportation Museum: housed in c.1869 Victorian railroad station.
Hours & Admission Prices: July-Aug. Sat. 1-4. Suggested Donation: Adults $2; members, school groups & children no charge. &
Attendance: 750 (estimated)

PAULINE E. GLIDDEN TOY MUSEUM, 49 Main St., Ashland, NH 03217. Mailing Address: P.O. Box 14, Ashland, NH 03217-0014. Tel.: 603-968-7524.
E-mail: willynorman57@gmail.com
Key Personnel: Pres. Historical Society, David Ruell; Dir. Toy Museum, Shirley Splaine.
Institution Type/Description: Early Toy Museum.
Hours & Admission Prices: July-Aug. Wed.-Fri. 1-4. Adults $2; children 12 & under no charge.
Attendance: 275 (actual)

WHIPPLE HOUSE MUSEUM, ASHLAND HISTORICAL SOCIETY, 14 Pleasant St., Ashland, NH 03217. Mailing Address: P.O. Box 175, Ashland, NH 03217-0175. Tel.: 603-968-7716. Fax: 603-968-7716.
E-mail: davidruell@gmail.com
Web Site: www.oldashlandnh.org
Key Personnel: Pres., David Ruell; Vice Pres., Jeanette Stewart; Treas., Robert Baker.
Institution Type/Description: Local History Museum: 1837 brick house, birthplace & childhood home of George Hoyt Whipple, winner of the Nobel Prize for medicine.
Hours & Admission Prices: July-Aug. Thurs. 1-4. Suggested Donation: adults $2; children, school groups & members no charge.
Attendance: 100 (estimated)

Auburn

MASSABESIC AUDUBON CENTER, 26 Audubon Way, Auburn, NH 03032-3109. Tel.: 603-668-2045.
E-mail: mac@nhaudubon.org
Web Site: www.nhaudubon.org
Institution Type/Description: Nature Center.
Hours & Admission Prices: Feb.-Nov. Tues.-Sat. 9-5; Dec.-Jan. Tues.-Fri. 9-5, Sat. 9-4.

Barrington

LITTLETON GRIST MILL, 79 Meadowbrook Dr., Barrington, NH 03825-7105. Mailing Address: P.O. Box 133, Barrington, NH 03825. Tel.: 603-259-3205.
E-mail: shop@littletongristmillonline.com
Web Site: www.littletongristmillonline.com
Institution Type/Description: Historic Building: built in 1797.
Hours & Admission Prices: Wed.-Sat. 10:30-3:30. No charge.

Bedford

BEDFORD HISTORICAL SOCIETY, 24 N. Amherst Rd., Bedford, NH 03110-5404. Tel.: 603-471-6336.
E-mail: info@bedfordhistoricalnh.org
Web Site: www.bedfordhistoricalnh.org
Key Personnel: Dir. Museum, Margaret Wiggin.
Institution Type/Description: History Museum.
Hours & Admission Prices: By appointment. No charge.

Berlin

THE MOFFETT HOUSE MUSEUM & GENEALOGY CENTER, 119 High St., Berlin, NH 03570-2062. Mailing Address: P.O. Box 52, Berlin, NH 03570-0052. Tel.: 603-752-7337. www.berlinnhhistoricalsociety.org.
E-mail: bcchs@hotmail.com
Key Personnel: Pres. (V), Renney Morneau; Vice Pres. (V), Walter Nadeau.
Institution Type/Description: Historic House: former home and office of Dr. and Mrs. Irving Moffett.
Hours & Admission Prices: Tues.-Sat. 12-4; other times by appointment. No charge; donations accepted. Closed major holidays.
Attendance: 800 (estimated)

NORTHERN FOREST HERITAGE PARK & BROWN HOUSE MUSEUM, 961 Main St., Berlin, NH 03570-3031. Tel.: 603-752-7202. Fax: 603-752-7222.
E-mail: heritage@ncia.net
Web Site: www.northernforestheritage.org
Key Personnel: Dir., Dick Huot; C.E.O., Joe Costello.
Institution Type/Description: Park & Historic House.
Hours & Admission Prices: Park: late May to early Oct. Tues.-Sat. 10-4. House: daily 9-4. Boat Tours: June-Oct. Tues.-Sat. 6pm. Tours: adult $15, children 5-11 $8; children under 5 no charge. ♿

Campton

CAMPTON HISTORICAL SOCIETY, Town House, 529 NH Rte. 175, Campton, NH 03223. Mailing Address: P.O. Box 160, Campton, NH 03223-0160. Tel.: 603-536-5140.
E-mail: camptonhistorical@gmail.com
Web Site: www.camptonhistorical.org
Institution Type/Description: Historical Society Museum: housed in the former Town Hall, library, and municipal court; built in 1855.
Hours & Admission Prices: Thurs. 9-4. No charge; donations accepted.

Canaan

CANAAN HISTORICAL SOCIETY AND MUSEUM, Canaan St., Canaan, NH 03741. Tel.: 603-523-9559.
E-mail: dfleethamjr@netzero.com
Web Site: www.canaannh.org
Key Personnel: Pres. (V), Daniel W. Fleetham, Jr.
Institution Type/Description: History Museum.
Hours & Admission Prices: June-Oct. Sat. 1-4. No charge; donations accepted.

Candia

FITTS MUSEUM, 185 High St., Candia, NH 03034. Mailing Address: c/o Town Office, 74 High St., Candia, NH 03034-2751. Tel.: 603-483-8881.
E-mail: fittsmuseum@comcast.net
Web Site: www.fittsmuseum.org
Institution Type/Description: Historic House Museum.
Hours & Admission Prices: May-Oct. third Sat. of the month 1-4; other times by appointment. No charge; donations accepted.
Attendance: 150 (estimated)

Canterbury

CANTERBURY SHAKER VILLAGE, INC., 288 Shaker Rd., Canterbury, NH 03224-2728. Tel.: 603-783-9511, ext. 200. Fax: 603-783-9362.
E-mail: info@shakers.org
Web Site: www.shakers.org
Key Personnel: Exec. Dir., Funi Burdick; Chm. (V), Deane Morrison; Archivist, Renee Fox; Museum Store Mgr., Dawn Demers.
Institution Type/Description: Historic Site & Village: 1792 preserved Shaker community consisting of 25 buildings on 694 acres.
Hours & Admission Prices: Call for hours & admissions prices. ♿
Attendance: 30,000 (estimated)

Center Sandwich

PATRICIA LADD CAREGA GALLERY, 69 Maple St., Center Sandwich, NH 03227. Mailing Address: P.O. Box 417, Center Sandwich, NH 03227. Tel.: 603-284-7728 & 6692.
Web Site: www.patricialaddcarega.com
Institution Type/Description: Art Gallery.
Hours & Admission Prices: Memorial Day to mid-Oct. Mon.-Sat. 10-5, Sun. 12-5.

SANDWICH HISTORICAL SOCIETY, 4 Maple St., Center Sandwich, NH 03227. Mailing Address: P.O. Box 244, Center Sandwich, NH 03227-0244. Tel.: 603-284-6269. Facebook.
E-mail: sandwichhistory@gmail.com
Web Site: www.sandwichhistorical.org
Key Personnel: Pres. (V), Geoff Burrows; Dir., Abby Hambrook.
Institution Type/Description: Local History Museum: housed in c.1850 Elisha Marston House; Quimby Barn Transportation Museum; Lower Corner School House; Grange Hall.
Hours & Admission Prices: late June to early Oct. Wed. - Sat. 10-4; other times by appointment. No charge; donations accepted.
Attendance: 2,000 (estimated)

Charlestown

CHARLESTOWN HISTORICAL SOCIETY, Town Hall, Archives Rm., 19 Summer St., Charlestown, NH 03603. Mailing Address: P.O. Box 159, Charlestown, NH 03603. Tel.: 603-826-9943.
E-mail: patricia@charlestown-nh.gov
Web Site: www.charlestown-nh.gov
Key Personnel: Pres., Joyce Higgins; Vice Pres., Pat Ahern; Treas., Judy Baraly; Sec., Cur. & Archivist, Marge Reed.
Institution Type/Description: Historical Society Museum.
Hours & Admission Prices: Memorial Day weekend & Columbus Day weekend; other times by appointment. Archives: Tues. 9am to noon. No charge; donations accepted. ♿
Attendance: 450 (estimated)

THE FORT AT NO. 4 LIVING HISTORY MUSEUM, 267 Springfield Rd., Rte. 11, Charlestown, NH 03603. Mailing Address: P.O. Box 1336, Charlestown, NH 03603-1336. Tel.: 603-826-5700.
E-mail: info@fortat4.com
Web Site: www.fortat4.org
Formerly: Old Fort Number 4 Associates
Key Personnel: Dir., Wendalyn Baker; Chm. (V), Albert St. Pierre.
Institution Type/Description: Historic Site Museum: granted in 1735 by Crown Province of Massachusetts, completed as a fortified village in 1744.
Hours & Admission Prices: Tours: April by appointment. Museum: May-Oct. daily 10-4:30. Adults $12, senior citizens 62 & over $10, children 6-17 $8; discounts to AAM & AAA members; members & children under 5 no charge. ♿
Attendance: 14,000 (estimated)

Claremont

THE CLAREMONT, NEW HAMPSHIRE HISTORICAL SOCIETY, INC., 26 Mulberry St., Claremont, NH 03743-2538. Mailing Address: P.O. Box 973, Claremont, NH 03470-0973. Tel.: 603-543-1400.
E-mail: claremont_historical@yahoo.com
Web Site: www.claremonthistoricalsociety.org
Key Personnel: Pres. & Chm. Bd. Trustees, Colin J. Sanborn.
Institution Type/Description: Local History Museum.
Hours & Admission Prices: mid-June to mid-Sept. Sat. 1-4; call for additional hours. Admission $1.

Colebrook

COLEBROOK AREA HISTORICAL MUSEUM, 17 Bridge St., 2nd Fl., Colebrook, NH 03576. Mailing Address: P.O. Box 32, Colebrook, NH 03576-0032. Tel.: 603-237-4470.
E-mail: agoodrum@myfairpoint.net
Web Site: colebrookareahistoricalsociety.weebly.com
Key Personnel: Pres., Arnold Goodrum.
Institution Type/Description: History Museum.
Hours & Admission Prices: Town Hall Museum: July-Aug. Sat. 10-1; other times by appointment. Tillotson Center Annex: open during center events; other times by appointment. No charge; donations accepted. &

Concord

ART CENTER IN HARGATE, ST. PAUL'S SCHOOL, 325 Pleasant St., Concord, NH 03301-2591. Tel.: 603-229-4643. Fax: 603-229-5696.
E-mail: ccallahan@sps.edu
Web Site: www.sps.edu
Key Personnel: Dir., Colin J. Callahan.
Institution Type/Description: Art Gallery.
Hours & Admission Prices: Sept.-May Tues.-Sat. 9:30-4. No charge. Closed spring break; Thanksgiving break; Christmas vacation. &
Attendance: 3,700 (estimated)

AUDUBON SOCIETY OF NEW HAMPSHIRE, 84 Silk Farm Rd., Concord, NH 03301-8311. Tel.: 603-224-9909. Fax: 603-226-0902.
E-mail: nha@nhaudubon.org
Web Site: www.nhaudubon.org
Key Personnel: C.E.O. & Pres., Michael Bartlett; Chm. (V), Paul Nickerson; Dir. Membership & Devel., Eric Berger; Museum Shop Mgr., Nancy Boisvert.
Institution Type/Description: Nature Center & Conservation Area.
Hours & Admission Prices: Mon.-Fri. 9-5. No charge; donations accepted. Closed legal holidays. &
Attendance: 100,000 (estimated)

KIMBALL JENKINS ESTATE, 266 N. Main St., Concord, NH 03301-5053. Tel.: 603-225-3932. Fax: 603-225-9288.
E-mail: arts@kimballjenkins.com
Web Site: www.kimballjenkins.com
Institution Type/Description: Art Gallery.
Hours & Admission Prices: Mon.-Fri. 9-4; other times by appointment.

MARY BAKER EDDY HISTORIC HOUSE, 62 N. State St., Concord, NH 03301-4330. Mailing Address: Longyear Museum, 1125 Boylston St., Chestnut Hill, MA 02467. Tel.: 603-225-3444. Facebook: Longyear Museum.
E-mail: marketing@longyear.org
Web Site: www.longyear.org
Key Personnel: Pres., Sandra J. Houston.
Institution Type/Description: Historic House: built c.1850.
Hours & Admission Prices: May-Oct. Mon.-Tues. & Sat. 10-4, Sun. 1-4; other times by appointment; Nov.-April by appointment. Suggested Donation: $7.

MCAULIFFE-SHEPARD DISCOVERY CENTER, 2 Institute Dr., Concord, NH 03301-7400. Tel.: 603-271-7827. Fax: 603-271-7832. Facebook: MS Discovery Center.
E-mail: epappas@starhop.com
Web Site: www.starhop.com
Formerly: Christa McAuliffe Planetarium
Key Personnel: Exec. Dir., Jeanne T. Gerulskis; Chm. (V), Paul A. Burkett, Esq.; C. F.O., Will Swyers; Dir. Education, Dr. Kimberley Duncan; Coord. Operations, Sherie Moore; Education Coord., R.P. Hale.
Institution Type/Description: Science Center.

Hours & Admission Prices: Summer & School Vacations: daily 10:30-4. Non-vacation weeks: Fri.-Sun. 10:30-4, 1st Fri. each month 6:30 pm-9 pm. Adults $10, seniors & students $9, children 3-12 $7; discounts to ASTC members; members and children 2 & under no charge. Planetarium: additional $5. Closed New Year's Day; Easter; Memorial Day; Independence Day; Labor Day; Thanksgiving; Christmas. &
Attendance: 40,721 (actual)

NEW HAMPSHIRE HISTORICAL SOCIETY, 30 Park St., Concord, NH 03301-4956. Tel.: 603-228-6688. Fax: 603-224-0463.
E-mail: jdesmarais@nhhistory.org
Web Site: www.nhhistory.org
Key Personnel: Pres., William H. Dunlap; Vice Pres., Joan E. Desmarais; Chm., Kurt M. Swenson; Dir. Education & Public Programs, Elizabeth Dubrulle; Dir. Collections & Exhibitions, Wesley Balla; Dir. Library, Sarah Gallagin; Dir. Finance, Michael E. Marr; Collections Mgr., Douglas Copeley.
Institution Type/Description: History Museum.
Hours & Admission Prices: Tues.-Sat. 9:30-5. Adults $7; members, children under 18, full-time students, active military & their families no charge. &
Attendance: 23,189 (actual)

NEW HAMPSHIRE STATE HOUSE AND VISITORS CENTER, 107 N. Main St., Concord, NH 03301. Tel.: 603-271-2154.
E-mail: virginia.drew@leg.state.nh.us
Web Site: gencourt.state.nh.us/nh_visitorcenter/default.htm
Institution Type/Description: Historic Building: built in 1819.
Hours & Admission Prices: Mon.-Fri. 8-4:15.

THE PIERCE MANSE, 14 Horseshoe Pond Lane, Concord, NH 03301-5028. Mailing Address: P.O. Box 425, Concord, NH 03302-0425. Tel.: 603-225-4555. Fax: 603-225-0540. Facebook: Pierce Manse.
E-mail: piercebrigade@gmail.com
Web Site: www.piercemanse.org
Key Personnel: Pres. (V), Joan Woodhead; Chm. (V), Joan Davis; Museum Shop Mgr., Maureen Rogers.
Institution Type/Description: Historic House Museum: 1842-1848 home of President Franklin Pierce.
Hours & Admission Prices: Pierce Manse: mid-June to Labor Day Tues.-Sat. 11-3; Labor Day to mid-Oct. Fri. & Sat. 12-3; groups of 10 or more by appointment. Family $15, adults $7, senior citizens $6, children & students $3; members no charge. Closed holidays. &
Attendance: 1,100 (actual)

Conway

EASTMAN LORD HOUSE, 100 Main St., Conway, NH 03818. Mailing Address: Conway Historical Society, P.O. Box 1949, Conway, NH 03818-1949. Tel.: 603-447-5551. Fax: 603-447-1991.
E-mail: conwayhistoricalsociety@gmail.com
Web Site: www.conwayhistoricalsociety.org
Key Personnel: Pres. (V), Ken Rancourt; Cur., Bob Cottrell.
Institution Type/Description: Historic House Museum: housed in the home of Conway mill owner, William Kimball Eastman, c.1818. Listed on the National Register of Historic Places
Hours & Admission Prices: Currently closed to public.
Attendance: 68 (actual)

Cornish

SAINT-GAUDENS NATIONAL HISTORIC SITE, 139 Saint Gaudens Rd., Cornish, NH 03745-4232. Tel.: 603-675-2175. Fax: 603-675-2701. Facebook: Saint Gaudens National Historic Site.
E-mail: rick_kendall@nps.gov
Web Site: www.nps.gov/saga
Key Personnel: Supt., Rick Kendall; Administrative Officer, April May Preston; Supvr. Interpretation, Chief Ranger, Volunteer Coord. & Museum Shop Mgr., Gregory C. Schwarz; Cur., Henry J. Duffy, Ph.D.; Facility Mgr., Steven Walasewicz.
Institution Type/Description: Art Museum: home & studio of Augustus Saint-Gaudens, American sculptor (1848-1907).
Hours & Admission Prices: late May to Oct. daily 9-4:30. Adults $7; discounts to US fee area, America the Beautiful, Senior Passes, National Park Pass, Golden Age, Golden Eagle & annual pass; children 15 & under and school groups no charge.
Attendance: 40,000 (estimated)

Derry

ROBERT FROST FARM, 122 Rockingham Rd., Rte. 28, Derry, NH 03038. Mailing Address: P.O. Box 1075, Derry, NH 03038-1075. Tel.: 603-432-3091.
E-mail: info@robertfrostfarm.org
Web Site: www.robertfrostfarm.org
Key Personnel: Co Chm., Cara Barlow; Co Chair, Robert Crawford; Historic Site Specialist, Ben Wilson; Museum Shop Mgr., William Gleed.
Institution Type/Description: Historic Site: 1900-1909 home of Robert Frost & setting for 43 of his poems.
Hours & Admission Prices: Call for hours and admission prices.
Attendance: 6,500 (estimated)

Dover

THE CHILDREN'S MUSEUM OF NEW HAMPSHIRE, 6 Washington St., Dover, NH 03820-3814. Tel.: 603-742-2002. Fax: 603-834-6275. Facebook: The Children's Museum of New Hampshire.
E-mail: questions@childrens-museum.org
Web Site: www.childrens-museum.org
Formerly: The Children's Museum of Portsmouth
Key Personnel: Pres., Jane Bard; Vice Pres. Devel. & Community Engagement, Paula Rais; Exhibit Dir., Mark Cuddy; Lead Educator, Meredith Lamothe; Gift Shop Mgr., Riley Batchelder; Dir. Visitor Svcs., Doug Tilton.
Institution Type/Description: Children's Museum.
Hours & Admission Prices: Tues.-Sat. 10-5, Sun. 12-5. Adults & children over one $9, seniors 65 & over $8; discounts to groups of 10 or more; ACM & ASTC members, museum members & children under one no charge. Closed New Year's Day; Easter; Labor Day; Thanksgiving; Christmas Eve & Day.
Attendance: 120,000 (estimated)

WOODMAN INSTITUTE MUSEUM, 182 Central Ave., Dover, NH 03820. Mailing Address: P.O. Box 1916, Dover, NH 03821-1916. Tel.: 603-742-1038.
E-mail: contact@woodmanmuseum.org
Web Site: www.woodmaninstitutemuseum.org
Institution Type/Description: History Museum.
Hours & Admission Prices: April-Nov. Wed.-Sun. 12-4:30. Adults $8, seniors 65 & over and students $6, children 6-15 $3; children 5 & under and members no charge. Closed holidays.

Durham

DURHAM HISTORIC ASSOCIATION MUSEUM, Rte. 108 & Main St., Durham, NH 03824-2815. Mailing Address: 21 Newmarket Rd., Durham, NH 03824-2815. Tel.: 603-868-2628.
E-mail: drsues1@gmail.com
Web Site: www.ci.durham.nh.us/community/durham-historic-association
Key Personnel: Pres., Richard Lord.
Institution Type/Description: Local History Museum: housed in c.1825 Town Hall.
Hours & Admission Prices: By appointment. No charge; donations accepted.
Attendance: 100 (estimated)

MUSEUM OF ART, UNH, Paul Creative Arts Center, 30 Academic Way, Durham, NH 03824-2617. Tel.: 603-862-3712. Fax: 603-862-2191.
E-mail: museum.of.art@unh.edu
Web Site: www.cola.unh.edu/moa
Key Personnel: Dir., Kristina Durocher; Pres. Bd. Advisors, Linda Chastney; Mgr. Exhibitions & Collections, Laura Calhoun; Education & Communication Mgr., Sara Zela; Administrative Asst., Cynthia Farrell.
Institution Type/Description: Art Museum.
Hours & Admission Prices: Sept.-May Mon.-Wed. 10-4, Thurs. 10-8, Sat.-Sun. 1-5. No charge; donations accepted. Closed university holidays.
Attendance: 6,297 (actual)

Enfield

ENFIELD SHAKER MUSEUM, 447 NH Rte. 4A, Enfield, NH 03748-3503. Tel.: 603-632-4346.
E-mail: info@shakermuseum.org
Web Site: www.shakermuseum.org
Formerly: Museum at Lower Shaker Village
Key Personnel: Exec. Dir., Dolores C. Struckhoff; Cur., Michael O'Connor; Coord. Events, Anna Guenther; Education Coord., Althea Goundrey.
Institution Type/Description: Historic Village: 1793 Shaker community.
Hours & Admission Prices: Jan.-May by appointment; May-Dec. Mon.-Sat. 10-4, Sun. noon-4. Adults $12, groups of 6 $10, youth 11-17 $8; children 6-10 $3;

children 5 & under no charge. Closed New Year's Eve & Day; Presidents' Day; Easter; Memorial Day; Independence Day; Labor Day; Thanksgiving & day after; Christmas Eve & Day.
Attendance: 5,000 (estimated)

LOCKEHAVEN SCHOOLHOUSE MUSEUM, Corner of Lockehaven Rd. & Ibey Rd., Enfield, NH 03748. Mailing Address: P.O. Box 612, Enfield, NH 03748-0612. Tel.: 603-632-7740.
Key Personnel: C.E.O., Paul Waehler; Vice Pres., Linda Jones; Treas., John P. Carr; Historian, Marjorie A. Carr.
Institution Type/Description: Historic Building: 1864 Lockehaven Schoolhouse.
Hours & Admission Prices: mid-June to Sept. Sun. 2-4. No charge.
Attendance: 150 (estimated)

Enfield Center

ENFIELD HISTORICAL SOCIETY MUSEUM, 1047 NH Rt. 4A, Enfield Center, NH 03749. Mailing Address: P.O. Box 612, Enfield, NH 03748-0612. Tel.: 603-632-7740.
Key Personnel: Pres., Paul Waehler; Vice Pres., Linda Jones; Treas., John P. Carr; Historian, Marjorie A. Carr.
Institution Type/Description: Historical Society Museum: housed in an 1851 structure that was used as a schoolhouse for 95 years.
Hours & Admission Prices: June-Sept. by appointment. No charge; donations accepted.
Attendance: 150 (estimated)

Epping

EPPING HISTORICAL SOCIETY, 11 Water St., Epping, NH 03802. Mailing Address: P.O. Box 348, Epping, NH 03042-0348. Tel.: 603-679-2944.
E-mail: joysgarden@hotmail.com
Key Personnel: Pres. (V) & Cur., Joy true.
Institution Type/Description: Historical Society Museum.
Hours & Admission Prices: Mon. 8-12; other times by appointment. No charge.
Attendance: 200 (estimated)

Exeter

AMERICAN INDEPENDENCE MUSEUM, One Governors Lane, Exeter, NH 03833-2420. Tel.: 603-772-2622. Fax: 603-772-0861.
E-mail: info@independencemuseum.org
Web Site: www.independencemuseum.org
Key Personnel: Exec. Dir., Julie Hall Williams; Pres., Susan Y. Desjardins; Museum Shop Mgr., Rachel Passannante.
Institution Type/Description: Historic House Museum: c.1721 Ladd-Gilman House & c.1775 Folsom Tavern.
Hours & Admission Prices: May-Nov. Tues.-Sat. 10-4. Adults $6, seniors 65 & over $5, students 6-18 $3; discounts to AAA & AAM members; children under 6 & members no charge.
Attendance: 5,023 (actual)

EXETER HISTORICAL SOCIETY, 47 Front St., Exeter, NH 03833-2707. Mailing Address: P.O. Box 924, Exeter, NH 03833-0924. Tel.: 603-778-2335. Facebook.
E-mail: info@exeterhistory.org
Web Site: www.exeterhistory.org
Key Personnel: Chm. (V), Ann Schieber; Cur., Barbara Rimkunas; Program Mgr., Laura Martin.
Institution Type/Description: Historical Society Museum: housed in the former public library; c. 1894.
Hours & Admission Prices: Tues. & Thurs. 2-4:30, Sat. 9:30 to noon. No charge; donations accepted.
Attendance: 1,200 (estimated)

GILMAN GARRISON, 12 Water St., Exeter, NH 03833-2431. Mailing Address: Historic New England Administrative Offices, Otis House, 141 Cambridge St., Boston, MA 02114-2702. Tel.: 603-436-3205.
E-mail: news@historicnewengland.org
Web Site: www.historicnewengland.org
Formerly: Gilman Garrison
Key Personnel: Pres., Carl R. Nold; Site Mgr., Linda Marshall.
Institution Type/Description: Historic House: 1709 Gilman Garrison House.
Hours & Admission Prices: June-Oct. 15 third Sat. 11-5. Adults $6, seniors $5, students $3; members no charge.
Attendance: 389 (actual)

THE LAMONT GALLERY, Phillips Exeter Academy, 11 Tan Lane, Exeter, NH 03833. Mailing Address: 20 Main St., Exeter, NH 03383. Tel.: 603-777-3461. Fax: 603-777-4371.
E-mail: gallery@exeter.edu
Web Site: www.exeter.edu/arts/8160.aspx
Key Personnel: Dir. & Cur., Lauren O'Neal; Gallery Mgr., Stacey Durand.
Institution Type/Description: Art Gallery.
Hours & Admission Prices: Academic Year: Mon. 1-5, Tues.-Sat. 9-5; July Tues.-Fri. 9-4. No charge. Closed school holidays. &
Attendance: 5,000 (estimated)

Fitzwilliam

FITZWILLIAM HISTORICAL SOCIETY & AMOS J. BLAKE HOUSE MUSEUM, 66 Rte. 119 - Village Green, Fitzwilliam, NH 03447. Mailing Address: P.O. Box 87, Fitzwilliam, NH 03447-0087. Tel.: 603-585-7742.
E-mail: info@fitzwilliamhistoricalsociety.org
Web Site: www.fitzwilliam.org/ftblake.htm
Key Personnel: Pres., Theresa Sillapaa.
Institution Type/Description: History Museum.
Hours & Admission Prices: Museum: Memorial Day to Labor Day Sat. 1-4; other times by appointment. Research: Thurs. 9-11. No charge; donations accepted. &
Attendance: 35 (estimated)

Franconia

FRANCONIA HERITAGE MUSEUM AND IRON FURNACE INTERPRETIVE CENTER, 553 Main St., Franconia, NH 03580. Mailing Address: P.O. Box 169, Franconia, NH 03580-0169. Tel.: 603-823-5000.
E-mail: heritagemuseum@myfairpoint.net
Web Site: www.franconianh.org
Key Personnel: Pres., Dot Wiggins; Vice Pres., Barbara Holt.
Institution Type/Description: Historic House Museum.
Hours & Admission Prices: Memorial Day to Oct. Sat. 1-4; other times by appointment. No charge; donations accepted. &
Attendance: 865 (actual)

THE FROST PLACE, 158 Ridge Rd., Franconia, NH 03580. Mailing Address: P.O. Box 74, Franconia, NH 03580-0074. Tel.: 603-823-5510. Facebook, Instagram, Twitter.
E-mail: frost@frostplace.org
Web Site: www.frostplace.org
Key Personnel: Exec. Dir., Maudelle Driskell; Chm. Bd. (V), Evan Hammond; Museum Shop Mgr., Paige Roberts.
Institution Type/Description: History Museum.
Hours & Admission Prices: Memorial Day to July 1 Thurs.-Sun. 1-5; July-Sept. Wed.-Mon. 1-5; Labor Day to Columbus Day Wed.-Mon. 10-5. Adults $5, seniors $4, children $3. &
Attendance: 3,500 (actual)

NEW ENGLAND SKI MUSEUM, 135 Tramway Drive, Franconia, NH 03580. Mailing Address: P.O. Box 267, Franconia, NH 03580-0267. Tel.: 603-823-7177. Fax: 603-823-9505.
E-mail: staff@skimuseum.org
Web Site: www.skimuseum.org
Key Personnel: Exec. Dir., Jeffrey R. Leich; Pres. (V), Bo Adams; Museum Shop Mgr. & Front Desk Staffer, Linda Bradshaw; Front Desk Staffer, Kay Kerr.
Institution Type/Description: Ski Museum.
Hours & Admission Prices: Memorial Day-March daily 10-5. Branch Museum: daily 9-4. No charge; donations accepted. Closed Thanksgiving; Christmas. &
Attendance: 21,910 (actual)

Franklin

DANIEL WEBSTER BIRTHPLACE, 131 North Rd., Franklin, NH 03235. Mailing Address: c/o NH Dept. of Resources & Economic Development, 172 Pembroke Rd., Concord, NH 03301-5791. Tel.: 603-934-5057.
E-mail: nhparks@dred.nh.gov
Web Site: www.nhstateparks.org
Key Personnel: Dir., Ben Wilson.
Institution Type/Description: Historic Site.
Hours & Admission Prices: June 21-Sept. 1. Sat.-Sun. 9-5. Adults $7, children 6-11 $3; New Hampshire residents & children 5 and under no charge.

FRANKLIN FIREFIGHTERS MUSEUM, 59 W. Bow St., Franklin, NH 03235. Tel.: 603-934-2205. Fax: 603-934-7408.

E-mail: firestaff@franklinnh.org
Web Site: http://franklinnh.vt-s.net/pages/FranklinNH_Fire/museum
Key Personnel: Pres. (V), Joshua A. Lee; Cur., Andrew Nadeay.
Institution Type/Description: Firefighters Museum.
Hours & Admission Prices: By appointment; No charge; donations accepted.
Attendance: 300 (estimated)

TARBIN GARDENS, 321 Salisbury Rd., Franklin, NH 03235-2503. Tel.: 603-934-3518.
E-mail: info@tarbingardens.com
Web Site: www.tarbingardens.com
Institution Type/Description: Gardens.
Hours & Admission Prices: May-Sept. Tues.-Sun. 10-6; other times by appointment. Guided Tours: daily 11am. Adults $9, children 4-17 and seniors 62 & over $7.50; children 3 & under no charge.

Gilford

THOMPSON-AMES HISTORICAL SOCIETY, 8 Belknap Mountain Rd., Gilford, NH 03249-6807. Tel.: 603-527-9009.
E-mail: thompsonames@gmail.com
Web Site: www.gilfordhistoricalsociety.org
Key Personnel: Pres. (V), Karin Landry; Vice Pres., Donna Shinlever; Sec., Walton Stockwell; Treas., Geoff Ruggles.
Institution Type/Description: Historical Society Museum.
Hours & Admission Prices: By appointment.

Gorham

GORHAM HISTORICAL SOCIETY AND RAIL MUSEUM, 25 Railroad St., Gorham, NH 03581-1638. Mailing Address: P.O. Box 351, Gorham, NH 03581-0351. Tel.: 603-466-5338. Facebook: Gorham Historical Society and Rail Museum.
E-mail: gorhamhistoricalsociety@gmail.com
Web Site: gorhamnewhampshire.com/Railroad_Museum.html
Key Personnel: Pres., Reuben Rajala.
Institution Type/Description: History Museum.
Hours & Admission Prices: Memorial Day to Columbus Day daily 10-2; other times by appointment. No charge.

Hampton

TUCK MUSEUM OF HAMPTON HISTORY, 40 Park Ave., Hampton, NH 03843-1601. Mailing Address: P.O. Box 1601, Hampton, NH 03843-1601. Tel.: 603-929-0781.
E-mail: info@hamptonhistoricalsociety.org
Web Site: www.hamptonhistoricalsociety.org
Key Personnel: Pres. (V), Robert Dennett; Dir., Betty Moore.
Institution Type/Description: Local History Museum: Tuck Museum, located on the site of the original settlement of Hampton in 1638.
Hours & Admission Prices: Wed., Fri. & Sun. 1-4; other times by appointment. No charge; donations accepted. &
Attendance: 1,200 (estimated)

Hancock

HANCOCK HISTORICAL SOCIETY & MUSEUM, 7 Main St., Hancock, NH 03449-6008. Mailing Address: P.O. Box 138, Hancock, NH 03449-0138. Tel.: 603-525-9379.
E-mail: history@hancockhistoricalsociety.org
Web Site: www.hancockhistoricalsociety.org
Key Personnel: C.E.O. & Pres. (V), Timothy J. Lord; Vice Pres., Neal Cass; Museum Committee Chair, Roberta D. Nylander.
Institution Type/Description: General Museum: housed in c.1809 Federal-style brick building which was possibly a tavern when built.
Hours & Admission Prices: Call for hours. No charge; donations accepted.
Attendance: 250 (estimated)

Hanover

HOOD MUSEUM OF ART, 6 E. Wheelock St., Dartmouth College, Hanover, NH 03755. Tel.: 603-646-2808. Fax: 603-646-1400. Facebook.
E-mail: hood.museum@dartmouth.edu
Web Site: hoodmuseum.dartmouth.edu
Key Personnel: Dir., John Stomberg.
Institution Type/Description: Art Museum.
Hours & Admission Prices: Temporarily closed. &
Attendance: 45,000 (actual)

HOPKINS CENTER FOR THE ARTS, 4 E. Wheelock St., Dartmouth College, Hanover, NH 03755. Mailing Address: 6041 Wilson Hall Lower Level, Dartmouth College, Hanover, NH 03755. Tel.: 603-646-2422.
E-mail: hopkins.center@dartmouth.edu
Web Site: hop.dartmouth.edu
Institution Type/Description: Art Gallery.
Hours & Admission Prices: Tues.-Sat. 12:30-10, Sun. 12:30-5:30.

Hebron

PARADISE POINT NATURE CENTER, 79 North Shore Rd., Hebron, NH 03241. Mailing Address: c/o NH Audubon, 84 Silk Farm Rd., Concord, NH 03301. Tel.: 603-224-9909. Fax: 603-744-3516.
E-mail: nha@nhaudubon.org
Web Site: www.nhaudubon.org
Institution Type/Description: Nature Center & Wildlife Sanctuary.
Hours & Admission Prices: July-Sept. Mon.-Sat. 10-4; other times by appointment. No charge; donations accepted.

Henniker

NEW ENGLAND COLLEGE GALLERY, 39 Main St., Henniker, NH 03242-6225. Tel.: 603-428-2329. Fax: 603-428-2266.
E-mail: dfurtkamp@nec.edu
Web Site: www.nec.edu
Key Personnel: Dir., Darryl Furtkamp.
Institution Type/Description: College Art Gallery.
Hours & Admission Prices: Academic Year: Tues.-Thurs. 11-6, Fri. 11-4. No charge. Closed Thanksgiving week; Christmas break. &
Attendance: 1,500 (estimated)

Hillsborough

THE FRANKLIN PIERCE HOMESTEAD STATE HISTORIC SITE, 301 Second NH Tpke., Hillsborough, NH 03244. Tel.: 603-478-3165. Fax: 603-464-3416.
E-mail: piercehomesteadhistoricsite@tds.net
Web Site: www.nhstateparks.org
Key Personnel: Dir., Benjamin Wilson; Mgr., Sara Dobrowolski; Administrator, Alan Dobrowolski.
Institution Type/Description: Historic House Museum: 1804 Mansion, built by Benjamin Pierce; childhood home of Franklin Pierce, 14th U.S. President.
Hours & Admission Prices: Memorial Day to Labor Day Fri.-Tues. 10-4; Sept. to Columbus Day Sat.-Sun. 10-4; last tour 3pm. Call for admission prices. Blue Star Museum. &
Attendance: 4,750 (estimated)

Holderness

SQUAM LAKES NATURAL SCIENCE CENTER, 23 Science Center Rd., Holderness, NH 03245. Mailing Address: P.O. Box 173, Holderness, NH 03245-0173. Tel.: 603-968-7194. Fax: 603-968-2229. Facebook: NH Wildlife.
E-mail: info@nhnature.org
Web Site: www.nhnature.org
Formerly: Science Center of New Hampshire
Key Personnel: Chm. Bd. (V), Kenneth H Evans, Jr.; Exec. Dir., Iain MacLeod; Dir. Operations, Elizabeth Rowe; Mgr. Mktg. & Visitor Svcs., Amanda Gillen.
Institution Type/Description: Natural Science Museum.
Hours & Admission Prices: May-Nov. daily 9:30-5. Adults $19; discounts to ANCA & AZA members; members no charge. &
Attendance: 79,946 (estimated)

Hollis

HOLLIS HISTORICAL SOCIETY - WHEELER HOUSE & ALWAYS READY ENGINE HOUSE, 20 Main St., Hollis, NH 03049. Mailing Address: P.O. Box 754, Hollis, NH 03049. Tel.: 603-465-3935. Facebook: @hollishistoricalsociety.
Web Site: www.hollishistoricalsociety.org
Key Personnel: Pres. (V), Bruce Hardy; Cur., Fredricka Olson.
Institution Type/Description: Historical Society Museum.
Hours & Admission Prices: June-Oct. Mon., Wed. and 1st & 3rd Sun. 1-4; Nov.-May Mon. & Wed. 1-4. No charge; donations accepted. Closed major holidays.

Hopkinton

HOPKINTON HISTORICAL SOCIETY, 300 Main St., Hopkinton, NH 03229-2627. Tel.: 603-746-3825. Facebook: Hopkinton Historical Society.
E-mail: nhas@tds.net
Web Site: www.hopkintonhistory.org
Formerly: New Hampshire Antiquarian Society
Key Personnel: Dir., Heather Mitchell; Pres. (V), Roxanne Benzel.
Institution Type/Description: Local History Museum.
Hours & Admission Prices: Thurs.-Fri. 9-4, Sat. 9-1. Admission charge for special exhibits & events only. Closed holidays. &
Attendance: 1,500 (estimated)

Intervale

HARTMANN MODEL R.R. & TOY MUSEUM, 15 Town Hall Rd., Intervale, NH 03845. Mailing Address: P.O. Box 165, Intervale, NH 03845-0165. Tel.: 603-356-9922. Fax: 603-356-9958.
E-mail: info@hartmannrr.com
Web Site: www.hartmannrr.com
Key Personnel: Pres., Nelly Hartmann.
Institution Type/Description: Model Railroad & Toy Museum.
Hours & Admission Prices: July-Aug. daily 10-5; Sept.-June Fri.-Mon. 10-5. Adults $6, seniors 60 & over $5, children $4; discounts to AAM & ICOM members. Closed Easter; Mother's Day; Thanksgiving; Christmas. &
Attendance: 10,000 (actual)

Jaffrey

JAFFREY CIVIC CENTER, 40 Main St., Jaffrey, NH 03452-6144. Tel.: 603-532-6527.
E-mail: info@JaffreyCivicCenter.com
Web Site: www.jaffreyciviccenter.com
Key Personnel: Exec. Dir., Dion Owens; Pres. (V), Lee S. Sawyer.
Institution Type/Description: Art Foundation & Historical Society.
Hours & Admission Prices: Tues. 10-6, Wed.-Fri. 1-5, Sat. 10-2. No charge; donations accepted. Closed national holidays.
Attendance: 12,000 (estimated)

MELVILLE ACADEMY MUSEUM, Thorndike Pond Rd., Jaffrey, NH 03452. Mailing Address: P.O. Box 722, Jaffrey, NH 03452-0722. Tel.: 603-532-4992.
E-mail: president@jcvis.org
Web Site: www.jcvis.org/museum/museum.php
Key Personnel: Cur., Sarah H Larsen.
Institution Type/Description: History Museum.
Hours & Admission Prices: July-Aug. Sat.-Sun. 2-4; other times by appointment. No charge; donations accepted.
Attendance: 240 (estimated)

Jefferson

JEFFERSON HISTORICAL MUSEUM, Rte. 2 900 Presidential Hwy., Jefferson, NH 03583. Mailing Address: P.O. Box 143, Jefferson, NH 03583.
E-mail: jeffersonhistsocy@gmail.com
Key Personnel: Pres., Winifred S. Ward; Sec., Marjorie Doan; Treas., Adele Woods.
Institution Type/Description: Historic Building: housed in an 1868 church.
Hours & Admission Prices: June to Columbus Day Thurs. & Sun. 1-4. No charge; donations accepted.
Attendance: 170 (estimated)

Keene

HISTORICAL SOCIETY OF CHESHIRE COUNTY, 246 Main St., Keene, NH 03431-4143. Mailing Address: P.O. Box 803, Keene, NH 03431-0803. Tel.: 603-352-1895. Facebook: Historical Society of Cheshire County.
E-mail: hscc@hsccnh.org
Web Site: www.hsccnh.org
Key Personnel: Dir., Alan F. Rumrill; Education Dir., Jennifer Carroll; Devel. Dir., Rick Swanson; Admin. Asst., Katharine Schillemat ; Museum Shop Mgr., Andrea Cheeney.
Institution Type/Description: Historical Society: housed in c.1870 Italianate Mansion.

Hours & Admission Prices: Tues. & Thurs.-Fri. 9-4, Wed. 9-9, 1st & 3rd Sat. each month 9-12. No charge. &
Attendance: 24,000 (estimated)

HORATIO COLONY HOUSE MUSEUM & NATURE PRESERVE, 199 Main St., Keene, NH 03431-3780. Tel.: 603-352-0460. Facebook: Horatio Colony Museum & Nature Preserve.
E-mail: colonymuseum@webryders.com
Web Site: horatiocolonymuseum.com
Key Personnel: C.E.O., Anita Carroll-Weldon; Pres. (V), Frank Coolidge.
Institution Type/Description: Historic Houses & Historic Buildings: c.1806 family home of collector & author Horatio Colony, II, grandson of Keene's first mayor & co-owners of the Keene's Woolen Mill.
Hours & Admission Prices: May to mid-Oct. Wed.-Sat. 11-4; other times by appointment. No charge.
Attendance: 3,000 (actual)

THORNE-SAGENDORPH ART GALLERY, Wyman Way, Keene, NH 03435-3501. Mailing Address: 229 Main St., Keene State College, Keene, NH 03435-3501. Tel.: 603-358-2720. Fax: 603-358-2238.
E-mail: thorne@keene.edu
Web Site: www.keene.edu/tsag
Institution Type/Description: Art Gallery.
Hours & Admission Prices: June-July Wed.-Thurs. 12-5, Fri. 3-8, Sat.-Sun. 12-5; Sept.-May Sun.-Wed. 12-5, Thurs.-Fri. 12-7, Sat. 12-8; other times by appointment. No charge; donations accepted. Closed academic holidays; semester breaks. &
Attendance: 6,000 (estimated)

THE WYMAN TAVERN, 339 Main St., Keene, NH 03431. Mailing Address: P.O. Box 803, Keene, NH 03431-0803. Tel.: 603-352-1895; 603-357-3855 (during open hrs.). Facebook: Wyman Tavern.
E-mail: hscc@hsccnh.org
Web Site: www.hsccnh.org
Key Personnel: Exec. Dir., Alan F. Rumrill; Pres., James Rousmaniere; Education Dir., Jennifer Carroll; Devel. Dir., Richard Swanson; Admin. Asst., Katharine Schillemat; Museum Shop Mgr., Andrea Cheeney.
Institution Type/Description: Historic Building: 1762 Wyman Tavern.
Hours & Admission Prices: June to Labor Day Thurs.-Sat. 11-4. Adults $3; children under 12 & members no charge.
Attendance: 1,500 (estimated)

Laconia

THE BELKNAP MILL SOCIETY, 25 Beacon St. East, The Mill Plaza, Laconia, NH 03246-3445. Tel.: 603-524-8813. Fax: 603-528-1228. Facebook: Historic Belknap Mill.
E-mail: information@belknapmill.org
Web Site: www.belknapmill.org
Institution Type/Description: Art & History Museum: housed in 1823 brick textile building.
Hours & Admission Prices: Mon.-Fri. 9-5, Sat. 9-3, call to confirm & for special events. Fees for special events; discounts to National Trust members. Closed New Year's Day; Memorial Day; Independence Day; Labor Day; Christmas. &
Attendance: 50,000 (actual)

LAKE WINNIPESAUKEE MUSEUM & HISTORICAL SOCIETY, 503 Endicott St. N., Rte. 3, Laconia, NH 03246-1725. Mailing Address: P.O. Box 5386, Weirs, NH 03247-5386. Tel.: 603-366-5950.
E-mail: info@lwhs.us
Web Site: www.lwhs.us
Key Personnel: Dir., Melanie Benton; Chm. (V), Robert Lawton; Pres. (V), Brian Vincent; Cur., Lynda Laflamme; Museum Shop Mgr., Vynnie Hale.
Institution Type/Description: Historic House Museum.
Hours & Admission Prices: May-Oct. Mon.-Sat. 10-4. No charge; donations accepted. &
Attendance: 1,000 (actual)

PRESCOTT FARM ENVIRONMENTAL EDUCATION CENTER, 928 White Oaks Rd., Laconia, NH 03246. Tel.: 603-366-5695. Fax: 603-366-5720.
E-mail: info@prescottfarm.org
Web Site: prescottfarm.org
Key Personnel: Jude Hamel.
Institution Type/Description: Education Center.
Hours & Admission Prices: Call for hours.

Lancaster

THE LANCASTER HISTORICAL SOCIETY, 226 Main St., Lancaster, NH 03584-3038. Mailing Address: P.O. Box 473, Lancaster, NH 03584-0473. Tel.: 603-788-3004.
E-mail: thelancasterhistoricalsociety@gmail.com
Key Personnel: Pres., Anne Morgan.
Institution Type/Description: Local History Museum: housed in 1780 Wilder-Holton House, first two-story house built in the county and Paul F. Smith Memorial Barn.
Hours & Admission Prices: Tours: summer by appointment. No charge; donations accepted. &

Lebanon

AVA GALLERY AND ART CENTER, 11 Bank St., Lebanon, NH 03766-1749. Tel.: 603-448-3117.
E-mail: info@avagallery.org
Web Site: www.avagallery.org
Key Personnel: Exec. Dir., Trip Anderson; Dir. Education, Adam Blue; Office Mgr., Margaret Burnett; Publications & Web, Carrie Fradkin; Coord. Exhibition, Jennifer Lay; Studio Mgr., Murray Ngoima; Bookkeeper, Abigail Murphy.
Institution Type/Description: Art Gallery.
Hours & Admission Prices: Tues.-Sat. 11-5; other times by appointment. No charge. &

Lisbon

LISBON AREA HISTORICAL SOCIETY, 6 'S. Main St., Lisbon, NH 03585. Mailing Address: P.O. Box 6, Lisbon, NH 03585. Tel.: 603-838-6146. Facebook.
E-mail: info@.lisbonareahistory.org
Web Site: www.lisbonareahistory.org
Institution Type/Description: Historical Society Museum.
Hours & Admission Prices: May-Oct. Fri.1-3, other times by appointment. No charge; donations accepted.

Londonderry

AVIATION MUSEUM OF NEW HAMPSHIRE, 27 Navigator Rd., Londonderry, NH 03053-4403. Tel.: 603-669-4877. Facebook: Aviation Museum of New Hampshire.
E-mail: jpappathan@nhahs.org
Web Site: www.nhahs.org
Key Personnel: Exec. Dir., Jessica Pappathan; Pres. (V), Robert Hough.
Institution Type/Description: Aviation History Museum.
Hours & Admission Prices: Fri.-Sat. 10-4, Sun. 1-4. Adults $5; members no charge. &
Attendance: 5,000 (estimated)

Manchester

ALVA DE MARS MEGAN CHAPEL ART CENTER, 100 Saint Anselm Dr., Saint Anselm College, Manchester, NH 03102-1308. Tel.: 603-641-7470. Fax: 603-641-7116.
E-mail: chapelartcenter@anselm.edu
Web Site: www.anselm.edu/chapelart
Key Personnel: Dir., Iain MacLellan, O.S.B.; Cur., Maggie Dimock; Administrative Asst., Pamela Condon.
Institution Type/Description: College Art Museum & Center: housed in the former college chapel; built in 1923.
Hours & Admission Prices: Tues.-Wed. & Fri.-Sat. 10-4, Thurs. 10-7. No charge. Closed holidays; college breaks; between exhibitions. &
Attendance: 5,000 (actual)

AMERICA'S CREDIT UNION MUSEUM, 420 Notre Dame Ave., Manchester, NH 03102. Tel.: 603-629-1553. Fax: 603-629-1595.
E-mail: ssmith@acumuseum.org
Web Site: www.acumuseum.org
Key Personnel: Exec. Dir., Stephanie Smith.
Institution Type/Description: History Museum.
Hours & Admission Prices: Mon.-Thurs. 9-3; Other times by appointment only. No charge. &

CURRIER MUSEUM OF ART, 150 Ash St., Manchester, NH 03104-4347. Tel.: 603-669-6144. Fax: 603-669-7194. Facebook: Currier Museum.
E-mail: visitor@currier.org
Web Site: www.currier.org

Key Personnel: Cur., Kurt Sundstrom; Asst. Cur., Samantha Cataldo; C.E.O. & Dir., Alan Chong; Pres. (V), David Jensen; Dir. Finance, Sherry Collins; Chief Cur., Andrew Spahr; Assoc. Cur., Aimie Westphal; Head Public Programs, Leah Fox; Art Center Dir., Bruce McColl; Museum Shop Mgr., Heidi Norton.
Institution Type/Description: Art Museum: housed in the former home of Isadore J. & Lucille Zimmerman; a Usonian home designed by Frank Lloyd Wright; built in 1950. Listed on the National Register of Historic Places.
Hours & Admission Prices: Sun.-Mon. & Wed.-Fri. 11-5, Sat. 10-5, 1st Thurs. of month 11-8. Adults $10, seniors $9, students $8; members & children under 18 no charge. &
Attendance: 66,339 (actual)

LAWRENCE L. LEE SCOUTING MUSEUM, 300 Blondin Rd., Manchester, NH 03109-5907. Mailing Address: 571 Holt Ave., Manchester, NH 03109-5213. Tel.: 603-669-8919, 603-625-6431. Fax: 603-625-2467.
E-mail: administrator@scoutingmuseum.org
Web Site: www.scoutingmuseum.org
Key Personnel: Scout Exec., Donald D. Shepard, Jr.; Chm. (V), Richard Zeloski.
Institution Type/Description: Scouting Museum.
Hours & Admission Prices: July-Aug. Sat. 10-4, call for additional hours; Sept.-June Sat. 10-4. No charge; donations accepted. Closed Independence Day; Christmas. &
Attendance: 2,500 (estimated)

MCININCH ART GALLERY - SOUTHERN NEW HAMPSHIRE UNIVERSITY, Robert Frost Hall, 2500 N. River Rd., Manchester, NH 03106. Tel.: 603-629-4622. Fax: 603-668-2211, ext. 2228.
E-mail: d.disston@snhu.edu
Web Site: www.snhu.edu/art
Key Personnel: Dir., Debbie Disston.
Institution Type/Description: Art Gallery.
Hours & Admission Prices: Academic Year: Mon.-Wed. & Fri.-Sat. 10-3, Thurs. 10-3 & 5-8. No charge; donations accepted. Closed university holidays & breaks. &
Attendance: 5,987 (actual)

MILLYARD MUSEUM, 200 Bedford St., Manchester, NH 03101. Mailing Address: 200 Bedford St., 1st Fl., Manchester, NH 03101-1132. Tel.: 603-622-7531. Fax: 603-641-8191.
E-mail: history@manchesterhistoric.org
Web Site: www.manchesterhistoric.org
Key Personnel: Exec. Dir., Aurore Eaton; Pres., Edward W. Brouder, Jr.; Cur. Museum Collection, Marylou Ashooh Lazos; Cur. Library Collection, Eileen O'Brien.
Institution Type/Description: Local History Museum.
Hours & Admission Prices: Museum: Wed.-Sat. 10-4. Research Center: Wed. & Sat. 10-4. Adults $6, seniors & college students $5, children 6-18 $2; discounts to AASLH & NEMA members; children under 6, members & library no charge. Closed New Year's Day; Independence Day; Veterans Day; Thanksgiving; Christmas Eve & Day. &
Attendance: 6,000 (estimated)

NEW HAMPSHIRE INSTITUTE OF ART, 148 Concord St., Manchester, NH 03104-4858. Tel.: 603-623-0313. Fax: 603-641-1832.
E-mail: CE@nhia.edu
Key Personnel: Pres., Kent Devereaux; Academic Dean, Patrick McCay; Dir. Devel., Jessica Kinsey; Dir. Admissions, Liam Sullivan; Vice Pres. Finance & Administration, Erik Gross; Shop Mgr., Joe Vivilecchia; Dir. Gallery, Alison Williams.
Institution Type/Description: Art Institute.
Hours & Admission Prices: Mon.-Fri. 9-5, Sat. 9-12. No charge. Closed legal holidays. &
Attendance: 27,500 (estimated)

SEE SCIENCE CENTER, 200 Bedford St., Manchester, NH 03101-1153. Tel.: 603-669-0400. Fax: 603-669-0400.
E-mail: info@see-sciencecenter.org
Web Site: www.see-sciencecenter.org
Key Personnel: Exec. Dir., Susan Howland; Education & Membership, Rebecca Mayhew; Operations & Design, Adele Maurier; Devel. Coord., Peter Gustafson.
Institution Type/Description: Science Museum.
Hours & Admission Prices: Mon.-Fri. 10-4, Sat.-Sun. 10-5. Admission $9; children 2 & under and members no charge. Closed New Year's Day; Easter; Memorial Day; Independence Day; Labor Day; Thanksgiving; Christmas Eve & Day. &
Attendance: 75,000 (estimated)

Melvin Village

TUFTONBORO HISTORICAL SOCIETY & MUSEUM, 449 GWH, Rte. 109, Melvin Village, NH 03850. Mailing Address: P.O. Box 372, Melvin Village, NH 03850-0372. Tel.: 603-544-7225, 603-544-2400.
Key Personnel: Dir., Margaret Bashe; Pres., Mary Antonucci.
Institution Type/Description: History Museum.
Hours & Admission Prices: July-Aug. Mon.-Fri. 2-4. No charge.

Meredith

MEREDITH CHILDREN'S MUSEUM, 28 Lang St., Meredith, NH 03253-5824. Tel.: 603-279-6307.
Institution Type/Description: Children's Museum.
Hours & Admission Prices: Daily 10-4. Admission $6. Closed Easter; Thanksgiving; Christmas.

Meriden

AIDRON DUCKWORTH ART MUSEUM, 21 Bean Rd., Meriden, NH 03770. Mailing Address: P.O. Box 61, Meriden, NH 03770-0061. Tel.: 603-469-3444. Facebook.
E-mail: info@aidronduckworthmuseum.org
Web Site: www.aidronduckworthmuseum.org
Key Personnel: Dir., Mila Pinigin; Trustee, Grace W. Harde.
Institution Type/Description: Art Museum.
Hours & Admission Prices: Fri.-Sun. 10-5; other times by appointment. No charge; donations accepted. &
Attendance: 1,500 (estimated)

Milton

NEW HAMPSHIRE FARM MUSEUM, INC., 1305 White Mountain Hwy., Milton, NH 03851. Mailing Address: P.O. Box 644, Rte. 125, Milton, NH 03851-0644. Tel.: 603-652-7840. Fax: 603-652-7840 (call first).
E-mail: info@farmmuseum.org
Web Site: www.farmmuseum.org
Key Personnel: Exec. Dir., Mark Foynes; Pres. (V), Otis Perry.
Institution Type/Description: Agriculture & Rural Life Museum: former Jones Farm with buildings dating from 1780s-1900s; the Plummer Homestead.
Hours & Admission Prices: Memorial Day to mid-Oct. Wed.-Sun. 10-4. Adults $7, children 4-17 $4; discount to NEMA members & groups of 10 or more; members no charge. &
Attendance: 4,000 (estimated)

Moultonborough

CASTLE IN THE CLOUDS, 455 Old Mountain Rd., Moultonborough, NH 03254. Mailing Address: P.O. Box 687, Moultonborough, NH 03254-0687. Tel.: 603-476-5900. Fax: 603-476-2512. Facebook.
E-mail: info@castleintheclouds.org
Web Site: castleintheclouds.org
Key Personnel: Dir., Charles Clark; Pres. (V), Frank Marcoux.
Institution Type/Description: Historic House: housed in Lucknow, the former estate of Tom & Olive Plant; built in 1914.
Hours & Admission Prices: May 6-June 2 Sat.-Sun. 10-4; June 3-Oct. 22 daily 10-4. Adults $16, seniors 65 & over $14, youth 5-15 $8; discounts to active military & veterans; children 4 & under no charge. &
Attendance: 52,000 (actual)

THE LOON CENTER AND MARKUS WILDLIFE SANCTUARY, 183 Lee's Mill Rd., Moultonborough, NH 03254. Mailing Address: P.O. Box 604, Moultonborough, NH 03254-0604. Tel.: 603-476-5666. Fax: 603-476-5497.
E-mail: info@loon.org
Web Site: www.loon.org
Institution Type/Description: Wildlife Sanctuary.
Hours & Admission Prices: Loon Center: mid-May to July 1 Mon.-Sat. 9-5; July to Columbus Day daily 9-5; Columbus Day to mid-May Thurs.-Sat. 9-5. Markus Sanctuary Walking Trails: daily dawn to dusk. No charge; donations accepted. Closed winter holidays; day after Thanksgiving. &
Attendance: 10,000 (estimated)

Nashua

JOHN M. HUNT MEMORIAL BUILDING, 6 Main St., Nashua, NH 03064-2712. Tel.: 603-594-3661. Facebook: The Hunt Memorial Building.
E-mail: derochea@nashuanh.gov
Key Personnel: Chm. (V), Joy Barrett.
Institution Type/Description: Historic Building: housed in the former Nashua Public Library. Listed on the National Register of Historic Buildings.
Hours & Admission Prices: Tours: by appointment. No charge; donations accepted. &
Attendance: 1,000 (estimated)

THE NASHUA HISTORICAL SOCIETY - ABBOT-SPALDING HOUSE MUSEUM AND FLORENCE SPEARE MEMORIAL MUSEUM, 5 Abbott St., Nashua, NH 03064-2119. Tel.: 603-883-0015. Fax: 603-889-8515.
E-mail: nashuahistorical@comcast.net
Key Personnel: Pres. (V), Joanne Ouellette; Cur., Beth McCarthy.
Institution Type/Description: House Museum.
Hours & Admission Prices: Abbot-Spalding Museum: by appointment. Florence H. Speare Memorial Museum: Tues.-Thurs. 10-4; other times by appointment. No charge; donations accepted. &
Attendance: 550 (estimated)

New Ipswich

BARRETT HOUSE, FOREST HALL, 79 Main St., New Ipswich, NH 03071-3716. Mailing Address: Historic New England, 143 Pleasant St., Portsmouth, NH 03801. Tel.: 603-436-3205.
E-mail: barretthouse@historicnewengland.org
Web Site: www.historicnewengland.org
Key Personnel: Pres., Carl Nold; Regl. Site Mgr., Craig Tuminaro.
Institution Type/Description: Historic House: c.1800 Barrett House, Forest Hall, Federal residence.
Hours & Admission Prices: June-Oct. 15 2nd & 4th Sat. of month 11-5; last tour at 4. Grounds: dawn to dusk. Adults $5, seniors $4, students $2.50; discounts to seniors, AAM, AAA, ICOM, WGBH members; New Ipswich residents & Historic New England members no charge.
Attendance: 840 (actual)

New London

NEW LONDON HISTORICAL SOCIETY, 179 Little Sunapee Rd., New London, NH 03257. Mailing Address: P.O. Box 965, New London, NH 03257-0965. Tel.: 603-526-6564. Facebook: @newlondonhistorical.
E-mail: info@newlondonhistoricalsociety.org
Web Site: www.newlondonhistoricalsociety.org
Key Personnel: Exec. Dir., Patricia McGoldnick; Pres. (V), Roger Smith.
Institution Type/Description: General Museum.
Hours & Admission Prices: Memorial Day to June & Sept. to Columbus Day Sun. & Tues. 12:30-3:30; July-Aug. Tues. 12:30-3:30; other times by appointment. Adults $6, members $4.
Attendance: 1,500 (estimated)

Newbury

THE FELLS, 456 Rte. 103A, Newbury, NH 03255. Mailing Address: P.O. Box 276, Newbury, NH 03255-0276. Tel.: 603-763-4789. Fax: 603-763-2452. Facebook: The Fells.
E-mail: info@thefells.org
Web Site: www.thefells.org
Key Personnel: Exec. Dir., Susan Warren; Chm. (V), John Ferries; Museum Shop Mgr., Mary Lou McCrave.
Institution Type/Description: Historic House & Gardens: former estate of American writer and diplomat John M. Hay. Listed on the National Register of Historic Places.
Hours & Admission Prices: Gardens & Trails: dawn to dusk. Main House: Memorial Day weekend-Columbus Day Sat.-Sun. & Mon. holidays 10-4; June 17 to Labor Day Wed.-Sun. 10-4. Main House Open: Families 2 adults & 2 or more children $25, adults $10, seniors 65 & over and students with ID $8, children 6-17 $4; discounts to AAM, AAA & Garden Conservancy members; members and children 5 & under no charge. Main House Closed: Families 2 adults & 2 or more children $15, adults $8, seniors 65 & over and students with ID $6, children 6-17 $3. &
Attendance: 10,000 (actual)

North Conway

CONWAY SCENIC RAILROAD, INC., 38 Norcross Circle, North Conway, NH 03860. Mailing Address: P.O. Box 1947, North Conway, NH 03860-1947. Tel.: 603-356-5251, 800-232-5251. Fax: 603-356-7606. Facebook: Conway Scenic Railroad.
E-mail: info@conwayscenic.com
Web Site: www.conwayscenic.com
Key Personnel: Gen. Mgr., David Swirk; Operations Mgr., Derek Palmieri; Mgr. Mktg. & Events, Susan Logan.
Institution Type/Description: Railroad Museum: housed in 1874 Victorian, wood-framed railroad station. A National Historic Landmark.
Hours & Admission Prices: See website for train schedules & fares. &
Attendance: 100,000 (actual)

EXTREME MOUNT WASHINGTON MUSEUM AND THE WEATHER DISCOVERY CENTER CLOSED, 2779 White Mountain Hwy., North Conway, NH 03860-5194. Mailing Address: P.O. Box 2310, North Conway, NH 03860-2310. Tel.: 603-356-2137, ext. 209. Fax: 603-356-0307.
E-mail: shop@mountwashington.org
Web Site: www.mountwashington.org
Key Personnel: Pres., Jack Middelton; Exec. Dir., Sharon Schilling; Dir. Museum Operations & Museum Shop Mgr., Samantha Brady; Dir. Education, Brian Fitzgerald.
Institution Type/Description: Park & Weather Museum: located on summit of Mount Washington.
Hours & Admission Prices: Extreme Mount Washington Museum: late-May to mid-Oct. daily 9-6. Weather Discovery Center: daily 10-5. Adults 18 & up $2, youth 7-17 $1; discounts to ASTC and MWOBS members; children 6 & under no charge. &
Attendance: 40,000 (estimated)

NEW ENGLAND SKI MUSEUM - EASTERN SLOPE BRANCH, 2628 White Mountain Hwy., North Conway, NH 03860-1673. Tel.: 603-730-5044.
Web Site: newenglandskimuseum.org
Institution Type/Description: Sports Museum.
Hours & Admission Prices: Daily 9-4. No charge. Closed Thanksgiving; Christmas.

North Hampton

FULLER GARDENS, 10 Willow Ave., North Hampton, NH 03862-2228. Tel.: 603-964-5414.
E-mail: fullergrdn@aol.com
Web Site: www.fullergardens.org
Key Personnel: C.E.O. & Dir., Jamie Colen; Museum Shop Mgr., Victoria Kaiser.
Institution Type/Description: Botanical Garden.
Hours & Admission Prices: mid-May to Oct. daily 10-5:30. Adults $9, senior citizens $8, children under 10 $4.50; discounts for groups of 10 or more; members & infants no charge. &
Attendance: 11,000 (estimated)

North Salem

AMERICA'S STONEHENGE, 105 Haverhill Rd., North Salem, NH 03073. Mailing Address: P.O. Box 84, North Salem, NH 03073-0084. Tel.: 603-893-8300.
E-mail: info@stonehengeusa.com
Web Site: www.stonehengeusa.com
Key Personnel: C.E.O. & Pres., Robert E. Stone; Gen. Mgr. & Public Rels., Dennis W. Stone; Operations Mgr., Patricia Stone.
Institution Type/Description: Archaeological Site: located on Mystery Hill, site of 4,000 year old archaeo-astronomical site.
Hours & Admission Prices: Daily 9-5. Adults $10, seniors $7, children 13-18 $6, children 6-12 $5. Closed Thanksgiving; Christmas. &
Attendance: 35,000 (estimated)

North Sutton

MUSTER FIELD FARM MUSEUM & THE MATTHEW HARVEY HOMESTEAD, Harvey Rd., North Sutton, NH 03260. Mailing Address: P.O. Box 118, North Sutton, NH 03260-0118. Tel.: 603-927-4276.
E-mail: musterfield@tds.net
Web Site: www.musterfieldfarm.com
Institution Type/Description: Farm Museum: housed in an 18th century farmhouse. Listed on the National Register of Historic Places.

Hours & Admission Prices: Farm Buildings: daily. Homestead: July-Oct. 3 Sun. 1-4. June Jam: $10 per person. Farm Days & Harvest Day: $5 per person; members & children under 6 no charge. Ice Day: no charge.

Peterborough

AQUARIUS NO. 1 FIRE MUSEUM, 16 Summer St., Peterborough, NH 03458. Mailing Address: Peterborough Fire & Rescue Assoc., Inc., P.O. Box 244, Peterborough, NH 03458. Tel.: 603-924-8090.
Web Site: www.firerescue.us
Institution Type/Description: Firefighting History Museum.
Hours & Admission Prices: By appointment.

MARIPOSA MUSEUM & WORLD CULTURE CENTER, 26 Main St., Peterborough, NH 03458-2420. Tel.: 603-924-4555. Fax: 603-924-7893.
E-mail: info@mariposamuseum.org
Web Site: www.mariposamuseum.org
Key Personnel: Dir., Karla Hostetler; Dir. Education, Melissa Brooks; Volunteer Coord., Douglas Ward; Admin., Tina Thaing; Museum Mgr., Nadiya Weidman.
Institution Type/Description: Art Museum.
Hours & Admission Prices: Summer: daily 11-5; Sept. to mid-June Tues.-Sun. 11-5; groups by appointment. Adults $6, senior $5, children $4; first Fri. of month 5-9 (call to confirm) & members no charge. Closed Federal holidays. &
Attendance: 5,000 (estimated)

THE MONADNOCK CENTER FOR HISTORY AND CULTURE, 19 Grove St., Peterborough, NH 03458-1422. Mailing Address: P.O. Box 58, Peterborough, NH 03458-0058. Tel.: 603-924-3235. Fax: 603-924-3200.
E-mail: director@monadnockcenter.org
Web Site: www.monadnockcenter.org
Formerly: Peterborough Historical Society
Key Personnel: Exec. Dir., Michelle M. Stahl.
Institution Type/Description: Historical Society Museum.
Hours & Admission Prices: Wed.-Sat. 10-4. Adults $3; members no charge. &
Attendance: 7,500 (estimated)

Plymouth

KARL DRERUP ART GALLERY, 150 Main St., Draper & Maynard Bldg., Plymouth, NH Mailing Address: 17 High St., MSC 73, Plymouth, NH 03264-1595. Tel.: 603-535-2614. Fax: 603-535-2938.
E-mail: kdag.art@plymouth.edu
Web Site: www.plymouth.edu/gallery/
Key Personnel: Gallery Dir., Cynthia Robinson.
Institution Type/Description: University Art Gallery.
Hours & Admission Prices: Sept.-May Mon.-Fri. 10-4, Wed. 10-8, Sat. 1-4. No charge. Closed holidays & PSU breaks. &
Attendance: 3,000 (estimated)

MUSEUM OF THE WHITE MOUNTAINS, 34 Highland St., Plymouth, NH 03264. Mailing Address: 17 High St., MSC 73, Plymouth, NH 03264. Tel.: 603-535-3210. Facebook.
E-mail: museum.wm@plymouth.edu
Web Site: www.plymouth.edu/museum-of-the-white-mountains
Institution Type/Description: History Museum.
Hours & Admission Prices: Mon.-Fri. 10-5, Sat. 11-4. No charge. Closed university holidays & between exhibits. &

Portsmouth

ALBACORE PARK SUBMARINE MUSEUM, 600 Market St., Portsmouth, NH 03801-7313. Tel.: 603-436-3680. Facebook: USS Albacore Submarine and Museum.
E-mail: albacorepark@myfairpoint.net
Web Site: www.ussalbacore.org
Key Personnel: Exec. Dir., John Maier; Pres. (V), Ken Herrick.
Institution Type/Description: Submarine Museum.
Hours & Admission Prices: Jan.-Feb. call for hours; March-Dec. daily 9:30-5:30. Family $16, adults $8, retired military (20 years) $5, children 7-17 $3; discounts to Historic Naval Ships Assoc. members & Tin Can Sailors; members, children under 7 & active duty no charge.
Attendance: 34,000 (actual)

BANKE MUSEUM, 14 Hancock St., Portsmouth, NH 03801. Mailing Address: P.O. Box 300, Portsmouth, NH 03802-0300. Tel.: 603-433-1100. Fax: 603-433-1129.
E-mail: info@strawberybanke.org
Web Site: www.strawberybanke.org
Key Personnel: Pres., Lawrence Yerdon; Chm. Overseers Committee (V), Gerald W.R. Ward; Chm. Bd. Trustees (V), Zachary Slater; Dir. Devel., Joe April; Cur., Elizabeth Farish; Dir. Special Projects, Rodney Rowland; Mgr. Education, Bekki Coppola; Dir. Mktg. & Communication, Stephanie Seacord; Events & Facilities Rental Mgr., Wendy McCoole; Archaeology, Alexandra Martin; Finance Mgr., Sarah Terenzio; Visitor Svcs. Mgr., Jonathan Brown; Restoration Carpenter, John Schnitzler; Cur. Historic Landscapes, Erik Wochholz; Mgr. Corporate Rels., Monique Deforge; Properties Coord., Michelle Gove.
Institution Type/Description: Historic Site: 17th-20th century Portsmouth & New England Seacoast.
Hours & Admission Prices: May-Oct. daily 10-5; outdoor ice skating rink & visitors center: daily 9-5. Family $48, adults $19.50, youth 5-17 $9; discounts to AAM, ICOM & NEMA members & groups of 10 or more; children under 5 & military families no charge. &
Attendance: 95,008 (actual)

GOVERNOR JOHN LANGDON HOUSE, 143 Pleasant St., Portsmouth, NH 03801-4506. Mailing Address: 141 Cambridge St., Boston, MA 02114-2702. Tel.: 603-436-3205, 617-227-3956. Facebook: Governor John Langdon House.
E-mail: langdonhouse@historicnewengland.org
Web Site: www.historicnewengland.org
Key Personnel: Pres. & C.E.O., Carl R. Nold; Site Mgr., Linda Marshall.
Institution Type/Description: National Historic House/Landmark: 1784 home of Governor John Langdon.
Hours & Admission Prices: June-Oct. 15 Fri.-Sun. 11-5. Adults $8; discounts to seniors, AAM, ICOM, AAA, WGBH members; Historic New England members no charge.
Attendance: 7,867 (actual)

HARBOR ARTS MUSEUM, 93 High St., Portsmouth, NH 03803. Tel.: 603-436-8596.
Key Personnel: Dir., Richard Smith; C.E.O., John Hansauldt.
Institution Type/Description: History Museum.
Hours & Admission Prices: Call for hours.
Attendance: 1,000 (estimated)

JACKSON HOUSE, 76 Northwest St., Portsmouth, NH 03801-3556. Mailing Address: 141 Cambridge St., Boston, MA 02114-2702. Tel.: 603-436-3205.
E-mail: news@historicnewengland.org
Web Site: www.historicnewengland.org
Key Personnel: Pres. & C.E.O., Carl R. Nold.
Institution Type/Description: Historic House: built c.1664 by Richard Jackson.
Hours & Admission Prices: June-Oct. 15 1st & 3rd Sat. of month 11-5, last tour at 4pm. Adults $6; discounts to AAM & ICOM members; members no charge.
Attendance: 666 (actual)

JOHN PAUL JONES HOUSE MUSEUM, 43 Middle St., Portsmouth, NH 03801-4302. Mailing Address: P.O. Box 728, Portsmouth, NH 03802-0728. Tel.: 603-436-8420.
E-mail: info@portsmouthhistory.org
Web Site: www.portsmouthhistory.org
Key Personnel: Pres., Ed Mallon; Exec. Dir., Kathleen Soldati; Cur., Gerald W.R. Ward.
Institution Type/Description: History Museum: housed in 1758 John Paul Jones House.
Hours & Admission Prices: Memorial Day to Oct. daily 11-5; tours by appointment. Adults $6, Portsmouth residents & AAA members $5; discounts to groups; children 12 and under & members no charge.
Attendance: 4,000 (estimated)

MOFFATT-LADD HOUSE AND GARDEN, 154 Market St., Portsmouth, NH 03801-3730. Tel.: 603-436-8221. Fax: 603-431-9063. Facebook: Moffatt-Ladd House & Garden.
E-mail: moffattladd@gmail.com
Web Site: moffattladd.com
Key Personnel: Dir. & Cur., Dr. Barbara M. Ward; Pres., Helen Ogden; Pres.-Elect, Mary Waples; Museum Shop Mgr., Ms. Virginia Guy.
Institution Type/Description: Historic House Museum: c.1763 house built by Captain John Moffatt.
Hours & Admission Prices: mid-June to mid-October Mon.-Sat. 11-5, Sun. 1-5. Adults $7, children 7-12 $2.50. Garden: $2; discounts for groups with appointment and NEMA & AAA members; children under 7, members & NSCDA no charge.
Attendance: 6,000 (actual)

NEW HAMPSHIRE ART ASSOCIATION, 136 State St., Portsmouth, NH 03801-3826. Tel.: 603-431-4230. Fax: 603-431-4230.
E-mail: nhartassociation@comcast.net
Web Site: nhartassociation.org
Formerly: Robert Lincoln Levy Gallery
Key Personnel: Dir., Billie Tooley; Pres. (V) Bd. Dir., David Hampson.
Institution Type/Description: Art Gallery.
Hours & Admission Prices: Wed.-Sat. 10-5, Sun. 12-4.
Attendance: 10,000 (estimated)

PORTSMOUTH ATHENAEUM, 9 Market Square, Portsmouth, NH 03801. Mailing Address: Box 848, Portsmouth, NH 03802-0848. Tel.: 603-431-2538. Fax: 603-431-7180.
E-mail: info@portsmouthathenaeum.org
Web Site: portsmouthathenaeum.org
Key Personnel: Keeper, Tom Hardiman; Pres., John Shaw; Librarian, Robin Silva.
Institution Type/Description: Library Museum: housed in 1805 Portsmouth Athenaeum building.
Hours & Admission Prices: Reference Library: Tues & Thurs. 1-4, Sat. 10-4; other times by appointment. Exhibition Gallery: Tues., Thurs. & Sat. 1-4. No charge; donations accepted. Call for holiday closings. &
Attendance: 2,500 (estimated)

PORTSMOUTH MUSEUM OF ART, 909 Islington St., Ste. 14, Portsmouth, NH 03801. Tel.: 603-436-0332.
E-mail: info@portsmouthmfa.org
Web Site: www.portsmouthmfa.org
Key Personnel: Dir., Chm. (V) & Museum Shop Mgr., Cathy Sununu.
Institution Type/Description: Art Museum.
Hours & Admission Prices: Temporarily closed.
Attendance: 5,500 (actual)

RUNDLET-MAY HOUSE, 364 Middle St., Portsmouth, NH 03801-5016. Mailing Address: 141 Cambridge St., Boston, MA 02114-2702. Tel.: 603-436-3205, 617-227-3956.
E-mail: rundletmayhouse@historicnewengland.org
Web Site: www.historicnewengland.org
Key Personnel: Pres. & C.E.O., Carl R. Nold; Site Mgr., Linda Marshall.
Institution Type/Description: Historic House: 1807 three-story Federal mansion with original outbuildings, courtyard & formal gardens.
Hours & Admission Prices: June-Oct. 15 1st & 3rd Sat. of month 11-5, (last tour at 4). Adults $8; discounts to seniors, AAM, ICOM & AAA members; Historic New England members no charge.
Attendance: 515 (actual)

WARNER HOUSE, 150 Daniel St., Portsmouth, NH 03801-3831. Mailing Address: Box 895, Portsmouth, NH 03802-0895. Tel.: 603-436-5909.
E-mail: housemanager@warnerhouse.org
Web Site: www.warnerhouse.org
Formerly: MacPheadris/Warner House
Key Personnel: Co Chm., Deborah Richards; Co Chm., Ronan Donohoe; Treas., Lorn Buxton; Sec., Elizabeth Farish; Cur., Carolyn Roy; Cur., Louise Richardson.
Institution Type/Description: Historic House Museum: c.1716 Macpheadris-Warner House.
Hours & Admission Prices: mid-June to mid-Oct. Wed.-Mon. 11-4; other times by appointment. Adults $7, senior citizens $4, children under 7-12 $3.50; discounts to groups, AAA members & Time Travelers; children under 7 & members no charge.
Attendance: 2,000 (estimated)

WENTWORTH-COOLIDGE MANSION, 375 Little Harbor Rd., Portsmouth, NH 03801. Mailing Address: 799 South St., Portsmouth, NH 03801. Tel.: 603-436-6607. Fax: 603-430-0025.
E-mail: info@wentworthcoolidge.org
Web Site: www.wentworthcoolidge.org
Key Personnel: Chm. (V), Noele Clews.
Institution Type/Description: Historic House: c.1750 home of first Royal Governor of New Hampshire.
Hours & Admission Prices: Tours: late June to early Sept. Wed.-Sun. 10-3; early Sept. to early Oct. Sat.-Sun. 10-3; other times by appointment.
Attendance: 7,763 (actual)

WENTWORTH LEAR HISTORIC HOUSES, 50 Mechanic St., Portsmouth, NH 03801. Mailing Address: P.O. Box 563, Portsmouth, NH 03802-0563. Tel.: 603-436-4406.
E-mail: wentworthlear@gmail.com
Web Site: wentworthlear.org

Formerly: Wentworth Gardner & Tobias Lear Houses Association
Key Personnel: Pres., Richard G. Adams; Treas., Fred Engelbach; Sec., Joseph Capobianco.
Institution Type/Description: Historic House: 1760 Wentworth Gardner House, Georgian mansion.
Hours & Admission Prices: June to Oct. 12 Wed.-Sun. 12-4. Adults $6, children $3; discount to groups & National Trust Affiliate; members no charge. &
Attendance: 910 (actual)

Raymond

RAYMOND HISTORICAL SOCIETY, 1 Depot Rd., Raymond, NH 03077. Mailing Address: P.O. Box 94, Raymond, NH 03077-0094. Tel.: 603-895-2866.
E-mail: ddgame@comcast.net
Web Site: www.raymondhistoricalsociety.org
Key Personnel: Pres. (V), Diane E. White; Museum Shop Mgr., Diane Debruyckere.
Institution Type/Description: Historical Society Museum: housed in the Old Raymond Train Depot.
Hours & Admission Prices: April 2 to mid-Dec. Sun. 1-5; other times by appointment. No charge; donations accepted.
Attendance: 300 (estimated)

Rye

SEACOAST SCIENCE CENTER, 570 Ocean Blvd., Rye, NH 03870-2131. Tel.: 603-436-8043. Fax: 603-433-2235. Facebook: @seacoastsciencecenter; Instagram: @seacoast_science_center; Twitter: @SeacoastSciCtr.
E-mail: info@sscnh.org
Web Site: seacoastsciencecenter.org
Key Personnel: Pres., Jim Chase; Vice Pres., Nichole Rutherford; Dir. Finance, Susan Bradbury; Dir. Programs, Henry Burke; Dir. Mission, Kate Leavitt; Dir. Exhibits, Jeremy LeClair; Dir. Mktg., Karen Provazza.
Institution Type/Description: Aquarium.
Hours & Admission Prices: April-Oct. daily 10-5; Nov.-March Sat.-Mon. 10-5. Adults $10, seniors & veterans $8, children 3-12 $5; discounts to Associated Nature Centers & New England Museum Assoc. members; members no charge. &
Attendance: 80,000 (actual)

Salisbury

SALISBURY HISTORICAL SOCIETY, Salisbury Heights, Rte. 4, Salisbury, NH 03268. Mailing Address: P.O. Box 263, Salisbury, NH 03268. Tel.: 603-648-2774.
E-mail: shscurator@gmail.com
Web Site: www.salisburyhistoricalsociety.org
Key Personnel: Cur., Linda Denoncourt; Pres., Al Romano.
Institution Type/Description: History Museum: housed in 1791 Old Baptist Church.
Hours & Admission Prices: April-Oct. Sat. 1-4. No charge; donations accepted.
Attendance: 250 (estimated)

Sandown

SANDOWN HISTORICAL SOCIETY AND MUSEUM, 6 Depot Rd., Sandown, NH 03873. Mailing Address: P.O. Box 300, Sandown, NH 03873-0373.
E-mail: sanhs@comcast.net
Web Site: www.sandownnhdepot.org
Key Personnel: Pres., Robert Driscoll; Vice Pres., Jon Wells; Treas., Robert Brouder; Cur., Sue Dupoy; Sec., Fran Rosenau; Historian, James Weber.
Institution Type/Description: Railroad & Local History Museum: housed in 1874 railroad station.
Hours & Admission Prices: May-Oct. Sat. 10-2. No charge; donations accepted. &
Attendance: 300 (estimated)

Sharon

THE SHARON ARTS CENTER, INC., 457 NH Rte. 123, Sharon, NH 03458-7116. Tel.: 603-924-7256. Fax: 603-924-6074.
E-mail: info@sharonarts.org
Web Site: www.sharonarts.org
Key Personnel: Exec. Dir., Keri Wiederspahn; Gallery & Store Dir., Camellia Sousa; Craft Gallery Coord., Gillie Dierauf.
Institution Type/Description: Art Gallery.
Hours & Admission Prices: Call for hours. &
Attendance: 36,000 (estimated)

South Sutton

SOUTH SUTTON OLD STORE MUSEUM, 12 Meeting House Hill Rd., South Sutton, NH 03273. Mailing Address: Sutton Historical Society, P.O. Box 457, South Sutton, NH 03273. Tel.: 603-927-4416.
E-mail: suttonnhhistory@gmail.com
Institution Type/Description: Historic Building: c.1850 general store.
Hours & Admission Prices: Call for hours. No charge; donations accepted.
Attendance: 100 (estimated)

Stewartstown

POORE FAMILY HOMESTEAD - HISTORIC FARM MUSEUM, 629 Hollow Rd. Rte. 145, Stewartstown, NH 03576. Mailing Address: 438 Fish Pond Rd., Colebrook, NH 03576. Tel.: 603-237-5500 & 5313. Facebook.
E-mail: info@poorefarm.org
Web Site: poorefarm.org
Key Personnel: Exec. Dir., Richard Johnsen; Dir., Mark J. Winer.
Institution Type/Description: Historic Building: housed in the Poore family homestead; c.1830.
Hours & Admission Prices: June-Sept. Fri.-Sun. 1-3. Suggested Donation: adults $10; active military & their families and children under 12 no charge. Blue Star Museum.
Attendance: 1,250 (estimated)

Sugar Hill

SUGAR HILL HISTORICAL MUSEUM, 1401 Rte. 117, Sugar Hill, NH 03586. Mailing Address: P.O. Box 591, Sugar Hill, NH 03586-0591. Tel.: 603-823-5336.
E-mail: kittyh41@gmail.com
Web Site: www.sugarhillnh.org
Key Personnel: Chm. (V), John E. Bigelow; Dir., Katharine N. Bigelow.
Institution Type/Description: History Museum.
Hours & Admission Prices: June 5-Oct.17 Fri.-Sat. 11-3. No charge; donations accepted.
Attendance: 1,789 (actual)

Sunapee

SUNAPEE HISTORICAL SOCIETY MUSEUM, 74 Main St., Sunapee Harbor, Sunapee, NH 03782. Mailing Address: P.O. Box 501, Sunapee, NH 03782-0501. Tel.: 603-763-9872.
E-mail: sunapeehistory@gmail.com
Web Site: sunapeehistoricalsociety.org
Key Personnel: Pres., Becky Rylander.
Institution Type/Description: History Museum.
Hours & Admission Prices: Summer: Tues. & Thurs.-Sun. 1-4, Wed. 7pm-9pm; Sept.-Oct. Sat.-Sun. 1-4. No charge; donations accepted.

Suncook

4-H NATURE CENTER, Bear Brook State Park & Campground, off Rte. 28, Allenstown, Suncook, NH 03275. Mailing Address: 157 Deerfield Rd., Allenstown, NH 03275-2503. Tel.: 603-485-9874. Fax: 603-485-4358.
Web Site: www.nhstateparks.com/bearbrook.html
Formerly: Bear Brook Nature Center.
Key Personnel: Park Mgr., David Evans.
Institution Type/Description: Natural History Museum.
Hours & Admission Prices: Memorial Day-Labor Day Fri.-Tues. 10-5. Museum: call for hours. Park Entrance Fee: adults $4, children 6-11 $2; children under 5 and NH residents 65 & over no charge.
Attendance: 1,500

Tamworth

REMICK COUNTRY DOCTOR MUSEUM AND FARM, 58 Cleveland Hill Rd., Tamworth, NH 03886. Tel.: 603-323-7591, 800-686-6117. Fax: 603-323-8382.
E-mail: info@remickmuseum.org
Web Site: www.remickmuseum.org
Key Personnel: Exec. Dir., Cara Sutherland; Chm. (V), Harold Cook; Museum Shop Mgr., Sharon Trott.
Institution Type/Description: Historic Site.
Hours & Admission Prices: Jan. 1-June 3 Mon.-Fri. 10-4; June 5-Sept. 2 Mon.-Fri. 9-5, Sat. 9-4; Sept. 5-Oct. 7 Mon.-Fri. 10-4, Sat. 10-3; Oct. 9-Dec. 30 Mon.-Fri.

10-4. Adults $5; discounts to AAM members; children 4 & under and members no charge. Closed major holidays.
Attendance: 11,000 (estimated)

Warner

THE LITTLE NATURE MUSEUM, 18 Highlawn Rd., Warner, NH 03278. Tel.: 603-746-6121.
E-mail: info@littlenaturemuseum.org
Web Site: www.littlenaturemuseum.org
Key Personnel: Dir., C.E.O. & Pres. (V), Sandra W. Martin.
Institution Type/Description: Natural History Museum.
Hours & Admission Prices: May-Oct. Sat.-Sun. call for hours & admission prices.

MT. KEARSARGE INDIAN MUSEUM, 18 Highlawn Rd., Warner, NH 03278. Mailing Address: P.O. Box 142, Warner, NH 03278-0142. Tel.: 603-456-2600 & 3244. Fax: 603-456-3092. Facebook: @Mt.KearsargeIndianMuseum.
E-mail: info@indianmuseum.org
Web Site: www.indianmuseum.org
Key Personnel: Exec. Dir., Patricia Violette; Chm. (V), David Salzberg; Deputy Dir., Emmons Cobb; Dir. Education, Liz Charlebois; Cur., Nancy Jo Chabot; Museum Shop Mgr., Debbie Moody.
Institution Type/Description: Native American History Museum.
Hours & Admission Prices: May-Oct. Mon.-Sat. 10-5, Sun. 12-5. Families $26; adults $9, senior citizens & students $8, children 6-12 $7; discounts to AAM, AAA & AARP members & Blue Star Museum participants; Native Americans, members & children under 6 no charge.
Attendance: 8,500 (estimated)

NEW HAMPSHIRE TELEPHONE MUSEUM, One Depot St., Warner, NH 03278-4421. Mailing Address: P.O. Box 444, Warner, NH 03278-0444. Tel.: 603-456-2234.
E-mail: info@nhtelephonemuseum.org
Web Site: www.nhtelephonemuseum.org
Key Personnel: Dir., Laura French; Pres. (V), Paul E. Violette; Program Coord., Graham Gifford.
Institution Type/Description: History Museum.
Hours & Admission Prices: March-April & Nov.-Dec. Tues. & Sat. 10-4; May-Oct. Tues.-Sat. 10-4; other times by appointment. Adults $5, seniors 60 & over $4, children grades 1-12 $3; discounts to AAA members; members no charge. Closed New Year's Day; Independence Day; Thanksgiving; Christmas.
Attendance: 1,200 (actual)

Waterville Valley

THE MARGARET AND H.A. REY CENTER AND CURIOUS GEORGE COTTAGE, 35 Village Rd., Bldg. C, Waterville Valley, NH 03215. Mailing Address: P.O. Box 286, Waterville Valley, NH 03215-0286. Tel.: 603-236-3308.
E-mail: info@thereycenter.org
Web Site: thereycenter.org/Welcome.html
Key Personnel: Exec. Dir., Leah Elliot.
Institution Type/Description: Art Museum: housed in the former summer home of Margaret and H.A. Rey, authors of the Curious George children's book series.
Hours & Admission Prices: July-Sept. 5 Wed.-Sat. 10-5; Sept. 6-June Sat. 10-5. No charge; donations accepted.

Wilton

FRYE'S MEASURE MILL, 12 Frye Mill Rd., Wilton, NH 03086. Tel.: 603-654-6581. Fax: 603-654-6103.
Web Site: www.fryesmeasuremill.com
Key Personnel: C.E.O., Archivist & Public Rels., Harland Savage, Jr.; Pres. (V) & Gift Shop Mgr., Pamela Savage.
Institution Type/Description: Industrial Museum: housed in 1858 measure mill. Listed on the National Register of Historic Places.
Hours & Admission Prices: Jan.-March Wed.-Sat. 10-4; April to mid-Dec. Tues.-Sat. 10-5, Sun. 12-5. Tours: Jan.-March call for hours; June-Oct. Sat. at 2. Adults $5.75; discount to groups; children under 12 no charge. Closed national holidays.

Wolfeboro

THE LIBBY MUSEUM, 755 N. Main St., Wolfeboro, NH 03894. Mailing Address: P.O. Box 629, Wolfeboro, NH 03894-0629. Tel.: 603-569-1035. Fax: 603-569-2246. Facebook, Twitter.
E-mail: director@thelibbymuseum.org
Web Site: thelibbymuseum.org

Key Personnel: Dir., Alana Albee.
Institution Type/Description: History & Natural History Museum.
Hours & Admission Prices: Memorial Day to Labor Day Tues.-Sat. 10-4; Sept. to Columbus Day Sat. 10-4, Sun. 12-4. Adults $5; children under 16 & veterans no charge. &
Attendance: 3,000 (actual)

WOLFEBORO HISTORICAL SOCIETY, 233 S. Main St., Wolfeboro, NH 03894. Mailing Address: P.O. Box 1066, Wolfeboro, NH 03894-1066. Tel.: 603-569-4997 (Clark House).
E-mail: lhorsken@gmail.com
Web Site: www.wolfeborohistoricalsociety.org
Key Personnel: Pres., Louise Horsken; Museum Opers., Mark Lush.
Institution Type/Description: Historical Society Museum.
Hours & Admission Prices: July-Aug. Wed.-Fri. 10-4, Sat. 10-2; Spring & Fall: by appointment. Call for admission prices. &
Attendance: 400 (estimated)

WRIGHT MUSEUM OF WORLD WAR II, 77 Center St., Rte. 28, Wolfeboro, NH 03894-4368. Mailing Address: P.O. Box 1212, Wolfeboro, NH 03894-1212. Tel.: 603-569-1212. Fax: 603-569-6326. Facebook: Wright Museum of World War II.
E-mail: info@wrightmuseum.org
Web Site: wrightmuseum.org
Key Personnel: Bd. Pres., Anne Blodget; Admin. Mgr, Donna Hamill; Exec. Dir., Dr. Michael Culver.
Institution Type/Description: History Museum.
Hours & Admission Prices: May-Oct. Mon.-Sat. 10-4, Sun. 12-4; other times by appointment. Adults $10, senior citizens & veterans $8, students $6; children 4 & under and members no charge. &
Attendance: 16,500 (actual)

Wolfeboro Falls

NEW HAMPSHIRE BOAT MUSEUM, 399 Center St., Wolfeboro Falls, NH 03896. Mailing Address: P.O. Box 1195, Wolfeboro Falls, NH 03896-1195. Tel.: 603-569-4554. Fax: 603-569-5931.
E-mail: museum@nhbm.org
Web Site: www.nhbm.org
Key Personnel: Exec. Dir., Lisa Simpson Lutts; Chm. (V), Joe DeChiaro; Museum Shop Mgr., Allison Gamble.
Institution Type/Description: Boat Museum.
Hours & Admission Prices: Memorial Day to Columbus Day Mon.-Sat. 10-4, Sun. 12-4. Adults $7, seniors 65 & over $4, students $3; discounts to AARP members; AAM & museum members, children 12 & under and museum staff no charge. &
Attendance: 6,200 (actual)

NEW JERSEY

(413 listings)

Absecon

HOWLETT HALL MUSEUM, 100 New Jersey Ave., Absecon, NJ 08201. Mailing Address: P.O. Box 1422, Absecon, NJ 08201-1422. Tel.: 609-659-9000.
E-mail: abseconplanner@gmail.com
Key Personnel: Pres., Rob Reid.
Institution Type/Description: History Museum.
Hours & Admission Prices: Sat. 11-2; call to confirm.

Allentown

HISTORIC WALNFORD, 62 Walnford Rd., Allentown, NJ 08501. Mailing Address: Monmouth County Park System, 805 Newmann Springs Rd., Lincroft, NJ 07738. Tel.: 609-259-6275, 732-842-4000. Fax: 609-259-0384. TDD: 732-219-9484.
E-mail: info@monmouthcountyparks.com
Web Site: www.monmouthcountyparks.com
Key Personnel: Park Mgr., William O'Shaughnessy; Historic Site Supvr., Sarah Bent.
Institution Type/Description: Historic Site: 20th-century colonial revival interpretation of 19th-century milling technology; 18th-century industrial village.
Hours & Admission Prices: Historic Buildings: daily 9-4; other times by appointment. Park: Memorial Day to Labor Day daily 8-7; Sept.-May daily 8-4:30. No charge; donations accepted. &
Attendance: 20,000 (actual)

Alloway

ALLOWAY HISTORY MUSEUM, Alloway Municipal Bldg., 49 S. Greenwich St., Alloway, NJ 08001. Mailing Address: P.O. Box 425, Alloway, NJ 08001. Tel.: 856-769-2632.
E-mail: flamingo22@comcast.net
Web Site: www.allowaytownship.com
Key Personnel: Co-Cur., Barbara Dawson; Co-Cur., Margaret Matthews.
Institution Type/Description: History Museum.
Hours & Admission Prices: last Sat. each month 9-12; other times by appointment.

RANCH HOPE CARRIAGE MUSEUM, 45 Sawmill Rd., Alloway, NJ 08001. Mailing Address: P.O. Box 571, Alloway, NJ 08001. Tel.: 856-935-1555.
Institution Type/Description: Carriage Museum.
Hours & Admission Prices: Mon.-Fri. 8:30-4:30 by appointment. No charge; donations accepted. &
Attendance: 100 (estimated)

Asbury Park

CRANE HOUSE, 508 4th Ave., Asbury Park, NJ 07712-6010. Tel.: 732-775-5682.
Institution Type/Description: Historic House Museum: housed in the former home of author, Stephen Crane; c.1877.
Hours & Admission Prices: Call for hours.

SILVERBALL MUSEUM ARCADE, 1000 Ocean Ave., Asbury Park, NJ 07712. Tel.: 732-774-4994. Facebook.
Web Site: silverballmuseum.com
Institution Type/Description: General Museum.
Hours & Admission Prices: Sun. 10-9, Mon.-Thurs. 11-9, Fri. 11 am to midnight, Sat. 10 to midnight. Admission $15-$20.

Atlantic City

ABSECON LIGHTHOUSE AND KEEPER'S HOUSE MUSEUM, 31 S. Rhode Island Ave., Atlantic City, NJ 08401-7760. Tel.: 609-449-1360. Fax: 609-449-1919.
E-mail: jean@abseconlighthouse.org
Web Site: www.abseconlighthouse.org
Institution Type/Description: History Museum & Historic Lighthouse: built in 1857.
Hours & Admission Prices: July-Aug. daily 10-5; Sept.-June Thurs.-Mon. 11-4. Adults $10, seniors 65 & over and college students $9, children 4-12 $6; children under 4 & active military no charge. Closed major holidays. &
Attendance: 28,000 (actual)

AFRICAN AMERICAN HERITAGE MUSEUM OF SOUTHERN NEW JERSEY, Noyes Arts Garage, 2200 Fairmount Ave., Atlantic City, NJ 08401. Tel.: 609-350-6662.
E-mail: info@aahmsnj.org
Web Site: www.aahmsnj.org
Key Personnel: Pres., Ralph Hunter; Exec. Dir., Stacey Hunter-Withers.
Institution Type/Description: History & Art Museum.
Hours & Admission Prices: Wed.-Sat. 11-6, Sun. 11-5. Branch Museum: Tues.-Fri. 10-3; other times by appointment. No charge; donations accepted.

ATLANTIC CITY AQUARIUM, 800 N. New Hampshire Ave., Atlantic City, NJ 08401-2900. Tel.: 609-348-2880. Fax: 609-345-4238.
Web Site: www.acaquarium.com
Formerly: Historic Gardner's Basin
Institution Type/Description: Maritime Village & Ocean Life Center: housed in pre-1900 waterfront homes, located on site where Atlantic City was founded.
Hours & Admission Prices: Daily 10-5. Adults $10, seniors 62 & over $7, children 4-12 $6; children 3 & under no charge. Closed New Year's Day; Thanksgiving; Christmas. &
Attendance: 90,000 (estimated)

ATLANTIC CITY ART CENTER, New Jersey Ave. & Boardwalk, Atlantic City, NJ 08401. Mailing Address: P.O. Box 845, Brigantine, NJ 08203-0845. Tel.: 609-347-5837 & 5838. Fax: 609-347-5844.
Institution Type/Description: Art Gallery.
Hours & Admission Prices: Summer: daily 10-4; Fall: Tues.-Sun. 10-4. No charge. Closed national holidays.

RIPLEY'S BELIEVE IT OR NOT! MUSEUM, 1441 Boardwalk, Atlantic City, NJ 08401-7144. Tel.: 609-347-2001.
E-mail: ripacac@aol.com
Web Site: www.ripleys.com/atlanticcity/
Key Personnel: Gen. Mgr., Chris Connelly.
Institution Type/Description: General Museum.
Hours & Admission Prices: Mon.-Tues. & Thurs.-Fri. 11-6, , Wed. 12-5, Sat. 10-8, Sun. 10-6. Adults 13 & over $18.99, children 5-12 $12.99; discounts to groups; children 4 & under no charge. &

Atlantic Highlands

ATLANTIC HIGHLANDS HISTORICAL SOCIETY - STRAUSS MANSION AND MUSEUM, 27 Prospect Circle, Atlantic Highlands, NJ 07716-1310. Mailing Address: P.O. Box 108, Atlantic Highlands, NJ 07716. Tel.: 732-291-1861. Facebook.
E-mail: ahhs123@comcast.net
Web Site: atlantichighlandshistory.com
Key Personnel: Acting Pres., Ken Frantz.
Institution Type/Description: Historical Society Museum.
Hours & Admission Prices: April-Dec. Sun. 1-4. No charge; donations accepted.

Avalon

AVALON HISTORICAL SOCIETY, 215 39th St., Avalon, NJ 08202-1648. Tel.: 609-967-0090.
E-mail: brisley@avalonhistoricalsociety.org
Web Site: www.avalonhistorycenter.com
Key Personnel: Pres. (V), Bob Penrose, Jr.
Institution Type/Description: History Museum.
Hours & Admission Prices: Mon.-Fri. 10-4, Sat. 11-4. No charge; donations accepted. &

Barnegat Light

BARNEGAT LIGHT HISTORICAL SOCIETY AND MUSEUM, 501 Central Ave., Barnegat Light, NJ 08006. Mailing Address: P. O. Box 386, Barnegat Light, NJ 08006. Tel.: 609-494-8578.
E-mail: klarson767@aol.com
Web Site: www.bl-hs.org/
Key Personnel: Pres. (V), Karen Larson.
Institution Type/Description: Historical Society Museum.
Hours & Admission Prices: June & Sept.-Oct. Sat.-Sun. 10-4; July-Aug. daily 10-4; tours by appointment. No charge; donations accepted. &
Attendance: 4,000 (estimated)

Basking Ridge

ENVIRONMENTAL EDUCATION CENTER, SOMERSET COUNTY PARK COMMISSION, 190 Lord Stirling Rd., Basking Ridge, NJ 07920-1329. Tel.: 908-722-1200, ext. 5002. Fax: 908-766-2687. Facebook.
E-mail: cspringer@scparks.org
Web Site: www.somersetcountyparks.org
Key Personnel: Mgr., Carrie Springer; Supvr., Kurt Bender.
Institution Type/Description: Environmental Education Center; located on site of Lord Stirling's Estate.
Hours & Admission Prices: Daily 9-5. Trails: daily sunrise to sunset. No charge; donations accepted. Closed major holidays. &
Attendance: 30,000 (estimated)

THE HISTORICAL SOCIETY OF THE SOMERSET HILLS, 15 W. Oak St., Basking Ridge, NJ 07920. Mailing Address: P.O. Box 136, Basking Ridge, NJ 07920. Tel.: 908-221-1770. Facebook.
E-mail: info@thssh.org
Web Site: thssh.org
Key Personnel: Chm. (V) & Cur., Sue Zibelli.
Institution Type/Description: Historical Society Museum; housed in the Brick Academy. Listed on the National Register of Historic Places.
Hours & Admission Prices: Museum: 1st Sun. each month 2-4. Research: by appointment only. No charge; donations accepted.
Attendance: 500 (estimated)

Bayonne

CHIEF JOHN T. BRENNAN FIRE MUSEUM, 10 W. 47th St., Bayonne, NJ 07002-4005. Mailing Address: c/o Fire Headquarters, 630 Avenue C, Bayonne, NJ 07002. Tel.: 201-858-6000.

Institution Type/Description: Firefighting History Museum; housed in the former fire department station; built in 1870. Listed on the National Register of Historic Places.
Hours & Admission Prices: Call for hours.

Bayville

BERKELEY TOWNSHIP HISTORICAL MUSEUM, 630 Rte. 9, Bayville, NJ 08721. Mailing Address: P.O. Box 303, Bayville, NJ 08721-0303. Tel.: 732-269-0643.
Key Personnel: Pres. (V), James Fosbre; Museum Shop Mgr., Dale Cottrell.
Institution Type/Description: History Museum.
Hours & Admission Prices: mid-June to mid-Sept. Wed. 6pm-8pm, Sun. 2-4; other times by appointment. No charge; donations accepted.
Attendance: 400 (actual)

Beach Haven

LONG BEACH ISLAND HISTORICAL ASSOCIATION, 129 Engleside Ave., Beach Haven, NJ 08008-1762. Mailing Address: P.O. Box 1222, Beach Haven, NJ 08008. Tel.: 609-492-0700. Fax: 609-492-3885.
E-mail: lbiha_museum@comcast.net
Formerly: Long Beach Island Historical Society
Key Personnel: Museum Shop Mgr., Kay Donelly.
Institution Type/Description: History Museum; housed in the former Holy Innocents' Episcopal Church built in 1882.
Hours & Admission Prices: June & Sept. Sat.-Sun. 12-4; July & Aug. daily 10-4. Suggested Donation: $3. &
Attendance: 2,300 (actual)

NEW JERSEY MARITIME MUSEUM, 528 Dock Rd., Beach Haven, NJ 08008-1833. Tel.: 609-492-0202. Fax: 609-492-7575. Facebook.
E-mail: info@njmm.org
Web Site: www.njmaritimemuseum.org
Formerly: Museum of New Jersey Maritime History
Key Personnel: Pres. & Treas., Deb Whitcraft; Exec. Dir., Jim Vogel.
Institution Type/Description: Maritime History Museum.
Hours & Admission Prices: June-Aug. daily 10-4; Sept.-May Fri.-Sun. 10-4; other times by appointment. No charge; donations accepted. &
Attendance: 9,000 (estimated)

Beachwood

JAKES BRANCH COUNTY PARK & NATURE CENTER, 1100 Double Trouble Rd., Beachwood, NJ 08722. Tel.: 732-281-2750.
E-mail: ocparks@co.ocean.nj.us
Key Personnel: Dir., Michael Mangum.
Institution Type/Description: Park & Nature Center.
Hours & Admission Prices: Call for hours.

Bedminster

JACOBUS VANDERVEER HOUSE & MUSEUM, 3055 River Rd., River Road Park, Bedminster, NJ 07921. Mailing Address: P. O. Box 723, Bedminster, NJ 07921-0723. Tel.: 908-396-6053. Facebook, Twitter, YouTube, Instagram.
E-mail: info@jvanderveerhouse.org
Web Site: www.jvanderveerhouse.org
Key Personnel: Pres., Robin Ray; Museum Coord., Taryn Nie.
Institution Type/Description: Historic House Museum.
Hours & Admission Prices: 2nd Sun. each month 1-4; call for special events hours. Adults $10; discounts to AAM & ICOM members; members and children 12 & under no charge. &

Belmar

OCEANSIDE GALLERY, 1010 Main St., Belmar, NJ 07719-2726. Tel.: 732-280-2167. Fax: 732-280-2167.
E-mail: gallery@oceansidegallery.com
Web Site: oceansidegallery.com
Institution Type/Description: Art Gallery.
Hours & Admission Prices: Tues. & Sat. 10-5, Wed. 10-8:30, Thurs. 10-6, Fri. 10-8; other times by appointment.

Belvidere

WARREN COUNTY HISTORICAL SOCIETY AND MUSEUM, 313 Mansfield St., Belvidere, NJ 07823. Mailing Address: P.O. Box 313, Belvidere, NJ 07823. Tel.: 908-475-4246.
Institution Type/Description: Historical Society Museum: house built c.1848.
Hours & Admission Prices: Sun. 2-4; groups by appointment. No charge; donations accepted.

Bernardsville

SCHERMAN HOFFMAN WILDLIFE SANCTUARY, 11 Hardscrabble Rd., Bernardsville, NJ 07924. Tel.: 908-396-6386. Fax: 908-766-7775.
E-mail: scherman-hoffman@njaudubon.org
Web Site: www.njaudubon.org
Key Personnel: Dir., Mike Anderson; Museum Shop Mgr., Susan Garretson Friedman.
Institution Type/Description: Wildlife Sanctuary.
Hours & Admission Prices: Tues.-Sat. 9-5, Sun. 12-5. No charge; donations accepted. Closed holidays. &
Attendance: 10,000 (estimated)

Blairstown

BLAIRSTOWN MUSEUM, 26 Main St., Blairstown, NJ 07825. Mailing Address: P.O. Box 109, Blairstown, NJ 07825. Tel.: 908-362-1371. Facebook.
E-mail: blairstownmuseum@gmail.com
Web Site: blairstownmuseum.com
Institution Type/Description: History Museum.
Hours & Admission Prices: Fri.-Sat. 11-5; groups of 8 or more by appointment. No charge; donations accepted.

FRIDAY THE 13TH MUSEUM, 27 Main St., Blairstown, NJ 07825. Mailing Address: P.O. Box 109, Blairstown, NJ 07825. Tel.: 908-362-1371.
Institution Type/Description: Movie Museum.
Hours & Admission Prices: Call for hours.

Bloomfield

HISTORICAL SOCIETY OF BLOOMFIELD NEW JERSEY, 90 Broad St., Bloomfield, NJ 07003-2585. Tel.: 973-566-6220 & 743-8844.
E-mail: info@hsob.org
Key Personnel: Pres. (V), Jean Kuras.
Institution Type/Description: Local History Museum: housed in Bloomfield Public Library.
Hours & Admission Prices: July-Aug. Wed. 2-4:30; Sept.-June Wed. 2-4:30, Sat. 10-12:30; other times by appointment. No charge; donations accepted. &
Attendance: 380 (estimated)

Boonton

BOONTON HISTORICAL SOCIETY, John Taylor Bldg., 210 Main St., Boonton, NJ 07005. Tel.: 973-402-8840.
E-mail: boontonhistory@boonton.org
Web Site: www.boonton.org
Institution Type/Description: Historical Society Museum.
Hours & Admission Prices: Sun. 1-4; other times by appointment.

NEW JERSEY FIREMEN'S HOME MUSEUM, 565 Lathrop Ave., Boonton, NJ 07005. Tel.: 973-334-0024.
E-mail: info@njfh.org
Web Site: www.njfh.org
Institution Type/Description: Firefighting History Museum.
Hours & Admission Prices: Daily 8-4. No charge; donations accepted. &
Attendance: 3,500 (estimated)

Bordentown

ARTFUL DEPOSIT GALLERY, 142 Farnsworth Ave., Bordentown, NJ 08505-1345. Tel.: 609-298-6970.
E-mail: artfuldeposit@gmail.com
Web Site: artfuldeposit.blogspot.com
Key Personnel: Dir., C.J. Mugavero.
Institution Type/Description: Art Gallery.

Hours & Admission Prices: mid-July to mid-Aug. Wed.-Thurs. & Sat. 1-6, Fri. 4-9, Sun. 1-5; mid-Aug to mid-July Wed.-Thurs. & Sat. 1-6, Sun. 1-5.

BORDENTOWN HISTORICAL SOCIETY, 302 Farnsworth Ave., Bordentown, NJ 08505. Mailing Address: P.O. Box 182, Bordentown, NJ 08505. Tel.: 609-298-1740 & 9181.
E-mail: bordentownhistoricalsociety@gmail.com
Web Site: bordentownhistory.org
Institution Type/Description: Historical Society Museum.
Hours & Admission Prices: Call for hours.

Bridgeton

BRIDGETON HALL OF FAME ALL SPORTS MUSEUM, Burt Avenue Recreation Center, Bridgeton, NJ 08302. Mailing Address: c/o City of Bridgeton Dept. of Recreation, 181 E. Commerce St., Bridgeton, NJ 08302. Tel.: 856-451-7300.
E-mail: kimga@co.cumberland.nj.us
Institution Type/Description: Sports Museum.
Hours & Admission Prices: Call for hours. No charge.

COHANZICK ZOO, 45 Mayor Aitken Dr., Bridgeton, NJ 08302. Tel.: 856-453-1658 & 1675.
Web Site: cohanzickzoo.org
Institution Type/Description: Zoo.
Hours & Admission Prices: Winter: daily 9-4; Summer: daily 9-5; groups by appointment. No charge; donations accepted. Closed Thanksgiving; Christmas. &

NAIL MILL MUSEUM, 1 Mayor Aitken Dr., Bridgeton, NJ 08302-1347. Tel.: 856-453-1675.
E-mail: kimga@co.cumberland.nj.us
Institution Type/Description: History Museum; housed in the former Cumberland Nail and Iron Company.
Hours & Admission Prices: Temporarily closed for renovations.

WOODRUFF MUSEUM OF INDIAN ARTIFACTS, 150 E. Commerce St., Bridgeton, NJ 08302-2613. Tel.: 856-451-2620. Fax: 856-455-1049.
E-mail: bpl@bridgetonlibrary.org
Web Site: www.bridgetonlibrary.org
Key Personnel: Library Dir., Linda McFadden.
Institution Type/Description: Native American History Museum.
Hours & Admission Prices: Museum: Wed. 1-4. Library: Tues.-Thurs. 10-8, Fri. 9-5, Sat. 9-4; other hours by appointment. No charge; donations accepted. Closed New Year's Day; Martin Luther King Jr. Day; Presidents' Day; Good Friday; Memorial Day; Independence Day; Labor Day; Veterans Day; Columbus Day; Election Day; Thanksgiving & day after; Christmas.
Attendance: 400 (estimated)

Bridgewater

SOMERSET COUNTY HISTORICAL SOCIETY - VAN VEGHTEN HOUSE, 9 Van Veghten Dr., Bridgewater, NJ 08807. Tel.: 908-218-1281.
E-mail: schs@schsnj.org
Web Site: www.schistoryweekend.com
Institution Type/Description: Historical Society Museum: house built in 1720. Listed on the National Register of Historic Places.
Hours & Admission Prices: Call for hours. No charge; donations accepted.

Brigantine

BRIGANTINE BEACH HISTORICAL MUSEUM & SOCIETY, 3607 Brigantine Blvd., Brigantine, NJ 08203-1001. Mailing Address: P.O. Box 833, Brigantine, NJ 08203. Tel.: 609-266-9339.
Key Personnel: Dir., Andrew Solari; Chm. (V), Linda Sayers; Museum Shop Mgr., Sue Van Nest.
Institution Type/Description: Historical Society Museum.
Hours & Admission Prices: Spring-Fall Sat. 11-2, Sun. 1-4; Summer Mon.-Sat. 11-2, Sun. 1-4. No charge; donations accepted.
Attendance: 2,300 (actual)

MARINE MAMMAL STRANDING CENTER - SEA LIFE MUSEUM, 3625 Brigantine Blvd., Brigantine, NJ 08203. Mailing Address: P.O. Box 773, Brigantine, NJ 08203. Tel.: 609-266-0538.
E-mail: mmsc@verizon.net
Web Site: www.marinemammalstrandingcenter.org

Key Personnel: Dir., Bob Schoelkopf.
Institution Type/Description: Marine Museum.
Hours & Admission Prices: Fall & Winter: Sat. 10-2; Summer: call for hours.

Burlington

BURLINGTON COUNTY HISTORICAL SOCIETY, 457 High
   St., Burlington, NJ 08016-4514. Tel.: 609-386-4773. Fax: 609-386-
   4828.
E-mail: burlcohistsoc@verizon.net
Web Site: www.burlingtoncountyhistoricalsociety.org
Key Personnel: Exec. Dir., Lisa Fox-Pfeiffer; Pres. (V), Gus Mosca; Dir. Education,
   Jeffrey J. Macechak; Librarian, Annie Brogan.
Institution Type/Description: Historical Society: historic house museums & local
   history museum.
Hours & Admission Prices: Houses, Museum & Children's History Center: Tues.-
   Sat. 10-5, groups by appointment. Library: Wed.-Thurs. 1-5. Adults $5, children
   under 12 $2.50; discounts to AAM members; members no charge. &
Attendance: 7,000 (actual)

CITY OF BURLINGTON HISTORICAL SOCIETY, 454 High
   St., Burlington, NJ 08016. Mailing Address: 457 High St.,
   Burlington, NJ 08016. Tel.: 609-386-4773. Facebook.
E-mail: burlcohistsoc@verizon.net
Key Personnel: Exec. Dir., Lisa Fox-Pfeiffer.
Institution Type/Description: Historical Society Museum: housed in c.1797 Hoskins
   House.
Hours & Admission Prices: Tours & History Center: Tues.-Sat. 10-5. Library:
   Wed.-Thurs. 1-5. Admission $5.
Attendance: 3,000

COLONIAL BURLINGTON FOUNDATION, INC., 213 Wood
   St., Burlington, NJ 08016. Mailing Address: P.O. Box 1552,
   Burlington, NJ 08016-7152. Tel.: 609-864-8152.
E-mail: applications@woodstreetfair.com
Web Site: www.colonialburlingtonfoundation.org/
Institution Type/Description: Historic House Museum: 1685 Thomas Revell House.
Hours & Admission Prices: first Sat. after Labor Day; other times by appointment.
   No charge; donations accepted.
Attendance: 12,000 (estimated)

Butler

BUTLER MUSEUM, 221 Main St., Butler, NJ 07405. Mailing
   Address: One Ace Rd., Butler, NJ 07405-1348. Tel.: 973-838-
   7222. Fax: 973-283-9895.
E-mail: butlermuseumnj@optonline.net
Web Site: www.butlermuseumnj.org
Key Personnel: Cur., Alan Bird.
Institution Type/Description: Military History Museum.
Hours & Admission Prices: 1st & 3rd Sat. 10-4. No charge. Closed holidays.

Caldwell

GROVER CLEVELAND BIRTHPLACE, 207 Bloomfield Ave.,
   Caldwell, NJ 07006-5115. Mailing Address: P.O. Box 183,
   Caldwell, NJ 07006. Tel.: 973-226-0001. Fax: 973-226-1810.
E-mail: gcmuseum@gmail.com
Web Site: clevelandbirthplace.org
Key Personnel: Dir. & Cur., Sharon Farrell.
Institution Type/Description: Historic House Museum: 1832 Old Manse of the
   Caldwell First Presbyterian Church; birthplace of President Grover Cleveland,
   22nd & 24th President of the United States.
Hours & Admission Prices: Wed.-Sat. 10-12 & 1-4, Sun. 1-4. No charge. Closed
   state & federal holidays.
Attendance: 6,000 (estimated)

Camden

ADVENTURE AQUARIUM, 1 Riverside Dr., Camden, NJ 08103-
   1060. Tel.: 856-365-3300; 844-474-3474. Fax: 856-365-3311.
Web Site: www.adventureaquarium.com
Formerly: New Jersey State Aquarium
Key Personnel: Public Rels. & Events Mgr., Deanna Sabec.
Institution Type/Description: Aquarium.
Hours & Admission Prices: Daily 10-5. Adults $31.99, children 2-12 $21.99; chil-
   dren under 2 no charge. &
Attendance: 510,000 (actual)

BATTLESHIP NEW JERSEY MUSEUM & MEMORIAL, 62
   Battleship Place, Camden, NJ 08103-3302. Tel.: 856-966-1652,
   ext. 211. Fax: 856-966-8228. Facebook.
E-mail: p.rowan@battleshipnewjersey.org
Web Site: www.battleshipnewjersey.org
Key Personnel: Chm., Marshall Spevak; Exec. Dir. & C.E.O., Philip Rowan.
Institution Type/Description: Naval Museum: one of the largest battleships ever
   built, the Iowa-class ship is our Nation's most decorated.
Hours & Admission Prices: May-Sept. 7 daily 9:30-5; Sept. 8-April daily 9:30-3.
   Fire Power Tour: adults $24.95, seniors, veterans, & children 5-11 $19.95, chil-
   dren 4 & under $5. Closed New Year's Day; Thanksgiving; Christmas. &
Attendance: 175,000 (estimated)

THE CAMDEN CHILDREN'S GARDEN, 3 Riverside Dr.,
   Camden, NJ 08103. Tel.: 856-365-8733.
E-mail: guestservices@camdenchildrensgarden.org
Institution Type/Description: Horticultural Garden.
Hours & Admission Prices: Thurs.-Fri. 10-3, Sat.-Sun. 10-4. Admission $9 per per-
   son, Camden Residence $6; children 1 & under no charge.

CAMDEN COUNTY HISTORICAL SOCIETY, 1900 Park Blvd.,
   Camden, NJ 08103-3697. Mailing Address: P.O. Box 378,
   Collingswood, NJ 08108-0378. Tel.: 856-964-3333. Fax: 856-964-
   0378.
E-mail: admin@cchsnj.com
Web Site: www.cchsnj.com
Key Personnel: Exec. Dir., Jack O'Byrne; Dir. Library, Bonny Beth Elwell; Dir.
   Collections, Josh Lisowski.
Institution Type/Description: History Museum.
Hours & Admission Prices: Museum & Library: Wed.-Fri. 10-4:30, Sun. 12-3.
   Pomona Hall: by appointment. Closed New Year's Eve & Day; Easter;
   Christmas; national holidays.
Attendance: 3,800 (actual)

STEDMAN GALLERY, Rutgers-Camden Center for the Arts, 314
   Linden St., Camden, NJ 08102-1403. Tel.: 856-225-6306. Fax:
   856-225-6597.
E-mail: arts@camden.rutgers.edu
Web Site: www.rutgerscamdenarts.org
Key Personnel: Dir., Cyril Reade; Assoc. Dir. Exhibitions, Nancy Maguire; Assoc.
   Dir. Education, Noreen Scott Garrity; Mgr. Community & Artist Programs,
   Carmen Pendleton.
Institution Type/Description: Art Museum.
Hours & Admission Prices: Sept.-April Mon.-Sat. 10-4; Summer: Mon.-Fri. 10-4.
   No charge; donations accepted. Closed New Year's Eve & Day; Memorial Day;
   Independence Day; Labor Day; Thanksgiving; Christmas Eve & Day; between
   exhibitions. &
Attendance: 18,300 (actual)

WALT WHITMAN HOUSE MUSEUM AND LIBRARY, 328
   Mickle Blvd., Camden, NJ 08103. Tel.: 856-964-5383. Fax: 856-
   964-1088.
Key Personnel: Cur., Richard Ryan.
Institution Type/Description: Historic Home Museum: 1884-1892 Walt Whitman
   home.
Hours & Admission Prices: Guided Tours: Wed.-Sat. 10-12 & 1-4, Sun. 1-4. No
   charge. Closed New Year's Day; Thanksgiving; Christmas.
Attendance: 3,000 (actual)

Canton

**LOWER ALLOWAYS CREEK HISTORIC LOG CABIN
   MUSEUM,** 736 Smick Rd., Canton, NJ 08001. Mailing Address:
   501 Locust Island Rd., P.O. Box 157, Hancocks Bridge, NJ 08038.
   Tel.: 856-935-1549.
Institution Type/Description: History Museum.
Hours & Admission Prices: March-May & Sept.-Nov. 3rd Sun. each month 1-4.

Cape May

HISTORIC COLD SPRING VILLAGE, 720 Rte. 9 S., Cape May,
   NJ 08204-4636. Tel.: 609-898-2300. Fax: 609-884-5926.
E-mail: 4info@hcsv.org
Web Site: www.hcsv.org
Key Personnel: Dir., Anne Salvatore; Mgr. Grants, Kate Devaney; Chief Admin.
   Officer, Clare Juechter.
Institution Type/Description: History Museum.

Hours & Admission Prices: June to Labor Day call for hours. Adults $14, children 3-12 $12; discounts to AAM members; children under 3 & members no charge. &

Attendance: 30,000

MID-ATLANTIC CENTER FOR THE ARTS & HUMANITIES/ EMLEN PHYSICK ESTATE/CAPE MAY LIGHTHOUSE/ FIRE CONTROL TOWER NO. 23, 1048 Washington St., Cape May, NJ 08204-1737. Mailing Address: P.O. Box 340, Cape May, NJ 08204-0340. Tel.: 609-884-5404, 800-275-4278. Fax: 609-884-5064.
E-mail: info@capemaymac.org
Web Site: www.capemaymac.org
Key Personnel: Mktg. Coord., Eliza Lotozo.
Institution Type/Description: Historic Building.
Hours & Admission Prices: Physick Estate Guided Tours: daily, Adults $15, children $8. Lighthouse: daily. Adults $10, children $5. Trolley Tours: daily. Adults $15, children $8. &
Attendance: 260,000 (actual)

NATURE CENTER OF CAPE MAY, 1600 Delaware Ave., Cape May, NJ 08204. Tel.: 609-898-8848. Fax: 609-898-8512.
E-mail: nccm@njaudubon.org
Web Site: www.njaudubon.org
Key Personnel: Dir., Gretchen Whitman.
Institution Type/Description: Nature Center.
Hours & Admission Prices: April-Oct. Mon.-Sat. 9-5; Sun. 11-4. No charge; donations accepted. &

NAVAL AIR STATION WILDWOOD AVIATION MUSEUM, 500 Forrestal Rd., Cape May Airport, Cape May, NJ 08242-2203. Tel.: 609-886-8787. Fax: 609-886-1942. Facebook: Naval Air Station Wildwood Aviation Museum.
E-mail: aviationmuseum@comcast.net
Institution Type/Description: Military Aviation Museum.
Hours & Admission Prices: April to Columbus Day daily 9-5; Oct.-Nov. daily 9-4; Dec.-March Mon.-Fri. 9-4. Adults $14, children 3-12 $10; children 2 & under and active military no charge. Closed New Year's Eve & Day; Thanksgiving; Christmas Eve & Day. &

Cape May Court House

CAPE MAY BIRD OBSERVATORY - THE CENTER FOR RESEARCH AND EDUCATION, 600 Rte. 47 N., Cape May Court House, NJ 08210. Tel.: 609-861-0700.
E-mail: cmbo2@njaudubon.org
Institution Type/Description: Bird Sanctuary.
Hours & Admission Prices: Observatory: April-Oct. daily 9:30-4:30; Nov.-March Wed.-Mon. 9:30-4:30. Center: April-May Tues.-Sat. 9:30-4:30.

CAPE MAY COUNTY HISTORICAL MUSEUM AND GENEALOGICAL SOCIETY, 504 Rte. 9 N., Cape May Court House, NJ 08210-1953. Tel.: 609-465-3535. Fax: 609-465-4274. Facebook.
E-mail: cmchgsmuseum@gmail.com
Web Site: www.cmcmuseum.org
Key Personnel: Dir., Donna M. Matalucci; Mktg. Coord., Deborah McGuire; Genealogist, Lois Broomell.
Institution Type/Description: History Museum: housed in the Cresse-Holmes House; built in 1704.
Hours & Admission Prices: Library & Museum: see website for hours & admission prices. &
Attendance: 3,000 (estimated)

CAPE MAY COUNTY PARK AND ZOO, 707 Rte. 9 N., Cape May Court House, NJ 08210. Mailing Address: 4 Moore Rd., DN 801, Cape May Court House, NJ 08210-1645. Tel.: 609-465-5271. Fax: 609-465-5421.
E-mail: info@cmczoo.com
Web Site: www.cmczoo.com
Key Personnel: Parks Dir., Edward Runyon; Zoo Dir., Dr. Hubert Paluch.
Institution Type/Description: Zoo.
Hours & Admission Prices: Zoo: Fall & Winter: daily 10-3:30; Spring & Summer: daily 10-4:30. Park: daily 7 am to dusk. No charge; donations accepted. Closed Christmas. &
Attendance: 700,000 (estimated)

CAPE MAY NATIONAL WILDLIFE REFUGE, 24 Kimbles Beach Rd., Cape May Court House, NJ 08210. Tel.: 609-463-0994.
E-mail: capemay@fws.gov
Web Site: www.fws.gov/refuge/cape_may/
Institution Type/Description: Wildlife Refuge.
Hours & Admission Prices: Headquarters: Mon.-Fri. 8-4:30. Refuge: dawn to dusk.

LEAMING'S RUN GARDEN & COLONIAL FARM, 1845 Rt. 9 N., Cape May Court House, NJ 08210-1436. Tel.: 609-465-5871. Facebook.
E-mail: info@leamingsrungardens.com
Web Site: www.leamingsrungardens.com
Key Personnel: C.E.O., Jack Aprill; Pres. (V), Emily Aprill; Dir., Gregg Aprill.
Institution Type/Description: Agricultural Museum: housed in last remaining whaler's house in New Jersey.
Hours & Admission Prices: mid-May to Sept. daily 9:30-5. Adults $8, children under 18 $4; discounts to groups; children 6 & under no charge. &
Attendance: 40,000

Cape May Point

CAPE MAY BIRD OBSERVATORY - THE NORTHWOOD CENTER, 701 E. Lake Dr., Cape May Point, NJ 08204. Mailing Address: P.O. Box 3, Cape May Point, NJ 08212. Tel.: 609-884-2736.
E-mail: cmbo1@njaudubon.org
Institution Type/Description: Bird Sanctuary.
Hours & Admission Prices: April-Oct. daily 9:30-4:30; Nov.-March Wed.-Mon. 9:30-4:30.

Cedar Grove

CEDAR GROVE HISTORICAL SOCIETY, 903 Pompton Ave., Cedar Grove, NJ 07009-1225. Mailing Address: P.O. Box 461, Cedar Grove, NJ 07009-0461. Tel.: 973-239-5414.
E-mail: info@cedargrovehistoricalsociety.org
Web Site: www.cedargrovehistoricalsociety.org
Institution Type/Description: Historical Society Museum: housed in mid 19th-century early Victorian vernacular Morgan family farmhouse.
Hours & Admission Prices: Wed. morning; other times by appointment. Volunteer work sessions: Wed. 10-1. No charge; donations accepted. &
Attendance: 500 (estimated)

Chatham

CHATHAM TOWNSHIP MUSEUM - THE RED BRICK SCHOOLHOUSE MUSEUM, 24 Southern Blvd., Chatham, NJ 07928. Mailing Address: P.O. Box 262, Chatham, NJ 07928-0262. Tel.: 973-635-0603. Facebook.
E-mail: museum@chathamtownshiphistoricalsociety.org
Web Site: www.chathamtownshiphistoricalsociety.org
Key Personnel: Director, Sheila M Goggins; Pres., Martha Wells; Vice Pres., Patricia Wells.
Institution Type/Description: History Museum.
Hours & Admission Prices: 1st Sun. of the month 2-4. No charge.
Attendance: 500 (estimated)

Cherry Hill

BARCLAY FARMSTEAD, 209 Barclay Ln., Cherry Hill, NJ 08034. Tel.: 856-795-6225.
E-mail: Info@BarclayFarmstead.org
Web Site: www.barclayfarmstead.org
Institution Type/Description: Historic House: built in 1816.
Hours & Admission Prices: March-Nov. Wed. 12-4, 1st Sun. each month 1-5; Dec.-Feb. Wed. 12-4; call to confirm. No charge; donations accepted.

GARDEN STATE DISCOVERY MUSEUM, 2040 Springdale Rd., Ste. 100, Cherry Hill, NJ 08003-2082. Tel.: 856-424-1233. Fax: 856-424-6516.
E-mail: roree@discoverymuseum.com
Web Site: www.discoverymuseum.com
Key Personnel: Dir., Kelly Lyons; Dir. Mktg. & Sales, Beverly Pak.
Institution Type/Description: Children's Museum.
Hours & Admission Prices: May-June & Sept. daily 9:30-5:30; July-Aug. Mon.-Thurs. 9:30-8:30, Fri.-Sun. 9:30-5:30; Oct.-April Sun.-Fri. 9:30-5:30, Sat. 9:30-8:30. Adults $13.95, senior citizens $12.95; discounts to military; children under one no charge. Closed Thanksgiving; Christmas. &
Attendance: 250,000 (estimated)

GOODWIN HOLOCAUST MUSEUM AND EDUCATION CENTER, 1301 Springdale Rd., Cherry Hill, NJ 08003. Tel.: 856-751-9500, ext. 1203.
E-mail: dsnyder@jfedsnj.org
Web Site: www.ghmec.org
Institution Type/Description: History Museum.
Hours & Admission Prices: Sun.-Fri.

Chester

COOPER GRISTMILL, 66 Washington Tpke., Chester, NJ 07930. Mailing Address: 66 Rte. 24, Chester, NJ 07930. Tel.: 908-879-5463.
E-mail: info@morrisparks.net
Institution Type/Description: Historic Building: built by Nathan Cooper in 1826.
Hours & Admission Prices: May-June & Sept.-Oct. Sat.-Sun. 10-5; July-Aug. Wed.-Sun. 10-5.

Clark

DR. WILLIAM ROBINSON PLANTATION & MUSEUM, 593 Madison Hill Rd., Clark, NJ 07066-3103. Mailing Address: Clark Historical Society, Municipal Bldg., 430 Westfield Ave., Clark, NJ 07066. Tel.: 732-340-1571.
E-mail: info@drrobinsonmuseum.org
Web Site: www.clarkhistoricalsociety.org
Key Personnel: Dir., Scott McCabe.
Institution Type/Description: Historic Society Museum; Historic House: c.1690, farmhouse with features of the Tudor period.
Hours & Admission Prices: March-June & Sept.-Dec. 3rd Sun. each month 12-4; other times by appointment. No charge; donations accepted.
Attendance: 1,000 (estimated)

Clayton

SCOTLAND RUN PARK NATURE CENTER, 980 Academy St., Clayton, NJ 08322. Mailing Address: c/o Gloucester Co. Parks & Recreation, 254 County House Rd., Clarksboro, NJ 08020. Tel.: 856-881-0845 & 856-251-6710.
E-mail: ltaylor@co.gloucester.nj.us
Web Site: www.gloucestercountynj.gov
Key Personnel: Park Naturalist, Dr. Daniel Duran.
Institution Type/Description: Nature Center.
Hours & Admission Prices: Park: dawn to dusk. Nature Center: Thurs. 1-6, Sat. 9-3; call to confirm.

Clifton

CLIFTON ARTS CENTER & SCULPTURE PARK, 900 Clifton Ave., Clifton, NJ 07013. Tel.: 973-472-5499. Fax: 973-470-8337. Facebook: Clifton Arts Center & Sculp.
E-mail: rcammilleri@cliftonnj.org
Web Site: www.cliftonnj.org
Key Personnel: Dir., Roxanne Cammilleri.
Institution Type/Description: Arts Center: housed in two early 20th century barns. Listed on the National Register of Historic Places.
Hours & Admission Prices: Wed.-Sat. 1-4. Adults $3.
Attendance: 35,000 (estimated)

HAMILTON VAN WAGONER MUSEUM, 971 Valley Rd., Clifton, NJ 07013-4028. Tel.: 973-744-2608.
E-mail: normaleeclf@aol.com
Web Site: cliftonj.com
Formerly: Hamilton House Museum-van Wagoner Museum
Institution Type/Description: Historic House Museum: 1815 Hamilton Van Wagoner House.
Hours & Admission Prices: Wed.-Sun. 10-5. Adults $5, children 6-16 $3; children under 6 no charge. Closed major holidays.
Attendance: 1,200 (estimated)

Clinton

HUNTERDON ART MUSEUM, 7 Lower Center St., Clinton, NJ 08809-1384. Tel.: 908-735-8415. Fax: 908-735-8416.
E-mail: info@hunterdonartmuseum.org
Web Site: www.hunterdonartmuseum.org
Key Personnel: Exec. Dir., Marjorie Frankel Nathanson; Pres. Bd. Trustees (V), Dr. Steve Sitrin; Dir. Educ., Joan Gavornik.

Institution Type/Description: Contemporary Art Museum: housed in 1836 restored stone grist mill.
Hours & Admission Prices: Tues.-Sun. 11-5. Suggested Donation: adults $7, seniors & students $5; discounts to NARM members; members and children 12 & under no charge.
Attendance: 33,000 (estimated)

RED MILL MUSEUM VILLAGE, 56 Main St., Clinton, NJ 08809-1328. Tel.: 908-735-4101. Fax: 908-735-0914. Facebook.
E-mail: director@theredmill.org
Web Site: theredmill.org
Formerly: Hunterdon Historical Museum
Key Personnel: Pres., Doug Hansen; Exec. Dir., Paul Muir; Collections Mgr., Elizabeth Cole.
Institution Type/Description: Historic Site & History Museum.
Hours & Admission Prices: Call for hours & admission prices.
Attendance: 18,000 (actual)

Closter

BELSKIE MUSEUM OF ART & SCIENCE, 280 High St., Closter, NJ 07624-1812. Tel.: 201-768-0286. Fax: 201-768-4220.
E-mail: belskiemuseum@hotmail.com
Web Site: www.belskiemuseum.com
Institution Type/Description: Art Museum.
Hours & Admission Prices: Sat.-Sun. 1-5; other times by appointment. No charge; donations accepted.
Attendance: 3,000 (estimated)

CLOSTER NATURE CENTER, 230 Ruckman Rd., Closter, NJ 07624. Mailing Address: P.O. Box 80, Closter, NJ 07624. Tel.: 201-750-2778.
E-mail: admin@closternaturecenter.org
Web Site: www.closternaturecenter.org
Institution Type/Description: Nature Center.
Hours & Admission Prices: Call for hours.

Columbus

MANSFIELD TOWNSHIP HISTORICAL SOCIETY - 1849 GEORGETOWN SCHOOL/MUSEUM & HISTORY OF MANSFIELD TOWNSHIP MUSEUM, 4 Fitzgerald Ln., Columbus, NJ 08022-2383. Tel.: 609-298-4174. Facebook: Mansfield Township Historical Society.
E-mail: agnname@aol.com
Key Personnel: Dir., Pearl J. Tusim; Pres., Roberta Kurtz; Pres. (V), Rita Puglia; Cur., James Soden; Sec., Laverne Cholewa.
Institution Type/Description: Historical Society Museum: housed in a rebuilt one-room school; Five Room Museum: located in the Mansfield Municipal Building.
Hours & Admission Prices: Open by appointment; call for reservations & admissions.
Attendance: 100 (estimated)

Cranbury

CRANBURY HISTORICAL & PRESERVATION SOCIETY, 4 Park Place E., Cranbury, NJ 08512-3208. Mailing Address: 6 S. Main St., Cranbury, NJ 08512-3112. Tel.: 609-655-1889.
E-mail: historycenter@comcast.net
Web Site: cranburyhistory.org
Key Personnel: Cur., Lisa Beach.
Institution Type/Description: Historical Society Museum: housed in restored 1834 Dr. Garrett Voorhees house.
Hours & Admission Prices: Cranbury Museum: Sun. 1-4. Elizabeth M. Wagner History Center: by appointment. No charge; donations suggested. Parsonage Barn: available for events; donations suggested.
Attendance: 1,000 (estimated)

NEW JERSEY AUDUBON SOCIETY'S PLAINSBORO PRESERVE & NATURE CENTER, 80 Scotts Corner Rd., Cranbury, NJ 08512. Tel.: 609-897-9400. Fax: 609-897-0287.
E-mail: plainsboro@njaudubon.org
Web Site: plainsboro.njaudubon.org
Key Personnel: Dir., Nancy Fiske.
Institution Type/Description: Nature Center.
Hours & Admission Prices: Nature Center: Tues.-Sat. 9-5, Sun. 12-5. Trails: daily sunrise to sunset. No charge. Closed holidays.

Cranford

CRANFORD HISTORICAL SOCIETY - THE HANSON HOUSE, 38 Springfield Ave., Cranford, NJ 07016-2144. Tel.: 908-276-0082.
E-mail: cranfordhistoricalsociety@verizon.net
Web Site: cranfordhistoricalsociety.org/
Institution Type/Description: Historical Society Museum.
Hours & Admission Prices: Mon.-Tues. 9 am-11:30 am & 2:30-5, Wed.-Thurs. 2:30-5; other times by appointment.

TOMASULO ART GALLERY - UNION COUNTY COLLEGE, Kenneth Campbell MacKay Library, 1033 Springfield Ave., Cranford, NJ 07016-1599. Tel.: 908-709-7155.
E-mail: tomasulogallery@ucc.edu
Key Personnel: Dir., Lisa Williamson.
Institution Type/Description: Art Gallery.
Hours & Admission Prices: Mon. 1-4, Tues.-Thurs. 1-4 & 6-9, Sat. 10-1. No charge.
Attendance: 1,000 (estimated)

Daretown

OLD PITTSGROVE PRESBYTERIAN CHURCH AND PITTSGROVE LOG COLLEGE, 312 Daretown Rd., Daretown, NJ 08318. Tel.: 856-358-1104.
E-mail: S_Shaner@comcast.net
Institution Type/Description: History Museum.
Hours & Admission Prices: By appointment.

Demarest

THE ART SCHOOL AT OLD CHURCH, 561 Piermont Rd., Demarest, NJ 07627-1615. Tel.: 201-767-7160. Fax: 201-767-0497.
E-mail: info@tasoc.org
Web Site: tasoc.org
Formerly: Old Church Cultural Center
Key Personnel: Exec. Dir., Lisa Beth Vettoso; Pres. (V), Edward Whittemore; Gallery Mgr., Emma Abad.
Institution Type/Description: Art & Cultural Center.
Hours & Admission Prices: Gallery & Office: Mon.-Fri. 9:30-5, Sat. 9:30-3. Please call for extended hours. No charge for exhibitions. Closed federal holidays; most Jewish holidays. &
Attendance: 2,200 (estimated)

Dennisville

DENNIS TOWNSHIP MUSEUM & HISTORY CENTER, 681 Petersburg Rd., Dennisville, NJ 08214. Tel.: 609-861-1899.
E-mail: dennistwpmuseum@comcast.net
Institution Type/Description: History Museum: housed in a former school house; built in 1874.
Hours & Admission Prices: 1st & 3rd Sat. 9-1. Closed national holidays.

Dover

DOVER AREA HISTORY SOCIETY, 55 W. Blackwell St., Dover, NJ 07801. Mailing Address: Dover Area Historical Society, P.O. Box 609, Dover, NJ 07802-0609. Tel.: 973-361-3525.
Web Site: www.dovernjhistory.org
Formerly: Dover History Museum
Key Personnel: Pres. (V), Mrs. Betty Inglis; Museum Shop Mgr., Richard Kelly.
Institution Type/Description: Historical Society Museum.
Hours & Admission Prices: Open by appointment and during previously announced open houses usually held Sun. 2-4. No charge; donations accepted.

East Brunswick

EAST BRUNSWICK MUSEUM CORPORATION, 16 Maple St., East Brunswick, NJ 08816-4450. Mailing Address: P.O. Box 875, East Brunswick, NJ 08816-0875. Tel.: 732-257-1508. Fax: 732-257-1508.
E-mail: ebmuseuminfo@gmail.com
Key Personnel: Pres., Karen Scott; Vice Pres., Martha Hess.
Institution Type/Description: Local & Regional History Museum: housed in 1860 Simpson Methodist Church & 1850 Appleby/Devoe House.
Hours & Admission Prices: Sat.-Sun. 1:30-4; groups at other times by appointment. No charge; donations accepted. Closed New Year's Day; Easter; Mother's Day;

Memorial Day; Father's Day; Independence Day; Labor Day; Thanksgiving; Christmas. &
Attendance: 8,000

Eastampton

HISTORIC SMITHVILLE MANSION, 803 Smithville Rd., Eastampton, NJ 08060. Mailing Address: c/o Friends of the Mansion at Smithville, P.O. Box 6000, Eastampton, NJ 08060. Tel.: 609-265-5858.
E-mail: info@smithvillemansion.org
Web Site: www.smithvillemansion.org
Institution Type/Description: Historic House Museum: built in 1840.
Hours & Admission Prices: Tours: early May to late Oct. Wed. & Sun. 1, 2, & 3. Adults $5, students $3; discounts to groups of 10 or more.

Edgewater Park

THE SHIPMAN MANSION, 221 Edgewater Ave., Edgewater Park, NJ 08010. Tel.: 609-387-9847.
E-mail: shipmanmansionfoundation@gmail.com
Web Site: www.shipmanmansion.org
Key Personnel: Chm. (V), Franklin P. Wood.
Institution Type/Description: Historic House Museum: built c.1869. Listed on the National Register of Historic Places.
Hours & Admission Prices: April-Nov. 1st Sat. 10-2, 1st Sun. 1-4.
Attendance: 300 (estimated)

Edison

THOMAS ALVA EDISON MEMORIAL TOWER AND MENLO PARK MUSEUM, 37 Christie St., Edison, NJ 08820-3860. Mailing Address: Edison Memorial Tower Corporation, P.O. Box 656, Edison, NJ 08818. Tel.: 732-549-3299. Fax: 732-494-4190.
E-mail: info@menloparkmuseum.org
Web Site: www.menloparkmuseum.com
Institution Type/Description: History Museum.
Hours & Admission Prices: Thurs.-Sat. 10-4; call to confirm. Suggested Donation: $5.

Egg Harbor City

EGG HARBOR CITY HISTORICAL SOCIETY - ROUNDHOUSE MUSEUM, 533 London Ave., Egg Harbor City, NJ 08215. Tel.: 609-965-9073 & 4677. Facebook.
E-mail: vf-6_felix@att.net
Key Personnel: Dir., Mark Maxwell; Pres. (V), Mark W. Maxwell.
Institution Type/Description: Historical Society Museum.
Hours & Admission Prices: Wed. & Sat. 1-4; call for special openings. No charge; donations accepted. Closed holidays. &
Attendance: 275 (estimated)

Elizabeth

BELCHER OGDEN MANSION, 1046 E. Jersey St., Elizabeth, NJ 07201-2504. Mailing Address: 1045 E. Jersey St., Ste. 101, Elizabeth, NJ 07201-2503. Tel.: 908-581-7555.
E-mail: jcosta@goelizabethnj.com
Institution Type/Description: Historic House Museum.
Hours & Admission Prices: By appointment.

BOXWOOD HALL, 1073 E. Jersey St., Elizabeth, NJ 07201. Mailing Address: c/o NJ Dept. of Environmental Protection State Park Svc., P.O. Box 402, Mail Code 501-04, Trenton, NJ 08625-0402. Tel.: 908-282-7617.
E-mail: jcosta@goelizabethnj.com
Web Site: ucnj.org/boxwood-hall
Institution Type/Description: Historic House Museum: built in 1750s by Elizabethtown's mayor, Samuel Woodruff later home to Elias Boudinot, a United States Congressman and then President of Congress.
Hours & Admission Prices: Mon.-Fri. 9-12 & 1-5.

Englishtown

BATTLEGROUND HISTORICAL SOCIETY - THE VILLAGE INN, 2 Water St., Englishtown, NJ 07726. Mailing Address: P.O. Box 61, Tennent, NJ 07763-0061. Tel.: 732-462-4947.
E-mail: thevillageinnenglishtown@verizon.net
Web Site: www.thevillageinn.org

Key Personnel: Pres., Hans Kernast; Treas., Kathy Doherty.
Institution Type/Description: Historic Building.
Hours & Admission Prices: 3rd Sun. each month 1-3. No charge; donations accepted.
Attendance: 200 (estimated)

Estell Manor

ESTELL MANOR HISTORICAL SOCIETY, 134 Cape May Ave., Estell Manor, NJ 08319. Mailing Address: P.O. Box 72, Estell Manor, NJ 08319-0072. Tel.: 609-476-2884.
E-mail: estellmanorhistoricalsociety@aol.com
Web Site: estellmanorhistoricalsociety.org
Key Personnel: Chm. (V), Robert Grant; Pres. (V), Tom Pogue; Museum Mgr., Diane Bassetti.
Institution Type/Description: Historical Society Museum: housed in a one room schoolhouse, Risley School. Listed on the National Register of Historic Places.
Hours & Admission Prices: Call for hours. No charge; donations accepted. &
Attendance: 350 (estimated)

Ewing

BENJAMIN TEMPLE HOUSE, Drake Farm Park, 27 Federal City Rd., Ewing, NJ 08638. Tel.: 609-883-2455. Fax: 609-883-2455.
Institution Type/Description: Historic House Museum: housed in the former home of Benjamin Temple, a farmer & early area settler; built c.1750.
Hours & Admission Prices: Wed. 10-2; other times by appointment.

KIDSBRIDGE TOLERANCE MUSEUM, 999 Lower Ferry Rd., Ewing, NJ 08628. Tel.: 609-771-0300.
E-mail: lynne@kidsbridgemuseum.org
Web Site: kidsbridgemuseum.org
Key Personnel: Exec. Dir., Lynne Azarchi; Chm. (V), Frank Lucchesi.
Institution Type/Description: Children's Museum.
Hours & Admission Prices: By appointment. &
Attendance: 2,500 (actual)

THE SARNOFF COLLECTION, The College of New Jersey, Roscoe West Hall, Ewing, NJ 08628. Tel.: 609-771-2654. Fax: 609-637-5193.
E-mail: sarnoff@tcnj.edu
Web Site: www.tcnj.edu/sarnoff
Key Personnel: Dir., Margaret Pezalla-Granlund.
Institution Type/Description: Communications History Museum: named in honor of David Sarnoff, Chairman of The Radio Corporation of America (RCA).
Hours & Admission Prices: Wed. 1-5, Sun. 1-3; groups by appointment. &
Attendance: 1,500

TCNJ ART GALLERY, Art & Interactive Multimedia Bldg., The College of New Jersey, Ewing, NJ 08628. Mailing Address: P.O. Box 7718, Ewing, NJ 08628-0718. Tel.: 609-771-2633. Fax: 609-637-5193. Facebook: TCNJ Art Gallery.
E-mail: tcag@tcnj.edu
Web Site: www.tcnj.edu/artgallery
Formerly: The College Art Gallery
Key Personnel: Dir., Margaret Pezalla-Granlund.
Institution Type/Description: Art Gallery.
Hours & Admission Prices: Tues.-Thurs. 12-7, Sun. 1-3. No charge. &
Attendance: 6,000 (estimated)

Fair Lawn

GARRETSON FARM, 4-02 River Rd., Fair Lawn, NJ 07410-1436. Tel.: 201-797-1775.
E-mail: info@garretsonfarm.org
Web Site: www.garretsonfarm.org
Institution Type/Description: Historic Homestead: built in 1719. Listed on the National Register of Historic Places.
Hours & Admission Prices: Call for hours.

Far Hills

UNITED STATES GOLF ASSOCIATION MUSEUM, 77 Liberty Corner Rd., Far Hills, NJ 07931-2570. Mailing Address: P.O. Box 708, Far Hills, NJ 07931-0708. Tel.: 908-234-2300, ext. 1057. Fax: 908-234-0242.
E-mail: museum@usga.org
Web Site: www.usgamuseum.com
Formerly: Golf House, Museum & Library

Key Personnel: Dir., Robert Williams; Sr. Historian, Mike Trostel; Film & Video Archivist, Shannon Doody; Librarian, Nancy Stulack; Mgr., Mktg. & Outreach, Kim Gianetti.
Institution Type/Description: Golf Museum & Library: housed in 1919 Georgian style home, designed by John Russell Pope.
Hours & Admission Prices: Tues.-Sun. 10-5. Adults $10, seniors $7, children 13-17 $5; discounts to veterans and AAA & museum members; children under 12 no charge. Closed major holidays. &
Attendance: 20,000 (estimated)

Farmingdale

ALLAIRE VILLAGE INC., 4265 Atlantic Ave., Farmingdale, NJ 07727. Mailing Address: 4263 Atlantic Ave., Farmingdale, NJ 07727. Tel.: 732-919-3500 & 938-2253. Fax: 732-938-3302. Facebook.
E-mail: info@allairevillage.org
Web Site: www.allairevillage.org
Formerly: Historic Allaire Village Inc.
Key Personnel: Exec. Dir., Hance M. Sitkus, CPA; Treas., Raymond O'Grady; Office Mgr., Kathy Geiser; Group Tours, Angela Larcara; Mgr. Volunteers & Educ. Prog., Gina Palmisano.
Institution Type/Description: Living History Museum & Preservation Project & Museum Complex: 1830s Howell iron works.
Hours & Admission Prices: Village & Historic Homes: April-May & Sept.-Nov. Sat.-Sun. 11-4; Memorial Day-Labor Day Wed.-Sun. 11-4; group tours by appointment. State Park: Spring & Fall daily 8-6; Memorial Day-Labor Day daily 8-8; Winter daily 8-4:30. Parking $5 per car Memorial Day-Labor Day; members no charge. &
Attendance: 300,000 (estimated)

Flemington

HUNTERDON COUNTY HISTORICAL SOCIETY, 114 Main St., Flemington, NJ 08822-1415. Tel.: 908-782-1091.
E-mail: hunterdonhistory@embarqmail.com
Web Site: www.hunterdonhistory.org
Key Personnel: Admin., David Harding; Cur. Manuscripts, Don Cornelius; Librarian, Pamela Robinson.
Institution Type/Description: General Museum: housed in the home of architect & builder, Mahlon Fisher; built in 1846.
Hours & Admission Prices: House: by appointment. Library: Thurs. & 4th Sat. 10-4, 4th Fri. 12-4; other times by appointment. No charge; donations accepted. Closed national holidays. &
Attendance: 2,500 (estimated)

NORTHLANDZ, 495 US 202, Flemington, NJ 08822. Tel.: 908-782-4022.
Web Site: northlandz.com
Institution Type/Description: Model Railroad & Doll Museum.
Hours & Admission Prices: July to early Sept. Mon. & Wed.-Fri. 10:30-4, Sat.-Sun. 10:30-5; early Sept. to June Mon. & Thurs.-Fri. 10:30-4, Sat.-Sun. 10:30-5. Adults $15.75, seniors $13.50, children $10.75; discounts to groups of 20 or more; children under 2 no charge.

SAMUEL FLEMING HOUSE MUSEUM & GARDENS, 5 Bonnell St., Flemington, NJ 08822-1311. Mailing Address: 38 Park Ave., Flemington, NJ 08822-1321. Tel.: 908-782-4607. Facebook: Samuel Fleming House Museum and Gardens.
E-mail: fleminghousemuseum@gmail.com
Web Site: fleminghousemuseum.org
Formerly: Fleming Castle Museum
Key Personnel: Pres. Bd. Trustees (V), Kelli Dockterman; Program Coord., Karen Larsen.
Institution Type/Description: Historic House Museum.
Hours & Admission Prices: 2nd Sat. of month 1-4. No charge; donations accepted.
Attendance: 1,150 (estimated)

Florham Park

IMAGINE THAT, A NEW JERSEY CHILDREN'S MUSEUM, 4 Vreeland Rd., Florham Park, NJ 07932-1555. Tel.: 973-966-8000. Fax: 973-966-8990.
E-mail: contactus@imaginethatmuseum.com
Web Site: www.imaginethatmuseum.com
Formerly: Imagine That Children's Museum
Key Personnel: Dir., Deborah Bodner.
Institution Type/Description: Interactive Children's Museum.
Hours & Admission Prices: Daily 10-5:30; groups by appointment. Children $10.95, adults $9.95; discounts to groups & AAA members; children under one no charge. Closed Thanksgiving; Christmas. &

Forked River

LACEY HISTORICAL SOCIETY, 126 S. Main St., Rte. 9, Forked River, NJ 08731. Mailing Address: Box 412, Forked River, NJ 08731-0412. Tel.: 609-971-0467.
E-mail: laceyhistsoc@verizon.net
Formerly: Old Schoolhouse Museum
Key Personnel: C.E.O. & Pres. (V), Elizabeth McGrath; Museum Shop Mgr., Mary Jensen.
Institution Type/Description: General Museum: housed in 1860 old schoolhouse.
Hours & Admission Prices: mid-June to Labor Day Wed. 1-3, Sat. 10 to noon; other times by appointment. No charge; donations accepted. &
Attendance: 1,000 (estimated)

POPCORN PARK ZOO, Humane Way at Lacey Rd., Forked River, NJ 08731. Mailing Address: P.O. Box 43, Forked River, NJ 08731-0043. Tel.: 609-693-1900. Fax: 609-693-8404.
Institution Type/Description: Zoo.
Hours & Admission Prices: Daily 11-5; groups by appointment. Adults $5, children under 12 & seniors $4; discounts to groups; children under 3 no charge. &

Fort Dix

ARMY RESERVE MOBILIZATION MUSEUM, 6501 Pennsylvania Ave., Fort Dix, NJ 08640-5300. Tel.: 609-562-6983. Fax: 609-562-2164.
E-mail: noelle.a.altamirano2.civ@mail.mil
Web Site: www.dix.army.mil
Formerly: Fort Dix Museum
Key Personnel: Dir. & Cur., Noelle Altamirano.
Institution Type/Description: Military Museum.
Hours & Admission Prices: Mon.-Fri. 8-4; general public by appointment. No charge. &
Attendance: 7,650 (actual)

Fort Hancock

GATEWAY, SANDY HOOK UNIT, NRA, 58 Magruder Rd., Fort Hancock, NJ 07732. Tel.: 732-872-5970.
Web Site: www.nps.gov/gate
Formerly: Sandy Hook National Seashore
Key Personnel: Historian, Thomas Hoffman; Museum Cur., Mary Rasa.
Institution Type/Description: National Park Museum: housed in the 1899 Fort Hancock Guard House or Post Stockade. Museum is part of Sandy Hook Historic Landmark.
Hours & Admission Prices: Visitor's Center: daily 10-5. Museum: Winter: Sat.-Sun. 1-5; Summer: daily 1-5. Historic House: Sat.-Sun. 1-5. Sandy Hook Lighthouse & Light Keepers Quarters: April-Oct. Mon.-Fri. 1-5, Sat.-Sun. 12-4:30; Nov. Sat.-Sun. 12-5. Parking: buses $25, cars $10; after Labor Day no charge. &
Attendance: 50,000

Fort Lee

FORT LEE HISTORIC PARK & MUSEUM, Hudson Terrace, Fort Lee, NJ 07024. Mailing Address: Palisades Interstate Park Commission, P.O. Box 155, Alpine, NJ 07620. Tel.: 201-461-1776. Fax: 201-461-7275.
E-mail: flhp@njpalisades.org
Web Site: www.njpalisades.org/fortlee
Key Personnel: Dir., Pres., Jim Hall; Museum Shop Mgr., J. Muller.
Institution Type/Description: History Museum: located in Historic Park.
Hours & Admission Prices: March-Dec. Wed.-Sun. 10-4:45. No charge. Metered Parking: daily 8-6. &
Attendance: 25,998 (actual)

Franklin

FRANKLIN MINERAL MUSEUM, 32 Evans St., Franklin, NJ 07416-1419. Mailing Address: P.O. Box 54, Franklin, NJ 07416-0054. Tel.: 973-827-3481. Fax: 973-827-0149. Facebook: Franklin Mineral Museum.
E-mail: info@franklinmineral.com
Web Site: franklinmineralmuseum.com
Key Personnel: Pres. (V), Mark A. Boyer; Treas., A. Lee Lowell.
Institution Type/Description: Geology & Mining Museum: adjacent to zinc mines, located in old mine engine house, built in late 19th century.
Hours & Admission Prices: April-Nov. Mon.-Fri. 10-4, Sat. 10-5, Sun. 11-5. Adults $7, seniors $6, children $5; members no charge. Closed Easter; Thanksgiving. &
Attendance: 20,000 (actual)

Franklin Lakes

THE GALLERY AT THE PRESBYTERIAN CHURCH AT FRANKLIN LAKES, 730 Franklin Lake Rd., Franklin Lakes, NJ 07417. Tel.: 201-891-0511. Fax: 201-891-0517.
E-mail: pcflmgr@yahoo.com
Web Site: pcfl.org
Key Personnel: Dir., Mary Guideth McColl.
Institution Type/Description: Art Gallery.
Hours & Admission Prices: Call for hours. No charge.

LORRIMER SANCTUARY, 790 Ewing Ave., Franklin Lakes, NJ 07417. Tel.: 201-891-2185.
E-mail: lorrimer@njaudubon.org
Web Site: www.njaudubon.org
Institution Type/Description: Nature Center: housed in a late 1700s house.
Hours & Admission Prices: Wed.-Fri. 9-5, Sat. 10-5, Sun. 1-5.

Freehold

COVENHOVEN HOUSE, 150 W. Main St., Freehold, NJ 07728. Mailing Address: Monmouth County Historical Assoc., 70 Court St., Freehold, NJ 07728-1710. Tel.: 732-462-1466.
E-mail: mcha@monmouthhistory.org
Institution Type/Description: Historic Building Museum: housed in the home of William & Elizabeth Covenhoven, built in 1753; later served as headquarters for British General Henry Clinton prior to the Battle of Monmouth in 1778.
Hours & Admission Prices: May-Sept. Thurs.-Sat. 1-4. No charge; donations accepted.

JEWISH HERITAGE MUSEUM OF MONMOUTH COUNTY, 310 Mounts Corner Dr., Freehold, NJ 07728. Tel.: 732-252-6990.
E-mail: info@jhmomc.org
Web Site: www.jhmomc.org
Key Personnel: Pres. (V), Vic Schioppo; Vice Pres. (V), Barbara Silvers.
Institution Type/Description: History Museum: housed in a former barn which was part of the Levi Solomon farm; c.1800.
Hours & Admission Prices: Tues.-Thurs. 10-3, Sun. 11-3. Adults $5, members $3. &
Attendance: 3,819 (actual)

MONMOUTH COUNTY HISTORICAL ASSOCIATION, 70 Court St., Freehold, NJ 07728-1710. Tel.: 732-462-1466. Fax: 732-462-8346. Facebook: Monmouth County Historical Association.
E-mail: emurphy@monmouthhistory.org
Web Site: www.monmouthhistory.org
Key Personnel: Interim Dir., Charles H. Jones, III; Dir. Collections, Joe Hammond; Dir. Devel. & Communications, Lisa Maher; Devel. & Communications Asst., Deanna Wilson.
Institution Type/Description: Historical Society Museums.
Hours & Admission Prices: Library: Wed.-Sat. 10-4. Museum: Tues.-Sat. 10-4; groups by appointment. Adults $5, senior citizens & children 6-18 $2.50; discounts to NARM & AAM members; members & children under 6 no charge. Historic Houses: call for information. Closed New Year's Day; Thanksgiving; Christmas Eve & Day. &
Attendance: 13,046 (actual)

Frenchtown

DECOYS & WILDLIFE GALLERY, 55 Bridge St., Frenchtown, NJ 08825-1229. Tel.: 908-996-6501, 888-996-6501 (Toll Free). Fax: 908-996-0807.
E-mail: decoys@decoyswildlife.com
Institution Type/Description: Art Gallery.
Hours & Admission Prices: Daily 10-6; other times by appointment. Closed Christmas.

Galloway

EDWIN B. FORSYTHE NATIONAL WILDLIFE REFUGE BRIGANTINE DIVISION, 800 E. Great Creek Rd., Galloway, NJ 08205. Mailing Address: P.O. Box 72, Oceanville, NJ 08231. Tel.: 609-652-1665.
E-mail: sandy_perchetti@fws.gov
Institution Type/Description: Wildlife Refuge.
Hours & Admission Prices: Call for hours.

STOCKTON UNIVERSITY ART GALLERY, 101 Vera King Farris Dr., Galloway, NJ 08205-9441. Mailing Address: K150/D. McGarvey, 101 Vera King Farris Dr., Galloway, NJ 08205-9441. Tel.: 609-652-4214. Fax: 609-652-4550. Facebook: Stockton University Art Gallery.
E-mail: denise.mcgarvey@stockton.edu
Web Site: www.stockton.edu/artgallery
Formerly: Richard Stockton College Art Gallery
Key Personnel: Exhibition Coord., Denise McGarvey.
Institution Type/Description: Art Gallery.
Hours & Admission Prices: May-Aug. Mon.-Thurs. 12-4; Sept.-April Mon.-Sat. 12-7:30, Sun. 12-4. No charge. &
Attendance: 6,000 (estimated)

Glassboro

GLASSBORO HERITAGE GLASS MUSEUM, 25 E. High St., Glassboro, NJ 08028-2519. Tel.: 856-881-7468.
E-mail: carollois@comcast.net
Key Personnel: Pres. (V), Carol Schoepske; Chm. (V), Rick Granda; Museum Shop Mgr., Linda Rudisill.
Institution Type/Description: Glass Museum.
Hours & Admission Prices: Wed. 12-3, Sat. 11-2, 4th Sun. 1-4. No charge; donations accepted.
Attendance: 1,000 (actual)

Greenwich

CUMBERLAND COUNTY HISTORICAL SOCIETY, 960 YeGreate St., Greenwich, NJ 08323. Mailing Address: P.O. Box 16, Greenwich, NJ 08323-0016. Tel.: 856-455-4055 & 8580. Fax: 856-455-8580. Facebook.
E-mail: cchistsoc@verizon.net
Web Site: www.cchistsoc.org
Key Personnel: Pres., Joseph DeLuca; Vice Pres., Linda S. Hruza-Jones; Sec., Ruth Ann Fox; Treas., Judith Uber; Dir. Library, Warren Q. Adams; Museum Shop Mgr., Kenneth Miller.
Institution Type/Description: Historical Society: housed in furnished 1730 Gibbon house.
Hours & Admission Prices: Gibbon House: April-Dec. Tues.-Sun. 1-4. Adults $3; society members no charge. Warren Lummis Gen. & Hist. Library: early Jan. to mid-Dec. Wed. 10-4, Sat.-Sun. 1-4. John Dubois Maritime Museum Sun. 1-4. Matthew Potter's Tavern & Old Stone Church: by appointment only. Prehistorical Museum: Wed. & Sat.-Sun. 12-4. No charge; donations accepted.
Attendance: 5,000 (estimated)

Hackensack

EDWARD WILLIAMS GALLERY - FAIRLEIGH DICKINSON UNIVERSITY, 150 Kotte Pl., Hackensack, NJ 07601-6112. Tel.: 201-692-2449. Fax: 201-692-2503.
E-mail: geraghty@fdu.edu
Key Personnel: Dir., Diana Soorikian.
Institution Type/Description: Art Gallery.
Hours & Admission Prices: Mon.-Fri. 8:30-2:30, Sat. 9:30-2:30. No charge.
Attendance: 2,000 (estimated)

NEW JERSEY NAVAL MUSEUM, 78 River St., Hackensack, NJ 07601-7110. Mailing Address: P.O. Box 207, Hackensack, NJ 07602-0207. Tel.: 201-342-3268. Fax: 201-342-3268.
E-mail: njnavalmuseum@yahoo.com
Web Site: www.njnm.org
Key Personnel: Acting Pres., Les Altschuler; Cur., Art Bischoff; Treas., Gwen Radloff.
Institution Type/Description: Naval Military Museum: located at World War II submarine USS Ling SS-297 in Hackensack River.
Hours & Admission Prices: Call for hours. Museum & Grounds: no charge. Tours: adults $12, senior citizens $7, children under 12 $6; discounts to veterans.
Attendance: 1,670 (actual)

Hackettstown

HACKETTSTOWN HISTORICAL SOCIETY MUSEUM & LIBRARY, 106 Church St., Hackettstown, NJ 07840-2206. Tel.: 908-852-8797.
E-mail: info@hackettstownhistory.com
Web Site: www.hackettstownhistory.com
Key Personnel: Archivist, Ray Lemasters.
Institution Type/Description: Local History & Genealogy Museum: housed in 1915 Theodore G. Plate House.

Hours & Admission Prices: Mon.-Tues. 9-2, Wed. & Fri. 9-4, Sun. 2-4; other times & groups by appointment. No charge; donations accepted. Closed major holidays.
Attendance: 250 (estimated)

Haddonfield

HISTORICAL SOCIETY OF HADDONFIELD, 343 Kings Hwy. E., Haddonfield, NJ 08033-1214. Tel.: 856-429-7375.
E-mail: info@haddonfieldhistory.org
Web Site: www.haddonfieldhistory.org
Key Personnel: Pres. (V), Carol Smith; Vice Pres., Doug Rauschenberger; Treas., Ellen Stone; Dir. Collections, Dianne Snodgrass; Archivist, Dana Dorman.
Institution Type/Description: Historical Society Museum: housed in Greenfield Hall, a Georgian style brick house, built in 1841. The Samuel Mickle House houses the Society's library. Both buildings listed on the National Register of Historic Places.
Hours & Admission Prices: Museum: Sept.-July Wed.-Fri. 1-4, 1st Sun. each month 1-3. Adults $5. Archive/Library: Sept.-July Tues. & Wed. 9:30-11:30, 1st Sun. of month 1-3 and by appointment. No charge. Closed major holidays.
Attendance: 1,100 (estimated)

INDIAN KING TAVERN, 233 Kings Hwy., Haddonfield, NJ 08033. Tel.: 856-429-6792.
E-mail: lhess141@gmail.com
Web Site: www.indiankingfriends.org
Institution Type/Description: Historic Building: built in 1750.
Hours & Admission Prices: By appointment.

MARKEIM ARTS CENTER, 104 Walnut St., Haddonfield, NJ 08033. Tel.: 856-429-8585.
E-mail: info@markeimartscenter.org
Web Site: markeimartscenter.org
Institution Type/Description: Art Center.
Hours & Admission Prices: Call for hours. &

Haledon

AMERICAN LABOR MUSEUM, BOTTO HOUSE NATIONAL LANDMARK, 83 Norwood St., Haledon, NJ 07508-1363. Tel.: 973-595-7953. Fax: 973-595-7291. Facebook: American Labor Museum / Botto House National Landmark.
E-mail: labormuseum@aol.com
Web Site: www.labormuseum.net
Key Personnel: Pres. (V), Michael Goodwin; Dir., Angelica M. Santomauro, Ed.D.; Project Mgr., Robert Leadlie; Financial Dir., Noel Christmas; Dir. Education & Museum Shop Mgr., Evelyn M. Hershey.
Institution Type/Description: Labor & Immigrant Studies Museum: housed in 1908 Botto House. A National Landmark.
Hours & Admission Prices: Wed.-Sat. 1-4; other times by appointment. Suggested Donation: adults $5; discounts to AAM & ICOM members; children under 12, AAA & museum members no charge. Closed major holidays except Labor Day. &
Attendance: 16,578 (estimated)

Hamilton

GROUNDS FOR SCULPTURE, 80 Sculptors Way, Hamilton, NJ 08619-3447. Tel.: 609-586-0616. Fax: 609-586-7303.
E-mail: info@groundsforsculpture.org
Web Site: www.groundsforsculpture.org
Key Personnel: Exec. Dir., Gary Garrido Schneider; C.F.O., Robert Gross; Chief Cur. & Artistic Dir., Tom Moran; Dir. Devel., Rhonda DiMascio; Dir. Opers., Richard Moskovitz; Dir. Mktg. & Communications, Coby Green Rifkin; Dir. Facilities, Matt Smith.
Institution Type/Description: Sculpture Park.
Hours & Admission Prices: Tues.-Sun. 10-6. Adults $16, seniors $13, students 6-17 with ID $10; members and children 5 & under no charge. Closed New Year's Day; Thanksgiving; Christmas. &
Attendance: 100,000 (estimated)

HISTORICAL SOCIETY OF HAMILTON TOWNSHIP JOHN ABBOTT II HOUSE, 2200 Kuser Rd., Hamilton, NJ 08690. Mailing Address: Historical Society of Hamilton Township, P.O. Box 11271, Hamilton, NJ 08620. Tel.: 609-585-1686.
Web Site: www.hamiltontownshiphistory.org
Institution Type/Description: Historical House: c.1730 farm house & 1840 addition.
Hours & Admission Prices: March-DSat.-Sun. 12-5 by appointment only. No charge; donations accepted. Closed Christmas.
Attendance: 4,000 (estimated)

JOHNSON ATELIER - THE SCULPTURE FOUNDATION, 60 Sculptors Way, Hamilton, NJ 08619. Tel.: 609-890-7777. Fax: 609-890-1816.
E-mail: info@atelier.org
Web Site: www.atelier.org
Institution Type/Description: Art Gallery.
Hours & Admission Prices: By appointment.

KUSER FARM MANSION, 390 Newkirk Ave., Hamilton, NJ 08610-4845. Mailing Address: 2090 Greenwood Ave., P.O. 00150, Hamilton, NJ 08609-2312. Tel.: 609-890-3630. Fax: 609-586-0678.
E-mail: PKrzywulak@hamiltonnj.com
Web Site: www.hamiltonnj.com
Institution Type/Description: Historic House: c.1896 Queen Anne style mansion & outbuildings, former summer home of Fred Kuser & his family.
Hours & Admission Prices: March-Oct. Sat.-Sun. 11-3:15 (last tour 2:30). Christmas Tours: Dec. first 2 weeks. Call to confirm hours. No charge, donations accepted.
Attendance: 2,500 (estimated)

Hammonton

BATSTO VILLAGE, 31 Batsto Rd., Hammonton, NJ 08037-5502. Tel.: 609-561-0024. Fax: 609-567-8116.
E-mail: info@batstovillage.org
Web Site: www.batstovillage.org
Formerly: Historic Batsto Village
Institution Type/Description: Historic Site Museum: Batsto Village, 33 historic buildings built in the 1800s.
Hours & Admission Prices: Batsto Mansion Tours: Wed.-Sun. 11, 1, 2 & 3. Visitor Center: daily 9-4. Grounds: daily dawn to dusk.; groups by appointment only. Tours: adults $3, children 6-11 $1; children under 6 no charge. Parking Fee: Sat.-Sun. & holidays Memorial Day to Labor Day Weekend $5. Closed New Year's Day; Thanksgiving; Christmas. ♿
Attendance: 100,000 (estimated)

Hancock's Bridge

HANCOCK HOUSE, 3 Front St., Hancock's Bridge, NJ 08038. Mailing Address: P.O. Box 139, Hancocks Bridge, NJ 08038-0139. Tel.: 856-935-4373. Fax: 856-935-2079.
E-mail: hancockhousenj@comcast.net
Web Site: www.state.nj.us/dep/parksandforests/historic/ hancockhouse/hancockhouse.index.htm
Key Personnel: Supt., Vince Bonica; Resource Interpretive Specialist, Alicia Bjornson.
Institution Type/Description: Historic House Museum: 1734 Hancock House, built by Judge William Hancock & scene of Revolutionary War's British Massacre March 21, 1778.
Hours & Admission Prices: Wed.-Sun. 9-4; call to confirm. No charge; donations accepted. Closed New Year's Day; Thanksgiving; Christmas.
Attendance: 4,000 (estimated)

Highlands

TWIN LIGHTS HISTORIC SITE, Lighthouse Rd., Highlands, NJ 07732. Tel.: 732-872-1814.
E-mail: twinlightshistoricalsociety@gmail.com
Web Site: twinlightslighthouse.com
Institution Type/Description: Lighthouse: built in 1862. Listed on the National Register of Historic Places.
Hours & Admission Prices: Memorial Day to Labor Day daily 10-4:30; Sept.-May Wed.-Sun. 10-4:30. No charge; donations accepted. Closed New Year's Day; Thanksgiving; Christmas; state holidays. ♿
Attendance: 80,000 (actual)

Hillsborough

DUKE FARMS, 1112 Dukes Pkwy. W., Hillsborough, NJ 08844. Tel.: 908-722-3700.
E-mail: info@dukefarms.org
Institution Type/Description: Historic Farm & Garden: housed in a former horse & dairy barn; built in 1906.
Hours & Admission Prices: Orientation Center & Trails: April to Dec. 1 Thurs.-Tues. 8:30-6. No charge.

Hillside

WOODRUFF HOUSE/EATON STORE MUSEUM/PHIL RIZZUTO SPORTS EXHIBIT, 111 Conant St., Hillside, NJ 07205-2801. Tel.: 908-353-8828.
E-mail: info@woodruffhouse.org
Web Site: www.hillsidehistoricalsociety.org
Key Personnel: Dir., Chm. & Pres. (V), Jacqueline Gradel; Devel., Ann Pettigrew; Treas., Helen Witting.
Institution Type/Description: Historical Society Museum.
Hours & Admission Prices: 3rd Sun. of month 2-4; other times by appointment. No charge; donations accepted.
Attendance: 900 (estimated)

Ho-Ho-Kus

THE HERMITAGE, Friends of the Hermitage, Inc., 335 N. Franklin Turnpike, Ho-Ho-Kus, NJ 07423-1035. Tel.: 201-445-8311. Fax: 201-445-0437. Facebook: The Hermitage.
E-mail: info@thehermitage.org
Web Site: www.thehermitage.org
Formerly: Friends of the Hermitage, Inc.
Key Personnel: Visitor Svcs. Mgr., Leslie Naghshineh; Exec. Dir., Victoria Harty; Pres. Friends of the Hermitage, Michael Orbe.
Institution Type/Description: Historic House Museum: farmhouse built in 1750s; renovated in Gothic Revival style 1840s. Visited by General Washington in 1778; site of Aaron Burr's marriage in 1782; home to the Rosencrantz family 1807-1970. A National Historic Landmark.
Hours & Admission Prices: Museum: Wed.-Fri. 10-4, Sat.-Sun. 1-4. House Tours: Wed.-Sun. 1:15, 2:15 & 3:15. Adults $7, students & seniors $5, children 6-12 $4; discounts to AAA members; children 5 & under no charge. ♿
Attendance: 15,000 (estimated)

Hoboken

BARSKY GALLERY, 48 Harrison St., Hoboken, NJ 07030. Tel.: 888-465-4949.
E-mail: info@barskygallery.com
Web Site: www.barskygallery.com
Institution Type/Description: Art Gallery.
Hours & Admission Prices: Thurs.-Sun. 11-6; other times by appointment.

HOBOKEN FIRE DEPARTMENT MUSEUM, 213 Bloomfield St., Hoboken, NJ 07030. Tel.: 201-420-2397.
E-mail: info@hobokenmuseum.org
Key Personnel: Cur., Bill Bergin; Asst. Cur., Joe Kennedy.
Institution Type/Description: Fire Fighting History Museum: housed in the city's former firehouse; built in 1870. Listed on the National Register of Historic Places.
Hours & Admission Prices: Spring to Fall Sat. 10-4, call to confirm; other times by appointment. No charge.

HOBOKEN HISTORICAL MUSEUM, 1301 Hudson St., Hoboken, NJ 07030-7427. Mailing Address: P.O. Box 3296, Hoboken, NJ 07030-1603. Tel.: 201-656-2240.
E-mail: info@hobokenmuseum.org
Web Site: www.hobokenmuseum.org
Key Personnel: Dir., Bob Foster.
Institution Type/Description: History Museum.
Hours & Admission Prices: Tues.-Thurs. 2-7, Fri. 1-5, Sat.-Sun. 12-5. Adults $4; members & children no charge.

Holmdel

HISTORIC LONGSTREET FARM, Holmdel Park, 44 Longstreet Rd., Holmdel, NJ 07733. Mailing Address: Monmouth County Park System, 805 Newmann Springs Rd., Lincroft, NJ 07738-1628. Tel.: 732-946-3758 & 842-4000. Fax: 732-946-0750. TDD: 732-219-9484.
E-mail: info@monmouthcountyparks.com
Web Site: www.monmouthcountyparks.com
Key Personnel: Site Mgr., Sandra Byard; Supvr., Sean O'Herron.
Institution Type/Description: Historic Farm: 1890 Longstreet Farm.
Hours & Admission Prices: Memorial Day to Labor Day daily 9-5; Sept.-May daily 10-4; groups by appointment. No charge; donations accepted. ♿
Attendance: 88,000 (actual)

HOLMES-HENDRICKSON HOUSE, 62 Longstreet Rd., Holmdel, NJ 07733. Mailing Address: Monmouth County Historical Assoc., 70 Court St., Freehold, NJ 07728-1710. Tel.: 732-462-1466.
Institution Type/Description: Historic House Museum: built in 1754.
Hours & Admission Prices: May-Sept. Thurs.-Sat. 1-4. No charge; donations accepted.

VIETNAM ERA MUSEUM & EDUCATIONAL CENTER, 1 Memorial Ln., Garden State Pkwy. Exit 116, Holmdel, NJ 07733. Mailing Address: P.O. Box 648, Holmdel, NJ 07733-0648. Tel.: 732-335-0033. Fax: 732-335-1107. Facebook.
E-mail: info@njvvmf.org
Web Site: www.njvvmf.org
Key Personnel: Exec. Dir., Bill Linderman; Cur., Sarah Hagarty; Admin., Lynn Duane.
Institution Type/Description: Historical & Military Museum.
Hours & Admission Prices: Tues.-Sat. 10-4. Adults $7, seniors & students $5; active & retired military and children under 10 no charge. &
Attendance: 20,000 (estimated)

Hope

HOPE HISTORICAL SOCIETY, 323 High St., Hope, NJ 07844. Mailing Address: P.O. Box 52, Hope, NJ 07844-0052. Tel.: 908-459-4277 & 4669.
Web Site: www.hopenjhistory.com/
Key Personnel: Pres., Peggy Schaedel; Vice Pres., Joy Fernbacher.
Institution Type/Description: General Museum: housed in early 1800s private home.
Hours & Admission Prices: Nov.-May Sun. 1-3; groups by appointment. No charge; donations accepted.
Attendance: 200 (estimated)

Hopewell

HOPEWELL MUSEUM, 28 E. Broad St., Hopewell, NJ 08525-1828. Tel.: 609-466-0103.
E-mail: mackart@verizon.net
Key Personnel: Pres., David M. Mackey; Cur., Beverly Weidl.
Institution Type/Description: General Museum.
Hours & Admission Prices: Mon., Wed. & Sat. 2-5. Research: Mon. & Wed. No charge; donations accepted. Closed national holidays.
Attendance: 960

MORPETH CONTEMPORARY ART STUDIO, 43 W. Broad St., Hopewell, NJ 08525-1901. Tel.: 609-333-9393.
E-mail: info@morpethcontemporary.com
Web Site: morpethcontemporary.com
Institution Type/Description: Art Gallery.
Hours & Admission Prices: Tues.-Sat. 11-6, Sun. 12-5.

Howell

HOWELL HISTORICAL SOCIETY & MACKENZIE MUSEUM, 427 Lakewood-Farmingdale Rd., Howell, NJ 07731-8723. Mailing Address: P.O. Box 444, Farmingdale, NJ 07727-0694. Tel.: 732-938-2212.
E-mail: howellhist@aol.com
Web Site: www.howellnj.com/historic/
Formerly: Howell Historical Society & Committee Museum
Key Personnel: Museum Shop Mgr., Virginia Krzyzanowski.
Institution Type/Description: Historical Society Museum: house built c.1807.
Hours & Admission Prices: Grist Miller's home: Sat. 9:30-12:30. Schoolhouse: last Sun. each month 1-4; other times by appointment. No charge; donations accepted.
Attendance: 1,000 (estimated)

MANASQUAN RESERVOIR ENVIRONMENTAL CENTER, 331 Georgia Tavern Rd., Howell, NJ 07731. Mailing Address: c/o Monmouth County Park System, 805 Newman Springs Rd., Lincroft, NJ 07738. Tel.: 732-751-9453.
Web Site: www.monmouthcountyparks.com
Institution Type/Description: Environmental Center.
Hours & Admission Prices: Memorial Day to Labor Day Fri. 10-8:30, Sat.-Thurs. 10-5; Sept.-May daily 10-4:30.

OLD ARDENA SCHOOLHOUSE - HOWELL HISTORICAL SOCIETY, Old Tavern & Preventorium Rds., Howell, NJ 07731. Mailing Address: P.O. Box 694, Farmingdale, NJ 07727-0694. Tel.: 732-938-2212.
Institution Type/Description: Historic Building: housed in a former schoolhouse; built c.1855.
Hours & Admission Prices: last Sun. each month 1-4.

Iselin

GARDEN FOR THE BLIND AND PHYSICALLY HANDICAPPED, 1081 Green St., Iselin, NJ 08830. Tel.: 732-283-1200.
E-mail: information@naturefortheblind.com
Web Site: www.naturefortheblind.com
Institution Type/Description: Garden.
Hours & Admission Prices: Mon.-Sat. 9-6.

Island Heights

THE JOHN F. PETO STUDIO MUSEUM, 102 Cedar Ave., Island Heights, NJ 08732. Mailing Address: P.O. Box 1022, Island Heights, NJ 08732-1022. Tel.: 732-929-4949.
E-mail: info@petomuseum.org
Web Site: petomuseum.org
Key Personnel: Exec. Dir., Raymond Salva.
Institution Type/Description: Art Museum.
Hours & Admission Prices: Sat.-Sun. 1-4; other times by appointment. Adults $10, children 12 & under $5; members no charge.

OCEAN COUNTY ARTISTS' GUILD, 22 Chestnut Ave., Island Heights, NJ 08732. Mailing Address: P.O. Box 1156, Island Heights, NJ 08732. Tel.: 732-270-3111.
E-mail: info@ocartistsguild.org
Web Site: www.ocartistguild.org
Institution Type/Description: Art Gallery.
Hours & Admission Prices: Tues.-Sun. 1-4.

Jackson

NEW JERSEY FOREST RESOURCE EDUCATION CENTER, 101 W. Veterans Hwy., Jackson, NJ 08527-3409. Tel.: 732-928-2360.
E-mail: FREC@dep.nj.gov
Web Site: http://www.state.nj.us/dep/parksandforests/forest/njfs_frep.html
Institution Type/Description: Education Center.
Hours & Admission Prices: Center: Mon.-Fri. 8-4. Trails: dawn to dusk.

Jamesburg

HISTORIC BUCKELEW MANSION, 203 Buckelew Ave., Jamesburg, NJ 08831. Mailing Address: P.O. Box 183, Jamesburg, NJ 08831. Tel.: 732-521-2040.
Institution Type/Description: Historic House Museum: built between 1685-1870.
Hours & Admission Prices: Temporarily closed.

Jersey City

AFRO-AMERICAN HISTORICAL SOCIETY MUSEUM, 1841 Kennedy Blvd., Jersey City, NJ 07305-2106. Tel.: 201-547-5262. Fax: 201-547-5392.
E-mail: anthony.olszewski@gmail.com
Web Site: www.cityofjerseycity.org/docs/afroam.shtml
Key Personnel: Dir., Neal E. Brunson.
Institution Type/Description: History Museum.
Hours & Admission Prices: Mon. & Wed.-Fri. 11-4, Tues. 12-5. No charge; donations accepted. Closed all legal holidays; election days.
Attendance: 7,500 (estimated)

CURIOUS MATTER, 272 5th St., Jersey City, NJ 07302-2304. Tel.: 201-659-5771. Facebook: Curious Matter.
E-mail: gallery@curiousmatter.org
Web Site: www.curiousmatter.org
Key Personnel: Dir., Raymond E. Mingst; Dir., Arthur Bruso.
Institution Type/Description: Art Gallery.
Hours & Admission Prices: Sun. 12-3; other times by appointment. No charge; donations accepted.

JERSEY CITY MUSEUM, 350 Montgomery St., Jersey City, NJ 07302-4041. Tel.: 201-413-0303; 201-413-6339 (TTY). Fax: 201-413-9922.
E-mail: info@jerseycitymuseum.org
Web Site: www.jerseycitymuseum.org
Institution Type/Description: Art Museum.
Hours & Admission Prices: Call for hours. &
Attendance: 21,000 (actual)

LIBERTY SCIENCE CENTER, Liberty State Park, 222 Jersey City Blvd., Jersey City, NJ 07305-4636. Tel.: 201-253-1201. Fax: 201-451-6949.
E-mail: phoffman@lsc.org
Web Site: www.lsc.org
Key Personnel: Pres. & C.E.O., Paul Hoffman; C.O.O., Jeff Sasson; Vice Pres. Finance, Janice Erzmoneit; Vice Pres. External Affairs, Christine Arnold-Schroeder.
Institution Type/Description: Science Center.
Hours & Admission Prices: April-June daily 9-5; July-Aug. Mon.-Fri. 9-4, Sat.-Sun. 9-5; Sept.-March Tues.-Fri. 9-4, Sat.-Sun. 9-5:30. Adults $21.75, senior citizens 62 & over $18.75, children 2-12 $17.75, teachers $11.75; discounts to AAM members; members no charge. Combination tickets available. &
Attendance: 650,000 (estimated)

THE MUSEUM OF RUSSIAN ART, 80 Grand St., Jersey City, NJ 07302-4522. Tel.: 201-332-9200.
E-mail: museumora@gmail.com
Web Site: www.moramuseum.org
Formerly: C.A.S.E. Museum of Russian Art in Exile
Key Personnel: Art Designer, Ozlem Mutaf Buyukar; Exhibitions & Partnerships Developer, Daria Gradusova; Media Adviser, Aleksandr Garber; IT Support, Glenn Makoushinski.
Institution Type/Description: Art Museum.
Hours & Admission Prices: Call for hours. Suggested Donation: adults $5; members no charge.

Kearny

KEARNY ART MUSEUM, 26 Howell Pl., Kearny, NJ 07032.
Key Personnel: Dir., John Daughty.
Institution Type/Description: Art Museum.
Hours & Admission Prices: By appointment. No charge; donations accepted.

KEARNY MUSEUM, Kearny Public Library, 318 Kearny Ave., Kearny, NJ 07032-2505. Tel.: 201-998-2666.
Web Site: www.kearnylibrary.org/museum.htm
Institution Type/Description: History Museum.
Hours & Admission Prices: Sept.-June Wed. 6:30-7:30, Sat. 10-12. No charge. &
Attendance: 400 (estimated)

Keyport

KEYPORT FIRE MUSEUM AND EDUCATION CENTER, 86 Broad St., Keyport, NJ 07735-1244. Mailing Address: P.O. Box 839, Keyport, NJ 07735. Tel.: 732-739-5362.
E-mail: popsqd@msn.com
Web Site: www.keyportfd.org
Key Personnel: Chm., Lawrence Stonerock; Museum Shop Mgr., Robert M. Poling.
Institution Type/Description: Fire-Fighting History Museum: built in 1900.
Hours & Admission Prices: April-Dec. Sat. 12-4, Sun. 11-3. No charge; donations accepted.
Attendance: 712 (actual)

Kingston

ROCKINGHAM, 84 Laurel Ave., Kingston, NJ 08528. Mailing Address: P.O. Box 496, Kingston, NJ 08528-0496. Tel.: 609-683-7132.
E-mail: rockingham1783@yahoo.com
Web Site: www.rockingham.net
Key Personnel: Dir., Lisa A. Flick.
Institution Type/Description: Historic House: 18th-century Berrien Mansion, Washington's final wartime headquarters while Continental Congress was in session in Princeton.
Hours & Admission Prices: Guided Tours: Wed.-Sat. 10, 11, 1, 2 & 3, Sun. 1, 2 & 3. No charge for walkins; donations accepted. Fee for group tours. &
Attendance: 4,000 (actual)

Lakehurst

NAVY LAKEHURST HISTORICAL SOCIETY & HERITAGE CENTER, Joint Base Lakehurst, Lakehurst, NJ 08733. Mailing Address: P.O. Box 328, Lakehurst, NJ 08733-0328. Tel.: 732-818-7520. Fax: 732-244-8897.
E-mail: tours2@nlhs.com
Web Site: nlhs.com
Key Personnel: Dir. & Pres. (V), Carl Jablonski; Museum Shop Mgr., John Niedzwiecki.
Institution Type/Description: History Museum: housed on the Naval Air Station and the site of the Hindenburg disaster.
Hours & Admission Prices: By appointment 2 weeks in advance. No charge; donations accepted.

Lakewood

JEWISH HISTORICAL SOCIETY OF OCEAN COUNTY, 1235A Route 70, Lakewood, NJ 08701. Tel.: 732-363-0530.
E-mail: federation@ocjf.org
Web Site: www.jewishoceancounty.org
Institution Type/Description: Jewish History Museum.
Hours & Admission Prices: Call for hours.

LAKEWOOD HERITAGE MUSEUM, 231 Third St., Municipal Bldg. 1st & 2nd Fls., Lakewood, NJ 08701-2882. Tel.: 732-276-7944.
E-mail: lakewoodmuseum@optonline.net
Web Site: www.twp.lakewood.nj.us/parkrec_cultur.htm
Institution Type/Description: History Museum.
Hours & Admission Prices: July-Aug. Tues. & Thurs. 2-5; Sept.-June Tues. & Thurs. 2-5, Sun. 2-4.

M. CHRISTINA GEIS ART GALLERY - GEORGIAN COURT UNIVERSITY, Arts & Science Center, 900 Lakewood Ave., Lakewood, NJ 08701-2600. Tel.: 732-364-2200, ext. 348.
E-mail: ksettles@georgian.edu
Institution Type/Description: Art Gallery.
Hours & Admission Prices: Mon.-Thurs. 9-8, Fri. 9-5. No charge.

Lambertville

HOLCOMBE-JIMISON FARMSTEAD MUSEUM, 1605 Daniel Bray Hwy. (Rte. 29), Lambertville, NJ 08530-2402. Tel.: 609-397-2752. Facebook: Holcombe-Jimison Farmstead Museum.
E-mail: holcombe.jimisonnj@gmail.com
Web Site: www.holcombe-jimison.org
Key Personnel: Pres. (V), Michael Judkins, Jr.
Institution Type/Description: Historic Building.
Hours & Admission Prices: May-Oct. Sun. 1-4, Wed. 9 am-12 pm; groups by appointment. Suggested Donation: adults $5, students $3, children under 5 no charge. &
Attendance: 2,100 (estimated)

HOWELL LIVING HISTORY FARM, 70 Woodens Lane, Lambertville, NJ 08530. Mailing Address: 101 Hunter Rd., Titusville, NJ 08560-1902. Tel.: 609-737-3299. Fax: 609-737-6524.
E-mail: pwatson@howellfarm.com
Web Site: www.howellfarm.org
Key Personnel: Admin., Pete Watson; Farm Mgr., Gary Houghton; Education, Susan DeVore; Program Coord., Kathy Brilla; Cur., Margaret Newman.
Institution Type/Description: Agricultural History Museum: living history farm where farm life & farming of 1900-1910 have been recreated.
Hours & Admission Prices: late Jan. to March Tues.-Sat. & early Dec. 10-4; April-Nov. Tues.-Sat. 10-4, Sun. 12-4. No charge; donations accepted. Closed legal holidays. &
Attendance: 50,000 (estimated)

JAMES WILSON MARSHALL HOUSE, 60 Bridge St., Lambertville, NJ 08530. Mailing Address: 60 Bridge St., P.O. Box 2, Lambertville, NJ 08530. Tel.: 609-397-0770.
Key Personnel: Chm. (V), Suzanne Gitomer.
Institution Type/Description: Historic House Museum: built in 1816. Listed on the National Register of Historic Places.
Hours & Admission Prices: April-Oct. Sat.-Sun. 1-4; other times by appointment.

Landing

LAKE HOPATCONG HISTORICAL MUSEUM, Hopatcong State Park, Landing, NJ 07850. Mailing Address: P.O. Box 668, Landing, NJ 07850-0668. Tel.: 973-398-2616. Facebook: Lake Hopatcong Historical Museum.
E-mail: lhhistory@att.net
Web Site: www.lakehopatconghistory.com
Key Personnel: Pres., Martin Kane; C.E.O., Robert Kays; Museum Shop Mgr., Laurie Martin.
Institution Type/Description: Local History Museum: housed in 19th century Morris Canal Lock Tender's house.
Hours & Admission Prices: March-May & Oct.-Dec. Sun. 12-4; Summer: call for hours. No charge; donations accepted. &
Attendance: 2,500 (actual)

Lawnside

BLACK HOLOCAUST MUSEUM OF SLAVERY, 327 White Horse Pike, Lawnside, NJ 08045. Mailing Address: P.O. Box 26846, Philadelphia, PA 19134. Tel.: 888-886-5378.
E-mail: info@lwfsm.com
Web Site: lwfsm.com
Institution Type/Description: History Museum.
Hours & Admission Prices: Wed.-Sun. 10-6.

PETER MOTT HOUSE - LAWNSIDE HISTORICAL SOCIETY, 26 Kings Court, Lawnside, NJ 08045. Mailing Address: P.O. Box 608, Lawnside, NJ 08045-0608. Tel.: 856-546-8850.
E-mail: lhs@petermotthouse.org
Web Site: www.petermotthouse.org
Institution Type/Description: Historical Society Museum: housed in a former station on the Underground Railroad; built in 1845. Listed on the National Register of Historic Places.
Hours & Admission Prices: Sat. 12-3; other times by appointment. Adults $5, students $2.

Lawrenceville

NATIONAL GUARD MILITIA MUSEUM OF NEW JERSEY - LAWRENCEVILLE, Armory, 151 Eggert Crossing Rd., Lawrenceville, NJ 08648. Tel.: 609-530-6802. Fax: 609-530-6807.
E-mail: ngmmnj-lv@outlook.com
Web Site: www.state.nj.us/military/museum/index.html
Key Personnel: Co-Cur., Col. Donald Kale; Co-Cur., Col. Jon Gribbin; Co-Cur., Ltc. William Kale.
Institution Type/Description: Military Heritage Museum.
Hours & Admission Prices: Call for hours. No charge, donations accepted. &
Attendance: 980 (estimated)

Lincroft

THE MONMOUTH MUSEUM, Newman Springs Rd., Brookdale C.C. Campus, 765 Newman Springs Rd., Lincroft, NJ 07738. Mailing Address: P.O. Box 359, Lincroft, NJ 07738-0359. Tel.: 732-747-2266. Fax: 732-747-8592.
E-mail: info@monmouthmuseum.org
Web Site: www.monmouthmuseum.org
Formerly: Monmouth Museum & Cultural Center
Key Personnel: Exec. Dir., Avis H. Anderson; Chm., Daniel J. Fenski, II.
Institution Type/Description: General Museum.
Hours & Admission Prices: Tues.-Thurs. & Sat. 10-5, Fri. 10-9, Sun. noon-5. Admission $8; discounts to AAM & PBS members; children 2 & under, members no charge. Closed New Year's Day; Easter; Memorial Day; Independence Day; Labor Day; Thanksgiving; Christmas. &
Attendance: 55,000 (actual)

Linwood

JAMES KIRK MARITIME MUSEUM, 301 Davis Ave., Linwood, NJ 08221. Tel.: 609-927-8293.
Institution Type/Description: Maritime Museum.
Hours & Admission Prices: Mon.-Thurs. 10-8, Fri. 10-5, Sat. 10-4.

LINWOOD HISTORICAL SOCIETY - LEEDSVILLE SCHOOLHOUSE, 16 Poplar Ave., Linwood, NJ 08221-1820. Tel.: 609-927-8293.

Institution Type/Description: Historical Society Museum: school building, built in 1873. Listed on the National Register of Historic Places.
Hours & Admission Prices: Call for hours. No charge; donations accepted.

Little Falls

YOGI BERRA MUSEUM & LEARNING CENTER, Montclair State Univ., 8 Yogi Berra Dr., Little Falls, NJ 07424-2161. Tel.: 973-655-2378. Fax: 973-655-6894.
E-mail: eve.yogi@montclair.edu
Web Site: www.yogiberramuseum.org
Key Personnel: Exec. Dir., Eve Schaenen; Pres. (V), Mark Markowitz; Vice Chair, Julie Jackson; Dir. Special Events, Joni Bronander; Finance Dir., Susan Walsh; Education Dir., Jenny Pollack; Office Mgr., Nikki Morton.
Institution Type/Description: Sports Museum.
Hours & Admission Prices: Wed.-Sun. 12-5. Adults $6, senior citizens $5, students & children $4; discounts to AAA, ICOM & AAM members; members & military no charge. Closed New Year's Eve & Day; Easter; Mother's Day; Memorial Day; Independence Day; Labor Day; Columbus Day; Christmas Eve & Day. &

Locust

HUBER WOODS ENVIRONMENTAL CENTER, 25 Brown's Dock Rd., Locust, NJ 07760. Tel.: 732-872-2670.
E-mail: info@monmouthcountyparks.com
Web Site: www.monmouthcountyparks.com
Institution Type/Description: Environmental Center.
Hours & Admission Prices: Mon.-Fri. 10-4, Sat.-Sun. 10-5.

Long Branch

LONG BRANCH HISTORICAL MUSEUM, 1260 Ocean Ave., Long Branch, NJ 07740-4550. Mailing Address: P.O. Box 2204, Elberon, NJ 07740-2204. Tel.: 732-223-0874.
E-mail: lbhma1879@gmail.com
Web Site: www.churchofthepresidents.org
Institution Type/Description: History Museum: housed in 1879 Saint James Episcopal Chapel, Church of the Presidents. Worshippers included: Presidents James A. Garfield, Ulysses S. Grant, Rutherford B. Hayes, Chester A. Arthur, Woodrow Wilson, Benjamin Harrison, William McKinley.
Hours & Admission Prices: Closed for restoration.

Longport

LONGPORT HISTORICAL SOCIETY MUSEUM, 2305 Atlantic Ave., Longport, NJ 08403. Tel.: 609-823-1115.
E-mail: lhsinfo2@yahoo.com
Institution Type/Description: Historical Society Museum: housed in a 1939 Coast Guard Station. Listed on the National Register of Historic Places.
Hours & Admission Prices: April-May & Oct.-Nov. Mon. 10-12; Summer: Sat. 9-12; Winter: Tues. 11-1; other times by appointment.

Loveladies

LONG BEACH ISLAND FOUNDATION OF THE ARTS & SCIENCES, 120 Long Beach Blvd., Loveladies, NJ 08008-6131. Tel.: 609-494-1241. Fax: 609-494-0662.
Key Personnel: Exec. Dir., Kristy Redford.
Institution Type/Description: Art, Craft, & Science Museum.
Hours & Admission Prices: Gallery: daily 9-4. Office: Mon.-Fri. 9-4, Sat.-Sun. 9-3.

Lumberton

AIR VICTORY MUSEUM, INC., 68 Stacy Haines Rd., Lumberton, NJ 08048-4106. Tel.: 609-267-4488. Fax: 609-702-1852.
E-mail: info@airvictorymuseum.com
Web Site: airvictorymuseum.com
Key Personnel: Pres. (V), Bob McGonigle; Museum Shop Mgr, Fred Koch.
Institution Type/Description: Aeronautics Museum.
Hours & Admission Prices: Wed.-Sat. 10-4, Sun. 11-4. Museum Aircraft: tours available. Adults $4, seniors 62 & over $3, children 4-12 $2; discounts to groups, military w/ID & AAA members; members and children 3 & under no charge. &
Attendance: 3,500 (actual)

Lyndhurst

NEW JERSEY MEADOWLANDS ENVIRONMENT CENTER, 2 DeKorte Park Plaza, Lyndhurst, NJ 07071. Tel.: 201-777-2431. Fax: 201-460-7836.

E-mail: info@njmeadowlands.gov
Web Site: www.njsea.com
Formerly: Hackensack Meadowlands Development Commission Environment Center & Museum
Key Personnel: Exec. Dir., Marcia A. Karrow; Environmental Education, Angela Cristini, Ph.D.; Operations Mgr. & Museum Shop Mgr., Donna Bocchino.
Institution Type/Description: Nature Center.
Hours & Admission Prices: Center: Mon.-Fri. 8-4, Sat.-Sun. 9-3. Store: daily 10-3. Trails: daily 8 to dusk. No charge; donations accepted. ఉ
Attendance: 50,000 (actual)

Madison

MUSEUM OF EARLY TRADES & CRAFTS, 9 Main St., Madison, NJ 07940-1819. Tel.: 973-377-2982, ext. 10. Fax: 973-377-7358.
E-mail: info@metc.org
Web Site: www.metc.org
Key Personnel: Chm., Thomas Judd; Vice Chair, Ginny Wilson; Dir., Deborah Farrar Starker; External Communications, Erin O'Donnell.
Institution Type/Description: New Jersey history museum housed in 1900 Richardsonian Romanesque style building, the former town library.
Hours & Admission Prices: Summer: Tues.-Sat. 10-4; Winter: Tues.-Sat. 10-4, Sun. 12-5. Adults $5, seniors, students, & children $3; AAM members & museum members no charge. Closed major holidays. ఉ
Attendance: 11,000 (estimated)

Mahwah

BERRIE CENTER FOR PERFORMING AND VISUAL ARTS, Ramapo College of NJ, 505 Ramapo Valley Rd., Mahwah, NJ 07430. Tel.: 201-684-7500.
E-mail: eeloi@ramapo.edu
Web Site: www.ramapo.edu/berriecenter
Institution Type/Description: Arts & Cultural Center.
Hours & Admission Prices: Tues. & Thurs.-Fri. 1-5, Wed. 1-7.

HINDU SAMAJ MANDIR - MUSEUM OF INDIA JOURNEY TO THE USA, 247 W. Ramapo Ave., Mahwah, NJ 07430. Tel.: 201-529-1277. Facebook: Hindu Samaj Mandir.
E-mail: ecommunication@hindusamajmandir.org
Web Site: www.hindusamajmandir.org
Institution Type/Description: India Heritage Museum: housed in a Hindu temple.
Hours & Admission Prices: Call for hours.

MAHWAH HISTORY SOCIETY, 201 Franklin Tpke., Mahwah, NJ 07430. Tel.: 201-512-0099. Facebook: Mahwah Museum.
E-mail: director@mahwahmuseum.org
Web Site: www.mahwahmuseum.org
Key Personnel: Pres. (V), Charles Carreras.
Institution Type/Description: History Museum.
Hours & Admission Prices: Sept.-June Wed., Sat. & Sun. 1-4. Admission $5; members no charge. ఉ
Attendance: 2,538

OLD STATION MUSEUM, 1871 Old Station Lane, Mahwah, NJ 07430. Mailing Address: Mahwah Museum Society, 201 Franklin Tpke., Mahwah, NJ 07430. Tel.: 201-512-0099.
E-mail: director@mahwahmuseum.org
Key Personnel: Pres. (V), Charles Carreras.
Institution Type/Description: Historic Building & Caboose: housed in the original station on the Erie Railroad in Mahwah; built in 1848.
Hours & Admission Prices: June-Sept. Sun. 2-4. Adults $5; members & children under 18 no charge.
Attendance: 100 (estimated)

Manalapan

MONMOUTH BATTLEFIELD STATE PARK, 20 Business Rte. 33, Manalapan, NJ 07726. Mailing Address: 347 Freehold - Englishtown Rd., Manalapan, NJ 07726. Tel.: 732-462-9616. Fax: 732-577-8816.
E-mail: mbshistory@yahoo.com
Institution Type/Description: Park Museum.
Hours & Admission Prices: Park: seasonal hours. Visitor Center: daily 9-4. Craig House: April-Dec. Sun. 1-4. ఉ

Manasquan

SQUAN VILLAGE HISTORICAL SOCIETY - BAILEY REED HOUSE, 105 South St., Manasquan, NJ 08736. Tel.: 732-223-6770. Fax: 732-223-6770.
E-mail: squanh@verizon.net
Web Site: www.squanvillagehistoricalsociety.org
Institution Type/Description: Historical Society Museum.
Hours & Admission Prices: By appointment.

Marlton

CENTER FOR THE ARTS IN SOUTHERN NEW JERSEY, 123 S. Elmwood Rd., Marlton, NJ 08053-2564. Tel.: 856-985-1009. Fax: 856-985-7555.
E-mail: cfasnj@yahoo.com
Web Site: www.cfasnj.com
Key Personnel: Exec. Dir., Ann M. Macready.
Institution Type/Description: Art Gallery: built in 1785 by Thomas and Mary Evens, the house was later occupied by the Ballinger family and then the Jaggard family. The Jaggard family built the golf course.
Hours & Admission Prices: Mon.-Tues. & Thurs.-Fri. 10-3, Wed. 10-3 & 7-9. No charge.

EVESHAM TOWNSHIP HISTORICAL SOCIETY, 10 Madison Court, Marlton, NJ 08053. Tel.: 856-988-6530.
E-mail: doughertypr@aol.com
Institution Type/Description: Historical Society Museum.
Hours & Admission Prices: Sept.-June 3rd Sat. each month 10-2.

Matawan

BURROWES MANSION MUSEUM, 94 Main St., Matawan, NJ 07747-2630. Mailing Address: Matawan Historical Society, P.O. Box 41, Matawan, NJ 07747. Tel.: 732-566-5605.
E-mail: info@burroesmansion.org
Web Site: burroesmansion.org
Key Personnel: Museum Shop Mgr. & Head Docent, Sarah Ellison; Historic Site Mgr., Howard Henderson.
Institution Type/Description: Historic House: 1723 Georgian half-house with gambrel roof, located on a Revolutionary War skirmish site.
Hours & Admission Prices: March-Dec. 1st & 3rd Sun. of each month 2-4; other times by appointment. Suggested Donation: $5. Closed Easter.
Attendance: 900 (actual)

CHEESEQUAKE STATE PARK INTERPRETIVE CENTER, 300 Gordon Rd., Matawan, NJ 07747. Tel.: 732-566-2161.
Institution Type/Description: Park & Interpretive Center.
Hours & Admission Prices: Memorial Day to Labor Day daily 8-4; Sept.-May Wed.-Sun. 8-4. ఉ

THOMAS WARNE HISTORICAL MUSEUM & LIBRARY, Mailing Address: 4216 Rte. 516, Matawan, NJ 07747. Tel.: 732-566-2108. Fax: 732-566-6943.
E-mail: info@thomas-warne-museum.com
Web Site: www.thomas-warne-museum.com
Key Personnel: Pres., Chris Aboia; Treas. (V), Richard Kujawinski.
Institution Type/Description: History Museum: housed in an 1885 one room school house. National Historic Site.
Hours & Admission Prices: Mon.-Fri. by appointment, Sat.-Sun. 12-4. No charge; donations accepted. Closed New Year's Day; Christmas. ఉ
Attendance: 200 (estimated)

Mauricetown

MAURICETOWN HISTORICAL SOCIETY - THE EDWARD COMPTON HOUSE, 1229 Front St., Mauricetown, NJ 08329. Mailing Address: P.O. Box 1, Mauricetown, NJ 08329. Tel.: 856-785-1137 & 1372.
Web Site: www.mauricetownhistoricalsociety.org
Key Personnel: Pres. (V), Carol D. Perrelli; Cur. & Museum Shop Mgr., Irene Ferguson.
Institution Type/Description: Historical Society Museum.
Hours & Admission Prices: 1st & 3rd Sun. of the month 1-4; other times by appointment. No charge; donations accepted. ఉ
Attendance: 1,200 (estimated)

Mays Landing

WARREN E. FOX NATURE CENTER, 109 Boulevard Rte. 50, Mays Landing, NJ 08330-4323. Tel.: 609-645-5960.
E-mail: barbiero_jerry@aclink.org
Key Personnel: Dir., Jerry Barbiero.
Institution Type/Description: Nature Center.
Hours & Admission Prices: Mon.-Fri. 8-4:30, Sat.-Sun. & holidays 8-4. No charge.

Medford

BARTON ARBORETUM & NATURE PRESERVE, One Medford Leas Way, Medford, NJ 08055. Tel.: 800-331-4302, 609-654-3000. Fax: 609-654-7894.
E-mail: communityrelations@medfordleas.net
Web Site: bartonarboretum.org
Key Personnel: Dir. Community Rel., Jane Weston.
Institution Type/Description: Arboretum.
Hours & Admission Prices: Arboretum: daily dawn to dusk. Trail Walks: by appointment.

MEDFORD HISTORICAL SOCIETY, 275 Church Rd., Medford, NJ 08055. Tel.: 609-654-7767.
E-mail: info@medfordhistory.org
Web Site: www.medfordhistory.org
Key Personnel: Pres. (V), William Stauts.
Institution Type/Description: Historical Society Museum: built in 1785.
Hours & Admission Prices: Call for hours. No charge; donations accepted.

WOODFORD CEDAR RUN WILDLIFE REFUGE, 4 Sawmill Rd., Medford, NJ 08055. Tel.: 856-983-3329. Facebook: Cedar Run.
E-mail: info@cedarrun.org
Web Site: www.cedarrun.org
Institution Type/Description: Wildlife Refuge.
Hours & Admission Prices: Mon.-Sat. 10-4, Sun. 12-4. Adults $5, children 4 & up $3. Closed Independence Day; Thanksgiving; Christmas; New Year's Day.

Mendham

RALSTON HISTORICAL ASSOCIATION, JOHN RALSTON MUSEUM, 313 Mendham Rd., W., Mendham, NJ 07945-1000. Tel.: 973-543-6878. Fax: 973-543-1149.
E-mail: pfr14@aol.com
Web Site: www.ralstonmuseum.org
Key Personnel: Pres. (V), Margaret Hogan.
Institution Type/Description: Historical Society Museum: housed in the oldest building used as a post office in the United States, 1780s.
Hours & Admission Prices: June-Oct. Sun. 2-5. No charge; donations accepted.
Attendance: 250 (estimated)

Metuchen

METUCHEN-EDISON HISTORICAL SOCIETY, Metuchen Public Library, 480 Middlesex Ave., Metuchen, NJ 08840-1457. Mailing Address: P.O. Box 61, Metuchen, NJ 08840. Tel.: 732-632-8526.
E-mail: info@metuchen-edisonhistsoc.org
Web Site: www.metuchen-edisonhistsoc.org
Institution Type/Description: Historical Society Museum.
Hours & Admission Prices: Call for hours.

Middletown

DEEP CUT GARDENS, 152 Red Hill Rd., Middletown, NJ 07748. Tel.: 732-671-6050.
E-mail: info@monmouthcountyparks.com
Institution Type/Description: Horticultural Park: housed in the former home of the Wihtol family.
Hours & Admission Prices: Daily 7am - 8:30.

MARLPIT HALL MUSEUM, 137 Kings Hwy., Middletown, NJ 07748-2003. Mailing Address: Monmouth County Historical Assoc., 70 Court St., Freehold, NJ 07728-1710. Tel.: 732-462-1466.
E-mail: info@monmouthhistory.org
Web Site: www.monmouthhistory.org
Institution Type/Description: Historic House Museum: built c.1756.
Hours & Admission Prices: Call for hours.

MOSES D. HEATH FARM MUSEUM, 219 Harmony Rd., Middletown, NJ 07748. Tel.: 732-671-0566.
E-mail: spradley18@aol.com
Institution Type/Description: Farm Museum.
Hours & Admission Prices: Call for hours.

PORICY PARK CONSERVANCY, 345 Oak Hill Rd., Middletown, NJ 07748. Mailing Address: Box 36, Middletown, NJ 07748-0036. Tel.: 732-268-7034.
E-mail: emhinckley@comcast.net
Web Site: www.poricypark.org
Formerly: Poricy Park Citizen's Committee
Key Personnel: Pres. Bd. Trustees, Elaine Hinckley; Treas., Victoria Massa; Gift Shop Mgr., Janet Delette.
Institution Type/Description: Nature Center: located on 250-acre nature preserve.
Hours & Admission Prices: Park: daily dawn to 10pm. Nature Center: Mon.-Fri. 8:30-4:30. No charge; donations accepted. Fees for special programs. Closed national holidays. &
Attendance: 22,000 (estimated)

TAYLOR-BUTLER HOUSE, 127 Kings Hwy., Middletown, NJ 07748-2003. Mailing Address: 70 Court St., Freehold, NJ 07728. Tel.: 732-462-1466.
E-mail: mcha@monmouthhistory.org
Web Site: www.monmouthhistory.org
Institution Type/Description: Historic House Museum: built in 1853.
Hours & Admission Prices: May-Sept. Thurs.-Sat. 1-4.

Milltown

EUREKA FIRE MUSEUM, 39 Washington Ave., Milltown, NJ 08850-1219. Tel.: 732-828-7207 & 7400.
E-mail: webmaster@milltownfire.org
Web Site: www.milltownfire.org/museum.htm
Key Personnel: Treas., Mark Steeber.
Institution Type/Description: Fire-Fighting Museum.
Hours & Admission Prices: By appointment only. No charge; donations accepted.
Attendance: 150 (estimated)

Millville

MILLVILLE ARMY AIR FIELD MUSEUM, 1 Leddon St., Millville Airport, Millville, NJ 08332-4822. Tel.: 856-327-2347. Fax: 856-327-5737. Facebook.
E-mail: museum@p47millville.org
Web Site: www.p47millville.org
Key Personnel: Dir., Lisa Jester; Chm. (V), Russell Davis; Pres. (V), Chuck Wyble.
Institution Type/Description: Military Museum.
Hours & Admission Prices: Mon. by appointment only, Tues.-Sun. 10-4; guided tours by appointment. No charge; donations accepted. &
Attendance: 4,000 (estimated)

MUSEUM OF AMERICAN GLASS AT WHEATON ARTS AND CULTURAL CENTER, 1000 Village Dr., Millville, NJ 08332. Mailing Address: 1501 Glasstown Rd., Millville, NJ 08332. Tel.: 856-825-6800. Fax: 856-825-2410.
E-mail: museum@wheatonarts.org
Web Site: www.wheatonarts.org
Formerly: Museum of American Glass at Wheaton Village
Key Personnel: Chm., Arnold Robinson; Exec. Dir., Susan Gogan; Dir. Exhibitions & Collections, Kristin Qualls; Assoc. Dir. Education & Programs, Pam Weichmann; Registrar, Elizabeth G. Wilk; Museum Shop Mgr., Catharine Nolan.
Institution Type/Description: American Glass Museum.
Hours & Admission Prices: Jan.-March call for hours; April-Dec. Tues.-Sun. 10-5. Adults $10, senior citizens $9, students $7; discounts to groups, AAM, ICOM & AAA members; members no charge. Closed New Year's Day; Easter; Thanksgiving; Christmas. &
Attendance: 57,000 (estimated)

RIVERFRONT RENAISSANCE CENTER FOR THE ARTS, 22 N. High St., Millville, NJ 08332-3830. Tel.: 856-327-4500. Fax: 856-327-9280.
E-mail: sean@rrcarts.com
Web Site: www.rrcarts.com
Key Personnel: Dir., Liz Nicklus.
Institution Type/Description: Art Gallery.
Hours & Admission Prices: Sun.-Thurs. 11-5, Fri. 11-8, Sat. 11-7. No charge; donations accepted. &
Attendance: 6,000 (actual)

Monmouth Beach

MONMOUTH BEACH CULTURAL CENTER, 128 Ocean Ave., Monmouth Beach, NJ 07750. Tel.: 732-229-4527.
E-mail: mbculturalcenter@comcast.net
Web Site: monmouthbeach.org
Institution Type/Description: History Museum.
Hours & Admission Prices: Call for hours.

Monroe Township

THE STONE MUSEUM, 608 Spotswood-Englishtown Rd., Monroe Township, NJ 08831-3222. Tel.: 732-521-2232. Fax: 732-521-3388.
E-mail: displayworld@erols.com
Web Site: www.thestonemuseum.com
Key Personnel: Dir., Pat Ciecko; Museum Shop Mgr., Barbara Thompson.
Institution Type/Description: Geology Museum.
Hours & Admission Prices: Sat.-Sun. 11-4. No charge. Closed New Year's Day; Memorial Day; Independence Day; Labor Day; Christmas. ら
Attendance: 20,000 (estimated)

Montclair

MONTCLAIR ART MUSEUM, 3 S. Mountain Ave., Montclair, NJ 07042. Tel.: 973-746-5555. Fax: 973-746-9118 & 0920. Facebook & Twitter: @mammontclair.
E-mail: curatorial@montclairartmuseum.org
Web Site: www.montclairartmuseum.org
Key Personnel: Pres., Frank Walter; Dir., Lora Urbanelli; Dir. Finance, Michael Frasco; Dir. Mktg. & Communications, Michael Gillespie; Chief Cur., Gail Stavitsky, Ph.D.; Cur. Native American Art, Pam Jardine; Museum Shop Mgr., Mari D'Alessandro.
Institution Type/Description: Art Museum: housed in Neo-classic brick & stone building.
Hours & Admission Prices: Wed.-Sun. 12-5. Adults $12, seniors & students with I. D. $10; discounts to AAM & ICOM members; members, children under 12 & Oct.-June first Thurs. of month 5-9 no charge. Closed major holidays. ら
Attendance: 64,506 (actual)

MONTCLAIR HISTORICAL SOCIETY - CLARK HOUSE & LIBRARY, 108 Orange Rd., Montclair, NJ 07042-2133. Tel.: 973-744-1796. Fax: 973-783-9419.
E-mail: mail@montclairhistorical.org
Web Site: www.montclairhistorical.org
Key Personnel: Exec. Dir., Jane Eliasof; Pres. (V), Elizabeth Hynes.
Institution Type/Description: Historic House Museum: housed in the former home of Dr. James Henry Clark & his wife Carrie Schenck; built in 1894. Listed on the National Register of Historic Places.
Hours & Admission Prices: Call for hours & admission prices. ら
Attendance: 4,800 (actual)

MONTCLAIR HISTORICAL SOCIETY - CHARLES SHULTZ HOUSE, 30 N. Mountain Ave., Montclair, NJ 07042. Mailing Address: 108 Orange Rd., Montclair, NJ 07042. Tel.: 973-744-1796.
E-mail: mail@montclairhistorical.org
Web Site: www.montclairhistory.org/charles-shultz-house-1/
Institution Type/Description: Historic House Museum: built in 1896. Listed on the National Register of Historic Places.
Hours & Admission Prices: April-Dec. 1st & 3rd Sun. each month 1-4. Adults $8, seniors & children $5; members no charge.

MONTCLAIR HISTORICAL SOCIETY - ISRAEL CRANE HOUSE & NATHANIEL CRANE HOUSE, 110 Orange Rd., Montclair, NJ 07042. Tel.: 973-744-1796.
E-mail: mail@montclairhistorical.org
Institution Type/Description: Historic Houses: Israel Crane House built in 1796; Nathaniel Crane House built in 1818.
Hours & Admission Prices: 1st & 3rd Sun. each month 1-4. Adults $8, seniors & children $5; members no charge.

NEW JERSEY ASSOCIATION OF MUSEUMS, c/o Montclair Art Museum, 3 S. Mountain Ave., Montclair, NJ 07042. Facebook: @NJMuseums.
E-mail: njassociationofmuseums@gmail.com
Web Site: www.njmuseums.org
Institution Type/Description: Museum Service Organization: represents 124 museums in the state.

Hours & Admission Prices: Mon.-Fri. 9-5.

VAN VLECK HOUSE & GARDENS, 21 Van Vleck St., Montclair, NJ 07042. Tel.: 973-744-4752. Fax: 973-746-1082.
E-mail: info@vanvleck.org
Web Site: www.vanvleck.org
Key Personnel: Exec. Dir., Charles Fischer.
Institution Type/Description: Historic House Museum: late 19th century home.
Hours & Admission Prices: House: Mon.-Fri. 10-3. Gardens: daily dawn to dusk. No charge.

Montville

MONTVILLE TOWNSHIP HISTORICAL MUSEUM, 6 Taylortown Rd., Montville, NJ 07045. Mailing Address: P.O. Box 519, Montville, NJ 07045. Tel.: 973-334-3665.
Web Site: www.montvillenj.org
Key Personnel: Pres., Kathleen Fisher.
Institution Type/Description: General Museum: housed in c. 1867 School House.
Hours & Admission Prices: Sept.-June Sun. 1-4. No charge; donations accepted. Closed national holidays.
Attendance: 1,200 (actual)

Moorestown

PERKINS CENTER FOR THE ARTS, 395 Kings Hwy., Moorestown, NJ 08057-2725. Tel.: 856-235-6488, 800-387-5226. Fax: 856-235-6624.
E-mail: create@perkinscenter.org
Web Site: www.perkinscenter.org
Key Personnel: Exec. Dir., Karen Chigounis.
Institution Type/Description: Art Center: housed in 1910 Tudor Revival House, designed by Herbert C. Wise, first editor of House & Garden magazine.
Hours & Admission Prices: Thurs.-Fri. 10-4, Sat.-Sun. noon to 4. No charge; donations accepted. ら
Attendance: 30,000 (estimated)

SMITH-CADBURY MANSION, 12 High St., Moorestown, NJ 08057-3504. Mailing Address: P.O. Box 477, Moorestown, NJ 08057. Tel.: 856-235-0353. Facebook.
Web Site: moorestownhistory.org
Institution Type/Description: Historic House Museum.
Hours & Admission Prices: Sept.-June: House Tours & Gift Shop: 2nd & 4th Sun. 1-3. Library: Tues. & 2nd Sun. each month 1-4. No charge; donations accepted.

Morganville

NEW JERSEY SCOUT MUSEUM, 705 Ginesi Dr., Morganville, NJ 07751-1235. Tel.: 732-862-1282.
E-mail: president@njsm.org
Web Site: www.njscoutmuseum.org
Key Personnel: Chm. (V), Fred Pachman.
Institution Type/Description: History Museum.
Hours & Admission Prices: Sept.-June Wed. 6pm-8pm; other times by appointment. No charge; donations accepted. ら
Attendance: 100 (estimated)

Morris Plains

THE STICKLEY MUSEUM AT CRAFTSMAN FARMS, 2352 Rt. 10 W., Manor Lane, Morris Plains, NJ 07950. Tel.: 973-540-0311 & 1165. Fax: 973-540-1167.
E-mail: info@stickleymuseum.org
Web Site: www.stickleymuseum.org
Formerly: Craftsman Farms Foundation
Key Personnel: Exec. Dir., Vonda Givens; Bd. Pres. (V), Barbara Weiskittel; Mgr. Education, Kristen McCauley; Mgr. Devel., Linda Blume; Coord. Visitor Svcs., Parker Sanchez; Registrar, Bernadette Rubbo; Office Mgr., Susie Traverso.
Institution Type/Description: Historic House & Site: 30 acre National Historic Landmark includes the Craftsman Log House of Gustav Stickley, one of America's leading proponents of the Arts & Crafts movement in the early 1900s.
Hours & Admission Prices: Thurs.-Sun. 12-4. Adults $10, seniors & students $7, children $4; members & children under 2 no charge. Closed major holidays. ら
Attendance: 11,108 (actual)

Morris Township

FOSTERFIELDS LIVING HISTORICAL FARM, 73 Kahdena Rd., Morris Township, NJ 07960-3524. Tel.: 973-326-7645. Fax: 973-631-5023.
E-mail: dhelmer@morrisparks.net
Web Site: www.morrisparks.net
Key Personnel: C.E.O., Dave Helmer; Asst. Dir. Historic Sites, Lynn Laffey; Pres. Park Comm., John Sette; Pres. Friends of Fosterfields, Anne Bukata; Farm Supvr., Rob Kibbe.
Institution Type/Description: Living Historical Farm & Agricultural Museum: located on a 230-acre farm site.
Hours & Admission Prices: Farm: April-July 1 Tues.-Sat. 10-5; July 2-Oct. Wed.-Sat. 10-5, Sun. 12-5. Adults $6, seniors $5, children 4-16 $4; discounts to AAA members; members & children under 3 no charge. &
Attendance: 24,000 (estimated)

THE GEORGE G. FRELINGHUYSEN ARBORETUM, 353 E. Hanover Ave., Morris Township, NJ 07960-3161. Mailing Address: P.O. Box 1295, Morristown, NJ 07962-1295. Tel.: 973-326-7600. Fax: 973-644-2726. TDD: 1-800-852-7899.
E-mail: info@parks.morris.nj.us
Web Site: www.arboretumfriends.org
Key Personnel: Dir. Park Maintenance, Ed Vath; Mgr. Horticulture, John Morse; Dir. Visitors Svcs., Denise Lanza.
Institution Type/Description: Arboretum: located on 1891 Whippany Farm Residence, summer home of George Griswold Frelinghuysen.
Hours & Admission Prices: Grounds: daily 8am-dusk. Education Center: daily 9-4:30. No charge; donations accepted. Closed New Year's Day; Thanksgiving; Christmas. &
Attendance: 400,000 (estimated)

Morristown

HISTORIC SPEEDWELL, 333 Speedwell Ave., Ste. A, Morristown, NJ 07960-9384. Tel.: 973-285-6550. Fax: 973-285-6541.
E-mail: msutherland@morrisparks.net
Web Site: www.morrisparks.net
Formerly: Historic Speedwell - Birthplace of the Telegraph
Key Personnel: Historic Sites Mgr., Mark Sutherland; Cur. Collections & Exhibits, Melanie Bump; Historic Education & Volunteer Supvr., Maressa McFarlane; Education Asst., Ashley Scotto; Education Asst., Marybeth Ginsberg.
Institution Type/Description: Historic site: 19th century homestead estate.
Hours & Admission Prices: April-June Tues.-Sat. 10-5; July-Oct. Wed.-Sat. 10-5, Sun. 12-5. Adults $4, seniors $3, students & children 4-16 $2; discounts to groups & AAM members; children under 4 no charge. &
Attendance: 6,000 (actual)

MACCULLOCH HALL HISTORICAL MUSEUM & GARDENS, 45 Macculloch Ave., Ste. 1, Morristown, NJ 07960-9374. Tel.: 973-538-2404. Fax: 973-538-9428. Instagram: @macullochhall.
E-mail: ppongracz@macullochhall.org
Web Site: www.macullochhall.org
Key Personnel: Exec. Dir., Dr. Patricia Pongracz; Cur. Collections F.M. Kirby, Ryan Hyman; Educator, Cynthia Winslow.
Institution Type/Description: Historic House: 1810 George Macculloch Home.
Hours & Admission Prices: Wed.-Thurs. & Sun. 1-4; groups by appointment. Adults $8, senior citizens & students over 12 $6, children 6-12 $4; discounts to AAM members; children under 5 & members no charge. Closed New Year's Eve & Day; Memorial Day; Independence Day; Labor Day; Thanksgiving & day after; Christmas Eve, Day & week.
Attendance: 4,362 (actual)

MORRIS COUNTY HISTORICAL SOCIETY (ACORN HALL HOUSE MUSEUM), 68 Morris Ave., Morristown, NJ 07960-4315. Tel.: 973-267-3465. Fax: 973-267-8773. Facebook: Acorn Hall.
E-mail: mchsacornhall@gmail.com
Web Site: morriscountyhistory.org
Key Personnel: Dir., Amy Curry.
Institution Type/Description: Historical Society Museum: housed in c.1853 Acorn Hall.
Hours & Admission Prices: Wed.-Thurs. 11-4, Sun. 1-4; groups by appointment. Adults $6, senior citizens $5, students $3; discounts to AAM members & active military and their families; children under 12 & members no charge. Closed New Year's Eve & Day; Christmas Eve, Day & week.
Attendance: 3,500 (estimated)

THE MORRIS MUSEUM, 6 Normandy Heights Rd., Morristown, NJ 07960-4627. Tel.: 973-971-3700. Facebook: Morris Museum.
E-mail: info@morrismuseum.org
Web Site: www.morrismuseum.org
Key Personnel: Exec. Dir. & C.E.O., Dr. Cleveland Johnson; Chm. (V), Gerri Horn; Dir. Finance, Constance Reed; Mgr. Collections, Maria Ribaudo; Artistic Dir. Bickford Theatre, Eric Hafen; Cur. Guinness Collection, Michelle Marinelli; Museum Shop Mgr., Kathleen Haviland.
Institution Type/Description: General Museum.
Hours & Admission Prices: Tues.-Sat. 11-5, 2nd & 3rd Thurs. 11-8, Sun. 12-5. Adults $10, senior citizens & children 3-12 $7; discounts to PBS members, AAM members & employees of other museums with ID; Thurs. 5-8 pay what you wish; children under 3 & members no charge. Closed major holidays. &
Attendance: 150,000 (actual)

MORRISTOWN NATIONAL HISTORICAL PARK, 30 Washington Place, Morristown, NJ 07960-4299. Tel.: 973-539-2016. Fax: 973-539-8361. TDD: 973-539-5072.
E-mail: jude_pfister@nps.gov
Web Site: nps.gov/morr
Key Personnel: Supt., Thomas Ross; Chief Interpretation, Vanessa Smiley; Museum Specialist, Joni Rowe; Chief Cultural Resources, Dr. Jude M. Pfister.
Institution Type/Description: Historic Site: 1777, 1779-1782 winter encampment sites of the Continental Army; 1779-1780 Washington's Headquarters.
Hours & Admission Prices: Daily 9-5. Adults $4; children under 16 no charge. Annual Family Pass: $15 Closed New Year's Day; Thanksgiving; Christmas. &
Attendance: 200,000 (estimated)

SCHUYLER-HAMILTON HOUSE, 5 Olyphant Place, Morristown, NJ 07960-4231. Tel.: 973-539-7502. Fax: 973-539-7502.
E-mail: abren8527@aol.com
Web Site: www.co.morris.nj.us/mchc/directory-museums.html#schuyler
Key Personnel: Dir., Patricia Sanftner; Co-1st Vice Regent, Kathleen Cruger; Co-2nd Vice Regent, Mariane Browne.
Institution Type/Description: Historic House Museum: 1760 home of Dr. Jabez Campfield, Revolutionary War army doctor. Site of Alexander Hamilton's engagement to Elizabeth Schuyler.
Hours & Admission Prices: Sun. 2-4; other times by appointment. Adults $5, children 12 to high school $2.50; children under 12 no charge.
Attendance: 1,000 (estimated)

Mount Holly

HISTORIC BURLINGTON COUNTY PRISON MUSEUM, 128 High St., Mount Holly, NJ 08060-1402. Mailing Address: Burlington County Division of Parks, P.O. Box 6000, Mount Holly, NJ 08060. Tel.: 609-265-5858 & 5476 (museum). Fax: 609-265-5797.
E-mail: parks@co.burlington.nj.us
Web Site: www.prisonmuseum.net
Key Personnel: Pres. (V) Historic Burlington County Prison Museum Assn., Janet L. Sozio; Supt. Burlington County Division of Parks, John H. Smith, Jr.; Site Attendant, Marisa Bozarth.
Institution Type/Description: Historic Building: 1810 Burlington County Prison. A National Historic Landmark.
Hours & Admission Prices: Thurs.-Sat. 10-4, Sun. noon-4. Adults $5, seniors over 55 & military $3, students $2; children under 5 no charge. Closed legal holidays. &
Attendance: 5,000 (actual)

JOHN WOOLMAN MEMORIAL, 99 Branch St., Mount Holly, NJ 08060-1866. Tel.: 609-267-3226.
E-mail: judyhynes@msn.com
Web Site: www.woolmancentral.com
Key Personnel: Dir., Jack Walz; Dir., Carol Walz.
Institution Type/Description: Historic Building & Site: 1783 John Woolman Memorial.
Hours & Admission Prices: Call for hours. No charge, donations requested. &
Attendance: 2,500 (estimated)

MOUNT HOLLY HISTORICAL SOCIETY - SHINN-CURTIS LOG HOUSE, 23 Washington St., Mount Holly, NJ 08060. Tel.: 609-267-2773.
Institution Type/Description: Historical Society Museum: housed in the former home of Thomas Shinn; c.1712.
Hours & Admission Prices: Call for hours.

THE OLD SCHOOLHOUSE, 35 Brainerd St., Mount Holly, NJ 08060. Mailing Address: 180 Burrs Rd., Westampton, NJ 08060. Tel.: 609-267-6996.

E-mail: colonialdamesnj@comcast.net
Web Site: www.colonialdamesnj.org
Institution Type/Description: Historic Building: housed in a former schoolhouse; built in 1756; listed on National Register of Historic Places.
Hours & Admission Prices: By appointment. &

Mount Laurel

PAWS FARM NATURE CENTER, 1105 Hainesport Rd., Mount Laurel, NJ 08054. Tel.: 856-778-8795.
E-mail: reservations@pawsdiscoveryfarm.com
Institution Type/Description: Nature Center.
Hours & Admission Prices: Wed.-Sun. 10-4. Adults $6, children $4; children under one no charge.

Mountainside

DEACON ANDREW HETFIELD HOUSE, Constitution Plaza, Watchung Ave., Mountainside, NJ 07092. Mailing Address: Mountainside Restoration Committee, 1385 Rte. 22 E., Mountainside, NJ 07092-2605. Tel.: 908-232-9282.
E-mail: hetfieldhouse1@yahoo.com
Institution Type/Description: Historic House Museum: built in 1760. Listed on the National Register of Historic Places.
Hours & Admission Prices: Call for hours.

TRAILSIDE NATURE AND SCIENCE CENTER, 452 New Providence Rd., Mountainside, NJ 07092-1409. Tel.: 908-789-3670. Fax: 908-789-3270.
E-mail: pbertsch@ucnj.org
Web Site: www.ucnj.org/trailside
Key Personnel: Dir., Patricia Bertsch; Asst. Dir., Karen Inzillo; Museum Shop Mgr., Lenore Mangan.
Institution Type/Description: Natural Science Museum.
Hours & Admission Prices: Visitor Center: daily 12-5. No charge; donations accepted. Closed New Year's Day; Easter; Independence Day; Thanksgiving & day after; Christmas Eve & Day. &
Attendance: 50,000 (estimated)

Mullica Hill

OLD TOWN HALL MUSEUM - THE HARRISON TOWNSHIP HISTORICAL SOCIETY, 62-64 S. Main St., Mullica Hill, NJ 08062. Mailing Address: P.O. Box 4, Mullica Hill, NJ 08062. Tel.: 856-478-4949.
E-mail: info@harrisonhistorical.com
Web Site: www.harrisonhistorical.com
Key Personnel: Chm. (V), Etta Jane Heiser; Pres. (V), Suzanne Grasso.
Institution Type/Description: Historical Society Museum: housed in the former town hall; built in 1871.
Hours & Admission Prices: Call for hours. No charge; donations accepted.
Attendance: 1,000 (estimated)

National Park

RED BANK BATTLEFIELD PARK & JAMES AND ANN WHITALL HOUSE, 100 Hessian Ave., National Park, NJ 08063. Mailing Address: P.O. Box 337, Woodbury, NJ 08096. Tel.: 856-853-5120. Fax: 856-853-0950. Facebook: Whitall House.
E-mail: jjanofsky@co.gloucester.nj.us
Web Site: www.whitall.org
Institution Type/Description: History Museum: housed in the home of James & Ann Whitall which also served as a Revolutionary War patriot headquarters and a field hospital; built in 1748. Listed on the National Register of Historic Places.
Hours & Admission Prices: House: April-Sept. Wed.-Sun. 1-4; Oct.-March Wed.-Fri. 9-12 & 1-4. no charge; donations accepted. &
Attendance: 6,000 (actual)

New Brunswick

AMERICAN HUNGARIAN FOUNDATION/MUSEUM OF THE AMERICAN HUNGARIAN FOUNDATION, 300 Somerset St., New Brunswick, NJ 08901-2248. Mailing Address: P.O. Box 1084, New Brunswick, NJ 08903-1084. Tel.: 732-846-5777. Fax: 732-249-7033.
E-mail: info@ahfoundation.org
Web Site: www.ahfoundation.org
Formerly: American Hungarian Foundation/Hungarian Heritage Center Museum

Key Personnel: Pres. & Acting Dir., Gergely Hajdu-Nemeth; Co Chm. Bd. (V), Zsolt Harsanyi; Co Chm. Bd. (V), August J. Molnar; Treas., Scott B. Lukacs; Librarian, Margaret Papai.
Institution Type/Description: Cultural Heritage Center.
Hours & Admission Prices: Tues.-Fri. 10-3, Sat. 9:30-1. Suggested Donation: $5. Closed New Year's Day; Easter; Memorial Day; Independence Day; Labor Day; Thanksgiving; Christmas. &
Attendance: 3,000 (estimated)

BUCCLEUCH MANSION, Buccleuch Park, 800 George St. (private driveway), (enter park from Easton Ave.), New Brunswick, NJ 08901. Mailing Address: Jersey Blue Chapter NSDAR, P.O. Box 27, New Brunswick, NJ 08903. Tel.: 732-745-5094.
E-mail: jkgennaro@aol.com
Key Personnel: Cur., Judy Gennaro.
Institution Type/Description: Historic House: 1739 three-story Colonial house, located on the site of 1776 Revolutionary War fortifications.
Hours & Admission Prices: June-Oct. last of month Sun. 1-4; groups by appointment year round. No charge; donations accepted. &
Attendance: 1,500 (estimated)

CENTER FOR LATINO ARTS & CULTURE, 122 College Ave., New Brunswick, NJ 08901-1165. Tel.: 732-932-1263. Fax: 732-932-1589.
E-mail: cafernan@echo.rutgers.edu
Web Site: clac.rutgers.edu
Key Personnel: Dir., Carlos Fernandez, Ph.D.; Program Coord., Silismar Suriel.
Institution Type/Description: Latino Arts & Culture.
Hours & Admission Prices: Mon.-Fri. 9-5; other times by appointment.

HENRY GUEST HOUSE, 58 Livingston Ave., New Brunswick, NJ 08901-2521. Mailing Address: 60 Livingston Ave., New Brunswick, NJ 08901-2520. Tel.: 732-745-5108. Fax: 732-846-0226.
E-mail: nbfpl@lmxac.org
Key Personnel: Dir., Robert Belvin.
Institution Type/Description: Historic House: 1760 Henry Guest House. Listed on the National Register of Historic Places.
Hours & Admission Prices: By appointment. No charge. &
Attendance: 2,000 (estimated)

JEWISH HISTORICAL SOCIETY OF CENTRAL JERSEY, 222 Livingston Ave., New Brunswick, NJ 08901. Tel.: 732-249-4894.
E-mail: info.jhscj@gmail.com
Web Site: www.jewishgen.org
Institution Type/Description: Jewish History Museum.
Hours & Admission Prices: Mon.-Fri. 9-1

RUTGERS GARDENS, 112 Ryders Ln., New Brunswick, NJ 08901-8519. Tel.: 732-932-8451. Fax: 732-932-7060.
E-mail: rugardens@aesop.rutgers.edu
Web Site: rutgersgardens.rutgers.edu
Key Personnel: Dir., Bruce Crawford; Volunteer Coord., Mary Ann McMillan; Supt., Matthew Jamicky.
Institution Type/Description: Research Arboretum.
Hours & Admission Prices: Daily 8:30 am-dusk. No charge; donations accepted.
Attendance: 20,000 (estimated)

RUTGERS UNIVERSITY GEOLOGY MUSEUM, Geology Hall, Old Queen Campus, 85 Somerset St., New Brunswick, NJ 08901. Tel.: 848-932-4243.
E-mail: museum@rci.rutgers.edu
Web Site: geologymuseum.rutgers.edu
Key Personnel: Co-Dir., Dr. Lauren Neitzke Adamo; Co-Dir., Dr. Patricia Irizarry.
Institution Type/Description: Geology Museum.
Hours & Admission Prices: Academic Year: Tues.-Thurs. 10-5, Fri. 10-4, Sat. 10-2; Summer: call for hours. No charge.

RUTGERS UNIVERSITY - MASON GROSS ART GALLERIES, 33 Livingston Ave., New Brunswick, NJ 08901. Tel.: 732-932-2222, ext. 798. Fax: 732-932-2217.
E-mail: artsonline@masongross.rutgers.edu
Web Site: www.masongross.rutgers.edu/contact
Institution Type/Description: Art Gallery.
Hours & Admission Prices: Call for hours.

ZIMMERLI ART MUSEUM AT RUTGERS UNIVERSITY, Rutgers, The State University of New Jersey, 71 Hamilton St., New Brunswick, NJ 08901-1248. Tel.: 848-932-7237. Fax: 732-932-8201.
E-mail: press@zimmerli.rutgers.edu
Web Site: www.zimmerlimuseum.rutgers.edu
Formerly: Jane Voorhees Zimmerli Art Museum
Key Personnel: Dir., Thomas Sokolowski; Chm., Joyce Glasgold; Mgr. Publications & Communications, Stacy Smith; Mgr. Business Affairs, Bernadette Clapsis; Operations, Security & Visitor Svcs. Mgr., Edward Schwab; Registrar, Leslie Kriff; Cur. American Art & Mellon Dir. Academic Programs, Donna Gustafson; Cur. Prints, Drawings & European Art, Christine Giviskos; Cur. Russian & Soviet Nonconformist Art, Julia Tulovsky; Research Cur. Soviet Nonconformist Art, Jane A. Sharp; Dir. Devel., Whitney Prendergast; Cur. Education & Interpretation, Amanda Potter; Asst. Cur. Prints & Drawings, Nicole Simpson; Communications Coord., Theresa Watson.
Institution Type/Description: Art Museum.
Hours & Admission Prices: Sept.-July Tues.-Fri. 10-4:30, Sat.-Sun. 12-5 & first Tues. most months 10-9. No charge; donations accepted. Closed major holidays; New Year's Day; Independence Day; Thanksgiving & day after; Christmas Eve & Day. ♿
Attendance: 56,727 (actual)

New Providence

NEW PROVIDENCE HISTORICAL SOCIETY, 1350 Springfield Ave., New Providence, NJ 07974. Mailing Address: New Providence Memorial Library, 377 Elkwood Ave., New Providence, NJ 07974-1837. Tel.: 908-665-1034. Facebook: @NewProvidenceHistoricalSociety.
E-mail: newprovhistorical@gmail.com
Web Site: www.newprovidencehistorical.com
Formerly: Saltbox Museum
Key Personnel: Pres. (V), Linda J. Kale.
Institution Type/Description: Historic House Museum.
Hours & Admission Prices: March-Nov. 1st & 3rd Sun. 1-3. No charge; donations accepted.
Attendance: 250 (estimated)

New Vernon

TUNIS-ELLICKS HISTORIC HOUSE AND MUSEUM, 16 Village Rd., New Vernon, NJ 07976. Mailing Address: P.O. Box 1777, New Vernon, NJ 07976. Tel.: 973-292-3661.
E-mail: hardinghist@comcast.net
Institution Type/Description: Historic House Museum.
Hours & Admission Prices: By appointment. No charge.

Newark

ALJIRA, A CENTER FOR CONTEMPORARY ART, 591 Broad St., Newark, NJ 07102-4403. Tel.: 973-622-1600. Fax: 973-622-6526.
E-mail: info@aljira.org
Web Site: www.aljira.org
Key Personnel: Exec. Dir., Dexter Wimberly.
Institution Type/Description: Art Center.
Hours & Admission Prices: Wed.-Fri. 12-6, Sat. 11-4.

CITY WITHOUT WALLS (CWOW), 6 Crawford St., Newark, NJ 07102. Tel.: 973-622-1188. Fax: 973-622-2941.
E-mail: info@cwow.org
Web Site: www.cwow.org
Key Personnel: Exec. Dir., Fayemi Shakur.
Institution Type/Description: Art Gallery.
Hours & Admission Prices: Wed.-Sat. 12-6; other times by appointment.

THE JEWISH MUSEUM OF NEW JERSEY, Congregation Ahavas Sholom, 145 Broadway, Newark, NJ 07104. Tel.: 973-485-2609.
E-mail: info@jewishmuseumnj.org
Web Site: jewishmuseumnj.org
Key Personnel: Pres., Max Herman.
Institution Type/Description: Jewish History Museum.
Hours & Admission Prices: Sun. 1-5; other times by appointment.

THE NEW JERSEY HISTORICAL SOCIETY, 52 Park Place, Newark, NJ 07102-4302. Tel.: 973-596-8500. Fax: 973-596-6957.
E-mail: contactnjhs@jerseyhistory.org

Web Site: www.jerseyhistory.org
Key Personnel: Exec. Dir., Steven Tettamanti; Library Specialist, James Amemasor; Dir. Education, Maribel Jusino-Iturralde.
Institution Type/Description: History Museum & Library.
Hours & Admission Prices: Museum: Tues.-Sat. 10-5. Library: Tues.-Sat. 12-5; school & group tours by appointment. Museum $3; Library $5; members no charge. Closed major holidays. ♿
Attendance: 20,000 (estimated)

THE NEWARK MUSEUM, 49 Washington St., Newark, NJ 07102-3176. Tel.: 973-596-6550. Fax: 973-642-0459. TDD: 973-596-6355.
E-mail: lbatitto@newarkmuseum.org
Web Site: www.newarkmuseum.org
Key Personnel: Co-Chair, Clifford Blanchard; Co-Chair, Christine C. Gilfillan; Dir. & C.E.O., Steven Kern; Deputy Dir. Finance & Admin., Beth Aron; Deputy Dir. Institutional Advancement, Deborah Kasindorf; Cur. Asia & the Pacific, Dr. Katherine Anne Paul; Cur. Decorative Arts, Ulysses G. Dietz; Cur. Africa & the Americas, Dr. Christa Clarke; Cur. American Art, Dr. Tricia Bloom; Astronomer, Kevin Conod; Dir. School Educational Program, Shirley Thomas; Deputy Dir. Educ., Sonnet Takahisa; Dir. Exhibits, Tim Wintemberg; Dir. Facilities Operations, David May; Librarian, Dr. William A. Peniston; Museum Shop Mgr., Sandy Ambar; Public Rels., Lisa Battito; Dir. Special Events, Carol Blunda.
Institution Type/Description: Art & Science Museum.
Hours & Admission Prices: Wed.-Sun. 12-5. Suggested Donation: adults $12; children, seniors & students $7; discounts to AAM members; members no charge. Public planetarium performances: adults $5, children under 12 $3. Closed New Year's Eve & Day; Independence Day; Thanksgiving; Christmas. ♿
Attendance: 948,663 (actual)

PAUL ROBESON GALLERIES-RUTGERS UNIVERSITY, Rutgers University - Newark, 350 Dr. Martin Luther King, Jr. Blvd., Paul Robeson Campus Center, Newark, NJ 07102. Tel.: 848-445-0515. Fax: 973-353-5912.
E-mail: galleryr@andromeda.rutgers.edu
Web Site: artgallery.newark.rutgers.edu
Key Personnel: Dir. & Cur., Anonda Bell.
Institution Type/Description: Art Gallery.
Hours & Admission Prices: Mon.-Thurs. 10-5, 1st Sat. each month 12-5. No charge. ♿
Attendance: 8,588 (actual)

Newfield

MATCHBOX ROAD MUSEUM, 15 Pearl St., Newfield, NJ 08344-2603. Mailing Address: P.O. Box 977, Newfield, NJ 08344. Tel.: 856-697-6900.
E-mail: mbroad@aol.com
Web Site: mbroad.com
Key Personnel: Everett Marshall, III.
Institution Type/Description: Toy Museum.
Hours & Admission Prices: By appointment. No charge; donations accepted. ♿

Newton

NEWTON FIRE DEPARTMENT MUSEUM, 150 Spring St., Newton, NJ 07860-2009. Tel.: 973-383-0396. Fax: 973-553-6806.
E-mail: info@newtonfiremuseum.org
Web Site: www.newtonfiremuseum.org
Key Personnel: Dir., Daniel Finkle.
Institution Type/Description: Fire-Fighting Museum: housed in an historic firehouse built in 1891.
Hours & Admission Prices: May-Oct. Thurs. 5pm-8pm, Sat. 11-3; groups by appointment.

SUSSEX COUNTY HISTORICAL SOCIETY, 82 Main St., Newton, NJ 07860. Mailing Address: P.O. Box 913, Newton, NJ 07860-0913. Tel.: 973-383-6010. Fax: 973-383-6010.
E-mail: sussexcountyhs@gmail.com
Web Site: sussexhistory.org
Key Personnel: Pres., Wayne T. McCabe; Vice Pres., Jay Docherty; Sec., Lisa Holder; Corresponding Sec., Peter Chletsos.
Institution Type/Description: Local Sussex County History & Genealogy Records Museum.
Hours & Admission Prices: Fri. 9-2. Museum: No charge; donations accepted. Library $15 daily; members no charge.
Attendance: 500 (estimated)

North Plainfield

THE FLEETWOOD MUSEUM, 614 Greenbrook Rd., North Plainfield, NJ 07063-1621. Mailing Address: 135 Sandford Ave., North Plainfield, NJ 07060. Tel.: 908-756-7810.
E-mail: naciampa@aim.com
Web Site: www.fleetwoodmuseum.org
Key Personnel: Dir. & Chm. (V), Nicholas A. Ciampa.
Institution Type/Description: Art Museum: housed in the Vermeule Mansion. Listed on the National Register of Historic Places.
Hours & Admission Prices: Sat. 10-4. No charge; donations accepted. Closed major holidays. &
Attendance: 1,200 (estimated)

North Wildwood

HEREFORD INLET LIGHTHOUSE, 111 N. Central Ave., North Wildwood, NJ 08260-5955. Mailing Address: P.O. Box 784, Rio Grande, NJ 08242-0784. Tel.: 609-522-4520. Fax: 609-522-8590.
Web Site: www.herefordlighthouse.org
Key Personnel: Pres., Tom Flud; Historic Site Mgr., Betty Mugnier; Chm., Steve Murray; Sec., Betty Mugnier.
Institution Type/Description: Historic Site & Maritime Museum: listed in the National Directory of Historic Places.
Hours & Admission Prices: May 5 to Oct. 24 daily 9-5. Tours: adults $5, children 11 & under $2; active Coast Guard & NJ Lighthouse Society members no charge.
Attendance: 30,000 (actual)

Northfield

NORTHFIELD MUSEUM, CASTO HOUSE & WEBB'S MILITARY SHED, Birch Grove Park, Burton Ave., Northfield, NJ 08225. Mailing Address: 1600 Shore Rd., Northfield, NJ 08225-2251. Tel.: 609-383-1505. Fax: 609-641-5901. Facebook: Northfield Museum and Casto House.
E-mail: northfieldmuseum@aol.com
Web Site: www.cityofnorthfield.org/main/castohouse.asp
Formerly: Northfield Bicentennial Museum
Key Personnel: Cur., Roy W. Clark.
Institution Type/Description: Local History Museum.
Hours & Admission Prices: Sun. & Wed. 1-3; other times by appointment. No charge; donations accepted. Photo prints $5. Closed some holidays. &
Attendance: 275 (estimated)

Nutley

NUTLEY HISTORICAL SOCIETY & MUSEUM, 65 Church St., Nutley, NJ 07110. Tel.: 973-667-1528.
E-mail: domtibaldo@aol.com
Web Site: nutleyhistoricalsociety.org
Key Personnel: Dir., John Simko; Pres. (V), Domenick Tibaldo; Dir. Art, Barry Lenson; Asst. Dir. & Museum Shop Mgr., Nancy Greulich.
Institution Type/Description: Historical Society Museum.
Hours & Admission Prices: By appointment. No charge.
Attendance: 3,000 (estimated)

Oak Ridge

JEFFERSON TOWNSHIP HISTORICAL SOCIETY, 315 Dover-Milton Rd., Oak Ridge, NJ 07438. Tel.: 973-697-0258.
E-mail: info@jthistoricalsociety.org
Key Personnel: Dir., Carol Keppel.
Institution Type/Description: Historical Society Museum: housed in the former home of Amos Chamberlain; c.1870.
Hours & Admission Prices: Call for hours.

Oakland

OAKLAND HISTORICAL SOCIETY - VAN ALLEN HOUSE, Franklin Ave., Oakland, NJ 07436. Mailing Address: P.O. Box 296, Oakland, NJ 07436. Tel.: 201-405-7726.
E-mail: ohs.inc1966@verizon.net
Web Site: www.oaklandhistoricalsociety.org
Institution Type/Description: Historical Society Museum: house built in 1777. Listed on the National Register of Historic Places.
Hours & Admission Prices: Feb.-June & Sept.-Oct. 3rd Sun. of the month 1-4; Dec. 1st Sun. 1-4. No charge; donations accepted.

Ocean City

DISCOVERY SEASHELL MUSEUM, 2721 Asbury Ave., Ocean City, NJ 08226-2329. Mailing Address: 2724 Central Ave., Ocean City, NJ 08226-2334. Tel.: 609-398-2316.
E-mail: seashellmuseum@gmail.com
Web Site: discoveryseashellmuseum.business.site
Institution Type/Description: Seashell Museum.
Hours & Admission Prices: Memorial Day to Dec. Mon.-Sat. 10-8, Sun. 12-6. No charge. &

OCEAN CITY ARTS CENTER, 1735 Simpson Ave., Ocean City, NJ 08226-3070. Tel.: 609-399-7628. Fax: 609-399-7089.
E-mail: info@oceancityartscenter.org
Web Site: www.oceancityartscenter.org
Key Personnel: Dir., Rosalyn Lifshin; Pres. (V), Dr. Jack Devine.
Institution Type/Description: Art Gallery.
Hours & Admission Prices: Mon.-Fri. 9-9, Sat. 9-3. No charge; donations accepted. &

OCEAN CITY HISTORICAL MUSEUM, INC., Cultural Community Center, 1735 Simpson Ave., Ocean City, NJ 08226-3070. Tel.: 609-399-1801. Fax: 609-399-0544.
E-mail: info@ocnjmuseum.org
Web Site: ocnjmuseum.org
Formerly: Friends of the Ocean City Historical Museum, Inc.
Key Personnel: Interim Exec. Dir., Johnette H. Halpin.
Institution Type/Description: Local History Museum.
Hours & Admission Prices: Mon.-Sat. 10-4. No charge; donations accepted. Closed major holidays. &
Attendance: 4,000 (estimated)

Ocean Grove

HISTORICAL SOCIETY OF OCEAN GROVE, NEW JERSEY, 50 Pitman Ave., Ocean Grove, NJ 07756-1557. Mailing Address: P.O. Box 446, Ocean Grove, NJ 07756-0446. Tel.: 732-774-1869. Fax: 732-774-1684.
E-mail: info@oceangrovehistory.org
Web Site: oceangrovehistory.org
Key Personnel: Pres., Samuel Oshan; Museum Shop Mgr., Jean Buckley.
Institution Type/Description: Historical Society Museum: located in Ocean Grove Historic District; emphasizing history of Ocean Grove & the history of the camp meeting.
Hours & Admission Prices: mid-May to mid-June Fri.-Sat. 10-4; mid-June to Sept. Mon.-Thurs. 10-4, Fri.-Sat. 10-5; Oct.-Dec. Sat. 10-4. No charge; donations accepted.
Attendance: 6,000 (actual)

Oceanville

THE NOYES MUSEUM OF ART, 733 Lily Lake Rd., Oceanville, NJ 08231. Tel.: 609-626-3420. Fax: 609-652-6166.
E-mail: info@noyesmuseum.org
Web Site: www.noyesmuseum.org
Key Personnel: Exec. Dir., Michael Cagno.
Institution Type/Description: Art Museum.
Hours & Admission Prices: Mon.-Sat. 10-4:30, Sun. 12-5. Adults $5, seniors & students over 12 $4; discounts to AAM, & N.J. Association of Museums members; children under 6, members & Stockton students, faculty & staff no charge. Closed national holidays. &
Attendance: 17,000 (estimated)

Ogdensburg

STERLING HILL MINING MUSEUM, INC., 30 Plant St., Ogdensburg, NJ 07439-1126. Tel.: 973-209-7212. Fax: 973-209-8505.
E-mail: info@sterlinghillminingmuseum.org
Web Site: www.sterlinghillminingmuseum.org
Key Personnel: C.E.O., Bill Kroth; Museum Shop Mgr., Rena Krause.
Institution Type/Description: Mining Museum: former New Jersey zinc company mine; national historic site.
Hours & Admission Prices: March by appointment; April-Nov. daily 10-3; Dec. Sat.-Sun. weather permitting. Adults $12, senior citizens $11, children 4-12 $9; discount to groups of 15 or more with reservations & AAA members; children 3 & under no charge. Closed New Year's Day; Easter; Thanksgiving; Christmas. &
Attendance: 45,000 (actual)

Oradell

HIRAM BLAUVELT ART MUSEUM, 705 Kinderkamack Rd., Oradell, NJ 07649-1504. Mailing Address: P.O. Box 443, Bedminster, NJ 07921. Tel.: 201-261-0012. Fax: 201-391-6418.
E-mail: info@blauveltartmuseum.com
Web Site: www.blauveltartmuseum.com
Key Personnel: Chm. Foundation, James L. Bellis, Sr.; Pres. Foundation, James Bellis, Jr.; Education Coord. & Registrar, Rosa Lara; Artist-in-Residence, Cary Sheeter.
Institution Type/Description: Art Museum: located in an 1893 shingle & turret-style carriage house.
Hours & Admission Prices: Wed.-Fri. 10-4, Sat.-Sun. 2-5. No charge. Closed holidays. ♿
Attendance: 2,000 (estimated)

Oxford

SHIPPEN MANOR, 8 Belvidere Ave., Oxford, NJ 07863-3014. Tel.: 908-453-4381. Fax: 908-453-4981.
E-mail: wcchc@nac.net
Web Site: www.wcchc.org
Key Personnel: Cur., Andy Drysdale.
Institution Type/Description: Historic House: listed on the National Register of Historic Places.
Hours & Admission Prices: Guided Tours: March-Nov. 1st & 3rd Sat. 1-4. No charge; donations accepted. Closed holidays.

Palmyra

PALMYRA COVE NATURE PARK, 1335 Rte. 73, Palmyra, NJ 08065. Tel.: 856-829-1900. Fax: 856-786-6138.
E-mail: KMEROLA@BCBRIDGES.ORG
Web Site: www.palmyracove.org/Home.aspx
Institution Type/Description: Park Museum & Discovery Center.
Hours & Admission Prices: Center: Mon.-Fri. 9-4, Sat.-Sun. 10-4.

Paramus

BERGEN COUNTY ZOOLOGICAL PARK, 216 Forest Ave., Paramus, NJ 07652-5349. Tel.: 201-262-3771. Fax: 201-986-1788.
E-mail: mvella@co.bergen.nj.us
Web Site: www.co.bergen.nj.us/parks/zoo.htm
Key Personnel: Dir., Marianne Vella; Cur. Education, Liz Carletta; Gen. Cur., Cindy Norton.
Institution Type/Description: Zoo.
Hours & Admission Prices: July-Aug. Thurs. 10-8, Fri.-Wed. 10-4:30; Sept.-June daily 10-4:30. Non-Residents: adults 15 & over $8, children 3-14 $5, seniors $2; Residents: adults 15 & over $4, children 3-14 $2, seniors $1; military & Nov.-April no charge. ♿
Attendance: 250,000 (estimated)

BUEHLER CHALLENGER & SCIENCE CENTER, 400 Paramus Rd., Parking Lot G, Paramus, NJ 07652-1508. Mailing Address: P. O. Box 647, Paramus, NJ 07653-0647. Tel.: 201-251-8589. Fax: 201-251-9049.
E-mail: missionservices@bcsc.org
Web Site: www.bcsc.org
Key Personnel: Mission Coord., Peggy Silverman.
Institution Type/Description: Science Museum.
Hours & Admission Prices: Call for further information. ♿

Park Ridge

PASCACK HISTORICAL SOCIETY, 19 Ridge Ave., Park Ridge, NJ 07656-1138. Mailing Address: P.O. Box 85, Park Ridge, NJ 07656-0285. Tel.: 201-573-0307. Fax: 201-666-8226.
E-mail: info@pascackhistoricalsociety.org
Web Site: www.pascackhistoricalsociety.org
Key Personnel: Pres. (V), Jacqueline A. Martin; Editor, Relics Newsletter, Kristin Bonnett Beuscher.
Institution Type/Description: General Museum: local history, housed in 1873 former Congregational Church.
Hours & Admission Prices: Wed. 10 am to noon, Sun. 1-4; other times by appointment. No charge. No charge, donations accepted. ♿
Attendance: 1,500 (estimated)

Paterson

PASSAIC COUNTY COMMUNITY COLLEGE, One College Blvd., Paterson, NJ 07505-1179. Tel.: 973-684-6555. Fax: 973-523-6085.
E-mail: jhaw@pccc.edu
Web Site: www.pccc.edu/art/gallery
Key Personnel: Exec. Dir. Cultural Affairs, Maria Mazziotti Gillan; Gallery Cur., Jane Haw; Assoc. Dir., Susan Balik.
Institution Type/Description: College Museum.
Hours & Admission Prices: June-Aug. Mon.-Thurs. 9-9; Sept.-May Mon.-Fri. 9-9, Sat. 9-5. No charge. ♿
Attendance: 54,000 (estimated)

PASSAIC COUNTY HISTORICAL SOCIETY AT LAMBERT CASTLE MUSEUM, 3 Valley Rd., Paterson, NJ 07503-2932. Tel.: 973-247-0085. Fax: 973-881-9434. Facebook: Passaic County Historical Society.
E-mail: info@lambertcastle.org
Web Site: lambertcastle.org
Key Personnel: Historic Site Mgr. & Cur., Heather Garside.
Institution Type/Description: Historical Society Museum: housed in 1893, Lambert Castle.
Hours & Admission Prices: Museum: Memorial Day to Labor Day Wed.-Sun. 12-4; Sept.-May Wed.-Sun. 1-4. Adults $5, seniors $4, children 5-17 $3; children under 5 & members no charge. ♿
Attendance: 27,500 (estimated)

THE PATERSON MUSEUM, 2 Market St., Ste. 202, Paterson, NJ 07501-1726. Tel.: 973-321-1260. Fax: 973-881-3435.
Key Personnel: Dir., Giacomo R. DeStefano; Cur. History, Bruce Balistrieri; Museum Attendant, Mohamed Khalil.
Institution Type/Description: History, Natural History & Science Museum: housed in 1871, Thomas Rogers Building, locomotive erecting shop.
Hours & Admission Prices: Tues.-Fri. 10-4, Sat.-Sun. 12:30-4:30. Suggested Donation: adults $2; discount to AAM & ICOM members; children no charge. Closed major holidays. ♿
Attendance: 17,500 (estimated)

Paulsboro

TINICUM REAR RANGE LIGHTHOUSE, 70 2nd St., Paulsboro, NJ 08066. Mailing Address: P.O. Box 176, Paulsboro, NJ 08066. Tel.: 856-423-1505.
E-mail: info@tinicumrearrangelighthouse.org
Web Site: www.tinicumrearrangelighthouse.org
Institution Type/Description: Historic Lighthouse: listed on the National Register of Historic Places.
Hours & Admission Prices: April-Oct. 3rd Sun. each month 12-4.

Pemberton

NORTH PEMBERTON RAILROAD STATION MUSEUM AND RAIL TRAIL, 3 Fort Dix Rd., Pemberton, NJ 08068-1439. Mailing Address: 500 Pemberton-Brown Mills Rd., Pemberton, NJ 08068-1539. Tel.: 609-894-0546. Fax: 609-894-0568.
E-mail: pthtrust@yahoo.com
Institution Type/Description: Historic Building: housed in a former railroad station; built in 1892. Listed on the National Register of Historic Sites.
Hours & Admission Prices: Temporarily closed. ♿

Pennington

STONY BROOK MILLSTONE WATERSHED ARBORETUM, 31 Titus Mill Rd., Pennington, NJ 08534. Tel.: 609-737-7592.
E-mail: jwaltman@thewatershed.org
Key Personnel: Exec. Dir., Jim Waltman.
Institution Type/Description: Arboretum.
Hours & Admission Prices: Dawn to dusk.

Penns Grove

HISTORICAL SOCIETY OF PENNS GROVE, CARNEY'S POINT, AND OLDMANS, 48 W. Main St., Penns Grove, NJ 08069. Tel.: 856-299-1556.
Web Site: www.upnhistory.org
Institution Type/Description: Historical Society Museum.
Hours & Admission Prices: March-Dec. Sun. 1-3.

Pennsauken

PENNSAUKEN HISTORICAL SOCIETY, 9201 Burrough Dover Ln., Pennsauken, NJ 08110-1000. Mailing Address: P.O. Box 56, Pennsauken, NJ 08110. Tel.: 856-662-3002.
E-mail: pennsaukenhistoricalsociety@gmail.com
Institution Type/Description: Historical Society Museum: housed in the Burrough-Dover house; built c.1710. Listed on the National Register of Historic Places.
Hours & Admission Prices: Call for hours.

Pennsville

CHURCH LANDING FARMHOUSE, 86 Church Landing Rd., Pennsville, NJ 08070-1203. Tel.: 856-678-4453.
E-mail: wmasten@pennsvillenb.com
Web Site: www.pvhistorical.njcool.net
Institution Type/Description: History Museum.
Hours & Admission Prices: Sun. 1-3; groups by appointment. Adults $2, seniors $1; members no charge.

Perth Amboy

THE KEARNY COTTAGE HISTORICAL ASSOCIATION, 63 Catalpa Ave., Perth Amboy, NJ 08861-4617. Tel.: 732-293-1090, 908-812-4549.
E-mail: kearnycottage@gmail.com
Web Site: www.kearnycottage.org
Formerly: The Kearny Cottage
Key Personnel: C.E.O., Paul W. Wang.
Institution Type/Description: Local History Museum.
Hours & Admission Prices: Mon., Thurs. & last Sun. each month 2-4. Admission by appointment. No charge; donations accepted.
Attendance: 260 (estimated)

PROPRIETARY HOUSE, THE ROYAL GOVERNOR'S MANSION, 149 Kearny Ave., Perth Amboy, NJ 08861-4700. Tel.: 732-826-5527. Fax: 732-826-8889.
E-mail: info@proprietaryhouse.org
Web Site: www.proprietaryhouse.org
Key Personnel: Pres., Lisa Nanton.
Institution Type/Description: Historic Building.
Hours & Admission Prices: Guided Tours: Wed. & Sun. 1-4. No charge; donations accepted. Closed New Year's Day; Easter; Mother's Day; Father's Day; Thanksgiving; Christmas Eve & Day. &
Attendance: 1,000 (estimated)

Phillipsburg

PHILLIPSBURG HISTORICAL SOCIETY, Municipal Bldg., Lower Level, 675 Corliss Ave., Phillipsburg, NJ 08865. Tel.: 908-454-0816.
E-mail: pburghistory@yahoo.com
Web Site: www.pburglib.com
Institution Type/Description: Historical Society Museum.
Hours & Admission Prices: Call for hours.

Piscataway

CORNELIUS LOW HOUSE/MIDDLESEX COUNTY MUSEUM, 1225 River Rd., Piscataway, NJ Mailing Address: 1050 River Rd., Piscataway, NJ 08854. Tel.: 732-745-4177. Fax: 732-745-4507.
E-mail: mark.nonestied@co.middlesex.nj.us
Web Site: www.middlesexcountynj.gov/Government/Departments/BDE/Pages/Office_ArtsandHistory.aspx
Key Personnel: Dept. Head, Business Devel. & Education, Kathaleen Shaw; Div. Head, Historic Sites & History Svcs., Mark Nonestied; Cur. Exhibitions, Katie Zavoski; Museum Educator & Facilities Management, Kenneth M. Helsby.
Institution Type/Description: History Museum & Historic House: housed in a c.1741 Georgian style home featuring a wainscoted central hall, original floors & staircase & Delft-tiled fireplaces.
Hours & Admission Prices: Museum: late April to May & Sept. to early Nov. Wed.-Fri. 10-4, Sat.-Sun. 12-4; June-Aug. Wed. & Fri. 10-4, Thurs. 10-8, Sat.-Sun. 12-4. Office: Mon.-Fri. 8:30-4:15, Sun. 1-4. &

EAST JERSEY OLDE TOWNE VILLAGE, 1050 River Rd., Piscataway, NJ 08855. Tel.: 732-745-3030. Fax: 732-463-1086.
E-mail: Mark.nonestied@co.middlesex.nj.us
Web Site: www.middlesexcountynj.gov/Government/Departments/BDE/Pages/Office_ArtsandHistory.aspx

Key Personnel: Division Head, Mark Nonestied.
Institution Type/Description: Historic Building District: 18th-century village.
Hours & Admission Prices: Village: late April to May & Sept. to early Nov. Wed.-Fri. 10-4, Sat.-Sun. 12-4; June-Aug. Wed. & Fri. 10-4, Thurs. 10-8, Sat.-Sun. 12-4. Office: Mon.-Fri. 8:30-4:15, Sun. 1-4. &
Attendance: 6,000 (estimated)

Plainfield

THE DRAKE HOUSE MUSEUM, 602 W. Front St., Plainfield, NJ 07060-1004. Tel.: 908-755-5831. Fax: 908-755-0132.
E-mail: drakehouseplainfieldnj@gmail.com
Web Site: drakehouseplainfieldnj.org
Key Personnel: Pres. (V), Nancy Piwowar; Chm. (V), Liz Rifino; 1st Vice Pres., Molly Banta; 2nd Vice Pres., Gail Scott Bey; Corresponding Sec., Sandy Gurshman; Museum Shop Mgr., Carlos Cardozo; Office Mgr., Danielle Franklin.
Institution Type/Description: History Museum: housed in 1746 Drake house.
Hours & Admission Prices: Sun. 2-4; other times by appointment. Suggested donation $5; members no charge. Closed holiday weekends. &
Attendance: 1,300 (actual)

Plainsboro

PLAINSBORO MUSEUM - WICOFF HOUSE, 641 Plainsboro Rd., Plainsboro, NJ 08536-2094. Tel.: 609-799-9040.
Institution Type/Description: Historical Society Museum.
Hours & Admission Prices: 1st & 3rd Sun. of the month 2-4:30.

Point Pleasant

NEW JERSEY MUSEUM OF BOATING, Johnson Bros. Boat Works, Bldg. #13, 1800 Bay Ave., Point Pleasant, NJ 08742-4584. Mailing Address: P.O. Box 155, Bay Head, NJ 08742. Tel.: 732-606-7605.
E-mail: kenmotz772@comcast.net
Web Site: njmb.org
Key Personnel: Chm. (V), William Birdsall; Pres. (V), Kenneth J. Motz; Museum Shop Mgr., Jon Palmer.
Institution Type/Description: Boating Museum.
Hours & Admission Prices: March-Nov. Wed.-Sun. 12-4. No charge; donations accepted. &
Attendance: 10,000 (estimated)

Point Pleasant Beach

JENKINSON'S AQUARIUM, 300 Ocean Ave., Point Pleasant Beach, NJ 08742. Tel.: 732-892-0600, ext. 130. Fax: 732-899-1717.
E-mail: jenkinsonsaquarium@comcast.net
Web Site: www.jenkinsons.com/aquarium
Key Personnel: Dir., Cindy Claus.
Institution Type/Description: Aquarium.
Hours & Admission Prices: Summer: daily 10-10; Winter: Mon.-Fri. 9:30-5, Sat.-Sun. 10-5. Adults $12, seniors 62 & over and children 3-12 $7; children 2 & under no charge. Closed New Year's Day; Thanksgiving; Christmas.
Attendance: 220,000 (actual)

Port Norris

BAYSHORE CENTER AT BIVALVE - DELAWARE BAY MUSEUM & FOLKLIFE CENTER, 2800 High St., Port Norris, NJ 08349-3126. Tel.: 856-785-2060. Fax: 856-785-2893.
E-mail: info@bayshorecenter.org
Web Site: www.bayshorecenter.org
Formerly: Bayshore Discovery Project
Key Personnel: Dir., Meghan E. Wren.
Institution Type/Description: Maritime Museum.
Hours & Admission Prices: Tues.-Sat. 11-4. Suggested Donations: adults $7, military $5. &

Princeton

DRUMTHWACKET - GOVERNORS MANSION, 354 Stockton St., Princeton, NJ 08540. Tel.: 609-683-0057.
E-mail: info@drumthwacket.org
Web Site: www.drumthwacket.org
Institution Type/Description: Historic Building: housed in the official residence of New Jersey governors.
Hours & Admission Prices: By appointment.

HISTORICAL SOCIETY OF PRINCETON, 354 Quaker Rd., Princeton, NJ 08540-4838. Tel.: 609-921-6748. Fax: 609-921-6939.
E-mail: information@princetonhistory.org
Web Site: www.princetonhistory.org
Key Personnel: Exec. Dir., Izzy Kasdin; Pres., Scott Sipprelle.
Institution Type/Description: History Museum: housed at the historic Updike Farmstead.
Hours & Admission Prices: Museum: Wed. & Fri.-Sun. 12-4, Thurs. 12-7. Adults $4; Thurs. 4-7 pm & members no charge. Closed New Year's Day; Easter; Independence Day; Thanksgiving; Christmas Eve & Day. &
Attendance: 18,500 (actual)

MORVEN MUSEUM & GARDEN, 55 Stockton St., Princeton, NJ 08540-6812. Tel.: 609-924-8144. Fax: 609-924-8331.
E-mail: info@morven.org
Web Site: www.morven.org
Formerly: Historic Morven
Key Personnel: Dir., Jill Barry; Pres. (V), Robert Wilson; Cur. Exhibitions, Elizabeth Allan; Museum Shop Mgr., Kathy O'Hara.
Institution Type/Description: Historic House Museum: former home of five New Jersey governors and a signer of the Declaration of Independence.
Hours & Admission Prices: Wed.-Sun. 10-4. Adults $10; seniors 60 & older and students $8; discounts to members. Closed New Year's Day; Independence Day; Thanksgiving; Christmas. &
Attendance: 15,000 (estimated)

PRINCETON UNIVERSITY ART MUSEUM, McCormack Hall, Princeton, NJ 08544-1018. Tel.: 609-258-3788. Fax: 609-258-3610.
E-mail: artmuseum@princeton.edu
Web Site: artmuseum.princeton.edu
Formerly: The Art Museum, Princeton University
Key Personnel: Dir., James C. Steward; Diane W. & James E. Burke Assoc. Dir. for Education, Caroline Harris; Assoc. Dir. Fin. & Operations, Karen Ohland; Assoc. Dir. Museum Development, Sally Bickerton; Assoc. Dir. Communications & Information, Stephen J. Kim; Assoc. Dir. Collections & Exhibitions, Chris Newth.
Institution Type/Description: Art Museum.
Hours & Admission Prices: Tues.-Wed. & Fri.-Sat. 10-5, Thurs. 10-9, Sun. 12-5. No charge; donations accepted. Closed national holidays. &
Attendance: 150,229 (actual)

PRINCETON UNIVERSITY MUSEUM OF NATURAL HISTORY, Princeton University, Guyot Hall, Princeton, NJ 08544. Mailing Address: 9 Eno Hall, Princeton University, Princeton, NJ 08544-0430. Tel.: 609-258-4102 & 3832. Fax: 609-258-1334.
E-mail: ehorn@princeton.edu
Key Personnel: Cur. Biological Collections, Elizabeth Horn.
Institution Type/Description: Natural History Museum.
Hours & Admission Prices: Open by appointment only. &
Attendance: 500 (estimated)

THOMAS CLARKE HOUSE/PRINCETON BATTLEFIELD STATE PARK, 500 Mercer Rd., Princeton, NJ 08540-4810. Tel.: 609-921-0074. Fax: 609-921-0074.
E-mail: pbsp@aol.com
Key Personnel: Cur., John K. Mills.
Institution Type/Description: Historic House: c.1772 Quaker Farm, field hospital after Battle of Princeton.
Hours & Admission Prices: Wed.-Sat. 10-12 & 1-4, Sun. 1-4. No charge; donations accepted. Closed New Year's Day; Thanksgiving; Christmas. &
Attendance: 90,000 (estimated)

Rahway

MERCHANT AND DROVERS TAVERN MUSEUM, 1632 St. Georges Ave., Rahway, NJ 07065-2006. Mailing Address: P.O. Box 1842, Rahway, NJ 07065-7842. Tel.: 732-381-0441.
E-mail: mdtavernmuseum@gmail.com
Web Site: www.merchantanddrovers.org
Key Personnel: Pres., Annette Satkowski; Vice Pres., Joseph Carpenter; Dir. Museum Operations, Alex Shipley; Program Mgr., Lisa Michaloski.
Institution Type/Description: Historic Building: built in c.1795. Listed on the National Register of Historic Places.
Hours & Admission Prices: Thurs.-Fri., and 1st & 3rd Sat. of month 10-4, 2nd & 4th Sun. of month 1-4; other times by appointment. Adults $5, members $4. &
Attendance: 2,300 (actual)

Randolph

HISTORICAL SOCIETY OF OLD RANDOLPH, 630 Millbrook Ave., Randolph, NJ 07869-3730. Mailing Address: P.O. Box 1776, Ironia, NJ 07845-1776. Tel.: 973-989-7095.
E-mail: hsor@juno.com
Web Site: www.randolphnj.org/get_to_know_us/historical_society
Key Personnel: Museum Shop Mgr., Joan Brembs.
Institution Type/Description: Historical Society Museum: housed in an 1860 farmhouse.
Hours & Admission Prices: early April to late Oct. Sun. 1-4; tours & other times by appointment. Adults $2; discounts to AAM & ICOM members; members no charge.
Attendance: 1,500 (estimated)

Readington

COLD BROOK SCHOOL, Potterstown Rd., Readington, NJ 08870. Mailing Address: 314 Rte. 12 County Complex, Bldg. #1, Planning Dept., P.O. Box 2900, Flemington, NJ 08822. Tel.: 908-236-2327. Fax: 908-236-2306.
E-mail: readingtonmuseums@gmail.com
Web Site: readingtontwp.org/ReadingtonMuseums/
Key Personnel: Program Dir., Margaret Smith.
Institution Type/Description: Historic Building: housed in a one-room school house, built in 1828.
Hours & Admission Prices: Call for hours.

Ridgewood

SCHOOLHOUSE MUSEUM OF THE RIDGEWOOD HISTORICAL SOCIETY, INC., 650 E. Glen Ave., Ridgewood, NJ 07450-1905. Tel.: 201-447-3242.
E-mail: ridgewoodhistoricalsociety@verizon.net
Web Site: www.ridgewoodhistoricalsociety.org
Key Personnel: Pres., Candace Latham.
Institution Type/Description: History Museum.
Hours & Admission Prices: Feb.-July & Sept.-Dec. Thurs. & Sat. 1-3, Sun. 2-4. Suggested Donation: adults $5. Closed Easter; Thanksgiving; Christmas.
Attendance: 800 (estimated)

Ringwood

NEW JERSEY BOTANICAL GARDEN AT SKYLANDS (NJBG), Morris Rd., Ringwood, NJ 07456. Mailing Address: P.O. Box 302, Ringwood, NJ 07456-0302. Tel.: 973-962-9534 & 7527. Fax: 973-962-1553.
E-mail: info@njbg.org
Web Site: www.njbg.org
Key Personnel: Pres., Dorothy Gall; Treas., Schuyler Jenks; Landscape Designer, Rich Flynn; Park Supvr., Eric Pain; Museum Shop Mgr., Sonja Vieth.
Institution Type/Description: Historic House & Site: 44-room Tudor-style manor house & 96-acre botanical garden.
Hours & Admission Prices: Gardens: daily 8-8. No charge. Manor House Tours: selected Sun. Adults $7, senior citizens $5, children 6-18 $3; children under 6 no charge.
Attendance: 98,000 (estimated)

RINGWOOD MANOR, Ringwood State Park, 1304 Sloatsburg Rd., Ringwood, NJ 07456-1706. Tel.: 973-962-2240. Fax: 973-962-2247. Facebook.
E-mail: rspris@verizon.net
Web Site: www.ringwoodmanor.org
Formerly: The Forges and Manor of Ringwood
Key Personnel: Supt., Eric Pain; Historic Preservationist, Sue Shutte; Museum Shop Mgr., Ralph Colfax.
Institution Type/Description: Historic House Museum.
Hours & Admission Prices: Wed.-Sun. 10-4. Adults $3, children 6-12 $1; children 5 & under no charge. Closed New Year's Day; Good Friday; Thanksgiving; Christmas. &
Attendance: 15,000 (actual)

River Edge

BERGEN COUNTY HISTORICAL SOCIETY, 1201-1209 Main St., River Edge, NJ 07661-2026. Mailing Address: P.O. Box 55, River Edge, NJ 07661-9998. Tel.: 201-343-9492.
E-mail: contactbchs@bergencountyhistory.org
Web Site: www.bergencountyhistory.org

Institution Type/Description: Local History Museum: housed in c.1713, 1752 Steuben House.
Hours & Admission Prices: Call for hours. Events by donation: adult $7, children $5. BCHS members no charge. Closed New Year's Day; Thanksgiving; Christmas. &
Attendance: 15,000

RIVER EDGE CULTURAL CENTER, 201 Continental Ave., River Edge, NJ 07661. Mailing Address: P.O. Box 416, River Edge, NJ 07661. Tel.: 201-634-0158.
E-mail: dunsay@juno.com
Web Site: www.recultural.org
Institution Type/Description: Cultural Center.
Hours & Admission Prices: Call for hours.

Roebling

ROEBLING MUSEUM, 100 Second Ave., Roebling, NJ 08554. Mailing Address: P.O. Box 9, Roebling, NJ 08554. Tel.: 609-499-7200. Fax: 609-499-7201.
E-mail: rmuseum@roeblingmuseum.org
Web Site: roeblingmuseum.org
Key Personnel: Exec. Dir., John Seitter; Pres. (V), Karl Darby.
Institution Type/Description: History Museum.
Hours & Admission Prices: April-Aug. Wed.-Sun. 11-4; Sept.-Dec. Thurs.-Sun. 11-4; other times by appointment. Adults $6, seniors & children 6-12 $5; members & children under 6 no charge. Closed New Year's Day; Thanksgiving; Christmas. &
Attendance: 5,000 (actual)

Roseland

ROSELAND HISTORICAL SOCIETY - THE HARRISON HOUSE, 126 Eagle Rock Ave., Roseland, NJ 07068. Mailing Address: P.O. Box 152, Roseland, NJ 07068. Tel.: 973-228-0742.
E-mail: info@roselandhistsocnj.org
Web Site: www.roselandhistsocnj.org
Institution Type/Description: Historical Society Museum: house built in 1824. Listed on the National and State Registers of Historic Places.
Hours & Admission Prices: Call for hours.

Roselle Park

ROSELLE PARK MUSEUM, 9 W. Grant Ave., Roselle Park, NJ 07204-1915. Tel.: 908-245-1776. Facebook.
E-mail: info@roselleparkhistoricalsociety.org
Web Site: roselleparkhistoricalsociety.com
Key Personnel: Pres., Patricia Butler.
Institution Type/Description: History Museum.
Hours & Admission Prices: Wed. 10-1. No charge; donations accepted.
Attendance: 1,020 (estimated)

Rutherford

MEADOWLANDS MUSEUM, 91 Crane Ave., Rutherford, NJ 07070-2539. Tel.: 201-935-1175.
E-mail: meadowlandsmuseum@verizon.net
Web Site: www.meadowlandsmuseum.com
Key Personnel: Bd. Pres., Robin Reenstra, Ph.D.
Institution Type/Description: Local History Museum: housed in Dutch Colonial farm house.
Hours & Admission Prices: Sat. 10-4; groups by appointment. Suggested donation: adults $5, children $3. Closed New Year's Day; Memorial Day; Independence Day; Labor Day; Thanksgiving; Christmas.
Attendance: 2,500 (estimated)

Salem

PSEG ENERGY & ENVIRONMENTAL RESOURCE CENTER, 244 Chestnut St., Salem, NJ 08079. Tel.: 856-339-3372.
E-mail: eerc@pseg.com
Web Site: www.pseg.com/family/power/eerc/index.jsp
Institution Type/Description: Energy Learning Center: housed in the former Nuclear Training Center.
Hours & Admission Prices: By appointment.

SALEM CITY FIRE MUSEUM, 166 E. Broadway, Salem, NJ 08079. Tel.: 856-362-1550.
Institution Type/Description: Fire Museum: housed in Union Fire Company's second firehouse; built in 1863.

Hours & Admission Prices: By appointment.

SALEM COUNTY HISTORICAL SOCIETY, 83 Market St., Salem, NJ 08079-1910. Tel.: 856-935-5004. Fax: 856-935-0728. Facebook: Salem County Historical Society.
E-mail: info@salemcountyhistoricalsociety.com
Web Site: www.salemcountyhistoricalsociety.com
Key Personnel: Pres., Barbara Smith Duffy; Administrative Librarian, Richard Guido; Admin. & Cur., Andrew Coldren.
Institution Type/Description: Historic Building, Site & History Museum.
Hours & Admission Prices: Tues.-Sat. 12-4. Adults $5; discounts to WHYY, AAA, AAM & ICOM members; members no charge. &
Attendance: 16,000 (estimated)

Scotch Plains

OSBORN CANNONBALL HOUSE, 1840 Front St., Scotch Plains, NJ 07076-1103. Mailing Address: P.O. Box 261, Scotch Plains, NJ 07076. Tel.: 908-322-6700, ext. 230.
Web Site: www.historicalsocietyspfnj.org
Key Personnel: Cur., Judy Terry; Pres. (V), Dave Bierman.
Institution Type/Description: Historic House: housed in the former home of Jonathan & Abigail Osborn; built c.1760.
Hours & Admission Prices: March-Dec. 1st Sun. of month 2-4; other times by appointment. No charge.
Attendance: 800 (estimated)

Sea Girt

NATIONAL GUARD MILITIA MUSEUM OF NEW JERSEY - SEA GIRT, National Guard Training Center, Rte. 71 & Sea Girt Ave., Sea Girt, NJ 08750. Mailing Address: P.O. Box 277, Sea Girt, NJ 08750-0277. Tel.: 732-974-5966.
Institution Type/Description: Military Heritage Museum.
Hours & Admission Prices: Tues. & Thurs. 10-3; other times by appointment. No charge; donations accepted.
Attendance: 3,141 (actual)

SEA GIRT LIGHTHOUSE, Beacon & Ocean Ave., Sea Girt, NJ 08750. Mailing Address: Sea Girt Lighthouse Citizens Committee, P.O. Box 83, Sea Girt, NJ 08750-0083. Tel.: 732-974-0514.
E-mail: support@seagirtlighthouse.com
Web Site: www.seagirtlighthouse.com
Institution Type/Description: Historic Building: housed in a live-in lighthouse; built in 1896.
Hours & Admission Prices: mid-April to Nov. 20 Sun. 2-4; other times by appointment.

Sea Isle City

SEA ISLE CITY HISTORICAL MUSEUM, 4800 Central Ave., Sea Isle City, NJ 08243. Mailing Address: P.O. Box 443, Sea Isle City, NJ 08243-0743. Tel.: 609-263-2992.
E-mail: seaislemuseum@outlook.com
Key Personnel: Acting Dir. & Pres. (V), Michael Stafford.
Institution Type/Description: Historical Museum.
Hours & Admission Prices: Mon.-Sat. 10-3. Donations accepted. &
Attendance: 10,000 (actual)

Seabrook

SEABROOK EDUCATIONAL AND CULTURAL CENTER, Upper Deerfield Twsp. Municipal Bldg., 1325 Hwy. 77, Seabrook, NJ 08302-5976. Tel.: 856-451-8393.
E-mail: seabrookhistory@gmail.com
Web Site: www.seabrookeducation.org
Institution Type/Description: History Museum.
Hours & Admission Prices: Mon.-Thurs. 9-12. No charge.
Attendance: 400 (estimated)

Short Hills

CORA HARTSHORN ARBORETUM AND BIRD SANCTUARY, 324 Forest Dr. S., Short Hills, NJ 07078-2308. Tel.: 973-376-3587. Fax: 973-379-5059.
E-mail: info@hartshornarboretum.com
Web Site: www.hartshornarboretum.com
Key Personnel: Dir., Tedor Whitman.
Institution Type/Description: Nature Center.

Hours & Admission Prices: Gardens & Grounds: dawn to dusk. Stone House: Mon.-Fri. 9-4:30, Sat.-Sun. 10-4. No charge; donations accepted. Closed New Year's Eve & Day; Christmas Eve, Day & week. &

MILLBURN-SHORT HILLS HISTORICAL SOCIETY, One Station Plaza, Short Hills, NJ 07078. Mailing Address: P.O. Box 243, Short Hills, NJ 07078. Tel.: 973-564-9519. Fax: 973-564-9519 (call first).
E-mail: mshhs@comcast.net
Web Site: www.mshhistsoc.org
Institution Type/Description: Historical Society Museum: housed in the Short Hills train station.
Hours & Admission Prices: Tues. 1-3, Wed. 3:30-5:30, Thurs. 5:30-7:30, 1st Sun. each month 2-4. No charge.

Shrewsbury

SHREWSBURY HISTORICAL SOCIETY MUSEUM, EDUCATION & RESEARCH CENTER, 419 Sycamore Ave., Shrewsbury, NJ 07702-0333. Mailing Address: P.O. Box 333, Shrewsbury, NJ 07702-0333. Tel.: 732-530-7974.
E-mail: donaldburden@verizon.net
Key Personnel: Pres., Donald W. Burden.
Institution Type/Description: Historical Society Museum.
Hours & Admission Prices: By appointment. No charge; donations accepted. &
Attendance: 384 (actual)

Somers Point

ATLANTIC COUNTY HISTORICAL SOCIETY, 907 Shore Rd., Somers Point, NJ 08244-0301. Mailing Address: P.O. Box 301, Somers Point, NJ 08244-0301. Tel.: 609-927-5218. Facebook.
E-mail: achsinfo@comcast.net
Web Site: www.atlanticcountyhistoricalsocietynj.org
Formerly: Atlantic Heritage Center
Key Personnel: Pres., Sid Parker; Cur., Joan Frankel; Librarian, Norman Goos.
Institution Type/Description: History Museum.
Hours & Admission Prices: Museum: temporarily closed. Library: Wed.-Sat. 10-3:30. Research: $5; members no charge. Closed New Year's Day; Good Friday & day after; Independence Day; Thanksgiving; Christmas. &
Attendance: 2,500

SOMERS MANSION, 1000 Shore Rd., Somers Point, NJ 08244. Mailing Address: 907 Shore Rd., Somers Point, NJ 08244. Tel.: 609-927-2212. Fax: 609-927-1827.
Key Personnel: Resource Interpretive Specialist-Historic Research, John Morsa.
Institution Type/Description: Historic House: 1720 Richard Somers House.
Hours & Admission Prices: Wed.-Sun. 10-12 & 1-4. No charge. Closed New Year's Day; Thanksgiving; Christmas.
Attendance: 3,500 (actual)

Somerset

COLONIAL PARK ARBORETUM AND GARDENS, 150 Mettlers Rd., Somerset, NJ 08873. Tel.: 732-873-2459.
E-mail: jvanpelt@scparks.org
Web Site: www.somersetcountyparks.org
Institution Type/Description: Arboretum & Gardens.
Hours & Admission Prices: Daily sunrise to sunset. No charge.

THE MEADOWS FOUNDATION - WYCKOFF-GARRETSON HOUSE, 215 S. Middlebush Rd., Somerset, NJ 08873. Mailing Address: P.O. Box 6321, Somerset, NJ 08873-6321. Tel.: 732-560-1977.
E-mail: info@themeadowsfoundation.org
Web Site: www.themeadowsfoundation.org
Institution Type/Description: Historic House Museum.
Hours & Admission Prices: Call for hours.

UKRAINIAN MUSEUM OF NEW JERSEY, INC., 135 Davidson Ave., Somerset, NJ 08873-1358. Tel.: 732-356-0090.
E-mail: info@UkrHEC.org
Web Site: www.ukrhec.org
Formerly: Museum of the Ukrainian Orthodox Memorial Church
Key Personnel: Dir., Archbishop Antony.
Institution Type/Description: Religious Museum.
Hours & Admission Prices: Call for hours.

Somerville

OLD DUTCH PARSONAGE, 71 Somerset St., Somerville, NJ 08876-2812. Tel.: 908-725-1015.
Key Personnel: Cur., Jim Kurzenberger.
Institution Type/Description: Historic House: 1751 old Dutch parsonage, home of Jacob Hardenbergh, founder of Rutgers University and its first president.
Hours & Admission Prices: Wed.-Sat. 10-12 & 1-4, Sun. 1-4; groups by appointment. No charge. Closed federal & state holidays.
Attendance: 5,000

SOMERVILLE FIRE DEPARTMENT MUSEUM, 15 N. Doughty Ave., Somerville, NJ 08876. Mailing Address: 25 West End Ave., Somerville, NJ 08876. Tel.: 908-526-7098 & 4828.
E-mail: mpellegrino@somervillefd.org
Institution Type/Description: History Museum.
Hours & Admission Prices: Sat. 10am-12pm; other times by appointment. No charge; donations accepted.
Attendance: 200 (estimated)

WALLACE HOUSE, 71 Somerset St., Somerville, NJ 08876-2812. Tel.: 908-725-1015.
E-mail: kerry.pflugh@dep.nj.gov
Key Personnel: Cur., Jim Kurzenberger.
Institution Type/Description: Historic House: 1778 Wallace House, Washington's headquarters during winter of 1778-79.
Hours & Admission Prices: Wed.-Sat. 10-12 & 1-4, Sun. 1-4. Groups of 10 or more by appointment only; school groups limited to 30 students at a time. Closed federal & state holidays.
Attendance: 5,000

South Orange

WALSH GALLERY, SETON HALL UNIVERSITY, 400 S. Orange Ave., South Orange, NJ 07079-2697. Tel.: 973-275-2033. Fax: 973-761-9550.
E-mail: jeanne.brasile@shu.edu
Web Site: library.shu.edu/gallery
Key Personnel: Dir., Jeanne Brasile.
Institution Type/Description: Art Gallery.
Hours & Admission Prices: Mon.-Fri. 10:30-4:30; call to confirm.

South River

SOUTH RIVER MUSEUM - OLD SCHOOL BAPTIST CHURCH, 64-66 Main St., South River, NJ 08882. Mailing Address: South River Historical & Preservation Society, Inc., P.O. Box 446, South River, NJ 08882. Tel.: 732-613-3078. Facebook.
E-mail: southriverhistory@gmail.com
Web Site: www.southriverhistory.org
Key Personnel: Pres. (V), Nan Whitehead.
Institution Type/Description: Historical & Preservation Society Museum: housed in a former Baptist church; built in 1805. Listed on the National & NJ Register of Historic Places.
Hours & Admission Prices: 1st Sun. each month 1:30-3:30, (2nd Sun. if the first is a holiday). No charge; donations accepted. &
Attendance: 300 (estimated)

Southampton

JACK ALLEN MEMORIAL EARLY COUNTY LIVING MUSEUM, 224 Landing St., Southampton, NJ 08088-8823. Tel.: 609-267-8382. Fax: 609-267-8382. Facebook.
E-mail: rallen2311@verizon.net
Web Site: www.jackallenmuseum.org
Institution Type/Description: History Museum.
Hours & Admission Prices: May-Oct. Sun. 1-4. Adults $3.

Sparta

FRIAR MOUNTAIN MODEL RAILROAD MUSEUM, 240 Demarest Rd., Sparta, NJ 07871. Tel.: 973-579-9833.
E-mail: wendy@fmmrm.com
Web Site: www.fmmrm.com
Institution Type/Description: Model Railroad Museum.
Hours & Admission Prices: Fri.-Sun. 10-5. Admission $6. &

Spring Lake

SPRING LAKE HISTORICAL SOCIETY, 423 Warren Ave., Spring Lake, NJ 07762. Mailing Address: P.O. Box 703, Spring Lake, NJ 07762. Tel.: 732-449-0772.
E-mail: djlau34@aol.com
Web Site: springlake.org
Key Personnel: Pres. (V), Mary Lou Oliva; Office Mgr., Nancy Smith.
Institution Type/Description: Historical Society Museum: housed in Spring Lake's Borough Hall; built in 1897.
Hours & Admission Prices: Thurs. & Sun. call for hours; other times by appointment. No charge. &
Attendance: 400 (estimated)

Springfield

SPRINGFIELD HISTORICAL SOCIETY, 126 Morris Ave., Springfield, NJ 07081. Mailing Address: 166 Milltown Rd., Springfield, NJ 07081-2313. Tel.: 973-376-4784 & 912-4464.
Web Site: www.springfield-nj.us/index.php?page=history
Institution Type/Description: Local History Museum: housed in The Cannon Ball House: built c.1741. Listed on the National Register of Historic Places.
Hours & Admission Prices: Call for hours. Closed holidays.
Attendance: 50 (estimated)

Stanton

BOUMAN-STICKNEY FARMSTEAD, 114 Dreahook Rd., Stanton, NJ 08885. Mailing Address: P.O. Box 216, Stanton, NJ 08885-0216. Tel.: 908-236-2327. Fax: 908-236-2306.
E-mail: readingtonmuseums@gmail.com
Web Site: www.readingtontwp.org/ReadingtonMuseums/
Key Personnel: Program Dir., Margaret Smith.
Institution Type/Description: Historic Buildings.
Hours & Admission Prices: Call for hours. No charge; donations accepted.
Attendance: 1,124 (estimated)

Stone Harbor

STONE HARBOR BIRD SANCTUARY, 11400 3rd Ave., Stone Harbor, NJ 08247. Tel.: 609-368-5102.
E-mail: info@stoneharborbirdsanctuary.org
Institution Type/Description: Wildlife Sanctuary.
Hours & Admission Prices: Call for hours.

THE WETLANDS INSTITUTE, 1075 Stone Harbor Blvd., Stone Harbor, NJ 08247-1424. Tel.: 609-368-1211. Fax: 609-368-3871.
E-mail: ltedesco@wetlandsinstitute.org
Web Site: www.wetlandsinstitute.org
Key Personnel: Exec. Dir., Dr. Lenore Tedesco; Chm., Raymond Burke.
Institution Type/Description: Nature Center.
Hours & Admission Prices: mid-May to mid-Oct. Mon.-Sat. 9:30-4:30, Sun. 10-4; mid-Oct. to mid-May Fri.-Sun. 9:30-4:30. Adults $8, children under 12 $6; discounts to seniors, military & groups; members no charge. Closed national holidays & two weeks at Christmas. &
Attendance: 50,000 (estimated)

Summit

THE CARTER HOUSE, 90 Butler Pkwy., Summit, NJ 07901-1617. Mailing Address: P.O. Box 464, Summit, NY 07902-0464. Tel.: 908-277-1747.
E-mail: president@summitnjhistory.org
Web Site: www.summitnjhistory.org
Key Personnel: Pres., Patricia E. Meola.
Institution Type/Description: Historic House: former home of Benjamin Carter; built in 1741.
Hours & Admission Prices: Sept.-June Tues. 9 am to noon, Wed. 1-4; other times by appointment. No charge.
Attendance: 1,500 (estimated)

REEVES-REED ARBORETUM, 165 Hobart Ave., Summit, NJ 07901-2908. Tel.: 908-273-8787. Fax: 908-273-6869.
E-mail: reevesreedarboretum@juno.com
Web Site: www.reeves-reedarboretum.org
Key Personnel: Exec. Dir., Gayle Petty-Johnson.
Institution Type/Description: Arboretum & Botanical Garden.

Hours & Admission Prices: Grounds & Visitor Center: April-Oct. daily 7-7; Nov.-March daily 9-4. Education Center: March-Nov. Tues.-Fri. 10-4, Sat. 9-1. Wisner House: Tues.-Fri. 10-4. No charge; donations accepted. &
Attendance: 46,003 (actual)

VISUAL ARTS CENTER OF NEW JERSEY, 68 Elm St., Summit, NJ 07901-3472. Tel.: 908-273-9121. Fax: 908-273-1457. Facebook: @VisualArtsCenterofNewJersey; Twitter & Instagram: @artcenternj.
E-mail: info@artcenternj.org
Web Site: www.artcenternj.org
Formerly: New Jersey Center for Visual Arts
Key Personnel: Exec. Dir., Melanie Cohn; Dir. Operations, Ernie Palatucci; Chm. Bd. Trustees, Marie Cohn.
Institution Type/Description: Visual Arts Center.
Hours & Admission Prices: Gallery: Mon.-Thurs. 10-8, Fri. 10-5, Sat.-Sun. 11-4; tours by appointment. Suggested Donation: adults $5, seniors & children $3; discounts to AAM & ICOM members; members, seniors & children under 12 no charge. Closed New Year's Eve & Day; Martin Luther King Jr. Day; Easter; Memorial Day; Independence Day; Labor Day; Columbus Day; Thanksgiving & day after; Christmas Eve & Day. &
Attendance: 30,000 (estimated)

Sussex

DAR VAN BUNSCHOOTEN MUSEUM, 1097 Rte. 23, Wantage, NJ 07461. Tel.: 973-875-4058 & 7634.
E-mail: bmatthews2564@hotmail.com
Key Personnel: Cur., Judy Smith; Regent, Bonnie Matthews; Museum Shop Mgr., Diana Matties.
Institution Type/Description: Historic House Museum: housed in the former home of Rev. Elias Van Bunschooten; built in 1787. Listed on the National Register of Historic Places.
Hours & Admission Prices: May-Oct. 2nd & 4th Sun. each month 1-4; groups by appointment. Adults $4, children $2; discounts to seniors on Thurs. & groups of 10 or more.
Attendance: 1,100 (estimated)

SPACE FARMS ZOO AND MUSEUM, 218 County Rd. 519, Sussex, NJ 07461-2800. Tel.: 973-875-3223. Fax: 973-875-9397.
E-mail: info@spacefarms.com
Web Site: www.spacefarms.com
Key Personnel: C.E.O., Parker Space; Museum Shop Mgr., Jill Space.
Institution Type/Description: General Museum and Zoo.
Hours & Admission Prices: April-Oct. daily 9-5. Adults $18, seniors 65 & over $16.50, children 3-12 $14.50; discounts to groups; children under 3 no charge. &
Attendance: 80,000 (actual)

Teaneck

PUFFIN CULTURAL FORUM, 20 Puffin Way, Teaneck, NJ 07666. Tel.: 201-836-3499.
E-mail: info@puffinfoundation.org
Web Site: www.puffinculturalforum.org
Key Personnel: Dir., Andrew Lee.
Institution Type/Description: Arts & Cultural Center.
Hours & Admission Prices: Tues.-Thurs. 12-4; other times by appointment.

Tenafly

AFRICAN ART MUSEUM OF THE S.M.A. FATHERS, 23 Bliss Ave., Tenafly, NJ 07670-3001. Tel.: 201-894-8611. Fax: 201-541-1280.
E-mail: museum@smafathers.org
Web Site: www.smafathers.org
Key Personnel: Pres., Rev. Michael Moran, S.M.A.; Dir., Robert J. Koenig; Registrar & Collections Mgr., Peter H. Cade.
Institution Type/Description: African Art Museum: located at the Society of African Missions, American Provincialate.
Hours & Admission Prices: Daily 10-5; group tours by appointment. No charge; donations accepted. Closed national & religious holidays. &
Attendance: 3,000 (estimated)

Teterboro

AVIATION HALL OF FAME AND MUSEUM OF NEW JERSEY, 400 Fred Wehran Dr., Teterboro, NJ 07608-1114. Tel.: 201-288-6344. Fax: 201-288-5666. Facebook: NJ Aviation Hall of Fame.
E-mail: njahof@verizon.net

Web Site: www.njahof.org
Key Personnel: Exec. Dir., Ralph C. Villecca, Sr.
Institution Type/Description: Aviation Museum.
Hours & Admission Prices: Tues.-Sun. 10-4. Adults $9, senior citizens & children
   $7. &
Attendance: 6,000 (actual)

Titusville

JOHNSON FERRY HOUSE MUSEUM, Washington Crossing
   State Park, 355 Washington Crossing Penn Rd., Titusville, NJ
   08560-1517. Tel.: 609-737-2515. TDD: 609-737-0623.
E-mail: nancy.ceperley@dep.nj.gov
Key Personnel: JFH - Resource Interpretive Specialist, Nancy Carter Ceperley; VC
   - Resource Interpretive Specialist, Clay Craighead.
Institution Type/Description: Historic Building Museum & Visitor Center; housed
   in a c.1740, ferry house in which George Washington & his officers met after
   crossing the Delaware River & before the march to Trenton.
Hours & Admission Prices: Ferry House: Wed.-Sat. 10-4, Sun. 1-4; groups by
   appointment only. No charge; donations accepted. Parking Fee: Memorial Day-
   Labor Day Sat.-Sun. $7 per car. Closed New Year's Day; Thanksgiving;
   Christmas. &
Attendance: 12,000 (actual)

Toms River

**CATTUS ISLAND COUNTY PARK - COOPER
   ENVIRONMENTAL CENTER,** 1170 Cattus Island Blvd., Toms
   River, NJ 08753. Tel.: 732-270-6960. Fax: 732-831-0406.
   Facebook.
E-mail: OCParks@co.ocean.nj.us
Web Site: www.ocparks.org
Institution Type/Description: Environmental Center.
Hours & Admission Prices: Park: daily dawn to dusk. Center: daily 8-4:30. &
Attendance: 20,000 (actual)

INSECTROPOLIS, 1761 Rte. 9, Toms River, NJ 08755-1296. Tel.:
   732-349-7090.
E-mail: info@insectropolis.com
Web Site: www.insectropolis.com
Key Personnel: Pres., Thomas Koerner.
Institution Type/Description: Bug Museum.
Hours & Admission Prices: Tues.-Sat. 10-3. Admission $7; discounts to groups of
   15 or more; children under 3 no charge. Closed holidays.

OCEAN COUNTY HISTORICAL SOCIETY, 26 Hadley Ave.,
   Toms River, NJ 08753-7540. Tel.: 732-341-1880. Fax: 732-341-
   4372. Facebook: Ocean County Historical Society.
E-mail: oceancounty.history@verizon.net
Web Site: www.oceancountyhistory.org
Key Personnel: Pres. & C.E.O., Franklin A. Reusch, Jr.; Museum Clerk, Donna
   Davis; Museum Shop Mgr., Ora Parks; Recording Sec., Kim Fleischer.
Institution Type/Description: History Museum.
Hours & Admission Prices: Office & Polly Miller exhibit room: Tues.-Fri. 9:30-4,
   1st Sat. of month 1-4; tours by appointment. Research Facilities: Tues.-Wed. &
   1st Sat. of month 1-4. Tours: no charge. Programs may require a fee; veterans
   no charge. &
Attendance: 5,000 (estimated)

**ROBERT J. NOVINS PLANETARIUM - OCEAN COUNTY
   COLLEGE,** College Dr., Rm. 100, Toms River, NJ 08754.
   Mailing Address: College Dr., P.O. Box 2001, Toms River, NJ
   08754-2001. Tel.: 732-255-0342 & 0343.
E-mail: planetarium@ocean.edu
Web Site: www.ocean.edu/campus/planetarium/index.htm
Institution Type/Description: Planetarium.
Hours & Admission Prices: Call for hours. &

TOMS RIVER SEAPORT SOCIETY & MARITIME MUSEUM,
   78 E. Water St., Toms River, NJ 08753-7554. Mailing Address: P.
   O. Box 1111, Toms River, NJ 08754-1111. Tel.: 732-349-9209.
   Fax: 732-349-2498.
E-mail: tomsriverssmm@yahoo.com
Web Site: www.tomsriverseaport.org
Key Personnel: Pres., Dan Crabbe.
Institution Type/Description: Maritime Museum.
Hours & Admission Prices: Tues., Thurs. & Sat. 10-2. No charge; donations
   accepted.
Attendance: 1,200 (estimated)

VIRGINIA PERLE ART GALLERY, 96 E. Water St., Toms River,
   NJ 08753. Tel.: 732-244-4300.
E-mail: virginiaperleartgallery@yahoo.com
Institution Type/Description: Art Gallery.
Hours & Admission Prices: Wed.-Sat. 12-4; other times by appointment.

Trenton

MEREDITH HAVENS FIRE MUSEUM OF TRENTON, Trenton
   Fire Dept. Headquarters, 244 Perry St., 1st Fl., Trenton, NJ 08618-
   3926. Tel.: 609-989-4038. Fax: 609-989-4280.
E-mail: firemuseum@trentonnj.org
Web Site: trentonfiremuseum.org
Key Personnel: Dir., Dennis M. Keenan.
Institution Type/Description: Fire Museum.
Hours & Admission Prices: Mon.-Fri. 9-5, Sat. 10-4; groups of 10 or more by
   appointment. &
Attendance: 700 (estimated)

NEW JERSEY OFFICE OF HISTORIC SITES, 501 E. State St.,
   Trenton, NJ 08625-0420. Mailing Address: NJ Div. of Parks &
   Forestry, State Park Svc., Mail Code 501-04, P.O. Box 420,
   Trenton, NJ 08625-0420. Tel.: 609-777-0238. Fax: 609-984-0503.
E-mail: beverly.weaver@dep.nj.gov
Web Site: www.njparksandforests.org/historic
Key Personnel: Admin., Beverly A. Weaver.
Institution Type/Description: Historic Sites & Villages.
Hours & Admission Prices: Wed.-Sat. 10-12 & 1-4, Sun. 1-4. Program fees might
   apply at certain locations. Closed New Year's Day; Thanksgiving; Christmas;
   Wed. after a Mon. holiday. &
Attendance: 970,000 (estimated)

NEW JERSEY STATE HOUSE, 125 W. State St., Trenton, NJ
   08608-1101. Mailing Address: State House Tour Office, State
   House Annex, P.O. Box 068, Trenton, NJ 08625-0068. Tel.: 609-
   847-3150. Fax: 609-292-1498.
E-mail: dapril@njleg.org
Web Site: www.njleg.state.nj.us
Key Personnel: Tour Program Coord., David April; Tour Program Educator, Sarah
   Schmidt.
Institution Type/Description: Historic Building: The New Jersey State House con-
   structed in 1792.
Hours & Admission Prices: Mon.-Fri. 10-3, Sat. 12-3. No charge. Closed state holi-
   days. &
Attendance: 39,277 (actual)

NEW JERSEY STATE MUSEUM, 205 W. State St., Trenton, NJ
   08608-1001. Mailing Address: P.O. Box 530, Trenton, NJ 08625-
   0530. Tel.: 609-292-6300 & 6464. Fax: 609-292-7636.
E-mail: njsm.info@sos.nj.us
Web Site: statemuseum.nj.gov
Key Personnel: Exec. Dir., Margaret M. O'Reilly; Foundation Exec. Dir., Nicole
   Jannotte.
Institution Type/Description: General Museum.
Hours & Admission Prices: Main Gallery: Tues.-Sun. 9-4:45. Auditorium Gallery:
   Tues.-Fri. 9-4:45. Museum: No charge; donations accepted. Planetarium: adults
   $7, seniors $6, children 12 & under $5; discounts to members & groups. Closed
   state holidays. &
Attendance: 158,000 (estimated)

OLD BARRACKS MUSEUM, 101 Barrack St., Trenton, NJ 08608-
   2007. Tel.: 609-396-1776. Fax: 609-777-4000.
E-mail: info@barracks.org
Web Site: www.barracks.org
Key Personnel: Exec. Dir., Richard Patterson; Pres. (V), John O'Sullivan; Office
   Mgr., Linda Mathies; Museum Shop Mgr., Vikki Bell; Chief Historical
   Interpreter, Gloria Bell; Tour Coord., Renee Kato.
Institution Type/Description: History Museum: housed in British military barracks
   built in 1758 during the French & Indian War.
Hours & Admission Prices: Mon.-Sat. 10-5. Adults $8, senior citizens & students
   $6; active military, children 5 & under and members no charge. Call ahead for
   handicap assistance. Closed New Year's Day; Thanksgiving; Christmas Eve &
   Day. &
Attendance: 23,552 (estimated)

THE 1719 WILLIAM TRENT HOUSE MUSEUM, 15 Market St.,
   Trenton, NJ 08611-2147. Tel.: 609-989-3027 & 0087. Fax: 609-
   278-7890. Facebook.
E-mail: office@williamtrenthouse.org

Web Site: www.williamtrenthouse.org
Formerly: William Trent House
Key Personnel: Dir., Trent House Association, Kate Nolan.
Institution Type/Description: Historic House: 1719 William Trent House.
Hours & Admission Prices: Daily 12:30-4; groups by appointment. Adults $4, senior citizens, students & children 12 and under $3; discounts to AAA & AAM members; members no charge. Closed holidays. ⑂
Attendance: 15,000 (estimated)

TRENTON CITY MUSEUM/TRENTON MUSEUM SOCIETY, 299 Parkside Ave., Trenton, NJ 08618. Mailing Address: P.O. Box 1034, Trenton, NJ 08606. Tel.: 609-989-3632 & 1191. Fax: 609-989-3624.
E-mail: info@ellarslie.org
Web Site: www.ellarslie.org
Key Personnel: Dir., Donna Carcaci Rhodes; Pres. (V), Richard Willinger; Museum Shop Mgr., Sally Baxter; Museum Shop Mgr., Jean Shaddow.
Institution Type/Description: General Museum: housed in c.1850 Ellarslie 34-room Tuscan Villa, designed by John Notman.
Hours & Admission Prices: Wed.-Sat. 12-4, Sun. 1-4. Suggested Donation: adults $5. Closed municipal holidays. ⑂
Attendance: 12,000 (estimated)

Tuckerton

GIFFORDTOWN SCHOOLHOUSE MUSEUM, 35 Leitz Blvd., Tuckerton, NJ 08087. Mailing Address: P.O. Box 43, Tuckerton, NJ 08087. Tel.: 609-294-1547.
E-mail: tuckertonhistoricalsociety@gmail.com
Web Site: tuckertonhistoricalsociety.org
Key Personnel: Pres. (V), Donald O. Caselli.
Institution Type/Description: Historic Building: housed in the former Giffordtown one-room schoolhouse.
Hours & Admission Prices: June-Sept. Wed. 10-4, Sat. 2-4; Oct.-May Wed. 10-4. Open Wed. all year; Sat. programs once a month all year. No charge; donations accepted.
Attendance: 480 (estimated)

TUCKERTON JUNCTION RAILROAD COMPANY, 213C E. Main St., Tuckerton, NJ 08087. Mailing Address: The Park at Bass River Twp., P.O. Box 331, New Gretna, NJ 08224. Tel.: 609-812-0300.
E-mail: info@tuckertonjunciton.com
Web Site: www.tuckertonjunction.com
Institution Type/Description: Hobby Museum.
Hours & Admission Prices: Wed.-Sun. call for hours.

TUCKERTON SEAPORT MUSEUM, 120 W. Main St., Tuckerton, NJ 08087-2237. Mailing Address: P.O. Box 52, Tuckerton, NJ 08087-0052. Tel.: 609-296-8868. Fax: 609-296-5810.
E-mail: info@tuckertonseaport.org
Web Site: www.tuckertonseaport.org
Formerly: Tuckerton Seaport A Project of Barnegat Bay Decoy & Baymen's Museum, Inc.
Key Personnel: Exec. Dir., Brooke Salvanto; Pres. (V), Jeff Daum, P.E.; Dir. Jersey Shore Folklife Center, Julie Hain; Museum Shop Mgr., Charlene Ackerman; Administrative Asst., Dot Dow.
Institution Type/Description: Maritime Museum.
Hours & Admission Prices: Daily 10-5. Adults $8, senior citizens 62 & over $6, children 6-12 $3; discounts to AAM members; members, children 5 & under no charge. Closed New Year's Eve & Day; Easter; Thanksgiving; Christmas. ⑂
Attendance: 30,000 (actual)

Union

CALDWELL PARSONAGE, 909 Caldwell Ave., Union, NJ 07083-6754. Tel.: 908-687-7977. Facebook.
E-mail: unionths@gmail.com
Web Site: www.unionnjhistory.com; www.unionhistory.org
Formerly: Reverend James and Hannah Caldwell Parsonage
Key Personnel: Dir., Thomas Haggerty; Chm. (V), Thomas Beisler; Pres. (V), Barbara La Mort; Vice Pres. (V), David Arminio; Sec. (V), Marie Canarelli.
Institution Type/Description: History & Culture Museum: housed in the former home of Presbyterian minister, Rev. James Caldwell; built in 1730, burned to the ground by the British Army in 1780; rebuilt in 1782. Listed on the National Register of Historic Places & the New Jersey State Register of Historic Places.
Hours & Admission Prices: Jan.-Feb., June & Oct. open houses; other times by appointment. No charge; donations accepted. ⑂
Attendance: 1,350 (actual)

KARL & HELEN BURGER GALLERY, Kean University, CAS Bldg., 1000 Morris Ave., Union, NJ 07083-7133. Tel.: 908-737-4452 & 0392. Fax: 908-737-4416.
E-mail: ntetkows@kean.edu
Web Site: www.kean.edu/~gallery/cas-gallery.html
Formerly: James Howe Gallery
Key Personnel: Dir. University Galleries, Neil Tetkowski.
Institution Type/Description: College Art Gallery.
Hours & Admission Prices: Sept.-May Mon.-Thurs. 10:30-4:30, Fri. 10:30-4. No charge. Closed college holidays. ⑂

LIBERTY HALL MUSEUM AT KEAN UNIVERSITY, 1003 Morris Ave., Union, NJ 07083-7120. Tel.: 908-527-0400. Fax: 908-352-8915. Facebook; Instagram; Twitter.
E-mail: libertyhall@kean.edu
Web Site: libertyhall.kean.edu
Key Personnel: C.E.O., John Kean, Sr.; Pres. (V), Joel D. Siegel, Esq.; Exec. Dir., Richard J. O'Neill; Dir. Operations, William P. Schroh, Jr.; Coord. Museum Programs, Lacey Bongard; Coord. School Programs, Maryellen McVeigh; Collection Mgr., Rachel Goldberg; Museum Store Mgr., Isbett Checo; Bldgs., Grounds & Maintenance, Jeff Eckert.
Institution Type/Description: Historic Building: c.1772 home of Gov. William Livingston, the first elected governor of New Jersey.
Hours & Admission Prices: March Fri.-Sun. 10-3; April-Dec. Wed.-Sun. 10-3. Adults $14, Kean Alumni $12, seniors, college students & children 3-7 $10; discounts to AAM members; Kean staff & students, children under 3 & members no charge. ⑂
Attendance: 25,000 (actual)

Upper Montclair

THE ESSEX COUNTY PRESBY MEMORIAL IRIS GARDENS, 474 Upper Mountain Ave., Upper Montclair, NJ 07043-1523. Tel.: 973-783-5974. Fax: 973-783-3833.
E-mail: info@presbyirisgardens.org
Web Site: presbyirisgardens.org
Key Personnel: Pres. (V), Nancy Skjei-Lawes; Garden Mgr., Dennis Hillerud.
Institution Type/Description: Iris Display Garden.
Hours & Admission Prices: mid-May to early June 10-8, Suggested Donation: $5. ⑂
Attendance: 10,000 (estimated)

MONTCLAIR STATE UNIVERSITY ART GALLERIES - GEORGE SEGAL GALLERY, Valley Rd. & Normal Ave., Upper Montclair, NJ 07043. Tel.: 973-655-3382. Fax: 973-655-7665.
E-mail: artgalleries@mail.montclair.edu
Web Site: www.montclair.edu/arts/galleries
Key Personnel: Dir., Teresa Rodriguez.
Institution Type/Description: University Art Gallery.
Hours & Admission Prices: Sept.-July Tues.-Wed. & Fri.-Sat. 10-5, Thurs. 12:30-7:30. No charge; donations accepted. Closed New Year's Day; Good Friday; Easter; Labor Day; Thanksgiving; Christmas. ⑂
Attendance: 5,000 (estimated)

Upper Saddle River

UPPER SADDLE RIVER HISTORICAL SOCIETY, 245 Lake St., Upper Saddle River, NJ 07458-1699. Tel.: 201-327-8644.
E-mail: prytter02@yahoo.com
Web Site: usrhistoricalsociety.org
Institution Type/Description: Historical Society Museum: housed in the Hopper-Goetschius House.
Hours & Admission Prices: July-Aug. Sun. 2-4; other times by appointment.

Vineland

VINELAND HISTORICAL AND ANTIQUARIAN SOCIETY, 108 S. Seventh St., Vineland, NJ 08360. Mailing Address: P.O. Box 35, Vineland, NJ 08362. Tel.: 856-691-1111. Facebook.
E-mail: vinelandhistory@gmail.com
Web Site: www.vinelandhistory1864.org
Key Personnel: Cur., Patricia A. Martinelli.
Institution Type/Description: History Museum.
Hours & Admission Prices: Tues.-Fri. 1-4 by appointment. Tours: Sat. 1-4. Visitors over 12 $1. Research Library: $10; members no charge. Closed holidays. ⑂

Wall

INFOAGE SCIENCE HISTORY LEARNING CENTER, 2201 Marconi Rd., Wall, NJ 07719. Tel.: 732-280-3000.
Key Personnel: Dir., Fred Carl.
Institution Type/Description: Science & History Center: housed on the site of Camp Evans, the former Marconi Belmar Trans-Atlantic Wireless station. Listed on the National Register of Historic Places.
Hours & Admission Prices: Wed. & Sat.-Sun. 1-5. Adults 13 & over $7, children 12 & under $4.

NEW JERSEY MUSEUM OF TRANSPORTATION, Allaire State Park, 4265 Atlantic Ave., Wall, NJ 07727-3715. Mailing Address: P.O. Box 622, Farmingdale, NJ 07727-0622. Tel.: 732-938-5524.
E-mail: office@njmt.org
Web Site: www.njmt.org
Institution Type/Description: Transportation Museum.
Hours & Admission Prices: Call for hours.

OLD WALL HISTORICAL SOCIETY, 1701 New Bedford Rd., Wall, NJ 07719. Mailing Address: P.O. Box 1203, Wall, NJ 07719. Tel.: 732-974-1430.
E-mail: oldwallhistorical@gmail.com
Key Personnel: Dir. & Pres. (V), Dr. De Hearn; Cur. & Museum Shop Mgr., Dennis Cirrito.
Institution Type/Description: Historical Society Museum.
Hours & Admission Prices: Call for hours. No charge.
Attendance: 600 (estimated)

Waretown

WELLS MILLS COUNTY PARK AND NATURE CENTER, 905 Wells Mills Rd., Waretown, NJ 08758. Tel.: 609-971-3085.
E-mail: OCParks@co.ocean.nj.us
Institution Type/Description: Park and Nature Center.
Hours & Admission Prices: Call for hours.

Warren

WAGNER FARM ARBORETUM AND GARDENS, 197 Mountain Ave., Warren, NJ 07059. Tel.: 908-350-7383.
Key Personnel: Office Mgr., Roslyn Nina-Cianfano.
Institution Type/Description: Arboretum.
Hours & Admission Prices: Office: Mon.-Fri. 10-2.

Washington

BLUE ARMY OF OUR LADY OF FATIMA AND THE IMMACULATE HEART OF MARY, 674 Mountain View Rd., Washington, NJ 07882. Tel.: 908-689-7200.
Institution Type/Description: Religious Museum.
Hours & Admission Prices: Call for hours.

MERRILL CREEK RESERVOIR, 34 Merrill Creek Rd., Washington, NJ 07882. Tel.: 908-454-1213. Fax: 908-454-2747.
E-mail: jmershon@merrillcreek.com
Web Site: www.merrillcreek.com
Key Personnel: On-site Coord., Jim Mershon.
Institution Type/Description: Nature Preserve.
Hours & Admission Prices: Visitors Center: Mon.-Fri. 8:30-4:30, Sat.-Sun. 10-4. Outdoor Areas: daily dawn to dusk. Closed New Year's Day; Easter; Thanksgiving & day after; Christmas Eve & Day.

Watchung

WATCHUNG ARTS CENTER, 18 Stirling Rd., Watchung, NJ 07069. Tel.: 908-753-0190.
E-mail: wacenter@optonline.net
Web Site: www.watchungarts.org
Key Personnel: Office Mgr., Shikha Sareen.
Institution Type/Description: Arts Center: housed in a former schoolhouse; c.1888.
Hours & Admission Prices: Tues.-Fri. 12-5, Sat. 10-3; other times by appointment. No charge; donations accepted.

Wayne

DEY MANSION MUSEUM, 199 Totowa Rd., Wayne, NJ 07470-3108. Tel.: 973-696-1776. Fax: 973-696-1365.
E-mail: deymansion@passaiccountynj.org

Formerly: Dey Mansion/Washington's Headquarters
Key Personnel: Dir., Kelly Ruffel; Cur., Margaret Puglia.
Institution Type/Description: Historic House Museum: headquarters of the Continental Army during July, October-November, 1780.
Hours & Admission Prices: Wed.-Fri. 1-4, Sat.-Sun. 1-4; group tours by appointment, last tour begins at 3:30. Adults $5, seniors 62 & older $4, kids 3-17 $3; under 3 no charge. Closed major holidays.
Attendance: 3,500 (actual)

UNIVERSITY GALLERIES - WILLIAM PATERSON UNIVERSITY, 300 Pompton Rd., Wayne, NJ 07470-2152. Tel.: 973-720-2654. Fax: 973-720-3270. Facebook, Twitter & Instagram: @WPUGalleries.
E-mail: evangelistak@wpunj.edu
Web Site: www.wpunj.edu/coac/gallery
Key Personnel: Gallery Dir., Kristen Evangelista; Public Rels., Mary Beth Zeman; Gallery Mgr., Emily Johnsen.
Institution Type/Description: College Art Gallery.
Hours & Admission Prices: Mon.-Fri. 10-5, Sun. call for hours; other times by appointment. No charge. Closed holidays.
Attendance: 10,000 (estimated)

WAYNE HISTORIC HOUSE MUSEUMS - VAN RIPER-HOPPER HOUSE MUSEUM, VAN DUYNE HOUSE MUSEUM, SCHUYLER-COLFAX HOUSE, 533 Berdan Ave., Wayne, NJ 07470-2026. Tel.: 973-694-7192, ext. 3375. Fax: 973-694-9100.
E-mail: dalessanc@waynetownship.com
Web Site: www.waynetownship.com/
Key Personnel: Chm. Wayne Historical Commission, Bob Monacelli; Coord. Museums, Carol D'Alessandro; Dir. Parks & Recreation, Russ Schubert.
Institution Type/Description: Historic House: 1786 Dutch Colonial Farmhouse restored.
Hours & Admission Prices: By appointment. Guided House Tour: adult $5, child $3; discounts to AAM & ICOM members; Blue Star active service military members with 5 family members no charge. Closed New Year's Day; Christmas.
Attendance: 1,800 (estimated)

West Long Branch

800 GALLERY & ROTARY ICE HOUSE GALLERY, Dept. Art & Design, Monmouth University, 400 Cedar Ave., West Long Branch, NJ 07764-1898. Tel.: 732-571-3428.
E-mail: etaormin@monmouth.edu
Web Site: www.monmouth.edu/academics/art/faculty/default.asp
Key Personnel: Dir. Galleries & Collections, Scott Knauer.
Institution Type/Description: Art Museum.
Hours & Admission Prices: Call for hours.

West Milford

LONG POND IRONWORKS MUSEUM, 1334 Greenwood Lake Tpke., West Milford, NJ 07421. Mailing Address: The Friends of Long Pond Ironworks, Inc., P.O. Box 809, Hewitt, NJ 07421. Tel.: 973-657-1688.
E-mail: info@longpondironworks.org
Web Site: www.longpondironworks.org
Key Personnel: Pres. (V), Paul Frost.
Institution Type/Description: History Museum.
Hours & Admission Prices: April-Nov. Sat.-Sun. 1-4, village tours every 2nd Sat.; other times by appointment. No charge; donations accepted.
Attendance: 2,500 (estimated)

WEST MILFORD MUSEUM, 1480 Union Valley Rd., West Milford, NJ 07480-1338. Tel.: 973-728-1823.
E-mail: museum@westmilford.org
Web Site: www.westmilfordmuseum.org
Key Personnel: Chairperson, Tonya Cubby.
Institution Type/Description: History Museum: built in 1860s, originally a Methodist Episcopal Church, later became West Milford's Town Hall 1912-1958.
Hours & Admission Prices: Sat. 1-4.

West Orange

ESSEX COUNTY'S TURTLE BACK ZOO, 560 Northfield Ave., West Orange, NJ 07052-2431. Tel.: 973-731-5800. Fax: 973-731-1059.
E-mail: info@turtlebackzoo.com

Web Site: www.turtlebackzoo.com
Key Personnel: Dir., Adam Kerins.
Institution Type/Description: Zoo.
Hours & Admission Prices: Daily 10-4:30. Adults $17, seniors 62 & over and children 2-12 $14; discounts to AZA members; children under 2 & members no charge. Closed Thanksgiving; Christmas. &
Attendance: 755,239 (actual)

THOMAS EDISON NATIONAL HISTORIC PARK, 211 Main St., West Orange, NJ 07052-5612. Tel.: 973-736-0550. Fax: 973-243-7172. TDD: 973-243-9122.
E-mail: edis_superintendent@nps.gov
Web Site: www.nps.gov/edis
Key Personnel: Supt., Thomas E. Ross.
Institution Type/Description: Historic Site: 20 historic structures from 1880-1887 including Glenmont home & laboratory of Thomas A. Edison.
Hours & Admission Prices: Estate: Fri.-Sun. 11-4. Grounds: 11:30-4. Laboratory: Wed.-Sun. 10-4; groups by appointment. Adults $10 (seven day pass); youth under 16 no charge. Annual Park Pass: $30. &
Attendance: 60,000 (estimated)

WEST ORANGE HISTORICAL SOCIETY, 425 Northfield Ave., Ste. 19, West Orange, NJ 07052.
E-mail: Josephfagan@westorangehistory.com
Key Personnel: Dir., Irene Manning.
Institution Type/Description: Historical Society.
Hours & Admission Prices: By appointment.

West Trenton

NEW JERSEY STATE POLICE MUSEUM, 1040 River Rd., West Trenton, NJ 08628-0068. Mailing Address: P.O. Box 7068, West Trenton, NJ 08628-0068. Tel.: 609-882-2000, ext. 6401. Fax: 609-882-0321.
Web Site: www.njsp.org/about/museum.shtml
Institution Type/Description: State Police History Museum.
Hours & Admission Prices: Mon.-Fri. 10-4, group tours by appointment. No charge. Closed state holidays. &

West Windsor

THE GALLERY, MERCER COUNTY COMMUNITY COLLEGE, Communications Center, 2nd Fl., 1200 Old Trenton Rd., West Windsor, NJ 08550-3407. Tel.: 609-586-4800, ext. 3589.
E-mail: gallery@mccc.edu
Web Site: www.mccc.edu/community-gallery.shtml
Key Personnel: Dir., Dylan Wolfe.
Institution Type/Description: Art Museum.
Hours & Admission Prices: Mon.-Wed. 11-3, Thurs. 11-7; call to confirm. No charge.

Westampton

HISTORIC PEACHFIELD, 180 Burrs Rd., Westampton, NJ 08060. Tel.: 609-267-6996.
E-mail: colonialdamesnj@comcast.net
Web Site: www.colonialdamesnj.org
Formerly: Peachfield Plantation
Institution Type/Description: Historic House Museum: listed on the National Register of Historic Places.
Hours & Admission Prices: By appointment. &

Westfield

MILLER-CORY HOUSE MUSEUM, 614 Mountain Ave., Westfield, NJ 07090-3044. Mailing Address: P.O. Box 455, Westfield, NJ 07091-0455. Tel.: 908-232-1776.
E-mail: millercorymuseum@gmail.com
Web Site: www.millercoryhouse.org
Key Personnel: C.E.O. & Chm. Bd. Governors, Lowell Schantz; Pres. (V), Patricia D'Angelo; Acquisitions, Joan Barna; Museum Shop Mgr., Debbie Bailey.
Institution Type/Description: Living Museum & Historic House: 1740 Miller-Cory House, two-story farmhouse.
Hours & Admission Prices: mid-Sept. to mid-June select Sundays only. Adults $4, children $3; members no charge. Closed holiday weekends.
Attendance: 1,700 (estimated)

Westhampton

RANCOCAS NATURE CENTER, 794 Rancocas Rd., Westhampton, NJ 08060. Tel.: 609-261-2495.
E-mail: info@rancocasnaturecenter.org
Institution Type/Description: Nature Center.
Hours & Admission Prices: Tues.-Sat. 9-5, Sun. 12-5.

Whippany

JEWISH HISTORICAL SOCIETY OF METROWEST, 901 Rte. 10 E., Whippany, NJ 07981-1156. Tel.: 973-929-2995.
E-mail: lforgosh@jhs-nj.org
Institution Type/Description: Jewish History Museum.
Hours & Admission Prices: Mon.-Fri. 9-1.

WHIPPANY RAILWAY MUSEUM, 1 Railroad Plaza, Rte. 10 W. & Whippany Rd., Whippany, NJ 07981-1505. Mailing Address: P. O. Box 16, Whippany, NJ 07981-0016. Tel.: 973-887-8177.
E-mail: info@whippanyrailwaymuseum.net
Web Site: www.whippanyrailwaymuseum.net
Key Personnel: Pres. (V), Steven P. Hepler.
Institution Type/Description: Railway Museum.
Hours & Admission Prices: April-Oct. Sun. 12-4. Adults $2, children under 12 $1.
Attendance: 25,000 (estimated)

Whitehouse

EVERSOLE-HALL HOUSE, 511 Rte. 523 S., Whitehouse, NJ 08888. Mailing Address: P.O. Box 216, Stanton, NJ 08885-0216. Tel.: 908-236-2327. Fax: 908-236-2306.
E-mail: readingtonmuseums@gmail.com
Web Site: www.readingtontwp.org/ReadingtonMuseum/evans_hall_house.html
Key Personnel: Museum Admin., Margaret Smith.
Institution Type/Description: Historic Buildings.
Hours & Admission Prices: Call for hours.
Attendance: 150 (estimated)

Wildwood

DOO WOP EXPERIENCE MUSEUM, 4500 Ocean Ave., Wildwood, NJ 08260. Mailing Address: c/o Doo Wop Preservation League, P.O. Box 1703, Wildwood, NJ 08260. Tel.: 609-523-1958.
E-mail: info@doowopusa.org
Web Site: www.doowopusa.org
Institution Type/Description: History Museum.
Hours & Admission Prices: Call for hours.

WILDWOOD HISTORICAL SOCIETY, INC., 3907 Pacific Ave., Wildwood, NJ 08260-4722. Tel.: 609-523-0277. Facebook: Wildwood Historical Society - George F. Boyer Museum.
E-mail: wildwoodhistoricalsociety@hotmail.com
Web Site: www.wildwoodhistoricalmuseum.com
Formerly: George F. Boyer Museum
Institution Type/Description: Historical Society Museum.
Hours & Admission Prices: April 13-May 13 & Oct. 5-Oct. 28: Thurs.-Sat. 9-2; May 15-Sept. Mon.-Sat. 9-2; No charge; donations accepted. Closed national holidays. &
Attendance: 2,500 (estimated)

WILDWOODS VIETNAM VETERANS REMEMBRANCE WALL, 4500 Ocean Dr., Wildwood, NJ 08260. Mailing Address: P.O. Box 481, Wildwood, NJ 08260. Tel.: 609-729-4000.
Web Site: www.wildwoodswall.com
Institution Type/Description: Veterans Memorial.
Hours & Admission Prices: Daily. No charge; donations accepted.

Wildwood Crest

WILDWOOD CREST HISTORICAL SOCIETY, 5800 Ocean Ave., Wildwood Crest, NJ 08260. Mailing Address: 2 Jefferson Ave., Somers Point, NJ 08244-1524. Tel.: 609-927-8002. Facebook: You're Probably From Wildwood Crest, NJ, If You Remember.
E-mail: kirkhastings5@aol.com
Web Site: cresthistory.org
Key Personnel: Pres., Kirk Hastings; Dir., Scott Hand; Sec., Sally Hastings.
Institution Type/Description: Historical Society Museum.

Hours & Admission Prices: Museum temporarily closed. Moving to a new location in 2017.

Williamstown

MONROE TOWNSHIP HISTORICAL SOCIETY - IRELAND HOFFER HOUSE, 313 S. Main St., Williamstown, NJ 08094. Tel.: 856-875-2943.
Institution Type/Description: Historical Society Museum.
Hours & Admission Prices: By appointment.

Woodbine

THE SAM AZEEZ MUSEUM OF WOODBINE HERITAGE OF STOCKTON UNIVERSITY, 610 Washington Ave., Woodbine, NJ 08270. Mailing Address: P.O. Box 517, Woodbine, NJ 08270-0517. Tel.: 609-861-5355. Facebook.
E-mail: Jane.Stark@sasi.stockton.edu
Web Site: www.thesam.org
Key Personnel: Exec. Dir., Jane Stark.
Institution Type/Description: History Museum.
Hours & Admission Prices: Wed.-Fri. & Sun. 10-4. No charge; donations accepted. Closed New Year's Day; Christmas Day.

Woodbridge

BARRON ARTS CENTER & MUSEUM, 582 Rahway Ave., Woodbridge, NJ 07095-3419. Tel.: 732-634-0413. Fax: 732-634-8633.
E-mail: barronarts@twp.woodbridge.nj.us
Web Site: www.twp.woodbridge.nj.us/barronarts/
Key Personnel: Dir., Barron Arts Center, Cynthia Knight.
Institution Type/Description: Art Museum, Gallery & Historic Building.
Hours & Admission Prices: Mon.-Fri. 11-4, Sat.-Sun. 2-4; call to confirm. No charge; donations accepted. Closed holidays. &
Attendance: 25,000 (estimated)

Woodbury

FRIENDSHIP FIRE COMPANY MUSEUM, 29 Delaware St., Woodbury, NJ 08096-5925. Tel.: 856-845-0066.
Institution Type/Description: Fire Fighting Museum.
Hours & Admission Prices: Mon.-Fri. 8-3.

GLOUCESTER COUNTY HISTORICAL SOCIETY, 58 N. Broad St., Woodbury, NJ 08096-4629. Mailing Address: 17 Hunter St., Woodbury, NJ 08096-4605. Tel.: 856-848-8531 (museum); 845-7881 (business office); 845-4771 (library). Fax: 856-845-4771.
E-mail: museumcoordinator@gchsnj.org
Web Site: www.gchsnj.org
Key Personnel: Pres., Lois Jenkins; Museum Coord., Kathleen Fleming; Library Coord., Barbara Price; Coord. Museum Collections, Patricia A. Hrynenko.
Institution Type/Description: Historical Society Museum; housed in the Hunter-Lawrence-Jessup House; built in 1765.
Hours & Admission Prices: Museum: Mon., Wed. & Fri. 1-4, last Sun. of month Sept.-April 2-5 pm; other times by appointment. Adults $5, children 6-18 $1; members & children under 5 no charge. Library: Tues. 6 pm-9:30 pm, Wed.-Fri. 10-4, last Sun. of month Sept.-April 2-5, first Sat. of month Oct.-May 10-4, Adults $5; member no charge. Closed national holidays. &
Attendance: 3,000 (estimated)

Woodstown

PILESGROVE-WOODSTOWN HISTORICAL SOCIETY, 42 N. Main St., Woodstown, NJ 08098. Tel.: 856-769-4588.
E-mail: pwhs@mhabookkeeping.com
Institution Type/Description: Historical Society Museum; housed in the 18th century Dickinson House.
Hours & Admission Prices: Sat. 10-1. No charge; donations accepted.

Wyckoff

JAMES A. MCFAUL ENVIRONMENTAL CENTER OF BERGEN COUNTY, 150 Crescent Ave., Wyckoff, NJ 07481-2751. Tel.: 201-891-5571. Fax: 201-891-5583. TDD: 201-343-7249.
E-mail: wildlifecenter@co.bergen.nj.us
Web Site: www.co.bergen.nj.us/parks

Key Personnel: C.E.O. & Dir., Raymond Dressler; Mgr., Peter Both.
Institution Type/Description: Nature Center; Park Museum.
Hours & Admission Prices: Programs: Mon.-Fri. 9:30-3:30. Park Grounds: Mon.-Fri. 8-sunset, Sat.-Sun. & holidays 8:30-sunset. No charge. &
Attendance: 50,000 (estimated)

NEW MEXICO

(209 listings)

Abiquiu

GHOST RANCH MUSEUMS, 280 Private Dr., #1708, Abiquiu, NM 87510. Tel.: 505-685-1006. Fax: 505-685-4519.
E-mail: gretcheng@ghostranch.org
Web Site: www.ghostranch.org
Key Personnel: Dir., Gretchen Gurtler; Chair (V), Charles Jaynes; Cur., Graham Burke; Archivist, John Perotto.
Institution Type/Description: History Museum.
Hours & Admission Prices: Mon.-Sat. 9-5, Sun. 1-5. No charge; donations accepted. Closed Thanksgiving; Christmas. &
Attendance: 18,075 (actual)

Acoma

SKY CITY CULTURAL CENTER & HAAK'U MUSEUM, Pueblo of Acoma, I-40 West, Exit 102, SPA 30 @ 32, Acoma, NM 87034. Mailing Address: c/o Pueblo of Acoma, P.O. Box 310, Acoma, NM 87034. Tel.: 800-747-0181, 505-552-7861. Fax: 505-552-7883. Facebook.
E-mail: friends@skycity.com
Web Site: www.acomaskycity.org
Formerly: Acoma Tourist & Visitation Center
Institution Type/Description: Indian Historical & Cultural Museum.
Hours & Admission Prices: Tours: early March-Nov. daily 9:30-3:30; Nov. to early March Fri.-Sun. 9:30-2:30. Adults $25, seniors, active duty military & college students $22, children & youth $17; discounts to groups, NTHP members & museum members. &
Attendance: 71,880 (actual)

Acoma Pueblo

ACOMA PUEBLO MUSEUM, NM 23 (12 miles SW of I-40), Acoma Pueblo, NM 87034. Mailing Address: P.O. Box 309, Acoma Pueblo, NM 87034-0309. Tel.: 505-252-1139.
Institution Type/Description: History Museum.
Hours & Admission Prices: Winter: 8-4:30. Summer: 8am-7pm.

Alamogordo

ALAMEDA PARK ZOO, 1321 N. White Sands Blvd., Alamogordo, NM 88310. Mailing Address: 1376 E. Ninth St., Alamogordo, NM 88310-5855. Tel.: 505-439-4290. Fax: 505-439-4103.
E-mail: sdiehl@ci.alamogordo.nm.us
Web Site: ci.alamogordo.nm.us
Key Personnel: Zoo Mgr., Johnny Crain; Cur., Kate Unterweger.
Institution Type/Description: Zoo; located in 1898 park.
Hours & Admission Prices: Daily 9-5. Adults 13-59 $4, senior citizens, military & children 5-12 $2.50; discounts to groups, AZA & AAZK members. Closed New Year's Day; Christmas. &
Attendance: 50,941 (actual)

NEW MEXICO MUSEUM OF SPACE HISTORY, 3198 State Route 2001, Alamogordo, NM 88310. Mailing Address: P.O. Box 5430, Alamogordo, NM 88311-5430. Tel.: 575-437-2840, Ext. 41153. Fax: 575-434-2245. Facebook, Twitter.
E-mail: msh.info@state.nm.us
Web Site: www.nmspacemuseum.org
Formerly: The Space Center
Key Personnel: Division Dir., Chris Orwoll; Deputy Dir., Billy Jones; Cur., Sue Taylor; Mktg. Dir., Cathy Harper; Education Dir., Dave Dooling.
Institution Type/Description: Space Museum; located near White Sands Missile Range, home of America's early space program.
Hours & Admission Prices: Mon., & Wed.-Sat. 10-5, Sun. 12-5. Adults $8, children 4-12 $6; discounts to ASTC members, senior citizens & military; members and children 3 & under no charge. Closed Thanksgiving; Christmas. &
Attendance: 92,000 (actual)

OLIVER LEE RANCH HOUSE MUSEUM, 409 Dog Canyon Rd., Alamogordo, NM 88310. Mailing Address: New Mexico State Parks, 1220 S. St. Francis Dr., Santa Fe, NM 87505. Tel.: 575-437-8284, 505-476-3355. Fax: 575-439-1290.
E-mail: howard.thomas@state.nm.us
Web Site: www.emnrd.state.nm.us
Institution Type/Description: History Museum.
Hours & Admission Prices: Tours: Sat.-Sun. 3pm by appointment. Day use $5, camping $8-10.

TOY TRAIN DEPOT MUSEUM AND TRAIN RIDE, 1991 N. White Sands Blvd., Alamogordo, NM 88310-6200. Tel.: 575-437-2855. Fax: 575-437-8169.
E-mail: toytraindepotnm@gmail.com
Web Site: toytraindepot.org
Key Personnel: Mgr. & Cur., John Koval.
Institution Type/Description: History Museum.
Hours & Admission Prices: Wed.-Thurs. & Sun. 12-5; Fri.-Sat. 10-5. Museum: $5. Train: $5. Combination: $8; discounts to military & groups with reservation; children 3 & under no charge. Closed Thanksgiving; Christmas.
Attendance: 10,272 (actual)

TULAROSA BASIN MUSEUM OF HISTORY, 1004 N. White Sands Blvd., Alamogordo, NM 88310-6659. Tel.: 575-434-4438.
E-mail: tbhs@zianet.com
Formerly: Alamogordo Museum of History
Key Personnel: Cur. & Museum Shop Mgr., Jean Ann Killer.
Institution Type/Description: Historical Society Museum.
Hours & Admission Prices: Mon.-Sat. 10-4. Closed federal holidays.
Attendance: 8,500 (actual)

WHITE SANDS NATIONAL MONUMENT, 19955 U.S. Hwy. 70, Alamogordo, NM 88310. Mailing Address: P.O. Box 1086, Holloman A.F.B., NM 88330-1086. Tel.: 505-679-2599. Fax: 505-479-4333.
E-mail: whsa_administration@nps.gov
Web Site: www.nps.gov/whsa
Institution Type/Description: Park Museum.
Hours & Admission Prices: Visitor Center: Winter: daily 9-5; Summer: daily 8-7. Monument: daily 7am to sunset. Adults $5; children 15 & under no charge. Closed Christmas.
Attendance: 470,921 (actual)

Albuquerque

ABQ BIOPARK BOTANIC GARDEN, 2601 Central Ave., N.W., Albuquerque, NM 87104. Tel.: 505-768-2000. Fax: 505-764-6281.
E-mail: biopark@cabq.gov
Web Site: www.cabq.gov/biopark
Formerly: Albuquerque Biological Park
Key Personnel: Dir., Rick Janser; Dir. Dept., Ray D. Darnell.
Institution Type/Description: Zoo, Aquarium & Botanical Garden.
Hours & Admission Prices: Daily 9-4:30. Adults $14.50, senior citizens 65 & over $7.50, children 3-12 $6; discount to AZA members; members & children 2 & under no charge. Closed New Year's Day; Thanksgiving; Christmas.
Attendance: 975,000 (actual)

ALBUQUERQUE MUSEUM OF ART & HISTORY, 2000 Mountain Rd., N.W., Albuquerque, NM 87104-1459. Tel.: 505-243-7255. Fax: 505-764-6546.
E-mail: clwright@cabq.gov
Web Site: www.cabq.gov/museum
Key Personnel: Dir., Cathy L. Wright; Asst. Dir., Cynthia Garcia; Cur. History, Deb Slaney; Cur. Art, Andrew Connors; Cur. Education, Elizabeth Becker; Museum Shop Mgr., Maureen Ryan.
Institution Type/Description: Art & History Museum.
Hours & Admission Prices: Tues.-Sun. 9-5. Adults $4, in-state residents $3; discounts to AAM & ICOM members; members no charge. Closed holidays.
Attendance: 135,148 (actual)

AMERICAN INTERNATIONAL RATTLESNAKE MUSEUM, 202 San Felipe, N.W., Suite A, Albuquerque, NM 87104-1426. Tel.: 505-242-6569. Fax: 505-242-6569 (call first).
E-mail: snakemuseum@aol.com
Web Site: www.rattlesnakes.com
Key Personnel: Dir., Bob Myers.
Institution Type/Description: Herpetology & Animal Conservation Museum.

** Hours & Admission Prices:** Summer: Mon.-Sat. 10-6, Sun. 1-5; Sept.-May Mon.-Fri. 11:30-5:30, Sat. 10-6, Sun. 1-5. Adults $6, seniors, military & students $5, kids $4. Closed New Year's Day; Easter; Thanksgiving; Christmas.
Attendance: 50,000 (actual)

ANDERSON/ABRUZZO ALBUQUERQUE INTERNATIONAL BALLOON MUSEUM, 9201 Balloon Museum Dr., N.E., Albuquerque, NM 87113-2425. Tel.: 505-880-0500. Fax: 505-768-6021.
E-mail: contact@balloonmuseum.com
Web Site: www.balloonmuseum.com
Key Personnel: Exec. Dir., Laurie Magovern; Mgr. Events & Membership, Deb Bains; Museum Shop Mgr., Ann Oishi.
Institution Type/Description: International Balloon Museum: named after Albuquerque balloon pilots Maxie Anderson and Ben Abruzzo, the first individuals to fly a balloon across the Atlantic.
Hours & Admission Prices: Tues.-Sun. 9-5. Adults $6, seniors 65 & over $4, children 6-17 $3; discount to New Mexico residents with ID; 1st Fri, each month, Sun. 9-1, ICOM, AAM, NMAM & Foundation members, and children 5 & under no charge. Closed New Year's Day; Thanksgiving; Christmas.
Attendance: 71,623 (actual)

CHIEF PAUL A. SHAVER POLICE MUSEUM, 400 Roma Ave., N.W., Albuquerque, NM 87102-2195. Tel.: 505-768-2200.
Institution Type/Description: History Museum.
Hours & Admission Prices: By appointment.

EXPLORA, 1701 Mountain Rd., N.W., Albuquerque, NM 87104-1396. Tel.: 505-224-8300. Fax: 505-224-8323.
E-mail: explora@explora.us
Web Site: www.explora.us
Formerly: Explora Science Center & Children's Museum of Albuquerque
Key Personnel: Exec. Dir., Joe Hastings; Deputy Dir., Kristin Leigh; Dir. Visitor Svcs., Tamara Grybko; Dir. Educational Svcs., Allison Brady; Dir. Admin., Alicia Borrego Pierce.
Institution Type/Description: Science Center & Children's Museum.
Hours & Admission Prices: Mon.-Sat. 10-6, Sun. 12-6. Adults $7, senior citizens 65 & over $5, children 1-11 $3; ASTC reciprocal membership program; children under 1 & members no charge. Closed New Year's Day; week after Labor Day; Independence Day; Thanksgiving; Christmas.
Attendance: 234,000 (estimated)

EXPO NEW MEXICO, 300 San Pedro, N.E., Albuquerque, NM 87108-2812. Mailing Address: P.O. Box 8546, Albuquerque, NM 87198-8546. Tel.: 505-222-9700. Fax: 505-266-7784.
E-mail: erin.thompson@state.nm.us
Web Site: exponm.com
Formerly: New Mexico State Fair Fine Arts Gallery
Key Personnel: Gen. Mgr., Dan Mourning; Sponsorship & Events Dir., Sabrina Garza.
Institution Type/Description: Art Gallery.
Hours & Admission Prices: Mon.-Fri. 8-5.

516 ARTS, 516 Central Ave., S.W., Albuquerque, NM 87102. Tel.: 505-242-1445. Fax: 505-244-4101.
E-mail: info@516arts.org
Web Site: www.516arts.org
Key Personnel: Pres. & Exec. Dir., Suzanne Sbarge.
Institution Type/Description: Art Gallery.
Hours & Admission Prices: Tues.-Sat. 12-5; other times by appointment. No charge; donations accepted.
Attendance: 13,000 (actual)

HOLOCAUST & INTOLERANCE MUSEUM OF NEW MEXICO, 616 Central Ave., S.W., Albuquerque, NM 87102. Mailing Address: P.O. Box 1762, Albuquerque, NM 87103-1762. Tel.: 505-247-0606. Fax: 505-247-0606 (call first).
E-mail: info@nmholocaustmuseum.org
Web Site: www.nmholocaustmuseum.org
Key Personnel: Admin., Lyn Berner; Pres. (V), Jennie L. Negin.
Institution Type/Description: History Museum.
Hours & Admission Prices: Tues.-Sat. 11-3:30. No charge; donations accepted. Closed major holidays.
Attendance: 3,893 (estimated)

INDIAN PUEBLO CULTURAL CENTER, 2401 12th St., N.W., Albuquerque, NM 87104-2397. Tel.: 505-843-7270. Fax: 505-842-6959.
E-mail: rsolimon@indianpueblo.com

Web Site: www.indianpueblo.org
Key Personnel: Dir., Monique Fragua; Continuing Education Mgr., March Becktell; Office Mgr., Stephanie Martinez; Gift Shop Mgr., Ira Wilson.
Institution Type/Description: Pueblo Cultural Museum.
Hours & Admission Prices: Daily 9-5. Adults $6, senior citizens $5.50, NM residents $4, students $3; discounts to groups of 10 or more; members and children 5 & under no charge. Closed New Year's Day; Memorial Day; Independence Day; Labor Day; Thanksgiving; Christmas. &
Attendance: 100,000 (estimated)

INSTITUTE OF METEORITICS METEORITE MUSEUM, 221 Yale Blvd., N.E., Albuquerque, NM 87131. Mailing Address: MSCO3 2050, 1 University of New Mexico, Albuquerque, NM 87131. Tel.: 505-277-2747. Fax: 505-277-3577.
E-mail: iom@unm.edu
Web Site: meteorite.unm.edu
Key Personnel: Dir. & Cur., Dr. Carl Agee.
Institution Type/Description: Meteorite Museum.
Hours & Admission Prices: Mon.-Fri. Call for hours. No charge; donations accepted. Closed university holidays. &
Attendance: 2,500 (estimated)

MAXWELL MUSEUM OF ANTHROPOLOGY, University of New Mexico, 500 University Blvd., N.E., Albuquerque, NM 87131. Mailing Address: MSCO1 1050, 1 University of New Mexico, Albuquerque, NM 87131. Tel.: 505-277-4405. Fax: 505-277-1547.
E-mail: maxwell@unm.edu
Web Site: maxwellmuseum.unm.edu
Key Personnel: Dir., Carla Sinopoli; Cur. Education, Amy Grochowski; Archives, Diane Tyink; Cur. Ethnology, Lea McChesney; Cur. Exhibits, Devorah Romanek.
Institution Type/Description: Science & Anthropology Museum.
Hours & Admission Prices: Tues.-Sat. 10-4. No charge; donations accepted. Closed holidays. &
Attendance: 26,000 (actual)

MUSEUM OF SOUTHWESTERN BIOLOGY, 302 Yale Blvd., N. E., CERIA 83, Rm. 204, Albuquerque, NM 87131. Mailing Address: 1 University of New Mexico/MSCO3 2020, Albuquerque, NM 87131. Tel.: 505-277-1360. Fax: 505-277-1351.
E-mail: cosborn@unm.edu
Web Site: msb.unm.edu
Key Personnel: Dir., Dr. Christopher Witt; Asst. Dir., Dr. Kelly Miller; Admin., Joanne Kuestner; Collections Mgr. Mammals, Dr. Jon Dunnum; Collection Mgr. Birds, Andrew B. Johnson; Cur. Amphibians & Reptiles, Dr. Howard L. Snell; Collection Mgr., Dr. Tom Giermakowski; Collection Mgr. Anthropods, Dr. David Lightfoot.
Institution Type/Description: Research Museum.
Hours & Admission Prices: Tours by appointment. No charge; donations accepted. &
Attendance: 1,500 (actual)

NATIONAL HISPANIC CULTURAL CENTER, ART MUSEUM, 1701 4th St., S.W., Albuquerque, NM 87102-4508. Tel.: 505-246-2261. Fax: 505-724-4760.
E-mail: rebecca.avitia@state.nm.us
Web Site: www.nhccnm.org
Key Personnel: Exec. Dir., Josefa Gonzalez-Mariscal; Deputy Dir., Alberto Cuessy; Dir. Performing Arts, Reeve Love.
Institution Type/Description: Art Museum.
Hours & Admission Prices: Tues.-Sun. 10-5. Adults $6; discounts to AAM & ICOM members; school groups, children under 16, members & Sun. no charge. Closed New Year's Day; Easter; Thanksgiving; Christmas. &
Attendance: 233,034 (actual)

NATIONAL MUSEUM OF NUCLEAR SCIENCE AND HISTORY, 601 Eubank Blvd., S.E., Albuquerque, NM 87123. Tel.: 505-245-2137. Fax: 505-242-4537.
E-mail: info@nuclearmuseum.org
Web Site: www.nuclearmuseum.org
Formerly: National Atomic Museum
Key Personnel: Dir., Jim Walther; Pres. (V), Wayne Laslie; Cur., David Hoover; Registrar, Sandra Fye; Dir. Mktg. & Public Rels., Jennifer Hayden; Dir. Education, Lisa Guida; Dir. Devel., Leslie Fraser; Museum Store Mgr., Molly Brunell.
Institution Type/Description: Nuclear Science & History Museum.
Hours & Admission Prices: Daily 9-5. Adults $14, senior citizens 60 & over $12, youth 6-17 $10; discounts to AAM members, groups, active military & veterans;

members and children 5 & under no charge. Closed New Year's Day; Easter; Thanksgiving; Christmas. &
Attendance: 60,000 (estimated)

NEW MEXICO MUSEUM OF NATURAL HISTORY & SCIENCE, 1801 Mountain Rd., N.W., Albuquerque, NM 87104-1375. Tel.: 505-841-2846. Fax: 505-841-2844. TDD: 505-841-2878.
E-mail: sherice.padilla@state.nm.us
Web Site: www.NMnaturalhistory.org
Key Personnel: Exec. Dir., Margie Marino; Deputy Dir., Gary Romero.
Institution Type/Description: Natural History & Science Museum.
Hours & Admission Prices: Daily 9-5. Museum: adults $8, seniors 60 & up $7, children 3-12 $5. Museum & Theater: adults $10, seniors 60 & up $9, children 3-12 $7. Planetarium: adults $7, seniors 60 & up $6, children 3-12 $4; discounts to AAM & ASTC members; members & children under 3 no charge. Combination packages available. Closed New Year's Day; Thanksgiving; Christmas. &
Attendance: 211,322 (actual)

NEW MEXICO VETERANS' MEMORIAL AND MUSEUM, 1100 Louisiana Blvd., S.E., Albuquerque, NM 87108. Mailing Address: P.O. Box 8389, Albuquerque, NM 87198-8389. Tel.: 505-256-2042. Fax: 505-256-2061.
E-mail: nmveteransmemorial@gmail.com
Web Site: nmvetsmemorial.org
Key Personnel: Cur., Mary Cox.
Institution Type/Description: Veterans Memorial & Museum.
Hours & Admission Prices: Visitor's Center & Museum: daily 9-3. No charge. Memorial: daily 6am-10pm. Closed New Year's Day; Christmas.

NORTH FOURTH ART CENTER & GALLERY, 4904 Fourth St., N.W., Albuquerque, NM 87107. Tel.: 505-345-2872. Fax: 505-345-2896.
E-mail: info@vsartsnm.org
Web Site: vsartsnm.org/gallery
Key Personnel: Exec. Dir., Marjorie Neset; Deputy Dir., Brynne Badeaux.
Institution Type/Description: Art Gallery.
Hours & Admission Prices: Mon.-Fri. 10-4.

PETROGLYPH NATIONAL MONUMENT, 6001 Unser Blvd., N. W., Albuquerque, NM 87120-2069. Tel.: 505-899-0205, ext. 331. Fax: 505-899-0207.
E-mail: petr_interpretation@nps.gov
Web Site: www.nps.gov/petr
Key Personnel: Dir., Joseph P. Sanchez; Museum Shop Mgr., Ed Dunn.
Institution Type/Description: National Park & Landmark.
Hours & Admission Prices: Daily 8-5. Sat.-Sun. $2, Mon.-Fri. $1. Closed holidays.
Attendance: 150,000 (estimated)

RIO GRANDE NATURE CENTER STATE PARK, 2901 Candelaria Rd., N.W., Albuquerque, NM 87107-2965. Tel.: 505-344-7240. Fax: 505-344-4505.
E-mail: friends@rgnc.org
Web Site: www.rgnc.org
Key Personnel: Pres., Dave Hutton; Park Supt., Beth Dillingham.
Institution Type/Description: Nature Center: preservation & protection of wetland and riverine resources in the Rio Grande Valley & the surrounding Bosque (woods); to educate visitors on the importance of wetlands and river resources in the arid Southwest.
Hours & Admission Prices: Park: daily 8-5. Visitor Center: daily 10-5. Parking Fee: car $3, van & buses $15. Closed New Year's Day; Thanksgiving; Christmas. &
Attendance: 2,000,000 (actual)

SAN FELIPE DE NERI CHURCH MUSEUM, San Felipe de Neri Parish, 2005 North Plaza N.W., Albuquerque, NM 87104. Mailing Address: P.O. Box 7007, Albuquerque, NM 87194-7007. Tel.: 505-243-4628. Fax: 505-224-9495.
E-mail: dgarcia@sanfelipedeneri.org
Web Site: www.sanfelipedeneri.org
Key Personnel: Mgr., Steve Torres.
Institution Type/Description: Historic Church.
Hours & Admission Prices: Mon.-Sat. 9-4:30. No charge.

SILVER FAMILY GEOLOGY MUSEUM - THE UNIVERSITY OF NEW MEXICO, Northrop Hall, Rm. #124, Albuquerque, NM 87131. Tel.: 505-277-4204.
E-mail: epsdept@unm.edu
Web Site: epswww.unm.edu/online-educational-resources/geology-museum

Institution Type/Description: Geology Museum.
Hours & Admission Prices: Mon.-Fri. 8-12 & 1-4:30. No charge. Closed university holidays.

TAMARIND INSTITUTE & GALLERY, University of New Mexico, 2500 Central Ave., S.E., Albuquerque, NM 87106. Mailing Address: University of New Mexico, MSC 04-2540, Albuquerque, NM 87131. Tel.: 505-277-3901. Fax: 505-277-3920.
E-mail: tamarind@unm.edu
Web Site: tamarind.unm.edu
Key Personnel: Dir., Diana Gaston.
Institution Type/Description: Art Gallery.
Hours & Admission Prices: 1st Fri. of the month 3:30. No charge.

TELEPHONE MUSEUM OF NEW MEXICO, 110 Fourth St., N. W., Albuquerque, NM 87102-3268. Mailing Address: P.O. Box 16174, Albuquerque, NM 87191-6174. Tel.: 505-842-2937. Fax: 505-332-4088.
E-mail: telmuseum@hotmail.com
Web Site: www.museumsusa.org
Key Personnel: Chair (V) & Pres. (V), Gigi Galassini; Dir. & Sec., Sue Stone; Treas., Sue Turner; Museum Shop Mgr., Sarah Church.
Institution Type/Description: Telephone & Communication Museum.
Hours & Admission Prices: Mon., Wed. & Fri. 10-2; large tours by appointment. Adults $2, children under 12 $1. Tours on off-hours: $4 per person. Closed holidays. &
Attendance: 2,500 (estimated)

TURQUOISE MUSEUM, 400 2nd St., N.W., Albuquerque, NM 87102. Tel.: 505-433-3684.
E-mail: turquoisemuseumabq@gmail.com
Web Site: turquoisemuseum.com
Key Personnel: Pres. & Cur., Joe Dan Lowry; Museum Shop Mgr., Katy Lowry.
Institution Type/Description: General Museum.
Hours & Admission Prices: Self-Guided Tours: Mon.-Sat. 10-4. Adults $20, senior citizens & children $15. Closed Independence Day; Thanksgiving; Christmas. &
Attendance: 9,375 (actual)

UNIVERSITY OF NEW MEXICO ART MUSEUM, UNM Center for the Arts, Cornell & Central N.E., Albuquerque, NM 87131. Mailing Address: UNM Art Museum, MSC04 2570, 1 University of New Mexico, Albuquerque, NM 87131. Tel.: 505-277-4001. Fax: 505-277-7315.
E-mail: artmuse@unm.edu
Web Site: www.unm.edu/~artmuse
Key Personnel: Dir., Arif Khan; Cur. Photographs & Prints, Michele Penhall; Cur. Raymond Jonson Gallery, Robert Ware; Mgr. Collections, Bonnie Verardo; Asst. Cur. Photographs & Prints, Sherri Sorensen; Curatorial Asst., Leilani Ringkvist; Preparator, Steven Hurley.
Institution Type/Description: Art Museum.
Hours & Admission Prices: Tues.-Sat. 10-4. No charge; donations accepted. Closed holidays. &
Attendance: 44,374 (actual)

WHEELS TRANSPORTATION MUSEUM, 1100 2nd S.W., Albuquerque, NM 87102-1535. Mailing Address: P.O. Box 95438, Albuquerque, NM 87199-5438. Tel.: 505-243-6269.
E-mail: info@wheelsmuseum.org
Web Site: www.wheelsmuseum.org
Key Personnel: Pres., Leba Freed.
Institution Type/Description: Transportation Museum.
Hours & Admission Prices: Call for hours. No charge; donations accepted. &

Angel Fire

DAVID WESTPHALL VETERANS FOUNDATION, 34 Country Rd., Angel Fire, NM 87710. Mailing Address: P.O. Box 608, Angel Fire, NM 87710. Tel.: 575-377-6900. Fax: 575-377-3223.
E-mail: info@vietnamveteransmemorial.org
Web Site: www.vietnamveteransmemorial.org
Institution Type/Description: Veterans Memorial & Museum.
Hours & Admission Prices: Visitors Center & Gift Shop: daily 9-5. Chapel: daily 24 hrs.
Attendance: 45,000

Artesia

ARTESIA HISTORICAL MUSEUM AND ART CENTER, 505 W. Richardson Ave., Artesia, NM 88210-2062. Tel.: 575-748-2390. Fax: 575-748-7345 (attn: Museum).
E-mail: artesiamuseum@artesianm.gov
Web Site: www.artesiann.gov
Key Personnel: Supvr., Michael Rebman.
Institution Type/Description: History Museum: located in 1904-05 Moore-Ward House.
Hours & Admission Prices: Tues.-Fri. 9-12 & 1-5, Sat. 1-5. No charge; donations accepted. Closed New Year's Day; Memorial Day; Independence Day; Labor Day; Thanksgiving & day after; Christmas Eve & Day. &
Attendance: 2,000 (actual)

Aztec

AZTEC MUSEUM AND PIONEER VILLAGE, 125 N. Main Ave., Aztec, NM 87410-1923. Tel.: 505-334-9829. Fax: 505-334-9829.
E-mail: info@aztecmuseum.org
Web Site: www.aztecmuseum.org
Key Personnel: Mgr., Jaima James.
Institution Type/Description: General Museum: housed in 1940 City Hall building; Pioneer Village including 16 buildings.
Hours & Admission Prices: May-Sept. Tues.-Sat. 10-5. Adults $5, students $3; discounts to school groups; children under 5 & members no charge. Closed New Year's Day; Good Friday; Memorial Day; Labor Day; Veterans Day; Independence Day; Thanksgiving; Christmas. &
Attendance: 4,000 (estimated)

AZTEC RUINS NATIONAL MONUMENT, Physical/Mailing Address: 725 Ruins Rd., Aztec, NM 87410. Tel.: 505-334-6174. Fax: 505-334-6372. TDD: 505-334-6174; Facebook: Aztec Ruins National Monument.
E-mail: azru_information@nps.gov
Web Site: www.nps.gov/azru
Key Personnel: Supt., Denise Robertson; Cur. & Chief Cultural Resources, Aron Adams; Chief Interpretation, Lauren Blacik.
Institution Type/Description: Archaeology Museum.
Hours & Admission Prices: mid-May to mid-Oct. daily 8-6; mid-Oct. to early May daily 9-5. Adults $5; children 15 & under no charge. Closed New Year's Day; Thanksgiving; Christmas. &
Attendance: 45,000 (actual)

Belen

BELEN HARVEY HOUSE MUSEUM, 104 N. 1st St., Belen, NM 87002-4302. Mailing Address: 333 Becker Ave., Belen, NM 87002-4337. Tel.: 505-966-2614. Facebook.
E-mail: harveyhousemuseum@gmail.com
Web Site: harveyhousemuseum.org
Key Personnel: Museum Shop Mgr., Heide Green.
Institution Type/Description: History Museum: housed in the former Harvey House Restaurant; built in 1910.
Hours & Admission Prices: Wed.-Fri. & Sun. 12-5, Sat. 10-5. No charge; donations accepted. Fee for groups of 25 or more.
Attendance: 10,000 (estimated)

Bernalillo

CORONADO STATE MONUMENT, 485 Kuaua Rd., Bernalillo, NM 87004-7099. Tel.: 505-867-5351, 800-419-3738. Fax: 505-867-1733.
E-mail: coronadohistoricsite@gmail.com
Web Site: www.nmmonuments.org
Key Personnel: Mgr., Angie Manning.
Institution Type/Description: Historic Site: Site of Tiwa Pueblo named Kuaua dating from AD 1300.
Hours & Admission Prices: Wed.-Mon. 8:30-5. Adults $3; discount to AAM & ICOM members and senior groups of 10 or more; seniors on Wed. with N.M.I. D., children 16 & under, school groups by appointment & New Mexico residents on Sun. no charge. Coronado Historic Site & Jemez Historic Site: two day pass $5 each site. Annual Site Pass: $10. Closed New Year's Day; Easter; Thanksgiving; Christmas. &
Attendance: 18,260 (actual)

SANDOVAL COUNTY HISTORICAL SOCIETY MUSEUM, 161 Edmond Rd., Bernalillo, NM 87004. Mailing Address: P.O. Box 692, Bernalillo, NM 87004-0692. Tel.: 505-867-2755.

E-mail: schsinfo@sandcohist.fatcow.com
Web Site: www.sandovalhistory.com/
Institution Type/Description: Historical Society Museum: housed in the former home of oil painter, Edmond DeLavy.
Hours & Admission Prices: Sept.-June Wed. 10-12, Sun. 2-4. Adults $5; members no charge. ♿
Attendance: 1,000 (actual)

Bloomfield

SAN JUAN COUNTY ARCHAEOLOGICAL RESEARCH CENTER AND LIBRARY AT THE SALMON RUIN/SAN JUAN COUNTY MUSEUM ASSOCIATION, 6131 U.S. Hwy. 64, Bloomfield, NM 87413. Mailing Address: P.O. Box 125, Bloomfield, NM 87413-0125. Tel.: 505-632-2013. Fax: 505-632-1707.
E-mail: sreducation@sisna.com
Web Site: www.salmonruins.com
Key Personnel: Pres., Kim Stradling; Exec. Dir., Larry L. Baker; Dir. Education, Nancy Sweet Espinosa; Acting Librarian & Museum Shop Mgr., Brandi Sargent.
Institution Type/Description: Archaeological and Cultural Museum, Library and Research Center.
Hours & Admission Prices: May-Oct. daily 8-5; Nov.-April Mon.-Sat. 8-5, Sun. 12-5. Adults 16 & over $4, senior citizens $3, children 6-15 $1; discounts to AAM members; children under 6, members & student groups no charge. Closed New Year's Day; Easter; Thanksgiving; Christmas. ♿
Attendance: 5,707 (actual)

Capitan

SMOKEY BEAR HISTORICAL PARK, 118 W. Smokey Bear Blvd., Capitan, NM 88316. Mailing Address: P.O. Box 591, Capitan, NM 88316-0891. Tel.: 575-354-2748. Fax: 575-354-6012.
E-mail: smokeybear.park@state.nm.us
Web Site: smokeybearpark.com/
Formerly: Smokey Bear Museum.
Institution Type/Description: General Museum.
Hours & Admission Prices: Daily 9-5, winter 9-4:30. Adults 13 & over $2, children 7-12 $1; children 6 & under no charge. Closed New Year's Day; Thanksgiving; Christmas. ♿
Attendance: 20,000 (actual)

Capulin

CAPULIN VOLCANO NATIONAL MONUMENT, 46 Volcano Rd., Capulin, NM 88414. Mailing Address: P.O. Box 40, Des Moines, NM 88418. Tel.: 505-278-2201. Fax: 505-278-2211.
E-mail: cavo_interpretation@nps.gov
Web Site: www.nps.gov/cavo/
Key Personnel: Dir., Christopher R. Moos; Park Ranger Interpretation, Lynn Cartmell.
Institution Type/Description: Natural Science Museum.
Hours & Admission Prices: Winter daily 8-4; Summer daily 7:30-6:30. Entrance fee: $10 per vehicle. All federal passes accepted. ♿
Attendance: 48,994 (actual)

Carlsbad

CARLSBAD CAVERNS NATIONAL PARK, 3225 National Parks Hwy., Carlsbad, NM 88220-5254. Tel.: 575-785-2232. Fax: 575-785-2133. TDD: 575-885-8884.
E-mail: erin_gearty@nps.gov
Web Site: www.nps.gov/cave
Institution Type/Description: Natural History & Archaeology Museum.
Hours & Admission Prices: Visitor Center: daily 8-5. Cave: Labor Day-Memorial Day call for hours. Adults 16 & over $15, senior citizens $5; discounts to National Parks pass holders, Golden Eagle Passport holders & Golden Age pass holders; youth 15 & under no charge. Ranger-guided Tours: $7-$20. Closed Thanksgiving; Christmas.
Attendance: 460,000 (actual)

CARLSBAD MUSEUM & ART CENTER, 418 W. Fox St., Carlsbad, NM 88220-5743. Tel.: 575-887-0276. Fax: 575-887-7191. Facebook: Carlsbad Museum and Art Center.
E-mail: museumstaff@cityofcarlsbadnm.com
Web Site: www.cityofcarlsbadnm.com/museum.cfm
Key Personnel: Dir., Dave Morgan.
Institution Type/Description: General Museum and Art Center.

Hours & Admission Prices: Tues.-Sat. 10-5. No charge; donations accepted. Closed New Year's Day; Martin Luther King, Jr. Day; Memorial Day; Independence Day; Labor Day; Veterans Day; Thanksgiving & day after; Christmas Eve & Day. ♿
Attendance: 11,301 (actual)

LIVING DESERT ZOO AND GARDENS STATE PARK, 1504 Miehls Dr., Carlsbad, NM 88220-3057. Mailing Address: P.O. Box 100, Carlsbad, NM 88221-0100. Tel.: 575-887-5516. Fax: 575-885-4478.
E-mail: adrian.stiteler@state.nm.us
Web Site: www.nmparks.com; www.livingdesertnm.org
Key Personnel: Zoo Dir., David Heckard; Animal Cur., Holly Payne; Museum Shop Mgr., Barbara Safley.
Institution Type/Description: Zoological & Botanical State Park.
Hours & Admission Prices: Memorial Day-Labor Day daily 8-5 (last entrance 3:30); Sept.-May daily 9-5 (last entrance 3:30). Adults $5, children 7-12 $3, organized youth groups $.50 per person; discounts to groups & AZA members; children 6 & under no charge. ♿
Attendance: 40,155 (actual)

Cedar Crest

MUSEUM OF ARCHAEOLOGY & MATERIAL CULTURE, 22 Calvary Rd., Cedar Crest, NM 87008-9314. Mailing Address: P.O. Box 582, Cedar Crest, NM 87008-0582. Tel.: 505-281-2005.
E-mail: info@museumarch.org
Web Site: www.turquoisetrail.org
Key Personnel: Dir., Bradley Bowman.
Institution Type/Description: Archaeology Museum.
Hours & Admission Prices: Call for hours and admission prices.

Cerrillos

CERRILLOS TURQUOISE MINING MUSEUM, 17 Waldo St. W., Cerrillos, NM 87010. Mailing Address: Box 131, Cerrillos, NM 87010. Tel.: 505-438-3008.
E-mail: brownp52@yahoo.com
Web Site: casagrandetradingpost.com
Key Personnel: Dir., Todd Brown; Museum Shop Mgr., Patricia Brown.
Institution Type/Description: Mining Museum.
Hours & Admission Prices: Daily 9-5. Admission: $2 per person; discounts to groups. ♿
Attendance: 10,000 (estimated)

Chimayo

CHIMAYO MUSEUM, Plaza del Cerro, Chimayo, NM 87522. Mailing Address: P.O. Box 727, Chimayo, NM 87522-0727. Tel.: 505-351-0945. Facebook.
E-mail: chimayomuseo@cybermesa.com
Key Personnel: Pres. (V), Brenda Romero.
Institution Type/Description: History Museum: former home of Jose Ramon & Petra Mestas Ortega.
Hours & Admission Prices: May-Oct. Wed.-Sat. 10-4. No charge; donations accepted.
Attendance: 2,000 (estimated)

Church Rock

RED ROCK PARK, 5757 Red Rock Park Dr., Church Rock, NM 87311. Mailing Address: P.O. Box 10, Church Rock, NM 87311-0010. Tel.: 505-722-3839. Fax: 505-905-1277.
E-mail: redrockpark@gallupnm.gov
Web Site: www.gallupnm.gov
Key Personnel: City Mgr., Maryann Ustick; Recreational Dir. Red Rock Park, Special Events & Projects, Ben Welch; Parks Specialist, Beverly Lovett.
Institution Type/Description: Anthropology & Natural History.
Hours & Admission Prices: Mon.-Fri. 8-5. No charge; donations accepted. Closed national holidays. ♿
Attendance: 200,000 (estimated)

Cimarron

PHILMONT MUSEUMS, Philmont Scout Ranch, 17 Deer Run Rd., Cimarron, NM 87714-9638. Tel.: 575-376-2281, ext. 1136. Fax: 575-376-2602.
E-mail: robin.taylor@scouting.org
Web Site: www.scouting.org/philmont/

Key Personnel: Dir., David Werhane; Librarian & Museum Shop Mgr., Robin Taylor.
Institution Type/Description: History & Art Museums: housed in Philmont Museum - Seton Memorial Library & Kit Carson Museum, located on the Philmont Scout Ranch.
Hours & Admission Prices: June-Aug. daily 8-5; Sept.-May Mon.-Sat. 8-12 & 1-5. Kit Carson Museum: Summer: daily 8-5. No charge; donations accepted. &
Attendance: 35,000 (estimated)

Clayton

HERZSTEIN MEMORIAL MUSEUM, 22 S. Second St., Clayton, NM 88415. Mailing Address: P.O. Box 75, Clayton, NM 88415-0075. Tel.: 575-374-2977. Fax: 575-374-2977.
E-mail: uchs@plateautel.net
Key Personnel: Dir., Victoria Baker.
Institution Type/Description: Regional Historical Museum.
Hours & Admission Prices: Tues.-Sat. 10-4; other times by appointment. No charge; donations accepted. Closed major holidays. &
Attendance: 700 (estimated)

Cleveland

CLEVELAND ROLLER MILL MUSEUM, Rte. 518, Cleveland, NM 87715. Mailing Address: P.O. Box 287, Cleveland, NM 87715-0287. Tel.: 575-387-2645. Facebook: Cleveland Roller Mill.
E-mail: dancas@nmnt.net
Web Site: www.clevelandrollermillmuseum.com
Key Personnel: Dir., Dan Cassidy.
Institution Type/Description: Historic Building.
Hours & Admission Prices: Memorial Day to Labor Day Sat.-Sun. 10-3. Museum: $3. Millfest: fee charged.
Attendance: 3,000 (estimated)

Cloudcroft

SACRAMENTO MOUNTAINS HISTORICAL MUSEUM, 1000 U.S. Hwy. 82, Cloudcroft, NM 88317. Mailing Address: P.O. Box 435, Cloudcroft, NM 88317-0435. Tel.: 575-682-2932. Facebook: Sacramento Mountains Historical Society and Museum.
E-mail: smhsmuseum@yahoo.com
Web Site: cloudcroftmuseum.com
Key Personnel: Pres. & Dir., Ed Woten.
Institution Type/Description: History Museum: a 2 1/2 acre pioneer village.
Hours & Admission Prices: Summer: Mon.-Tues. & Fri.-Sat. 10-4, Sun. 1-4; Winter: Fri.-Sat. 10-4. Adults $5, children 6-12 $3; discounts to military; members & children under 6 no charge. Closed holidays. &
Attendance: 3,000 (estimated)

Clovis

CLOVIS DEPOT MODEL TRAIN MUSEUM, 221 W. First St., Clovis, NM 88101-7409. Tel.: 575-762-0066, 888-762-0064. Fax: 575-762-0066 (call first).
E-mail: philipw@3lefties.com
Web Site: www.clovisdepot.com/
Key Personnel: Dir, Cur, Phil Williams.
Institution Type/Description: Model Train Museum.
Hours & Admission Prices: March-Aug. & Oct.-Jan. Wed.-Sun. 12-5; call for additional hours.

EULA MAE MUSEUM & ART GALLERY, Clovis Community College, 417 Schepps Blvd., Clovis, NM 88101-8345. Tel.: 505-769-4115.
E-mail: carolyn.lindsey@clovis.edu
Web Site: www.clovis.edu
Institution Type/Description: Art Gallery and Museum.
Hours & Admission Prices: Mon.-Fri. 8-4:30; groups by appointment. No charge.

HILLCREST PARK ZOO, 1208 N. Norris, Clovis, NM 88101. Mailing Address: P.O. Box 760, Clovis, NM 88102. Tel.: 575-769-7873. Fax: 575-763-9666. Facebook.
E-mail: zoo1@cityofclovis.org
Web Site: www.hillcrestparkzoo.info
Key Personnel: Dir., Vince Romero; Asst. Dir., Mark Yannotti.
Institution Type/Description: Zoo.
Hours & Admission Prices: Tues.-Sun. 9-4. Adults $4, seniors $3, children 3-11 $2; discounts to military; members and children 2 & under no charge. Closed major holidays. &

NORMAN & VI PETTY ROCK & ROLL MUSEUM, 105 E. Grand Ave., Clovis, NM 88101-7509. Tel.: 575-763-3435.
E-mail: staff@clovisnm.com
Web Site: www.pettymuseum.com
Institution Type/Description: History Museum.
Hours & Admission Prices: Mon.-Fri. 8-12 & 1-5, Sat. & group tours by appointment. Adults $6.

Columbus

COLUMBUS HISTORICAL SOCIETY MUSEUM, Hwy. 9 & 11, Columbus, NM 88029. Mailing Address: P.O. Box 562, Columbus, NM 88029-0562. Tel.: 575-531-2620.
E-mail: columbusnmmuseum@yahoo.com
Key Personnel: Acting Cur., Betty Dean; Pres. (V), Richard Dean.
Institution Type/Description: Historical Society Museum.
Hours & Admission Prices: Sept.-April daily 10-4; May-Aug. daily 10-1. No charge; donations accepted. Closed most holidays.

PANCHO VILLA STATE PARK, 400 W. Hwy. 9, Columbus, NM 88029. Mailing Address: P.O. Box 450, Columbus, NM 88029-0450. Tel.: 575-531-2711. Fax: 575-531-2115. Facebook: Pancho Villa State Park.
E-mail: john.read@state.nm.us
Web Site: www.emnrd.state.nm.us/spd/panchovillastatepark.html; www.panchovillastateparkfriendsgroup.org
Key Personnel: Park Mgr., John Read.
Institution Type/Description: State Park: located on the grounds of the former Camp Furlong.
Hours & Admission Prices: Daily 9-4 (closed noon to 1 for lunch); call for holiday hours. Exhibit Hall: $5 per day per vehicle; no charge for paid campers. &
Attendance: 50,000 (estimated)

Corrales

CASA SAN YSIDRO, 973 Old Church Rd., Corrales, NM 87048. Mailing Address: 2000 Mountain Rd., N.W., Albuquerque, NM 87104-1459. Tel.: 505-898-3915. Fax: 505-897-8828.
E-mail: clwright@cabq.gov
Web Site: albuquerquemuseum.org/art-history/casa-san-ysidro
Institution Type/Description: Historic House: housed in the home of the Gutierrez family; built in 1870.
Hours & Admission Prices: Tours: Feb.-May & Sept.-Nov. Tues.-Fri. 9:30 & 1:30, Sat. 10:30, 12 & 1:30; June-Aug. Tues.-Sat. 10:30, 12, & 1:30. Adults $6, seniors & students $5, children 12 & under $4.

Deming

DEMING LUNA MIMBRES MUSEUM, 301 S. Silver St., Deming, NM 88030-3761. Tel.: 575-546-2382.
E-mail: dlmm@qwestoffice.net
Web Site: www.lunacountyhistoricalsociety.com
Key Personnel: Dir., Suzanne Stewart.
Institution Type/Description: Historical Society Museum & Historic House: housed in 1916 Deming National Armory; it once housed the unit that marched against Pancho Villa after his raid on Columbus NM & in 1941 housed men who were in the Bataan Death march; The Custom House, belonged to Seaman Field, an early custom agent.
Hours & Admission Prices: Mon.-Sat. 9-4; groups by appointment. No charge; donations accepted. Closed New Year's Day; Easter; Thanksgiving; Christmas. &
Attendance: 21,000 (actual)

Edgewood

WILDLIFE WEST NATURE PARK, 87 N. Frontage Rd., Edgewood, NM 87015. Mailing Address: P.O. Box 1359, Edgewood, NM 87015-1359. Tel.: 505-281-7655, 877-981-9453. Fax: 505-281-7170.
E-mail: info@wildlifewest.org
Web Site: www.wildlifewest.org
Institution Type/Description: Wildlife Nature Park.
Hours & Admission Prices: mid-March to Oct. daily 10-6; Nov. to mid-March daily 12-4. Adults $9, seniors $7, students $5; children under 5 no charge. &
Attendance: 25,000 (estimated)

Espanola

BOND HOUSE MUSEUM, 706 Bond St., Espanola, NM 87532-2727. Mailing Address: 405 N. Paseo De Onate, Espanola, NM 87532-2619. Tel.: 505-747-8535.
E-mail: mail@plazadeespanola.com
Institution Type/Description: Historic House: former home of Frank Bond & his family. Listed on the National Register of Historic Places.
Hours & Admission Prices: Mon.-Fri. 12-4, Sat. 11-3. No charge.

Farmington

BOLACK MUSEUM OF FISH AND WILDLIFE AND BOLACK ELECTROMECHANICAL MUSEUM, B Square Ranch, 3901 Bloomfield Hwy., Farmington, NM 87401-2831. Tel.: 505-325-4275.
Web Site: www.bolackmuseum.com
Key Personnel: Dir., Owner & Cur., Tommy Bolack.
Institution Type/Description: Fish and Wildlife Museum.
Hours & Admission Prices: Mon.-Sat. 9-3. No charge. Closed holidays.
Attendance: 22,000 (estimated)

E3 CHILDREN'S MUSEUM & SCIENCE CENTER, 302 N. Orchard Ave., Farmington, NM 87401-6227. Tel.: 505-599-1425.
E-mail: cpowell@fmtn.org
Key Personnel: Dir., Bart Wilsey; Museum Coord., Cherie D. Powell; Museum Shop Mgr., Kandy LeMoine.
Institution Type/Description: Children's Museum and Science Center.
Hours & Admission Prices: Tues.-Sat. 10-5. No charge; donations accepted. &

FARMINGTON MUSEUM, 3041 E. Main St., Farmington, NM 87402-7621. Tel.: 505-599-1174. Fax: 505-326-7572.
E-mail: bwilsey@fmtn.org
Web Site: www.farmingtonmuseum.org
Key Personnel: Dir., Bart Wilsey; Cur. Exhibits, Tom Cunningham; Volunteer Coord., Kandy LeMoine.
Institution Type/Description: General Museum.
Hours & Admission Prices: Mon.-Sat. 8-5. No charge; donations accepted. Closed New Year's Day; Thanksgiving; Christmas. &
Attendance: 106,000 (actual)

HARVEST GROVE FARM & ORCHARDS EXHIBIT BARN, Animas Park off Browning Pkwy., Farmington, NM 87402. Mailing Address: 3041 E. Main St., Farmington, NM 87402-7621. Tel.: 505-599-1423.
E-mail: bwilsey@fmtn.org
Web Site: www.farmingtonmuseum.org
Institution Type/Description: Historic House.
Hours & Admission Prices: By appointment.

RIVERSIDE NATURE CENTER, Animas Park off Browning Pkwy., Farmington, NM 87401. Mailing Address: 3041 E. Main St., Farmington, NM 87402-7621. Tel.: 505-599-1422. Fax: 505-599-1429.
E-mail: dthatcher@fmtn.org
Web Site: www.farmingtonmuseum.org
Key Personnel: Museum Specialist, Donna Thatcher.
Institution Type/Description: Nature Center.
Hours & Admission Prices: April-Sept. Tues.-Sat. 9-6, Sun. 1-5; Oct.-March Tues.-Sat. 9-5, Sun. 1-4. No charge; donations accepted. Closed New Year's Day; Easter; Thanksgiving; Christmas.

Folsom

FOLSOM MUSEUM, INC., Main Street, Folsom, NM 88419. Mailing Address: P.O. Box 454, Folsom, NM 88419-0454. Tel.: 575-278-2122.
E-mail: museum@folsomvillage.com
Web Site: www.folsommuseum.org
Key Personnel: Pres., Linda Behrendsen.
Institution Type/Description: Archaeology Museum: housed in the 1896 Doherty Mercantile Store Building.
Hours & Admission Prices: May Sat.-Sun. 10-5; Memorial Day to Sept. daily 10-5; other times by appointment. Adults $1.50, children 6-12 $.50; members & children under 6 no charge. &
Attendance: 2,000 (estimated)

Fort Stanton

FORT STANTON MUSEUM, 104 Kit Carson Rd., Fort Stanton, NM 88323. Mailing Address: P.O. Box 1, Fort Stanton, NM 88323-0001. Tel.: 575-354-0341.
E-mail: info@fortstanton.org
Key Personnel: Pres. (V), Larry Auld; Museum Shop Mgr., Charlotte Rowe.
Institution Type/Description: Military History Museum.
Hours & Admission Prices: April-Nov. Mon. & Thurs.-Sat. 10-4, Sun. 12-4; Dec.-March Sat. 10-4, Sun. 12-4. No charge; donations accepted.
Attendance: 11,000 (estimated)

Fort Sumner

BILLY THE KID MUSEUM LLC, 1435 E. Sumner Ave., Fort Sumner, NM 88119-9606. Tel.: 575-355-2380. Fax: 575-355-1380.
E-mail: info@billythekidmuseumfortsumner.com
Web Site: billythekidmuseumfortsumner.com
Key Personnel: Owner, Donald E. Sweet; Museum Shop Mgr., Tim Sweet; Museum Shop Mgr., Lula Sweet.
Institution Type/Description: Local History Museum.
Hours & Admission Prices: May 15-Oct. 1 daily 8:30-5; Oct.-May 15 Mon.-Sat. 8:30-5. Adults $5, senior citizens 62 & over $4, children 7-15 $3; children 6 & under no charge. Closed Thanksgiving; Christmas. &
Attendance: 16,000 (actual)

BOSQUE REDONDO MEMORIAL FORT SUMNER STATE MONUMENT, 3647 Billy the Kid Rd., Fort Sumner, NM 88119-0356. Mailing Address: Box 356, Fort Sumner, NM 88119-0356. Tel.: 575-355-2573. Fax: 575-355-2575.
E-mail: josephine.lucero@state.nm.us
Web Site: www.nmmonuments.org
Formerly: Fort Sumner State Monument
Key Personnel: Pres. (V) & Museum Shop Mgr., MaryAnn Cortese.
Institution Type/Description: Historic Site: 1862-1869 frontier fort; control & supply station for Bosque Redondo Indian Reservation; relocation site of the Mescalero, Apache & Navajo peoples in the early 1860s; destination of The Long Walk.
Hours & Admission Prices: Daily 8:30-5. Adults $3; AAM members, school groups & children 17 & under no charge. Closed New Year's Day; Easter; Thanksgiving; Christmas. &
Attendance: 10,126 (actual)

Gallup

REX MUSEUM, 301 W. Historic 66 Ave., Gallup, NM 87301. Tel.: 505-863-1363.
E-mail: rexmuseum@ci.gallup.nm.us
Key Personnel: Pres. Gallup Historical Society (V), Dale Underwood.
Institution Type/Description: History Museum.
Hours & Admission Prices: Mon.-Fri. 9-5. No charge; donations accepted. Closed legal holidays. &
Attendance: 2,100 (estimated)

STORYTELLER MUSEUM, 201 E. Hwy. 66, Gallup, NM 87301-6126. Tel.: 505-863-4131.
E-mail: kent@cia-g.com
Web Site: ggsc.wnmu.edu/mcf/museums/storyteller.html
Key Personnel: Dir., Ken Hodges.
Institution Type/Description: Native American History.
Hours & Admission Prices: Mon.-Fri. 9-4. No charge. &

Glencoe

RUIDOSO RIVER MUSEUM, 26897 U.S. Highway 70E, Glencoe, NM 88324. Tel.: 575-257-0296.
Institution Type/Description: History Museum.
Hours & Admission Prices: Sun.-Mon. & Thurs. 10-5. Adults $5, children 6-15 $2.50; children 5 & under no charge.

Grants

NEW MEXICO MINING MUSEUM, 100 N. Iron Ave., Grants, NM 87020-3657. Mailing Address: P.O. Box 297, Grants, NM 87020-0297. Tel.: 505-287-4802, 800-748-2142. Fax: 505-287-8224.
E-mail: discover@grants.org
Web Site: www.grants.org
Key Personnel: Exec. Dir., Star Gonzales.
Institution Type/Description: Mining Museum.

Hours & Admission Prices: Mon.-Sat. 9-4. Adults 19-59 $3, seniors 60 & over and youth 7-18 $2; children 6 & under no charge. Closed holidays. &

Hillsboro

BLACK RANGE MUSEUM, Hwy. NM 152, Hillsboro, NM 88042. Mailing Address: P.O. Box 454, Hillsboro, NM 88042-0454. Tel.: 575-895-5685.
E-mail: blackrangemusuem@gmail.com
Key Personnel: Dir., June Anders.
Institution Type/Description: History Museum.
Hours & Admission Prices: Fri.-Sun. 11-4. No charge; donations accepted. Closed Easter; Thanksgiving; Christmas.
Attendance: 800 (estimated)

Hobbs

WESTERN HERITAGE MUSEUM AND LEA COUNTY COWBOY HALL OF FAME, 5317 Lovington Hwy., NMJC Campus, Hobbs, NM 88240-9121. Tel.: 575-392-6730 & 492-2678. Fax: 575-492-2680. Facebook.
E-mail: themuseum@nmjc.edu
Web Site: www.nmjc.edu/museum
Key Personnel: Exec. Dir., Erin Anderson; Dir. Education, Mary Lyle; Administrative Sec., Mari Pankratz.
Institution Type/Description: History & Educational Museum.
Hours & Admission Prices: Tues.-Sat. 10-5, Sun. 1-5; tours by appointment. Adults $5, seniors & students 6-18 $3; discount to AAM & NMAM members; children 5 & under, NMJC students & members no charge. Closed major holidays; college holidays; reduced hours during Spring & Christmas break. &
Attendance: 25,227 (actual)

Jemez Springs

JEMEZ HISTORIC SITE, 18160 Hwy. 4, Jemez Springs, NM 87025. Mailing Address: P.O. Box 143, Jemez Springs, NM 87025-0143. Tel.: 575-829-3530, 800-495-1279. Fax: 505-829-3534. Facebook.
E-mail: matthew.barbour@state.nm.us
Web Site: nmhistoricsites.org
Formerly: Jemez State Monument
Key Personnel: Regional Mgr., Matthew Barbour; Instructional Coord., Marlon Magdalena; Ranger, Brenda Tafoya.
Institution Type/Description: Historic Site: ruins of Giusewa Pueblo, ancestral Jemez Village, occupied 1280-1680; ruins of Spanish mission, San Jose de los Jemez.
Hours & Admission Prices: Wed.-Sun. 8:30-5. Adults $5; NM seniors on Wed., NM residents on 1st Sun. of month and children 16 & under no charge. Coronado & Jemez 2 Day Pass $7. Annual Site Pass $10. Annual Museum & Monument Pass $25. Closed New Year's Day; Thanksgiving; Christmas. &
Attendance: 18,000 (estimated)

Kingston

HISTORIC PERCHA BANK MUSEUM, 119B Main St., Kingston, NM 88042. Tel.: 575-895-5652.
E-mail: info@perchabankmuseum.org
Web Site: www.perchabankmuseum.org
Key Personnel: Dir., Mark Nero.
Institution Type/Description: Historic Bank Museum.
Hours & Admission Prices: Summer: Fri.-Sun. 11-3; other times by appointment. No charge; donations accepted.
Attendance: 650 (estimated)

Lamy

LAMY RAILROAD & HISTORY MUSEUM, 151 Old Lamy Trail, Lamy, NM 87540. Tel.: 505-466-6154.
Institution Type/Description: History Museum: housed in the former Pflueger general store; built in 1881. Listed on the National Register of Historic Places.
Hours & Admission Prices: By appointment.

Las Cruces

THE BRANIGAN CULTURAL CENTER, 501 N. Main St., Las Cruces, NM 88001. Mailing Address: P.O. Box 20000, Las Cruces, NM 88004. Tel.: 575-541-2154. Fax: 575-541-2152.
E-mail: rslaughter@las-cruces.org
Web Site: www.las-cruces.org/public-services/museums
Formerly: Las Cruces Historical Museum & Cultural Center

Key Personnel: Dir., Rebecca Slaughter; Cur. Education, Andrew Albertson.
Institution Type/Description: Cultural Center and Art & History Museum: housed in the former city library built in 1934. Listed on the National Register of Historic Places.
Hours & Admission Prices: Tues.-Fri. 10-4:30, Sat. 9-4:30. No charge; donations accepted. Closed New Year's Day; Martin Luther King Jr. Day; Presidents' Day; Memorial Day; Independence Day; Labor Day; Columbus Day; Veterans Day; Thanksgiving & day after; Christmas Eve & Day. &
Attendance: 18,294 (actual)

CITY OF LAS CRUCES MUSEUM SYSTEM ADMINISTRATION, 700 N. Main, Las Cruces, NM 88001. Mailing Address: P.O. Box 20000, Las Cruces, NM 88004. Tel.: 575-541-2000. Fax: 575-525-8587.
E-mail: wticknor@las-cruces.org
Web Site: www.las-cruces.org/public-services/museums
Key Personnel: City Mgr., Robert Garza.
Institution Type/Description: Art & History Museums: Branigan Cultural Center is listed on the National & State Register of Historic Places. Railroad Museum: housed in the Santa Fe Depot; listed on the National Register of Historic Places. Rio Grande Theatre, built 1926, listed on the National Register of Historic Places.
Hours & Admission Prices: See individual museum listings. &
Attendance: 78,952 (actual)

DONA ANA COUNTY SHERIFF'S DEPARTMENT MUSEUM, 845 N. Motel Blvd., Las Cruces, NM 88007-8100. Tel.: 575-525-8847.
Web Site: donaanacounty.org/sheriff/history
Institution Type/Description: History Museum.
Hours & Admission Prices: Mon.-Fri. 8-5. Closed holidays.

HISTORIC RIO GRANDE THEATRE, 211 N. Main St., Las Cruces, NM 88001. Mailing Address: P.O. Box 1721, Las Cruces, NM 88004. Tel.: 575-523-6403. Fax: 575-523-4760.
E-mail: infodaac@daarts.org
Web Site: www.riograndtheatre.com
Key Personnel: Exec. Dir., Kathleen Albers; Operations Mgr., Daniel Delaney.
Institution Type/Description: Historic Building: built in 1926.
Hours & Admission Prices: Tours: call for hours. No charge; donations accepted. &

LAS CRUCES MUSEUM OF ART, 491 N. Main St., Las Cruces, NM 88001. Mailing Address: P.O. Box 20000, Las Cruces, NM 88004. Tel.: 575-541-2137. Fax: 575-541-2371.
E-mail: moa@las-cruces.org
Web Site: las-cruces.org/museums
Key Personnel: Museum Admin., Jennifer Robles.
Institution Type/Description: Art Museum.
Hours & Admission Prices: Tues.-Fri. 10-4:30, Sat. 9-4:30. No charge; donations accepted. Closed city holidays. &
Attendance: 17,546 (actual)

LAS CRUCES MUSEUM OF NATURAL HISTORY, Mesilla Valley Mall, 700 S. Telshor, Las Cruces, NM 88011. Mailing Address: P.O. Box 20000, Las Cruces, NM 88004. Tel.: 575-522-3120. Fax: 575-532-3370.
E-mail: mwalczak@las-cruces.org
Web Site: www.las-cruces.org/public-services/museums
Key Personnel: Dir., Michael Walczak; Naturalist, Richard Quick; Cur. Education, Kim Hanson.
Institution Type/Description: Science & Nature Museum.
Hours & Admission Prices: Mon.-Thurs. & Sat. 10-5, Fri. 10-8, Sun. 1-5. No charge; donations accepted. Closed New Year's Day; Martin Luther King Jr. Day; Presidents' Day; Memorial Day; Independence Day; Labor Day; Columbus Day; Veterans Day; Thanksgiving & day after; Christmas Eve & Day. &
Attendance: 169,126 (actual)

LAS CRUCES RAILROAD MUSEUM, 351 Mesilla St., Las Cruces, NM 88001. Mailing Address: P.O. Box 20000, Las Cruces, NM 88004. Tel.: 575-647-4480. Fax: 575-647-4304.
E-mail: gcourts@las-cruces.org
Web Site: www.las-cruces.org/public-services/museums
Key Personnel: Dir., Garland Courts; Education, Joanne Beer.
Institution Type/Description: Railroad History Museum: housed in the Santa Fe Depot; built in 1909. Listed on the National Register of Historic Places.
Hours & Admission Prices: Thurs.-Sat. 9-4:30. No charge; donations accepted. Closed New Year's Day; Martin Luther King Jr. Day; Presidents' Day; Memorial Day; Independence Day; Labor Day; Columbus Day; Veterans Day; Thanksgiving & day after; Christmas Eve & Day. &
Attendance: 10,993 (actual)

NEW MEXICO FARM & RANCH HERITAGE MUSEUM, 4100 Dripping Springs Rd., Las Cruces, NM 88011-5067. Tel.: 575-522-4100. Fax: 575-522-3085. Facebook.
E-mail: frhm@state.nm.us
Web Site: www.nmfarmandranchmuseum.org
Key Personnel: Dir., Mark Santiago; Collections Mgr., Holly Radke; Education, LuAnn Kilday; Public Rels., Craig Massey; Museum Shop Mgr., Maria Massey.
Institution Type/Description: Agriculture, History & Science Museum.
Hours & Admission Prices: Mon.-Sat. 9-5, Sun. 12-5. Adults $5, seniors $4, children 4-17 $3, veterans $2; members no charge. Closed New Year's Day; Thanksgiving; Christmas. &
Attendance: 75,000 (actual)

PAUL W. KLIPSCH MUSEUM, NEW MEXICO STATE UNIVERSITY, College of Engineering, 1060 Frenger Mall, Engineering Complex 111, Las Cruces, NM 88033. Mailing Address: Engineering Complex 111, P.O. Box 30001, Las Cruces, NM 88033-8001. Tel.: 575-646-2913.
E-mail: engrdean@nmsu.edu
Web Site: nmsu.edu
Institution Type/Description: History Museum.
Hours & Admission Prices: By appointment.

UNIVERSITY ART GALLEREY, NEW MEXICO STATE UNIVERSITY, 1390 E. University Ave., Las Cruces, NM 88003-8001. Mailing Address: Box 30001, Dept. Box 3572, Las Cruces, NM 88003-8001. Tel.: 505-646-2545. Fax: 505-646-8036. Facebook, Instagram.
E-mail: artglry@nmsu.edu
Web Site: uag.nmsu.edu
Key Personnel: Dir., Marisa Sage; Gallery Mgr., Jasmine Woodul.
Institution Type/Description: University Art Gallery.
Hours & Admission Prices: Tues.-Sat. 10-4, Wed. 12-4 & 6-8. No charge; donations accepted. Closed university holidays. &
Attendance: 23,000 (actual)

UNIVERSITY MUSEUM, NEW MEXICO STATE UNIVERSITY, Univ. Ave. at Solano Dr., Kent Hall, Las Cruces, NM 88003. Mailing Address: P.O. Box 30001, MSC 331, Las Cruces, NM 88003. Tel.: 575-646-5161. Fax: 575-646-1419. TDD: 505-646-3739.
E-mail: museum@nmsu.edu
Web Site: www.nmsu.edu/~museum/
Key Personnel: Dir., Dr. Fumi Arakawa; Cur., Dr. Anna Stvankman.
Institution Type/Description: University Anthropology Museum.
Hours & Admission Prices: Tues.-Sat. 10-4. No charge; donations accepted. Closed major and university holidays. &
Attendance: 21,000 (estimated)

THE ZUHL MUSEUM: HOME OF THE ZUHL COLLECTION, NMSU Alumni and Visitors Center, 775 College Dr., Las Cruces, NM 88003. Mailing Address: Dept. Geological Sciences, MSC 3AB, NMSU, P.O. Box 30001, Las Cruces, NM 88003-8001. Tel.: 575-646-3616 & 4714. Fax: 575-646-6123. Facebook: Zuhl Museum.
E-mail: zuhl@nmsu.edu
Web Site: www.nmsu.edu/zuhl
Key Personnel: Dir. & Cur., Tiffany Holder-Santos.
Institution Type/Description: Art Gallery & Natural History Museum.
Hours & Admission Prices: Mon.-Fri. 8-5. Closed holidays. &
Attendance: 1,000 (estimated)

Las Vegas

CITY OF LAS VEGAS MUSEUM AND ROUGH RIDER MEMORIAL COLLECTION, 727 Grand Ave., Las Vegas, NM 87701. Mailing Address: 1700 N. Grand Ave., Las Vegas, NM 87701-4731. Tel.: 505-426-3205. Facebook: City of Las Vegas Museum and Rough Rider Memorial Collection.
E-mail: museum@desertgate.com
Web Site: lasvegasmuseum.org
Key Personnel: Admin., Kristin Hsueh.
Institution Type/Description: History Museum: Santa Fe Trail interpretive site.
Hours & Admission Prices: Tues.-Sat. 10-4. No charge; donations accepted. Closed most holidays. &
Attendance: 3,500 (actual)

THE RAY DREW GALLERY-NEW MEXICO HIGHLANDS UNIVERSITY, National Ave., Las Vegas, NM 87701. Tel.: 505-454-3338 & 3332. Fax: 505-454-0026.
E-mail: gallery@nmhu.edu
Formerly: The Fine Arts Gallery-New Mexico Highlands University
Key Personnel: C.E.O., Dr. Jim Fries; Dir., Bob Read.
Institution Type/Description: Art Museum.
Hours & Admission Prices: Mon.-Fri. 8-5. No charge. Closed major holidays.
Attendance: 9,000 (estimated)

Lincoln

LINCOLN HISTORIC SITE, Hwy. 380, Lincoln, NM 88338. Mailing Address: P.O. Box 36, Lincoln, NM 88338-0036. Tel.: 575-653-4372. Facebook: Lincoln Historic Site.
E-mail: charles.ruberson@state.nm.us
Web Site: www.nmhistoricsites.org
Formerly: Old Lincoln County Courthouse Museum & Lincoln State Monument
Key Personnel: Monument Mgr., Gary Cozzens; Dir., Richard Sims.
Institution Type/Description: History Museum.
Hours & Admission Prices: Daily 8:30-4:30; groups by appointment. Adults $5; discounts to senior groups and AAM & ICOM members; children under 16 no charge. Closed New Year's Day; Easter; Thanksgiving; Christmas. &
Attendance: 40,000 (actual)

Lordsburg

LORDSBURG-HIDALGO COUNTY MUSEUM, 710 E. 2nd St., Lordsburg, NM 88045. Mailing Address: 316 E. 10th St, Lordsburg, NM 88045. Tel.: 575-542-9086.
E-mail: countymanager@hidalgocounty.org
Web Site: www.lordsburghidalgocounty.net
Institution Type/Description: History Museum.
Hours & Admission Prices: Mon.-Fri. 1-5.

SHAKESPEARE GHOST TOWN, 2 1/2 Miles South of Main St., Lordsburg, NM 88045. Mailing Address: P.O. Box 253, Lordsburg, NM 88045-0253. Tel.: 575-542-9034.
E-mail: visit@shakespeareghosttown.com
Web Site: www.shakespeareghosttown.com
Key Personnel: Pres. & Dir., Emanuel D. Hough.
Institution Type/Description: History Museum.
Hours & Admission Prices: Tours: 2nd weekend of month 10-12 & 2-4. Adults $7, children 6-12 $3. Living History Events: 4th weekend in April, June, Aug. & Oct. 10-12 & 2-4. Adults $5, children 6-12 $4. &
Attendance: 3,000 (actual)

Los Alamos

THE ART CENTER AT FULLER LODGE, 2132 Central Ave. Front, Los Alamos, NM 87544-4013. Mailing Address: P.O. Box 1295, Espanola, NM 87532-1295. Tel.: 505-662-1635. Fax: 505-662-9334.
E-mail: director@artful.org
Web Site: artfulnm.org
Key Personnel: Exec. Dir., Ken Nebel; Museum Shop Mgr., Samantha Gregory.
Institution Type/Description: Art Center & Gallery.
Hours & Admission Prices: Mon.-Sat. 10-4. No charge; donations accepted. Closed New Year's Day; Thanksgiving; Christmas. &
Attendance: 18,000 (actual)

BANDELIER NATIONAL MONUMENT, 15 Entrance Rd., Los Alamos, NM 87544-9508. Tel.: 505-672-3861 & 0343. Fax: 505-672-9607.
E-mail: band-administration@nps.gov
Web Site: www.nps.gov/band
Key Personnel: Park Supt., Brad Traver; Chief Protection, Fred Patton; Chief Interpretation, Lynne Dominy; Chief Facility Management, Liza Ermelling; Park Archeologist, Rory Gauthier; Museum Technician, Gary Roybal.
Institution Type/Description: National Park & Archaeological Site Museum.
Hours & Admission Prices: Winter: daily 8-4:30; Spring & Fall 9-5:30; Summer: 8-6. Admission $12 per car; call park for commercial vehicle fees. Annual Pass: seniors 62 & over $10; Bandelier pass $30; inter-agency pass $80. Closed New Year's Day; Christmas. &
Attendance: 300,000 (actual)

BRADBURY SCIENCE MUSEUM, 1350 Central Ave., Los Alamos, NM 87544. Mailing Address: MSC330, P.O. Box 1663, Los Alamos, NM 87545. Tel.: 505-667-4444. Fax: 505-665-6932.

E-mail: web-bsm@lanl.gov
Web Site: www.lanl.gov/museum
Key Personnel: Dir., Linda Deck; Collections, Wendy Strohmeyer; Exhibits Designer, Omar Juveland.
Institution Type/Description: Science & History Museum.
Hours & Admission Prices: Sun.-Mon. 1-5, Tues.-Sat. 10-5. No charge. Closed New Year's Day; Thanksgiving; Christmas. &
Attendance: 80,000 (actual)

LOS ALAMOS HISTORY MUSEUM, 1050 Bathtub Row, Los Alamos, NM 87544. Mailing Address: P.O. Box 43, Los Alamos, NM 87544-0043. Tel.: 505-662-6272 (weekdays 10-4) & 4493. Facebook: Los Alamos History Museum.
E-mail: info@losalamoshistory.org
Web Site: www.losalamoshistory.org
Key Personnel: Exec. Dir., Elizabeth Martineau; Archivist, Rebecca Collinsworth; Museum Shop Mgr., Todd Nickols.
Institution Type/Description: Local History Museum.
Hours & Admission Prices: Exhibit Hall: Mon.-Fri. 9-5, Sat.-Sun. 10-4; Archives: Mon.-Fri. 10-4. Admission $5; members, Los Alamos County residents, children 18 & under and active-duty military no charge. Tours: adults $15; children & school groups no charge. Museum shop discounts to members. Closed New Year's Day; Thanksgiving; Christmas. &
Attendance: 34,700 (actual)

MESA PUBLIC LIBRARY ART GALLERY, 2400 Central Ave., Los Alamos, NM 87544-4014. Tel.: 505-662-8240. Fax: 505-662-8245.
Web Site: www.losalamosnm.us
Key Personnel: Dir., Charlie Kalogeros-Chattan; Dir., Carol Meine.
Institution Type/Description: Art Gallery.
Hours & Admission Prices: Mon.-Thurs. 10-9, Fri. 10-6, Sat. 10-5, Sun. 12-5.

Los Ranchos

THE UNSER RACING MUSEUM, 1776 Montano N.W., Los Ranchos, NM 87107-3245. Tel.: 505-341-1776.
E-mail: susan@unserracingmuseum.com
Web Site: www.unserracingmuseum.com
Key Personnel: Dir., Susan Unser; Pres. (V), Al Unser; Museum Shop Mgr., Janet deVesty.
Institution Type/Description: Racing Museum.
Hours & Admission Prices: Daily 10-4. Adults $10, seniors & military $6; discounts to groups of 20 or more and Blue Star members; children under 16 no charge. Closed New Year's Day; Easter; Thanksgiving; Christmas. &
Attendance: 20,000 (estimated)

Lovington

LEA COUNTY MUSEUM, 103 S. Love St., Lovington, NM 88260-4218. Tel.: 575-396-4805. Fax: 575-396-4805.
E-mail: leacomuseum@leaco.net
Web Site: www.leacountymuseum.org
Key Personnel: Dir., Jim Harris.
Institution Type/Description: History Museum.
Hours & Admission Prices: Tues.-Sat. 9-5; other times by appointment. No charge. Closed New Year's Day; Independence Day; Thanksgiving; Christmas.

Madrid

OLD COAL MINE MUSEUM, 2846 State Hwy. 14, (on the Turquoise Trail), Madrid, NM 87010. Tel.: 505-438-3780, 505-473-0743 (schedule tour).
E-mail: ocm@themineshafttavern.com
Web Site: www.themineshafttavern.com
Key Personnel: Dir. & C.E.O., Lori Lindsey.
Institution Type/Description: Mine Museum.
Hours & Admission Prices: Fri.-Mon. 10-5; other times by appointment weather permitting. Adults $5; discounts to seniors & children under 10. Closed Thanksgiving; Christmas.
Attendance: 3,575 (estimated)

Magdalena

BOX CAR MUSEUM, 108 N. Main St., Magdalena, NM 87825. Mailing Address: P.O. Box 145, Magdalena, NM 87825. Tel.: 575-854-2361. Fax: 575-854-2273. Facebook: Magdalena Public Library.
E-mail: mpl@gilanet.com
Web Site: www.magdalenapubliclibrary.org

Key Personnel: Cur., Judith Shamosh.
Institution Type/Description: History Museum.
Hours & Admission Prices: Mon.-Tues. & Thurs. 11-6, Wed. 12:30-8, Sat. 12-4. No charge; donations accepted.
Attendance: 300 (estimated)

Mesilla

GADSDEN MUSEUM, 1875 Boutz Rd., Mesilla, NM 88046. Mailing Address: Box 147, Mesilla, NM 88046-0147. Tel.: 575-526-6293.
E-mail: gadsden.museum@yahoo.com
Web Site: gadsdenmuseummesilla.com
Key Personnel: Dir., Mary F. Bird.
Institution Type/Description: History Museum.
Hours & Admission Prices: Wed.-Sat. by appointment. Adults $8, children 5 & up $5. Closed New Year's Day; Easter; Independence Day; Thanksgiving; Christmas. &
Attendance: 100 (estimated)

Moriarty

MORIARTY HISTORICAL SOCIETY & MUSEUM, 202 Broadway St., Moriarty, NM 87035. Mailing Address: P.O. Box 1366, Moriarty, NM 87035-1366. Tel.: 505-832-0839.
E-mail: momuseum@yahoo.com
Web Site: www.moriartymuseum.org
Key Personnel: Pres., Rosalyn Sammie Pachta; Cur. & Archivist, Barbara Takiguchi.
Institution Type/Description: General Museum.
Hours & Admission Prices: Tues.-Fri. 10-5, Sat. 10-2; other times by appointment. No charge; donations accepted. Closed New Year's Day; Memorial Day; Independence Day; Thanksgiving; Christmas. &
Attendance: 11,000 (actual)

U.S. SOUTHWEST SOARING MUSEUM, 918 E. Old Hwy. 66, Moriarty, NM 87035. Mailing Address: P.O. Box 3626, Moriarty, NM 87035-3626. Tel.: 505-832-9222.
E-mail: usssm1@yahoo.com
Web Site: www.swsoaringmuseum.org
Institution Type/Description: History Museum.
Hours & Admission Prices: May-Oct. Mon.-Sat. 9-4; Nov.-April Mon. & Wed. 10-3, Tues. & Thurs.-Sat. 10-3. Adults $7.50, seniors $6.50, youth 7-18 $4.50; children 6 & under no charge.

Mountainair

SALINAS PUEBLO MISSIONS NATIONAL MONUMENT, 102 S. Ripley St., Mountainair, NM 87036. Mailing Address: P.O. Box 517, Mountainair, NM 87036-0517. Tel.: 505-847-2585. Fax: 505-847-2441.
E-mail: sapu_superintendent@nps.gov
Web Site: www.nps.gov/sapu/index.htm
Formerly: Gran Quivira National Monument
Key Personnel: Supt., Thomas L. Betts; Chief Ranger & Chief Interpretation, Norma Pineda.
Institution Type/Description: Archaeology Museums: located near the sites of Abo, gran Quivira & Quarai, prehistoric pithouses c.800 A.D.; prehistoric Indian ruins c.1100-1670 A.D.; four Spanish mission ruins c.1622-1672.
Hours & Admission Prices: Headquarters: daily 8-5. Monument: Memorial Day to Labor Day daily 9-6; Sept.-May daily 9-5. No charge; donations accepted. Closed New Year's Day; Thanksgiving; Christmas. &
Attendance: 30,000 (estimated)

Nageezi

CHACO CULTURE NATIONAL HISTORICAL PARK, 1808 County Rd. 7950, Nageezi, NM 87037. Mailing Address: P.O. Box 220, Nageezi, NM 87037-0220. Tel.: 505-786-7014. Fax: 505-786-7061.
Web Site: www.nps.gov/chcu
Institution Type/Description: Archaeology Museum.
Hours & Admission Prices: Park: daily 7-sunset. Entrance Fees 2016: vehicle $16, motorcycle $12, Individual $8. Closed New Year's Day; Thanksgiving; Christmas. &
Attendance: 100,000 (estimated)

Organ

THE SPACE MURALS MUSEUM, 12450 Hwy. 70 E., Organ, NM 88052. Mailing Address: P.O. Box 243, Organ, NM 88052-0243. Tel.: 575-382-0977.
E-mail: spacemuralsmuseum@gmail.com
Web Site: www.zianet.com
Institution Type/Description: Space Museum.
Hours & Admission Prices: Mon.-Sat. 9-5, Sun. 10-6. No charge.

Pecos

PECOS NATIONAL HISTORICAL PARK, State Rd. 63, 2 mi. south of Pecos, Pecos, NM 87552. Mailing Address: P.O. Box 418, Pecos, NM 87552-0418. Tel.: 505-757-7200. Fax: 505-757-7207.
E-mail: peco_visitor_information@nps.gov
Web Site: www.nps.gov/peco
Key Personnel: Supt., Dennis Carruth; Chief Education, Visitor Svcs. & Cultural Resources, Christine Beekman; Cur., Heather Young.
Institution Type/Description: Cultural & Natural Historic Site.
Hours & Admission Prices: Memorial Day-Labor Day: daily 8-6; Sept.-May daily 8-5. Adult $3; children under 16 no charge. Closed New Year's Day; Thanksgiving; Christmas. Senior Pass, Interagency Pass & Access Pass available.
Attendance: 40,000 (actual)

Pinos Altos

PINOS ALTOS HISTORICAL MUSEUM, 33 Main St., Pinos Altos, NM 88053. Mailing Address: P.O. Box 505, Silver City, NM 88062. Tel.: 575-388-1882.
E-mail: info@pinosaltoscabins.com
Web Site: www.pinosaltos.org/museum/schaferlogcabin.html
Institution Type/Description: History Museum: housed in the Schafer Log Cabin c.1860.
Hours & Admission Prices: Daily 10-5.

Portales

BLACKWATER DRAW MUSEUM, 1500 S. Ave K, Lea Hall, Portales, NM 88130. Mailing Address: Eastern NM Univ., 1500 S. Ave K, Station 53, Portales, NM 88130. Tel.: 575-562-2202, 575-356-8900. Fax: 575-562-2291. Facebook.
E-mail: bwdarchaeology@enmu.edu
Web Site: www.bwdarchaeology.com
Key Personnel: Dir., Brendon Asher, Ph.D.; Cur., Jenna Domeischel.
Institution Type/Description: Archaeological Site: 1932 America's first multi-cultural, paleoindian archaeological site.
Hours & Admission Prices: Tues.-Sat. 9-12 & 1-5, Sun. 12-5. Adults $3, seniors 60 & up $2, students & children 6-15 $1; discounts to school groups; children under 6 no charge. Closed school holidays. ♿
Attendance: 7,000 (estimated)

DR. ANTONIO "TONY" GENNARO NATURAL HISTORY MUSEUM, Roosevelt Hall, 1500 S. Ave. K, Eastern New Mexico University, Portales, NM 88130. Tel.: 575-562-2706, 2753 & 2862. Fax: 575-562-2192.
E-mail: drgennaromuseum@gmail.com
Web Site: www.enmu.edu/natural-history-museum
Formerly: Natural History Museum
Key Personnel: Dir. & Cur. Exhibits, Ivana Mali; Head Cur. Collections, Darren A. Pollock.
Institution Type/Description: Natural History Museum: housed in Roosevelt Hall, originally used as a men's dormitory.
Hours & Admission Prices: Mon.-Fri. 8-5. No charge. ♿

MILES MINERAL MUSEUM, Eastern New Mexico University Campus, Roosevelt Hall, Portales, NM 88130. Mailing Address: 1500 S. Ave. K, STA 33, Portales, NM 88130. Tel.: 575-562-2651 & 2174. Fax: 575-562-2192.
E-mail: jim.constantopoulos@enmu.edu
Web Site: www.enmu.edu/about/general-information/local-events-and-info/arts-and-culture/miles-mineral-museum
Key Personnel: Dir. & Cur., Dr. Jim Constantopoulos.
Institution Type/Description: Geology Museum.
Hours & Admission Prices: Mon.-Fri. 8-5. No charge; donations accepted. ♿
Attendance: 4,936 (actual)

ROOSEVELT COUNTY MUSEUM, Eastern New Mexico Univ., Station 9, Portales, NM 88130. Mailing Address: 1200 W. University, Portales, NM 88130. Tel.: 575-562-2592. Fax: 575-562-2362.
E-mail: enmu.rcm@enmu.edu
Web Site: www.enmu.edu/services/museums/roosevelt-county/
Key Personnel: Cur., Mark Romero.
Institution Type/Description: History Museum.
Hours & Admission Prices: Mon.-Fri. 8-5, Sat. 10-4, Sun. 1-4. No charge; donations accepted. Closed university Christmas break; national holidays.
Attendance: 2,000 (estimated)

Quemado

DIA CENTER FOR THE ARTS, Quemado, NM 87829. Mailing Address: P.O. Box 7416, Albuquerque, NM 87194. Tel.: 505-898-3335.
E-mail: reservations@lightningfield.org
Web Site: www.diacenter.org
Key Personnel: Admin., Kathleen Shields.
Institution Type/Description: Art Museum.
Hours & Admission Prices: May-June & Sept.-Oct. $150 per person; July-Aug. $250 per person; discounts to students & children. Email for reservations & information.

Radium Springs

FORT SELDEN STATE MONUMENT, 1280 Ft. Selden Rd., Radium Springs, NM 88054. Mailing Address: P.O. Box 2087, Santa Fe, NM 87504. Tel.: 575-526-8911.
E-mail: leslie.bergloff@state.nm.us
Web Site: www.nmmonuments.org/fort-selden
Key Personnel: Dir. NM Historic Sites, Patrick Moore; Site Mgr., Leslie Bergloff.
Institution Type/Description: Military Museum: located on site of 1865-1891 army fort; 1884-1886 home of Douglas MacArthur.
Hours & Admission Prices: Wed.-Sun. 8:30-5. Admission $5; children 16 and under no charge. Closed New Year's Day; Easter; Thanksgiving; Christmas. ♿

Ramah

EL MORRO NATIONAL MONUMENT, Hwy. 53-42 mi. S.W. of Grants, Ramah, NM 87321. Mailing Address: HC 61 Box 43, Ramah, NM 87321-9603. Tel.: 505-783-4226. Fax: 505-783-4689. Facebook: El Morro National Monument.
E-mail: mitzi_frank@nps.gov
Web Site: www.nps.gov/elmo
Key Personnel: Supt., Mitzi Frank.
Institution Type/Description: National Monument, Historical & Archaeological Site Museum: located at site of Inscription Rock, bearing inscriptions dating from 1605-1906; prehistoric Pueblo Ruins.
Hours & Admission Prices: Daily 9-5. No charge; donations accepted. Closed New Year's Day; Thanksgiving; Christmas. ♿
Attendance: 80,000 (actual)

WILD SPIRIT WOLF SANCTUARY, 378 Candy Kitchen Rd., Ramah, NM 87321. Mailing Address: HC 61, P.O. Box 28, Ramah, NM 87321-9601. Tel.: 505-775-3304. Fax: 505-775-3824.
E-mail: info@wildspiritwolfsanctuary.org
Web Site: www.wildspiritwolfsanctuary.org
Key Personnel: Exec. Dir., Leyton Cougar; Memberships, Education & Admin., Cheryl Vaughn; Newsletter, Advertising, Publications, Georgia Cougar.
Institution Type/Description: Wildlife Sanctuary.
Hours & Admission Prices: Tues.-Sun. 10:30-4:30. Tours: daily 11:30, 1:30 & 3:30. Adults $7, senior citizens $6, children $4.

Raton

BOY SCOUT MUSEUM, 400 S. 1st St., Raton, NM 87740-4063. Tel.: 505-445-1413.
E-mail: info@santafetrailnm.org
Web Site: www.santafetrailnm.org/site558.html
Key Personnel: Owner & Cur., Dennis Downing; Owner & Cur., Sue Downing.
Institution Type/Description: History Museum.
Hours & Admission Prices: Daily 10-5; other times by appointment.

COLFAX COUNTY SOCIETY OF ART, HISTORY AND ARCHAEOLOGY, 108 S. 2nd St., Raton, NM 87740-3906. Tel.: 575-445-8979.
E-mail: ratonmuseum@gmail.com

Web Site: www.theratonmuseum.org
Key Personnel: Pres., Kathy McQueary; Archivist, Roger Sanchez.
Institution Type/Description: General Museum.
Hours & Admission Prices: Summer: May-Sept. Tues.-Sat. 9-5; Winter: Oct.-April Wed.-Sat. 10-4. Admission $5; discounts to groups over 20 people; members no charge. donations accepted. &

Attendance: 6,000 (actual)

RATON MUSEUM, 108 S. 2nd St., Raton, NM 87740-3906. Tel.: 505-445-8979.
E-mail: ratonmuseum@gmail.com
Web Site: www.theratonmuseum.org
Key Personnel: C.E.O., Roger Sanchez; Pres. (V), Kathy McQueary.
Institution Type/Description: Historical Society Museum.
Hours & Admission Prices: May-Aug. Tues.-Sat. 9-5; Sept.-April Wed.-Sat. 10-4; will open for special groups. Adults $5; discounts to groups of 20 or more; members no charge. Closed New Year's Day; Memorial Day; Independence Day; Thanksgiving; Christmas. &
Attendance: 6,000 (actual)

Rio Rancho

J&R VINTAGE AUTO MUSEUM, 3650 NM Hwy. 528, Rio Rancho, NM 87144-7524. Tel.: 505-867-2881.
E-mail: info@jrvintageautos.com
Web Site: www.jrvintageautos.com
Institution Type/Description: Auto Museum.
Hours & Admission Prices: Mon.-Sat. 10-5. Adults $6, senior citizens $5, children 6-12 $3; discounts to groups; children under 6 no charge.

Roswell

ANDERSON MUSEUM OF CONTEMPORARY ART, 409 E. College Blvd., Roswell, NM 88201-7524. Tel.: 575-623-5600. Fax: 575-623-5603. Facebook.
E-mail: email@roswellamoca.org
Web Site: www.roswellamoca.org
Key Personnel: Dir., C.E.O. & Chm. (V), Donald B. Anderson; Exec. Vice Pres., Dameron Midgette; Education, Cymantha Liakos; Public Rels., Nancy Fleming; Museum Shop Mgr., Nancy Fleming.
Institution Type/Description: Contemporary Art Museum.
Hours & Admission Prices: Mon.-Fri. 9-4, Sat.-Sun. 1-5. No charge; donations accepted. Closed New Year's Day; Independence Day; Thanksgiving; Christmas. &
Attendance: 10,000 (estimated)

THE GENERAL DOUGLAS L. MCBRIDE MUSEUM, NEW MEXICO MILITARY INSTITUTE, 101 W. College Blvd., Roswell, NM 88201-5100. Tel.: 505-624-8220. Fax: 505-624-8258.
E-mail: klopfer@nmmi.edu
Web Site: www.nmmi.cc.nm.us/museum
Key Personnel: Dir., Col. Jerry Klopfer; Administrative Asst., Liz Bolin.
Institution Type/Description: Military Museum: housed in c.1912 Luna Natatorium.
Hours & Admission Prices: Mon.-Fri. 8-4; other times by appointment. No charge; donations accepted. Closed national holidays. &
Attendance: 4,000

HISTORICAL CENTER FOR SOUTHEAST NEW MEXICO, 200 N. Lea Ave., Roswell, NM 88201-4655. Tel.: 575-622-8333. Fax: 575-623-8746. Facebook: Historical Center for Southeast New Mexico.
E-mail: history@dfn.com
Web Site: www.hssnm.net
Key Personnel: Pres., Judy Smith; Administrative Dir. & Museum Dir., Tina Williams; Museum Shop Mgr. & Administrative Asst., Amy Davis; Librarian & Archivist, Elvis E. Fleming.
Institution Type/Description: Historical Museum & Archives Center: housed in 1910-12 J.P. White, Sr. House.
Hours & Admission Prices: Daily 1-4. No charge; donations accepted. Closed New Year's Day; Easter; Independence Day; Thanksgiving; Christmas Eve & Day.
Attendance: 3,500 (actual)

INTERNATIONAL UFO MUSEUM AND RESEARCH CENTER, 114 N. Main St., Roswell, NM 88203-4706. Tel.: 505-625-9495. Fax: 505-625-1907.
E-mail: director@roswellufomuseum.com
Web Site: roswellufomuseum.com
Key Personnel: Exec. Dir., Jim Hill; Deputy Dir., Karen Jarmillo.
Institution Type/Description: UFO museum.

Hours & Admission Prices: Daily 9-5. Adults $5, seniors 65 & over and military $3, children 5-15 $2; discounts to tour groups with reservation; student groups, members and children 4 & under no charge. &
Attendance: 167,500 (actual)

ROSWELL MUSEUM AND ART CENTER, 100 West 11th, Roswell, NM 88201-4998. Tel.: 505-624-6744. Fax: 505-624-6765. Facebook: Roswell Museum and Art Center.
E-mail: rmac@roswellmuseum.org
Web Site: www.roswellmuseum.org
Key Personnel: Exec. Dir., Caroline Brooks; Pres. (V), Peggy Krantz; Cur., Sara Woodbury; Cur. Education, Amanda Nicholson; Membership Coord., Colette Speer; Planetarium Dir., Jeremy Howe; Museum Shop Mgr., Charles Bentley.
Institution Type/Description: General & Art Museum.
Hours & Admission Prices: Tues.-Sat. 9-5, Sun. & holidays 1-5. No charge; donations accepted. Closed New Year's Day; Thanksgiving; Christmas. &
Attendance: 37,281 (actual)

SPRING RIVER PARK & ZOO, College & Atkinson Sts., Roswell, NM 88201-9506. Mailing Address: P.O. Drawer 1838, Roswell, NM 88202-1838. Tel.: 507-624-6760. Fax: 507-624-6941.
E-mail: roswellzoo@dfn.com
Web Site: www.roswellmysteries.com
Key Personnel: Dir. Parks & Recreation, Kim Elliott; Dir. Zoo, Elaine Mayfield; Pres. (V), Rita Kane-Doerhoefer.
Institution Type/Description: Zoo.
Hours & Admission Prices: Summer: 10-8; Winter: 10-5:30, weather permitting. No charge; donations accepted. &
Attendance: 90,000 (estimated)

WALKER AVIATION MUSEUM, Roswell Intl. Air Center Terminal, 1 Jerry Smith Cir., Roswell, NM 88203. Tel.: 575-347-2464.
Web Site: www.wafbmuseum.org
Institution Type/Description: Military Museum.
Hours & Admission Prices: Mon.-Sat. 9-3:30.

Ruidoso Downs

THE HUBBARD MUSEUM OF THE AMERICAN WEST, 26301 Hwy. 70 W., Ruidoso Downs, NM 88346. Mailing Address: P.O. Box 40, Ruidoso Downs, NM 88346-0040. Tel.: 575-378-4142. Fax: 575-378-4166.
E-mail: info@hubbardmuseum.org
Web Site: www.hubbardmuseum.org
Formerly: Museum of the Horse
Key Personnel: Museum Dir., Jim Kofakis; Cur. Exhibits, David Mandel.
Institution Type/Description: History Museum.
Hours & Admission Prices: Thurs.-Mon. 9-5. Adults $7, senior citizens over 65 & military $5, children 6-16 $2; members & children under 6 no charge. Closed Thanksgiving; Christmas. &
Attendance: 30,000 (actual)

San Antonio

EL CAMINO REAL HISTORIC TRAIL SITE, 300 E. County Rd., San Antonio, NM 87832. Mailing Address: P.O. Box 175, Socorro, NM 87801-0175. Tel.: 505-854-3600.
E-mail: chris.hanson@state.nm.us
Web Site: www.elcaminoreal.org
Formerly: El Camino Real International Heritage Center
Institution Type/Description: History Museum.
Hours & Admission Prices: Wed.-Sun. 8:30-5. Adults $5; military veterans & children under 18 no charge. Closed New Year's Day; Easter; Thanksgiving; Christmas. &

Sandia Park

TINKERTOWN MUSEUM, 121 Sandia Crest Rd., Sandia Park, NM 87047. Mailing Address: P.O. Box 303, Sandia Park, NM 87047-0303. Tel.: 505-281-5233. Facebook.
Web Site: www.tinkertown.com
Key Personnel: Dir., Carla Ward.
Institution Type/Description: Folk Art Museum.
Hours & Admission Prices: April to Nov. 1 daily 9-6. Adults $4, senior citizens $3.50, children $2; discounts to groups, and AAM & ICOM members.
Attendance: 26,200 (actual)

Santa Fe

ALLAN HOUSER GALLERY & SCULPTURE GARDEN, 125 Lincoln Ave., Ste. 112, Santa Fe, NM 87501. Tel.: 505-982-4705. Facebook & Instagram: @AllanHouserGallery; Twitter: @Haozous.
E-mail: fineart@allanhouser.com
Web Site: allanhouser.com
Key Personnel: Dir. Production, Eric Vance.
Institution Type/Description: Art Gallery; Sculpture Garden: located at 26 Haozous Rd., Santa Fe, NM 87508.
Hours & Admission Prices: Gallery: Mon.-Sat. 10-5; Sculpture Garden: open by appointment only.

BELLAS ARTES, 653 Canyon Rd., Santa Fe, NM 87501. Tel.: 505-983-2745.
E-mail: bc@bellasartesgallery.com
Web Site: www.bellasartesgallery.com
Key Personnel: Founder, Charlotte Kornstein.
Institution Type/Description: Art Gallery.
Hours & Admission Prices: Tues.-Sat. 11-5.

CHARLOTTE JACKSON FINE ART, 554 S. Guadalupe, Santa Fe, NM 87501. Tel.: 505-989-8688. Fax: 505-989-9898. Facebook & Instagram: @CharlotteJacksonFineArt; Twitter: @CJFASantaFe.
E-mail: press554@charlottejackson.com
Web Site: www.charlottejackson.com
Key Personnel: Dir., Charlotte Jackson.
Institution Type/Description: Art Gallery.
Hours & Admission Prices: Tues.-Fri. 10-5:30, Sat. 10-5; Sun. by appointment.

EL RANCHO DE LAS GOLONDRINAS MUSEUM, 334 Los Pinos Rd., Santa Fe, NM 87507-4363. Tel.: 505-471-2261. Fax: 505-471-5623. Facebook: El Rancho de Las Golondrinas Museum.
E-mail: mail@golondrinas.org
Web Site: www.golondrinas.org
Key Personnel: Chm. (V), Steve Machen, Ph.D.; Interim Dir., Daniel Goodman; Deputy Admin., Michael King; Interim Asst. Dir., Sean Paloheimo; Education & Volunteer Mgr., Laura Gonzales-Meredith; Cur. Agriculture, Julie Anna Lopez; Site Rental Mgr., Vic Macias; Dir. Devel., Kathryn Carey; Front Desk Mgr. & Tour Coord., Amy Munoz-Sotelo.
Institution Type/Description: Living History Museum: housed on 1700-1885 Las Golondrinas Ranch.
Hours & Admission Prices: Museum: June-Sept. Wed.-Sun. 10-4. Adults $6-$13, seniors & military $4; members & children under 5 no charge. Admission varies for weekends & special events. Closed Labor Day.
Attendance: 55,000 (actual)

GEORGIA O'KEEFFE MUSEUM, 217 Johnson St., Santa Fe, NM 87501-1826. Tel.: 505-946-1000. Fax: 505-946-1091. Facebook: @georgiaokeeffemuseum; Instagram & Twitter: @okeefemuseum.
E-mail: info@okeeffemuseum.org
Web Site: www.okeeffemuseum.org
Key Personnel: Dir., Robert A. Kret; Chm., Roxanne Decyk; Sr. Dir. Collections & Interpretation, Cody Hartley; Cur., Carolyn Kastner; Dir. Employee & Organizational Devel., Cathy Ullery; Communications Mgr., Mara Christian Harris.
Institution Type/Description: Art Museum.
Hours & Admission Prices: Sun.-Thurs. & Sat. 10-5, Fri. 10-7. Adults $13, students with ID $11; discounts to AAM & ICOM members; reciprocal museum members, students 17 & under & members no charge. Closed New Year's Day; Easter; Thanksgiving; Christmas.
Attendance: 172,877 (actual)

GERALD PETERS GALLERY, 1005 Paseo de Peralta, Santa Fe, NM 87501-2735. Tel.: 505-954-5700. Fax: 505-954-5754. Facebook: Gerald Peters Gallery; Instagram: @gerald_peters_gallery; Twitter@GPGallery.
E-mail: info@gpgallery.com
Web Site: www.gpgallery.com
Key Personnel: Pres., Gerald P. Peters; Dir., Elizabeth Hubbard Hook; Dir. Contemporary, Evan Feldman; Dir. Naturalism, Maria Hajic; Registrar, Lindsey Lutz.
Institution Type/Description: Art Gallery.
Hours & Admission Prices: Mon.-Sat. 10-5. No charge.

GIB SINGLETON MUSEUM OF FINE ART, Plaza Mercado, 112 W. San Francisco St., Santa Fe, NM 87501. Tel.: 505-995-9713.
E-mail: info@gibsingletonmuseum.com
Web Site: gibsingletonmuseum.org
Key Personnel: Dir., John Goekler.
Institution Type/Description: Art Museum.
Hours & Admission Prices: Mon.-Fri. 10-6.

THE GOVERNOR'S GALLERY, State Capitol, Rm. 400, 491 Old Santa Fe Trail, Santa Fe, NM 87501-2753. Mailing Address: P.O. Box 2087, Santa Fe, NM 87504. Tel.: 505-476-5072. Fax: 505-476-5076. Facebook: NewMexicoMuseumArt.
E-mail: merry.scully@state.nm.us
Web Site: www.nmartmuseum.org
Key Personnel: Head Curatorial Affairs, Merry Scully.
Institution Type/Description: Art Gallery: housed in State Capitol on Old Santa Fe Trail.
Hours & Admission Prices: Mon.-Fri. 8-5. No charge.
Attendance: 30,000 (actual)

HUNTER KIRKLAND CONTEMPORARY, 200-B Canyon Rd., Santa Fe, NM 87501. Tel.: 505-984-2111. Fax: 505-984-8111. Facebook: Hunter Kirkland Contemporary; Instagram: @hunterkirklandcontemporary; Twitter: @HKC_ArtGallery.
E-mail: hunterkirkland@earthlink.net
Web Site: www.hunterkirklandcontemporary.com
Key Personnel: Owner, Dir., Nancy Hunter.
Institution Type/Description: Art Gallery.
Hours & Admission Prices: Open daily, call for hours.

IAIA MUSEUM OF CONTEMPORARY NATIVE ARTS, 108 Cathedral Pl., Santa Fe, NM 87501. Tel.: 505-983-8900.
E-mail: pphillips@iaia.edu
Web Site: www.iaia.edu
Key Personnel: Dir., Patsy Phillips.
Institution Type/Description: Art Museum.
Hours & Admission Prices: Call for hours.

IAIA MUSEUM OF CONTEMPORARY NATIVE ARTS, 108 Cathedral Pl., Santa Fe, NM 87501-2027. Tel.: 505-983-8900. Fax: 505-983-1222. Facebook, Twitter.
E-mail: museum@iaia.edu
Web Site: www.iaia.edu/museum
Key Personnel: Dir., Patsy Phillips; Administrative Coord., Marcella Apodaca; Facilities & Security Mgr., Thomas Atencio; Membership & Program Mgr., Andrea Hanley; Preparator & Exhibitions, Mattie Reynolds; Chief Cur., Manuela Well-Off-Man; Cur. Collections, Tatiana Lomahaftewa Singer; Graphic Designer, Sallie Wesaw Sloan.
Institution Type/Description: Culturally Specific.
Hours & Admission Prices: Mon. & Wed.-Sat. 10-5, Sun. 12-5. Adults $10, students & senior citizens with ID $5; discounts to AAM members; children 16 & under, members, & Native Americans no charge. Closed New Year's Day; Easter; Thanksgiving; Christmas.
Attendance: 39,761 (actual)

KENNETH E. BRASEL CENTENNIAL MUSEUM, New Mexico School for the Deaf, 1060 Cerrillos Rd., Santa Fe, NM 87505. Tel.: 505-476-6300. Facebook: @NMSchoolDeaf.
E-mail: kerilynn11@msn.com
Web Site: www.nmsd.k12.nm.us
Key Personnel: NMSD Supt., Dr. Rosemary J. Gallegos.
Institution Type/Description: History Museum.
Hours & Admission Prices: By appointment only. No charge.

MARTHA KEATS GALLERY, 644 Canyon Rd., Santa Fe, NM 87501. Mailing Address: P.O. Box 1, Santa Fe, NM 87504. Tel.: 505-982-6686.
E-mail: artworkinquiries@marthakeatsgallery.com
Web Site: www.marthakeatsgallery.com
Institution Type/Description: Art Gallery.
Hours & Admission Prices: Call for hours.

MONROE GALLERY OF PHOTOGRAPHY, 112 Don Gaspar, Santa Fe, NM 87501. Tel.: 505-992-0800. Fax: 505-992-0810. Facebook & Twitter: @monroegallery.
E-mail: info@monroegallery.com
Web Site: www.monroegallery.com
Key Personnel: Owner, Sidney Monroe; Owner, Michelle Monroe.
Institution Type/Description: Art Gallery.
Hours & Admission Prices: Call for hours.

MORNING STAR GALLERY, 513 Canyon Rd., Santa Fe, NM 87501. Tel.: 505-982-8187. Fax: 505-984-2368. Facebook: @morningstargallery.
E-mail: indian@morningstargallery.com
Web Site: www.morningstargallery.com
Key Personnel: Owner, Nedra Matteucci.
Institution Type/Description: Art Gallery.
Hours & Admission Prices: Call for hours.

MUNOZ WAXMAN GALLERY - CENTER FOR CONTEMPORARY ARTS, 1050 Old Pecos Trail, Santa Fe, NM 87505. Tel.: 505-982-1338. Facebook, Instagram, Twitter.
E-mail: curator@ccasantafe.org
Web Site: www.ccasantafe.org
Key Personnel: Exec. Dir., Stuart Ashman.
Institution Type/Description: Art Gallery.
Hours & Admission Prices: Thurs.-Sun. noon to 5.

MUSEUM OF INDIAN ARTS & CULTURE, 710 Camino Lejo, Santa Fe, NM 87505-7511. Mailing Address: P.O. Box 2087, Santa Fe, NM 87504-2087. Tel.: 505-476-1269. Fax: 505-476-1330. Faceboook: @IndianArtsCulture; Twitter: @NMM_IndianArts.
E-mail: miac.info@state.nm.us
Web Site: www.indianartsandculture.org
Key Personnel: Dir., Della Warrior; Deputy Dir., Marla Redcorn-Miller; Cur. Archaeological Research Collections, Julia Clifton; Cur. Individually Cataloged Collections, Valerie Verzuh; Archivist, Diana Bird; Dir. Education, Joyce Begay-Foss; Librarian, Allison Colborne.
Institution Type/Description: Native American Arts & Culture Museum: Laboratory of Anthropology is housed in 1931 Spanish-Pueblo revival architecture designed by John Gaw Meem.
Hours & Admission Prices: May-Oct. daily 10-5; Nov.-April Tues.-Sun. 10-5. Adults $12, students w/ID $11; discounts AAM members; children 16 & under and members no charge. Closed New Year's Day; Easter; Thanksgiving; Christmas. ♿
Attendance: 48,446 (actual)

MUSEUM OF INTERNATIONAL FOLK ART, 706 Camino Lejo, Santa Fe, NM 87505. Mailing Address: P.O. Box 2087, Santa Fe, NM 87504-2087. Tel.: 505-476-1200. Fax: 505-476-1300. Facebook: @InternationalFolkArt; Twitter: @NMM_IntFolkArt.
E-mail: info.moifa@state.nm.us
Web Site: www.internationalfolkart.org
Key Personnel: Dir., Khristaan Villela; Deputy Dir., Aurelia Gomez; Dir. Collections, Polina J. Smutko; Cur. Latin American & Caribbean Collections, Amy Groleau; Cur. Latino, Hispano & Spanish Colonial Collections, Nicolasa Chavez; Cur. Textiles & Costumes, Carrie Hertz; Cur. European & American Folk Art, Laura Addison; Sr. Cur. & Cur. Asian & Oceanic Folk Art, Felicia Katz-Harris; Librarian & Archivist, Caroline Dechert; Special Events & Public Rels. Coord., Laura Lovejoy-May; Outreach Educator, Patricia Sigala; Exec. Sec., Chris Vitagliano.
Institution Type/Description: International Folk Art Museum.
Hours & Admission Prices: May-Oct. daily 10-5; Nov.-April Tues.-Sun. 10-5. Adults & Seniors $12, students w/ID $6; discounts to New Mexico residents and AAM & ICOM members; children 16 & under, school groups, museum foundation members no charge. Closed New Year's Day; Easter; Thanksgiving; Christmas. ♿
Attendance: 85,000 (actual)

MUSEUM OF NEW MEXICO, 725 Camino Lejo, Santa Fe, NM 87505-7516. Mailing Address: P.O. Box 2087, Santa Fe, NM 87504-2087. Tel.: 505-982-6366. Fax: 505-476-1127. Facebook: @MONMF.
E-mail: steve.cantrell@state.nm.us
Web Site: www.museumofnewmexico.org
Key Personnel: Dir. NM History Museum, Andrew Wulf; Dir. Museum of Indian Arts & Culture, Della Warrior; Dir. NM Museum of Arts, Mary Kershaw; Dir. Museum of International Folk Art, Khristaan Villela; Public Rels. Mgr., Steve Cantrell.
Institution Type/Description: History, Art, Folk Art & Anthropology Museums.
Hours & Admission Prices: NM History Museum, Museum of Art, Museum of International Folk Art and Museum of Indian Arts & Cultures: daily 10-5. Admission $12, students w/ID $6, Cultural Pass: $30; discounts to NM residents & groups; Museum of New Mexico Foundation members & children under 16 no charge. Closed Mondays Nov.-April; New Year's Day; Easter; Thanksgiving; Christmas. ♿
Attendance: 642,100 (actual)

NEDRA MATTEUCCI GALLERIES, 1075 Paseo de Peralta, Santa Fe, NM 87501. Tel.: 505-982-4631. Fax: 505-984-0199. Facebook & Instagram: @nedramatteuccigalleries.
E-mail: inquiry@matteucci.com
Web Site: www.matteucci.com
Key Personnel: Owner, Nedra Matteucci.
Institution Type/Description: Art Gallery.
Hours & Admission Prices: Mon.-Sat. 9-5.

NEW MEXICO HISTORY MUSEUM/PALACE OF THE GOVERNORS, 113 Lincoln Ave., (NMHM), Santa Fe, NM 87501. 105 W. Palace Ave., (Palace), Santa Fe, NM 87501. Mailing Address: P.O. Box 2087, Santa Fe, NM 87504-2087. Tel.: 505-476-5100 (Palace) & 5200 (NMHM). Fax: 505-476-5104. Facebook, Twitter.
E-mail: andrew.wulf@state.nm.us
Web Site: www.nmhistorymuseum.org; www.palaceofthegovernors.org
Key Personnel: Interim Dir., Billy Garrett; Opers. Mgr., Seth McFarland; Collections & Education Mgr., Rene Harris; Registrar, Deborah King; Finance Mgr., Andrea Chavez; Curator, Cathy Notarnicola; Curator, Alicia Romero.
Institution Type/Description: Palace: housed in c.1610 Spanish-style government building.
Hours & Admission Prices: May-Oct. daily 10-5; Nov.-April Tues.-Sun. 10-5. Adults $12, New Mexico residents $7; discounts AAM members; children 16 & under and members no charge. Closed New Year's Day; Easter; Thanksgiving; Christmas. ♿
Attendance: 100,000 (estimated)

NEW MEXICO MUSEUM OF ART, 107 W. Palace Ave., Santa Fe, NM 87501-2014. Mailing Address: P.O. Box 2087, 107 W. Palace Ave., Santa Fe, NM 87504-2087. Tel.: 505-476-5072. Fax: 505-476-5076.
E-mail: rebecca.potance@state.nm.us
Web Site: nmartmuseum.org
Formerly: Museum of Fine Arts
Key Personnel: Dir., Mary Kershaw; Librarian, Rebecca Potance; Head Education & Visitor Experience, Rebecca Aubin; Head Registration & Collections, Michelle Gallagher-Roberts; Cur. Photography, Kate Ware; Preparator, Sam Rykels; Head, Curatorial Affairs, Merry Scully; Cur. 20th Century Art, Christian Waguespack; Mgr. Collections, Erica Prater; Museum Educator & Volunteer Coord., Chris Nail; Security Captain, Dominic Martinez.
Institution Type/Description: Art Museum: housed in an architectural structure patterned after New Mexico mission churches.
Hours & Admission Prices: Winter: Tues.-Sun. 10-5; Summer: daily 10-5. Single non-resident $12, single NM residents $7; discounts to AAM & ICOM members; school groups, NM residents on 1st Sun. of month, seniors 60 & over on Wed., 1st Fri. each month 5-7 & museum members no charge. Annual Culture Pass: $30 (allows 1 visit to each State Museum & Historic Site). Closed New Year's Day; Easter; Thanksgiving; Christmas. ♿
Attendance: 125,000 (actual)

NEW MEXICO NATIONAL GUARD MUSEUM, 1050 Old Pecos Tr., Santa Fe, NM 87505-2688. Tel.: 505-474-1670. Facebook: @nmngmuseum.
E-mail: nmngbmf@gmail.com
Web Site: www.bataanmuseum.com
Formerly: Bataan Memorial Museum
Key Personnel: Dir., Maj. Gen. (Ret.) Frank Schober.
Institution Type/Description: Military Museum.
Hours & Admission Prices: Tues.-Fri. 10-4. No charge; donations accepted. Closed holidays.

NUART GALLERY, 670 Canyon Rd., Santa Fe, NM 87501. Tel.: 505-988-3888. Facebook, Instagram & Twitter: @nuartgallery.
E-mail: fineart@nuartgallery.com
Web Site: www.nuartgallery.com
Key Personnel: Owner, Juan Kelly; Owner, Kim Kelly.
Institution Type/Description: Art Gallery.
Hours & Admission Prices: Daily 10-5.

OWEN CONTEMPORARY, 225 Canyon Rd., Santa Fe, NM 87501. Tel.: 505-820-0807. Fax: 505-820-7080. Facebook & Instagram: @owencontemporary; Twitter @owengallery.
E-mail: art@owencontemporary.com
Web Site: owencontemporary.com
Formerly: Karan Ruhlen Gallery
Key Personnel: Owner, Tim Owen; Sales, Suann Sinclair.
Institution Type/Description: Art Gallery.
Hours & Admission Prices: Mon.-Sat. 10-5, Sun. 11-4.

PEYTON WRIGHT GALLERY, 237 E. Palace Ave., Santa Fe, NM 87501. Tel.: 505-989-9888, 800-879-8898. Fax: 505-989-9889. Facebook: Peyton Wright Gallery; INstagram: @peytonwrightgallery; Twitter: @PWGallerySF.
E-mail: info@peytonwright.com
Web Site: peytonwright.com
Key Personnel: Gallery Owner, John Wright Schaefer.
Institution Type/Description: Art Gallery: housed in the Spiegelberg House. Listed on the National Register of Historic Places.
Hours & Admission Prices: Mon.-Sat. 9:30-5; Sun. by appointment.

PIPPIN CONTEMPORARY, 409 Canyon Rd., Santa Fe, NM 87501. Tel.: 505-795-7476. Facebook: @PippinAbstractArt; Twitter: @PippinArt.
E-mail: pippincontemporary@gmail.com
Web Site: pippincontemporary.com
Key Personnel: Owner, Tom Ross; Gallery Dir., Rebecca Haines.
Institution Type/Description: Art Gallery.
Hours & Admission Prices: Sat.-Thurs. 10-5:30, Fri. 10-7.

POEH CULTURAL CENTER, 78 Cities of Gold Rd., Santa Fe, NM 87506-0918. Tel.: 505-455-5041. Facebook: @poehculturalcenter.
E-mail: info@poehcenter.org
Web Site: poehcenter.org
Key Personnel: Exec. Dir., Karl Duncan.
Institution Type/Description: Tribal Museum.
Hours & Admission Prices: Mon.-Fri. 9-5, Sat. 10-5. No charge; donations accepted. Closed Thanksgiving; Feast Day; Christmas. &
Attendance: 750 (estimated)

SITE SANTA FE, 1606 Paseo de Peralta, Santa Fe, NM 87501-3724. Tel.: 505-989-1199. Fax: 505-989-1188. Facebook: @sitesantafe.
E-mail: info@sitesantafe.org
Web Site: www.sitesantafe.org
Key Personnel: Phillips Dir. & Chief Cur., Irene Hofmann; Deputy Dir. & C.F.O., Catherine Putnam; Bd. Chair, Andrew Wallerstein; Bd. Vice Chair, Steve Berkowitz; Bd. Sec., Courtney Finch Taylor; Pres. Emeritus, John L. Marion; Dir. Education & Outreach, Joanne Lefrak; Dir. External Affairs, Anne Wrinkle.
Institution Type/Description: Contemporary Art Museum.
Hours & Admission Prices: Temporarily closed for renovations until Fall 2017. Adults $10, seniors, students & children $5; discounts to museum staff, AAM & ICOM members; members & Fri. no charge. Closed national holidays. &
Attendance: 25,000 (actual)

SAN ILDEFONSO PUEBLO MUSEUM, 02 Tunyo PO Rd., Santa Fe, NM 87506. Tel.: 505-455-3549. Fax: 505-455-7351.
E-mail: governorsassistant@sanipueblo.org
Web Site: www.sanipueblo.org
Key Personnel: Tourism Mgr., Denise Moquino.
Institution Type/Description: History Museum.
Hours & Admission Prices: Mon.-Fri. 8-45. Vehicles $10 (includes museum admission).

SAN MIGUEL MISSION CHURCH, 401 Old Santa Fe Trail, Santa Fe, NM 87501-2746. Tel.: 505-983-3974.
E-mail: sanmiguelsantafe@yahoo.com
Web Site: sanmiguelchapel.org
Institution Type/Description: Historic Building: built in 1610.
Hours & Admission Prices: Open during the week for prayer & visitors. Latin Mass: Sun. 2pm; Ordinary Mass: Sun. 5pm. &
Attendance: 65,000 (actual)

SANTA FE BOTANICAL GARDEN, 715 Camino Lejo, Santa Fe, NM 87505. Mailing Address: P.O. Box 23343, Santa Fe, NM 87502-3343. Tel.: 505-471-9103. Facebook: @SantaFeBotanicalGarden.
E-mail: info@santafebotanicalgarden.org
Web Site: www.santafebotanicalgarden.org
Key Personnel: C.E.O., Clayton Bass; Horticulture & Special Projects Dir., Scott Canning; Finance Dir., George Jones; Devel. Dir., Rebecca Jensen; Education Dir., Mollie Parsons; Public Affairs Dir., Sarah Spearman; Collections Mgr., Cristina Salvador; Adult Education & Volunteer Coord., Shawna Jones.
Institution Type/Description: Botanical Garden.
Hours & Admission Prices: April-Dec. daily 9-5. Jan.-March Wed.-Sun. 10-3. April-Dec. adults $10, NM resident adults $9, seniors 65 & over and active military $8, students w/ID and children 6 & over $7; children under 6 & members no charge. Jan.-March adults $7, seniors 65 & over and active military $6, students w/ID and children 6 & over $5; children under 6 & members no charge. Tours available. Closed New Year's Day; Thanksgiving; Christmas.

SANTA FE CHILDREN'S MUSEUM, 1050 Old Pecos Trail, Santa Fe, NM 87505-2688. Tel.: 505-989-8359. Fax: 505-989-7506. Facebook: @santafechildrensmuseum; Instagram & Twitter: @SFCMuseum.
E-mail: children@santafechildrensmuseum.org
Web Site: www.santafechildrensmuseum.org
Key Personnel: Exec. Dir., Susan Lynn; Bd. Pres., Sharon Woods; Sec. & Gift Shop Mgr., Meri Frauwirth.
Institution Type/Description: Children's Museum: located in Santa Fe's historic district.
Hours & Admission Prices: Wed. 9-5, Thurs. 10-6:30; Fri. & Sat. 10-5, Sun. 12-5. Adults $7.50, children $5; children under 1 no charge. Closed New Year's Day; Easter; Independence Day; Thanksgiving; Christmas. &
Attendance: 45,000 (actual)

SANTA FE CLAY CONTEMPORARY CERAMICS, 545 Camino de La Familia, Santa Fe, NM 87501. Tel.: 505-984-1122. Facebook: Santa Fe Clay; Twitter: @SantaFeClay.
E-mail: sfc@santafeclay.com
Web Site: www.santafeclay.com
Key Personnel: Owner, Dir. & Cur., Avra Leodas.
Institution Type/Description: Art Gallery.
Hours & Admission Prices: Mon.-Sat. 9-5.

SANTUARIO DE NUESTRA SENORA DE GUADALUPE, 100 S. Guadalupe St., Santa Fe, NM 87501. Tel.: 505-983-8868. Fax: 505-983-4304.
Key Personnel: Santuario Dir., Gail Delgado.
Institution Type/Description: Religious Museum & Historic Site: housed in c.1780 church built by the Franciscans.
Hours & Admission Prices: Mon.-Sat. 9-12 & 1-4. No charge; donations accepted. &
Attendance: 21,000

SCHOOL FOR ADVANCED RESEARCH, INDIAN ARTS RESEARCH CENTER, 660 Garcia St., Santa Fe, NM 87505-2858. Mailing Address: P.O. Box 2188, Santa Fe, NM 87504-2188. Tel.: 505-954-7200. Facebook: @schoolforadvancedresearch.org.
E-mail: info@sarsf.org
Web Site: www.sarweb.org
Formerly: School of American Research
Key Personnel: SAR Pres., Michael F. Brown; Dir., Brian D. Valllo; Vice Pres. Finance & Admin., Sharon Tison; Collections Mgr., Lisa Hsu Barrera; Cur. Education, Elysia Poon; Registrar, Jennifer Day.
Institution Type/Description: Art Research Center.
Hours & Admission Prices: June to Sept. Wed. & Fri. 2pm by appointment only. Admission $15; members no charge. Closed federal holidays. &
Attendance: 1,000 (estimated)

SELBY FLEETWOOD GALLERY, 600 Canyon Rd., Santa Fe, NM 87501. Tel.: 505-992-8877, 800-992-6855.
E-mail: art@selbyfleetwoodgallery.com
Web Site: www.selbyfleetwoodgallery.com
Institution Type/Description: Art Gallery.
Hours & Admission Prices: Daily 10-5.

SPANISH COLONIAL ARTS SOCIETY, 750 Camino Lejo, Santa Fe, NM 87505-7511. Mailing Address: P.O. Box 5378, Santa Fe, NM 87502-5378. Tel.: 505-982-2226. Fax: 505-982-4585. Facebook: @spanishcolonialarts.
E-mail: admissions@spanishcolonial.org
Web Site: www.spanishcolonial.org
Key Personnel: Exec. Dir. Society, David F. Setford; Pres., Larry Jujan; Chief Cur., Jana Gottshalk.
Institution Type/Description: Spanish Colonial Art Museum.
Hours & Admission Prices: May-Sept. daily 10-5; Oct.-April Tues.-Sun. 10-5. Admission $8; discounts to AAM members; children under 16, N.M. residents on Sun. & members no charge. &
Attendance: 100,000 (estimated)

TAI MODERN, 1601 Paseo de Peralta, Santa Fe, NM 87501. Tel.: 505-984-1387. Facebook & Instagram: @taimodernsantafe.
E-mail: gallery@taimodern.com
Web Site: www.taimodern.com
Key Personnel: Dir., Margo Thoma; Assoc. Dir., Jaquelin Loyd; Dir. Japanese Art, Koichiro Okada; Collections Mgr., Steve Halvorsen; Dir. Communications, Celia Luz Santos.
Institution Type/Description: Art Gallery: housed in an 1860s farmhouse.
Hours & Admission Prices: Mon.-Sat. 10-5.

VENTANA FINE ART, 400 Canyon Rd., Santa Fe, NM 87501. Tel.: 800-746-8815. Facebook.
E-mail: info@ventanafineart.com
Web Site: ventanafineart.com
Key Personnel: Owner, Connie Axton.
Institution Type/Description: Art Gallery.
Hours & Admission Prices: Mon.-Sat. 9:30-5, Sun. 10-4. No charge. Closed Easter; Thanksgiving; Christmas. ♿

THE VISUAL ARTS GALLERY, SANTA FE COMMUNITY COLLEGE, 6401 Richards Ave., Santa Fe, NM 87508. Tel.: 505-428-1501.
E-mail: clark.baughn@sfcc.edu
Web Site: www.sfcc.edu/offices/visual-arts-gallery
Key Personnel: Dir. Galleries & Assoc. Prof., Clark Baughan.
Institution Type/Description: Art Gallery.
Hours & Admission Prices: Call for hours.

THE WHEELWRIGHT MUSEUM OF THE AMERICAN INDIAN, 704 Camino Lejo, Santa Fe, NM 87505-7511. Mailing Address: P.O. Box 5153, Santa Fe, NM 87502-5153. Tel.: 505-982-4636 & 1-800-607-4636. Fax: 505-989-7386.
E-mail: info@wheelwright.org
Web Site: www.wheelwright.org
Key Personnel: Dir. & C.E.O., Jonathan Batkin; Cur., Cheri Falkenstien-Doyle; Fiscal Officer, Jaclyn Gomez; Mgr. Case Trading Post, Ken Williams.
Institution Type/Description: Anthropology & Art Museum.
Hours & Admission Prices: Daily 10-5. Admission $8; members no charge. Closed New Year's Day; Thanksgiving; Christmas. ♿
Attendance: 33,000 (actual)

WIFORD GALLERY & SCULPTURE GARDEN, 403 Canyon Rd., Santa Fe, NM 87501. Tel.: 505-982-2403. Fax: 505-982-1076. Facebook: Wiford Gallery; Twitter: @wifordgallery.
E-mail: art@wifordgallery.com
Web Site: www.wifordgallery.com
Key Personnel: Founder, C.E.O., Tim Wiford.
Institution Type/Description: Art Gallery.
Hours & Admission Prices: Mon.-Sat. 9-6.

WINTEROWD FINE ART, 701 Canyon Rd., Santa Fe, NM 87501. Tel.: 505-992-8878. Facebook: @WinterowdFineArt; Instagram & Twitter: @WinterowdArt.
E-mail: info@fineartsantafe.com
Web Site: fineartsantafe.com
Key Personnel: Dir., Karla Winterowd.
Institution Type/Description: Art Gallery.
Hours & Admission Prices: Mon.-Sat. 10-5, Sun. noon to 4.

Santa Rosa

ROUTE 66 AUTO MUSEUM, 2866 Will Rogers Ave., (Historic Rte. 66), Santa Rosa, NM 88435. Tel.: 505-472-1966.
E-mail: info@route66automuseum.com
Web Site: www.route66automuseum.com
Key Personnel: Owner, Bozo Cordova.
Institution Type/Description: Car Museum.
Hours & Admission Prices: April-Oct. Mon.-Sat. 7:30am-6pm, Sun. 10-5; Nov.-March Mon.-Sat. 8-5, Sun. 10-5. Adults $5; discount to family & groups.

Santa Teresa

WAR EAGLES AIR MUSEUM, 8012 Airport Rd., Santa Teresa, NM 88008. Tel.: 575-589-2000. Facebook: War Eagles Air Museum.
E-mail: mail@war-eagles-air-museum.com
Web Site: www.war-eagles-air-museum.com/
Key Personnel: Dir., Bob Dockendorf; Operations Mgr., George Guerra; Gift Shop Mgr., Kathy Barnicoat.
Institution Type/Description: Military Aviation History.
Hours & Admission Prices: Tues.-Sun. 10-4. Adults $5, seniors & military $4; students & children no charge. ♿
Attendance: 15,000 (actual)

Silver City

FRANCIS MCCRAY GALLERY, Western NM Univ., 1000 College Ave., Silver City, NM 88062. Mailing Address: Western NM Univ., P.O. Box 680, Silver City, NM 88062-0680. Tel.: 575-538-6517. Fax: 575-538-6619.
Web Site: www.wnmu.edu
Key Personnel: Professor, Michael Metcalf.
Institution Type/Description: University Art Gallery
Hours & Admission Prices: Sept.-May Mon.-Fri. 10-4:30; other times by appointment. No charge; donations accepted. Closed university holidays. ♿
Attendance: 2,400 (estimated)

SILVER CITY MUSEUM, 312 W. Broadway, Silver City, NM 88061-4921. Tel.: 575-538-5921. Fax: 575-388-1096.
E-mail: info@silvercitymuseum.org
Web Site: www.silvercitymuseum.org
Key Personnel: Dir., Carmen Vendelin.
Institution Type/Description: History Museum: housed in the former home of H. B. Ailman; 1881.
Hours & Admission Prices: Tues.-Fri. 9-4:30, Sat.-Sun. 10-4. Suggested Donation: $5; members no charge. Closed New Year's Day; Thanksgiving; Christmas. ♿
Attendance: 11,000 (estimated)

WESTERN NEW MEXICO UNIVERSITY MUSEUM, 1000 W. College St., (Top of 10th St., within the University), Silver City, NM 88061. Mailing Address: P.O. Box 680, Silver City, NM 88062-0680. Tel.: 575-538-6386.
E-mail: cynthia.bettison@wnmu.edu
Web Site: museum.wnmu.edu
Key Personnel: Dir., Dr. Cynthia Ann Bettison, Ph.D, R.P.A.
Institution Type/Description: Anthropology Museum.
Hours & Admission Prices: Fleming Hall, the home of WNMU Museum, is closed for a multi-million-dollar transformation. Follow WNMU Staff "behind-the-scenes" on Facebook or at museum.wnmu.edu as we document the return to Fleming Hall, plans for various exhibition spaces, progress in creating, developing and installing new exhibitions. Grand Re-Opening Celebration of WNMU Museum (in Fleming Hall) to be determined in 2019. ♿
Attendance: (actual)

Socorro

HAMMEL MUSEUM, 500 Sixth St., Socorro, NM 87801-4227. Mailing Address: P.O. Box 923, Socorro, NM 87801-0923. Tel.: 575-835-3183.
Web Site: socorrohistory.org
Key Personnel: Dir., Debra Dean.
Institution Type/Description: History Museum: housed in the former Hammel Brewery & later operated as an ice house and soft drink bottling plant until the 1950s.
Hours & Admission Prices: First Sat. of month 9-12. No charge.

NEW MEXICO BUREAU OF GEOLOGY MINERAL MUSEUM, New Mexico Tech, 801 Leroy Place, Socorro, NM 87801-4681. Tel.: 505-835-5140 & 5420. Fax: 505-835-6333.
E-mail: vwlueth@nmt.edu
Web Site: geoinfo.nmt.edu
Formerly: New Mexico Bureau of Mines Mineral Museum
Key Personnel: Cur., Virgil W. Lueth, Ph.D.
Institution Type/Description: Mineral Museum.
Hours & Admission Prices: Mon.-Fri. 8-5, Sat.-Sun. 10-3; other times by appointment. No charge; donations accepted. Closed state holidays. ♿
Attendance: 13,136 (actual)

Springer

SANTA FE TRAIL MUSEUM, 516 Maxwell Ave., Springer, NM 87747. Tel.: 505-483-5554.
Institution Type/Description: History Museum: housed in the former Colfax County Court House, built in 1881.
Hours & Admission Prices: Memorial Day-Labor Day daily 10-4. No charge; donations accepted.
Attendance: 400 (actual)

Taos

GOVERNOR BENT MUSEUM, 117 Bent St., Taos, NM 87571. Mailing Address: P.O. Box 153, Taos, NM 87571-0153. Tel.: 505-758-2376. Fax: 505-758-2376.
E-mail: thn52@yahoo.com
Key Personnel: C.E.O. & Museum Shop Mgr., Tom Noeding.
Institution Type/Description: History Museum: housed in c.1825 home belonging to Charles Bent, first American Governor of New Mexico territory, site of his death in 1847 during an uprising.

Hours & Admission Prices: Daily 10-5. Adults $3, children 8-15 $1; discount to groups; children under 8 with parents no charge.
Attendance: 7,000 (estimated)

THE HARWOOD MUSEUM OF ART OF THE UNIVERSITY OF NEW MEXICO, 238 Ledoux St., Taos, NM 87571-7009. Tel.: 505-758-9826. Fax: 505-758-1475.

E-mail: info@hartwoodmuseum.org
Web Site: www.harwoodmuseum.org
Formerly: The Harwood Foundation of the University of New Mexico
Key Personnel: Dir., Susan Longhenry; Pres., Linda Warning; Vice Pres., Gus Foster; Devel. Officer, Juniper Manley; Cur., Jina Brenneman; Cur. Education, Lucy Perera; Museum Shop Mgr., Carolyn Hinske; Finance, Sherry Carlton.
Institution Type/Description: Art Museum.
Hours & Admission Prices: Tues.-Sat. 10-5, Sun. 12-5. Adults $8; discounts to members, groups & AAM members; children under 12 no charge. Closed major holidays. ♿
Attendance: 20,276 (actual)

KIT CARSON HOME & MUSEUM, INC., 113 Kit Carson Rd., Taos, NM 87571-5949. Tel.: 505-758-4945.

E-mail: directorkchm@yahoo.com
Web Site: www.kitcarsonmuseum.org
Institution Type/Description: Historic House Museum: home of Kit & Josefa Carson, 1843-1865.
Hours & Admission Prices: Nov. -Feb. daily 10-4; March-Oct. daily 10-5. Adults 20-61 $7, seniors 62 & over $6, teens $5, discounts to groups, active military, scouts & Freemasons. children 12 & under, members and students with teachers no charge. Closed New Year's Day; Easter; Thanksgiving; Christmas. ♿
Attendance: 23,500 (actual)

MILLICENT ROGERS MUSEUM, 1504 Millicent Rogers Rd., Taos, NM 87571. Mailing Address: P.O. Box 1210, Taos, NM 87571-1210. Tel.: 575-758-2462. Fax: 575-758-2462. Facebook: @MillicentRogersMuseum.

E-mail: mrm@millicentrogers.org
Web Site: www.millicentrogers.org
Formerly: Millicent Rogers Museum of Northern New Mexico
Key Personnel: Exec. Dir., Caroline Jean Fernald; Bd. Pres., Laurie Mitchell Dunn; Cur. Collections, Carmela Quinto; Museum Shop Mgr., Nancy Colvert.
Institution Type/Description: Ethnology & Art Museum.
Hours & Admission Prices: April-Oct. daily 10-5; Nov.-March Tues.-Sun. 10-5. Family $18, adults $10, seniors $8, students $6, New Mexican residents $5, children under 16 $2; discounts to AAM members; members no charge. Tours 10 & over $4 with 24 hr. notice. Closed New Year's Day; Easter; Memorial Day; Independence Day; Labor Day; San Geronimo Day (Sept. 30, Taos Pueblo feast day); Thanksgiving; Christmas. ♿
Attendance: 25,000 (actual)

TAOS ART MUSEUM, 227 Paseo del Pueblo Norte, Taos, NM 87571-7316. Mailing Address: P.O. Box 1848, Taos, NM 87571-1848. Tel.: 575-758-2690. Fax: 575-758-7320.

E-mail: director@taosartmuseum.org
Web Site: www.taosartmuseum.org
Formerly: Fechin Institute
Key Personnel: Exec. Dir., Erion Simpson; Pres. (V), Jerry Geist; Museum Shop Mgr., Vickie Snyder.
Institution Type/Description: Art Museum: housed in the former home & studio of Nicolai I. Fechin; built 1927-1933.
Hours & Admission Prices: Tues.-Sun. 10-5. Adults $8; members & Taos County residents on Sun. no charge.
Attendance: 10,000 (estimated)

TAOS COUNTY HISTORICAL SOCIETY, INC., 104 N. Plaza, Taos, NM 87571-4110. Mailing Address: P.O. Box 2447, Taos, NM 87571-2447. Tel.: 575-770-0681. Facebook: Taos County Historical Society.

E-mail: tchsmail@taosnet.com
Web Site: www.taoscountyhistoricalsociety.org
Key Personnel: Pres. (V), L.A. Lindquist.
Institution Type/Description: Historical Society.
Hours & Admission Prices: Mon., Wed. & Fri. 1-3. No charge.
Attendance: 264 (estimated)

TAOS HISTORIC MUSEUMS, 222 Ledoux St., Taos, NM 87571-5944. Tel.: 575-758-0505. Fax: 575-758-0330.

E-mail: director@taoshistoricmuseums.org
Web Site: www.taoshistoricmuseums.org
Formerly: Kit Carson Historic Museums
Key Personnel: Dir., Kathryn Ritter.

Institution Type/Description: History & Art Museum.
Hours & Admission Prices: Blumenschein Home & Martinez Hacienda: Summer Mon.-Sat. 10-5, Sun. 12-5; Winter: Mon.-Sat. 10-4, Sun. 12-4. Adults $8, seniors $7; discounts to groups & families; members no charge. Combination tickets for all sites: $12. Closed New Year's Day; Thanksgiving; Christmas.
Attendance: 31,957 (actual)

Tijeras

MUSEUM OF THE AMERICAN MILITARY FAMILY & LEARNING CENTER, 546B State Hwy. 333, Tijeras, NM 87059. Tel.: 505-504-6830.

E-mail: militaryfamilymuseum@comcast.net
Web Site: militaryfamilymuseum.org
Key Personnel: Exec. Dir., Dr. Circe Olson Woessner, ND.
Institution Type/Description: Military History Museum.
Hours & Admission Prices: Summer: Sat.-Wed. 10:30-5; Winter: Sat.-Sun. 11-4. No charge; by appointment

Tome

TOME PARISH MUSEUM, 7 Church Loop, Tome, NM 87060-6001. Mailing Address: P.O. Box 100, Tome, NM 87060-0100. Tel.: 505-865-7497. Fax: 505-865-7622 (call first).

E-mail: mabaca@icchurchtome.org
Web Site: www.icchurchtome.org
Key Personnel: Museum Coord., Elena Calles.
Institution Type/Description: Religious Museum.
Hours & Admission Prices: Tues.-Sat. 9-1. No charge; donations accepted. ♿

Truth or Consequences

GERONIMO SPRINGS MUSEUM, 211 Main St., Truth or Consequences, NM 87901-2838. Tel.: 575-894-6600. Fax: 575-894-2888. Facebook: Geronimo Springs Museum.

E-mail: info@geronimospringsmuseum.com
Web Site: geronimospringsmuseum.com
Key Personnel: Dir. & Museum Shop Mgr., Marilyn Pope; Pres. (V), Don Armijo.
Institution Type/Description: History Museum.
Hours & Admission Prices: Mon.-Sat. 9-5, Sun. 12-5. Adults $6, members $5, students under 18 $3; discounts to senior citizens, AAM, ICOM, AARP, & AAA members, military, college students, children & organizations. Closed New Year's Day; Easter; Independence Day; Thanksgiving; Christmas. ♿
Attendance: 12,500 (actual)

Tucumcari

MESALANDS COMMUNITY COLLEGE'S DINOSAUR MUSEUM AND NATURAL SCIENCES LABORATORY, 222 E. Laughlin, Tucumcari, NM 88401-2730. Mailing Address: 911 S. Tenth St., Tucumcari, NM 88401-3390. Tel.: 575-461-3466. Fax: 575-461-1901. Facebook.

E-mail: gretcheng@mesalands.edu
Web Site: www.mesalands.edu
Key Personnel: Dir., Gretchen Gurtler; Cur., Axel Hungerbuchler, Ph.D.; Museum Shop Mgr., Linda Morris.
Institution Type/Description: Natural Science Museum.
Hours & Admission Prices: March to Labor Day Tues.-Sat. 10-6; Sept.-Feb. Tues.-Sat. 12-5. Adults $6.50, senior citizens $5.50, college students & educators $4.50, children $4; discounts to members, active military & groups. Closed New Year's Day; Thanksgiving; Christmas. ♿
Attendance: 13,863 (actual)

TUCUMCARI HISTORICAL MUSEUM, 416 S. Adams, Tucumcari, NM 88401-2718. Tel.: 505-461-4201.

E-mail: museum@cityoftucumcari.com
Web Site: www.cityoftucumcari.com
Key Personnel: Pres., Alan Daugherty; Vice Pres., Danny Wallace; 2nd Vice Pres., Randall Rush; Sec., Cynthia Lathrom; Treas., Barbara Hicklin.
Institution Type/Description: History & Folk Art Museum: housed in 1903 school.
Hours & Admission Prices: Tues.-Sat. 9-3; Memorial Day - Labor Day Tues.-Sat. 9-6. Adults $5, seniors 65 & over $4, children 6-15 $1; discounts to groups of 10 or more; children 5 & under no charge. Closed holidays. ♿
Attendance: 5,000 (estimated)

Watrous

FORT UNION NATIONAL MONUMENT, I 25 Exit 366, 8 mi on Hwy. 161, Watrous, NM 87753. Mailing Address: P.O. Box 127,

Watrous, NM 87753-0127. Tel.: 505-425-8025. Fax: 505-454-1155.
E-mail: foun_administration@nps.gov
Web Site: www.nps.gov/foun/
Key Personnel: Supt., Marie Sauter; Museum Shop Mgr., Jessica Gonzales.
Institution Type/Description: Historic Site & Building.
Hours & Admission Prices: Memorial Day to Labor Day daily 8-5; Sept.-May 8-4; tours by appointment. Adults 16 & over $3; senior citizens with Golden Age Passport & children under 16 no charge. Closed New Year's Day; Thanksgiving; Christmas. &
Attendance: 15,782 (actual)

White Oaks

WHITE OAKS SCHOOLHOUSE MUSEUM, Schoolhouse Rd, White Oaks, NM 88301. Mailing Address: c/o Lincoln County Historical Society, P.O. Box 91, Lincoln, NM 88301-0091. Tel.: 575-648-2394, ext. 137.
Institution Type/Description: Historic Building: built in 1895.
Hours & Admission Prices: Memorial Day to Labor Day Sat.-Sun. 10-4.

White Sands

WHITE SANDS MISSILE RANGE MUSEUM, 200 Headquarters Ave., White Sands, NM 88002. Tel.: 575-647-1116.
E-mail: darren.l.court.civ@mail.mil
Web Site: www.wsmr-history.org
Institution Type/Description: History Museum.
Hours & Admission Prices: Mon.-Fri. 8-4, Sat. 10-3. No charge. Closed holidays.

Zuni

A:SHIWI A:WAN MUSEUM AND HERITAGE CENTER, 02E Ojo Caliente Rd., Zuni, NM 87327. Mailing Address: P.O. Box 339, Zuni, NM 87327. Tel.: 505-782-4403. Fax: 505-782-4503. Facebook.
E-mail: curtis.quam@ashiwi.org
Web Site: ashiwi-museum.org
Key Personnel: Exec. Dir., Jim Enote; Museum Technician, Curtis Quam.
Institution Type/Description: Native American Museum.
Hours & Admission Prices: Mon.-Fri. 8-5. General Admission: no charge. Tours: fee charged. Closed major holidays. &
Attendance: 7,000 (estimated)

NEW YORK

(866 listings)

Akron

KNIGHT-SUTTON MUSEUM - NEWSTEAD HISTORICAL SOCIETY, 123 Main St., Akron, NY 14001. Mailing Address: P. O. Box 222, Akron, NY 14001. Tel.: 716-542-7022.
Key Personnel: Dir., Marybeth Whiting.
Institution Type/Description: Historical Society Museum.
Hours & Admission Prices: Call for hours.

RICH-TWINN OCTAGON HOUSE - NEWSTEAD HISTORICAL SOCIETY, 145 Main St., Akron, NY 14001. Mailing Address: P.O. Box 222, Akron, NY 14001-0222. Tel.: 716-542-7022.
Institution Type/Description: Historic House: housed in an octagon shaped house built by Charles B. Rich in the late 1840s. Listed on the National Register of Historic Places.
Hours & Admission Prices: March-Oct. 1st & 3rd Sun. of the month 1-3; Nov. 1st Sun. of the month 1-3; Dec. call for hours.

Albany

ALBANY HERITAGE AREA VISITORS CENTER, 25 Quackenbush Square, Albany, NY 12207-2311. Tel.: 518-434-0405. Fax: 518-434-0887.
E-mail: accvb@albany.org
Web Site: albany.org
Key Personnel: Dir. & Museum Shop Mgr., Kathy Quandt; C.E.O., Michele Vennard; Chm. (V), Bob Belber.
Institution Type/Description: History Museum & Visitor Center.

Hours & Admission Prices: Mon.-Fri. 9-4, Sat. 10-3, Sun. 11-3. No charge; donations accepted. &
Attendance: 16,000 (actual)

ALBANY INSTITUTE OF HISTORY & ART, 125 Washington Ave., Albany, NY 12210-2296. Tel.: 518-463-4478. Fax: 518-462-1522.
E-mail: information@albanyinstitute.org
Web Site: www.albanyinstitute.org
Key Personnel: Dir., Tammis K. Groft; Bd. Chm. (V), George R. Hearst, III; Chief Cur., W. Douglas McCombs; Dir. Finance & HR, Susan Hsu; Dir. Education, Erika Sanger; Dir. Facilities Operations, Joe Benassi; Museum Shop Mgr., Elizabeth Bechand.
Institution Type/Description: History & Art Museum.
Hours & Admission Prices: Wed., Fri. & Sat. 10-5, Thurs. 10-8, Sun. 12-5. Adults $10, senior citizens & students $8, children 6-12 $6; discounts to AAM, ICOM, NARM, AAA, Empire State reciprocal & North American reciprocal members; children under 6 & members no charge. Closed major holidays. &
Attendance: 90,000 (estimated)

ALBANY PINE BUSH DISCOVERY CENTER, 195 New Karner Rd., Albany, NY 12205-4605. Tel.: 518-456-0655.
E-mail: info@albanypinebush.org
Web Site: www.albanypinebush.org
Key Personnel: Exec. Dir., Christopher Hawver; Dir. Communications & Outreach, Wendy Craney.
Institution Type/Description: Nature Center.
Hours & Admission Prices: Tues.-Fri. 9-4, Sat.-Sun. 10-4. No charge. Closed New Year's Day; Thanksgiving; Christmas.

DESTROYER ESCORT HISTORICAL MUSEUM, Broadway & Quay Sts., Albany, NY 12202. Mailing Address: P.O. Box 1926, Albany, NY 12201. Tel.: 518-431-1943. Fax: 518-432-1123. Facebook, Twitter.
E-mail: info@ussslater.org
Web Site: www.ussslater.org
Key Personnel: Dir., Timothy C. Rizzuto; Chm. (V), Bartley Costello, III; Pres. (V), Anthony Esposito; Business Mgr., Rosehn M. Gipe.
Institution Type/Description: Military History Museum: housed on the destroyer escort, USS Slater.
Hours & Admission Prices: April-Nov. Wed.-Sun. 10-4. Adults $9, senior citizens $8, children under 14 $7; discounts to groups; members no charge. Closed Easter; Thanksgiving.
Attendance: 15,000 (estimated)

ESTHER MASSRY GALLERY, 1002 Madison Ave., Albany, NY 12208. Mailing Address: 432 Western Ave., Albany, NY 12203. Tel.: 518-485-3902 & 337-2390. Fax: 518-337-4967.
E-mail: flanagaj@strose.edu
Web Site: www.strose.edu/gallery
Formerly: The College of Saint Rose Art Gallery
Key Personnel: Dir. & Cur., Jeanne Flanagan.
Institution Type/Description: College Art Gallery.
Hours & Admission Prices: Sept.-April Mon.-Tues. & Fri.-Sat. 12-5; Wed.-Thurs. 12-8; June-July Tues.-Fri. 12-5. No charge; donations accepted. Closed school holidays; winter & spring break; between exhibitions. &
Attendance: 10,000 (actual)

HISTORIC CHERRY HILL, 523 1/2 S. Pearl St., Albany, NY 12202-1111. Tel.: 518-434-4791. Fax: 518-434-4806.
E-mail: info@historiccherryhill.org
Web Site: www.historiccherryhill.org
Key Personnel: C.E.O. & Dir., Liselle LaFrance; Pres., Michael R. Beiter; Dir. Education, Rebecca Watrous; Cur., Deborah Emmons-Andarawis; Business Mgr., Lauren Mastin; Program Asst. & Facilities Support Asst., Aine Leader-Nagy; Manuscript Specialist & Communications Coord., Mary Doehla.
Institution Type/Description: Historic House: 1787 Cherry Hill.
Hours & Admission Prices: Tours: Wed. at 1, 2, & 3, Sat. at 2 & 3.
Attendance: 10,400 (actual)

IRISH AMERICAN HERITAGE MUSEUM, 370 Broadway, Albany, NY 12207. Tel.: 518-427-1916. Fax: 518-427-1915.
E-mail: irishamermuseum@cs.com
Web Site: irishamericanheritagemuseum.org
Key Personnel: C.E.O. & Chm. (V), Edward Collins; Financial Dir., David Stack.
Institution Type/Description: Heritage Museum.
Hours & Admission Prices: Museum: Wed.-Fri. 11-4, Sat. 10-4, Sun. 12-4. Library: Mon.-Fri. 8:30-4; groups by appointment. No charge; donations accepted. East Durham Museum: Memorial Day to Labor Day Wed.-Sun. 12-4; groups by appointment. Suggested Donations: adults $3, seniors $2; children 14 & under

no charge. Empire State Museum Reciprocal Program; North American Reciprocal Museum Program. &

Attendance: 25,000 (estimated)

THE LITTLE GALLERY, SAGE COLLEGE OF ALBANY, 140 New Scotland Ave., Rathbone Hall, Albany, NY 12208-3491. Tel.: 518-292-8625.

Key Personnel: Faculty Advisor, Janice Medina.
Institution Type/Description: Art Gallery.
Hours & Admission Prices: Sun.-Fri. 1-5.

NEW YORK STATE - EMPIRE STATE PLAZA ART COLLECTION, 2978 Corning Tower, 1 Empire State Plaza, Albany, NY 12242. Tel.: 518-473-7521. Fax: 518-474-0984.

E-mail: curatorial.services@ogs.state.ny.us
Institution Type/Description: Art Collection.
Hours & Admission Prices: Concourse & Plaza: Mon.-Fri. 89:30-5. Corning Tower: Mon.-Fri. 7-6. By appointment. No charge.

NEW YORK STATE MUSEUM, Cultural Education Center, 222 Madison Ave., Albany, NY 12230. Tel.: 518-474-5877. Fax: 518-486-3696.

E-mail: nysmdirector@nysed.gov
Web Site: www.nysm.nysed.gov
Key Personnel: Dir., Mark A. Schaming; Dir. Research & Collections, Dr. John Hart; State Archaeologist & Dir. Cultural Resource Survey Program, Dr. Christina B. Rieth.
Institution Type/Description: General Museum.
Hours & Admission Prices: Museum: Tues.-Sun. 9:30-5; Discovery Place & Carousel: Tues.-Sun. 10-4:30. Suggested Donation: family $10, individual $5. Closed New Year's Day; Independence Day; Thanksgiving; Christmas. &
Attendance: 719,205 (actual)

OPALKA GALLERY, SAGE COLLEGE OF ALBANY, 140 New Scotland Ave., Albany, NY 12208-3491. Tel.: 518-292-7742. Fax: 518-292-1903. Facebook: Opalka Gallery.

E-mail: opalka@sage.edu
Web Site: www.sage.edu/opalka
Key Personnel: Dir., Elizabeth Greenberg; Asst. to the Dir., Jacqueline Smith.
Institution Type/Description: Art Gallery.
Hours & Admission Prices: Winter: Mon.-Fri. 10-8, Sun. 12-4; Summer: Mon.-Fri. 10-4; other times by appointment. No charge. &

SCHUYLER MANSION STATE HISTORIC SITE, 32 Catherine St., Albany, NY 12202-1605. Tel.: 518-434-0834. Fax: 518-434-3821.

E-mail: heidi.hill@parks.ny.gov
Web Site: www.nysparks.com/hist
Key Personnel: Historic Site Mgr., Heidi Hill; Educator, Michelle Mavigliano.
Institution Type/Description: Historic Building & Site: 1761 home of American Revolution Major Gen. Philip Schuyler and his family. Listed on the National Register of Historic Places.
Hours & Admission Prices: mid-May to Oct. Wed.-Sun. 11-5; Nov. to mid-May by appointment; groups by appointment. Adults $5, senior & students $4; children 12 & under & members no charge. Closed New Year's Day; Thanksgiving; Christmas. &
Attendance: 10,000 (actual)

SHAKER HERITAGE SOCIETY, Mailing Address: 25 Meeting House Rd., Albany, NY 12211. Tel.: 518-456-7890. Fax: 518-452-7348.

E-mail: shakerdirector@gmail.com
Web Site: www.shakerheritage.org
Key Personnel: Exec. Dir., Starlyn D'Angelo; Pres., Jessica Ansert Klami; Education Dir., Dr. Michelle Arthur; Gift Shop Mgr., Tara Needham; Spl. Events Coord., Kelly Ballard.
Institution Type/Description: Historical Society Museum: housed in c.1848 meeting house.
Hours & Admission Prices: March-Oct. Tues.-Sat. 10-4; Nov. to mid-Dec. Mon.-Sat. 10-4. Adults $5. Closed major holidays. &
Attendance: 13,000 (actual)

TEN BROECK MANSION - ALBANY COUNTY HISTORICAL ASSOCIATION, 9 Ten Broeck Place, Albany, NY 12210-2524. Tel.: 518-436-9826. Fax: 518-436-1489.

E-mail: achadirector@onecommail.com
Web Site: www.tenbroeckmansion.org

Key Personnel: Exec. Dir., Jillian Altenburg; Pres., Marie Erkes; First Vice Pres., Jennifer Dorsey; Second Vice Pres., Joanne Justice; Treas., Stephanie Ferentinos; Sec., Sharon Calka.
Institution Type/Description: Historic House Museum: 1798 Arbor Hill, Federal style mansion, home of General Abraham Ten Broeck & later the Olcott family.
Hours & Admission Prices: May-Oct. Thurs.-Fri. 10-4, Sat.-Sun. 1-4: Adults $5, students & seniors $4, children $3; children under 5 & members no charge. Closed all major holidays.
Attendance: 5,925 (actual)

UNIVERSITY ART MUSEUM, UNIVERSITY AT ALBANY, State University of New York, 1400 Washington Ave., Albany, NY 12222. Tel.: 518-442-4035. Fax: 518-442-5075. Facebook.

E-mail: museum@albany.edu
Web Site: www.albany.edu/museum
Key Personnel: Dir., Janet Riker; Assoc. Dir., Corinna Ripps Schaming; Exhibit Designer, Zheng Hu; Preparator, Jeffrey Wright-Sedam; Exhibition & Outreach Coord., Naomi Lewis; Registrar, Darcie Abbatiello; Admin. Asst., Joanne Lue; Admin. Asst., Alana Akacki.
Institution Type/Description: Contemporary Art.
Hours & Admission Prices: Summer: Tues.-Sat. 11-4; Sept.-June Tues. 10-8, Wed.-Fri. 10-5, Sat. 12-4. No charge. Closed major holidays & during installations. &
Attendance: 37,500 (estimated)

Albertson

CLARK BOTANIC GARDEN, 193 I.U. Willets Rd., Albertson, NY 11507-2298. Tel.: 516-484-8600 & 2208. Fax: 516-625-3718.

E-mail: darcyj@northhempstead.com
Web Site: www.clarkbotanic.org
Institution Type/Description: Botanical Garden.
Hours & Admission Prices: Summer: daily 10-4; Winter: Mon.-Fri. 10-4. No charge; donations accepted. &
Attendance: 20,000 (estimated)

Alden

ALDEN HISTORICAL SOCIETY, INC., 13213 Broadway, Alden, NY 14004-1312. Mailing Address: 1594 Westcott Ave., Alden, NY 14004-1122. Tel.: 716-937-3700.

E-mail: aldenhistsoc@gmail.com
Web Site: www.alden.erie.gov
Key Personnel: Archivist, Karen Muchow.
Institution Type/Description: History Museum: housed in 1859 Alden Historical Society House.
Hours & Admission Prices: March-Dec. 1st & 3rd Sun. 1-3; other times by appointment. No charge; donations accepted. &
Attendance: 500 (estimated)

Alfred

THE SCHEIN-JOSEPH INTERNATIONAL MUSEUM OF CERAMIC ART, Binns-Merrill Hall, Top Fl., Alfred University Campus, Alfred, NY 14802. Mailing Address: 2 Pine St., Alfred, NY 14802-1214. Tel.: 607-871-2421. Fax: 607-871-2615.

E-mail: ceramicsmuseum@alfred.edu
Web Site: ceramicsmuseum.alfred.edu
Key Personnel: Dir., Wayne Higby; Museum Asst., Grace Tessein; Collections Mgr., Susan Kowalczyk.
Institution Type/Description: Ceramic Museum.
Hours & Admission Prices: Wed.-Fri. 10-4. Call for exhibition information. No charge; donations accepted. Closed school holidays. &
Attendance: 2,000 (estimated)

Almond

ALMOND HISTORICAL SOCIETY/HAGADORN HOUSE MUSEUM, 7 N. Main St., Almond, NY 14804. Mailing Address: 1 Park St., Box 234, Almond, NY 14804-0234. Tel.: 607-288-2833.

E-mail: almondhistoricalsociety@gmail.com
Web Site: almondhistory.wordpress.com
Key Personnel: Pres., Louise Schwartz; Vice Pres., Helen Spencer; Sec., Donna Ryan; Treas., Teresa Johnson.
Institution Type/Description: Historical Society Museum: housed in 1830 Hagadorn House.
Hours & Admission Prices: Fri. 2-4; other times by appointment. No charge; donations accepted. &
Attendance: 1,500 (estimated)

Amagansett

EAST HAMPTON TOWN MARINE MUSEUM, 301 Bluff Rd.,
Amagansett, NY 11930. Mailing Address: 101 Main St., East
Hampton, NY 11937-2714. Tel.: 631-324-6850. Fax: 631-324-
9885.
E-mail: info@easthamptonhistory.org
Web Site: www.easthamptonhistory.org
Key Personnel: Pres. (V), Hollis Forbes; Exec. Dir., Richard Barons.
Institution Type/Description: Marine Museum.
Hours & Admission Prices: Memorial Day to Columbus Day Sat.-Sun. 10-5. Adults
$4, senior citizens $3, students $1; discounts to AAM, AAA & military mem-
bers; members & preschoolers no charge.
Attendance: 8,000 (estimated)

Amenia

WETHERSFIELD ESTATE AND GARDENS, 214 Pugsley Hill
Rd., Amenia, NY 12501-5032. Tel.: 845-373-8037.
E-mail: info@hlfoundation.org
Web Site: www.wethersfieldgarden.org
Key Personnel: Mgr., Kevin Malloy.
Institution Type/Description: Historic House Museum.
Hours & Admission Prices: June-Sept. Wed. & Fri.-Sat. 12-5 by appointment. Call
for admission prices. &
Attendance: 3,000

Amherst

BUFFALO NIAGARA HERITAGE VILLAGE, 3755 Tonawanda
Creek Rd., Amherst, NY 14228-1599. Tel.: 716-689-1440. Fax:
716-689-1409. Facebook & Twitter: @bnhvillage; Instagram:
@bnhvillage.
E-mail: info@bnhv.org
Web Site: www.bnhv.org
Formerly: Amherst Museum
Key Personnel: Exec. Dir., Herbert Schmidt; Pres., Beth Roehling Flynn.
Institution Type/Description: Historical Museum: features 10 historic buildings.
Hours & Admission Prices: Wed. & Fri. 9:30-4:30, Thurs. 9:30-8, Sat. 12-4:30.
Adults $8, seniors, active military & students $6, children $4; members no
charge. Closed holidays. &
Attendance: 40,000 (estimated)

MUSEUM OF DISABILITY HISTORY, 3826 Main St., Amherst,
NY 14226. Tel.: 716-629-3606. Fax: 716-629-3624.
E-mail: dplatt@people-inc.org
Web Site: www.museumofdisability.org
Key Personnel: Dir., Theresa Fraser; Educator, Elizabeth Marotta; Cur., Douglas A.
Platt; Research Specialist, Reid Dunlavey; Museum Shop Mgr., Lacy Abbott.
Institution Type/Description: Disability History Museum.
Hours & Admission Prices: Mon.-Fri. 10-4; other times by appointment. No charge;
donations accepted. Closed municipal holidays. &
Attendance: 400

Amityville

LAUDER MUSEUM - AMITYVILLE HISTORICAL SOCIETY,
170 Broadway, Amityville, NY 11701-2704. Mailing Address: P.
O. Box 764, Amityville, NY 11701-0764. Tel.: 631-598-1486. Fax:
631-598-1486.
E-mail: wtl20mp@aol.com
Web Site: www.amityvillehistoricalsociety.com
Key Personnel: C.E.O., William T. Lauder; Pres., Caroline D'Antonio; Treas.,
Martha Peterson; Cur., Seth Purdy.
Institution Type/Description: Historical Museum: 1909 brick edifice formally used
for a bank.
Hours & Admission Prices: Tues. & Fri.-Sun. 2-4. No charge; donations accepted.
Closed New Year's Day; Easter; Independence Day; Christmas. &
Attendance: 3,500 (estimated)

Amsterdam

WALTER ELWOOD MUSEUM, 100 Church St., Amsterdam, NY
12010-4243. Tel.: 518-843-5151. Fax: 518-843-6098. Facebook:
Walter Elwood Museum.
E-mail: info@walterelwoodmuseum.org
Web Site: www.walterelwoodmuseum.org
Key Personnel: Exec. Dir., Ann M. Peconie; Pres. (V), Suzanna Hunter; Museum
Shop Mgr., Chasity George.
Institution Type/Description: General Museum.

Hours & Admission Prices: Mon.-Fri. 9-4; groups by appointment. Adults $3,
seniors $2; discounts to AAM & ICOM members; members and children 12 &
under no charge. Closed most major & school holidays
Attendance: 5,000 (actual)

Angola

**EVANS HISTORICAL SOCIETY AND 1857 SCHOOL HOUSE
MUSEUM,** 8787 Erie Rd., Angola, NY 14006-9620. Tel.: 716-
549-6139.
E-mail: evanshistsoc@aol.com
Institution Type/Description: Historical Society Museum: housed in a two-story
brick school; built in 1857.
Hours & Admission Prices: July-Aug. Sun. 2-4; Sept.-June 1st Sun. of month 2-4.

Annandale-on-Hudson

**CENTER FOR CURATORIAL STUDIES, BARD COLLEGE
AND THE HESSEL MUSEUM OF ART,** Bard College, 33
Garden Rd., Annandale-on-Hudson, NY 12504. Mailing Address:
Bard College, P.O. Box 5000, Annandale-on-Hudson, NY 12504-
5000. Tel.: 845-758-7598. Fax: 845-758-2442.
E-mail: ccs@bard.edu
Web Site: www.bard.edu/ccs
Key Personnel: Exec. Dir., Tom Eccles; Dir. Graduate Program & Chief Cur.,
Lauren Cornell; Dir. Library & Archives, Ann Butler; Dir. External Affairs,
Ramona Rosenberg; Dir. Colls. Research, Andrew Blackley; Graduate Program
Coord., Amanda Bard; Administrative & Devel. Coord., Karlene King;
Registrar, Amy Linker; Preparator, Mark DeLura; Librarian, Bronwen Bitetti;
Administrative Asst., Trian Mort; Mgr. Security, Harry Jaycox.
Institution Type/Description: Art Museum.
Hours & Admission Prices: Center: call for hours. Museum: Thurs.-Sun. 11-6.
Administration: Mon.-Fri. 9-5. Library: Sept.-June: Mon.-Wed. 10-7, Thurs.-Fri.
10-5, Sat. 1-5, Sun. 1-7. Summer: Mon.-Fri. 1-5. No charge. Closed New Year's
Day; Independence Day; Thanksgiving; Christmas. &
Attendance: 12,000 (actual)

Arcade

ARCADE HISTORICAL SOCIETY, 331 W. Main St., Arcade, NY
14009-1110. Mailing Address: P.O. Box 236, Arcade, NY 14009-
0236. Tel.: 585-492-4466. Facebook: Arcade Historical Society.
E-mail: office@arcadehistoricalsociety.org
Web Site: www.arcadehistoricalsociety.org
Key Personnel: Pres. (V), Joanne Haskell; Operations Mgr., Susan Andrews.
Institution Type/Description: Historical Society Museum: housed in 1903 Queen
Anne-style house.
Hours & Admission Prices: Thurs. 1-8, Fri. 9-4; other times by appointment. No
charge; donations accepted. Closed January; New Year's Day; Thanksgiving;
Christmas.
Attendance: 1,700 (estimated)

Arden

ORANGE COUNTY HISTORICAL SOCIETY, 21 Clove Furnace
Dr., Arden, NY 10910. Mailing Address: P.O. Box 55, Arden, NY
10910-0055. Tel.: 845-351-4696.
E-mail: info@orangecountyhistoricalsociety.org
Web Site: www.orangecountyhistoricalsociety.org
Institution Type/Description: Historical Society Museum.
Hours & Admission Prices: Mon.-Fri. 8-4:30.

Ardsley

ARDSLEY HISTORICAL SOCIETY, 9 American Legion Dr.,
Library 2nd Fl., Ardsley, NY 10502. Tel.: 914-693-6027.
E-mail: info@ardsleyhistoricalsociety.org
Web Site: www.ardsleyhistoricalsociety.org
Institution Type/Description: Historical Society Museum.
Hours & Admission Prices: Tues. 10 to noon; other times by appointment.

**COUNTY OF WESTCHESTER, DEPARTMENT OF PARKS,
RECREATION AND CONSERVATION,** 450 Saw Mill River
Rd., Ardsley, NY 10502. Tel.: 914-231-4500. Fax: 914-864-7053.
E-mail: countycenterres@westchestergov.com
Web Site: www.westchestergov.com/parks
Key Personnel: County Exec., Robert P. Astorino; Commissioner, Kathleen
O'Connor; Naturalist, John Baker.
Institution Type/Description: Nature Centers, Sanctuaries & Historic Sites.

Hours & Admission Prices: Washington's Headquarters by appointment only. Trailside Museum & Marshlands Conservancy: call for hours. No charge. Cranberry Lake Preserve: Tues.-Sun. 9-5. Lenoir Preserve: Tues.-Sun. 9-5. Silver Lake Preserve: daily 9-4. Lasdon Bird Sanctuary: daily dawn-dusk. Read Natural Park & Wildlife Sanctuary: Tues.-Sun. 9-5. Tarrytown Lighthouse: by appointment only.

Armonk

THE NORTH CASTLE HISTORICAL SOCIETY, 440 Bedford Rd., Armonk, NY 10504-2502. Tel.: 914-273-4510.
E-mail: NorthCastleHistoricalSociety@gmail.com
Web Site: northcastlehistoricalsociety.org
Key Personnel: Pres., Anna Marie Marrone; Town Historian, Public Rels. & Publications Dir., Sharon Tomback; Museum Shop Mgr., Jodie Burns.
Institution Type/Description: Historical Society Museum.
Hours & Admission Prices: April-Dec. Sun. 2-5, Wed. 2-4; other times by appointment. Suggested Donations: adults $5, member adults $3, children $1. &
Attendance: 750 (estimated)

Astoria

HAMMER PICTURES, 22-27 Crescent St., Astoria, NY 11105. Tel.: 917-353-9398; 718-204-7941.
E-mail: thepeoplesmuseum@hotmail.com
Web Site: thepeoplesmuseum.org
Key Personnel: Chm. & Pres., Mark Allen Sepanski; Vice Pres., April D. Sepanski; Bd. Sec., Dr. Pamela E. Ransom, Ph.D.; Bd. Treas., Howard S. Rose; Clerk, Marie T. Sepanski; Bd. Member, Norma Quarles; Bd. Member, Martin Berkowitz, CPA; Bd. Member, Henry Galiano; Bd. Member, Paul L. Sieswerda; Bd. Member, Jeffrey R. Myers; Bd. Member, Fred D. Wilson; Bd. Member, Brandon Ballengee.
Institution Type/Description: Film History Museum.
Hours & Admission Prices: By appointment. No charge; donations accepted.
Attendance: 350

MUSEUM OF THE MOVING IMAGE, 3601 35 Ave. (at 37 St.), Astoria, NY 11106. Tel.: 718-777-6800. Fax: 718-784-4681.
E-mail: info@movingimage.us
Web Site: www.movingimage.us
Key Personnel: Exec. Dir., Carl Goodman; Co Chm. (V), Ivan Lustig; Co Chm. (V), Michael Barker; Deputy Dir. Operations, Exhibitions & Design, Wendell Walker; Deputy Dir. Administration & C.F.O., Lise Suino; Dir. Education, Jordan Smith; Chief Cur., David Schwartz; Retail Mgr., Jonathan Bencosme.
Institution Type/Description: Art, History & Technology Museum of Film, Television & Digital Media.
Hours & Admission Prices: Wed.-Thurs. 10:30-5, Fri. 10:30-8, Sat.-Sun. 11:30-7. Adults $15, seniors 65 & up and college students with valid ID $11, youth 3-17 $7; members, children under 3, AAM & ICOM members, Fri. 4-8 no charge. Closed Memorial Day; Independence Day; Labor Day; Thanksgiving; Christmas. &
Attendance: 234,477 (actual)

THE PEOPLE'S MUSEUM, 22-27 Crescent St., Astoria, NY 11105-3105. Tel.: 718-204-7941; 917-353-9398. Facebook.
E-mail: thepeoplesmuseum@hotmail.com
Web Site: thepeoplesmuseum.org
Key Personnel: Dir., Chm. & Pres., Mark Allen Sepanski; Devel., Education & Public Rels., April D. Sepanski; Treas., Howard S. Rose; Sec., Dr. Pamela Estelle Ransom, Ph.D.; Registrar, Brandon Ballengee; Cur., Paul L. Sieswerda; Archivist & Artist, Fred Douglas Wilson; Trustee, Henry Galiano; Trustee, Jeffrey R. Myers; Accounting CPA Partner at Lutz & Carr, Martin Berkowitz.
Institution Type/Description: General Museum.
Hours & Admission Prices: By appointment. No charge; donations accepted. &

Auburn

CAYUGA MUSEUM & CASE RESEARCH LAB MUSEUM, 203 Genesee St., Auburn, NY 13021-3304. Tel.: 315-253-8051. Fax: 315-253-9829.
E-mail: cayugamuseum@verizon.net
Web Site: www.cayuganet.org/cayugamuseum
Key Personnel: Dir., Eileen McHugh; Cur., Kirsten Wise.
Institution Type/Description: Local History Museum.
Hours & Admission Prices: Feb.-Dec. Tues.-Sun. 12-5. Adults $5; children under 12 & members no charge. Closed holidays. &
Attendance: 9,300 (actual)

THE HARRIET TUBMAN HOME, 180 South St., Auburn, NY 13021-5636. Tel.: 315-252-2081.

E-mail: khill@harriethouse.org
Web Site: www.harriethouse.org
Key Personnel: Exec. Dir., Karen V. Hill.
Institution Type/Description: History Museum.
Hours & Admission Prices: Tues.-Fri. 10-4, Sat. 10-3.

SCHWEINFURTH MEMORIAL ART CENTER, 205 Genesee St., Auburn, NY 13021-3304. Tel.: 315-255-1553. Fax: 315-255-0871.
E-mail: mail@schweinfurthartcenter.org
Web Site: www.myartcenter.org
Key Personnel: Exec. Dir., Donna Lamb; Pres. (V), Anthony Bartolotta; Program Dir., Deirdre Aureden.
Institution Type/Description: Cultural Art Center.
Hours & Admission Prices: Tues.-Sat. 10-5, Sun. 1-5. Suggested admission $6; children under 12 & members no charge. Closed holidays. &
Attendance: 20,000 (actual)

SEWARD HOUSE MUSEUM, 33 South St., Auburn, NY 13021-3929. Tel.: 315-252-1283. Fax: 315-253-3351.
E-mail: director@sewardhouse.org
Web Site: sewardhouse.org
Key Personnel: Pres., Daniel Fisher; Exec. Dir., Billye J. Chabot; Facilities Mgr., Andrew Roblee; Dir. Education, John Kingsley.
Institution Type/Description: Historic House: 1816 home of William H. Seward.
Hours & Admission Prices: Feb.-June & mid-Oct. to Dec. Tues.-Sat. 10-4; July to mid-Oct. Tues.-Sat. 10-4, Sun. 1-4. Adults $7, senior citizens $6, students $2; discounts to AAM & ICOM members; members no charge. Closed major holidays. &
Attendance: 16,000 (actual)

WARD W. O'HARA AGRICULTURAL & COUNTRY LIVING MUSEUM & DR. JOSEPH F. NARPINSKI EDUCATIONAL CENTER, 6880 E. Lake Rd., Auburn, NY 13021. Tel.: 315-252-7644. Fax: 315-253-5199.
Key Personnel: C.E.O., Chm. (V) & Pres. (V), Norman Riley; Dir. & Museum Shop Mgr., Timothy J. Quill.
Institution Type/Description: Agricultural Museum.
Hours & Admission Prices: mid-May to mid-Sept. daily 11-4; other times by appointment. No charge; donations accepted. &
Attendance: 15,000 (estimated)

Ausable Chasm

NORTH STAR UNDERGROUND RAILROAD MUSEUM, 1131 Mace Chasm Rd., Ausable Chasm, NY 12911-1704. Tel.: 518-834-5180.
E-mail: ugr@frontier.com
Web Site: northcountryundergroundrailroad.com
Key Personnel: Pres., Jacqueline Madison.
Institution Type/Description: Underground Railroad Museum.
Hours & Admission Prices: May-June & Sept.-Oct. daily 11-4; July-Aug. daily 11-5; other times by appointment. No charge; donations accepted.
Attendance: 6,000 (actual)

Austerlitz

EDNA ST. VINCENT MILLAY SOCIETY, 440 E. Hill Rd., Austerlitz, NY 12017. Tel.: 518-392-3362.
E-mail: info@millay.org
Web Site: millay.org
Institution Type/Description: Historic House: housed in the former home of writer and Pulitzer Prize-winning poet, Edna St. Vincent Millay; built in 1892.
Hours & Admission Prices: Office: Mon.-Fri. 9-5. Tours: May to Nov. 1 Fri.-Mon. by appointment. Gallery: May to Nov. 1 Fri.-Mon. 10-4:30.

Baldwin

BALDWIN HISTORICAL SOCIETY AND MUSEUM, 1980 Grand Ave., Baldwin, NY 11510-2836. Facebook: @baldwinlihistoricalsociety.
E-mail: baldwinhistoricalsociety@gmail.com
Web Site: www.baldwinhistoricalsociety.com
Key Personnel: C.E.O., Dir., & Pres. (V), Gary Farkash; Vice Pres. & Public Rels., Karen Montalbano.
Institution Type/Description: Historical Society Museum.
Hours & Admission Prices: By appointment. No charge; donations accepted. Closed New Year's Day; Easter; Christmas. &
Attendance: 200 (estimated)

Ballston Spa

NATIONAL BOTTLE MUSEUM, 76 Milton Ave., Ballston Spa, NY 12020-1405. Tel.: 518-885-7589. Fax: 518-885-0317. Facebook.
E-mail: nbm@nycap.rr.com
Web Site: www.nationalbottlemuseum.org
Key Personnel: Dir., Gary Moeller; Pres. (V), Eleanor Dillon.
Institution Type/Description: History Museum.
Hours & Admission Prices: Jan.-Feb. Thurs.-Sat. 10-4; March-May & Oct.-Dec. Tues.-Sat. 10-4; June-Sept. Fri.-Tues. 10-4. No charge; donations accepted. Closed New Year's Day; Christmas.
Attendance: 3,750 (estimated)

SARATOGA COUNTY HISTORICAL SOCIETY, BROOKSIDE MUSEUM, 6 Charlton St., Ballston Spa, NY 12020-1707. Tel.: 518-885-4000. Fax: 518-885-4055.
E-mail: info@brooksidemuseum.org
Web Site: www.brooksidemuseum.org
Formerly: Brookside, Saratoga County Historical Society
Key Personnel: Exec. Dir., Joy Houle; Pres. (V), Jeanne Obermayer; Dir. Education, Anne Clothier; Cur., Kathleen Coleman.
Institution Type/Description: General Museum: housed in 1792 Aldridge House & Resort Hotel.
Hours & Admission Prices: Tues.-Fri. 10-4, Sat. 10-2. Family $5, adults $2, senior citizens $1.50, students & children $1; museum, AASLH & MANY members no charge. Closed New Year's Day; Easter; Thanksgiving; Christmas.
Attendance: 11,000 (actual)

Batavia

THE HOLLAND LAND OFFICE MUSEUM, 131 W. Main St., Batavia, NY 14020-2021. Tel.: 585-343-4727. Facebook: The Holland Land Office Museum.
E-mail: info@hollandlandoffice.com
Web Site: www.hollandlandoffice.com
Key Personnel: Dir., Jeffrey E. Donahue; Pres. (V), Robert Purk; Museum Shop Mgr., Corinne Iwanicki.
Institution Type/Description: General Museum: housed in 1815 cut-stone structure erected for use as the office of Holland Land Co. where land was offered for sale in 1800s.
Hours & Admission Prices: Jan.-May & Sept.-Nov. Tues.-Sat. 10-4; Memorial Day to Labor Day Mon.-Sat. 10-4; late-Nov. to Dec. Tues.-Sat. 10-4, Sun. 12:30-4:30. No charge; donations accepted. Closed legal holidays.
Attendance: 6,500 (actual)

Bath

MAGEE HOUSE - STEUBEN COUNTY HISTORICAL SOCIETY, 1 Cohocton St., Bath, NY 14810. Tel.: 607-776-9930.
E-mail: steuben349@yahoo.com
Web Site: www.steubenhistoricalsociety.org
Key Personnel: Dir., Kirk House; Chm. (V), Helen K. Brink.
Institution Type/Description: Historical Society Museum.
Hours & Admission Prices: Mon.-Fri. 10-3. No charge; donations accepted. Closed holidays.

Bay Shore

SAGTIKOS MANOR HISTORICAL SOCIETY, Montauk Hwy. & Manor Ln., Bay Shore, NY 11706. Mailing Address: P.O. Box 5344, Bay Shore, NY 11706. Tel.: 631-854-0939. Facebook: Sagtikos Manor Historical Society.
E-mail: info@sagtikosmanor.com
Web Site: sagtikosmanor.com
Key Personnel: Pres., Sarah Faye Meurer; Museum Shop Mgr., Maria Pecorale.
Institution Type/Description: Historical Society Museum: housed in the former home of the Thompson-Gardiner family; built in 1697. The estate served as the British Army's local headquarters during the Revolutionary War. President George Washington stayed in the manor during his tour of Long Island in 1790.
Hours & Admission Prices: June Sat.-Sun. 1-3:30; July-Aug. Fri.-Sun. 1-3:30; Sept. Sat.-Sun. 1-3:30; groups by appointment. Adults $9, seniors over 60 & K-12 $5.
Attendance: 1,500 (estimated)

Bayport

BAYPORT AERODROME, Vitamin Dr., Bayport, NY 11705-1115. Mailing Address: P.O. Box 728, Bayport, NY 11705.
E-mail: flyhulls@aol.com

Key Personnel: Chm. (V), Kevin Kilroy; Pres. (V), John C. Hess; Museum Shop Mgr., Bob Mott.
Institution Type/Description: Aviation History Museum.
Hours & Admission Prices: June-Sept. 10-4. No charge; donations accepted.
Attendance: 1,800 (actual)

Bayside

BAYSIDE HISTORICAL SOCIETY, 208 Totten Ave. - Fort Totten, Bayside, NY 11359. Tel.: 718-352-1548. Fax: 718-352-3904.
E-mail: info@baysidehistorical.org
Web Site: www.baysidehistorical.org
Key Personnel: Exec. Dir., Alison McKay.
Institution Type/Description: Historical Society Museum: housed in the Castle, built in 1887 for the U.S. Army Corps of Engineers as their Officersï¿½ Mess Hall & Club.
Hours & Admission Prices: Tues.-Fri. 10-4, Sat.-Sun. 12-4. Admission $5; discounts to groups.

QCC ART GALLERY/CUNY, 222-05 56th Ave., Bayside, NY 11364-1497. Tel.: 718-631-6396. Fax: 718-631-6620.
E-mail: qccartgallery@qcc.cuny.edu
Web Site: www.qccartgallery.org
Key Personnel: Dir., Mr. Faustino Quintanilla; Asst. Dir., Deanne DeNyse.
Institution Type/Description: College Art Gallery.
Hours & Admission Prices: Tues. & Fri. 10-5, Wed.-Thurs. 10-7, Sat.-Sun. 12-5. No charge; donations accepted. Closed major holidays.
Attendance: 35,000 (estimated)

Beacon

BEACON HISTORICAL SOCIETY, 477 Main St., Beacon, NY 12508-3819. Mailing Address: P.O. Box 89, Beacon, NY 12508-0089. Tel.: 845-831-0514.
Web Site: www.beaconhistoricalsociety.org
Key Personnel: Pres. (V), Robert Murphy.
Institution Type/Description: Historical Museum.
Hours & Admission Prices: Thurs. 10-12, Sat. 1-3. Archival Research: 4th Tues. of each month. Open Meetings 7:30pm. No charge.
Attendance: 500 (estimated)

DIA:BEACON, 3 Beekman St., Beacon, NY 12508-2521. Mailing Address: c/o Dia Art Foundation, 535 W. 22nd St., 4th Fl., New York, NY 10011. Tel.: 845-440-0100. Fax: 845-440-0092. Facebook.
E-mail: info@diaart.org
Web Site: www.diaart.org
Key Personnel: Chm. (V), Nathalie de Gunzburg; Dir., Jessica Morgan; Mng. Dir., Susan Sayre Batton; Financial Dir., Ashley Mitchell; Cur., Yasmil Raymond; Dir. Operations, Jim Schaeufele; Mgr. Visitor Svcs., Caroline Schneider; Arts Education Assoc., Meagan Mattingly; Sr. Registrar, Elizabeth Peck; Mgr. Human Resources, Molsey Lare; Group Tours & Events Mgr., Kathleen Anderson; Museum Shop Mgr., Jill Rogers.
Institution Type/Description: Art Museum.
Hours & Admission Prices: Jan.-March Fri.-Mon. 11-4; April-Oct. Thurs.-Mon. 11-6; Nov.-Dec. Thurs.-Mon. 11-4. Adults $15, senior citizens 65 & over & students $12; discounts to other museum staff, and AAM & ICOM members; members, children under 12 & Beacon residents on Sat.-Sun. no charge. Bookstore & Cafe: 10:30am until closing. Closed New Year's Day; Thanksgiving; Christmas Eve & Day.
Attendance: 80,000 (actual)

THE MADAM BRETT HOMESTEAD, 50 Van Nydeck Ave., Beacon, NY 12508-3326. Tel.: 845-831-6533.
E-mail: gonzo4851@aol.com
Web Site: melzingah.awardspace.com/id5.htm
Key Personnel: Regent (V), Helen Walker; Cur., Anne Thomas; Dir. Tours, Anne Thomas.
Institution Type/Description: Historic Site: c.1709 & c.1740 Madam Brett Homestead.
Hours & Admission Prices: April-Dec. 2nd Sat. of month. Adults $5, students $2.
Attendance: 400 (estimated)

MOUNT GULIAN HISTORIC SITE, 145 Sterling St., Beacon, NY 12508-1483. Tel.: 845-831-8172. Fax: 845-831-7376. Facebook: Mount Gulian Historic Site.
E-mail: info@mountgulian.us
Web Site: www.mountgulian.org
Key Personnel: Exec. Dir., Elaine Hayes.

Institution Type/Description: Historic Site Museum: housed in an 18th century Dutch Colonial Homestead.
Hours & Admission Prices: Wed.-Fri. & Sun. 1-5; group tours by appointment. Adults $8, seniors $6, youth 6-18 $4; AAM & Mount Gulian members no charge.
Attendance: 5.000 (estimated)

Bear Mountain

BEAR MOUNTAIN TRAILSIDE MUSEUMS AND ZOO, Bear Mountain State Park, Bear Mountain, NY 10911. Mailing Address: Palisades Interstate Park Commission, P.O. Box 427, Bear Mountain, NY 10911-0427. Tel.: 845-786-2701, ext. 263. Fax: 845-786-7157.
E-mail: mcgowan@parksny.gov
Web Site: palisadesparksconservancy.org
Key Personnel: Exec. Dir., Ed McGowan.
Institution Type/Description: Natural History Museum.
Hours & Admission Prices: Daily 10-4:30. No charge; donations accepted. Parking in state park $8. Closed Thanksgiving; Christmas. &

Bedford

MUSEUM OF THE BEDFORD HISTORICAL SOCIETY, 612 Old Post Rd., Bedford, NY 10506. Mailing Address: P.O. Box 491, Bedford, NY 10506-0491. Tel.: 914-234-9751. Fax: 914-234-5461. Facebook: Museum of the Bedford Historical Society.
E-mail: info@bedfordhistoricalsociety.org
Web Site: www.bedfordhistoricalsociety.org
Key Personnel: Exec. Dir., Evelyne H. Ryan; Chm. (V), Kirtley Cameron; Pres. (V), Stacy E. Albanese.
Institution Type/Description: Local History Museum.
Hours & Admission Prices: Museum: Thurs.-Sat. 12-3; other times by appointment. Adult $5, members no charge. &
Attendance: 200 (estimated)

Bedford Corners

WESTMORELAND SANCTUARY, INC., 260 Chestnut Ridge Rd., Bedford Corners, NY 10549-4812. Tel.: 914-666-8448. Fax: 914-242-1175.
E-mail: westsanc@optonline.net
Web Site: westmorelandsanctuary.org
Key Personnel: Dir. & Naturalist, Stephen Ricker.
Institution Type/Description: Nature Sanctuary.
Hours & Admission Prices: Trails: daily dawn-dusk. Museum: Mon.-Sat. 9-5, Sun. 10:30-5. No charge; donations accepted.
Attendance: 40,000 (estimated)

Bellport

BELLPORT-BROOKHAVEN HISTORICAL SOCIETY AND MUSEUM, 31 Bellport Lane, Bellport, NY 11713-2739. Tel.: 631-286-0888.
E-mail: president@bbhsmuseum.org
Web Site: www.bbhsmuseum.org
Institution Type/Description: Local History Museum.
Hours & Admission Prices: Memorial Day to Labor Day Fri.-Sun. 1-4; other times by appointment. Adults $5, seniors citizens 65 & over and children 13-17 $4; discounts to AAM & ICOM members; children 12 & under and members no charge. Exchange Shop: Collectibles Consignment Shop: May-Dec. Fri.-Sun. 11-4. &
Attendance: 975 (estimated)

Belmont

ALLEGANY COUNTY MUSEUM, 11 Wells St., Belmont, NY 14813-1052. Mailing Address: Court House Court St., Belmont, NY 14813. Tel.: 585-268-9293. Fax: 716-268-9446.
E-mail: historian@alleganyco.com
Key Personnel: Dir., Craig R. Braack.
Institution Type/Description: History Museum: housed in 1842 Greek Revival Church.
Hours & Admission Prices: Mon.-Fri. 9-4:30; other times by appointment. No charge; Closed holidays. &

Bergen

BERGEN MUSEUM OF LOCAL HISTORY, 7547 Lake Rd., Bergen, NY 14416. Mailing Address: 10 Hunter St., Bergen, NY 14416. Tel.: 585-494-0080, 494-1121 & 704-4119 (cell). Fax: 585-494-1488.
Key Personnel: Mgr. & Museum Shop Mgr., Peggy Denton; Pres., Teresa Alexander; Vice Pres., Tracy Miller; Sec., Nancy Charcolla; Sec., Jean Stewart; Treas., Lisa Teremy.
Institution Type/Description: Local History Museum: housed in 1843 schoolhouse.
Hours & Admission Prices: June-Oct. by appointment. No charge; donations accepted. Closed legal holidays. &
Attendance: 175 (estimated)

HARFORD BARN MUSEUM, 15 S. Lake Ave., Bergen, NY 14416. Mailing Address: 10 Hunter St., Bergen, NY 14416. Tel.: 585-494-0080.
E-mail: historian@bergenny.org
Key Personnel: Dir., Thomas M. Tiefel.
Institution Type/Description: Historic Building: housed in a restored barn; built in the 1800s.
Hours & Admission Prices: June-Oct. by appointment. No charge; donations accepted. &
Attendance: 325 (estimated)

Bethel

THE MUSEUM AT BETHEL WOODS, 200 Hurd Rd., Bethel, NY 12720. Mailing Address: P.O. Box 222, Liberty, NY 12754-0222. Tel.: 845-583-2075. Fax: 845-583-4242. Facebook.
E-mail: wlawrence@bethelwoodscenter.org
Web Site: www.bethelwoodscenter.org
Key Personnel: Dir. & Sr. Cur., Wade Lawrence; C.E.O., Darlene Fedun; Assoc. Cur., Megan Culbert; Registrar, Robin Green; Museum Shop Mgr., Lori McBride.
Institution Type/Description: History Museum & Historic Site: at the site of the 1969 Woodstock Music and Art Fair.
Hours & Admission Prices: April-Dec. see website for hours. Adults $15; discounts to military, AAM & ICOM members. Closed Thanksgiving; Christmas Eve & Day. &
Attendance: 40,000 (estimated)

Big Flats

BIG FLATS HISTORICAL SOCIETY MUSEUM, 258 Hibbard Rd., Big Flats, NY 14814. Mailing Address: P.O. Box 232, Big Flats, NY 14814. Tel.: 607-562-7460.
Key Personnel: Pres. (V), Linda L. Patrick.
Institution Type/Description: Historical Society Museum.
Hours & Admission Prices: Tues. 9am to noon; other times by appointment. No charge; donations accepted. &
Attendance: 1,630 (estimated)

Binghamton

BINGHAMTON UNIVERSITY ART MUSEUM, 4400 Vestal Pkwy. East, Binghamton, NY 13902-6000. Mailing Address: P.O. Box 6000, Binghamton, NY 13902-6000. Tel.: 607-777-2634. Fax: 607-777-2613.
E-mail: hogan@binghamton.edu
Web Site: artmuseum.binghamton.edu
Key Personnel: Dir., Diane Butler; Dir. Asst., Jacqueline Hogan; Registrar, Silvia Ivanova.
Institution Type/Description: Art Museum.
Hours & Admission Prices: Summer: Tues.-Fri. 12-4; Sept.-June Tues.-Wed. & Fri.-Sat. 12-4, Thurs. 12-7; other times by appointment. No charge; donations accepted. Closed holidays. &

BINGHAMTON ZOO AT ROSS PARK, 60 Morgan Rd., Binghamton, NY 13903-3667. Mailing Address: 185 Park Ave., Binghamton, NY 13903-3643. Tel.: 607-724-5461. Facebook; Twitter; Instagram..
E-mail: office@rosspark.com
Web Site: www.rossparkzoo.com
Formerly: Ross Park Zoo
Key Personnel: Exec. Dir., Phillip Ginter.
Institution Type/Description: Zoo.
Hours & Admission Prices: Early May to mid-Sept. daily 10-4; see website for season hours. Adults $9, seniors 55 & over, college students and military with ID

$8, children 3-11 $7; discount to groups; children 2 & under and members no charge. &
Attendance: 60,000 (estimated)

THE BROOME COUNTY HISTORICAL SOCIETY, 185 Court St., Binghamton, NY 13901-3503. Tel.: 607-778-3572. Fax: 607-778-6429.
E-mail: localhistory@bclibrary.info
Web Site: www.bclibrary.info/history.htm
Key Personnel: Pres. (V), David J. Dixon.
Institution Type/Description: History Museum: housed in Roberson Museum.
Hours & Admission Prices: Mon. & Wed.-Fri. 9-5, Tues. 12-8. No charge; donations accepted. &
Attendance: 25,000 (estimated)

THE BUNDY MUSEUM OF HISTORY AND ART, 129 Main St., Binghamton, NY 13905-2742. Mailing Address: Visitors Center, 127 Main St., Binghamton, NY 13905. Tel.: 607-772-9179. Facebook: Bundy Museum.
E-mail: info@bundymuseum.org
Web Site: www.bundymuseum.org
Formerly: The Bundy Arts & Victorian Museum
Key Personnel: Dir., Janna Rudler; Chm. (V), Charles Gilinsky.
Institution Type/Description: History Museum.
Hours & Admission Prices: Tues.-Sat. 11-5. Adults $7, students & senior citizens $5; discount to AAM members; children 10 & under no charge.
Attendance: 1,100 (estimated)

CUTLER BOTANIC GARDEN, 840 Upper Front St., Binghamton, NY 13905-1542. Tel.: 607-772-8953. Fax: 607-723-5951.
E-mail: broome@cornell.edu
Web Site: www.cce.cornell.edu/broome
Key Personnel: C.E.O., David A. Bradstreet; Program Assoc., Brian Aukema.
Institution Type/Description: Botanical Garden.
Hours & Admission Prices: June-Oct. daily during daylight hours. No charge; donations accepted. &
Attendance: 15,000 (estimated)

THE DISCOVERY CENTER OF THE SOUTHERN TIER, 60 Morgan Rd., Binghamton, NY 13903-3667. Tel.: 607-773-8750 & 8661, ext. 206. Fax: 607-773-8019.
E-mail: director@thediscoverycenter.org
Web Site: www.thediscoverycenter.org
Key Personnel: C.E.O., Margaret S. Crocker; Pres., Nicola R. Chanecka; Financial Dir., Catherine Fiacco; Asst. Dir., Donna Jones-Wright; Dir. Mktg., Martha J. Steed; Museum Shop Mgr., Jennifer Fiala.
Institution Type/Description: Children's Museum: located in historic Ross Park. Discovery Center chartered in 1984.
Hours & Admission Prices: July-Aug. Mon.-Fri. 10-4, Sat. 10-5, Sun. 12-5; Sept.-June Tues.-Fri. 10-4, Sat. 10-5, Sun. 12-5. Children 2 & over $6, adults $5; discounts to groups, ACM members; children 1 & under and members no charge. &
Attendance: 53,420 (actual)

ROBERSON MUSEUM AND SCIENCE CENTER, 30 Front St., Binghamton, NY 13905-4779. Tel.: 607-772-0660. Fax: 607-771-8905. Facebook: Roberson Museum.
E-mail: blake@roberson.org
Web Site: www.roberson.org
Key Personnel: C.E.O., Terry McDonald; Pres. (V), Glenn Small; Exhibition Devel., Peter Klosky; Registrar, Shannon Lindridge.
Institution Type/Description: General Museum.
Hours & Admission Prices: Wed.-Thurs. & Sat.-Sun. 12-5, Fri. 12-9. Adults $8, seniors & students $6, $20 family maximum (6 people maximum), reciprocal agreement with ASTC, Arnot Art Museum & 19 other New York State museums; discount to AAM & ICOM members; members no charge. Closed major holidays. &
Attendance: 35,000 (estimated)

Bloomfield

ANTIQUE WIRELESS MUSEUM, 6925 State Route 5, Bloomfield, NY 14469. Mailing Address: P.O. Box 421, Bloomfield, NY 14469. Tel.: 585-257-5119.
E-mail: n2evg@arrl.net
Web Site: www.antiquewireless.org
Formerly: A.w.a. Electronic-communication Museum
Key Personnel: Dir., Thomas Peterson; Deputy Dir., Robert Hobday; Cur., Lynn Bisha; Treas., Stan Avery.

Institution Type/Description: museum of the history of technology used to communicate.
Hours & Admission Prices: Tues. 10-3, Sat. 1-5. Closed holidays. &
Attendance: 2,000 (estimated)

Blue Mountain Lake

ADIRONDACK EXPERIENCE, THE MUSEUM ON BLUE MOUNTAIN LAKE, 9097 State Rte. 30, Blue Mountain Lake, NY 12812-0099. Mailing Address: P.O. Box 99, Blue Mountain Lake, NY 12812-0099. Tel.: 518-352-7311. Fax: 518-352-7653.
E-mail: info@theadkx.org
Web Site: www.theadkx.org
Key Personnel: Exec. Dir., David M. Kahn; Chief Cur., Laura S. Rice; Mktg. Dir., Ausra Angermann.
Institution Type/Description: Regional History & Art Museum.
Hours & Admission Prices: Museum: Memorial Day to mid-Oct. daily 10-5 including holidays. Adults $20, seniors 62 & over $18, student with ID & children 6-12 $12; discounts to groups of 15 or more, AAM & MANY members; members, active military and children 5 & under no charge. Library: Mon.-Fri. 9-5 by appointment. &
Attendance: 59,380 (actual)

Bolton Landing

BOLTON HISTORICAL MUSEUM, 4924 Main St., Bolton Landing, NY 12814. Mailing Address: P.O. Box 441, Bolton Landing, NY 12814-0441. Tel.: 518-644-9960.
E-mail: jga4679@gmail.com
Web Site: www.boltonhistorical.org
Institution Type/Description: History Museum: housed in a former church; built in 1890.
Hours & Admission Prices: Call for hours. No charge; donations accepted. &
Attendance: 5,000 (actual)

THE SEMBRICH, MARCELLA SEMBRICH OPERA MUSEUM, 4800 Lake Shore Dr. (Rte. 9N), Bolton Landing, NY 12814. Mailing Address: P.O. Box 417, Bolton Landing, NY 12814-0417. Tel.: 518-644-2431 (Office); 518-644-9839 (Museum). Fax: 518-644-9531. Facebook.
E-mail: office@thesembrich.org
Web Site: www.thesembrich.org
Key Personnel: Pres., William Hubert; Vice Pres., Lisa Hall; Sec., Rebecca Smith; Treas., Elizabeth Spinelli; Exec. Dir., Elizabeth Barton-Navitsky; Artistic Dir., Richard Wargo.
Institution Type/Description: Opera Museum, Music Venue & Historic Building: 1923 The Sembrich Studio, former teaching studio of Madame Marcella Sembrich, opera singer, teacher & director of the vocal departments at the Curtis Institute & the Juilliard School.
Hours & Admission Prices: June 15-Sept. 15 daily 10-12:30 & 2-5; No charge; donations accepted. &
Attendance: 2,500 (estimated)

Brewster

SOUTHEAST MUSEUM ASSOCIATION, INC., 67 Main St., Brewster, NY 10509-1416. Tel.: 845-279-7500. Fax: 845-279-1992.
E-mail: sem@bestweb.net
Web Site: www.southeastmuseum.org
Key Personnel: Exec. Dir., Amy Campanaro; Pres. (V), Elizabeth Ryder; Cur., Joan Crawford; Museum Shop Mgr., Eleanor Keefe.
Institution Type/Description: Historical Museum.
Hours & Admission Prices: April-Dec. Tues.-Sat. 10-4. No charge; donations accepted.
Attendance: 4,500 (estimated)

Bridgehampton

THE BRIDGEHAMPTON MUSEUM, 2368 Main St. & Corwith Ave., Bridgehampton, NY 11932-0977. Mailing Address: P.O. Box 977, Bridgehampton, NY 11932-0977. Tel.: 631-537-1088. Fax: 631-537-4225.
E-mail: bhhs@optonline.net
Web Site: bhmuseum.org
Formerly: The Bridgehampton Historical Society
Key Personnel: Exec. Dir., John Eilertsen; Pres., Walter Miller.
Institution Type/Description: General Museum.

Hours & Admission Prices: Mon.-Fri. 10-3; other times by appointment. Adults $5; members no charge. Closed legal holidays. &
Attendance: 5,000 (actual)

CHILDREN'S MUSEUM OF THE EAST END, 376 Bridgehampton/Sag Harbor Turnpike, Bridgehampton, NY 11932. Mailing Address: P.O. Box 316, Bridgehampton, NY 11932-0316. Tel.: 631-537-8250. Fax: 631-537-2413.
E-mail: steve@cmee.org
Web Site: www.cmee.org
Key Personnel: Dir., Steve Long.
Institution Type/Description: Children's Museum.
Hours & Admission Prices: Wed.-Mon. 9-5; groups by appointment. Admission $10; members & children under one no charge. &

Brockport

CAPEN HOSE COMPANY NO. 4 - FIRE MUSEUM, 237 S. Main St., Brockport, NY 14716. Mailing Address: 36 Cherry Dr., Brockport, NY 14420-1104. Tel.: 716-637-4713 & 2512.
E-mail: webmaster@brockportfire.org
Web Site: brockportfire.org/Museum/Museum.html
Institution Type/Description: Firefighting History Museum.
Hours & Admission Prices: By appointment.

TOWER FINE ARTS GALLERY (SUNY BROCKPORT), Tower Fine Arts Bldg., 180 Holley St., Brockport, NY 14420-2985. Mailing Address: 350 New Campus Dr., Brockport, NY 14420-2985. Tel.: 585-395-2805. Fax: 585-395-2588.
E-mail: tmassey@brockport.edu
Web Site: www.brockport.edu/finearts/
Key Personnel: Chm., Phyllis Kloda; Dir., Timothy Massey.
Institution Type/Description: Art Museum.
Hours & Admission Prices: Academic Year: Mon.-Fri. 10-5, Sun. 1-4. No charge. &
Attendance: 6,000 (estimated)

Bronx

BARTOW-PELL MANSION MUSEUM, CARRIAGE HOUSE & GARDENS, 895 Shore Rd., Pelham Bay Park, Bronx, NY 10464-1030. Tel.: 718-885-1461. Fax: 718-885-9164.
E-mail: info@bpmm.org
Web Site: www.bartowpellmansionmuseum.org
Key Personnel: Exec. Dir., Alison McKay; Museum Admin., Susan M. Chesloff.
Institution Type/Description: Historic House Museum: 1842-1888 Bartow-Pell Mansion, Greek-Revival mansion.
Hours & Admission Prices: Wed. & Sat.-Sun. 12-4. Adults $8, seniors & students $6; discounts for AAM & ICOM members & groups; children under 6 & members no charge. Closed New Year's Eve & Day; Easter; Thanksgiving weekend; Christmas.
Attendance: 15,000 (estimated)

THE BRONX COUNTY HISTORICAL SOCIETY, 3309 Bainbridge Ave., Bronx, NY 10467-2850. Tel.: 718-881-8900. Fax: 718-881-4827.
E-mail: angel@bronxhistoricalsociety.org
Web Site: www.bronxhistoricalsociety.org
Key Personnel: C.E.O., Dr. Gary D. Hermalyn; Pres. (V), Jacqueline Kutner; Cur. & Mgr. Edgar Allan Poe Cottage, Kathleen A. McAuley; Assoc. Librarian, Laura Tosi; Valentine-Varian House Mgr., Marcus Hickman; Dir. Bronx Latino History Project, Angel Hernandez; Education Outreach, Daniel Richards; Historian, Prof. Lloyd Ultan; Researcher, Dr. Stephen Stertz; Journal Editor, Dr. Elizabeth Beirne.
Institution Type/Description: Historical Society.
Hours & Admission Prices: Mon.-Fri. 9-5, Sat. 10-4, Sun. 1-5. Adults $5, senior citizens, children & students $3; discounts to AAM members; members no charge. &
Attendance: 85,000 (estimated)

THE BRONX MUSEUM OF THE ARTS, 1040 Grand Concourse, Bronx, NY 10456-3901. Tel.: 718-681-6000. Fax: 718-681-6181.
E-mail: info@bronxmuseum.org
Web Site: www.bronxmuseum.org
Key Personnel: Exec. Dir., Holly Block; Dir. Finance & Operations, Alan Highet; Dir. Programs, Sergio Bessa; Dir. External Affairs, Allison Chernow; Public Liaison, Miriam Tabb.
Institution Type/Description: Art Museum.

Hours & Admission Prices: Thurs. & Sat.-Sun. 11-6, Fri. 11-8. No charge; donations accepted. Closed New Year's Day; Thanksgiving; Christmas. &
Attendance: 75,000 (estimated)

BRONX ZOO, 2300 Southern Blvd., Bronx, NY 10460-1090. Tel.: 718-220-5100. Fax: 718-220-2685.
E-mail: PR@wcs.org
Web Site: www.wcs.org
Key Personnel: Pres. & C.E.O., Cristian Samper; Exec. Vice Pres. & C.O.O., Robert G. Menzi; Exec. Vice Pres. & Gen. Dir. Zoos & Aquarium & Jonathan Little Cohen Dir. of Bronx Zoo, James J. Breheny; Exec. Vice Pres. Public Affairs, John F. Calvelli; Exec. Vice Pres. Global Resources, Bertina Ceccarelli; Exec. Vice Pres. Conservation & Science & Joan O. L. Tweey Chair in Conservation Strategy, John G. Robinson; Sr. Vice Pres. Communications, Mary A. Dixon; Sr. Vice Pres., Gen. Counsel & Deputy Sec., Christopher J. McKenzie, Esq.; Sr. Vice Pres. & C.F.O., Laura Stolzenthaler; Vice Pres. & Gen. Cur., Assoc. Dir. Bronx Zoo, Patrick R. Thomas; Chief Veterinarian & Dir. Zoological Health, Paul P. Calle.
Institution Type/Description: Zoo.
Hours & Admission Prices: Mon.-Fri. 10-5, Sat.-Sun. & holidays 10-5:30; Adults 13 & up $33.95, senior 65 & up $28.95, child 3-12 $23.95; discounts to AAA members; members, children 2 & under, & Wed. no charge. Additional fees for parking, some exhibits & rides. &
Attendance: 1,932,638 (actual)

CITY ISLAND NAUTICAL MUSEUM, City Island, 190 Fordham St., Bronx, NY 10464. Mailing Address: P.O. Box 82, Bronx, NY 10464-0082. Tel.: 718-885-0008 & 0507. Fax: 718-885-0507. Facebook: City Island Nautical Museum.
E-mail: cihs@cityislandmuseum.org
Web Site: www.cityislandmuseum.org
Key Personnel: Pres. & Cur., Tom Nye; Treas., Fred Ramftl; Vice Pres., Barbara Dolensek; Sec., Jane Protzman; Museum Shop Mgr., Barbara Hoffman.
Institution Type/Description: Nautical Museum: housed in 1897-98, P.S. 17 school building.
Hours & Admission Prices: Sat.-Sun. 1-5; other times by appointment. Admission $5; members no charge. &
Attendance: 2,700 (estimated)

EDGAR ALLAN POE COTTAGE, Poe Park, Grand Concourse at E. Kingsbridge Rd., Bronx, NY 10458. Mailing Address: Bronx County Historical Society, 3309 Bainbridge Ave., Bronx, NY 10467-2840. Tel.: 718-881-8900. Fax: 718-881-4827.
E-mail: kmcauley@bronxhistoricalsociety.org
Web Site: www.bronxhistoricalsociety.org
Key Personnel: C.E.O., Dr. Gary Hermalyn; Pres. (V), Jacqueline Kutner; Dir. Museums, Kathleen A. McAuley.
Institution Type/Description: Historic House: housed in the former residence of poet Edgar Allan Poe; built in 1812.
Hours & Admission Prices: Thurs. & Fri. 10-3, Sat. 10-4, Sun. 1-5; group tours by appointment. Adults $5, seniors, students & children $3; discounts to AAM & ICOM members; members & Historic House Trust of NYC members no charge.
Attendance: 44,829 (actual)

THE HALL OF FAME FOR GREAT AMERICANS, Bronx Community College, 2155 University Ave., Rm. 26, Bronx, NY 10453-2804. Tel.: 718-289-5160 & 5146. Fax: 718-289-5160.
E-mail: therese.lemelle@bcc.cuny.edu
Web Site: www.bcc.cuny.edu/halloffame
Key Personnel: Dir., Therese LeMelle; Tour Guide, Remo Cosentino.
Institution Type/Description: Art & History Museum.
Hours & Admission Prices: Daily 10-5; guided tours by appointment. Guided Tours: $5 per person; school groups & self-guided tours no charge.
Attendance: 25,000 (estimated)

LEHMAN COLLEGE ART GALLERY, 250 Bedford Park Blvd. W., Bronx, NY 10468-1589. Tel.: 718-960-8731, Fax: 718-960-6991.
E-mail: susan@lehman.cuny.edu
Web Site: www.lehman.edu/gallery
Key Personnel: Dir., Susan Hoeltzel; Chm. (V), Virginia Cupiola; Devel. Assoc., Mary Ann Siano.
Institution Type/Description: College Art Museum.
Hours & Admission Prices: June-Aug. open by appointment; Sept.-June Tues.-Sat. 10-4. No charge. &
Attendance: 30,000 (estimated)

LONGWOOD ART GALLERY AT HOSTOS CENTER FOR THE ARTS & CULTURE, 450 Grand Concourse, at 149th St., Bronx, NY 10451. Tel.: 718-518-4455.

E-mail: longwood@bronxarts.org
Web Site: www.bronxarts.org/lag.asp
Institution Type/Description: Art Gallery.
Hours & Admission Prices: Mon.-Sat. 10-6.

MARITIME INDUSTRY MUSEUM AT FORT SCHUYLER, 6
Pennyfield Ave., Bronx, NY 10465-4127. Tel.: 718-409-7218.
E-mail: museum@sunymaritime.edu
Web Site: sunymaritime.edu
Key Personnel: Dir., Capt. Eric J. Johansson; Chm., Capt. James J. McNamara;
Treas., Matthew Bonvento; Cur., William Sokol, Jr.; Admin. Asst., Patricia
Perez.
Institution Type/Description: Maritime Museum.
Hours & Admission Prices: Mon.-Sat. 9-4. No charge; donations accepted. Closed
on holidays.
Attendance: 15,000 (estimated)

NEW YORK BOTANICAL GARDEN, 2900 Southern Blvd.,
Bronx, NY 10458. Tel.: 718-817-8700. Fax: 718-220-6504.
E-mail: tskoda@nybg.org
Web Site: www.nybg.org
Key Personnel: Chm. Bd. (V), Maureen K. Chilton; C.E.O. & the William C. Steere
St. Pres., Carrie Rebora Barratt, Ph.D.; Dir., J.V. Cossaboom; Vice Pres.
Botanical Svcs. and Dir. & Phileocology Cur. Economic Botany, Michael J.
Balick, Ph.D.; Stavros Niarchos Foundation Vice Pres. Children's Education,
James Boyer, Ph.D.; Vice Pres. Continuing & Public Education, Barbara
Corcoran; Arthur Ross Vice Pres. Horticulture & Living Collections, Todd
Forrest; Thomas J. Hubbard Vice Pres. & Dir. LuEsther T. Mertz Library, Susan
Fraser; Vice Pres. Capital Projects, Ursula Hoskins; Vice Pres. Communications,
Melinda Manning; Vice Pres. Retail & Business Devel., Richard Pickett; Vice
Pres. Membership & Visitor Experience, Marci Silverman; Vice Pres. &
Cullman Cur., Dennis W. Stevenson, Ph.D.; Vice Pres. Landscape &
Glasshouses, Brian Sullivan; Vice Pres. Patricia K. Holmgren Dir. of the
William & Lynda Steere Herbarium and Cur. Bryophytes, Barbara M. Thiers,
Ph.D.; Vice Pres. Conservation Strategy, Brian M. Boom, Ph.D.; Vice Pres.
Gov. & Comm. Relations, Aaron Bouska; C.F.O., Sarah Gillman; Gen. Counsel,
Justin Jamail; Vice Pres. IT, Christian Keck; Chief Advancement Officer, J. Tim
Landi; Vice Pres. Site Ops. & Chief Sustainability Officer, John McEnrue; Vice
Pres. HR & Chief Diversity Officer, Raquel Nazario; Vice Pres. Garden
Experience & Chief Marketing Officer, Lauren Turchio.
Institution Type/Description: Botanical Garden & Nature Center.
Hours & Admission Prices: Tues.-Sun. 10-6. Mon.-Fri.: adults $23, senior citizens
65 & up & students w/I.D. $20, children 2-12 $10; children under 2 & members
no charge. Sat.-Sun.: adults $28, senior citizens 65 & up & students w/I.D. $25,
children 2-12 $12; discounts to New York City residents (grounds only),
American Horticulture Society, American Public Gardens Association, Museum
Council of New York City, American Assoc. of Museums, Macauly Honors
College at CUNY, Cultural Passport Program & AAM members; children under
2 & members no charge. Closed Thanksgiving; Christmas. &
Attendance: 820,000 (actual)

NEW YORK YANKEES MUSEUM, Yankee Stadium, One E.
161st St., Bronx, NY 10451-2100. Tel.: 646-977-8687.
Key Personnel: Cur., Brian Richards.
Institution Type/Description: Baseball Museum.
Hours & Admission Prices: Museum: Game Day - from the time the gates open
until the end of the 8th inning. No charge. Non-Game Days: museum access is
part of the Yankee Stadium tour. Yankee Stadium Tours: May-Sept. call for
hours. Tours: adults $20-$25, children 14 & under and seniors 60 & over $20-
$23; children 3 & under no charge.

**VALENTINE-VARIAN HOUSE/MUSEUM OF BRONX
HISTORY,** Varian House Park, 3266 Bainbridge Ave. at E. 208th
St., Bronx, NY 10467. Mailing Address: Bronx County Historical
Society, 3309 Bainbridge Ave., Bronx, NY 10467-2850. Tel.: 718-
881-8900. Fax: 718-881-4827.
E-mail: kmcauley@bronxhistoricalsociety.org
Web Site: www.bronxhistoricalsociety.org
Key Personnel: C.E.O., Dr. G. Hermalyn; Pres. (V), Jacqueline Kutner; Dir.
Museums, Kathleen McAuley; Dir. Operations & Devel., Dimitris Raptopoulos;
Educator, Angel Hernandez.
Institution Type/Description: Historical House: second oldest house in the Bronx
built by Isaac Valentine in 1758; sold to Isaac Varian in 1792.
Hours & Admission Prices: Sat. 10-4, Sun. 1-5, Mon.-Fri. tours by appointment.
Adults $5, seniors, students & children $3; discounts to AAM & ICOM mem-
bers; members & Historic House Trust of NYC no charge.
Attendance: 43,606 (estimated)

VAN CORTLANDT HOUSE MUSEUM, Van Cortlandt Park,
Broadway at 246th St., Bronx, NY 10471. Mailing Address: 6393

Broadway, Bronx, NY 10471-2798. Tel.: 718-543-3344. Fax: 718-
543-3315. TDD: 800-281-5722.
E-mail: info@vancortlandhouse.org
Web Site: www.vancortlandhouse.org
Key Personnel: Dir., Laura Carpenter; Pres., Ann Crawford; Museum Shop Mgr.,
Juana Vasquez.
Institution Type/Description: Historic House: c.1748 house built by Frederick Van
Cortlandt.
Hours & Admission Prices: Tues.-Fri. 10-3, Sat.-Sun. 11-4; groups by appointment.
Adults $5, senior citizens & students $3; discounts to AAM members; children
under 12, Wed. & members of Colonial Dames no charge. Closed major holi-
days.
Attendance: 8,600 (actual)

WAVE HILL, W 249th St. & Independence Ave., Bronx, NY 10471-
2899. Mailing Address: 675 W. 252nd St., Bronx, NY 10471-2899.
Tel.: 718-549-3200. Fax: 718-884-8952. Facebook, Twitter,
Instagram: Wave Hill or @wavehill.
E-mail: information@wavehill.org
Web Site: www.wavehill.org
Key Personnel: Exec. Dir. & Pres., Karen Meyerhoff; Co, Chair, Sarah G. Gund;
Co Chair, Richard S. Zinman; Vice Pres. & Chief Opers. Officer, Michele
Rossetti; Sr. Dir. Horticulture, Louis Bauer; Dir. Mktg. & Communications,
Mary Weitzman; Dir Visitor Svcs., Michael Wiertz; Dir. Devel., Barbara
Giordano; Sr. Dir. Arts, Education & Programs, Jennifer McGregor; Dir.
Education, Alix Cotumaccio; Dir. Facilities & Capital Projects, Frank Perrone;
Shop Mgr., Jenah Barry.
Institution Type/Description: Public Garden and Cultural Center.
Hours & Admission Prices: March 15-Oct. 31 Tues.-Sun. 9-5:30; Nov. 1-March 14
Tues.-Sun. 9-4:30. Adults $8, seniors 65 & over and students $4, children 6-18
$2; children under 6, Tues. & Sat. 9-12 and members no charge. Closed New
Year's Day; Thanksgiving; Christmas. &
Attendance: 163,402 (estimated)

Bronxville

**EASTCHESTER HISTORICAL SOCIETY - 1835 MARBLE
SCHOOLHOUSE,** 390 California Rd., Bronxville, NY 10708.
Mailing Address: P.O. Box 37, Eastchester, NY 10709-0037. Tel.:
914-793-1900. Facebook: Eastchester Historical Society.
E-mail: marbleschoolhouse@yahoo.com
Web Site: www.eastchesterhistoricalsociety.org
Key Personnel: Pres. (V), Annmarie Flannery; Cur., Lissa Halen.
Institution Type/Description: Historical Society Museum: housed in c.1835 Marble
School House & separate library building.
Hours & Admission Prices: By appointment. No charge; donations accepted.
Attendance: 300 (estimated)

Brooklyn

A.I.R. GALLERY, 155 Plymouth St., Brooklyn, NY 11201-1150.
Tel.: 212-255-6651. Fax: 212-255-6653. Facebook; Twitter;
Instgram.
E-mail: info@airgallery.org
Web Site: airgallery.org
Key Personnel: Exec. Dir., Roxana Fabius; Assoc. Dir. & Dir. Fellowship,
Jacqueline Ferrante.
Institution Type/Description: Art Gallery.
Hours & Admission Prices: Wed.-Sat. 12-6. No charge; donations accepted. &
Attendance: 84,000 (estimated)

AMOS ENO GALLERY, 56 Bogart St., Brooklyn, NY 11206. Tel.:
718-237-3001. Facebook: Amos Eno Gallery.
E-mail: amosenogallery@gmail.com
Web Site: www.amoseno.org
Key Personnel: Dir., Mary Gagler.
Institution Type/Description: Art Gallery.
Hours & Admission Prices: Thurs.-Sun. 12-6.

BAC GALLERY, Mailing Address: Brooklyn Arts Council, 20 Jay
St., Ste. 616, Brooklyn, NY 11201. Tel.: 718-625-0080. Facebook:
@BrooklynArtsCouncil; Twitter: @BKArtsCouncil.
E-mail: gallery@brooklynartscouncil.org
Web Site: www.brooklynartscouncil.org/bacgallery
Key Personnel: Exec. Dir., Charlotte Cohen; Arts in Education Dir., Philip
Alexander; Assoc. Dir. Devel. & External Affairs, Jasmine Wagner.
Institution Type/Description: Art Gallery.
Hours & Admission Prices: Mon.-Fri. 10-5. No charge; donations accepted. Closed
holidays.

BLACK & WHITE GALLERY / PROJECT SPACE, 56 Bogart St., Brooklyn, NY 11206. Tel.: 718-599-8775. Fax: 347-881-9033. Facebook: Black and White Gallery; Instagram: @bwg_ps; Twitter: @BWGallery.
E-mail: info@blackandwhiteartgallery.com
Web Site: www.blackandwhiteartgallery.com
Key Personnel: Founder & Dir., Tatyana Okshteyn; Co-Dir. & Cur., Sasha Okshteyn.
Institution Type/Description: Art Gallery.
Hours & Admission Prices: Fri.-Sun. 1-6; other times by appointment

BRIC, 647 Fulton St., Brooklyn, NY 11217. Tel.: 718-683-5600. Fax: 718-802-9095. Facebook, Instagram & Twitter: @bricartsmedia.
E-mail: bric@bricartsmedia.org
Web Site: www.bricartsmedia.org
Formerly: BRIC Contemporary Art
Key Personnel: Pres., Leslie G. Schultz; Exec. Vice Pres., Betsy Smulyan; Vice Pres. Contemporary Art, Elizabeth Ferrer; Vice Pres. Performing Arts, Jack Walsh; Dir. Devel., Elaine Bowen; Dir. Education, Jackie Chang; Dir. Finance, Lexi Robertson; Sr. Mktg. Mgr., Abigail Clark; Asst. Cur., Jenny Gerow; Gallery Mgr., Dennis Witkin.
Institution Type/Description: Art Museum.
Hours & Admission Prices: Tues.-Fri. 10-8, Sat.-Sun. 10-6. No charge; donations accepted. &
Attendance: 12,000 (actual)

BROOKLYN BOTANIC GARDEN, 990 Washington Ave., Brooklyn, NY 11225-1099. Mailing Address: 1000 Washington Ave., Brooklyn, NY 11225. Tel.: 718-623-7200. Fax: 718-857-2430. Facebook & Instagram: @BrooklynBotanic; Twitter: @bklynbotanic.
E-mail: feedback@bbg.org
Web Site: www.bbg.org
Key Personnel: Pres., Scot Medbury; Sr. Vice Pres. Institutional Advancement, Leslie Findlen; Vice Pres. Education & Interpretation, Sonal Bhatt; Vice Pres. Visitor Experience & Mktg., Samantha Campbell; Vice Pres. Planning, Design & Construction, Tracey Faireland; Vice Pres. Finance & C.F.O., Dorota Rashid; Vice Pres. Horticulture & Facilities, Melanie Sifton.
Institution Type/Description: Arboretum & Botanical Garden.
Hours & Admission Prices: General Grounds: March-Oct. Tues.-Fri. 8-6, Sat.-Sun. 10-6; Nov. Tues.-Fri. 8-4:30, Sat.-Sun. 10-4:30; Dec.-Feb. Tues.-Sun. 10-4:30. Adults $15, seniors 65 & over and students 12 & over $8; children under 12, members, school groups, & Tues. no charge. Closed New Year's Day; Labor Day; Thanksgiving; Christmas. &
Attendance: 685,000 (estimated)

BROOKLYN CHILDREN'S MUSEUM, 145 Brooklyn Ave., Brooklyn, NY 11213-1900. Tel.: 718-735-4400. Fax: 718-604-7442. Facebook: @BrooklynChildrensMuseum; Instagram: @bcmkids; Twitter: @BrooklynKids.
E-mail: swilchfort@brooklynkids.org
Web Site: www.brooklynkids.org
Key Personnel: Pres. & C.E.O., Stephanie Hill Wilchfort; Dir. Exhibits & Interpretation, Hana Elwell; Dir. Govt. & Community Affairs, Margaret Walton.
Institution Type/Description: General Children's Museum.
Hours & Admission Prices: Tues.-Wed. & Fri. 10-5, Thurs. 10-6, Sat.-Sun. 10-7. Admission $13; discounts to AAM, ASTC & ACM members; members & children under 12 months no charge. Closed New Year's Day; Thanksgiving; Christmas. &
Attendance: 250,000 (actual)

BROOKLYN HISTORICAL SOCIETY, 128 Pierrepont St., Brooklyn, NY 11201-2711. Tel.: 718-222-4111. Fax: 718-222-3794. Facebook, Instagram & Twitter: @BrooklynHistory.
E-mail: jcodes@brooklynhistory.org
Web Site: www.brooklynhistory.org
Formerly: Long Island Historical Society
Key Personnel: Pres., Deborah Schwartz; Chm. (V), James Rossman; Dir. Education, Emily Potter-Ndiaye; Dir. Finance & Operations, Jason Pietrangeli; Retail & Visitor Svcs Mgr., Patrcik Valentine.
Institution Type/Description: History Museum: housed in building designed by architect, George B. Post.
Hours & Admission Prices: Wed.-Sun. 12-5. Adults $10, students & seniors $6; discounts to AAM & ICOM members; members no charge. Closed New Year's Day; Independence Day; Thanksgiving; Christmas. &
Attendance: 49,770 (actual)

BROOKLYN MUSEUM, 200 Eastern Pkwy., Brooklyn, NY 11238-6099. Tel.: 718-638-5000. Fax: 718-501-6136. Facebook, Instagram & Twitter: @brooklynmuseum.
E-mail: information@brooklynmuseum.org
Web Site: www.brooklynmuseum.org
Formerly: Brooklyn Museum of Art
Key Personnel: Chm., Barbara M. Vogelstein; Vice Chm., Stephanie Ingrassia; Shelby White & Leon Levy Dir., Anne Pasternak; Pres. & C.O.O., David Berliner; Dir. Exhibitions & Strategic Initiatives, Sharon Matt Atkins; Dir. Collections & Curatorial Affairs, Susan Fisher; Cur. European Art, Lisa Small; Sr. Cur. Egyptian, Classical & Ancient Near Eastern Art, Edward Bleiberg; Sr. Cur. Lisa & Bernard Selz, Asian Art, Joan Cummins; Sackler Sr. Cur., Elizabeth A. Sackler Ctr. for Feminist Art, Catherine J. Morris; John & Barbara Vogelstein Sr. Cur., Contemporary Art, Eugenie Tsai; Andrew W. Mellon Sr. Cur., Arts of the Americas, Nancy Rosoff; Assoc. Cur. Egyptian Art, Yekaterina Barbash; Asst. Cur. Contemporary Art, Ashley James; Assoc. Cur. Elizabeth A. Sackler Ctr. for Feminist Art, Carmen Hermo; Andrew W. Mellon Senior Cur. American Art, Jane Dini; Phillip Leonian & Edith Rosenbaum Leonian Cur., Photography, Drew Sawyer; Curator Emeritus, Kevin Stayton; Hagop Kevorkian Assoc. Curator Islamic Art, Aysin Yoltar-Yildirim; Dir. Public Programs, Lauren Argentina Zelaya.
Institution Type/Description: Art Museum.
Hours & Admission Prices: Wed. & Fri.-Sun. 11-6, Thurs. 11-10, first Sat. every month 11-11. Suggested Donations: adults $16, students & senior citizens 62 & up $10; discounts to AAM & ICOM members; ages 19 & under & members no charge. Closed New Year's Day; Thanksgiving; Christmas. &
Attendance: 325,501 (actual)

BROOKLYN WATERFRONT ARTISTS COALITION (BWAC), 499 Van Brunt St., Redhook, Brooklyn, NY 11231. Mailing Address: BWAC c/o OHM, 76 Degraw St., Brooklyn, NY 11231. Tel.: 718-596-2506 & 2507. Facebook: @BWAC.ART.
E-mail: bwacinfo@aol.com
Web Site: bwac.org
Key Personnel: Arts Admin., Jane Gutterman; Accountant, Jay Weissman; Gallery Supvr., Judith Eloise Hopper.
Institution Type/Description: Art Gallery: housed in a pre-Civil War-era warehouse.
Hours & Admission Prices: Sat.-Sun. 1-6.
Attendance: 18,000 (estimated)

THE CITY RELIQUARY MUSEUM, 370 Metropolitan Ave., Brooklyn, NY 11211. Tel.: 718-782-4842. Facebook.
E-mail: info@cityreliquary.org
Web Site: cityreliquary.org
Key Personnel: Founder, Dave Herman.
Institution Type/Description: History Museum.
Hours & Admission Prices: Thurs.-Sun. 12-6. Adults $7, college students, educators, & seniors $5; discounts to groups; children 12 & under no charge. Closed New Year's Day; Thanksgiving; Christmas.

CONEY ISLAND MUSEUM, 1208 Surf Ave., Brooklyn, NY 11224-2816. Tel.: 718-372-5159. Fax: 718-372-5101. Facebook & Twitter: @coneyislandusa; Instagram: #coneyislandmuseum.
E-mail: museum@coneyisland.com
Web Site: www.coneyisland.com/museum.shtml
Key Personnel: Founder & Artistic Dir., Dick D. Zigun; Cur., Lisa Mangels-Schaefer.
Institution Type/Description: History Museum.
Hours & Admission Prices: Mid-June to Labor Day Wed.-Sat. 12-6, Sun. 2-6; Labor Day to mid-June Sat. 12-6, Sun. 2-6. Adults $5, seniors & children under 12 $3; discounts to local residents.

DIEU DONNE, Building 3, Ste. 602, 63 Flushing Ave. Unit 112, Brooklyn, NY 11205. Tel.: 212-226-0573. Fax: 212-226-6088.
E-mail: kflynn@dieudonne.org
Web Site: www.dieudonne.org
Key Personnel: Exec. Dir., Kathleen Flynn.
Institution Type/Description: Art Gallery.
Hours & Admission Prices: Tues.-Fri. 10-6, Sat. 12-6; other times by appointment.

FRANKLIN FURNACE ARCHIVE, INC., Pratt Institute, 200 Willoughby Ave., Brooklyn, NY 11205-7501. Tel.: 718-687-5800. Fax: 718-687-5830.
E-mail: mail@franklinfurnace.org
Web Site: www.franklinfurnace.org
Key Personnel: Founding Dir., Martha Wilson; Sr. Archivist, Michael Katchen; Program Coord., Jenny Korns; Deputy Dir., Harley Spiller.
Institution Type/Description: Art Museum.
Hours & Admission Prices: Mon.-Fri. 10-6. No charge.

HARBOR DEFENSE MUSEUM, US Army Garrison Fort Hamilton, 101st St. & Fort Hamilton Pkwy., Brooklyn, NY 11252-9523. Tel.: 718-630-4349. Facebook: @USAGFortHamilton.

Web Site: www.hamilton.army.mil
Key Personnel: Dir. & Cur., Gus Keilers.
Institution Type/Description: Military Museum: housed in 1825-1831 Fort Hamilton.
Hours & Admission Prices: Mon.-Fri. 10-4, Sat. 10-2. No charge. Closed Federal holidays. &
Attendance: 24,000 (estimated)

JEWISH CHILDREN'S MUSEUM, 792 Eastern Pkwy., Brooklyn, NY 11213-3502. Tel.: 718-467-0600. Fax: 718-467-1300. Facebook: Jewish Children's Museum.
E-mail: info@jcm.museum
Web Site: www.jcm.museum
Key Personnel: Program Dir., Goldie Moskowitz.
Institution Type/Description: Children's Museum.
Hours & Admission Prices: Mon.-Thurs. 10-4, Sun. 10-6; school & youth groups call 718-907-8888 for group bookings. Admission $13, seniors $10; children under 2 no charge.

KENTLER INTERNATIONAL DRAWING SPACE, 353 Van Brunt St., Brooklyn, NY 11231. Tel.: 718-875-2098. Facebook: @kentlergallery; Instagram & Twitter: @kentlerdrawing.
E-mail: info@kentlergallery.org
Web Site: www.kentlergallery.org
Key Personnel: Co-Founder & Exec. Dir., Florence Neal; Programs Mgr., Sallie Mize.
Institution Type/Description: Art Gallery.
Hours & Admission Prices: Thurs.-Sun. 12-5. No charge.

KLOMPCHING GALLERY, 89 Water St., Brooklyn, NY 11201. Tel.: 212-796-2070. Facebook & Twitter: @klompching; Instagram: @klompchinggallery.
E-mail: info@klompching.com
Web Site: www.klompching.com
Key Personnel: Dir., Debra Klomp Ching; Dir., Darren Ching.
Institution Type/Description: Art Gallery.
Hours & Admission Prices: Wed.-Sat. 11-6; other times by appointment. No charge.
Attendance: 5,200 (estimated)

LEFFERTS HISTORIC HOUSE, Flatbush Ave., Prospect Park, Brooklyn, NY 11215-3709. Mailing Address: Prospect Park Alliance, 95 Prospect Park W., Brooklyn, NY 11215-3709. Tel.: 718-965-8951. Fax: 718-789-4724.
E-mail: info@prospectpark.org
Web Site: www.prospectpark.org
Formerly: Lefferts Homestead
Key Personnel: Pres. & Park Admin., Sue Donoghue.
Institution Type/Description: Historic House: built c.1783 Dutch-American architecture.
Hours & Admission Prices: April-June & Sept.-Nov. Thurs.-Sun. & holidays 12-5; July-Aug. Thurs.-Sun. 12-6; Dec.-March Sat.-Sun. & school holidays 12-4. Suggested donation $3. Closed New Year's Day; Thanksgiving; Christmas Eve & Day. &
Attendance: 45,000 (actual)

LESBIAN HERSTORY EDUCATIONAL FOUNDATION, INC. AKA LESBIAN HERSTORY ARCHIVES, 484 14th St., Brooklyn, NY 11215-5702. Tel.: 718-768-3953. Fax: 718-768-4663. Facebook: @herstoryarchives.
E-mail: lesbianherstoryarchives@gmail.com
Web Site: www.lesbianherstoryarchives.org
Key Personnel: Treas., Deborah Edel.
Institution Type/Description: Lesbian History & Culture Museum.
Hours & Admission Prices: See website for hours. No charge; donations accepted. &
Attendance: 3,000 (estimated)

MINUS SPACE, 16 Main St., Ste. A, Brooklyn, NY 11201-1020. Tel.: 718-801-8095. Facebook & Twitter: @minusspace; Instagram: @minus_space.
E-mail: info@minusspace.com
Web Site: www.minusspace.com
Key Personnel: Dir., Matthew Deleget; Dir., Rossana Martinez.
Institution Type/Description: Art Gallery.
Hours & Admission Prices: Wed.-Sat. 11-5; other times by appointment. Closed federal holidays; Thanksgiving week; Christmas week; New Year's week.

MOCADA - THE MUSEUM OF CONTEMPORARY AFRICAN DIASPORAN ARTS, 80 Hanson Pl., Brooklyn, NY 11217-1506. Tel.: 718-230-0492. Fax: 718-230-0246. Facebook: @MoCADAmuseum.
E-mail: info@mocada.org
Web Site: mocada.org
Key Personnel: Exec. Dir., James Bartlett; Operations & Finance Dir., Cherise Jones; Assoc. Devel. Dir., Tiasia O'Brien; Programs Coord., Atisha Fordyce; Events & Visitor Svcs. Assoc., Geraldine Leibot.
Institution Type/Description: Art Museum.
Hours & Admission Prices: Wed., Fri. & Sat. noon to 7, Thurs. noon to 8, Sun. noon to 6. Adults $8, seniors 65 & over and students $4; children under 12 no charge.

MOMENTA ART, 56 Bogart St., 1P, Brooklyn, NY 11206. Tel.: 718-218-8058.
E-mail: contact@momentaart.org
Web Site: www.momentaart.org
Key Personnel: Chairperson, Elisabeth Kley; Founder & Exec. Dir., Eric Heist; Program & Admin. Dir., Kikuko Tanaka.
Institution Type/Description: Art Gallery.
Hours & Admission Prices: Sat. & Sun. noon to 6.

MUSEUM OF FOOD AND DRINK LAB, 62 Bayard St., Brooklyn, NY 11222. Tel.: 718-387-2845.
E-mail: info@mofad.org
Web Site: www.mofad.org
Institution Type/Description: Food & Drink Museum.
Hours & Admission Prices: Wed.-Thurs. 12-5, Fri. 12-8, Sat.-Sun. 12-6. Adults $10, students & seniors $8, children 6-17 $5; children under 5 no charge.

NEW YORK AQUARIUM, Surf Ave. & W. 8th St., Brooklyn, NY 11224-3495. Mailing Address: c/o Wildlife Conservation Society, 2300 Southern Blvd., Bronx, NY 10460. Tel.: 718-265-2663, 718-220-5103. Facebook, Instagram & Twitter: @nyaquarium.
E-mail: guestrelations@wcs.org
Web Site: nyaquarium.org
Key Personnel: Pres. & C.E.O., Cristian Samper; Dir., Jon F. Dohlin; Exec. Dir. New Project Administration, Ray Davis; Gen. Cur. & Dir. Animal Operations, Dave DeNardo; Dir. Communications, Max Pulsinelli.
Institution Type/Description: Aquarium.
Hours & Admission Prices: Memorial Day-Labor Day Mon.-Fri. 10-5, Sat.-Sun. & holidays 10-7; Sept.-May daily 10-4:30. Admission 3 & up $11.95; discount to active duty and reserve members of U.S. military; children 2 & under no charge. &
Attendance: 767,026 (actual)

NORTE MAAR, 88 Pine St., Brooklyn, NY 12941. Tel.: 646-361-8512. Facebook & Twitter: @nortemaar.
E-mail: nortemaar@gmail.com
Web Site: www.nortemaar.org
Key Personnel: Dir., Jason Andrew.
Institution Type/Description: Art Gallery.
Hours & Admission Prices: Call for hours.

NURTUREART, 56 Bogart St., Brooklyn, NY 11206. Tel.: 718-782-7755. Fax: 718-569-2086.
E-mail: gallery@nurtureart.org
Web Site: nurtureart.org
Key Personnel: Exec. Dir., William Penrose; Education Dir., Molly O'Brien; Gallery Mgr., Ivan Gilbert.
Institution Type/Description: Art Gallery.
Hours & Admission Prices: Thurs.-Sun. noon to 6; other times by appointment.

PROSPECT PARK ZOO, 450 Flatbush Ave., Brooklyn, NY 11225-3707. Mailing Address: c/o Wildlife Conservation Society, 2300 Southern Blvd., Bronx, NY 10460. Tel.: 718-399-7339. Fax: 718-399-7337. Facebook.
E-mail: mpulsinelli@wcs.org
Web Site: www.prospectparkzoo.com
Formerly: Prospect Park Wildlife Center
Key Personnel: Dir., Denise McClean; Dir. Communications, Max Pulsinelli.
Institution Type/Description: Zoo.
Hours & Admission Prices: Winter: daily 10-4:30; Summer: Mon.-Fri. 10-5, Sat.-Sun. 10-5:30. Adults $8, senior citizens 65 & up $6, children 3-12 $5; members and children 2 & under no charge. &
Attendance: 232,426 (actual)

ROBERT LEHMAN GALLERY AT URBANGLASS, 647 Fulton St., Brooklyn, NY 11217. Tel.: 718-625-3685. Fax: 718-625-3889. Facebook & Twitter: @UrbanGlass; Instagram: @urbanglass_-ware.
E-mail: info@urbanglass.org
Web Site: urbanglass.org
Key Personnel: Exec. Dir., Cybele Maylone; Dir. Operations, Brian Kibler; Dir. Finance, Jeff Bush; Dir. Education, Ben Wright.
Institution Type/Description: Art Gallery.
Hours & Admission Prices: Tues.-Fri. noon to 7, Sat. 11-7, Sun. 11-6. No charge.

THE RUBELLE & NORMAN SCHAFLER GALLERY, Pratt Institute, 200 Willoughby Ave., Brooklyn, NY 11205-3802. Tel.: 718-636-3517. Fax: 718-399-4230. Facebook: Schafler Gallery, Pratt Institute.
E-mail: exhibits@pratt.edu
Web Site: www.pratt.edu/exhibitions
Key Personnel: Dir. Exhibitions, Nick Battis; Asst. Dir. Exhibitions, Kirsten Nelson.
Institution Type/Description: Art & University Museum.
Hours & Admission Prices: Fall/Spring Semester: Mon.-Fri. 9-5, Sat. noon to 5; Summer: Mon.-Fri. 9-4. No charge. Closed major holidays.
Attendance: 10,000 (estimated)

SLAG GALLERY, 56 Bogart St, Brooklyn, NY 11206. Tel.: 212-967-9818. Fax: 212-967-9819. Facebook: Slag Gallery; Twitter & Instagram: @SLAGgallery.
E-mail: info@slaggallery.com
Web Site: slaggallery.com
Key Personnel: Owner & Dir., Irina Protopopescu.
Institution Type/Description: Art Gallery.
Hours & Admission Prices: Thurs.-Sun. 1-6; other times by appointment.

SMACK MELLON GALLERY, 92 Plymouth St., Brooklyn, NY 11201. Tel.: 718-834-8761. Fax: 718-834-5233. Facebook, Instagram & Twitter: @SmackMellon.
E-mail: info@smackmellon.org
Web Site: smackmellon.org
Key Personnel: Exec. Dir., Kathleen Gilrain; Pres. Bd. Dirs., Sherri Marton; Cur. & Dir. Exhibitions, Gabriel de Guzman; Gallery & Studios Mgr., Eva Mayhabal Davis.
Institution Type/Description: Art Gallery.
Hours & Admission Prices: Wed.-Sun. noon to 6. &

SOUTHFIRST, 60 N. 6th St., Brooklyn, NY 11211. Tel.: 718-599-4884.
E-mail: info@southfirst.org
Web Site: www.southfirst.org
Key Personnel: Co-Founder, Owner & Dir., Maika Pollack.
Institution Type/Description: Art Gallery.
Hours & Admission Prices: Sat. & Sun. noon to 6; other times by appointment.

WATERFRONT MUSEUM, 290 Conover St., Pier 44, Brooklyn, NY 11231-1020. Tel.: 718-624-4719. Fax: 888-320-2485. Facebook: @thewaterfrontmuseum; Twitter: @MuseumBarge.
E-mail: dsharps@waterfrontmuseum.org
Web Site: www.waterfrontmuseum.org
Formerly: Hudson Waterfront Museum
Key Personnel: Pres., David Sharps; Chm. (V), Kristy Krivitsky.
Institution Type/Description: Maritime Museum: housed aboard the 1914 Lehigh Valley Railroad Barge #79 used during the Lighterage Era 1860-1960, when goods were transferred from port docks to railhead terminals by tug & barge. Listed on the National Register of Historic Places.
Hours & Admission Prices: Thurs. 4-8, Sat. 1-5; call to confirm; groups by appointment. Suggested Donation: $5. &
Attendance: 10,000 (estimated)

WYCKOFF HOUSE MUSEUM, 5816 Clarendon Rd., Brooklyn, NY 11203-5444. Tel.: 718-629-5400. Facebook, Instagram & Twitter: @wyckoffmuseum.
E-mail: info@wyckoffmuseum.org
Web Site: wyckoffmuseum.org
Formerly: The Pieter Claesen Wyckoff House Museum
Key Personnel: Museum Dir., Melissa Branfman; Docent, Lucie Chin.
Institution Type/Description: Historic House: c.1652 Dutch Colonial farmhouse.
Hours & Admission Prices: Grounds: Fri.-Sat. 12-4; Guided House Tours; Fri.-Sat. 1 p.m. & 3 p.m. Adults $5, senior citizens, students & children $3; museum members no charge.
Attendance: 10,000 (estimated)

Brooklyn Heights

NEW YORK TRANSIT MUSEUM, Corner of Boerum Pl. & Schermerhorn St., Brooklyn Heights, NY 11201. Mailing Address: 130 Livingston St., 10th Fl., Brooklyn, NY 11201-5106. Tel.: 718-694-1600 & 1873. Fax: 718-694-1791.
E-mail: regina.asborno@nyct.com
Web Site: www.mta.info/museum
Key Personnel: Chm. (V), Susan Gilbert; Deputy Dir., Regina Asborno; Tour Coord., Luz Montano; Asst. Dir. & Devel. Officer, Sarah Landreth; Admin. Mgr., Angela Agard Solomon; Operations Mgr., Jesus Albino; Sr. Mgr. Exhibits, Robert Del Bagno; Mgr. Education, Elyse Newman; Cur., Brigid Harmon; Assoc. Cur., Chandra Buie; Education Specialist, Virgil Talaid; Collection Mgr., Carey Stumm; Mgr. Retail & MTA Products Devel., Gail Goldberg; Educator Coord., Kristin Fields; Asst. Mgr. Retail Operations, Dorla Arnold; Retail Mgr., Ilana Stollman.
Institution Type/Description: Urban Transportation Museum: located in a decommissioned subway station c.1936.
Hours & Admission Prices: Tues.-Fri. 10-4, Sat.-Sun. 12-5. Adults $6, senior citizens & children under 17 $4; discounts to AAM, ICOM & ASTC members; members no charge. GCT Annex: Mon.-Fri. 8-8, Sat.-Sun. 10-6. No charge. Closed New Year's Eve & Day; Memorial Day; Independence Day; Labor Day Weekend; Thanksgiving; Christmas. &
Attendance: 458,656 (actual)

Brookville

STEINBERG MUSEUM OF ART - LONG ISLAND UNIVERSITY, Hillwood Commons, 2nd Fl., 720 Northern Blvd., Brookville, NY 11548-1319. Tel.: 516-299-4073. Fax: 516-299-2787.
E-mail: museum@cwpost.liu.edu
Web Site: www.liu.edu/museum
Formerly: Hillwood Art Museum
Institution Type/Description: Art Museum & Public Art Program.
Hours & Admission Prices: June-July Mon.-Fri. 9-4:30; Sept.-May Mon.-Wed. & Fri. 9:30-4:30, Thurs. 9:30-8, Sat. 11-3. No charge; donations accepted. &
Attendance: 15,000 (actual)

Brownville

GENERAL JACOB BROWN HISTORICAL SOCIETY, 116 E. Main St., Brownville, NY 13615. Tel.: 315-782-4508. Fax: 315-786-1178.
Institution Type/Description: Historical Society Museum: housed in 1811-1815 General Brown Mansion.
Hours & Admission Prices: By appointment only. No charge; donations accepted.

Buffalo

ALBRIGHT-KNOX ART GALLERY, 1285 Elmwood Ave., Buffalo, NY 14222-1096. Tel.: 716-882-8700; 716-270-8297 (TTY). Fax: 716-882-8773. Facebook: Albright-Knox Art Gallery.
E-mail: info@albrightknox.org
Web Site: www.albrightknox.org
Key Personnel: Peggy Pierce Elfvin Dir., Dr. Janne Siren; Deputy Dir., Joe Lin-Hill; Pres. (V), Alice F. Jacobs; Godin-Spaulding Cur. & Cur. of the Collection, Holly E. Hughes; Chief Cur., Cathleen Chaffee; Dir. Communications, Maria Scully-Morreale.
Institution Type/Description: Art Museum.
Hours & Admission Prices: Tues.-Sun. 10-5, first Fri. every month 10-10. Adults $12, seniors 62 & up and students 13 & up $8, children 6-12 $5; discounts to AAM members & groups; active duty U.S. & Canadian military personnel, CIMAM members, children 5 & under & museum members no charge. Closed New Year's Day; Independence Day; Thanksgiving; Christmas Day. &
Attendance: 143,653 (actual)

THE BENJAMIN & DR. EDGAR R. COFELD JUDAIC MUSEUM OF TEMPLE BETH ZION, 805 Delaware Ave., Buffalo, NY 14209-2005. Mailing Address: 700 Sweet Home Rd., Buffalo, NY 14226-1444. Tel.: 716-836-6565. Fax: 716-831-1126.
E-mail: rabbifreirich@tbz.org
Web Site: www.tbz.org
Institution Type/Description: Judaic Museum.
Hours & Admission Prices: Mon.-Fri. 9-4, Sat. 11-12; tours by appointment. No charge; donations accepted. &
Attendance: 16,000

BIG ORBIT, 30 Essex St., Buffalo, NY 14213. Tel.: 716-856-2717.
Web Site: www.cepagallery.org

Institution Type/Description: Art Gallery.
Hours & Admission Prices: Fri.-Sun. 12-6.

BUFFALO AND ERIE COUNTY BOTANICAL GARDENS,
2655 South Park Ave., Buffalo, NY 14218-1526. Tel.: 716-827-1584 ext. 212. Fax: 716-828-0091. Facebook: Buffalo and Erie County Botanical Gardens.
E-mail: info@buffalogardens.com
Web Site: www.buffalogardens.com
Key Personnel: Pres. & C.E.O., David J. Swarts; Chm. (V), Joseph DiDomineco; Sr. Dir. Operations, Julie DeCarolis; Guest Svcs. & Gift Shop Mgr., Denise Nichols.
Institution Type/Description: Botanical Garden.
Hours & Admission Prices: Daily 10-5. Adults $11, seniors 62 & up $10; students 13 & up $9, children 3-12 $6; discounts to American Horticulture Society's reciprocal program; members and children 2 & under no charge. Closed Thanksgiving; Christmas. &
Attendance: 102,000 (actual)

BUFFALO AND ERIE COUNTY HISTORICAL SOCIETY DBA THE BUFFALO HISTORY MUSEUM,
One Museum Ct., Buffalo, NY 14216-3119. Tel.: 716-873-9644. Fax: 716-873-8754. Instagram, Twitter.
E-mail: ccaldwell@buffalohistory.org
Web Site: buffalohistory.org
Key Personnel: Exec. Dir., Melissa Brown; Pres., Steven P. McCarville; Dir. Museum Collections, Walter Mayer; Asst. Librarian, Amy Miller.
Institution Type/Description: Local/Regional History Museum: housed in the only permanent building constructed for the 1901 Pan American Exposition. National Historic Landmark.
Hours & Admission Prices: Museum: Tues. & Thurs.-Sat. 10-5, Wed. 10-8, Sun. 12-5. Adults $7, senior citizens & students 13-21 $4, children 7-12 $2.50; discounts for groups, AAM & ICOM members; veterans, children under 7 & members no charge. Reference Library: Wed.-Sat. 1-5. Non-members $6. Closed New Year's Day; Thanksgiving; Christmas. &
Attendance: 65,000 (estimated)

BUFFALO AND ERIE COUNTY NAVAL & MILITARY PARK,
One Naval Park Cove, Buffalo, NY 14202. Tel.: 716-847-1773. Fax: 716-847-6405.
E-mail: info@buffalonavalpark.org
Web Site: buffalonavalpark.org
Key Personnel: Chm. (V), Donald A. Alessi; Exec. Dir., Captain Brian W. Roche, USCG (Ret.); Supt. Ships, John Branning; Office Mgr., JoAnn Drozdzak; Gift Shop Mgr., JoAnn Thomas.
Institution Type/Description: Historical Ships & Military Museum.
Hours & Admission Prices: April-Oct. daily 10-5; Nov. Sat.-Sun. 10-4. Adults $10, senior citizens & children 6-16 $6; discounts to groups, active military personnel, AAM & ICOM members; children 5 & under and members no charge. &
Attendance: 55,000 (estimated)

BUFFALO ARTS STUDIO,
Tri-Main Ctr., 2495 Main St., Ste. 500, Buffalo, NY 14214. Tel.: 716-833-4450.
E-mail: cori@buffaloartsstudio.org
Web Site: buffaloartsstudio.org
Institution Type/Description: Art Gallery.
Hours & Admission Prices: June-Aug. Tues.-Fri. 11-5; Sept.-May Tues.-Fri. 11-5, Sat. 10-2. Suggested Donation: $3.

BUFFALO FIRE HISTORICAL SOCIETY & MUSEUM,
1850 William St., Buffalo, NY 14206. Tel.: 716-892-8400.
E-mail: bfhsmuseum@verizon.net
Web Site: www.bfhsmuseum.com
Institution Type/Description: Firefighting History Museum.
Hours & Admission Prices: Sat. 10-4; groups by appointment. &

BUFFALO HARBOR MUSEUM,
66 Erie St., Buffalo, NY 14202. Tel.: 716-849-0914. Fax: 716-849-0914.
E-mail: info@llmhs.org
Web Site: www.llmhs.org
Formerly: Lower Lakes Marine Historical Society
Institution Type/Description: Marine Historical Society Museum.
Hours & Admission Prices: Thurs. & Sat. 10-3. No charge; donations accepted. &
Attendance: 1,500 (estimated)

BUFFALO MUSEUM OF SCIENCE,
1020 Humboldt Pkwy., Buffalo, NY 14211-1293. Tel.: 716-896-5200, 866-291-6660. Fax: 716-897-6723. Facebook: Buffalo Museum of Science.
E-mail: mwigglesworth@sciencebuff.org
Web Site: www.sciencebuff.org
Formerly: Buffalo Society of Natural Sciences
Key Personnel: Pres. & C.E.O., Marisa Wigglesworth; Chm. (V), Judith A. Feld; Dir. Learning & Interpretation, Karen Wallace; C.F.O., Hope Kianka; Exhibits Dir., David Cinquino; Dir. Collections & Special Projects, Kathryn Leacock; Operations Mgr., Jerry Silvis.
Institution Type/Description: Natural History Museum.
Hours & Admission Prices: Mon.-Tues. 10-4, Wed. 10-9, Thurs.-Sun. 10-4. Adults $11, senior citizens 62 & over $9, children 2-17, students & military with ID $8; discounts to ASTC members, Buffalo & Erie county Public Library cardholders, and NFTA pass cardholders; members & children under 2 no charge. &
Attendance: 111,225 (actual)

BUFFALO TRANSPORTATION PIERCE-ARROW MUSEUM & 1927 BUFFALO FILLING STATION BY FRANK LLOYD WRIGHT,
263 Michigan Ave., Buffalo, NY 14203-2900. Mailing Address: 24 Myrtle Ave., Buffalo, NY 14204-2048. Tel.: 716-853-0084. Facebook: @PierceArrowMuseum.
E-mail: piercemuseum@roadrunner.com
Web Site: pierce-arrow.com
Formerly: Buffalo Transportation Pierce-Arrow Museum
Key Personnel: Dir., James T. Sandoro.
Institution Type/Description: Transportation Museum.
Hours & Admission Prices: Call for hours. Adults $10. &
Attendance: 10,000 (estimated)

BUFFALO ZOO,
300 Parkside Ave., Buffalo, NY 14214-1999. Tel.: 716-837-3900, ext. 100. Fax: 716-833-3743. Facebook, Twitter.
E-mail: dschaefer@buffalozoo.org
Web Site: www.buffalozoo.org
Formerly: Buffalo Zoological Gardens
Key Personnel: Pres., Norah Fletchall; Chm., Jonathan Dandes; Dir. Finance, Denise Schaefer; Gen. Cur., Malia L. Somerville; Veterinarian, Kurt Volle, D.V. M.; Dir. Mktg. & Membership, Todd Geise; Service Systems Assoc., Nicole Wurstner.
Institution Type/Description: Zoological Gardens & Children's Zoo.
Hours & Admission Prices: Winter: Gates daily 10-4; Grounds 10-5; Summer: Gates daily 10-4; Grounds daily 10-5. Regular 13-64 $12, youth 2-12 $10, senior citizens 65 & over $9, discounts to AZA members & groups; children under 2 & zoo members no charge. Closed Thanksgiving; Christmas. &
Attendance: 538,100 (actual)

BURCHFIELD-PENNEY ART CENTER,
Buffalo State College, 1300 Elmwood Ave., Buffalo, NY 14222-1004. Tel.: 716-878-6011. Fax: 716-878-6003.
E-mail: burchfld@buffalostate.edu
Web Site: www.burchfieldpenney.org
Key Personnel: Chm., Carol Kociela; C.O.O., Carolyn A. Morris Hunt, CFRE; Assoc. Dir. & Chief Cur., Scott Propeack; Assoc. Dir. Programs, Donald J. Metz; Dir. Mktg. & Public Rels., Kathleen McMorrow Heyworth; Burchfield Scholar, Nancy Weekly; Curatorial Assoc., Kathy Gaye Shiroki; Museum Store Mgr., Mia Schachel.
Institution Type/Description: Art Museum: housed on the State University College at Buffalo Campus.
Hours & Admission Prices: Tues.-Wed. & Fri.-Sat. 10-5, Thurs. 10-9, Sun. 1-5. Adults $10, seniors 62 & up $8, students w/I.D. $5; discounts to AAM & NARM members; active military & their families, children 10 & under & members no charge. Closed New Year's Day, Independence Day; Thanksgiving day; Christmas Day. &
Attendance: 70,000 (actual)

CEPA GALLERY,
617 Main St., Buffalo, NY 14203. Tel.: 716-856-2717. Fax: 716-270-0184.
Web Site: www.cepagallery.org
Key Personnel: Exec. Dir. & Cur., Lawrence Brose; Pres. (V), Biff Henrich; Education Dir., Lauren Tent; Artistic Dir., David Mitchell; Exec. Asst., Lynda Kaszubski.
Institution Type/Description: Art Gallery.
Hours & Admission Prices: Mon.-Fri. 9-5, Sat. 12-4.
Attendance: 300,000 (estimated)

CENTER FOR EXPLORATORY AND PERCEPTUAL ART,
617 Main St., #201, Buffalo, NY 14203-1400. Tel.: 716-856-2717. Fax: 716-270-0184.
E-mail: info@cepagallery.com
Web Site: www.cepagallery.org
Key Personnel: Exec. Dir., Lawrence Brose; Dir. Education, Lauren Tent; Exec. Asst., Lynda Kaszubski.
Institution Type/Description: Art Gallery.

Hours & Admission Prices: Mon.-Fri. 9-5, Sat. 12-4; other times by appointment. No charge; donations accepted. &
Attendance: 1,000,000 (estimated)

FRANK LLOYD WRIGHT'S MARTIN HOUSE, 125 Jewett Pkwy., Buffalo, NY 14214-2301. Mailing Address: 143 Jewett Pkwy., Buffalo, NY 14214-2301. Tel.: 716-856-3858. Fax: 716-856-4009. Facebook: www.facebook.com/pages/Darwin-Martin-House/104684288914; Twitter: twitter.com/TheMartinHouse.

E-mail: info@martinhouse.org
Web Site: www.martinhouse.org
Key Personnel: Exec. Dir., Mary F. Roberts; Pres. (V), Keith Stolzenburg; Dir. Programs, Angela Laviano-Hamister.
Institution Type/Description: Historic House: housed in the former home of Darwin & Isabelle Martin; designed by Frank Lloyd Wright; built in 1904. A National Historic Landmark.
Hours & Admission Prices: Open year round. See website for detailed tour times and prices. &
Attendance: 40,000 (actual)

HALLWALLS CONTEMPORARY ARTS CENTER, 341 Delaware Ave., Buffalo, NY 14202. Tel.: 716-854-1694. Fax: 716-854-1696.

E-mail: polly@hallwalls.org
Web Site: www.hallwalls.org
Key Personnel: Exec. Dir., Edmund Cardoni; Deputy Dir. Finance & Devel., Polly Little; Cur. Visual Arts, John Massier; Dir. Music, Steven Bczkowski.
Institution Type/Description: Interdisciplinary Arts Center and Gallery.
Hours & Admission Prices: Tues.-Fri. 11-6, Sat. 11-2.

SHEA'S PERFORMING ARTS CENTER, 646 Main St., Buffalo, NY 14202. Mailing Address: P.O. Box 1130, Buffalo, NY 14205. Tel.: 716-847-1410. Fax: 716-847-1644.

E-mail: mmurphy@sheas.org
Web Site: www.sheas.org
Key Personnel: Pres., Michael Murphy.
Institution Type/Description: Historic Building: built in 1926. A National Historic Site.
Hours & Admission Prices: Tours: Tues., Thurs. & Sat. 10 & 1; during non-show days; groups by appointment. Adults $8, children, students & seniors $4; discounts to groups of 20 or more.

THEODORE ROOSEVELT INAUGURAL NATIONAL HISTORIC SITE, 641 Delaware Ave., Buffalo, NY 14202-1079. Tel.: 716-884-0095. Fax: 716-884-0330.

E-mail: stanton_hudson@partner.nps.gov
Web Site: trsite.org
Key Personnel: Exec. Dir. & Site Supt., Stanton H. Hudson, Jr.; Pres. (V), Donald A. Ogilvie; Vice Pres. (V), Karen Gaughan Scott; Dir. Admin. & Special Projects, Paul Zwirecki; Cur. & Dir. Public Programming, Lenora Henson; Education Dir., Mark Lozo; Administrative Asst., Shannon Lyons; Deputy Dir., Janice Kuzan; Facilities Mgr., Dan Dietrich; Interpreter, Mark Comito.
Institution Type/Description: Historic Building & Site: the site of the inauguration of Pres. Theodore Roosevelt in 1901.
Hours & Admission Prices: Tours: daily. Adults $10; discounts to National Park Pass holders; members no charge. Closed New Year's Eve & Day; Easter; Memorial Day; Independence Day; Labor Day; Thanksgiving; Christmas Eve & Day. &
Attendance: 26,000 (actual)

UNIVERSITY AT BUFFALO ART GALLERIES, UB Art Galleries, Center for the Arts, 201 Center for the Arts, Buffalo, NY 14260-6000. Tel.: 716-645-6913. Fax: 716-645-6753. Facebook: UB Art Galleries.

E-mail: rscalise@buffalo.edu
Web Site: www.ubartgalleries.org
Key Personnel: Acting & Deputy Dir., Robert Scalise; Sr. Cur., Rachel Adams; Tech. Asst., Jim Snider; Head Preparator, Ken Short; Asst. Preparator, Tom Andersen; Maintenance Supvr., Paul Wilcox; Finance & Gen. Opers. Mgr., Lynn Lasota.
Institution Type/Description: University Art Gallery & Museum.
Hours & Admission Prices: UB Art Gallery: Tues.-Fri. 11-5, Sat. 1-5; UB Anderson Gallery: Wed.-Sat. 11-5, Sun. 1-5. No charge; donations accepted. Closed New Year's Day; Memorial Day; Independence Day; Labor Day; Thanksgiving Day; Christmas; during installations. &
Attendance: 10,000 (estimated)

Burt

VAN HORN MANSION - NEWFANE HISTORICAL SOCIETY, Rt. 78, Burt, NY 14028. Mailing Address: P.O. Box 115, Newfane, NY 14108-0115. Tel.: 716-778-7197. Facebook: Town of Newfane Historical Society; The Van Horn Mansion.

E-mail: info@newfanehistoricalsociety.com
Web Site: www.newfanehistoricalsociety.com
Key Personnel: Dir., Jill Heck; Pres. (V), Bill Neidlinger.
Institution Type/Description: Historic House Museum: housed in the former home of James Van Horn; built in 1823. Listed on the National Registry of Historical Buildings.
Hours & Admission Prices: April-Dec. Sun. 1-4. No charge; donations accepted.
Attendance: 3,000 (estimated)

Byron

BYRON HISTORICAL MUSEUM, 6407 Town Line Rd., Byron, NY 14422. Mailing Address: 6451 Mill Pond Rd., Byron, NY 14422-9758. Tel.: 585-548-9008.

E-mail: byron-historian@juno.com
Web Site: www.byronny.com/history.html
Key Personnel: Historian, Beth Wilson; Historian, Bob Wilson.
Institution Type/Description: General Museum.
Hours & Admission Prices: Memorial Day to Labor Day Sun. 2-4; other times by appointment. No charge.
Attendance: 235

Caledonia

BIG SPRINGS MUSEUM, 3095 Main St., Caledonia, NY 14423-1237. Mailing Address: Box 41, Caledonia, NY 14423-0041. Tel.: 585-538-9880. Facebook.

E-mail: bigspringshistoricalsociety@gmail.com
Web Site: www.bigspringsmuseum.org
Key Personnel: Pres. (V), Janice Grattan; Cur., Patty Garrett; Docent, Mike LaFave.
Institution Type/Description: General Museum.
Hours & Admission Prices: Sun. 1-4, Mon. 9-12; call for additional hours. No charge; donations accepted. Closed Easter; Memorial Day; Independence Day; Christmas. &
Attendance: 1,800 (estimated)

Calverton

GRUMMAN MEMORIAL PARK, Rte. 25 & 25A, Calverton, NY 11933. Mailing Address: P.O. Box 147, Calverton, NY 11933-0147. Tel.: 631-369-1826.

E-mail: gmpark@optonline.net
Web Site: www.grummanpark.org
Formerly: East End Aircraft L.I. Corp.
Key Personnel: Chm. (V), Joe Van de Wetering.
Institution Type/Description: Military Museum.
Hours & Admission Prices: Daily 9-5. No charge. &
Attendance: 15,000 (estimated)

Camden

QV HISTORICAL SOCIETY AT CARRIAGE HOUSE MUSEUM, 2 N. Park St., Camden, NY 13316-1306. Mailing Address: P.O. Box 38, Camden, NY 13316-0038. Tel.: 315-245-4652.

E-mail: historycamden@verizon.net
Key Personnel: Pres. (V), J.C. Kuttruff.
Institution Type/Description: Historical Society Museum.
Hours & Admission Prices: May-Oct. Wed. & Fri.-Sat. 1-4; call to confirm; other times by appointment. No charge; donations accepted. Closed holidays.
Attendance: 500 (estimated)

Camillus

WILCOX OCTAGON HOUSE MUSEUM, 5420 W. Genesee St., Camillus, NY 13031. Mailing Address: 4600 W. Genesee St., Camillus, NY 13219. Tel.: 315-488-7800.

E-mail: octagonhouseofcamillus@gmx.com
Web Site: www.octagonhouseofcamillus.org
Institution Type/Description: Historic House Museum: built in 1856. Listed on the National Register of Historic Places.
Hours & Admission Prices: April-Dec. Sun. 1-5; other times by appointment. No charge; donations accepted.
Attendance: 1,500 (estimated)

Canaan

CANAAN HISTORICAL SOCIETY, INC., 13 Warner Crossing Rd., Canaan, NY 12029. Mailing Address: 84 Old Hudson Turnpike, Canaan, NY 12029-2801. Tel.: 518-781-4228.
E-mail: nyvetcounsil@yahoo.com
Key Personnel: Pres., Gary Flaherty; Cur., Tammy Flaherty.
Institution Type/Description: Historic Building: 1829 former Meeting House, Presbyterian Society.
Hours & Admission Prices: July-Aug. Sat. 1-4; other times by appointment. No charge; donations accepted. &
Attendance: 115 (estimated)

Canajoharie

ARKELL MUSEUM, 2 Erie Blvd., Canajoharie, NY 13317-1198. Tel.: 518-673-2314. Fax: 518-673-5243. Facebook: Arkell Museum.
E-mail: info@arkellmuseum.org
Web Site: www.arkellmuseum.org
Formerly: Canajoharie Library and Art Gallery
Key Personnel: Dir. & Chief Cur., Diane Forsberg; Pres., Charles Tallent.
Institution Type/Description: American Art Museum.
Hours & Admission Prices: Tues.-Fri. 10-5, Sat.-Sun. 1-5. Adults $8, students & seniors $6; members and children 11 & under no charge. Closed New Year's Day, Thanksgiving, Christmas. &
Attendance: 44,500 (actual)

Canandaigua

THE GRANGER HOMESTEAD SOCIETY, INC., 295 N. Main St., Canandaigua, NY 14424-1228. Tel.: 585-394-1472. Fax: 585-394-6958.
E-mail: info@grangerhomestead.org
Web Site: www.grangerhomestead.org
Key Personnel: Exec. Dir., Martha Herbik; Pres. (V), David Sauter; Administrative Asst., Libby Campbell; Museum Shop Mgr., Bonnie Kelly; Facilities Mgr., James Catalfamo.
Institution Type/Description: Historic House Museum: 1816 Gideon Granger Mansion.
Hours & Admission Prices: June-Oct. Tues.-Wed. & Sat.-Sun. 1-5, Thurs.-Fri. 11-5. Adults $6, senior citizens $5, children $2; discounts to groups, AAA and AAM members & Sonnenberg Gardens visitors; members no charge. Additional charge for special events. Closed New Year's Eve & Day; Presidents' Day; Memorial Day; Independence Day; Labor Day; Columbus Day; Thanksgiving; Christmas Eve, Day & week. &
Attendance: 16,000 (estimated)

ONTARIO COUNTY HISTORICAL SOCIETY, 55 N. Main St., Canandaigua, NY 14424-1438. Tel.: 585-394-4975. Fax: 716-394-9351.
E-mail: director@ochs.org
Web Site: www.ochs.org
Key Personnel: Exec. Dir. & Museum Shop Mgr., Edward Varno; Pres. (V), Christopher Hubler; Bookkeeper, Ernest Mor; Cur., Wilma T. Townsend; Educator, Dr. Prestone E. Pierce; Library Mgr., Linda Alexander; Museum Shop Mgr., Maureen O'Connell Baker.
Institution Type/Description: Historical Society Museum.
Hours & Admission Prices: Jan.-April Tues.-Fri. 10-4:30, Sat. 11-3; May-Dec. Tues. & Thurs.-Fri. 10-4:30, Wed. 10-9, Sat. 11-3. No charge; donations accepted. Research Room: by appointment. Research: $7.50. Research by Mail: $35 per hour. Closed national holidays. &
Attendance: 15,000 (actual)

SONNENBERG GARDENS & MANSION STATE HISTORIC PARK, 151 Charlotte St., Canandaigua, NY 14424-1363. Tel.: 585-394-4922. Fax: 585-394-2192.
E-mail: director@sonnenberg.org
Web Site: www.sonnenberg.org
Key Personnel: Chm. (V), Kristen Fragnoli; Dir., David Hutchings.
Institution Type/Description: Historic House & Botanical Garden: housed in the summer estate of Frederick Ferris & Mary Clark Thompson; built in 1887.
Hours & Admission Prices: May & Sept.-Oct. daily 9:30-4:30; Memorial Day to Labor Day 9:30-5:30. Adults $14, seniors 60 & over $12, military & students w/ ID $7, children 4-12 $2; discounts to AAA members; members and children 3 & under no charge. American Horticultural Society reciprocal admission program. See website for details on combination passes with other historic & cultural sites. &
Attendance: 36,500 (actual)

Canastota

INTERNATIONAL BOXING HALL OF FAME, 1 Hall of Fame Dr., Canastota, NY 13032. Mailing Address: 1 Hall of Fame Dr., 360 N. Peterboro St., Canastota, NY 13032. Tel.: 315-697-7095. Fax: 315-697-5356.
Institution Type/Description: Boxing Hall of Fame.
Hours & Admission Prices: Mon.-Fri. 9-5, Sat.-Sun. 10-4.

Canisteo

KANESTIO HISTORICAL SOCIETY, 23 Main St., Canisteo, NY 14823. Mailing Address: P.O. Box 35, Canisteo, NY 14823-0035. Tel.: 607-698-2086.
E-mail: kanestiohs@gmail.com
Key Personnel: Co Pres., Larry Stephens; Co Pres., Sue Babbatt.
Institution Type/Description: Historical Society Museum.
Hours & Admission Prices: Wed.-Fri. 1-3. Programs: 3rd Tues. each month 7pm. No charge.
Attendance: 192 (actual)

Canton

PIERREPONT MUSEUM, 864 State Hwy. 68, Canton, NY 13617-3468. Mailing Address: 872 State Hwy. 68, Canton, NY 13617-3468. Tel.: 315-386-8311 & 379-0804. Fax: 315-379-0415.
E-mail: bjbryant@twc.com
Key Personnel: Historian, Barbara J. Daniels.
Institution Type/Description: Antiques Museum: housed in early 1800 district school house.
Hours & Admission Prices: Memorial Day-Labor Day Sat. 10-1; other times by appointment. No charge; donations accepted. &
Attendance: 150 (estimated)

ST. LAWRENCE COUNTY HISTORICAL ASSOCIATION - SILAS WRIGHT HOUSE, 3 E. Main, Canton, NY 13617-1416. Mailing Address: P.O. Box 8, Canton, NY 13617-0008. Tel.: 315-386-8133. Fax: 315-386-8134. Facebook: SLC Historical Association.
E-mail: info@slcha.org
Web Site: www.slcha.org
Key Personnel: Exec. Dir., Susanne Longshore.
Institution Type/Description: Preservation Project: housed in 1834 home of Governor Silas Wright.
Hours & Admission Prices: Museum & Archives: Tues.-Thurs. 12-4, Fri. 12-6, Sat. 10-4. Museum: no charge. Archives: adults $5, college students $2.50; discounts to AAM & ICOM members; members & children no charge. Closed New Year's Eve & Day; Martin Luther King, Jr. Day; Presidents' Day; Memorial Day; Independence Day; Labor Day; Columbus Day; Thanksgiving & day after; Christmas Eve, Day and week. &
Attendance: 4,000 (estimated)

ST. LAWRENCE UNIVERSITY - RICHARD F. BRUSH ART GALLERY AND PERMANENT COLLECTION, 23 Romoda Dr., Canton, NY 13617-1501. Tel.: 315-229-5174. Fax: 315-229-7425. Facebook.
E-mail: ctedford@stlawu.edu
Web Site: www.stlawu.edu/gallery
Key Personnel: Dir., Catherine L. Tedford; Asst. Dir., Carole Mathey; Arts Programming Coord., Juli Pomainville.
Institution Type/Description: University Art Gallery.
Hours & Admission Prices: Mon.-Thurs. 12-8, Fri.-Sat. 12-5. No charge. Closed college recesses. &
Attendance: 20,000 (estimated)

Cape Vincent

CAPE VINCENT HISTORICAL MUSEUM, James St., Cape Vincent, NY 13618. Mailing Address: P.O. Box 376, Cape Vincent, NY 13618-0376. Tel.: 315-654-4400.
Key Personnel: Pres. (V), Jeanne Thompson; Dir., Nancy Knapp; Dir. & Town Historian, Jeanie Ebert.
Institution Type/Description: General Museum: housed in a stone building used as barracks in the War of 1812.
Hours & Admission Prices: July-Aug. Mon.-Sat. 10-4, Sun. 1-3. Historical research & family histories by appointment. No charge; donations accepted. &
Attendance: 3,000 (estimated)

TIBBETTS POINT LIGHTHOUSE, 33439 County Rte. 6, Cape Vincent, NY 13618. Mailing Address: P.O. Box 683, Cape Vincent, NY 13618. Tel.: 315-654-3450 & 2700.
E-mail: tibbettspointlighthouse@gmail.com
Web Site: www.capevincent.org/lighthouse
Institution Type/Description: Lighthouse: built 1854. Listed on the National Register of Historic Places.
Hours & Admission Prices: Lighthouse: May 22 to June 22 & Sept. 8-Oct. 12 Fri.-Mon. 10-7; June 26-Sept. 2 daily 10-7. Hostel: early June to early Sept.

Castile

WILLIAM PRYOR LETCHWORTH MUSEUM, One Letchworth State Park, Castile, NY 14427-9714. Tel.: 585-493-3600. Fax: 716-493-5272. TDD: 716-493-3070.
E-mail: brian.scriven@parks.ny.gov
Web Site: www.nysparks.state.ny.us
Key Personnel: Park Mgr., Roland Beck; Museum Dir. & Historic Site Mgr., Brian Scriven.
Institution Type/Description: State Park Museum.
Hours & Admission Prices: May-Oct. daily 10-5. No charge; donations accepted. &
Attendance: 25,000 (actual)

Cattaraugus

CATTARAUGUS AREA HISTORICAL CENTER, 23 Main St., Cattaraugus, NY 14719-1032. Mailing Address: P.O. Box 93, Cattaraugus, NY 14719-0093. Tel.: 716-257-5189.
E-mail: bjmcclellan@cattco.org
Web Site: www.cattco.org/museum
Key Personnel: Pres. (V), Laura Land; Sec., Heather Gunther; Corresponding Sec., James Land.
Institution Type/Description: Historical Society Museum: housed in historic building owned by Village of Cattaraugus.
Hours & Admission Prices: 2nd Sun. each month 1:30-3:30; other times by appointment. No charge; donations accepted.
Attendance: 150 (estimated)

Cazenovia

CAZENOVIA COLLEGE - ART GALLERY AT REISMAN HALL ART & DESIGN CENTER, Cazenovia College, 6 Sullivan St., Cazenovia, NY 13035-1085. Tel.: 315-655-7138. Fax: 315-655-2190.
E-mail: jpepper@cazenovia.edu
Web Site: www.cazenovia.edu
Formerly: Cazenovia College - Art & Design Gallery
Key Personnel: Dir., Jen Pepper.
Institution Type/Description: Art Gallery.
Hours & Admission Prices: Spring, Fall & Winter: Mon.-Thurs. 1-4 & 7-9, Fri. 1-4, Sat.-Sun. 2-6. Summer hours vary. No charge; donations accepted. Closed during college holidays & breaks. &
Attendance: 1,000 (estimated)

LORENZO STATE HISTORIC SITE, 17 Rippleton Rd., Cazenovia, NY 13035-9601. Tel.: 315-655-3200. Fax: 315-655-4304.
E-mail: barbara.bartlett@parks.ny.gov
Web Site: www.lorenzony.org
Key Personnel: Dir., Barbara Bartlett; Cur. Asst., Jackie Vivirito.
Institution Type/Description: Historic House Museum: 1807 Federal-style mansion built for John Lincklaen, land agent for the Holland Land Co.
Hours & Admission Prices: May-Oct. Wed.-Sun. 10-4:30; other times by appointment. Adults $5, tour groups & NY state senior citizens $4; Friends of Lorenzo & members no charge. &
Attendance: 32,000 (estimated)

ROTHSCHILD PETERSEN PATENT MODEL MUSEUM, 4796 W. Lake Rd., Cazenovia, NY 13035-9670.
E-mail: museum@patentmodel.org
Web Site: www.patentmodel.org
Key Personnel: Owner, Alan Rothschild.
Institution Type/Description: General Museum.
Hours & Admission Prices: By appointment only.

STONE QUARRY HILL ART PARK, INC., 3883 Stone Quarry Rd., Cazenovia, NY 13035-8447. Mailing Address: P.O. Box 251, Cazenovia, NY 13035-0251. Tel.: 315-655-3196. Fax: 315-655-5742.

E-mail: office@stonequarryhillartpark.org
Web Site: www.sqhap.org
Key Personnel: Exec. Dir., Emily Zaengle; Pres., Anne Ferguson; Vice Pres., Sandra Hund.
Institution Type/Description: Art Park.
Hours & Admission Prices: Daily dawn to dusk. Admission $5 per person; children 16 & under and members no charge. &
Attendance: 10,000 (estimated)

Centerport

CENTERPORT FIRE MUSEUM, 9 Park Circle, Centerport, NY 11721. Tel.: 631-261-5916.
E-mail: chiefscfd@gmail.com
Web Site: centerportfd.org
Institution Type/Description: Firefighting History Museum.
Hours & Admission Prices: By appointment.

SUFFOLK COUNTY VANDERBILT MUSEUM AND PLANETARIUM, 180 Little Neck Rd., Centerport, NY 11721-1145. Mailing Address: P.O. Box 0605, Centerport, NY 11721-0605. Tel.: 631-854-5579. Fax: 631-854-5594.
E-mail: info@vanderbiltmuseum.org
Web Site: www.vanderbiltmuseum.org
Key Personnel: Exec. Dir., Lance Reinheimer; Pres. Bd. Trustees (V), Ronald A. Beattie; Assoc. Dir., Elizabeth Wayland-Morgan; Planetarium Technical & Production Coord., Dave Bush; Dir. Curatorial Affairs, Stephanie Gress; Education, Beth Laxer-Limmer; Museum Shop & Business Office, Barbara Oster.
Institution Type/Description: Historical Site; Marine & Natural History Museum & Planetarium. 1910-36, Spanish Revival mansion located on 43-acre landscaped estate of William K. Vanderbilt, II.
Hours & Admission Prices: June 25-Sept. 2 Tues.-Sat. 11-5, Sun. 12-5; Sept. 3-Oct. 30 Tues. & Fri.-Sat. 11-5, Sun. 12-5; Oct. 31.-June 24 Tues. & Sat.-Sun. 12-5; call for school holiday hours. Planetarium Shows: Fri.-Sat. 8pm, 9pm & 10pm. General Admission: adults $7; members no charge. Guided Mansion Tour or Planetarium Show: $6 additional fee. Closed New Year's Eve & Day; Easter; Memorial Day; Independence Day; Labor Day; Thanksgiving; Christmas Eve & Day.
Attendance: 100,000 (actual)

Chappaqua

NEW CASTLE HISTORICAL SOCIETY - HORACE GREELEY HOUSE, 100 King St., Chappaqua, NY 10514-3433. Mailing Address: P.O. Box 55, 100 King St., Chappaqua, NY 10514-0055. Tel.: 914-238-4666. Fax: 914-238-1296.
E-mail: director@newcastlehs.org
Web Site: www.newcastlehs.org
Key Personnel: Museum Shop Mgr., Lois Danneckar; Pres., Betsy Guardenter; Exec. Dir., Betsy Towl.
Institution Type/Description: History Museum: housed in the Horace Greeley family country home, 1864-1872.
Hours & Admission Prices: Aug. Tues.-Thurs. 1-4; Sept.-July Tues.-Thurs. & Sat. 1-4. No charge; donations accepted. Closed New Year's Day; Thanksgiving; Christmas. &
Attendance: 4,741 (actual)

Chazy

THE ALICE T. MINER COLONIAL COLLECTION, 9618 Main St., Chazy, NY 12921. Mailing Address: P.O. Box 628, Chazy, NY 12921-0628. Tel.: 518-846-7336. Facebook: The Alice; Twitter: @TheAliceTMuseum.
E-mail: director@minermuseum.org
Web Site: www.minermuseum.org
Key Personnel: C.E.O., Pres. (V) & Chm. (V), Dana B. Grant; Dir. & Cur., Ellen E. Adams.
Institution Type/Description: Colonial Revival Museum: housed in 1824 limestone building. Listed on the National Register of Historic Places.
Hours & Admission Prices: April by appointment only; May-Dec. Tues.-Sat. 10-4, guided tours at 10, noon & 2. Adults $3, seniors $2, students $1; student groups no charge. Closed Jan.-March; Independence Day; Thanksgiving; Christmas Eve & Day.
Attendance: 515 (estimated)

Cherry Valley

CHERRY VALLEY MUSEUM, 49 Main St., Cherry Valley, NY 13320. Mailing Address: P.O. Box 115, Cherry Valley, NY 13320-0115. Tel.: 607-264-3303 & 3098. Fax: 607-264-9320.
E-mail: museum@celticart.com
Web Site: www.cherryvalleymuseum.com
Key Personnel: Dir., Chm. (V) & Museum Shop Mgr., Barbara Bell; Pres. (V), James Johnson.
Institution Type/Description: History Museum: housed in 1832 home.
Hours & Admission Prices: Memorial Day to mid-Oct. daily 10-5. Adults $6, senior citizens 60 & over $5.50; discounts to groups of 10 or more & AAA members; children under 11 & members no charge. Closed Independence Day. &
Attendance: 700 (estimated)

Chester

CHESTER HISTORICAL SOCIETY, 47 Main St., Chester, NY 10918. Tel.: 845-469-2388. Facebook.
E-mail: chester_historical@mac.com
Web Site: www.chesterhistoricalsociety.com
Key Personnel: Pres. (V), Debby Lu Vadala-Adams; Chair (V), Norma Stoddard.
Institution Type/Description: Historical Society Museum.
Hours & Admission Prices: Tues. 10 to noon. No charge; donations accepted.
Attendance: 250 (estimated)

CHESTER HISTORY MUSEUM - 1915 ERIE RAILROAD STATION, 19 Winkler Pl., Chester, NY 10918-1259. Mailing Address: 47 Main St., Chester, NY 10918. Tel.: 845-469-2591. Facebook.
E-mail: chester_historical@mac.com
Web Site: www.chesterhistoricalsociety.com
Key Personnel: Pres. (V), Bill Schilling.
Institution Type/Description: Historical Society Museum: housed in restored Erie Railroad Station; built in 1915.
Hours & Admission Prices: May-Oct. Sat. 9-1; groups by appointment. No charge; donations accepted. &
Attendance: 2,000 (estimated)

Chittenango

CHITTENANGO LANDING CANAL BOAT MUSEUM, 717 Lakeport Rd., Chittenango, NY 13037-8584. Tel.: 315-687-3801. Facebook: Chittenango Landing Canal Boat Museum.
E-mail: info@clcbm.org
Web Site: clcbm.org
Key Personnel: Exec. Dir., Christine O'Neil.
Institution Type/Description: Transportation Museum: housed in a 19th century structure.
Hours & Admission Prices: May-June & Sept.-Oct. Sat.-Sun. 1-4; July-Aug. daily 11-3. Family $20, adults $6, senior citizens $5, children 4-12 $3. Closed New Year's Day; Easter; Thanksgiving; Christmas. &
Attendance: 12,000 (estimated)

Clarence

HISTORICAL SOCIETY OF THE TOWN OF CLARENCE, 10465 Main St., Clarence, NY 14031-1617. Mailing Address: P.O. Box 86, Clarence, NY 14031-0086. Tel.: 716-759-8575.
E-mail: clarencehistoricalmuseum@gmail.com
Web Site: clarencehistory.com
Key Personnel: Pres., Thomas Steffan; Cur., Mrs. Alicia L. Braaten.
Institution Type/Description: Historical Society & Genealogy Museum.
Hours & Admission Prices: Call for hours. No charge; donations accepted. Closed holidays. &
Attendance: 2,300 (actual)

Clayton

THE ANTIQUE BOAT MUSEUM, 750 Mary St., Clayton, NY 13624-1119. Tel.: 315-686-4104. Fax: 315-686-2775.
E-mail: info@abm.org
Web Site: www.abm.org
Formerly: Thousand Islands Shipyard Museum
Key Personnel: Exec. Dir., Frederick H. Hager; Dir. Public Programming, Lora Nadolski; Cur., Emmett Smith; Curatorial Asst., Claire Wakefield; Educator, Julie Broadbent; Watercraft Conservator, Mike Corrigan; Coord. Events, Margaret Hummel; Dir. Endowment, John MacLean; Dir. Leadership Gifts, Barbara Maddocks; Assoc. Dir. Endowment, Christine Brown; C.F.O., Dale Corsa; Accounting Clerk, Norma Zimmer; Museum Shop Mgr., Charlotte

Brooks; Administrative Asst., Kirsti Touhey; Supvr. Facilities, Bud Gray; Maintenance Asst., Jim Mellowship; Maintenance Asst., Sam Hopkins.
Institution Type/Description: Antique Boat Museum.
Hours & Admission Prices: mid-May to mid-Oct. daily 9-5; other times by appointment. Adults $13, youth $6.50; discounts to seniors, AAA, & groups; military and children under 6 & members no charge. &
Attendance: 33,295 (actual)

THOUSAND ISLANDS ARTS CENTER HOME OF THE HANDWEAVING MUSEUM, 314 John St., Clayton, NY 13624-1017. Tel.: 315-686-4123.
E-mail: leslie@tiartscenter.org
Web Site: www.tiartscenter.org
Formerly: American Handweaving Museum and Thousand Islands Craft School
Key Personnel: Exec. Dir., Leslie Rowland; Chm. (V), Barbara Thomas; Events Coord., Joy Rhinebeck; Education Coord., Marcia Rogers; Curatorial Specialist, Marina Loew.
Institution Type/Description: Textile Museum: housed in late 19th-century two-story frame home.
Hours & Admission Prices: Museum: Mon.-Fri. 9-5, Sat. 10-4; Adults $5; members no charge. Pottery Studio: Thurs. 6-9 & Sat. noon-5. Closed major holidays. &
Attendance: 1,200 (estimated)

THOUSAND ISLANDS MUSEUM, 312 James St., Clayton, NY 13624-1012. Mailing Address: P.O. Box 27, Clayton, NY 13624-0027. Tel.: 315-686-5794. Fax: 315-686-4867.
E-mail: info@timuseum.org
Web Site: www.timuseum.org
Key Personnel: Pres. (V), Thomas Humberstone; Museum Shop Mgr., April Ingerson.
Institution Type/Description: Local & Regional History Museum.
Hours & Admission Prices: May-Sept. Mon.-Fri. 10-5, Sat.-Sun. 10-4; Oct.-Dec. Tues.-Sun. 10-4. No charge; donations accepted. &
Attendance: 15,000 (actual)

Clinton

CLINTON HISTORICAL SOCIETY, One Fountain St., Clinton, NY 13323. Mailing Address: P.O. Box 42, Clinton, NY 13323. Tel.: 315-859-1392.
E-mail: clintonhistoricalsociety1@gmail.com
Web Site: clintonhistory.org
Institution Type/Description: Historical Society Museum: housed in the former Clinton Baptist Church.
Hours & Admission Prices: Wed. & Sat. 1-4. No charge. &
Attendance: 800 (estimated)

THE RUTH AND ELMER WELLIN MUSEUM OF ART, Hamilton College, 198 College Hill Rd., Clinton, NY 13323-1218. Tel.: 315-859-4396. Fax: 315-859-4060. Facebook: Wellin Museum.
E-mail: wellin@hamilton.edu
Web Site: www.hamilton.edu/wellin
Formerly: The Emerson Gallery
Key Personnel: Dir., Tracy Adler; Assoc. Dir. & Cur., Susanna White; Mgr. Educational Programming & Outreach, Megan Austin; Bldg. Mgr. & Preparator, Christopher Harrison; Gen. Contact & Office Asst., Amy Sylvester; Collection & Exhibitions Specialist, Katherine Alcauskas; Andrew W. Mellon Educator for School & Community Programs, Amber Spadea.
Institution Type/Description: Art Museum.
Hours & Admission Prices: Tues.-Sun. 11-5. No charge. Closed New Year's Day; Memorial Day; Independence Day; Christmas. &
Attendance: 8,000 (estimated)

Cohocton

COHOCTON HISTORICAL SOCIETY, Main St., Cohocton, NY 14826. Mailing Address: P.O. Box 177, Cohocton, NY 14826. Tel.: 585-384-5729. Fax: rjtowner@yahoo.com.
Web Site: www.townofcohocton.com
Key Personnel: Pres., Ron Towner.
Institution Type/Description: Historical Society Museum.
Hours & Admission Prices: Summer: 1st Sat. of the month 9-1.

Cold Spring

CONSTITUTION ISLAND ASSOCIATION, 1700 Rte. 9D, Cold Spring, NY 10516. Mailing Address: P.O. Box 126, Cold Spring, NY 10516-0216. Tel.: 845-265-2501.
E-mail: ciaatwp@gmail.com

Web Site: www.constitutionisland.org
Key Personnel: Office Mgr., Drea Kaplon; Chm. (V), Frederick Osborn, III.
Institution Type/Description: Historic House Museum: c.1800 Victorian home of writers Susan & Anna Warner on Constitution Island, site of several Revolutionary War fortification ruins; traditional 19th century gardens.
Hours & Admission Prices: Tours: late April to June 15 schools only, by reservation; June 21 to early Oct. Wed.-Thurs. 1 & 2. Adults $10, senior citizens & children under 16 $9; discounts to AAM & ICOM members; children 6 & under no charge.
Attendance: 2,000 (estimated)

PUTNAM COUNTY HISTORICAL SOCIETY & FOUNDRY SCHOOL MUSEUM, 63 Chestnut St., Cold Spring, NY 10516-2613. Tel.: 845-265-4010. Fax: 845-265-2884.
E-mail: office@pchs-fsm.org
Web Site: www.pchs-fsm.org
Key Personnel: Exec. Dir., Mindy Krazmien; Cur., Trudie Alexis Grace; Dir. Administration, Kara Shier; Coord. Outreach, Kendall Helbock; Office Mgr., Helen Brown; Curatorial Asst., Anne Saunders.
Institution Type/Description: Local History Museum: housed in 1828 Foundry Schoolhouse.
Hours & Admission Prices: March-Dec. Wed.-Sun. 11-5. No charge; donations accepted. &
Attendance: 1,800 (estimated)

Cold Spring Harbor

PRESERVATION LONG ISLAND, 161 Main St., Cold Spring Harbor, NY 11724-0148. Mailing Address: P.O. Box 148, Cold Spring Harbor, NY 11724-0148. Tel.: 631-692-4664. Fax: 631-692-5265. Facebook: Preservation Long Island.
E-mail: info@preservationlongisland.org
Web Site: preservationlongisland.org
Key Personnel: Pres., Daniel W. White; Exec. Dir., Alexandra P. Wolfe; Education Dir., Darren St. George; Property Mgr., Mark Agosta; Cur., Lauren Brincat.
Institution Type/Description: Gallery & Office Headquarters: housed in the former Methodist Episcopal Church; built in 1842.
Hours & Admission Prices: Custom House: May-June & Sept.-Oct. Sat.-Sun. 10-5; July-Aug. daily 10-5; groups by appointment. Joseph Lloyd Manor: Memorial Day to Columbus Day Sun. 1-5; groups by appointment. Sherwood-Jayne Farm: June-Oct. 1st Sat. each month 12-3; other times by appointment. Custom House: adults $6, seniors $5, children 7-14 $3. Joseph Lloyd Manor & Sherwood-Jayne Houses: adults $5, seniors & children 7-14 $3. Gallery for Changing Exhibitions: call for hours. Suggested admission: $5. &
Attendance: 7,450 (estimated)

THE WHALING MUSEUM & EDUCATION CENTER OF COLD SPRING HARBOR, 301 Main St., Cold Spring Harbor, NY 11724. Mailing Address: 279 Main St., Cold Spring Harbor, NY 11724-0025. Tel.: 631-367-3418. Fax: 631-692-7037.
E-mail: kkelly@cshwhalingmuseum.org
Web Site: www.cshwhalingmuseum.org
Key Personnel: Exec. Dir., Nomi Dayan; Events & Mktg., Jennifer Donatelli; Business Mgr., Katie Kelly; Coord. Education, Cindy Grimm; Pres. (V), Art Brings; Museum Shop Mgr., Joan Lowenthal.
Institution Type/Description: Whaling Museum.
Hours & Admission Prices: Memorial Day-Labor Day daily 11-5; Sept.-May Tues.-Sun. 11-5; adults $6, senior citizens & students 5-18 $5; discounts to CAMM & ICOM members, & other museum professionals; active military, members & children under 3 no charge. Sun. special programs. &
Attendance: 22,000 (actual)

Commack

LONG ISLAND CULTURE HISTORY LAB & MUSEUM, Hoyt Farm Park, 200 New Hwy., Commack, NY 11725. Mailing Address: c/o Suffolk County Archaeological Assn., P.O. Box 1542, Stony Brook, NY 11790. Tel.: 631-929-8725. Fax: 631-929-8725.
E-mail: SCArchaeology@gmail.com
Web Site: www.scaa-ny.org
Key Personnel: Pres. (V), Douglas DeRenzo; Dir., Gaynell Stone, Ph.D.
Institution Type/Description: Historical Site: prehistoric park with an 18th-century house & 20th-century outbuildings. Site 1: Native American complex. Site 2: 18th- & 19th-century house & outbuildings; Dutch architecture.
Hours & Admission Prices: Sept.-June Mon.-Fri. 10-2 by appointment. Call for admission prices. &
Attendance: 10,000 (actual)

Cooperstown

COOPERSTOWN HEROES OF BASEBALL WAX MUSEUM, 99 Main St., Cooperstown, NY 13326. Tel.: 607-547-1273.
E-mail: info@baseballwaxmuseum.com
Web Site: www.baseballwaxmuseum.com
Institution Type/Description: Wax Museum.
Hours & Admission Prices: Daily 9-9. Adults $9.95, seniors 65 & over and children 4-12 $7.95.

THE FARMERS' MUSEUM, INC., 5775 State Hwy. 80, Cooperstown, NY 13326. Mailing Address: P.O. Box 30, Cooperstown, NY 13326-0030. Tel.: 607-547-1450. Fax: 607-547-1499.
E-mail: info@nysha.org
Web Site: www.farmersmuseum.org
Key Personnel: Pres. & C.E.O., Paul S. D'Ambrosio, Ph.D.
Institution Type/Description: Village Museum: housed in early 19th-century Village including 29 buildings.
Hours & Admission Prices: April to mid-May & Oct. Tues.-Sun. 10-4; mid-May to Columbus Day daily 10-5; Nov.-Dec. open for special programs only. Adults 13-64 $12, seniors 65 & over $10.50, children 7-12 $6; discounts to AAM members; members, children under 6 & under & New York State Historical Association members no charge. &
Attendance: 60,000 (estimated)

HYDE HALL, INC., 267 Glimmerglass State Park Rd., Cooperstown, NY 13326. Mailing Address: P.O. Box 721, Cooperstown, NY 13326-0721. Tel.: 607-547-5098 & 6129. Fax: 607-547-8462. Facebook: Hyde Hall.
E-mail: jonathanmaney@hydehall.org
Web Site: www.hydehall.org
Formerly: Friends of Hyde Hall, Inc.
Key Personnel: Exec. Dir., Jonathan Maney; Tours & Collections Coord., Larry Smith; Operations Asst. & Special Events, Stacey Michael; Museum Shop Mgr., Randy Lamb.
Institution Type/Description: Historic House Museum.
Hours & Admission Prices: Tours: Mother's Day to Oct. daily 10-5, last tour at 4pm. Adults $12, seniors 65 & over and children 6-12 $8; children under 6 no charge. &
Attendance: 5,000 (actual)

NATIONAL BASEBALL HALL OF FAME AND MUSEUM, 25 Main Street, Cooperstown, NY 13326. Tel.: 607-547-7200. Fax: 607-547-0398. Facebook, Twitter, Instagram.
E-mail: info@baseballhall.org
Web Site: baseballhall.org
Key Personnel: Pres., Jeffrey Idelson; Chm. (V), Jane Forbes Clark; Sr. Vice Pres. Finance & Administration, Jeff Jones; Vice Pres. Retail Mktg. & Licensing, Sean J. Gahagen; Vice Pres. Communications & Education, Jon Shestakofsky; Vice Pres. Sponsorship & Devel., Kenneth Meifort; Vice Pres. Exhibitions & Collections, Erik Strohl; Sr. Cur., Tom Shieber.
Institution Type/Description: Sports Museum.
Hours & Admission Prices: Daily 9-5. Adults $25, senior citizens 65 & up $20, veterans $18; children 7-12 $15; discount to AAM members & groups with advance reservations; active & career retired military, children 6-7 under and members no charge. Closed New Year's Day; Thanksgiving; Christmas. &
Attendance: 301,755 (actual)

NEW YORK STATE HISTORICAL ASSOCIATION - FENIMORE ART MUSEUM, 5798 St. Hwy. 80, Cooperstown, NY 13326. Mailing Address: P.O. Box 800, Cooperstown, NY 13326-0800. Tel.: 607-547-1400. Fax: 607-547-1404.
E-mail: info@nysha.org
Web Site: www.fenimoreartmuseum.org
Key Personnel: Chm. Bd., Dr. Douglas E. Evelyn; Pres. & C.E.O., Paul S. D'Ambrosio, Ph.D.; Dir. Finance, Marnie Auld; Vice Pres. Operations, Joseph Siracusa; Sr. Dir. Human Resources, Barbara Fischer; Dir. Cooperstown Graduate Program, Gretchen Sorin; Dir. Collections, Erin Richardson; Dir. Exhibitions, Michelle Murdock; Dir. Mktg., Todd Kenyon; Registrar, Christine Olsen; Museum Shop Mgr., Sue deBruijn.
Institution Type/Description: Art Museum & Historical Association.
Hours & Admission Prices: April to mid-May & Oct.-Dec. Tues.-Sun. 10-4; mid-May to Columbus Day daily 10-5. Adults 13-64 $12, seniors 65 & over $10.50; discounts to AAM members; members and children 12 & under no charge. Closed Thanksgiving; Christmas. &
Attendance: 41,700 (estimated)

THE SMITHY, 55 Pioneer St., Cooperstown, NY 13326. Tel.: 607-547-8671.

E-mail: gallery@smithyarts.org
Web Site: www.smithyarts.org
Formerly: Smithy Center for the Arts
Key Personnel: Exec. Dir., Janet Erway.
Institution Type/Description: Art Gallery.
Hours & Admission Prices: May-Sept. Tues.-Sat. 10-5, Sun. 12-5.

Corning

THE CORNING MUSEUM OF GLASS, One Museum Way, Corning, NY 14830-2253. Tel.: 607-937-5371.
E-mail: info@cmog.org
Web Site: www.cmog.org
Key Personnel: Chm. (V), James B. Flaws; Pres. & Exec. Dir., Karol Wight; C.O. O., Alan Eusden; Sr. Dir. Creative Svcs. & Mktg., Robert K. Cassetti; Dir. Human Resources & Safety, Ellen Corradini; Dir. Mktg. & Community Rels., Beth Duane; Deputy C.O.O., Nancy J. Earley; Librarian, James Galbraith; Chief Digital Officer, Scott Sayre; Dir. The Studio, Amy Schwartz; Dir. Finance, David Togni; Dir. Education & Interpretation, Kris Wetterlund; Collections & Exhibitions Mgr., Warren Bunn; Sr. Mgr. Hot Glass Programs, Steve Gibbs; Chief Conservator, Stephen Koob; Operations Mgr., Dave Murray; GlassMarket Mgr., Victor Nemard; Head of Publications, Richard Price; IT Mgr., Randy Vargason; Cur. Science & Technology, Marvin Bolt; Cur. American Glass, Kelly Conway.
Institution Type/Description: Glass Art Museum.
Hours & Admission Prices: May-Sept. daily 9-8; Sept.-May daily 9-5. Adults $18; discounts to local residents, senior citizens, college students, military, AAA, AAM & ICOM; members & age 17 & under no charge. Closed New Year's Day; Thanksgiving Day; Christmas Eve & Day. &
Attendance: 420,000 (actual)

HORNBY HISTORICAL SOCIETY, P.O. Box 892, Corning, NY 14830-0892. Tel.: 607-962-5775. Facebook: Hornby Historical Society.
Key Personnel: Pres. (V), Andy Hakes; Sec., Hazel Russell; Treas., Eunice Taggert.
Institution Type/Description: Local History Museum: housed in a small country schoolhouse.
Hours & Admission Prices: July-Aug. Sun. 1-3; other days by appointment. No charge; donations accepted.
Attendance: 74 (actual)

PATTERSON INN MUSEUM/CORNING - PAINTED POST HISTORICAL SOCIETY - HERITAGE VILLAGE OF THE SOUTHERN FINGER LAKES, 59 W. Pulteney St., Corning, NY 14830-2212. Mailing Address: 73 W. Pulteney St., Corning, NY 14830. Tel.: 607-937-5281. Fax: 607-937-5281.
E-mail: cpphs@heritagevillagesfl.com
Web Site: www.heritagevillagesfl.org
Formerly: The Benjamin Patterson Inn Museum
Key Personnel: Pres. (V), Leon Golder.
Institution Type/Description: Historic Buildings.
Hours & Admission Prices: Mon.-Sat. 10-4; other times by appointment. Family $14, adults $6, senior citizens 60 & over $4, students $2; discounts to groups over 10 & AAA members; preschool children & members no charge. Closed major holidays. &
Attendance: 5,000 (estimated)

THE ROCKWELL MUSEUM, 111 Cedar St., Corning, NY 14830-2632. Tel.: 607-937-5386. Fax: 607-974-4536.
E-mail: info@rockwellmuseum.org
Web Site: www.rockwellmuseum.org
Key Personnel: Exec. Dir., Kristin Swain; C.E.O. & Chm. (V), Beth Dann; Dir. Education, Gigi Alvare; Programs & Events Planner, Brett Smith; Dir. Mktg. & Communications, Beth Manwaring; Controller, Andrew Braman.
Institution Type/Description: American Western & Native American Art Museum.
Hours & Admission Prices: Memorial Day to Labor Day daily 9-8; Sept.-May daily 9-5. Adults $9, senior citizens $8; discounts to groups, NARM & Museums West Consortium members; members & youth under 19 no charge. Closed New Year's Day; Thanksgiving; Christmas Eve & Day. &
Attendance: 38,833 (actual)

WEST END GALLERY, 12 W. Market St., Corning, NY 14830. Tel.: 607-936-2011.
E-mail: info@westendgallery.net
Web Site: www.westendgallery.net
Key Personnel: Co-Owner & Exec. Dir., Jesse Gardner; Co Owner & Financial Dir., John Gardner; Sales Mgr., Lin Gardner.
Institution Type/Description: Fine Arts and Glass Gallery.
Hours & Admission Prices: All events are free and open to the public. Winter: Mon.-Fri. 10-5:30, Sat. 10-4, Sun. by appointment; Summer Hours: Mon.-Thurs. 10-5:30, Fri. 10-8, Sat. 10-5, Sun. 2-5.

Cornwall

HUDSON HIGHLANDS NATURE MUSEUM, 120 Muser Dr., Cornwall, NY 12518. Mailing Address: P.O. Box 451, Cornwall, NY 12518. Tel.: 845-534-5506. Fax: 845-534-4581. Facebook: @hhnaturemuseum.
E-mail: jreisner@hhnm.org
Web Site: www.hhnm.org
Formerly: Museum of the Hudson Highlands
Key Personnel: Exec. Dir., Jacqueline Grant; Chm. (V), Susan W. Christensen; Vice Pres., Fred Osborn; Dir. Education, Jennifer Brinker; Mgr. Mktg., Joanne Reisner; Operations Mgr., Ron Lipkin; Wildlife Center, Emily Nestlerode; Dir. Preschool, Kerrilee Hunter.
Institution Type/Description: Nature & Environmental Museum.
Hours & Admission Prices: Wildlife Education Center: Fri.-Sun. noon-4; Outdoor Discovery Center: mid-April to mid-Nov. Sat.-Sun. 10-4; Meet the Animals Sat.-Sun. 1pm & 2:30pm. Wildlife Education Center: admission $3; members no charge. Outdoor Discovery Center: $3; members no charge. &
Attendance: 40,000 (estimated)

Corona

LOUIS ARMSTRONG HOUSE & ARCHIVES, 34-56 107th St., Corona, NY 11368-1226. Tel.: 718-997-3670 & 478-8274.
Web Site: www.louisarmstronghouse.org
Key Personnel: Dir., Michael Cogswell.
Institution Type/Description: Historic House Museum.
Hours & Admission Prices: Tues.-Fri. 10-5, Sat.-Sun. 12-5; groups by appointment. Adults $10, seniors, students & children $7; discounts to groups; members & children under 4 no charge.

QUEENS ZOO, 53-51 111th St., Corona, NY 11368. Tel.: 718-271-1500, ext 126. Facebook; Twitter; Instagram..
E-mail: guestrelations@wcs.org
Web Site: www.queenszoo.org
Key Personnel: Pres. & C.E.O. WCS, Cristian Samper; Exec. Vice Pres. Zoos & Aquariums for WCS, James J. Breheny.
Institution Type/Description: Zoo.
Hours & Admission Prices: April 6-Nov. 2 Mon.-Fri. 10-5, Sat.-Sun. & holidays 10-5:30; Nov.-April daily 10-4:30. Adults $9.95, seniors 65 & up $7.95, children 3-12 $6.95; members & children 2 & under no charge. &
Attendance: 208,389 (actual)

Cortland

BOWERS SCIENCE MUSEUM, State Univ. of New York Cortland, 356 Bowers Hall, Cortland, NY 13045. Tel.: 607-753-2900. Fax: 607-753-2927.
Key Personnel: Dir. & Cur., Dr. Peter K. Ducey.
Institution Type/Description: Science Museum.
Hours & Admission Prices: Summer: Mon.-Fri. 8-4; Sept.-June Mon.-Fri. 9-6; special group tours by appointment with Biology Dept. or Science Bldg. Coord. No charge. Closed holidays. &
Attendance: 4,000

CORTLAND COUNTY HISTORICAL SOCIETY, 25 Homer Ave., Cortland, NY 13045-2056. Tel.: 607-756-6071.
E-mail: cortlandcountyhistoricalsociety@centralny.twcbc.com
Web Site: www.cortlandhistory.com
Key Personnel: Pres., Diane Ames; Dir., Mindy Leisenring; Mgr. Collections, Anita Wright.
Institution Type/Description: Historical Society Museum: housed in 1882 Suggett House built by James Suggett, holder of patents on the driven well.
Hours & Admission Prices: Museum: Tues.-Sat. 1-5. Library: Tues.-Sat. 1-5. Gift Shop: Tues.-Sat. 9:30-5. Museum Tours: adults $3. Research Library $8 & $5; members no charge. Closed New Year's Day; Independence Day; Thanksgiving; Christmas. &
Attendance: 3,200 (actual)

DOWD GALLERY, STATE UNIVERSITY OF NEW YORK COLLEGE AT CORTLAND, SUNY Cortland, Dowd Fine Arts Center, Rm. 162, Cortland, NY 13045. Mailing Address: SUNY Cortland, P.O. Box 2000, Cortland, NY 13045-0900. Tel.: 607-753-4216. Fax: 607-753-5934.
E-mail: dowd.gallery@cortland.edu
Web Site: www2.cortland.edu/departments/art/dowd-gallery/
Key Personnel: Interim Dir., Bryan Thomas; Gallery Mgr., Jaroslava Prihodova.
Institution Type/Description: University Art Gallery.

Hours & Admission Prices: Mon.-Fri. 10-4; other times by appointment. No charge; donations accepted. Closed major & university holidays. ♿
Attendance: 3,500 (estimated)

THE 1890 HOUSE-MUSEUM & CENTER FOR ARTS, 37 Tompkins St., Cortland, NY 13045-2555. Tel.: 607-756-7551. Fax: 607-756-7551 (call first).
E-mail: the1890house@gmail.com
Web Site: www.the1890house.org
Key Personnel: Dir., Meg Hutchins.
Institution Type/Description: Historic House: 1890 Victorian chateauesque style mansion.
Hours & Admission Prices: Thurs.-Sat. 12-4. Adults $8, students & senior citizens $5; discounts to groups; children under 10 & members no charge. ♿
Attendance: 5,000 (estimated)

Coxsackie

BRONCK MUSEUM, 90 County Rte. 42, Coxsackie, NY 12051-3022. Mailing Address: P.O. Box 44, Coxsackie, NY 12051-0044. Tel.: 518-731-6490.
E-mail: gchsbm@mhcable.com
Web Site: www.gchistory.org/
Key Personnel: Site Mgr., Shelby Mattice; Pres., Robert Hallock; Chm., Joseph Warren; Museum Shop Mgr., Jennifer Barnhart.
Institution Type/Description: Historic House Museum: 1663 home of Pieter Bronck, cousin of the first settler north of the Harlem River for whom Bronx Borough of New York was named.
Hours & Admission Prices: Memorial Day to Oct. 15 Wed.-Fri. 12-4, Sat. 10-4, Sun. 1-4. Adults $6, youth 12-15 $3, children 5-11 $2; children under 5 & members no charge.
Attendance: 2,209 (actual)

Croghan

AMERICAN MAPLE MUSEUM, 9756 Main St., Croghan, NY 13327. Mailing Address: P.O. Box 81, Croghan, NY 13327-0081. Tel.: 315-346-1107. Facebook.
E-mail: americanmaplemuseum@frontier.com
Web Site: www.americanmaplemuseum.org
Key Personnel: Pres., Donald Moser; Treas., Jane Yancey; Sec., Eleanor Allen; Site Admin. & Museum Shop Mgr., Gail Britton.
Institution Type/Description: Agricultural Museum.
Hours & Admission Prices: June Mon. & Fri.-Sat. 11-4; July to Labor Day Mon.-Sat. 11-4; groups & other times by appointment. Family $10, adults $5, children 5-14 $2; children under 5 no charge. ♿
Attendance: 1,710 (estimated)

Cropseyville

BRUNSWICK HISTORICAL SOCIETY - GARFIELD SCHOOL, 605 Brunswick Rd., Cropseyville, NY 12052. Mailing Address: P.O. Box 1776, Cropseyville, NY 12052. Tel.: 518-279-4024.
E-mail: president@bhs-ny.org
Web Site: www.bhs-ny.org
Key Personnel: Pres. (V), Tracy Broderick.
Institution Type/Description: Historic Building: housed in a two-room schoolhouse; built in 1881.
Hours & Admission Prices: Wed. 1-3, Sat. 10-3.
Attendance: 200 (estimated)

Cross River

TRAILSIDE NATURE MUSEUM, Ward Pound Ridge, Rte. 35 & Rte. 121, Cross River, NY 10518. Mailing Address: P.O. Box 236, Cross River, NY 10518-0236. Tel.: 914-864-7322.
E-mail: mqs5@westchestergov.com
Web Site: www.friendsoftrailside.org
Key Personnel: Cur., Melinda Quintero.
Institution Type/Description: Natural History Museum.
Hours & Admission Prices: Winter: Tues.-Sat. 9-4; Summer: Mon.-Fri. 9-4. No charge. Parking Fee: $5 with resident permit, $10 without permit. Closed holidays. ♿
Attendance: 20,000 (estimated)

Crown Point

CROWN POINT STATE HISTORIC SITE, 21 Grandview Dr., Crown Point, NY 12928-2852. Tel.: 518-597-4666. Fax: 518-597-4668. Facebook: Crown Point State Historic Site.
E-mail: michael.roets@parks.ny.gov
Web Site: www.nysparks.com
Key Personnel: Mgr. Historic Site, Michael Roets; Pres. (V), Jeff Kauffman.
Institution Type/Description: Historic Site: 1734 remains of French fort, 1759 British Fort Crown Point & Outwork fortifications controlling Lake Champlain.
Hours & Admission Prices: Museum: mid-May-mid-Oct. Thurs.-Mon. 9:30-5; other times by appointment. Adults $4, senior citizens & students $3. Grounds: Summer 7 am-8 pm. ♿

Cuddebackville

NEVERSINK VALLEY MUSEUM OF HISTORY AND INNOVATION, 26 Hoag Rd., Cuddebackville, NY 12729. Mailing Address: P.O. Box 263, Cuddebackville, NY 12729-0263. Tel.: 845-754-8870. Fax: 845-754-8870.
E-mail: nvam@frontiernet.net
Web Site: neversinkmuseum.org
Formerly: Neversink Valley Area Museum
Key Personnel: C.E.O. & Pres. (V), Stephen Skye; Exec. Dir., Seth Goldman; Asst. Exec. Dir., David H. Lawrence.
Institution Type/Description: Preservation Project & History Museum: housed in 2 buildings including a 1790, salt box-type house, part of the Delaware & Hudson Canal Park Historic Landmark.
Hours & Admission Prices: Thurs.-Sun. 12-4. Adults $3, children $1.50; children under 6 & members no charge. ♿
Attendance: 7,000 (actual)

Delhi

DELAWARE COUNTY HISTORICAL ASSOCIATION & FLETCHER DAVIDSON LIBRARY AND ARCHIVES, 46549 State Hwy. 10, Delhi, NY 13753. Tel.: 607-746-3849.
E-mail: dcha@delhi.net
Web Site: dcha-ny.org
Institution Type/Description: History Museum.
Hours & Admission Prices: Library & Archives: Tues.-Wed. 10-3; other times by appointment. Requested Donation: $5. Buildings & Galleries: Memorial Day to mid-Oct. Tues.-Sun. 11-4; Winter: Mon.-Fri. 10-3. Adults $4, children $1.50; members no charge.
Attendance: 4,500 (actual)

Derby

GRAYCLIFF CONSERVANCY, 6472 Old Lake Shore Rd., Derby, NY 14047-9731. Mailing Address: P.O. Box 823, Derby, NY 14047-0823. Tel.: 716-947-9217. Fax: 716-947-2086.
E-mail: Graycliff@verizon.net
Web Site: graycliffestate.org
Key Personnel: Exec. Dir., Reine Hauser; Pres. (V), Diane Schrenk; Group Tour Coord., Shannon Lyons; Museum Shop Mgr., Ryan Gravell.
Institution Type/Description: Historic House Museum: summer home of Isabelle and Darwin Martin; estate designed by Frank Lloyd Wright, 1926-1931.
Hours & Admission Prices: See website for information. ♿
Attendance: 10,000 (actual)

Dobbs Ferry

DOBBS FERRY HISTORICAL SOCIETY - THE MEAD HOUSE, 12 Elm St., Dobbs Ferry, NY 10522. Tel.: 914-674-1007.
E-mail: dfhistory@optimum.net
Web Site: www.dobbsferryhistory.org/Home.html
Key Personnel: Pres. (V), Mary S. Donovan.
Institution Type/Description: Historical Society Museum.
Hours & Admission Prices: Tues. 10 to noon; other times by appointment. No charge; donations accepted.
Attendance: 500 (estimated)

Douglaston

ALLEY POND ENVIRONMENTAL CENTER, INC., 228-06 Northern Blvd., Douglaston, NY 11362-1096. Tel.: 718-229-4000, ext. 0. Fax: 718-229-0376.
E-mail: info@alleypond.com
Web Site: www.alleypond.com
Key Personnel: Exec. Dir., Irene V. Scheid; Pres. (V), Rita Sherman.

Institution Type/Description: Nature & Environmental Center.
Hours & Admission Prices: Mon.-Sat. 9-4:30, Sun. 9-3:30. Environmental Center: no charge; donations accepted. Nominal fee for special programs. Closed New Year's Eve & Day; Martin Luther King Jr. Day; Presidents' Day; Easter; Mother's Day; Independence Day; Labor Day; Columbus Day; Thanksgiving & day after; Christmas Eve & Day. &
Attendance: 62,000 (actual)

Dresden

ROBERT GREEN INGERSOLL BIRTHPLACE MUSEUM, 61 Main St., Dresden, NY 14441. Mailing Address: Ingersoll Memorial Committee, P.O. Box 664, Amherst, NY 14226. Tel.: 315-536-1074.
E-mail: tflynn@centerforinquiry.net
Web Site: www.secularhumanism.org/ingersoll
Key Personnel: Dir., Thomas Flynn; C.E.O., Robyn Blumner; Chm. (V), Jeff Ingersoll; Museum Shop Mgr., Frances Emerson.
Institution Type/Description: Historic House Museum: housed in the birthplace of Robert Green Ingersoll; born Aug. 11, 1833.
Hours & Admission Prices: Memorial Day to Oct. Sat.-Sun. 12-5. Suggested Donation: $5 per person. &
Attendance: 450 (actual)

Earlville

EARLVILLE GALLERIES, 18 E. Main St., Earlville, NY 13332. Mailing Address: P.O. Box 111, Earlville, NY 13332. Tel.: 315-691-3550. Facebook.
E-mail: info@earlvilleoperahouse.com
Web Site: www.earlvilleoperahouse.com
Formerly: Earlville Opera House Galleries
Key Personnel: Exec. Dir., Michelle Connelly.
Institution Type/Description: Art Gallery: housed in the historic Earlville Opera House; built in 1892.
Hours & Admission Prices: Tues.-Fri. 10-5, Sat. 12-3. No charge; donations accepted. &
Attendance: 7,277 (actual)

East Aurora

AURORA HISTORICAL SOCIETY, 363 Oakwood Ave., East Aurora, NY 14052-2319. Mailing Address: P.O. Box 472, East Aurora, NY 14052-0472. Tel.: 716-652-4735. Facebook: Aurora Historical Society New York.
E-mail: ahs1951@verizon.net
Web Site: www.aurorahistoricalsociety.com
Key Personnel: Pres., Susan McBurney; Dir. & Town Historian, Robert Lowell Goller; Cur. Elbert Hubbard Museum, Tom Alcamo; Cur. Elbert Hubbard Museum, Don Meade; Cur. Millard Fillmore House, Kathy Frost.
Institution Type/Description: Museum Complex & Historic District: national landmark known as Roycroft Campus, originated c.1896 by Elbert Hubbard as a haven to promote all types of arts & crafts; still in operation.
Hours & Admission Prices: June-Oct. Wed. & Sat.-Sun. 1-4. Fillmore & Hubbard museums $10 each location; members no charge.
Attendance: 1,000 (estimated)

ELBERT HUBBARD-ROYCROFT MUSEUM, 363 Oakwood Ave., East Aurora, NY 14052-2319. Mailing Address: P.O. Box 472, East Aurora, NY 14052-0472. Tel.: 716-652-4735. Facebook: Aurora Historical Society New York.
E-mail: ahs1951@verizon.net
Web Site: www.aurorahistoricalsociety.com
Key Personnel: Dir., Robert Lowell Goller; Co-Cur., Tom Alcamo; Co-Cur., Don Meade.
Institution Type/Description: Library and History Museum: housed in 1910 Scheide Mantel Home.
Hours & Admission Prices: June-Oct. Wed. & Sat.-Sun. 1-4. Adults $10, school children $5; Aurora Historical Society members no charge.
Attendance: 2,000 (estimated)

EXPLORE & MORE CHILDREN'S MUSEUM, 300 Gleed Ave., East Aurora, NY 14052-2983. Tel.: 716-655-5131. Fax: 716-655-5466. Facebook: Explore & More Children's Museum.
E-mail: info@exploreandmore.org
Web Site: www.exploreandmore.org
Key Personnel: C.E.O., Douglas Love; Chm., Barry Swartz; Mktg. Mgr., Jennifer Fee; Interpretive Programs, Amelia Blake; Museum Shop Mgr., Andy Powrie.
Institution Type/Description: Children's Museum.

Hours & Admission Prices: Wed.-Sat. 10-5, Sun. 12-5, first Fri. of month 10-8, Mon.-Tues. large groups by appointment. Admission $7; ACM reciprocal; members, families on WIC, Arts Access & SNAP/EBT cardholders no charge. Closed New Year's Day; Easter; Independence Day; Thanksgiving; Christmas. &
Attendance: 56,709 (actual)

MILLARD FILLMORE PRESIDENTIAL SITE, 24 Shearer Ave., East Aurora, NY 14052. Mailing Address: Box 472, East Aurora, NY 14052-0472. Tel.: 716-652-8875 & 2432. Facebook: Aurora Historical Society New York.
E-mail: ahs1951@verizon.net
Web Site: www.aurorahistoricalsociety.com
Formerly: Millard Fillmore House
Key Personnel: Pres., Susan McBurney; Cur., Kathy Frost; Dir., Robert Lowell Goller.
Institution Type/Description: Historical Society Museum: housed in 1826 home of the 13th U.S. President, Millard Fillmore.
Hours & Admission Prices: June-Oct. 15 Wed. & Sat.-Sun. 1-4; other times & tours by appointment. Adults $10; members & children under 12 no charge.
Attendance: 900 (estimated)

ROYCROFT CAMPUS, 31 S. Grove St., East Aurora, NY 14052-2325. Tel.: 716-655-0261. Fax: 716-655-8498.
E-mail: info@roycroftcampuscorp.com
Web Site: www.roycroftcampuscorporation.com
Formerly: Copper Shop Gallery
Key Personnel: Exec. Dir., Curt Maranto.
Institution Type/Description: History Museum.
Hours & Admission Prices: Daily 10-5. No charge; donations accepted. &
Attendance: 250,000 (estimated)

East Bloomfield

BLOOMFIELD ACADEMY MUSEUM, 8 South Ave., East Bloomfield, NY 14443. Mailing Address: P.O. Box 212, E. Bloomfield, NY 14443-0212. Tel.: 585-657-7244. Fax: 585-657-7244.
E-mail: director@ebhs1838.org
Web Site: www.ebhs1838.org
Key Personnel: Cur., Stephen Beaulieu; Museum Shop Mgr., Richard Delong.
Institution Type/Description: Historic Agency: housed in 1838 Bloomfield Academy Building.
Hours & Admission Prices: April-Dec. Wed.-Fri. 9-2, Sat. 9-12. No charge; donations accepted. Closed major holidays.
Attendance: 1,000 (estimated)

East Durham

DURHAM CENTER MUSEUM/RESEARCH LIBRARY, State Rte. 145, East Durham, NY 12423. Mailing Address: P.O. Box 192, East Durham, NY 12423-0192. Tel.: 518-239-8461 & 4081. Fax: 518-239-4081.
E-mail: durhamcentermu@aol.com
Institution Type/Description: General Museum.
Hours & Admission Prices: Museum: Memorial Day to Columbus Day Thurs.-Sun. 1-4. Adults $2.50, children under 12 $1.50; discount to AAM & ICOM members; children under 5 accompanied by adult no charge. &
Attendance: 500 (estimated)

East Hampton

ARTSOLAR CONTEMPORARY ART & DESIGN, 44 Davids Ln., East Hampton, NY 11937. Tel.: 631-907-8422. Fax: 631-329-5150. Facebook: @ArtSolarContemporary.
E-mail: info@artsolar.com
Web Site: www.artsolar.com
Key Personnel: Dir., Esperanza Leon.
Institution Type/Description: Art Gallery.
Hours & Admission Prices: Call for hours.

CLINTON ACADEMY MUSEUM, 151 Main St., East Hampton, NY 11937-2716. Mailing Address: 101 Main St., East Hampton, NY 11937-2714. Tel.: 631-324-6850. Fax: 631-324-9885.
E-mail: info@easthamptonhistory.org
Web Site: www.easthamptonhistory.org
Key Personnel: Pres. (V), Hollis Forbes; Exec. Dir., Richard Barons.
Institution Type/Description: History Museum: housed in a former school; built in 1784. Listed on the National Register of Historic Places.

Hours & Admission Prices: Call for hours. No charge; donations accepted. &
Attendance: 1,800 (estimated)

EAST HAMPTON HISTORICAL SOCIETY, INC., 101 Main St., East Hampton, NY 11937-2714. Tel.: 631-324-6850. Fax: 631-324-9885.
E-mail: info@easthamptonhistory.org
Web Site: www.easthamptonhistory.org
Key Personnel: Exec. Dir., Richard Barons; Pres. (V), Holllis Forbes.
Institution Type/Description: Historical Society Museum.
Hours & Admission Prices: Office: Tues.-Sat. 10-5. Adults $4; discounts to AAM & military members; members no charge.
Attendance: 10,000 (estimated)

GUILD HALL MUSEUM, 158 Main St., East Hampton, NY 11937-2795. Tel.: 631-324-0806. Fax: 631-324-2722.
E-mail: museum@guildhall.org
Web Site: www.guildhall.org
Key Personnel: Exec. Dir., Ruth Stevens Appelhof, Ph.D.; Chm. Bd. (V), Marty Cohen; Chm. (V), Sue Sylvor; Museum Dir. & Chief Cur., Christina M Strassfield; Museum Shop Mgr., Elaine Dangio.
Institution Type/Description: Art Museum.
Hours & Admission Prices: Independence Day to Labor Day daily 11-5; Sept.-May Mon. & Fri.-Sat. 11-5, Sun. 12-5. Suggested Donation: $7 per person; discounts to AAM & ICOM members; members no charge. Closed New Year's Day; Thanksgiving; Christmas. &
Attendance: 50,000 (actual)

HOME SWEET HOME MUSEUM, 14 James Lane, East Hampton, NY 11937-2710. Mailing Address: East Hampton Village Hall, 86 Main St., East Hampton, NY 11937. Tel.: 631-324-0713 & 4150 & 267-6834. Fax: 631-324-0713 & 4189.
E-mail: hking@easthamptonvillage.org
Web Site: www.easthampton.com/homesweethome.org
Key Personnel: Historic Site Mgr., Hugh King.
Institution Type/Description: Historic House: mid-18th century saltbox dedicated to the memory of John Howard Payne, 19th-century actor, playwright & author of Home Sweet Home.
Hours & Admission Prices: May-Sept. Mon.-Sat. 10-4, Sun. 2-4; Oct.-Nov. Fri.-Sun.; other times by appointment. Adults $4, children $2. Closed New Year's Day; Thanksgiving; Christmas. &
Attendance: 500 (actual)

LONGHOUSE RESERVE, 133 Hands Creek Rd., East Hampton, NY 11937-3808. Tel.: 631-329-3568. Fax: 631-329-4299.
E-mail: info@longhouse.org
Web Site: www.longhouse.org
Key Personnel: Exec. Dir., Matko Tomicic; Founder, Jack Lenor Larsen; Pres., Dianne Benson; Treas., Mark Levine; Cur., Wendy Van Deusen; Museum Shop Mgr., Kate D'Arcy.
Institution Type/Description: General Museum.
Hours & Admission Prices: April 21-June & Sept. Mon., Wed. & Sat. 2-5; July-Aug. Wed.-Sat. 2-5; mid-Oct. to Nov. Sat. 12-3; Adults $10, senior citizens $8; children & members no charge. &
Attendance: 10,000 (actual)

MULFORD FARM MUSEUM, 10 James Lane, East Hampton, NY 11937-2714. Mailing Address: East Hampton Historical Society, 101 Main St., East Hampton, NY 11937-2714. Tel.: 631-324-6850. Fax: 631-324-9885.
E-mail: info@easthamptonhistory.org
Web Site: www.easthamptonhistory.org
Key Personnel: Exec. Dir., Richard Barons; Pres. (V), Hollis Forbes.
Institution Type/Description: Historic Farm Complex: c.1680 frame salt box farm house and c.1720 barn with several outbuildings, continuously belonging to eight generations of the Mulford family 1710-1948 located on 3 acres.
Hours & Admission Prices: Memorial Day-June & Sept.-Columbus Day Sat. 10-5, Sun. 12-5; July-Aug. Fri.-Sat. 10-5, Sun. 12-5. Adults $4, seniors $3, students $2; discounts to military, AAM & AAA members; members no charge.
Attendance: 8,000 (estimated)

OSBORN-JACKSON HOUSE, 101 Main St., East Hampton, NY 11937-2714. Mailing Address: East Hampton Historical Society, 101 Main St., East Hampton, NY 11937. Tel.: 631-324-6850. Fax: 631-324-9885.
E-mail: info@easthamptonhistory.org
Web Site: www.easthamptonhistory.org
Key Personnel: Exec. Dir., Richard Barons; Pres. (V), Hollis Forbes.
Institution Type/Description: History Museum: housed in a two-story home; built in 1720.

Hours & Admission Prices: Tues.-Sat. 10-5. No charge.
Attendance: 800 (estimated)

East Islip

ISLIP ART MUSEUM, 50 Irish Lane, East Islip, NY 11730-2003. Tel.: 631-224-5402. Fax: 631-224-5417.
E-mail: lynda@isliparts.org
Web Site: islipartmuseum.org
Key Personnel: Exec. Dir., Lynda A. Moran; Cur., Beth Giacummo; Asst. Cur., Jason Schuck; Museum Shop Mgr. & Administrative Asst., Rosa Ramos.
Institution Type/Description: Art Museum.
Hours & Admission Prices: Wed.-Sat. 10-4, Sun. 12-4. No charge; donations accepted. Closed New Year's Day; Easter; Memorial Day; Independence Day; Labor Day; Thanksgiving & day after; Christmas. &
Attendance: 12,000 (actual)

East Meadow

NASSAU COUNTY, DIVISION OF MUSEUM SERVICES, DEPARTMENT OF RECREATION, PARKS & MUSEUMS, Eisenhower Park, East Meadow, NY 11554. Tel.: 516-572-0200. Fax: 516-572-0260.
E-mail: mdambrosio@nassaucountyny.gov
Web Site: nassaucountyny.gov/parks
Institution Type/Description: Preservation Project: Old Bethpage Village, farm community of pre-Civil War era, 45 historic structures; Jericho historic preserve, six structures from early 1800s, Sands Point Preserve, four early 1900s Gold Coast estate structures.
Hours & Admission Prices: Call for information.
Attendance: 767,019 (actual)

East Meredith

HANFORD MILLS MUSEUM, 73 County Hwy. 12, Corner of County Hwys. 10 & 12, East Meredith, NY 13757. Mailing Address: P.O. Box 99, East Meredith, NY 13757-0099. Tel.: 607-278-5744. Fax: 607-278-6299.
E-mail: info@hanfordmills.org
Web Site: www.hanfordmills.org
Key Personnel: Dir., Elizabeth Callahan; Chm. (V), Katie Boardman; Asst. Dir., Caroline de Marrais; Cur., Suzanne Soden; Mill Operations Foreman, Dawn Raudibaugh; Museum Shop Mgr., Louise Storey.
Institution Type/Description: Historic Site & Industrial Museum: housed in water powered mill & 16 historic structures.
Hours & Admission Prices: mid-May to mid-Oct. Wed.-Sun. 10-5; other times by appointment. Adults $8.50, seniors 65 & over $6.50, military $4.25; discounts to AAA & AAM members; members and children 12 & under no charge. Buses welcome. &
Attendance: 8,200 (estimated)

Eden

KAZOO FACTORY & MUSEUM, 8703 S. Main St., Eden, NY 14057. Tel.: 716-992-3960.
E-mail: edenkazoo@gmail.com
Institution Type/Description: History Museum.
Hours & Admission Prices: Mon.-Thurs. & Sat. 10-5, Fri. 10-6.

Elizabethtown

ADIRONDACK HISTORY CENTER, 7590 Court St., Elizabethtown, NY 12932. Mailing Address: P.O. Box 428, Elizabethtown, NY 12932-0428. Tel.: 518-873-6466.
E-mail: echs@adkhistorycenter.org
Web Site: adkhistorycenter.org
Key Personnel: Pres. (V), Carol Blakeslee-Collin; Dir., Margaret Gibbs.
Institution Type/Description: History Museum.
Hours & Admission Prices: Memorial Day to Columbus Day daily 10-5. Adults $5, seniors $4, students $4; discounts to AAM members; members, school groups & children under 6 no charge.
Attendance: 10,000 (estimated)

Elma

ELMA TOWN MUSEUM - ELMA HISTORICAL SOCIETY INC., 3011 Bowen Rd., Elma, NY 14059. Mailing Address: P.O. Box 84, Elma, NY 14059. Tel.: 716-655-0046.
E-mail: elmahistory@aol.com
Web Site: www.elmanyhistory.com

Formerly: Elma Town Museum - Elma Historical Inc.
Key Personnel: Pres., Marlene Baumgartner.
Institution Type/Description: Historical Houses & Sites.
Hours & Admission Prices: Thurs. 1-4, 1st & 3rd Sun. each month 1-4; other times by appointment and for special events. No charge; donations accepted. Closed holidays. &
Attendance: 3,000 (estimated)

Elmira

ARNOT ART MUSEUM, 235 Lake St., Elmira, NY 14901-3191. Tel.: 607-734-3697. Fax: 607-734-5687.
E-mail: rick@arnotartmuseum.org
Web Site: arnotartmuseum.org
Key Personnel: Exec. Dir., Rick Pirozzolo; Business Mgr., Lynda Williams; Mgr. Education Programs, Meghan O'Loughlin; Mgr. Collections, Laura Wetmore; Dir. Tour Svcs., Wendy Taylor; Facilities Caretaker, Gregg Leavenworth.
Institution Type/Description: Art Museum: housed in 1833 Greek Revival style home of Matthias H. Arnot with 1985 Graham Gund Addition, and Carriage House Education Center.
Hours & Admission Prices: Tues.-Fri. 10-5, Sat. 12-5. Adults $7; discounts to AAM & ICOM members; members no charge; reciprocal membership with 15 New York State museums. Closed national holidays. &
Attendance: 17,000 (actual)

CHEMUNG COUNTY HISTORICAL SOCIETY, 415 E. Water St., Elmira, NY 14901-3410. Tel.: 607-734-4167 & 4168. Fax: 607-734-1565.
E-mail: cchs@chemungvalleymuseum.org
Web Site: www.chemungvalleymuseum.org
Key Personnel: Pres., Russell Smith; Dir., Bruce Whitmarsh; Cur., Erin Doane; Coord. Education, Kerry Lippincott; Archivist, Rachel Dworkin; Administrative Asst., Christine Gunderson; Journal Editor, Joe Lemak.
Institution Type/Description: Historical Society Museum.
Hours & Admission Prices: Museum: Mon.-Sat. 10-5. Office: Mon.-Fri. 9-5. Library & Research: Mon.-Fri. 1-5. Tours: adults $3; discounts to AAM & museum members. Personal Tours: adults $4. Closed holidays. &
Attendance: 10,000 (estimated)

MARK TWAIN ARCHIVES - GANNETT-TRIPP LIBRARY - ELMIRA COLLEGE, One Park Place, Elmira, NY 14901. Tel.: 607-735-1869. Fax: 607-735-1712.
E-mail: mwoodhouse@elmira.edu
Institution Type/Description: Library & Archives.
Hours & Admission Prices: By appointment.

MARK TWAIN STUDY & EXHIBIT - ELMIRA COLLEGE, One Park Place, Cowles Hall, Elmira, NY 14901. Tel.: 607-735-1941. Fax: 607-735-1756.
E-mail: twaincenter@elmira.edu
Institution Type/Description: History Museum.
Hours & Admission Prices: Study: May to Labor Day Mon.-Sat. 9:30-4:30; Sept. to mid-Oct. Sat. 9:30-5:30; or by appointment.

NATIONAL SOARING MUSEUM, Harris Hill, 51 Soaring Hill Dr., Elmira, NY 14903-9204. Tel.: 607-734-3128. Fax: 607-732-6745.
E-mail: info@soaringmuseum.org
Web Site: www.soaringmuseum.org
Key Personnel: Exec. Dir., Trafford L. Doherty; Pres. Bd., W. Stuart Schweizer; Dir. Museum Svcs., Mary D. Flasphaler; Museum Shop Mgr., Lisa C. Bartlett.
Institution Type/Description: Aeronautics Museum: located on the site of the earliest soaring contests in the United States.
Hours & Admission Prices: Daily 10-5. Adults $7.50, senior citizens $6.50, youth 7-17 $4.50; discounts to groups & AAA members; members & children under 6 no charge. &
Attendance: 22,000 (estimated)

TANGLEWOOD NATURE CENTER AND MUSEUM, 443 Coleman Ave., Elmira, NY 14903-9311. Tel.: 607-732-6060. Fax: 607-732-6210.
E-mail: elainems@stny.rr.com
Web Site: www.tanglewoodnaturecenter.com
Key Personnel: Office Mgr. & Museum Shop Mgr., Deanna Soper; Pres. Bd., Linda Hillman; Exec. Dir., Elaine Farwell; Volunteer Coord., Ian Martin; Cur., Valerie Heywood; Grounds & Bldg., Rich Gridley.
Institution Type/Description: Nature Center.

Hours & Admission Prices: Museum: May-Oct. Tues.-Sat. 8:30-4:30; Nov.-April Tues.-Sat. 9-4. Trails: daily dawn to dusk. No charge; donations accepted. Closed holidays. &
Attendance: 30,000 (estimated)

Elmsford

GREATER HUDSON HERITAGE NETWORK, 2199 Saw Mill River Rd., Elmsford, NY 10523-3812. Tel.: 914-592-6726. Fax: 914-592-6946.
E-mail: info@greaterhudson.org
Web Site: www.greaterhudson.org
Formerly: Lower Hudson Conference of Historical Agencies and Museums
Key Personnel: C.E.O. & Exec. Dir., Priscilla Brendler; Pres. (V), Jacquetta Haley; Project Mgr., Dianne Macpherson.
Institution Type/Description: Museum Service Organization
Hours & Admission Prices: Mon.-Fri. 9-4. No charge. Fees for training programs. Workshop & seminar fee discount to GHHN member organizations & individuals. Closed Westchester County & New York state holidays. &
Attendance: 500 (estimated)

WESTCHESTER COUNTY HISTORICAL SOCIETY, 2199 Saw Mill River Rd., Elmsford, NY 10523-3812. Tel.: 914-592-4323. Fax: 914-231-1510.
E-mail: info@westchesterhistory.com
Web Site: www.westchesterhistory.com
Key Personnel: Exec. Dir., Susanne Pandich; Chm. (V), Lee Pollock; Librarian, Patrick Raftery.
Institution Type/Description: Historical Society Library & Research Center.
Hours & Admission Prices: Research Library: Tues.-Wed. 9-4. No charge. &
Attendance: 2,500 (estimated)

Esperance

GEORGE LANDIS ARBORETUM, 174 Lape Rd., Esperance, NY 12066. Mailing Address: P.O. Box 186, Esperance, NY 12066-0186. Tel.: 518-875-6935. Fax: 518-875-6394. Facebook: George Landis Arboretum.
E-mail: info@landisarboretum.org
Web Site: www.landisarboretum.org
Key Personnel: Exec. Dir., Fred Breglia; Pres. (V), James Paley; Science Educator, George Steele.
Institution Type/Description: Arboretum & Botanical Garden.
Hours & Admission Prices: Daily dawn to dusk. No charge; donations accepted.
Attendance: 8,000 (estimated)

Fairport

FAIRPORT HISTORICAL MUSEUM, Perinton Historical Society, 18 Perrin St., Fairport, NY 14450-2122. Tel.: 585-223-3989. Facebook: Perinton Historical Society.
E-mail: info@perintonhistoricalsociety.org
Web Site: www.perintonhistoricalsociety.org
Key Personnel: Dir., Vicki Masters Profitt.
Institution Type/Description: Local History Museum.
Hours & Admission Prices: March-Dec. Sun. & Tues. 2-4, Thurs. 7pm-9pm, Sat. 9am-11am. No charge; donations accepted. Closed major holidays. &
Attendance: 1,223 (estimated)

Farmingdale

AMERICAN AIRPOWER MUSEUM, 1230 New Hwy., Farmingdale, NY 11735. Mailing Address: c/o Cockpit USA, 15 W. 39th St., 12th Fl., New York, NY 10018. Tel.: 631-293-6398.
E-mail: info@americanairpowermuseum.org
Web Site: www.americanairpowermuseum.org
Key Personnel: Pres., Jeff Clyman; Museum Shop Mgr., Jacky Clyman.
Institution Type/Description: History Museum.
Hours & Admission Prices: Thurs.-Sun. 10:30-4. Adults $10, seniors & veterans $8, children 4-12 $5, children under 4 no charge. &
Attendance: 15,000 (estimated)

Fayetteville

MATILDA JOSLYN GAGE FOUNDATION & HOME, 210 E. Genesee St., Fayetteville, NY 13066. Tel.: 315-637-9511.
E-mail: foundation@matildajoslyngage.org
Web Site: www.matildajoslyngage.org
Key Personnel: Site Dir., Sarah Flick; Founder, Sally Roesch Wagner, Ph.D.
Institution Type/Description: Historic Home: built c.1820.

Hours & Admission Prices: Mon.-Tues. & Thurs.-Fri. 10-4. Adults $8, seniors 62 & over $6, students $5; discounts to groups of 10 or more; pre-school children no charge.

THE STICKLEY MUSEUM, 300 Orchard St., 2nd Fl., Fayetteville, NY 13066. Mailing Address: 1 Stickley Dr., P.O. Box 480, Manlius, NY 13104-0480. Tel.: 315-682-5500. Fax: 315-682-6306. Facebook.
E-mail: amanda.clifford@stickley.com
Web Site: www.stickleymuseum.com
Key Personnel: Dir., Amanda L. Clifford.
Institution Type/Description: Furniture Museum.
Hours & Admission Prices: Tues. 9-5, Sat. 10-5; other times by appointment. No charge. &
Attendance: 1,393 (actual)

Fineview

THE MINNA ANTHONY COMMON NATURE CENTER AT WELLESLEY STATE PARK, 44927 Cross Island Rd., Fineview, NY 13640-3105. Tel.: 315-482-2479. Facebook.
Web Site: www.macnaturecenter.com
Key Personnel: Dir., Gabriela Padewska.
Institution Type/Description: Nature Center.
Hours & Admission Prices: Museum: daily 8-4. Trails: sunrise to sunset. Closed Thanksgiving; Christmas. &
Attendance: 50,000 (estimated)

Fishkill

VAN WYCK HOMESTEAD MUSEUM - FISHKILL HISTORICAL SOCIETY, 504 Rte. 9, Fishkill, NY 12524. Mailing Address: P.O. Box 133, Fishkill, NY 12524-0133. Tel.: 845-896-9560.
E-mail: vanwyckhomestead@aol.com
Web Site: www.fishkillhistoricalsociety.org
Key Personnel: Pres. (V), Steve Lynch; Museum Shop Mgr., Helga Mackenzie.
Institution Type/Description: Historic House Museum: housed in a former Dutch Colonial Homestead built in 1732; officers' headquarters during the Revolutionary War for northern supply depot 1776-83.
Hours & Admission Prices: Memorial Day to Oct. Sat.-Sun. 1-4. No charge; donations accepted.
Attendance: 2,000 (estimated)

Flanders

THE BIG DUCK, 1012 Flanders Rd., Flanders, NY 11901. Mailing Address: P.O. Box 144, West Sayville, NY 11796. Tel.: 631-852-3377.
E-mail: mudda1@optonline.net
Institution Type/Description: Historic Building: listed on the National Register of Historic Places.
Hours & Admission Prices: Tues.-Sat. 10-5, Sun. 2-5, call to confirm. No charge.

Floral Park

QUEENS COUNTY FARM MUSEUM, 73-50 Little Neck Pkwy., Floral Park, NY 11004-1129. Tel.: 718-347-3276, ext. 303. Fax: 718-347-3243. TDD: 800-281-5722.
E-mail: amy@queensfarm.org
Web Site: www.queensfarm.org
Key Personnel: Exec. Dir. & Events Coord., Amy Fischetti Boncardo; Pres. (V), James A. Trent; Chm. (V), Samuel Shapiro; Cur., Renee Tone; Dir. Education, Interpreter & Museum Shop Mgr., Diane Miller; Dir. Agriculture, Gary Mitchell; Dir. Horticultural, Annemarie Gero; Administrative Asst., Fran Erato; Interpreter, Mary Mifsud; Museum Shop Mgr., Sarah Meyer.
Institution Type/Description: Historic House: c.1772 Adriance Farmhouse.
Hours & Admission Prices: Outdoors: daily 10-5. House Tours: Sat.-Sun. 10-5. General Admission: no charge. School tours $4-$8 per person. School Workshops $5-$8 per person. Special Events $4-$9 per person. &
Attendance: 500,000 (actual)

Flushing

THE BOWNE HOUSE HISTORICAL SOCIETY, 37-01 Bowne St., Flushing, NY 11354-5628. Tel.: 718-359-0528. Fax: 718-359-0873.
E-mail: office@bownehouse.org
Web Site: www.bownehouse.org
Key Personnel: Pres., Rosemary Vietor.

Institution Type/Description: Historic House Museum: 1661 home of John Bowne, religious freedom advocate.
Hours & Admission Prices: Museum is under restoration. Please call for appointment. &

THE GODWIN-TERNBACH MUSEUM, Queens College, 405 Klapper Hall, 65-30 Kissena Blvd., Flushing, NY 11367-1575. Tel.: 718-997-4747. Fax: 718-997-4734.
E-mail: gtmuseum@qc.cuny.edu
Web Site: www.qc.cuny.edu/godwin_ternbach
Formerly: Frances Godwin & Joseph Ternbach Museum
Key Personnel: Dir. & Cur., Dr. Amy Winter; Chm. (V), Margaret Zeuschner.
Institution Type/Description: Art Museum.
Hours & Admission Prices: Mon.-Thurs. 11-7, Sat. 11-5. No charge; donations accepted. &
Attendance: 9,500 (estimated)

LEWIS H. LATIMER HOUSE MUSEUM, 34-41 137th St., Flushing, NY 11354. Tel.: 718-961-8585. Facebook.
E-mail: lewislatimerhouse@gmail.com
Web Site: latimernow.org
Institution Type/Description: Historic House Museum: housed in the former home of Lewis Howard Latimer, an African-American inventor & electrical pioneer and the son of fugitive slaves; built 1887-1889.
Hours & Admission Prices: Wed., Fri. & Sun. 12-5; groups by appointment. No charge; donations accepted. &

METS HALL OF FAME & MUSEUM, Citi Field, Roosevelt Ave., Flushing, NY 11368-1699. Tel.: 718-507-8499.
E-mail: mlbexecutiverelations@website.mlb.com
Web Site: newyork.mets.mlb.com
Institution Type/Description: Sports Museum & Hall of Fame.
Hours & Admission Prices: During Home Games: when gates open to the end of the game. No charge. Non-game Days: access with Citi Field tour. Tickets: adults $10, children 12 & under and seniors 60 & over $7; discounts to groups; military no charge.

QUEENS BOTANICAL GARDEN, 43-50 Main St., Flushing, NY 11355-4758. Tel.: 718-886-3800. Fax: 718-463-0263.
E-mail: info@queensbotanical.org
Web Site: www.queensbotanical.org
Key Personnel: Chm., Rovena Schirling; Exec. Dir., Susan Lacerte; Dir. Finance & Admin., Wai Li; Maintenance Supvr., Peter Sansone; Dir. Mktg. & Devel., Stephanie Ehrlich; Sr. Attendant Guard, James Adams.
Institution Type/Description: Botanical Garden and Arboretum.
Hours & Admission Prices: April-Oct. Tues.-Sun. 8-6; Nov.-March Tues.-Sun. 8-4:30. April-Oct. adults $6, seniors 62 & over and students $4, children 4-12 $2; children 3 & under, APGA, American Horticultural Society & garden members no charge. &
Attendance: 220,202 (actual)

QUEENS HISTORICAL SOCIETY, 143-35 37th Ave., Flushing, NY 11354-5729. Tel.: 718-939-0647. Fax: 718-539-9885. Facebook: Queens Historical Society.
E-mail: info@queenshistoricalsociety.org
Web Site: www.queenshistoricalsociety.org
Key Personnel: Mgr. Collections, Richard Hourahan; Education & Outreach, Andrea Zrake; Pres., Patricia B. Sherwood; Vice Pres. History, James Driscoll; Treas., Carol Gillen Costello; Membership Sec., Catherine Williams.
Institution Type/Description: Historic Site: c.1785 Kingsland Homestead, located in Weeping Beech Park.
Hours & Admission Prices: Office: Mon.-Fri. 9-4:30. Museum: Tues. & Sat.-Sun. 2:30-4:30. Adults $5, senior citizens & students $3; members no charge. Closed major holidays. &
Attendance: 6,000 (estimated)

VOELKER ORTH MUSEUM, 149-19 38th Ave., Flushing, NY 11354. Tel.: 718-359-6227.
E-mail: info@vomuseum.org
Web Site: www.vomuseum.org
Institution Type/Description: Historic House: built c.1890.
Hours & Admission Prices: Office: Mon.-Fri. 9-4. Tours: Tues. & Sat.-Sun. 1-4. Closed Easter; Mother's Day.

Fonda

NATIVE AMERICAN EXHIBIT, NATIONAL KATERI SHRINE, 3636 State Hwy. 5, Fonda, NY 12068. Mailing Address: P.O. Box 627, Fonda, NY 12068-0627. Tel.: 518-853-3646.
E-mail: saintkateri@katerishrine.com

Web Site: www.katerishrine.com
Key Personnel: Dir., Rita Gullion; Chap., Rev. Timothy Lyons, O.F.M.Conv.
Institution Type/Description: Religious Shrine & Historic Archaeological Site: 1666-1693 staked out Mohawk Indian castle & 1666-1676 residence of Kateri Tekakwitha.
Hours & Admission Prices: May-Oct. daily 9-6; other times by appointment. No charge; donations accepted. Mass schedule: Sat. 4:30, Sun. 10:30. &
Attendance: 5,000 (estimated)

Fort Edward

OLD FORT HOUSE MUSEUM, 29 Broadway, Fort Edward, NY 12828. Mailing Address: P.O. Box 106, Fort Edward, NY 12828-0106. Tel.: 518-747-9600. Fax: 518-747-7790. Facebook, Twitter.
E-mail: oldfort@albany.twc.bc.com
Web Site: www.oldforthousemuseum.com
Key Personnel: C.E.O. & Historian, R. Paul McCarty; Pres. (V), Mary R. Smith; Dir. Education & Sec., Rebecca Gallagher.
Institution Type/Description: Local History Museum: housed in 1772-73 Old Fort House.
Hours & Admission Prices: June-Aug. daily 1-5; Sept. to Columbus Day Tues.-Sun. 1-5. Adults $5, youth 13-18 $3; discounts to AAA members; members & children 12 & under no charge. Closed national holidays. &
Attendance: 3,805 (actual)

Fort Hunter

SCHOHARIE CROSSING STATE HISTORIC SITE, 129 Schoharie St., Fort Hunter, NY 12069-0140. Mailing Address: P.O. Box 140, Fort Hunter, NY 12069-0140. Tel.: 518-829-7516. Fax: 518-829-7491. Facebook: Schoharie Crossing State Historic Site.
E-mail: schohariecrossing@parks.ny.gov
Web Site: nysparks.com
Key Personnel: Historic Site Mgr., Janice M. Fontanella.
Institution Type/Description: Historic Site.
Hours & Admission Prices: Daily during daylight hours, weather permitting. Visitor Center: May-Oct. Wed.-Sat. 10-5, Sun. 1-5. No charge; donations accepted. &
Attendance: 80,000 (estimated)

Fort Johnson

OLD FORT JOHNSON, Rte. 5, Fort Johnson, NY 12070. Mailing Address: Fort Johnson, P.O. Box 196, Fort Johnson, NY 12070-0196. Tel.: 518-843-0300.
E-mail: museum@oldfortjohnson.org
Web Site: www.oldfortjohnson.org
Key Personnel: Pres., Philip V. Cortese.
Institution Type/Description: General Museum: housed in 1749 Fort Johnson, home of Sir William Johnson, Supt. of Indian affairs & general of the Royal Militia & scene of Indian councils, military assemblies & Indian administration for British colonies.
Hours & Admission Prices: May 15-Oct. 15 Wed.-Sat. 10-4, Sun. 1-5. Adults $4; members & children under 12 no charge.
Attendance: 3,500 (estimated)

Fort Montgomery

FORT MONTGOMERY STATE HISTORIC SITE, 690 Rte. 9 W., Fort Montgomery, NY 10922. Mailing Address: P.O. Box 213, Fort Montgomery, NY 10922. Tel.: 845-446-2134. Fax: 845-446-2403.
Institution Type/Description: Historic Site: scene of the Revolutionary War battle for control of the Hudson River.
Hours & Admission Prices: Call for hours.

Fort Plain

FORT PLAIN MUSEUM, 389 Canal St., Fort Plain, NY 13339-1160. Mailing Address: P.O. Box 324, Fort Plain, NY 13339-0324. Tel.: 518-993-2527. Facebook: Fort Plain Museum.
E-mail: fortplainmuseum@yahoo.com
Web Site: www.fortplainmuseum.com
Key Personnel: Chm., Norm Bollen; Vice Chm., Wayne Lenig; Museum Shop Mgr., Brian Mack.
Institution Type/Description: History Museum: housed in restored 19th-century farmhouse.
Hours & Admission Prices: May-Aug. daily 1-5; Sept.-Oct. Fri.-Sun. 1-5; Nov.-April by appointment. Admission: $5 per person. &
Attendance: 2,500 (estimated)

Franklinville

ISCHUA VALLEY HISTORICAL SOCIETY, INC., 9 Pine St., Franklinville, NY 14737-1111. Mailing Address: P.O. Box 153, Franklinville, NY 14737. Tel.: 716-676-2590.
E-mail: maidlynn@aol.com
Web Site: ischuavalleyhistoricalsociety.org
Key Personnel: Pres., Bruce D. Fredrickson; Treas., Duane Walker; Sec., Ida Gardner; Cur., Maggie Fredrickson.
Institution Type/Description: Historical Society Museum: listed on State & National Historic Registers.
Hours & Admission Prices: Miner's Cabin: Memorial Day-Labor Day Sun. 2-5. Howe-Prescott House: by appointment only. No charge; donations accepted.
Attendance: 700 (estimated)

Fredonia

CATHY & JESSE MARION ART GALLERY, State University College, Fredonia, NY 14063. Tel.: 716-673-4897. Fax: 716-673-4990. Facebook: Cathy & Jesse Marion Art Gallery.
E-mail: tina.hastings@fredonia.edu
Web Site: www.fredonia.edu/rac
Formerly: Rockefeller Arts Center Art Gallery
Key Personnel: Gallery Dir., Tina Hastings.
Institution Type/Description: Art Gallery.
Hours & Admission Prices: Academic School Year: Tues.-Thurs. & Sun. 12-4, Fri.-Sat. 12-6. No charge. Closed holidays; college breaks. &
Attendance: 3,109 (actual)

D.R. BARKER HISTORICAL MUSEUM, 20 E. Main St., Fredonia, NY 14063. Mailing Address: 7 Day St., Fredonia, NY 14063-1813. Tel.: 716-672-2114.
E-mail: barkermu@netsync.net
Web Site: www.barkermuseum.net
Formerly: Historical Museum of the D.R. Barker Library
Key Personnel: Dir. Library, Sara Hart.
Institution Type/Description: Genealogy Library & History Museum: housed in 1821 Leverett Barker Home.
Hours & Admission Prices: Tues. 4-8, Sat. 1-5. No charge; donations accepted. Closed national holidays. &
Attendance: 3,958 (actual)

Fultonville

SHRINE OF OUR LADY OF MARTYRS AKA THE NATIONAL SHRINE OF THE NORTH AMERICAN MARTYRS, 136 Shrine Rd., Fultonville, NY 12072. Tel.: 518-853-3033. Fax: 518-853-3051.
E-mail: office@martyrsshrine.org
Web Site: www.martyrsshrine.org
Key Personnel: Dir., Rev. George H. Belgarde, S.J.; Museum Mgr. & Media Rep., Elizabeth Lynch; Supvr. Operations, Larry Steiger; Gift Shop Mgr., Joanne Wiesner.
Institution Type/Description: Museum Complex & Historic Site: housed in c.1900 frame structure, located on the site of the 1646 martyrdom of Father Isaac Jogues, French Jesuit priest & 1656 birthplace of Kateri Tekakwitha.
Hours & Admission Prices: Museum: Mon.-Fri. 12-4, Sat.-Sun. 10-4. Visitor Center: May-Oct. Sun.-Fri. 10-5, Sat. 10-5:30. Mass Schedule: Mon.-Sat. 11:30 & 4, Sun. 9, 11 & 4. No charge; donations accepted. &
Attendance: 75,000 (estimated)

Garden City

CRADLE OF AVIATION MUSEUM, Charles Lindbergh Blvd., Garden City, NY 11530. Mailing Address: One Davis Ave., Garden City, NY 11530-6743. Tel.: 516-572-4111. Fax: 516-572-4065.
E-mail: aparton@cradleofaviation.org
Web Site: www.cradleofaviation.org
Key Personnel: Exec. Dir., Andrew Parton; Chm. Bd. (V), Marc MacDonell; Deputy Dir., Jennifer Baxmeyer; Dir. Education, Catherine Bingham; Financial Dir., Dan Boehm; Cur., Joshua Stoff; Dir. Museum Operations, Gary Monti.
Institution Type/Description: Air and Space Museum & Educational Center.
Hours & Admission Prices: Daily 9:30-5. Museum: adult $15, seniors 62 & over and children 4-12 $13; additional fees for other attractions. Closed Thanksgiving; Christmas. &
Attendance: 300,000 (actual)

FIREHOUSE ART GALLERY, NASSAU COMMUNITY COLLEGE, One Education Dr., Garden City, NY 11530-6793. Tel.: 516-572-7162, ext. 25073. Fax: 516-572-7005.
E-mail: gallery@ncc.edu
Web Site: firehouse.ncc.edu
Key Personnel: Dir., Lynn Rozzi.
Institution Type/Description: College Art Gallery.
Hours & Admission Prices: Mon.-Tues, 11:30-7, Wed. 8:30-2, Thurs. 8:30-7, Fri.-Sat. 11:30-2. No charge. Closed college holidays. ♿
Attendance: 12,000 (estimated)

LONG ISLAND CHILDREN'S MUSEUM, Charles Lindbergh Blvd., Garden City, NY 11530. Mailing Address: 11 Davis Ave., Garden City, NY 11530-6745. Tel.: 516-224-5800. Fax: 516-302-8188.
E-mail: development@licm.org
Web Site: www.licm.org
Key Personnel: Exec. Dir., Suzanne LeBlanc; Co Chm. (V), Robert S. Lemle; Co Chm. (V), Scott Rechler; Asst. Museum Shop Mgr., Tanya Skachinsky.
Institution Type/Description: Children's Museum.
Hours & Admission Prices: July-Aug. daily 10-5; Sept.-June Tues.-Sun. 10-5. Admission $12, seniors 65 & over $11; discounts to educators, military, AAM, AAA, ACM & ASTC members; members & children under one no charge. ♿
Attendance: 275,375 (actual)

NASSAU COUNTY FIREFIGHTERS MUSEUM, One Davis Ave., Garden City, NY 11530. Tel.: 516-572-4177 & 4066. Facebook.
Web Site: www.ncfiremuseum.org
Institution Type/Description: Firefighting History Museum.
Hours & Admission Prices: July-Aug. daily 10-5; Sept.-June Tues.-Sun. 10-5. Adults $5, senior citizens 62 & over, volunteer firemen and children $4.
Attendance: 25,000 (actual)

RUTH S. HARLEY UNIVERSITY CENTER GALLERY, 1 South Ave., Garden City, NY 11530. Tel.: 516-877-3126.
E-mail: augalleries@gmail.com
Web Site: art-galleries.adelphi.edu
Key Personnel: Dir. Exhibitions, Eliz Alahverdian.
Institution Type/Description: Art Gallery.
Hours & Admission Prices: Mon.-Fri. 11-7, Sat.-Sun. 11-5.

Gardiner

MOHONK PRESERVE, INC., 3197 Rte. 44/55, Gardiner, NY 12525. Mailing Address: P.O. Box 715, New Paltz, NY 12561-0715. Tel.: 845-255-0919. Fax: 845-255-5646.
E-mail: info@mohonkpreserve.org
Web Site: mohonkpreserve.org
Key Personnel: Pres. Bd. Dir. (V), James L. Hoover; Exec. Dir., Glenn D. Hoagland; Dep. Exec. Dir., David Toman; Dir. Mktg. & Communs., Gretchen Reed; Dir. Cons. Science, Dr. Elizabeth Long; Deputy Exec. Dir., Joe Alfano; Dir. Education, Kathy Ambrosini; Dir. Land Protection & Stewartship, Emily Hague; Museum Shop Mgr., Ken Halpern.
Institution Type/Description: Historic Site & Nature Center: located in the Shawangunk Mountains.
Hours & Admission Prices: Preserve: daily sunrise-sunset. Visitor Center: Mon.-Fri. 9-5. Adults: climbers & bikers $17, hikers $12; discount to ANCA members & groups with reservations; members & children under 13 no charge. Closed New Year's Day; Thanksgiving; Christmas Eve & Day. ♿
Attendance: 150,000 (estimated)

Garnerville

GARNER ARTS CENTER, Garnerville Arts & Industrial Center, 55 W. Railroad Ave., Garnerville, NY 10923. Tel.: 845-947-7108.
E-mail: info@garnerartscenter.org
Web Site: garnerartscenter.org
Formerly: GAGA Arts Center
Key Personnel: Pres., Robin Rosenberg; Exec. Dir., James Tyler; Program Dir., Christine Olivier de Molina.
Institution Type/Description: Art Gallery: housed in a 19th century textile mill.
Hours & Admission Prices: Call for hours.

Garrison

BOSCOBEL HOUSE & GARDENS, 1601 Rte. 9D, Garrison, NY 10524-4406. Tel.: 845-265-3638. Fax: 845-265-4405.
E-mail: info@boscobel.org
Web Site: www.boscobel.org
Key Personnel: Exec. Dir., Steven Miller; Pres. (V), Barnabas McHenry; Mktg. & Events Mgr., Donna Blaney; Museum Educator, Lisa DiMarzo; Museum Shop Mgr., Renate Smoller; Cur., Jennifer Carlquist; Maintenance Supvr., John Malone.
Institution Type/Description: Historic House Museum: c.1808 New York Federal style home built by States Morris Dyckman.
Hours & Admission Prices: April-Oct. Wed.-Mon. 9:30-5; Nov.-Dec. Wed.-Mon. 9:30-4. House & Grounds: Family of 4 $45; adults $17, senior citizens 62 & over $14; children 6-14 $8. Grounds: Family of 4 $30, adults $11, children 6-14 $5; discounts to groups of 12 or more & AAM members; museum employees of local museums in Hudson Valley with proper ID & Friends of Boscobel no charge. Closed Thanksgiving; Christmas. ♿
Attendance: 55,000 (actual)

GARRISON ART CENTER, 23 Garrison's Landing, Garrison, NY 10524-3648. Mailing Address: P.O. Box 4, Garrison, NY 10524-0004. Tel.: 845-424-3960. Fax: 845-424-4711.
E-mail: director@garrisonartcenter.org
Web Site: www.garrisonartcenter.org
Key Personnel: Exec. Dir., Carinda Swann.
Institution Type/Description: Art Center.
Hours & Admission Prices: Tues.-Sun. 12-5. No charge; donations accepted. ♿
Attendance: 20,000 (estimated)

MANITOGA/THE RUSSEL WRIGHT DESIGN CENTER, 584 Rte. 9D, Garrison, NY 10524. Mailing Address: P.O. Box 249, Garrison, NY 10524-0249. Tel.: 845-424-3812. Fax: 845-424-4043.
E-mail: info@russelwrightcenter.org
Key Personnel: Pres. (V), David McAlpin; Asst. Dir. & Museum Shop Mgr., Lori Moss.
Institution Type/Description: Historic House Museum: housed in the former home & studio of designer Russel Wright. A National Historic Landmark.
Hours & Admission Prices: Tours: May-Oct. Mon.-Fri. call for hours, Sat.-Sun. 11 & 1:30; groups by appointment. Adults $15; discounts to American Horticultural Society, Long House Preserve members; members no charge.
Attendance: 3,500 (estimated)

Geneseo

BERTHA V.B. LEDERER GALLERY, SUNY Geneseo, Brodie Hall, 1 College Circle, Geneseo, NY 14454-1401. Tel.: 585-245-5814.
E-mail: hawkins@geneseo.edu
Key Personnel: Dir., Cynthia Hawkins.
Institution Type/Description: Art Gallery.
Hours & Admission Prices: Mon.-Thurs. 12-4, Fri.-Sat. 12-6. No charge; donations accepted. Closed Thanksgiving; Christmas, fall & spring breaks. ♿
Attendance: 1,000

LIVINGSTON COUNTY HISTORICAL SOCIETY MUSEUM, 30 Center St., Geneseo, NY 14454-1204. Tel.: 585-243-9147.
E-mail: lchistory@frontier.com
Web Site: www.livingstoncountyhistoricalsociety.com
Formerly: Cobblestone Museum
Key Personnel: Pres., Sally Wood; Dir., Anna Kowalchuk.
Institution Type/Description: Historical Society Museum: housed in former district #5 schoolhouse.
Hours & Admission Prices: May-Dec. 1 Thurs. & Sun. 2-5; call for information or appointments. No charge; donations accepted.
Attendance: 2,500 (actual)

1941 HISTORICAL AIRCRAFT GROUP MUSEUM, 3489 Big Tree Ln., Geneseo, NY 14454. Mailing Address: P.O. Box 185, Geneseo, NY 14454. Tel.: 585-243-2100. Fax: 585-245-9802.
E-mail: editor.1941hag@gmail.com
Web Site: www.1941hag.org/index.html
Institution Type/Description: Military Aviation History Museum.
Hours & Admission Prices: April-Sept. daily 10-4; Oct.-March Mon., Wed. & Fri.-Sat. 10-4. Adults $4, children 5-12 $1; children under 5 no charge. Closed New Year's Day; Thanksgiving; Christmas.

Geneva

THE DAVIS GALLERY AT HOUGHTON HOUSE, 1 King's Ln., Geneva, NY 14456. Mailing Address: c/o Hobart and William Smith Colleges, 300 Pultney St., Geneva, NY 14456. Tel.: 315-781-3483.
E-mail: kvaughn@hws.edu
Web Site: www.hws.edu/academics/davisgallery

Key Personnel: Cur., Kathryn Vaughn.
Institution Type/Description: Art Gallery.
Hours & Admission Prices: mid-Aug. to mid-May Mon.-Fri. 9:30-4:30, Sat. 1:30-4:30.

GENEVA HISTORY MUSEUM, 543 S. Main St., Geneva, NY 14456-3194. Tel.: 315-789-5151. Fax: 315-789-0314.
E-mail: info@genevahistoricalsociety.com
Web Site: genevahistoricalsociety.com
Key Personnel: Dir., Kerry Lippincott; Rose Hill Education Coord., Alice Askins; Cur. Collections & Exhibits, John C. Marks; Archivist, Karen D. Osburn; Dir. Education & Public Info, Anne F. Dealy; Office Mgr., Jeanine Housman; Facilities Mgr., David Knitter.
Institution Type/Description: Local History Museum & Historic Houses.
Hours & Admission Prices: Geneva History Museum: May-Oct. Mon.-Fri. 9:30-4:30, Sat. 12-5; Nov.-April Tues.-Fri. 9:30-4:30, Sat. 1:30-4:30. Suggested donation $3. Rose Hill Mansion: May-Oct. Tues.-Sat. 10-4, Sun. 1-5. Adults $10, seniors 62 & over $7, children 10-18 $6; children 9 & under no charge. Johnston House: May-Oct. Sat. 10-4, Sun. 1-5. Suggested donation $3. All museums closed major holidays.
Attendance: 12,040

Germantown

CLERMONT STATE HISTORIC SITE, One Clermont Ave., Germantown, NY 12526-5632. Tel.: 518-537-4240 & 8687. Fax: 518-537-6240.
E-mail: fofc@valstar.net
Web Site: www.friendsofclermont.org
Key Personnel: Dir., Susan Boudreau; Pres. (V), Carl Brandt; Dir. Education, Kjirsten Gustavson; Administrative Asst., Roberta Nolan; Bd. Coord., Audrey Reifler; Historic Horticulturist, Jane Lehmuller.
Institution Type/Description: Historic House Museum & Estate Grounds: located on 500-acre Hudson Valley estate, with c.1730 home belonging to seven generations of the Livingston family.
Hours & Admission Prices: House: April-Oct. Tues.-Fri. 11-5 (last tour 4:30); Nov.-March Sat.-Sun. 11-4. Adults $5, seniors over 62 $4; children under 12 no charge. Visitor Center: Jan. 2-April 1 Sat.-Sun. Grounds: daily 8:30-sunset. Visitor Center & Grounds no charge. Closed holidays. &
Attendance: 100,000 (estimated)

Ghent

THE FIELDS SCULPTURE PARK AT OMI INTERNATIONAL ARTS CENTER, 1405 Cty. Rte. 22, Ghent, NY 12075-3809. Tel.: 518-392-4747. Fax: 518-392-4740.
E-mail: bmaynes@artomi.org
Web Site: www.omiartscenter.org
Key Personnel: Dir., Ruth Adams.
Institution Type/Description: Sculpture Park.
Hours & Admission Prices: Daily dawn to dusk. No charge; donations accepted. &
Attendance: 13,000 (estimated)

Glen Cove

GARVIES POINT MUSEUM & PRESERVE, 50 Barry Dr., Glen Cove, NY 11542-1765. Tel.: 516-571-8010.
E-mail: vnatale@nassaucountyny.gov
Web Site: www.garviespointmuseum.com
Institution Type/Description: Natural History Museum.
Hours & Admission Prices: Tues.-Sat. 10-4. Adults $3, children 5-12 $2 (with parent or guardian); Friends of Garvies Point Museum & Preserve members no charge. Closed holidays. &

HOLOCAUST MEMORIAL AND TOLERANCE CENTER, Welwyn Preserve, 100 Crescent Beach Rd., Glen Cove, NY 11542. Tel.: 516-571-8040. Facebook: Holocaust Memorial and Tolerance Center.
E-mail: info@hmtcli.org
Web Site: www.hmtcli.org
Key Personnel: Sr. Dir. Education & Community Affairs, Beth Lilach; Dir. Devel., Judy Vladimir.
Institution Type/Description: History Museum.
Hours & Admission Prices: Mon.-Fri. 10-4:30, Sat.-Sun. & holidays 12-4. No charge; donations accepted. Special Events: discounts to AAM & ICOM members. Closed major holidays. &
Attendance: 50,000 (estimated)

NORTH SHORE HISTORICAL MUSEUM, 140 Glen St., Glen Cove, NY 11542. Mailing Address: P.O. Box 217, Glen Cove, NY 11542-0217. Tel.: 516-801-1191. Fax: 516-656-9725.
E-mail: director@northshorehistoricalmuseum.org
Web Site: www.northshorehistoricalmuseum.org
Institution Type/Description: History Museum.
Hours & Admission Prices: Wed. 2-6, Sat. 11-3; groups by appointment. Adults $5, seniors 65 & over and youth 13-17 $4; members and children 12 & under no charge.

Glens Falls

THE CHAPMAN HISTORICAL MUSEUM, 348 Glen St., Glens Falls, NY 12801-3520. Tel.: 518-793-2826. Fax: 518-793-2831.
E-mail: director@chapmanmuseum.org
Web Site: chapmanmuseum.org
Key Personnel: Exec. Dir., Timothy Weidner; Cur., Jillian Mulder; Educator, Andrea Kinderman.
Institution Type/Description: Regional History Museum: housed in c.1868 Zopher Isaac DeLong House & attached Carriage House Gallery.
Hours & Admission Prices: Tues.-Sat. 10-4, Sun. 12-4. Adults $5, seniors 65 & over and students $4; children under 12 & members no charge. Closed major holidays. &
Attendance: 15,000 (actual)

THE HYDE COLLECTION, 161 Warren St., Glens Falls, NY 12801-4562. Tel.: 518-792-1761. Fax: 518-792-9197. Facebook; Instagram.
E-mail: adminassist@hydecollection.org
Web Site: www.hydecollection.org
Key Personnel: C.E.O., Norman Dascher, Jr.; Registrar & Collections Mgr., Barbara Bertucio; Membership, Chelsea Sears; Dir. Curatorial Affairs & Programming, Jonathan Canning; Cur. Museum Education & Programming, Jenny Hutchinson; Administrative Asst., Melissa Montgomery; Events Coord., Kayla Romanowski.
Institution Type/Description: Art Museum.
Hours & Admission Prices: Please see website for hours. Adults 18 & over $12, seniors 60 & over $10; students with ID, members, children under 13, veterans, and active duty military & their family no charge. Closed most national holidays. &
Attendance: 26,142 (actual)

WORLD AWARENESS CHILDREN'S MUSEUM, 89 Warren St., Glens Falls, NY 12801-4509. Tel.: 518-793-2773. Fax: 518-761-2071. Facebook: World Awareness Children's Museum.
E-mail: admin@worldchildrensmuseum.org
Web Site: www.worldchildrensmuseum.org
Key Personnel: Dir., Heather E. Hickland; Bd. Pres., Jane Thompson; Bd. Vice Pres., Lynn Shanks.
Institution Type/Description: Children's Museum.
Hours & Admission Prices: Thurs.-Sat. 9:30-5, Sun. 12-5. Admission $5; children under 3 no charge.

Glenville

EMPIRE STATE AEROSCIENCES MUSEUM, 250 Rudy Chase Dr., Glenville, NY 12302-7104. Tel.: 518-377-2191, ext. 10. Fax: 518-377-1959.
E-mail: esam@esam.org
Web Site: www.esam.org
Key Personnel: Pres. (V), James Liguori; Museum Shop Mgr., Joyce Newkirk.
Institution Type/Description: Aerosciences & Airplane Museum.
Hours & Admission Prices: Sept.-June Fri.-Sun. 10-4; other times by appointment. Adults $8, seniors & military $6, youth 6-16 $5; members & children under 6 no charge. Closed New Year's Day; Thanksgiving; Christmas. &
Attendance: 15,000 (estimated)

Gloversville

FULTON COUNTY MUSEUM, 237 N. Kingsboro Ave., Gloversville, NY 12078-1428. Mailing Address: P.O. Box 711, Gloversville, NY 12078-0711. Tel.: 518-725-2203.
E-mail: fultoncohist@frontier.com
Web Site: www.fultoncountymuseum.com
Key Personnel: Pres. (V), Mark Pollack; Suprv., Donna Terranova.
Institution Type/Description: Historical Society & Industrial Craft Museum: housed in Old Kingsborough School, located on the site of the original Kingsborough Academy built in 1831.

Hours & Admission Prices: May 20 to Columbus Day Thurs.-Sun. 12-4. No charge; donations accepted. Closed Independence Day. &

Attendance: 1,470 (actual)

Goshen

THE HARNESS RACING MUSEUM AND HALL OF FAME, 240 Main St., Goshen, NY 10924-2157. Tel.: 845-294-6330. Fax: 845-294-3463. Facebook: Harness Racing Museum & Hall of Fame.

E-mail: info@harnessmuseum.com

Web Site: www.harnessmuseum.com

Formerly: Trotting Horse Museum/Hall of Fame of the Trotter

Key Personnel: Dir., Janet Terhune; Pres., Lawrence S. DeVan.

Institution Type/Description: Sports Museum: housed in 1913 Tudor-styled stable located next to Historic Track.

Hours & Admission Prices: General Admission: no charge. Docent Guided Group Tours: $4. &

Attendance: 15,629 (actual)

Gouverneur

GOUVERNEUR HISTORICAL ASSOCIATION, 30 Church St., Gouverneur, NY 13642-1416. Tel.: 315-287-0570.

E-mail: gouverneurmuseum@centralny.twcbc.com

Web Site: gouverneurmuseum.com

Key Personnel: Pres. (V) & Cur. History & Acquisitions, Joseph Laurenza; Vice Pres., Jon Jackson; Treas., R. Joseph Weekes.

Institution Type/Description: Historical Society Museum: housed in 1890 Presbyterian Manse.

Hours & Admission Prices: Wed. & Sat. 1-3; other times by appointment. No charge; donations accepted. Closed New Year's Day; Christmas. &

Attendance: 1,093 (actual)

Grand Island

GRAND ISLAND HISTORICAL SOCIETY - RIVER LEA, Beaver Island State Park, Grand Island, NY 14072. Mailing Address: P.O. Box 135, Grand Island, NY 14072. Tel.: 716-773-3271.

E-mail: jodi@giecom.net

Web Site: www.isledegrande.com

Key Personnel: Pres. (V), C. Nestark.

Institution Type/Description: Historical Society Museum.

Hours & Admission Prices: By appointment. Park: entrance fee. River Lea: no charge.

Attendance: 500 (actual)

Granville

PEMBER MUSEUM OF NATURAL HISTORY, 33 W. Main St., Granville, NY 12832-1320. Tel.: 518-642-1515. Facebook.

E-mail: pember@roadrunner.com

Web Site: www.thepember.com

Key Personnel: Pres. (V), Mary J. King; Treas., Robert Tatko; Educator, Cur. & Museum Shop Mgr., Bernadette Hoffman.

Institution Type/Description: Natural History Museum, Nature Center & Conservation Area.

Hours & Admission Prices: Tues.-Fri. 1-5, Sat. 10-3. No charge; donations accepted. Closed holidays.

Attendance: 5,000 (actual)

SLATE VALLEY MUSEUM, 17 Water St., Granville, NY 12832-1316. Tel.: 518-642-1417. Fax: 518-642-1417.

E-mail: mail@slatevalleymuseum.org

Web Site: www.slatevalleymuseum.org

Key Personnel: Exec. Dir., Mary Lou Willits; Bd. Pres. (V), David P. Bridges; Treas., Gladys Frustaci; Asst. Dir. & Educator, Sarah Benway.

Institution Type/Description: History Museum.

Hours & Admission Prices: Tues.-Fri. 1-5, Sat. 10-4. Adults $5; discounts to ICOM & AAM members; members, children 12 & under and Slate company employees no charge. Closed New Year's Eve & Day; Independence Day; Thanksgiving; Christmas Eve & Day. &

Attendance: 7,000 (actual)

Great River

BAYARD CUTTING ARBORETUM, 440 Montauk Hwy., Great River, NY 11739. Mailing Address: P.O. Box 907, Great River,

NY 11739-0907. Tel.: 631-581-1002. Fax: 631-581-1031. Facebook: Bayard Cutting Arboretum.

E-mail: nelson.sterner@parks.ny.gov

Web Site: www.bayardcuttingarboretum.com

Key Personnel: Dir., Nelson Sterner; Dir. Grounds, John Krzyminski; Bd. Chm., Prof. Barbara Schaedler.

Institution Type/Description: Arboretum: located on 1886 National Register Historic Site.

Hours & Admission Prices: April-Oct. daily 10-5; Nov.-March daily 10-4. Buses: $35-$75, Car: $8; discounts to senior citizens & handicapped persons with New York State park passes.

Attendance: 150,000 (estimated)

Greece

GREECE HISTORICAL SOCIETY & MUSEUM, 595 Long Pond Rd., Greece, NY 14612. Mailing Address: P.O. Box 16249, Greece, NY 14616. Tel.: 585-225-7221. Facebook.

E-mail: greecehistoricalsociety@yahoo.com

Web Site: www.greecehistoricalsociety.org

Key Personnel: Pres. (V), Bill Sauers; Museum Shop Mgr., Wendy Peeck.

Institution Type/Description: Local Town Historical Society Museum: house built in 1870s.

Hours & Admission Prices: Museum: Sun. 1:30-4; tours by appointment. Office: Mon. 9:30-12:30. No charge; donations accepted. &

Attendance: 1,600 (estimated)

Greenport

EAST END SEAPORT MUSEUM AND MARINE FOUNDATION, 3rd St. at Ferry Dock, Greenport, NY 11944. Mailing Address: P.O. Box 624, Greenport, NY 11944-0624. Tel.: 631-477-2100. Fax: 631-477-0004.

E-mail: director@eastendseaport.org

Web Site: www.eastendseaport.org

Key Personnel: Chm. (V), Ron Breuer; Museum Shop Mgr., Mary Herrick.

Institution Type/Description: Maritime Museum: housed in c.1894 historic Long Island Railroad Station depicting maritime heritage & seaport history of Eastern Long Island.

Hours & Admission Prices: May 17-June Sat.-Sun. 11-5; July-Sept. Wed.-Mon. 11-5. Suggested Donation: $2. &

Attendance: 9,500 (actual)

RAILROAD MUSEUM OF LONG ISLAND, 440-4th St., Greenport, NY 11944-0726. Mailing Address: P.O. Box 726, Greenport, NY 11944-0726. Tel.: 631-727-7920 (Riverhead) & 477-0439 (Greenport). Fax: 631-765-2757. Facebook: Railroad Museum of Long Island.

E-mail: info@rmli.org

Web Site: www.rmli.org

Key Personnel: Pres., Don Fisher; Vice Pres., Dennis DeAngelis; Trustee, Dennis Harrington; Sec., James Werner; Treas., Al Schick; Museum Shop Mgr., Richard Horn.

Institution Type/Description: Railroad Museum.

Hours & Admission Prices: Riverhead: Memorial Day to Columbus Day Sat.-Sun. 10-4; Oct.-May Sat. 10-4. Greenport: Memorial Day to Oct. Sat.-Sun. 11-4. Adults $7, children 5-12 $4; discounts to NRHS members & active or veteran military with ID; children under 5 & members no charge. &

Attendance: 8,000 (estimated)

Greenwich

WASHINGTON COUNTY FAIR FARM MUSEUM, 392 Old Schuylerville Rd., Greenwich, NY 12834-4615. Tel.: 518-692-2464. Fax: 518-692-1021.

E-mail: markwashfair@aol.com

Web Site: washingtoncountyfair.com

Key Personnel: Fair Mgr., Mark St. Jacques, C.F.E.; Education, Joan Prouty.

Institution Type/Description: History Museum.

Hours & Admission Prices: May-Oct. call for schedule; other times by appointment. No charge; donations accepted. &

Attendance: 25,000 (estimated)

Hamburg

HAMBURG HISTORICAL SOCIETY - THE DUNN HOUSE, 5902 Gowanda State Rd., Hamburg, NY 14075. Mailing Address: P.O. Box 400, Hamburg, NY 14075-0400. Tel.: 716-646-6460.

Institution Type/Description: Historical Society Museum.

Hours & Admission Prices: Wed.-Thurs. 9:30-1:30; other times by appointment.

Hamilton

LONGYEAR MUSEUM OF ANTHROPOLOGY, Colgate Univ.,
13 Oak Dr., 116 Alumni Hall, Hamilton, NY 13346. Tel.: 315-228-
7184.
E-mail: longyear@colgate.edu
Web Site: www.colgate.edu/campus-life/ arts-on-campus/longyearmuseum
Key Personnel: Sr. Cur., Carol Ann Lorenz.
Institution Type/Description: History Museum.
Hours & Admission Prices: Academic Year: Mon.-Thurs. 9:30-4:30; other times by
appointment.

THE PICKER ART GALLERY, Colgate University, 13 Oak Dr.,
Hamilton, NY 13346-1398. Tel.: 315-228-7634. Fax: 315-228-
7932.
E-mail: pickerart@colgate.edu
Web Site: www.colgate.edu/picker
Key Personnel: Dir., Anja Chavez; Educator, Melissa Davies; Registrar, Sarisha
Guarneiri; Administrative Asst., Jasmine Kellogg; Senior Cur. Collections, Jill
Shaw; Curatorial Asst., Sarah Horowitz; Preparator, Aaron Kakos.
Institution Type/Description: Art Gallery.
Hours & Admission Prices: No charge. See website for hours. &
Attendance: 5,187 (actual)

Hammondsport

GLENN H. CURTISS MUSEUM, 8419 State Rte. 54,
Hammondsport, NY 14840-9795. Tel.: 607-569-2160. Fax: 607-
569-2040.
E-mail: info@glennhcurtissmuseum.org
Web Site: www.glennhcurtissmuseum.org
Key Personnel: C.E.O. & Dir., Trafford L. Doherty; Pres., Richard Honeyman;
Cur., Rick Leisenring; Museum Shop Mgr., Lynne Mason.
Institution Type/Description: Aviation & Local History Museum.
Hours & Admission Prices: June-Oct. Mon.-Sat. 9-5, Sun. 10-5; Nov.-May daily
10-4. Adults $8.50, senior citizens $7, students $5.50; discounts to groups of 10
or more & AAA members; children 6 & under and members no charge. Closed
New Year's Day; Easter; Thanksgiving; Christmas. &
Attendance: 25,000 (estimated)

THE WINE MUSEUM OF GREYTON H. TAYLOR, 8843
Greyton H. Taylor Memorial Dr., Hammondsport, NY 14840-
9635. Mailing Address: P.O. Box 458, Hammondsport, NY 14840-
0458. Tel.: 607-868-4814 & 3610. Fax: 607-868-3205.
E-mail: info@bullyhill.com
Web Site: www.bullyhill.com
Key Personnel: Pres., Lillian Taylor; Dir. & Museum Shop Mgr., Paul N. Sprague.
Institution Type/Description: Technology Museum: housed in 1880 Greyton H.
Taylor Wine building.
Hours & Admission Prices: Daily 11-5. No charge; donations requested. &
Attendance: 6,500 (estimated)

Harpursville

OLD ONAQUAGA HISTORICAL SOCIETY, 42 Maple St.,
Harpursville, NY 13787. Mailing Address: P.O. Box 318,
Harpursville, NY 13787-0318. Tel.: 607-775-1190.
Key Personnel: Pres., Eileen Rugieri; Historian-Colesville, Val La Clair.
Institution Type/Description: History Museum: housed in 1828 Episcopal Church.
Hours & Admission Prices: May-Oct. 2nd Sun. 2-5; other times by appointment.
No charge; donations accepted from non-Colesville residents.
Attendance: 450 (estimated)

Hastings-on-Hudson

HASTINGS HISTORICAL SOCIETY, 407 Broadway, Hastings-
on-Hudson, NY 10706. Tel.: 914-478-2249.
E-mail: hhscottage@hastingshistorical.org
Key Personnel: Pres. (V), Natalie Barry; Archivist, Muriel Olsson.
Institution Type/Description: Historical Society Museum: housed in the former
Henry Draper observatory.
Hours & Admission Prices: July-Aug. Mon. & Thurs. 10-2; Sept.-June 1st Sat. each
month 2-4; other times by appointment. No charge; donations accepted.

UPSTREAM GALLERY, 8 Main St., Hastings-on-Hudson, NY
10706. Tel.: 914-674-8548.
E-mail: upstreamgallery26@gmail.com
Web Site: upstreamgallery.com
Institution Type/Description: Art Gallery.

Hours & Admission Prices: April-Oct. Thurs.-Fri. 12:30-5:30, Sat.-Sun. 10-5:30;
Nov.-March Thurs.-Sun. 12:30-5:30.

Hempstead

AFRICAN AMERICAN MUSEUM OF NASSAU COUNTY, 110
N. Franklin St., Hempstead, NY 11550-3029. Tel.: 516-572-0730.
Fax: 516-572-0732.
E-mail: taags.aam@gmail.com
Web Site: www.theamuseum.org
Formerly: Black History Exhibit Center
Key Personnel: Chm. (V), Joysetta Pearse; Pres. (V), Julius O. Pearse; Art Dir.,
Fatimah White; Cur., Minna Dunn; Receptionist, Dementria Jones.
Institution Type/Description: African American Museum.
Hours & Admission Prices: Tues.-Sat. 10-5. Adults $5. &
Attendance: 5,583 (actual)

HOFSTRA UNIVERSITY MUSEUM, 112 Hofstra University,
Hempstead, NY 11549-1120. Tel.: 516-463-5672. Fax: 516-463-
4743.
E-mail: beth.e.levinthal@hofstra.edu
Web Site: www.hofstra.edu/museum
Key Personnel: Exec. Dir., Beth E. Levinthal; Dir. Museum Education, Nancy
Richner; Assoc. Dir. Exhibitions & Collections, Karen Albert; Public Rels.,
Ginny Greenberg; Coord. Devel. & Membership, Tiffany Jordan.
Institution Type/Description: Art Museum.
Hours & Admission Prices: Tues.-Fri. 11-4, Sat.-Sun. 12-4. No charge; donations
accepted. Closed Independence Day; Thanksgiving Recess; Christmas Recess;
all university recesses. &
Attendance: 25,301 (actual)

Herkimer

HERKIMER COUNTY HISTORICAL SOCIETY, 400 N. Main
St., Herkimer, NY 13350-1955. Tel.: 315-866-6413. Facebook:
Herkimer County Historical Society.
E-mail: herkimerhistory@yahoo.com
Web Site: www.rootsweb.ancestry.com/~nyhchs/
Key Personnel: Pres., Kathleen Huxtable; Exec. Dir., Susan R. Perkins;
Administrative Asst., Caryl Hopson; Dir. Outreach, Russeen Young.
Institution Type/Description: Local History Museum.
Hours & Admission Prices: July-Aug. Mon.-Fri. 10-4, Sat. 10-3; Sept.-June Mon.-
Fri. 10-4. No charge; donations accepted. Closed Mon. in Jan & Feb. and
national holidays. &
Attendance: 4,000 (estimated)

Hicksville

THE HICKSVILLE GREGORY MUSEUM, 1 Heitz Place,
Hicksville, NY 11801-3101. Tel.: 516-822-7505. Fax: 516-822-
3227.
E-mail: mail@gregorymuseum.org
Web Site: gregorymuseum.org
Key Personnel: Pres., Richard Althaus; Cur. & Museum Shop Mgr., Donald Curran.
Institution Type/Description: Earth Science Museum.
Hours & Admission Prices: Tues.-Fri. 9:30-4:30, Sat.-Sun. 1-5. Adults $5, students
& senior citizens $3; members no charge. Closed major holidays. &
Attendance: 6,000 (estimated)

High Falls

**DELAWARE AND HUDSON CANAL HISTORICAL SOCIETY
AND MUSEUM,** 23 Mohonk Rd., High Falls, NY 12440. Mailing
Address: P.O. Box 23, High Falls, NY 12440-0023. Tel.: 845-687-
9311. Fax: 845-687-9311. Facebook: DH Canal Museum.
E-mail: info@canalmuseum.org
Web Site: www.canalmuseum.org
Key Personnel: Pres., Bill Merchant.
Institution Type/Description: Transportation Museum: housed in 1885 Episcopal
Church.
Hours & Admission Prices: May-Oct. Sat.-Sun. 11-5. Adults $5, children under 12
$2; members no charge. &
Attendance: 1,000 (estimated)

Hogansburg

AKWESASNE MUSEUM, 321 State Rte. 37, Hogansburg, NY
13655-3114. Tel.: 518-358-2240 & 2461. Fax: 518-358-2649.
E-mail: akwmuse@northnet.org
Web Site: www.akwesasneculturalcenter.org

Key Personnel: C.E.O., Glory Cole; Pres. (V), Irving Papineau; Museum Shop Mgr., Sue Ellen Herne.

Institution Type/Description: Cultural Center.

Hours & Admission Prices: Mon.-Fri. 9-4, Sat. by appointment; guided tours by appointment only. Adults $2, children $1; Native Americans & children 5 & under no charge. Closed all major holidays. ♿

Attendance: 2,034 (actual)

Homer

HOMEVILLE ANTIQUE FIRE DEPARTMENT MUSEUM, 32 Center St., Homer, NY 13077. Tel.: 607-749-4466.

Institution Type/Description: Firefighting History Museum.

Hours & Admission Prices: Call for hours.

Hoosick Falls

BENNINGTON BATTLEFIELD STATE HISTORIC SITE, 30 Caretaker's Rd., Hoosick Falls, NY 12090-4801. Tel.: 518-860-9094 & 686-7109. Fax: 518-279-1902. Facebook.

E-mail: david.pitlyk@parks.ny.gov

Web Site: www.nysparks.state.ny.us

Key Personnel: Historic Site Asst., David Pitlyk; Pres. Friends of Bennington Battlefield, Peter Schaaphok.

Institution Type/Description: Historic Site: 1777 Revolutionary War battle site includes monuments to participating states, map of actual battle & panorama display of the battle site.

Hours & Admission Prices: May to mid-Nov. daily 8am to sunset. ♿

Attendance: 19,066 (actual)

LOUIS MILLER MUSEUM - HOOSICK TOWNSHIP HISTORICAL SOCIETY, 166 Main St., P.O. Box 536, Hoosick Falls, NY 12090. Tel.: 518-686-4682.

E-mail: staff@hoosickhistory.com

Web Site: www.hoosickhistory.com

Key Personnel: Dir., Charles Filkins.

Institution Type/Description: History Museum.

Hours & Admission Prices: Mon.-Fri. 11-3; other times by appointment.

Hornell

HORNELL ERIE DEPOT RAILROAD MUSEUM, 82 Main St., Hornell, NY 14843. Tel.: 607-324-7421. Fax: 607-324-3150.

E-mail: historian@cityofhornell.com

Web Site: www.hornellny.us/museum.htm

Key Personnel: Chm. (V), Gene Baker; Pres. (V), Doug Smith; Coord. Collections, Collette Cornish.

Institution Type/Description: History Museum.

Hours & Admission Prices: Wed.-Fri. 6pm-8pm, Sat. 12:30-3. No charge; donations accepted.

Attendance: 1,000 (estimated)

Horseheads

HORSEHEADS HISTORICAL SOCIETY MUSEUM AT THE DEPOT, 312 W. Broad St., Horseheads, NY 14845. Tel.: 607-739-3938.

E-mail: info@horseheadshistorical.org

Web Site: www.horseheadshistorical.com

Key Personnel: Pres. (V), Richard Margeson.

Institution Type/Description: Historical Society Museum: housed in the former railroad depot; built in 1866.

Hours & Admission Prices: April-Dec. Tues., Thurs. & Sat. 12-3; other times by appointment. No charge. ♿

Attendance: 1,000 (estimated)

WINGS OF EAGLES DISCOVERY CENTER, 339 Daniel Zenker Dr., Horseheads, NY 14845-1102. Tel.: 607-358-4247. Fax: 607-358-4248. Facebook: Wings of Eagles Discovery Center.

E-mail: bbenza@wingsofeagles.com

Web Site: www.wingsofeagles.com

Formerly: National Warplane Museum

Key Personnel: C.E.O. & Pres., Michael S. Hall; Chm. (V) & Museum Shop Mgr., Brenda Benza; Pres. (V), Donald Keddell; Dir. Restoration, Ed Knitter; Cur., Edward Flesch.

Institution Type/Description: Aviation & Aerospace Museum.

Hours & Admission Prices: Tues.-Sat. 10-4. Adults $7, senior citizens $5.50, children 6-17 $4; discounts to military, Women in Aviation, families, AAM, ICOM,

ASTC & AAA members; children under 6 & members no charge. Closed New Year's Day; Easter; Thanksgiving; Christmas. ♿

Attendance: 80,000 (estimated)

ZIM'S HOUSE, HORSEHEADS HISTORICAL SOCIETY, 601 Pine St., Horseheads, NY 14845. Mailing Address: Horseheads Historical Society, 312 W. Broad St., Horseheads, NY 14845. Tel.: 607-739-3938.

E-mail: rmargeson1@yahoo.com

Web Site: www.horseheadshistorical.com

Key Personnel: Pres. (V), Richard Margeson.

Institution Type/Description: Historic House Museum: housed in the former home of political caricaturist of the late 1800s & early 1900s, Eugene Zimmerman. Listed on the National Register of Historic Places.

Hours & Admission Prices: By appointment. No charge.

Attendance: 200 (estimated)

Howes Cave

IROQUOIS INDIAN MUSEUM, 324 Caverns Rd., Howes Cave, NY 12092. Mailing Address: P.O. Box 7, Howes Cave, NY 12092-0007. Tel.: 518-296-8949. Fax: 518-296-8955. Facebook.

E-mail: info@iroquoismuseum.org

Web Site: www.iroquoismuseum.org

Key Personnel: Dir., Stephanie Shultes; Chair & Pres., Christina Hanks.

Institution Type/Description: Anthropology Museum & Site: focus on Iroquois art and culture.

Hours & Admission Prices: April & Nov. Thurs.-Sat. 10-4, Sun. 12-4; May-Oct. Tues.-Sat. 10-5, Sun. 12-5. Adults $8, seniors & youths 13-17 $6.50, children 5-12 $5; discounts to groups, AAM & ICOM members; children under 5 & members no charge. Closed Easter; Thanksgiving; Christmas Eve & Day. ♿

Attendance: 8,000 (actual)

Hudson

FASNY MUSEUM OF FIRE FIGHTING, 117 Harry Howard Ave., Hudson, NY 12534-1601. Tel.: 518-822-1875, ext. 11. Fax: 518-822-8520.

E-mail: jamie@fasnyfiremuseum.com

Web Site: www.fasnyfiremuseum.org

Formerly: American Museum of Fire Fighting

Key Personnel: Pres. Bd. Dirs., Evan Schlem; Vice Pres., Neal Van Deusen; Dir., Jamie Smith Quinn; Museum Shop Mgr., Lori Decker.

Institution Type/Description: Fire-Fighting Antiques Museum.

Hours & Admission Prices: Daily 10-5. Family $20, adults $7, children 3 & over $5; museum, FASNY, NARM & ESRP members and children 2 & under no charge. Closed major holidays. ♿

Attendance: 30,000 (actual)

OLANA STATE HISTORIC SITE, 5720 Rte. 9-G, Hudson, NY 12534. Tel.: 518-828-0135. Fax: 518-828-6742.

E-mail: linda.mclean@oprhp.state.ny.us

Web Site: www.olana.org; www.nysparks.com

Key Personnel: Dir. Olana State Historic Site, Linda E. McLean; Dir. Education, Carri L. Manchester; Chief Cur., Evelyn Trebilcock; Assoc. Cur., Valerie Balint; Archivist & Librarian, Ida Brier; Historic Site Asst., Roberta Bennett; Maintenance Chief, Timothy Dodge; Pres. Olana Partnership, Sara Griffen; Chm. (V) The Olana Partnership, Richard Sharp; Chm. (V), Susan Eastman; Vice Pres. Devel. of The Olana Partnership, Bob Burns; Public Rels. & Admin. Olana Partnership, Nelson Sterner; Museum Shop Mgr., Rachel Patton.

Institution Type/Description: Historic House: 1870 Persian style villa residence of 19th-century landscape artist, Frederic E. Church.

Hours & Admission Prices: Grounds: daily 8 to sunset. House Tours: April to late Nov. Tues.-Sun. & Mon. holidays 10-5; late Nov. to March Fri.-Sun. 11-4; groups by appointment. Standard House Tour: adults $9, seniors & students $8; children under 12 no charge. Second Floor & Gallery: adults $9, seniors & students $8; children under 12 no charge. Combined House & Second Floor: adults $12, seniors & students $10; members of the Olana Partnership no charge. Vehicle Fee: May-Oct. Sat.-Sun. $5. Closed New Year's Day; Easter; Thanksgiving; Christmas. ♿

Attendance: 33,495 (actual)

PARKER-O'MALLEY AIR MUSEUM, 435 Old Rte. 20, Hudson, NY 12075. Mailing Address: P.O. Box 216, Ghent, NY 12075-0216. Tel.: 518-392-7200. Fax: 518-392-2227.

E-mail: jmcmahon@parkeromalley.org

Key Personnel: C.E.O., James E. McMahon.

Institution Type/Description: Aeronautics Museum.

Hours & Admission Prices: By appointment only. Adults $5, children $3. ♿

Huntington

DAVID CONKLIN FARMHOUSE, 2 High St., Huntington, NY 11743-3416. Mailing Address: 209 Main St., Huntington, NY 11743-6907. Tel.: 631-427-7045. Fax: 631-427-7056.
E-mail: rkissam@huntingtonhistoricalsociety.org
Web Site: www.huntingtonhistoricalsociety.org
Key Personnel: Exec. Coord., Robert "Toby" Kissam; Pres. (V), Carl Lawrence.
Institution Type/Description: Historic Site.
Hours & Admission Prices: Fri. & Sun. 1-4; other times by appointment. Adults $5, students & seniors $3; discounts to AAM members; children under 5 & museum members no charge. Closed holidays. &
Attendance: 10,500 (estimated)

DR. DANIEL W. KISSAM HOUSE, 434 Park Ave., Huntington, NY 11743. Mailing Address: 209 Main St., Huntington, NY 11743-6907. Tel.: 631-427-7045. Fax: 631-427-7056.
E-mail: rkissam@huntingtonhistoricalsociety.org
Web Site: www.huntingtonhistoricalsociety.org
Formerly: Kissam House
Key Personnel: Exec. Coord., Robert "Toby" Kissam; Pres. (V), Carl Lawrence.
Institution Type/Description: Historic House: c.1795 Federal shingled house with added c.1830 kitchen wing.
Hours & Admission Prices: Sun. 1-4. Adults $5, children under 12 $3; discounts to AAM members; members no charge. Closed New Year's Day; Easter; Thanksgiving; Christmas. &
Attendance: 10,500 (estimated)

THE HECKSCHER MUSEUM OF ART, 2 Prime Ave., Huntington, NY 11743-7702. Tel.: 631-351-3250. Fax: 631-423-2145.
E-mail: info@heckscher.org
Web Site: www.heckscher.org
Key Personnel: Chm., Beverly J. Bell; Exec. Dir. & C.E.O., Michael W. Schantz, Ph.D.; Cur., Lisa Chalif; Registrar, Andrew Schaeffer; Dir. Education, Joy Weiner; Office Mgr., Nancy O'Brien; Dir. Devel., Deborah Johnson.
Institution Type/Description: Art Museum: building built in 1920.
Hours & Admission Prices: Wed.-Fri. 10-5, 1st Fri. each month 5-8:30, Sat.-Sun. 11-5. Adults $8, seniors 62 & over $6, students 10 & over $5; discount to AAM members & Huntington residents; active military, veterans & their family, children under 10 & members no charge. Closed Thanksgiving; Christmas. &
Attendance: 20,862 (actual)

HUNTINGTON SEWING & TRADE SCHOOL, 209 Main St., Huntington, NY 11743-6907. Tel.: 631-427-7045. Fax: 516-427-7056.
E-mail: cmaguire@huntingtonhistoricalsociety.org
Web Site: www.huntingtonhistoricalsociety.org
Key Personnel: Exec. Dir., Carol A. Maguire; Pres. (V), Kevin Arloff.
Institution Type/Description: Historical Building: c.1905, 2 1/2 story Jacobean Revival Trade School designed by Cady, Berg & See.
Hours & Admission Prices: Office: Mon.-Fri. 9:30-5. Archives & Library: Wed.-Thurs. 1-4. Adult $4; discounts to AAM members; members no charge. Call for special exhibit fees. Closed New Year's Day; Easter; Thanksgiving; Christmas. &
Attendance: 10,500 (estimated)

SOLDIERS & SAILORS MEMORIAL BUILDING, 228 Main St., Huntington, NY 11743-6915. Tel.: 631-427-7045. Fax: 631-427-7056.
E-mail: rkissam@huntingtonhistoricalsociety.org
Web Site: www.huntingtonhistoricalsociety.org
Formerly: Huntington Historical Society
Key Personnel: Exec. Coord., Robert "Toby" Kissam; Pres. (V), Carl Lawrence.
Institution Type/Description: History Museum: housed in 1892 Civil War Memorial building & 1st community library.
Hours & Admission Prices: Call for hours.
Attendance: 12,000 (estimated)

Huntington Station

WALT WHITMAN BIRTHPLACE STATE HISTORIC SITE AND INTERPRETIVE CENTER, 246 Old Walt Whitman Rd., Huntington Station, NY 11746-4148. Tel.: 631-427-5240. Fax: 631-427-5247. Facebook.
E-mail: director@waltwhitman.org
Web Site: www.waltwhitman.org
Key Personnel: Exec. Dir. & Public Rels., Cynthia Shor; Pres. (V), William T. Walter, Ph.D.; Archivist, Richard A. Ryan.

Institution Type/Description: Historic House: c.1810 birthplace & early home of Walt Whitman, born in 1819.
Hours & Admission Prices: Summer: Mon.-Fri. 11-4, Sat.-Sun. 11-5; Winter: Wed.-Fri. 1-4, Sat.-Sun. 11-4. Adults $6, senior citizens, veterans & children under 18 $5, college students $4; discounts to AAM & ICOM members; members and children 5 & under no charge. Closed New Year's Day; Easter; Thanksgiving; Christmas. &
Attendance: 8,000 (actual)

Hurleyville

SULLIVAN COUNTY HISTORICAL SOCIETY, INC., 265 Main St., Hurleyville, NY 12747-0247. Mailing Address: P.O. Box 247, Hurleyville, NY 12747-0247. Tel.: 845-434-8044.
E-mail: schs@sullivancountyhistory.org
Web Site: www.sullivancountyhistory.org
Key Personnel: Pres. (V), Suzanne Cecil; Finance Officer, Judy Wolkoff; Genealogy, Suzanne Cecil; Cur. & Archivist, Arthur Hessinger; Museum Shop Mgr., W.F. Burns.
Institution Type/Description: Historical Society Museum.
Hours & Admission Prices: Museum: Tues.-Sat. 10-4:30, Sun. 1-4:30. No charge; donations accepted; Archives: Wed. 10-4:30. Modest fee for extended genealogical research; veterans & spouses no charge. Closed New Year's Day; Thanksgiving; Christmas. &
Attendance: 8,500 (actual)

Hyde Park

ELEANOR ROOSEVELT NATIONAL HISTORIC SITE, 54 Val Kill Park Rd., Hyde Park, NY 12538-1917. Tel.: 877-444-6777. Fax: 845-229-0739.
E-mail: scott_rector@nps.gov
Web Site: www.nps.gov/elro/
Key Personnel: Museum Shop Mgr., Anne Meisner.
Institution Type/Description: Historic House: Val-Kill, home of Eleanor Roosevelt from 1945-1962.
Hours & Admission Prices: May-Oct. Thurs.-Mon. 9-5; Nov.-April Thurs.-Mon. 1 & 3. Adults $10; children under 15 no charge. Reservation for tours call 800-967-2283. Closed New Year's Day; Thanksgiving; Christmas. &
Attendance: 58,000 (actual)

FRANKLIN D. ROOSEVELT PRESIDENTIAL LIBRARY-MUSEUM, 4079 Albany Post Rd., Hyde Park, NY 12538-1999. Tel.: 800-337-8474, 845-486-7770. Fax: 845-486-1147. Facebook, YouTube, Twitter.
E-mail: roosevelt.library@nara.gov
Web Site: www.fdrlibrary.marist.edu
Key Personnel: Dir., Paul Sparrow; Supervisory Cur., Herman Eberhardt; Supervisory Archivist, Kirsten Carter; Education Specialist, Jeff Urbin; Public Affairs Specialist, Cliff Laube; Museum Store Mgr., Amy Northup.
Institution Type/Description: Presidential Library.
Hours & Admission Prices: April-Oct. daily 9-6; Nov.-March daily 9-5. Combination Museum & Roosevelt Home: adults $18; discounts to Senior Pass, Access Pass, Annual Pass for U.S. Military; children 16 & under and school groups no charge. Closed New Year's Day; Thanksgiving; Christmas. &
Attendance: 175,000 (actual)

HOME OF FRANKLIN D. ROOSEVELT NATIONAL HISTORIC SITE, 4097 Albany Post Rd., Hyde Park, NY 12538. Tel.: 845-229-9115. Fax: 845-229-7115.
E-mail: scott_rector@nps.gov
Web Site: www.nps.gov/hofr
Key Personnel: Supt., Sarah Olson.
Institution Type/Description: Historic House: Hudson River home of F.D.R.
Hours & Admission Prices: Daily 9-5. Adults $18 (includes admission to the FDR Presidential Library & Museum); discounts to Golden Age Passport & National Park Pass holders; children under 15 & school groups no charge. Reservation required for motorcoach tours & school groups, call 800-967-2283. Closed New Year's Day; Thanksgiving; Christmas. &
Attendance: 105,000 (actual)

VANDERBILT MANSION NATIONAL HISTORIC SITE, 119 Vanderbilt Park Rd., Hyde Park, NY 12538. Mailing Address: 4097 Albany Post Rd., Hyde Park, NY 12538-1917. Tel.: 800-337-8474. Fax: 845-229-0739.
Web Site: www.nps.gov/vama
Key Personnel: Supt., Sarah Olson; Museum Shop Mgr., Anne Meisner.
Institution Type/Description: Historic House Museum: 1896-1899 Beaux-Arts style Mansion, designed by McKim, Mead, & White.

Hours & Admission Prices: Tours: May-Oct. daily 9:15, 10, 11, 12, 1, 2, 3, & 4; Nov.-April daily 10, 12, 2, 4. Adults $10; discounts to National Park Golden Age & Access card holders; children 15 & under and school groups no charge. Closed New Year's Day; Thanksgiving; Christmas. &
Attendance: 359,000 (actual)

Ilion

REMINGTON FIREARMS MUSEUM AND COUNTRY STORE, 14 Hoefler Ave., Ilion, NY 13357-1888. Tel.: 315-895-3200 & 3301. Fax: 315-895-3543.
E-mail: sheila.claus@remington.com
Web Site: www.remington.com
Key Personnel: Cur. & Archives Coord., Fred Supry; Museum Shop Mgr., John Balio.
Institution Type/Description: Firearms Museum.
Hours & Admission Prices: Mon.-Fri. 8:30-4:30, closed 12:00-1:00. Closed two weeks annually for maintenance as well as all major holidays. Call 315-895-3200 for more information. &
Attendance: 50,000 (estimated)

Interlaken

INTERLAKEN HISTORICAL SOCIETY, Main St., Interlaken, NY 14847. Mailing Address: P.O. Box 270, Interlaken, NY 14847-0270. Tel.: 607-532-4213.
E-mail: orchardland@zoom-dsl.com
Web Site: www.interlakenhistory.org
Key Personnel: Pres. (V), Diane Bassette Nelson; Vice Pres., Bill Schaffner; Sec., Ann Buddle; Treas., Karen King.
Institution Type/Description: Historical Society & Farmers Museum: housed in 1826 Lockwood Hinman House and relocated grain cradle factory.
Hours & Admission Prices: July-Aug. Sun. 1-3, Sat. 10-1; other times by appointment. No charge; donations accepted. &
Attendance: 400 (estimated)

Irvington

IRVINGTON HISTORICAL SOCIETY & HISTORY CENTER - THE MCVICKAR HOUSE, 131 Main St., Irvington, NY 10533. Mailing Address: P.O. Box 23, Irvington, NY 10533-0023. Tel.: 914-591-1020.
E-mail: comments@irvingtonhistoricalsociety.org
Web Site: www.irvingtonhistoricalsociety.org
Institution Type/Description: Historical Society Museum: housed in the former home of Rev. William McVickar, first rector of the Church of St. Barnabas; built in 1853. Listed on the National Register of Historic Places.
Hours & Admission Prices: Thurs. & Sat. 1-4. No charge. &

Ithaca

CORNELL PLANTATIONS, One Plantations Rd., Ithaca, NY 14850-2799. Tel.: 607-255-2400. Fax: 607-255-2404.
E-mail: plantations@cornell.edu
Web Site: www.cornellplantations.org
Key Personnel: Dir., Christopher Dunn; Dir. Education, Sonja Skelly; Dir. Devel., Beth Anderson.
Institution Type/Description: Botanical Garden, Arboretum, Natural Preserves.
Hours & Admission Prices: Daily sunrise-sunset. Guided tours by appointment. No charge; donations accepted.
Attendance: 60,000 (estimated)

HANDWERKER GALLERY, 1170 Gannett Center, Ithaca College, Ithaca, NY 14850-7276. Tel.: 607-274-3018. Facebook.
E-mail: mbaldwin@ithaca.edu
Web Site: www.ithaca.edu/handwerker
Key Personnel: Dir., Mara Baldwin.
Institution Type/Description: Art Gallery & College Museum.
Hours & Admission Prices: Mon., Wed. & Fri. 10-6, Thurs. 10-9, Sat. -Sun. 12-5. No charge. Closed vacation breaks. &
Attendance: 8,900 (estimated)

HERBERT F. JOHNSON MUSEUM OF ART, Cornell University, Ithaca, NY 14853. Mailing Address: 114 Central Ave., Ithaca, NY 14853. Tel.: 607-255-6464. Fax: 607-255-9940. Facebook, Twitter, Instagram.
E-mail: museum@cornell.edu
Web Site: www.museum.cornell.edu
Key Personnel: Dir., Stephanie L. Wiles; Chm. (V), Gary Davis; Assoc. Dir. Finance Admin., Peter Gould; Chief Cur. & Cur. Asian Art, Ellen Avril; Cur.

Prints & Drawings 1800-1945, Nancy Green; Cur. Modern & Contemporary Art, Andrea Inselmann; Ames Assoc. Dir. & Cur. Education, Cathy Klimaszewski; Coord. School & Children's Programs, Carol Hockett; Registrar, Matthew Conway; Chief of Security, Holly Fairlie; Chief Preparator, David Ryan; Dir. Devel., Matt Braun; Editorial Mgr., Andrea Potochniak; Cur. Earlier European & American Art, Andrew Weislogel.
Institution Type/Description: Art Museum.
Hours & Admission Prices: Tues.-Sun. 10-5. No charge; donations accepted. Closed Memorial Day; Independence Day; Labor Day; Thanksgiving; Christmas to New Year's Day. &
Attendance: 89,000 (estimated)

THE HISTORY CENTER IN TOMPKINS COUNTY, 401 E. State St., Ste. 100, Ithaca, NY 14850-4400. Tel.: 607-273-8284. Facebook: The History Center in Tompkins County.
E-mail: director@thehistorycenter.net
Web Site: www.thehistorycenter.net
Formerly: DeWitt Historical Society of Tompkins County & Tompkins County Museum
Key Personnel: Exec. Dir., Rod Howe; Pres. Bd. (V), Gwen Seaquist; Photographer, Carl Koski; Visitor Svcs. Mgr., Ksenia Ionova; Archivist, Donna Eschenbrenner; Elementary Education, Carole West.
Institution Type/Description: Historical Society Museum.
Hours & Admission Prices: Tues., Thurs. & Sat. 11-5. Museum: no charge; donations accepted. Research Library: call for fees. See website for days closed. &
Attendance: 15,000 (estimated)

L.H. BAILEY HORTORIUM, 412 Mann Library, Cornell University, Ithaca, NY 14853-4301. Tel.: 607-255-2131. Fax: 607-255-5407.
E-mail: wlc1@cornell.edu
Web Site: www.plantbio.cornell.edu
Key Personnel: Chm. & Professor, William Crepet; Assoc. Professor, Melissa Luckow; Professor, David M. Bates; Professor, Eloy Rodriguez; Adjunct Professor, James L. Reveal; Assoc. Professor & Cur., Kevin C. Nixon; Assoc. Professor, Jerrold I. Davis; Professor, Jeffrey J. Doyle; Assoc. Cur., Anna M. Stalter; Asst. Cur. & Librarian, Peter Fraissinet.
Institution Type/Description: Horticulture & Botanical Museum.
Hours & Admission Prices: Mon.-Fri. 9-5. No charge. Closed national holidays. &
Attendance: 1,000 (estimated)

MCGRAW HALL MUSEUM AND ANTHROPOLOGY COLLECTIONS, 150 McGraw Hall, Cornell University, Ithaca, NY 14853-4601. Tel.: 607-254-8688. Facebook: @anthrocollects.
E-mail: f.gleach@cornell.edu
Web Site: anthrocollections.library.cornell.edu/about
Key Personnel: Cur., Frederic W. Gleach.
Institution Type/Description: Anthropology Museum.
Hours & Admission Prices: Call for hours.
Attendance: 500 (estimated)

MUSEUM OF THE EARTH, 1259 Trumansburg Rd., Ithaca, NY 14850-1398. Tel.: 607-273-6623, ext. 26. Fax: 607-273-6620.
E-mail: marketing@museumoftheearth.org
Web Site: www.museumoftheearth.org
Formerly: Museum of the Earth and Cayuga Nature Center
Key Personnel: Dir., Dr. Warren D. Allmon; Dir. Exhibits, Beth Stricker; Assoc. Dir. Institutional Advancement, Elizabeth Brando; Dir. Collections, Greg Dietl; Assoc. Dir. Science, Paula Mikkelsen; Assoc. Dir. Outreach, Robert Ross; Chm. (V), Linda Irany; Museum Shop Mgr., Alicia Michael.
Institution Type/Description: Natural History Museum.
Hours & Admission Prices: Memorial Day to Labor Day Mon.-Sat. 10-5, Sun. 11-5; Sept.-May Mon. & Thurs.-Sat. 10-5, Sun. 11-5. Adults $8, seniors & college students $5, children 4-17 $3; discounts to ASTC members; members and children 3 & under no charge. Closed New Year's Day; Thanksgiving; Christmas. &
Attendance: 30,000 (estimated)

SCIENCENTER, 601 First St., Ithaca, NY 14850-3507. Tel.: 607-272-0600. Fax: 607-277-7469.
E-mail: info@sciencenter.org
Web Site: www.sciencenter.org
Key Personnel: Exec. Dir., Charles H. Trautmann; Deputy Dir., Tim Scott; Dir. Guest Rels. & Operations, Josh Giblin; Dir. Education, Michelle Kortenaar; Exhibits Mgr., Robin Burlingham; Finance Dir., Chris Fagan.
Institution Type/Description: Science & Technology Museum.
Hours & Admission Prices: July-Aug. Mon.-Sat. 10-5, Sun. 12-5; Sept.-June Tues.-Sat. 10-5, Sun. 12-5. Adults $8, senior citizens $7, children 3-17 $6; discount to AAM members; members, reciprocal ASTC & ACM members; children under 3 & members no charge. Closed New Year's Day; Thanksgiving; Christmas. &
Attendance: 100,000 (actual)

Jamaica

JAMAICA CENTER FOR ARTS & LEARNING (JCAL), 161-04 Jamaica Ave., Jamaica, NY 11432-6112. Tel.: 718-658-7400, ext. 123. Fax: 718-658-7922.
E-mail: info@jcal.org
Web Site: www.jcal.org
Key Personnel: Exec. Dir., Cathy Hung.
Institution Type/Description: Multidisciplinary Art Center.
Hours & Admission Prices: Galleries: Mon.-Sat. 10-6. No charge; donations accepted. Closed major national holidays. &
Attendance: 35,000 (estimated)

KING MANOR MUSEUM, 150-03 Jamaica Ave., King Park, Jamaica, NY 11432. Mailing Address: 9004 161st St., Ste. 704, Jamaica, NY 11432-6101. Tel.: 718-206-0545. Fax: 718-206-0541.
E-mail: nwilliams@kingmanor.org
Web Site: www.kingmanor.org
Key Personnel: C.E.O., Nadezhda Williams; Pres. (V), Gerald J. Caliendo.
Institution Type/Description: Historic Building/Site; History Museum: Now the centerpiece of an 11-acre historic park, King Manor was the home of Rufus King from 1805-1827. King was a signer of the U.S. Constitution, senator from NY State and ambassador to Great Britain under four presidents, and outspoken opponent of slavery. 1819 & 1820, King led the Senate debate against admission of Missouri as a slave state.
Hours & Admission Prices: Thurs.-Fri. 12-2, Sat.-Sun. 1-5; groups of 10 or more by appointment. Suggested Admission: adults $5, seniors & students $3; discounts to groups, AAM, ICOM and NYC Historic House Trust members; children 16 & under and members no charge.
Attendance: 8,558 (actual)

Jamestown

FENTON HISTORY CENTER-MUSEUM & RESEARCH CENTER, 67 Washington St., Jamestown, NY 14701-6697. Tel.: 716-664-6256. Facebook.
E-mail: information@fentonhistorycenter.org
Web Site: www.fentonhistorycenter.org
Key Personnel: Pres. (V), Richard Lundquist; Dir., Joni Blackman; Dir. Education, Sara Reale; Mgr. Collections, Norman P. Carlson; Archivist, Karen E. Livsey; Membership, Office & Gift Shop Mgr., Paula Bechmann.
Institution Type/Description: History Museum: housed in 1863 Italian villa style mansion of Reuben E. Fenton, U.S. Congressman, Senator, NY. State Governor & founder of NYS Republican Party.
Hours & Admission Prices: Mon.-Sat. 10-4. Adults $10, children 5-12 $4; discounts to AAA, AAM & ICOM members; children under 5 & members no charge. Closed New Year's Day; Memorial Day; Independence Day; Labor Day; Thanksgiving; Christmas.
Attendance: 5,245 (actual)

JAMES PRENDERGAST LIBRARY ASSOCIATION, ART GALLERY, 509 Cherry St., Jamestown, NY 14701-5098. Tel.: 716-484-7135. Fax: 716-487-1148.
E-mail: prendergastlibrary@yahoo.com
Web Site: www.prendergastlibrary.org
Key Personnel: Acting Dir., Tina A. Scott; Gallery Coord., Anne Plyler.
Institution Type/Description: Art Museum & Gallery.
Hours & Admission Prices: Mon.-Fri. 9-8:30, Sat. 9-5, Sun. 1-5. No charge; donations accepted. &
Attendance: 5,599 (actual)

LUCILE M. WRIGHT AIR MUSEUM, 300 N. Main St., Jamestown, NY 14701-5109. Tel.: 716-664-9500.
E-mail: wrightairmuseum@gmail.com
Web Site: wrightairmuseum.org
Key Personnel: Pres. (V), Richard Fessenden.
Institution Type/Description: Aviation History Museum.
Hours & Admission Prices: Tues.-Sat. call for hours. No charge; donations accepted. Closed holidays. &
Attendance: 2,209 (actual)

LUCILLE BALL DESI ARNAZ CENTER, 2 W. Third St., Jamestown, NY 14701. Tel.: 716-484-0800. Fax: 716-484-9373. Facebook.
E-mail: info@lucy-desi.com
Web Site: www.lucy-desi.com; www.lucycomdyfest.com
Formerly: Lucille Ball Desi Arnaz Center for Comedy
Key Personnel: Exec. Dir., Journey Gunderson; Pres. (V), George Panebianco.
Institution Type/Description: General Museum.

Hours & Admission Prices: Mon.-Sat. 10-5, Sun. 11-4. Adults $15, seniors $14; discounts to AARP, NARM, AAA members; members no charge. &
Attendance: 20,000 (estimated)

ROGER TORY PETERSON INSTITUTE OF NATURAL HISTORY, 311 Curtis St., Jamestown, NY 14701-9620. Tel.: 716-665-2473, 800-758-6841. Fax: 716-665-3794.
E-mail: information@rtpi.org
Web Site: www.rtpi.org
Key Personnel: Pres., Twan Leenders; Conservation Tech., Elyse Henshaw; Visitor & Admin. Svcs. Asst., Amy Hudson; Exhibits & Public Progs. Coord., Jane Johnson; Conservation & Outreach Coord., Scott Kruitbosch; Devel. Dir.., Linda Pierce; Communications Coord., Melanie Smith.
Institution Type/Description: Natural History Museum & Art Gallery: building was designed by Robert A.M. Stern.
Hours & Admission Prices: Tues.-Sat. 10-4, Sun. 1-5. Family $30; adults $12, seniors & military $10; students & children $8. Closed national holidays. &
Attendance: 12,747 (actual)

THE WEEKS GALLERY AT JAMESTOWN COMMUNITY COLLEGE, 525 Falconer St., Jamestown, NY 14701-1920. Mailing Address: P.O. Box 20, Jamestown, NY 14702-0020. Tel.: 716-338-1300. Fax: 716-338-1451.
E-mail: weeksgallery@mail.sunyjcc.edu
Web Site: weeksgallery.sunyjcc.edu
Formerly: The CCC Weeks Gallery
Key Personnel: Dir. & Cur., Patricia Briggs; Arts Admin., Collin Shaffer.
Institution Type/Description: Art Gallery.
Hours & Admission Prices: Mon.-Thurs. 11-5, Fri. 11-3; Summer: Tues.-Fri. 11-4. No charge. Closed college holidays. &
Attendance: 8,500 (estimated)

Johnstown

JOHNSON HALL STATE HISTORIC SITE, 139 Hall Ave., Johnstown, NY 12095-1615. Tel.: 518-762-8712. Fax: 518-762-2330.
E-mail: wade.wells@parks.ny.gov
Web Site: www.nysparks.com
Key Personnel: Historic Site Mgr., Wade Wells; Pres. (V) & Museum Shop Mgr., Wanda Burch.
Institution Type/Description: Historic site; Historic House Museum: 1763 home of Sir William Johnson, Superintendent of Indian Affairs of the Six Nations Confederacy.
Hours & Admission Prices: Call for hours. Adults $4, seniors & groups $3, children 12 & under $1; members no charge. Closed most holidays. &
Attendance: 34,232 (estimated)

JOHNSTOWN HISTORICAL SOCIETY, 17 N. William St., Johnstown, NY 12095-2115. Tel.: 518-762-7076.
Key Personnel: Pres. (V), Catherine Levee; Cur., James F. Morrison.
Institution Type/Description: Historical Society Museum.
Hours & Admission Prices: Memorial Day to Labor Day Sat.-Sun. 1-4; other times by appointment. No charge; donations accepted. Closed New Year's Day; Memorial Day; Independence Day; Labor Day; Thanksgiving; Christmas.
Attendance: 794 (actual)

Katonah

CARAMOOR CENTER FOR MUSIC & THE ARTS, INC., 149 Girdle Ridge Rd., Katonah, NY 10536-3815. Mailing Address: Box 816, Katonah, NY 10536-0816. Tel.: 914-232-5035, ext. 221. Fax: 914-232-5521.
E-mail: museum@caramoor.org
Web Site: www.caramoor.org
Key Personnel: Chm. Bd. (V), Jim Attwood; C.E.O., Jeffrey P. Haydon; Managing Dir., Paul Rosenblum; Vice Pres. & Chief Devel. Officer, Nina Curley; Museum Mgr. & Dir. Programs, Mercedes Santos-Miller; Archivist, Hilton Bailey; Vice Pres. & C.F.O, Tammy Belanger; Dir. Education, Scott Ellison; Exec. Asst. & Bd. Liaison, Afton Battle; Dir. Annual Giving, Alithia Dutschke; Dir. Individual Gifts, Talia Bennick; Dir. Special Events & Rentals, Christine Bosco; Dir. Mktg., Sal Vaccard.
Institution Type/Description: House Museum: housed in 54 room Mediterranean style villa.
Hours & Admission Prices: May-Oct. Wed.-Sun. 1-4, last tour at 3 except during festival on Sat. 1-5, last tour at 4; Nov.-April Tues.-Fri. by appointment only. Adults $10; discounts to AAM members; members, children 16 & under no charge. &
Attendance: 60,000 (estimated)

JOHN JAY HOMESTEAD STATE HISTORIC SITE, 400 Rte. 22, Katonah, NY 10536. Mailing Address: P.O. Box 832, Katonah, NY 10536-0832. Tel.: 914-232-5651. Fax: 914-232-8085. TDD: 845-889-4100.
E-mail: heather.iannucci@oprhp.state.ny.us
Web Site: www.nysparks.com
Key Personnel: C.E.O. & Historic Site Mgr., Heather Iannucci; Interpretive Programs Asst., Allan Weinreb.
Institution Type/Description: Historic House Museum: federal style country home reflects the residence of U.S. Chief Justice & New York state Governor John Jay & family living here in the first third of the 19th century.
Hours & Admission Prices: April-Nov. Tues.-Sat. 10-4, Sun. 11-4. Grounds: daily 8-dusk. Adults $7, senior citizens $5; Friends and children 12 & under no charge. &
Attendance: 60,721 (actual)

KATONAH MUSEUM OF ART, 134 Jay St., Katonah, NY 10536-3737. Tel.: 914-232-9555, ext. 0. Fax: 914-232-3128.
E-mail: info@katonahmuseum.org
Web Site: www.katonahmuseum.org
Key Personnel: Pres. Bd. Trustees, Deborah Mullin, Ph.D.; Exec. Dir., Darsie Alexander; Deputy Dir. Institutional Advancement & Administration, Jennifer Berry; Assoc. Dir. Devel., Gary Ryan; Registrar, Nancy Hitchcock; Cur. Learning Center, Naomi Leiseroff; Cur. Education, Program Dept., Margaret Adasko; Assoc. Cur., Elizabeth Rooklidge.
Institution Type/Description: Art Museum.
Hours & Admission Prices: Tues.-Sat. 10-5, Sun. 12-5. Adults $10, students & seniors $5; members & children under 12 no charge. &
Attendance: 40,000 (estimated)

STEPPING STONES, 62 Oak Rd., Katonah, NY 10536-1810. Tel.: 914-232-4822. Fax: 914-232-2580.
E-mail: info@steppingstones.org
Web Site: www.steppingstones.org
Key Personnel: Dir., Annah Perch; Pres. (V), Michael Kelly.
Institution Type/Description: Historic House Museum: housed in the former home of Bill & Lois Wilson, co-founders of Alcoholics Anonymous and Al-Anon.
Hours & Admission Prices: Daily by appointment. Suggested Donations: $10 per person. Closed Easter; Thanksgiving; Christmas.
Attendance: 1,800 (actual)

Kinderhook

COLUMBIA COUNTY HISTORICAL SOCIETY, INC., 5 Albany Ave., Kinderhook, NY 12106-0311. Mailing Address: P.O. Box 311, Kinderhook, NY 12106-0311. Tel.: 518-758-9265. Fax: 518-758-2499.
E-mail: cchs@cchsny.org
Web Site: www.cchsny.org
Key Personnel: Acting Exec. Dir., David H. Smith; Pres., James Guidera.
Institution Type/Description: Historic House Museums: c.1820 Vanderpoel House of History; 1737 Luykas Van Alen House; c.1850 Ichabod Crane School House (interpretation date c.1925). History Museum: Columbia County Museum.
Hours & Admission Prices: Museum: Thurs.-Fri. 10-4, Sat.-Sun. 12-4. Adults $5, senior citizens $2. Historic Properties: Memorial Day to Columbus Day Sat.-Sun. 12-4; group tours by appointment. Adults $5, students & senior citizens 55 & over $3; discounts to AAM, NARM & ICOM members; children under 12 & members no charge.
Attendance: 24,500 (actual)

MARTIN VAN BUREN NATIONAL HISTORIC SITE, Rt. 9H, Kinderhook, NY 12106. Mailing Address: 1013 Old Post Rd., Kinderhook, NY 12106-3605. Tel.: 518-758-9689. Fax: 518-758-6986.
Web Site: www.nps.gov/mava
Key Personnel: C.E.O., Dan Dattilio; Cur., Dr. Patricia West; Chief Interpretation, James A. McKay.
Institution Type/Description: Historic House: home of President Martin Van Buren.
Hours & Admission Prices: mid-May to Oct. daily 9-4. Family $12, adults $5; children under 16 & members no charge. &
Attendance: 21,000 (actual)

Kings Park

KINGS PARK HERITAGE MUSEUM, Ralph J. Osgood Intermediate School, 101 Church St., Kings Park, NY 11754. Mailing Address: 99 Old Dock Rd., Kings Park, NY 11754. Tel.: 631-269-3305.
E-mail: kpheritagemuseumnet@gmail.com
Web Site: kpheritagemuseum.net

Key Personnel: Pres. (V) & Cur., Leo P. Ostebo; Treas., Roy Conforte; Historian, Ed Dumala; Historian, Joann Gallettatlahn.
Institution Type/Description: Local History Museum: housed in elementary school.
Hours & Admission Prices: Mon.-Fri. 10-2, Sat. 10-1 by appointment only. No charge; donations encouraged. Closed school holidays. &
Attendance: 4,500 (estimated)

Kings Point

AMERICAN MERCHANT MARINE MUSEUM, United States Merchant Marine Academy, Kings Point, NY 11024-1699. Mailing Address: US Merchant Marine Academy, 300 Steamboat Road, Kings Point, NY 11024-1699. Tel.: 516-726-6047.
E-mail: museum@usmma.edu
Web Site: www.usmma.edu/museum
Key Personnel: Interim Dir., Joshua M. Smith.
Institution Type/Description: Maritime Museum: American Merchant Marine.
Hours & Admission Prices: Tues.-Fri. 10-3. No charge; donations accepted. Closed federal holidays. &
Attendance: 4,000 (estimated)

Kingston

FRIENDS OF HISTORIC KINGSTON, FRED J. JOHNSTON HOUSE MUSEUM, 63 Main St., Kingston, NY 12401-3801. Mailing Address: P.O. Box 3763, Kingston, NY 12402-3763. Tel.: 845-339-0720.
E-mail: fohk@verizon.net
Web Site: www.fohk.org
Key Personnel: Dir., Jane Kellar; Pres. (V), Patricia Murphy.
Institution Type/Description: History Museum.
Hours & Admission Prices: May-Oct. Sat.-Sun. 1-4; other times by appointment. Adults $5, children $2; members no charge. &
Attendance: 4,100 (estimated)

HUDSON RIVER MARITIME MUSEUM, 50 Rondout Landing, Kingston, NY 12401-6092. Tel.: 845-338-0071, ext. 12. Fax: 845-338-0583.
E-mail: rlange@hrmm.org
Web Site: www.hrmm.org
Key Personnel: Bd. Pres., Robert Burhans; Exec. Dir., Lisa Cline; Dir. Education, Sarah Wassberg Johnson; Devel. & Collections Mgr., Ellie Burhans; Digital Archivist & Collections Mgr., Carla Lesh.
Institution Type/Description: Maritime Museum interpreting the maritime and industrial heritage of the Hudson River and it's tributaries.
Hours & Admission Prices: May-Nov. daily 11-5; mid-Nov. to April Thurs.-Sun. 11-5. Museum: adults $7, seniors & children $5; discounts to active military & CAMM members; members no charge. Blue Star Museum. &
Attendance: 20,000 (estimated)

SENATE HOUSE STATE HISTORIC SITE, 296 Fair St., Kingston, NY 12401-3836. Tel.: 845-338-2786. Fax: 845-334-8173.
E-mail: thomas.kernan@parks.ny.gov
Web Site: www.nysparks.com
Key Personnel: Mgr. Historic Site, Thomas Kernan.
Institution Type/Description: Historic Site.
Hours & Admission Prices: April 15-Oct. Wed.-Sat. 10-5, Sun. 1-5; other times by appointment. Adults $4, seniors & groups $3; children under 12 no charge. Closed most holidays. &
Attendance: 25,000 (estimated)

TROLLEY MUSEUM OF NEW YORK, 89 E. Strand, Kingston, NY 12401-6001. Mailing Address: P.O. Box 2291, Kingston, NY 12402-2291. Tel.: 845-331-3399.
E-mail: admin@tmny.org
Web Site: tmny.org
Key Personnel: Pres. (V), Jon McGrew; Archivist, Evan Jennings; Treas., William Brandt; Admin., Steve Ladin; Museum Shop Mgr., Glendon Moffett.
Institution Type/Description: Transportation Museum.
Hours & Admission Prices: early May to mid-Oct. Sat.-Sun. & holidays 12-5. Also open for special events. Adults $6, senior citizens 62 & over and children 6-12 $4; discounts to AAM members; children 6 & under no charge.
Attendance: 5,000 (estimated)

ULSTER COUNTY HISTORICAL SOCIETY, 2682 State Rte. 209, Kingston, NY 12401. Mailing Address: P.O. Box 279, Stone Ridge, NY 12484-0279. Tel.: 845-338-5614.
E-mail: director@bevierhousemuseum.org
Web Site: www.ulstercountyhistoricalsociety.org

Key Personnel: Dir., Jessica Phinney; Pres., Suzanne Hauspurg.
Institution Type/Description: Bevier House: stone farm house owned by the Bevier family from 1715-1938; registered county historic landmark & National Historic Register.
Hours & Admission Prices: May-Oct. Thurs.-Sun. 12-5. Adults $5, seniors $4, children $3; AAM & ICOM members no charge.
Attendance: 500 (estimated)

VOLUNTEER FIREMEN'S MALL AND MUSEUM OF KINGSTON, 265 Fair St., Kingston, NY 12401-3807. Mailing Address: P.O. Box 1501, Kingston, NY 12402-1501. Tel.: 845-331-0866. Facebook: Volunteer Firemen's Mall and Museum of Kingston.
E-mail: vfmuseumofkingston@gmail.com
Key Personnel: Pres. (V), Billy J. Knowles.
Institution Type/Description: Fire-Fighting Museum.
Hours & Admission Prices: April-May & Sept.-Oct. Fri. 11-3, Sat. 10-4; June-Aug. Wed.-Fri. 11-3, Sat. 10-4. No charge; donations accepted.
Attendance: 2,500 (estimated)

LaFargeville

NORTHERN NEW YORK AGRICULTURAL HISTORICAL SOCIETY, AGRICULTURAL MUSEUM AT STONE MILLS, 30950 NYS Rte. 180, LaFargeville, NY 13656. Mailing Address: P.O. Box 108, LaFargeville, NY 13656-0108. Tel.: 315-658-2353. Facebook: Stone Mills Agricultural Museum.
E-mail: agstonemills@yahoo.com
Web Site: www.stonemillsmuseum.org
Key Personnel: Dir., Gail Marsh; Dir., Tom Gardner; Pres. (V), Michael LaDue.
Institution Type/Description: Agricultural History Museum Complex.
Hours & Admission Prices: May-Sept. by appointment except events. Adult $5; discounts to AAM members; children 16 & under and life members no charge. &
Attendance: 10,000 (estimated)

Lake George

FORT WILLIAM HENRY MUSEUM, 48 Canada St., Lake George, NY 12845-1600. Tel.: 518-668-5471 & 964-6647. Fax: 518-964-6659.
E-mail: kathryn@fortwilliamhenry.com
Web Site: www.fwhmuseum.com
Key Personnel: Pres., Robert Flacke; Dir., Melodie Viele; C.F.O., Kathy Muncil.
Institution Type/Description: Historic Site Museum: restored c.1750 Fort William Henry.
Hours & Admission Prices: May-Oct. daily 9-5. Adults $16.95, senior citizens $13.95, children 3-11 $7.95; discount to groups; children under 5 & military with ID no charge.
Attendance: 43,150 (estimated)

HOUSE OF FRANKENSTEIN WAX MUSEUM, 213 Canada St., Lake George, NY 12845-1401. Tel.: 518-668-3377.
E-mail: doctor@frankensteinwaxmuseum.com
Web Site: frankensteinwaxmuseum.com
Institution Type/Description: Wax Museum.
Hours & Admission Prices: Call for hours. Adults $9.30, students 13-17 $8.36, children 6-12 $4.65.

LAKE GEORGE HISTORICAL ASSOCIATION MUSEUM, Old Warren County Courthouse, 290 Canada St., Lake George, NY 12845. Mailing Address: P.O. Box 472, Lake George, NY 12845-0472. Tel.: 518-668-5044.
E-mail: lgha@verizon.net
Web Site: lakegeorgehistorical.org
Key Personnel: Pres. Bd. Trustees (V), Alex Parrott; Dir., Maggie McClure.
Institution Type/Description: Historical Society Museum: housed in 1845 Warren County Courthouse, located in the region of famous battles of the French & Indian War and American Revolution.
Hours & Admission Prices: late May to mid-June & Oct. 1 to Columbus Day Sat.-Sun. 11-4; July-Aug. Tues. & Fri.-Sat. 11-4, Wed.-Thurs. 3-8; Sept. Fri.-Sun. 11-4. No charge.
Attendance: 3,500

Lake Placid

THE HISTORY MUSEUM, LAKE PLACID-NORTH ELBA HISTORICAL SOCIETY, 242 Station St., Lake Placid, NY 12946-1949. Mailing Address: P.O. Box 189, 242 Station St., Lake Placid, NY 12946-0189. Tel.: 518-523-1608. Facebook, Instagram.

E-mail: info@lakeplacidhistory.com
Web Site: lakeplacidhistory.com
Key Personnel: Dir., Courtney Bastian; Pres., Patricia Clark.
Institution Type/Description: Historic House: 1904 D&H train station.
Hours & Admission Prices: Memorial Day to mid-June & Labor Day to mid-Sept. Sat.-Sun. 10-4; mid-June to Sept. & mid-Sept. to Columbus Day Wed.-Sun. 10-4. No charge; donations accepted.
Attendance: 1,685 (estimated)

JOHN BROWN FARM STATE HISTORIC SITE, 115 John Brown Rd., Lake Placid, NY 12946-3248. Tel.: 518-523-3900. Fax: 518-523-3951.
E-mail: brendan.mills@oprhp.state.ny.us
Web Site: nysparks.state.ny.us/sites/info.asp?siteid=14
Key Personnel: Historic Site Asst., Brendan Mills.
Institution Type/Description: Historic House Museum: 1855 frame house occupied by John Brown & his family while he carried on his anti-slavery campaigns; the burial place of John Brown.
Hours & Admission Prices: May-Oct. Wed.-Mon. 10-5. Adults $2, seniors & children $1; children under 12 no charge. &
Attendance: 37,000 (actual)

LAKE PLACID OLYMPIC MUSEUM, 2634 Main St., Lake Placid, NY 12946. Mailing Address: P.O. Box 2002, Lake Placid, NY 12946. Tel.: 518-523-1655, ext. 226. Fax: 518-523-9275.
E-mail: museum@orda.org
Web Site: www.lpom.org
Formerly: 1932 & 1980 Lake Placid Winter Olympics Museum
Key Personnel: Dir., Alison Haas; Chm. (V), Matthew Norfolk.
Institution Type/Description: Sports Museum.
Hours & Admission Prices: Daily 10-5. Adults $7, seniors & juniors $5; children 6 & under no charge. Closed Ironman Sunday in July; Thanksgiving; Christmas. &
Attendance: 28,000 (estimated)

LeRoy

LEROY HOUSE & JELL-O GALLERY, 23 E. Main St., LeRoy, NY 14482-1209. Tel.: 585-768-7433. Fax: 585-768-7579.
E-mail: info@jellogallery.org
Web Site: www.jellomuseum.com
Key Personnel: Dir. & Cur., Lynne J. Belluscio; Pres. (V), Jim Newkirk; Museum Shop Mgr., Carolyn Bolin.
Institution Type/Description: Historical Society Museum.
Hours & Admission Prices: Leroy House: call for hours. Jell-O Gallery: Jan.-March Mon.-Fri. 10-4; April-Dec. Mon.-Sat. 10-4, Sun. 1-4. Adults $4, children 6-11 $1.50; discounts to groups, tours, AAM & AAA members; children 5 & under and members no charge. Closed New Year's Day; Thanksgiving; Christmas.
Attendance: 11,000 (estimated)

Lewiston

CASTELLANI ART MUSEUM OF NIAGARA UNIVERSITY, 5795 Lewiston Rd., Lewiston, NY 14109. Mailing Address: P.O. Box 1938, Niagara University, NY 14109-1938. Tel.: 716-286-8200. Fax: 716-286-8289.
E-mail: kjk@niagara.edu
Web Site: www.niagara.edu/cam/
Key Personnel: Dir., Kate Koperski; Gallery & Installation Mgr., Kurt Von Voetsch; Cur. Collections & Exhibitions, Michael Beam; Cur. Folk Arts, Carrie Hertz; Registrar, Kathleen Fraas; Educ. Coord., Marian Granfield; Coord. Events, Public Rels. & Membership, Susan Clements; Museum Shop Mgr., Carla Castellani; Office Coord., Daphne Wyse; Weekend & Special Events Mgr., Celia Rodino.
Institution Type/Description: University & Art Museum.
Hours & Admission Prices: Tues.-Sat. 11-5, Sun. 1-5. No charge; donations accepted. Closed Good Friday; Easter; Thanksgiving; Christmas; university holidays. &
Attendance: 20,000 (actual)

NYPA NIAGARA POWER VISTA, 5777 Lewiston Rd., Lewiston, NY 14092-2152. Tel.: 716-286-6661. Fax: 716-286-6654.
E-mail: npvista@nypa.gov
Web Site: www.nypa.gov/vc/niagara.htm
Key Personnel: Dir. Community Affairs, Lou Paonessa; Sr. Community Rels. Rep., Teresa Martinez.
Institution Type/Description: Electricity & Technology Museum.
Hours & Admission Prices: Daily 9-5. No charge. Closed New Year's Eve & Day; Thanksgiving; Christmas Eve & Day. &
Attendance: 80,000 (actual)

Lily Dale

LILY DALE MUSEUM, 16-18 Library St., Lily Dale, NY 14752. Mailing Address: 5 Second St., P.O. Box 145, Lily Dale, NY 14752. Tel.: 716-969-4825. Fax: 716-595-2442. Facebook.
E-mail: ronnagylilydale@gmail.com
Web Site: www.lilydaleassembly.org
Institution Type/Description: History Museum: housed in a former one-room school; built in 1890.
Hours & Admission Prices: Call or see website for hours. No charge; donations accepted. ♿
Attendance: 5,000 (estimated)

Lindenhurst

OLD VILLAGE HALL MUSEUM, 215 S. Wellwood Ave., Lindenhurst, NY 11757-4904. Mailing Address: P.O. Box 296, Lindenhurst, NY 11757-0296. Tel.: 631-957-4385.
Key Personnel: Chm. (V) & Dir., Johanna Sandy.
Institution Type/Description: Local History Museum.
Hours & Admission Prices: Wed. & Fri.-Sat. 2-4; museum relocating, call to confirm hours. No charge; donations accepted. Closed holidays.
Attendance: 1,129 (actual)

Little Falls

HERKIMER HOME STATE HISTORIC SITE, 200 State Rte. 169, Little Falls, NY 13365-5818. Tel.: 315-823-0398. Fax: 315-823-0587.
E-mail: karen.sheckells@parks.ny.gov
Web Site: www.herkimerhomeacademy.org
Key Personnel: Dir., Karen Sheckells.
Institution Type/Description: Historic House: housed in the former home & gravesite of Gen. Nicholas Herkimer; built c.1760.
Hours & Admission Prices: Memorial Day to Labor Day Wed.-Sat. 10-5, Sun. & Mon. holidays 1-5. Adults $4, seniors & students $3; children 12 & under no charge.
Attendance: 29,316 (actual)

LITTLE FALLS HISTORICAL SOCIETY MUSEUM, 319 S. Ann St., Little Falls, NY 13365-1362. Tel.: 315-823-0643.
E-mail: info@lfhistoricalsociety.com
Web Site: www.lfhistoricalsociety.com
Key Personnel: Pres. (V), Jeffrey Gressler; Museum Shop Mgr., Eileen Zak.
Institution Type/Description: Local History Museum: housed in 1833 Greek Revival bank building.
Hours & Admission Prices: June-Oct. Mon.-Fri. 1-4, Sat. 9-12. No charge, donations accepted. Closed July 4 & Labor Day. ♿
Attendance: 1,200 (actual)

MOHAWK VALLEY CENTER FOR THE ARTS, INC., 401 Canal Pl., Little Falls, NY 13365. Tel.: 315-823-0808. Fax: 315-823-0805.
E-mail: director@mohawkvalleyarts.org
Web Site: ww.mohawkvalleyarts.org
Key Personnel: Dir., Barbara Boucher.
Institution Type/Description: Art Gallery.
Hours & Admission Prices: Tues.-Sat. 11-4

Liverpool

SAINTE MARIE AMONG THE IROQUOIS, 6680 Onondaga Lake Pkwy., Liverpool, NY 13088-5061. Mailing Address: 106 Lake Dr., Liverpool, NY 13088-5118. Tel.: 315-453-6768. Fax: 315-453-6772.
E-mail: stemarie1657@yahoo.com
Web Site: onondagacountyparks.com
Key Personnel: Park Supt., Dale Grinolds.
Institution Type/Description: History Museum: housed in re-created 1657 French Mission which stood on the shores of Onondaga Lake.
Hours & Admission Prices: mid-May to mid-Oct. Mon.-Fri. 9-3, Sat.-Sun. 12-5; mid-Oct. to mid-May Mon.-Fri. 9-3. Mid-May to mid-Oct. adults $3, senior citizens 62 & over $2.50, children 6-17 $2; children 5 & under no charge. Mid-Oct. to mid-May no charge; donations accepted.

SALT MUSEUM, 106 Lake Dr., Onondaga Lake Park, Liverpool, NY 13088. Mailing Address: 106 Lake Dr., Liverpool, NY 13088-5118. Tel.: 315-453-6715; 6712. Fax: 315-453-6764.
E-mail: olp@ongov.net
Web Site: www.onondagacountyparks.com/parks/olp/salt-museum.php
Key Personnel: Park Supt., Dale Grinolds; Museum Shop Mgr., Rhoda Sikes.
Institution Type/Description: Historic Site: salt block; reconstruction & exhibit gallery.
Hours & Admission Prices: mid-May to mid-Oct. weekends 1-6. No charge; donations accepted. ♿
Attendance: 20,000 (actual)

Livingston Manor

CATSKILL FLY FISHING CENTER & MUSEUM, 1031 Old Rte. 17, Livingston Manor, NY 12758. Mailing Address: P.O. Box 1295, Livingston Manor, NY 12758-1295. Tel.: 845-439-4810.
E-mail: office@cffcm.com
Web Site: www.cffcm.com
Key Personnel: Exec. Dir., Glenn Pontier; Pres. (V), Kelly E. Buchta; Vice Pres., Miriam Stone; Treas., Grant Jones; Office Mgr. & Museum Shop Mgr., Samantha Mango.
Institution Type/Description: Fly Fishing Museum.
Hours & Admission Prices: April-Oct. daily 10-4; Nov.-March Tues.-Fri. 10-1, Sat. 10-4. Adults $10; members no charge. Closed New Year's Day; Thanksgiving; Christmas. ♿
Attendance: 9,000 (actual)

Lockport

NIAGARA COUNTY HISTORICAL SOCIETY DBA THE HISTORY CENTER OF NIAGARA COUNTY, 215 Niagara St., Lockport, NY 14094-2605. Tel.: 716-434-7433. Fax: 716-434-3309. Niagara History Center.
Web Site: niagarahistory.org
Key Personnel: C.E.O. & Dir., Melissa L. Dunlap; Pres. (V), David Caldwell; Dir. Erie Canal Discovery Center, Dir. Devel. Niagara County Historical Society & Museum Shop Mgr., Ray Wigle; Education Coord. & Asst. Dir., Ann Marie Linnabery; Cur., Tori Pellish; Mktg. & Public Rels., Patricia Kibler-Fries.
Institution Type/Description: History Museum.
Hours & Admission Prices: Niagara County Historical Society: Mon.-Sat. 9-5. Closed holidays. Erie Canal Discovery Center: May-Oct. daily 9-5, Nov.-April Fri.-Sat. 10-3. Col. Bond/Jessee Hawley House: call for hours. The Penney Gallery: May-Oct. daily 9-5, Nov.-April Thurs.-Sat. 10-3. Adult $6, group $4, discounts to military, members no charge.
Attendance: 33,478 (actual)

Long Eddy

BASKET HISTORICAL SOCIETY MUSEUM HALL, Rte. 97, Long Eddy, NY 12760. Mailing Address: P.O. Box 199, Long Eddy, NY 12760. Tel.: 845-887-5417.
E-mail: baskethistsociety@gmail.com
Institution Type/Description: Historical Society Museum.
Hours & Admission Prices: Call for hours.

Long Island City

DORSKY GALLERY CURATORIAL PROGRAMS, 11-03 45th Ave., at corner of 11th St., Long Island City, NY 11101-5109. Tel.: 718-937-6317. Fax: 718-937-7469.
E-mail: info@dorsky.org
Web Site: www.dorsky.org
Key Personnel: Dir., David A. Dorsky.
Institution Type/Description: Alternative Exhibition Space.
Hours & Admission Prices: Thurs.-Mon. 11-6; other times by appointment. No charge; donations accepted. ♿

FISHER LANDAU CENTER FOR ART, 38-27 30th St., Long Island City, NY 11101-2716. Tel.: 718-937-0727.
E-mail: info@flcart.org
Web Site: www.flcart.org
Institution Type/Description: Art Center.
Hours & Admission Prices: Thurs.-Mon. 12-5. No charge. ♿

ISAMU NOGUCHI GARDEN MUSEUM, 9-01 33rd Rd., (at Vernon Blvd.), Long Island City, NY 11106. Mailing Address: 32-37 Vernon Blvd., Long Island City, NY 11106-4926. Tel.: 718-204-7088. Fax: 718-278-2348.
E-mail: museum@noguchi.org
Web Site: www.noguchi.org
Key Personnel: Chm., Samuel Sachs, II; Dir., Jenny Dixon; Dir. Devel., Jennifer Burlenski; Head Education, Heather Brady; Finance Mgr., Zehava Fishman;

Admin. Dir., Amy Hau; Registrar, Larry Giacoletti; Dir. Collections Cur., Bonnie Rychlak; Museum Shop Mgr., Peter Scibetta.
Institution Type/Description: Art Museum; housed in former studio of Isamu Noguchi.
Hours & Admission Prices: Wed.-Fri. 10-5, Sat.-Sun. 11-6. Adults $10, students & seniors $5; discounts to AAM & ICOM members and employees of NYC Museum Council Institutions. Pay what you wish 1st Fri. of month. &
Attendance: 26,000 (estimated)

LAGUARDIA AND WAGNER ARCHIVES, 31-10 Thomson Ave., Rm. E-238, Long Island City, NY 11101-3007. Tel.: 718-482-5065. Fax: 718-482-5069. Facebook: LaGuardia and Wagner Archives.
E-mail: richardli@lagcc.cuny.edu
Web Site: www.laguardiawagnerarchive.lagcc.cuny.edu
Key Personnel: Dir., Richard K. Lieberman; Archivist, Douglas DiCarlo.
Institution Type/Description: History Museum.
Hours & Admission Prices: Exhibits: Mon.-Fri. 7am-10pm, Sat.-Sun. 7-5. Research & Archives: Summer: Mon.-Thurs. 9:30-4:30; Fall, Winter & Spring: Mon.-Fri. 9:30-4:30. No charge. Closed major holidays. &
Attendance: 2,000 (estimated)

MOMA PS1, 22-25 Jackson Ave., Long Island City, NY 11101-4309. Tel.: 718-784-2084. Fax: 718-482-9454.
E-mail: mail_ps1@moma.org
Web Site: momaps1.org
Formerly: P.S. 1 Contemporary Art Center
Key Personnel: Dir., Klaus Biesenbach; Chm., Agnes Gund; C.O.O., Jenni Kim; Dir. Finance & Administration, Robert Wayne; Cur. & Assoc. Dir. Exhibitions & Programs, Peter Eleey; Assoc. Cur., Jenny Schlenzka; Asst. Cur., Mia Locks; Communications Dir., Allison Rodman; Dir. Devel., Angela Goding; Sr. Mgr. Visitor Services, Zachary Bowman; Mgr. Building Operations, Kevin Kulick.
Institution Type/Description: Contemporary Art Museum; housed in 19th-century Romanesque Revival schoolhouse.
Hours & Admission Prices: Thurs.-Mon. noon-6. Adults $10, students & senior citizens $5; discounts to AAM & ICOM members; youth 16 & under & MoMA members no charge. Closed New Year's Day; Memorial Day; Independence Day; Thanksgiving; Christmas. &
Attendance: 133,000

SCULPTURECENTER, 44-19 Purves St., Long Island City, NY 11101-2907. Tel.: 718-361-1750. Fax: 718-786-9336. Facebook; Instagram.
E-mail: info@sculpture-center.org
Web Site: www.sculpture-center.org
Key Personnel: Exec. Dir., Mary Ceruti; Associate Dir., Ben Whine; Cur., Ruba Katrib; Dir. Devel., Allison Derusha.
Institution Type/Description: Art Gallery.
Hours & Admission Prices: Thurs.-Mon. 11-6. Suggested Donation: $5. &
Attendance: 12,181 (actual)

SOCRATES SCULPTURE PARK, 32-01 Vernon Blvd. (at Broadway), Long Island City, NY 11106. Mailing Address: P.O. Box 6259, Long Island City, NY 11106-0259. Tel.: 718-956-1819. Fax: 718-626-1533. Facebook: Socrates Sculpture Park.
E-mail: info@socratessculpturepark.org
Web Site: socratessculpturepark.org
Key Personnel: Dir., John Hatfield; Pres. (V), Stuart Match Suna; Dir. Public Programs & Community Rels., Shaun Leonardo; Facilities & Studio Mgr., Lars Fisk; Dir. Devel. & Communications, Katie Denny Horowitz; Dir. Exhibitions, Elissa Goldstone.
Institution Type/Description: Sculpture Park.
Hours & Admission Prices: Daily 8:30 to sunset. No charge. &
Attendance: 100,000 (estimated)

Lowville

LEWIS COUNTY HISTORICAL SOCIETY MUSEUM, 7552 S. State St., Lowville, NY 13367-1529. Mailing Address: P.O. Box 446, Lowville, NY 13367-0446. Tel.: 315-376-8957.
E-mail: lewiscountyhistoricalsociety@gmail.com
Web Site: lewiscountyhistory.org
Key Personnel: Pres., Marian Opela; Sec., Lida Perfetto; Vice Pres., Christopher Miller; Treas., Sharon Sears; Museum Shop Mgr., Linda Hornig.
Institution Type/Description: History Museum.
Hours & Admission Prices: Historical Society: June to mid-Oct. Tues.-Fri. 10-4, Sat. 10-12; mid-Oct. to June Tues.-Thurs. 10-4. Lewis County Research Center: June to mid-Oct. Tues.-Thurs. 10-4; mid-Oct. to June Tues.-Wed. 10-4. No charge; donations accepted. Closed federal holidays. &
Attendance: 1,900 (estimated)

Lyons

WAYNE COUNTY HISTORICAL SOCIETY'S MUSEUM OF WAYNE COUNTY HISTORY, 21 Butternut St., Lyons, NY 14489-1124. Tel.: 315-946-4943. Fax: 315-946-0069.
E-mail: info@waynehistory.org
Web Site: www.waynehistory.org
Formerly: Wayne County Historical Society
Key Personnel: Exec. Dir., Larry Ann Evans; Museum Mgr., Karen Schwab.
Institution Type/Description: Historical Society Museum.
Hours & Admission Prices: Tues.-Fri. & Sat. June-Aug. 10-4. Adults $4, children $2; members no charge. Closed legal holidays.
Attendance: 8,000 (actual)

Macedon

MACEDON HISTORICAL SOCIETY, INC., 1185 Macedon Center Rd., Macedon, NY 14502. Mailing Address: P.O. Box 303, Macedon, NY 14502-0303. Facebook: Macedon NY History.
E-mail: macedon_historical_society@outlook.com
Web Site: www.macedonhistoricalsociety.org
Key Personnel: Pres. (V), Kathleen Murphy; Vice Pres. (V), Jay Murphy; Treas. & Cur., Carmen Pagano; Sec. & Cur., Linda Braun.
Institution Type/Description: Historical Society Museum.
Hours & Admission Prices: Summer: call for hours; other times by appointment. No charge; donations accepted. &
Attendance: 150 (estimated)

Mahopac

THE PUTNAM CHILDREN'S DISCOVERY CENTER, 854 Rte. 6, Mahopac, NY 10541-1721. Mailing Address: P.O. Box 222, Carmel, NY 10512-0222. Tel.: 845-621-1260. Fax: 914-205-3623.
E-mail: jnewman@discoveryctr.org
Web Site: discoveryctr.org
Key Personnel: Exec. Dir., Janice Newman.
Institution Type/Description: Children's Museum.
Hours & Admission Prices: Call for hours.

Malone

FRANKLIN COUNTY HISTORICAL & MUSEUM SOCIETY, 51 Milwaukee St., Malone, NY 12953-1916. Mailing Address: P. O. Box 388, Malone, NY 12953-0388. Tel.: 518-483-2750. Facebook.
E-mail: fcohms@northnet.org
Web Site: www.franklinhistory.org
Key Personnel: Pres. (V), Cheryl Learned.
Institution Type/Description: County History Museum.
Hours & Admission Prices: Research: June-Aug. Tues.-Fri. 1-4; Winter: by appointment. Museum Tours: by appointment. Tours: adults $5; discounts to AASLH members; members no charge. Research: adults $10; members no charge. Closed holidays.
Attendance: 1,500 (estimated)

Mamaroneck

KOSLOWE JUDAICA GALLERY, 175 Rockland Ave., Mamaroneck, NY 10543. Tel.: 914-698-2960. Fax: 914-698-3610.
E-mail: executive@wjcenter.org
Web Site: www.wjcenter.org/community
Key Personnel: Exec. Dir., Susan Lurie.
Institution Type/Description: Jewish Art & History Museum.
Hours & Admission Prices: Call for hours. No charge; donations accepted. &

LARCHMONT HISTORICAL SOCIETY, 740 W. Boston Post Rd., Ste. 301, Mamaroneck, NY 10543-3345. Mailing Address: P. O. Box 742, Larchmont, NY 10538-0742. Tel.: 914-381-2239 & 834-5136.
E-mail: archives@larchmonthistory.org
Web Site: www.larchmonthistory.org
Key Personnel: Pres. (V), Colette Rodbell; Treas., Jim Sweeney; Archivist, Lynne Crowley; Membership Coord., Lauren Gottfried.
Institution Type/Description: Historical Society Museum.
Hours & Admission Prices: Tues. & Thurs. 9-2; other times by appointment. No charge. &
Attendance: 300 (estimated)

Manhasset

HISTORICAL SOCIETY OF THE TOWN OF NORTH HEMPSTEAD, 220 Plandome Rd., Manhasset, NY 11030-2326. Mailing Address: P.O. Box 3000, Manhasset, NY 11030-3000. Tel.: 516-627-0590.
E-mail: feedback@northhempsteadny.gov
Web Site: www.northhempstead.com
Key Personnel: Pres., Hon. Dolores Sedacca.
Institution Type/Description: Historical Society Museum.
Hours & Admission Prices: by appointment. No charge.

SCIENCE MUSEUM OF LONG ISLAND, Leeds Pond Preserve, 1526 N. Plandome Rd., Manhasset, NY 11030. Mailing Address: P.O. Box 908, Plandome, NY 11030-0908. Tel.: 516-627-9400, ext. 11. Fax: 516-365-8927. Facebook: Science Museum of Long Island.
E-mail: smli@optonline.net
Web Site: smli.org
Key Personnel: Dir., John T. Tanacredi, Ph.D.; Pres. (V), Carlo Manganillo.
Institution Type/Description: Science Center.
Hours & Admission Prices: Office: Mon.-Fri. 9-3:30. Call for information on charges & activities; discount to museum members.
Attendance: 15,000 (estimated)

Manlius

MANLIUS HISTORICAL SOCIETY AND MUSEUM/ MANLIUS MUSEUM, 109 Pleasant St., Manlius, NY 13104. Mailing Address: P.O. Box 28, Manlius, NY 13104-0028. Tel.: 315-682-6660. Facebook.
E-mail: manliushistory@gmail.com
Web Site: www.manliushistory.org
Key Personnel: Dir., Chris Malmgren.
Institution Type/Description: Historical Society Museum.
Hours & Admission Prices: Museum: June-Sept. Sat. 1-4; groups & other times by appointment. Research Center: Wed.-Fri. 10-4; other times by appointment. No charge; donations accepted. Closed Easter; Thanksgiving; Christmas.
Attendance: 450 (estimated)

Marcellus

MARCELLUS HISTORICAL SOCIETY, 18 North St., Marcellus, NY 13108. Mailing Address: P.O. Box 165, Marcellus, NY 13108-0165.
E-mail: PEGANOLAN1@HOTMAIL.COM
Web Site: http://marcellushistoricalsociety.org/
Key Personnel: Pres. (V), Doug Nightingale; Vice Pres., Kathy McLaughlin; Treas., Patricia Sanborn; Sec., Carrie Beth Pottinger.
Institution Type/Description: History Museum: housed in early 1830s house.
Hours & Admission Prices: Sun. 1-3, Thurs. 1-4; other times by appointment. No charge; donations accepted. Closed holidays.
Attendance: 833 (estimated)

Marilla

MARILLA HISTORICAL SOCIETY MUSEUM, 1810 Two Rod Rd., Marilla, NY 14102. Mailing Address: P.O. Box 36, Marilla, NY 14102-0036. Tel.: 716-652-1827 & 2436.
E-mail: info@townofmarilla.com
Web Site: townofmarilla.com/historical-society/
Key Personnel: Pres., Mary Beth Serafin; Vice Pres., Cindy Petrinec; Treas., John Foss; Sec., Judy Mees.
Institution Type/Description: Local History Museum.
Hours & Admission Prices: Jan.-June & Sept.-Nov. 3rd Sun. each month 2-4; call for special event hours. No charge; donations accepted.
Attendance: 200 (estimated)

Marlboro

GOMEZ MILL HOUSE MUSEUM AND HISTORIC SITE, 11 Mill House Rd., Marlboro, NY 12542-6514. Tel.: 845-236-3126.
E-mail: gomezmillhouse@gomez.org
Web Site: www.gomez.org
Key Personnel: Exec. Dir., Ruth K. Abrahams, Ph.D.; Pres. (V), Robert Jacobs, Jr.; Museum Site Asst., Richard Rosencrans.
Institution Type/Description: Historic House & Living History Museum.
Hours & Admission Prices: mid-April to Nov. Wed.-Sun. 10-4. Adults $10, seniors 55 & over $7, children & students 6-18 $4; discount to groups of 10 or more,

WNET, AAM & Channel 13 members; members & children under 6 no charge. Closed Easter; Thanksgiving; Jewish holidays; Christmas; national holidays.
Attendance: 3,000 (estimated)

Mastic Beach

FIRE ISLAND NATIONAL SEASHORE, William Floyd Estate, 245 Park Dr., Mastic Beach, NY 11951. Mailing Address: 120 Laurel St., Patchogue, NY 11772-3596. Tel.: 631-399-2030. Fax: 631-399-0017.
Web Site: www.nps.gov/fiis
Key Personnel: Cur., Steven Czarniecki.
Institution Type/Description: National Park.
Hours & Admission Prices: Grounds: Memorial Day to Oct. Fri.-Sun. 9-6. William Floyd Estate: Memorial Day to Veterans Day Fri.-Sun. 10-4. No charge. Closed holidays.
Attendance: 8,000

Mattituck

MATTITUCK LAUREL HISTORICAL SOCIETY AND MUSEUMS, 18300 Main Rd., Mattituck, NY 11952. Mailing Address: P.O. Box 766, Mattituck, NY 11952. Tel.: 631-298-5248.
E-mail: webmaster@mlhistoricalsociety.org
Key Personnel: Pres. (V), Lauren Brigham; Museum Shop Mgr., Norman Wamback.
Institution Type/Description: History Museum.
Hours & Admission Prices: May-Sept. Sat.-Sun. 1-4. Adults $5.
Attendance: 60 (estimated)

Mayville

DART AIRPORT AVIATION MUSEUM, 6167 Plank Rd., Mayville, NY 14757. Mailing Address: P.O. Box 211, Mayville, NY 14757. Tel.: 716-753-2160.
Institution Type/Description: Aviation History Museum.
Hours & Admission Prices: May-Nov. 1 Tues.-Sun. 10-5.

Medina

MEDINA RAILROAD MUSEUM, 530 West Ave., Medina, NY 14103-1554. Tel.: 585-798-6106. Fax: 585-798-1086. Facebook.
E-mail: office@railroadmuseum.net
Web Site: www.railroadmuseum.net
Key Personnel: Pres. (V), Frederick Henn; Exec. Dir., Janien Klotzbach.
Institution Type/Description: Railroad Museum.
Hours & Admission Prices: Tues.-Sun. 11-5. Adults $9, senior citizens $8, children under 18 $7; discounts to AAM members; members & children under 2 no charge. Closed major holidays.
Attendance: 33,000 (estimated)

Middlesex

MIDDLESEX HERITAGE GROUP & HISTORICAL SOCIETY MUSEUM, Town Hall, Main St., Middlesex, NY 14507. Mailing Address: P.O. Box 147, Middlesex, NY 14507. Tel.: 585-554-3607, Ext. 1006.
E-mail: middlesexheritagegroup@gmail.com
Key Personnel: Historian, Daniel Robeson.
Institution Type/Description: Historical Society Museum.
Hours & Admission Prices: Wed. 9 to noon. No charge; donations accepted.
Attendance: 220 (estimated)

Middletown

HISTORICAL SOCIETY OF MIDDLETOWN AND THE WALLKILL PRECINCT, INC., 25 East Ave., Middletown, NY 10940-5818. Mailing Address: P.O. Box 34, Middletown, NY 10940-0034. Tel.: 845-342-0941.
E-mail: enjine@aol.com
Key Personnel: Pres., Gerald Kleiner; Vice Pres., Peter Laskaris; Sec., Dorothy Hunt-Ingrassia; Treas., Gwen Deserto; Cur., Marvin H. Cohen.
Institution Type/Description: Local History Museum: housed in 1886 building.
Hours & Admission Prices: Wed. 1-5; other times call 845-343-4219 for appointment. No charge.
Attendance: 300 (estimated)

Millbrook

MILLBROOK SCHOOL, TREVOR ZOO, 131 Millbrook School Rd., Millbrook, NY 12545-4932. Tel.: 845-677-3704.
E-mail: trevorzoo@millbrook.org
Web Site: www.trevorzoo.org
Key Personnel: Dir., Alan Tousignant, Ph.D.; Dir. Prog., Jessica Bennett; Animal Care Coord., Kyleen Parajon; Registrar, Julie Herman; Dir. Media, Daniel Cohen.
Institution Type/Description: Zoo.
Hours & Admission Prices: Daily 8:30-5. Adults $5, children $3; discounts to groups. Summer Family Pass $40. &
Attendance: 22,000 (estimated)

Monroe

MUSEUM VILLAGE, 1010 Rte. 17 M, Monroe, NY 10950-1625. Tel.: 845-782-8248. Fax: 845-782-6432.
E-mail: info@museumvillage.org
Web Site: www.museumvillage.org
Key Personnel: Exec. Dir., Michael Sosler; Chm. (V), Paul Campanella; Collections Mgr., Chris Cantrell; Education Coord., Lori Siccardi; Museum Shop Mgr., Virginia Mina.
Institution Type/Description: Living History Museum.
Hours & Admission Prices: Call for hours. Adults $10, senior citizens & children 4-12 $8; discounts to AASLH partner institutions; members & children under 4 no charge.
Attendance: 30,757 (actual)

Montauk

MONTAUK POINT LIGHTHOUSE MUSEUM, 2000 Montauk Hwy., Montauk, NY 11954-5600. Mailing Address: P.O. Box 943, Montauk, NY 11954. Tel.: 631-668-2544. Fax: 631-668-2546.
E-mail: keeper@montauklighthouse.com
Web Site: www.montauklighthouse.com
Key Personnel: Dir. Site Management & Museum Dir., Ms. Johnson Nordlinger; Museum Shop Mgr., Fran Haak.
Institution Type/Description: Lighthouse Museum.
Hours & Admission Prices: Call for hours. Adults $10, senior citizens $8, children $4; discounts to groups. Children must meet a minimum height requirement of 41 inches. &
Attendance: 80,000 (estimated)

Montgomery

BRICK HOUSE, 850 Rte. 17K, Montgomery, NY 12549. Mailing Address: P.O. Box 462, Montgomery, NY 12549. Tel.: 845-457-4921. Fax: 845-615-3830.
Web Site: www.hillholdandbrickhouse.org
Key Personnel: Park Commissioner, Richard Rose; Dir., Susan Tucker.
Institution Type/Description: Historic House: 1768 Georgian style house, built by Nathaniel Hill.
Hours & Admission Prices: May-Oct. Sat.-Sun. 10-4:30. Family $7, adults $3, children $2; discounts to groups. Closed Memorial Day; Independence Day; Labor Day. &
Attendance: 4,000 (actual)

HILL-HOLD MUSEUM, 128 Rte. 416, Montgomery, NY 12549. Mailing Address: P.O. Box 462, Montgomery, NY 12549. Tel.: 845-291-2404. Fax: 845-615-3830.
Web Site: www.hillholdandbrickhouse.org
Key Personnel: Parks Commissioner, Richard Rose; Dir., Susan Tucker.
Institution Type/Description: Historic House: housed in a Georgian style stone house; built in 1769.
Hours & Admission Prices: mid-May to mid-Oct. Wed.-Sun. 10-4:30; groups by appointment. Family $7, adults $3, children $2. Closed Memorial Day; Independence Day; Labor Day. &
Attendance: 8,000

ORANGE COUNTY FIREFIGHTERS MUSEUM, 141 Clinton St., Montgomery, NY 12549. Mailing Address: P.O. Box 688, Montgomery, NY 12549. Tel.: 845-457-9654.
E-mail: enjine@aol.com
Web Site: www.ocfm.us
Key Personnel: Chm. & Pres., F. Edward Devitt; Treas., Walter Karsten; Education, John Conner; Cur., James Bair; Public Rels., Marvin H. Cohen.
Institution Type/Description: Firefighting History Museum: housed in an early fire-house.

Hours & Admission Prices: Sat. 1-4; other times by appointment. No charge; donations accepted.
Attendance: 1,200 (estimated)

Montour Falls

SCHUYLER COUNTY HISTORICAL SOCIETY, INC., 108 N. Catharine, Montour Falls, NY 14865. Mailing Address: P.O. Box 651, Montour Falls, NY 14865-0651. Tel.: 607-535-9741. Facebook, Twitter.
E-mail: director@schuylerhistory.org
Web Site: www.schuylerhistory.org
Key Personnel: Dir., Julie Morris; Pres., Jean Hubsch; Vice Pres., Allen Buddle.
Institution Type/Description: Local History Museum.
Hours & Admission Prices: April to mid-Dec. Tues.-Fri. 10-4, Sat. call for hours; other times by appointment. No charge; donations accepted. Research room: $5 per hour. Closed holidays. &
Attendance: 2,000 (actual)

Moravia

CAYUGA-OWASCO LAKES HISTORICAL SOCIETY, 14 W. Cayuga, Moravia, NY 13118. Mailing Address: P.O. Box 247, Moravia, NY 13118-0247. Tel.: 315-497-3906.
E-mail: colhs@localnet.com
Web Site: www.colhs.org
Key Personnel: Pres., Roger Phillips; Sec., Sandy Morehouse.
Institution Type/Description: Local History & Genealogy Museum: housed in pre-1850 History House.
Hours & Admission Prices: House Tours: Sat. 10-2. Research: Mon. 9-12; other times by appointment. No charge; donations accepted. Closed holidays. &
Attendance: 400 (estimated)

Mumford

GENESEE COUNTRY VILLAGE & MUSEUM, 1410 Flint Hill Rd., Mumford, NY 14511-0310. Mailing Address: P.O. Box 310, Mumford, NY 14511-0310. Tel.: 585-538-6822. Fax: 585-538-2887 & 6927. Facebook: @GCVMuseum.
E-mail: info@gcv.org
Web Site: www.gcv.org
Key Personnel: Pres. & C.E.O., Becky Wehle; Chm., Gayle A.G. Stiles; C.F.O., Stacy L. Kehrer; Dir. Retail & Visitor Svcs., Robin Lott; Dir. Education Svcs., Jennifer Haines; Dir. Interpretation, Brian Nagel; Sr. Dir. Guest Rels. & Administration, Christine M. Rovet.
Institution Type/Description: Art Gallery, Nature Center, Recreated Village & Living History Museum.
Hours & Admission Prices: mid-May to Labor Day Tues.-Sun. 10-4; Sept. to Columbus Day Wed.-Sun. 10-4. Adults $18, senior citizens over 62 & students $15, veterans with ID $14, youth 4-16 $10; members & children under 4 no charge. Closed week after Labor Day. Additional fee for special events. &
Attendance: 85,978 (actual)

Munnsville

FRYER MEMORIAL MUSEUM, William St., Munnsville, NY 13409. Mailing Address: Town of Stockbridge, P.O. Box 87, Munnsville, NY 13409. Tel.: 315-495-5451.
Institution Type/Description: Local History Museum: housed in 1886 Munnsville Post Office. Specialize in genealogical & local history research.
Hours & Admission Prices: By appointment. No charge; donations accepted.
Attendance: 200 (estimated)

Naples

CUMMING NATURE CENTER, 6472 Gulick Rd., Naples, NY 14512. Tel.: 585-374-6160. Fax: 585-374-8286.
E-mail: heidi_luizzi@rmsc.org
Web Site: www.rmsc.org/cummingnaturecenter
Institution Type/Description: Nature Center.
Hours & Admission Prices: Wed.-Fri. 9-3:30, Sat.-Sun. 9-4:30. Closed Labor Day; Columbus Day. Requested Donation: family $10, adults $3; members no charge.

Narrowsburg

FORT DELAWARE MUSEUM OF COLONIAL HISTORY, 6615 State Rt. 97, Narrowsburg, NY 12764. Mailing Address: P.O. Box 5012, Monticello, NY 12701-5192. Tel.: 845-252-6660. Fax: 845-807-0335.
E-mail: brian.scardefield@co.sullivan.ny.us

Web Site: co.sullivan.ny.us
Institution Type/Description: History Museum: 1755-1785 a reconstruction of Cushetunk, the first stockaded settlement in the upper Delaware Valley.
Hours & Admission Prices: Memorial Day to June Sat. 10-5, Sun. 12-5; late June to Labor Day Mon. & Fri.-Sat. 10-5, Sun. 12-5. Adults $7, seniors $5, children 5-14 $4. &
Attendance: 5,000 (actual)

New City

HISTORICAL SOCIETY OF ROCKLAND COUNTY, 20 Zukor Rd., New City, NY 10956-4388. Tel.: 845-634-9629. Fax: 845-634-8690.
E-mail: info@rocklandhistory.org
Web Site: www.rocklandhistory.org
Key Personnel: Exec. Dir., Erin L. Martin; Pres. (V), Dr. Thomas F.X. Casey.
Institution Type/Description: History Museum.
Hours & Admission Prices: Daily 1-5. Adults $7, children $3; members no charge. Closed major holidays. &
Attendance: 12,000 (estimated)

New Hartford

NEW HARTFORD HISTORICAL SOCIETY, 2 Paris Rd., New Hartford, NY 13413. Mailing Address: P.O. Box 238, New Hartford, NY 13413-0238. Tel.: 315-724-7258.
E-mail: historicalnh@yahoo.com
Web Site: nhnyhistorical.com
Key Personnel: Pres. (V) & Museum Shop Mgr., Barbara Couture; Archivist, Julie Cully.
Institution Type/Description: Historical Museum.
Hours & Admission Prices: Mon. 1-3, Sat. 10-1. No charge; donations accepted. &
Attendance: 45 (estimated)

New Lebanon

SHAKER MUSEUM/MOUNT LEBANON, 202 Shaker Rd., New Lebanon, NY 12125. Mailing Address: P.O. Box 630, New Lebanon, NY 12125. Tel.: 518-794-9100, ext. 218. Fax: 518-794-8621. Facebook, Twitter, Instagram.
E-mail: contact@shakerml.org
Web Site: www.shakerml.org
Formerly: Shaker Museum and Library
Key Personnel: Pres., David Stocks; Exec. Dir., Lacy Schutz; Dir. Research, Jerry Grant; Mgr. Programs & Operations, Wyatt Erchak; Chm. Bd. Trustees, Jeff Daly.
Institution Type/Description: Shaker History & Culture Museum.
Hours & Admission Prices: June-Oct. open for special programs; call for hours. Guided Tours: $10 per person. Exhibits: donation requested.
Attendance: 2,000 (estimated)

New Paltz

HISTORIC HUGUENOT STREET, 81 Huguenot St., New Paltz, NY 12561-1415. Mailing Address: 88 Huguenot St., New Paltz, NY 12561-1415. Tel.: 845-255-1660. Fax: 845-255-0376. Facebook, Instagram & Twitter: Huguenot Street.
E-mail: info@huguenotstreet.org
Web Site: www.huguenotstreet.org
Formerly: The Huguenot Historical Society
Key Personnel: Exec. Dir., Josephine Bloodgood; Bd. Chair (V), Mary Etta Schneider; Librarian & Archivist, Carrie Allmendinger; Dir. Pub. Programming, Kara Gaffken; Communications & Mktg. Mgr., Kaitlin Gallucci; Museum Shop Mgr., Kristine Gillespie; Dir. Devel., Kay Flamino.
Institution Type/Description: Historic Site & Historic House Museum: c.1680-1890, stone houses.
Hours & Admission Prices: Grounds: dawn to dusk. Visitor's Center, Museum Shop & Tours: April & Nov.-Dec. Sat.-Sun. 10-5; May-Oct. Thurs.-Tues. 10-5; guided tours & school group tours by appointment. Guided Tours: adults $15; discounts to seniors, veterans & Friends of museum; children 12 & under no charge. School Tours & Activity: $8 per student. School Tour: $5 per student. &
Attendance: 15,000 (estimated)

SAMUEL DORSKY MUSEUM OF ART, STATE UNIVERSITY OF NEW YORK AT NEW PALTZ, 1 Hawk Dr., New Paltz, NY 12561-2447. Tel.: 845-257-3844. Fax: 845-257-3854.
E-mail: sdma@newpaltz.edu
Web Site: www.newpaltz.edu/museum
Key Personnel: Chm. (V), David A. Dorsky; Mgr. Art Collections, Wayne Lempka; Dir. Neil C. Trager, Sara J. Pasti; Museum Educator, Judi Esmond; Cur., Daniel

Belasco; Assoc. Cur. Collections, Dr. Jaimee Uhlenbrock; Preparator, Robert Wagner; Coord. Visitor Svcs., Amy Pickering.
Institution Type/Description: Art Gallery.
Hours & Admission Prices: Aug. Sat.-Sun. 11-5; Sept.-July Wed.-Sun. 11-5. Suggested Donations $5. Closed legal & school holidays. &
Attendance: 16,000 (estimated)

New Rochelle

COLLEGE OF NEW ROCHELLE CASTLE GALLERY, 29 Castle Place, New Rochelle, NY 10805. Tel.: 914-654-5423. Fax: 914-654-5014.
E-mail: castlegallery@cnr.edu
Web Site: castlegallery.cnr.edu
Key Personnel: Dir., Katrina Rhein; Gallery Mgr., Michelle Jammes.
Institution Type/Description: Art Gallery: housed in Leland Castle; built in 1855. Listed on the National Register of Historic Places.
Hours & Admission Prices: Sept.-June Tues. & Thurs.-Fri. 10-5, Wed. 10-8, Sat.-Sun. 12-4. No charge. Closed holidays.

New Windsor

NATIONAL PURPLE HEART HALL OF HONOR, 374 Temple Hill Rd., New Windsor, NY 12553. Mailing Address: P.O. Box 207, Vails Gate, NY 12584-0207. Tel.: 845-561-1765, 877-284-6667. Fax: 845-569-0382.
E-mail: anita.pidala@parks.ny.gov
Web Site: www.thepurpleheart.com
Key Personnel: Dir., Anita Pidala; Program Dir., Peter Bedrossian.
Institution Type/Description: Military History Museum: commemorates America's military personnel that were wounded or killed by enemy action.
Hours & Admission Prices: Tues.-Sat. 10-5, Sun. 1-5. No charge; donations accepted. Closed most holidays. &
Attendance: 23,031 (actual)

NATIONAL TEMPLE HILL ASSOCIATION, INC., Edmonston House, Headquarters, 1042 Rte. 94, New Windsor, NY 12553. Mailing Address: Edmonston House, Headquarters, P.O. Box 315, Vails Gate, NY 12584-0315. Tel.: 845-561-5073. Fax: 845-561-5073.
Key Personnel: Pres. (V), Daniel S. Lucia.
Institution Type/Description: Historic House: c.1755 Edmonston House served as headquarters during Revolutionary War for General Horatio Gates & Maj. Gen. Arthur St. Clair.
Hours & Admission Prices: Edmonston House: July-Sept. Sun. 2-5. Last Encampment of the Continental Army: late April to Oct. daylight hours; Guides Thurs.-Sun. 12-4:30. No charge; donations accepted.
Attendance: 1,200 (estimated)

NEW WINDSOR CANTONMENT STATE HISTORIC SITE, 374 Temple Hill Rd., Rte. 300, New Windsor, NY 12553. Mailing Address: P.O. Box 207, Vails Gate, NY 12584-0207. Tel.: 845-561-1765. Fax: 845-561-6577.
E-mail: michael.mcgurty@parks.ny.gov
Web Site: www.nysparks.com
Key Personnel: Historic Site Mgr., Michael S. McGurty.
Institution Type/Description: Historic Site: living history museum located on site of last encampment of Washington's northern Continental Army, 1782-1783.
Hours & Admission Prices: Mon.-Sat. 10-5, Sun. 1-5. Admission for group tours & educational programs. Closed New Year's Day; Columbus Day; Thanksgiving; Christmas. &
Attendance: 23,000 (actual)

STORM KING ART CENTER, 1 Museum Rd., New Windsor, NY 12553. Tel.: 845-534-3115. Fax: 845-534-4457. Facebook: Storm King Art Center.
E-mail: info@stormkingartcenter.org
Web Site: stormking.org
Key Personnel: Pres., John P. Stern; Chm., James H. Ottaway, Jr.; Dir. & Cur., David R. Collens; Dir. Finance, Dwayne Jarvis; Dir. Devel., Rachel Coker; Dir. Education & Public Programs, Victoria Lichtendorf.
Institution Type/Description: Art Museum & Sculpture Park.
Hours & Admission Prices: Wed.-Sun. 10-4:30. Adults $15, senior citizens 65 & up $12, college students w/I.D. & youth 5-18 $8; discounts to AAM & ICOM members and bus groups of 15 or more with 2-week advance reservations; children 4 & under and members no charge. Closed Thanksgiving Day. &
Attendance: 76,000 (estimated)

New York

ACA GALLERIES - AMERICAN CONTEMPORARY ARTISTS, 529 W. 20th St., 5th Fl., New York, NY 10011. Tel.: 212-206-8080. Facebook; Instagram; Twitter.
E-mail: info@acagalleries.com
Web Site: www.acagalleries.com
Key Personnel: Contact, Dorian Bergen.
Institution Type/Description: Art Gallery.
Hours & Admission Prices: Tues.-Sat. 11-6; other times by appointment. No charge.

Attendance: 7,500 (estimated)

THE AKC MUSEUM OF THE DOG, 101 Park Ave., New York, NY 10178. Tel.: 212-696-8360. Facebook.
Web Site: www.museumofthedog.org
Key Personnel: Exec. Dir., Alan Fausel.
Institution Type/Description: Fine Arts Museum.
Hours & Admission Prices: Tues.-Sun. 10-5. Adults $15, seniors 65 & up, students 13-24 and active/retired military $10, children under 12 $5. Closed holidays.
Attendance: (actual)

ABRONS ARTS CENTER/HENRY STREET SETTLEMENT, 466 Grand St., New York, NY 10002-4804. Tel.: 212-598-0400. Fax: 212-505-8329.
E-mail: jdurham@henrystreet.org
Web Site: www.abronsartscenter.org
Formerly: The Main Gallery of Henry Street Settlement/Abrons Art Center
Key Personnel: Artistic Dir., Craig T. Peterson; Chm. (V), Scott L. Swid; Pres. (V), Ian D. Highet; House Mgr., Carl Johnson; Dir. Engagement & Visual Arts, Carolyn Sickles; Engagement Mgr. Visual Arts, Chantra Ellis; Registrar, Kim Cox.
Institution Type/Description: Arts Center.
Hours & Admission Prices: Tues.-Sat. 12-6. No charge; donations accepted. Closed national holidays.
Attendance: 40,000 (actual)

THE AFRICA CENTER, 1280 5th Ave., Ste. 7H, New York, NY 10029-7815. Tel.: 212-444-9795.
E-mail: info@theafricacenter.org
Web Site: www.theafricacenter.org
Formerly: The Museum for African Art
Key Personnel: CEO, Uzodinma M. Iweala; COO & CFO, Jenny Hourihan; Controller, Velky Valentin; Assoc. Cur, Evelyn Owen; Dir. Progs., Alana Hairston.
Institution Type/Description: African Art Center.
Hours & Admission Prices: Tues.-Thurs. 8-7, Fri. 8am-9pm, Sat. 9-9, Sun. 9-7. No charge.

AMERICAN ACADEMY OF ARTS AND LETTERS, 633 W. 155th St., New York, NY 10032-7501. Tel.: 212-368-5900.
E-mail: academy@artsandletters.org
Web Site: www.artsandletters.org
Key Personnel: Exec. Dir., Cody Upton; Deputy Dir., Ardith Holmgrain; Cur., Exhibs, Art Awards & Purchases, Souhad Rafey; Sr. Dir., Facilities & Construction, Jay Rahhali.
Institution Type/Description: Art Museum & Library.
Hours & Admission Prices: Galleries: Thurs.-Sun. 1-4, when exhibitions are held. No charge. Office: Mon.-Fri. 9:30-5. Closed holidays.
Attendance: 2,500

AMERICAN FOLK ART MUSEUM, 2 Lincoln Sq., Columbus Ave. @ W. 66th St., New York, NY 10023. Mailing Address: 4729 32nd Pl., Long Island City, NY 11101-2409. Tel.: 212-595-9533.
E-mail: info@folkartmuseum.org
Web Site: www.folkartmuseum.org
Key Personnel: Exec. Dir., Dr. Anne-Imelda Radice; Pres., Edward V. Blanchard, Jr.; Deputy Dir. Administration & Chief Fin. Officer, Kathleen Hayes; Deputy Dir. Curatorial Affairs, Chief Cur. & Dir. Exhibitions, Stacy Hollander; Cur. Art of the Self-Taught & Art Brut, Dr. Valerie Rousseau; Dir. Education, Rachel Rosen; Dir. Exhibition Production & Chief Registrar, Ann-Marie Reilly; Dir. Communications & Mktg., Kate Merlino; Deputy Dir. Devel., Karley Klopfenstein; Dir. Retail & Visitor Services, Stefanie Levinson; Coord. Public Programs, Rachel Heidenry.
Institution Type/Description: Folk Art Museum.
Hours & Admission Prices: Mon.-Thurs. & Sat. 11:30-7, Fri. noon-7:30, Sun. 12-6; guided tours by appointment. No charge.
Attendance: 150,000 (estimated)

AMERICAN IRISH HISTORICAL SOCIETY, 991 5th Ave., New York, NY 10028-0101. Tel.: 212-288-2263. Fax: 212-628-7927. Facebook: American Irish Historical Society.
E-mail: aihs@aihs.org
Web Site: www.aihs.org
Key Personnel: Pres. Gen., Thomas Dowling; Exec. Dir., Christopher P. Cahill.
Institution Type/Description: Research Library: housed in c.1900 townhouse.
Hours & Admission Prices: Mon.-Fri. 10-5. No charge; donations accepted.
Attendance: 3,000 (estimated)

AMERICAN JEWISH HISTORICAL SOCIETY, 15 W. 16th St., New York, NY 10011-6301. Tel.: 212-294-6160. Fax: 212-294-6161.
E-mail: info@ajhs.org
Web Site: www.ajhs.org
Key Personnel: Exec. Dir., Annie Polland, Ph.D.; DIr. Emeritus, Bernard Wax; Dir., Colls. & Engagement, Melani Meyers; Dir., Progs. & Opers., Chelsea Bracci.
Institution Type/Description: Ethnic History Museum.
Hours & Admission Prices: Center: Mon. & Wed. 9:30-8, Tues. & Thurs. 9:30-5, Fri. 9:30-4, Sun. 11-5. Reading Room: Mon.-Thurs. 9:30-6, Fri. 9:30-2, Sun. by appointment. No charge. Closed national holidays & major Jewish holidays.
Attendance: 2,000 (estimated)

AMERICAN MUSEUM OF NATURAL HISTORY, Central Park West at 79th St., New York, NY 10024-5193. Tel.: 212-769-5100. Facebook: @naturalhistory; Instagram & Twitter: @amnh.
E-mail: visitorinfo@amnh.org
Web Site: www.amnh.org
Key Personnel: Pres., Ellen V, Futter; Cur. in Charge, Herpetology, Frank T. Burbrink; Cur. in Charge, Earth & Planetary Sciences, Denton Ebel; Cur. in Charge, Mordecai-Mark Mac Low; Cur. in Charge, Scott A. Schaefer; Cur. in Charge, Nancy B. Simmons.
Institution Type/Description: Natural History Museum.
Hours & Admission Prices: Daily 10-5:45. Adults $23, students & seniors $18, children 2-12 $13. Additional fees for special exhibitions. Closed Thanksgiving; Christmas.
Attendance: 5,000,000 (estimated)

AMERICAN NUMISMATIC SOCIETY, 75 Varick St., Ste. 1101, New York, NY 10013-1917. Tel.: 212-571-4470. Facebook: American Numismatic Society.
E-mail: membership@numismatics.org
Web Site: www.numismatics.org
Key Personnel: Exec. Dir., Gilles Bransbourg; Collections Mgr., Dr. Elena Stolyarik.
Institution Type/Description: Numismatics History Museum.
Hours & Admission Prices: Library: Mon.-Fri. 9:30-4. $20 per day, members & students no charge. Curational & Archives: by appointment. Curatorial: $50 per day; archives $20 per day, government photo ID required; students with valid ID no charge.
Attendance: 1,300 (estimated)

AMERICAS SOCIETY, 680 Park Ave., (at 68th St.), New York, NY 10065-5072. Tel.: 212-249-8950.
E-mail: artgallery@as-coa.org
Web Site: www.as-coa.org/visual-arts
Formerly: Center for Inter-American Relations
Key Personnel: Pres. & CEO, Susan Segal; Dir. & Chief Cur. Visual Arts, Aime Iglesias Lukin.
Institution Type/Description: Art Gallery.
Hours & Admission Prices: Wed.-Sat. 12-6. See website for hours. Closed major holidays.
Attendance: 12,000 (estimated)

ANTHOLOGY FILM ARCHIVES, 32 Second Ave. (at 2nd. St.), New York, NY 10003-8631. Tel.: 212-505-5181. Fax: 212-477-2714.
Web Site: www.anthologyfilmarchives.org
Key Personnel: Pres. (V) & Dir., Jonas Mekas; Bd. Chm., Barney Oldfield; Dir. & Sec., John Mhiripiri; Dir. Publications, Wendy Dorsett; Archivist, John Klacsmann.
Institution Type/Description: Film Museum.
Hours & Admission Prices: Jan. to 3rd week in Aug. & Sept. to 3rd week in Dec. Film Screenings: Mon.-Fri. 6-11, Sat.-Sun. 3-11. Adults $9, senior citizens & students $5; members no charge.
Attendance: 50,000 (estimated)

APERTURE FOUNDATION, 547 W. 27th St., 4th Fl., New York, NY 10001-5511. Tel.: 212-505-5555. Fax: 212-979-7759. Facebook, Instagram, Twitter.
E-mail: info@aperture.org
Web Site: www.aperture.org
Key Personnel: Exec. Dir., Chris Boot; Creative Dir., Lesley A. Martin; Chair, Cathy Kaplan; Dir. Sales & Mktg., Kellie McLaughlin.
Institution Type/Description: Photography Foundation.
Hours & Admission Prices: Mon.-Sat. 10-6; call for extended hours. No charge. Closed New Year's Eve & Day; Martin Luther King Jr. Day; Presidents' Day; Memorial Day; Independence Day; Labor Day; Thanksgiving & day after; Christmas Eve, Day & week.
Attendance: 16,887 (actual)

ARSENAL GALLERY, Arsenal Bldg., Central Park, Fifth Ave. & 64th St., New York, NY 10065. Mailing Address: New York City Dept. of Parks & Recreation, The Arsenal, Central Park, Rm. 20, New York, NY 10065. Tel.: 212-360-8163. Fax: 212-360-1329.
E-mail: artandantiquities@parks.nyc.gov
Web Site: www.nyc.gov/parks/art
Institution Type/Description: Art Gallery.
Hours & Admission Prices: Mon.-Fri. 9-5. No charge.

ARTHUR A. HOUGHTON JR. GALLERY & THE GREAT HALL GALLERY, 7 E. 7th St., Foundation Bldg., New York, NY 10003-8128. Mailing Address: The Cooper Union School of Art, 30 Cooper Square, New York, NY 10003-7120. Tel.: 212-353-4200.
E-mail: artschool@cooper.edu
Web Site: www.cooper.edu/about/galleries-auditoriums
Key Personnel: Acting Dean of Art School, Michael Essl.
Institution Type/Description: Art Gallery.
Hours & Admission Prices: Mon.-Fri. 12-7, Sat. 12-5. No charge.

ARTISTS SPACE, 55 Walker St., New York, NY 10013-2505. Tel.: 212-226-3970. Fax: 212-226-7036. Facebook: Artists Space.
E-mail: info@artistsspace.org
Web Site: www.artistsspace.org
Key Personnel: Exec. Dir., Jay Sanders.
Institution Type/Description: Art Gallery.
Hours & Admission Prices: Wed.-Sun. 12-6. Suggested Donation $5; members no charge. Closed New Year's Eve & Day; Independence Day; Thanksgiving; Christmas Eve & Day.
Attendance: 10,000 (estimated)

ASIA SOCIETY MUSEUM, 725 Park Ave., New York, NY 10021-5088. Tel.: 212-288-6400.
E-mail: info@asiasociety.org
Web Site: www.asiasociety.org
Formerly: Asia Society Galleries
Key Personnel: Pres. & CEO, Josette Sheeran; Exec. Vice Pres., Tom Nagorski; Museum Dir., Boon Hui Tan.
Institution Type/Description: Asian Art Museum.
Hours & Admission Prices: July to Labor Day Tues.-Thurs. & Sat.-Sun. 11-6; Sept.-June Tues.-Thurs. & Sat.-Sun. 11-6, Fri. 11-9. Adults $7; members, disabled persons & companion, children under 16 accompanied by a parent & Fri. 6-9 no charge.
Attendance: 84,580 (estimated)

ASIAN AMERICAN ARTS CENTRE, 111 Norfolk St., Ofc 1, New York, NY 10002-3394. Tel.: 212-233-2154. Fax: 360-283-2154.
E-mail: aaacinfo@artspiral.org
Web Site: www.artspiral.org
Key Personnel: Exec. Dir. & Cur., Robert Lee; Chm. (V), Eleanor Yung.
Institution Type/Description: Contemporary American Culture Art Museum.
Hours & Admission Prices: Tues.-Fri. 12:30-6:30, Sat. 1:30-4:30. No charge; donations accepted.
Attendance: 5,000 (estimated)

BABCOCK GALLERIES, 525 W. 25th St., 11th Fl., New York, NY 10001-5501. Tel.: 212-767-1852. Fax: 212-767-1857.
E-mail: info@babcockgalleries.com
Web Site: www.babcockgalleries.com
Key Personnel: Owner, John Driscoll, Ph.D.; Dir., Kate Deatly-Peluso; Senior Assoc., Lisa Koonce; Sr. Assoc. & Cur. John Frederick Kensett Catalogue Raisonne, Huntley Platt; Gallery Asst., Daniella Hansen.
Institution Type/Description: Art Gallery.
Hours & Admission Prices: Mon.-Fri. 10-5, Sat. by appointment. No charge.

BARD GRADUATE CENTER; DECORATIVE ARTS, DESIGN HISTORY, MATERIAL CULTURE, 18 W. 86th St., New York, NY 10024-3602. Tel.: 212-501-3023. Fax: 212-501-3079. TDD: 212-501-3012 (for public programs only).
E-mail: gallery@bgc.bard.edu
Web Site: www.bgc.bard.edu
Key Personnel: Dir. & Founder, Dr. Susan Weber; Dean, Dr. Peter N. Miller; Dean Academic Admin. & Student Affairs, Elena Pinto Simon; Gallery Dir., Nina Stritzler-Levine; Editor West 86th: A Journal of Decorative Arts, Design History and Material Culture, Paul Stirton.
Institution Type/Description: Decorative Art Academic Institution & Gallery.
Hours & Admission Prices: Tues.-Wed. & Fri.-Sun. 11-5, Thurs. 11-8. Adults $7, senior citizens & students $5; discounts to AAM & ICOM members and museum staff; Thurs. after 5pm & children under 12 no charge. Closed New Year's Day; Martin Luther King Jr. Day; Easter; Memorial Day; Independence Day; Labor Day; Thanksgiving & day after; Christmas.
Attendance: 3,000 (estimated)

BELVEDERE CASTLE, Mid-Park at 79th St., New York, NY 10021. Mailing Address: Central Park Conservancy, 14 E. 60th St., New York, NY 10022. Tel.: 212-772-0288. Fax: 212-772-0214.
Web Site: www.centralparknyc.org
Key Personnel: Assoc. Vice Pres. Institute for Urban Parks, Terry Carta.
Institution Type/Description: Historic Site & Preservation Project: 1872 Gothic tower within 843 acre landmark park designed by Frederick Law Olmsted and Calvert Vaux.
Hours & Admission Prices: Sat.-Sun. 10-5. No charge; donations accepted. Closed New Year's Day; Thanksgiving; Christmas.
Attendance: 100,000 (actual)

BERNARD JUDAICA MUSEUM, CONGREGATION EMANU-EL OF THE CITY OF NEW YORK, 1 E. 65th St., New York, NY 10065-6501. Tel.: 212-744-1400. Fax: 212-570-0826.
E-mail: info@emanuelnyc.org
Web Site: www.emanuelnyc.org/museum
Key Personnel: Pres., John H. Streicker; Dir. Devel., Robyn W. Cimbol.
Institution Type/Description: Judaica Museum: housed in 1929 synagogue.
Hours & Admission Prices: Sun.-Thurs. 10-4:30; docent tours by appointment. No charge. Closed Jewish holidays.

BOWERY GALLERY, 530 W. 25th St., 4th Fl., New York, NY 10001-5545. Tel.: 646-230-6655.
E-mail: info@bowerygallery.org
Web Site: www.bowerygallery.org
Institution Type/Description: Art Gallery.
Hours & Admission Prices: Tues.-Sat. 11-6.

BOXING HALL OF CHAMPIONS, 8022 S. Rainbow Blvd., Las Vegas, NV 89139-6477. Tel.: 702-582-7040.
E-mail: info@bhoc.com
Institution Type/Description: Boxing History Museum.
Hours & Admission Prices: Call for hours.

CASTLE CLINTON NATIONAL MONUMENT, Battery Park, New York, NY 10004. Mailing Address: 26 Wall St., New York, NY 10005-1996. Tel.: 212-344-7220. Fax: 212-285-6874.
E-mail: shirley_mckinney@nps.gov
Web Site: www.nps.gov/cacl
Key Personnel: Supt., Shirley McKinney.
Institution Type/Description: Historic Site.
Hours & Admission Prices: Daily 7:45-5. No charge. Closed Christmas.
Attendance: 2,433,250 (actual)

THE CATHEDRAL OF ST. JOHN THE DIVINE, 1047 Amsterdam Ave. & 112th St., New York, NY 10025-1798. Tel.: 212-316-7540.
E-mail: info@stjohndivine.org
Web Site: www.stjohndivine.org
Key Personnel: Dean, Very Rev. Dr. Clifton Daniel, III.
Institution Type/Description: Historic Building & Religious Museum: housed in a Romanesque & neo-Gothic Cathedral.
Hours & Admission Prices: Daily 7:30-6. Visitor Center & Pop-Up Show: daily 9-5. Suggested Donation: adults $10, seniors & students $8.
Attendance: 1,000,000 (estimated)

CAUSEY CONTEMPORARY GALLERY, 15 Broad St. #1428, New York, NY 10005. Tel.: 917-328-3140.
E-mail: info@causeycontemporary.com
Web Site: causeycontemporary.com

Key Personnel: Owner & Dir., Tracy Causey-Jeffery; Assoc. Dir., M. Quinton Jeffery.
Institution Type/Description: Art Gallery.
Hours & Admission Prices: Call for hours.

CENTER FOR BOOK ARTS, 28 W. 27th St., 3rd Fl., New York, NY 10001-6906. Tel.: 212-481-0295. Fax: 866-708-8994.
E-mail: info@centerforbookarts.org
Web Site: centerforbookarts.org
Key Personnel: Chair, Stephen Bury; Exec. Dir., Alexander Campos.
Institution Type/Description: Contemporary Book Arts Museum.
Hours & Admission Prices: Mon.-Fri. 11-6, Sat. 10-5. No charge; donations accepted. Closed New Year's Day; Passover-Easter weekend; Memorial Day; Independence Day; Labor Day; Yom Kippur; Christmas. &
Attendance: 20,000 (estimated)

CENTRAL PARK ZOO, 64th St. & 5th Ave., New York, NY 10065. Mailing Address: c/o Wildlife Conservation Society, 2300 Southern Blvd., Bronx, NY 10460. Tel.: 212-439-6500.
E-mail: cpzinfo@wcs.org
Web Site: centralparkzoo.com
Key Personnel: Dir., Craig Piper; Cur. Animals, Susan Cardillo.
Institution Type/Description: Zoo.
Hours & Admission Prices: April to Nov. Mon.-Fri. 10-5, weekends & holidays 10-5:30; Nov.-March daily 10-4:30. Adult $12, senior $9, child 3-12 $7; discounts to WCS members & Total Experience tickets purchased online; child 2 & under no charge.

CHANCELLOR ROBERT R. LIVINGSTON MASONIC LIBRARY & MUSEUM, 71 W. 23rd St., New York, NY 10010-4102. Tel.: 212-337-6620. Fax: 212-633-2639.
E-mail: info@nymasoniclibrary.org
Web Site: www.nymasoniclibrary.org
Key Personnel: Dir., Thomas M. Savini; Pres. (V), Bruce Renner; Head Librarian, Jo-Ann E. Wong; Cur., Catherine M. Walter.
Institution Type/Description: History Museum: located in Masonic Hall.
Hours & Admission Prices: Mon., Wed. & Fri. 8:30-4:30, Tues. & Thurs. 12-8. No charge; donations accepted. Closed legal holidays. &
Attendance: 3,200 (actual)

CHILDREN'S CULTURAL CENTER OF NATIVE AMERICA, 203 W. 107th St., Ste B, New York, NY 10025. Tel.: 646-330-2125. Fax: 646-707-0414.
E-mail: center@cccona.nyc
Web Site: www.cccona.nyc
Formerly: Children's Museum of the Native American
Key Personnel: Dir., Irma LaGuerre.
Institution Type/Description: Children's Museum.
Hours & Admission Prices: Sept.-June Mon.-Fri. 10:30-1 by appointment. Admission $9.

CHILDREN'S MUSEUM OF MANHATTAN, The Tisch Building, 212 W. 83rd St., New York, NY 10024-4901. Tel.: 212-721-1223.
E-mail: info@cmom.org
Web Site: www.cmom.org
Key Personnel: CEO & Dir., Aileen Hefferren; COO, Jacques M. Brunswick; Deputy Dir. Education & Guest Services, Leslie Bushara; CAO, Jane McIntosh.
Institution Type/Description: Children's Museum: housed in former elementary school building.
Hours & Admission Prices: Tues.-Fri. & Sun. 10-5, Sat. 10-7. Admission $15, senior citizens & persons with disabilities $12; children under one & members no charge. Closed New Year's Day; Thanksgiving; Christmas. &
Attendance: 340,000 (estimated)

CHILDREN'S MUSEUM OF THE ARTS, 103 Charlton St., New York, NY 10014-3645. Tel.: 212-274-0986. Fax: 212-274-1776. Facebook: Children's Museum of the Arts.
E-mail: info@cmany.org
Web Site: www.cmany.org
Key Personnel: Exec. Dir., Barbara Hunt McLanahan; Deputy Dir., Erica Freyberger; Dir. Fine Arts & Cur., Jil Weinstock; Dir. Community Progs., Michelle Lopez; Dir. WEE Arts & Early Childhood Progs., Tom Burnett; Media Lab Mgr., Chloe Sun.
Institution Type/Description: Children's Museum.
Hours & Admission Prices: Mon. 12-5, Thurs.-Fri. 12-6, Sat. -Sun. 10-5. Children & Adults $12; Thurs. 4-6 and seniors 66 & over pay as you wish; children under one no charge. Closed Memorial Day; Independence Day; Labor Day; Thanksgiving; Christmas Day. &
Attendance: 110,000 (actual)

CHINA INSTITUTE GALLERY, CHINA INSTITUTE IN AMERICA, 100 Washington St., New York, NY 10006-1707. Tel.: 212-744-8181. Fax: 212-628-4159.
E-mail: gallery@chinainstitute.org
Web Site: www.chinainstitute.org
Key Personnel: Gallery Dir., Willow Weilan Hai; Pres., James B. Heimowitz; Asst. Dir., Insher Pan.
Institution Type/Description: Art Gallery.
Hours & Admission Prices: Mon.-Wed & Fri.-Sat. 10-5, Thurs. 10-8. Adults $10, students & seniors $5; Thurs. 5-8, members & children under 16 no charge. Closed major holidays; between exhibitions. &
Attendance: 12,000 (actual)

CHOCO-STORY NEW YORK, 350 Hudson St., New York, NY 10014. Tel.: 917-261-4252. Facebook.
E-mail: chocostoryny@mrchocolate.com
Web Site: mrchocolate.com/pages/museum
Key Personnel: Owner, Jacques Torres.
Institution Type/Description: Chocolate Museum.
Hours & Admission Prices: Wed.-Sun. 10-5. Adults $15, students, Seniors & military $12, children 4-12 $10; discount to groups of 20 or more with reservation.

THE COLLECTORS CLUB, INC., 22 E. 35th St., New York, NY 10016-3806. Tel.: 212-683-0559. Fax: 212-481-1269.
E-mail: info@collectorsclub.org
Web Site: www.collectorsclub.org
Key Personnel: Pres., Lawrence Haber; Vice Pres., Joan Harmer; Treas., Roger S. Brody; Sec., Matthew Healey.
Institution Type/Description: Historic House and Library: housed in 1902, five-story brownstone rowhouse, former residence of Thomas B. Clark; neo-Georgian architecture designed by Stanford White.
Hours & Admission Prices: Mon.-Fri. 10-5, call first. No charge. Closed major holidays.

THE CONSERVATORY GARDEN, Fifth Ave. at 105th St., New York, NY 10029. Mailing Address: Central Park Conservancy, 14 E. 60th St., New York, NY 10022. Tel.: 212-310-6600. Fax: 212-360-1388.
E-mail: press@centralparknyc.org
Web Site: www.centralparknyc.org
Key Personnel: Dir. & C.E.O. & Central Park Admin., Douglas Blonsky; C.O.O. & Chief Landscape Architect, Christopher Nolan.
Institution Type/Description: Botanical & Aquatic Gardens: six acre formal garden.
Hours & Admission Prices: Daily 8-dusk. No charge. &
Attendance: 10,000 (estimated)

COOPER HEWITT, SMITHSONIAN DESIGN MUSEUM, 2 E. 91st St., New York, NY 10128-0669. Tel.: 212-849-8400. Fax: 212-849-8401. Facebook, Twitter, Instagram.
E-mail: cooperhewitt@si.edu
Web Site: www.cooperhewitt.org
Formerly: Cooper-Hewitt, National Design Museum, Smithsonian Institution
Key Personnel: Dir., Caroline Baumann; Chm. (V), Barbara A. Mandel; Pres. (V), Beth Comstock; Cur. Dir., Cara McCarty; Cur. Product Design & Decorative Arts, Sarah Coffin; Cur. Contemporary Design, Ellen Lupton; Cur. Wallcoverings, Gregory Herringshaw; Librarian, Stephen H. Van Dyk; Dir. Retail, Robert Nachman.
Institution Type/Description: Design Museum: housed in 1901 Andrew Carnegie Mansion.
Hours & Admission Prices: Sun.-Fri. 10-6, Sat. 10-9. Adults $18, seniors $12, students $9; members and 18 & under no charge. Closed Thanksgiving; Christmas. &
Attendance: 418,000 (actual)

CZECH CENTER NEW YORK, 321 E. 73rd St., New York, NY 10021. Tel.: 646-422-3399. Fax: 646-422-3383. Facebook: @CzechCenterNewYork.
E-mail: info@czechcenter.com
Web Site: www.czechcenter.com
Key Personnel: Dir., Mrs. Barbara Karpetova.
Institution Type/Description: Civic Art & Culture Center Museum.
Hours & Admission Prices: Mon. & Wed.-Fri. 10-6, Tues. 10-7. No charge; donations accepted. Closed New Year's Day; Christmas Eve, Day & day after. &
Attendance: 10,000 (estimated)

DAVID RICHARD GALLERY - NEW YORK, 211 E. 121st St., New York, NY 10035. Tel.: 212-882-1705.
E-mail: d@davidrichardgallery.com
Web Site: www.davidrichardgallery.com
Key Personnel: Co Dir., David Eichholtz; Co. Dir., Richard Barger.

Institution Type/Description: Art Gallery.
Hours & Admission Prices: Wed.-Sat. 10-6; other times by appointment.

DIA ART FOUNDATION, 535 W. 22nd St., 4th Fl., New York, NY 10011-1119. Tel.: 212-989-5566. Fax: 212-989-4055. Facebook: Dia Art Foundation.
E-mail: info@diaart.org
Web Site: www.diaart.org
Key Personnel: Dir., Jessica Morgan; Chm. Bd. (V), Nathalie de Gunzburg; Dir. Operations, James P. Schaeufele; Dir. Digital Media, Sara Tucker; Dir. Publications, Stephen Hoban.
Institution Type/Description: Art Center.
Hours & Admission Prices: See website for individual listings. Discounts to other museum staff, AAM & ICOM members. &

DILLON GALLERY, 487 W. 22nd St., New York, NY 10011-2501. Tel.: 212-727-8585. Fax: 212-727-8705.
E-mail: mail@dillongallery.com
Web Site: www.dillongallery.com
Institution Type/Description: Art Gallery.
Hours & Admission Prices: Call for hours.

DISCOVERY TIMES SQUARE, 226 W. 44th St., New York, NY 10036. Tel.: 866-987-9692.
E-mail: info@tsxnyc.com
Web Site: www.discoverytsx.com
Institution Type/Description: General Museum.
Hours & Admission Prices: Sun.-Thurs. 10-8, Fri.-Sat. 10-9. Adults $19-$27, Seniors 65 & over $16.50-$23.50, children 4-12 $14.50-$19.50. &

THE DRAWING CENTER, 35 Wooster St., New York, NY 10013-5300. Tel.: 212-219-2166. Fax: 888-380-3362.
E-mail: info@drawingcenter.org
Web Site: www.drawingcenter.org
Key Personnel: Exec. Dir., Brett Littman; Co Chm., Jane Dresner Sadaka; Co Chm., Rhiannan Kubicka; Exec. Editor of the Drawing Center's Publications, Noah Chasin; Dir. Education & Community Prog., Aimee Good; Mng. Editor, Joanna Berman Ahlberg; Chief Cur., Claire Gilman; Cur, Open Sessions, Lisa Sigal; Communications Dir., Molly Gross; Coord. Operations, Dan Gillespie; Dir. Finance & Admin., Champ Knecht; Dir. Devel., DeLana Dameron-John; Mng. Exhibitions, Olga Tetkowski; Asst. Cur., Amber Harper; Devel. Assoc., Carlos Bernabe.
Institution Type/Description: Art Museum: housed in c.1866 historic cast iron building.
Hours & Admission Prices: Wed. & Fri.-Sun. 12-6, Thurs. 12-8. Adults $5, students & seniors $3; discounts to AAM & ICOM members; members no charge. Closed New Year's Day; Thanksgiving; Christmas. &
Attendance: 55,000 (actual)

DYCKMAN FARMHOUSE MUSEUM AND PARK, 4881 Broadway, (at 204th St.), New York, NY 10034-3101. Tel.: 212-304-9422.
E-mail: info@dyckmanfarmhouse.org
Web Site: www.dyckmanfarmhouse.org
Key Personnel: Exec. Dir., Meridith Horsford; Dir. Education, Fabiola Caceres.
Institution Type/Description: Historic House: 1784 Dyckman House, old Dutch-American farmhouse.
Hours & Admission Prices: April-Sept. Thurs. 11-7, Fri.-Sat. 11-4; Oct.-March Fri. & Sun. 11-4. Museum: donation requested. Gardens no charge.
Attendance: 12,924 (actual)

EL MUSEO DEL BARRIO, 1230 Fifth Ave., New York, NY 10029-9962. Tel.: 212-831-7272. Fax: 212-831-7927. Facebook; Twitter.
E-mail: info@elmuseo.org
Web Site: www.elmuseo.org
Key Personnel: Chairwoman, Maria Eugenia Maury; Exec. Dir., Patrick Charpenel; Dir. Govt. & Community Affairs, Ana Chireno; Dir. Finance, Evelyn Rivera; Cur., Rocio Aranda-Alvarado; Permanent Collection Mgr., Noel Valentin; Head Retail & Visitor Services, Monika A. Garcia.
Institution Type/Description: Caribbean, Latino and Latin American Art Museum.
Hours & Admission Prices: Wed.-Sat. 11-6, Sun. 12-5. Suggested Donation: adults $9, senior citizens & students $5; discount to AAM & ICOM members; 3rd Sat. each month, seniors on Wed., members & children under 12 no charge. Closed New Year's Day; Independence Day; Thanksgiving; Christmas Day. &
Attendance: 300,000 (estimated)

FEDERAL HALL NATIONAL MEMORIAL, 26 Wall St., New York, NY 10005-1996. Tel.: 212-825-6990. Fax: 212-668-2899. Facebook: Federal Hall National Memorial.

E-mail: shirley_mckinney@nps.gov
Web Site: www.nps.gov/feha/
Key Personnel: Supt., Shirley McKinney.
Institution Type/Description: History Museum.
Hours & Admission Prices: Mon.-Fri. 9-5. No charge. Closed Thanksgiving & Christmas Day. &
Attendance: 148,601 (actual)

FRAUNCES TAVERN(R) MUSEUM, 54 Pearl St., New York, NY 10004-4300. Tel.: 212-425-1778. Fax: 212-509-3467.
E-mail: exd@frauncestavernmuseum.org
Web Site: www.frauncestavernmuseum.org
Key Personnel: Exec. Dir., Jessica B. Phillips; Marketing Coord., Amy Kennard; Membership Mgr., Colyn Hunt.
Institution Type/Description: History Museum: housed in 1907 renovated & restored 18th-century tavern & four adjacent 19th-century buildings.
Hours & Admission Prices: Daily 12-5. Adults $7, seniors, students & children 8-6 $4; children under 6, members & active military no charge. Closed New Year's Day; Thanksgiving; Christmas. &
Attendance: 26,000 (actual)

THE FRICK COLLECTION, 1 East 70th St., New York, NY 10021-4981. Tel.: 212-288-0700. Fax: 212-628-4417.
E-mail: info@frick.org
Web Site: www.frick.org
Key Personnel: Dir., Ian Wardropper; Chief Cur., Xavier Salomon; Gen. Counsel & Asst. Sec., Alison Lonshein; Deputy Dir. & C.O.O., Joseph Shatoff; C.F.O. & Asst. Treas., Michael Paccione; Chief HR Officer, Dana Spencer Winfield; Deputy Dir. External Affairs, Tia Chapman; Librarian, Stephen J. Bury.
Institution Type/Description: Art Museum: formerly private home, c.1913-1914 building designed by Carrere & Hastings.
Hours & Admission Prices: Collection: Tues.-Sat. 10-6, Sun. 11-5. Reference Library; Sept.-May. Mon.-Fri. 10-5, Sat. 10-2; June-July Mon.-Fri. 10-5; August Tues.-Thurs. 10-5. Adults $22, persons with disabilities & seniors 65 & over $17, youth 10-17 $12; members no charge. Children under 10 not admitted. Closed New Year's Day; Martin Luther King Jr. Day; Lincoln's Birthday; Presidents' Day; Memorial Day; Independence Day; Labor Day; Columbus Day; Thanksgiving; Christmas. &
Attendance: 290,992 (actual)

GALLERY 456, Chinese American Arts Council, 456 Broadway, 3rd Fl., New York, NY 10013. Tel.: 212-431-9740. Fax: 212-431-9789. Facebook & Twitter: @caacarts.
E-mail: info@caacarts.org
Web Site: www.caacarts.org
Key Personnel: Dir. & C.E.O., Alan Chow.
Institution Type/Description: Art Gallery.
Hours & Admission Prices: Mon.-Fri. 12-5. No charge; donations accepted.
Attendance: 2,000 (estimated)

GENERAL GRANT NATIONAL MEMORIAL, W. 122nd St. & Riverside Dr., New York, NY 10027-2522. Mailing Address: 26 Wall St., New York, NY 10005. Tel.: 212-670-7251.
E-mail: shirley_mckinney@nps.gov
Web Site: www.nps.gov/gegr/
Key Personnel: Supt., Shirley McKinney; Deputy Supt., Lorena Harris; Supervisory Park Ranger, Ramon Mangual; Lead Park Ranger, Christopher (Sierra) Willoughby.
Institution Type/Description: Historical Museum: housed in 1897 building.
Hours & Admission Prices: Visitor Center: Wed.-Sun. 9-5. Mausoleum: Wed.-Sun. 10-5. No charge. Closed New Year's Day; Thanksgiving; Christmas.
Attendance: 118,000 (actual)

THE GRACIE MANSION CONSERVANCY, E. 88th st. & East End Ave, New York, NY 10028. Tel.: 212-570-4751. Fax: 212-570-4493.
E-mail: gracieinfo@cityhall.nyc.gov
Web Site: www.nyc.gov/gracie
Key Personnel: Exec. Dir., Roxanne John.
Institution Type/Description: Historic House: 1799 Archibald Gracie country house. Designated the mayoral residence of New York City in 1942.
Hours & Admission Prices: Tours: by appointment. &
Attendance: 40,000 (estimated)

GREY ART GALLERY, NEW YORK UNIVERSITY, 100 Washington Square E., New York, NY 10003-6688. Tel.: 212-998-6780. Fax: 212-995-4024. Facebook, Instagram, Twitter.
E-mail: greyartgallery@nyu.edu
Web Site: greyartgallery.nyu.edu

Key Personnel: Dir., Lynn Gumpert; Assoc. Dir., Head Exhibitions & Collections, Michele Wong; Head Education & Public Programs, Lucy Oakley; Head Admin., Jodi Hanel; Asst. to Dir./Press Officer, Ally Mintz; Administrative Asst., Amber Lynn; Chief Preparator, Richard Wager; Preparator, Noah Landfield.
Institution Type/Description: Fine Arts Museum: housed in Main Building of New York University on Washington Square, historic center of early New York City.
Hours & Admission Prices: Tues. & Thurs.-Fri. 11-6, Wed. 11-8, Sat. 11-5. Suggested Donation: $3 per person. Closed Memorial Day weekend; Independence Day; Thanksgiving weekend. &
Attendance: 25,000 (estimated)

GROLIER CLUB LIBRARY, 47 E. 60th St., New York, NY 10022. Tel.: 212-838-6690 ext. 5. Fax: 212-838-2445. Facebook: Grolier Club Library.
E-mail: mconstantinou@grolierclub.org
Web Site: www.grolierclub.org
Key Personnel: Librarian, Meghan Constantinou.
Institution Type/Description: Library.
Hours & Admission Prices: Sept.-July Mon.-Sat. 10-5. No charge. Closed holidays.

GROUND ZERO MUSEUM WORKSHOP, 420 W. 14th St., Fl. 2, New York, NY 10014. Tel.: 212-924-1040.
E-mail: groundzeromuseum@aol.com
Web Site: groundzeromuseumworkshop.org
Key Personnel: Dir., Marlon Suson.
Institution Type/Description: History Museum.
Hours & Admission Prices: Tours: Sun.-Mon. 12-2, Tues. & Thurs.-Fri. 11-1, Sat. 11, 1, & 3. Adults $25, seniors & children $19; family members of 9/11 victims & active FDNY, PAPD & NYDP no charge.
Attendance: 15,000 (estimated)

HAMILTON GRANGE NATIONAL MEMORIAL, 414 W. 141st St., New York, NY 10031. Mailing Address: c/o Federal Hall NM, 26 Wall St., New York, NY 10005. Tel.: 646-548-2310.
E-mail: shirley_mckinney@nps.gov
Web Site: www.nps.gov/hagr
Key Personnel: Supt., Shirley McKinney.
Institution Type/Description: History Museum & Historic House: home of Alexander Hamilton.
Hours & Admission Prices: Wed.-Sun. 9-5. No charge. Closed Thanksgiving; Christmas Day. &
Attendance: 11,478 (actual)

HAMPDEN-BOOTH THEATRE LIBRARY AT THE PLAYERS, 16 Gramercy Park S., New York, NY 10003-1705. Tel.: 212-228-1861.
E-mail: hampdenboo@aol.com
Web Site: hampdenbooth.org
Key Personnel: Cur. & Librarian, Raymond Wemmlinger.
Institution Type/Description: Art & Theater Museum: housed in remodeled Gothic Revival townhouse.
Hours & Admission Prices: Mon.-Fri. 9-5 by appointment only. No charge; donations accepted.

HISPANIC SOCIETY MUSEUM & LIBRARY, 155th St. & Broadway, New York, NY 10032. Mailing Address: 613 W. 155th St., New York, NY 10032-7597. Tel.: 212-926-2234. Fax: 212-690-0743.
E-mail: info@hispanicsociety.org
Web Site: www.hispanicsociety.org
Formerly: The Hispanic Society of America
Key Personnel: Exec. Dir. & Pres., Mitchell A. Codding; Asst. Dir. & Cur. Decorative Arts, Margaret E. Connors McQuade; Cur. Manuscripts & Rare Books, Dr. John O'Neill; Sr. Cur. Paintings, Drawings & Metalwork, Marcus B. Burke; Cur. Prints & Photographs, Patrick Lenaghan; Cur. Sculpture, Archaeology & Textiles, Constancio del Alamo; Education, Cristina Domeneca.
Institution Type/Description: Art Museum & Research Library.
Hours & Admission Prices: See website for hours. No charge; donations accepted. Closed holidays; New Year's Eve & Day; Thanksgiving weekend; Christmas Eve, Day & week.
Attendance: 25,000 (estimated)

HISTORIC HOUSE TRUST OF NEW YORK CITY, The Arsenal, 830 Fifth Ave., Rm. 203, New York, NY 10065-7001. Tel.: 212-360-8282. Fax: 212-360-8201. Facebook: The Official Historic House Trust of New York City.
E-mail: hhtinfo@parks.nyc.gov
Web Site: www.historichousetrust.org

Key Personnel: Exec. Dir., John Krawchuk; Chair, John Gustafsson; Sec., Gary Ross; Treas., Lisa Ackerman.
Institution Type/Description: Historic Agency: created in 1989 to preserve and promote 23 Historic House museums located on Park land in the five boroughs.
Hours & Admission Prices: Visit website for information.
Attendance: 815,619 (actual)

HUNTER COLLEGE ART GALLERIES, 695 Park Ave., New York, NY 10065-5085. Tel.: 212-772-4991. Fax: 212-772-4554.
E-mail: hcag@hunter.cuny.edu
Web Site: www.hunter.cuny.edu/art/galleries
Key Personnel: Dir., Joachim Pissarro; Head Preparator, Phi Nguyen; Dir. Exhibitions & Cur., Sarah Watson.
Institution Type/Description: Art Galleries.
Hours & Admission Prices: Sept.-June: Bertha and Karl Leubsdorf Art Gallery: Tues.-Sat. 1-6. Times Square Gallery: Tues.-Sat. 1-6. No charge. Closed Christmas; New Year's Day. &
Attendance: 10,000 (estimated)

ILDIKO BUTLER GALLERY, FORDHAM UNIVERSITY, Lincoln Center Campus, 113 W. 60th St., New York, NY 10023. Mailing Address: Fordham University, Dept. of Theatre & Visual Arts, 113 W. 60th St., Rm. 423, New York, NY 10023. Tel.: 212-636-6073. Fax: 212-636-6788.
E-mail: contact@fordhamuniversitygalleries.com
Web Site: ildikobutlergallery.com
Formerly: Center Gallery, Fordham University
Key Personnel: Dir., Stephan Apicella-Hitchcock.
Institution Type/Description: Art Gallery.
Hours & Admission Prices: Call for hours. No charge. &

THE INTERCHURCH CENTER, 475 Riverside Dr., New York, NY 10115-0003. Tel.: 212-870-2200. Fax: 212-870-2440.
E-mail: admin@interchurch-center.org
Web Site: www.interchurch-center.org
Key Personnel: Pres. & Exec. Dir., Paula M. Mayo; Chm. (V), Louis Barbarin; Cur., Frank DeGregorie; Ecumenical Librarian, Tracey Del Duca.
Institution Type/Description: Library with Exhibits.
Hours & Admission Prices: Mon.-Fri. 10-5. No charge. Closed legal holidays; Good Friday; day after Thanksgiving; Christmas Eve. &
Attendance: 5,000

INTERNATIONAL CENTER OF PHOTOGRAPHY MUSEUM, 79 Essex St., New York, NY 10002. Tel.: 212-857-0000. Facebook; Instagram; Twitter.
E-mail: info@icp.org
Web Site: www.icp.org
Key Personnel: Exec. Dir., Mark Lubell; Chm. Bd. (V), Caryl S. Englander; Pres. (V), Jeffrey A. Rosen; Controller, Victor Quinones; Chief Devel. Officer, Kirra Steel; Sr. Dir. Operations & Visitor Engagement, Karen Eckhaus; Dir. Exhibitions & Collections, Erin Barnett.
Institution Type/Description: Photography Museum.
Hours & Admission Prices: Wed. & Fri.-Mon. 11-7, Thurs. 11-9. Adults $16, seniors 62 & over, military, students with ID and visitors with disabilities $12; discounts to SNAP/EBT members; ICP members & students, children 18 & under and caregivers of disabled no charge. &
Attendance: 100,000 (estimated)

INTERNATIONAL PRINT CENTER NEW YORK (IPCNY), 508 W. 26th St. Room 5A, New York, NY 10001. Tel.: 212-989-5090. Fax: 212-989-6069.
E-mail: contact@ipcny.org
Web Site: www.ipcny.org
Key Personnel: Dir., Judy Hecker; Public Programs Mgr., Stephanie Trejo; Marketing & Communications Specialist, Anne Osherson.
Institution Type/Description: Print Exhibition Space.
Hours & Admission Prices: July Mon.-Fri. 11-6; Sept.-June Tues.-Sat. 11-6. No charge. Closed national holidays. &
Attendance: 24,000 (estimated)

INTREPID SEA, AIR & SPACE MUSEUM, Pier 86, W. 46th St. & 12th Ave., New York, NY 10036-4103. Tel.: 212-245-0072. Fax: 212-245-1547.
Web Site: www.intrepidmuseum.org
Key Personnel: Pres., Susan Marenoff-Zausner; Exec. Vice Pres., David A. Winters; C.F.O. & C.A.O., Patricia Beene-Colasanti; Sr. Vice Pres. Exhibits, Education & Programming, Elaine Charnov; Vice Pres. IT, Vincent Forino; Vice Pres. Education, Lynda Kennedy; Sr. Vice Pres. Business Devel., Marc Lowitz; Vice Pres. Mktg., Mike Onysko; Sr. Vice Pres. Facilities, Engineering & Security, Matt Woods; Vice Pres. Institutional Advancement, Alexis Marion.

Institution Type/Description: Armed Forces Museum: 900 ft. long aircraft carrier.
Hours & Admission Prices: April-Oct. Mon.-Fri. 10-5, Sat.-Sun. & holidays 10-6; Nov.-March daily 10-5. Adults $24, seniors 62 & up & college students w/I.D. $20, youth 7-17 $ 19, veterans $17, child 3-9 $12; children under 3, active duty & retired military & members no charge. Closed Thanksgiving; Christmas. &
Attendance: 700,000 (estimated)

ITALIAN AMERICAN MUSEUM, 155 Mulberry St., New York, NY 10013-4721. Tel.: 212-965-9000. Fax: 212.965.9004.
E-mail: info@italianamericanmuseum.org
Web Site: www.italianamericanmuseum.org
Key Personnel: C.E.O., Chm. (V), Pres. (V) & Cur., Dr. Joseph V. Scelsa; Devel., Maria Fosco; Treas., Richard LaGreca; Museum Shop Mgr., Daniella Day.
Institution Type/Description: Cultural Heritage Museum.
Hours & Admission Prices: Fri.-Sun noon-6; other times by appointment. No charge; donations accepted. Closed legal holidays. &
Attendance: 10,000 (estimated)

JAPAN SOCIETY GALLERY, 333 E. 47th St., New York, NY 10017-2399. Tel.: 212-832-1155. Fax: 212-715-1262. Facebook: Japan Society Gallery.
E-mail: gallery@japansociety.org
Web Site: www.japansociety.org
Key Personnel: Pres., Motoatsu Sakurai; Gallery Dir., Yukie Kamiya; Chm. & C.E.O., Stanley M. Bergman.
Institution Type/Description: Art Museum.
Hours & Admission Prices: Spring & Fall: Tues.-Thurs. 11-6, Fri. 11-9, Sat.-Sun. 11-5. Adults $12, seniors & students $10; discounts to AAM, ICOM, NYC Council of Museums & museum members; Closed major holidays. &
Attendance: 25,000 (actual)

THE JEWISH MUSEUM, 1109 Fifth Ave. at 92nd St., New York, NY 10128-0118. Tel.: 212-423-3200. Fax: 212-423-3232. Facebook, Instagram, Twitter.
E-mail: info@thejm.org
Web Site: www.thejewishmuseum.org
Key Personnel: Dir., Claudia Gould; Chm. (V), Robert Pruzan; Chief of Staff, David Goldberg; Deputy Dir. Finance & Administration, Joseph Rorech; Deputy Dir. Program Administration, Ruth Beesch; Dir. Education, Nelly Silagy Benedek; Deputy Dir. Devel., Elyse Buxbaum; Dir. Membership, Jenna Bastian; Sr. Cur., Susan L. Braunstein; Deputy Dir. Mktg. & Communications, Sarah Supcoff; Sr. Dir. Communications, Anne Scher; Dir. Merchandising, Stacey Zaleski; Mgr. Collections, Katharine Danalakis; Chief Counsel & Talent Officer, Cindy Caplan; Sr. Dir. Operations & Exhibition Svcs., Al Lazarte.
Institution Type/Description: Art Museum: housed in 1908 Felix Warburg Mansion, a seven-story French Gothic structure.
Hours & Admission Prices: Thurs. 11-8, Fri.-Tues. 11-5:45. Adults $15 senior citizens $12, students $7.50; discounts to members & AAM members; members, children 18 & under and Sat. no charge. Closed Rosh Hashanah; Yom Kippur; Thanksgiving. &
Attendance: 200,000 (actual)

KEHILA KEDOSHA JANINA SYNAGOGUE & MUSEUM, 280 Broome St., New York, NY 10002-3702. Tel.: 212-431-1619. Fax: 212-673-4441.
E-mail: info@kkjsm.org
Web Site: www.kkjsm.org
Key Personnel: Dir., Marcia Haddad Ikonomopoulos; Pres., Marvin Marcus.
Institution Type/Description: Jewish History Museum.
Hours & Admission Prices: Museum: Sun. 11-4; other times by appointment. Shabbat Services: Sat. 9am.
Attendance: 5,000 (actual)

KENKELEBA GALLERY, 214 E. 2nd St., New York, NY 10009-8031. Tel.: 212-674-3939. Fax: 212-505-5080.
Key Personnel: Artistic Dir., Joe Overstreet; Dir., Corrine Jennings.
Institution Type/Description: Art Gallery.
Hours & Admission Prices: Wed.-Sat. 11-6. No charge.

KGB ESPIONAGE MUSEUM CLOSED, 245 W. 14th St., New York, NY 10011. Tel.: 917-388-2332. Facebook; Twitter; Instagram.
E-mail: info@kgbespionagemuseum.org
Web Site: kgbespionagemuseum.org
Institution Type/Description: History Museum.
Hours & Admission Prices: Daily 10-8. Adults $22, seniors 65 & over and students $17, children 7-17 $13; children 6 & under no charge.

LACRASIA'S GLOVE MUSEUM, 270 W. 38th St., Ste. 1202, New York, NY 10018. Tel.: 212-686-5428.

E-mail: info@wingweftgloves.com
Web Site: www.lacrasiagloves.com
Key Personnel: Dir., Jay G. Ruckel; Museum Shop Mgr., Lacrasia Duchein.
Institution Type/Description: General Museum.
Hours & Admission Prices: By appointment only. No charge; donations accepted.
Attendance: 1,000 (estimated)

LESLIE-LOHMAN MUSEUM OF GAY AND LESBIAN ART, 26 Wooster St., New York, NY 10013. Tel.: 212-431-2609. Fax: 212-431-2666. Facebook: @LeslieLohmanMuseum.
E-mail: info@leslielohman.org
Web Site: www.leslielohman.org
Key Personnel: Founder, Charles W. Leslie; Dir., Gonzalo Casals; Bd. Pres., Cynthia Powell.
Institution Type/Description: Museum.
Hours & Admission Prices: Wed. & Fri.-Sun. 12-6, Thurs. 12-8. Suggested donation $9. &
Attendance: 25,000 (actual)

LIPANI GALLERY, FORDHAM UNIVERSITY, Lincoln Center Campus, 113 W. 60th St., Sub Level, Visual Arts Complex, New York, NY 10023. Mailing Address: Fordham University, Dept. Theatre & Visual Arts, 113 W. 60th St., Rm. 423, New York, NY 10023-6594. Tel.: 212-636-6073. Fax: 212-636-6788.
E-mail: contact@fordhamuniversitygalleries.com
Web Site: lipanigallery.com
Formerly: Push Pin Gallery Fordham University
Key Personnel: Dir., Stephan Apicella-Hitchcock.
Institution Type/Description: Art Gallery.
Hours & Admission Prices: Call for hours. No charge. &

LOWER EAST SIDE TENEMENT MUSEUM, 91 Orchard St., New York, NY 10002-3132. Tel.: 212-431-0233; 212-431-0714 (TTY). Fax: 212-431-0402. Facebook & Twitter: @tenementmuseum; Instagram: @thetenementmuseum.
E-mail: lestm@tenement.org
Web Site: www.tenement.org
Key Personnel: Pres., Kevin Jennings; Co-Chm., Scott Metzner; Co-Chm., Merryl Snow Zegar; Exec. Vice Pres. & C.O.O., Barry Roseman; Sr. Vice Pres. Education & Programming, Annie Polland; Vice Pres. Mktg. & Communications, David Eng; Vice Pres. Devel., Julie A. Davidson; Vice Pres. Devel., Julie Davidson.
Institution Type/Description: Immigrant History Museum: housed in c.1863 pre Old-Law tenement building.
Hours & Admission Prices: Daily 10-6:30. Thurs. 10-8:30. Adults $25, students & seniors 65 & above $20; discounts to AAM members, Natl. Trust Historic Preservation, Museum Assoc. NY, Amex, Bloomberg, Con Edison, MET Life, Morgan Stanley; children under 5 (Meet Victoria Tour only) & members no charge. Foods of Lower East Side: adults $45, Students & Seniors $40, members $22. Closed New Year's Day; Thanksgiving; Christmas. &
Attendance: 218,000 (actual)

MERCHANT'S HOUSE MUSEUM, 29 E. Fourth St., New York, NY 10003-7003. Tel.: 212-777-1089. Fax: 212-777-1104.
E-mail: nyc1832@merchantshouse.org
Web Site: www.merchantshouse.com
Key Personnel: Chm., Nicholas B.A. Nicholson; Exec. Dir., Margaret Halsey Gardiner; Sec., Anthony Bellov.
Institution Type/Description: Historic House: 1832 example of late Federal & Greek Revival architecture.
Hours & Admission Prices: Self-Guided Tours: Thurs.-Mon. 12-5. Guided Tours: Thurs.-Mon. 2pm. Adults $10, senior citizens & students $5; children under 12 & members no charge. Closed New Year's Eve & Day; Easter; Independence Day; Thanksgiving; Christmas Eve & Day.
Attendance: 6,000 (estimated)

THE MET BREUER, 945 Madison Ave., New York, NY 10021. Tel.: 212-731-1675.
Institution Type/Description: Art Museum.
Hours & Admission Prices: Tues.-Thurs. & Sun. 10-5:30, Fri.-Sat. 10-9; groups by appointment. Suggested Admission: adults $25, seniors 65 & over $17, students $12; members & children under 12 no charge. Ticket includes same-day admission to The met Fifth Ave., The Met Breuer & The Met Cloisters. Closed New Year's Day; Thanksgiving; Christmas. &

THE MET CLOISTERS, 99 Margaret Corbin Dr., Fort Tryon Park, New York, NY 10040-1198. Tel.: 212-923-3700.
E-mail: cloisters@metmuseum.org
Web Site: www.metmuseum.org/visit/met-cloisters

Key Personnel: Administrator, Christina Alphonso; Michel David-Weill Cur. in Charge, C. Griffith Mann; Paul & Jill Rudduck Sr. Cur., Barbara Boehm; Sr. Research Assoc., Christine Brennan; Cur., Melanie Holcomb.
Institution Type/Description: Art Museum.
Hours & Admission Prices: March-Oct. daily 10-5:15; Nov.-Feb. daily 10-4:45. Recommended Admission: adults $25, seniors $17, students $12; members & children under 12 accompanied by an adult no charge. Closed Thanksgiving Day; Christmas Day; New Year's Day. &
Attendance: 240,000 (estimated)

THE METROPOLITAN MUSEUM OF ART, 1000 Fifth Ave., New York, NY 10028-0113. Tel.: 212-535-7710. Fax: 212-570-3879. Facebook, Instagram & Twitter: @metmuseum.
E-mail: communications@metmuseum.org
Web Site: www.metmuseum.org
Key Personnel: Chm. Bd., Daniel Brodsky; Pres. & Interim C.E.O., Daniel H. Weiss; Sr. Vice Pres. Sec. & Gen. Counsel, Sharon H. Cott.
Institution Type/Description: Art Museum.
Hours & Admission Prices: Closed until Oct. 21, 2019 &
Attendance: 7,000,000 (estimated)

MEXICAN CULTURAL INSTITUTE OF NEW YORK, 27 E. 39th St., 3rd Fl., New York, NY 10016. Tel.: 212-217-6400. Fax: 212-217-6425.
E-mail: ctoscano@consulmexny.mx
Web Site: www.mciny.org/
Key Personnel: Exec. Dir., Caterina Toscano.
Institution Type/Description: Mexican History Museum.
Hours & Admission Prices: Call for hours.

MIRIAM & IRA D. WALLACH ART GALLERY, 116th St. & Broadway, Schermerhorn Hall, 8th Fl., New York, NY 10027. Mailing Address: Columbia University, 926 Schermerhorn Hall, 1190 Amsterdam Ave. MC 5502, New York, NY 10027-7054. Tel.: 212-854-6800. Fax: 212-854-7800.
E-mail: wallach@columbia.edu
Web Site: www.columbia.edu/cu/wallach
Key Personnel: Dir. & Cur., Deborah Cullen-Morales.
Institution Type/Description: Art Gallery: housed in Schermerhorn Hall.
Hours & Admission Prices: During the academic year Wed.-Sat. 1-5. No charge. &
Attendance: 5,000 (estimated)

MMUSEUMM, 4 Cortlandt Alley, Between Franklin St. & White St., New York, NY 10013. Mailing Address: 368 Broadway #512, New York, NY 10013. Tel.: 888-763-8839. Twitter; Instagram.
E-mail: info@mmuseumm.com
Web Site: www.mmuseumm.com
Formerly: Cortlandt Alley
Key Personnel: Dir., Alex Kalman.
Institution Type/Description: Modern History Museum.
Hours & Admission Prices: Fri. 6pm-9pm, Sat.-Sun. 12-6. Viewing Windows: daily 24 hrs. No charge; donations accepted. Closed major holidays. &

THE MORGAN LIBRARY & MUSEUM, 225 Madison Ave., New York, NY 10016-3405. Tel.: 212-685-0008. Fax: 212-481-3484. Facebook & Twitter: Morgan Library; Instagram: The Morgan Library.
E-mail: media@themorgan.org
Web Site: www.themorgan.org
Key Personnel: Dir., Colin B. Bailey; Pres., Lawrence R. Ricciardi; Deputy Dir., Jessica Ludwig; Dir. Finance & Administration, Kristina W. Stillman; Cur. Robert H. Taylor & Dept. Head, Declan Kiely; Cur. & Dept. Medieval & Renaissance Manuscripts, Roger S. Wieck; Cur. Charles Engelhard & Head Dept. Drawings & Prints, John Marciari; Astor Cur. & Dept. Head, Printed Books & Bindings, John Bidwell; Dir. Institutional Advancement, Lauren Stakias; Cur. Seals & Tablets & Dept. Head, Sidney Babcock; Acting Dir. Thaw Conservation Center & Drue Heinz Book Conservator, Margaret Holben Ellis; Paper Conservator, Reba Snyder; Dir. Education, Linden Chubin; Dir. Communications & Mktg., Patrick Milliman; Dir. Merchandising Svcs., Sean Hayes; Publications Mgr., Karen Banks.
Institution Type/Description: Library & Art Museum: housed in the 1906 library built by McKim, Mead, & White for Pierpont Morgan.
Hours & Admission Prices: Tues.-Thurs. 10:30-5, Fri. 10:30-9, Sat. 10-6, Sun. 11-6. Adults $18, youth 13-16, students w/ I.D. & seniors $12; discounts to AAM & ICOM members; members no charge. Closed New Year's Day; Thanksgiving; Christmas. &
Attendance: 208,000 (estimated)

MORRIS-JUMEL MANSION, 65 Jumel Ter., New York, NY 10032-5360. Tel.: 212-923-8008. Fax: 212-923-8947.

Web Site: www.morrisjumel.org
Key Personnel: Pres., Pamela Palanque North, Esq.; Vice Pres., Wayne Benjamin; Co-Exec. Dir, Alexis Marnel; Co-Exec. Dir., Christopher Davalos; Mgr. School & Family Prog., Michael Whitten.
Institution Type/Description: Historic House: 1765 Morris-Jumel Mansion, oldest residence in Manhattan; used as Gen. Washington's headquarters during the Revolution; purchased by the Jumel family in 1810; Eliza Jumel married Aaron Burr in the front parlor.
Hours & Admission Prices: Wed.-Sun. 10-4; other times by appointment. Adults $5, students & senior citizens $4, school groups $1.50 per child; Historic House Trust of New York City, Museum Council of New York City, museum, children under 12, AAM & ICOM members no charge. Group tours available. Closed New Year's Day; Memorial Day; Independence Day; Labor Day; Thanksgiving; Christmas.
Attendance: 35,000 (estimated)

MOUNT VERNON HOTEL MUSEUM & GARDEN, 421 E. 61st St., New York, NY 10065-8736. Tel.: 212-838-6878. Facebook: Mount Vernon Hotel Museum.
E-mail: info@mvhm.org
Web Site: www.mvhm.org
Formerly: Abigail Adams Smith Museum
Key Personnel: Dir., Terri Daly; Cur. Education, Natalia Sokolova; Cur. Collections, Ruth Osborne.
Institution Type/Description: Historic House Museum: Built in 1799 interiors from 1826.
Hours & Admission Prices: Tues.-Sun. 11-4. Adults $8, students & senior citizens $7; children under 12 & members no charge. Closed New Year's Day; Independence Day; Thanksgiving; Christmas.
Attendance: 30,000 (estimated)

THE MUNICIPAL ART SOCIETY OF NEW YORK, 488 Madison Ave., Ste. 1900, New York, NY 10022. Tel.: 212-935-3960. Fax: 212-753-1816.
E-mail: info@mas.org
Web Site: www.mas.org
Key Personnel: Pres., Elizabeth Goldstein.
Institution Type/Description: Advocacy, planning & preservation organization dedicated to improving livability in New York.
Hours & Admission Prices: By appointment. No charge; donations accepted. &
Attendance: 65,000 (estimated)

MUSEUM AT ELDRIDGE STREET, 12 Eldridge St., New York, NY 10002-6204. Tel.: 212-219-0888. Fax: 212-966-4782.
E-mail: contact@eldridgestreet.org
Web Site: www.eldridgestreet.org
Key Personnel: Exec. Dir., Bonnie Dimun; Chm. (V), Michael Weinstein; Pres. (V), Steven Walsey; Dir. Education, Judith Greenspan; Vice Pres. Institutional Advancement, Eva Brune; Dir. Mktg. & Audience Outreach, Chelsea Dowell.
Institution Type/Description: Historic Site, Cultural Center & Museum: a national historic landmark.
Hours & Admission Prices: Synagogue Tours: Sun.-Thurs. 10-5, Fri. 10-3. Adults $10, senior citizens & students $8, children 5-18 $6; discounts to AAM members; members & children under 5 no charge. Closed Jewish & national holidays. &
Attendance: 35,000 (actual)

THE MUSEUM AT FIT, 227 W. 27th St., New York, NY 10001-5992. Tel.: 212-217-4530. Fax: 212-217-4531. Facebook, Instagram & Twitter: @themuseumatfit.
E-mail: museuminfo@fitnyc.edu
Web Site: www.fitnyc.edu/museum
Key Personnel: Dir. & Chief Cur., Dr. Valerie Steele; Head Conservator, Ann Coppinger; Deputy Dir., Patricia Mears; Registrar, Sonia Dingilian; Mgr. Exhibits, Michael Goitia; Sr. Cur., Fred Dennis; Cur. Education, Tanya Melendez.
Institution Type/Description: Fashion Museum.
Hours & Admission Prices: Tues.-Fri. 12-8, Sat. 10-5. No charge. Closed legal holidays. &
Attendance: 100,000 (actual)

MUSEUM OF AMERICAN FINANCE, New York, NY 10005. Tel.: 212-908-4110. Fax: 212-742-0573.
E-mail: kaguilera@moaf.org
Web Site: www.moaf.org
Formerly: Museum of American Financial History
Key Personnel: Chm. (V), Dr. Richard Sylla; Pres. & C.E.O., David J. Cowen; Deputy Dir., Kristin Aguilera; Dir. Exhibits, Maura Ferguson; Managing Dir. Visitor Svcs. & Building Operations, Linda Rapacki.

Institution Type/Description: Financial Museum and de facto Visitor Center for the New York Stock Exchange.
Hours & Admission Prices: Temporarily closed. &
Attendance: 50,000 (estimated)

THE MUSEUM OF AMERICAN ILLUSTRATION AT THE SOCIETY OF ILLUSTRATORS, 128 E. 63rd St., New York, NY 10065-7303. Tel.: 212-838-2560. Fax: 212-838-2561.
E-mail: info@societyillustrators.org
Web Site: www.societyillustrators.org
Formerly: Society of Illustrators Museum of American Illustration
Key Personnel: Pres., Tim O'Brien; Exec. Dir., Anelle Miller.
Institution Type/Description: Art Museum & Gallery.
Hours & Admission Prices: Gallery: Sept.-July Tues. 10-8, Wed.-Fri. 10-5, Sat. 12-4. No charge; donations accepted. Closed legal holidays.
Attendance: 30,000 (estimated)

MUSEUM OF ARTS AND DESIGN, 2 Columbus Cir., New York, NY 10019-1800. Tel.: 212-299-7777.
E-mail: info@madmuseum.org
Web Site: www.madmuseum.org
Formerly: American Craft Museum
Key Personnel: Dir., Chris Scoates.
Institution Type/Description: Art Museum.
Hours & Admission Prices: Tues.-Wed. & Sat.-Sun. 10-6, Thurs. & Fri. 10-9. Adults $18, seniors $14, students $12; Thurs. 6-9 pay what you wish; discounts to groups; youth 18 & under & members no charge. Closed major holidays. &
Attendance: 500,000 (estimated)

MUSEUM OF CHINESE IN AMERICA, Physical/Mailing Address: 215 Centre St., New York, NY 10013. Tel.: 855-955-MOCA. Fax: 212-619-4720.
E-mail: info@mocanyc.org
Web Site: www.mocanyc.org
Formerly: Museum of Chinese In the Americas
Key Personnel: Pres., Nancy Yao Maasbach; Vice Pres. Prog. & Museum Experience, Beatrice Chen.
Institution Type/Description: History Museum: housed in a former public school; built in 1893.
Hours & Admission Prices: Tues.-Wed., Fri.-Sun. 11-6, Thurs. 11-9. Adults $10, seniors 65 & over and students $5; discount to AAM & ICOM members; children under 12 in groups less than 8 & members no charge. Closed Mon.; New Year's Day; Thanksgiving; Christmas Day. &
Attendance: 30,000 (actual)

MUSEUM OF COMIC AND CARTOON ART, 128 E. 63rd St, New York, NY 10065. Tel.: 212-838-2560. Fax: 212-838-2561.
E-mail: info@societyillustrators.org
Web Site: www.societyillustrators.org
Key Personnel: Exec. Dir., Anelle Miller; Chm. (V); Ellen Weinstein.
Institution Type/Description: Art Museum.
Hours & Admission Prices: Tues. 10-8, Wed.-Fri. 10-5, Sat. 12-4. Adults $5; discounts to groups; children 12 & under no charge.

MUSEUM OF JEWISH HERITAGE-A LIVING MEMORIAL TO THE HOLOCAUST, 36 Battery Place, New York, NY 10280-1502. Tel.: 646-437-4202. Fax: 646-437-4311. Facebook: Museum of Jewish Heritage.
E-mail: info@mjhnyc.org
Web Site: www.mjhnyc.org
Key Personnel: Chm., Bruce C. Ratner; Vice Chm., Peter S. Kalikow; Vice Chair, Abraham H. Foxman; Vice Chm., Stephen E. Kaufman; Pres. & C.E.O., Michael S. Glickman; Deputy Dir., Elissa Cohen; Vice Pres. Operations, Michael Stafford; Vice Pres. Education, Elizabeth Edelstein; Dir. Foundation & Corporate Grants, Sharon Steinbach; Dir. Finance, Demetria Tsialas; Dir. Admin. & Human Resources, Tammy Chiu; Sr. Registrar & Mgr. Traveling Exhibitions, Erica Blumenfeld; Museum Shop Asst. Mgr., Peter Mones.
Institution Type/Description: Jewish History Museum: 20th-century memorial to the Holocaust.
Hours & Admission Prices: Daylight Savings Time: Sun.-Tues. & Thurs. 10-5:45, Wed. 10-8, Fri. 10-5; Eastern Standard Time & Eve of Jewish Holidays: Sun.-Tues. & Thurs. 10-5:45, Wed. 10-8, Fri. 10-3. Adults $12, seniors $10, students $7; discounts to AAM & ICOM members; members, children under 12 & Wed. 4-8 no charge. Closed Jewish holidays; Thanksgiving. &
Attendance: 153,993 (actual)

THE MUSEUM OF MODERN ART, 11 W. 53rd St., New York, NY 10019-5401. Tel.: 212-708-9400. Fax: 212-708-9889. Facebook; Twitter.
Web Site: www.moma.org

Key Personnel: Chm., Leon D. Black; Pres., Ronnie Heyman; Dir., Glenn Lowry; Asst. Treas., James Gara; Treas., Richard E. Salomon; Sr. Deputy Dir. External Affairs, Todd Bishop; Sr. Deputy Dir. Exhibitions & Collections, Ramona Bannanan; Deputy Dir. Education, Wendy Woon; Chief Cur. Drawings & Prints, Christophe Cherix; Chief Cur. Painting & Sculpture, Ann Temkin; Chief Cur. Photography, Quentin Bajac; Chief Cur. Architecture & Design, Martino Stierli; Chief Cur. Film, Rajendra Roy; Chief Cur. Media & Performance, Stuart Comer.
Institution Type/Description: Art Museum.
Hours & Admission Prices: Fri. 10-9, Sat.-Thurs. 10-5:30. Museum: adults $25, seniors 65 & over $18, full-time students with ID $14; discounts to AAM & ICOM members; children 16 & under. MoMA members & Fri. 5:30pm-9pm no charge. Additional charge for film & media programs. Closed Thanksgiving; Christmas. &
Attendance: 2,219,554 (estimated)

MUSEUM OF SEX, 233 5th Ave., New York, NY 10016. Tel.: 212-689-6337. Fax: 646-349-1333.
E-mail: info@museumofsex.com
Web Site: museumofsex.com
Institution Type/Description: History Museum.
Hours & Admission Prices: Sun.-Thurs. 10-8, Fri.-Sat. 10-9; groups by appointment. Adults $17.50, seniors and students 18 & over $15.25; discounts to groups of 10 or more; children under 18 not admitted. Closed Thanksgiving; Christmas. &
Attendance: 200,000 (actual)

MUSEUM OF THE CITY OF NEW YORK, 1220 Fifth Ave, at 103rd St., New York, NY 10029. Tel.: 212-534-1672. Fax: 212-534-0687.
E-mail: info@mcny.org
Web Site: www.mcny.org
Key Personnel: Ronay Menschel Dir. & Pres., Whitney Donhauser; Chm. (V), James G. Dinan; Deputy Dir. & Chief Cur., Sarah M. Henry; C.O.O., Jerry Gallagher; C.F.O., Osman C. Kurtulus; Dir. Collections, Lindsay Turley; Dir. Frederick A.O. Schwarz Ctr., Franny Kent; Mgr. Visitor Services & Retail, Kate Ludwig; Communications Mgr., Jacob Tugendrajch.
Institution Type/Description: General Museum.
Hours & Admission Prices: Daily 10-6. Suggested Admissions: adults $14, senior citizens & students $10; discounts to AAM members; children under 12 & members no charge. Closed New Year's Day; Thanksgiving; Christmas. &
Attendance: 243,841 (actual)

NATIONAL ACADEMY MUSEUM & SCHOOL, 1083 Fifth Ave., New York, NY 10128-0114. Tel.: 212-369-4880. Fax: 212-426-1711.
E-mail: mpellegrin@nationalacademy.org
Web Site: www.nationalacademy.org
Key Personnel: Exec. Dir., Maura Reilly; Dir. Collections & Curatorial Affairs, Diana Thompson; Head of Security, Sherwin Angel; Dean, Maurizio Pellegrin.
Institution Type/Description: American Art Museum, School of Fine Arts, Academy of Artists & Architects.
Hours & Admission Prices: Wed.-Sun. 11-6; see website for additional hours. Adults $15, senior citizens 65 & over and students with ID $10; members, children under 12 & National Academy School students no charge. Closed New Year's Day; Independence Day; Thanksgiving; Christmas. &
Attendance: 20,000 (estimated)

NATIONAL ARTS CLUB, 15 Gramercy Park S., New York, NY 10003-1796. Tel.: 212-475-3424. Fax: 212-475-3692.
E-mail: info@nationalartsclub.org
Web Site: www.nationalartsclub.org
Key Personnel: Exec. Dir., Linda Zagaria.
Institution Type/Description: Art Museum: housed in 1840s, former mansion of Governor Samuel Tilden.
Hours & Admission Prices: Call for confirmation of hours of exhibition galleries. No charge.

NATIONAL AUDUBON SOCIETY, 225 Varick St., Fl. 7, New York, NY 10014-4396. Tel.: 212-979-3196. Fax: 212-979-3188.
E-mail: audubon@emailcustomerservice.com
Web Site: www.audubon.org
Institution Type/Description: Wildlife & Wildlife Habitat Protection Society.
Hours & Admission Prices: Contact individual sanctuaries for hours. &
Attendance: 125,000

NATIONAL JAZZ MUSEUM IN HARLEM, 58 W 129th St., New York, NY 10027. Tel.: 212-348-8300.
E-mail: tsmith@jmih.org
Web Site: jazzmuseuminharlem.org/

Key Personnel: Co-Artistic Dir., Jonathan Batiste; Co-Artistic Dir., Chritian McBride; Mng. Dir., Jasna Radonjic.
Institution Type/Description: Jazz Museum.
Hours & Admission Prices: Thurs.-Mon. 11-5; groups of 10 or more by appointment. Suggested Donation: adults $10; children under 12 & members no charge. Closed federal holidays. ♿

NATIONAL MUSEUM OF MATHEMATICS, 11 E. 26th St., New York, NY 10010. Mailing Address: 134 W. 26th St., Ste. 4S, New York, NY 10001. Tel.: 212-542-0566.
E-mail: info@momath.org
Web Site: momath.org
Key Personnel: Exec. Dir. & CEO, Cindy Lawrence.
Institution Type/Description: Hands-on Science Center.
Hours & Admission Prices: Daily 10-5. Adults $15, children 12 & over, students and seniors 65 & over $9; children under 2 no charge.
Attendance: 129,000 (actual)

NATIONAL MUSEUM OF THE AMERICAN INDIAN GEORGE GUSTAV HEYE CENTER, SMITHSONIAN INSTITUTION, Alexander Hamilton U.S. Custom House, One Bowling Green, New York, NY 10004. Tel.: 212-514-3794. Fax: 212-514-3800.
E-mail: nmai-ny@si.edu
Web Site: americanindian.si.edu
Key Personnel: Dir. National Museum of the American Indian, Kevin Gover; Public Affairs Specialist, Joshua Voda.
Institution Type/Description: Anthropology & Indian Museum.
Hours & Admission Prices: Thurs. 10-8, Fri.-Wed. 10-5. No charge; donations accepted. Closed Christmas. ♿
Attendance: 474,000 (estimated)

NATIONAL SEPTEMBER 11 MEMORIAL & MUSEUM, 180 Greenwich St., New York, NY 10007. Mailing Address: 200 Liberty St., 16th Fl., New York, NY 10281. Tel.: 212-312-8800. Fax: 212-227-7931. Facebook: 911 Memorial.
E-mail: info@911memorial.org
Web Site: www.911memorial.org
Key Personnel: Pres. & C.E.O., Alice Greenwald; Exec. Vice Pres. & Dep. Dir. of Strategy & Advancement, Allison Blais; Exec. Vice Pres. & Dep. Dir. External Affairs, Michael Frazier; Exec. Vice Pres. & Dep. Dir. Museum Prog., Clifford Chanin.
Institution Type/Description: History Museum & Memorial: housed on the World Trade Center site.
Hours & Admission Prices: Memorial: daily 7:30-9. No charge. Museum: daily, advanced reservations recommended; groups by appointment. Adults $24, seniors 65 & over, U.S. veterans, and U.S. college students $18, youth 7-17 $15; discounts to U.S. military, FDNY, NYPD, PAPD and AAM members; 9/11 family members, rescue & recovery workers and Tues. 5-8 no charge. Tours: Museum $20 additional fee; Memorial $15 additional fee. ♿
Attendance: 1,820,000 (actual)

NEUE GALERIE NEW YORK, 1048 Fifth Ave., New York, NY 10028-0111. Tel.: 212-628-6200. Fax: 212-628-8824. Facebook: Neue Galerie New York.
E-mail: museum@neuegalerie.org
Web Site: www.neuegalerie.org
Key Personnel: Dir., Renee Price; Book Store Dir., Bruno Keusch; Design Shop Dir., Paul Landy.
Institution Type/Description: Art Museum: housed in a landmark building on Museum Mile designed by Carrere & Hastings and completed in 1914.
Hours & Admission Prices: Thurs.-Mon. 11-6. Adults $20, seniors $15, students $10; museum professionals, members of the press, AAM & ICOM members & 1st Fri. each month 6pm-8pm no charge. Children under 12 not admitted. ♿
Attendance: 120,000

NEW MUSEUM, 235 Bowery, New York, NY 10002-1218. Tel.: 212-219-1222. Fax: 212-431-5328. Facebook, Instagram, Twitter: @newmuseum.
E-mail: info@newmuseum.org
Web Site: www.newmuseum.org
Key Personnel: Dir., Lisa Phillips; Chm. Bd. Trustees, Saul Dennison; Pres. Bd. Trustees, James Keith Brown; Deputy Dir., Karen Wong; Artistic Dir., Massimiliano Gioni; Assoc. Dir. Institutional Advancement, Dennis Szakacs.
Institution Type/Description: Art Museum.
Hours & Admission Prices: Wed. & Fri.-Sun. 11-6, Thurs.-11-9. Adult $16, seniors $14, students $10; members & youth under 18 no charge. Closed all major holidays. ♿
Attendance: 300,000

NEW YORK CITY FIRE MUSEUM, 278 Spring St., New York, NY 10013-1405. Tel.: 212-691-1303. Fax: 212-352-3117. Facebook: New York City Fire Museum.
E-mail: director@nycfiremuseum.org
Web Site: nycfiremuseum.org
Key Personnel: Exec. Dir., Gary Urbanowicz; Colls. Mgr. & Cur., Sean P. Britton; Asst. Dir. & Event Coord., Noemi Bourdier.
Institution Type/Description: Fire-Fighting Museum: housed in 1904 firehouse.
Hours & Admission Prices: Daily 10-5. Adults $10, students with ID, firefighters, federally disabled, AAA members & seniors $8, children $5. Closed New Year's Day, Easter, Memorial Day, Independence Day, Thanksgiving; Christmas Day.
Attendance: 40,000 (estimated)

THE NEW YORK CITY POLICE MUSEUM, 100 Old Slip, New York, NY 10005-3539. Tel.: 212-480-3100, ext. 105. Fax: 212-480-9757.
E-mail: jbose@nycpm.org
Web Site: www.nycpm.org
Key Personnel: C.E.O., Julie Bose; Pres., Rick Friedberg; Museum Shop Mgr., Iris Stephen.
Institution Type/Description: Police History Museum.
Hours & Admission Prices: Mon.-Sat. 10-5, Sun. 12-5; school groups by appointment. Adults $8, seniors $5; discounts to AAM members; NYPD personnel & members no charge. Closed New Year's Day; Thanksgiving; Christmas. ♿
Attendance: 81,500 (actual)

NEW-YORK HISTORICAL SOCIETY, 170 Central Park West, New York, NY 10024-5194. Tel.: 212-873-3400. Fax: 212-595-5707.
E-mail: info@nyhistory.org
Web Site: www.nyhistory.org
Key Personnel: Pres. & C.E.O., Louise Mirrer; Chm. (V), Pam B. Schafler; Vice Pres. & Library Dir., Michael Ryan; Vice Pres. & Museum Dir., Margi Hofer; Vice Pres. Communications, Ines Aslan; Vice Pres. Devel., Matt Spiegel; Vice Pres. Education, Mia Nagawiecki; Vice Pres. Education Emerita, Sharon Dunn; Vice Pres. Public Programs, Dale Gregory; Vice Pres., Chief Historian & Dir, Center for Women's History, Valerie Paley; Vice Pres. History Exhibitions, Marci Reaven; C.F.O., Richard Shein; Vice Pres. & Dir. DiMenna Children's History Museum, Alice Stevenson; Dir. IT, Armando Lopez; Dir. Visitor Svcs., Nick Mancini; Dir. Security, Bill Montgomery; Dir. Devel., Cheryl Morgan; Dir. Library Operations, Nina Nazionale; Dir. Merchandise Operations, Ione Saroyan; Dir. Exhibitions & Creative Dir., Gerhard Schlanzky; Dir. Special Events, Anne VanderWal; Asst. Vice Pres. Opers., Yashiris Moreta; General Counsel, Freddy Taveras; Snr. Dir. Resources & Programs, Jean W. Ashton; Snr. Art Historian & Museum Dir. Emerita, Linda S. Ferber; Deputy Museum Dir., Emily Croll; Art Dir., Kira Hwang; Dir. Audio & Visual Technology, Luke Johnson; Dir. Human Resources, Frank DiMaiolo; Dir. Individual Giving, Jeanne Thompson; Dir. Special Events, Karen Roshevsky; Dir. Library Digital Program, Henry Raine.
Institution Type/Description: Historical Society.
Hours & Admission Prices: Museum: Tues.-Thurs. & Sat. 10-6, Fri. 10-8, Sun. 11-5. Library: Tues.-Fri. 10-4:45. Adults $21, seniors, educators & active military $16, students $13, children 5-13 $6; discounts to AAM members; members and children 4 & under no charge. Fri. 6pm-8pm pay what you wish. Closed Labor Day; Thanksgiving; Christmas. ♿
Attendance: 310,000 (estimated)

THE NEW YORK PUBLIC LIBRARY, ASTOR, LENOX AND TILDEN FOUNDATIONS, Stephen A. Schwarzman Building, 476 Fifth Avenue (42nd St and Fifth Ave), New York, NY 10018. Tel.: 917-275-6975.
Web Site: www.nypl.org
Key Personnel: Chm. Bd. Trustees, Evan R. Chesler; Pres. & C.E.O., Anthony W. Marx; Chief Branch Library Officer, Christopher Platt; Vice Pres., Gen. Counsel & Sec., Michele Coleman Mayes; C.O.O. & Treas., Iris Weinshall; Chief External Rels. Officer, Carrie Welch; Vice Pres. HR, Louise Shea.
Institution Type/Description: Public Library: housed in 1911 Central Building on the site of the Croton Reservoir.
Hours & Admission Prices: Daily. Call for branch hours. No charge; donations accepted. Closed holidays. ♿
Attendance: 18,000,000 (actual)

THE NEW YORK PUBLIC LIBRARY FOR THE PERFORMING ARTS, 40 Lincoln Center Plaza (65th St and Columbus Ave), New York, NY 10023-7486. Mailing Address: Stephen A. Schwarzman Building, 476 Fifth Avenue (42nd St and Fifth Ave), New York, NY 10018. Tel.: 917-275-6975.
Web Site: www.nypl.org
Key Personnel: Pres., Anthony Marx.
Institution Type/Description: History Museum of Performing Arts.

Hours & Admission Prices: Mon. & Thurs. 12-8, Tues.-Wed. & Fri. 12-6, Sat. 2-6. No charge. Closed national holidays. &
Attendance: 350,000 (actual)

THE NEW YORK STUDIO SCHOOL OF DRAWING, PAINTING & SCULPTURE, 8 W. 8th St., New York, NY 10011-9084. Tel.: 212-673-6466. Fax: 212-777-0996.
E-mail: info@nyss.org
Web Site: www.nyss.org
Key Personnel: Dean, Graham Nickson; Coord. Gallery & Recruitment, Rachel Rickert.
Institution Type/Description: Art Institute: located in a federally landmarked building, site of studios of sculptors Daniel Chester French & Gertrude Vanderbilt Whitney; original site of the Whitney Museum of American Art.
Hours & Admission Prices: Daily 10-10. Weekly Evening Lecture Series: Tues.-Wed. 6:30 pm-8 pm. No charge; donations accepted. Closed national holidays & school vacations, depending on exhibition schedule.
Attendance: 10,000 (estimated)

NICHOLAS ROERICH MUSEUM, 319 W. 107th St., New York, NY 10025-2799. Tel.: 212-864-7752.
E-mail: inquiries@roerich.org
Web Site: www.roerich.org
Key Personnel: Exec. Dir., Gvido Trepsa; Archivist, Nataliya Fomin; Dir. Cultural Activities, Jean Fletcher.
Institution Type/Description: Art Museum.
Hours & Admission Prices: Tues.-Fri. 12-4, Sat. & Sun. 2-5. No charge; donations accepted. Closed select holidays. &
Attendance: 6,000 (estimated)

9/11 TRIBUTE MUSEUM, 92 Greenwich St., New York, NY 10006. Mailing Address: c/o September 11th Families Assn., 22 Cortlandt, Ste. 801, New York, NY 10007. Tel.: 866-737-1184. Facebook; Instagram; Twitter.
E-mail: info@911tributemuseum.com
Web Site: 911tributemuseum.org
Formerly: Tribute WTC Visitor Center
Key Personnel: C.E.O. & Co-Founder, Jennifer Adams-Webb; Bd. Pres., Lee Ielpi.
Institution Type/Description: History Museum.
Hours & Admission Prices: Memorial: daily 7:30 am-9 pm. No charge. Museum: Sun.-Thurs. 9-8, Fri.-Sat. 9-9. Adults $24, youth 13-17, seniors & college students $20, children 7-12 $15; 9/11 family members, rescue & recovery workers, military, children under 7 and museums members no charge. Additional fee for guided tour. Closed New Year's Day; Easter; Thanksgiving; Christmas.
Attendance: 500,000 (estimated)

NYC BARBERSHOP MUSEUM, 290 Columbus Ave., New York, NY 10023. Tel.: 646-476-3525. Facebook.
E-mail: welcome@nycbarbershopmuseum.com
Web Site: nycbarbershopmuseum.com
Key Personnel: Owner, Arthur Rubinoff.
Institution Type/Description: History Museum: housed in a working barbershop.
Hours & Admission Prices: Mon.-Tues. & Fri. 10-7, Wed.-Thurs. 10-8, Sat. 10-6, Sun. 11-5.

THE PALEY CENTER FOR MEDIA, 25 W. 52nd St., New York, NY 10019-6129. Tel.: 212-621-6600.
E-mail: mreidy@paleycenter.org
Web Site: www.paleycenter.org
Formerly: The Museum of Television & Radio
Key Personnel: Pres. & C.E.O., Maureen Reidy; Exec. Vice Pres. Programming, Diane Lewis; Vice Pres. Devel., Susan Madden; Vice Pres. Finance & Operations, David Schoer.
Institution Type/Description: Digital Media Museum.
Hours & Admission Prices: NY: Wed. & Fri.-Sun. 12-6, Thurs. 12-8. LA: Wed.-Sun. 12-5. Suggested Donation: adults $10, senior citizens & students $8, children under 14 $5; discounts to groups. Closed New Year's Day; Independence Day; Thanksgiving; Christmas. &
Attendance: 120,000 (actual)

PRATT MANHATTAN GALLERY, 144 W. 14th St., 2nd Fl., New York, NY 10011-7301. Tel.: 212-647-7778.
E-mail: exhibits@pratt.edu
Web Site: www.pratt.edu/exhibitions
Key Personnel: Dir., Nick Battis; Asst. Dir., Olivia Good.
Institution Type/Description: Art Museum & Center.
Hours & Admission Prices: Tues.-Sat. 11-6. No charge. Closed major holidays. &
Attendance: 30,000

THE RENEE AND CHAIM GROSS FOUNDATION, 526 LaGuardia Place, New York, NY 10012-1401. Tel.: 212-529-4906. Fax: 212-529-1966.
E-mail: info@rcgrossfoundation.org
Web Site: www.rcgrossfoundation.org
Key Personnel: Pres., Mimi Gross; Interim Dir. & Cur. of Collections, Sasha Davis; Bookkeeper, Celeste Baker.
Institution Type/Description: Museum: housed in a late 19th century structure with cast iron facade that served as Chaim Gross' home and studio for more than 30 years.
Hours & Admission Prices: Tues.-Fri. 10-5 by appointment. No charge; donation requested. Closed national holidays. &

THE ROSE MUSEUM AT CARNEGIE HALL, 154 W. 57th St., 2nd Fl., New York, NY 10019-3321. Mailing Address: 881 7th Ave., New York, NY 10019-3210. Tel.: 212-903-9629.
E-mail: archives@carnegiehall.org
Web Site: www.carnegiehall.org
Key Personnel: C.E.O. Carnegie Hall & Artistic Dir., Clive Gillinson; Dir. & Archivist, Gino Francesconi; Pres., Sanford I. Weill; Archives Mgr., Robert Hudson.
Institution Type/Description: Theatre Museum: housed in c.1891 Carnegie Hall building.
Hours & Admission Prices: Sept. 15-June daily 11-4:30, open to concert-goers before concerts & during intermission. No charge. &
Attendance: 25,000 (estimated)

RUBIN MUSEUM OF ART, 150 W. 17th St., New York, NY 10011-5402. Tel.: 212-620-5000. Fax: 212-620-0628. Facebook; Twitter; Instagram.
E-mail: info@rubinmuseum.org
Web Site: rubinmuseum.org
Key Personnel: Co-Chm., Donald Rubin; Co-Chm., Shelley F. Rubin; Exec. Dir., Patrick Sears; Pres. Bd., Robert M. Baylis; Dir. Finance & Administration, Marilena Christodoulou; Sr. Mgr. Museum Operations, Steven Battaglia; Dir. Programs & Engagement, Tim McHenry; Head Collections Mgmt. & Registration, Michelle Bennett Simorella; Head Mktg. & Communications, Elke Dehner; Head Exhibition Design, John Monaco; Head Individual Giving & Major Gifts, Nicky Combs; Head Institutional Giving, Gabrielle Mertz; Head IT Implementation & Operations, Harvard Lim; HR Mgr., Hazel King; Finance Mgr., Julio C. Quintero; Museum Shop Mgr., Prisanee Suwanwatana; Sr. Cur. Collections & Research, Karl Debreczeny; Cur. Modern & Contemporary Art, Beth Citron; Cur. Exhibitions, Risha Lee; Cur. Himalayan Art, Elena Pakhoutova.
Institution Type/Description: Art Museum.
Hours & Admission Prices: Mon. & Thurs. 11-5, Wed. 11-9, Fri. 11-10, Sat.-Sun. 11-6. Adults $15, seniors & students $10; Museum Council of NYC, Caregiver, AAM, NARM & ICOM members, children 12 & under, members and Fri. 6pm-10pm no charge. Closed New Year's Day; Thanksgiving; Christmas. &
Attendance: 190,000 (actual)

SALMAGUNDI CLUB GALLERY, 47 5th Ave., New York, NY 10003-4396. Tel.: 212-255-7740. Fax: 212-229-0172. Facebook & Instagram: @salmagundiclub; Twitter: @Salmagundi.
E-mail: info@salmagundi.org
Web Site: www.salmagundi.org
Key Personnel: Chm. (V), Tim Newton; Pres. (V), Robert Pillsbury.
Institution Type/Description: Art Gallery.
Hours & Admission Prices: Mon.-Fri. 1-6, Sat.-Sun. 1-5. No charge; donations accepted.
Attendance: 20,000 (estimated)

THE SCHOMBURG CENTER FOR RESEARCH IN BLACK CULTURE, THE NEW YORK PUBLIC LIBRARY, The New York Public Library, 515 Malcolm X. Blvd., New York, NY 10037-1801. Tel.: 917-275-6975.
E-mail: schomburgtours@nypl.org
Web Site: www.nypl.org/locations/schomburg
Key Personnel: Dir., Kevin Young.
Institution Type/Description: History Museum & Reference Library.
Hours & Admission Prices: Mon.-Wed. 12-8, Thurs.-Sat. 10-6. No charge; donations accepted. Closed New Year's Day, Martin Luther King, Jr. Day, Presidents' Day, Easter, Memorial Day weekend, Independence Day, Labor Day weekend, Columbus Day, Veterans Day, Thanksgiving Day, Christmas Day. &
Attendance: 134,186 (actual)

THE SHED, W. 30th St. between 10th & 11th Avenues, New York, NY 10001. Tel.: 646-455-3494. Twitter, Facebook, Instagram.
E-mail: info@theshed.org

Key Personnel: CEO & Artistic Dir., Alex Poots; C.O.O., Maryann Jordan; C.F.O., Peter Gee; Chief Mktg. & Communications Officer, Jeff Levine; Dir. Devel. Operations, Hemmendy Nelson; Dir. Mktg., Gretchen Scott; Sr. Cur., Emma Enderby.
Institution Type/Description: Arts Center
Hours & Admission Prices: Tues.-Wed. & Sat. 11-6, Thurs.-Sat. 11-8. Admission varies; discounts to groups of 10 or more. &

SHEILA C. JOHNSON DESIGN CENTER, Parsons The New School for Design, 66 Fifth Ave. at 13th St., New York, NY 10011. Mailing Address: 2 W. 13th St., Rm. Z101, New York, NY 10011. Tel.: 212-229-8919.
E-mail: sjdc@newschool.edu
Web Site: www.newschool.edu/parsons/sheila-c-johnson-design-center
Institution Type/Description: Art Gallery.
Hours & Admission Prices: Thurs. 12-8, Fri.-Wed. 12-6. No charge. Closed major holidays.

SIDNEY MISHKIN GALLERY OF BARUCH COLLEGE, 135 E. 22nd St., New York, NY 10010-5505. Tel.: 646-660-6652.
E-mail: mishkingallery@baruch.cuny.edu
Web Site: www.baruch.cuny.edu/mishkin/gallery.html
Key Personnel: Dir. & Cur., Alaina Claire Feldman, Ph.D.; Asst. Cur., Dino Dincer Sirin.
Institution Type/Description: University Gallery: housed in 1939 Family Court Building erected by WPA.
Hours & Admission Prices: Mon.-Wed. & Fri. 11-6 Thurs. 11-7. No charge. Closed university holidays. &

THE SKYSCRAPER MUSEUM, 39 Battery Place, New York, NY 10280-1501. Tel.: 212-968-1961. Fax: 212-732-3039. Facebook: The Skyscraper Museum.
E-mail: info@skyscraper.org
Web Site: www.skyscraper.org
Key Personnel: C.O.O., William Havemeyer; Pres. & Dir., Carol Willis; Sec. & Counsel, Jed Marcus; Treas., Owen Gutfreund.
Institution Type/Description: Architecture Museum.
Hours & Admission Prices: Wed.-Sun. 12-6. Adults $5, students & seniors $2.50; discounts to AAM & ICOM members; members no charge. &
Attendance: 25,000 (estimated)

SOLOMON R. GUGGENHEIM MUSEUM, 1071 Fifth Ave. at 89th St., New York, NY 10128-0112. Tel.: 212-423-3500. Fax: 212-423-3787.
E-mail: info@guggenheim.org
Web Site: www.guggenheim.org
Key Personnel: Dir. Solomon R. Guggenheim Museum & Foundation, Richard Armstrong; Sr. Deputy Dir. & C.O.O., Marc Steglitz; Deputy Dir. & Officer for Global Strategies, Juan Ignacio Vidarte; Deputy Dir., Gen. Council & Asst. Sec., Sarah G. Austrian; Deputy Dir., Global Communications, Tina Vaz; Deputy Dir., Advancement, Catherine Carver Dunn; Deputy Dir. & Engelberg Dir. Education, Kim Kanatani; Deputy Dir. & Jennifer and David Stockman Chief Cur., Nancy Spector; Deputy Dir. & Chief Conservator, Carol Stringari; Dir. Emeritus Peggy Guggenheim Collection & Foundation Dir. for Italy, Philip Rylands; Sr. Cur. Collections & Exhibitions, Susan Davidson; Samsung Sr. Cur. Asian Art & Sr. Advisor Global Arts, Alexandra Munroe; Sr. Cur. Photography, Jennifer Blessing; Sr. Cur., Jeffrey Weiss; Sr. Cur. 19th & early 20th Century Art, Vivien Greene; Sr. Cur. Collections & Exhibitions, Tracey Bashkoff; Dir. Curatorial Affairs, Joan Young; Cur. & Mgr., Curatorial Affairs, Abu Dhabi Project, Solomon R. Guggenheim Foundation, Valerie Hillings; Cur. Contemporary Art, Katherine Brinson; Cur. Architecture & Digital Initiatives, Troy Conrad Therrien; Cur. Performance & Media, Nat Trotman; Dir. Peggy Guggenheim Collection, Karole Vail; Cur. Modern Art & Provenance, Megan Fontanella; Asst. Cur. Collections, Lauren Hinkson; Asst. Cur., Abu Dhabi Project, Sarah Kalter-Wasserman; Asst. Cur. Abu Dhabi Project, Solomon R. Guggenheim Foundation, Fawz Kabra; Asst. Cur., Susan Thompson; Cur. at Large, Latin America, Pablo Leon de la Barra; Guggenheim UBS MAP Cur., Middle East & North Africa, Sara Raza; Asst. Cur., Amara Antilla; Sr. Conservator, Collections & Exhibitions, Julie Barten; Conservator, Objects, Esther Chao; Conservator, Panza Collection, Francesca Esmay; Assoc. Chief Conservator for Collection, Gillian McMillan; Sr. Conservator, Objects, Nathan Otterson; Conservator Time-Based Media, Joanna Phillips; Conservator, Paper & Photographs, Jeffrey Warda; Assoc. Dir. Education & Community Engagement, Rose Demir; Dir. Education, School & Family Programs, Sharon Vatsky; Dir. Education, Public Programs, Christina Yang.
Institution Type/Description: Art Museum: housed in building designed by Frank Lloyd Wright.
Hours & Admission Prices: Sun.-Wed. 10-5:45, Fri.-Sat. 10-7:45. Adults $25, seniors & students $18; discounts to AAM & ICOM members; children under 12 & members no charge. Pay What You Wish: Sat. 5:45pm-7:45pm. Closed Christmas. &
Attendance: 1,000,000 (estimated)

SOUTH STREET SEAPORT MUSEUM, 12 Fulton St., New York, NY 10038-2109. Tel.: 212-748-8600. Facebook: South Street Seaport Museum.
E-mail: info@seany.org
Web Site: www.southstreetseaportmuseum.org
Formerly: Seaport Museum of New York
Key Personnel: Exec. Dir., Capt. Jonathan Boulware; Deputy Exec. Dir., Yvonne Simons.
Institution Type/Description: Maritime History Museum.
Hours & Admission Prices: Museum: see website for hours. Bowne Printers & Bowne & Co. Stationers: daily 11-7. Schooner Pioneer: call for reservations & fee. Closed major holidays. Discounts to CAMM & AAM members; children under 2 no charge.
Attendance: 62,000 (actual)

STATUE OF LIBERTY MUSEUM, Liberty Island, New York, NY 10004. Tel.: 212-363-3200. Facebook.
Web Site: nps.gov
Institution Type/Description: History Museum.
Hours & Admission Prices: Museum: no charge. Ferry: adults $18, seniors $14, children 4-12 $9. &

STATUE OF LIBERTY NATIONAL MONUMENT & ELLIS ISLAND IMMIGRATION MUSEUM, Statue of Liberty National Monument, New York, NY 10004. Tel.: 212-363-3200. Fax: 212-363-6304.
E-mail: stli_info@nps.gov
Web Site: www.nps.gov/stli
Key Personnel: Supt., John Piltzecker.
Institution Type/Description: Statue of Liberty: housed in 1886 151-ft. copper statue bearing torch of freedom was gift of French people to commemorate alliance of U.S. & France; monument includes two exhibits on the Statue of Liberty; World Heritage Site. Ellis Island: over 12 million immigrants were processed here between 1892-1954; exhibits on Ellis Island, American immigration, film, learning center, library & oral history program; access to both islands by ferry.
Hours & Admission Prices: Liberty Island & Ellis Island: open daily except for Christmas Day. Access to sites by ferry only, advanced reservations suggested. Contact Statue Cruises: (877) LADY-TIX or www.statuecruises.com. &
Attendance: 3,408,560 (actual)

STOREFRONT FOR ART AND ARCHITECTURE, 97 Kenmare St., New York, NY 10012. Tel.: 212-431-5795.
E-mail: info@storefrontnews.org
Web Site: www.storefrontnews.org
Key Personnel: Chief Cur. & Exec. Dir., Eva Franch.
Institution Type/Description: Art Gallery.
Hours & Admission Prices: Tues.-Sat. 11-6.

THE STUDIO MUSEUM IN HARLEM, 144 W. 125th St., New York, NY 10027-4423. Tel.: 212-864-4500. Fax: 212-864-4800.
E-mail: pr@studiomuseum.org
Web Site: www.studiomuseum.org
Key Personnel: Dir. & Chief Cur., Thelma Golden; Chm., Raymond J. McGuire.
Institution Type/Description: Contemporary Art Museum: sculpture garden; collection, documentation, preservation & interpretation of the art & artifacts of Black American & the African Diaspora.
Hours & Admission Prices: Thurs. & Fri. 12-9, Sat. 10-6, Sun. 12-6. Suggested Donation: adults $7, students & senior citizens $3; discounts to AAM members; members & children under 12 no charge. Closed major holidays. &
Attendance: 90,831 (estimated)

T.F. CHEN CULTURAL CENTER/NEW WORLD ART CENTER, 250 Lafayette St., Fl. 5, New York, NY 10012-4040. Tel.: 212-966-4363. Fax: 212-966-5285.
E-mail: chen@tfchen.com
Web Site: www.tfchen.com
Key Personnel: C.E.O. & Pres. (V), Lucia Chen; Chm. (V), Dr. T.F. Chen; Financial Dir., Ted Chen; Public Rels. & Cur., Julie Chen.
Institution Type/Description: Art Museum.
Hours & Admission Prices: By appointment only. No charge; donations accepted. Closed New Year's Day; Christmas.
Attendance: 200 (estimated)

THEODORE ROOSEVELT BIRTHPLACE NATIONAL HISTORIC SITE, 28 E. 20th St., New York, NY 10003-1311. Tel.: 212-260-1616. Fax: 212-677-3587.
Web Site: www.nps.gov/thrb/
Key Personnel: Supt., Shirley McKinney; Chief of Interpretation, Education & Visitor Services, Barbara Applebaum; Chief of Facilities, Hector Fonseca.

Institution Type/Description: Historic Site Museum: housed in 1919-1923 reconstructed Theodore Roosevelt birthplace.
Hours & Admission Prices: Tues.-Sat. 9-5. No charge. Closed Thanksgiving; Christmas.
Attendance: 40,000 (actual)

TRINITY MUSEUM OF THE PARISH OF TRINITY CHURCH,
74 Trinity Pl., New York, NY 10006. Mailing Address: c/o Trinnty Wall St. Archives, 120 Broadway, 38th Fl., New York, NY 10271. Tel.: 212-602-0800 & 0872. Fax: 212-602-9648.
E-mail: archives@trinitywallstreet.org
Web Site: www.trinitywallstreet.org/history/
Institution Type/Description: Religious & History Museum: housed in 1846 Trinity Church, on site first used in 1697.
Hours & Admission Prices: Mon.-Fri. 9-11:45 & 1-5:30, Sat.-Sun. 9-3:45; St. Paul's: Mon.-Sat. 10-6, Sun. 7-6. No charge; donations accepted. Closed holidays. &
Attendance: 33,000 (estimated)

THE UKRAINIAN MUSEUM, 222 E. 6th St., New York, NY 10003-8201. Tel.: 212-228-0110. Fax: 212-228-1947. Facebook: @UkrainianMuseum; Twitter: @UkrMuseum.
E-mail: info@ukrainianmuseum.org
Web Site: www.ukrainianmuseum.org
Key Personnel: Dir., Maria Shust; Pres. Bd. Trustees, Chryzanta Hentisz, Esq.
Institution Type/Description: Culturally Specific Museum.
Hours & Admission Prices: Wed.-Sun. 11:30-5. Adults $8, students with valid ID & senior citizens $6; members & children under 12 no charge. Closed New Year's Day; Ukrainian Christmas & Easter; Easter; Independence Day; Ukrainian Independence Day; Thanksgiving; Christmas. &
Attendance: 25,000 (estimated)

UNION FOR REFORM JUDAISM, 633 Third Ave., New York, NY 10017-6706. Tel.: 212-650-4040. Fax: 212-650-4239.
E-mail: urj@urj.org
Web Site: www.urj.org
Formerly: Union of American Hebrew Congregation
Key Personnel: Pres., Rabbi Rick Jacobs.
Institution Type/Description: Religious Library & Museum.
Hours & Admission Prices: Mon.-Thurs. 9-4, Fri. 9-5. Closed Jewish holidays & festivals.

UNITED NATIONS VISITOR CENTRE, Visitor Check-in Office, 801 1st Ave. at 45th St., New York, NY 10017. Tel.: 212-963-8687. Facebook; Twitter.
E-mail: toursunhq@un.org
Web Site: visit.un.org
Institution Type/Description: International History Center.
Hours & Admission Prices: Visitor Center: Jan.-Feb. Mon.-Fri. 9-4:45; March-Dec. daily 9-4:45. Guided Tours: Mon.-Fri. 9-4:45; children under 5 not permitted. Adults $20, senior and student 13 & over $13, children 5-12 $11. Closed New Year's Day; Presidents' Day; Good Friday; Memorial Day; Eid al-Fitr; Independence Day; Eid al-Adha; Labor Day; Thanksgiving; Christmas. &
Attendance: 1,000,000 (estimated)

VAN DOREN WAXTER GALLERY, 23 E. 73rd St., New York, NY 10021. Tel.: 212-445-0444. Fax: 212-445-0442.
E-mail: info@vandorenwaxter.com
Web Site: www.vandorenwaxter.com/
Formerly: Greenberg Van Doren Gallery
Key Personnel: Exec. Dir., Elizabeth Sadeghi.
Institution Type/Description: Art Gallery.
Hours & Admission Prices: Tues.-Sat. 10-6.

THE VILCEK FOUNDATION, 85 Broad St., 27th Fl., New York, NY 10004. Tel.: 212-472-2500. Fax: 212-472-4720. Facebook & Instagram: @vilcekfoundation; Twitter: @vilcek.
E-mail: info@vilcek.org
Web Site: www.vilcek.org
Key Personnel: Co-Founder, C.E.O. & Chm., Dr, Jan T. Vilcek; Pres., Rick Alan Kinsel; Cur., Emily Schuchardt Navratil, Ph.D.
Institution Type/Description: Art Gallery.
Hours & Admission Prices: During Exhibitions: Wed.-Sat. 12-6; other times by appointment. No charge.
Attendance: 796 (actual)

VISUAL ARTS GALLERY, 601 W. 26th St., 15th Fl., New York, NY 10001-1138. Mailing Address: 209 E. 23rd St., New York, NY 10010-3994. Tel.: 212-592-2145. Fax: 646-638-2110.

E-mail; gallery@sva.edu
Web Site: www.schoolofvisualarts.edu
Key Personnel: Dir., Francis Di Tommaso; Asst. Dir., Richard Brooks.
Institution Type/Description: Art Museum.
Hours & Admission Prices: Mon.-Sat. 10-6. No charge. &
Attendance: 8,158 (actual)

WHITNEY MUSEUM OF AMERICAN ART, 99 Gansevoort St., New York, NY 10014-1404. Tel.: 212-570-3600. Fax: 212-606-0207.
E-mail: info@whitney.org
Web Site: whitney.org
Key Personnel: Alice Pratt Brown Dir., Adam D. Weinberg; Deputy Dir. Intl. Initiatives & Sr. Cur., Donna DeSalvo; Deputy Dir. Programs & Nancy & Steve Crown Family Chief Cur., Scott Rothkopf; Deputy Dir. Advancement, Alexandra Wheeler; C.O.O., John S. Stanley.
Institution Type/Description: Art Museum.
Hours & Admission Prices: Sun., Mon., Wed., Thurs. 10:30-6, Fri.-Sat. 10:30-10. Adults $22, senior citizens 62 & over and students $18; members & children under 18 no charge. Closed New Year's Day; Thanksgiving; Christmas. &
Attendance: 650,000 (estimated)

YESHIVA UNIVERSITY MUSEUM AT THE CENTER FOR JEWISH HISTORY, 15 W. 16th St., New York, NY 10011-6301. Tel.: 212-294-8330. Fax: 212-294-8335. Facebook: @YeshivaUniversityMuseum; Instagram & Twitter: @yumuseum.
E-mail: info@yum.cjh.org
Web Site: www.yumuseum.org
Key Personnel: Dir., Dr. Jacob Wisse; Cur. Collection, Bonni-Dara Michaels; Dir. Educator, Ilana Benson.
Institution Type/Description: Religious & Cultural Museum: with the purpose of preserving, enriching & interpreting Jewish life as it is reflected in the arts, history & sciences.
Hours & Admission Prices: Mon. 5-8, Tues., Thurs. & Sun. 11-5, Wed. 11-8, Fri. 11-2:30. Tours available by appointment. Adults $8, senior citizens & students $6; discounts to AAM members; students, staff & alumni of Yeshiva University, members, Mon. & Wed. 5-8, Fri. 11-2:30 no charge. Closed Jewish holidays. &
Attendance: 40,000 (estimated)

Newark Valley

BEMENT-BILLINGS FARMSTEAD, 9241 Rte. 38, Newark Valley, NY 13811. Mailing Address: P.O. Box 222, Newark Valley, NY 13811-0222. Tel.: 607-642-9516. Fax: 607-642-9516.
E-mail: nvhistory@stny.rr.com
Web Site: nvhistory.org
Key Personnel: Farmstead Dir., Ed Nizalowski; Bd. Trustee Chm., Ross McGraw.
Institution Type/Description: Historic Site: c.1840 Bement-Billings Farmstead Museum.
Hours & Admission Prices: July to early Oct. Sat.-Sun. 12-4; other times by appointment. Adults $2, students $1; members no charge.
Attendance: 2,000 (estimated)

NEWARK VALLEY DEPOT MUSEUM, 9241 Rte. 38, Newark Valley, NY 13811. Tel.: 607-642-9516. Fax: 607-642-9516.
E-mail: nvhistory@stny.rr.com
Web Site: www.nvhistory.org
Key Personnel: Dir., Ed Nizalowski; Bd. Pres., Ross McGraw.
Institution Type/Description: Railroad Museum; 1869 Depot restored in 1910.
Hours & Admission Prices: July to early Oct. Sat.-Sun. 12-4; other times by appointment. Adults $2, students $1; members no charge. &
Attendance: 10,000 (estimated)

Newburgh

HISTORICAL SOCIETY OF NEWBURGH BAY AND THE HIGHLANDS - CAPTAIN DAVID CRAWFORD HOUSE, 189 Montgomery St., Newburgh, NY 12550-3636. Tel.: 845-561-2585. Facebook: Newburgh Historical Society.
E-mail: historicalsocietynb@gmail.com
Web Site: www.newburghhistoricalsociety.com
Key Personnel: Bd. Pres., Jim Hoekema; Vice Pres., Glenn T. Marshall; Dir., Matthew Colon.
Institution Type/Description: Historic House: housed in the former home of Captain David Crawford; built in 1830.
Hours & Admission Prices: April-Oct. Sun. 1-4; other times by appointment. Suggested Donation: $5. Closed major holidays. &
Attendance: 3,000 (estimated)

MOTORCYCLEPEDIA, 250 Lake St., Newburgh, NY 12550-5262. Tel.: 845-569-9065. Facebook.
E-mail: info@motorcyclepediamuseum.org
Web Site: www.motorcyclepediamuseum.org
Key Personnel: Museum Coord., Chris Knasiak.
Institution Type/Description: Motorcycle Museum.
Hours & Admission Prices: Fri.-Sun. 10-5. Adults $15, seniors, active military & veterans $12, students $10, youth $5; children under 7 no charge. ♿
Attendance: 12,000 (actual)

WASHINGTON'S HEADQUARTERS STATE HISTORIC SITE, Corner of Liberty & Washington Sts., Newburgh, NY 12551-1476. Mailing Address: P.O. Box 1783, Newburgh, NY 12551-1783. Tel.: 845-562-1195. Fax: 845-561-1789.
E-mail: elyse.goldberg@parks.ny.gov
Web Site: nysparks.state.ny.us/historic-sites/17/details.aspx
Key Personnel: Historic Site Mgr., Elyse B. Goldberg.
Institution Type/Description: Historic House Museum: housed in Jonathan Hasbrouck House, used as Gen. George Washington's headquarters, 1782-1783; built in 1750.
Hours & Admission Prices: Call for hours. Adults $4, seniors 62 & over $3; discount to groups; children 12 & under and FSHSHH members no charge. Braille tours available.
Attendance: 21,203 (actual)

Niagara Falls

AQUARIUM OF NIAGARA, 701 Whirlpool St., Niagara Falls, NY 14301-1094. Tel.: 716-285-3575, ext. 204. Fax: 716-285-8513.
E-mail: aquariumnf@aol.com
Web Site: www.aquariumofniagara.org
Key Personnel: Exec. Dir., Gary Siddall; Pres., Richard Torcasio; Cur. Education, Sarah Courtney; Museum Shop Mgr., Terri Sherman.
Institution Type/Description: Aquarium.
Hours & Admission Prices: Daily 9-5. Adults $13, senior citizens $11.25, children 4-12 $9; discounts to AAA members & special groups; children under 4 & members no charge. State Park Pass Program. Closed Thanksgiving; Christmas. ♿
Attendance: 275,000 (actual)

NIAGARA AEROSPACE MUSEUM, 9900 Porter Rd., Niagara Falls Intl. Airport, Niagara Falls, NY 14304. Mailing Address: 2221 Niagara Falls Blvd., Ste. 7, Niagara Falls, NY 14304-1696. Tel.: 716-297-1323. Facebook: Niagara Aerospace Museum.
E-mail: niagaerospacemu@verizon.net
Web Site: www.wnyaerospace.org
Key Personnel: Exec. Dir., Jack Wysocki.
Institution Type/Description: Aviation History Museum.
Hours & Admission Prices: Sat.-Sun. 11-4. Adults $6, senior citizens 62 & over and students $5, children 12 & under $2; discount to groups; members no charge. Closed New Year's Eve & Day; Thanksgiving; Christmas Eve & Day. ♿

NIAGARA GORGE DISCOVERY CENTER, New York State Parks, Niagara Region, Robert Moses State Pkwy. near Main St., Niagara Falls, NY 14303-0132. Mailing Address: P.O. Box 1132, Niagara Falls, NY 14303. Tel.: 716-278-1796 & 1770. Fax: 716-278-0838.
Web Site: www.niagarafallsstatepark.com
Formerly: Schoellkopf Geological Museum.
Key Personnel: Park Mgr., Tom Watt; Mktg. & Public Affairs, Angela P. Berti.
Institution Type/Description: Natural & Local History Museum: located on the brink of the Niagara Gorge.
Hours & Admission Prices: Call for hours. Adults $3, children 6-12 $2; children 5 & under no charge. Closed New Year's Day; Thanksgiving; Christmas. ♿
Attendance: 68,551 (actual)

North Blenheim

LANSING MANOR HOUSE MUSEUM, 1378 State Rte. 30, North Blenheim, NY 12131. Mailing Address: P.O. Box 898, 1378 State Rte. 30, N. Blenheim, NY 12131-0898. Tel.: 800-724-0309. Fax: 518-287-6381. Facebook: NYPA Energy.
E-mail: samantha.vanness@nypa.gov
Web Site: www.nypa.gov/html/vcblenhe.html
Key Personnel: Supvr., Samantha Clark.
Institution Type/Description: Historic House: 1819 Lansing Manor House, Federal Manor house built by Chancellor John Lansing Jr., occupied by his son-in-law Jacob Sutherland as manager of the Blenheim Patent 1783-1853.
Hours & Admission Prices: May-Oct. Wed.-Mon. 10-5 by appointment. No charge. ♿
Attendance: 12,400 (actual)

North Salem

HAMMOND MUSEUM AND JAPANESE STROLL GARDEN, 28 Deveau Rd., North Salem, NY 10560-2115. Mailing Address: P.O. Box 326, 28 Deveau Rd., North Salem, NY 10560-2115. Tel.: 914-669-5033.
E-mail: gardenprogram@yahoo.com
Web Site: www.hammondmuseum.org.
Key Personnel: Dir., Lorraine Laken; Chm. Bd., Evelyn S. Tapani-Rosenthal; Business Mgr., Judy Schurmacher.
Institution Type/Description: Cross-Cultural Center.
Hours & Admission Prices: Wed.-Sat. 12-4. Adults $5, seniors & students $4; discounts to AAM & AAA members & seniors; members & children under 12 no charge.
Attendance: 5,800 (estimated)

North Tonawanda

HERSCHELL CARROUSEL FACTORY MUSEUM, 180 Thompson St., North Tonawanda, NY 14120-5420. Tel.: 716-693-1885. Fax: 716-743-9018. Facebook; Herschell Carrousel Factory Museum.
E-mail: hcfm@carrouselmuseum.org
Web Site: www.carrouselmuseum.org
Key Personnel: Dir. (V), Raphaelle A. Proefrock; Pres. (V), Charles W. Proefrock; Museum Shop Mgr., Maureen Schumacher.
Institution Type/Description: Company Museum: housed in 1916 Allan Herschell Company factory building. Listed on the National Register of Historic Places.
Hours & Admission Prices: April-June 11 & Sept.-Dec. Wed.-Sun. 12-4; June 14 to Labor Day Mon.-Sat. 10-4, Sun. 12-4. Adults $5, senior citizens $4, children 2-12 $2.50; discounts to active military, AAM, AARP & AAA members; members no charge. Closed Easter; Thanksgiving; Christmas. ♿
Attendance: 11,000 (estimated)

NORTH TONAWANDA HISTORY MUSEUM, 54-60 Webster St., North Tonawanda, NY 14120-5814. Tel.: 716-213-0554.
E-mail: nthistorymuseum@aol.com
Web Site: www.nthistorymuseum.org
Key Personnel: Exec. Dir., Donna Zellner Neal.
Institution Type/Description: History Museum.
Hours & Admission Prices: Memorial Day to Labor Day Mon.-Sat. 10-4; Sept.-May Tues.-Sat. 10-4. Adults $5, seniors & veterans $3; members no charge. Closed holidays. ♿
Attendance: 20,000 (actual)

Northport

NORTHPORT HISTORICAL SOCIETY, 215 Main St., Northport, NY 11768. Mailing Address: P.O. Box 545, Northport, NY 11768-0545. Tel.: 631-757-9859. Fax: 631-757-9398.
E-mail: info@northporthistorical.org
Web Site: www.northporthistorical.org
Key Personnel: Dir., Heather Johnson; Pres. (V), Steven King; Museum Educator, Marion Munch; Museum Shop Mgr., Lois Howe.
Institution Type/Description: History Museum.
Hours & Admission Prices: Tues.-Sun. 1-4:30. Suggested Donation: $5; discounts to Smithsonian Museum Day members. Closed New Year's Day; Easter; Independence Day; Thanksgiving; Christmas.
Attendance: 4,342 (actual)

Norwich

CHENANGO COUNTY HISTORICAL SOCIETY MUSEUM, 45 Rexford St., Norwich, NY 13815-1121. Tel.: 607-334-9227. Fax: 607-334-7809.
E-mail: estuscchs@roadrunner.com
Web Site: www.chenangohistorical.org
Key Personnel: Dir., Alan V. Estus; Pres., Linda M. Green; Sec., Mary Pat Laufair; Vice Pres., Walter O. Rogers; Treas., Howard Fogel; Cur., Meghan Molloy; Museum Shop Mgr., Liz Welch.
Institution Type/Description: Historical Society Museum.
Hours & Admission Prices: Jan.-March Mon.-Fri. 1-4; April-Dec. Sun.-Fri. 1-4; other times by appointment. No charge; donations accepted. Closed legal holidays.
Attendance: 1,500 (estimated)

NORTHEAST CLASSIC CAR MUSEUM, 24 Rexford St., Norwich, NY 13815-1172. Tel.: 607-334-2886. Fax: 607-336-6745.
E-mail: info@classiccarmuseum.org

Web Site: www.classiccarmuseum.org
Key Personnel: Exec. Dir., Robert M. Jeffrey; Pres., RC Woodford; Mktg., Heather Calkins.
Institution Type/Description: Classic Car Museum.
Hours & Admission Prices: Daily 9-5. Adults $10, children 6-18 $5; members & children under 6 no charge. Closed Easter; Thanksgiving; Christmas. &
Attendance: 16,000 (estimated)

Norwood

NORWOOD HISTORICAL ASSOCIATION AND MUSEUM, 39 N. Main St., Norwood, NY 13668-1123. Mailing Address: P.O. Box 163, Norwood, NY 13668-0163. Tel.: 315-353-2751.
E-mail: glacomb@twcny.rr.com
Key Personnel: Dir., Richard Boprey; Chm. (V), Dick Boyle; Sec., Rose Valyo.
Institution Type/Description: General Museum.
Hours & Admission Prices: May-Oct. Tues. & Thurs. 2-4, other times by appointment. No charge; donations accepted.
Attendance: 300

Nyack

EDWARD HOPPER HOUSE ART CENTER, 82 N. Broadway, Nyack, NY 10960-2628. Tel.: 845-358-0774. Fax: 845-358-0774.
E-mail: info@hopperhouse.org
Web Site: www.hopperhouse.org
Key Personnel: Exec. Dir., Carole Perry; Pres., Victoria Hertz.
Institution Type/Description: Art Center: boyhood home of renowned American Realist painter, Edward Hopper.
Hours & Admission Prices: Thurs.-Sun. 1-5. Adults $5, seniors $3; children, students, Whitney Museum & center members no charge. &
Attendance: 4,000 (estimated)

Oceanside

MARINE NATURE STUDY AREA, 500 Slice Dr., Oceanside, NY 11572. Tel.: 516-766-1580.
E-mail: michfar@tohmail.org
Web Site: mnsa.info
Institution Type/Description: Marine Nature Study.
Hours & Admission Prices: Tues.-Sat. 9-5.

Ogdensburg

FREDERIC REMINGTON ART MUSEUM, 303 Washington St., Ogdensburg, NY 13669-1517. Tel.: 315-393-2425. Fax: 315-393-4464. Facebook: Frederic Remington Art Museum.
E-mail: info@fredericremington.org
Web Site: www.fredericremington.org
Key Personnel: Exec. Dir., Laura A. Foster; Administrative Aide, Shannon Ghize; Pres., Juliann Cliff; Education Specialist, Laura Desmond; Account Clerk, Debbie Ormasen; Dir. Devel. & Museum Shop Mgr., Melanie Flack.
Institution Type/Description: Art Museum: housed in 1809-10 Mansion with modern gallery addition.
Hours & Admission Prices: May 15-Oct. 15 Mon.-Sat. 10-5, Sun. 1-5; Oct. 16-May 14 Wed.-Sat. 11-5, Sun. 1-5. Adults $9, seniors and students 16 & over $8; discounts to AAM, NARM, AAA members & military; children 15 & under and members no charge. Closed New Year's Day; Easter; Thanksgiving; Christmas. &
Attendance: 10,000 (actual)

Old Bethpage

OLD BETHPAGE VILLAGE RESTORATION, 1303 Round Swamp Rd., Old Bethpage, NY 11804-1199. Tel.: 516-572-8401. Fax: 516-572-8439.
E-mail: karena@nassaucountyny.gov
Web Site: www.obvrnassau.com
Key Personnel: Site Dir., Sue Bennett; Supvr. Volunteers, Judy Pockriss.
Institution Type/Description: Living History Village Museum: 15 historic site units which include houses, shops, barns, outbuildings, tavern, church & schoolhouse.
Hours & Admission Prices: April-Dec. Wed.-Sun. 10-4. Adults $10, seniors & children $7; discounts to groups; children under 5 no charge. Closed New Year's Eve; Veterans Day; Thanksgiving & day after; Christmas Eve & Day.
Attendance: 89,505 (actual)

Old Westbury

OLD WESTBURY GARDENS, 71 Old Westbury Rd., Old Westbury, NY 11568-1603. Mailing Address: P.O. Box 430, Old Westbury, NY 11568-0430. Tel.: 516-333-0048. Fax: 516-333-6807.
E-mail: emccauley@oldwestburygardens.org
Web Site: oldwestburygardens.org
Key Personnel: C.E.O. & Pres., John Norbeck; Chm. (V), Mary S. Phipps; Dir. Devel., Doreen Banks; Dir. Visitor Svcs., Collections Mgmt. & Museum Shop Mgr., Paul Hunchak; Dir. Public Rels., Vincent Kish; Dir. Horticulture, Maura M. Brush; Walled Garden Supvr., Kimberly Johnson; Greenhouse Supvr., Scott Lucas.
Institution Type/Description: Historic House & Public Horticultural Display Garden: 1906 Charles II style mansion furnished with 18th-century decorative & fine arts.
Hours & Admission Prices: Grounds: late April to Oct. Wed.-Mon. 10-5. House: late April to Oct. Wed.-Mon. 11-5; Nov.-Dec. call for hours. House & Gardens: adults $10, senior citizens over 62 $8, children 7-17 $5; members and children 6 & under no charge, except during special events. &
Attendance: 60,000 (actual)

Onchiota

SIX NATIONS INDIAN MUSEUM, 1462 County Rte. 60, Onchiota, NY 12989-2102. Tel.: 518-891-2299.
E-mail: info@sixnationsindianmuseum.com
Web Site: www.sixnationsindianmuseum.com
Key Personnel: Dir., John Fadden; Museum Shop Mgr. & Asst., Elizabeth E. Fadden.
Institution Type/Description: Indian Museum, with emphasis on Iroquois.
Hours & Admission Prices: July-Aug. Tues.-Sun. 10-5; June & Sept. by appointment. Adults $4, children $2; Indians & special non-Indian friends no charge.
Attendance: 2,000 (estimated)

Oneida

MADISON COUNTY HISTORICAL SOCIETY-COTTAGE LAWN, 435 Main St., Oneida, NY 13421-2440. Tel.: 315-363-4136 & 361-9735. Fax: 315-361-9735. Facebook: Madison County Historical Society.
E-mail: history@mchs1900.org
Web Site: www.mchs1900.org
Key Personnel: C.E.O. & Exec. Dir., Sydney L. Loftus; Pres. (V), Mishell Magnusson.
Institution Type/Description: Historical Society Museum: housed in Gothic Revival 1849 Cottage Lawn designed by Alexander Jackson Davis.
Hours & Admission Prices: Mon.-Fri. 10-4. Tours: adults $5, seniors $2; discount to AAM members; children 12 & under and members no charge. Research: adults $10; members no charge.
Attendance: 12,000 (estimated)

ONEIDA COMMUNITY MANSION HOUSE, 170 Kenwood Ave., Oneida, NY 13421-2820. Tel.: 315-363-0745. Fax: 315-361-4580.
E-mail: ocmh@oneidacommunity.org
Web Site: www.oneidacommunity.org
Key Personnel: Exec. Dir., Kevin Coffee; Cur. Education, Molly Jessup; Museum Shop Mgr., Pauline Caputi.
Institution Type/Description: Historic Home: National Historic Landmark comprising four 19th & early 20th century masonry buildings designed in Italianate & Victorian Gothic styles.
Hours & Admission Prices: Self-Guided Tours: Mon.-Sat. 10-4, Sun. 1-4. Guided Tours: Wed.-Sat. 10 & 2, Sun. 2; groups by appointment. Adults $5, students $3; discounts to AAM, ICOM, AASLH, VHA & NARM members & groups; children & members no charge. Closed major holidays. &
Attendance: 9,843 (actual)

SHAKO:WI CULTURAL CENTER, Oneida Indian Nation, 5 Territory Rd., Oneida, NY 13421-9304. Tel.: 315-829-8801. Fax: 315-829-8805.
E-mail: kwatson@oneida-nation.org
Web Site: www.oneida-nation.net
Key Personnel: Dir., Kandice Watson.
Institution Type/Description: Tribal Museum.
Hours & Admission Prices: Mon.-Sat. 9-5. No charge. Closed holidays; American Indian Day.
Attendance: 3,600 (estimated)

Oneonta

ONEONTA WORLD OF LEARNING - OWL, 277 Main St., Oneonta, NY 13820. Tel.: 607-431-8543.
E-mail: worldoflearning@live.com
Web Site: oneontaworldoflearning.org
Institution Type/Description: Children's Museum.
Hours & Admission Prices: Mon.-Tues. 9-2, Thurs. & Sat. 10-2, Sun. 12-4. Admission $5; members no charge.

SCIENCE DISCOVERY CENTER OF ONEONTA, State University New York College, Bugbee Hall, 3rd Fl., Oneonta, NY 13820-4015. Tel.: 607-436-2011. Fax: 607-436-2654.
E-mail: scdisc@oneonta.edu
Web Site: www.oneonta.edu/academics/sdc
Key Personnel: Dir., Hugh Gallagher, Jr.
Institution Type/Description: Science Museum.
Hours & Admission Prices: July-Aug. Mon.-Sat. 12-4; Sept.-June Thurs.-Sat. 12-4; groups by appointment. No charge; donations accepted. Closed Thanksgiving; Christmas. &
Attendance: 5,720 (actual)

THE YAGER MUSEUM OF ART & CULTURE, One Hartwick Dr., Oneonta, NY 13820-4000. Mailing Address: P.O. Box 4020, Oneonta, NY 13820-4000. Tel.: 607-431-4480. Fax: 607-431-4468.
E-mail: museum@hartwick.edu
Web Site: www.hartwick.edu/campus-life/arts-culture/yager-museum
Key Personnel: College Pres., Dr. Margaret L. Drugovich; Coord., Dr. Douglas Kendall; Cur. Anthropological Collection, Dr. David Anthony; Collections Mgr., Dr. Quintin Lewis; Program & Bus. Mgr., Anne Salluzzo.
Institution Type/Description: General Museum.
Hours & Admission Prices: Tues.-Sat. 12-4:30; collection research by appointment only. No charge, donations accepted. Closed school holidays. &

Ontario

HERITAGE SQUARE MUSEUM, 7147 Ontario Center Rd., Ontario, NY 14519. Mailing Address: Town of Ontario Historical & Landmark Preservation Society, P.O. Box 462, Ontario, NY 14519-0462. Tel.: 315-524-5356. Fax: 315-524-9709.
E-mail: jimandverag@rochester.rr.com
Web Site: heritagesquaremuseum.org
Key Personnel: Pres. & Museum Shop Mgr., Vera Graves; Vice Pres., Ann Welker; Sec., Marguerite Manning; Treas., Ed Kushall.
Institution Type/Description: Historical Society Museum Complex: housed on the site of the Pease farm of fruit & vegetables.
Hours & Admission Prices: June 2-Oct. 7 Sat.-Sun. 1:30-4; other times by appointment. School & group tours by bus are welcome. Adults $6, seniors & children $5; members no charge. Closed Memorial Day weekend; Independence Day weekend; Labor Day weekend. &
Attendance: 21,400 (estimated)

Orangeburg

ORANGETOWN HISTORICAL MUSEUM AND ARCHIVES - SALYER HOUSE AND DEPEW HOUSE, 196 Chief Bill Harris Way, (formerly Blaisdell Rd.), Orangeburg, NY 10962-2011. Mailing Address: 26 Orangeburg Rd., Orangeburg, NY 10962-1706. Tel.: 845-398-1302. Fax: 845-398-8919. Facebook: Orangetown Museum; Instagram @otownmuse.
E-mail: otownmuseum@optonline.net
Web Site: www.orangetownmuseum.com
Key Personnel: Dir., Mary R. Cardenas; Chm. (V), Luise Weischowsky; Supvr., Andy Stewart; Cur., Elizabeth Skrabonja; Public Rels., Sandi Miller; Registrar, Joseph Barbieri; Museum Shop Mgr., Aruna Shah.
Institution Type/Description: History Museum.
Hours & Admission Prices: Sun. 1-4, Tues. & Sat. 10-2; other times by appointment. No charge; donations accepted. Closed holidays. &
Attendance: 621 (actual)

Orchard Park

ORCHARD PARK HISTORICAL SOCIETY, 4287 S. Buffalo St., Orchard Park, NY 14127. Mailing Address: 4100 N. Freeman Rd., Orchard Park, NY 14127-2525. Tel.: 716-662-2185.
E-mail: ophsjolls@gmail.com
Web Site: ophistoricalsociety.wordpress.com
Key Personnel: C.E.O. & Pres., Dennis J. Mill; Cur., Yasabel N. Gibson.

Institution Type/Description: Historical Society Museum: housed in the Jolls house; built in 1870.
Hours & Admission Prices: Spring-Oct. 1st & 3rd Sat. 2-4; Nov. 28-Dec. 20 Sat.-Sun. 2-4; groups by appointment. Admission: $2. &
Attendance: 425 (estimated)

Orient

OYSTERPONDS HISTORICAL SOCIETY: MUSEUM & ARCHIVE OF ORIENT & EAST MARION HISTORY, 1555 Village Lane, Orient, NY 11957. Mailing Address: P.O. Box 70, Orient, NY 11957-0070. Tel.: 631-323-2480. Fax: 631-323-3719.
E-mail: ohsorient@optonline.net
Web Site: www.oysterpondshistoricalsociety.org
Institution Type/Description: History Village Museum Complex.
Hours & Admission Prices: July-Oct. Thurs. & Sat.-Sun. 2-5; other times by appointment. Adults $5, children under 16 $.50; discounts to AASLH members; members no charge. &
Attendance: 5,000 (estimated)

Oriskany

ORISKANY BATTLEFIELD STATE HISTORIC SITE, 7801 State Rt. 69, Oriskany, NY 13424-4115. Tel.: 315-768-7224. Fax: 315-337-3081.
E-mail: nancy.demyttenaere@oprhp.state.ny.us
Web Site: www.nysparks.com
Key Personnel: Regl. Historic Preservation Supvr., Nancy Demyttenaere; Second in Command, Bill Acomb.
Institution Type/Description: Historic Site: Revolutionary War Battlefield & Memorial Park, site of Aug. 6, 1777 ambush of Colonial Militia & Oneida allies by Loyalist forces.
Hours & Admission Prices: April-Oct. daily 10-4. No charge; donations accepted.
Attendance: 23,000 (actual)

Ossining

OSSINING HISTORICAL SOCIETY MUSEUM, 196 Croton Ave., Ossining, NY 10562-4504. Tel.: 914-941-0001. Fax: 914-941-0001.
E-mail: ohsm@bestweb.net
Web Site: www.ossininghistorical.org
Key Personnel: Pres., Joseph Burton; Vice Pres., Deborah Van Steen; Treas., Greg Fratianni.
Institution Type/Description: Local History Museum & Fine Arts Collection.
Hours & Admission Prices: By appointment. No charge; donations accepted. &
Attendance: 1,500 (estimated)

Oswego

FORT ONTARIO STATE HISTORIC SITE, One E. 4th St., Oswego, NY 13126-1233. Mailing Address: P.O. Box 5379, Oswego, NY 13126. Tel.: 315-343-4711.
E-mail: fortontariofriends@gmail.com
Web Site: www.fortontario.com
Key Personnel: Pres. (V), Charles Harrington; Site Mgr., Paul Lear; Asst., Richard LaCrosse; Cur., Jennifer Emmons; Sec., Roberta Elmer; Maintenance Supvr., Robert Clarke.
Institution Type/Description: Military Museum: housed in 1839-1844 fortifications situated at the outlet of Oswego River into Lake Ontario.
Hours & Admission Prices: May-Oct. 15 Tues.-Sun. & Mon. holidays 10-4:30; groups by appointment. Adults $4, seniors & students with I.D. $3; children 12 & under & Friends of Fort Ontario no charge.
Attendance: 15,000 (actual)

H. LEE WHITE MARINE MUSEUM, W. 1st St. Pier, Oswego, NY 13126. Mailing Address: P.O. Box 101, Oswego, NY 13126-0101. Tel.: 315-342-0480. Fax: 315-343-5778. Facebook: HLWMM.
E-mail: info@hleewhitemarinemuseum.com
Web Site: hleewhitemarinemuseum.com
Key Personnel: Exec. Dir., Mercedes Niess; Retail & Visitor Experience Mgr., Susan Wild; Public Rels. Asst., Shelia Weldin.
Institution Type/Description: Maritime Museum.
Hours & Admission Prices: July-Aug. daily 10-5; Sept.-June daily 1-5. Adults $7, teenagers $3; discounts to SUNY students, HNSA, AAA, AAM & ICOM members, active duty military; museum members & children under 13 no charge. Closed New Year's Eve & Day; Easter; Thanksgiving; Christmas Eve, Day & week.
Attendance: 28,700 (actual)

JOHN D. MURRAY FIREFIGHTER'S MUSEUM, 35 E. Cayuga St., Oswego, NY 13126. Tel.: 315-529-1393.
Institution Type/Description: Firefighting History Museum.
Hours & Admission Prices: Call for hours.

RICHARDSON-BATES HOUSE MUSEUM, 135 E. 3rd St., Oswego, NY 13126-2655. Tel.: 315-343-1342.
E-mail: ochs@rbhousemuseum.org
Web Site: www.rbhousemuseum.org
Key Personnel: Pres. (V), Justin White.
Institution Type/Description: Historic House Museum: Richardson-Bates house, built 1867-90.
Hours & Admission Prices: April-Dec. Thurs.-Sat. 1-5; research library by appointment. Family $12; adults $5, students & seniors $3, children $2; discounts to American Assoc. for State & Local History, NY State Historical Assoc. & AAM members; members no charge. Closed holidays.
Attendance: 2,500 (estimated)

SAFE HAVEN HOLOCAUST REFUGEE SHELTER MUSEUM, 2 E. 7th St., Oswego, NY 13126-1197. Mailing Address: P.O. Box 846, Oswego, NY 13126-0846. Tel.: 315-342-3003. Fax: 315-342-1411.
E-mail: safehavenmuseum@gmail.com
Web Site: www.oswegohaven.org
Formerly: Safe Haven Museum and Education Center
Key Personnel: C.E.O. & Pres., George R. DeMass.
Institution Type/Description: History Museum.
Hours & Admission Prices: Memorial Day-Labor Day daily 11-4; Labor Day-Memorial Day Thurs.-Sun. 11-4. Adults $5, children $3, students $2; members no charge.
Attendance: 2,500 (estimated)

TYLER ART GALLERY, State University of New York College of Arts & Science, 7060 State Rte. 104, 123 Tyler Hall, Oswego, NY 13126-3599. Tel.: 315-312-2113. Fax: 315-312-5642. Facebook: Tyler Gallery.
E-mail: michael.flanagan@oswego.edu
Web Site: www.oswego.edu/other_campus/tylerart/index.html
Key Personnel: Dir., Michael Flanagan; Administrative Aide, Traci Terpening.
Institution Type/Description: Art Gallery.
Hours & Admission Prices: Sept.-May Tues.-Sat. 11:30-3. No charge; donations accepted. Closed during college vacation periods.
Attendance: 18,650 (actual)

Ovid

OVID HISTORICAL SOCIETY, 7203 Main St., Ovid, NY 14521. Mailing Address: P.O. Box 374, Ovid, NY 14521. Tel.: 607-869-5222.
E-mail: ovidhs67@yahoo.com
Institution Type/Description: Historical Society Museum.
Hours & Admission Prices: Thurs. 10 to noon, Sat. 10-1.

Owego

TIOGA COUNTY HISTORICAL SOCIETY, 110 Front St., Owego, NY 13827-1519. Tel.: 607-687-2460. Fax: 607-687-2460. Facebook: Tioga County Historical Society.
E-mail: museum@tiogahistory.org
Web Site: www.tiogahistory.org
Key Personnel: Exec. Dir., Kevin Lentz.
Institution Type/Description: History Museum.
Hours & Admission Prices: Wed.-Sat. 10-4. No charge; donations accepted. Closed New Year's Day; Independence Day; Thanksgiving; Christmas.
Attendance: 7,168 (actual)

Oyster Bay

COE HALL, 1395 Planting Fields Rd., Oyster Bay, NY 11771-1302. Mailing Address: P.O. Box 660, Oyster Bay, NY 11771-0660. Tel.: 516-922-9210. Fax: 516-922-9226.
E-mail: scherenfant@plantingfields.org
Web Site: plantingfields.org
Key Personnel: Exec. Dir., Henry Joyce; Chm. (V), Michael D. Coe; Pres. (V), G. Morgan Brown; Business Mgr., Sherley Cherenfant; Cur., Marianne Della Croce; Volunteer Coord. & Museum Shop Mgr., Katherine Sterner; Weekend Coord., Elsa Eisenberg; Coord. Membership & Dir. Devel., Patrice Panza; Field Trip Coord., Melissa Valencia; Garden Librarian, Rose Marie Papayanopulos;

Asst. Cur., Kristy Caratzola; Dir. Special Events, Jennifer Lavella; Education Asst., Tracy Potavin.
Institution Type/Description: Historic House: 1918-1921 Tudor Revival Mansion.
Hours & Admission Prices: April-Sept. daily 12-3:30; groups by appointment. Guided Tours: adults $3.50; discounts to AAM & AAA members; children 6-12 & members no charge. Arboretum: $6 per car. Closed legal holidays.
Attendance: 200,000 (actual)

OYSTER BAY HISTORICAL SOCIETY, 20 Summit St., Oyster Bay, NY 11771-2317. Mailing Address: P.O. Box 297, Oyster Bay, NY 11771-0297. Tel.: 516-922-5032.
E-mail: obhsdirector@optonline.net
Web Site: www.oysterbayhistorical.org
Key Personnel: Exec. Dir., Philip Blocklyn; Collections Mgr., Melanie Derschowitz; Museum Shop Mgr., Elizabeth Roosevelt.
Institution Type/Description: Historical Society Museum: housed in c.1720 Earle-Wightman House.
Hours & Admission Prices: Tues.-Fri. 10-2, Sat. 11-3, Sun. 1-4. No charge; donations requested. Closed major holidays.
Attendance: 4,000 (estimated)

OYSTER BAY RAILROAD MUSEUM, 102 Audrey Ave., Oyster Bay, NY 11771. Mailing Address: P.O. Box 335, Oyster Bay, NY 11771-0335. Tel.: 516-558-7036.
E-mail: info@obrm.org
Web Site: www.obrm.org
Institution Type/Description: Railroad Museum.
Hours & Admission Prices: Call for hours.
Attendance: 2,000 (estimated)

PLANTING FIELDS ARBORETUM STATE HISTORIC PARK, 1395 Planting Fields Rd., Oyster Bay, NY 11771-1302. Mailing Address: P.O. Box 58, Oyster Bay, NY 11771-0058. Tel.: 516-922-8600. Fax: 516-922-8610.
E-mail: henry.joyce@plantingfields.org
Web Site: www.plantingfields.org
Key Personnel: Exec. Dir., Henry B. Joyce; Chm. Planting Fields Foundation, G. Morgan Browne; Dir. Mktg. & Special Events, Jennifer L. Lavella; Cur., Gwendolyn L. Smith.
Institution Type/Description: Arboretum.
Hours & Admission Prices: Daily 9-5. $8 per car, April 1-Labor Day; no charge during winter. Coe Hall: see separate listing. Closed Christmas Day.
Attendance: 262,360 (estimated)

RAYNHAM HALL MUSEUM, 20 W. Main St., Oyster Bay, NY 11771-2216. Tel.: 516-922-6808. Fax: 516-922-7640.
E-mail: info@raynhamhallmuseum.org
Web Site: www.raynhamhallmuseum.org
Key Personnel: Exec. Dir., Harriet Gerard Clark; Asst. Dir., Theresa Skvarla; Pres. (V), Kay Hutchins Sato; Coord. Education, Jessica M. Semins; Collections Mgr., Jennifer Ladd.
Institution Type/Description: c.1738 Historic House Museum: 1851 Gothic Revival addition.
Hours & Admission Prices: Memorial Day to Labor Day Sat.-Sun. 10-5; Sept.-May Tues.-Sun. 1-5; group tours by appointment. Adults $5, students with ID & senior citizens $3; discounts to AAM members; children under 6 & members no charge. Closed New Year's Day; Thanksgiving; Christmas; most national holidays.
Attendance: 10,032 (actual)

SAGAMORE HILL NATIONAL HISTORIC SITE, 20 Sagamore Hill Rd., Oyster Bay, NY 11771-1899. Tel.: 516-922-4788. Fax: 516-922-4792.
E-mail: sahi_information@nps.gov
Web Site: www.nps.gov/sahi
Key Personnel: Supt., Thomas Ross; Cur., Amy Verone; Museum Shop Mgr., Debbie Bulck.
Institution Type/Description: Historic House Museum: 1885 Sagamore Hill, home of Theodore Roosevelt.
Hours & Admission Prices: Memorial Day to Labor Day daily 9:30-5; Winter: Wed.-Sun. 9:30-5; groups by appointment. Adults $10; children under 16 & scheduled educational groups no charge. Closed New Year's Day; Thanksgiving; Christmas.
Attendance: 65,000 (actual)

Painted Post

PAINTED POST - ERWIN MUSEUM AT THE DEPOT, 277 Steuben St., Painted Post, NY 14870. Mailing Address: 73 W.

Pulteney St., Corning, NY 14830-2212. Tel.: 607-654-7981; 937-5281 (for appts.). Fax: 607-937-5281.
E-mail: cpphs@stny.rr.com
Web Site: www.heritagevillagesfl.org
Key Personnel: Pres., Leon Golder; Vice Pres., Zachary Houseworth.
Institution Type/Description: General Museum.
Hours & Admission Prices: June-Aug. Mon.-Fri. 10-4, Sat. 10-2; Sept.-Oct. Sat. 10-2; other times by appointment. No charge, donations accepted. &
Attendance: 500 (estimated)

Palmyra

ALLING COVERLET MUSEUM, 122 William St., Palmyra, NY 14522-1030. Mailing Address: 132 Market St., Palmyra, NY 14522-1136. Tel.: 315-597-6981. Fax: 315-597-6981.
E-mail: bjfhpinc@rochester.rr.com
Web Site: www.historicpalmyrany.com
Key Personnel: Chm., Becke Tomkiewicz; Exec. Dir., Bonnie J. Hays; Museum Shop Mgr., Steve Hays.
Institution Type/Description: American Coverlet Museum.
Hours & Admission Prices: May-Oct. Mon. 1-4, Tues.-Sat. 10:30-4:30; Nov.-April Mon.-Sat. 1-4. No charge; donations accepted. &
Attendance: 13,000 (actual)

ERIE CANAL DEPOT MUSEUM, 132-140 1/2 Market St., Palmyra, NY 14522. Mailing Address: 132 Market St., Palmyra, NY 14522-1136. Tel.: 315-597-6981. Fax: 315-597-6981.
E-mail: bjfhpinc@rochester.rr.com
Web Site: www.historicpalmyrany.com
Formerly: Historic Palmyra's Print Shop
Key Personnel: C.E.O. & Chm. (V), Becke Tomkiewicz; Exec. Dir., Bonnie J. Hays; Museum Shop Mgr., Steve Hays.
Institution Type/Description: History Museum: housed in an Erie Canal tenant house.
Hours & Admission Prices: May-Oct. Tues.-Sat. 10:30-4:30; Nov.-April Tues.-Thurs. 11-4. Individual Museum: adults $3; members no charge. Trail Pass: family $20, adults $10, students & senior citizens $7; children 10 & under and members no charge. &
Attendance: 13,000 (estimated)

HILL CUMORAH VISITORS CENTER & HISTORIC SITES, 603 State Rte. 21 S., Palmyra, NY 14522-9301. Tel.: 315-597-5851. Facebook.
E-mail: hcvc@ldschurch.org
Web Site: www.lds.org/locations/hill-cumorah-visitors-center
Key Personnel: Dir., Dale H. Bradford.
Institution Type/Description: Religious Museums & Historic Sites: 5 historical sites & places of historic significance in connection with the founding of the Church of Jesus Christ of Latter-day Saints.
Hours & Admission Prices: Mon.-Sat. 9-9, Sun. 12:30-9. No charge. Closed Christmas. &
Attendance: 150,000 (estimated)

HISTORIC PALMYRA'S WILLIAM PHELPS GENERAL STORE, 140 Market St., Palmyra, NY 14522-1136. Mailing Address: 132 Market St., Palmyra, NY 14522-1136. Tel.: 315-597-6981. Fax: 315-597-6981.
E-mail: bjfhpinc@rochester.rr.com
Web Site: www.historicpalmyrany.com
Formerly: Historic Palmyra Inc.
Key Personnel: Chm. & Pres. (V), Becke Tomkiewicz; Exec. Dir., Bonnie J. Hays; Museum Shop Mgr., Steve Hays.
Institution Type/Description: Erie Canal Store & Home: housed in c.1826 building.
Hours & Admission Prices: May-Oct. Tues.-Sat. 10:30-4:30; Nov.-April Tues.-Thurs. 11-4. Individual Pass: adults $3; members no charge. Trail Pass: family $14, adults $7, students & senior citizens $5; children 10 & under and members no charge. Closed Independence Day; Labor Day. &
Attendance: 13,000 (actual)

PALMYRA HISTORICAL MUSEUM, 132 Market St., Palmyra, NY 14522-1136. Tel.: 315-597-6981. Fax: 315-597-6981.
E-mail: bjfhpinc@rochester.rr.com
Web Site: www.historicpalmyrany.com
Key Personnel: C.E.O. & Chm. (V), Becke Tomkiewicz; Exec. Dir., Bonnie J. Hays; Museum Shop Mgr., Steve Hays.
Institution Type/Description: Historic Building: housed in a former 26 room hotel, c.1826.
Hours & Admission Prices: May-Oct. Tues.-Sat. 10:30-4:30; Nov.-April Tues.-Thurs. 11-4. Individual Museum: adults $3; members no charge. Trail Pass: fam-

ily $14, adults $7, student & senior citizen $5; children 10 & under and members no charge.
Attendance: 13,000 (estimated)

Parishville

PARISHVILLE MUSEUM, 1785 Main St., Parishville, NY 13672. Mailing Address: c/o Town of Parishville, P.O. Box 246, Parishville, NY 13672. Tel.: 315-265-4232. Facebook: Parishville Museum.
E-mail: josephm73@yahoo.com
Key Personnel: Pres., Joseph McGill; Vice Pres., Sherry Remington.
Institution Type/Description: History Museum: located in 1800 home.
Hours & Admission Prices: July-Aug. Tues. & Thurs. 1-3; other times by appointment. No charge; donations accepted.
Attendance: 250 (estimated)

Pawling

GUNNISON MUSEUM OF NATURAL HISTORY, 378 Old Quaker Hill Rd., Pawling, NY 12564-3449. Mailing Address: P.O. Box 345, Pawling, NY 12564-0345. Tel.: 845-855-5099.
Key Personnel: Pres., Elizabeth P. Allen; Cur., Mrs. James Mandracchia.
Institution Type/Description: Natural History Museum.
Hours & Admission Prices: May-Oct. Fri.-Sun. 1-4. Admission by donation.
Attendance: 2,000 (actual)

HISTORICAL SOCIETY OF QUAKER HILL & PAWLING, 126 E. Main St., Pawling, NY 12564-1428. Mailing Address: P.O. Box 99, Pawling, NY 12564-0099. Tel.: 845-855-5395.
E-mail: johnbetsyb@comcast.net
Web Site: www.pawling-history.org
Formerly: Historical Society of Quaker Hill & Pawling/John Kane House
Key Personnel: Pres. (V), John Brockway; Membership, Rachel Davis; Museum Shop Mgr., Mrs. Jeanne Kelly.
Institution Type/Description: Historical Society.
Hours & Admission Prices: May 15-Oct. 15 Sat.-Sun. 2-4. Special opening 2nd weekend in Dec. No charge; donations accepted.
Attendance: 642 (actual)

Peekskill

THE PEEKSKILL MUSEUM, 124 Union Ave., Peekskill, NY 10566-3429. Mailing Address: P.O. Box 84, Peekskill, NY 10566-0084. Tel.: 914-736-0473.
Web Site: www.peekskillmuseum.com
Key Personnel: Pres. (V), John Curran; Vice Pres., William Stillman; Treas., Paula Connolly; Corresponding Sec., Dolores Ubben.
Institution Type/Description: Historic Building & History Museum: housed in 1876-77 Dwight Herrick House.
Hours & Admission Prices: April-Oct. Sat. 1-4; Nov.-March Sat. 1-3. Adults $2, children $1; members no charge. &
Attendance: 500

Pelham

PELHAM ART CENTER, 155 Fifth Ave., Pelham, NY 10803-1503. Tel.: 914-738-2525. Fax: 914-738-2686.
E-mail: info@pelhamartcenter.org
Web Site: www.pelhamartcenter.org
Key Personnel: Dir., Lynn Honeysett; Chm., Barbara Carden; Pres., Anna Riehl.
Institution Type/Description: Art Center.
Hours & Admission Prices: Tues.-Fri. 12-5, Sat. 10-4. No charge; donations accepted. Closed New Year's Day; Memorial Day; Independence Day; Columbus Day; Thanksgiving; Christmas. &
Attendance: 13,000 (estimated)

Penn Yan

THE AGRICULTURAL MEMORIES MUSEUM, 1110 Townline Rd., Penn Yan, NY 14527-9002. Tel.: 315-536-1206.
E-mail: jrjensen@copper.net
Web Site: www.agriculturalmemoriesmuseum.com
Key Personnel: Owner, Jennifer R. Jensen; Asst., Hilbert J. Jensen.
Institution Type/Description: Agricultural Museum.
Hours & Admission Prices: June-Oct. by appointment. Adults $4, students & children 2-12 $1; discounts to groups; children under 2 no charge.
Attendance: 250 (estimated)

YATES COUNTY HISTORY CENTER, 107 Chapel St., Penn Yan, NY 14527-1128. Tel.: 315-536-7318. Fax: 315-536-0976. Facebook: Yates County Genealogical and Historical Society.
E-mail: ycghs@yatespast.org
Web Site: www.yatespast.org
Formerly: Yates County Genealogical and Historical Society and Oliver House Museum and L. Caroline Underwood Museum
Key Personnel: Exec. Dir. & Cur., Tricia Noel; Administrative Asst., Lisa Harper.
Institution Type/Description: History Museum.
Hours & Admission Prices: July-Aug. Tues.-Fri. 9-4, Sat. 10-2; Sept.-June Tues.-Fri. 9-4. Admission $5. Research Center: $5 per hr. Closed major holidays. &
Attendance: 5,000 (estimated)

Peru

BABBIE RURAL & FARM LEARNING MUSEUM, 250 River Rd., Peru, NY 12972. Tel.: 518-643-8052.
E-mail: babbieag309@babbiemuseum.org
Web Site: www.babbiemuseum.org
Key Personnel: C.E.O., Leeward Babbie.
Institution Type/Description: History Museum.
Hours & Admission Prices: Call for hours. Adults $7; members no charge. &
Attendance: 1,400 (estimated)

Piffard

TOWN OF YORK HISTORICAL SOCIETY - WARREN HOMESTEAD, 2431 Dow Rd., Piffard, NY 14533. Mailing Address: P.O. Box 464, York, NY 14592-0464. Tel.: 585-243-2027.
E-mail: gcox8@rochester.rr.com
Web Site: www.yorkwines.org
Key Personnel: Pres. (V), Gary A. Cox.
Institution Type/Description: Historical Society Museum: housed in the former home of Samuel Warren, a successful commercial winemaker of the Finger Lakes & New York state; built c.1830.
Hours & Admission Prices: Spring to Fall 1st & 3rd Sun. each month. No charge; donations accepted.
Attendance: 200 (estimated)

Pittsford

HISTORIC PITTSFORD, 18 Monroe Ave., Pittsford, NY 14534-1928. Tel.: 585-381-2941.
E-mail: historicpittsford@gmail.com
Web Site: www.historicpittsford.com
Key Personnel: Dir., Peggy Brizee.
Institution Type/Description: Historic House: 1820 lawyer's office.
Hours & Admission Prices: Wed. & Sat. 9-12; other times by appointment. No charge.
Attendance: 350 (estimated)

Plattsburgh

CLINTON COUNTY HISTORICAL ASSOCIATION & MUSEUM, 98 Ohio Ave., Plattsburgh, NY 12903-4401. Tel.: 518-561-0340. Fax: 518-561-0340.
E-mail: director@clintoncountyhistorical.org
Web Site: www.clintoncountyhistorical.org
Key Personnel: Pres., Helen Nerska; Dir., Melissa A. Peck; Vice Pres., William Laundry; Sec., Jan Couture; Treas., Maurica Gilbert; Museum Shop Mgr., James Bailey.
Institution Type/Description: Historical Society Museum.
Hours & Admission Prices: Wed.-Sat. 10-3. Adults $5, seniors $3, students $2; discounts to AAA, AAM & ICOM members; school groups, Historical Association & members no charge. Closed legal holidays. &
Attendance: 1,000 (estimated)

KENT-DELORD HOUSE MUSEUM, 17 Cumberland Ave., Plattsburgh, NY 12901-1849. Tel.: 518-561-1035. Facebook: Kent - Delord House Museum.
E-mail: kentdelord@primelink1.net
Web Site: www.kentdelordhouse.org
Key Personnel: Pres., Trevor Laughlin; Dir., Donald Wickman.
Institution Type/Description: Historic House Museum: c.1797, Kent-Delord home.
Hours & Admission Prices: Tues.-Fri. 12-2, Sat. call for hours; guided tours & group tours by appointment. Adults $5, students $3, children under 12 $2; discounts for groups; members no charge. &
Attendance: 7,500 (estimated)

PLATTSBURGH STATE ART MUSEUM S.U.N.Y., State University of New York, 101 Broad St., Plattsburgh, NY 12901-2637. Mailing Address: State University of New York, Myers Room 235, 101 Broad St., Plattsburgh, NY 12901-2637. Tel.: 518-564-2474 & 2178. Fax: 518-564-2473.
E-mail: ceil.esposito@plattsburgh.edu
Web Site: clubs.plattsburgh.edu/museum
Key Personnel: Dir. & Cur., Cecilia M. Esposito; Museum Educator, Samantha Bellinger; Mgr. Collections, Candace Truso.
Institution Type/Description: Art Museum & Galleries.
Hours & Admission Prices: Jan. 2-Dec. 23 daily 12-4. No charge; donations accepted. Closed legal holidays. &
Attendance: 20,000 (estimated)

Pocantico Hills

HISTORIC HUDSON VALLEY, 639 Bedford Rd., Pocantico Hills, NY 10591. Tel.: 914-631-8200. Fax: 914-631-0089. Facebook: Historic Hudson Valley; Twitter: @hhvalley.
E-mail: info@hudsonvalley.org
Web Site: www.hudsonvalley.org
Key Personnel: Pres., Waddell W. Stillman.
Institution Type/Description: Preservation Project.
Hours & Admission Prices: See website for up-to-date tour times & admission prices. &
Attendance: 243,000 (actual)

Port Jefferson

HISTORICAL SOCIETY OF GREATER PORT JEFFERSON, 115 Prospect St., Port Jefferson, NY 11777-1812. Mailing Address: P.O. Box 586, Port Jefferson, NY 11777-0586. Tel.: 631-473-2665.
E-mail: info@portjeffhistorical.org
Web Site: www.portjeffhistorical.org
Key Personnel: Pres. (V), Nick Acampora; Museum Shop Co-Mgr., Eileen Coen.
Institution Type/Description: Maritime Museum: housed in c.1840 John R. Mather homestead & out buildings.
Hours & Admission Prices: Memorial Day to Columbus Day Wed.-Sun. 12-4. Family $5, adults $3; children & members no charge. &
Attendance: 1,600 (estimated)

Port Jervis

MINISINK VALLEY HISTORICAL SOCIETY, 125-133 W. Main St., Port Jervis, NY 12771. Mailing Address: P.O. Box 659, Port Jervis, NY 12771-0659. Tel.: 845-856-2375. Facebook: Minisink Valley Historical Society.
E-mail: history@minisink.org
Web Site: www.minisink.org
Key Personnel: Exec. Dir., Nancy Conod; Pres., Robert Shultz.
Institution Type/Description: Historical Society Museum: housed in 1793 stone home.
Hours & Admission Prices: Library: Thurs. 1-4; other times by appointment. Suggested Donation $4; discounts to members. Museum: July-Oct. Sat. 10-4. No charge; donations accepted. &
Attendance: 15,000

Port Washington

COW NECK PENINSULA HISTORICAL SOCIETY SANDS-WILLETS HOUSE, 336 Port Washington Blvd., Port Washington, NY 11050-4530. Tel.: 516-365-9074.
E-mail: info@cowneck.org
Web Site: www.cowneck.org
Key Personnel: Pres. (V), Fred Blumlein; Treas., Richard Coyle; Cur., Harrison Hunt; Dir. Education, Mary Alice Puglise; Museum Shop Mgr., Evelyn Fitzsimmons.
Institution Type/Description: Historical Society Museum.
Hours & Admission Prices: Sands-Willets House: May-Oct. 1st & 3rd Sun. 2pm; other times by appointment. Dodge House: May-Sept. 4th Sun. 2pm; other times by appointment. Suggested Donation: $5. Closed holidays.
Attendance: 3,000 (estimated)

POLISH AMERICAN MUSEUM, 16 Belleview Ave., Port Washington, NY 11050-3607. Tel.: 516-883-6542.
E-mail: basia1979@aol.com
Web Site: polishamericanmuseum.com
Key Personnel: Pres., Barbara Szydlowski; 1st Vice Pres., Steve Szachacz; 2nd Vice Pres., Irene Wierbicki; Treas., Michael Levchuck; Recording Sec., Wilma Wierbicki; Cur., Gerald Kochan; Historian, Cynthia Stockla.

Institution Type/Description: Folk Art Museum & Library.
Hours & Admission Prices: Wed.-Fri. 10-2, Sat.-Sun. by appointment. No charge; donations accepted. Closed legal holidays. &
Attendance: 1,200 (estimated)

THE SALGO TRUST FOR EDUCATION, 95 Middle Neck Rd., Port Washington, NY 11050-1218. Tel.: 516-767-3654. Fax: 516-767-7881.
Web Site: salgotrust.org
Key Personnel: Trustee, Miklos Salgo; Trustee, Christina Salgo; Collection Mgr., Eileen Baral.
Institution Type/Description: Art Museum.
Hours & Admission Prices: By appointment only. No charge.

Potsdam

POTSDAM PUBLIC MUSEUM, 2 Park St. at Civic Center, Potsdam, NY 13676. Mailing Address: P.O. Box 5168, Potsdam, NY 13676-5168. Tel.: 315-265-6910. Fax: 315-265-3149. Facebook.
E-mail: museum@vi.potsdam.ny.us
Web Site: www.potsdampublicmuseum.org
Key Personnel: Dir. & Cur., Mimi Van Deusen; Pres., Jan Wojcik; Vice Pres., Tom Baker.
Institution Type/Description: Local History Museum: housed in 1876 sandstone church.
Hours & Admission Prices: Tues.-Sat. 10-4. Suggested Donation: $2. Closed state & national holidays. &
Attendance: 3,050 (actual)

ROLAND GIBSON GALLERY, 44 Pierrepont Ave., State Univ. of New York at Potsdam, Potsdam, NY 13676-2200. Tel.: 315-267-3290. Fax: 315-267-4884.
E-mail: vasherak@potsdam.edu
Web Site: www.potsdam.edu/gibson/gibson.html
Key Personnel: Dir., April Vasher-Dean; Mgr. Collections, Romi Sebald-Chudzinski; Administrative Asst., Claudette Fefee.
Institution Type/Description: University Art Museum.
Hours & Admission Prices: Summer: Wed.-Sat. 12-4; Academic Year: Mon. & Fri. 12-5, Tues. & Thurs. 12-7, Sat. 12-4. No charge; donations accepted. Closed college recesses; public holidays. &
Attendance: 14,000 (estimated)

Poughkeepsie

ART GALLERY MARIST COLLEGE, 3399 North Rd., Poughkeepsie, NY 12601-1387. Tel.: 845-575-3000, ext. 2308. Fax: 845-471-6213.
E-mail: edward.smith@marist.edu
Web Site: www.marist.edu/commarts/art/gallery.html
Key Personnel: Dir., Edward Smith; Chm. Art Dept., Richard Lewis.
Institution Type/Description: Art Museum.
Hours & Admission Prices: Sept.-May Mon.-Sat. 12-5. No charge. &
Attendance: 2,000 (estimated)

DUTCHESS COUNTY HISTORICAL SOCIETY, Clinton House, 549 Main St., Poughkeepsie, NY 12601. Mailing Address: P.O. Box 88, Poughkeepsie, NY 12602-0088. Tel.: 845-471-1630. Fax: 845-471-1634.
E-mail: dchistorical@verizon.net
Web Site: www.dutchesscountyhistoricalsociety.org
Key Personnel: Exec. Dir., Patty Moore; Pres., Denise Van Buren.
Institution Type/Description: Historical Society Museum: housed in c.1765 Clinton House, used as NY state capitol during the Revolutionary War.
Hours & Admission Prices: Tues.-Thurs. 10-3. Library research: $20; members no charge. Closed New Year's Eve & Day; Memorial Day; Independence Day; Labor Day; Thanksgiving & day after; Christmas Eve & Day. &
Attendance: (estimated)

THE FRANCES LEHMAN LOEB ART CENTER, 124 Raymond Ave., Vassar College, Poughkeepsie, NY 12604. Mailing Address: Box 703, Vassar College, Poughkeepsie, NY 12604. Tel.: 845-437-5237 & LOEB (5632). Fax: 845-437-5955.
E-mail: jamundy@vassar.edu
Web Site: fllac.vassar.edu
Key Personnel: The Ann Hendricks Bass Dir., James Mundy; The Emily Hargroves Fisher '57 & Richard B. Fisher Cur. & Asst. Dir. Strategic Planning, Mary-Kay Lombino; The Philip & Lynn Strauss Cur. Prints & Drawings, Patricia Phagan; The Andrew W. Mellon Cur. Academic Programs, Elizabeth Nogrady; Cur.

Public Education, Margaret Vetare; Collections Mgr. & Registrar, Joann Potter; Assoc. Registrar, Karen Hines; Preparator, Bruce Bundock; Asst. Collections Mgr., Eleanor White; Coord. Membership, Events & Volunteer Svcs., Francine Brown.
Institution Type/Description: Art Museum.
Hours & Admission Prices: Tues.-Wed. & Fri.-Sat. 10-5, Thurs. 10-9, Sun. 1-5. No charge. Closed New Year's Eve & Day; Thanksgiving Day; Christmas Eve, Day & week. &
Attendance: 36,000 (estimated)

LOCUST GROVE ESTATE, 2683 South Rd., Poughkeepsie, NY 12601-5275. Tel.: 845-454-4500, ext. 211. Fax: 845-485-7122.
E-mail: info@lgny.org
Web Site: www.lgny.org
Formerly: Locust Grove, The Samuel Morse Historic Site
Key Personnel: Exec. Dir., Kenneth Snodgrass.
Institution Type/Description: Historic Site: 200 acre estate.
Hours & Admission Prices: Visitor Center: Jan.-March Mon.-Fri. 10-5; May-Dec. daily 10-5. Tours: April & Nov.-Dec. Sat.-Sun. 10-5; May-Oct. daily 10-5; groups by appointment only. Adults $11, youth 6-18 $6; discounts to AAM members; Friends members no charge.
Attendance: 90,000 (actual)

MID-HUDSON CHILDREN'S MUSEUM, 75 N. Water St., Poughkeepsie, NY 12601-1720. Tel.: 845-471-0589. Fax: 845-471-0415.
E-mail: info@mhcm.org
Web Site: www.mhcm.org
Key Personnel: Dir., Lara Litchfield-Kimber; Chm. (V), Steve Loehr.
Institution Type/Description: Children's Museum.
Hours & Admission Prices: Tues.-Sat. 9:30-5, Sun. 11-5. Admission $8; members & children under one no charge. Discounts to ADM & ASTC members, active military & grandparent days. &
Attendance: 50,000 (estimated)

Pound Ridge

POUND RIDGE HISTORICAL SOCIETY - THE POUND RIDGE MUSEUM, 255 Westchester Ave., Pound Ridge, NY 10576. Mailing Address: Pound Ridge Historical Society, P.O. Box 51, Pound Ridge, NY 10576-0051. Tel.: 914-764-4333 (museum).
E-mail: info@poundridgehistorical.org
Web Site: www.poundridgehistorical.org
Key Personnel: Chm. (V) & Pres. (V), Joyce Butterfield; Treas., Joyce Matern.
Institution Type/Description: Historical Society & Local History Museum: housed in an 1853 wooden frame building.
Hours & Admission Prices: April-Dec. Sat.-Sun. 2-4; researchers & groups by appointment. No charge; donations accepted. Closed holidays.
Attendance: 425 (estimated)

Prattsburgh

NARCISSA PRENTISS HOUSE, 7225 County Rte. 75, Prattsburgh, NY 14873. Mailing Address: P.O. Box 201, Prattsburgh, NY 14873. Tel.: 607-522-4537 (July & Aug. only).
E-mail: sandconl48@yahoo.com
Key Personnel: Dir. & Pres. (V), Sandra L. Conley; Chm. (V), Joan Georgia.
Institution Type/Description: Historic House: c.1805 birthplace of Narcissa Prentiss Whitman, missionary & one of the first two non-Indian women to cross the Rockies.
Hours & Admission Prices: July & Aug. Sat.-Sun. 1-4; other times by appointment. No charge; donations accepted. Closed Independence Day; Labor Day.
Attendance: 140 (estimated)

Prattsville

ZADOCK PRATT MUSEUM, Main St., Rte. 23, Prattsville, NY 12468-0333. Mailing Address: P.O. Box 333, Prattsville, NY 12468-0333. Tel.: 518-299-3395 & 3258.
E-mail: prattmuseum@hotmail.com
Web Site: zadockprattmuseum.com
Key Personnel: Exec. Dir., Carolyn Bennett.
Institution Type/Description: Historic House: housed in the former home of Zadock Pratt, Prattsville town founder; built in c.1828. Listed on the National Register of Historic Places.
Hours & Admission Prices: Memorial Day to Columbus Day Thurs.-Sun. 1-5. Suggested Donation: $3.

Pultneyville

WILLIAMSON-PULTNEYVILLE HISTORICAL SOCIETY, 4130 Mill St., Pultneyville, NY 14538. Mailing Address: P.O. Box 92, Pultneyville, NY 14538. Tel.: 315-589-9892.
E-mail: info@w-phs.org
Web Site: www.w-phs.org
Key Personnel: Museum Shop Mgr., Suzi Goodrich.
Institution Type/Description: Historical Society Museum.
Hours & Admission Prices: By appointment. No charge; donations accepted. &
Attendance: 600 (estimated)

Purchase

ARTHUR M. BERGER ART GALLERY - MANHATTANVILLE COLLEGE, 2900 Purchase St., Purchase, NY 10577. Tel.: 914-694-2200.
E-mail: ADMISSIONS@MVILLE.EDU
Web Site: www.mville.edu/tags/arthur-m-berger-gallery
Key Personnel: Dir., Charles McGill.
Institution Type/Description: Art Gallery.
Hours & Admission Prices: Tues. & Thurs.-Fri. 11-6, Wed. 11-7, Sat. 12-4; other times by appointment.

BROWNSON GALLERY - MANHATTANVILLE COLLEGE, Brownson Hall, 2nd Fl., Purchase, NY 10577. Tel.: 914-694-2200.
E-mail: tim.ross@mville.edu
Web Site: www.mville.edu
Institution Type/Description: Art Gallery.
Hours & Admission Prices: Call for hours. No charge. &

NEUBERGER MUSEUM OF ART, PURCHASE COLLEGE, STATE UNIVERSITY OF NEW YORK, 735 Anderson Hill Rd., Purchase, NY 10577-1402. Tel.: 914-251-6100. Fax: 914-251-6101.
E-mail: nma@purchase.edu
Web Site: www.neuberger.org
Key Personnel: Dir.l., Tracy Fitzpatrick; Mktg. Assoc., Suzanne Grady.
Institution Type/Description: University Art Museum.
Hours & Admission Prices: Tues.-Sun. 12-5. Adults $5, seniors 62 & over & students $3; discounts to AAM, ICOM, AAMD & Channel 13; members, children 12 & under & Purchase College falculty, staff & students no charge. Closed major holidays. &
Attendance: 56,500 (actual)

Queens

NEW YORK HALL OF SCIENCE, 47-01 111th St., Queens, NY 11368-2999. Tel.: 718-699-0005. Fax: 718-699-1341.
E-mail: mrecord@nysci.org
Web Site: www.nysci.org
Key Personnel: Pres. & C.E.O., Margaret Honey.
Institution Type/Description: Science Museum.
Hours & Admission Prices: Mon.-Fri. 9:30-5, Sat.-Sun. 10-6; groups by appointment. Adults 18 & over $15, children, senior citizens & college students $12; discounts to AAM & ASTC members; members no charge. Closed Labor Day; Thanksgiving; Christmas. &
Attendance: 500,000 (estimated)

QUEENS MUSEUM OF ART, New York City Bldg., Flushing Meadows Corona Park, Queens, NY 11368-3398. Tel.: 718-592-9700. Fax: 718-592-5778.
E-mail: info@queensmuseum.org
Web Site: www.queensmuse.org
Key Personnel: Exec. Dir., Tom Finkelpearl; Pres., Gretchen Werwaiss; Dir. Finance, Julie Lou; Dir. Education, Lauren Schloss; Dir. Exhibitions, Hitomi Iwasaki; Museum Shop Mgr., Betty Abramowitz.
Institution Type/Description: Art & Cultural Center.
Hours & Admission Prices: Wed.-Fri. 10-5, Sat.-Sun. 12-5. Suggested Donations: adults $5, senior citizens & students $2.50; discounts to AAM & ICOM members; members & children under 5 no charge. Closed New Year's Day; Thanksgiving; Christmas. &
Attendance: 85,216 (actual)

Queensbury

WARREN COUNTY HISTORICAL SOCIETY, 195 Sunnyside Rd., Queensbury, NY 12804-7762. Tel.: 518-743-0734. Fax: 518-824-5861. Facebook: Warren County Historical Society.
E-mail: mail@warrencountyhistoricalsociety.org

Web Site: warrencountyhistoricalsociety.org
Institution Type/Description: Historical Society Museum.
Hours & Admission Prices: Call for hours. No charge; donations accepted. &
Attendance: 500 (estimated)

Red Hook

RHINEBECK AERODROME MUSEUM, 9 Norton Rd., Red Hook, NY 12572. Mailing Address: P.O. Box 229, Rhinebeck, NY 12572-0229. Tel.: 845-752-3200. Fax: 845-758-6481.
E-mail: info@oldrhinebeck.org
Web Site: www.oldrhinebeck.org
Key Personnel: Pres. (V), Michael DiGiacomio.
Institution Type/Description: Aeronautics & Space Museum.
Hours & Admission Prices: Museum: May-Oct. daily 10-5. Air Show: June- Oct. Sat.-Sun. 2 pm. Mon.-Fri.: adults $12, children 6-17, military and seniors 65 & over $8; children 5 & under no charge. Museum & Airshow: Sat.-Sun.: adults $25, children 6-17, military and seniors 65 & over $20; children 5 & under no charge.
Attendance: 40,000 (estimated)

Remsen

STEUBEN MEMORIAL STATE HISTORIC SITE, Starr Hill Rd., Remsen, NY 13438. Mailing Address: c/o Oriskany Battlefield SHS, 7801 State Rte. 69, Oriskany, NY 13424-4115. Tel.: 315-768-7224. Fax: 315-337-3081.
E-mail: nancy.demyttenaere@oprhp.state.ny.us
Web Site: www.nysparks.com
Key Personnel: Regl. Historic Preservation Supv., Nancy Denyttenaere; Second in Command, Bill Acomb.
Institution Type/Description: Historic Site: burial site of Baron Friederich Wilhelm von Steuben, Drillmaster of American Army, located on land granted by New York State for services in the American Revolution.
Hours & Admission Prices: Memorial Day to Sept. 1 daily dawn to dusk. No charge; donations accepted. &
Attendance: 6,785 (actual)

Rensselaer

CRAILO STATE HISTORIC SITE, 9 1/2 Riverside Ave., Rensselaer, NY 12144-2927. Tel.: 518-463-8738. Fax: 518-433-1860.
E-mail: maryellen.grimaldi@oprhp.state.ny.us
Key Personnel: Historic Site Mgr., Heidi Hill.
Institution Type/Description: Historic Building: c.1704, brick dwelling belonging to the Van Rensselaer family; used as museum of Dutch culture in the upper Hudson Valley.
Hours & Admission Prices: Nov.-March Mon.-Fri. 11-4 by appointment. Adults $5, seniors & students $4; discounts to groups; children 12 & under no charge. &
Attendance: 10,000 (actual)

Richfield Springs

PETRIFIED CREATURES MUSEUM OF NATURAL HISTORY, U.S. Rte. 20, Richfield Springs, NY 13439. Mailing Address: P.O. Box 751, Richfield Springs, NY 13439-0751. Tel.: 315-858-2868. Fax: 315-858-2868.
E-mail: petrifiedcreaturesmuseum@yahoo.com
Web Site: www.petrifiedcreatures.com
Key Personnel: C.E.O., Dir. & Museum Shop Mgr., Stella C. Mlecz; Education & Cur., Richard S. Mlecz; Public Rels. & Treas., Sally E. Kennedy; Archivist, Frank Maiocco; Security, Michael Vesely.
Institution Type/Description: Nature & Science Museum.
Hours & Admission Prices: May 15-June & Sept. 1-Sept. 15 Thurs.-Mon. 10-5; July-Aug. daily 10-5. Adults $9, senior citizens $7, children 5-11 $5; discount to AAM & ICOM members; children under 5 no charge. &
Attendance: 7,500 (estimated)

Ridge

BROOKHAVEN VOLUNTEER FIREFIGHTERS MUSEUM, Rte. 25 (Middle Country Rd.), Ridge, NY 11961. Mailing Address: P.O. Box 367, Ridge, NY 11961. Tel.: 631-924-8114.
E-mail: bmc8ashctsel@hotmail.com
Web Site: www.brookhavenfiremuseum.org
Key Personnel: Dir., Herb Petersen; Chm. (V), Paul Callegari.
Institution Type/Description: Firefighting History Museum: housed in the former Center Moriches Firehouse; built in 1889.

Hours & Admission Prices: May 2nd-Oct. Sat. 10-4, Sun. 12-4; other times by appointment. No charge; donations accepted. Closed holidays. &

Attendance: 2,000 (estimated)

Riverdale

DERFNER JUDAICA MUSEUM + THE ART COLLECTION AT THE HEBREW HOME AT RIVERDALE, 5901 Palisade Ave., Riverdale, NY 10471-1253. Tel.: 718-581-1596. Fax: 718-581-1980.

E-mail: schevlowe@hebrewhome.org

Web Site: riverspringhealth.org/art

Key Personnel: Dir. & Chief Cur., Susan Chevlowe; Assoc. Cur., Emily O'Leary; Educator, Elana Kaplan.

Institution Type/Description: Judaica and Modern/Contemporary Art Museum.

Hours & Admission Prices: Sun.-Thurs. 10:30-4:30. No charge; donations accepted. Closed federal & Jewish holidays. &

Attendance: 7,749 (actual)

Riverhead

HALLOCKVILLE MUSEUM FARM, 6038 Sound Ave., Riverhead, NY 11901-5609. Tel.: 631-298-5292. Fax: 631-298-0144.

E-mail: hallockv@optonline.net

Web Site: hallockville.com

Key Personnel: Exec. Dir., Herbert Strobel.

Institution Type/Description: Historic Site: located on c.1765 Hallock Homestead.

Hours & Admission Prices: Guided Tours: May-Dec. weekends 11-4. Adults $7, seniors & children $5; members no charge. Closed New Year's Day; Easter; Thanksgiving; Christmas Eve & Day. &

Attendance: 10,000 (estimated)

THE LONG ISLAND SCIENCE CENTER, 11 W. Main St., Riverhead, NY 11901-2818. Tel.: 631-208-8000. Fax: 631-208-8304.

E-mail: programs@lisciencecenter.org

Web Site: www.lisciencecenter.org

Key Personnel: Contact Person, Wendy Werner.

Institution Type/Description: Science Center.

Hours & Admission Prices: July-Aug. Tues.-Sat. 11-4; Sept.-June Sat. 11-4. Admission: $5; discounts to ASTC members; members no charge. &

SUFFOLK COUNTY HISTORICAL SOCIETY, 300 W. Main St., Riverhead, NY 11901-2894. Tel.: 631-727-2881. Fax: 631-727-3467.

E-mail: schsociety@optonline.net

Web Site: www.suffolkcountyhistoricalsociety.org

Key Personnel: Pres., Bob Baraukas; Dir., Kathryn M. Curran; Museum Shop Mgr., Lee Thumser.

Institution Type/Description: Historical Museum.

Hours & Admission Prices: Museum: Tues.-Sat. 12:30-4:30. Adults $5; members no charge. Library: Wed.-Sat. 12:30-4:30. Library: $2. Closed legal holidays.

Attendance: 12,000 (estimated)

Rochester

ARTISANWORKS, 565 Blossom Rd., Ste. L, Rochester, NY 14610. Tel.: 585-288-7170. Fax: 585-288-7186.

E-mail: victoria@artisanworks.com

Web Site: www.artisanworks.net

Key Personnel: Dir. Events, Victoria Benz-Gehrke.

Institution Type/Description: Art Space.

Hours & Admission Prices: Fri.-Sat. 11-6, Sun. 12-5. Adults $12, students and seniors 60 & over $8; members no charge.

CHARLOTTE-GENESEE LIGHTHOUSE HISTORICAL SOCIETY, 70 Lighthouse St., Rochester, NY 14612. Tel.: 585-621-6179.

E-mail: info@geneseelighthouse.org

Web Site: www.geneseelighthouse.org

Key Personnel: Pres. (V), Phillip R. Hurwitz; Chm. (V), Virginia Kobylarz.

Institution Type/Description: Historical Society Museum: lighthouse built in 1822.

Hours & Admission Prices: May-Nov. Fri.-Mon. 1-5. Adults $3; members no charge.

Attendance: 5,200 (estimated)

GATES HISTORICAL SOCIETY - HINCHEY HOMESTEAD, 634 Hinchey Rd., Rochester, NY 14624. Tel.: 585-464-9740.

E-mail: jsswingle@aol.com

Web Site: gateshistory.org

Institution Type/Description: Historical Society Museum.

Hours & Admission Prices: Wed. 12-3. Suggested Donation: $5. Call for tours.

GENESEE WARBIRDS AVIATION HISTORY MUSEUM, 16 W. Main St., Ste. 310, Rochester, NY 14614. Tel.: 585-234-5387.

E-mail: admin@geneseewarbirds.org

Web Site: www.geneseewarbirds.org

Institution Type/Description: Military Aviation History Museum.

Hours & Admission Prices: By appointment. Adults $4, senior citizens 60 & over $3, children under 12 $2; members no charge.

GEORGE EASTMAN MUSEUM, 900 East Ave., Rochester, NY 14607-2298. Tel.: 585-271-3361. Fax: 585-271-3970. Facebook.

E-mail: info@eastman.org

Web Site: www.eastman.org

Key Personnel: Chm. (V), Steven Schwartz; Vice Pres. Operations & Finance, Thomas Combs; Dir., Bruce Barnes, Ph.D.; Sr. Cur. Motion Picture Collection, Paolo Cherchi Usai; Cur. George Eastman Collection, Kathy Connor; Cur. Tech., Todd Gustavson; Community Engagement, Laura Sadowski; Publications Mgr., Amy Schelemanow; Dir. Communications & Visitor Svcs., Eliza Benington Kozlowski; Dir. Commercial Devel., Peter Briggs; Dir. Conservation, Taina Meller.

Institution Type/Description: Photography and Cinematography Museum: housed in 1905 George Eastman home; historic house museum & gardens.

Hours & Admission Prices: Tues.-Sat. 10-5, Sun. 11-5. Adults $14, senior citizens $12, students $5; children 12 & under no charge. Closed Thanksgiving; Christmas. &

Attendance: 131,759 (actual)

HIGHLAND BOTANICAL PARK, 171 Reservoir Ave., Rochester, NY 14620-2728. Tel.: 585-753-7275. Fax: 585-753-7284.

E-mail: webmaster@monroecounty.gov

Web Site: www2.monroecounty.gov/parks-highland.php

Key Personnel: Supt., Mark Quinn.

Institution Type/Description: Arboretum.

Hours & Admission Prices: Highland Park: April-Oct. daily 7a.m.-11p.m., Nov.-March Mon.-Thurs. 7-4. Lamberton Conservatory: daily 10-4. Adults $3, seniors 62 & over and youth 6-18 $2; children 5 & under no charge. Closed Christmas Day. &

Attendance: 50,000

IRONDEQUOIT CHAPTER DAR HERVEY ELY HOUSE, 11 Livingston Park, Rochester, NY 14608-2047. Mailing Address: 138 Troup St., Rochester, NY 14608-2032. Tel.: 585-232-4509.

Key Personnel: Regent, Susan Leighton.

Institution Type/Description: Historic House Museum: 1837 Hervey Ely House, example of Greek revival architecture.

Hours & Admission Prices: 2nd Wed. each month 10-12, 3rd Wed. each month 10:30-3:30; other times by appointment. Adults $1.50, children $.75. &

THE LANDMARK SOCIETY OF WESTERN NEW YORK, 133 S. Fitzhugh St., Rochester, NY 14608-2204. Tel.: 585-546-7029, ext. 10. Fax: 585-546-4788.

E-mail: info@landmarksociety.org

Web Site: www.landmarksociety.org

Key Personnel: Exec. Dir., Wayne Goodman; Dir. Public Programs, Cindy Boyer; Pres. (V), Castelein Ludwig.

Institution Type/Description: Preservation Project: housed in 1840 Hoyt-Potter House. Historic House Museums: Stone-Tolan Houses.

Hours & Admission Prices: Stone-Tolan House: March-Dec. Fri.-Sat. 12-4; groups by appointment. Adults $3, children 8-18 $1; discounts to AAM members; members no charge. Ellwanger Garden: 2nd week in May (lilac festival) by appointment. Wenrich Library: by appointment; no charge. Closed national holidays. &

Attendance: 21,420 (estimated)

MEMORIAL ART GALLERY OF THE UNIVERSITY OF ROCHESTER, 500 University Ave., Rochester, NY 14607-1484. Tel.: 585-276-8900. Fax: 585-473-6266. TDD: 585-473-6152; Facebook MAG Rochester.

E-mail: maginfo@mag.rochester.edu

Web Site: mag.rochester.edu

Key Personnel: Mary W. & Donald R. Clark Dir., Jonathan Binstock; Exhibitions Coord., Margot Muto; Cur. European Art, Nancy Norwood; Public Rels., Social Media & Webmaster, Meg Colombo; Permanent Collection Registrar, Courtney Lippa; Exhibitions Registrar, Dan Knerr; Dir. Principal & Major Gifts, Joseph Carney; Dir. Academic Programs, Marlene Hamann-Whitmore; C.O.O. & Dep. Dir., Patti Giordano; Gallery Store Mgr., Loretta Fritsch.

Institution Type/Description: Art Museum: housed in a 1913 Italian Renaissance style building with additions in 1926, 1968 & 1987; located on the site of the original campus of University of Rochester.
Hours & Admission Prices: Wed. & Fri.-Sun. 11-5, Thurs. 11-9. Adults $14, senior citizens 62 & up and active-duty military $10, college students with ID & children 6-18 $5; discounts to New York Consortium members and Thurs. 5-9pm; University of Rochester students, members and children 5 & under no charge. Closed New Year's Day; Independence Day; Thanksgiving; Christmas. &
Attendance: 219,145 (actual)

MONROE COMMUNITY COLLEGE, MERCER GALLERY, 1000 E. Henrietta Rd., Brighton Campus, Rochester, NY 14623-5701. Tel.: 585-292-2021. Fax: 585-292-3120.
E-mail: kfarrell@monroecc.edu
Web Site: www.monroecc.edu
Key Personnel: Dir., Kathleen M. Farrell.
Institution Type/Description: Art Gallery.
Hours & Admission Prices: Mon., Wed., Fri.10-5, Thurs. 10-5; other times by appointment. No charge.

ROCHESTER CONTEMPORARY ART CENTER, 137 East Ave., Rochester, NY 14604. Tel.: 585-461-2222. Fax: 585-4461-2223.
E-mail: info@rochestercontemporary.org
Web Site: www.rochestercontemporary.org
Formerly: Pyramid Arts Center
Institution Type/Description: Art Gallery.
Hours & Admission Prices: Wed.-Thurs. & Sat.-Sun. 1-5, Fri. 1-10. Adults $1; members no charge. &
Attendance: 18,000 (actual)

ROCHESTER HISTORICAL SOCIETY, 121 Lincoln Ave., Rochester, NY 14611. Tel.: 585-623-8285.
Web Site: www.rochesterhistory.org
Key Personnel: Christy Lou Zuhlke; Pres. (V), Carolyn Vacca, Ph.D.
Institution Type/Description: Historical Society Museum.
Hours & Admission Prices: Adults $3; members no charge. &

ROCHESTER MEDICAL MUSEUM & ARCHIVES, 1441 East Ave., Rochester, NY 14610. Tel.: 585-922-1847. Fax: 585-922-0018.
E-mail: vacarchives@rochesterregional.org
Web Site: rochestergeneral.org/archives
Formerly: ViaHealth Archives Consortium
Key Personnel: Pres. & C.E.O., Eric Bieber, MD.
Institution Type/Description: Medical Museum.
Hours & Admission Prices: Mon.-Fri. 10-4; other times by appointment. No charge; donations accepted. &
Attendance: 1,000 (estimated)

ROCHESTER MUSEUM & SCIENCE CENTER, 657 East Ave., Rochester, NY 14607-2177. Tel.: 585-271-4320. Fax: 585-271-5935. Facebook: Rochester Museum & Science Center.
E-mail: katebennett@rmsc.org
Web Site: www.rmsc.org
Key Personnel: C.E.O. & Pres., Kate Bennett; Chm. Bd. (V), Anthony J. Adams, Jr., Esq.; Dir. Strasenburgh Planetarium, Steve Fentress; Dir. Cumming Nature Center, Nathan Hayes; Dir. Member & Visitor Services, Heidi Luizzi; Sr. Dir. Collections & Exhibits, Kathryn Murano Santos; HR Mgr., Bonnie Turner; Admin. Asst. Operations, Elizabeth Dugdale; Vice Pres. Advancement, Pam Jackson; Assoc. Dir. Youth & Family Programs, Joelle Adolfi.
Institution Type/Description: Science & Technology, Natural Sciences & Cultural Heritage Museum.
Hours & Admission Prices: Science Museum: Mon.-Sat. 9-5, Sun. 11-5. Adults $13, senior citizens & college students w/I.D. $12, children 3-18 $11; museum members and children under 3 no charge. Strasenburgh Planetarium: contact for show times & admission prices. Science Museum & Planetarium Combined Admission: Adults $17, senior citizens & college students w/I.D. $15, children 3-18 $14. Museum & Planetarium: closed Thanksgiving Day; Christmas Day. Nature Center: Wed.-Fri. 9-3:30, Sat.-Sun. 9-4:30. Suggested Donation: $3; members no charge. Nature Center: closed early Nov. to late Dec. &
Attendance: 388,931 (actual)

SENECA PARK ZOO, 2222 St. Paul St., Rochester, NY 14621-1097. Tel.: 585-336-7200. Fax: 585-342-1477.
E-mail: shanson@senecazoo.org
Web Site: www.senecaparkzoo.org
Key Personnel: Exec. Dir. Zoo Society, Pamela Reed Sanchez; Dir. County Zoo, Larry Sorel.
Institution Type/Description: Zoo.

Hours & Admission Prices: April-Oct. daily 10-4. Adults $12, seniors 63 & over $11, youth 3-11 $9; Nov.-March daily 10-3. Adults $10, seniors 63 & over $9, youth 3-11 $7. Members and children 2 & under no charge. Closed New Year's Day; Thanksgiving; Christmas. &
Attendance: 336,000 (actual)

THE STRONG, NATIONAL MUSEUM OF PLAY, One Manhattan Square, Rochester, NY 14607-3941. Tel.: 585-263-2700; 585-423-0746 (TDD). Fax: 585-263-2493. Facebook: @the-strongmuseum; Twitter: @museumofplay.
E-mail: info@museumofplay.org
Web Site: www.museumofplay.org
Formerly: Strong National Museum of Play
Key Personnel: Pres. & C.E.O., Steve Dubnik; Chm., Laura Saxby Lynch; Exec. Vice Pres. Mktg. & Communications, Suzanne Y. Seldes; Vice Pres. Institutional Advancement, Lisa M. Feinstein; Vice Pres. Collections, Christopher Bensch; Vice Pres. Exhibit, Jon-Paul Dyson, Ph.D.; Vice Pres. Finance & Facilities, Trudy Quartley; Vice Pres. Play Studies, Scott G. Eberle, Ph.D.
Institution Type/Description: History Museum.
Hours & Admission Prices: Mon.-Thurs. 10-5, Fri.-Sat. 10-8, Sun. 12-5; groups of 20 or more by appointment. Museum: $14.50; children under 2 & members no charge. Museum & Butterfly Garden: admission $19.50; discounts to AAM & museum members and school groups; children under 2 no charge. Closed Thanksgiving; Christmas. &
Attendance: 550,000 (actual)

Rome

EMPIRE STATE HERITAGE PARK LLC, 5789 Rome-New London Rd., Rome, NY 13440-8338. Mailing Address: P.O. Box 4413, Rome, NY 13442. Tel.: 315-337-3999. Fax: 315-337-3999.
E-mail: mandm2000@twcny.rr.com
Web Site: www.eriecanalvillage.net
Formerly: Erie Canal Village
Key Personnel: Owner, Ronald Trottier; Mgr., Melody Milewski.
Institution Type/Description: Outdoor Living History Museum.
Hours & Admission Prices: Call for hours. &
Attendance: 20,000 (estimated)

FORT STANWIX NATIONAL MONUMENT, 100 N. James St., Rome, NY 13440-5816. Mailing Address: 112 E. Park St., Rome, 13440. Tel.: 315-338-7730. Fax: 315-334-5051.
E-mail: fost_superintendent@nps.gov
Web Site: www.nps.gov/fost
Key Personnel: Dir. & Supt., Frank Barrows; Chief Visitor Experience, Michelle Riter; Cur., Keith Routley.
Institution Type/Description: National Monument.
Hours & Admission Prices: Fort: April-Nov. daily 10-4. No charge; donations accepted. Closed Thanksgiving. Visitor Center: daily 9-5. No charge. Closed New Year's Day; Thanksgiving; Christmas. &
Attendance: 71,263 (actual)

ROME ART AND COMMUNITY CENTER, 308 W. Bloomfield St., Rome, NY 13440-4197. Tel.: 315-336-1040. Fax: 315-336-1090.
E-mail: executivedirector@romeart.org
Web Site: www.romeart.org
Key Personnel: Exec. Dir., Kelly Fleming; Chm. Bd. (V), Ann Lynch.
Institution Type/Description: Art Center.
Hours & Admission Prices: Tues.-Thurs. 10-5, Fri. 10-2; other times by appointment. No charge; donations accepted. Closed National holidays. &
Attendance: 25,000 (estimated)

ROME HISTORICAL SOCIETY MUSEUM, 200 Church St., Rome, NY 13440-5872. Tel.: 315-336-5870. Fax: 315-336-5912.
E-mail: info@romehistoricalsociety.org
Web Site: www.romehistoricalsociety.org
Key Personnel: Pres. (V), Michael Kohli; Dir., Arthur L. Simmons, III.
Institution Type/Description: Historical Society Museum.
Hours & Admission Prices: Museum: Tues.-Fri. 9-3, Sat. 10-2. No charge; donations accepted. Library by appointment. Research Fee: non-member $20 per hour, members $5 per hour; students no charge. Closed holidays. &
Attendance: 4,000 (estimated)

Roosevelt Island

FRANKLIN D. ROOSEVELT FOUR FREEDOMS PARK, 1 FDR Four Freedoms Park, Roosevelt Island, NY 10044. Tel.: 212-204-8831.

E-mail: tours@fdrffp.org
Web Site: www.fdrfourfreedomspark.org
Institution Type/Description: Memorial Park.
Hours & Admission Prices: April-Sept. Wed.-Mon. 9-7; Oct.-March Wed.-Mon. 9-5. No charge.

Rosendale

CENTURY HOUSE HISTORICAL SOCIETY - A.J. SNYDER ESTATE, 668 Rte. 213, Rosendale, NY 12472-0150. Mailing Address: P.O. Box 150, Rosendale, NY 12472-0150. Tel.: 845-658-9900.
E-mail: info@centuryhouse.org
Web Site: www.centuryhouse.org
Key Personnel: Pres. (V), Anne Gorrick; Museum Shop Mgr., Althea Doris Werner.
Institution Type/Description: Historic House: 1809 old stone Century House, built by Christopher Snyder for his son, Jacob L. Snyder, pioneer in cement manufacturing. Historic Site: Snyder Estate Natural Cement Historic District, on state & national registers of historic places.
Hours & Admission Prices: Memorial Day to Labor Day Sun. 1-4; other times by appointment. Suggested Donation $3, children $1; members no charge. &
Attendance: 4,325 (actual)

Roslyn

ROSLYN LANDMARK SOCIETY, 221 Main St., Roslyn, NY 11576-2168. Mailing Address: Roslyn Landmark Society, Box 234, 36 Main St., Roslyn, NY 11576. Tel.: 516-625-4363. Fax: 516-625-4363.
E-mail: rlsinfo@optonline.net
Web Site: www.roslynlandmarks.org/index.html
Formerly: Van Nostrand Starkins House
Key Personnel: Exec. Dir., Anne B. Tinder.
Institution Type/Description: Historical Building & Site: c.1680 earliest surviving building in Roslyn; site contains a 17th-century well & has had 4 archaeological investigations.
Hours & Admission Prices: June-Oct. Sat.-Sun. 1-4. Adults $4, children $2.
Attendance: 600 (estimated)

Roslyn Harbor

NASSAU COUNTY MUSEUM OF ART, One Museum Dr., Roslyn Harbor, NY 11576-1138. Tel.: 516-484-9337. Fax: 516-484-0710.
E-mail: kwillers@nassaumuseum.org
Web Site: nassaumuseum.org
Key Personnel: Dir., Karl Emil Willers, Ph.D.; Pres. (V), Angela Susan Anton; Deputy Dir. & Chief Registrar, Fernanda Bennett; Asst. to the Dir. & Office Mgr., Rita Mack; Dir. Devel., Monica Reischmann; Accountant, Diane Roedel; Dir. Education, Laura Lynch; Dir. Volunteers, Nancy Barone; Asst. Cur. & Asst. Registrar, Rhianna Lee Ellis; Retail Merchandise Mgr., Meryl Gordon; Property Supvr. & Facility Rental Mgr., Frances Diesu.
Institution Type/Description: Art Museum: housed in c.1900 three story neo-Georgian brick mansion, former estate of Childs Frick.
Hours & Admission Prices: Tues.-Sun. 11-4:45. Adults $10, seniors 62 & up $8, children 4-12 & students $4; members no charge. Closed New Year's Day; Independence Day; Thanksgiving; Christmas Day. &
Attendance: 200,000 (actual)

Rotterdam Junction

MABEE FARM HISTORIC SITE, 1100 Main St., Rotterdam Junction, NY 12150. Tel.: 518-887-5073. Fax: 518-214-0029. Facebook: Mabee Farm Historic Site.
E-mail: mabeefarm@gmail.com
Web Site: www.mabeefarm.org
Formerly: Historic Mabee Farm Site
Key Personnel: Pres., Merritt Glennon; Chm., Marianne Blanchard.
Institution Type/Description: History Museum.
Hours & Admission Prices: Tues.-Sat. 10-4. House Tours or Exhibits: adults $5, $8 for both tours; members no charge. Closed New Year's Eve & Day; Martin Luther King Jr. Day; Labor Day; Memorial Day; Independence Day; Labor Day; Columbus Day; Election Day; Thanksgiving & day after; Christmas Eve & Day. &
Attendance: 17,000 (estimated)

Roxbury

JOHN BURROUGHS MEMORIAL STATE HISTORIC SITE, Burroughs Memorial Rd., Roxbury, NY 12474. Mailing Address: Mine Kill State Park, Rte. 30, P.O. Box 923, North Blenheim, NY 12131-0923. Tel.: 518-827-6111, ext. 91. Fax: 518-827-6782.
E-mail: christopher.kenyon@parks.ny.gov
Web Site: www.nysparks.com
Key Personnel: Park Mgr., Chris Kenyon.
Institution Type/Description: Historic Site: burial site of naturalist John Burroughs.
Hours & Admission Prices: Daily dawn to dusk. No charge.
Attendance: 2,500 (estimated)

Rye

JAY HERITAGE CENTER, 20 Boston Post Rd., Rye, NY 10580. Tel.: 914-698-9275.
E-mail: jayheritagecenter@gmail.com
Institution Type/Description: Historic House Museum: housed in the boyhood home of New York State's native founding father, John Jay; built in 1838. A National Historic Landmark.
Hours & Admission Prices: Call for hours.

THE RYE HISTORICAL SOCIETY SQUARE HOUSE MUSEUM AND KNAPP HOUSE ARCHIVES, One Purchase St., Rye, NY 10580-3002. Tel.: 914-967-7588. Fax: 914-967-6253. Facebook; Instagram.
E-mail: jplick@ryehistoricalsociety.org
Web Site: ryehistory.org
Institution Type/Description: History Museum: housed in c.1730 Square House.
Hours & Admission Prices: Tues.-Fri. 9-4, Sat. 10-3. No charge; donations accepted.

Sackets Harbor

SACKETS HARBOR BATTLEFIELD STATE HISTORIC SITE, 504 W. Main St., Sackets Harbor, NY 13685. Mailing Address: P. O. Box 27, Sackets Harbor, NY 13685-0027. Tel.: 315-646-3634. Fax: 315-646-1203.
E-mail: constance.barone@oprhp.state.ny.us
Web Site: www.nysparks.com
Key Personnel: Site Mgr., Constance B. Barone; Interpretive Programs Asst., Stephen Wallace.
Institution Type/Description: Historic U.S. Navy Yard & Battlefield complex: housed in six buildings, 1818 Union Hotel; restored 1849 Commandant's & Master's houses; 1848 stable; 1850 ice house; 1832 farmhouse; located on site of 19th-century U.S. naval base, which played an important part in the War of 1812; Maritime Museum; restored 1850-60 navy yard building complex; War of 1812 battlefield in upstate N.Y.
Hours & Admission Prices: Grounds: daily sunrise to sunset. Facilities: see website for hours. Adults $3, students 13-21 with ID, seniors 62 & over, military with ID $2; children 12 & under no charge. &
Attendance: 112,280 (actual)

Sag Harbor

SAG HARBOR WHALING & HISTORICAL MUSEUM, 200 Main St., Sag Harbor, NY 11963-3009. Mailing Address: P.O. Box 1327, Sag Harbor, NY 11963-0050. Tel.: 631-725-0770. Fax: 631-725-5638.
E-mail: info@sagharborwhalingmuseum.org
Web Site: www.sagharborwhalingmuseum.org
Key Personnel: Co Pres. (V), Barbara Lobosco; Co Pres. (V), Linley Pennytaker Hagen; Business Mgr., Vanessa Petruccelli; Museum Shop Mgr., Michael Butler.
Institution Type/Description: Whaling Museum: housed in 1845 Greek Revival mansion, Benjamin Huntting House.
Hours & Admission Prices: mid-May to mid-Oct. daily 10-5. Adults $6, senior citizens & students $5, children 3-11 $2; discount to groups; tour guides, members & bus drivers no charge. &
Attendance: 8,500 (estimated)

Saint Bonaventure

THE REGINA A. QUICK CENTER FOR THE ARTS, St. Bonaventure Univ., Rte. 417, Cornelius Welch Dr., Saint Bonaventure, NY 14778. Mailing Address: P.O. Drawer B.H., Saint Bonaventure, NY 14778. Tel.: 716-375-2494. Fax: 716-375-2690.

E-mail: quick@sbu.edu
Web Site: www.sbu.edu/quickcenter.aspx?id=2012
Formerly: St. Bonaventure Art Collection
Key Personnel: Exec. Dir., Joseph A. LoSchiavo.
Institution Type/Description: Art Museum.
Hours & Admission Prices: Summer: Tues.-Sat. 12-5. Winter: Mon.-Fri. 10-5, Sat.-Sun. 12-4. No charge; donations accepted. Closed New Year's Day; Easter; Thanksgiving; Christmas. ♿
Attendance: 20,000 (actual)

Saint Johnsville

FORT KLOCK HISTORIC RESTORATION, 7214 State Hwy. 5, Saint Johnsville, NY 13452-4502. Mailing Address: P.O. Box 42, Saint Johnsville, NY 13452-0042. Tel.: 518-568-7779.
E-mail: fortklock@gmail.com
Web Site: fortklockrestoration.org
Key Personnel: Chm. (V), Frank Arduini; Pres. (V), Eugene Wagner.
Institution Type/Description: Historic House Museum: 1750 Klock Homestead.
Hours & Admission Prices: Memorial Day to mid-Oct. Tues.-Sun. 9-5; tours & special demonstration by appointment. Adults $3, children $1. ♿
Attendance: 2,000 (estimated)

Salamanca

SALAMANCA RAIL MUSEUM, 170 Main St., Salamanca, NY 14779-1574. Tel.: 716-945-3133. Fax: 716-945-3133. Facebook: Salamanca Rail Museum.
E-mail: salarail@verizon.net
Key Personnel: C.E.O., Chm. (V) & Cur., Gerald J. Fordham; Treas., Robert W. Irwin; Public Rels., Kevin Burleson; Museum Shop Mgr., Barbara A. Fordham.
Institution Type/Description: Transportation Museum: housed in a 1912 restored passenger depot constructed by the Buffalo, Rochester and Pittsburgh Railway.
Hours & Admission Prices: April-Dec. Mon.-Sat. 10-5, Sun. 12-5. Tours: $1 donation per person. Closed Thanksgiving; Christmas. ♿
Attendance: 7,705 (actual)

SENECA-IROQUOIS NATIONAL MUSEUM, 814 Broad St., Salamanca, NY 14779-1378. Mailing Address: 252 Rochester St., Salamanca, NY 14779-1509. Tel.: 716-945-1760. Fax: 716-945-1624.
E-mail: sue.grey@sni.org
Web Site: www.senecamuseum.org
Key Personnel: Acting Dir., David L. George-Shongo, Jr.; Cur., Marissa Corwin; Mgr. Collections, Johnna Crouse; Museum Shop Mgr., Eva Aidman.
Institution Type/Description: Anthropology & Ethnology Museum.
Hours & Admission Prices: Mon. 12-5, Tues.-Sun. 9-5. Adults $5, senior citizens & college students $3, children 7-16 $2; discounts to AAM & AAA members; children under 7 no charge. Closed SNI observed holidays. ♿
Attendance: 15,000 (estimated)

Sanborn

SANBORN AREA HISTORICAL SOCIETY, 2822 Niagara St., Sanborn, NY 14132-9282. Mailing Address: P.O. Box 172, Sanborn, NY 14132-0172. Tel.: 716-731-9510.
E-mail: sanborngerry@gmail.com
Web Site: sanbornhistory.org
Key Personnel: Pres., William Read; Chm. (V), Hilda Snyder; Sec., Gerald E. Treichler; Public Rels. & Treas., Glenn Wienke; Archivist, Jane Schultz; Cur., Bonnie Haskell.
Institution Type/Description: History Museum.
Hours & Admission Prices: School House Museum: April-Nov. Sun. 2-4; Dec.-March 1st Sun. 2-4; other times by appointment. Farm Museum: April-Oct. Wed. 1-4, Sun. 2-4; other times by appointment. No charge; donations accepted. ♿
Attendance: 5,300 (estimated)

SANBORN FARM MUSEUM, 2660 Saunders Settlement Rd., Sanborn, NY 14132. Mailing Address: P.O. Box 172, Sanborn, NY 14132. Tel.: 716-990-6909.
E-mail: info@sanbornhistory.org
Web Site: www.sanbornhistory.org/farmmuseum.htm
Key Personnel: Cur., Bonnie Haskell.
Institution Type/Description: History Museum.
Hours & Admission Prices: mid-April to mid-Oct. Wed. 1-4, Sun. 2-4; other times by appointment. No charge; donations accepted. ♿

Saranac Lake

ROBERT LOUIS STEVENSON MEMORIAL COTTAGE, 44 Stevenson Lane, Saranac Lake, NY 12983-1975. Mailing Address: P.O. Box 607, Saranac Lake, NY 12983-0607. Tel.: 518-891-1462.
E-mail: pennypiper@verizon.net
Web Site: www.robertlouisstevensonmemorialcottage.org
Key Personnel: Pres., William Delahant; Vice Pres., Thomas Delahant; Cur., Mike Delahant; Sec., Melinda Hadley; Treas., Les Hershhorn.
Institution Type/Description: Literary Museum: housed in 1887 home of Robert Louis Stevenson.
Hours & Admission Prices: July to Columbus Day Tues.-Sun. 9:30-12 & 1-4:30; other times by appointment. Adults $5; children under 12 & members no charge.
Attendance: 500 (estimated)

SARANAC LABORATORY MUSEUM, 89 Church St., Ste. 2, Saranac Lake, NY 12983. Tel.: 518-891-4606.
E-mail: mail@historicsaranaclake.org
Web Site: historicsaranaclake.org
Key Personnel: Exec. Dir., Amy Catania.
Institution Type/Description: History Museum.
Hours & Admission Prices: Mon.-Fri. 9-3 by appointment.

Saratoga Springs

THE CHILDREN'S MUSEUM AT SARATOGA, 69 Caroline St., Saratoga Springs, NY 12866-3202. Tel.: 518-584-5540. Fax: 518-584-6059.
E-mail: info@cmssny.org
Web Site: www.cmssny.org
Key Personnel: Chm. (V), Michael Mihaly; Dir., Michelle Smith.
Institution Type/Description: Children's Museum.
Hours & Admission Prices: July-Labor Day Mon.-Sat. 9:30-4:30; Labor Day-June Tues.-Sat. 9:30-4:30, Sun. 12-4:30. Admission $6; children under one no charge. Closed New Year's Day; Easter; Memorial Day; Independence Day; Thanksgiving; Christmas Eve & Day. ♿
Attendance: 35,339 (actual)

FRANCES YOUNG TANG TEACHING MUSEUM AND ART GALLERY, Skidmore College, 815 N. Broadway, Saratoga Springs, NY 12866-1632. Tel.: 518-580-8080. Fax: 518-580-5069.
E-mail: tang@skidmore.edu
Web Site: www.skidmore.edu/tang
Institution Type/Description: Art Museum.
Hours & Admission Prices: Tues.-Sun. 12-5. Suggested Donations: adults $5; discounts to AAM & ICOM members; members no charge. Closed New Year's Day; Thanksgiving; Christmas. ♿
Attendance: 50,000 (actual)

HISTORICAL SOCIETY OF SARATOGA SPRINGS, The Casino, Congress Park, Saratoga Springs, NY 12866. Mailing Address: P.O. Box 216, Saratoga Springs, NY 12866-0216. Tel.: 518-584-6920. Fax: 518-581-1477.
E-mail: info@saratogahistory.org
Web Site: www.saratogahistory.org
Key Personnel: Dir., James D. Parillo; Pres., Lisa Millis; Cur., Becky Codner; Research Asst., John Conors; Archivist, Doris Lamont; Museum Shop Mgr., Ted Waite.
Institution Type/Description: Local History Museum: housed in 1871 gambling casino, a designated National Landmark.
Hours & Admission Prices: Wed.-Sun. 10-4. Adults $5, senior citizens $4; discounts to AAM members; children under 12, members, Ann Grey Gallery, Bolster Collection Archives no charge.
Attendance: 12,000 (estimated)

NATIONAL MUSEUM OF DANCE & HALL OF FAME, 99 S. Broadway, Saratoga Springs, NY 12866-4557. Tel.: 518-584-2225, ext. 3001. Fax: 518-584-4515. Facebook: Dance Museum.
E-mail: info@dancemuseum.org
Web Site: www.dancemuseum.org
Key Personnel: Dir., Raul Martinez; Chm. Bd. Dir. (V), Michele Riggi; Exhibition Coord. & Designer, Laura Dirado; Rental Coord., Jo Ambrosio; Programming & Outreach Coord., Jessica Munson.
Institution Type/Description: Dance Museum.
Hours & Admission Prices: March-Nov. Tues.-Sun. 10-4:30. Adults $6.50, senior citizens & students $5, children under 12 $3; discounts to AAM members; members no charge. Office closed New Year's Eve, day & week; Christmas Eve, Day & week. ♿
Attendance: 15,000 (estimated)

NATIONAL MUSEUM OF RACING AND HALL OF FAME, 191 Union Ave., Saratoga Springs, NY 12866-3556. Tel.: 518-584-0400, 800-562-5394. Fax: 518-584-4574.
E-mail: info@racingmuseum.org/nmrmedia@racingmuseum.net
Web Site: racingmuseum.org
Key Personnel: Dir., Christopher Dragone; Pres., Stella F. Thayer; Asst. Dir. & Membership, Cathy Maguire.
Institution Type/Description: National Thoroughbred Racing Museum.
Hours & Admission Prices: Racing Season daily 9-5; Off Season: Mon.-Sat. 10-4, Sun. 12-4. Adults $7, students & senior citizens with ID $5; discounts to groups, AAM & ICOM members; members & children under 5 no charge. Closed New Year's Day; Easter; Thanksgiving; Christmas. &
Attendance: 60,000 (actual)

NEW YORK STATE MILITARY MUSEUM AND VETERANS RESEARCH CENTER, 61 Lake Ave., Saratoga Springs, NY 12866-2315. Tel.: 518-581-5100. Fax: 518-581-5111.
E-mail: historians@ny.ngb.army.mil
Web Site: www.nysmm.org
Key Personnel: Dir., Michael Aikey; Registrar, Christopher Morton; Chief Cur., Courtney Burns; Archivist, Jim Gandy.
Institution Type/Description: Military Museum.
Hours & Admission Prices: Tues.-Sat. 10-4. No charge. Closed New York state holidays. &
Attendance: 12,000 (estimated)

SARATOGA AUTOMOBILE MUSEUM, 110 Avenue of the Pines, Saratoga Springs, NY 12866-6220. Tel.: 518-587-1935. Fax: 518-587-4149.
E-mail: info@saratogaautomuseum.org
Web Site: www.saratogaautomuseum.org
Key Personnel: Dir., Jean Hoffman; Dir. Devel., Richard Selikoff; Education & Public Rels., Alan Edstrom.
Institution Type/Description: Automobile Museum.
Hours & Admission Prices: June-Sept. daily 10-5; Columbus Day to May Tues.-Sun. 10-5. Adults $8, senior citizens, active military & students 17 & over $5, children 6-16 $3.50; discounts to groups; children under 6 no charge. Closed New Year's Eve & Day; Thanksgiving; Christmas. &
Attendance: 30,000 (actual)

THE SCHICK ART GALLERY, SKIDMORE COLLEGE, 815 N. Broadway, Saisselin Art Bldg., Fl. 2, Saratoga Springs, NY 12866-1698. Tel.: 518-580-5049.
E-mail: mjablons@skidmore.edu
Web Site: www.skidmore.edu/schick
Key Personnel: Dir., Paul Sattler; Curatorial Asst., Rebecca Shepard.
Institution Type/Description: Art Gallery.
Hours & Admission Prices: Sept.-May Mon.-Thurs. 10-6, Fri. 10-4, Sat.-Sun. 1-4:30; Summer: call for hours. No charge. &
Attendance: 25,000 (estimated)

Saugerties

OPUS 40 SCULPTURE PARK AND MUSEUM, 50 Fite Rd., Saugerties, NY 12477-3260. Tel.: 845-246-3400. Facebook: Opus 40.
E-mail: patopus40@hotmail.com
Web Site: www.opus40.org
Formerly: Opus 40 and the Quarryman's Museum
Key Personnel: Pres., Pat Richards; Sec., Tad Richards.
Institution Type/Description: Art Museum & Sculpture Park.
Hours & Admission Prices: May-Oct. Thurs.-Sun. 11-5:30. Adults $10, senior citizens & students $7, school age children $3; members & children under 5 no charge.
Attendance: 15,000 (estimated)

Sayville

SAYVILLE HISTORICAL SOCIETY, Edwards St. & Collins Ave., Sayville, NY 11782. Mailing Address: P.O. Box 41, Sayville, NY 11782-0041. Tel.: 631-563-0186 & 567-1289.
E-mail: sayvillehistorical@gmail.com
Web Site: www.sayville.com/historicalsociety
Key Personnel: Admin., Linda Conron; Pres. (V), Constance Currie; Treas., Cathy Foudy.
Institution Type/Description: Historical Society Museum.
Hours & Admission Prices: Oct.-June 1st & 3rd Sun. 2-4. No charge; donations accepted. Closed when holiday falls on Open House Sunday. &
Attendance: 830 (actual)

Scarsdale

THE GREENBURGH NATURE CENTER, 99 Dromore Rd., Scarsdale, NY 10583-1705. Tel.: 914-723-3470. Fax: 914-725-6599.
E-mail: mtjimosgoldberg@greenburghnaturecenter.org
Web Site: www.greenburghnaturecenter.org
Key Personnel: Exec. Dir., Margaret Tjimos Goldberg; Dir. Finance, Jocelyn Lim; Dir. Operations & Visitor Svcs., Penny Berman; Dir. Conservation Education, Anne Jaffe Holmes; Dir. Education & Living Collections, Travis Brady; Dir. Mktg., IT & Communications, Vicki Seiden Sherman.
Institution Type/Description: Nature Center: located on a 33-acre greenspace, former Nunataks Estate.
Hours & Admission Prices: Grounds: daily dawn-dusk. Manor House: Mon.-Thurs. 9:30-4:30, Sat.-Sun. 10-4:30. Adults $7, children 2-12 $5; discounts to NYSAM members; Greenburgh residents, Westchester County Parks Pass; members no charge except for special events & programs. &
Attendance: 80,000 (estimated)

THE SCARSDALE HISTORICAL SOCIETY, 937 Post Rd., Scarsdale, NY 10583-5656. Mailing Address: P.O. Box 431, Scarsdale, NY 10583-0431. Tel.: 914-723-1744. Fax: 914-723-2185.
E-mail: history@cloud9.net
Web Site: scarsdalehistory.org
Key Personnel: Pres., Bill Doescher; Exec. Dir., Cindy Krossman; Treas., Gloria Forte; Museum Shop Mgr., Greta Fisher; Museum Shop Mgr., Etta Parker.
Institution Type/Description: Historical Society: housed in 1828 Quaker Meeting House, a 19th-century farm house of modest means.
Hours & Admission Prices: Mon.-Fri. 9-4; other times by appointment. Museum: adults $3, senior citizens & students $2; discounts to AAM members; members no charge. Cudner Hyatt House: adults $5, seniors & students $3; discounts to AAM members; members no charge. Closed national holidays.
Attendance: 10,000 (actual)

WEINBERG NATURE CENTER, 455 Mamaroneck Rd., Scarsdale, NY 10583-7727. Tel.: 914-722-1289. Fax: 914-723-4784 (call first). Facebook: Weinberg Nature Center.
E-mail: info@weinbergnaturecenter.org
Web Site: www.weinbergnaturecenter.org
Key Personnel: Pres., Dr. Melissa Grigione; Program Dir., Cindy Polera.
Institution Type/Description: Nature Center.
Hours & Admission Prices: Summer: Mon.-Fri. 9-5; Fall, Winter & Spring: Mon., Wed. & Fri. 10-5, Tues. & Thurs. 10-2, see website to confirm. Charge for some weekend programs. Closed village holidays. &
Attendance: 20,000 (estimated)

Schenectady

MANDEVILLE GALLERY, UNION COLLEGE, Nott Memorial, 807 Union St., Schenectady, NY 12308. Mailing Address: 807 Union St., Union College, Schaffer Library, Rm. 212, Schenectady, NY 12308-3103. Tel.: 518-388-6004. Facebook: @MandevilleGallery.UnionCollege.
E-mail: mandevillegallery@union.edu
Web Site: www.union.edu/gallery
Key Personnel: Cur. Art Collections & Exhibitions, Julie Lohnes.
Institution Type/Description: College Museum.
Hours & Admission Prices: Daily 10-6. No charge; donations accepted. Closed New Year's Eve & Day; Independence Day; Thanksgiving & day after; Christmas week. &
Attendance: 5,000 (estimated)

MISCI, 15 Nott Terrace Heights, Schenectady, NY 12308-3198. Tel.: 518-382-7890. Fax: 518-382-7893. Facebook: Schenectady Museum.
E-mail: communications@misci.org
Web Site: www.misci.org
Formerly: Schenectady Museum and Suits-Bueche Planetarium
Key Personnel: Pres., Dr. William "Mac" Sudduth; Chm. Bd., Tony Farah; Museum Shop Coord., Lindsay Sheehan.
Institution Type/Description: History, Science & Technology Museum and Planetarium.
Hours & Admission Prices: Mon.-Sat. 9-5, Sun. 12-5. Adults $10.50, seniors $9, children 3-12 $7.50; discounts to AAM, ICOM & AAA members; ASTC, Empire State Reciprocal Program members, museum members & children under 4 no charge. Planetarium Programs: Tues.-Fri. 2 pm, Sat. 1, 2 & 3. Planetarium: additional $5 per person. Closed New Year's Day; Independence Day; Thanksgiving; Christmas. &
Attendance: 86,428 (actual)

THE MUSEUM OF PRINTS AND PRINTMAKING, 150 Barrett St., Schenectady, NY 12305. Tel.: 518-449-4756.
E-mail: semowich@gmail.com
Web Site: pcaprint.org
Key Personnel: Pres. (V), Thomas Andress; Vice Pres., Joe Galu; Cur., Charles Semowich.
Institution Type/Description: Print Museum.
Hours & Admission Prices: By appointment only. No charge. &

SCHENECTADY COUNTY HISTORICAL SOCIETY, 32 Washington Ave., Schenectady, NY 12305-1600. Tel.: 518-374-0263. Fax: 518-688-2825.
E-mail: curator@schist.org
Web Site: www.schenectadyhistorical.org
Key Personnel: Pres., Marianne Blanchard; Cur., Mary Zawacki; Librarian, Michael Maloney.
Institution Type/Description: General Museum & Historic House Site: located within area of original Schenectady stockade built by the Dutch in 1661.
Hours & Admission Prices: Museum & Library: Mon.-Fri. 10-5, Sat. 10-2. Mabee Farm: Tues.-Sat. 10-4; Summer: call for additional hours. Museum: adults $5; students & members no charge. Farm: adults $8; students & members no charge. Closed national holidays. &
Attendance: 17,000 (actual)

Schoharie

OLD STONE FORT MUSEUM COMPLEX, 145 Fort Rd., Schoharie, NY 12157-4705. Tel.: 518-295-7192. Fax: 518-295-7187.
E-mail: office@theoldstonefort.org
Web Site: www.theoldstonefort.org
Key Personnel: C.E.O. & Dir., Carle J. Kopecky; Pres., Michael West; Treas., Anne Hendrix; Cur. & Education, Daniel Beams; Office & Museum Shop Mgr., Laura Spickerman.
Institution Type/Description: General Museum: housed in 1772 church, later used as a fort.
Hours & Admission Prices: May-Oct. Mon.-Sat. 10-5, Sun. 12-5. Adults $7, senior citizens $6, children $2; discounts to AAM & ICOM members; Schoharie County Schools & members no charge. &
Attendance: 4,900 (actual)

SCHOHARIE COLONIAL HERITAGE ASSOCIATION, Palatine House, Spring St., Schoharie, NY 12157. Mailing Address: P.O. Box 554, Schoharie, NY 12157-0554. Tel.: 518-295-7505 & 7585. Fax: 518-295-6001.
E-mail: scha@midtel.net
Web Site: www.midtel.net/~scha
Key Personnel: C.E.O., Sarah Sherman; Pres., Jean Harra; Vice Pres., Ruth Anne Keese; Treas., Donna McCabe.
Institution Type/Description: Historic Building: housed in 1743 Palatine House, old Lutheran parsonage.
Hours & Admission Prices: May group tours only; June-Oct. Thurs.-Sun. 1-4. Donations: adults $2.50, students $1; discounts to groups; members first visit no charge. RR Museum: Memorial Day to Columbus Day Sat.-Sun. 12-4.
Attendance: 750 (estimated)

Scotia

FLINT HOUSE, 421 Reynolds St., Scotia, NY 12302-1601. Mailing Address: 13 Larkin St., Scotia, NY 12302. Tel.: 518-374-2371.
Institution Type/Description: Historic House & Museum: housed in a 1735 salt box house.
Hours & Admission Prices: Call for a guided tour, 518-374-2871. No charge; donations accepted.
Attendance: 875 (actual)

Sea Cliff

SEA CLIFF VILLAGE MUSEUM, 95 Tenth Ave., Sea Cliff, NY 11579-1127. Mailing Address: P.O. Box 72, Sea Cliff, NY 11579. Tel.: 516-671-0090. Fax: 516-671-2530.
E-mail: seacliffmuseum@aol.com
Web Site: seacliffmuseum.com
Key Personnel: Dir. & Cur., Sara Reres; Museum Technician, James Reres.
Institution Type/Description: Village Museum: housed in the former Sea Cliff Methodist Church, built in 1913.
Hours & Admission Prices: Oct.-June Sun. 2-5. Adults $1.
Attendance: 1,000 (actual)

Seaford

SEAFORD HISTORICAL MUSEUM, 3890 Waverly Ave., Seaford, NY 11783-2614. Mailing Address: Seaford Historical Society, P.O. Box 1254, Seaford, NY 11783. Tel.: 516-221-2851.
E-mail: info@seafordhistoricalsociety.org
Web Site: www.seafordhistoricalsociety.org
Key Personnel: Pres. (V), Judith Bongiovi.
Institution Type/Description: History Museum: housed in 1893 two-room schoolhouse.
Hours & Admission Prices: July-Aug. Sun. 12-3. Presentations: $5; 2nd Sun. each month no charge. &
Attendance: 2,000 (estimated)

Selden

SUFFOLK CENTER ON THE HOLOCAUST, DIVERSITY & HUMAN UNDERSTANDING, Suffolk County Community College, Huntington Library, 2nd Fl., 533 College Rd., Selden, NY 11784-2851. Tel.: 631-451-4700. Fax: 631-451-4697.
E-mail: chdhu@sunysuffolk.edu
Web Site: www.chdhu.org
Institution Type/Description: History Museum.
Hours & Admission Prices: Mon.-Thurs. 10-2; other times by appointment.

Selkirk

BETHLEHEM HISTORICAL ASSOCIATION, 1003 River Rd., Selkirk, NY 12158-4033. Mailing Address: P.O. Box 263, Selkirk, NY 12158-0263. Tel.: 518-767-9432.
E-mail: correspondingsecretary@bethlehemhistorical.org
Web Site: bethlehemhistorical.org
Key Personnel: Pres., George Lenhardt; Registrar, Valerie Thompson.
Institution Type/Description: General Museum: housed in 1859 Cedar Hill school.
Hours & Admission Prices: June-Aug. Sun. 2-5. No charge; donations accepted. &
Attendance: 375 (actual)

Seneca Falls

NATIONAL WOMEN'S HALL OF FAME, 76 Fall St., Seneca Falls, NY 13148-1451. Mailing Address: P.O. Box 335, Seneca Falls, NY 13148-0335. Tel.: 315-568-8060. Fax: 315-568-2976.
E-mail: admin@womenofthehall.org
Web Site: www.greatwomen.org
Key Personnel: C.E.O., Jill S. Tietjen, P.E.; Bd. Pres., Jeanne Giovannini; Cur. & Educator, Merrill Amos; Admin., Pat Alnes.
Institution Type/Description: Historic Building & Site: 1920s Victorian style bank building.
Hours & Admission Prices: Feb.-April & Oct.-Dec. Wed.-Sat. 11-5; May-Sept. Mon.-Sat. 10-5, Sun. 12-5. Family $7, adults $3, students & seniors $1.50; discounts to veterans; members & children under 5 no charge. Closed New Year's Day; Easter; Memorial Day; Independence Day; Labor Day; Thanksgiving; Christmas. &
Attendance: 15,000 (actual)

SENECA FALLS HISTORICAL SOCIETY, 55 Cayuga St., Seneca Falls, NY 13148-1222. Tel.: 315-568-8412. Fax: 315-568-8426.
E-mail: sfhis@rochester.rr.com
Web Site: www.sfhistoricalsociety.org
Key Personnel: Dir., Frances T. Barbieri; Pres. (V), Kay Irland.
Institution Type/Description: Local History Museum: 23 room Victorian Mansion.
Hours & Admission Prices: Business: Mon.-Fri. 9-4. Tours: June-Sept. Mon.-Sat. 10-3. Family $30, adults $15; discounts to AAM, ICOM, AAA & AARP members; members no charge. Closed New Year's Day; Martin Luther King Jr. Day; Presidents' Day; Memorial Day; Independence Day; Veterans Day; Columbus Day; Thanksgiving & day after; Christmas week.
Attendance: 18,000 (actual)

SENECA MUSEUM OF WATERWAYS AND INDUSTRY, 89 Fall St., Seneca Falls, NY 13148. Mailing Address: P.O. Box 388, Seneca Falls, NY 13148. Tel.: 315-568-1510. Fax: 315-568-1504.
E-mail: info@senecamuseum.com
Web Site: www.senecamuseum.com
Key Personnel: Dir., Linda Solan; Chm. (V), Don Gentilcore; Museum Shop Mgr., Barb Dorvee.
Institution Type/Description: History Museum.

Hours & Admission Prices: Jan.-Feb. Tues.-Sat. 10-4; March-Dec. Mon.-Sat. 10-4, Sun. 12-1; groups by appointment. Guided Tours: adults $5; children under 14 no charge. ⅃
Attendance: 17,000 (actual)

WOMEN'S RIGHTS NATIONAL HISTORICAL PARK, 136 Fall St., Seneca Falls, NY 13148. Tel.: 315-568-0024.
Institution Type/Description: History Museum: housed in the former Village Hall; built in 1915.
Hours & Admission Prices: Daily 9-5. Closed New Year's Day; Thanksgiving; Christmas.

Setauket

GALLERY NORTH, 90 N. Country Rd., Setauket, NY 11733-1352. Tel.: 631-751-2676. Fax: 631-751-0180.
E-mail: info@gallerynorth.org
Web Site: www.gallerynorth.org
Key Personnel: Pres. & Chm., Nancy Goroff; Dir. & Cur., Judith Levy.
Institution Type/Description: Art Gallery.
Hours & Admission Prices: mid-Jan. to Dec. Tues.-Sat. 10-5, Sun. 12-5. No charge. Closed Easter; Thanksgiving; Christmas. ⅃
Attendance: 17,500 (estimated)

THREE VILLAGE HISTORICAL SOCIETY, 93 N. Country Rd., Setauket, NY 11733-1347. Tel.: 631-751-3730. Fax: 631-751-3936.
E-mail: info@tvhs.org
Web Site: threevillagehistoricalsociety.org
Key Personnel: Exec. Dir., Judith Estes; Pres., Patricia Yantz; Archivist, Karen Martin; Office Asst., Suzie Roberts; Office Asst., Maryanne Vigneaux.
Institution Type/Description: Historical Society.
Hours & Admission Prices: Mon.-Fri. 10-3, Sat.-Sun. by appointment. Adults $5, children & members $3. ⅃
Attendance: 3,000 (estimated)

Shelter Island

SHELTER ISLAND HISTORICAL SOCIETY, 16 S. Ferry Rd., Shelter Island, NY 11964. Mailing Address: P.O. Box 847, Shelter Island, NY 11964. Tel.: 631-749-0025. Fax: 631-749-1825. Facebook: Shelter Island Historical Society.
E-mail: info@shelterislandhistorical.org
Web Site: shelterislandhistorical.org
Key Personnel: Exec. Dir., Nanette Lawrenson; Pres. (V), Elizabeth Pedersen; Vice Pres., Janet D'Amato; Treas., Belle Lareau; Sec., Donna Clark; Business Mgr. & Museum Shop Mgr., Alexandra M. Binder.
Institution Type/Description: Historic House Museum: 1743 James Havens house.
Hours & Admission Prices: Call for hours. Archival Department: by appointment only. Closed New Year's Day; Columbus Day; Thanksgiving; Christmas.
Attendance: 5,500 (estimated)

Sidney

SIDNEY HISTORICAL ASSOCIATION, 21 Liberty St., Rm. 218, Sidney, NY 13838-1246. Mailing Address: 21 Liberty St., Box 8, Sidney, NY 13838-1266. Tel.: 607-563-2542.
E-mail: sidneyhistorical@stny.rr.com
Web Site: www.sidneyonline.com/sha.htm
Key Personnel: Pres., Mike Wood; Vice Pres., Joelene Cole; Cur., Graydon Ballard; Treas., Bonnie Curtis; Sec., Karen Cycon.
Institution Type/Description: Regional History Museum.
Hours & Admission Prices: Sept.-July Wed. 4pm-6pm, Thurs. 9am-11:30am; other times by appointment. No charge. Closed holidays. ⅃
Attendance: 779 (actual)

Skaneateles

THE JOHN D. BARROW ART GALLERY, Skaneateles Library, 49 E. Genesee St., Skaneateles, NY 13152-1314. Tel.: 315-685-5135. Facebook: Barrow Art Gallery.
E-mail: jdbag1900@aol.com
Web Site: www.barrowgallery.org
Key Personnel: Dir., Margaret Whitehouse.
Institution Type/Description: Art Gallery.
Hours & Admission Prices: Memorial Day to Labor Day Mon.-Fri. 1-4, Sat. 11-4; Sept.-May Thurs.-Fri. 11-4. Tours by appointment. No charge; donations accepted. Closed holidays.
Attendance: 5,000 (estimated)

Smithtown

SMITHTOWN HISTORICAL SOCIETY, 239 Middle Country Rd., Smithtown, NY 11787-2807. Tel.: 631-265-6768. Fax: 631-979-4694.
E-mail: info@smithtownhistorical.org
Web Site: www.smithtownhistorical.org
Key Personnel: Dir., Kiernan Lannon; Pres. (V), Brad Harris; Dir. Education, Elizabeth Jenks.
Institution Type/Description: Historical Society Museums.
Hours & Admission Prices: Caleb Smith House: Mon.-Fri. 9-5, Sat. by appointment. Historic Houses: by appointment. No charge; donations accepted. ⅃
Attendance: 25,000 (estimated)

Sodus Point

SODUS BAY LIGHTHOUSE MUSEUM, 7606 N. Ontario St., Sodus Point, NY 14555-9536. Mailing Address: P.O. Box 94, Sodus Point, NY 14555-0094. Tel.: 315-483-4936.
E-mail: info@sodusbaylighthouse.org
Web Site: www.sodusbaylighthouse.org
Key Personnel: Museum Dir., Joseph O'Toole; Pres. (V), Laurie Hayden; Vice Pres. (V), Shelley Usiatynski; Museum Shop Mgr., Matt Clingerman.
Institution Type/Description: Historical Society Museum: housed in an 1870 lighthouse.
Hours & Admission Prices: May 1-Oct. 31 Tues.-Sun. & Mon. holidays 10-5. Adults $5, students (K-12) $2.50; members & preschool children no charge. ⅃
Attendance: 21,000 (estimated)

Somers

SOMERS HISTORICAL SOCIETY, Elephant Hotel, Rte. 100 & 202, Somers, NY 10589. Mailing Address: P.O. Box 336, Somers, NY 10589-0336. Tel.: 914-277-4977.
E-mail: somershistoricalsoc@yahoo.com
Web Site: www.somershistoricalsoc.org
Formerly: Somers Historical Society Museum and Museum of the Early American Circus
Key Personnel: Pres. (V), Emil Antonaccio.
Institution Type/Description: Circus & Local History Museum: housed in 1825 Elephant Hotel built by Hachaliah Bailey.
Hours & Admission Prices: Thurs. 2-4; other times by appointment. No charge.
Attendance: 1,000 (estimated)

Southampton

SHINNECOCK NATION CULTURAL CENTER AND MUSEUM, 100 Montauk Hwy. & W. Gate Rd., Southampton, NY 11969. Mailing Address: P.O. Box 5059, Southampton, NY 11969-5059. Tel.: 631-287-4923. Fax: 631-287-7153.
E-mail: office@shinnecockmuseum.org
Web Site: www.shinnecockmuseum.org
Institution Type/Description: Native American Museum.
Hours & Admission Prices: Thurs.-Sun. 11-5; tours by appointment. Adults $8, seniors 55 & over and students $5.50, children 5-12 $4.75; members & children under 5 no charge.

SOUTHAMPTON HISTORICAL MUSEUM, Rogers Mansion, 17 Meeting House Lane, Southampton, NY 11968-4911. Mailing Address: P.O. Box 303, Southampton, NY 11969-0303. Tel.: 631-283-2494.
E-mail: info@southamptonhistoricalmuseum.org
Web Site: southamptonhistoricalmuseum.org
Formerly: Southampton Colonial Society
Key Personnel: Exec. Dir., Tom Edmonds; Pres., Bob Beck; Asst. to Exec. Dir., Nicole Hart; Mgr. Research Center, Mary Cummings; Education & Gift Shop Mgr., Laurie Collins; Business Mgr., Sally Van Allen Halsey; Historic Sites Mgr., Connor Flanagan.
Institution Type/Description: History Museum.
Hours & Admission Prices: Rogers Mansion: March-Dec. Wed.-Sat. 11-4. Thomas Halsey Homestead: July to mid-Oct. Sat. 11-4. Adults $4; children 17 & under and members no charge. ⅃
Attendance: 39,405 (actual)

Southold

SOUTHOLD HISTORICAL SOCIETY AND MUSEUM, 54325 Main Rd., Southold, NY 11971-4646. Mailing Address: P.O. Box 1, Southold, NY 11971. Tel.: 631-765-5500. Fax: 631-765-8510.
E-mail: info@southoldhistorical.org

Web Site: southoldhistoricalsociety.org
Key Personnel: Exec. Dir., Deanna Witte-Walker; Pres., Overton Day.
Institution Type/Description: General Museum.
Hours & Admission Prices: July-Aug. Sat.-Sun. 1-4. Admission $5.
Attendance: 9,000 (estimated)

SOUTHOLD INDIAN MUSEUM, 1080 Bayview Rd., Southold, NY 11971. Mailing Address: P.O. Box 268, Southold, NY 11971-0268. Tel.: 631-765-5577. Fax: 631-765-5577.
E-mail: indianmuseum@aol.com
Web Site: southoldindianmuseum.org
Key Personnel: Pres. (V), Ellen Barcel; Membership, Education & Museum Shop Mgr., Martha Waide.
Institution Type/Description: Archaeology & Indian Museum.
Hours & Admission Prices: Sun. 1:30-4:30. Adults $4; members no charge. Closed New Year's Day; Easter; Thanksgiving; Christmas.
Attendance: 3,000 (estimated)

Spencerport

OGDEN HISTORICAL SOCIETY, 568 Colby St., Spencerport, NY 14559. Mailing Address: P.O. Box 777, Adams Basin, NY 14410-0777. Tel.: 585-352-3672. Facebook: Ogden Historical Society.
E-mail: historian@ogdenny.com
Key Personnel: Town Historian, Carol Coburn.
Institution Type/Description: Historic House: 1811 Eastman-Colby House.
Hours & Admission Prices: Sun. 2-4, group tours by appointment. No charge; donations accepted. &
Attendance: 500 (estimated)

Springville

CONCORD HISTORICAL SOCIETY, WARNER MUSEUM AND THE LUCY BENSLEY CENTER GENEALOGY RESEARCH CENTER, 23 N. Buffalo St., Springville, NY 14141. Tel.: 716-592-0094.
E-mail: lucybensleycenter@gmail.com
Web Site: www.concordnyhistoricalsociety.org
Key Personnel: Pres. & Historian, David Batterson; Vice Pres., Joel Maul; Treas., Jeanne Fornes; Sec., Mel Miller.
Institution Type/Description: Local History Museum.
Hours & Admission Prices: Lucy Bensley Center: Tues.-Thurs. 9-3, 2nd & 4th Sun. each month 2-4. Concord Mercantile & The Heritage: Tues. & Thurs. 7pm-9pm, Wed. & Sat. 10-2; other times by appointment. No charge; donations accepted. &
Attendance: 650 (estimated)

Staatsburg

STAATSBURGH STATE HISTORIC SITE, 75 Mills Mansion Dr., Rd. #1, Staatsburg, NY 12580-5911. Mailing Address: P.O. Box 308, Staatsburg, NY 12580-0308. Tel.: 845-889-8851. Fax: 845-889-8843. Facebook: Staatsburgh SHS.
E-mail: staatsburghshs@parks.ny.gov
Web Site: nysparks.com
Formerly: Mills Mansion State Historic Site
Key Personnel: Historic Site Mgr., Pamela Malcolm.
Institution Type/Description: Historic House Museum: 1895 65-room Neo-classical Revival mansion designed by Stanford White.
Hours & Admission Prices: Call for hours & admission prices. &
Attendance: 24,206 (actual)

Staten Island

ALICE AUSTEN HOUSE MUSEUM, 2 Hylan Blvd., Staten Island, NY 10305-2002. Tel.: 718-816-4506. Fax: 718-815-3959.
E-mail: info@aliceausten.org
Web Site: www.aliceausten.org
Key Personnel: Exec. Dir., Janice Monger; Dir. Education, Annmarie McDonnell; Visitor Svcs. Mgr., Shiloh Aderhold.
Institution Type/Description: Historic House: c.1690 one of the oldest in New York, home of photographer Alice Austen.
Hours & Admission Prices: March-Dec. Thurs.-Sun. 11-5; other times by appointment. Adults $3; discounts to AAM members; members no charge. Closed holidays. &
Attendance: 19,000 (estimated)

THE CONFERENCE HOUSE, 298 Satterlee St., Staten Island, NY 10307. Tel.: 718-984-6046. Fax: 718-984-7760.

E-mail: service@conferencehouse.org
Web Site: www.conferencehouse.org
Key Personnel: Pres., Linda Jensen; Office Operations Mgr., Amanda Granberg; Caretaker, Deborah Woodbridge.
Institution Type/Description: Historic House Museum: housed in 1675 Conference House or Billopp House, built by Capt. Christopher Billopp, English Navy. Site of peace conference during Revolutionary War between Ben Franklin, John Adams & Edward Rutledge with Lord Admiral Richard Howe, Sept. 11, 1776.
Hours & Admission Prices: April to mid-Dec. Fri.-Sun. 1-4. Adults $4, children & seniors $3; discounts to military; members no charge. Closed New Year's Day; Independence Day; Thanksgiving; Christmas.
Attendance: 3,906 (actual)

GARIBALDI-MEUCCI MUSEUM, 420 Tompkins Ave., Staten Island, NY 10305-1704. Tel.: 718-442-1608. Fax: 718-442-8635.
E-mail: info@garibaldimeuccimuseum.org
Web Site: garibaldimeuccimuseum.org
Formerly: Garibaldi and Meucci Museum of the Order Sons of Italy In America
Key Personnel: Dir. & Admin., Michela Traetto; Pres., Joseph Rondinelli; Co-Chm., Joseph Sciame; Co-Chm., Luigi Squillante; Coord. Publicity, Bonnie McCourt.
Institution Type/Description: Historic House: 1845 country home of inventor Antonio Meucci. Italian Patriot, General Giuseppe Garibaldi also occupied house 1850-53.
Hours & Admission Prices: Wed.-Sat. 1-5. School Programs: daily 9:30-11:30. Suggested Donation: $5; discounts to AAM & ICOM members; children under 10 & members no charge. Closed bank holidays.
Attendance: 10,000 (estimated)

HISTORIC RICHMOND TOWN - STATEN ISLAND HISTORICAL SOCIETY, 441 Clarke Ave., Staten Island, NY 10306-1196. Tel.: 718-351-1611. Fax: 718-351-6057. Facebook: Historic Richmond Town.
E-mail: info@historicrichmondtown.org
Web Site: www.historicrichmondtown.org
Key Personnel: Exec. Dir., Ed Wiseman; Pres. (V), Kevin Fisher; Chief Cur., Maxine Friedman; Dir. Education, Felicity Beil.
Institution Type/Description: Historical Society Museum & Historic Village: housed in 1848-1917 County Clerk's & Surrogate's office; site includes nearly 40 historic structures.
Hours & Admission Prices: Wed.-Sun. 1-5. Tours: Wed.-Fri. 2:30pm. Adults $8, senior citizens & students 12-17 $6, children 4-11 $5; active military, SIHS & museum members, children under 3 and Friday no charge. Closed New Year's Day; Easter; Thanksgiving; Christmas.
Attendance: 116,000 (actual)

JACQUES MARCHAIS MUSEUM OF TIBETAN ART, 338 Lighthouse Ave., Staten Island, NY 10306-1217. Tel.: 718-987-3500. Fax: 718-351-0402. Facebook.
E-mail: mventrudo@tibetanmuseum.org
Web Site: www.tibetanmuseum.org
Key Personnel: C.E.O., Meg Ventrudo; Chm. (V), Helaine Dandrea; Bookkeeper, Jayne Catalfo; Museum Asst., Alison Baldassano.
Institution Type/Description: Tibetan Art Museum: Buddhist art, primarily Tibetan, as well as other Asian objects exhibited in a traditional Tibetan style building.
Hours & Admission Prices: Wed.-Sun. 1-5; other times by appointment. Adults $6, seniors & students $4; discounts to AAM, Museum Council of NY & Cool Culture members; members no charge. Closed major holidays.
Attendance: 5,200 (actual)

THE NOBLE MARITIME COLLECTION, 1000 Richmond Terr., Staten Island, NY 10301-1181. Tel.: 718-447-6490. Fax: 718-447-6056.
E-mail: erinurban@noblemaritime.org
Web Site: www.noblemaritime.org
Formerly: The John A. Noble Collection
Key Personnel: Exec. Dir., Erin Urban; Asst. Dir., Ciro Galeno; Dir. Programs, Dawn Daniels; Cur., Megan Beck; Museum Shop Mgr., Nick Dowen.
Institution Type/Description: Art & Maritime History Museum.
Hours & Admission Prices: Thurs.-Sun. 1-5. Adults $5, seniors, students & educators $3; discounts to AAM members; children under 10 & members no charge. Closed New Year's Day; Thanksgiving & Day after; Christmas. &
Attendance: 30,000 (actual)

SEQUINE MANSION, 440 Seguine Ave., Staten Island, NY 10309-3936. Mailing Address: 830 Fifth Ave., The Arsenal, Rm. 203, New York, NY 10065-7001. Tel.: 718-967-3542.
E-mail: lindabsl10@aol.com
Web Site: www.historichousetrust.org
Formerly: Seguine-Burke Plantation
Key Personnel: Exec. Dir. Historic House Trust, Franklin D. Vagnone.

Institution Type/Description: Historic House: 1837 two-story Greek Revival mansion built by businessman Joseph A. Seguine.
Hours & Admission Prices: By appointment only. No charge.

SNUG HARBOR CULTURAL CENTER & BOTANICAL GARDEN, 1000 Richmond Ter., Staten Island, NY 10301-1114. Tel.: 718-425-3504. Fax: 718-815-0198. Facebook: Snug Harbor Cultural Center and Botanical Garden.

E-mail: info@snug-harbor.org
Web Site: snug-harbor.org
Key Personnel: Chm. Bd. Directors, Mark Lauria; Pres. & C.E.O., Lynn B. Kelly; C.F.O., Jefrey Manzer; Dir. Devel., Kirstin Swanson.
Institution Type/Description: Cultural Center & Botanical Garden: housed in a former retirement home for sailors.
Hours & Admission Prices: Grounds: daily dawn to dusk. Visitor's Center & Newhouse Center: Wed.-Sun. 12-5. Garden: Tues.-Sun. 10-5. Adults $5, seniors & students $4; children under 12 no charge. Gardens & Galleries: adults $8, seniors & students $7; children under 12 no charge. Special Events & Performances prices may vary. Closed New Year's Day; Thanksgiving; Christmas. &
Attendance: 300,000 (estimated)

STATEN ISLAND CHILDREN'S MUSEUM, 1000 Richmond Terr. at Snug Harbor, Staten Island, NY 10301. Tel.: 718-273-2060. Fax: 718-273-2836.

E-mail: info@sichildrensmuseum.org
Web Site: www.sichildrensmuseum.org
Key Personnel: Exec. Dir., Dina R. Rosenthal; Business Mgr., Roxanne Burke; Exhibits Mgr., Renee Wasser.
Institution Type/Description: Children's Museum.
Hours & Admission Prices: School Year: Tues.-Fri. 11-5, Sat.-Sun. 10-5; Summer: Tues. & Thurs.-Sun. 10-5, Wed. 10-7. Admission: over 1 $8; discounts to AAM, ICOM, AYM & ASTC members; members, Wed. 3-5; grandparents on Wed. no charge. Closed New Year's Day; Easter; Memorial Day; Independence Day; Labor Day; Thanksgiving; Christmas. &
Attendance: 175,000 (actual)

STATEN ISLAND MUSEUM, 1000 Richmond Terr., Bldg. A, Staten Island, NY 10301. Tel.: 718-727-1135, ext. 114. Fax: 718-273-5683. Facebook; Instagram; Twitter.

E-mail: info@statenislandmuseum.org
Web Site: www.statenislandmuseum.org
Formerly: Staten Island Institute of Arts & Sciences (SIIAS)
Key Personnel: Pres. & C.E.O., Janice Monger; Chm. Bd., David Businelli; Vice Pres. Finance, Dorothy Pinkston; Archivist, Gabriella Leone; Vice Pres. External Affairs & Advancement, Henryk Behnke; Vice Pres. Exhibitions & Programs, Diane Matyas; Acting Mgr. Education, Susan Hogan; Mgr. Communications, Rachel Somma; Registrar/Collections Mgr., Audrey Malachowsky; Visitor Svcs. Mgr., Renee Bushelle; Mgr. Devel., Amanda Straniere; Mgr. Programs, Rylee Eterginoso.
Institution Type/Description: General Museum.
Hours & Admission Prices: Tues.-Sun. 11-5. Adults $8, students & seniors $5, children 2-12 $2; discounts to AAM members; children under 2 & members no charge. Closed New Year's Day; Memorial Day; Independence Day; Thanksgiving; Christmas. &
Attendance: 41,923 (estimated)

STATEN ISLAND ZOO, 614 Broadway, Staten Island, NY 10310-2896. Tel.: 718-442-3100 & 3101. Fax: 718-981-8711.

E-mail: kmitchell@statenislandzoo.org
Web Site: www.statenislandzoo.org
Key Personnel: Exec. Dir., Kenneth C. Mitchell; Pres., William J. Frew, Jr.; Gen. Cur., Dr. Marc Valitutto, VMD.
Institution Type/Description: Zoo.
Hours & Admission Prices: Daily 10-4:45. Adults $8, seniors 60 & over $6, children 3-14 $5, disabled $3; members, children under 3, members of reciprocal zoos & every Wed. 2-4:45 no charge. Closed New Year's Day; Thanksgiving; Christmas. &
Attendance: 157,178 (actual)

Sterling Center

STERLING HISTORICAL SOCIETY AND LITTLE RED SCHOOLHOUSE MUSEUM, 1294 State Rte. 104A, Sterling Center, NY 13156. Mailing Address: P.O. Box 114, Sterling, NY 13156. Tel.: 315-564-6721.

E-mail: sterlinghistory@lakeontario.net
Web Site: www.lakeontario.net/sterlinghistory
Key Personnel: Pres., Patricia Shortslef; Sec. & Trustee, Susan Parsons; Treasurer & Trustee, James Chaffee; Trustee, Mr. Marion Teachout; Trustee, Leigh Shortslef; Town Clerk, Lisa Cooper; Museum Shop Mgr., Susan Allen.

Institution Type/Description: Historical Society Museum: housed in The Little Red School House, an original wood frame, two-story structure.
Hours & Admission Prices: weekend after July 4th to weekend before Labor Day Sat.-Sun. 1-4. No charge; donations accepted.
Attendance: 180 (estimated)

Stillwater

SARATOGA NATIONAL HISTORICAL PARK, 648 Rte. 32, Stillwater, NY 12170-1604. Tel.: 518-664-9821, ext. 224. Fax: 518-664-3349.

E-mail: sara_info@nps.gov
Web Site: www.nps.gov/sara
Key Personnel: Supt., Joe Finan; Program Dir., Gina Johnson.
Institution Type/Description: Military Museum: located on the site of the Battles of Saratoga, Sept. 19 and Oct. 7, 1777.
Hours & Admission Prices: Visitor Center: daily 9-5. Tour Road: April to early Dec. daily 9am to sunset. Park: no charge. Tour Road: $5. Closed New Year's Day; Thanksgiving; Christmas. &
Attendance: 150,000 (actual)

Stony Brook

LONG ISLAND MUSEUM OF AMERICAN ART, HISTORY & CARRIAGES, 1200 Rte. 25A, Stony Brook, NY 11790-1992. Tel.: 631-751-0066, ext. 0. Fax: 631-751-0353. Facebook.

E-mail: mail@longislandmuseum.org
Web Site: www.longislandmuseum.org
Formerly: The Museums at Stony Brook
Key Personnel: Exec. Dir., Neil Watson; Chm. (V), Thomas M. Buonaiuto; Dir. Devel., Deirdre Doherty; Dir. Collections & Interpretation, Joshua Ruff; Dir. Education, Lisa Unander; Dir. Communications, Julie Diamond; Bldgs. & Grounds Exhibition Designer & Preparator, Joe Esser; Collections, Christine Marzano; Museum Shop Mgr., Dori Portes.
Institution Type/Description: General Museum.
Hours & Admission Prices: Call for hours. Adults $10, senior citizens $7, children $4; discounts to AAM members; members no charge. Closed New Year's Day; Easter; Thanksgiving; Christmas Eve & Day. &
Attendance: 26,750 (actual)

MUSEUM OF LONG ISLAND NATURAL SCIENCES, Earth & Space Sciences Bldg.-State University of New York at Stony Brook, Stony Brook, NY 11794. Tel.: 631-632-8230. Fax: 631-632-8240. www.museumoflongislandnaturalsciences.org.

E-mail: Pamela.Stewart@sunysb.edu
Web Site: www.geosciences.stonybrook.edu/museum
Key Personnel: Dir., Pamela Stewart; Cur. Geology, Steven E. Englebright.
Institution Type/Description: Natural Science Museum.
Hours & Admission Prices: Mon.-Fri. 9-5. No charge; donations accepted. Closed national holidays. &
Attendance: 20,000 (estimated)

PAUL W. ZUCCAIRE GALLERY, STONY BROOK UNIVERSITY, Staller Center for the Arts, Stony Brook, NY 11794-5425. Tel.: 631-632-7240. Facebook, Twitter.

E-mail: zuccairegallery@stonybrook.edu
Web Site: zuccairegallery.stonybrook.edu
Formerly: University Art Gallery
Key Personnel: Dir., Karen Levitov.
Institution Type/Description: University Art Gallery.
Hours & Admission Prices: early Sept. to May Tues.-Fri. 12-4, Sat. 7-9. No charge. Closed holidays. &
Attendance: 12,000 (estimated)

Stony Point

STONY POINT BATTLEFIELD STATE HISTORIC SITE, 44 Battlefield Rd., Stony Point, NY 10980. Mailing Address: Box 182, Stony Point, NY 10980-0182. Tel.: 845-786-2521. Fax: 845-786-0463. Facebook.

Web Site: www.palisadesparksconservancy.org
Key Personnel: Historic Site Mgr., Julia M. Warger.
Institution Type/Description: Historic Site & Military Museum: located on the site of raid on British stronghold by Brigadier Gen. Anthony Wayne on July 16, 1779.
Hours & Admission Prices: mid-April to Oct. Wed.-Sun. 10-5, Sun. 12-5. Museum & Lighthouse: fees charged for evening tours, lantern walks, special events, & programs.
Attendance: 36,000 (estimated)

Syracuse

COMMUNITY FOLK ART CENTER, 805 E. Genesee St., Syracuse, NY 13210-1507. Tel.: 315-442-2230. Fax: 315-442-2972. Facebook: Community Folk Art Center.
E-mail: cfac@syr.edu
Web Site: communityfolkartcenter.org
Key Personnel: Sr. Admin., Josette Burgos.
Institution Type/Description: Art Center.
Hours & Admission Prices: Tues.-Fri. 10-5, Sat. 11-5. No charge; donations accepted.

ERIE CANAL MUSEUM, 318 Erie Blvd., E., Syracuse, NY 13202-1106. Tel.: 315-471-0593. Fax: 315-471-7220.
E-mail: contactus@eriecanalmuseum.org
Web Site: www.eriecanalmuseum.org
Key Personnel: Exec. Dir., Diana Goodsight; Pres. (V), Steve Kelly; Cur., Daniel Franklin Ward; Devel. & Public Rels. Dir., Vicki Krisak; Mgr. Operations, Steve Caraccuo.
Institution Type/Description: History Museum: housed in 1850 Greek Revival style Weighlock Building, a monument to Erie Canal architecture; Syracuse Heritage Area Visitors Center.
Hours & Admission Prices: Mon.-Sat. 10-5, Sun. 10-3. No charge; donations accepted. Library by appointment only. Closed New Year's Day; Independence Day; Thanksgiving; Christmas. ᠔
Attendance: 25,000 (estimated)

EVERSON MUSEUM OF ART, 401 Harrison St., Syracuse, NY 13202-3091. Tel.: 315-474-6064. Fax: 315-474-6943. Facebook: Everson Museum of Art.
E-mail: everson@everson.org
Web Site: www.everson.org
Formerly: Everson Museum of Art of Syracuse & Onondaga County
Key Personnel: Chair, Gary Grossman; Pres. & C.E.O., Elizabeth Dunbar; Pres. (V), Ellen Hardy; Cur. Education, Kimberly Griffiths; Archivist & Librarian, Mary Iversen; Asst. Dir., Sarah Massett; Museum Shop Mgr., Sheila Goldie; Museum Shop Mgr., Karen Williams.
Institution Type/Description: Art Museum.
Hours & Admission Prices: Tues.-Fri. & Sun. 12-5, Thurs. 12-8, Sat. 10-5. Suggested Donation: $5 per person. Closed New Year's Day; Independence Day; Thanksgiving; Christmas. ᠔
Attendance: 80,000 (estimated)

MILTON J. RUBENSTEIN MUSEUM OF SCIENCE & TECHNOLOGY, 500 S. Franklin St., Syracuse, NY 13202-1245. Tel.: 315-425-9068. Fax: 315-425-9072.
E-mail: tonimartin@most.org
Web Site: www.most.org
Key Personnel: Pres., Toni Martin; Exec. Vice Pres., Lauren Kochian; Chief Program Officer, Peter Plumley.
Institution Type/Description: Science & Technology Museum.
Hours & Admission Prices: Wed.-Sun. 10 am-4 pm. Adults $12, seniors 65 & over and children 2-11 $10; discounts to ASTC members; members no charge. ᠔
Attendance: 120,000 (estimated)

ONONDAGA HISTORICAL MUSEUM, 321 Montgomery St., Syracuse, NY 13202-2098. Tel.: 315-428-1864. Fax: 315-471-2133.
E-mail: karen.cooney@cnyhistory.org
Web Site: www.cnyhistory.org
Key Personnel: Exec. Dir., Gregg Tripoli; Dir. Finance, Joseph Scro; Cur. Collections, Thomas Hunter; Pres. (V), Lee DeAmicis; Cur. History, Robert Searing; Education Assoc., Scott Peal; Archivist, Pamela Priest; Research Specialist, Sarah Kozma; Devel. Officer, Jon Zella; Devel. Associate, Shannon Kieb; Support Svcs. Admin., Karen Cooney; Museum Shop Mgr., Renee Ross.
Institution Type/Description: Local Historical Museum.
Hours & Admission Prices: Museum: Wed.-Fri. 10-4, Sat.-Sun. 11-4. No charge; donations accepted. Research Center: Wed.-Fri. 10-2 Sat. 11-3:30. Non-members: Adults $7, students $4; members no charge. Closed national holidays. ᠔
Attendance: 30,000 (estimated)

ROSAMOND GIFFORD ZOO AT BURNET PARK, 1 Conservation Place, Syracuse, NY 13204-2590. Tel.: 315-435-8511. Fax: 315-435-8517. Facebook & Twitter: @syracusezoo.
E-mail: rgzoo@ongov.net
Web Site: www.rosamondgiffordzoo.org
Formerly: Burnet Park Zoo
Key Personnel: Dir., Ted Fox; Society Pres., Janet Agostini; Dir. Education, Nathan Keefe; Dir. Food & Beverage, Jim Mahler; Dir. Mktg., Maria Simmons; Dir.

Public Rels., Jaime Alverez; Volunteer Svcs. Mgr., Ellen Vaughn; Museum Shop Mgr., Jessica Bumpus.
Institution Type/Description: Zoo.
Hours & Admission Prices: Daily 10-4:30. Jan.-Feb. adults $4, seniors 62 & over $2.50, youth 3-18 $2; members and children 2 & under no charge. March-Dec. adults $8, senior citizens 62 & over $5, youth 3-18 $4; members and children 2 & under no charge. Closed New Year's Day; Thanksgiving; Christmas. ᠔
Attendance: 350,737 (actual)

SKA-NONH - GREAT LAW OF PEACE CENTER, 321 Montgomery St., Syracuse, NY 13202.
E-mail: nicole.abrams@cnyhistory.org
Key Personnel: Dir., Nicole Abrams; C.E.O., Gregg A. Tripoli; Devel., Jon Zella; Education, Scott Peal; Public Rels., Jon Zella; Treas., Joseph Scro; Registrar, Thomas Hunter; Cur., Robert Searing; Archivist, Pamela Priest; Museum Shop Mgr., Renee Ross.
Institution Type/Description: History Museum.
Hours & Admission Prices: Wed.-Fri. 10-4, Sat.-Sun. 11-4. Adults $5, senior citizens & students $4. Closed major holidays. ᠔
Attendance: 25,000 (estimated)

SUART GALLERIES - SYRACUSE UNIVERSITY, Shaffer Art Bldg., Syracuse University, Syracuse, NY 13244. Tel.: 315-443-4097. Fax: 315-443-9225.
E-mail: suart@syr.edu
Web Site: suart.syr.edu
Formerly: Syracuse University Art Collection
Key Personnel: Dir., Domenic J. Iacono; Assoc. Dir., David Prince; Registrar, Laura Wellner; Asst. Dir. Museum Operations, Andrew J. Saluti; Coord. Collection & Exhibition, Emily Dittman; Sec. & Office Coord., Alex Hahn.
Institution Type/Description: Art Gallery.
Hours & Admission Prices: Tues.-Sun. 11-4:30; other times by appointment. No charge. Closed New Year's Eve & Day; Thanksgiving & weekend after; Christmas Eve, Day & week. ᠔
Attendance: 12,000 (estimated)

Tappan

TAPPANTOWN HISTORICAL SOCIETY, Main St., Tappan, NY 10983. Mailing Address: P.O. Box 71, Tappan, NY 10983-0071. Tel.: 845-359-1149 & 2730.
Web Site: tappantown.org
Institution Type/Description: Historical Society & Historic District: approximately 20 18th- & 19th-century homes.
Hours & Admission Prices: No charge.

Tarrytown

THE HISTORICAL SOCIETY, SERVING SLEEPY HOLLOW AND TARRYTOWN, One Grove St., Tarrytown, NY 10591-4122. Tel.: 914-631-8374. Facebook: The Historical Society, serving Sleepy Hollow and Tarrytown.
E-mail: historyatgrove@aol.com
Web Site: www.thehistoricalsociety.net
Formerly: The Historical Society of Tarrytowns, Inc.
Key Personnel: Pres., Scott C. Monje; Admin. & Cur., Sara Mascia.
Institution Type/Description: History Museum.
Hours & Admission Prices: Wed.-Thurs. & Sat. 2-4. No charge; donations accepted. Archives: by appointment. Closed holidays.
Attendance: 2,500 (estimated)

LYNDHURST, 635 S. Broadway, Tarrytown, NY 10591-6499. Tel.: 914-631-4481, ext. 0. Fax: 914-631-5634.
E-mail: lyndhurst@nthp.org
Web Site: www.lyndhurst.org
Key Personnel: Events & Rentals, Christine Plazas; Preservation Mgr., Krystyn Hastings-Silver; Bldgs. & Grounds Mgr., David Ware; Visitor Svcs., Lisa Buckley.
Institution Type/Description: Historic House Museum: 19th-century Gothic Revival residence of William Paulding, George Merritt & Jay Gould family, designed by Alexander Jackson Davis.
Hours & Admission Prices: May-Dec. see website for hours. Adults $15, members $7.50, discounts to AAM members. ᠔
Attendance: 67,510 (estimated)

Ticonderoga

FORT TICONDEROGA, 100 Fort Ti Rd., Rte 74 E., Ticonderoga, NY 12883. Mailing Address: P.O. Box 390, Ticonderoga, NY 12883-0390. Tel.: 518-585-2821. Fax: 518-585-2210.

E-mail: info@fort-ticonderoga.org
Web Site: www.fort-ticonderoga.org
Key Personnel: Pres. & C.E.O., Beth L. Hill; Chm. (V), Sanford Morehouse; Dir. Education, Richard Strum; Sr. Dir. Interpretation, Stuart Lilie; Business Mgr., Sydney Collier; Communications Officer & Group Tour Coord., Lauren MacLeod; Devel. Officer & Membership Coord., Martha Strum; Collections Mgr., Miranda Peters; Cur., Matthew BP Keagle.
Institution Type/Description: Military History Museum: housed in 1755 barracks of reconstructed Colonial & Revolutionary fortress; restored formal garden c.1920.
Hours & Admission Prices: early May to mid-Oct. 9:30-5, mid-Oct. to Nov. 10-4. Adults $17.50-$19.50, seniors 62 & over $16-$17, children 5-12 $8; discounts to AAM members; children 4 & under and members no charge. &
Attendance: 74,081 (estimated)

Tonawanda

HISTORICAL SOCIETY OF THE TONAWANDAS, INC., 113 Main St., Tonawanda, NY 14150-2129. Tel.: 716-694-7406.
E-mail: tonahist@gmail.com
Web Site: www.tonawandashistory.org
Key Personnel: Pres. (V), Alice Roth.
Institution Type/Description: Historical Society Museums: housed in 1870 brick New York Central Railroad Station & 1829 Long Homestead.
Hours & Admission Prices: Museum: Wed. 12-4:30, Thurs. 10-6, Sat. 10-2. No charge. Long Homestead: Memorial Day to Labor Day Sun.1-4; other times by appointment. Admission $4; children under 12 & members no charge. Closed holidays.
Attendance: 4,000 (estimated)

Troy

THE ARTS CENTER OF THE CAPITAL REGION, 265 River St., Troy, NY 12180. Tel.: 518-273-0552. Fax: 518-273-4591.
E-mail: info@artscenteronline.org
Web Site: www.artscenteronline.org
Institution Type/Description: Art Gallery.
Hours & Admission Prices: Mon.-Thurs. 11-7, Fri.-Sat. 9-5, Sun. 12-4. No charge.

THE CHILDREN'S MUSEUM OF SCIENCE AND TECHNOLOGY, 250 Jordan Rd., Troy, NY 12180-8394. Tel.: 518-235-2120. Fax: 518-235-6836.
E-mail: museum@sunypoly.edu
Web Site: www.cmost.org
Formerly: The Junior Museum
Key Personnel: Interim Dir., Catherine Gilbert.
Institution Type/Description: Children's Museum & Science Center.
Hours & Admission Prices: July-Aug. Mon.-Sat. 10-5; Sept.-June Tues.-Sun. 9-4; other times by appointment. Toddler Explore & More Time: Sept.-June Wed. 1-5. Admission 2 & over $8; discounts to ASTC members; members & children under 2 no charge. Closed New Year's Day; Easter; Memorial Day; Independence Day; Labor Day; Thanksgiving; Christmas. &
Attendance: 65,000 (actual)

LANSINGBURGH HISTORICAL SOCIETY - THE MELVILLE HOUSE AND MUSEUM, 2 114th St., Troy, NY 12182-2712. Mailing Address: P.O. Box 219, Troy, NY 12182-0219. Tel.: 518-235-3501. Facebook.
E-mail: lhssecretary@gmail.com
Web Site: www.lansingburghhistoricalsociety.org
Key Personnel: Acting Pres. (V), John Ward; Acting Pres. (V), Mary Ellen Ward.
Institution Type/Description: Historical Society Museum: housed in home built by Stephan Gorham, the first postmaster in the region; built in 1786.
Hours & Admission Prices: By appointment. No charge; donations accepted.
Attendance: 500 (estimated)

RENSSELAER COUNTY HISTORICAL SOCIETY, 57 Second St., Troy, NY 12180-3928. Tel.: 518-272-7232. Fax: 518-273-1264.
E-mail: info@rchsonline.org
Web Site: www.rchsonline.org
Key Personnel: Pres., Joyce Chupka; Cur., Stacy Pomeroy Draper; Registrar, Kathryn Sheehan.
Institution Type/Description: History & Art Museum: 1927 Hart-Cluett House;
Hours & Admission Prices: Feb.-Dec. 23 Tues.-Sat. 12-5. Adults $5; members no charge. &
Attendance: 8,000 (estimated)

Tupper Lake

NATURAL HISTORY MUSEUM OF THE ADIRONDACKS/ THE WILD CENTER, 45 Museum Dr., Tupper Lake, NY 12986-9712. Tel.: 518-359-7800. Fax: 518-359-3253. Facebook: The Wild Center.
E-mail: info@wildcenter.org
Web Site: www.wildcenter.org
Key Personnel: Exec. Dir., Stephanie Ratcliffe; Bd. Pres. (V), Lynn S. Birdsong; Dir. Devel., Hillarie Logan-Dechene; Dir. Programs, Jennifer Kretser; Public Rels., Tracey Legat; Cur., Leah Valerie; Dir. Facilities, David St. Onge; Museum Shop, Josh Pratt.
Institution Type/Description: Natural History Museum.
Hours & Admission Prices: Memorial Day-Labor Day daily 10-6; Sept. to Columbus Day daily 10-5; Oct. to May Fri.-Sun. 10-5. Adults $20, senior citizens $18, children $13; discounts to groups; members & children under 4 no charge. Closed New Year's Day; Thanksgiving; Christmas. &
Attendance: 60,000 (actual)

Ulster Park

KLYNE ESOPUS MUSEUM, 764 Rte. 9W, Ulster Park, NY 12487. Mailing Address: P.O. Box 751, Port Ewen, NY 12466-0751. Tel.: 845-338-8109.
E-mail: klyneesopusmuseumhistorical@gmail.com
Web Site: klyneesopusmuseum.us
Key Personnel: Pres., Rosane Balistreri.
Institution Type/Description: Local History Museum: housed in c.1827 Old Dutch Church.
Hours & Admission Prices: last week of May to 1st week of Dec. Fri.-Tues. 1-4; groups by appointment only. No charge; donations accepted. &
Attendance: 650 (estimated)

Union Springs

FRONTENAC HISTORICAL SOCIETY AND MUSEUM, 178 Cayuga St., Union Springs, NY 13160. Mailing Address: P.O. Box 338, Union Springs, NY 13160. Tel.: 315-889-7273.
E-mail: frontenac@rochester.twcbc.com
Web Site: freepages.history.rootsweb.ancestry.com/~frontenac/
Institution Type/Description: History Museum.
Hours & Admission Prices: Call for hours.

Upton

BROOKHAVEN NATIONAL LABORATORY-SCIENCE LEARNING CENTER, Brookhaven National Laboratory, Upton, NY 11973-5000. Mailing Address: P.O. Box 5000, Bldg. 400, Upton, NY 11973-5000. Tel.: 631-344-2838 & 4495. Fax: 631-344-5832.
E-mail: oep@bnl.gov
Web Site: www.bnl.gov/slc
Formerly: BNL Science Museum
Key Personnel: Supvr., Gail Donoghue; Coord., Bernadette Uzzi.
Institution Type/Description: Science Museum: dedicated to using inquiry methods to teach science to students in grades K-12.
Hours & Admission Prices: Open to school groups, scouts & teachers by appointment only. No charge. &
Attendance: 37,000 (actual)

Utica

MUNSON-WILLIAMS-PROCTOR ARTS INSTITUTE MUSEUM OF ART, 310 Genesee St., Utica, NY 13502-4799. Tel.: 315-797-0000, ext. 2168. Fax: 315-797-5608.
E-mail: rschneid@mwpai.org
Web Site: www.mwpai.org
Key Personnel: Dir. & Chief Cur., Anna T. D'Ambrosio; Pres., Anthony J. Spiridigloizzi; Cur. Modern & Contemporary Art, Mary Murray; Registrar & Exhibition Mgr., Michael D. Somple; Head Librarian, Kathryn Corcoran; Museum Educator, April Oswald.
Institution Type/Description: Art Museum.
Hours & Admission Prices: Tues.-Sat. 10-5, Sun. 1-5. Charge for special exhibitions; members no charge. Closed New Year's Day; Martin Luther King Jr. Day; Independence Day; Thanksgiving; Christmas. &
Attendance: 73,684 (actual)

ONEIDA COUNTY HISTORY CENTER, 1608 Genesee St., Utica, NY 13502-5425. Tel.: 315-735-3642. Fax: 315-732-0806. Facebook.

E-mail: ochs@oneidacountyhistory.org
Web Site: www.oneidacountyhistory.org
Key Personnel: Exec. Dir., Brian J. Howard; Coord. Community Outreach, Rebecca McLain; Chm. Bd., Andrew Weimer; Museum Shop Mgr., George Abel.
Institution Type/Description: History Museum.
Hours & Admission Prices: June-Sept. Mon.-Fri. 10-4; Oct.-May Tues.-Fri. 10-4 & Sat. 10-2. No charge; donations accepted. Closed national holidays. &
Attendance: 3,500 (estimated)

UTICA CHILDREN'S MUSEUM, 311 Main St., Utica, NY 13501-1282. Tel.: 315-724-6129.
E-mail: jbickfordmanson@uticacm.org
Web Site: uticacm.org
Formerly: Children's Museum of History, Natural History and Science at Utica, New York
Key Personnel: Exec. Dir., Elizabeth Brando.
Institution Type/Description: Children's Museum.
Hours & Admission Prices: Wed.-Sat. 10-4:30. Adults $8; members no charge. &
Attendance: 18,500 (estimated)

UTICA ZOO, 1 Utica Zoo Way, Utica, NY 13501. Tel.: 315-738-0472. Fax: 315-738-0475. Facebook: Utica Zoo: Instagram & Twitter: @uticazoo.
E-mail: info@uticazoo.org
Web Site: www.uticazoo.org
Key Personnel: Exec. Dir., Andria Heath; Mgr. Education, Mary Hall; Dir. Animal Opers., Chris Grassl; Supt. Bldgs. & Grounds, Gary Mundschenk; Veterinarian, Ellen Hilton, D.V.M.; Gift Shop Mgr., Melissa Ellis.
Institution Type/Description: Zoo.
Hours & Admission Prices: April 1-Oct. 31 daily 10-4:45. Adults $8, seniors 62 & up $6.75, children 3-12 $4.75. Nov. 1-March 31 daily 10-4. Adults $4.25, seniors 62 & up $3.50, children 3-12 $2.50; discounts to groups of 10 or more; children 2 & under no charge. &
Attendance: 73,000 (actual)

Vails Gate

KNOX HEADQUARTERS STATE HISTORIC SITE, 289 Forge Hill Rd., Vails Gate, NY 12584. Mailing Address: P.O. Box 207, Vails Gate, NY 12584-0207. Tel.: 845-561-1765, ext. 22. Fax: 845-561-6577.
E-mail: michael.mcgurty@parks.ny.gov
Web Site: www.nysparks.com
Key Personnel: Historic Site Mgr., Michael S. McGurty.
Institution Type/Description: Historic House Museum: 1754 John Ellison home, used as Continental Army officers' headquarters.
Hours & Admission Prices: Tours: Memorial Day-Labor Day Wed.-Fri. 11 & 3, Sat. 10-5, Sun. 1-5; other times by appointment. No charge; donations accepted.
Attendance: 8,500 (estimated)

Vestal

KOPERNIK OBSERVATORY & SCIENCE CENTER, 698 Underwood Rd., Vestal, NY 13850. Tel.: 607-748-3685. Fax: 607-748-3222.
E-mail: info@kopernik.org
Web Site: www.kopernik.org
Key Personnel: Dir., Drew Deskur, BSEE, M.B.A.
Institution Type/Description: Observatory & Science Center.
Hours & Admission Prices: March-Nov. Fri. 7:30pm; Dec.-Feb. call for hours; other times by appointment.

THE VESTAL MUSEUM, 328 Vestal Pkwy. E., Vestal, NY 13850. Mailing Address: 605 Vestal Pkwy. W., Vestal, NY 13850-1437. Tel.: 607-748-1432. Facebook: The Vestal Museum.
E-mail: crosales@vestalny.com
Web Site: www.vestalnyu.com/residents/museum/index.php
Key Personnel: Dir., Cherese Wiesner-Rosales.
Institution Type/Description: Historic Building: DL&W Vestal Railroad Depot; built in 1881.
Hours & Admission Prices: Call or see website for hours. No charge; donations accepted. &
Attendance: 1,800 (estimated)

Victor

GANONDAGAN STATE HISTORIC SITE, 1488 Victor Bloomfield Rd. at State Rte. 444, Victor, NY 14564. Mailing Address: P.O. Box 239, Victor, NY 14564-0239. Tel.: 585-924-5848 & 5414. Fax: 585-742-1732.

E-mail: info@ganondagan.org
Web Site: www.ganondagan.org
Key Personnel: Historic Site Mgr., Peter Jemison; Interpretive Programs, Michael Galban; Office Admin., Ronnie Reitter; Pres. Friends Ganondagan (V), Daniel Rundberg.
Institution Type/Description: Historic Site: late 17th-century Seneca Indian town settlement.
Hours & Admission Prices: Visitors Center: May-Oct. Tues.-Sun. 9-5. Longhouse: Tues.-Sun. 10-4:30. Trails: 8-sunset, weather permitting. Adults $3, children $2; discounts to AAM members.
Attendance: 37,000 (actual)

VALENTOWN MUSEUM, 7370 Valentown Rd., Victor, NY 14564. Mailing Address: Victor Historical Society, P.O. Box 472, Victor, NY 14564-0472. Tel.: 585-924-4170. Fax: 585-924-0523.
E-mail: info@valentown.org
Web Site: valentown.org
Institution Type/Description: History Museum: housed in 1879 Valentown Hall, 19th century community center, located on site of camp area for War of 1812 soldiers & on Seneca Indian Trail of the 1600s used by fur traders, explorers & missionaries.
Hours & Admission Prices: June-Sept. Sun. 1-4; other times by appointment. Adults $6, seniors & students $4; members & children under 6 no charge.
Attendance: 4,000 (estimated)

Walden

HISTORICAL SOCIETY OF WALDEN & WALLKILL VALLEY, 34 N. Montgomery St., Walden, NY 12586-1117. Mailing Address: P.O. Box 48, Walden, NY 12586-0048. Tel.: 845-778-1173.
E-mail: hswwv@adprose.org
Web Site: www.thewaldenhouse.org
Key Personnel: Pres. (V), Barbara Imbasciani.
Institution Type/Description: Historic House Museum: late 18th-century Jacob T. Walden House.
Hours & Admission Prices: Open by appointment only. No charge; donations accepted.
Attendance: 150 (estimated)

Wantagh

WANTAGH PRESERVATION SOCIETY, 1700 Wantaugh Ave., Wantagh, NY 11793. Mailing Address: P.O. Box 132, Wantagh, NY 11793-0132. Tel.: 516-826-8767. Facebook: Wantagh Preservation Society.
E-mail: wantaghmuseum@gmail.com
Web Site: www.wantagh.li/museum
Key Personnel: Pres., Bob Meagher; Vice Pres., Elaine Yarris.
Institution Type/Description: History Museum.
Hours & Admission Prices: Sun. 2-4. No charge; donations accepted.
Attendance: 3,000 (estimated)

Wappinger Falls

SPORTS MUSEUM OF DUTCHESS COUNTY, Wheeler Hill Rd., Wappinger Falls, NY 12590. Mailing Address: P.O. Box 7, Poughkeepsie, NY 12602-0007. Tel.: 845-297-9308.
E-mail: d5softball@aol.com
Web Site: www.sportsmuseumofdcny.org
Institution Type/Description: Sports Museum.
Hours & Admission Prices: Summer: Sat. 11-4, Sun. 1-4; see website for additional hours. No charge; donations accepted. &
Attendance: 607 (actual)

Warsaw

WARSAW HISTORICAL MUSEUM, 15 Perry Ave., Warsaw, NY 14569-1205. Tel.: 585-786-5240. Fax: 585-786-5240.
E-mail: gateshouse1@frontier.com
Web Site: warsawhistory.org
Key Personnel: WHS Pres., Robert Heubusch.
Institution Type/Description: Historic Building Museum: c.1824 building.
Hours & Admission Prices: Mon.-Fri. 10-2; other times by appointment. No charge; donations accepted.
Attendance: 945 (actual)

Warwick

THE HISTORICAL SOCIETY OF THE TOWN OF WARWICK, A.W. Buckbee Center, 2 Colonial Ave., Warwick, NY 10990. Mailing Address: P.O. Box 353, Warwick, NY 10990-0353. Tel.: 845-986-3236.
E-mail: info@warwickhistoricalsociety.org; whs@warwick.net
Web Site: www.warwickhistoricalsociety.org
Key Personnel: Pres., Michael Bertolini.
Institution Type/Description: General Museum.
Hours & Admission Prices: July-Oct. Thurs.-Sun. 12-4. Admission $5, family $10.
Attendance: 3,000 (estimated)

PACEM IN TERRIS, 96 Covered Bridge Rd., Warwick, NY 10990-2854. Tel.: 845-986-4329. Fax: 845-986-4329.
E-mail: paceminterris@frontiernet.net
Web Site: frederickfranck.org
Key Personnel: Pres. & Dir., Lukas Franck; Asst., Frances Jennick.
Institution Type/Description: Historic House: c.1780 water mill ruin & c.1840 country inn, McCanns Hotel & Saloon.
Hours & Admission Prices: May-Oct. Mon.-Fri. 11-4, Sat.-Sun. & holidays 11-6. No charge; donations accepted.
Attendance: 3,000 (estimated)

Water Mill

PARRISH ART MUSEUM, 279 Montauk Hwy., Water Mill, NY 11976. Tel.: 631-283-2118. Fax: 631-283-7006.
E-mail: info@parrishart.org
Web Site: www.parrishart.org
Key Personnel: Dir., Terrie Sultan; Public Rels. & Mktg. Dir., Mark Segal; Deputy Dir., Scott Howe; Special Events & Membership Dir., Nina Madison; Dir. Education, Cara Conklin-Wingfield; Asst. Finance, Susan Swiatocha; Chief Cur. Art & Education, Alicia Longwell; Bldg. Mgr., Walter Gallagher; Museum Shop Mgr., Damian Wolfe.
Institution Type/Description: Art Museum: built in 1897, under the direction of Grosvenor Atterbury, in the style of the Latin Cross.
Hours & Admission Prices: May 15-Sept. 15 Fri. 11-9, Sat.-Thurs. 11-6; Sept. 16-May 14 Wed.-Thurs. & Sat.-Mon. 11-6, Fri. 11-8. Adults $10, senior citizens $8; discounts to guests of members; students, members, & children under 18 no charge. Closed New Year's Day; Easter; Independence Day; Thanksgiving; Christmas. &
Attendance: 60,000 (estimated)

WATER MILL MUSEUM, 41 Old Mill Rd., Water Mill, NY 11976. Mailing Address: P.O. Box 63, Water Mill, NY 11976-0063. Tel.: 631-726-4625. Facebook: Water Mill Museum.
E-mail: info@watermillmuseum.org
Web Site: www.watermillmuseum.org
Key Personnel: Pres. (V), Jeanne White; Museum Shop Mgr., Joan Wilson.
Institution Type/Description: Historic Building Museum: oldest commercial structure on the east end of Long Island. A water-powered working grist mill.
Hours & Admission Prices: May 20 to Columbus Day Thurs.-Mon. 11-5. No charge; donations accepted. Closed Independence Day.
Attendance: 700 (estimated)

Waterford

NEW YORK STATE OPRHP, BUREAU OF HISTORIC SITES, Peebles Island, Waterford, NY 12188. Mailing Address: P.O. Box 219, Waterford, NY 12188-0219. Tel.: 518-237-8643, ext. 3202. Fax: 518-235-4248.
Web Site: www.nysparks.state.ny.us
Institution Type/Description: State Agency.
Hours & Admission Prices: Office: Mon.-Fri. 8-5. Refer to individual site listings for hours & admission fees. &
Attendance: 500,000 (estimated)

WATERFORD HISTORICAL MUSEUM AND CULTURAL CENTER, 2 Museum Lane, Waterford, NY 12188-2639. Tel.: 518-238-0809. Facebook: @waterforhmcc; Instagram: @waterfordmuseum; LinkedIn: Waterford Historical Museum and Cultural Center.
E-mail: info@waterfordmuseum.com
Web Site: www.waterfordmuseum.com
Key Personnel: Dir., Anastasia Garceau; Vice Pres., Michael Dack; Pres., Patricia Burke; Treas., Nancy Spretty.
Institution Type/Description: Local History Museum & Cultural Center: housed in 1830 Hugh White homestead.

Hours & Admission Prices: Museum: May-Oct. Tues.-Sat. 10-3, Sun. 12:30-3; other times by appointment. Adults $6; children & seniors $5; children 6 & under, members and military with ID no charge. Permanent Exhibit: Jan.-April Wed.-Fri. 10-3. George & Anabel O'Connor Research Library and Archive: Tues.-Fri. 10-3 by appointment only. Fee $5. Closed New Year's Day; Memorial Day weekend; Independence Day weekend; Labor Day weekend; Thanksgiving; Christmas. &
Attendance: 230 (estimated)

Waterloo

M'CLINTOCK HOUSE, 14 E. Williams St., Waterloo, NY 13165-1411. Mailing Address: 136 Fall St., Seneca Falls, NY 13148. Tel.: 315-568-0024.
E-mail: wori_information_desk@nps.gov
Institution Type/Description: Historic House: housed in the former home of Thomas and Mary M'Clintock; the site of the drafting of the Declaration of Sentiments for the Women's Rights Convention; built in 1836.
Hours & Admission Prices: Memorial Day to Labor Day Fri.-Mon.

NATIONAL MEMORIAL DAY MUSEUM, 35 E. Main St., Waterloo, NY 13165-1430. Mailing Address: 31 E. Williams, Waterloo, NY 13165-1410. Tel.: 315-539-0533 & 9611. Fax: 315-539-7798. Facebook: National Memorial Day Museum.
E-mail: waterloolib@gmail.com
Web Site: www.wlhs-ny.org
Key Personnel: Pres. (V), Coreen Lowry.
Institution Type/Description: Memorial Day Museum: housed in c.1836 home.
Hours & Admission Prices: Memorial Day to Columbus Day 12-5; other times by appointment. Tours by request. Requested Donations: family $5, adults $3, senior citizens $2, students $1; members & children under 12 no charge. Closed Labor Day.
Attendance: 1,300 (actual)

PETER WHITMER FARM & FAYETTE CHAPEL, 1451 Aunkst Rd., Waterloo, NY 13165-9736. Mailing Address: Hill Cumorah, 603 State Rte. 21 S., Palmyra, NY 14522-9301. Tel.: 315-539-2552. Facebook.
E-mail: info@hillcumorah.org
Web Site: www.lds.org/locations/peter-whitmer-log-home
Key Personnel: Dir., Dale H. Bradford.
Institution Type/Description: Historic House: located on site of organization of The Church of Jesus Christ of Latter-Day Saints (Mormon), 1830.
Hours & Admission Prices: Summer: Mon.-Sat. 9-9, Sun. 12:30-9; Winter: daily 9-5. No charge. Closed Christmas. &
Attendance: 70,000 (estimated)

Watertown

JEFFERSON COUNTY HISTORICAL SOCIETY, 228 Washington St., Watertown, NY 13601-3379. Tel.: 315-782-3491. Fax: 315-782-2913. Facebook: Jefferson County History.
E-mail: director@jeffersoncountyhistory.org
Web Site: jeffersoncountyhistory.org
Key Personnel: Exec. Dir., Diane Page Jordan; Cur. Education, Melissa Widrick; Office Mgr., Donna Koniz.
Institution Type/Description: History Museum: housed in 1876 Paddock Mansion.
Hours & Admission Prices: Tues.-Fri. 10-5, Sat. 9-4. Adults $6; members no charge. Closed national holidays. &
Attendance: 11,000 (estimated)

SCI-TECH CENTER OF NORTHERN NEW YORK, 154 Stone St., Watertown, NY 13601-3250. Tel.: 315-788-1340. Fax: 315-788-2738 (call first).
E-mail: scitech@scitechcenter.org
Web Site: www.scitechcenter.org
Key Personnel: C.E.O., Stephen Karon; Pres. (V), Paul Barben.
Institution Type/Description: Science & Technology Museum.
Hours & Admission Prices: Mon. holidays & Tues.-Sat. 10-4. Adults $4, children $3, seniors $2; discounts to AAM, ICOM & ASTC Passport members & groups with reservations; children under 3 & members no charge. Closed Thanksgiving; Christmas. &
Attendance: 8,061 (actual)

Watkins Glen

INTERNATIONAL MOTOR RACING RESEARCH CENTER AT WATKINS GLEN, 610 S. Decatur St., Watkins Glen, NY 14891-1613. Tel.: 607-535-9044. Fax: 607-535-9039.
E-mail: research@racingarchives.org

Web Site: www.racingarchives.org
Formerly: Watkins Glen Motor Racing Research Library
Key Personnel: Pres., J.C. Argetsinger; Chm. (V), Syd Silverman; Dir. Admin., Max Neal.
Institution Type/Description: Sports Museum & Research Library.
Hours & Admission Prices: Mon.-Fri. 9-5, Sat. 10-2; other times by appointment. No charge; donations accepted. Closed New Year's; Independence Day; Memorial Day; Thanksgiving; Christmas. ♿
Attendance: 7,500 (estimated)

Weedsport

HALL OF FAME & CLASSIC CAR MUSEUM, 1 Speedway Dr., Weedsport, NY 13166-9544. Mailing Address: P.O. Box 240, Weedsport, NY 13166-0240. Tel.: 315-374-3661. Fax: 315-834-9734.
E-mail: jspeno2@gmail.com
Web Site: www.dirthalloffame-classiccarmuseum.com
Key Personnel: Treas., Gary Spaid; Cur., Jack Speno; Museum Shop Mgr., Harry Elkema.
Institution Type/Description: Motorsports Museum.
Hours & Admission Prices: May to Columbus Day Tues.-Sun. 12-5; other times by appointment. Adults $7, senior citizens & students $5; discounts to groups of 10 or more, AAM & ICOM members. Closed Easter; Mother's Day. ♿
Attendance: 5,000 (estimated)

OLD BRUTUS HISTORICAL SOCIETY, INC., 8943 N. Seneca St., Weedsport, NY 13166. Mailing Address: P.O. Box 516, Weedsport, NY 13166-0516. Tel.: 315-834-9342.
E-mail: drandal3@twcny.rr.com
Key Personnel: Pres. (V) Elvin Dolph; Dir. (V), Dennis Randall; Historian, Jeanne Baker; Treas., Jean Saroodis; Sec., Barbara Ward.
Institution Type/Description: Local Historical Society & Museum.
Hours & Admission Prices: Mon.-Tues. 9-12; other times by appointment. No charge; donations accepted. Closed New Year's Day; Easter; Memorial Day; Independence Day; Labor Day; Thanksgiving; Christmas. ♿
Attendance: 1,500 (estimated)

West Henrietta

NEW YORK MUSEUM OF TRANSPORTATION, 6393 E. River Rd., West Henrietta, NY 14586-9575. Mailing Address: P.O. Box 136, West Henrietta, NY 14586-0136. Tel.: 585-533-1113.
E-mail: info@nymtmuseum.org
Web Site: www.nymtmuseum.org
Key Personnel: Pres. (V), Charles Lowe; Vice Pres. & Museum Shop Mgr., Douglas Anderson; Sec., James E. Dierks; Treas., Robert Achilles.
Institution Type/Description: Transportation Museum.
Hours & Admission Prices: mid-May to Oct. Sun. 11-5; groups & other times by appointment; Nov. to mid-May call for hours. Mid-May to Oct. adults $8, seniors 65 & over $7, students 3-12 $6; members & military no charge; Nov. to mid-May call for admission fees. Closed New Year's Day; Easter; Christmas. ♿
Attendance: 4,785 (actual)

West Park

JOHN BURROUGHS ASSOCIATION, INC., Off John Burroughs Dr., West Park, NY 12493. Mailing Address: John Burroughs Assoc., Inc., 15 W. 77th St., New York, NY 10024-5153. Tel.: 212-769-5169. Fax: 212-313-7182.
E-mail: breslof@amnh.org
Web Site: research.amnh.org/burroughs/
Formerly: Slabsides
Key Personnel: Pres., David Liddell; Sec., Lisa Breslof.
Institution Type/Description: Historic House Museum: 1895-1896 house built by naturalist John Burroughs in Nature Sanctuary.
Hours & Admission Prices: By appointment. Trails: dawn to dusk daily. No charge; donations accepted.
Attendance: 800 (estimated)

West Point

WEST POINT MUSEUM, United States Military Academy, Bldg. 2110, West Point, NY 10996. Tel.: 845-938-2203 & 3590. Fax: 845-938-7478. Facebook: West Point Museum.
E-mail: museum@usma.edu
Web Site: www.usma.edu/museum
Key Personnel: Dir., David M. Reel; Cur. Arms, Leslie D. Jensen; Cur. Uniforms & Military History, Michael J. McAfee; Exhibit Specialist, Jose Cartagena; Museum Specialist Conservator, Paul R. Ackermann; Cur. Art, Marlana Cook;

Museum Shop Mgr., Amber Sabotka; Registrar, Brian Rayca; Security Chief, Gloria Johnson.
Institution Type/Description: Military History Museum.
Hours & Admission Prices: Daily 10:30-4:15. No charge; donations accepted. Closed New Year's Day; Thanksgiving; Christmas. No charge; donations accepted. ♿
Attendance: 215,000 (actual)

West Sayville

LONG ISLAND MARITIME MUSEUM, 88 West Ave., West Sayville, NY 11796-1908. Tel.: 631-854-4974. Fax: 631-854-4979.
E-mail: limm@limaritime.org
Web Site: www.limaritime.org
Key Personnel: Dir., Stephen M. Jones; Chm. (V), Michael Eagan; Asst. Dir., Terry Blitman; Sailing Program Dir., Capt. Mike Caldwell; Registrar, Arlene Balcewicz; Librarian, Barbara Forde; Admin. Coord., Brianne Musselwhite.
Institution Type/Description: Maritime History Museum.
Hours & Admission Prices: Mon.-Sat. 10-4, Sun. 12-4. Adults $6, senior citizens & children under 12 $4; discounts for AAM & ICOM members; CAMM members no charge. ♿
Attendance: 85,000 (estimated)

West Seneca

FIREMEN'S MEMORIAL EXHIBIT CENTER OF WESTERN NEW YORK, 4141 Seneca St., West Seneca, NY 14224-3040. Tel.: 716-712-0413.
Institution Type/Description: Firefighting History Museum.
Hours & Admission Prices: Call for hours.

WEST SENECA HISTORICAL SOCIETY, 919 Mill Rd., West Seneca, NY 14224-3038. Tel.: 716-674-4283. Fax: 716-674-4283.
E-mail: historicalsociety@twsny.org
Web Site: www.westsenecahistory.com
Key Personnel: Pres. (V), Frances Deppeler.
Institution Type/Description: Historical Society Museum: housed an original Lower Ebenezer Society house; built in 1850. Listed on the New York and Federal Registries of Historical Places.
Hours & Admission Prices: Tues. 10-4, 1st Sun. of month 2-4. No charge; donations accepted.
Attendance: 920 (actual)

Westfield

CHAUTAUQUA COUNTY HISTORICAL SOCIETY, MCCLURG MUSEUM, Rts. 20 & 394 (Main & Portage Sts.), Westfield, NY 14787. Mailing Address: P.O. Box 7, Westfield, NY 14787-0007. Tel.: 716-326-2977. Facebook: Chautauqua County Historical Society.
E-mail: cchs@mcclurgmuseum.org
Web Site: www.Clurgmuseum.org
Key Personnel: Pres., Cristie Herbst; Vice Pres., Dr. David Brown; Office Mgr., Shari Gollnitz.
Institution Type/Description: County History Museum: housed in 1820 Mansion, built by James McClurg, an early settler.
Hours & Admission Prices: Tues.-Sat. 10-4. Adults $5; discounts to groups; students & members no charge. Closed holidays.
Attendance: 2,500 (estimated)

White Plains

WHITE PLAINS MUSEUM GALLERY, 100 Martine Ave., 2nd Fl., White Plains, NY 10601. Mailing Address: 5 Sylvan Place, New Rochelle, NY 10801. Tel.: 914-632-8226.
E-mail: david@davidobey.com
Web Site: www.davidtobey.com
Institution Type/Description: Art Gallery.
Hours & Admission Prices: Call for hours.

Williamsville

WILLIAMSVILLE MEETING HOUSE & MUSEUM, 5658 Main St., Williamsville, NY 14221. Mailing Address: c/o 120 N. Ellicott St., Williamsville, NY 14221. Tel.: 716-626-4406.
E-mail: kpoules@village.williamsville.ny.us
Web Site: walkablewilliamsville.com
Key Personnel: Pres. (V), Mary E. Lowther.
Institution Type/Description: Historic Building: built in 1871. Listed on the National Register of Historic Places.

Hours & Admission Prices: Sept.-June 2nd Sun. each month 1-3. No charge; donations accepted.
Attendance: 250

Wilson

WILSON HISTORICAL MUSEUM, 645 Lake St., Wilson, NY 14172. Mailing Address: P.O. Box 830, Wilson, NY 14172-0830. Tel.: 716-751-9886. Fax: 716-751-6141.
E-mail: agaffiliat@aol.com
Web Site: www.wilsonnewyork.com/hist_society.html
Key Personnel: Pres., Kyle Andrews.
Institution Type/Description: General & Historical Society Museum: housed in 1912 Railroad Depot.
Hours & Admission Prices: May-Nov. Sun. 2-4. No charge; donations accepted.
Attendance: 1,200 (estimated)

Wilton

ULYSSES S. GRANT COTTAGE STATE HISTORIC SITE, Mount McGregor, Wilton, NY 12831. Mailing Address: P.O. Box 2294, Wilton, NY 12831-5294. Tel.: 518-584-4353.
E-mail: info@grantcottage.org
Web Site: www.grantcottage.org
Key Personnel: Admin. & Pres. (V), Tim Welch; Dir., Jonathan Duda; Chm. (V), Bob Conner; Museum Shop Mgr., Dave Hubbard.
Institution Type/Description: Historic House: 1878 cottage where Gen. Ulysses S. Grant spent the last six weeks of his life in June/July 1885; completed his personal memoirs.
Hours & Admission Prices: Memorial Day-Labor Day Wed.-Sun. 10-4; Sept. to Columbus Day Sat.-Sun. 10-4. Adults $5, senior citizens & students $4; children 5 & under and members no charge. &
Attendance: 3,300 (estimated)

Windsor

OLD STONE HOUSE MUSEUM, 22 Chestnut St., Windsor, NY 13865-4105. Tel.: 607-655-1491.
E-mail: info@theoldstonehouse.org
Key Personnel: Dir., Luella F. English.
Institution Type/Description: History Museum: housed in Federal period house of Major Jed Hotchkiss, C.S.A.
Hours & Admission Prices: Sat.-Sun. 10-5; other times by appointment. No charge; donations accepted.
Attendance: 300 (estimated)

Woodside

TOPAZ ARTS, INC., 55-03 39th Ave., Woodside, NY 11377. Tel.: 718-505-0440.
E-mail: info@topazarts.org
Web Site: www.topazarts.org
Key Personnel: Co Founder, Todd B. Richmond; Co Founder, Paz Tanjuaquio.
Institution Type/Description: Art Gallery.
Hours & Admission Prices: Call for hours.

Woodstock

CENTER FOR PHOTOGRAPHY AT WOODSTOCK, 59 Tinker St., Woodstock, NY 12498-1236. Tel.: 845-679-9957.
E-mail: info@cpw.org
Web Site: www.cpw.org
Key Personnel: Exec. Dir., Hannah Frieser; Program Mgr., Jan Nagle.
Institution Type/Description: Photography Museum.
Hours & Admission Prices: Gallery: Wed.-Sun. 12-5. Office: Mon.-Fri. 10-6. Lecture series: adults $7; discount to members, seniors & students. Gallery: no charge; donations accepted. &
Attendance: 50,000 (estimated)

WOODSTOCK ARTISTS ASSOCIATION & MUSEUM, 28 Tinker St., Woodstock, NY 12498-1233. Tel.: 845-679-2940.
E-mail: info@woodstockart.org
Web Site: www.woodstockart.org
Key Personnel: Exec. Dir. & Cur., Janice La Motta; Assoc. Dir., Bryana Devine.
Institution Type/Description: Art Association & Museum.
Hours & Admission Prices: Thurs.-Mon. 12-5; other times by appointment. Suggested Donation: adults $5; discounts to AAM & ICOM members; members no charge. Closed New Year's Day; Labor Day; Thanksgiving; Christmas. &
Attendance: 25,000 (actual)

Wyoming

MIDDLEBURY HISTORICAL SOCIETY, 22 S. Academy St., Wyoming, NY 14591-9801. Mailing Address: P.O. Box 198, Wyoming, NY 14591-0198. Tel.: 585-495-6420. Facebook.
Key Personnel: Pres., Mr. Douglas Norton.
Institution Type/Description: Historical Society Museum: housed in 1817 Middlebury Academy.
Hours & Admission Prices: Memorial Day-last weekend in Sept. Sun. 2-5. No charge; donations accepted. &
Attendance: 691 (actual)

Yonkers

HUDSON RIVER MUSEUM, 511 Warburton Ave., Yonkers, NY 10701-1899. Tel.: 914-963-4550. Fax: 914-963-8558. Facebook: www.facebook.com/HudsonRivMuseum; Twitter: twitter.com/HudsonRivMuseum; Instagram: www.instagram.com/hudsonriver-museum.
E-mail: info@hrm.org
Web Site: www.hrm.org
Key Personnel: Dir., Masha Turchinsky; Chair, Bd. Trustees, Thomas D'Auria; Deputy Dir. Advancement, Communications & Administration, Samantha Hoover; Asst. Dir. Finance & Human Resources, Marion Freedman; Chair, Curatorial Dept., Laura Vookles; Asst. Dir. Education, Saralinda Lichtblau.
Institution Type/Description: General Museum.
Hours & Admission Prices: Museum: Wed.-Sun. 12-5. Adults $7, senior citizens & students $6, children $5; discounts for Metro-North Railroad commuters, FWMA & Channel 13 members; members no charge. Planetarium: Sat.-Sun. 12:30, 2:00, 3:30; school groups & tours by appt. Adults $4, seniors & students $3, children $2; members no charge. Closed New Year's Day; Thanksgiving; Christmas. &
Attendance: 65,000 (estimated)

PHILIPSE MANOR HALL STATE HISTORIC SITE, 29 Warburton Ave., (& Dock St.), Yonkers, NY 10701-2721. Tel.: 914-965-4027. Fax: 914-965-6485.
Web Site: www.nysparks.state.ny.us/historic-sites/37/details.aspx
Key Personnel: Dir., Kimberly Flook; Commissioner, Carol Ash; Pres. (V), Joan Jennings.
Institution Type/Description: Art & History Museum: housed in early 18th-century Georgian style manor house.
Hours & Admission Prices: April-Oct. Tues.-Sat. 10-5; Nov.-March Tues.-Sat. 10-4; other times by appointment. Adults $5, seniors & students $3; members & children under 12 no charge. Closed holidays. &
Attendance: 25,000 (estimated)

Yorktown Heights

TOWN OF YORKTOWN MUSEUM, YCCC Building - Top Fl., 1974 Commerce St., Yorktown Heights, NY 10598-4433. Tel.: 914-962-2970. Fax: 914-962-4379.
E-mail: museum@yorktownny.org
Web Site: www.yorktownmuseum.org
Key Personnel: C.E.O., Alice Roker; Tour Coord., Nancy Augustowski; Asst. Cur. & Museum Shop Mgr., Adele Hobby.
Institution Type/Description: General Museum.
Hours & Admission Prices: Tues. & Thurs. 11-4, Sat. 1-4. Tours: adults $5, children $2; discounts to members. Closed Easter; Thanksgiving; Christmas. &
Attendance: 5,000 (actual)

Youngstown

OLD FORT NIAGARA, Fort Niagara State Park, Youngstown, NY 14174. Mailing Address: P.O. Box 169, Youngstown, NY 14174-0169. Tel.: 716-745-7611. Fax: 716-745-9141.
E-mail: remerson@oldfortniagara.org
Web Site: www.oldfortniagara.org
Key Personnel: Exec. Dir., Robert L. Emerson; Pres., Bruce Newton; Asst. Dir. & Cur., Jerome Brubaker; Museum Shop Mgr., Patricia Fitzpatrick.
Institution Type/Description: Military Historic Site.
Hours & Admission Prices: July-Aug. daily 9-7; Sept.-June daily 9-5. Adults $12, senior citizens $11, children 6-12 $8; discounts to groups & Museum Assoc. of New York members; members no charge. Closed New Year's Day; Thanksgiving; Christmas. &
Attendance: 219,000 (actual)

NORTH CAROLINA

(540 listings)

Aberdeen

MALCOLM BLUE FARM MUSEUM, 1177 Bethesda Rd., Aberdeen, NC 28315. Mailing Address: P.O. Box 785, Aberdeen, NC 28315-0785. Tel.: 910-944-7558. Fax: 910-944-7558.
E-mail: aprd@townofaberdeen.net
Web Site: townofaberdeen.net
Institution Type/Description: Farm Museum.
Hours & Admission Prices: By appointment only. No charge; donations accepted.
Attendance: 3,000 (estimated)

Albemarle

MORROW MOUNTAIN STATE PARK, 49104 Morrow Mountain Rd., Albemarle, NC 28001-7886. Tel.: 704-982-4402. Fax: 704-982-5323.
E-mail: morrow.mountain@ncmail.net
Web Site: www.ncparks.gov
Key Personnel: Park Supt., Greg Schneider.
Institution Type/Description: Park Museum.
Hours & Admission Prices: Daily 10-5. No charge. Closed Christmas. &
Attendance: 201,970 (estimated)

STANLY COUNTY HISTORIC PRESERVATION COMMISSION AND MUSEUM, 245 E. Main St., Albemarle, NC 28001-4919. Tel.: 704-986-3777. Fax: 704-986-3778.
E-mail: junderwood@co.stanly.nc.us
Web Site: www.stanlycountymuseum.com
Key Personnel: Dir., Jonathan A. Underwood; Chm., Christy Stoner; Cur., Lessie Huneycutt.
Institution Type/Description: History Museum & Visitor Center.
Hours & Admission Prices: Wed.-Fri. 10-5, Sat. 10-4. No charge; donations accepted. Closed major holidays. &
Attendance: 5,881 (actual)

Asheboro

AMERICAN CLASSIC MOTORCYCLE MUSEUM, 1170 US Hwy. 64 W., Asheboro, NC 27205. Tel.: 336-629-9564.
Institution Type/Description: Motorcycle Museum.
Hours & Admission Prices: Mon. 6am-2pm, Tues.-Fri. 6am-5:30pm, Sat. 6am-4pm. No charge.

NORTH CAROLINA AVIATION MUSEUM, 2222-G Pilots View Rd., Asheboro, NC 27204. Tel.: 336-625-0170. Fax: 336-625-2984.
E-mail: info@ncaviationmuseumhalloffame.com
Web Site: www.ncairmuseum.org
Institution Type/Description: Aviation Museum.
Hours & Admission Prices: Thurs.-Sun. 11-5. Adults $10, seniors $8, students under 18 $5; children 5 & under no charge.

NORTH CAROLINA ZOOLOGICAL PARK, 4401 Zoo Pkwy., Asheboro, NC 27205-1425. Tel.: 800-488-0444, 336-879-7000. Fax: 336-879-2891.
E-mail: rod.hackney@nczoo.org
Web Site: www.nczoo.org
Key Personnel: Chm. Zoological Park Council, Scott Reed; Dir., Dr. David M. Jones; Business Officer, Mary Joan Pugh; Human Resources Officer, Cami Bunting; Gen. Cur., Ken Reininger; Cur. Horticulture, Virginia Wall; Design Cur., Ellen Greer; Assoc. Cur. Mammals, Guy Lichty; Cur. Herpetology, John Groves; Public Rels. Mgr., Rod Hackney; Veterinarian, Michael R. Loomis; Museum Shop Mgr., David Whitaker.
Institution Type/Description: Zoo.
Hours & Admission Prices: Daily 9-5; groups by appointment. Adults $12, senior citizens & college students $10, children 2-12 $8; discounts for groups, AZA & selected zoological institutions; North Carolina school groups in grades K-12, members & children under 2 no charge. &
Attendance: 761,964 (actual)

Asheville

ANTIQUE CAR MUSEUM AT GROVEWOOD VILLAGE, 111 Grovewood Rd., Asheville, NC 28804-2858. Tel.: 828-253-7651. Fax: 828-254-2489.
E-mail: automuseum@grovewood.com

Web Site: www.grovewood.com
Formerly: Estes-Winn Antique Car Museum
Key Personnel: Mgr., Tom Anders; Pres., Barbara Blomberg.
Institution Type/Description: Transportation Museum: located on the grounds of c.1917 Biltmore Homespun Shops.
Hours & Admission Prices: April-Dec. Mon.-Sat. 10-5:30, Sun. 11-5:30. No charge; donations accepted. &
Attendance: 25,000 (estimated)

ASHEVILLE ART MUSEUM, 2 S. Pack Square, Asheville, NC 28801-3521. Mailing Address: P.O. Box 1717, Asheville, NC 28802-1717. Tel.: 828-253-3227. Fax: 828-257-4503.
E-mail: mailbox@ashevilleart.org
Web Site: www.ashevilleart.org
Key Personnel: C.E.O., Pamela L. Myers; Cur., Carolyn Grosch; Asst. Cur., Cole Hendrix; Mgr. Education Programs, Sharon McRorie; Financial Officer, Lindsay G. Rosson; Preparator, Jay Milnar; Mktg. & Public Rels., Jen Swangon; Campaign Mgr., Rebecca Lynch-Maass; Mgr. School & Family Programs, Erin Shope; Mgr. Adult Programs, Krist McMillan; Membership & Events Mgr., Joanna K. Miller; Museum Shop & Visitor Svcs. Mgr., Laura Wheeler; Museum Shop & Events Coord., Lauren Bacchus; Registrar, Myra Scott; Mgr. Grants, Mark Jackson.
Institution Type/Description: Art Museum.
Hours & Admission Prices: Tues.-Sat. 10-5, Sun. 1-5; special evening hours available. Adults $8, senior citizens & students $7; discounts to AAM & ICOM members; children under 5 & members no charge. Southeastern & North American reciprocal members. Closed New Year's Day; Independence Day; Labor Day; Thanksgiving; Christmas. &
Attendance: 129,500 (actual)

THE ASHEVILLE HISTORY CENTER AT THE SMITH-MCDOWELL HOUSE, 283 Victoria Rd., Asheville, NC 28801-4817. Tel.: 828-253-9231. Fax: 828-253-5518.
E-mail: smh@wnchistory.org
Web Site: www.wnchistory.org
Key Personnel: Dir., Ali Mangkang; Pres., Richard Graham; Coord. Education, Lisa Whitfield; Volunteer Coord., Elaine Blake.
Institution Type/Description: Historic Building & Local History Museum: housed in 1840 Smith-McDowell House.
Hours & Admission Prices: Wed.-Sat. 10-4, Sun. 12-4. Adults $9, children 8-18 $5; discounts to groups, AAA & AASLH members; members no charge. &
Attendance: 2,500 (estimated)

ASHEVILLE MUSEUM OF SCIENCE, 43 Patton Ave, Asheville, NC 28801. Tel.: 828-254-7162.
E-mail: info@ashevillescience.org
Web Site: www.ashevillescience.org
Formerly: Colburn Gem & Mineral Museum, Inc.
Key Personnel: Exec. Dir., Anna Priest; Devel. Dir., Alison Gooding.
Institution Type/Description: Geology, Mineralogy & Paleontology Museum & Earth Science.
Hours & Admission Prices: Mon.-Sat. 10-5, Sun. 1-5. Adults $8, children $7; discount to groups, AAM, ASTC & SEMC members; children under 4 & members no charge. Closed major holidays. &
Attendance: 27,232 (actual)

BILTMORE ESTATE, One Approach Rd., Asheville, NC 28803-8900. Tel.: 828-255-1333, 800-411-3812. Fax: 828-225-6383.
E-mail: rking@biltmore.com
Web Site: www.biltmore.com
Key Personnel: Vice Pres., Richard King; Sr. Vice Pres. Attraction, Tom Ruff; Vice Pres. Finance & Controller, Stephen Watson; Vice Pres. Agricultural Svcs., Ted Katsigianis; Pres. Wine Company, Jerry Douglass; Vice Pres. Winemaker, Bernard Delille; Vice Pres. Sales, Jim Owens; Group Sales Mgr., Paula Wilbur.
Institution Type/Description: Historic House, Conservatory & Gardens: 1895 Biltmore House.
Hours & Admission Prices: Welcome Center: Mon.-Thurs. 8:30-3, Fri.-Sat. 8:30-4. House: seasonal hours. See website for admission fees. &
Attendance: 902,000 (actual)

BLACK MOUNTAIN COLLEGE MUSEUM + ARTS CENTER, 56 Broadway, Asheville, NC 28801-2916. Mailing Address: P.O. Box 18912, Asheville, NC 28814-0912. Tel.: 828-350-8484. Fax: 828-350-8484.
E-mail: bmcmac@bellsouth.net
Web Site: www.blackmountaincollege.org
Key Personnel: Dir., Katherine Devine; Program Dir., Alice Sebrell.
Institution Type/Description: Art Museum.
Hours & Admission Prices: Tues.-Wed. 12-4, Thurs.-Sat. 11-5. No charge; donations accepted. &

BLUE RIDGE PARKWAY VISITOR CENTER, 199 Hemphill Knob Rd., Asheville, NC 28803-8686. Tel.: 828-348-3400.
E-mail: angie@blueridgeheritage.com
Web Site: www.blueridgeheritage.com
Formerly: Blue Ridge Parkway Destination Center
Key Personnel: Exec. Dir., Angie Chandler.
Institution Type/Description: History Museum.
Hours & Admission Prices: Daily 9-5. No charge. Closed New Year's Day; Thanksgiving; Christmas.
Attendance: 93,434 (estimated)

BOTANICAL GARDENS AT ASHEVILLE, 151 W. T. Weaver Blvd., Asheville, NC 28804-3414. Tel.: 828-252-5190.
E-mail: bgardens@bellsouth.net
Web Site: ashevillebotanicalgardens.org
Key Personnel: Pres., Gwen Wisler; Vice Pres. & Museum Shop Mgr., Suzanne Wodek; Garden Mgr. & Horticulture Chm., Jay Kranyik; Administrative Asst., Heather Rayburn.
Institution Type/Description: Botanical Gardens: includes site of earthen battlements of the Civil War, Battle of Asheville.
Hours & Admission Prices: Visitor Center: mid-March-Dec. daily 10-4. Grounds: daily. No charge; donations accepted.
Attendance: 35,000 (estimated)

THE NORTH CAROLINA ARBORETUM, 100 Frederick Law Olmsted Way, Asheville, NC 28806-9315. Tel.: 828-665-2492. Fax: 828-665-2371.
E-mail: info@ncarboretum.org
Web Site: www.ncarboretum.org
Key Personnel: Dir., George Briggs; Museum Shop Mgr., Tracy Grazette.
Institution Type/Description: Arboretum.
Hours & Admission Prices: Mon.-Sat. 9-5, Sun. 12-5. Vehicle: $14. Closed New Year's Day; Thanksgiving; Christmas.

THE SOUTHERN APPALACHIAN RADIO MUSEUM, A-B Technical Community College, 340 Victoria Rd. Elm Bldg., Rm. 315, Asheville, NC 28801. Tel.: 828-299-1276.
E-mail: info@blueridgeheritage.com
Web Site: blueridgeheritage.com/attractions-destinations/southern-appalachian-radio-museum
Key Personnel: Pres., John Travis; Vice Pres., Norman Harrill; Sec. & Treas., Clint Gorman.
Institution Type/Description: History Museum.
Hours & Admission Prices: Feb.-Nov. Fri. 1-3; other times by appointment. No charge; donations accepted. Closed school holidays.

SOUTHERN HIGHLAND CRAFT GUILD, Milepost 382, Blue Ridge Pkwy., Asheville, NC 28805. Mailing Address: P.O. Box 9545, Asheville, NC 28815-0545. Tel.: 828-298-7928. Fax: 828-298-7962. Facebook: Folk Art Center.
E-mail: info@craftguild.org
Web Site: www.southernhighlandguild.org
Formerly: Folk Art Center
Key Personnel: Exec. Dir., Tom Bailey.
Institution Type/Description: Southern Appalachian Craft Museum.
Hours & Admission Prices: Jan.-March daily 9-5; April-Dec. daily 9-6. No charge; donations accepted. Closed New Year's Day; Thanksgiving; Christmas.
Attendance: 281,000 (actual)

THOMAS WOLFE MEMORIAL, 52 N. Market St., Asheville, NC 28801-8105. Tel.: 828-253-8304. Fax: 828-252-8171. Facebook: Thomas Wolfe Memorial.
E-mail: contactus@wolfememorial.com
Web Site: www.wolfememorial.com
Key Personnel: Dir., Tom Muir.
Institution Type/Description: Historic House: built in 1883 Thomas Wolfe boarding house, The Old Kentucky Home.
Hours & Admission Prices: Tues.-Sat. 9-5. Adults $5, students $2. Closed state holidays.
Attendance: 18,000 (actual)

WESTERN NORTH CAROLINA NATURE CENTER, 75 Gashes Creek Rd., Asheville, NC 28805-2529. Tel.: 828-298-5600, ext. 303. Fax: 828-298-2644.
E-mail: staff@wildwnc.org
Web Site: www.wncnaturecenter.org
Key Personnel: Dir., Chris Gentile; Dir. Education, Keith Mastin; Cur. Animals, Allison Ballentine; Museum Shop Mgr., Mischa Trinks.
Institution Type/Description: Zoological Park.

Hours & Admission Prices: Daily 10-5. Adults $8, senior citizens $7, children 3-14 $4; discounts to ASTC & AZA members; members and children 2 & under no charge. Closed major winter holidays.
Attendance: 92,408 (actual)

YMI CULTURAL CENTER, 39 S. Market St., Asheville, NC 28801-3726. Mailing Address: P.O. Box 7301, Asheville, NC 28802-7301. Tel.: 828-257-4540. Fax: 828-257-4539. Facebook: YMI Cultural Center.
E-mail: ymicc@att.net
Web Site: www.ymicc.org
Institution Type/Description: Art & History Gallery.
Hours & Admission Prices: By appointment.
Attendance: 1,000 (estimated)

Atlantic Beach

FORT MACON STATE PARK, 2303 E. Fort Macon Rd., Atlantic Beach, NC 28512-5638. Tel.: 252-726-3775. Fax: 252-726-2497.
E-mail: fort.macon@ncparks.gov
Web Site: friendsoffortmacon.org
Key Personnel: Park Supt., Randall Newman; Dir., Michael A. Murphy; Park Ranger, Kevin Bleck; Park Ranger, Paul R. Branch; Chief Maintenance, John Schell; Maintenance Mechanic, Robert Taber; Ranger, Benjamin Fleming; Ranger, Paul Terry; Office Asst. III, Cleta Buck; Museum Shop Mgr., Cathy Imhoff.
Institution Type/Description: Museum & Historic Building: 1834 brick casemated, irregular pentagon shape, outer & inner walls with moat, Fort Macon.
Hours & Admission Prices: Daily 9-5:30. No charge; donations accepted. Closed Christmas.
Attendance: 1,250,000 (estimated)

Aurora

AURORA FOSSIL MUSEUM FOUNDATION, INC., 400 Main St., Aurora, NC 27806-0352. Mailing Address: P.O. Box 352, Aurora, NC 27806-0352. Tel.: 252-322-4238. Fax: 252-322-2220.
E-mail: info@aurorafossilmuseum.org
Web Site: www.aurorafossilmuseum.org
Formerly: Aurora Fossil Museum
Key Personnel: Dir., Cynthia D. Crane.
Institution Type/Description: Geology & Paleontology Museum.
Hours & Admission Prices: March to Labor Day Mon.-Sat. 9-4:30, Sun. 12:30-4:30; Sept.-Feb. Mon.-Sat. 9-4:30; groups of 10 or more by appointment. No charge; donations accepted.
Attendance: 25,000 (estimated)

Bailey

THE COUNTRY DOCTOR MUSEUM, 6642 Peele Rd., Bailey, NC 27807. Mailing Address: P.O. Box 34, Bailey, NC 27807-0034. Tel.: 252-235-4165. Fax: 252-235-2372.
E-mail: andersonan@ecu.edu
Web Site: www.countrydoctormuseum.org
Institution Type/Description: Rural Medical & Pharmacology Museum with emphasis on Eastern North Carolina from 1850-1960.
Hours & Admission Prices: Tues.-Sat. 10-4. Adults $5, senior citizens & AAA members $4, students $3. Closed holidays.
Attendance: 2,000 (estimated)

Bald Head Island

OLD BALDY LIGHTHOUSE & SMITH ISLAND MUSEUM, 101 Lighthouse Wynd, Bald Head Island, NC 28461. Tel.: 910-457-7481.
Web Site: oldbaldy.org
Institution Type/Description: Historic Lighthouse: c.1850.
Hours & Admission Prices: Bald Head Island is accessible by passenger ferry from Deep Point Marina, 1301 Ferry Rd., Southport, NC. See website for ferry schedule & admission prices. Lighthouse & Museum: Mon.-Sat. 9-5, Sun. 11-5. Adults 13 & over $5, youth 3-12 $3; children 2 & under no charge.

Bath

HISTORIC BATH STATE HISTORIC SITE, 207 Carteret St., Bath, NC 27808. Mailing Address: P.O. Box 148, Bath, NC 27808-0148. Tel.: 252-923-3971. Fax: 252-923-3971.
E-mail: bath@ncdcr.gov
Web Site: www.bath.nchistoricsites.org
Key Personnel: Site Mgr., Leigh Swane; Gift Shop Mgr., Robyn Jackson.

Institution Type/Description: Visitor Center.
Hours & Admission Prices: Tues.-Sat. 9-5. Two house tour: adults $2, students $1; discount to groups. Closed winter holidays. ♿
Attendance: 30,600 (estimated)

Beaufort

BEAUFORT HISTORIC SITE, 138 Turner St., Beaufort, NC 28516-2139. Mailing Address: 150 Turner St., Beaufort, NC 28516-2139. Tel.: 252-728-5225. Fax: 252-728-4966.
E-mail: beauforthistoricsite@earthlink.net
Web Site: www.beauforthistoricsite.org
Key Personnel: Exec. Dir., Patricia Suggs; Chm. (V), Polly Hagle; Pres. (V), Bill Kaeser; Vice Pres., Larry Jones; Vice Pres., Dick Bierly; Treas., Lucia Stanley; Museum Shop Mgr., Diane Donovan.
Institution Type/Description: Historical & Preservation Society.
Hours & Admission Prices: Mon.-Sat. 9:30-5; group tours by appointment. Adults $8, children under 12 $4. English Bus Tours: Mon. & Wed.-Sat. Adults $8. Old Burying Ground Tour: Tues.-Thurs. 2:30 Adults $8; discounts to AAA members & groups of 30 or more. Closed Easter; Thanksgiving; Christmas Eve & Day. ♿
Attendance: 65,000 (estimated)

NORTH CAROLINA MARITIME MUSEUM, 315 Front St., Beaufort, NC 28516-2124. Tel.: 252-728-7317. Fax: 252-728-2108.
E-mail: maritime@ncdcr.gov
Web Site: www.ncmaritimemuseum.org
Key Personnel: Dir., Joe Schwarzer; Pres., Elwyn Wood; Cur. Education, John Hairr; Dir. Opers., Brent Creelman; Dir. Devel. & Communications, Gina G. Holland.
Institution Type/Description: Natural & Maritime History Museum.
Hours & Admission Prices: Mon.-Fri. 9-5, Sat. 10-5, Sun. 1-5. No charge; donations accepted. Closed New Year's Day; Thanksgiving; Christmas Eve & Day. ♿
Attendance: 205,285 (actual)

Belhaven

BELHAVEN MEMORIAL MUSEUM, INC., 211 E. Main St., Belhaven Town Hall, 2nd Fl., Belhaven, NC 27810-1413. Mailing Address: P.O. Box 220, Belhaven, NC 27810-0220. Tel.: 252-943-6817. Fax: 252-943-2357.
Web Site: www.beaufort-county.com/Belhaven/museum/Belhaven.htm
Key Personnel: Pres., Ed Harris.
Institution Type/Description: Local History Museum.
Hours & Admission Prices: Mon.-Tues & Thurs.-Sun. 1-5. No charge; donations accepted.
Attendance: 5,000 (estimated)

Belmont

DANIEL STOWE BOTANICAL GARDEN, 6500 S. New Hope Rd., Belmont, NC 28012-8788. Tel.: 704-825-4490. Fax: 704-829-1240.
E-mail: larkin@dsbg.org
Web Site: www.dsbg.org
Key Personnel: Exec. Dir., Kara Newport; Dir. Mktg. & Guest Svcs., Jim Hoffman, APR.
Institution Type/Description: Botanical Garden.
Hours & Admission Prices: Daily 9-5. Adults $12, seniors 60 & over $11, children 4-12 $6; discounts to AAA members; members & children under 4 no charge. Closed New Year's Day; Thanksgiving; Christmas. ♿

Benson

BENSON MUSEUM OF LOCAL HISTORY, 102 W. Main St., Benson, NC 27504-1504. Tel.: 919-894-3825. Facebook: Benson Museum of Local History.
E-mail: thobgood@townofbenson.com
Key Personnel: Dir., Terry Hobgood; Chm. (V), Hampton Whittington.
Institution Type/Description: History Museum.
Hours & Admission Prices: Wed.-Sat. tours vary. No charge; donations accepted. ♿
Attendance: 400 (estimated)

Bethania

HISTORIC BETHANIA VISITOR CENTER, 5480 Bethania Rd., Bethania, NC 27010. Mailing Address: P.O. Box 259, Bethania, NC 27010. Tel.: 336-922-0434.
E-mail: visitorcenter@townofbethania.org
Web Site: www.townofbethania.org

Institution Type/Description: Visitor Center.
Hours & Admission Prices: Call for hours.

Black Mountain

SWANNANOA VALLEY MUSEUM & HISTORY CENTER, 223 W. State St., Black Mountain, NC 28711-3408. Mailing Address: P.O. Box 306, Black Mountain, NC 28711-0306. Tel.: 828-669-9566. Facebook: @svmuseum.
E-mail: info@swannanoavalleymuseum.org
Web Site: www.swannanoavalleymuseum.org
Key Personnel: Dir., Anne Chesky Smith; Chm. (V), Wendell Begley; Asst. Dir., Katherine Cutshall.
Institution Type/Description: History Museum.
Hours & Admission Prices: March-Dec. Tues.-Sat. 10-5. No charge; donations accepted. ♿
Attendance: 7,227 (estimated)

Blowing Rock

APPALACHIAN HERITAGE MUSEUM, 175 Mystery Hill Lane, Blowing Rock, NC 28605. Tel.: 828-264-2792. Fax: 828-262-3292.
E-mail: mysteryhillnc@gmail.com
Web Site: www.mysteryhill-nc.com
Institution Type/Description: History Museum.
Hours & Admission Prices: June-Aug. daily 9-8; Sept.-May daily 9-5. Adults 13-59 $9, seniors 60 & over $8, children 5-12 $7; discounts to groups; children 4 & under no charge.
Attendance: 40,000 (estimated)

BLOWING ROCK ART AND HISTORY MUSEUM (BRAHM), 159 Chestnut St., Blowing Rock, NC 28605. Mailing Address: P.O. Box 828, Blowing Rock, NC 28605. Tel.: 828-295-9099. Fax: 828-295-9029.
E-mail: director@blowingrockmuseum.org
Web Site: www.blowingrockmuseum.org
Key Personnel: Exec. Dir., Lee Carol Giduz.
Institution Type/Description: Art & History Museum.
Hours & Admission Prices: June-Oct. Tues.-Wed. & Fri.-Sat. 10-5, Thurs. 10-7, Sun. 1-5; Nov.-May Tues.-Wed. & Fri.-Sat. 10-5, Thurs. 10-7. Adults $7, seniors $6, children & students $4; discounts to NARM members; active military, museum members and children 4 & under no charge. ♿
Attendance: 10,000 (actual)

MYSTERY HILL - HERITAGE & NATIVE ARTIFACT MUSEUM, 129 Mystery Hill Lane, Blowing Rock, NC 28605-9549. Tel.: 828-264-2792.
E-mail: mysteryhillnc@gmail.com
Web Site: www.mysteryhill-nc.com
Institution Type/Description: Historic House Museum: built in 1903.
Hours & Admission Prices: June-Aug. daily 9-8; Sept.-May 9-5. Adults 13-59 $9, seniors 60 & over $8, children 5-12 $7; discounts to groups; children 4 & under no charge.

Boone

THE CHILDREN'S PLAYHOUSE, 400 Tracy Circle, Boone, NC 28607-3846. Tel.: 828-263-0011.
E-mail: kathyparham@gmail.com
Web Site: www.goplayhouse.org/
Key Personnel: Exec. Dir., Kathy Parham.
Institution Type/Description: Children's Museum.
Hours & Admission Prices: June-July Tues.-Sat. 10-5; Aug.-May Tues.-Fri. 10-5, Sat. 10-3. Admission $5; children one & under and members no charge.

DANIEL BOONE NATIVE GARDENS, 651 Horn in the West Dr., Boone, NC 28607. Mailing Address: P.O. Box 1705, Boone, NC 28607-1705. Facebook.
E-mail: danielboonegardens1963@gmail.com
Web Site: danielboonenativegardens.org
Institution Type/Description: Native Gardens.
Hours & Admission Prices: May-Oct. daily 10-6. Adults 16 & over $2.

HICKORY RIDGE LIVING HISTORY MUSEUM, 591 Horn in the West Dr., Boone, NC 28607-4283. Mailing Address: P.O. Box 295, Boone, NC 28607-0295. Tel.: 828-264-2120. Fax: 828-264-9089. Facebook: Hickory Ridge Living History Museum.
E-mail: saha.museum@gmail.com

Web Site: www.hickoryridgemuseum.com
Formerly: Hickory Ridge Homestead
Key Personnel: Cur., Dave Davis.
Institution Type/Description: History Museum.
Hours & Admission Prices: May-Oct. Sat. 9-1; late June to mid-Aug. Tues.-Sun. 5:30-8. Admission by donation; charge for private group tours.

TURCHIN CENTER FOR THE VISUAL ARTS, 423 W. King St., Boone, NC 28607-3523. Mailing Address: ASU Box 32139, Boone, NC 28608. Tel.: 828-262-3017. Fax: 828-262-7546. Facebook: Turchin Center.
E-mail: turchincenter@appstate.edu
Web Site: www.tcva.org
Key Personnel: Dir., Hank T. Foreman.
Institution Type/Description: Art Gallery.
Hours & Admission Prices: Tues.-Thurs. & Sat. 10-6, Fri. 12-8. No charge; donations accepted.
Attendance: 81,205 (actual)

Brevard

SILVERMONT MANSION 2ND FLOOR HOUSE MUSEUM, 364 E. Main St., Brevard, NC 28712. Tel.: 828-884-3156.
E-mail: info@silvermont.org
Key Personnel: Co-Chm. (V), Jan Osborne; Co-Chm. (V), Lee Stewart.
Institution Type/Description: Historic House Museum: built in 1917. Listed on the National Register of Historic Places.
Hours & Admission Prices: Call for hours. No charge; donations accepted.
Attendance: 500 (estimated)

SPIERS GALLERY, Sims Art Center, Brevard College, 1 Brevard College Dr., Brevard, NC 28712-4283. Tel.: 828-884-2243.
E-mail: bbyers@brevard.edu
Web Site: www.Brevard.edu
Key Personnel: Dir., Bill Byers.
Institution Type/Description: Art Gallery.
Hours & Admission Prices: Sept.-May Mon.-Fri. 8-3. No charge. &
Attendance: 1,000 (estimated)

TRANSYLVANIA HERITAGE MUSEUM, 40 W. Jordan St., Brevard, NC 28712-3641. Mailing Address: P.O. Box 2347, Brevard, NC 28712-2347. Tel.: 828-884-2347.
Key Personnel: Exec. Dir., Rebecca Suddeth.
Institution Type/Description: History Museum.
Hours & Admission Prices: Wed.-Sat. 10-5. No charge.

Bryson City

SMOKY MOUNTAIN TRAINS, 100 Greenlee St., Bryson City, NC 28713. Mailing Address: P.O. Box 1490, Bryson City, NC 28713-1490. Tel.: 828-488-5200, 866-914-5200. Fax: 828-488-3162.
E-mail: info@smokymountaintrains.com
Web Site: www.smokymountaintrains.com
Key Personnel: C.E.O. & Cur., Timothy O. Cooper.
Institution Type/Description: Train Museum.
Hours & Admission Prices: Mon.-Sat. 9:30-5; call to confirm. Adults $9, children 3-11 $5; children under 3 no charge. Closed New Year's Day; Thanksgiving; Christmas. &
Attendance: 30,000 (actual)

Burgaw

BURGAW TRAIN DEPOT, 115 S. Dickerson St., Burgaw, NC 28425. Mailing Address: P.O. Box 1096, Burgaw, NC 28425. Tel.: 910-259-9817. Fax: 910-300-6116.
E-mail: info@burgawchamber.com
Institution Type/Description: Historic Building: housed in the former train depot; c.1850. Listed on the National Register of Historic Places.
Hours & Admission Prices: Daily 9-5.

PENDER COUNTY MUSEUM, 200 W. Bridgers St., Burgaw, NC 28425. Mailing Address: P.O. Box 1380, Burgaw, NC 28425-1380. Tel.: 910-259-8543.
E-mail: penderhist@hotmail.com
Web Site: pendercountymuseum.webs.com
Key Personnel: Chm. (V), Jeanette Jones; Pres. (V), Jeanette Jones.
Institution Type/Description: Local History Museum.

Hours & Admission Prices: Thurs.-Fri. 1-4, Sat. 10-2. No charge; donations accepted.
Attendance: 500 (estimated)

Burlington

ALAMANCE BATTLEGROUND STATE HISTORIC SITE, 5803 South N.C. 62, Burlington, NC 27215. Tel.: 336-227-4785. Fax: 336-227-4787. Facebook: Alamance Battleground State Historic Site.
E-mail: alamance@ncdcr.gov
Web Site: www.alamancebattleground.nchistoricsites.org
Key Personnel: Historic Interpreter, Bill Thompson; Historic Site Asst., Lisa Cox.
Institution Type/Description: Historic Site.
Hours & Admission Prices: Tues.-Sat. 9-5. No charge; donations accepted. Closed major holidays. &
Attendance: 11,588 (actual)

ALAMANCE COUNTY HISTORICAL MUSEUM, 4777 S. Hwy. 62, Burlington, NC 27215-9295. Tel.: 336-226-8254. Facebook: Alamance County Historical Museum.
E-mail: achm@triad.twcbc.com
Web Site: www.alamancemuseum.org
Key Personnel: C.E.O. & Dir., William Vincent, Ph.D.; Pres. (V), Frances Powell Barnes.
Institution Type/Description: Historic House Museum: housed in the former home of E.M. Holt.
Hours & Admission Prices: Tues.-Fri. 9-4, Sat. 10:30-4, Sun. 1-4. No charge; donations accepted. Closed federal holidays.
Attendance: 15,000 (actual)

CEDAROCK HISTORICAL FARM, 4242 R. Dean Coleman Rd., Burlington, NC 27215. Mailing Address: c/o Friends of Cedarock Historical Farm, 5949 Lindley Mill Rd., Graham, NC 27253. Tel.: 336-570-6759.
Web Site: www.alamance-nc.com
Institution Type/Description: Historical Farm: housed on the site of John & Polly Garrett 1830 farm.
Hours & Admission Prices: Call for hours.

CONSERVATORS' CENTER, 676 E. Hughes Mill Rd., Burlington, NC 27217. Mailing Address: P.O. Box 882, Mebane, NC 27302. Tel.: 336-421-0065, 800-979-3370.
E-mail: nfo@conservatorscenter.org
Web Site: www.conservatorscenter.org
Key Personnel: Co Founder, Doug Evans; Co Founder, Mindy Stinner.
Institution Type/Description: Wildlife Refuge & Conservation Center.
Hours & Admission Prices: By appointment.

TEXTILE HERITAGE MUSEUM AT GLENCOE, 2406 Glencoe St., Burlington, NC 27217. Mailing Address: 2314 Westover Ter., Burlington, NC 27215-4789. Tel.: 336-260-0038.
E-mail: textileheritage@triad.rr.com
Web Site: www.textileheritagemuseum.org
Key Personnel: Dir., Jerrie Nall; Sec. & Treas., Kathy Barry; Archivist, Fred Archer.
Institution Type/Description: Historic Building Museum: housed in the former 1880 Glencoe Mill Company Store and Office in the Glencoe Mill Village.
Hours & Admission Prices: Sat.-Sun. 1-4; groups by appointment. No charge; donations accepted. Closed New Year's Eve & Day; Easter; Thanksgiving; Christmas. &
Attendance: 10,000 (estimated)

WHISTLESTOP EXHIBIT AT COMPANY SHOPS STATION, 101 N. Main St., Burlington, NC 27217. Tel.: 336-570-1444.
E-mail: raillines@ncrr.com
Web Site: www.whistlestopncrr.com
Institution Type/Description: Railroad History Museum.
Hours & Admission Prices: Daily 7:30-7; other times by appointment. No charge. &

Burnsville

MOUNT MITCHELL STATE PARK & MUSEUM, 2388 Hwy. 128, Burnsville, NC 28714. Tel.: 828-675-4611.
E-mail: mount.mitchell@ncparks.gov
Institution Type/Description: Park Museum.

Hours & Admission Prices: Museum: May-Oct. daily 0-6. Park: March & Oct. daily 8-7; April & Sept. daily 8-8; May-Aug. daily 8-9; Nov.-Feb. daily 8-6. Closed Christmas.

YANCEY HISTORY ASSOCIATION - RUSH WRAY MUSEUM, McElroy House, 11 Academy St., Burnsville, NC 28714. Mailing Address: 3 Academy St., Burnsville, NC 28714-2944. Tel.: 828-678-9587.
E-mail: yhmuseum@frontier.com
Key Personnel: Pres. (V), Elaine Boone; Museum Shop Mgr., C. Carter.
Institution Type/Description: History Museum: housed in the McElroy House; c.1840. Dr. Lloyd Bailey Annex Museum.
Hours & Admission Prices: Wed.-Sat. 10-4. Adults $5; members no charge. &
Attendance: 5,000 (estimated)

Buxton

HATTERAS ISLAND VISITOR CENTER, Cape Hatteras Light Station, Buxton, NC 27920. Mailing Address: 1401 National Park Dr., Manteo, NC 27954-9451. Tel.: 252-473-2111 & 995-4474. Fax: 252-995-4633.
E-mail: caha_information@nps.gov
Web Site: www.nps.gov/caha
Key Personnel: Supt., Dave Hallac.
Institution Type/Description: Park Museum.
Hours & Admission Prices: Center: Fri. before Memorial Day to Labor Day 9-6, Labor Day to Memorial Day weekend 9-5. No charge. Lighthouse: 3rd Fri. in April to Columbus Day 9-4:30. Adults $8, seniors 62 & over and children 12 & under $4; members no charge. Closed Christmas. &
Attendance: 4,500,000 (estimated)

Camden

CAMDEN COUNTY HERITAGE MUSEUM, 117 N. NC Hwy. 343, Camden, NC 27976. Tel.: 252-771-8333, 877-771-8333.
E-mail: camdenmuseum1777@gmail.com
Institution Type/Description: Historic Building: housed in the former Camden County jailhouse; c.1910.
Hours & Admission Prices: Mon.-Fri. 8-12 & 1-5; groups by appointment.

Cameron

ALOHA SAFARI ZOO, 159 Mini Lane, Cameron, NC 28348. Tel.: 919-770-7109.
E-mail: alohasafarizoonc@gmail.com
Web Site: alohasafarizoo.org
Institution Type/Description: Zoo.
Hours & Admission Prices: Sat.-Sun. 10-5. Admission $5.

Canton

CANTON AREA HISTORICAL MUSEUM, 36 Park St., Canton, NC 28716-4324. Tel.: 828-646-3412.
E-mail: cponton@cantonnc.com
Key Personnel: Cur., Caroline Ponton; Chm. (V), Cole Smathers.
Institution Type/Description: History Museum.
Hours & Admission Prices: Mon. & Tues. 1-5, Fri. & Sat. 10-3. No charge; donations accepted. &
Attendance: 100 (estimated)

Carrboro

THE ARTSCENTER, 300-G E. Main St., Carrboro, NC 27510-2359. Tel.: 919-929-2787, ext. 201. Fax: 919-969-8574. Facebook: ArtsCenter Live.
E-mail: info@artscenterlive.org
Web Site: www.artscenterlive.org
Formerly: The Art School
Institution Type/Description: Art Gallery.
Hours & Admission Prices: Call for hours. No charge.
Attendance: 98,000 (actual)

Carthage

BRYANT HOUSE, 3361 Mt. Carmel Rd., Carthage, NC 28327-8337. Mailing Address: P.O. Box 324, Southern Pines, NC 28388-0324. Tel.: 910-692-2051. Fax: 910-692-2051.
E-mail: moorehistory@connectnc.net
Web Site: moorehistory.com

Institution Type/Description: Historic House: built c.1820.
Hours & Admission Prices: May-Oct. 2nd & 4th Sun. of month 2-4; other times by appointment.
Attendance: 500 (estimated)

CARTHAGE MUSEUM, 202 Rockingham St., Carthage, NC 28327. Mailing Address: Town of Carthage Government, 4396 Hwy. 15501, Carthage, NC 28327. Tel.: 910-947-2331.
Institution Type/Description: History Museum.
Hours & Admission Prices: By appointment.

Cary

PAGE-WALKER ARTS & HISTORY CENTER, 119 Ambassador Loop, Cary, NC 27512. Mailing Address: P.O. Box 8005, Cary, NC 27512-8005. Tel.: 919-460-4963. Fax: 919-388-1141.
E-mail: kris.carmichael@townofcary.org
Web Site: www.townofcary.org
Key Personnel: Dir., Kristina Carmichael; Chm. (V), Bob Myers.
Institution Type/Description: History Museum: housed in a former hotel; built in 1868. Listed on the National Register of Historic Places.
Hours & Admission Prices: Mon.-Thurs. 10-9:30, Fri. 10-5, Sat. 10-1; other times by appointment. No charge. &
Attendance: 25,000 (estimated)

STEVENS NATURE CENTER, 2616 Kildaire Farm Rd., Cary, NC 27518-9612. Mailing Address: P.O. Box 8005, Cary, NC 27512-8005. Tel.: 919-387-5980.
Institution Type/Description: Nature Center.
Hours & Admission Prices: May-Sept. Mon.-Sat. 10-7, Sun. 1-7; Oct.-April Mon.-Sat. 10-5, Sun. 1-5. Closed holidays.

Cashiers

MORDECAI ZACHARY HOUSE, 1940 Hwy. 107 S., Cashiers, NC 28717. Mailing Address: P.O. Box 104, Cashiers, NC 28717-0104. Tel.: 828-743-7710. Fax: 828-743-7169. Facebook: Zachary-Tolbert House.
E-mail: info@cashiershistoricalsociety.org
Web Site: www.cashiershistoricalsociety.org/
Formerly: Zachary-Tolbert House
Key Personnel: Exec. Dir., Alan Rhew; Volunteer Chm., Gayle Eby.
Institution Type/Description: Historic House Museum.
Hours & Admission Prices: May-Oct. Fri.-Sat. 11-3. Tours: no charge; donations accepted. &
Attendance: 1,750 (estimated)

Caswell Beach

OAK ISLAND LIGHTHOUSE, 300-A Caswell Beach Rd., Caswell Beach, NC 28465. Mailing Address: Friends of Oak Island Lighthouse, 1100 Caswell Beach Rd., Caswell Beach, NC 28465.
E-mail: oakislandlighthouse@gmail.com
Web Site: oakislandlighthouse.org
Institution Type/Description: Historic Lighthouse.
Hours & Admission Prices: Tours to 2nd level of lighthouse: Memorial Day to Labor Day Wed. & Sat. 10-2. Tours to top of lighthouse: by appointment.

Catawba

HISTORIC MURRAY'S MILL, 1489 Murray's Mill Rd., Catawba, NC 28609. Mailing Address: P.O. Box 73, Newton, NC 28658. Tel.: 828-241-4299.
E-mail: cchajlml@gmail.com
Institution Type/Description: History Museum.
Hours & Admission Prices: Sat. 9-5, Sun. 1-5. Adults $5; discounts to groups.

Cedar Mountain

GLASS FEATHER STUDIO & GARDENS, 200 Glass Feather Dr., Cedar Mountain, NC 28718-0241. Mailing Address: P.O. Box 241, Cedar Mountain, NC 28718-0241. Tel.: 828-885-8457.
E-mail: info@glassfeather.com
Web Site: glassfeather.com
Key Personnel: Owner, Patricia Travis, M.A.
Institution Type/Description: Art Gallery.
Hours & Admission Prices: April-Dec. 21 Wed.-Sat. 10-5.

Chadbourn

1910 A.C.L. DEPOT, 1st Ave. & Colony St., Chadbourn, NC 28431. Mailing Address: P.O. Box 100, Chadbourn, NC 28431-0100.
E-mail: hildaf28431@yahoo.com
Key Personnel: Dir., Edna T. Yates; Treas., Hilda Bullard.
Institution Type/Description: History Museum; housed in a former train depot built in 1910. Listed on the Register of Historic Places.
Hours & Admission Prices: Tues. 1-5, Sun. 2-5; other times by appointment. No charge; donations accepted.
Attendance: 1,000 (estimated)

Chapel Hill

ACKLAND ART MUSEUM, The University of North Carolina at Chapel Hill, 101 S. Columbia St. near Franklin St., Chapel Hill, NC 27514. Mailing Address: Campus Box 3400, The University of North Carolina at Chapel Hill, Chapel Hill, NC 27599-3400. Tel.: 919-966-5736. Fax: 919-966-1400. TDD: 919-962-0837; Facebook: Ackland Art Museum.
E-mail: ackland@email.unc.edu
Web Site: www.ackland.org
Key Personnel: Dir., Katie Ziglar; Deputy Dir. Curatorial Affairs, Peter Nisbet; Dir. Academic Programs, Carolyn Allmendinger; Asst. Dir. Collections, Lauren Turner; Mgr. School & Community Programs, Jenny Marvel; Dir. Communications, Emily Bowles; Registrar, Scott Hankins; Museum Shop Mgr., Alice Southwick; Cur. Asian Art, Bradley M. Bailey.
Institution Type/Description: Art Museum.
Hours & Admission Prices: See website for hours. No charge; donations accepted. &
Attendance: 60,000 (estimated)

CAROLINA BASKETBALL MUSEUM, 450 Skipper Bowles Dr., Chapel Hill, NC 27599. Tel.: 919-962-6000. Fax: 919-962-6002. Facebook: Carolina Basketball Museum.
E-mail: candrews@uncaa.unc.edu
Web Site: goheels.com
Key Personnel: Dir., Clara A. Perry.
Institution Type/Description: Sports Museum.
Hours & Admission Prices: Tues.-Fri. 10-4, Sat. 9-1; groups by appointment. No charge; donations accepted.
Attendance: 60,000 (actual)

CHARLES KURALT LEARNING CENTER & MUSEUM, Univ. of North Carolina Chapel Hill, School of Journalism, Carroll Hall, 2nd Fl., Chapel Hill, NC 27599-3365. Tel.: 919-962-1204.
E-mail: mjschool@unc.edu
Web Site: mj.unc.edu
Institution Type/Description: History Museum.
Hours & Admission Prices: Tues. & Thurs. 2-4; other times by appointment.

COKER ARBORETUM OF THE NORTH CAROLINA BOTANICAL GARDEN, 100 Old Mason Farm Rd., Chapel Hill, NC 27514. Mailing Address: The University of North Carolina at Chapel Hill, CB #3375 Totten Center, Chapel Hill, NC 27599-3375. Tel.: 919-962-0522. Fax: 919-962-3531.
E-mail: ncbg@unc.edu
Web Site: www.ncbg.unc.edu
Key Personnel: Dir., Dr. Peter White; Cur., Dan Stern.
Institution Type/Description: Arboretum.
Hours & Admission Prices: June-Aug. Mon.-Fri. 8-6, Sat. 9-6, Sun. 1-6; Sept.-May Mon.-Fri. 8-5, Sat. 9-5, Sun. 1-5. No charge; donations accepted. &
Attendance: 10,000 (estimated)

HORACE WILLIAMS HOUSE, 610 E. Rosemary St., Chapel Hill, NC 27514-3720. Tel.: 919-942-7818. Facebook: Preservation Chapel Hill.
E-mail: info@preservationchapelhill.org
Web Site: www.preservationchapelhill.com
Key Personnel: Dir., Cheri Szcodronski; Pres. (V), Megan Wooley-Ousdahl.
Institution Type/Description: Historic House Museum; built c.1854.
Hours & Admission Prices: Tues.-Fri. 10-4; other times by appointment. No charge; donations accepted.
Attendance: 6,000 (estimated)

JORDAN LAKE EDUCATIONAL STATE FOREST, 2832 Big Woods Rd., Chapel Hill, NC 27514. Tel.: 919-542-1154.
E-mail: jordanlakeesf.ncfs@ncagr.gov
Web Site: www.ncesf.org
Institution Type/Description: State Forest.
Hours & Admission Prices: July-Aug. Tues.-Fri. 9-5, Sat.-Sun. 11-8; Sept.-June Tues.-Fri. 9-5, Sat.-Sun. 11-5.

KIDZU CHILDREN'S MUSEUM, 201 S. Estes Dr., Ste. A9, Chapel Hill, NC 27514. Tel.: 919-933-1455.
E-mail: info@kidzuchildrensmuseum.org
Web Site: www.kidzuchildrensmuseum.org
Key Personnel: Dir., Lisa Van Deman; Chair, Betsy Bennett.
Institution Type/Description: Children's Museum.
Hours & Admission Prices: Tues.-Sat. 10-5, Sun. 1-5. Admission one & over $7.50; discounts to Association of Children's Museum members; members & children under one no charge.
Attendance: 90,000 (estimated)

MOREHEAD PLANETARIUM AND SCIENCE CENTER, 250 E. Franklin St., Chapel Hill, NC 27514. Mailing Address: CB #3480 UNC, Chapel Hill, NC 27599. Tel.: 919-962-1236. Fax: 919-962-1238.
E-mail: mhplanet@unc.edu
Web Site: www.moreheadplanetarium.org
Key Personnel: Dir., Todd Boyette; Dir. Advancement, Jeff Hill; Dir. Experiential Design, Jay Heinz; Dir. Finance, Susan Durham; Dir. Programs & Strategic Initiatives, Crystal Harden.
Institution Type/Description: Planetarium and Science Center.
Hours & Admission Prices: See website for hours. Adults $7.68, students, children & senior citizens $6.51; members no charge. &
Attendance: 146,000 (estimated)

NORTH CAROLINA BOTANICAL GARDEN, 100 Old Mason Farm Rd., Chapel Hill, NC 27517. Mailing Address: The University of North Carolina at Chapel Hill, CB 3375, Chapel Hill, NC 27599-3375. Tel.: 919-962-0522. Fax: 919-962-3531.
E-mail: ncbg@unc.edu
Web Site: www.ncbg.unc.edu
Key Personnel: C.E.O. & Dir., Dr. Peter S. White; Pres. (V), Thomas W. Earnhardt, Ph.D.; Assoc. Dir. Devel., Charlotte Jones-Roe; Asst. Dir. Conservation, John L. Randall.
Institution Type/Description: Botanical Garden.
Hours & Admission Prices: June-Aug. Mon.-Fri. 8-5, Sat. 9-6, Sun. 1-6; Sept.-May Mon.-Fri. 8-5, Sat. 9-5, Sun. 1-5. No charge; donations accepted. Closed New Year's Day; Martin Luther King Jr. Day; Thanksgiving; Christmas. &
Attendance: 100,000 (estimated)

NORTH CAROLINA COLLECTION GALLERY, Wilson Library, 200 South Rd., Chapel Hill, NC 27514. Mailing Address: The University of NC at Chapel Hill, North Carolina Collection, Campus Box 3930, Chapel Hill, NC 27514-8890. Tel.: 919-962-0104.
E-mail: ljacobso@email.unc.edu
Web Site: library.unc.edu/wilson/gallery.html
Key Personnel: Dir., Linda Jacobson.
Institution Type/Description: History Museum.
Hours & Admission Prices: Mon.-Fri. 9-5, Sat. 9-1, Sun. 1-5. No charge. Closed major holidays. &
Attendance: 13,000 (estimated)

PATTERSON'S MILL COUNTRY STORE, 5109 Farrington Rd., Chapel Hill, NC 27517. Tel.: 919-493-8149.
Institution Type/Description: History Museum.
Hours & Admission Prices: Call for hours. No charge; donations accepted.

Charlotte

BECHTLER MUSEUM OF MODERN ART, 420 S. Tryon St., Charlotte, NC 28202. Tel.: 704-353-9200. Fax: 704-353-9299. Facebook, Instagram & Twitter: @thebechtler.
E-mail: info@bechtler.org
Web Site: bechtler.org
Key Personnel: C.E.O. & Pres., John Boyer; Chm. (V), Cyndee Paterson; Museum Shop Mgr., Patty Stevens; Dir. Mktg., Sharon Holm.
Institution Type/Description: Art Museum.
Hours & Admission Prices: Mon. & Wed.-Sat. 10-5, Sun. 12-5. Adults $8, seniors 65 & up, college students, & educators $6, youth 11-18 $4; children 10 & under and members no charge. Closed major holidays. &
Attendance: 48,269 (actual)

BILLY GRAHAM LIBRARY, 4330 Westmont Dr., Charlotte, NC 28217-1001. Tel.: 704-401-3200. Facebook, Instagram, Twitter.

E-mail: LibraryStudents@billygraham.org
Web Site: billygrahamlibrary.org
Key Personnel: Vice Pres., Tom Phillips.
Institution Type/Description: Library & Historic Home: childhood home of Billy Graham has been restored & moved to this location.
Hours & Admission Prices: Mon.-Sat. 9:30-5; groups of 15 or more by appointment. No charge. Closed New Year's Day; Thanksgiving; Christmas Eve & Day. &

CAROLINAS AVIATION MUSEUM, 4672 First Flight Dr., Charlotte, NC 28208-5770. Tel.: 704-997-3770. Fax: 704-469-3193. Facebook: @ft1549; Instagram: @carolinasaviationmuseum.
E-mail: 1549@carolinasaviation.org
Web Site: www.carolinasaviation.org
Formerly: Carolinas Historic Aviation Compassion
Key Personnel: Pres., Katie Swaringen; Controller, Lynn Wyles; Museum Store Mgr., Carrie Howard; Events, Jan Black; Education Coord., Kent Lupton; Facilities Mgr., Kyle Karbowski.
Institution Type/Description: Aviation Museum.
Hours & Admission Prices: Mon.-Fri. 10-4, Sat. 10-5, Sun. 1-5. Adults $12, senior citizens $10, students $8; discounts to groups & military; children 5 & under no charge. Closed New Year's Day; Easter; Thanksgiving; Christmas Eve & Day. &
Attendance: 460,000 (estimated)

CHARLOTTE MECKLENBURG LIBRARY, 310 N. Tryon St., Charlotte, NC 28202-2139. Tel.: 704-416-0100. Facebook, Instagram & Twitter: @cmlibrary.
Web Site: www.cmlibrary.org
Key Personnel: C.E.O., Lenoir C. Keesler, Jr.; Dir. Libraries, David Singleton; Dir. Mktg., Communications & Advocacy, Cordelia Anderson; Dir. Financing & Funding, Angie Myers; Dir. Technology & Innovation, Seth Ervin; Dir. Human Resources, Deanna Griffin; Dir. Real Estate, Frank Blair; Exec. Dir. Charlotte Mecklenburg Library Foundation, Jenni Gaisbauer.
Institution Type/Description: Public Library.
Hours & Admission Prices: Mon.-Thurs. 9-8, Fri.-Sun. 1-5. No charge. Closed national holidays. &

CHARLOTTE MUSEUM OF HISTORY, 3500 Shamrock Dr., Charlotte, NC 28215-3214. Tel.: 704-568-1774. Fax: 704-566-1817. Facebook: @charlottemuseumofhistory; Twitter: @CLThistory.
E-mail: info@charlottemuseum.org
Web Site: www.charlottemuseum.org
Key Personnel: Pres. & C.E.O., Kay Peninger; Chm. (V), Mary Turk-Meena.
Institution Type/Description: History Museum.
Hours & Admission Prices: Museum: Tues.-Sat. 10-5, Sun. 1-5; Guided Tours: Tues.-Sat. every hour noon-4. Adult $10, children 6-17 & seniors 62 & up $7; discounts to military & groups; children under 6 & members no charge. &
Attendance: 54,928 (actual)

CLAYWORKS GALLERY, 4506 Monroe Rd., Charlotte, NC 28205-7716. Tel.: 704-344-0795. Fax: 704-344-4842. Facebook & Twitter: @claywrsclt; Instagram: @claywrksclt.
E-mail: adellinger@clayworksinc.org
Web Site: clayworksinc.org
Key Personnel: Exec. Dir., Adrienne Dellinger; Studio Mgr., Kimberly Tyrrell; Community Impact Coord., Susan Hughes.
Institution Type/Description: Art Gallery.
Hours & Admission Prices: By appointment.

DISCOVERY PLACE NATURE, 1658 Sterling Rd., Charlotte, NC 28209-1599. Tel.: 704-372-6261. Facebook: @DiscoveryPlaceNature; Twitter: @DPNature.
E-mail: info@discoveryplace.org
Web Site: nature.discoveryplace.org
Formerly: Charlotte Nature Museum
Key Personnel: Dir., Marvin Bouknight; C.E.O. & Pres., Catherine Wilson Horne; Chm. (V), Mark McGoldrick.
Institution Type/Description: Nature Museum.
Hours & Admission Prices: Tues.-Fri. 9-4, Sat. 9-5, Sun. noon to 5. Admission $8; discounts to military & groups of 15 or more; children under 2 & members no charge. ASTC reciprocal. Closed New Year's Day; Easter; Independence Day; Thanksgiving; Christmas Eve & Day. &
Attendance: 69,000 (actual)

DISCOVERY PLACE SCIENCE, 301 N. Tryon St., Charlotte, NC 28202-2138. Tel.: 704-372-6261. Facebook, Instagram & Twitter: @DiscoveryPlace.
E-mail: info@discoveryplace.org
Web Site: science.discoveryplace.org

Key Personnel: Pres. & C.E.O., Catherine Wilson Horne; Chm. (V), Mark McGoldrick; Chief Advancement Officer, Sarah Bordy; C.F.O. & Vice Pres. Business Affairs, Deanna Dycus; Vice Pres. Talent Mgmt., Ervine Gourdine; Vice Pres. Exhibitions & Operations, Joanie Vandenburg Philipp; Vice Pres. Mktg. & Communications, Debra Smul.
Institution Type/Description: Science & Technology Center.
Hours & Admission Prices: Mon.-Fri. 9-4, Sat. 9-5, Sun. noon to 5. Museum: adults $17, seniors $15, children $13; members no charge. IMAX: adults $10, seniors & children $9; combination tickets available. Closed Easter; Thanksgiving; Christmas Eve & Day. &
Attendance: 665,473 (actual)

ELDER GALLERY, 1520 S. Tryon St., Charlotte, NC 28203. Tel.: 704-370-6337. Facebook: @eldergallery; Instagram: @elder_art.
E-mail: lelder@elderart.com
Web Site: www.elderart.com
Key Personnel: Founder, Larry Elder.
Institution Type/Description: Art Gallery.
Hours & Admission Prices: Wed.-Fri. 10-5:30, Sat. 10-2; other times by appointment.

HARVEY B. GANTT CENTER FOR AFRICAN AMERICAN ARTS + CULTURE, 551 S. Tryon St., Charlotte, NC 28202. Tel.: 704-547-3700. Fax: 704-547-3770. Facebook, Instagram & Twitter: @hbganttcenter.
E-mail: info@ganttcenter.org
Web Site: www.ganttcenter.org
Formerly: Afro-American Cultural Center
Key Personnel: Pres. & C.E.O., David R. Taylor; C.O.O., Bonita Buford; Dir. Special Events & Merchandising, Chanel M. Davis; Creative Dir., Jessica Gaynelle Moss; Mktg. Mgr., Loan Sewer; Membership & Annual Giving Mgr., Shannon Walker; Asst. Registrar, Alexys Taylor; Museum Shop Assoc., Priscilla Walters; Database Mgr., Mark Garrison; Guest Svcs. Mgr., Herman Marigny; Mktg. Specialist, Kimberly H. Noble.
Institution Type/Description: Cultural Center: housed in an AIA award winning facility.
Hours & Admission Prices: Tues.-Sat. 10-5, Sun. 1-5. Adults $9, college students, educators, seniors & military $7, youth 6-17 $7; discounts to groups of 10 or more; children 5 & under and members no charge. Closed New Year's Day; Easter; Independence Day; Thanksgiving; Christmas. &
Attendance: 50,000 (estimated)

HISTORIC DOWD HOUSE, 2216 Monument St., Charlotte, NC 28208. Mailing Address: c/o Mecklenburg County Park & Recreation, 5841 Brookshire Blvd., Charlotte, NC 28216. Tel.: 704-336-7600.
E-mail: park-admin@mecklenburgcountync.gov
Web Site: charmeck.org/mecklenburg/county/ParkandRec
Key Personnel: Dir. Parks & Recreation, Jim Garges; Deputy Dir. Parks & Recreation, Michael Kirschman.
Institution Type/Description: Historic House: housed in the former Headquarters for Camp Greene Army Training Base during WWI; built in 1879.
Hours & Admission Prices: 3rd day each month by appointment.

HISTORIC ROSEDALE PLANTATION, 3427 N. Tryon St., Charlotte, NC 28206-2052. Tel.: 704-335-0325. Fax: 704-335-0384.
E-mail: dhunter@historicrosedale.org
Web Site: historicrosedale.org
Key Personnel: Exec. Dir., Deborah A. Hunter; Pres., Hugh Dussek, Ph.D.; Vice Pres., Dusty Holcomb; Education Cur., Allison Varriale.
Institution Type/Description: General Museum.
Hours & Admission Prices: Tours: Thurs.-Sun. 1:30 & 3; groups of 15 or more by appointment. Adults $10, senior citizens 65 & up and children 4-18 $8; discounts to AAA members; members and children 3 & under with guardian no charge. Closed major holidays.
Attendance: 10,000 (actual)

IMAGINON: THE JOE & JOAN MARTIN CENTER, 300 E. Seventh St., Charlotte, NC 28202. Tel.: 704-416-4600. Facebook & Instagram: @ImaginOn.
Web Site: www.imaginon.org
Key Personnel: C.E.O., Lee Keesler.
Institution Type/Description: Children's Museum.
Hours & Admission Prices: Mon.-Thurs. 9-8, Fri. & Sat. 9-5, Sun. 1-5.

JERALD MELBERG GALLERY, 625 S. Sharon Amity Rd., Charlotte, NC 28211-2811. Tel.: 704-365-3000. Facebook: @JeraldMelbergGallery; Instagram: @jeraldmelberg.
E-mail: gallery@jeraldmelberg.com

Web Site: www.jeraldmelberg.com
Key Personnel: Dir., Jerald Melberg.
Institution Type/Description: Art Gallery.
Hours & Admission Prices: Mon.-Fri. 10-6, Sat. 10-4; other times by appointment.
&

LEVINE MUSEUM OF THE NEW SOUTH, 200 E. Seventh St., Charlotte, NC 28202-2508. Tel.: 704-333-1887. Fax: 704-333-1896. Facebook, Instagram & Twitter: @LevineMuseum.
E-mail: khill@museumofthenewsouth.org
Web Site: www.museumofthenewsouth.org
Key Personnel: Pres. & C.E.O., Kathryn Hill; Sr. Vice Pres. Audience Engagement, Dan Spock; Sr. Vice Pres. Mktg. & Communications, Mandy Drakeford; C.F.O., Lisa Hordlt; Mktg. & Communications, Melody Gross; Museum Shop Mgr., Bertha Tillman.
Institution Type/Description: History Museum.
Hours & Admission Prices: Mon.-Sat. 10-5, Sun. 12-5. Adults $9, seniors 62 & over, educators, college students & active military $7, children 6-18 $5, members & children 5 & under no charge. Closed New Year's Day; Easter; Memorial Day; Independence Day; Labor Day; Thanksgiving; Christmas Eve & Day. &
Attendance: 50,000 (estimated)

THE LIGHT FACTORY, 1817 Central Ave., Charlotte, NC 28205-5109. Tel.: 704-333-9755. Facebook & Twitter: @TheLightFactory.
E-mail: info@lightfactory.org
Web Site: lightfactory.org
Key Personnel: Exec. Dir., Kay Tuttle; Dir. Education, Laurie Schorr; Dir. Community Engagement, Eric Pickersgill.
Institution Type/Description: Photography & Film Gallery.
Hours & Admission Prices: Wed.-Sat. noon to 6; other times by appointment. No charge; donations accepted. Closed New Year's Day; Easter; Independence Day; Thanksgiving; Christmas; major holidays. &
Attendance: 70,000 (estimated)

MCDOWELL NATURE CENTER AND PRESERVE, 15222 York Rd., Charlotte, NC 28278. Tel.: 704-588-5224.
E-mail: chris.matthews@mecklenburgcountync.gov
Web Site: charmeck.org/mecklenburg/county/ParkandRec
Key Personnel: Division Dir., Nature Preserves & Natural resources, Chris Matthews; Environmental Education Mgr., Stephen Hutchinson.
Institution Type/Description: Nature Center.
Hours & Admission Prices: Nature Center: Mon.-Sat. 9-5, Sun. 1-5. Nature Preserve: daily 7am to sunset. No charge.

MINT MUSEUM RANDOLPH, 2730 Randolph Rd., Charlotte, NC 28207-2031. Tel.: 704-337-2000. Fax: 704-337-2101.
E-mail: info@mintmuseum.org
Web Site: www.mintmuseum.org
Formerly: Mint Museum of Art
Key Personnel: Interim Pres. & C.E.O., Bruce Larowe; Chm., Richard T. Williams; C.F.O., Gary Blankemeyer; Dir. Learning & Engagement, Cynthia Moreno; Dir. Collections & Exhibitions, Michele Leopold; Chief Registrar, Katherine Steiner; Dir. Library & Archives, Joyce Weaver; Dir. Facilities, Cindy Clayton; Dir. Public Rels. & Publications, Leigh Dyer; Dir. Community Rels., Rubie Britt-Height; Sr. Cur. American, Modern & Contemporary Art, Dr. Jonathan Stuhlman; Sr. Cur. Craft, Design & Fashion, Annie Carlano; Cur. Decorative Arts, Brian D. Gallagher; Mgr. & Buyer, Retail Operations, Amy Grigg.
Institution Type/Description: Art Museum: housed in 1835 first branch of the U.S. Mint, expanded in 1967 & 1985.
Hours & Admission Prices: Wed. 11-9, Thurs.-Sat. 11-6, Sun. 1-5. Adults $12, seniors & students $9; members no charge. Closed major holidays. &
Attendance: 118,000 (estimated)

MINT MUSEUM UPTOWN, 500 S. Tryon St., Charlotte, NC 28202. Tel.: 704-337-2000. Fax: 704-337-2101.
E-mail: info@mintmuseum.org
Web Site: www.mintmuseum.org
Formerly: Mint Museum of Craft + Design
Key Personnel: Interim Pres. & CEO, Bruce Larowe; Chm. (V), Richard T. Williams; C.F.O., Gary Blankemeyer; Dir. Learning & Engagement, Cynthia Moreno; Dir. Collections & Exhibitions, Michele Leopold; Chief Registrar, Katherine Steiner; Dir. Library & Archives, Joyce Weaver; Dir. Facilities, Cindy Clayton; Dir. Community Rels., Rubie Britt-Height; Dir. Public Rels. & Publications, Leigh Dyer; Sr. Cur. American, Modern & Contemporary Art, Dr. Jonathan Stuhlman; Sr. Cur. Craft, Design & Fashion, Annie Carlano; Cur. Decorative Arts, Brian D. Gallagher; Mgr. & Buyer, Retail Operations, Amy Grigg.
Institution Type/Description: Arts & Crafts Museum.
Hours & Admission Prices: Wed. 11-9, Thurs.-Sat. 11-6, Sun. 1-5. Adults $12, seniors & students $9; members no charge. Closed major holidays. &

NASCAR HALL OF FAME, 400 E. Martin Luther King, Jr. Blvd., Charlotte, NC 28202. Tel.: 704-654-4400. Facebook, Instagram & Twitter: @nascarhall.
E-mail: guestservices@nascarhall.com
Web Site: www.nascarhall.com
Key Personnel: Exec. Dir., Winston Kelley; C.E.O., Tom Murray.
Institution Type/Description: Sports Museum & Hall of Fame.
Hours & Admission Prices: Daily 10-6. Adult $19.95, military & seniors $17.95, children $12.95. High Octane Combo Packages: adults $27-$38. &
Attendance: 170,500 (actual)

PROVIDENCE GALLERY, 601-A Providence Rd., Charlotte, NC 28207. Tel.: 704-333-4535. Twitter: @charlottencarts.
E-mail: providenceframes@bellsouth.net
Web Site: www.providencegallery.net
Key Personnel: Resident Artist, Rod Wimer.
Institution Type/Description: Art Gallery.
Hours & Admission Prices: Mon.-Fri. 9-5, Sat. 10-2; other times by appointment.

SHAIN GALLERY, 2823 Selwyn Ave., Charlotte, NC 28209. Tel.: 704-334-7744. Facebook: @ShainGallery.
E-mail: shainart@earthlink.net
Web Site: www.shaingallery.com
Key Personnel: Owner, Gaby Shain; Dir., Sybil Godwin.
Institution Type/Description: Art Gallery.
Hours & Admission Prices: Mon.-Sat. 10-5; other times by appointment.

SPIRIT SQUARE CENTER FOR ARTS AND EDUCATION, 345 N. College St., Charlotte, NC 28202-2113. Tel.: 704-372-1000.
E-mail: marketingvp@ncbpac.org
Web Site: www.blumenthalarts.org
Key Personnel: Pres., Tom Gabbard; Vice Pres. Operations, Bill Dantos; Vice Pres. Mktg., Wendy Oglesby; Vice Pres. Devel., Cindy Rice; Vice Pres. Education, Ralph Beck.
Institution Type/Description: Art Gallery.
Hours & Admission Prices: Call for hours.
Attendance: 298,729 (estimated)

UNC CHARLOTTE BOTANICAL GARDENS, 9201 University City Blvd., Charlotte, NC 28223. Tel.: 704-687-8622. Facebook & Instagram: UNCCharlotteGardens.
E-mail: jgillman@uncc.edu
Web Site: gardens.uncc.edu
Key Personnel: Dir., Dr. Jeff Gillman; Asst. Dir., Paula Gross; Office Mgr., Amparo Gill; Greenhouse Mgr., Tammy Blume; Greenhouse Mgr., John Denti; Susie Harwood Garden Mgr., Teri Edwards; Van Landingham Glen Mgr., Meredith Hebden; Mktg. Mgr., Chris Claudio.
Institution Type/Description: Botanical Gardens.
Hours & Admission Prices: Gardens: daily dawn to dusk. Greenhouse: Mon.-Sat. 9-4, Sun. 1-4. No charge; donations accepted.
Attendance: 25,000 (estimated)

WELLS FARGO HISTORY MUSEUM CLOSED, 401 S. Tryon St., Charlotte, NC 28202. Mailing Address: Wells Fargo Historical Svcs., 420 Montgomery St., MAC-A0101-022, San Francisco, CA 94163. Tel.: 704-715-1866. Fax: 704-715-1867. Facebook: Wells Fargo.
E-mail: wfmuseum.clt@wellsfargo.com
Web Site: www.wellsfargohistory.com
Key Personnel: Museum Mgr., Sharon Robinson; Cur., Michelle Colandro.
Institution Type/Description: Company History Museum: housed in the Wells Fargo Bldg. adjacent to the Levine Cultural Campus.
Hours & Admission Prices: Tues.-Sat. 9-5. No charge. Closed bank holidays. &

WING HAVEN, 260 Ridgewood Ave., Charlotte, NC 28209-1632. Tel.: 704-331-0664. Facebook; Instagram; Twitter.
E-mail: admin@winghavengardens.org
Web Site: winghavengardens.org
Key Personnel: Exec. Dir., Barrett Sloan Ranson; Devel. Dir., Susan Little Evans; Garden Cur., Andrea Sprott; Garden Mgr., Ginny Barr; Volunteer Coord., Lydia Skardon.
Institution Type/Description: Public Garden.
Hours & Admission Prices: Wed.-Sat. 10-5. Adults $10; members and children under 10 no charge. Closed major holidays. &
Attendance: 20,000 (actual)

Cherokee

CHEROKEE HISTORICAL ASSOCIATION, 564 Tsali Blvd., Cherokee, NC 28719. Mailing Address: P.O. Box 398, Cherokee, NC 28719. Tel.: 828-497-2111, 866-554-4557. Fax: 828-497-6987.
E-mail: cherokeehistorical.info@gmail.com
Web Site: www.cherokeehistorical.org
Key Personnel: Exec. Dir., John Tissue; Village Dir., Laura Blythe; Opers. Mgr., Christopher McCoy; Program Coord., Philenia Walkingstick.
Institution Type/Description: History Museum: re-created 18th century Oconaluftee Indian Village.
Hours & Admission Prices: Tours: May to mid-Oct. Mon.-Sat. 9-4. Adults $18, children $14; children 5 & under no charge.

MOUNTAIN FARM MUSEUM-GREAT SMOKY MOUNTAINS NATIONAL PARK, 1194 Newfound Gap Rd., Cherokee, NC 28719-8249. Tel.: 828-497-1900 & 1904. Fax: 828-497-1910.
E-mail: grsm_smokies_information@nps.gov
Web Site: nps.gov/grsm
Key Personnel: Site Supvr., Lynda Doucette.
Institution Type/Description: Park Visitor Center.
Hours & Admission Prices: Call for hours. No charge; donations accepted. Closed Christmas. &
Attendance: 100,000 (estimated)

MUSEUM OF THE CHEROKEE INDIAN, 589 Tsali Blvd., Cherokee, NC 28719. Mailing Address: P.O. Box 1599, Cherokee, NC 28719-1599. Tel.: 828-497-3481. Fax: 828-497-4985.
E-mail: littlejohn@cherokeemuseum.org
Web Site: www.cherokeemuseum.org
Key Personnel: Management, Bo Taylor; Education, Barbara Duncan; Museum Shop Mgr., Sharon Littlejohn; Membership, Joyce Cooper.
Institution Type/Description: Cherokee Indian Museum.
Hours & Admission Prices: Memorial Day to Labor Day Mon.-Sat. 9-7, Sun. 9-5; Sept.-May daily 9-5. Adults $11, children 6-12 $7; complimentary subscription to Journal for members; discounts for AAA & AARP members Jan.-May, groups & AAM members; members & children 5 & under no charge. Closed New Year's Day; Thanksgiving; Christmas. &
Attendance: 150,000

Cherryville

C. GRIER BEAM TRUCK MUSEUM, 111 N. Mountain St., Cherryville, NC 28021-2940. Mailing Address: P.O. Box 238, Cherryville, NC 28021-0238. Tel.: 704-435-3072.
E-mail: info@beamtruckmuseum.com
Web Site: www.beamtruckmuseum.com
Key Personnel: C.E.O. & Chm. (V), Michael N. Beam; Pres., Sandra B. Dismukes; Museum Shop Mgr., Joseph C. Dismukes.
Institution Type/Description: Transportation Museum.
Hours & Admission Prices: Thurs. & Sat. 10-3, Fri. 10-5. No charge; donations accepted. Closed New Year's Day; Independence Day; Christmas Eve & Day. &
Attendance: 3,000 (estimated)

CHERRYVILLE HISTORICAL MUSEUM, 109 E. Main St., Cherryville, NC 28021-3406. Mailing Address: P.O. Box 307, Cherryville, NC 28021-0307. Tel.: 704-435-8011.
E-mail: chvhistorical@att.net
Key Personnel: Dir., Pat Sherrill; Pres. (V), Darrell Carpenter; Museum Shop Mgr., Katherine Goins.
Institution Type/Description: Historic Building: built in 1911.
Hours & Admission Prices: Sat. 10-2. No charge; donations accepted.
Attendance: 1,200 (estimated)

Clayton

CLEMMONS EDUCATIONAL STATE FOREST, 2411 Old U.S. 70 W., Clayton, NC 27520. Tel.: 919-553-5651.
E-mail: clemmonsesf.ncfs@ncagr.gov
Web Site: www.ncesf.org
Institution Type/Description: State Forest.
Hours & Admission Prices: March 1 to Nov. 30 Tues.-Fri. 9-5, Sat.-Sun. 11-5. No charge; donations accepted. &
Attendance: 56,000 (estimated)

Clemmons

ARBORETUM AT TANGLEWOOD, 4201 Manor House Cir., Clemmons, NC 27012. Mailing Address: 4061 Clemmons Rd., Clemmons, NC 27012. Tel.: 336-703-6400.
E-mail: sanderjp@forsyth.cc
Institution Type/Description: Arboretum.
Hours & Admission Prices: 7am to sunset. Entrance Fee: $2 per person. Closed Christmas.

Clinton

SAMPSON COUNTY HISTORY MUSEUM, 313 Lisbon St., Clinton, NC 28328. Mailing Address: P.O. Box 786, Clinton, NC 28329-0786. Tel.: 910-590-0007. Fax: 910-590-0007. Facebook: @SampsonHistory.
E-mail: schm@intrstar.net
Web Site: www.sampsonhmc.com
Key Personnel: Dir., Chris Woodson; Pres. (V), Kay Raynor; Cur., Ruth Pope; Asst., Brittany Hayes.
Institution Type/Description: History Museum.
Hours & Admission Prices: Thurs.-Sat. 10-4. No charge; donations accepted. &
Attendance: 5,000 (actual)

Columbia

COLUMBIA THEATER CULTURAL RESOURCES CENTER, 304 Main St., Columbia, NC 27925. Mailing Address: P.O. Box 55, Columbia, NC 27925. Tel.: 252-766-0200, 888-737-0437. Fax: 252-766-0202.
E-mail: ctcrcenter@embarqmail.com
Institution Type/Description: Historic Building: housed in the former Columbia Theater built in 1938 by German immigrant Fred Schlez.
Hours & Admission Prices: Wed.-Fri. 10-4.

POCOSIN LAKES NATIONAL WILDLIFE REFUGE - WALTER B. JONES, SR. CENTER FOR THE SOUNDS, 205 S. Ludington Dr., Columbia, NC 27925. Mailing Address: P.O. Box 55, Columbia, NC 27925. Tel.: 252-796-3004 & 3008. Fax: 252-796-3196.
E-mail: pocosinlakes@fws.gov
Web Site: www.fws.gov/pocosinlakes
Institution Type/Description: Wildlife Refuge & Visitor Center.
Hours & Admission Prices: Refuge: daily daylight hours. Center: May-Sept. Tues.-Sat. 10-4; Oct.-April Wed.-Sat. 10-4.
Attendance: 63,000

Columbus

HOUSE OF FLAGS MUSEUM, 33 Gibson St., Columbus, NC 28722. Mailing Address: P.O. Box 1090, Columbus, NC 28722. Tel.: 828-894-5640.
E-mail: flagmuseum@gmail.com
Web Site: www.houseofflags.org
Institution Type/Description: Flag History Museum.
Hours & Admission Prices: March-Nov. Tues. & Thurs. 10-1, Sat. 10-4; other times by appointment. No charge; donations accepted.

POLK COUNTY HISTORICAL ASSOCIATION MUSEUM, 60 Walker St., Columbus, NC 28722. Mailing Address: P.O. Box 503, Columbus, NC 28722-0503. Tel.: 828-894-3351.
Web Site: www.polkcounty.org; www.polknc.org
Key Personnel: Pres. (V), Ted Owens.
Institution Type/Description: History Museum.
Hours & Admission Prices: Tues. & Thurs. 10-1, Sat. 10-4; other times by appointment. No charge; donations accepted. &
Attendance: 1,500 (estimated)

Concord

BACKING UP CLASSICS AUTO MUSEUM, 4545 Concord Pkwy. S., Concord, NC 28027-4618. Tel.: 704-788-9500.
E-mail: info@morrisonmotorco.com
Web Site: www.morrisonmotorco.com
Key Personnel: Dir., Lindsay Morrison Hartman.
Institution Type/Description: Classic Car Museum.
Hours & Admission Prices: Mon.-Tues. & Thurs.-Sat. 10-5.

BOST GRIST MILL, 4701 Hwy. 200, Concord, NC 28025-8170. Tel.: 704-782-1600.
E-mail: bostgristmill@netzero.com
Web Site: www.bostgristmill.com
Institution Type/Description: Historic Grist Mill.
Hours & Admission Prices: By appointment. &

CHARLOTTE MOTOR SPEEDWAY, 5555 Concord Pkwy., S., Concord, NC 28027. Mailing Address: P.O. Box 600, Concord, NC 28026. Tel.: 704-455-3200, 800-455-3267.
E-mail: tickets@charlottemotorspeedway.com
Web Site: www.charlottemotorspeedway.com
Institution Type/Description: Sports Museum.
Hours & Admission Prices: Feel the Thrill Speedway Tour: Mon.-Sat. 9:30, 10:30, 11:30, 1:30, 2:30 & 3:30, Sun. 1:30, 2:30 & 3:30. Tours not available on race days. Adults $12, seniors 55 & over, military, EMS/Fire/Police personnel and children 9 & under $10. Over the Wall Tour: Mon.-Sat. 10:30 & 1:30, Sun. groups only. Adults $20, seniors 55 & over, military, EMS/Fire/Police personnel and children 9 & under $18.

HENDRICK MOTORSPORTS MUSEUM, 4400 Papa Joe Hendrick Blvd., Concord, NC 28262. Tel.: 704-455-3400, 877-467-4890 (Toll Free).
Institution Type/Description: Sports Museum.
Hours & Admission Prices: Mon.-Fri. 9-5, Sat. 10-4. No charge.

ROUSH FENWAY RACING MUSEUM, 4600 Roush Pl., N.W., Concord, NC 28027.
E-mail: roushracing@roushracing.com
Institution Type/Description: Auto Racing Museum.
Hours & Admission Prices: Mon.-Fri. 8-5.

SAM BASS GALLERY, 4030 Concord Pkwy. S., Concord, NC 28027-5024. Tel.: 800-556-5464. Fax: 704-455-6916.
E-mail: info@sambass.com
Web Site: www.sambass.com
Institution Type/Description: Art Gallery.
Hours & Admission Prices: Tues.-Fri. 10-12:30 & 1:30-5; groups by appointment.

Conover

CATAWBA COUNTY FIREFIGHTER'S MUSEUM, 3957 Herman Sipe Rd., Conover, NC 28613. Mailing Address: 100 A S. W. Blvd., Newton, NC 28658. Tel.: 828-466-0911 & 465-8238.
E-mail: mpettit@catawbacountync.gov
Institution Type/Description: Fire-Fighting Museum.
Hours & Admission Prices: Sat. 11-4, Sun. 1-4; other times by appointment.

Cooleemee

MILL HOUSE MUSEUM, 163 Cross St., Cooleemee, NC 27014. Mailing Address: P.O. Box 667, Cooleemee, NC 27014-0667. Tel.: 336-284-6040.
E-mail: blinky1@yadtel.net
Key Personnel: Dir., Lynn Rumley; Pres. (V), Tony Steele.
Institution Type/Description: History Museum.
Hours & Admission Prices: Guided Tours by appointment. Adults $4, seniors $3. &
Attendance: 3,000 (estimated)

TEXTILE HERITAGE MUSEUM, 131 Church St., Cooleemee, NC 27014. Mailing Address: P.O. Box 667, Cooleemee, NC 27014-0667. Tel.: 336-284-6040.
E-mail: blinky1@yadtel.net
Web Site: cooleemee.org
Key Personnel: Dir., Lynn Rumley; Pres. (V), Tony Steele.
Institution Type/Description: History Museum.
Hours & Admission Prices: Wed.-Sat. 10-4. No charge; donations accepted. &
Attendance: 3,000 (estimated)

Cornelius

THE COMMUNITY ARTS PROJECT GALLERY, 20700 N. Main St., Unit 112, Cornelius, NC 28031. Mailing Address: P.O. Box 1166, Davidson, NC 28036-1166. Tel.: 704-896-8980.
Institution Type/Description: Art Gallery.
Hours & Admission Prices: Mon.-Thurs. 9-5, Fri. 9-12.

MICHAEL WALTRIP RACING HEADQUARTERS, 20310 Chartwell Center Dr., Cornelius, NC 28031. Mailing Address: P.O. Box 640, Cornelius, NC 28031-0640. Tel.: 704-897-5555 & 655-9550.
Web Site: michaelwaltripracing.com
Institution Type/Description: Sports Museum.
Hours & Admission Prices: Mon.-Fri. 9-5.

Corolla

CURRITUCK BEACH LIGHTHOUSE, 1101 Corolla Village Rd., Corolla, NC 27927. Mailing Address: P.O. Box 58, Corolla, NC 27927. Tel.: 252-453-4939.
E-mail: info@currituckbeachlight.com
Web Site: www.currituckbeachlight.com
Institution Type/Description: Historic Lighthouse: built in 1875.
Hours & Admission Prices: late March to May & Sept. to late Nov. daily 9-5; Memorial Day to Labor Day Wed.-Thurs. 9-8, Fri.-Tues. 9-5. Admission $7; children 7 & under no charge. Closed Thanksgiving.

THE WHALEHEAD CLUB, 1100 Club Rd., Corolla, NC 27927. Mailing Address: P.O. Box 307, Corolla, NC 27927-0307. Tel.: 252-453-9040. Fax: 252-457-0129.
E-mail: director@whaleheadclub.com
Web Site: whaleheadclub.org
Key Personnel: Pres. (V), Jeanne Melggs; Public Rels., Shannon O'Sullivan; Treas., Kimberley Hoey; Cur., Jill Landen; Museum Shop Mgr., Donna Strartak.
Institution Type/Description: Historic House Museum: listed on the National Register of Historic Sites.
Hours & Admission Prices: Mon.-Sat. 9-5. Adults $9; discounts to AAM members, groups of 15 or more and children 8 & under no charge. Closed New Year's Day; Martin Luther King Jr. Day; Easter; Thanksgiving; Christmas Eve, Day & day after.
Attendance: 20,000 (estimated)

WILD HORSE MUSEUM, 1129 Corolla Village Rd., Corolla, NC 27927. Tel.: 252-453-8002. Fax: 252-453-8073.
E-mail: info@corollawildhorses.com
Web Site: www.corollawildhorses.com
Institution Type/Description: Horse Museum.
Hours & Admission Prices: Call for hours.

Creswell

PETTIGREW STATE PARK, 2252 Lake Shore Rd., Creswell, NC 27928. Tel.: 252-797-4475.
E-mail: pettigrew@ncparks.gov
Institution Type/Description: Park & American Indian History Museum.
Hours & Admission Prices: Call for hours.

SOMERSET PLACE STATE HISTORIC SITE, 2572 Lake Shore Rd., Creswell, NC 27928-9174. Tel.: 252-797-4560. Fax: 252-797-4171.
E-mail: somerset@ncdcr.gov
Web Site: www.nchistoricsites.org/somerset/somerset.htm
Key Personnel: Site Mgr., Karen Hayes.
Institution Type/Description: Plantation.
Hours & Admission Prices: Tues.-Sat. 9-5. No charge, donations accepted. Closed holidays. &
Attendance: 23,407 (actual)

Crossnore

CROSSNORE FINE ARTS GALLERY, Crossnore School, 205 Johnson Lane, Crossnore, NC 28616. Mailing Address: P.O. Box 249, Crossnore, NC 28616. Tel.: 828-733-3144 & 387-1695.
E-mail: artgallery@crossnoreschool.org
Web Site: www.crossnoregallery.org
Key Personnel: Mgr., Heidi Fisher.
Institution Type/Description: Art Gallery.
Hours & Admission Prices: Mon.-Sat. 9-5.

CROSSNORE WEAVERS AND GALLERY: A WORKING MUSEUM, 205 Johnson Ln., Crossnore, NC 28616. Mailing Address: P.O. Box 249, Crossnore, NC 28616-0249. Tel.: 828-733-4660. Fax: 828-733-3250.
E-mail: weavingroom@crossnoreschool.org
Web Site: www.crossnoreschool.org
Formerly: The Weaving Room.
Key Personnel: Dir., Martha Hill; Chm. (V), Freda Nichols.
Institution Type/Description: History Museum: listed on the National Register of Historical Places.
Hours & Admission Prices: Mon.-Sat. 9-5. No charge; donations accepted. Closed Easter; Thanksgiving; Christmas. &
Attendance: 5,500 (estimated)

Cullowhee

FINE ARTS MUSEUM - JOHN W. BARDO FINE AND PERFORMING ARTS CENTER, 199 Centennial Dr., Cullowhee, NC 28723. Tel.: 828-227-3591.
E-mail: ddrury@wcu.edu
Web Site: www.fineartmuseum.wcu.edu
Formerly: Fine Arts Museum - Western Carolina University Fine & Performing Arts Center
Key Personnel: Interim Dir., Denis Drury; Museum Technician, Kevin Kirkpatrick; Museum Attendant, Dawn Behling.
Institution Type/Description: Fine Arts Museum.
Hours & Admission Prices: Mon.-Wed. & Fri. 10-4, Thurs. 10-7. No charge; donations accepted. Closed university holidays. ㅎ
Attendance: 7,627 (actual)

MOUNTAIN HERITAGE CENTER, 176 Central Dr., Western Carolina University, Cullowhee, NC 28723. Tel.: 828-227-7129.
E-mail: atlane@email.wcu.edu
Web Site: www.wcu.edu/mhc
Key Personnel: Dir. & Cur., Pamela Meister; Education Specialist, Peter Koch; Coord. Events, Trina Royar; Administrative Support, Anne Lane.
Institution Type/Description: History Museum.
Hours & Admission Prices: Mon.-Wed. & Fri. 10-4, Thurs. 10-7. No charge; donations accepted. Closed university holidays. ㅎ
Attendance: 30,000 (estimated)

Currie

MOORES CREEK NATIONAL BATTLEFIELD, 40 Patriots Hall Dr., Currie, NC 28435. Tel.: 910-283-5591. Fax: 910-283-5351.
E-mail: jonathan_grubbs@nps.gov
Web Site: www.nps.gov/mocr
Key Personnel: Park Ranger, Jonathan Grubbs.
Institution Type/Description: Military Museum: located on the site of the Feb. 27, 1776 Battle of Moores Creek Bridge.
Hours & Admission Prices: Daily 9-5. No charge. Closed New Year's Day; Thanksgiving; Christmas. ㅎ
Attendance: 48,988 (actual)

Dallas

GASTON COUNTY MUSEUM OF ART AND HISTORY, 131 W. Main St., Dallas, NC 28034-2021. Mailing Address: P.O. Box 429, Dallas, NC 28034-0429. Tel.: 704-922-7681. Fax: 704-922-7683.
E-mail: gaston.museum@gastongov.com
Web Site: www.gastoncountymuseum.org
Key Personnel: Dir., Jeff Pruett; Trustee Chm., Vann Noblett; Administrative Asst., Elaine Jackson; Cur., Stephanie Elliott; Registrar, Regan Brooks.
Institution Type/Description: Art and History Museum: housed in 1852 Hoffman Hotel.
Hours & Admission Prices: Tues.-Fri. 10-5, Sat. 10-3; other times by appointment. No charge; donations accepted. Closed holidays. ㅎ
Attendance: 27,000 (estimated)

Danbury

J.E. PRIDDY'S GENERAL STORE, 2121 Sheppard Mill Rd., Danbury, NC 27016. Tel.: 336-593-8786.
Web Site: priddysgeneralstore.com
Institution Type/Description: Historic Building Museum: built in 1888.
Hours & Admission Prices: Mon.-Sat. 8-6.

Davidson

VAN EVERY/SMITH GALLERIES, 315 N. Main St., Davidson College Visual Arts Center, Davidson, NC 28036-9404. Mailing Address: P.O. Box 7117, Davidson, NC 28035-7117. Tel.: 704-894-2520 & 2519. Fax: 704-894-2691.
E-mail: brthomas@davidson.edu
Web Site: www.davidson.edu
Key Personnel: Dir., Brad Thomas.
Institution Type/Description: College Art Gallery.
Hours & Admission Prices: Sept.-May Mon.-Fri. 10-5, Sat.-Sun. 12-4. No charge. Closed college & national holidays. ㅎ
Attendance: 4,000 (actual)

Dunn

AVERASBORO BATTLEFIELD AND MUSEUM, 3300 Hwy. 82, Dunn, NC 28334-6571. Mailing Address: P.O. Box 1811, Dunn, NC 28335. Tel.: 910-891-5019.
E-mail: bpearce7@nc.rr.com
Institution Type/Description: History Museum.
Hours & Admission Prices: Call for hours. No charge; donations accepted. ㅎ
Attendance: 12,000 (estimated)

GENERAL WILLIAM C. LEE AIRBORNE MUSEUM, 209 W. Divine St., Dunn, NC 28334. Mailing Address: P.O. Box 1111, Dunn, NC 28334-1111. Tel.: 910-892-1947. Facebook.
E-mail: info@generalleeairbornemuseum.org
Web Site: generalleeairbornemuseum.org
Key Personnel: Pres., Oscar Harris.
Institution Type/Description: Military History Museum.
Hours & Admission Prices: Mon.-Fri. 8:30-4:30, Sat. 11-4; groups by appointment. No charge; donations accepted. Closed holidays.
Attendance: 1,500 (estimated)

Durham

BENNETT PLACE STATE HISTORIC SITE, 4409 Bennett Memorial Road, Durham, NC 27705-2307. Tel.: 919-383-4345. Facebook, Twitter.
E-mail: bennett@ncdcr.gov
Web Site: www.bennettplacehistoricsite.com
Formerly: Bennett Farm
Key Personnel: Site Mgr., Diane Smith; Pres. Support Group, Karen Edwards.
Institution Type/Description: Military Museum & Historic Farm: reconstructed c.1850 Bennett House.
Hours & Admission Prices: Tues.-Sat. 9-5. No charge; donations accepted. Closed major holidays. ㅎ
Attendance: 22,000 (estimated)

DUKE HOMESTEAD STATE HISTORIC SITE, 2828 Duke Homestead Rd., Durham, NC 27705-2726. Tel.: 919-627-6990.
E-mail: duke@ncdcr.gov
Web Site: dukehomestead.org
Key Personnel: Site Mgr., Jessica Shillingsford.
Institution Type/Description: Historic House: 1852 homestead of Washington Duke, founder of the American Tobacco Co.
Hours & Admission Prices: Tues.-Sat. 9-5. No charge; donations accepted. Closed New Year's Day; Thanksgiving; Christmas Eve & Day. ㅎ
Attendance: 22,500

HISTORIC STAGVILLE, 5828 Old Oxford Hwy., Durham, NC 27712-9758. Tel.: 919-620-0120. Facebook.
E-mail: info@stagville.org
Web Site: www.stagville.org
Institution Type/Description: Historic House.
Hours & Admission Prices: Halls: Tues.-Sat. 9-5. Tours: Tues.-Sat. 11, 1 & 3. No charge; donations accepted. Closed New Year's Day; Martin Luther King Jr. Day; Good Friday; Memorial Day; Independence Day; Labor Day; Veterans Day; Thanksgiving; Christmas. ㅎ
Attendance: 14,000 (estimated)

HISTORY OF MEDICINE COLLECTIONS, Duke University Medical Center Library, 411 Chapel Dr., 3rd Fl., Durham, NC 27710. Mailing Address: DUMC Box 90185, Durham, NC 27708. Tel.: 919-684-8549. Fax: 919-660-5934.
E-mail: mclhistory@mc.duke.edu
Web Site: www.mclibrary.duke.edu/hmc
Key Personnel: Cur., Rachel Ingold.
Institution Type/Description: University Library.
Hours & Admission Prices: By appointment. No charge. ㅎ
Attendance: 2,000 (estimated)

LYDA MOORE MERRICK GALLERY - THE HAYTI HERITAGE CENTER, 804 Old Fayetteville St., Durham, NC 27707. Tel.: 919-683-1709. Fax: 919-682-5869.
E-mail: info@hayti.org
Web Site: www.hayti.org
Institution Type/Description: Art Gallery.
Hours & Admission Prices: By appointment.

MUSEUM OF LIFE AND SCIENCE, 433 Murray Ave., Durham, NC 27704-3101. Tel.: 919-220-5429. Fax: 919-220-5575.

Web Site: lifeandscience.org
Formerly: North Carolina Museum of Life and Science
Key Personnel: Pres. & C.E.O., Barry Van Deman; Bd. Chm., Tracey Martin.
Institution Type/Description: Science & Technology Center.
Hours & Admission Prices: Tues.-Sat. 10-5, Sun. 12-5. Adults $14, senior citizens 65 & over and military with ID $11, children 3-12 $10; discounts to AAA members; members and children 2 & under no charge. Train Rides $3. Closed New Year's Day; Thanksgiving; Christmas. &
Attendance: 300,000 (actual)

NCCU ART MUSEUM, North Carolina Central University, Lawson St. (Btw. Fine Arts Bldg. & Music Bldg.), Durham, NC 27707. Mailing Address: P.O. Box 19555, Durham, NC 27703. Tel.: 919-530-6211. Fax: 919-560-5649.
Web Site: web.nccu.edu/artmuseum
Key Personnel: Dir., Kenneth G. Rodgers; Registrar, Pat Jones.
Institution Type/Description: University Art Museum.
Hours & Admission Prices: Tues.-Fri. 9-4:30, Sun. 2-4. No charge. &

NASHER MUSEUM OF ART AT DUKE UNIVERSITY, 2001 Campus Dr., Durham, NC 27705-1003. Mailing Address: P.O. Box 90732, Durham, NC 27708-0732. Tel.: 919-684-5135. Fax: 919-681-8624.
E-mail: nasherinfo@duke.edu
Web Site: www.nasher.duke.edu
Formerly: Duke University Museum of Art
Key Personnel: Dir., James H. Semans.
Institution Type/Description: Art Museum.
Hours & Admission Prices: Tues.-Wed. & Fri.-Sat. 10-5, Thurs. 10-9, Sun. 12-5. Suggested Donation: adults $5, seniors & Duke Alumni $4, non-Duke students $3; children under 16, members, Duke students, faculty & staff no charge. Closed New Year's Day; Independence Day; Thanksgiving; Christmas Eve & Day. &
Attendance: 115,000 (actual)

SARAH P. DUKE GARDENS, Duke University West Campus, 420 Anderson St., Durham, NC 27708. Mailing Address: Duke University, P.O. Box 90341, Durham, NC 27708-0341. Tel.: 919-684-3698.
E-mail: bill.lefevre@duke.edu
Key Personnel: Exec. Dir., William M. LeFevre.
Institution Type/Description: Gardens.
Hours & Admission Prices: Daily. No charge; donations accepted.
Attendance: 300,000

21C MUSEUM HOTEL DURHAM, 111 N. Corcoran St., Durham, NC 27701. Tel.: 919-956-6700.
E-mail: nfortunegreeley@21cMuseum.org
Web Site: www.21cmuseumhotels.com/durham/
Key Personnel: Museum Mgr., Nell Fortune-Greeley.
Institution Type/Description: Contemporary Art Gallery.
Hours & Admission Prices: See website for hours. No charge.

Edenton

CHOWAN ARTS COUNCIL GALLERY - THE GALLERY, 504 S. Broad St., Edenton, NC 27932. Tel.: 252-482-8005.
E-mail: CACEDENTON@GMAIL.COM
Web Site: www.chowanarts.com
Key Personnel: Dir., Murielle Harmon; Gallery Liaison, Mary Altman.
Institution Type/Description: Art Gallery.
Hours & Admission Prices: Mon.-Fri. 11-4, Sat.-Sun. 10-2. No charge; donations accepted. &

EDENTON NATIONAL FISH HATCHERY, 1102 W. Queen St., Edenton, NC 27932. Tel.: 252-482-4118. Fax: 252-482-2106.
E-mail: stephen_jackson@fws.gov
Web Site: www.fws.gov/edenton
Key Personnel: Hatchery Mgr., Stephen C. Jackson.
Institution Type/Description: Aquarium.
Hours & Admission Prices: By appointment.

HISTORIC EDENTON STATE HISTORIC SITE, 108 N. Broad St., Edenton, NC 27932. Tel.: 252-482-2637. Fax: 252-482-3499. Facebook: Historic Edenton SHS.
E-mail: edenton@ncdcr.gov
Web Site: www.edenton.nchistoricsites.org
Formerly: James Iredell House State Historic Site

Key Personnel: Site Mgr., Karen Ipock; Operations Mgr., Judith W. Chilcoat; Historic Interpreter, Keith Furlough; Historic Interpreter, Sharon K. Keeter; Historic Interpreter, Charles Boyette; Historic Interpreter, Carolyn A. Owens; Maintenance Mechanic, Blake S. Harmon.
Institution Type/Description: Historic House Museum.
Hours & Admission Prices: Tues.-Sat. 9-5. Guided Walking and Trolley Tours: $2-$10; discounts to children 12 & under. Visitor Center: no charge. Closed state holidays. &
Attendance: 24,821 (actual)

Elizabeth City

THE JAQUELIN JENKINS GALLERY, 516 E. Main St., Elizabeth City, NC 27907. Tel.: 252-338-6455. Fax: 252-338-3156.
E-mail: info@artsaoa.com
Web Site: www.artsaoa.com
Institution Type/Description: Art Gallery.
Hours & Admission Prices: Call for hours.

MUSEUM OF THE ALBEMARLE, 501 S. Water St., Elizabeth City, NC 27909-4863. Tel.: 252-335-1453. Fax: 252-335-0637.
E-mail: moa@ncdcr.gov
Web Site: www.museumofthealbemarle.com
Key Personnel: Admin., William J. McCrea; Administrative Officer, Mary Cherry Tirak; Cur., Wanda Lassiter; Coord. Education, Charlotte Patterson; Facilities Mgr., Wayne Mathews; Lighting, Electronics & Interactive Technician, Lynette Sawyer; Educator, Lori Meads; Utility Worker, William Seymore; Museum Shop Mgr., Mary Temple; Office Asst., Rhiana Srebro; Public Information Asst., Lisa Doepker; Exhibit Designer, Jamie McCargo; Carpenter, Matthew Ferrell; Utility Worker, Ben Shipley; Collections Specialist, Clay Swindell.
Institution Type/Description: History Museum.
Hours & Admission Prices: Tues.-Sat. 10-4. No charge; donations accepted. Closed state holidays. &
Attendance: 42,627 (actual)

PORT DISCOVER: NORTHEASTERN NORTH CAROLINA'S CENTER FOR HANDS-ON SCIENCE, 611 E. Main St., Elizabeth City, NC 27909. Tel.: 252-338-6117. Facebook: @portdiscoverNC.
E-mail: mike@portdiscover.org
Web Site: portdiscover.wildapricot.org
Key Personnel: Dir., Robin Kelly-Goss; Dir. Membership & Mktg., Dana Parker.
Institution Type/Description: Science Center.
Hours & Admission Prices: Tues.-Fri. 1-5, Sat. 10-4; groups by appointment. No charge; donations accepted.

Ellerbe

RANKIN MUSEUM OF AMERICAN HERITAGE, 131 W. Church St., Ellerbe, NC 28338. Tel.: 910-652-6378. Fax: 910-652-6130. Facebook; Instagram.
E-mail: rankinmuseum@gmail.com
Web Site: www.rankinmuseum.org
Key Personnel: Dir., Emilie Cobb; Pres., Brett Webb; Vice Pres., Julian Carter; Financial Dir., Jim Chavis.
Institution Type/Description: General Museum.
Hours & Admission Prices: Mon.-Tues. & Thurs.-Sat. 9-5, Sun. 2-5. Adults $4, AAA travel members $3, students $1; discounts to groups; members and children 4 & under no charge. Closed New Year's Day; Easter; Thanksgiving; Christmas Eve & Day. &
Attendance: 3,000 (estimated)

Farmville

MAY MUSEUM & PARK, 3802 S. Main, Farmville, NC 27828-8548. Mailing Address: P.O. Box 623, Farmville, NC 27828-0086. Tel.: 252-753-6725. Cell: 252-327-8859.
E-mail: maymuseum@farmville-nc.com
Key Personnel: Dir., Deb Higgins.
Institution Type/Description: History Museum.
Hours & Admission Prices: Mon.-Fri. 9-5. No charge; donations accepted. &
Attendance: 2,000 (estimated)

Fayetteville

ARTS COUNCIL OF FAYETTEVILLE/CUMBERLAND COUNTY, 301 Hay St., Fayetteville, NC 28301-5535. Mailing Address: P.O. Box 318, Fayetteville, NC 28302-0318. Tel.: 910-323-1776. Fax: 910-323-1727.

E-mail: admin@theartscouncil.com
Web Site: www.theartscouncil.com
Key Personnel: Exec. Dir., Deborah Martin Mintz; Gen. Mgr., Nancy Silver; Dir. Opers., Robert Pinson; Dir. Mktg., Mary Kinney; Exec. Asst., Jennifer Gilbertson.
Institution Type/Description: Arts Center: housed in c.1910 former Post Office & Library.
Hours & Admission Prices: Mon.-Thurs. 8:30-5, Fri. 8:30-Noon; other times by appointment. No charge. Closed New Year's Day; Good Friday; Memorial Day; Independence Day; Labor Day; Thanksgiving; Christmas. &
Attendance: 85,000 (estimated)

CAPE FEAR BOTANICAL GARDEN, 536 N. Eastern Blvd., Fayetteville, NC 28301. Mailing Address: P.O. Box 53485, Fayetteville, NC 28305. Tel.: 910-486-0221. Fax: 910-486-4209.
E-mail: info@capefearbg.org
Web Site: www.capefear.org
Institution Type/Description: Botanical Garden.
Hours & Admission Prices: March to mid-Dec. Mon.-Sat. 10-5, Sun. 12-5; mid-Dec. to Feb. Mon.-Sat. 10-5. Adults $6, children 6-12 $1; children 5 & under and members no charge.

DAVID MCCUNE INTERNATIONAL ART GALLERY - METHODIST UNIVERSITY, William F. Bethune Center for Visual Arts, 5400 Ramsey St., Fayetteville, NC 28311. Tel.: 910-425-5379.
E-mail: sfoti@davidmccunegallery.org
Web Site: www.davidmccunegallery.org
Key Personnel: Exec. Dir., Silvana M. Foti.
Institution Type/Description: Art Gallery.
Hours & Admission Prices: Tues.-Fri. 11-5 & Sat. 12-4. No charge. Closed Sunday, Monday & holidays.

FASCINATE-U CHILDREN'S MUSEUM, 116 Green St., Fayetteville, NC 28301-5024. Mailing Address: P.O. Box 2671, Fayetteville, NC 28302-2671. Tel.: 910-829-9171. Fax: 910-433-1639.
E-mail: webmail@fascinate-u.com
Web Site: www.fascinate-u.com
Institution Type/Description: Children's Museum.
Hours & Admission Prices: Tues. & Thurs.-Fri. 9-5, Wed. 9-7, Sat. 10-5, Sun. 12-5. Children $4, adults $3. Closed New Year's Day; Easter; Thanksgiving; Christmas Eve & Day.

FAYETTEVILLE AREA TRANSPORTATION AND LOCAL HISTORY MUSEUM, 325 Franklin St., Fayetteville, NC 28301. Mailing Address: 121 Lamon St., Fayetteville, NC 28301-4953. Tel.: 910-433-1457.
Web Site: www.fayettevillenc.net/sites/st_trainstation2.htm
Institution Type/Description: Local History Museum.
Hours & Admission Prices: Call for hours.

FAYETTEVILLE INDEPENDENT LIGHT INFANTRY ARMORY & MUSEUM, 210 Burgess St., Fayetteville, NC 28301. Mailing Address: 227 Hillside Ave., Fayetteville, NC 28301. Tel.: 910-433-1457, 800-255-8217.
Institution Type/Description: Military History Museum.
Hours & Admission Prices: By appointment. No charge.

MUSEUM OF THE CAPE FEAR HISTORICAL COMPLEX, 801 Arsenal Ave., Fayetteville, NC 28305. Mailing Address: P.O. Box 53693, Fayetteville, NC 28305-3693. Tel.: 910-486-1330. Fax: 910-486-1585.
E-mail: david.reid@ncdcr.gov
Web Site: museumofthecapefear.ncdcr.gov
Key Personnel: Admin., David E. Reid; Assoc. Cur. Education, Leisa Greathouse; Exhibit Designer, Margaret Shearin; Carpenter & Exhibit Builder, Jim Frederickson; Assoc. Cur. Research, Kathryn A. Beach; 1897 Poe House Educator, Megan Maxwell; Arsenal Park Educator, Chris Woodson; Historic Interpreter, Jim Brisson; Collections Asst., Bill Surface.
Institution Type/Description: History Museum: octagonal structure & building foundations from the federal arsenal in Arsenal Park.
Hours & Admission Prices: Tues.-Sat. 10-5, Sun. 1-5. No charge; donations accepted. Closed New Year's Day; Easter; Independence Day; Thanksgiving; Christmas Eve & Day. &
Attendance: 25,000 (actual)

NORTH CAROLINA VETERANS PARK & VISITORS CENTER, 300 Bragg Blvd., Fayetteville, NC 28301. Tel.: 910-433-1547.
Web Site: www.ncveteranspark.org
Institution Type/Description: Military Veterans Memorial.
Hours & Admission Prices: Tues.-Sat. 10-5, Sun. 12-5.

U.S. ARMY AIRBORNE & SPECIAL OPERATIONS MUSEUM, 100 Bragg Blvd., Fayetteville, NC 28301-4806. Tel.: 910-643-2766. Fax: 910-643-2792.
E-mail: jim.bartlinski.civ@mail.mil
Web Site: www.asomf.org
Key Personnel: Dir., Jim Bartlinski.
Institution Type/Description: Military Museum.
Hours & Admission Prices: Mon. Federal holidays & Tues.-Sat. 10-5, Sun. 12-5. No charge; donations accepted. Closed New Year's Day; Easter; Thanksgiving; Christmas. &
Attendance: 148,000 (actual)

Ferguson

WHIPPOORWILL ACADEMY AND VILLAGE, 11928 NC Hwy. 268 W., Ferguson, NC 28624. Mailing Address: P.O. Box 458, Ferguson, NC 28624. Tel.: 336-973-3237. Facebook: Whippoorwill Academy.
E-mail: whippoorwillvillage@gmail.com
Key Personnel: Co-Dir., Margaret Martine; Co-Dir., Sharon Underwood; Mgr., Collee Riddle.
Institution Type/Description: History Museum.
Hours & Admission Prices: April-mid Nov. Sat. 1-5; Wed.-Fri. groups of 10 or more by appointment. Adults $3, children 5-12 $1; children under 5 no charge. &
Attendance: 6,000 (estimated)

Flat Rock

CARL SANDBURG HOME NATIONAL HISTORIC SITE, 81 Carl Sandburg Lane, Flat Rock, NC 28731-8635. Tel.: 828-693-4178. Fax: 828-693-4179.
E-mail: carl_administration@nps.gov
Web Site: www.nps.gov/carl
Key Personnel: Park Supt., Mr. Tyrone Brandyburg.
Institution Type/Description: Historic House: 1838 home of Confederate Sec. of Treasury C. G. Memminger & later acquired by Carl Sandburg in 1945.
Hours & Admission Prices: Daily 9-5. Adults $5; children under 17 no charge. &
Attendance: 100,000 (estimated)

Fontana Dam

FONTANA DAM & VISITORS CENTER, Hwy. 28 S., Fontana Dam, NC 28733-9700. Mailing Address: Tennessee Valley Authority, 400 W. Summit Hill Dr., Knoxville, TN 37902. Tel.: 800-467-1388, 828-498-2234.
E-mail: lsmith@tva.gov
Web Site: www.tva.com/sites/fontana.htm
Key Personnel: Site Mgr., Laura Smith.
Institution Type/Description: History Museum.
Hours & Admission Prices: Visitor Center: April-Oct. daily 9-7. &

Forest City

RUTHERFORD COUNTY FARM MUSEUM, 240 Depot St., Forest City, NC 28043-3654. Tel.: 828-248-1248.
Key Personnel: Dir., Wilbur Burgin.
Institution Type/Description: Farm Museum.
Hours & Admission Prices: Wed.-Sat. 10-4. Adults $2; children no charge. &
Attendance: 300 (estimated)

Fort Bragg

82ND AIRBORNE DIVISION MUSEUM, Bldg. C-6841, 5108 Ardennes St., Fort Bragg, NC 28310. Mailing Address: P.O. Box 70119, Fort Bragg, NC 28307-0119. Tel.: 910-432-3443 & 5307. Fax: 910-432-1642.
Web Site: www.bragg.army.mil/18abn/museums.htm
Key Personnel: Dir. & Cur., John W. Aarsen; Chm. (V), Richard O'Hore; Registrar, Betty J. Rucker; Archivist, Jimmie Hallis; Museum Shop Mgr., Shantay McQueen.
Institution Type/Description: Military History Museum.

Hours & Admission Prices: Tues.-Sat. 10-4:30 (valid photo ID required). No charge; donations accepted. Closed New Year's Day; Thanksgiving; Christmas. &

Attendance: 65,000 (actual)

JFK SPECIAL WARFARE MUSEUM, Ardennes & Marion Sts., Bldg. D-2502, Fort Bragg, NC 28307. Mailing Address: JFK SW/ SF Branch Museum, P.O. Box 70060, Fort Bragg, NC 28307-5000. Tel.: 910-432-1533 & 4272. Fax: 910-432-4062.
E-mail: merrittr@soc.mil
Web Site: www.soc.mil/swcs/museum/html
Key Personnel: Cur., Roxanne M. Merritt; Museum Assn. Pres., Col. William Palmer, (USA Ret.); Gift Shop Mgr., Betty Amaker.
Institution Type/Description: U.S. Army Military Museum.
Hours & Admission Prices: Tues.-Fri. 10:30-4., Sat. 11-4. No charge; donations accepted. Closed most federal holidays. &
Attendance: 56,750 (actual)

Four Oaks

BENTONVILLE BATTLEFIELD STATE HISTORIC SITE, 5466 Harper House Rd., Four Oaks, NC 27524-9125. Tel.: 910-594-0789. Fax: 910-594-0027.
E-mail: bentonville@ncdcr.gov
Web Site: www.bentonvillebattlefield.nchistoricsites.org
Key Personnel: Site Mgr., Donald B. Taylor; Site Asst. Mgr., Derrick Brown; Site Interpreter, Jeff Fritzinger.
Institution Type/Description: Historic Site.
Hours & Admission Prices: Tues.-Sat. 9-5. No charge; donations accepted. Closed most major holidays.
Attendance: 28,000 (actual)

HOWELL WOODS ENVIRONMENTAL LEARNING CENTER, 6601 Devil's Racetrack Rd., Four Oaks, NC 27524. Tel.: 919-938-0115.
E-mail: mamassengill@johnstoncc.edu
Web Site: www.johnstoncc.edu/howellwoods
Key Personnel: Dir., Jordan Astoske.
Institution Type/Description: Wildlife & Nature Center.
Hours & Admission Prices: Call for hours.

Franklin

FRANKLIN GEM & MINERAL MUSEUM, 25 Phillips St., Franklin, NC 28734-3029. Tel.: 828-369-7831 & 8915.
E-mail: franklingemsociety@gmail.com
Key Personnel: Pres. (V), Al Pribble; Museum Shop Mgr., John Hayes.
Institution Type/Description: Gem & Mineral Museum: housed in the former Macon County Public Jail; built in 1850.
Hours & Admission Prices: May-Oct. Mon.-Sat. 12-4; Nov.-April Sat. 12-4; groups by appointment. No charge. Closed Independence Day.
Attendance: 9,000 (estimated)

MACON COUNTY HISTORICAL SOCIETY & MUSEUM, 36 W. Main, Franklin, NC 28734. Tel.: 828-524-9758.
E-mail: fund43@aol.com
Key Personnel: Dir., R. Steven Rice; Chm. (V), Robert Poindexter.
Institution Type/Description: History Museum: housed in the Pendergrass Building, c.1904.
Hours & Admission Prices: May-Oct. Tues.-Fri. 10-5, Sat. 1-5; Nov.-April Tues.-Fri. 10-4, Sat. 1-4; other times by appointment. No charge; donations accepted.
Attendance: 5,000 (estimated)

THE SCOTTISH TARTANS MUSEUM, 86 E. Main St., Franklin, NC 28734-3026. Tel.: 828-524-7472.
E-mail: tartans@scottishtartans.org
Web Site: www.scottishtartans.org/
Institution Type/Description: General Museum.
Hours & Admission Prices: Mon.-Sat. 10-5. Adults $2, children $1.

UPTOWN GALLERY, 30 E. Main St., Franklin, NC 28734. Tel.: 828-349-4607.
E-mail: info@uptowngalleryoffranklin.com
Web Site: www.uptowngalleryoffranklin.com
Institution Type/Description: Art Gallery.
Hours & Admission Prices: Jan.-April Mon.-Sat. 11-3; May-Dec. Mon.-Sat. 10-5; other times by appointment.

WILDERNESS TAXIDERMY & OUTFITTERS MUSEUM, 5040 Highlands Rd., Franklin, NC 28734-4009. Tel.: 828-524-3677. Fax: 828-349-4200.
E-mail: fuchs@dnet.net
Web Site: www.wildernesstaxidermy.com
Institution Type/Description: Taxidermy Museum.
Hours & Admission Prices: Mon.-Tues. & Thurs.-Fri. 8-5, Sat. 8 am-12 pm.

Fremont

CHARLES B. AYCOCK BIRTHPLACE STATE HISTORIC SITE, 264 Governor Aycock Rd., Fremont, NC 27830-7906. Tel.: 919-242-5581. Fax: 919-242-6668.
E-mail: aycock@ncdcr.gov
Web Site: www.ah.dcr.state.nc.us/hs/Aycock/Aycock.htm
Key Personnel: Site Mgr., Leigh V. Strickland; Museum Shop Mgr., Sarah Pittman.
Institution Type/Description: History Museum.
Hours & Admission Prices: Mon.-Sat. 9-5. No charge; donations accepted. Closed Martin Luther King Jr. Day; Memorial Day; Independence Day; Labor Day; Veterans Day; Thanksgiving; Christmas Eve & Day. &
Attendance: 19,198 (actual)

Frisco

FRISCO NATIVE AMERICAN MUSEUM AND NATURAL HISTORY CENTER, 53536 Hwy. 12, Frisco, NC 27936. Mailing Address: P.O. Box 399, Frisco, NC 27936-0399. Tel.: 252-995-4440. Fax: 252-995-4030. Facebook: Frisco Native American Museum.
E-mail: admin@nativeamericanmuseum.org
Web Site: www.nativeamericanmuseum.org
Key Personnel: Exec. Dir., Carl Bornfriend; Chm. & Pres., James Goes; Chm. (V), Elvin Hooper; Asst. Dir., Ronnie Francisco; Education & Public Rels., Joyce Bornfriend; Museum Shop Mgr., Amber Roth; Maintenance, Charles Donald Carmen, III; Maintenance, David Rivera.
Institution Type/Description: History Museum: located on Hatteras Island, the central building is more than 100 years old with a history of use as a village post office & general store.
Hours & Admission Prices: Summer: Tues.-Sun. 10:30-5, Mon. by appointment; Winter: call for hours. Family $15, adults $5, senior citizens $3; discount to AAM members. Closed Thanksgiving; Christmas. &
Attendance: 35,000 (estimated)

Gastonia

AMERICAN MILITARY MUSEUM, 109 W. Second Ave., Gastonia, NC 28052. Tel.: 704-866-6068.
E-mail: jimboi812@carolina.rr.com
Institution Type/Description: Military Museum.
Hours & Admission Prices: Sun. 1-5; other times by appointment.

THE SCHIELE MUSEUM OF NATURAL HISTORY AND JAMES H. LYNN PLANETARIUM, 1500 E. Garrison Blvd., Gastonia, NC 28054-5133. Tel.: 704-866-6900. Fax: 704-866-6041.
E-mail: annt@cityofgastonia.com
Web Site: www.schielemuseum.org
Key Personnel: Dir., Dr. Ann Tippitt; Dir. Planetarium, Jim Craig; Accountant, Janice Edge; Asst. Dir. Operations, Karl McKinnon; Advancement Dir., Tricia Griffin; Mktg. Dir., Philip McGinnis; Collections Mgr., Carrie V. Duran; Research Coord. & Cur. Archaeology, Dr. J. Alan May; Adj. Cur. Life Sciences, Dawn Flynn; Security Mgr., Mark Rudisill.
Institution Type/Description: Natural History Museum.
Hours & Admission Prices: Mon.-Sat. 9-5, Sun. 1-5. Museum: City Residents: adults $5, children, students & seniors $4. Non-Residents: adults $7, children, students & seniors $6. Planetarium: $3. Members & ASTC members no charge. Closed Easter; Thanksgiving; Christmas Eve & Day. &
Attendance: 89,356 (actual)

Gold Hill

HISTORIC GOLD HILL, 735 St. Stephens Church Rd., Gold Hill, NC 28071. Mailing Address: P.O. Box 206, Gold Hill, NC 28071. Tel.: 704-960-6457.
E-mail: vivian@historicgoldhill.com
Web Site: historicgoldhill.com
Institution Type/Description: Historic Buildings.
Hours & Admission Prices: Call for hours.

Goldsboro

ARTS COUNCIL OF WAYNE COUNTY, 102 N. John St., Goldsboro, NC 27530. Tel.: 919-736-3300.
E-mail: wendy@artsinwayne.org
Web Site: artsinwayne.org
Formerly: Community Arts Council, Inc.
Key Personnel: Exec. Dir., Wendy Snow Walker; Gallery & Education Dir., Becca Scott Reynolds.
Institution Type/Description: Art Gallery.
Hours & Admission Prices: Mon.-Thurs. 9-5, Fri. 9-7, Sat. 10-3. No charge; donations accepted. Closed New Year's Day & day after; Good Friday; Easter; Memorial Day; Independence Day; Labor Day; Thanksgiving & day after; Christmas Eve, Day & week. ♿

CHERRY HOSPITAL MUSEUM, 201 Stevens Mill Rd., Goldsboro, NC 27530. Tel.: 919-580-2936. Fax: 919-731-3418.
E-mail: tanya.rollins@dhhs.nc.gov
Institution Type/Description: History Museum: housed in a hospital building that was opened by the state in 1880 for African Americans with mental illness.
Hours & Admission Prices: Mon.-Fri. by appointment. No charge; donations accepted. ♿
Attendance: 500 (estimated)

GOLDSBOROUGH BRIDGE BATTLEFIELD, Old Mt. Olive Hwy., Goldsboro, NC 27530. Mailing Address: 103 S. George St., Goldsboro, NC 27530. Tel.: 919-736-4423.
E-mail: info@goldsborough.bridge.com
Web Site: www.goldsboroughbridge.com
Institution Type/Description: Historic Site: battlefield where 15,000 soldiers fought in Dec. 1862.
Hours & Admission Prices: Daily sunrise to Sunset. No charge; donations accepted.

SEYMOUR JOHNSON AIR FORCE BASE, 1510 Wright Brothers Ave., Ste. 200, Goldsboro, NC 27534. Tel.: 919-734-2241 & 722-0027.
Web Site: seymourjohnson.af.mil
Institution Type/Description: Military Museum.
Hours & Admission Prices: last Thurs. each month by appointment.

WAYNE COUNTY MUSEUM, 116 N. William St., Goldsboro, NC 27530. Tel.: 919-734-5023. Facebook; Instagram.
E-mail: info@waynemuseum.org
Web Site: waynemuseum.org
Key Personnel: Exec. Dir., Jennifer Kuykendall; Asst. Dir., Marie Ballentine Shafer; Pres. Bd., Nancy Dalia; Military Cur., Kenneth Gambill.
Institution Type/Description: History Museum.
Hours & Admission Prices: Tues.-Sat. 11-4; other times by appointment. No charge; donations accepted. Closed most federal holidays. ♿
Attendance: 5,000 (actual)

WAYNESBOROUGH HISTORICAL VILLAGE & VISITOR CENTER, 801 US Hwy. 117 Bypass S., Goldsboro, NC 27530. Tel.: 919-731-1653.
E-mail: information@waynesboroughhistoricalvillage.com
Web Site: www.waynesboroughhistoricalvillage.com
Institution Type/Description: Historical Village.
Hours & Admission Prices: Summer: Mon.-Sat. 11-5, Sun. 1-5; Winter: Mon.-Sat. 10-4, Sun. 1-4. No charge.

Graham

CHILDREN'S MUSEUM OF ALAMANCE COUNTY, 217 S. Main St., Graham, NC 27253. Mailing Address: P.O. Box 1178, Graham, NC 27253-1176. Tel.: 336-228-7997.
E-mail: info@childrensmuseumofalamance.org
Web Site: www.childrensmuseumofalamance.org
Institution Type/Description: Children's Museum.
Hours & Admission Prices: Sat. 10-5, Sun. 1-5. Adults $5; discounts to ACM reciprocal members; members no charge. ♿

GRAHAM HISTORICAL MUSEUM, 135 W. Elm St., Graham, NC 27253. Mailing Address: 637 Johnson Ave., Graham, NC 27253. Tel.: 336-513-4773 & 226-4794.
E-mail: jandrews@cityofgraham.com
Institution Type/Description: History Museum.
Hours & Admission Prices: Sun. 2-5; other times by appointment. No charge; donations accepted.

Grantsboro

PAMLICO COUNTY MUSEUM & HERITAGE CENTER, 10642 Hwy. 55 E., Grantsboro, NC 28529. Mailing Address: P.O. Box 33, Grantsboro, NC 28529. Tel.: 252-745-2239. Fax: 252-745-2242. Facebook: Pamlico County Museum & Heritage Center.
E-mail: pcha@pamlico.net
Web Site: pamlicocountyhistorymuseum.com
Key Personnel: Dir., Pat Prescott; Pres. (V), Terry Cannan.
Institution Type/Description: History Museum.
Hours & Admission Prices: Tues.-Fri. 10-4. No charge. ♿
Attendance: 5,000 (actual)

Greensboro

ACC HALL OF CHAMPIONS, 1921 W. Lee St., Greensboro, NC 27403. Tel.: 336-315-8411.
Web Site: acchallofchampions.net
Institution Type/Description: Sports Museum.
Hours & Admission Prices: Thurs.-Sat. 10-4. Adults $5, children 2-12 $3; discounts to groups of 4 or more.

AFRICAN AMERICAN ATELIER, INC., Greensboro Cultural Center, 200 N. Davie St., Ste. 14, Greensboro, NC 27401-2865. Tel.: 336-333-6885. Fax: 336-373-4826. Facebook: African American Atelier; Twitter: AAAtelier.
E-mail: info@africanamericanatelier.org
Web Site: www.africanamericanatelier.org
Key Personnel: Bd. Pres., Eresterine Guidry; Co-Gallery Mgr., Lou Mecia Koonce; Co-Gallery Mgr., Angela Fitzgerald; Youth Dir., LeSheri Clemons.
Institution Type/Description: Art Gallery.
Hours & Admission Prices: Aug.-June Tues.-Sat. 10-5, Sun. 2-5. No charge; donations accepted. ♿
Attendance: 30,000 (estimated)

ANNE RUDD GALYON & IRENE CULLIS GALLERIES, GREENSBORO COLLEGE, College Pl., Cowan Humanities Bldg., Greensboro, NC 27401. Mailing Address: 815 W. Market St., Greensboro, NC 27401. Tel.: 336-272-7102. Fax: 336-217-7245.
E-mail: langerj@greensboro.edu
Web Site: www.greensboro.edu/about/galleries
Key Personnel: Gallery Dir., James Langer.
Institution Type/Description: College Art Gallery.
Hours & Admission Prices: Mon.-Fri. 9-5, Sat. by appointment. No charge. Closed college holidays. ♿
Attendance: 3,000 (estimated)

BLANDWOOD MANSION, 447 W. Washington St., Greensboro, NC 27401-2348. Mailing Address: P.O. Box 13136, Greensboro, NC 27415-3136. Tel.: 336-272-5003. Facebook: Blandwood.
E-mail: bbriggs@blandwood.org
Web Site: www.blandwood.org/
Key Personnel: Exec. Dir., Benjamin Briggs.
Institution Type/Description: Historic House: former home of North Carolina Governor John Motley Moorehead, c.1790. A National Historic Landmark.
Hours & Admission Prices: Tues.-Sat. 11-4, Sun. 2-5; groups of 20 or more by appointment. Adults $8, seniors $7, children under 12 $5; discounts to AAA members & groups; school groups no charge. Closed holidays.

BROCK HISTORICAL MUSEUM, Greensboro College, Main Bldg., 815 W. Market St., Greensboro, NC 27401-1875. Tel.: 336-272-7102, ext. 283. Fax: 336-271-6634.
E-mail: ehenry@greensboro.edu
Web Site: www.greensboro.edu/museum
Institution Type/Description: History Museum.
Hours & Admission Prices: Mon.-Fri. 9-4 by appointment.

CENTER FOR VISUAL ARTISTS - GREENSBORO, 200 N. Davie St., Box 13, Greensboro, NC 27401-2819. Tel.: 336-333-7485. Fax: 336-333-7477.
E-mail: info@greensboroart.org
Web Site: www.greensboroart.org
Formerly: Greensboro Artists' League
Key Personnel: Pres., Martha Mason; Dir. Education, Katie Lank; Education Asst., Christie Gulley; Cur., Kristy Thomas; Programming Asst., Melanie Greene.
Institution Type/Description: Art Gallery: located in the Greensboro Cultural Center.

Hours & Admission Prices: Tues. & Thurs.-Sat. 10-5, Wed. 10-7, Sun. 2-5. No charge; donations accepted. Closed legal holidays. &
Attendance: 90,000 (estimated)

COLONIAL HERITAGE CENTER AT GUILFORD COURTHOUSE NATIONAL MILITARY PARK, 2332 New Garden Rd., Greensboro, NC 27410-2355. Tel.: 336-545-5315. Fax: 336-545-5314.
E-mail: guco_administration@nps.gov
Web Site: www.nps.gov/guco
Formerly: Tannenbaum Historic Park
Key Personnel: Dir., Charles Cranfield.
Institution Type/Description: Historic Site.
Hours & Admission Prices: Fri.-Sat. 8:30-5. No charge.
Attendance: 20,000 (estimated)

GREENHILL, 200 N. Davie St., Greensboro, NC 27401. Mailing Address: 200 N. Davie St., Box 4, Greensboro, NC 27401. Tel.: 336-333-7460. Fax: 336-333-2612. Facebook: Greenhill Art.
E-mail: laura.way@greenhillnc.org
Web Site: www.greenhillnc.org
Formerly: Green Hill Center for North Carolina Art
Key Personnel: Exec. Dir. & C.E.O., Laura Way; Pres. (V), Adam Tarleton; Dir., Curatorial & Artistic Programs, Edie Carpenter; Dir. Operations, Emily Shank; Dir. Programs, Lynn Sanders-Bustle; Dir. Adult & Youth Education Programs, Jaynile Meyer; Art Educator, Laura Maruzzella; Mktg. & Design Specialist, Lauren Gordon; Devel. & Logistics Assoc., Bethany Barnes; Museum Shop Mgr. & Registrar, Toni Tronu; Curatorial Asst., Carol Groover.
Institution Type/Description: Art Gallery.
Hours & Admission Prices: The Gallery & The Shop: Tues. & Thurs.-Sat. 10-5, Wed. 10-7, Sun. 2-5. Suggested Donation: $5. ArtQuest: Tues., Thurs. & Sat. 1-5, Wed. 1-7, Fri. 10-5. Admission $6; children 1 & under, Wed. 5pm-7pm, & members no charge. Closed legal holidays. &
Attendance: 40,000 (estimated)

GREENSBORO CHILDREN'S MUSEUM, 220 N. Church St., Greensboro, NC 27401-2918. Tel.: 336-574-2898. Fax: 336-574-3810.
E-mail: info@gcmuseum.com
Web Site: www.gcmuseum.com
Key Personnel: C.E.O., Betsy Grant; Chm. (V), John Cross; Mktg., Steffany Reeve.
Institution Type/Description: Children's Museum.
Hours & Admission Prices: Mon. 9-12 (members only), Tues.-Thurs. & Sat. 9-5, Fri. 9-8, Sun. 1-5. Adults $6, seniors $5; discounts to groups of 10 or more, Fri. 5-8 & Sun. 1-5; members & children under one no charge. Closed New Year's Day; Easter; Memorial Day; Independence Day; Labor Day; Thanksgiving; Christmas Eve & Day. &
Attendance: 140,000 (actual)

GREENSBORO HISTORICAL MUSEUM, INC., 130 Summit Ave., Greensboro, NC 27401-3016. Tel.: 336-373-2043 & 2982 (before 10am & Mon.). Fax: 336-373-2204.
E-mail: carol.hart@greensboro-nc.gov
Web Site: www.greensborohistory.org
Key Personnel: Pres., Margaret Benjamin; Cur. & Registrar, Susan Webster; Cur. Collections, Jon Zachman; Community Historian, Linda Evans; Archivist, Elise Allison; Museum Shop Mgr., Cynthia Kennard.
Institution Type/Description: Local History Museum.
Hours & Admission Prices: Tues.-Sat. 10-5, Sun. 2-5. No charge; donations accepted. Closed city of Greensboro holidays. &

GREENSBORO SCIENCE CENTER, 4301 Lawndale Dr., Greensboro, NC 27455-1899. Tel.: 336-288-3769. Fax: 336-288-2531.
E-mail: marketing@greensboroscience.org
Web Site: www.greensboroscience.org
Formerly: The Natural Science Center of Greensboro
Key Personnel: C.E.O., Glenn Dobrogosz; Mktg. Mgr., Erica Brown; Museum Shop Mgr., Josh Rothrock; Chm. (V), Susan Wiseman.
Institution Type/Description: Natural History, Science Museum, Aquarium, Planetarium & Zoo.
Hours & Admission Prices: Daily 9-5, zoo closes at 4 seasonally. Adults $13.50, seniors 65 & over and children 3-13 $12.50; discounts to Greensboro residents, military, AAM & AZA members; members and children 2 & under no charge. OmniSphere Theater: $3-$5. Closed Thanksgiving; Christmas. &
Attendance: 434,718 (actual)

GUILFORD COLLEGE ART GALLERY, 5800 W. Friendly Ave., Greensboro, NC 27410-4108. Tel.: 336-316-2438. Fax: 336-316-2950.

E-mail: thammond@guilford.edu
Web Site: www.library.guilford.edu/art-gallery
Key Personnel: Dir. & Cur., Theresa N. Hammond.
Institution Type/Description: College Art Gallery: located in Hege Library.
Hours & Admission Prices: Main Gallery: Mon.-Fri. 9-5, Sun. 2-5. Atrium Galleries: Mon.-Thurs. 8:30-2am, Fri. 8:30-6, Sat. 10-9, Sun. 12-2am. No charge. Closed college holidays. &
Attendance: 7,500 (estimated)

GUILFORD COURTHOUSE NATIONAL MILITARY PARK, 2332 New Garden Rd., Greensboro, NC 27410-2355. Tel.: 336-288-1776. Fax: 336-282-2296.
E-mail: guco_administration@nps.gov
Web Site: www.nps.gov/guco
Key Personnel: Supt., Charles Cranfield; Museum Shop Mgr., Nancy Stewart.
Institution Type/Description: Military Museum.
Hours & Admission Prices: Visitor Center open Tues.-Sat. 8:30-5. Tour road closed to vehicles Sun. No charge, donations accepted. Closed New Year's Day; Thanksgiving & Christmas. &
Attendance: 70,000 (actual)

GUILFORD NATIVE AMERICAN ART GALLERY, 200 N. Davie St., Greensboro, NC 27402. Tel.: 336-273-6605.
E-mail: gallery7@bellsouth.net
Web Site: greensboro.nc.gov
Institution Type/Description: Art Gallery.
Hours & Admission Prices: Tues.-Sat. 10-5, Sun. 2-5.

INTERNATIONAL CIVIL RIGHTS CENTER & MUSEUM, 134 S. Elm St., Greensboro, NC 27401. Tel.: 336-274-9199, 800-748-7116. Fax: 336-274-6244.
E-mail: info@sitinmovement.org
Web Site: www.sitinmovement.org
Key Personnel: C.E.O., John L. Swaine; Coord. Exhibition Tours, Anita Johnson; Museum Shop Assoc. & Docent, Jean Dulin; Curatorial Program Assoc., Nakia Hoskins; Special Events & Membership Coord., La Toya Wiley; Museum Shop Assoc., Shirley Tate; Facilities Coord., Tyrone Cook.
Institution Type/Description: History Museum.
Hours & Admission Prices: Guided Tours: April-Sept. Mon.-Thurs. 9-6, Fri.-Sat. 9-7; Oct.-March Mon.-Sat. 10-6. Adults $12, seniors 65 & over and students $10, children 6-12 $8; discounts to AAM, AARP, AAA, & military member; children under 6 & AAM members no charge. &
Attendance: 70,000 (actual)

NORTH CAROLINA A&T STATE UNIVERSITY GALLERIES, Corner of Bluford and Dudley Sts., Greensboro, NC 27411. Mailing Address: Dudley Bldg., 1601 E. Market St., Greensboro, NC 27411-0002. Tel.: 336-334-3209. Fax: 336-334-4378.
E-mail: sharris@ncat.edu
Web Site: www.ncat.edu/~museum/
Formerly: Mattye Reed African Heritage Center
Key Personnel: Cur., Christi Pemberton; Administrative Asst., Lisa Phillips.
Institution Type/Description: University Museum.
Hours & Admission Prices: Mon.-Fri. 10-5; other times by appointment. No charge; donations accepted. Closed university holidays.
Attendance: 10,000 (estimated)

WEATHERSPOON ART MUSEUM, Spring Garden & Tate St., Univ. of NC at Greensboro, Greensboro, NC 27402-6170. Mailing Address: P.O. Box 26170, Greensboro, NC 27402-6170. Tel.: 336-334-5770. Fax: 336-334-5907. Facebook.
E-mail: weatherspoon@uncg.edu
Web Site: weatherspoon.uncg.edu
Formerly: Weatherspoon Art Gallery
Key Personnel: Dir., Nancy Doll; C.E.O., Dr. Dana Dunn; Pres., Hillary Meredith; Public & Community Rels. Officer, Loring Martensen; Cur. Collections, Elaine D. Gustafson; Cur. Education, Ann Grimaldi; Cur. Exhibitions, Emily Stamey; Assoc. Cur. Education, Terri Dowell-Dennis.
Institution Type/Description: University Art Museum.
Hours & Admission Prices: Tues.-Wed. & Fri. 10-5, Thurs. 10-9, Sat.-Sun. 1-5. No charge; donations accepted. Closed university holidays. &
Attendance: 37,757 (actual)

Greenville

GREENVILLE MUSEUM OF ART, INC., 802 S. Evans St., Greenville, NC 27834-3268. Tel.: 252-758-1946.
E-mail: info@gmoa.org
Web Site: www.gmoa.org

Key Personnel: Bd. Pres., Melissa Goldstein; Exec. Dir., Ned Puchner; Collections & Exhibitions Mgr., Paige Hackler; Office Coord., Alyssa Morales.
Institution Type/Description: NC Artists & American Landscapes Museum
Hours & Admission Prices: Tues.-Fri. 10-4:30, Sat. 1-4. Tours: Wed.-Fri. between 10 & 12. No charge; donations accepted. Closed major holidays. ♿
Attendance: 17,000 (actual)

WALTER L. STASAVICH SCIENCE AND NATURE CENTER, River Park N., 1000 Mumford Rd., Greenville, NC 27858. Tel.: 252-329-4560. Fax: 252-329-4547.
E-mail: chorrigan@greenvillenc.gov
Web Site: www.greenvillenc.gov
Key Personnel: Park Coord., Christopher Horrigan.
Institution Type/Description: Science & Nature Center.
Hours & Admission Prices: Tues.-Sat. 9:30-5, Sun. 1-5.

WELLINGTON B. GRAY GALLERY, East Carolina Univ., Jenkins Fine Arts Ctr., Greenville, NC 27858-4353. Tel.: 252-328-6336. Fax: 252-328-6441.
E-mail: braswellg@ecu.edu
Web Site: www.ecu.edu/art/home/html
Key Personnel: Dir., Tom Braswell.
Institution Type/Description: Art Gallery.
Hours & Admission Prices: Mon.-Fri. 10-4, Sat. 10-2. No charge; donations accepted. Closed university holidays. ♿
Attendance: 20,102 (actual)

Grifton

GRIFTON MUSEUM AND CATECHNA INDIAN VILLAGE, 437 A Creekshore Dr., Grifton, NC 28530. Mailing Address: P.O. Box 85, Grifton, NC 28530. Tel.: 252-524-0190.
E-mail: gkg28530@gmail.com
Institution Type/Description: American Indian Village & Museum.
Hours & Admission Prices: 1st & 3rd Sun. 1-5; other times by appointment.

Grover

PRESIDENTIAL CULINARY MUSEUM & U.S. PRESIDENTIAL SERVICE CENTER, 301 Cleveland Ave., Grover, NC 28073. Tel.: 704-937-2940. Facebook: The Inn of the Patriots.
E-mail: curator@presidentialculinarymuseum.org
Web Site: www.presidentialculinarymuseum.org
Formerly: Presidential Culinary Museum
Key Personnel: Dir. & Pres., Martin C.J. Mongiello; C.E.O. & Chm., Michael C. Mongiello, Jr.; Chm. (V), Allan B. Miller; Pres. (V), Rick E. Scott; Museum Shop Mgr., Stormy L. Mongiello.
Institution Type/Description: History Museum: housed in The Inn of the Patriots.
Hours & Admission Prices: Guided Tours: daily 9:30am; bus tours & specialty groups by appointment. Adults $7, senior citizens & military $5; discounts to AAM & ICOM members; children under 12 no charge.
Attendance: 6,872 (actual)

Halifax

HISTORIC HALIFAX STATE HISTORIC SITE, 25 St. David St., Halifax, NC 27839. Mailing Address: P.O. Box 406, Halifax, NC 27839-0406. Tel.: 252-583-7191. Fax: 252-583-9421. Facebook: Historic Halifax State Historic Site.
E-mail: halifax@ncdcr.gov
Web Site: www.halifax.nchistoricsites.org
Key Personnel: Sites Mgr., Monica Moody; Chm., Wrenn Phillips; Museum Shop Mgr., Sarah Hill.
Institution Type/Description: Preservation Project & Visitor Center.
Hours & Admission Prices: Tues.-Sat. 9-5. No charge; donations accepted. Closed holidays. ♿
Attendance: 40,000 (estimated)

Hamilton

FORT BRANCH CONFEDERATE EARTHEN FORT CIVIL WAR SITE, 2883 Fort Branch Rd., Hamilton, NC 27840. Mailing Address: P.O. Box 355, Hamilton, NC 27840. Tel.: 800-776-8566.
E-mail: fort.branch.nc@gmail.com
Web Site: www.fortbranchcivilwarsite.com
Institution Type/Description: Civil War Site: housed on the site of the Confederate Army in 1861.
Hours & Admission Prices: April to early Nov. Sat.-Sun. 1:30-5:30; other times by appointment.

Hamlet

NATIONAL RAILROAD MUSEUM AND HALL OF FAME, INC., 120 E. Spring St., Bus Hwy. 74 E, Hamlet, NC 28345. Mailing Address: P.O. Box 1583, Hamlet, NC 28345-1583. Tel.: 910-582-3555.
E-mail: nrrmhof@yahoo.com
Key Personnel: Pres., Tim Nevinger; Vice Pres., William Billingsley; Sec. & Treas., Kay Cavendish.
Institution Type/Description: Railroad Museum.
Hours & Admission Prices: Sat.-Sun. 1-4; other times by appointment. No charge; donations accepted. Closed Christmas. ♿
Attendance: 6,500 (estimated)

Harkers Island

CAPE LOOKOUT LIGHTHOUSE & LIGHT STATION VISITOR CENTER AND KEEPERS QUARTERS MUSEUM, 131 Charles St., Harkers Island, NC 28516. Tel.: 252-728-2250. Fax: 252-728-2160. Facebook: Cape Lookout.
E-mail: CALO_Information@nps.gov
Web Site: www.nps.gov/calo/learn/historyculture/lths.htm
Key Personnel: Superintendent, Jeff West.
Institution Type/Description: Historic Lighthouse: built in 1859.
Hours & Admission Prices: Lighthouse: Wed.-Sat. 10-3:45; groups by appointment; call for holiday hours. Adults $8, children 12 & over and seniors 62 & over $4. Ferry transportation not included in fees.

CORE SOUND WATERFOWL MUSEUM & HERITAGE CENTER, 1785 Island Rd., Harkers Island, NC 28531-9670. Mailing Address: P.O. Box 556, Harkers Island, NC 28531-0556. Tel.: 919-728-1500. Fax: 919-728-1742.
E-mail: museum@coresound.com
Web Site: www.coresound.com
Key Personnel: Dir., Karen Willis Amspacher; Chm. (V), Charles S. Jones; Museum Shop Mgr., Jennifer Taylor.
Institution Type/Description: Heritage Center.
Hours & Admission Prices: Mon.-Sat. 10-5, Sun. 2-5. No charge; donations accepted. Closed New Year's Day; Easter; Thanksgiving; Christmas. ♿
Attendance: 25,000 (estimated)

Harrisburg

U.S. LEGEND CARS INTERNATIONAL, 5245 Hwy. 49 S., Harrisburg, NC 28075. Tel.: 704-455-3896. Fax: 704-455-3820.
E-mail: gechapman@uslegendcars.com
Web Site: 600racing.com
Institution Type/Description: Race Car Manufacturer.
Hours & Admission Prices: Call for hours.

Hatteras

GRAVEYARD OF THE ATLANTIC MUSEUM, 59200 Museum Dr., Hatteras, NC 27943. Mailing Address: P.O. Box 284, Hatteras, NC 27943-0191. Tel.: 252-986-2995. Fax: 252-986-1212.
E-mail: museum@graveyardoftheatlantic.com
Web Site: www.graveyardoftheatlantic.com
Institution Type/Description: Maritime History Museum.
Hours & Admission Prices: Mon.-Fri. 10-4. No charge; donations accepted. ♿
Attendance: 50,000 (actual)

Havelock

EASTERN CAROLINA AVIATION HERITAGE FOUNDATION, 201 Tourist Center Dr., Havelock, NC 28532. Mailing Address: P.O. Box 368, Havelock, NC 28532. Tel.: 252-444-4348.
E-mail: aohlensenlen@havelocknc.us
Web Site: ecaviationheritage.com
Institution Type/Description: Military Aviation History Museum.
Hours & Admission Prices: Mon.-Fri. 8-5, Sat. 10-5. No charge; donations accepted. ♿

Haw River

CHILDREY HOUSE, WORLD WAR II, HOME FRONT MUSEUM, 309 E. Main St., Haw River, NC 27258. Mailing Address: c/o Haw River Historical Association, P.O. Box 936, Haw River, NC 27258. Tel.: 336-578-0784 & 684-1002.

Key Personnel: Dir., Gail Knauff; Dir., Cathy Wilson; Dir., Buddy Boggs.
Institution Type/Description: History Museum.
Hours & Admission Prices: Veterans Day weekend & Memorial Day weekend; other times by appointment. No charge; donations accepted.
Attendance: 150 (estimated)

HAW RIVER HISTORICAL MUSEUM, 201 E. Main St., Haw River, NC 27258. Mailing Address: P.O. Box 936, Haw River, NC 27258-0936. Tel.: 336-578-0784; 684-1002 & 266-4391. Facebook: Haw River Museum.
E-mail: gaknauff@yahoo.com
Key Personnel: Dir., Gail Knauff; Dir., Cathy Wilson; Treas., Buddy Boggs.
Institution Type/Description: History Museum.
Hours & Admission Prices: Sat.-Sun. 1-4; other times by appointment. No charge; donations accepted.
Attendance: 600 (estimated)

Hawk

DELLINGER GRIST MILL ON CANE CREEK, 4020 Cane Creek Rd., Hawk, NC 27949. Mailing Address: P.O. Box 1125, Bakersville, NC 28705. Tel.: 828-688-1009.
E-mail: jackdellinger@bellsouth.net
Web Site: www.dellingermill.com
Key Personnel: Owner, Jack Dellinger.
Institution Type/Description: Grist Mill: built in 1867. Listed on The National Register of Historic Places.
Hours & Admission Prices: Call for hours; groups by appointment.

Hayesville

CLAY COUNTY HISTORICAL AND ARTS COUNCIL MUSEUM, 21 Davis Loop, Hayesville, NC 28904. Mailing Address: P.O. Box 5, Hayesville, NC 28904-0005. Tel.: 828-389-6814.
E-mail: mike@hayesville.org
Web Site: clayhistoryarts.org
Institution Type/Description: History Museum: housed in a former county jail; built in 1912.
Hours & Admission Prices: Memorial Day to Labor Day Tues.-Sat. 10-4; Sept.-Oct. Fri.-Sat. 10-4. No charge; donations accepted. &
Attendance: 1,800 (actual)

Henderson

HENDERSON INSTITUTE HISTORICAL MUSEUM, 629 W. Rockspring St., Henderson, NC 27536. Mailing Address: P.O. Box 2081, Henderson, NC 27536. Tel.: 252-430-0616. Facebook: @hihistoricalmuseum.net1.
E-mail: edsco1128@gmail.com
Web Site: historicalmuseum.net
Key Personnel: Cur., Edna Scott.
Institution Type/Description: Historic Building: housed in the former secondary school for African Americans in Vance County; built in 1887.
Hours & Admission Prices: Wed.-Sat. 1-4; other times by appointment. No charge. &
Attendance: 300 (estimated)

Hendersonville

HENDERSON COUNTY HERITAGE MUSEUM, 1 Historic Courthouse Sq., Main St., Hendersonville, NC 28792. Tel.: 828-694-1619.
E-mail: museumoffice@hendersoncountync.org
Web Site: www.hendersoncountymuseum.com
Key Personnel: Exec. Dir., Anne Ridings; Supvr., Kaleb Shuller.
Institution Type/Description: Heritage Museum.
Hours & Admission Prices: Wed.-Sat. 10-5, Sun. 1-5.

HISTORIC JOHNSON FARM, 3346 Haywood Rd., Hendersonville, NC 28791-9721. Tel.: 828-891-6585. Fax: 828-890-7001. Facebook: Historic Johnson Farm; Twitter: @hcpsjohnsonfarm.
E-mail: jfarm@hcpsnc.org
Web Site: www.historicjohnsonfarm.org
Key Personnel: Dir., Jay Owens; Pres. (V), Bunny Wilson.
Institution Type/Description: Historic Farm: housed on a late 19th-century tobacco farm. Listed on the National Register of Historic Places.

Hours & Admission Prices: Tours: June-Aug. Mon.-Thurs. 10:30am & 1:30pm; Sept.-May Mon.-Fri. 10:30am & 1:30pm. Adults $5, students K-12 $3; children under 5 no charge.
Attendance: 6,200 (estimated)

HOLMES EDUCATIONAL STATE FOREST, 1299 Crab Creek Rd., Hendersonville, NC 28739-8440. Tel.: 828-692-0100.
E-mail: holmesESF.ncfs@ncagr.gov
Institution Type/Description: State Forest.
Hours & Admission Prices: mid-March to late Nov. Tues.-Sun.

MINERAL AND LAPIDARY MUSEUM OF HENDERSON COUNTY INC., 400 N. Main St., Hendersonville, NC 28792-4901. Tel.: 828-698-1977. Fax: 828-698-1977.
E-mail: info@mineralmuseum.org
Web Site: www.mineralmuseum.org
Key Personnel: C.E.O. & Pres., Jerry Howe; Dir., Diane Lapp; Treas., Zeb Palmer.
Institution Type/Description: Mineral & Lapidary Museum.
Hours & Admission Prices: Mon.-Fri. 1-5, Sat. 10-5. No charge; donations accepted. Closed New Year's Day; Thanksgiving; Christmas. &
Attendance: 31,865 (actual)

MOUNTAIN FARM AND HOME MUSEUM, 101 Brookside Camp Rd., Hendersonville, NC 28792-1101. Tel.: 828-697-8846.
Key Personnel: Pres. (V), A.B. Wexler.
Institution Type/Description: History Museum.
Hours & Admission Prices: Mon.-Fri. 9-3. No charge; donations accepted. &
Attendance: 500 (estimated)

WESTERN NORTH CAROLINA AIR MUSEUM, 1340 E. Gilbert St., Hendersonville, NC 28792. Mailing Address: P.O. Box 2343, Hendersonville, NC 28793-2343. Tel.: 828-698-2482. Facebook: Western North Carolina Air Museum.
Key Personnel: Pres. (V), Joseph Lilley; Vice Pres. (V), William Howe.
Institution Type/Description: Aviation Museum.
Hours & Admission Prices: April-Oct. Sun. & Wed. 12-5, Sat. 10-5; Nov.-March Wed. & Sat.-Sun. 12-5. No charge; donations accepted. &

Hertford

THE JIM "CATFISH" HUNTER BASEBALL MUSEUM, 118 W. Market St., Hertford, NC 27944-1151. Tel.: 252-426-5657. Fax: 252-426-7542. Facebook: Perquimans Chamber.
E-mail: director@visitperquimans.com
Web Site: www.visitperquimans.com
Key Personnel: Exec. Dir. Chamber of Commerce, J. Sid Eley.
Institution Type/Description: Sports Museum.
Hours & Admission Prices: Mon.-Fri. 9:30-4:30, Sat. 10-12; other times by appointment. No charge; donations accepted. &
Attendance: 3,500 (actual)

NEWBOLD WHITE HOUSE HISTORIC SITE, 151 Newbold-White Rd., Hertford, NC 27944-8240. Mailing Address: P.O. Box 103, Hertford, NC 27944-0103. Tel.: 252-426-7567. Facebook: Newbold White House.
E-mail: nbwh1730@embarqmail.com
Web Site: www.perquimansrestoration.org
Key Personnel: Pres. (V), Sandy Stevenson; Museum Shop Mgr., Darla Matthews.
Institution Type/Description: Historic Site.
Hours & Admission Prices: April-Oct. Thurs.-Sat. 10-4; other times by appointment. Adults $5.50, children 6 & up $3.50; discounts to groups; members & children under 6 no charge. &
Attendance: 1,056 (actual)

Hickory

CATAWBA SCIENCE CENTER, 243 3rd Ave., N.E., Hickory, NC 28601-5168. Mailing Address: P.O. Box 2431, Hickory, NC 28603-2431. Tel.: 828-322-8169, ext. 300. Fax: 828-322-8169. Facebook.
E-mail: info@catawbascience.org
Web Site: www.catawbascience.org
Key Personnel: Dir., Alan Barnhardt; Asst. Dir., Tricia Little; Pres. (V), Kelle Huffman; Dir. Programs, Erin Graves; Museum Shop Mgr., Nadia Scopes.
Institution Type/Description: Science & Technology Center.
Hours & Admission Prices: Tues.-Fri. 10-5, Sat. 10-4, Sun. 1-4. Adults $8, senior citizens 62 and over, military with ID & youth 3-18 $6; children under 3, mem-

bers & ASTC Passport Program Participants no charge. Closed major holidays. &

Attendance: 84,500 (actual)

HARPER HOUSE/HICKORY HISTORY CENTER, 310 N. Center St., Hickory, NC 28601-5031. Tel.: 828-324-7294. Fax: 828-465-9813. Facebook: Harper House HHC.
E-mail: cchakreese@gmail.com
Web Site: catawbahistory.org
Key Personnel: Site Mgr., Kendall Reese; Dir., Dr. Amber Clawson.
Institution Type/Description: History Museum.
Hours & Admission Prices: Fri.-Sat. 10-5; other times by appointment. Tours: Harper House: $5; members no charge. Bonniwell-Lyerly House: no charge.
Attendance: 1,000 (estimated)

HICKORY AVIATION MUSEUM, Hickory Regional Airport, 3101 9th Ave. Dr., N.W., Hickory, NC 28601-8646. Tel.: 828-323-7408.
E-mail: lindajhill@bellsouth.net
Web Site: hickoryaviationmuseum.org
Institution Type/Description: Aviation History Museum.
Hours & Admission Prices: Sat. 10-5, Sun. 1-5; other times by appointment.

HICKORY FURNITURE MART MUSEUM, 2220 Hwy. 70 S.E., Level 1, West Entrance, Hickory, NC 28602. Tel.: 800-462-6278.
E-mail: info@hickoryfurniture.com
Web Site: hickoryfurniture.com
Institution Type/Description: Furniture Museum.
Hours & Admission Prices: Mon.-Sat. 9-6.

HICKORY LANDMARKS SOCIETY-PROPST HOUSE AND MAPLE GROVE MUSEUMS, 542 Second St., N.E., Hickory, NC 28601. Mailing Address: P.O. Box 2341, Hickory, NC 28603-2341. Tel.: 828-322-4731. Fax: 828-327-9096.
E-mail: pdaily@hickorylandmarks.org
Web Site: www.hickorylandmarks.org
Key Personnel: Exec. Dir. & C.E.O., Patrick T. Daily; Cur. Collections & Education Coord., Leslie Keller.
Institution Type/Description: Three Victorian House museums (1882-1895).
Hours & Admission Prices: Propst St. House Museum: March 15-Dec. 15 Thurs. & Sun. 1:30-4:30. Maple Grove Museum: Mon.-Fri. 9-5. No charge; donations accepted.
Attendance: 6,300 (estimated)

THE HICKORY MUSEUM OF ART, 243 Third Ave., N.E., Hickory, NC 28601-5168. Tel.: 828-327-8576. Fax: 828-327-7281.
E-mail: info@hickorymuseumofart.org
Web Site: www.hickoryart.org
Key Personnel: Exec. Dir., Lise C. Swensson; Pres. (V), Alan Jackson; Dir. Education, Virginia Zellmer; Communications Mgr., Mary Katherine Creel; Membership Coord., Amanda Price; Museum Shop Mgr., Clarissa Starnes.
Institution Type/Description: Art Museum.
Hours & Admission Prices: Tues.-Sat. 10-4, Sun. 1-4. No charge; donations accepted. Closed New Year's Day; Easter; Independence Day; Thanksgiving; Christmas. &
Attendance: 32,010 (actual)

Hiddenite

HIDDENITE CENTER, INC., 316 Church St., Hiddenite, NC 28636. Mailing Address: P.O. Box 311, Hiddenite, NC 28636-0311. Tel.: 828-632-6966. Fax: 828-632-5756.
E-mail: info@hiddenitecenter.com
Web Site: www.hiddenitecenter.com
Key Personnel: Exec. Dir., James W. Woods; Asst. Dir., Karen B. Walker; Dir. Education, Allison S. Houchins; Museum Shop Mgr., Peggy Martin.
Institution Type/Description: General Museum & Art Center: housed in 1900 James Paul Lucas Mansion.
Hours & Admission Prices: Tues.-Fri. 10-4:30, Sat. 10-3. Museum: adults $4, seniors & students $3; discounts to AAM members & NC Museums Council; children under 6, members, Art Center, gallery & doll collection no charge. Closed Easter & day after; Independence Day; Labor Day; Thanksgiving; Christmas. &
Attendance: 25,000 (estimated)

High Point

ALL-A-FLUTTER FARMS LLC, 7850-B Clinard Farms Rd., High Point, NC 27265. Tel.: 336-454-5651. Facebook: All A Flutter.

E-mail: allaflutterfarms@gmail.com
Web Site: www.all-a-flutter.com
Formerly: All-A-Flutter Butterfly Farm
Institution Type/Description: Butterfly Farm
Hours & Admission Prices: By appointment. Admission $7; children under 2 no charge. &

BERNICE BIENENSTOCK FURNITURE LIBRARY, 1009 N. Main St., High Point, NC 27262. Tel.: 336-883-4011.
E-mail: info@furniturelibrary.com
Web Site: www.furniturelibrary.com
Institution Type/Description: Historic Building: housed in the Grayson House; built in 1923. Listed on the National Register of Historic Places.
Hours & Admission Prices: Daily 9-5.

HIGH POINT MUSEUM, 1859 E. Lexington Ave., High Point, NC 27262-3499. Tel.: 336-885-1859. Fax: 336-883-3284. Facebook: High Point Museum; Twitter: @HighPointMuseum.
E-mail: hpmuseum@highpointnc.gov
Web Site: www.highpointmuseum.org
Key Personnel: Dir., Edith Brady; Pres. (V), Donna Kaiser; Registrar, Corinne Midgett; Community Rel., Teresa Loflin; Cur. Collections, Marian Inabinett; Cur. Education, Michael Scott; Museum Shop Mgr., Mary Barnett.
Institution Type/Description: History Museum.
Hours & Admission Prices: Museum: Tues.-Sat. 10-4:30. Historical Park: Sat. 10-4:30. No charge; donations accepted. Closed New Year's Day; Martin Luther King Jr. Day; Easter; Memorial Day; Independence Day; Labor Day; Thanksgiving & day after; Christmas Eve & Day. &
Attendance: 16,000 (estimated)

MILLIS REGIONAL HEALTH EDUCATION CENTER, 600 N. Elm St., High Point, NC 27261. Mailing Address: P.O. Box HP-5, High Point, NC 27261-1899. Tel.: 336-878-6713. Fax: 336-878-6163.
E-mail: hpmilliscenter@unchealth.unc.edu
Web Site: www.millishealth.com
Key Personnel: Dir., Tessa Grogan; C.E.O. & Pres., Ernie Borio.
Institution Type/Description: Health Education Center.
Hours & Admission Prices: Mon.-Fri. 8:30-5 by appointment. Student $5; adult chaperones no charge.
Attendance: 7,535 (actual)

PIEDMONT ENVIRONMENTAL CENTER, 1220 Penny Rd., High Point, NC 27265-9182. Tel.: 336-883-8531. Fax: 336-883-8537.
E-mail: dick.thomas@highpointnc.gov
Web Site: www.piedmontenvironmental.com
Key Personnel: Exec. Dir., Richard Thomas.
Institution Type/Description: Environmental & Nature Center.
Hours & Admission Prices: Mon.-Fri. 9-5. No charge; donations accepted. Closed New Year's Day; Easter; Independence Day; Thanksgiving; Christmas. &
Attendance: 80,000 (estimated)

ROSETTA C. BALDWIN MUSEUM, 1408 R.C. Baldwin Ave., High Point, NC 27260. Tel.: 336-289-1942.
E-mail: hpafmuseum@yahoo.com
Web Site: rosettacbaldwinfoundation.com
Key Personnel: Dir., C.E.O. & Chm. (V), Julius Clark.
Institution Type/Description: Historic House: housed in the former home of Rosetta Baldwin who turned her home into a school for African American children in 1942.
Hours & Admission Prices: Tues. & Thurs. 10-4; other times by appointment. No charge; donations accepted.
Attendance: 150 (estimated)

SPRINGFIELD MUSEUM OF OLD DOMESTIC LIFE, 555 E. Springfield Rd., High Point, NC 27263-1843. Mailing Address: 803 Kingston Dr., High Point, NC 27262-7047. Tel.: 336-889-4911.
E-mail: bgh@northstate.net
Key Personnel: Dir. & Chief Cur., Brenda Haworth; Asst. Cur., Dan Warren.
Institution Type/Description: General Museum: housed in a former Quaker Meetinghouse built in 1858.
Hours & Admission Prices: By appointment. No charge; donations accepted.
Attendance: 100 (estimated)

THEATRE ART GALLERIES - TAG, 220 E. Commerce Ave., High Point, NC 27260. Tel.: 336-887-2137. Fax: 336-887-3415.
E-mail: jeffhorney@tagart.org

Web Site: www.tagart.org
Key Personnel: Exec. Dir., Jeff Horney.
Institution Type/Description: Art Gallery.
Hours & Admission Prices: Call for hours.

Highlands

THE BASCOM, 323 Franklin Rd., Highlands, NC 28741. Mailing Address: P.O. Box 766, Highlands, NC 28741-0766. Tel.: 828-526-4949. Fax: 828-526-0277.
E-mail: info@thebascom.org
Web Site: www.thebascom.org
Key Personnel: Exec. Dir., Linda Steigleder.
Institution Type/Description: Art Gallery.
Hours & Admission Prices: Call for hours. No charge.

MUSEUM OF AMERICAN CUT AND ENGRAVED GLASS, 472 Chestnut St., Highlands, NC 28741. Mailing Address: 218 Whiteside Mountain Rd., Highlands, NC 28741-7357. Tel.: 828-526-3415 & 3427.
E-mail: geobon@hcgexpress.net
Key Personnel: Dir., C.E.O. & Museum Shop (V), George E. Siek, Sr.
Institution Type/Description: Glass Museum.
Hours & Admission Prices: May-Oct. Tues., Thurs. & Sat. 1-4; Dec.-April by appointment. No charge; donations accepted. Closed Independence Day unless it falls on Tues., Thurs., or Sat. No charge; donations accepted. &
Attendance: 1,000 (estimated)

Hillsborough

AYR MOUNT AND POET'S WALK, 376 St. Mary's Rd., Hillsborough, NC 27278-2523. Tel.: 919-732-6886. Fax: 919-732-4524.
E-mail: ayrmount@classicalamericanhomes.org
Web Site: classicalamericanhomes.org
Institution Type/Description: Historic House Museum: housed in the former home of William Kirkland of Ayr, Scotland; c.1815.
Hours & Admission Prices: House Guided Tours: March 15-Dec. 15 Wed. 11am, Thurs.-Sat. 11am & 2 pm, Sun. 2 pm; other times by appointment. $12 per person. Poet's Walk: March-April & Sept.-Oct. daily 9-6; May & Aug. daily 9-7; June-July daily 9-8; Nov.-Feb. daily 9-5. No charge.
Attendance: 40,000 (estimated)

BURWELL SCHOOL HISTORIC SITE, 319 North Churton St., Hillsborough, NC 27278. Mailing Address: P.O. Box 922, Hillsborough, NC 27278-0922. Tel.: 919-732-7451. Fax: 919-644-7577.
E-mail: info@burwellschool.org
Web Site: burwellschool.org
Institution Type/Description: Historic Building: housed in the former home of Robert & Anna Burwell, c.1821.
Hours & Admission Prices: Wed.-Sat. 11-4, Sun. 1-4. No charge.
Attendance: 7,200 (estimated)

THE GARDENS OF MONTROSE, St. Marys Rd., Hillsborough, NC 27278. Mailing Address: P.O. Box 957, Hillsborough, NC 27278-0957. Tel.: 919-732-7787.
E-mail: montrosegdn@embarqmail.com
Web Site: www.gardenconservancy.org
Institution Type/Description: Garden Conservancy.
Hours & Admission Prices: Guided Tours: Tues. & Thurs. 10am, Sat. 10am & 2pm, by appointment. Tours: adults 12 & over $10; children 6-11$5; children under 6 no charge.

HILLSBOROUGH VISITORS CENTER - ALEXANDER DICKSON HOUSE, 150 E. King St., Hillsborough, NC 27278-2685. Tel.: 919-732-7741. Facebook.
E-mail: sarah@historichillsborough.org
Web Site: www.visithillsboroughnc.com
Formerly: Orange County Visitor's Center - Alexander Dickson House
Key Personnel: Dir., Sarah DeGennaro.
Institution Type/Description: Visitor's Center & Historic House: site includes an office used by Confederate Gen. Joseph E. Johnston before he surrendered his troops to Union Gen. William T. Sherman in April 1865.
Hours & Admission Prices: Center: Mon.-Sat. 10-4, Sun. 12-4. No charge; donations accepted. Closed major holidays.
Attendance: 6,000 (estimated)

MOOREFIELDS, 2201 Moorefields Rd., Hillsborough, NC 27278. Tel.: 919-732-4941.
E-mail: moorefields@earthlink.net
Web Site: www.moorefields.org
Institution Type/Description: Historic House Museum: housed in the former summer home of U.S. Supreme Court Justice Alfred Moore; built in 1785. Listed on the National Register of Historic Places.
Hours & Admission Prices: By appointment. No charge; donations accepted.

ORANGE COUNTY HISTORICAL MUSEUM, 201 N. Churton St., Hillsborough, NC 27278-2535. Tel.: 919-732-2201. Facebook: Orange County Historical Museum.
E-mail: info@orangenchistory.org
Web Site: www.orangecountymuseum.org
Key Personnel: Exec. Dir., Brandie Fields; Historic Interpreter, Carol Yavelak.
Institution Type/Description: Local History Museum.
Hours & Admission Prices: Jan. Tues.-Sun. 1-4; Feb.-Dec. Tues.-Sat. 11-4, Sun. 1-4; group tours by appointment. No charge; donations accepted. Blue Star Museum.
Attendance: 10,766 (actual)

RUFFIN-ROUHLAC HOUSE, 101 E. Orange St., Hillsborough, NC 27278. Tel.: 919-732-1270. Fax: 919-644-2390.
E-mail: info@visithillsboroughnc.com
Web Site: visithillsboroughnc.com
Institution Type/Description: Historic Building: housed in the former home of Chief Justice Thomas Ruffin; presently houses the Town Hall.
Hours & Admission Prices: Mon.-Fri. 9-5. No charge.

Huntersville

CAROLINA RAPTOR CENTER, 6000 Sample Rd., Huntersville, NC 28078. Mailing Address: P.O. Box 16443, Charlotte, NC 28297-6443. Tel.: 704-875-6521. Fax: 704-875-8814. Facebook: Carolina Raptor Center.
E-mail: raptors@carolinaraptorcenter.org
Web Site: www.carolinaraptorcenter.org
Key Personnel: Exec. Dir., Tim Warren; Chm. Bd. (V), Doug Bowman; Assoc. Exec. Dir., Michele Miller Houck; Museum Shop Mgr., Kelsey Hoke.
Institution Type/Description: Living Museum.
Hours & Admission Prices: Mon.-Sat. 10-5, Sun. 12-5. Adults $10, seniors, military & teachers $8, students 5 & over $6; discounts to groups of 15 or more; members and children 4 & under no charge. Closed New Year's Day; Thanksgiving; Christmas.
Attendance: 40,000 (estimated)

DISCOVERY PLACE KIDS - HUNTERSVILLE, 105 Gilead Rd., Huntersville, NC 28078. Tel.: 704-372-6261. Facebook & Twitter: @DPKHuntersville.
E-mail: info@discoveryplace.org
Web Site: kids.discoveryplace.org
Key Personnel: Chm. (V), Mark McGoldrick; Pres. & C.E.O., Catherine Wilson Horne.
Institution Type/Description: Children's Museum.
Hours & Admission Prices: Tues.- Fri. 9-4, Sat. 9-5, Sun. noon to 5. Admission $8; children under one & members no charge. Closed Easter; Thanksgiving; Christmas Eve & Day.

ENERGY EXPLORIUM, 13339 Hagers Ferry Rd., Huntersville, NC 28078. Tel.: 980-875-5600, 800-777-0003.
Web Site: www.duke-energy.com
Institution Type/Description: Science Museum.
Hours & Admission Prices: Mon.-Fri. 9-5, Sat. 12-5; groups of 10 or more by appointment. Closed New Year's Day; Easter; Thanksgiving; Christmas Eve & Day. &

HISTORIC LATTA PLANTATION, 5225 Sample Rd., Huntersville, NC 28078-9107. Tel.: 704-875-2312. Fax: 704-875-1724. Facebook.
E-mail: dclay@lattaplantation.org
Web Site: www.lattaplantation.org
Key Personnel: Exec. Dir., David Clay; Bd. Pres., Bill Crosby; Dir. Education, Heather Lineberger; Visitor Svcs. Mgr., Maureen Steine.
Institution Type/Description: Historic House Museum: 1800 house.
Hours & Admission Prices: Tues.-Sat. 10-5, Sun. 1-5. Adults $8, seniors 62 & over and students $7; discount to groups of 15 or more & AAM members; members & children under 5 no charge. Closed major holidays.
Attendance: 30,000 (actual)

HISTORIC RURAL HILL, INC., 4431 Neck Rd., Huntersville, NC 28078-8342. Mailing Address: P.O. Box 1009, Huntersville, NC 28070-1009. Tel.: 704-875-3113. Fax: 704-875-3193. Facebook.
E-mail: office@ruralhill.net
Web Site: www.ruralhill.net
Formerly: Catawba Valley Scottish Society
Key Personnel: Exec. Dir., Jeff Fissel; Dir. Education, Zac Vinson.
Institution Type/Description: Historic Site: housed on the former farm of Major John & Violet Davidson, one of the original signers of the Mecklenburg Declaration of Independence.
Hours & Admission Prices: Mon.-Fri. 9-4, Sat. call for hours. Adults 13 & over $6, children 5-12 $4; children 4 & under no charge. &
Attendance: 90,000 (estimated)

LATTA PLANTATION NATURE PRESERVE, 6211 Sample Rd., Huntersville, NC 28078. Tel.: 704-875-1391. Fax: 704-875-1394.
Web Site: www.mecknc.gov/ParkandRec/StewardshipServices/NatureCenters/Pages/Latta.aspx
Institution Type/Description: Nature Preserve.
Hours & Admission Prices: Mon.-Sat. 9-5, Sun. 1-5. No charge.

METROLINA GREENHOUSES, 16400 Huntersville Concord Rd., Huntersville, NC 28078. Tel.: 704-875-1371, 800-543-3915. Fax: 704-875-6741.
Web Site: www.metrolinagreenhouses.com
Institution Type/Description: Agricultural Museum.
Hours & Admission Prices: By appointment.

Jacksonville

LYNNWOOD PARK ZOO, 1071 Wells Rd., Jacksonville, NC 28540. Tel.: 910-938-5848.
Web Site: www.lynnwoodparkzoo.com
Institution Type/Description: Zoo.
Hours & Admission Prices: Fri.-Mon. 10-5; groups by appointment. Adults $9, children 2-12 $7.

MONTFORD POINT MARINES MUSEUM, Bldg. M101 East Wing, Marine Corps Base, Camp Gilbert H. Johnson, Jacksonville, NC 28540. Mailing Address: MPMA, Inc., P.O. Box 711, Quantico, VA 22134. Tel.: 910-554-0808.
E-mail: museumdirector@montfordpointmarines.org
Web Site: montfordpointmarines.org
Key Personnel: Natl. Pres., Dr. James T. Averhart, Jr.
Institution Type/Description: Military History Museum: housed on the former training facility for black Marines from 1842-1949.
Hours & Admission Prices: Tues. & Thurs. 11-4; groups by appointment.

Jamestown

MENDENHALL HOMEPLACE, 603 W. Main St., Jamestown, NC 27282. Mailing Address: P.O. Box 512, Jamestown, NC 27282-0512. Tel.: 336-454-3819. Facebook: Mendenhall Homeplace.
E-mail: director@mendenhallhomeplace.com
Web Site: www.mendenhallplantation.org
Formerly: Mendenhall Plantation
Key Personnel: Dir., Shawn M. Rogers; Pres. (V), Shirley Haworth.
Institution Type/Description: Historic House Museum: home built in 1811. Listed on the National Register of Historic Places.
Hours & Admission Prices: early Jan.-Feb. Fri.-Sat. 1-4; March to late Dec. Tues.-Fri. 11-3, Sat. 1-4. Adults $5, seniors, students & children over 13 $3, children under 13 $2.
Attendance: 3,000 (estimated)

Kenansville

COWAN MUSEUM OF HISTORY AND SCIENCE, 411 S. Main St., Kenansville, NC 28349. Mailing Address: P.O. Box 950, Kenansville, NC 28349-0950. Tel.: 910-296-2149. Fax: 910-296-2107. Facebook; Twitter.
E-mail: curator@cowanmuseum.org
Web Site: www.cowanmuseum.org
Formerly: Cowan Museum
Key Personnel: Dir., Robin Grotke; Museum Asst., Kawan Allen.
Institution Type/Description: History & Science Museum.
Hours & Admission Prices: Tues.-Sat. 10-4. No charge; donations accepted. Closed holidays; holiday weekend. &
Attendance: 2,500 (estimated)

LIBERTY HALL PLANTATION, 409 S. Main St., Kenansville, NC 28349. Mailing Address: P.O. Box 634, Kenansville, NC 28349. Tel.: 910-296-2175.
E-mail: libertyhalltours@embarqmail.com
Web Site: www.libertyhallnc.org
Institution Type/Description: Historic House Museum: housed in an 11 room Southern plantation; built in the early 1800s.
Hours & Admission Prices: Tues.-Sat. 10-4. Admission $5; groups by appointment. Closed major holidays.

Kenly

TOBACCO FARM LIFE MUSEUM, INC., Hwy. 301 N., 709 Church St., Kenly, NC 27542. Mailing Address: P.O. Box 88, Kenly, NC 27542-0088. Tel.: 919-284-3431. Fax: 919-284-9788. Facebook.
E-mail: curator@tobaccofarmlifemuseum.org
Web Site: www.tobaccofarmlifemuseum.org.
Key Personnel: Mgr. & Cur., Melody Worthington.
Institution Type/Description: Agriculture Museum.
Hours & Admission Prices: mid-Jan. to Dec. Tues.-Sat. 9:30-5. Adults $8, senior citizens $7, students $6; discounts to AAM, AAA & NCMC members; members & children 2 & under no charge. Closed Easter; Thanksgiving; Christmas & day after. &
Attendance: 6,000 (actual)

Kernersville

KORNER'S FOLLY, 413 S. Main St., Kernersville, NC 27284-2737. Mailing Address: P.O. Box 2091, Kernersville, NC 27285. Tel.: 336-996-7922. Facebook: Korner's Folly.
E-mail: dale@kornersfolly.org
Web Site: www.kornersfolly.org
Key Personnel: Exec. Dir., Dale Pennington; Pres., Ray Smith; Treas., Tom McDaniel.
Institution Type/Description: Historic House: c.1880 Victorian home.
Hours & Admission Prices: Wed.-Sat. 10-4, Sun. 1-4. Adults $10, children $6; children under 6 & members no charge. Closed New Year's Day; Easter; Fourth of July; Thanksgiving; Christmas.
Attendance: 8,500 (actual)

PAUL J. CIENER BOTANICAL GARDEN, 215 S. Main St., Kernersville, NC 27284. Tel.: 336-996-7888.
E-mail: jwhisnant@pjcbg.org
Web Site: cienerbotanicalgarden.org
Key Personnel: Exec. Dir., John Whisnant; Chm. (V), David Ciener; Prog. Coord., Toni Hays; Museum Shop Mgr., Kim Babyak; Cur., Adrienne Roethling.
Institution Type/Description: Botanical Garden.
Hours & Admission Prices: Gardens: daily dawn to dusk. Welcome Center: Mon.-Fri. 9-5. No charge; donations accepted.
Attendance: 15,000 (estimated)

Kill Devil Hills

WRIGHT BROTHERS NATIONAL MEMORIAL, 1000 Croatan Hwy., Kill Devil Hills, NC 27948. Mailing Address: 1401 National Park Dr., Manteo, NC 27954. Tel.: 252-473-2111. Fax: 252-473-2595.
E-mail: caha_public_affairs@nps.gov
Web Site: www.nps.gov/wrbr
Key Personnel: Supt., Dave Hallac.
Institution Type/Description: Located on the site of the Wright Brothers first powered flight in 1903. Centennial Pavilion: reconstructed Wright camp buildings & 60 ft. memorial shaft atop Big Kill Devil Hill.
Hours & Admission Prices: Daily 9-5. Admission $7; children 15 & under no charge. Closed Christmas. &
Attendance: 496,500 (actual)

Kings Mountain

CROWDERS MOUNTAIN STATE PARK, 522 Park Office Lane, Kings Mountain, NC 28086-7902. Tel.: 704-853-5375. Fax: 704-853-5391.
E-mail: crowders.mountain@ncdenr.gov
Key Personnel: Park Supt., Larry Hyde.
Institution Type/Description: Park & Visitors Center.
Hours & Admission Prices: Park: March-April & Sept.-Oct. daily 8-8; May-Aug. daily 8-9; Nov.-Feb. daily 8-6. No charge. Closed Christmas. &
Attendance: 349,000 (actual)

KINGS MOUNTAIN HISTORICAL FIRE MUSEUM, 211 Cleveland Ave., Kings Mountain, NC 28086. Mailing Address: c/o Kings Mountain Fire Dept., P.O. Box 429, Kings Mountain, NC 28086-0429. Tel.: 704-734-0555. Fax: 704-734-4468.
E-mail: frankb@cityofkm.com
Web Site: kmfire.com
Key Personnel: Chm. (V), Frank Burns.
Institution Type/Description: Fire Museum.
Hours & Admission Prices: Call for hours. No charge.
Attendance: 350 (estimated)

KINGS MOUNTAIN HISTORICAL MUSEUM, 100 E. Mountain St., Kings Mountain, NC 28086. Mailing Address: P.O. Box 552, Kings Mountain, NC 28086. Tel.: 704-739-1019. Fax: 704-734-4537.
E-mail: director@kingsmountainmuseum.org
Web Site: www.kingsmountainmuseum.org
Key Personnel: Dir. & Cur., Adria L. Focht.
Institution Type/Description: History Museum.
Hours & Admission Prices: Tues.-Sat. 10-4; groups by appointment. No charge; donations accepted. Closed New Year's Day; Independence Day; Thanksgiving; Christmas Eve & Day. &
Attendance: 5,500 (actual)

Kinston

CSS NEUSE STATE HISTORIC SITE AND GOV. RICHARD CASWELL MEMORIAL, 100 N. Queen St., Kinston, NC 28504-4928. Tel.: 252-522-2091. Fax: 252-527-7036.
E-mail: cssneuse@ncdcr.gov
Web Site: www.cssneuse.nchistoricsites.org
Key Personnel: Historic Site Mgr., Guy Smith; Historic Interpreter III, Morris Bass; Historic Interpreter II & Museum Shop Mgr., Holly Weaver; Historic Site Asst., Thomas R. Dawson; Office Asst. III, Sharon Clements; Maintenance Mechanic II, Gaston Davis.
Institution Type/Description: Historic Site.
Hours & Admission Prices: Mon.-Sat. call for hours. No charge; donations accepted. Closed major state holidays. &
Attendance: 13,000 (estimated)

CSS NEUSE II, 118 W. Heritage St., Kinston, NC 28502. Mailing Address: C.S.S. Neuse Foundation, Inc., P.O. Box 251, Kinston, NC 28502-0251. Tel.: 252-560-2150.
E-mail: info@cssneuseii.org
Web Site: www.cssneuseii.org
Key Personnel: Dir., David Mooring.
Institution Type/Description: Military History Museum.
Hours & Admission Prices: Sat. 10-4; other times by appointment. No charge; donations accepted.

CASWELL CENTER MUSEUM AND VISITOR CENTER, 2415 W. Vernon Ave., Kinston, NC 28504. Tel.: 252-208-3780. Fax: 252-208-3771.
E-mail: caswell.center@ncmail.net
Institution Type/Description: History Museum.
Hours & Admission Prices: No charge; donations accepted.

CASWELL NO. 1 FIRE STATION MUSEUM, 118 S. Queen St., Kinston, NC 28501. Mailing Address: 1005 Oriental Ave., Kinston, NC 28504. Tel.: 252-522-4676 & 527-1566. Facebook.
E-mail: director@prideofkinston.org
Institution Type/Description: Historic Building: housed in the city's original fire station; built in 1895. Listed on the National Register of Historic Places.
Hours & Admission Prices: Tues., Thurs. & Sat. 10-4. No charge.

EXCHANGE NATURE CENTER, 401 W. Caswell St., Kinston, NC 28501. Tel.: 252-939-3367.
Institution Type/Description: Nature Center.
Hours & Admission Prices: Tues.-Sat. 9:30-5, Sun. 1-5.

HARMONY HALL, 109 E. King St., Kinston, NC 28501. Mailing Address: P.O. Box 3171, Kinston, 28502. Tel.: 252-522-0421. Facebook.
E-mail: harmony.hall.kinston@gmail.com
Web Site: www.harmonyhallkinston.com
Institution Type/Description: Historic House: built in 1772.
Hours & Admission Prices: Wed.-Sat. 10-4. No charge; donations accepted.
Attendance: 500 (estimated)

KINSTON COMMUNITY COUNCIL FOR THE ARTS, 400 N. Queen St., Kinston, NC 28501. Tel.: 252-527-2517. Fax: 252-527-8280.
E-mail: slandis@kinstoncca.com
Web Site: www.kinstoncca.com
Formerly: Kinston Arts Council, Inc.
Key Personnel: Exec. Dir., Sandy Landis; Opers. Mgr., Jo Anna Dail.
Institution Type/Description: Arts Council: housed in historic building.
Hours & Admission Prices: Tues.-Fri. 10-6, Sat. 10-2. No charge, donations accepted. Closed state holidays. &
Attendance: 10,000

NEUSEWAY PLANETARIUM, HEALTH & SCIENCE MUSEUM, 403 W. Caswell St., Kinston, NC 28501. Tel.: 252-939-3302.
Web Site: www.neusewaypark.com
Institution Type/Description: Science Museum & Planetarium.
Hours & Admission Prices: Museum: Tues.-Sat. 9:30-5, Sun. 1-5. Planetarium: Tues.-Fri. 1 & 4, Sat. 11am, 1 & 4, Sun. 2 & 4.

Kitty Hawk

OUTER BANKS CHILDREN AT PLAY, 3810 N. Croatan Hwy., Kitty Hawk, NC 27949. Tel.: 252-261-0290.
E-mail: info@childrenatplayobx.com
Web Site: www.childrenatplayobx.com
Key Personnel: Dir., Alyssa Hannon; Pres. (V), Diane Wehner.
Institution Type/Description: Children's Museum.
Hours & Admission Prices: Tues.-Sat. 10-5. Children $7, adults $5, 12 months & under no charge. Closed Thanksgiving; Christmas Eve, Day & day after. &
Attendance: 8,000 (actual)

Kure Beach

FORT FISHER STATE HISTORIC SITE, U.S. Hwy. 421-1610 Fort Fisher Blvd., S. of Kure Beach, Kure Beach, NC 28449. Tel.: 910-458-5538. Fax: 910-458-0477.
E-mail: fisher@ncdcr.gov
Web Site: www.nchistoricsites.org/fisher
Key Personnel: Dir., Jim Steele; Support Group CEO, Paul Laird.
Institution Type/Description: Historic Site & Visitor Center.
Hours & Admission Prices: Tues-Sat 9-5, Sun. noon-5. No charge, donations accepted. Closed most state holidays. &
Attendance: 800,000 (actual)

NORTH CAROLINA AQUARIUM AT FORT FISHER, 900 Loggerhead Rd., Kure Beach, NC 28449-3786. Mailing Address: c/o NC Aquarium Society, 3125 Poplarwood Ct., Ste. 160, Raleigh, NC 27604. Tel.: 910-458-8257. Fax: 910-458-6812.
E-mail: ffmail@ncaquariums.com
Web Site: www.ncaquariums.com/fort-fisher
Key Personnel: Dir., Peggy Sloan; Pres., Neal Conoley; Aquariums Dir., David Griffin; Cur. Exhibits, David Barney; Cur. Education, Jennifer Metzler-Fiorino; Dive Safety Officer, Brian Germick; Business Mgr., Angie Leary; Visitor & Member Svcs. Coord., Joanna Zazzali; Media Technician, Bob Griffin; Public Rels. Coord., Robin Nalepa; Museum Shop Mgr., Jill Kennen.
Institution Type/Description: Aquarium: aquatic life & habitats of North Carolina.
Hours & Admission Prices: Daily 9-5. Adults 13-61 $10.95, seniors 62 & over & military $9.95, children 3-12 $8.95; discounts to AAM members; children 2 & under, registered school groups & NCAS members no charge. Closed New Year's Day; Thanksgiving; Christmas. &
Attendance: 420,176 (actual)

Lake Junaluska

WORLD METHODIST MUSEUM, 575 N. Lakeshore Dr., Lake Junaluska, NC 28745-9742. Mailing Address: P.O. Box 518, Lake Junaluska, NC 28745-0518. Tel.: 828-456-7242. Fax: 828-456-9433. Facebook.
E-mail: jbolden@worldmethodistcouncil.org
Web Site: www.methodistmuseum.org
Key Personnel: Gen. Sec. World Methodist Council, Bishop Ivan Abrahams; Asst. to Gen. Sec., Barbara Bowser; Museum Dir., Jackie R. Bolden.
Institution Type/Description: Religious History Museum.
Hours & Admission Prices: Tues.-Sat. 9-4, special groups by appointment. No charge; donations accepted. Closed holidays. &
Attendance: 12,500 (actual)

Lake Waccamaw

LAKE WACCAMAW DEPOT MUSEUM, 201 Flemington Ave., Lake Waccamaw, NC 28450. Mailing Address: P.O. Box 386, Lake Waccamaw, NC 28450-0386. Tel.: 910-646-1992. Facebook: Lake Waccamaw Depot Museum.
E-mail: info@lakewaccamawdepotmuseum.com
Web Site: lakewaccamawdepotmuseum.com
Key Personnel: Chm. (V), Nancy Sigmon; Treas., Jackie Brooks; Cur., Rebecca Lane; Museum Shop Mgr., Charlotte Hollingsworth.
Institution Type/Description: Marine Science & History Museum; housed in c.1904 railroad station.
Hours & Admission Prices: Wed.-Fri. 10-3, Sat. 10-1. No charge; donations accepted. &
Attendance: 3,600 (estimated)

Laurinburg

JOHN BLUE HOUSE AND MUSEUM, 13040 X-Way Rd., Laurinburg, NC 28352. Mailing Address: P.O. Box 152, Laurinburg, NC 28353. Tel.: 910-280-0435.
E-mail: walkeramj@bellsouth.net
Web Site: johnbluecottonfestival.com
Key Personnel: Museum Shop Mgr., Jim Walker.
Institution Type/Description: Historic House: built in the early 1890s by businessman, farmer & inventor, John Blue Sr.
Hours & Admission Prices: Call for hours. No charge; donations accepted. &
Attendance: 5,000 (estimated)

MUSEUM OF SCOTLAND COUNTY, 13043 X Way Rd., Laurinburg, NC 28353. Mailing Address: c/o Scotland Co. Tourism & Development Authority, 507 W. Covington St., Laurinburg, NC 28353. Tel.: 910-276-2496.
Web Site: www.scotlandcounty-museum.com
Institution Type/Description: History Museum.
Hours & Admission Prices: Call for hours.

ST. ANDREWS PRESBYTERIAN COLLEGE ART GALLERY, 1700 Dogwood Mile, Laurinburg, NC 28352-5521. Tel.: 910-277-5555. Fax: 910-277-5020.
Institution Type/Description: Art Gallery.
Hours & Admission Prices: Mon.-Fri. 9-4:30. No charge.

SCOTTISH HERITAGE CENTER, St. Andrews Presbyterian College, DeTamble Library, 1700 Dogwood Mile, Laurinburg, NC 28352. Tel.: 910-277-5236. Fax: 910-277-5020.
E-mail: bagpipe@sapc.edu
Web Site: www.sapc.edu
Key Personnel: Dir., Bill Caudill.
Institution Type/Description: Heritage Center.
Hours & Admission Prices: Call for hours.

Lenoir

CALDWELL ARTS COUNCIL, 601 College Ave., Lenoir, NC 28645-5406. Mailing Address: P.O. Box 1613, Lenoir, NC 28645-1613. Tel.: 828-754-2486. Fax: 828-754-2440. Facebook: Caldwell Arts Council.
E-mail: info@caldwellarts.com
Web Site: www.caldwellarts.com
Key Personnel: Dir., Adrienne Roellgen.
Institution Type/Description: Cultural Arts Museum.
Hours & Admission Prices: Tues.-Fri. 9-5, Sat. 10-2. No charge.

CALDWELL HERITAGE MUSEUM, INC., 112 Vaiden St., S.W., Lenoir, NC 28645-5670. Tel.: 828-758-4004. Fax: 828-758-4242. Facebook: @CaldwellHeritageMuseum.
E-mail: caldwellheritagemuseum@yahoo.com
Web Site: www.caldwellheritagemuseum.org
Key Personnel: Dir., Jeff H. Stepp; Chm. (V), Mike Gibbons.
Institution Type/Description: History Museum.
Hours & Admission Prices: Tues.-Fri. 10-4:30, Sat. 10-3. No charge; donations accepted. &
Attendance: 3,200 (estimated)

FORT DEFIANCE, 1792 Fort Defiance Dr., Lenoir, NC 28645-6606. Tel.: 828-758-1671.
E-mail: fortdefiancenc@gmail.com
Web Site: fortdefiancenc.org
Institution Type/Description: Historic Building: former home of Revolutionary War hero, Gen. William Lenoir; built in 1792.
Hours & Admission Prices: April-Oct. Thurs.-Sat. 10-5, Sun. 1-5; Nov.-March Sat.-Sun. by appointment.

TUTTLE EDUCATIONAL STATE FOREST, 3420 Playmore Beach Rd., Lenoir, NC 28655. Tel.: 828-757-5608.
E-mail: tuttleESF.DFR@ncagr.gov
Institution Type/Description: Park Museum.
Hours & Admission Prices: mid-March to mid-Nov. Tues.-Sun. call for hours.

Level Cross

RICHARD PETTY MUSEUM, 311 Branson Mill Rd., Level Cross, NC 27317. Mailing Address: 311 Branson Mill Rd., Randleman, NC 27317. Tel.: 336-495-1143. Fax: 336-495-1543.
E-mail: info@rpmuseum.com
Web Site: www.rpmuseum.com
Key Personnel: Exec. Dir., Jean Wilson; C.E.O., Richard Petty; Museum Shop Mgr., Bonnie Davis.
Institution Type/Description: Petty Family & History Museum.
Hours & Admission Prices: Wed.-Sat. 9-5. Adults $10, seniors $8, students $5; discounts to groups & military families; children 6 & under and military no charge. Closed Thanksgiving; Christmas. &
Attendance: 3,500 (estimated)

Lexington

DAVIDSON COUNTY HISTORICAL MUSEUM, 2 S. Main St., Old Courthouse on the Square, Lexington, NC 27292-3320. Tel.: 336-242-2035. Fax: 336-242-2871.
E-mail: choffmann@co.davidson.nc.us
Web Site: www.co.davidson.nc.us/HistoricalMuseum
Key Personnel: Library Dir., Ruth Ann Copley; Cur., Catherine Hoffmann.
Institution Type/Description: Local History Museum: housed in the county's oldest existing courthouse; built in 1858. Listed on the National Register of Historic Places.
Hours & Admission Prices: Tues.-Fri. 10-4, first Sun. of month 2-4. No charge; donations accepted. Closed holidays. &
Attendance: 18,000 (actual)

Lincolnton

LINCOLN COUNTY MUSEUM OF HISTORY, 403 E. Main St., Lincolnton, NC 28092-3305. Tel.: 704-748-9090. Fax: 704-732-9057.
E-mail: lcmh@bellsouth.net
Web Site: www.lincolncountyhistory.com
Key Personnel: Exec. Dir., Jason L. Harpe; Cur. Archaeology & Collections, January W. Porter; Administrative Asst., Tina Guffey.
Institution Type/Description: History Museum.
Hours & Admission Prices: Tues. & Thurs. 1-5, Sun. 2-5. No charge; donations accepted. &
Attendance: 4,000 (estimated)

Linville

GRANDFATHER MOUNTAIN, 2050 Blowing Rock Hwy., Linville, NC 28646. Mailing Address: P.O. Box 129, Linville, NC 28646. Tel.: 800-468-7325. Fax: 828-733-2608. Facebook.
E-mail: nature@grandfather.com
Web Site: www.grandfather.com
Key Personnel: Dir., Jesse Pope.
Institution Type/Description: Nature Center.
Hours & Admission Prices: Early Spring: Mon.-Fri. 9-5, Sat.-Sun. 9-6; Spring: daily 9-6; Summer: daily 8-7; Fall: daily 9-7; Winter: daily 9-5. Adults $18, seniors 60 & over $15, children 4-12 $8; discounts to AAA members; children under 4 no charge. &
Attendance: 250,000 (estimated)

Littleton

BUCK SPRING - NATHANIEL MACON HOMEPLACE, 217 Nathaniel Macon Dr., Littleton, NC 27850. Mailing Address: c/o Warren County Historic Preservation Commission, 542 W. Ridgeway St., Warrenton, NC 27589. Tel.: 252-257-3640. Fax: 252-257-5616.
E-mail: paulapulley@warrencountync.gov
Institution Type/Description: History Museum.

Hours & Admission Prices: Call for hours.

Louisburg

LOUISBURG COLLEGE ART GALLERY, 501 N. Main St., Louisburg, NC 27549-2399. Tel.: 919-497-3238. Fax: 919-496-1788.
E-mail: whinton@louisburg.edu
Web Site: www.louisburg.edu/news/art.html
Key Personnel: Dir. & Cur., William Hinton; Business Officer, Belinda Faulkner; Public Rels. & Publications Dir., Amy McManus.
Institution Type/Description: Art Gallery: housed in 1787 Louisburg College auditorium theatre complex.
Hours & Admission Prices: Mon.-Fri. 9-5. No charge. Closed holidays. &
Attendance: 10,000

Lumberton

EXPLORATION STATION, 104 N. Chestnut St., Lumberton, NC 28358. Mailing Address: 210 E. Second St., Lumberton, NC 28358. Tel.: 910-738-1114. Fax: 910-738-4379.
E-mail: info@explorationstation.co
Web Site: www.robesonpartnership.org
Key Personnel: Exec. Dir., Dr. Jessica Lowery.
Institution Type/Description: Children's Museum.
Hours & Admission Prices: Wed. 10-5, Thurs. & Fri. 10-7, Sat. 10-5, Sun. 1-5. Children over 1 $4, adults $3; discounts to ACM members; members no charge.
Attendance: 383 (estimated)

ROBESON COUNTY HISTORY MUSEUM, P.O. Box 2503, Lumberton, NC 28359. Mailing Address: P.O. Box 2503, Lumberton, NC 28359. Tel.: 910-738-7979.
E-mail: richardmonroe@nc.rr.com
Web Site: robesoncountyhistory.org
Key Personnel: Cur., Blake Tyner; Pres. (V), Richard H. Monroe.
Institution Type/Description: History Museum: housed in the Southern Express Building.
Hours & Admission Prices: Tues. & Thurs. 10 to noon, Sun. 2-4. No charge; donations accepted. Closed holidays. &

ROBESON PLANETARIUM AND SCIENCE CENTER, 420 Caton Rd., Lumberton, NC 28358. Tel.: 910-735-2147. Fax: 910-671-6017. Facebook.
E-mail: brandt@uncp.edu
Web Site: www.robeson.k12.nc.us/domain/47
Key Personnel: Dir., Ken Brandt.
Institution Type/Description: Planetarium & Science Center.
Hours & Admission Prices: Call for hours & admission. No charge. &
Attendance: 9,000 (estimated)

Maggie Valley

WHEELS THROUGH TIME MUSEUM, INC., 62 Vintage Ln., Maggie Valley, NC 28751. Mailing Address: P.O. Box 790, Maggie Valley, NC 28751-0790. Tel.: 828-926-6266. Fax: 828-926-9158.
E-mail: info@wheelsthroughtime.com
Web Site: www.wheelsthroughtime.com
Institution Type/Description: Motorcycle & Automobile Museum.
Hours & Admission Prices: April-Nov. Thurs.-Mon. 9-5. Adults $15, seniors 65 & over $12, children 6-14 $7. &
Attendance: 50,000 (estimated)

Manteo

ALLIGATOR RIVER NATIONAL WILDLIFE REFUGE & VISITOR CENTER, 100 Conservation Way, Manteo, NC 27954. Mailing Address: P.O. Box 1969, Manteo, NC 27954. Tel.: 252-473-1131. Fax: 252-473-1668.
E-mail: alligatorriver@fws.gov
Web Site: www.fws.gov/refuge/alligator-river
Key Personnel: Refuge Mgr., Mike Bryant; Deputy Refuge Mgr., Scott Lanier; Visitor Svcs. Mgr., Bonnie Strawser; Visitor Ctr. Mgr., Mary Grindlay.
Institution Type/Description: Wildlife Refuge.
Hours & Admission Prices: Refuge: daily daylight hours. Visitor Center: Mon.-Sat. 9-4, Sun. 12-4. No charge; donations accepted.

DARE COUNTY REGIONAL AIRPORT MUSEUM, 410 Airport Rd., Manteo, NC 27954. Mailing Address: P.O. Box 429, Manteo, NC 27954. Tel.: 252-475-5570. Fax: 252-473-1196.
E-mail: museum@darenc.com
Web Site: www.darenc.com/airport/museum.htm
Key Personnel: Dir. Airport, David Daniels.
Institution Type/Description: Aviation History Museum.
Hours & Admission Prices: Daily 8-7.

ELIZABETHAN GARDENS, 1411 National Park Dr., Manteo, NC 27954. Tel.: 252-473-3234. Fax: 252-473-3244.
E-mail: tours@elizabethangardens.org
Web Site: www.elizabethangardens.org
Key Personnel: Exec. Dir., Carl Curnutte, III.
Institution Type/Description: Gardens.
Hours & Admission Prices: March & Oct.-Nov. daily 9-5; April-May & Sept. daily 9-6; June-Aug. daily 9-7; Dec. daily 10-4. Adults $9, youth 6-17 $6, children 5 & under and pets $3, members no charge. Closed New Year's Eve & Day; Thanksgiving; Christmas Eve & Day. &

FORT RALEIGH NATIONAL HISTORIC SITE, 1401 National Park Dr., Manteo, NC 27954. Tel.: 252-473-5772. Fax: 252-473-1049.
E-mail: caha_information@nps.gov
Web Site: www.nps.gov/fora
Key Personnel: Supt., Barclay Trimble; Archives Technician, Jami P. Lanier; Volunteer Coord., Mary Doll; Museum Shop Mgr., Rulaine Kegerris.
Institution Type/Description: Historic Park Museum: located on the site of the 1585-1587 Roanoke Island Colony attempts.
Hours & Admission Prices: Park: daily sunrise to sunset. Visitor Center: daily 9-5. Closed Christmas. &
Attendance: 170,780 (estimated)

NORTH CAROLINA AQUARIUM ON ROANOKE ISLAND, 374 Airport Rd., Manteo, NC 27954-9485. Mailing Address: P.O. Box 967, Manteo, NC 27954. Tel.: 252-475-2300. Fax: 252-473-1980. Facebook & Instagram: North Carolina Aquarium on Roanoke Island.
E-mail: rimail@ncaquariums.com
Web Site: www.ncaquariums.com
Key Personnel: Dir., Maylon White; C.E.O. & Business Mgr., Deborah Edelman.
Institution Type/Description: Aquarium.
Hours & Admission Prices: Daily 9-5. Adults $10.95, senior citizens 62 & over $9.95, children 3-12 $8.95; children 2 & under, members, NC Aquarium society, NC school groups, Martin Luther King Day, & Veterans Day no charge. Closed Thanksgiving; Christmas. &
Attendance: 184,998 (actual)

PEA ISLAND NATIONAL WILDLIFE REFUGE, 100 Conservation Way, Manteo, NC 27954. Mailing Address: P.O. Box 1969, Manteo, NC 27954. Tel.: 252-473-1131. Fax: 252-473-1668.
E-mail: alligatorriver@fws.gov
Web Site: www.fws.gov/refuge/pea_island
Key Personnel: Refuge Mgr., Mike Bryant.
Institution Type/Description: Wildlife Refuge.
Hours & Admission Prices: Daily 9-4. No charge; donations accepted.
Attendance: 2,500,000 (actual)

ROANOKE ISLAND FESTIVAL PARK, One Festival Park, Manteo, NC 27954-9396. Tel.: 252-475-1500. Fax: 252-475-1507.
E-mail: festivalparkinformation@ncdcr.gov
Web Site: www.roanokeisland.com
Key Personnel: Exec. Dir., Kim Sawyer; Chm. (V), Ellen Newbold; Pres. (V), Friends of Elizabeth II, Tod Clissold; Operations Mgr., Amy Hinnant; Facilities Mgr., Carroll Williams; Communications Mgr., Tanya Young.
Institution Type/Description: History Museum: living history 1585 settlement site & replica 16th century ship.
Hours & Admission Prices: March 2-Dec. daily 9-5. Adults $10, students $7; discounts to groups; members & children under 5 no charge. &
Attendance: 135,000 (actual)

ROANOKE ISLAND MARITIME MUSEUM, 104 Fernando St., On the Manteo Waterfront, Manteo, NC 27954. Mailing Address: c/o Town of Manteo, P.O. Box 246, Manteo, NC 27954. Tel.: 252-475-1750.
E-mail: wickre@townofmanteo.com
Web Site: www.townofmanteo.com
Institution Type/Description: Maritime Museum.
Hours & Admission Prices: Temporarily closed.

ROANOKE MARSHES LIGHTHOUSE, Queen Elizabeth Ave., Manteo, NC 27954. Mailing Address: P.O. Box 246, Manteo, NC 27954. Tel.: 252-475-1750.
E-mail: FestivalParkInformation@ncdcr.gov
Institution Type/Description: History Museum.
Hours & Admission Prices: Temporarily closed.

Marion

HISTORIC CARSON HOUSE, 1805 US Hwy. 70 W., Marion, NC 28752. Tel.: 828-724-4948.
E-mail: info@historiccarsonhouse.com
Web Site: www.historiccarsonhouse.com
Key Personnel: Chm., Dr. James Haney; Exec. Dir., Sara Bryant; Treas., Leslie Morgan; Sec., Ann McNutt.
Institution Type/Description: History Museum: housed in 1793 Col. John Carson House.
Hours & Admission Prices: April-Nov. Wed.-Sat. 10-4, Sun. 2-5; groups by appointment. Adults $5; members & children under 12 no charge. ⑀
Attendance: 3,000 (estimated)

LINVILLE CAVERNS, 19929 US 221 N., Marion, NC 28752. Tel.: 800-419-0540. Fax: 828-756-4171.
E-mail: info@linvillecaverns.com
Institution Type/Description: Geology Museum.
Hours & Admission Prices: March & Nov. daily 9-4:30; April-May & Sept.-Oct. daily 9-5; June to Labor Day daily 9-6; Dec.-Feb. Sat.-Sun. 9-4:30. Adults $7.50, seniors 62 & over $6.50, children 5-12 $5.50; children under 5 no charge.

Mars Hill

RURAL LIFE MUSEUM, Mars Hill College, Montague Bldg., Cascade & College Sts., Mars Hill, NC 28754. Mailing Address: Mars Hill College, P.O. Box 6706, Mars Hill, NC 28754-5000. Tel.: 828-689-1262.
E-mail: lreker@mhu.edu
Web Site: www.mhu.edu/museum
Institution Type/Description: History Museum.
Hours & Admission Prices: By appointment. No charge.

Mayodan

MAYO RIVER STATE PARK, 500 Old Mayo Park Rd., Mayodan, NC 27027. Tel.: 336-427-2530.
E-mail: mayo.river@ncparks.gov
Web Site: ncparks.gov/visit/parks/mari/main.php
Institution Type/Description: Park Museum.
Hours & Admission Prices: Call for hours.

McLeansville

REPLACEMENTS, LTD. MUSEUM, 1089 Knox Rd., McLeansville, NC 27301. Tel.: 800-737-5223.
E-mail: inquire@replacements.com
Institution Type/Description: China Museum.
Hours & Admission Prices: Tours: daily 9:30-6.

Midland

REED GOLD MINE STATE HISTORIC SITE, 9621 Reed Mine Rd., Midland, NC 28107-9673. Tel.: 704-721-4653. Facebook: Reed Gold Mine State Historic Site.
E-mail: larry.neal@ncdcr.gov
Web Site: www.nchistoricsites.org/reed
Key Personnel: Site Mgr., Larry K. Neal, Jr.; Museum Shop Mgr., Susan Smith.
Institution Type/Description: Historic Site: 1799 site of the first documented discovery of gold in the United States.
Hours & Admission Prices: Tues.-Sat. 9-5. No charge; donations accepted. Gold panning: $3 per person. Closed state holidays. ⑀
Attendance: 48,000 (actual)

Montreat

PRESBYTERIAN HERITAGE CENTER, 318 Georgia Ter., Montreat, NC 28757. Mailing Address: P.O. Box 207, Montreat, NC 28757-0207. Tel.: 828-669-6556.
E-mail: info@phcmontreat.org
Web Site: www.phcmontreat.org
Key Personnel: Exec. Dir., Ron Vinson.

Institution Type/Description: History Museum.
Hours & Admission Prices: Thurs.-Fri. 10-4, Sat. 1-4; other times by appointment. No charge. ⑀

Mooresville

DALE EARNHARDT INC. MUSEUM, 1675 Dale Earnhardt Hwy. 3, Mooresville, NC 28115. Tel.: 704-662-8000. Fax: 704-663-7945.
E-mail: mlucas@dei-zone.com
Institution Type/Description: Sports Museum.
Hours & Admission Prices: Mon.-Fri. 9-5. No charge.

JR MOTORSPORTS, 349 Cayuga Dr., Mooresville, NC 28117. Tel.: 866-576-8883.
E-mail: shoptours@jrmracing.com
Web Site: jrmotorsport.com
Institution Type/Description: Dale Earnhardt Jr.'s Race Shop.
Hours & Admission Prices: Tours: Thurs.-Fri. 9-4:30 by appointment. (email request for tour).

KYLE BUSCH MOTORSPORTS, 351 Mazeppa Rd., Mooresville, NC 28115.
E-mail: web@kylebusch.com
Web Site: www.kylebuschmotorsports.com
Institution Type/Description: Motorsports Museum.
Hours & Admission Prices: Mon.-Fri. 9-4.

LAZY 5 RANCH, 15100 Mooresville Rd., Mooresville, NC 28115-7245. Tel.: 704-663-5100. Fax: 704-664-1549.
E-mail: lazy5ranch@aol.com
Web Site: www.lazy5ranch.com
Institution Type/Description: Zoo.
Hours & Admission Prices: Mon.-Sat. 9 to dusk. Adults $8.50, children 2-11 and seniors 60 & over $5.50; discounts to groups. Wagon Rides: adults $5, children 2-11 and seniors 60 & over $3; discounts to groups.

MEMORY LANE MUSEUM, 769 River Hwy., Mooresville, NC 28117. Tel.: 704-662-3673, 877-270-3509. Fax: 704-662-8515. Facebook: Memory Lane Museum.
E-mail: memorylanemuseum@gmail.com
Web Site: www.memorylaneautomuseum.com
Key Personnel: Dir., Sam Alex Beam; Chm. (V), Sam A. Beam, III; Museum Shop Mgr., Michele Tilton.
Institution Type/Description: Automobile & Racing History Museum.
Hours & Admission Prices: Summer: Mon.-Sat. 10-5; Winter: Mon.-Sat. 10-5. Race Week: May & Oct. Sun. 9-5. Adults $10, children 6-12 $6; children under 6 no charge. ⑀

NORTH CAROLINA AUTO RACING HALL OF FAME, 119 Knob Hill Rd., Lakeside Park, Mooresville, NC 28117-6847. Tel.: 704-663-5331.
E-mail: donna@ncarhof.com
Web Site: www.ncarhof.com
Key Personnel: Mgr., Donna DeNardo.
Institution Type/Description: Auto Racing Museum.
Hours & Admission Prices: Mon.-Fri. 10-5, Sat. 10-3. Adults $6, seniors 55 & over and children 6-12 $4.

PENSKE RACING, 200 Penske Way, Mooresville, NC 28115. Tel.: 704-664-2300.
Web Site: www.raceshops.com
Institution Type/Description: Racing Facility.
Hours & Admission Prices: Mon.-Fri. 9-5; call to confirm. No charge.

Morehead City

HISTORY MUSEUM OF CARTERET COUNTY, 1008 Arendell St., Morehead City, NC 28557-4143. Tel.: 252-247-7533. Fax: 252-247-2756.
E-mail: museumdirector.cchs@gmail.com
Web Site: www.carterethistory.org
Formerly: Carteret County Museum of History & Art
Key Personnel: Pres. (V), Jan Buckingham; Librarian, Pat Edwards; Exec. Dir., Steve Anderson; Museum Shop Mgr., Stacey Veros.
Institution Type/Description: History Museum.
Hours & Admission Prices: Summer: Tues.-Sat. 10-4; Winter: Tues.-Fri. & 1st Sat. each month 10-4. Non-members $3, members $1. Closed holidays. ⑀
Attendance: 5,000 (actual)

Morganton

HERITAGE MUSEUM, 102 E. Union St., Morganton, NC 28655-3448. Mailing Address: P.O. Box 915, Morganton, NC 28680. Tel.: 828-437-4104. Facebook.
E-mail: historicburke@gmail.com
Web Site: www.historicburke.org
Institution Type/Description: History Museum: housed in the Old Burke County Courthouse; built in 1837.
Hours & Admission Prices: Tues.-Fri. 10-4. Suggested Donation: $5. &
Attendance: 2,000 (estimated)

THE HISTORY MUSEUM OF BURKE COUNTY, 201 W. Meeting St., Morganton, NC 28655. Mailing Address: P.O. Box 416, Morganton, NC 28655. Tel.: 828-437-1777.
E-mail: thehistorymuseum@directus.net
Web Site: www.thehistorymuseumofburke.org
Institution Type/Description: History Museum.
Hours & Admission Prices: Call for hours.

MCDOWELL HOUSE AT QUAKER MEADOWS, 119 St. Mary's Church Rd., Morganton, NC 28680. Mailing Address: P.O. Box 915, Morganton, NC 28680-0915. Tel.: 828-437-4104. Facebook: Historic Burke Foundation.
E-mail: historicburke@compascable.net
Web Site: www.historicburke.org
Institution Type/Description: Historic House Museum: built in 1812 by Captain Charles McDowell, Jr.
Hours & Admission Prices: April-Oct. Sun. 2-4; other times by appointment. No charge; donations accepted. &

SENATOR SAM J. ERVIN, JR. LIBRARY AND MUSEUM, Western Piedmont Community College, 1001 Burkemont Ave., Morganton, NC 28655. Tel.: 828-438-6152.
E-mail: library@wpcc.edu
Web Site: www.samervinlibrary.org
Key Personnel: Cur., Daniel R. Smith; Asst. Cur., Nancy Daniel.
Institution Type/Description: History Museum.
Hours & Admission Prices: Mon.-Fri. 8-5. No charge.

Mount Airy

THE ANDY GRIFFITH MUSEUM, 218 Rockford St., Mount Airy, NC 27030. Tel.: 336-786-1604.
E-mail: arts@surryarts.org
Web Site: www.andygriffithmuseum.com
Institution Type/Description: History Museum.
Hours & Admission Prices: Mon.-Sat. 9-5, Sun. 1-5; groups by appointment. Closed Thanksgiving; Christmas.

GERTRUDE SMITH HOUSE, 708 N. Main St., Mount Airy, NC 27030. Mailing Address: 615 N. Main St., Mount Airy, NC 27030-3723. Tel.: 336-786-6856, 336-755-3283.
E-mail: gilmersmith708@gmail.com
Key Personnel: Chm., David Beal; Supvr. Buildings & Grounds, Cindy Puckett; Sec. Foundation, Tom Fawcett.
Institution Type/Description: Cultural & Enrichment Center: housed in the former Jefferson Davis Smith family home; built in 1903. Listed on the National Register of Historic Places.
Hours & Admission Prices: April-Dec. Mon., Wed. & Fri.-Sat. 11-4; other times by appointment, call 336-786-6856. No charge; Closed holidays. &
Attendance: 8,947 (actual)

MOORE HOUSE, 202 Moore Ave., Mount Airy, NC 27030. Mailing Address: c/o Mount Airy Restoration Foundation, PO Box 447, Mount Airy, NC 27030. Tel.: 336-786-6116, 800-948-0949.
Institution Type/Description: Historic House: built in 1862.
Hours & Admission Prices: Call for hours.

MOUNT AIRY MUSEUM OF REGIONAL HISTORY, 301 N. Main St., Mount Airy, NC 27030-3811. Tel.: 336-786-4478, 336-786-1666. Facebook: Mt. Airy Museum.
E-mail: mamrh@northcarolinamuseum.org
Web Site: www.northcarolinamuseum.org
Key Personnel: Dir., Matthew J. Edwards; Chm. (V), J. M. Petelle; Cur. Collections, Amy Snyder; Museum Shop Mgr., Nancy Davis.
Institution Type/Description: History Museum.

Hours & Admission Prices: April-Oct. Mon.-Sat. 10-5, Sun. 1-5; Nov.-March Tues.-Sat. 10-5. Adults $6, senior citizens $5, students $4; discounts to groups. &
Attendance: 15,000 (estimated)

Mount Gilead

TOWN CREEK INDIAN MOUND STATE HISTORIC SITE, 509 Town Creek Mound Rd., Mount Gilead, NC 27306-8506. Tel.: 910-439-6802. Fax: 910-439-6441.
E-mail: towncreek@ncdcr.gov
Web Site: www.towncreekindianmound.com
Key Personnel: Site Mgr., Rich Thompson.
Institution Type/Description: Historic Site & Visitor Center: Mississippian period Ceremonial Center restored; temple on top of earth mound, priest's dwelling, burial house & mud-plastered palisade surrounding temple.
Hours & Admission Prices: Tues.-Sat. 9-5, Sun. 1-5. No charge; donations accepted. Closed holidays. &
Attendance: 22,000 (actual)

Mount Ulla

KERR MILL AT SLOAN PARK, 550 Sloan Rd., Mount Ulla, NC 28125. Tel.: 704-637-7776.
Web Site: co.rowan.nc.us
Institution Type/Description: Historic Building: housed in a former grist mill; built in 1823.
Hours & Admission Prices: Sat.-Sun. 1-7; other times by appointment.

Murfreesboro

BRADY C. JEFCOAT MUSEUM OF AMERICANA, 201 W. High St., Murfreesboro, NC 27855-1819. Mailing Address: P.O. Box 3, Murfreesboro, NC 27855. Tel.: 252-398-5922, 910-358-1202.
E-mail: mha@murfreesboronc.org
Web Site: murfreesboronc.org
Key Personnel: Dir., Colon Ballance.
Institution Type/Description: History Museum.
Hours & Admission Prices: Sat. 11-4, Sun. 2-5; groups by appointment. Adults $8, students $6. &
Attendance: 2,000 (estimated)

THE MURFREESBORO HISTORICAL ASSOCIATION, INC., 116 E. Main St., Murfreesboro, NC 27855-1407. Mailing Address: P.O. Box 3, Murfreesboro, NC 27855-0003. Tel.: 252-398-5922.
E-mail: mha@murfreesboronc.org
Web Site: www.murfreesboronc.org
Key Personnel: Pres., Lamar Van Brackle.
Institution Type/Description: Historical Association: housed in the Roberts-Vaughan House; built in 1790.
Hours & Admission Prices: Mon.-Fri. 9-1. Tours: by appointment. Roberts-Vaughan House no charge. Jefcoat Museum: adults $8, students $6.
Attendance: 1,500 (estimated)

Murphy

CHEROKEE COUNTY HISTORICAL MUSEUM, INC., 87 Peachtree St., Murphy, NC 28906-2940. Tel.: 828-837-6792. Fax: 828-837-6792.
E-mail: cchistoricalmuseum@gmail.com
Key Personnel: Dir. & Museum Shop Mgr., Wanda Stalcup; Pres., Glenda Fisher; Vice Pres., Mary Ann Thompson.
Institution Type/Description: History Museum.
Hours & Admission Prices: Mon.-Fri. 9-5; group tours by appointment. Adults $3, children $1. Closed New Year's Day; Good Friday through Easter Monday; Memorial Day; Independence Day; Labor Day; Thanksgiving; Christmas. &
Attendance: 7,000 (estimated)

FIELDS OF THE WOOD, 10000 Hwy. 294, Murphy, NC 28906. Mailing Address: P.O. Box 2910, Cleveland, TN 37320. Tel.: 828-494-7855. Facebook: COGOP Heritage.
E-mail: fieldsofthewood@cogop.org
Web Site: fieldsofthewood.net
Key Personnel: Dir., Paul Holt.
Institution Type/Description: History Museum.
Hours & Admission Prices: Sunrise to sunset. No charge; donations accepted.

New Bern

ATTMORE-OLIVER HOUSE MUSEUM, 511 Broad St., New Bern, NC 28560. Mailing Address: 511 Broad St., New Bern, NC 28560. Tel.: 252-638-8558. Fax: 252-638-5773. Facebook: New Bern Historical Society.
E-mail: lynne@newbernhistorical.org
Web Site: www.newbernhistorical.org
Key Personnel: Exec. Dir., Lynne Harakal; Pres. (V), Nelson McDaniel.
Institution Type/Description: Historic House Museum: c.1790.
Hours & Admission Prices: By appointment. No charge; donations accepted.
Attendance: 7,000 (estimated)

THE BIRTHPLACE OF PEPSI-COLA STORE, 256 Middle St., New Bern, NC 28560. Tel.: 252-636-5898.
Institution Type/Description: History Museum: housed in the birthplace of Pepsi-Cola; invented by Caleb Bradham in his pharmacy in 1898.
Hours & Admission Prices: Jan.-Feb. Mon.-Sat. 10-6; March-Dec. Mon.-Sat. 10-6, Sun. 12-4.

FRIENDS OF FIREMEN'S MUSEUM, 420 Broad St., New Bern, NC 28560. Tel.: 252-636-4087. Fax: 252-636-4087.
E-mail: firechief-nb@admin.ci.new-bern.nc.us
Formerly: New Bern Firemen's Museum
Key Personnel: C.E.O., Charles Williams; Sec. & Treas., Richard M. Register; Museum Shop Mgr., Ben Gaskill.
Institution Type/Description: Fire-Fighting Museum.
Hours & Admission Prices: Mon.-Sat. 10-4. Adults $7, students $4; children under 6 no charge. Closed New Year's Day; Thanksgiving; Christmas.
Attendance: 14,000 (estimated)

TRYON PALACE, 529 S. Front St., New Bern, NC 28562. Mailing Address: P.O. Box 1007, New Bern, NC 28563-1007. Tel.: 252-639-3500, 800-767-1560. Fax: 252-514-4876. Facebook: Tryon Palace.
E-mail: info@tryonpalace.org
Web Site: www.tryonpalace.org
Formerly: Tryon Palace Historic Sites & Gardens
Key Personnel: Chm., William C. Cannon, Jr.; Exec. Dir., Lee Johnson; Coord. Human Resources & Admin. Suppor, Laurie Bowles; Dir. Collections, Alyson Rhodes-Murphy; Controller, Susan L. Flowers; Conservator, Richard Baker; Foundation Coord., Erin Langley; African American Outreach Coord., Sharon C. Bryant; Security Coord., Sean Creamer; Security Coord., Orlando Venters; Museum Store Mgr., Susan Briley; Volunteer Coord., Pam Stevens.
Institution Type/Description: History Museum.
Hours & Admission Prices: Jan.-June Mon.-Sat. 9-5, Sun. 12-5, last tour at 4. Gardens: June-Aug. Mon.-Sat. 9-7, Sun. 12-5, last tour at 4. One Day Pass: adults $20, students grades 1-12 $10; Two Day Pass: adults $26, students $13; discounts to seniors 62 & over, military, AAM & AAA members, college students and groups. Galleries: adults $12, students $4. Gardens: adults $6, students $3. Closed New Year's Day; Thanksgiving; Christmas Eve, Day & day after. ⅋
Attendance: 150,000 (actual)

New Hill

HARRIS ENERGY AND ENVIRONMENTAL CENTER, 3932 New Hill, New Hill, NC 27562. Tel.: 919-362-3261. Fax: 919-362-3446.
Web Site: progress-energy.com/harris
Institution Type/Description: Environmental Center.
Hours & Admission Prices: By appointment. Closed holidays.

NORTH CAROLINA RAILWAY MUSEUM, 5121 Daisy St., New Hill, NC 27562. Mailing Address: P.O. Box 40, New Hill, NC 27562-0040. Tel.: 919-362-5416.
E-mail: info@triangletrain.com
Web Site: www.triangletrain.com
Institution Type/Description: Railway Museum.
Hours & Admission Prices: Sat.-Sun. 9-5. No charge.

Newland

AVERY COUNTY MUSEUM, 1829 Schultz Circle, Newland, NC 28657. Mailing Address: P.O. Box 266, Newland, NC 28657-0266. Tel.: 828-733-7111.
E-mail: averymuseum@gmail.com
Web Site: averymuseum.com
Key Personnel: Exec. Dir., Michael Hardy.
Institution Type/Description: County Museum.

Hours & Admission Prices: May-Oct. Fri. 10-4, Sat. 11-3; other times by appointment. No charge; donations accepted.
Attendance: 1,000 (estimated)

Newton

CATAWBA COUNTY MUSEUM OF HISTORY, 30 N. College Ave., Newton, NC 28658. Mailing Address: P.O. Box 73, Newton, NC 28658-0073. Tel.: 828-465-0383. Fax: 828-465-9813.
E-mail: mherzognc@gmail.com
Web Site: www.catawbahistory.org
Key Personnel: C.E.O. & Dir., Melinda Herzog; Pres. (V) & Chm. (V), Shuford Abernethy, III; Cur., Kendall Reese; Mktg. Dir., Joshua Cummings; Registrar & Site Mgr., Jennifer Marquart-Leach; Business Officer, Doris Teague; Registrar, John Powers; Librarian, Marian Stearns.
Institution Type/Description: History Museum: housed in former 1924 Catawba Courthouse.
Hours & Admission Prices: Museum of History: Tues.-Sat. 9-4. Guided Tour $3.50. Murray's Mill: Thurs.-Sat. 9-5, Sun. 1-5. Admission $5, guided tour $6. Bunker Hill Covered Bridge: daily sunrise to sunset. No charge. Harper House: Thurs.-Sat. 10-5, Sun. 1-5. Admission $5. Closed major holidays. ⅋
Attendance: 43,480 (estimated)

North Wilkesboro

WILKES ART GALLERY, 913 C St., North Wilkesboro, NC 28659-4119. Tel.: 336-667-2841. Fax: 336-667-9264.
E-mail: info@wilkesartgallery.org
Web Site: wilkesartgallery.org
Key Personnel: C.E.O., Kara Minton-Elmore; Pres., Madeline Johnson; Vice Pres., John Harwell; Office Mgr., Eric Blahnik.
Institution Type/Description: Art Gallery.
Hours & Admission Prices: Tues.-Fri. 10-5, Sat. 10-2. No charge; donations accepted. Closed New Year's Day; Easter & day after; Memorial Day; Independence Day; Labor Day; Thanksgiving; Christmas Eve & Day. ⅋
Attendance: 12,000 (estimated)

Oak Island

OAK ISLAND NATURE CENTER, 52nd St., N.E. & Yacht Dr., Oak Island, NC 28465. Mailing Address: 4601 E. Oak Island Dr., Oak Island, NC 28465. Tel.: 910-278-5011.
E-mail: info@oak-islandnc.com
Institution Type/Description: Nature Center.
Hours & Admission Prices: Memorial Day to Labor Day Wed.-Sun. 12-3; Sept.-May Fri.-Sun. 12-3.

Oak Ridge

OLD MILL OF GUILFORD, 1340 NC Hwy. 68 N., Oak Ridge, NC 27310. Tel.: 336-643-4783.
E-mail: olmill@triad.rr.com
Web Site: www.oldmillofguilford.com
Institution Type/Description: Historic Building: housed in a working gristmill; built in 1767. Listed on the National Register of Historic Places.
Hours & Admission Prices: Daily 9-5.

Oakboro

OAKBORO REGIONAL MUSEUM OF HISTORY, 231 N. Main St., Oakboro, NC 28129. Mailing Address: P.O. Box 565, Oakboro, NC 28129. Tel.: 704-485-4222.
E-mail: oakboromuseum@aol.com
Key Personnel: Chm. (V), Bob Barbee; Pres. (V), Judy Tucker; Museum Shop Mgr., Jane Barnhardt.
Institution Type/Description: History Museum.
Hours & Admission Prices: Sun.-Mon. 2-4, Thurs. 10am-12pm; groups of 8 or more by appointment; call for additional hours. ⅋
Attendance: 825 (estimated)

Ocean Isle Beach

MUSEUM OF COASTAL CAROLINA, 21 E. Second St., Ocean Isle Beach, NC 28469. Tel.: 910-579-1016. Fax: 910-575-4770.
E-mail: minfo@museumplanetarium.org
Web Site: www.museumplanetarium.org
Key Personnel: Exec. Dir., Terry Bryant; Chm. & Pres., Jerry Rothenberg; Dir. Planetarium, Will Snyder; Membership Svcs., Deb Boyce; Educator, Maria Knapik; Museum Shop Mgr., Karen Nelson; Planetarium Asst., Janice Rhodes.
Institution Type/Description: Natural History Museum.

Hours & Admission Prices: Summer: 10-8; Fall: Thurs.-Sat. 10-3; Winter & Spring: Fri.-Sat. 10-3. Adults $9.50, seniors 62 & over $8.50, children 3-12 $7.50; children 2 & under no charge.
Attendance: 37,601 (actual)

Ocracoke

OCRACOKE ISLAND VISITOR CENTER, Hwy. 12, Ocracoke, NC 27960. Mailing Address: 1401 National Park Dr., Manteo, NC 27954-9451. Tel.: 252-473-2111 & 928-4531. Fax: 252-473-2595.
E-mail: caha_information@nps.gov
Web Site: www.nps.gov/caha
Key Personnel: Supt., Barclay Trimble; Archives Technician, Jami P. Lanier.
Institution Type/Description: Park Museum & Visitor Center.
Hours & Admission Prices: mid-June to Labor Day daily 9-6; Sept.-June daily 9-5. No charge. ♿
Attendance: 54,600 (actual)

OCRACOKE PRESERVATION SOCIETY MUSEUM - THE DAVID WILLIAMS HOME, 49 Water Plant Rd., Ocracoke, NC 27960. Mailing Address: P.O. Box 1240, Ocracoke, NC 27960-1240. Tel.: 252-928-7375. Facebook: Ocracoke Preservation Society.
E-mail: info@ocracokepreservation.org
Web Site: www.ocracokepreservation.org
Key Personnel: Dir., Andrea Powers; Asst. Dir., Mary Bryant.
Institution Type/Description: Historic House Museum: c.1900. Listed on the National Register of Historic Places.
Hours & Admission Prices: Call for hours. No charge; donations accepted.
Attendance: 15,000 (estimated)

Old Fort

MOUNTAIN GATEWAY MUSEUM, 24 Water St., Old Fort, NC 28762. Mailing Address: P.O. Box 1286, Old Fort, NC 28762-1286. Tel.: 828-668-9259. Fax: 828-668-0041.
E-mail: mgm@ncdcr.gov
Web Site: mountaingatewaymuseum.org
Key Personnel: Dir., RoAnn Bishop.
Institution Type/Description: History Museum.
Hours & Admission Prices: Mon. 12-5, Tues.-Sat. 9-5, Sun. 2-5. No charge. Closed state holidays.
Attendance: 20,000 (actual)

OLD FORT RAILROAD MUSEUM, 25 Hwy. 70 W., Old Fort, NC 28762. Mailing Address: 38 Catawba Ave., Old Fort, NC 28762. Tel.: 828-668-4282.
Institution Type/Description: Historic Building: housed in a former deport; built in 1890.
Hours & Admission Prices: Call for hours.

Oriental

ORIENTAL'S HISTORY MUSEUM, 802 Broad St., Oriental, NC 28571. Mailing Address: P.O. Box 103, Oriental, NC 28571.
E-mail: museum@dockline.net
Key Personnel: Cur., Marsha Shirk.
Institution Type/Description: History Museum.
Hours & Admission Prices: Fri. 11-3, Sat.-Sun. 1-4. No charge; donations accepted.

Oxford

GRANVILLE COUNTY HISTORICAL SOCIETY MUSEUM, 1 Museum Ln., Oxford, NC 27565. Mailing Address: P.O. Box 1433, Oxford, NC 27565-1433. Tel.: 919-693-9706. Fax: 919-693-9706.
E-mail: webmail@granvillemuseumnc.org
Web Site: www.granvillemuseumnc.org
Key Personnel: Dir. & Museum Shop Mgr., Pam Thornton; Asst. Dir., Valerie Heinssen; Pres. (V), Dr. Richard Taylor.
Institution Type/Description: History & Science Museum.
Hours & Admission Prices: Wed.-Fri. 10-4, Sat. 11-3. No charge; donations accepted. Closed Easter; Thanksgiving; Christmas. ♿
Attendance: 6,932 (actual)

SALLIE MAE LIGON MUSEUM & ARCHIVES, Cobb Ctr. at Dunn Cottage, 600 college St., Oxford, NC 27565. Tel.: 919-603-3904. Facebook, Twitter, Flickr.
E-mail: ssmith@mhc-oxford.org
Web Site: www.salliemaeligon.org

Key Personnel: Dir., Stacey Smith.
Institution Type/Description: History Museum: housed in a former residential home for children; built in 1873.
Hours & Admission Prices: Mon.-Fri. 9-4 by appointment. No charge; donations accepted. ♿

Pembroke

NATIVE AMERICAN RESOURCE CENTER, University of North Carolina at Pembroke, Pembroke, NC 28372. Mailing Address: P.O. Box 1510, Pembroke, NC 28372-1510. Tel.: 910-521-6282.
E-mail: nativemuseum@uncp.edu
Web Site: www.uncp.edu/nativemuseum/
Key Personnel: Dir., Dr. Stanley Knick; Business Officer, Neil R. Hawk; Publications & Public Rels. Dir., Amber Rach.
Institution Type/Description: Native American Museum: housed in 1923 Old Main Building.
Hours & Admission Prices: Mon.-Sat. 8-5; groups by appointment. No charge. Closed state holidays. ♿
Attendance: 10,000 (actual)

Penland

PENLAND GALLERY & VISITORS CENTER, 3135 Conley Rdige Rd., Penland, NC 28765. Mailing Address: P.O. Box 37, Penland, NC 28765. Tel.: 828-765-6211. Instagram.
E-mail: gallery@penland.org
Web Site: penland.org/gallery
Key Personnel: Dir., Kathryn Gremley.
Institution Type/Description: Fine Craft Gallery & Visitors Center located at Penland School of Crafts.
Hours & Admission Prices: March to early Dec. Tues.-Sat. 10-5, Sun. 12-5. No charge. ♿
Attendance: 13,000 (estimated)

Pine Knoll Shores

NORTH CAROLINA AQUARIUM AT PINE KNOLL SHORES, One Roosevelt Dr., Pine Knoll Shores, NC 28512. Mailing Address: One Roosevelt Blvd., Pine Knoll Shores, NC 28512. Tel.: 252-247-4003. Fax: 252-247-0663.
E-mail: pksmail@ncaquariums.com
Web Site: www.ncaquariums.com
Key Personnel: Dir., Allen Monroe; Dir. Husbandry & Operations, Stuart May; Cur. Education, Windy Arey Kent; Coord. Public Rels., Julie Powers.
Institution Type/Description: Aquarium.
Hours & Admission Prices: Adults $8, seniors 62 & over $7, children 3-12 $6; children under 3 & members no charge. Closed New Year's Day; Thanksgiving; Christmas. ♿
Attendance: 403,769 (actual)

Pinehurst

GIVEN MEMORIAL LIBRARY AND TUFTS ARCHIVES, 150 Cherokee Rd., Pinehurst, NC 28374. Mailing Address: P.O. Box 159, Pinehurst, NC 28370. Tel.: 910-295-6022 & 3642.
E-mail: info@giventufts.com
Institution Type/Description: Library & Archives.
Hours & Admission Prices: Mon.-Fri. 9:30-5, Sat. 9:30-12:30. No charge; donations accepted.

SANDHILLS HORTICULTURAL GARDENS, 3395 Airport Rd., Pinehurst, NC 28374-8778. Tel.: 910-695-3882. Fax: 910-695-3894.
E-mail: johnsond@sandhills.edu
Web Site: www.sandhillshorticulturalgardens.com
Key Personnel: Dir., Dee Johnson; Chm. (V), Andy Auman.
Institution Type/Description: Botanical Garden.
Hours & Admission Prices: Visitor Center: daily 8-5. Gardens: dawn to sunset. No charge; donations accepted. ♿
Attendance: 7,500 (estimated)

Pineville

PRESIDENT JAMES K. POLK STATE HISTORIC SITE, 12031 Lancaster Hwy., Pineville, NC 28134. Mailing Address: P.O. Box 475, Pineville, NC 28134-0475. Tel.: 704-889-7145. Fax: 704-889-3057. Facebook: President James K. Polk State Historic site.

E-mail: polk@ncdcr.gov
Web Site: www.polk.nchistoricsites.org
Key Personnel: Site Mgr., Scott Warren; Pres. (V), Sharon Van Kuren.
Institution Type/Description: Historic Buildings & Visitor Center.
Hours & Admission Prices: Tues.-Sat. 9-5. No charge; donations accepted. Closed New Year's Day; Memorial Day; Independence Day; Labor Day; Thanksgiving; Christmas Eve & Day. &
Attendance: 16,048 (actual)

Pinnacle

HORNE CREEK LIVING HISTORICAL FARM, 308 Horne Creek Farm Rd., Pinnacle, NC 27043. Tel.: 336-325-2298. Fax: 336-325-3150.
E-mail: hornecreek@ncmail.net
Institution Type/Description: History Museum.
Hours & Admission Prices: Tues.-Sat. 9-5. No charge; donations accepted. Closed most major holidays.

Pisgah Forest

ALLISON-DEAVER HOUSE MUSEUM, 200 Hwy. 280, Pisgah Forest, NC 28768. Mailing Address: Transylvania County Historical Society, P.O. Box 2061, Brevard, NC 28712-2061. Tel.: 828-884-5137 & 8570.
E-mail: tchsociety@yahoo.com
Web Site: www.preservingourpast.org
Key Personnel: Exec. Dir., Kaye Myers.
Institution Type/Description: Historic House Museum: listed on the National Register of Historic Places.
Hours & Admission Prices: mid-May to mid-Oct. Sat. 10-4, Sun. 1-4.

FOREST DISCOVERY CENTER AND CRADLE OF FORESTRY HISTORIC SITE, 11250 Pisgah Hwy., Pisgah Forest, NC 28768. Mailing Address: 1600 Pisgah Hwy., Pisgah Forest, NC 28768. Tel.: 828-877-3130.
Institution Type/Description: History Museum.
Hours & Admission Prices: mid-April to early Nov. daily 9-5. Adults 16 & over $5; children 15 & under and Tues. no charge.

PISGAH CENTER FOR WILDLIFE EDUCATION, 1401 Fish Hatchery Rd., Pisgah Forest, NC 28768. Mailing Address: P.O. Box 1600, Pisgah Forest, NC 28768. Tel.: 828-877-4423. Fax: 828-877-4792.
E-mail: lee.sherrill@ncwildlife.org
Web Site: www.ncwildlife.org/Learning/EducationCenters/Pisgah.aspx
Key Personnel: Program Coord., Lee Sherrill.
Institution Type/Description: Wildlife Center.
Hours & Admission Prices: April-Nov. Mon.-Sat. 8-4:45; Dec.-March Mon.-Fri. 8-4:45. No charge; donations accepted. Closed New Year's Day, Martin Luther King, Jr. Birthday, Easter weekend, Veteran's Day, Thanksgiving weekend, Christmas. &
Attendance: 125,000 (actual)

Pittsboro

CAROLINA TIGER RESCUE, 1940 Hanks Chapel Rd., Pittsboro, NC 27312-9794. Tel.: 919-542-4684. Fax: 919-542-4454.
E-mail: info@carolinatigerrescue.org
Web Site: www.carolinatigerrescue.org
Institution Type/Description: Wildlife Refuge.
Hours & Admission Prices: Advance ticket purchase required. See website for information. Adults $18, youth 4-12 $11; children 3 & under no charge.

Plymouth

GOD'S WILDLIFE CREATIONS, 111 W. Water St., Plymouth, NC 27962. Mailing Address: P.O. Box 706, Plymouth, NC 27962. Tel.: 252-793-6600. Fax: 252-793-3500.
E-mail: tourism@washingtoncountygov.com
Web Site: www.visitwashingtoncountync.com
Formerly: Wildlife Museum & Gallery
Institution Type/Description: General Museum.
Hours & Admission Prices: Mon.-Fri. 9-4. Adults $5, youth 5-12 $3; children 4 & under no charge. &
Attendance: 800 (estimated)

PORT-O-PLYMOUTH MUSEUM, 302 E. Water St., Plymouth, NC 27962. Mailing Address: P.O. Box 296, Plymouth, NC 27962-0296. Tel.: 252-793-1377. Fax: 252-741-9501. Facebook.
E-mail: admin@portoplymouthmuseum.org
Web Site: portoplymouthmuseum.org
Key Personnel: Cur., David Bennett; Pres. (V), George Waters; Museum Shop Mgr., Dorothy Irvine.
Institution Type/Description: History Museum.
Hours & Admission Prices: Tues.-Sat. 9-4. Adults $3.50. &
Attendance: 1,500 (estimated)

ROANOKE RIVER LIGHTHOUSE & MARITIME MUSEUM, 206 W. Water St., Plymouth, NC 27962. Tel.: 252-217-2204.
E-mail: info@roanokeriverlighthouse.org
Web Site: www.roanokeriverlighthouse.org
Institution Type/Description: History Museum.
Hours & Admission Prices: Tues.-Sat. 11-3; other times by appointment.

Pollocksville

FOSCUE PLANTATION HOUSE, 7509 N. U.S. 17 Hwy., Pollocksville, NC 28573. Mailing Address: 909 Rockford Rd., Highpoint, NC 27262. Tel.: 252-224-1803.
Web Site: www.foscueplantation.com
Institution Type/Description: Historic House Museum: housed in the former home of Simon Foscue, Jr.; built in 1824.
Hours & Admission Prices: Thurs. 10-4; other times by appointment.

Princeton

POWELL'S GARDEN, 9468 U.S. Hwy. 70, Princeton, NC 27569. Tel.: 919-936-4421.
Institution Type/Description: Garden.
Hours & Admission Prices: Mon.-Sat. 10-6.

Purlear

RENDEZVOUS MOUNTAIN EDUCATIONAL STATE FOREST, 1956 Rendezvous Mountain Rd., Purlear, NC 28665. Tel.: 336-667-5072.
E-mail: rendezvousmountainesf.ncfs@ncagr.gov
Web Site: www.ncesf.org/rmesf/home.htm
Institution Type/Description: Park Museum.
Hours & Admission Prices: March to late Nov. call for hours.

Raleigh

AFRICAN AMERICAN CULTURAL COMPLEX, 119 Sunnybrook Rd., Raleigh, NC 27610-1827. Tel.: 919-250-9336. Fax: 919-212-3598.
E-mail: info@aaccmuseum.com
Web Site: www.aaccmuseum.com
Formerly: Black Heritage Park
Key Personnel: Chm., Dr. Prezell Robinson; Treas., Rhonda Russell; C.E.O., Dr. Elliott B. Palmer; Program Coord., Juanita B. Palmer.
Institution Type/Description: History Museum.
Hours & Admission Prices: By appointment.

ARTSPACE, 201 E. Davie St., Raleigh, NC 27601. Tel.: 919-821-2787. Fax: 919-821-0383. Facebook & Twitter: @artspacenc.
E-mail: info@artspacenc.org
Web Site: www.artspacenc.org
Key Personnel: Pres. & C.E.O., Mary Poole; Dir. Artistic Programs, Annah Lee; Dir. Devel. & Communications, Ileana Rodriguez; Education & Outreach Coord., Angela Lombardi.
Institution Type/Description: Art Museum & Gallery.
Hours & Admission Prices: Tues.-Wed. & Fri.-Sat. 10-6, Thurs. 10-7. No charge; donations accepted. Closed New Year's Day; Christmas. &
Attendance: 150,000 (estimated)

CAM RALEIGH - CONTEMPORARY ART MUSEUM RALEIGH, 409 W. Martin St., Raleigh, NC 27603. Tel.: 919-261-5920. Facebook & Twitter: @camraleigh; Instagram: @cam_raleigh.
E-mail: info@camraleigh.org
Web Site: www.camraleigh.org
Key Personnel: Exec. Dir., Gab Smith; Exhibitions Dir., Eric Gaard; Assoc. Dir. Exhibitions, Nell Fortune-Greeley; Events & Facilities Mgr., Kelsey Melville;

Assoc. Dir. Operations & Museum Educator, Melissa Roth; Gallery Educator, Mollie Earls.
Institution Type/Description: Contemporary Art.
Hours & Admission Prices: Mon. by appointment, Wed.-Fri. 11-6:30, Sat.-Sun. 12-5. Adults $5; children under 10, NARM, Mod/Co, active duty military, veterans & their families, teachers, first responders, area college students, NC State College of Design students, staff & faculty, CAM members & first Fri. of month no charge. Closed New Year's Day; Martin Luther King, Jr. Day; Good Friday; Memorial Day; Independence Day; Labor Day; Christmas. ᕦ
Attendance: 33,000 (estimated)

CITY OF RALEIGH MUSEUM, 220 Fayetteville St., Raleigh, NC 27601-1358. Tel.: 919-832-3775. Fax: 919-832-3085. Facebook: @CORMuseum.
E-mail: cormuseum@gmail.com
Web Site: www.cityofraleighmuseum.org
Formerly: Raleigh City Museum
Key Personnel: Museum Dir., Ernest Dollar.
Institution Type/Description: History Museum.
Hours & Admission Prices: Tues.-Sat. 9-4, Sun. 1-4, also open first Fri. of month 6-9. No charge; donations accepted. Closed New Year's Day; Thanksgiving; Christmas Eve & Day. ᕦ
Attendance: 23,918 (actual)

DR. MARTIN LUTHER KING JR. MEMORIAL GARDENS, 1215 Martin Luther King Jr. Blvd., Raleigh, NC 27610. Mailing Address: c/o Raleigh Parks, Recreation and Cultural Resources Dept., P.O. Box 590, Raleigh, NC 27601. Tel.: 919-996-3000.
E-mail: diane.b.sauer@raleighnc.gov
Web Site: wwww.raleighnc.gov/parks
Key Personnel: Dir. Parks, Recreation & Cultural Resources, Diane Sauer.
Institution Type/Description: Memorial Garden.
Hours & Admission Prices: Dawn to dusk.

GREGG MUSEUM OF ART & DESIGN AT NORTH CAROLINA STATE UNIVERSITY, 1903 Hillsborough St., Raleigh, NC 27607. Mailing Address: Campus Box 7330, Raleigh, NC 27695. Tel.: 919-515-3503. Fax: 919-515-6163.
E-mail: gregg@ncsu.edu
Web Site: gregg.arts.ncsu.edu
Formerly: North Carolina State University Gallery of Art & Design
Key Personnel: Dir., Roger Manley; Pres., Shawn Brewster; Cur. Education & Resources, Zoe Starling; Art Preparator, Matt Gay; Registrar, Mary Hauser; Museum Ops. Mgr., Hilary Kinlaw; Asst. Registrat, Jordan Cao; Collections Asst., Janine LeBlanc; Asst. Dir. Devel., Mona Fitzpatrick; Events & Facilities Coord., Tamar Harris Warren; Visitor Svcs. & Security Coord., Jeannifer Sandoval.
Institution Type/Description: Art Museum.
Hours & Admission Prices: Tues.-Wed. & Fri.-Sat. 10-5, Thurs. 10-9, Sun. 1-5, 1st Fri. each month 10-7. No charge. ᕦ
Attendance: 47,323 (estimated)

HAYWOOD HALL HOUSE AND GARDENS, 211 New Bern Place, Raleigh, NC 27601. Mailing Address: P.O. Box 10461, Raleigh, NC 27605. Tel.: 919-832-8357. Facebook: Haywood Hall.
E-mail: haywoodhall@bellsouth.net
Web Site: www.haywoodhall.org
Key Personnel: Resident Mgr., Greg Hatem.
Institution Type/Description: Historic House: housed in the former home of State Treasurer John Haywood; built in 1799.
Hours & Admission Prices: By appointment.

HISTORIC OAK VIEW COUNTY PARK, 4028 Carya Dr., Raleigh, NC 27610-2913. Wake County Dept. Parks & Recreation, P.O. 550, Raleigh, NC 27602. Tel.: 919-250-1013. Fax: 919-250-1119. Facebook: @oakviewpark.
E-mail: oakview@wakegov.com
Web Site: www.wakegov/parks/oakview
Key Personnel: Park Mgr., Emily Catherman Fryar; Asst. Park Mgr. Education, Abby Jones.
Institution Type/Description: Historic Farmstead.
Hours & Admission Prices: Park Grounds: daily 8 to sunset; Park Buildings: Mon.-Sat. 8:30-5, Sun. 1-5. No charge. Closed New Year's Day; Thanksgiving; Christmas Eve & Day. ᕦ
Attendance: 100,000 (estimated)

HISTORIC YATES MILL COUNTY PARK, 4620 Lake Wheeler Rd., Raleigh, NC 27603. Tel.: 919-856-6675. Fax: 919-856-6674. Facebook: @yatesmill.

E-mail: yatesmill@wakegov.com
Web Site: www.wakegov.com/parks/yatesmill
Key Personnel: Park Mgr., Tim Lisk; Dir. Programs, Rebeccah Waff Cope; Asst. Mgr. Operations, Dick Shannon; Park Technician Operations, Richard Smith; Park Technician Group Programs, Ashley Martin; Park Technician Public History & Volunteer Coord., Laura Ketcham; Park Technician Public Programs, Amy Dombrowski Juliana.
Institution Type/Description: History Museum & Historic Site: housed in a gristmill built in 1760s.
Hours & Admission Prices: Park: 8am to dusk; A.E. Finley Visitor Center: daily 8:30-5; Tours: March to Nov. Sat. & Sun. Park: no charge; Tours: adults $5, seniors 60 & over $4, children 7-16 $3; children 6 & under no charge.
Attendance: 113,929 (estimated)

JC RAULSTON ARBORETUM AT NC STATE UNIVERSITY, 4415 Beryl Rd., Raleigh, NC 27695. Mailing Address: Dept. Horticultural Science, Campus Box 7522, Raleigh, NC 27695. Tel.: 919-515-3132. Fax: 919-515-5361. Facebook: @jcraulstonarboretum; Twitter: @jcraulstonarb.
E-mail: mark_weathington@ncsu.edu
Web Site: jcra.ncsu.edu
Key Personnel: Dir., Mark Weathington; Asst. Dir., Arlene Calhoun; Business Svcs. Coord., Kathy Field; Programs & Educaton Coord., Christopher Todd Glenn; Dir. Devel., Sonia Murphy; Membership & Volunteer Coord., Kathryn Wall.
Institution Type/Description: Arboretum.
Hours & Admission Prices: April-Oct. daily 8-8; Nov.-March daily 8-5. No charge; donations accepted. ᕦ
Attendance: 35,000 (estimated)

JOEL LANE MUSEUM HOUSE, 728 W. Hargett St., Raleigh, NC 27603-1618. Mailing Address: P.O. Box 10884, Raleigh, NC 27605-0884. Tel.: 919-833-3431. Fax: 919-833-9431. Facebook: Joel Lane Museum House; Twitter: @JoelLaneMuseum.
E-mail: joellane@bellsouth.net
Web Site: www.joellane.org
Key Personnel: Pres. (V), Claudia Brown; Dir., Meaghan Nappo; Asst. Dir., Kathy Ruse; Docent, Lanie Hubbard.
Institution Type/Description: Raleigh Historic Site: housed in the former home of Colonel Joel Lane. Listed on the National Register of Historic Places.
Hours & Admission Prices: Tours: March to mid-Dec. Wed.-Fri. 10, 11, 12, & 1, Sat. 1, 2 & 3; other times by appointment; Jan.-Feb. Sat. 1, 2 & 3; other times by appointment. Adults $8, seniors 65 & over $7, students $4; discounts to Time Travelers & AAA members; members & children under 6 no charge.
Attendance: 4,750 (actual)

MARBLES KIDS MUSEUM, 201 E. Hargett St., Raleigh, NC 27601-1437. Tel.: 919-834-4040. Fax: 919-834-3516. Facebook: @marbleskidsmuseum; Twitter: @MarblesRaleigh.
E-mail: info@marbleskidsmuseum.org
Web Site: www.marbleskidsmuseum.org
Formerly: Exploris
Key Personnel: Chm. Bd. (V), Steve Pretzer; Pres. & C.E.O., Sally Edwards; Vice Pres. Mktg. & Communications, Pickel Tannenbaum; Vice Pres. Play Experience, Pam Hartley; Vice Pres. Operations, Tim Hazlehurst; Vice Pres. Team & Guest Rels., Britt Thomas.
Institution Type/Description: Children's Museum.
Hours & Admission Prices: Thurs. 9-7, Fri.-Wed. 9-5. Admission $5; children under 1 & members no charge. Closed Easter; Thanksgiving; Christmas. ᕦ
Attendance: 546,000 (estimated)

MORDECAI HISTORIC PARK, 1 Mimosa St., Raleigh, NC 27604-1203. Mailing Address: c/o City of Raleigh Parks Recreation & Cultural Resources, P.O. Box 590, Raleigh, NC 27602. Tel.: 919-857-4364. Fax: 919-834-7314.
E-mail: joshua.ingersoll@raleighnc.gov
Web Site: www.raleighnc.gov/mordecai
Key Personnel: Dir., Joshua Ingersoll.
Institution Type/Description: Historic Houses: housed in the birthplace of Andrew Johnson.
Hours & Admission Prices: Tues.-Sat. 10-3, Sun. 1-3, last tour 3. Tours: adults $5, seniors & youth $3; members & children 6 & under no charge. ᕦ
Attendance: 11,000 (actual)

NORTH CAROLINA EXECUTIVE MANSION, 200 N. Blount St., Raleigh, NC 27601. Mailing Address: NC State Capitol, 4624 Mail Service Center, Raleigh, NC 27699-4624. Tel.: 919-733-4994. Fax: 919-715-4030.
E-mail: ncsites@ncdcr.gov
Web Site: www.nchistoricsites.org/capitol/

Key Personnel: Interpretive Specialist, Rachel Moore.
Institution Type/Description: Historic Mansion: housed in the home of North Carolina's governors since 1891.
Hours & Admission Prices: Tours: by appointment.

NORTH CAROLINA MUSEUM OF ART, 2110 Blue Ridge Rd., Raleigh, NC 27607-6494. Mailing Address: 4630 Mail Service Center, Raleigh, NC 27699-4600. Tel.: 919-839-6262. Fax: 919-733-8034. Facebook, Instagram, Twitter.
Web Site: www.ncartmuseum.org
Key Personnel: Dir., Lawrence J. Wheeler, Ph.D.
Institution Type/Description: Art Museum.
Hours & Admission Prices: Tues.-Sun. 10-5. No charge. Closed Thanksgiving; Christmas. &
Attendance: 400,000 (estimated)

NORTH CAROLINA MUSEUM OF HISTORY, 5 E. Edenton St., Raleigh, NC 27601-1011. Tel.: 919-807-7900. Fax: 919-733-8655. Facebook, Instagram, Twitter.
E-mail: webmaster_moh@ncdcr.gov
Web Site: ncmuseumofhistory.org
Key Personnel: Dir., Ken Howard.
Institution Type/Description: History Museum.
Hours & Admission Prices: Mon.-Sat. 9-5, Sun. 12-5. No charge; donations accepted. Closed New Year's Day; Easter; Thanksgiving; Christmas Eve & Day. &
Attendance: 342,000 (actual)

NORTH CAROLINA MUSEUM OF NATURAL SCIENCES, 11 W. Jones St., Raleigh, NC 27601-1029. Mailing Address: Mail Service Center 1626, Raleigh, NC 27699-1600. Tel.: 919-707-9800. Fax: 919-733-1573. Facebook, Instagram & Twitter: @naturalsciences.
E-mail: betsy.m.bennett@ncdenr.gov
Web Site: naturalsciences.org
Key Personnel: Dir., Emlyn Koster; Dir., Friends of the Museum, Angela Baker-James; Dir. Exhibits & Digital Media, Roy G. Campbell; Dir. School & Lifelong Education, Liz Baird; Head Communications, Jonathan Pishney; Head Mktg., Imogen Hoyle; Museum Store & Nature Art Gallery Mgr., Heather Heath; Head Fish & Invertebrates, Dr. Raquel Fagundo; Research Cur. Geology, Dr. Christopher Tacker; Research Cur. Herpetology, Dr. Bryan Stuart; Research Cur. Paleontology, Mary Schweitzer; Research Cur. Ornithology, John Gerwin; Research Cur. Mammalogy, Lisa J. Gatens.
Institution Type/Description: Natural Science Museum.
Hours & Admission Prices: Museum: Mon.-Sat. 9-5, Sun. noon to 5. Nature Center: Mon.-Sat. 9-5, Sun. noon to 5. No charge; donations accepted. &
Attendance: 724,000 (actual)

NORTH CAROLINA OFFICE OF ARCHIVES AND HISTORY, 109 E. Jones St., Raleigh, NC 27601-1023. Mailing Address: 4610 Mail Service Center, Raleigh, NC 27699-4610. Tel.: 919-807-7280. Fax: 919-733-8807.
E-mail: ahweb@ncdcr.net
Web Site: www.ncdcr.gov/node/5466
Key Personnel: Deputy Sec., Dr. Kevin Cherry; Dir. Historical Resources, Dr. Ramona Bartos; State Archivist, Sarah Koonts; Dir. Historic Sites, Michelle Lanier; Dir. NC Museum of History, Ken Howard.
Institution Type/Description: Historic House & Site.
Hours & Admission Prices: Archives Research Room: Tues.-Fri. 8-5, Sat. 9-4. State Historic Sites: call for hours. State Capitol: Mon.-Fri. 8-5, Sat. 9-5, Sun. 1-5. Admission at most sites no charge. Closed national holidays. &

NORTH CAROLINA SPORTS HALL OF FAME, 5 E. Edenton St., Raleigh, NC 27622. Mailing Address: P.O. Box 31524, Raleigh, NC 27622. Tel.: 919-845-3455. Facebook: @ncshof.
E-mail: dfish@ncsportshalloffame.org
Web Site: www.ncshof.org
Key Personnel: Exec. Dir., Don Fish; Assoc. Dir., Kevin Brafford.
Institution Type/Description: Sports Museum.
Hours & Admission Prices: Mon.-Sat. 9-5, Sun. 12-5. No charge.

NORTH CAROLINA STATE CAPITOL, 1 E. Edenton St., Raleigh, NC 27601. Mailing Address: 4624 Mail Service Center, Raleigh, NC 27699-4624. Tel.: 919-733-4994 & 807-7950. Fax: 919-715-4030. Facebook & Twitter: @NCStateCapitol.
E-mail: state.capitol@ncdcr.gov
Web Site: www.nchistoricsites.org/capitol
Key Personnel: Interpretive Specialist, Rachel Moore.

Institution Type/Description: Historic Building: built in 1840. A National Historic Landmark.
Hours & Admission Prices: Self-Guided Tours: Mon.-Fri. Guided Tours: Sat. 11-2; groups by appointment. No charge; donations accepted.

RAY PRICE LEGENDS OF HARLEY-DAVIDSON DRAG RACING MUSEUM, 1126 S. Saunders St., Raleigh, NC 27603-2204. Tel.: 919-832-2261. Facebook: @RayPriceHarley; Twitter: @RayPriceHD.
E-mail: hdweb@rayprice.ocm
Web Site: www.rayprice-hd.com
Key Personnel: Gen. Mgr., Mark Hendrix.
Institution Type/Description: Drag Racing Museum.
Hours & Admission Prices: Mon.-Tues. & Thurs.-Fri. 8-6, Sat. 8-4.

WILLIAM B. UMSTEAD STATE PARK, 8801 Glenwood Ave., Raleigh, NC 27617. Tel.: 919-571-4170. Facebook & Instagram: @williamumsteadstatepark; Twitter: @UmsteadStPk.
E-mail: william.umstead@ncparks.gov
Web Site: www.ncparks.gov/william-b-umstead-state-park
Institution Type/Description: State Park & Visitor Center.
Hours & Admission Prices: Park Office & Visitor Center: daily 8-5. Closed Christmas Day.

Ramseur

MILLSTONE CREEK ORCHARDS, 506 Parks Crossroad Church Rd., Ramseur, NC 27316. Tel.: 336-824-5263.
E-mail: info@millstonecreekorchards.com
Web Site: millstonecreekorchards.com
Institution Type/Description: Working Orchard.
Hours & Admission Prices: mid-May to Nov. Mon.-Sat. 9-6, Sun. 1-5:30; groups by appointment.

Richlands

ONSLOW COUNTY MUSEUM, 301 S. Wilmington St., Richlands, NC 28574-8326. Tel.: 910-324-5008. Fax: 910-324-2897.
E-mail: museum@onslowcountync.gov
Web Site: www.onslowcountync.gov/museum
Key Personnel: Division Head, Lisa Whitman-Grice; Pres., Arthine Thomas; Chm., John Chandler; Collections Mgr., Patricia Hughey; Education Coord., Chancellor Mellman; Exhibits Facilitator, Kenneth Barbee; Office Asst., Cacelia Davis.
Institution Type/Description: General Museum.
Hours & Admission Prices: Tues.-Fri. 10-4:30, Sat. 10-4; school groups by appointment. Adults $2, students & youth 3-18 $1; children 3 & under no charge. Closed New Year's Day; Martin Luther King Jr. Day; Good Friday; Easter; Independence Day; Labor Day; Veterans Day; Thanksgiving & day after; Christmas. &
Attendance: 10,000 (estimated)

Roanoke Rapids

ROANOKE CANAL MUSEUM AND TRAIL, 15 Jackson St. Ext., Roanoke Rapids, NC 27870-1901. Tel.: 252-537-2769. Facebook.
E-mail: rnewsome@roanokerapidsnc.com
Web Site: www.roanokecanal.com/museum
Key Personnel: Cultural Resources Leader, Ryan Newsome.
Institution Type/Description: History Museum: listed on the National Register of Historic Places.
Hours & Admission Prices: Museum: Tues.-Sat. 10-4. Trail: daily dawn to dusk. Admission: $4; children 8 & under no charge.

ROANOKE VALLEY VETERANS MUSEUM, 1620 E. 10th St., Roanoke Rapids, NC 27870. Tel.: 252-537-2514, 800-522-4282.
E-mail: rrvetcenter@yahoo.com
Web Site: roanokevalleyveteransmuseum.com
Institution Type/Description: Military History Museum.
Hours & Admission Prices: Tues.-Sat. 10-4. No charge; donations accepted.

Robbinsville

JUNALUSKA MEMORIAL AND MUSEUM, 1 Junaluska Dr., Hwy. 143, Robbinsville, NC 28771. Mailing Address: P.O. Box 1209, Robbinsville, NC 28771. Tel.: 828-479-4727.
E-mail: friendsofjuno@dnet.net
Web Site: www.junaluska.com
Key Personnel: Mgr., Thomas Holland.
Institution Type/Description: History Museum.

Hours & Admission Prices: Mon.-Fri. 8-4. No charge.

Rockingham

DISCOVERY PLACE KIDS - ROCKINGHAM, 233 E. Washington St., Rockingham, NC 28379. Tel.: 910-997-5266. Facebook & Twitter: @DPKRockingham.
E-mail: info@discoveryplace.org
Web Site: kids.discoveryplace.org
Key Personnel: Dir., Katie Rohleder; Chm. (V), Mark McGoldrick; Pres. & C.E.O., Catherine Wilson Horne.
Institution Type/Description: Children's Museum.
Hours & Admission Prices: Tues.-Fri. 9-4, Sat. 9-5, Sun. noon to 5. Admission $8; discounts to military; children under one & members no charge. Closed Easter; Thanksgiving; Christmas Eve & Day.

Rocky Mount

IMPERIAL CENTRE FOR THE ARTS & SCIENCES, 270 Gay St., Rocky Mount, NC 27804-5442. Mailing Address: P.O. Box 1180, Rocky Mount, NC 27802-1180. Tel.: 252-972-1266. Fax: 252-972-1563. Facebook.
E-mail: kelvin.yarrell@rockymountnc.gov
Web Site: www.imperialcentre.org
Formerly: Rocky Mount Arts Center
Key Personnel: Supvr. Programs, Sheila Long; Box Office Mgr., Adrienne Lynch; Mgr. Theatre, Brooke Edwards; Arts Cur., Alicyn Wiedrich; Education Coord., Tracy Grosner; Cur. Museum Education, Leigh White; Cur. Museum Exhibits, Steve Armstrong; Space Science Educator, Steve Schmidt; Technical Dir. Theatre, James Zervus; Special Events Coord., Susan Phelps; Admin. Sec., Eva Satterwhite.
Institution Type/Description: Children's Museum & Science Center.
Hours & Admission Prices: Tues.-Sat. 10-5, Sun. 1-5. Gallery & Art Center: no charge. Productions: call for prices. Children's Museum & Science Center: $6 per person. Closed Easter; Thanksgiving; Christmas. ♿
Attendance: 92,858 (actual)

ROCKY MOUNT CHILDREN'S MUSEUM AND SCIENCE CENTER, INC., 270 Gay St., Rocky Mount, NC 27804-5442. Tel.: 252-972-1167. Fax: 252-972-1535.
E-mail: museum@imperialcentre.org
Web Site: museum.imperialcentre.org
Key Personnel: Dir., Candy L. Madrid; Space Science Educator, Steve Schmidt; Cur. Education, Leigh White; Cur. Exhibits, Frank Armstrong; Sec., Tabitha Richardson.
Institution Type/Description: Science Museum.
Hours & Admission Prices: Tues.-Sat. 10-5, Sun. 1-5. Adults $5, children 2-15 $4, senior citizens 60 & over $3; museum & ASTC members, children one & under and residents on Sun. 1-5 no charge. Planetarium: $5. Combination pricing available. Closed Thanksgiving; Christmas. ♿
Attendance: 100,000 (actual)

ROCKY MOUNT FIRE MUSEUM, 404 S. Church St., Rocky Mount, NC 27804-5809. Tel.: 252-972-1376.
Institution Type/Description: Fire Museum: housed in the original Fire Station No. 2; built in 1924.
Hours & Admission Prices: Mon.-Fri. 8:30-5; other times by appointment.

STONEWALL MANOR, 1331 Stonewall Lane, Rocky Mount, NC 27804. Mailing Address: P.O. Box 9028, Rocky Mount, NC 27804. Tel.: 252-442-0063. Fax: 252-443-0137.
E-mail: stonewalllf@embarqmail.com
Web Site: www.stonewallmanor.org
Key Personnel: Pres. (V), Morris Wilder; Nash County Historical Coord., Lauren Filliettaz; Tour Guide, Mary Dyer; Tour Guide, Barbara Hardison Privette; Treas., Stewart Gibson.
Institution Type/Description: Historic House & Site.
Hours & Admission Prices: Call for hours. Adults $5, seniors $3, children under 12 $2; discounts to groups of 6 or more; children 4 & under no charge. ♿
Attendance: 1,000 (estimated)

Rodanthe

CHICAMACOMICO LIFE-SAVING STATION HISTORIC SITE AND MUSEUM, 23645 N.C. Hwy. 12, Rodanthe, NC 27968. Mailing Address: P.O. Box 5, Rodanthe, NC 27968. Tel.: 252-987-1552. Fax: 252-987-1559.
E-mail: clss@embarqmail.com
Web Site: www.chicamacomico.net
Key Personnel: Pres. (V), John Griffin; Site Mgr., Dinah Beveridge.

Institution Type/Description: History Museum.
Hours & Admission Prices: April-Nov. Mon.-Fri. 10-5. Adults $8, seniors 65 & over $7, students 4-17 $6; discounts to groups of 20 or more; USCG members no charge.

Roxboro

PERSON COUNTY MUSEUM OF HISTORY, 309 N. Main St., Roxboro, NC 27573-5326. Mailing Address: P.O. Box 1792, Roxboro, NC 27573-1792. Tel.: 336-597-2884.
E-mail: pcmuseum@roxboro.net
Web Site: www.visitroxboronc.com/heritage/museum.htm
Institution Type/Description: History Museum.
Hours & Admission Prices: Wed.-Fri. 10-4, Sat. 10-2; other times by appointment.

Rutherford

GREEN RIVER PLANTATION, 6333 Coxe Rd., Rutherford, NC 28139. Tel.: 828-286-1461.
E-mail: greenriver@wildblue.net
Web Site: greenriverplantation.wordpress.com/
Institution Type/Description: Historic House Museum: housed in a 42 room mansion; built in 1807. Listed on the National Register of Historic Places.
Hours & Admission Prices: Daily call for hours; groups by appointment. Adults 12 & over $20, seniors 65 & over $18, children under 12 $10; discounts to groups; children under 4 no charge.

Rutherfordton

BROAD RIVER GEMS AND MINING COMPANY, 218 River Landing, Rutherfordton, NC 28139-7390. Tel.: 828-286-1220.
E-mail: earl.-nospam@broadrivergems.com.com
Web Site: broadrivergems.com
Institution Type/Description: Mining Museum.
Hours & Admission Prices: Daily 10-6.

KIDSENSES CHILDREN'S MUSEUM, 172 N. Main St., Rutherfordton, NC 28139-2502. Mailing Address: P.O. Box 150, Rutherfordton, NC 28139-0150. Tel.: 828-286-2120.
E-mail: info@kidsenses.org
Web Site: www.kidsenses.com
Key Personnel: Exec. Dir., Willard Whitson.
Institution Type/Description: Children's Museum.
Hours & Admission Prices: Tues.-Thurs. & Sat. 9-5, Fri. 9-8. Adults $5, seniors 55 & over and Mon.-Fri. after 3 pm $3; discounts to Catawba Science Center & Chimney Rock State Park members.
Attendance: 33,500 (actual)

Salisbury

DAN NICHOLAS PARK NATURE CENTER, 6800 Bringle Ferry Rd., Salisbury, NC 28146-7144. Tel.: 704-216-7803. Fax: 704-639-0947.
E-mail: bringled@co.rowan.nc.us
Web Site: www.dannicholas.net
Key Personnel: Parks & Recreation Dir., Dan Bringle; County Mgr., Gary Page; Nature Center Dir., Bob Pendergrass; Asst. Naturalist, David Jones.
Institution Type/Description: Zoo & Nature Center Museum.
Hours & Admission Prices: April-Oct. Mon.-Thurs. 8-5, Fri.-Sun. 8-8; Nov.-March daily 9-5. Petting Barn $.50. ♿
Attendance: 100,000

DR. JOSEPHUS HALL HOUSE, 226 S. Jackson St., Salisbury, NC 28144-4838. Mailing Address: P.O. Box 4221, Salisbury, NC 28145-4221. Tel.: 704-636-0103. Facebook: Historic Salisbury Foundation.
E-mail: office@historicsalisbury.org
Web Site: www.historicsalisbury.org
Institution Type/Description: Historic House Museum: housed in a former school; built in 1820. Listed on the National Register of Historic Places.
Hours & Admission Prices: Sat.-Sun. 1-4; other times by appointment. Adults $5, children 6-12 $1; children under 6 no charge.

HORIZONS UNLIMITED SUPPLEMENTARY EDUCATIONAL CENTER, 1636 Parkview Circle, Salisbury, NC 28144-2461. Tel.: 704-639-3004. Fax: 704-639-3015.
E-mail: ellisra@rss.k12.nc.us
Web Site: www.rssed.org

Key Personnel: Dir. & Space Science Specialist, Lisa Wear; Science Specialist & Dir. Planetarium, Patsy Wilson; History Specialist, Theresa Pierce.
Institution Type/Description: General Museum.
Hours & Admission Prices: By appointment. &
Attendance: 21,850

ROWAN MUSEUM, INC., 202 N. Main St., Salisbury, NC 28144-4356. Tel.: 704-633-5946. Fax: 704-633-9858.
E-mail: rowanmuseum@carolina.rr.com
Web Site: rowanmuseum.org
Key Personnel: Exec. Dir., Kaye Brown Hirst; Pres., Paul Brown.
Institution Type/Description: History Museum.
Hours & Admission Prices: Utzman-Chambers House: April-Nov. Sat.-Sun. 1-4. Rowan Museum: Mon.-Fri. 10-4, Sat.-Sun.1-4; other times by appointment. Old Stone House: April-Dec. Thurs.-Sun. 1-4. Adults $3, students $1.50, children $1; discounts to AAM members. &
Attendance: 5,000 (estimated)

WATERWORKS VISUAL ARTS CENTER, 123 E. Liberty St., Salisbury, NC 28144-5038. Tel.: 704-636-1882. Fax: 704-636-1895.
E-mail: admin@waterworks.org
Web Site: waterworks.org
Key Personnel: Exec. Dir., Anne Scott Clement.
Institution Type/Description: Art Museum.
Hours & Admission Prices: Mon.-Fri. 10-5, Sat. 10-2. No charge; donations accepted. Closed major holidays. &
Attendance: 20,000 (estimated)

Saluda

PEARSON'S FALLS, 2748 Pearson Falls Rd., Saluda, NC 28773. Tel.: 828-749-3031.
E-mail: info@pearsonsfalls.org
Web Site: www.pearsonsfalls.org
Institution Type/Description: Nature & Wildlife Preserve.
Hours & Admission Prices: Feb. & Nov.-Dec. Mon.-Sat. 10-5, Sun. 12-5; March-Oct. Mon.-Sat. 10-6, Sun. 12-6. Adults 13 & up $5, youth 6-12 $1; children under 6 no charge. Closed Thanksgiving; Christmas.

Sanford

HOUSE IN THE HORSESHOE STATE HISTORIC SITE, 288 Alston House Rd., Sanford, NC 27330-8712. Tel.: 910-947-2051. Fax: 910-947-2051. Facebook: House in the Horseshoe.
E-mail: horseshoe@ncdcr.gov
Web Site: www.nchistoricsites.org/horsesho
Key Personnel: Site Mgr., Kimberly Mozingo.
Institution Type/Description: Historic House: housed in the former home of North Carolina Governor Benjamin Williams; built in 1772; site of Revolutionary War militia skirmish.
Hours & Admission Prices: Tues.-Sat. 9-5. No charge; donations accepted. Closed state holidays. &
Attendance: 17,064 (actual)

MUSEUM OF RAILROAD HOUSE HISTORICAL ASSOCIATION MUSEUM INC., 110 Charlotte Ave., Sanford, NC 27330-4304. Mailing Address: P.O. Box 1023, Sanford, NC 27331-1023. Tel.: 919-776-7479.
Web Site: www.railroadhouse.org
Key Personnel: Pres. (V), Oliver Crawley.
Institution Type/Description: Historic House: 1872 Railroad House, Gothic Revival, oldest house in Sanford, home of the first mayor & site of first school.
Hours & Admission Prices: Sat.-Sun. 1-5; other times by appointment. No charge; donations accepted.
Attendance: 2,000 (estimated)

Scotland Neck

SYLVAN HEIGHTS BIRD PARK, 500 Sylvan Heights Pkwy., Scotland Neck, NC 27874. Mailing Address: P.O. Box 368, Scotland Neck, NC 27874. Tel.: 252-826-3186. Fax: 252-826-3273.
E-mail: info@shwpark.com
Web Site: shwpark.com
Key Personnel: Exec. Dir., Mike Lubbock; Cur., Brad Hazelton; Opers. Mgr., Ali Lubbock; Retail Mgr., JoAnn Josey; Education Coord., Lee Peoples; Membership & Devel., Brent Lubbock.
Institution Type/Description: Bird Park.

Hours & Admission Prices: April-Oct. Tues.-Sun. 9-5; Nov.-March Tues.-Sun. 9-4. Adults $9, senior citizens 62 & over $7, children 3-12 $5; children under 3 no charge. Closed Thanksgiving; Christmas.

Seagrove

MUSEUM OF NC TRADITIONAL POTTERY, 127 E. Main St., Seagrove, NC 27341. Mailing Address: P.O. Box 500, Seagrove, NC 27341. Tel.: 336-873-7887. Facebook: Museum of NC Traditional Pottery.
E-mail: ncpottery122@gmail.com
Web Site: www.seagrovepotterymuseum.net
Key Personnel: Pres. (V), Phil Morgan; Museum Shop Mgr., Teresa Milks.
Institution Type/Description: Pottery History Museum.
Hours & Admission Prices: No charge; donations accepted.

NORTH CAROLINA POTTERY CENTER, 233 East Ave., Seagrove, NC 27341-0531. Mailing Address: P.O. Box 531, Seagrove, NC 27341-0531. Tel.: 336-873-8430. Fax: 336-873-8530.
E-mail: manager@ncpotterycenter.org
Web Site: www.ncpotterycenter.org
Key Personnel: Pres., Linda Carnes-McNaughton; Mgr., Paulett Badgett.
Institution Type/Description: Pottery Center.
Hours & Admission Prices: Tues.-Sat. 10-4. Adults $2, students 9th-12th grade $1; students K-8th grade & members no charge. &
Attendance: 12,000 (actual)

SEAGROVE ORCHIDS, 3451 Brower Mill Rd., Seagrove, NC 27341. Tel.: 336-879-6677.
Institution Type/Description: Working Nursery.
Hours & Admission Prices: Tues.-Sat. 10-5; other times by appointment.

Sedalia

CHARLOTTE HAWKINS BROWN MUSEUM, 6136 Burlington Rd., Sedalia, NC 27249. Mailing Address: P.O. Box B, Sedalia, NC 27342-0190. Tel.: 336-449-4846. Fax: 336-449-0176.
E-mail: chb@ncdcr.gov
Web Site: www.nchistoricsites.org/chb/chb.htm
Institution Type/Description: History Museum.
Hours & Admission Prices: Mon.-Sat. 9-5. No charge; donations accepted. Closed most major state holidays. &
Attendance: 13,000 (actual)

Seven Springs

CLIFFS OF THE NEUSE STATE PARK, 240 Park Entrance Rd., Seven Springs, NC 28578-8968. Tel.: 919-778-6234. Fax: 919-778-7447.
E-mail: cliffs.neuse@ncmail.net
Web Site: www.ncparks.gov/Visit/parks/clne/main.php
Key Personnel: Park Supt., Lyden Sutton; Dist. Naturalist, Jeanne Peacock.
Institution Type/Description: Park Museum.
Hours & Admission Prices: March-May & Sept.-Nov. daily 8-8; June-Aug. daily 8-9; Dec.-Feb. daily 8-6. No charge. Closed Christmas.
Attendance: 70,000 (estimated)

Shelby

CLEVELAND COUNTY ARTS CENTER, 111 S. Washington St., Shelby, NC 28150. Tel.: 704-484-2787. Fax: 704-481-1822.
E-mail: info@ccartscouncil.org
Web Site: www.ccartscouncil.org
Key Personnel: Pres., Shearra Miller; Mktg. Coord., Violet Arth.
Institution Type/Description: Arts Center: housed in the former post office building.
Hours & Admission Prices: Mon.-Fri. 9-5:30.

EARL SCRUGGS CENTER, 103 S. Lafayette St., Shelby, NC 28150. Mailing Address: P.O. Box 2063, Shelby, NC 28151. Tel.: 704-487-6233. Facebook: Earl Scruggs Center.
E-mail: info@earlscruggscenter.org
Web Site: earlscruggscenter.org
Key Personnel: Dir., Emily Epley; Cur. & Collections Mgr., Adrienne Nirde.
Institution Type/Description: History Museum.
Hours & Admission Prices: Wed. 10-6, Thurs.-Sat. 10-4, Sun. 1-5. Adults $12, seniors & college students $8, children 6-17 $5; discounts to groups; children 5 & under no charge. Closed New Year's Day; Easter; Memorial Day; Independence Day; Labor Day; Thanksgiving; Christmas Eve & Day.

INTERNATIONAL LINEMANS MUSEUM, 529 Caleb Rd., Shelby, NC 28152. Mailing Address: P.O. Box 1740, Shelby, NC 28152. Tel.: 704-482-7638. Facebook: Lineman Museum.
E-mail: ilm@linemanmuseum.com
Web Site: www.linemanmuseum.com
Key Personnel: C.E.O., Andy Price.
Institution Type/Description: History Museum.
Hours & Admission Prices: Mon.-Fri. 8-5; other times by appointment. No charge.
Attendance: 200 (estimated)

Siler City

THE FARM AT CELEBRITY DAIRY, 2106 Mt. Vernon - Hickory Mountain Rd., Siler City, NC 27344. Tel.: 877-742-5176.
E-mail: theinn@celebritydairy.com
Web Site: www.celebritydairy.com
Institution Type/Description: Dairy Farm.
Hours & Admission Prices: By appointment.

Smithfield

ARBORETUM AT JOHNSTON COMMUNITY COLLEGE, 1240 E. Market St., Smithfield, NC 27577. Mailing Address: P.O. Box 2350, Smithfield, NC 27577. Tel.: 919-209-2052.
Web Site: www.johnstoncc.edu/arboretum
Institution Type/Description: Arboretum.
Hours & Admission Prices: Call for hours.

AVA GARDNER MUSEUM, 325 E. Market St., Smithfield, NC 27577-3919. Tel.: 919-934-5830.
E-mail: avainfo@avagardner.org
Web Site: www.avagardner.org
Key Personnel: Dir., Lynell Seabold; Chm., Don Duggin.
Institution Type/Description: Film Museum.
Hours & Admission Prices: Mon.-Sat. 9-5, Sun. 2-5. Adults $10, seniors 65 & over, military & teens 13-17 $9, children 6-12 $6; discount to groups of 10 or more; children under 6 no charge. &
Attendance: 10,000 (actual)

Snow Camp

SNOW CAMP HISTORICAL SOCIETY, 301 Drama Rd., Snow Camp, NC 27349. Mailing Address: P.O. Box 535, Snow Camp, NC 27349-0535. Tel.: 336-376-6948.
E-mail: snowcampot@aol.com
Web Site: www.snowcampdrama.com
Key Personnel: Chm. (V), James Shields.
Institution Type/Description: History Museum.
Hours & Admission Prices: May-Aug. Mon.-Fri. 9-5. No charge. &
Attendance: 10,000 (estimated)

South Mills

DISMAL SWAMP STATE PARK & VISITORS CENTER, 2294 US 17 N., South Mills, NC 27976. Tel.: 252-771-6593 & 6582. Fax: 252-771-9944.
E-mail: dismal.swamp@ncparks.gov
Web Site: www.ncparks.gov/visit/parks/disw/main.php
Key Personnel: Supt., Adam Carver.
Institution Type/Description: State Park & Visitors Center.
Hours & Admission Prices: Park: March-Oct. daily 8-6; Nov.-Feb. daily 8-5. Visitors Center: Mon.-Fri. 8-4:30, Sat.-Sun. 9:30-4:30. No charge. Closed Christmas.
Attendance: 121,813 (actual)

South Nags Head

BODIE ISLAND LIGHT STATION, Bodie Island Lighthouse, South Nags Head, NC 27959. Mailing Address: 1401 National Park Dr., Manteo, NC 27954-9451. Tel.: 252-473-2111 & 441-5711. Fax: 252-449-0788.
E-mail: caha_information@nps.gov
Web Site: www.nps.gov/caha
Formerly: Bodie Island Visitor Center
Key Personnel: Supt., Barclay Trimble; Archives Technician, Jami P. Lanier.
Institution Type/Description: Park Museum & Visitor Center.
Hours & Admission Prices: Daily 9-5. No charge; donations accepted. &
Attendance: (estimated)

Southern Pines

ARTS COUNCIL OF MOORE COUNTY - CAMPBELL HOUSE, 482 E. Connecticut Ave., Southern Pines, NC 28387-5624. Mailing Address: P.O. Box 405, Southern Pines, NC 28388-0405. Tel.: 910-692-2787. Fax: 910-693-1217.
E-mail: acmc@mooreart.net
Web Site: www.mooreart.net
Institution Type/Description: Art Museum.
Hours & Admission Prices: Mon.-Fri. 9-5, 3rd Sat. of select months 2-4. No charge.

SHAW HOUSE, 110 Morganton Rd., Southern Pines, NC 28387. Mailing Address: P.O. Box 324, Southern Pines, NC 28388-0324. Tel.: 910-692-2051. Fax: 910-692-2051.
E-mail: moorehistory@connectnc.net
Web Site: moorehistory.com
Institution Type/Description: Historic House Museum: built c.1820.
Hours & Admission Prices: Tours: Tues.-Fri. 1-4; other times by appointment. No charge.
Attendance: 1,500 (estimated)

TAXIDERMY HALL OF FAME OF NORTH CAROLINA/ ANTIQUE TOOL MUSEUM/CREATION MUSEUM, 156 N. W. Broad St., Southern Pines, NC 28387. Tel.: 910-692-3471.
E-mail: community@creationmuseum.org
Web Site: thecreationmuseum.org
Institution Type/Description: History Museum.
Hours & Admission Prices: Call for hours.

WEYMOUTH WOODS-SANDHILLS NATURE PRESERVE MUSEUM, 1024 Fort Bragg Rd., Southern Pines, NC 28387-7319. Tel.: 910-692-2167. Fax: 910-692-8042.
E-mail: weymouth.woods@ncparks.gov
Web Site: www.ncparks.gov/Visit/parks/wewo/main.php
Key Personnel: Ranger, Kim Hyre.
Institution Type/Description: Natural History & Science Museum.
Hours & Admission Prices: Daily 9-5. No charge; donations accepted. Closed Christmas.
Attendance: 22,295 (estimated)

Southport

DUKE ENERGY BRUNSWICK NUCLEAR PLANT VISITOR CENTER, 8470 River Rd. S.E., Southport, NC 28461. Tel.: 910-457-2418.
Institution Type/Description: Energy Museum.
Hours & Admission Prices: Call for hours. No charge. Closed major holidays.

FORT JOHNSON - SOUTHPORT MUSEUM, 203 E. Bay St., Southport, NC 28461. Tel.: 910-457-7927.
E-mail: tourism@southportnc.org
Web Site: southportnc.org
Institution Type/Description: Military History Museum: housed on the site of Fort Johnston; built in 1748.
Hours & Admission Prices: Mon.-Sat. 10-4, Sun. call for hours.

NORTH CAROLINA MARITIME MUSEUM AT SOUTHPORT, 204 E. Moore St., Southport, NC 28461-3928. Tel.: 910-457-0003.
Institution Type/Description: Maritime History Museum.
Hours & Admission Prices: Temporarily closed.

Sparta

DOUGHTON PARK - BRINEGAR CABIN AND CAUDILL FAMILY HOMESTEAD, Blue Ridge Pkwy., MP 240, Sparta, NC 28675. Mailing Address: c/o Blue Ridge Parkway Assn., P.O. Box 2136, Asheville, NC 28802-2136. Tel.: 336-372-8877.
Institution Type/Description: Historic House Museum & Park.
Hours & Admission Prices: May-Oct. call for hours. No charge.

Spencer

NORTH CAROLINA TRANSPORTATION MUSEUM, 411 S. Salisbury Ave., Spencer, NC 28159-2238. Tel.: 704-636-2889. Fax: 704-639-1881.
E-mail: nctrans@nctrans.org

Web Site: www.nctrans.org
Key Personnel: Exec. Dir., Samuel Wegner; Museum Foundation Pres. (V), Roy Johnson; Facility Mgr., Brian Howell; Public Information Officer, Mark Brown; C.F.O., Marlene Minshew; Education Programming Coord., Brian Moffitt; Volunteer Coord., LeAnne Johnson; Volunteer Coord., Vickie Peacock; Exhibits Coord., Bob Hopkins; Historian, Walter Turner.
Institution Type/Description: Historic Transportation Museum; housed in 1896, Southern Railway steam primary staging & repair facility complex containing 20 structures, 37 bay roundhouse, turntable & 90,000 feet back shop.
Hours & Admission Prices: Jan.-March Tues.-Sat. 9-5; April-Aug. Mon.-Sat. 9-5, Sun. 1-5; Sept.-Dec. Tues.-Sat. 9-5, Sun. 1-5. Museum: adults $5, seniors & active military $4, children 3-12 $3. Museum & Train Ride: adults $10, children 3-12 $6, seniors & active military $4; discounts to AAA members & groups; children 2 & under no charge. Closed New Year's Day; Easter; Veterans Day; Thanksgiving; Christmas. &
Attendance: 80,000 (estimated)

Spruce Pine

EMERALD VILLAGE - NORTH CAROLINA MINING MUSEUM, 331 McKinney Mine Rd., Spruce Pine, NC 28777. Mailing Address: P.O. Box 98, Little Switzerland, NC 28749. Tel.: 828-765-6463. Fax: 828-765-6329.
E-mail: info@emeraldvillage.com
Web Site: www.emeraldvillage.com
Institution Type/Description: Mining Museum.
Hours & Admission Prices: April daily 10-4; May & Sept.-Oct. daily 9-5; Memorial Day to Labor Day daily 9-6. Mine Tour: adults $8, senior citizens 60 & over $7, students $6; discounts to groups; preschool children no charge. Gold Panning: $10 & up.

MUSEUM OF NORTH CAROLINA MINERALS, Milepost 331, Blue Ridge Pkwy. at Hwy. 226, Spruce Pine, NC 28777. Mailing Address: Blue Ridge Pkwy. Foundation, 717 S. Marshall St., Ste. 105 B, Winston-Salem, NC 27101-5865. Tel.: 828-765-2761. Fax: 828-765-0202.
Key Personnel: District Ranger, Tim Francis.
Institution Type/Description: Mineral & Mineral Industry Museum.
Hours & Admission Prices: Daily 9-5. No charge. Closed New Year's Day; Thanksgiving; Christmas. &
Attendance: 254,000 (estimated)

Stanley

BREVARD STATION MUSEUM, 112 S. Main St., Stanley, NC 28164-1750. Tel.: 704-263-9801. Facebook: Brevard Station Museum.
E-mail: brevardstation@gmail.com
Web Site: www.brevardstation.com
Key Personnel: Admin., Joyce J. Handsel; Bd. Pres. (V), W. Barry Smith.
Institution Type/Description: History Museum.
Hours & Admission Prices: Tues.-Thurs. 10-4; other times by appointment. No charge.
Attendance: 500 (estimated)

Statesville

ALLISON WOODS OUTDOOR LEARNING CENTER, 2106 Turnersburg Hwy., Statesville, NC 28625. Mailing Address: P.O. Box 211, Statesville, NC 28687-0211. Tel.: 704-873-5976.
E-mail: selena@allisonwoodslivinghistory.org
Web Site: www.allisonwoodslivinghistory.org
Institution Type/Description: Historic Buildings & Gardens: listed on the National Register of Historic Places.
Hours & Admission Prices: Call for hours.

FORT DOBBS STATE HISTORIC SITE, 438 Fort Dobbs Rd., Statesville, NC 28625-1915. Tel.: 704-873-5882. Fax: 704-873-5995.
E-mail: richard.douglas.brown@ncdcr.gov
Web Site: www.fortdobbs.org
Key Personnel: Historic Site Mgr., Doug Brown; Chm. (V), Ralph Bentley; Historic Interpreter, Scott Douglas.
Institution Type/Description: Historic Site.
Hours & Admission Prices: Tues.-Sat. 9-5. No charge; donations accepted. &
Attendance: 32,000 (actual)

GREGORY CREEK HOMESTEAD, 1335 Museum Rd., Statesville, NC 28625. Mailing Address: P.O. Box 223, Statesville, NC 28687-0223. Tel.: 704-873-4734.
Institution Type/Description: History Museum.
Hours & Admission Prices: By appointment.

IREDELL MUSEUMS, 134 Court St., Statesville, NC 28677. Mailing Address: P.O. Box 223, Statesville, NC 28687-0223. Tel.: 704-873-7347. Facebook.
E-mail: ajohnston@iredellmuseums.org
Web Site: www.iredellmuseums.org
Key Personnel: Dir., Melinda Herzog; Pres. (V), Amy Lawton.
Institution Type/Description: General Museum.
Hours & Admission Prices: Tues.-Sat. 10-5. Admission 3 & over $5; members no charge. Closed national holidays. &
Attendance: 25,000 (estimated)

Sunset Beach

INGRAM PLANETARIUM, 7625 High Market St., Sunset Beach, NC 28468. Tel.: 910-575-0033. Fax: 910-575-0031.
E-mail: pinfo@museumplanetarium.org
Web Site: www.museumplanetarium.org
Key Personnel: Exec. Dir., Terry Bryant; Planetarium Dir., Mark Jankowski; Mktg., Susan Silk; Educational Svcs. Coord., Allison Smith; Membership Svcs., Deb Boyce; Gift Shop Mgr., Lynn Wiedman.
Institution Type/Description: Planetarium.
Hours & Admission Prices: Hours & programs are seasonal, check website. Adults $8, seniors 60 & over and students $6, children 3-4 $4; children 2 & under no charge.

Tarboro

BLOUNT-BRIDGERS HOUSE/HOBSON PITTMAN MEMORIAL GALLERY, 130 Bridgers St., Tarboro, NC 27886-3868. Tel.: 252-823-4159. Fax: 252-823-6190.
Web Site: edgecombearts.com
Formerly: Blount-Bridgers House/Edgecombe Country Art Museum
Key Personnel: Dir., Carol Banks; Pres. (V), Ashley Stancil.
Institution Type/Description: Art Museum: housed in c.1808 Blount-Bridgers plantation house.
Hours & Admission Prices: Summer: Tues.-Fri. 10-4, By appointment only for weekends. Groups by appointment. Adults $5, children under 12 $2; members no charge. Closed New Year's Day; Good Friday; Easter; Memorial Day; Independence Day; Labor Day; Thanksgiving; Christmas. &
Attendance: 4,000 (estimated)

Thomasville

1870 TRAIN DEPORT, 44 W. Main St., Thomasville, NC 27360. Tel.: 800-611-9907.
E-mail: Visit@TvilleNC.com
Web Site: thomasvilletourism.com
Institution Type/Description: Historic Building: built in 1870. Listed on the National Register of Historic Places.
Hours & Admission Prices: Mon.-Fri. 9-5, Sat. 9-1. No charge. &

Thurmond

PRECIOUS ALPACA FARM, 2930 S. Center Church Rd., Thurmond, NC 28683. Tel.: 336-957-3581.
E-mail: bbrown7568@aol.com
Institution Type/Description: Farm.
Hours & Admission Prices: Sat. 9-5, Sun. 1-5; groups by appointment.

Tillery

TILLERY HISTORY HOUSE MUSEUM, 321 Community Center Rd., Tillery, NC 27887. Mailing Address: P.O. Box 61, Tillery, NC 27887. Tel.: 252-826-3017. Fax: 252-826-3244.
E-mail: tillery@aol.com
Web Site: www.cct78.org
Key Personnel: Dir. & Chm. (V), Gary R. Grant; Chm. (V), Gary Redding.
Institution Type/Description: Historic House Museum: housed on former plantation land worked by generations of African-American slaves.
Hours & Admission Prices: By appointment. No charge; donations accepted. &
Attendance: 1,500 (actual)

Topsail Island

MISSILES & MORE MUSEUM, 720 Channel Blvd., Topsail Island, NC 28460. Mailing Address: c/o Historical Society of Topsail Island, P.O. Box 475, Holly Ridge, NC 28445. Tel.: 800-626-2780, 910-328-2488.
Web Site: missilesandmoremuseum.org
Institution Type/Description: History Museum: housed in the Assembly Building; built in 1946.
Hours & Admission Prices: April to mid-May & Sept. to mid-Oct. Mon.-Fri. 2-5; Memorial Day to Labor Day Mon.-Sat. 2-5.

Trinity

LINBROOK HERITAGE ESTATE, 5507 Snyder Country Rd., Trinity, NC 27370. Tel.: 336-861-6959.
E-mail: info@linbrookheritageestate.com
Web Site: www.linbrookheritageestate.com
Institution Type/Description: History Museum: estate comprises Linbrook Hall, the Historic Hoover House, and the Neal Agricultural and Industrial Museum.
Hours & Admission Prices: Tues.-Sat. 9-5, Sun. 2-5; groups by appointment. Linbrook Hall: adults $20, seniors 65 & over and youth 12-17 $15; children under 12 no charge. Historic Hoover House, Neal Agricultural & Industrial Museum: adults $5, seniors 65 & over and youth 12-17 $3; children under 12 no charge.

NEAL JOHN DEERE TRACTOR MUSEUM, 5507 Snyder Country Rd., Trinity, NC 27370. Tel.: 336-861-6959.
E-mail: johndeer@northstate.net
Web Site: nealsjohndeeretractors.com
Institution Type/Description: Tractor Museum.
Hours & Admission Prices: Sat. 9-5, Sun. 2-5.

Tryon

FOOTHILLS EQUESTRIAN NATURE CENTER (FENCE), 3381 Hunting County Rd., Tryon, NC 28782. Tel.: 828-859-9021.
E-mail: info@fence.org
Web Site: www.fence.org
Institution Type/Description: Nature Center.
Hours & Admission Prices: Call for hours.

TOY MAKERS HOUSE MUSEUM, 43 E. Howard St., Tryon, NC 28782-2400. Tel.: 828-290-6600.
Institution Type/Description: Toy History Museum.
Hours & Admission Prices: Call for hours.

Valdese

WALDENSIAN HERITAGE MUSEUM, 208 Rodoret St., Valdese, NC 28690-2841. Mailing Address: P.O. Box 111, Valdese, NC 28690-0111. Tel.: 828-874-1111& 879-2531. Fax: 828-874-1111.
E-mail: museum@waldensianpresbyterian.org
Web Site: www.waldensianpresbyterian.org
Formerly: Museum of Waldensian History
Key Personnel: Exec. Dir. & Museum Shop Mgr., Gretchen Costner; Pres. (V), Jewell Bounous.
Institution Type/Description: Religious Museum.
Hours & Admission Prices: Summer during outdoor drama: Fri.-Sat. 4-6. Tours: Tues.-Fri. 11 & 2; other times by appointment. Adults $2, students $1. Closed New Year's Day; Easter; Memorial Day; Labor Day; Thanksgiving; Christmas. &
Attendance: 2,000 (estimated)

WALDENSIAN TRAIL OF FAITH, 401 Church St., N.W., Valdese, NC 28690. Mailing Address: P.O. Box 1256, Valdese, NC 28690. Tel.: 828-874-1893, 800-635-4778. Facebook: Waldensian Trail of Faith.
E-mail: trailoffaith1893@gmail.com
Web Site: www.waldensiantrailoffaith.org
Key Personnel: Dir., Anthony Collins; Pres. (V), Jim Jacumin.
Institution Type/Description: History Museum.
Hours & Admission Prices: Mon.-Fri. 9-5, Sat.-Sun. 2-5. Self Guided Tours: adults $7, seniors $6, teachers & students $4; guided tours available for groups of 10 or more by appointment $2 per person. Closed New Year's Day; Thanksgiving; Christmas. &
Attendance: 5,000 (actual)

Wadesboro

ANSON COUNTY HISTORICAL SOCIETY, INC., 206 E. Wade St., Wadesboro, NC 28170-2229. Tel.: 704-694-6694.
E-mail: ansonhistorical@windstream.net
Web Site: www.ansonhistoricalsociety.org
Key Personnel: Pres. (V), Tommy Allen.
Institution Type/Description: General Museum.
Hours & Admission Prices: Tues.-Sat. 9-1; groups by appointment only. Mon.-Fri. 9-1. No charge; donations accepted. &
Attendance: 1,050 (estimated)

PEE DEE NATIONAL WILDLIFE REFUGE, 5770 U.S. Hwy. 52 N., Wadesboro, NC 28170. Tel.: 704-694-4424. Fax: 704-694-6570.
E-mail: jeffrey_bricken@fws.gov
Web Site: www.fws.gov/peedee
Key Personnel: Refuge Mgr., J.D. Bricken; Asst. Refuge Mgr., Greg Walmsley.
Institution Type/Description: Wildlife Refuge.
Hours & Admission Prices: Call for hours.
Attendance: 35,000

Wake Forest

THE WAKE FOREST HISTORICAL MUSEUM, 414 N. Main St., Wake Forest, NC 27587. Mailing Address: P.O. Box 494, Wake Forest, NC 27588-0494. Tel.: 919-556-2911. Fax: 919-556-2991. Facebook: Wake Forest Museum.
E-mail: morrisce@wfu.edu
Web Site: www.wakeforestmuseum.org
Formerly: Wake Forest College Birthplace Society, Inc.
Key Personnel: Exec. Dir., Ed Morris; Pres. (V), Tom Parrish; Vice Pres., Durward Matheny; Asst. Dir., Jennifer Smart.
Institution Type/Description: Historic Society Museum: housed in the first home of Wake Forest University; built in 1820.
Hours & Admission Prices: Tues.-Fri. 9-12 & 1:30-4:30, Sun. 2-5; tours by appointment. No charge. Closed major holidays. &
Attendance: 8,000 (estimated)

Warsaw

DUPLIN COUNTY VETERANS MEMORIAL MUSEUM, 119 E. Hill St., Warsaw, NC 28398-1917. Mailing Address: P.O. Box 137, Warsaw, NC 28398. Tel.: 910-293-2190.
E-mail: dcveteransmuseum@yahoo.com
Web Site: duplincountyveteransmuseum.com
Key Personnel: Cur., Earl Rouse; Chm. (V), Jene Thompson.
Institution Type/Description: Military Museum: housed in the L. P. Best house; built in 1894. Listed on the National Register of Historic Places.
Hours & Admission Prices: Thurs.-Fri. 1-4, Sat. by appointment. Adults $2; members no charge. &
Attendance: 100 (estimated)

Washington

NORTH CAROLINA ESTUARIUM, 223 E. Water St., Washington, NC 27889. Tel.: 252-948-0000.
E-mail: estuarium@embarqmail.com
Institution Type/Description: Environmental Center.
Hours & Admission Prices: Tues.-Sat. 10-4. Adults $4, students K-12 $2; children 4 & under no charge.

Waxhaw

MEXICO CARDENAS MUSEUM, 6403 Davis Rd., Waxhaw, NC 28173. Mailing Address: P.O. Box 248, Waxhaw, NC 28173-0248. Tel.: 704-843-6045.
E-mail: mexico_cardenas_museum_jaars@jaars.org
Web Site: www.jaars.org
Key Personnel: Financial Dir., Roy Self; Public Rels., Jeff Park.
Institution Type/Description: History Museum.
Hours & Admission Prices: Mon.-Sat. 9-12 & 1-4. No charge; donations accepted. &
Attendance: 3,242 (actual)

THE MUSEUM OF THE ALPHABET, 6409 Davis Rd., The JAARS Center, Waxhaw, NC 28173. Mailing Address: P.O. Box 248, Waxhaw, NC 28173-0248. Tel.: 704-843-6066. Fax: 704-843-6200.

E-mail: info@jaars.org
Web Site: www.jaars.org/museum/alphabet/index.htm
Key Personnel: Financial Dir., Roy Self; Public Rels., Jeff Park.
Institution Type/Description: Alphabet Museum.
Hours & Admission Prices: Mon.-Sat. 9-12 & 1-4. No charge; donations accepted. Closed government holidays. &
Attendance: 4,723 (actual)

MUSEUM OF THE WAXHAWS & ANDREW JACKSON MEMORIAL, 8215 Waxhaw Hwy. - Hwy. 75, Waxhaw, NC 28173. Mailing Address: P.O. Box 7, Waxhaw, NC 28173-1038. Tel.: 704-843-1832. Fax: 704-843-1832.
E-mail: mwaxhaw@museumofthewaxhaws.org
Web Site: www.museumofthewaxhaws.com/
Key Personnel: Dir., Sharon Murrer.
Institution Type/Description: Regional History Museum focus on settlement period, American Revolution & Andrew Jackson's life.
Hours & Admission Prices: Fri.-Sat. 10-5, Sun. 2-5. Adults $5, seniors 60 & over $4, children 6-12 $2; members and children 5 & under no charge. Closed New Year's Day; Thanksgiving; Christmas. &
Attendance: 3,000 (actual)

Waynesville

MUSEUM OF NORTH CAROLINA HANDICRAFTS, INC., 49 Shelton St., Waynesville, NC 28786. Tel.: 828-452-1551.
E-mail: info@sheltonhouse.org
Web Site: www.sheltonhouse.org
Institution Type/Description: Historic House Museum: housed in the former home of Stephen Jehu Shelton and then his son, William Taylor Shelton; built in 1875. Listed on the National Register of Historic Places.
Hours & Admission Prices: April-Oct. Tues.-Sat. 11-4; Winter: open for group tours & events by appointment. Adults $6, students $5; discounts to groups of 10 or more; children under 5 no charge.
Attendance: 700 (estimated)

Weaverville

ZEBULON B. VANCE BIRTHPLACE STATE HISTORIC SITE, 911 Reems Creek Rd., Weaverville, NC 28787-8710. Tel.: 828-645-6706. Fax: 828-645-0936.
E-mail: vance@ncdcr.gov
Web Site: www.nchistoricsites.org/vance/vance.htm
Key Personnel: Site Mgr., Michael Moore.
Institution Type/Description: Park Museum Visitor Center.
Hours & Admission Prices: Tues.-Sat. 9-5. No charge; donations accepted. Closed major holidays. &
Attendance: 11,764 (actual)

Welcome

RICHARD CHILDRESS RACING MUSEUM, 236 Industrial Dr., Welcome, NC 27374. Mailing Address: P.O. Box 360, Welcome, NC 27374. Tel.: 366-731-3334.
E-mail: jkiser@rcrracing.com
Web Site: www.rcrracing.com
Key Personnel: Licensing & Retail Mgr., Jessica Kiser.
Institution Type/Description: Sports Museum.
Hours & Admission Prices: Museum: Thurs.-Sat. 10-6; Team Store: Tues.-Wed. 10-5, Thurs.-Sat. 10-6.

West Jefferson

ASHE ARTS CENTER, 303 School Ave., West Jefferson, NC 28694. Tel.: 336-846-2787.
E-mail: jane@ashecountyarts.org
Web Site: www.ashecountyarts.org/galleryshop.htm
Key Personnel: Exec. Dir., Jane Lonon; Dir. Opers., Linda Dreyer; Dir. Programs, Rebecca Williams.
Institution Type/Description: Art Gallery.
Hours & Admission Prices: Jan.-March Mon.-Fri. 9-4; April-Dec. Mon.-Fri. 9-4, Sat. 10-4.

ASHE COUNTY CHEESE PLANT & STORE, 106 E. Main St., West Jefferson, NC 28694. Mailing Address: P.O. Box 447, West Jefferson, NC 28694. Tel.: 800-445-1378, 336-246-2501.
E-mail: info@ashecountycheese.com
Web Site: www.ashecountycheese.com
Institution Type/Description: Cheese Plant.
Hours & Admission Prices: Mon.-Sat. 8:30-5. &

BLUFF MOUNTAIN NATURE PRESERVE, Edwards Rd., West Jefferson, NC 28694. Mailing Address: 334 Blackwell St., Ste. 300, Durham, NC 27701. Tel.: 336-497-1972.
E-mail: bluffmountainpreserve@gmail.com
Web Site: www.blueridgeheritage.com
Key Personnel: Guide, Kim Hadley.
Institution Type/Description: Nature Preserve.
Hours & Admission Prices: By appointment.

Whiteville

NORTH CAROLINA MUSEUM OF NATURAL SCIENCES AT WHITEVILLE, 415 S. Madison St., Whiteville, NC 28472-4125. Tel.: 910-914-4185. Fax: 910-641-0385. Facebook & Twitter: @NCMNSWhiteville.
E-mail: whiteville@naturalsciences.org
Key Personnel: Pres. Bd., Bill Thompson; Dir., Emlynn Koster, Ph.D.; Exhibit Coord., Sara Capps; Educator, Kellie Lewis; Administrative Asst., Rhonda Billeaud; Gift Shop/Museum Store Mgr., Marlene Cartrette.
Institution Type/Description: Natural Science Museum.
Hours & Admission Prices: Tues.-Sat. 9-5. No charge. Closed state holidays. &
Attendance: 18,686 (actual)

Wilkesboro

WILKES HERITAGE MUSEUM, 100 E. Main St., Wilkesboro, NC 28697. Mailing Address: P.O. Box 935, Wilkesboro, NC 28697-0935. Tel.: 336-667-3171.
E-mail: info@wilkesheritagemuseum.com
Web Site: www.wilkesheritagemuseum.com
Key Personnel: Dir., Jennifer Furr.
Institution Type/Description: History Museum.
Hours & Admission Prices: Mon.-Fri. 10-4. Admission $6; children 5 & under no charge. Closed major holidays.

Willard

PENDERLEA HOMESTEAD MUSEUM, 284 Garden Rd., Willard, NC 28478-6780. Mailing Address: P.O. Box 1783, Burgaw, NC 28425-1783. Tel.: 910-259-5344.
E-mail: info@penderleahomesteadmuseum.org
Web Site: www.penderleahomesteadmuseum.org
Key Personnel: Pres. Bd. Dirs., Pattye M. Ebert; Vice Pres., David Haase; Cur., Ann Southerland Cottle.
Institution Type/Description: History Museum.
Hours & Admission Prices: Sat. 1-4. No charge; donations accepted. &
Attendance: 250 (actual)

Williamston

ASA BIGGS HOUSE - MARTIN COUNTY HISTORICAL SOCIETY, 100 E. Church St., Williamston, NC 27892. Mailing Address: P.O. Box 851, Williamston, NC 27892. Tel.: 252-792-6605. Fax: 252-792-8710.
E-mail: tourism@visitmartincounty.com
Institution Type/Description: Historical Society Museum: housed in the former home of attorney, federal judge & U.S. Senator Asa Biggs; built in 1831. Listed on the National Register of Historic Places.
Hours & Admission Prices: Call for hours.

Wilmington

AIRLIE GARDENS, 300 Airlie Rd., Wilmington, NC 28403-3706. Tel.: 910-798-7700.
E-mail: airlieinfo@nhcgov.com
Institution Type/Description: Gardens.
Hours & Admission Prices: Jan.-March 19 Mon.-Sat. 9-5; March 20-April 2 & May 18-Dec. daily 9-5; April 3-May 17 Sun.-Wed. 9-5, Thurs.-Sat. 9-7. Adults $8, county residents & military $5, children 4-12 $3. Closed New Year's Day.

BATTLESHIP NORTH CAROLINA, 1 Battleship Rd., Wilmington, NC 28401. Mailing Address: P.O. Box 480, Wilmington, NC 28402-0480. Tel.: 910-399-9100. Fax: 910-251-5807. Facebook, Instagram.
E-mail: michelle.robinson@ncdcr.gov
Web Site: www.battleshipnc.com
Key Personnel: Exec. Dir., Capt. Terry Bragg; Asst. Dir. Operations, Chris Vargo; Comptroller, Elizabeth Haynes; Dir. Promotions, Meaghan Holmes;

Maintenance Dir., Terry Kuhn; Cur., Kim Robinson Sincox; Cur., Mary Ames Booker; Dir. Sales, Leesa McFarlane; Dir. Programs, Danielle Wallace.
Institution Type/Description: Historic Ship Museum.
Hours & Admission Prices: Memorial Day to Labor Day daily 8-8; Sept.-May daily 8-5. Adults $14, seniors & military $10, children 6-11 $6; discounts to groups; Friends of the Battleship & children under 5 no charge.
Attendance: 200,000 (actual)

BELLAMY MANSION MUSEUM OF HISTORY AND DESIGN ARTS, 503 Market St., Wilmington, NC 28401-4634. Tel.: 910-251-3700, ext. 102. Fax: 910-763-8154.
E-mail: info@bellamymansion.org
Web Site: www.bellamymansion.org
Key Personnel: Exec. Dir., Beverly Ayscue; Chm., Sharon Stone; Dir. Mktg. & Facilities, Gene Ayscue; Dir. Public Education, Madeline Flagler.
Institution Type/Description: Historic House Museum: housed in c.1861 Bellamy Mansion, a 22-room Greek Revival and Italianate residence built by free and enslaved African Americans that includes original slave quarters.
Hours & Admission Prices: Tues.-Sat. 10-5, Sun. 1-5. Adults $10, children 5-12 $4; discounts to groups, Preservation North Carolina & Friends of Bellamy Mansion Museum members; members & National Trust for Historic Preservation members no charge. Closed New Year's Day; Easter; Memorial Day; Independence Day; Thanksgiving; Christmas.
Attendance: 15,000 (actual)

THE BURGWIN-WRIGHT MUSEUM AND GARDENS, 224 Market St., Wilmington, NC 28401-4444. Tel.: 910-762-0570. Fax: 910-762-8650. Facebook: The Burgwin-Wright Museum.
E-mail: info@burgwinwrighthouse.com
Web Site: www.burgwinwrighthouse.com
Key Personnel: Museum Mgr., Christine Lamberton; Exec. Dir. & C.E.O., Joy Allen.
Institution Type/Description: Historic House Museum: housed in 1771 Burgwin-Wright House & Garden.
Hours & Admission Prices: Tues.-Sat. 10-4, last tour at 3. Adults $10, students 4-18 or with college ID $5; discount for multiple house ticket; children 3 & under; active military & members no charge. Closed national holidays.
Attendance: 4,500 (estimated)

CAMERON ART MUSEUM, 3201 S. 17th St., Wilmington, NC 28412-6554. Tel.: 910-395-5999. Fax: 910-395-5030.
E-mail: kkelly@cameronartmuseum.org
Web Site: www.cameronartmuseum.org
Formerly: St. John's Museum of Art
Key Personnel: Dir., Anne Brennan; Chm. (V), Frances Goodman; Cur. Public Programs, Daphne Holmes; Property Mgr., Johnnie McKoy; Cur. Education, Georgia Mastroieni; Resident Master Artist, Hiroshi Sueyoshi; Registrar, Holly Tripman; Museum Shop Mgr., Nan Pope.
Institution Type/Description: Art Museum.
Hours & Admission Prices: Tues.-Wed. & Fri.-Sun. 10-5, Thurs. 10-9. Adults $8; discount to students, senior citizens, NARM & AAM members; members no charge. Closed holidays.
Attendance: 40,000 (actual)

CAPE FEAR MUSEUM OF HISTORY AND SCIENCE, 814 Market St., Wilmington, NC 28401-4752. Tel.: 910-798-4350. Fax: 910-798-4382. Facebook & Twitter: capefearmuseum.
E-mail: amangus@nhcgov.com
Web Site: www.capefearmuseum.com
Key Personnel: Dir., Sheryl Mays; Chair, Mike Hudson; Pres. (V) CFM Associates, Inc., Stuart Borrett; Administrative Asst., Jessica Sisco; Cur., Barbara L. Rowe; Mgr. Education, Amy Thornton; Public Rels. Specialist, Amy Mangus; Educator, Tom Osborne; Educator, Jameson McDermott; Educator, Pepper Hill; Mgr. Exhibits, Adrienne Garwood; Exhibits Designer, John Timmerman; Registrar, Heather Yenco; Historian, Janet Davidson; Dir. Donor Rels., Kitty Yerkes.
Institution Type/Description: History & Science Museum.
Hours & Admission Prices: May-Sept. Mon.-Sat. 9-5, Sun. 1-5; Sept.-May Tues.-Sat. 9-5, Sun. 1-5. Adults $8, seniors, college students & military $7, children 6-17 $5; discounts to ASTC, NARM & SEMC members; children under 5 & members no charge. Closed major holidays.
Attendance: 40,680 (actual)

CAPE FEAR SERPENTARIUM, 20 Orange St., Wilmington, NC 28401-4419. Tel.: 910-762-1669. Fax: 910-762-1669.
E-mail: reptileeducation@gmail.com
Web Site: www.capefearserpentarium.com
Key Personnel: Dir., Dean Ripa.
Institution Type/Description: Herpetology Museum.
Hours & Admission Prices: Summer: Sun.-Fri. 11-5, Sat. 11-6; Winter: call for hours. Admission $9; discounts to groups; children 2 & under no charge.

THE CHILDREN'S MUSEUM OF WILMINGTON, 116 Orange St., Wilmington, NC 28401-4421. Tel.: 910-254-3534. Fax: 910-254-3565. Facebook: The Children's Museum of Wilmington.
E-mail: info@playwilmington.org
Web Site: www.playwilmington.org
Key Personnel: Dir., Jim Karl.
Institution Type/Description: Children's Museum.
Hours & Admission Prices: Labor Day-Memorial Day Tues.-Sat. 9-5, Sun. 1-5; Memorial Day-Labor Day Mon.-Sat. 9-5, Sun. 1-5; admission $9.75; discounts to military & seniors; children under one no charge. Closed Easter; Thanksgiving; Christmas Eve & Day.
Attendance: 54,000 (actual)

LOWER CAPE FEAR HISTORICAL SOCIETY, INC., 126 S. Third St., Wilmington, NC 28401-4556. Tel.: 910-762-0492 & 2976. Fax: 910-763-5869. Facebook: Latimer House Lower Cape Fear Historical Society.
E-mail: info@latimerhouse.org
Web Site: www.hslcf.org
Key Personnel: Chm. (V), Pat Hardee; Pres. (V), John Golden; Vice Pres., Clauston Jenkins; Office Mgr., Brittany Bennett; Archives Representative, James Rush Beeler; Archivist, Candace McGreevy.
Institution Type/Description: Decorative Arts Museum: housed in 1852 Latimer House, on National Register of Historic Places.
Hours & Admission Prices: Mon.-Sat. 10-3. Adults $10, children & students $5; discounts to AAA members; members no charge.
Attendance: 3,000 (actual)

MUSEUM OF THE BIZARRE, 201 S. Water St., Wilmington, NC 28401. Tel.: 910-399-2641.
Web Site: museumbizarre.com
Institution Type/Description: Science Museum.
Hours & Admission Prices: Daily 11-8. Admission $3; children under 3 no charge.

MUSEUM OF WORLD CULTURES/UNIVERSITY OF NORTH CAROLINA AT WILMINGTON, William M. Randall Library, UNC at Wilmington, 601 S. College Rd., Wilmington, NC 28403-5649. Tel.: 910-962-3276.
E-mail: parnellg@uncw.edu
Web Site: library.uncw.edu/museum
Key Personnel: Coord. Special Collections, Jerry Parnell.
Institution Type/Description: University Museum.
Hours & Admission Prices: Call for hours.

POPLAR GROVE HISTORIC PLANTATION, 10200 U.S. Hwy. 17 N., Wilmington, NC 28411-6854. Tel.: 910-686-9518. Fax: 910-686-4309.
E-mail: pgp@poplargrove.org
Web Site: www.poplargrove.org
Key Personnel: Pres. (V), Chris Wilcox; Dir., Caroline Lewis; Museum Shop Mgr. & Volunteer Coord., Felicia Greene.
Institution Type/Description: Historic House & Site: housed in 1850 Greek Revival Plantation Manor House.
Hours & Admission Prices: Mar.-Oct. Mon.-Sat. 9-3:30. Adults $12, senior citizens & Military $10, students $6; discount to groups of 15 or more & AAA members; members & children under 5 no charge. Closed Easter; Thanksgiving; Christmas.
Attendance: 40,000 (estimated)

WILMINGTON RAILROAD MUSEUM, 505 Nutt St., Ste. 6, Wilmington, NC 28401-3316. Tel.: 910-763-2634.
E-mail: wrrmnc@bellsouth.net
Web Site: www.wrrm.org
Key Personnel: Exec. Dir., Mark W. Koenig; Pres. (V), William Bryden.
Institution Type/Description: Railroad Museum: housed in 1883 freight warehouse building.
Hours & Admission Prices: Call or visit website for confirmation of hours. Adults $8.50, military & seniors 60 & over $7.50, children 2-12 $4.50; discounts to groups, AAM & ICOM members; members & children under 2 no charge. Closed New Year's Eve & Day; Easter; Thanksgiving; Christmas Eve & Day.
Attendance: 21,675 (actual)

Wilson

ARTS COUNCIL OF WILSON, 124 Nash St., S.W., Wilson, NC 27893. Tel.: 252-291-4329. Fax: 252-234-0049.
E-mail: acw@wilsonarts.com
Web Site: www.wilsonarts.com
Institution Type/Description: Art Gallery.
Hours & Admission Prices: Call for hours.

BARTON ART GALLERIES, Whitehead & Gold St., Wilson, NC 27893. Mailing Address: Art Dept., Barton College, P.O. Box 5000, 704A College St., Wilson, NC 27893-7000. Tel.: 252-399-6477 & 6300.
E-mail: artgalleries@barton.edu
Web Site: www.barton.edu
Key Personnel: Dir., Susan Fecho.
Institution Type/Description: Art Gallery.
Hours & Admission Prices: mid-Aug. to mid-May Mon.-Fri. 10-4. No charge. Closed New Year's Day; Martin Luther King; Good Friday; Thanksgiving; Christmas; fall & spring breaks. &
Attendance: 800 (estimated)

IMAGINATION STATION SCIENCE AND HISTORY MUSEUM, 224 E. Nash St., Wilson, NC 27893. Mailing Address: P.O. Box 2127, Wilson, NC 27894-2127. Tel.: 252-291-5113. Fax: 252-291-2968.
E-mail: mail@imaginescience.org
Web Site: scienceandhistory.org
Key Personnel: C.E.O., Nancy Van Dolsen; Pres., Woody Harrison.
Institution Type/Description: Science & History Museum.
Hours & Admission Prices: Tues.-Sat. 9-5, Sun. 1-4. Adults $5, seniors & students $4; discounts to AAM & ASTC members; children under 4 & members no charge. Closed Thanksgiving; Christmas. &
Attendance: 30,000 (actual)

NORTH CAROLINA BASEBALL MUSEUM, Fleming Stadium, 300 Stadium St., Wilson, NC 27893. Tel.: 252-296-3048. Facebook: North Carolina Baseball Museum.
Web Site: ncbaseballmuseum.com
Institution Type/Description: Baseball Museum.
Hours & Admission Prices: During home games & by appointment. Adults $3, children 17 & under and seniors 65 & over $1; discounts to groups.
Attendance: 8,000 (estimated)

OLIVER NESTUS FREEMAN ROUND HOUSE MUSEUM, 1202 Nash St., Wilson, NC 27893. Tel.: 252-296-3056.
E-mail: gigmaster4@gmail.com
Web Site: olivernestusfreemanroundhouse.com
Key Personnel: Dir., Bill Myers.
Institution Type/Description: History Museum: housed in the former home of Freeman; built in 1946.
Hours & Admission Prices: Tues.-Fri. 9-1, Sat. 12-4; other times by appointment. No charge; donations accepted. &
Attendance: 3,000 (estimated)

VOLLIS SIMPSON WHIRLIGIG PARK, 305 Barnes St., Wilson, NC 27894. Mailing Address: P.O. Box 2882, Wilson, NC 27894. Tel.: 252-243-8440.
E-mail: whirligigpark@gmail.com
Web Site: www.wilsonwhirligigpark.com
Institution Type/Description: Sculpture Garden.
Hours & Admission Prices: Mon.-Thurs. 9-5.

WILSON BOTANICAL GARDENS, 1806 S.W. Goldsboro St., Wilson, NC 27893. Tel.: 252-237-0113. Fax: 252-237-0114. Facebook: Wilson Botanical Gardens.
E-mail: info@wilsonbotanicalgardens.org
Web Site: www.wilsonbotanicalgardens.org
Key Personnel: Pres. (V), Linda May.
Institution Type/Description: Botanical Garden.
Hours & Admission Prices: Daily dawn to dusk. No charge; donations accepted. &

WILSON ROSE GARDEN, 1800 Herring Ave., Wilson, NC 27893-6727. Tel.: 252-399-2261. Fax: 252-399-2196.
E-mail: hbass@wilsonnc.org
Web Site: www.wilsonrosegarden.com
Institution Type/Description: Gardens.
Hours & Admission Prices: Dawn to dusk. No charge.

Windsor

HISTORIC HOPE FOUNDATION, INC., 132 Hope House Rd., Windsor, NC 27983-7458. Tel.: 252-794-3140. Fax: 252-794-5583. Facebook.
E-mail: info@hopeplantation.org
Web Site: www.hopeplantation.org
Key Personnel: Pres. (V), Turner B. Sutton.

Institution Type/Description: Historic House Museum: located on the Hope Plantation.
Hours & Admission Prices: April-Dec. 20 Mon.-Sat. 10-4, Sun. 2-5; other times by appointment. Adults $11, seniors $10, children & students $6; discount to AAA, AAM & ICOM members; members & Bertie County students no charge. Blue Star museum. Closed Thanksgiving; Christmas.
Attendance: 17,500 (estimated)

ROANOKE/CASHIE RIVER CENTER, 112 W. Water St., Windsor, NC 27983. Tel.: 252-794-2001. Fax: 252-794-5202.
E-mail: roanoke_cashierc@embarqmail.com
Institution Type/Description: History Museum.
Hours & Admission Prices: Wed.-Fri. 10-4, Sat. 10-2.

Wingate

JESSE HELMS CENTER, 3910 U.S. 74 E., Wingate, NC 28174. Mailing Address: P.O. Box 247, Wingate, NC 28174-0247. Tel.: 704-233-1776. Fax: 704-233-1787.
E-mail: info@jessehelmscenter.org
Web Site: jessehelmscenter.org
Key Personnel: Facility Coord., Ladonna Snodgrass.
Institution Type/Description: History Museum.
Hours & Admission Prices: Mon.-Fri. 9-5. No charge.

Winnabow

BRUNSWICK TOWN/FORT ANDERSON STATE HISTORIC SITE, 8884 St. Philips Rd., S.E., Winnabow, NC 28479-5035. Tel.: 910-371-6613. Fax: 910-383-3806.
E-mail: brunswick@ncdcr.gov
Web Site: www.nchistoricsites.org/brunswic/brunswic.htm
Key Personnel: Regl. Supvr. East Region, James A. Bartley.
Institution Type/Description: Historic Site: 1726-1776 excavated foundations of port town; earthen Confederate Fort Anderson.
Hours & Admission Prices: Tues.-Sat. 9-5. No charge; donations accepted. Closed Thanksgiving; Christmas Eve & Day. &
Attendance: 54,680 (actual)

Winston-Salem

CHARLOTTE AND PHILIP HANES ART GALLERY, WAKE FOREST UNIVERSITY, Art Dept., 1834 Wake Forest Rd., Winston-Salem, NC 27106. Mailing Address: P.O. Box 7232, Winston-Salem, NC 27109. Tel.: 336-758-5795 & 5585. Fax: 336-758-6014.
E-mail: brightpb@wfu.edu
Web Site: www.wfu.edu/Academic-departments/Art/gall_index.html
Formerly: Wake Forest University Fine Arts Gallery.
Key Personnel: Dir., Paul Bright.
Institution Type/Description: Art Museum.
Hours & Admission Prices: Sept.-May Mon.-Fri. 10-5, Sat.-Sun. 1-5. No charge. Closed university holidays. &
Attendance: 6,500

CHILDREN'S MUSEUM OF WINSTON-SALEM, 390 S. Liberty St., Winston-Salem, NC 27101-5260. Tel.: 336-723-9111. Fax: 336-723-9469.
E-mail: info@childrensmuseumofws.org
Web Site: www.childrensmuseumofws.org
Key Personnel: Exec. Dir., Elizabeth Dampier; Dir. Mktg., Brandy Hall; Dir. Programming, Christine Simonson; Dir. Guest Svcs., Lesa Pierce.
Institution Type/Description: Children's Museum.
Hours & Admission Prices: Memorial Day to Labor Day Mon.-Sat. 10-4, Sun. 1-5; Sept.-May Tues.-Sat. 10-4, Sun. 1-5. Admission one & over $7, seniors 62 & over $6; discounts to groups of 15 or more; members, educators & children under one no charge. ACM reciprocal membership. Closed New Year's Day; Easter; Thanksgiving; Christmas. &
Attendance: 70,000 (estimated)

DAVIS GALLERY - SAWTOOTH SCHOOL FOR VISUAL ART, 251 N. Spruce Street, Winston-Salem, NC 27101. Tel.: 336-723-7395. Fax: 336-773-0132. Facebook: Sawtooth School for Visual Art.
E-mail: info@sawtooth.org
Web Site: www.sawtooth.org
Key Personnel: Exec. Dir., JoAnne Vernon.
Institution Type/Description: Art Gallery.
Hours & Admission Prices: Mon.-Fri. 9-7, Sat. 9-4. No charge; donations accepted. &

DELTA ARTS CENTER, 2611 New Walkertown Rd., Winston-Salem, NC 27101-1948. Tel.: 336-722-2625.
E-mail: delta2611@bellsouth.net
Web Site: www.deltafinearts.org/
Key Personnel: Interim Exec. Dir., Daphne Holmes-Johnson.
Institution Type/Description: Arts Center.
Hours & Admission Prices: Tues.-Fri. 10-5, Sat. 11-3; groups by appointment. No charge. Closed New Year's Eve, Day & day after; Thanksgiving & day after; Christmas Eve, Day & week.

DIGGS GALLERY AT WINSTON-SALEM STATE UNIVERSITY, 601 Martin Luther King Jr. Dr., Winston-Salem, NC 27110-0003. Tel.: 336-750-2458. Fax: 336-750-2463.
E-mail: diggsinfo@wssu.edu
Web Site: www.wssu.edu
Key Personnel: Dir., Cur. & Devel., Belinda Tate; Cur. Education, Dara Silver; Office Asst., Monica Scott.
Institution Type/Description: University Art Gallery.
Hours & Admission Prices: Gallery: Tues.-Sat. 11-5. Office: Mon.-Fri. 8-5. No charge. Closed New Year's Eve & Day; Martin Luther King Jr. Day; Good Friday; Memorial Day; Independence Day; Labor Day; Veterans Day; Thanksgiving; Christmas Eve, Day & week.
Attendance: 14,700 (actual)

HISTORIC BETHABARA PARK, 2147 Bethabara Rd., Winston-Salem, NC 27106-2701. Tel.: 336-924-8191. Fax: 336-924-0535.
E-mail: vfulton@triadbiz.rr.com
Web Site: www.bethabarapark.org
Key Personnel: Dir., Victoria M. Fulton; Chm. (V), Heather Smith, Jr.; Museum Shop Mgr., Diana B. Overbey.
Institution Type/Description: Historic Site & Wilderness Preserve: 1753 site of the first Moravian Settlement in North Carolina.
Hours & Admission Prices: Visitor Center & Buildings: April to mid-Dec. Tues.-Fri. 10:30-4:30, Sat.-Sun. 1:30-4:30. Grounds: daily. Adults $4, children $1.
Attendance: 141,000 (estimated)

HISTORIC OAK GROVE SCHOOL MUSEUM, 2637 Oak Grove Circle, Winston-Salem, NC 27106. Mailing Address: 313 Indera Mills Ct., Winston-Salem, NC 27101. Tel.: 336-722-5138, ext. 225.
Institution Type/Description: Historic Building Museum: housed in a former school built in the early 1900s for African American students. Listed on the National Register of Historic Places.
Hours & Admission Prices: By appointment.

MUSEUM OF ANTHROPOLOGY, WAKE FOREST UNIVERSITY, 1834 Wake Forest Rd., Winston-Salem, NC 27106. Mailing Address: P.O. Box 7267, Winston-Salem, NC 27109-7267. Tel.: 336-758-5282. Fax: 336-758-5116. Facebook: WFUMOA.
E-mail: moa@wfu.edu
Web Site: moa.wfu.edu
Formerly: Museum of Man
Key Personnel: Academic Dir., Dr. Andrew Gurstelle; Asst. Dir., Sara Cromwell; Educator, Tina Smith; Collections Mgr., Stormy Harrell.
Institution Type/Description: Anthropology Museum.
Hours & Admission Prices: Tues.-Sat. 10-4:30; groups by appointment only. No charge; donations accepted.
Attendance: 10,140 (actual)

MUSEUM OF EARLY SOUTHERN DECORATIVE ARTS (MESDA), 924 S. Main St., Winston-Salem, NC 27101-5335. Tel.: 336-721-7360. Fax: 336-721-7367.
E-mail: research@oldsalem.org
Web Site: www.mesda.org
Key Personnel: C.E.O. & Pres., Lee French; C.F.O., Eric Hoyle; Vice Pres. & Chief Cur., Robert Leath; Dir. Research, June Lucas; Dir. Education & Special Programs, Sally Gant; Assoc. Cur., Daniel Ackermann; Dir. Devel., Frances Beasley; Dir. Collections & Cur., Johanna M. Brown; Collections Mgr., Abigail Linville; Office Admin., Martha Ashley; Photographer, Wes Stewart; Librarian, Michele Doyle; Vice Pres. Publications, Gary Albert.
Institution Type/Description: Decorative Arts Museum.
Hours & Admission Prices: Tues.-Sat. 9:30-4:30, Sun. 1-5. Adults $21, children 6-16 $10; discounts to AAM & ICOM members. Closed Easter; Thanksgiving; Christmas Eve & Day.
Attendance: 19,176 (actual)

NEW WINSTON MUSEUM, 713 S. Marshall St., Winston-Salem, NC 27101-5808. Tel.: 336-724-2842.
E-mail: info@newwinston.org
Web Site: newwinston.org
Key Personnel: Exec. Dir., Chris Jordan; Devel. & Prog. Mgr., Alanna Meltzer-Holderfield.
Institution Type/Description: History Museum.
Hours & Admission Prices: Mon.-Fri. 12-5, Sat. 10-2. No charge; donations accepted. Closed New Year's Day; Good Friday; Independence Day; Labor Day; Thanksgiving; Christmas.
Attendance: 2,700 (actual)

OLD SALEM MUSEUMS & GARDENS, 900 Old Salem Rd., Winston-Salem, NC 27101-5329. Mailing Address: 600 S. Main St., Winston-Salem, NC 27101-5329. Tel.: 336-721-7300, 888-653-7253. Fax: 336-721-7335.
E-mail: info@oldsalem.org
Web Site: www.oldsalem.org
Formerly: Historic Town of Salem
Key Personnel: Pres. & C.E.O., Frank Vagnone.
Institution Type/Description: Historic Restoration Village: 1766 Moravian Congregation Town.
Hours & Admission Prices: Visitor Center: Tues.-Sat. 9-5, Sun. 12:30-5. Town: Tues.-Sat. 9:30-4:30, Sun. 1-4:30. Adults $27, children $13. Closed New Year's Day; Easter; Thanksgiving; Christmas Eve & Day.
Attendance: 450,000 (estimated)

REYNOLDA GARDENS OF WAKE FOREST UNIVERSITY, 100 Reynolda Village, Winston-Salem, NC 27106-5123. Tel.: 336-758-5593. Fax: 336-758-4132.
E-mail: gardens@wfu.edu
Web Site: www.reynoldagardens.org
Key Personnel: Mgr., Preston Stockton; Asst. Mgr., John Kiger; Cur. Education, Camilla Wilcox.
Institution Type/Description: Conservatory: housed in 1912 building.
Hours & Admission Prices: Greenhouses: Jan. & July Mon.-Fri. 10-5; Feb.-June & Aug.-Dec. Mon.-Sat. 10-5. Grounds: daily sunrise-sunset. No charge.
Attendance: 100,000 (estimated)

REYNOLDA HOUSE MUSEUM OF AMERICAN ART, 2250 Reynolda Rd., Winston-Salem, NC 27106-5117. Mailing Address: P.O. Box 7287, Winston-Salem, NC 27109-7287. Tel.: 336-758-5150, 888-663-1149. Fax: 336-758-5704. Facebook; Twitter; Instagram.
E-mail: reynolda@reynoldahouse.org
Web Site: reynoldahouse.org
Key Personnel: Dir., Allison C. Perkins; Chm. (V), Barbara Smith; Pres. (V), John W. Davis, III; Business Mgr., Kim Hampton; Dir. Devel., Stephan Dragisic; Dir. Education, Kathleen F.G. Hutton; Dir. Collections Management, Rebecca Eddins; Dir. External Rels., Sarah R. Smith; Dir. Program & Interpretation, Philip Archer; Museum Shop Mgr., Cindy Byrd.
Institution Type/Description: Art Museum: housed in 1917 home of R.J. Reynolds, founder of R.J. Reynolds Tobacco Company.
Hours & Admission Prices: Feb.-Dec. Tues.-Sat. 9:30-4:30, Sun. 1:30-4:30; see website for additional hours. Adults $18; discounts for AAM; children, students with current ID, Wake Forest Univ. faculty & staff, military with ID, NARM or SERM reciprocal & members no charge. Closed month of Jan.; New Year's Day; Thanksgiving; Christmas Eve & Day.
Attendance: 55,400 (actual)

SCIWORKS, 400 Hanes-Mill Rd., Winston-Salem, NC 27105-9667. Tel.: 336-767-6730. Fax: 336-661-1777.
E-mail: info@sciworks.org
Web Site: sciworks.org
Key Personnel: Exec. Dir., Paul Kortenaar; Bd. Chm., Jonathan M. Cochrane; Vice Pres. Finance, Sam Hancock; Vice Pres. Education & Programs, Kelli Isenhour; Vice Pres. Exhibits, Tom Wilson; Vice Pres. Facilities, Carl Nisbet; Devel. Coord., Jennifer Hudson; Mktg. Coord., Ally McCauley; Science Shop Mgr., Bobbie Tucker.
Institution Type/Description: Science & Technology Museum.
Hours & Admission Prices: Labor Day to June Tues.-Fri. 10-4, Sat. 10-5, Sun. noon-5; June to Labor Day Mon.-Sat. 10-5, Sun. noon-5. Adults $11, youth 3-19 & seniors 62 & up $9; discounts for ASTC & AAM members; children under 3 & members no charge. Closed New Year's Day; Thanksgiving; Christmas.
Attendance: 79,000 (actual)

SINGLE SISTERS HOUSE MUSEUM, 601 S. Church St., Winston-Salem, NC 27101. Tel.: 336-721-2600.
Web Site: www.salem.edu
Institution Type/Description: Historic Building: established in 1772 by early Moravian settlers, dedicated to the education of women; built in 1785.
Hours & Admission Prices: Mon.-Fri. 9-4:30, Sat. 9-noon. No charge; donations accepted.

SOUTHEASTERN CENTER FOR CONTEMPORARY ART

(SECCA), 750 Marguerite Dr., Winston-Salem, NC 27106-5861. Tel.: 336-725-1904. Fax: 336-722-9142. Facebook, Instagram.
E-mail: info@secca.org
Web Site: www.secca.org
Key Personnel: Exec. Dir., Gordon Peterson; Cur. Contemporary Art, Cora Fisher; Advisory Bd. Chair, Chris Oldham.
Institution Type/Description: Contemporary Art.
Hours & Admission Prices: Tues.-Wed. & Fri.-Sat. 10-5, Thurs. 10-8, Sun. 1-5. No charge. Closed major holidays. ⬥
Attendance: 30,000 (estimated)

WINSTON CUP MUSEUM, 1355 N. Martin Luther King Jr. Dr.,

Winston-Salem, NC 27101. Tel.: 336-724-4557. Fax: 336-724-4558.
E-mail: wcminfo@winstoncupmuseum.com
Web Site: www.winstoncupmuseum.com
Key Personnel: Dir., Bill Soper; C.E.O., William Spencer; Museum Shop Mgr., Kathleen Allen.
Institution Type/Description: History Museum.
Hours & Admission Prices: Tues.-Sat. 10-5. Adults $8, children 5-12 $4; children under 5 no charge.
Attendance: 2,000 (estimated)

Winton

C.S. BROWN REGIONAL CULTURAL ARTS CENTER &

MUSEUM, 511 S. Main St., Winton, NC 27986. Mailing Address: P.O. Box 435, Winton, NC 27986. Tel.: 252-209-7284.
E-mail: csbrownculturalartscenter@gmail.com
Web Site: csbrownculturalartscenter.weebly.com
Formerly: C.S. Brown School Auditorium Restoration Association, Inc.
Key Personnel: Dir., Mary Harrell-Sessoms.
Institution Type/Description: History Museum: housed in Brown Hall; built in 1926. Listed on the National Register of Historic Places.
Hours & Admission Prices: Call for hours. No charge; donations accepted. ⬥

WINTON CENTURY POST OFFICE MUSEUM, 404 N. Main

St., Winton, NC 27986. Mailing Address: c/o Hertford Co. Administration, 115 Justice Dr., Ste. 1, Winton, NC 27986. Tel.: 252-358-5788 & 3041.
E-mail: loria.williams@hertfordcountync.gov
Institution Type/Description: Historic Building Museum: housed in the former town post office building.
Hours & Admission Prices: Call for hours.

Wrightsville Beach

WRIGHTSVILLE BEACH MUSEUM OF HISTORY, 303 W.

Salisbury St., Wrightsville Beach, NC 28480-1819. Mailing Address: P.O. Box 584, Wrightsville Beach, NC 28480-0584. Tel.: 910-256-2569. Fax: 910-256-2569.
E-mail: info@wbmuseum.com
Web Site: www.wbmuseum.com
Key Personnel: Dir., Madeline Flagler.
Institution Type/Description: History Museum: housed in Myer's Cottage.
Hours & Admission Prices: Tues.-Fri. 10-4, Sat. 12-5, Sun. 1-5. No charge; donations accepted.
Attendance: 5,426 (actual)

Yanceyville

RICHMOND-MILES HISTORY MUSEUM, 15 Main St.,

Yanceyville, NC 27379. Mailing Address: c/o CCHA, P.O. Box 278, Yanceyville, NC 27379. Tel.: 336-694-4965.
E-mail: caswellmuseum@embarqmail.com
Key Personnel: Pres. (V), Sallie Smith.
Institution Type/Description: History Museum: housed in the Graves-Florance-Gatewood House; built in 1822.
Hours & Admission Prices: Wed.-Fri. 12-4; other times by appointment. No charge; donations accepted.
Attendance: 75 (estimated)

NORTH DAKOTA

(161 listings)

Abercrombie

FORT ABERCROMBIE STATE HISTORIC SITE, 935

Broadway, Abercrombie, ND 58001. Mailing Address: P.O. Box 148, Abercrombie, ND 58001-0148. Tel.: 701-553-8513 & 328-2666. Fax: 701-328-3710. Facebook.
E-mail: histsoc@nd.us
Web Site: www.history.nd.gov/historicsites/abercrombie
Key Personnel: Site Supvr., Thomas Casler.
Institution Type/Description: Historic Site: This site preserves the military post that served from 1857 to 1877 as the gateway to the Dakota frontier. It was besieged by the Sioux during the Dakota conflict of 1862.
Hours & Admission Prices: May 16-Sept. 15 daily 8-5. Adults $5, children 6-14 $2.50, student in groups $1; discounts to groups of 20 or more. ⬥
Attendance: 10,000 (estimated)

Adams

KNUDT SALLE LOG CABIN, Rt. 1, Adams, ND 58210. Mailing

Address: 323 3rd St., Minto, ND 58261. Tel.: 701-944-2792.
Institution Type/Description: Preservation Project: housed in 1884 log cabin located in city park.
Hours & Admission Prices: Memorial Day-Labor Day Sun. 2-5; other times by appointment. No charge; donations accepted. ⬥
Attendance: 60 (estimated)

Alexander

LEWIS AND CLARK TRAIL MUSEUM, US Hwy. 85, Alexander,

ND 58831. Mailing Address: P.O. Box 343, Alexander, ND 58831-0343. Tel.: 701-828-3157.
Institution Type/Description: History Museum: housed in 1914 school building.
Hours & Admission Prices: Call for hours. No charge; donations accepted.

Almont

ALMONT HERITAGE PARK AND MUSEUM, Main St., Almont,

ND 58520. Mailing Address: 5370 County Rd. 137, Almont, ND 58520. Tel.: 701-843-7927.
Key Personnel: Chm. (V) & Pres. (V), Tracy Larson; Co-Chm. (V), Nancy Doll.
Institution Type/Description: History Museum.
Hours & Admission Prices: Memorial Day to Labor Day. No charge.

Ashley

MCINTOSH COUNTY HISTORICAL SOCIETY, 615 Center

Ave. N., Ashley, ND 58413-7011. Tel.: 701-288-3374.
Key Personnel: Pres. (V), Ronald J. Meidinger.
Institution Type/Description: Historical Museum.
Hours & Admission Prices: June-Sept. Sun. 2-4; other times by appointment. No charge; donations accepted. ⬥
Attendance: 250 (estimated)

Beach

GOLDEN VALLEY COUNTY MUSEUM, 186 1st Ave., S.E.,

Beach, ND 58621. Mailing Address: P.O. Box 384, Beach, ND 58621-0384. Tel.: 701-872-3938.
E-mail: skogy@midstate.net
Key Personnel: Pres. (V), Judy M. Ridenhower.
Institution Type/Description: History Museum.
Hours & Admission Prices: May 30 to Labor Day Tues.-Fri. 1-4; other times by appointment. No charge; donations accepted. ⬥
Attendance: 200

Berthhold

UPPER SOURIS NATIONAL WILDLIFE REFUGE, 17705 212th

Ave., N.W., Berthhold, ND 58718-9666. Tel.: 701-468-5467. Fax: 701-468-5600. Facebook: Upper Souris National Wildlife Refuge.
E-mail: uppersouris@fws.gov
Web Site: www.fws.gov/uppersouris
Institution Type/Description: Wildlife Refuge.
Hours & Admission Prices: Refuge: daily 5am-10pm. Visitor Center: Mon.-Fri. 8-4:30. No charge. ⬥

Beulah

HELMUTH PFENNIG WILDLIFE MUSEUM, 6148 3rd St., N. W., Beulah, ND 58523-9488. Tel.: 701-873-4889.
Institution Type/Description: Natural History Museum.
Hours & Admission Prices: Call for hours.

MERCER COUNTY MUSEUM, 108 Seventh St., N.E., Beulah, ND 58523. Mailing Address: P.O. Box 1134, Beulah, ND 58523-1134. Tel.: 701-873-5070.
E-mail: mchs@westriv.com
Key Personnel: Pres. (V), Blake Wiedrich.
Institution Type/Description: General Museum.
Hours & Admission Prices: Memorial Day to Labor Day Sun. 1-4; other times by appointment. No charge; donations accepted. &
Attendance: 500 (estimated)

Bismarck

BISMARCK ART & GALLERIES ASSOCIATION, 422 E. Front Ave., Bismarck, ND 58504-5641. Tel.: 701-223-5986. Fax: 701-223-8960.
E-mail: baga@midconetwork.com
Web Site: www.bismarck-art.org
Key Personnel: Exec. Dir., Linda Christman.
Institution Type/Description: Art Gallery.
Hours & Admission Prices: Tues.-Fri. 10-5, Sat. 1-3.

BUCKSTOP JUNCTION, MISSOURI VALLEY HISTORICAL SOCIETY, E. Bismarck Expwy., Bismarck, ND 58501. Mailing Address: P.O. Box 941, Bismarck, ND 58502-0941. Tel.: 701-250-8575.
E-mail: marlette@bis.midco.net
Web Site: www.BuckstopJunction.org
Key Personnel: Pres. (V), Larry Strand; Museum Shop Mgr., Marlette Pittman.
Institution Type/Description: Historic Village.
Hours & Admission Prices: Office & Shoppe: May to mid-Sept. Fri.-Sat. 12-4. Guided Tours: June-Aug. Sat. 1pm; other times by appointment. Adults $5; members no charge.
Attendance: 9,300 (estimated)

CAMP HANCOCK STATE HISTORIC SITE, 101 E. Main Ave., Bismarck, ND 58301. Tel.: 701-328-9528.
E-mail: histsoc@nd.gov
Web Site: history.nd.gov/historicsites/hancock/
Key Personnel: Site Supvr., Johnathan Campbell.
Institution Type/Description: Historic Site: preserves part of military installation originally established as Camp Greeley in 1872 to protect work gangs building the Northern Pacific Railroad.
Hours & Admission Prices: May 15-Sept. 16, Fri.-Sun. 1-5; other times by appointment. No charge; donations accepted.
Attendance: 2,000 (actual)

THE CLELL AND RUTH GANNON GALLERY AT BISMARCK STATE COLLEGE, Library Bldg., 1500 Edwards Ave., Bismarck, ND 58501-1276. Tel.: 701-391-9840.
E-mail: bsc.library@bismarckstate.edu
Key Personnel: Dir., Andrea Fagerstrom.
Institution Type/Description: Art Museum.
Hours & Admission Prices: Mon.-Thurs. 7am-9pm, Fri. 7-4, Sun. 4-8. No charge.

DAKOTA ZOO, 602 Riverside Park Rd., Bismarck, ND 58502. Mailing Address: P.O. Box 711, Bismarck, ND 58502-0711. Tel.: 701-223-7543. Fax: 701-258-8350. Facebook: Dakota Zoo.
E-mail: director@dakotazoo.org
Web Site: www.dakotazoo.org
Key Personnel: Dir., Terry Lincoln; Pres. (V), Kristy Entzi; Museum Shop Mgr., Jace Schacher.
Institution Type/Description: Zoo.
Hours & Admission Prices: May-Sept. daily 10-7. Adults $7.25, children 12 & under $4.25; discounts to AZA members; members no charge. &
Attendance: 150,278 (actual)

THE ELSE FORDE GALLERY AT BISMARCK STATE COLLEGE, Schafer Hall, 1500 Edwards Ave., Bismarck, ND 58501-1276. Tel.: 701-224-5601.
E-mail: barbara.jirges@bsc.nodak.edu
Web Site: www.ndga.org/galleries/bscg.html
Key Personnel: Dir., Barbara Jirges.
Institution Type/Description: Art Gallery.
Hours & Admission Prices: Mon.-Thurs. 7am-9pm, Fri. 7-4, Sun. 6pm-9pm.

FORMER GOVERNORS' MANSION STATE HISTORIC SITE, 320 E. Ave. B, Bismarck, ND 58501-3676. Mailing Address: State Historical Society of North Dakota, North Dakota Heritage Center, 612 E. Boulevard Ave., Bismarck, ND 58505. Tel.: 701-328-9528.
E-mail: histsoc@nd.gov
Web Site: histroy.nd.gov/historicsites/fgm/
Key Personnel: Site Supvr., Johnathan Campbell, Jr.
Institution Type/Description: Historic Site: housed in the restored Victorian house which served as residence for 21 governors of North Dakota from 1893 to 1960; built in 1884
Hours & Admission Prices: mid-May to mid-Sept. Mon.-Fri. 10-5, Sat.-Sun. 12-4; Oct.-May 2nd Fri.-Sat. each month 1-5; other times by appointment. No charge; donations accepted.
Attendance: 3,500

GARY'S GALLERY, 3000 N. 4th St., Unit 122, Bismarck, ND 58503-5557. Tel.: 701-258-0060.
E-mail: info@garypmillerart.com
Web Site: garymillerart.com
Institution Type/Description: Art Museum.
Hours & Admission Prices: Call for hours.

GATEWAY TO SCIENCE, 1810 Schafer St., Ste. 1, Bismarck, ND 58501-1218. Tel.: 701-258-1975. Fax: 701-222-7515.
E-mail: gscience@gscience.org
Web Site: www.gatewaytoscience.org
Key Personnel: Exec. Dir., Elisabeth Demke; Pres. (V), Tim Lervick.
Institution Type/Description: Science Museum.
Hours & Admission Prices: Mon.-Thurs. 12-7, Fri.-Sat. 10-5. Adults $7, students 4-17 $4; discount to ASTC members; members, Gateway to Science members & children under 4 no charge. Closed New Year's Eve & Day; Easter; Independence Day; Thanksgiving; Christmas Eve & Day. &
Attendance: 27,958 (actual)

NORTH DAKOTA STATE CAPITOL, 600 E. Boulevard Ave., Bismarck, ND 58505. Tel.: 701-328-2480 & 2471. Fax: 701-328-0121.
Institution Type/Description: Historic Building: built in 1933.
Hours & Admission Prices: Tours: Memorial Day to Labor Day Mon.-Fri. 8-4, Sat. 9-4, Sun. 1-4; Sept.-May Mon.-Fri. 8-4. No charge.

STATE HISTORICAL SOCIETY OF NORTH DAKOTA AND NORTH DAKOTA HERITAGE CENTER & STATE MUSEUM, North Dakota Heritage Center, 612 E. Blvd., Bismarck, ND 58505. Tel.: 701-328-2666. Fax: 701-328-3710. TDD: 800-366-6888.
E-mail: histsoc@state.nd.us
Web Site: www.history.nd.gov
Key Personnel: Dir., Bill Peterson; Asst. Dir., Andrea Wike; Dir. Communications & Education, Kimberly Jondahl; Dir. State Archives, Ann Jenks; Dir. Historic Preservation & Deputy State Historic Preservation Officer, Fern Swenson.
Institution Type/Description: History Museum.
Hours & Admission Prices: Heritage Center: Mon.-Fri. 8-5, Sat.-Sun. 10-5. Research Library: Mon.-Fri. 8-4:30, 2nd Sat. each month 10-4:30. No charge; donations accepted. Closed New Year's Day; Easter; Thanksgiving; Christmas. &
Attendance: 250,000 (estimated)

UTTC CULTURAL ARTS INTERPRETIVE CENTER, United Tribes Technical College, Bismarck, ND 58504. Tel.: 701-255-3285.
Institution Type/Description: Native American Museum.
Hours & Admission Prices: Mon.-Fri. 8-5 by appointment.

Bowdon

BOWDON CENTENNIAL MUSEUM, 232 40th Ave., N.E., Bowdon, ND 58418. Tel.: 701-962-3736.
E-mail: lindawidicker@daktel.com
Key Personnel: Pres. (V) & Museum Shop Mgr., Rod L. Widicker; Treas., Vivian Miller; Security, Laurel Jones.
Institution Type/Description: History Museum.
Hours & Admission Prices: late May to late Oct. Wed.-Sun. 1-5; other times by appointment. No charge; donations accepted. &
Attendance: 350 (estimated)

Bowman

PIONEER TRAILS REGIONAL MUSEUM, 12 First Ave., N.E., Bowman, ND 58623-4010. Mailing Address: P.O. Box 78, Bowman, ND 58623-0078. Tel.: 701-523-3600.
E-mail: ptrm@ptrm.org
Web Site: ptrm.org
Key Personnel: Pres. (V), Dean Pearson; Admin., Jean Nudell.
Institution Type/Description: History Museum.
Hours & Admission Prices: May-Sept. Mon.-Sat. 9-5; Oct.-April Mon.-Fri. 10-4. Adults 14 & over $5, youth 3-17 $3; children 6 & under and members no charge. Closed federal holidays. &
Attendance: 2,000 (estimated)

Cando

CANDO ARTS CENTER, 502 4th Ave., Cando, ND 58324-6161. Mailing Address: Cando Arts Council, P.O. Box 368, Cando, ND 58324. Tel.: 701-968-3655.
E-mail: candoarts@gmail.com
Web Site: candoarts.weebly.com
Key Personnel: Dir., Shelley Lord.
Institution Type/Description: Art Center.
Hours & Admission Prices: Tues. 1-6:30, Wed.-Fri. 1-4 and by appointment.

CANDO PIONEER FOUNDATION, INC., 502 Main St., Cando, ND 58324-0142. Mailing Address: P.O. Box 142, Cando, ND 58324-0142. Tel.: 701-968-3943 & 3490.
E-mail: slarson@gondtc.com
Formerly: Pioneer Museum
Key Personnel: Pres. (V), James Slusser; Museum Shop Mgr., Vicki Lingen.
Institution Type/Description: History Museum.
Hours & Admission Prices: By appointment. No charge; donations accepted. &
Attendance: 750 (estimated)

Carrington

FOSTER COUNTY MUSEUM, 2nd St. S. & 16th Ave., Carrington, ND 58421. Mailing Address: c/o Foster County Historical Society, 756 Main St., Carrington, ND 58421. Tel.: 701-652-1313; 701-652-3363 & 674-3270 (tours).
Key Personnel: Cur., Ralph Harmon; Cur., Henry Gussiaas.
Institution Type/Description: History Museum.
Hours & Admission Prices: Sun. afternoons & by appointment. No charge; donations accepted.

Cavalier

PEMBINA COUNTY HISTORICAL SOCIETY AND MUSEUM, 13572 Hwy. 5, Cavalier, ND 58220. Tel.: 701-265-4941.
E-mail: pchsm@polarcomm.com
Web Site: ndpchs.com/museum.htm
Key Personnel: Admin., Zelda Hartje.
Institution Type/Description: Historical Society Museum.
Hours & Admission Prices: By appointment. No charge.

PIONEER HERITAGE CENTER, 13571 Hwy. 5, Cavalier, ND 58220-9545. Tel.: 701-265-4561. Fax: 701-265-4443.
E-mail: isp@nd.gov
Web Site: www.parkrec.nd.gov
Key Personnel: Pres. (V), Alfred Byron; Park Mgr., Justin Robinson; Park Ranger & Interpretive Coord., Char Binstock; Museum Shop Mgr., Lorraine Schroeder.
Institution Type/Description: State Park Museum.
Hours & Admission Prices: Center: Memorial Day-Labor Day daily 9-5; Fall, Winter & Spring Mon.-Fri. 9-5, Sun. 1-5. $5 per vehicle; $25 per year; members no charge. Closed New Year's Day; Easter; Mother's Day; Thanksgiving; Christmas. &
Attendance: 4,000 (actual)

Cayuga

TEWAUKON NATIONAL WILDLIFE REFUGE, 9754 143 1/2 Ave., S.E., Cayuga, ND 58013-9764. Tel.: 701-724-3598. Fax: 701-724-3683.
E-mail: tewaukon@fws.gov
Web Site: www.fws.gov/tewaukon
Institution Type/Description: Wildlife Refuge.
Hours & Admission Prices: Refuge: daily 5am-10pm. Office & Visitor Center: Mon.-Fri. 8-4:30.

Center

FORT CLARK TRADING POST STATE HISTORIC SITE, 1074 27th Ave., S.W., Center, ND 58530-9429. Mailing Address: 612 E. Blvd. Ave., Bismarck, ND 58505. Tel.: 701-328-2666.
E-mail: fswenson@nd.gov
Web Site: www.state.nd.us/hist
Key Personnel: Agency Dir., Claudia Berg, Jr.; Dir. Historic Preservation, Fern Swenson; Historic Sites Mgr., Guinn Hinmann.
Institution Type/Description: Historic Site Museum: built in 1830-1831, the fort was burned down in 1861.
Hours & Admission Prices: mid-May to mid-Sept. daily 8-5. No charge; donations accepted. Society's Museum Stores: discounts to members.
Attendance: 10,000 (actual)

Coleharbor

AUDUBON NATIONAL WILDLIFE REFUGE, 3275 11th St., N. W., Coleharbor, ND 58531-9419. Tel.: 701-442-5474. Fax: 701-442-5546.
E-mail: audubon@fws.gov
Web Site: www.fws.gov/audubon/
Key Personnel: Dist. Mgr., Kathy Baer.
Institution Type/Description: Wildlife Refuge.
Hours & Admission Prices: Mon.-Fri. 8-4:30. No charge. Closed federal holidays.

Cooperstown

GRIGGS COUNTY HISTORICAL MUSEUM, 203 12th St., S.E., Cooperstown, ND 58425. Mailing Address: P.O. Box 242, Cooperstown, ND 58425-0242.
Institution Type/Description: History Museum.
Hours & Admission Prices: May-Sept. Sun. 1-4:30; other times by appointment. Adults $5, students $2; children under 5 no charge.

RONALD REAGAN MINUTEMAN MISSILE STATE HISTORIC SITE, 555 113 1/2 Ave., N.W., Hwy. 45, Cooperstown, ND 58425-0006. Mailing Address: P.O. Box 6, Cooperstown, ND 58425-0006. Tel.: 701-797-3691. Fax: 701-797-3693.
E-mail: histsoc@nd.gov
Web Site: www.history.nd.gov
Key Personnel: Mark Sundlov.
Institution Type/Description: Historic Sites: housed on the former Oscar-Zero Missile Alert Facility and November-33 Launch Facility which were part of the nation's minuteman missile force.
Hours & Admission Prices: March to mid-May & mid-Sept. to Oct. Mon. & Wed.-Sat. 10-6, Sun. 1-5; mid-May to mid-Sept. daily 10-6; Nov.-Feb. by appointment. Adults $10, students $3; discounts to groups of 20 or more; children & members no charge. &
Attendance: 8,500 (estimated)

Crosby

DIVIDE COUNTY HISTORICAL SOCIETY MUSEUM, 300 Second Ave., N.E., Crosby, ND 58730. Mailing Address: P.O. Box 130, Crosby, ND 58730-0130. Tel.: 701-339-0059.
E-mail: dctthreshingbee@gmail.com
Key Personnel: Pres. (V), John Tysse.
Institution Type/Description: Village Museum.
Hours & Admission Prices: Tours by appointment, call for information. No charge; donations accepted. Facilities: $12 for 3 days.
Attendance: 3,600 (estimated)

Devils Lake

LAKE REGION HERITAGE CENTER, 502 4th St., N.E., Devils Lake, ND 58301-0245. Mailing Address: P.O. Box 245, Devils Lake, ND 58301. Tel.: 701-662-3701. Facebook: Lake Region Heritage Center.
E-mail: lrhc@gondtc.com
Web Site: www.lrhcmuseum.com
Key Personnel: Dir., John M. Grochowski; Museum Asst., Jackie Johnson; Pres. (V), George Zenk.
Institution Type/Description: Heritage Center.
Hours & Admission Prices: June-Sept. Tues.-Fri. 9-5, Sat. 10-4; Oct.-May Tues.-Sat. 10-4. Adults $5, seniors & students $3; veterans & active military no charge.
Attendance: 1,000 (estimated)

LAKE REGION HERITAGE HOUSE MUSEUM, 416 Sixth St., Devils Lake, ND 58301-0626. Mailing Address: P.O. Box 245, Devils Lake, ND 58301-0245. Tel.: 701-662-3701 & 7080.
E-mail: lrhc@gondtc.com
Web Site: www.lrhcmuseum.com
Institution Type/Description: Historic House Museum.
Hours & Admission Prices: Wed.-Sun. 1-4; other times by appointment. Adults $3; seniors & students $2; children under 6 no charge.

NORTH DAKOTA MARITIME MUSEUM, 503 8th St., Devils Lake, ND 58301-0626. Tel.: 701-662-7031. Fax: 701-662-7049.
Institution Type/Description: Maritime Museum.
Hours & Admission Prices: Sun. 2-5 by appointment.

Dickinson

DSU ART GALLERY, Klinefelter Hall, Dickinson State Univ., Dickinson, ND 58601-4896. Mailing Address: Klinefelter Hall, Box 28, Dickinson State Univ., Dickinson, ND 58601-4896. Tel.: 800-279-HAWK.
E-mail: greg.walter@dickinsonstate.edu
Web Site: www.dickinsonstate.edu
Key Personnel: Dir., Greg Walter.
Institution Type/Description: Art Gallery.
Hours & Admission Prices: Mon.-Fri. 8-5. No charge.

DICKINSON MUSEUM CENTER, 188 Museum Dr. E., Dickinson, ND 58601-4088. Tel.: 701-456-6225.
E-mail: info@dickinsonmuseumcenter.org
Web Site: www.dickinsonmuseumcenter.org
Formerly: Joachim Regional Museum
Key Personnel: Dir., Robert Fuhrman; Cur. Paleontology, Dr. Denver Flower, Ph. D.; Cur. History, Allison Hinman; Museum Education Coord., Jessica Stratton; Museum Svcs. Coord., Teresa Bolke.
Institution Type/Description: Museum Center: Joachim Regional Museum, Badlands Dinosaur Museum, Prairie Outpost Park, Pioneer Machinery Hall.
Hours & Admission Prices: Memorial Day to Labor Day Mon.-Sat. 9-5, Sun. 12-5; Sept.-May Mon.-Sat. 9-5. Adults $6, seniors 65 & over $5, children 3-12 $4; children 2 & under no charge. &
Attendance: 12,213 (actual)

UKRAINIAN CULTURAL INSTITUTE, 1221 W. Villard, Dickinson, ND 58601-4849. Mailing Address: P.O. Box 6, Dickinson, ND 58602-0006. Tel.: 701-483-1486. Fax: 701-483-4366.
E-mail: uci@ndsupernet.org
Key Personnel: Dir., Teresa Kessel.
Institution Type/Description: Ukrainian History Museum.
Hours & Admission Prices: Mon.-Wed. 9-3, Thurs. 9-8. No charge; donations accepted.

Drayton

DRAYTON UNITED METHODIST CHURCH, 203 N. Main St., Drayton, ND 58225-0327. Mailing Address: P.O. Box 327, Drayton, ND 58225-0327. Tel.: 701-454-3880.
E-mail: umc@polarcomm.com
Formerly: Methodist Episcopal Church
Institution Type/Description: Historic Building: housed in a church built in 1905. Listed on the National Register of Historic Places.
Hours & Admission Prices: Tours: by appointment. No charge.

Dresden

CAVALIER COUNTY MUSEUM, 10123 95th St., Dresden, ND 58249. Mailing Address: 324 8th Ave., Langdon, ND 58249. Tel.: 701-283-5417.
Web Site: museumatdresden.wordpress.com
Institution Type/Description: History Museum.
Hours & Admission Prices: Memorial Day to Labor Day Sun.-Mon., Wed. & Fri. 1-5. No charge; donations accepted.

Dunn Center

DUNN COUNTY HISTORICAL SOCIETY & MUSEUM, 153 Museum Trail, Dunn Center, ND 58626. Mailing Address: P.O. Box 145, Killdeer, ND 58640-0145. Tel.: 701-548-8111.
E-mail: dunncountymuseum@ndsupernet.com
Web Site: www.dunncountymuseum.org

Institution Type/Description: Historical Society Museum
Hours & Admission Prices: By appointment. Call for admission prices. &
Attendance: 500 (estimated)

Dunseith

INTERNATIONAL PEACE GARDEN, 10939 Hwy. 281, Dunseith, ND 58329-9445. Mailing Address: R.R. 1 Box 116, Dunseith, ND 58329-9445. Tel.: 701-263-4390, 888-432-6733. Fax: 701-263-3169.
E-mail: kathy@peacegarden.com
Web Site: www.peacegarden.com
Key Personnel: C.E.O. & C.O.O., Doug Hevenor; Pres. (V), Ed Anderson; Vice Pres., Tyrone Langager; Finance Mgr., Leonard Richard.
Institution Type/Description: Arboretum.
Hours & Admission Prices: Garden: daily. Peak time for flowers: July 15-Aug. 15. Gate: late May to mid-Sept. daily 9-7. Office: Mon.-Fri. 80-4. Donations: $125 per tour bus, $25 season pass, $20 per vehicle a season, $10 per vehicle a day, $5 pedestrian. &
Attendance: 150,000

Edmore

WHEATLAND MANOR, 405 S. Grant St., Edmore, ND 58330. Mailing Address: P.O. Box 8, Edmore, ND 58330-0008. Tel.: 701-644-2291 & 2453.
Institution Type/Description: History Museum.
Hours & Admission Prices: Memorial Day-Labor Day Sun. 1-3; other times by appointment.

Egeland

TOWNER COUNTY HISTORICAL MUSEUM, Main St., Egeland, ND 58331. Mailing Address: 108 4th Ave., Munich, ND 58352. Tel.: 701-682-5106.
E-mail: dabar@utma.com
Key Personnel: Pres. (V), Anita Barrett; Museum Shop Mgr., David Barrett.
Institution Type/Description: Historical Society Museums.
Hours & Admission Prices: By appointment. Museum: $5, donations accepted. Special Events: fees vary.
Attendance: 60 (estimated)

Ellendale

COLEMAN MUSEUM, Southeast Corner of Main St. & Railroad Ave., Ellendale, ND 58436. Mailing Address: 8836 92nd St., S.E., Ellendale, ND 58436.
Institution Type/Description: Historical Society Museum.
Hours & Admission Prices: June-Sept. Tues. & Fri. 1-5. No charge; donations accepted.

Enderlin

ENDERLIN HISTORICAL SOCIETY AND MUSEUM, 315 Railway St., Enderlin, ND 58027. Mailing Address: 13296 55th St. S.E., Enderlin, ND 58027. Tel.: 701-437-3205.
E-mail: info@enderlinmuseum.org
Web Site: www.enderlinmuseum.org
Institution Type/Description: Historical Society Museum.
Hours & Admission Prices: May-Sept. Thurs.-Fri. 1-4, Sat. 9 to noon; other times by appointment.

Epping

BUFFALO TRAILS MUSEUM, Main St., Epping, ND 58843. Mailing Address: P.O. Box 22, Epping, ND 58843-0022. Tel.: 701-859-4361 (June-Aug.).
E-mail: buffalotrailmuseum@yahoo.com
Web Site: epping.govoffice.com
Key Personnel: Pres., Duane Syverson.
Institution Type/Description: Regional History Museum.
Hours & Admission Prices: May-July Tues.-Sat. 10-4, Sun. 12-5. Adults $5, students & groups over 10 $2; discounts to groups; life members no charge.
Attendance: 275 (estimated)

Fargo

THE CHILDREN'S MUSEUM AT YUNKER FARM, 1201 28th Ave. N., Fargo, ND 58102-1337. Tel.: 701-232-6102. Fax: 701-232-4605.
E-mail: info@childrensmuseum-yunker.org
Web Site: childrensmuseum-yunker.org
Key Personnel: Exec. Dir., Yvette Nasset.
Institution Type/Description: Children's Museum
Hours & Admission Prices: Summer: Mon.-Sat. 10-5, Sun. 1-5; School Year: Tues.-Sat. 10-5, Sun. 1-5. Admission $5; children under one & members no charge. &
Attendance: 46,000 (estimated)

FARGO AIR MUSEUM, 1609 19th Ave. N., Fargo, ND 58102-1886. Tel.: 701-293-8043. Fax: 701-293-8103.
Web Site: fargoairmuseum.org
Key Personnel: Exec. Dir., Fran Brummund; Chm., Rex Hammarback.
Institution Type/Description: Air & Space Museum.
Hours & Admission Prices: Memorial Day to Labor Day Mon.-Sat. 9-5, Sun. 12-4; Sept.-May Tues.-Sat. 9-5, Sun. 12-4. Adults $6, senior citizens $5, children 5-12 $4; discounts to groups; members no charge. Closed New Year's Day; Easter; Thanksgiving; Christmas.
Attendance: 30,000 (estimated)

FARGO THEATRE, 314 Broadway, Fargo, ND 58102-4715. Tel.: 701-239-8385.
E-mail: emily@fargotheatre.org
Web Site: fargotheatre.org
Institution Type/Description: Historic Building: housed in a fully-restored art deco theatre built in 1926 to host Vaudeville & silent movies.
Hours & Admission Prices: Tours: call for hours. Films: Mon.-Fri, 5, 7 & 9pm, Sat.-Sun. 1, 3, 5, 7, & 9pm. Closed Christmas Eve. &

GALLERY 4, LTD, 114 Broadway N., Ste. G2, Fargo, ND 58102-4942. Tel.: 701-237-6867.
E-mail: gallery4ltd@gmail.com
Web Site: www.gallery4fargo.com
Institution Type/Description: Art Gallery.
Hours & Admission Prices: Tues.-Wed. & Fri.-Sat. 11-5, Thurs. 11-7. &

MAURY WILLS MUSEUM, 1515 15th Ave. N., Ground Fl., Fargo, ND 58102-5701. Tel.: 701-235-6161. Fax: 701-297-9247.
E-mail: redhawks@fmredhawks.com
Institution Type/Description: Sports Museum.
Hours & Admission Prices: Mon.-Fri. 9-5, No charge. &

MEMORIAL UNION GALLERY, 258 Memorial Union, North Dakota State Univ., Fargo, ND 58105-5476. Mailing Address: North Dakota State University, Dept. 5340, P.O. Box 6050, Fargo, ND 58108-6050. Tel.: 701-231-8239. Fax: 701-231-7866. Facebook: Memorial Union Gallery.
E-mail: ndsu.mugallery@ndsu.edu
Web Site: www.mu.ndsu.edu/gallery/exhibits_and_artists
Key Personnel: Gallery Coord., Netha Cloeter.
Institution Type/Description: Art Gallery.
Hours & Admission Prices: mid-May to mid-Aug. Tues.-Fri. 11-4; Aug. 15 to mid-May Tues.-Wed. & Fri.-Sat. 11-5, Thurs. 11-8. No charge. Closed holidays. &
Attendance: 2,300 (actual)

PLAINS ART MUSEUM, 704 First Ave. N., Fargo, ND 58102-4904. Tel.: 701-551-6100. Fax: 701-293-1082.
E-mail: museum@plainsart.org
Web Site: plainsart.org
Key Personnel: Interim Dir. & C.E.O., Mark Henze.
Institution Type/Description: Art Museum.
Hours & Admission Prices: Tues.- Wed. & Fri. 11-5, Thurs. 11-9, Sat. 10-5; tours by appointment. No charge. Closed New Year's Day; Memorial Day; Labor Day; Thanksgiving; Christmas. &
Attendance: 59,748 (actual)

RED RIVER ZOO, 4255 23rd Ave., S., Fargo, ND 58104-8603. Tel.: 701-277-9240. Fax: 701-277-9238.
E-mail: director@redriverzoo.org
Key Personnel: Dir., Sally Jacobson; Pres. (V), Brad Dahl; Guest Svcs. Mgr., Jeremiah Gard.
Institution Type/Description: Zoo.
Hours & Admission Prices: May-Sept. daily 10-7; Oct.-April Sat.-Sun. 10-5. Adults $9.75, seniors over 60 $8.75, children 2-14 $7.75; children under 2 no charge. &
Attendance: 125,000 (actual)

ROGER MARIS MUSEUM, West Acres Shopping Center, 3902 13th Ave. S., Fargo, ND 58103-3357. Mailing Address: c/o West Acres Mall, 3902 13th Ave. S., Ste. 3717, Fargo, ND 58103. Tel.: 701-282-2222, 800-783-6450.
E-mail: westacres@westacres.com
Web Site: www.rogermarismuseum.com
Institution Type/Description: Sports Museum.
Hours & Admission Prices: Mon.-Sat. 10-9, Sun. 12-6. No Charge. Closed Easter; Thanksgiving; Christmas.

Fessenden

WELLS COUNTY HISTORICAL SOCIETY MUSEUM, 903 4th St. N.E., Fessenden, ND 58438. Tel.: 701-547-3684.
E-mail: wchs.news2014@mail.com
Formerly: Wells County Museum
Key Personnel: Pres., Carol Beck; Vice Pres., Pat Lenz; Sec., Judy Martin; Treas., Betty Hirschkorn.
Institution Type/Description: Historic Building: housed in a 1919 2-room school house.
Hours & Admission Prices: By appointment. No charge.
Attendance: 350 (estimated)

Forman

SARGENT COUNTY MUSEUM, 8987 Hwy. 32, Forman, ND 58032. Mailing Address: 300 3rd St., S.W., Forman, ND 58032-9709. Tel.: 701-724-3194.
E-mail: sargentcountymuseum@yahoo.com
Web Site: sargentcountymuseum.org
Institution Type/Description: History Museum.
Hours & Admission Prices: Memorial Day to Labor Day Mon.-Fri. 10-4, Sun. 1-4; other times by appointment. No charge; donations accepted. &
Attendance: 500 (actual)

Fort Ransom

RANSOM COUNTY HISTORICAL SOCIETY, 101 Mill Road, S. E., Fort Ransom, ND 58033-9740. Mailing Address: P.O. Box 5, Fort Ransom, ND 58033-0005. Tel.: 701-680-0916.
Web Site: rchsmuseum.tripod.com
Key Personnel: Pres. (V), Richard Birklid.
Institution Type/Description: History Museum: housed in 1867-1872 U.S. Military Fort.
Hours & Admission Prices: Memorial Day to Oct. 1 Sat.-Sun. 1-5; other times by appointment. Adults $1; members & children no charge.
Attendance: 5,000 (estimated)

Fort Totten

FORT TOTTEN STATE HISTORIC SITE, 417 Cavalry Cir., Fort Totten, ND 58335. Mailing Address: P.O. Box 224, Fort Totten, ND 58335-0224. Tel.: 701-766-4441. Fax: 701-766-1382.
E-mail: ngronseth@nd.gov
Web Site: www.discovernd.com/hist
Key Personnel: Dir. State Historical Society of North Dakota, Merl Paaverud; Div. Dir. Historic Sites, Fern Swenson; Eastern Rgnl. Site Mgr., Diane Rogness; Site Supvr. & Museum Store Mgr., Jack Mattson.
Institution Type/Description: Historic Site & Outdoor Museum: 1868-1890 Military Post; Pioneer Daughters Museum; 1891-1959 Indian School, consisting of 17 structures.
Hours & Admission Prices: Visitor Center & P.W. Museum Facilities: mid-May to mid-Sept. daily 8-5; mid-Sept. to mid-May Mon.-Fri. by appointment. Adults $5, children 6-15 $1.50; discounts to school groups, NDHF & FFTHS members; members & children under 6 no charge. Bus: $40, Season Passes: Family $20, Individual $10. &
Attendance: 15,000 (estimated)

Fullerton

ROSEBUD SCHOOL MUSEUM, Main St., Fullerton, ND 58441. Mailing Address: P.O. Box 27, Fullerton, ND 58441-0027. Tel.: 701-375-7521.
E-mail: jglynn@drtel.net
Institution Type/Description: Historic Building: housed in a former one-room schoolhouse; built in 1901.
Hours & Admission Prices: May-Oct. by appointment.

Garrison

HERITAGE PARK MUSEUM, First St. & First Ave., N.W., Garrison, ND 58540. Mailing Address: Garrison Convention & Visitors' Bureau, P.O. Box 1000, Garrison, ND 58540-0850. Tel.: 701-463-2546.
Web Site: www.garrisonnd.com/?id=81
Key Personnel: Dir., Garrison Convention & Visitors' Bureau, McKaila Matteson.
Institution Type/Description: History Museum.
Hours & Admission Prices: Memorial Day to Labor Day Mon. 11-4; other times by appointment.

NORTH DAKOTA FIREFIGHTER'S MUSEUM & HALL OF FAME, 52 N. Main St., Garrison, ND 58540. Mailing Address: P. O. Box 1000, Garrison, ND 58540. Tel.: 701-463-2345, 800-799-4242.
E-mail: ndfm@restel.com
Web Site: www.ndfm.org
Institution Type/Description: Fire Fighters Museum.
Hours & Admission Prices: Mon.-Fri. 8-5. No charge.

NORTH DAKOTA FISHING HALL OF FAME AND MUSEUM, 4034 Hwy. 37 Bypass, Garrison, ND 58540. Mailing Address: 4034 Hwy. 37 Bypass, Garrison, ND 58540. Tel.: 701-463-2600.
E-mail: ndfm@restel.com
Web Site: www.ndfishinghalloffame.org
Institution Type/Description: Fishing Museum.
Hours & Admission Prices: Mon.-Fri. 1-6, Sat.-Sun. 11-5.

Glen Ullin

GLEN ULLIN MUSEUM, 207 S. 10th St., Glen Ullin, ND 58631. Mailing Address: 6315 46th St., Glen Ullin, ND 58631-9734. Tel.: 701-348-3295.
Key Personnel: Pres. (V), Lance Gartner; Dir., Mike Schirado; Dir., Laura Gartner; Dir., Viola Weindhart.
Institution Type/Description: Historic Buildings.
Hours & Admission Prices: By appointment. No charge; donations accepted.
Attendance: 750 (estimated)

Goodrich

PIONEER HISTORICAL SOCIETY OF SHERIDAN COUNTY, 840 22nd Ave., N.E., Goodrich, ND 58444. Tel.: 701-884-2752.
Key Personnel: Pres. (V) Jerry Reiswig.
Institution Type/Description: Historic Buildings.
Hours & Admission Prices: By appointment. No charge; donations accepted.
Attendance: 50 (estimated)

Grafton

HERITAGE VILLAGE & JUGVILLE MUSEUM, 695 W. 12th St., Grafton, ND 58237-2115. Tel.: 701-360-0088 & 520-1207.
E-mail: vernaaasand@gmail.com
Web Site: www.walshcountyhistorical.com
Key Personnel: Pres., Ken Hoffmann; Office Mgr., Verna Aasand.
Institution Type/Description: History Museum.
Hours & Admission Prices: Memorial Day to Labor Day by appointment. No charge; donations accepted.
Attendance: 100 (estimated)

HISTORIC ELMWOOD HOUSE, Stephen Ave. & 2nd St., Grafton, ND 58237. Mailing Address: Chamber of Commerce, 432 Hill Ave., Grafton, ND 58237-1002. Tel.: 701-352-0152.
Institution Type/Description: Historic House Museum: housed in the former home of North Dakota's second Attorney General, Cam Spencer; built in 1895. Listed on the National Register of Historic Places.
Hours & Admission Prices: By appointment. No charge; donations accepted.

Grand Forks

BROWNING ARTS, 23 S. Fourth St., Grand Forks, ND 58201-4733. Tel.: 701-746-5090.
Institution Type/Description: Art Gallery.
Hours & Admission Prices: Jan. to late Nov. Mon.-Fri. 9-5:30; Thanksgiving to Christmas Mon.-Sat. 9-5:30.

GRAND FORKS COUNTY HISTORICAL SOCIETY, 2405 Belmont Rd., Grand Forks, ND 58201-7505. Tel.: 701-775-2216.
E-mail: gfhistory@midconetwork.com
Web Site: grandforkshistory.com
Key Personnel: Pres., Greg Vettel; Dir., Leah Byzewski; Treas., Wallace Bloom.
Institution Type/Description: Historical Society Museum: located on the former farmsite belonging to Tom Campbell, the agriculturalist.
Hours & Admission Prices: Grounds: May 15-Sept. 15 daily 1-5. Office: Summer Mon.-Fri. 9-12; Winter by appointment. Adults 16 & over $5, children 10-15 $3; children under 10 & members no charge. Closed Independence Day.
Attendance: 5,000 (estimated)

NORTH DAKOTA MUSEUM OF ART, 261 Centennial Dr., Stop 7305, Grand Forks, ND 58202-6003. Tel.: 701-777-4195. Fax: 701-777-4425. www.facebook.com/ndmoa.
E-mail: ndmoa@ndmoa.com
Web Site: www.ndmoa.com
Key Personnel: Dir. & Chief Cur., Laurel J. Reuter; Pres. Bd. Trustees, Julie Blehm, M.D.; Exhibition Coord. & Registrar, Greg Vettel; Dir. Education, Matt Anderson; Dir. Rural Art, Matthew Wallace; Accountant, Brad Werner; Office Mgr. & Volunteer Coord., Sungyee Joh; Collection Care Specialist, Danielle Masters; Mgr. Cafe, Heather Schneider; Museum Shop Mgr., Sheila Dalgliesh.
Institution Type/Description: Art Museum.
Hours & Admission Prices: Mon.-Fri. 9-5, Sat.-Sun. 1-5. No charge; donations accepted.
Attendance: 50,000 (estimated)

UNIVERSITY OF NORTH DAKOTA ART COLLECTIONS GALLERY AT THE EMPIRE ARTS CENTER, 415 Demers Ave., Grand Forks, ND 58201. Mailing Address: Hughes Fine Arts Center, 3350 Campus Rd., Stop 7099, Grand Forks, ND 58202-7099. Tel.: 701-777-2257. Fax: 701-777-2903.
E-mail: art.jones@und.edu
Key Personnel: Dir., Dr. Arthur Jones.
Institution Type/Description: University Art Collection Gallery.
Hours & Admission Prices: Mon.-Fri. 11-4. No charge; donations accepted.

UNIVERSITY OF NORTH DAKOTA ZOOLOGY MUSEUM, Dept. of Biology, Stop 9019, Grand Forks, ND 58202. Tel.: 701-777-2621. Fax: 701-777-2623.
E-mail: susan.felege@email.und.edu
Web Site: www.und.edu/dept/biology/undergrad
Key Personnel: Cur. Vertebrates, Susan Ellis-Felege; Cur. Invertebrates, Dr. Jefferson Vaughan.
Institution Type/Description: Natural History Museum.
Hours & Admission Prices: Mon.-Fri. 8-4:30 by appointment. No charge. Closed national holidays.
Attendance: 200 (estimated)

Grand Rapids

LAMOURE COUNTY MUSEUM, Memorial Park, Grand Rapids, ND 58458. Mailing Address: P.O. Box 128, LaMoure, ND 58458-0128. Tel.: 701-883-5301.
Institution Type/Description: Historical Building.
Hours & Admission Prices: Memorial Day to Labor Day: call for times.

Grassy Butte

GRASSY BUTTE HISTORIC POST OFFICE, 101 Museum Dr., Grassy Butte, ND 58634. Mailing Address: 581 Highway 85 S, Grassy Butte, ND 58634. Tel.: 701-863-6604.
E-mail: xrranch@ndsupernet.com
Formerly: Old Sod Post Office
Key Personnel: Pres. (V) & Museum Shop Mgr., Gail Chinn; Chm. (V), Lois Flick; Dir., Rose Eschenko.
Institution Type/Description: History Museum: built in 1912 of logs & sod, housed Grassy Butte Post Office from 1914 until 1964. Listed on the National Register of Historic Places.
Hours & Admission Prices: Memorial Day to June Sat.-Sun. 9-4; July to Labor Day daily 9-4. No charge; donations accepted.
Attendance: 535 (actual)

Hanks

PIONEER TRAILS MUSEUM, 9 miles west junction Hwy. 85 & Hwy. 50, Hanks, ND 58856. Mailing Address: 2310 University Ave., Williston, ND 58801. Tel.: 701-572-4759.
E-mail: ptrm@ptrm.org

Institution Type/Description: History Museum.
Hours & Admission Prices: June-Sept. Sun. 1-5, Mon.-Fri. by appointment. No charge; donations accepted.
Attendance: 85 (estimated)

Hatton

HATTON-EIELSON MUSEUM & HISTORICAL ASSOCIATION, 405 Eielson St., Hatton, ND 58240. Mailing Address: P.O. Box 278, Hatton, ND 58240-0278. Tel.: 701-543-3725.
E-mail: bholt@gra.midco.net
Web Site: www.hattonmuseum.org
Key Personnel: Pres., Gary Lillemoen; Vice Pres., Loretta Larson; Public Rels., Treas. & Museum Shop Mgr., Eileen Holt.
Institution Type/Description: Historic Building: c.1900 Victorian home of aviator-explorer Carl Ben Eielson.
Hours & Admission Prices: June-Aug. Sun. 1-4 or by appointment. Adults $5, children $1; preschool no charge.
Attendance: 600 (estimated)

Hebron

HEBRON HISTORICAL AND ART SOCIETY, 606 Lincoln Ave., Hebron, ND 58638. Mailing Address: P.O. Box V, Hebron, ND 58638-0452. Tel.: 701-878-4060.
Web Site: www.hebronnd.org/live_historical.html
Key Personnel: Dir. & Pres. (V), Robyn Renalds; Chm., Lyle Hoerauf; Vice Pres., Claudia Meberg; Museum Shop Mgr., Henry Mische.
Institution Type/Description: History Museum.
Hours & Admission Prices: By appointment. No charge; donations accepted. &
Attendance: 200 (estimated)

Hillsboro

TRAILL COUNTY HISTORICAL SOCIETY, 306 Caledonia W. Ave., Hillsboro, ND 58045. Mailing Address: P.O. Box 173, Hillsboro, ND 58045-0173. Tel.: 701-636-5571.
E-mail: chrismcinnes@co.traill.nd.us
Key Personnel: Pres., Dallas Hammond; Vice Pres., Chris McInnes; Cur., Michelle Hammond.
Institution Type/Description: General Museum: housed in 1897 three-story brick mansion.
Hours & Admission Prices: June-Aug. Sat.-Sun. 2-5; other times by appointment. Suggested Donation: $2.
Attendance: 1,000 (estimated)

Hope

STEELE COUNTY HISTORICAL SOCIETY, 301 Steele Ave., Hope, ND 58046. Mailing Address: P.O. Box 144, Hope, ND 58046-0144. Tel.: 701-945-2394. Fax: 701-945-2394.
E-mail: scmuseum@invisimax.com
Web Site: www.steelecomuseum.com
Formerly: Steele County Museum
Key Personnel: Pres. (V), Homer Wennerston; Dir., Sue Johnson.
Institution Type/Description: Historical Society Museum.
Hours & Admission Prices: May-Sept. Tues.-Fri. 9-5, Sun. 2-5; Oct.-April Tues.-Fri. 9-5. Suggested Donation: adults $5, seniors & children $3; students & members no charge. &
Attendance: 1,800 (estimated)

Jamestown

THE ARTS CENTER, 115 2nd St., S.W., Jamestown, ND 58401-4114. Mailing Address: P.O. Box 363, Jamestown, ND 58402-0363. Tel.: 701-251-2496. Fax: 701-251-1749.
E-mail: tbarnes@jamestownarts.com
Web Site: www.jamestownarts.com
Key Personnel: Dir., Taylor Barnes; Mgr. Gallery, Sally Jeppson.
Institution Type/Description: Art Museum.
Hours & Admission Prices: Mon.-Fri. 9-5, Sat. 10-2. No charge; donations accepted. &
Attendance: 9,000 (estimated)

FORT SEWARD MUSEUM, 605 10th Ave., N.W., Jamestown, ND 58401-2027. Mailing Address: 4145 91st Ave., S.E., Ypsilanti, ND 58497. Tel.: 701-251-1875.
Institution Type/Description: Military History Museum: housed on the original site of the military fort, 1872-1877.

Hours & Admission Prices: Museum: Memorial Day to Labor Day daily 10-6. Grounds: daily.

FRONTIER VILLAGE ASSOCIATION, INC., 17th St., S.E., Jamestown, ND 58401. Mailing Address: P.O. Box 324, Jamestown, ND 58402-0324. Tel.: 701-252-6307. Fax: 701-252-5455.
E-mail: mhager@unisonbank.com
Key Personnel: Pres., Charles Tanata.
Institution Type/Description: History Museum.
Hours & Admission Prices: Memorial Day-Labor Day daily 9-9. No charge; donations accepted. &
Attendance: 150,000 (estimated)

NATIONAL BUFFALO MUSEUM, 500 17th St., S.E., Jamestown, ND 58401-6456. Tel.: 701-252-8648; 800-807-1511. Fax: 701-253-5803.
E-mail: director@buffalomuseum.com
Web Site: www.buffalomuseum.com/
Key Personnel: Exec. Dir., Kim Penrod; Museum Shop Mgr., Jessica Manson.
Institution Type/Description: Buffalo Museum.
Hours & Admission Prices: May & Sept.-Oct. Mon.-Fri. 9-5, Sat. 10-5, Sun. 12-5; Memorial Day to Labor Day daily 8-8; Nov.-April Mon.-Fri. 9-5, Sat. 10-5. Adults $5, seniors $4, students 7-18 $1; discounts to groups of 15 or more, AAA, AAM & ICOM members; members, military & children 6 & under no charge. National Park members no charge, donations accepted. &
Attendance: 18,898 (actual)

NORTH DAKOTA SPORTS HALL OF FAME, 212 3rd Ave., N. E., Jamestown, ND 58401. Tel.: 701-252-4835. Fax: 701-252-8089. Facebook.
E-mail: cschafer@daktel.com
Web Site: jamestownciviccenter.com
Key Personnel: Dir., Pamela Fosse; Pres. (V), Robert King.
Institution Type/Description: Sports Hall of Fame.
Hours & Admission Prices: Mon.-Fri. 8-5. No charge. &
Attendance: 150,000 (estimated)

STUTSMAN COUNTY MEMORIAL MUSEUM, 321 3rd Ave., S. E., Jamestown, ND 58401-4208. Mailing Address: P.O. Box 1002, Jamestown, ND 58402-1002. Tel.: 701-252-6741 & 4809. Facebook: Stutsman Museum.
Web Site: stutsmanmuseum.org
Key Personnel: C.E.O. & Pres. (V), Harold Sahr; Cur., Alden Kollman.
Institution Type/Description: Historic Building: built in 1907.
Hours & Admission Prices: Memorial Day to Sept. Mon.-Fri. 10-5, Sat.-Sun. 1-5; tours by appointment. No charge; donations accepted. &
Attendance: 1,800 (estimated)

Kenmare

LAKE COUNTY HISTORICAL SOCIETY'S PIONEER VILLAGE, Hwy. 52, Kenmare, ND 58746. Mailing Address: P.O. Box 324, Kenmare, ND 58746. Tel.: 701-385-4287.
Institution Type/Description: Village Museum.
Hours & Admission Prices: Wed.-Fri. 4-7, Sat.-Sun. 2-5; other times by appointment.

Kulm

WHITESTONE HILL BATTLEFIELD STATE HISTORIC SITE, 7310 86th St., S.E., Kulm, ND 58456-9555. Tel.: 701-328-3508.
E-mail: histsoc@nd.gov
Web Site: history.nd.gov/historicsites/whitestone/
Key Personnel: Site Supvr., James E. Hill; Historic Sites Mgr., Diane Rogness.
Institution Type/Description: Historic Site Museum: army troops under General Alfred Sully battled Sioux warriors in 1863.
Hours & Admission Prices: May 16 to Sept. 15 Thurs.-Mon. 10-5. No charge; donations accepted.
Attendance: 2,000 (actual)

LaMoure

LAMOURE COUNTY MUSEUM, Memorial Park, 9797 66th St., S.E., LaMoure, ND 58458. Mailing Address: P.O. Box 42, LaMoure, ND 58458. Tel.: 701-883-6040.
Institution Type/Description: History Museum.
Hours & Admission Prices: mid-May to mid-Nov. Sat. 2-4.

TOY FARMER MUSEUM, 7496 106th Ave., SE, LaMoure, ND 58458-9404. Tel.: 701-883-5206, 800-533-8293. Fax: 701-883-5209.
E-mail: info@toyfarmer.com
Web Site: www.toyfarmer.com/museum
Key Personnel: C.E.O., Cathy Scheibe.
Institution Type/Description: Toy Farmer Museum.
Hours & Admission Prices: May-Sept. Mon.-Fri. 10-6, Sat.-Sun. 12-5; Oct-April Mon.-Fri. 10-5, Sat.-Sun. 12-5. No charge. Closed New Year's Day; Easter; Thanksgiving; Christmas.

Lakota

A.M. TOFTHAGEN LIBRARY & MUSEUM AKA LAKOTA CITY LIBRARY, 116 W. B Ave., Lakota, ND 58344. Mailing Address: P.O. Box 307, Lakota, ND 58344-0307. Tel.: 701-247-2543.
E-mail: lakotalibrary@polarcomm.com
Key Personnel: Dir., Angela Jutila.
Institution Type/Description: Library & History Museum: listed on the National Register of Historic Places.
Hours & Admission Prices: Mon & Tues. 12-5, Thurs. 10-3. No charge; donations accepted.
Attendance: 2,152 (actual)

Larimore

LARIMORE COMMUNITY MUSEUM, 310 Towner Ave., Larimore, ND 58251. Mailing Address: P.O. Box 524, Larimore, ND 58251-0524. Tel.: 701-397-5723.
Key Personnel: Pres., Hazel Sletten; Treas., Janna Phelps.
Institution Type/Description: History Museum.
Hours & Admission Prices: Memorial Day to Labor Day. Suggested Donations: adults $1, students $.50.
Attendance: 100 (estimated)

Lidgerwood

LIDGERWOOD COMMUNITY MUSEUM, 10 Third Ave., SE, Lidgerwood, ND 58053. Mailing Address: P.O. Box 36, Lidgerwood, ND 58053. Tel.: 701-538-4466.
E-mail: lmuseum@rrt.net
Key Personnel: Dir., Annette Smykowski.
Institution Type/Description: History Museum.
Hours & Admission Prices: 1st & 3rd Sun. each month 1-5. No charge; donations accepted.

Linton

EMMONS COUNTY MUSEUM, NW First and Oak, Linton, ND 58552. Mailing Address: P.O. Box 862, Linton, ND 58552-0862. Tel.: 701-254-4399.
Key Personnel: Pres. (V), Mary Ann Gefroh.
Institution Type/Description: History Museum: housed in St. James Episcopal Church.
Hours & Admission Prices: Fri. & Sun. 2-4; other times by appointment. No charge; donations accepted. &
Attendance: 225 (estimated)

Litchville

LITCHVILLE COMMUNITY MUSEUM, Fifth St., Litchville, ND 58461. Tel.: 701-762-4475.
E-mail: bchistoricalsociety@hotmail.com
Institution Type/Description: Historic House Museum: built in 1901.
Hours & Admission Prices: Memorial Day to Labor Day daily 2-4. No charge; donations accepted.

Makoti

MAKOTI THRESHERS' MUSEUM, 106 7th Ave. W., Makoti, ND 58756. Mailing Address: 30000 338th St. S.W., Ryder, ND 58779-9522. Tel.: 701-726-5656.
Key Personnel: Pres. (V), Merle Dreher.
Institution Type/Description: History Museum.
Hours & Admission Prices: June-Sept. by appointment. No charge; donations accepted.
Attendance: 3,000 (actual)

Mandan

FORT ABRAHAM LINCOLN STATE PARK, 4480 Ft. Lincoln Rd., Mandan, ND 58554-7947. Tel.: 701-667-6340. Fax: 701-667-6349.
E-mail: falsp@nd.gov
Web Site: www.parkrec.nd.gov
Key Personnel: Park Mgr., Dan Schelske.
Institution Type/Description: State Park Museum.
Hours & Admission Prices: May-Oct. daily 9-5; other times by appointment. Park Vehicle Fee: $5. Custer House Tours: adults $6, students $4. &
Attendance: 150,000 (estimated)

NORTH DAKOTA STATE RAILROAD MUSEUM, 3102 37th St., N.W., Mandan, ND 58554. Mailing Address: P.O. Box 1001, Mandan, ND 58554-7001. Tel.: 701-663-9322. Facebook: North Dakota State Railroad Museum.
E-mail: ndstaterrmuseum@gmail.com
Web Site: www.ndsrm.org
Key Personnel: Pres. (V), Wes Wenger.
Institution Type/Description: Railroad History Museum.
Hours & Admission Prices: Memorial Day to Labor Day daily 1-5. No charge; donations accepted. &
Attendance: 2,750 (estimated)

Manvel

MANVEL MUSEUM, Main St., Manvel, ND 58256. Mailing Address: 3286 Hwy. 81, Ardoch, ND 58261-9510. Tel.: 701-696-2279.
Institution Type/Description: History Museum.
Hours & Admission Prices: By appointment.

Marmarth

UNIQUE ANTIQUE AUTO MUSEUM, 305 1st St., W., Marmarth, ND 58643. Tel.: 701-279-5904.
E-mail: vanhorn1159@n.d.supernet.com
Web Site: www.uniqueantiquemuseum.com
Key Personnel: Owner, J.D. VanHorn; Museum Shop Mgr., Janice M Abraham.
Institution Type/Description: Auto Museum.
Hours & Admission Prices: May 7-Sept. 7 daily 9-5. Adults $7; Lifetime members no charge. &

Medora

BILLINGS COUNTY MUSEUM, 475 Fourth St., Medora, ND 58645. Mailing Address: P.O. Box 364, Medora, ND 58645. Tel.: 701-623-4829.
E-mail: bcm@midstate.net
Web Site: www.billingscountymuseum.com
Institution Type/Description: History Museum: housed in the former Billings County Courthouse.
Hours & Admission Prices: mid-May to mid-Sept. daily 9-5. Adults $3, seniors $2, students $1.

CHATEAU DE MORES STATE HISTORIC SITE, 3448 Chateau Rd., Medora, ND 58645. Mailing Address: c/o State Historical Society of North Dakota, 612 E. Boulevard Ave., Bismarck, ND 58505. Tel.: 701-623-4355. Fax: 701-623-4921.
E-mail: shschateau@nd.gov
Web Site: www.history.nd.gov/historicsites/chateau
Key Personnel: Dir. State Historical Society of ND, Claudia J. Berg; Chateau Site Mgr., Samuel Kerr.
Institution Type/Description: Historic Site: housed in a 26 two-story chateau built as the summer residence for the Marquis de Mores family.
Hours & Admission Prices: mid-May to mid-Sept. daily 8:30-5:30. Interpretive Center: mid-Sept. to mid-May Wed.-Sun. 9-5. Adults $10, children 6-15 $5; discounts to groups of 20 or more; active military & preschoolers no charge. Season Pass: $20. Closed Easter; Thanksgiving; Christmas. &
Attendance: 85,000 (actual)

NORTH DAKOTA COWBOY HALL OF FAME, 250 Main St., Medora, ND 58645. Mailing Address: P.O. Box 1211, Dickinson, ND 58602-1211. Tel.: 701-623-2000. Fax: 701-623-2001. Facebook: North Dakota Cowboy Hall of Fame.
E-mail: heritage@northdakotacowboy.com
Web Site: www.northdakotacowboy.com
Key Personnel: Exec. Dir., Phil Baird.

Institution Type/Description: History Museum.
Hours & Admission Prices: May 15-Sept. 15 daily 9-6; off-season by appointment. Discounts to military members. &

THEODORE ROOSEVELT NATIONAL PARK-VISITOR CENTER, 315 2nd Ave., Medora, ND 58645. Mailing Address: P. O. Box 7, Medora, ND 58645-0007. Tel.: 701-623-4466. Fax: 701-623-4840. Facebook: Theodore Roosevelt National Park.
E-mail: eileen_andes@nps.gov
Web Site: www.nps.gov/thro
Key Personnel: Park Supt., Wendy Ross.
Institution Type/Description: Visitor Center & National Park.
Hours & Admission Prices: Park: daily. Visitor Centers: daily 8-4:30; Summer: 8-6, call or see website to confirm hours. Park: Vehicle $10, Individual $5. Annual Pass $80. Closed New Year's Day; Thanksgiving; Christmas. &
Attendance: 630,319 (actual)

VON HOFFMAN HOUSE, 485 Broadway, Medora, ND 58645. Mailing Address: P.O. Box 198, Medora, ND 58645-0198. Tel.: 800-633-6721.
E-mail: medora@medora.com
Web Site: www.medora.com
Formerly: Medora Doll House
Key Personnel: Dir., Kinley R. Slauter.
Institution Type/Description: Historic House Museum; built in 1884.
Hours & Admission Prices: Memorial Day to Labor Day daily 10-7. No charge; donations accepted.

Minnewaukan

MINNEWAUKAN MUSEUM, Old U.S. 281, 210 C Ave. S., Minnewaukan, ND 58351. Mailing Address: P.O. Box 183, Minnewaukan, ND 58351-0183. Tel.: 701-473-5669.
Key Personnel: Pres. (V), Cathy Nord.
Institution Type/Description: History Museum.
Hours & Admission Prices: By appointment. No charge; donations accepted.
Attendance: 20 (estimated)

Minot

DAKOTA TERRITORY AIR MUSEUM, 100 34th Ave., N.E., Minot, ND 58703. Mailing Address: P.O. Box 195, Minot, ND 58702-0195. Tel.: 701-852-8500. Facebook.
E-mail: airmuseum@minot.com
Web Site: dakotaterritoryairmuseum.com/
Key Personnel: Chm. (V), Don Larson; Dir., Glenn Blackaby.
Institution Type/Description: Aviation History Museum.
Hours & Admission Prices: mid-May to mid-Oct. Mon.-Sat. 10-5, Sun. 1-5; other times by appointment. Family $20, adults $10, children 6-17 $5; discounts to active military; members no charge. &
Attendance: 5,800 (estimated)

NORTH DAKOTA ART GALLERY ASSOCIATION, #2 11th Ave., N.W., Minot, ND 58701-6420. Tel.: 701-858-3242. Fax: 701-858-3894.
E-mail: ndaga@ndaga.org
Web Site: www.ndaga.org
Key Personnel: Dir., Linda A. Olson.
Institution Type/Description: Art Gallery.
Hours & Admission Prices: Mon.-Fri. 9-5.

NORTHWEST ART CENTER, Minot State University, 11th Ave. N.W., Minot, ND 58707. Mailing Address: 500 University Ave. W., Minot, ND 58707. Tel.: 701-858-3264.
E-mail: nac@minotstateu.edu
Web Site: www.minotstateu.edu/nac
Formerly: Hartnett Hall Gallery
Key Personnel: Dir., Avis Veikley.
Institution Type/Description: Art Center.
Hours & Admission Prices: Mon.-Fri. 8-4:30; other times by appointment. No charge; donations accepted. &
Attendance: 5,000 (estimated)

OLD SOO DEPOT TRANSPORTATION MUSEUM, 15 N. Main St., Minot, ND 58703-3103. Mailing Address: P.O. Box 2148, Minot, ND 58702. Tel.: 701-852-2234.
E-mail: soodepot@srt.com
Institution Type/Description: Historic Building: housed in the restored 1912 Soo Line Depot.

Hours & Admission Prices: Call for hours. No charge.

RAILROAD MUSEUM OF MINOT, 19 First St., N.E., Minot, ND 58701-3960. Mailing Address: P.O. Box 74, Minot, ND 58702-0074. Tel.: 701-852-7091. Facebook: Railroad Museum of Minot.
E-mail: railroadmuseum@srt.com
Key Personnel: Dir., James Huston; Museum Shop Mgr., Roger Burchill.
Institution Type/Description: Railroad Museum.
Hours & Admission Prices: Sat. 10-2; other times by appointment. No charge; donations accepted. &
Attendance: 2,000 (estimated)

ROOSEVELT PARK ZOO, 1219 Burdick Expwy., E., Minot, ND 58701. Mailing Address: P.O. Box 549, Minot, ND 58702-0549. Tel.: 701-857-4166. Fax: 701-857-4169. Facebook: RP Zoo.
E-mail: info@srt.com
Web Site: www.rpzoo.com
Key Personnel: Chm., Bob Petry; Dir., David Merritt; Pres. (V), Jenny Steckler; Museum Shop Mgr., Jennifer Fry.
Institution Type/Description: Zoo.
Hours & Admission Prices: May-Sept. daily 10-8. Adults $7, Adults 55 & over $6.50, children 4-12 $3.75; discounts to groups; AZA members and children 3 & under no charge. Season passes available. &
Attendance: 75,000 (actual)

SCANDINAVIAN HERITAGE PARK, 1020 S. Broadway, Minot, ND 58701-4660. Mailing Address: P.O. Box 862, Minot, ND 58702-0862. Tel.: 701-852-9161.
E-mail: scandha@srt.com
Web Site: www.scandinavianheritage.org
Key Personnel: Pres., Gail S. Peterson.
Institution Type/Description: Cultural Heritage Museum.
Hours & Admission Prices: mid-May to first weekend in Oct. Mon.-Fri. 10-4. Buildings: summer Sat.-Sun. when volunteers are present, please call for hours. No charge. &

TAUBE MUSEUM OF ART, 2 N. Main St., Minot, ND 58703-3104. Tel.: 701-838-4445. Fax: 701-838-6471.
E-mail: taube@srt.com
Web Site: www.taubemuseum.org
Formerly: Taube Museum of Art and Minot Art Association
Key Personnel: Exec. Dir. & Museum Shop Mgr., Asher Noel; Pres., Mandi Carroll; Gallery Coord., Rachel Alfaro; Education Coord., Margaret Lee.
Institution Type/Description: Art Museum: housed in renovated bank building.
Hours & Admission Prices: Tues.-Fri. 10:30-5:30, Sat. 11-4; other times by appointment. No charge; donations accepted. Closed holidays. &
Attendance: 21,452 (estimated)

WARD COUNTY HISTORICAL SOCIETY, 2005 Burdick Expwy. E., Minot, ND 58702. Mailing Address: P.O. Box 994, Minot, ND 58702-0994. Tel.: 701-839-0785. Facebook: Ward County Historical Society.
E-mail: wchs@wchsnd.org
Web Site: www.wchsnd.org
Key Personnel: Dir., Sue Bergan; Pres. (V), Bruce Brooks.
Institution Type/Description: Historic Building & Site.
Hours & Admission Prices: Memorial Day-Labor Day Tues.-Sat. 1-6; extended hours during ND State Fair. No charge; donations accepted. &
Attendance: 6,000 (actual)

Minto

WALSH COUNTY HISTORICAL MUSEUM, 323 3rd St., Minto, ND 58261. Tel.: 701-248-3237 & 3414.
E-mail: historian@walshhistory.org
Institution Type/Description: History Museum.
Hours & Admission Prices: Memorial Day to Labor Day Sun. 1-4; other times by appointment. Adults 18 & over $5, students $3; preschool no charge.

Mohall

RENVILLE COUNTY HISTORICAL SOCIETY, 504 First St., N. E., Mohall, ND 58761-4200. Mailing Address: 204 Central Ave., Apt. 2D, Mohall, ND 58761-0163. Tel.: 701-240-7015. Facebook: Renville County Historical Society.
E-mail: trevor_hoyt@hotmail.com
Key Personnel: Pres., Trevor Hoyt; Sec., Betty Johnson; Treas., Joyce Lunde.
Institution Type/Description: General Museum: housed in a pioneer church from Norma, ND & first depot built in Mohall, ND.

Hours & Admission Prices: mid-June to mid-Sept. Thurs. 2-5. No charge; donations accepted. &

Attendance: 38 (estimated)

Mooreton

BAGG BONANZA HISTORICAL FARM, 8025 169th Ave., S.E., Mooreton, ND 58061. Mailing Address: P.O. Box 702, Mooreton, ND 58061. Tel.: 701-274-8989 & 642-2411.

Web Site: www.baggfarm.com

Key Personnel: Chm. (V) & Pres. (V), Norma Nosek; Museum Shop Mgr., Sandy Link.

Institution Type/Description: History Museum.

Hours & Admission Prices: Summer: Fri.-Sun. 12-5; other times by appointment. Adults $5, children under 12 $3.50; members & children under 6 no charge. &

Attendance: 5,000 (estimated)

Mott

MOTT GALLERY OF HISTORY & ART, Brown Ave., Mott, ND 58646. Mailing Address: 508 Minn Ave., Mott, ND 58646. Tel.: 701-824-2552.

Institution Type/Description: Art Gallery & History Museum: housed in the historic bank building.

Hours & Admission Prices: Summer: Sun. & Thurs. 1-4. No charge; donations accepted. &

Attendance: 586 (actual)

Napoleon

LOGAN COUNTY MUSEUM, 207 Lake St. W., Napoleon, ND 58561. Mailing Address: 208 E. 5th St., Napoleon, ND 58561-7217. Tel.: 701-754-2640 & 2221.

Key Personnel: Dir. & Pres. (V), Charles Weigel.

Institution Type/Description: Historical Society Museum.

Hours & Admission Prices: Sun., Memorial Day, Independence Day & Labor Day 1-4; other times by appointment. No charge; donations accepted.

Attendance: 150 (estimated)

New Rockford

EDDY COUNTY MUSEUM, 1115 1st Ave N, New Rockford, ND 58356. Mailing Address: P.O. Box 135, New Rockford, ND 58356. Tel.: 701-947-2205. Facebook.

E-mail: dillon1348@gmail.com

Key Personnel: Pres. (V), Jessica Dillon.

Institution Type/Description: History Museum.

Hours & Admission Prices: Labor Day-Memorial Day Sun. 1-4. No charge; donations accepted. &

Attendance: 400 (estimated)

New Salem

NEW SALEM HISTORICAL SOCIETY/CUSTER TRAIL MUSEUM, N. 8th St., New Salem, ND 58563. Mailing Address: 4248 43rd Ave., New Salem, ND 58563. Tel.: 701-843-7384.

Key Personnel: Chm. (V), Sharon Hartmann.

Institution Type/Description: Historical Society Museum.

Hours & Admission Prices: Sun. 1-4; other times by appointment. No charge; donations accepted.

New Town

THREE TRIBES MUSEUM, 302 Frontage Rd., New Town, ND 58763. Mailing Address: P.O. Box 147, New Town, ND 58763-0147. Tel.: 701-627-4477. Fax: 701-627-3805.

E-mail: tatmuseum@restel.net

Institution Type/Description: Native American Museum.

Hours & Admission Prices: May-Oct. Mon.-Fri. 10-4. Adults $3, seniors & children 12-18 $2; children 11 & under no charge.

Attendance: 5,000 (actual)

Oakes

DICKEY COUNTY HISTORICAL SOCIETY, 424 Main Ave., Oakes, ND 58474. Mailing Address: 9225 104th St., S.E., Oakes, ND 58474-9449. Tel.: 701-742-30234. Fax: 701-783-4485.

E-mail: lane.bredeson@gmail.ciom

Web Site: dickeycohistoricalsociety.com

Key Personnel: Chm. (V), Lane Bredeson; Pres. (V), Mary Ann Kunrath.

Institution Type/Description: History Museum: housed in the former First National Bank, built in 1902.

Hours & Admission Prices: By appointment. No charge; donations accepted. &

Attendance: 400 (estimated)

Parshall

PAUL BROSTE ROCK MUSEUM, 508 Main St. N., Parshall, ND 58770. Mailing Address: P.O. Box 184, Parshall, ND 58770-0184. Tel.: 701-862-3264.

Institution Type/Description: Rock Museum.

Hours & Admission Prices: May to Labor Day Wed.-Sat. 12-4. Adults $4, students $2. &

Pekin

STUMP LAKE VILLAGE PIONEER MUSEUM, Stump Lake Village, ND Hwy. #1, Pekin, ND 58361. Mailing Address: Nelson County Historical Society, P.O. Box 141, Pekin, ND 58361. Tel.: 701-247-2374.

E-mail: elfmans55@hotmail.com

Web Site: www.stumplakepark.com

Institution Type/Description: Village Museum.

Hours & Admission Prices: June to Labor Day Sun. 1-5.

Pembina

PEMBINA STATE MUSEUM, 805 State Hwy. 59, Pembina, ND 58271-0456. Mailing Address: P.O. Box 456, Pembina, ND 58271-0456. Tel.: 701-825-6840. Fax: 701-825-6383.

E-mail: jblanchard@nd.gov

Web Site: history.nd.gov

Key Personnel: Museum Site Supvr., Jeff Blanchard.

Institution Type/Description: History Museum.

Hours & Admission Prices: Memorial Day to Labor Day Mon.-Sat. 9-6, Sun. 1-6; Sept.-May Mon.-Sat. 9-5, Sun. 1-5. Museum: no charge; donations accepted. Tower: $2; SHSND Foundation no charge. Closed New Year's Day; Easter; Thanksgiving; Christmas. &

Attendance: 3,671 (actual)

Plaza

PLAZA COMMUNITY MUSEUM, 502 5th Ave., Plaza, ND 58771. Mailing Address: P.O. Box 188, Plaza, ND 58771-0188. Tel.: 701-497-3724.

E-mail: snowwhite@restel.com

Institution Type/Description: History Museum: housed in a church.

Hours & Admission Prices: By appointment. No charge; donations accepted.

Portland

GOOSE RIVER HERITAGE CENTER, 14714 1st St., N.E., Portland, ND 58274-9440. Tel.: 612-716-5672.

Key Personnel: Pres., Eric Strand; Dir., Grace Woldem.

Institution Type/Description: History Museum.

Hours & Admission Prices: Memorial Day to Labor Day Sat.-Sun. 12-3; other times by appointment. Adult $5. &

Attendance: 140 (actual)

Ray

RAY OPERA HOUSE MUSEUM, 119 Main St., Ray, ND 58849. Mailing Address: 420 4th Ave. E., Ray, ND 58849. Tel.: 701-568-3578.

E-mail: tricodev@nccray.com

Key Personnel: Pres., Gordon Lokken; Dir., Jerry Engel.

Institution Type/Description: History Museum.

Hours & Admission Prices: June-Oct. Sun. 2-4; other times by appointment. No charge; donations accepted. &

Attendance: 50 (estimated)

Regent

HETTINGER COUNTY HISTORICAL SOCIETY, Main Street, Regent, ND 58650. Mailing Address: P.O. Box 151, Regent, ND 58650-0151. Tel.: 701-563-4643.

E-mail: museum1@ndsupernet.com

Web Site: hettingercomuseum.org

Key Personnel: Chm. (V), Jess Kouba; Pres. (V), Gary Greff; Sec. & Treas., Paula Anderson.
Institution Type/Description: Local History Museum.
Hours & Admission Prices: Memorial Day to Labor Day daily 9-5; other times by appointment. Adults $5, children $3; discount to groups. &
Attendance: 400 (estimated)

Riverdale

GARRISON DAM NATIONAL FISH HATCHERY & VISITOR CENTER, Hatchery Rd., Riverdale, ND 58565. Mailing Address: P.O. Box 530, Riverdale, ND 58565-0530. Tel.: 701-654-7451.
E-mail: garrisondam@fws.gov
Web Site: www.fws.gov/mountain-prairie/fisheries/garrisonDam.php
Key Personnel: Mgr., Rob Holm.
Institution Type/Description: Fish Hatchery & Visitor Center.
Hours & Admission Prices: Visitor Center: Labor Day to Memorial Day daily 8-3:30. Hatchery: daily.

Rugby

PRAIRIE VILLAGE MUSEUM, 102 Hwy. 2, S.E., Rugby, ND 58368-2424. Mailing Address: P.O. Box 232, Rugby, ND 58368-0232. Tel.: 701-776-6414, 701-681-9342. Facebook: Prairie Village Museum.
E-mail: prairievillagemuseum@gmail.com
Web Site: www.prairievillagemuseum.com
Key Personnel: Exec. Dir., Catherine Jelsing; Pres. (V), Roger Sitter.
Institution Type/Description: History Museum.
Hours & Admission Prices: May 15-Sept. 15 Mon.-Sat. 8:30-5, Sun. noon-5; groups by appointment. Adults $7, students and seniors 65 & over $6, children 7-17 $3; active military & reserves and their families and children 6 & under no charge.
Attendance: 4,000 (actual)

VICTORIAN DRESS MUSEUM, 312 Second Ave., S.W., Rugby, ND 58368-1708. Tel.: 701-776-2189.
Institution Type/Description: Dress Museum: housed in the former Saint Paul's Episcopal Church. Listed on the National Register of Historic Places.
Hours & Admission Prices: By appointment.

Ryder

RYDER HISTORICAL SOCIETY MUSEUM, 33200 331st Ave., S.W., Ryder, ND 58779. Tel.: 701-726-5663.
E-mail: jwarner@restel.com
Key Personnel: Pres. (V), John Warner; Museum Shop Mgr., Faye Karna.
Institution Type/Description: Historical Society Museum.
Hours & Admission Prices: June-Sept. call for hours; other times by appointment. No charge; donations accepted. &
Attendance: 150 (estimated)

Saint John

ROLETTE COUNTY HISTORICAL SOCIETY MUSEUM, Main St., Saint John, ND 58369. Mailing Address: P.O. Box 377, Saint John, ND 58369-0377. Tel.: 701-263-4564.
Institution Type/Description: Historical Society Museum.
Hours & Admission Prices: Memorial Day to Labor Day Sun. 2-4.

Saint Michael

SULLYS HILL NATIONAL GAME PRESERVE, 2107 Park Dr., Saint Michael, ND 58370. Mailing Address: 221 2nd St. N.W., Ste. 2, Devils Lake, ND 58301. Tel.: 701-766-4272. Fax: 701-766-4096. Facebook.
E-mail: sullyshill@fws.gov
Web Site: sullyshill.fws.gov
Institution Type/Description: Wildlife Preserve.
Hours & Admission Prices: Auto Tour: May-Oct. daily 8 am to sunset. Visitor Center: May-Sept. No charge. &
Attendance: 75,000 (estimated)

Stanley

FLICKERTAIL VILLAGE AND MUSEUM, 5th St., S.E. off U.S. 2, Stanley, ND 58784. Mailing Address: 1012 E. LaSalle Dr., Bismarck, ND 58503-8895. Tel.: 701-628-3335 & 2802.
Key Personnel: Dir., Robert G. Liebl.

Institution Type/Description: History Museum.
Hours & Admission Prices: June-Aug. Wed. 6:30pm-8:30pm, Sun. 2-4; other times by appointment. Adults $3, children 11 & under $1.

Stanton

KNIFE RIVER INDIAN VILLAGES NATIONAL HISTORIC SITE, 564 County Rd. 37, Stanton, ND 58571-9422. Mailing Address: P.O. Box 9, Stanton, ND 58571-0009. Tel.: 701-745-3300. Fax: 701-745-3708.
E-mail: knri_information@nps.gov
Web Site: www.nps.gov/knri
Key Personnel: Supt., Wendy Ross.
Institution Type/Description: Historic Site.
Hours & Admission Prices: Memorial Day to Labor Day daily 8-6; Sept.-May 8-4:30. No charge. Closed New Year's Day; Thanksgiving; Christmas. &
Attendance: 24,704 (actual)

Steele

KIDDER COUNTY MUSEUM, 103 W. Broadway, Steele, ND 58482-7110. Mailing Address: 2571 37th St., S.E., Steele, ND 58482. Tel.: 701-475-2133 & 2741.
Key Personnel: Pres. (V), Glen DeKrey; Vice Pres., Eleanore Wolbaum; Sec., Rachel DeKrey; Treas., Bev Johnson.
Institution Type/Description: History Museum.
Hours & Admission Prices: Mon.-Fri. 9-12; other times by appointment. No charge.

Strasburg

PIONEER HERITAGE, INC. - LAWRENCE WELK HOUSE, 845 88th St., S.E., Strasburg, ND 58573. Mailing Address: P.O. Box 52, Strasburg, ND 58573-0052. Tel.: 701-336-7777, 701-254-4439.
E-mail: ndsu.library.archives@ndsu.edu
Formerly: Ludwig Welk Farmstead
Key Personnel: Pres. (V), Adam Baumstarck.
Institution Type/Description: Historic House Museum: housed in the boyhood home of Lawrence Welk.
Hours & Admission Prices: Memorial Day to Labor Day Thurs.-Sun. 10-5. Adults $5, children 6-12 $3; children under 6 no charge. &
Attendance: 898 (actual)

Tioga

NORSEMAN MUSEUM, 17 N.E. 2nd St., Tioga, ND 58852. Mailing Address: P.O. Box 273, Tioga, ND 58852-0273.
Key Personnel: Pres. (V), Ronnie Lund.
Institution Type/Description: History Museum.
Hours & Admission Prices: June-Aug. Sun. 1-4; other times by appointment. No charge; donations accepted.
Attendance: 350 (actual)

Valley City

BARNES COUNTY HISTORICAL MUSEUM, 315 Central Ave. N., Valley City, ND 58072-2954. Tel.: 701-845-0966. Fax: 701-845-5223 (Attn: Wes).
E-mail: bchistoricalsociety@hotmail.com
Web Site: www.hellovalley.com
Key Personnel: Cur., Wes Anderson.
Institution Type/Description: History Museum.
Hours & Admission Prices: Mon.-Sat. 10-4, Sun. by appointment. No charge; donations accepted. Closed national holidays. &
Attendance: 10,000 (actual)

Wahpeton

CHAHINKAPA ZOO, 1004 R.J. Hughes Dr., Wahpeton, ND 58075. Mailing Address: P.O. Box 1325, Wahpeton, ND 58074-1325. Tel.: 701-642-8709. Fax: 701-642-9285. Facebook: Chahinkapa Zoo.
E-mail: administration@chahinkapazoo.org
Web Site: www.chahinkapazoo.org
Key Personnel: Zoo Dir., Kathy Diekman; Cur., Tom Schmaltz; Lead Keeper, Trainer & Registrar, Addy Paul; Pres. (V), Wade Harty.
Institution Type/Description: Zoo.

Hours & Admission Prices: mid-April to Aug. daily 10-7; Sept. to mid-Oct. daily 10-5. Adults 13 & over $8, seniors 60 & over and military with ID $7, children 4-12 $5; members and children 3 & under no charge. Prairie Rose Carousel: $2.
Attendance: 66,000 (actual)

RICHLAND COUNTY HISTORICAL MUSEUM, 2nd St. and 7th Ave. N., Wahpeton, ND 58075. Mailing Address: P.O. Box 1292, Wahpeton, ND 58074-1292. Tel.: 701-642-3075. Facebook.
E-mail: richco.museum@702com.net
Web Site: richlandcountymuseumnd.org
Key Personnel: Pres. (V) Lois Berndt; Sec. & Treas., Corrie Myhre.
Institution Type/Description: Historical Society Museum.
Hours & Admission Prices: mid-April to Oct. Tues., Thurs. & Sat. 1-4. No charge; donations accepted. Closed Easter; Independence Day; Labor Day. &
Attendance: 1,300 (estimated)

Walhalla

GINGRAS TRADING POST STATE HISTORIC SITE, 12882 105th St., N.E., Walhalla, ND 58282-9757. Mailing Address: C/o Pembina State Museum, 805 Hwy. 59, P.O. Box 456, Pembina, ND 58271. Tel.: 701-549-2775. Fax: 701-825-6383.
E-mail: jblanchard@nd.gov
Web Site: history.nd.gov
Key Personnel: Site Supvr., Jeff Blanchard.
Institution Type/Description: Historic Site Museum.
Hours & Admission Prices: May 16-Sept. 15 daily 10-5. No charge; donations accepted.
Attendance: 537 (actual)

Washburn

MCLEAN COUNTY HISTORICAL SOCIETY MUSEUM, 602 Main Ave., Washburn, ND 58577. Mailing Address: P.O. Box 124, Washburn, ND 58577. Tel.: 701-462-3660.
E-mail: mcleancounty.nd.museum@hotmail.com
Web Site: www.washburnnd.com
Key Personnel: Chm. (V) & Pres. (V), Jenell Olson; Cur., Rhonda Johnson.
Institution Type/Description: Historical Society Museum.
Hours & Admission Prices: May-Sept. Mon.-Fri. 10-4, Sat. 1-4; other times by appointment. No charge; donations accepted. &
Attendance: 800 (estimated)

THE NORTH DAKOTA LEWIS & CLARK INTERPRETIVE CENTER, 2876 N. 8th St., S.E., Washburn, ND 58577. Mailing Address: P.O. Box 607, Washburn, ND 58577-0607. Tel.: 701-462-8535, 877-462-8535. Fax: 701-462-3316. Facebook: The North Dakota Lewis & Clark Interpretive Center.
E-mail: info@fortmandan.org
Web Site: www.fortmandan.com
Key Personnel: Pres., David Borlaug; Dir., Clay Jenkinson; Membership Dir. & Exec. Asst., Nancy Krebsbach; Mktg. Coord., Nicolette Borlaug; Museum Store Mgr., Sarah Trandahl.
Institution Type/Description: History Museum.
Hours & Admission Prices: Memorial Day to Labor Day daily 9-5; Sept.-May Mon.-Sat. 9-5, Sun. 12-5; groups by appointment. Adults $7.50, students $3; members no charge. &

Watford City

PIONEER MUSEUM OF MCKENZIE COUNTY, 100 2nd Ave., S.W., Watford City, ND 58854. Mailing Address: P.O. Box 126, Watford City, ND 58854-0126. Tel.: 701-444-2990. Facebook: McKenzie County History.
E-mail: museum@ruggedwest.com
Web Site: www.4eyes.net
Key Personnel: Pres. (V), Jennifer Sorenson; Dir., Charlotte Schilke; Sec. & Treas., Jan Dodge.
Institution Type/Description: Pioneer Museum.
Hours & Admission Prices: Mon.-Sat. 10-6. No charge; donations accepted. &
Attendance: 1,000 (estimated)

West Fargo

THE ARTSPLACE, 234 30th Ave. E, West Fargo, ND 58078-7934. Tel.: 701-746-6479.
Institution Type/Description: Art Gallery.

Hours & Admission Prices: Mon.-Sat. 10-5; other times by appointment. No charge; donations accepted.
Attendance: 1,173 (actual)

CASS COUNTY HISTORICAL SOCIETY AT BONANZAVILLE, 1351 W. Main Ave., West Fargo, ND 58078-1321. Tel.: 701-282-2822. Fax: 701-282-7606.
E-mail: info@bonanzaville.org
Web Site: www.bonanzaville.org
Key Personnel: Pres., John Lund; Exec. Dir., Brenda Warren; Facilities Mgr., Roger Ward.
Institution Type/Description: Pioneer Village & Museum Complex: consisting of 43 buildings.
Hours & Admission Prices: Call for seasonal hours. Adults $12, seniors & military $10, children $6; members no charge. &
Attendance: 100,000 (estimated)

Williston

FORT BUFORD STATE HISTORIC SITE, 15349 39th Lane, N. W., Williston, ND 58801-8677. Tel.: 701-572-9034. Fax: 701-572-9033.
E-mail: shsbuford@nd.gov
Web Site: www.nd.gov/hist
Key Personnel: Dir. State Historical Society of ND, Merl Paaverud; Div. Dir. Historic Sites, Fern Swenson; Mgr. Historic Sites, Diane Rogness; Site Supvr., Steven Reidburn; Asst. Site Supvr., Kerry Finsaas; Museum Shop Mgr., Rhonda Brown.
Institution Type/Description: Historic Site: housed in 1871 officers quarters of Fort Buford, at confluence of Yellowstone and Missouri Rivers; site of Sitting Bull's surrender July 20, 1881.
Hours & Admission Prices: May 16-Sept. 15 daily 8-6. Confluence Center: Sept. 16 to May 15 Wed.-Sun. 9-4. Adults $5, children 6-15 $2.50, school groups $1 each; discounts to SHSND foundation members; members and children 5 & under no charge. Tour Bus: $40 per bus. Annual Site Pass: $20. Closed New Year's Day, Easter, Thanksgiving, Christmas. &
Attendance: 14,753 (actual)

FORT UNION TRADING POST NATIONAL HISTORIC SITE, 15550 Hwy. 1804, Williston, ND 58801-8680. Tel.: 701-572-9083. Fax: 701-572-7321.
E-mail: fred_macvaugh@nps.gov
Web Site: www.nps.gov/fous
Key Personnel: Supt., Andrew Banta.
Institution Type/Description: Park & Historic Site: reconstructed American Fur Company fur trade post at the historic confluence of the Missouri & Yellowstone Rivers.
Hours & Admission Prices: Winter: daily 9-5:30; Summer: daily 8-6:30. No charge; donations accepted. Closed New Year's Day; Thanksgiving; Christmas. &
Attendance: 15,000 (estimated)

FRONTIER MUSEUM, 6330 2nd Ave. W., Williston, ND 58801. Tel.: 701-577-4504.
E-mail: jimr@co.williams.nd.us
Key Personnel: Pres., Jim Ryen.
Institution Type/Description: General Museum.
Hours & Admission Prices: By appointment. Adults $3, children $1.50. &
Attendance: 2,000 (estimated)

MISSOURI-YELLOWSTONE CONFLUENCE INTERPRETIVE CENTER, 15349 39th Lane, N.W., Williston, ND 58801. Tel.: 701-572-9034. Fax: 701-328-3710.
E-mail: shsbuford@nd.gov
Institution Type/Description: History Museum.
Hours & Admission Prices: mid-May to mid-Sept. daily 9-7; mid-Sept. to mid-May Wed.-Sat. 9-4, Sun. 1-5. Adults $5, children $2.50.

Wimbledon

MIDLAND CONTINENTAL DEPOT TRANSPORTATION MUSEUM, 401 Railway St., Wimbledon, ND 58492. Tel.: 701-320-1020 & 435-2875.
E-mail: midlandcontinentaldepot@gmail.com
Web Site: www.midlandcontinentaldepot.com
Institution Type/Description: Transportation Museum: housed in the former home of Peggy Lee. Listed on the National Register of Historic Places.
Hours & Admission Prices: Memorial Day to Labor Day daily 1-4; other times by appointment. No charge. &

WIMBLEDON COMMUNITY MUSEUM INC., 301 Center St., Wimbledon, ND 58492. Mailing Address: P.O. Box 223, Wimbledon, ND 58492. Tel.: 701-435-2239.
E-mail: midlandcontinentaldepot@gmail.com
Web Site: www.midlandcontinentaldepot.com
Institution Type/Description: History Museum.
Hours & Admission Prices: Memorial Day to Labor Day daily 1-4; other times by appointment. No charge; donations accepted. &

Wolford

DALE & MARTHA HAWK MUSEUM, 4839 78 St., Wolford, ND 58385-9402. Tel.: 701-583-2381.
E-mail: dmhawk@gondtc.com
Web Site: www.hawkmuseum.org
Key Personnel: Dir. & Pres. (V), Richard Noyes; Cur., Gordon Thingvold.
Institution Type/Description: History Museum.
Hours & Admission Prices: May-Oct. daily 9-5. Adults $5, children under 12 $1.50. &
Attendance: 3,500 (estimated)

Woodworth

MELZER MUSEUM, Main St., Woodworth, ND 58476. Tel.: 701-752-4119.
Institution Type/Description: History Museum.
Hours & Admission Prices: By appointment.

OHIO
(489 listings)

Akron

AKRON ART MUSEUM, One South High, Akron, OH 44308-1801. Tel.: 330-376-9185. Fax: 330-376-1180.
E-mail: mail@akronartmuseum.org
Web Site: www.akronartmuseum.org
Key Personnel: Dir. & C.E.O., Mark Masuoka; Pres. (V), Christine Myeroff; Dir. Education, Alison Caplan; Assoc. Educator, Gina Thomas McGee; Collections Mgr., Arnold Tunstall; Chief Curator, Janice T. Driesbach; Museum Shop Mgr., Laura Firestone; Special Projects, Jennifer Shipman.
Institution Type/Description: Art Museum.
Hours & Admission Prices: Administrative Office: Mon.-Fri. 9-5; Gallery: Wed. & Fri.-Sun. 11-5, Thurs. 11-9. Adults $7, students and seniors 65 & over $5; discounts to AAM, NARM, & Metro RTA members; children 12 & under, members and Thurs. no charge. Ohio Reciprocal Program. Closed New Year's Day; Memorial Day; Independence Day; Labor Day; Thanksgiving; Christmas Eve & Day. &

AKRON POLICE MUSEUM, Harold K. Stubbs Justice Center, 217 S. High St., #508A, Akron, OH 44308-1636. Tel.: 330-375-2390.
Institution Type/Description: Police History Museum.
Hours & Admission Prices: Mon.-Fri. 8-3:30; groups by appointment.

AKRON ZOOLOGICAL PARK, 504 Euclid Ave., Akron, OH 44307. Mailing Address: 500 Edgewood Ave., Akron, OH 44307. Tel.: 330-375-2550. Fax: 330-375-2575.
E-mail: info@akronzoo.org
Web Site: www.akronzoo.org
Key Personnel: Pres. & C.E.O., L. Patricia Simmons; Dir. Mktg. & Guest Svcs., David Barnhardt; Dir. Devel., Pamela Webb.
Institution Type/Description: Zoo.
Hours & Admission Prices: May-Oct. daily 10-5; Nov.-April daily 11-4. Summer: adults $11, senior citizens 62 & up $9, children 2-14 $8; Winter: admission $7; discounts to groups & AZA members; members & children under 2 no charge. Closed New Year's Day; Thanksgiving; Christmas Eve & Day. &
Attendance: 255,000 (estimated)

BETHLEHEM CAVE AND NATIVITY MUSEUM, Nativity of The Lord Jesus Catholic Church, 2425 Myersville Rd., Akron, OH 44312. Tel.: 330-699-5086. Fax: 330-699-4299.
E-mail: nativity@neohio.twcbc.com
Web Site: www.nativityofthelord.org/museum.asp
Institution Type/Description: Religious Museum.
Hours & Admission Prices: Mon.-Fri. 9-4, Sat. 4-6, Sun. 8-12:30. No charge; donations accepted. &

EMILY DAVIS GALLERY - UNIVERSITY OF AKRON, Myers School of Art, 150 E. Exchange St., Akron, OH 44325-7801. Mailing Address: 302 Buchtel Commons, Akron, OH 44325. Tel.: 330-972-5950.
E-mail: ua.art@uakron.edu
Web Site: www.uakron.edu/art/galleries
Institution Type/Description: Art Gallery.
Hours & Admission Prices: Mon.-Tues. & Fri.-Sat. 10-5, Wed.-Thurs. 10-9.

HOWER HOUSE, University of Akron, 60 Fir Hill, Akron, OH 44325-2401. Tel.: 330-972-6909. Fax: 330-384-2635.
E-mail: howerhouse@uakron.edu
Web Site: howerhouse.org
Key Personnel: Dir., Cindy Bussey.
Institution Type/Description: Historic House Museum: former home of John Henry Hower, a leading Akron industrialist; c.1871.
Hours & Admission Prices: Feb.-Dec. Wed.-Sat. 12-3:30; groups by appointment. Adults $8, senior citizens 65 & over $6, students & children $2; discounts to groups; children 6 & under no charge. Closed major holidays.

STAN HYWET HALL AND GARDENS, INC., 714 N. Portage Path, Akron, OH 44303-1399. Tel.: 330-836-5533. Fax: 330-836-2680.
E-mail: info@stanhywet.org
Web Site: www.stanhywet.org
Key Personnel: Pres & Exec. Dir., Sean Joyce; Vice Pres. Outreach & Communications, Gailmarie Fort; Vice Pres. Events & Personnel, Valerie Still.
Institution Type/Description: Historic House Museum: 1912-15 65-room Tudor Revival: manor house and country estate of Frank A. Seiberling, co-founder of Goodyear Tire & Rubber Co.
Hours & Admission Prices: April-Nov. Tues.-Sun. 10-6, last entry 4:30; Dec. call for hours. Tours prices vary. Closed New Year's Eve & Day; Easter; Thanksgiving; Christmas Eve & Day. &
Attendance: 200,000 (estimated)

THE SUMMIT COUNTY HISTORICAL SOCIETY OF AKRON, OHIO, 550 Copley Rd., Akron, OH 44320-2398. Tel.: 330-535-1120. Fax: 330-535-0250. Facebook: @summitcountyhistoricalsociety; Instagram: @summit_history; Twitter: @schistorical.
E-mail: schs@summithistory.org
Web Site: summithistory.org
Key Personnel: Pres. & C.E.O., Leianne Neff Heppner; Business Mgr., Denise Lundell; Education Coord., Claire Lucas; Admin. Asst., Mary Conley; Museum Svcs. Coord., Charlotte Gingert.
Institution Type/Description: History Museum.
Hours & Admission Prices: Wed.-Sat. 1-4. Adults $8, students $2; members no charge. Closed national holidays.
Attendance: 14,000 (estimated)

Alliance

MABEL HARTZELL HISTORICAL HOME, 840 N. Park Ave., Alliance, OH 44601-1728. Mailing Address: P.O. Box 2044, Alliance, OH 44601-0044. Tel.: 330-821-8972. Facebook.
E-mail: alliancehistory@yahoo.com
Web Site: www.alliancehistory.org
Key Personnel: Pres., Michelle Dillon; Vice Pres., Joseph Zelasko; Treas., Stephen Stone; Sec., Jennifer Crist.
Institution Type/Description: Historic House: an 1867 Italianate home built by Matthew Earley, a prominent businessman & politician; restored to 1880s period with original furnishings.
Hours & Admission Prices: By appointment only. Admission $5; children under 12 no charge.
Attendance: 400 (estimated)

Amherst

AMHERST HISTORICAL SOCIETY, 113 S. Lake St., Amherst, OH 44001. Tel.: 440-988-7255. Fax: 440-988-2951.
E-mail: amhersthistory@centurytel.net
Web Site: amhersthistoricalsociety.org
Key Personnel: Cur., Ronald Sauer.
Institution Type/Description: Historical Society Museum.
Hours & Admission Prices: May to early Dec. Wed. 10-12, Sun. 2-4.
Attendance: 1,000 (estimated)

Archbold

SAUDER VILLAGE, 22611 State Rte. 2, Archbold, OH 43502-9452. Mailing Address: P.O. Box 235, Archbold, OH 43502-0235. Tel.: 419-446-2541, 800-590-9755. Fax: 419-445-5251. TDD: 419-445-9610.
E-mail: info@saudervillage.org
Web Site: www.saudervillage.org
Key Personnel: Pres. & C.E.O., Debbie Sauder David; Dir. Historic Operations, Kris Jemmott; Cur. Education, Chris Lankenau; Cur. Collections, Tracie Evans; Business Officer, Corey Smeltzer; Dir. Mktg., Jeanette Smith.
Institution Type/Description: Living History Village: a 37-building pioneer village.
Hours & Admission Prices: May & Sept.-Oct. Tues.-Fri. 10-3:30, Sat. 10-5, Sun. 12-4; Memorial Day to Labor Day Tues.-Sat. 10-5, Sun. 12-4. Adults $16, students 6-16 $10; discount to seniors, AAA members & groups; members and children 5 & under no charge. &
Attendance: 100,000 (actual)

Ashland

ASHLAND COUNTY HISTORICAL SOCIETY, 420 Center St., Ashland, OH 44805-3247. Tel.: 419-289-3111. Fax: 419-207-8153.
E-mail: ashlandhistory@zoominternet.net
Web Site: www.ashlandhistory.org
Key Personnel: Dir., Chris Box.
Institution Type/Description: Historical Society Museum.
Hours & Admission Prices: Tours: April-Dec. Mon. & Wed. 11-2; other times by appointment. No charge.
Attendance: 4,000 (estimated)

Ashtabula

ASHTABULA ARTS CENTER, 2928 West 13th St., Ashtabula, OH 44004-2498. Tel.: 440-964-3396. Fax: 440-964-3396.
E-mail: info@ashtabulaartscenter.org
Web Site: ashtabulaartscenter.org
Key Personnel: Exec. Dir., Lori Robishaw; Pres. (V), Debbi Waring; Dir. Visual Arts, Meeghan Humphrey; Dir. Finance, Cindy Rimpela; Theater & Music Dir., Kimberly Godfrey; Dance Dir., Shelagh Dubsky.
Institution Type/Description: Art Museum Center.
Hours & Admission Prices: Mon.-Thurs. 9-9, Fri. 9-4, Sat. 9-1. No charge. Closed holidays. &
Attendance: 15,000 (estimated)

ASHTABULA MARITIME AND SURFACE TRANSPORTATION MUSEUM, 1071 Walnut Blvd., Ashtabula, OH 44005-1546. Mailing Address: Ashtabula Maritime Museum, P.O. Box 1546, Ashtabula, OH 44005-1546. Tel.: 440-997-5370; 964-6847.
E-mail: bobanne@windstream.net
Web Site: www.ashtabulamaritimemuseum.org
Key Personnel: Exec. Dir., Robert Frisbie.
Institution Type/Description: Marine Museum: housed in the former residence of the Lighthouse Keepers and the Coast Guard Chief, built in 1871/1898.
Hours & Admission Prices: Memorial Day to Labor Day Fri.-Sun. 12-5; Sept. Sat. & Sun. 12-5. Adults $5, children 6-16 $3; US military in uniform, members & children under 6 no charge. &
Attendance: 5,000 (actual)

Athens

ATHENS COUNTY HISTORICAL SOCIETY AND MUSEUM, Southeast Ohio History Center, 24 W. State St., Athens, OH 45701-2567. Tel.: 740-592-2280. Fax: 740-594-8352.
E-mail: tom@athenshistory.org
Key Personnel: Exec. Dir., Tom O'Grady.
Institution Type/Description: Historical Society Museum.
Hours & Admission Prices: Tues.-Sat. 12-4. No charge; donations accepted. &
Attendance: 3,220 (actual)

THE DAIRY BARN ARTS CENTER, 8000 Dairy Lane, Athens, OH 45701-9393. Mailing Address: P.O. Box 747, Athens, OH 45701-0747. Tel.: 740-592-4981. Fax: 740-592-5090.
E-mail: artsinfo@dairybarn.org
Web Site: www.dairybarn.org
Formerly: The Dairy Barn Southeastern Ohio's Cultural Arts Center
Key Personnel: Dir., Andrea Lewis; Museum Shop Mgr., Claire White.
Institution Type/Description: Arts Center: housed in a former dairy barn; built in 1914. Listed on the National Register of Historic Places.

Hours & Admission Prices: Tues.-Sun. 12-5. Admission $5; members, children under 12 & Wed. no charge. &
Attendance: 22,000 (actual)

KENNEDY MUSEUM OF ART, Ohio University, Lin Hall, Athens, OH 45701-2979, Tel.: 740-593-1304. Fax: 740-593-1305.
E-mail: kennedymuseum@ohio.edu
Web Site: www.ohiou.edu/museum
Key Personnel: Dir., Edward Pauley; Cur. Education, Sally Delgado; Cur., Petra Kralickova; Registrar, Jeffrey Carr; Mktg., Public Rels. & Guest Svcs., Lori Spencer.
Institution Type/Description: University Art Museum.
Hours & Admission Prices: Gallery: Mon.-Wed. & Fri. 10-5, Thurs. 10-8, Sat.-Sun. 1-5. Cafe: Mon.-Fri. 8-3. No charge; donations accepted. &
Attendance: 10,000 (actual)

OHIO UNIVERSITY ART GALLERY, 528 Seigfred Hall, Athens, OH 45701. Tel.: 740-593-0796. Fax: 740-593-1305. Facebook.
E-mail: kesselc@ohio.edu
Web Site: www.ohiou.edu/art/ougallery.html
Key Personnel: Dir. Exhibition, Courtney Kessel; Dir., Davie LaPalombara.
Institution Type/Description: University Art Gallery.
Hours & Admission Prices: Mon.-Wed. & Fri.-Sat. 10-4, Thurs. 10-8. No charge. &
Attendance: 15,000 (estimated)

Aurora

AURORA HISTORICAL SOCIETY, 115 E. Pioneer Trail, Aurora Memorial Library Bldg., Aurora, OH 44202-7922. Tel.: 330-995-3336.
E-mail: aurorahist@windstream.net
Web Site: aurorahistorical.org
Key Personnel: Pres., John Kudley; Dir., Marcelle R. Wilson, Ph.D.; Museum Shop Mgr., Josephine Smalley.
Institution Type/Description: General Museum.
Hours & Admission Prices: Mon. & Wed. 2-4; other times by appointment. No charge. &
Attendance: 1,400 (actual)

Bainbridge

DR. JOHN HARRIS DENTAL MUSEUM, 208 West Main St., Bainbridge, OH 45612. Mailing Address: Bainbridge Historical Society, P.O. Box 424, Bainbridge, OH 45612-0424. Tel.: 740-634-2228; 626-7266.
Web Site: www.bainbridgedentalmuseum.com
Key Personnel: Pres., Mr. David Tillis.
Institution Type/Description: Dental History Museum: housed in 1827 former office of Dr. John Harris.
Hours & Admission Prices: April-May & Sept.-Oct. Sat.-Sun. 12-4; June-Aug. Tues.-Sun. 12-4. Adults $5; children under 12 & members no charge. &
Attendance: 350 (estimated)

Barnesville

BELMONT COUNTY VICTORIAN MANSION MUSEUM, 532 N. Chestnut St., Barnesville, OH 43713-1274. Mailing Address: P. O. Box 434, Barnesville, OH 43713-0434. Tel.: 740-425-1457.
E-mail: estewart336@comcast.net
Web Site: www.barnesvilleohio.com/belmontcountymuseum
Formerly: Gay 90's Mansion Museum
Key Personnel: C.E.O. & Pres., Emery C. Stewart; Dir. & Treas., Rebecca J. Thomas.
Institution Type/Description: General Museum: housed in 1890 Richardsonian mansion.
Hours & Admission Prices: May-Sept. Wed.-Sun. & holidays 1-4; special tours by appointment. Adults $5, children 6-18 $2; discounts to groups & AAA members.
Attendance: 1,058 (actual)

Batavia

TRI-STATE WARBIRD MUSEUM, 4021 Borman Ave., Batavia, OH 45103. Tel.: 513-735-4500.
E-mail: deldridge.tswm@fuse.net
Web Site: www.tri-statewarbirdmuseum.org/museum.html
Institution Type/Description: Military Aviation Museum.
Hours & Admission Prices: Wed. 4-7, Sat. 10-3. Adults $12, student & veteran $7.

Bath

HALE FARM AND VILLAGE, 2686 Oak Hill Rd., Bath, OH 44210. Mailing Address: P.O. Box 296, Bath, OH 44210-0296. Tel.: 330-666-3711. Fax: 330-666-9497.
E-mail: info@wrhs.org
Web Site: www.halefarm.org
Key Personnel: Pres. & C.E.O., Kelly Falcone-Hall, WRHS; Bd. Chm., Glenn Anderson, Jr., WRHS; Dir., Jason Klein.
Institution Type/Description: Village Museum.19th century agrarian & village communities in the Western Reserve.
Hours & Admission Prices: June-Aug. Wed.-Sun. 10-5; Sept.-Oct. Sat.-Sun. 10-5; school groups by appointment; Nov.-May by appointment only. Adults $10, children 3-12 $5; discounts to groups and AAM & ICOM members; members no charge. Closed New Year's Day; Memorial Day; Independence Day; Labor Day; Thanksgiving; Christmas. &
Attendance: 60,000 (actual)

Bay Village

BAYARTS, 28795 Lake Rd., Bay Village, OH 44140-1399. Tel.: 440-871-6543. Facebook.
E-mail: info@bayarts.net
Web Site: www.bayarts.net
Formerly: Baycrafters, Inc.
Key Personnel: Exec. Dir., Nancy Heaton; Gen. Mgr., Beth Milli; Artistic Dir., Karen Petkovic; Dir. Education, Linda Goik.
Institution Type/Description: Art Center: housed in two historic houses & Playhouse.
Hours & Admission Prices: Office & Shop: Mon.-Wed. & Fri.-Sat. 9-5, Thurs. 9-8. Fuller House: Mon.-Sat. 9-3. No charge; donations accepted. Closed holidays.
Attendance: 24,000

LAKE ERIE NATURE & SCIENCE CENTER, 28728 Wolf Rd., Bay Village, OH 44140-1350. Tel.: 440-871-2900. Fax: 440-871-2901.
E-mail: info@lensc.org
Web Site: www.lensc.org
Formerly: Lake Erie Junior Museum
Key Personnel: Exec. Dir., Catherine Timko; Pres. (V), Colleen Lowmiller; Museum Shop Mgr., Sheryl Caine.
Institution Type/Description: Nature Center.
Hours & Admission Prices: Daily 10-5; groups by appointment only. No charge; donations accepted. Closed New Year's Day; Easter; Memorial Day; Independence Day; Labor Day; Thanksgiving; Christmas. &
Attendance: 180,000 (estimated)

ROSE HILL MUSEUM, 27715 Lake Rd., Bay Village, OH 44140. Mailing Address: P.O. Box 40187, Bay Village, OH 44140-0187. Tel.: 440-871-7338 & 835-2718.
E-mail: mail@bayhistorical.com
Web Site: www.bayhistorical.com
Key Personnel: Pres. (V), Cathy Flament; Vice Pres., Steve Ruscher; Corresponding Sec., Cindi Lindgren; Treas., Abigail Sammon; Accessions & Museum Shop Mgr., Janet Zvara.
Institution Type/Description: History Museum: housed in 1818 Western Reserve farmhouse belonging to the Cahoon Family, first settlers in Dover Township.
Hours & Admission Prices: Sun. 2-4:30, call for special tours. No charge; donations accepted.
Attendance: 1,500 (estimated)

Beachwood

MALTZ MUSEUM OF JEWISH HERITAGE, 2929 Richmond Rd., Beachwood, OH 44122-3270. Tel.: 216-593-0575. Fax: 216-593-0576. Facebook: Maltz Museum; Twitter; @maltzmuseum.
E-mail: info@mmjh.org
Web Site: maltzmuseum.org
Key Personnel: Mng. Dir., David Schafer; Dir. Finance, Susan Friedman; Dir. External Affairs, Dahlia Fisher; Dir. Opers., Laurie Hughes; Mgr. Public Programs & Stop the Hate, Ben Becker; Mgr. Education & Outreach, Courtney Krieger; Mgr. Volunteers & Visitor Svcs., Wesley Aaron Bane; Mgr. Collections & Exhibitions, Lindsay Miller; Devel. Mgr., Michelle Feinberg; Exec. Asst. & Grant Writer, Renee Leonard; Museum Shop Mgr., Helen Fineberg.
Institution Type/Description: Jewish Heritage Museum.
Hours & Admission Prices: Tues. & Thurs.-Sun. 11-5, Wed. 11-9. Adults $12, students & seniors $10; children 5-11 $5; discounts to NARM & CAJM members. &
Attendance: 100,000 (estimated)

Bedford

BEDFORD HISTORICAL SOCIETY MUSEUM AND LIBRARY, 30 S. Park St. (Squire Place), Bedford, OH 44146. Mailing Address: P.O. Box 46282, Bedford, OH 44146-0282. Tel.: 440-232-0796.
E-mail: museum@bedfordohiohistory.org
Web Site: www.bedfordohiohistory.org
Formerly: Bedford Museum
Key Personnel: C.E.O., Janet Caldwell; Pres., Robert Schroeter, Sr.; Archivist, Debra Grubb; Librarian, Paul Pojman; Mgr., Doris Shriver.
Institution Type/Description: History Museum.
Hours & Admission Prices: Mon. & Wed. 7:30pm-10pm, Thurs. 10am-4pm; Second Sun. of the month 2-5. No charge; donations accepted. &
Attendance: 10,000 (actual)

Bellaire

THE NATIONAL IMPERIAL GLASS MUSEUM, 3200 Belmont St., Bellaire, OH 43906-1521. Mailing Address: P.O. Box 534, Bellaire, OH 43906-0534. Tel.: 740-671-3971.
E-mail: info@imperialglass.org
Web Site: www.imperialglass.org/museum.htm
Key Personnel: Admin., Rosalie Wenckoski; Chm. (V), Paul Douglas.
Institution Type/Description: Glass Museum.
Hours & Admission Prices: April-Oct. Thurs.-Sat. 11-3. Admission: $3; NIGCS members no charge. Closed Independence Day. &
Attendance: 480 (estimated)

UNOFFICIAL LEGO & TOY MUSEUM, 4597 Noble St., Bellaire, OH 43906. Tel.: 740-671-8890.
E-mail: toymuseum@hotmail.com
Web Site: danstoymuseum.blogspot.com
Institution Type/Description: Toy Museum.
Hours & Admission Prices: Wed.-Sun. 12-7. Adults $8, children $6; children 4 & under no charge.

Bellbrook

BELLBROOK HISTORICAL MUSEUM, 42 N. Main St., Bellbrook, OH 45305-2009. Mailing Address: 3640 Ferry Rd., Bellbrook, OH 45305-0285. Tel.: 937-848-4666.
E-mail: brx4bellmu@yahoo.com
Web Site: www.cityofbellbrook.org
Key Personnel: Chm. (V), Dwight W. Bartlett.
Institution Type/Description: History Museum: housed in The Crowl Building, a former mortuary.
Hours & Admission Prices: Sat. 12-5. No charge; donations accepted. Closed holidays. &
Attendance: 500 (estimated)

Bellefontaine

LOGAN COUNTY HISTORY CENTER, 521 E. Columbus Ave., Bellefontaine, OH 43311-2401. Tel.: 937-593-7557.
E-mail: historycenter@loganhistory.org
Web Site: www.loganhistory.org
Formerly: Logan County Historical Society Museum
Key Personnel: Dir. & Cur., Todd McCormick; Pres. (V), Dan Bratka.
Institution Type/Description: Historical Society Museum.
Hours & Admission Prices: Wed.-Sun. 1-4. No charge; donations accepted. Orr Mansion not handicapped accessible. &
Attendance: 7,500 (estimated)

Bellevue

HISTORIC LYME VILLAGE ASSOCIATION, 5001 State Rte. 4, Bellevue, OH 44811. Mailing Address: P.O. Box 342, Bellevue, OH 44811-0342. Tel.: 419-483-4949.
E-mail: info@lymevillage.org
Web Site: www.lymevillage.org
Key Personnel: Dir., Ely Beachy; Chm. (V) & Museum Shop Mgr., Ray Parker; Pres., Roger Kinney; Vice Pres., Bill Drown; Treas., Dennis Bauer.
Institution Type/Description: History Museum.
Hours & Admission Prices: June-Aug. Tues.-Sat. 10-4, Sun. 12-4; Sept. Sun. 12-4. Adults $9, senior citizens 60 & over $8, children 6-12 $5; members no charge. &
Attendance: 7,000 (estimated)

MAD RIVER & NKP RAILROAD MUSEUM, 253 Southwest St., Bellevue, OH 44811-1377. Mailing Address: 233 York St., Bellevue, OH 44811-1377. Tel.: 419-483-2222.
E-mail: madriver@onebellevue.com
Web Site: madrivermuseum.org
Key Personnel: Pres. (V), Christopher Beamer.
Institution Type/Description: Railroad History Museum.
Hours & Admission Prices: May & Sept.-Oct. Sat.-Sun. 12-4; Memorial Day to Labor Day daily 12-4. Adults $7, seniors 60 & over $6, children 3-12 $4; members & children under 3 no charge.
Attendance: 4,500 (estimated)

Belpre

BELPRE HISTORICAL SOCIETY/FARMER'S CASTLE MUSEUM, 509 Ridge St., Belpre, OH 45714. Mailing Address: P. O. Box 731, Belpre, OH 45714-0731. Tel.: 740-423-7588.
E-mail: info@belprehistory.com
Web Site: belprehistory.com
Key Personnel: Pres., Nancy Sams.
Institution Type/Description: History Museum.
Hours & Admission Prices: April-Oct. Wed. & Sat. 1-4. Adults $4, students $1.

Berea

FAWICK ART GALLERY, Kleist Center for Art & Drama, 95 E. Bagley Rd., Berea, OH 44017. Tel.: 440-826-2152.
Institution Type/Description: Art Gallery.
Hours & Admission Prices: Mon.-Fri. 2-5; other times by appointment.

Beverly

THE OLIVER TUCKER MUSEUM, 441 5th St., Beverly, OH 45715. Mailing Address: 70 Maple Circle, Waterford, OH 45786-5321. Tel.: 740-984-2489.
Web Site: olivertuckermuseum.com
Key Personnel: Pres. (V), Susan Trotter; Bd. Trustee, Wayne Fansworth; Bd. Trustee & Vice Pres., Francis M. Sampson.
Institution Type/Description: Historic Buildings.
Hours & Admission Prices: June-Aug. Sat.-Sun. 1-4; groups & other times by appointment. No charge; donations accepted. &
Attendance: 425 (estimated)

Bexley

BEXLEY HISTORICAL SOCIETY, 2080 Clifton Ave., Bexley, OH 43209-1405. Tel.: 614-559-4360.
E-mail: info@bexleyhistory.org
Web Site: www.bexleyhistory.org
Key Personnel: Pres., Mike Kilbourne; Cur., Edie Mae Herrel.
Institution Type/Description: Local History Museum.
Hours & Admission Prices: 1st Thurs. of month 10-2, 1st Sun. of month 1-4; other times by appointment. No charge; donations accepted. Closed holidays. &
Attendance: 500 (estimated)

Blanchester

BLANCHESTER AREA HISTORICAL SOCIETY MUSEUM, 206 W. Main St., Blanchester, OH 45107. Tel.: 937-382-1965.
E-mail: info@clintoncountyohio.com
Institution Type/Description: Historical Society Museum.
Hours & Admission Prices: Wed. & Sat. 1-4. Adults $5; members and children 13 & under no charge.

Bluffton

THE LION AND LAMB PEACE ARTS CENTER, Bluffton University, Spring St., Bluffton, OH 45817-2104. Mailing Address: Bluffton University, 1 University Dr. - 50, Bluffton, OH 45817-2104. Tel.: 419-358-3207.
E-mail: lionlamb@bluffton.edu
Web Site: www.bluffton.edu/lionlamb
Key Personnel: Dir., Louise Matthews.
Institution Type/Description: Arts & Literature Center.
Hours & Admission Prices: Academic Year: Tues.-Thurs. 9-5, Fri. 9-12; other times by appointment. No charge. &
Attendance: 4,000 (estimated)

Bolivar

FORT LAURENS HISTORIC SITE, 11067 Fort Laurens Rd., N. W., Bolivar, OH 44612. Mailing Address: P.O. Box 621, Zoar, OH 44697-0508. Tel.: 330-874-2059. Fax: 330-874-2936. Facebook.
E-mail: fortlaurens@gmail.com
Web Site: fortlaurens.org
Key Personnel: Dir., Tammi Mackey Shrum; Museum Shop Mgr., Megan Clevenger.
Institution Type/Description: Military Fort Museum: site of the only Revolutionary War fort in Ohio; the site of the Tomb of the Unknown Patriot of the Revolutionary War.
Hours & Admission Prices: Museum: May Sat. 11-4, Sun. 12-4; June-Aug. Wed.-Sat 11-4, Sun. 12-4; Sept.-Nov. Fri.-Sat. 11-4, Sun. 12-4. Adults $5, children 5-17 $3; military with ID no charge. &
Attendance: 3,873 (actual)

Bowling Green

BOWLING GREEN STATE UNIVERSITY FINE ARTS CENTER GALLERIES, 1303 Fine Arts Center, Bowling Green State University, Bowling Green, OH 43403. Tel.: 419-372-8525. Fax: 419-372-2544. Facebook: BGSU Art Galleries.
E-mail: galleries@bgsu.edu
Web Site: gallery.bgsu.edu
Key Personnel: Gallery Dir., Jacqueline S. Nathan.
Institution Type/Description: Art Gallery.
Hours & Admission Prices: School Year: Tues.-Wed. & Fri.-Sat. 11-4, Thurs. 11-4 & 6pm-9pm, Sun. 1-4; Summer: call for hours. No charge; donations accepted. Closed university holidays. &
Attendance: 9,000 (estimated)

NATIONAL CONSTRUCTION EQUIPMENT MUSEUM, 16623 Liberty Hi Rd., Bowling Green, OH 43402-9309. Tel.: 419-352-5616.
E-mail: info@hcea.net
Web Site: www.hcea.net
Key Personnel: Chm. (V), Dare Geis; Pres. (V), Larry Kotkowski; Museum Shop Mgr., Dan Frahtz.
Institution Type/Description: History Museum.
Hours & Admission Prices: Mon.-Fri. 1-5. Adults $7; discounts to seniors & groups; members no charge.
Attendance: 200 (estimated)

WOOD COUNTY HISTORICAL CENTER AND MUSEUM, 13660 County Home Rd., Bowling Green, OH 43402-9281. Tel.: 419-352-0967. Fax: 419-352-6220. Facebook: Wood County History.
E-mail: director@woodcountyhistory.org
Web Site: www.woodcountyhistory.org
Key Personnel: Dir., Dana Nemeth; Coord. Education, Michael McMaster; Coord. Mktg. & Events, Kelli Kling; Cur., Holly Hartlerode; Technician, Michael Ginnetti; Devel. Coord., Kelsey Kleine.
Institution Type/Description: Regional History Museum: housed in a former county infirmary or poor farm on 50-acre site.
Hours & Admission Prices: Feb. Mon. 10-4, Sat.-Sun. 1-4. Suggested Donation: adults $5, children $1; discounts to AAM & AAA members; members no charge. Closed county holidays. &
Attendance: 25,000 (estimated)

Bradford

BRADFORD OHIO RAILROAD MUSEUM, 200 N. Miami Ave., Bradford, OH 45308-1164. Mailing Address: P.O. Box 101, Bradford, OH 45308-0101. Tel.: 937-552-2196. Fax: 740-654-0505. Facebook.
E-mail: bornrr@yahoo.com
Web Site: bradfordrrmuseum.org
Key Personnel: C.E.O., Pres. (V) & Museum Shop Mgr., Sandy Edminson; Devel., Marilyn Kosier; Chm. (V), Don Wick; Education, Jeremy Martin; Public Rels., Sue Vickroy; Treas., Jordon Ingle; Archivist, Bill Haines.
Institution Type/Description: History & Railroad Museum.
Hours & Admission Prices: April-Oct. Sat. 10-4. Adults $5. &
Attendance: 2,000 (estimated)

Brecksville

CUYAHOGA VALLEY NATIONAL PARK, 15610 Vaughn Rd., Brecksville, OH 44141-3097. Tel.: 440-417-3890. Fax: 440-546-5989.

E-mail: cuva_info@nps.gov
Web Site: www.nps.gov/cuva
Formerly: Cuyahoga Valley National Recreation Area
Key Personnel: Supt., Craig Kenkel.
Institution Type/Description: Park Museum.
Hours & Admission Prices: Park: daily. Towpath Trail daily 24 hours; other trails dawn to dusk. Park Visitor Centers: call for hours. No charge; donations accepted. &
Attendance: 2,300,000 (actual)

Brimfield

THE KELSO HOUSE MUSEUM, 4158 State Route 43, Brimfield, OH 44240. Tel.: 330-673-1058.
E-mail: curator@kelsohouse.org
Web Site: www.kelsohouse.org
Key Personnel: Cur., Judi Allen.
Institution Type/Description: Regional History Museum: housed in the former home of William R. Kelso originally the Union Inn & Tavern; built in 1833.
Hours & Admission Prices: Thurs. & Sat. 12-4; other times by appointment. No charge; donations accepted. &
Attendance: 500 (estimated)

Brooklyn

BROOKLYN HISTORICAL SOCIETY, 4442 Ridge Rd., Brooklyn, OH 44144-3353. Mailing Address: P.O. Box 44422, Brooklyn, OH 44144-0422. Tel.: 216-941-0160. Facebook: Brooklyn Historical Society.
E-mail: groundhogsgarden@wowway.com
Key Personnel: Pres. (V), Barbara Stepic; Vice Pres., John Geralds.
Institution Type/Description: Local History Museum.
Hours & Admission Prices: Tues. 10-2. No charge; donations accepted. Closed holiday weekends.
Attendance: 1,200 (estimated)

Bryan

SPANGLER STORE & MUSEUM, 400 N. Portland St., Bryan, OH 43506-1200. Mailing Address: 71P.O. Box, Bryan, OH 43506-0071. Tel.: 419-633-6439, 888-636-4221.
E-mail: info@spanglercandy.com
Institution Type/Description: Company Museum.
Hours & Admission Prices: Memorial Day to Labor Day Mon.-Fri. 10-3; Winter: Wed.-Fri. 10-3; other times by appointment. Museum: no charge. Tours: adults $5, seniors $4, children 6-18 $3; children 5 & under no charge. Closed New Year's Eve & Day; Good Friday; Memorial Day; Independence Day; Thanksgiving & day after; Christmas Eve & Day.

Bucyrus

BUCYRUS HISTORICAL SOCIETY, 202 S. Walnut St., Bucyrus, OH 44820-2326. Mailing Address: P.O. Box 493, Bucyrus, OH 44820-0493. Tel.: 419-562-6386 & 9073.
E-mail: Curator@bucyrushistoricalsociety.org
Web Site: www.bucyrusonline.com/bhs
Key Personnel: C.E.O., Dr. John K. Kurtz; Cur., Mary Ellen Lust; Cur., Don Lust.
Institution Type/Description: Historical Society Museum: housed in 1839 Scroggs Family Home.
Hours & Admission Prices: Mon. 1-4; tours by appointment. No charge; donations accepted. Closed holidays.
Attendance: 600 (estimated)

CRAWFORD AGRICULTURAL MUSEUM, 610 Whetstone St., Bucyrus, OH 44820. Mailing Address: c/o Crawford Antique Farm Machinery Assn., P.O. Box 105, Bucyrus, OH 44820. Tel.: 419-562-1123.
E-mail: rhaas5@columbus.rr.com
Key Personnel: Treas., Dorothy E. Haas; Pres. (V), Michael McCracken.
Institution Type/Description: Agricultural Museum.
Hours & Admission Prices: May-Sept. 1st & 3rd Sun. 1-4, No charge; donations accepted. &

Burton

CENTURY VILLAGE MUSEUM, 14653 E. Park St., Burton, OH 44021. Mailing Address: P.O. Box 153, Burton, OH 44021-0153. Tel.: 440-834-1492. Fax: 440-834-4012.
E-mail: info@geaugahistorical.org

Key Personnel: Pres. (V), Kurt Updegraff; Site Mgr. & Museum Shop Mgr., Cheryl McNulty; Office Mgr., Terry Kwasniewski; Dir. Tours, Rosemary Kneale; Maintenance Supvr., William Troyer.
Institution Type/Description: Historic Village Museum.
Hours & Admission Prices: April-Nov. Public Tours: Sat.-Sun. 1 & 3. School Tours: by appointment. Adults $7, children 6-12 $4; discounts to AAA & Golden Buckeye members; children under 6 no charge.
Attendance: 30,000 (estimated)

Cadiz

CLARK GABLE MUSEUM, 138 Charleston St., Cadiz, OH 43907. Mailing Address: P.O. Box 65, 138 Charleston St., Cadiz, OH 43907. Tel.: 740-942-4989. Fax: 740-942-4989.
E-mail: clarkgablefoundation1901@gmail.com
Web Site: clarkgablefoundation.com
Key Personnel: Exec. Dir. & Museum Shop Mgr., Nan Mattern; Pres. (V), Dr. Gary Barker.
Institution Type/Description: Historic House Museum: housed in the birthplace of Clark Gable.
Hours & Admission Prices: May & Sept. Wed.-Sat. 10-4; June to Labor Day Wed.-Sat. 10-4, Sun. 1:30-4; Oct.-Nov. Wed.-Fri. 10-4. Adults $5.50, seniors $4.75, children $3; discounts to AAM members & groups of 15 or more; members no charge. Closed major holidays. &
Attendance: 1,200 (estimated)

HARRISON COUNTY HISTORY OF COAL MUSEUM, Puskarich Public Library, 200 E. Market St., Cadiz, OH 43907-1214. Tel.: 740-942-2623.
E-mail: puskrich@oplin.lib.oh.us
Institution Type/Description: History Museum.
Hours & Admission Prices: Mon.-Sat. 9-5, Sun. special hours by group appointment. No charge.

Cambridge

GUERNSEY COUNTY MUSEUM, 218 N. 8th St., Cambridge, OH 43725-1840. Mailing Address: P.O. Box 741, Cambridge, OH 43725-0741. Tel.: 740-439-5884.
E-mail: guernseyhistory@yahoo.com
Web Site: www.gcohmuseum.org
Key Personnel: Pres., Madelyn Joseph; Vice Pres., Diane Krall; Sec., Diana Wetzel; Treas., Mary Jane Downerd; Cur., Judy Clay.
Institution Type/Description: General Museum: housed in 1831 McFarland Home.
Hours & Admission Prices: April-Dec. Tues., Thurs. & Sat. 12-3; other times by appointment. Adults $5, children $3.
Attendance: 189 (actual)

NATIONAL MUSEUM OF CAMBRIDGE GLASS, 136 S. Ninth St., Cambridge, OH 43725-2453. Mailing Address: P.O. Box 416, Cambridge, OH 43725-0416. Tel.: 740-432-4245.
E-mail: nocglass@yahoo.com
Web Site: www.cambridgeglass.org
Key Personnel: Chm. (V), Cynthia Arent; Pres. (V), David Ray.
Institution Type/Description: Glass Museum.
Hours & Admission Prices: April-Oct. Wed.-Sat. 9-4, Sun. 12-4. Adults $5, senior citizens & AAA members; children under 12 no charge. Closed Easter; Independence Day. &

Canal Fulton

CANAL FULTON HERITAGE SOCIETY, 116 S. Canal St., Canal Fulton, OH 44614-1317. Tel.: 330-854-3808.
E-mail: cfhs@discovercanalfulton.com
Web Site: www.cfheritage.org
Key Personnel: Pres., Ed Shuman.
Institution Type/Description: Historical & Preservation Society.
Hours & Admission Prices: Museum: May-Oct. Sat.-Sun. 12-4. Admission: $2.
Attendance: 2,000 (estimated)

Canal Winchester

NATIONAL BARBER MUSEUM AND HALL OF FAME, 135 Franklin St., Canal Winchester, OH 43110. Mailing Address: P.O. Box 15, Canal Winchester, OH 43110. Tel.: 614-833-1846 & 837-8400.
E-mail: maippoliti@insight.rr.com
Web Site: www.nationalbarbermuseum.org
Formerly: Ed Jeffers Barber Museum
Key Personnel: Dir., Mike Ippoliti.

Institution Type/Description: History Museum.
Hours & Admission Prices: By appointment. Adults $5, seniors $4, students $3; discounts to groups and AAM & ICOM members. ♿
Attendance: 500 (estimated)

SLATE RUN LIVING HISTORICAL FARM, METRO PARKS, 1375 State Rte. 674 N., Canal Winchester, OH 43110-9406. Tel.: 614-833-1880. Fax: 614-834-1220. TDD: 614-895-6240.
E-mail: info@metroparks.net
Web Site: www.metroparks.net/ParksSlateRunFarm.aspx
Key Personnel: Exec. Dir., John O'Meara.
Institution Type/Description: Historic Site: 1856 house; 1881 barn.
Hours & Admission Prices: April-May & Sept.-Oct. Tues.-Sat. 9-4, Sun. 11-4; June-Aug. Tues.-Thurs. 9-4, Fri.-Sat. 9-6, Sun. 11-6; Nov.-March Wed.-Sat. 9-4, Sun. 11-4. No charge. Closed New Year's Day; Thanksgiving; Christmas. ♿
Attendance: 40,000 (estimated)

Canfield

THE WAR VET MUSEUM, 23 E. Main St., Canfield, OH 44406-1360. Tel.: 330-533-6311.
E-mail: warvetmuseum@gmail.com
Web Site: www.warvetmuseum.org
Key Personnel: Owner & Operator, Lew Speece.
Institution Type/Description: Military Museum.
Hours & Admission Prices: Call for hours. No charge; donations accepted. Closed Easter; Thanksgiving; Christmas.

Canton

CANTON CLASSIC CAR MUSEUM, 123 6th St., S.W., Canton, OH 44702-2111. Mailing Address: 612 Market Ave. S., Canton, OH 44702-2114. Tel.: 330-455-3603. Fax: 330-455-0363.
E-mail: char@cantonclassiccar.org
Web Site: www.cantonclassiccar.org
Key Personnel: Dir., Char Lautzenheiser; Chm. (V), Florence Belden; Pres. (V), Marshall Belden, Jr.; Financial Dir., Timothy Belden; Cur., Norman Munson; Museum Shop Mgr., Lanny Nicholson.
Institution Type/Description: Automobile Museum.
Hours & Admission Prices: Daily 10-5. Adults $7.50, senior citizens $6, children 6-18 $5; discounts to AAA, tour & family groups; members & children under 6 no charge. Closed New Year's Day; Easter; Thanksgiving; Christmas. ♿
Attendance: 10,000 (estimated)

CANTON MUSEUM OF ART, 1001 Market Ave. N., Canton, OH 44702-1075. Tel.: 330-453-7666. Fax: 330-453-1034. Facebook: Canton Museum of Art.
E-mail: info@cantonart.org
Web Site: www.cantonart.org
Key Personnel: Exec. Dir., Max R. Barton, II; Dir. Finance, Kristina Belliveau; Chief Cur., Lynnda Arrasmith; Mgr. Education, Erica Emerson; Dir. Devel., Linda Woit; Dir. Mktg., Rob Lehr; Asst. Registrar, Kayleigh Pisani-Page.
Institution Type/Description: Art Center and Museum.
Hours & Admission Prices: Tues.-Thurs. 10-8, Fri.-Sat. 10-5, Sun. 1-5. Adults $8, senior citizens & college students $6; discounts to AAM members & Blue Star Museum; Thur., children 12 & under and members no charge. Closed New Year's Day; Memorial Day; Independence Day; Labor Day; Thanksgiving; Christmas. ♿
Attendance: 30,000 (estimated)

MCKINLEY PRESIDENTIAL LIBRARY & MUSEUM, 800 McKinley Monument Dr., N.W., Canton, OH 44708-4800. Tel.: 330-455-7043. Fax: 330-455-1137. Facebook: McKinley Presidential Library & Museum.
E-mail: info@mckinleymuseum.org
Web Site: www.mckinleymuseum.org
Key Personnel: Dir., Joyce Yut; Pres. (V), Robert F. Belden; Vice Pres., Don Deitemyer; Asst. Dir. & Cur., Kimberly Kenney; Sec., Robert Leibensperger; Treas., Mark Wright; Asst. Sec., Treas. & Museum Shop Mgr., Cindy Sober; Dir. Planetarium, David Richards; Dir. Education, Chris Kenney; Dir. Science, Lynette Reiner; Volunteer Dir., Carol Paris; Archivist, Mark Holland; Office Mgr., Linnea Schmucker.
Institution Type/Description: History, Science & Comprehensive Family Museum.
Hours & Admission Prices: Mon.-Sat. 9-4, Sun. 12-4. Adults $9, senior citizens $8, children 3-18 $7; discounts to adult groups over 20 & ASTC reciprocity members; museum members & children under 3 no charge. Closed New Year's Day; Easter; Memorial Day; Labor Day; Thanksgiving; Christmas. ♿
Attendance: 51,229 (actual)

NATIONAL FIRST LADIES' LIBRARY, 331 S. Market Ave., Canton, OH 44702-2107. Tel.: 330-452-0876. Fax: 330-445-2008.
E-mail: pkrider@firstladies.org
Web Site: www.firstladies.org
Key Personnel: Exec. Dir., Patricia Krider.
Institution Type/Description: History Museum.
Hours & Admission Prices: Guided Tours: June-Aug. Tues.-Sat. 9:30, 10:30, 12:30, 1:30 & 2:30, Sun. 12:30, 1:30, 2:30; Sept.-May Tues.-Sat. 9:30, 10:30, 12:30, 1:30 & 2:30. Adults $7, senior citizens $6, students $5. Closed New Year's Eve & Day; Presidents' Day; Memorial Day; Independence Day; Labor Day; Thanksgiving; Christmas Eve & Day. ♿
Attendance: 8,500 (estimated)

NATIONAL FOOTBALL MUSEUM, INC., 2121 George Halas Dr., N.W., Canton, OH 44708-2630. Tel.: 330-456-8207. Fax: 330-588-3801. Facebook.
E-mail: jason.aikens@profootballhof.com
Web Site: www.profootballhof.com
Key Personnel: Pres. & Exec. Dir., David Baker; Chm., Randy Hunt; Chief Administration Officer, Steve Strawbridge; C.F.O., Scott Emerick; Exec. Vice Pres. Museums, Selection Process & Chief Communications Officer, Joe Horrigan; Registrar, Christy Davis; Vice Pres. Communications & Chief of Staff, Pete Fierle; Vice Pres. Operations & Facilities, Kevin Shiplet; Education Mgr., Jerry Csaki; Cur. Collections, Jason Aikens; Vice Pres. Exhibits & Museum Svcs., Saleem Choudhry; Archivist, Jon Kendle; Museum Shop Mgr., Michelle Hunt; Communications Asst., Chris Schilling; Dir. Technology, Chad Reese; Hospitality Mgr., Brian Proud.
Institution Type/Description: Professional Football Museum.
Hours & Admission Prices: Memorial Day to Labor Day daily 9-8; Sept.-May daily 9-5. Adults $26, senior citizens 65 & up $22, children 6-12 $19; discount to groups & AAM members; children 6 & under, members and Insider's Club members no charge. Closed Thanksgiving; Christmas. ♿
Attendance: 214,000 (actual)

Carroll

HISTORICAL AIRCRAFT SQUADRON MUSEUM, Fairfield County Airport, 3266 Old Columbus Rd. N.W., Carroll, OH 43112-9723. Tel.: 740-653-4778. Fax: 740-653-2387.
E-mail: dabell31@yahoo.com
Web Site: www.historicalaircraftsquadron.com
Key Personnel: Pres. (V), Eric Meister.
Institution Type/Description: Aviation History Museum.
Hours & Admission Prices: Wed.-Sat. 10-4. No charge.
Attendance: 1,200 (estimated)

Carrollton

ASHTON HOUSE MUSEUM, 120 3rd St., N.W., Carrollton, OH 44615. Mailing Address: c/o John H. & Evelyn L. Ashton Preservation Assoc., 60 W. Main St., Carrollton, OH 44615. Tel.: 330-627-2682.
E-mail: curator@ashtonhousemuseum.com
Web Site: ashtonhousemuseum.com
Key Personnel: Cur., Jim Painting.
Institution Type/Description: History Museum.
Hours & Admission Prices: April-Dec. Wed.-Sat. 10-5, Sun. 1-5; other times by appointment. Adults $3, children 4-12 $2; children 3 & under no charge. Blue Star Museum. ♿

BLUEBIRD FARM TOY MUSEUM, 190 Alamo Rd., Carrollton, OH 44615-9581. Tel.: 330-627-8046.
E-mail: dalexander@ccparkdistrict.org
Institution Type/Description: Toy Museum.
Hours & Admission Prices: Mon.-Fri. 11-3.

MCCOOK HOUSE, CIVIL WAR MUSEUM, 15 S. Lisbon St., Carrollton, OH 44615. Mailing Address: c/o Carrol County Historical Society, P.O. Box 174, Carrollton, OH 44615-0174. Tel.: 330-627-3345, 800-600-7172. Fax: 330-627-5366.
E-mail: info@ohiohistory.org
Web Site: www.ohiohistory.org/museums-and-historic-sites/museum–historic-sites-by-name/mccook-house
Key Personnel: Mgr., Cur. & Museum Shop Mgr., Shirley Anderson; Pres. (V), David McMahon; Vice Pres., Ann Myers; Sec., Diane George; Treas., Jennifer Cramer.
Institution Type/Description: History Museum.
Hours & Admission Prices: Memorial Day to Labor Day & 2nd weekend in Oct. Fri.-Sat. 10-5, Sun. 1-5; Sept. to 1st weekend in Oct. Sat. 10-5, Sun. 1-5; tours

by appointment. Adults $3, children $1; Carroll Co. Historical Society & Ohio Historical Society members no charge.
Attendance: 1,195 (actual)

SUSIE'S MUSEUM OF CHILDHOOD, Bluebird Farm Park, 190 Alamo Rd., Carrollton, OH 44615. Tel.: 330-627-8046. Fax: 330-627-8046.
E-mail: info@ccparkdistrict.org
Web Site: www.ccparkdistrict.org
Institution Type/Description: History Museum.
Hours & Admission Prices: April-Dec. Tues.-Sun. 11-4.

Celina

MERCER COUNTY HISTORICAL MUSEUM, THE RILEY HOME, 130 E. Market, Celina, OH 45822-1731. Mailing Address: P.O. Box 512, Celina, OH 45822-1731. Tel.: 419-678-2614.
E-mail: histalig@bright.net
Key Personnel: Pres. (V), Joyce L. Alig.
Institution Type/Description: Historical Society Museum: housed in 1896 the Riley home.
Hours & Admission Prices: By appointment only. No charge.
Attendance: 6,000 (actual)

Centerville

CENTERVILLE - WASHINGTON TOWNSHIP HISTORICAL SOCIETY & ASAHEL WRIGHT COMMUNITY CENTER, 26 N. Main St., Centerville, OH 45459-4619. Tel.: 937-291-2223. Fax: 937-432-9296.
Web Site: www.mvcc.net/centerville/histsoc
Key Personnel: Exec. Dir., Vickie Bondi; Bookkeeper, Peggy Brooker; Cur., Susan Ross; Coord. Education, Cheryl Meyer.
Institution Type/Description: Historic House Museum: housed in the former home of the Wright Brothers great uncle.
Hours & Admission Prices: House: Tues.-Fri. 12-4. No charge; donations accepted. Closed New Year's Day; Thanksgiving; Christmas.
Attendance: 1,500 (estimated)

CENTERVILLE - WASHINGTON TOWNSHIP HISTORICAL SOCIETY & WALTON HOUSE MUSEUM, 89 W. Franklin St., Centerville, OH 45459-4735. Tel.: 937-433-0123. Fax: 937-424-4629.
E-mail: cwths@sbcglobal.net
Web Site: www.mvcc.net/centerville/histsoc
Key Personnel: Dir., Vickie Bondi; Pres., Susan Ross.
Institution Type/Description: History Museum.
Hours & Admission Prices: Tues.-Fri. 12-4, Sat. by appointment. No charge; donations accepted.
Attendance: 5,000 (estimated)

Chagrin Falls

CHAGRIN FALLS HISTORICAL SOCIETY, 87 E. Washington St., Chagrin Falls, OH 44022-3001. Tel.: 440-247-4695.
E-mail: chaghist@gmail.com
Web Site: www.chagrinhistorical.org
Key Personnel: Pres., John Bourisseau; Dir., Jane Babinsky; Cur., Pat E. Zalba; Photograph Collection, Zo Sykora; Librarian, Laura Gorretta; Volunteer Coord., Jean Hood.
Institution Type/Description: Historical Society Museum.
Hours & Admission Prices: Museum & Research Center: Thurs. 2-7, Sat. 11-3; other times by appointment. Research: $10 per day; members no charge. Closed holidays.
Attendance: 2,500 (estimated)

Chillicothe

ADENA MANSION AND GARDENS, 847 Adena Rd., Chillicothe, OH 45601-1380. Tel.: 740-772-1500, 800-319-7248. Fax: 740-775-2746.
E-mail: info@adenamansion.com
Web Site: www.adenamansion.com
Formerly: Adena State Memorial, The Home of Thomas Worthington
Key Personnel: C.E.O., Ed Behanna; Dir., Kathy Styer.
Institution Type/Description: Historic House Restoration: 1806-1807 original mansion of Ohio's sixth governor & first senator, Thomas Worthington.
Hours & Admission Prices: April-Oct. Wed.-Sat. 9-5, Sun. 12-5; Nov.-March for special events only. Adults $8, children 6-12 $4; discounts to senior citizens &

AAM members; OHS members and children 5 & under no charge. Closed Easter.
Attendance: 11,000 (actual)

THE FRIENDS OF LUCY HAYES HERITAGE CENTER, 90 W. Sixth St., Chillicothe, OH 45601-3838. Mailing Address: P.O. Box 1790, Chillicothe, OH 45601-5790. Tel.: 740-775-5829 (center). Fax: 740-775-5829.
E-mail: lucy@lucyhayes.org
Web Site: www.lucyhayes.org
Key Personnel: Pres. (V), Paul Thacker; Treas., Linda Barrett; Sec., Melody Smith.
Institution Type/Description: General Museum: restored birthplace of First Lady Lucy Hayes.
Hours & Admission Prices: April-Sept. Mon. 10-2, Sat. 1-4; other times by appointment. Adults $4, children $2; members no charge. Closed Good Friday; Memorial Day weekend.
Attendance: 502 (actual)

HOPEWELL CULTURE NATIONAL HISTORICAL PARK, 16062 State Rte. 104, Chillicothe, OH 45601-9701. Tel.: 740-774-1126. Fax: 740-774-1140. Facebook: Hopewell Culture National Historical Park.
E-mail: hocu_superintendent@nps.gov
Web Site: www.nps.gov/hocu
Formerly: Mound City Group National Monument
Institution Type/Description: Park Museum: 200 B.C.-500 A.D., Hopewell Indian earthwork.
Hours & Admission Prices: Visitor's Center: Memorial Day to Labor Day daily 8:30-6; Sept.-May daily 8:30-5. No charge; donations accepted. Closed New Year's Day; Thanksgiving; Christmas.
Attendance: 30,000 (actual)

JAMES M. THOMAS TELEPHONE MUSEUM, 68 E. Main St., Chillicothe, OH 45601. Tel.: 740-772-8200.
Institution Type/Description: History Museum.
Hours & Admission Prices: Mon.-Fri. 8:30-4:30.

ROSS COUNTY HISTORICAL SOCIETY, INC., 45 W. 5th St., Chillicothe, OH 45601-3227. Tel.: 740-772-1936. Facebook: Ross County Historical Society Inc.
E-mail: info@rosscountyhistorical.org
Web Site: www.rosscountyhistorical.org
Key Personnel: C.E.O., Dir. & Museum Shop Mgr., Thomas G. Kuhn; Pres. (V), Ronald Bowen.
Institution Type/Description: General Museum.
Hours & Admission Prices: Jan.-March by appointment only; April-Dec. Tues.-Sat. 1-5. Adults $4, senior citizens & students $2; discounts to AAM, ICOM & AAA members; members & Ross County School classes no charge. Closed major holidays.
Attendance: 5,000 (actual)

Cincinnati

AMERICAN CLASSICAL MUSIC HALL OF FAME, Mailing Address: 1 W. 4th St., Ste. 1550, Cincinnati, OH 45202. Tel.: 513-621-3263.
E-mail: classicalhalloffame@gmail.com
Web Site: classicalwalkoffame.org
Key Personnel: Chm., Chris Phelps; Sec., Lindsey NeCamp; Treas., James Donnellon.
Institution Type/Description: Virtual Museum.

AMERICAN SIGN MUSEUM, 1330 Monmouth St., Cincinnati, OH 45225. Tel.: 513-541-6366. Fax: 513-701-2190.
E-mail: info@americansignmuseum.org
Web Site: www.signmuseum.org
Key Personnel: Founder, Tod Swormstedt; Mng. Dir., Brad Huberman.
Institution Type/Description: Sign Museum.
Hours & Admission Prices: Museum: Wed.-Sat. 10-4, Sun. 12-4. Guided Tours: Wed.-Sat. 11am & 2pm, sun. 2pm. Adults $15, seniors, students & military $10; discounts to groups; children 12 & under no charge. Closed New Year's Day; Thanksgiving; Christmas Eve & Day.
Attendance: 2,196 (actual)

THE BETTS HOUSE, 416 Clark St., Cincinnati, OH 45203-1423. Tel.: 513-651-0734.
E-mail: info@thebettshouse.org
Web Site: thebettshouse.org

Key Personnel: House Mgr., Cora Arney; Pres. (V), Carrie VanDerzee; Vice Pres. (V), Cynthia Cole; Treas., Kinney Moore.
Institution Type/Description: Historic Building: 1804 farm house on original foundation with mid- & late-19th-century additions.
Hours & Admission Prices: Wed. & Fri.-Sat. 12-5; other times by appointment. Adults $5, children $2; members no charge. Closed federal holidays.
Attendance: 1,400 (estimated)

CARY COTTAGE, Clovernook Center for the Blind and Visually Impaired, 7000 Hamilton Ave., Cincinnati, OH 45231-5240. Tel.: 513-522-3860. Fax: 513-728-3946. TDD: 513-522-3860.
E-mail: clovernook@clovernook.org
Web Site: www.clovernook.org
Institution Type/Description: Historic House: 1832 home of poets Alice & Phoebe Cary.
Hours & Admission Prices: Tours: Mon.-Fri. by appointment. No charge; donations accepted.
Attendance: 100 (estimated)

CINCINNATI ART GALLERIES, 225 E. Sixth St., 1st Fl., Cincinnati, OH 45202-3209. Tel.: 513-381-2128. Facebook.
E-mail: hausrath@cincyart.com
Web Site: www.cincyart.com
Institution Type/Description: Art Gallery.
Hours & Admission Prices: Mon.-Fri. 9-4, Sat. 10-4. No charge. &

CINCINNATI ART MUSEUM, 953 Eden Park Dr., Cincinnati, OH 45202-1596. Tel.: 513-721-2787. Fax: 513-721-0129.
E-mail: information@cincyart.org
Web Site: www.cincinnatiartmuseum.org
Key Personnel: Dir., Cameron Kitchin; C.F.O., Carol Edmondson; Chm. (V), Jon R. Moeller; Pres. (V), Andrew E. DeWitt; Chief Administrative Officer, Dave Linnenberg; Asst. to the Dir., Kristen Vincenty; Dir. Devel., Kirby Neumann; Dir. Learning & Interpretation, Emily Holtrop; Chief Cur. and Cur. Fashion Arts & Textiles, Cynthia Amneus; Cur. Prints, Kristin Spangenberg; Cur. American Art, Julie Aronson; Cur. Decorative Art & Design, Amy Dehan; Cur. Asian Art, Hou-mei Sung; Assoc. Cur. European Paintings, Sculpture & Drawings, Peter Bell; Cur. South Asian Art, Islamic Art & Antiquities, Ainsley Cameron; Assoc. Cur. Photography, Nathaniel Stein; Museum Shop Mgr., Connie Newman.
Institution Type/Description: Art Museum.
Hours & Admission Prices: Tues.-Wed. & Fri.-Sun. 11-5, Thurs. 11-8. General admission & parking: no charge. Special Exhibitions: pricing may vary. Closed New Year's Day; Independence Day; Thanksgiving; Christmas. &
Attendance: 272,352 (actual)

CINCINNATI AVIATION HERITAGE SOCIETY & MUSEUM, 262 Wilmer Ave., Rm. 26, Cincinnati, OH 45226. Tel.: 513-321-0492.
E-mail: history@cahslunken.com
Institution Type/Description: History Museum.
Hours & Admission Prices: Mon. & Fri. 10-2.

CINCINNATI FIRE MUSEUM, 315 W. Court St., Cincinnati, OH 45202-1073. Tel.: 513-621-5553. Fax: 513-621-1456.
E-mail: info@cincyfiremuseum.com
Web Site: www.cincyfiremuseum.com
Institution Type/Description: History & Fire-Fighting Museum: housed in 1906 fire-house.
Hours & Admission Prices: Tues.-Sat. 10-4. Adults $8, senior citizens 65 & over $7, children 7-17 $6; discounts to AAM members & groups; children 6 & under and members no charge. Closed major holidays. &
Attendance: 20,000 (actual)

CINCINNATI MUSEUM CENTER AT UNION TERMINAL, 1301 Western Ave., Cincinnati, OH 45203-1123. Mailing Address: 250 W. Court St., Ste. 300E, Cincinnati, OH 45202. Tel.: 513-287-7000, 800-733-2077; 800-750-0750 (TTY). Facebook: Cincy Museum.
E-mail: information@cincymuseum.org
Web Site: www.cincymuseum.org
Key Personnel: C.E.O. & Pres., Elizabeth Pierce; Chm., Edward Diller; Vice Pres. Finance & Admin. and C.F.O., Jill Berkemeier; Vice Pres. Featured Experiences, David Duszynski; Asst. Vice Pres. Collections & Research, Dr. Glenn Storrs; Chief Learning Officer, Whitney Owens; Dir. Volunteer Svcs., Angie Smorey; Assoc. Vice Pres. Facility Operations, Steve Terheiden; Registrar, Jennifer Jensen; Dir. Exhibits, Chris Novy; Dir. Nature Preserve, Christopher Bedel.
Institution Type/Description: History Museum: housed in a 1933 Art Deco building. A National Historic Landmark.

Hours & Admission Prices: Cincinnati Union Terminal under renovation until Oct. 2018. CHM & MNH are closed. Mon.-Sat. 10-5, Sun. 11-6. Adults $10.50, senior citizens 60 & over and children 3-12 $9.50; discount to AAM & ICOM members; members no charge. Closed Thanksgiving; Christmas. &
Attendance: 1,449,000 (actual)

CINCINNATI REDS HALL OF FAME & MUSEUM, 100 Joe Nuxhall Way, Cincinnati, OH 45202. Tel.: 513-765-7000. Fax: 513-765-7847.
E-mail: rwalls@reds.com
Web Site: redsmuseum.org
Key Personnel: Exec. Dir., Rick Walls; Pres. (V), Tyler McMullen; Museum Shop Mgr., Karen Mahon.
Institution Type/Description: Sports Museum.
Hours & Admission Prices: Daily 10-5; extended hours on Reds game days. Adults $10, seniors 60 & over and students $8, active military & veterans $6; children 4 & under no charge. Closed New Year's Day; Thanksgiving; Christmas.
Attendance: 80,000 (actual)

CINCINNATI SKIRBALL MUSEUM HEBREW UNION COLLEGE-JEWISH INSTITUTE OF RELIGION, 3101 Clifton Ave., Cincinnati, OH 45220-2488. Tel.: 513-487-3098. Fax: 513-221-0321. Facebook.
E-mail: jmendelson@huc.edu
Web Site: www.huc.edu/museums/cn
Key Personnel: Dir., Abby Schwartz.
Institution Type/Description: Art and Jewish History Museum.
Hours & Admission Prices: Tues. & Thurs. 11-4, Sun. 1-5; other times by appointment. No charge; donations accepted. &
Attendance: 1,500 (actual)

CINCINNATI ZOO & BOTANICAL GARDEN, 3400 Vine St., Cincinnati, OH 45220-1333. Tel.: 513-281-4700, ext. 0 & 559-7724. Fax: 513-487-3336. TDD: 513-559-2730.
E-mail: info@cincinnatizoo.org
Web Site: www.cincinnatizoo.org
Key Personnel: Exec. Dir., Thane Maynard; C.O.O., Dave Jenike; Vice Pres. Mktg. & Communications, Chad Yelton; Veterinarian, Mark Campbell, D.V.M.; Dir. Human Resources, Jeff Walton; Dir. Membership, T.R. Amrine.
Institution Type/Description: Zoo.
Hours & Admission Prices: Winter: daily 10-5; Summer: daily 10-6. General Admission: adults $19, seniors 62 & over and children 2-12 $13. Parking $10; discounts to groups of 25 or more and AAM & ICOM members; museum members & AZA members no charge. &
Attendance: 1,300,000 (estimated)

CIVIC GARDEN CENTER OF GREATER CINCINNATI, 2715 Reading Rd., Cincinnati, OH 45206-1617. Tel.: 513-221-0981. Fax: 513-221-0961.
E-mail: info@civicgardencenter.org
Web Site: www.civicgardencenter.org
Key Personnel: Exec. Dir., Vickie Ciotti; Coord. Youth Education, Mary Dudley; Horticulturist, Bennett Dowling; Exec. Asst., Terry Houston; Coord. Community Gardens, Greg Potter; Vol. Coord., Jan Simms.
Institution Type/Description: Horticultural Center.
Hours & Admission Prices: Mon.-Fri. 9-5, Sat. 9-4. No charge; donations accepted. &
Attendance: 10,000 (estimated)

THE CONTEMPORARY ARTS CENTER, 44 E. Sixth St., Cincinnati, OH 45202-3998. Tel.: 513-345-8400. Fax: 513-721-7418.
E-mail: admin@cacmail.org
Web Site: www.contemporaryartscenter.org
Key Personnel: Dir., Raphaela Platow.
Institution Type/Description: Art Museum.
Hours & Admission Prices: Wed.-Fri. 10-9, Sat.-Mon. 10-4. No charge. &
Attendance: 177,000 (actual)

DAAP GALLERIES, University of Cincinnati, 2624 Clifton Ave., Cincinnati, OH 45221. Mailing Address: Univ. of Cincinnati, P.O. Box 210016, Cincinnati, OH 45221-0016. Tel.: 513-556-2839. Fax: 513-556-3288.
E-mail: daapgalleries@us.edu
Web Site: www.daap.uc.edu/Gallery/gallery.htm
Key Personnel: Collections Asst., Jonathan Nolting; Mgr. Meyers Gallery, Rob Anderson; Mgr. University Galleries on Sycamore, Maria Seda-Reeder.
Institution Type/Description: Art Gallery.

Hours & Admission Prices: Reed Gallery & Meyers Gallery: Sun.-Thurs. 10-5. University Galleries on Sycamore Tues.-Fri. 11-5, Sat. 11-4. No charge. Closed university holidays. &
Attendance: 10,000 (estimated)

THE DELHI HISTORICAL SOCIETY MUSEUM, 468 Anderson Ferry Rd., Cincinnati, OH 45238-5281. Tel.: 513-451-4313. Fax: 513-451-4300.
E-mail: info.delhi.hs@gmail.com
Web Site: delhihistoricalsociety.org
Institution Type/Description: Historical Society Museum; formerly the Joe Witterstaetter Homestead, built in the 1880s.
Hours & Admission Prices: Tues., Thurs. & Sun. 12-3.

GREATER CINCINNATI POLICE MUSEUM, 308 Reading Rd., Cincinnati, OH 45202. Mailing Address: 308 Reading Rd., Ste. 201, Cincinnati, OH 45202. Tel.: 513-300-3664.
E-mail: director@police-museum.org
Web Site: www.gcphs.com
Key Personnel: Dir., Lt. Stephen R. Kramer, (Ret.); Cur., Richard W. Gross.
Institution Type/Description: History Museum.
Hours & Admission Prices: Tues., Thurs. & Sat. 10-4. No charge; donations accepted. &
Attendance: 1,200 (estimated)

HARRIET BEECHER STOWE HOUSE, 2950 Gilbert Ave., Cincinnati, OH 45206. Tel.: 513-751-0651.
E-mail: friendsharrietbeecherstowe@gmail.com
Web Site: www.stowehousecincy.org
Institution Type/Description: Historic House Museum: housed in the former of Harriet Beecher Stowe, author of Uncle Tom's Cabin.
Hours & Admission Prices: March 4 to Dec. 10 Fri.-Sun. 12-4; group tours & other times by appointment. Adults $4, children 6-18 $2. Closed Federal holidays.
Attendance: 2,600 (actual)

INDIAN HILL HISTORICAL SOCIETY, 8100 Given Rd., Cincinnati, OH 45243-1520. Tel.: 513-891-1873. Fax: 513-891-1873.
E-mail: ihhist@cinci.rr.com
Web Site: www.indianhill.org
Key Personnel: Pres. (V), Susan Holzapfel; Admin., Lawre Bonekemper.
Institution Type/Description: Local History Museum.
Hours & Admission Prices: By appointment only. No charge. &
Attendance: 500 (estimated)

KROHN CONSERVATORY, 1501 Eden Park Dr., Cincinnati, OH 45202-6030. Tel.: 513-421-5707. TDD: 513-352-3380.
E-mail: andrea.schepmann@cincinnati.oh.gov
Web Site: www.cineypark.com
Key Personnel: Dir. & Museum Shop Mgr., Andrea Schepmann.
Institution Type/Description: Botanical Garden & Conservatory.
Hours & Admission Prices: Tues.-Sun. 10-5; special evening hours during Christmas Show. Adults $4, children 5-12 $2; admission prices may change with seasonal shows.
Attendance: 185,000 (actual)

MOUNT AIRY ARBORETUM, 5083 Colerain Ave., Cincinnati, OH 45223-1072. Tel.: 513-541-8176 or 2510. Fax: 513-541-8176.
E-mail: paula.miller@cincinnati-oh.gov
Web Site: www.cincinnati-oh.gov/parks
Key Personnel: Supvr. Mt. Airy, Larry Parker.
Institution Type/Description: Botanical Garden: located on the site of Mount Airy Forest, the first municipal reforestation project in the U.S., started in 1911.
Hours & Admission Prices: Forest: daily 6am-10pm. Arboretum daily 7:30-dark. No charge. All facilities require reservations; call 513-352-4080.

NATIONAL UNDERGROUND RAILROAD FREEDOM CENTER, 50 E. Freedom Way, Cincinnati, OH 45202. Tel.: 513-333-7500, 877-648-4838 (toll free).
E-mail: communications@nurfc.org
Web Site: www.freedomcenter.org
Key Personnel: Vice Pres. & Provost, Michael Battle, D.Min.; Dir. Museum Experience, Richard Cooper; Dir. Devel. Opers., Sherri Fillingham; Dir. Institutional Effectiveness, Yolanda Sherrer; Dir. Mktg. & Communications, Jamie Glavic.
Institution Type/Description: History Museum.
Hours & Admission Prices: Tues.-Sat. 11-5. Adults $15, seniors 60 & over $13, children 3-12 $10.50; discounts to groups of 10 or more with reservation; children under 3 no charge. Closed Thanksgiving; Christmas. &

STUDIO SAN GIUSEPPE ART GALLERY, College of Mt. St. Joseph, 5701 Delhi Rd., Cincinnati, OH 45233-1670. Tel.: 513-244-4314. Fax: 513-244-4942.
E-mail: Jerry_Bellas@mail.msj.edu
Web Site: www.msj.edu/about/facilities/studio-san-giuseppe-art-gallery/
Key Personnel: Dir., Gerald M. Bellas.
Institution Type/Description: Art Gallery: housed in the Dorothy Meyer Ziv Art Building.
Hours & Admission Prices: Academic Year: Mon.-Fri. 10-5, Sat.-Sun. 1-5. No charge. Closed major holidays. &
Attendance: 5,000 (estimated)

TAFT MUSEUM OF ART, 316 Pike St., Cincinnati, OH 45202-4293. Tel.: 513-241-0343. Fax: 513-241-7762.
E-mail: taftmuseum@taftmuseum.org
Web Site: www.taftmuseum.org
Key Personnel: Pres. & C.E.O., Deborah Emont Scott; Dir. Finance, Beth K. Siler; Dir. Mktg. & Public Rels., Emma Caro; Dir. Curatorial Affairs, Lynne D. Ambrosini, Ph.D.; Dir. Devel., Lindsey NeCamp; Mgr. School & Docent Programs, Lisa Morrisette; Mgr. Events, Jenna Wilson; Assoc. Cur., Tammy Muente; Chief Preparator & Exhibition Designer, Mark Rohling; Registrar, Joan C. Hendricks; Mgr. Visitor Experience, Brooke Sherritt.
Institution Type/Description: Art Museum: housed in 1820 Baum-Longworth-Taft House.
Hours & Admission Prices: Tues.-Fri. 11-4, Sat.-Sun. 11-5. Adults $10, youth 6-17 $5; discounts to AAM & ICOM members; members, children 5 & under and Sun. no charge. No charge on Sunday. Closed New Year's Day; Independence Day; Thanksgiving; Christmas. &
Attendance: 45,665 (actual)

TRAILSIDE NATURE CENTER, 3400 Brookline Ave., Cincinnati, OH 45220. Mailing Address: 950 Eden Park Drive, Cincinnati, OH 45202. Tel.: 513-751-3679.
Web Site: www.cincinnatiparks.com
Formerly: Trailside Nature Center & Museum
Key Personnel: Dir. Parks, Wade Walcutt; CIT Coordinator, Erin Morris.
Institution Type/Description: Park Museum.
Hours & Admission Prices: No charge; donations accepted. Closed holidays. &
Attendance: 20,000 (estimated)

21C MUSEUM HOTEL CINCINNATI, 609 Walnut St., Cincinnati, OH 45202. Tel.: 513-578-6600.
E-mail: mhurst@21cMuseum.org
Web Site: www.21cmuseumhotels.com/cincinnati/
Key Personnel: Museum Mgr., Michael Hurst.
Institution Type/Description: Contemporary Art Gallery.
Hours & Admission Prices: See website for hours. No charge.

WILLIAM HOWARD TAFT NATIONAL HISTORIC SITE, 2038 Auburn Ave., Cincinnati, OH 45219-3025. Tel.: 513-684-3262. Fax: 513-684-3627.
Web Site: www.nps.gov/wiho/index.html
Key Personnel: Supt., Brenda M. Waters; Museum Shop Mgr. & Chief of Interpretation & Resources Mgmt., Kerry Wood.
Institution Type/Description: Historic House Museum: c.1857 birthplace & boyhood home of William Howard Taft, 27th President of the U.S. & 10th Chief Justice.
Hours & Admission Prices: Daily 8-4. No charge; donations accepted. Closed New Year's Day; Thanksgiving; Christmas. &
Attendance: 24,500 (actual)

XAVIER UNIVERSITY ART GALLERY, 1658 Herald Ave., Cincinnati, OH 45207-1035. Tel.: 513-745-3811 & 1919. Fax: 513-745-1098. TDD: 513-745-3811.
E-mail: uetz@xavier.edu
Web Site: xavier.edu/art/gallery.cfm
Key Personnel: Dir., Katherine Uetz.
Institution Type/Description: Art Gallery.
Hours & Admission Prices: Academic Year: Mon.-Fri. 10-4. No charge. Closed official & university holidays. &
Attendance: 1,800

Cleveland

ARTISTS ARCHIVES OF THE WESTERN RESERVE, 1834 E. 123rd St., Cleveland, OH 44106-1910. Tel.: 216-721-9020. Facebook: @ArtistsArchivesoftheWesternReserve.
E-mail: info@artistsarchives.org
Web Site: www.artistsarchives.org

Key Personnel: Exec. Dir., Mindy Tousley; Pres. (V), Philip Bautista; Gallery Coord. & Archival Asst., Megan Alves.
Institution Type/Description: Regional Visual Art.
Hours & Admission Prices: Wed.-Fri. 10-4, Sat. 12-4. No charge; donations accepted. &
Attendance: 5,000 (actual)

ARTNEO, 1305 W. 80th St., Cleveland, OH 44102-6204. Tel.: 216-227-9507.
E-mail: info@artneo.org
Web Site: artneo.org
Formerly: Cleveland Artists Foundation at Beck Center for the Arts
Key Personnel: Cur. & Collection Mgr., Christopher Richards; Pres. Bd. Dirs., Sabine Kretzschmar.
Institution Type/Description: Art Museum.
Hours & Admission Prices: Summer: Tues.-Fri. 1-5; Sept.-May Tues.-Thurs. 1-5, Fri.-Sat. 1-8. No charge; donations accepted. Closed major holidays. &
Attendance: 30,000 (estimated)

THE CHILDREN'S MUSEUM OF CLEVELAND, 3813 Euclid Ave., Cleveland, OH 44115. Tel.: 216-791-7114. Fax: 216-791-8838. Facebook: @CMCCleveland; Twitter: @CMC_Cleveland.
E-mail: info@cmcleveland.org
Web Site: cmcleveland.org
Formerly: Rainbow Children's Museum and TRW Early Learning Center
Key Personnel: Exec. Dir., Maria Camparnelli; Chm. Bd., Maria Cashy; Dir. Exhibitions, Karen Katz; Dir. Visitor Svcs., Collections Mgr. & Registrar, Shannon Post; Dir. Facilities, Leland Merk; Membership Coord., Lisa Merk; Dir. Education & Lead Grant Writer, Kelsey Tarase; Volunteer Coord., Amanda Halmes; Maintenance Supvr., Chris Beal.
Institution Type/Description: Children's Museum.
Hours & Admission Prices: Mon. & Wed.-Fri. 9-4; Sat. 10-5, Sun. noon-5. Admission $12; members & children under 1 no charge. Closed major holidays. &
Attendance: 96,331 (actual)

CLEVELAND BOTANICAL GARDEN, 11030 East Blvd., Cleveland, OH 44106-1706. Tel.: 216-721-1600, ext. 194. Fax: 216-721-2056.
E-mail: info@bcgarden.org
Web Site: www.cbgarden.org
Key Personnel: Interim Pres. & C.E.O., Paul Abbey; Exec. Asst., Deborah Ryan; Interim Chief Advancement Officer, Tara Turner; Vice. Pres. Education, Marian Williams; Vice Pres. Community Engagement, Paul Spector; Vice Pres. Opers., Patricia Roberts; Vice Pres. Brand Experience, Dave Lowery; Dir. Horticulture & Conservation, Roger Gettig; Dir. Finance, Jim Ansberry; Dir. Facilities, Mike Logsdon.
Institution Type/Description: Botanical Garden.
Hours & Admission Prices: Tues. & Thurs.-Sat. 10-5, Wed. 10-9 Sun. 12-5. Adults $12, children 3-12 $8; children 2 & under and members no charge. Closed New Year's Day; Thanksgiving; Christmas. &
Attendance: 140,000 (actual)

CLEVELAND GRAYS ARMORY MUSEUM, 1234 Bolivar Rd., Cleveland, OH 44115. Tel.: 216-621-5938. Fax: 216-621-5941. Facebook: Cleveland Grays Armory Museum.
E-mail: info@graysarmory.com
Web Site: www.graysarmory.com
Key Personnel: Pres. (V), William A. Roediger.
Institution Type/Description: Historic Building: built in 1893. Listed on the National Register of Historic Places.
Hours & Admission Prices: By appointment. Donations accepted. &

CLEVELAND HISTORY CENTER, 10825 East Blvd., Cleveland, OH 44106-1788. Tel.: 216-721-5722. Fax: 216-721-0891. Twitter.
E-mail: info@wrhs.org
Web Site: www.wrhs.org
Formerly: Western Reserve Historical Society History Center
Key Personnel: Dir., Angie Lowrie; Bd. Chm. (V), Glenn G. Anderson, Jr.; Sr. Vice Pres. Research & Publications, John Grabowski; Pres. & C.E.O., Kelly Falcone-Hull; CFO, Hilary Frank Beatrez.
Institution Type/Description: History Museum.
Hours & Admission Prices: Cleveland History Center: Tues.-Sat. 10-5, Sun. 12-5. Research Library: Thurs.-Sat. 10-5. Adults $10, seniors 62 & over $9, children 3-12 $5; members and children 2 & under no charge. Closed New Year's Day; Easter; Memorial Day; Independence Day; Labor Day; Thanksgiving; Christmas Eve & Day. &
Attendance: 70,500 (actual)

CLEVELAND METROPARKS OUTDOOR EDUCATION DIVISION, 4101 Fulton Parkway, Cleveland, OH 44144. Tel.: 216-635-3200. Facebook: @clevelandmetroparks; Instagram & Twitter: @clevemetroparks.
E-mail: generalinfo@clevelandmetroparks.com
Web Site: www.clevelandmetroparks.com
Key Personnel: CEO, Brian M. Zimmerman; CFO, Karen Fegan; COO, Joseph Roszak; Chief Devel. Officer, Natalie Ronayne; Chief Mktg. Officer, Kelly Manderfield; Exec. Dir., Cleveland Metroparks Zoo, Christopher Kuhar; Exec. Dir., Golf Opers., Sean McHugh; Ranger Chief, John Betori.
Institution Type/Description: Nature Center & Conservation Area.
Hours & Admission Prices: Trails: daily 6am-11pm. Nature Centers: daily 9:30-5. No charge. Nature Centers: closed New Year's Day; Easter; Thanksgiving; Christmas. &
Attendance: 473,508 (estimated)

CLEVELAND METROPARKS ZOO, 3900 Wildlife Way, Cleveland, OH 44109-3132. Tel.: 216-661-6500, ext. 0. Fax: 216-661-3312.
E-mail: zooinfo@clevelandmetroparks.com
Web Site: www.clemetzoo.com
Key Personnel: Dir. Facility Operations, Christopher Lowe; Dir. Revenue, Tim Savona; Dir. Conservation Education, Victoria Searles; Exec. Dir. Zoo Society, Elizabeth Fowler; Dir. Animal & Veterinary Programs, Andi Kornak.
Institution Type/Description: Zoo.
Hours & Admission Prices: Memorial Day-Labor Day Mon.-Fri. 10-5, Sat.-Sun. & holidays 10-7; Sept.-May daily 10-5. Zoo & Rainforest: adults 12 & over $13.25, seniors 62 & over $12.25, youth 2-11 $9.25; Mon. residents of Cuyahoga County & Hinckley Township, children under 2 no charge. Closed New Year's Day; Christmas. &
Attendance: 1,123,660 (actual)

THE CLEVELAND MUSEUM OF ART, 11150 East Blvd., Cleveland, OH 44106-1797. Tel.: 216-421-7350 or 1-877-262-4748. Fax: 216-421-0411. TDD: 216-421-0018.
E-mail: info@clevelandart.org
Web Site: www.clevelandart.org
Key Personnel: Dir. & Pres., William M. Griswold; Chm. (V), Peter Raskind.
Institution Type/Description: Art Museum.
Hours & Admission Prices: Tues.-Sun. 10-5. No charge; donations accepted. Closed New Year's Day; Independence Day; Thanksgiving; Christmas. &
Attendance: 308,000 (actual)

THE CLEVELAND MUSEUM OF NATURAL HISTORY, 1 Wade Oval Dr., University Circle, Cleveland, OH 44106-1767. Tel.: 216-231-4600. Fax: 216-231-5919. TDD: 216-231-7777; Facebook: Cleveland Museum of Natural History.
E-mail: tconnors@cmnh.org
Web Site: www.cmnh.org
Key Personnel: Exec. Dir. & C.E.O., Evalyn Gates, Ph.D.; Chief Mktg. & Communications Officer, Thomas E. Connors; C.F.O.O., Todd Welki; Cur. Invertebrate Paleontology, Dr. Joseph Hannibal; Cur. Vertebrate Zoology, Dr. Timothy Matson; Cur. Paleobotany & Paleoecology, Dr. Denise Su; Cur. Vertebrate Paleontology, Dr. Michael Ryan; Cur. Mineralogy, Dr. David Saja; Cur. Ornithology, Dr. Andrew Jones; Dir. Education, Carin Miller; Dir. Conservation & Cur. Botany, James Bissell, L.H.D.; Dir. Wildlife Resources, Harvey Webster; Cur. Archaeology, Dr. Brian Redmond; Dir. GreenCityBlueLake Institute, David Beach.
Institution Type/Description: Natural History Museum.
Hours & Admission Prices: Mon.-Tues. & Thurs.-Sat. 10-5, Wed. 10-10, Sun. 12-5. Adults $14, youth, college students & senior citizens $10; discount to AAM members; children 2 & under & members no charge. Planetarium: $5. Closed New Year's Day; Memorial Day; Independence Day; Labor Day; Thanksgiving; Christmas. &
Attendance: 263,000 (actual)

CLEVELAND POLICE HISTORICAL SOCIETY & MUSEUM, 1300 Ontario St., Cleveland, OH 44113-1600. Tel.: 216-623-5055 & 5056. Fax: 216-623-5145. Facebook: @clevelandpolicemuseum.
E-mail: clevelandpolicemuseum@gmail.com
Web Site: www.clevelandpolicemuseum.org
Key Personnel: Museum Shop Mgr., Geraldine Diemert; Office Mgr., Marilyn Jech; Pres. (V), Tom Armelli.
Institution Type/Description: Police Museum: presently housed in Cleveland police headquarters.
Hours & Admission Prices: Mon.-Fri. 10-4. No charge; donations accepted. Closed New Year's Day; Memorial Day; Independence Day; Labor Day; Thanksgiving; Christmas. &
Attendance: 4,108 (actual)

CRAWFORD AUTO AVIATION MUSEUM OF THE WESTERN RESERVE HISTORICAL SOCIETY, 10825 East Blvd., Cleveland, OH 44106-1703. Tel.: 216-721-5722. Fax: 216-721-0891.
E-mail: alowrie@wrhs.org
Web Site: www.wrhs.org
Key Personnel: Pres. & C.E.O., Kelly Falcone-Hall; Cur. Transportation History, Derek Moore; Dir. Cleveland History Ctr., Angie Lowrie; CFO, Hilary Frank Beatrez.
Institution Type/Description: Automobile & Aircraft Museum.
Hours & Admission Prices: Tues.-Sat. 10-5, Sun. 12-5. Adults $10, senior citizens 62 & over $9, children 3-12 $5; discounts to tours & groups; members and children 2 & under no charge. Closed New Year's Day; Easter; Independence Day; Thanksgiving; Christmas Eve & Day.
Attendance: 205,000 (actual)

DITTRICK MUSEUM OF MEDICAL HISTORY, 11000 Euclid Ave., Cleveland, OH 44106-1714. Tel.: 216-368-3648. Fax: 216-368-0165. Facebook: Dittrick Museum of Medical History.
E-mail: james.edmonson@case.edu
Web Site: www.case.edu/artsci/dittrick/museum
Key Personnel: Chief Cur., James M. Edmonson; Museum Registrar & Archivist, Jennifer K. Nieves; Public Engagement, Brandy L. Schillace; Website Design & Photography, Laura Travis.
Institution Type/Description: Medical History Museum.
Hours & Admission Prices: Mon.-Fri. 10-5. No charge; donations accepted. Closed New Year's Day; Memorial Day weekend; Independence Day; Labor Day weekend; Thanksgiving; Christmas Eve & Day.
Attendance: 15,000 (estimated)

DUNHAM TAVERN MUSEUM, 6709 Euclid Ave., Cleveland, OH 44103-3913. Tel.: 216-431-1060.
E-mail: dunhamtavern@sbcglobal.net
Web Site: www.dunhamtavern.org
Key Personnel: Pres., Douglas Bunker; Treas., Barbara Peterson; Caretaker, Tyrone Hatcher.
Institution Type/Description: General Museum: housed in 1824 Dunham Tavern.
Hours & Admission Prices: Wed. & Sun. 1-4. Adults $3, children under 12 $2; discounts to AAM members; members no charge; group tours call for appointment. Closed New Year's Day; Easter; Thanksgiving; Christmas.
Attendance: 4,200 (estimated)

GALLERIES AT CLEVELAND STATE UNIVERSITY, 1307 Euclid Ave., Cleveland, OH 44115. Mailing Address: 2121 Euclid Ave., AG 116, Cleveland, OH 44115-2226. Tel.: 216-687-2103 & 2000. Fax: 216-687-9340. TDD: 216-687-2000.
E-mail: t.knapp@csuohio.edu
Web Site: www.csuohio.edu/artgallery
Key Personnel: Dir. & Cur., Robert Thurmer; Chm., Martin Bleeke; Chm., Irina Koukhanova; Pres., Ronald Berkman; Asst. Dir., Tim Knapp; Devel., Teri Kocevar; Public Rels., William Dube.
Institution Type/Description: University Art Gallery.
Hours & Admission Prices: Sept.-May Mon.-Fri. 10-5, Sat. 12-4. No charge; donations accepted. Closed federal, state & university holidays.
Attendance: 18,231 (actual)

GREAT LAKES SCIENCE CENTER, 601 Erieside Ave., Cleveland, OH 44114-1021. Tel.: 216-694-2000. Fax: 216-696-2140. Facebook: @greatlakessciencecenter; Twitter: @GLScienceCtr.
E-mail: glscinfo@glsc.org
Web Site: www.greatscience.com
Key Personnel: Chm. Bd., David Peace; Pres. & C.E.O., Kirsten Ellenbogen, Ph.D.; C.F.O., Kenneth J. Sinchak; Vice Pres. Exhibitions, Valence Davillier, III; Vice Pres. Mktg., Communications & Sales, Susan Allen; Vice Pres. Devel., Patrick Ertle.
Institution Type/Description: Technology & Science Museum.
Hours & Admission Prices: Summer: April-Oct. Mon.-Sat. 10-5, Sun. noon-5; Winter: Oct.-April Tues.-Sat. 10-5, Sun. noon-5. Adults $15, youth 2-12 $12; discounts to seniors, students & AAM members. Closed Easter; Thanksgiving; Christmas; during Cleveland Browns home games.
Attendance: 310,000 (actual)

INTERNATIONAL WOMEN'S AIR & SPACE MUSEUM, INC., 1501 N. Marginal Rd., Rm. 165, Cleveland, OH 44114-3726. Tel.: 216-623-1111. Fax: 216-623-1113. Instagram.
E-mail: cluhta@iwasm.org
Web Site: www.iwasm.org
Key Personnel: Pres. (V), Caroline Luhta; Exec. Dir., Heather Alexander; Operations Mgr., Katie Brinager.

Institution Type/Description: Women's Aeronautics Museum: housed at an airport.
Hours & Admission Prices: Mon.-Fri. 9-4; other times by appointment. No charge; donations accepted. Closed holidays.
Attendance: 10,000 (estimated)

LEARNING CENTER AND MONEY MUSEUM, Federal Reserve Bank of Cleveland, 1455 E. Sixth St., Cleveland, OH 44114. Tel.: 216-579-3188. Fax: 216-579-2150.
E-mail: learningcenter@clev.frb.org
Key Personnel: Mgr., Jennifer Ransom.
Institution Type/Description: money; economics & personal finance.
Hours & Admission Prices: Mon.-Thurs. 9:30-2:30; groups by appointment. Visitors 16 & over must present a valid driver's license or other photo ID to enter. No charge. Closed bank holidays.
Attendance: 10,000 (estimated)

MUSEUM OF CONTEMPORARY ART CLEVELAND, 11400 Euclid Ave., Ste. 100, Cleveland, OH 44106-5923. Tel.: 216-421-8671. Fax: 216-421-0737.
E-mail: info@mocacleveland.org
Web Site: www.mocacleveland.org
Formerly: Cleveland Center for Contemporary Art
Key Personnel: Dir., Jill Snyder; Bd. Pres., Harriet Warm; Community Rels. Mgr., Jude Goergen; Emily Hall Tremaine Curatorial Fellow, Megan Lykins; Dir. Mktg. & Communications, Peter Vertes; Dir. Finance, Grace Garver; Sr. Cur., Andrea Hickey; Graphic Designer, Danielle Rini Uva; Visitor Svcs. Mgr. & Museum Shop Mgr., Heather Young; School Programs & Tour Coord., Dara Sepkoski; Dir. Devel., John Grayson; Registrar & Cur. Coord., Ann Albano; Mgr. Member Rels., Rob Sikora; Exhibitions Mgr., Ray Juaire; Asst. Preparator, Paul Sydorenko; Finance Asst. & IT Mgr., Terri Tokar; Asst. Cur., Ana Vejzovic; Administrative Asst., Andrea Kormos.
Institution Type/Description: Art Museum.
Hours & Admission Prices: Tues. & Thurs.-Sun. 11-5, Wed. 11-8. Adults $4, students & seniors $3; discounts to AAM & ICOM members; children under 12, members and MOCA members no charge. Closed New Year's Day; Easter; Independence Day; Thanksgiving; Christmas.
Attendance: 20,000

NASA GLENN RESEARCH & VISITOR CENTER, Lewis Field, 21000 Brookpark Rd., Cleveland, OH 44135-3191. Tel.: 216-433-9653.
E-mail: mack.g.thomas@nasa.gov
Web Site: www.nasa.gov/centers/glenn/events/index.html
Institution Type/Description: Space Science.
Hours & Admission Prices: April-Oct. by appointment. Government-issued photo ID required for entry.

THE NATURE CENTER AT SHAKER LAKES, 2600 S. Park Blvd., Cleveland, OH 44120-1699. Tel.: 216-321-5935, ext. 227. Fax: 216-321-1869.
E-mail: naturecenter@shakerlakes.org
Web Site: www.shakerlakes.org
Key Personnel: Exec. Dir., Kay Carlson; Bd. Pres., Jeffrey D. Kadlic; Financial Officer, Christopher Hall; Mgr. Visitor & Administrative Svcs., Brittany Coffin.
Institution Type/Description: Nature Center.
Hours & Admission Prices: Mon.-Sat. 10-5, Sun. 1-5. No charge; donations accepted. Closed New Year's Day; Easter; Memorial Day; Independence Day; Labor Day; Thanksgiving; Christmas.
Attendance: 30,000 (estimated)

REINBERGER GALLERIES AT THE CLEVELAND INSTITUTE OF ART, 11610 Euclid Ave., Cleveland, OH 44106-1710. Tel.: 216-421-7407.
E-mail: nwoods@cia.edu
Web Site: www.cia.edu/exhibitions/about-the-reinberger-gallery
Key Personnel: Dir., Nichole Woods; Gallery Asst., Samantha Konet.
Institution Type/Description: Art Gallery.
Hours & Admission Prices: Mon.-Thurs. & Sat. 10-5, Fri. 10-9, Sat. & Sun. noon-5.

THE ROCK AND ROLL HALL OF FAME AND MUSEUM, Physical/Mailing Address: 1100 Rock and Roll Blvd., Cleveland, OH 44114. Tel.: 216-781-7625. Fax: 216-781-1832. Facebook: @rockandrollhalloffame; Instagram & Twitter: @rockhall.
E-mail: info@rockhall.org
Web Site: www.rockhall.com
Key Personnel: C.E.O. & Pres., Greg Harris; Pres. & C.E.O. Rock and Roll Hall of Fame Foundation, Joel Peresman; Exec. Vice Pres. & C.F.O., Brian Kenyon; Vice Pres. Education & Visitor Engagement, Jason Hanley; Vice Pres. Devel. & External Rels., Caprice Bragg; Vice Pres. Mktg. & Communications, Todd

Mesek; Vice Pres. Collections & Curatorial Affairs, Karen L. Herman; Vice Pres. Technology, Marc Check.
Institution Type/Description: Rock and Roll Music Museum.
Hours & Admission Prices: Daily 10-5:30, Wed. 10-9. Adults $23.50, senior citizens 65 & over $21.50, children 6-12 $13.75; discounts to NE Ohio residents, military, college students & member guests; children 5 & under and members no charge. Closed Thanksgiving; Christmas. ♿
Attendance: 500,000 (estimated)

ROMANIAN ETHNIC ART MUSEUM, St. Mary's Romanian Orthodox Cathedral, 3256 Warren Rd., Cleveland, OH 44111-1144. Tel.: 216-521-8449. Fax: 216-941-3068.
E-mail: st.mary.cathedral@sbcglobal.net
Web Site: www.smroc.org/culture.php
Key Personnel: Pres. & Dir., Rev. Remus Grama.
Institution Type/Description: Folk Art Museum.
Hours & Admission Prices: Museum: by appointment. Office: Mon.-Fri. 9-5. No charge; donations accepted.
Attendance: 1,500 (estimated)

SPACES GALLERY, 2220 Superior Viaduct, Cleveland, OH 44113. Tel.: 216-621-2314.
E-mail: contact@spacesgallery.org
Web Site: spacesgallery.org
Key Personnel: Exec. Dir., Christina Vassallo.
Institution Type/Description: Art Gallery.
Hours & Admission Prices: Tues.-Wed. & Fri.-Sun. 12-5, Thurs. 12-8. No charge; donations accepted.

THE TEMPLE MUSEUM OF JEWISH ART, RELIGION AND CULTURE, University Circle at Silver Park, 1855 Ansel Rd., Cleveland, OH 44106. Mailing Address: 26000 Shaker Blvd., Beachwood, OH 44122-7199. Tel.: 216-831-3233. Fax: 216-831-4216.
E-mail: whelfand@tti.org
Web Site: www.tti.org
Formerly: The Temple Museum of Religious Art
Key Personnel: Dir., Bob Allenick; Dir. Temple Museums, Sue Koletsky.
Institution Type/Description: Religious Judaica Museum.
Hours & Admission Prices: Museum Tours: Mon.-Fri. 9-4 by appointment. No charge; donations accepted. Closed Jewish & legal holidays.
Attendance: 4,000 (estimated)

UKRAINIAN MUSEUM-ARCHIVES, INC., 1202 Kenilworth Ave., Cleveland, OH 44113-4417. Tel.: 216-781-4329. Fax: 216-781-5844.
E-mail: staff@umacleveland.org
Web Site: www.umacleveland.org
Key Personnel: Dir., Taras Szmagala, Sr.; Chm. Bd. Dirs., Daria Kowcz Jakubowycz, Sr.; Treas. Bd. Dirs., Zenon Holubec; Cur., Aniza Kraus.
Institution Type/Description: Ukrainian History, Culture & Art Museum.
Hours & Admission Prices: Tues.-Sat. 10-3. No charge; donations accepted. Closed holidays.
Attendance: 2,500 (estimated)

THE WESTERN RESERVE FIRE MUSEUM AND EDUCATION CENTER, 310 Carnegie Ave., Cleveland, OH 44115. Tel.: 216-664-6312. Fax: 216-664-3490.
E-mail: info@wrfmc.com
Web Site: www.wrfmc.com
Key Personnel: Exec. Dir., Dan Hayden; Historian & Cur., Paul Nelson.
Institution Type/Description: Fire Museum.
Hours & Admission Prices: Wed.-Sat. 10-4. Adults $8, children $3; discounts to AAM & ICOM members; members no charge. Visit website for special events. Closed holidays.
Attendance: 2,500 (actual)

Clyde

CLYDE MUSEUM & MCPHERSON HOUSE, 124 W. Buckeye St., Clyde, OH 43410-1934. Mailing Address: P.O. Box 97, Clyde, OH 43410-0097. Tel.: 419-547-7946. Fax: 419-547-7946. Facebook.
E-mail: curator@clydemuseum.org
Web Site: www.clydemuseum.org
Key Personnel: Cur. & Dir., Gene A. Smith.
Institution Type/Description: History Museum.
Hours & Admission Prices: Feb.-Nov. Thurs. 1-5, Sat. 10-1; other times by appointment. No charge; donations accepted. ♿
Attendance: 500 (estimated)

Columbiana

THE LOG HOUSE MUSEUM OF THE HISTORICAL SOCIETY OF COLUMBIANA-FAIRFIELD TOWNSHIP, 10 E. Park Ave., Columbiana, OH 44408-1350. Tel.: 330-482-2983.
E-mail: museum@loghousemuseum.info
Web Site: www.loghousemuseum.info/contact-us/
Formerly: The Historical Society of Columbiana-Fairfield Township
Key Personnel: Cur. & Historian, Nora Salmen; Genealogist, Beverly J. Richardson.
Institution Type/Description: Local History Museum: housed in original log house on site of 1807 post office.
Hours & Admission Prices: Memorial Day to early Sept. Fri.-Sat. 2-4. Tours by appointment. No charge; donations accepted.
Attendance: 1,000 (estimated)

Columbus

BILLY IRELAND CARTOON LIBRARY & MUSEUM - THE OHIO STATE UNIVERSITY, Sullivant Hall, 1813 N. High St., Columbus, OH 43210. Tel.: 614-292-0538. Fax: 614-292-9101.
E-mail: cartoons@osu.edu
Web Site: cartoons.osu.edu
Key Personnel: Cur. & Assoc. Prof., Jenny Robb; Assoc. Cur., Collections & Asst. Prof., Wendy Pflug; Assoc. Cur., Outreach & Asst. Prof., Caitlin McGurk; Asst. Cur., Susan Liberator; Asst. Cur., Marilyn Scott; Asst. Cur., Ann Lennon.
Institution Type/Description: Cartoon Art Museum.
Hours & Admission Prices: Tues.-Sun. 1-5. Closed holidays.

BUNTE GALLERY, Franklin University-Alumni Hall, 301 E. Rich St., Columbus, OH 43215-4960.
Web Site: franklin.edu/news-community/community-relations/bunte-gallery
Institution Type/Description: Art Gallery. Built in honor of Dr. Frederick J. Bunte, Franklin University's second president.
Hours & Admission Prices: Mon.-Thurs. 8-5.

COSI, 333 W. Broad St., Columbus, OH 43215-2738. Tel.: 614-228-2674. Fax: 614-629-3226.
E-mail: call_center@cosi.org
Web Site: www.cosi.org
Key Personnel: Pres. & C.E.O., Frederic Bertley, Pd.D.; C.F.O. & Sr. Vice Pres., Admin. & Finance, Francis Pompey; Sr. Vice Pres., Engagement & Impact, Azuka MuMin; Vice Pres. Experience Div., Andy Zakrasjek.
Institution Type/Description: Science/Technology Center.
Hours & Admission Prices: See website for hours & admission pricing. ♿
Attendance: 627,833 (actual)

CENTRAL OHIO FIRE MUSEUM, 260 N. 4th St., Columbus, OH 43215-2511. Tel.: 614-464-4099.
E-mail: cofmuseum@aol.com
Web Site: www.centralohiofiremuseum.com
Institution Type/Description: Fire Museum: housed in restored 1908 engine house. Listed on the National Register of Historic Places.
Hours & Admission Prices: Tues.-Sat. 10-4; groups by appointment. Adults $6, seniors $5, children $4; discounts to groups. Closed holidays. ♿
Attendance: 10,000 (estimated)

COLUMBUS CULTURAL ARTS CENTER, 139 W. Main St., Columbus, OH 43215-5044. Tel.: 614-645-7047. TDD: 614-645-3317.
E-mail: tmcamp@columbus.gov
Web Site: www.culturalartscenteronline.org
Key Personnel: Arts Admin., Geoffrey Martin; Asst. Arts Admin., Todd Camp; Main Gallery Coord., Tom Baillieul; Conversations & Coffee Coord., Ellen O'Shaughnessy; Gift Shop Mgr., Ann Jelett.
Institution Type/Description: Center for Cultural & Visual Arts.
Hours & Admission Prices: Mon. 1-4 & 7pm-10pm, Tues.-Thurs. 9-4 & 7pm-10pm, Fri.-Sat. 9-4. No charge; donations accepted. ♿
Attendance: 50,000

COLUMBUS MUSEUM OF ART, 480 E. Broad St., Columbus, OH 43215-3886. Tel.: 614-221-6801. Fax: 614-221-0226. Facebook, Instagram & Twitter: @columbusmuseum.
E-mail: info@cmaohio.org
Web Site: www.columbusmuseum.org
Key Personnel: Pres., Michael Martz; 2nd Vice Pres., Joy Gonsiorowski; Exec. Dir., Nannette V. Maciejunes; Exec. Deputy Dir., Sarah J. Rogers; Deputy Dir. Operations & Chief Registrar, Rod Bouc; Exec. Asst. Dir. & Dir., Learning, Cindy M. Foley; Exec. Deputy Dir. Finance & Admin., Kimberly Aufdencamp; Dir. Devel., Lucy Ackley; Dir. Mktg. & Communications, Melissa E. Ferguson;

Dir. Special Events Sales, Susan Brehm; Dir. Visitor Experience, Kim Hopcraft; Dir. Retail Opers., Pam Edwards; Dir. Facilities, David A. Leach; Chief Cur., David Stark; William J. & Sarah Ross Soter Assoc. Cur. of Photography, Drew Sawyer; Cur. Contemporary Art, Tyler Cann; Curator-at-Large, Carole Genshaft.
Institution Type/Description: Art Museum.
Hours & Admission Prices: Tues.-Wed. & Fri.-Sun. 10-5 & Thurs.10-9. Adults $14, senior citizens 60+ & students 18+ $8, students 6-17 $5; children 5 & under, members and Sun. no charge. Closed Independence Day; Thanksgiving; Christmas. &
Attendance: 200,000 (estimated)

THE FRANK W. HALE, JR. BLACK CULTURAL CENTER,
154 W. 12th Ave., Columbus, OH 43210-1389. Tel.: 614-292-0074. Fax: 614-292-2737.
E-mail: odihbcc@osu.edu
Web Site: odi.osu.edu/hale-black-cultural-center
Key Personnel: Dir., Larry Williamson, Jr.; Program Mgr., Phillip G. Mayo.
Institution Type/Description: Cultural Center.
Hours & Admission Prices: Winter: Mon.-Fri. 8am-10pm, Sat. 11-7, Sun. 12-8; Summer: Mon.-Fri. 7:30-5.

FRANKLIN PARK CONSERVATORY AND BOTANICAL GARDENS,
1777 E. Broad St., Columbus, OH 43203-2040. Tel.: 614-715-8000, 800-214-7275. Fax: 614-715-8199.
E-mail: info@fpconservatory.org
Web Site: www.fpconservatory.org
Key Personnel: Pres., Patrick Henthorne.
Institution Type/Description: Conservatory.
Hours & Admission Prices: Daily 10-5; call for extended hours. Adults $19, seniors 60 & over $16, children 3-12 $12; discounts to groups; children 2 & under and members no charge. Closed Thanksgiving; Christmas. &
Attendance: 275,000 (estimated)

GLADYS KELLER SNOWDEN GALLERY,
1787 Neil Ave., Campbell Hall, Rm. 175, Columbus, OH 43210. Tel.: 614-292-3090. Fax: 614-688-8133.
E-mail: strege.2@osu.edu
Web Site: costume.osu.edu/visit-us
Key Personnel: Cur., Gayle Strege.
Institution Type/Description: Art Gallery.
Hours & Admission Prices: Academic Year: Tues.-Thurs. 10-5, Fri. 10-4, Sat. 12-4, call to confirm. No charge; donations accepted. Closed university holidays.

GRANGE INSURANCE AUDUBON CENTER,
505 W. Whittier St., Columbus, OH 43215. Tel.: 614-545-5475.
E-mail: dtabata@audubon.org
Web Site: grange.audubon.org
Key Personnel: Exec. Dir., Dawn Tabata; Conservation & Outreach Mgr., Michael Goldman; Education Program Mgr. & Vol. Coord., Allison Clark.
Institution Type/Description: Audubon Center.
Hours & Admission Prices: Tues.-Thurs. 10-5, Fri.-Sat. 9-3, Sun. 12-5. No charge; donations accepted.

HISTORIC COSTUME & TEXTILES COLLECTION,
1787 Neil Ave., Columbus, OH 43210-1220. Tel.: 614-292-3090. Fax: 614-688-8133.
E-mail: strege.2@osu.edu
Web Site: costume.osu.edu
Key Personnel: Cur., Gayle Strege; Asst. Cur., Marlise Schoeny.
Institution Type/Description: Costume & Textile Museum.
Hours & Admission Prices: Tues.-Thurs. 10-5, Fri. 10-4, Sat. 12-4; other times by appointment. No charge, donations accepted. Closed university holidays. &
Attendance: 1,000 (estimated)

HOPKINS HALL GALLERY - THE OHIO STATE UNIVERSITY,
128 N. Oval Mall, Columbus, OH 43210. Tel.: 614-292-0234.
E-mail: artsinitiative@osu.edu
Web Site: hhg.osu.edu
Key Personnel: Exec. Dir., Valarie Williams; Deputy Dir., Facilities & Programming, Christopher Gose; Deputy Dir., Exhibitions & Curatorial Practice, Merijn van der Heijden; Dir. Communications, Erik Pepple; Sr. Preparator, Jeremy Stone; Opers. & Program Mgr., Emily Smith Oilar.
Institution Type/Description: Art Gallery.
Hours & Admission Prices: Academic Year: Mon.-Fri. 11-5; Summer: Tues.-Fri. 11-4. No charge. Closed New Year's Eve & Day; Thanksgiving week; Christmas Eve, Day & week.

JACK NICKLAUS MUSEUM,
2355 Olentangy River Rd., Columbus, OH 43210-1032. Tel.: 614-247-5959. Fax: 614-247-5906.
E-mail: info@nicklausmuseum.org
Web Site: www.nicklausmuseum.org
Key Personnel: Cur., Steve Auch; Events Mgr., Barbara Hartley.
Institution Type/Description: Sports Museum.
Hours & Admission Prices: Tues.-Sat. 9-5. Adults $10, students $5.

JUBILEE MUSEUM AND CATHOLIC CULTURAL CENTER,
57 S. Grubb St., Columbus, OH 43215-2747. Tel.: 614-600-0054.
E-mail: info@jubileemuseum.org
Web Site: www.jubileemuseum.org
Formerly: Jubilee Museum at Holy Family
Key Personnel: Cur., Rev. Kevin F. Lutz.
Institution Type/Description: Religious Museum: housed in the former Holy Family High School.
Hours & Admission Prices: Mon.-Sat. 10-4, Sun. 1-4. Adults $10, seniors, students & children $5.
Attendance: 3,500 (estimated)

KELTON HOUSE MUSEUM & GARDEN,
586 E. Town St., Columbus, OH 43215-4888. Tel.: 614-464-2022.
E-mail: keltonhouse@cs.com
Web Site: www.keltonhouse.com
Key Personnel: Chm., Hayley Roberts; Pres., Beth Daly; Dir., Georgeanne Reuter.
Institution Type/Description: Historic House Museum.
Hours & Admission Prices: Sun. 1-4 (docent-led tour), Mon.-Fri. 10-4 (audio tour), Sat. 1-4 (audio tour). Adults $6, senior citizens $5, college students $4, children grades K-12 $3; members no charge. Closed Easter; Christmas. &
Attendance: 9,035 (actual)

MUSEUM OF CLASSICAL ARCHAEOLOGY - THE OHIO STATE UNIVERSITY,
028 Dulles Hall, 230 W. 17th Ave., Columbus, OH 43210. Tel.: 614-247-4470.
E-mail: gregory.4@osu.edu
Web Site: moca.osu.edu
Key Personnel: Dir., Timothy Gregory.
Institution Type/Description: Archaeology Museum.
Hours & Admission Prices: See website for hours. Closed summers & university holidays & breaks.

THE OHIO CRAFT MUSEUM,
1665 W. Fifth Ave., Columbus, OH 43212-2315. Tel.: 614-486-4402. Facebook.
E-mail: btalbott@ohiocraft.org
Web Site: www.ohiocraft.org
Key Personnel: Dir., Betty Talbott; Opers. Mgr., John Barr.
Institution Type/Description: Craft Museum.
Hours & Admission Prices: Mon.-Fri. 10-5, Sat.-Sun. 1-4. No charge. Closed holidays.

OHIO HISTORY CONNECTION,
800 E. 17th Ave., Columbus, OH 43211-2474. Tel.: 614-297-2300 & 2350, 800-686-6124. Fax: 614-297-2352. TDD: 800-750-0750; Facebook.
E-mail: info@ohiohistory.org
Web Site: www.ohiohistory.org
Formerly: Ohio Historical Society
Key Personnel: Exec. Dir. & C.E.O., Burt Logan; Pres. Bd., Thomas V. Chema; Dir. World Heritage, Jen Aultman; Chief Development Officer, Hillary Bates; Deputy Exec. Dir. & Chief Learning Officer, Ben Garcia; Snr. Advisor CEO, Stephen George; Dir. American Indian Relations, Stacey Halfmoon; Dir. State Historic Preservation Office, Amanda Schraner; Dir. National Afro-American Museum & Cultural Center, Charles Wash; Dir. Membership, Erin Wingfield; Dir. Cultural Resources, Megan Wood; Chief Mktg. Officer, Jamison Pack; Dir. Outreach, Stacia Kuceyeski; Division Dir., Jen Cassidy; C.F.O., Jeff Ward; Dir. Community & Govt. Rels., Todd Kleismit.
Institution Type/Description: History Museum.
Hours & Admission Prices: Ohio Historical Center & Museum Store: Wed.-Sat. 10-5, Sun. 12-5. Archives & Library: Wed.-Sat. 10-5. Ohio Village & Branch Sites: call 800-686-6124 for hours. Adults $10, seniors $9, children 6-12 $5, students $4; discounts to Golden Buckeye, OLHA, AAA, AARP, AAM & ICOM members; OHS members & children under 6 no charge. Closed New Year's Eve & Day; Thanksgiving; Christmas Eve & Day; Monday holidays. &
Attendance: 440,000 (actual)

THE OHIO STATE UNIVERSITY FACULTY CLUB,
181 S. Oval Dr., Columbus, OH 43210. Tel.: 614-292-2262. Fax: 614-292-1144.
E-mail: lisa@ohio-statefacultyclub.com
Web Site: www.ohio-statefacultyclub.com

Key Personnel: Art Coord., Lisa Craig Morton.
Institution Type/Description: University Art Gallery & Club.
Hours & Admission Prices: Mon.-Fri. 8-5.

OHIO STATEHOUSE MUSEUM EDUCATION CENTER, 1 Capitol Sq., Columbus, OH 43215. Tel.: 614-752-9777.
E-mail: visitors@ohiostatehouse.org
Web Site: ohiostatehouse.org/museum/museum-education-center
Key Personnel: Cur., Chris Matheney; Tours, Katie Montgomery.
Institution Type/Description: Historic Building: built 1861.
Hours & Admission Prices: Statehouse: Mon.-Fri. 9-4, Sat.-Sun. 12-4. Guided Tours: Mon.-Fri. 10-3, Sat. Sun. 12-3. Closed state holidays.

OHIO WOMEN'S HALL OF FAME, 274 E. First Ave., Ste. 300, Columbus, OH 43201. Tel.: 614-466-3847. Fax: 614-728-6974.
E-mail: ohioana@ohioana.org
Web Site: jfs.ohio.gov/women/index.stm
Key Personnel: Exec. Dir., David Weaver.
Institution Type/Description: History Museum.
Hours & Admission Prices: Closed in 2017 for relocation.

ORTON GEOLOGICAL MUSEUM, OHIO STATE UNIVERSITY, 155 S. Oval Mall, Columbus, OH 43210-1308. Tel.: 614-292-6896. Fax: 614-292-1496.
E-mail: gnidovec.1@osu.edu
Web Site: ortongeologicalmuseum.osu.edu
Key Personnel: Dir. & Professor, Bill Ausich; Mgr. Collection & Cur., Dale Gnidovec.
Institution Type/Description: College Geology Museum: housed in Orton Hall.
Hours & Admission Prices: Mon.-Fri. 9-5; other times by appointment. No charge; donations accepted. &
Attendance: 11,927 (actual)

THE SCHUMACHER GALLERY, CAPITAL UNIVERSITY, 1 College and Main, Columbus, OH 43209-2394. Tel.: 614-236-6319. Fax: 614-236-6490.
E-mail: dgentili@capital.edu
Web Site: www.schumachergallery.org
Key Personnel: Dir., Dr. Cassandra Tellier; Asst. to Dir., David Gentilini.
Institution Type/Description: University Art Museum.
Hours & Admission Prices: Sept.-May Mon.-Sat. 1-5. No charge; donations accepted. Closed university holidays. &
Attendance: 10,000

THE SNOWDEN-GRAY HOUSE, 530 E. Town St., Columbus, OH 43215-4820. Tel.: 614-228-6515, 866-554-1870.
E-mail: kkgfnd@kkg.org
Web Site: www.kappa.org/heritagemuseum
Formerly: Heritage Museum of Kappa Kappa Gamma
Key Personnel: Archivist & Cur., Kylie Towers Smith.
Institution Type/Description: History Museum: former home of an Ohio governor, built in 1852. Listed on the National Register of Historic Places.
Hours & Admission Prices: Wed.-Thurs. 1-4; other times by appointment. Suggested donations: adults $5, seniors & students $3; children under 5 no charge.
Attendance: 1,000 (estimated)

WEXNER CENTER FOR THE ARTS, The Ohio State University, 1871 N. High St., Columbus, OH 43210-1105. Tel.: 614-292-0330. Fax: 614-292-3639.
E-mail: info@wexarts.org
Web Site: www.wexarts.org
Key Personnel: Dir., Sherri Geldin; Deputy Dir., Jack Jackson.
Institution Type/Description: Contemporary Arts Center.
Hours & Admission Prices: Tues.-Wed. & Sun. 11-6, Thurs.-Sat. 11-8. Closed New Year's Day; Martin Luther King Day; Memorial Day; Independence Day; Labor Day; Veterans' Day; Thanksgiving; Christmas. &
Attendance: 190,380 (actual)

Conneaut

CONNEAUT RAILROAD MUSEUM, Depot St., Conneaut, OH 44030. Mailing Address: P.O. Box 643, Conneaut, OH 44030-0643. Tel.: 440-599-7878.
E-mail: ronbgrumpy@suite224.net
Key Personnel: Natl. Dir., Ronald Brundage, Jr.; Vice Pres., Ed Trenn; Sec., Michelle Jewel; Treas., Norman Gross.
Institution Type/Description: Antique Railroad Museum: housed in 1900 former New York Central depot.

Hours & Admission Prices: Memorial Day-Labor Day daily 12-5. No charge; donations accepted. &
Attendance: 10,000 (estimated)

Copley

AKRON FOSSILS & SCIENCE CENTER, 2080 S. Cleveland-Massillon Rd., Copley, OH 44321. Tel.: 330-665-3466. Fax: 330-666-9801.
E-mail: info@akronfossils.com
Web Site: www.akronfossils.com
Institution Type/Description: Science Center.
Hours & Admission Prices: Memorial Day to Labor Day Tues.-Sat. 10-5; Sept.-May Sat. 10-5. Admission $10, children 3 & under no charge. Closed New Year's Eve & Day; Memorial Day; Independence Day; Christmas Eve & Day. &

Coshocton

HISTORIC ROSCOE VILLAGE, 600 N. Whitewoman St., Coshocton, OH 43812. Tel.: 740-622-7644. Fax: 740-623-6555. Facebook, Twitter, Pinterest, Instagram.
E-mail: rvmarketing@roscoevillage.com
Web Site: www.roscoevillage.com
Institution Type/Description: Historic Site: more than 23 restored buildings; Greek Revival structures.
Hours & Admission Prices: Visitor's Center: April-Dec. Mon.-Sat. 10-4, Sun. 12-5. Toll House: Jan.-March daily 12-4; April-Dec. Mon.-Sat. 10-4, Sun. 12-5. Museum: family $11, adults $4, student $3; discounts to groups. Living History Tours: adults $9.95, youth $4.95; children 5 & under no charge. Closed New Year's Day, Easter, Thanksgiving, Christmas. &
Attendance: 70,000 (estimated)

JOHNSON-HUMRICKHOUSE MUSEUM, Roscoe Village, 300 N. Whitewoman St., Coshocton, OH 43812-1061. Tel.: 740-622-8710. Fax: 740-622-8710 *51.
E-mail: jhmuseum@jhmuseum.org
Web Site: www.jhmuseum.org/default.htm
Key Personnel: Dir., Patti Malenke.
Institution Type/Description: General Museum.
Hours & Admission Prices: May-Oct. daily 12-5; Nov.-April Tues.-Sun. 1-4:30. Adults $3, youth $2; members no charge. Closed New Year's Day; Easter; Thanksgiving; Christmas Eve & Day. &
Attendance: 9,831 (actual)

POMERENE CENTER FOR THE ARTS, 317 Mulberry St., Coshocton, OH 43812-2037. Tel.: 740-622-0326. Facebook.
E-mail: pomerenearts@gmail.com
Web Site: www.pomerenearts.org/index.htm
Key Personnel: C.O.O., Donovan Rice; Dir., Anne Cornell.
Institution Type/Description: Art Gallery/Community Art Center: housed in an 1836 Greek Revival home.
Hours & Admission Prices: Tues.-Sat. 1-5; Sun.-Mon. by appointment. No Charge; donations accepted. &
Attendance: 2,500 (estimated)

Covington

FORT ROWDY MUSEUM, 101 Spring St., Covington, OH 45318. Tel.: 937-473-2270.
Institution Type/Description: Historical Society Museum: built in 1850.
Hours & Admission Prices: By appointment.

Crestline

CRESTLINE SHUNK MUSEUM, 211 N. Thoman St., Crestline, OH 44827-1444. Mailing Address: P.O. Box 456, Crestline, OH 44827-0456. Tel.: 419-683-3410.
Institution Type/Description: Local History Museum: housed in 1860 Victorian home.
Hours & Admission Prices: May-Sept. last full weekend each month; other times by appointment. No charge; donations accepted.
Attendance: 200 (estimated)

LOWE-VOLK PARK NATURE CENTER, Crawford Park District, 2401 State Rte. 598, Crestline, OH 44827. Tel.: 419-683-9000. Fax: 419-683-6281. Facebook: Crawford Park District.
E-mail: bfisher@crawfordparkdistrict.org
Web Site: www.crawfordparkdistrict.org
Key Personnel: Park Dir., Bill Fisher.

Institution Type/Description: Nature Center.
Hours & Admission Prices: Mon.-Sat. 8-4.

Dalton

DALTON COMMUNITY HISTORICAL SOCIETY, 115 E. Main
St., Dalton, OH 44618. Mailing Address: P.O. Box 273, Dalton,
OH 44618. Tel.: 330-828-2221.
E-mail: daltonhistoricalsociety@gmail.com
Key Personnel: Pres., Vickie Slater.
Institution Type/Description: Historical Society Museum: housed in the former Old
Eagle Hotel and Tavern; built in 1821.
Hours & Admission Prices: 1st Sun. of month 1-4. No charge; donations accepted.

Dayton

AULLWOOD AUDUBON CENTER AND FARM, 1000 Aullwood
Rd., Dayton, OH 45414-1129. Tel.: 937-890-7360. Fax: 937-890-
2382. Facebook & Twitter: Aullwood Audubon.
E-mail: askus@aullwood.org
Web Site: www.aullwood.org
Key Personnel: Pres. & C.E.O., David Yarnold.
Institution Type/Description: Environmental Education Facility & Working
Educational Farm.
Hours & Admission Prices: Mon.-Sat. 9-5, Sun. 1-5. Adults $5, children 2-18 $3;
ANCA, National Audubon Society & Friends of the Aullwood members and
children under 2 no charge. Closed winter holidays. &
Attendance: 120,000 (actual)

BOONSHOFT MUSEUM OF DISCOVERY, 2600 DeWeese
Pkwy., Dayton, OH 45414-5499. Tel.: 937-275-7431. Fax: 937-
275-5811. Facebook, Instagram & Twitter: @BoonshoftMuseum.
E-mail: info@boonshoftmuseum.org
Web Site: www.boonshoftmuseum.org
Key Personnel: C.F.O. & Interim C.E.O., Douglas Hull; Chm. (V), Greg Hoffbauer;
Vice Pres. Education, Dawn Kirchner; Vice Pres. Devel., Bethany Deines; Dir.
Astronomy, Jason Heaton; Dir. Facilities Mgmt., Ron Puterbaugh; Sun Watch
Indian Village/Archaeological Park Site Mgr. & Site Anthropologist, Andrew
Sawyer; Site Mgr. Fort Ancient, Jack Blosser; Acting Cur. Live Animals,
Stephanie Hylinsky; Sr. Cur., William Kennedy; Museum Shop Mgr., Angela
Shaffer.
Institution Type/Description: Natural History Museum, Science Center, Zoo,
Children's Museum.
Hours & Admission Prices: Boonshoft (Dayton): Mon.-Sat. 9-5, Sun. 12-5. Adults
$14.50, seniors $12.50, children 3-17 $11.50; members, ACM, AZA & ASTC
reciprocity no charge. Call for show information. Closed New Year's Eve &
Day; Easter; Thanksgiving; Christmas Eve & Day. &
Attendance: 214,000 (actual)

COX ARBORETUM METROPARK, 6733 Springboro Pike,
Dayton, OH 45449-3496. Tel.: 937-434-9005. Fax: 937-438-1221.
TDD: 937-275-PARK.
E-mail: diane.hart@metroparks.org
Web Site: www.metroparks.org/parks/coxarboretum
Formerly: Cox Arboretum & Gardens MetroPark
Key Personnel: Acting Dir., Rosie Melia; Horticulturist, Richmond Pearson; Family
& Children's Education, Katrina Arnold; Garden Store Mgr., Diane Hart.
Institution Type/Description: Arboretum & Gardens.
Hours & Admission Prices: Grounds: April-Oct. daily 8am-10pm; Nov.-March
daily 8am-8pm. Buildings: Mon.-Fri. 8-5, Sat.-Sun. 11-4. No charge; donations
accepted. Closed New Year's Day; Christmas. &
Attendance: 360,000 (estimated)

DAYTON ART INSTITUTE, 456 Belmonte Park N., Dayton, OH
45405-4700. Tel.: 937-223-5277. Fax: 937-223-3140. Facebook:
Dayton Art Institute.
E-mail: info@daytonart.org
Web Site: www.daytonartinstitute.org
Key Personnel: Dir. & C.E.O., Michael R. Roediger; Chm., Bear Monita; Dir.
External Affairs, Alexis Larsen; Cur. Education, Susan Martis; Chief Cur.,
Aimee Marcereau DeGalan; Museum Shop Mgr., Diane Haskell.
Institution Type/Description: Art Museum.
Hours & Admission Prices: Tues.-Wed. & Fri.-Sat. 11-5, Thurs. 11-8, Sun. 12-5.
Suggested Admission: adults $8, seniors 60 & over, active military and groups
$5; college students with ID 18 & over, youth 17 & under and members no
charge. Special exhibition fee charged. Closed major holidays. &
Attendance: 114,600 (actual)

DAYTON HISTORY AT CARILLON PARK, 1000 Carillon
Blvd., Dayton, OH 45409-2023. Tel.: 937-293-2841; ext. 100. Fax:
937-293-5798.
E-mail: info@daytonhistory.org
Web Site: www.carillonpark.org
Formerly: Carillon Historical Park
Key Personnel: Pres. & C.E.O., Brady Kress.
Institution Type/Description: Historical Museum Complex.
Hours & Admission Prices: Mon.-Sat. 9:30-5, Sun. 12-5. Adults $8, senior citizens
$7, students 3-17 $5; discounts to AASLH members; children under 3 & mem-
bers no charge. &
Attendance: 160,000 (estimated)

DAYTON INTERNATIONAL PEACE MUSEUM, 208 W.
Monument Ave., Dayton, OH 45402-3015. Tel.: 937-227-3223.
Fax: 937-224-2713.
E-mail: info@daytonpeacemuseum.org
Web Site: www.daytonpeacemuseum.org
Formerly: Dayton Peace Museum
Key Personnel: Exec. Dir., Jerry Leggett; Chm. (V), Bill Shaw.
Institution Type/Description: Peace Museum: house listed on the National Register
of Historic Places.
Hours & Admission Prices: Wed.-Sat. 10-5, Sun. 1-5. No charge; donations
accepted. Closed major holidays. &
Attendance: 4,000 (estimated)

DAYTON VISUAL ARTS CENTER, 118 N. Jefferson St., Dayton,
OH 45402. Tel.: 937-224-3822.
E-mail: dvac@daytonvisualarts.org
Web Site: www.daytonvisualarts.org
Key Personnel: Exec. Dir., Eva Buttacavoli.
Institution Type/Description: Art Gallery.
Hours & Admission Prices: Tues.-Sat. 11-6, 1st Fri. each month 11-8.

PATTERSON HOMESTEAD, 1815 Brown St., Dayton, OH 45409-
2414. Mailing Address: c/o Dayton History, 1000 Carillon Blvd.
#D, Dayton, OH 45409-2023. Tel.: 937-222-9724, 973-293-2841.
Fax: 937-222-0345. FacebooK: Patterson Homestead.
E-mail: info@daytonhistroy.org
Web Site: www.daytonhistroy.org
Key Personnel: Dir., Denise L. Darling.
Institution Type/Description: Historic House: Patterson Homestead, a vernacular
Ohio Federal style farmhouse built between 1816-1850.
Hours & Admission Prices: Thurs.-Sat. 10-4. Suggested Donation: $2 per person.
Closed legal holidays. &
Attendance: 1,280 (actual)

PAUL LAURENCE DUNBAR STATE MEMORIAL, 219 N. Paul
Laurence Dunbar St., Dayton, OH 45402-6502. Mailing Address:
1000 Carillon Blvd., Dayton, OH 45409. Tel.: 937-313-2010.
E-mail: education@daytonhistory.org
Web Site: www.ohiohistory.org/places/dunbar
Key Personnel: Pres. (V), Benette DeCoux; Program Mgr., Josh Cain.
Institution Type/Description: Historic House: housed in the home of African
American poet, Paul Laurence Dunbar.
Hours & Admission Prices: Fri.-Sat. 10-4, Sun. 12-4. Adults $6, children 3-17 $3;
discounts to active military, AAA members, seniors 65 & over & groups;
Dayton History & Ohio Historical Society members & National Park Service
Pass holders no charge. Closed New Year's Eve & Day; Thanksgiving;
Christmas Eve & Day. &
Attendance: 1,200 (actual)

ROBERT AND ELAINE STEIN GALLERIES, 3640 Colonel
Glenn Hwy., 128-CAC, Dayton, OH 45435. Tel.: 937-775-2978.
Fax: 937-775-4082.
E-mail: artgalleries@wright.edu
Web Site: liberal-arts.wright.edu/art-galleries
Formerly: Wright State University Art Galleries
Key Personnel: Gallery Coord., Tess Cortes.
Institution Type/Description: University Art Gallery.
Hours & Admission Prices: Tues.-Wed. & Fri. 10-4, Thurs. 10-7, Sat.-Sun. 12-4.
No charge. Closed holidays. &
Attendance: 12,000 (actual)

SUNWATCH INDIAN VILLAGE/ARCHAEOLOGICAL PARK,
2301 W. River Rd., Dayton, OH 45417. Tel.: 937-268-8199. Fax:
937-268-1760.
E-mail: sunwatch@sunwatch.org
Web Site: www.sunwatch.org

Formerly: Sunwatch Prehistoric Indian Village
Key Personnel: C.F.O. & Interim C.E.O., Douglas Hull; Chm. (V), Greg Hoffbauer; Dir. Education, Jean Copas; Site Mgr., Andrew Sawyer.
Institution Type/Description: Historic Site: reconstructed 800 year old village built by the Fort Ancient Indians. A National Historic Landmark.
Hours & Admission Prices: Tues.-Sat. 9-5, Sun. 12-5. Adults $7, senior citizens 60 & over and students 6-17 $6; members no charge. Closed New Year's Eve & Day; Easter; Thanksgiving; Christmas Eve & Day. &
Attendance: 15,000 (actual)

Defiance

AUGLAIZE VILLAGE, 12296 Krouse Rd., Defiance, OH 43512. Mailing Address: P.O. Box 801, Defiance, OH 43512-0801.
E-mail: villageauglaize@gmail.com
Web Site: www.auglaizevillagemuseum.org
Key Personnel: Pres. (V), Scott Lantow; Vice Pres., Pat Wise; Museum Shop Mgr., Deb Kutzli.
Institution Type/Description: Village Museum.
Hours & Admission Prices: May-Oct. event weekends & by appointment. Adults $4, seniors $3, children 6-18 $2; children under 12 with an adult & members no charge. &
Attendance: 6,000 (estimated)

Delaware

DELAWARE COUNTY HISTORICAL SOCIETY - NASH HOUSE MUSEUM, 157 E. William St., Delaware, OH 43015-2165. Tel.: 740-369-3831.
E-mail: info@delawareohiohistory.org
Web Site: www.delawareohiohistory.org
Institution Type/Description: Historic House. Built in the 1878.
Hours & Admission Prices: mid-March to mid-Nov. Wed. & Sat.-Sun. 2-4:30, Thurs. 10-4:30; mid-Nov. to mid-March. Sun. 2-4:30. No charge; donations accepted. Closed major holidays.

RICHARD M. ROSS ART MUSEUM, Ohio Wesleyan University, 60 S. Sandusky St., Delaware, OH 43015-2333. Tel.: 740-368-3606. Fax: 740-368-3515.
E-mail: ramuseum@owu.edu
Key Personnel: Dir., Justin Kronewetter; Sr. Asst., Tammy Wallace; Gallery Asst., Stephen Perakis.
Institution Type/Description: Art Museum.
Hours & Admission Prices: Tues.-Wed. & Fri. 10-5, Thurs. 10-9, Sun. 1-5. No charge; donations accepted.

Delphos

DELPHOS CANAL COMMISSION MUSEUM, 241 Main St., Delphos, OH 45833-1764. Mailing Address: P.O. Box 256, Delphos, OH 45833-0256. Tel.: 419-695-7737. Facebook: Delphos Canal Commission Museum.
E-mail: info@delphoscanalcommission.com
Web Site: www.delphoscanalcommission.com
Key Personnel: Pres. (V), Lou Hohman.
Institution Type/Description: History Museum.
Hours & Admission Prices: Thurs. 9-12, Sat.-Sun. 1-3; groups by appointment. No charge; donations accepted. &
Attendance: 2,000 (estimated)

DELPHOS POSTAL MUSEUM, 339 N. Main St., Delphos, OH 45833-0174. Mailing Address: P.O. Box 174, Delphos, OH 45833-0174. Tel.: 419-303-5482.
E-mail: mphdelphos@gmail.com
Web Site: www.postalhistorymuseum.org
Key Personnel: Dir., Gary S. Levitt; Pres. (V), Rev. David Howell.
Institution Type/Description: History Museum: housed in a former horse avery; built in 1902.
Hours & Admission Prices: Call for hours. No charge; donations accepted.
Attendance: 4,000 (estimated)

Dennison

THE DENNISON RAILROAD DEPOT MUSEUM, 400 Center St., Dennison, OH 44621-1402. Mailing Address: P.O. Box 11, Dennison, OH 44621-0011. Tel.: 740-922-6776. Fax: 740-922-4929. Facebook: @DennisonRailroadDepotMuseum; Twitter: @DennisonDepot; Instagram: @dennisondepot; Pinterest: /dennisondepot.

E-mail: director@dennisondepot.org
Web Site: www.dennisondepot.org
Key Personnel: Dir., Wendy R. Zucal; Bd. Pres., April Berni; Mgr., Brand Rels. & Consumer Experience, Jacob Masters; Cur., Kim Turkovic; Membership Coord., Kerri Silverthorn; Experience Coord., Curtis Moreland; Experience Coord., Alicia Miller; Experience Coord., Chealsey Cunningham; Museum Shop Mgr., Rose Pancher.
Institution Type/Description: National Historic Landmark: housed in 1873 Pennsylvania Railroad Depot.
Hours & Admission Prices: Tues.-Fri. 10-5, Sat. 11-4, Sun. 11-3. Adults $8, senior citizens $6, students 7-17 $4; discounts to AAM & AAA members; children under 7 & members no charge. Closed New Year's Day; Easter; Independence Day; Thanksgiving; Christmas. &
Attendance: 85,000 (estimated)

Dover

J.E. REEVES VICTORIAN HOME, 325 E. Iron Ave., Dover, OH 44622-2105. Tel.: 330-343-7040, 800-815-2794. Fax: 330-343-6290. Facebook: J.E. Reeves Victorian Home.
E-mail: director@reevesmuseum.org
Web Site: www.doverhistory.org
Key Personnel: Dir., Shelagh Pruni; Pres., Greg Bair; Vice Pres., Patti Feller.
Institution Type/Description: General Historical Society Museum: housed in 19th-century restored Victorian mansion, home of J.E. Reeves.
Hours & Admission Prices: June-Oct. Tues.-Sun. noon-4; Nov. 11-Dec. 22 daily 1-7. Adults $8, seniors $7, children 5-18 $3; discounts to AAA members; members no charge. .
Attendance: 4,000 (estimated)

WARTHER MUSEUM INC., 331 Karl Ave., Dover, OH 44622-2767. Mailing Address: PO Box 686, Dover, OH 44622-0686. Tel.: 330-343-7513. Facebook.
E-mail: carol@thewarthermuseum.com
Web Site: www.thewarthermuseum.com
Key Personnel: Pres., Carol Moreland.
Institution Type/Description: Arts & Crafts Museum.
Hours & Admission Prices: Daily 9-5. Adults $13.50, students $5; discounts to groups. Closed New Year's Day; Easter; Thanksgiving; Christmas. &
Attendance: 100,000 (estimated)

Doylestown

CHIPPEWA-ROGUES HOLLOW HISTORICAL SOCIETY, 17500 Galehouse Rd., Doylestown, OH 44230-9773. Mailing Address: P.O. Box 283, Doylestown, OH 44230. Tel.: 330-882-3375. Facebook: Chippewa-Rogues Hollow Historical Society.
E-mail: marymertic@juno.com
Web Site: www.chippewarogueshollow.org
Key Personnel: Pres. (V), Earl Kerr; Vice Pres., Mary Mertic.
Institution Type/Description: Historical Society Museum.
Hours & Admission Prices: June-Sept. Sun. 2-4. &
Attendance: 500 (estimated)

Dublin

WORLD'S FIRST WENDY'S RESTAURANT, One Dave Thomas Blvd., Dublin, OH 43017-5452. Tel.: 888-824-8140.
E-mail: mediarelations@wendys.com
Key Personnel: Senior Dir. Internal Communication, Bob Bertini; Pres. & C.E.O., Emil J. Brolick; Chief Mktg. Officer, Craig S. Bahner; Chief Communications Officer, Liliana M. Esposito.
Institution Type/Description: General Museum: housed in the first Wendy's Restaurant opened in 1969; named after his daughter Melinda (Wendy) Thomas, a nickname given to her by her siblings.
Hours & Admission Prices: Mon.-Fri. 10-8, Sat. 10-7, Sun. 11-6. No charge.

East Liverpool

LOU HOLTZ/UPPER OHIO VALLEY HALL OF FAME, 120 E. Fifth St., East Liverpool, OH 43920-3031. Tel.: 330-386-5443. Fax: 330-382-0244.
E-mail: director@louholtzhalloffame.com
Web Site: www.louholtzhalloffame.com
Key Personnel: Pres., Frank C. Dawson; Treas., Jackman Vodrey; Dir., Robin Webster.
Institution Type/Description: Hall of Fame.
Hours & Admission Prices: Mon.-Fri. 10-5, Sat. 10-1. No charge; donations accepted. Closed legal holidays. &
Attendance: 2,500 (estimated)

MUSEUM OF CERAMICS, 400 E. 5th St. at Broadway, East Liverpool, OH 43920-3134. Tel.: 330-386-6001, 800-600-7180. Facebook: Museum of Ceramics.
E-mail: museumofceramics@gmail.com
Web Site: www.TheMuseumOfCeramics.org
Key Personnel: Dir. & Museum Shop Mgr., S.W. Vodrey; Historic Site Technician, Philip L. Rickerd.
Institution Type/Description: History Museum: housed in 1909 Old City Post Office.
Hours & Admission Prices: Tues.-Sat. 9:30-3:30. Adults $4, students $2; discounts to AAA members & Time Travelers; children 5 & under and members no charge. Closed federal holidays. &
Attendance: 1,900 (estimated)

THOMPSON HOUSE MANSION, 305 Walnut St., East Liverpool, OH 43920. Mailing Address: East Liverpool Historical Society, P. O. Box 476, East Liverpool, OH 43920. Tel.: 330-386-5964. Fax: 330-386-9279.
E-mail: brookeslaw@sbcglobal.net
Web Site: www.eastliverpoolhistoricalsociety.net
Key Personnel: President, Tim Brookes; Treas., Wm. Gray.
Institution Type/Description: Historic House Museum: housed in the former home of C.C. Thompson, built in 1876. Listed on the National Register of Historical Places.
Hours & Admission Prices: Call for hours. No charge; donations accepted.
Attendance: 350

Eastlake

CROATIAN HERITAGE MUSEUM & LIBRARY - OUR CROATIA, INC., 34900 Lakeshore Blvd., Eastlake, OH 44095-3575. Tel.: 440-946-2044 (museum) & 316-7211. Fax: 216-991-2310.
E-mail: croatianmuseum@sbcglobal.net
Web Site: www.croatianmuseum.com
Key Personnel: Chm. (V), Pres. (V) & Cur., Branka M. Malinar; Treas., Kathy Kuhar; Archivist & Librarian, Jerry Malinar; Devel., Judith Zivic; Public Rels., Suzanne Jerin.
Institution Type/Description: Folk Art Museum.
Hours & Admission Prices: Fri. 12-6; other times by appointment. No charge; donations accepted. Closed New Year's Day; Christmas. &
Attendance: 9,000 (estimated)

Elmore

SCHEDEL ARBORETUM & GARDENS, 19255 W. Portage River S. Rd., Elmore, OH 43416-9743. Tel.: 419-862-3182. Facebook: Schedel Arboretum Gardens.
E-mail: info@schedel-gardens.org
Web Site: www.schedel-gardens.org
Key Personnel: Dir., Rodney Noble; Grounds Supt., Jeff Saffran; Events Coord. & Exec. Asst., Veronica Sheets; Asst. Grounds Supt., Kendra Schwartz.
Institution Type/Description: Arboretum.
Hours & Admission Prices: May-Oct. Tues.-Sat. 10-4, Sun. 12-4. Adults $10, seniors 60 & up $9, children 6-12 $6; discounts to AAA members; children 5 & under and members no charge. Closed Memorial Day; Independence Day; Labor Day.
Attendance: 15,000 (actual)

Elyria

THE LORAIN COUNTY HISTORICAL SOCIETY - THE HICKORIES, 509 Washington Ave., Elyria, OH 44035-5128. Mailing Address: 284 Washington Ave., Elyria, OH 44035. Tel.: 440-322-3341. Fax: 440-322-2817.
E-mail: lchs@lchs.org
Web Site: lchs.org
Key Personnel: Exec. Dir. & C.E.O., William Bird; Pres. (V), Clarence Wills; Office Mgr., Kelsey Voit; Collections & Research Asst., Donna McGuire; Education Coord., Anne Michael; Education Coord., Janet Bird; Education Coord., Jim Smith; Archivist, Eric Greenly.
Institution Type/Description: History Museum.
Hours & Admission Prices: Tours: Jan.-April Thurs.-Fri. 1-4, Sat. 1-3; May-Dec. Tues.-Fri. 1-4, Sat. 1-3; group & school tours by appointment. Adults $5, youth 13-18 $3, children 6-12 $2; discounts to groups; members of Northeastern Ohio Inter Museum Council, LCHS members and employees & their immediate family no charge. Closed holidays.
Attendance: 4,000 (estimated)

THE LORAIN COUNTY HISTORICAL SOCIETY - THE LORAIN COUNTY HISTORY CENTER, 284 Washington Ave., Elyria, OH 44035. Tel.: 440-322-3341. Fax: 440-322-0893.
E-mail: lchs@lchs.org
Web Site: lchs.org
Key Personnel: Dir., William Bird; Pres. (V), Clarence Wills.
Institution Type/Description: History Center: housed in an Italianate-style mansion; built in 1857. Listed on the National Register of Historic Places.
Hours & Admission Prices: Tues.-Fri. 10-4, Sat. 1-3; other times by appointment. Adults $5, youth 13-18 $3, children 6-12 $2; children under 6, NEDIMC & museum members no charge. &
Attendance: 957 (actual)

Euclid

EUCLID HISTORY MUSEUM, 21129 North St., Euclid, OH 44117. Tel.: 216-289-8577.
Institution Type/Description: History Museum: housed in the former Euclid Township High School; built in 1894.
Hours & Admission Prices: Tues.-Sat. 1-4.

NATIONAL CLEVELAND-STYLE POLKA HALL OF FAME AND MUSEUM, 605 E. 222nd St., Euclid, OH 44123-2031. Tel.: 216-261-3263. Fax: 216-261-4134.
E-mail: polkashop@aol.com
Web Site: www.polkafame.com
Key Personnel: C.O.O. & Pres., Joseph Valencic.
Institution Type/Description: Music History Museum.
Hours & Admission Prices: Tues.-Wed. & Fri. 12-5, Sat. 10-3. No charge; donations accepted.

Fairport Harbor

FAIRPORT HARBOR LIGHTHOUSE & MUSEUM, 129 Second St., Fairport Harbor, OH 44077-5816. Tel.: 440-354-4825. Facebook: Community Fine Arts Center.
E-mail: keeper@fairportharborlighthouse.org
Web Site: www.fairportharborlighthouse.org
Formerly: Fairport Marine Museum
Key Personnel: Pres. (V) & Museum Shop Mgr., Mary Alyce Gladding.
Institution Type/Description: Marine Museum: housed in the 1871 Fairport Lighthouse & keeper's residence.
Hours & Admission Prices: Memorial Day to mid-Sept. Wed., Sat.-Sun. & legal holidays 1-6; group tours by appointment. Adults $5, senior citizens $4, children 6-12 $3; discounts to AAM, ICOM & Intermuseum Council members; members, military & children under 6 no charge. &
Attendance: 4,500 (actual)

FINNISH HERITAGE MUSEUM, 301 High St., Fairport Harbor, OH 44077. Mailing Address: P.O. Box 1121, Fairport Harbor, OH 44077. Tel.: 440-352-8301. Facebook: Finnish Heritage Museum.
E-mail: info@finnishheritagemuseum.org
Web Site: finnishheritagemuseum.org
Key Personnel: Pres. (V), Lasse Hiltunen; Museum Shop Mgr., Sue Troutman.
Institution Type/Description: Heritage Museum.
Hours & Admission Prices: Spring, Summer & Fall Wed. & Sun. 1-4, Sat. 9-3; Winter Sat. 9-3. Adults $3, youth 13-17 $1.50; children 12 & under no charge.
Attendance: 1,500 (estimated)

Findlay

HANCOCK HISTORICAL MUSEUM, 422 W. Sandusky St., Findlay, OH 45840-3222. Tel.: 419-423-4433. Fax: 419-423-2154.
E-mail: ssisser@hancockhistoricalmuseum.org
Web Site: www.hancockhistoricalmuseum.org
Key Personnel: Exec. Dir., Sarah Sisser; Pres., Roger Criblez; Archivist, Joy Bennett; Accountant, Carrie Glass.
Institution Type/Description: Local History Museum.
Hours & Admission Prices: Wed.-Sat. 10-4, Sun. 1-4; tours available by appointment. Adults $5, seniors $3, children $2; members no charge. &
Attendance: 40,000 (actual)

MAZZA MUSEUM, Gardner Fine Arts Pavilion, University of Findlay, Findlay, OH 45840-3653. Mailing Address: The University of Findlay, 1000 N. Main St., Findlay, OH 45840-3653. Tel.: 800-472-9502, ext. 5521. Fax: 419-434-6480.
E-mail: teeple@findlay.edu
Web Site: www.mazzamuseum.org
Key Personnel: Dir., Benjamin E. Sapp; Museum Shop Mgr., Lee Myers.
Institution Type/Description: Art Museum.

Hours & Admission Prices: Wed.-Fri. 12-5, Sun. 1-4; other times by appointment. No charge; donations accepted. Closed major holidays. &
Attendance: 10,000 (actual)

Fort Recovery

FORT RECOVERY MUSEUM, 1 Fortsite St., Fort Recovery, OH 45846. Mailing Address: P.O. Box 533, Fort Recovery, OH 45846. Tel.: 419-375-4649.
E-mail: fortrecoverystatemuseum@yahoo.com
Web Site: www.fortrecoverymuseum.com
Key Personnel: Pres. (V), Helen LeFevre.
Institution Type/Description: Military & Indian Museum: housed in partially reconstructed Anthony Wayne fort with two blockhouses.
Hours & Admission Prices: May & Sept. Sat.-Sun. 12-5; June-Aug. daily 12-5. Adults $3, students $1; members, OHS members, children 5 & under no charge.
Attendance: 3,346 (estimated)

Fostoria

FOSTORIA AREA HISTORICAL MUSEUM, 123 W. North St., Fostoria, OH 44830-2232. Mailing Address: P.O. Box 142, Fostoria, OH 44830-0142. Tel.: 419-435-3588.
Institution Type/Description: General Museum.
Hours & Admission Prices: May-Oct. Sat. 1:30-4:30; other times by appointment. &
Attendance: 1,000 (estimated)

GLASS HERITAGE GALLERY, 109 N. Main St., Fostoria, OH 44830-2215. Tel.: 419-435-5077. Facebook.
E-mail: museum@fostoriaglass.com
Web Site: fostoriaglass.com
Key Personnel: Pres. (V), William King.
Institution Type/Description: Glass Museum.
Hours & Admission Prices: March Thurs.-Sat. 10-3; April-Dec. Wed.-Sat. 10-4; other times by appointment. No charge; donations accepted. &
Attendance: 300 (estimated)

Franklin

HARDING MUSEUM OF THE FRANKLIN AREA HISTORICAL SOCIETY, 302 Park Ave., Franklin, OH 45005-3549. Tel.: 937-746-8295.
E-mail: franklinohhistory@gmail.com
Web Site: www.franklinohmuseums.org
Key Personnel: Pres., Elizabeth Buchanan; Museum Mgr., Mary Nenninger.
Institution Type/Description: Local History Museum: housed in 1901 home of Major General E.F. Harding located in Franklin's Mackinaw Historic District.
Hours & Admission Prices: May-Nov. Sat. 11-3; other times by appointment. Adults $3; discounts to AAM & ICOM; members no charge.
Attendance: 1,000 (estimated)

Fremont

RUTHERFORD B. HAYES PRESIDENTIAL LIBRARY AND MUSEUM, Spiegel Grove, Fremont, OH 43420-2796. Tel.: 419-332-2081. Fax: 419-332-5424. Facebook: Hayes Presidential Center.
E-mail: cweininger@rbhayes.org
Web Site: www.rbhayes.org
Key Personnel: Exec. Dir., Christie Weininger; Pres. (V), Stephen A. Hayes; Cur. Manuscript, Nan Card; Head Librarian, Rebecca Hill; Head Photographic Resources, Gilbert Gonzalez; Dir. Devel., Kathy Boukissen; Museum Shop Mgr., Lisa Stuart.
Institution Type/Description: U.S. Library & Museum.
Hours & Admission Prices: Museum & Residence: Mon.-Sat. 9-5, Sun. & holidays 12-5. Adults $13, children 6-12 $5; discounts to groups with appointment, senior citizens, active military & their families, AAA members, Civil War Trust & Natl. Historical Society; children under 6, AAM, AASLH, OHS & HPC members & grounds no charge. Closed New Year's Day; Easter; Thanksgiving; Christmas. Library: Mon.-Sat. 9-5. No charge. Closed holidays. &
Attendance: 40,137 (actual)

SANDUSKY COUNTY HISTORICAL SOCIETY - HOLDERMAN HOUSE, 514 Birchard Ave., Fremont, OH 43420. Tel.: 419-332-0303.
E-mail: f.recktenwald@aol.com
Formerly: Sandusky County Pioneer and Historical Association
Key Personnel: Pres. (V), Fred W. Recktenwald.
Institution Type/Description: Historical Society Museum.

Hours & Admission Prices: May-Nov. Wed. & Sun. 1-4; other times by appointment. Adults 16 & over $2. Closed Thanksgiving. &
Attendance: 500 (estimated)

Gahanna

THE CENTER FOR CIVIL WAR PHOTOGRAPHY, Gahanna, OH 43230. Mailing Address: 947 E. Johnstown Rd. #161, Gahanna, OH 43230-1851. Tel.: 614-656-2297.
E-mail: info@civilwarphotography.org
Web Site: www.civilwarphotography.org
Key Personnel: Co Founder & Pres., Bob Zeller; Vice Pres., Garry Adelman; Co Founder & Dir. Devel., Charles Morrongiello; Exec. Dir., Jennifer Kon; Dir. Membership, Justin A. Shaw; Dir. Imaging, John Richter.
Institution Type/Description: Virtual Museum.
Hours & Admission Prices: Online museum.

Galion

GALION HISTORICAL MUSEUM, 132 S. Union St., Galion, OH 44833-2524. Mailing Address: P.O. Box 125, Galion, OH 44833-0125. Tel.: 419-468-9338. Facebook: Galion Historical Society.
E-mail: galionhistory@gmail.com
Web Site: www.galionhistory.com
Key Personnel: Pres., Mary Court.
Institution Type/Description: History Museum.
Hours & Admission Prices: June-Oct. Sun. 1-4. House Tour: $5; discount to Blue Start Museum members. &
Attendance: 500 (estimated)

GALION HISTORICAL SOCIETY & BROWNELLA COTTAGE, 201 S. Union St., Galion, OH 44833-2524. Mailing Address: P.O. Box 125, Galion, OH 44833-0125. Tel.: 419-468-9338.
E-mail: galionhistory@gmail.com
Web Site: www.galionhistory.com
Key Personnel: Pres., Marcia Yunker; Vice Pres., Mike Mateer; Office Mgr., Tanesha Pickering.
Institution Type/Description: Historic House: Home & Study of Bishop William Montgomery Brown; Galion Historical Museum.
Hours & Admission Prices: June-Sept. Sun. by appointment; groups by appointment year-round. Adults $5, students $3.
Attendance: 1,500 (actual)

Gallipolis

FRENCH ART COLONY, 530 First Ave., Gallipolis, OH 45631-1245. Mailing Address: P.O. Box 472, Gallipolis, OH 45631-0472. Tel.: 740-446-3834. Fax: 740-446-3834.
E-mail: info@frenchartcolony.org
Web Site: www.frenchartcolony.org
Key Personnel: Bd. Member, Jan Thaler; Bd. Member, Peggy Evans; Exec. Dir., Joseph Wright; Chm. (V), Amy Weaver.
Institution Type/Description: Art Gallery: housed in 1855 Holzer Family Home.
Hours & Admission Prices: Galleries: Tues.-Fri. 9-4, Sat. 10-3, Sun. 1-5. No charge; donations accepted. &
Attendance: 7,000 (estimated)

OUR HOUSE TAVERN STATE MEMORIAL, 432 First Ave., Gallipolis, OH 45631. Mailing Address: P.O. Box 607, Gallipolis, OH 45631-0607. Tel.: 740-446-0586.
E-mail: amasara@suddenlink.net
Web Site: ohiohistory.org/places/ourhouse
Key Personnel: Pres., Sara Sheets; Chm. (V), Carol Warren; Site Mgr., Becky Pasquale.
Institution Type/Description: History Museum: housed in 1819 restored Ohio River tavern.
Hours & Admission Prices: Memorial Day-Labor Day Wed.-Sat. 10-4, Sun. 1-4. No charge; donations accepted.
Attendance: 500 (estimated)

Galloway

TRAP HISTORY MUSEUM, 6106 Bausch Rd., Galloway, OH 43119-9382. Mailing Address: P.O. Box 94, Galloway, OH 43119. Tel.: 614-878-6011.
E-mail: traphistorymuseum@gmail.com
Web Site: www.traphistorymuseum.com
Key Personnel: Dir., Tom Parr.
Institution Type/Description: History Museum.

Hours & Admission Prices: By appointment only. No charge; donations accepted.
Attendance: 50 (estimated)

Gambier

GUND GALLERY AT KENYON COLLEGE, 101 1/2 College Dr., Gambier, OH 43022. Tel.: 740-427-5969.
E-mail: gundgallery@kenyon.edu
Web Site: www.thegundgallery.org
Key Personnel: Dir., Natalie Marsh, M.F.A., Ph.D.; Asst. Dir., Christopher Yates, M.F.A.; Mgr. Collections & Registrar, Robin Goodman.
Institution Type/Description: Art Gallery.
Hours & Admission Prices: Tues.-Wed. & Fri. 1-7, Thurs. 1-10, Sat.-Sun. 1-5. No charge. Closed New Year's Eve & Day; Easter; Memorial Day; Independence Day; Thanksgiving; Christmas Eve & Day.

Gates Mills

GATES MILLS HISTORICAL SOCIETY, 7580 Old Mill Rd., Gates Mills, OH 44040. Mailing Address: P.O. Box 191, Gates Mills, OH 44040-0191. Tel.: 440-423-1040.
E-mail: manselmo@roadrunner.com
Web Site: gatesmillshistoricalsociety
Key Personnel: Pres. (V), Marcia Anselmo; Treas., Helen Gelbach; Sec., Sherry Levering.
Institution Type/Description: History Museum.
Hours & Admission Prices: By appointment. No charge; donations accepted.
Attendance: 500 (estimated)

Geneva

PLATT R. SPENCER MEMORIAL ARCHIVES AND SPECIAL COLLECTIONS AREA AT THE GENEVA PUBLIC LIBRARY, Geneva Public Library, 860 Sherman St., Geneva, OH 44041-9101. Tel.: 440-466-4521, ext. 284. Fax: 440-466-0162.
E-mail: schneima@acdl.info
Web Site: www.acdl.info/archives
Key Personnel: Dir., William Tokarczyk; Archivist, Mary Schneider.
Institution Type/Description: Archive.
Hours & Admission Prices: Call for hours. Private tours on Tues. by appointment. No charge; donations accepted. Closed New Year's Eve & Day; Easter; Memorial Day; Independence Day; Labor Day; Thanksgiving; Christmas Eve & Day.
Attendance: 1,000 (estimated)

SHANDY HALL, 6333 S. Ridge Rd. W., Geneva, OH 44041-8377. Mailing Address: Western Reserve Historical Society, 10825 East Blvd., Cleveland, OH 44106. Tel.: 216-721-5722.
E-mail: info@wrhs.org
Web Site: www.wrhs.org
Key Personnel: Pres. & C.E.O., Kelly Falcone-Hall, WRHS; Bd. Chm., Glenn Anderson, Jr.., WRHS.
Institution Type/Description: Historic House: 1815 Shandy Hall, early Western Reserve home.
Hours & Admission Prices: Temporary closed.

Geneva-on-the-Lake

ASHTABULA COUNTY HISTORICAL SOCIETY, 5865 Lake Rd., Geneva-on-the-Lake, OH 44041-9427. Mailing Address: P.O. Box 36, Jefferson, OH 44047-0036. Tel.: 440-466-7337.
E-mail: nan@alltel.net
Web Site: www.ashtcohs.com
Institution Type/Description: House Museum & Landmark: 1811 Blakeslee Log Cabin, 1823 Jennie Munger Gregory Memorial Museum, Geneva-on-the-Lake; 1823 Joshua R. Giddings law office.
Hours & Admission Prices: May & July-Sept. Wed.-Fri. 12-4; June Wed.-Sat. 12-4. Adults $4, children $2.
Attendance: 1,000 (estimated)

Georgetown

US GRANT BOYHOOD HOME, 219 E. Grant Ave., Georgetown, OH 45121. Mailing Address: US Grant Homestead Association, 112 N. Water St., Georgetown, OH 45121. Tel.: 937-378-3087, 877-372-8177.
E-mail: baileyho@frontier.com
Web Site: usgrantboyhoodhome.org
Key Personnel: Pres. (V), Stan Purdy; Dir., Nancy Purdy; Museum Shop Mgr., Joye White.
Institution Type/Description: Historic House Museum: housed in the boyhood home of Ulysses S. Grant from 1823-1839. Listed on the National Register of Historic Places.
Hours & Admission Prices: Boyhood Home & Schoolhouse: May-Oct. Wed.-Sun. 12-5. Adults $5, students $3; discounts to AAM & ICOM members; members no charge. Admission covers both Grant Boyhood Home & Grant Schoolhouse.
Attendance: 1,000 (estimated)

US GRANT SCHOOLHOUSE, 508 S. Water St., Georgetown, OH 45121. Mailing Address: US Grant Homestead Association, 112 N. Water St., Georgetown, OH 45121. Tel.: 937-378-3087, 877-372-8177 (toll-free).
E-mail: baileyho@frontier.com
Web Site: usgrantboyhoodhome.org
Key Personnel: Pres. (V), Stan Purdy; Dir., Nancy Purdy; Museum Shop Mgr., Joye White.
Institution Type/Description: Historic Building: housed in the one room schoolhouse that Ulysses attended from the ages of 6 to 13; built in 1829.
Hours & Admission Prices: Schoolhouse & Boyhood Home: May-Oct. Wed.-Sun. 12-5. Adults $5, students $3; discounts to AAM & ICOM members; members no charge. Admission covers both Grant Schoolhouse & Grant Boyhood Home.
Attendance: 1,000 (estimated)

Glenford

FLINT RIDGE STATE MEMORIAL MUSEUM, 15300 Flint Ridge Rd., Glenford, OH 43739-9639. Tel.: 740-787-2476, 800-283-8707.
E-mail: meweingartner@ohiohistory.org
Key Personnel: Mgr., M.E. Weingartner; Education Specialist, Hapi Cummons.
Institution Type/Description: Natural History Museum: located on the site of prehistoric flint pit.
Hours & Admission Prices: Memorial Day-Labor Day Sat.-Sun. 12-5. Adults $4, children 6-12 $3; discounts to school groups, seniors & AAA members; members and children 5 & under 6 no charge.
Attendance: 7,158 (actual)

Gnadenhutten

GNADENHUTTEN HISTORICAL PARK & MUSEUM, 352 S. Cherry St., Gnadenhutten, OH 44629. Mailing Address: 156 Spring St., Gnadenhutten, OH 44629. Tel.: 740-254-4143. Fax: 740-254-4992.
E-mail: gnadmuse@gnaden.com
Web Site: www.gnaden.com/?cat=31
Institution Type/Description: Historical Park Museum.
Hours & Admission Prices: May Tues. & Sun. 1-5, Sat. 10-5; June-Oct. Tues.-Sat. 10-5, Sun. 1-5; other times by appointment. No charge, donations accepted.
Attendance: 10,000 (estimated)

Gomer

GOMER WELSH COMMUNITY MUSEUM, 7365 Gomer Rd., Gomer, OH 45809. Tel.: 419-999-5820 & 642-5911.
Institution Type/Description: History Museum.
Hours & Admission Prices: 2nd & 4th Sun. each month 1:30-4. No charge.

Granville

DENISON MUSEUM, 240 W. Broadway, Granville, OH 43023-1120. Mailing Address: P.O. Box 810, Granville, OH 43023-0810. Tel.: 740-587-6255. Fax: 740-587-5628. Facebook, Twitter.
E-mail: museum@denison.edu
Web Site: denisonmuseum.org
Formerly: Denison University Art Gallery
Key Personnel: Dir., Rebecca Futo Kennedy; Cur. Collections & Research, Sarah Baker; Cur. Education & Exhibits, Megan Hancock.
Institution Type/Description: University Museum.
Hours & Admission Prices: Mon.-Fri. 12-5. No charge. Closed university holidays.
Attendance: 3,008 (actual)

GRANVILLE, OHIO, HISTORICAL SOCIETY MUSEUM, 115 E. Broadway, Granville, OH 43023-1303. Mailing Address: P.O. Box 129, Granville, OH 43023-0129. Tel.: 740-587-3951. Facebook: Granville Ohio Historical Society.
E-mail: granvillehistorical@gmail.com
Web Site: www.granvillehistory.org
Key Personnel: Pres. (V), Thomas Martin; Vice Pres. (V), Cynthia Cort.
Institution Type/Description: History Museum: housed in 1816 Alexandrian Bank.

Hours & Admission Prices: mid-April to May Sat 12-4 & Sun. 1-3; June-Aug. Fri. 1-3, Sat. 12-4, Sun. 1-3; Sept.-Oct. Sat. 12-4 & Sun. 1-3. No charge; donations accepted. Closed Independence Day weekend. &
Attendance: 3,800 (actual)

ROBBINS HUNTER MUSEUM, AVERY-DOWNER HOUSE, 221 E. Broadway, Granville, OH 43023-1305. Mailing Address: P. O. Box 183, Granville, OH 43023-0183. Tel.: 740-587-0430.
E-mail: annlowder@robbinshunter.org
Web Site: www.robbinshunter.org
Key Personnel: Pres., Kevin Kerr; Dir., Ann K. Lowder.
Institution Type/Description: Historic House: 1842 American Greek Revival house, designed by Minard Lafever.
Hours & Admission Prices: April 4-Dec. 28 Wed.-Sat. 1-4. No charge; donations accepted. Closed Independence Day; Thanksgiving; Christmas. &
Attendance: 13,000 (estimated)

Greenville

GARST MUSEUM, 205 N. Broadway, Greenville, OH 45331-2222. Tel.: 937-548-5250. Fax: 937-548-7645.
E-mail: information@garstmuseum.org
Web Site: www.garstmuseum.org
Formerly: Darke County Historical Society
Key Personnel: Chm., Rodney Oda; Vice Chm., Steve Gruber, Ph.D.; CEO, Clay Johnson, Ph.D.; Treas., Susan Barker; Museum Shop Mgr., Brenda Arnett; Program Mgr., Jenny Clark.
Institution Type/Description: History Museum: housed in 1852 Inn.
Hours & Admission Prices: Feb.-Dec. Tues.-Sat. 10-4, Sun. 1-4. Adults $10, senior citizens 60 & over $9, youth 6-17 $7; discounts to AAA members; members & children under 5 no charge. Closed New Year's Eve & Day; Easter; Independence Day; Thanksgiving; Christmas Eve & Day. &
Attendance: 20,000 (actual)

Groveport

MOTTS MILITARY MUSEUM, 5075 S. Hamilton Rd., Groveport, OH 43125-9336. Tel.: 614-836-1500.
E-mail: info@mottsmilitarymuseum.org
Web Site: www.mottsmilitarymuseum.org
Key Personnel: Dir. & Archivist, Warren E. Motts; Chm. (V), Bo Hindall; Financial Dir., Ronald Albers; Devel., Gerrit Vanstraten; Public Rels. & Museum Shop Mgr., Daisy Motts; Museum Shop Mgr., Ken Macklin.
Institution Type/Description: Military Museum.
Hours & Admission Prices: Tues.-Sat. 9-5, Sun. 1-5. Adults $10, senior citizens & veterans $8, students $5; discounts to active military, & groups; members and children 5 & under no charge. Closed national holidays. &
Attendance: 12,000 (actual)

Hamilton

BUTLER COUNTY HISTORICAL SOCIETY, 327 N. 2nd St., Hamilton, OH 45011-1651. Tel.: 513-896-9930. Fax: 513-896-9936.
E-mail: bcomuseum@fuse.net
Web Site: www.bchistoricalsociety.com
Formerly: Butler County Museum
Key Personnel: Pres. (V), Curtis Ellison; Dir., Kathy Creighton.
Institution Type/Description: History Museum: housed in Benninghofen mansion; built 1861.
Hours & Admission Prices: Tues.-Wed. 11-4, Fri. 9-4, Sat. 9-2; groups by appointment. No charge; donations accepted. &
Attendance: 1,500 (estimated)

PYRAMID HILL SCULPTURE PARK & MUSEUM, 1763 Hamilton Cleves Rd., St. Rd. 128, Hamilton, OH 45013-9601. Tel.: 513-868-1234.
E-mail: pyramid@pyramidhill.org
Web Site: www.pyramidhill.org
Key Personnel: Exec. Dir., Sean FitzGibbons.
Institution Type/Description: Sculpture Park & Museum.
Hours & Admission Prices: April-Oct. Mon.-Fri. 8-5, Sat.-Sun. 8-6; Nov.-March Mon.-Fri. 8-5, Sat.-Sun. 10-5. Adults $8, children 6-12 $3; children 5 & under no charge.
Attendance: 112,366 (actual)

Harrison

AMERICAN WATCHMAKERS-CLOCKMAKERS INSTITUTE, 701 Enterprise Dr., Harrison, OH 45030-2164. Tel.: 513-367-9800. Fax: 513-367-1414. Facebook: My AWCI.
E-mail: jordan@awci.com
Web Site: www.awci.com
Key Personnel: Exec. Dir., Jordan Ficklin; Chm. (V), Jack Kurdzionak.
Institution Type/Description: Horological Display.
Hours & Admission Prices: Mon.-Fri. 8-5 by appointment only. Adults $3, senior citizens $2; discounts to AAM & ICOM members; school groups, children 12 & under, AWCI members no charge. Closed national holidays. &
Attendance: 300 (estimated)

VILLAGE HISTORICAL SOCIETY OF HARRISON, INC., Governor Othniel Looker Home, 10580 Marvin Rd., Harrison, OH 45030. Mailing Address: 115 N. Walnut St., Harrison, OH 45030-1140. Tel.: 513-367-9285.
Key Personnel: Pres. (V), Teri Becker.
Institution Type/Description: Historic House: 1804 Othniel Looker Home. Listed on the National Register of Historic Places.
Hours & Admission Prices: May-Sept. third Sun. of each month 1:30-4; other times & tours by appointment. No charge; donations accepted.

Heath

THE GREAT CIRCLE EARTHWORKS, 455 Hebron Rd., Heath, OH 43056. Tel.: 740-344-0498; 800-589-8224.
E-mail: communications@ohiohistory.org
Web Site: ohiohistory.org/visit/museum-and-site-locator/newark-earthworks
Formerly: Moundbuilders State Memorial & Museum
Institution Type/Description: Prehistoric Indian Art Museum & Historical Site: embankment 1,200 feet in diameter with earthen walls 8-14 feet in height enclosing 26 acres; comprise The Great Circle Earthworks, ceremonial grounds of prehistoric Hopewell Indians, 1000 B.C.-700 A.D.
Hours & Admission Prices: Winter: Mon.-Fri. 8:30-5, Sat. 10-5, Sun. 1-5. Memorial Day to Labor Day Mon.-Fri. 8:30-5, Sat. 10-4, Sun. 12-4. No charge; donations accepted. Closed New Year's Day; Martin Luther King Jr. Day; Columbus Day; Easter; Veterans Day; Thanksgiving & day after; December 23-25; December 29-31. &
Attendance: 7,000 (estimated)

Hilliard

EARLY TELEVISION FOUNDATION AND MUSEUM, 5396 Franklin St., Hilliard, OH 43026. Tel.: 614-771-0510.
E-mail: info@earlytelevision.org
Institution Type/Description: Communication Museum.
Hours & Admission Prices: Sat. 10-6, Sun. 12-5. Suggested Donations: adults $5, children over 6 $2.

Hillsboro

HIGHLAND HOUSE MUSEUM, 151 E. Main St., Hillsboro, OH 45133-1450. Tel.: 937-393-3392.
Institution Type/Description: Historic House: 1844 Highland House.
Hours & Admission Prices: Fri. 1-5, Sun. 1-4; other times by appointment. No charge; donations accepted.
Attendance: 1,500 (estimated)

Holland

J.H. FENTRESS ANTIQUE POPCORN MUSEUM, 7922 Hill Ave., Holland, OH 43528. Tel.: 419-308-4812.
E-mail: info@antiquepopcornmuseum.com
Web Site: www.antiquepopcornmuseum.com
Key Personnel: Dir., Jim Fentress.
Institution Type/Description: History Museum.
Hours & Admission Prices: By appointment. No charge.

Hudson

HUDSON LIBRARY AND HISTORICAL SOCIETY, 96 Library St., Hudson, OH 44236-5122. Tel.: 330-653-6658. Fax: 330-650-3373.
E-mail: archives3@hudson.lib.oh.us
Web Site: www.hudson.lib.oh.us
Key Personnel: Exec. Dir., E. Leslie Polott; Asst. Dir., Ellen Smith; Facilities Mgr., Kathy Hamad.
Institution Type/Description: Regional History Museum.

Hours & Admission Prices: Mon.-Thurs. 9-9, Fri. 9-1, Sat. 9-5, Sun. 12-5. No charge. Closed New Year's Eve & Day; Easter; Memorial Day; Independence Day; Labor Day; Thanksgiving; Christmas Eve & Day.

Ironton

LAWRENCE COUNTY GRAY HOUSE MUSEUM, 506 S. 6th St., Ironton, OH 45638-1825. Mailing Address: P.O. Box 73, Ironton, OH 45638-0073. Tel.: 740-532-1222.
Institution Type/Description: General Museum.
Hours & Admission Prices: mid-April to mid-Dec. Fri.-Sun. 1-5. No charge, donations accepted. &
Attendance: 1,723 (actual)

Jackson

LILLIAN JONES MUSEUM, 75 Broadway St., Jackson, OH 45640-1610. Tel.: 740-286-2556.
E-mail: director@jonesmuseum.com
Web Site: www.jonesmuseum.com
Key Personnel: Dir., Megan Malone; Cur., Rhonda Woolum.
Institution Type/Description: History Museum.
Hours & Admission Prices: Tues.-Thurs. 10-3; other times by appointment. No charge; donations accepted. Closed major holidays. &
Attendance: 500 (actual)

Kalida

PUTNAM COUNTY HISTORICAL SOCIETY MUSEUM, 201 E. Main St., Kalida, OH 45853. Mailing Address: P.O. Box 264, Kalida, OH 45853-0264. Tel.: 419-532-3008. Fax: 419-532-2944.
E-mail: pchs@bright.net
Web Site: www.bright.net/~pchs/
Key Personnel: Pres., Joe Balbaugh; Vice Pres., Janis Lentz; Chm. (V) & Cur., Carol Wise; Recording Sec., Ruth Oglesbee; Corresponding Sec., Lori Ann Hemenway; Treas., Shirley Berelsman; Membership, Deb Carder.
Institution Type/Description: Historical Building: housed in 1901 old Methodist church.
Hours & Admission Prices: Sun. 1-4, Wed. 9-12. No charge; donations accepted. &
Attendance: 2,000 (estimated)

Kent

KENT STATE UNIVERSITY MUSEUM, 515 Hilltop Dr., Kent, OH 44242. Mailing Address: P.O. Box 5190, Kent, OH 44242. Tel.: 330-672-3450. Fax: 330-672-3218.
E-mail: museum@kent.edu
Web Site: www.kent.edu/museum/
Key Personnel: Dir., Jean Druesedow; Mgr. Collections & Museum Registrar, Joanne Fenn; Cur., Sara Hume; Exhibition Designer, Jim Williams; Administrative Asst., Mary Gilbert.
Institution Type/Description: Costume & Decorative Arts Museum: housed in 1927 building, first library of the University.
Hours & Admission Prices: Wed. & Fri.-Sat. 10-4:45, Thurs. 10-8:45, Sun. 12-4:45. Adults $5, senior citizen $4, children $3; discounts to AAM & ICOM members; children under 7 no charge. Annual pass $25. Closed university & national holidays. &
Attendance: 9,270 (actual)

KENT STATE UNIVERSITY, SCHOOL OF ART GALLERIES, Kent, OH 44242. Mailing Address: P.O. Box 5190, Kent, OH 44242. Tel.: 330-672-7853. Fax: 330-672-4729.
E-mail: galleries@kent.edu
Web Site: galleries.kent.edu
Key Personnel: Dir., Christine Havice.
Institution Type/Description: Art School and Gallery.
Hours & Admission Prices: Tues.-Fri. 11-5. No charge; donations accepted. Closed school holidays. &
Attendance: 26,000 (actual)

Kenton

HARDIN COUNTY HISTORICAL MUSEUMS, INC., 223 N. Main St., Kenton, OH 43326-1505. Tel.: 419-673-7147.
E-mail: hardincountymuseums@windstream.net
Web Site: www.hardinmuseums.org
Key Personnel: Dir., Linda Iams.
Institution Type/Description: History Museum.

Hours & Admission Prices: Tues.-Fri. 1-4. No charge; donations accepted. Closed holidays. &
Attendance: 500 (estimated)

Kettering

SOCIETY FOR THE PRESERVATION OF BRITISH TRANSPORTATION IN AMERICA, INC. DBA BRITISH TRANSPORTATION MUSEUM, 2304 Wrenside Lane, Kettering, OH 45440-2324. Tel.: 937-985-7204; 434-1750.
E-mail: britishcarmuseum@ameritech.net
Web Site: www.britishtransportationmuseum.org
Key Personnel: Pres. (V), Peter Stroble; Vice Pres. & Public Rels., Mike Barton; Treas., Archivist & Museum Shop Mgr., Richard R. Smith; Educ., Amanda Hawker; Member-at-Large, J. Colb; Member-at-Large, Mike Edgerton.
Institution Type/Description: Transportation Museum.
Hours & Admission Prices: Dec.-March call for hours. No charge; donations accepted.
Attendance: 475 (estimated)

Kidron

KIDRON SONNENBERG HERITAGE CENTER, 13153 Emerson Rd., Kidron, OH 44636-0234. Mailing Address: P.O. Box 234, Kidron, OH 44636. Tel.: 330-857-9111.
E-mail: kidronheritagecenter@hotmail.com
Web Site: kidronhistoricalsociety.org
Key Personnel: Dir., Dick Wolf.
Institution Type/Description: History Museum.
Hours & Admission Prices: April-Nov. Thurs. & Sat. 11-3, Dec.-March by appt. No charge; donations accepted.

Kirtland

THE HOLDEN ARBORETUM, 9500 Sperry Rd., Kirtland, OH 44094-5172. Tel.: 440-946-4400. Fax: 440-602-3857.
E-mail: holden@holdenarb.org
Web Site: www.holdenarb.org
Key Personnel: Pres. & C.E.O., Clem Hamilton; Chm. Bd. (V), Joe Mahovlic; Assoc. Dir. Devel. & Dir. Planned Giving, Alicia Soss; Dir. Finance, Jim Ansberry; Dir. Horticulture & Conservation, Roger Gettig; Dir. Education, Paul C. Spector; Dir. Human Resources, Nancy Spellman.
Institution Type/Description: Arboretum.
Hours & Admission Prices: Daily 9-5. Non-members $10, children 6-18 $4; discounts to seniors on Tues., groups & AAM members; members & children under 5 no charge. Closed Thanksgiving; Christmas. &
Attendance: 87,437 (actual)

N. K. WHITNEY STORE MUSEUM, 7800 Kirtland Chardon Rd., Kirtland, OH 44094. Tel.: 440-256-9805. Fax: 440-256-2692. Facebook.
E-mail: vckirtland@ldschurch.org
Institution Type/Description: History Museum: housed in a restored 1830s country store & post office.
Hours & Admission Prices: Mon.-Sat. 9am to dusk, Sun. 11:30 to dusk. No charge.
Attendance: 75,000 (actual)

Lakeside

HERITAGE HALL MUSEUM, 238 Maple Ave., Lakeside, OH 43440. Mailing Address: Lakeside Heritage Society, Inc., 324 W. Third St., Lakeside, OH 43440. Tel.: 419-798-5519.
E-mail: contact@hamiltonheritagehall.org
Web Site: www.hamiltonheritagehall.org/McCloskey_Museum/Home.html
Institution Type/Description: History Museum: housed in the former Lakeside Methodist Church; built in 1875.
Hours & Admission Prices: June to Labor Day Tues.-Sat. 10-12 & 1-4:30, Sun. 1:30-4:30; groups by appointment. No charge.

LAKESIDE HERITAGE ARCHIVES, 324 W. Third St., Lakeside, OH 43440. Tel.: 419-798-5519.
E-mail: manager@lakesideheritagesociety.com
Web Site: www.lakesideheritagesociety.org
Institution Type/Description: Archives.
Hours & Admission Prices: May-Aug. Tues.-Sat. 10-2; other times by appointment.

Lakewood

OLDEST STONE HOUSE MUSEUM, 14710 Lake Ave., Lakewood, OH 44107-1353. Tel.: 216-221-7343. Fax: 216-221-0320.
E-mail: museum@lakewoodhistory.org
Web Site: www.lakewoodhistory.org
Key Personnel: Pres. (V), Kathy Haber, Jr.; Dir., Greg Palumbo.
Institution Type/Description: Historic House Museum: 1838 Old Stone House.
Hours & Admission Prices: Feb.-Nov. Wed. 1-4, Sun. 2-5. No charge; donations accepted. Closed national holidays.
Attendance: 2,500 (actual)

Lancaster

DECORATIVE ARTS CENTER OF OHIO, 145 E. Main St., Lancaster, OH 43130-3713. Tel.: 740-681-1423. Fax: 740-681-2713.
E-mail: hill@decartsohio.org
Web Site: www.decartsohio.org
Key Personnel: Exec. Dir., Brian O. Hill, M.A.; Pres., Justin Ristay; Devel. Dir., Denise Mitchell; Dir. Education, Trisha Clifford-Sprouse; Communications Mgr., Angela Morrison; Visitor Svcs., Cathy Kessler; Museum Shop Mgr., Bianca Gery.
Institution Type/Description: Decorative Arts Museum.
Hours & Admission Prices: Tues.-Sat. 10-4, Sun. 1-4. General Admission: no charge; donations accepted. Groups of 10 or more $3. Closed major holidays. &
Attendance: 16,105 (actual)

THE GEORGIAN MUSEUM, 105 E. Wheeling St., Lancaster, OH 43130-3706. Tel.: 740-654-9923. Fax: 740-654-9121.
E-mail: info@fairfieldheritage.org
Web Site: www.fairfieldheritage.org
Key Personnel: Exec. Dir., Andrea Brookover; Office Mgr., Mary Lawrence; Asst. Office Mgr., Kady Wolfe.
Institution Type/Description: Historical Society Museum: housed in 1830-1832 The Georgian, Federal-style house with Regency features.
Hours & Admission Prices: Mon.-Fri. 9-4:30. Adults $6, students 6-18 $2; discount to groups & seniors; children under 6, active duty military personnel with ID & members no charge. Closed holidays. &
Attendance: 7,500 (estimated)

OHIO GLASS MUSEUM & GLASS BLOWING STUDIO, 124 W. Main St., Lancaster, OH 43130-3756. Mailing Address: P.O. Box 794, Lancaster, OH 43130. Tel.: 740-687-0101. Fax: 740-687-0140.
E-mail: museum@ohioglassmuseum.org
Web Site: ohioglassmuseum.org
Formerly: The Ohio Glass Museum & Glass Blowing Studio
Key Personnel: Dir., Douglas Ingram.
Institution Type/Description: Glass Museum.
Hours & Admission Prices: March-Oct. Tues.-Sun. 1-4; Nov.-Feb. Tues.-Sat. 1-4; other times by appointment. Adults $6, seniors $5, students 6-18 $3; members no charge. &
Attendance: 8,358 (actual)

SHERMAN HOUSE MUSEUM, 137 E. Main St., Lancaster, OH 43130-3713. Mailing Address: 105 E. Wheeling St., Lancaster, OH 43130-3706. Tel.: 740-687-5891; 654-9923. Fax: 740-654-9121.
E-mail: fairheritage@greenapple.com
Web Site: www.shermanhouse.com
Key Personnel: Exec. Dir., Andrea Brookover; Office Mgr., Mary Lawrence; Asst. Office Mgr, Kady Wolfe.
Institution Type/Description: Historical House.
Hours & Admission Prices: April to mid-Dec. Tues.-Sun. 12-4. Adults $6; students under 18 $2; discount to groups, seniors, students and AAA & AAM members; children under 6 & members no charge. Closed holidays. &
Attendance: 11,000 (estimated)

Lebanon

GLENDOWER HISTORIC MANSION, 105 Cincinnati Ave., Lebanon, OH 45036-2117. Mailing Address: 105 S. Broadway, Lebanon, OH 45036-1707. Tel.: 513-932-1817. Fax: 513-932-8560.
E-mail: wchs@wchsmuseum.org
Web Site: wchsmuseum.org
Formerly: Glendower State Memorial
Key Personnel: Exec. Dir., Victoria Van Harlingen.

Institution Type/Description: Historic Building Museum: restored Greek revival house.
Hours & Admission Prices: June to Labor Day Wed.-Sat. 12-4; call for Christmas hours; groups by appointment. Adults $8, seniors 65 & over $7, students under 18 $5; WCHS members no charge.
Attendance: 1,384 (estimated)

WARREN COUNTY HISTORY CENTER, 105 S. Broadway, Lebanon, OH 45036-1707. Tel.: 513-932-1817. Fax: 513-932-8560.
E-mail: wchs@wchsmuseum.org
Web Site: wchsmuseum.org
Key Personnel: Exec. Dir., Victoria Van Harlingen; Head Cur., Mary Klei; Dir. Education, John Zimkus; Cur. Exhibits, Jeanne Doan.
Institution Type/Description: Local History Museum.
Hours & Admission Prices: Tues.-Fri. 9-4, Sat. 10-5. Adults $7, senior citizens 65 & over $6, children 5-18 $4; members no charge. Closed some holidays. &
Attendance: 6,800 (estimated)

Lexington

RICHLAND COUNTY MUSEUM, 51 W. Church St., Lexington, OH 44904-1258. Mailing Address: P.O. Box 3153, Lexington, OH 44904-0153. Tel.: 419-884-2230.
E-mail: woodsiewoman@yahoo.com
Web Site: www.richlandcountymuseum.org
Institution Type/Description: General Museum: housed in c.1850 school building.
Hours & Admission Prices: May-Oct. Sun. 1:30-4:30; group tours by appointment. No charge; donations accepted. &
Attendance: 2,000 (estimated)

Lima

ALLEN COUNTY MUSEUM, 620 W. Market St., Lima, OH 45801-4665. Tel.: 419-222-9426. Fax: 419-222-0649.
E-mail: acraft@wcoil.com
Web Site: www.allencountymuseum.org
Key Personnel: Dir., Amy Craft; Pres., William C. Timmermeister; Vice Pres., Richard Boehr; Cur. Manuscripts & Archives, Anna B. Selfridge; Cur. Education, Sarah Rish; Asst. Cur., Charles Bates; Museum Shop Mgr., Joann Park; Admin. Asst. & Bookkeeper, Donna Collins.
Institution Type/Description: History Museum.
Hours & Admission Prices: Museum: Tues.-Sat. 1-5, Sun. 1-4. Children's Discovery Center: Tues.-Sun. 1-5. Museum: Suggested Donation: $5. MacDonell House: admission 11 & over $3; members no charge. Closed holidays. &
Attendance: 64,000 (estimated)

ARTSPACE/LIMA, 65 Town Square, Lima, OH 45801-4950. Tel.: 419-222-1721.
E-mail: artspacelima@woh.rr.com
Web Site: www.artspacelima.com
Key Personnel: Operations Mgr., Bill Sullivan; Assoc. Mgr., Kay Van Meter.
Institution Type/Description: Art Gallery.
Hours & Admission Prices: Tues.-Fri. 10-5, Sat. 10-2.

LIMA FIRE FIGHTERS MEMORIAL MUSEUM, Lima Municipal Center, 50 Town Sq., Lima, OH 45801. Tel.: 419-221-5164.
E-mail: treasurer@LimaFireFighters.org
Institution Type/Description: Fire Fighters Museum.
Hours & Admission Prices: By appointment. No charge.

Lisbon

LISBON HISTORICAL SOCIETY, 117/119 E. Washington St., Lisbon, OH 44432. Mailing Address: P.O. Box 191, Lisbon, OH 44432-0191. Tel.: 330-424-1861.
E-mail: lisbonhs@epohi.com
Web Site: www.lisbonhistory.org
Key Personnel: Co Chm., Kenneth Everett; Pres. (V), Heidi Blosser; Co Chm. & Head Cur., Gene Krotky.
Institution Type/Description: General Museum.
Hours & Admission Prices: Tues. 10-3; other times by appointment. No charge; donations accepted. Closed holidays.
Attendance: 1,500 (estimated)

Lithopolis

THE WAGNALLS MEMORIAL, 150 E. Columbus St., Lithopolis, OH 43136. Mailing Address: P.O. Box 217, Lithopolis, OH 43136.

Tel.: 614-837-4765. Fax: 614-833-4767. FaceBook: The Wagnalls Memorial.
E-mail: leisel@wagnalls.org
Web Site: www.wagnalls.org
Key Personnel: Dir., John K. Bitler; Chm. (V), Jared McGill.
Institution Type/Description: Library & Community Center; Foundation.
Hours & Admission Prices: Mon.-Thurs. 10:30-7:30, Sat. 10-2. No charge; donations accepted. Closed national holidays. ₺

Logan

PENCIL SHARPENER MUSEUM - HOCKING HILLS REGIONAL WELCOME CENTER, 13178 State Rte. 664 S., Logan, OH 43138-8560. Tel.: 740-753-4634.
E-mail: request@explorehockinghills.com
Key Personnel: Owner, Charlotte A. Johnson; Dir., Karen Raymore.
Institution Type/Description: General Museum.
Hours & Admission Prices: By appointment. No charge.

Lorain

LORAIN HISTORICAL SOCIETY, 329 W. 10th St., Lorain, OH 44052-1972. Tel.: 440-245-2563.
E-mail: info@lorainhistory.org
Web Site: www.lorainhistory.org
Formerly: Black River Historical Society of Lorain
Key Personnel: Pres., Ben Norton; Vice Pres., Jack Gaudry; Dir. & Museum Shop Mgr., Barbara Piscopo; Treas., Al Harsar; Cur., Ron Sauer; Sec., Terri Frederick; Education, Rodney Beals.
Institution Type/Description: City History Museum.
Hours & Admission Prices: Carnegie Center Administrative Office: Tues.-Fri. 10-3; 2nd & 4th Sat. 11-2. Tours: Tues.-Thurs. 1-3. Sun. by appointment. Adults $3, students 6-18 $1; discounts to NEOIMC; children under 5 & members no charge. Closed major holidays. ₺
Attendance: 1,500 (estimated)

Loudonville

CLEO REDD FISHER MUSEUM, 203 E. Main St., Loudonville, OH 44842-1214. Tel.: 419-994-4050. Facebook: Cleo Redd Fisher Museum.
E-mail: crfmuseum.com
Web Site: www.crfmuseum.com
Key Personnel: Pres., Jeanne Griffin; Cur., Kenny Libben.
Institution Type/Description: Local History Museum.
Hours & Admission Prices: By appointment; call for holiday weekend hours. No charge; donations accepted. ₺
Attendance: 10,000 (estimated)

Loveland

GREATER LOVELAND HISTORICAL SOCIETY MUSEUM, 201 Riverside Dr., Loveland, OH 45140-2303. Tel.: 513-683-5692.
E-mail: glhsm@fuse.net
Web Site: www.lovelandmuseum.org
Key Personnel: Dir., Janet Beller; Pres., Norman Neal; Librarian, Jo Funke; Museum Shop Co-Mgr., Nancy Garfinkel.
Institution Type/Description: Local History Museum; housed in c.1861 two-story frame structure, 1797 log house, 1879 gazebo & herb garden.
Hours & Admission Prices: Sat.-Sun. 1-4 & other times by appointment. No charge; donations accepted. Closed Easter; Christmas. ₺
Attendance: 1,000 (estimated)

Lucas

MALABAR FARM STATE PARK, 4050 Bromfield Rd., Lucas, OH 44843-9745. Tel.: 419-892-2784. Fax: 419-892-3988.
E-mail: malabar.farm.parks@dnr.state.oh.us
Web Site: www.malabarfarm.org
Key Personnel: C.E.O. & Museum Shop Mgr., Jason Wesley; Chm. (V) & Museum Shop Mgr., Sybil Burskey; Park Mgr., Korre Boyer; Asst. Park Mgr., Siera D. Marth.
Institution Type/Description: Park Museum; housed in The Big House, former home of author Louis Bromfield.
Hours & Admission Prices: Check website for hours. House Tours: Adults $4, seniors 55 & over $3.60, children 7 & over 2. Farm Wagon Tours: $2 per person 7 & over; seniors 55 & over $1.80. Closed major holidays. ₺
Attendance: 400,000 (estimated)

Mansfield

BIBLE WALK, 500 Tingley Ave., Mansfield, OH 44905-1234. Tel.: 800-222-0139. Fax: 419-524-2002.
E-mail: lbmjulia@richnet.net
Web Site: www.biblewalk.us
Formerly: Living Bible Museum
Key Personnel: Dir., Julia Mott-Hardin.
Institution Type/Description: Religious Museum.
Hours & Admission Prices: Mon.-Sat. 9-6, Sun. 3-7. Various tours available. Call for prices. ₺

ELEMENT OF ART STUDIO & GALLERY, 96 N. Main St., Mansfield, OH 44902. Tel.: 419-522-2965. Facebook: Element of Art Studio & Gallery.
Web Site: www.eoastudiogallery.com
Institution Type/Description: Art Gallery.
Hours & Admission Prices: Tues.-Fri. 10-5, Sat. 10-3. No charge.

KINGWOOD CENTER, 900 Park Ave., W., Mansfield, OH 44906-2999. Tel.: 419-522-0211. Fax: 419-522-0211.
E-mail: info@kingwoodcenter.org
Web Site: www.kingwoodcenter.org
Key Personnel: C.E.O., Charles T. Gleaves.
Institution Type/Description: Botanical Garden.
Hours & Admission Prices: Grounds & Gardens: March & Nov. daily 8-5; April-Oct. daily 8-7. Kingwood Hall: April-Oct. Sat. 1-5; Dec. call for extended hours. Greenhouse: March-Oct. daily 8-4:20. Parking: April 14-Oct. 14 $5; members no charge. American Horticultural Society reciprocal program. Closed holidays.
Attendance: 250,000 (estimated)

LITTLE BUCKEYE CHILDREN'S MUSEUM, 44 W. Fourth St., Mansfield, OH 44902. Tel.: 419-522-2332.
E-mail: info@littlebuckeye.org
Web Site: www.littlebuckeye.org
Institution Type/Description: Children's Museum.
Hours & Admission Prices: Wed.-Sat. 10-6, Sun. 1-6. Admission 2 & over $7. Closed New Year's Eve & Day; Easter; Mother's Day; Father's Day; Thanksgiving; Christmas Eve & Day.

THE MANSFIELD ART CENTER, 700 Marion Ave., Mansfield, OH 44906-5006. Tel.: 419-756-1700. Fax: 419-756-0860. Facebook: The Mansfield Art Center.
E-mail: info@mansfieldartcenter.org
Web Site: www.mansfieldartcenter.org
Key Personnel: Exec. Dir., George Whitten; Pres. (V), David Kalish; Museum Shop Mgr., Roger Coulton.
Institution Type/Description: Art Gallery.
Hours & Admission Prices: Tues.-Sun. 11-5. No charge; donations accepted. Gift Shop: discount to NARM members. Closed national holidays. ₺
Attendance: 80,000 (actual)

MANSFIELD FIRE MUSEUM, 1265 W. Fourth St., Mansfield, OH 44906. Tel.: 419-529-2573.
E-mail: mansfieldfiremuseum@yahoo.com
Institution Type/Description: Fire Museum.
Hours & Admission Prices: June-Sept. 1 Sat.-Wed. 1-4; Sept.-May Sat.-Sun. 1-4.

MANSFIELD MEMORIAL MUSEUM, 34 Park Ave., W., Mansfield, OH 44902-1603. Tel.: 419-525-2491.
E-mail: sschaut@richnet.net
Key Personnel: Owner, Julia Hardin; Gen. Mgr., Scott Cater.
Institution Type/Description: History Museum.
Hours & Admission Prices: Feb.-Dec. Sat. 10-4, Sun. 12-4. No charge; donations accepted.

THE OHIO STATE REFORMATORY, 100 Reformatory Rd., Mansfield, OH 44905. Tel.: 419-522-2644.
E-mail: info@mrps.org
Web Site: www.mrps.org
Institution Type/Description: Historic Building; a former prison which housed over 155,000 inmates from 1896-1990. Also the setting for a number of television shows, videos & films including Shawshank Redemption.
Hours & Admission Prices: April-Sept. 1 daily 11-4. Guided Tours: adults $14, students 7-17, seniors 60 & over, college students and military $12. Self-Guided Tours: adults $9, students 7-17, seniors 60 & over, college students and military $7; discounts to members & groups. Audio Wand: $5. Closed major holidays.

Marblehead

MARBLEHEAD LIGHTHOUSE HISTORICAL SOCIETY MUSEUM, 9999 E. Bayshore Rd., Marblehead, OH 43440. Mailing Address: P.O. Box 144, Marblehead, OH 43440. Tel.: 419-734-4424, ext. 2. Facebook.
E-mail: marbleheadlighthousehs@gmail.com
Web Site: marbleheadlighthouseohio.org
Institution Type/Description: Historic Buildings.
Hours & Admission Prices: Park: daily. Historic Buildings: Memorial Day to Labor Day daily 12-4. Tower: admission 6 & over $3; children under 6 no charge. House & Station: no charge.

Marietta

CAMPUS MARTIUS MUSEUM, 601 2nd St., Marietta, OH 45750-2122. Tel.: 740-373-3750, 800-860-0145. Fax: 740-373-3680. Facebook.
E-mail: info@campusmartiusmuseum.org
Web Site: mariettamuseums.org
Key Personnel: Museum Admin., Le Ann Hendershot.
Institution Type/Description: History Museum.
Hours & Admission Prices: Mon. & Wed.-Sat. 9:30-5, Sun. & holidays 12-5. Adults $7, students $4; OHS members and children 5 & under no charge. Closed New Year's Day; Easter; Thanksgiving; Christmas. &
Attendance: 10,550 (actual)

THE CASTLE, 418 Fourth St., Marietta, OH 45750-2003. Tel.: 740-373-4180. Fax: 740-373-4233.
E-mail: castle@mariettacastle.org
Web Site: www.mariettacastle.org
Key Personnel: Dir., Scott Britton; Pres., Judy Grize; Treas., Molly Frye.
Institution Type/Description: Historic House: c.1855 Gothic Revival-style home.
Hours & Admission Prices: Jan.-March group tours only; April-May & Sept.-Dec. Mon. & Thurs.-Sat. 10-4, Sun. 1-4; June-Aug. Mon.-Tues. & Thurs. 10-4, Sun. 1-4. Adults $7, senior citizens $6.50, students $4; discounts to groups, AARP, AAM & AAA members; children under 6 & members no charge. Closed New Year's Day; Easter; Thanksgiving; Christmas. &
Attendance: 6,023 (actual)

THE CHILDREN'S TOY & DOLL MUSEUM, 206 Gilman St., Marietta, OH 45750-2837. Mailing Address: P.O. Box 4034, Marietta, OH 45750-7034. Tel.: 740-373-5900.
Key Personnel: Pres. (V), Donna Kern.
Institution Type/Description: Children's Museum.
Hours & Admission Prices: May-Nov. 1 Sat.-Sun. 1-4; other times by appointment. Family $10, adults $4, children $2; discount to families; members no charge.

OHIO RIVER MUSEUM, 601 Front St., Marietta, OH 45750. Mailing Address: 601 Second St., Marietta, OH 45750-2122. Tel.: 740-373-3750, 800-860-0145. Fax: 614-373-3680. Facebook.
E-mail: info@campusmartiusmuseum.org
Web Site: campusmartiusmuseum.org
Key Personnel: Museum Admin., Le Ann Hendershot.
Institution Type/Description: History Museum & Historic Ship: 1918 stern-wheel Steamer, W.P. Snyder Jr., a National Historic Landmark.
Hours & Admission Prices: April to Labor Day Mon. & Wed.-Sat. 9:30-5, Sun. & holidays 12-5; Sept.-Oct. Sat. 9:30-5, Sun. & holidays 12-5; tours by appointment. Adults $7, students $4; OHS members & children 5 and under no charge. &
Attendance: 4,200 (estimated)

PEOPLES MORTUARY MUSEUM, 408 Front St., Marietta, OH 45750. Tel.: 740-373-1111. Fax: 740-373-1112.
E-mail: bill@cawleyandpeoples.com
Web Site: www.cawleyandpeoples.com
Key Personnel: Dir., C.E.O. & Chm., Bill Peoples.
Institution Type/Description: History Museum.
Hours & Admission Prices: By appointment. No charge. &
Attendance: 500 (estimated)

Marion

BUCKEYE TELEPHONE MUSEUM AKA THE CLARE E. WILLIAMS TELEPHONE MUSEUM ASSOCIATION, CWA Union Hall, 581 Bellefontaine Ave., Marion, OH 43302. Mailing Address: 6075 Marion Edison Rd., Caledonia, OH 43314-9413. Tel.: 419-947-8676, 800-371-6688; 740-389-7990 (Marion County Visitors Bureau).

E-mail: jekosto@frontier.com
Key Personnel: Dir., John E. Kosto; C.E.O., Jerron Reeder.
Institution Type/Description: History Museum.
Hours & Admission Prices: By appointment. Suggested Donation: $2. &
Attendance: 250 (estimated)

HARDING HOME AND MUSEUM, 380 Mt. Vernon Ave., Marion, OH 43302-4120. Tel.: 740-387-9630, 800-600-6894. Fax: 740-387-9630 (call first).
E-mail: shall@hardinghome.org
Web Site: www.hardinghome.org
Key Personnel: Site Mgr., S. Hall.
Institution Type/Description: History Museum: housed in 1920 cottage, press corps center for Harding's Campaign.
Hours & Admission Prices: Memorial Day weekend to Sept. Wed.-Sun. 12-5; Sept.-Oct. weekends 12-5 and by appointment on weekdays; Nov.-May by appointment only. Adults $7, seniors 60 & up $6, students 12-17 $4, children 6-11 $3; discounts AAA members; Ohio Historical Society, Marion Technical College student with ID and active military & families with ID no charge. &
Attendance: 6,000 (estimated)

HUBER MACHINERY MUSEUM, 220 E. Fairground St., Marion, OH 43302. Mailing Address: P.O. Box 6010, Marion, OH 43301-6010. Tel.: 740-389-1098.
E-mail: fjd1@roadrunner.com
Institution Type/Description: Machinery Museum.
Hours & Admission Prices: March-Dec. Sat. 1-4; other times by appointment. No charge; donations accepted. &
Attendance: 2,500 (actual)

THE MARION COUNTY HISTORICAL SOCIETY MUSEUM, 169 E. Church St., Ste. A, Marion, OH 43302-3826. Tel.: 740-387-4255. Fax: 740-387-0117.
E-mail: mchs@marionhistory.com
Web Site: www.marionhistory.com
Key Personnel: Dir., C.E.O. & Museum Shop Mgr., Gale E. Martin; Pres., Randy Windland; Treas., Diane Mault; Museum Shop Mgr., Meredithe Predmore.
Institution Type/Description: History Museum.
Hours & Admission Prices: March-April & Nov.-Dec. Sat.-Sun. 1-4; May-Oct. Wed.-Sun. 1-4; group tours by appointment. Adults $5, seniors $4, children 6-12 $2; discounts to AAA & Golden Buckeye members; members & children under 6 no charge. &
Attendance: 8,000 (actual)

STENGEL-TRUE MUSEUM, 504 S. State St., Marion, OH 43302-5036. Tel.: 740-387-6140.
E-mail: info@visitmarionohio.com
Key Personnel: Chm. (V), Kevin Hall.
Institution Type/Description: Historical Society Museum: housed in c.1860 Judge Ozias Bowen home.
Hours & Admission Prices: By appointment. Requested Donation: $1. Closed holidays.
Attendance: 2,400 (estimated)

WYANDOT POPCORN MUSEUM, Heritage Hall, 169 E. Church St., Ste. B, Marion, OH 43302-3826. Tel.: 740-387-4255. Fax: 7404-387-0117.
E-mail: mchs@marionhistory.com
Web Site: www.marionhistory.com
Key Personnel: Dir., Gale E. Martin; Pres. (V), Brooks Brown; Museum Shop Mgr., Meredithe Predmore.
Institution Type/Description: Popcorn Museum.
Hours & Admission Prices: May-Oct. Wed.-Sun. 1-4; Nov.-April Sat.-Sun. 1-4. Adults $5, seniors $4, children 6-12 $2; discounts to AAA & Golden Buckeye members; members & children under 6 no charge. Closed New Year's Day; Easter; Memorial Day; Independence Day; Labor Day; Thanksgiving; Christmas Eve & Day. &
Attendance: 6,000 (estimated)

Marshallville

MARSHALLVILLE HISTORICAL SOCIETY, 4 E. Church St., Marshallville, OH 44645. Tel.: 330-855-4041.
Institution Type/Description: Historical Society Museum.
Hours & Admission Prices: By appointment.

Marysville

THE UNION COUNTY HISTORICAL SOCIETY, 246 W. Sixth St., Marysville, OH 43040-1531. Mailing Address: P.O. Box 303, Marysville, OH 43040-0303. Tel.: 937-644-0568.
E-mail: rwparrott@embarqmail.com
Web Site: www.historyohio.com/
Key Personnel: Pres., Robert W. Parrott; Vice Pres., Stephen W. Badenhop; Treas., John Woerner.
Institution Type/Description: Historical Society Museum: housed in the Henry W. Morey home; built in 1891.
Hours & Admission Prices: April-Nov. Wed. 1-4; other times by appointment. No charge. Adults $5; members no charge. Closed New Year's Day; Thanksgiving; Christmas.
Attendance: 2,500 (estimated)

Mason

MASON HISTORICAL SOCIETY - ALVERTA GREEN MUSEUM, 207 W. Church St., Mason, OH 45040. Tel.: 513-398-6750.
E-mail: masonhistorical@yahoo.com
Web Site: www.masonhistoricalsociety.org
Key Personnel: Cur., Letha Hendrickson.
Institution Type/Description: History Museum.
Hours & Admission Prices: Thurs.-Fri. 1-4. No charge; donations accepted.

Massillon

MASSILLON MUSEUM, 121 Lincoln Way, E., Massillon, OH 44646-6633. Tel.: 330-833-4061. Fax: 330-833-2925.
E-mail: ancoon@massillonmuseum.org
Web Site: www.massillonmuseum.org
Key Personnel: Exec. Dir., Alexandra Nicholis Coon; Chm. (V), Gloria Pope; Archivist, Mandy Pond; Operations Officer, Scot Phillips.
Institution Type/Description: History & Art Museum.
Hours & Admission Prices: Tues.-Sat. 9:30-5, Sun. 2-5; evenings by appointment. No charge; donations accepted. Closed legal holidays. &
Attendance: 23,746 (actual)

SPRING HILL HISTORIC HOME, 1401 Springhill Ln., N.E., Massillon, OH 44646. Tel.: 330-833-6749. Facebook: Spring Hill Historic Home.
E-mail: info@springhillhistorichome.org
Web Site: www.springhillhistorichome.org
Key Personnel: Dir., Samantha Kay Smith.
Institution Type/Description: Historic House: housed in the former home of Thomas & Charity Rotch; built in 1821.
Hours & Admission Prices: Call for hours. Adults $5, seniors 65 & over and students 6-17 $4; members and children 5 & under no charge.

Maumee

WOLCOTT HOUSE MUSEUM COMPLEX, 1031 River Rd., Maumee, OH 43537-3460. Tel.: 419-893-9602. Fax: 419-893-3108.
E-mail: mvhs@buckeye-access.com
Web Site: www.wolcotthouse.org
Key Personnel: Pres., Paul Sullivan; Exec. Dir., Jack Hiles; Museum Shop Mgr., Judy Walrod.
Institution Type/Description: Historic Structures: 1836 Wolcott House; c.1850 log cabin; c.1840 saltbox style farmhouse; c.1880 train depot; c.1901 country church; c.1840 Greek Revival townhouse; c.1850 one room county schoolhouse.
Hours & Admission Prices: Museum Guided Tours: Thurs.-Sun. 12:30 & 2:30. Adults $5, seniors $4, students $2.50; discounts to AAA members; members no charge. Gift Shop: April-Dec. Thurs.-Sun. 12-4:30.
Attendance: 10,000 (estimated)

McCutchenville

MCCUTCHEN OVERLAND INN, 283 State Hwy. 53 N., McCutchenville, OH 44844. Mailing Address: P.O. Box 372, Upper Sandusky, OH 43351-0372. Tel.: 419-981-2052.
E-mail: curator@wyandothistory.org
Institution Type/Description: Historic House: housed in a former stage coach stop built by Col. Joseph McCutchen in 1829.
Hours & Admission Prices: June-Oct. Sat.-Sun. 1-4:30. Adults $2, children 13 & under $1. &

Medina

MEDINA COUNTY HISTORICAL SOCIETY, THE JOHN SMART HOUSE, 206 N. Elmwood St., Medina, OH 44256-1829. Mailing Address: P.O. Box 306, Medina, OH 44258-0306. Tel.: 330-722-1341.
E-mail: mchs@zoominternet.net
Web Site: www.medinahistorical.com
Key Personnel: Co-Pres., Mary Jane Brewer; Co-Pres., Thomas D. Hilberg; Vice Pres., Brian Feron; Treas., Carole Feron.
Institution Type/Description: Historical Society Museum: located in 14-room Victorian home.
Hours & Admission Prices: Tues. 9-4, 1st Sun. of the month 1-4; other times by appointment. No charge; donations accepted.
Attendance: 2,300 (estimated)

MEDINA TOY AND TRAIN MUSEUM, 7 Public Square, Medina, OH 44256-2203. Tel.: 330-764-4455. Fax: 330-722-2205.
E-mail: ormandys@zoominternet.net
Institution Type/Description: Toy & Train Museum.
Hours & Admission Prices: Mon.-Sat. 10-5, Sun. 12-5. Adults 10 & over $3.
Attendance: 5,500 (estimated)

Mentor

JAMES A. GARFIELD NATIONAL HISTORIC SITE, 8095 Mentor Ave., Mentor, OH 44060-5753. Tel.: 440-255-8722. Fax: 440-974-2045. Facebook: Garfield NPS.
E-mail: jaga_interpretation@nps.gov
Web Site: www.nps.gov/jaga
Institution Type/Description: Historic House: c.1880 home of former Pres. James Garfield.
Hours & Admission Prices: May-Oct. daily 10-5; Nov.-April Fri-Sun. 10-5. Guided Tours: $7; children 15 & under and NPS Pass holders no charge. Guided tour of Garfield Home $7, 15 & under no charge. Closed New Year's Day; Thanksgiving; Christmas. &
Attendance: 30,000 (actual)

MENTOR FIRE MUSEUM, 7262 Jackson St., Mentor, OH 44060. Tel.: 440-299-0202.
E-mail: museum@mentorsafetyvillage.com
Web Site: www.mentorsafetyvillage.com
Key Personnel: Dir. & Cur., Don Zimmerman; Treas., Gabe Zelinka; Archivist, Jeremy Szydlowski.
Institution Type/Description: Firefighting History Museum: housed in a former fire station; built in 1940s.
Hours & Admission Prices: By appointment. No charge; donations accepted.
Attendance: 50 (estimated)

Miamisburg

MIAMISBURG HISTORICAL SOCIETY, 4 N. Main St., Miamisburg, OH 45342-2313. Mailing Address: P.O. Box 774, Miamisburg, OH 45343-0774. Tel.: 937-859-5000.
E-mail: mhsociety@att.net
Web Site: www.miamisburg.org
Key Personnel: Dir., Randy Staley; Pres., Paul Schultz; Cur., Larry Suttman; Museum Shop Mgr., Judy Frizzell.
Institution Type/Description: Historical Society Museum.
Hours & Admission Prices: Wed. & Sat. 1-4; other times by appointment. No charge; donations accepted. &
Attendance: 800 (estimated)

WRIGHT "B" FLYER, INC., 10550 Springboro Pike, Miamisburg, OH 45342. Tel.: 937-885-2327. Fax: 937-885-3310.
E-mail: wbflyer@dayton.net
Web Site: www.wright-b-flyer.org/about-us.html
Formerly: Wright "B" Flyer's Hangar and Museum
Key Personnel: Chm. (V), Jay Jabour.
Institution Type/Description: Aviation History Museum.
Hours & Admission Prices: Tues., Thurs. & Sat. 9-2:30; other times by appointment. No charge.

Middletown

CANAL MUSEUM, 1605 N. Verity Pkwy., Middletown, OH 45042. Mailing Address: c/o Middletown Historical Society, P.O. Box 312, Middletown, OH 45042. Tel.: 513-424-5539. Facebook: Canal Museum.
E-mail: themiddletownhistoricalsociety@gmail.com

Web Site: middletownhistoricalsociety.com
Key Personnel: Pres. (V), Sam Ashworth; Archivist, Phyllis Ashworth.
Institution Type/Description: History Museum.
Hours & Admission Prices: Summer: Sun. 2-4. No charge; donations accepted.
Attendance: 300 (estimated)

MIDDLETOWN ARTS CENTER, 130 N. Verity Pkwy., Middletown, OH 45042. Mailing Address: P.O. Box 441, Middletown, OH 45042. Tel.: 513-424-2417.
E-mail: pattbelisle@middletownartscenter.com
Web Site: www.middletownartscenter.com
Key Personnel: Dir., Patt Belisle; Pres. (V), Jackie Philips; Asst. Dir., Kim Minor; Program Coord., Leslie Pinto; Administrative Asst. & Volunteer Coord., Cheryl Landen.
Institution Type/Description: Art Gallery.
Hours & Admission Prices: Mon. 9-12pm, Tues & Thurs. 1-9, Wed. 9am-9pm, Sat. 9am-12pm. No charge; donations accepted. Closed President's Day; Memorial Day; 4th of July; Labor Day; Nov. 26-Nov. 30; Dec. 9-Jan. 4, 2015. &
Attendance: 4,750 (estimated)

MIDDLETOWN HISTORICAL SOCIETY - SHARTLE HOUSE, 120 N. Verity Pkwy., Middletown, OH 45042. Mailing Address: P. O. Box 312, Middletown, OH 45042. Tel.: 513-424-5539. Facebook: Middletown Historical Society - Shartle House.
E-mail: themiddletownhistoricalsociety@gmail.com
Web Site: middletownhistoricalsociety.com
Key Personnel: Pres. (V), Sam Ashworth.
Institution Type/Description: Historical Society Museum.
Hours & Admission Prices: Wed. 10-2. No charge; donations accepted. &
Attendance: 500 (estimated)

Milan

MILAN HISTORICAL MUSEUM, INC., 10 Edison Dr., Milan, OH 44846-9319. Mailing Address: P.O. Box 308, Milan, OH 44846-0308. Tel.: 419-499-2968. Fax: 419-499-9004.
E-mail: museum@milanhistory.org
Web Site: www.milanhistory.org
Key Personnel: Pres. (V), Mr. Sparky Weilnam; C.E.O. & Dir., Ann Basilone-Jones.
Institution Type/Description: General Museum: housed in 1846 home of Dr. Lehman Galpin who assisted in the birth of Thomas A. Edison.
Hours & Admission Prices: April-May & Sept.-Oct. Sat.-Sun. 1-5; June-Aug. Tues.-Sat. 10-5, Sun. 1-5; other times by appointment. Adults $7, Senior Citizens $6, children 6-12 $4; discount to AAM members & groups; members no charge. Closed Labor Day weekend. &
Attendance: 5,700

THOMAS EDISON BIRTHPLACE MUSEUM, 9 N. Edison Dr., Milan, OH 44846-0451. Mailing Address: P.O. Box 451, Milan, OH 44846-0451. Tel.: 419-499-2135. Fax: 419-499-2135 (call first). Facebook: Edison Birthplace Association.
E-mail: director@tomedison.org
Web Site: www.tomedison.org
Key Personnel: C.E.O. & Pres. (V), Robert K.L. Wheeler; Exec. Dir., Lois J. Wolf.
Institution Type/Description: Historic House Museum: 1841 birthplace & home of Thomas A. Edison.
Hours & Admission Prices: Feb.-March & Nov.-Dec. Fri.-Sun. 1-5 (last tour 4:30); April-May & Sept.-Oct. Tues.-Sun. 1-5; June-Aug. Tues.-Sat. 10-5, Sun. 1-5 (last tour 4:30). Family $20, adults $7, senior citizens $6, youth 5-17 $5; discount to groups of 10 or more; military families from Memorial Day to Labor Day & military members all year no charge. Blue Star Museums Program. Closed New Year's Day; Easter; Labor Day weekend; Thanksgiving; Christmas.
Attendance: 6,000 (actual)

Milford

PROMONT HOUSE MUSEUM, Greater Milford Area Historical Society Inc., 906 Main St., Milford, OH 45150-1767. Tel.: 513-248-0324. Fax: 513-248-2304.
E-mail: info@milfordhistory.net
Web Site: www.milfordhistory.net
Key Personnel: Administrator, Donna Amann.
Institution Type/Description: Historical Society Museum: housed in 1865, Italianate 3-story brick home.
Hours & Admission Prices: March-Dec. 2nd Sat. & 2nd Sun. of month 1-4; special groups by appointment. Adults $5, children $1; members no charge.
Attendance: 1,800 (estimated)

Millersburg

AMISH & MENNONITE HERITAGE CENTER, 5798 County Rd. 77, Millersburg, OH 44654. Tel.: 877-858-4634.
E-mail: director@amheritagecenter.com
Web Site: www.behalt.com
Institution Type/Description: Heritage Center.
Hours & Admission Prices: Mon.-Sat. 9-5. Adults $8.75-$12.50; members no charge. &
Attendance: 23,000 (estimated)

HOLMES COUNTY HISTORICAL SOCIETY, 484 Wooster Rd., Millersburg, OH 44654. Mailing Address: P.O. Box 126, Millersburg, OH 44654-0126. Tel.: 330-674-0022, 888-201-0022. Facebook: Victorian House Museum.
E-mail: info@holmeshistory.com
Web Site: www.victorianhouse.org, www.holmeshistory.com
Key Personnel: Exec. Dir., Mark Boley; Pres., Camille Nowels; Vice Pres., Susan Helal; Sec., Pat Shrock; Treas., Bonnie Self; Cur., Candi Barnhart.
Institution Type/Description: Historical Society Museum: housed in 1902 Victorian-style house.
Hours & Admission Prices: March Sat.-Sun. 1-4; April-Oct. Tues.-Sun. 1-4; group tours by appointment. Adults $8, seniors 65 & over $7, students $3; discounts to groups; children under 12 & members no charge.
Attendance: 5,000 (estimated)

Minster

LAKE LORAMIE HERITAGE MUSEUM, Lake Loramie State Park, State Rte. 362, 4401 Fort Loramie Swanders Rd., Minster, OH 45865-9306. Mailing Address: Lake Loramie State Park, 12774 St. Rt. 235 N, Lakeview, OH 43331. Tel.: 937-295-3900. Fax: 937-295-2119.
E-mail: jason.whitman@dnr.state.oh.us
Web Site: www.dnrstate.oh.us
Institution Type/Description: History Museum.
Hours & Admission Prices: Summer: Sat. 1-4. No charge; donations accepted.
Attendance: 230 (estimated)

MINSTER HISTORICAL SOCIETY AND MUSEUM, 112 W. Fourth St., Minster, OH 45865. Tel.: 419-628-4600.
E-mail: mhs1832@frontier.com
Web Site: minsterhistoricalsociety.com
Institution Type/Description: History Museum.
Hours & Admission Prices: Tues. 10-2, Sun. 1-3; groups by appointment. Closed major holidays.

Monroe

MONROE HISTORICAL SOCIETY, 10 E. Elm St., Monroe, OH 45050. Mailing Address: P.O. Box 82, Monroe, OH 45050. Tel.: 513-539-2270. Facebook: Monroe Historical Society.
E-mail: info@monroeoh-historicalsociety.org
Web Site: www.monroeoh-historicalsociety.org
Formerly: Chickahominy House Museum
Key Personnel: Pres. (V), Christina McElfresh; Museum Shop Mgr., James Price.
Institution Type/Description: Historical Society Museum.
Hours & Admission Prices: Mon. 10am-12pm; other times by appointment. No charge; donations accepted.
Attendance: 450 (estimated)

1910 GENERAL STORE MUSEUM, 2 E. Elm St., Monroe, OH 45050. Mailing Address: Monroe Historical Society, P.O. Box 82, Monroe, OH 45050. Tel.: 513-539-2270.
E-mail: info@monroeohhistoricalsociety.org
Web Site: www.monroeoh-historicalsociety.org
Key Personnel: Cur., Dorothy Smith; Asst. Cur., Jo Hutsenpiller; Dir., Facilities, Jim Price; Dir. Special Events, Anna Hale.
Institution Type/Description: Historical Society Museum.
Hours & Admission Prices: Main Street Campus: Mon. 10-12 & by appointment. Log Cabin: by appointment. No charge.
Attendance: 400 (estimated)

Montpelier

WILLIAMS COUNTY HISTORICAL MUSEUM, 611 E. Main St., Williams County Fairgrounds, Montpelier, OH 43543. Mailing Address: P.O. Box 415, Montpelier, OH 43543-0415. Tel.: 419-485-8200.

E-mail: wchs@williams-net.com
Web Site: williamscountyhistory.org
Key Personnel: Exec. Dir. & Cur., Pam Schroeder.
Institution Type/Description: General Museum.
Hours & Admission Prices: May-Oct. Mon.-Thurs. 1-4; other times & tours by
   appointment. Adults $2, children 6-18 $1; members no charge. Closed holidays.
   &
Attendance: 1,500 (estimated)

Mount Pleasant

**FRIENDS (QUAKER) YEARLY MEETING HOUSE STATE
   MEMORIAL,** 298 Market St., Mount Pleasant, OH 43939.
   Mailing Address: 69670 Sunset Dr., Bridgeport, OH 43912. Tel.:
   800-752-2631.
E-mail: jamela85@aol.com
Key Personnel: Site Operations Mgr., Sherry Sawchuk.
Institution Type/Description: Historic House Museum: built in 1814.
Hours & Admission Prices: May-Oct. by appointment. Meeting House: adults $7,
   children 6-12 $4; discounts to groups; OHS members & children under 5 no
   charge. Six Building Tour: adults $15, students 6-12 $7; discounts to groups;
   children under 5 no charge.
Attendance: 500 (estimated)

MOUNT PLEASANT HISTORICAL SOCIETY, 342 Union St.,
   Mount Pleasant, OH 43939. Mailing Address: 69670 Sunset Dr.,
   Bridgeport, OH 43912. Tel.: 800-752-2631. Facebook.
E-mail: jamela85@aol.com
Key Personnel: C.E.O. & Pres. (V), Angela Feenerty.
Institution Type/Description: General Museum.
Hours & Admission Prices: May-Oct. by appointment. Adults $15, children 6-12
   $7; discount to groups of 20 or more; children under 5 no charge.
Attendance: 400 (estimated)

Mount Vernon

KNOX COUNTY AGRICULTURAL MUSEUM, Knox County
   Fairgrounds, State Rte. 3, Mount Vernon, OH 43050. Mailing
   Address: Knox County Agriculture Association, P.O. Box 171,
   Mount Vernon, OH 43050. Tel.: 740-397-1423.
E-mail: info@theagmuseum.org
Web Site: www.theagmuseum.org
Institution Type/Description: Agriculture Museum.
Hours & Admission Prices: By appointment.

KNOX COUNTY HISTORICAL SOCIETY, 875 Harcourt Rd.,
   Mount Vernon, OH 43050-4325. Mailing Address: P.O. Box 522,
   Mount Vernon, OH 43050-0522. Tel.: 740-393-5247.
E-mail: kchs@knoxhistory.org
Web Site: www.knoxhistory.org/about.htm
Key Personnel: Dir., James K. Gibson.
Institution Type/Description: Historical Society Museum.
Hours & Admission Prices: Wed. 6pm-8pm, Thurs.-Sun. 2-4.

Napoleon

DR. BLOOMFIELD HOME AND CARRIAGE HOUSE, West
   Clinton & Webster Sts., Napoleon, OH 43545. Mailing Address:
   Henry County Historical Society, P.O. Box 443, Napoleon, OH
   43545. Tel.: 419-758-3262.
Institution Type/Description: Historic House Museum: c.1879.
Hours & Admission Prices: May-Oct. Sun. 2-4; other times by appointment.

HENRY COUNTY HISTORICAL SOCIETY, Henry County
   Fairgrounds, Napoleon, OH 43545. Mailing Address: P.O. Box
   443, Napoleon, OH 43545. Tel.: 419-758-3262.
E-mail: jamesrebar@roadrunner.com
Institution Type/Description: Historical Society Museum.
Hours & Admission Prices: By appointment.

Nelsonville

STUART'S OPERA HOUSE, 52 Public Sq., Nelsonville, OH
   45764-1133. Mailing Address: P.O. Box 217, Nelsonville, OH
   45764-0217. Tel.: 740-753-1924. Fax: 740-753-1982.
E-mail: info@stuartsoperahouse.org
Web Site: www.stuartsoperahouse.org
Formerly: Hocking Valley Museum of Theatrical History, Inc.

Key Personnel: Pres., Miki Brooks; Dir., Tim Peacock; C.O.O., Adam Fischer.
Institution Type/Description: Theater Museum: housed in 1879 Stuart's Opera
   House.
Hours & Admission Prices: Mon.-Fri. 10-5. No charge; donations accepted. &
Attendance: 20,000 (estimated)

New Athens

FRANKLIN MUSEUM, 187 N. Main St., New Athens, OH 43981.
   Tel.: 740-968-1042 & 4066.
Institution Type/Description: History Museum: housed in the former Franklin
   College building. Listed on the National Register of Historic Places.
Hours & Admission Prices: May-Sept. Tues.-Thurs. 12-4; other times by appoint-
   ment. Adults $5.

New Bremen

THE BICYCLE MUSEUM OF AMERICA, 7 W. Monroe St., New
   Bremen, OH 45869-1146. Tel.: 419-629-9249. Fax: 419-629-3256.
   Facebook: Bicycle Museum.
E-mail: jessica.howison@crown.com
Web Site: www.bicyclemuseum.com
Key Personnel: Cur., Public Rels. & Museum Shop Mgr., Jessica Howison.
Institution Type/Description: Bicycle Museum.
Hours & Admission Prices: June-Sept. Mon.-Fri. 9-7, Sat. 10-2; Oct.-May Mon.-
   Fri. 9-5, Sat. 10-2. Adults $3, senior citizens $2, students $1; drivers of groups &
   children under 6 no charge.
Attendance: 10,000 (estimated)

New Carlisle

HONEY CREEK FIRE MUSEUM, 315 N. Adams St., New
   Carlisle, OH 45344. Tel.: 937-845-0480.
Institution Type/Description: Firefighting History Museum.
Hours & Admission Prices: By appointment.

New Philadelphia

HISTORIC SCHOENBRUNN VILLAGE, 1984 W. High Ave.,
   New Philadelphia, OH 44663. Mailing Address: P.O. Box 11,
   Dennison, OH 44621-0011. Tel.: 740-922-6776, 800-752-2711.
   Fax: 740-922-4929. Facebook: Historic Schoenbrunn Village.
E-mail: director@dennisondepot.org
Web Site: www.ohiosfirstvillage.com
Formerly: Schoenbrunn Village State Memorial
Key Personnel: Dir., Wendy Zucal; Site Mgr., Rata Williamson; Garden &
   Volunteer Coord., Michelle Hallman; Mgr. Brand Rels. & Consumer
   Engagement, Jacob Masters; Gift Shop Mgr., Joan Beorn.
Institution Type/Description: Museum Village Complex.
Hours & Admission Prices: Memorial Day-Labor Day Tues.-Sat. 9:30-5, Sun. 12-5;
   Sept.-Oct. Sat. 9:30-5, Sun. 12-5. Adults $7, seniors $5, children $4; discounts to
   groups & AAM members; members no charge. &
Attendance: 12,500 (estimated)

Newark

THE DAWES ARBORETUM, 7770 Jacksontown Rd., S.E.,
   Newark, OH 43056-9380. Tel.: 740-323-2355 & 800-44-DAWES.
E-mail: jarrasmith@dawesarb.org
Web Site: www.dawesarb.org
Institution Type/Description: Arboretum & Nature Center.
Hours & Admission Prices: Grounds: March & Sept.-Oct. daily 7am to 6:30pm;
   April-Aug. daily 7am to 8pm; Nov.-Feb. daily 7-5. Visitor Center: Mon.-Sat. 8-
   5, Sun. & holidays 12-5. No charge. Closed New Year's Day; Thanksgiving;
   Christmas. Daweswood House Museum Tours: May-Oct. Fri.-Sun. 12 & 2.
   March-April Sat.-Sun. 12 & 2. Adults $2, youth $1; members no charge.
Attendance: 260,000 (estimated)

LICKING COUNTY ARTS, 50 S. 2nd St., Newark, OH 43055.
   Tel.: 740-349-8031 & 350-7490.
E-mail: lcagalleryonsecond@gmail.com
Web Site: www.lickingcountyarts.com
Key Personnel: Museum Shop Cur., Mary Helen Fernandez Stewart.
Institution Type/Description: Art Gallery; Exhibition Gallery.
Hours & Admission Prices: Tues.-Sat. 11-4; school tours by appointment. No
   charge; donations accepted. Closed holidays. &
Attendance: 2,500

LICKING COUNTY HISTORICAL SOCIETY, Veterans Park, N. 6th St., Newark, OH 43058. Mailing Address: P.O. Box 785, Newark, OH 43058-0785. Tel.: 740-345-4898. Fax: 740-345-4898 (call first).
E-mail: LCHS@ALINK.COM
Web Site: www.lchsohio.org
Key Personnel: Pres. (V), John Crissinger; Cur., Emily Larson.
Institution Type/Description: Historic Buildings.
Hours & Admission Prices: Office & Library: by appointment. Library: no charge.
Attendance: 3,200 (estimated)

NATIONAL HEISEY GLASS MUSEUM, 169 W. Church St., Newark, OH 43055-4945. Tel.: 740-345-2932. Fax: 740-345-9638.
E-mail: business@heiseymuseum.org
Web Site: www.heiseymuseum.org
Key Personnel: Dir., Larry Burge.
Institution Type/Description: Glass Museum: housed in 1831 King House.
Hours & Admission Prices: Jan.-Feb. Tues.-Sat. 10-4; March-Dec. Tues.-Sat. 10-4, Sun. 1-4. Adults $4; discount to groups of 10 or more; members & children under 18 accompanied by adult no charge. Blue Star Museum. Closed holidays. &
Attendance: 3,500 (estimated)

SHERWOOD-DAVIDSON HOUSE, Veterans Park, 31 N. 6th St., Newark, OH 43058-0785. Mailing Address: P.O. Box 785, Newark, OH 43058-0785. Tel.: 740-345-4898. Fax: 740-345-4898 (call first). Facebook.
E-mail: sherwooddavidson@yahoo.com
Web Site: www.lchsohio.org
Key Personnel: Pres., John Crissinger, Jr.; Cur., Emily Larson.
Institution Type/Description: Historic House Museum: c.1820 Sherwood-Davidson house-a federal style home built by Buckingham Sherwood.
Hours & Admission Prices: May to mid-Dec. Tues., Thurs. & Sat. 1-3. Adults $3; members no charge. Closed holidays.
Attendance: 900 (estimated)

WEBB HOUSE MUSEUM, 303 Granville St., Newark, OH 43055-4480. Tel.: 740-345-8540.
E-mail: webbhouse@windstream.net
Web Site: lchsohio.org
Key Personnel: Cur., Mindy Honey Nelson.
Institution Type/Description: Historic House Museum & Gardens.
Hours & Admission Prices: Thurs.-Fri. 1-4; other times by appointment. No charge; donations accepted. Tour groups $2 per person.
Attendance: 200 (estimated)

THE WORKS: OHIO CENTER FOR HISTORY, ART & TECHNOLOGY, 55 S. First St., Newark, OH 43055-5429. Tel.: 740-349-9277. Fax: 740-345-7252.
E-mail: kimdowns@attheworks.org
Web Site: www.attheworks.org
Formerly: Institute of Industrial Technology
Key Personnel: C.E.O., Marcia W. Downes; Chm., John Hinderer; Museum Shop Mgr., Kim Downs.
Institution Type/Description: Science & History Museum.
Hours & Admission Prices: Jan.-March Tues.-Sat. 10-6; April-Dec. Tues.-Sat. 9-5. Adults $9, senior citizens $7, children $5; discounts to ASTC, History Traveler, & Smithsonian Affiliate members; members no charge. Closed Memorial Day; Labor Day; Thanksgiving; Christmas. &
Attendance: 54,975 (actual)

Newcomerstown

OLDE MAIN STREET MUSEUM & SOCIAL CENTER, 213 W. Canal St., Newcomerstown, OH 43832-1101. Mailing Address: P. O. Box 443, Newcomerstown, OH 43832-0443. Tel.: 740-498-7735.
E-mail: newcomerstownmuseums@gmail.com
Web Site: www.newcomerstownmuseums.com
Key Personnel: Pres., Vane Scott; Vice Pres. & Historian, Harley Dakin; Sec., Sue Scott; Treas., Sue Bowman; Coord. Social Events, BJ McFadden.
Institution Type/Description: History Museum.
Hours & Admission Prices: Memorial Day to Oct. Tues.-Sat. 11-4, Sun. 1-4. Adults $3. &
Attendance: 2,000 (actual)

TEMPERANCE TAVERN, 221 W. Canal St., Newcomerstown, OH 43832-1101. Mailing Address: P.O. Box 443, Newcomerstown, OH 43832-0443. Tel.: 740-498-7735.

E-mail: newcomerstownmuseums@gmail.com
Web Site: www.newcomerstownmuseums.com
Key Personnel: Pres., Vane Scott; Vice Pres. & Historian, Harley Dakin; Sec., Sue Scott; Treas., Sue Bowman; Coord. Social Events, B.J. McFadden; Museum Shop Mgr., Kris Goss.
Institution Type/Description: Historical Society Museum: housed in c.1841 Temperance Tavern.
Hours & Admission Prices: Memorial Day to Oct. Tues.-Sat. 11-4, Sun. 1-4; tours by appointment. Adults $3; donations accepted. &
Attendance: 2,000 (estimated)

Niles

MCKINLEY BIRTHPLACE HOME AND RESEARCH CENTER, 40 S. Main St., Niles, OH 44446-5012. Tel.: 330-652-1704. Fax: 330-652-5788.
E-mail: mckinley@mcklib.org
Web Site: www.mckinley.lib.oh.us
Formerly: National McKinley Birthplace Memorial & McKinley Birthplace Home
Key Personnel: Pres. (V), J. Terrance Dull; Vice Pres., James Yuhasz; Dir. Library, Michelle Alleman; Museum Shop Mgr., Kadie Bowen.
Institution Type/Description: housed on the site of the building where president William McKinley was born.
Hours & Admission Prices: Check website for hours; other times by appointment. No charge; donations accepted. Closed holidays. &
Attendance: 2,576 (actual)

WARD-THOMAS MUSEUM, 503 Brown St., Niles, OH 44446. Mailing Address: P.O. Box 368, Niles, OH 44446. Tel.: 330-544-2143.
E-mail: curator@nileshistoricalsociety.org
Key Personnel: Pres. (V), Nancy Malone; Cur., Audrey John.
Institution Type/Description: Historical Society Museum: housed in the former home of James Ward and John & Margaret Thomas, two prominent Niles industrial families; built in 1862.
Hours & Admission Prices: 1st Sun. each month; other times by appointment. No charge; donations accepted.

North Canton

HOOVER HISTORICAL CENTER, 1875 E. Maple St., North Canton, OH 44720-3331. Tel.: 330-490-7435. Facebook.
E-mail: ahaines@walsh.edu
Web Site: www.walsh.edu/hoover-historical-center
Key Personnel: Chm. (V), Operations Coord. & Museum Shop Mgr., Ann Haines; Cur., Megan Pellegrino.
Institution Type/Description: Company & History Museum: housed in 1853 Hoover family home.
Hours & Admission Prices: March to mid-Dec. Wed.-Sat. 1-4; groups of 8 or more by appointment. Adults $5; discounts to veterans with military ID during veterans' week; children under 12 no charge. Closed major holidays. &
Attendance: 2,000 (estimated)

MILITARY AVIATION PRESERVATION SOCIETY AIR MUSEUM, 2260 International Pkwy., North Canton, OH 44720. Tel.: 330-896-6332.
E-mail: kovesci.kim@mapsairmuseum.org
Web Site: mapsairmuseum.org
Key Personnel: Dir., Kim Kovesci; Chm. (V), Robert Schwartz; Museum Shop Mgr., Robert Johnston.
Institution Type/Description: Military History Museum.
Hours & Admission Prices: Tues.-Sat. 9-4:30, Sun. 11:30-4. Closed New Year's Day; Easter; Memorial Day; Independence Day; Labor Day; Thanksgiving; Christmas. &
Attendance: 27,000 (actual)

OHIO SOCIETY OF MILITARY HISTORY, 2260 International Pkwy., North Canton, OH 44720-1375. Tel.: 330-832-5553.
E-mail: osmh@sssnet.com
Institution Type/Description: Military History Museum.
Hours & Admission Prices: March 15-Dec. 15 Wed.-Fri. 10-5, Sat. 10-3. No charge; donations accepted. &
Attendance: 884 (actual)

Northfield

PALMER HOUSE, HISTORICAL SOCIETY OF OLDE NORTHFIELD, 9390 Olde Eight Rd., Northfield, OH 44067. Mailing Address: P.O. Box 99, Northfield, OH 44067. Tel.: 330-468-0909. Fax: 330-468-1163. Facebook.

E-mail: hson@worldnet.att.net
Web Site: www.hson.info
Key Personnel: Treas., Jill Potter.
Institution Type/Description: Historical Society Museum.
Hours & Admission Prices: April-Oct. 2nd & 4th Sun. 2-4; other times by appointment. No charge.
Attendance: 20 (estimated)

Norwalk

FIRELANDS HISTORICAL SOCIETY MUSEUM & LANING-YOUNG RESEARCH CENTER, 4 Case Ave., Norwalk, OH 44857-1404. Mailing Address: P.O. Box 572, Norwalk, OH 44857-0572. Tel.: 419-668-6038. Facebook.
E-mail: curator@firelandsmuseum.com
Web Site: www.firelandsmuseum.com
Institution Type/Description: History Museum: housed in 1836 Preston-Wickham House.
Hours & Admission Prices: May & Sept.-Oct. Sat. 10-3, Sun. 12-4; June-Aug. Tues.-Sat. 10-3, Sun. 12-4; other times by appointment. Adults $5, senior $4, youth 12-18 $3; discounts to groups of 10 or more and Lake Erie Shores & Islands members; members & children under 12 no charge.
Attendance: 550 (estimated)

Norwich

NATIONAL ROAD/ZANE GREY MUSEUM, 8850 E. Pike, Norwich, OH 43767-9785. Mailing Address: P.O. Box 107, New Concord, OH 43762-0107. Tel.: 740-872-3143, Fax: 740-872-3510.
E-mail: jmuseum@newconcord-oh.gov
Web Site: johnglenn.org
Key Personnel: Dir. Operatioins, Debbie Allender; Exec. Dir., Keith Eberly; Mgr., Kathryn Miller; Educ. Spec., JoAnna Duncan; Admin., Laura Holmes.
Institution Type/Description: General Museum.
Hours & Admission Prices: May-Sept. Wed.-Sat. 10-4, Sun. 1-4. Adult $7, seniors $6, students $3; discounts to groups and AAA, & Blue Star Museum member; children 5 & under and member no charge. Closed holidays.
Attendance: 5,112 (actual)

Norwood

DRAKE PLANETARIUM, 2020 Sherman Ave., Norwood, OH 45212-2616. Tel.: 513-396-5578. Fax: 513-396-6486.
E-mail: pbowers@drakeplanetarium.org
Web Site: www.drakeplanetarium.org
Key Personnel: Dir., Pamela Bowers; Business Mgr., Carolyn Steger.
Institution Type/Description: Planetarium.
Hours & Admission Prices: Call for hours.

DRAKE SCIENCE CENTER, 2020 Sherman Ave., Norwood, OH 45212-3100. Tel.: 513-396-5578. Fax: 513-396-6486.
E-mail: csteger@drakeplanetarium.org
Web Site: www.drakeplanetarium.org/contact.html
Key Personnel: Business Mgr., Carolyn Steger.
Institution Type/Description: Science Center.
Hours & Admission Prices: Call for hours. Discounts to AAM members.

Oak Hill

WELSH-AMERICAN HERITAGE MUSEUM, 412 E. Main St., Oak Hill, OH 45656-1229. Mailing Address: 225 S. Front St., Oak Hill, OH 45656-1244. Tel.: 740-682-7057.
E-mail: jjindra@rio.edu
Web Site: jacksonohio.org/welshmuseum.htm
Key Personnel: Cur., Mildred Bangert.
Institution Type/Description: History Museum.
Hours & Admission Prices: By appointment. No charge; donations accepted.

Oberlin

ALLEN MEMORIAL ART MUSEUM, 87 N. Main St., Oberlin, OH 44074-1161. Tel.: 440-775-8665. Fax: 440-775-6841.
E-mail: mharding@oberlin.edu
Web Site: www.oberlin.edu/amam
Key Personnel: Dir. The John G.W. Cowles, Andria Derstine; Dir. Communs., Megan Harding; Registrar, Lucille Stiger; Cur. Education, Jill Greenwood; Cur. Academic Programs, Liliana Milkova; Administrative Asst., Sally Moffitt.
Institution Type/Description: Art Museum.

Hours & Admission Prices: Tues.-Sat. 10-5, Sun. 1-5. No charge; donations accepted. Closed major holidays; New Year's Eve; Christmas Day and week.
Attendance: 35,000 (actual)

OBERLIN HERITAGE CENTER, 73-1/2 S. Professor St., Oberlin, OH 44074. Mailing Address: P.O. Box 0455, Oberlin, OH 44074-0455. Tel.: 440-774-1700. Facebook: Oberlin Heritage Center.
E-mail: liz.schultz@oberlinheritage.org
Web Site: www.oberlinheritagecenter.org
Formerly: Oberlin Heritage Center/O.H.I.O. (Oberlin Historical and Improvement Organization)
Key Personnel: Dir. & C.E.O., Elizabeth Schultz; Pres. (V), Gail Wood; Business Mgr., Bethany Hobbs.
Institution Type/Description: Historical Society Museum.
Hours & Admission Prices: Guided Tours: Tues., Thurs. & Sat. 10:30 & 1:30; other times by appointment. Drop-in tours available during office hours. Adults $6; discounts to AAM, ICOM, AAA, AASLH & Time Traveler's members; members, students & children accompanied by adult no charge. Closed major holidays. Gift Shop Office (at Monroe House): Tues.-Sat. 10-3.
Attendance: 10,690 (actual)

WELTZHEIMER/JOHNSON HOUSE, 534 Morgan St., Oberlin, OH 44074. Mailing Address: Oberlin College, 87 N. Main St., Oberlin, OH 44074. Tel.: 440-775-8671.
Institution Type/Description: Historic House Museum: housed in a Frank Lloyd Wright Usonian house; completed in 1949.
Hours & Admission Prices: April-Nov. 1st Sun. each month 12-5; groups of 10 or more by appointment. Adults $5; college students & children under 18 no charge.

Oregon

OREGON-JERUSALEM HISTORICAL SOCIETY, 1133 Grasser St., Oregon, OH 43616-7632. Mailing Address: P.O. Box 167632, Oregon, OH 43616-7632. Tel.: 419-693-7052. Fax: 419-693-7052.
E-mail: connieisbell72@gmail.com
Web Site: www.ojhs.org
Key Personnel: Pres. (V), Connie Isbell; Museum Shop Mgr., Jo Ann Flanagan.
Institution Type/Description: General Museum.
Hours & Admission Prices: Thurs. 10-2; other times by appointment. No charge; donations accepted.
Attendance: 1,500 (actual)

Oregonia

FORT ANCIENT EARTHWORKS & NATURE PRESERVE, 6123 State Rt. 350, (Exit 32 & 36 off I-71), Oregonia, OH 45054-9708. Tel.: 513-932-4421. Fax: 513-932-4843, 800-860-0141.
E-mail: jblosser@fortancient.org
Web Site: fortancient.org
Formerly: Fort Ancient Museum
Key Personnel: C.F.O. & Interim C.E.O., Douglas Hull; Area Mgr., Jack K. Blosser.
Institution Type/Description: Prehistoric Site Museum.
Hours & Admission Prices: April-Nov. Tues.-Sat. 10-5, Sun. 12-5; Dec.-March Sat. 10-5, Sun. 12-5; other times by appointment. Adults $7, seniors 60 & over and students $6; discounts to AAA, AAM & ICOM members; OHC & DSNH members and children under 5 no charge.
Attendance: 22,500 (estimated)

Orrville

ORRVILLE HISTORICAL MUSEUM, 142 Depot St., Orrville, OH 44667. Mailing Address: P.O. Box 437, Orrville, OH 44667. Tel.: 330-930-0113.
Institution Type/Description: History Museum: housed in the former Manhattan Restaurant.
Hours & Admission Prices: Feb.-Nov. Wed. 9-12, 2nd & 4th Sat. each month 1-4; other times by appointment.

Oxford

HEFNER MUSEUM OF NATURAL HISTORY, 100 Upham Hall, Miami Univ., Oxford, OH 45056. Tel.: 513-529-4617. Fax: 513-529-6900.
E-mail: sulliv55@miamioh.edu
Web Site: www.miamioh.edu/hefnermuseum
Formerly: Hefner Zoology Museum
Key Personnel: Dir., Steven M. Sullivan; Education, Julie Robinson.
Institution Type/Description: Natural History Museum.

Hours & Admission Prices: June-Aug. Mon.-Fri. 9-4; Sept.-May Mon.-Fri. 9-5. No charge; donations accepted. Closed university holidays. &
Attendance: 5,000 (estimated)

HIESTAND GALLERIES, 401 Maple St., Oxford, OH 45056. Tel.: 513-529-1883.
E-mail: taulbeae@miamioh.edu
Web Site: miamioh.edu/hiestand.galleries
Key Personnel: Dir., Ann Taulbee.
Institution Type/Description: Art Gallery.
Hours & Admission Prices: Mon.-Fri. 9-4:30; other times by appointment. No charge.

MIAMI UNIVERSITY ART MUSEUM, 801 S. Patterson Ave., Oxford, OH 45056-3435. Tel.: 513-529-2232. Fax: 513-529-6555. TDD: 513-529-1541.
E-mail: wicksrs@miamioh.edu
Web Site: www.miamioh.edu/art-museum
Key Personnel: Dir., Robert S. Wicks, Ph.D.; Cur. Exhibitions, Jason Shaiman; Cur. Education, Cynthia C. Collins; Registrar, Laura Stewart; Program Assoc., Susan V. Gambrell; Preparator & Operations Mgr., Mark DeGennaro; Mktg. & Communications Coord., Sherri Krazl.
Institution Type/Description: University Museum.
Hours & Admission Prices: Tues.-Fri. 10-5, Sat. 12-5; additional hours during evening programs & events. No charge. Closed national & university holidays. &
Attendance: 30,000 (estimated)

WILLIAM HOLMES MCGUFFEY MUSEUM, 401 E. Spring St., Oxford, OH 45056-3646. Tel.: 513-529-8380. Fax: 513-529-2637.
E-mail: mcguffeymuseum@miamioh.edu
Web Site: www.miamioh.edu/mcguffeymuseum
Key Personnel: Pres. (V), Dr. Sue Jones; Dir., Robert Wicks; Cur., Stephen C. Gordon.
Institution Type/Description: Historic House Museum: 1833 home of William Holmes McGuffey.
Hours & Admission Prices: Thurs.-Sat. 1-5. No charge; donations accepted. Closed university holidays. &
Attendance: 1,500 (actual)

Painesville Township

LAKE COUNTY HISTORICAL SOCIETY, 415 Riverside Dr., Painesville Township, OH 44077-5321. Tel.: 440–639-2945. Fax: 440-639-2947. Facebook.
E-mail: collections@lakehistory.org
Web Site: www.lakehistory.org
Key Personnel: Exec. Dir., Kathie Purmal; Pres., Morris W. Beverage, III; Pres. (V) & Museum Shop Mgr., Annie Hitchcock.
Institution Type/Description: History Museum.
Hours & Admission Prices: Museum: May-Oct. Tues.-Sat. 10-2, Sun. 1-4; Nov.-April Tues.-Sat. 10-2. Research Library: Tues.-Sat. 10-2, other times by appointment. Museum Self-Guided Tour: $3. Research Library: adults $7; discount to AAM & ICOM members; members no charge.
Attendance: 28,000 (estimated)

Parma

CRILE ARCHIVES - CUYAHOGA COMMUNITY COLLEGE - WESTERN CAMPUS, 11000 Pleasant Valley Rd., Parma, OH 44130-5199. Tel.: 216-987-5594.
E-mail: james.banks@tri-c.edu
Web Site: www.tri-c.edu/crile-archive
Key Personnel: Dir., Dr. James Banks; Archivist, Jennifer Pflaum.
Institution Type/Description: Archives.
Hours & Admission Prices: By appointment.

STEARNS HOMESTEAD, 6975 Ridge Rd., Parma, OH 44129. Mailing Address: P.O. Box 29002, Parma, OH 44129. Tel.: 440-845-9770. Facebook.
E-mail: stearnshomestead@gmail.com
Web Site: stearnshomestead.com
Key Personnel: Pres. (V), Ruth Fay; Museum Shop Mgr., Carol Werner.
Institution Type/Description: Historic Homestead.
Hours & Admission Prices: May to mid-Oct. Sat.-Sun. 12-4. No charge; donations accepted. &
Attendance: 5,000 (estimated)

Peebles

DAVIS MEMORIAL NATURE PRESERVE, 2715 Davis Memorial Rd., Peebles, OH 45660. Mailing Address: 3677 David Memorial Rd., Peebles, OH 45660. Tel.: 866-749-0701.
E-mail: OHIOSTATEPARKS@DNR.STATE.OH.US
Web Site: http://naturepreserves.ohiodnr.gov/davismemorial
Institution Type/Description: Nature Preserve.
Hours & Admission Prices: Daily sunrise to sunset. No charge. &

SERPENT MOUND MUSEUM, 3850 State Rte. 73, Peebles, OH 45660-9128. Mailing Address: c/o Arc of Appalacia Preserve System, 7660 Cave Rd., Bainbridge, OH 45612. Tel.: 937-587-2796. Fax: 937-587-1116. Facebook: Arc of Appalacia Preserve System.
E-mail: serpentmound@arcofappalachia.org
Web Site: www.arcofappalachia.org
Key Personnel: Dir., Nancy Stranahan.
Institution Type/Description: Indian Museum.
Hours & Admission Prices: Park & Earthworks: daily dawn-dusk. Museum & Gift Shop: March & Nov.-Dec. Sat.-Sun. 10-4; April daily 10-4; May & Sept.-Oct. Thurs.-Mon. 10-4, Fri.-Sun. 9-5; June-Aug. Mon.-Thurs. 10-4, Fri.-Sun. 10-6. Parking $8; OHS members no charge.
Attendance: 40,000 (actual)

Perrysburg

FORT MEIGS: OHIO'S WAR OF 1812 BATTLEFIELD, 29100 W. River Rd., Perrysburg, OH 43551-6019. Mailing Address: P.O. Box 3, Perrysburg, OH 43552. Tel.: 419-874-4121. Facebook.
E-mail: aphlipot@fortmeigs.org
Web Site: www.fortmeigs.org/
Formerly: Fort Meigs State Memorial
Key Personnel: Dir., Rick Finch; Chm. (V), George Jones, III; Programs Mgr., Dan Woodward; Museum Shop Mgr., Barb Brauer; Office Mgr., Ashley Phlipot.
Institution Type/Description: Military Fort Museum: reconstructed 1813 fort from the War of 1812; History Museum.
Hours & Admission Prices: Museum & Visitors Center: daily. Fort: April-Oct. Wed.-Sat. 9:30-5, Sun. 12-5. Adults $8, seniors 60 & over $7, students $4; members & children 5 and under no charge.
Attendance: 30,000 (actual)

OWENS COMMUNITY COLLEGE/WALTER E. TERHUNE GALLERY, Center for Fine & Performing Arts, 30335 Oregon Rd., Perrysburg, OH 43551-4593. Mailing Address: P.O. Box 10000, Toledo, OH 43699-1947. Tel.: 567-661-2721. Fax: 567-661-7011.
E-mail: art_gallery@owens.edu
Web Site: www.owens.edu
Institution Type/Description: Art Museum.
Hours & Admission Prices: Mon.-Tues. & Fri.-Sat. 10-4, Wed.-Thurs. 10-7. No charge. Closed major holidays; school breaks. &
Attendance: 7,000 (actual)

Pickerington

AMA MOTORCYCLE HALL OF FAME MUSEUM, 13515 Yarmouth Dr., Pickerington, OH 43147-8214. Tel.: 614-856-2222, ext. 1234. Fax: 614-856-2221. Facebook.
E-mail: info@motorcyclemuseum.org
Web Site: www.motorcyclemuseum.org
Formerly: Motorcycle Heritage Museum.
Key Personnel: Pres. & C.E.O., Rob Dingman; C.O.O., Jeff Massey; Program Specialist, Paula Schremser.
Institution Type/Description: Sports Museum & Hall of Fame.
Hours & Admission Prices: Daily 9-5. Adults $10, seniors $8, students 12-17 $3; discounts to AMA, National Motorcycle Organizations & Clubs, AAA, and veterans. Closed New Year's Day; Easter; Thanksgiving; Christmas Eve & Day. &
Attendance: 15,000 (actual)

Piqua

JOHNSTON FARM & INDIAN AGENCY, 9845 N. Hardin Rd., Piqua, OH 45356-9707. Tel.: 937-773-2522. Fax: 937-773-4311.
E-mail: ahite@ohiohistory.org
Web Site: www.johnstonfarmohio.com
Formerly: Piqua Historical Area State Memorial
Key Personnel: Site Mgr., Andy Hite; Groundskeeper, Rob Cline; Museum Shop Mgr., Diana Jacobs; Lead Interpreter, Marla Fair.
Institution Type/Description: History Museum.

Hours & Admission Prices: April-May. & Sept.-Oct. Mon.-Fri. 9-2 by appointment; June-Aug. Thurs.-Fri. 10-5, Sat.-Sun. 12-5. Adults $9, students 6-12 $4; discounts to seniors, AAA members & groups with advanced reservation; OHS, members, Johnston Farm Friends no charge. &
Attendance: 20,000 (actual)

Point Pleasant

GRANT'S BIRTHPLACE STATE MEMORIAL, 1551 State Rte. 232, Point Pleasant, OH 45153-9301. Mailing Address: P.O. Box 2, New Richmond, OH 45157-0002. Tel.: 513-553-4911, 800-283-8932. Fax: 614-297-2352.
E-mail: robertsgtkj@juno.com
Web Site: www.ohiohistory.org/places/grantbir
Key Personnel: Museum Attendant, Greg Roberts.
Institution Type/Description: Historic House: 1821 restored cottage, birthplace of Ulysses S. Grant.
Hours & Admission Prices: April-Oct. Wed.-Sat. 9:30-12 & 1-5, Sun. 1-5; groups by appointment. Adults $2.50, seniors $2, children 6-12 $1.50; children 5 & under and OHS members no charge. &
Attendance: 6,000

Pomeroy

MEIGS COUNTY MUSEUM, 144 Butternut Ave., Pomeroy, OH 45769-1260. Mailing Address: P.O. Box 145, Pomeroy, OH 45769-0145. Tel.: 740-992-3810. Fax: 740-992-3810. Facebook: Meigs County Historical Society and Museum.
E-mail: meigscohistorical@frontier.net
Web Site: meigscohistorical.org
Key Personnel: Pres., Margaret Parker.
Institution Type/Description: Local History Museum.
Hours & Admission Prices: Tues.-Fri. 10-3. Closed federal holidays. &
Attendance: 3,000

Port Clinton

AFRICAN SAFARI WILDLIFE PARK, 267 S Lightner Rd., Port Clinton, OH 43452. Tel.: 419-732-3606. Fax: 419-734-1919. Facebook: African Safari Wildlife Park.
E-mail: Info@africansafariwildlifepark.com
Web Site: www.africansafariwildlifepark.com
Institution Type/Description: Wildlife Park.
Hours & Admission Prices: late Feb. to May & Sept.-Nov. daily 10-5; Memorial Day to Labor Day daily 9-7. Summer: admission 7 & up $23.95, children 3-6 $15.95; discounts to seniors 55 & over and veterans; children 2 & under no charge. Spring & Fall: admission 7 & up $17.95, children 3-6 $11.95; discounts to seniors 55 & over and veterans; children 2 & under no charge. Camel rides: Adults (up to 300 lbs.) $10. children $5. &

OTTAWA COUNTY MUSEUM, 126 W. 3rd. St., Port Clinton, OH 43452-1842. Mailing Address: P.O. Box 845, Port Clinton, OH 43452-0845. Tel.: 419-732-2273.
E-mail: ochm@cros.net
Key Personnel: Cur., Peggy Debien.
Institution Type/Description: History Museum.
Hours & Admission Prices: Winter: Wed. 12-3; Summer: Tues.-Thurs. 12-3; other times by appointment. No charge; donations accepted. &
Attendance: 600 (estimated)

Portsmouth

SOUTHERN OHIO MUSEUM, 825 Gallia St., Portsmouth, OH 45662-0990. Mailing Address: 825 Gallia St., P.O. Box 990, Portsmouth, OH 45662-0990. Tel.: 740-354-5629. Fax: 740-354-4090.
E-mail: mark@somacc.com
Web Site: www.somacc.com
Key Personnel: Exec. Dir., Mark Chepp; Artistic Dir., Charlotte Gordon.
Institution Type/Description: Museum & Cultural Center.
Hours & Admission Prices: Tues.-Fri. 10-5, Sat. 1-5. no charge; gift shop discount to AAM & NARM members; Closed national holidays. &
Attendance: 31,000 (estimated)

Powell

COLUMBUS ZOO AND AQUARIUM, 4850 W. Powell Rd., Powell, OH 43065-0400. Mailing Address: P.O. Box 400, Powell, OH 43065-0400. Tel.: 614-645-3400. Fax: 614-645-3465.

E-mail: info@columbuszoo.org
Web Site: www.columbuszoo.org
Formerly: Columbus Zoological Park Association, Inc.
Key Personnel: C.E.O. & Pres., Tom Stalf.
Institution Type/Description: Zoology Museum.
Hours & Admission Prices: Summer daily 9-7; Winter daily 10-5. Adults $17.99, seniors 60 & over $12.99, children 3-9 $9.99; discounts to Franklin County residents; members & children under 3 no charge. Parking: $8. Closed Thanksgiving; Christmas Eve & Day. &
Attendance: 2,322,934 (actual)

Put-in-Bay

ANTIQUE CAR MUSEUM, 979 Catawba Ave., Put-in-Bay, OH 43456-0708. Mailing Address: P.O. Box 708, Put-in-Bay, OH 43456-0708. Tel.: 419-285-2283.
E-mail: fun@perryscave.com
Institution Type/Description: Car Museum.
Hours & Admission Prices: April & Oct. Sat.-Sun. 11-5; May-Sept. daily 10:30-6. No charge.

LAKE ERIE ISLANDS HISTORICAL SOCIETY, 25 Town Hall Place, Put-in-Bay, OH 43456. Mailing Address: P.O. Box 25, Put-in-Bay, OH 43456-0025. Tel.: 419-285-2804.
E-mail: director@leihs.org
Web Site: leihs.org
Key Personnel: Dir., Dan Savage.
Institution Type/Description: Historical Society Museum.
Hours & Admission Prices: mid-May to Oct. daily 11-5; groups by appointment. Adults & children $3, seniors 65 & over $2.50; members & veterans no charge. &

PERRY'S CAVE, 979 Catawba Ave., Put-in-Bay, OH 43456. Mailing Address: P.O. Box 708, Put-in-Bay, OH 43456-0708. Tel.: 419-285-2283.
E-mail: zoe@putinbaytrans.com
Web Site: www.perryscave.com
Institution Type/Description: Geology Museum: an Ohio Natural Landmark.
Hours & Admission Prices: April & Oct. Sat.-Sun. 11-5; May-Sept. daily 10-6. Adults $8, children 6-12 $4.50; children under 6 no charge.

PERRY'S VICTORY & INTERNATIONAL PEACE MEMORIAL, 93 Delaware Ave., Put-in-Bay, OH 43456. Mailing Address: 93 Delaware Ave., P.O. Box 549, Put-in-Bay, OH 43456-0549. Tel.: 419-285-2184. Fax: 419-285-2516. Facebook: Perrys Victory and International Peace Memorial.
E-mail: jeff_helmer@nps.gov
Web Site: www.nps.gov/pevi/
Key Personnel: Acting Supt., Barbara Fearon; Chief of Interpretation, Jeff Helmer.
Institution Type/Description: Park Museum; History Museum.
Hours & Admission Prices: mid-May & mid-Sept. to late-Oct. daily 10-6; mid-Sept.-Oct. 10-5; Oct.: Fri.-Mon. 10-5. closed Tues., Wed., Thurs. Adults $3, children under 16 no charge. Interagency passes may be purchased on site. &
Attendance: 150,000 (estimated)

STONEHENGE ESTATE, 808 Langram Rd., Put-in-Bay, OH 43456. Tel.: 419-285-6134 & 2585.
E-mail: info@stonehenge-put-in-bay.com
Institution Type/Description: Historic House Museum: housed in a stone farmhouse. Listed on the National Register of Historic Places.
Hours & Admission Prices: By appointment.

Ravenna

PORTAGE COUNTY HISTORICAL SOCIETY, 6549 N. Chestnut St., Ravenna, OH 44266-3907. Tel.: 330-296-3523.
E-mail: pchsohio@neo.rr.com
Web Site: www.portagecountyhistoricalsociety.org
Key Personnel: Pres. (V), Wayne Enders; Museum Shop Mgr., Barbara Petroski.
Institution Type/Description: General Museum.
Hours & Admission Prices: Thurs. & Sat. 2-5. Museum Tours: $3. Grounds: $5. Closed holidays. &
Attendance: 1,200 (estimated)

Reading

READING HISTORICAL SOCIETY MUSEUM, 22 W. Benson St., Reading, OH 45215-3202. Tel.: 513-733-2787.
Key Personnel: Pres. (V), James J. Lichtenberg.

Institution Type/Description: Historical Society Museum; 1905 house built by local tinsmith.
Hours & Admission Prices: first Sun. of each month 1-3; other times by appointment. No charge; donations accepted.
Attendance: 100 (estimated)

Rio Grande

ESTHER ALLEN GREER MUSEUM - UNIVERSITY OF RIO GRANDE, W. College Ave., 2nd Fl., Rio Grande, OH 45674. Tel.: 740-245-7364.
E-mail: bdavies@rio.edu
Web Site: www.rio.edu/fine-arts/greer-museum.cfm
Institution Type/Description: Art Museum.
Hours & Admission Prices: Tues.-Fri. 1-5.

Ripley

RANKIN HOUSE STATE MEMORIAL, 6152 Rankin Hill Rd., Ripley, OH 45167-1044. Mailing Address: P.O. Box 176, Ripley, OH 45167-0176. Tel.: 937-392-1627. Fax: 937-392-4044.
E-mail: ripleyohio@aol.com
Web Site: www.ripleyohio.net
Key Personnel: Dir., Betty Campbell.
Institution Type/Description: Historic Site: restored home of abolitionist Rev. John Rankin, 1828; Underground Railroad site.
Hours & Admission Prices: May-Oct. Wed.-Sat. 10-5, Sun. 12-5; groups by appointment. Adults $4, students 6-18 $2, Golden Buckeye card holders $3.20; members and children 5 & under no charge.
Attendance: 5,000

Rittman

RITTMAN HISTORICAL SOCIETY, 28 Gish Rd., Rittman, OH 44270. Mailing Address: P.O. Box 583, Rittman, OH 44270-0583. Tel.: 330-485-9885. Facebook: Rittman Historical Society / Pioneer Cemetery.
E-mail: rittmanhistory@outlook.com
Key Personnel: Pres., Jack Rice; Vice Pres., Helen Becerra; Treas., Fred Winkler; Sec., Rose Brouse.
Institution Type/Description: Historic House Museum.
Hours & Admission Prices: By appointment only. No charge; donations accepted.
Attendance: 150 (estimated)

Roseville

CLAY CENTER OF OHIO, 7327 Ceramic Rd., N.E., Roseville, OH 43777-9694. Mailing Address: P.O. Box 200, Crooksville, OH 43731-0200. Tel.: 740-697-7021. Facebook.
E-mail: ceramicmseuem@gmail.com
Formerly: Ohio Ceramic Museum and Heritage Center
Key Personnel: Dir., Dale Hague; Pres., Linda Sawyers; Vice Pres., Joan Spring; Museum Shop Mgr., James Burns.
Institution Type/Description: Arts & Crafts Museum.
Hours & Admission Prices: April-Oct. Thurs.-Sun. 12-4; other times by appointment. Adults $4, senior citizens $3.50, students $2; discounts to AAM & ICOM members; children under 5 & members no charge. &
Attendance: 5,000 (estimated)

Saint Marys

AUGLAIZE COUNTY HISTORICAL SOCIETY, Daniel Mooney Museum, 223 S. Main St., Saint Marys, OH 45885-2208. Tel.: 419-393-8532 & 738-9328.
Web Site: www.auglaizecountyhistory.org/
Key Personnel: Pres. (V), Karen Dietz; Vice Pres., George Neargarder; Treas., James Heinrich.
Institution Type/Description: General Museum: housed in c.1876 home of Civil War Officer Major Charles Hipp.
Hours & Admission Prices: Mon. & Wed.-Fri. 8-5, Tues. 8-7, Sat. 1-4. No charge; donations accepted. Closed holidays.
Attendance: 1,500 (estimated)

Salem

SALEM HISTORICAL SOCIETY AND MUSEUM, Physical/Mailing Address: 208 S. Broadway Ave., Salem, OH 44460-3004. Tel.: 330-337-8514. Facebook.
E-mail: thesalemhistoricalsociety@gmail.com
Web Site: www.salemhistoricalsociety.org

Key Personnel: Pres. (V), Virginia Maria Grilli; Dir., David C. Stratton; Cur., David J. Shivers; Gift Shop Chm., Dixie Gordon.
Institution Type/Description: Local History Museum.
Hours & Admission Prices: Tours: May-Oct. Sun. 1-4; other times call for appointment. Adults $6, children 5-17 $3; discounts to groups of 10 or more & museum affiliates; children under 5 no charge. Research & Administration: Mon. & Wed.-Thurs. 9am to noon; other times by appointment. No charge. Offices: closed major holidays.
Attendance: 3,500 (estimated)

Sandusky

COOKE-DORN HOUSE, 1415 Columbus Ave., Sandusky, OH 44870. Tel.: 419-627-0640.
E-mail: tour@oldhouseguild.org
Formerly: Eleutheros Cooke House and Garden
Key Personnel: C.E.O. & Pres. (V), Richard Keller; Chm. (V), Ann Marie Flood.
Institution Type/Description: Historic House Museum: housed in the former home of Eleutherus Cooke, Sandusky's first lawyer & politician serving in the Ohio Legislature and U.S. Congress; built c.1840.
Hours & Admission Prices: April-Dec. Tues.-Fri. 12-3, Sat. 10-1; other times by appointment. No charge; donations accepted.
Attendance: 626 (actual)

JOHNSON'S ISLAND MUSEUM & INFORMATION CENTER, Ohio Veterans Home, I.F. Mack Bldg., 3416 Columbus Ave., Sandusky, OH 44870. Mailing Address: P.O. Box 1865, Marblehead, OH 43440.
E-mail: jipres@johnsonsisland.org
Web Site: www.johnsonsisland.org
Key Personnel: Pres. & Cur., Donald Young.
Institution Type/Description: History Museum.
Hours & Admission Prices: Memorial Day to Labor Day Sat.-Sun. & holidays 1-4; other times by appointment.

MARITIME MUSEUM OF SANDUSKY, 125 Meigs St., Sandusky, OH 44870-2834. Tel.: 419-624-0274.
E-mail: sanduskymaritime@bex.net
Web Site: www.sanduskymaritime.org
Institution Type/Description: Maritime History Museum.
Hours & Admission Prices: June-Aug. Tues.-Sat. 10-4, Sun. 12-4; Sept.-May Fri.-Sat. 10-4, Sun. 12-4. Adults $4, senior citizens & children under 12 $3. Closed major holidays. &
Attendance: 24,417 (actual)

THE MERRY-GO-ROUND MUSEUM, 301 Jackson St., Sandusky, OH 44870. Tel.: 419-626-6111. Fax: 419-626-1297.
E-mail: merrygoround39@peoplepc.com
Web Site: merrygoroundmuseum.org
Key Personnel: Dir., Veronica VandenBout.
Institution Type/Description: Carousel Museum.
Hours & Admission Prices: Feb. Sat. 11-5, Sun. 12-5; March-May & Sept.-Dec. Wed.-Sat. 11-5, Sun. 12-5; June to Labor Day Mon.-Sat. 10-5, Sun. 12-5. Adults $6, seniors 60 & over $5, children 4-14 $4; children 3 & under no charge.
Attendance: 25,000 (estimated)

MUSEUM OF CAROUSEL ART & HISTORY, 301 Jackson St., Sandusky, OH 44870-2621. Tel.: 419-626-6111. Fax: 419-626-1297.
E-mail: merrygoround39@peoplepc.com
Web Site: www.merrygoroundmuseum.org
Formerly: Merry Go Round Museum
Key Personnel: C.E.O., Veronica Vanden Bout; Pres. (V) & Chm. (V), Gary Mortus; Financial Dir., Bridget Castle; Museum Shop Mgr., Carol Brown.
Institution Type/Description: Carousel Art & History Museum.
Hours & Admission Prices: Jan.-Feb. Sat. 11-5, Sun. 12-5; March-May & Sept.-Dec. Wed.-Sat. 11-5, Sun. 12-5; Memorial Day-Labor Day Mon.-Sat. 10-5, Sun. 12-5. Adults $5, senior citizens $4, children $3, discounts to groups of 10 or more; member adults no charge. Closed New Year's Eve & Day; Easter; Thanksgiving; Christmas Eve & Day. &
Attendance: 21,232 (estimated)

OHIO VETERANS HOMES MUSEUM, 3416 Columbus Ave., Sandusky, OH 44870. Tel.: 419-625-2454, ext. 1447.
Key Personnel: Dir., Kimberly Lewallen.
Institution Type/Description: Military Museum.
Hours & Admission Prices: Fri.-Sun. 12-4; other times by appointment. No charge.

SANDUSKY LIBRARY FOLLETT HOUSE MUSEUM, 404 Wayne St., Sandusky, OH 44870-2751. Mailing Address: Sandusky Library, 114 W. Adams St., Sandusky, OH 44870-2751. Tel.: 419-625-3834. Fax: 419-625-4574. Facebook: Follett House Museum.
E-mail: museumservices@sandusky.lib.oh.us
Web Site: www.sandusky.lib.oh.us/
Key Personnel: Museum Admin., Maggie Marconi; Dep. Dir., Dennis McMullen; Archives Librarian, Ron Davidson.
Institution Type/Description: Local History Museum: housed in the 1834-37 Greek Revival home of Oran Follett.
Hours & Admission Prices: April-May & Oct.-Dec. Sat. 12-4; June-Aug. Wed. & Fri. 12-4, Sat. 10-1; Sept. Sat. 10-1; group tours by appointment. No charge; donations accepted. Closed Easter; Thanksgiving; Christmas.
Attendance: 3,000 (estimated)

Seville

NORTHERN OHIO RAILWAY MUSEUM, 5515 Buffham Rd., Seville, OH 44273. Mailing Address: P.O. Box 458, Chippewa Lake, OH 44215-0458. Tel.: 330-769-5501.
E-mail: wstoner001@neo.rr.com
Institution Type/Description: Railway Museum.
Hours & Admission Prices: May 15 to Oct. Sat. 10-4. No charge; donations accepted.

Shaker Heights

THE SHAKER HISTORICAL SOCIETY, 16740 S. Park Blvd., Shaker Heights, OH 44120-1641. Tel.: 216-921-1201. Fax: 216-921-2615.
E-mail: shakerhistory@shakerhistory.org
Web Site: www.shakerhistory.org
Key Personnel: Pres. (V), Keith Arian; Exec. Dir., Ware Petznick.
Institution Type/Description: Historical Society Museum: located on land once owned by North Union Colony of Shakers, in a historic 1910 house.
Hours & Admission Prices: Tues.-Fri. 11-5, Sun. 2-5; other times by appointment. Adults $5, children 6-12 $3; children 5 & under, Ohio History Connection & museum members no charge. Closed holidays.
Attendance: 2,500 (actual)

Sharonville

HISTORIC SOUTHWEST OHIO, INC., Heritage Village, 11450 Lebanon Pike, Rte. 42, Sharonville, OH 45241. Mailing Address: P.O. Box 62475, Cincinnati, OH 45262-0475. Tel.: 513-563-9484. Fax: 513-563-0914.
E-mail: wdichtl@heritagevillagecincinnati.org
Web Site: www.heritagevillagecincinnati.org
Key Personnel: Pres. (V), Rob Carter; Dir., William J. Dichtl; Dir. Education, Steve Preston.
Institution Type/Description: Historic Village Museum.
Hours & Admission Prices: Heritage Village: May-Sept. Tues.-Sat. 10-5, Sun. 1-5; Oct.-April Wed.-Fri. 1-4. May-Sept. adults $5, children $3; members no charge. Oct.-April call for pricing. &

Attendance: 15,000 (actual)

Sheffield Lake

103RD OHIO VOLUNTEER INFANTRY CIVIL WAR MUSEUM, 5501 E. Lake Rd., Sheffield Lake, OH 44054-1900. Tel.: 440-949-2790.
E-mail: museum@103ovi.com
Web Site: www.103ovi.com
Formerly: 103rd Ohio Volunteer Infantry Memorial Foundation
Key Personnel: Pres., Christine Stair; Cur., Deborah Wagner; Museum Shop Mgr., Darlene Grubaugh.
Institution Type/Description: Military Museum: housed in c.1900 Elfordilno frame structure located on 4-acre site purchased in 1866 by the 103rd Ohio Volunteer Infantry.
Hours & Admission Prices: Call for appointment. Suggested Donation: adults $2, students $1; members no charge.
Attendance: 500 (estimated)

Sidney

SHELBY COUNTY HISTORICAL SOCIETY, 201 N. Main Ave., Sidney, OH 45365. Mailing Address: P.O. Box 376, Sidney, OH 45365-0376. Tel.: 937-498-1653. Facebook: Shelby County Historical Society, Sidney, OH.

E-mail: info@shelbycountyhistory.org
Web Site: www.shelbycountyhistory.org
Key Personnel: Dir., Tilda Phlipot; Pres. (V), Julie Gilardi.
Institution Type/Description: Historical Society Museum.
Hours & Admission Prices: Mon.-Fri. 1-5, Sat. 9-12. No charge. Closed holidays.
Attendance: 15,000 (actual)

Smithville

SMITHVILLE COMMUNITY HISTORICAL SOCIETY, 381 E. Main St., Smithville, OH 44677. Mailing Address: P.O. Box 12, Smithville, OH 44677. Tel.: 330-669-9308.
E-mail: schsmill@gmail.com
Web Site: sohchs.org
Institution Type/Description: Historical Society Museum.
Hours & Admission Prices: Mill: Wed. 1:30-4. Buildings: June-Oct. 2nd & 4th Sun. 1:30-4.

Springfield

CLARK COUNTY HISTORICAL SOCIETY - HERITAGE CENTER OF CLARK COUNTY, 117 S. Fountain Ave., Springfield, OH 45502-1207. Tel.: 937-324-0657. Fax: 937-324-1992.
E-mail: rsherrock@heritagecenter.us
Web Site: www.heritagecenter.us
Key Personnel: C.E.O., Roger Sherrock; Pres., William A. Kinnison; Cur., Kasey Eichensehr.
Institution Type/Description: History Museum.
Hours & Admission Prices: Gallery: Tues.-Sat. 9-5. Library & Archives: Wed.-Sat. 10-5. Suggested Donations: Gallery & Museum $10 per family, $5 per person. Library & Archives: $4 per day; members no charge. Closed national holidays. &
Attendance: 28,401 (actual)

PENNSYLVANIA HOUSE MUSEUM, 1311 W. Main St., Springfield, OH 45504-2815. Tel.: 937-322-7668.
E-mail: pl92on@hotmail.com
Web Site: www.pennsylvaniahousemuseum.info
Key Personnel: Chm. (V), Patricia Nowicki; Museum Shop Mgr., Marilyn Thompson.
Institution Type/Description: Historic House Museum: housed in a Federal-style home built by David Snively in 1839; former home of Dr. Isaac K. Funk of Funk & Wagnalls.
Hours & Admission Prices: March-Dec. Sat.-Sun. 1-3; groups by appointment. Adults $10, children $3; children under 5 no charge. Closed holidays.
Attendance: 800 (estimated)

SPRINGFIELD MUSEUM OF ART, 107 Cliff Park Rd., Springfield, OH 45504-2501. Tel.: 937-325-4673. Fax: 937-325-4674.
E-mail: smoa@main-net.com
Web Site: www.springfieldart.museum
Key Personnel: Exec. Dir., Angus Randolph; Bd. Pres., Andy Inck; Cur., Charlotte Gordon; Dir. Mktg., Katherine Denney; Facilities Mgr., James Brewer; Systems Mgr., Ken Pinkham.
Institution Type/Description: Art Museum.
Hours & Admission Prices: Tues.-Sat. 9-5, Sun. 12:30-4:30. Adults $5; discounts to AAM members; members & Sun. no charge. Closed New Year's Day; Memorial Day; Independence Day; Labor Day; Christmas. &
Attendance: 39,989 (actual)

THE WESTCOTT HOUSE FOUNDATION, 1340 E. High St., Springfield, OH 45505-1166. Tel.: 937-327-9291. Fax: 937-327-9074.
E-mail: info@westcotthouse.org
Web Site: www.westcotthouse.org
Key Personnel: Chm., Mark Chepp; Dir. Devel., Jenny Montgomery; Cur., Marta Wojcik; Volunteer Coord., Erik Lindsjo; Facilities Mgr., Tom Fyffe.
Institution Type/Description: Historic House Museum: housed in Frank Lloyd Wright's only Prairie Style home in Ohio.
Hours & Admission Prices: House Guided Tours: May-Oct. Wed.-Sat. 11, 12, 1, 2, 3, 4, Sun. 1, 2, 3, 4; Nov.-April Wed.-Fri. 11, 1, 3, Sat. 11, 12, 1, 2, 3, 4, Sun. 1, 2, 3, 4. Adults $15, seniors 65 & over and students $12; discounts to groups; members no charge. Frank Lloyd Wright reciprocal membership. &
Attendance: 9,003 (actual)

Steubenville

THE JEFFERSON COUNTY HISTORICAL ASSOCIATION,
426 Franklin Ave., Steubenville, OH 43952-1818. Mailing
Address: Box 4268, Steubenville, OH 43952-8268. Tel.: 740-283-
1133.
E-mail: jeffcohist@gmail.com
Web Site: www.jeffcountyhistorical.org
Key Personnel: Pres., Judy Brancazio; 1st Vice Pres., Eleanor Naylor; 2nd Vice
   Pres. & Library Dir., Charles Green.
Institution Type/Description: Historical Society Museum: housed in 1918 mansion.
Hours & Admission Prices: mid-March to late Nov. Wed.-Thurs. 10-3; other times
   by appointment. Suggested Donation: adults $2; members no charge. Blue Star
   Museum. Closed holidays.
Attendance: 1,000 (estimated)

Strongsville

GARDENVIEW HORTICULTURAL PARK, 16711 Pearl Rd. Rte.
42, 1 1/2 miles S. of Rte. 82, Strongsville, OH 44136-6048. Tel.:
440-238-6653.
E-mail: gardenviewhp@gmail.com
Web Site: sites.google.com/site/gvhortpk
Key Personnel: Dir. & Chm. (V), Joseph P. Tooman.
Institution Type/Description: Public Horticultural Park.
Hours & Admission Prices: March-Nov. 1 Sat.-Sun. 12-6; groups & members year-
   round by appointment. Adults $5, children $3; members no charge.
Attendance: 700 (estimated)

Sugar Grove

WAHKEENA NATURE PRESERVE, 2200 Pump Station Rd.,
Sugar Grove, OH 43155-9665. Tel.: 740-746-8695, 800-297-1883.
E-mail: wahkeena@att.net
Web Site: ohsweb.ohiohistory.org/places/c13/
Key Personnel: Site Mgr., Thomas Shisler.
Institution Type/Description: Nature Center.
Hours & Admission Prices: April-Oct. Sat.-Sun. 8-4:30. $2 per car; AAM & ICOM
   members no charge.
Attendance: 3,500

Sugarcreek

ALPINE HILLS HISTORICAL MUSEUM, 106 W. Main St.,
Sugarcreek, OH 44681. Mailing Address: P.O. Box 293,
Sugarcreek, OH 44681-0293. Tel.: 888-609-7592. Facebook:
Alpine Hills Museum.
E-mail: alpinehillsmuseum@yahoo.com
Web Site: www.alpinehills.webstarts.com
Key Personnel: Dir. & Museum Shop Mgr., Kelly Kuhn; Pres. (V), Lowell
   Youngen.
Institution Type/Description: History Museum.
Hours & Admission Prices: April-Oct. Mon.-Thurs. 9-4:30, Fri.-Sat. 9-6. No
   charge; donations accepted.
Attendance: 12,000 (actual)

JOHN S. YODER HOME, 116 Andreas Dr., N.E., Sugarcreek, OH
44681. Mailing Address: P.O. Box 508, Sugarcreek, OH 44681.
Tel.: 330-852-4644.
E-mail: alpinehillsmuseum@yahoo.com
Institution Type/Description: Historic House Museum: housed in an Amish home
   built in 1869.
Hours & Admission Prices: May-Oct. Fri.-Sat. 12-5. No charge; donations
   accepted.

Sylvania

**SYLVANIA HISTORICAL VILLAGE & HERITAGE CENTER
MUSEUM,** 5717 N. Main St., Sylvania, OH 43560. Tel.: 419-882-
4865.
E-mail: hist.village@sev.org
Key Personnel: Cur., Joyce Armstrong.
Institution Type/Description: History Museum: housed in the former home of Dr.
   Uriah A. Cooke.
Hours & Admission Prices: Museum: Wed. 3-7, Sat.-Sun. 1-4. Village: by appoint-
   ment.

Tiffin

AMERICAN CIVIL WAR MUSEUM OF OHIO, 217 S.
Washington, Tiffin, OH 44883. Tel.: 419-455-9551.
E-mail: info@acwmo.org
Web Site: www.acwmo.org
Key Personnel: Dir., Pres. (V) & Museum Shop Mgr., Gary C. Dundore.
Institution Type/Description: Military History Museum.
Hours & Admission Prices: 1st Wed. March to mid-Dec. Adults $6, seniors 55 &
   over $5, students $3; children under 6 & members no charge. Closed holidays. &
Attendance: 3,500 (actual)

**THE ENCHANTED MOMENT DOLL MUSEUM/GALLERY
INC.,** 174 Jefferson St., Tiffin, OH 44883. Tel.: 419-443-0038.
Web Site: www.theenchantedmomentdolls.com
Key Personnel: Dir. & Museum Shop Mgr., Jean A. Berlekamp; C.E.O. & Museum
   Shop Mgr., Myrna L. Riedel.
Institution Type/Description: Doll Museum.
Hours & Admission Prices: Wed.-Fri. 10-3, Sat. 10-2:30; other times by appoint-
   ment. Admission $6. &
Attendance: 400 (estimated)

SENECA COUNTY MUSEUM, 28 Clay St., Tiffin, OH 44883-
2259. Tel.: 419-447-5955. Fax: 419-443-7940.
Key Personnel: Dir., Rosalie Adams; Pres. (V), Barry Porter.
Institution Type/Description: Historic House: 1853 Rezin W. Shawhan residence &
   carriage house.
Hours & Admission Prices: Tues.-Thurs. 1-4; other times by appointment. Closed
   holidays.
Attendance: 7,000

TIFFIN GLASS MUSEUM, 25 S. Washington St., Tiffin, OH
44883-2347. Mailing Address: P.O. Box 554, Tiffin, OH 44883-
0554. Tel.: 419-448-0200. Facebook: Tiffin Glass Collectors and
Museum.
E-mail: museum@tiffinglass.org
Web Site: www.tiffinglass.org
Key Personnel: Dir. & Museum Shop Mgr., Ruth Hemminger.
Institution Type/Description: Glass History Museum.
Hours & Admission Prices: Tues.-Sat. 1-5; other times by appointment. No charge;
   donations accepted. Closed New Year's Day; Easter; Independence Day;
   Thanksgiving; Christmas. &
Attendance: 2,100 (actual)

Toledo

BLAIR MUSEUM OF LITHOPHANES, 5403 Elmer Dr., Toledo,
OH 43615-2803. Tel.: 419-245-1356. Fax: 419-535-5770.
E-mail: ksheehan@lithophanmuseum.org
Web Site: www.lithophanemuseum.org
Key Personnel: Dir. & Cur., Kelly Sheehan, Ph.D.
Institution Type/Description: Decorative Arts Museum.
Hours & Admission Prices: May-Oct. Sat.-Sun. 1-4; other times by appointment.
   No charge; donations accepted. Special Tours: $5 per person. &
Attendance: 3,000 (actual)

IMAGINATION STATION, 1 Discovery Way, Toledo, OH 43604-
1579. Tel.: 419-244-2674. Fax: 419-255-2674.
E-mail: pmorin@istscience.org
Web Site: imaginationstationtoledo.org
Formerly: COSI Toledo
Key Personnel: C.E.O., Lori Hauser; Chm. (V), David Waterman; Dir. Operations,
   Amy Hering; Chief Scientist, Carl Nelson; Corporate Devel. Officer, Karen
   George; Dir. STEM Education, Sloan Eberly Mann; Asst. Dir. Mktg., Stephanie
   Brinkman; Public Rel. Coord., Emily Garcia; Asst. Dir. Operations, Patrice
   James.
Institution Type/Description: Science Museum.
Hours & Admission Prices: Tues.-Sat. 10-5, Sun. noon-5. Big Kids 13-64 $11,
   seniors 65 & up $10, kids 3-12 $9; kids 2 & under and members no charge. &
Attendance: 203,084 (actual)

NATIONAL MUSEUM OF GREAT LAKES, 1701 Front St.,
Toledo, OH 43605. Mailing Address: P.O. Box 8218, Toledo, OH
43605. Tel.: 419-214-5000.
E-mail: glhs1@inlandseas.org
Web Site: www.inlandseas.org
Key Personnel: Exec. Dir., Christopher Gillchrist; C.O.O., John McCarty; Dir.
   Devel., Anna Kolin; Archaeological Dir., Carrie Sowden; Education Mgr., Ellen
   Kennedy.
Institution Type/Description: History Museum.

Hours & Admission Prices: Museum: Jan.-March Wed.-Sat. 10-5, Sun. 12-5; April-Dec. Tues.-Sat. 10-5, Sun. 12-5. Memorial Day & Labor Day: call for hours. SS Col. James M. Schoonmaker: May-Oct. Museum: adults $11, senior 65 & over, AAA and military $10, youth 6-17 $8; members and children 5 & under no charge. Museum & Schoonmaker: adults $15, seniors 65 & over, AAA and military $14, youth 6-17 $12; members and children 5 & under no charge. Closed New Year's Day; Easter; Thanksgiving; Christmas. &
Attendance: 25,000 (estimated)

TOLEDO BOTANICAL GARDEN, 5403 Elmer Dr., Toledo, OH 43615-2803. Tel.: 419-536-5566. Fax: 419-536-5574.
E-mail: membership@toledogarden.org; carol.gray@toledogarden.org
Web Site: www.toledogarden.org
Formerly: Crosby Gardens
Key Personnel: Dir., Karen Ranney Wolkins; Pres. (V), Jennifer Scroggs.
Institution Type/Description: Botanical Garden.
Hours & Admission Prices: Daily dawn to dusk. No charge; donations accepted. &
Attendance: 130,000 (estimated)

TOLEDO FIREFIGHTERS MUSEUM, 918 Sylvania Ave., Toledo, OH 43612-1343. Tel.: 419-478-3473. Fax: 419-245-3293.
E-mail: toledofiremuseum@bex.net
Institution Type/Description: Firefighters History Museum: housed in Old Number 18 Fire House.
Hours & Admission Prices: Sat. 12-4; other times by appointment. Call for admission prices. &
Attendance: 2,500 (estimated)

THE TOLEDO MUSEUM OF ART, 2445 Monroe St., Toledo, OH 43620-1500. Mailing Address: P.O. Box 1013, Toledo, OH 43697-1013. Tel.: 419-255-8000. Fax: 419-255-5638. TDD: 419-255-8000; Facebook: The Toledo Museum of Art.
E-mail: info@toledomuseum.org
Web Site: www.toledomuseum.org
Key Personnel: Chm. Bd., David K. Welles, Jr.; Dir., Brian Kennedy, Ph.D.; C.O.O., Carol Bintz; C.F.O., Mary Siefke; William Hutton Sr. Cur. European Paintings & Sculpture Before 1900, Lawrence W. Nichols; Cur. Glass & Decorative Arts, Jutta-Annette Page; Assoc. Dir., Amy Gilman; Registrar, Andrea Mall; Head Librarian, Alison Huftalen; Dir. Devel., Todd Ahrens; Dir. Communications, Kelly Fritz Garrow; Museum Shop Mgr., Heather Blankenship; Asst. Dir., Adam Levine; Emma Leah Bippus Dir. Education & Engagement, Mike Deetsch; Assoc. Cur. Contemporary Art & Head Visitor Engagement, Halona Norton-Westbrook.
Institution Type/Description: Art Museum.
Hours & Admission Prices: Tues.-Wed. 10-4, Thurs.-Fri. 10-9, Sat. 10-5, Sun. 12-5. No charge. Closed occasional holidays. &
Attendance: 457,000 (actual)

THE TOLEDO ZOO, 2700 Broadway St., Toledo, OH 43609-3100. Mailing Address: P.O. Box 140130, Toledo, OH 43614-0130. Tel.: 419-385-5721. Fax: 419-389-8670.
E-mail: info@toledozoo.org
Web Site: www.toledozoo.org
Key Personnel: Exec. Dir., Jeff Sailer; Pres. (V), Lamont Thurston; Veterinarian & Dir. Animal Health Nutrition, Ric Berlinski; Dir. Human Resources, Nancy Foley; Dir. Conservation & Research, Dr. Peter Tolson; Dir. Horticulture, Nancy Bucher; Cur. Fishes, Jay F. Hemdal; Cur. Graphic & Exhibit Design, Alex DeBeukelaer; Asst. Program Dir. & Cur. Herpetology, Andy Odum; Volunteer Mgr., Bill Davis; Registrar, Wyn Hall; Merchandise Buyer, Deborah L. Noward; Assoc. Cur. Birds, Monica Blackwell; Assoc. Cur. Birds, Chuck Cerbini; Cur. Education, Mitchell Magdich; Asst. Dir. Program Animals, Randi Meyerson; Dir. Facilities & Planning, Rick Payeff.
Institution Type/Description: Zoo.
Hours & Admission Prices: May-Sept. daily 10-6; Oct.-April daily 10-5. Adults $17, seniors over 60 & children 2-11 $14; discounts to groups, county residents, AZA members; members with card & children under 2 no charge. Parking: RV's, campers & motor coaches $15, cars & field trip buses $7. Closed New Year's Day; Thanksgiving; Christmas. &
Attendance: 994,424 (actual)

UNIVERSITY OF TOLEDO STRANAHAN ARBORETUM, 4131 Tantara Dr., Toledo, OH 43623. Tel.: 419-841-1007. Fax: 419-530-4421.
E-mail: daryl.dwyer@utoledo.edu
Web Site: www.utoledo.edu/nsm/arboretum/
Key Personnel: Dir., Dr. Daryl Dwyer.
Institution Type/Description: Arboretum.
Hours & Admission Prices: Mon.-Thurs. 9-6, Fri. 9-3.

WILDWOOD MANOR HOUSE, 5100 W. Central Ave., Toledo, OH 43615-2106. Tel.: 419-461-0520, 419-277-0107.
E-mail: heather.norris@metroparkstoledo.com
Web Site: www.metroparkstoledo.com
Key Personnel: Dir. Programming, Heather Norris; Program/Manor House Staff, Susan Roberts-McGlade; Rental Facilities Coord., Grace Peoples.
Institution Type/Description: Historic House: c.1938.
Hours & Admission Prices: Jan.-March Sat.-Sun. 12-5; April-June Thurs.-Sat. 12-5; July-Sept Tues.-Fri. 12-5; Oct. to mid-Nov. Thurs.-Fri. & Sun. 12-5; First full week of Dec. 10-8. No charge; donations accepted. Closed holidays. &
Attendance: 30,000 (actual)

Trenton

CHRISHOLM HISTORIC FARMSTEAD, 2070 Woodsdale Rd., Trenton, OH 45067-9752. Mailing Address: Metroparks of Butler County, 2051 Timberman Rd., Hamilton, OH 45013. Tel.: 513-867-5835.
E-mail: friendsofchrisholm@yahoo.com
Web Site: www.chrisholmhistoricfarmstead.org
Key Personnel: Pres. (V) Friends of Chrisholm, Bill McKnight.
Institution Type/Description: Historic Site: housed in the Samuel Augspurger farmhouse, built in 1874. Listed on the National Register of Historic Places.
Hours & Admission Prices: Park: daily 8am to dusk. Home: Summer call for hours; other times by appointment. Park Permit: Non-Residents $10 annual, $5 daily; Butler County Residents no charge. Home: no charge; donations accepted.
Attendance: 1,360 (estimated)

Troy

BRUKNER NATURE CENTER, 5995 Horseshoe Bend Rd., Troy, OH 45373-9485. Tel.: 937-698-6493.
E-mail: info@bruknernaturecenter.com
Web Site: www.bruknernaturecenter.com
Institution Type/Description: Nature Center.
Hours & Admission Prices: Mon.-Sat. 9-5, Sun. 12:30-5. Adults $1, children $.25.

MIAMI VALLEY VETERANS MUSEUM, 107 W. Main St., Troy, OH 45373. Mailing Address: P.O. Box 154, Troy, OH 45373. Tel.: 937-332-8852.
E-mail: director@theyshallnotbeforgotten.org
Web Site: www.theyshallnotbeforgotten.org
Key Personnel: Exec. Dir., Mitch Fogle.
Institution Type/Description: Military History Museum.
Hours & Admission Prices: Tues. 1-4, Wed. & Sat. 9-1, Thurs. 1-5.

MUSEUM OF TROY HISTORY, 124 E. Water St., Troy, OH 45373. Tel.: 937-339-5155.
E-mail: museumoftroyhistory124@gmail.com
Web Site: museumoftroyhistory.org
Institution Type/Description: History Museum: housed in the former home of John Kitchen.
Hours & Admission Prices: Sat.-Sun. 2-4. No charge.

OVERFIELD TAVERN MUSEUM, 201 E. Water St., Troy, OH 45373-3438. Tel.: 937-335-4019.
E-mail: info@overfieldtavernmuseum.com
Web Site: www.overfieldtavernmuseum.com/index.htm
Key Personnel: Dir., Robert Patton; Asst. Cur., Busser Howell; Cur., Kelly Smith.
Institution Type/Description: Historic Building Museum: housed in 1808 Overfield Tavern a 2-story, hewed-log building, which served as the first courthouse in Troy, Ohio.
Hours & Admission Prices: April-Oct. Sat.-Sun. 1-4; other times by appointment. No charge; donations accepted. Closed New Year's Eve & Day; Easter; Independence Day; Thanksgiving.

TROY-HAYNER CULTURAL CENTER, 301 W. Main St., Troy, OH 45373-3241. Tel.: 937-339-0457. Fax: 937-335-6373.
E-mail: troyhaynercenter@troyhayner.org
Web Site: www.troyhayner.org
Key Personnel: Pres., Cam Armstrong; Dir., Linda Lee Jolly; Asst. Dir., David Wion.
Institution Type/Description: Cultural Center: housed in c.1914 Mary Jane Hayner House, built in the Norman-Romanesque Revival style of architecture.
Hours & Admission Prices: Mon. 5pm-9pm, Tues.-Thurs. 9-9, Fri.-Sat. 9-5, Sun. 1-5. No charge; donations accepted. Closed holidays. &
Attendance: 41,534 (estimated)

WACO AIR MUSEUM & LEARNING CENTER, 1865 S. County Rd. 25A, Troy, OH 45373. Tel.: 937-335-9226. Fax: 937-335-4357. Facebook; Instagram.
E-mail: admin@wacoairmuseum.org
Web Site: www.wacoairmuseum.org/index.html
Formerly: WACO Historical Society & Learning Center
Key Personnel: Dir., Gretchen Hawk; Dir. Learning Center, Nancy Royer; Pres. (V), John Schilling; Museum Shop Mgr., Patty Wagner.
Institution Type/Description: Historical Society Museum.
Hours & Admission Prices: Mon.-Fri. 9-1:30, Sat.-Sun. 12-5. Adults $6, military with ID $5, children 7-17 $3; children under 7 & members no charge. &
Attendance: 3,500 (estimated)

Twinsburg

TWINSBURG HISTORICAL SOCIETY, 8996 Darrow Rd., Twinsburg, OH 44087-2127. Mailing Address: P.O. Box 7, Twinsburg, OH 44087-0007. Tel.: 330-487-5565.
E-mail: akancler@windstream.net
Web Site: lwkweb.com/twinsburghistoricalsociety/
Key Personnel: Pres., Audrey Kancler; Vice Pres., Sue Graham; Sec., Bonnie Williams; Corresponding Sec., Lea Bissell; Treas., Dan Simecek.
Institution Type/Description: General Museum: housed in 1865 school.
Hours & Admission Prices: Feb.-Dec. last Sun. each month 2-5; other times by appointment. No charge; donations accepted. &
Attendance: 500 (estimated)

Uhrichsville

THE UHRICHSVILLE MUSEUM OF CLAY INDUSTRY & FOLKART, 330 N. Main St., Uhrichsville, OH 44683. Mailing Address: P.O. Box 11, Dennison, OH 44621. Tel.: 740-922-6776 & 5455. Fax: 740-922-4929.
E-mail: claymuseum@dennisondepot.org
Web Site: claymuseum.com
Formerly: Uhrichsville Clay Museum
Key Personnel: Dir., Wendy Zucal.
Institution Type/Description: History Museum.
Hours & Admission Prices: Tues.-Fri. 9-5, Sat. 11-4. Adults $3, seniors $2, students $1; discounts to groups of 20 or more. Closed major holidays.
Attendance: 2,500 (estimated)

Upper Sandusky

INDIAN MILL MUSEUM STATE MEMORIAL, 7417 Co. Hwy. 47, Upper Sandusky, OH 43351-1430. Mailing Address: c/o Wyandot County Museum, P.O. Box 372, Upper Sandusky, OH 43351-0372. Tel.: 419-294-3857.
E-mail: info@ohiohistory.org
Web Site: www.ohiohistory.org/indianmill
Institution Type/Description: Historic Site.
Hours & Admission Prices: Memorial Day to Labor Day Fri.-Sun. 1-6; Sept.-Oct. Sat.-Sun. 1-6; groups by appointment. Admission 13 & over $1, children 6-12 $.50; children under 6 & Ohio Historical Society members no charge. &
Attendance: 2,245 (actual)

WYANDOT COUNTY HISTORICAL SOCIETY, 130 S. 7th St., Upper Sandusky, OH 43351-1339. Mailing Address: P.O. Box 372, Upper Sandusky, OH 43351-0372. Tel.: 419-294-3857. Facebook: Wyandot County Historical Society.
E-mail: curator@wyandothistory.org
Web Site: www.wyandothistory.org
Key Personnel: Dir. & Cur., Ronald I. Marvin, Jr.
Institution Type/Description: General Museum.
Hours & Admission Prices: Museum: May-Oct. Fri.-Sun. 1-4:30. Adults $2, students & children $1. &

Urbana

CEDAR BOG NATURE PRESERVE, 980 Woodburn Rd., Urbana, OH 43078-9417. Mailing Address: P.O. Box 510, Urbana, OH 43078-0510. Tel.: 937-484-3744, 800-860-0147.
E-mail: cedarbog@ctcn.net
Web Site: www.cedarbognp.org
Key Personnel: Site Mgr., Tracy Bleim.
Institution Type/Description: Nature Preserve: post-glacial alkaline bog in Ohio.
Hours & Admission Prices: Wed.-Sat. 10-4; other times by appointment. Adults $5, children 6-12 $4, AAA & Golden Buckeye discount $1; members no charge. &
Attendance: 5,000 (actual)

CHAMPAIGN AVIATION MUSEUM, Urbana Grimes Airport I74, 1652 N. Main St., Urbana, OH 43078. Tel.: 937-652-4710.
Institution Type/Description: Aviation Museum.
Hours & Admission Prices: Tues.-Sat. 9-4; other times by appointment. No charge; donations accepted. &
Attendance: 15,000 (estimated)

CHAMPAIGN COUNTY HISTORICAL MUSEUM, 809 E. Lawn Ave., Urbana, OH 43078. Mailing Address: P.O. Box 65, Urbana, OH 43078-0065. Tel.: 937-653-6721. Facebook.
E-mail: champhistmus@ctcn.net
Web Site: www.champaigncountyhistoricalmuseum.org
Key Personnel: Pres. (V), Dan Walter; Treas., Howard Brust.
Institution Type/Description: Historical Society Museum: housed in 1912 school for Champaign County Children's Home.
Hours & Admission Prices: Mon.-Tues. 10-4; other times by appointment. No charge; donations accepted. &
Attendance: 1,600 (actual)

GRIMES FLYING LABORATORY MUSEUM, Grimes Field, 1636 N. Main St., Urbana, OH 43078. Tel.: 937-873-5764 & 652-4319.
E-mail: info@aviationheritagearea.org
Institution Type/Description: History Museum.
Hours & Admission Prices: Sat. 9-1; other times by appointment.

JOHNNY APPLESEED EDUCATIONAL CENTER & MUSEUM, 579 College Way, Urbana University, Urbana, OH 43078-2081. Tel.: 937-484-1303. Fax: 937-772-9297.
E-mail: cheryl.ogden@urbana.edu
Web Site: www.urbana.edu/index.php/alumni_and_friends/appleseed_society/museum/
Formerly: Johnny Appleseed Society Museum
Key Personnel: Dir. & Museum Shop Mgr., Cheryl Ogden; Chm (V), Dr. Francis Hazard.
Institution Type/Description: History Museum.
Hours & Admission Prices: Tues.-Fri. 10-3, Sat. 11-4; other times by appointment. $3 12 & over, 12 & under no charge. &
Attendance: 1,350 (estimated)

Utica

VELVET ICE CREAM COMPANY MUSEUM & MILLING MUSEUM, 11324 Mt. Vernon Rd., Utica, OH 43080. Mailing Address: P.O. Box 588, Utica, OH 43080. Tel.: 800-589-500, 740-892-3921. Fax: 740-892-4339.
E-mail: info@velveticecream.com
Web Site: www.velveticecream.com
Institution Type/Description: Ice Cream & Milling Museums.
Hours & Admission Prices: Museum & Parlor: May, June-Aug. & Sept. daily 11-7; Oct. daily 11-6. Mill & Factory Tours: Mon.-Fri. 11-3. &
Attendance: 150,000 (estimated)

Van Wert

CENTRAL INSURANCE FIRE MUSEUM, 800 S. Washington St., Van Wert, OH 45891-2357. Tel.: 419-238-1010.
E-mail: agibson@central-insurance.com
Web Site: www.central-insurance.com/docs/fire-museum.htm
Institution Type/Description: Fire-Fighting Museum.
Hours & Admission Prices: 3rd Fri. of each month 1-3; other times by appointment. No charge.

VAN WERT COUNTY HISTORICAL SOCIETY, 602 N. Washington St., Van Wert, OH 45891-1265. Mailing Address: P.O. Box 621, Van Wert, OH 45891-0621. Tel.: 419-771-9851.
E-mail: vwc.historicalsociety@gmail.com
Web Site: www.vanwert.com/museum
Key Personnel: Pres. (V), Jon Amundson.
Institution Type/Description: Historic House Museum: housed in the former home of John O. & Tacey Viella Clark; built in 1895.
Hours & Admission Prices: March-Nov. Sun. 2-4:30; groups by appointment. No charge; donations accepted. &
Attendance: 3,500 (estimated)

Vandalia

TRAPSHOOTING HALL OF FAME & MUSEUM, 601 W. National Rd., Vandalia, OH 45377-1036. Mailing Address: P.O. Box 281, Vandalia, OH 45377. Tel.: 937-660-5663. Fax: 937-660-5664.
E-mail: staff@traphof.org
Web Site: www.traphof.org
Institution Type/Description: Trapshooting Museum.
Hours & Admission Prices: Mon.-Fri. 9-3. No charge. Closed New Year's Day; Memorial Day; Independence Day; Labor Day; Thanksgiving; Christmas.

Wapakoneta

ARMSTRONG AIR & SPACE MUSEUM, 500 Apollo Dr., Wapakoneta, OH 45895. Mailing Address: P.O. Box 1978, Wapakoneta, OH 45895-0978. Tel.: 419-738-8811.
E-mail: info@armstrongmuseum.org
Web Site: www.armstrongmuseum.org
Key Personnel: Dir., Chris Burton; Pres. (V), Tom Finkelmeier, Jr.
Institution Type/Description: Aeronautics & Space Museum.
Hours & Admission Prices: Tues.-Sat. 9:30-5, Sun. 12-5. Adults $8, children $4; discount to groups, Golden Buckeye & AAA members; members & children under 5 no charge. Closed New Year's Day, Thanksgiving & Christmas. &
Attendance: 50,000 (actual)

Warren

JOHN STARK EDWARDS HOUSE & MUSEUM, 303 Monroe St., N.W., Warren, OH 44483. Mailing Address: P.O. Box 1907, Warren, OH 44482-1907. Tel.: 330-394-4653. Fax: 330-394-4653.
E-mail: museum@trumbullcountyhistory.org
Web Site: www.trumbullcountyhistory.org
Key Personnel: Pres. (V), Robt. Smith; Cur., Eileen Blaney; Cur., Trish Scarmuzzi.
Institution Type/Description: Historic House: 1807 John Stark Edwards house.
Hours & Admission Prices: April-Dec. 1st Sun. each month 2-5; groups by appointment. No charge; donations accepted. Closed holidays.
Attendance: 2,100 (actual)

NATIONAL PACKARD MUSEUM, 1899 Mahoning Ave., N.W., Warren, OH 44483-2081. Tel.: 330-394-1899. Fax: 330-394-7796.
E-mail: national@packardmuseum.org
Web Site: www.packardmuseum.org
Key Personnel: C.E.O., Cur. & Archivist, Mary Ann Porinchak; Dir. Operations, Charlie Ohlin, Esq.; Event Mgr., Christine Bobco.
Institution Type/Description: History Museum.
Hours & Admission Prices: Tues.-Sat. 12-5, Sun. 1-5; varied hours for special events & prearranged tours. Adults $8, senior citizens & students $5; discounts to groups, AARP & AAA members; members & children under 7 no charge. Closed New Year's Eve & Day; Easter; Memorial Day; Independence Day; Labor Day; Thanksgiving; Christmas Eve & Day. &
Attendance: 20,000 (estimated)

SUTLIFF MUSEUM, 444 Mahoning Ave., N.W., Warren, OH 44483. Tel.: 330-395-6575.
E-mail: info@sutliffmuseum.org
Web Site: www.sutliffmuseum.org
Key Personnel: Dir., Melissa Karman; Cur., Aimee Wehmeyer.
Institution Type/Description: History Museum.
Hours & Admission Prices: Wed.-Sat. 2-4; other times by appointment. No charge. &

Washington Court House

FAYETTE COUNTY MUSEUM, 517 Columbus Ave., Washington Court House, OH 43160-1427. Tel.: 740-335-2953.
E-mail: fayettecountyhistory@gmail.com
Web Site: www.fayette-co-oh.com/museum.html
Key Personnel: Pres. (V), Warren Craig; Financial Dir., Craig Breedlove; Sec. Bd. Trustees, Donald J. Moore.
Institution Type/Description: History Museum: housed in a 14 room Victorian mansion.
Hours & Admission Prices: May-Sept. Sat.-Sun. 1-4. No charge; donations accepted.
Attendance: 1,350 (actual)

Wauseon

FULTON COUNTY HISTORICAL MUSEUM, 229 Monroe St., Wauseon, OH 43567-1127. Mailing Address: P.O. Box 104, Wauseon, OH 43567-0104. Tel.: 419-337-7922. Facebook.
E-mail: museum@fultoncountyhs.org
Web Site: www.fultoncountyhs.org
Key Personnel: Pres. (V), Carl Buehrer; Dir., John D. Swearingen, Jr.
Institution Type/Description: History Museum.
Hours & Admission Prices: April-Nov. Tues.-Fri. 10-4, Sat. 10-2; other times by appointment. Adults $4, seniors $3, students $2; members no charge. Closed holidays. &
Attendance: 850 (estimated)

Waynesville

CAESAR'S CREEK PIONEER VILLAGE, Caesar's Creek State Park, 3999 Pioneer Village Rd., Waynesville, OH 45068-8630. Mailing Address: P.O. Box 652, Waynesville, OH 45068. Tel.: 513-897-1120.
E-mail: ccpioneervillage@aol.com
Web Site: www.caesarscreekpioneervillage.org
Institution Type/Description: History Museum.
Hours & Admission Prices: Call for hours. Adults $5; children no charge.
Attendance: 30,000 (estimated)

Wellington

SPIRIT OF '76 MUSEUM, 201 N. Main St., Wellington, OH 44090. Mailing Address: P.O. Box 76, Wellington, OH 44090-0076. Tel.: 440-647-4367 & 4576.
E-mail: thespiritof76museum@gmail.com
Web Site: thespiritof76museum.org
Key Personnel: Pres., John Perry.
Institution Type/Description: Historical Society Museum: housed in 1872 building.
Hours & Admission Prices: April-Oct. Sat.-Sun. 2:30-5 by appointment; groups of 10 or more by appointment. No charge; donations accepted. &
Attendance: 950 (actual)

Wellston

BUCKEYE FURNACE HISTORIC SITE, 123 Buckeye Park Rd., T167, Wellston, OH 45692-9511. Mailing Address: Friends of Buckeye Furnace, Inc., P.O. Box 475, Jackson, OH 45640-0475. Tel.: 740-384-3537. Facebook: Buckeye Furnace State Memorial.
E-mail: jmeach42@gmail.com
Web Site: www.buckeyefurnace.com
Formerly: Buckeye Furnace State Memorial
Key Personnel: Pres. (V), J. Michael Stroth; Museum Shop Mgr., Tammie Mash; Museum Attendant, Jan McKibben.
Institution Type/Description: History Museum: 1851 restored Iron Furnace Complex.
Hours & Admission Prices: Memorial Day to Oct. call for hours; other times by appointment. No charge; donations accepted.
Attendance: 5,000 (actual)

Wellsville

RIVER MUSEUM, 1003 Riverside Ave., Wellsville, OH 43968-1374. Mailing Address: P.O. Box 13, Wellsville, OH 43968-0013. Facebook: Wellsville Historical Society.
E-mail: wellsvillerivermuseum@hotmail.com
Key Personnel: Pres., Robert Lloyd; Vice Pres., Tom Davidson; Treas., Jeff Weekley; Sec., Janet Taggart.
Institution Type/Description: History Museum: housed in c.1870 home of Dr. John Hammond.
Hours & Admission Prices: June-Sept. Sun. 1-4:30; private tours available all year. Charge for special tours only. &
Attendance: 1,200 (estimated)

West Liberty

PIATT CASTLES, 10051 Township Rd. 47, West Liberty, OH 43357. Mailing Address: P.O. Box 497, West Liberty, OH 43357-0497. Tel.: 937-465-2821 & 844-3480. Fax: 937-465-7774. Facebook.
E-mail: mpcastle@aol.com
Web Site: www.piattcastles.org
Key Personnel: C.E.O. & Pres., Margaret Piatt; Vice Pres. & Dir. Opers., James White; Dir. Mktg. & Communications, Kate Piatt-Eckert.

Institution Type/Description: Historic House Museums: Mac-A-Cheek completed in 1871; Norman-French style home with several generations of Piatt Family furnishings & objects; Mac-O-Chee Castle completed in 1881 Flemish style home with American furnishings & objects.
Hours & Admission Prices: Spring & Fall Sat.-Sun. 11-4; Memorial Day-Labor Day daily 11-5. Single Castle: adults $12, seniors 65 & up $11, youth 5-15 $7. Two Castles: adults $20, seniors 65 & up $18, youth 5-15 $12; discounts to AAA members & groups.
Attendance: 1,200 (actual)

Westerville

ANTI-SALOON LEAGUE MUSEUM, Westerville Public Library, 126 S. State St., Westerville, OH 43081-2029. Tel.: 614-259-5028. Fax: 614-882-5369.
E-mail: bweinhar@westervillelibrary.org
Web Site: www.westervillelibrary.org/antisaloon
Key Personnel: Archivist, Beth Weinhardt.
Institution Type/Description: History Museum: housed in the building that served as League headquarters.
Attendance: 3,000 (estimated)

FISHER GALLERY - OTTERBEIN UNIVERSITY, Roush Hall, 27 S. Grove St., Westerville, OH 43081. Tel.: 614-823-1792.
E-mail: kyoung@otterbein.edu
Institution Type/Description: Art Gallery.
Hours & Admission Prices: Academic Year: daily 9-9.

FRANK MUSEUM OF ART - OTTERBEIN UNIVERSITY, 39 S. Vine St., Westerville, OH 43081-1643. Mailing Address: c/o Dept. of Art, 33 Collegeview Rd., A123, Westerville, OH 43081. Tel.: 614-818-9716.
E-mail: jglowski@otterbein.edu
Web Site: www.otterbein.edu
Key Personnel: Museum & Galleries Dir., Janice Glowski.
Institution Type/Description: Art Museum: housed in the former Salem Evangelical Church; built in 1877.
Hours & Admission Prices: Academic Year: Wed.-Fri. 11-3.

HANBY HOUSE, 160 W. Main St., Westerville, OH 43081. Mailing Address: P.O. Box 1063, Westerville, OH 43086-7063. Tel.: 614-891-6289, 800-600-6843.
E-mail: hanbyhouse@yahoo.com
Web Site: www.hanbyhouse.org
Key Personnel: Site Mgr. & Museum Shop Mgr., Pamela Allen.
Institution Type/Description: Historic House: 1853 pre-Civil War home of Bishop William Hanby, father of composer & author Benjamin R. Hanby. Listed on the National Park Service Network to Freedom Underground Railroad sites.
Hours & Admission Prices: March-April & Oct.-Dec. by appointment; May-Sept. Sat.-Sun. 1-4. Adults $3, children 6-17 $1; discounts to senior citizens, Golden Buckeye & Ohio Historical Society members; Hanby Club members & children under 6 no charge.
Attendance: 2,200 (estimated)

INNISWOOD METRO GARDENS, 940 S. Hempstead Rd., Westerville, OH 43081-3612. Tel.: 614-895-6216. Fax: 614-895-6352.
Web Site: www.inniswood.org
Institution Type/Description: Botanical Garden: former estate of Grace and Mary Innis.
Hours & Admission Prices: Daily 7am to dusk. No charge. &
Attendance: 360,000 (actual)

MILLER GALLERY - OTTERBEIN UNIVERSITY, 33 Collegeview Rd., Westerville, OH 43081-1643. Tel.: 614-823-1792.
E-mail: kyoung@otterbein.edu
Institution Type/Description: Art Gallery.
Hours & Admission Prices: Academic Year: Mon.-Fri. 8-4, Sat.-Sun. 1-4. Closed holidays.

WEITKAMP OBSERVATORY AND PLANETARIUM, Otterbein College, 155 W. Main St., Westerville, OH 43081-1430. Tel.: 614-823-1316. Fax: 614-823-1968.
E-mail: ewerwa@otterbein.edu
Web Site: www.otterbein.edu/physics/weitkamp-observatory.asp
Key Personnel: Dir., Uwe Trittmann.
Institution Type/Description: Observatory & Planetarium.

Hours & Admission Prices: Call for hours.
Attendance: 200 (estimated)

Whitehouse

THE BUTTERFLY HOUSE, Wheeler Farms, 11266 Obee Rd., Whitehouse, OH 43571-9208. Tel.: 419-877-2733.
E-mail: info@thestablesonobee.com
Web Site: www.wheelerfarms.com/butterfly-house
Key Personnel: Owner, Duke Wheeler.
Institution Type/Description: Butterfly Museum.
Hours & Admission Prices: May-Aug. Mon.-Sat. 10-5, Sun. 12-5; Sept. Thurs.-Sat. 10-5, Sun. 12-5; Oct. Sat.-Sun. 12-5. Adults $9, seniors 65 & up $8, children 4-11 $7; children 3 & under no charge.

Wilberforce

NATIONAL AFRO-AMERICAN MUSEUM & CULTURAL CENTER, 1350 Brush Row Rd., Wilberforce, OH 45384-0578. Mailing Address: P.O. Box 578, Wilberforce, OH 45384-0578. Tel.: 937-376-4944, ext. 122. Fax: 937-376-2007.
E-mail: infonaamcc@ohiohistory.org
Key Personnel: Dir., Dr. Charles Wash.
Institution Type/Description: African American History Museum: located on grounds of c.1856 Wilberforce University campus.
Hours & Admission Prices: Tues.-Sat. 9-5. Adults $4, seniors $3.60, children & students $1.50; discounts to AAM & Assoc. of African American Museum members; members no charge. Closed major holidays. &
Attendance: 2,500 (actual)

PAUL ROBESON CULTURAL AND PERFORMING ARTS CENTER, Central State University, 1400 Brush Row Rd., Wilberforce, OH 45384. Mailing Address: P.O. Box 1004, Wilberforce, OH 45384-1004. Tel.: 937-376-6403.
Web Site: www.centralstate.edu/academics/art_science/fine_performing_arts
Key Personnel: Chm., James Smith; Asst. Prof., Kenneth Pointer; Assoc. Prof., Dr. Ronald Claxton; Assoc. Prof., Dwayne Daniel.
Institution Type/Description: Art Gallery.
Hours & Admission Prices: Call for hours. No charge.

Willoughby

INDIAN MUSEUM OF LAKE COUNTY, OHIO, 7519 Mentor Ave., Ste. A112, Mentor, OH 44060. Tel.: 440-951-3813. Fax: 440-951-3813.
Web Site: indianmuseumoflakecounty.org
Key Personnel: Dir. & Museum Shop Mgr., Ann L. Dewald; Pres. (V), Douglas R. Divish; Treas., John Brewster.
Institution Type/Description: Native American Museum.
Hours & Admission Prices: Mon.-Fri. 10-4, Sat.-Sun. 1-4. Adults $4, seniors $3, students K-12 $2; discounts to AAM members; members & preschoolers no charge. Closed major holiday weekends; winter & spring breaks. &
Attendance: 3,000 (estimated)

KIRTLAND TEMPLE VISITOR CENTER, 7809 Joseph St., Willoughby, OH 44094-9255. Tel.: 440-256-1830. Fax: 440-256-1929.
E-mail: info@kirtlandtemple.org
Web Site: www.kirtlandtemple.org
Key Personnel: C.E.O., Ronald Romig; Pres., Stephen Veazey.
Institution Type/Description: Historic Site: house of worship; 1833-1836.
Hours & Admission Prices: Feb. by appointment; March-April Mon.-Sat. 10-4, Sun. 1-5; May-Oct. Mon.-Sat. 9-5, Sun. 1-5; Nov.-Dec. Mon.-Sat. 10-4, Sun. 1-4; groups by appointment. Tours: $3. Closed New Year's Day; Easter; Thanksgiving; Christmas Eve & Day.
Attendance: 30,000 (actual)

Wilmington

CLINTON COUNTY HISTORICAL SOCIETY, 149 E. Locust St., Wilmington, OH 45177-2338. Mailing Address: P.O. Box 529, Wilmington, OH 45177-0529. Tel.: 937-382-4684. Fax: 937-382-5634.
E-mail: kay@clintoncountyhistory.org
Web Site: clintoncountyhistory.org
Key Personnel: Dir., Kay Fisher.
Institution Type/Description: Historical Society Museum: housed in an 1835 Greek Revival mansion.

Hours & Admission Prices: Museum: March-Dec. Wed.-Fri. 1-4. Library: March-Nov. Wed.-Fri. 1-4. Adults $5; members no charge. &

Attendance: 1,200 (estimated)

QUAKER HERITAGE CENTER OF WILMINGTON COLLEGE, College St. & Douglas St., Wilmington, OH 45177. Mailing Address: Wilmington College of Ohio, 1870 Quaker Way, Wilmington, OH 45177. Tel.: 937-382-6661, ext. 719.
E-mail: qhc@wilmington.edu
Web Site: www2.wilmington.edu
Institution Type/Description: History Museum.
Hours & Admission Prices: Mon.-Fri. 9-4; other times by appointment. No charge.

Wilmot

THE WILDERNESS CENTER INC., 9877 Alabama Ave., S.W., Wilmot, OH 44689. Mailing Address: P.O. Box 202, Wilmot, OH 44689-0202. Tel.: 330-359-5235. Fax: 330-359-7898.
E-mail: gordon@wildernesscenter.org
Web Site: www.wildernesscenter.org
Key Personnel: Exec. Dir., Gordon T. Maupin; Pres., C. Andrew Haag; Dir. Education, Joann L. Ballbach; Caretaker / Naturalist, Kenneth R. Schlegel, Jr.; Naturalist, Carrie Elvey; Naturalist, Lynda A. Price; Dir. Devel., Barbara Vitcosky; Dir. Land Stewardship, Gary Popotnik; Bookstore & Office Mgr., Rebecca Cyphert; Staff Accountant, Gina Mast; Mktg. & Public Rels., Vicki L. Capps; Custodian, Paul Lyon.
Institution Type/Description: Nature Center & Land Trust.
Hours & Admission Prices: Interpretive Building: Tues.-Sat. 9-5, Sun. 1-5. Nature Center: daily dawn-dusk. No charge; donations accepted; discounts to ANCA members. &

Attendance: 80,000 (actual)

Woodsfield

PARRY PARK MUSEUMS, 217 Eastern Ave., Woodsfield, OH 43793. Mailing Address: Monroe County Historical Society, P.O. Box 538, Woodsfield, OH 43793. Tel.: 740-472-1933. Facebook: Friend Monroe County Historical Society.
E-mail: moncohissoc@att.net
Web Site: www.rootsweb.ancestry.com/~ohmchs
Key Personnel: Dir. & Pres. (V), Joyce Wiggins; Museum Shop Mgr., Bart Wiggins.
Institution Type/Description: History Museum.
Hours & Admission Prices: Museums: June-Oct. call for hours or appointment. No charge; donations accepted. Senior Center Office: Mon.-Tues. 9-4, Fri. 10-2. Member discount for publications. &

Attendance: 300 (estimated)

Woodville

WOODVILLE HISTORICAL SOCIETY MUSEUM, 107 E. Main St., Woodville, OH 43469. Tel.: 419-849-2349.
E-mail: m.k.o@embarqmail.com
Key Personnel: Pres. (V), Michael K. O'Connor.
Institution Type/Description: Historical Society Museum.
Hours & Admission Prices: Call for hours. No charge; donations accepted.
Attendance: 350 (estimated)

Wooster

THE COLLEGE OF WOOSTER ART MUSEUM, Ebert Art Center, 1220 Beall Ave., Wooster, OH 44691. Tel.: 330-263-2495. Fax: 330-263-2633. Facebook: College of Wooster Art Museum.
E-mail: kzurko@wooster.edu
Web Site: wooster.edu/cwam
Key Personnel: Dir., Kitty McManus Zurko; Preparator, Douglas McGlumphy.
Institution Type/Description: College Art Gallery.
Hours & Admission Prices: Tues.-Fri. 11-4, Sat.-Sun. 1-4. No charge. Closed college breaks. &

Attendance: 9,500 (actual)

WAYNE CENTER FOR THE ARTS, 237 S. Walnut St., Wooster, OH 44691-4753. Tel.: 330-264-2787. Fax: 330-264-9314.
E-mail: waynectr@wayneartscenter.org
Web Site: www.wayneartscenter.org
Key Personnel: Exec. Dir., Robb Hyde; Pres. (V), Matthew Long; Bookkeeper, Marge Yochheim; Education Coord., Liza Zemancik; Museum Shop Mgr., Kristin Larson.
Institution Type/Description: Art Center.

WAYNE COUNTY HISTORICAL SOCIETY, 546 E. Bowman St., Wooster, OH 44691-3110. Tel.: 330-264-8856.
E-mail: host@waynehistoricalohio.org
Web Site: www.waynehistorical.org
Key Personnel: Pres., David Broehl; Office Admin., Lucy Drabenstott.
Institution Type/Description: General Museum: Housed in the original home of General Reasin Beall built between 1815 & 1817 on a land grant signed by Pres. James Madison.
Hours & Admission Prices: Feb.-Oct. Wed.-Sun. 2-4:30; Nov.-Jan. by appointment. Adults $5; members & students no charge. Closed national holidays; Christmas. &

Attendance: 10,000 (estimated)

Worthington

OHIO RAILWAY MUSEUM, 990 Proprietors Rd., Worthington, OH 43085. Tel.: 614-885-7345. Facebook.
E-mail: info@ohiorailwaymuseum.org
Web Site: www.ohiorailwaymuseum.org
Key Personnel: Pres. & Maintenance Mgr., Gary Anagnostis; Museum Shop Mgr., Linda Moore; Vice Pres., Public Opers. Mgr & Volunteer Coord., Dan Reed.
Institution Type/Description: Transportation Museum.
Hours & Admission Prices: Sun. 12-4; groups by appointment. Adults $8, military & seniors 65 & over $7, children 4-12 $6; children 3 & under no charge.
Attendance: 4,000 (estimated)

WORTHINGTON HISTORICAL SOCIETY, 50 W. New England Ave., Worthington, OH 43085-3536. Tel.: 614-885-1247. Facebook: Worthington Historical Society.
E-mail: info@worthingtonhistory.org
Web Site: www.worthingtonhistory.org
Key Personnel: Dir., Kate LaLonde; Pres. Worthington Historical Society (V), Jutta C. Pegues; Cur., Sue Whitaker; Museum Shop Mgr., Karen Cantlon.
Institution Type/Description: Historic House Museums: 1811-1819, Orange Johnson House & Garden; The Doll Museum, 1845 Classical Revival Manse & Society Headquarters.
Hours & Admission Prices: Orange Johnson House: April-Dec. Sun. 2-5; other times by appointment. Adults $5, children 6-16 $3; members & children 5 & under no charge. The Doll Museum: Tues.-Fri. 1-4, Sat. 10-2. Library: 1st & 3rd Wed. 1:30-4. Gift Shop: Tues.-Fri. 1-4, Sat. 10-2. Closed holidays.
Attendance: 3,900 (estimated)

Wright-Patterson Air Force Base

NATIONAL MUSEUM OF THE UNITED STATES AIR FORCE, 1100 Spaatz St., Wright-Patterson Air Force Base, OH 45433-7102. Tel.: 937-255-3286. Fax: 937-255-0523.
E-mail: nationalmuseum.mu@us.af.mil
Web Site: www.nationalmuseum.af.mil
Key Personnel: Dir., Lt. Gen. John L. "Jack" Hudson, USAF Ret.; Senior Cur., Krista Strider; Education, Judith Wehn; Public Rels., Diana Bachert; Collection Mgr., Roberta Carothers; Research/Archives, Wes Henry; Operations, John Marang; Air Force Museum Foundation, Mike Imhoff; Museum Shop Mgr., Melinda Lawrence.
Institution Type/Description: Military Aviation Museum: located at historic Wright Field, site of early aviation pioneering.
Hours & Admission Prices: Daily 9-5. Museum: no charge. IMAX Theatre: call for admission prices. Closed New Year's Day; Thanksgiving; Christmas. &

Attendance: 1,000,000 (estimated)

Xenia

GREENE COUNTY HISTORICAL SOCIETY, 74 W. Church St., Xenia, OH 45385-2902. Tel.: 937-372-4606. Fax: 372-372-5660 (call first).
E-mail: gchsxo@yahoo.com
Key Personnel: Exec. Dir., Catherine Wilson.
Institution Type/Description: Historical Society Museum.
Hours & Admission Prices: Tues.-Fri. 12-4, Sat. 12-3:30. Adults $3, youth under 18 $2. Closed New Year's Day; Independence Day; Thanksgiving; Christmas Eve & Day. &

Attendance: 3,000 (estimated)

Yellow Springs

GLEN HELEN ECOLOGY INSTITUTE TRAILSIDE MUSEUM, 405 Corry St., Yellow Springs, OH 45387-1843. Mailing Address: 1075 State Rt. 343, Yellow Springs, OH 45387. Tel.: 937-769-1902. Fax: 937-767-6655.
E-mail: rjaramillo@antioch-college.edu
Web Site: www.glenhelen.org
Key Personnel: Exec. Dir., Nick Boutis.
Institution Type/Description: Natural History Museum & Nature Center.
Hours & Admission Prices: Call for hours.
Attendance: 12,000

Youngstown

THE ARMS FAMILY MUSEUM OF LOCAL HISTORY, 648 Wick Ave., Youngstown, OH 44502-1289. Tel.: 330-743-2589. Fax: 330-743-7210.
E-mail: mvhs@mahoninghistory.org
Web Site: www.mahoninghistory.org
Key Personnel: Pres., William J. Cleary, Jr., M.D.; Dir., H. William Lawson; Mgr. Education & External Rels. and Museum Shop Mgr., Leann Rich; Registrar, T. Lea Mollman; Mgr. Collections & Curatorial Svcs., Jessica D. Trickett; Archivist, Pamela Speis.
Institution Type/Description: Local History Museum.
Hours & Admission Prices: Tues.-Sun. 1-5. Adults $4, college students & senior citizens $3, students under 18 $2; discounts for AAM, ICOM; members no charge. Closed national holidays. &
Attendance: 15,000 (actual)

THE BUTLER INSTITUTE OF AMERICAN ART, 524 Wick Ave., Youngstown, OH 44502-1286. Tel.: 330-743-1711. Fax: 330-743-9567.
E-mail: info@butlerart.com
Web Site: www.butlerart.com
Key Personnel: Dir., Louis A. Zona; Pres., Thomas J. Cavalier; Asst. Dir., M. Susan Carfano; Dir. Education, Joyce Mistovich; Business Mgr., Amy Kaufman; Dir. Information, Wendy Swick; Museum Shop Mgr., Renee Sheakoski.
Institution Type/Description: American Art Museum.
Hours & Admission Prices: Tues.-Sat. 11-4, Sun. 12-4. No charge; donations accepted. Closed New Year's Day; Easter; Independence Day; Thanksgiving; Christmas. &
Attendance: 140,000 (estimated)

FORD NATURE EDUCATION CENTER, 840 Old Furnace Rd., Youngstown, OH 44511-1470. Mailing Address: Mill Creek MetroParks, P.O. Box 596, Canfield, OH 44406. Tel.: 330-740-7107. Fax: 330-740-7133.
E-mail: generalinfo@millcreekmetroparks.com
Web Site: www.millcreekmetroparks.com/visit/places/mill-creek-park/ford-nature-center/
Key Personnel: Exec. Dir., Dennis Miller; Outdoor Education Mgr., Raymond Novotny; Pres., Louis Schiavoni.
Institution Type/Description: Nature Center: housed in 1912, 13-room stone mansion.
Hours & Admission Prices: Tues.-Sat. 10-5, Sun. 12-5. No charge; donations accepted. Closed New Year's Day; Thanksgiving; Christmas. &
Attendance: 20,000 (actual)

MCDONOUGH MUSEUM OF ART, Youngstown State University, 525 Wick Ave., Youngstown, OH 44555. Mailing Address: One University Plaza, Youngstown, OH 44555. Tel.: 330-941-1400. Fax: 330-941-1492.
E-mail: labrothers@ysu.edu
Web Site: www.mcdonoughmuseum.ysu.edu
Key Personnel: Dir., Leslie A. Brothers; Asst. Dir., Angela DeLucia; Exhibition Design & Production Mgr., Robyn Maas.
Institution Type/Description: Contemporary Art Center.
Hours & Admission Prices: Tues.-Sat. 11-4. No charge; donations accepted. Closed all major holidays. &
Attendance: 18,000 (estimated)

OH WOW! THE ROGER & GLORIA JONES CHILDREN'S CENTER FOR SCIENCE & TECHNOLOGY, 11 W. Federal St., Youngstown, OH 44503. Tel.: 330-744-5914. Fax: 330-259-0258.
E-mail: info@ohwowkids.org
Web Site: ohwowkids.org
Formerly: Children's Museum of the Valley
Key Personnel: Dir., Suzanne Barbati.

Institution Type/Description: Children's Museum.
Hours & Admission Prices: Tues.-Fri. 10-4:30, Sat. 12-4:30. Adults $5, senior citizens $4; discounts to groups & ACM reciprocal members; first Wed. of month & children under 3 no charge. Closed New Year's Day; Independence Day; Christmas Eve & Day. &
Attendance: 18,000 (estimated)

YOUNGSTOWN HISTORICAL CENTER OF INDUSTRY & LABOR, 151 W. Wood St., Youngstown, OH 44503-1034. Mailing Address: History Dept. - YSU, One University Plaza, Youngstown, OH 44555. Tel.: 330-941-1314, 800-262-6137. Fax: 330-941-2304.
E-mail: mipallante@ysu.edu
Key Personnel: Site Mgr., Martha Pallante.
Institution Type/Description: History Museum.
Hours & Admission Prices: Wed.-Fri. 10-4, Sat. 12-4. Adults $7, children 6-12 $3; discount to AAA members, seniors & active military; children 5 & under, YSU students & employees, and Ohio History Connection members no charge. Closed New Year's Day; Independence Day; Labor Day; Thanksgiving; Christmas. &
Attendance: 10,000 (estimated)

Zanesville

DR. INCREASE MATHEWS HOUSE, 304 Woodlawn Ave., Zanesville, OH 43701-4940. Mailing Address: 115 Jefferson St., Zanesville, OH 43701-4905. Tel.: 740-454-9500.
E-mail: phsomc@sbcglobal.net
Web Site: www.muskingumhistory.org
Key Personnel: Dir., Jim Geyer; Pres., Bob Jenkins.
Institution Type/Description: Historical Society Museum: housed in 1805 Dr. Increase Matthews House.
Hours & Admission Prices: May – Sept. Sun. 1-4; other times by appointment. Adults $5, students $1.
Attendance: 534 (estimated)

PUTNAM UNDERGROUND RAILROAD EDUCATION CENTER, 522 Woodlawn Ave., Zanesville, OH 43701. Tel.: 740-450-3100.
Institution Type/Description: History Museum.
Hours & Admission Prices: Temporarily closed.

THE STONE ACADEMY, 115 Jefferson St., Zanesville, OH 43701. Tel.: 740-454-9500.
E-mail: phsomc@sbcglobal.net
Web Site: www.muskingumhistory.org
Key Personnel: Dir., Jim Geyer.
Institution Type/Description: Historic House Museum: housed in the childhood home of Elizabeth Robins, late 19th century actress, author & activist; built in 1809.
Hours & Admission Prices: Tues.-Fri. 12-4.

ZANESVILLE MUSEUM OF ART, 620 Military Rd., Zanesville, OH 43701-1533. Tel.: 740-452-0741. Fax: 740-452-0797.
E-mail: vanessa@zanesvilleart.org
Web Site: www.zanesvilleart.org
Formerly: Zanesville Art Center
Key Personnel: Pres. (V), Richard Duncan; Operations Technician, Fred Orr; Temporary Operations Mgr., Andrew Near; Administrative Asst., Vanessa Brosie.
Institution Type/Description: Art Museum.
Hours & Admission Prices: Wed. & Fri.-Sat. 10-5, Thurs. 10-7:30. Adults $6, seniors $4; members no charge. Reciprocity with Ohio Art Museums. Closed holidays. &
Attendance: 24,000 (estimated)

Zoar

ZOAR COMMUNITY ASSOCIATION, 198 Main St., Zoar, OH 44697. Mailing Address: P.O. Box 621, Zoar, OH 44697-0508. Tel.: 330-874-3011 & 2646, 800-262-6195. Fax: 330-874-3211. Facebook.
E-mail: zoarinfo@historiczoarvillage.com
Web Site: www.historiczoarvillage.com
Formerly: Zoar State Memorial
Key Personnel: Dir., Tammi Mackey Shrum; Pres. (V), Jon Elsasser.
Institution Type/Description: Historic Site: 12 restored buildings of 1817 German religious communal sect.

Hours & Admission Prices: April-May & Oct. Sat. 11-4, Sun. 12-4; June-Sept. Wed.-Sat. 11-4, Sun. 12-4. Adults $8, children 4-17 $4; Time Travelers, ZCA & OHS members no charge. &
Attendance: 23,956 (actual)

OKLAHOMA
(329 listings)

Ada

ADA ARTS AND HERITAGE CENTER, 400 S. Rennie, Ada, OK 74820. Tel.: 580-332-7302.
E-mail: adaarts_heritage@yahoo.com
Web Site: adaartsandheritagecenter.com
Key Personnel: Dir., Sarah Hilton.
Institution Type/Description: Historic Building: housed in the former Ada Public Library; built in 1939. Listed on the National Register of Historic Places.
Hours & Admission Prices: Mon.-Fri. 10-2.

CHICKASAW NATIONAL HEADQUARTERS & CULTURAL CENTER, 520 E. Arlington, Ada, OK 74821. Mailing Address: P. O. Box 1548, Ada, OK 74821. Tel.: 580-436-2603.
Web Site: www.chickasawculturalcenter.com
Institution Type/Description: Native American Museum.
Hours & Admission Prices: Tues.-Fri. 9-5. No charge.

Afton

NATIONAL ROD & CUSTOM CAR HALL OF FAME MUSEUM, 55251 E. Hwy. 85A, Afton, OK 74331-2774. Tel.: 918-257-4234. Fax: 918-257-4234.
E-mail: dstarbird@wavelinx.net
Web Site: darrylstarbird.com
Key Personnel: Dir., Donna Starbird; C.E.O., Darryl Starbird.
Institution Type/Description: Automobile Museum.
Hours & Admission Prices: March-Nov. Wed.-Mon. 10-5; other times by appointment. Adults 13 & over $10, seniors 65 & over $9, children 8-12 $5, children 7 & under & members no charge. &

Aline

SOD HOUSE MUSEUM, 4628 State Hwy. 8, Aline, OK 73716-5629. Tel.: 580-463-2441.
E-mail: sodhouse@okhistory.org
Web Site: www.okhistory.org/sodhouse
Key Personnel: Historic Properties Mgr., Renee Trindle.
Institution Type/Description: Historic House: built 1894, following the opening of the Cherokee Outlet.
Hours & Admission Prices: mid-Jan. to Dec. Tues.-Sat. 9-5. Adults $5, seniors $4, students 6-18 $3; members no charge. Closed legal holidays. &
Attendance: 6,500 (actual)

Altus

MORGAN DOLL MUSEUM, 909 E. Broadway, Altus, OK 73521. Tel.: 580-482-2387.
Key Personnel: Dir., Mary Morgan.
Institution Type/Description: Doll Museum.
Hours & Admission Prices: Tues., Thurs. & Sat.-Sun. 1-5; other times by appointment. No charge. &
Attendance: 700 (estimated)

MUSEUM OF THE WESTERN PRAIRIE, 1100 Memorial Dr., Altus, OK 73521-2600. Tel.: 580-482-1044. Fax: 580-482-0128.
E-mail: jbuchanan@okhistory.org
Web Site: www.okhistory.org/sites/westernprairie
Key Personnel: Pres. (V), Dennis Vernon; Dir., Jennie Buchanan; Museum Shop Mgr., Mary Jane Winsett.
Institution Type/Description: General & Historical Society Museum.
Hours & Admission Prices: Tues.-Sat. 10-5. Adults $4, seniors & military $3, children 6-18 $1; society members no charge. Closed state holidays. &
Attendance: 4,037 (actual)

Alva

ALVA REGIONAL AIRPORT MUSEUM, 2875 College Blvd., Alva, OK 73717. Tel.: 580-327-2898. Fax: 580-327-4965.
E-mail: alvaair@sbcglobal.net
Web Site: alvaok.org/ara.htm

Institution Type/Description: History Museum.
Hours & Admission Prices: Daily 8-5. No charge.

CHEROKEE STRIP MUSEUM, 901 14th St., Alva, OK 73717-2500. Tel.: 580-327-2030. Facebook.
E-mail: cherokeestripmuseumalva@gmail.com
Web Site: www.cherokeestripmuseumalva.org
Key Personnel: C.E.O. & Chm. (V), Don Lynch; Cur., Beth Smith.
Institution Type/Description: General Museum: housed in the Alva General Hospital building; built in 1932.
Hours & Admission Prices: Tues.-Sun. 1-5; groups by appointment. Adults $5; members no charge. Closed Easter; Christmas. &
Attendance: 3,000 (estimated)

NORTHWESTERN OKLAHOMA STATE UNIVERSITY MUSEUM, Jesse Dunn Bldg., 709 Oklahoma Blvd., Alva, OK 73717-2749. Tel.: 580-327-1700, ext. 8513 & 8564. Fax: 580-327-8556.
E-mail: sdthompson@nwosu.edu
Web Site: www.nwosu.edu
Key Personnel: Co Dir., Dr. Steven Thompson; Co Dir., Dr. Aaron Place.
Institution Type/Description: Natural History Museum.
Hours & Admission Prices: Call for hours. No charge; donations accepted. Closed college holidays.
Attendance: 600 (estimated)

Ames

AMES ASTROBLEME MUSEUM, 109 E. Main St., Ames, OK 73718. Mailing Address: P.O. Box 568, Ames, OK 73718. Tel.: 580-753-4624. Fax: 580-753-4221.
E-mail: bawells@aoghs.org
Web Site: aoghs.org
Institution Type/Description: History Museum: housed on the site of a meteor crash that occurred 450 million years ago.
Hours & Admission Prices: Daily 24 hours. No charge.
Attendance: 400 (estimated)

HAJEK MOTORSPORTS MUSEUM, RR 1, Ames, OK 73718. Mailing Address: P.O. Box 106, Ames, OK 73718. Tel.: 580-753-4611. Fax: 580-753-4266.
Institution Type/Description: Motorsports Museum.
Hours & Admission Prices: Call for hours.

Anadarko

ANADARKO HERITAGE MUSEUM, 311 E. Main St., Anadarko, OK 73005-3023. Tel.: 405-247-3240. Fax: 405-247-3240.
E-mail: anadarkomuseum@netride.net
Formerly: Philomathic Museum
Key Personnel: C.E.O. & Pres. (V), Betty Bell; Co-Cur., Wilson Daingkau; Co-Cur., Cathy Crowell.
Institution Type/Description: General Museum.
Hours & Admission Prices: Mon.-Fri. 10-4, Sat. by appointment. No charge; donations accepted. Closed legal holidays. &
Attendance: 1,000 (estimated)

DELAWARE NATION MUSEUM, 31064 State Hwy. 281, Anadarko, OK 73005. Tel.: 405-247-2448, ext. 1181. Fax: 405-247-8905.
E-mail: jross@delawarenation.com
Web Site: www.delawarenation.com
Formerly: Delaware Tribal Museum
Key Personnel: Museum Shop Mgr., Gina Wooster.
Institution Type/Description: Native American Museum.
Hours & Admission Prices: Mon.-Fri. 8-5. No charge; donations accepted. Closed holidays. &

INDIAN CITY U.S.A. CULTURAL CENTER, 2 1/2 Miles S. on Hwy. 8, Anadarko, OK 73005. Mailing Address: Kiowa Tribe, P. O. Box 369, Carnegie, OK 73015. Tel.: 580-654-2300.
Institution Type/Description: Natural History Museum: located on 1887 site of Tonkawa Massacre.
Hours & Admission Prices: Temporarily closed. &
Attendance: 38,471 (estimated)

NATIONAL HALL OF FAME FOR FAMOUS AMERICAN INDIANS, Hwy. 62, E., Anadarko, OK 73005. Mailing Address: P.O. Box 548, Anadarko, OK 73005-0548. Tel.: 405-247-5555 & 3331. Fax: 405-247-5571.
Key Personnel: C.E.O. (V), Joe McBride, Jr.; Sec., Carolyn N. McBride.
Institution Type/Description: Native American Museum.
Hours & Admission Prices: Mon.-Sat. 9-5, Sun. 1-5. No charge; donations accepted. Closed New Year's Day; Thanksgiving; Christmas. &
Attendance: 20,000 (estimated)

PHILOMATHIC PIONEER MUSEUM, 311 E. Main St., Anadarko, OK 73005-3023. Tel.: 405-247-3240.
Institution Type/Description: History Museum.
Hours & Admission Prices: Tues.-Fri. 10-5, Sat.-Sun. 1-5. No charge.

SOUTHERN PLAINS INDIAN MUSEUM, 801 E. Central Blvd., Anadarko, OK 73005-4437. Mailing Address: P.O. Box 749, Hwy. 62, E., Anadarko, OK 73005-0749. Tel.: 405-247-6221. Fax: 405-247-7593.
E-mail: feedback@ios.doi.gov
Web Site: www.doi.gov
Key Personnel: Cur., Bambi Allen.
Institution Type/Description: Indian Art Museum.
Hours & Admission Prices: Mon.-Fri. 10-4. No charge. Closed federal holidays. &
Attendance: 25,000 (estimated)

Antlers

WILDLIFE HERITAGE CENTER MUSEUM, 610 S.W. D St., Antlers, OK 74523. Tel.: 580-298-9933.
E-mail: antlersdeerfestival@yahoo.com
Web Site: www.wildlifeheritagecenter.org
Key Personnel: Pres. (V), Tracy Stephanson; Museum Shop Mgr., Verne Jackson.
Institution Type/Description: Wildlife Museum.
Hours & Admission Prices: Mon.-Fri. 9-4, Sat. 10-2. No charge; donations accepted. Closed holidays. &
Attendance: 4,000 (actual)

Apache

APACHE HISTORICAL SOCIETY MUSEUM, 101 W. Evans, Apache, OK 73006. Mailing Address: P.O. Box 101, Apache, OK 73006-0101. Tel.: 580-588-3392. Fax: 580-588-3393.
Key Personnel: Chm. & Pres. (V), Danny Swanda; Mgr., Mary Joyce Swanda.
Institution Type/Description: Historical Society Museum.
Hours & Admission Prices: Mon.-Fri. 12-4. No charge; donations accepted. Closed holidays. &
Attendance: 400 (estimated)

Ardmore

CHARLES B. GODDARD CENTER FOR VISUAL AND PERFORMING ARTS, 401 First Ave., S.W., Ardmore, OK 73401-4725. Mailing Address: P.O. Box 1624, Ardmore, OK 73402-1624. Tel.: 580-226-0909. Fax: 580-226-8891. Facebook: Charles B. Goddard The Goddard Center.
E-mail: goddardcenter@yahoo.com
Web Site: www.goddardcenter.org
Key Personnel: Exec. Dir., Ken Bohannon; Chm. (V), Jan Tindale; Treas. (V), Andrew Harlow; Cur. & Preparator, Cory Blankenship.
Institution Type/Description: Center for Visual & Performing Arts.
Hours & Admission Prices: Tues.-Fri. 9-5, Sat. 1-4. No charge; donations accepted. Closed national holidays. &
Attendance: 10,000 (estimated)

ELIZA CRUCE HALL DOLL COLLECTION, 320 E. St., N.W., Ardmore, OK 73401-4304. Tel.: 580-223-8290.
E-mail: belhaggerty@ardmorelibrary.org
Key Personnel: Dir., Daniel R. Gibbs.
Institution Type/Description: Antique Doll Museum.
Hours & Admission Prices: Mon.-Thurs. 10-8, Fri. 10-6, Sat.-Sun. 1-5. No charge; donations accepted. Closed legal holidays. &
Attendance: 10,000 (estimated)

GREATER SOUTHWEST HISTORICAL MUSEUM, 35 Sunset Dr., Ardmore, OK 73401-2852. Tel.: 580-226-3857. Fax: 580-226-3357. Facebook: @gshmuseum.
E-mail: thegreatersouthwest@gshm.org

Web Site: www.gshm.org
Key Personnel: Dir., Wesley Hull; Office & Museum Shop Mgr., Lisa Allen.
Institution Type/Description: History Museum.
Hours & Admission Prices: Tues.-Sat. 10-5. No charge; donations accepted. &
Attendance: 10,000 (estimated)

TUCKER TOWER NATURE CENTER, c/o Lake Murray State Park, 13528 Scenic State Hwy. 77, Ardmore, OK 73401-7083. Tel.: 580-223-2109. Fax: 580-223-4052. Facebook: Lake Murray State Park.
E-mail: lakemurrayresort@oklahomaresorts.com
Web Site: www.oklahomaparks.com
Key Personnel: Park Naturalist, Mark Teders.
Institution Type/Description: Park Museum: built 1933-35 by WPA & CCC for a Governor's Retreat.
Hours & Admission Prices: Feb.-May & Sept.-Nov. Wed.-Sun. 9-5; Memorial Day-Labor Day daily 9-7. Any donation for admission. &
Attendance: 35,000 (actual)

Atoka

CONFEDERATE MEMORIAL MUSEUM, 2902 US Hwy. 69 N., Atoka, OK 74525. Mailing Address: P.O. Box 245, Atoka, OK 74525-0245. Tel.: 580-889-7192. Fax: 580-889-7192.
E-mail: atokamuseum@yahoo.com
Web Site: www.civilwaralbum.com/atoka
Key Personnel: Site Mgr., Gwen Walker; Museum Dir., Cindy Wallis; Pres. (V), Katie Hardman.
Institution Type/Description: Military Museum.
Hours & Admission Prices: Mon.-Fri. 9-4. No charge; donations accepted. Closed national holidays. &
Attendance: 9,000 (estimated)

Barnsdall

BIGHEART MUSEUM, 616 W. Main, Barnsdall, OK 74002. Mailing Address: P.O. Box 475, Barnsdall, OK 74002-0475. Tel.: 918-847-2397.
Key Personnel: Cur., Joe Williams; Cur., Faye Wickware.
Institution Type/Description: History Museum: named after Osage Chief James Bigheart.
Hours & Admission Prices: Tues.-Fri. 12-4, Sat. 9-1. No charge.

Bartlesville

BARTLESVILLE AREA HISTORY MUSEUM, 401 S. Johnstone Ave., City Bldg., 5th Fl., Bartlesville, OK 74003-6619. Tel.: 918-338-4290. Fax: 918-338-4264. Facebook: Bartlesville Area History Museum.
E-mail: jacrabtr@cityofbartlesville.org
Web Site: www.bartlesvillehistorycom
Key Personnel: Dir., Shelly McGill; Registrar, Matthew Clapper; Volunteer Coord. & Public Rels., Jo Crabtree; Collections Mgr., Debbie Neece.
Institution Type/Description: History Museum.
Hours & Admission Prices: Mon.-Fri. 10-4. Suggested Donation: adults $3. Closed major holidays. &
Attendance: 5,000 (estimated)

FRANK LLOYD WRIGHT'S PRICE TOWER, 510 S. Dewey, Bartlesville, OK 74003-3560. Mailing Address: P.O. Box 2464, Bartlesville, OK 74005-2464. Tel.: 918-336-4949. Fax: 918-336-7117. Facebook: Price Tower Arts Center.
E-mail: info@pricetower.org
Web Site: www.pricetower.org
Formerly: Price Tower Arts Center
Key Personnel: Exec. Dir., Timothy Boruff; Chm. (V), C.J. Silas; Pres. (V), Brad Doenges; Assoc. Cur., Deshane Atkins; Docent Coord., Judy DuVall; Dir. Mktg. & Public Rels., Amy Haley.
Institution Type/Description: Art, Architecture & Design Museum: housed in Price Tower, designed by Frank Lloyd Wright.
Hours & Admission Prices: Gallery: Tues.-Sat. 10-5, Sun. 12-5. Adults $5, seniors $4; discounts to AAM, ICOM, NARM members, & Frank Lloyd Wright public sites; members and students 16 & under no charge. Tower Tours: Tues.-Sat. 11 & 2, Sun. 2; reservations recommended. Tours: adults $12, seniors $10, children 18 & under $10. Closed New Year's Day; Thanksgiving; Christmas. &
Attendance: 32,000 (actual)

FRANK PHILLIPS HOME, 1107 S. Cherokee, Bartlesville, OK 74003-5027. Tel.: 918-336-2491. Fax: 918-336-3529. Facebook: Frank Phillips Home.
E-mail: jgoss@okhistory.org
Web Site: www.frankphillipshome.org
Key Personnel: Dir. & Cur., Jim L. Goss.
Institution Type/Description: Historic House: 1909 Frank Phillips home.
Hours & Admission Prices: Tours: Wed.-Fri. 10, 11, 2, 3, & 4, Sat. 10, 11, 1, 2, 3, 4. Adults $5. Behind the Scenes Director's Tour: Wed.-Fri. 9am-10:30am. Adults $10. Closed major holidays. &
Attendance: 4,895 (actual)

PHILLIPS PETROLEUM COMPANY MUSEUM, 410 Keeler, Bartlesville, OK 74004. Tel.: 855-631-8687.
E-mail: lorrie.l.rockman@conocophillips.com
Web Site: www.phillips66museum.com
Key Personnel: Dir., Stan Baughn.
Institution Type/Description: History and Technology Museum.
Hours & Admission Prices: Mon.-Sat. 10-4. No charge. Closed holidays.

WOOLAROC MUSEUM, 1925 Woolaroc Ranch Rd., Bartlesville, OK 74003-7171. Mailing Address: P.O. Box 1647, Bartlesville, OK 74005. Tel.: 918-336-0307, ext. 10, 888-WOOLAROC. Fax: 918-336-0084.
E-mail: lstone@woolaroc.org
Web Site: www.woolaroc.org
Key Personnel: Dir., Kenneth Meek; C.E.O., Bob Fraser; Cur. Art, Linda Stone; Bldg. Supt., Tim Sydebotham; Museum Shop Mgr., Beth Greene.
Institution Type/Description: Art & History Museum.
Hours & Admission Prices: Memorial Day to Labor Day Tues.-Sun. 10-5; Sept.-May Wed.-Sun. 10-5. Adults $10; senior citizens 65 & over $8; discounts to AAM members, special needs groups & organized school groups; members & children 11 & under no charge. Closed Thanksgiving; Christmas. &
Attendance: 100,000 (actual)

Beaver

JONES AND PLUMMER TRAIL MUSEUM, Fairgrounds, S. Douglas St., Beaver, OK 73932. Tel.: 580-625-4439. Facebook: Jones Plummer Trail Museum.
E-mail: jplummermuseum@yahoo.com
Institution Type/Description: History Museum.
Hours & Admission Prices: Tues.-Sat. 11-3, Sun. 1-4. No charge. &

Bethany

OKLAHOMA MUSEUM OF FLYING, 7110 Millionaire Dr., Bethany, OK 73008. Tel.: 405-535-9565.
E-mail: greg-p51@cox.net
Institution Type/Description: History Museum.
Hours & Admission Prices: Mon.-Fri. 9-4, Sat. 10-2. No charge; donations accepted.

Billings

DR. RENFROW-MILLER MUSEUM, 201 S. Broadway St., Billings, OK 74630. Mailing Address: 2100 Ranch, Billings, OK 74630. Tel.: 580-725-3258 & 3487.
Institution Type/Description: Historic House Museum: housed in the former home and office of pioneer doctor, Thomas F. Renfrow; built in 1901. Listed on the National Register of Historic Places.
Hours & Admission Prices: By appointment. No charge; donations accepted.

HENRY AND SHIRLEY BELLMON LIBRARY & MUSEUM, Main & Broadway, Billings, OK 74630. Mailing Address: 2500 Zig Zag, Billings, OK 74630-2003. Tel.: 580-725-3487.
Institution Type/Description: Library & Museum: c.1900 building. Listed on the National Register of Historic Places.
Hours & Admission Prices: By appointment. No charge.

Binger

CADDO HERITAGE MUSEUM, Caddo Nation Complex, Hwy. 281 & 152, Binger, OK 73009. Mailing Address: P.O. Box 478, Binger, OK 73009. Tel.: 405-658-2344.
E-mail: pcross@caddonation.org
Web Site: caddonation-nsn.gov
Institution Type/Description: History Museum.
Hours & Admission Prices: Mon.-Fri. 9-4. No charge. &

Bixby

BIXBY HISTORICAL SOCIETY MUSEUM, 24 E. McKennon Ave., Bixby, OK 74008-4332. Mailing Address: P.O. Box 1046, Bixby, OK 74008-1046. Tel.: 918-366-1200.
E-mail: bixby.okhs@cox.net
Web Site: www.rootsweb.ancestry.com/~okbhs/index.html
Institution Type/Description: Historical Society Museum.
Hours & Admission Prices: Wed. & 1st Sat. of each month 11-2; tours by appointment.

Blackwell

TOP OF OKLAHOMA HISTORICAL SOCIETY MUSEUM, 303 S. Main St., Blackwell, OK 74631-3347. Tel.: 580-363-0209. Facebook.
E-mail: tohsmuseum@outlook.com
Key Personnel: Dir., Melissa Hudson; Pres., Dianne Braden; Sec., Fredda Ganer.
Institution Type/Description: Local History Museum: housed in c.1912 Electric Park Pavilion.
Hours & Admission Prices: Mon.-Sat. 10-4, No charge; donations accepted. Closed major holidays. &
Attendance: 1,150 (estimated)

Boise City

CIMARRON HERITAGE CENTER MUSEUM, 1300 N. Cimarron, Boise City, OK 73933. Mailing Address: P.O. Box 214, Boise City, OK 73933-0441. Tel.: 580-544-3479. Facebook: Cimarron Heritage Center Museum.
E-mail: museum@ptsi.net
Web Site: www.chcmuseumok.com
Key Personnel: Dir., Jody Risley; Pres. (V), Beverly Baker.
Institution Type/Description: History Museum.
Hours & Admission Prices: Mon.-Sat. 10-12 & 1-4. No charge; donations accepted. Closed major holidays.
Attendance: 5,700 (estimated)

Bokchito

MUSEUM OF CREATION TRUTH, 3290 State Rd. 22, Bokchito, OK 74726. Tel.: 580-924-0803.
Key Personnel: Dir., Billy Gordon; Dir., Delie Gordon.
Institution Type/Description: Natural History Museum.
Hours & Admission Prices: Sat. 10-4; other times by appointment. No charge. &
Attendance: 300 (estimated)

Boley

BOLEY HISTORICAL MUSEUM, 10 W. Grant St., Boley, OK 74829. Mailing Address: P.O. Box 627, Boley, OK 74829. Tel.: 918-667-3711, 405-567-5738. Fax: 918-667-3331.
E-mail: hhicks@wwtech.edu
Key Personnel: Chm. (V), Henrietta Hicks; Museum Shop Mgr., Addie Miller.
Institution Type/Description: History Museum.
Hours & Admission Prices: By appointment. Adults $2; members no charge. &
Attendance: 1,100 (estimated)

Bristow

BRISTOW HISTORICAL MUSEUM, 1 Railroad Place, Bristow, OK 74010-3040. Mailing Address: P.O. Box 127, Bristow, OK 74010-0127. Tel.: 918-367-5151.
E-mail: info@visitbristowok.com
Web Site: www.visitbristowok.com/museums.htm
Institution Type/Description: History Museum: housed in 1923 restored depot.
Hours & Admission Prices: Mon.-Fri. 9-4.

Broken Arrow

BROKEN ARROW HISTORICAL SOCIETY, 400 S. Main, Broken Arrow, OK 74012. Tel.: 918-258-2616.
E-mail: llewis.bamuseum@yahoo.com
Web Site: www.bahistoricalsociety.com
Key Personnel: Dir., Lori Lewis.
Institution Type/Description: Historical Society Museum.
Hours & Admission Prices: Tues.-Fri. 10-4, Sat. 10-2. Adults $5; children under 18 no charge. &

Broken Bow

BEAVERS BEND WILDLIFE MUSEUM, RR 4, Broken Bow, OK 74728. Mailing Address: P.O. Box 10, Broken Bow, OK 74728. Tel.: 580-494-6497.
E-mail: information@beaversbend.com
Web Site: www.beaversbend.com
Institution Type/Description: Wildlife Museum.
Hours & Admission Prices: Mon.-Sat. 9-5. Adults & children over 12 $6, senior citizens 65 & over $5, children 12 & under $3.50; discounts to groups.

GARDNER MANSION & MUSEUM, 6745 E. U.S. Hwy. 70, Broken Bow, OK 74728-5507. Tel.: 580-584-6588. Fax: 580-584-6588.
Key Personnel: Museum Shop Mgr., Lewis R. Stiles.
Institution Type/Description: Historic House Museum: housed in the former home of the Choctaw Indian Chief; built in 1884.
Hours & Admission Prices: Summer: Mon.-Sat. 10-5.
Attendance: 2,000 (estimated)

INDIAN MEMORIAL MUSEUM, 402 E. 2nd St., Broken Bow, OK 74728. Tel.: 580-584-6531.
Institution Type/Description: History Museum.
Hours & Admission Prices: Mon.-Fri. 9-6.

OKLAHOMA FOREST HERITAGE CENTER MUSEUM, Beavers Bend State Park, US-259A, Broken Bow, OK 74728. Mailing Address: P.O. Box 157, Broken Bow, OK 74728-0157. Tel.: 580-494-6497. Fax: 580-494-6689. Facebook: Forest Heritage Center.
E-mail: fhc@beaversbend.com
Web Site: www.forestry.ok.gov/fhc
Key Personnel: Dir., Doug Zook.
Institution Type/Description: Forestry Museum.
Hours & Admission Prices: Daily 8-5. No charge; donations accepted. &
Attendance: 150,000 (estimated)

Buffalo

BUFFALO MUSEUM, 108 S. Hoy, Buffalo, OK 73834. Mailing Address: P.O. Box 224, Buffalo, OK 73834. Tel.: 580-735-2628.
Key Personnel: Pres. (V), Sydney B. Malt.
Institution Type/Description: History Museum.
Hours & Admission Prices: May-Oct. Fri.-Sat. 1-4, Sun. 2-4; other times by appointment. No charge; donations accepted. &

Cache

QUANAH PARKER STAR HOUSE/EAGLE PARK GHOST TOWN, Rte. 2 (SH-115 at US-62), Cache, OK 73527. Mailing Address: 810 N. 8th St., Cache, OK 73527-9630. Tel.: 580-429-3420.
Key Personnel: Mgr., Kathy Threadwell; Mgr., Wayne Gipson.
Institution Type/Description: History Museum.
Hours & Admission Prices: By appointment only.

Caddo

CADDO INDIAN TERRITORY MUSEUM AND LIBRARY, 110 Buffalo St., Caddo, OK 74729. Mailing Address: P.O. Box 105, Caddo, OK 74729. Tel.: 580-367-2787.
E-mail: caddomuseum@yahoo.com
Key Personnel: Cur., Dorthy McGrath.
Institution Type/Description: History Museum.
Hours & Admission Prices: Tues.-Sat. 11-5; other times by appointment. No charge; donations accepted.
Attendance: 1,200 (estimated)

Carnegie

KIOWA CULTURE PRESERVATION AUTHORITY, Hwy. 9 W., Carnegie, OK 73015. Mailing Address: P.O. Box 369, Carnegie, OK 73015. Tel.: 580-654-2300, ext. 370.
Formerly: Kiowa Tribe Museum and Resource Center
Key Personnel: Chm. (V), David Sullivan; Sec. & Treas., Tommie Louise Doyebi.
Institution Type/Description: American Indian Museum.
Hours & Admission Prices: Mon.-Fri. 8-4:30. No charge; donations accepted. &
Attendance: 1,500 (actual)

Catoosa

ARKANSAS RIVER HISTORICAL SOCIETY MUSEUM, 5350 Cimarron Rd., Catoosa, OK 74015-3027. Tel.: 918-266-2291. Fax: 918-226-7678.
Institution Type/Description: Historical Society Museum.
Hours & Admission Prices: Mon.-Fri. 8-4:30. No charge; donations accepted.

CATOOSA HISTORICAL SOCIETY MUSEUM, 207 N. Cherokee, Catoosa, OK 74015. Mailing Address: c/o Catoosa Historical Society, P.O. Box 738, Catoosa, OK 74015. Tel.: 918-266-3296. Fax: 918-266-7156.
E-mail: georgiamcafee@yahoo.com
Institution Type/Description: Historical Society Museum.
Hours & Admission Prices: Tues. & Fri. 10-3. No charge; donations accepted. &
Attendance: 250 (estimated)

D.W. CORRELL MUSEUM, 19934 E. Pine St., Catoosa, OK 74015. Mailing Address: P.O. Box 190, Catoosa, OK 74015. Tel.: 918-266-3612. Facebook: D.W. Correll Museum.
E-mail: ehamshar@cityofcatoosa.org
Web Site: cityofcatoosa.org/index.php/d-w-correll-museum
Key Personnel: Dir., Eric Hamshar.
Institution Type/Description: History Museum.
Hours & Admission Prices: Tues. & Thurs. 11-7, Wed. & Fri.-Sat. 9-5. Adults 18 & over $3, seniors 62 & over $2; military, school & nursing home groups and youth 17 & under no charge. Closed government holidays.

Chandler

LINCOLN COUNTY HISTORICAL SOCIETY AND MUSEUM OF PIONEER HISTORY, 717 Manvel Ave., Chandler, OK 74834-2842. Tel.: 405-258-2425.
E-mail: lincolncountyhs@sbcglobal.net
Web Site: www.pioneermuseumok.org
Key Personnel: Pres. (V), Michelle Keller; Vice Pres., Dee Douglas; Treas., Susan Morton; Sec., Liz Hellams; Museum Shop Mgr., Carol Beckman.
Institution Type/Description: Local History Museum.
Hours & Admission Prices: Wed.-Sat. 10-4. No charge; donations accepted. &
Attendance: 3,954 (actual)

Cheyenne

PIONEER MUSEUM, CITY PARK, 107 Pioneer Park Way, Cheyenne, OK 73628. Mailing Address: P.O. Box 34, Cheyenne, OK 73628. Tel.: 580-497-3882.
E-mail: tdale55@aol.com; lmad43@hotmail.com
Web Site: www.rogermills.org
Key Personnel: Dir., Barbara Little.
Institution Type/Description: Park & Museum Complex: consists of a 1903 One Room School, Pioneer Museum, Minnie Slief Community Museum, Veterans Display, Santa Fe Depot, Chapel, & early 1900s Kendall House Log Cabin.
Hours & Admission Prices: Museum: March 1-Oct. 31 Tues.-Sat. 10-4; Roll I-Room School: open all-year; April, May, Sept. & Oct. call for hours. No charge; donations accepted. &
Attendance: 2,000 (estimated)

WASHITA BATTLEFIELD NATIONAL HISTORIC SITE, 18555 Hwy. 47 A, Cheyenne, OK 73628. Mailing Address: 18555 Hwy 47A, Ste. A, Cheyenne, OK 73628. Tel.: 580-497-2742. Fax: 580-497-2712.
E-mail: kevin_bowles_mohr@nps.gov
Web Site: www.nps.gov/waba
Institution Type/Description: Historic Site: site of the Southern Cheyenne village of Chief Black Kettle and where the Battle of Washita occurred in 1868.
Hours & Admission Prices: Overlook & Trail: daily dawn to dusk. Visitor Center: daily 8-5. Closed New Year's Day; Thanksgiving; Christmas.

Chickasha

GRADY COUNTY HISTORICAL SOCIETY, 415 W. Chickasha Ave., Chickasha, OK 73018. Mailing Address: P.O. Box 495, Chickasha, OK 73023. Tel.: 405-224-6480. Facebook: Grady County Historical Society.
E-mail: gradycomuseum@gmail.com
Web Site: www.gradycountyhistorical.org
Institution Type/Description: Historical Society Museum: housed in the former department store, The Dixie; built in 1907.
Hours & Admission Prices: Mon.-Fri. 10-3. No charge; donations accepted. &

Claremore

BELVIDERE MANSION, 121 N. Chickasaw Ave., Claremore, OK 74017-7418. Tel.: 918-342-1127.
E-mail: belvidereclaremore@gmail.com
Web Site: www.belvideremansion.com
Institution Type/Description: Historic Mansion: built in 1907.
Hours & Admission Prices: Mansion & Gift Shop: Tues.-Sat. 10-3. Tea Room: Tues.-Sat. 11-2. No charge; donations accepted.

J.M. DAVIS ARMS & HISTORICAL MUSEUM, 330 N. J.M. Davis Blvd., Claremore, OK 74017-7066. Tel.: 918-341-5707. Fax: 918-341-5771.
E-mail: info@thegunmuseum.com
Web Site: www.thegunmuseum.com
Key Personnel: Exec. Dir., Wayne McCombs; Cur., Jason Schubert; Chm. (V), William Higgins; Tourism Coord., Kimberly Thompson.
Institution Type/Description: Firearms & Historical Museum.
Hours & Admission Prices: Tues.-Sat. 10-5. No charge; donations requested. Closed New Year's Day; Thanksgiving; Christmas.

OKLAHOMA MILITARY ACADEMY MUSEUM, Rogers State Univ., Meyer Hall, 2nd Fl., 1701 W. Will Rogers Blvd., Claremore, OK 74017. Tel.: 918-343-7777, 800-256-7511.
E-mail: admissions@rsu.edu
Web Site: www.rsu.edu/alumni/oklahoma-military-academy/oma-museum/
Key Personnel: Exec. Dir., Dr. Danette Boyle.
Institution Type/Description: Military School History Museum.
Hours & Admission Prices: Mon.-Fri. 8-5. Closed holidays.

WILL ROGERS MEMORIAL MUSEUM, 1720 W. Will Rogers Blvd., Claremore, OK 74017-3208. Mailing Address: P.O. Box 157, Claremore, OK 74018-0157. Tel.: 918-341-0719. Fax: 918-343-8119.
E-mail: wrinfo@willrogers.com
Web Site: www.willrogers.com
Key Personnel: Dir., Tad Jones; Asst. Dir., Jacob Krumwiede.
Institution Type/Description: History Museum.
Hours & Admission Prices: Memorial: Daily 10-5. Off season hours (Nov. 11-Mar. 1) - closed Mon. & Tues. Closed Thanksgiving and Christmas. Adults $7, Seniors 62 & over and military $5; discounts to NARM members; Children 6-17 $3, Children 5 & under Free. Birthplace: Daily 10-5. Off season hours (Nov. 11-Mar. 1) Closed; Closed Thanksgiving and Christmas. No charge; donations encouraged.
Attendance: 152,026 (actual)

Clinton

CHEYENNE CULTURAL CENTER, 2250 N.E. Rte. 66, Clinton, OK 73601. Tel.: 580-323-6224.
Institution Type/Description: Native American History Museum.
Hours & Admission Prices: Call for hours.

MOHAWK LODGE INDIAN STORE, 22702 Rte. 66 N., Clinton, OK 73601-7526. Tel.: 580-323-2360.
Key Personnel: Owner, Pat Henry.
Institution Type/Description: American Indian Museum: trading post opened in 1892.
Hours & Admission Prices: Mon.-Sat. 9-5. No charge; donations accepted.
Attendance: 3,500 (estimated)

OKLAHOMA ROUTE 66 MUSEUM, 2229 W. Gary Blvd., Clinton, OK 73601-5305. Tel.: 580-323-7866. Fax: 580-323-2870.
E-mail: rt66mus@okhistory.org
Web Site: www.route66.org
Key Personnel: C.E.O., Bob Blackburn; Dir., Pat Smith; Cur., Andy Watson.
Institution Type/Description: History Museum.
Hours & Admission Prices: Mon.-Sat. 9-5, Sun. 1-5. Adults $4, senior citizens $3, students 6-18 $1.
Attendance: 34,000 (actual)

Coalgate

COAL COUNTY HISTORICAL & MINING MUSEUM, 212 S. Broadway, Coalgate, OK 74538. Tel.: 580-927-2360.
Institution Type/Description: History Museum.
Hours & Admission Prices: Tues.-Thurs. 10-3:30, Sat. 10-1. No charge.

Colbert

COLBERT HISTORICAL MUSEUM, 100 N. Burney, Colbert, OK 74733. Mailing Address: P.O. Box 1299, Colbert, OK 74733. Tel.: 580-296-2385.
E-mail: wyotahannan@cherokeetel.com
Web Site: wyotahannan.cherokeecomm.com
Key Personnel: Dir. & Pres. (V), Wyota Hannan.
Institution Type/Description: History Museum.
Hours & Admission Prices: By appointment. No charge; donations accepted.
Attendance: 100 (estimated)

Colcord

TALBOT LIBRARY AND MUSEUM, 500 S. Colcord Ave., Colcord, OK 74338. Mailing Address: P.O. Box 349, Colcord, OK 74338. Tel.: 918-326-4532.
E-mail: talbotlibrary@earthlink.net
Web Site: talbotlibrary.org
Institution Type/Description: Library.
Hours & Admission Prices: Wed.-Sat. 10-4.

Collinsville

COLLINSVILLE DEPOT MUSEUM, 115 S. 10th St., Collinsville, OK 74021-3124. Mailing Address: 337 N. 20th St., Collinsville, OK 74021. Tel.: 918-371-3540.
E-mail: wttkitty@sbcglobal.net
Formerly: Santa Fe Railroad Depot & Caboose
Key Personnel: Pres., Historical Society, William Terrill Thomas; Dir., Ronald G. Evans; Owner Collinsville Newspaper, Ted Wright; Museum Shop Mgr., Thomas Evans Wright.
Institution Type/Description: Antiques Museum: housed in 90-year-old depot.
Hours & Admission Prices: by appointment only. No charge; donations accepted.
Attendance: 300 (estimated)

NEWSPAPER MUSEUM, 1110 W. Main St., Collinsville, OK 74021-3113. Tel.: 918-798-1804.
E-mail: wrightted@aol.com
Web Site: www.cvilleok.com/museum.html
Key Personnel: Dir., Ted Wright.
Institution Type/Description: History Museum.
Hours & Admission Prices: By appointment. Tours: adults $1.

Cordell

WASHITA COUNTY MUSEUM, 115 E. 1st St., Cordell, OK 73632. Mailing Address: P.O. Box 153, Cordell, OK 73632. Tel.: 580-832-5270.
E-mail: yrwd49@hintonet.net
Key Personnel: Pres. (V), Landon Jones; Vice Pres. (V), Lavern Berry; Sec. & Treas., Lonnie Yearwood.
Institution Type/Description: History Museum: housed in the Carnegie Library; built in 1911.
Hours & Admission Prices: Fri. 2-4; other times by appointment. No charge; donations accepted. Closed holidays.
Attendance: 800 (estimated)

Coweta

MISSION BELL MUSEUM, 204 S. Bristow Ave., Coweta, OK 74429-2301. Mailing Address: P.O. Box 850, Coweta, OK 74429-0850. Tel.: 918-486-2189. Fax: 918-486-2513.
Institution Type/Description: Historical Society Museum: housed in a former Presbyterian Church; built in 1907.
Hours & Admission Prices: Tues. & Thurs. open four hours & by appointment only. No charge; donations accepted.
Attendance: 200 (estimated)

Crescent

FRONTIER COUNTRY MUSEUM, 500 N. Grand St., Crescent, OK 73028. Mailing Address: P.O. Box 856, Crescent, OK 73028. Tel.: 405-969-3660. Fax: 405-969-3660.
E-mail: frontiercountrymuseum@gmail.com
Web Site: www.frontiercountrymuseum.org
Key Personnel: Pres. (V), Sandra Voskuhl; Museum Shop Mgr., Carol Oltmanns.
Institution Type/Description: History Museum.
Hours & Admission Prices: Tues.-Fri. 10-4. Adults $5, seniors 55 & over $3, children 1st to 12 grade $2; members no charge.

Cushing

RICHARD O. DODRILL'S MUSEUM OF ROCKS, MINERALS & FOSSILS, 914 E. 2nd St., Cushing, OK 74023-4135. Mailing Address: 1400 E. McElroy Rd., Unit 207, Stillwater, OK 74075-7338.
Key Personnel: Dir. & Cur., Richard O. Dodrill.
Institution Type/Description: History Museum.
Hours & Admission Prices: Tues.-Sat. 10-4. No charge. &

Cyril

CYRIL HERITAGE HOUSE MUSEUM, 3rd & Main St., Cyril, OK 73029. Mailing Address: Historical Society of Oklahoma, 470 288 Hwy. 101, Sallisaw, OK 74955. Tel.: 580-583-5333.
E-mail: okhc@okhistory.org
Institution Type/Description: History Museum: built in 1910.
Hours & Admission Prices: By appointment. No charge.

Davis

ARBUCKLE HISTORICAL SOCIETY MUSEUM, 12 Main St., Davis, OK 73030. Tel.: 580-369-2518.
Institution Type/Description: Historical Society Museum.
Hours & Admission Prices: Daily 10-4. No charge.

Dewey

DEWEY HOTEL MUSEUM, 801 N. Delaware, Dewey, OK 74029-1609. Tel.: 918-534-0215.
E-mail: info@wchs-ok.org
Institution Type/Description: Historic Building: 1899 Victorian-style wood frame hotel built for Jacob H. Bartles.
Hours & Admission Prices: April-Nov. Tues.-Sat. Adults $3, students 13-18 $1.50; members and children 12 & under no charge. Closed holidays.
Attendance: 6,000 (actual)

TOM MIX MUSEUM, 721 N. Delaware, Dewey, OK 74029-2307. Mailing Address: P.O. Box 190, Dewey, OK 74029-0190. Tel.: 918-534-1555.
E-mail: tommix@cableone.net
Web Site: tommixmuseum.com
Key Personnel: Museum Shop Mgr., Fawn Lassiter; Museum Shop Asst. Mgr., Karen Michno.
Institution Type/Description: History Museum.
Hours & Admission Prices: Jan.-Feb. Thurs.-Sat. 10-4:30; March-Dec. Tues.-Sat. 10-4:30. Suggested Donation: adults $3, children $.50. Closed legal holidays. &
Attendance: 5,500 (estimated)

Drumright

DRUMRIGHT HISTORICAL SOCIETY MUSEUM, 301 E. Broadway, Drumright, OK 74030-3805. Mailing Address: P.O. Box 441, Drumright, OK 74030. Tel.: 918-352-3002. Facebook: Drumright Historical Society Museum.
E-mail: curator@drumrighthistoricalsociety.org
Web Site: www.drumrighthistoricalsociety.org
Formerly: Drumright Oil Museum
Key Personnel: Cur., Tammy Posey; Pres. (V), Lela Willey; Vice Pres. (V), Angie Bengston; Treas., Sarah Mattox; Sec., Deborah Wilson.
Institution Type/Description: History Museum: housed in a 1915 Santa Fe Depot. Listed on the National Register of Historic Places.
Hours & Admission Prices: Winter: Thurs. 9-2, Fri. 9-5, Sat. 10-5. Summer: Thurs. 3-7, Fri.-Sat. 9-5; groups by appointment. No charge; donations accepted.
Attendance: 1,112 (actual)

Duncan

CHISHOLM TRAIL HERITAGE CENTER & GARIS GALLERY OF THE AMERICAN WEST, 1000 N. Chisholm Trail Pkwy., Duncan, OK 73533-1539. Tel.: 580-252-6692. Fax: 580-252-6567. Facebook: www.facebook.com/onthechisholmtrail.
E-mail: info@onthechisholmtrail.com
Web Site: www.onthechisholmtrail.com
Formerly: On The Chisholm Trail Statue & Museum
Key Personnel: Exec. Dir., Stacy Cramer Moore; Education Coord., Leah Mulkey; Public Rels. & Mktg. Coord., Toni Hopper; Gift Shop Mgr., Syvonna Davis.
Institution Type/Description: History Museum.

Hours & Admission Prices: Mon.-Sat. 10-5, Sun. 1-5. Adults $6, seniors 55 & over $5, youth 5-17 $4; discount to groups. Closed Thanksgiving; Christmas. &
Attendance: 20,000 (estimated)

STEPHENS COUNTY HISTORICAL SOCIETY AND MUSEUM, Hwy. 81 & Beech, Fuqua Park, Duncan, OK 73533. Mailing Address: P.O. Box 1294, Duncan, OK 73534-1294. Tel.: 580-252-0717.
E-mail: covahurstwilliams@gmail.com
Key Personnel: Dir., Cova Williams; Chm. & Asst. Dir. (V), Vickie Zimmerman; Assoc. Dir., Louise Elliott; Assoc. Dir., Marge Rigdon; Assoc. Dir., Sharleen Johns.
Institution Type/Description: History Museum.
Hours & Admission Prices: Tues. & Thurs.-Sat. 1-5. No charge; donations accepted. Closed New Year's Eve & Day; Easter; Thanksgiving; Christmas. &
Attendance: 6,894 (actual)

W.T. FOREMAN PRAIRIE HOUSE FOUNDATION, 814 W. Oak, Duncan, OK 73533. Mailing Address: P.O. Box 2094, Duncan, OK 73534. Tel.: 580-252-1780 & 251-0027. Facebook: The Prairie House.
E-mail: gloafman@cableone.net
Web Site: theprairiehouse.com
Key Personnel: Dir., Kathy Smith; C.E.O., Gail Loafman.
Institution Type/Description: Historic House Museum: built in 1918. Listed on the National Register of Historic Places.
Hours & Admission Prices: Tues. & Thurs. 1-4; other times by appointment. No charge; donations accepted. &

Durant

FORT WASHITA, 3348 State Rd. 199, Durant, OK 74701-9443. Tel.: 580-924-6502.
E-mail: ftwashita@okhistory.org
Web Site: www.okhistory.org/sites/fortwashita
Key Personnel: Site Mgr., Jim Argo; Historic Interpreter, Ron Petty.
Institution Type/Description: Historic Site: 1842-1865 frontier military fort.
Hours & Admission Prices: Tues.-Sat. 9-4:30; Sun. 1-4:30. No charge; donations accepted. Closed national holidays.
Attendance: 25,000 (actual)

THREE VALLEY MUSEUM, 401 W. Main St., Durant, OK 74701-5026. Tel.: 580-920-1907.
E-mail: 3valleymuseumok@gmail.com
Web Site: www.threevalleymuseum.com
Key Personnel: Pres., Greg Phillips.
Institution Type/Description: History Museum.
Hours & Admission Prices: Tues.-Fri. 1-5, Sat. 11-3; other times by appointment. No charge; donations accepted. Closed Thanksgiving; Christmas.
Attendance: 2,000 (estimated)

Durham

BREAK O' DAY FARM AND METCALFE MUSEUM, EW 86, Durham, OK 73642. Mailing Address: 8647 N. 1745 Rd., Durham, OK 73642. Tel.: 580-655-4467. Fax: 580-655-4654.
E-mail: metcalfe@dobsonteleco.com
Web Site: www.metcalfemuseum.org
Key Personnel: Dir., Roger Lester; Dir., Lloydelle Lester; Pres. (V), Janna Montgomery; Museum Shop Mgr., Becky Buster.
Institution Type/Description: Art Museum.
Hours & Admission Prices: March-Nov. Tues.-Sat. 10-5. No charge; donations accepted. Closed holidays.

Edmond

EDMOND HISTORICAL SOCIETY & MUSEUM, 431 S. Boulevard, Edmond, OK 73034-3873. Tel.: 405-340-0078. Fax: 405-340-2771.
E-mail: edmondhistory@edmondhistory.org
Web Site: edmondhistory.org
Key Personnel: Exec. Dir., Anita Schlaht; Pres., Betsy Mantor; Treas., Robert Austin; Museum Shop Mgr., Jill Courter.
Institution Type/Description: Historical Society Museum: housed in 1936 native stone armory.
Hours & Admission Prices: Tues.-Fri. 10-5, Sat. 1-4. No charge; donations accepted. Closed major holidays. &
Attendance: 20,000 (actual)

LABORATORY OF HISTORY MUSEUM, University of Central Oklahoma, Department of History & Geography, 100 N. University Dr., Edmond, OK 73034-5207. Tel.: 405-974-4669.
E-mail: historymuseum@uco.edu
Web Site: sites.uco.edu
Key Personnel: Dir., Heidi Vaughn.
Institution Type/Description: History Museum.
Hours & Admission Prices: Call for hours. No charge; donations accepted.

El Reno

CANADIAN COUNTY HISTORICAL MUSEUM, 300 S. Grand, El Reno, OK 73036-3610. Tel.: 405-262-5121. Fax: 405-262-9397.
E-mail: vptrishane@aol.com
Web Site: www.elreno.org
Key Personnel: Pres., Vicki Proctor; Cur., Pat Reuter; Gift Shop Mgr., Marguerite Stoakes.
Institution Type/Description: Historical Society Museum: housed in 1906 Rock Island Railway Station on 98th Meridian.
Hours & Admission Prices: Wed.-Sat. 9-5, Sun. 1-5. No charge; donations accepted. Closed New Year's Day; Independence Day; Thanksgiving; Christmas. &

FORT RENO VISITOR CENTER, 7107 W. Cheyenne St., El Reno, OK 73036. Tel.: 405-262-3987. Fax: 405-262-0133.
E-mail: info@fortreno.org
Web Site: www.fortreno.org
Key Personnel: Dir. & Museum Shop Mgr., Sarah Overholser; Chair (V), Theleda Fuller; Pres. (V), David VonTuglin.
Institution Type/Description: Visitor Center.
Hours & Admission Prices: Daily 10-4. Adults $5. &
Attendance: 22,000 (estimated)

Elk City

ANADARKO BASIN MUSEUM OF NATURAL HISTORY, 204 N. Main St., Elk City, OK 73644-4754. Tel.: 580-243-0437.
Institution Type/Description: Natural History Museum: housed in the former Casa Grande Hotel; built in the late 1920s. Listed on the National Register of Historic Places.
Hours & Admission Prices: Temporarily closed.

NATIONAL ROUTE 66 MUSEUM AND OLD TOWN COMPLEX, 2717 W. Hwy. 66, Elk City, OK 73644. Mailing Address: P.O. Box 5, Elk City, OK 73648-0005. Tel.: 405-225-6266. Fax: 580-225-3234.
E-mail: jacksom@elkcity.com
Web Site: www.elkcity.com
Key Personnel: Chm., L.V. Baker, Jr.; Dir., Basil Weatherly; Cur., Wanda Queenan; Museum Shop Mgr., Maxine Jackson.
Institution Type/Description: General Museum.
Hours & Admission Prices: Memorial Day to Labor Day Mon.-Sat. 9-5, Sun. 2-5; Sept.-May Mon.-Sat. 9-5, Sun. 2-5. Adults $5, seniors & children over 6 $4; discounts to groups, AAA members, bus tours, members, senior & school groups. Closed New Year's Day; Easter; Thanksgiving; Christmas Eve & Day. &
Attendance: 35,000 (actual)

TRANSPORTATION MUSEUM, Old Hwy. 66 N., Elk City, OK 73648. Mailing Address: P.O. Box 5, Elk City, OK 73648. Tel.: 580-225-6266.
Institution Type/Description: Transportation History Museum.
Hours & Admission Prices: Mon.-Sat. 9-5, Sun. 2-5; other times by appointment.

Enid

CHEROKEE STRIP REGIONAL HERITAGE CENTER, 507 S. 4th St., Enid, OK 73701-5835. Tel.: 580-237-1907. Fax: 580-234-1055.
E-mail: aholland@okhistory.org
Web Site: csrhc.org
Formerly: Museum of the Cherokee Strip
Key Personnel: Pres., Andrea Holland.
Institution Type/Description: Regional History Museum.
Hours & Admission Prices: Museum: Tues.-Sat. 10-5, Sun. 1-5. Families $13, adults $5, seniors 62 & over, students $3; discounts to groups; children 5 & under, members and active duty military & veterans no charge. Closed New Year's Day; Easter; Thanksgiving; Christmas. &
Attendance: 15,000 (actual)

HUMPHREY HERITAGE VILLAGE, 507 S. 4th St., Enid, OK 73701. Tel.: 580-237-1907.
E-mail: csrhcinfo@okhistory.org
Web Site: www.csrhc.org/humphrey-village.html
Institution Type/Description: Historic Village Museum.
Hours & Admission Prices: Tues.-Fri. 9-5, Sat.-Sun. 2-5; other times by appointment. No charge. Closed state holidays.

LEONA MITCHELL SOUTHERN HEIGHTS HERITAGE CENTER AND MUSEUM, 616 Leona Mitchell Blvd., Enid, OK 73701. Tel.: 580-402-2524. Fax: 580-223-7062.
E-mail: achoctaw1866@aol.com
Web Site: www.leonamitchellsouthernheightsindianmuseum.org
Key Personnel: Exec. Dir., Barbara Finley.
Institution Type/Description: Heritage Center.
Hours & Admission Prices: Tues.-Fri. 10-4, Sat. 10-2; other times by appointment. Adults $8, children 5-17 $5.

LEONARDO'S CHILDREN'S MUSEUM, 200 E. Maple, Enid, OK 73701. Mailing Address: P.O. Box 348, Enid, OK 73702. Tel.: 580-233-2787.
E-mail: marketing@leonardos.org
Web Site: www.leonardos.org
Formerly: Leonardo's Discovery Warehouse
Key Personnel: Exec. Dir., Tracy Bittle; Chm. (V), Molly Shepherd.
Institution Type/Description: Children's Museum.
Hours & Admission Prices: Mon.-Sat. 10-5, Sun. 1-5. Admission $9; discounts to groups & Oklahoma Museum Network members; children under 2 no charge. &
Attendance: 96,000 (actual)

MIDGLEY MUSEUM, 1001 Sequoyah Dr., Enid, OK 73703. Tel.: 580-234-7265.
Institution Type/Description: Historic House: housed in a home built of petrified wood & rock.
Hours & Admission Prices: Wed.-Fri. 1-5, Sat. 2-5. No charge; donations accepted.

RAILROAD MUSEUM OF OKLAHOMA, 702 N. Washington, Enid, OK 73701-3138. Tel.: 580-233-3051.
E-mail: railroad_museum@att.net
Institution Type/Description: Railroad Museum.
Hours & Admission Prices: Tues.-Fri. 1-4, Sat. 9-1, Sun. 2-5. Suggested Donations: $3 per person. Closed holidays. &

SIMPSON'S OLD TIME MUSEUM & MOVIE STUDIO, 228 E. Randolph Ave., Enid, OK 73701. Tel.: 580-234-4998.
E-mail: rick@skeletoncreekproductions.com
Institution Type/Description: History Museum.
Hours & Admission Prices: Mon.-Sat. 8-11 & 1-4. No charge.

Erick

ROGER MILLER MUSEUM, Corner of Roger Miller Blvd. & Sheb Wooley Ave., Erick, OK 73645. Mailing Address: P.O. Box 464, Erick, OK 73645-0464. Tel.: 580-526-3833. Facebook: Roger Miller Museum.
E-mail: rettasnowden@yahoo.com
Web Site: www.rogermillermuseum.com
Institution Type/Description: History Museum.
Hours & Admission Prices: Wed.-Sat. 9-5; other times by appointment. Adults $3, seniors & students $2. Closed holidays.
Attendance: 5,000 (estimated)

Fairview

MAJOR COUNTY HISTORICAL SOCIETY, State Hwy. 58, Fairview, OK 73737. Mailing Address: P.O. Box 555, Fairview, OK 73737. Tel.: 580-227-2265.
E-mail: office@mchsok.net
Web Site: www.mchsok.net
Key Personnel: Pres., Don Voth; Mgr., Nate Conley.
Institution Type/Description: Historical Society Museum.
Hours & Admission Prices: Tues.-Fri. 1-5, Sat. 10-2. No charge; donations accepted. Closed holidays. &
Attendance: 2,500 (estimated)

Fort Gibson

FORT GIBSON HISTORIC SITE, 907 N. Garrison Ave., Fort Gibson, OK 74434. Mailing Address: P.O. Box 457, Fort Gibson, OK 74434-0457. Tel.: 918-478-4088. Fax: 918-478-4089.
E-mail: fortgibson@okhistory.org
Web Site: www.fortgibson.com/historical_sites.htm
Key Personnel: Dir., David Fowler; Museum Shop Mgr., Omar Reed.
Institution Type/Description: Military Museum Complex.
Hours & Admission Prices: Tues.-Sat. 10-5. Adults $3, senior citizens $2.50, students 6-18 $1; discounts to AAM members; children 5 & under & veterans no charge.
Attendance: 60,432 (actual)

Fort Sill

FORT SILL NATIONAL HISTORIC LANDMARK AND MUSEUM, 435 Quanah Rd., Fort Sill, OK 73503-5100. Tel.: 580-442-5123. Fax: 580-442-0552. Facebook.
E-mail: usarmy.sill.fcoe.mbx.fort-sill-museum@mail.mil
Key Personnel: Dir., Scott A. Neel, Ph.D.
Institution Type/Description: Military Museum: housed in the 1869-75 original stone buildings of Fort Sill's Indian Territory.
Hours & Admission Prices: Tues.-Sat. 8:30-5. No charge; donations accepted. Closed New Year's Eve & Day; Thanksgiving; Christmas Eve & Day. ♿
Attendance: 35,000 (estimated)

Fort Towson

FORT TOWSON HISTORIC SITE, HC 63, Fort Towson, OK 74735-9273. Mailing Address: P.O. Box 1580, Fort Towson, OK 74735-9273. Tel.: 580-873-2634. Fax: 580-873-9385.
E-mail: fttowson@okhistory.org
Web Site: www.okhistory.org/military/forttowson.html
Formerly: Fort Towson Military Park
Key Personnel: Site Mgr. & Dir., John Davis; Interim Cur., Keith Reese.
Institution Type/Description: Historic Site & Ruins.
Hours & Admission Prices: Mon.-Fri. 9-5, Sat.-Sun. 1-5. No charge; donations accepted. Closed state holidays.
Attendance: 29,454 (actual)

Frederick

CRAWFORD COLLECTION, 115 W. Main St., Frederick, OK 73542. Tel.: 580-335-3211.
Institution Type/Description: General Museum.
Hours & Admission Prices: 2nd Sat. each month 11-2. No charge. ♿

PIONEER HERITAGE TOWNSITE CENTER, 201 N. 9th St., Frederick, OK 73542. Tel.: 580-335-5844.
E-mail: pioneer@okhistory.org
Institution Type/Description: History Museum: housed in a pioneer village including 8 structures.
Hours & Admission Prices: Mon.-Fri. 9-3, 2nd Sat. 10-1; other times by appointment. No charge.

Freedom

FREEDOM MUSEUM, 405 Main St., Freedom, OK 73842. Mailing Address: P.O. Box 145, Freedom, OK 73842. Tel.: 580-621-3533.
Institution Type/Description: History Museum.
Hours & Admission Prices: Tues.-Fri. 11-4. No charge; donations accepted.
Attendance: 1,200 (actual)

Gate

GATEWAY TO THE PANHANDLE, Main St., Gate, OK 73844. Mailing Address: P.O. Box 27, Gate, OK 73844-0027. Tel.: 580-934-2004.
E-mail: emaphet@ptsi.net
Key Personnel: Dir., Pres. (V) & Museum Shop Mgr., L. Ernestine Maphet; Cur. & Librarian, Peggy Whiteman; Deputy Dir., Karen Bond; Deputy Dir., Valerie Spurgeon; Asst. Dir., Louise Hein.
Institution Type/Description: Historic Buildings.
Hours & Admission Prices: Mon.-Sat. 11-4, Sun. & holidays by appointment. No charge; donations accepted. Closed Thanksgiving; Christmas. ♿
Attendance: 450 (estimated)

Geary

CANADIAN RIVERS HISTORICAL SOCIETY MUSEUM, 717 S. Broadway, Geary, OK 73040. Mailing Address: c/o Geary Historical Society, P.O. Box 216, Geary, OK 73040. Tel.: 405-884-2608.
Institution Type/Description: Historical Society Museum.
Hours & Admission Prices: By appointment. No charge.

Gene Autry

GENE AUTRY OKLAHOMA MUSEUM, 47 Prairie St., Gene Autry, OK 73436. Mailing Address: P.O. Box 92, Gene Autry, OK 73436-0044. Tel.: 580-294-3335 & 768-5559. Facebook: Gene Autry Oklahoma Museum.
E-mail: geneautryoklahomamuseum@gmail.com
Web Site: www.geneautryokmuseum.org
Key Personnel: Dir., Leslei Fisher; Pres. (V), Micele Garrison.
Institution Type/Description: General Museum.
Hours & Admission Prices: Thurs.-Sat. 10-5, Sun. 12-5 by appointment. No charge; donations accepted. ♿
Attendance: 2,000 (estimated)

Goodwell

NO MAN'S LAND HISTORICAL SOCIETY, 214 E. Ave., Goodwell, OK 73939. Mailing Address: P.O. Box 278, Goodwell, OK 73939-0278. Tel.: 580-349-2670. Fax: 580-349-2670.
E-mail: nmlhs@outlook.com
Web Site: www.nmlhs.org
Key Personnel: Dir., Sue Weissinger; Pres. (V), Ron Kincannon.
Institution Type/Description: Historical Society Museum.
Hours & Admission Prices: Tues.-Fri. 10-12 & 1-4, Sat. 10-4. No charge; donations accepted. Closed legal holidays. ♿
Attendance: 4,000 (estimated)

Grove

HAR-BER VILLAGE MUSEUM, 4404 W. 20th St., Grove, OK 74344-5136. Tel.: 918-786-6446 & 3488. Fax: 918-786-6213. Facebook: Har-Ber Village On Grand Lake O' The Cherokees.
E-mail: director@har-bervillage.com
Web Site: www.har-bervillage.com
Key Personnel: Exec. Dir., Amelia Chamberlain; Bd. Trustees, Robert Carter.
Institution Type/Description: Pioneer-era Village Museum.
Hours & Admission Prices: 3rd Sat. March to 1st Sat. Nov. Thurs.-Mon. 9-3:30; call or see website for updated information. Adults $10, seniors 62 & over $7.50, children 6-14 $5; discounts to veterans, AAM members & groups of 10 or more; members and children 5 & under no charge. School Tours: $3 per student. ♿
Attendance: 18,000 (actual)

Guthrie

NATIONAL LIGHTER MUSEUM, 5715 S. Sooner Rd., Guthrie, OK 73044-6739. Tel.: 405-282-3025.
E-mail: tballard8@cox.net
Web Site: www.nationallightermuseum.com
Key Personnel: Owner & Cur., Ted C. Ballard.
Institution Type/Description: History Museum.
Hours & Admission Prices: By appointment. No charge.

OKLAHOMA FRONTIER DRUG STORE MUSEUM, 214 W. Oklahoma, Guthrie, OK 73044. Tel.: 405-282-1895.
E-mail: drugstoremuseum@aol.com
Web Site: www.drugmuseum.org
Key Personnel: Dir., G. Mark Ekiss, R.PH.
Institution Type/Description: Drugstore & Pharmacy Museum.
Hours & Admission Prices: Tues.-Sat. 10-5. No charge; donations accepted. Closed New Year's Day; Christmas.
Attendance: 10,000 (estimated)

OKLAHOMA TERRITORIAL MUSEUM, 406 E. Oklahoma Ave., Guthrie, OK 73044-3317. Tel.: 405-282-1889.
E-mail: guthriecomplex@okhistory.org
Web Site: www.oklahomaterritorialmuseum.org
Key Personnel: Dir., Nathan Turner; Cur. Collections, Erin Brown; Main Tech, James Ray; Clerk, Sharen Bowers.
Institution Type/Description: History Museum: housed in the Fred Pfeiffer Memorial Museum building & the Carnegie Library.

Hours & Admission Prices: By appointment. Closed holidays. &
Attendance: 16,685 (actual)

OWENS ARTS PLACE MUSEUM, 1202 E. Harrison Ave., Guthrie, OK 73044. Tel.: 405-260-0204.
E-mail: mail@owensmuseum.com
Web Site: www.owensmuseum.com
Key Personnel: Dir. & C.E.O., Wallace Owens.
Institution Type/Description: Art Museum.
Hours & Admission Prices: Tues.-Thurs. 10-4, Sun. 1-4. No charge. Closed holidays. &
Attendance: 1,500 (estimated)

TERRITORIAL CAPITAL SPORTS MUSEUM, 315 W. Oklahoma Ave., Guthrie, OK 73044-3107. Tel.: 405-260-1342. Fax: 405-260-1342. Facebook: Territorial Capital Sports Museum.
E-mail: oklasportsmuseum@sbcglobal.net
Web Site: territorialcapitalsportsmuseum.org
Formerly: Oklahoma Sports HOF Museum-Guthrie
Key Personnel: Dir., Richard Hendricks; Pres. (V), Jack Herron.
Institution Type/Description: Sports Museum.
Hours & Admission Prices: Tues.-Sat. 10-4, Sun. by appointment. Adults $5; members no charge. &
Attendance: 1,500 (estimated)

Harrah

HARRAH HISTORY CENTER AND RAILROAD DEPOT MUSEUM, 20881 E. Main St., Harrah, OK 73045. Mailing Address: P.O. Box 846, Harrah, OK 73045. Tel.: 405-454-6911.
E-mail: harrahhsitorycente@att.net
Web Site: www.harrahhistorycenter.com
Formerly: Harrah Historical Society
Key Personnel: Pres. (V), Tom Barron.
Institution Type/Description: Historical Society Museum.
Hours & Admission Prices: Tues.-Thurs. 10-4; other times by appointment. No charge; donations accepted. &
Attendance: 400 (estimated)

Hartshorne

TWIN CITIES HERITAGE MUSEUM, 929 Pennsylvania Ave., Hartshorne, OK 74547. Tel.: 918-297-7220.
Institution Type/Description: History Museum.
Hours & Admission Prices: Wed.-Sat. 10-3 by appointment. No charge.

Healdton

HEALDTON OIL MUSEUM, 315 E. Main St., Hwy. 76, Healdton, OK 73438-1714. Mailing Address: c/o Oklahoma Historical Society, 800 Nazih Zuhdi Dr., Oklahoma City, OK 73105. Tel.: 580-229-0900.
Web Site: www.okhistory.org/sites/healdtonoil
Key Personnel: Mgr., Melanie Williams.
Institution Type/Description: Technology Museum.
Hours & Admission Prices: Mon.-Fri. 9-4. No charge; donations accepted. Closed legal holidays. &
Attendance: 2,411 (estimated)

Heavener

HEAVENER RUNESTONE STATE PARK, 18365 Runestone Rd., Heavener, OK 74937-7493. Mailing Address: 103 E. Avenue B, Heavener, OK 74937-2601. Tel.: 918-653-2241. Fax: 918-653-3435.
E-mail: heavener@oklahomaparks.com
Key Personnel: Park Mgr., Rick Sanders; Maintenance & Repair Tech., William Rowland.
Institution Type/Description: Historic Site: Runestone inscription, Glome Valley.
Hours & Admission Prices: March-Oct. daily 8-dusk; Nov.-Feb. daily 8-dusk. No charge; donations accepted. &
Attendance: 90,000 (actual)

PETER CONSER HOME, 47114 Conser Creek Rd., Heavener, OK 74937-9022. Mailing Address: Oklahoma Historical Center, 800 Nazih Zuhdi Dr., Oklahoma City, OK 73105. Tel.: 918-653-2493.
Key Personnel: C.E.O., Dr. Bob Blackburn; Site Mgr., A.G. Hembree.

Institution Type/Description: Historic House: 1894 Peter Conser House; a captain of the Lighthorsemen of the Moshulatubbe District, a noted law enforcement group of the Choctaw Nation.
Hours & Admission Prices: Wed.-Sat. 10-5, Sun. 1-5. No charge; donations accepted. Closed national holidays. &
Attendance: 6,000 (estimated)

Henryetta

HENRYETTA TERRITORIAL MUSEUM, 410 W. Moore, Henryetta, OK 74437-5255. Mailing Address: P.O. Box 220, Henryetta, OK 74437-0220. Tel.: 918-652-7112. Fax: 918-652-7112.
E-mail: mdcak46@sbcglobal.net
Web Site: www.territorialmuseum.net
Key Personnel: Pres., Marsha Smith; Pres. (V), Mike Doak.
Institution Type/Description: History Museum.
Hours & Admission Prices: Wed.-Sat. 11-3; other times by appointment. No charge; donations accepted. Closed holidays.
Attendance: 1,500 (estimated)

Hinton

HINTON HISTORICAL MUSEUM & PARKER HOUSE, 801 S. Broadway, Hinton, OK 73047. Tel.: 405-542-3181.
E-mail: eoh@blogoklahoma.net
Institution Type/Description: History Museum.
Hours & Admission Prices: Mon.-Sat. 10-4.

Hobart

GENERAL TOMMY FRANKS LEADERSHIP INSTITUTE AND MUSEUM, 507 S. Main, Hobart, OK 73651. Mailing Address: P.O. Box 222, Hobart, OK 73651-0222. Tel.: 580-726-5900. Fax: 580-726-5901.
E-mail: museum@tommyfranksmuseum.org
Web Site: tommyfranksmuseum.org
Key Personnel: Chm., Tom Talley; Dir., D'Lese Travis; Mgr. Museum, Scott Cumm; Deputy Dir., Nikki Jones; Mgr. Finance, Adalita Cumm.
Institution Type/Description: History Museum.
Hours & Admission Prices: Mon.-Sat. 10-12 & 1-5. No charge; donations accepted. Closed holidays. &
Attendance: 4,500 (estimated)

KIOWA COUNTY HISTORICAL MUSEUM, 518 S. Main, Hobart, OK 73651. Tel.: 580-726-6202. Fax: 580-726-6202.
E-mail: kiowacomuseum@cableone.net
Institution Type/Description: History Museum; housed in the former Rock Island Depot; built in 1909. Listed on the National Register of Historic Places.
Hours & Admission Prices: Mon.-Fri. 10-12 & 1-4. No charge; donations accepted. Closed holidays.
Attendance: 400 (estimated)

Hollis

HARMON COUNTY HISTORICAL MUSEUM, 102 W. Broadway St., Hollis, OK 73550. Tel.: 580-688-9545.
E-mail: harcomuseum@pldi.net
Key Personnel: Cur., Sue Harris.
Institution Type/Description: History Museum; Harmon County named after Judson Harmon, a U.S. Attorney General from Ohio.
Hours & Admission Prices: Tues.-Fri. 11-4; other times by appointment.

Hominy

DRUMMOND HOME, 305 N. Price, Hominy, OK 74035-1007. Tel.: 918-885-2374. Facebook: Drummond Home of the Oklahoma Historical Society.
E-mail: bwhitcomb@okhistory.org
Key Personnel: Site Mgr., Beverly Whitcomb.
Institution Type/Description: Historic House: 1905 Drummond Home.
Hours & Admission Prices: Wed.-Sat. 9-5, Sun. 1-5. Tours: 10-4. Adults $3, seniors $2.50, children 6-18 $1; discounts to groups; children 5 & under no charge. Closed state holidays.
Attendance: 1,800 (estimated)

FIELD HISTORICAL PRINTING MUSEUM, 109 W. Main St., Hominy, OK 74035-1031. Mailing Address: c/o Hominy Heritage

Association, 121 West Main, Hominy, OK 74035. Tel.: 918-885-2688.
E-mail: welcome2@bleeenterprises.com
Institution Type/Description: History Museum.
Hours & Admission Prices: By appointment. No charge.

Hugo

CHOCTAW COUNTY HISTORICAL SOCIETY, 307 North B St., Hugo, OK 74743-3325. Mailing Address: P.O. Box 577, Hugo, OK 74743-0577. Tel.: 580-326-6630. Facebook.
E-mail: friscodepot@live.com
Web Site: www.friscodepot.org
Key Personnel: Dir. & CEO, Norm Pence.
Institution Type/Description: Historical Museum: housed in 1912 Frisco Railroad Depot; original Harvey House restaurant.
Hours & Admission Prices: Tues.-Sat. 10-4; tours by appointment. Museum: no charge; donations accepted. Closed Thanksgiving; Christmas.
Attendance: 2,096 (actual)

Idabel

BARNES-STEVENSON HOUSE - MCCURTAIN COUNTY HISTORICAL SOCIETY, 302 S.E. Adams Ave., Idabel, OK 74745. Tel.: 580-212-3639.
E-mail: ksivard1987@gmail.com
Institution Type/Description: Historical Society Museum.
Hours & Admission Prices: By appointment.

MUSEUM OF THE RED RIVER, 812 E. Lincoln Rd., Idabel, OK 74745-7815. Tel.: 508-286-3616. Fax: 508-286-3616.
E-mail: motr@hotmail.com
Web Site: www.museumoftheredriver.org
Key Personnel: Dir., Henry Moy; Pres. (V) Herron Foundation, Donald A. Herron; Pres. (V) Idabel Museum Society, Judy Petre; Volunteer Coord., Sallie Webb; Keeper of Collections, Daniel Vick; Cur. Assoc., Mario Rivera; Museum Asst., John Malin; Business Mgr., Vickie Smith; Museum Shop Mgr., Sherron Mitchell.
Institution Type/Description: General Museum.
Hours & Admission Prices: Tues.-Sat. 10-5, Sun. 1-5. No charge; donations accepted. Closed New Year's Day; Memorial Day; Independence Day; Thanksgiving; Christmas. &
Attendance: 11,900 (actual)

Indiahoma

WICHITA MOUNTAINS WILDLIFE REFUGE, 32 Refuge Headquarters, Indiahoma, OK 73552-2478. Tel.: 580-429-3222.
E-mail: Quinton_Smith@fws.gov
Web Site: www.fws.gov/refuge
Institution Type/Description: Wildlife Refuge.
Hours & Admission Prices: Mon.-Fri. 8-4:30.

Indianola

OLD CHOATE HOUSE MUSEUM, 403 Walnut St., Indianola, OK 74442. Tel.: 918-823-4421.
Institution Type/Description: Historic House Museum: housed in the former home of a Choctaw Senate President.
Hours & Admission Prices: By appointment. No charge.

Inola

MIKE FULLER'S AUTO & GAS MUSEUM, 22 N. Broadway, Inola, OK 74036. Tel.: 918-906-5192. Fax: 918-543-3999.
Institution Type/Description: History Museum.
Hours & Admission Prices: Daily 10-8. No charge.

Jay

DELAWARE COUNTY HISTORICAL SOCIETY & MARIEE WALLACE MUSEUM, 538 Krause St., Jay, OK 74346. Mailing Address: P.O. Box 855, Jay, OK 74346-0855. Tel.: 918-253-4345.
E-mail: jaymuseum@brightok.net
Web Site: dchsmuseumok.com/contact-us
Key Personnel: Dir. & Museum Shop Mgr., Jackie Coatney; Pres. (V), Becki Farley.
Institution Type/Description: Historical Society Museum.

Hours & Admission Prices: Summer: Mon.-Tues. & Thurs.-Fri. 9-5, Wed. 1:30-5; Winter: Mon.-Fri. 9-2. No charge; donations accepted.
Attendance: 3,000 (estimated)

Jenks

OKLAHOMA AQUARIUM AND THE KARL AND BEVERLY WHITE NATIONAL FISHING TACKLE MUSEUM, 300 Aquarium Dr., Jenks, OK 74037-4148. Mailing Address: P.O. Box 910, Jenks, OK 74037-0910. Tel.: 918-296-3474. Fax: 918-296-3467.
E-mail: events@okaquarium.org
Web Site: okaquarium.org
Key Personnel: Exec. Dir., Teri Bowers.
Institution Type/Description: Aquarium.
Hours & Admission Prices: Tues. 10-9, Wed.-Mon. 10-6. Adults $15.95, senior citizens & military $13.95, children 3-12 $11.95; children 2 & under no charge. Closed Christmas.

Jones

JONES HISTORICAL SOCIETY MUSEUM, 145 N.W. First St., Jones, OK 73049. Mailing Address: PO Box 515, Jones, OK 73049. Tel.: 405-399-2228.
Web Site: jonesoklahomahistoricalsociety.org
Key Personnel: Chm., John McEwen.
Institution Type/Description: Historical Society Museum.
Hours & Admission Prices: By appointment.

Kaw City

KANZA MUSEUM, 698 Grandview Dr., Kaw City, OK 74641. Mailing Address: Drawer 50, Kaw City, OK 74641. Tel.: 580-269-2552. Fax: 580-269-2301.
E-mail: cdouglas@kawnation.com
Web Site: www.kawnation.com
Key Personnel: Dir., Crystal Douglas; C.E.O., Guy Monroe.
Institution Type/Description: Native American Museum.
Hours & Admission Prices: Mon.-Fri. 8-5. No charge. &

KAW CITY MUSEUM, 910 Washunga Dr., Kaw City, OK 74641. Mailing Address: P.O. Box 56, Ponca City, OK 74602. Tel.: 580-269-2366.
E-mail: susanrutledge@mac.com
Web Site: kawcitymuseum.com
Institution Type/Description: History Museum: housed in a former train depot; built in 1902.
Hours & Admission Prices: May to Labor Day Mon.-Tues. & Thurs.-Fri. 1-5, Sat.-Sun. 2-5. No charge. &

Kenton

KENTON MUSEUM, 100 E. Main, Kenton, OK 73946. Tel.: 580-261-7479.
Institution Type/Description: History Museum: housed in the former home of Dr. Lane; built in 1902.
Hours & Admission Prices: Memorial Day to Labor Day Fri.-Sun. 9-5. No charge.

Keota

OVERSTREET-KERR HISTORICAL FARM, 28878 Kerr-Overstreet Rd., Keota, OK 74941-6817. Tel.: 918-966-3396. Fax: 918-966-3396.
E-mail: mailbox@kerrcenter.com
Web Site: www.kerrcenter.com
Institution Type/Description: Farm Museum.
Hours & Admission Prices: Mon.-Sat. by appointment. &
Attendance: 5,000 (estimated)

Kingfisher

CHISHOLM TRAIL MUSEUM, 605 Zellers Ave., Kingfisher, OK 73750-4228. Tel.: 405-375-5176.
E-mail: ctmus@pldi.net
Web Site: www.chisholmandseay.com
Key Personnel: Pres., Jeremy Ingle; Dir., Adam Lynn; Museum Shop Mgr., Marvin Reames.
Institution Type/Description: General Museum.

Hours & Admission Prices: Tues.-Sat. 10-5. Adults $4, children 6-18 $2; children 5 & under no charge. Closed state holidays. &

Attendance: 8.500 (estimated)

GOVERNOR SEAY MANSION, 605 Zellers Ave., Kingfisher, OK 73750-4228. Tel.: 405-375-5176. Fax: 405-375-5176.

E-mail: chisholmtrail@okhistory.org

Web Site: www.chisholmandseay.com

Key Personnel: C.E.O., Bob Blackburn; Dir., Adam Lynn; Pres., Jeremy Ingle; Cur., Renee Mitchell; Museum Shop Mgr., Marvin Reames.

Institution Type/Description: Historic House: Built-in 1892 restored mansion of second territorial Gov. A.J. Seay.

Hours & Admission Prices: Tues.-Sat. 10-5. Adults $4, children 6-18 $2; children under 5 no charge. Closed state holidays. &

Attendance: 7,000 (estimated)

Krebs

KREBS HERITAGE MUSEUM, 85 S. Main St., Krebs, OK 74554. Mailing Address: P.O. Box 1493, Krebs, OK 74554-1493. Tel.: 918-426-0377.

E-mail: krebsmuseum@yahoo.com

Web Site: krebsmuseum.com

Key Personnel: C.E.O., Dir. & Chm. (V), Steve DeFrange; Museum Shop Mgr., Deborah Young.

Institution Type/Description: Historical Museum.

Hours & Admission Prices: Call for hours. No charge; donations accepted. &

Attendance: 875 (estimated)

Langston

MELVIN B. TOLSON BLACK HERITAGE CENTER, Langston University, Sanford Hall, Langston, OK 73050. Mailing Address: P.O. Box 1500, Langston, OK 73050. Tel.: 405-466-3346. Fax: 405-466-2979.

Key Personnel: Dir., Jameka B. Lewis.

Institution Type/Description: Black Heritage Center.

Hours & Admission Prices: Mon.-Fri. 8-5. No charge.

Lawton

CAMERON UNIVERSITY ART GALLERY, Louise D. McMahon Fine Arts Complex, Rm. 125, Lawton, OK 73505-6377. Tel.: 580-581-2211.

E-mail: scottk@cameron.edu

Web Site: www.cameron.edu

Institution Type/Description: Art Gallery.

Hours & Admission Prices: No charge.

COMANCHE NATIONAL MUSEUM AND CULTURAL CENTER, 701 N.W. Ferris Ave., Lawton, OK 73507-5442. Tel.: 580-353-0404.

E-mail: info@comanchemuseum.com

Web Site: comanchemuseum.com

Key Personnel: Dir., Candy Morgan; Collections Mgr., Nicki Hise.

Institution Type/Description: Native American Museum.

Hours & Admission Prices: Mon.-Fri. 8-5, Sat. 10-2. No charge; donations accepted. Closed Thanksgiving; Christmas. &

Attendance: 10,000 (estimated)

LESLIE POWELL FOUNDATION AND GALLERY, 620 S.W. D Ave., Lawton, OK 73501-4508. Tel.: 580-357-9526. Fax: 580-357-9526. Facebook: Leslie Powell Foundation and Gallery.

E-mail: 1partgallery@gmail.com

Web Site: www.lpgallery.org

Key Personnel: Exec. Dir. & Cur., Matthew D. Hughes.

Institution Type/Description: Art Gallery.

Hours & Admission Prices: Mon.-Sat. 12-4. No charge. Closed holidays. &

Attendance: 3,000 (actual)

MATTIE BEAL HOME, 1008 S.W. 5th St., Lawton, OK 73501. Mailing Address: Lawton Heritage Assn., Inc., P.O. Box 311, Lawton, OK 73502. Tel.: 580-678-3156.

E-mail: contact@lawtonheritage.org

Web Site: www.lawtonheritage.org

Institution Type/Description: Historic House Museum: built in 1907. Listed on the National Register of Historic Places.

Hours & Admission Prices: Feb.-Dec. Thurs.-Sun. 12-3. Closed Thanksgiving; Christmas.

MUSEUM OF THE GREAT PLAINS, 601 NW Ferris Ave., Lawton, OK 73507-5443. Tel.: 580-581-3460.

E-mail: info@discovermgp.org

Web Site: www.discovermgp.org

Key Personnel: Exec. Dir. & Cur. Exhibits, John Hernandez; Chm. (V), Janice Bell; Sr. Cur. & Cur. Special Collections, Deborah Baroff; Living History Interpreter, Tim Poteete; Registrar & Collections Mgr., Jim Whiteley; Cur. Educator, Jana Brown; Deputy Dir. & Dir. Devel., Bart McClenny; Museum Shop Mgr., Rebecca Royal; Exec. Asst., Mary Owensby; Bldg. Mgr., Larry Holland; Receptionist & Weekend Clerk, Dean Keiser; Office Asst., Margaret Tatum.

Institution Type/Description: Regional History Museum.

Hours & Admission Prices: Mon.-Sat. 10-5, Sun. 1-5, Federal holidays 10-4. Adults $10, senior citizens 62 & over and military $9, children 3-12 $8; members and children 2 & under no charge. Closed New Year's Day; Thanksgiving; Christmas. &

Attendance: 31,453 (actual)

Leedey

BOSWELL MUSEUM, Main & Broadway, Leedey, OK 73654. Mailing Address: P.O. Box 128, Leedey, OK 73654. Tel.: 580-488-3616. Fax: 580-488-3376.

Institution Type/Description: History Museum.

Hours & Admission Prices: By appointment. No charge; donations accepted.

Attendance: 50 (estimated)

Lindsay

MURRAY-LINDSAY MANSION & PIKES PEAK SCHOOL, Hwy. 76 S., Lindsay, OK 73052-0282. Mailing Address: P.O. Box 282, Lindsay, OK 73052-0282. Tel.: 405-756-2121.

Key Personnel: Pres. (V), Shawn Bridwell.

Institution Type/Description: Historic Buildings.

Hours & Admission Prices: Wed.-Fri. & Sun. 1-4, Sat. 10-2; other times by appointment. No charge; donations accepted. Closed all holidays. &

Attendance: 2,500 (estimated)

Locust Grove

ZOO SAFARI, 5301 Earbob Rd., Locust Grove, OK 74352. Tel.: 918-386-2203. Facebook: Zoo Safari.

E-mail: thelearningzoo@ymail.com

Web Site: www. zoosafariusa.org

Key Personnel: Dir., Maria Jinks; Pres. (V), John Jinks.

Institution Type/Description: Zoo.

Hours & Admission Prices: Summer: daily 10-8; Winter: daily 10-4. No charge, donations accepted.

Attendance: 300 (estimated)

Madill

MARSHALL COUNTY OF OKLAHOMA GENEALOGICAL & HISTORICAL SOCIETY & THE MUSEUM OF SOUTHERN OKLAHOMA, 400 W. Overton, Rm. #3, Madill, OK 73446. Mailing Address: 800 Nazih Zuhdi Dr., Oklahoma City, OK 73105. Tel.: 580-795-5060.

E-mail: genealogic4@gmail.com

Web Site: www.themoso.com

Key Personnel: Pres., Doris Albin; Vice Pres. & Cur., Marcia Jones; Treas. & Sec., Dan Heltzer.

Institution Type/Description: History Museum.

Hours & Admission Prices: Mon.-Fri. 10-4, Sat. 10-2 by appointment. No charge; donations accepted. Closed New Year's Day; Independence Day; Memorial Day; Labor Day; Piomingo Day; Thanksgiving; Christmas. &

Attendance: 750 (estimated)

Mangum

OLD GREER COUNTY MUSEUM & HALL OF FAME, 222 W. Jefferson St., Mangum, OK 73554-4000. Mailing Address: P.O. Box 2, Mangum, OK 73554-0002. Tel.: 580-782-2851. Facebook: Old Greer County Museum & Hall of Fame.

E-mail: oldgreercountymuseum@yahoo.com

Web Site: oldgreercountymuseum.com

Institution Type/Description: History Museum.

Hours & Admission Prices: Thurs.-Fri. 9-3, 1st & 3rd Sat. 9-2. No charge; donations accepted. Closed legal holidays. &

Attendance: 1,000 (estimated)

Marietta

LOVE COUNTY MILITARY MUSEUM, 408 1/2 W. Chickasaw St., Marietta, OK 73448. Tel.: 580-276-3192.
Institution Type/Description: Military History Museum.
Hours & Admission Prices: Thurs.-Sat. 9-2. No charge. &

LOVE COUNTY PIONEER MUSEUM, 409 W. Chickasaw, Marietta, OK 73448. Mailing Address: P.O. Box 134, Marietta, OK 73448. Tel.: 580-276-9020.
Institution Type/Description: History Museum.
Hours & Admission Prices: Thurs.-Sat. 10-2; groups by appointment. No charge. &

NORTON'S INDIAN TERRITORY MUSEUM, 115 W. Main, Marietta, OK 73448. Mailing Address: P.O. Box 23, Marietta, OK 73448. Tel.: 580-276-2568. Fax: 580-276-5249.
E-mail: nortsmooth@yahoo.com
Key Personnel: Owner, Ronnie Norton.
Institution Type/Description: History Museum.
Hours & Admission Prices: Tues.-Fri. 10-5, Sat. 10-1. No charge.
Attendance: 8,000 (estimated)

Marlow

MARLOW AREA MUSEUM, 127 W. Main St., Marlow, OK 73055. Mailing Address: 223 W. Main, Marlow, OK 73055. Tel.: 580-658-2212. Facebook.
E-mail: marlowchamber@cableone.net
Web Site: marlowchamber.org
Institution Type/Description: History Museum.
Hours & Admission Prices: Call for hours. No charge; donations accepted.

Maud

MAUD HISTORICAL MUSEUM, 130 E. Main, Maud, OK 74854. Mailing Address: P.O. Box A, E. Main, Maud, OK 74854. Tel.: 405-374-2880.
Institution Type/Description: History Museum: housed in the former Irby Drug Building; built in 1928.
Hours & Admission Prices: June-Dec. Sat.-Sun. 2-4; other times by appointment. No charge.

McAlester

J.G. PUTERBAUGH HOUSE & GARRARD ARDENEUM, 345 E. Adams, McAlester, OK 74501-4651. Mailing Address: McAlester Chamber of Commerce, P.O. Box 759, McAlester, OK 74502. Tel.: 918-423-0314.
Institution Type/Description: Historic House Museum: housed in the former home of J.G. Puterbaugh, one of the founding fathers of McAlester's coal business.
Hours & Admission Prices: By appointment.

J. J. MCALESTER MANSION, 14 E. Smith, McAlester, OK 74501-2648. Tel.: 918-423-8620.
Institution Type/Description: Historic House Museum: built in 1870. Listed on the National Register of Historic Places.
Hours & Admission Prices: Fri. by appointment. $2 per person.

MCALESTER SCOTTISH RITE MASONIC CENTER, 305 N. 2nd St., McAlester, OK 74501-4648. Mailing Address: P.O. Box 609, McAlester, OK 74502-0609. Tel.: 918-423-6360. Fax: 918-423-6362.
Web Site: www.mcalesterscottishrite.org
Key Personnel: Gen. Sec., L.R. (Jerry) Grubbs.
Institution Type/Description: History Museum.
Hours & Admission Prices: Masonic Center: Mon.-Fri. 8-12 & 1-5. Tours: Mon.-Fri. 9-12 & 1-4. No charge; donations accepted. &
Attendance: 150 (estimated)

OKLAHOMA PRISONS' HISTORICAL MUSEUM, Stonewall & West St., McAlester, OK 74501-4651. Mailing Address: P.O. Box 97, McAlester, OK 74502-0097. Tel.: 918-423-4700.
E-mail: dale.cantrell@doc.state.ok.us
Key Personnel: Pres. (V), Dale Cantrell.
Institution Type/Description: Prison History Museum.
Hours & Admission Prices: Call for hours. No charge.
Attendance: 200 (estimated)

OKLAHOMA TROLLEY MUSEUM, 21 E. Monroe, McAlester, OK 74501-4651. Mailing Address: P.O. Box 145, McAlester, OK 74501. Tel.: 918-423-2446.
Institution Type/Description: Trolley Museum.
Hours & Admission Prices: Call for hours.

PITTSBURGH COUNTY GENEALOGICAL AND HISTORICAL SOCIETY, INC., 113 E. Carl Albert Pkwy., McAlester, OK 74501-5039. Tel.: 918-426-0388.
E-mail: choctawnationit@sbcglobal.net
Web Site: www.pittsburghcogenealogical.org
Formerly: Pittsburgh County Historical Museum
Key Personnel: Pres. (V), Christina Thurber.
Institution Type/Description: History Museum.
Hours & Admission Prices: Mon.-Fri. 9-3. No charge; donations accepted. Closed major holidays.

TANNEHILL MUSEUM, 450 W. Stonewall, McAlester, OK 74501-2346. Mailing Address: P.O. Box 3215, McAlester, OK 74502. Tel.: 918-470-5755. Fax: 918-423-7720.
Institution Type/Description: Gun Museum.
Hours & Admission Prices: By appointment. No charge; donations accepted. &
Attendance: 500 (estimated)

McLoud

MCLOUD HISTORICAL SOCIETY MUSEUM AND HERITAGE CENTER, 421 W. Broadway, McLoud, OK 74851. Mailing Address: P.O. Box 1292, McLoud, OK 74851. Tel.: 405-964-5169.
E-mail: mcloudmuseum@gmail.com
Web Site: www.mcloudhistoricalsociety.org
Key Personnel: Dir., Glenda Kuhn; Treas., Jim Metcalf; Cur., Sylvia Metcalf.
Institution Type/Description: Historical Society Museum: housed in c.1932 Ford dealership building.
Hours & Admission Prices: Feb.-June & Aug.-Dec. Tues. & Fri. 10-3. No charge; donations accepted.
Attendance: 500 (estimated)

Medford

GRANT COUNTY MUSEUM, Main & Cherokee Sts., Medford, OK 73759. Mailing Address: P.O. Box 241, Medford, OK 73759. Tel.: 580-395-2342. Fax: 580-395-2343.
Institution Type/Description: General Museum.
Hours & Admission Prices: By appointment only. No charge; donations accepted. &
Attendance: (estimated)

Meeker

CARL HUBBELL MUSEUM, 510 W. Carl Hubbell Blvd., Meeker, OK 74855. Mailing Address: P.O. Box 186, Meeker, OK 74855. Tel.: 405-279-3813.
Key Personnel: Chm. (V), Vernon Markwell.
Institution Type/Description: Baseball Museum.
Hours & Admission Prices: Mon.-Fri. 8-5. No charge; donations accepted.
Attendance: 550 (estimated)

Miami

DOBSON MUSEUM, 110 A St. S.W., Miami, OK 74354-6806. Mailing Address: P.O. Box 242, Miami, OK 74355. Tel.: 918-542-5388.
E-mail: ochs@dobsonmuseum.com
Web Site: www.dobsonmuseum.com
Key Personnel: Dir., Jordan Boyd.
Institution Type/Description: History Museum.
Hours & Admission Prices: Sun., Wed. & Fri. 1-4. No charge; donations accepted.
Attendance: 1,000 (estimated)

Midwest City

ATKINSON HERITAGE CENTER, 1001 N. Midwest Blvd., Midwest City, OK 73110-2799. Mailing Address: c/o Rose State College Foundation, 6420 S.E. 15th St., Midwest City, OK 73110. Tel.: 405-732-5832.
E-mail: atkinson@rose.edu

Web Site: www.rose.edu/atkinson-heritage-center
Institution Type/Description: Historic House Museum: housed in the former home of Midwest city founder, W.P. "Bill" Atkinson; built in 1955.
Hours & Admission Prices: By appointment.

Minco

MINCO HISTORICAL SOCIETY AND MUSEUM, 304 N.W. Main St., Minco, OK 73059. Tel.: 405-352-4480.
E-mail: mwoodworth@cox.net
Web Site: www.minco-ok.com/history
Institution Type/Description: Historical Society Museum.
Hours & Admission Prices: Thurs.-Fri. 10-3; other times by appointment.

Muskogee

ATALOA LODGE MUSEUM, 2299 Old Bacone Rd., Muskogee, OK 74403-1568. Tel.: 918-683-4581, ext. 283, 888-682-5514, ext. 7283. Fax: 918-687-5913.
Web Site: www.bacone.edu/ataloa
Key Personnel: Museum Dir., John Timothy.
Institution Type/Description: Indian Artifacts Museum.
Hours & Admission Prices: Wed.-Sat. 8:30-5, Sun. 1-5. No charge; donations accepted. Closed national holidays except by appointment. &
Attendance: 6,000

THE FIVE CIVILIZED TRIBES MUSEUM, 1101 Honor Heights Dr., Muskogee, OK 74401-1321. Tel.: 918-683-1701. Fax: 918-683-3070.
E-mail: 5tribesdirector@sbcglobal.net
Web Site: www.fivetribes.org
Key Personnel: Exec. Dir., Sean Barney.
Institution Type/Description: American Indian Museum & Art Gallery: housed in 1875 Union Indian Agency Building; pertains to the Cherokee, Chickasaw, Choctaw, Creek & Seminole tribal histories & American Indian Territory History.
Hours & Admission Prices: Mon.-Fri. 10-5, Sat. 10-2. Adults $4, seniors 62 & up $3, students $2. &
Attendance: 28,728 (actual)

MUSKOGEE WAR MEMORIAL PARK & MILITARY MUSEUM, 3500 Batfish Rd., Muskogee, OK 74403. Tel.: 918-682-6294. Fax: 918-682-1642.
E-mail: info@warmemorialpark.org
Web Site: warmemorialpark.org
Formerly: USS Batfish
Key Personnel: Exec. Dir., Brent Trout.
Institution Type/Description: Maritime Naval Museum: War Memorial & WWII Submarine, U.S.S. Batfish.
Hours & Admission Prices: mid-March to mid-Oct. Wed.-Sat. 10-6, Sun. 1-6. Adult $6, senior citizens $4, children $3; discounts available for groups, military & AAA and AAM members. Closed Easter; Thanksgiving; Christmas.
Attendance: 30,000 (actual)

OKLAHOMA MUSIC HALL OF FAME & MUSEUM, 401 S. 3rd St., Muskogee, OK 74401. Mailing Address: P.O. Box 3221, Muskogee, OK 74402-3221. Tel.: 918-687-0800. Fax: 918-687-0900.
E-mail: okmusic@omhof.com
Web Site: omhof.com
Key Personnel: Dir., Jim P. Blair; Chm. (V), Sue Harris; Museum Shop Mgr., Ronald Boren.
Institution Type/Description: History Museum & Hall of Fame.
Hours & Admission Prices: Tues.-Sat. 10-5. &
Attendance: 10,000 (estimated)

THOMAS-FOREMAN HOME, 1419 W. Okmulgee, Muskogee, OK 74401-6740. Tel.: 918-686-6624. Fax: 918-682-3477. Facebook: Thomas-Foreman Historic Home.
E-mail: 3riversmuseum@sbcglobal.net
Web Site: www.thomas-foremanhistorichome.com
Key Personnel: Chm. (V), Sue Tolbert; Pres. (V), Judy Dotson.
Institution Type/Description: Historic House: 1898 Home of Judge John R. Thomas and Grant & Carolyn Thomas Foreman.
Hours & Admission Prices: Fri.-Sat. 10-5; tours by appointment. Adults $2, seniors & students $1. Closed national holidays.
Attendance: 1,200

THREE RIVERS MUSEUM, 220 Elgin, Muskogee, OK 74401-7019. Tel.: 918-686-6624. Fax: 918-682-3477. Facebook: Three Rivers Museum.
E-mail: 3riversmuseum@sbcglobal.net
Web Site: www.3riversmuseum.com
Key Personnel: Chm., Roger Bell; Dir., Sue Tolbert.
Institution Type/Description: History Museum: housed in restored 1916 Midland Valley Railroad Depot.
Hours & Admission Prices: Wed.-Sat. 10-5. Adults $3, students $1.50; children under 6 no charge. &
Attendance: 2,000 (estimated)

Mustang

MUSTANG HISTORICAL MUSEUM, 470 W. State Hwy. 152, Mustang, OK 73064. Mailing Address: P.O. Box 464, Mustang, OK 73064. Tel.: 405-745-3365.
E-mail: kathy.nowlin49@gmail.com
Key Personnel: Pres. (V), Glen Muse.
Institution Type/Description: History Museum.
Hours & Admission Prices: Sat. 10-2; other times by appointment. No charge; donations accepted.
Attendance: 90 (actual)

Newkirk

NEWKIRK COMMUNITY HISTORICAL MUSEUM, 101 S. Maple, Newkirk, OK 74647-4026. Tel.: 580-362-2377. Fax: 580-362-3390.
Institution Type/Description: History Museum.
Hours & Admission Prices: Sun. 2-4; other times by appointment. No charge.

Noble

TIMBERLAKE ROSE ROCK MUSEUM, 419 S. Hwy. 77, Noble, OK 73068-0663. Mailing Address: P.O. Box 663, Noble, OK 73068-0663. Tel.: 405-872-9838.
E-mail: okart73071@yahoo.com
Key Personnel: Museum Shop Mgr., Nancy Stine.
Institution Type/Description: Natural History Museum.
Hours & Admission Prices: Tues.-Fri. 10-6, Sat. 10-4. No charge.
Attendance: 4,000 (estimated)

Norman

FIREHOUSE ART CENTER, 444 S. Flood Ave., Norman, OK 73069-5513. Tel.: 405-329-4523. Fax: 405-292-9763. Facebook: Firehouse Art Center.
E-mail: info@normanfirehouse.com
Web Site: www.normanfirehouse.com
Key Personnel: Exec. Dir., Douglas Shaw Elder; Pres., Byron Jackson; Creative Dir., Emily Smart; Receptionist, Sally Frech; Exec. Asst., Kristyn Brigance.
Institution Type/Description: Art Center.
Hours & Admission Prices: Mon.-Fri. 9:30-5:30, Sat. 10-4. No charge; donations accepted. Closed federal holidays. &
Attendance: 5,000 (estimated)

FRED JONES JR. MUSEUM OF ART, University of Oklahoma, 555 Elm Ave., Norman, OK 73019-3003. Tel.: 405-325-3272 & 0843. Fax: 405-325-7696. Facebook: Fred Jones Jr. Museum of Art.
E-mail: museuminfo@ou.edu
Web Site: www.ou.edu/fjjma
Key Personnel: Dir. Wylodean & Bill Saxon, Mark A. White, Ph.D.; Cur. Eugene B. Adkins, Hadley Jerman; Dir. Communications, Kaylee Kain; Dir. Audience Devel., Lesha Maag; Dir. Learning & Engagement, Melissa Ski; Community Learning Coord., Karen Bowles; Community Outreach Coord., Amanda Boehm-Garcia; Tour Coord., Reagan Suddeth; Mgr. Administration & Financial Operations, Tanya Denton; Visitor Svc. Rep., Rex Beal; Museum Store Mgr. & Buyer, Jin Jo Garton; Asst. Mgr., Museum Store, Amanda Roberts; Chief Registrar, Tracy Bidwell; Assoc. Registrar, Selena Capraro; Chief Preparator & Exhibition Designer, Brad Stevens; Assoc. Preparator, Christopher Mackie; Mgr. Facilities & Special Events, John Fowler; Chief Security Supvr., John Paul; Asst. Security Supvr., Scott Crow; Asst. Security Supvr., Johnny McKee.
Institution Type/Description: Art Museum.
Hours & Admission Prices: Tues.-Wed. & Fri.-Sat. 10-5, Thurs. 10-9, Sun. 1-5. No charge. &
Attendance: 45,000 (actual)

MOORE-LINDSAY HISTORICAL HOUSE MUSEUM, 508 N. Peters, Norman, OK 73069-7251. Tel.: 405-321-0156. Facebook: The Moore-Lindsay House.
E-mail: mlhhmuseum@gmail.com
Web Site: www.normanmuseum.org
Formerly: The Norman Cleveland County Historical Museum
Key Personnel: Mgr., Stephanie Hixon; Bd. Pres. (V), Sue Schrems.
Institution Type/Description: Historical Society Museum: housed in 1899 Queen Anne style urban house.
Hours & Admission Prices: Tues.-Sat. 11-4. Guided Tours: 11, 1, & 3. No charge; donations accepted. Closed holidays.
Attendance: 2,000 (estimated)

NATIONAL WEATHER CENTER, 120 David L. Boren Blvd., Norman, OK 73072. Tel.: 405-325-3095. Fax: 405-325-1180. Facebook; Twitter..
E-mail: dopplerdepot@nwc.ou.edu
Web Site: ou.edu/mnwc/visit/tours
Institution Type/Description: Weather Center.
Hours & Admission Prices: Public Tours: Mon., Wed. & Fri. 1 pm. Group & School Tours: Tues. & Thurs. 10 am & 1 pm. All tours by appointment only. No charge.

ROBERT BEBB HERBARIUM, 770 Van Vleet Oval, Rm. 206, Norman, OK 73019-6155. Mailing Address: Department of Botany & Microbiology, Univ. of Oklahoma, 206 Cross Hall, Norman, OK 73019. Tel.: 405-325-7533. Fax: 405-325-7619.
E-mail: bebbherbarium@ou.edu
Web Site: www.biosurvey.ou.edu/bebb/bebbhome.html
Key Personnel: Cur., Wayne J. Elisens; Collections Mgr., Amy Buthod.
Institution Type/Description: Herbarium.
Hours & Admission Prices: Mon.-Fri. 9-5. No charge. Closed university holidays.

SAM NOBLE OKLAHOMA MUSEUM OF NATURAL HISTORY, University of Oklahoma, 2401 Chautauqua Ave., Norman, OK 73072-7029. Tel.: 405-325-4712. Fax: 405-325-7699.
E-mail: snomnh@ou.edu
Web Site: www.snomnh.ou.edu
Key Personnel: Dir. & Cur. Mammals, Dr. Michael A. Mares; Assoc. Cur. Paleontology, Dr. Richard Lupia; Cur. Herpetology, Dr. Cameron Siler; Cur. Archeology, Dr. Marc Levine; Cur. Invertebrate Paleontology, Dr. Stephen Westrop; Cur. Mammals, Dr. Janet K. Braun; Cur. Vertebrate Paleontology, Dr. Nicholas Czaplewski; Head Finance, Technology and HR, Paul King; Registrar & Repatriation Specialist, Elsbeth Dowd; Cur. Ichthyology, Dr. Janet Brown; Assoc. Cur. Ethnology, Dr. Daniel C. Swan; Head Education, Dr. Jes Cole; Museum Shop Mgr., Ksenia Goode.
Institution Type/Description: General Museum.
Hours & Admission Prices: Museum: Mon.-Sat. 10-5, Sun. 1-5. Office: Mon.-Fri. 8-5. Adults $8, seniors 65 & over $6, children 4-17 $5; discounts for AAM & ICOM members, military and AAA members; members, OU students and children 3 & under no charge. Closed New Year's Day; Thanksgiving; Christmas.
Attendance: 151,007 (actual)

Nowata

NOWATA COUNTY HISTORICAL SOCIETY MUSEUM, 136 S. Dak, Nowata, OK 74048-3413. Mailing Address: P.O. Box 87, Nowata, OK 74048. Tel.: 918-273-1191. Facebook: Nowata County Historical Society Museum.
Web Site: nowatamuseum.org
Key Personnel: Dir. & Chm. (V), Carroll K. Craun.
Institution Type/Description: Historical Society Museum: housed in former Nowata grocery store.
Hours & Admission Prices: Tues.-Sat. 1-4; other times by appointment. No charge; donations accepted.
Attendance: 2,050 (estimated)

Okemah

OKFUSKEE COUNTY HISTORY CENTER, 407 W. Broadway St., Okemah, OK 74859. Mailing Address: P.O. Box 409, Okemah, OK 74859. Tel.: 918-623-2440. Fax: 918-623-2440.
E-mail: ron.gott@vosdic.com
Web Site: okemahok.com
Formerly: Okfuskee County Historical Society
Key Personnel: Dir. & Pres. (V), Ron Gott; Museum Shop Mgr., Wayland Bishop.
Institution Type/Description: Historical Society Museum: housed in a Masonic temple; built in 1926.

Hours & Admission Prices: Call for hours. No charge; donations accepted.
Attendance: 6,000 (estimated)

Oklahoma City

ASA NATIONAL SOFTBALL HALL OF FAME AND MUSEUM COMPLEX, 2801 N.E. 50th, Oklahoma City, OK 73111-7200. Tel.: 405-424-5266. Facebook.
Web Site: teamusa.org/USA-Softball/ASA-Hall-of-Fame-Complex
Key Personnel: Exec. Dir., Craig Cress; Pres. (V), Warren Jones; Hall of Fame Svcs. Mgr., Codi Warren.
Institution Type/Description: Sports Museum.
Hours & Admission Prices: May-Sept. Mon.-Fri. 8-4:30, Sat. 10-4, Sun. 1-4; Oct.-April Mon.-Fri. 8-5. No charge; donations accepted. Closed New Year's Day; Independence Day; Thanksgiving & day after; Christmas.
Attendance: 150,000 (estimated)

AMERICAN BANJO MUSEUM, 9 East Sheridan Ave., Oklahoma City, OK 73104. Tel.: 405-604-2793. Fax: 405-601-1821.
E-mail: events@americanbanjomuseum.com
Web Site: americanbanjomuseum.com
Formerly: National Four-String Banjo Hall of Fame Museum
Key Personnel: Exec. Dir., Johnny Baier.
Institution Type/Description: Musical Instrument Museum.
Hours & Admission Prices: Tues.-Sat. 11-6, Sun. 12-5. Family $15, adults $6, seniors $5, children 6-17 $4.

AMERICAN PIGEON MUSEUM & LIBRARY, 2300 N.E. 63rd, Oklahoma City, OK 73111-8208. Tel.: 405-478-5155.
E-mail: theamericanpigeonmuseum@gmail.com
Web Site: www.theamericanpigeonmuseum.org
Key Personnel: Cur., Lorrie Monteiro.
Institution Type/Description: Pigeon History Museum.
Hours & Admission Prices: Museum/Library: Fri.-Sat. 10-4; other times by appointment. No charge; donations accepted. Closed holidays.
Attendance: 3,000 (estimated)

[ARTSPACE] AT UNTITLED, 1 N.E. 3rd St., Oklahoma City, OK 73104. Tel.: 405-815-9995.
E-mail: artspace@1ne3.org
Web Site: www.artspaceatuntitled.org
Key Personnel: Founder & Creative Dir., Laura Warriner.
Institution Type/Description: Contemporary Art Center.
Hours & Admission Prices: Tues.-Fri. 10-5, Sat. 10-4. No charge.

BETTY PRICE GALLERY, Oklahoma State Capitol, 2300 N. Lincoln Blvd. Ste. 640, Oklahoma City, OK 73105. Mailing Address: P.O. Box 52001-2001, Oklahoma City, OK 73152-2001. Tel.: 405-521-2931. Fax: 405-521-6418. Facebook.
E-mail: okarts@arts.ok.gov
Web Site: www.arts.ok.gov/Art_at_the_Capitol/Betty_Price_Gallery.html
Institution Type/Description: Art Gallery.
Hours & Admission Prices: Closed for renovations; call for information.
Attendance: 35,000 (estimated)

CLASSEN HIGH SCHOOL MUSEUM, 1901 N. Ellison, Oklahoma City, OK 73137. Mailing Address: P.O. Box 270905, Oklahoma City, OK 73137. Tel.: 405-608-3455.
E-mail: info@classen.org
Web Site: classen.org
Institution Type/Description: History Museum: built in 1920.
Hours & Admission Prices: Temporarily closed.

45TH INFANTRY DIVISION MUSEUM, 2145 N.E. 36th, Oklahoma City, OK 73111-5396. Tel.: 405-424-5313. Fax: 405-424-3748. Facebook.
E-mail: curator@45thdivisionmuseum.com
Web Site: www.45thdivisionmuseum.com
Key Personnel: Dir., Col. Dave Brown, (Ret.); Cur., Michael E. Gonzales; Museum Shop Mgr., Jan Brian; Vehicle & Weapons Specialist, SSG Clark Briand, (Ret.).
Institution Type/Description: Military History Museum.
Hours & Admission Prices: Tues.-Fri. 9-4:15, Sat. 10-4:15, Sun. 1-4:15. No entry within 45 minutes of closing, park gates locked no later than 5. No charge; donations accepted. Closed holidays; open patriotic holidays.
Attendance: 51,000 (estimated)

HARN HOMESTEAD MUSEUM, 1721 N. Lincoln Blvd., Oklahoma City, OK 73105-4911. Tel.: 405-235-4058. Fax: 405-235-4041.

E-mail: info@harnhomestead.com
Web Site: www.harnhomestead.com
Formerly: Harn Homestead and 1889er Museum
Key Personnel: Pres., Paula Love; Exec. Dir., Melessa Gregg.
Institution Type/Description: Historic House: housed in 1904 Victorian house & barn located on the site of 10-acre tract which was part of 1889 Land Run.
Hours & Admission Prices: Mon.-Fri. 10-4. Adults $5, seniors & military $4; members and children 3 & under no charge. Closed Federal holidays. &
Attendance: 25,000 (actual)

INTERNATIONAL GYMNASTICS HALL OF FAME, OmniPlex Ctr., 2100 N.E. 52nd St., Oklahoma City, OK 73111. Tel.: 405-602-6664.
E-mail: reservations@sciencemuseumok.org
Web Site: www.ighof.com
Institution Type/Description: Sports Museum.
Hours & Admission Prices: Mon.-Fri. 9-5, Sat. 9-6, Sun. 11-6. Adults $12.95, seniors & children 3-12 $10.95; admission includes entry to Science Museum Oklahoma.

JIM THORPE MUSEUM & OKLAHOMA SPORTS HALL OF FAME, 20 S. Mickey Mantle Dr., Oklahoma City, OK 73104. Tel.: 405-427-1400.
E-mail: info@oksportshof.org
Web Site: oklahomasportshalloffame.org
Key Personnel: Pres., Mike James; Museum Cur., Justin Lenhart; Dir. Advancement, Olivia James.
Institution Type/Description: Sports Museum located on the Chickasaw Bricktown Ballpark site.
Hours & Admission Prices: Tues.-Sat. 10-5. No charge; donations accepted. &
Attendance: 11,000 (actual)

MELTON ART REFERENCE LIBRARY, 4300 N. Sewell, Oklahoma City, OK 73118-8010. Tel.: 405-613-5177. Fax: 405-525-0396.
E-mail: meltonart@aol.com
Web Site: www.marl-okc.org
Key Personnel: C.E.O. & Pres., Robynne Mulcahy; Dir., Suzanne Silvester.
Institution Type/Description: Art Resource Library.
Hours & Admission Prices: Mon.-Fri. 10-5. No charge; donations accepted. Closed holidays. &
Attendance: 1,500

MYRIAD BOTANICAL GARDENS, 301 W. Reno Ave., Oklahoma City, OK 73102. Tel.: 405-445-7080. Fax: 405-297-3620.
E-mail: emcfall@myriadgardens.org
Web Site: www.oklahomacitybotanicalgardens.com
Key Personnel: Exec. Dir., Maureen Heffernan; Dir. Facilities, Matthew Maly; Dir. Devel., Susan Grossman; Deputy Dir. & Dir. Myriad Gardens Foundation Community Bd., Debora Morey; Dir. Public Relations & Mktg., Leslie A. Spears; Dir. Horticulture, Nate Tschaenn; C.F.O., Chuck Davis.
Institution Type/Description: Botanical Gardens.
Hours & Admission Prices: June to Labor Day Mon.-Sat. 9-5, Sun. 11-7; Sept.-May Mon.-Sat. 9-5, Sun. 11-5. Adults $7, seniors 62 & over and students $6, children 4-12 $4; children 3 & under no charge. &
Attendance: 1,000,000

NATIONAL COWBOY & WESTERN HERITAGE MUSEUM, 1700 N.E. 63rd St., Oklahoma City, OK 73111-7997. Tel.: 405-478-2250. Fax: 405-478-4714. Facebook, Twitter: @ncwhm; Instagram: @nationalcowboymuseum; YouTube: NCWHMuseum.
E-mail: info@nationalcowboymuseum.org
Web Site: www.nationalcowboymuseum.org
Formerly: National Cowboy Hall of Fame and Western Heritage Center
Key Personnel: Asst. to the Pres., Jamie Schuermann; Chief of Curatorial Affairs & Asst. Dir., Mike Leslie; C.F.O. & Interim Pres., Gary Moore; Chief Devel. Officer, Jan Taylor; Sr. Mktg. Dir., Kirsten Holder; Research Center Librarian, Karen Spilman; Dir. Education, Gretchen Jeane; Dir. Operations, Doug Lane; IT Security Systems Admin., Alan Brown; Cur. Ethnology, Eric Singleton; Emeritus Cur. History, Richard Rattenbury; McCasland Chair Cowboy Culture, Don Reeves; Visitor Services, Shannon Strain; Traffic & Graphic Mgr., Steven Schmidt; Chief Public Experience Officer, Inez Wolins; Registrar, Melissa Owens; Museum Shop Mgr., Laney Carey; Facility Sales Mgr., Charlene Ferris; Dir. Accounting, Michael Meyers; Devel. & Membership Assoc., Trent Riley; Mgr. Human Resources, Jennifer Nuckols; Sr. Events Mgr., Jacy Gentry; Dir. Annie Oakley Society, Diana Fields; Digital & Manuscript Archivists, Kera Newby; Digital & Manuscript Archivists, Holly Hasenfratz; Cur. Archival & Photographic Collections, Kimberly Roblin; Cur. Special Exhibits, Susan Patterson; Mechanical Opers. Mgr., Cody Wells; Chief Preparator, Hal Prestwood; Asst. Registrar, Tobie Cunningham; Assoc. Registrar, Sheri Duncan.

Institution Type/Description: Art & History Museum.
Hours & Admission Prices: Daily 10-5. Adults $12.50, senior citizens & students $9.75, children $5.75; discount to groups, Blue Star Museum participants & AAM members; members no charge. Closed New Year's Day; Thanksgiving; Christmas.
Attendance: 197,279 (actual)

NINETY-NINES MUSEUM OF WOMEN PILOTS, 4300 Amelia Earhart Rd., Oklahoma City, OK 73159-1106. Tel.: 405-685-9990.
E-mail: museum@ninety-nines.org
Web Site: museumofwomenpilots.org
Institution Type/Description: History Museum.
Hours & Admission Prices: Call for hours.

THE OKLAHOMA BLACK MUSEUM AND PERFORMING ARTS CENTER, 4701 N. Lincoln Blvd., Oklahoma City, OK 73105-3318. Tel.: 405-213-8077.
E-mail: info@okafterschool.org
Web Site: okafterschool.org/all-event-list/the-oklahoma-black-museum-and-performing-arts-center-presents-steam/
Institution Type/Description: Black History Museum.
Hours & Admission Prices: Call for hours.

OKLAHOMA CITY MUSEUM OF ART, 415 Couch Dr., Oklahoma City, OK 73102-2214. Tel.: 405-236-3100, ext. 200. Fax: 405-236-3122.
E-mail: info@okcmoa.com
Web Site: www.okcmoa.com
Key Personnel: C.E.O. & Pres., E. Michael Whittington; Chm., J. Edward Barth; HR Coord., Aysha Shahid; Curatorial Asst., Jessica Provencher; Dir. Curatorial Affairs, Michael Anderson, Ph.D.; Project & Film Asst., John "Dudley" Marshall; Mgr. Outreach & Early Learning, Amanda Harmer; Dir. Learning & Engagement, Tracy Trvels; Mgr. Tours & Adult Learning, Bryon Chambers; Tour & Studio Coord., Neely Simms; Dir. Facilities Operations, Jack Madden; IT Mgr., Bert Boan; Dir. Mktg. & Communications, Becky Weintz; Head Design & Installation, Ernesto Sanchez; Chief Preparator, Trent Lawson; Preparator, Randall Barnes; Registrar, Maury Ford; Finance Asst., Sonia Ceballos; Visitor Svcs. Assoc., Marsha Jones; Chief Safety & Security, Steve Thompson; Museum Shop Mgr., Richard Bruner; Mgr. Museum Cafe, Ahmad Farnia; Museum Cafe Mgr., Lauren Cates.
Institution Type/Description: Art Museum.
Hours & Admission Prices: Tues.-Wed. & Fri.-Sat. 10-5, Thurs. 10-9, Sun. 12-5. Adults $12, senior citizens & students $10, military $5; discounts to groups of 15 or more & AAM members; members and children 5 & under no charge. Closed New Year's Day; Easter; Independence Day; Thanksgiving; Christmas. &
Attendance: 135,000 (actual)

OKLAHOMA CITY NATIONAL MEMORIAL & MUSEUM, 620 N. Harvey, Oklahoma City, OK 73102-3032. Mailing Address: P.O. Box 323, Oklahoma City, OK 73101-0323. Tel.: 405-235-3313. Fax: 405-235-3315.
E-mail: kariwatkins@oklahomacitynationalmemorial.org
Web Site: www.oklahomacitynationalmemorial.org
Key Personnel: Exec. Dir., Kari F. Watkins; C.F.O., Laurie Barton; Chm. (V), Mike Turpen; Travel Mktg Consultant & Group Sales, Tina Gilliland.
Institution Type/Description: Historic Foundation.
Hours & Admission Prices: Mon.-Sat. 9-6, Sun. 12-6. Adults $15, seniors 62 & over, students 6-17 & military $12; children 5 & under no charge, discounts to groups. Closed New Year's Day; Easter; Thanksgiving; Christmas Eve & Day.
Attendance: 389,246 (actual)

OKLAHOMA CITY ZOO, 2000 Remington Pl., Oklahoma City, OK 73111-7199. Mailing Address: 2101 N.E. 50th St., Oklahoma City, OK 73111. Tel.: 405-424-3344.
E-mail: crennels@okczoo.org
Web Site: www.okczoo.com
Key Personnel: C.E.O. & Exec. Dir., Dwight Lawson.
Institution Type/Description: Zoo.
Hours & Admission Prices: Daily 9-5. Adults $8, children 3-11 & senior citizens 65 & over $5; discounts to groups of 15 or more, active-duty & retired military and their families; members and children 2 & under no charge. Closed New Year's Day; Thanksgiving; Christmas. &
Attendance: 787,717 (actual)

OKLAHOMA CONTEMPORARY ARTS CENTER, 3000 General Pershing Blvd., Oklahoma City, OK 73107-6202. Tel.: 405-951-0000. Fax: 405-951-0003. Facebook, Twitter, Instagram.
Web Site: www.oklahomacontemporary.org

Formerly: City Arts Center
Key Personnel: Chm. & Pres., Christian Keesee; Exec. Dir., Donna Rinehart-Keever; Artistic Dir., Jeremiah Matthew Davis; Dir. Devel., Jennifer Thurman; Dir. Education & Public Programming, Erin Oldfield; Curatorial & Exhibitions Dir., Jennifer Scanlan; Dir. Communications, Lori Brooks; Dir. Finance, Salvador Ontiveros; Exhibits Mgr., Steve Boyd; Visitor Svcs. Facility Mgr., Laura Rice; Education Coord., Christine Gibson; Education Assoc., Alyssa DeVane; Annual Fund Mgr., Meredith McCormick.
Institution Type/Description: Art Center.
Hours & Admission Prices: Mon.-Thurs. 9am-10pm, Fri.-Sat. 9-5. No charge; donations accepted. Closed major holidays. ♿
Attendance: 3,000 (estimated)

OKLAHOMA FIREFIGHTERS MUSEUM, 2716 N.E. 50th St., Oklahoma City, OK 73111-7299. Tel.: 405-424-3440, 800-308-5336. Fax: 405-424-1032.
E-mail: geneb@osfa.info
Web Site: osfa.info
Key Personnel: Mgr., Gene C. Brown.
Institution Type/Description: Fire-Fighting History Museum.
Hours & Admission Prices: Mon.-Sat. 9-4:30, Sun. 1-4:30. Adults $6, senior citizens $5, children 6-12 $3; discounts to AAM, ICOM & AAA members; members & children under 6 no charge. Closed major holidays. ♿
Attendance: 7,000 (actual)

OKLAHOMA HALL OF FAME AT THE GAYLORD-PICKENS MUSEUM, 1400 Classen Dr., Oklahoma City, OK 73106-6614. Tel.: 405-235-4458. Fax: 405-235-2714. Facebook: Oklahoma Hall of Fame.
E-mail: info@oklahomahof.com
Web Site: oklahomahof.com
Formerly: Gaylord-Pickens Oklahoma Heritage Museum
Key Personnel: Pres., Shanon L. Rich; Chm. (V), Mark A. Stansbury; Dir. Mktg. & Communications, Shelley Rowan.
Institution Type/Description: Heritage Museum.
Hours & Admission Prices: Tues.-Fri. 9-5, Sat. 10-5. Adults $7, seniors citizens 62 & up and students 6-17 $5; discounts to groups of 15 or more; members no charge. Closed New Year's Day; Thanksgiving; Christmas. ♿
Attendance: 8,000 (actual)

OKLAHOMA HISTORICAL SOCIETY, 800 Nazih Zuhdi Dr., Oklahoma City, OK 73105-7917. Tel.: 405-522-0765. Facebook, Twitter.
E-mail: admissions@okhistory.org
Web Site: www.okhistory.org
Key Personnel: Exec. Dir., Dr. Bob Blackburn; Deputy Dir., Jeff Briley; Dir. Research, Chad Williams; Oklahoma Museum of History Dir., Dan Provo; Dir. Museums & Historic Sites Div., Kathy Dickson; Dir. Publications, Elizabeth Bass; Deputy Dir., Terry Howard; Deputy State Historic Preservation Officer, Lynda Ozan; Dir. Visitor Svcs., Jera Winters.
Institution Type/Description: State Historical Society Museums.
Hours & Admission Prices: Oklahoma History Center: Mon.-Sat. 10-5. Research Center: Tues.-Sat. 10-4:45. History Center: family $18, adults $7, seniors 62 & over $5, students $4; children 5 & under and active military & veterans with ID no charge. Closed New Year's Day; Thanksgiving; Christmas. ♿
Attendance: 297,543 (actual)

OKLAHOMA MUSEUM OF HISTORY, 800 Nazih Zuhdi Dr., Oklahoma City, OK 73105. Tel.: 405-522-3602. Fax: 405-521-5402.
E-mail: bblackburn@okhistory.org
Web Site: www.okhistory.org
Formerly: The State Museum of History
Key Personnel: Exec. Dir. & C.E.O., Dr. Bob Blackburn; Museum Dir., Dan Provo; Asst. Museum Dir., Jeff Briley; Dir. Education, Sarah Dumas.
Institution Type/Description: State History Museum.
Hours & Admission Prices: Mon.-Sat. 10-5. Families $18, adults $7, seniors 62 & over $5, students $4; discount to AAM members, Time Travelers Network and Smithsonian Institute & affiliate members; children 5 & under and members no charge. Closed New Year's Day; Thanksgiving; Christmas. ♿
Attendance: 185,000 (actual)

OKLAHOMA MUSEUM OF TELEPHONE HISTORY, 111 Dean A McGee Ave., Rm. 178, Oklahoma City, OK 73102. Tel.: 405-236-6153.
E-mail: oktelmuseum@yahoo.com
Web Site: attpioneervolunteers.org/chapter-41/oklahoma-chapter-41-museum
Institution Type/Description: History Museum.
Hours & Admission Prices: Mon. & Wed. 10-2. No charge. ♿
Attendance: 800 (actual)

OKLAHOMA MUSEUMS ASSOCIATION, 2020 Remington Pl., Oklahoma City, OK 73111-7103. Tel.: 405-424-7757. Fax: 405-427-5068.
E-mail: info@okmuseums.org
Web Site: www.okmuseums.org
Key Personnel: Exec. Dir., Brenda Granger; Pres., Jennifer Holt.
Institution Type/Description: Museum Service Organization.
Hours & Admission Prices: Call for hours. ♿

OKLAHOMA RAILWAY MUSEUM, 3400 N.E. Grand Blvd., Oklahoma City, OK 73111-4417. Tel.: 405-424-8222. Fax: 405-424-0504. Facebook: Oklahoma Railway Museum.
E-mail: info@oklahomarailwaymuseum.org
Web Site: www.oklahomarailwaymuseum.org
Key Personnel: Pres. (V), Eric Dillbeck; Sec., Drake Rice.
Institution Type/Description: Railway Museum.
Hours & Admission Prices: Thurs.-Sat. 9-4. Museum: no charge; donations accepted. Train Rides: April-Sept. first & third Sat. adults 13 & over $12, children 3-12 $5; discounts to NRHS, ARM & TRAIN members; children under 3 no charge.
Attendance: 20,368 (estimated)

OKLAHOMA STATE CAPITOL, 2300 N. Lincoln Blvd., Oklahoma City, OK 73105. Tel.: 405-521-3356.
Institution Type/Description: Historic Building: built in 1917.
Hours & Admission Prices: Guided Tours: Mon.-Fri. 9am, 10am, 11am, 1pm, 2pm, & 3pm; groups of 10 or more by appointment. No charge. Closed Christmas. ♿

OKLAHOMA VISUAL ARTS COALITION, 730 W. Wilshire Blvd., Ste. 104, Oklahoma City, OK 73116-7738. Tel.: 405-232-6991. Fax: 405-316-5611.
E-mail: director@ovac-ok.org
Web Site: www.ovac-ok.org
Key Personnel: Exec. Dir., Krystle Brewer; Prog. Coord., Sterling Smith.
Institution Type/Description: Art Museum.
Hours & Admission Prices: Call for hours.

OVERHOLSER MANSION, 405 N.W. 15th, Oklahoma City, OK 73103-3503. Tel.: 405-525-5325. Facebook: Henry Overholser Mansion.
E-mail: overholsermansion@preservationok.org
Web Site: overholsermansion.org
Key Personnel: Exec. Dir., David Pettyjohn.
Institution Type/Description: Historic House: 1902-04 Overholser Mansion.
Hours & Admission Prices: Tours: Feb.-Dec. Tues.-Sat. 10, 11, 12, 1, & 2. Adults $10, senior citizens $7, students & children $5; children under 6 no charge. Closed legal holidays.
Attendance: 1,000 (estimated)

RED EARTH ART CENTER, 6 Santa Fe Plaza, Oklahoma City, OK 73102-9027. Tel.: 405-427-5228. Fax: 405-427-8079. Facebook: Red Earth Inc..
E-mail: info@redearth.org
Web Site: www.redearth.org
Formerly: Red Earth Museum
Key Personnel: Chm. (V), Vickie L. Norick; Pres. (V), Teri Stanek; Dir. Mktg. & Public Relations, Eric Oesch; Dir. Devel. & Admin., Christy Alcox.
Institution Type/Description: Native American Art Center.
Hours & Admission Prices: Mon.-Fri. 10-5. No charge; donations accepted. ♿
Attendance: 50,000 (estimated)

SCIENCE MUSEUM OKLAHOMA, 2020 Remington Pl., Oklahoma City, OK 73111. Tel.: 405-602-6664. Fax: 405-602-3767. Facebook: Science Museum Oklahoma.
E-mail: reservations@sciencemuseumok.org
Web Site: sciencemuseumok.org
Formerly: Omniplex Science Museum
Key Personnel: Pres. & CEO, Sherry Marshall; Chm. Bd. of Trustees, Colin Fitzsimons; Vice Pres. Operations & Finance, Kevin Wilson; Vice Pres. Organizational Devel. & Community Engagement, Linda Maisch; Guest Rels., Melody Muniz.
Institution Type/Description: Science & Technology Museum.
Hours & Admission Prices: Mon.-Fri. 9-5, Sat. 9-6, Sun. 11-6. Adults 13-64 $15.95, senior citizens & children 3-12 $12.95; discounts to ASTC & AAA members and military; members no charge. Closed Thanksgiving; Christmas Eve & Day. ♿
Attendance: 492,434 (actual)

SKELETONS: MUSEUM OF OSTEOLOGY, 10301 S. Sunnylane Rd., Oklahoma City, OK 73160. Tel.: 405-814-0006. Fax: 405-794-6985.
E-mail: info@museumofosteology.org
Web Site: www.skeletonmuseum.com
Key Personnel: Founder, Jay Villemarette; Mktg. & Sale Dir., Samantha Tutor; Dir. Education, Ashley Mason-Burns-Meerschaert.
Institution Type/Description: Science Museum.
Hours & Admission Prices: Mon.-Fri. 8-5, Sat. 11-5, Sun. 1-5. Adults $10, children 3-13 $8; discounts to groups of 10 or more; children under 3 no charge. Closed Easter; Thanksgiving; Christmas. ♿
Attendance: 75,000 (actual)

21C MUSEUM HOTEL OKLAHOMA CITY, 900 W. Main St., Oklahoma City, OK 73106. Tel.: 405-982-6900.
E-mail: mslavid@21cMuseum.org
Web Site: www.21cmuseumhotels.com/oklahomacity/
Key Personnel: Museum Mgr., Michaela Slavid.
Institution Type/Description: Contemporary Art Gallery.
Hours & Admission Prices: See website for hours. No charge.

THE WORLD ORGANIZATION OF CHINA PAINTERS, 2700 N. Portland Ave, Oklahoma City, OK 73107-5408. Tel.: 405-521-1234. Fax: 405-521-1265.
E-mail: wocporg@theshop.net
Web Site: www.wocporg.com
Key Personnel: Exec. Dir., Patricia Dickerson; World Show Vice Pres., Mary Ann Clarin; Exhibit Clerk, Michelle Richardson.
Institution Type/Description: Porcelain Museum.
Hours & Admission Prices: Mon.-Thurs. 9-5, Sat.-Sun. call for hours. No charge; donations accepted. Closed New Year's Eve & Day; Memorial Day; Independence Day; Labor Day; Thanksgiving; Christmas. ♿
Attendance: 2,500

Okmulgee

CREEK COUNCIL HOUSE MUSEUM, 106 W. 6th St., Okmulgee, OK 74447-5014. Mailing Address: P.O. Box 918, Okmulgee, OK 74447-0918. Tel.: 918-756-2324. Fax: 918-756-3671. Facebook: Creek Council House Museum.
E-mail: creekmuseum@sbcglobal.net
Key Personnel: Cur., Clint Sago.
Institution Type/Description: Muscogee Creek History Museum: housed in 1878 Creek Council House.
Hours & Admission Prices: Tues.-Fri. 10-4, Sat. 10-3. No charge; donations accepted. Closed legal holidays. ♿
Attendance: 7,843 (actual)

Oologah

OOLOGAH HISTORICAL SOCIETY, 202 W. Cooweescoowee Ave., Oologah, OK 74053. Mailing Address: P.O. Box 185, Oologah, OK 74053-0185. Tel.: 918-443-2934. Fax: 918-443-2934. Facebook.
E-mail: oolagahhistorical@atlasok.com
Web Site: www.oologah.com/oologah/ohmuseum.htm
Key Personnel: Pres. (V), Mike Branen; Museum Shop Mgr., Pat Simerly.
Institution Type/Description: Historical Society Museum.
Hours & Admission Prices: Mon.-Fri. 11-4. No charge; donations accepted. ♿
Attendance: 450 (estimated)

WILL ROGERS BIRTHPLACE RANCH, 9501 E. 380 Rd., Oologah, OK 74053. Tel.: 918-275-4201.
E-mail: wrinfo@willrogers.com
Web Site: www.willrogers.com
Institution Type/Description: Historic Ranch: built in 1875.
Hours & Admission Prices: Daily 8-5. No charge; donations accepted. Closed Thanksgiving; Christmas.

Owasso

OWASSO HISTORICAL MUSEUM, 26 S. Main St., Owasso, OK 74055-3109. Mailing Address: Owasso Historical Society, P.O. Box 1481, Owasso, OK 74055. Tel.: 918-272-4966.
E-mail: mhinkle@cityofowasso.com
Web Site: cityofowasso.com/museum/index.html
Key Personnel: Dir., Marcia Boutwell.
Institution Type/Description: Historical Society Museum: housed in the Komma Building, built in 1928.
Hours & Admission Prices: Tues.-Fri. 12-4, Sat. 10-4. No charge; donations accepted.

Park Hill

CHEROKEE NATIONAL MUSEUM, 21192 S. Keeler Dr., Park Hill, OK 74451. Mailing Address: P.O. Box 515, Tahlequah, OK 74465-0515. Tel.: 918-456-6007. Fax: 918-456-6165.
E-mail: info@cherokeeheritage.org
Web Site: www.cherokeeheritage.org
Key Personnel: Exec. Dir., Carey Tilley; Cur., I. Mickel Yantz; Archivist, Tom Mooney; Dir. Devel., Penny L. Moore; Museum Shop Mgr., Kathryn Roastingear.
Institution Type/Description: History Museum: site of 1851 Cherokee Female Seminary, burned in 1887.
Hours & Admission Prices: Feb.-April & Sept.-Dec. Mon.-Sat. 9-5; May-Labor Day daily 9-5. Adults $8.50, seniors 55 & over and college students $7.50, youth 5-18 $5; discounts to groups of 10 or more; children 5 & under and Cherokee National Historical Society, Inc. members no charge. Closed New Year's Eve; Easter; Thanksgiving; Christmas Eve & Day. ♿
Attendance: 21,000 (estimated)

JOHN ROSS MUSEUM, 22366 S. 530 Rd., Park Hill, OK 74451. Mailing Address: c/o Cherokee Nation Cultural Tourism, 777 W. Cherokee St., Catoosa, OK 74015. Tel.: 877-779-6977.
E-mail: julie-hubbard@cherokee.org
Web Site: cherokeetourismok.com
Institution Type/Description: History Museum: housed in an early rural school-house; built in 1913.
Hours & Admission Prices: Tues.-Sat. 10-4. Adults $3, seniors & students $2; discounts to groups; children under 5 no charge.

MURRELL HOME, 19479 E. Murrell Home Rd., Park Hill, OK 74451-2001. Tel.: 918-456-2751. Fax: 918-456-2751. Facebook.
E-mail: murrellhome@okhistory.org
Web Site: www.okhistory.org/murrellhome
Key Personnel: Site Mgr., David Fowler; Historical Interpreter, Jennifer Frazee.
Institution Type/Description: Historic House: Murrell Home built c.1845.
Hours & Admission Prices: Tues.-Sat. 10-5. Family (up to 6 people) $18, adult $7, senior 62 & up $5, students 6-18 $4; discounts to groups of 10 or more; veterans & active military w/ I.D., children 5 & under and OHS members no charge. Closed state legal holidays. ♿
Attendance: 18,107 (actual)

Pauls Valley

PAULS VALLEY HISTORICAL SOCIETY - SANTA FE DEPOT MUSEUM, 204 S. Santa Fe, Pauls Valley, OK 73075. Tel.: 405-238-2244 & 2779.
Key Personnel: Dir., Adrienne Grimmett.
Institution Type/Description: Historic Building Museum: depot built in 1905.
Hours & Admission Prices: Tues.-Sat. 9-4:30; other times by appointment. No charge; donations accepted. Closed holidays. ♿
Attendance: 2,750 (estimated)

TOY & ACTION FIGURE MUSEUM, 111 S. Chickasaw St., Pauls Valley, OK 73075. Mailing Address: P.O. Box 314, Pauls Valley, OK 73075. Tel.: 405-238-6300. Fax: 405-238-6301.
E-mail: director@actionfiguremuseum.com
Web Site: actionfiguremuseum.com
Key Personnel: Dir., Jodi Wood; Bd. Pres., Ryan Mayberry; Cur., Kevin Stark.
Institution Type/Description: Toy Museum.
Hours & Admission Prices: Memorial Day to Labor Day Mon.-Thurs. 10-5, Fri.-Sat. 10-7, Sun. 1-5; Sept.-May Mon.-Sat. 10-5, Sun. 1-5. Adults $7, children $5; discounts to seniors & military.

Pawhuska

OSAGE COUNTY HISTORICAL SOCIETY MUSEUM, 700 N. Lynn Ave., Pawhuska, OK 74056-3238. Tel.: 918-287-9119.
E-mail: ochs@att.net
Web Site: www.osagecohistoricalmuseum.com
Key Personnel: Pres. (V), Mrs. Shirley Roberts; Museum Shop Mgr., Garrett Hartness; Museum Shop Mgr., Mary K. Warren.
Institution Type/Description: Historic Building: 1923 Santa Fe Depot Building.
Hours & Admission Prices: Tues.-Sat. 10-4. No charge; donations accepted. Closed Thanksgiving; Christmas. ♿
Attendance: 2,500 (actual)

OSAGE NATION MUSEUM, 819 Grandview Ave., Pawhuska, OK 74056-3203. Mailing Address: P.O. Box 779, Pawhuska, OK 74056-0779. Tel.: 918-287-5441. Fax: 918-287-5227. Facebook: www.facebook.com/OsageNationMuseum.
E-mail: museum@osagenation-nsn.gov
Web Site: www.osagenation-nsn.gov/museum
Key Personnel: Dir. & Cur., Hallie Winter; Collections Mgr., Dawn Rewolinski; Guest Svcs. Rep., Pauline Allred; Program Asst., Kimberly McCauley.
Institution Type/Description: Native American History Museum.
Hours & Admission Prices: Tues.-Sat. 8:30-5. No charge; donations accepted. Closed federal holidays. ♿
Attendance: 5,000 (estimated)

Pawnee

PAWNEE BILL RANCH AND MUSEUM, 1141 Pawnee Bill Rd., Pawnee, OK 74058-3563. Mailing Address: P.O. Box 493, Pawnee, OK 74058-0493. Tel.: 918-762-2513. Fax: 918-762-2514. Facebook: Pawnee Bill Ranch and Museum.
E-mail: pawneebill@okhistory.org
Web Site: www.pawneebillranch.org
Key Personnel: Dir., Ron Brown; Historical Collections Specialist, Erin Brown.
Institution Type/Description: Historic House: 1910 restored house. Home of Wild West showman and bison ranch.
Hours & Admission Prices: April-Oct. Sun.-Mon. 1-4, Tues.-Sat. 10-5; Nov.-March Wed.-Sat. 10-5, Sun. 1-4. Adults $5, senior citizens 65 & over $4, students 6-18 $3; discounts to groups; OHS Ranch & Association members and children 5 & under no charge. Closed state holidays. ♿
Attendance: 45,681 (actual)

PAWNEE COUNTY HISTORICAL SOCIETY MUSEUM AND DICK TRACY HEADQUARTERS, 513 6th St., Pawnee, OK 74058. Tel.: 918-762-4681. Facebook: Pawnee County Historical Society.
E-mail: pawnee@pawneechs.org
Web Site: www.pawneechs.org
Institution Type/Description: Historical Society Museum.
Hours & Admission Prices: Tues.-Fri. 10-4; call to confirm. No charge; donations accepted. ♿

Perkins

OKLAHOMA TERRITORIAL PLAZA, 750 N. Main St., Perkins, OK 74059. Mailing Address: P.O. Box 667, Perkins, OK 74059. Tel.: 405-547-2777.
E-mail: info@okterritory.org
Web Site: www.okterritory.org
Formerly: Old Church Center and Museum
Key Personnel: Dir., W. David Sasser.
Institution Type/Description: Historic Buildings.
Hours & Admission Prices: Buildings: Sat. 1-4; other times by appointment. Park: daily. No charge; donations accepted. ♿
Attendance: 7,300 (estimated)

Perry

CHEROKEE STRIP MUSEUM AND ROSE HILL SCHOOL, 2617 W. Fir St., Perry, OK 73077-7903. Tel.: 580-336-2405. Fax: 580-336-2064.
E-mail: csmuseum@okhistory.org
Web Site: cherokee-strip-museum.org
Formerly: Cherokee Strip Museum
Key Personnel: Dir., Kelly Houston.
Institution Type/Description: History Museum.
Hours & Admission Prices: mid-Jan. to Dec. Tues.-Fri. 9-5, Sat. 10-4. Adults $5, senior citizens 62 & over $4, children 6-17 $3; children 5 & under no charge. Closed legal holidays. ♿
Attendance: 8,000 (estimated)

THE HERITAGE CENTER AND DITCH WITCH(R) MUSEUM, 6th & Cedar St., Perry, OK 73077. Mailing Address: P.O. Box 1902, Perry, OK 73077. Tel.: 580-572-3344, 844-572-1902.
Institution Type/Description: Industrial Museum: housed in the original Charles Machine Works, Inc. Company building, a manufacturer of Ditch Witch underground construction equipment.
Hours & Admission Prices: By appointment. No charge.

Piedmont

PIEDMONT HISTORICAL SOCIETY, 101 Monroe Ave., N.W., Piedmont, OK 73078. Mailing Address: P.O. Box 233, Piedmont, OK 73078. Tel.: 405-373-1424 & 1233.
E-mail: piedmonthistoricalsociety@ymail.com
Institution Type/Description: Historical Society Museum: housed in Piedmont's first two story brick building which housed the Piedmont State Bank; built in 1917.
Hours & Admission Prices: By appointment. No charge; donations accepted.

Ponca City

CANN MEMORIAL BOTANICAL GARDEN, 1500 E. Grand, Ponca City, OK 74604-5209. Mailing Address: 905 W. Hartford, Ponca City, OK 74601-1162. Tel.: 580-767-0430.
Institution Type/Description: Botanical Garden.
Hours & Admission Prices: Daily dawn to dusk. No charge; donations accepted.

CONOCO MUSEUM, 501 W. South Ave., Ponca City, OK 74601-6105. Tel.: 580-765-8687. Fax: 580-767-2147.
E-mail: oneilcm@p66.com
Web Site: www.conocomuseum.com
Key Personnel: Dir., Carla O'Neill.
Institution Type/Description: History Museum.
Hours & Admission Prices: Mon.-Sat. 10-5, Sun. 1-5. No charge. Closed holidays. ♿
Attendance: 5,000 (actual)

MARLAND MANSION ESTATE, 901 Monument Rd., Bldg. 2, Ponca City, OK 74604-3600. Tel.: 580-767-0420, 800-422-8340. Fax: 580-763-8054.
E-mail: marlandmansion@poncacityok.gov
Web Site: www.marlandmansion.com
Key Personnel: Exec. Dir., David Keathly.
Institution Type/Description: Historic House Museum: housed in a 55-room Italian Renaissance villa, c.1925.
Hours & Admission Prices: Mon.-Sat. 10-5, Sun. 1-5. Adults $7, seniors 65 & over and students 12-17 $5, students 6-11 $4.

MARLAND'S GRAND HOME, 1000 E. Grand, Ponca City, OK 74601-5607. Tel.: 580-767-0427.
E-mail: dettejc@poncacityok.gov
Web Site: marlandgrandhome.com
Formerly: Ponca City Cultural Center Museum
Key Personnel: Dir., David Keathly.
Institution Type/Description: Cultural Center & Ethnology Museum.
Hours & Admission Prices: Tues.-Sat. 10-5. Adults $5, military and seniors 65 & over $4, youth 6-17 $3. Closed holidays.
Attendance: 8,500 (actual)

PIONEER WOMAN STATUE & MUSEUM, 701 Monument Rd., Ponca City, OK 74604-3910. Tel.: 580-765-6108. Fax: 580-762-2498. Facebook: Pioneer Woman Museum.
E-mail: piown@okhistory.org
Web Site: www.pioneerwomanmuseum.com
Key Personnel: Dir., Robbin Davis; Chm. (V), Mary Beth Moore; Historical Interpreter, Keith Fagan.
Institution Type/Description: Women's History Museum.
Hours & Admission Prices: Tues.-Sat. 10-5. Adults $4, senior citizens $3, students 6-18 $1; discounts to Oklahoma Museums Assoc., Oklahoma Historical Society, Mountain Plains Museums Assoc., AAM & AAA members. Closed state holidays. ♿
Attendance: 5,000 (actual)

PONCA CITY ART CENTER, 819 E. Central, Ponca City, OK 74601-5506. Tel.: 580-765-9746.
E-mail: pcartcenter@sbcglobal.net
Web Site: www.poncacityartcenter.com
Institution Type/Description: Art Museum: housed in Soldani Mansion. Listed on the National Register of Historic Places.
Hours & Admission Prices: Wed.-Sun. 1-5. No charge; donations accepted. Closed Independence Day; Thanksgiving, Christmas.

STANDING BEAR MUSEUM AND EDUCATION CENTER, Standing Bear Park, 601 Standing Bear Pkwy., Ponca City, OK 74601. Mailing Address: P.O. Box 247, Ponca City, OK 74602. Tel.: 580-762-1514.
E-mail: info@standingbearpark.com
Institution Type/Description: Native American History Museum.

Hours & Admission Prices: Mon.-Fri. 9-5, Sat. 10-2. No charge. &

Poteau

LEFLORE COUNTY HISTORICAL SOCIETY, 303 Dewey Ave., Poteau, OK 74953. Mailing Address: P.O. Box 457, Poteau, OK 74953. Tel.: 918-647-9330.
E-mail: leflorecountyhistoricalsociety@windstream.net
Web Site: leflorecountyhistoricalsocietymuseum.webs.com
Institution Type/Description: Historical Society Museum: housed in the former Hotel Lowrey; built in 1922.
Hours & Admission Prices: Wed.-Thurs. 9-6; other times by appointment.

ROBERT S. KERR MUSEUM, 23009 Kerr Mansion Rd., Poteau, OK 74953-8119. Tel.: 918-647-8221. Fax: 918-647-3952.
E-mail: cburleigh@carlalbert.edu
Web Site: www.casc.cc.ok.us/kerr_center
Key Personnel: Dir., Cheryl Burleigh.
Institution Type/Description: Oklahoma History Museum.
Hours & Admission Prices: Mon.-Sun. upon request or by appointment. No charge; donations accepted. Closed Jan-March & major holidays. &
Attendance: 3,556 (actual)

Prague

PRAGUE HISTORICAL MUSEUM, 815 N. Jim Thorpe Blvd., Prague, OK 74864-4522. Tel.: 405-567-4750.
E-mail: office@praguechamber.org
Institution Type/Description: History Museum.
Hours & Admission Prices: Mon., Wed. & Fri. 1-4; groups by appointment. No charge; donations accepted.

Purcell

MCCLAIN COUNTY HISTORICAL MUSEUM, 203 W. Washington, Purcell, OK 73080-4227. Tel.: 405-701-3171. Facebook: McClain County Museum.
E-mail: mcmuseum@mail.com
Key Personnel: Chm. (V), Dir. & Cur., Maria Pope; Pres. (V), Pam Hobbs.
Institution Type/Description: History Museum.
Hours & Admission Prices: Thurs.-Fri. 1-4; other times by appointment. Call for current information. No charge; donations accepted. Closed some holidays.
Attendance: 170 (estimated)

Quapaw

QUAPAW TRIBAL MUSEUM, 905 Whitebird St., Quapaw, OK 74363. Tel.: 918-674-2619. Fax: 918-674-2581.
E-mail: khildreth@quapawtribe.com
Institution Type/Description: Native American History Museum.
Hours & Admission Prices: Mon.-Thurs. 8-5, Fri. 8-4.

Ripley

WASHINGTON IRVING TRAIL & MUSEUM, 3918 S. Mehan Rd., Ripley, OK 74062-6278. Mailing Address: P.O. Box 1852, Stillwater, OK 74076. Tel.: 405-624-9130.
E-mail: cchlouber@aol.com
Web Site: www.washingtonirvingtrailmuseum.com
Key Personnel: Dir., Cur. & Museum Shop Mgr., Dale Chlouber; Chm. (V) & Pres. (V), John Wilson.
Institution Type/Description: History Museum.
Hours & Admission Prices: Wed.-Sat. 11-5, Sun. 1-5. No charge; donations accepted. &
Attendance: 5,000 (estimated)

Sallisaw

14 FLAGS MUSEUM, 400 E. Cherokee, Sallisaw, OK 74955. Mailing Address: Echo Rider, 105274 S. 4690 Rd., Sallisaw, OK 74955. Tel.: 918-775-2608. Fax: 918-775-9550.
E-mail: chamber@sallisawok.org
Institution Type/Description: History Museum: housed in a log cabin; built in 1845.
Hours & Admission Prices: Daily 9-5. No charge.

SEQUOYAH CABIN, 470288 Hwy. 101, Sallisaw, OK 74955-9744. Tel.: 918-775-2413. Fax: 918-775-2413.
E-mail: seqcabin@okhistory.org
Formerly: Sequoyah Home Site

Key Personnel: C.E.O., Bob Blackburn; Cur. & Museum Shop Mgr., Jerry Dobbs.
Institution Type/Description: Historic Building & Site: housed in 1829, Sequoyah Log Cabin.
Hours & Admission Prices: Tues.-Fri. 9-5, Sat.-Sun. 2-5, adults $5, seniors (65 & over $4, student 6-18 veterans, & military with ID $3; group rate (10 or more) scheduled in advance. Closed holidays. &
Attendance: 20,000 (estimated)

Sand Springs

SAND SPRINGS CULTURAL & HISTORICAL MUSEUM, 9 E. Broadway St., Sand Springs, OK 74063. Mailing Address: P.O. Box 1807, Sand Springs, OK 74063-1807. Tel.: 918-246-2509. Fax: 918-245-7101.
E-mail: museum@sandspringsok.org
Web Site: www.sandspringsmuseum.org
Key Personnel: C.E.O., Dir. & Museum Shop Mgr., Dr. Stacy Reaves; Chm. (V), Jerry Hanner; Chm. (V), Ed Dubie; Pres. (V), Cynthia Phillips; Public Events, Ruth Ellen Henry.
Institution Type/Description: Cultural and Historical Museum: housed in the Page Memorial Library.
Hours & Admission Prices: Tues.-Fri. 1-5; other times by appointment. No charge; donations accepted. &
Attendance: 5,000 (estimated)

Sapulpa

SAPULPA HISTORICAL MUSEUM, 100 E. Lee, Sapulpa, OK 74066-4216. Tel.: 918-224-4871. Fax: 918-224-7765. Facebook: Sapulpa Historical Society Museum.
E-mail: sapulpahistsoc@tulsacoxmail.com
Web Site: sapulpahistoricalsociety.com
Key Personnel: Dir., Mike Jeffries; Pres. (V), Rick Woolery; Vice Pres., Larry White; Treas., Russell Crosby; Sec., Belinda Crosby; Gift Shop Mgr. & Administrative Asst., Shanna Rutledge.
Institution Type/Description: History Museum: housed in three-story, 1910 Wills Building, which was renovated in 1982.
Hours & Admission Prices: Sept. to late Aug. Tues.-Sat. 10-3; group tours by appointment. No charge; donations accepted. Closed major holidays. &
Attendance: 1,800 (actual)

WAITE PHILLIPS FILLING STATION MUSEUM, 26 E. Lee Ave., Sapulpa, OK 74066. Mailing Address: 100 E. Lee Ave., Sapulpa, OK 74066. Tel.: 918-224-4871. Fax: 918-224-7765.
Institution Type/Description: Historic Building Museum: built in 1923.
Hours & Admission Prices: Tues. & Thurs.-Sat. 10-4, Wed. 10-12 & 1-4. No charge; donations accepted. Closed New Year's Day; Memorial Day; Independence Day; Labor Day; Thanksgiving; Christmas Day & week.

Sayre

RS & K RAILROAD MUSEUM, 411 N. 6th St., Sayre, OK 73662-263. Tel.: 580-928-3525.
Institution Type/Description: Toy Museum.
Hours & Admission Prices: Daily 9-9 by appointment. &

SHORTGRASS COUNTRY MUSEUM SOCIETY, 106 E. Poplar Ave., Sayre, OK 73662-2933. Mailing Address: P.O. Box 260, Sayre, OK 73662-0260.
E-mail: mikeblevins@cableone.net
Key Personnel: Chm. (V), Mike Blevins; Pres. (V), Kenny Bibb; Business Advisor & Dir., Bunny Neff.
Institution Type/Description: Historic Building Museum: housed in the former Rock Island Depot; built in 1901.
Hours & Admission Prices: Closed for renovations. No charge; donations accepted. &
Attendance: 350 (estimated)

Seiling

REDINGER FUNERAL MUSEUM, 105 E. Gary England Ave., Seiling, OK 73663. Mailing Address: P.O. Box 236, Seiling, OK 73663-0236. Tel.: 580-922-4226. Fax: 580-922-4228.
E-mail: rredinger@pldi.net
Web Site: www.redingerfuneralhome.com
Institution Type/Description: History Museum.
Hours & Admission Prices: By appointment. No charge.

Seminole

JASMINE MORAN CHILDREN'S MUSEUM, 1714 Hwy. 9 W., Seminole, OK 74868. Tel.: 405-382-0950. Fax: 405-382-3707.
E-mail: mdonaho@jasminemoran.com
Web Site: www.jasminemoran.com/frameset.html
Key Personnel: Exec. Dir., Marci Donato.
Institution Type/Description: Children's Museum.
Hours & Admission Prices: Tues.-Sat. 10-5, Sun. 1-5. Admission 3-60 $8, seniors over 60 $7; children under 3 no charge. Closed major holidays.

OKLAHOMA OIL MUSEUM, 1800 Hwy. 9 West, (Wrangler Blvd.), Seminole, OK 74868. Mailing Address: P.O. Box 202, Seminole, OK 74818-0202.
E-mail: okoil@att.net
Formerly: Seminole Historical & Oil Museum
Key Personnel: Pres. (V), Chuck Chadick; Dir., Kristy Burgess; Museum Shop Mgr., Barbara Ross.
Institution Type/Description: Seminole County Oil History Museum.
Hours & Admission Prices: Mon.-Thurs. 10-4, Fri.-Sat. 10-2. Adults $4, children $2; discounts to school groups. Closed holidays. &
Attendance: 2,000 (estimated)

Shattuck

SHATTUCK WINDMILL MUSEUM & PARK, 1100 S. Main, Shattuck, OK 73858. Mailing Address: P.O. Box 227, Shattuck, OK 73858-0227. Tel.: 580-938-5291.
Web Site: www.shattuckwindmillmuseum.org
Key Personnel: Dir., Phillis Ballew; Pres. (V), Edgar Longhofer; Museum Shop Mgr., Naomi Bradley.
Institution Type/Description: History Museum.
Hours & Admission Prices: Daily. No charge; donations accepted. &
Attendance: 1,500 (actual)

Shawnee

CITIZEN POTAWATOMI NATION CULTURAL HERITAGE CENTER, 1899 S. Gordon Cooper Dr., Shawnee, OK 74801-9004. Tel.: 405-878-5830, 800-880-9880. Fax: 405-878-5840.
E-mail: scoon@potawatomi.org
Web Site: www.potawatomi.org
Formerly: Citizen Potawatomi Museum
Key Personnel: Chm., John A. "Rocky" Barrett; Mgr. Collections, Stacy S. Coon; Facilities & Operations Mgr., Cindy Stewart.
Institution Type/Description: Native American Museum.
Hours & Admission Prices: Tues.-Fri. 8-5, Sat. 10-3. No charge; donations accepted. Closed holidays. &
Attendance: 21,000 (estimated)

MABEE-GERRER MUSEUM OF ART, 1900 W. MacArthur, Shawnee, OK 74804-2403. Tel.: 405-878-5300. Fax: 405-878-5133.
E-mail: info@mgmoa.org
Web Site: www.mgmoa.org
Key Personnel: Dir. & Chief Cur., Dane Pollei; Dir. Devel., Tonya Ricks; Cur. Collections & Museum Shop Mgr., Delaynna Trim; Cur. Education, Donna Merkt.
Institution Type/Description: Art Museum.
Hours & Admission Prices: Tues.-Sat. 10-5, Sun. 1-4. Adults $5, Seniors $4, children 6-17 $3; discount to AAM members; members & children under 5 no charge. Closed major holidays. &
Attendance: 30,000 (estimated)

POTTAWATOMIE COUNTY MUSEUM AND HISTORICAL SOCIETY, 614 E. Main St., Shawnee, OK 74801. Mailing Address: P.O. Box 114, Shawnee, OK 74801. Tel.: 405-275-8412. Fax: 405-273-1210. Facebook: Pottawatomie County Oklahoma Historical Society.
E-mail: info@pottcountymuseum.org
Web Site: www.pottcountymuseum.org
Formerly: Santa Fe Depot Museum
Key Personnel: Pres. (V), Tom Terry; Dir., Ken Landry; Museum Shop Mgr., Cherita Landry.
Institution Type/Description: History Museum.
Hours & Admission Prices: Tues.-Sat. 10-4. Suggested Donation: adults $2, children & students $1; discounts to groups. Closed holidays. &
Attendance: 3,834 (actual)

Skiatook

SKIATOOK MUSEUM, 115 S. Broadway, Skiatook, OK 74070-1540. Tel.: 918-396-7558.
Key Personnel: Pres., Donna Sue Jones; Vice Pres., John Reynolds.
Institution Type/Description: History Museum: housed in a former doctor's home, built in 1912.
Hours & Admission Prices: Tues.-Fri. 1-4. No charge; donations accepted. Closed legal holidays.

Spiro

SPIRO MOUNDS ARCHAEOLOGICAL CENTER, 18154 1st St., Spiro, OK 74959-4463. Tel.: 918-962-2062. Fax: 918-962-2062. Facebook: @SpiroMoundsArchaeologicalCenter.
E-mail: spiro@okhistory.org
Web Site: www.okhistory.org
Key Personnel: Historic Property Mgr., Dennis Peterson.
Institution Type/Description: Archaeological Site.
Hours & Admission Prices: Wed.-Sat. 9-5, Sun. 12-5. Adults $7, senior citizens $6, children $3; discounts to Oklahoma Historical Society members. Closed state holidays. &
Attendance: 10,000 (estimated)

Stigler

HASKELL COUNTY HISTORICAL SOCIETY MUSEUM, American Legion Hut, 204 E. Main St., Stigler, OK 74462. Mailing Address: P.O. Box 481, Stigler, OK 74462-0481. Tel.: 918-967-2161.
E-mail: stiglermuseum@yahoo.com
Institution Type/Description: Historical Society Museum.
Hours & Admission Prices: Mon., Wed. & Fri. 9:30-2.

Stillwater

GALLAGHER-IBA ARENA - HERITAGE HALL SPORTS MUSEUM, Oklahoma State University, Stillwater, OK 74078. Tel.: 405-744-3864. Fax: 405-744-4535.
E-mail: shelly.parke@okstate.edu
Institution Type/Description: Sports Museum.
Hours & Admission Prices: Mon.-Fri. 9-5. No charge. &
Attendance: 5,500 (estimated)

GARDINER ART GALLERY, Oklahoma State University, Stillwater, OK 74078. Mailing Address: 108 Bartlett Center, Stillwater, OK 74078-4084. Tel.: 405-744-6016. Fax: 405-744-5767.
Web Site: art.okstate.edu
Key Personnel: Gallery Mgr., Teresa Holder, M.A.
Institution Type/Description: Art Museum.
Hours & Admission Prices: Mon. & Wed.-Fri. 8-5, Tues. 8-8. No charge. Closed national holidays. &
Attendance: 10,000 (estimated)

NATIONAL WRESTLING HALL OF FAME & MUSEUM, 405 W. Hall of Fame Ave., Stillwater, OK 74075-5025. Tel.: 405-377-5243. Fax: 405-377-5244.
E-mail: info@nwhof.org
Web Site: www.nwhof.org
Key Personnel: C.E.O., Lee Roy Smith; Chm. (V), Terry Shockley; Office Mgr. & Museum Shop Mgr., Maghan Cawlfield.
Institution Type/Description: Sports Museum: located near campus of Oklahoma State University.
Hours & Admission Prices: Mon.-Fri. 9-4; other times by appointment. Adults $5, students $2 Closed holidays. &
Attendance: 10,000 (estimated)

OKLAHOMA STATE UNIVERSITY BOTANICAL GARDEN, 360 Agricultural Hall, Stillwater, OK 74078-6025. Tel.: 405-744-5414. Fax: 405-744-9709.
E-mail: botanicgarden@okstate.edu
Web Site: hortla.okstate.edu
Key Personnel: Dir., Dr. Dale M. Maronek; Education, Mr. David Hillock; Cur., Dr. Mike Schnelle.
Institution Type/Description: Botanical Garden.
Hours & Admission Prices: Mon.-Fri. 8-5. No charge; donations accepted.
Attendance: 12,000 (estimated)

OKLAHOMA STATE UNIVERSITY MUSEUM OF ART, 720 S. Husband St., Stillwater, OK 74074. Tel.: 405-744-2780. Fax: 405-744-2800.
E-mail: museum@okstate.edu
Web Site: museum.okstate.edu
Key Personnel: Dir. & Chief Cur., Victoria Berry; Coord. Mktg. & Communications, Hayley Bondank.
Institution Type/Description: Art Museum.
Hours & Admission Prices: Tues. & Fri.-Sat. 11-4, Wed.-Thurs. 11-7. No charge. ♿

SHEERAR MUSEUM OF STILLWATER HISTORY, 702 S. Duncan St., Stillwater, OK 74074-4443. Tel.: 405-377-0359. Facebook.
E-mail: info@sheerarmuseum.org
Web Site: www.sheerarmuseum.org
Formerly: The Sheerar and Cultural Heritage Center
Key Personnel: Dir., Roger Moore; Pres. (V), Pat Jaynes.
Institution Type/Description: History Museum.
Hours & Admission Prices: Tues.-Fri. 11-5, Sat.-Sun. 1-4. No charge; donations accepted. Closed major holidays. ♿
Attendance: 12,000 (estimated)

STILLWATER AIRPORT MEMORIAL MUSEUM, 2020 W. Airport Rd., Stillwater, OK 74075. Tel.: 405-372-7881. Fax: 405-372-8460.
Institution Type/Description: Airport Museum.
Hours & Admission Prices: Museum: by appointment. Lobby: daily 7am-10pm. No charge. ♿

Stroud

THE SAC AND FOX NATIONAL PUBLIC LIBRARY AND CULTURAL CENTER, 920883 S. Hwy. 99, Stroud, OK 74079. Mailing Address: Administration Bldg., 920883 S. Hwy. 99 Bldg. A, Stroud, OK 74079. Tel.: 918-968-3526, ext. 2020. Fax: 918-968-0705. Facebook.
E-mail: library@sacandfoxnation-nsn.gov
Key Personnel: Dir., Kathy Platt; Historical Researcher, Catherine Walker.
Institution Type/Description: library; Native American.
Hours & Admission Prices: Mon.-Fri. 8:30-5. No charge. Closed National holidays. ♿
Attendance: 1,500 (estimated)

Sulphur

ARBUCKLE HISTORICAL SOCIETY MUSEUM, 402 W. Muskogee Ave., Sulphur, OK 73086-4614. Tel.: 580-622-5593.
Institution Type/Description: Historical Society Museum: housed in the former Sulphur City Hall; built in 1917.
Hours & Admission Prices: Fri.-Sun. 12-5; groups by appointment.

CHICKASAW HOLISSO RESEARCH CENTER, 867 Cooper Memorial Dr., Sulphur, OK 73086-8697. Tel.: 580-622-7130.
E-mail: ccc@chickasaw.net
Institution Type/Description: Research Center.
Hours & Admission Prices: Mon.-Sat. 10-5, Sun. 12-5.

CHICKASAW NATIONAL RECREATION AREA, 901 W. 1st St., Sulphur, OK 73086. Tel.: 580-622-7234. TDD: 580-622-3165.
Web Site: www.nps.gov/chic
Formerly: Platt National Park
Key Personnel: Chief Interpreter, Ron Parker.
Institution Type/Description: Nature Center.
Hours & Admission Prices: Park: daily. Nature Center: Memorial Day-Labor Day daily 9-5:30; Sept.-May daily 9-4:30. No charge; donations accepted. Closed New Year's Day; Thanksgiving; Christmas. ♿
Attendance: 36,000 (actual)

NATIONAL MUSEUM OF HORSE SHOEING TOOLS AND HALL OF HONOR, 7781 U.S. Hwy. 177, Sulphur, OK 73086. Tel.: 580-622-4644. Fax: 580-622-4669.
E-mail: carousel@brightok.net
Web Site: www.horseshoeingmuseum.com
Key Personnel: Dir., Lee Liles.
Institution Type/Description: History Museum.
Hours & Admission Prices: By appointment. No charge.

Tahlequah

CHEROKEE NATIONAL PRISON MUSEUM, 124 E. Choctaw St., Tahlequah, OK 74464. Tel.: 918-207-3640.
Institution Type/Description: Historic Building Museum: built in 1875.
Hours & Admission Prices: Tues.-Sat. 10-4. Adults $5, seniors & students $3; children under 5 no charge.

CHEROKEE NATIONAL SUPREME COURT MUSEUM, 122 E. Keetoowah St., Tahlequah, OK 74464. Tel.: 918-207-3508.
E-mail: communications@cherokee.org
Institution Type/Description: Historic Building Museum: built in 1844.
Hours & Admission Prices: Tues.-Sat. 10-4. Adults $5, seniors & students $3; children under 5 no charge.

Tecumseh

TECUMSEH HISTORICAL SOCIETY MUSEUM, 114 S. Broadway, Tecumseh, OK 74873. Mailing Address: P.O. Box 292, Tecumseh, OK 74873-0292.
E-mail: tecumsehhistory@hotmail.com
Key Personnel: Pres. (V), Jane Fleming.
Institution Type/Description: Historical Society Museum: housed in the former Dickson & Legg Buildings.
Hours & Admission Prices: Sat. 10-2; other times by appointment. No charge; donations accepted. ♿
Attendance: 481 (actual)

Tishomingo

CHICKASAW BANK MUSEUM & JOHNSTON COUNTY MUSEUM, 413 E. Main St., Tishomingo, OK 73460. Mailing Address: P.O. Box 804, Tishomingo, OK 73460-0804. Tel.: 580-371-3141. Fax: 580-371-3141.
E-mail: INFO@CHICKASAWCOUNTRY.COM
Key Personnel: Pres. (V), Jackie Baker; Museum Shop Mgr., Letha Clark.
Institution Type/Description: History Museum: housed in a Chickasaw Tribe bank building; built in 1902. Listed on the National Register of Historic Places.
Hours & Admission Prices: Tues.-Fri. 9-5, Sat. 9:30-4:30; other times by appointment. No charge; donations accepted. ♿
Attendance: 3,024 (actual)

CHICKASAW COUNCIL HOUSE MUSEUM, 209 N. Fisher, Tishomingo, OK 73460-1717. Mailing Address: P.O. Box 1548, Ada, OK 74821-1548. Tel.: 580-371-3351.
E-mail: museum@chickasaw.net
Web Site: www.chickasaw.net
Key Personnel: Mgr., Flora Fink.
Institution Type/Description: Native American Museum.
Hours & Admission Prices: Mon.-Fri. 9-6, Sat. 10-4. No charge; donations accepted. Closed legal holidays. ♿

Tonkawa

A.D. BUCK HISTORY & WELCOME CENTER, 1220 E. Grand, Tonkawa, OK 74653. Mailing Address: P.O. Box 310, Tonkawa, OK 74653-0310. Tel.: 580-628-3318 & 6473. Fax: 405-628-6209.
E-mail: jill.green@noc.edu
Web Site: www.noc.edu
Formerly: The A.D. Buck Museum of Natural History & Science
Key Personnel: Vice Pres. Devel. & Community Rels., Sheri Snyder; Dir. Alumni & Community Rels., Jill Green.
Institution Type/Description: History Museum.
Hours & Admission Prices: By appointment. No charge. ♿
Attendance: 59 (actual)

MCCARTER MUSEUM OF TONKAWA HISTORY, 220 E. Grand Ave., Tonkawa, OK 74653. Mailing Address: P.O. Box 467, Tonkawa, OK 74653. Tel.: 580-628-2898.
E-mail: marilee@kskc.net
Key Personnel: Pres., Evelyn Coyle; Past Pres., Marille Helton.
Institution Type/Description: History Museum.
Hours & Admission Prices: Tues.-Sat. 1-3; other times by appointment. No charge.

TONKAWA TRIBAL MUSEUM, 10951 Allen Dr., Tonkawa, OK 74653. Mailing Address: 1 Rush Buffalo Rd., Tonkawa, OK 74653. Tel.: 580-628-2561. Fax: 580-628-2279, 580-279-6515. Facebook: Tonkawa Tribe.
E-mail: info@tonkawatribe.com

Web Site: www.tonkawatribe.com
Key Personnel: Dir., Russell L. Martin; Museum Shop Mgr., Miranda Myer.
Institution Type/Description: Native American Museum.
Hours & Admission Prices: Mon.-Fri. 8:30-4:30. No charge. Closed all federal holidays. &

Tulsa

ALEXANDRE HOGUE GALLERY - UNIVERSITY OF TULSA, 2930 E. 5th St., Tulsa, OK 74104. Tel.: 918-631-2739. Fax: 918-631-3423.
E-mail: mark-lewis@utulsa.edu
Institution Type/Description: Art Gallery.
Hours & Admission Prices: Mon.-Fri. 8-5. No charge.

ELSING MUSEUM, LRC 137B, 7777 S. Lewis Ave., Tulsa, OK 74171. Tel.: 918-495-6262.
E-mail: rbush@oru.edu
Web Site: elsing.oru.edu
Key Personnel: Dir., Cur. & Museum Shop Mgr., Roger Bush; Education Dir., Dr. Catherine Klehm.
Institution Type/Description: Geology Museum.
Hours & Admission Prices: Wed.-Sat. 1:30-4:30; call to confirm during holiday season. No charge; donations accepted. Closed holidays. &
Attendance: 600 (estimated)

GILCREASE MUSEUM - THOMAS GILCREASE INSTITUTE OF AMERICAN HISTORY & ART, 1400 N. Gilcrease Museum Rd., Tulsa, OK 74127-2100. Tel.: 918-596-2700, 888-655-2278 (Toll Free). Fax: 918-596-2770.
E-mail: sandi-freeman@utulsa.edu
Web Site: gilcrease.org
Key Personnel: Exec. Dir., Susan Neal; Chm. (V), Marc C. Maun; Dir. Opers., Sandra Freeman; Rights & Reproduction, Diana Cox; Membership Coord., Rachel Johnson; Sr. Dir. Devel., Frank Mulhern; Dir. Collections & Acting Chief Registrar, Susan Buchanan; Dir. Museum Shop & Visitor Services, Melanie Rosencutter; Event Coord., Nick Kindelt; Mgr. Communications, Lacy Wulfers; Volunteer Svcs., Donna Gainey; Dir. Learning & Community Engagement, Alison Rossi; Dir. Digitization Collections, Diana Folsom; Sr. Cur. & Cur. Art, Laura Fry; Coord. Membership, Rachel Johnson; Librarian, Renee Harvey.
Institution Type/Description: American History & Art Museum.
Hours & Admission Prices: Tues.-Sun. 10-5. Adults $8, seniors 62 & over and active duty U.S. military $6, college students $5; discounts to groups of 10 or more, Western Reciprocal, Museums West Consortium & North American Reciprocal members; children 18 & under, museum members, University of Tulsa students w/ I.D., K-12 grade school tours; 1st Tues. & 3rd Sun. of each month no charge. Closed Christmas. &
Attendance: 76,366 (actual)

MABEL B. LITTLE HERITAGE HOUSE MUSEUM, 322 N. Greenwood Ave., Tulsa, OK 74120-1026. Tel.: 918-596-1006. Fax: 918-583-2770.
E-mail: mlmackey@sbcglobal.net
Institution Type/Description: Historic House.
Hours & Admission Prices: Mon.-Fri. 9-5, Sat. by appointment.

PHILBROOK DOWNTOWN, 116 E. Brady St., Tulsa, OK 74103. Tel.: 918-749-7941.
E-mail: mbrown@philbrook.org
Web Site: www.philbrook.org
Institution Type/Description: Art Museum.
Hours & Admission Prices: Wed.-Sat. 12-7, Sun. 12-5. Adults $9, students & senior citizens $7; youth under 17 & members no charge. Closed New Year's Day; Independence Day; Thanksgiving; Christmas.

THE PHILBROOK MUSEUM OF ART, INC., 2727 S. Rockford Rd., Tulsa, OK 74114-4104. Mailing Address: P.O. Box 52510, Tulsa, OK 74152-0510. Tel.: 918-749-7941. Fax: 918-743-4230. TDD: 918-749-7941 (public info. line).
E-mail: mbrown@philbrook.org
Web Site: www.philbrook.org
Key Personnel: Exec. Dir., Pres. & C.E.O., Scott Stulen; Chm., Bill Thomas; Deputy Dir., Paul Nelson; Facility Mgr., Charisse Cooper; Librarian, Tom Young; Museum Shop Mgr., Susan Shrewder; Dir. Communications, Tricia Milford-Hoyt; Dir. Finance, Donna Durrin; Cur. Native American & Non-Western Art, Christina Burke; Chief Cur. & Cur. American Art, Catherine Whitney; Nancy E. Meinig Cur. Modern & Contemporary Art, Sienna Brown.
Institution Type/Description: Art Museum & Gardens.

Hours & Admission Prices: Tues.-Wed. & Fri.-Sun. 10-5, Thurs. 10-8. Adults $9, senior citizens & higher education students $7; discounts to military, chaperones & groups of 10 or more; children 18 & under, members, and 2nd Sat. each month no charge. &
Attendance: 161,000 (estimated)

THE SHERWIN MILLER MUSEUM OF JEWISH ART, 2021 E. 71st St., Tulsa, OK 74136-5408. Tel.: 918-492-1818. Fax: 918-492-1888. Facebook, Twitter, Instagram, Yelp.
E-mail: info@jewishmuseum.net
Web Site: www.jewishmuseum.net
Formerly: Fenster Museum of Jewish Art
Key Personnel: Exec. Dir., Drew Diamond; Chm. (V), Nancy Lobo; Dir. Collections & Exhibits, Mickel Yantz; Dir. Devel & Programs, Tracey Herst-Woods.
Institution Type/Description: Judaica Art Museum.
Hours & Admission Prices: Adults $6.50, senior citizens $5.50, students $3.50; discounts to groups of 10 or more, ICOM & AAM members; law enforcement, uniform services, military, teachers, Blue Star members & museum members no charge. &
Attendance: 14,000 (estimated)

SOCIETY OF EXPLORATION GEOPHYSICISTS - GEOSCIENCE CENTER, 8801 S. Yale, Tulsa, OK 74137-3573. Mailing Address: P.O. Box 702740, Tulsa, OK 74170-2740. Tel.: 918-497-5555. Fax: 918-497-5557.
E-mail: members@seg.org
Web Site: seg.org
Institution Type/Description: Earth Science Center.
Hours & Admission Prices: Call for hours.

TULSA AIR AND SPACE MUSEUM & PLANETARIUM, 3624 N. 74th E. Ave., Tulsa, OK 74115-3622. Tel.: 918-834-9900. Fax: 918-834-6723.
E-mail: sstgeorge@tulsamuseum.org
Web Site: www.tulsaairandspacemuseum.org
Formerly: Tulsa Air and Space Center
Key Personnel: Exec. Dir., Sheryl St. George; Dir. Education, Jared Casci; Chm. (V), Bill Christiansen; Comptroller, Lori Moffitt.
Institution Type/Description: Space Museum & Planetarium.
Hours & Admission Prices: Mon.-Sat. 10-4. Adults $15, seniors, students & military $12, youth $10; children 4 & under and members no charge. Closed holidays. &
Attendance: 62,000 (actual)

TULSA CHILDREN'S MUSEUM DISCOVERY LAB, 560 N. Maybelle Ave., Tulsa, OK 74127. Tel.: 918-295-8144.
E-mail: info@tulsachildrensmuseum.org
Web Site: tulsachildrensmuseum.org
Key Personnel: Exec. Dir., Ray Vandiver, Ph.D.
Institution Type/Description: Children's Museum.
Hours & Admission Prices: Mon.-Sat. 9:30-5, Sun. 11:30-5. Admission 2 & over $6; discounts to groups; members & children under 2 no charge. Closed Thanksgiving; Christmas.

TULSA HISTORICAL SOCIETY AND MUSEUM, 2445 S. Peoria, Tulsa, OK 74114-1326. Tel.: 918-712-9484. Fax: 918-712-1939. Facebook: Tulsa History.
E-mail: ths@tulsahistory.org
Web Site: tulsahistory.org
Key Personnel: Exec. Dir., Michelle Place; Communications & Facilities Mgr., Britni Worley; Dir. Education & Exhibits, Maggie Brown; Cur. Collections & Archivist, Ian Swart; Dir. Devel., Maggie Jewell; Education Dir., Neal Pascoe.
Institution Type/Description: Historical Society Museum: housed in the Sam Travis Mansion.
Hours & Admission Prices: Tues.-Sat. 10-4. Adults $5, seniors $3, members, students & children no charge. Closed holidays. &

TULSA ZOO & LIVING MUSEUM, 6421 E. 36th St., N., Tulsa, OK 74115-2100. Tel.: 918-669-6600 & 6202. Fax: 918-669-6260.
E-mail: info@tulsazoo.org
Web Site: tulsazoo.org
Institution Type/Description: Zoo & Natural History Museum.
Hours & Admission Prices: Daily 9-5. Adults $10, senior citizens 65 & over $8, children 3-11 $6; discounts to AZA members; children 2 & under & members no charge. Closed Christmas; third Fri. in June. &
Attendance: 630,000 (estimated)

WOODY GUTHRIE CENTER, 102 E. Brady St., Tulsa, OK 74103. Tel.: 918-574-2710.

E-mail: info@woodyguthriecenter.org
Web Site: woodyguthriecenter.org
Key Personnel: Exec. Dir., Deana McCloud.
Institution Type/Description: History Museum.
Hours & Admission Prices: Tues.-Sun. 10-6, 1st Fri. each month 10-9. Adults $8, seniors 55 & over and college students $7, youth 5-17 $6; discounts to groups & military; children under 5 no charge.

Tuskahoma

CHOCTAW NATION OF OKLAHOMA CAPITOL MUSEUM, Council House Rd., Tuskahoma, OK 74574. Tel.: 918-569-4465. Fax: 918-569-4465.
E-mail: suefolsom@choctawnation.com
Institution Type/Description: History Museum: housed in the capitol building; built in 1884.
Hours & Admission Prices: Mon.-Fri. 8-4:30. No charge. Closed holidays.

Tuttle

TIGER SAFARI, 963 County St. 2930, Tuttle, OK 73089. Tel.: 405-381-9453 & 414-9365.
E-mail: tigersafari@me.com
Web Site: www.tigersafari.us
Key Personnel: Owner, Bill Meadows.
Institution Type/Description: Zoo.
Hours & Admission Prices: Spring: daily 8-6; Memorial Day to Labor Day Tues.-Sun. 9-5:30. Adults $8, children $7; children under 2 no charge.

Vinita

EASTERN TRAILS MUSEUM, 215 W. Illinois, Vinita, OK 74301-3129. Tel.: 918-256-2115.
E-mail: etmuseum@junct.com
Web Site: www.vinitapl.okpls.org/museum.htm
Key Personnel: Cur., Wanda Norton.
Institution Type/Description: History Museum.
Hours & Admission Prices: Mon.-Fri. 1-4, Sat. 1-3. No charge; donations accepted. &

Wagoner

CITY OF WAGONER HISTORICAL MUSEUM, 122 S. Main, Wagoner, OK 74467-5221. Mailing Address: P.O. Box 406, Wagoner, OK 74477-0406. Tel.: 918-485-9111. Facebook.
E-mail: lizmcmahon@windstream.net
Key Personnel: Dir., Jerry Hickman.
Institution Type/Description: History Museum.
Hours & Admission Prices: Tues.-Sat. 10-3. No charge; donations accepted. &
Attendance: 700 (estimated)

Wakita

TWISTER THE MOVIE MUSEUM, 101 W. Main St., Wakita, OK 73771. Mailing Address: P.O. Box 285, Wakita, OK 73771-0285. Tel.: 580-594-2312.
E-mail: info@twistercountry.com
Web Site: www.twistercountry.com
Institution Type/Description: Movie Museum: located in the town where the movie Twister was filmed.
Hours & Admission Prices: April-Aug. Tues.-Sat. 1-5. No charge. Closed holidays.

Walters

COTTON COUNTY MUSEUM, 116 N. Broadway, Walters, OK 73572. Mailing Address: P.O. Box 244, Walters, OK 73572. Tel.: 580-875-3335.
E-mail: garrison1940@sbcglobal.net
Institution Type/Description: History Museum: housed in the former Grand Theatre.
Hours & Admission Prices: Mon.-Thurs. 9-12 & 1-3; other times by appointment.

Warner

WALLIS MUSEUM, 1000 College Rd., Warner, OK 74469-9700. Mailing Address: Rte. 1, Box 1000, Warner, OK 74469-9700. Tel.: 918-463-6236. Fax: 918-463-6314.
E-mail: nrigney@connorsstate.edu
Web Site: www.connorsstate.edu

Formerly: Rural Farming & Agriculture Museum
Key Personnel: C.E.O., Dr. Tim Faltyn.
Institution Type/Description: University Museum.
Hours & Admission Prices: Closed for relocation. &

Warwick

SEABA STATION MOTORCYCLE MUSEUM, 336992 E. Hwy. 66, Warwick, OK 74834. Tel.: 405-258-9141 & 365-1744.
E-mail: JERRY@SEABASTATION.COM
Web Site: http://www.seabastation.com/
Institution Type/Description: Motorcycle Museum: housed in the former Seaba Filling Station; built in 1921. Listed on the National Register of Historic Places.
Hours & Admission Prices: Thurs.-Tues. 10-5; other times by appointment. No charge.

Watonga

T.B. FERGUSON HOME, 519 N. Weigle Ave., Watonga, OK 73772. Tel.: 580-623-5069. Facebook: Friends of the T.B. Ferguson Home.
E-mail: historic.tbferguson@gmail.com
Web Site: www.okhistory.org/sites/tbferguson
Key Personnel: Site Dir., Cindy Pitts.
Institution Type/Description: Historic House: c.1901 T.B. Ferguson Home, home of sixth territorial Governor.
Hours & Admission Prices: Mon. & Thurs. 11-4, Fri. 12:30-5:30, Sat. 10:30-3:30. No charge; donations accepted. Closed state holidays.
Attendance: 4,320 (estimated)

Waurika

ROCK ISLAND DEPOT MUSEUM, 105 S. Meridian, Waurika, OK 73573. Mailing Address: 122 S. Main St., Waurika, OK 73573-3054. Tel.: 590-228-3274. Fax: 590-228-2907.
E-mail: museum@waurika.lib.ok.us
Key Personnel: Museum Bd. Pres., Nancy Way; Librarian & Cur., Cathy Dumas.
Institution Type/Description: History Museum.
Hours & Admission Prices: Tues.-Sat. 10-5.

Waynoka

WAYNOKA HISTORY MUSEUM & INFORMATION CENTER, 1383 S. Cleveland St., Waynoka, OK 73860. Tel.: 580-824-1886. Fax: 580-824-0921.
Institution Type/Description: History Museum: housed in the 1910 Harvey House and 1910 Santa Fe Depot. Listed on the National Register of Historic Places.
Hours & Admission Prices: Tues.-Sat. 12:30-4:30. &

Weatherford

HEARTLAND OF AMERICA MUSEUM, 1600 S. Frontage Rd., Weatherford, OK 73096-6119. Tel.: 580-774-2212.
E-mail: heartland@oklahomaheartlandmuseum.com
Web Site: oklahomaheartlandmuseum.com
Key Personnel: Dir., Rick Lundquist; C.E.O. & Pres. (V), Everett Swearengin; Museum Shop Mgr., Jewrell Crall.
Institution Type/Description: History Museum.
Hours & Admission Prices: Tues.-Fri. 9-5, Sun. 1-5; other times by appointment. Adults 19 & over $6, students 6-18 $2; discount on Veteran's Day & to groups of 10 or more. Closed New Year's Day; Easter; Memorial Day; Independence Day; Labor Day; Thanksgiving; Christmas. &
Attendance: 1,000 (estimated)

STAFFORD AIR & SPACE MUSEUM, 3000 Logan Rd., Weatherford, OK 73096-2681. Tel.: 580-772-5871.
E-mail: director@staffordmuseum.org
Web Site: www.staffordmuseum.org
Institution Type/Description: Air & Space Museum.
Hours & Admission Prices: Mon.-Sat. 9-5, Sun. 1-5. Adults 19-54 $7, seniors 55 & over $5, children & students $2. Closed New Year's Day; Easter; Memorial Day; Independence Day; Labor Day; Thanksgiving; Christmas. &
Attendance: 25,000 (estimated)

Webbers Falls

WEBBERS FALLS HISTORICAL SOCIETY AND MUSEUM, Commercial & Main, Webbers Falls, OK 74470. Mailing Address: P.O. Box 5, Webbers Falls, OK 74470. Tel.: 918-464-2728.
E-mail: wfmuseum@crosstel.net

Web Site: www.webbersfallsok.org
Institution Type/Description: Historical Society Museum: town named in honor of Chief Walter Webber who settled here in 1828.
Hours & Admission Prices: Call for hours.

Weleetka

OLD CITY HALL & JAIL, State Hwy. 75 & Seminole, Weleetka, OK 74880. Mailing Address: P.O. Box 733, Weleetka, OK 74880. Tel.: 405-786-2501 & 3251.
Formerly: Weleetka Town Hall and Jail
Key Personnel: Dir., Anna Gordon.
Institution Type/Description: Historic Building: housed in the former City Hall building; built in 1910. Listed on the National Register of Historic Places.
Hours & Admission Prices: By appointment. No charge.
Attendance: 15 (actual)

Wewoka

SEMINOLE NATION MUSEUM, 524 S. Wewoka Ave., Wewoka, OK 74884-3239. Mailing Address: Box 1532, Wewoka, OK 74884-1532. Tel.: 405-257-5580. Fax: 405-257-5580.
E-mail: director@theseminolenationmuseum.org
Web Site: www.theseminolenationmuseum.org
Key Personnel: C.E.O. & Pres. (V), William Wantland; Exec. Dir. & Chief Cur., Richard Ellwanger; Asst. Cur., Lewis Johnson; Physical Plant, Noah Hail; Registrar, Karen Smith.
Institution Type/Description: History Museum.
Hours & Admission Prices: Mon.-Sat. 10-5. No charge; donations accepted. Closed Federal holidays. &
Attendance: 10,000 (estimated)

Wilburton

LUTIE COAL MINER'S MUSEUM, 2307 E. Main St., Wilburton, OK 74578. Tel.: 918-465-2216.
Institution Type/Description: Mining Museum: housed in the former Hailey Ola Coal Company house; built in 1901.
Hours & Admission Prices: By appointment. No charge.

ROBBERS CAVE NATURE CENTER, Hwy. 2 N., Wilburton, OK 74578. Mailing Address: P.O. Box 9, Wilburton, OK 74578-0009. Tel.: 918-465-2562, 800-654-8240. Fax: 918-465-2781. Facebook: Robbers Cave State Park.
E-mail: robberscave@travelok.com
Web Site: www.TravelOK.com/RobbersCave
Key Personnel: Park Mgr., Merle Cox; Park Naturalist, Jacque Martin.
Institution Type/Description: Nature Center.
Hours & Admission Prices: Sun.-Thurs. 8-6, Fri.-Sat. 8-8. No charge.

Wilson

WILSON HISTORICAL MUSEUM, 1270 8th St., Wilson, OK 73463. Tel.: 580-668-2505.
E-mail: whm@wilsonhistoricalmuseum.org
Web Site: www.wilsonhistoricalmuseum.org
Key Personnel: Pres. (V), Carole Gandy Pinches.
Institution Type/Description: History Museum: housed in the Dr. Darling/Wilson Post-Democrat building; built in 1926.
Hours & Admission Prices: Tues. & Thurs.-Sat. 10-4; other times by appointment. No charge; donations accepted. &
Attendance: 1,100

Woodward

FORT SUPPLY HISTORIC SITE, 2009 Williams Ave., Woodward, OK 73801-5717. Tel.: 580-766-3767.
E-mail: shayn1023@gmail.com
Web Site: www.okhistory.org
Key Personnel: Dir., Shayne House.
Institution Type/Description: Historic Site: housed on the site of the army supply camp used during the winter against the Plains Indians in western Indian Territory.
Hours & Admission Prices: Tues.-Sat. 9-4 by appointment. Closed state holidays.

PLAINS INDIANS & PIONEERS MUSEUM, 2009 Williams Ave., Woodward, OK 73801-5717. Tel.: 580-256-6136. Fax: 580-256-2577.
E-mail: contact@pipm1.org

Web Site: www.pipm1.org
Key Personnel: Dir., Robert Roberson; Cur., Tammy Hawbaker; Gift Shop Mgr., Jo Simmons.
Institution Type/Description: Regional History Museum.
Hours & Admission Prices: Tues.-Sat. 10-5. No charge; donations accepted. Closed major holidays. &
Attendance: 9,000 (actual)

Wynnewood

ESKRIDGE HOTEL MUSEUM, 114 E. Robert S. Kerr Blvd., Wynnewood, OK 73098-6621. Mailing Address: c/o Wynnewood Historical Society, P.O. Box 428, Wynnewood, OK 73098-0428. Tel.: 405-238-4567. Fax: 405-665-4619. Facebook: The Eskridge Hotel Museum.
E-mail: theeskridgehotel@yahoo.com
Web Site: www.eskridgehotelmuseum.org
Key Personnel: Dir., Sandy Campbell.
Institution Type/Description: History Museum: built by Pinckney Reid Eskridge in 1907.
Hours & Admission Prices: Mon.-Thurs. 11-4; other times by appointment. Adults $4, seniors 55 & over $3, students $2; discounts to groups; children 5 & under and school groups & military veterans no charge.

Yale

JIM THORPE HOME, 706 E. Boston Ave., Yale, OK 74085-4004. Tel.: 918-387-2815.
E-mail: frick.linda@yahoo.com
Key Personnel: Cur., Linda C. Frick; Cur., Virginia Stanford.
Institution Type/Description: History Museum.
Hours & Admission Prices: Wed.-Sat. 10-5. No charge. Closed major holidays. &
Attendance: 1,200 (estimated)

Yukon

YUKON HISTORICAL SOCIETY MUSEUM & ART CENTER, 601 Oak, Yukon, OK 73099-2538. Tel.: 405-354-5079.
Web Site: www.thestagedoorinc.org
Key Personnel: Pres., John Knuppel.
Institution Type/Description: History & Art Museum: housed in a 1910 school building.
Hours & Admission Prices: By appointment. Museum: no charge. Art Center: call for admission prices.

YUKON'S BEST RAILROAD MUSEUM, 410 Oak Ave., Yukon, OK 73099-2640. Tel.: 405-354-5079.
Key Personnel: Pres. & Cur., John Knuppel; Cur., Jack Austerman.
Institution Type/Description: Railroad Museum.
Hours & Admission Prices: By appointment. No charge; donations accepted.

OREGON

(203 listings)

Agness

AGNESS-ILLAHE MUSEUM, INC., 34470 Agness-Illaha Rd., P. O. Box 36, Agness, OR 97406-9701. Mailing Address: 29419 Ellensburg, P.O. Box 1598, Gold Beach, OR 97444. Tel.: 541-247-2014.
E-mail: ptl@dishmail.net
Web Site: www.agnessmuseum.com
Key Personnel: Dir., Linda Graves; C.E.O., Dennis Graves.
Institution Type/Description: History Museum.
Hours & Admission Prices: May-Sept. daily 11-2. No charge; donations accepted. &
Attendance: 1,000 (estimated)

Albany

ALBANY REGIONAL MUSEUM, 136 Lyon St., S., Albany, OR 97321-2703. Tel.: 541-967-7122. Facebook: Albany Regional Museum.
E-mail: armuseum@peak.org
Web Site: www.armuseum.com
Key Personnel: Chm. (V), Darrel Tedisch; Exec. Dir., Keith Lohse; Collections & Exhibits Mgr., Amy Bozorth; Membership & Visitor Svcs. Coord., Erica Broad; Membership & Visitor Svcs. Asst., Kathwren Hayes.
Institution Type/Description: Historical Museum.

Hours & Admission Prices: Tues.-Fri. 11-4, Sat.10-2. Adults $2; members no charge. Closed New Year's Day; Labor Day; Thanksgiving; Christmas. &
Attendance: 7,527 (actual)

THE MONTEITH HOUSE MUSEUM, 518 Second Ave., S.W., Albany, OR 97321-2239. Mailing Address: Monteith Historic Society, P.O. Box 965, Albany, OR 97321-0362. Tel.: 541-928-0911. Facebook: Monteith House Museum.
E-mail: info@albanyvisitors.com
Web Site: www.monteithhouse.org
Key Personnel: Pres. (V), Chet Houser.
Institution Type/Description: Historic House: built in 1849. Listed on the National Register of Historic Places.
Hours & Admission Prices: June 15-Sept. 15 Wed.-Sat. 12-4. No charge, donations accepted.
Attendance: 2,000 (estimated)

Ashland

HANSON HOWARD GALLERY, 89 Oak St., Ashland, OR 97520-1802. Tel.: 541-488-2562.
E-mail: hhgall@mind.net
Web Site: hansonhowardgallery.com
Institution Type/Description: Art Gallery.
Hours & Admission Prices: Call for hours.

SCHNEIDER MUSEUM OF ART, Southern Oregon University, 1250 Siskiyou Blvd., Ashland, OR 97520-5001. Tel.: 541-552-6245. Fax: 541-552-8241. Facebook, Twitter, Instagram.
E-mail: sma@sou.edu
Web Site: www.sou.edu/sma
Key Personnel: Acting Dir., Scott Malbaurn.
Institution Type/Description: Art Museum.
Hours & Admission Prices: Mon.-Sat. 10-4. No charges; donations accepted. Closed state holidays; university holidays. &
Attendance: 15,000 (estimated)

SCIENCEWORKS HANDS-ON MUSEUM, 1500 E. Main St., Ashland, OR 97520-1312. Tel.: 541-482-6767. Fax: 541-482-5716.
E-mail: info@scienceworksmuseum.org
Web Site: www.scienceworksmuseum.org
Key Personnel: Interim Exec. Dir., Susan Unger; Interim Education Dir., Zoey Belyea; Exhibition Dir., Leo Palombo.
Institution Type/Description: Science Museum.
Hours & Admission Prices: Academic Year: Wed.-Sun. 12-5; Memorial Day to Labor Day daily 11-6. Adults $12.50, children 2-12 $10.50; discounts to groups of 10 or more; children under 2 no charge. Closed New Year's Day; Easter; Independence Day; Thanksgiving; Christmas. &
Attendance: 60,000 (actual)

SOUTHERN OREGON UNIVERSITY MUSEUM OF VERTEBRATE NATURAL HISTORY, 1250 Siskiyou Blvd., Ashland, OR 97520-5001. Mailing Address: Southern Oregon University, Dept. of Biology, Ashland, OR 97520. Tel.: 541-552-6749 & 6341. Fax: 541-552-6415.
E-mail: stonek@sou.edu
Key Personnel: Cur., Dr. Karen Stone; Sec. Biology Dept., Colleen Martin.
Institution Type/Description: Vertebrate Biology Museum.
Hours & Admission Prices: By appointment only. No charge; donations accepted.

Astoria

COLUMBIA RIVER MARITIME MUSEUM, 1792 Marine Dr., Astoria, OR 97103-3525. Tel.: 503-325-2323. Fax: 503-325-2331.
E-mail: information@crmm.org
Web Site: www.crmm.org
Key Personnel: Exec. Dir., Sam Johnson; Deputy Dir., Bruce Jones; Chm. (V), Michael Haglund; Cur., Jeff Smith; Museum Shop Mgr., Blue Anderson.
Institution Type/Description: History & Maritime Museum.
Hours & Admission Prices: Daily 9:30-5. Adults $14, senior citizens $12, children 6-17 $5; members & children under 6 no charge. Reciprocal admission with participating Council of American Maritime Museums. Closed Thanksgiving; Christmas. &
Attendance: 115,080 (actual)

FLAVEL HOUSE MUSEUM, 441 8th St., Astoria, OR 97103-4620. Mailing Address: P.O. Box 88, Astoria, OR 97103-0088. Tel.: 503-325-2203. Fax: 503-325-7727.
E-mail: cchs@cumtux.org

Web Site: www.cumtux.org
Formerly: Captain George Flavel House Museum
Key Personnel: Exec. Dir., McAndrew Burns; Archivist, Liisa Penner; Business Mgr., Emily Gray; Dir. Mktg. & Devel., W. Sam Rascoe; Cur., Chelsea Vaughn.
Institution Type/Description: Historic House Museum.
Hours & Admission Prices: May-Sept. daily 10-5; Oct.-April daily 11-4. Adults $7, seniors citizens $6, youth 6-17 $2; children under 6 & members no charge. Closed New Year's Day; Thanksgiving; Christmas Eve & Day.
Attendance: 23,000 (estimated)

THE HERITAGE MUSEUM, 1618 Exchange St., Astoria, OR 97103-3615. Mailing Address: P.O. Box 88, Astoria, OR 97103-0088. Tel.: 503-325-2203.
E-mail: cchs@cumtux.org
Web Site: www.cumtux.org
Key Personnel: Exec. Dir., McAndrew Burns; Business Mgr., Martha L. Dahl; Dir. Mktg., Sam Rascoe; Archivist, Liisa Penner; Cur., Amber Glen.
Institution Type/Description: Historical Society Museum.
Hours & Admission Prices: May-Sept. Tues.-Sat. 10-5; Oct.-April Tues.-Sat. 11-4. Adults $4, children 6-17 $2; members no charge. Closed New Year's Eve & Day; Thanksgiving; Christmas Eve & Day. &
Attendance: 6,500 (estimated)

LEWIS & CLARK NATIONAL HISTORICAL PARK, 92343 Fort Clatsop Rd., Astoria, OR 97103. Tel.: 503-861-2471. Fax: 503-861-2585. TDD: 503-861-1620.
E-mail: lewi_superintendent@nps.gov
Web Site: www.nps.gov/lewi
Formerly: Fort Clatsop National Memorial
Key Personnel: Supt., Jon Burpee; Chief Visitor Svcs., Jill Harding; Chief Resource Mgmt., Chris Clatterbuck; Chief Facility Mgmt., Andrew Rasmussen.
Institution Type/Description: Historic Fort: replica of the 1805-1806, winter encampment of the Lewis & Clark Expedition; objects relating to the Lewis & Clark expedition.
Hours & Admission Prices: Mid-June to Labor Day daily 9-6; after Labor Day to mid-June daily 9-5. 7-day entrance fee 16 & up $3; children 15 & under no charge. Closed Christmas. &
Attendance: 226,000 (actual)

UPPERTOWN FIREFIGHTERS MUSEUM, 2986 Marine Dr., Astoria, OR 97103. Mailing Address: Clatsop County Historical Society, P.O. Box 88, Astoria, OR 97103-0088. Tel.: 503-325-2203. Fax: 503-325-7727.
E-mail: cchs@cumtux.org
Web Site: www.cumtux.org
Key Personnel: Exec. Dir., McAndrew Burns; Business Mgr., Martha L. Dahl; Dir. Mktg. & Devel., W. Sam Rascoe; Archivist, Liisa Penner.
Institution Type/Description: Firefighters Museum.
Hours & Admission Prices: June-Aug. by appointment. &
Attendance: 3,000 (estimated)

Aurora

AURORA COLONY HISTORICAL SOCIETY, 15018 2nd St., N. E., Aurora, OR 97002. Mailing Address: P.O. Box 202, Aurora, OR 97002-0202. Tel.: 503-678-5754. Fax: 503-678-5756.
E-mail: info@auroracolony.org
Web Site: www.auroracolony.org
Key Personnel: Pres. (V), Kenneth Hartley.
Institution Type/Description: Historical Society Museum.
Hours & Admission Prices: Feb.-Dec. Tues.-Sat. 11-4, Sun. 12-4. Adults $6, seniors 60 & over $5, students $4, youth $3; discounts to AAA & AAM members; children 5 & under and members no charge. Closed major holidays. &
Attendance: 5,000 (estimated)

Baker City

ADLER HOUSE MUSEUM, 2305 Main St., Baker City, OR 97814. Mailing Address: 2480 Grove St., Baker City, OR 97814. Tel.: 541-523-9308.
E-mail: museum@bakercounty.org
Web Site: www.bakerheritagemuseum.com/adler-house.html
Institution Type/Description: Historic House Museum: housed in the former home of philanthropist, Leo Adler; built in 1889.
Hours & Admission Prices: Memorial Day to Labor Day Fri.-Sat. 10-3:30; other times by appointment. Adults $6; children 12 & under no charge.

BAKER HERITAGE MUSEUM, 2480 Grove St., Baker City, OR 97814-2719. Tel.: 541-523-9308. Fax: 541-523-9308. Facebook: Baker Heritage Museum.

E-mail: museum@bakercounty.org
Web Site: www.bakerheritagemuseum.com
Formerly: Oregon Trail Regional Museum
Key Personnel: Dir., Lea Gettle; Chm. (V), Steve Bogart.
Institution Type/Description: History Museum.
Hours & Admission Prices: mid-March to Oct. daily 9-4; see website for additional winter hours. Family $20; adults $6, senior citizens 60 & over and youth 13-17 $5; discounts to groups; children 12 & under and members no charge. &
Attendance: 20,000 (actual)

NATIONAL HISTORIC OREGON TRAIL INTERPRETIVE CENTER, 22267 Oregon Hwy. 86, Baker City, OR 97814. Mailing Address: P.O. Box 987, Baker City, OR 97814-0987. Tel.: 541-523-1843. Fax: 541-523-1834.
E-mail: or_nhotic_mail@blm.gov
Web Site: www.blm.gov/or/oregontrail/
Key Personnel: Center Dir., Sarah LeCompte; Museum Shop Mgr., Mary Kolb; Maintenance Lead, John-Luc Metz; Park Ranger, Kelly Burns; Visitor Information Asst., Cheri Garver; Visitor Information Asst., Calvin Henshaw; Exhibit Specialist, Gypsy Burks.
Institution Type/Description: History Museum & Interpretive Center: interpretive center along Oregon Trail; historic gold mining site.
Hours & Admission Prices: Feb. 16-March & Nov. daily 9-4; April-Oct. daily 9-6; Dec.-Feb. 15 Thurs.-Sun. 9-4. April-Oct. adults $8, senior citizens 62 & over $4.50; discounts to groups & tours; Inter-Agency Pass, NHOTIC Individual & Family members, schools and children under 16 no charge; Nov.-March adults $5, seniors $3.50; discounts to groups & tours; Inter-Agency Pass, NHOTIC Individual & family members, schools and children under 16 no charge. Closed New Year's Day; Thanksgiving; Christmas. &
Attendance: 69,852 (actual)

Bandon

BANDON HISTORICAL SOCIETY MUSEUM, 270 Fillmore & Hwy. 101, Bandon, OR 97411. Mailing Address: P.O. Box 737, Bandon, OR 97411-0737. Tel.: 541-347-2164. Fax: 541-347-2164.
E-mail: bandonhistoricalmuseum@yahoo.com
Web Site: bandonhistoricalmuseum.org
Formerly: Coquille River Museum/Bandon Historical Society
Key Personnel: Exec. Dir. & Museum Shop Mgr., Judy Knox; Pres. (V), Dean Conyes; Vice Pres. & Education, Jim Proehl; Sec., Faye Albertson; Treas., Nancy Murphy.
Institution Type/Description: History Museum.
Hours & Admission Prices: Feb.-May & Oct.-Dec. Mon.-Sat. 10-4; June-Sept. Mon.-Sun. 10-4. Adults $3; children under 12 & society members no charge. Closed New Year's Day; Thanksgiving; Christmas Eve & Day. &
Attendance: 3,500 (estimated)

COQUILLE RIVER LIGHTHOUSE/BULLARDS BEACH STATE PARK, 2 miles N. of Bandon, Hwy. 101, Bandon, OR 97411. Mailing Address: P.O. Box 569, Bandon, OR 97411-0569. Tel.: 541-347-2209. Fax: 541-347-4656.
E-mail: Beth.Wilson@oregon.gov
Web Site: www.oregonstateparks.org/park_71.php
Key Personnel: Park Mgr., Ben Fisher; Park Ranger, Eric Cook.
Institution Type/Description: Historic Building Museum: housed in 1896 lighthouse.
Hours & Admission Prices: Coquille River Lighthouse: May-Oct. daily 11-5. No charge; donations accepted.
Attendance: 28,380 (actual)

Beaverton

OREGON SPORTS HALL OF FAME AND MUSEUM, 4840 S. W. Western Ave. Ste. 600, Beaverton, OR 97005. Tel.: 503-227-7466. Fax: 503-235-5688.
E-mail: info@oregonsportshall.org
Web Site: www.oregonsportshall.org
Formerly: State of Oregon Sports Hall of Fame
Key Personnel: Pres. (V), Chuck Richards; Exec. Dir., Mike Rose.
Institution Type/Description: Sports Museum.
Hours & Admission Prices: Temporarily closed for relocation. &

Bend

DESCHUTES HISTORICAL MUSEUM, 129 N.W. Idaho Ave., Bend, OR 97703. Tel.: 541-389-1813. Fax: 541-317-9345.
E-mail: info@deschuteshistory.org
Web Site: www.deschuteshistory.org
Key Personnel: Exec. Dir., Kelly Cannon-Miller; Museum Mgr., Vanessa Ivey; Collections Mgr., Shey Hyatt; Membership Officer, Tracy Alexander.

Institution Type/Description: History Museum: housed in 1914 Reid School.
Hours & Admission Prices: Tues.-Sat. 10-4:30; other times by appointment. Adults $5, children 13-17 $2; children 12 & under, members & Independence Day no charge. Closed New Year's Day; Thanksgiving; Christmas. &
Attendance: 8,000 (estimated)

HIGH DESERT MUSEUM, 59800 S. Hwy. 97, Bend, OR 97702-7963. Tel.: 541-382-4754. Fax: 541-382-5256. Facebook.
E-mail: info@highdesertmuseum.org
Web Site: www.highdesertmuseum.org
Key Personnel: Exec. Dir., Dr. Dana Whitelaw; Dir. Programs, Dr. Christina Cid; Cur. Western History, Dr. Laura Ferguson; Cur. Natural History, Louise Shirley; Cur. Living History, Linda Evans; Devel., Gail Hodge; Dir. Communications, Heidi Hagemeier; Museum Shop Mgr., Julie Sturges.
Institution Type/Description: Natural & Cultural History Museum.
Hours & Admission Prices: Summer: daily 9-5; Winter: daily 10-4. May-Oct. adults 13-64 $15, seniors 65 & over $12, children 5-12 $9; discounts to groups & AAM members; members and children 4 & under no charge. Nov.-March adults 13-64 $10, seniors 65 & over $9, children 5-12 $6; discounts to Blue Star Program & AAM members; children 4 & under no charge. Closed Independence Day; Thanksgiving; Christmas. &
Attendance: 169,926 (actual)

Brookings

CHETCO VALLEY HISTORICAL MUSEUM, 15461 Museum Rd., Brookings, OR 97415. Mailing Address: P.O. Box 2004, Brookings, OR 97415. Tel.: 541-469-6651.
E-mail: julie@ross-insurance.com
Web Site: www.chetcomuseum.org
Institution Type/Description: Historic House Museum: housed in the Blake house; built in 1857.
Hours & Admission Prices: Memorial Day to Oct. Sat.-Sun. 12-4. No charge; donations accepted. Closed legal holidays.

Brooks

ANTIQUE CATERPILLAR MACHINERY MUSEUM, 3995 Brooklake Rd., N.E., Brooks, OR 97303-9732. Tel.: 503-538-3935.
Web Site: antiquecaterpillarmuseum.org
Key Personnel: Pres., Don Leffler.
Institution Type/Description: Machinery Museum.
Hours & Admission Prices: Call for hours.

PACIFIC NORTHWEST TRUCK MUSEUM, 3995 Brooklake Rd., N.E., Brooks, OR 97305. Mailing Address: P.O. Box 9087, Brooks, OR 97305-0087. Tel.: 503-312-0039 & 463-8701.
E-mail: office@pacificnwtruckmuseum.org
Web Site: www.pacificnwtruckmuseum.org
Key Personnel: Pres. (V), Terry Dovre; Chm. (V), Doug Delano; Treas., Craig Vogel; Museum Shop Mgr., Jerry Crume.
Institution Type/Description: Truck Museum.
Hours & Admission Prices: Museum: April-Sept. Sat.-Sun. 10-4:30; other times by appointment. Donation: adults $5; members no charge. Truck Show: admission $10; children under 12 no charge. Closed New Year's Day; Christmas. &
Attendance: 18,000 (estimated)

Brownsville

LINN COUNTY HISTORICAL MUSEUM AND MOYER HOUSE, 101 Park Ave., Brownsville, OR 97327. Mailing Address: Box 607, Brownsville, OR 97327-0607. Tel.: 541-466-3390. Facebook: Linn County Historical Museum.
E-mail: lchm@co.linn.or.us
Web Site: linnmuseum.com
Key Personnel: C.E.O., Brian Carrol; Chm. Trust (V), Glenn Harrison; Pres. Friends (V), Roger Geeting; Museum Coord., Mandy Cole; Museum Shop Mgr., Joni Nelson.
Institution Type/Description: Local History Museum: arranged to represent 1800s city with exhibits of businesses operating in the community showing life-style pursuits in other fields such as agriculture, mining & timber; early travel 1850-1920s. Historic House: 1881 Italianate Victorian, Moyer House.
Hours & Admission Prices: Summer: Mon.-Sat. 11-4, Sun. 1-5; Winter: Mon.-Sat. 11-4. Moyer House Guided Tours $5. Closed New Year's Day; Easter; Thanksgiving; Christmas. &
Attendance: 8,298 (estimated)

Burns

HARNEY COUNTY HISTORICAL MUSEUM, 18 W. D St., Burns, OR 97720-1226. Mailing Address: P.O. Box 388, Burns, OR 97720-0388. Tel.: 541-573-5618.
E-mail: harneymuseum@centurytel.net
Web Site: hchistoricalsociety.com
Key Personnel: Pres., Mildred Fine.
Institution Type/Description: General Museum.
Hours & Admission Prices: April -Sept. Tues.-Sat. 10-4. Suggested Donation: family of 5 $15 (additional children $.50 each), couples $8, single $5, senior citizens $3, children 6-17 $.50; discounts to groups; members no charge. &
Attendance: 823 (actual)

Canby

CANBY HISTORICAL SOCIETY, 888 N.E. 4th Ave., Canby, OR 97013-2300. Mailing Address: P.O. Box 160, Canby, OR 97013-0160. Tel.: 503-266-6712.
E-mail: depotmuseum@canby.com
Web Site: www.canbyhistoricalsociety.org
Formerly: Canby Depot Museum
Key Personnel: Pres., Nora Clark; Vice Pres., Cheryl Rahn.
Institution Type/Description: History Museum: housed in an 1891 railroad depot.
Hours & Admission Prices: March-Dec. Thurs.-Sun. 1-4. No charge, suggested Donation: adults $2. Closed holidays; holiday weekends. &
Attendance: 1,100 (estimated)

Cannon Beach

CANNON BEACH HISTORY CENTER AND MUSEUM, 1387 S. Spruce St., Cannon Beach, OR 97110. Mailing Address: P.O. Box 1005, Cannon Beach, OR 97110-1005. Tel.: 503-436-9301. Fax: 503-436-0490.
E-mail: info@cbhistory.org
Web Site: www.cbhistory.org
Key Personnel: Dir., Elaine Trucke; Pres. (V), Kimberley Speer-Miller; Museum Shop Mgr., Liz Johnson.
Institution Type/Description: History Museum.
Hours & Admission Prices: Wed.-Mon. 1-5. No charge; donations accepted. &
Attendance: 3,500 (actual)

Canyon City

GRANT COUNTY HISTORICAL MUSEUM, 101 S. Canyon City Blvd., Hwy. 395, Canyon City, OR 97820. Mailing Address: P.O. Box 464, Canyon City, OR 97820-0464. Tel.: 541-575-0362. Fax: 541-575-0515.
E-mail: museum@ortelco.net
Web Site: www.gchistoricalmuseum.com
Key Personnel: Dir., Jayne Primrose.
Institution Type/Description: Local History Museum: located in Canyon City, site of active gold mining area in 1862.
Hours & Admission Prices: May-Sept. Tues.-Sat. 9-4:30; other times by appointment. Adults $4, senior citizens & veterans $3.50, children 7-16 $2; children under 7 no charge.
Attendance: 1,046 (actual)

Cascade Locks

CASCADE LOCKS HISTORICAL MUSEUM, 1 Marine Dr., Cascade Locks, OR 97014. Mailing Address: P.O. Box 321, Cascade Locks, OR 97014-0307. Tel.: 541-374-8535.
E-mail: rare@portofcascadelocks.org
Web Site: portofcascadelocks.org
Key Personnel: Dir. & Museum Shop Mgr., Pat Power; Chm. (V), Bill Hanket.
Institution Type/Description: History Museum.
Hours & Admission Prices: May-Sept. Tues.-Sun. 12-5. Family $5, adults $3, seniors & children $2; members no charge.
Attendance: 2,202 (actual)

Central Point

CRATER ROCK MUSEUM, 2002 Scenic Ave., Central Point, OR 97502-2185. Mailing Address: P.O. Box 3999, Central Point, OR 97502-0041. Tel.: 541-664-6081. Fax: 541-664-3848.
E-mail: roxyanngems@msn.com
Institution Type/Description: Earth Sciences Museum.
Hours & Admission Prices: Tues.-Sat. 10-4. Adults $4, seniors, students & children $2.

Chiloquin

COLLIER MEMORIAL STATE PARK & LOGGING MUSEUM, 46000 Hwy. 97 N., Chiloquin, OR 97624-9631. Tel.: 541-783-2471. Fax: 541-783-2707.
E-mail: todd.honeywell@oregon.gov
Web Site: oregonstateparks.org/index.cfm?do=parkPage. dsp_parkPage&parkId=165
Key Personnel: Park Mgr., Todd Honeywell.
Institution Type/Description: Logging, Pioneer & Lumber Museum & Village.
Hours & Admission Prices: Museum: daily 8-4. Park: daily dawn-dusk. Office: Mon.-Fri. 8-4:30. No charge; donations accepted. &
Attendance: 88,164

Clackamas

BRIGADIER GENERAL JAMES B. THAYER OREGON MILITARY MUSEUM, Camp Withycombe, 15300 S.E. Minuteman Way, Clackamas, OR 97015. Tel.: 503-683-5359, Fax: 503-683-4913.
E-mail: terese.m.thoennes.civ@mail.mil
Web Site: www.oregonmilitarymuseum.org
Key Personnel: Cur., Tracy Thoennes.
Institution Type/Description: Military History Museum.
Hours & Admission Prices: Temporarily closed for renovation. &
Attendance: 3,500 (actual)

Columbia City

CAPLES HOUSE MUSEUM, 1915 1st St., Columbia City, OR 97018. Mailing Address: Caretaker, Caples Museum, P.O. Box 263, Columbia City, OR 97018-0263. Tel.: 503-397-5390.
E-mail: capleshouse@comcast.net
Web Site: www.rootsweb.com/~orossdar/Caples.htm
Institution Type/Description: Historic House Museum.
Hours & Admission Prices: March-Oct. Fri. 11-4, Sat. 11-3, Sun. 1-3; Nov.-Feb. by appointment. Adults $4, children $3; discounts to members.

Condon

GILLIAM COUNTY HISTORICAL SOCIETY & MUSEUM COMPLEX, Hwy. 19 at Burns Park, Condon, OR 97823. Mailing Address: P.O. Box 377, Condon, OR 97823-0377. Tel.: 541-384-4233.
E-mail: gillamcohistoricalsociety@gmail.com
Web Site: gilliamcountyhistory.org
Key Personnel: Pres. (V), Karen Wilde; Treas., M'Liss Jamieson; Museum Shop Mgr., Sue Dalzell.
Institution Type/Description: History Museum.
Hours & Admission Prices: May-Oct. Wed.-Sun. 1-5; call for holiday hours. No charge; donations accepted. &
Attendance: 882 (actual)

Coos Bay

COOS ART MUSEUM, 235 Anderson, Coos Bay, OR 97420-1610. Tel.: 541-267-3901 & 4877. Fax: 541-267-4877 (please call 267-3901). Facebook.
E-mail: sbroocks@coosart.org
Web Site: www.coosart.org
Key Personnel: Dir., Steven Broocks; Pres. (V), Herb Yussim.
Institution Type/Description: Art Museum: housed in 1935 Post Office building.
Hours & Admission Prices: Tues.-Fri. 10-4, Sat. 1-4. Adults $5, seniors & students $2; discount to veterans; members no charge. &
Attendance: 13,842 (actual)

MARSHFIELD SUN PRINTING MUSEUM, 1049 Front St., Coos Bay, OR 97420. Mailing Address: P.O. Box 783, Coos Bay, OR 97420-0148. Tel.: 541-267-6152.
E-mail: gtinker1@frontier.com
Key Personnel: Pres. (V), George Tinker.
Institution Type/Description: Historic Building Museum: housed in the former Marshfield Sun newspaper building.
Hours & Admission Prices: Memorial Day to Labor Day Tues.-Sat. 10-4; other times by appointment. No charge; donations accepted. &
Attendance: 573 (actual)

Corbett

FRIENDS OF VISTA HOUSE, Crown Point State Park, 40700 E. Historic Columbia River Hwy., Corbett, OR 97019. Mailing Address: Friends of Vista House, P.O. Box 204, Corbett, OR 97019-0204. Tel.: 503-695-2230 & 2240.
E-mail: friends@vistahouse.com
Web Site: www.vistahouse.com
Key Personnel: Exec. Dir., Marguerite Perry.
Institution Type/Description: Historic Building Museum: built in 1916. Listed on the National Register of Historic Places.
Hours & Admission Prices: March-Oct. daily; Nov.-Feb. Sat.-Sun. call for hours. No charge; donations accepted. &
Attendance: 1,000,000 (estimated)

Corvallis

CORVALLIS ARTS CENTER, DBA THE ARTS CENTER, 700 S.W. Madison Ave., Corvallis, OR 97333. Tel.: 541-754-1551. Fax: 541-754-1552. Facebook.
E-mail: info@theartscenter.net
Web Site: theartscenter.net
Formerly: Corvallis Arts Center
Key Personnel: Dir., Cynthia Spencer; Chm. (V), Jeff Gunn; Museum Shop Mgr., Krista Rich.
Institution Type/Description: Art Gallery.
Hours & Admission Prices: Tues.-Sat. 12-5. No charge; donations accepted. &
Attendance: 13,000 (actual)

OREGON STATE UNIVERSITY MEMORIAL UNION CONCOURSE GALLERY, Jefferson St., OSU, Corvallis, OR 97331. Mailing Address: 10 Memorial Union E., Corvallis, OR 97331-8592. Tel.: 541-737-6371. Fax: 541-737-1565.
E-mail: susan.bourque@oregonstate.edu
Web Site: www.osumu.org/about_art.htm
Key Personnel: Dir., Kent Sumner; Coord. Exhibits, Susan Bourque.
Institution Type/Description: Art Institute.
Hours & Admission Prices: June-Aug. Mon.-Fri. 8-5; Sept.-May Mon.-Thurs. 7-11, Fri. 7-12, Sat. 7:30-12, Sun. 8:30-11. No charge. Closed national holidays. &
Attendance: 36,000 (estimated)

Cottage Grove

BOHEMIA GOLD MINING MUSEUM, 308 S. 10th St., Cottage Grove, OR 97424. Mailing Address: P.O. Box 1658, Cottage Grove, OR 97424. Tel.: 541-942-5022.
E-mail: bohemiagoldminingmuseum@gmail.com
Key Personnel: Dir., Sara Smith.
Institution Type/Description: Mining History Museum.
Hours & Admission Prices: Closed for relocation. Call for hours. Suggested Donation: $2.
Attendance: 3,200 (estimated)

COTTAGE GROVE MUSEUM & ANNEX, 147 H St. & Birch Ave., Cottage Grove, OR 97424. Mailing Address: P.O. Box 142, Cottage Grove, OR 97424-0005. Tel.: 541-942-4269 & 968-2254. Facebook: @CottageGroveMuseum.
E-mail: b_bvenice@msn.com
Key Personnel: Chm. (V), Becky Venice; Coord., Tara Sue Hughart; Museum Shop Mgr., Joanne Skelton.
Institution Type/Description: General Museum: housed in former 1896 octagonal Roman Catholic Church.
Hours & Admission Prices: Summer: Fri.-Sun. 1-4; Winter: Sat.-Sun. 1-4. No charge; donations accepted. &
Attendance: 1,500 (estimated)

OREGON AVIATION HISTORICAL SOCIETY, 2475 Jim Wright Way, Cottage Grove, OR 97424. Mailing Address: P.O. Box 553, Cottage Grove, OR 97424. Tel.: 541-767-0244. Facebook.
E-mail: oregonaviation.org@gmail.com
Web Site: www.oregonaviation.org
Key Personnel: Pres. (V), Douglas Kindred.
Institution Type/Description: Historical Society Museum.
Hours & Admission Prices: May-Sept. Sat. 10-4; other times by appointment. No charge; donations accepted. &

Crater Lake

CRATER LAKE NATIONAL PARK, Hwy. 62, Crater Lake, OR 97604. Mailing Address: P.O. Box 7, Crater Lake, OR 97604-0007. Tel.: 541-594-3000.
E-mail: mary_merryman@nps.gov
Web Site: www.nps.gov/crla
Key Personnel: Supt., Craig Ackerman; Administrative Officer, Shawn Parratt.
Institution Type/Description: National Park Museum & Archive.
Hours & Admission Prices: Park Visitor Center: daily 10-4:30. Park entry fee. &
Attendance: 500,000

Depoe Bay

OREGON COAST SPORTS MUSEUM & INTERNATIONAL SPORTS HALL OF FAME AND OLYMPIC MUSEUM, 110 N.E. Hwy. 101, Depoe Bay, OR 97341. Mailing Address: P.O. Box 166, Depoe Bay, OR 97341-0166. Tel.: 541-765-2923, 702-346-1776.
Web Site: www.olympicsource.org
Key Personnel: Exec. Dir. & Museum Shop Mgr., Heidi E. Nash.
Institution Type/Description: Sports Museum.
Hours & Admission Prices: By appointment. Adults $5, children under 12 $3; discounts to groups, AAM & ICOM members; members no charge. &

Echo

CHINESE HOUSE/O.R. & N. MUSEUM & ST. PETER'S CATHOLIC CHURCH, 230 W. Bridge & 33208 Marble, Echo, OR 97826. Mailing Address: P.O. Box 426, Echo, OR 97826-0426. Tel.: 541-376-8411. Fax: 541-376-8218.
E-mail: ecpl@centurytel.net
Web Site: www.echo-oregon.com
Key Personnel: C.E.O., Diane Berry.
Institution Type/Description: History Museum.
Hours & Admission Prices: Call for hours & appointment. No charge; donations accepted.
Attendance: 75 (estimated)

FORT HENRIETTA PARK, 10 W. Main St., Echo, OR 97826. Mailing Address: P.O. Box 9, Echo, OR 97826-0009. Tel.: 541-571-3597.
E-mail: ecpl@centurytel.net
Web Site: www.echo-oregon.com/fort.html
Institution Type/Description: History Museum & Interpretive Center.
Hours & Admission Prices: Park: Mon.-Fri. dawn-dusk. Library: Mon.-Fri. 8:30-4:30. No charge; donations accepted. &

OREGON TRAIL ARBORETUM, 1 Neely Lane, Echo, OR 97826. Mailing Address: 20 S. Bonanza, P.O. Box 9, Echo, OR 97826-0009. Tel.: 541-376-8411. Fax: 541-376-8218.
E-mail: ecpl@centurytel.net
Web Site: www.echo-oregon.com
Key Personnel: Records, Diane Berry; Mayor, Richard Winter, Ph.D.
Institution Type/Description: Arboretum.
Hours & Admission Prices: Mon.-Fri. dawn-dusk. No charge; donations accepted. &

Eugene

CASCADES RAPTOR CENTER, 32275 Fox Hollow Rd., Eugene, OR 97405. Mailing Address: P.O. Box 5386, Eugene, OR 97405. Tel.: 541-485-1320. Fax: 541-485-4586. Facebook: Cascades Raptor Center.
E-mail: info@cascadesraptorcenter.org
Web Site: www.cascadesraptorcenter.org
Key Personnel: Exec. Dir., Louise Shimmel; Pres. (V), Stephanie Hand.
Institution Type/Description: Nature Center.
Hours & Admission Prices: April-Oct. Tues.-Sun. 10-6; Nov.-March Tues.-Sun. 10-4. Adults $8, teens & seniors $7, children under 12 $5; discounts to Assoc. of Nature Center Admin; members no charge.
Attendance: 25,000 (actual)

CONGER STREET CLOCK MUSEUM, 730 Conger St., Eugene, OR 97402. Tel.: 541-344-6359. Fax: 541-338-0869.
Institution Type/Description: Clock History Museum.
Hours & Admission Prices: Mon.-Sat. 10-5:30. No charge.

EUGENE SCIENCE CENTER, 2300 Leo Harris Pkwy., Eugene, OR 97401-8834. Mailing Address: P.O. Box 1518, Eugene, OR 97440-1518. Tel.: 541-682-7888. Fax: 541-484-9027. Facebook.
E-mail: info@eugenesciencecenter.org
Web Site: www.eugenesciencecenter.org
Formerly: Science Factory Children's Museum & Exploration Dome
Key Personnel: Exec. Dir., Tim Scott; Dir. Devel., Scott Rogers; Dir. Operations, Elena Aguero.
Institution Type/Description: Science Museum.
Hours & Admission Prices: July-Aug. daily 10-4; Sept.-June Tues.-Sun. 10-4. Exhibits: adults $5, seniors $4; children 2 & under and members no charge. Planetarium: adults $5, seniors $4; discounts for members; children 2 & under no charge. Combination: adults $8, seniors $6; children 2 & under no charge. Closed New Year's Day; Easter; Independence Day; Thanksgiving; Christmas Eve & Day. ♿
Attendance: 35,000 (actual)

JORDAN SCHNITZER MUSEUM OF ART, 1430 Johnson Lane, Eugene, OR 97403. Mailing Address: 1223 University of Oregon, Eugene, OR 97403-1223. Tel.: 541-346-3027 & 0973. Fax: 541-346-0976.
E-mail: jschnitz@uoregon.edu
Web Site: jsma.uoregon.edu
Formerly: University of Oregon Museum of Art
Key Personnel: Exec. Dir., Jill Hartz; Administrative Asst., Angie Canaday; Leadership Council Pres., Jim Walker; Chief Cur. Collections, Asian Art & Academic Support, Anne Rose Kitagawa; Assoc. Dir. Operations, Exhibits & Museum Shop Mgr., Kurt Neugebauer; Security Mgr., Anthony Cranford; Business Mgr., Karri Pargeter; Accounting, Lisa Montgomery; Dir. Education, Lisa Abia-Smith; Mgr. Collections, Chris White; Chief Preparator, Joey Capadona; Registrar, Miranda Callander; Mgr. Communications, Debbie Williamson-Smith; Visitor Svcs., Jamie Leaf.
Institution Type/Description: Art Museum.
Hours & Admission Prices: Wed. 11-8, Thurs.-Sun. 11-5. Adults $5, seniors $3; discounts to AAM, ICOM & NARM members; Univ. of Oregon students, faculty & staff; high school & non-UO college students, children 13 & under and members no charge. ♿
Attendance: 50,233 (estimated)

LANE COMMUNITY COLLEGE ART GALLERY, 4000 E. 30th Ave., Eugene, OR 97405-0640. Tel.: 541-463-3431. Fax: 541-463-4185.
E-mail: salzmanj@lanecc.edu
Web Site: www.lanecc.edu/artgallery
Key Personnel: Gallery Dir., Jennifer Salzman.
Institution Type/Description: Art Gallery.
Hours & Admission Prices: Sept.-June Mon.-Thurs. 8-9, Fri. 8-4. No charge. Closed New Year's Day; Presidents' Day; Memorial Day; Labor Day; Thanksgiving; Christmas. ♿
Attendance: 12,500 (actual)

LANE COUNTY HISTORICAL SOCIETY & MUSEUM, 740 W. 13th Ave., Eugene, OR 97402-4010. Mailing Address: P.O. Box 5407, Eugene, OR 97405. Tel.: 541-682-4242. Fax: 541-682-7361. Facebook: Lane County Historical Society & Museum.
E-mail: officemanager@lchm.org
Web Site: www.lchm.org
Formerly: Lane County Pioneer Museum
Key Personnel: Dir., Robert L. Hart; Office Mgr., Adrienne Gaudette.
Institution Type/Description: History Museum.
Hours & Admission Prices: Tues.-Sat. 10-4. Adults $5, seniors 60 & over $3, youth 15-17 $1; children under 14 & members no charge. Closed national holidays.
Attendance: 7,000 (actual)

MAUDE I. KERNS ART CENTER, 1910 E. 15th Ave., Eugene, OR 97403-2094. Tel.: 541-345-1571. Fax: 541-345-6248.
E-mail: staff@mkartcenter.org
Web Site: www.mkartcenter.org
Key Personnel: Bd. Pres. (V), David Wade; Exec. Dir., Karen Pavelec; Assoc. Dir., Sabrina Hershey; Exhibits Coord., Michael Fisher; Publicity Coord., Marsha Shankman; Administrative Asst., Kelly McCormick.
Institution Type/Description: Art Museum: housed in 1895 historic landmark church building.
Hours & Admission Prices: Mon.-Fri. 10-5:30, Sat. 12-4. Suggested Donations: family $5, individual $2. ♿
Attendance: 60,000 (estimated)

MOUNT PISGAH ARBORETUM, 34901 Frank Parrish Rd., Eugene, OR 97405-9673. Tel.: 541-747-3817. Fax: 541-741-4904.
E-mail: office@mountpisgaharboretum.org

Web Site: www.mountpisgaharboretum.org
Key Personnel: Exec. Dir., Brad van Appel; Pres. Bd., Lann Leslie; Site Mgr., Tom LoCascio; Education Mgr., Jenny Laxton.
Institution Type/Description: Arboretum-Botanical Garden.
Hours & Admission Prices: Daily dawn-dusk. No charge; donations accepted. ♿
Attendance: 400,000 (estimated)

OREGON AIR & SPACE MUSEUM, 90377 Boeing Dr., Eugene, OR 97402-9536. Tel.: 541-461-1101. Fax: 541-461-1101.
E-mail: charalyn@charink.com
Web Site: oasm.info
Key Personnel: Pres. (V), Bruce Lamont; Dir. Operations & Museum Shop Mgr., Charalyn Glade.
Institution Type/Description: Aviation & Space Museum.
Hours & Admission Prices: April-Oct. Wed.-Sun. 12-4; Nov.-March Wed.-Sat. 12-4. Adults $7, senior citizens 62 & up $6, children 6-17 $3; children 5 & under, members, Pearson Air Museums, Seattle Museums of Flight, Lane Community College, Civil Air Patrol & LEC Aviation Academy members no charge; group rates available; rental rates negotiable. Closed some holidays. ♿
Attendance: 4,000 (estimated)

SHELTON MCMURPHEY JOHNSON HOUSE, 303 Willamette St., Eugene, OR 97405. Tel.: 541-484-0808. Facebook.
E-mail: director@smjhouse.org
Web Site: www.smjhouse.org
Institution Type/Description: Historic House Museum: built in 1888.
Hours & Admission Prices: Tues.-Fri. 10-1, Sat.-Sun. 1-4. Adults $6, children $3; discounts to AAA, seniors, students & groups.
Attendance: 3,800 (actual)

UNIVERSITY OF OREGON MUSEUM OF NATURAL AND CULTURAL HISTORY, 1680 E. 15th Ave., Eugene, OR 97403-1224. Mailing Address: 1224 University of Oregon, Eugene, OR 97403-1224. Tel.: 541-346-3024. Fax: 541-346-5334. Facebook.
E-mail: mnch@uoregon.edu
Web Site: natural-history.uoregon.edu
Key Personnel: Exec. Dir., Jon M. Erlandson; Assoc. Dir., Scott Fitzpatrick; Archeological Research Dir., Thomas J. Connolly; Exhibitions & Public Programs, Ann Craig; Anthropological Collections Dir., Pamela Endzweig; Condon Fossil Collection Dir., Greg Retallack; Oregon Folklife Network Dir., Riki Saltzman.
Institution Type/Description: Natural History Museum. (Association of Science - Associated member with ASTC Technology Centers).
Hours & Admission Prices: Tues.-Sun. 11-5. Family $12, adults $6, seniors & youth $4; discounts to EBT cardholders through Museums for All Program; UO students, faculty & staff and MNCH members no charge. ASTC & NARM reciprocal benefits. Closed New Year's Day; Independence Day; Thanksgiving; Christmas. ♿
Attendance: 29,000 (estimated)

Fairview

EAST COUNTY HISTORICAL ORGANIZATION (ECHO), 60 Main St., Fairview, OR 97024. Mailing Address: P.O. Box 946, Fairview, OR 97024-0946. Tel.: 503-618-0946. Facebook; Twitter; Istagram.
E-mail: info@echohistory.org
Web Site: www.echohistory.org
Formerly: Zimmerman House and Heslin House Museums
Formerly: Fairview-Rockwood-Wilkes Historical Society
Key Personnel: Pres., Peggy Olin; Treas., Twila Mysinger.
Institution Type/Description: Heslin House with gardens; historic jailhouse.
Hours & Admission Prices: Tours: 3rd Sat. of month 12-4. Adults $2; Fairview residents, ECHO members & children under 13 no charge. ♿

Florence

SIUSLAW PIONEER MUSEUM, 278 Maple St., Florence, OR 97439. Mailing Address: P.O. Box 2637, Florence, OR 97439-0164. Tel.: 541-997-7884.
E-mail: museum@winfinity.com
Web Site: www.siuslawpioneermuseum.com
Key Personnel: Chm. (v), Del Phelps; Pres. (V), Stephen Skidmore.
Institution Type/Description: History Museum.
Hours & Admission Prices: Feb.-Nov. Tues.-Sun. 12-4. Adults $3; children under 16 & members no charge. Closed Easter; Thanksgiving; Christmas.
Attendance: 2,458 (actual)

Forest Grove

PACIFIC UNIVERSITY MUSEUM, Pacific University, 2043 College Way, Forest Grove, OR 97116-1756. Tel.: 503-352-2211. Fax: 503-352-2252.
E-mail: deni@pacificu.edu
Web Site: www.pacificu.edu
Key Personnel: Pres., Dr. Lesley M. Hallick.
Institution Type/Description: History Museum housed in: 1850 Old College Hall.
Hours & Admission Prices: First Wed. 1-4, or by appointment. No charge; donations accepted. Closed university vacations & holidays.
Attendance: 1,500 (estimated)

VALLEY ART GALLERY, 2022 Main St., Forest Grove, OR 97116. Mailing Address: P.O. Box 333, Forest Grove, OR 97116. Tel.: 503-357-3703. Facebook: Valley Art Association.
E-mail: office@valleyart.org
Web Site: www.valleyart.org
Key Personnel: Pres., Dana Zurcher.
Institution Type/Description: Art Gallery.
Hours & Admission Prices: Mon.-Sat. 11-5:30. No charge. Closed New Year's Day; Thanksgiving; Christmas.
Attendance: 1,000 (estimated)

Fort Rock

FORT ROCK VALLEY HISTORICAL HOMESTEAD MUSEUM, 64696 Fort Rock Rd., Fort Rock, OR 97735. Mailing Address: Fort Rock Valley Historical Society, P.O. Box 84, Fort Rock, OR 97735-0084. Tel.: 541-576-2207.
E-mail: frmuseum@centurylink.net
Institution Type/Description: Historic Buildings: eleven buildings in a village setting.
Hours & Admission Prices: mid-May to mid-Sept. Fri.-Sun. 10-4. Admission 12 & over $1.

Fossil

FOSSIL MUSEUM, 501 First St., Fossil, OR 97830. Mailing Address: P.O. Box 465, Fossil, OR 97830-0465. Tel.: 541-763-2113. Fax: 541-763-2026. Facebook: Fossil Museum, Fossil, Oregon.
E-mail: mgg1939@centurytel.net
Key Personnel: Pres. (V), Donna D. Hopper; Chmn. (V), Marilyn G. Garcia.
Institution Type/Description: History Museum.
Hours & Admission Prices: Memorial Day to Labor Day Mon. & Wed.-Sun. 1-4. No charge; donations accepted
Attendance: 1,054 (actual)

Garibaldi

GARIBALDI MUSEUM, 112 Garibaldi Ave., Garibaldi, OR 97118. Mailing Address: P.O. Box 5, Garibaldi, OR 97118. Tel.: 503-322-8411. Fax: 503-322-8411.
E-mail: info@garibaldimuseum.org
Web Site: www.garibaldimuseum.org
Key Personnel: Dir. & Museum Shop Mgr., Anna Rzuczek; Pres. (V), Christine Bacon.
Institution Type/Description: Maritime Museum.
Hours & Admission Prices: March-Nov. Thurs.-Mon. 10-4; other times by appointment. Admission 10 & over $4, seniors $3; discounts to groups of 10 or more; children 10 & under no charge.
Attendance: 4,000 (actual)

Gold Beach

ROGUE RIVER MUSEUM, 29880 Harbor Dr., Gold Beach, OR 97444. Mailing Address: P.O. Box 1011, Gold Beach, OR 97444-1011. Tel.: 541-247-4571.
E-mail: jerrys@roguejets.com
Web Site: www.roguejets.com/museum.php
Institution Type/Description: History Museum.
Hours & Admission Prices: July-Aug. daily 9-9; Sept.-June Mon.-Sat. 9-6, Sun. 10-5.

Government Camp

MT. HOOD CULTURAL CENTER & MUSEUM, 88900 E. Hwy. 26, Business Loop, Government Camp, OR 97028. Mailing Address: P.O. Box 55, Government Camp, OR 97028-0055. Tel.: 503-272-3301. Facebook: Mt. Hood Museum.
E-mail: info@mthoodmuseum.org
Web Site: www.mthoodmuseum.org
Key Personnel: Pres. (V), Lloyd Musser; Museum Shop Mgr., Cheryl Maki.
Institution Type/Description: History Museum.
Hours & Admission Prices: Daily 9-5. No charge; donations accepted. Closed Thanksgiving; Christmas.
Attendance: 20,000 (actual)

Grand Ronde

CHACHALU TRIBAL MUSEUM & CULTURAL CENTER, 9615 Grand Ronde Rd., Grand Ronde, OR 97347-9712. Tel.: 503-879-2248. Fax: 503-879-2126.
E-mail: david.lewis@grandronde.org
Web Site: www.grandronde.org
Formerly: Confederated Tribes of Grand Ronde Cultural Resources Department Museum & Cultural Center
Key Personnel: Education & Outreach, Kathy Cole; Coord. Site Protection & Tribal Historic Preservation Officer, Eirik Thorsgard; Language & Cultural Specialist, Bobby Mercier; Interpretive Specialist, Julie Brown; Cultural Resources Specialist, Brian Krehbiel; Tribal Historian, David Lewis; Cultural Collections Specialist, Veronica Montano; Site Protection Specialist, David Harrelson; Archaeologist, Briece Edwards; Land & Culture Mgr., Jan Rubach; Sec., Flicka Lucero.
Institution Type/Description: Tribal Museum.
Hours & Admission Prices: Offices: Mon.-Fri. 8-5. Closed New Year's Day; Presidents' Day; Independence Day; Labor Day; Veterans Day; Thanksgiving; Christmas; National Indian Day; Restoration Day.

Grants Pass

GRANTS PASS MUSEUM OF ART, 229 S.W. G St., Grants Pass, OR 97526-2415. Mailing Address: P.O. Box 966, Grants Pass, OR 97528-0081. Tel.: 541-479-3290. Facebook.
E-mail: museum@gpmuseum.com
Web Site: www.gpmuseum.com
Key Personnel: Exec. Dir., Hyla Lipson; Pres. (V), Nancy Yonally Coleman; Museum Shop Mgr., Cindy Kahoun.
Institution Type/Description: Art Museum.
Hours & Admission Prices: Tues.-Sat. 10-5. No charge; donations accepted. Closed New Year's Day; Easter; Memorial Day; Independence Day; Labor Day; Thanksgiving; Christmas.
Attendance: 21,346 (actual)

SCHMIDT HOUSE MUSEUM & RESEARCH LIBRARY, 508 & 512 S.W. 5th St., Grants Pass, OR 97526-2804. Mailing Address: 512 S.W. 5th St., Grants Pass, OR 97526-2804. Tel.: 541-479-7827.
E-mail: jchistoricalsociety@gmail.com
Web Site: www.jocohistorical.org
Key Personnel: Dir., Rose Scott; Chm. (V) & Pres. (V), Joan Momsen; Museum Shop Mgr., Martha Metcalf.
Institution Type/Description: Historic House & Research Library.
Hours & Admission Prices: Tues.-Fri. 10-4. Admission $10; discount to AAA members.
Attendance: 1,500 (estimated)

WISEMAN & FIREHOUSE GALLERIES, ROGUE COMMUNITY COLLEGE, 3345 Redwood Hwy., Grants Pass, OR 97527-9291. Tel.: 541-956-7241. Fax: 503-471-3588.
E-mail: kbrake@roguecc.edu
Web Site: www.roguecc.edu/galleries
Key Personnel: Dir., Karl Brake; Pres. Rogue Community College, Cathy Kemper-Pelle; Gallery Coord., Heather Green.
Institution Type/Description: Art Galleries: the FireHouse Gallery is housed in the firehouse portion of historic city hall; the Wiseman Gallery is located on the Redwood Campus & Rogue Community College campus in the Wiseman Center.
Hours & Admission Prices: Wiseman Gallery: Mon.-Thurs. 8-7, Fri. 8-3. FireHouse Gallery: Tues.-Fri. 11:30-4:30. No charge. Closed national holidays & between college quarters. Call for summer hours.
Attendance: 19,000 (estimated)

Gresham

ECHO-THE ZIMMERMAN HOUSE, 17111 N.E. Sandy Blvd., Gresham, OR 97230. Mailing Address: P.O. Box 946, Fairview, OR 97024-0946. Tel.: 503-618-0946. Facebook; Twitter; Instagram.
E-mail: info@echohistory.org
Web Site: www.echohistory.org
Key Personnel: Pres., Peggy Olin; Treas., Twila Mysinger.
Institution Type/Description: Historic House Museum: built in 1874.
Hours & Admission Prices: 3rd Sat. each month 12-4. Adults $7, seniors $5; ECHO members & children under 13 no charge.

GRESHAM HISTORY MUSEUM, 410 N. Main Ave., Gresham, OR 97030-7212. Mailing Address: P.O. Box 65, Gresham, OR 97030-0011. Tel.: 503-661-0347. Facebook.
E-mail: greshamhistorical@gmail.com
Web Site: www.greshamhistoricalsociety.org
Formerly: Gresham Pioneer Museum
Key Personnel: Pres., David Baumann; Museum Coord., Matt Holland; Collections Mgr., Silvie Andrews.
Institution Type/Description: Historical Society Museum: housed in 1913 Carnegie library.
Hours & Admission Prices: Tues. & Thurs. 10-4, Fri. 2-8, Sat. 10-2. Donations requested. &
Attendance: 2,948 (actual)

Haines

EASTERN OREGON MUSEUM, 610 Third St., Haines, OR 97833-6388. Mailing Address: 14514 Muddy Creek Lane, Haines, OR 97833-6388. Tel.: 541-856-3233. Facebook: Eastern Oregon Museum.
E-mail: riderm622@gmail.com
Formerly: Eastern Oregon Museum on the Old Oregon Trail
Key Personnel: Pres. & Chm (V), Barbara Campbell; Vice Pres., Viola Perkins; Treas., Mary Rider; Sec., Teri Johnson.
Institution Type/Description: General Museum: housed in a 1931 old school gym.
Hours & Admission Prices: May 15-Sept. 15 Thurs.-Sun. & holidays 10-3:30; other times by appointment. Family $5, adult $3. &
Attendance: 4,000 (actual)

Hammond

FORT STEVENS HISTORIC MILITARY SITE & MUSEUM, Fort Stevens State Park, 100 Peter Iredale Rd., Hammond, OR 97121-9712. Tel.: 503-861-2000. Facebook: Fort Stevens Historic Military Site.
E-mail: foofs@teleport.com
Key Personnel: Pres. (V), Teri Buckmeir; Museum Shop Mgr., Laura Neal.
Institution Type/Description: Historic Site: listed on the National Register of Historic Places.
Hours & Admission Prices: June-Sept. daily 10-6; Oct.-May daily 10-4. No charge; donations accepted. Closed New Year's Day; Christmas.
Attendance: 46,296 (actual)

Heppner

AGRICULTURAL EQUIPMENT MUSEUM, Riverside & A Sts., Heppner, OR 97836. Mailing Address: P.O. Box 515, Heppner, OR 97836. Tel.: 541-676-5546.
Institution Type/Description: History Museum.
Hours & Admission Prices: May-Sept. Tues.-Fri. 1-5, Sat. 11-3.

MORROW COUNTY MUSEUM, 444 N. Main St., Heppner, OR 97836. Mailing Address: P.O. Box 1153, Heppner, OR 97836. Tel.: 541-676-5524.
E-mail: heritagemuseum@hotmail.com
Institution Type/Description: History Museum.
Hours & Admission Prices: May-Sept. Tues.-Fri. 1-5, Sat. 11-3; other times by appointment. No charge; donations accepted.

Hillsboro

CLASSIC AIRCRAFT AVIATION MUSEUM, 3005 N.E. Cornell Rd., Hillsboro, OR 97124-6316. Mailing Address: P.O. Box 91430, Portland, OR 97291-0430. Tel.: 503-693-1414.
E-mail: donkel@classicaircraft.org
Web Site: www.classicaircraft.org

Key Personnel: Dir., Doug Donkel, Ph.D.
Institution Type/Description: Aviation Museum.
Hours & Admission Prices: Mon.-Thurs. 9-4.

RICE NORTHWEST MUSEUM OF ROCKS AND MINERALS, 26385 N.W. Groveland Dr., Hillsboro, OR 97124-9351. Tel.: 503-647-2418.
E-mail: info@ricenorthwestmuseum.org
Web Site: www.ricenorthwestmuseum.org
Key Personnel: Exec. Dir., Melena Wallace.
Institution Type/Description: Geology Museum.
Hours & Admission Prices: Wed.-Sun. 1-5; groups by appointment. Adults $7, seniors $6, students 5-17 $5; members & children under 5 no charge. Closed New Year's Day; Independence Day; Thanksgiving; Christmas. &
Attendance: 30,000 (actual)

Hood River

THE HISTORY MUSEUM OF HOOD RIVER COUNTY, 300 E. Port Marina Dr., Hood River, OR 97031-1198. Mailing Address: P.O. Box 781, Hood River, OR 97031-0026. Tel.: 541-386-6772. Fax: 541-386-6772.
E-mail: heritagecouncil@gmail.com
Web Site: hoodriverhistorymuseum.org
Formerly: Hood River County Historical Museum
Key Personnel: Chm. Hood River County Heritage Council, Deborah Chenoweth; Vice Chm., Roberta Schweller; Exec. Dir., Lynn Federle Orr, Ph.D.; Museum Shop, Elaine Johnson.
Institution Type/Description: General Museum.
Hours & Admission Prices: Mon.-Sat. 11-4. Admission $5; military & their families, children under 10 & members no charge. Closed major holidays. &
Attendance: 5,300 (estimated)

WESTERN ANTIQUE AEROPLANE & AUTOMOBILE MUSEUM, Ken Jernstedt Airfield 4S2, 1600 Air Museum Rd., Hood River, OR 97031-9800. Tel.: 541-308-1600. Fax: 541-308-1601.
E-mail: info@waaamuseum.org
Web Site: www.waaamuseum.org
Key Personnel: Pres. & Founder, Terry Brandt; Dir., Judy Newman; Dir. Restorations, Jakonah Matson Bell.
Institution Type/Description: Transportation History Museum.
Hours & Admission Prices: Daily 9-5. Adults $14, senior citizens & veterans $12, students 5-18 $6; children 4 & under and active military with ID no charge. Closed New Year's Day; Thanksgiving; Christmas. &
Attendance: 40,000 (actual)

Independence

HERITAGE MUSEUM SOCIETY, 112 S. 3rd St., Independence, OR 97351. Mailing Address: P.O. Box 7, Independence, OR 97351-0007. Tel.: 503-838-4989.
Web Site: orheritage.org
Key Personnel: Dir., Robin Puccetti; Cur., Peggy Smith; Society Pres., Kathy Pomeroy; Aide, Shannon Cockayne.
Institution Type/Description: Historical Society Museum & Historic Site.
Hours & Admission Prices: Wed.-Sat. 1-5; groups of 10 or more by appointment. Admission $3; members no charge.
Attendance: 1,837 (actual)

John Day

KAM WAH CHUNG STATE HERITAGE SITE, Ing Hay Way, John Day, OR 97845. Mailing Address: P.O. Box 115, John Day, OR 97845-0115. Tel.: 541-575-2800, 800-551-6949.
E-mail: park.info@oregon.gov
Web Site: www.oregonstateparks.org
Formerly: Kam Wah Chung & Co. Museum
Key Personnel: Dir., Lisa Sumption; Cur., Don Merritt.
Institution Type/Description: Chinese Heritage Museum.
Hours & Admission Prices: Museum Tours: May-Oct. daily 9-12 & 1-5. No charge.
Attendance: 9,000 (actual)

Joseph

WALLOWA COUNTY MUSEUM, 110 S. Main, Joseph, OR 97846. Mailing Address: P.O. Box 430, Joseph, OR 97846-0430. Tel.: 541-432-6095.
E-mail: sroberts@co.wallowa.or.us
Key Personnel: Bd. Chm., Caryl Coppin; Cur., Ann Hayes.

Institution Type/Description: History Museum.
Hours & Admission Prices: Memorial Day to late Sept. daily 10-5; other times by appointment. Adults $4, seniors 65 & over $3, children 7-17 $2; children 6 & under no charge.

Junction City

JUNCTION CITY HISTORICAL SOCIETY, 655 Holly St., Junction City, OR 97448-1631. Tel.: 541-952-0900.
E-mail: cgoodin253@msn.com
Web Site: www.junctioncity.com/history
Key Personnel: Pres., Linda VanOrden; Vice Pres., Dale Rowe; Cur., Kitty Goodin.
Institution Type/Description: History Museum & House: housed in 1872 Dr. Norman Lee house, first doctor in Junction City.
Hours & Admission Prices: Thurs. 3-5, first Sat. of month 1-4. No charge; donations accepted.
Attendance: 1,424 (actual)

Keizer

KEIZER HERITAGE MUSEUM, 980 Chemawa Rd., N.E., Keizer, OR 97307-3716. Mailing Address: P.O. Box 20845, Keizer, OR 97307-0845. Tel.: 503-393-9660. Fax: 503-393-0209.
E-mail: heritage@wvi.com
Web Site: www.keizerheritage.org
Key Personnel: Co Dir., Evelyn Franz; Co Dir., Ray Hanson; Pres. (V), Judy Peterson.
Institution Type/Description: History Museum.
Hours & Admission Prices: Tues. & Thurs. 2-4, Sat. 10-4. No charge; donations accepted. &
Attendance: 1,317 (actual)

Kerby

KERBYVILLE MUSEUM, 24195 Redwood Hwy., Kerby, OR 97531. Mailing Address: P.O. Box 3003, Kerby, OR 97531-3003. Tel.: 541-592-5252.
Key Personnel: Pres., Dennis Strayer; Vice Pres., Lloydeen K. Davis; Sec., Donna Tellyer; Treas., Chuck Rigby.
Institution Type/Description: History Museum: part of which is housed in 1880s Old Naucke Residence located on the site of the Old Town of Kerbyville.
Hours & Admission Prices: mid-May to mid-Sept. Thurs.-Tues. 11-3. Adults $4, seniors $3, children 6-16 $2; discount to school groups & families; children under 6 no charge. &
Attendance: 1,000 (estimated)

Kimberly

JOHN DAY FOSSIL BEDS NATIONAL MONUMENT, 32651 Hwy. 19, Kimberly, OR 97848-6228. Tel.: 541-987-2333 (administrative). Fax: 541-987-2336. TDD: 541-987-2334.
E-mail: joda_paleontology@nps.gov
Web Site: www.nps.gov/joda
Key Personnel: Supt., Sheley Hall; Collections Mgr., Chris Schierup; Chief Interpretation, Jeff Axel; Cur., Joshua Samuels; Preparator, Jennifer Cavin.
Institution Type/Description: Park Museum.
Hours & Admission Prices: Daily 9-5. No charge; donations accepted. Closed federal holidays. &
Attendance: 30,000 (estimated)

Klamath Falls

FAVELL MUSEUM INC., 125 W. Main St., Klamath Falls, OR 97601-4287. Tel.: 541-882-9996.
E-mail: favellmuseum@gmail.com
Web Site: www.favellmuseum.org
Formerly: Favell Museum of Western Art and Indian Artifacts
Key Personnel: Dir., Janann Loetscher; Cur., Patsy McMillan; Museum Shop Mgr., Misti Chamberlain.
Institution Type/Description: Indian History & Fine Arts Museum: located on an old Indian camp.
Hours & Admission Prices: Tues.-Sat. 10-5. Adults $10, children 6-16 $5; members and children 5 & under no charge.
Attendance: 4,000 (estimated)

KLAMATH COUNTY MUSEUM, 1451 Main St., Klamath Falls, OR 97601-5989. Tel.: 541-883-4208. Fax: 541-883-5710.
E-mail: tkepple@co.klamath.or.us
Web Site: www.co.klamath.or.us/museum/index.htm

Key Personnel: Mgr., Todd Kepple; Cur., Lynn Jeche; Museum Shop Mgr., Nancy Sieverts; Museum Asst., Susan Rambo.
Institution Type/Description: History & Natural History Museum.
Hours & Admission Prices: Klamath County Museum: Tues.-Sat. 9-5. Adults 13 & over $5, seniors & students $4; children 12 & under no charge. Baldwin Hotel Museum: June-Sept. Wed.-Sat. 10-4. Adults $10. Ft. Klamath Museum: June to Labor Day Thurs.-Mon. 10-6. No charge; donations accepted. Closed major holidays.
Attendance: 15,000 (estimated)

SENATOR GEORGE BALDWIN HOTEL, 31 Main St., Klamath Falls, OR 97601-3174. Mailing Address: 1451 Main St., Klamath Falls, OR 97601-5915. Tel.: 541-883-4208. Fax: 541-883-5170.
Key Personnel: Mgr., Todd Kepple; Cur., Lynn Jeche.
Institution Type/Description: Historic Houses & Historic Buildings Museum: Victorian 3 story structure built in 1906.
Hours & Admission Prices: June-Sept. Tues.-Sat. 10-4. Adults $2, seniors & students $1; children 6 and under & members no charge.
Attendance: 4,500 (estimated)

La Grande

EASTERN OREGON FIRE MUSEUM & LEARNING CENTER, 207 Depot St., La Grande, OR 97850-2618. Tel.: 541-963-8588. Fax: 541-963-3936.
Institution Type/Description: Fire Museum: housed in the former fire station of downtown La Grande. Listed on the National Register of Historic Places.
Hours & Admission Prices: Memorial Day to Labor Day Mon.-Fri. 9-5, Sat. 9-3; Sept.-May Mon.-Fri. 9-5; other times by appointment. No charge; donations accepted.

Lakeview

SCHMINCK MEMORIAL MUSEUM, 128 S. E St., Lakeview, OR 97630-1721. Mailing Address: 1069 Piper Sonoma St., Eugene, OR 97404-3810. Tel.: 541-947-3134.
E-mail: dandlschminck@centurytel.net
Key Personnel: Dir., Monica Lawson.
Institution Type/Description: History Museum: housed in the former home of pioneers, Dalph & Lula Schminck; home is a Sears Craftsmen Built house ordered from Sears Catalog 1922.
Hours & Admission Prices: March-Oct. Wed.-Sat. 11-4. Adults & teens $4, seniors $3; children under 13 no charge. Closed holidays.
Attendance: 800 (estimated)

Lincoln City

NORTH LINCOLN COUNTY HISTORICAL MUSEUM, 4907 S. W. Hwy. 101, Lincoln City, OR 97367-1417. Tel.: 541-996-6614. Fax: 541-996-1244.
E-mail: mlchmdirector@gmail.com
Web Site: northlincolncountyhistoricalmuseum.org
Key Personnel: Exec. Dir., Anne Hall; Museum Shop Mgr., Cindy Weitzel.
Institution Type/Description: History Museum.
Hours & Admission Prices: Feb.-May & Sept.-Dec. 15 Wed.-Sat. 12-5; June-Aug. Wed.-Sun. 12-5. No charge. Closed holidays. &
Attendance: 7,200 (actual)

Madras

ERICKSON AIRCRAFT COLLECTION, Mailing Address: 2408 NW Berg Dr., Madras, OR 97741. Tel.: 541-460-5065. Fax: 541-460-5014.
E-mail: info@ericksoncollection.com
Web Site: www.ericksoncollection.com
Formerly: Tillamook Naval Air Station Museum
Key Personnel: Gen. Mgr., Mike Oliver; Asst. Mgr., Michelle Forster; Museum Shop Mgr., Michelle Forster.
Institution Type/Description: General Museum.
Hours & Admission Prices: Daily 9-5. Adults $9, senior citizens & military with active ID $8, youth 6-17 $5; children 5 & under no charge. Closed Thanksgiving; Christmas. &
Attendance: 80,000 (actual)

Marylhurst

THE ART GYM, Marylhurst University, 17600 Pacific Hwy. 43, Marylhurst, OR 97036-0261. Mailing Address: P.O. Box 261, Marylhurst, OR 97036-0261. Tel.: 503-699-6243 & 636-8141. Fax: 503-636-9526.

E-mail: artgym@marylhurst.edu
Web Site: www.marylhurst.edu
Formerly: The Art Gym at Marylhurst University
Key Personnel: Dir. & Cur., Terri M. Hopkins.
Institution Type/Description: University Museum.
Hours & Admission Prices: Jan.-June & Sept.-Nov. Tues.-Sun. 12-4. No charge; donations accepted. Closed on holidays. &
Attendance: 5,000 (actual)

McMinnville

EVERGREEN AVIATION & SPACE MUSEUM, 500 N.E. Captain Michael King Smith Way, McMinnville, OR 97128-8877. Tel.: 503-434-4180 & 4185. Fax: 503-434-4188.
E-mail: publicity@sprucegoose.org
Web Site: www.evergreenmuseum.org
Formerly: Evergreen Airventure Museum
Key Personnel: Exec. Dir., Larry Wood; Dir. Operations, Philip Jaeger; Dir. Public Rels. & Mktg., Kasey Richter; Chm. (V), Delford M. Smith; Dir. Special Events, Melissa Grace; Dir. Finance, Olga Mery; Cur., Stewart Bailey.
Institution Type/Description: Aeronautics & Space Museum.
Hours & Admission Prices: Daily 9-5. Museum: adults 17-64 $20, seniors 65 & over $19, youth 5-16 $18; members no charge. Museum & 3D Theater: adults $27, seniors 65 & over $26, youth 5-16 $25; discounts to ASTC members; members no charge. Closed holidays. &
Attendance: 250,000 (estimated)

Medford

KID TIME!, 106 N. Central Ave., Medford, OR 97501. Tel.: 541-772-9922. Fax: 541-773-5713.
E-mail: kidtimediscoverymedford@gmail.com
Web Site: www.kid-time.org
Formerly: Kids' Imagination Discovery Space
Institution Type/Description: Children's Museum.
Hours & Admission Prices: Mon.-Sat. 10-5, Sun. 12-5. Children $6, adults $3; children under 1 & members no charge.

ROGUE GALLERY & ART CENTER, 40 S. Bartlett, Medford, OR 97501-7216. Tel.: 541-772-8118. Fax: 541-772-0294.
E-mail: director@roguegallery.org
Web Site: www.roguegallery.org
Key Personnel: Exec. Dir., Kim Hearon; Administrative Asst., Rachel Barrett; Dir. Education, Brooke Nuckles Genteko.
Institution Type/Description: Visual Art Center & Art Gallery.
Hours & Admission Prices: Tues.-Fri. 10-5, Sat. 11-3. No charge; donations accepted. Closed national holidays. &
Attendance: 20,000 (estimated)

SOUTHERN OREGON HISTORICAL SOCIETY, 106 N. Central Ave., Medford, OR 97501. Tel.: 541-773-6536. Fax: 541-776-7994.
E-mail: communicate@sohs.org
Web Site: www.sohs.org
Key Personnel: Devel. Dir., Diana Drews; Archivist, Pat Harper; Educational Program Asst., Joelle Jorissen; Assoc. Cur. Collections, Tina Reuwsaat; Exhibitions Cur., Amy Drake; Library Mgr., Billie Taylor.
Institution Type/Description: History Museum & Historic Sites.
Hours & Admission Prices: Call 541-773-6536 for hours & admission prices. Members no charge. Closed New Year's Day; Thanksgiving; Christmas. &
Attendance: 269,867 (actual)

Milton Freewater

FRAZIER FARMSTEAD MUSEUM, 1403 Chestnut St., Milton Freewater, OR 97862. Mailing Address: P.O. Box 764, Milton Freewater, OR 97862-0764. Tel.: 541-938-4636 & 3480.
E-mail: frazier1868@gmail.com
Web Site: www.frazierfarmsteadmuseum.org
Institution Type/Description: Historic Farmstead: housed in the former home of community founder, W.S. Frazier; built in 1892. Listed on the National Register of Historic Places.
Hours & Admission Prices: April-Dec. Thurs.-Sat. 11-4; other times by appointment. No charge; donations accepted.

Milwaukie

MILWAUKIE MUSEUM, 3737 S.E. Adams St., Milwaukie, OR 97222-5917. Tel.: 503-659-5780.
E-mail: tutumom@msn.com

Web Site: milwaukiemuseum.tripod.com
Key Personnel: Pres. (V), Adele Wilder.
Institution Type/Description: Historic House Museum: housed in the former home of the George Wise family, built in 1865.
Hours & Admission Prices: Sat. 1-5. No charge; donations accepted. Closed Easter; Christmas. &
Attendance: 650 (estimated)

Moro

SHERMAN COUNTY HISTORICAL MUSEUM, 200 Dewey St., Moro, OR 97039. Mailing Address: P.O. Box 173, Moro, OR 97039. Tel.: 541-565-3232. Facebook: Sherman County Historical Society & Museum.
E-mail: info@shermanmuseum.org; director@shermanmuseum.org
Web Site: www.shermanmuseum.org
Institution Type/Description: Historical Society Museum.
Hours & Admission Prices: May-Oct. daily 10-5. Adults $5, children $1; discounts to groups & Blue Star Museum members. &
Attendance: 2,050 (actual)

Myrtle Point

COOS COUNTY LOGGING MUSEUM, 705 Maple St., Myrtle Point, OR 97458. Mailing Address: P.O. Box 325, Myrtle Point, OR 97458-0325. Tel.: 541-572-1014.
E-mail: manager@ci.myrtlepoint.or.us
Key Personnel: Pres. (V), Richard Bushnell.
Institution Type/Description: Logging Museum.
Hours & Admission Prices: Mon.-Sat. 10-4, Sun. 1-4. No charge; donations accepted. &
Attendance: 4,800 (estimated)

Newberg

HOOVER-MINTHORN HOUSE MUSEUM, 115 S. River St., Newberg, OR 97132-3153. Mailing Address: P.O. Box 1212, Newberg, OR 97132-8212. Tel.: 503-538-6629. Facebook.
E-mail: hooverminthornhousemuseum@gmail.org
Web Site: www.hooverminthorn.org
Key Personnel: Dir., Sarah B. Munro; Chm. (V), Anita Barbey; Pres. (V), Nancy Pedersen.
Institution Type/Description: Historic House Museum: housed in the boyhood home of President Herbert Hoover, 1885-1888; built in 1881. Listed on the National Register of Historic Places.
Hours & Admission Prices: Feb. & Dec. Sat.-Sun. 1-4; March-Nov. Wed.-Sun. 1-4. Family $20 maximum, adults $5, students & seniors $3; discounts to veterans and AAM & ICOM members; children under 10 & cultural partners no charge. Closed holidays.
Attendance: 1,200 (estimated)

Newport

LINCOLN COUNTY HISTORICAL SOCIETY, Pacific Maritime Heritage Center, 333 S.E. Bay Blvd., Newport, OR 97365-4726. Mailing Address: 545 S.W. 9th St., Newport, OR 97365-4726. Tel.: 541-265-7509. Fax: 541-265-3992. Facebook.
E-mail: lchs@oregoncoasthistory.org
Web Site: www.oregoncoasthistory.org
Formerly: Oregon Coast History Center
Key Personnel: Dir., Steve Wyatt; Pres. (V), Robert Olson; Finance & Museum Shop Mgr., Colleen Tod.
Institution Type/Description: History Museums.
Hours & Admission Prices: Pacific Maritime Heritage Center and Burrows House: Thurs.-Sun. 11-4. Center: adults $5; children under 12 no charge. Burrows House: by donation. Closed New Year's Day; Independence Day; Thanksgiving; Christmas. &
Attendance: 15,000 (actual)

NEWPORT VISUAL ARTS CENTER, 777 N.W. Beach Dr., Newport, OR 97365. Tel.: 541-265-6540. Facebook.
E-mail: twebb@coastarts.org
Web Site: www.coastarts.org
Key Personnel: Dir., Tom Webb; C.E.O., Catherine Rickbone.
Institution Type/Description: Art Gallery.
Hours & Admission Prices: Runyan Gallery: Tues.-Sun. 11-6. Upstairs Gallery: Tues.-Sat. 12-4. No charge; donations accepted.
Attendance: 16,000 (actual)

OREGON COAST AQUARIUM, 2820 S.E. Ferry Slip Rd., Newport, OR 97365-5269. Tel.: 541-867-3474. Fax: 541-867-6846.
E-mail: info@aquarium.org
Web Site: www.aquarium.org
Key Personnel: Pres. & C.E.O., Carrie E. Lewis.
Institution Type/Description: Aquarium.
Hours & Admission Prices: Memorial Day to Labor Day daily 9-6; Sept.-May daily 10-5. Adult 18-64 $19.95, seniors 65 & over $17.95, young adult 13-17 $16.95; children 3-12 $12.95; children 2 & under no charge. ♿
Attendance: 448,579 (actual)

YAQUINA BAY LIGHTHOUSE, 842 Government St., Newport, OR 97365. Mailing Address: Friends of Yaquina Lighthouses, 750 N.W. Lighthouse Dr., #7, Newport, OR 97365. Tel.: 541-265-5679.
Web Site: www.yaquinalights.org
Institution Type/Description: Historic Lighthouse: built in 1871. Listed on the National Register of Historic Places.
Hours & Admission Prices: Summer: daily 11-5; Winter: daily 12-4. No charge; donations accepted.

YAQUINA HEAD LIGHTHOUSE AND INTERPRETIVE CENTER, 750 Lighthouse Dr. #7, Newport, OR 97365. Tel.: 541-574-3145. Fax: 541-574-3140.
E-mail: jmoeller@blm.gov
Web Site: www.blm.gov/resources/recreation/yaquina/index.php
Institution Type/Description: Historic Lighthouse & Museum.
Hours & Admission Prices: Interpretive Center: Summer: 10-4:30; Winter: 10-4. Lighthouse: call for hours. Site: sunrise to sunset. $7 per car. ♿
Attendance: 340,000 (actual)

North Bend

COOS HISTORICAL & MARITIME MUSEUM, 1220 Sherman, North Bend, OR 97459-3666. Mailing Address: Coos County Historical Society, 1220 N. Front St., Coos Bay, OR 97420. Tel.: 541-756-6320. Fax: 541-756-6320.
E-mail: info@cooshistory.org
Web Site: www.cooshistory.org
Formerly: Coos County Historical Society Museum
Key Personnel: C.E.O. & Dir., Annie Donnelly; Pres., Steve Greif; Pres. (V), Jennifer Groth.
Institution Type/Description: General History Museum.
Hours & Admission Prices: Tues.-Sat. 10-4. Adults $4, senior citizens & students $2; members no charge. Closed Thanksgiving; Christmas. ♿
Attendance: 3,800 (actual)

Nyssa

OREGON TRAIL AGRICULTURAL MUSEUM, 117 Good Ave., Nyssa, OR 97913-3833. Mailing Address: P.O. Box 2303, Nyssa, OR 97913-0303. Tel.: 541-372-3193. Fax: 541-272-3193.
E-mail: dndeboer@fmtc.com
Key Personnel: Chm. (V), Jerry Deira; Chm. (V), Nancy Deboer; Dir., Nancy DeBoer.
Institution Type/Description: Agriculture Museum.
Hours & Admission Prices: Summer: Sat. 10-4, Sun. 1-4. No charge; donations accepted. ♿
Attendance: 233 (actual)

Oakland

OAKLAND MUSEUM, 130 Locust St., Oakland, OR 97462. Mailing Address: P.O. Box 624, Oakland, OR 97462-0624. Tel.: 541-459-3087.
Web Site: www.historicoaklandoregon.com
Key Personnel: Dir., Louise J. Stearns.
Institution Type/Description: Local History Museum.
Hours & Admission Prices: Daily 12:30-3:30. No charge; donations accepted. Closed holidays.
Attendance: 2,550 (actual)

Oakridge

OAKRIDGE-WESTFIR PIONEER MUSEUM, 76433 Pine St., Oakridge, OR 97463. Mailing Address: P.O. Box 807, Oakridge, OR 97463-0807. Tel.: 541-782-2402.
Institution Type/Description: History Museum.

Hours & Admission Prices: Call for hours.

Ontario

FOUR RIVERS CULTURAL CENTER & MUSEUM, 676 S.W. 5th Ave., Ontario, OR 97914-3436. Tel.: 541-889-8191. Fax: 541-889-7628.
E-mail: info@4rcc.com
Web Site: www.4rcc.com
Key Personnel: Chm. (V), Cathy Yasuda; Pres. (V), Diana Garcia; Exec. Dir., Matthew Stringer; Museum Shop Mgr., Lela Rogers.
Institution Type/Description: History Museum.
Hours & Admission Prices: Mon.-Sat. 10-5. Adults $4, seniors $3; discounts to groups over 20; members no charge. ♿
Attendance: 45,000 (actual)

Oregon City

MCLOUGHLIN MEMORIAL ASSOCIATION, 713 Center St., Oregon City, OR 97045-1948. Tel.: 503-656-5146. Fax: 503-557-4637.
E-mail: mcloughlinmemorial@gmail.com
Web Site: www.mcloughlinhouse.org
Institution Type/Description: Historic House Museum: housed in the former home of Dr. John McLoughlin, Chief Factor of the Hudson Bay Company; built in 1846. Listed on the National Register of Historic Places.
Hours & Admission Prices: Feb.-Dec. Fri.-Sat. 10-4. No charge; donations accepted. ♿
Attendance: 4,486 (actual)

MUSEUM OF THE OREGON TERRITORY - CLACKAMAS COUNTY HISTORICAL SOCIETY, 211 Tumwater Dr., Oregon City, OR 97045-2900. Mailing Address: P.O. Box 2211, Oregon City, OR 97045-0054. Tel.: 503-655-5574. Fax: 503-655-0035.
E-mail: manager@clackamashistory.org
Web Site: clackamashistory.org
Institution Type/Description: Oregon Territory Museum.
Hours & Admission Prices: Wed.-Sat. 10:30-4:30. Family (2 adults & 2 children) $20, adults $8, seniors 65 & up $7, children 5-17 $5; members, children under 5, retired military and active military & their family no charge.

STEVENS CRAWFORD MUSEUM, 603 6th St., Oregon City, OR 97045-2232. Tel.: 503-655-2866.
E-mail: volunteers@clackamashistory.org
Web Site: clackamashistory.org
Institution Type/Description: Historic House Museum: built in 1908.
Hours & Admission Prices: Wed.-Fri. 12-4, Sat. 1-4. Adults $4, seniors $3, students $2; children under 5 no charge.

THE WILLIAM L. HOLMES HOUSE AT THE HOLMES HOUSE, 536 Holmes Ln., Oregon City, OR 97045. Mailing Address: 713 Center St., Oregon City, OR 97045. Tel.: 503-656-5146. Facebook.
E-mail: mcloughlinmemorial@gmail.com
Web Site: www.mcloughlinhouse.org
Institution Type/Description: Historic House Museum: housed in the former home of William & Louisa Holmes; built in 1847.
Hours & Admission Prices: Check website for hours. Adults $3, seniors & youth 6-17 $3; MMA & reciprocal members and children 6 & under no charge.
Attendance: 350 (estimated)

Parkdale

INTERNATIONAL MUSEUM OF CAROUSEL ART, 4976 Alexander Dr., Parkdale, OR 97041-7604. Mailing Address: P.O. Box 1522, Hood River, OR 97031. Tel.: 541-806-8068. Fax: 541-387-8797.
E-mail: dsperron@gmail.com
Web Site: www.carouselmuseum.com
Key Personnel: Chm. (V), Duane S. Perron.
Institution Type/Description: General Museum.
Hours & Admission Prices: Temporarily closed for renovation. ♿

Pendleton

CHILDREN'S MUSEUM OF EASTERN OREGON, 400 S. Main St., Pendleton, OR 97801-2248. Tel.: 541-276-1066.
E-mail: director@cmeo.org
Web Site: www.cmeo.org

Key Personnel: Exec. Dir., Heidi Anderson; Pres., Mike Heriza.
Institution Type/Description: Children's Museum.
Hours & Admission Prices: Mon.-Sat. 10-5; groups by appointment. Admission $4; discounts to groups of 15 or more; children under one no charge.
Attendance: 11,628 (actual)

HERITAGE STATION, UMATILLA COUNTY HISTORICAL SOCIETY MUSEUM, 108 S.W. Frazer, Pendleton, OR 97801-2138. Mailing Address: P.O. Box 253, Pendleton, OR 97801-0253. Tel.: 541-276-0012. Fax: 541-276-7989. Facebook.
E-mail: membership@heritagestationmuseum.org
Web Site: www.heritagestationmuseum.org
Key Personnel: Exec. Dir., Barbara Lund-Jones; Dir. Devel. & Membership, Kari Brooks.
Institution Type/Description: Historical Society Museum: located in a 1909 train depot.
Hours & Admission Prices: Call for hours. Family $10; adults $5, seniors $4, students $2; discount to AAM members & groups; children under 5 & members no charge. Closed New Year's Day; Thanksgiving; Christmas. ♿
Attendance: 5,500 (estimated)

PENDLETON CENTER FOR THE ARTS, 214 N. Main St., Pendleton, OR 97801. Tel.: 541-278-9201.
E-mail: info@pendletonarts.org
Web Site: www.pendletonarts.org
Key Personnel: Exec. Dir., Roberta Lavadour.
Institution Type/Description: Art Gallery: housed in the former Carnegie Library; built in 1916.
Hours & Admission Prices: Call for hours.

PENDLETON ROUND-UP AND HAPPY CANYON HALL OF FAME, 1114 S.W. Court Ave., Pendleton, OR 97801. Mailing Address: 1205 S.W. Court Ave., Pendleton, OR 97801. Tel.: 541-278-0815. Fax: 541-276-9776.
E-mail: ruphalloffame@gmail.com
Web Site: pendletonhalloffame.com
Key Personnel: Chm. (V), Corinne Swearingen; Pres. (V), Robert Pahl.
Institution Type/Description: History Museum & Hall of Fame.
Hours & Admission Prices: Mon.-Sat. 10-4. Adults $5, seniors $4, children 10 & under $2. ♿
Attendance: 3,956 (estimated)

TAMASTSLIKT CULTURAL INSTITUTE, 47106 Wildhorse Blvd., Pendleton, OR 97801-3379. Tel.: 541-429-7700. Fax: 541-429-7709. Facebook: Tamastslikt Cultural Institute.
E-mail: info@tamastslikt.org
Web Site: www.tamastslikt.org
Key Personnel: Dir., Roberta Conner; Education, Cassandra Franklin; Mktg., Michelle Liberty; Registrar & Cur., Randall Melton; Room Bookings, Alice Johnson; Mgr. Research & Collections, Malissa Minthorn Winks; Museum Shop Mgr., Hilda Alexander.
Institution Type/Description: History Museum.
Hours & Admission Prices: Mon.-Sat. 10-5. Adults $10; discounts to NARM, AAM & AAA members; CTUIR members, Fort Walla Walla Museum members, Blue Star families & first Fri. of the month no charge. Closed New Year's Day; Thanksgiving; Christmas. ♿
Attendance: 34,000 (estimated)

Philomath

BENTON COUNTY HISTORICAL MUSEUM, 1101 Main St., Philomath, OR 97370. Mailing Address: P.O. Box 35, Philomath, OR 97370-0035. Tel.: 541-929-6230. Fax: 541-929-6261.
E-mail: info@bentoncountymuseum.org
Web Site: www.bentoncountymuseum.org
Key Personnel: Exec. Dir., Irene Zenev.
Institution Type/Description: History Museum & Art Gallery: housed in c.1867 brick building, originally used as the Philomath College building.
Hours & Admission Prices: Philomath: Tues.-Sat. 10-4:30. No charge; donations accepted. Closed major holidays. ♿
Attendance: 8,000 (estimated)

Port Orford

CAPE BLANCO HERITAGE SOCIETY, 92331 Coast Guard Hill Rd., Port Orford, OR 97465. Mailing Address: Cape Blanco Heritage Society, P.O. Box 1132, Port Orford, OR 97465-1132. Tel.: 541-332-0521.
E-mail: president@capeblancoheritagesociety.com
Web Site: www.capeblancoheritagesociety.com

Formerly: Point Orford Heritage Society
Key Personnel: Pres., Dave Holman; Museum Shop Mgr., Steve Roemen.
Institution Type/Description: Coast Guard History Museum.
Hours & Admission Prices: April-Oct. Wed.-Mon. 10-3:30; other times by appointment. No charge; donations accepted.
Attendance: 4,400 (estimated)

Portland

BLUE SKY, THE OREGON CENTER FOR THE PHOTOGRAPHIC ARTS, 122 N.W. 8th Ave., Portland, OR 97209. Tel.: 503-225-0210. Fax: 503-225-2990.
E-mail: bluesky@blueskygallery.org
Web Site: www.blueskygallery.org
Key Personnel: Exec. Dir., Lisa DeGrace.
Institution Type/Description: Art Gallery.
Hours & Admission Prices: Tues.-Sun. 12-5; groups of 12 or more by appointment. No charge; donations accepted. Closed New Year's Day; Independence Day; Thanksgiving; Christmas. ♿
Attendance: 20,000 (estimated)

THE DOUGLAS F. COOLEY MEMORIAL ART GALLERY, REED COLLEGE, 3203 S.E. Woodstock Blvd., Portland, OR 97202-8199. Tel.: 503-771-7251. Fax: 503-788-6691 (Reed College).
E-mail: snyders@reed.edu
Web Site: reed.edu/gallery
Key Personnel: Dir. & Cur., Stephanie Snyder; Registrar & Program Coord., Colleen Gotze; Coord. Education Outreach, Gregory MacNaughton.
Institution Type/Description: Exhibition Gallery.
Hours & Admission Prices: Sept.-June Tues.-Sun. 12-5. No charge. ♿
Attendance: 5,500

HELLENIC AMERICAN CULTURAL CENTER & MUSEUM OF OREGON & SW WASHINGTON, 3131 N.E. Glisan, Portland, OR 97232-2501. Tel.: 503-858-8567. Facebook: Hellenic-American Cultural Center & Museum (HACCM).
E-mail: haccmpdx@gmail.com
Web Site: www.hellenicamericancc.org
Key Personnel: Chm. (V), Nick Fkiaras; Administrative Asst., Katherine Karafotias.
Institution Type/Description: Cultural Center.
Hours & Admission Prices: Tues. 11-3, Sun. noon-1; other times by appointment. No charge; donations accepted. ♿
Attendance: 3,000 (estimated)

HOYT ARBORETUM, 4000 S.W. Fairview Blvd., Portland, OR 97221-2706. Tel.: 503-865-8733.
Web Site: www.hoytarboretum.org
Key Personnel: Exec. Dir. Hoyt Arboretum Friends, Anna Goldrich; Opers. & Volunteer Coord., Becky Schreiber; Cur., Martin Nicholson; Horticulturist, Mark McKinney; Plant Taxonomist & Herbarium Cur., Mandy Tu.
Institution Type/Description: Arboretum.
Hours & Admission Prices: Park: daily 5am-9:30pm. Visitor Center: Mon.-Fri. 9-4, Sat.-Sun. 11-3. No charge; donations accepted. Closed New Year's Day; Thanksgiving; Christmas. ♿
Attendance: 350,000 (estimated)

LEACH BOTANICAL GARDEN, 6704 S.E. 122nd Ave., Portland, OR 97236. Tel.: 503-823-9503.
E-mail: INFO@LEACHGARDEN.ORG
Web Site: www.leachgarden.org
Institution Type/Description: Botanical Garden.
Hours & Admission Prices: Tues.-Sat. 9-4, Sun. 1-4. No charge; donations accepted. Closed New Year's Day; Easter; Independence Day; Thanksgiving; Christmas.

LITTMAN & WHITE GALLERIES, 1825 S.W. Broadway #250, Portland, OR 97201-3256. Mailing Address: P.O. Box 751-SD, Portland, OR 97207. Tel.: 503-725-5656. Fax: 503-725-5680.
E-mail: littmanandwhite@gmail.com
Web Site: littmanwhite.tumblr.com/
Formerly: Portland State University Galleries
Key Personnel: Dir., Sasha Jones; Co-Cur., Carlin Brown; Co-Cur., Paul Maziar; Preparator, Holly Richwine; Publicity Coord., Andrew Jankowski.
Institution Type/Description: Art Gallery.
Hours & Admission Prices: Littman Gallery: Mon.-Wed. noon-5, Thurs. & Fri. noon-6. No charge. White Gallery: Mon.-Fri. 8-10, Sat. 9-7. No charge. Closed federal holidays; campus closures. ♿
Attendance: 52,386 (actual)

THE NATIONAL HAT MUSEUM, 1928 S.E. Ladd Ave., Portland, OR 97214-4737. Tel.: 503-232-0433; 503-319-0799 (Mobile).
E-mail: info@thehatmuseum.com
Web Site: www.thehatmuseum.com
Key Personnel: Dir., LuAnn Trotebas; Office Mgr., Bernard Trotebas.
Institution Type/Description: Hat Museum: housed in the Ladd-Reingold House; built in 1910. Listed on the National Register of Historic Places.
Hours & Admission Prices: Reservations required. Tour & Hat Program Tickets: $35; maximum group size 5. Closed Thanksgiving; Christmas.
Attendance: 1,100 (estimated)

THE OLD CHURCH SOCIETY, INC., 1422 S.W. 11th Ave., Portland, OR 97201-3304. Tel.: 503-222-2031. Fax: 503-222-2981.
E-mail: staff@theoldchurch.org
Web Site: theoldchurch.org
Key Personnel: Exec. Dir., Amanda Stark.
Institution Type/Description: Historical Society: housed in 1882 Calvary Presbyterian Church.
Hours & Admission Prices: Tues.-Fri. 11-3; other times by appointment. No charge; donations accepted.. &
Attendance: 50,000 (estimated)

OREGON HISTORICAL SOCIETY, 1200 S.W. Park Ave., Portland, OR 97205-2483. Tel.: 503-222-1741. Facebook.
E-mail: orhist@ohs.org
Web Site: www.ohs.org
Key Personnel: Pres., Emily Rogers; Vice Pres., Jennifer Sitton.
Institution Type/Description: History Museum.
Hours & Admission Prices: Museum: Mon.-Sat. 10-5, Sun. 12-5. Library: Tues. 1-5, Wed.-Sat. 10-5. See website for admission prices. Closed New Year's Day; Presidents' Day; Memorial Day; Independence Day; Labor Day; Thanksgiving; Christmas Eve & Day. &
Attendance: 40,000 (estimated)

OREGON JEWISH MUSEUM AND CENTER FOR HOLOCAUST EDUCATION, 724 N.W. Davis St., Portland, OR 97209. Tel.: 503-226-3600. Fax: 503-226-1800. Facebook: @OregonJewishMuseum.
E-mail: info@ojmche.org
Web Site: www.ojmche.org
Formerly: Oregon Jewish Museum
Key Personnel: Exec. Dir., Judith Margles; Pres. (V), Elaine Coughlin; Gift Shop Mgr., Judi Brodkin.
Institution Type/Description: Jewish Museum.
Hours & Admission Prices: Temporarily closed until 2017 for relocation to a new, permanent space. &
Attendance: 5,500 (estimated)

OREGON MARITIME MUSEUM, 198 S.W. Naito Pkwy., Portland, OR 97204. Mailing Address: 115 S.W. Ash St., Ste. 400C, Portland, OR 97204-3568. Tel.: 503-224-7724.
E-mail: info@oregonmaritimemuseum.org
Web Site: oregonmaritimemuseum.org
Institution Type/Description: Maritime Museum.
Hours & Admission Prices: Wed. & Fri.-Sat. 11-4. Adults $7, seniors 62 & over $5, students 13-18 with ID $4, youth 6-12 $3; active military with ID & children under 6 no charge. &
Attendance: 2,500 (estimated)

OREGON MUSEUM OF SCIENCE AND INDUSTRY, 1945 S.E. Water Ave., Portland, OR 97214-3356. Tel.: 800-955-6674. Facebook.
E-mail: info@omsi.edu
Web Site: www.omsi.edu
Key Personnel: Pres., Nancy Stueber; C.O.O., Erin Graham; Vice Pres. Finance & Analysis, Tim Mack; Vice Pres. Learning Experiences, Deb Mumm-Hill; Vice Pres. Devel., Love Centerwall.
Institution Type/Description: Science & Technology Center.
Hours & Admission Prices: See website for hours. Adults $14, senior $10.75, youth 3-13 $9.75; discounts to groups of 12 or more; members no charge. Special pricing for premier featured exhibits. Closed Thanksgiving; Christmas. &
Attendance: 750,000 (estimated)

OREGON NIKKEI ENDOWMENT/OREGON NIKKEI LEGACY CENTER, 121 N.W. 2nd Ave., Portland, OR 97209-3903. Tel.: 503-224-1458.
E-mail: info@oregonnikkei.org
Web Site: www.oregonnikkei.org
Key Personnel: Exec. Dir., Lynn Longfellow.
Institution Type/Description: Japanese Heritage Museum.

Hours & Admission Prices: Tues.-Sat. 11-3, Sun. 12-3. Adults $5; seniors 62 & over and students $3; members & children 11 and under no charge. &

OREGON ZOO, 4001 S.W. Canyon Rd., Portland, OR 97221-2799. Tel.: 503-226-1561. Fax: 503-226-6836.
Web Site: www.oregonzoo.org
Key Personnel: Dir., Dr. Don Moore; Assoc. Dir. Finance & Operations, Jody Brassfield-English; Exec. Dir. Oregon Zoo Foundation, Julie Fitzgerald.
Institution Type/Description: Zoo.
Hours & Admission Prices: Memorial Day to Labor Day daily 9:30-6; Sept. to May daily 9:30-4. Adults $11.50, senior citizens 65 & over $10, children 3-11 $8.50; discounts to groups & AZA members; members & children 2 & under no charge. Closed Christmas. &
Attendance: 1,494,315 (actual)

PITTOCK MANSION, 3229 N.W. Pittock Dr., Portland, OR 97210-5099. Tel.: 503-823-3623. Fax: 503-823-3626.
E-mail: mbones@pittockmansion.org
Web Site: www.pittockmansion.org
Key Personnel: Exec. Dir., Marta Bones; Cur. & Program Mgr., Patricia Larkin.
Institution Type/Description: Historic House: 1909-1914 French Renaissance, Pittock Mansion.
Hours & Admission Prices: Feb.-June & Sept.-Jan. 1st daily 11-4; July-Aug. daily 10-5. Adults $10, senior citizens $9, children 6-18 $7; discounts to military & AAA members; children 5 & under & members no charge. Closed Thanksgiving; Christmas. &
Attendance: 90,000 (actual)

PORTLAND ART MUSEUM, 1219 S.W. Park Ave., Portland, OR 97205-2486. Tel.: 503-226-2811.
E-mail: info@pam.org
Web Site: www.portlandartmuseum.org
Key Personnel: Dir. & Chief Cur., Brian Ferriso.
Institution Type/Description: Art Museum.
Hours & Admission Prices: Tues.-Wed. & Sat.-Sun. 10-5, Thurs.-Fri. 10-8, groups by appointment. Adults $19.99, seniors 62 & over and college students 18 & over with student ID $16.99; discounts for adult groups; school groups, children 17 & under and members no charge. Additional fee for special exhibitions. Closed Thanksgiving; Christmas. &
Attendance: 325,000 (estimated)

PORTLAND CHILDREN'S MUSEUM, 4015 S.W. Canyon Rd., Portland, OR 97221-2759. Tel.: 503-223-6500. Facebook.
Web Site: www.portlandcm.org
Formerly: CM2-Children's Museum 2nd Generation
Key Personnel: Exec. Dir., Ruth Shelly; Dir. Facilities, Kyle Dhristoph; Dir. Teaching & Learning, Susan Harris MacKay; Dir. Museum Experience, Jeremiah Sazdanoff; Dir. Exhibits, Somya Singh; Dir. External Affairs, Stephanie Tolk.
Institution Type/Description: Children's Museum.
Hours & Admission Prices: Museum: daily 9-5. Admission $10.75, military and seniors 55 & over $9.75; members & children under one no charge. &
Attendance: 320,000 (estimated)

PORTLAND JAPANESE GARDEN, 611 S.W. Kingston Ave., Portland, OR 97205. Mailing Address: P.O. Box 3847, Portland, OR 97208-3847. Tel.: 503-223-1321. Fax: 503-223-8303.
E-mail: info@japanesegarden.com
Web Site: japanesegarden.com
Key Personnel: C.E.O., Stephen D. Bloom; Deputy Dir., Cynthia Johnson Haruyama; C.O.O., Cheryl Ching; Chief Devel. Officer, Tom Cirillo; Dir. Mktg. & Communs., Lisa Christy.
Institution Type/Description: Garden.
Hours & Admission Prices: mid-March to Sept. Mon. 12-7, Tues.-Sun. 10-7; Oct. to mid-March Mon. 12-4, Tues.-Sun. 10-4. Adults $9.50, seniors 65 & over and college students with ID $7.75, youth 6-17 $6.75; children 5 & under no charge.

PORTLAND POLICE MUSEUM, 1111 S.W. 2nd Ave., Portland, OR 97204-3231. Tel.: 503-823-0019. Facebook.
E-mail: info@portlandpolicemuseum.com
Web Site: www.portlandpolicemuseum.com
Institution Type/Description: Police Museum.
Hours & Admission Prices: Tues.-Fri. 10-3. No charge; donations accepted. &
Attendance: 4,000 (actual)

PORTLAND PUPPET MUSEUM, 906 S.E. Umatilla St., Portland, OR 97202. Tel.: 503-233-7723. Facebook.
E-mail: news@puppetmuseum.com
Web Site: puppetmuseum.com
Hours & Admission Prices: Thurs.-Sun. 2-8.

RONNA AND ERIC HOFFMAN GALLERY OF CONTEMPORARY ART, 0615 S.W. Palatine Hill Rd., MSC 95, Portland, OR 97219. Tel.: 503-768-7687. Fax: 503-768-7682.
E-mail: gallery@lclark.edu
Web Site: www.lclark.edu/hoffman_gallery
Key Personnel: Dir., Linda Tesner.
Institution Type/Description: Art Gallery.
Hours & Admission Prices: Tues.-Sun. 11-4. No charge.

STARK'S VACUUM MUSEUM, 107 N.E. Grand Ave., Portland, OR 97232. Tel.: 503-232-4101. Fax: 503-235-9723. Facebook.
E-mail: info@starks.com
Web Site: starks.com/vacuum-museum
Key Personnel: Mgr., Ted Burk.
Institution Type/Description: Vacuum Museum.
Hours & Admission Prices: Mon.-Fri. 8-6, Sat. 9-6, Sun. 10-5. No charge.

WASHINGTON COUNTY MUSEUM, 17677 N.W. Springville Rd., Portland, OR 97229. Tel.: 503-645-5353. Fax: 503-640-7195.
E-mail: info@washingtoncountymuseum.org
Web Site: www.washingtoncountymuseum.org
Formerly: Washington County Historical Society
Key Personnel: Pres., Douglas Johnson; Treas., AJ Wheeler.
Institution Type/Description: History Museum.
Hours & Admission Prices: Wed.-Thurs. 10-4. No charge. Research Library: Mon.-Fri. by appointment. Closed major holidays. &
Attendance: 4,839 (actual)

WELLS FARGO HISTORY MUSEUM CLOSED, 1300 S.W. Fifth Ave., Portland, OR 97201-5688. Mailing Address: Wells Fargo Historical Services, 420 Montgomery St., MAC-A0101-022, San Francisco, CA 94163. Tel.: 503-886-1102. Fax: 503-886-2676. Facebook: Wells Fargo.
E-mail: wfmuseum.or@wellsfargo.com
Web Site: www.wellsfargohistory.com
Key Personnel: Museum Mgr., Steve Greenwood.
Institution Type/Description: Company History Exhibit: housed in the Portland Wells Fargo Ctr. Downtown.
Hours & Admission Prices: Mon.-Fri. 9-5. No charge. Closed bank holidays. &

WORLD FORESTRY CENTER DISCOVERY MUSEUM, 4033 S.W. Canyon Rd., Portland, OR 97221-2798. Tel.: 503-228-1367.
Web Site: www.worldforestry.org
Key Personnel: Interim Exec. Dir., Sara Wu.
Institution Type/Description: Global Forestry Museum.
Hours & Admission Prices: Memorial Day to Labor Day daily 10-5; winter Thurs.-Mon. 10-5. Adult $7, senior citizens $6, children 3-18 $5; children 2 & under and members no charge. Closed Thanksgiving; Christmas Eve & Day. &
Attendance: 70,000 (actual)

YALE UNION CLOSED, 800 S.E. 10th Ave., Portland, OR 97214. Tel.: 503-236-7996.
E-mail: yu@yaleunion.org
Web Site: www.yaleunion.org
Formerly: YU Contemporary Art Center
Key Personnel: Dir., Curtis Knapp.
Institution Type/Description: Art Gallery.
Hours & Admission Prices: Call for hours. &
Attendance: 30,000 (estimated)

Prairie City

DEWITT MUSEUM, 425 S. Main St., Prairie City, OR 97869. Mailing Address: P.O. Box 370, Prairie City, OR 97869. Tel.: 541-820-3330 & 3605.
E-mail: pchall@ortelco.net
Web Site: www.prairiecityoregon.com
Key Personnel: Dir., Kathy Smith; Chm., Jay Waterhouse.
Institution Type/Description: History Museum: housed in the former Sumpter Valley Railway Station; built in 1910. Listed on the National Register of Historic Places.
Hours & Admission Prices: mid-May to mid-Oct. Wed.-Sun. 10-5. &

Princeton

BENSON MEMORIAL MUSEUM, MALHEUR NATIONAL WILDLIFE REFUGE, 36391 Sodhouse Lane, Princeton, OR 97721-9523. Tel.: 541-493-2612. Fax: 541-493-2405.
E-mail: malheur@fws.gov

Web Site: www.fws.gov/malheur
Key Personnel: Visitor Services Mgr., Carey Goss.
Institution Type/Description: Wildlife Refuge & Bird Sanctuary.
Hours & Admission Prices: Daily sunrise-sunset. Visitor Center: Mon.-Fri. 8-4, Sat.-Sun. call for hours. No charge; donations accepted. &
Attendance: 60,000 (estimated)

Prineville

A.R. BOWMAN MEMORIAL MUSEUM, 246 N. Main St., Prineville, OR 97754-1852. Tel.: 541-447-3715. Fax: 541-447-3715 (call first).
E-mail: bowmuse@netscape.net
Web Site: www.bowmanmuseum.org
Key Personnel: Dir. & C.E.O., Gordon Gillespie; Pres., Ruthie McKenzie.
Institution Type/Description: Local History Museum: housed in 1910 bank building.
Hours & Admission Prices: Feb.-May & Sept.-Dec. Tues.-Fri. 10-5, Sat. 11-4; June-Aug. Mon.-Fri. 10-5, Sat.-Sun. 11-4. No charge; donations accepted. Closed major holidays.
Attendance: 10,882 (estimated)

Reedsport

UMPQUA DISCOVERY CENTER, 409 Riverfront Way, Reedsport, OR 97467-1495. Tel.: 541-271-4816. Fax: 541-271-4816. Facebook: Umpqua Discovery Center.
E-mail: info@umpquadiscoverycenter.com
Web Site: www.umpquadiscoverycenter.com
Key Personnel: Dir. & Museum Shop Mgr., Diane Novak.
Institution Type/Description: History Museum.
Hours & Admission Prices: June-Sept. Mon.-Sat. 10-5, Sun. 12-4; Oct.-May Mon.-Sat. 10-4, Sun. 12-4. Adults $8, children 5-16 $4; group & school rates available; members no charge. Closed New Year's Day; Thanksgiving; Christmas. &
Attendance: 17,000 (estimated)

UMPQUA RIVER LIGHTHOUSE MUSEUM, 1020 Lighthouse Rd., Reedsport, OR 97467. Tel.: 541-271-4361. Facebook: Umpqua River Light.
E-mail: grbradle@codouglas.or.us
Key Personnel: Museum Mgr. & Lighthouse Keeper, Gaylyn Bradley.
Institution Type/Description: History Museum: housed in a 4-story former US Coast Guard Station; built in 1939.
Hours & Admission Prices: March-April & Nov.-Dec. Fri.-Sun. 10-4; May-Oct. daily 10-4:30. Museum: no charge; donations accepted. Guided Lighthouse Tours: adults $5, seniors & students $3; active duty military & their families and children 3-5 no charge.
Attendance: 23,412 (actual)

Rickreall

POLK COUNTY MUSEUM, 560 S.W. Pacific Hwy., Rickreall, OR 97371. Mailing Address: P.O. Box 67, Monmouth, OR 97361-0067. Tel.: 503-623-6251.
E-mail: pchsoregon@gmail.com
Web Site: polkcountyhistoricalsociety.com
Key Personnel: C.E.O., C.F. Stevens.
Institution Type/Description: History Museum.
Hours & Admission Prices: Mon. & Wed.-Sat. 1-5. Adults $5, seniors $3, students $1; members & children under 5 no charge. &
Attendance: 1,992 (actual)

Rogue River

WOODVILLE MUSEUM, INC., 199 First St., Rogue River, OR 97537. Mailing Address: P.O. Box 128, Rogue River, OR 97537-0128. Tel.: 541-582-3088.
Key Personnel: Chm., Samuel D. Evensizer; Treas., Shirley O. Allen.
Institution Type/Description: History Museum: housed in Hatch House, c.1909.
Hours & Admission Prices: Tues.-Sat. 12-4. No charge; donations accepted. Closed legal holidays.
Attendance: 2,000 (estimated)

Roseburg

DOUGLAS COUNTY MUSEUM OF HISTORY AND NATURAL HISTORY, 123 Museum Dr., Roseburg, OR 97471-5308. Tel.: 541-957-7007. Fax: 541-957-7017.
E-mail: museum@co.douglas.or.us
Web Site: www.co.douglas.or.us/museum

Key Personnel: C.E.O., Gardner Chappell; Cur., Jena Mitchell; Exhibit Preparator, James Davis; Research Librarian & Museum Shop Mgr., Karen Bratton.
Institution Type/Description: General Museum.
Hours & Admission Prices: Jan.-Oct. Mon.-Fri. 9-5, Sat. 10-5, Sun. 12-5; Nov.-Dec. Tues.-Fri. 9-5, Sat. 10-5. Adults $4, seniors $3, children 4-17 & college students $2; children under 4 & members no charge. Closed legal holidays. &
Attendance: 12,000 (actual)

FLOED-LANE HOUSE, 544 S.E. Douglas Ave., Roseburg, OR 97470. Mailing Address: P.O. Box 2534, Roseburg, OR 97470-0430. Tel.: 541-900-3858.
E-mail: webmaster@douglascountyhistoricalsociety.org
Web Site: douglascountyhistoricalsociety.org
Formerly: Douglas County Pioneer Museum
Key Personnel: Pres. (V), Peggy A. Rowe-Snyder; Chm. (V), Ken Deatherage.
Institution Type/Description: Historic House Museum: Floed-Lane House & Douglas County Pioneer Museum.
Hours & Admission Prices: Sat.-Sun. 1-4; other times by appointment. No charge; donations accepted. Closed Easter; Independence Day; Labor Day; Thanksgiving; Christmas. &
Attendance: 320 (actual)

Saint Benedict

MOUNT ANGEL ABBEY MUSEUM, One Abbey Dr., Saint Benedict, OR 97373. Tel.: 503-845-3030. Fax: 503-845-3594.
E-mail: info@mountangelabbey.org
Web Site: www.mountangelabbey.org/monastery/museum.html
Institution Type/Description: Religious Museum.
Hours & Admission Prices: Daily 10-11:30 & 1-5.

Saint Paul

CHAMPOEG STATE HERITAGE AREA VISITOR CENTER, 8239 Champoeg Rd., N.E., Saint Paul, OR 97137-9796. Mailing Address: 7679 Champoeg Rd. NE, Saint Paul, OR 97137-9525. Tel.: 503-678-1251, ext. 221. Fax: 503-678-6142.
Web Site: www.oregonstateparks.org/park_113.php
Key Personnel: Park Mgr., Bryan Nielsen.
Institution Type/Description: Park Museum Visitor Center: at location of first provisional government in the Pacific Northwest (1843).
Hours & Admission Prices: Summer: daily 9-5; Fall & Winter: Mon.-Fri. 11-4, Sat.-Sun. 10-5. Car parking $5. No charge; donations accepted. Closed Thanksgiving; Christmas. &
Attendance: 17,250

OSSDAR NEWELL PIONEER VILLAGE, 8089 Champoeg Rd., N.E., Saint Paul, OR 97137-9709. Tel.: 503-266-3944.
E-mail: info@newellpioneervillage.com
Web Site: www.newellpioneervillage.com
Formerly: Robert Newell House, DAR Museum and Pioneer Mothers Memorial Cabin
Key Personnel: Dir., Judy Van Atta; State Cur. and DAR State Chm. Bldgs. & Grounds, Barbara Kieffer; Bldgs. & Grounds Chair, Marilyn Olson.
Institution Type/Description: Historic House: 1959 restoration of 1852 Robert E. Newell House and 1931 pioneer cabin.
Hours & Admission Prices: March-Sept. Fri.-Sun. 1-5; private tours by appointment. Adults $4, children under 12 $2; discounts to members & seniors.
Attendance: 6,500 (estimated)

Salem

A.C. GILBERT'S DISCOVERY VILLAGE, 116 Marion St., N.E., Salem, OR 97301-3437. Tel.: 503-371-3631, 800-208-9514. Fax: 503-316-3485.
E-mail: info@acgilbert.org
Web Site: www.acgilbert.org
Formerly: Gilbert House Children's Museum
Key Personnel: Exec. Dir., Pamela Vorachek; Pres. (V), Shannon Martinez.
Institution Type/Description: Historic Houses: home of Andrew T. Gilbert, banker; home of C.S. Rockenfield, nurseryman; home of J.L. Parrish, businessman & minister.
Hours & Admission Prices: Mon.-Sat. 10-5, Sun. 12-5. Adults 3-59 $6, seniors 60 & over $4.50, children 1-2 $3; discounts to ASTC & AAA members; members no charge. Closed New Year's Day; Easter; Thanksgiving; Christmas. &
Attendance: 82,000 (actual)

B-17 ALLIANCE MUSEUM & RESTORATION HANGAR, Salem McNary Airfield (enter at Main Terminal), 3278 25th St., S. E., Salem, OR 97302. Mailing Address: 13515 S.E. McLaughlin Blvd., Milwaukie, OR 97222. Tel.: 971-803-2428. Facebook.
E-mail: terrys@b17alliance.com
Web Site: www.B17Alliance.com
Formerly: Wings of Freedom Showcase
Key Personnel: Exec. Dir. & Museum Shop Mgr., Theresa Scott; C.E.O., Jayson R. Scott; Chm. (V), Dr. Fred Bremner.
Institution Type/Description: WWII Memorial Museum & B-17 Restoration Hangar.
Hours & Admission Prices: Tues., Thurs. & Sat. 10-2; other times by appointment. Suggested Donation $10. &
Attendance: 3,500 (actual)

DEEPWOOD MUSEUM & GARDEN, 1116 Mission St., S.E., Salem, OR 97302-6207. Tel.: 503-363-1825. Fax: 503-363-3586.
E-mail: info@historicdeepwoodestate.org
Web Site: www.deepwoodmuseum.org
Formerly: Historic Deepwood Estate
Key Personnel: Exec. Dir., Lynne Richardson; Site Mgr., Deborah McNair; Museum Mgr., Sarah Pearson; Volunteer Coord., Melanie Jones; Pres. (V), Cassandra Ferder.
Institution Type/Description: Historical Museum.
Hours & Admission Prices: May-Sept.: Wed.-Sat. 9-12; Oct.-April Wed.-Sat. 12-3. Adults $6, seniors $5, students $4, youth 6-15 $3; members & children under 5 no charge.
Attendance: 26,891 (actual)

HALLIE FORD MUSEUM OF ART, Willamette University, 700 State St., Salem, OR 97301. Mailing Address: Willamette University, 900 State St., Salem, OR 97301-3922. Tel.: 503-370-6855. Fax: 503-375-5458. Facebook: Hallie Ford Museum of Art.
E-mail: museum-art@willamette.edu
Web Site: www.willamette.edu/arts/hfma
Key Personnel: Dir. & C.E.O., John Olbrantz; Cur. Collections, Jonathan Bucci; Cur. Education, Elizabeth Garrison; Designer & Preparator, Silas Cook; Membership & Public Rels. Mgr., Andrea Foust.
Institution Type/Description: Art Museum.
Hours & Admission Prices: Tues.-Sat. 10-5, Sun. 1-5. Adults $6, senior citizens 55 & over $4 students 18 & over with ID $3; discounts to groups and AAM, AIA, AAA, & NARM members; members and children & students 17 & under no charge. Closed New Year's Eve & Day; Easter; Independence Day; Thanksgiving & day after; Christmas Eve, Day & week. &
Attendance: 30,000 (estimated)

OREGON ELECTRIC RAILWAY HISTORICAL SOCIETY, INC., 3395 Brooklake Rd., N.E., Salem, OR 97303. Tel.: 971-701-6327.
E-mail: apmaoffice@eschelon.com
Web Site: www.oerhs.org
Key Personnel: Museum Dir., Greg Bonn.
Institution Type/Description: Electric Railway Museum.
Hours & Admission Prices: Museum: Sat. 11-5, Sun. 12-4. Trolley: adults $5, youth 12-18 $3; children 11 & under no charge. &
Attendance: 6,856 (actual)

OREGON FIRE SERVICE MUSEUM, 1284 Court St., N.E., Salem, OR 97301. Tel.: 888-313-6873. Facebook: Oregon Fire Service museum.
E-mail: oregonfiremuseum@gmail.com
Web Site: www.oregonfiremuseum.org
Key Personnel: Pres. Bd. Dirs., Greg Musil; Vice Pres. Bd. Dirs., Stewart R. Parker; Sec. Bd. Dirs., Vickie Musil; Cur. & Historian, Shirley Tormey.
Institution Type/Description: Firefighting History Museum.
Hours & Admission Prices: By appointment. No charge; donations accepted.

OREGON STATE CAPITOL, 900 Court St., N.E., Salem, OR 97301. Tel.: 503-986-1388.
Institution Type/Description: Historic Building: built in 1938. Listed on the National Register of Historic Places.
Hours & Admission Prices: Tours: Memorial Day to Labor Day Mon.-Fri. 9-4; other times by appointment. No charge.

PREWITT-ALLEN ARCHAEOLOGICAL MUSEUM AT CORBAN UNIVERSITY, 5000 Deer Park Dr., S.E., Salem, OR 97317-9392. Tel.: 503-589-8128.
E-mail: adjeffers@corban.edu
Web Site: inside.corban.edu/archeological-museum

Institution Type/Description: Archaeology Museum.
Hours & Admission Prices: Academic Year: Mon.-Thurs. 8:30am-10pm, Fri. 8-5:30, Sat. 10:30-5; other times by appointment; call to confirm hours. No charge; donations accepted. &

SALEM ART ASSOCIATION-BUSH HOUSE MUSEUM AND BUSH BARN ART CENTER, 600 Mission St., S.E., Salem, OR 97302-6203. Tel.: 503-581-2228. Fax: 503-371-3342.
E-mail: info@salemart.org
Web Site: www.salemart.org
Key Personnel: Exec. Dir., Sandra Burnett; Chm. Salem Art Assoc. Bd. of Directors, Paula Kanarek; Dir. Bush Barn Art Center, Catherine Alexander; Dir. Community Arts Education, Kathy Dinges-Rice; Dir. Bush House Museum, Ross Sutherland; Dir. Fundraising, Debbie Leahy.
Institution Type/Description: Historic House Museum: housed in 1878 Asahel Bush, II house. Historic Barn: home of the Salem Art Association.
Hours & Admission Prices: Bush House Tours: March-Dec. 23 Wed.-Sun. 1, 2, 3, & 4pm. Adults $6, seniors 62 & over $5, students 16 & over $4, youth 6-15 $3; SAA members and children 5 & under no charge. Bush Barn Art Center: Tues.-Fri. 10-5, Sat.-Sun. 12-5. &
Attendance: 85,000 (estimated)

WILLAMETTE HERITAGE CENTER, 1313 Mill St., S.E., Salem, OR 97301-6591. Tel.: 503-585-7012. Fax: 503-588-9902. Facebook: Willamette Heritage Center.
E-mail: info@willametteheritage.org
Web Site: www.willametteheritage.org
Formerly: Willamette Heritage Center at the Mill
Key Personnel: Exec. Dir., Bob H. Reinhardt; Pres. (V), Dr. Jennifer Jopp; Devel. Dir., Michelle Cordova; Cur., Kylie Pine; Operations Dir., Sean O'Hara; Office & Accounts Mgr., Holly Klaus; Educ. & Outreach Dir., Kathleen Schulte.
Institution Type/Description: History Museum.
Hours & Admission Prices: Mon.-Sat. 10-5. Adults $7, seniors 65 & up $6, college students $5, youth 6-17 $3; discounts to veterans & AAA members; children under 5 & members no charge. Closed New Year's Day; Thanksgiving; Christmas. &
Attendance: 65,171 (actual)

Scio

SCIO HISTORICAL SOCIETY & DEPOT MUSEUM, 39004 N. E. 1st Ave., Scio, OR 97374. Mailing Address: P.O. Box 226, Scio, OR 97374-0226. Tel.: 503-394-2199.
E-mail: maintrain1800@smt-net.com
Key Personnel: Pres. (V), Stephanie Bates.
Institution Type/Description: History Museum.
Hours & Admission Prices: May-Oct. Sat.-Sun. 1-4. No charge; donations accepted.

Seaside

SEASIDE AQUARIUM, 200 N. Prom, Seaside, OR 97138-5945. Tel.: 503-738-6211.
E-mail: aquarium@seasideaquarium.com
Web Site: www.seasideaquarium.com
Institution Type/Description: Aquarium.
Hours & Admission Prices: Call for hours. Adults $8, senior citizens 64 & over $6.75, children 6-13 $4; children 5 & under no charge.

SEASIDE MUSEUM & HISTORICAL SOCIETY, 570 Necanicum Dr., Seaside, OR 97138-6040. Tel.: 503-738-7065. Fax: 503-738-7065.
E-mail: seasidemuseum@hotmail.com
Web Site: www.seasidemuseum.org/
Key Personnel: Pres., Chris Gonzalez; Chm. (V), Roger Waller; Museum Shop Mgr., Val Smith.
Institution Type/Description: History Museum.
Hours & Admission Prices: Mon.-Sat. 10-3; groups by appointment. Adults $3, senior citizens $2, students $1; members and children 6 & under no charge. Closed New Year's Day; Easter; Mother's Day; Memorial Day; Father's Day; Labor Day; Thanksgiving; Christmas. &
Attendance: 1,777 (actual)

Springfield

HISTORIC VILLAGE AT DORRIS RANCH, 205 Dorris St., Springfield, OR 97477. Tel.: 541-736-4544. Fax: 541-736-4529.
Web Site: willamalane.org
Institution Type/Description: Historic Farm: listed on the National Register of Historic Places.
Hours & Admission Prices: Daily 6am to dusk.

SPRINGFIELD MUSEUM, 590 Main St., Springfield, OR 97477-5469. Tel.: 541-726-3677. Fax: 541-726-3688.
E-mail: museumdirector@springfield.or.us
Web Site: www.springfieldmuseum.com
Key Personnel: Exec. Dir., Jim Cupples; Pres. of Board, Mike Walker; Cur. & Registrar, Jan McKee.
Institution Type/Description: General Museum: housed in 1911 building.
Hours & Admission Prices: Tues.-Fri. 10-4, Sat. 12-4. Adults $2; discounts to OMA & AAM members; members no charge. Closed legal holidays. &
Attendance: 8,978 (actual)

Sweet Home

EAST LINN MUSEUM, 746 Long St., Sweet Home, OR 97386-3303. Tel.: 541-367-4580.
E-mail: eastlinnmuseum@yahoo.com
Key Personnel: Pres. (V), Gail Gregory; Museum Shop Mgr., Glenda Hopkins.
Institution Type/Description: History Museum.
Hours & Admission Prices: Feb.- Nov. Thurs.-Sat. 11-4, Sun. 1-4. Closed Easter; Memorial Day; Independence Day. No charge; donations accepted. &
Attendance: 2,500 (estimated)

The Dalles

COLUMBIA GORGE DISCOVERY CENTER AND WASCO COUNTY MUSEUM, 5000 Discovery Dr., The Dalles, OR 97058-9755. Tel.: 541-296-8600. Fax: 541-298-8660.
E-mail: cpurcell@gorgediscovery.org
Web Site: www.gorgediscovery.org
Key Personnel: Chm. (V), William G. Dick, II; Exec. Dir., Carolyn Purcell; Office Admin., Marie Bailey; Dir. Education, Steve Thompson; Museum Shop Mgr., Shawn McCleary.
Institution Type/Description: Interpretive Center & Museum.
Hours & Admission Prices: Daily 9-5. Adults $9, senior citizen $7, children $5; discounts to groups & active military; members no charge. Closed New Year's Day; Thanksgiving; Christmas. &
Attendance: 36,000 (actual)

THE DALLES ART ASSOCIATION, 220 E. 4th St., The Dalles, OR 97058-2206. Mailing Address: P.O. Box 1026, The Dalles, OR 97058-9026. Tel.: 541-296-4759.
E-mail: thedallesart@earthlink.net
Web Site: thedallesartcenter.org
Key Personnel: Dir., Carmen Toll.
Institution Type/Description: Art Association Gallery.
Hours & Admission Prices: Tues.-Sat. 11-5. No charge; donations accepted. Closed New Year's Day; Independence Day; Thanksgiving; Christmas. &
Attendance: 5,000 (estimated)

FORT DALLES MUSEUM/ANDERSON HOMESTEAD, 500 W. 15th St., The Dalles, OR 97058-1527. Mailing Address: c/o Fort Dalles Museum/Anderson Homestead Foundation, P.O. Box 591, The Dalles, OR 97058-0591. Tel.: 541-296-4547.
E-mail: fortdallesmuseum@gmail.com
Web Site: fortdallasmuseum.org
Key Personnel: Museum Dir., Cal McDermid.
Institution Type/Description: Historic Building Museum: 1856 Fort Dalles Surgeon's quarters.
Hours & Admission Prices: May 15-Sept. 15 daily 10-5; other times by appointment. Adults $5, seniors 55 & over $4, students 7-17 $1; discounts to groups; members no charge. Closed winter holidays.
Attendance: 2,750 (actual)

Tillamook

LATIMER QUILT AND TEXTILE CENTER, 2105 Wilson River Loop Rd., Tillamook, OR 97141. Tel.: 503-842-8622. Fax: 503-842-8692.
E-mail: latimertextile@centurylink.net
Web Site: www.latimerquiltandtextile.com
Institution Type/Description: Textile Museum.
Hours & Admission Prices: April-Oct. Mon.-Sat. 10-5, Sun. 12-4; Nov.-March Mon.-Sat. 10-4. Adults $4, seniors 62 & up $3; discounts to groups; members & children under 12 no charge. Closed New Year's Day; Easter; Independence Day; Thanksgiving; Christmas. &

TILLAMOOK CHEESE FACTORY & VISITOR'S CENTER, 4175 Hwy. 101 N., Tillamook, OR 97141-7770. Tel.: 503-815-1300. Fax: 503-815-1305.
Web Site: www.tillamook.com

Key Personnel: Pres. & C.E.O., Patrick Criteser.
Institution Type/Description: Visitor Center.
Hours & Admission Prices: mid-June to Labor Day daily 8-8; Labor Day to mid-June daily 8-6. No charge. Closed Thanksgiving; Christmas. &
Attendance: 950,000

TILLAMOOK COUNTY PIONEER MUSEUM, 2106 Second St., Tillamook, OR 97141-2399. Tel.: 503-842-4553. Fax: 503-842-4553. Facebook: Tillamook County Pioneer Museum.
E-mail: director@tcpm.org
Web Site: www.tcpm.org
Key Personnel: Dir., Gary E. Albright; Chm. (V), Phyllis Wustenberg; Museum Shop Mgr., Ruby Fry-Matson.
Institution Type/Description: Historical Museum: housed in 1905 Old Courthouse.
Hours & Admission Prices: Tues.-Sun. 10-4. Research Library: Tues.-Fri. 10-4 by appointment. Adults $4, seniors 62 & over $3, students 10-17 $1; discounts to active military members & their families; members & children under 10 no charge. Blue Star Museum. Closed major holidays. &
Attendance: 11,000 (actual)

Toledo

TOLEDO HISTORY CENTER, 208 S. Main St., Toledo, OR 97391-1203. Mailing Address: P. O. Box 213, Toledo, OR 97391-0213. Tel.: 541-336-1203.
E-mail: laedmondson@newportnet.com
Formerly: Toledo Historical Museum at Toledo City Hall
Key Personnel: Pres. (V), Ann Edmondson; Treas., Jim Franklin.
Institution Type/Description: History Museum.
Hours & Admission Prices: Wed.-Sun. 12-4. No charge; donations accepted. Closed holidays. &
Attendance: 1,500 (estimated)

YAQUINA PACIFIC RAILROAD HISTORICAL SOCIETY, 100 N.W. A St., Toledo, OR 97391-1570. Mailing Address: P.O. Box 119, Toledo, OR 97391-0119. Tel.: 541-336-5256.
E-mail: yprhs@peak.org
Web Site: www.yaquinapacificrr.org
Key Personnel: Pres., Alan Holzapfel; Exec. Dir., Dean Tingey.
Institution Type/Description: Railroad History Museum.
Hours & Admission Prices: Summer: Tues.-Sat. 10-4; Winter: Tues.-Sat. 10-2. No charge; donations accepted.
Attendance: 1,994 (actual)

YAQUINA RIVER MUSEUM OF ART, 151 N.E. Alder St., Toledo, OR 97391-1521. Tel.: 541-336-1907. Fax: 541-336-1907. Facebook: Yaquina River Museum of Art.
E-mail: yrmaoffice@qwestoffice.net
Web Site: www.michaelgibbons.net/museum.htm
Key Personnel: Chm. & Cur., Michael Gibbons; Museum Shop Mgr., Judy Gibbons.
Institution Type/Description: Art Museum.
Hours & Admission Prices: Wed.-Sun. 12-4. No charge; donations accepted.
Attendance: 4,000 (estimated)

Trail

TRAIL TAVERN MUSEUM, 144 Old Hwy. 62, Trail, OR 97541. Tel.: 541-621-4462.
E-mail: trapperjackv@gmail.com
Key Personnel: Chm. (V), Jim Collier.
Institution Type/Description: History Museum: housed in a former tavern.
Hours & Admission Prices: April 15-Sept. Thurs.-Sun. 12:30-4:30, Oct. Sat.-Sun. 12:30-4:30; tours by appointment. No charge; donations accepted. &
Attendance: 446 (actual)

Troutdale

TROUTDALE HISTORICAL SOCIETY, 732 E. Historic Columbia River Hwy., Troutdale, OR 97060-2061. Mailing Address: 219 E. Historic Columbia River Hwy., Troutdale, OR 97060-2078. Tel.: 503-661-2164.
E-mail: info@troutdalehistory.org
Web Site: www.troutdalehistory.org
Key Personnel: Pres., Bettianne Goetz; Vice Pres., Margaret Rice; Treas., Marilee Thompson; Sec., Norm Thompson; Exec. Dir., LeAnn Stephan; Historian, Sharon Nesbit; Photo Librarian, Julie Stewart; Cur., Dee Dee Hansen.
Institution Type/Description: Historical Society Museums.
Hours & Admission Prices: Rail Depot: Fri. 10-2. Harlow House: Summer Sun. 1-4; Winter Sun. 1-3. Barn Exhibit Hall: Summer Mon.-Sat. 9-4, Sun. 1-4; Winter

Wed.-Sat. 10-3, Sun. 1-3. Rail Depot & Harlow House: No charge; donations accepted. Barn Exhibit Hall: adults 12 & over $5; Multnomah County residents no charge. Closed all federal holidays. &
Attendance: 3,600 (estimated)

Umatilla

UMATILLA MUSEUM & HISTORICAL FOUNDATION, 911 Sixth St., Umatilla, OR 97882. Mailing Address: P.O. Box 975, Umatilla, OR 97882-0975. Tel.: 541-922-0209.
E-mail: yakka1@msn.com
Key Personnel: Pres. (V), Keith Harding; Dir. & Chm. (V), Marge Nelson; Museum Shop Mgr., Larry Nelson.
Institution Type/Description: History Museum: housed in the former city hall building.
Hours & Admission Prices: Call for hours. No charge; donations accepted. &
Attendance: 1,000 (estimated)

Union

UNION COUNTY MUSEUM, 311 S. Main St., Union, OR 97883. Mailing Address: P.O. Box 190, Union, OR 97883-0190. Tel.: 541-562-6003. Facebook.
Web Site: www.ucmuseumoregon.org
Key Personnel: Pres. (V), Sharon Hohstadt; Museum Shop Mgr., Carol Mulvany.
Institution Type/Description: History Museum: housed in 1881 former First National Bank of Union building.
Hours & Admission Prices: Mother's Day-Columbus Day Mon.-Sat. 10-4; other times by appointment. Adults $5, senior citizens $4, students $3; members no charge. &
Attendance: 300 (estimated)

Vale

MALHEUR HISTORICAL PROJECT, STONEHOUSE MUSEUM, 255 Main St., Vale, OR 97918. Mailing Address: P.O. Box 413, Vale, OR 97918-0413. Tel.: 541-473-2070.
Key Personnel: Pres. (V), Gary Fugate; Treas., Charlotte Fugate.
Institution Type/Description: Historic House: 1872 stone house built as a wayside house on the Oregon Trail.
Hours & Admission Prices: May-Oct. Tues.-Sat. 12-4. No charge; donations accepted. &
Attendance: 2,000 (estimated)

Vernonia

VERNONIA PIONEER MUSEUM, 511 E. Bridge St., Vernonia, OR 97064-1406. Mailing Address: P.O. Box 26, Vernonia, OR 97064-0026. Tel.: 503-429-3713, 503-705-2173. Facebook: Vernonia Pioneer Museum.
E-mail: vernoniamuseum@gmail.com
Web Site: vernoniahandsonart.org
Formerly: Columbia County History Museum
Key Personnel: Pres. (V), Jay Anderson; Vice Pres., Ralph Keasey; Treas., Tobie Finzel; Sec., Barbara Larsen.
Institution Type/Description: Historical Museum: housed in the old Oregon American Mill office built in the late 1920s; listed on the National Register of Historic Places.
Hours & Admission Prices: June-Aug. Fri.-Sun. 1-4; Sept.-May Sat.-Sun. 1-4. No charge; donations accepted. Closed New Year's Day; Easter; Mother's Day; Independence Day; Independence Day; Christmas. &
Attendance: 625 (actual)

Waldport

WALDPORT HERITAGE MUSEUM, 320 N.E. Grant St., Waldport, OR 97394. Mailing Address: P.O. Box 822, Waldport, OR 97394-0822. Tel.: 541-563-7092.
E-mail: waldportmuseum@peak.org
Web Site: waldportmuseum.org
Key Personnel: Pres., Colleen Nickerson; Pres. (V), Judy Gibbs.
Institution Type/Description: History Museum.
Hours & Admission Prices: Wed.-Fri. 12-4, Sat.-Sun. 10-4. No charge; donations accepted. &
Attendance: 849 (actual)

Warm Springs

THE MUSEUM AT WARM SPRINGS, 2189 Hwy. 26, Warm Springs, OR 97761. Mailing Address: P.O. Box 909, Warm Springs, OR 97761-0909. Tel.: 541-553-3331. Fax: 541-553-3338.
E-mail: maws@museumatwarmsprings.org
Web Site: www.museumatwarmsprings.org
Key Personnel: Exec. Dir., Carol Leone; Operations Mgr. & Bd. Treas., Sunmiet Maben; Pres., Doug Goe; Vice Pres., Bill Nicholson; Devel. Officer, Debra Stacona; Receptionist & Devel. Asst., Angela A. Smith; Cur., Natalie Kirk; Museum Shop Mgr., Lucinda Sohappy.
Institution Type/Description: Tribal Museum.
Hours & Admission Prices: Tues.-Sat. 9-5. Adults $7, seniors $6, children $3; discount to groups, AAA, AAM, NARMA, Western Museums Assoc., OMA & AASLH members; members no charge. Closed New Year's Day; Thanksgiving; Christmas. &
Attendance: 8,000 (estimated)

Winston

WILDLIFE SAFARI, 1790 Safari Rd., Winston, OR 97496. Mailing Address: P.O. Box 1600, Winston, OR 97496-1600. Tel.: 541-679-6761. Fax: 541-679-1148. Facebook: Wildlife Safari.
E-mail: guestservices@wildlifesafari.net
Web Site: www.wildlifesafari.net
Key Personnel: Dir., Dan Van Slyke; Chm. (V), Pat Markham.
Institution Type/Description: Zoo.
Hours & Admission Prices: Drive-thru daily 9-5. Adults $17.99, seniors 60 & over $14.99, children 4-12 $11.99.
Attendance: 150,000 (estimated)

Woodburn

WOODBURN ART CENTER - GLATT HOUSE GALLERY, 2551 N. Boones Ferry Rd., Woodburn, OR 97071-9669. Tel.: 503-982-6450.
E-mail: Woodburnartcenter@live.com
Institution Type/Description: Art Gallery.
Hours & Admission Prices: Call for hours.

WOODBURN HISTORICAL MUSEUM, 455 N. Front St., Woodburn, OR 97071. Mailing Address: 270 Montgomery St., Woodburn, OR 97071-4730. Tel.: 503-982-9531.
E-mail: kristin.wierenga@ci.woodburn.or.us
Web Site: www.woodburn-or.gov/communitydevelopment/history/default.aspx
Formerly: Woodburn Museum.
Key Personnel: Dir., Kristin Wierenga.
Institution Type/Description: History Museum.
Hours & Admission Prices: Sat.-Sun. 11-3; other times by appointment. No charge; donations accepted.
Attendance: 500 (estimated)

Yachats

LITTLE LOG CHURCH & MUSEUM, 328 W. Third St., Yachats, OR 97498. Mailing Address: P.O. Box 712, Yachats, OR 97498-0712. Tel.: 541-547-3976.
Key Personnel: Dir., Karl Christianson.
Institution Type/Description: Historic Building Museum: housed in the former Little Log Church; built in the shape of a cross.
Hours & Admission Prices: Fri.-Wed. 12-3.

PENNSYLVANIA

(562 listings)

Abington

BRIAR BUSH NATURE CENTER, 1212 Edge Hill Rd., Abington, PA 19001-3203. Tel.: 215-887-6603. Fax: 215-887-9079.
E-mail: greta@briarbush.org
Web Site: www.briarbush.org
Key Personnel: Exec. Dir., Greta Brunschwyler; Chm. (V), Patrick Hromison; Dir. Devel., Karen Serfass; Dir. Public Programs, Melissa Eldridge; Dir., Greta Brunschwyler; Environmental Educator, Ehren Gross; Environmental Educator, Katie McAfee; Treas., Michele Kaczalek; Sr. Naturalist, Mark Fallon; Museum Shop Mgr., Patti Platt.
Institution Type/Description: Nature Center.
Hours & Admission Prices: Observatory & Museum: Mon.-Sat. 9-5, Sun. 1-5. Nature Trails sunrise-sunset. Adults $3, children $2; township residents, and

AAM & museum members no charge. Closed New Year's Day; Independence Day; Thanksgiving; Christmas. &
Attendance: 65,000 (actual)

Academia

TUSCARORA ACADEMY MUSEUM - JUNIATA COUNTY HISTORICAL SOCIETY, Academia Rd. & Academy Rd., Academia, PA 17082. Mailing Address: 498 Jefferson St., Ste. B, Mifflintown, PA 17059. Tel.: 717-436-5152.
E-mail: jchs1931@juniatacountyhistoricalsociety.org
Web Site: www.juniatacountyhistoricalsociety.org
Key Personnel: Pres., Audrey R. Sizelove.
Institution Type/Description: Historic Building: housed in a former boarding school; built in 1816.
Hours & Admission Prices: June-Aug. Sun. 1:30-4; other times by appointment. No charge; donations accepted.
Attendance: 200 (estimated)

Alexandria

HARTSLOG HERITAGE MUSEUM, Alexandria Public Library, 2nd Fl., Main St., Alexandria, PA 16611. Mailing Address: P.O. Box 3, Alexandria, PA 16611-0003. Tel.: 814-207-1410.
E-mail: hartslogday@verizon.net
Institution Type/Description: History Museum.
Hours & Admission Prices: 1st Sun. of month 2-4; other times by appointment. No charge; donations accepted.

Allentown

ALLENTOWN ART MUSEUM, 31 N. 5th St., Allentown, PA 18101-1605. Tel.: 610-432-4333. Fax: 610-434-7409. Facebook: Allentown Art Museum.
E-mail: info@allentownartmuseum.org
Web Site: allentownartmuseum.org
Key Personnel: Pres. & C.E.O., David Mickenberg; Chm. Bd. Trustees, Dolores A. Laputka, Esq.; Vice Pres. Curatorial & Education, Elaine Mehalakes Lucks; Vice Pres. Devel. & Communications, Maureen Wendling; Devel. Officer, Tara Craig; Museum Shop Mgr., Sharon Yurkanin; Bldg. Operations Mgr., Tom Edge; Registrar, Beverly Hoover.
Institution Type/Description: Art Museum.
Hours & Admission Prices: Wed.-Sat. 11-4, Sun. 12-4. Adults $12, students, seniors and children 6 & over $10; children 5 & under, members, active military & Sun. no charge. NARM reciprocal. Closed national holidays. &
Attendance: 117,500 (actual)

AMERICA ON WHEELS MUSEUM, 5 North Front St., Allentown, PA 18102-5303. Tel.: 610-432-4200. Fax: 610-432-3670.
E-mail: director@americaonwheels.org
Web Site: www.americaonwheels.org
Formerly: America On Wheels
Key Personnel: Exec. Dir. & Museum Shop Mgr., Linda Merkel; Pres. (V), Jack Curcio; Exhibit Chair, Alan Gross.
Institution Type/Description: Transportation Museum.
Hours & Admission Prices: Jan.-Feb. Wed.-Sat. 10-5, Sun. 12-5; March-Dec. Tues.-Sat. 10-5, Sun. 12-5. Adults $10, seniors 62 & over $7, children 6-16 $5; children 12 & under no charge every Sun.; discount to AOW & AAA members. Closed New Year's Day; Independence Day; Thanksgiving; Christmas. &
Attendance: 50,000 (actual)

DA VINCI SCIENCE CENTER, 3145 Hamilton Blvd. Bypass, Allentown, PA 18103-3686. Tel.: 484-664-1002. Fax: 484-664-1022. Facebook.
E-mail: ask@davincisciencecenter.org
Web Site: www.davincisciencecenter.org
Key Personnel: Exec. Dir. & C.E.O., Lin Erickson; Chm. (V), Vincent Sergi; Dir. Business Devel., Brian Strohecker.
Institution Type/Description: Science Center.
Hours & Admission Prices: Mon.-Sat. 10-5, Sun. 12-5. Admission $12.95; discounts to groups of 10 or more; children 2 & under and ASTC & museums members no charge. Closed New Year's Day; Easter; Thanksgiving; Christmas. &
Attendance: 101,907 (actual)

LEHIGH VALLEY HERITAGE MUSEUM, 432 W. Walnut St., Allentown, PA 18102-5428. Tel.: 610-435-1074, ext. 19. Fax: 610-435-9812.
E-mail: j_garrera@lehighvalleyheritagemuseum.org
Web Site: www.lchs.museum

Formerly: Lehigh County Historical Society
Key Personnel: Exec. Dir., Joseph Garrera.
Institution Type/Description: Historical Society.
Hours & Admission Prices: Museum: Tues.-Sat. 10-4, Sun. 12-4. Adults $8, children $3; members no charge. Closed major holidays. ⅃
Attendance: 36,500 (estimated)

MACK TRUCKS HISTORICAL MUSEUM, 2402 Lehigh Pkwy. S., Allentown, PA 18103. Tel.: 610-351-8999. Fax: 610-351-8756.
E-mail: mack.museum@macktrucks.com
Web Site: macktruckshistoricalmuseum.org
Key Personnel: Cur., Don Schumaker.
Institution Type/Description: Company History Museum.
Hours & Admission Prices: Call for hours. No charge. ⅃
Attendance: 6,000 (actual)

MARTIN ART GALLERY, Baker Center for the Arts, Muhlenberg College, Allentown, PA 18104. Mailing Address: 2400 Chew St., Allentown, PA 18104. Tel.: 484-664-3467. Fax: 484-664-3113.
E-mail: kburke@muhlenberg.edu
Web Site: www.muhlenberg.edu/
Institution Type/Description: College Art Gallery.
Hours & Admission Prices: Tues.-Sat. 12-8. No charge. Closed all major holidays; semester breaks. ⅃
Attendance: 7,000 (estimated)

MUSEUM OF INDIAN CULTURE, 2825 Fish Hatchery Rd., Allentown, PA 18103-9214. Tel.: 610-797-2121. Fax: 610-797-2801. Facebook: Museum Indian Culture.
E-mail: info@museumofindianculture.org
Web Site: www.museumofindianculture.org
Formerly: Lenni Lenape Historical Society
Key Personnel: Exec. Dir., Pat Rivera; Cur., Archivist & Registrar, Lee Hallman.
Institution Type/Description: History Museum.
Hours & Admission Prices: June 22-Sept. 8 Thurs.-Sun. 10-4, Sept. 8-June 22 Fri.-Sun. 10-4. Adults $5, seniors & children 12-17 $4; members no charge. Closed national holidays. ⅃
Attendance: 14,000 (estimated)

Allenwood

CLYDE PEELING'S REPTILAND, 18628 U.S. Route 15, Allenwood, PA 17810-9731. Tel.: 570-538-1869. Fax: 570-538-1714.
E-mail: info@reptiland.com
Web Site: reptiland.com
Key Personnel: Dir., Clyde Peeling; Operations Mgr., Chad Peeling; Dir. Mktg. & Guest Svcs., Kalin Palmatier; Museum Shop Mgr., Melody Drick; Exhibit Designer, Elliot Peeling; Zoological Mgr., Jeff Cook.
Institution Type/Description: Zoo.
Hours & Admission Prices: April-May & Sept.-Oct. Mon.-Fri. 10-5, Sat.-Sun. 10-6; Memorial Day-Labor Day daily 9-6; Nov.-March daily 10-5. Adults 12 & over $16, children 3-11 $14; children 2 & under and members no charge. Closed New Year's Day; Thanksgiving; Christmas. ⅃
Attendance: 60,000 (estimated)

Allison Park

DEPRECIATION LANDS MUSEUM, 4743 S. Pioneer Rd., Allison Park, PA 15101-2400. Mailing Address: P.O. Box 174, Allison Park, PA 15101-0174. Tel.: 412-486-0563.
E-mail: depreciationlands@gmail.com
Web Site: www.depreciationlandsmuseum.org
Institution Type/Description: Living History Museum, village & cemetery: Includes c. 1837 Covenanter Church, c. 1803 log house, one room school, blacksmith shop, carriage house & 18th c. style mercantile.
Hours & Admission Prices: May-Oct. Sun. 1-4; Nov.-April by appointment. Adults $3. ⅃
Attendance: 5,000 (estimated)

Altoona

BAKER MANSION HISTORY MUSEUM, 3419 Oak Ln., Altoona, PA 16602. Mailing Address: P.O. Box 1083, Altoona, PA 16603-1083. Tel.: 814-942-3916. Fax: 814-942-7078.
E-mail: info@blairhistory.org
Web Site: www.blairhistory.org
Formerly: Blair County History Center at Baker Mansion
Key Personnel: Exec. Dir. & C.E.O., Joe DeFrancesco; Chm. (V), Jared Frederick.

Institution Type/Description: History Museum & Historic Mansion: housed in the former home of ironmaster Elias Baker and his family; built in 1849.
Hours & Admission Prices: Tours: Memorial Day to Labor Day Tues.-Sun. 12-4; Sept.-May by appointment. Research: by appointment. Adults $8.
Attendance: 10,000 (estimated)

QUAINT CORNER CHILDREN'S MUSEUM, 2000 Union Ave., Altoona, PA 16601-2059. Tel.: 814-944-6830.
E-mail: quaintcorner@verizon.net
Web Site: www.quaintcorner.org
Institution Type/Description: Children's Museum: housed in the former home of Daniel O'Rorke; built 1893.
Hours & Admission Prices: Fri.-Sat. 10-5. Family $5.

RAILROADERS MEMORIAL MUSEUM, 1300 9th Ave., Altoona, PA 16602-2487. Tel.: 814-946-0834. Fax: 814-946-9457. Facebook.
E-mail: admin@railroadcity.com
Web Site: www.railroadcity.com
Key Personnel: Exec. Dir., Larry Salone; Chm. (V), Dr. Andy Mulhollen; C.O.O., Cynthia Hershey.
Institution Type/Description: Railroad Museum.
Hours & Admission Prices: Museum: March 16-April 29 Fri.-Sat. 9-5, Sun. 11-5; April 30-Oct. 28 Mon.-Sat. 9-5, Sun. 11-5; Nov. 2-Nov. 18 Fri.-Sat. 9-5, Sun. 11-5. Adults 12-61 $11, seniors 62 & over and military $10, children 2-11 $9; discounts to groups; children under 2 no charge. Closed Easter; Thanksgiving. Horseshoe Curve: March 16-Oct. 28 Mon.-Sat. 9-6, Sun. 11-6; Nov. 2-Nov. 18 Fri.-Sat. 9-5, Sun. 11-5. Admission 2 & over $8; discounts to groups; children under 2 no charge. Closed Easter; Thanksgiving. ⅃
Attendance: 39,485 (actual)

SOUTHERN ALLEGHENIES MUSEUM OF ART AT ALTOONA, 1210 11th Ave., Altoona, PA 16601. Tel.: 814-946-4464. Fax: 814-946-3131. Facebook: Southern Alleghenies Museum of Art at Altoona.
E-mail: altoona@sama-art.org
Web Site: www.sama-art.org
Key Personnel: Dir., Gary Moyer.
Institution Type/Description: Art Museum.
Hours & Admission Prices: Tues.-Fri. 10-5, Sat. 1-5. No charge; donations accepted. ⅃
Attendance: 72,427 (actual)

Ambler

THE STOOGEUM, 904 Sheble Ln., Ambler, PA 19002. Mailing Address: P.O. Box 747, Gwynedd Valley, PA 19437-0747. Tel.: 267-468-0810.
E-mail: garystooge@aol.com
Web Site: www.stoogeum.com
Key Personnel: Cur., Gary Lassin.
Institution Type/Description: Comedy Museum.
Hours & Admission Prices: See website for hours. Admission $10; children 12 & under no charge. ⅃
Attendance: 2,500 (estimated)

Ambridge

OLD ECONOMY VILLAGE, 270 Sixteenth St., Ambridge, PA 15003-2225. Tel.: 724-266-4500. Fax: 724-266-3010.
E-mail: miknecht@pa.gov
Web Site: www.oldeconomyvillage.org
Key Personnel: Site Dir., Michael Knecht; Pres. (V), Bob Clendennen; Office Coord., Jason Weber.
Institution Type/Description: Historic Village Museum: 18 buildings of the original town of Economy (now Ambridge), PA, built between 1824 & 1831.
Hours & Admission Prices: April-Dec. Wed.-Sat. 10-5, Sun. 12-5. Adults $10, senior citizens 65 & over $9, children 3-11 $6; discount to AAA members; children under 2 & members no charge. Closed major holidays. ⅃
Attendance: 13,100 (actual)

Annville

SUZANNE H. ARNOLD ART GALLERY, LEBANON VALLEY COLLEGE, 101 N. College Ave., Annville, PA 17003-1404. Tel.: 717-867-6445. Fax: 717-867-6124.
E-mail: mcnulty@lvc.edu
Web Site: www.lvc.edu/gallery
Key Personnel: Dir., Barbara McNulty, Ph.D.; Chm. (V), Dr. Grant Taylor; Registrar & Cur., Crista Detweiler.

Institution Type/Description: Art Museum.
Hours & Admission Prices: Wed. 5-8pm, Thurs.-Fri. 1-4:30, Sat.-Sun. 11-5. No charge; donations accepted. Closed during college holidays. &
Attendance: 4,500 (estimated)

Apollo

W.C.T.U. BUILDING - APOLLO AREA HISTORICAL SOCIETY MUSEUM, 317 N. 2nd St., Apollo, PA 15613. Mailing Address: P.O. Box 434, Apollo, PA 15613. Tel.: 724-478-2899. Facebook: @apollohistory.
E-mail: apollopahistory@gmail.com
Web Site: apollopahistory.wordpress.com
Institution Type/Description: Historical Society Museum: housed in the former home of the Women's Christian Temperance Union and the home of the first public library in Armstrong County; built in 1909.
Hours & Admission Prices: April-Dec. Wed. & Sat. 11-2. No charge; donations accepted. &

Ashland

PIONEER TUNNEL COAL MINE & STEAM TRAIN, 19th & Oak Sts., Ashland, PA 17921. Tel.: 570-875-3850. Fax: 570-875-3301. Facebook: Official Pioneer Tunnel Coal Mine.
E-mail: ashpa@ptd.net
Web Site: www.pioneertunnel.com
Key Personnel: Gen. Mgr., Keith Neidig; Business Mgr., Chastity Moran; Pres. (V), Robert Snyder.
Institution Type/Description: Mining Museum.
Hours & Admission Prices: Mine Tours: April daily 11, 12:30 & 2; May & Sept.-Oct. Mon.-Fri. 11, 12:30 & 2, Sat.-Sun. 10-5; Memorial Day to Labor Day: daily 10-5. Coal Mine Tours: adult $10.50, children 2-11 $7.50; discounts to groups. Steam Train Ride: adult $8.50, children 2-11 $6.60; discounts to groups. Combination Ticket: adults $17.10, children 2-11 $12.60. &
Attendance: 29,172 (actual)

Athens

TIOGA POINT MUSEUM, 724 S. Main St., P.O. Box 143, Athens, PA 18810. Tel.: 570-888-7225. Facebook: Tioga Point Museum.
E-mail: tpointmuseum@stny.rr.com
Web Site: www.tiogapointmuseum.org
Key Personnel: Dir., Margaret Boritz; Pres., Todd Babcock.
Institution Type/Description: General Museum.
Hours & Admission Prices: Tues. & Thurs. 12-8, Sat. 10-1; other times by appointment. No charge; donations accepted. Closed national holidays. &
Attendance: 1,423 (actual)

Audubon

JOHN JAMES AUDUBON CENTER AT MILL GROVE, 1201 Pawlings Rd., Audubon, PA 19403-2242. Tel.: 610-666-5593. Fax: 484-831-5305. Facebook.
E-mail: millgrove@audubon.org
Web Site: johnjames.audubon.org
Formerly: Mill Grove, The Audubon Wildlife Sanctuary
Key Personnel: Dir., Jean Bochnowski; Chm. (V), Leigh Altadonna; Senior Cur., Nancy S. Powell; Facilities Coord., Nathan Roberts; Administrative Coord., Mary MacFarland; Education Coord., Barron Ashley.
Institution Type/Description: Art Museum, Wildlife Refuge & Historic Site: built in 1762; first home in America of artist/naturalist John James Audubon (1803-1806). A National Historic Landmark.
Hours & Admission Prices: Tues.-Sat. 10-4, Sun. 1-4; guided tours by appointment. Adults $5, seniors 60 & over $4, children 6-17 $3; members no charge. Grounds: 7 am to dusk, no charge. Closed New Year's Eve & Day; Easter; Independence Day; Thanksgiving; Christmas Eve & Day; major holidays.
Attendance: 20,000 (actual)

Avella

MEADOWCROFT ROCKSHELTER AND HISTORIC VILLAGE, 401 Meadowcroft Rd., Avella, PA 15312-2759. Tel.: 724-587-3412. Fax: 724-587-3414.
E-mail: socialmedia@heinzhistorycenter.org
Web Site: www.heinzhistorycenter.org
Formerly: Meadowcroft Rockshelter and Museum of Rural Life
Key Personnel: Dir., David R. Scofield; Cur., Bonnie Reese; Dir. Education, Dr. John Boback; Visitor Svcs. Mgr., Fran Skariot.
Institution Type/Description: History Museum: 275-acre history village with 19th century rural village recreation; 17th century eastern woodlands Indian village recreation. A National Historic Landmark-Meadowcroft Rockshelter.

Hours & Admission Prices: May & Sept.-Oct. Sat. 12-5, Sun. 1-5; Memorial Day to Labor Day Wed.-Sat. 12-5, Sun. 1-5. Adults $12, children 6-17 $6; discounts to AAM members; members & children under 6 no charge. &
Attendance: 15,608 (actual)

Beaver Falls

AIR HERITAGE, INC., 35 Piper St., Beaver Falls, PA 15010-1043. Tel.: 724-843-2820. Fax: 724-847-4581.
E-mail: airheritage1@verizon.net
Web Site: www.airheritage.org
Key Personnel: Pres. (V), Bill Schillig; Museum Shop Mgr., Lois Wyke.
Institution Type/Description: Aviation History Museum.
Hours & Admission Prices: Mon.-Sat. 10-5, Sun. by appointment. No charge; donations accepted. Closed major holidays. &
Attendance: 1,400 (estimated)

BEAVER FALLS HISTORICAL SOCIETY AND MUSEUM, 1301 7th Ave., Beaver Falls, PA 15010-4219. Mailing Address: P. O. Box 493, Beaver Falls, PA 15010. Tel.: 724-494-2439.
Key Personnel: Pres. (V), Kenneth Britten.
Institution Type/Description: Historical Society Museum.
Hours & Admission Prices: Mon.-Thurs. 10-2. No charge; donations accepted. &
Attendance: 995 (actual)

Bedford

BEDFORD COUNTY HISTORICAL SOCIETY, 6441 Lincoln Hwy., Bedford, PA 15522. Tel.: 814-623-2011. Facebook: Bedford County Historical Society.
E-mail: bedfordhistory@embarqmail.com
Web Site: www.bedfordpahistory.com
Key Personnel: Dir., Gillian K. Leach.
Institution Type/Description: Historical Society Museum.
Hours & Admission Prices: Mon.-Fri. 9-4. &
Attendance: 1,500 (actual)

FORT BEDFORD MUSEUM, 110 Fort Bedford Dr., Bedford, PA 15522. Mailing Address: 244 W. Penn St., Bedford, PA 15522. Tel.: 814-623-8891.
E-mail: info@fortbedfordmuseum.org
Web Site: www.fortbedfordmuseum.org
Key Personnel: Mgr. & Museum Shop Mgr., Lisa Merritt; Cur., Larry Yantz.
Institution Type/Description: History Museum.
Hours & Admission Prices: April-Oct. Wed.-Sun. 11-5; other times by appointment. Adults $5, senior citizens 65 & over $4.50, students 6-18 $3; children under 6 no charge.
Attendance: 2,870 (actual)

THE NATIONAL MUSEUM OF THE AMERICAN COVERLET, 322 S. Juliana St., Bedford, PA 15522-1734. Tel.: 814-623-1588. Facebook: National Museum of the American Coverlet.
E-mail: info@coverletmuseum.org
Web Site: www.coverletmuseum.org
Key Personnel: Museum Dir., Melinda Zongor.
Institution Type/Description: Coverlet Museum.
Hours & Admission Prices: Mon.-Sat. 10-5, Sun. 12-4. Adults $10; discounts to groups; members no charge.

Bellefonte

CENTRE COUNTY LIBRARY AND HISTORICAL MUSEUM, 203 N. Allegheny St., Bellefonte, PA 16823-1601. Tel.: 814-355-1516. Fax: 814-355-2700.
E-mail: paroom@centrecountylibrary.org
Web Site: www.centrecountylibrary.org
Key Personnel: Library & Museum Colls. Asst., Erin Hicks.
Institution Type/Description: Historic Library & Local History Museum.
Hours & Admission Prices: Mon., Wed., Fri. 10-5, Tues. & Thurs. 12-5, 3rd Sat. each month 10-2. No charge; donations accepted. Closed national holidays.
Attendance: 962 (actual)

Benwood

CASTLE HALLOWEEN MUSEUM, 2028 Broad Ave., Altoona, PA 16601. Mailing Address: 2024-2026-2028 Broad Ave., Altoona, PA 16601. Tel.: 814-940-1031.
E-mail: castlehalloween@atlanticbb.net

Web Site: www.castlehalloween.com
Key Personnel: Owner, Pamela Apkarian-Russell.
Institution Type/Description: Halloween Social History Museum.
Hours & Admission Prices: By appointment only. Tours: $8. &

Bethel

GOLDEN AGE AIR MUSEUM, Grimes Airfield, 371 Airport Rd., Bethel, PA 19507. Tel.: 717-933-9566.
E-mail: info@goldenageair.org
Web Site: www.goldenageair.org
Institution Type/Description: Aviation History.
Hours & Admission Prices: May-Oct. Sat. 10-4, Sun. 11-4. Adults $5, children 6-12 $3; discounts to groups; members no charge.

Bethlehem

BANANA FACTORY, 25 W. Third St., Bethlehem, PA 18015-1238. Tel.: 610-332-1300.
E-mail: info@fest.com
Web Site: www.bananafactory.org
Key Personnel: Dir., Debra Miller.
Institution Type/Description: Art Gallery.
Hours & Admission Prices: Gallery: daily 11-4. Building: Mon.-Fri. 8am-9:30pm, Sat.-Sun. 8:30-5. No charge. Closed New Year's Day; Thanksgiving; Christmas. &
Attendance: 12,000 (estimated)

BURNSIDE PLANTATION, INC., 1461 Schoenersville Rd., Bethlehem, PA 18018-1889. Mailing Address: 74 W. Broad St., Ste. 260, Bethlehem, PA 18018-5738. Tel.: 610-882-0450. Fax: 610-882-0460.
E-mail: info@historicbethlehem.org
Web Site: www.historicbethlehem.org
Key Personnel: Pres., Charlene Donchez Mowers; Vice Pres. & Mng. Dir., LoriAnn Wukitsch; Finance, Tom Homanick; Chm., Joseph Kochanasz; Cur., Caitlin Harvey.
Institution Type/Description: Historic Site.
Hours & Admission Prices: Fri.-Sat. 11-4, Sun. 12-4; activities offered throughout the day with Pass Into History purchase.
Attendance: 4,000 (estimated)

COLONIAL INDUSTRIAL QUARTER, Main St. and Church St., Bethlehem, PA 18018. Mailing Address: 74 W. Broad St., Ste. 260, Bethlehem, PA 18018. Tel.: 610-882-0450. Fax: 610-882-0460.
E-mail: info@historicbethlehem.org
Web Site: www.historicbethlehem.org
Formerly: Historic Bethlehem Inc.
Key Personnel: Pres., Charlene Donchez Mowers; Vice Pres. & Mng. Dir., LoriAnn Wukitsch; Finance, Thomas Homanick; Chm., Joseph Kochanasz; Cur., Caitlin Harvey.
Institution Type/Description: Historical Site.
Hours & Admission Prices: Colonial Industrial Quarter Smithy: Summer & Fall Fri.-Sun. 12-4. Grounds: daily. Goundie House: Tues.-Sat. 10-5, Sun. 12-5. Visitors Center: Jan.-Nov. Tues.-Sat. 10-5, Sun. 12-5; Nov. 25-Dec. 23 Sun.-Wed. 10-6, Thurs.-Sat. 10-8; Dec. 26-Dec. 31 Mon.-Fri. 10-8, Sat. 10-3. &
Attendance: 10,000 (estimated)

KEMERER MUSEUM OF DECORATIVE ARTS, 427 N. New St., Bethlehem, PA 18018-5802. Mailing Address: c/o Historic Bethlehem, 74 W. Broad St., Ste. 260, Bethlehem, PA 18018. Tel.: 610-882-0450. Fax: 610-882-0460.
E-mail: info@historicbethlehem.org
Web Site: www.historicbethlehem.org
Key Personnel: Pres., Charlene Donchez Mowers; Vice Pres. & Mng. Dir., LoriAnn Wukitsch; Finance, Thomas Homanick; Chm., Joseph Kochanasz; Cur., Caitlin Harvey; Museum Site Mgr., Marissa Zondag.
Institution Type/Description: Regional Decorative Arts Museum.
Hours & Admission Prices: Fri.-Sun. 12-4, holiday Thurs.-Fri. & Sun. 12-5, Sat. 10-5. Adults $5, senior citizens $4, youth 6-12 $2.50; discount to AAA members; HBP members no charge. &
Attendance: 10,000 (estimated)

LEHIGH UNIVERSITY ART GALLERIES TEACHING MUSEUM, Zoellner Arts Center, 420 E. Packer Ave., Bethlehem, PA 18015-3010. Tel.: 610-758-3615. Fax: 610-758-4580.
E-mail: db01@lehigh.edu
Web Site: www.luag.org
Key Personnel: Curatorial Asst. Exhibitions, Collections & Publications, Mark Wonsidler; Operations Admin., Denise Stangl; Social Media & Dept. Coord.,

Alexandria Wismer; Collections Mgr. & Registrar, Vasti DeEsch; Head Preparator & Exhibition Design, Jeffrey Ludwig-Dicus; Preparator, Khalil Allaik; Visitor Svcs. & Museum Education, Patricia McAndrew.
Institution Type/Description: University Museum.
Hours & Admission Prices: Zoellner Arts Center Galleries: Wed.-Sat. 11-5, Sun. 1-5. DuBois Gallery & Maginnes Hall: Mon.-Fri. 9-10, Sat. 9-12. Siegel Gallery & Iacocca Hall: Mon.-Thurs. 9-10, Fri. 9-5. Gallery at Rauch Business Center: Mon.-Fri. 8-10, Sat. 8-5. Call for Summer hours. No charge; donations accepted. Closed national holidays; school holidays. &
Attendance: 15,000 (estimated)

MORAVIAN MUSEUM OF BETHLEHEM, INC., 66 W. Church St., Bethlehem, PA 18018. Mailing Address: 74 W. Broad St., Ste. 260, Bethlehem, PA 18018-5738. Tel.: 610-882-0450. Fax: 610-882-0460.
E-mail: cdm@historicbethlehem.org
Web Site: www.historicbethlehem.org
Key Personnel: Pres., Charlene Donchez Mowers; Finance, Thomas Homanick; Chm., Anne Zug; Cur., Caitlin Harvey; Site Coord., Melanie Depcinski.
Institution Type/Description: Historic Site Museum: housed in 1741 Gemeinhaus. A National Historic Landmark.
Hours & Admission Prices: Jan.-March Sat. 11-4, Sun. 12-4; April-Nov. Fri. & Sat. 11-4, Sun. 12-4; Nov. & Dec. extended hours. Admission $12-$20 depending on the amount of sites to be visited. Closed New Year's Day; Thanksgiving; Christmas Eve & Day.
Attendance: 5,000 (estimated)

NATIONAL MUSEUM OF INDUSTRIAL HISTORY, 602 E. 2nd St., Ste. 70, Bethlehem, PA 18015. Tel.: 610-694-6644. Fax: 610-694-6641. Facebook.
E-mail: info@nmih.org
Web Site: www.nmih.org
Key Personnel: Dir., Pres. & C.E.O., Amy Hollander; Chm., L. Charles Marcon; Museum Shop Mgr., Deedee Riffle.
Institution Type/Description: History Museum: housed on the site of the former Bethlehem Steel plant.
Hours & Admission Prices: Wed.-Sun. 10-5. Adults $12; discounts to Smithsonian affiliates & NARM members; members no charge. &
Attendance: 50,000

SUN INN PRESERVATION ASSOCIATION INC., 556 Main St., 2nd Fl., Bethlehem, PA 18018-5861. Tel.: 610-866-1758. Fax: 590-694-3521.
E-mail: suninn@rcn.com
Web Site: www.suninnbethlehem.org/
Key Personnel: Pres., Seth Cornish; Vice Pres., Randi Mantz; Treas., Gary Dologite.
Institution Type/Description: Historical Museum: housed in a Germanic stone building which hosted the military leaders, statesmen and the Founding Fathers during the American Revolution.
Hours & Admission Prices: Sat.-Sun. 1-4. No charge; donations accepted. &
Attendance: 11,500 (actual)

Biglerville

NATIONAL APPLE MUSEUM, 154 W. Hanover St., Biglerville, PA 17307. Mailing Address: P.O. Box 656, Biglerville, PA 17307-0656. Tel.: 717-677-4556.
E-mail: info@nationalapplemuseum.com
Web Site: nationalapplemuseum.com
Key Personnel: Pres. (V), Harold L. Griffie; Archivist, Tim Smith.
Institution Type/Description: Local History & Agriculture Museum: housed in restored Civil War barn.
Hours & Admission Prices: May-Oct. Sat. 11-4, Sun. 1-4; groups & other times by appointment. Adults $3, seniors 60 & over $2, children 6-16 $1.50; discounts to AAM & ICOM members. &
Attendance: 3,500 (estimated)

Birdsboro

DANIEL BOONE HOMESTEAD, 400 Daniel Boone Rd., Birdsboro, PA 19508-8735. Tel.: 610-582-4900. Fax: 610-582-1744.
E-mail: info@danielboonehomestead.org
Web Site: www.danielboonehomestead.org
Institution Type/Description: Open Air Museum: located on site of Daniel Boone's birth.
Hours & Admission Prices: Recreation: Tues.-Fri. 10-4, Sat. 10-4:45, Sun. 12-3:45. Visitor Center & Historic Area: see website for seasonal hours. Adults $7, AAA

& senior citizens (65 & over) $6; children 5-11 $4; members and children 4 & under no charge. Closed New Year's Day; Thanksgiving; Christmas Eve & Day. *Attendance:* 45,000 (estimated)

Blairsville

HISTORICAL SOCIETY OF BLAIRSVILLE, 116 E. Campbell St., Blairsville, PA 15717-1310. Tel.: 724-459-0580.
Institution Type/Description: Historical Society Museum: housed in the former home of Nellie Stitt; built in 1909.
Hours & Admission Prices: Tues.-Sat. 10-2; other times by appointment.

Bloomsburg

BILL'S OLD BIKE BARN, 7145 Columbia Blvd., Bloomsburg, PA 17815-8635. Tel.: 570-759-7030. Fax: 570-759-9684.
E-mail: billsbikebarn@uplink.net
Web Site: www.billsbikebarn.com
Key Personnel: Dir., William Morris; Museum Shop Mgr., Judy E. Laubach.
Institution Type/Description: History Museum.
Hours & Admission Prices: Thurs.-Fri. 10-6, Sat. 9:30-3, Sun. 1-5. Adults $5.

THE CHILDREN'S MUSEUM, INC., 2 W. Seventh St., Bloomsburg, PA 17815-2603. Tel.: 570-389-9206.
E-mail: info@the-childrens-museum.org
Web Site: www.the-childrens-museum.org
Key Personnel: Dir., Shawna Meiser.
Institution Type/Description: Children's Museum.
Hours & Admission Prices: Tues.-Sat. 10-4. Adults $6.50; members no charge. Closed major holidays. &
Attendance: 17,000 (actual)

COLUMBIA COUNTY HISTORICAL AND GENEALOGICAL SOCIETY, 225 Market St., Bloomsburg, PA 17815-0360. Mailing Address: P.O. Box 360, Bloomsburg, PA 17815-0360. Tel.: 570-784-1600.
E-mail: research@colcohist-gensoc.org
Web Site: www.colcohist-gensoc.org
Key Personnel: Pres., John R. Thomas; Exec. Dir., Bonnie Farver; Museum Dir., Alex Dubil.
Institution Type/Description: Historical Society Museum.
Hours & Admission Prices: Tues. & Fri. 9-3, Thurs. 1-7:30, Sat. 9am-11:30am. Library Research: $2 per hour; members no charge. &
Attendance: 2,600 (estimated)

HAAS GALLERY OF ART - BLOOMSBURG UNIVERSITY, Haas Center for the Arts & Mitrani Hall, 2nd Fl., Bloomsburg, PA 17815. Mailing Address: Dept. of Art & Art History, 400 E. Second St., Bloomsburg, PA 17815. Tel.: 570-389-4708.
E-mail: rmorgan@bloomu.edu
Key Personnel: Gallery Assoc., Rebecca Rugg.
Institution Type/Description: Art Gallery.
Hours & Admission Prices: Mon.-Fri. 9-4, Sat. 12-2. No charge. Closed university holidays. &

Blue Bell

WISSAHICKON VALLEY HISTORICAL SOCIETY, 799 Skippack Pike, Blue Bell, PA 19422. Mailing Address: P.O. Box 96, Ambler, PA 19002-0096. Tel.: 215-646-6541.
E-mail: info@wvalleyhs.org
Web Site: www.wvalleyhs.org
Institution Type/Description: Historical Society Museum: housed in the former Whitpain Public School; built 1895. Listed on the National Register of Historic Places.
Hours & Admission Prices: Call for hours.

Boalsburg

BOALSBURG HERITAGE MUSEUM, 304 E. Main St., Boalsburg, PA 16827. Mailing Address: P.O. Box 346, Boalsburg, PA 16827. Tel.: 814-466-3035.
Web Site: www.boalsburgheritagemuseum.org
Institution Type/Description: History Museum.
Hours & Admission Prices: Tues. & Sat. 2-4; other times by appointment. No charge; donations accepted.

COLUMBUS CHAPEL, BOAL MANSION MUSEUM, 163 Boal Estate Dr., Boalsburg, PA 16827. Mailing Address: P.O. Box 116, Boalsburg, PA 16827-0116. Tel.: 814-466-6210.
E-mail: office@boalmuseum.com
Web Site: boalmuseum.com
Key Personnel: Dir., Bob Cameron.
Institution Type/Description: Historic House Museum: 1809, Boal Mansion.
Hours & Admission Prices: May & Sept.-Oct. Tues.-Sun. 1:30-5; Summer: Tues.-Sat. 10-5, Sun. 12-5. Adults $10, children $6; discount to prearranged group tours over 10. &
Attendance: 25,000 (estimated)

PENNSYLVANIA MILITARY MUSEUM AND 28TH DIVISION SHRINE, 602 Boalsburg Pike, Boalsburg, PA 16827-1251. Mailing Address: P.O. Box 160A, Boalsburg, PA 16827-0660. Tel.: 814-466-6263. Fax: 814-466-6618.
E-mail: karlsmith@pa.gov
Web Site: www.pamilmuseum.org
Key Personnel: Dir. & Cur., Chuck Smith; Pres., Steve Schroder; Business Mgr. & Museum Shop Mgr., Danielle Hughs; Museum Educator, Joseph Horvath.
Institution Type/Description: Military Museum.
Hours & Admission Prices: Museum: call for hours. Shrine & Museum Grounds: Summer Tues.-Sat. 9-5, Sun. 12-5; Winter call for hours. Adults 12-64 $6, seniors & groups $5.50, youths 3-11 $4; discounts to AAM members; children under 3 & members no charge. Closed New Year's Day; Thanksgiving; Christmas. &
Attendance: 15,000 (estimated)

Boyertown

BOYERTOWN AREA HISTORICAL SOCIETY, 43 S. Chestnut St., Boyertown, PA 19512-1508. Tel.: 610-367-5255.
E-mail: boyertownhistory@windstream.net
Web Site: www.boyertownhistory.org
Key Personnel: Pres. (V), Brian Quigley; Dir. Collections, Lindsay Dierolf.
Institution Type/Description: Historical Society Museum: housed in the former home of George Unger & later the St. Columbkill Roman Catholic Church; built in 1902.
Hours & Admission Prices: Thurs. 1-9; other times by appointment. Adults $5; discounts to students under 18; members no charge. &
Attendance: 1,000 (estimated)

BOYERTOWN MUSEUM OF HISTORIC VEHICLES, 85 S. Walnut St., Boyertown, PA 19512-1462. Tel.: 610-367-2090. Fax: 610-367-9712.
E-mail: mail@boyertownmuseum.org
Web Site: boyertownmuseum.org
Key Personnel: Exec. Dir., David V. Beard; Chm. Exec. Committee (V), Robert H. Dare; Pres. (V), Bernard Hofmann; Operations Mgr., Loretta Wolf; Facilities Supvr., Roderick Reinert; Cur., Kendra Cook; Museum Receptionist, Darlene Brunner.
Institution Type/Description: Transportation Museum.
Hours & Admission Prices: Tues.-Sun. 9:30-4. Adults $6, seniors $5, students $4; discounts to AAA & AAM members; children under 6 no charge. Closed major holidays. &
Attendance: 4,900 (actual)

Bradford

ZIPPO/CASE VISITORS CENTER, 1932 Zippo Dr., Bradford, PA 16701-5414. Mailing Address: 33 Barbour St., Bradford, PA 16701-1998. Tel.: 814-368-1932 & 2711. Fax: 814-368-2874.
E-mail: lmeabon@zippo.com
Web Site: www.zippo.com
Key Personnel: C.E.O. & Pres. Zippo Mfg. Co., Gregory W. Booth; Dir., Patrick Grandy; Cur. & Archivist, Linda Meabon; Museum Shop Mgr., Jesse Noga.
Institution Type/Description: Company Museum.
Hours & Admission Prices: Mon.-Sat. 9-5, Sun. 11-4. No charge. Closed New Year's Day; Easter; Thanksgiving; Christmas. &
Attendance: 50,000 (estimated)

Bridgeville

WOODVILLE PLANTATION, 1375 Washington Pike, Bridgeville, PA 15017-2821. Tel.: 412-221-0348.
E-mail: nevillehouseassociates@gmail.com
Institution Type/Description: History Museum: housed in the former home of John & Presley Neville; c.1780.
Hours & Admission Prices: Self-Guided Tours: Wed.-Sat. 10-6. Guided Tours: Sun. 1-4.

Bristol

MARGARET R. GRUNDY MEMORIAL MUSEUM, 610 Radcliffe St., Bristol, PA 19007. Tel.: 215-788-9432 & 7891.
E-mail: bl@grundyfoundation.com
Web Site: www.grundyfoundation.com
Institution Type/Description: History Museum.
Hours & Admission Prices: Tues.-Sat. 1-4; groups by appointment. No charge. Closed major holidays.

Brodheadsville

HERITAGE CENTER OF THE WESTERN POCONO COMMUNITY LIBRARY, 149 Bond Lane, Brodheadsville, PA 18322-0318. Mailing Address: P.O. Box 318, Brodheadsville, PA 18322-6318. Tel.: 570-402-1906. Fax: 570-992-7915.
E-mail: wpcl10@ptd.net
Web Site: www.wpcl.lib.pa.us
Key Personnel: Dir., Carol Kern; Devel., Education & Pub. Rels., Jessica Reitz; Treas., Shereen Eckhart.
Institution Type/Description: Local History Museum.
Hours & Admission Prices: Tues.-Sat. 10-4. No charge; donations accepted. Closed New Year's Day; Independence Day; Thanksgiving; Christmas. ♿
Attendance: 151 (actual)

Brookville

JEFFERSON COUNTY HISTORY CENTER, 172-176 Main St., P.O. Box 51, Brookville, PA 15825-0051. Tel.: 814-849-0077.
E-mail: jchc@windstream.net
Web Site: www.jchconline.org
Key Personnel: Exec. Dir., Ken Burkett; Cur., Carole Briggs.
Institution Type/Description: History Center.
Hours & Admission Prices: Wed.-Sat. 12-5.

Bryn Athyn

GLENCAIRN MUSEUM: ACADEMY OF THE NEW CHURCH, 1001 Cathedral Rd., Bryn Athyn, PA 19009-0757. Mailing Address: Box 757, Bryn Athyn, PA 19009-0757. Tel.: 267-502-2600 & 2990. Fax: 267-502-2986. Facebook: Glencairn Museum.
E-mail: info@glencairnmuseum.org
Web Site: www.glencairnmuseum.org
Key Personnel: Dir. Emeritus, Stephen H. Morley; Dir., Brian Henderson; Cur., C. Edward Gyllenhaal; Asst. Dir., Bret Bostock; Coord. Education, Christine McDonald; Mktg. & Public Rels., Joralyn Glenn; Tours & Rental Events, Leah Smith; Museum Shop Mgr. and Mgr. Operations & Membership, Peter Childs; Chief Custodian, Edwin Steiner.
Institution Type/Description: Religious Art Museum: housed in a Romanesque style building crafted in stained glass, mosaic, & sculptured granite; c.1939.
Hours & Admission Prices: Museum: Tues.-Fri. 8-5, Sat.-Sun. 1-4:30. Tours: Tues.-Fri. 2:30, Sat. & Sun. 1, 1:45, 2:30 & 3; reservations suggested. Christmas in the Castle Tours: Nov. 27-Jan. 10 Mon.-Fri. 1:30 & 2:30, Sat.-Sun. 1, 1:30 & 2:30; reservations recommended. Adults $12, seniors & students $10; discounts for Basic members, and AAM & NARM members; children 3 & under and Gold members no charge. Closed national holidays. ♿
Attendance: 17,600 (estimated)

Butler

BUTLER COUNTY HISTORICAL SOCIETY - SENATOR WALTER LOWRIE HOUSE, 123 W. Diamond St., Butler, PA 16001. Tel.: 724-283-8116. Fax: 724-283-2505.
E-mail: society@butlerhistory.com
Web Site: www.butlerhistory.com
Key Personnel: Dir., Patricia M. Collins; Pres. (V), Brett W. Ligo.
Institution Type/Description: Historic House Museum: home built in 1828.
Hours & Admission Prices: Tours: by appointment. Office: Tues.-Fri. 10-4. Adults $5, children 16 & under $2. Closed legal holidays.
Attendance: 3,000 (estimated)

MARIDON MUSEUM, 322 N. McKean St., Butler, PA 16001-4913. Tel.: 724-282-0123. Fax: 724-282-0567.
E-mail: info@maridon.org
Web Site: www.maridon.org
Key Personnel: Pres. Bd., Kenneth Bronder; Dir., Roxann D. Booser.
Institution Type/Description: History Museum.
Hours & Admission Prices: Wed.-Sat. 11-4. Adults $4, senior citizens & students $3; members and children 8 & under no charge. Closed New Year's Day; Easter; Memorial Day; Independence Day; Labor Day; Thanksgiving; Christmas. ♿
Attendance: 2,100 (estimated)

California

THE GALLAGHER HOUSE - CALIFORNIA AREA HISTORICAL SOCIETY, 429 Wood St. @ 5th St., California, PA 15419. Mailing Address: P.O. Box 624, California, PA 15419-0624. Tel.: 724-938-3250. Facebook: California PA Historical Society.
E-mail: calpahistoricalsociety@gmail.com
Institution Type/Description: Historic House: built in 1903.
Hours & Admission Prices: Tues.-Thurs. 9-4; other times by appointment. No charge; donations accepted. Closed holidays.

Camp Hill

THE FRIENDS OF PEACE CHURCH, St. John's and Trindle Roads, Camp Hill, PA 17011. Mailing Address: P.O. Box 3034, Shiremanstown, PA 17011-3034. Tel.: 717-737-6492.
Web Site: www.historicpeacechurch.org
Key Personnel: Pres., Vernon Cleary; Vice Pres., James Bower; Treas., Earnest Kepner; Sec., Charlene Cleary; Property Placement Officer, Janice Mullen; Museum Shop Mgr., Betty O'Neill.
Institution Type/Description: Historic Site & Building: 1799 Georgian style stone church.
Hours & Admission Prices: June-Sept. Sun. 2-5. No charge; donations accepted. ♿
Attendance: 9,290 (actual)

Carbondale

CARBONDALE HISTORICAL SOCIETY AND MUSEUM, One N. Main St., 3rd Fl., Carbondale, PA 18407. Mailing Address: P.O. Box 151, Carbondale, PA 18407-0151. Tel.: 570-282-0385.
E-mail: info@carbondalehistorical.org
Institution Type/Description: Historical Society Museum: housed in the Carbondale City Hall building. Listed on the National Register of Historic Places.
Hours & Admission Prices: Mon.-Fri. 12-5. No charge; donations accepted. ♿

Carlisle

CUMBERLAND COUNTY HISTORICAL SOCIETY, THE HAMILTON LIBRARY, THE TWO MILE HOUSE AND HISTORY ON HIGH THE SHOP, 21 N. Pitt St., Carlisle, PA 17013-2945. Tel.: 717-249-7610. Fax: 717-258-9332.
E-mail: info@historicalsociety.com
Web Site: www.historicalsociety.com
Key Personnel: Exec. Dir., Linda F. Witmer.
Institution Type/Description: Local History Library & Museum.
Hours & Admission Prices: Mon. 4-8, Tues.-Fri. 10-4, Sat. 10-2. Library: adults $5. Museum & Exhibits no charge; donations accepted. Closed New Year's Day; Memorial Day; Independence Day; Labor Day; Martin Luther King, Jr. Day; Presidents' Day; Thanksgiving; Christmas & day after. ♿
Attendance: 60,000 (actual)

THE TROUT GALLERY, 240 W. High St., Carlisle, PA 17013. Mailing Address: Dickinson College, P.O. Box 1773, Carlisle, PA 17013-2896. Tel.: 717-245-1344. Fax: 717-254-8929.
E-mail: trout@dickinson.edu
Web Site: www.troutgallery.org
Key Personnel: Dir., Dr. Phillip Earenfight; Registrar & Exhibition Preparator, James Bowman; Asst. Dir. Design Svcs., Neil Mills; Dir. Design Svcs., Amanda DeLorenze.
Institution Type/Description: Art Museum.
Hours & Admission Prices: Tues.-Sat. 10-4. No charge. Closed national holidays; New Year's Day; Memorial Day; Independence Day; Thanksgiving break; Christmas break. ♿
Attendance: 11,479 (actual)

UNION FIRE COMPANY MUSEUM, 35 W. Louther St., Carlisle, PA 17013. Tel.: 717-243-2123.
E-mail: irw98@comcast.net
Web Site: www.unionfireco.org/museum
Institution Type/Description: Firefighting History Museum: housed in the former fire station built in 1888.
Hours & Admission Prices: Daily 10-8; groups by appointment. No charge; donations accepted.
Attendance: 500 (estimated)

UNITED STATES ARMY HERITAGE AND EDUCATION CENTER - ARMY HERITAGE MUSEUM, 950 Soldiers Dr., Carlisle, PA 17013-5021. Tel.: 717-245-3972. Fax: 717-245-4370 (COM) & 242-4370 (DSN).
E-mail: usarmy.carlisle.awc.mbx-cpa@mail.mil
Web Site: www.usahec.org
Key Personnel: Dir., Col. Peter D. Crean; Deputy Dir., Ltc. Scott T. Clutter; Dir. US Army Military History Institute, Mr. James Scudieri; Dir. Army Heritage Museum, John Leighow; Dir. Visitor & Education Svcs., John Giblin; Dir. USAWC Library, Ms. Greta Braungard.
Institution Type/Description: Military Museum.
Hours & Admission Prices: Mon.-Sat. 10-5, Sun. 12-5. No charge. Closed some federal holidays. &
Attendance: 180,000 (actual)

Catawissa

CATAWISSA RAILROAD CO., 119 Pine St., Catawissa, PA 17820-1239. Tel.: 570-356-2345. Fax: 570-356-7876.
E-mail: walt@caboosenut.com
Web Site: caboosenut.com
Institution Type/Description: Railroad Museum.
Hours & Admission Prices: Daily 8-5. No charge.
Attendance: 2,000 (estimated)

Centre Hall

PENN'S CAVE & WILDLIFE PARK, 222 Penns Cave Rd., Centre Hall, PA 16828-8103. Tel.: 814-364-1664. Fax: 814-364-8778. Facebook: Penn's Cave 1885.
E-mail: info@pennscave.com
Web Site: www.pennscave.com
Institution Type/Description: Cavern & Wildlife Park.
Hours & Admission Prices: Call for hours. Wildlife Park: adults $19.95, senior citizens 65 & over $18.95, children 2-12 $11.95; discounts to military; children under 2 no charge. Cave: adults $16.95, senior citizens 65 & over $15.95, children 2-12 $8.95; discounts to military. Cave & Wildlife Park: adults $30.95, seniors citizens 65 & over $29.95, children 2-12 $16.95; discounts to military; children under 2 no charge. &

Chadds Ford

BRANDYWINE BATTLEFIELD PARK, 1491 Baltimore Pike, Chadds Ford, PA 19317-7369. Mailing Address: Brandywine Battlefield Park Assoc., P.O. Box 202, Chadds Ford, PA 19317. Tel.: 610-459-3342, ext. 3001. Fax: 610-459-9586. Facebook: Brandywine Battlefield.
E-mail: judythorpe@verizon.net
Web Site: www.brandywinebattlefield.org
Key Personnel: Pres. (V), George Thorpe; Site Admin., Michael Bertheaud.
Institution Type/Description: Historic Site: site of the Battle of the Brandywine.
Hours & Admission Prices: March 12-March 31 Fri.-Sat. 9-4, Sun. 12-4; April-Nov. Wed.-Sat. 9-4, Sun. 12-4. Tours: adults $8, senior citizens & youth 6-14 $5; children under 6 & military no charge. Park: no charge.
Attendance: 20,000 (estimated)

BRANDYWINE RIVER MUSEUM OF ART, U.S. Rte. 1, at Hoffman's Mill Rd., Chadds Ford, PA 19317. Mailing Address: P. O. Box 141, Chadds Ford, PA 19317-0141. Tel.: 610-388-2700. Fax: 610-388-1197.
E-mail: inquiries@brandywine.org
Web Site: www.brandywinemuseum.org
Key Personnel: Exec. Dir., Virginia A. Logan.
Institution Type/Description: Art Museum: housed in 1864 Hoffman's Mill located on the Brandywine River.
Hours & Admission Prices: Daily 9:30-4:30. Adults $15, senior citizens $10, students & children 6-18 $6; discounts to AAM, ICOM & AAMD members; children under 5 & members no charge. Closed Thanksgiving; Christmas. &
Attendance: 101,000 (actual)

CHADDS FORD HISTORICAL SOCIETY, 1736 Creek Rd., Chadds Ford, PA 19317. Mailing Address: P.O. Box 27, Chadds Ford, PA 19317-0027. Tel.: 610-388-7376.
E-mail: info@chaddsfordhistory.org
Web Site: www.chaddsfordhistory.org
Key Personnel: Exec. Dir., Nadia Barakat; Pres. (V), Kendal Reynolds; Education Coord. & Collections Mgr., Lynda Gillow; Program & Devel. Mgr., Allison Schell.
Institution Type/Description: Historical Society Museum.

Hours & Admission Prices: House Tours & Visitor's Center: Wed.-Sat. 11-4:30. Barn: no charge. Each House: $5 per person; members no charge.
Attendance: 20,000 (estimated)

THE CHRISTIAN C. SANDERSON MUSEUM, 1755 Creek Rd., Chadds Ford, PA 19317. Mailing Address: P.O. Box 153, Chadds Ford, PA 19317-0153. Tel.: 610-388-6545.
E-mail: info@sandersonmuseum.org
Web Site: www.sandersonmuseum.org
Key Personnel: Pres. (V), Susan M. Minarchi; Cur., Charles E. Ulmann.
Institution Type/Description: History Museum.
Hours & Admission Prices: March-Nov. Thurs.-Sun. 12-4; groups by appointment. Adults $5; members no charge. Closed Easter; Thanksgiving; Christmas.
Attendance: 1,000 (estimated)

Chambersburg

CHAMBERSBURG VOLUNTEER FIREMAN'S MUSEUM, 441 Broad St., Chambersburg, PA 17201. Tel.: 717-263-5872.
E-mail: cfdinfo@chambersburgpa.gov
Web Site: www.chambersburgfire.com
Institution Type/Description: Firefighting History Museum.
Hours & Admission Prices: By appointment. No charge; donations accepted.

Cheltenham

CHELTENHAM CENTER FOR THE ARTS, 439 Ashbourne Rd., Cheltenham, PA 19012. Tel.: 215-379-4660. Fax: 215-663-1946.
E-mail: info@cheltenhamarts.org
Web Site: cheltenhamarts.org
Institution Type/Description: Art Gallery.
Hours & Admission Prices: Call for hours.

Chester

WIDENER UNIVERSITY ART COLLECTION AND GALLERY, 14th & Chestnut Sts. (University Center), Chester, PA 19013. Mailing Address: One University Pl., Chester, PA 19013-5792. Tel.: 610-499-1189 & 4000. Fax: 610-499-4425.
E-mail: rmwarda@widener.edu
Web Site: www.widener.edu/artgallery
Key Personnel: Collections Mgr., Rebecca M. Warda.
Institution Type/Description: University Art Museum.
Hours & Admission Prices: Sept.-May Tues. 10-7, Wed.-Sat. 10-4:30; June-Aug. call for hours. No charge. Closed major holidays. &
Attendance: 4,000 (estimated)

Clarion

CLARION COUNTY HISTORICAL SOCIETY, SUTTON-DITZ HOUSE MUSEUM, 17 S. Fifth Ave., Clarion, PA 16214-1501. Tel.: 814-226-4450. Fax: 814-226-7106. Facebook: Clarion County Historical Society.
E-mail: clarionhistory@comcast.net
Web Site: www.clarioncountyhistoricalsociety.org
Key Personnel: Dir. & Cur., Mary Lea Lucas; Chm. (V), Rudy Jannazzo; Museum Shop Mgr., Karen Slack.
Institution Type/Description: County History Museum: located in c.1850 home, renovated in 1909.
Hours & Admission Prices: Museum: Tues.-Fri. 10-4; other times by appointment. No charge; donations accepted. Closed major holidays. &
Attendance: 1,800 (estimated)

UNIVERSITY GALLERIES, Clarion Univ. of Pennsylvania, Carlson Library A-4, Clarion, PA 16214. Tel.: 814-393-2523. Fax: 814-393-2168.
E-mail: gallery@clarion.edu
Formerly: Sandford Gallery
Institution Type/Description: Art Gallery.
Hours & Admission Prices: Tues.-Thurs. & Sat. 12-5. No charge. Closed university holidays. &
Attendance: 1,500 (estimated)

Clearfield

CLEARFIELD COUNTY HISTORICAL SOCIETY, 511 Van Valzah Ave., Clearfield, PA 16830-2521. Tel.: 814-765-6125.
Web Site: www.clearfieldcountyhistoricalsociety.net

Key Personnel: Pres., Denny Shaffner; 1st Vice Pres., Susan Williams; Sec., Mary Kay Royer; Membership, Cathie Hughes; Treas., Brent Thomas; Museum Shop Mgr., Warren Fox.
Institution Type/Description: Local History Museum: housed in c.1880, 3-story brick building.
Hours & Admission Prices: May-Oct. Thurs. & Sun. 1:30-4:30; other times by appointment. No charge; donations accepted.
Attendance: 1,300 (actual)

Coalport

COALPORT AREA COAL MUSEUM, 961 Forest St., Coalport, PA 16627. Mailing Address: P.O. Box 248, Coalport, PA 16627-0248. Tel.: 814-672-4378 & 312-8620.
E-mail: rwsnyder@windstream.net
Web Site: www.coalportmuseum.org
Formerly: Coalport Area Museum Commission
Key Personnel: Pres. (V), Robert J. Counsman, Jr.; Cur., Richard W. Snyder, II.
Institution Type/Description: History Museum.
Hours & Admission Prices: Mon.-Wed. 10-5, Thurs. 10-6. Sun. 1-5. No charge; donations accepted.
Attendance: 1,000 (estimated)

Coatesville

NATIONAL IRON & STEEL HERITAGE MUSEUM, 50 S. 1st Ave., Coatesville, PA 19320. Tel.: 610-384-9282.
E-mail: admin@steelmuseum.org
Web Site: www.steelmuseum.org
Key Personnel: Exec. Dir., James D. Ziegler; Pres., Scott G. Huston.
Institution Type/Description: History Museum.
Hours & Admission Prices: Mon.-Sat. 10-4; groups by appointment. ♿
Attendance: 2,300 (actual)

Collegeville

PHILIP AND MURIEL BERMAN MUSEUM OF ART AT URSINUS COLLEGE, 601 E. Main St., Collegeville, PA 19426-1000. Mailing Address: P.O. Box 1000, Collegeville, PA 19426-1000. Tel.: 610-409-3500. Fax: 610-409-3664.
E-mail: lhanover@ursinus.edu
Web Site: www.ursinus.edu/berman
Key Personnel: Dir., Lisa Tremper Hanover; Administrative Asst., Suzanne Calvin; Collections Mgr., Julie Choma.
Institution Type/Description: Art Museum.
Hours & Admission Prices: Tues.-Fri. 10-4, Sat.-Sun. 12-4:30. No charge; donations accepted. Closed college holidays. ♿
Attendance: 32,000 (estimated)

Columbia

COLUMBIA MUSEUM OF HISTORY - COLUMBIA HISTORIC PRESERVATION SOCIETY, 19-21 N. Second St., Columbia, PA 17512. Mailing Address: P.O. Box 578, Columbia, PA 17512.
E-mail: cverachps@gmail.com
Key Personnel: Dir. & Pres. (V), Christopher Vera.
Institution Type/Description: History Museum: housed in the former First Evangelical Lutheran Church; built in 1853.
Hours & Admission Prices: Sat.-Sun. 1-4; other times by appointment. No charge; donations accepted.
Attendance: 2,000 (estimated)

FIRST NATIONAL BANK MUSEUM, 170 Locust St., Columbia, PA 17512-1109. Tel.: 717-684-8864, 717-341-7229. Fax: 717-684-8048. Facebook: First National Bank Museum.
E-mail: bankmuseum@yahoo.com
Key Personnel: Owner & Cur., Nora Motter Stark; Owner & Cur., Michael Stark.
Institution Type/Description: History Museum.
Hours & Admission Prices: Call for hours. Suggested donation $8-$10.

THE NATIONAL WATCH & CLOCK MUSEUM, 514 Poplar St., Columbia, PA 17512-2124. Tel.: 717-684-8261. Fax: 717-684-0878.
E-mail: museumoftime@nawcc.org
Web Site: www.museumoftime.org
Key Personnel: Exec. Dir., J. Steven Humphrey; Museum Dir., Noel Poirier; Cur., Kim Jovinelli; Library Dir., Sara Butler-Dockery; Librarian, Nancy Dyer; Archivist, Kate Van Riper.
Institution Type/Description: Horological Museum.

Hours & Admission Prices: April & Sept.-Nov. Tues.-Sat. 10-5, Sun. 12-4; Memorial Day to Labor Day Mon.-Sat. 10-5, Sun. 12-4; Dec.-March Tues.-Sat. 10-4. Adults $9; discounts to children, senior citizens, groups, AAA & AAM members; ASTC passport & NAWCC members no charge. Closed holidays. ♿
Attendance: 15,000 (estimated)

TURKEY HILL EXPERIENCE, 301 Linden St., Columbia, PA 17512. Tel.: 844-847-4884. Facebook; Twitter; Pinterest..
Web Site: turkeyhillexperience.com
Institution Type/Description: Company Museum.
Hours & Admission Prices: Daily seasonal hours. Basic Experience Tour: adults $10.50, seniors 62 & over and children 4-12 $10; military and children 3 & under no charge. Taste Lab & Tea Discovery areas require an additional fee. Closed Thanksgiving; Christmas.

WRIGHT'S FERRY MANSION, 38 S. Second St., Columbia, PA 17512-1402. Mailing Address: P.O. Box 68, Columbia, PA 17512-0068. Tel.: 717-684-4325.
E-mail: info@lancastercountymuseums.org
Key Personnel: Exec. Dir., Thomas Cook; Cur., Elizabeth Meg Schaefer.
Institution Type/Description: Historic House: 1738 Susanna Wright House.
Hours & Admission Prices: May-Oct. Tues.-Wed. & Fri.-Sat. 10-3 (last tour begins at 3). Adults $5, children 6-18 $2.50; discount to groups. Closed holidays.
Attendance: 2,000

Concordville

PIERCE-WILLITS MAIN HOUSE, Smithbridge Rd., Concordville, PA 19331. Mailing Address: Concord Township Historical Society, P.O. Box 152, Concordville, PA 19331. Tel.: 610-459-8911.
Institution Type/Description: Historical Society Museum.
Hours & Admission Prices: By appointment.

Conshohocken

MONTGOMERY COUNTY GUILD OF PROFESSIONAL ARTISTS (MCGOPA), Inquirer Bldg., Rte. 23, Conshohocken, PA 19428. Mailing Address: P.O. Box 60736, King of Prussia, PA 19406. Tel.: 610-803-3248.
E-mail: mcgopa@comcast.net
Key Personnel: Dir., Maria Lourdes Solomon.
Institution Type/Description: Art Gallery.
Hours & Admission Prices: Call for hours.

Coolspring

COOLSPRING POWER MUSEUM, 179 Coolspring Rd., Coolspring, PA 15730. Tel.: 814-849-6883.
E-mail: cpm@coolspringpowermuseum.org
Web Site: www.coolspringpowermuseum.org
Key Personnel: Dir., Vance Packard; Dir., Paul Harvey, M.D.; Dir., Chris Austin; Dir., Douglas Fye, Jr.; Dir. & Financial Dir., Jennifer Fye; Pres., Clark Colby; Dir., John Hanley; Dir., Kim Himes; Dir., Kevin Kusel; Dir., Lee Caylor; Dir., Glenn Anthony; Dir., Michael Murphy; Dir., Tommy Turner; Chm. (V) & Membership, Gail Lavender; Museum Shop Mgr., Fran Colby.
Institution Type/Description: Historical Museum.
Hours & Admission Prices: April-Oct. 3rd Sat.-Sun. each month 10-5; other times by appointment. Adult $6, senior citizen, children under 12 & students $1; discounts to groups; children & members no charge. ♿
Attendance: 19,125 (estimated)

Cornwall

CORNWALL IRON FURNACE, 94 Rexmont Rd., Cornwall, PA 17016. Mailing Address: P.O. Box 251, Cornwall, PA 17016-0251. Tel.: 717-272-9711. Fax: 717-272-0450.
E-mail: ssomers@pa.gov
Web Site: www.cornwallironfurnace.org
Key Personnel: Historic Site Admin., Stephen G. Somers.
Institution Type/Description: Industrial Museum.
Hours & Admission Prices: Tues.-Sat. 9-5, Sun. 12-5. Adults $6, senior citizens 65 & over $5.50, youth 3-12 $4; discounts to AAM members; children under 6 no charge. Closed New Year's Day; Martin Luther King Jr. Day; Presidents' Day; Columbus Day; Veterans Day; Thanksgiving & day after; Christmas. ♿
Attendance: 9,000 (estimated)

Corry

CORRY AREA HISTORICAL SOCIETY, INC., 945 Mead Ave., Corry, PA 16407. Tel.: 814-664-4749. Facebook: Corry Area Historical Society.
E-mail: admin@corryareahistoricalsociety.org
Web Site: www.corryareahistoricalsociety.org
Key Personnel: C.E.O., Ann Clark; Vice Pres., Nancy Mason; 2nd Vice Pres., Connie Burkhart; Sec., Loretta Beckerink; Treas., Cherie Dickey; Cur., Alisa Puckly.
Institution Type/Description: Local History Museum.
Hours & Admission Prices: Memorial Day-Labor Day Thurs. 10-2, Sun. 2-4; groups & tours at other times by appointment. No charge; donations accepted.
Attendance: 5,500 (estimated)

Coudersport

POTTER COUNTY HISTORICAL SOCIETY, 308 N. Main St., Coudersport, PA 16915-1626. Mailing Address: P.O. Box 605, Coudersport, PA 16915-0605. Tel.: 814-274-4410. Fax: 814-274-4411.
E-mail: pottercohist@zitomedia.net
Web Site: www.paintedhills.org
Key Personnel: Pres., David Castano; 1st Vice Pres., Charles Nelson; 2nd Vice Pres., Donna Batterson; Sec. & Treas., Lucille Church; Librarian, Diane Caudell.
Institution Type/Description: Historical Society Museum.
Hours & Admission Prices: Museum Tours & Research: Mon. & Fri. 10:30-4. No charge; donations accepted.
Attendance: 1,800 (estimated)

Cresson

ADMIRAL PEARY MONUMENT, 7468 Admiral Peary Hwy., Rte. 2014, Cresson, PA 16630-1717. Mailing Address: Bureau of Historic Sites & Museums-Commonwealth Keystone Building, 400 North St., Harrisburg, PA 17120-0053. Tel.: 717-705-0559.
Key Personnel: Property Placement Div. Chief, Robert N. Sieber.
Institution Type/Description: State Monument: dedicated to Admiral Robert E. Peary, discoverer of the North Pole in 1909.
Hours & Admission Prices: Daily dawn-dusk. No charge.

Dallas

PAULY FRIEDMAN ART GALLERY, Misericordia University, 301 Lake St., Dallas, PA 18612-1008. Tel.: 570-674-6250. Fax: 570-674-6416.
E-mail: dposatko@misericordia.edu
Web Site: www.misericordia.edu
Formerly: MacDonald Art Gallery
Key Personnel: Dir., Dona Posatko; Cur. & Gallery Asst., Dona Posatko.
Institution Type/Description: Art Gallery, part of the university.
Hours & Admission Prices: Mon.-Thurs. 10:30-8, Sat.-Sun. 1-5. No charge.

Dayton

MARSHALL HOUSE MUSEUM, 107 N. State St., Dayton, PA 16222. Mailing Address: P.O. Box 447, Dayton, PA 16222-0447. Tel.: 814-257-8846.
E-mail: innkeeper@marshallhouse.com
Web Site: www.marshallhouse.com
Institution Type/Description: Historic House Museum: built in 1868. Listed on the National Register of Historic Places.
Hours & Admission Prices: Memorial Day to mid-Oct. Sat. 2-4; other times by appointment.
Attendance: 200 (estimated)

Delaware Water Gap

ANTOINE DUTOT MUSEUM & GALLERY, 24 Main St., (Rte. 611), Delaware Water Gap, PA 18327. Mailing Address: P.O. Box 484, Delaware Water Gap, PA 18327-0484. Tel.: 570-476-4240.
Web Site: www.dutotmuseum.com
Institution Type/Description: History Museum & Art Gallery: housed in a former school house; c.1850.
Hours & Admission Prices: Memorial Day to Columbus Day Sat.-Sun. 1-5. Suggested Donation: adults $2; children under 12 no charge.

Devault

GREAT VALLEY NATURE CENTER, 4251 State Rd., Devault, PA 19432. Mailing Address: P.O. Box 82, Devault, PA 19432. Tel.: 610-935-9777. Fax: 610-935-0130.
E-mail: gvnature@gmail.com
Web Site: www.gvnc.org/home
Key Personnel: Exec. Dir., Tom Pascocello.
Institution Type/Description: Nature Center.
Hours & Admission Prices: By appointment.

Devon

JENKINS ARBORETUM & GARDENS, 631 Berwyn Baptist Rd., Devon, PA 19333-1001. Tel.: 610-647-8870.
E-mail: webinfo@jenkinsarboretum.org
Web Site: www.jenkinsarboretum.org
Key Personnel: Dir., Dr. Harold E. Sweetman.
Institution Type/Description: Arboretum: on grounds of former home of H. Lawrence Jenkins & Elisabeth Phillippe Jenkins.
Hours & Admission Prices: Daily 8am to sunset. No charge; donations accepted.
Attendance: 30,000 (estimated)

Dillsburg

DILL'S TAVERN & PLANTATION, 227 N. Baltimore St., Dillsburg, PA 17019. Mailing Address: P.O. Box 340, Dillsburg, PA 17019. Tel.: 717-502-1440.
E-mail: nychaps@northernyorkhistorical.org
Web Site: northenyorkhistorical.org
Institution Type/Description: Living history museum housed in the Dills Tavern built between 1794-1819. Listed on the National Register of Historic Places.
Hours & Admission Prices: Mon.-Fri. 10-2. Tours: April-Oct. Sun. 2-4 or by appointment. Adults $10; Family $15.

Doylestown

BUCKS COUNTY CIVIL WAR MUSEUM & LIBRARY, 32 N. Broad St., Doylestown, PA 18901-4317. Tel.: 215-822-1562, 215-822-3857.
E-mail: civilwarmuseumdoylestown@gmail.com
Web Site: www.civilwarmuseumdoylestown.org
Key Personnel: Exec. Dir., Dee Ann Smith; Pres. (V), Greg Munson.
Institution Type/Description: History Museum.
Hours & Admission Prices: Sat. 10:30-2; other times by appointment. No charge; donations accepted.
Attendance: 820 (estimated)

DOYLESTOWN HISTORICAL SOCIETY, 56 S. Main St., Doylestown, PA 18901-0550. Tel.: 215-345-9430. Fax: 215-345-5119.
E-mail: info@doylestownhistorical.org
Web Site: www.doylestownhistorical.org
Key Personnel: C.E.O., Chm. (V) & Pres. (V), Stu Abramson; Admin. & Museum Shop Mgr., Fletcher Walls.
Institution Type/Description: Historical Society Museum.
Hours & Admission Prices: Jan.-March 15 Sat. 10-4; March 16-Dec. Sat. 10-4, Sun. 12-4; other times by appointment. No charge.
Attendance: 5,000 (estimated)

FONTHILL MUSEUM, E. Court St. & Rte. 313, Doylestown, PA 18901. Mailing Address: 84 S. Pine St., Doylestown, PA 18901-4930. Tel.: 215-348-9461. Fax: 215-348-9462.
E-mail: fhmail@fonthillmuseum.org
Web Site: www.fonthillmuseum.org
Formerly: Fonthill Museum of the Bucks County Historical Society
Key Personnel: C.E.O., Doug Dolan; Chm., William Maeghin; Site Admin., Edward L. Reidell.
Institution Type/Description: Historic House Museum & National Historic Landmark: Fonthill, a 44-room concrete castle-like building built 1908-1912, was the home of Henry C. Mercer (1856-1930), noted archaeologist, collector and arts & crafts movement tilemaker.
Hours & Admission Prices: Mon.-Sat. 10-5, Sun. 12-5; guided tour only, reservations suggested. Adults $14. See website for current admission fees. Discounts to AAM & ICOM members. Closed New Year's Day; Thanksgiving; Christmas.
Attendance: 30,000 (estimated)

HERITAGE CONSERVANCY, 85 Old Dublin Pike, Doylestown, PA 18901-2468. Tel.: 215-345-7020. Fax: 215-345-4328. Facebook: Heritage Conservancy.

E-mail: info@heritageconservancy.org
Web Site: www.heritageconservancy.org
Key Personnel: C.O.O., Linda Cacossa; Chm., Marvin L. Woodall; Pres., Jeffrey Marshall.
Institution Type/Description: Headquarters housed in 1927, Tudor Revival Style Aldie Mansion; emphasis on land conservation and historic preservation.
Hours & Admission Prices: By appointment only. Adults $4; children 12 & under no charge. &
Attendance: 23,000 (estimated)

JAMES A. MICHENER ART MUSEUM, 138 S. Pine St., Doylestown, PA 18901-4931. Tel.: 215-340-9800. Fax: 215-340-9807.
E-mail: rrosen@michenerartmuseum.org
Web Site: www.michenerartmuseum.org
Key Personnel: Dir. & C.E.O., Lisa Tremper Hanover; Chm. Bd. Trustees (V), Kevin Putman; Pres. Bd. Trustees (V), Louis Della Penna; C.F.O., Dorothy Landes; Dir. Operations, Hollie Brown; Dir. Programs, Zoriana Siokalo; Cur. Education, Adrienne Romano; Librarian & Database Coord., Birgitta Bond; Assoc. Dir. Mkgt. & Communications, Christine Hensel Triantos; Preparator, Bryan Brems; Exec. Asst., Rebecca Rosen; Facility Mgr., Mike Jayne.
Institution Type/Description: Art Museum.
Hours & Admission Prices: Tues.-Fri. 10-4:30, Sat. 10-5, Sun. 12-5. Adults $18, seniors $17, college students $16; children 6-18 $8; discounts to AAM members; members & children under 6 no charge. &
Attendance: 150,000 (actual)

MERCER MUSEUM OF THE BUCKS COUNTY HISTORICAL SOCIETY, 84 S. Pine St., Doylestown, PA 18901-4930. Tel.: 215-345-0210. Fax: 215-230-0823.
E-mail: info@mercermuseum.org
Web Site: www.mercermuseum.org
Key Personnel: C.E.O. & Pres., Douglas C. Dolan; Exec. Vice Pres., Molly W. Lowell; Vice Pres. Collections & Interpretation, Cory Amsler.
Institution Type/Description: History, Historical Technology & Folk Art Museum: housed in 1916 concrete castle-like building. A National Historic Landmark.
Hours & Admission Prices: Museum: Sun. 12-5, Mon.-Sat. 10-5. Library: call for hours. Adults $14, senior citizens $12, youth $8; discounts to groups, AAA, AAM & ICOM members; children under 5 & members no charge. Closed New Year's Day; Thanksgiving; Christmas. &
Attendance: 65,000 (estimated)

MORAVIAN POTTERY & TILE WORKS, 130 Swamp Rd., Doylestown, PA 18901-2451. Tel.: 215-348-6098. Fax: 215-345-1361.
E-mail: mptw@buckscounty.org
Web Site: www.buckscounty.org/visitors
Key Personnel: Dir., Charles Yeske.
Institution Type/Description: Historic Building: a National Historic Landmark.
Hours & Admission Prices: Tours: daily 10-4:45. Adults $5, senior citizens $4, children 7-17 $3; discounts to AAM members. Tile Shop: no charge. Closed major holidays. &
Attendance: 26,387 (actual)

DuBois

WINKLER GALLERY OF FINE ART, 36 N. Brady St., DuBois, PA 15801-2256. Tel.: 814-375-5834.
E-mail: winklergallery@gmail.com
Institution Type/Description: Art Gallery.
Hours & Admission Prices: Tues.-Thurs. 11-5, Fri.-Sat. 11-8. No charge.

Eagles Mere

EAGLES MERE MUSEUM, 288 Eagles Mere Ave., Eagles Mere, PA 17731. Mailing Address: P.O. Box 440, Eagles Mere, PA 17731. Tel.: 570-525-3155. Facebook: Eagles Mere Museum.
E-mail: emmuseuminfo@gmail.com
Web Site: eaglesmeremuseum.com
Key Personnel: Pres., Joan Werner; Shop Mgr. & Sec., Lisa Frey; Museum Shop Mgr., Joyce Igoe.
Institution Type/Description: History Museum.
Hours & Admission Prices: Memorial Day-Labor Day Mon.-Fri. 10-5, Sat.-Sun. 10-4; Sept.-May Sat.-Sun. 10-4; other times by appointment. No charge; donations accepted. Closed New Year's Day; Thanksgiving; Christmas. &
Attendance: 9,495 (actual)

East Brady

BRADY'S BEND HISTORICAL SOCIETY, St. Stephen's Old Stone Church, Rte. 68, East Brady, PA 16029. Mailing Address: P. O. Box 451, East Brady, PA 16029. Tel.: 724-526-5693.
E-mail: dmcc1018@aol.com
Web Site: www.bradysbendhistoricalsociety.org
Institution Type/Description: Historical Society Museum.
Hours & Admission Prices: By appointment.

East Stroudsburg

POCONO INDIAN MUSEUM, 5905 Milford Rd., Rte. 209, East Stroudsburg, PA 18302. Mailing Address: P.O. Box 1222, Bushkill, PA 18324. Tel.: 570-588-9338.
E-mail: dream38@ptd.net
Web Site: poconoindianmuseum.com
Institution Type/Description: American Indian Museum.
Hours & Admission Prices: Memorial Day to Labor Day 10-6; Winter: 10-5:30. Adults $6, children 6-12 $3; discounts to AAM members; children under six no charge.
Attendance: 10,000 (estimated)

Easton

CRAYOLA EXPERIENCE, 30 Centre Square, Easton, PA 18042. Tel.: 610-515-8000.
E-mail: eastonexperience@crayolaexperience.com
Web Site: crayolaexperience.com
Institution Type/Description: Children's Center.
Hours & Admission Prices: Daily 10-6. Admission 3 & over $21.99, seniors 65 & over $17.99; discounts to groups of 15 or more & military members; children 2 & under no charge. &

LAFAYETTE COLLEGE ART GALLERIES, 317 Hamilton St., Easton, PA 18042-1768. Mailing Address: 111 Quad Dr., Easton, PA 18042-1768. Tel.: 610-330-5361. Fax: 610-330-5642.
E-mail: artgallery@lafayette.edu
Web Site: galleries.lafayette.edu
Key Personnel: Pres. Lafayette College, Alison Byerly; Dir., Lafayette Arts, Jennifer Kelly; Vice Pres., Finance & Admin., Roger Demareski; Dir. Lafayette Art Galleries, Michiko Okaya; Collections Mgr. & Registrar, David Burnhauser; Dir. Security, Jeff Troxell.
Institution Type/Description: College Art Galleries and Collections.
Hours & Admission Prices: Williams Center Gallery: Sept.-May Mon.-Wed. & Fri. 11-5, Thurs. 11-8, Sat.-Sun. 12-5. Grossman Gallery: Sept.-May Tues.-Sat. 11-4. No charge. Closed school holidays. &
Attendance: 6,000 (estimated)

MIXSELL HOUSE MUSEUM & TEXTILE RESEARCH CENTER, S. 4th & Ferry Sts., Easton, PA 18042. Mailing Address: 342 Northampton St., Easton, PA 18042. Tel.: 610-253-1222.
E-mail: khc1861@yahoo.com
Web Site: northamptonctymuseum.org
Institution Type/Description: Historic House Museum.
Hours & Admission Prices: By appointment.

NATIONAL CANAL MUSEUM, DELAWARE AND LEHIGH NATIONAL HERITAGE CORRIDOR, INC., 2750 Hugh Moore Park Rd., Easton, PA 18042-7120. Tel.: 610-923-3548. Fax: 610-923-0537.
E-mail: lovetta@delawareandlehigh.org
Web Site: canals.org
Formerly: National Canal Museum, Hugh Moore Historical Park and Museums
Key Personnel: Chm., Nick Forte; C.E.O., Elissa Garofalo; Museum Shop Manager, Esther Tews.
Institution Type/Description: Transportation and Industrial Museum.
Hours & Admission Prices: Museum: Memorial Day to Labor Day Wed.-Sun. 12-5; Sept.-May see website for hours. Boat: May-Sept. Museum & Boat Ride: adults $12, seniors & military $11, children $9. &
Attendance: 20,000 (estimated)

NORTHAMPTON COUNTY HISTORICAL AND GENEALOGICAL SOCIETY AT THE SIGAL MUSEUM, 342 Northampton St., Easton, PA 18042. Tel.: 610-253-1222. Fax: 610-253-4701.
E-mail: andrewzf@northamptonctymuseum.org
Web Site: sigalmuseum.org

Key Personnel: Exec. Dir., Andrew A. Zellers-Frederich; Pres. (V), L. Anderson Daub; Museum Shop Mgr., Helaine Sigal.
Institution Type/Description: History Museum.
Hours & Admission Prices: By appointment. Adults $7; members no charge. &
Attendance: 8,000 (estimated)

1753 BACHMANN PUBLICK HOUSE, 2nd & Northampton Sts., Easton, PA 18042. Mailing Address: 342 Northampton St., Easton, PA 18042. Tel.: 610-253-1222.
E-mail: c.birgel@northamptonctymuseum.org
Web Site: northamptonctymuseum.org
Institution Type/Description: Historic House Museum: housed in the former home of Jacob & Katrinna Bachmann; built in 1753.
Hours & Admission Prices: Call for hours.

Ebensburg

CAMBRIA COUNTY HISTORICAL SOCIETY, 615 N. Center, Ebensburg, PA 15931-1122. Mailing Address: P.O. Box 278, Ebensburg, PA 15931-0278. Tel.: 814-472-6674. Facebook: Cambria County Historical Society.
E-mail: awbuck@verizon.net
Web Site: www.cambriacountyhistorical.com
Key Personnel: C.E.O. & Pres. (V), Dave Huber; Cur., Kathy Jones.
Institution Type/Description: General Museum: housed in the 1889 A.W. Buck house.
Hours & Admission Prices: March-Jan. Tues.-Fri. 10-4, Sat. 9-1. No charge; donations accepted; Research Library: $3 non members. &
Attendance: 2,000 (estimated)

Eckley

ECKLEY MINERS' VILLAGE, Main St., Eckley, PA 18255. Mailing Address: 2 Eckley Main St., Weatherly, PA 18255-5030. Tel.: 570-636-2070. Fax: 570-636-2938. TDD: 800-654-5988.
E-mail: eckleymuseum@gmail.com
Web Site: www.eckleyminersvillagemuseum.com
Key Personnel: Dir., Bode J. Morin, Ph.D.; Pres. (V), Margie Bogash; Museum Shop Mgr., Melissa Stachaz.
Institution Type/Description: Historic Village: 54 houses built in the 1850s as coal patch town including Roman Catholic Church, Episcopal Church, doctor's office; coal breaker, visitor's center & mule barn.
Hours & Admission Prices: Mon.-Sat. 9-5, Sun. 12-5. Adults $8, senior citizens 60 & over $7, children 6-12 $6; discounts to AAM, ICOM members, PHML Trails of History & all professional organizations; members no charge. Walking Tours: $2 per person. Closed Martin Luther King Jr. Day; Veterans Day; Columbus Day; Thanksgiving, Christmas. &
Attendance: 20,000 (estimated)

Eldred

ELDRED WORLD WAR II MUSEUM, 201 Main St., Eldred, PA 16731. Mailing Address: P.O. Box 273, Eldred, PA 16731-0273. Tel.: 814-225-2220, 866-686-9944 (Toll Free). Fax: 814-225-4407. Facebook: Eldred WWII Museum.
E-mail: info@eldredpawwiimuseum.com
Web Site: www.eldredpawwiimuseum.com
Key Personnel: Dir., Steve Appleby; Business Mgr., Frances Carner.
Institution Type/Description: Military History Museum.
Hours & Admission Prices: Sun. 1-4, Tues.-Sat. 10-4. Adults $5; discounts to groups; children 18 & under no charge. Closed New Year's Eve & Day; Independence Day; Thanksgiving & day after; Christmas Eve, Day & day after. &

Elizabethtown

WINTERS HERITAGE HOUSE MUSEUM, 41-47 E. High St., Elizabethtown, PA 17022. Mailing Address: P.O. Box 14, Elizabethtown, PA 17022-0014. Tel.: 717-367-4672. Fax: 717-367-9991.
E-mail: n.landis@embarqmail.com
Web Site: www.elizabethtownhistory.org
Key Personnel: Dir., Nancy Landis; Pres. (V), Phil Clark.
Institution Type/Description: Historic House Museum: c.1750.
Hours & Admission Prices: March to mid-Dec. Wed.-Fri. 9;30-3; other times by appointment. Museum: adults $2; members no charge. Research: adults $5 daily. Closed holidays.
Attendance: 1,000 (estimated)

Elkins Park

RICHARD WALL HOUSE MUSEUM - THE IVY, 1 Wall Park Dr., Elkins Park, PA 19027. Mailing Address: 8230 Old York Rd., Elkins Park, PA 19027-1589. Tel.: 215-887-9159 & 6200, ext. 114. Fax: 215-887-1561.
E-mail: sfries@cheltenham-township.org
Web Site: www.cheltenhamtownship.org
Key Personnel: Chm., Jack Washington; Vice Chm., Thomas Wieckowski, Ph.D.; Cur., Louise Cohen; Township Mgr., Bryan T. Havir.
Institution Type/Description: Historic House Museum: listed on the National Register of Historic Places.
Hours & Admission Prices: By appointment. No charge; donations accepted. &
Attendance: 315 (estimated)

THE TEMPLE JUDEA MUSEUM, 8339 Old York Rd., Elkins Park, PA 19027-1515. Tel.: 215-887-2027. Fax: 215-887-1070. Facebook: The Temple Judea Museum; Instagram: @templejudea-museum.
E-mail: tjmuseum@kenesethisrael.org
Web Site: www.kenesethisrael.org/museum; templejudeamuseum.pastperfectonline.com
Key Personnel: Dir. & Cur., Rita Rosen Poley; Chm. (V), Karen Shain Schloss.
Institution Type/Description: Art & History Museum.
Hours & Admission Prices: Mon.-Fri. 10-6, Sun. 10-1; other times by appointment. No charge. Closed Jewish holidays; legal holidays. &
Attendance: 2,000 (estimated)

Elverson

HOPEWELL FURNACE NATIONAL HISTORIC SITE, 2 Mark Bird Lane, Elverson, PA 19520-9535. Tel.: 610-582-8773. Fax: 610-582-2768. Facebook.
E-mail: hofu_superintendent@nps.gov
Web Site: www.nps.gov/hofu
Formerly: Hopewell Village National Historic Site
Key Personnel: Site Dir., David Blackburn; Facility Mgr., Butch Shermer; Pres. Friends of Hopewell Furnace NHS, Jim McClelland; Cultural Resource Mgr., Rebecca Ross; Museum Shop Mgr., Christine Hawthorne; Volunteer Coord., Frank Hebblethwaite.
Institution Type/Description: Industrial Museum.
Hours & Admission Prices: Visitor Center & Village: Oct.-May Wed.-Sun. 9-5; June-Sept. daily 9-5. No charge; donations accepted. Closed New Year's Day; Martin Luther King Jr. Day; Presidents' Day; Thanksgiving; Christmas. &
Attendance: 51,852 (estimated)

Emlenton

PUMPING JACK MUSEUM, Crawford Center on Hill St., Hill St., Emlenton, PA 16373. Mailing Address: P.O. Box 25, Emlenton, PA 16373-0025. Tel.: 724-867-0030.
E-mail: pjmuseum@gmail.com
Web Site: www.pumpingjack.com
Key Personnel: Pres. (V), Joyce Beikert.
Institution Type/Description: History Museum.
Hours & Admission Prices: May-Oct. Sat.-Sun. 12-3; other times by appointment. No charge; donations accepted. &
Attendance: 100 (estimated)

Emmaus

SHELTER HOUSE SOCIETY, 601 S. 4th St., Emmaus, PA 18049-3934. Mailing Address: Box 254, Emmaus, PA 18049-0254. Tel.: 610-965-9258.
E-mail: jwmaulfair@verizon.net
Key Personnel: Chm., Noreen Yamamoto; Pres., Jane Maulfair; Museum Shop Mgr., Dean Bortz; Asst. Sec., Ruth L. Grohol.
Institution Type/Description: Historic House: 1734-1741 Shelter House.
Hours & Admission Prices: Daily by appointment only; closed Christmas. No charge; donations accepted.
Attendance: 400 (estimated)

Ephrata

EICHER ARTS CENTER AND INDIAN MUSEUM, 409 Cocalico St., Ephrata, PA 17522. Mailing Address: P.O. Box 601, Ephrata, PA 17522. Tel.: 717-738-3084. Fax: 717-738-4196.
E-mail: eacims@dejazzd.com
Web Site: www.eicherartscenter.com
Key Personnel: Coord., James DeFilippis.

Institution Type/Description: History Museum: built in 1733 by members of the Ephrata Cloister Brotherhood.
Hours & Admission Prices: By appointment. No charge.

EPHRATA CLOISTER, 632 W. Main St., Ephrata, PA 17522-1717. Tel.: 717-733-6600.
E-mail: ephrata1732@gmail.com
Web Site: www.ephratacloister.org
Key Personnel: Dir., Elizabeth Bertheaud; Pres., Drew Myers; Museum Shop Mgr., Susan Shober.
Institution Type/Description: Historic Site: comprising of 9 mid-18th century buildings of Germanic architectural style, located on original site of a celibate religious community.
Hours & Admission Prices: Jan.-Feb. Thurs.-Sat. 9-5, Sun. 12-5; March-Dec. Tues.-Sat. 9-5, Sun. 12-5. Adults $10, senior citizens 65 & over $9, youth 3-11 $6; discounts to groups, all motor clubs, National Historical Society, AAM & ICOM members; members no charge. Closed New Year's Day; Easter; Columbus Day; Veterans Day; Thanksgiving & day after; Christmas.
Attendance: 16,000 (actual)

HISTORICAL SOCIETY OF THE COCALICO VALLEY, 237/ 249 W. Main St., Ephrata, PA 17522. Mailing Address: P.O. Box 193, Ephrata, PA 17522-0193. Tel.: 717-733-1616.
E-mail: cjmarquet@gmail.com
Web Site: www.cocalicovalleyhs.org
Key Personnel: Pres. (V), Lowell Haws; Librarian, Cynthia J. Marquet.
Institution Type/Description: History Museum.
Hours & Admission Prices: Museum: Sat. 10-4. No charge; donations accepted. Library & Research Center: Mon. & Wed.-Thurs. 9:30-6, Sat. 8:30-5. Research: $3.
Attendance: 900 (estimated)

Erie

ERIE ART MUSEUM, 411 State St., Erie, PA 16501-1106. Tel.: 814-459-5477. Fax: 814-452-1744. Facebook.
E-mail: christine@erieartmuseum.org
Web Site: www.erieartmuseum.org
Formerly: Erie Art Center, Art Club of Erie
Key Personnel: Exec. Dir., Susan Black; Pres., Stephen Porter; Cur., Susan Barnett; Dir. Mktg. & Events, Emily Dauber; Dir. Finance, Mary Pruchniewski; Dir. Devel., Christine Eddy; Devel. Asst., Laura Paris; Dir. Education & Folk Art, Kelly Armor; Frame Shop Mgr., James Pearson; Sr. Designer, Andrea Krivak; Education Coord., Ally Thomas; Facility Operations & Events Mgr., Tavon Markov; Registrar, Vance Lupher.
Institution Type/Description: Art Museum: housed in the former Erie branch of the US Bank of Pennsylvania; built in 1839.
Hours & Admission Prices: Tues.-Sat. 11-5, Sun. 1-5. Adults $9, students & senior citizens $7; Wed., children under 5 and AAM, ICOM & museum members no charge. Closed New Year's Day; Easter; Independence Day; Thanksgiving; Christmas. &
Attendance: 42,300 (estimated)

ERIE MARITIME MUSEUM & U.S. BRIG NIAGARA, Bayview Commons, 150 E. Front St., Ste. 100, Erie, PA 16507-1594. Tel.: 814-452-2744. Fax: 814-455-6760.
E-mail: info@flagshipniagara.org
Web Site: www.eriemaritimemuseum.org
Formerly: Erie Maritime Museum & Flagship Niagara
Key Personnel: Chm. PHMC, Andrew E. Masich; Exec. Dir. PHMC, James M. Vaughan; Pres. Flagship Niagara League, Jim Scheider; Site Admin. & Sr. Captain, Walter Rybka; Museum Shop Mgr., Barbara Corbett; Museum Shop Mgr., Judy Tucci.
Institution Type/Description: Historic Ship & Maritime History Museum.
Hours & Admission Prices: April-Sept. Mon.-Sat. 9-5, Sun. 12-5; Oct. Mon.-Sat. 9-5; Nov.-March Thurs.-Sat. 9-5; closed all major holidays with exception of Memorial Day, July 4 & Labor Day. Closed day after Thanksgiving. Adults $10, senior citizens $8, youth 3-11 $5; discounts to AAA, AAM, ICOM, PHMC Associates; active duty military & family, children under 3, Flagship Niagara League members, PA Heritage members, no charge. &
Attendance: 25,000 (estimated)

ERIE PLANETARIUM, Penn State Behrend, School of Science, 4205 College Dr., 1 Prischak Bldg., Erie, PA 16563-0203. Tel.: 814-898-6105. Fax: 814-898-6213.
E-mail: echs@eriecountyhistory.org
Web Site: www.eriecountyhistory.org/erie-planetarium
Key Personnel: Dir., Caleb Pifer; Dir. Operations & Visitor Member Svcs., Melanie Kuebel-Stankey; Planetarium Coord., Jim Gavio.
Institution Type/Description: Planetarium.

Hours & Admission Prices: Call for hours. Family $10, adults $5, senior $4, children $3; discounts to AAM members & groups; members no charge. &
Attendance: 5,500 (estimated)

ERIE ZOO, 423 W. 38th St., Erie, PA 16508-2701. Mailing Address: P.O. Box 3268, Erie, PA 16508-0268. Tel.: 814-864-4091. Facebook.
E-mail: info@eriezoo.org
Web Site: www.eriezoo.org
Formerly: Erie Zoological Park & Botanical Gardens of Northwestern Pennsylvania
Key Personnel: Pres. & C.E.O., Scott Mitchell.
Institution Type/Description: Zoo & Botanical Garden.
Hours & Admission Prices: March-Nov. daily 10-5. Adults 13 & over $10, senior citizens 62 & over $8, children 2-12 $6; children under 2 no charge. &
Attendance: 462,100 (estimated)

EXPERIENCE CHILDREN'S MUSEUM, 420 French St., Erie, PA 16507-1541. Tel.: 814-453-3743. Facebook; Instagram.
E-mail: info@eriechildrensmuseum.org
Web Site: www.eriechildrensmuseum.org
Key Personnel: Exec. Dir., Ainslie Brosig.
Institution Type/Description: Children's/Youth Museum.
Hours & Admission Prices: Tues., Thurs. & Sat. 9-11, 12-2 & 3-5. Admission 2 & over $8; discount to ACM members; members and children one & under no charge. Closed New Year's Day, Easter, Memorial Day; Independence Day; Labor Day; Thanksgiving; Christmas Eve & Day. &
Attendance: 37,200 (actual)

FIREFIGHTERS HISTORICAL MUSEUM, 428 Chestnut St., Erie, PA 16507-1224. Tel.: 814-456-5969.
E-mail: mfahey@erie.pa.us
Web Site: firefightershistoricalmuseum.com
Institution Type/Description: Firefighting History Museum.
Hours & Admission Prices: June-July Sat. 11-4, Sun. 1-4; Sept.-Oct. Sat.-Sun. 1-4. Adults $4, senior citizens & firefighters $2.50, children 6-12 $1.

PRESQUE ISLE LIGHTHOUSE, Tom Ridge Environmental Center, 301 Peninsula Dr., Erie, PA 16505. Tel.: 814-833-3604. Facebook.
E-mail: presqueislelightstation@gmail.com
Web Site: presqueislelighthouse.org
Institution Type/Description: Lighthouse: built 1873. Listed on the National Register of Historic Places.
Hours & Admission Prices: Memorial Day to Labor Day. Tower: $6. House $3.

THOMAS HAGEN HISTORY CENTER - HISTORICAL SOCIETY OF ERIE COUNTY, 356 W. 6th St., Erie, PA 16507. Tel.: 814-454-1813. Fax: 814-454-6890.
E-mail: echs@eriehistory.org
Web Site: www.eriehistory.org
Formerly: Erie County History Center & Cashier's House
Key Personnel: Exec. Dir., Caleb Pifer; Deputy Dir. & Cur., Drew Ulrich; Operations Dir., Melanie Kuebel-Stankey.
Institution Type/Description: Historical Society Museum.
Hours & Admission Prices: Tues.-Sat. 11-5. Adults $9, children $6; discounts to AAM & AASLH members; society members no charge. Closed holidays. &
Attendance: 10,000 (estimated)

WATSON-CURTZE MANSION, 356 W. Sixth St., Erie, PA 16507-1245. Tel.: 814-871-5790 & 454-1813. Fax: 814-454-6890.
E-mail: echs@eriecountyhistory.org
Web Site: www.eriecountyhistory.org
Formerly: Erie Historical Museum and Planetarium
Key Personnel: Dir., Caleb Pifer.
Institution Type/Description: Historic House.
Hours & Admission Prices: Wed.-Sat. 11-4, Sun. 1-4. Family $10, Adults $5, seniors $4, children 2-12 $3; discounts to AAM members & Wed.; members & children under 2 no charge.
Attendance: 5,075 (actual)

Fallsington

HISTORIC FALLSINGTON, INC., 4 Yardley Ave., Fallsington, PA 19054-1117. Tel.: 215-295-6567. Fax: 215-295-6567.
E-mail: info@historicfallsington.org
Web Site: www.historicfallsington.org
Key Personnel: Exec. Dir., Erica Armour.
Institution Type/Description: 17th to 20th-Century Quaker Village.
Hours & Admission Prices: mid-May to mid-Oct. Tues.-Sat. 10:30-3:30; mid-Oct. to mid-May Tues.-Fri. by appointment. Adults $7, senior citizens $6, children 6-

12 $3; discounts to AAA members; members & children 5 and under no charge. Closed New Year's Day; Presidents' Day; Easter; Memorial Day; Independence Day; Labor Day; Christmas.
Attendance: 7,500 (estimated)

Farmington

FORT NECESSITY NATIONAL BATTLEFIELD, One Washington Pkwy., Farmington, PA 15437-9501. Tel.: 724-329-5819. Fax: 724-329-8682.
E-mail: lawren_dunn@nps.gov
Web Site: www.nps.gov/fone
Key Personnel: Supt., Keith Newlin; Unit Mgr., Chief Law Enforcement Ranger, Norman W. Nelson; Cultural Resource Mgr. & Cur., Lawren Dunn; Museum Shop Mgr., James Tomasek.
Institution Type/Description: History Museum.
Hours & Admission Prices: Grounds: daily dawn to dusk. Center: daily 9-5. Adults 16 & over $5. Closed New Year's Day; Martin Luther King Jr. Day; Thanksgiving; Christmas. &
Attendance: 125,000 (estimated)

Fayetteville

PENNSYLVANIA FOREST FIRE MUSEUM, 3050 Lincoln Way E., Fayetteville, PA 17222-9556. Mailing Address: P.O. Box 176, Fayetteville, PA 17222-0176. Tel.: 717-352-2815.
E-mail: info@paforestheritage.org
Web Site: www.paforestheritage.org
Institution Type/Description: Forest Fire History Museum.
Hours & Admission Prices: Call for hours.

Fort Loudoun

STATE HISTORIC SITE OF FORT LOUDOUN, 1720 Brooklyn Rd., Fort Loudoun, PA 17724. Mailing Address: P.O. Box 181, Fort Loudoun, PA 17224-0181. Tel.: 717-369-3318. Fax: 717-783-1073.
E-mail: secretary@fortloudoun-pa.com
Web Site: www.fortloudoun-pa.com/
Institution Type/Description: Historic Site: site of Fort Loudoun, erected in 1756 by the British.
Hours & Admission Prices: Memorial Day to Labor Day Sat.-Sun. 12-5; other times by appointment. No charge; donations accepted.

Fort Washington

THE HIGHLANDS, 7001 Sheaff Lane, Fort Washington, PA 19034-2005. Tel.: 215-641-2687. Fax: 215-641-2556.
E-mail: mbb@highlandshistorical.org
Web Site: www.highlandshistorical.org
Key Personnel: Pres., George Anthony Smith; Dir., Margaret Bleecker Blades; Cur. Education, Elizabeth Gavrys.
Institution Type/Description: Historic Site: 1796 Georgian country house built by Anthony Morris, Speaker of the Pennsylvania Senate; Gardens designed by Wilson Eyre.
Hours & Admission Prices: Tours: Mon.-Fri. 1:30; other times by appointment. Adults $5; discounts to AAM & ICOM members; AABGA members no charge.
Attendance: 12,000 (actual)

HISTORICAL SOCIETY OF FORT WASHINGTON, 473 Bethlehem Pike, Fort Washington, PA 19034-2313. Tel.: 215-646-6065.
Key Personnel: Pres. (V), H. Roy Thompson; Treas., Ingrid Rivel; Librarian, William Amey.
Institution Type/Description: Historical Society & Genealogical Library: housed in 1801 Clifton House.
Hours & Admission Prices: Sept.-June Wed. 2-4; other times by appointment. No charge; donations accepted. Closed holidays.
Attendance: 800 (estimated)

HOPE LODGE AND MATHER MILL, 553 S. Bethlehem Pike, Fort Washington, PA 19034. Tel.: 215-646-1595.
E-mail: hopelodgepa@gmail.com
Web Site: www.historichopelodge.org
Key Personnel: Pres. (V) Friends of Hope Lodge, Kevin Horan; Museum Shop Mgr., Coleen Bant.
Institution Type/Description: Historic Buildings: 1743, Hope Lodge, built for Samuel Morris; c.1820 Mather mill, stone grist mill built on the site of former 17th-century mill by Edward Farmar.

Hours & Admission Prices: June-Oct. see website for hours & admission prices. Discounts to PA Trail of History, PA Heritage Foundation members & Friends of Hope Lodge. Closed New Year's Day; Martin Luther King Jr. Day; Presidents' Day; Columbus Day; Veterans Day; Thanksgiving & day after; Christmas. &
Attendance: 3,000 (estimated)

Forty Fort

NATHAN DENISON HOUSE, 35 Denison St., Forty Fort, PA 18704-4311. Mailing Address: c/o Luzerne County Historical Society, 49 S. Franklin St., Wilkes-Barre, PA 18701. Tel.: 570-823-6244 ext. 3.
Web Site: luzernehistory.org
Institution Type/Description: Historic House: 1790 Denison House, Connecticut style architecture, built in the Wyoming Valley; home of Col. Nathan Denison, 1790-1809.
Hours & Admission Prices: Tours by appointment. Admission $5.
Attendance: 1,000 (actual)

Franklin

DEBENCE ANTIQUE MUSIC WORLD, 1261 Liberty St., Franklin, PA 16323-1361. Tel.: 814-432-8350. Fax: 814-437-7193. Facebook.
E-mail: debencemuseum@verizon.net
Web Site: www.debencemusicworld.com
Key Personnel: Dir. & Chm. (V), Prescott Greene; Museum Shop Mgr., Mary C. Nicklin.
Institution Type/Description: Musical Instruments Museum.
Hours & Admission Prices: April-Oct. Tues.-Sat. 11-4, Sun. 12:30-4; Nov.-March by appointment. Adults $8, senior citizens $7, students $5, youth 3-14 $3; discounts to AAA & WDUQ members and groups of 10 or more; children under 3, local 4th graders & basement exhibits no charge. &
Attendance: 3,000 (actual)

VENANGO COUNTY HISTORICAL SOCIETY, 301 S. Park St., Franklin, PA 16323-1238. Mailing Address: P.O. Box 301, Franklin, PA 16323. Tel.: 814-437-2275. Fax: 814-432-8620.
E-mail: vchistory@neohio.twcbc.com
Web Site: venango.pa-roots.com/venangohistoricalsociety.html
Key Personnel: Pres., Rainy Linn.
Institution Type/Description: Historical Society: housed in the Hoge-Osmer House, built c.1865.
Hours & Admission Prices: April Sat. 10-2; May-Dec. Tues.-Thurs. & Sat. 10-2. Research fee $5.

Gallitzin

ALLEGHENY PORTAGE RAILROAD NATIONAL HISTORIC SITE AND JOHNSTOWN FLOOD NATIONAL MEMORIAL, 110 Federal Park Rd., Gallitzin, PA 16641-2000. Tel.: 814-886-6116. Fax: 814-884-0206.
E-mail: nancy_smith@nps.gov
Web Site: www.nps.gov/alpo
Key Personnel: Supt., Keith Newlin; Cur., Nancy Smith; Museum Shop Mgr., Doug Bosley.
Institution Type/Description: Visitor Center.
Hours & Admission Prices: Daily 9-5. Adults $4; children under 16 no charge. Closed holidays in winter. &
Attendance: 140,000

Gettysburg

ADAMS COUNTY HISTORICAL SOCIETY, 368 Springs Ave., Gettysburg, PA 17325-1718. Mailing Address: P.O. Box 4325, Gettysburg, PA 17325-4325. Tel.: 717-334-4723, ext. 201. Fax: 717-334-0722.
E-mail: info@achs-pa.org
Web Site: www.achs-pa.org
Key Personnel: Dir., Benjamin Neely.
Institution Type/Description: Historical Society Museum.
Hours & Admission Prices: Wed. & Fri.-Sat. 9-12 & 1-4, Thurs. 9-12, 1-4 & 6-9. Research: adults $5; members no charge. Closed holidays.
Attendance: 2,100 (estimated)

THE DAVID WILLS HOUSE, 8 Lincoln Sq., Gettysburg, PA 17325-2205. Mailing Address: 1195 Baltimore St., Gettysburg, PA 17325. Tel.: 877-874-2478. Fax: 717-334-5796.

E-mail: info@gettysburgfoundation.org
Web Site: www.gettysburgfoundation.org
Key Personnel: Mgr., Sheilla Combs.
Institution Type/Description: History Museum.
Hours & Admission Prices: Call for hours. ♿

EISENHOWER NATIONAL HISTORIC SITE, 1195 Baltimore
Pike, Ste. 100, Gettysburg, PA 17325-7034. Tel.: 877-874-2478.
Fax: 717-338-0821. TDD: 717-334-1382.
E-mail: bob_kirby@nps.gov
Web Site: www.nps.gov/eise
Key Personnel: Supt., Bob Kirby; Museum Cur., Michael R. Florer; Supervisory
Historian, Carol A. Hegeman; Museum Shop Mgr., Lisa Kamps.
Institution Type/Description: Historic Site: presidential & retirement home of
Dwight D. Eisenhower, 34th President of the U.S. & Supreme Commander of
Allied forces in Europe during World War II.
Hours & Admission Prices: Visitor Center: daily 8-5. House: daily 9-4. Tours via
shuttle bus only. Adults $7.50, children 6-12 $5; discounts to groups of 16 or
more. Closed New Year's Day; Thanksgiving; Christmas. ♿
Attendance: 70,000 (actual)

GETTYSBURG FIRE DEPARTMENT MUSEUM, 35 N. Stratton
St., Gettysburg, PA 17325. Tel.: 717-334-8300.
Institution Type/Description: Firefighting History Museum.
Hours & Admission Prices: Call for hours.

GETTYSBURG NATIONAL MILITARY PARK, 1195 Baltimore
Pike, Ste. 100, Gettysburg, PA 17325-7034. Tel.: 877-874-2478.
Fax: 717-334-1891. TDD: 717-334-1382.
E-mail: gett_superintendent@nps.gov
Web Site: www.gettysburgfoundation.org
Key Personnel: Chief Cur. Museum, Greg Goodell.
Institution Type/Description: Military Museum & Battlefield.
Hours & Admission Prices: Museum & Visitor Center: April-Oct. daily 8-6; Nov.-
March daily 8-5. Grounds: April-Oct. daily 6am-10pm; Nov.-March 5am-7pm.
David Wills House: call for hours. Closed New Year's Day; Thanksgiving;
Christmas. ♿
Attendance: 1,900,000 (actual)

LINCOLN TRAIN MUSEUM, 425 Steinwehr Ave., Gettysburg, PA
17325-2930. Tel.: 717-334-5678. Fax: 717-334-0224. Facebook.
E-mail: gettysburglincolntrain@gmail.com
Web Site: www.lincolntrain.com
Key Personnel: Museum Shop Mgr., Karen Saylor.
Institution Type/Description: History Museum.
Hours & Admission Prices: Spring & Fall Sun.-Thurs. 9-7, Fri.-Sat. 9-9; June-July
daily 9-9; Dec.-March Thurs.-Mon. & holidays 10-6. Adults $7, adult members
$6, children 6-12 $4, discounts to AAA members, seniors, police, fire, EMS &
military & reenactors in period dress; children 5 & under no charge. Prices sub-
ject to change. Closed New Year's Day, Thanksgiving; Christmas.
Attendance: 30,000 (estimated)

SCHMUCKER ART GALLERY, Gettysburg College, 300 N.
Washington St., Gettysburg, PA 17325-1483. Mailing Address:
Box 2452, Gettysburg, PA 17325. Tel.: 717-337-6080. Fax: 717-
337-6099. Facebook: Schmucker Art Gallery.
E-mail: segan@gettysburg.edu
Web Site: www.gettysburg.edu/gallery
Key Personnel: Dir., Shannon Egan, Ph.D.
Institution Type/Description: Art Gallery.
Hours & Admission Prices: Tues.-Sat. 10-4. No charge; donations accepted. Closed
college holidays. ♿
Attendance: 4,000 (estimated)

SHRIVER HOUSE MUSEUM, 309 Baltimore Ave., Gettysburg,
PA 17325-2602. Tel.: 717-337-2800. Facebook.
E-mail: mail@shriverhouse.org
Web Site: www.shriverhouse.org
Key Personnel: Dir. & Chm. (V), Nancie W. Gudmestad; Pres. (V), Del
Gudmestad.
Institution Type/Description: Historic House Museum: housed in the former home
of George & Hettie Shriver; built in 1860.
Hours & Admission Prices: March Sat.-Sun. 10-5; April-Oct. Sun.,-Thurs. 10-5, Fri.
-Sat. 10-6; Nov. 12-5; Thanksgiving 5-10; Dec. Sat. 12-10; other times by
appointment. Adults $8.95, children 7-12 $6.95; discounts to military & groups
of 10 or more. Closed Christmas Eve, Day & week.
Attendance: 30,000 (actual)

Girard

THE BATTLES MUSEUMS OF RURAL LIFE, 436 Walnut St.,
Girard, PA 16417-1650. Tel.: 814-454-1813. Fax: 814-454-6890.
E-mail: echs@eriecountyhistory.org
Web Site: www.eriecountyhistory.org
Key Personnel: Dir., Caleb Pifer; Operations Dir., Melanie Kuebel-Stankey;
Pres. (V), Jack Watts.
Institution Type/Description: Historic & Agriculture Museum: housed on 130 acres
of farmland & woodland.
Hours & Admission Prices: By appointment. Family $10, Adults $5, senior citizens
$4, children $3; discounts to AAM members; members & children under 6 no
charge. ♿
Attendance: 3,562 (actual)

HAZEL KIBLER MEMORIAL MUSEUM, 522 Main St., E.,
Girard, PA 16417-1713. Mailing Address: 21 S. Park Row, Girard,
PA 16417-1629. Tel.: 814-774-4168.
E-mail: swinick@aol.com
Key Personnel: Pres., Stephanie Wincik.
Institution Type/Description: History Museum.
Hours & Admission Prices: Memorial Day-Labor Day Sun. 2-4; groups by appoint-
ment. Adults $2, children $1.

Gladwyne

HENRY FOUNDATION FOR BOTANICAL RESEARCH, 801
Stony Lane, Gladwyne, PA 19035-1460. Mailing Address: P.O.
Box 7, Gladwyne, PA 19035-0007. Tel.: 610-525-2037. Fax: 610-
525-4024.
E-mail: susan@henrybotanicgarden.org
Key Personnel: Pres. & Exec. Dir., Susan P. Treadway.
Institution Type/Description: Botanical Garden.
Hours & Admission Prices: Tues.-Thurs. 10-3 by appointment. Admission $5.
Attendance: 8,000 (estimated)

RIVERBEND ENVIRONMENTAL EDUCATION CENTER,
1950 Spring Mill Rd., Gladwyne, PA 19035-1000. Tel.: 610-527-
5234. Fax: 610-527-1161.
E-mail: info@riverbendeec.org
Web Site: www.riverbendeec.org
Key Personnel: Exec. Dir., Laurie Bachman; Chm. (V) & Pres. (V), Beverly
Galloway.
Institution Type/Description: Nature Center.
Hours & Admission Prices: Grounds: daily dawn to dusk. Center: Mon.-Fri. 9-5.
Fee for camp & school programs. Walking Trails: no charge. Closed national
holidays. ♿
Attendance: 12,000 (estimated)

Glenside

ARCADIA UNIVERSITY ART GALLERY, Church & Easton
Rds., Glenside, PA 19038. Mailing Address: 450 S. Easton Rd.,
Glenside, PA 19038-3295. Tel.: 215-572-2133, 2131 & 2900. Fax:
215-881-8774.
E-mail: torchiar@arcadia.edu
Web Site: www.arcadia.edu
Formerly: Beaver College Art Gallery
Key Personnel: Pres., Jerry Griener; Dir., Richard Torchia; Vice Pres. Institutional
Advancement, Nick Costa; Public Rels., Lori Bauer.
Institution Type/Description: Art Gallery: housed in c.1893 historic building.
Hours & Admission Prices: Sept.-May Tues.-Wed. & Fri. 10-3, Thurs. 10-8, Sat.-
Sun. 12-4. No charge; donations accepted. Closed Thanksgiving; Christmas.
Attendance: 6,500 (estimated)

Green Lane

GOSCHENHOPPEN FOLKLIFE LIBRARY AND MUSEUM,
116 Gravel Pike, Red Men's Hall, Green Lane, PA 18054-0476.
Mailing Address: P.O. Box 476, Green Lane, PA 18054-0476. Tel.:
215-234-8953.
E-mail: redmens_hall@goschenhoppen.org
Web Site: www.goschenhoppen.org
Key Personnel: C.E.O. & Chm., George Spotts; Pres. (V), Edward C. Johnson;
Chm. Museum & Library, D.F. Abe Roan; Sec., Susan Cook; Office Mgr., Jodie
Ritto.
Institution Type/Description: Folklife Museum: housed in c.1900 three-story brick
Red Men's Hall; Country Store Museum: a recreation of a country store c.1870-
1930; Henry Antes House: a restored 1736 Germanic house containing two

floors in the attic & located on the site of the Pottsgrove encampment of the Continental Army, September, 1777.
Hours & Admission Prices: Museum: April-Oct. Sun. 1:30-4; other times by appointment. No charge; donations accepted. Library: by appointment only. &
Attendance: 7,850 (estimated)

Greencastle

ALLISON-ANTRIM MUSEUM, INC., 365 S. Ridge Ave., Greencastle, PA 17225-1157. Tel.: 717-597-9010.
E-mail: aamuseum@greencastlemuseum.org
Web Site: www.greencastlemuseum.org
Key Personnel: Pres., Bonnie A. Shockey; Treas., David McCarney.
Institution Type/Description: General Museum.
Hours & Admission Prices: Mon.-Fri. 12-4; other times by appointment. No charge; donations accepted. Closed major holidays. &
Attendance: 1,000 (actual)

Greensburg

BALTZER MEYER HISTORICAL SOCIETY, 642 Baltzer Meyer Pike, Greensburg, PA 15601-9711. Tel.: 724-836-6915.
E-mail: baltzermeyer@juno.com
Web Site: baltzermeyer.pa-roots.com/Pages/home.html
Institution Type/Description: Historical Society Museum.
Hours & Admission Prices: mid-April to mid-Oct. Mon. & Wed. 10-2; mid-Oct. to mid-April Wed. 10-2, call to confirm. Closed New Year's Eve; Christmas Eve.

WESTMORELAND COUNTY HISTORICAL SOCIETY, 362 Sand Hill Rd., Ste. 1, Greensburg, PA 15601. Tel.: 724-532-1935. Fax: 724-532-1938.
E-mail: history@westmorelandhistory.org
Web Site: www.westmorelandhistory.org
Key Personnel: Dir., Lisa C. Hays; Chm. (V), Susan M. Sommers, Ph.D.; Museum Shop Mgr., Joan DeRose.
Institution Type/Description: Historical Society Museum: located on a Revolutionay War era National Register site.
Hours & Admission Prices: Tues.-Fri. 9-5; other times by appointment. $5. Library: Tues.-Fri. 9-5, evenings by appointment. $5; Historic Hanna's Town: May-Oct. $5; discounts to seniors, students, AAA & Blue Star Museum members. &

WESTMORELAND MUSEUM OF AMERICAN ART, 221 N. Main St., Greensburg, PA 15601. Tel.: 724-837-1500. Facebook.
E-mail: info@thewestmoreland.org
Web Site: www.thewestmoreland.org
Key Personnel: C.E.O. & The Richard M. Scaife Dir., Judith H. O'Toole; Pres., Ellen Swank; Chief Cur., Barbara L. Jones; Deputy Dir. & Dir. Devel., Catena Bergevin; Dir. Budget & Finance, Suzanne Wright; Dir. Education & Visitor Svcs., Joan McGarry; Dir. Mktg. & Public Rels., Claire Ertl; Mgr. Collections, Douglas W. Evans; Museum Shop Mgr., Carol Sullivan.
Institution Type/Description: American Art Museum.
Hours & Admission Prices: Tues. & Thurs.-Sun. 11-5, Wed. 11-7. Suggested Donation: adults $15, seniors 65 & over $10; members, students, children 18 & under and veterans & their families no charge. Closed New Year's Day; Easter; Thanksgiving; Christmas. &
Attendance: 19,821 (actual)

Greenville

GREENVILLE RAILROAD PARK AND MUSEUM, 314 Main St., Greenville, PA 16125-2615. Tel.: 724-588-4009.
E-mail: greenvillerailroadpark@gmail.com
Web Site: www.greenvilletrainmuseum.org
Institution Type/Description: Railroad Museum.
Hours & Admission Prices: May & Sept.-Oct. Sat.-Sun. 1-5; mid-June to Labor Day Tues.-Sun. 1-5. No charge; donations accepted.

Grove City

GROVE CITY AREA HISTORICAL SOCIETY, 111 College Ave., Grove City, PA 16127. Mailing Address: P.O. Box 764, 111 College Ave., Grove City, PA 16127. Tel.: 724-458-1798. Facebook: Grove City Area Historical Society.
E-mail: gcahs@zoominternet.net
Web Site: grovecityhistoricalsociety.org
Key Personnel: Pres. (V), Kathy Jack; Treas., Thomas Armour.
Institution Type/Description: Historical Society Museum: housed in the former Traveler's Hotel.
Hours & Admission Prices: Tues.-Sat. 12-3. No charge; donations accepted. &
Attendance: 1,400 (actual)

Halifax

LAKE TOBIAS WILDLIFE PARK, 760 Tobias Rd., Halifax, PA 17032-9474. Tel.: 717-362-9126. Fax: 717-362-9993. Facebook: Lake Tobias Wildlife Park.
E-mail: info@laketobias.com
Web Site: laketobias.com
Key Personnel: Park Mgr., Ern Tobias; Public Rels. & Mktg., Jan Tobias-Kieffer.
Institution Type/Description: Zoo.
Hours & Admission Prices: May to Labor Day Mon.-Fri. 10-6, Sat.-Sun. 10-7; Sept.-Oct. Sat.-Sun. 10-6. Park: 3 & over $6; children under 3 no charge. Safari: 3 & over $6; children under 3 no charge. &
Attendance: 160,000 (estimated)

Hamburg

READING RAILROAD HERITAGE MUSEUM, 500 S. Third St., Hamburg, PA 19526. Mailing Address: P.O. Box 15143, Reading, PA 19612-5143. Tel.: 610-562-5513.
E-mail: museum@readingrailroad.org
Web Site: www.readingrailroad.org
Key Personnel: Devel., John Brown; Chm. (V), Dale Woodland; Pres. (V), Duane E. Engle; Treas., Jim Adams; Archivist, Richard Bates.
Institution Type/Description: Transportation Museum.
Hours & Admission Prices: March to mid-Jan. Sat. 10-4, Sun. 12-4. Adults $7, seniors 65 & over and children 5-12 $3; discounts to active military; children under 5 & members no charge. &
Attendance: 3,000 (estimated)

Hanover

GREATER HANOVER AREA FIRE MUSEUM, 134 E. Hanover St., Hanover, PA 17331. Tel.: 717-637-6674 & 6671.
E-mail: egsfm@yahoo.com
Web Site: www.hanoverfiremuseum.com
Formerly: Hanover Fire Museum
Key Personnel: Pres. (V), Edmund G. Schwartz; Vice Pres. (V), James A. Roth; Sec., Christopher Lockard; Asst. Sec., Darlene Schwartz; Treas., W. Hal Wyatt; Asst. Treas., Anthony F. Funk; Cur., Wayne A. Bollinger.
Institution Type/Description: Firefighting History Museum.
Hours & Admission Prices: Tues. and 1st & 3rd Sat. each month 9-3. No charge; donations accepted.

UTZ POTATO CHIP FACTORY TOUR, 900 High St., Hanover, PA 17331. Tel.: 800-367-7629.
E-mail: tours@utzsnacks.com
Web Site: utzsnacks.com
Institution Type/Description: Company History & Tour.
Hours & Admission Prices: Mon.-Thurs. 10-3:30; groups of 10 or more by appointment. Closed New Year's Day; Easter; Memorial Day; Independence Day; Labor Day; Thanksgiving; Christmas.

Harleysville

MENNONITE HERITAGE CENTER, 565 Yoder Rd., Harleysville, PA 19438-1020. Tel.: 215-256-3020. Fax: 215-256-3023. Facebook: Mennonite Heritage Center.
E-mail: info@mhep.org
Web Site: www.mhep.org/
Key Personnel: Dir., Sarah Wolfgang Heffner; Asst. Dir., Rose A. Moyer; Pres. (V), Chris Detweiler; Cur. & Librarian, Joel D. Alderfer; Archivist, Forrest Moyer; Dir. Advancement, Steve Diehl; Volunteer Coord., Tim Kennel.
Institution Type/Description: Heritage Center.
Hours & Admission Prices: Tues.-Fri. 10-5, Sat. 10-2. Donation requested. Closed New Year's Day; Good Friday; Easter; Independence Day; Thanksgiving; Christmas. &
Attendance: 7,000 (estimated)

Harrisburg

ART ASSOCIATION OF HARRISBURG, 21 N. Front St., Harrisburg, PA 17101-1625. Tel.: 717-236-1432. Fax: 717-236-6631. Facebook.
E-mail: carrie@artassocofhbg.com
Web Site: www.artassocofhbg.com
Key Personnel: Dir., Pres. & Museum Shop Mgr., Carrie Wissler Thomas; Chm. (V), David Volkman.
Institution Type/Description: Art: 1810 four-story Italianate-style home housing the Art Association building.

Hours & Admission Prices: Mon.-Thurs. 9:30-9, Fri. 9:30-4, Sat. 10-4, Sun. 2-5. No charge. Closed New Year's Day; Easter; Thanksgiving; Christmas.
Attendance: 12,000 (estimated)

BENJAMIN OLEWINE III NATURE CENTER, 100 Wildwood Way, Harrisburg, PA 17110-2914. Tel.: 717-221-0292. Fax: 717-221-0318.
E-mail: friendsofww@wildwoodlake.org
Web Site: www.wildwoodlake.org
Institution Type/Description: Nature Center.
Hours & Admission Prices: Park: daily dawn to dusk. Center: Tues.-Sun. 10-4. Closed holidays. &
Attendance: 85,000 (estimated)

FORT HUNTER MANSION & PARK, 5300 N. Front St., Harrisburg, PA 17110-1718. Tel.: 717-599-5751. Fax: 717-599-5838.
E-mail: jhair@dauphinc.org
Web Site: www.forthunter.org
Key Personnel: Mansion Mgr., Mary Trost; Park Mgr., Julia Hair; Educator, Elizabeth Johnson.
Institution Type/Description: Historic House & Park: housed in 1814 Federal style stone mansion, on the site of French & Indian War fort.
Hours & Admission Prices: May-Dec. Tues.-Sat. 10-5, Sun. 12-5. Adults $5, senior citizens $4, children $3; members no charge. &
Attendance: 9,000 (estimated)

THE HISTORICAL SOCIETY OF DAUPHIN COUNTY, The John Harris/Simon Cameron Mansion, 219 S. Front St., Harrisburg, PA 17104-1619. Tel.: 717-233-3462. Fax: 717-233-6059. Facebook: Dauphin County History.
E-mail: office@dauphincountyhistory.org
Web Site: www.dauphincountyhistory.org
Key Personnel: Exec. Dir., Nicole Smith; Cur., Janet Bowen; Librarian, Ken Frew.
Institution Type/Description: Historic House Museum: 1766 built by John Harris, Jr., founder of Harrisburg; renovated in 1863 by Simon Cameron, Lincoln's first secretary of war.
Hours & Admission Prices: Tours: Mon.-Thurs. 1-4, last tour begins at 3. Tour: adults $8, senior citizens $7, children 6-12 $6; discounts to groups; children under 6 & members no charge. Library: Mon.-Thurs. 1-4. Adults $10. Closed most holidays. &
Attendance: 2,500 (estimated)

THE NATIONAL CIVIL WAR MUSEUM, One Lincoln Center at Reservoir Park, Harrisburg, PA 17103. Tel.: 717-260-1861. Fax: 717-260-9599.
E-mail: info@nationalcivilwarmuseum.org
Web Site: www.nationalcivilwarmuseum.org
Key Personnel: C.E.O., Wayne E. Motts; Chm. (V), Paul Wipple; Museum Shop Mgr., Kate McDermott.
Institution Type/Description: Military & History Museum.
Hours & Admission Prices: Mon.-Tues. & Thurs.-Sat. 10-5, Wed. 10-8, Sun. 12-5. Family $35, adults $10, senior citizens $9, students $8, closed New Year's Day, Easter, Thanksgiving & Christmas. &
Attendance: 40,000 (actual)

PENNSYLVANIA FEDERATION OF MUSEUMS AND HISTORICAL ORGANIZATIONS, 234 N. 3rd St., Harrisburg, PA 17101-1516. Tel.: 717-909-4950. Fax: 717-909-3996.
E-mail: pamuseums@pamuseums.org
Web Site: www.pamuseums.org
Key Personnel: Exec. Dir., Rusty Baker; Dir. Programming, Chrisoula Randas Perdziola.
Institution Type/Description: Museum Service Organization.
Hours & Admission Prices: Mon.-Fri. 8:30-5. Closed federal & state holidays. &

PENNSYLVANIA HISTORICAL & MUSEUM COMMISSION, 300 North St., Harrisburg, PA 17120-0101. Tel.: 717-787-2891. Fax: 717-783-1073. Facebook.
E-mail: amacdonald@pa.gov
Web Site: www.phmc.pa.gov
Key Personnel: Exec. Dir., James M. Vaughan; Chair, Nancy Moses; Dir. Bureau of Historic Sites & Museums, Brenda Reigle; Bureau Dir. PA State Archives, David Carmicheal; Acting Dir. Bureau of The State Museum of Pennsylvania, Beth Hager; Bureau Dir. Management Svcs., Pam Roche; Bureau Dir. State Historic Preservation Office, Andrea MacDonald; Div. Chief Historic Sites & Museums, Michael Bertheaud; Div. Chief Architecture & Preservation, Andrea Lowery; Div. Chief Historic Sites & Museums, Charles Fox.
Institution Type/Description: State Agency; Conservation Center.

Hours & Admission Prices: See individual listings for museums, historic sites, & houses; discounts for active military & their families and AAM & ICOM members; PA Heritage Foundation, State Legislature, media, State Museum of Pennsylvania members, teachers, tour leaders & children under 3 no charge. &
Attendance: 1,100,000 (estimated)

THE PENNSYLVANIA NATIONAL FIRE MUSEUM, 1820 N. 4th St., Harrisburg, PA 17110. Tel.: 717-232-8915. Fax: 717-232-8916.
E-mail: info@pnfm.org
Web Site: www.pnfm.org
Key Personnel: Pres. (V), Dave Houseal; Museum Shop Mgr., John Wagner.
Institution Type/Description: Fire Museum: housed in the 1899 Victorian firehouse Reily Hose Company No. 10.
Hours & Admission Prices: Tues.-Sat. 10-4, Sun. 1-4. Adults $7, seniors $6, student $5; discounts to groups. Closed holidays.
Attendance: 5,000 (estimated)

PENNSYLVANIA STATE ARCHIVES, 350 North St., Harrisburg, PA 17120-0090. Tel.: 717-783-3281.
E-mail: ra-statearchives@pa.gov
Web Site: www.portal.state.pa.us
Institution Type/Description: Archives.
Hours & Admission Prices: Wed.-Fri. 9-4, Sat. 9-12 & 1-4. Closed state holidays.

PENNSYLVANIA STATE CAPITOL, Commonwealth Ave., Harrisburg, PA 17120. Mailing Address: 501 N. 3rd St., Harrisburg, PA 17120-0302. Tel.: 800-868-7672.
E-mail: jfetter@os.pasen.gov
Web Site: www.pacapitol.com
Institution Type/Description: Historic Building: built in 1906.
Hours & Admission Prices: Mon.-Fri. 8:30-4, Sat.-Sun. 9am, 11am, 1pm & 3pm.

ROSE LEHRMAN ART GALLERY, Rose Lehrman Art Center, Harrisburg Area Community College, 1 HACC Dr., Harrisburg, PA 17110-2903. Tel.: 717-780-2478.
E-mail: smwillia@hacc.edu
Web Site: www.hacc.edu/RoseLehrmanArtsCenter/ArtGallery/index.cfm
Key Personnel: Cur., Shawn Williams.
Institution Type/Description: Art Gallery.
Hours & Admission Prices: Summer & Fall: Mon., Wed. & Fri. 11-3, Tues. & Thurs. 11-3 and 5-7; other times by appointment.

THE STATE MUSEUM OF PENNSYLVANIA, 300 North St., Harrisburg, PA 17120-0101. Tel.: 717-787-4980. Fax: 717-783-4558.
E-mail: FriendsOfStateMuseumPA@gmail.com
Web Site: www.statemuseumpa.org
Key Personnel: Museum Dir., Beth Hager.
Institution Type/Description: General Museum.
Hours & Admission Prices: Wed.-Sat. 9-5, Sun. 12-5. Adults $7, seniors 65 & up $6, children 1-11 $5; PA Heritage Society members & military no charge. &
Attendance: 300,000 (estimated)

SUSQUEHANNA ART MUSEUM, 1401 N. 3rd St., Harrisburg, PA 17102-1909. Tel.: 717-233-8668. Fax: 717-233-8155.
E-mail: info@sqart.org
Web Site: www.sqart.org
Key Personnel: Exhibitions Mgr., Amy Hammond; Dir. Outreach Education, Wendy Sweigart; Museum Operations Coord., Susan Bennett.
Institution Type/Description: Art Museum.
Hours & Admission Prices: Call for hours & admission prices. &
Attendance: 10,000 (estimated)

WHITAKER CENTER FOR SCIENCE AND THE ARTS, 222 Market St., Harrisburg, PA 17101-2113. Mailing Address: 225 Market St., 2nd Fl., Harrisburg, PA 17101-2126. Tel.: 717-214-ARTS (2787). Fax: 717-221-8208. Facebook: Whitaker Center Hbg.
E-mail: info@whitakercenter.org
Web Site: www.whitakercenter.org
Formerly: Museum of Scientific Discovery
Key Personnel: Pres. & C.E.O., Michael L. Hanes; Vice Pres. Science & Cinema Programs, Steve Bishop; C.F.O., Meghan Clark; Bd. Chm., Gary St. Hilaire; Dir. Finance, Margaret Freedman; Vice Pres. Operations, Lisa Kreider; Museum Shop Mgr., Teresa Griffin.
Institution Type/Description: Science Center.
Hours & Admission Prices: Science Center: Tues.-Sat. 9:30-5, Sun. 11:30-5. Adults $16, senior citizens (55+) & military with valid ID $14, junior (3-17) $12.50,

discounts to ASTC members; members & children under 3 no charge. Hollywood Movies: adults $13.75, senior citizens (55+) & military with valid ID $12.75, juniors (3-17) $11.75. Cinema Documentaries: adults $9.50, junior (3-17), senior citizens (55+) & military with valid ID $8; discounts to members. Combo: adults $19.75, senior (55+) & military with valid ID $18, junior (3-17) $16.75. Holiday hours vary. &
Attendance: 400,000 (estimated)

Hartsville

WARWICK TOWNSHIP HISTORICAL SOCIETY & MOLAND HOUSE HISTORIC PARK, 1641 Old York Rd., Hartsville, PA 18974. Mailing Address: P.O. Box 107, Jamison, PA 18929-0107. Tel.: 215-918-1754. Facebook: The Moland House.
E-mail: events@moland.org
Web Site: www.moland.org
Formerly: Moland House
Key Personnel: Pres., J. David Mullen; Museum Shop Mgr., JoAnne Mullen.
Institution Type/Description: Historical House Museum: housed in Moland family's farmhouse which was used as George Washington's headquarters from August 10, 1777 to August 23, 1777.
Hours & Admission Prices: Call for hours. No charge, donations accepted. &
Attendance: 1,000 (estimated)

Hatboro

AMY B. YERKES MUSEUM - MILLBROOK SOCIETY, 32 N. York Rd., Hatboro, PA 19040. Mailing Address: P.O. Box 506, Hatboro, PA 19040. Tel.: 215-957-1877. Facebook: The Millbrook Society.
E-mail: millbrooksociety@gmail.com
Web Site: www.millbrooksociety.org
Key Personnel: Dir., Mary Porter; Pres. (V), D. Shannon.
Institution Type/Description: History Museum.
Hours & Admission Prices: Wed. 7:30pm-9:30pm. No charge; donations accepted.
Attendance: 10 (estimated)

Haverford

CANTOR FITZGERALD GALLERY - HAVERFORD COLLEGE, Whitehead Campus Center, 370 Lancaster Ave., Haverford, PA 19041. Tel.: 610-896-1287.
E-mail: hcexhibits@gmail.com
Web Site: www.haverford.edu/exhibits
Key Personnel: Assoc. Dir. Cantor Fitzgerald Gallery & Campus Exhibitions, Matthew Seamus Callinan.
Institution Type/Description: Art Gallery.
Hours & Admission Prices: Mon.-Tues. & Thurs.-Fri. 11-5, Wed. 11-8, Sat.-Sun. 12-5. No charge.

HAVERFORD COLLEGE ARBORETUM, 370 Lancaster Ave., Haverford, PA 19041-1392. Tel.: 610-896-1405. Fax: 610-896-1095.
E-mail: arbor@haverford.edu
Web Site: www.haverford.edu/Arboretum
Key Personnel: Dir., William Astifan; Cur., Martha Van Artsdalen.
Institution Type/Description: Arboretum: Haverford College is a Quaker institution, the architecture reflects a simple style starting in 1833.
Hours & Admission Prices: Daily dawn-dusk. No charge; donations accepted. &

MAIN LINE ART CENTER, 746 Panmure Rd., Haverford, PA 19041-1218. Tel.: 610-525-0272. Fax: 610-525-5036.
E-mail: info@mainlineart.org
Key Personnel: Exec. Dir., Judy Herman.
Institution Type/Description: Art Gallery.
Hours & Admission Prices: Call for hours.

Havertown

HAVERFORD TOWNSHIP HISTORICAL SOCIETY, Karakung Dr., Powder Mill Valley Park, Havertown, PA 19083. Mailing Address: Box 825, Havertown, PA 19083-0825. Tel.: 484-452-3382. Facebook: Haverford Historical.
E-mail: info@haverfordhistoricalsociety.org
Web Site: www.haverfordhistoricalsociety.org
Key Personnel: Cur., Kelly Brennan; Pres. & Treas., Irene Coffey.

Institution Type/Description: Local History Museum: housed in c.1710 Lawrence Cabin, adjoining c.1810 Nitre Hall home of the Powder Master & c.1797 Federal School.
Hours & Admission Prices: May-Sept. last Sun. each month 10-1. Free will donation.
Attendance: 3,700 (estimated)

Hazleton

GREATER HAZLETON HISTORICAL SOCIETY & MUSEUM, 55 N. Wyoming St., Hazleton, PA 18201-6069. Tel.: 570-455-8576. Facebook: Greater Hazleton Historical Society and Museum.
E-mail: hazletonmuseum@gmail.com
Web Site: hazletonmuseum.org
Key Personnel: Pres., Thomas Gabos.
Institution Type/Description: Historical Society Museum.
Hours & Admission Prices: By appointment only. &
Attendance: 1,000 (estimated)

Hellertown

GILMAN MUSEUM, 726 Durham St., at the Cave, Hellertown, PA 18055. Mailing Address: P.O. Box M, Hellertown, PA 18055-0220. Tel.: 610-838-8767. Fax: 610-838-2961.
E-mail: museum@alton.nh.gov
Web Site: www.lostcave.com
Key Personnel: Dir., C.E.O. & Chief Cur., Beverly L. Rozewicz; Chm. (V), Robert Gilman.
Institution Type/Description: Natural History & Antique Weapons: located on the site of an old Limestone Quarry, at the entrance of a natural underground series of caverns.
Hours & Admission Prices: Memorial Day to Labor Day daily 9-6; 1st Tues. in Sept. to last Thurs. in May daily 9-5. Cavern Tours: adults $13.95, children 3-12 $8.95. Closed New Year's Day; Thanksgiving; Christmas.
Attendance: 25,000 (estimated)

LOWER SAUCON TOWNSHIP HISTORICAL SOCIETY - LUTZ FRANKLIN SCHOOL, 4216 Countryside Lane, Hellertown, PA 18055. Mailing Address: P.O. Box 176, Hellertown, PA 18055. Tel.: 610-625-8771. Facebook: Lutz-Franklin Schoolhouse.
E-mail: lshistorical@yahoo.com
Web Site: www.lutzfranklin.com
Key Personnel: Pres. (V), Susan Horiszny.
Institution Type/Description: History Museum: housed in a former schoolhouse, c.1826.
Hours & Admission Prices: Call for hours. No charge; donations accepted. &
Attendance: 900 (estimated)

Hershey

AACA MUSEUM - ANTIQUE AUTOMOBILE CLUB OF AMERICA MUSEUM, 161 Museum Dr., Hershey, PA 17033-2462. Tel.: 717-566-7100. Fax: 717-566-7300. Twitter.
E-mail: info@aacamuseum.org
Web Site: aacamuseum.org
Key Personnel: Pres. (V), Henry "Hank" W. Hallowell, III; Museum Shop Mgr., Hillary Carter.
Institution Type/Description: Automobile Museum.
Hours & Admission Prices: Daily 9-5. Adults $12, seniors 61 & over $11, children 4-12 $9; discounts to AAA members; members and children 3 & under no charge. Closed New Year's Day; Thanksgiving; Christmas Eve & Day. &
Attendance: 60,000 (actual)

HERSHEY-DERRY TOWNSHIP HISTORICAL SOCIETY, 40 Northeast Dr., Hershey, PA 17033-2732. Tel.: 717-520-0748.
E-mail: hdths@hersheyhistory.org
Web Site: hersheyhistory.org
Institution Type/Description: History Museum.
Hours & Admission Prices: Mon., Wed. & Fri. 9-4:30, Sat. 9-1. Adults $3. &

HERSHEY GARDENS, 170 Hotel Rd., Hershey, PA 17033-9507. Tel.: 717-534-3492. Fax: 717-533-5095.
E-mail: info@hersheygardens.org
Web Site: www.hersheygardens.org
Key Personnel: Exec. Dir. M.S. Hershey Foundaiton, Don Papson; Dir. Communs. & Public Rels., Jill Manley; Assoc. Dir., Jamie Shiffer.
Institution Type/Description: Arboretum/ Botanical Gardens & Horticultural Society: retains original 1937 landscape design & structures.

Hours & Admission Prices: Call for seasonal hours. Adults $12.50, seniors 62 & over $11.50, children 3-12 $9; discounts to groups; children 2 & under and members no charge. Closed Thanksgiving; Christmas. &
Attendance: 120,800 (actual)

THE HERSHEY STORY, 63 W. Chocolate Ave., Hershey, PA 17033-1558. Tel.: 717-534-3439. Fax: 717-534-8940.
E-mail: info@hersheymuseum.org
Web Site: www.hersheystory.org
Formerly: Hershey Museum
Key Personnel: Interim Dir., Don Papson; Assoc. Dir., Amy Bischof; Mgr. Public Programs, Lois Miklas; Dir. Education, Mariella Trosko; Mgr. Chocolate Lab, Kyle Nagurny; School Programs Supvr., Beth Hiner; Mgr. Collections, Valerie Seiber; Mgr. Visitor Experience, Lisa Morelli; Trips & Excursions Consultant, Janet Hester; Mgr. Systems, Information & Accounting, Sharon Smith; Coord. Membership, Barb Latz.
Institution Type/Description: History Museum.
Hours & Admission Prices: Daily 9-5:30. Adults $10, senior citizens 62 & over $9, youth 3-12 $7.50; discounts to groups, ICOM, AAM & AAA members; members no charge. Closed Thanksgiving; Christmas. &
Attendance: 90,215 (actual)

HERSHEY'S CHOCOLATE WORLD, 101 Chocolate World Way, Hershey, PA 17033. Tel.: 717-534-4900.
Web Site: hersheypa.com/chocolateworld
Institution Type/Description: Company History Museum & Tour.
Hours & Admission Prices: Daily seasonal hours. Chocolate World & Tour: no charge. Trolley Works, Create Your Own Candy Bar, Hershey's Unwrapped & 4D Chocolate Movie: individual or combination pricing available.

THE MUSEUM OF BUS TRANSPORTATION, INC., 161 Museum Dr., Hershey, PA 17033-2462. Tel.: 717-566-7100, ext. 119. Fax: 717-566-7300.
Web Site: busmuseum.org
Key Personnel: C.E.O., Pres. & Mgr., J. Thomas Collins; Vice Pres., Robert Smith; Treas., Edwin P. Wolf; Museum Shop Mgr., O.J. Ogden.
Institution Type/Description: Transportation Museum.
Hours & Admission Prices: Summer: daily 9-5; Labor Day to Memorial Day Wed.-Sun. 9-5. Adults $7; discount to members. Closed New Year's Day; Thanksgiving; Christmas. &
Attendance: 50,000 (actual)

ZOOAMERICA NORTH AMERICAN WILDLIFE PARK, 201 Park Ave., Hershey, PA 17033. Mailing Address: 100 W. Hershey Park Dr., Hershey, PA 17033. Tel.: 717-534-3900. Fax: 717-534-3151.
E-mail: zooamerica@hersheypa.com
Web Site: www.zooamerica.com
Key Personnel: Dir., Troy E. Stump; Cur., Dale Snyder; Supvr. Southern Swamps, Pat McCann; Supvr. Great Southwest, Katie Govern; Cur. Educatioin, Elaine Gruin; Supvr. Exterior Exhibits, Tal Wenrich; Supvr. Exterior Exhibits, Tim Becker; Administrative Support, Dee Nixon.
Institution Type/Description: Zoological Park.
Hours & Admission Prices: Call for hours. Adults $11, senior citizens, children 3-8 $9; discounts to AZA members; children under 2 no charge. Closed New Year's Day; Thanksgiving; Christmas. &
Attendance: 623,848 (actual)

Honesdale

HONESDALE FIRE MUSEUM, Protection Engine Company No. 3, 1205 Main St., Honesdale, PA 18431.
E-mail: srpratt@verizon.net
Web Site: www.engine3.org/Museum.html
Institution Type/Description: Fire Museum.
Hours & Admission Prices: By appointment.

WAYNE COUNTY HISTORICAL SOCIETY, 810 Main, Honesdale, PA 18431. Mailing Address: P.O. Box 446, Honesdale, PA 18431. Tel.: 570-253-3240. Fax: 570-253-5204.
E-mail: wchs@ptd.net
Web Site: www.waynehistorypa.org
Key Personnel: Exec. Dir., Carol Dunn; Pres., Kelly Alogna; 1st Vice Pres., Tracy Schwarz; Sec., Dorothy Kieff; Treas., Thomas Colbert; Museum Shop Mgr., Jane Brooks; Librarian, Kay Stephenson.
Institution Type/Description: History Museum.
Hours & Admission Prices: Call for hours. Adults $5; discounts to groups & AAA members; members, children 3-18 & students no charge. Closed New Year's Day; Thanksgiving; Christmas. &
Attendance: 5,000 (estimated)

Horsham

GRAEME PARK, 859 County Line Rd., Horsham, PA 19044-1401. Tel.: 215-343-0965. Fax: 215-343-2223. Facebook: Graeme Park Horsham.
E-mail: ra-graemepark@pa.gov
Web Site: www.graemepark.org
Key Personnel: Pres. (V), Beth McCausland; Dir., Office Mgr. Historic Site Admin. & Museum Educator, Carla Loughlin; Museum Shop Mgr., Carol Brunner.
Institution Type/Description: Historic House: 1722, Keith Mansion, located within 42 acres at Graeme Park.
Hours & Admission Prices: Fri.-Sat. 10-4, Sun. 12-4; last tours are one hour before closing. Admission $6, seniors 65 & over and groups $5, youth 3-11 $3; discounts to PHMC Trail of History & AAA members; PA Heritage members, members & children under 3 no charge. Closed New Year's Day; Martin Luther King Jr. Day; Presidents' Day; Easter; Columbus Day; Veterans Day; Thanksgiving & day after; Christmas.
Attendance: 8,311 (estimated)

THE HAROLD F. PITCAIRN WINGS OF FREEDOM AVIATION MUSEUM, 1155 Easton Rd., Horsham, PA 19044. Mailing Address: P.O. Box 747, Horsham, PA 19044. Tel.: 215-672-2277. Facebook: Wings of Freedom Aviation Museum.
E-mail: dvhaa@wingsoffreedommuseum.org
Web Site: www.wingsoffreedommuseum.org
Key Personnel: Pres., John Rehfuss; Vice Pres., Mark Horwitz; Chm. (V), Gen. Ronald Nelson; Museum Shop Mgr., Shirley Luvender.
Institution Type/Description: Aviation Museum.
Hours & Admission Prices: Wed.-Fri. 10:30-3, Sat.-Sun. 10:30-4. No charge; donations accepted. &
Attendance: 12,000 (actual)

Howard

CURTIN VILLAGE AT EAGLE IRONWORKS HISTORICAL SITE, 251 Curtin Village Rd., Howard, PA 16841. Tel.: 814-355-1982 & 4071.
E-mail: curtinvillage@verizon.net
Web Site: www.curtinvillage.com
Institution Type/Description: Historic Site: housed on the iron plantation site operated by Roland Curtin and his family from 1810-1921.
Hours & Admission Prices: last weekend in May to Oct. Sat. 10-4, Sun. 11-4; groups & other times by appointment. Adults $4, children 12 & under $1.

Hummelstown

HUMMELSTOWN AREA HISTORICAL SOCIETY MUSEUM AND PARISH HOUSE, Rosanna St. & N. Alley, Hummelstown, PA 17036. Mailing Address: 32 W. Main St., Hummelstown, PA 17036-1515. Tel.: 717-566-6314.
E-mail: hahs@hummelstownhistoricalsociety.org
Web Site: www.hummelstownhistoricalsociety.org
Key Personnel: Pres., Chad Lister.
Institution Type/Description: Historical Society Museum: housed in a former Zion Lutheran Church; built in 1815.
Hours & Admission Prices: Museum: by appointment. Library: Mon. & Wed. 10-4, Thurs. 10-2. Museum: no charge. Library: $5. &
Attendance: 1,000 (estimated)

Huntingdon

HUNTINGDON COUNTY HISTORICAL SOCIETY, 106 4th St., Huntingdon, PA 16652-1418. Mailing Address: P.O. Box 305, Huntingdon, PA 16652-0305. Tel.: 814-643-5449. Facebook.
E-mail: hchsmail@gmail.com
Web Site: www.huntingdonhistory.org
Key Personnel: Exec. Dir., Kelley Kroecker.
Institution Type/Description: County Historical Society Museum: housed in a Victorian house.
Hours & Admission Prices: Victorian House Museum & Library: April-Nov. Wed.-Fri. 9-4; other times by appointment. Office: Tues.-Fri. 10-4. House Tours: $5 per person. Library: $10 per person per day; members no charge.
Attendance: 1,000 (estimated)

ISETT ACRES MUSEUM, Stone Creek Ridge Rd., Huntingdon, PA 16652. Mailing Address: P.O. Box 419, Huntingdon, PA 16652. Tel.: 814-643-9600.
E-mail: isetthmuseum@gmail.com
Web Site: isettacres.com
Key Personnel: Mgr., Justina Hall.

Institution Type/Description: History Museum.
Hours & Admission Prices: Mon.-Sat. 8-5, Sun. 12-5. Adults $6, students $4. &

JUNIATA COLLEGE MUSEUM OF ART, 1700 Moore St., Huntingdon, PA 16652. Tel.: 814-641-3505. Fax: 814-641-3607. Facebook: Juniata College Museum of Art.
E-mail: blake@juniata.edu
Web Site: www.juniata.edu/services/museum
Key Personnel: Dir., Kathryn Blake; Cur., Jennifer Streb.
Institution Type/Description: Art Museum: housed in former Carnegie Library built in 1906; Beaux-Arts style, Greek cross with rotunda & stained glass windows.
Hours & Admission Prices: May-Aug. Wed.-Fri. 12-4; Sept.-April Mon.-Fri. 10-4, Sat. 12-4. No charge. Closed major holidays; college holidays. &
Attendance: 2,000 (estimated)

SWIGART MUSEUM, 12031 William Penn Hwy., Museum Park, Rte. 22 E., Huntingdon, PA 16652. Mailing Address: P.O. Box 214, Huntingdon, PA 16652-0214. Tel.: 814-643-0885. Fax: 814-643-2857.
E-mail: tours@swigartmuseum.com
Web Site: www.swigartmuseum.com
Key Personnel: Dir. & Museum Shop Mgr., Marjorie E. Cutright; Pres. (V), Patricia B. Swigart.
Institution Type/Description: Automotive Museum.
Hours & Admission Prices: Memorial Day-Oct. daily 10-5. Adults $8, senior citizens $7.50, children 6-12 $4; discounts to AAM members & groups of 20 or more; children 5 & under no charge. &

Indiana

HISTORICAL AND GENEALOGICAL SOCIETY OF INDIANA COUNTY, 621 Wayne Ave., Indiana, PA 15701-3072. Tel.: 724-463-9600. Fax: 724-463-9899.
E-mail: ichistoricalsociety@gmail.com
Web Site: www.hgsic.org
Key Personnel: Pres., Thomas Crumm; Chm., JoAnne McQuilkin.
Institution Type/Description: Local History Museum.
Hours & Admission Prices: Tues.-Fri. 9-4, Sat. 10-3. Library: $3 per person; members & students no charge. &
Attendance: 2,300 (actual)

THE JIMMY STEWART MUSEUM, 835 Philadelphia St., Indiana, PA 15701-3907. Mailing Address: P.O. Box One, Indiana, PA 15701. Tel.: 724-349-6112, 800-83-JIMMY. Fax: 724-349-6140.
E-mail: tharley@jimmy.org
Web Site: www.jimmy.org
Key Personnel: C.E.O., Dir. & Pres. of Foundation, Timothy F. Harley; Board Chm., Jeffrey Tobin; Vice Chm. (V), Carson Greene, Jr.; Treas., Gerald Thomchick; Museum Shop Mgr., Nancy Empfield.
Institution Type/Description: History & Audio-Visual Film Museum.
Hours & Admission Prices: Mon.-Sat. 10-4, Sun. 12-4. Adults $8, senior citizens & students $7, children $6; discounts to AAM members; children under 7 & members no charge. Closed New Year's Day; Martin Luther King, Jr. Day; President's Day Easter; Memorial Day, Independence Day; Labor Day; Thanksgiving; Christmas. &
Attendance: 5,600 (estimated)

KIPP GALLERY AT INDIANA UNIVERSITY OF PENNSYLVANIA, College of Fine Arts, Sprowls Hall, 1st Fl., 470 S. 11th St., Indiana, PA 15705. Tel.: 724-357-2530. Fax: 724-357-7778.
E-mail: lively-arts@iup.edu
Web Site: www.iup.edu/livelyarts/series/kippgallery
Key Personnel: Dean College of Fine Arts, Michael Hood; Dir., Kyle Houser.
Institution Type/Description: University Art Gallery.
Hours & Admission Prices: Academic Year: Tues.-Fri. 11-4, Sat. 1-4; Summer: Mon.-Tues. & Thurs. 11-4. No charge. Closed university holidays. &

THE UNIVERSITY MUSEUM, Sutton Hall, Indiana University of Pennsylvania, 1011 South Dr., Indiana, PA 15705. Mailing Address: Sutton Hall, Indiana Univ. of Penn., Room 111, Indiana, PA 15705. Tel.: 724-357-2397. Fax: 724-357-7778.
E-mail: mhood@iup.edu
Web Site: www.iup.edu/museum
Key Personnel: Exhibitions Coord., William Double; Dean, Michael Hood; Pres. (V), Myron H. Tomb.
Institution Type/Description: Art & History Museum: National Historic Landmark Site.

Hours & Admission Prices: Tues.-Wed. & Fri. 2-6:30, Thurs. 12-7:30, Sat. 12-4. No charge. Closed university holidays. &
Attendance: 5,000

Jamestown

PYMATUNING DEER PARK, 804 E. Jamestown Rd., Jamestown, PA 16134. Mailing Address: 842 E. Jamestown Rd., Jamestown, PA 16134-9502. Tel.: 724-932-3200. Fax: 724-932-3198.
E-mail: info@pymatuningdeerpark.com
Web Site: www.pymatuningdeerpark.com
Institution Type/Description: Zoo.
Hours & Admission Prices: Memorial Day to Labor Day daily 10-6; Sept. Sat.-Sun. 10-6. Adults 13 & over $8, senior citizens $7, children 2-12 $6; children under 2 no charge. Train Ride: $2; children under 2 no charge.

Jeannette

BUSHY RUN BATTLEFIELD, 1253 Bushy Run Rd., Jeannette, PA 15644. Mailing Address: P.O. Box 468, Harrison City, PA 15636-0468. Tel.: 724-527-5584. Fax: 724-527-5610.
E-mail: info@bushyrunbattlefield.com
Web Site: www.bushyrunbattlefield.com
Key Personnel: Pres. (V), Bonnie Ramus.
Institution Type/Description: Military Museum: located on the site of Bushy Run Battlefield, used during Pontiac's Rebellion, 1763.
Hours & Admission Prices: Visitor's Center: May-Oct. Wed.-Sat 9-5, Sun. 12-5. Park: Wed.-Sun. 9-5; groups by appointment. Adults $5, seniors & AAA members $4.50, children 6-17 $3; members no charge. &
Attendance: 33,000 (estimated)

Jenkintown

ABINGTON ART CENTER, 515 Meetinghouse Rd., Ste. 1, Jenkintown, PA 19046-2964. Tel.: 215-887-4882. Fax: 215-887-5789.
E-mail: info@abingtonartcenter.org
Web Site: www.abingtonartcenter.org
Key Personnel: Exec. Dir., Laura Burnham; Asst. Dir., Heather Rutledge; Chm. (V), Eric Weckel.
Institution Type/Description: Art Center & Sculpture Park.
Hours & Admission Prices: Wed. & Fri. 10-5, Thurs. 10-7, Sat.-Sun. 10-3. No charge; donations accepted. Closed New Year's Eve & Day; Independence Day; Thanksgiving; Christmas week. &
Attendance: 31,421 (actual)

OLD YORK ROAD HISTORICAL SOCIETY, 515 Meetinghouse Rd., Jenkintown, PA 19046-2964. Tel.: 215-886-8590.
E-mail: oldyorkroadhistory@gmail.com
Web Site: www.oyrhs.org
Key Personnel: Pres. (V), David B. Rowland; Photo Archivist, Leslie Bell; Archivist, Linda Stanley.
Institution Type/Description: Local History Research Library.
Hours & Admission Prices: Mon. 7pm-9pm, Tues. 11-2, Wed. 11-3; other times by appointment. No charge; donations accepted.
Attendance: 350 (actual)

Jersey Shore

JERSEY SHORE HISTORICAL SOCIETY, 200 S. Main St., Jersey Shore, PA 17740-1812. Tel.: 717-398-1973.
Web Site: jshistory.org
Institution Type/Description: Historical Society Museum: housed in the Samuel Moss House.
Hours & Admission Prices: Call for hours.

Jim Thorpe

ASA PACKER MANSION, Packer Hill, Jim Thorpe, PA 18229-0108. Mailing Address: P.O Box 108, Jim Thorpe, PA 18229-0108. Tel.: 570-325-3229.
E-mail: abretzik@yahoo.com
Web Site: www.asapackermansion.com
Key Personnel: Dir. & Historian, Ava Bretzik.
Institution Type/Description: Historic Building: 1860 Victorian mansion.
Hours & Admission Prices: April-May Sat.-Sun. 11-4:15; Memorial Day-Nov. 1. daily 11-4:15. Adults $8, senior citizens 55 & over $7, students & children 6-18 $5; children under 5 no charge. &
Attendance: 30,000

Johnstown

JOHNSTOWN AREA HERITAGE ASSOCIATION, 201 6th Ave., Johnstown, PA 15906-2500. Mailing Address: P.O. Box 1889, Johnstown, PA 15907-1889. Tel.: 814-539-1889. Fax: 814-535-1931.
E-mail: info@jaha.org
Web Site: www.jaha.org
Formerly: Johnstown Flood Museum
Key Personnel: Exec. Dir., Richard A. Burkert; Pres. (V), Mark Pasquerilla; Designer & Archivist, Marcia Kelly; Dir. Visitor Svcs., Kim Baxter; Cur., Kaytlin Sumner.
Institution Type/Description: History Museum.
Hours & Admission Prices: Jan.-March Tues.-Sun. 10-5; April-Dec. daily 10-5. Two Sites: adults $8, senior citizens $7, children $6; discounts to AAM & ICOM members; members & children no charge. &
Attendance: 68,000 (actual)

SOUTHERN ALLEGHENIES MUSEUM OF ART AT JOHNSTOWN, Pasquerilla Performing Arts Center, University of Pittsburgh at Johnstown, 450 Schoolhouse Rd., Johnstown, PA 15904-2912. Tel.: 814-269-7234. Fax: 814-269-7240.
E-mail: johnstown@sama-art.org
Web Site: www.sama-art.org
Key Personnel: Exec. Dir., G. Gary Moyer; Coord. Education, Jessica Campbell.
Institution Type/Description: Art Museum.
Hours & Admission Prices: Mon.-Fri. 9-5. No charge; donations accepted. Closed major holidays. &
Attendance: 50,428 (actual)

Kempton

ALBANY TOWNSHIP HISTORICAL SOCIETY, 404 Old Philly Pike, Kempton, PA 19529-9306. Mailing Address: P.O. Box 95, Kempton, PA 19529. Tel.: 610-756-6144.
E-mail: info@albanyths.org
Web Site: albanyths.org
Institution Type/Description: Historical Society Museum: housed in a former grain & feed warehouse; built in 1917.
Hours & Admission Prices: By appointment. No charge. &
Attendance: 450 (estimated)

HAWK MOUNTAIN SANCTUARY, 1700 Hawk Mountain Rd., Kempton, PA 19529-9379. Tel.: 610-756-6961. Fax: 610-756-4468.
E-mail: info@hawkmountain.org
Web Site: www.hawkmountain.org
Key Personnel: Pres., Jerry Regan; Museum Shop Mgr., Mary Therese Grob.
Institution Type/Description: Nature Center.
Hours & Admission Prices: Sept.-Nov. daily 8-5; Dec.-Aug. daily 9-5. Adults $5 ($7 on autumn weekends), children 6-12 $3; members no charge. &
Attendance: 70,000 (estimated)

Kennett Square

LONGWOOD GARDENS, 1001 Longwood Rd., Kennett Square, PA 19348. Mailing Address: P.O. Box 501, Kennett Square, PA 19348-0501. Tel.: 610-388-1000. Fax: 610-388-2294.
E-mail: questions@longwoodgardens.org
Web Site: www.longwoodgardens.org
Key Personnel: Dir., Paul Redman; Dir. Horticulture, Sharon Loving; Dir. Administration & C.F.O., Dennis Fisher; Dir. Mktg., Marnie Conley; Dir. Education, Doug Needham.
Institution Type/Description: Arboretum & Horticultural Display Garden.
Hours & Admission Prices: April-Aug. daily 9-6; Sept.-March daily 9-5. Illuminated evening fountain display: June-Aug. Thurs.-Sat. evenings at dusk. Nonpeak Days: adults $20, seniors 62 & over $17, youth 5-18 $10; children 4 & under no charge. &
Attendance: 1,024,000 (actual)

King of Prussia

VALLEY FORGE NATIONAL HISTORICAL PARK, 1400 N. Outer Line Dr., King of Prussia, PA 19406-1009. Tel.: 610-783-1037. Fax: 610-783-1038.
E-mail: dona_medermott@nps.gov
Web Site: www.nps.gov/vafo
Key Personnel: Supt., Kate Hammond; Museum Shop Mgr., Daria Fink.
Institution Type/Description: Historic Site: c.1777-1778 site of Continental Army winter encampment.

Hours & Admission Prices: Daily 9-5. No charge. Closed New Year's Day; Thanksgiving; Christmas. &
Attendance: 2,100,000 (estimated)

Kinzers

ROUGH & TUMBLE ENGINEERS HISTORICAL ASSOCIATION, 4997 Lincoln Hwy. E., Kinzers, PA 17535. Mailing Address: Box 9, Kinzers, PA 17535-0009. Tel.: 717-442-4249.
E-mail: info@roughandtumble.org
Web Site: www.roughandtumble.org
Key Personnel: Pres., Arthur Astle; Cur., David Adams.
Institution Type/Description: Agricultural & Mechanical Technology & History.
Hours & Admission Prices: Call for hours & admission. &

Kittanning

ARMSTRONG COUNTY HISTORICAL MUSEUM AND GENEALOGICAL SOCIETY, INC., 300 N. McKean St., Kittanning, PA 16201-1373. Mailing Address: P.O. Box 735, Kittanning, PA 16201-0735. Tel.: 724-548-5707.
E-mail: achgs@windstream.net
Web Site: achmgs.yolasite.com
Formerly: McCain House - Armstrong County Historical Society
Key Personnel: Pres. (V), Lee J. Calarie.
Institution Type/Description: Historic House Museum: built in 1842.
Hours & Admission Prices: April to mid-Nov. Thurs. & 1st Sun. of month 12-4, other times by appointment. No charge, donations accepted.
Attendance: 650 (estimated)

WINDBER COAL HERITAGE CENTER CLOSED, 301 Market St., Kittanning, PA 16201-1504. Tel.: 814-467-6680, 877-826-3933. Fax: 814-467-8715.
E-mail: wchc@adelphia.net
Web Site: www.echf.windberpa.org
Institution Type/Description: Mining History Museum.
Hours & Admission Prices: Call for hours. Discount to members & group tours over 20. &

Knoxville

KNOXVILLE PUBLIC LIBRARY, 112 Main St., Knoxville, PA 16928-0277. Mailing Address: P.O. Box 277, Knoxville, PA 16928-0277. Tel.: 814-326-4448. Fax: 814-326-4448.
E-mail: kpblibrary@gmail.com
Web Site: www.knoxvillepubliclibrary.com
Key Personnel: Pres. (V), Teressa Sasserson; Sherrie, Vitulli ; Librarian, Ellen Williams; Asst. Librarian, Bonnie McCormack.
Institution Type/Description: History Museum.
Hours & Admission Prices: Mon. 9-8:30, Wed. & Fri. 9-6:30, Sat. 9-5. No charge.
Attendance: 100 (estimated)

Kutztown

OLD SPOKES AUTO MUSEUM, 10399 Old Rte. 22, Kutztown, PA 19530-8531. Tel.: 484-554-7517.
E-mail: bthompson@oldspokes.com
Web Site: www.oldspokes.com
Institution Type/Description: Auto Museum.
Hours & Admission Prices: Call for hours.

PENNSYLVANIA GERMAN CULTURAL HERITAGE CENTER AT KUTZTOWN UNIVERSITY, 22 Luckenbill Rd., Kutztown, PA 19530-9203. Tel.: 610-683-1589, 484-646-4165 (Library) & 4166 (office). Fax: 610-683-1330.
E-mail: heritage@kutztown.edu
Web Site: www.kutztown.edu/community/PGCHC
Formerly: Pennsylvania Dutch Folk Culture Society, Inc.
Key Personnel: Dir., Dr. Robert Reynolds; Registrar, Patty Frandsen; Bldg. Conservator & Exhibit Specialist, Patrick Donmoyer; Coord. Public Rels., Amanda Richardson.
Institution Type/Description: Folk Culture Museum.
Hours & Admission Prices: Mon.-Fri. 10-4; tours by appointment. Adults $5; members no charge. Closed most holidays. &
Attendance: 12,000 (estimated)

Lackawaxen

ZANE GREY MUSEUM, 135 Scenic Dr., Lackawaxen, PA 18435. Mailing Address: 274 River Rd., Beach Lake, PA 18405-4046. Tel.: 570-685-4871. Fax: 570-729-8565. Facebook; Instagram.
E-mail: upde_interpretation@nps.gov
Web Site: www.nps.gov/upde
Key Personnel: Supt., Kristina Heister.
Institution Type/Description: History Museum.
Hours & Admission Prices: Memorial Day to Labor Day daily 10-5; Sept. to mid-Oct. Sat.-Sun. 10-5. No charge.
Attendance: 8,000 (actual)

Lake Ariel

CLAWS 'N' PAWS WILD ANIMAL PARK, 1475 Ledgedale Rd., Lake Ariel, PA 18436-5589. Tel.: 570-698-6154.
Web Site: www.clawsnpaws.com
Institution Type/Description: Zoo.
Hours & Admission Prices: May to mid-Oct. daily 10-6. Adults 12 & over $14.95, seniors 65 & over $13.95, children 2-11 $10.95; children one & under no charge.

Lakeville

SCULPTED ICE WORKS FACTORY TOUR & NATURAL ICE HARVEST MUSEUM, Rte. 590, Lakeville, PA 18438. Mailing Address: 311 Purdytown Tpke., Lakeville, PA 18438. Tel.: 570-226-6246.
E-mail: sales@sculptediceworks.com
Web Site: sculptediceworks.com
Key Personnel: Owner & Sculptor, Mark S. Crouthamel; Mktg., Event Coord. & Designer, Kathryn Bauer; Production Mgr., Roy Witten.
Institution Type/Description: Company History Museum.
Hours & Admission Prices: Office: Mon.-Fri. 9-4. Tours for groups of 20 or more. Call for reservation.

Lancaster

THE AMISH FARM & HOUSE, 2395 Lincoln Hwy. E., Lancaster, PA 17602-1174. Mailing Address: 2395 Covered Bridge Dr., Lancaster, PA 17602-1174. Tel.: 717-394-6185. Fax: 717-394-4857. Facebook: Amish Farm & House.
E-mail: info@amishfarmandhouse.com
Web Site: www.amishfarmandhouse.com
Key Personnel: Gen. Mgr., Mark Andrews; Dir. Mktg., Eric Conner; Operations Mgr., Hope Byers; Museum Shop Mgr., Dawn Sutton.
Institution Type/Description: Historic House Museum.
Hours & Admission Prices: Jan.-March daily 10-4; April-May & Sept.-Oct. daily 9-5; June-Aug. daily 9-6; Nov.-Dec. daily 9-4. General Admission: adults 12 & over $9.50, seniors 60 & over $8.50, children 5-11 $6.50; children 5 & under no charge. Closed New Year's Day; Thanksgiving; Christmas.

DEMUTH MUSEUM, 120 E. King St., Lancaster, PA 17602-2832. Tel.: 717-299-9940. Fax: 717-299-9749.
E-mail: info@demuth.org
Web Site: www.demuth.org
Key Personnel: Dir., Anne M. Lampe.
Institution Type/Description: Art Museum.
Hours & Admission Prices: Feb.-Dec. Tues.-Sat. 10-4, Sun. 1-4. No charge; donations accepted.

HANDS-ON HOUSE, CHILDREN'S MUSEUM OF LANCASTER, 721 Landis Valley Rd., Lancaster, PA 17601-4888. Tel.: 717-569-KIDS. Fax: 717-581-9283. Facebook: Hands-on House, Children's Museum of Lancaster.
E-mail: info@handsonhouse.org
Web Site: handsonhouse.org
Key Personnel: Exec. Dir., Lynne Morrison.
Institution Type/Description: Children's Museum.
Hours & Admission Prices: Memorial Day to Labor Day Mon.-Thurs. & Sat. 10-5, Fri. 10-8, Sun. 12-5; Sept.-May Tues.-Thurs. 11-4, Fri. 11-8, Sat. 10-5, Sun. 12-5. Admission $9.50; discounts to groups & ACM members; members no charge. Closed New Year's Day; Easter; Memorial Day; Independence Day; Labor Day; Thanksgiving; Christmas Eve & Day.
Attendance: 65,000 (estimated)

HERITAGE CENTER OF LANCASTER COUNTY, INC., 126 E. King St., Lancaster, PA 17602-2832. Tel.: 717-299-6440. Fax: 717-299-6916.
E-mail: info@lancasterheritage.com
Web Site: www.lancasterheritage.com
Key Personnel: Exec. Dir., Wendy Nagle; Cur., Wendell Zercher; Museum Shop Mgr., Sue Schumann.
Institution Type/Description: General Museum.
Hours & Admission Prices: Temporarily closed. Quilt Museum: adults $6; children no charge. Heritage Center: no charge. Closed New Year's Day; Easter; Memorial Day; Independence Day; Labor Day; Thanksgiving; Christmas.
Attendance: 75,000 (actual)

LANCASTER MUSEUM OF ART, 135 N. Lime St., Lancaster, PA 17602-2952. Tel.: 717-394-3497.
E-mail: generalmuseummanager@gmail.com
Web Site: www.Lmapa.org
Key Personnel: Gen. Museum Mgr., Genine E. Antonelli; Exec. Dir., Anne M. Lampe.
Institution Type/Description: Regional Visual Arts Museum.
Hours & Admission Prices: Feb.-Dec. Tues.-Sat. 10-4, Sun. 12-4. No charge; donations requested. Closed national holidays.
Attendance: 35,000 (estimated)

LANCASTER SCIENCE FACTORY, 454 New Holland Ave., Lancaster, PA 17602. Tel.: 717-509-6363. Fax: 717-509-6386.
E-mail: info@tlsf.org
Web Site: www.lancastersciencefactory.org
Key Personnel: Exec. Dir., Bob Herbert.
Institution Type/Description: Science Museum.
Hours & Admission Prices: May-Aug. Mon.-Sat. 10-5, Sun. 12-5; Sept.-April Tues.-Sat. 10-5, Sun. 12-5. Adults $8, seniors 60 & over $7, children 3-15 $6.50; discounts to groups of 10 or more; ASTC members and children 2 & under no charge. Closed New Year's Day; Easter; Thanksgiving; Christmas.

LANCASTERHISTORY.ORG - LANCASTER COUNTY'S HISTORICAL SOCIETY & PRESIDENT JAMES BUCHANAN'S WHEATLAND, 230 N. President Ave., Lancaster, PA 17603-3125. Tel.: 717-392-4633. Facebook: Lancaster History.
E-mail: info@lancasterhistory.org
Web Site: www.lancasterhistory.org
Key Personnel: Pres. & C.E.O., Thomas R. Ryan; Vice Pres., Robin Sarratt; Dir. Wheatland, Patrick Clarke; Cur., Wendell Zercher; Dir. Library Svcs., Marjorie Bardeen; Archivist, Heather Tennies; Genealogist, Kevin Shue.
Institution Type/Description: Historical Society Archives, Library & Exhibitions.
Hours & Admission Prices: Mon., Wed. & Fri.-Sat. 9:30-5, Tues. & Thurs. 9:30-8. Library: adults $7; discounts to AAM members; members no charge. Exhibitions: adults $7; members no charge. Wheatland Tours: $10; members no charge. Combo pricing available. Closed national holidays.
Attendance: 35,000 (actual)

LANDIS VALLEY VILLAGE AND FARM MUSEUM, 2451 Kissel Hill Rd., Lancaster, PA 17601-4809. Tel.: 717-569-0401, ext. 216 & 208. Fax: 717-560-2147.
E-mail: jlewars@pa.gov
Web Site: landisvalleymuseum.org
Key Personnel: Bd. Pres., Brandon Harter; Dir., James A. Lewars; Events Coord., Cindy Kirby-Reedy; Maintenance & Security, Kyle Hake; Farm & Garden Mgr., Joseph Schott; Coord. Heirloom Seed Project, Joanne Dirks; Cur., Bruce Bomberger; Interpretation Supvr., Karen Cunningham; Museum Educator, Tim Essig; Museum Educator, Mike Emery; Dir. Group Sales, Joyce Perkinson; Scholar in Residence, Dr. Irwin Richman.
Institution Type/Description: Rural Life & Culture Village Museum Complex.
Hours & Admission Prices: Mon.-Sat. 9-5, Sun. 12-5. Adults $12, senior citizens $10, youth 6-12 $8; discount to groups, AAA, AAM & ICOM members, student groups & for tickets from other state sites & local museums; children under 6 & members no charge. Closed New Year's Day; Thanksgiving; Christmas.
Attendance: 87,000 (actual)

NORTH MUSEUM OF NATURE & SCIENCE, 400 College Ave., Lancaster, PA 17603-3393. Tel.: 717-291-3941. Fax: 717-358-4504. Facebook, Instagram & Twitter: North Museum.
E-mail: info@northmuseum.org
Web Site: www.northmuseum.org
Formerly: North Museum of Natural History & Science
Key Personnel: Interim Exec. Dir., Terry Kraft; Bd. Pres. (V), Rick Seavey.
Institution Type/Description: Natural History & Science Museum.
Hours & Admission Prices: Seasonal hours, visit northmuseum.org for current schedule. Museum: adults $9, junior 3-17 and seniors 65 & over $8; discounts to

ASTC & Blue Star Museum Program members; members and children 2 & under no charge. Museum & Planetarium: adults $13, junior 3-17 and seniors 65 & over $12; discounts to ASTC & Blue Star Museum Program members; members and children 2 & under no charge. Closed New Year's Day; Easter; Independence Day; Labor Day; Thanksgiving; Christmas. &
Attendance: 30,000 (estimated)

THE PHILLIPS MUSEUM OF ART, FRANKLIN & MARSHALL COLLEGE, 700 College Ave., Lancaster, PA 17604. Mailing Address: P.O. Box 3003, Lancaster, PA 17604-3003. Tel.: 717-358-3879. Fax: 717-358-4441.
E-mail: claire.giblin@fandm.edu
Web Site: www.fandm.edu/phillips-museum
Key Personnel: Dir., Eliza J. Reilly; Cur. Exhibitions, Claire Giblin; Registrar & Collections Mgr., Maureen Lane; Exhibition Coord., Russell O'Connell; Cur. Exhibitions & Academic Affairs, Julia Marsh.
Institution Type/Description: Art Museum.
Hours & Admission Prices: Academic Year: Tues.-Fri. 11:30-4:30, Sat.-Sun. 12:30-4:30; Summer: call for hours. No charge. Closed legal holidays. &
Attendance: 5,000 (estimated)

ROCK FORD PLANTATION, 881 Rockford Rd., Lancaster, PA 17602-1225. Tel.: 717-392-7223.
E-mail: director@rockfordplantation.org
Web Site: www.rockfordplantation.org
Formerly: Historic Rock Ford
Key Personnel: Exec. Dir., Samuel C. Slaymaker; Pres., Pamela Stoner; Asst. to Dir., Nancy Bradley; Cur., Sarah Alberico.
Institution Type/Description: Historic House: 1794 Georgian mansion of Gen. Edward Hand.
Hours & Admission Prices: April-Oct. Tues.-Sun. 10-3; tours on the hour, last tour begins at 3. Adults $8, seniors & youth 6-17 $7; children 5 & under no charge.
Attendance: 3,000 (estimated)

SEHNER-ELLICOTT-VON HESS HOUSE, 123 N. Prince St., Lancaster, PA 17603-3525. Tel.: 717-291-5861. Fax: 717-291-2251.
E-mail: tas@hptrust.org
Web Site: www.hptrust.org
Key Personnel: Exec. Dir., Timothy Smedick; Pres. (V), Gary Klinger.
Institution Type/Description: Historic House: c.1787.
Hours & Admission Prices: Mon.-Fri. 9-3:30. No charge; donations accepted. Closed holidays.

WOLF MUSEUM OF MUSIC AND ART, 423 W. Chestnut Ave., Lancaster, PA 17603-3405. Mailing Address: P.O. Box 701, Lancaster, PA 17608-0701. Tel.: 717-392-6382.
Web Site: wolfmuseum.net
Institution Type/Description: Music & Art Museum: housed in the former home & studio of Dr. William A. Wolf & his wife Frances; built in 1886.
Hours & Admission Prices: By appointment & for public recitals.

Landisville

AMOS HERR HOUSE FOUNDATION AND HISTORIC SOCIETY, 1756 Nissley Rd., Landisville, PA 17538-1360. Mailing Address: P.O. Box 52, Landisville, PA 17538-0052. Tel.: 717-898-8822.
E-mail: info@herrhomestead.org
Web Site: www.herrhomestead.org
Key Personnel: Pres. (V) & Museum Shop Mgr., John Houston; Treas., Catherine Glass; Cur. & Archivist, Eileen Johns; Sec., Mrs. Millie Brubaker.
Institution Type/Description: History Museum.
Hours & Admission Prices: April-Oct. Sat.-Sun. 1-4; private tours by appointment. No charge; donations accepted. Closed New Year's Day; Easter; Memorial Day; Independence Day; Labor Day; Thanksgiving; Christmas. &
Attendance: 197 (actual)

Langhorne

HISTORIC LANGHORNE ASSOCIATION, 160 W. Maple Ave., Langhorne, PA 19047-2820. Tel.: 215-757-1888 & 6158. Fax: 215-741-5767.
E-mail: historiclanghorne1@verizon.net
Web Site: historiclanghorne.org
Key Personnel: Pres., James Maier; Vice Pres. & Archivist, Lawrence Langhans; Treas., Jack Fulton; Librarian, Jean Noble; Archivist, Museum Shop Mgr. & Recording Sec., Evelyn Aicher.
Institution Type/Description: Historical Association.

Hours & Admission Prices: Wed. & Sat. 10-12 & 7-9; other times by appointment. No charge; donations accepted. &
Attendance: 1,200 (actual)

Lansdale

JENKINS HOMESTEAD AND LANSDALE HISTORICAL RESEARCH CENTER, 137 Jenkins Ave., Lansdale, PA 19446. Tel.: 215-855-1872 & 393-8919.
E-mail: info@lansdalehistory.org
Key Personnel: Dir., Clarence Kinsey, Jr.
Institution Type/Description: History Museum.
Hours & Admission Prices: Wed.-Thurs. 11-4, Sat. 9-12. No charge; donations accepted.

Lansford

NO. 9 COAL MINE & MUSEUM, 9 Dock St., Lansford, PA 18232-1202. Mailing Address: P.O. Box 287, Lansford, PA 18232-1202. Tel.: 570-645-7074.
E-mail: no.9minemuseum@gmail.com
Web Site: no9minemuseum.wixsite.com/museum
Key Personnel: Pres., Zachary Petroski.
Institution Type/Description: Underground Coal Mining Museum.
Hours & Admission Prices: Museum: Wed.-Sun. 10-4. Mine Tours: April & Oct.-Nov. Fri.-Sun. 11-3; May-Sept. Wed.-Sun. 11-3. Museum: $3 per person. Mine Tour & Museum: adults $10, children $7; discounts to AAA members & groups of 20 or more. &
Attendance: 10,000 (estimated)

Latrobe

KLBE LATROBE AIR MUSEUM, Arnold Palmer Rgnl. Airport, 148 Aviation Lane, Latrobe, PA 15650. Tel.: 724-787-8396.
Key Personnel: Dir., Dave Austin; Dir., Sam Schrecengost.
Institution Type/Description: Aviation History Museum.
Hours & Admission Prices: Summer: Sat.-Sun. 10-2; other times by appointment. No charge.

Laughlintown

COMPASS INN MUSEUM, 1382 Rte. 30 E., Laughlintown, PA 15655. Mailing Address: P.O. Box 167, Laughlintown, PA 15655-0167. Tel.: 724-238-6818. Fax: 724-238-3968. Facebook: Compass Inn Museum.
E-mail: tgrohall@compassinn.org
Web Site: www.compassinn.org
Key Personnel: Pres. (V), Cindy Purnell; Exec. Dir., Theresa Gay Rohall; Innkeeper, Malori Stevenson; Business Office Coord., Cathy Cummings.
Institution Type/Description: History Museum: housed in a restored stagecoach inn; built in 1799. Listed on the National Register of Historic Places.
Hours & Admission Prices: May-Oct. Tues.-Sat. 11-4, Sun. 1-5; groups of 10 or more by appointment. Adults $9, students $6; discounts to AASLH members, senior citizens & active military; members and children 5 & under no charge.
Attendance: 5,083 (actual)

Lebanon

LEBANON COUNTY HISTORICAL SOCIETY, 924 Cumberland St., Lebanon, PA 17042-5186. Tel.: 717-272-1473. Fax: 717-272-7474.
E-mail: office@lchsociety.org
Web Site: lchsociety.org
Formerly: The Stoy Museum of the Lebanon County Historical Society
Key Personnel: Pres., Ed Dannels; Treas., Carol Christ; Archivist & Librarian, Adam T. Bentz, Ph.D.
Institution Type/Description: Historical Society Museum.
Hours & Admission Prices: Museum: Tues.-Fri. 10-5, Sat. 10-2. Tours: Sat. 11, other times by appointment. Adults $6, senior citizens $5, children 6-18 $3; members & children 5 & under no charge. Library: adults $6; students & members no charge. Union Canal Rides: May-Oct. Sun. 12:30-4. Adults $8, children 6-18 $4. Closed national holidays.
Attendance: 2,000 (actual)

Leechburg

DAVID LEECH HOUSE - LEECHBURG AREA MUSEUM AND HISTORICAL SOCIETY, 118 First St., Leechburg, PA 15656-1304. Mailing Address: P.O. Box 156, Leechburg, PA 15656-0156. Tel.: 724-845-8914.

E-mail: lamahs@windstream.net
Web Site: www.leechburgmuseum.org
Institution Type/Description: Historic House Museum: housed in the home of Leechburg founder, David Leech; c.1830.
Hours & Admission Prices: March-Dec. Wed. & Sat. 12-3.

Lewisburg

PACKWOOD HOUSE MUSEUM, 8 Market St., Lewisburg, PA 17837. Mailing Address: 15 N. Water St., Lewisburg, PA 17837-1569. Tel.: 570-524-0323. Fax: 570-524-0548.
E-mail: info@packwoodhousemuseum.com
Web Site: www.packwoodhousemuseum.com
Key Personnel: Admin., Jennifer Snyder; Chm. (V), Sue Hornberger; Museum Shop Mgr., Sue Hornberger.
Institution Type/Description: Historic House Museum: housed in a former log tavern (1790-1830), hotel (1830-1886), apartments (1893-1936) and later residence of John & Edith Fetherston.
Hours & Admission Prices: Gallery: Tues.-Sat. 10-5. Museum: by appointment. Adults $10, senior citizens & students $7; discounts to AAM, ICOM & AASLH members; members & children under 12 no charge. Closed holidays.
Attendance: 3,678 (actual)

SAMEK ART GALLERY, Elaine Langone Center, Bucknell University, Lewisburg, PA 17837. Tel.: 570-577-3981. Fax: 570-577-3215.
E-mail: peltier@bucknell.edu
Web Site: www1.bucknell.edu/samek/
Formerly: Bucknell Art Gallery
Key Personnel: Operations Mgr., Cynthia Peltier.
Institution Type/Description: University Art Museum.
Hours & Admission Prices: Aug.-May Mon.-Wed. & Fri. 11-5, Thurs. 11-8, Sat.-Sun. 1-5; call to confirm show. No charge. Closed major holidays; university breaks. &
Attendance: 24,853 (actual)

SLIFER HOUSE MUSEUM, 80 Magnolia Dr., Lewisburg, PA 17837-6312. Tel.: 570-524-2245. Facebook: @SliferHouseMuseum.
E-mail: jessica.owens@albrightcare.org
Web Site: www.sliferhouse.org
Key Personnel: Dir., Jessica Owens Pastuszek.
Institution Type/Description: Historic House: 1861 Tuscan villa, designed by architect Samuel Sloan for secretary of the Commonwealth of PA, Eli Slifer.
Hours & Admission Prices: 3rd week of April through 2nd week of Dec. Thurs.-Sat. 1-4pm. Adults $7, senior citizens 60 & up $6, college students with ID $5; youth under 18 & members no charge. Closed Easter; Thanksgiving; Christmas.
Attendance: 3,200 (actual)

UNION COUNTY HISTORICAL SOCIETY, Union County Courthouse, 2nd and St. Louis Sts., Lewisburg, PA 17837-1903. Mailing Address: Union County Courthouse, 103 S. 2nd St., Lewisburg, PA 17837-1903. Tel.: 570-524-8666. Fax: 570-524-8743. Facebook: Union County PA Historical Society.
E-mail: info@unioncountyhistoricalsociety.org
Web Site: www.unioncountyhistoricalsociety.org
Key Personnel: Pres., Bruce Teeple; Vice Pres., Doug Hovey; Sec., Margaret Kastner; Treas., Kim Ranck.
Institution Type/Description: Historical Society Museum: housed in the Dale Engle-Walker house; built in 1793.
Hours & Admission Prices: Mon.-Fri. 8:30-12 & 1-4:30. Suggested Donation: adults $5. &
Attendance: 1,300 (estimated)

Lewistown

MCCOY HOUSE, 17 N. Main St., Lewistown, PA 17044-1746. Mailing Address: One W. Market St., Lewistown, PA 17044. Tel.: 717-242-1022 & 248-4711. Fax: 717-242-3488. Facebook.
E-mail: info@mifflincountyhistoricalsociety.org
Web Site: www.mccoyhouse.com
Key Personnel: Pres., Forest K. Fisher; Administrative Asst., Laura M. Shope.
Institution Type/Description: Historic House: birthplace of Major General Frank McCoy, who served in the Army from the Spanish-American War through World War II.
Hours & Admission Prices: Museum: mid-May to Oct. Tues. & 2nd Sat. each month 11-2. No charge; donations accepted. Library: March to mid-Nov. Tues.-Wed. 10-4. Admission $5; members no charge.
Attendance: 1,500 (estimated)

Ligonier

ANTIOCHIAN HERITAGE MUSEUM, Rte. 711, Ligonier, PA 15658. Mailing Address: 140 Church Camp Trail, Bolivar, PA 15923. Tel.: 724-238-3677. Fax: 724-238-2102.
E-mail: info@antiochianvillage.org
Web Site: www.antiochianvillage.org/center/heritage/museum.html
Key Personnel: Cur., Julia Ritter.
Institution Type/Description: History Museum.
Hours & Admission Prices: Winter: Mon.-Fri. 10-4; Summer: call for extended hours; other times by appointment. No charge; donations accepted. &

FORT LIGONIER ASSOCIATION, 200 S. Market St., Ligonier, PA 15658-1242. Tel.: 724-238-9701. Fax: 724-238-9732.
E-mail: office@fortligonier.org
Web Site: www.fortligonier.org
Key Personnel: Dir., J. Martin West; Cur. Education, Penelope A. West.
Institution Type/Description: History Museum.
Hours & Admission Prices: April 15-Nov. 15 Mon.-Sat. 10-4:30, Sun. 12-4:30. Adults $7, seniors $6, children 6-14 $4; discounts to groups, AAM & ICOM members; children under 5 & members no charge. &
Attendance: 37,112 (actual)

SOUTHERN ALLEGHENIES MUSEUM OF ART AT LIGONIER VALLEY, One Boucher Lane, Rte. 711, Ligonier, PA 15658-2110. Tel.: 724-238-6015. Fax: 724-238-6281.
E-mail: ligonier@sama-art.org
Web Site: ww.sama-art.org
Institution Type/Description: Art Museum.
Hours & Admission Prices: Tues.-Fri. 10-5, Sat.-Sun. 1-5. No charge; donations accepted. Closed holidays.
Attendance: 6,000 (estimated)

Limerick

LIMERICK TOWNSHIP HISTORICAL SOCIETY - THE HUNSBERGER HOUSE, 545 W. Ridge Pike, Limerick, PA 19468-1417. Tel.: 610-495-5229.
Web Site: limerickpahistory.org
Key Personnel: Chm. (V), William Miller; Pres. (V), Dorothy L. Jones.
Institution Type/Description: Historical Society Museum: housed in the home of Isaac Tyson Hunsberger; built in 1827. Listed on the National Register of Historic Places.
Hours & Admission Prices: Wed. 9-4, 2nd Sun. each month 1-4. No charge; donations accepted.
Attendance: 20 (estimated)

Lititz

JULIUS STURGIS PRETZEL BAKERY AND MUSEUM, 219 E. Main St., Lititz, PA 17543. Tel.: 717-626-4354. Facebook; Instagram.
E-mail: info@juliussturgis.com
Web Site: juliussturgis.com
Key Personnel: CEO, Tom Sturgis; Pres., Tim Snyder; Gen. Mgr., Kurt Van Gilder.
Institution Type/Description: Company Museum: housed in the home and commercial pretzel bakery of Julius Sturgis; built in 1784. Listed on the National Register of Historic Places.
Hours & Admission Prices: Tours: late Jan. to Dec. Mon.-Sat. 9:30-4:30, Sun. 12-3:30; groups of 10 or more by appointment. Adults $3.75, children 4-12 $2.75; children under 4 no charge. Closed New Year's Day; Easter; Thanksgiving; Christmas. &

LITITZ HISTORICAL FOUNDATION MUSEUM & MUELLER HOUSE, 137-145 E. Main St., Lititz, PA 17543-2009. Mailing Address: P.O. Box 65, Lititz, PA 17543. Tel.: 717-627-4636.
E-mail: lhf@dejazzd.com
Web Site: www.lititzhistoricalfoundation.com
Institution Type/Description: Historic House Museum: built in 1793.
Hours & Admission Prices: Memorial Day to Labor Day Mon.-Fri. 10-4. Museum: no charge; donations accepted. House Tours: adults $5, students $3; discount to AAA members; children under 10 & members no charge.
Attendance: 6,300 (actual)

WILBUR CHOCOLATE CANDY AMERICANA ANTIQUE COLLECTIONS & CANDY STORE, 48 N. Broad St., Lititz, PA 17543-1005. Tel.: 888-294-5287 (Toll Free), 717-626-3249 (Store).

Web Site: www.wilburbuds.com
Key Personnel: Mgr., Amy Weik.
Institution Type/Description: Candy Museum.
Hours & Admission Prices: Mon.-Sat. 10-5. No charge. &

Lock Haven

HEISEY MUSEUM, CLINTON COUNTY HISTORICAL SOCIETY, 362 E. Water St., Lock Haven, PA 17745-1418. Tel.: 570-748-7254. Facebook: Clinton County Historical Society.
E-mail: heisey@clintoncountyhistory.com
Web Site: www.clintoncountyhistory.com
Key Personnel: Pres. (V), JoAnn Bowes.
Institution Type/Description: Historical Society Museum.
Hours & Admission Prices: Wed.-Thurs. 10-3. No charge; donations accepted. Groups: $3 per person; members no charge. Closed Thanksgiving; Christmas.
Attendance: 4,850 (estimated)

PIPER AVIATION MUSEUM FOUNDATION, One Piper Way, Lock Haven, PA 17745-2266. Tel.: 570-748-8283. Fax: 570-893-8357.
E-mail: pipermuseum@comcast.net
Web Site: www.pipermuseum.com
Key Personnel: Pres., John B. Bryerton; Treas., John Bryerton; Cur., Lou Bernard; Historian, Roger Peperell; Public Rels., Stacy Young.
Institution Type/Description: Aviation Museum.
Hours & Admission Prices: Mon.-Fri. 9-4, Sat.-Sun. 12-4. Adults $7, seniors $6, children 7-16 $4. Closed major holidays. &
Attendance: 3,500 (estimated)

Loretto

SOUTHERN ALLEGHENIES MUSEUM OF ART AT LORETTO, Saint Francis University Mall, 112 Franciscan Way, Loretto, PA 15940-9709. Mailing Address: P.O. Box 9, Loretto, PA 15940-0009. Tel.: 814-472-3920. Fax: 814-472-4131.
E-mail: loretto@sama-art.org
Web Site: www.sama-art.org
Key Personnel: Exec. Dir., G. Gary Moyer; Cur., Scott Dimond.
Institution Type/Description: Visual Art Museum: located on the Mall of St. Francis University.
Hours & Admission Prices: Tues.-Fri. 10-5, Sat.-1-5. No charge; donations accepted. Closed holidays. &
Attendance: 75,000 (estimated)

Malvern

THE WHARTON ESHERICK MUSEUM, 1520 Horseshoe Tr., Malvern, PA 19355. Mailing Address: P.O. Box 595, Paoli, PA 19301-0595. Tel.: 610-644-5822. Fax: 610-644-2244. Facebook: The Wharton Esherick Museum.
E-mail: information@whartonesherickmuseum.org
Web Site: www.whartonesherickmuseum.org
Key Personnel: Pres. (V), Laurence A. Liss; Exec. Dir. & Cur., Julie Gannaway; Cur., Laura Heemer; Cur., Laura Heemer.
Institution Type/Description: Art & Woodworking Museum: housed in Wharton Esherick's handcrafted residence & studio. National Historic Landmark.
Hours & Admission Prices: Guided Tours: March-Dec. Tues.-Fri. groups only 10-4, Sat. 10-5, Sun. 1-5; tours by appointment. Adults $15, seniors $13, children under 12 $8; discounts to AAM members; members no charge. Closed holidays. &
Attendance: 5,500 (estimated)

Manheim

MANHEIM FIRE COMPANY MUSEUM, 83 S. Main St., Manheim, PA 17545-1645. Tel.: 717-665-3661.
Institution Type/Description: Firefighting History Museum.
Hours & Admission Prices: Call for hours.

McKeesport

MCKEESPORT REGIONAL HISTORY & HERITAGE CENTER, 1832 Arboretum Dr., McKeesport, PA 15132. Tel.: 412-678-1832. Fax: 412-678-7130.
E-mail: mckheritage@yahoo.com
Web Site: www.mckeesportheritage.org
Formerly: McKeesport Heritage Center
Key Personnel: Dir., Robyn Tedesco; Pres. (V), Evette Wivagg.
Institution Type/Description: History Museum.

Hours & Admission Prices: Tues.-Fri. 10-4, Sat. 9-3. No charge; donations accepted. &
Attendance: 3,753 (estimated)

Meadville

ALLEGHENY COLLEGE ART GALLERIES (BOWMAN, PENELEC & MEGAHAN GALLERIES), N. Main St., Meadville, PA 16335-3902. Mailing Address: Box 23, Meadville, PA 16335. Tel.: 814-332-4365. Fax: 814-332-6238. Facebook: Doane Hall.
E-mail: darren.miller@allegheny.edu
Web Site: www.allegheny.edu/artgalleries
Key Personnel: Dir., Darren Miller.
Institution Type/Description: Art Gallery.
Hours & Admission Prices: Tues.-Fri. 12:30-5, Sat. 1:30-5, Sun. 2-4. No charge. &
Attendance: 5,000 (estimated)

BALDWIN-REYNOLDS HOUSE MUSEUM, 639 Terrace St., Meadville, PA 16335-1733. Mailing Address: 411 Chestnut St., Meadville, PA 16335. Tel.: 814-724-6080.
E-mail: museum@baldwinreynolds.org
Web Site: www.baldwinreynolds.org
Key Personnel: Chm. (V), Bruce Barrett; Pres. (V), Beth Rekas; Cur., Joshua F. Sherretts.
Institution Type/Description: Historic House: 1841-43 Baldwin-Reynolds Mansion.
Hours & Admission Prices: mid-May to Aug. Wed.-Sun. 12-4. Tours: June-Aug. 12, 1, 2, 3. Adults $5, children $3; members no charge.
Attendance: 4,000 (estimated)

Mechanicsburg

M. LOUISE AUGHINBAUGH GALLERY AT MESSIAH COLLEGE, Climenhaga Fine Arts Ctr., One College Ave., Ste. 3400, Mechanicsburg, PA 17055. Mailing Address: Messiah College School of the Arts, One College Ave., Ste. 3004, Mechanicsburg, PA 17055. Tel.: 717-766-2511, ext. 2486.
E-mail: cforsyth@messiah.edu
Web Site: messiah.edu
Key Personnel: Dir., Christine A. Forsythe.
Institution Type/Description: Art Museum.
Hours & Admission Prices: Mon.-Thurs. 9-4, Fri. 9-9, Sun. 2-5. No charge. &

MECHANICSBURG MUSEUM ASSOCIATION, 2 W. Strawberry Alley, Mechanicsburg, PA 17055-6213. Tel.: 717-697-6088. Fax: 717-697-6285.
E-mail: mechanicsburgmuseum@gmail.com
Web Site: www.mechanicsburgmuseum.org
Key Personnel: Dir. & Museum Shop Mgr., Steven B. Zimmerman; Archivist & Pres. (V), Beverly Bone; Membership, Jean Souder; Membership, Fay GeeGee; Education, Jean Layne; Public Rels., Grace Rarick; Chm. (V), Fern Oram; Security, Leroy Weaver.
Institution Type/Description: Local History & Railroad Museum.
Hours & Admission Prices: Wed.-Sat. 12-3; other times by appointment. Frankeberger Tavern: May-Sept. Sat. 12-3. No charge; donations accepted. Closed holidays. &
Attendance: 3,500 (estimated)

THE OAKES MUSEUM OF NATURAL HISTORY AT MESSIAH COLLEGE, One College Ave., Ste. 3029, Mechanicsburg, PA 17055. Tel.: 717-691-6082; 717-691-2357. Fax: 717-691-6046.
E-mail: oakesmuseum@messiah.edu
Web Site: www.messiah.edu/Oakes
Key Personnel: Dir., Kenneth D. Mark; Education Coord., Helena Cicero; Education Coord., Beth Erikson; Treas., David Walker; Cur. Herpetology & Ornithology, Dr. Erik Lindquist; Cur. Botany & Entomology, Dr. David Foster; Cur. Geology, Mr. Edwin Charles; Cur. Concology, Mrs. Ruth Bierbower; Cur. Mycology, Dr. Gary Emberger; Cur. Archaeology, Dr. David Pettegrew.
Institution Type/Description: Natural History Museum.
Hours & Admission Prices: Sat. 1-5. Adults $6.50, senior citizens, students and children 3-12 $4; discounts to groups & AAM members. Closed major holidays. &
Attendance: 21,278 (actual)

Media

DELAWARE COUNTY INSTITUTE OF SCIENCE, 11 Veterans Sq., Media, PA 19063-3201. Tel.: 610-566-5126.

E-mail: info.delcoscience@gmail.com
Web Site: www.delcoscience.org
Key Personnel: Pres. Pro-tem, Roger Mitchell.
Institution Type/Description: Science Museum.
Hours & Admission Prices: Mon., Thurs. & Sat. 9 to noon. No charge.
Attendance: 2,000 (estimated)

TYLER ARBORETUM, 515 Painter Rd., Media, PA 19063. Tel.:
610-566-9134. Fax: 610-891-1490.
E-mail: info@tylerarboretum.org
Web Site: www.tylerarboretum.org
Key Personnel: Exec. Dir., Richard A. Colbert; Dir. Horticulture, Mike Karkowski.
Institution Type/Description: Arboretum.
Hours & Admission Prices: Seasonal hours, see website. Adults $7, seniors 65 &
over $6, children 3-15 $4; discounts to AABGA members; children under 3 &
members no charge; participates in AHS reciprocal admissions program.
Attendance: 52,000 (estimated)

Mercer

MERCER COUNTY HISTORICAL SOCIETY, 119 S. Pitt St.,
Mercer, PA 16137-1211. Tel.: 724-662-3490. Facebook: Mercer
County Historical Society.
E-mail: info@mchspa.org
Web Site: www.mchspa.org
Key Personnel: Exec. Dir., William C. Philson; Pres. & C.E.O., Robert F. Lark.
Institution Type/Description: Historical Society Museum: housed in 1825 Magoffin
House.
Hours & Admission Prices: Tues.-Fri. 10-4:30, Sat. 10-3; group tours by appoint-
ment only. No charge; donations accepted. Closed national holidays. &
Attendance: 3,000 (estimated)

Merion Station

SAINT JOSEPH'S UNIVERSITY - UNIVERSITY GALLERY,
Merion Hall, Maguire Campus, 355 N. Latches Ln., Merion
Station, PA 19066. Mailing Address: 5600 City Ave., Philadelphia,
PA 19131. Tel.: 610-660-1840. Fax: 610-660-2278. Facebook;
Instagram; Twitter.
E-mail: jbracy@sju.edu
Web Site: www.sju.edu/gallery
Key Personnel: Chm. Art Dept., Bruce Wells, Ph.D.; Gallery Cur., Jeanne Bracy.
Institution Type/Description: University Art Museum.
Hours & Admission Prices: Mon.-Fri. 9-7, Sat. 10-1. No charge. Closed national
holidays; University holidays. &
Attendance: 2,000 (estimated)

Middleburg

THE SNYDER COUNTY HISTORICAL SOCIETY, 30 E. Market
St., Middleburg, PA 17842-1017. Mailing Address: P.O. Box 276,
Middleburg, PA 17842-0276. Tel.: 570-837-6191. Fax: 570-837-
4282.
E-mail: schs@snydercounty.org
Key Personnel: C.E.O. & Pres. (V), Teresa J. Berger; Editor, Ruth Roush; Sec., Lee
E. Knepp.
Institution Type/Description: Historical Society Museum.
Hours & Admission Prices: Museum: May-Sept. Sun. 1:30-5; other times by
appointment. Library: March-April & Oct.-Dec. Mon. & Thurs.-Fri. 10-3.30;
May-Sept. Sun. 1:30-5, Mon. & Thurs.-Fri. 10-3:30. No charge; donations
accepted. &
Attendance: 2,000 (estimated)

Mifflinburg

MIFFLINBURG BUGGY MUSEUM ASSOCIATION, INC., 598
Green St., Mifflinburg, PA 17844-1241. Tel.: 570-966-1355.
Facebook.
E-mail: mifflinburgbuggymuseum@gmail.com
Web Site: www.buggymuseum.org
Key Personnel: Dir., Bronwen Sanders; Pres. (V), Peter N. Gardner.
Institution Type/Description: Industrial Museum.
Hours & Admission Prices: Museum: April-Oct. Thurs.-Sat. 10-5, Sun. 1-5; call for
winter hours. Adults $10, children $5; discounts to groups of 20 or more and
AAA & AARP members; members no charge. Visitor Center: no charge; dona-
tions accepted. Closed major holidays. &
Attendance: 2,000 (estimated)

Milford

PIKE COUNTY HISTORICAL SOCIETY, 608 Broad St.,
Milford, PA 18337-1704. Mailing Address: P.O. Box 915, Milford,
PA 18337-0915. Tel.: 570-296-8126.
E-mail: pikemuse@ptd.net
Web Site: www.pikecountyhistoricalsociety.org
Key Personnel: Dir., Lori Strelicki.
Institution Type/Description: Local History Museum.
Hours & Admission Prices: Columns Museum: July-Aug. Wed.-Sun. 1-4; Sept.-
June Wed & Sat.-Sun. 1-4; other times by appointment. Adults $5, students $3;
children & members no charge.
Attendance: 3,000 (estimated)

Mill Run

FALLINGWATER, 1478 Mill Run Rd., Mill Run, PA 15464-1542.
Mailing Address: P.O. Box R, Mill Run, PA 15464-0167. Tel.:
724-329-8501.
E-mail: fallingwater@paconserve.org
Web Site: www.fallingwater.org
Key Personnel: Pres., Thomas Saunders; Dir. & Vice Pres., Lynda S. Waggoner;
Museum Shop Mgr., Betsy Poole.
Institution Type/Description: Historic House: designed by Frank Lloyd Wright in
1935 for the Edgar Kaufmann family, built over a waterfall.
Hours & Admission Prices: mid-March to Nov. Thurs.-Tues. 10-4; reservations
essential. Adults $25-$27, youth 6-12 $17-$20. Grounds only: adults $8. In-
depth tours: adults $72; discounts to school groups, ICOM & AAM members,
Western Pennsylvania Conservancy & Frank Lloyd Wright Building
Conservancy members. &
Attendance: 167,270 (actual)

Millersburg

**HISTORICAL SOCIETY OF MILLERSBURG & UPPER
PAXTON TOWNSHIP MUSEUM,** 330 Center St., Millersburg,
PA 17061. Mailing Address: P.O. Box 171, Millersburg, PA
17061-0171. Tel.: 717-692-4084.
E-mail: mbghist@epix.net
Key Personnel: Dir., Don Smith; Dir., Leslie Smith.
Institution Type/Description: Local History Museum: housed in 1919 fire house &
municipal building.
Hours & Admission Prices: May-Oct. Sat. 10-2, Sun. 2-4. No charge; donations
accepted.
Attendance: 1,000 (actual)

NED SMITH CENTER FOR NATURE AND ART, 176 Water
Company Rd., Millersburg, PA 17061-0033. Tel.: 717-692-3699.
Fax: 717-692-0977.
E-mail: info@nedsmithcenter.org
Web Site: www.nedsmithcenter.org
Institution Type/Description: Art Gallery.
Hours & Admission Prices: Gallery & Shop: Tues.-Sat. 10-4. Office: Mon.-Fri.
8:30-4:30. Adults $7, seniors 65 & over $2; members & children under 12 no
charge.

Montrose

**SUSQUEHANNA COUNTY HISTORICAL SOCIETY & FREE
LIBRARY ASSOCIATION,** Two Monument Sq., Montrose, PA
18801-1115. Mailing Address: 18 Monument St., Montrose, PA
18801. Tel.: 570-278-1881. Fax: 570-278-9336. Facebook:
Susquehanna County Historical Society.
E-mail: info@susqcohistsoc.org
Web Site: www.susqcohistsoc.org
Key Personnel: Administrator & Librarian, Susan Stone; Chm. Historical
Committee, Carol Korutz; Chm. Bd., Tom Kurosky; Cur., Elizabeth A. Smith.
Institution Type/Description: History Museum.
Hours & Admission Prices: Museum & Genealogy Reference Room: May-Sept.
Mon.-Thurs. 9-5; Oct.-April Mon. & Thurs. 9-5, Tues.-Wed. 12-5. Public
Library: Mon.-Thurs. 9-9, Sat. 9-4. No charge; donations accepted. Genealogy
Reference Room: $10 research fee for visiting non-members; $85 for all mailed
requests. Closed national holidays. &
Attendance: 2,700 (estimated)

Morrisville

PENNSBURY MANOR, 400 Pennsbury Memorial Rd., Morrisville,
PA 19067-6797. Tel.: 215-946-0400. Fax: 215-310-1011. TDD:
215-310-1016.

E-mail: willpenn17@aol.com
Web Site: www.pennsburymanor.org
Key Personnel: Dir., Douglas Miller; Museum Education, Mary Ellyn Kunz; Pres., Ron Schmid; Cur., Todd Galle; Volunteer Coord., Hannah Howard; Horticulturist, Mike Johnson; Mgr. & Public Rels., Tabitha Dardes; Supt. Bldgs. & Grounds, Joseph Cameli.
Institution Type/Description: Historic House Museum: 1683 Pennsbury Manor, residence of William Penn, reconstructed in 1939.
Hours & Admission Prices: Tues.-Sat. 9-5, Sun. 12-5. Adults $9, senior citizens 65 & over $7, children 3-11 $5; discounts to AAM & ICOM members. Grounds Pass: $3. Closed New Year's Day; Veterans Day; Columbus Day; Thanksgiving & day after; Christmas. &
Attendance: 27,500 (actual)

Mountainhome

CRESCO STATION MUSEUM, Rte. 390 & Sand Spring Rd., Mountainhome, PA 18342. Mailing Address: P.O. Box 358, Mountainhome, PA 18342-0358. Tel.: 570-595-2279.
E-mail: stationmuseum@verizon.net
Web Site: www.barretthistory.org
Institution Type/Description: History Museum.
Hours & Admission Prices: Memorial Day to June & Sept.-Oct. 12 Sun. 1-4; July-Aug. Wed. & Sat.-Sun. 1-4. No charge.
Attendance: 500 (estimated)

Muncy

MUNCY HISTORICAL SOCIETY, 40 N. Main St., Muncy, PA 17756. Mailing Address: P.O. Box 11, Muncy, PA 17756. Tel.: 570-546-5917.
E-mail: muncyhistorical@aol.com
Web Site: muncyhistoricalsociety.org
Institution Type/Description: Historical Society Museum.
Hours & Admission Prices: March-Nov. Mon.-Fri. 9-3; other times by appointment. Closed holidays.

Narberth

SWEET MABEL FOLK ART & FINE CRAFT GALLERY, 41 N. Narberth Ave., Narberth, PA 19072-2347. Tel.: 610-667-3041.
E-mail: sweetmabelart@aol.com
Institution Type/Description: Art Gallery.
Hours & Admission Prices: Tues.-Fri. 11-6, Sat. 10-5, Sun. 12-5.

Nazareth

MARTIN GUITAR MUSEUM, 510 Sycamore St., Nazareth, PA 18064. Mailing Address: P.O. Box 329, Nazareth, PA 18064-0329. Tel.: 610-759-2837. Fax: 610-759-6360.
E-mail: dboak@martinguitar.com
Web Site: www.martinguitar.com
Institution Type/Description: Guitar Museum.
Hours & Admission Prices: Museum & Visitor Center: Mon.-Fri. 8-5. Factory: Mon.-Fri. 9-4. No charge; donations accepted. Closed national holidays. &
Attendance: 40,000 (estimated)

MORAVIAN HISTORICAL SOCIETY, 214 E. Center St., Nazareth, PA 18064-2209. Tel.: 610-759-5070. Facebook.
E-mail: info@moravianhistoricalsociety.org
Web Site: www.moravianhistoricalsociety.org
Key Personnel: Dir., Megan van Ravensway; Pres., Steven Krawiec; Vice Pres., Bryan Lobach; Shop Mgr., Colleen McMahon.
Institution Type/Description: History Museum: housed in 1740/1743 Whitefield House.
Hours & Admission Prices: Daily 1-4. Adults $5; children under 5 & members no charge. Closed Easter; Thanksgiving; Christmas Eve.
Attendance: 8,000 (estimated)

PENNSYLVANIA LONGRIFLE MUSEUM AND JOHN JOSEPH HENRY HOUSE MUSEUM, 402 Henry Rd., Nazareth, PA 18064. Mailing Address: P.O. Box 345, Nazareth, PA 18064-0345. Tel.: 610-759-9029. Fax: 610-759-9029. Facebook: Pennsylvania Longrifle Museum.
E-mail: jacobsburg@rcn.com
Web Site: www.jacobsburghistory.com
Key Personnel: Exec. Dir., Ira Hiberman.
Institution Type/Description: History Museum.

Hours & Admission Prices: May-Oct. Sat.-Sun. 12-4. Adults $5; members & children under 12 no charge. Blue Star Museum.
Attendance: 5,000 (estimated)

New Brighton

THE MERRICK ART GALLERY, 1100 Fifth Ave., New Brighton, PA 15066. Mailing Address: P.O. Box 312, New Brighton, PA 15066-0312. Tel.: 724-846-1130.
E-mail: merrickartgallery@verizon.net
Web Site: www.merrickartgallery.org
Key Personnel: Dir. & Education Dir., Cynthia A. Kundar; Trustee, Karen Capper.
Institution Type/Description: Art Museum.
Hours & Admission Prices: Winter & Spring: Tues.-Sat. 10-4:30, Sun. 1-4; Summer & Fall: Wed.-Sat. 10-4, every other Sun. 1-4. No charge; donations accepted; docent guided tours $2. Closed New Year's Eve & Day; Memorial Day; Independence Day; Labor Day; Thanksgiving; Christmas to mid-Jan.; holiday weekends. &
Attendance: 4,200 (estimated)

New Castle

ARTS & EDUCATION AT THE HOYT CENTER FOR THE ARTS/HOYT INSTITUTE OF FINE ARTS, 124 E. Leasure Ave., New Castle, PA 16101-2398. Tel.: 724-652-2882. Fax: 724-657-8786. Facebook: Arts & Education at the Hoyt.
E-mail: hoyt@hoytartcenter.org
Web Site: www.hoytartcenter.org
Formerly: Hoyt Center for the Arts
Key Personnel: C.E.O. & Exec. Dir., Kimberly B. Koller-Jones; Pres., Maria McKee; Exhibitions Coord., Patricia McLatchy; Program Dir., Robert Presnar; Mktg. Dir., Melissa Maiella.
Institution Type/Description: Art Museum: housed in two early 20th-century mansions, Greek Revival style & Tudor Revival style.
Hours & Admission Prices: Tues. & Thurs. 11-8, Wed. & Fri.-Sat. 11-4, Sun. for special events; guided tours by appointment. East Mansion no charge. West Mansion Guided Tours $5, discounts to AAM members. Closed New Year's Day; Easter; Memorial Day; Independence Day; Labor Day; Thanksgiving; Christmas. &
Attendance: 78,449 (estimated)

LAWRENCE COUNTY HISTORICAL SOCIETY, 408 N. Jefferson St., New Castle, PA 16101. Mailing Address: P.O. Box 1745, New Castle, PA 16103. Tel.: 724-658-4022. Fax: 724-658-8885. Facebook: Lawrence County Historical Society.
E-mail: info@lawrencechs.com
Web Site: www.lawrencechs.com
Key Personnel: Pres (V), Paul P. Lynch; Dir., Anna Mary Mooney.
Institution Type/Description: Historical Society Museum; 1904 18 room mansion.
Hours & Admission Prices: Tues., Thurs. & Sat. 11-4; other times by appointment. Adults $5; members no charge. &
Attendance: 300 (estimated)

New Holland

NEW HOLLAND HISTORICAL SOCIETY MUSEUM, 207 E. Main St., P.O. Box 464, New Holland, PA 17557-0464.
E-mail: info@nhhistorical.com
Web Site: www.nhhistorical.com
Key Personnel: Chm. (V), Donald Welsh.
Institution Type/Description: Historical Society Museum: housed in the historic Kauffman Hardware bldg.
Hours & Admission Prices: Thurs.-Sat. 10-2; other times by appointment. No charge; donations accepted. &
Attendance: 500 (estimated)

New Hope

BOWMAN'S HILL WILDFLOWER PRESERVE, 1635 River Rd. (PA Rte. 32), New Hope, PA 18938. Mailing Address: P.O. Box 685, New Hope, PA 18938-0685. Tel.: 215-862-2924. Fax: 215-862-1846.
E-mail: bhwp@bhwp.org
Web Site: www.bhwp.org
Key Personnel: Dir., A. Miles Arnott; Chm. (V), Allison Hamilton; Coord. Education, Kelly Joslin; Visitor Svcs. Coord., Liz Poole Lamb.
Institution Type/Description: Botanical Garden.

Hours & Admission Prices: Jan. 3-Dec. 23 daily 9-5. Adults $6, seniors 65 & over and students $4, children 3-14 $3; children under 3 & members no charge. Closed Thanksgiving. &
Attendance: 40,000 (estimated)

THE PARRY MANSION MUSEUM, 45 S. Main St., New Hope, PA 18938. Mailing Address: New Hope Historical Society, P.O. Box 41, New Hope, PA 18938-0041. Tel.: 215-862-6729. Fax: 215-862-8227.
E-mail: newhopehs@verizon.net
Web Site: www.newhopehs.org
Key Personnel: Pres., Dee Dee Bowman; Exec. Dir., Deborah Lang; Treas., Chuck Mintzer.
Institution Type/Description: Decorative Arts Museum.
Hours & Admission Prices: May-Nov. Sat.-Sun. 1:30-5. No charge.
Attendance: 2,300 (estimated)

Newtown

HICKS ART CENTER GALLERY - BUCKS COUNTY COMMUNITY COLLEGE, 275 Swamp Rd., Newtown, PA 18940-4106. Tel.: 215-504-8531.
E-mail: fran.orlando@bucks.edu
Web Site: www.bucks.edu/gallery
Key Personnel: Dir., Fran Orlando.
Institution Type/Description: Art Gallery.
Hours & Admission Prices: Mon. & Fri. 9-4, Tues.-Thurs. 9-8, Sat. 9-12. No charge.

NEWTOWN HISTORIC ASSOCIATION, 105 Court St., Newtown, PA 18940. Mailing Address: P.O. Box 303, Newtown, PA 18940-0303. Tel.: 215-968-4004.
E-mail: dcnhh@comcast.net
Web Site: www.newtownhistoric.org
Key Personnel: Pres., Barry Fleck; Pres. (V), Head Research Library & Cur., Harriet Beckert; Treas., Marjorie Torongo; Museum Shop Mgr., Geno Peruzzi.
Institution Type/Description: Local History Museum: housed in early 1700s Half Moon Inn.
Hours & Admission Prices: June-Aug. Tues. 9-3, Thurs. 7-9, Sun. 2-4; Sept.-May Tues. 9-3, Thurs. 7-9. No charge; donations accepted. Closed holidays.
Attendance: 2,200 (estimated)

Newtown Square

COLONIAL PENNSYLVANIA PLANTATION, 3900 N. Sandy Flash Dr., Newtown Square, PA 19073. Mailing Address: P.O. Box 158, Gradyville, PA 19039. Tel.: 610-566-1725. Facebook: Colonial Pennsylvania Plantation.
E-mail: info@colonialplantation.org
Web Site: www.colonialplantation.org
Key Personnel: Pres., James Adams; Treas., Ted Jacquet; Vice Pres. & Dir. Devel., Charles Barr; Office Mgr., Suzanne Gault.
Institution Type/Description: Historical Museum: housed in c.18th-century Quaker farm.
Hours & Admission Prices: Groups Tours: April-Nov. Mon.-Fri. Public Tours: Sat.-Sun. 11-5. Adults $10, children 4-12 $6; members & children under 4 no charge. Special weekend events may have different pricing. &
Attendance: 27,000 (actual)

Norristown

ELMWOOD PARK ZOO, 1661 Harding Blvd., Norristown, PA 19401. Tel.: 610-277-3825. Fax: 610-292-0332. Facebook: Elmwood Park Zoo.
E-mail: guestservices@elmwoodparkzoo.org
Web Site: www.elmwoodparkzoo.org
Institution Type/Description: Zoo.
Hours & Admission Prices: March-Oct. daily 10-5; Nov.-Feb. daily 10-4. See website for admission & membership prices.

HISTORICAL SOCIETY OF MONTGOMERY COUNTY, 1654 DeKalb St., Norristown, PA 19401-5415. Tel.: 610-272-0297. Fax: 610-272-2609.
E-mail: contact@hsmcpa.org
Web Site: www.hsmcpa.org
Key Personnel: Exec. Dir., Barry Rauhauser; Cur., Kristine Walsh; Archivist, Nancy Sullivan.
Institution Type/Description: Historical Society Museum.
Hours & Admission Prices: Mon. & Thurs. 10-5, Tues.-Wed. 1-8, Sat. 10-2. Adults $5; members no charge. &

North Huntingdon

BIG MAC MUSEUM, 9061 Rte. 30, North Huntingdon, PA 15642-2792. Tel.: 724-863-9837.
Web Site: www.bigmacmuseum.com
Institution Type/Description: History Museum.
Hours & Admission Prices: Store: Mon.-Fri. 4:30am-12am, Sat. 4:30am-1am, Sun. 5:30am-11pm. Group Tours: by appointment.

North Wales

ROTH LIVING FARM MUSEUM OF DELAWARE VALLEY COLLEGE, 1260 Welsh Rd., North Wales, PA 19545. Tel.: 215-699-3560.
E-mail: rothmuseum@delval.edu
Web Site: www.delval.edu/roth
Institution Type/Description: Living Farm Museum.
Hours & Admission Prices: Call for hours. Prices vary by program.
Attendance: 1,153

Northumberland

JOSEPH PRIESTLEY HOUSE, 472 Priestley Ave., Northumberland, PA 17857-1226. Mailing Address: P.O. Box 226, Northumberland, PA 17857-0226. Tel.: 570-473-9474.
E-mail: info@josephpriestleyhouse.org
Web Site: www.josephpriestleyhouse.org
Key Personnel: Pres. (V), Dee Ann Casteel.
Institution Type/Description: Historic House Museum: housed in the former home of Joseph Priestley; built in 1798.
Hours & Admission Prices: Visitor Center: mid-March to Nov. Sat.-Sun. Tours: 1, 2 & 3. Adults $6, senior citizens & groups $5.50, youth 3-11 $4; discounts to PHMC, AAM, ICOM & Federation members; members and active military & their family no charge. Closed Easter; Mother's Day.
Attendance: 900 (actual)

Nottingham

HERR'S SNACK FACTORY TOUR, 271 Old Baltimore Pike, Nottingham, PA 19362-9788. Mailing Address: 20 Herr Dr., P.O. Box 300, Nottingham, PA 19362. Tel.: 800-284-7488.
Web Site: herrs.com/snackfactorytours
Institution Type/Description: Company Museum.
Hours & Admission Prices: Live Tours: Mon.-Wed. 9-3. Video Tours: Thurs. 9-3 & Fri. 9-11 Adults $4, children 4-17 $3; children 3 & under no charge. Closed New Year's Eve & Day; Good Friday; Memorial Day; Independence Day; Labor Day; Thanksgiving; Christmas Eve & Day. &

Oakdale

PITTSBURGH BOTANIC GARDEN, 799 Pinkerton Run Rd., Oakdale, PA 15071. Tel.: 412-444-4464.
E-mail: info@pittsburghbotanicgarden.org
Web Site: pittsburghbotanicgarden.org
Key Personnel: Pres., Greg Nace; C.O.O., Christine Koebley; Dir. Opers., Kitty Vagley; Cur. Plant Collections, Susan Beck Meyers.
Institution Type/Description: Botanical Garden.
Hours & Admission Prices: Summer: Thurs. 9-8; Fri.-Wed. 9-5; Winter: Thurs.-Sun. 9-5. Adults $9, seniors 62 & over and students $8, children 3-18 $6; members and children 3 & under no charge. Closed Thanksgiving; Christmas Eve & Day.

Oaks

AMERICAN TREASURE TOUR MUSEUM, 1 American Treasure Way, Oaks, PA 19456-0616. Mailing Address: P.O. Box 616, Oaks, 19456-0616. Tel.: 866-970-8687.
E-mail: info@americantreasuretour.com
Web Site: americantreasuretour.com
Institution Type/Description: General Museum.
Hours & Admission Prices: Thurs.-Sun. 10-3. Lage group tours daily by appointment. &

Oil City

VENANGO MUSEUM OF ART, SCIENCE & INDUSTRY, 270 Seneca St., Oil City, PA 16301-1304. Tel.: 814-676-2007. Fax: 814-678-6719.
E-mail: venangomuseum@verizon.net
Web Site: www.venangomuseum.org

Key Personnel: Pres. (V), Mary Balas; Financial Dir., Albert Abramovic; Exec. Dir., Security & Museum Shop Mgr., Betsy Kellner.
Institution Type/Description: Art, Science & Industry Museum: housed in c.1905 Beau Arts style Post Office Building.
Hours & Admission Prices: April-Dec. Tues.-Sun. 10-4. Adults $7, senior citizens & students $5, children under 12 $3; members no charge. Closed New Year's Day; Easter; Memorial Day; Independence Day; Labor Day; Thanksgiving; Christmas. &
Attendance: 3,000 (estimated)

Orwell

HOME TEXTILE TOOL MUSEUM, 1819 Orwell Hill Rd., Orwell, PA 18837. Mailing Address: P.O. Box 153, Rome, PA 18837. Tel.: 570-247-7175.
E-mail: info@httm.org
Web Site: www.httm.org
Institution Type/Description: History Museum.
Hours & Admission Prices: Call for hours. Adults $5. &

Paradise

NATIONAL CHRISTMAS CENTER AND MUSEUM, 3427 Lincoln Hwy. E., Paradise, PA 17562-9621. Tel.: 717-442-7950. Fax: 717-442-9304. Facebook: The National Christmas Center.
E-mail: info@nationalchristmascenter.com
Web Site: www.nationalchristmascenter.com
Key Personnel: Exec. Dir. & Museum Shop Mgr., Mandy Brown; Cur., Jim Morrison; Museum & Mktg. Dir., Heidi Brennan.
Institution Type/Description: Christmas History Museum.
Hours & Admission Prices: March-April Sat.-Sun. 10-6; May-Jan. 1 daily 10-6; other times by appointment. Call for extended holiday hours. Adults $12.50, children 3-12 $5. Closed New Year's Day; Easter; Thanksgiving; Christmas. &
Attendance: 30,000 (estimated)

Pennsburg

SCHWENKFELDER LIBRARY & HERITAGE CENTER, 105 Seminary St., Pennsburg, PA 18073-1898. Tel.: 215-679-3103. Fax: 215-679-8175.
E-mail: info@schwenkfelder.com
Web Site: schwenkfelder.com
Key Personnel: Exec. Dir., David W. Luz; Pres., Jerry Heebner; Administrative Asst., Joanne Jalowy; Cur. Collections, Candace K. Perry; Archivist, Hunt Schenkel; Educator, Maggie Buckwalter; Assoc. Dir. Research, Dr. L. Allen Viehmeyer; Assoc. Dir. Theology, Dr. Peter C. Erb.
Institution Type/Description: History Museum.
Hours & Admission Prices: Tues.-Wed. & Fri. 9-4, Thurs. 9-8, Sat. 10-3, Sun. 1-4. No charge, donations accepted. &
Attendance: 10,466 (actual)

Pennsylvania Furnace

PASTO AGRICULTURAL MUSEUM, 2710 W. Pine Grove Rd., Gate K, Pennsylvania Furnace, PA 16865. Mailing Address: 137 Agricultural Admin. Bldg., University Park, PA 16802. Tel.: 814-863-1383.
E-mail: pastoagmuseum@psu.edu
Web Site: agsci.psu.edu/pasto
Key Personnel: Cur., Rita Graef.
Institution Type/Description: Agriculture Museum.
Hours & Admission Prices: mid-March to mid-Nov. by appointment. &

Perkasie

THE PEARL S. BUCK HOUSE, 520 Dublin Rd., Perkasie, PA 18944-3000. Tel.: 215-249-0100. Fax: 215-249-9657.
E-mail: info@pearlsbuck.org
Web Site: www.pearlsbuck.org
Key Personnel: C.E.O., Janet C. Mintzer; C.F.O. & C.O.O., Jill Reeder; Chief Mktg. Officer, Linda J. Bishop; Vice Pres. Relationship Devel., Tony Luna; Vice Pres. Programs, Laura Lomax; Cur., Marie Toner.
Institution Type/Description: Historic House Museum: housed in pre-1825 stone farmhouse. Home of author, humanitarian, & activist, Peral S. Buck and her family. A National Historic Landmark.
Hours & Admission Prices: Tours: Jan.-Feb. Mon.-Fri. 1 pm, Sat. 11 am, 1 pm, 2 pm, Sun. 1 pm & 2 pm; March-Nov. 11 Mon.-Sat. 11 am, 1 pm & 2 pm, Sun. 1 pm & 2 pm. Adults $15, senior citizens $12, students $7; members no charge. Closed New Year's Eve & Day; Easter; Memorial Day; Independence Day; Labor Day; Veterans Day; Thanksgiving; Christmas Eve & Day. &
Attendance: 23,431 (actual)

Philadelphia

THE ACADEMY OF NATURAL SCIENCES OF DREXEL UNIVERSITY, 1900 Ben Franklin Pkwy., Philadelphia, PA 19103-1101. Tel.: 215-299-1000. Fax: 215-299-1028. Facebook.
E-mail: belardo@ansp.org
Web Site: www.ansp.org
Formerly: The Academy of Natural Sciences
Key Personnel: Chm. Bd. Trustees, David E. Griffith; Pres. & C.E.O., Scott Cooper, Ph.D.; Dir. Library & Archives, Ted Daeschler, Ph.D.; Vice. Pres. Education, Jacquie Genovesi, Ph.D.; Dir. Center for Systemic Biology & Evolution, Richard McCourt, Ph.D.; C.F.O. & C.O.O., Lisa Miller; Snr. Fellow, Robert M. Peck; Chief Learning & Engagement Officer, Niki Ciccotelli Stewart; Vice Pres. Mktg., Jane Taylor; Vice Pres. Center Academy Science, David Velinsky, Ph.D.; Dir. Patrick Center Environmental Research, Roland Wall.
Institution Type/Description: Natural Science Museum.
Hours & Admission Prices: Mon.-Fri. 10-4:30, Sat.-Sun. & holidays 10-5. Admission 13 & over $22, children 2-12 $18; discounts to groups; members & children under 2 no charge. Closed New Year's Day; Thanksgiving; Christmas. &
Attendance: 250,000 (actual)

THE AFRICAN AMERICAN MUSEUM IN PHILADELPHIA, 701 Arch St., Philadelphia, PA 19106-1504. Tel.: 215-574-0380, ext. 230. Fax: 215-818-1072. Facebook: African American Museum in Philadelphia.
E-mail: info@aampmuseum.org
Web Site: www.aampmuseum.org
Key Personnel: Pres. & C.E.O., Patricia Wilson Aden; Vice Pres. Finance & Admin., Leonie Alexandre; Vice Pres. Programming, Ivan Henderson; Membership & Volunteer Coord., Gillian Golson; Artist-In-Residence, Richard Watson; Mgr. Visitor Svcs., Deborah Johnson.
Institution Type/Description: Historical & Cultural Museum. This African American Museum in Philadelphia (AAMP) is dedicated to collecting, preserving and interpreting the material and intellectual culture of African Americans.
Hours & Admission Prices: Thurs.-Sat. 10-5, Sun. 12-5. Adults $14, children, students, & seniors $10; discounts to groups, AAM & ICOM members; members no charge. Closed national holidays. &
Attendance: 80,000 (estimated)

AMERICAN CATHOLIC HISTORICAL SOCIETY, 263 S. 4th St., Philadelphia, PA 19106-3819. Tel.: 215-925-5752.
E-mail: americancatholichistsoc@gmail.com
Web Site: www.amchs.org
Key Personnel: Exec. Dir., Rev. Msgr. James P. McCoy; Pres., Michael H. Finnegan; Vice Pres., Dr. Thomas Rzeznik; Treas., Edgar F. Welsh; Recording Sec., Kathleen Oxx; Corresponding Sec., Nicholas Rademacher.
Institution Type/Description: Religious & American History Museum.
Hours & Admission Prices: Open by appointment. No charge; donations accepted.
Attendance: 1,000 (estimated)

AMERICAN PHILOSOPHICAL SOCIETY (APS) MUSEUM, Philosophical Hall, 104 S. Fifth St., Philadelphia, PA 19106. Mailing Address: Richardson Hall, 431 Chestnut St., Philadelphia, PA 19106-2426. Tel.: 215-440-3442. Fax: 215-238-0340. Facebook: @americanphilosophicalsociety; Twitter & Instagram: @amphilsociety.
E-mail: museum@amphilsoc.org
Web Site: www.apsmuseum.org
Key Personnel: C.E.O., Keith Thomson; Dir., Merrill Mason; Pres., Clyde Barker; Education, Michael Madeja; Treas., John Wolfe.
Institution Type/Description: History, Art & Science Museum.
Hours & Admission Prices: April 7 to Dec. 30. Thurs.-Sun. 10-4. Suggested donation $2. Closed Thankgiving; Christmas. &
Attendance: 95,000 (actual)

AMERICAN SWEDISH HISTORICAL MUSEUM, 1900 Pattison Ave., Philadelphia, PA 19145-5999. Tel.: 215-389-1776. Fax: 215-389-7701. Facebook, Twitter, Instagram.
E-mail: info@americanswedish.org
Web Site: www.americanswedish.org
Key Personnel: Exec. Dir., Tracey Beck; Chm., Bo Bergqvist; Education & Public Progs., Lauren Burnham; Cur., Carrie Hogan; Coord. Membership & Mktg., Caroline Rossy; Maintenance, Frank Sanders.
Institution Type/Description: Swedish-American History & Art Museum: located on 17th-century Queen Christina land grant.
Hours & Admission Prices: Tues.-Fri. 10-4, Sat.-Sun. 12-4. Adults $8, senior citizens & students $6, children 5-11 $4; discounts to AAA & AAM members; members & children under 5 no charge. Closed holidays. &
Attendance: 13,000 (actual)

ANTHONY J. DREXEL PICTURE GALLERY & RINCLIFFE GALLERY - DREXEL UNIVERSITY, 3141 Chestnut St., Main Bldg., 3rd Fl., Philadelphia, PA 19104. Tel.: 215-895-2414.
E-mail: drexelcollection@drexel.edu
Web Site: drexel.edu/drexelcollection
Institution Type/Description: Art Galleries.
Hours & Admission Prices: Drexel: Mon.-Fri. 3:30-5; other times by appointment. Rincliffe: Mon.-Fri. 8-8:30. No charge. Closed New Year's Day; Martin Luther King Jr. Day; Memorial Day; Independence Day; Labor Day; Columbus Day; Thanksgiving & day after; University breaks.

ARTHUR ROSS GALLERY, UNIVERSITY OF PENNSYLVANIA, 220 S. 34th St., Philadelphia, PA 19104-3808. Mailing Address: Box 5, College Hall, Philadelphia, PA 19104-6303. Tel.: 215-898-2083 & 1479. Fax: 215-573-2045. Facebook: Arthur Ross Gallery; Twitter: @Arthur_Ross.
E-mail: arg@pobox.upenn.edu
Web Site: www.arthurrossgallery.org
Key Personnel: Dir. & Univ. Cur., Lynn Marsden-Atlass; Assoc. Dir., Dejay B. Duckett; Asst. Dir. Devel. & Mktg., Sara Stewart.
Institution Type/Description: Art Gallery: housed in a building designed by Frank Furness in 1891 as the University of Pennsylvania main library. A National Historical Landmark.
Hours & Admission Prices: Tues.-Fri. 10-5, Sat.-Sun. 12-5. No charge. Closed some holidays. &
Attendance: 12,000 (estimated)

THE ATHENAEUM OF PHILADELPHIA, 219 S. 6th St., E. Washington Square, Philadelphia, PA 19106-3794. Tel.: 215-925-2688. Fax: 215-925-3755.
E-mail: conn@philaathenaeum.org
Web Site: www.philathenaeum.org
Key Personnel: Exec. Dir., Dr. Peter Conn; Pres. Bd. Dirs., Robert E. Linck; Cur. Architecture, Bruce Laverty; Circulation Librarian, Jill L. Lee; Digital Center Supvr., Michael Senaca.
Institution Type/Description: Library with Art Collections: housed in 1845-1847, Athenaeum of Philadelphia (national historic landmark), John Notman (1810-1865), architect.
Hours & Admission Prices: Mon.-Fri. 9-5, Sat. 11-3. Research: by appointment. No charge; donations accepted. Closed bank holidays. &
Attendance: 20,000 (estimated)

AWBURY ARBORETUM, Francis Cope House, One Awbury Rd., Philadelphia, PA 19138-1505. Tel.: 215-849-2855. Fax: 215-849-0213.
E-mail: awbury@awbury.org
Web Site: www.awbury.org
Key Personnel: Gen. Mgr., Christopher R. van de Velde; Chm., Mark Sellers.
Institution Type/Description: Arboretum & Cultural Landscape: 1860 Francis Cope House.
Hours & Admission Prices: Grounds: daily dawn-dusk. Francis Cope House: Spring-Fall Mon.-Fri. 9-5; Winter: Tues.-Fri. 9-5. No charge; donations accepted. &
Attendance: 10,000 (estimated)

BARNES FOUNDATION, 2025 Benjamin Franklin Pkwy., Philadelphia, PA 19103. Tel.: 215-278-7000. Facebook: @barnesfoundation; Twitter: @the_barnes.
E-mail: info@barnesfoundation.org
Web Site: www.barnesfoundation.org
Key Personnel: Exec. Dir. & Pres., Thomas Collins; Exec. Vice Pres., C.F.O. & C.O.O., Margaret Zminda.
Institution Type/Description: Art Foundation: 18th-century historic site.
Hours & Admission Prices: Wed.-Mon. 11-5. Adults $25, seniors $23, college students with ID & youth 13-18 $5; children 12 & under and members no charge. &
Attendance: 200,000 (estimated)

BARTRAM'S GARDEN, 5400 Lindbergh Blvd., Philadelphia, PA 19143. Tel.: 215-729-5281. Fax: 215-729-1047. Facebook & Twitter: @BartramsGarden.
E-mail: info@bartramsgarden.org
Web Site: bartramsgarden.org
Key Personnel: Pres. Bd. Dirs., Elizabeth Bressi-Stoppe; Exec. Dir., Maitreyi Roy; Asst. Dir., Stephanie Phillips; Dir. Admin., Andrea Taylor; Dir. Landscapes & Facilities, Tom Reber; Land Mgr., Todd Greenberg; Cur., Joel Fry.
Institution Type/Description: Historic House & Botanical Garden: c.1731 Bartram House.

Hours & Admission Prices: April-Dec. Mon.-Fri. 10-4, Sat.-Sun. 10-6. Adults $12, senior citizens & youth $10; discounts to AAM members; children 2 & under and members no charge. Closed holidays.
Attendance: 40,000 (estimated)

BETSY ROSS HOUSE, 239 Arch St., Philadelphia, PA 19106-1999. Mailing Address: c/o Historic Philadelphia, Inc., 150 S. Independence Mall W., Ste. 550, Philadelphia, PA 19106. Tel.: 215-629-4026. Facebook: @betsyrosshouse.
E-mail: info@historicphiladelphia.org
Web Site: www.historicphiladelphia.org/betsy-ross-house
Key Personnel: Pres. & CEO Historic Philadelphia, Inc., Amy Needle; Publicist, Heather Kincaid.
Institution Type/Description: Historic House: 1773-1786 home of Betsy Ross, seamstress of the first American flag.
Hours & Admission Prices: March-Nov. daily 10-5; Dec.-Feb. Tues.-Sun. 10-5. Audio Tours: adults $7, children, seniors, students & military $6; Self-Guided Tours: adults $5, children, seniors, students & military $4; discounts to AAM & ICOM members; members no charge. Audio Tour: adults $7, children, seniors, students & military $6. Closed New Year's Day; Thanksgiving; Christmas. &
Attendance: 315,459 (actual)

THE CAROLYN AND HOWARD ALBER GALLERY AT ALLENS LANE ART CENTER, 601 W. Allens Lane, Philadelphia, PA 19119. Tel.: 215-248-0546. Fax: 215-248-0559.
E-mail: info@allenslane.org
Web Site: www.allenslane.org/gallery.htm
Key Personnel: Exec. Dir., Craig Stover.
Institution Type/Description: Art Gallery.
Hours & Admission Prices: Mon.-Fri. 10-5; other times by appointment.

CHESTNUT HILL CONSERVANCY, 8708 Germantown Ave., Philadelphia, PA 19118-2717. Tel.: 215-247-9329.
E-mail: info@chhist.org
Web Site: www.chconservancy.org
Formerly: Chestnut Hill Historical Society
Key Personnel: Exec. Dir., Lori Salganicoff; Devel. Dir., Kristin Hagar Southall; Business Mgr., Leah Silverstein; Cur. & Archivist, Liz Jarvis; Archivist, Alex Bartlett.
Institution Type/Description: Historical Society Museum: housed in an 1870s Victorian house.
Hours & Admission Prices: Archives: Wed. 9:30-2:30, Thurs. 9:30-12:30, Sat. 11-4, appointments preferred. Admission & Research $15; members no charge.
Attendance: 800 (estimated)

THE CLAY STUDIO, 137-139 N. Second St., Philadelphia, PA 19106. Mailing Address: 137 N. Second St., Philadelphia, PA 10106. Tel.: 215-925-3453. Facebook: @theclaystudio.phl; Twitter: @theclaystudio.
E-mail: info@theclaystudio.org
Web Site: www.theclaystudio.org
Key Personnel: Pres., Chris Taylor; Vice Pres., Jennifer Martin; Cur. Artistic Programs, Jennifer Zwilling; Dir. Devel., Lesly Attarian; Dir. Education, Josie Bockelman; Events & Mktg. Coord., Eva Piatek; Gallery & Retail Coord., Dominique Ellis.
Institution Type/Description: Art Gallery.
Hours & Admission Prices: Mon.-Sat. 11-6, Sun. 12-6. No charge.
Attendance: 8,791 (actual)

CLIVEDEN, 6401 Germantown Ave., Philadelphia, PA 19144. Tel.: 215-848-1777. Fax: 215-438-2892. Facebook: @TheCliveden.
E-mail: info@cliveden.org
Web Site: www.cliveden.org
Key Personnel: Exec. Dir., Dr. David Young; Bd. Chair, Theodore Reed; Preservation Dir., Libbie Hawes; Education Dir., Carolyn Wallace.
Institution Type/Description: Historic House Museum: 1763-1767 residence built by Benjamin Chew & site of the Battle of Germantown, Oct. 4, 1777.
Hours & Admission Prices: April-Dec. Thurs.-Sun. 12-4; other times by appointment. Adults & seniors $10, students $8; discounts to AAA & National Trust members; members no charge. Closed New Year's Day; Thanksgiving; Christmas. &
Attendance: 60,000 (estimated)

THE DESIGN CENTER AT PHILADELPHIA UNIVERSITY, 4201 Henry Ave., Philadelphia, PA 19144. Tel.: 215-951-2722. Facebook: @thedesigncenterphilau.
E-mail: thedesigncenter@philau.edu
Web Site: thedesigncenter.tumblr.com
Formerly: The Design Center at Philadelphia University
Key Personnel: Cur. Collections, Jade Papa.

Institution Type/Description: Design Museum: housed in Goldie Paley House.
Hours & Admission Prices: Galleries: Mon.-Fri. 10-4. Textile Collection: by appointment. No charge. Closed major & school holidays. ♿
Attendance: 6,000 (estimated)

EASTERN STATE PENITENTIARY HISTORIC SITE, 2027 Fairmount Ave., Philadelphia, PA 19130. Tel.: 215-236-3300. Fax: 215-236-5289.
E-mail: info@easternstate.org
Web Site: www.easternstate.org
Key Personnel: Pres. & CEO, Sara Jane Elk; Sr. Vice Pres., Dir. Interpretation & Public Programming, Sean Kelley; Vice Pres., Dir. Operations, Brett Bertolino; Assoc. Dir. Events & Operations, Amy Hollaman; Assoc. Dir. Visitor Svcs. & Operations, Shelly Sickbert; Assoc. Dir. Design & Facility Engineering, James Travis, III; Assoc. Dir. Mktg. & Communications, Nicole Fox Frankhouser; Dir. Education & Tour Programs, Lauren Zalut; Dir. Advancement, Elyssa Kane.
Institution Type/Description: Historic Site.
Hours & Admission Prices: Daily 10-5. Adults $14, senior citizens $12, students & children 7-12 $10; members no charge. Not recommended for children under 7. Closed New Year's Eve & Day; Easter; Thanksgiving; Christmas Eve & Day.
Attendance: 190,000 (estimated)

THE EBENEZER MAXWELL MANSION, INC., 200 W. Tulpehocken St., Philadelphia, PA 19144-3210. Tel.: 215-438-1861. Fax: 215-438-0133. Facebook: @EbenezerMaxwellMansion; Twitter: @EMaxwellMansion.
E-mail: emaxwellmansion@yahoo.com
Web Site: ebenezermaxwellmansion.org
Key Personnel: Exec. Dir., Diane S. Richardson; Pres., Mark Frazier Lloyd.
Institution Type/Description: Historic House: 1859 Victorian Villa.
Hours & Admission Prices: Thurs.-Sat. 12-4; groups by appointment. Adults $7, students & children 18 & under $5; members no charge. Closed national holidays.
Attendance: 980 (actual)

EDGAR ALLAN POE NATIONAL HISTORIC SITE, 532 N. Seventh St., Philadelphia, PA 19123. Mailing Address: 143 S. 3rd St., Philadelphia, PA 19106-2818. Tel.: 215-597-8780 & 8787. Fax: 215-861-4950. TDD: 215-597-8780.
E-mail: karie_diethorn@nps.gov
Web Site: www.nps.gov/edal
Key Personnel: Mgr., Patricia Jones; Cur., Karie Diethorn; Superintendent, Cynthia Macleod; Chief Cultural Resources, Doris Fanelli; Chief Asset Preservation & Maintenance, Matt Hess; Deputy Superintendent, B J Dunn.
Institution Type/Description: Historic Site; c.1843 Edgar Allan Poe brick house.
Hours & Admission Prices: Check website for hours.

ELFRETH'S ALLEY ASSOCIATION, 124-126 Elfreths Alley, Philadelphia, PA 19106-2006. Tel.: 215-627-8680.
E-mail: elfrethsdirector@gmail.com
Web Site: www.elfrethsalley.org
Key Personnel: Pres., Neil Frauenglass; Vice Pres., Kelly Murphy; Treas., Eric Silverman.
Institution Type/Description: Historic House.
Hours & Admission Prices: April-Oct. Fri.- Sun. 12-5. Guided tours: adults $8, children 7-12 $2; children under 7 no charge.
Attendance: 44,300 (actual)

ESTHER KLEIN GALLERY AT THE UNIVERSITY CITY SCIENCE CENTER (EKG), 3600 Market St., Philadelphia, PA 19104-2641. Mailing Address: 3711 Market St., Ste. 800, Philadelphia, PA 19104-5504. Tel.: 215-966-6188. Fax: 215-966-6001. Facebook: @EstherKleinGallery1; Instagram: @esther_-klein_gallery.
E-mail: gallery@sciencecenter.org
Web Site: http://www.sciencecenter.org/discover/ekg
Formerly: Esther M. Klein Art Gallery at University City Science Center
Key Personnel: C.E.O. & Pres., Dr. Stephen Tang; Cur., Angela McQuillan.
Institution Type/Description: Art Gallery.
Hours & Admission Prices: Mon.-Sat. 9-5. No charge; donations accepted. ♿
Attendance: 100,000 (estimated)

THE FABRIC WORKSHOP AND MUSEUM, 1214 Arch St., Philadelphia, PA 19107-2816. Tel.: 215-561-8888. Fax: 215-561-8887. Facebook: Fabric Workshop; Twitter: fabricworkshop.
E-mail: info@fabricworkshopandmuseum.org
Web Site: www.fabricworkshopandmuseum.org
Key Personnel: Exec. Dir., Susan Lubowsky Talbott; Pres. (V), Katherine Sokolnikoff; Head Exhibitions & Publications, Stephanie Alison Greene; Mgr. Printing Production & Master Printer, Kate Abercrombie; Devel. Asst., Rebekah Atkins; Dir. Photography & Registrar, Carlos Avendano; Mgr. Technology & Visual Media, Aaron Billheimer; Art Museum Sales Shop Dir. & Building Dir., Tracey Blackman; Asst. to the Dirs. & Public Rels., Michele Bregande; Registrar, Justin Hall; Teaching Artist, Apprentice Program, Shelby Donnelly; Study Tour Coord. & Visitor Svcs. Asst., Petra Floyd; Videographer, Tyler Henry; Sewing & Construction Technician & Project Coord., Andrea Landau; Master Printer, Virgil Marti; Teaching Artist, Apprentice Program, Ryan Parker; Head Education & Master Printer, Christina Roberts; Mgr. Family & Community, Sophie Sanders; Administrative & Publicity Coord., Alexander Unkovic; Mgr. Studio Operations & Projects Mgr., Nami Yamamoto; Studio Asst., Anthony Bowers; Studio Asst. & Construction, Paige Fetchen; Studio Asst. & Printer, Joy Ude.
Institution Type/Description: Contemporary Art Museum & Studio focusing on work in new material & new media.
Hours & Admission Prices: Mon.-Fri. 10-6, Sat.-Sun. 12-5; groups by appointment. No charge; donations accepted. Closed on some federal holidays. ♿
Attendance: 10,000 (estimated)

THE FAIRMOUNT PARK CONSERVANCY, 1617 John F. Kennedy Blvd., Ste. 1670, Philadelphia, PA 19103. Tel.: 215-988-9334. Fax: 215-988-9335.
E-mail: info@myphillypark.org
Web Site: myphillypark.org
Key Personnel: Exec. Dir., Rick Magder; Sr. Dir. Operations & Planning, Tim Clair; Sr. Dir. Preservation & Project Mgmt., Lucy Strackhouse; Sr. Dir. Devel., Meg Holscher; Sr. Dir. Civic Initiatives, Jennifer Mahar; Sr. Dir. Strategy & Planning, Ellen Ryan; Sr. Dir. Public Partnerships, Jamie Gauthier.
Institution Type/Description: City Park System: consisting of West Fairmount Park, East Fairmount Park, Benjamin Franklin Parkway, various cultural institutions, historic sites & landmarks and numerous neighborhood & watershed parks.
Hours & Admission Prices: Please visit website for complete list of parks, cultural sites, historic sites & landmarks and other activities. ♿

FAIRMOUNT WATER WORKS, 640 Water Works Dr., Philadelphia, PA 19130. Tel.: 215-685-0723. Fax: 215-685-0718.
E-mail: info@fairmountwaterworks.org
Web Site: fairmountworks.com
Key Personnel: Exec. Dir., Karen Young.
Institution Type/Description: Historic Site: housed on the site of Philadelphia's former pumping station; c.1815.
Hours & Admission Prices: Tues.-Sat. 10-5, Sun. 1-5; groups by appointment.
Attendance: 460,000

FIREMAN'S HALL MUSEUM, 147 N. 2nd St., Philadelphia, PA 19106-2097. Tel.: 215-923-1438.
E-mail: pfdhc@firemanshallmuseum.org
Web Site: www.firemanshallmuseum.org
Formerly: Philadelphia Fire Museum
Key Personnel: Pres. (V), Richard A. Coppola; Cur., Alberto Gonzalez; Museum Shop Mgr., Frank Schiazza.
Institution Type/Description: Fire-Fighting Museum: housed in 1900 Philadelphia firehouse.
Hours & Admission Prices: Tues.-Sat. 10-4:30. No charge; donations accepted. Closed city holidays. ♿
Attendance: 26,000

FORT MIFFLIN ON THE DELAWARE, 1 Fort Mifflin Rd., Philadelphia, PA 19153. Tel.: 215-685-4167. Facebook, Twitter.
E-mail: fortmifflininfo@gmail.com
Web Site: www.fortmifflin.us
Key Personnel: Exec. Dir., Elizabeth Beatty; Chm. Bd., Chester Wichowski; Site & Program Mgr., Joseph Nevin.
Institution Type/Description: Historic Site: 1777 fort.
Hours & Admission Prices: March to mid-Dec. Wed.-Sun. 10-4; other times by appointment. Adults $8, seniors $6, children 6-12 $4; members, active duty military w/ID and children 5 & under no charge. ♿
Attendance: 16,000 (actual)

THE FRANKLIN INSTITUTE, 222 N. 20th St., Philadelphia, PA 19103-1190. Tel.: 215-448-1200. Facebook: TheFranklinInstitute; Twitter: @TheFranklin.
E-mail: guestservices@fi.edu
Web Site: www.fi.edu
Key Personnel: Pres. & C.E.O., Larry Dubinski; Chm. (V), Donald Morel, Jr., Ph. D.; Sr. Digital Officer, Susan Poulton; Vice Pres. Strategic Initiatives, Julie A. March; Vice Pres. Finance, Siobhan Keefe; Vice Pres. External Affairs, Mark Mills; Vice Pres. Operations & Capital Projects, Richard Rabena; Vice Pres. Human Resources, Reid Styles.
Institution Type/Description: Science & Technology Museum, Planetarium & Omniverse Theater.

Hours & Admission Prices: Daily 9:30-5. General Admission: adults $19.95, children 3-11 $15.95; discounts to AAM & ASTC members; members and children 2 & under no charge. Additional fee for special exhibitions & IMAX theater. Closed New Years Day; Thanksgiving; Christmas. &
Attendance: 900,000 (estimated)

FRED WOLF, JR. GALLERY AND SHOPPE/KLEINLIFE, 10100 Jamison Ave., Philadelphia, PA 19116-3832. Tel.: 215-698-7300. Fax: 215-673-7447.
E-mail: pactman@phillyjcc.com
Formerly: Fred Wolf, Jr. Gallery/Klein Branch Jewish Community Center
Key Personnel: C.E.O. KleinLife, Andre Krug.
Institution Type/Description: Art Gallery.
Hours & Admission Prices: Mon.-Thurs. 10-4, Fri. & Sun. 10-2. No charge. Closed Jewish holidays. &
Attendance: 45,000 (estimated)

FREE LIBRARY OF PHILADELPHIA RARE BOOK DEPARTMENT, 1901 Vine St., Philadelphia, PA 19103-1189. Tel.: 215-686-5416. Facebook: @flprarebooks.
E-mail: erefrbd@freelibrary.org
Web Site: www.freelibrary.org/rarebooks
Key Personnel: Chief, Special Collections Div., Janine Pollock.
Institution Type/Description: Public Library.
Hours & Admission Prices: Mon.-Sat. 9-5, daily tour starts at 11. &

FRIENDS OF HISTORIC SEDGELEY, Mailing Address: 15 Kelly Dr., Philadelphia, PA 19130. Facebook.
E-mail: info@friendsofhistoricsedgeley.org
Web Site: friendsofhistoricsedgeley.org
Institution Type/Description: Historic Buildings: listed on the National Register of Historic Places.
Hours & Admission Prices: See website for hours.

THE GALLERIES AT MOORE, 20th St. & The Parkway, Philadelphia, PA 19103. Mailing Address: 1925 Cherry St., Philadelphia, PA 19103. Tel.: 215-965-4027. Fax: 215-568-5921. Facebook: The Galleries at Moore.
E-mail: galleries@moore.edu
Web Site: moore.edu/the-galleries-at-moore
Key Personnel: Interim Dir., Gabrielle L. Suzenski; Education & Pub. Engagement Coord., Matt Kalasky.
Institution Type/Description: Art Gallery.
Hours & Admission Prices: Mon.-Sat. 11-5, No charge; donations accepted. Closed all academic & legal holidays. &
Attendance: 49,500 (estimated)

THE GENEALOGICAL SOCIETY OF PENNSYLVANIA, 2100 Bayberry Rd., Ste. 111, Philadelphia, PA 19116. Tel.: 267-686-2296. Facebook: PAGenealogy.
E-mail: info@genpa.org
Web Site: www.genpa.org
Key Personnel: Pres., Carol M. Sheaffer, M.D.; Vice Pres., Susan S. Koelble; Vice Pres., Deborah Coombe; Sec., Valerie-Anne Lutz; Treas., Nancy C. Janyszeski.
Institution Type/Description: Genealogical Society Library.
Hours & Admission Prices: Call for hours. &
Attendance: 900 (actual)

GLEN FOERD MANSION, 5001 Grant Ave., Philadelphia, PA 19114-3154. Tel.: 215-632-5330.
E-mail: info@glenfoerd.org
Web Site: www.glenfoerd.org
Key Personnel: Exec. Dir., Meg Sharp Walton.
Institution Type/Description: Historic House: built in 1850.
Hours & Admission Prices: Fri.-Sun. 11-3. Guided Tours: 11am & 12:30pm. Tours: $5 per person; discounts to groups.

GRAND ARMY OF THE REPUBLIC MUSEUM & LIBRARY, 4278 Griscom St., Philadelphia, PA 19124-3954. Tel.: 215-289-6484.   Facebook: @GrandArmyOfTheRepublicMuseumAndLibrary.
E-mail: garmuslib@verizon.net
Web Site: garmuslib.org
Key Personnel: Pres., Hugh Boyle; Vice Pres., Anthony Waskie; Sec., Mary Ann Hartner; Treas., Mike Peter; Communications Dir., Courtney Lee Malpass; Librarian, Joseph Perry.
Institution Type/Description: Civil War Museum: housed in 1796 late Georgian-style house.

Hours & Admission Prices: Tues. 12-4, Sun. 12-5; other times by appointment. No charge; donations accepted. &
Attendance: 3,200

HISTORIC GERMANTOWN, 5501 Germantown Ave., Philadelphia, PA 19144-2291. Tel.: 215-844-1683. Fax: 215-844-2831. Facebook.
E-mail: programs@freedomsbackyard.com
Web Site: www.freedomsbackyard.com
Formerly: Germantown Historical Society
Key Personnel: Exec. Dir., Trapeta Mayson; Pres. (V), Loretta Witt; Librarian & Archivist, Alex Bartlett.
Institution Type/Description: Local History Museum & Library.
Hours & Admission Prices: Tues. 9-1, Thurs. 1-5, 1st Sun. each month by appointment. Adults $10, students $5; discounts to AAM, AAA, ICOM & Philadelphia card members; members no charge. &
Attendance: 4,500 (estimated)

HISTORIC ST. GEORGE'S MUSEUM & ARCHIVES, 235 N. Fourth St., Philadelphia, PA 19106-1194. Tel.: 215-925-7788.
E-mail: office@historicstgeorges.org
Web Site: www.historicstgeorges.org/museum
Key Personnel: Admin., Donna Miller.
Institution Type/Description: Religious Museum: housed in 1763 St. George's United Methodist Church, built of British brick & located on the original site of construction.
Hours & Admission Prices: Museum & Archives: Summer: Wed.-Fri. 10-4; Fall & Winter: Mon.-Fri. 10-4; Sat. group tours 10 A.M. by appointment. No charge; donations accepted.
Attendance: 2,000 (estimated)

HISTORICAL SOCIETY OF PENNSYLVANIA, 1300 Locust St., Philadelphia, PA 19107-5661. Tel.: 215-732-6200. Fax: 215-732-2680. Facebook, Twitter.
E-mail: library@hsp.org
Web Site: hsp.org
Key Personnel: Pres. & C.E.O., Charles T. Cullen; Bd. Chm. (V), Eric W. Noll; Sr. Dir. Library & Collections & C.O.O., Lee Arnold; C.F.O., Dennis Williams; Business Opers. Mgr., Joaquin Moreland-Sender; Acting Dir. Devel., Jon-Chris Hatalski; Dir. Preservation & Conservation Svcs., Tara O'Brien; Dir. Archives, Cary Hutto; Dir. Research Svcs., David Haugaard; Historian & Head Reference Svcs., Daniel Rolph; Dir. Cataloguing, Anthony DiGiovanni.
Institution Type/Description: Historical Research Library.
Hours & Admission Prices: Tues. & Thurs. 12:30-5:30, Wed. 12:30-8:30, Fri. 10-5:30. Library: adults $8; members, students & military w/ valid ID no charge. Closed national holidays. &
Attendance: 8,682 (actual)

INDEPENDENCE NATIONAL HISTORICAL PARK, 143 S. 3rd St., Philadelphia, PA 19106-2818. Tel.: 215-965-2305 & 597-8787. Fax: 215-861-4950. Facebook, Twitter.
E-mail: cynthia_macleod@nps.gov
Web Site: www.nps.gov/inde
Key Personnel: Supt., Cynthia MacLeod; Chief Cultural Resources Management, Doris Fanelli; Chief Historian, Jed Levin; Chief Asset Preservation & Maintenance, Matthew Hess; Chief Resource & Visitor Protection, Patrick Suddath.
Institution Type/Description: General Museum.
Hours & Admission Prices: Park: daily 9-5. Independence Visitor Center: 8:30-6. Independence Hall Tours: March-Dec. $1.50 per person; Jan.-Feb. no charge. &
Attendance: 5,500,000 (actual)

INDEPENDENCE SEAPORT MUSEUM, Penn's Landing Waterfront, 211 S. Columbus Blvd., Philadelphia, PA 19106-3101. Tel.: 215-413-8655. Fax: 215-925-6713. Facebook, Instagram & Twitter: @phillyseaport.
E-mail: visitorservices@phillyseaport.org
Web Site: www.phillyseaport.org
Formerly: Philadelphia Maritime Museum
Key Personnel: Pres. & C.E.O., John Brady; Chm., Peter H. Havens; Vice Pres. External Affairs, Michele Blazer; Vice Pres. Interpretation & Visitor Experience, Michael J. Flynn; Chief Cur., Craig Bruns; Digital Content Mgr., Gina Rullo; Dir. J. Welles Henderson Archive & Library, Terry Potter; Supt. Boats & Docks, Travis Davis; Dir. Workshop on the Water, Mark Donohue; Dir. Devel., Ellen Fleurov; Dir. Education, Olivia Thomas; Dir. Hospitality, Dena Rose; Controller, Brandon Maake; Dir. Technology, John Laurino.
Institution Type/Description: Maritime Museum.
Hours & Admission Prices: Daily 10-5. Adults $16, seniors 65 & up, children 3-12, college students & military $12; discounts to members, AAM, AAA & WHYY

members and groups of 10 or more; members & children under 2 no charge. Closed Thanksgiving; Christmas. &

Attendance: 88,570 (actual)

INSTITUTE OF CONTEMPORARY ART, UNIVERSITY OF PENNSYLVANIA, 118 S. 36th St., Philadelphia, PA 19104-3289. Tel.: 215-898-7108 & 5911. Fax: 215-898-5050.

E-mail: info@icaphila.org
Web Site: www.icaphila.org
Key Personnel: Dir., Amy Sadao; Chief Cur., Anthony Elms; Assoc. Cur., Kate Kraczon; Dorothy & Stephen R. Weber Cur., Alex Klein; Dir. Devel., Samantha Gibb Roff; Business Admin., Shannon Freitas; Dir. Mktg. & Communications, Jill Katz; Dir. Curatorial Affairs, Robert Chaney; Head Preparator & Building Admin., Paul Swenbeck; Registrar, Mandy Bartram; Coord. Visitor Svcs. & Program Tech, William Hidalgo; Communications Assoc. & Digital Editor, Heather Holmes; Assoc. Dir. Devel. Individual Gifts, Jeffrey Bussmann; Curatorial Admin., Lauren Downing; Spiegel-Wilks Curatorial Fellow, Gee Wesley; Asst. to Dir., Eliza Coviello.
Institution Type/Description: Contemporary Art Gallery.
Hours & Admission Prices: Wed. 11-8, Thurs.-Fri. 11-6, Sat.-Sun. 11-5. No charge; donations accepted. Closed New Year's Day; Easter; Thanksgiving; Christmas. &
Attendance: 22,000 (actual)

JOHNSON HOUSE HISTORIC SITE, 6306 Germantown Ave., Philadelphia, PA 19144-1908. Tel.: 215-438-1768, 215-438-5510.

E-mail: info@johnsonhouse.org
Web Site: www.johnsonhouse.org
Formerly: Johnson House Underground Railroad Museum
Key Personnel: Exec. Dir., Cornelia Swinson.
Institution Type/Description: Historic House: built c.1768. Listed on the National Register of Historic Places.
Hours & Admission Prices: Mon.-Wed. by appointment only, Thurs.-Fri. 10-4. Adults $8, seniors $6, children $4; discounts to National Park Service.
Attendance: 8,000 (estimated)

LA SALLE UNIVERSITY ART MUSEUM, 1900 W. Olney Ave., Philadelphia, PA 19141-1199. Tel.: 215-951-1000. Fax: 215-951-5096. Facebook: @LaSalleUniversityArtMuseum; Twitter: @LSUAM.

E-mail: artmuseum@lasalle.edu
Web Site: www.lasalle.edu/museum
Key Personnel: Dir. & Chief Cur., Klare Scarborough, Ph.D.; Chm. (V), William E. Kelly, Jr.; Cur. Education & Public Programs, Miranda Clark-Binder; Collections Mgr. & Registrar, Rebecca Oviedo.
Institution Type/Description: Art Museum.
Hours & Admission Prices: Academic Year: Mon.-Fri. 10-4; Summer: Mon.-Thurs. 9-5; other times by appointment only. No charge; donations accepted. &
Attendance: 7,657 (actual)

LEST WE FORGET BLACK HOLOCAUST MUSEUM OF SLAVERY, 3650 Richmond St., Philadelphia, PA 19134. Tel.: 215-205-4324; 397-6060. Facebook: @LestWeForgetPhila.

E-mail: info@lwsfm.com
Web Site: lwsfm.com
Key Personnel: Pres. & Cur., J. Justin Ragsdale; Co-Cur., Gwen Ragsdale.
Institution Type/Description: History Museum.
Hours & Admission Prices: Daily 10-6 by appointment only. Adults, seniors & students $10; members and children 5 & under no charge.

LIBRARY COMPANY OF PHILADELPHIA, 1314 Locust St., Philadelphia, PA 19107-5698. Tel.: 215-546-3181. Fax: 215-546-5167.

E-mail: laugust@librarycompany.org
Web Site: www.librarycompany.org
Key Personnel: Dir., Dr. Michael J. Barsanti; Pres. (V), Hal Rosenberg; Librarian, James N. Green; Cur. Prints, Sarah Weatherwax; Chief Conservation, Jennifer Woods Rosner; Chief Reference, Cornelia S. King; Cur. Arts & Artifacts, Linda August; Cur. Printed Books, Rachel D'Agostino.
Institution Type/Description: Library of Rare Books.
Hours & Admission Prices: Mon.-Fri. 9-4:45. No charge. Closed major holidays. &
Attendance: 5,875 (actual)

MANAYUNK-ROXBOROUGH ART CENTER, 419 Green Ln. (Rear), Philadelphia, PA 19128-3325. Tel.: 215-482-3363. Facebook, Twitter.

E-mail: mrac.arts@gmail.com
Web Site: www.mrartcenter.org
Formerly: Manayunk Art Center

Key Personnel: Vice Pres., Mike Muir; Dir. Programming, Krista Niles; Dir. Humanities, Peter Krok.
Institution Type/Description: Art Gallery.
Hours & Admission Prices: Sat.-Sun. 11-3. No charge except for classes & workshops; donations accepted.
Attendance: 2,000

MARIAN ANDERSON HISTORICAL SOCIETY & MUSEUM, 762 S. Martin St., Philadelphia, PA 19146. Tel.: 215-779-4219; 267-908-3790. Facebook: @NationalMarianAndersonMuseum; Twitter: @NationalMAHSMus.

E-mail: marianandersonhistoricsociety@gmail.com
Web Site: marianandersonhistoricalsociety.weebly.com
Key Personnel: Founder & C.E.O., Blanche Burton Lyles.
Institution Type/Description: Historical Society Museum: housed in the former home of singer Marian Anderson. Listed on the National Register of Historic Places.
Hours & Admission Prices: Mon.-Sat. 10-4. Admission $10.

MARIO LANZA INSTITUTE/MUSEUM, 712 Montrose St., Philadelphia, PA 19147-3944. Mailing Address: P.O. Box 54624, Philadelphia, PA 19148-0624. Tel.: 215-238-9691. Fax: 215-238-9694.

E-mail: mariolanzainstitute@verizon.net
Web Site: www.mariolanzainstitute.org
Key Personnel: Pres., Publicity Dir. & Sec., William J. Ronayne; Treas. & Vice Pres., Jeanette Frese; Bd. Member, Ray Katz; Bd. Member, Dorothy Todaro; Bd. Member, Giovanna Cavaliere; Legal Counsel, Joseph Caruso, Esq.
Institution Type/Description: Specialized Museum: one block from museum is the Mario Lanza Birthplace.
Hours & Admission Prices: See website for hours; other times by appointment. Admission: $5 per person; members no charge.
Attendance: 2,500 (estimated)

MARVIN SAMSON CENTER FOR HISTORY OF PHARMACY, Griffith Hall, 600 S. 43rd St., Philadelphia, PA 19104-4495. Tel.: 215-596-8721.

E-mail: m.brody@usciences.edu
Web Site: www.usp.edu
Key Personnel: Dir. & Cur., Michael Brody.
Institution Type/Description: Pharmacy Museum.
Hours & Admission Prices: Mon.-Fri. 9-5. No charge.
Attendance: 5,000

THE MASONIC, TEMPLE, LIBRARY AND MUSEUM OF PENNSYLVANIA, The Grand lodge of Pennsylvania, 1 N. Broad St., Philadelphia, PA 19107-2598. Tel.: 215-988-1917.

E-mail: GIR@pagrandlodge.org
Web Site: www.pamasonictemple.org
Key Personnel: Chm., Raymond T. Dietz; Librarian, Glenys A. Waldman; Asst. Librarian, Catherine L. Giaimo; Cur., Dennis P. Buttleman, Jr.
Institution Type/Description: History Museum: housed in c.1873 Masonic Temple.
Hours & Admission Prices: Masonic Temple Tours: Tues.-Sat. 10, 11, 1, 2 & 3; Library & Museum: Tues.-Fri. 9-5, Sat. 9-1; other times by appointment. Masonic Temple Tours: family (up to 6 people $35, adults $15, groups, senior citizens 65 & up and students w/ID $10; Library & Museum Only $7; PA Masons w/ID and active military & children under 5 no charge. Closed national holidays. &
Attendance: 30,000 (estimated)

MORRIS ARBORETUM OF THE UNIVERSITY OF PENNSYLVANIA, 100 E. Northwestern Ave., Philadelphia, PA 19118-2697. Tel.: 215-247-5777. Fax: 215-248-4439. Facebook: Morris Arboretum.

E-mail: cranesj@upenn.edu
Web Site: www.morrisarboretum.org
Key Personnel: Exec. Dir., Paul W. Meyer; Dir. Facilities & Finance, Kevin Schrecengost; Dir. Devel., Mira Zergani; Dir. Botany, Dr. Timothy Block; Dir. Mktg., Susan Crane; Dir. Facilities, Tom Wilson; Dir. Public Programs, Robert Gutowski; Museum Shop Mgr., Christopher Dorman.
Institution Type/Description: Arboretum.
Hours & Admission Prices: April-Oct. Mon.-Fri. 10-4, Sat.-Sun. 10-5; Nov.-March 10-4 daily. Adults $17, senior citizens $15, students & youth 3-18 $9; discounts to PHS, AHS, AAA, WHYY, WXPN, PCVB members; Penn students, staff, & alumni and members no charge. Closed New Year's Day; Thanksgiving; Christmas Eve & Day. &
Attendance: 138,962 (actual)

MUMMERS MUSEUM, 1100 S. 2nd St. (at Washington Ave.), Philadelphia, PA 19147-5497. Tel.: 215-336-3050. Fax: 215-389-5630. Facebook: Mummers Museum.
E-mail: mummersmus@aol.com
Web Site: mummersmuseum.com
Key Personnel: Pres. (V), Tom Loomis; Cur. & Coord., Mark Montanaro; Mgr., Eileen Garbarino.
Institution Type/Description: Audio-Visual Film & Costume Museum: located on 1600-1800s site of original route of Mummers.
Hours & Admission Prices: Wed.-Sat. 9:30-4:30. No charge; donations accepted. Closed all holidays. &
Attendance: 12,000 (estimated)

MUSEUM AT CHF, 315 Chestnut St., Philadelphia, PA 19106-2793. Tel.: 215-925-2222. Facebook & Twitter: @ChemHeritage.
E-mail: museum@chemheritage.org
Web Site: www.chemheritage.org/museum-at-chf
Key Personnel: Museum Dir., Erin McLeary; Museum Operations Mgr., Ann Elizabeth Wiener; Museum Collections Mgr., Stephanie Lampkin; Exhibitions Projects Mgr., Christy Schneider; Digital Projects Mgr., Charles McGhee Hassrick.
Institution Type/Description: Science Museum.
Hours & Admission Prices: Tues.-Sat. 10-5, 1st Fri. each month March-Dec. 10-8. No charge. Closed New Year's Day; Memorial Day; Independence Day; Labor Day; Thanksgiving; Christmas. &

THE MUSEUM OF NURSING HISTORY, INC., LaSalle Univ., St. Benilde Tower - 3rd Fl., 1900 W. Olney Ave., Philadelphia, PA 19141-1199. Tel.: 215-831-7819. Facebook: Museum Nursing History.
E-mail: sandrahresdavis@gmail.com
Web Site: www.nursinghistory.org
Key Personnel: Pres. (V) & Nurse Historian, Sandra Davis, Ed.D., R.N.; Treas., Jane Early.
Institution Type/Description: Nursing History: originally located in Pennsylvania Hospital, the first hospital in the U.S. (1751).
Hours & Admission Prices: Mon.-Fri. 9-5, special arrangements for group tours. No charge; donations accepted. &
Attendance: 250 (estimated)

MUSEUM OF THE AMERICAN REVOLUTION, 101 S. Third St., Philadelphia, PA 19106. Tel.: 215-253-6731; 877-740-1776. Facebook.
E-mail: info@amrevmuseum.org
Web Site: www.amrevmuseum.org
Formerly: The American Revolution Center
Key Personnel: Pres. & C.E.O., Michael E. Quinn; C.O.O., ZeeAnn Mason; Vice Pres. Advancement, Claudia Stowers; Dir. Construction & Design, John McDevitt; Dir. Devel., Kristian Smith; Dir. Mktg. & Public Rels., Christine Spencer; Dir. Collections & interpretation, R. Scott Stephenson; Dir. Learning & Engagement, Mary Jane Taylor; Historian & Cur., Philip Mead; Dir. Human Resources, Sue Nicol; Dir. Finance, Maureen O'Ryan.
Institution Type/Description: History Museum: located in historic Philadelphia.
Hours & Admission Prices: Museum closed until April 19, 2017. Adults $19, students $17, children 6 & up $12; children 5 & under no charge. Closed New Year's Day; Thanksgiving; Christmas. &
Attendance: (actual)

MUTTER MUSEUM OF THE COLLEGE OF PHYSICIANS OF PHILADELPHIA, 19 S. 22nd St., Philadelphia, PA 19103-3097. Tel.: 215-560-8564. Facebook, Instagram & Twitter: @muttermuseum.
E-mail: info@collegeofphysicians.org
Web Site: muttermuseum.org
Key Personnel: Dir. & C.E.O., The Thomas W. Langfitt Chair, George M. Wohlreich, M.D.; Dir. Mutter Museum & Historical Medical Library & William Maul measey Chair for the History of Medicine, Robert Hicks; Dir. Mutter Institute & Cur. Mutter Museum, Anna Dhody; Mutter Museum Educator, Marcy Engleman; Collections Mgr., Lowell Flanders; Exhibits Designer, Michael Keys.
Institution Type/Description: Medical Museum.
Hours & Admission Prices: Museum: daily 10-5; Library: by appointment. Adults $18, senior citizens 65 & up $16, military w/ID $15, students w/ID & children 6-17 $13; discounts to groups, AAM & ICOM members; children under 5 & members no charge. Closed New Year's Day; Thanksgiving; Christmas Eve & Day. &
Attendance: 130,000 (estimated)

NAOMI WOOD COLLECTION AT WOODFORD MANSION, 33rd & Dauphin St., E. Fairmount Park, Philadelphia, PA 19132. Tel.: 215-229-6115. Facebook: @WoodfordMansion.
E-mail: memoffat@gmail.com
Web Site: www.woodfordmansion.org
Key Personnel: Site Mgr., Martha Moffat.
Institution Type/Description: Historic House Museum: 1756 Woodford Mansion.
Hours & Admission Prices: Tues.-Sun. 10-4. Adults $8, senior citizens 65 & up, students w/ID & youth 13-17 $5; children under 12 no charge. Closed New Year's Eve & Day; Christmas Eve & Day.
Attendance: 5,000 (actual)

NATIONAL ARCHIVES AT PHILADELPHIA, 14700 Townsend Rd., Philadelphia, PA 19154-2044. Tel.: 215-305-2044. Fax: 215-305-2038. Facebook: @NARAatPhiladelphia.
E-mail: philadelphia.archives@nara.gov
Web Site: www.archives.gov/philadelphia
Formerly: National Archives and Records Administration - Mid-Atlantic Region
Key Personnel: Field Support Officer, David Roland; Admin. Officer, Brenda Bernard; Dir., Federal Records Center, Aaron Swann; Teacher Workshops & School Programs, Andrea Reidell.
Institution Type/Description: Archives: housed in 1938 Works Project Administration Construction building.
Hours & Admission Prices: Mon.-Fri. 8:30-3:30. No charge; donations accepted. Closed federal holidays. &
Attendance: 12,000 (actual)

NATIONAL CONSTITUTION CENTER, 525 Arch St., Independence Mall, Philadelphia, PA 19106-1595. Tel.: 215-409-6600. Facebook, Instagram & Twitter: @constitutionctr.
E-mail: visitorcomments@constitutioncenter.org
Web Site: constitutioncenter.org
Key Personnel: Pres. & C.E.O., Jeffrey Rosen; C.O.O., Vince Stango; Dir. Bd. Rels., Christina Chagin; Vice Pres. Finance, Christine Donnelly; Distinguished Prof. Constitutional Law, Michael Gerhardt; Vice Pres. Exhibitions, Stephanie Reyer; Vice Pres. Visitor Experience & Education, Kerry Sautner.
Institution Type/Description: History Museum.
Hours & Admission Prices: Mon.-Sat. 9:30-5, Sun. 12-5. Adults $14.50, senior citizens 65 & over and students w/ID $13, youth 6-18 $11; active military, children 5 & under and members no charge. Closed New Year's Day; Thanksgiving; Christmas.

NATIONAL LIBERTY MUSEUM, 321 Chestnut St., Philadelphia, PA 19106-2707. Tel.: 215-925-2800. Fax: 215-925-3800. Facebook & Instagram: @NationalLibertyMuseum; Twitter: @LibertyMuseum.
E-mail: liberty@libertymuseum.org
Web Site: www.libertymuseum.org
Key Personnel: C.E.O., Gwen Borowsky; Pres., Thomas Caramanico; Vice Pres. Institutional Advancement, Peggy Sweeney; Vice Pres. Programs, Kevin O'Rangers; Public Rels. & Outreach Dir., Jan Griesemer; Press, Sherry Hawk.
Institution Type/Description: Art Museum.
Hours & Admission Prices: Winter: Mon.-Fri. 11-4, Sat. 10-5, Sun. 12-5; Spring & Fall: daily 10-5; Summer: daily 10-6. Adults $7, seniors $6, students $5, children 5-17 w/adult $2; discounts to AAA members; children under 5 & members no charge. Closed Christmas. &
Attendance: 62,000 (estimated)

NATIONAL MUSEUM OF AMERICAN JEWISH HISTORY CLOSED, 101 South Independence Mall East, Philadelphia, PA 19106-2517. Tel.: 215-923-3811. Fax: 215-923-0763.
E-mail: nmajh@nmajh.org
Web Site: www.nmajh.org
Key Personnel: Pres. & C.E.O., Ivy L. Barsky; Co-Chm., Ronald Rubin; Dir. Finance, Don Maedche; Deputy Dir. Programming & Museum Historian, Josh Perelman; Dir. Mktg. & Commun., Yael Eytan; Retail Sales Mgr., Kristen Kreider.
Institution Type/Description: Social & Ethnic History Museum: located on Independence Mall.
Hours & Admission Prices: Tues.-Fri. 10-5; Sat.-Sun. 10-5:30. Adults $12, seniors & youth $11; members, active duty military & children no charge. Closed New Year's Day; Thanksgiving. &
Attendance: 250,000 (estimated)

PAINTED BRIDE ART CENTER, 230 Vine St., Philadelphia, PA 19106-1293. Tel.: 215-925-9914. Fax: 215-925-7402.
E-mail: info@paintedbride.org
Web Site: paintedbride.org
Key Personnel: Exec. Dir., Laurel Raczka; Assoc. Dir., Lisa Nelson-Haynes.
Institution Type/Description: Art Center.

Hours & Admission Prices: Tues.-Sat. 12-6 & during performances.

PAUL PECK ALUMNI CENTER GALLERY - DREXEL UNIVERSITY, 32nd & Market Sts., 3141 Chestnut St., Philadelphia, PA 19104. Tel.: 215-895-2414.
E-mail: drexelcollection@drexel.edu
Web Site: drexel.edu/drexelcollection
Institution Type/Description: Art Gallery: housed in the former Centennial Bank's bookkeeping room; built in 1876. Listed on the National Register of Historic Places.
Hours & Admission Prices: Mon.-Fri. 9-5.

THE PAUL ROBESON HOUSE, c/o West Philadelphia Cultural Alliance, 4949/4951 Walnut St., Philadelphia, PA 19139-4228. Tel.: 215-747-4675.
E-mail: wphlca@gmail.com
Web Site: paulrobesonhouse.org
Key Personnel: Bd. Chm., Mitchell Swann; Cur., Vernoca Michael.
Institution Type/Description: Historical House Museum: housed in the former home of Paul Robeson.
Hours & Admission Prices: By appointment. Adults $10, groups of 10 or more $6, children $5.

PENNSYLVANIA ACADEMY OF THE FINE ARTS, 118-128 N. Broad St., Philadelphia, PA 19102-1424. Tel.: 215-972-7600. Facebook, Instagram & Twitter: @PAFAcademy.
E-mail: pafa@pafa.org
Web Site: www.pafa.org
Key Personnel: Chm. (V), Kevin F. Donohoe; Pres. & C.E.O., David R. Brigham; Dean School Fine Arts, Clint Jukkala; Vice Pres. HR & Admin., James Gaddy; Exec. Vice Pres. Devel., Melissa D. Kaiser; Exec. Vice Pres. Mktg. & Communications, Heike Rass; C.F.O., Anthony DeCocinis.
Institution Type/Description: Art Museum & School: housed in 1876 Centennial building designed by Furness & Hewitt.
Hours & Admission Prices: Tues.-Thurs. 10-5, Wed. 10-9, Sat.-Sun. 11-5. Permanent Collection: adults $15, senior citizens 60 & up and students w/ID $12, youth 13-18 $8; discounts to AAM members; members & children 12 & under no charge. Combination: adults $15, seniors & students with ID $12, youth 13-18 $10; discounts to AAM members; members and children 12 & under no charge. Closed major holidays. &
Attendance: 132,532 (actual)

THE PHILADELPHIA ART ALLIANCE, 251 S. 18th St., Philadelphia, PA 19103-6168. Tel.: 215-545-4302. Fax: 215-545-0767. Facebook: @philartalliance.
E-mail: info@philartalliance.org
Web Site: www.philartalliance.org
Key Personnel: Exec. Dir., Thora Jacobson; Chief Cur., Melissa Caldwell; Membership Coord., Flora Ward; Events Coord., Mary Kay Kaminsky.
Institution Type/Description: Multi-Disciplinary Arts Center: housed in c.1906 home, designed by Klauder of the architectural firm Day & Klauder; located on Rittenhouse Square.
Hours & Admission Prices: Tues.-Sun. 12-6. Adults $5, seniors $3; members no charge. Closed national holidays.
Attendance: 20,000 (estimated)

PHILADELPHIA DOLL MUSEUM, 2253 N. Broad St., Philadelphia, PA 19132. Tel.: 215-787-0220.
E-mail: dollmuse@aol.com
Web Site: www.philadollmuseum.com
Key Personnel: Exec. Dir., Barbara Whiteman.
Institution Type/Description: Doll Museum.
Hours & Admission Prices: Thurs.-Sat. 10-4, Sun. 12-4. Adults $4, seniors, students & children under 12 $3; discounts to groups.

PHILADELPHIA HISTORY MUSEUM, 15 S. 7th St., Philadelphia, PA 19106-2313. Tel.: 215-685-4830. Fax: 215-685-4837. Facebook: @PhiladelphiaHistoryMuseum; Instagram & Twitter: @philahistory.
E-mail: info@philadelphiahistory.org
Web Site: www.philadelphiahistory.org
Formerly: Atwater Kent Museum of Philadelphia dba Philadelphia History Museum
Key Personnel: C.E.O. & Exec. Dir., Charles Croce; Bd. Pres., David S. Rasner, Esq.; Dir. Collection & Exhibitions, Kristen Froehlich; Registrar & Collections Mgr., Joshua Blay; Visitor Svcs. & Membership Mgr., Joanne Gasienski; Historian, Cynthia Little, Ph.D.; Dir. External Rels. & Special Events, Kelly Murphy.
Institution Type/Description: History Museum: housed in 1826 building designed by John Haviland.

Hours & Admission Prices: Tues.-Sat. 10:30-4:30. Adults $10, seniors $8, students & teens 13-18 $6; members, active military, children 12 & under no charge. &
Attendance: 15,000 (estimated)

PHILADELPHIA MUSEUM OF ART, 2600 Benjamin Franklin Pkwy., Philadelphia, PA 19130. Mailing Address: P.O. Box 7646, Philadelphia, PA 19101-7646. Tel.: 215-763-8100. Fax: 215-236-4465. Facebook, Instagram & Twitter: @philamuseum.
E-mail: visitorservices@philamuseum.org
Web Site: www.philamuseum.org
Key Personnel: Chair Bd. Trustees, Leslie Anne Miller; The George D. Widener Dir. & C.E.O., Timothy Rub; Pres. & C.O.O., Gail M. Harrity; The Pappas-Sarbanes Deputy Dir. Collections & Programs, Alice Beamesderfer; Gen. Counsel & Asst. Sec., Jeffrey Blair; C.F.O., Robert Rambo; The Robert L. McNeil, Jr. Sr. Cur. American Art & Dir. Center for American Art, Kathleen A. Foster; The H. Richard Dietrich, Jr. Cur. American Decorative Arts, David Barquist; The Montgomery-Garvan Assoc. Cur. American Decorative Arts, Alexandra Alevizatos Kirtley; The Susan Gray Detweiler Cur. American Art & Mgr. Center of American Art, Jessica Smith; The Nancy M. McNeil Assoc. Cur. American Modern & Contemporary Crafts & Decorative Arts, Elisabeth Agro; The Keith L. & Katherine Sachs Cur. Contemporary Art, Carlos Basualdo; The Jack M. & Annette Y. Friedland Sr. Cur. Costume & Textiles, Dilys E. Blum; The Le Vine Assoc. Cur. Costume & Textiles & Supervising Cur. Study Room & Academic Rels., H. Kristina Haugland; The Luther W. Brady Cur. Japanese Art & Cur. East Asian Art, Felice Fischer; The Maxine & Howard Lewis Assoc. Cur. Korean Art, Hyunsoo Woo; The J.J. Medveckis Assoc. Cur. Arms & Armor, Dirk H. Breiding; The J. Mahlon Buck, Jr. Family Sr. Cur. European Decorative Arts after 1700, Kathryn Bloom Hiesinger; The Gloria & Jack Drosdick Cur. European Painting & Cur. John G. Johnson Collection, Jennifer Thompson; The Audrey & William H. Helfand Sr. Cur. Prints, Drawings, & Photographs, Innis Howe Shoemaker; The Kathy & Ted Fernberger Cur. Prints, John Ittmann; The Mainwaring Cur. Drawings, Ann Percy; The Brodsky Cur. Photographs, Alfred Stieglitz Ctr., Peter Barberie; The Stella Kramrisch Cur. Indian & Himalayan Art, Darielle Mason; The Neubauer Family Dir. Conservation, Mark S. Tucker; The John & Chara Haas Sr. Conservator Decorative Arts & Sculpture, Sally Malenka; The Aron Sr. Conservator Paintings, Teresa Lignelli; The Theodore Siegl Conservator Modern & Contemporary Paintings, Cindy Albertson; The Charles K. Williams, II Sr. Conservator Works of Art on Paper, Nancy Ash; The Elaine S. Harrington Sr. Conservator Furniture & Woodwork, Behrooz Salimnejad; The Penny & Bob Fox Sr. Conservator Costumes & Textiles, Sara Reiter; Dir. Devel., Jonathan Peterson; Deputy Dir. Devel., Individual Giving & Gifts or Works of Art, David Blackman; Dir. Institutional Support, Nico Hartzell; Dir. Corporate Rels., Elizabeth Tawadros; The Kathleen C. Sherrerd Sr. Cur. Education, Marla K. Shoemaker; The Zoe & Dean Pappas Cur. Education, Public Programs, Emily Schreiner; The Constance Williams Cur. Education, School & Teacher Programs, Barbara A. Bassett; The Park Family Dir. Exhibition Design, Jack Schlechter; Dir. Exhibition Planning, Suzanne F. Wells; Dir. Engineering, Facilities & Operations, Al Shaikoli, P.Eng.; Dir. Human Resources, Greer Diefenderfer; The John H. McFadden & Lisa D. Kabnick Dir. Information Svcs., William Weinstein; The Arcadia Dir. Library & Archives, Kristen Regina; The Martha Hamilton Morris Archivist, Susan Anderson; Exec. Dir. Mktg & Communications, Norman Keyes; Creative & Brand Management Dir., Luis Bravo; Dir. Visitor Operations & Memberships, Jessica Sharpe; Dir. Visitor Services, Kevin Wonder; The William T. Ranney Dir. Publishing, Sherry Babbitt; Dir. Registration, Irene Taurins; Dir. Retail, James F. Cincotta; Dir. Special Events, Camille Focarino.
Institution Type/Description: Art Museum: located in Fairmount Park.
Hours & Admission Prices: Main Bldg.: Tues., Thurs. & Sat.-Sun. 10-5, Wed. & Fri. 10-8:45. Perelman Bldg.: Tues.-Sun. 10-5. Adults $20, senior citizens 65 & over $18, students w/ID & youth 13-18 $14; discounts to AAM & ICOM members; members and children 12 & under no charge. General admission does not include special ticketed exhibitions. Closed Independence Day; Thanksgiving; Christmas. &
Attendance: 792,936 (estimated)

PHILADELPHIA MUSEUM OF JEWISH ART/ CONGREGATION RODEPH SHALOM, 615 N. Broad St., Philadelphia, PA 19123-2417. Tel.: 215-627-6747. Facebook: Philadelphia Museum of Jewish Art.
E-mail: info@rodephshalom.org
Web Site: www.rodephshalom.org
Key Personnel: Dir., Wendi Furman.
Institution Type/Description: Religious Museum: housed in the oldest German synagogue in the Western hemisphere.
Hours & Admission Prices: Mon.-Thurs. 10-4, Fri. 10-2. No charge; donations accepted. Closed Jewish & public holidays. &
Attendance: 6,000

PHILADELPHIA SOCIETY FOR THE PRESERVATION OF LANDMARKS, 321 S. Fourth St., Philadelphia, PA 19106-4218.

Tel.: 215-925-2251. Fax: 215-925-7909. Facebook: @PhilaLandmarks1931; Instagram & Twitter: @PhilaLandmarks.
E-mail: info@philalandmarks.org
Web Site: www.philalandmarks.org
Key Personnel: Exec. Dir., Jonathan Burton; Chm. (V), Charles P. Keates, Esq.; PhilaLandmarks Road Scholar Dir., Margaret M. Biddle; Admin., Jorja Fullerton; Devel. & Communications Dir., Mickey Herr; Outreach Coord., Sarah Sutton.
Institution Type/Description: Historic Building/Site.
Hours & Admission Prices: Powel House: April-Nov. Thurs.-Sat. 11-3, Sun. noon to 3, March & Dec. weekends by appointment only; Hill-Physick House: closed for restorations; private tours & rentals by appointment only; Historic Waynesborough: Thurs.-Sun. 1-3. Grumblethorpe: April-Oct. 2nd Sat. of month noon to 4 & by appointment. Family $20, adults $8, students & senior citizens $6; discounts for groups; Landmarks' members no charge.
Attendance: 21,000 (estimated)

PHILADELPHIA ZOO, 3400 W. Girard Ave., Philadelphia, PA 19104-1139. Tel.: 215-243-1100, ext. 0. Fax: 215-243-5385. Facebook: @philadelphiazoo; Twitter: @phillyzoo.
E-mail: lombardo.dana@phillyzoo.org
Web Site: www.philadelphiazoo.org
Formerly: The Philadelphia Zoo and Zoological Garden
Key Personnel: Chm. Bd., F. William McNabb, III; C.E.O. & Pres., Vikram H. Dewan; C.O.O., Andrew Baker, Ph.D.; C.F.O., Matthew Malek; Sec., M. Rita Burke; Dir. Communications, Dana Lombardo.
Institution Type/Description: Zoo.
Hours & Admission Prices: March-Oct. daily 9:30-5; Nov.-Feb. daily 9:30-4. March-Oct. adult $23, child 2-11 $19; Nov.-Feb. admission $16; discounts to groups with advanced reservations; children under 2 & members no charge. Closed New Year's Eve & Day; Thanksgiving; Christmas Eve & Day. &
Attendance: 1,200,000 (actual)

PIZZA BRAIN'S MUSEUM OF PIZZA CULTURE, 2313 Frankford Ave., Philadelphia, PA 19125. Tel.: 215-291-2965. Facebook; Instagram.
Web Site: pizzabrain.org/museum
Institution Type/Description: History Museum.
Hours & Admission Prices: Mon.-Thurs. 11-9, Fri.-Sat. 11-10, Sun. 12-9.

PLEASE TOUCH MUSEUM, Memorial Hall, Fairmount Park, 4231 Ave. of the Republic, Philadelphia, PA 19131-3719. Tel.: 215-581-3181. Fax: 215-581-3182.
E-mail: info@pleasetouchmuseum.org
Web Site: www.pleasetouchmuseum.org
Key Personnel: Pres. & C.E.O., Patricia Wellenbach; Chm. Bd., Sally Stetson; Vice Pres. Admin. & Finance, Michael Armento; Vice Pres. Visitor Engagement, Leslie Walker; Cur. Collections, Stacey Swigart; Dir. Sales, Beth Kirk; Exec. Asst., Lisa Toole.
Institution Type/Description: Children's Museum.
Hours & Admission Prices: Mon.-Sat. 9-5, Sun. 11-5. Admission $17; discounts to AAM & ACM members; children under one no charge. Closed Thanksgiving; Christmas. &
Attendance: 497,494 (estimated)

PRESBYTERIAN HISTORICAL SOCIETY, 425 Lombard St., Philadelphia, PA 19147-1516. Tel.: 215-627-1852. Fax: 215-627-0115.
E-mail: refdesk@history.pcusa.org
Web Site: www.history.pcusa.org
Key Personnel: Exec. Dir., Beth Hessel.
Institution Type/Description: Religious Museum.
Hours & Admission Prices: Mon.-Fri. 8:30-4:30. No charge. Closed national holidays. &
Attendance: 1,000

THE PRINT CENTER, 1614 Latimer St., Philadelphia, PA 19103-6308. Tel.: 215-735-6090. Facebook; Twitter; Instagram.
E-mail: info@printcenter.org
Web Site: www.printcenter.org
Key Personnel: Exec. Dir., Elizabeth F. Spungen; Asst. to Dir., Mikaela Hawk; Chm. (V), Frances G. Gerson; Pres. (V), Hester Stinnett; Cur., John Caperton; Sales & Program Mgr., Evan Laudenslager; Communications & Special Events Mgr., Michele Bregande.
Institution Type/Description: Arts Center.
Hours & Admission Prices: Tues.-Sat. 11-6. No charge; donations accepted. Closed major holidays.
Attendance: 8,000 (estimated)

RODIN MUSEUM, 2151 Benjamin Franklin Pkwy., Philadelphia, PA 19130. Mailing Address: c/o Philadelphia Museum of Art, P.O. Box 7646, Philadelphia, PA 19101-7646. Tel.: 215-763-8100. Fax: 215-235-0050.
E-mail: visitorservices@philamuseum.org
Web Site: www.rodinmuseum.org
Key Personnel: The Gloria & Jack Drosdick Cur. European Painting & Sculpture and Cur. John C. Johnson Collection, Jennifer Thompson; The Muriel & Philip Berman Cur. Modern Art, Matthew Affron; The Agnes & Jack Mulroney Assoc. Cur. European Painting & Sculpture, Christopher Atkins.
Institution Type/Description: Art Museum.
Hours & Admission Prices: Wed.-Mon. 10-5. Suggested Admission: adults $10, seniors 65 & over $8, youth 13-18 & students with valid ID $7; members and children 12 & under no charge. Closed Independence Day; Thanksgiving; Christmas. &
Attendance: 52,480 (actual)

ROSENBACH MUSEUM & LIBRARY, 2008-2010 DeLancy Place, Philadelphia, PA 19103-6584. Tel.: 215-732-1600. Fax: 215-545-7529.
E-mail: info@rosenbach.org
Web Site: www.rosenbach.org
Key Personnel: Chm., Susan B. Miller; John C. Haas Dir., Derick Dreher; Assoc. Dir. & Dir. Devel., Kelsey Scouten Bates; Cur. & Dir. Collections, Judith M. Guston; Hirsig Family Dir. Education, Emilie Parker; Mgr. Advancement, Alicia Thomas; Exec. Asst., Cathleen Chandler; Librarian, Elizabeth E. Fuller; Facilities Mgr., Christina Doe; Registrar, Jobi Zink.
Institution Type/Description: Rare Books & Library Museum.
Hours & Admission Prices: Tues. & Fri. 12-5, Wed.-Thurs. 12-8, Sat. & Sun. 12-6. Guided Tours: adults $10, senior citizens 65 & over $8, children & students $5; discounts to groups; AAM, ICOM & NARM members, children under 5 & members no charge. Closed national holidays. &
Attendance: 11,500 (actual)

RYERSS MUSEUM & LIBRARY, Burholme Park, 7370 Central Ave., Philadelphia, PA 19111-3059. Tel.: 215-685-0544 & 0599. Facebook: Ryerss Museum & Library.
E-mail: ryerssmuseum@gmail.com
Web Site: ryerssmuseum.org
Key Personnel: Park Historian & Admin. Supvr., Theresa Stuhlman.
Institution Type/Description: Decorative Art & General Museum; housed in 1859 Victorian House.
Hours & Admission Prices: Fri.-Sun. 10-4. No charge; donations accepted. Closed New Year's Day; Easter; Thanksgiving; Christmas. &
Attendance: 6,171 (actual)

SAMUEL S. FLEISHER ART MEMORIAL, 719 Catharine St., Philadelphia, PA 19147-2811. Tel.: 215-922-3456, ext. 300.
E-mail: info@fleisher.org
Web Site: www.fleisher.org
Key Personnel: Dir., Elizabeth Grimaldi; Pres. (V), Jolley Christman; Museum Shop Mgr., Fred Kelley.
Institution Type/Description: Art Museum.
Hours & Admission Prices: Mon.-Thurs. 9-9:30, Fri. 9-5, Sat. 9-3. No charge. &
Attendance: 20,000

SCHMIDT-DEAN GALLERY, 1719 Chestnut St., Philadelphia, PA 19103. Tel.: 215-569-9433. Fax: 215-569-9434. Facebook: Schmidt/Dean Gallery.
E-mail: schmidtdean@netzero.net
Web Site: schmidtdean.com
Key Personnel: Christopher Schmidt.
Institution Type/Description: Art Gallery.
Hours & Admission Prices: Tues.-Sat. 10:30-6, Mon. by appointment. No charge.

THE SCHUYLKILL CENTER FOR ENVIRONMENTAL EDUCATION, 8480 Hagy's Mill Rd., Philadelphia, PA 19128-1998. Tel.: 215-482-7300, ext. 110. Fax: 215-482-8158. Facebook & Instagram: @schuylkillcenter; Twitter: @SchuylkillCtr.
E-mail: scee@schuylkillcenter.org
Web Site: www.schuylkillcenter.org
Key Personnel: Exec. Dir., Mike Weilbacher; Pres. Bd. Trustees, Timothy Szuhaj; Dir. Education, Elisabeth Zafiris; Dir. Wildlife Rehabilitation, Rick Schubert; Dir. Art Programs, Christian Catanese; Dir. Land & Facilities, Steve Goin; Dir. Devel., Casey Combs; Dir. Finance & Admin., Donna Struck; Gift Shop Mgr., Michelle Havens.
Institution Type/Description: Nature Center.

Hours & Admission Prices: Center: Mon.-Sat. 9-5. Trails: daily dawn to dusk. No charge; donations accepted. Closed New Year's Day; Easter; Memorial Day; Independence Day; Labor Day; Thanksgiving; Christmas. &

Attendance: 55,500 (actual)

SIMEONE FOUNDATION AUTOMOTIVE MUSEUM, 6825 Norwitch Dr., Philadelphia, PA 19153-3412. Tel.: 215-365-7233. Fax: 215-365-8230. Facebook: @SimeoneAutomotiveMuseum; Twitter: @SimeoneMuseum.

E-mail: amanda@simeonemuseum.org

Web Site: www.simeonemuseum.org

Formerly: Simeone Automotive Museum

Key Personnel: Exec. Dir., Fred Simeone; Operations Admin., Amanda Jimenez; Dir. Education, Rick Adams; Cur., Kevin Kelly; Facilities Mgr., Chris Neapolitan; Public Rels & Mktg., Ron Spangler.

Institution Type/Description: Sports Museum.

Hours & Admission Prices: Tues.-Fri. 10-6, Sat.-Sun. 10-4. Adults $12, seniors $10, students $8; discounts to AAM members; members & children under 8 no charge.

Attendance: 12,778 (actual)

THE STEPHEN GIRARD COLLECTION, Girard College #116, 2101 S. College Ave., Philadelphia, PA 19121-4857. Tel.: 215-787-4434. Fax: 215-787-4404.

E-mail: elaurent@girardcollege.edu

Web Site: www.girardcollege.edu

Key Personnel: Dir. Historical Resources, Kathy Haas; Pres. Girard College, Clarence D. Armbrister.

Institution Type/Description: Period Furniture & Decorative Arts Museum: located in Founder's Hall, Greek Revival Building designed by Thomas U. Walter, on the grounds of Girard College.

Hours & Admission Prices: Thurs. 9-2; group by appointment. No charge for individuals & small groups.

Attendance: 5,000 (actual)

TALLER PUERTORRIQUENO, 2721 N. 5th St., Philadelphia, PA 19133. Tel.: 215-426-3311. Fax: 215-426-5682. Facebook: @tallerpr.org; Twitter: @TallerPR.

E-mail: cfebo@tallerpr.org

Web Site: tallerpr.org

Formerly: Lorenzo Homar Gallery

Key Personnel: Exec. Dir., Dr. Carmen Febo-San Miguel, M.D.; Bd. Chair, Edgardo Gonzalez; Cur. & Exhibitions Mgr., Rafael Damast; Education Dir., Asdrey Irizarry; Cultural Enrichment Program Mgr., Adela Rivera-Rodriguez; Youth Artist Program Mgr. & Outreach Support, Daniel de Jesus; Cultural Enrichment & Education Facility Mgr., Carlos Pardo; Gift Shop Mgr., Aida Devine.

Institution Type/Description: Art Gallery.

Hours & Admission Prices: Mon.-Fri. 9-5, Sat. 9-4. No charge, donations accepted.

TEMPLE CONTEMPORARY, TYLER SCHOOL OF ART OF TEMPLE UNIVERSITY, 2001 N. 13th St., Philadelphia, PA 19122-6016. Tel.: 215-777-9138. Fax: 215-777-9143.

E-mail: sarah.biemiller@temple.edu

Web Site: tyler.temple.edu/temple-contemporary

Key Personnel: Dir., Robert Blackson; Asst. Dir., Sarah Biemiller.

Institution Type/Description: Art Gallery.

Hours & Admission Prices: Wed.-Sat. 11-6; other times by appointment. No charge. &

Attendance: 20,000 (estimated)

TREASURY OF FAITH MUSEUM, 830 N. Franklin St., Philadelphia, PA 19123. Tel.: 215-627-3389.

E-mail: tofmuseum@ukrcap.org

Web Site: www.ukrarcheparchy.us/index.php?categoryid=23

Institution Type/Description: Religious Museum.

Hours & Admission Prices: Call for hours. No charge; donations accepted.

U.S. MINT - PHILADELPHIA, 5th and Arch Sts., Philadelphia, PA 19106. Mailing Address: 151 N. Independence Mall E., Philadelphia, PA 19106-1886. Tel.: 215-408-0112.

Web Site: www.usmint.gov

Key Personnel: Acting Principal Deputy Dir., David Motl; Plant Mgr., Marc Landry.

Institution Type/Description: Numismatics Museum.

Hours & Admission Prices: Mon.-Fri. 9-4:30. No charge. Closed federal holidays. &

Attendance: 240,000 (actual)

UNIVERSITY OF PENNSYLVANIA MUSEUM OF ARCHAEOLOGY AND ANTHROPOLOGY, 3260 South St., Philadelphia, PA 19104-6324. Tel.: 215-898-4000. Fax: 215-898-0657.

E-mail: info@pennmuseum.org

Web Site: www.penn.museum

Key Personnel: Williams Dir., Julian Siggers, Ph.D.; Exec. Dir. Advancement, Amanda Mitchell-Boyask; Merle-Smith Dir. Learning & Public Engagement, Ellen M. Owens; Dir. Exhibits & Special Programs, Kate Quinn; C.O.O., Melissa P. Smith, C.F.A.; Deputy Dir. & Chief Cur., Stephen J. Tinney, Ph.D.

Institution Type/Description: University Archaeology & Anthropology Museum.

Hours & Admission Prices: Tues.-Sun. 10-5, first Wed. each month 10-8. Adults $18, seniors 65 & above $16, children 6-17; discounts to AAM & ICOM members; active military, children 5 & under, Penn Card holders & members no charge. Closed holidays. &

Attendance: 145,000 (estimated)

THE UNIVERSITY OF THE ARTS - ROSENWALD-WOLF GALLERY, 333 S. Broad St., Philadelphia, PA 19107-5839. Mailing Address: 320 S. Broad St., Philadelphia, PA 19102-4994. Tel.: 215-717-6480. Fax: 215-717-6468. Facebook: @uarts-rwg.

E-mail: ssachs@uarts.edu

Web Site: www.uarts.edu/about/rosenwald-wolf-gallery

Key Personnel: Dir., Sid Sachs.

Institution Type/Description: University Art Gallery.

Hours & Admission Prices: Mon.-Fri. 10-5, Sat.-Sun. 12-5. No charge. Closed academic holidays. &

Attendance: 30,000 (estimated)

THE VICTORIAN SOCIETY IN AMERICA, 1636 Sansom St., Philadelphia, PA 19103-5404. Tel.: 215-636-9872. Fax: 215-636-9873.

E-mail: info@victoriansociety.org

Web Site: www.victoriansociety.org

Key Personnel: Pres. (V), Kevin Rose; Business Mgr., Sue Verzella; Historian, C. Dudley Brown.

Institution Type/Description: Historical Society: housed in an1899 Victorian church.

Hours & Admission Prices: Mon.-Fri. 9-5. No charge. Closed New Year's Day; Memorial Day; Independence Day; Labor Day; Thanksgiving; Christmas.

WAGNER FREE INSTITUTE OF SCIENCE, 1700 W. Montgomery Ave., Philadelphia, PA 19121-3227. Tel.: 215-763-6529. Fax: 215-763-1299. Facebook: @WagnerFreeInstitute.

E-mail: info@wagnerfreeinstitute.org

Web Site: www.wagnerfreeinstitute.org

Key Personnel: Dir., Susan Glassman; Librarian & Archivist, Lynn Dorwaldt; Dir. Children's Education, Dana Semos; Children's Educator, Holly Clark.

Institution Type/Description: Natural History & Natural Science Museum.

Hours & Admission Prices: Museum: Tues.-Fri. 9-4. Museum: $10 suggested donation. Guided Tours: adults $15, seniors $10, children $5; discounts to members & groups. Education Programs: no charge. Closed national holidays.

Attendance: 18,000 (estimated)

WELLS FARGO HISTORY MUSEUM CLOSED, 123 S. Broad St., Philadelphia, PA 19109. Mailing Address: Wells Fargo Historical Svcs., 420 Montgomery St., MAC-A0101-022, San Francisco, CA 94163. Tel.: 215-670-6123. Fax: 215-670-6128. Facebook: Wells Fargo.

E-mail: historicalservices@wellsfargo.com

Web Site: www.wellsfargohistory.com

Key Personnel: Museum Mgr., Patrick Wittwer; Cur., Mandi Magnuson-Hung.

Institution Type/Description: Company History Museum: housed in a historic c.1928 Beaux-Arts building.

Hours & Admission Prices: Mon.-Thurs. 9-5, Fri. 9-6. No charge. Closed bank holidays. &

WOODMERE ART MUSEUM, 9201 Germantown Ave., Philadelphia, PA 19118-2618. Tel.: 215-247-0476. Fax: 215-247-2387. Facebook: @WoodmereArtMuseum; Twitter: @WoodmereArt.

E-mail: info@woodmereartmuseum.org

Web Site: www.woodmereartmuseum.org

Key Personnel: The Patricia Van Burgh Allison Dir. & C.E.O., William Valerio, Ph.D.; Pres., James Alexandre; Deputy Dir. Collections & Registrar, Sally Larson; Deputy Dir. Exhibitions, Rick Ortwein; Dir. Communications, Gabrielle Turgoose; The Klorfine Foundation Dir. Devel., Anne Standish; Dir. Finance, Nick Yzzi; The Robert L. McNeil, Jr. Cur. Education, Hildy Tow; Dir.

Foundation & Government Rels., Pamela Loos; Dir. Members Rels., Natalie Greene; Dir. Guest Svcs., Joe Pompilii; Dir. Museum Store, Stephen Kersner.

Institution Type/Description: Art Museum: housed in 1867 Victorian mansion with modern additions.

Hours & Admission Prices: Tues.-Thurs. & Sun. 10-5, Fri. 10-8:45, Sat. 10-6. Special Exhibitions: adults $10, senior citizens $7; discounts to AAM & ICOM members & Cultural Pass holders; Sun., members, children & college students with ID no charge. Closed selected holidays. &

Attendance: 48,000 (estimated)

WYCK, 6026 Germantown Ave., Philadelphia, PA 19144-2191. Tel.: 215-848-1690. Fax: 215-848-1612. Facebook: @wyckhousegarden; Instagram: @wyckhouse; Twitter: @Wyck_House.

E-mail: wyck@wyck.org

Web Site: www.wyck.org

Key Personnel: Exec. Dir., Jennifer L. Carlson; Co-Chair, Emily Lind Baker; Co-Chair, James Query; Devel. & Programs Mgr., Mariel Rosati; Home Farm Mgr., Kripa Dholakia.

Institution Type/Description: Historic Building Museum: housed in 18th-century building.

Hours & Admission Prices: April-Nov. Thurs.-Sat. noon to 4. Family $10, adults & children $5, senior citizens $4; discounts to AAM & ICOM members; members no charge. Closed New Year's Day; Independence Day; Christmas; Thanksgiving. &

Attendance: 3,681 (actual)

Phoenixville

HISTORICAL SOCIETY OF THE PHOENIXVILLE AREA, 204 Church St., Phoenixville, PA 19460-3414. Tel.: 610-933-7646.

E-mail: hspa@verizon.net

Web Site: www.hspa-pa.org

Key Personnel: Pres., Susan C. Marshall; Treas., Duane Parker; Devel., Richard Lusch; Public Rels., Martha Parker; Archivist, John R. Ertell; Office Mgr., Robert Deger.

Institution Type/Description: Historical Society Museum.

Hours & Admission Prices: Wed.-Fri. 9-3, 1st Sun. of month 1-4; other times by appointment. No charge; donations accepted. &

Attendance: 750 (actual)

Pittsburgh

THE ANDY WARHOL MUSEUM, 117 Sandusky St., Pittsburgh, PA 15212-5890. Tel.: 412-237-8300. Fax: 412-237-8340.

E-mail: information@warhol.org

Web Site: www.warhol.org

Key Personnel: Dir., Patrick Moore; Chair, Michele Fabrizi.

Institution Type/Description: Art Museum: industrial warehouse with ornate terra cotta clad facade, built 1911-22.

Hours & Admission Prices: Tues.-Thurs. & Sat.-Sun. 10-5, Fri. 10-10. Adults $20, students & children 3-18 $10; discounts Fri. 5-10 and AAM & ICOM members; members of Carnegie Museums of Pittsburgh no charge. Closed Memorial Day; Independence Day; Labor Day; Thanksgiving; Christmas. &

Attendance: 92,000

ASSOCIATED AMERICAN JEWISH MUSEUMS, 4905 Fifth Ave., Pittsburgh, PA 15213-2941. Tel.: 412-621-6566. Fax: 412-621-5475.

E-mail: jacob@rodefshalom.org

Key Personnel: C.E.O. & Pres. (V), Walter Jacob; Financial Dir., Jeff Herzog; Education, F. Pomerantz; Public Rels., Francine Rickenbach.

Institution Type/Description: Ethnic History Association.

Hours & Admission Prices: No charge; donations accepted.

Attendance: 5,000 (estimated)

AUGUST WILSON CENTER FOR AFRICAN AMERICAN CULTURE, 980 Liberty Ave., Pittsburgh, PA 15222-3736. Mailing Address: c/o Pittsburgh Cultural Trust, 803 Liberty Ave., Pittsburgh, PA 15222. Tel.: 412-258-2700 & 338-8725. Fax: 412-258-2701.

Web Site: culturaldistrict.org

Key Personnel: Co-Exec. Dir., Oliver Byrd; Co-Exec. Dir., Sala Udin; Chm. (V), Aaron Walton.

Institution Type/Description: Cultural Center.

Hours & Admission Prices: Tues.-Sat. 11-6. Adults $8, teachers $6, seniors & students $4; discounts to groups; members & NARM members no charge. Closed major holidays. &

Attendance: 27,000 (estimated)

BAYERNHOF MUSEUM, 225 St. Charles Pl., Pittsburgh, PA 15215. Tel.: 412-782-4231.

Web Site: bayernhofmuseum.com

Institution Type/Description: General Museum.

Hours & Admission Prices: By appointment. Admission 12 & over $10. Children under 12 not admitted. Closed major holidays.

BICYCLE HEAVEN BIKE MUSEUM, 1800 Preble & Columbus Ave., Pittsburgh, PA 15233. Tel.: 412-734-4034. Facebook.

E-mail: bikeheaven@comcast.net

Web Site: bicycleheaven.org

Key Personnel: Owner, Craig Morrow; Owner, Mindy Morrow.

Institution Type/Description: Bicycle Museum.

Hours & Admission Prices: Daily 10-7. No charge; donations accepted.

CARNEGIE MUSEUM OF ART, 4400 Forbes Ave., Pittsburgh, PA 15213-4080. Tel.: 412-622-3131. Fax: 412-622-5787. Facebook: Carnegie Museum of Art.

E-mail: visitorservices@carnegiemuseums.org

Web Site: www.cmoa.org

Key Personnel: Chm., Martin G. McGuinn; Dir. The Henry J. Heinz II, Lynn Zelevansky; Deputy Dir., Sarah Minnaert; Chief Cur., Catherine Evans; Cur. Fine Arts, Louise Lippincott; Cur. Architecture, Tracy Myers; Cur. Architecture, Raymund Ryan; Cur. Education, Marilyn M. Russell; Cur. Dec. Arts, Rachel Delphia; Chief Preparator, Kurt Christian; Chief Conservator, Ellen Baxter; Dir. Publications, Katie Reilly; Chief Registrar, Orian Neumann; Dir. Devel., Jamie McMahon; Dir. Mktg., Brad Stephenson; Media Rels. Mgr., Jonathan Gaugler; Mgr. Mktg. & Communications, Dacia Massengill.

Institution Type/Description: Art Museum: housed in 1896-1907, Alden and Harlow American Renaissance-style building & 1974 Edward Larrabee Barnes addition.

Hours & Admission Prices: Mon. & Wed.-Sat. 10-5, Thurs. 10-8, Sun. 12-5. Adults $19.95, seniors 65 & over $14.95, students w/ID & children 3-18 $11.95; discounts to AAM & ICOM members; members and children 2 & under no charge. Closed New Year's Day; Easter; Thanksgiving; Christmas. &

Attendance: 327,800 (actual)

CARNEGIE MUSEUM OF NATURAL HISTORY, 4400 Forbes Ave., Pittsburgh, PA 15213-4080. Tel.: 412-622-3131. Fax: 412-622-8837.

E-mail: cmnhweb@carnegiemnh.org

Web Site: www.carnegiemnh.org

Key Personnel: Interim Leadership Team & Interim Dir. Education and Visitor Experience, Jessica Lausch; Interim Leadership Team, Carnegie Museum of Natural History, Maureen Rolla; Dir. Finance, Robert Spoharski; Section Head & Collection Mgr., Marc Wilson; Collection Mgr. Amphibians & Reptiles, Stephen Rogers; Assoc. Cur. Botany, Dr. Cynthia Morton; Assoc. Cur., Invertebrate Zoology, Dr. John E. Rawlins; Assoc. Cur. Mollusks, Timothy Pearce; Cur. Public Programs, Mary Ann Steiner; Dir. Powdermill Nature Reserve, Dr. John Wenzel; Mgr. Library, Xianghua Sun; Vice Pres. CMP Devel., Dolores F. Ellenberg.

Institution Type/Description: Natural History & Anthropology Museum: housed in c.1896 American Renaissance style building.

Hours & Admission Prices: Mon., Wed. & Fri.-Sat. 10-5, Thurs. 10-8, Sun. 12-5; call to confirm. Adults $19.95, senior citizens 65 & over $14.95, students with ID & children 3-18 $11.95; discounts to AAM & ICOM members and Thurs. after 4 pm; members and children 2 & under no charge. Closed legal holidays. &

Attendance: 900,000 (estimated)

CARNEGIE MUSEUMS OF PITTSBURGH (CARNEGIE INSTITUTE), 4400 Forbes Ave., Pittsburgh, PA 15213-4080. Tel.: 412-622-3131.

E-mail: hannonj@carnegiemuseums.org

Web Site: www.carnegiemuseums.org

Key Personnel: Pres. & C.E.O., Jo Ellen Parker; C.F.O., Kevin D. Hiles; Vice Pres. Devel., Dolores F. Ellenberg; Vice Pres. Facilities, Planning & Operations, Tony Young; Dir. Corporate Human Resources, Beverly McGrath; Co-Dir. Henry Buhl, Jr., Carnegie Science Center, Ronald Baillie; Co-Dir. Henry Buhl, Jr., Carnegie Science Center, Ann Metzger; Mng. Dir. The Andy Warhol Museum, Patrick Moore; The Henry J. Heinz II Dir. Carnegie Museum of Art, Lynn Zelevansky; Dir., Carnegie Museum of Natural History, Eric Dorfman.

Institution Type/Description: General Museum.

Hours & Admission Prices: See The Andy Warhol Museum, Carnegie Museum of Art, Carnegie Museum of Natural History and Carnegie Science Center for hours & admission prices. &

Attendance: 1,407,373 (actual)

CARNEGIE SCIENCE CENTER, One Allegheny Ave., Pittsburgh, PA 15212-5895. Tel.: 412-237-3326. Fax: 412-237-3319. Facebook: Carnegie Science Center.

E-mail: reynoldsm@carnegiesciencecenter.org

Web Site: www.carnegiesciencecenter.org
Key Personnel: Henry Buhl, Jr. Co Dir., Ann Metzger; Henry Buhl, Jr. Co Dir., Ronald J. Baillie; Dir. Visitor Experience, Jessica Lausch; C.F.O., Kevin D. Hiles; Dir. Finance, Carol Casey; Vice Pres. Devel., Dolores F. Ellenberg; Sr. Dir. Devel. & Campaign Dir., Danni Piccolo; Museum Shop Mgr., Donna Riedford.
Institution Type/Description: Science and Technology Center.
Hours & Admission Prices: Sun.-Thurs. 10-5, Fri.-Sat. 10-7; call to confirm. Adults $19.95, children $11.95; discounts to groups, AAM, ASTC & ICOM members; members no charge. Closed Thanksgiving; Christmas; occasional Steelers home game days. &
Attendance: 541,207 (actual)

CENTER FOR AMERICAN MUSIC, University of Pittsburgh, Stephen Foster Memorial, 4301 Forbes Ave., Pittsburgh, PA 15260. Tel.: 412-624-4100. Fax: 412-624-7447.
E-mail: dir@pitt.edu
Web Site: www.pitt.edu/~amerimus/CAM1.htm
Key Personnel: Dir., Deane L. Root; Assoc. Dir., Kathryn Miller Haines.
Institution Type/Description: Music History Museum.
Hours & Admission Prices: By appointment only. Closed university holidays. &
Attendance: 3,497 (estimated)

CHILDREN'S MUSEUM OF PITTSBURGH, 10 Children's Way, Pittsburgh, PA 15212-5250. Tel.: 412-322-5058. Fax: 412-322-4932. Facebook.
E-mail: hi@pittsburghkids.org
Web Site: www.pittsburghkids.org
Formerly: Pittsburgh Children's Museum
Key Personnel: Exec. Dir., Jane Werner; Dir. External Affairs, Gina Evans; Pres., Michael Duckworth; Vice Pres., Karen Larimer; Sec., Winston Simmonds; Treas., Robert Denove; Dir. Finance, Christine Koebley; Dir. Visitor Svcs., Admissions & Museum Shop Mgr., George Brzezinski; Dir. Mktg., Bill Schlageter; Dir. Education, Chip Lindsey; Dir. New Media, Suzanne McCaffrey; Dir. Learning & Research, Lisa Brahms; Dir. Design, Anne Fullenkamp.
Institution Type/Description: Children's Museum.
Hours & Admission Prices: Daily 10-5. Adults $16, senior citizens and children 2 & over 2 $14; discounts to ASTC & ACM reciprocal memberships; members & children under 2 no charge. Closed New Year's Day; Memorial Day; Independence Day; Labor Day; Thanksgiving; Christmas. &
Attendance: 306,098 (actual)

CONTEMPORARY CRAFT, 2100 Smallman St., Pittsburgh, PA 15222-4440. Tel.: 412-261-7003. Fax: 412-261-1941. Facebook: Contemporary Craft.
E-mail: info@contemporarycraft.org
Web Site: www.contemporarycraft.org
Key Personnel: Exec. Dir., Janet L. McCall; Dir. Exhibitions, Kate Lydon; Finance Dir., Yu-San Cheng; Dir. Devel., Aaron Martin; Mktg. Mgr., Stephanie Sun.
Institution Type/Description: Contemporary Craft Museum.
Hours & Admission Prices: Mon.-Sat. 10-5. No charge; donations accepted. Closed major holidays. &
Attendance: 145,000 (estimated)

THE FORT PITT BLOCK HOUSE, 601 Commonwealth Pl., Bldg. C, Pittsburgh, PA 15222. Mailing Address: 101 Commonwealth Pl., Ste. 1, Point State Pk., Pittsburgh, PA 15222-1249. Tel.: 412-471-1764.
Web Site: www.fortpittblockhouse.com
Key Personnel: Pres. (V), Fort Pitt Society, Elizabeth Wheatley; Cur. & Museum Shop Mgr., James Haltturen.
Institution Type/Description: Historic Building: house in the Fort Pitt Block House; built in 1764.
Hours & Admission Prices: April-Oct. Wed.-Sun. 10:30-4:30; Nov.-March Fri.-Sun. 10:30-4:30. No charge; donations accepted. Closed most legal holidays. &
Attendance: 10,000 (estimated)

THE FRICK ART & HISTORICAL CENTER, 7227 Reynolds St., Pittsburgh, PA 15208-2919. Tel.: 412-371-0600. Fax: 412-371-6104.
E-mail: info@thefrickpittsburgh.org
Web Site: www.thefrickpittsburgh.org
Key Personnel: Dir., Robin Nicholson, Jr.; Chm., Carolyn Reed; Finance Mgr., Lisa Macioce; Dir. External Affairs, Susan S. Neszpaul; Dir. Operations & Visitor Svcs., Bill Nichols; Dir. Education, Amanda D. Gillen; Dir. Curatorial Affairs, Sarah Hall; Museum Store Mgr., Victoria Sumney.
Institution Type/Description: Art & History Museums.
Hours & Admission Prices: Tues.-Thurs. & Sat.-Sun. 10-5, Fri. 10-9. Clayton Tour: adults $12, seniors & students $10; discounts to AAM & ICOM members; members no charge. Other Venues: no charge; donations accepted; special exhibitions

charge may apply. Closed New Year's Day; Independence Day; Thanksgiving; Christmas Eve & Day. &
Attendance: 130,749 (actual)

HARTWOOD MANSION, 200 Hartwood Acres, Pittsburgh, PA 15238-1193. Tel.: 412-767-9200. Fax: 412-767-0171.
E-mail: patti.benaglio@alleghenycounty.us
Web Site: www.county.allegheny.pa.us/parks
Key Personnel: Manager, Patti Benaglio.
Institution Type/Description: Historic House Museum: housed in the former estate of John and Mary Flinn Lawrence, daughter of state Sen. William Flinn; built in 1929.
Hours & Admission Prices: Mon.-Sat. 10-3, Sun. 12-4. Adults $6, senior citizens 60 & over and children 13-17 $4, children 6-12 $2, children 5 & under $1. Public Holiday Teas: $33. Closed holidays.
Attendance: 3,000 (estimated)

HUNT INSTITUTE FOR BOTANICAL DOCUMENTATION, Carnegie Mellon University, 5000 Forbes Ave., Pittsburgh, PA 15213-3815. Tel.: 412-268-2434. Fax: 412-268-5677.
E-mail: huntinst@andrew.cmu.edu
Web Site: www.huntbotanical.org
Key Personnel: Dir., Dr. T. D. Jacobsen; Business Officer & Sales Mgr., Amy Ashley-Matta; Art Cur., Lugene B. Bruno; Librarian, Charlotte A. Tancin; Archivist, J. Dustin Williams.
Institution Type/Description: Science Art Institute.
Hours & Admission Prices: Mon.-Fri. 8:30-12 & 1-5, Sun. 1-4. No charge. Closed holidays.

MATTRESS FACTORY, LTD., 500 Sampsonia Way, Pittsburgh, PA 15212-4444. Tel.: 412-231-3169. Fax: 412-322-2231. Facebook: Mattress Factory.
E-mail: info@mattress.org
Web Site: www.mattress.org
Key Personnel: Co Dir. & Pres., Barbara Luderowski; Co Dir., Michael Olijnyk; Fundraising & Donor Relations Officer, Caitlin Harpster; Museum Shop Mgr., Sam Ditch.
Institution Type/Description: Art Museum.
Hours & Admission Prices: Tues.-Sat. 10-5, Sun. 1-5; other times by appointment. Adults $20, senior citizens & students $15; discounts to North American Reciprocal members; members & children under 6 no charge. Closed New Year's Day; Easter; Memorial Day; Thanksgiving; Christmas. &
Attendance: 75,000 (actual)

THE MILLER GALLERY AT CARNEGIE MELLON, Purnell Center for the Arts, Carnegie Mellon University, Pittsburgh, PA 15213-3890. Mailing Address: 5000 Forbes Ave., Pittsburgh, PA 15213-3890. Tel.: 412-268-3618. Fax: 412-268-4746.
E-mail: miller-gallery@andrew.cmu.edu
Web Site: www.cmu.edu/millergallery
Formerly: Regina Gouger Miller Gallery
Key Personnel: Asst. Dir., Margaret Cox.
Institution Type/Description: Art Gallery.
Hours & Admission Prices: Tues.-Sun. 12-6. No charge; donations accepted. &
Attendance: 15,000 (estimated)

NATIONAL AVIARY IN PITTSBURGH, INC., Allegheny Commons West, 700 Arch St., Pittsburgh, PA 15212-5248. Tel.: 412-323-7235. Fax: 412-321-4364. Facebook: National Aviary.
E-mail: info@aviary.org
Web Site: www.aviary.org
Key Personnel: Mng. Dir., Cheryl Tracy; Museum Shop Mgr., Lori Urbowitz.
Institution Type/Description: Aviary.
Hours & Admission Prices: Daily 10-5. Adults $14, seniors 60 & up $13, children 2-12 $12; discounts to AZA Reciprocal members; members & children 2 & under no charge. Closed Thanksgiving; Christmas Eve & Day. &
Attendance: 140,000 (actual)

PHIPPS CONSERVATORY AND BOTANICAL GARDENS, 1 Schenley Park, Pittsburgh, PA 15213-3830. Mailing Address: 1059 Shady Ave., Pittsburgh, PA 15232-2912. Tel.: 412-622-6914. Fax: 412-622-7363.
E-mail: info@phipps.conservatory.org
Web Site: www.phipps.conservatory.org
Key Personnel: Dir., Richard Piacentini; Chm. (V), Scott Lammie.
Institution Type/Description: Conservatory.
Hours & Admission Prices: Fri. 9:30am-10pm, Sat.-Thurs. 9:30-5. Adult $15, seniors & children 2-18 $11; discounts to groups of 15 or more & AAA mem-

bers; children under 2 & members no charge. Closed Thanksgiving; Christmas. &
Attendance: 368,826 (estimated)

PITTSBURGH FILMMAKERS/PITTSBURGH CENTER FOR THE ARTS, 6300 Fifth Ave., Pittsburgh, PA 15232-2922. Tel.: 412-361-0873 & 0455. Fax: 412-361-8338.
E-mail: info@pittsburgharts.org
Web Site: www.pittsburgharts.org
Key Personnel: CEO, Germaine Williams; Dir. Special Events, Joy Sato.
Institution Type/Description: Contemporary Arts Center.
Hours & Admission Prices: Tues.-Fri. 10-5, Sat. 10-3, Sun. 12-4. Adults $5, seniors 62 & over $4, students $3; children 12 & under, members, and CMU faculty & staff no charge. Closed Christmas. &
Attendance: 36,067 (actual)

PITTSBURGH ZOO AND PPG AQUARIUM, One Wild Place, Pittsburgh, PA 15206. Tel.: 412-665-3639, ext. 0. Fax: 412-665-3661.
E-mail: bbaker@pittsburghzoo.org
Web Site: www.pittsburghzoo.org
Key Personnel: C.E.O. & Pres., Dr. Barbara T. Baker.
Institution Type/Description: Zoo & Aquarium.
Hours & Admission Prices: Spring & Fall daily 9-5 (gates close at 4); Winter daily 9-4 (gates close at 3); Summer daily 9-6 (gates close at 4:30). Adults $15, senior citizens $14, children 2-13 $13; discount to groups; children under 24 months, military w/I.D. & members no charge. Closed New Year's Day; Thanksgiving; Christmas. &
Attendance: 941,116 (actual)

RODEF SHALOM BIBLICAL BOTANICAL GARDEN, 4905 5th Ave., Pittsburgh, PA 15213-2941. Tel.: 412-621-6566. Fax: 412-621-5475.
E-mail: wjacob303@aol.com
Web Site: www.biblicalgardenpittsburgh.org
Key Personnel: C.E.O., Harlan Stone; Dir., Walter Jacob.
Institution Type/Description: Biblical Botanical Garden.
Hours & Admission Prices: June to mid-Sept. Sun.-Tues. & Thurs. 10-2, Wed. 7-9, Sat. 12-1. No charge. &
Attendance: 3,500 (estimated)

SENATOR JOHN HEINZ HISTORY CENTER, 1212 Smallman St., Pittsburgh, PA 15222-4200. Tel.: 412-454-6000. Fax: 412-454-6031.
E-mail: nschano@heinzhistorycenter.org
Web Site: www.heinzhistorycenter.org
Formerly: Senator John Heinz Pittsburgh Regional History Center
Key Personnel: Pres. & C.E.O., Andrew E. Masich; Senior Vice Pres., Betty Arenth; Dir. Mktg. & Communications, Ned Schano; Dir. Human Resources, Renee Falbo; Chief Archivist, Matthew Strauss; Education & Enterprise, Sandra Smith; Education Mgr., Mariruth Leftwich; Dir. Events, Maura Minteer.
Institution Type/Description: History Museum.
Hours & Admission Prices: History Center & Sports Museum: daily 10-5. Adults $16, senior citizen 62 & over $14, retired & active military, students with valid ID, children 6-17 $6.50, children under 5 & members no charge. Closed New Year's Day; Easter; Thanksgiving; Christmas. &
Attendance: 160,000 (estimated)

SILVER EYE CENTER FOR PHOTOGRAPHY, 1015 E. Carson St., Pittsburgh, PA 15203-1109. Tel.: 412-431-1810. Fax: 412-431-5777.
E-mail: info@silvereye.org
Web Site: www.silvereye.org
Institution Type/Description: Art Gallery.
Hours & Admission Prices: Tues.-Sat. 12-6. No charge; donations accepted. &

SOLDIERS & SAILORS MILITARY MUSEUM & MEMORIAL, 4141 Fifth Ave., Pittsburgh, PA 15213. Tel.: 412-621-4253. Fax: 412-683-9339.
E-mail: curator@soldiersandsailorshall.org
Key Personnel: C.E.O., John F. McCabe.
Institution Type/Description: Military History Museum.
Hours & Admission Prices: Mon.-Sat. 10-4. Adults $5-$8; members, military & veterans no charge. Closed New Year's Day; Independence Day; Labor Day; Thanksgiving; Christmas. &

THEATRE HISTORICAL SOCIETY OF AMERICA, 461 Cochran Rd., Ste 1, Pittsburgh, PA 15228-1253. Tel.: 630-782-1800. Fax: 630-782-1802.

E-mail: execdirector@historictheatres.org
Web Site: historictheatres.org
Key Personnel: Exec. Dir., Richard Fosbrink; Dir. Archives, Kathy McLeister; Pres. (V), Karen Colizzi Noonan.
Institution Type/Description: Historical Society Museum.
Hours & Admission Prices: Tues.-Fri. 9-4 by appointment. No charge; donations accepted.
Attendance: 1,500 (estimated)

UNIVERSITY ART GALLERY, UNIVERSITY OF PITTSBURGH, 650 Schenley Dr., Frick Fine Arts Bldg., Rm. 104, University of Pittsburgh, Pittsburgh, PA 15260-7601. Tel.: 412-648-2423. Fax: 412-648-2792. Facebook: University Art Gallery, University of Pittsburgh.
E-mail: uag@pitt.edu
Web Site: www.haa.pitt.edu/collections/university-art-gallery
Key Personnel: Dept. Chm., Barbara McCloskey.
Institution Type/Description: Art Gallery; housed in 1965 building by Helen Clay Frick.
Hours & Admission Prices: Academic Year: Mon.-Fri. 10-4; other times by appointment. No charge. Closed holidays; university breaks. &
Attendance: 5,100 (actual)

WOOD STREET GALLERIES, 601 Wood St., Pittsburgh, PA 15222-2503. Tel.: 412-471-5605. Fax: 412-232-3262. Facebook: Wood St Galleries; Twitter: woodstreetpgh.
E-mail: info@woodstreetgalleries.org
Web Site: www.woodstreetgalleries.org
Key Personnel: Cur., Murray Horne; Asst. Cur., Amy Staggs; Preparator, George Dun; Preparator, Chris Korch; Preparator, Craig Smith; Preparator, Dave Zak; Preparator, Nate Curtiss; Preparator, Stephanie Defelice.
Institution Type/Description: Contemporary Gallery.
Hours & Admission Prices: Wed.-Thurs. 11-6, Fri.-Sat. 11-8, Sun. 11-5. No charge; donations accepted. &
Attendance: 10,000 (estimated)

Pleasantville

PITHOLE VISITOR CENTER, 14118 Pithole Rd., Pleasantville, PA 16341. Mailing Address: c/o Drake Well Museum, 202 Museum Ln., Titusville, PA 16354-7658. Tel.: 814-827-2797 (Drake Well). Fax: 814-827-4888 (Drake Well).
E-mail: drakewell@verizon.net
Key Personnel: C.E.O., James M. Vaughan; Chm., Stephen Miller; Site Mgr., Barbara Zolli.
Institution Type/Description: Oil Well Museum.
Hours & Admission Prices: Call for hours.
Attendance: 2,000 (estimated)

Plymouth

PLYMOUTH HISTORICAL SOCIETY, INC., 115 Gaylord Ave., Plymouth, PA 18651-2200. Mailing Address: 157 Nottingham St., Plymouth, PA 18651. Tel.: 570-779-5840.
E-mail: georgettapotoski@aol.com
Web Site: www.locallivinghistorypa.com/phs/home.htm
Key Personnel: Dir. & Pres. (V), Stephen Kondrad; Treas., Helen Yonells; Public Rels., Chris Pagoda; Museum Shop Mgr., Mary Langdon.
Institution Type/Description: Historical Society Museum.
Hours & Admission Prices: Thurs. & Sat. 12-4; other times by appointment. No charge; donations accepted.
Attendance: 500 (actual)

Point Marion

FRIENDSHIP HILL NATIONAL HISTORIC SITE, 223 New Geneva Rd., Point Marion, PA 15474. Mailing Address: 1 Washington Pkwy., Farmington, PA 15437-9501. Tel.: 724-725-9190. Fax: 724-725-1999.
E-mail: lawren_dunn@nps.gov
Web Site: www.nps.gov/frhi
Key Personnel: Deputy Supt., Keith Newlin; Supt., Jeffrey P. Reinbold; Unit Mgr. & Chief Law Enforcement Ranger, Norman W. Nelson; Cultural Resource Mgr. & Cur., Lawren Dunn; Museum Shop Mgr., James Tomasek.
Institution Type/Description: History Museum.
Hours & Admission Prices: Park: daily dawn to dusk. Building: Summer: daily 9-5; Winter: Sat.-Sun. 9-5. No charge; donations accepted. Closed Federal holidays; New Year's Day; Martin Luther King Jr. Day; George Washington's Birthday; Veterans Day; Thanksgiving; Christmas. &
Attendance: 50,000 (estimated)

Pottstown

POTTSGROVE MANOR, 100 W. King St., Pottstown, PA 19464-6318. Tel.: 610-326-4014. Fax: 610-326-9618. Facebook: Pottsgrove Manor.
E-mail: pottsgrovemanor@montcopa.org
Web Site: www.montcopa.org/pottsgrovemanor
Key Personnel: Region Mgr., Michelle Harris; Cur., Amy Reis.
Institution Type/Description: Historic House: 1752 Pottsgrove Manor.
Hours & Admission Prices: Tues.-Sat. 10-4, Sun. 1-4. No charge; donations accepted. Closed New Year's Day; Easter; Independence Day; Thanksgiving; Christmas. &
Attendance: 5,000 (estimated)

Pottsville

JEWISH MUSEUM OF EASTERN PENNSYLVANIA, 2400 W. End Ave., Pottsville, PA 17901. Tel.: 570-622-5890.
Institution Type/Description: Jewish History Museum.
Hours & Admission Prices: By appointment only. No charge. &

SCHUYLKILL COUNTY HISTORICAL SOCIETY, 305 N. Centre St., Pottsville, PA 17901-2512. Mailing Address: P.O. Box 1356, Pottsville, PA 17901-7356. Tel.: 570-622-7540. Facebook.
E-mail: sch.hist@comcast.net
Web Site: www.schuylkillhistory.org
Key Personnel: Exec. Dir., Thomas Drogalis; Chm. (V), R. Jay Zane, Esq.; Museum Shop Mgr., Diana Prosymchak.
Institution Type/Description: Historical Society Museum.
Hours & Admission Prices: Wed.-Fri. 10-4, Sat. 10-2. Adults $3; members no charge. &
Attendance: 1,000 (estimated)

Prospect Park

MORTON HOMESTEAD, 100 Lincoln Ave., Prospect Park, PA 19076. Mailing Address: 923 7th Ave., Prospect Park, PA 19076-2307. Facebook: Prospect Park Historical Society.
E-mail: PPHS19076@gmail.com
Key Personnel: Pres. & C.E.O., Glen J. Schwenke; Vice Pres., John R. Shemeluk; Sec. & Treas., Patricia J. Schwenke.
Institution Type/Description: History Museum: housed in late 17th-century Morton Homestead.
Hours & Admission Prices: Temporarily closed. &
Attendance: 2,000 (estimated)

Punxsutawney

PUNXSUTAWNEY AREA HISTORICAL & GENEALOGICAL SOCIETY, 400-401 W. Mahoning St., Punxsutawney, PA 15767. Mailing Address: P.O. Box 286, Punxsutawney, PA 15767-0286. Tel.: 814-938-2555.
E-mail: punxsutawneyhistory@verizon.net
Web Site: punxsutawneyhistory.org
Key Personnel: Chm. (V), Elmer Reed; Pres. (V), Nancy Anthony; Museum Shop Mgr., Karen Curry.
Institution Type/Description: Historical Society Museum.
Hours & Admission Prices: Bennis House & Lattimer House: Thurs.-Sun. 1-4. Genealogy: Lattimer House Thurs. & Sat. 10-1. No charge; donations accepted. &
Attendance: 1,000 (estimated)

PUNXSUTAWNEY WEATHER DISCOVERY CENTER, 201 N. Findley St., Punxsutawney, PA 15767. Tel.: 814-938-1000. Facebook.
E-mail: info@weatherdiscovery.org
Web Site: www.weatherdiscovery.org
Institution Type/Description: Science Museum.
Hours & Admission Prices: Jan.-March Mon. & Thurs.-Sat. 10-4; April-May & Sept. Mon.-Tues. & Thurs.-Sat. 10-4; June-Aug. Mon.-Sat. 10-4. Adults $6; children 2 & under no charge. &

Quarryville

SOUTHERN LANCASTER COUNTY HISTORICAL SOCIETY, INC. A/K/A SOLANCO HISTORICAL SOCIETY, 1932 Robert Fulton Hwy., P.O. Box 33, Quarryville, PA 17566. Mailing Address: P.O. Box 33, Quarryville, PA 17566-0033. Tel.: 717-548-2679. Facebook.

E-mail: solancohistorical@gmail.com
Web Site: southernlancasterhistory.org
Key Personnel: Pres., Stanley White; Vice Pres., George A. Stiles; Dir., Robert Highfield; Dir., Barclay Richards.
Institution Type/Description: Historic House: c.1760 Robert Fulton birthplace.
Hours & Admission Prices: Birthplace: Memorial Day-Labor Day Sat. & holidays 11-4. SLCHS Archives: June-Aug. Wed. 9-12; Sept.-May Wed. 9-12, 2nd & 4th Sat. 9-12. Guided Tours: Sept.-May: Adults $5, Youth 6-18 $3 (2 for $5); members & children under 6 no charge. &
Attendance: 1,000 (estimated)

Reading

BERKS COUNTY HERITAGE CENTER, 1102 Red Bridge Rd., Reading, PA 19605. Mailing Address: 2201 Tulpehocken Rd., Wyomissing, PA 19610-1020. Tel.: 610-374-8839. Fax: 610-373-7049. Facebook: Berks county Parks and Recreation.
E-mail: cwegener@countyofberks.com
Web Site: www.co.berks.pa.us/parks/cwp
Key Personnel: Dir., Cathy L. Wegener.
Institution Type/Description: History Museum.
Hours & Admission Prices: May-Oct. Tues.-Sat. 10-4, Sun. 12-5. Adults $5, senior citizens 60 & over $4, students 7-18 $3; children under 7 no charge. &
Attendance: 10,000 (estimated)

CENTRAL PENNSYLVANIA AFRICAN AMERICAN MUSEUM, Old Bethel African Methodist Episcopal Church, 119 N. Tenth St., Reading, PA 19601-3704. Tel.: 610-371-8713.
E-mail: CPAAM@verizon.net
Web Site: www.cpaam.net
Key Personnel: Dir., C.E.O. & Pres. (V), Frank L. Gilyard, Sr.
Institution Type/Description: History Museum.
Hours & Admission Prices: Wed. & Fri. 10:30-1:30, Sat. 1-3 by appointment. Adults $8, senior citizens $6, children 5-12 $4; discounts to groups of 20 or more; children 4 & under no charge.
Attendance: 300

FREEDMAN GALLERY-ALBRIGHT COLLEGE, 13th St. & Bern St., Reading, PA 19604. Mailing Address: Box 15234, Reading, PA 19612-5234. Tel.: 610-921-7541. Fax: 610-921-7768.
E-mail: gallery@alb.org
Web Site: www.albright.edu/freedman
Key Personnel: Dir. Center for the Arts, David M. Tanner; Cur., Erin Riley-Lopez; Cur. Education, Beth Krumholz; Collections Mgr. & Preparator, Nancy Sarangoulis.
Institution Type/Description: College Art Gallery.
Hours & Admission Prices: Sept.-May Tues.-Fri. 10-5, Sat.-Sun. 1-4; Summer: call for hours. No charge; donations accepted. Closed major holidays & college breaks. &
Attendance: 4,457 (actual)

HISTORICAL SOCIETY OF BERKS COUNTY DBA BERKS HISTORY CENTER, 940 Centre Ave., Reading, PA 19601-2198. Tel.: 610-375-4375. Fax: 610-375-4376.
E-mail: history@berkshistory.org
Web Site: www.berkshistory.org
Key Personnel: Pres., Susan Yatron; Dir., Sime B. Bertolet; Communications, Alexis Campbell.
Institution Type/Description: History Museum & Archive.
Hours & Admission Prices: Museum: Tues.-Fri. 10-3, Sat. 9-3. Library: Wed.-Fri. 8-5, Sat. 8-4. Adults $7, senior citizens $5, children $4; members no charge. &
Attendance: 15,000 (estimated)

MID ATLANTIC AIR MUSEUM, 11 Museum Dr., Reading, PA 19605-9407. Tel.: 610-372-7333. Fax: 610-372-1702.
E-mail: maam@maam.org
Web Site: www.maam.org
Key Personnel: Pres., Russell A. Strine; Office Mgr., Brenda Saylor.
Institution Type/Description: Aviation Museum.
Hours & Admission Prices: Daily 9:30-4. Adults $10, seniors $8, children 6-12 $3; members & children 5 and under no charge. Closed New Year's Eve & Day; MLK Day; Presidents' Day; Easter; Memorial Day; Independence Day; Thanksgiving; Christmas Eve & Day. &
Attendance: 30,000 (actual)

NEAG PLANETARIUM AT THE READING PUBLIC MUSEUM, 1211 Parkside Dr. S., Reading, PA 19611-1441. Mailing Address: 500 Museum Rd., Reading, PA 19611-1425. Tel.: 610-371-5850, ext. 244. Fax: 610-371-5632.
E-mail: planetarium@readingpublicmuseum.org

Web Site: www.readingpublicmuseum.org/planetarium
Key Personnel: Chm. (V), Rolf D. Schmidt; 1st Vice Chm. (V), Kathleen W. Kleppinger; 2nd Vice Chm. (V), Donald Bristol; Dir. Planetarium, Mark J. Mazurkiewicz.
Institution Type/Description: Planetarium.
Hours & Admission Prices: Tues.-Thurs. & Sat. 11-5, Fri. 11-8, Sun. 12-5. Museum: adults $7, children $5. Star Shows: adults $6, seniors, children & students $4; discounts to AAM & ICOM members; children under 4 & members no charge. Closed New Year's Day; Martin Luther King Jr. Day; Labor Day; Thanksgiving; Christmas. &
Attendance: 17,000 (actual)

READING AREA FIREFIGHTERS MUSEUM, INC., 501 S. 5th St., Reading, PA 19602. Tel.: 610-655-6080.
E-mail: rdgfiremuseum@gmail.com
Web Site: www.readingareafirefightersmuseum.com
Key Personnel: Pres. (V), William H. Rehr, III.
Institution Type/Description: Firefighting History Museum.
Hours & Admission Prices: Call for hours. No charge; donations accepted.

READING PUBLIC MUSEUM, 500 Museum Rd., Reading, PA 19611-1425. Tel.: 610-371-5850. Fax: 610-371-5632. Facebook: Reading Public Museum.
E-mail: info@readingpublicmuseum.org
Web Site: www.readingpublicmuseum.org
Key Personnel: Chm., David Meas; Dir. & C.E.O., John Graydon Smith; Planetarium Dir., Mark Mazurkiewicz; Cur. Art & Civilization, Scott Schweigert; Collections Mgr. & Registrar, Ashley Hamilton Houston; Mgr. Education, Wendy Koller; Mgr. Mktg., Emily Moore.
Institution Type/Description: Art & Science Museum.
Hours & Admission Prices: Daily 11-5. Adults $10, children 4-17, seniors & college students $6; discounts as part of ASTC reciprocal agreement; children 3 & under & members no charge. Closed New Year's Day; Thanksgiving; Christmas. &
Attendance: 70,000 (estimated)

Rockhill Furnace

ROCKHILL TROLLEY MUSEUM, 430 Meadow St., Rockhill Furnace, PA 17249. Mailing Address: P.O. Box 203, Rockhill Furnace, PA 17249. Tel.: 814-447-9576 (weekends), 610-437-0448 (weekdays). Facebook: Rockhill Trolley.
E-mail: info@rockhilltrolley.org
Web Site: www.rockhilltrolley.org
Key Personnel: Pres., Joel Salomon; Archivist, Douglas Peters; Museum Shop Mgr., Charles T. Kumpas.
Institution Type/Description: Transportation Museum.
Hours & Admission Prices: June-Oct. Sat.-Sun. 11-4. Adults $7, children 2-12 $4; discounts to groups, AAA & AARP members; members no charge.
Attendance: 5,000 (estimated)

Rome

P. P. BLISS GOSPEL SONGWRITERS MUSEUM, Main St., Rome, PA 18837. Mailing Address: P.O. Box 84, Rome, PA 18837. Tel.: 570-247-2228.
E-mail: ppbmuseum@cableracer.com
Key Personnel: Dir., Deborah Barrett.
Institution Type/Description: History Museum: housed in the former home of Mr. Bliss' parents.
Hours & Admission Prices: Memorial Day to Labor Day Wed. & Sat. 1-4; other times by appointment.

Russell

SHED MUSEUM, 7159 Scandia Rd., Russell, PA 16345-6941. Tel.: 814-757-4443.
E-mail: thehedscandia@verizon.net
Web Site: www.theshedscandia.com
Key Personnel: Dir., Debbie Fitzsimmons.
Institution Type/Description: History Museum.
Hours & Admission Prices: May-Oct. Fri.-Sun. 11-5 & by appointment. No charge.
Attendance: 400 (estimated)

Saint Marys

HISTORICAL SOCIETY OF ST. MARYS AND BENZINGER TOWNSHIP, 99 Erie Ave., Saint Marys, PA 15857-1408. Tel.: 814-834-6525.
E-mail: stmaryshistoricalsociety@windstream.net

Web Site: smhistoricalsociety.com
Key Personnel: Cur., Alice Beimel.
Institution Type/Description: History Museum.
Hours & Admission Prices: Tues. 10-4, Thurs. 1-4 & 6-8; other times by appointment. No charge. &
Attendance: 1,500 (estimated)

Schaefferstown

HISTORIC SCHAEFFERSTOWN, INC., 106 N. Market St., Schaefferstown, PA 17088. Mailing Address: P.O. Box 307, Schaefferstown, PA 17088-0307. Tel.: 717-949-2444.
E-mail: info@hsimuseum.org
Web Site: www.hsimuseum.org
Key Personnel: Pres., Alice Oskam; Museum Shop Mgr., Betty Fromm.
Institution Type/Description: Village Museum.
Hours & Admission Prices: Alexander Schaeffer Farm Museum: April-Oct. 4 1st Sat. of month 10-4. Festivals: 10-5. Adults $5; children under 12 & members no charge. Brendle Museum & Gemberling Rex House: April 4 to Oct. 4 Tues. 1-4, 1st Sat. of month 10-4; other times by appointment. Adults $3 per site; discounts to AAM & ICOM members; members no charge.
Attendance: 4,863 (actual)

Schnecksville

LEHIGH VALLEY ZOO, 5150 Game Preserve Rd., Schnecksville, PA 18078-0519. Mailing Address: P.O. Box 519, Schnecksville, PA 18078-0519. Tel.: 610-799-4171. Fax: 610-799-4170.
E-mail: mborland@lvzoo.org
Web Site: lvzoo.org
Key Personnel: Pres. & CEO, Melissa Borland; Dir. Devel., Doreen Carl; Dir. Education, Cher Vatalaro; Dir. Guest Svcs., Melissa Rosevear; Dir. Veterinary Svcs. & Chief Veterinian, Scott Rosenbloom, VMD; Gen. Curator, Richard Rosevear; Mgr. Facilities & Grounds, Josh Stettler.
Institution Type/Description: Zoo.
Hours & Admission Prices: April-Oct. daily 10-4; Nov.-March daily 10-3. March: admission $10; children under 2 no charge; April-Oct.: adults $13, seniors 65 & over $12, children 2-11 $11; children under 2 no charge; Nov.-Feb.: admission $8; children under 2 no charge. &
Attendance: 213,814 (estimated)

Schwenksville

PENNYPACKER MILLS, 5 Haldeman Rd., Schwenksville, PA 19473-1844. Mailing Address: c/o Montgomery County Parks, Trails, & Historic Sites, P.O. Box 311, Norristown, PA 19404-0311. Tel.: 610-287-9349. Fax: 610-287-9657. Facebook Pennypacker Mills.
E-mail: pennypackermills@montcopa.org
Web Site: www.montcopa.org/pennypackermills
Key Personnel: Historic Site Administrator, Ella Aderman.
Institution Type/Description: Historic House: c.1901-1916 colonial revival building.
Hours & Admission Prices: Tues.-Sat. 10-4, Sun. 1-4; last tour 3:30. Suggested Donation: $2. Closed New Year's Eve & Day; Easter; Independence Day; Thanksgiving; Christmas Eve & Day. &
Attendance: 25,000 (actual)

Scottdale

WEST OVERTON MUSEUMS, 109 West Overton Rd., Scottdale, PA 15683. Tel.: 724-887-7910.
E-mail: info@westovertonvillage.org
Web Site: www.westovertonvillage.org
Formerly: Westmoreland Fayette Historical Society
Key Personnel: Pres. Bd., Brian Corcoran; Dir., Kelly Linn; Asst. Dir., Jessica Kadie-Barclay.
Institution Type/Description: Museum Complex: c.1850 rural industrial village.
Hours & Admission Prices: Call or see website for information. &
Attendance: 5,000 (estimated)

Scranton

ELECTRIC CITY TROLLEY MUSEUM, 300 Cliff Ave., Scranton, PA 18503. Tel.: 570-963-6590. Fax: 570-963-6447.
E-mail: webmaster@ectma.org
Web Site: ectma.org
Institution Type/Description: Trolley Museum: housed in a late 19th century mill building.

Hours & Admission Prices: Museum: daily 9-4. Trolley Excursions: May-Oct. Thurs.-Sun. 10:30, 12, 1:30 & 3; Dec. call for hours. Closed New Year's Day; Thanksgiving; Christmas. &
Attendance: 30,000 (actual)

EVERHART MUSEUM: NATURAL HISTORY, SCIENCE AND ART, 1901 Mulberry St., Scranton, PA 18510-2390. Tel.: 570-346-7186. Fax: 570-346-0652.
E-mail: general.information@everhart-museum.org
Web Site: www.everhart-museum.org
Key Personnel: C.E.O. & Dir., Cara A. Sutherland; Chm. Bd., Joseph F. Cortin; Dir. Interpretive Programs, Stefanie Colarusso; Cur., Nezka Pfeifer; Museum Shop Mgr., Deb Burke; Administrative Asst., Nancy Casey; Dir. Resources, Deborah L. Pann.
Institution Type/Description: Art, Science & Natural History Museum.
Hours & Admission Prices: Feb.-Dec. Mon. & Thurs.-Fri. 12-4, Sat. 10-5, Sun. 12-5. Adults $7, students & seniors $5, children $3; discounts to AAM & ICOM members; children under 6 & members no charge. &
Attendance: 30,000 (estimated)

THE HOUDINI MUSEUM & THEATER, 1433 N. Main Ave., Scranton, PA 18508-1822. Mailing Address: 229 Willow Ave., Olyphant, PA 18447-1443. Tel.: 570-342-5555.
E-mail: magicus@comcast.net
Web Site: www.houdini.org
Key Personnel: Devel., Penny Wilkes; Public Rels., Dick Brooks; Education, Dorothy Dietrich.
Institution Type/Description: History Museum.
Hours & Admission Prices: July to Labor Day daily 1-6; Sept.-June Sat.-Sun. 1-6; other times by appointment.
Attendance: 40,000 (estimated)

THE LACKAWANNA HISTORICAL SOCIETY AT THE CATLIN HOUSE, 232 Monroe Ave., Scranton, PA 18510-2104. Tel.: 570-344-3841. Fax: 570-344-3815.
E-mail: lackawannahistory@gmail.com
Web Site: lackawannahistory.org
Key Personnel: Exec. Dir., Mary Ann Moran-Savakinus; Pres., Michael Gilmartin; Treas., Douglas Forrer; Sec., William Conlogue; Museum Asst., Sarah Piccini.
Institution Type/Description: Historic Society Museum: housed in The Catlin House, a late Victorian mansion in English Tudor Revival architecture.
Hours & Admission Prices: Tues.-Fri. 10-5, Sat. 12-3. Guided Tours: Tues.-Fri. 1-3, Sat. 12-3 or by appointment. Museum: $2 per person; donations accepted. Library: $5 per person. Closed New Year's; Good Friday; Memorial Day; Independence Day; Labor Day; Thanksgiving; Christmas Eve & Day. &
Attendance: 4,000 (estimated)

PENNSYLVANIA ANTHRACITE HERITAGE MUSEUM, 22 Bald Mountain Rd., McDade Park, Scranton, PA 18504. Tel.: 570-963-4804. Fax: 570-963-4194.
E-mail: ckulesa@state.pa.us
Web Site: anthracitemuseum.org
Key Personnel: Site Admin., Chester Kulesa.
Institution Type/Description: History Museum.
Hours & Admission Prices: April-Nov. Mon.-Sat. 9-5, Sun. 12-5; Dec.-March Tues.-Sat. 9-5, Sun. 12-5. Adults 12-64 $7, senior citizens 65 & over $6, youth 3-11 $5; discounts to AAM & ICOM; active military, family, children under 6 & members no charge. Closed New Year's Day; Martin Luther King, Jr. Day; Presidents' Day; Columbus Day; Veterans Day; Thanksgiving & day after; Christmas. &
Attendance: 20,000 (actual)

STEAMTOWN NATIONAL HISTORIC SITE, 350 Cliff St. off Lackawanna Ave., Scranton, PA 18503. Mailing Address: 150 S. Washington Ave., Scranton, PA 18503-2079. Tel.: 570-340-5206 & 5200. Fax: 570-340-5196.
E-mail: kathy_lang@nps.gov
Web Site: www.nps.gov/stea
Institution Type/Description: Railroad History Museum: housed on a working railroad yard.
Hours & Admission Prices: Jan. 6-March 29 daily 10-4; March 30-Jan. 5 daily 9-5. Fee charged for special events. Train Excursion Rides: call for information & prices. Closed New Year's Day; Thanksgiving; Christmas. &
Attendance: 100,000 (actual)

SURACI GALLERY, MAHADY GALLERY, AND THE MASLOW COLLECTION, 2300 Adams Ave., Scranton, PA 18509-1598. Tel.: 570-348-6278, ext. 2428. Fax: 570-340-6023.
E-mail: gallery@marywood.edu
Web Site: www.themaslowcollection.org

Formerly: Marywood University Art Galleries (Suraci Gallery and Contemporary Gallery)
Key Personnel: C.E.O. & Pres., Sister Anne Munley, I.H.M., Ph.D.; Dir., Sandra Ward Povse.
Institution Type/Description: University Art Gallery.
Hours & Admission Prices: Winter: Mon. & Thurs.-Fri. 9-4, Tues.-Wed. 9-8, Sat.-Sun. 1-4. Summer: Mon.-Fri. 12-3. No charge. Closed major holidays; semester breaks. &
Attendance: 17,525 (estimated)

TIMMY'S TOWN CENTER, The Mall at Steamtown, 2nd Fl., Scranton, PA 18503. Mailing Address: 240 Penn Ave., Scranton, PA 18503-1932. Tel.: 570-341-1511. Fax: 540-504-3209.
E-mail: timmystowncenter@verizon.net
Web Site: www.timmystowncenter.org
Key Personnel: Dir., Megan Swann; C.E.O., Alexis Kelly.
Institution Type/Description: Children's Museum.
Hours & Admission Prices: Thurs.-Sat. 10-4, Sun. 12-4. Admission $3; discounts to ACM members; members & children under 2 no charge.
Attendance: 10,000 (actual)

Selinsgrove

LORE DEGENSTEIN GALLERY, Susquehanna University, 514 University Ave., Selinsgrove, PA 17870-1001. Tel.: 570-372-4059. Fax: 570-372-2775.
E-mail: gallery@susqu.edu
Web Site: www.susqu.edu/art_gallery
Key Personnel: Dir., Daniel Olivetti.
Institution Type/Description: Art Gallery.
Hours & Admission Prices: Daily 11-4; by appointment when classes are not in session. No charge. Closed university holidays & breaks. &
Attendance: 3,592 (actual)

Sewickley

SEWICKLEY VALLEY HISTORICAL SOCIETY, 200 Broad St., Sewickley, PA 15143-1525. Tel.: 412-741-5315.
E-mail: sewickleyhistory@verizon.net
Web Site: www.sewickleyhistory.org
Key Personnel: Exec. Dir., Harton S. Semple, Jr.; Assoc. Dir., Susan Holton.
Institution Type/Description: Historical Society Museum.
Hours & Admission Prices: Tues.-Fri. 10-2; other times by appointment.

Shenandoah

SCHUYLKILL HISTORICAL FIRE SOCIETY, 105 S. Jardin St., Shenandoah, PA 17976. Tel.: 570-462-4400.
E-mail: mkitsock@ptd.net
Key Personnel: Pres. (V), Michael Kitsock.
Institution Type/Description: Firefighting History Museum: housed in 1870 Fire Station.
Hours & Admission Prices: By appointment. No charge; donations accepted. &
Attendance: 1,000 (estimated)

Shippensburg

FASHION ARCHIVES AND MUSEUM OF SHIPPENSBURG UNIVERSITY, 1871 Old Main Dr., Davis House, Shippensburg, PA 17257. Tel.: 717-477-1239. Facebook: Shippensburg University Fashion Archives & Museum.
E-mail: fasharch@ship.edu
Web Site: www.fashionarchives.org
Key Personnel: Dir., Dr. Karin J. Bohleke.
Institution Type/Description: University Costume Museum.
Hours & Admission Prices: Academic Year: Mon.-Thurs. 12-4; other times by appointment. Adults $5, seniors & students $4; children 12 & under no charge. Closed holidays. &
Attendance: 900 (estimated)

SHIPPENSBURG HISTORICAL SOCIETY MUSEUM, 52 W. King St., Shippensburg, PA 17257-0539. Mailing Address: P.O. Box 539, Shippensburg, PA 17257-0539. Tel.: 717-532-6727. Facebook: Shippensburg Historical Society.
E-mail: shiphist@pa.net
Web Site: www.shippenburghistory.org
Key Personnel: Pres., Lizzie Bailey; Vice Pres., Bruce Hockersmith; Dir., Tiffany Weaver; Cur., John McCorriston.
Institution Type/Description: General Museum.

Hours & Admission Prices: Wed. & Fri.-Sat. 1-4 & by appointment. No charge; donations accepted.
Attendance: 1,800 (estimated)

Somerset

HISTORICAL AND GENEALOGICAL SOCIETY OF SOMERSET COUNTY, 10649 Somerset Pike, Somerset, PA 15501-7357. Tel.: 814-445-6077. Fax: 814-443-6621.
E-mail: c-mware@pa.gov
Web Site: www.somersethistoricalcenter.org
Key Personnel: Dir., Mark Ware; Cur., Jacob Miller; Education Coord, Katie Cordek; Prog. Aide & Sec., Debbie Miller.
Institution Type/Description: Local History Museum; SW Pennsylvania rural history.
Hours & Admission Prices: April - Oct. Tues.-Sat. 9-5, Sun. 12-5; Nov.-March Tues.-Sat. 9-5. Adults $6, seniors $5.50, youth 3-11 $3; discounts for groups; members & children under 3 no charge. Closed most holidays.
Attendance: 23,000 (actual)

LAUREL ARTS, 214 S. Harrison Ave., Somerset, PA 15501-1803. Mailing Address: P.O. Box 414, Somerset, PA 15501. Tel.: 814-443-2433. Fax: 814-443-3870.
E-mail: arts@laurelarts.org
Web Site: www.laurelarts.org
Key Personnel: Pres. (V), Hank Parke.
Institution Type/Description: Art Museum.
Hours & Admission Prices: Tues.-Thurs. 10-6, Fri. 10-4, Sat. 12-4. No charge. Closed New Year's Day; Easter; Memorial Day; Independence Day; Labor Day; Veterans Day; Thanksgiving & day after; Christmas week.
Attendance: 51,015 (estimated)

SOMERSET HISTORICAL CENTER, 10649 Somerset Pike, Somerset, PA 15501-7357. Tel.: 814-445-6077. Fax: 814-443-6621.
E-mail: c-mware@pa.gov
Web Site: www.somersethistoricalcenter.org
Key Personnel: Dir., Mark Ware; Education Coord., Katie Cordek; Cur., Jacob Miller; Maintenance, Eric Sadler.
Institution Type/Description: History Museum.
Hours & Admission Prices: April-Oct. Tues.-Sat. 9-5, Sun. 12-5; Nov.-March Tues.-Sat. 9-5. Adults 18-60 $6, seniors $5.50, youth $3; discounts to groups, tickets from other PHMC sites, AAA, ICOM & AAM members; members no charge. Closed major holidays.
Attendance: 23,000 (actual)

South Fork

JOHNSTOWN FLOOD NATIONAL MEMORIAL, 733 Lake Rd., South Fork, PA 15956-3602. Tel.: 814-495-4643. Fax: 814-495-7463.
Web Site: www.nps.gov/jofl
Key Personnel: Supt., Jeff Reinbold.
Institution Type/Description: Park Museum Memorial: located at the site of the dam which collapsed May 31, 1889, causing the Johnstown Flood.
Hours & Admission Prices: Memorial Day-Labor Day daily 9-5. Adults 15 & over $5. Closed New Year's Day; Martin Luther King Jr. Day; Presidents' Day; Veterans Day; Thanksgiving; Christmas.
Attendance: 190,000

South Williamsport

WORLD OF LITTLE LEAGUE: PETER J. MCGOVERN MUSEUM AND OFFICIAL STORE, 525 U.S. Rte. 15, (Montgomery Pike), South Williamsport, PA 17702. Mailing Address: P.O. Box 3485, Williamsport, PA 17701-0485. Tel.: 570-326-3607. Fax: 570-326-2267. Facebook: Little League Museum.
E-mail: lvanauken@littleleague.org
Web Site: www.littleleague.org
Key Personnel: Pres. & C.E.O., Stephen D. Keener; Vice Pres. & Exec. Dir., Lance W. Van Auken; Dir. Public Programming & Outreach, Janice L. Ogurcak; C.F.O., David Housenknecht; Cur. & Asst. Dir., Adam Thompson.
Institution Type/Description: Little League Baseball & Softball Museum.
Hours & Admission Prices: Daily 9-5. Adults $5, seniors $3, children $2; discounts to AAM members. Closed New Year's Eve & Day; Easter; Thanksgiving; Christmas Eve & Day.
Attendance: 24,029 (actual)

Springdale

RACHEL CARSON HOMESTEAD, 613 Marion Ave., Springdale, PA 15144-1242. Mailing Address: Box 46, Springdale, PA 15144. Tel.: 724-274-5459. Fax: 724-275-1259.
E-mail: info@rachelcarsonhomested.org
Web Site: rachel_carson_homestead.myupsite.com
Key Personnel: Pres. (V), Rev. David L.H. Carlisle; Exec. Dir., Jeanne Cecil.
Institution Type/Description: Historic House: located at the birthplace & childhood home of ecologist & Silent Spring author Rachel Carson.
Hours & Admission Prices: By appointment. Adults $10, senior citizens & children 5-12 $5; discounts to groups of ten or more & members. Closed major holidays.
Attendance: 2,000 (estimated)

Springs

SPRINGS MUSEUM, 134 River Rd., Springs, PA 15562. Mailing Address: P.O. Box 62, Springs, PA 15562-0062. Tel.: 814-662-2625.
E-mail: jfb@qcol.net
Web Site: www.springspa.org
Key Personnel: Pres. (V), Joseph Bender.
Institution Type/Description: General Museum.
Hours & Admission Prices: Memorial Day to Labor Day Wed.-Fri. 1-5, Sat. 9-2. No Charge; donations accepted.
Attendance: 5,000 (estimated)

State College

CENTRE COUNTY HISTORICAL SOCIETY, Centre Furnace Mansion, 1001 E. College Ave., State College, PA 16801-6898. Tel.: 814-234-4779.
E-mail: info@centrecountyhistory.org
Web Site: www.centrehistory.org
Key Personnel: Pres. (V), Dr. Kathleen O'Toole; Pres. Emeritus, Jacqueline J. Melander; Exec. Dir., Mary Sorensen; Coord. Mktg. & Events, Johanna Sedgwick; Administrative Asst., Christine Tate.
Institution Type/Description: Historic House Museum.
Hours & Admission Prices: Tours: Sun., Wed. & Fri. 1-4. Library & Archives: by appointment. No charge; donations accepted. Closed New Year's Eve & Day; Easter; Memorial Day; Independence Day; Labor Day; Thanksgiving; Christmas Eve, Day & week.
Attendance: 7,000 (estimated)

DISCOVERY SPACE OF CENTRAL PENNSYLVANIA, 112 W. Foster Ave., Ste. 1, State College, PA 16801. Tel.: 814-234-0200.
E-mail: info@mydiscoveryspace.org
Web Site: mydiscoveryspace.org
Key Personnel: Exec. Dir., Allayn Beck; Dir. Educ., Michele Crowl.
Institution Type/Description: Children's Museum.
Hours & Admission Prices: Wed.-Sat. 10-5, Sun. 12-5. Adults $6; discounts to groups; children under two no charge; discounts to ASTC & AAA members. Closed New Year's Eve & Day; Easter; Memorial Day; Thanksgiving; Christmas Eve & Day.
Attendance: 17,000 (actual)

Sterling Run

LITTLE MUSEUM - CAMERON COUNTY HISTORICAL SOCIETY, Rte. 120, Sterling Run, PA 15834. Mailing Address: P.O. Box 433, Emporium, PA 15834-0433. Tel.: 814-486-0213.
E-mail: info@thelittlemuseum.org
Web Site: thelittlemuseum.org
Institution Type/Description: Historical Society Museum.
Hours & Admission Prices: Wed. & Sat.-Sun. 1-4; other times by appointment.

Stewartstown

STEWARTSTOWN HISTORICAL SOCIETY, 17 Mill St., Stewartstown, PA 17363. Mailing Address: P.O. Box 82, Stewartstown, PA 17363. Tel.: 717-993-5003.
E-mail: stewhist@yahoo.com
Web Site: www.stewhist.org
Key Personnel: Pres. (V), Donald Linebaugh, Ph.D.
Institution Type/Description: Historical Society Museum.
Hours & Admission Prices: Sun. 2-4. No charge; donations accepted.
Attendance: 500 (actual)

Strasburg

THE NATIONAL TOY TRAIN MUSEUM, 300 Paradise Ln., Strasburg, PA 17579-0248. Mailing Address: P.O. Box 248, Strasburg, PA 17579-0248. Tel.: 717-687-8976 & 8623. Fax: 717-687-0742. Facebook: National Toy Train Museum.
E-mail: tca-office@traincollectors.org
Web Site: www.nttmuseum.org
Key Personnel: Dir., Tammy Hersh; Pres., Joseph Fanara; Past Pres., Charles Anyan; Quarterly Editor, Mark Boyd; Publications Editor, Timothy Stier.
Institution Type/Description: Toy & Model Train Museum.
Hours & Admission Prices: April-May & Sept.-Dec. Sat.-Sun. 10-5; Memorial Day to Labor Day daily 10-5. Family $22, adults $7, seniors 65 & over $6, children 6-12 $4; discount to groups of 20 or more; members & children under 6 no charge. Season Pass: $21 per person. ♿
Attendance: 53,000 (actual)

RAILROAD MUSEUM OF PENNSYLVANIA, 300 Gap Rd., Strasburg, PA 17579. Mailing Address: P.O. Box 15, Strasburg, PA 17579-0015. Tel.: 717-687-8629 & 8628, ext. 3001. Fax: 717-687-0876.
E-mail: info@rrmuseumpa.org
Web Site: www.rrmuseumpa.org
Key Personnel: Dir., Jeffrey Bliemeister; Pres., Al Giannantonio; Education, Patrick Morrison; Librarian & Archivist, Nick Zmijewski; Restoration Mgr., Allan Martin; Security, Dennis Keperling; Gift Shop Mgr., Laura Martin.
Institution Type/Description: History & Transportation Museum.
Hours & Admission Prices: April-Oct. Mon.-Sat. 9-5, Sun. 12-5; Nov.-March Tues-Sat. 9-5, Sun. 12-5. Adults $8, senior citizens $7, children 6-17 $6; discounts to AAM & AAA members; children 5 and under & members no charge. Closed New Year's Day; Thanksgiving; Christmas. ♿
Attendance: 133,500 (actual)

Strongstown

DANE CASTLE, Frederick Rd., Strongstown, PA 15957. Mailing Address: P.O. Box 10, Route 403 North, Strongstown, PA 15957-0010. Tel.: 814-749-7341.
Web Site: www.danecastle.com
Institution Type/Description: History Museum.
Hours & Admission Prices: April-Nov. 1st by appointment. Admission $5. ♿

Stroudsburg

MONROE COUNTY HISTORICAL ASSOCIATION/STROUD MANSION, 900 Main St., Stroudsburg, PA 18360-1604. Tel.: 570-421-7703. Fax: 570-421-9199.
E-mail: mcha@ptd.net
Web Site: www.monroehistorical.org
Formerly: Stroud Mansion/Monroe County Historical Association
Key Personnel: Pres., Russell D. Scott, III; Exec. Dir., Amy Leiser.
Institution Type/Description: Local History Museum: housed in the 1795 Strond Mansion built by Jacob Stroud, founder of Stroudsburg.
Hours & Admission Prices: Tues.-Fri. 10-4, 1st & 3rd Sat. 10-4. Guided Tours: 11am & 2pm. Adults $8; discounts to AAM members; members no charge. Closed major holidays.
Attendance: 1,243 (actual)

QUIET VALLEY LIVING HISTORICAL FARM, 347 Quiet Valley Rd., Stroudsburg, PA 18360-9455. Tel.: 570-992-6161. Fax: 570-992-9587.
E-mail: farm@quietvalley.org
Web Site: www.quietvalley.org
Key Personnel: Bd. Pres., Maryellen Mross; Dir., Janet F. Mishkin.
Institution Type/Description: Living Farm Museum: housed on the 1765 site of a Pennsylvania homestead.
Hours & Admission Prices: 3rd Sat. in June to Labor Day Tues.-Sat. 10-5, Sun. 12-5; school groups by appointment. Adults $10, children 3-12 $5; discounts to groups, AAA members & Blue Star active military; members no charge. Special Events: Farm Animal Frolic: adults $8, children 3-12 $5. Harvest Festival: adults $10, children 3-12 $5. Old Time Christmas: adults $10, children 3-12 $5. ♿
Attendance: 27,000 (estimated)

Sunbury

THE NORTHUMBERLAND COUNTY HISTORICAL SOCIETY, 1150 N. Front St., Sunbury, PA 17801-1126. Tel.: 570-286-4083.
E-mail: nchs1756@gmail.com
Web Site: www.northumberlandcountyhistoricalsociety.org
Key Personnel: Pres., Connie Tressler; Office Mgr., Charlotte Rhinehart.
Institution Type/Description: Historic Site: 1756-94, frontier outpost; 1852, Hunter Mansion.
Hours & Admission Prices: Mon., Wed. & Fri. 1-4. Museum: no charge; donations accepted. Library $5; members no charge. ♿
Attendance: 3,900 (estimated)

Swarthmore

SCOTT ARBORETUM OF SWARTHMORE COLLEGE, 500 College Ave., Swarthmore, PA 19081-1306. Tel.: 610-328-8025. Fax: 610-328-7755. Facebook: Scott Arboretum.
E-mail: scott@swarthmore.edu
Web Site: www.scottarboretum.org
Formerly: The Scott Foundation
Key Personnel: Dir., Claire Sawyers; Pres. (V), Laura Fetterman; Education Coord., Julie Jenny; Horticultural Coord., Jeff Jabco; Public Rels. Coord. (V), Becky Robert; Cur., Andrew Bunting; Office Mgr., Jacqui West.
Institution Type/Description: Arboretum.
Hours & Admission Prices: Arboretum: daily dawn-dusk. Main office: Mon.-Fri. 8:30-12 & 1-4:30. No charge; donations accepted. Office closed New Year's Eve & Day; Independence Day; Thanksgiving; Christmas Eve, Day & week. ♿
Attendance: 30,000 (estimated)

Tarentum

ALLEGHENY-KISKI VALLEY HISTORICAL SOCIETY AND HERITAGE MUSEUM, 224 E. Seventh Ave., Tarentum, PA 15084-1513. Tel.: 724-224-7666. Facebook: Allegheny-Kiski Valley Historical Society and Heritage Museum.
E-mail: akvhs@salsgiver.com
Web Site: akvhs.org
Formerly: Allegheny-Kiski Valley Historical Society
Key Personnel: Pres. (V), Dolly Mistrik.
Institution Type/Description: Heritage Museum: housed in the former home of American Legion Post 85; built in 1931.
Hours & Admission Prices: Wed. & Sat. 11-3. Adults $5; members & veterans no charge. ♿
Attendance: 4,000 (estimated)

Tidioute

SIMPLER TIMES MUSEUM, 111 Simpler Times Lane, St. U.S. Rte. 62, Tidioute, PA 16351. Tel.: 814-484-3483.
Key Personnel: Pres. (V), Bruce E. Ziegler.
Institution Type/Description: Local History Museum.
Hours & Admission Prices: Call for hours. Adults $4, children 16 & under $1; 4-H, Girl Scouts, Boy Scouts, & church groups no charge.
Attendance: 4,500 (estimated)

Tionesta

FOREST COUNTY HISTORICAL SOCIETY, 206 Elm St., Tionesta, PA 16353. Mailing Address: P.O. Box 546, Tionesta, PA 16353-0546. Tel.: 814-755-4422.
Institution Type/Description: Historical Society Museum.
Hours & Admission Prices: late May to late Sept. Mon.-Sat. 10-4; other times by appointment.

Titusville

DRAKE WELL MUSEUM, 202 Museum Lane, Titusville, PA 16354-8902. Tel.: 814-827-2797. Fax: 814-827-4888. Facebook: Drake Well Museum.
E-mail: drakewell@verizon.net
Web Site: www.drakewell.org
Key Personnel: C.E.O., James M. Vaughan; Pres. (V), Harry Wilmoth; Museum Shop Mgr., Sheri Hamilton.
Institution Type/Description: Industrial Oil Museum: located on site of first commercially successful oil well.
Hours & Admission Prices: Jan.-March Wed.-Sat. 9-5, Sun. 12-5; April-Dec. Tues.-Sat. 9-5, Sun. 12-5. Adults 12-64 $10, senior citizens 65 & over $8, youth 3-11 $5; discounts to AAA members; children under 3 no charge. Closed New Year's Day; Martin Luther King Jr. Day; Presidents' Day; Columbus Day; Veterans Day; Thanksgiving & day after; Christmas. ♿
Attendance: 42,000 (estimated)

Towanda

BRADFORD COUNTY HISTORICAL SOCIETY, 109 Pine St., Towanda, PA 18848-1701. Tel.: 570-265-2240.
E-mail: info@bradfordhistory.com
Web Site: www.bradfordhistory.com
Key Personnel: Mng. Cur., Matthew Carl.
Institution Type/Description: Historical Society Museum: Bradford County jail building.
Hours & Admission Prices: Library: Wed.-Fri. 10-4, 1st Sat. 10-2. Museum: Memorial Day to Labor Day Wed.-Fri. 10-4, 1st Sat. each month 10-2; groups by appointment. No charge; donations accepted. Genealogy Research: $10 daily; members no charge. Closed Federal holidays. &
Attendance: 1,500

FRENCH AZILUM, INC., 469 Queens Rd., Towanda, PA 18848-9107. Tel.: 570-265-3376.
E-mail: frenchazilum@epix.net
Web Site: www.frenchazilum.com
Key Personnel: Pres. Bd., Phillip Swank; Site Mgr., Danielle Lambert.
Institution Type/Description: Historic House & Site: 1793-1803 Refuge of the French Royalists; 1836 Laporte House.
Hours & Admission Prices: May 23-Sept. 7 Fri.-Mon. 11-5; 1st tour at 12pm, last tour at 4pm; Sept. 13-Oct. 5 Sat.-Sun. 11-5; other times by appointment. Adults $5, students $3; children under 12 & members no charge. &
Attendance: 3,750 (estimated)

Trappe

HENRY MUHLENBERG HOUSE, 201 W. Main St., Trappe, PA 19426. Mailing Address: P.O. Box 26708, Collegeville, PA 19426-0708. Tel.: 610-489-7560.
E-mail: info@trappehistoricalsociety.org
Institution Type/Description: Historic House Museum: built in 1776. Listed on the National Register of Historic Places.
Hours & Admission Prices: Call for hours.

THE HISTORICAL SOCIETY OF TRAPPE, COLLEGEVILLE, PERKIOMEN VALLEY, INC., 301 W. Main St., Trappe, PA 19426. Mailing Address: P.O. Box 26708, Collegeville, PA 19426-0708. Tel.: 610-489-7560. Fax: 610-489-7560.
E-mail: info@trappehistoricalsociety.org
Web Site: www.trappehistoricalsociety.org
Key Personnel: Historian, Rev. Judith A. Meier.
Institution Type/Description: Local History Museum: housed in early 18th- & 19th-century Dewees Tavern.
Hours & Admission Prices: House & Tavern: Spring, Summer & Fall 2nd & 4th Sun. 1:30-4. Donations: $2.
Attendance: 1,100 (estimated)

Ulysses

PENNSYLVANIA LUMBER MUSEUM, 5660 U.S. Rte. 6, MP 188, Ulysses, PA 16948. Mailing Address: P.O. Box 239, Galeton, PA 16922-0239. Tel.: 814-435-2652. Fax: 814-435-6361. Facebook: Pennsylvania Lumber Museum.
E-mail: pberberich@pa.gov
Web Site: www.lumbermuseum.org
Key Personnel: Site Admin., Josh Roth; Pres., Robert Miller; Shop Attendant, Barb Peters; Records Mgr., Patricia Berberich.
Institution Type/Description: History and Lumber Museum.
Hours & Admission Prices: Wed.-Sun. 9-5. Adults $8, senior citizens 65 & over $7, children 3-11 $5; discounts to AAM & AAA members; members & active military no charge. Closed most State & Federal holidays. &
Attendance: 15,000 (estimated)

University Park

EARTH & MINERAL SCIENCES MUSEUM AND ART GALLERY, 19 Deike Burrows Rd., University Park, PA 16802-5000. Mailing Address: 207 Deike Bldg., Pennsylvania State University, University Park, PA 16802-5000. Tel.: 814-865-6336.
E-mail: rgraham@ems.psu.edu
Web Site: www.ems.psu.edu/museum
Key Personnel: C.E.O. & Dir., Russell W. Graham; Asst. Dir., Julianne Snider.
Institution Type/Description: Natural History, Science & Art Museum.
Hours & Admission Prices: Mon.-Fri. 9:30-5. No charge; donations accepted. Closed legal holidays; university's recess. &
Attendance: 8,000 (estimated)

THE FROST ENTOMOLOGICAL MUSEUM, DEPT. OF ENTOMOLOGY, THE PENNSYLVANIA STATE UNIVERSITY, Headhouse #3, Curtin Rd., University Park, PA 16802-1009. Tel.: 814-863-2865. Fax: 814-865-3048.
E-mail: kck@psu.edu
Web Site: ento.psu.edu/facilities/frost
Key Personnel: Cur. Emeritus, Dr. Ke Chung Kim.
Institution Type/Description: Specialized Natural History Museum.
Hours & Admission Prices: Mon.-Fri. 9:30-4:30. No charge; donations accepted. &
Attendance: 5,000 (estimated)

MATSON MUSEUM OF ANTHROPOLOGY, 409 Carpenter Bldg., Pennsylvania State University, University Park, PA 16802-3401. Tel.: 814-865-3853.
E-mail: anthropology@la.psu.edu
Web Site: www.anthro.psu.edu/matson_museum/index.shtml
Key Personnel: Dir., Dr. Clair McHale Milner.
Institution Type/Description: Anthropology Museum.
Hours & Admission Prices: Academic Year: Mon.-Thurs. 9-4, Fri. 9-3; Summer: Mon.-Fri. 11-4. No charge.

PALMER MUSEUM OF ART, THE PENNSYLVANIA STATE UNIVERSITY, The Pennsylvania State University, Curtin Rd., University Park, PA 16802-2507. Tel.: 814-865-7672. Fax: 814-863-8608.
E-mail: palmermuseum@psu.edu
Web Site: www.palmermuseum.psu.edu
Key Personnel: Dir., Erin M. Coe; Advisory Bd. Chm., Ron Rumford; Asst. Dir & Cur., Joyce Robinson, Ph.D.; Cur. American Art, Adam Thomas; Charles V. Hallman Sr. Cur., Patrick J. McGrady, Ph.D.; Assoc. Dir. Membership & Donor Rels., Amber Krieg; Educator, Brandi Breslin; Registrar, Beverly Balger Sutley; Interim Administrative Coord., Sheryl Shaffer; Sr. Exhibition Preparator, Richard Hall; Preparator, Craig Witter; Museum Security & Facility Mgr., Jeremy R. Warner; Asst. Museum Security & Facility Mgr., Daniel Esposito; Museum Store Mgr., Steve Artz.
Institution Type/Description: Art Museum.
Hours & Admission Prices: Tues.-Sat. 10-4:30, Sun. 12-4. No charge; donations accepted. Closed national holidays; New Year's Eve & Day; Christmas Eve, Day & week. &
Attendance: 35,688 (actual)

PENN STATE ALL-SPORTS MUSEUM, Beaver Stadium, University Park, PA 16802. Tel.: 814-865-0044.
E-mail: krh132@psu.edu
Web Site: www.gopsusports.com/museum
Key Personnel: Dir., Ken Hickman; Programming & Education, Aimee Brown.
Institution Type/Description: Sports Museum.
Hours & Admission Prices: Tues.-Sat. 10-4, Sun. 12-4; call for additional hours. Adults $5, seniors citizens 65 & over, students and children under 14 $3. Closed New Year's Eve & Day; Easter; Memorial Day; Thanksgiving; Christmas Eve & Day. &
Attendance: 22,000 (estimated)

Upland

THE FRIENDS OF THE CALEB PUSEY HOUSE, INC., 15 Race St., Upland, PA 19015. Mailing Address: P.O. Box 1183, Upland, PA 19015-0183. Tel.: 610-874-5665.
E-mail: calebpuseyhouse@comcast.net
Institution Type/Description: General Museum: housed in Caleb Pusey House; built in 1683. Listed on the National Register of Historical Places.
Hours & Admission Prices: May-Oct. Sat. 1-4; groups by special arrangement. No charge; donations accepted. &
Attendance: 1,500 (estimated)

Upper Leacock Township

MASCOT ROLLER MILLS AND RESSLER FAMILY HOME, Stumptown Rd. & Newport Rd., Upper Leacock Township, PA 17572. Mailing Address: 443 W. Newport Rd., Ronks, PA 17572-9717. Tel.: 717-656-7616.
E-mail: resslermill@gmail.com
Web Site: resslermill.com
Institution Type/Description: Historic Site: housed in the 1855 Ressler family home and 1865 mill.
Hours & Admission Prices: May to 3rd Sat. Oct. Mon.-Sat. 10-4. No charge.
Attendance: 9,000 (estimated)

Vandergrift

VICTORIAN VANDERGRIFT MUSEUM & HISTORICAL SOCIETY, 184 Sherman Ave., Vandergrift, PA 15690-1136. Tel.: 724-568-1990.
E-mail: vvmhs@comcast.net
Web Site: www.vvmhs.org
Key Personnel: Dir., Elizabeth Caporali; Pres. (V), Anthony Ferrante.
Institution Type/Description: Historical Society Museum: housed in the former Sherman School building.
Hours & Admission Prices: Mon.-Sat. 10-3. No charge; donations accepted.

Wallingford

FAY FREEDMAN GALLERY, 414 Plush Mill Rd., Wallingford, PA 19086. Tel.: 610-566-1713. Fax: 610-566-0547.
E-mail: info@communityartscenter.org
Web Site: www.communityartscenter.org
Key Personnel: Exec. Dir., Deborah R. Yoder.
Institution Type/Description: Art Gallery.
Hours & Admission Prices: Call for hours.

Warren

WARREN COUNTY HISTORICAL SOCIETY, 210 Fourth Ave., Warren, PA 16365-2318. Mailing Address: P.O. Box 427, Warren, PA 16365-0427. Tel.: 814-723-1795.
E-mail: warrenhistory@kinzua.net
Web Site: www.warrenhistory.org
Key Personnel: Mng. Dir., Michelle Gray.
Institution Type/Description: Local History Museum: housed in second empire mansion.
Hours & Admission Prices: May-Sept. Mon.-Fri. 8:30-4:30, Sat. 9-12; Oct.-April Mon.-Fri. 8:30-4:30; other times by appointment. Adults $1; members & children no charge. Closed national holidays. ♿
Attendance: 10,500 (estimated)

Washington

DAVID BRADFORD HOUSE, 175 S. Main St., Washington, PA 15301-4948. Mailing Address: P.O. Box 537, Washington, PA 15301-0537. Tel.: 724-222-3604. Facebook: David Bradford House.
E-mail: bradfordhouse@verizon.net
Web Site: www.bradfordhouse.org
Key Personnel: Pres., William Price; Historical Consultant, John Tecklenburg; Admin., Tracie Liberatore; Museum Shop Mgr., Denise Cummins.
Institution Type/Description: Historic House: housed in c.1788 restored home of a 1794 Whiskey Tax Rebellion leader.
Hours & Admission Prices: April-Dec. Wed. 11-3. Adults $5, seniors $4, students 6-18 $3; children under 6 & members no charge.
Attendance: 1,500 (estimated)

PENNSYLVANIA TROLLEY MUSEUM, 1 Museum Rd., Washington, PA 15301-6133. Tel.: 724-228-9256. Fax: 724-228-9675.
E-mail: ptm@pa-trolley.org
Web Site: www.patrolley.org
Key Personnel: Chm. (V) & Pres. (V), Dennis Bockus; Exec. Dir., Scott R. Becker; Sec., Ralph Ciccone; Treas., Joe Stelmack.
Institution Type/Description: Railway Museum.
Hours & Admission Prices: April-May & Sept. to mid-Dec. Sat.-Sun. 10-4; June-Aug. Tues.-Sun. 10-4. Adults $10, seniors 62 & over $9, children 3-15 $7; children 2 & under no charge. ♿
Attendance: 32,627 (actual)

WASHINGTON COUNTY HISTORICAL SOCIETY - LEMOYNE HOUSE, 49 E. Maiden St., Washington, PA 15301-4941. Tel.: 724-225-6740. Facebook.
E-mail: wchs@wchspa.org
Web Site: www.wchspa.org
Key Personnel: Dir., Clayton Kilgore; Pres. Bd. (V), Bracken Burns; Cur., Katie West; Research Librarian, Charles Edgar; Administrative Asst., Kathy Dzikowski.
Institution Type/Description: Historic House: historic house & doctor's office used as part of the Underground Railroad. A National Historic Landmark.
Hours & Admission Prices: Tues.-Fri. 11-4. Adults $5, students $4; discounts to AAA & AAM members; members no charge. Closed holidays. ♿
Attendance: 8,000 (estimated)

Washington Crossing

WASHINGTON CROSSING HISTORIC PARK, 1112 River Rd., Washington Crossing, PA 18977-1202. Mailing Address: P.O. Box 103, Washington Crossing, PA 18977-0103. Tel.: 215-493-4076. Fax: 215-493-4820.
E-mail: info@washingtoncrossingpark.org
Web Site: www.ushistory.org/washingtoncrossing
Key Personnel: Exec. Dir., Joseph Capone; Site Admin., Joan Hauger; Museum Cur., Kimberly McCarty; Historic Interpreter & Museum Shop Coord., Connie Unangst.
Institution Type/Description: Historic Site & Recreational Park Land.
Hours & Admission Prices: Daily 10-4. Bowman's Hill Tower: daily 10-4, weather permitting. Single Site: adults & children 4 & up $6; discounts to AAM members; children under 4, military & members no charge. Three Sites: adults $11; Grounds: no charge. Closed New Year's Day; Martin Luther King Jr. Day; Presidents' Day; Columbus Day; Thanksgiving. ♿
Attendance: 350,000 (estimated)

Waterford

FORT LEBOEUF MUSEUM, 123 S. High St., Waterford, PA 16441. Mailing Address: P.O. Box 622, Waterford, PA 16441. Tel.: 814-796-4014.
E-mail: msgrnjns1@aol.com
Web Site: www.fortleboeufhistoricalsociety.org
Key Personnel: Property Placement Officer & Pres. (V), Judy Nelson; Chm. (V) & Museum Shop Mgr., Jim Edwards.
Institution Type/Description: History Museum: located at the site of a succession of three forts, all named Fort LeBoeuf; built by the French in 1753; rebuilt by the British in 1760; rebuilt by the governor of Pennsylvania in 1795.
Hours & Admission Prices: Thurs. 10-3, Sat. 10-4, Sun. 1-4. Adults $4, students $1.
Attendance: 1,000 (estimated)

Watsontown

HISTORIC WARRIOR RUN CHURCH, Intersection Susquehanna Trail & 8th St., Watsontown, PA 17777. Mailing Address: Fort Freeland Heritage Society, P.O. Box 26, Turbotville, PA 17772-0026. Tel.: 570-538-1308.
E-mail: info@freelandfarm.org
Web Site: www.freelandfarm.org/warrior_run_church.php
Key Personnel: Pres., E. Jane Koch.
Institution Type/Description: Historic Building & Site: 1835 Country Greek Revival Style Church; Revolutionary War Graveyard.
Hours & Admission Prices: Tours by appointment. No charge; donations accepted. ♿
Attendance: 3,000 (estimated)

Wayne

CHANTICLEER FOUNDATION, 786 Church Rd., Wayne, PA 19087-4713. Tel.: 610-687-4163. Fax: 610-293-0149.
E-mail: admin@chanticleergarden.org
Web Site: www.chanticleergarden.org
Key Personnel: Exec. Dir., R. William Thomas.
Institution Type/Description: Garden.
Hours & Admission Prices: April-Oct. Wed.-Sun. 10-5; groups tours by appointment. Adults $10; discounts to museum & library members; garden professionals & children under 13 no charge. Season Pass: 1 Person $30, 2 Person $50, 3 Person $75. ♿
Attendance: 40,000 (actual)

THE FINLEY HOUSE, 113 W. Beech Tree Lane, Wayne, PA 19087-3212. Tel.: 610-688-2668.
E-mail: info@radnorhistory.org
Web Site: radnorhistory.org
Key Personnel: Pres. (V), Ted Pollard.
Institution Type/Description: Historical Society Museum: housed in c.1789 Finley House.
Hours & Admission Prices: Tues. & Sat. 2-4; other times by appointment. No charge; donations accepted.
Attendance: 400 (estimated)

Waynesboro

OLLER HOUSE, 138 W. Main St., Waynesboro, PA 17268-1564. Tel.: 717-762-1747.
E-mail: waynesborohistory@comcast.net
Web Site: www.waynesborohistory.com

Key Personnel: Mgr., Ken Beam.
Institution Type/Description: Historic House; built in 1892.
Hours & Admission Prices: Wed. 1-5, Thurs. & Sat. 10-4, Fri. 10-1; other times by appointment. No charge; donations accepted.

RENFREW MUSEUM & PARK, 1010 E. Main St., Waynesboro, PA 17268-2338. Tel.: 717-762-4723. Fax: 717-762-6384.
E-mail: renfrew@innernet.net
Web Site: www.renfrewmuseum.org
Key Personnel: C.E.O., Douglas Tengler; Chm. (V), David Hykes; Admin., Bonnie Iseminger; Supvr. Grounds, John H. Frantz; Museum Shop Mgr., Cheryl Keyser.
Institution Type/Description: Decorative Arts Museum; housed in 1812 Pennsylvania German farm house.
Hours & Admission Prices: April-Oct. Tues.-Fri. 12-4, Sat.-Sun. 1-4; other times by appointment. Adults $5, seniors $4.50, children 7-12 $3.50; discount to groups; children 6 & under and members no charge. Closed Mother's Day; Memorial Day; Father's Day; Independence Day; Labor Day.
Attendance: 14,500 (estimated)

Waynesburg

GREENE COUNTY HISTORICAL MUSEUM, 918 Rolling Meadows Rd., Waynesburg, PA 15370-3470. Tel.: 724-627-3204. Fax: 724-627-3204.
E-mail: gchrmuseum@greenecountyhistory.com
Web Site: www.greencountyhistory.com
Key Personnel: Dir., Eben Williams; Pres., Candace Tustin; Vice Pres., George Blystone; Treas., Deborah Wilson; Sec., Joyce Winters.
Institution Type/Description: Historical Society Museum; housed in 1861 former county home.
Hours & Admission Prices: Tues.-Sat. 10-4, Sun. by appointment. Adults $7, seniors over 60 & children 6-12 $5; discount to AAA members; NARM members, children under 6 & members no charge. Closed Easter; Thanksgiving; Christmas. &
Attendance: 5,000 (estimated)

PAUL R. STEWART MUSEUM, Waynesburg University, 51 W. College St., Waynesburg, PA 15370-1258. Tel.: 724-852-3214.
E-mail: cdennis@waynesburg.edu
Web Site: www.waynesburg.edu/museum
Key Personnel: Assoc. Dir., Courtney Dennis.
Institution Type/Description: History, Cultural & Geological Heritage Museum.
Hours & Admission Prices: Self-Guided Tours: Mon.-Fri. 8:30-4:30 call to confirm. Guided Tours & Groups: by appointment. No charge. Closed holidays & university breaks.

Wescosville

BARTHOLOMEW CENTER FOR THE PRESERVATION OF LOWER MACUNGIE TOWNSHIP HISTORY, 3120 S. Cedar Crest Blvd., Emmaus, PA 18049. Mailing Address: P.O. Box 3722, Wescosville, PA 18106. Facebook.
E-mail: lmthistory@yahoo.com
Web Site: lmthistory.org
Institution Type/Description: History Museum.
Hours & Admission Prices: Sun. 1-4; other times by appointment. No charge. Closed holidays.

West Chester

AMERICAN HELICOPTER MUSEUM & EDUCATION CENTER, 1220 American Blvd., West Chester, PA 19380-4268. Tel.: 610-436-9600.
E-mail: info@americanhelicopter.museum
Web Site: www.americanhelicopter.museum
Key Personnel: Exec. Dir., Sarah Sands, Jr.; Chm. Bd., Marc Sheffler; Dir. Museum Svcs. & Mktg., Robyn Morgan; Bookkeeper & Public Rels. Coord., Jan Feighner; Education Coord., Erica Zwilling; Major Gift Assoc., Greg Coin; Gift Shop, Gary Brenner; Helicopter Pilot, Frank Zook.
Institution Type/Description: Aeronautics Museum.
Hours & Admission Prices: Wed.-Sat. 10-5, Sun. noon-5. Adults $10, seniors, students w/I.D. & children under 12 $8; members and children under 2 no charge. Closed New Year's Day; Easter; Memorial Day; Thanksgiving; Christmas. &
Attendance: 30,000 (estimated)

CHESTER COUNTY HISTORICAL SOCIETY, 225 N. High St., West Chester, PA 19380-2658. Tel.: 610-692-4800. Fax: 610-692-4357. Facebook: Chester County Historical Society.
E-mail: cchs@chestercohistorical.org
Web Site: www.chestercohistorical.org

Key Personnel: Pres., Elizabeth Laurent; Chm. (V), James Sargent; Photo Archivist, Pamela C. Powell; Dir. Collections & Cur., Ellen Endslow; Librarian, Jasmine Smith.
Institution Type/Description: History Museum.
Hours & Admission Prices: Museum & Library: Tues.-Sat. 9:30-4:30. Museum & Library: adults $8, seniors $6, students $5; discounts to AAA& AAM members; CCHS members, active military, county court jurors no charge. Closed New Year's Day; Memorial Day; Independence Day; Labor Day; Thanksgiving; Christmas. &
Attendance: 33,000 (estimated)

White Mills

DORFLINGER-SUYDAM WILDLIFE SANCTUARY & GLASS MUSEUM, Elizabeth St. & Long Ridge Rd., White Mills, PA 18473. Mailing Address: P.O. Box 356, White Mills, PA 18473-0356. Tel.: 570-253-1185. Fax: 570-253-5196.
E-mail: suydam@ptd.net
Web Site: www.dorflinger.org
Key Personnel: Exec. Dir., Joan G. Gillner.
Institution Type/Description: Wildlife Sanctuary & Glass Museum.
Hours & Admission Prices: Sanctuary: daily dawn to dusk. Museum: May-Oct. Wed.-Sat. 10-4, Sun. 1-4. Adults $5, seniors 55 & over $4; discounts to members.
Attendance: 3,000 (estimated)

Wilkes-Barre

LUZERNE COUNTY HISTORICAL SOCIETY, 49 S. Franklin St., Wilkes-Barre, PA 18701. Mailing Address: 49 S. Franklin St., Wilkes-Barre, PA 18701-1290. Tel.: 570-823-6244. Fax: 570-823-9011.
E-mail: info@luzernehistory.org
Web Site: www.luzernehistory.org
Formerly: Wyoming Historical and Geological Society
Key Personnel: Exec. Dir., Aimee E Newell, Ph.D.; Dir. Operations, Mark J. Riccetti; Dir. Library & Archives, Amanda Fontenova.
Institution Type/Description: History Museum.
Hours & Admission Prices: Library: Wed & Fri. 12-5, Thur. 12-6, Sat. 10-2; Museum: Wed.-Fri. 2-6, Sat. 10-2. Adults $5, children $3.
Attendance: 12,000 (estimated)

SORDONI ART GALLERY, Wilkes University, 141 S. Main St., Wilkes-Barre, PA 18702. Tel.: 570-408-4325. Fax: 570-408-7733. Facebook; Instagram; Twitter.
E-mail: heather.sincavage@wilkes.edu
Web Site: wilkes.edu/sordoniartgallery
Key Personnel: Dir., Heather Sincavage.
Institution Type/Description: Art Gallery.
Hours & Admission Prices: Tues.-Wed. & Fri. 10-5, Thurs. 10-7, Sat.-Sun. 12-5. No charge. Closed major holidays. &
Attendance: 5,000 (actual)

Williamsport

PETER HERDIC TRANSPORTATION MUSEUM, 810 Nichols Place, Williamsport, PA 17701. Mailing Address: 1500 W. 3rd St., Williamsport, PA 17701. Tel.: 570-601-3455.
E-mail: kmurphy@rideRVT.com
Institution Type/Description: Transportation Museum.
Hours & Admission Prices: Tues.-Sat. 10-3; other times by appointment.

THE THOMAS T. TABER MUSEUM OF THE LYCOMING COUNTY HISTORICAL SOCIETY, 858 W. 4th St., Williamsport, PA 17701-5824. Tel.: 570-326-3326. Fax: 570-326-3689.
E-mail: lchsmuseum@verizon.net
Web Site: www.tabermuseum.org
Formerly: Lycoming County Historical Society and Museum
Key Personnel: Dir., Gary W. Parks; Chm. (V), Charles Luppert; Cur., Scott Sagar; Museum Store Mgr., Anne Persun.
Institution Type/Description: Regional History Museum.
Hours & Admission Prices: May-Oct. Tues.-Fri. 9:30-4, Sat. 11-4, Sun. 1-4; Nov.-April Tues.-Fri. 9:30-4, Sat. 11-4. Adults $7.50, senior citizens 65 & over $6, children 3-12 $5; discount to military and AAM & AAA members; members no charge. Closed national holidays. &
Attendance: 13,000 (actual)

Willow Street

1719 HANS HERR HOUSE & MUSEUM, 1849 Hans Herr Dr., Willow Street, PA 17584-9536. Tel.: 717-464-4438.
E-mail: info@hansherr.org
Web Site: www.hansherr.org
Key Personnel: Dir., Becky Gochnauer; Administrative Asst., Donnalee Mylin; Museum Shop Mgr., Starla Hess.
Institution Type/Description: Historic House: 1719 Herr House.
Hours & Admission Prices: April to 1st week Dec. Mon.-Sat. 9-4. Adults $8, children 7-12 $4; discounts to groups of 10 or more. Closed Good Friday; Thanksgiving.
Attendance: 8,200 (estimated)

Womelsdorf

CONRAD WEISER HOMESTEAD AND MEMORIAL PARK, 30 Weiser Lane, Womelsdorf, PA 19567-9768. Tel.: 610-589-2934. Fax: 610-589-9458.
E-mail: info@conradweiserhomestead.org
Web Site: www.conradweiserhomestead.org
Key Personnel: Pres. (V), David G. Sonnen; Groundskeeper, Arnel Greth; Museum Shop Mgr., Brian Beamesderfer.
Institution Type/Description: Historic House: 1729-1760 Conrad Weiser homestead.
Hours & Admission Prices: Grounds: dawn to dusk. Homestead: April-Nov. 1st Sun. each month 12-5. No charge; donations accepted. &
Attendance: 25,000 (estimated)

Worcester

PETER WENTZ FARMSTEAD, 2030 Shearer Rd., Worcester, PA 19490. Mailing Address: P.O. Box 240, Worcester, PA 19490-0240. Tel.: 610-584-5104. Fax: 610-584-6860.
E-mail: peterwentzfarmstead@mail.montcopa.org
Web Site: www.montcopa.org
Key Personnel: Pres. (V), Kathy Yost; Admin., Dianne M. Cram; Farm Mgr., James Nichols; Cur., Mark Turdo; Educator, Kimberly Boice; Asst. Farm Mgr., Jay Ryan.
Institution Type/Description: Historic Building & Site: 1758 farmstead belonging to Peter Wentz; used twice by General Washington where he planned the Battle of Germantown & received the word of victory at Saratoga.
Hours & Admission Prices: Tues.-Sat. 10-4, Sun. 1-4. No charge; donations accepted. Closed county holidays. &
Attendance: 12,000 (estimated)

Wrightsville

WRIGHTSVILLE HISTORICAL MUSEUM, 309 Locust St., Wrightsville, PA 17368-1221. Tel.: 717-252-1169. Facebook.
E-mail: hwistaff@historicwrightsv.comcast.net
Web Site: www.historicwrightsvillepa.org
Key Personnel: Exec. Dir., Madeline Flagler; Pres., Lori Rosbrugh.
Institution Type/Description: History Museum.
Hours & Admission Prices: Sun. 1-4; other times by appointment. No charge; donations accepted.

Wyalusing

WYALUSING VALLEY MUSEUM, 25 Main St., Wyalusing, PA 18853. Mailing Address: P.O. Box 301, Wyalusing, PA 18853-0301. Tel.: 570-746-3979.
E-mail: info@wyalusingmuseum.com
Web Site: www.wyalusingmuseum.com
Key Personnel: Pres. (V), Mary Skillings; Treas., Karl Peterson; Cur., Morgan Clinton.
Institution Type/Description: History Museum.
Hours & Admission Prices: May-Oct. Sat.-Sun. 12-4; other times by appointment. No charge; donations accepted.

York

HARLEY-DAVIDSON VEHICLE OPERATIONS TOUR CENTER, 1425 Eden Rd., York, PA 17402. Tel.: 717-852-6440.
Web Site: harley-davidson.com
Institution Type/Description: Company Museum.
Hours & Admission Prices: Tour Center: Mon.-Fri. 8-4. Freedom Factory Tour: Mon.-Fri. 8 am. No charge. Classic Factory Tour: Mon.-Fri. 9 am, 10 am, 12:30 pm, 2 pm. Adults $10; discount to group of 10 or more. Steel Toe Tour: Mon.-Fri. 9:15 am & 12 pm. Adults $38; discounts to groups of 16 or more. Children under 12 not admitted on factory tours. Closed New Year's Eve & Day; Independence Day; Thanksgiving & day after; Christmas Eve, Day & week.

POLICE HERITAGE MUSEUM, 54 W. Market St., York, PA 17401-1228. Mailing Address: P.O. Box 1582, York, PA 17405-1582. Tel.: 717-845-2677.
E-mail: info@policeheritagemuseum.com
Institution Type/Description: History Museum.
Hours & Admission Prices: Temporarily closed for relocation.

YORK BARBELL MUSEUM AND USA WEIGHTLIFTING HALL OF FAME, 3300 Board Rd., York, PA 17406-8409. Tel.: 717-767-6481. Fax: 717-764-0044. Facebook: @YorkBarbellUSA.
E-mail: asmith@yorkbarbell.com
Web Site: www.yorkbarbell.com
Key Personnel: Controller, Zachary Shenk.
Institution Type/Description: Sports Museum.
Hours & Admission Prices: Mon.-Thurs. & Sat. 9:30-4:30, Fri. 9:30-6. No charge; donations accepted. &
Attendance: 4,000 (estimated)

YORK COLLEGE GALLERIES, Wolf Hall, 441 Country Club Rd., York, PA 17403-3643. Tel.: 717-815-1354 & 1528. Facebook: York College Galleries.
E-mail: mclayrob@ycp.edu
Web Site: www.ycp.edu
Key Personnel: Gallery Dir., Matthew Clay-Robison.
Institution Type/Description: Art Gallery.
Hours & Admission Prices: Mon.-Tues. & Fri. 9-5, Wed.-Thurs. 9-9, Sat. 10-4. No charge. &

YORK COUNTY HERITAGE TRUST, 250 E. Market St., York, PA 17403. Tel.: 717-848-1587. Facebook.
E-mail: nsmith@yorkhistorycenter.org
Web Site: www.yorkhistorycenter.org
Institution Type/Description: History Museum.
Hours & Admission Prices: Ag & Industrial Museum: Tues.-Sat. 10-4. Society Museum, Library & Archives Tues.-Sat. 9-5. Colonial Complex: April-Nov. Tues.-Sat. guided tours, see website. Bonham House: seasonal hours, see website. Fire Museum: April-Nov. see website. Adults $15, children 6-18 $7, children 5 & under no charge. Closed New Year's Day; Easter; Memorial Day; Independence Day; Labor Day; Thanksgiving; Christmas.

YORK COUNTY HERITAGE TRUST, AGRICULTURAL AND INDUSTRIAL MUSEUM, 217 W. Princess St., York, PA 17403-2013. Mailing Address: 250 E. Market St., York, PA 17403-2013. Tel.: 717-846-6452. Fax: 717-812-1204.
E-mail: info@yorkheritage.org
Web Site: www.yorkheritage.org
Key Personnel: Dir., Joan Mummert; Collections Mgr., Janie Kreines; Dir. Education, Daniel Roe; Dir. Library & Archives, Lila Fourhman-Shaull.
Institution Type/Description: Agriculture & Industrial Museum; 1874-1955 former industrial complex.
Hours & Admission Prices: Agricultural & Industrial Museum: Tues.-Sat. 10-4. Colonial Complex: Tours Tues.-Sat. see website for schedule. Historical Society Museum: Tues.-Sat. 9-5. Fire Museum: Sat. 10-4. York County Heritage Sites: adults $15, students 6-18 $7, discounts for military, AAA, ICOM & AAM members; children 5 & under & members no charge. Library $6. Closed New Year's Day; Easter; Memorial Day; Independence Day; Labor Day; Thanksgiving; Christmas. &
Attendance: 48,250 (actual)

YORK COUNTY HERITAGE TRUST - BONHAM HOUSE, 250 E. Market St., York, PA 17403. Tel.: 717-846-6452.
E-mail: jmummert@yorkheritage.org
Institution Type/Description: Historic House Museum: housed in the former home of Horace & Rebekah Bonham, built in 1875.
Hours & Admission Prices: April-Dec. Sat. 10-4 by appointment. Adults $15, students 6-18 $7; children 5 & under no charge.

YORK COUNTY HERITAGE TRUST, FIRE MUSEUM OF YORK COUNTY, 757 W. Market St., York, PA 17401-3650. Mailing Address: 250 E. Market St., York, PA 17403-2013. Tel.: 717-848-1587. Fax: 717-812-1204.
E-mail: info@yorkheritage.org
Web Site: www.yorkheritage.org
Key Personnel: Pres. & CEO, Joan Mummert; Collections Mgr., Janie Kreines; Dir. Education, Daniel Roe; Dir. Library & Archives, Lila Fourhman-Shaull.

Institution Type/Description: Fire-fighting Museum: housed in 1903-1904 Royal Fire Station #6.

Hours & Admission Prices: Fire Museum: Sat. 10-4; tours by appointment. Historical Society Museum & Agricultural and Industrial Museum: Tues.-Sat. 10-4. Colonial Complex: Guided Tours Tues.-Sat. 10-4. Bonham House: by appointment. York County Heritage Trust Sites: adults $15, students 6-18 $7, discounts to groups, seniors, military, AAA, ICOM & AAM members; children 5 & under & members no charge. Library $6. Closed New Year's Day; Easter; Memorial Day; Independence Day; Labor Day; Thanksgiving; Christmas. &

Attendance: 48,250 (actual)

YORK COUNTY HISTORY CENTER, 250 E. Market St., York, PA 17403-2013. Tel.: 717-848-1587. Fax: 717-812-1204.

E-mail: info@yorkhistorycenter.org
Web Site: yorkhistorycenter.org
Formerly: The Historical Society of York County
Key Personnel: Pres. & C.E.O., Joan Mummert; Chm. Bd., Rob Kinsley; Dir. Education, Par Bowman; Dir. Library & Archives, Lila Fourhman-Shaull; Museum Shop Buyer, Judy Bono.
Institution Type/Description: History Museum.
Hours & Admission Prices: Historical Society Museum: Tues.-Sat. 10-4. Adult $15, children 6-18 $7, children 5 & under no charge. Library & Archives: Tues.-Sat. 9-5. Library & Archives: adults $8. Closed New Year's Day; Easter Monday; Memorial Day; Independence Day; Labor Day; Thanksgiving; Christmas. &
Attendance: 40,244 (actual)

York Springs

EASTERN MUSEUM OF MOTOR RACING, 100 Baltimore Rd., York Springs, PA 17372. Mailing Address: P.O. Box 688, Mechanicsburg, PA 17055-0688. Tel.: 717-528-8279. Facebook: Eastern Museum of Motor Racing Group.

E-mail: admin@emmr.org
Web Site: www.emmr.org
Key Personnel: Administrative Coord., Amanda J. Eshenour; Museum Shop Mgr., Larry Garland; Museum Shop Mgr., Kim Garland.
Institution Type/Description: General Museum.
Hours & Admission Prices: April-Oct. Fri.-Sun. 10-4. No charge; donations accepted.

Zelienople

ZELIENOPLE HISTORICAL SOCIETY, 243 S. Main St., Zelienople, PA 16063-1151. Tel.: 724-452-9457.

E-mail: zhs@zelienoplehistoricalsociety.com
Web Site: www.zelienoplehistoricalsociety.com
Key Personnel: C.E.O., Elizabeth Kelleher; Pres. (V), Janet Rogan; Museum Shop Mgr., Mary Cameron.
Institution Type/Description: Historic Houses: Passavant House c.1808 Federal-Georgian brick & frame structure; c.1805 Buhl House.
Hours & Admission Prices: Tours: Mon.-Fri. 9:30am; other times by appointment. Adults $5, students $3; members no charge. Office: Mon.-Fri. 9-12. Library: by appointment. &
Attendance: 1,000 (estimated)

RHODE ISLAND

(120 listings)

Adamsville

GRAY'S STORE, 4 Main St., Adamsville, RI 02801. Mailing Address: P.O. Box 53, Adamsville, RI 02801-0053. Tel.: 401-635-4566.

Key Personnel: Owner, Grayton T. Waite.
Institution Type/Description: Historic Building: housed in a general store built by Samuel Church in 1788; also includes first post office in Little Compton (1804).
Hours & Admission Prices: Mon.-Sat. 9-5, Sun. & holidays 12-4. No charge; donations accepted.

Barrington

BARRINGTON PRESERVATION SOCIETY & MUSEUM, Barrington Public Library, Lower Level, 281 County Rd., Barrington, RI 02806-2406. Tel.: 401-289-0802. Facebook: Barrington Preservation.

E-mail: information@barringtonpreservation.org
Web Site: www.barringtonpreservation.org
Key Personnel: Pres. (V), Nathaniel Taylor.
Institution Type/Description: History Museum.

Hours & Admission Prices: Wed. & Sat. 1-4; other times by appointment. No charge. &

Attendance: 400 (estimated)

Block Island

BLOCK ISLAND HISTORICAL SOCIETY MUSEUM, 18 Old Town Rd., Block Island, RI 02807. Mailing Address: P.O. Box 79, Block Island, RI 02807-0079. Tel.: 401-864-4357.

E-mail: blockhistory@me.com
Web Site: www.blockislandtimes.com/listings/2867912/the-block-island-historical-society
Key Personnel: Exec. Dir., Pamela Gasner; Pres., Dr. Gerald Abbott.
Institution Type/Description: Historical Society Museum.
Hours & Admission Prices: Summer: daily 11-4; Spring & Fall: Sat.-Sun. 11-4. Adults $5.50, seniors & students $3; members & children 16 & under no charge.

Bristol

AUDUBON SOCIETY OF RHODE ISLAND ENVIRONMENTAL EDUCATION CENTER, 1401 Hope St., Bristol, RI 02809-1153. Mailing Address: 12 Sanderson Rd., Smithfield, RI 02917-2606. Tel.: 401-245-7500. Fax: 401-245-9339. Facebook: Audubon RI.

E-mail: adimonti@asri.org
Web Site: www.asri.org
Key Personnel: Exec. Dir., Lawrence Taft; Pres., Cynthia Warren; Treas., Mark Carrison; Sr. Dir. Advancement, Jeffery Hall; Dir., Anne DiMonti; Museum Shop Mgr., Tim Parker.
Institution Type/Description: Natural History Museum.
Hours & Admission Prices: mid-April to mid-Oct. daily 9-5; mid-Oct. to mid-April Wed.-Sat. 9-5, Sun. 12-5. Adults $6, children 4-12 $4; children under 4 & members no charge. &
Attendance: 33,000 (actual)

BLITHEWOLD MANSION, GARDENS & ARBORETUM, 101 Ferry Rd., (Rt. 114), Bristol, RI 02809-2902. Tel.: 401-253-2707. Fax: 401-253-0412.

E-mail: info@blithewold.org
Web Site: www.blithewold.org
Key Personnel: Exec. Dir., Karen Binder; Chm. (V), Curt Ley; Chm. Emeritus (V), Noreen Ackerman; Dir. Special Events, Karen Bellavance; Grounds Mgr., Fred Perry; Mgr. Education & Programs, Julie Christina; Dir. Communications & Visitor Experience, Tree Callanan; Cur., Margaret Whitehead; Museum Shop Mgr., Sue Legault.
Institution Type/Description: Historic Building & Arboretum: 1908 English manor house & summer residence of Augustus Van Wickle.
Hours & Admission Prices: Mansion: April to Columbus Day & day after Thanksgiving to New Year's Day Tues.-Sun. 10-4. Grounds: April to Columbus Day & day after Thanksgiving to New Year's Day daily 10-5. Family $24, adults $12, seniors, military & students $10, children 6-17 $3; discounts to AAA members; children 5 & under and members no charge. Closed New Year's Eve & Day; Christmas Eve & Day. &
Attendance: 32,500 (actual)

COGGESHALL FARM MUSEUM INC., 1 Colt Dr., Bristol, RI 02809-1019. Mailing Address: 1 Colt Dr., Bristol, RI 02809-1019. Tel.: 401-253-9062. Facebook: Coggeshall Farm Museum Inc..

E-mail: info@coggeshallfarm.org
Web Site: www.coggeshallfarm.org
Key Personnel: Pres. (V), Cindy Elder; Interim Exec. Dir., Casey Duckett.
Institution Type/Description: Living History Museum.
Hours & Admission Prices: mid-April to mid-Dec. Tues.-Sun. 10-4; mid-Dec. to mid-April daily 10-4. Adults $5, children 3-12 & seniors $3; members & children under 3 no charge. Sat.-Sun. adults $7, children 3-12 & seniors $5; members & children under 3 no charge. Closed selected holidays. &
Attendance: 10,500 (estimated)

HERRESHOFF MARINE MUSEUM/AMERICA'S CUP HALL OF FAME, One Burnside St., Bristol, RI 02809. Mailing Address: P.O. Box 450, Bristol, RI 02809-0420. Tel.: 401-253-5000. Fax: 401-253-6222. Facebook: Herreshoff Marine Museum.

E-mail: info@herreshoff.org
Web Site: www.herreshoff.org
Key Personnel: Chm. Bd. (V), David Ford; C.E.O., Wm. H. Dyer Jones; C.O.O., Lawrence D. Lavers.
Institution Type/Description: Maritime Museum: located at the site of the former Herreshoff Manufacturing Company.

Hours & Admission Prices: April 28-Oct. daily 10-5; Nov.-Dec. call for hours. Adults $12, senior citizens $10, military $8, students 10 & over $5; children 9 & under, CAMM & museum members no charge. Closed Independence Day. &
Attendance: 8,000 (actual)

LINDEN PLACE, 500 Hope St., Bristol, RI 02809-1808. Tel.: 401-253-0390. Fax: 401-253-4106.
E-mail: info@lindenplace.org
Web Site: www.lindenplace.org
Key Personnel: Exec. Dir., James Burke Connell; Tour Dir., Joan Doyle Roth; Site Admin., Susan E. Battle.
Institution Type/Description: Historic Buildings: housed in an 1810 Federal-style mansion built by General George De Wolf; the estate was featured in the film The Great Gatsby.
Hours & Admission Prices: May to Columbus Day Tues.-Sat. 10-4; other times by appointment. Adults $8, seniors & students $6, children 6-12 $5; discounts to PBS, AAA, & NE Museum members.

MOUNT HOPE FARM, 250 Metacom Ave., Bristol, RI 02809-5180. Mailing Address: P.O. Box 66, Bristol, RI 02809-0066. Tel.: 401-254-1745. Fax: 401-254-1270.
E-mail: gina@mounthopefarm.org
Web Site: www.mounthopefarm.com
Key Personnel: Dir. & Pres. (V), James W. Farley.
Institution Type/Description: Historic Site & Building: housed in Governor Bradford House, c.1745. Listed on the National Register of Historic Places.
Hours & Admission Prices: May-Oct. & Dec. Wed.-Sat. 12-4. Admission $6.

Charlestown

CHARLESTOWN HISTORICAL SOCIETY, 4417B Old Post Rd., Charlestown, RI 02813. Mailing Address: P.O. Box 100, Charlestown, RI 02813. Tel.: 401-364-1838.
E-mail: info@charlestownhistorical.org
Web Site: charlestownhistorical.org
Institution Type/Description: Historical Society Museum.
Hours & Admission Prices: By appointment.

Chepachet

GLOCESTER HERITAGE SOCIETY, 1181 Putnam Pike, Chepachet, RI 02814. Mailing Address: P.O. Box 269, Chepachet, RI 02814-0269. Tel.: 401-568-8967.
E-mail: info@glocesterheritagesociety.org
Web Site: www.glocesterheritagesociety.org
Formerly: Job Armstrong Store
Key Personnel: Pres., Marie Sweet.
Institution Type/Description: Historic Building: housed in an early 1800s store.
Hours & Admission Prices: By appointment. No charge; donations accepted.

Coventry

GENERAL NATHANAEL GREENE HOMESTEAD, 50 Taft St., Coventry, RI 02816-5314. Tel.: 401-821-8630.
E-mail: nathanaelgreenehmst@gmail.com
Web Site: nathanaelgreenehomestead.org
Institution Type/Description: Historic House Museum: built in 1770. Listed on the National Register of Historic Places.
Hours & Admission Prices: May-Oct. Mon., Wed. & Sat. 10-5, Sun. 1-5; other times by appointment. Adults $5, children $3.

PAINE HOUSE, 7 Station St., Coventry, RI 02816. Mailing Address: Western Rhode Island Civic Historical Society, P.O. Box 2, Coventry, RI 02816. Tel.: 914-633-1776.
E-mail: painecottage@optonline.net
Key Personnel: Dir., John R. Wright.
Institution Type/Description: Historic House Museum.
Hours & Admission Prices: Thurs. & Sat.-Sun 10-5, other times by appointment. Suggested donation Adults $5, children 12 & under $3.

WESTERN RHODE ISLAND CIVIC HISTORICAL SOCIETY, 7 Station St., Coventry, RI 02816. Mailing Address: P.O. Box 2, Coventry, RI 02816. Tel.: 401-385-9997.
E-mail: info@westernrihistory.org
Web Site: westernrihistory.org
Key Personnel: Pres., Norma Smith; Vice Pres., Marilyn Nagy; Sec., Katie McDonald.
Institution Type/Description: Local History Museum.

Hours & Admission Prices: May-Dec. Sat. 1-4 by appointment. Adults $3, students & children $1; members no charge.
Attendance: 75 (estimated)

Cranston

GOVERNOR SPRAGUE MANSION, 1351 Cranston St., Cranston, RI 02920. Tel.: 401-944-9226.
E-mail: smoyer3@verizon.net
Web Site: www.cranstonhistoricalsociety.org
Key Personnel: Pres. (V), Sandra Moyer.
Institution Type/Description: Historic House Museum: housed in the former home of the Sprague family, built in 1790.
Hours & Admission Prices: Call for hours. Adults 12 & over $10, children under 12 $5. &
Attendance: 2,000 (estimated)

JOY HOMESTEAD, 156 Scituate Ave., Cranston, RI 02921. Mailing Address: Cranston Historical Society, 1351 Cranston St., Cranston, RI 02920-6721. Tel.: 401-944-9226.
Key Personnel: Pres. (V), Sandra Moyer.
Institution Type/Description: Historic House: housed in the former home of Job Joy; built in 1764. Listed on the National Register of Historic Places.
Hours & Admission Prices: Call for hours.
Attendance: 750 (estimated)

PROVIDENCE JEWELRY MUSEUM, 1 Spectacle St., Cranston, RI 02910. Tel.: 401-274-0999 & 781-3100. Facebook: @provjewelrymuseum; Twitter: @ProvJwlryMuseum.
E-mail: info@providencejewelrymuseum.com
Web Site: www.providencejewelrymuseum.com
Key Personnel: Dir., Peter DiCristofaro.
Institution Type/Description: Jewelry Museum.
Hours & Admission Prices: By appointment only.

East Greenwich

JAMES MITCHELL VARNUM HOUSE AND MUSEUM, 57 Pierce St., East Greenwich, RI 02818. Mailing Address: 6 Main St., East Greenwich, RI 02818. Tel.: 401-884-1776.
E-mail: k8bcm@cox.net
Web Site: www.varnumcontinentals.org
Key Personnel: Dir., Col. Bruce C. MacGunnigle; Caretaker, Barlow B. Healy; Cur., Skip Healy.
Institution Type/Description: Historic House Museum: 1773 home of Major General James Mitchell Varnum.
Hours & Admission Prices: June-Aug. Sat.-Sun. 10-4; call to confirm hours. Suggested Donations: $5; discounts to AAM & ICOM members. &
Attendance: 600 (estimated)

NEW ENGLAND WIRELESS & STEAM MUSEUM INC., 1300 Frenchtown Rd., East Greenwich, RI 02818-1329. Mailing Address: P.O. Box 883, East Greenwich, RI 02818-0883. Tel.: 401-885-0545.
E-mail: newsm@newsm.org
Web Site: www.newsm.org
Key Personnel: Emeritus Pres., Robert W. Merriam; Pres., Frederick L. Jaggi.
Institution Type/Description: History Museum: listed on the National Register of Historic Places.
Hours & Admission Prices: Groups by appointment only. Adults $15; students $7; discount to groups of 10 or more. &
Attendance: 3,000 (estimated)

VARNUM MEMORIAL ARMORY & MILITARY MUSEUM, 6 Main St., East Greenwich, RI 02818-3827. Tel.: 401-884-4110.
E-mail: armory@varnumcontinentals.org
Web Site: www.varnumcontinentals.org
Key Personnel: C.E.O., Col. John F. Cuddy; Cur., Maj. Donald Marcum.
Institution Type/Description: Military Museum: 1913 medieval-style armory; headquarters of Varnum Continentals military command dating from 1775, built 1913 in Medieval style & occupied by Varnum Continentals.
Hours & Admission Prices: By appointment only. No charge; donations accepted.
Attendance: 600 (estimated)

East Providence

HUNT HOUSE MUSEUM - EAST PROVIDENCE HISTORICAL SOCIETY, 65 Hunts Mills Rd., East Providence, RI 02916. Mailing Address: P.O. Box 4774, East Providence, RI 02916. Tel.: 401-438-1750.
E-mail: info@ephist.org
Web Site: ephist.org
Key Personnel: Pres., Nancy Moore.
Institution Type/Description: Historic House Museum.
Hours & Admission Prices: March-June & Sept.-Dec. 2nd Sun. each month 1-3:30; other times by appointment. No charge; donations accepted.
Attendance: 350 (actual)

Exeter

TOMAQUAG INDIAN MEMORIAL MUSEUM, Arcadia Village, 390 A Summit Rd., Exeter, RI 02822-1808. Tel.: 401-491-9063. Fax: 401-491-9063. Facebook: Tomaquag Museum.
E-mail: lorenspears@tomaquagmuseum.com
Web Site: www.tomaquagmuseum.com
Key Personnel: Dir., Loren Spears; Chm. (V), Maria Lawrence, Ph.D.
Institution Type/Description: Native American Museum.
Hours & Admission Prices: Spring, Summer & Fall: Wed. 10-5, Sat. 10-2; tours, groups & winter by appointment. Adults $5, students & seniors $4, children $3; discounts to Blue Star Museum members; military families Memorial Day-Labor Day no charge. &
Attendance: 2,000 (estimated)

Foster

BORDERS FARM MUSEUM, Borders Farm Preservation, Inc., 31 North Rd., Foster, RI 02825. Tel.: 401-647-5689.
E-mail: farmer@bordersfarm.org
Web Site: www.bordersfarm.org
Key Personnel: Owner, Mary Thomas.
Institution Type/Description: Farm Museum.
Hours & Admission Prices: Daily 8-5; call to confirm.

FOSTER TOWN HOUSE, 181 Howard Hill Rd., Foster, RI 02825-1226. Tel.: 401-392-9200. Fax: 401-702-5010.
E-mail: clsholly@townoffoster.com
Web Site: townoffoster.com
Key Personnel: Dir., Carol Sholly.
Institution Type/Description: Historic House: built in 1781
Hours & Admission Prices: Summer: Mon.-Thurs. 8:30-5:30. No charge. &
Attendance: 300 (estimated)

Jamestown

BEAVERTAIL LIGHTHOUSE MUSEUM, Beavertail State Park, Jamestown, RI 02835. Mailing Address: Beavertail Lighthouse Museum Association, P.O. Box 83, Jamestown, RI 02835-0083. Tel.: 401-423-3270.
E-mail: info@beavertaillight.org
Web Site: www.beavertaillight.org
Key Personnel: Pres. (V), Guy Archambault; Museum Shop Mgr., Dorrie Lynn.
Institution Type/Description: Lighthouse Museum: the third oldest lighthouse on the Atlantic seacoast.
Hours & Admission Prices: May 24 to mid-June & Sept. to Columbus Day Sat.-Sun. 12-3; June 16 to Labor Day daily 10-4. No charge; donations accepted.
Attendance: 27,000 (estimated)

JAMESTOWN FIRE DEPARTMENT MEMORIAL MUSEUM, 50 Narragansett Ave., Jamestown, RI 02835-1167. Tel.: 401-423-0062. Fax: 401-423-7278.
E-mail: jamestownfd@msn.com
Web Site: www.jamestownfd.com/museum.htm
Key Personnel: Museum & Web, Kenneth H. Caswell.
Institution Type/Description: Fire Fighting Museum.
Hours & Admission Prices: Call for hours.

JAMESTOWN MUSEUM, 92 Narragansett Ave., Jamestown, RI 02835-1174. Mailing Address: P.O. Box 156, Jamestown, RI 02835-0156. Tel.: 401-423-0784. Facebook: Jamestown Historical Society.
E-mail: info@jamestownhistoricalsociety.org
Web Site: jamestownhistoricalsociety.org
Key Personnel: Pres., Mary Heath.

Institution Type/Description: Local History Museum: housed in 19th-century schoolhouse.
Hours & Admission Prices: June to early Sept. Wed.-Sun. 1-4; early Sept.-Oct. Sat.-Sun. 1-4. No charge; donations accepted. &
Attendance: 1,000 (estimated)

SYDNEY L. WRIGHT MUSEUM, Jamestown Philomenian Library, 26 North Rd., Jamestown, RI 02835-1434. Tel.: 401-423-7281.
Web Site: www.jamestownri.com/library/museum.htm
Institution Type/Description: Archaeology Museum.
Hours & Admission Prices: mid-May to mid-June Mon.-Tues. 10-9, Wed. 10-5 & 7pm-9pm, Thurs. 12-5 & 7pm-9pm, Fri.-Sat. 10-5; June 15-Sept. 15 Mon.-Tues. 10-9, Wed. 10-5 & 7pm-9pm, Thurs. 12-5 & 7pm-9pm, Fri. 10-5, Sat. 10-2; mid-Sept. to mid-May Mon.-Tues. 10-9, Wed. 10-5 & 7pm-9pm, Thurs. 12-5 & 7pm-9pm, Fri.-Sat. 10-5, Sun. 1-5. &

WATSON FARM, 455 North Rd., Jamestown, RI 02835-2238. Tel.: 401-423-0005. Fax: 401-423-2554.
E-mail: Watsonfarm1796@yahoo.com
Web Site: jamestowncommunityfarm.com/watson_farm/index.htm
Key Personnel: Pres., Carl Nold; Farm Mgr., Don Minto; Farm Mgr., Heather Minto.
Institution Type/Description: Historic Farm: c.1796 Watson Farm, 285-acre working farm.
Hours & Admission Prices: June-Oct. 15 Tues., Thurs. & Sun. 1-5. Adults $4; discounts to seniors, WGBH, AAA, AAM & ICOM members; Historic New England members no charge. Call for further information.
Attendance: 3,059 (actual)

Johnston

CLEMENCE-IRONS HOUSE, 38 George Waterman Rd., Johnston, RI 02919. Mailing Address: 141 Cambridge St., Boston, MA 02114. Tel.: 401-728-9696.
E-mail: clemenceirons@historicnewengland.org
Web Site: www.historicnewengland.org/property/clemence-irons-house/
Key Personnel: Pres. & C.E.O., Carl R. Nold; Site Mgr., Dan Santos.
Institution Type/Description: Historic House Museum: housed in the former home of Richard Clemence; built in 1691.
Hours & Admission Prices: June-Oct. second Sat. 12-3 & by appointment. Adults $6, seniors $5, students $3; members & Johnston residents no charge.
Attendance: 327 (actual)

ELIJAH ANGELL HOUSE/JOHNSTON HISTORY MUSEUM, 101 Putnam Pike, Johnston, RI 02919. Tel.: 401-231-3380.
E-mail: info@johnstonhistorical.org
Key Personnel: Pres. (V), Louis H. McGowan.
Institution Type/Description: Historic House Museum: housed in a farm house built in 1824. Listed on the National Register of Historic Places.
Hours & Admission Prices: Mon. 6:30pm-8:30pm, Fri. 2-5. No charge; donations accepted. &

Kingston

FAYERWEATHER HOUSE, 1859 Mooresfield Rd., Kingston, RI 02881-1715. Mailing Address: P.O. Box 222, Wakefield, RI 02880. Tel.: 401-789-9072. Facebook.
E-mail: info@fayerweathercraftguild.com
Web Site: www.fayerweatherhouse.com/
Key Personnel: Pres. (V), Cynthia Smythe.
Institution Type/Description: Historic House Museum: built in 1820. Listed on the National Register of Historic Places.
Hours & Admission Prices: May-Dec. Tues.-Sat. 10-4. No charge.

FINE ARTS CENTER MAIN GALLERY, 105 Upper College Rd., Kingston, RI 02881. Tel.: 401-874-5821. Fax: 401-874-2729.
E-mail: artdept@etal.uri.edu
Web Site: www.uri.edu/artsci/art/galleries.html
Key Personnel: Dir., Ronald Hutt.
Institution Type/Description: Art Gallery.
Hours & Admission Prices: Mon.-Sat. 12-4. No charge; donations accepted.
Attendance: 10,262 (actual)

HELME HOUSE GALLERY, 2587 Kingstown Rd., Kingston, RI 02881-1605. Tel.: 401-783-2195.
E-mail: socart@verizon.net
Web Site: www.southcountyart.org
Key Personnel: Dir., Jason Fong.
Institution Type/Description: Art Gallery.

Hours & Admission Prices: Wed.-Sun. 1-5. Closed holidays.

PETTAQUAMSCUTT HISTORICAL SOCIETY, 2636 Kingstown Rd., Kingston, RI 02881-1624. Tel.: 401-783-1328. Facebook: Pettaquamscutt Historical.
E-mail: washingtoncountyhistory@gmail.com
Web Site: www.washingtoncountyhistory.org
Key Personnel: Exec. Dir., Erica Luke; Pres. (V), Jeffrey Taber.
Institution Type/Description: Historical Society Museum: housed in 1858 & 1861 Old Washington County Jail.
Hours & Admission Prices: Feb.-Dec. Thurs. & Sat. 11-4; other times by appointment. Adults $5, students & seniors $3; discounts to AAM members; members and children 12 & under no charge.
Attendance: 2,000 (estimated)

Lincoln

ARNOLD HOUSE, 487 Great Rd., Lincoln, RI 02865. Mailing Address: Historic New England, 141 Cambridge St., Boston, MA 02114-2702. Tel.: 401-728-9696.
E-mail: arnoldhouse@historicnewengland.org
Web Site: www.historicnewengland.org
Key Personnel: Site Mgr., Dan Santos.
Institution Type/Description: National Historic House/Landmark: built in 1693.
Hours & Admission Prices: Sat.-Sun. 11-5. Adults $8; discounts to AAM & ICOM members; Historic New England members no charge.
Attendance: 4,014 (actual)

CAPTAIN WILBUR KELLY HOUSE, Blackstone River State Park, Lower River Rd., Lincoln, RI 02865. Mailing Address: Blackstone Heritage Corridor, 670 Linwood Ave., Whitinsville, MA 01588-2068. Tel.: 401-333-0295.
E-mail: dem.riparks@dem.ri.gov
Web Site: www.riparks.com
Institution Type/Description: Historic House Museum: housed in the former home of canal boat captain & mill owner Wilbur Kelly.
Hours & Admission Prices: April-Oct. daily 9-5. No charge.

FRIENDS OF HEARTHSIDE, INC., 677 Great Rd., Lincoln, RI 02865-1401. Mailing Address: 404 Front St., Lincoln, RI 02865. Tel.: 401-726-0597.
E-mail: kathy.hartley@hearthsidehouse.org
Web Site: www.hearthsidehouse.org
Key Personnel: Chm. (V), Kathryn A. Hartley; Vice Pres., Site Mngmt., John Scanlon.
Institution Type/Description: Historic House: housed in an 1810 mansion.
Hours & Admission Prices: March-Dec. see website for hours. Adults $8, seniors $6, children 10-17 $4; members & children under 10 no charge.
Attendance: 1,000 (estimated)

NORTH GATE, 1873 Old Louisquisset Pike, Lincoln, RI 02865. Mailing Address: Blackstone Valley Historical Society, P.O. Box 125, Lincoln, RI 02865. Tel.: 401-725-2847.
E-mail: bvhsri@gmail.com
Web Site: www.bvhsri.org
Institution Type/Description: Historic Building: housed in a former toll-gate house for the Louisquisset Tpke. Co., built in 1807; served as a hotel in mid-1800s.
Hours & Admission Prices: By appointment.

Little Compton

LITTLE COMPTON HISTORICAL SOCIETY, 548 W. Main Rd., Little Compton, RI 02837-1123. Mailing Address: P.O. Box 577, Little Compton, RI 02837-0577. Tel.: 401-635-4035. Fax: 401-635-4035.
E-mail: lchistory@littlecompton.org
Web Site: www.littlecompton.org
Key Personnel: Mng. Dir., Marjory O'Toole; Pres. (V), Dora Atwater Millikin; Admin., Nancy Carignan; Mgr. Collections, Fred Bridge.
Institution Type/Description: History Museum: housed in 1850 Wilbor Barn & 1690-1860 Wilbor House.
Hours & Admission Prices: late June to Labor Day Thurs.-Sun. 1-5; Sept.-Oct. Sat.-Sun. 1-5; other times by appointment. Adults $7.50, children $5; discounts to NEMA members; reciprocal membership; members no charge.
Attendance: 2,750 (estimated)

Middletown

NORMAN BIRD SANCTUARY, 583 Third Beach Rd., Middletown, RI 02842-5738. Tel.: 401-846-2577. Fax: 401-846-2772.
E-mail: nharrison@normanbirdsanctuary.org
Web Site: www.normanbirdsanctuary.org
Key Personnel: Exec. Dir., Natasha Harrison; Dir. Properties, Joseph McLaughlin; Dir. Education, Kim Botelho; Coord. Education, Rachel Holbert; Coord. Education, Nicole Lavoie; Administrative Dir., Lesley Muir; Dir. Devel., Suzanne Garvin; Devel. Asst., Erika Gibb.
Institution Type/Description: Bird Sanctuary.
Hours & Admission Prices: Daily 9-5. Trail: adults $6, children 3-12 $3; children under 3 & members no charge. Closed major holidays.
Attendance: 40,000 (estimated)

PRESCOTT FARM, 2009 W. Main Rd., Middletown, RI 02842-7963. Mailing Address: Newport Restoration Foundation, 51 Touro St., Newport, RI 02840. Tel.: 401-849-7300.
Web Site: www.newportrestoration.org/visit/prescott_farm/
Key Personnel: Exec. Dir., Pieter Roos.
Institution Type/Description: History Museum.
Hours & Admission Prices: June-Sept. Tues.-Sat. 10-3. Guided Tour: adults $5; children under 12 no charge. Grounds: no charge.

SACHUEST POINT NATIONAL WILDLIFE REFUGE, 769 Sachuest Point Rd., Middletown, RI 02842. Mailing Address: 50 Bend Rd., Charlestown, RI 02813-2503. Tel.: 401-847-5511. Fax: 401-619-2680.
Web Site: www.fws.gov/refuge/Sachuest_Point
Institution Type/Description: Wildlife Refuge.
Hours & Admission Prices: Visitor Center: daily 10-4.
Attendance: 65,000 (estimated)

WHITEHALL MUSEUM HOUSE, 311 Berkeley Ave., Middletown, RI 02842-5392. Mailing Address: P.O. Box 4144, Middletown, RI 02842-0144. Tel.: 401-846-3116.
E-mail: jrmcd1951@aol.com
Web Site: whitehallmuseumhouse.org
Key Personnel: Chm. (V) & Pres. (V), Eleanor Burgess; Museum Shop Mgr., Maris Humphreys.
Institution Type/Description: Historic House Museum: housed in the former home of Anglican Bishop, George Berkeley; built in 1729.
Hours & Admission Prices: July-Aug. Tues.-Sun. 10-4; other times by appointment. Adults $5; discounts to AAA & International Berkeley Society members and Anglican clergy; members no charge.
Attendance: 534 (actual)

Narragansett

SOUTH COUNTY MUSEUM INC., 115 Strathmore St., Narragansett, RI 02882. Mailing Address: Box 709, Narragansett, RI 02882-0709. Tel.: 401-783-5400. Fax: 401-783-0506.
E-mail: info@southcountymuseum.org
Web Site: www.southcountymuseum.org
Key Personnel: Pres., Daryl Anne Anderson; Vice Pres., Doris Manganaro; Staff Dir., Jim Crothers; Business Mgr., Carolyn Shea.
Institution Type/Description: History Museum.
Hours & Admission Prices: May-June & Sept. Fri.-Sat. 10-4; July-Aug. Wed.-Sat. 10-4. Adults $6, seniors $5, children 6-12 $2; discounts to AAM, AAA, NEMA, & AASLH members; children under 6 & members no charge.
Attendance: 3,017 (actual)

Newport

ARTILLERY COMPANY OF NEWPORT MILITARY MUSEUM, 23 Clarke St., Newport, RI 02840-3023. Mailing Address: P.O. Box 14, Newport, RI 02840. Tel.: 401-846-8488.
E-mail: info@newportartillery.org
Web Site: www.newportartillery.org
Key Personnel: Colonel Commanding, Col. Craig Mulvey; Exec. Officer, LTC Seth Chiaro; Operations Officer, Major Robert Beebe; Adjutant & Communications Officer, Capt. Kenneth L. Pike; Finance Officer, 2nd Lt. Corinne Edenbach.
Institution Type/Description: Military Museum: housed in c.1836 Armory.
Hours & Admission Prices: May-Oct. Sat. 10-4. No charge; donations accepted.

CARROT MUSEUM - ARMISTEAD COTTAGE, 55 Hunter Ave., Newport, RI 02840. Tel.: 401-848-7123. Fax: 401-848-0977.
E-mail: romana@armisteadcottage.com

Key Personnel: Owner, Romana Zawarti.
Institution Type/Description: Carrot Museum: housed in Armistead Cottage Bed & Breakfast.
Hours & Admission Prices: Call for hours.

COLONY HOUSE, Washington Square, Newport, RI 02840. Mailing Address: c/o Newport Historical Society, 82 Touro St., Newport, RI 02840-2931. Tel.: 401-846-0813. Fax: 401-846-1853.
Web Site: newporthistory.org
Institution Type/Description: Historic State House Building: 1739 Colony House. Listed on the National Register of Historic Places.
Hours & Admission Prices: Call for hours. &
Attendance: 2,750 (estimated)

EDWARD KING HOUSE, 35 King St., Newport, RI 02840-3595. Tel.: 401-846-7426.
E-mail: info@edwardkinghouse.org
Web Site: www.edwardkinghouse.org
Institution Type/Description: Historic House: former home of China Trade merchant, Edward King; built in c.1845.
Hours & Admission Prices: Tours: Mon.-Fri. 9-4; other times by appointment.

FORT ADAMS STATE PARK, 90 Fort Adams Dr., Newport, RI 02840. Tel.: 401-841-0707. Fax: 401-841-0790.
E-mail: fort@fortadams.org
Web Site: www.fortadams.org
Key Personnel: Exec. Dir., Joe Dias.
Institution Type/Description: Park & History Museum.
Hours & Admission Prices: Memorial Day to Columbus Day 10-4. Adults $10, children 6-17 $5; discounts to groups; children 5 & under no charge.
Attendance: 20,000 (estimated)

FRIENDS MEETING HOUSE (QUAKER), 30 Marlborough St., Newport, RI 02840. Mailing Address: Newport Historical Society, 82 Touro St., Newport, RI 02840-2931. Tel.: 401-846-0831 (Historical Society).
Institution Type/Description: Historic House: built in 1704
Hours & Admission Prices: Call for hours.

INTERNATIONAL TENNIS HALL OF FAME & MUSEUM, 194 Bellevue Ave., Newport, RI 02840-3586. Tel.: 401-849-3990, 800-457-1144. Fax: 401-849-8780 & 851-7920 (Research Center).
E-mail: newport@tennisfame.com
Web Site: www.tennisfame.com
Key Personnel: C.E.O., Todd Martin; Dir., Douglas Stark; Chm., John Arnhold; Pres., Stan Smith; Retail Merchandising & Sales Mgr., Julie Suazo.
Institution Type/Description: Sports Museum: housed in the 1880 Newport Casino, site of the first national tennis championships, held in 1881.
Hours & Admission Prices: Daily 9:30-5. Adults $12, seniors, military & student $10; discounts to USTA, AAA, NEMA, ISHA, ICOM & AAM members; members and children 16 & under no charge. Closed Thanksgiving; Christmas. &
Attendance: 25,000 (estimated)

MUSEUM OF YACHTING, Fort Adams State Park, 449 Thames St., Newport, RI 02840-6720. Tel.: 401-848-5777.
E-mail: info@iyrs.edu
Web Site: iyrs.edu
Key Personnel: Pres., Terry Nathan; C.O.O. & C.F.O., Rebeka Mazzone.
Institution Type/Description: Yachting Museum: located in Fort Adams State Park.
Hours & Admission Prices: Tues.-Sat. 12-5. Adults $5; discounts to groups; members, students & children under 18 no charge.
Attendance: 8,000 (actual)

NATIONAL MUSEUM OF AMERICAN ILLUSTRATION, 492 Bellevue Ave., Newport, RI 02840-4127. Tel.: 401-851-8949. Fax: 401-851-8974.
E-mail: art@americanillustration.org
Web Site: www.americanillustration.org
Key Personnel: Dir. & Co-Founder, Judy Goffman Cutler; C.E.O. & Chair, Laurence S. Cutler; Admin. Interior & Museum Shop Mgr., Jill Perkins; Exec. Asst., Shelley Shaw; Exec. Asst., Lauren Scrima; Groundskeeper, Craig Knowles.
Institution Type/Description: Art Museum.
Hours & Admission Prices: Memorial Day Weekend to Labor Day Thurs.-Sun. 11-5; Labor Day to Memorial Day Weekend Fri. 11-5. Adults $20, senior citizens 60 & over and military with ID $18, students with ID $14, children 5-12 $10; AAM members no charge. Children under 5 not admitted.
Attendance: 10,000 (estimated)

NAVAL WAR COLLEGE MUSEUM, 686 Cushing Rd., Newport, RI 02841-1207. Tel.: 401-841-4052. Fax: 401-841-7074.
E-mail: museum@usnwc.edu
Web Site: www.usnwc.edu/NWC-museum
Key Personnel: Dir., Dr. David Kohnen; Mng. Dir., Ryan Meyer; Dir. Education, Liz DeLucia; Cur., Rob Doane; Mgr. Collections, Walter Nicolds.
Institution Type/Description: Naval Museum: housed in 1820 Founders Hall, a National Historic Landmark.
Hours & Admission Prices: Mon.-Fri. 10-4; advanced reservation required for visitors without base access. No charge. Closed Federal holidays. &
Attendance: 25,000 (estimated)

NEWPORT ART MUSEUM & ART ASSOCIATION, 76 Bellevue Ave., Newport, RI 02840-7411. Tel.: 401-848-8200. Fax: 401-848-8205. Facebook: Newport Art Museum.
E-mail: info@newportartmuseum.org
Web Site: www.newportartmuseum.org
Key Personnel: Exec. Dir., Norah Diedrich; Pres., Sandra Craig; Cur., Francine Weiss; Dir. Education, Maggie Anderson.
Institution Type/Description: Art Museum.
Hours & Admission Prices: Tues.-Sat. 10-4, Sun. 12-4. Open holiday Mondays. Adults $10, seniors 65+ $8, active military with ID & students $6, children 5 & under & members no charge, discounts to AAA & NARM members; Sat. 11-12 no charge. &
Attendance: 19,619 (actual)

NEWPORT HISTORICAL SOCIETY & THE MUSEUM OF NEWPORT HISTORY, 127 Thames St., Newport, RI 02840-6627. Mailing Address: 82 Touro St., Newport, RI 02840-2931. Tel.: 401-846-0813 & 841-8770. Fax: 401-846-1853.
E-mail: info@newporthistorical.org
Web Site: newporthistory.org
Key Personnel: Exec. Dir., Ruth Taylor; Pres. (V), Thomas Goddard; Reference Librarian & Genealogist, Bertram Lippincott, III; Dir. of Education, Ingrid Peters.
Institution Type/Description: History Museum.
Hours & Admission Prices: Newport Historical Society Library & Gallery: Tues.-Fri. 9:30-4:30, Sat. 9:30-12. No charge. Museum of Newport History: Winter: daily 10-5. Summer: Mon.-Sat. 10-6, Sun. 10-5. Suggested Donation: adults $4, children $2; discounts to AAM & ICOM members; members & children under 5 no charge.
Attendance: 30,000 (estimated)

NEWPORT RESTORATION FOUNDATION, 51 Touro St., Newport, RI 02840-2932. Tel.: 401-849-7300. Fax: 401-849-0125. Facebook: Newport Restoration Foundation.
E-mail: info@newportrestoration.org
Web Site: newportrestoration.org
Key Personnel: Interim Exec. Dir., Wendy Nicholas; Dir. Finance & Administration, Amy Winsor; Dir. Preservation, Shantia Anderheggen; Public Programs Mgr., Kelsey Mullen; Mktg. Coord., Meaghan Barry; Cur., Kristen Costa; Human Resources Admin., Maeve Sheehan.
Institution Type/Description: Historic House Museum.
Hours & Admission Prices: Rough Point: mid-March to mid-May Thurs.-Sun. 10-2; mid-May to early Nov. Tues.-Sun. 10-3:45. Adults $25; discounts to AAM members; children 12 & under no charge. Whitehorne House: May-Oct. Thurs.-Sun. 10:30-3. Adults $6; discounts to AAM members; children 12 & under no charge. Guided Tours: 10:30 & 3. Adults $12; discounts to AAM members. Prescott Farm Grounds: daily dawn to dusk. No charge. &
Attendance: 21,455 (estimated)

THE PRESERVATION SOCIETY OF NEWPORT COUNTY/ THE NEWPORT MANSIONS, 424 Bellevue Ave., Newport, RI 02840-6924. Tel.: 401-847-1000.
E-mail: info@newportmansions.org
Web Site: www.newportmansions.org
Key Personnel: C.E.O. & Exec. Dir., Trudy Coxe; Chm., Monty M. Burnham; Chief of Staff, Terry Dickinson; Dir. Museum Affairs, Lise Dubé-Scherr; Dir. Devel., Maureen Sheridan; Dir. Finance, Jim Burress; Dir. Museum Experience, John Rodman; Dir. Gardens & Grounds, Jeff Curtis; Dir. Retail Sales, Cynthia O'Malley; Dir. Properties, Christopher Daly; Dir. Special Events, Philip Pelletier.
Institution Type/Description: 11 historic house museums on 88 acres & arboretum c.1748-1902.
Hours & Admission Prices: Visit website for hours. Adults $15-$35, children 6-17 $7.50-$12; discounts to groups of 20 or more & AAM members; members no charge. Closed Thanksgiving; Christmas. &
Attendance: 1,017,586 (actual)

REDWOOD LIBRARY AND ATHENAEUM, 50 Bellevue Ave., Newport, RI 02840-3292. Tel.: 401-847-0292. Fax: 401-841-5680.
E-mail: redwood@redwoodlibrary.org
Web Site: www.redwoodlibrary.org
Key Personnel: Exec. Dir., Benedict Leca; Pres. (V), Edwin G. Fischer, M.D.
Institution Type/Description: Historic Building: c.1750 designed by architect, Peter Harrison.
Hours & Admission Prices: Mon.-Wed. & Fri.-Sat. 9:30-5:30, Thurs. 9:30-8, Sun. 1-5; Admission $10; members, students under 18 & first Sun. of the month no charge. Closed holidays. ⅊
Attendance: 20,000 (estimated)

ROSE ISLAND LIGHTHOUSE, One Washington St, Newport, RI 02840. Mailing Address: Rose Island Lighthouse Foundation, P.O. Box 1419, Newport, RI 02840-0014. Tel.: 401-847-4242. Fax: 401-847-7262.
E-mail: david@roseisland.org
Web Site: www.roseisland.org
Key Personnel: Exec. Dir., David McCurdy.
Institution Type/Description: Lighthouse Museum: listed on the National Register of Historic Places.
Hours & Admission Prices: July to Labor Day daily 10-4; other times by appointment. Island accessible by ferry. Museum: adults $5, seniors 65 & over and children 6-12 $4.

SAVE THE BAY EXPLORATION CENTER AND AQUARIUM, 100 Save The Bay Drive, Newport, RI 02905. Tel.: 401-272-3540. Fax: 401-273-7151. Facebook: Save the Bay Exploration Center and Aquarium.
E-mail: savebay@savebay.org
Web Site: www.savebay.org/aquarium
Institution Type/Description: Marine Science Learning Center.
Hours & Admission Prices: Memorial Day to Labor Day daily 10-4; Labor Day-Memorial Day Fri.-Sun. 10.-4. Adults $8, seniors & military $$7; children 3 & under no charge. ⅊
Attendance: 24,000 (actual)

TOURO SYNAGOGUE, 85 Touro St., Newport, RI 02840-2969. Tel.: 401-847-4794.
E-mail: meryle@tourosynagogue.org
Web Site: www.tourosynagogue.org
Key Personnel: Admin., Meryle Cawley.
Institution Type/Description: Historic Building: built in 1763. A National Historic Site.
Hours & Admission Prices: See website for hours. Adults $12, seniors $10, students, military, National Trust & Park Service with ID $8; discounts to groups of 10 or more; children 13 & under no charge.
Attendance: 30,000 (estimated)

North Kingstown

QUONSET AIR MUSEUM, North Kingstown, RI 02852-7406. Mailing Address: P.O. Box 1571, North Kingstown, RI 02852-0629. Tel.: 401-294-9540. Fax: 401-294-9887.
E-mail: support@quonsetairmuseum.com
Web Site: quonsetairmuseum.com
Key Personnel: Pres., David Stecker; Dir. & Museum Shop Mgr., David H. Payne.
Institution Type/Description: Air Museum.
Hours & Admission Prices: Temporarily closed. ⅊
Attendance: 8,500 (estimated)

RHODE ISLAND COMPUTER MUSEUM, 310 Compass Cir., Bldg. 310, Bay C, North Kingstown, RI 02852. Mailing Address: 1130 Ten Rod Rd., Bldg. D, Ste. 103A, North Kingstown, RI 02852. Tel.: 401-603-3321.
E-mail: rhodeislandcomputermuseum@gmail.com
Web Site: www.ricomputermuseum.org
Institution Type/Description: Computer Museum.
Hours & Admission Prices: By appointment.

SEABEE MUSEUM AND MEMORIAL PARK, 21 Iafrate Way, North Kingstown, RI 02852-1792. Tel.: 401-294-7233. Fax: 401-294-9501.
E-mail: info@seabeemuseum.com
Web Site: www.seabeemuseum.com
Key Personnel: Pres. (V), Nicholas Fisch; Museum Shop Mgr., Robert Schwab.
Institution Type/Description: Military Museum.

Hours & Admission Prices: May-Oct. daily 9:30-2; Nov.-April Wed. & Sat.-Sun. 9:30-2; other times by appointment. No charge; donations accepted.
Attendance: 3,500 (estimated)

Pawtucket

DAGGETT HOUSE, Slater Memorial Park, Next to Loof Carousel, Pawtucket, RI 02861. Mailing Address: 16 Second St., Pawtucket, RI 02861-3133. Tel.: 401-722-6931.
E-mail: darpawtucket@hotmail.com
Institution Type/Description: Historic House: housed in the restored former home of John Daggett, Jr.; built 1685. Listed on the National Register of Historic Places.
Hours & Admission Prices: Tours: May to mid-Dec. by appointment.
Attendance: 700 (estimated)

OLD SLATER MILL NATIONAL HISTORIC LANDMARK, 67 Roosevelt Ave., Pawtucket, RI 02860-2127. Mailing Address: P.O. Box 696, Pawtucket, RI 02862-0696. Tel.: 401-725-8638. Fax: 401-722-3040.
E-mail: info@slatermill.org
Web Site: www.slatermill.org
Key Personnel: Exec. Dir., Lori Urso; Program Dir., Erika Davis; Facilities Coord., Jay Brunelle; Booking Agent, Joyce Neves.
Institution Type/Description: History Museum of Textile Industry.
Hours & Admission Prices: March-April & Nov. Sat.-Sun. 11-3; May-June & Sept.-Oct. Wed. Sun. & Mon. holidays 10-4; July 4th to Labor Day Tues. 10-4; Dec.-Jan. groups by appointment. Adults $12, senior citizens 65 & over and students $10, children 6-12 $8.50; members, Blue Star museum members & children under 6 no charge. ⅊
Attendance: 30,000 (estimated)

Peace Dale

MUSEUM OF PRIMITIVE ART AND CULTURE, 1058 Kingstown Rd., Ste. 5, Peace Dale, RI 02879-2487. Tel.: 401-783-5711. Facebook: Museum of Primitive Art and Culture.
E-mail: mpaac@verizon.net
Web Site: www.primitiveartmuseum.org
Key Personnel: Pres. (V), Virginia Williams.
Institution Type/Description: Anthropology Museum.
Hours & Admission Prices: Wed. 10-2; other times by appointment. Suggested Donation $1; discounts to AAM, ICOM & NEMA members; members no charge. Closed holidays.
Attendance: 3,000 (estimated)

Portsmouth

PORTSMOUTH HISTORICAL SOCIETY, 870 E. Main Rd. & Union St., Portsmouth, RI 02871. Mailing Address: P.O. Box 834, Portsmouth, RI 02871-0834. Tel.: 401-683-9178. Facebook.
E-mail: phsinfo@portsmouthhistorical.org
Web Site: www.portsmouthhistorical.org
Key Personnel: Pres., James E. Garman.
Institution Type/Description: Local History Museum: housed in 1865 former Portsmouth Christian Union Church. Listed on the National Historic Register.
Hours & Admission Prices: Memorial Day to Columbus Day Sun. 2-5; other times by appointment. No charge; donations accepted.
Attendance: 600 (estimated)

Providence

ANNMARY BROWN MEMORIAL, 21 Brown St., Box A, Providence, RI 02912-9005. Tel.: 401-863-2942.
E-mail: peter_harrington@brown.edu
Web Site: library.brown.edu/about/amb
Key Personnel: Head, Business & Facilities, Barbara Schulz; Cur., Peter Harrington.
Institution Type/Description: Art Museum.
Hours & Admission Prices: Labor Day to Memorial Day Mon.-Fri. 1-5, during the academic year. No charge. Closed national holidays.

BERT GALLERY, 24 Bridge St., Providence, RI 02903. Tel.: 401-751-2628. Facebook & Twitter: @BertGallery.
E-mail: info@bertgallery.com
Web Site: www.bertgallery.com
Key Personnel: Dir. & Owner, Catherine Little Bert.
Institution Type/Description: Art Gallery.
Hours & Admission Prices: Open by appointment only.

BETSY WILLIAMS COTTAGE, Roger Williams Park, 1000 Williams Ave., Providence, RI 02907. Tel.: 401-785-9450. Fax: 401-941-5920.
Key Personnel: Park Supt., Wendy Nilsson.
Institution Type/Description: Historic House: housed in the former home of Betsy Williams; built in 1773 by Nathaniel Williams for his son James, the father of Betsy. The home is located in Roger Williams Park, named after the founder of the city of Providence and one of the founders of RI.
Hours & Admission Prices: Call for information.

CHAZAN GALLERY AT WHEELER, 228 Angell St., Providence, RI 02906. Tel.: 401-421-9230. Facebook: @chazangallery.org.
E-mail: info@chazangallery.org
Web Site: chazangallery.org
Key Personnel: Dir., Liz Kilduff; Asst. Dir., Elena Lledo.
Institution Type/Description: Art Gallery.
Hours & Admission Prices: Sept.-May Tues.-Sat. 11-4, Sun. 2-4. No charge.
Attendance: 3,000 (estimated)

DAVID WINTON BELL GALLERY, List Art Center, Brown University, 64 College St., Providence, RI 02912. Tel.: 401-863-2932. Fax: 401-863-9323. Facebook: @BellGallery.
E-mail: jo-ann_conklin@brown.edu
Web Site: www.brown.edu/bellgallery
Key Personnel: Dir., Jo-Ann Conklin; Cur., Ian Alden Russell; Admin., Terrance Abbott; Preparator, Ian Budish; Preparator, Naushon Hale.
Institution Type/Description: University Art Gallery.
Hours & Admission Prices: Mon.-Wed. & Fri. 11-4, Thurs. 1-9, Sat. & Sun. 1-4. No charge; donations accepted. Closed Dr. Martin Luther King, Jr. Day; Memorial Day; Independence Day; Labor Day; Thanksgiving & day after; Christmas. &
Attendance: 10,000 (estimated)

EDWARD MITCHELL BANNISTER GALLERY, Rhode Island College - Roberts Hall, 124, 600 Mt. Pleasant Ave., Providence, RI 02908. Tel.: 401-456-9765.
E-mail: bannistergallery@ric.edu
Web Site: www.ric.edu/bannister/Pages/default.aspx
Key Personnel: Dir., James Montford.
Institution Type/Description: Art Gallery.
Hours & Admission Prices: Academic Year: Tues.-Fri. noon to 8; Summer: Mon.-Wed. 11-5, Thurs. noon to 8. No charge. Closed holidays. &

GOVERNOR HENRY LIPPITT HOUSE MUSEUM, 199 Hope St., Providence, RI 02906-2136. Mailing Address: c/o Preserve Rhode Island, 957 N. Main St., Providence, RI 02904. Tel.: 401-453-0688. Facebook & Twitter: @lippitthouse; Instagram: @lippitthousemuseum.
E-mail: lippitthouse@preserveri.org
Web Site: www.preserveri.org/lippitt-house-museum
Key Personnel: Museum Dir., Carrie Taylor; Cur. Education, Jaclyn Delamatre; Museum Rentals Mgr., Kristen Minsky.
Institution Type/Description: Historic House: 1865 renaissance-revival mansion; a National Historic Landmark.
Hours & Admission Prices: Mon.-Fri. 9-4; other times by appointment. Adults $10, students w/ID $5; discount to groups & AAM members; children 12 & under & active military w/ID no charge. Closed all holidays.
Attendance: 1,350 (estimated)

HAFFENREFFER MUSEUM OF ANTHROPOLOGY, BROWN UNIVERSITY, 21 Prospect St., Providence, RI 02912. Mailing Address: 300 Tower St., Bristol, RI 02809. Tel.: 401-863-2065. Fax: 401-253-1198. Facebook; Twitter; Instagram.
E-mail: haffenreffermuseum@brown.edu
Web Site: www.brown.edu/Facilities/Haffenreffer/index.html
Key Personnel: Dir., Robert Preucel; Pres. Friends Bd., Jeffrey Schreck; Deputy Dir. & Chief Cur., Kevin P. Smith; Cur., Thierry Gentis; Registrar, Dawn Kimbrel; Exhibit Designer & Photographic Archivist, Rip Gerry; Museum Opers. & Communications Coord., Emily Jackson; Cur. Education, Geralyn Ducady.
Institution Type/Description: Anthropology Museum.
Hours & Admission Prices: Manning Hall Gallery: Tues.-Sun. 10-4. No charge; donations accepted. Closed federal holidays; university breaks. &
Attendance: 17,000 (estimated)

HUNT-CAVANAGH GALLERY, PROVIDENCE COLLEGE, 63 Eaton St., Providence, RI 02918. Tel.: 401-865-2400.
E-mail: pcgalleries@providence.edu
Web Site: pcgalleries.providence.edu
Key Personnel: Dir. & Cur., Jamilee Lacy.

Institution Type/Description: Art Gallery.
Hours & Admission Prices: During Exhibitions: Wed.-Sat. noon to 6; other times by appointment. No charge. Closed college holidays.

JOHN HAY LIBRARY, BROWN UNIVERSITY, 20 Prospect St., Box A, Providence, RI 02912. Tel.: 401-863-2146.
E-mail: hay@brown.edu
Web Site: library.brown.edu/hay
Key Personnel: Dir. John Hay Library & Special Collections, Christopher Geissler; Univ. Archivist & Asst. Dir. Special Collections, Jennifer Betts; Univ. Cur., Robert Emlen.
Institution Type/Description: Library.
Hours & Admission Prices: Mon.-Thurs. 10-10, Fri. 10-5, Sun. noon to 10. No charge; donations accepted. &

JOHN NICHOLAS BROWN CENTER FOR PUBLIC HUMANITIES AND CULTURAL HERITAGE, Nightingale Brown House, 357 Benefit St., Providence, RI 02903. Mailing Address: c/o Brown University, Box 1880, Providence, RI 02912-1880. Tel.: 401-863-1177. Fax: 401-863-7777. Facebook: John Nicholas Brown Center for Public Humanities & Cultural Heritage.
E-mail: publichumanities@brown.edu
Web Site: www.brown.edu/jnbc
Key Personnel: Dir., Susan Smulyan; Asst. Dir. Professional Programs & Cur., Ronald Potvin; Asst. Dir. Programs, Marissa Brown; Ctr. Mgr., Sabina Griffin.
Institution Type/Description: Brown University Public Humanities MA Program.
Hours & Admission Prices: Labor Day to Memorial Day Mon.-Fri. 9-5; Memorial Day to Labor Day 9-4.
Attendance: 1,500 (estimated)

MEETING HOUSE OF THE FIRST BAPTIST CHURCH IN AMERICA, 75 N. Main St., Providence, RI 02903-1307. Tel.: 401-454-3418.
E-mail: fbc_inamerica@verizon.net
Web Site: www.fbcia.org
Key Personnel: Minister, Rev. Jamie Washam; Moderator, Dr. Joanne Schneider.
Institution Type/Description: Historic Building: a National Historic Landmark.
Hours & Admission Prices: Mon.-Fri. 10-12 & 1-3; groups by appointment. Guided Tours: Sun. after church services. $2 per person. Closed National holidays. &
Attendance: 9,000 (estimated)

MUSEUM OF NATURAL HISTORY AND CORMACK PLANETARIUM, Roger Williams Park, 1000 Elmwood Ave., Providence, RI 02907. Tel.: 401-680-7221. Fax: 401-461-5146. Facebook: @museumofnaturalhistoryandplanetarium.
E-mail: info@musnathist.com
Web Site: providenceri.com/museum
Formerly: Museum of Natural History, Roger Williams Park
Key Personnel: Dir., Renee Gamba.
Institution Type/Description: Natural History Museum.
Hours & Admission Prices: Museum: daily 10-4. General admission $2; discounts to AAM & AAA members; children under 4 no charge. Planetarium: Sat.-Sun. 2 pm. Admission $3; discounts to AAM & AAA members; children under 4 not permitted. Closed holidays. &
Attendance: 100,000 (estimated)

PROVIDENCE ATHENAEUM, 251 Benefit St., Providence, RI 02903-2799. Tel.: 401-421-6970. Fax: 401-421-2860. Facebook: @ProvidenceAthenaeum; Instagram & Twitter: @pvdAth.
E-mail: info@providenceathenaeum.org
Web Site: www.providenceathenaeum.org
Key Personnel: Exec. Dir., Matt Burriesci; Business Mgr., Ken Garrepy; Bldg. & Grounds Mgr., Leslie Myers; Dir. Collections & Library Svcs., Kate Wodehouse; Dir. Membership & Devel., Danielle Kemsley; Dir. Programs, Holly Gaboriault.
Institution Type/Description: Historic Building: built in 1838.
Hours & Admission Prices: Mon.-Thurs. 9-7, Fri. & Sat. 9-5, Sun. 1-5; Memorial Day to Labor Day Mon.-Thurs. 10-6, Fri.-Sat. 9-5, Sat. 10-2. No charge; donations accepted. Closed New Year's Day; Martin Luther King Jr. Day; Presidents' Day; Easter; Memorial Day; Independence Day; Victory Day; Labor Day; Columbus Day; Veterans Day; Thanksgiving; Christmas Eve & Day.

PROVIDENCE CHILDREN'S MUSEUM, 100 South St., Providence, RI 02903-4749. Tel.: 401-273-5437. Fax: 401-273-1004. Facebook: @ProvidenceChildrensMuseum; Twitter: @ProvCM.
E-mail: info@childrenmuseum.org
Web Site: www.childrenmuseum.org

Key Personnel: Exec. Dir., Caroline Payson O'Donnell; Assoc. Dir. & Dir. Communications, Megan Fischer; Dir. Finance & Opers., Marvin Ronning; Dir. Devel., Jennifer Laurelli; Dir. Education, Kristin Read; Visitor Experience Mgr., Turenne Bedell; Program Dir., Heidi Brinig; Membership & Mktg. Coord., Jocelyn Hopkins.
Institution Type/Description: Children's Museum.
Hours & Admission Prices: April to August daily 9-6; Sept.-March Tues.-Sun. 9-6. Admission $9; discounts to groups and AAM, ICOM & NEMA members; members, ACM members, children under 12 months no charge. Closed Thanksgiving; Christmas Eve & Day. &
Attendance: 144,684 (actual)

PROVIDENCE CITY HALL, 25 Dorrance St., Providence, RI 02903-1738. Mailing Address: c/o Providence Dept. of Art, Culture + Tourism, 444 Westminster St., 3rd Fl., Providence, RI 02903. Tel.: 401-421-7740. Fax: 401-274-8240.
E-mail: sfortunato@providenceri.com
Web Site: www.providenceri.com
Key Personnel: Dir. Art, Culture + Tourism, Stephanie Fortunato.
Institution Type/Description: Historic Building: built in 1878. Listed on the National Register of Historic Places.
Hours & Admission Prices: Summer: Mon.-Fri. 8:30-4; Winter: Mon.-Fri. 8:30-4:30. Tours by appointment.

PROVIDENCE PRESERVATION SOCIETY, 24 Meeting St., Providence, RI 02903-1214. Tel.: 401-831-7440. Fax: 401-831-8583. Facebook: @pvdpreservation.
E-mail: info@ppsri.org
Web Site: www.ppsri.org
Key Personnel: Exec. Dir., Brent Runyon; Office Mgr. & Membership Coord., Kate Blankenship; Dir. Donor Rels. & Trustee Liaison, Angela Kondon; Dir. Devel. & External Affairs, Sarah Santos; Preservation & Public Engagement Officer, Marena Wisniewski.
Institution Type/Description: Preservation Society: housed in 1772 Shakespeare's Head House & Garden.
Hours & Admission Prices: Office: Mon.-Fri. 9-5. Closed all major holidays. &

PROVIDENCE PUBLIC LIBRARY, 150 Empire St., Providence, RI 02903-3219. Tel.: 401-455-8000. Facebook: @providence.public; Instagram: @providencepubliclibrary; Twitter: @provlib.
E-mail: pplref@provlib.org
Web Site: www.provlib.org
Key Personnel: Exec. Dir., Jack Martin; Assoc. Dir., Aaron Peterman; Head Cur. Collections, Jordan Goffin.
Institution Type/Description: Library.
Hours & Admission Prices: Mon. & Wed. 12:30-8:30, Tues. 9:30-5:30, Thurs. & Fri. 12:30-5:30, Sat. 9:30-2:30, Sun. 1-5, other times by appointment. No charge. &

RHODE ISLAND HISTORICAL PRESERVATION AND HERITAGE COMMISSION, Old State House, 150 Benefit St., Providence, RI 02903-1209. Tel.: 401-222-2678; 800-745-5555 (TTY). Fax: 401-222-2968.
E-mail: hphc.info@preservation.ri.gov
Web Site: www.preservation.ri.gov
Key Personnel: Acting Dir., Jeffrey Emidy.
Institution Type/Description: Historical Preservation Commission: housed in 1762 Old State House.
Hours & Admission Prices: Office: Mon.-Fri. 9-4. No charge. Closed state holidays.

RHODE ISLAND HISTORICAL SOCIETY, 110 Benevolent St., Providence, RI 02906-3103. Tel.: 401-331-8575. Fax: 401-351-0127.
E-mail: execdirector@rihs.org
Web Site: www.rihs.org
Key Personnel: Exec. Dir., C. Morgan Grefe, Ph.D.; Chair, Luther W. Spoehr, Ph. D.; Deputy Exec. Dir. Finance, Charmyne Goodfellow; Deputy Exec. Dir. Collections, Richard J. Ring; Librarian, Phoebe Bean; Dir. Education, Geralyn Ducady; Dir. Museum Work & Culture, Anne Conway; Dir. Advancement, Elizabeth Wood.
Institution Type/Description: Historical Society Museums.
Hours & Admission Prices: Library: Wed.-Fri. 10-5, 2nd Sat. of the month 10-5. Adults $8, students & seniors over 65 $5; RI residents, members & children under 12 no charge. John Brown House: April-June & Sept.-Nov. Tues.-Fri. 1-4, Sat. 10-4; Summer: Tues.-Thurs. 1-4, Fri.-Sat. 10-4; Dec.-March Sat. 10-4. Adults $10, students & senior citizens $8, children 10-17 $6; members & children under 10 no charge. Museum of Work & Culture: Tues.-Fri. 9:30-4, Sat. 10-4, Sun. 1-4. Adults $8, senior citizens & students $6; discounts groups of 10

or more; children under 10 with adult & RIHS members no charge. Closed New Year's Day; Easter; Independence Day; Thanksgiving; Christmas. &
Attendance: 30,000 (actual)

RHODE ISLAND STATE ARCHIVES, 337 Westminster St., Providence, RI 02903-3302. Tel.: 401-222-2353. Fax: 401-222-3199.
E-mail: statearchives@sos.ri.gov
Web Site: sos.ri.gov/archives
Key Personnel: State Archivist, R. Gwenn Stearn.
Institution Type/Description: State Archives.
Hours & Admission Prices: Mon.-Fri. 8:30-4:30. No charge. &

RHODE ISLAND STATE HOUSE, 82 Smith St., Providence, RI 02903. Mailing Address: 82 Smith St., Rm. 38, Providence, RI 02903. Tel.: 401-222-3983. Fax: 401-22-1404.
E-mail: tourcoordinator@sos.ri.gov
Web Site: sos.ri.gov
Institution Type/Description: Historic Building: built 1895-1904.
Hours & Admission Prices: Tours: Mon.-Fri. 9am, 10am, 11am, 1pm & 2pm. No charge. &
Attendance: 13,000 (estimated)

RISD MUSEUM, RHODE ISLAND SCHOOL OF DESIGN, 224 Benefit St., Providence, RI 02903-2723. Tel.: 401-454-6500. Fax: 401-454-6556. Facebook, Instagram & Twitter: @RISDMuseum;.
E-mail: museum@risd.edu
Web Site: www.risdmuseum.org
Key Personnel: Dir., John W. Smith; Chm., William Tsiaras, M.D.; Deputy Dir. Exhibitions, Education & Programs, Sarah Ganz; Mgr. Business & Finance, Glenn Stinson; Cur. Painting & Sculpture, Maureen O'Brien; Cur. Ancient Art, Gina Borromeo; Cur. Costume & Textiles, Kate Irvin; Chief Cur. & Houghton P. Metcalf, Jr. Cur. Prints, Drawings & Photographs, Jan Howard; Richard Brown Baker Cur. Contemporary Art, Dominic Molon; David & Peggy Rockefeller Cur. Decorative Arts & Design, Elizabeth A. Williams; Dir. Devel. & External Affairs, Amee Spondike; Mgr. Special Events, Pam Kimel; Mktg. & Public Rels. Assoc., Matthew Berry; Head Registrar, Joseph Leduc; Mgr. Visitor Svcs., Colleen Mullaly; Mgr. Safety, Security & Facilities, Philip Lessard; Store Dir., Charles Flora.
Institution Type/Description: Art Museum.
Hours & Admission Prices: Tues.-Sun. 10-5, 3rd Thurs. of month 10-9. Adults $15, senior citizens 62 & over $12, college students w/ID $8; discounts to AAA, AAM & ICOM members; RISD staff, faculty & students w/ID, children 18 & under and members no charge. Closed New Year's Eve & Day; Independence Day; Thanksgiving; Christmas Eve & Day. &
Attendance: 100,987 (actual)

ROGER WILLIAMS NATIONAL MEMORIAL, 282 N. Main St., Providence, RI 02903-1240. Tel.: 401-521-7266. Facebook: @RogerWilliamsNPS.
Web Site: www.nps.gov/rowi
Key Personnel: Supt., Meghan Kish; Mgmt. Asst., Jennifer Smith; Admin. Officer, Michelle Spink; Chief Interpretation & Education, Joshua Boles.
Institution Type/Description: Historic Site.
Hours & Admission Prices: Summer: daily 9-5; Fall: daily 9-4:30; Winter: Wed.-Sun. 9-4:30. No charge; donations accepted. Closed New Year's Day; Thanksgiving; Christmas. &
Attendance: 121,960 (estimated)

ROGER WILLIAMS PARK ZOO, 1000 Elmwood Ave., Providence, RI 02907-3659. Tel.: 401-785-3510. Fax: 401-941-3988. Facebook: RPW Zoo.
E-mail: info@rwpzoo.org
Web Site: www.rwpzoo.org
Key Personnel: Exec. Dir. Zoo & RI Zoological Society, Jeremy Goodman, D.V. M.; Chm. (V), Maribeth Williamson; Dir. Education, Shareen Knowlton; Veterinarian, Michael McBride, D.V.M.; Deputy Dir. Animal Care, Tim French.
Institution Type/Description: Zoo.
Hours & Admission Prices: April-Sept. daily 10-5; Oct.-March daily 10-4. Adults $14.95, senior citizens 62 & over $12.95, children 3-12 $9.95; children 2 & under no charge. Closed Thanksgiving; Christmas Eve & Day. &
Attendance: 646,752 (actual)

STAGES OF FREEDOM, 101 Dyer St., 2nd Fl., Providence, RI 02903. Tel.: 401-421-0606. Facebook.
E-mail: rickman@rickmangroup.com
Web Site: ribhs.org
Formerly: Rhode Island Black Heritage Society
Key Personnel: Pres., William Bundy; Exec. Dir., Ray Rickman.
Institution Type/Description: History Museum.

Hours & Admission Prices: Mon.-Fri. 10:30-3:30; other times by appointment. Special collections research by appointment only. Fee charged for searches & archival assistance; discount to AAM members. No charge; donations accepted. Closed holidays. &
Attendance: 3,500 (actual)

STEPHEN HOPKINS HOUSE, Benefit St., Providence, RI 02903. 15 Hopkins St., Providence, RI 02903. Tel.: 401-421-0694. Facebook.
E-mail: shh1707@gmail.com
Web Site: www.stephenhopkins.org
Key Personnel: Chair, Kim N. Clark.
Institution Type/Description: Historic Museum House: 1707 Governor Stephen Hopkins home.
Hours & Admission Prices: April-Nov. Wed. 11-2, Sat. 10-4; Dec.-March Wed. 11-2; other times by appointment. Recommended donation $5.
Attendance: 4,000 (actual)

Saunderstown

CASEY FARM, Route 1A, 2325 Boston Neck Rd., Saunderstown, RI 02874. Mailing Address: 141 Cambridge St., Boston, MA 02114-2702. Tel.: 401-295-1030, 617-227-3956.
E-mail: info@historicnewengland.org
Web Site: www.historicnewengland.org
Key Personnel: Pres. & C.E.O., Carl R. Nold.
Institution Type/Description: Historic Homestead: c.1750, homestead still functioning as a working farm.
Hours & Admission Prices: June-Oct. 15 Tues. & Thurs. 1-5, Sat. 9-2. Adult $6; discount to seniors, AAM, ICOM, AAA & WGBH members; Historic New England members no charge. Call for further information.
Attendance: 41,601 (actual)

THE GILBERT STUART BIRTHPLACE AND MUSEUM, 815 Gilbert Stuart Rd., Saunderstown, RI 02874-2911. Tel.: 401-294-3001. Fax: 401-294-3869.
E-mail: info@gilbertstuartmuseum.org
Web Site: gilbertstuartmuseum.org
Key Personnel: Dir. & Museum Shop Mgr., Margaret O'Connor.
Institution Type/Description: Historic House Museum: 1755 birthplace of artist Gilbert Stuart.
Hours & Admission Prices: May & Sept. Thurs.-Mon. 10-4; mid-June to Aug. daily 10-4. Adults $10, children 6-12 $6.
Attendance: 5,400 (estimated)

Smithfield

AUDUBON SOCIETY OF RHODE ISLAND, 12 Sanderson Rd., Smithfield, RI 02917-2600. Tel.: 401-949-5454. Fax: 401-949-5788.
E-mail: audubon@asri.org
Web Site: www.asri.org
Key Personnel: Exec. Dir., Lawrence Taft; Bd. Pres. (V), Candace E. Powell; Financial Dir., Susan Mansolillo; Cur., Eugenia Marks; Sr. Dir. Educational Programs, Kristen Swanberg; Publications Asst., Hope Foley; Museum Shop Mgr., Jan Weyant.
Institution Type/Description: Nature Conservation Center.
Hours & Admission Prices: Mon.-Fri. 9-5. No charge; donations accepted for use of trails. Closed New Year's Day; Thanksgiving; Christmas. &
Attendance: 25,000 (estimated)

SMITH-APPLEBY HOUSE, 220 Stillwater Rd., Smithfield, RI 02917-1849. Tel.: 401-231-7363.
E-mail: contact@smithapplebyhouse.org
Web Site: www.smithapplebyhouse.org
Institution Type/Description: Historic House Museum: housed in an 18th century farm house.
Hours & Admission Prices: By appointment.

Tiverton

BUTTERFLY ZOO, 409 Bulgarmarsh Rd., Tiverton, RI 02878. Mailing Address: 1151 Aquidneck Ave., Middletown, RI 02842. Tel.: 401-849-9519.
E-mail: info@familydaysout.com
Key Personnel: Owner, Marc Schenck.
Institution Type/Description: Butterfly Zoo.
Hours & Admission Prices: Memorial Day to Labor Day Mon.-Sat. 11-4, Sun. 12-4. Adults $6, children $4; children under 3 no charge.

CHASE-CORY HOUSE, 3908 Main Rd., Tiverton, RI 02878-4809. Mailing Address: P.O. Box 98, Adamsville, RI 02801. Tel.: 401-624-2096.
E-mail: info@tivertonfourcorners.com
Web Site: www.tivertonfourcorners.com
Institution Type/Description: Historic Houses.
Hours & Admission Prices: By appointment. No charge.

EMILIE RUECKER WILDLIFE REFUGE, Seapowet Ave., Tiverton, RI 02878. Mailing Address: Audubon Society of Rhode Island, 12 Sanderson Rd., Smithfield, RI 02917. Tel.: 401-949-5454.
E-mail: jhall@asri.org
Web Site: asri.org
Institution Type/Description: Wildlife Refuge.
Hours & Admission Prices: Call for hours.

FORT BARTON, Lawton & Highland Aves., Tiverton, RI 02878-4401. Mailing Address: Town Hall, 343 Highland Rd., Tiverton, RI 02878-4499. Tel.: 401-625-6700 & 624-2549.
E-mail: administrator@tiverton.ri.gov
Key Personnel: Co Chm., Garry Plunkett; Co Chm., Brian Janes.
Institution Type/Description: History Museum: site was the staging area for the invasion of Aquidneck Island & named after Lt. Col. William Barton. Listed on the National Register of Historic Places.
Hours & Admission Prices: Call for hours.

Wakefield

EDWARD EVERETT HALE HOUSE, 2625A Commodore Perry Hwy., Wakefield, RI 02879. Mailing Address: c/o Pettaquamscutt Historical Society, 2636 Kingstown Rd., Kingston, RI 02881. Tel.: 401-783-1328.
E-mail: halehouseri@gmail.com
Web Site: halehouseri.org
Institution Type/Description: Historic House Museum: housed in the former summer home of Rev. Dr. Edward Everett Hale; built in 1873.
Hours & Admission Prices: July-Aug. Fri.-Sat. 12-4.

Warren

CHARLES W. GREENE MUSEUM, George Hail Free Library, 530 Main St., Warren, RI 02885-4368. Tel.: 401-245-7686. Facebook.
E-mail: epatricrn@yahoo.com
Web Site: www.georgehail.org/cwgMuseum.htm
Key Personnel: Dir., E. Patricia Redfearn; Chm. (V), John Chaney.
Institution Type/Description: History Museum.
Hours & Admission Prices: Museum: Wed. 2-4 or by appointment. Library: July-Aug. Mon.-Thurs. 10-8, Fri. 10-5, Sat. 10-3; Sept.-June Mon.-Thurs. 10-8, Fri.-Sat. 10-5. No charge; donations accepted.
Attendance: 125 (estimated)

FIREMEN'S MUSEUM, 38 Baker St., Warren, RI 02885-3107. Mailing Address: 1 Joyce St., Warren, RI 02885-3238. Tel.: 401-245-7600.
Key Personnel: Dir., Chief Galinelli.
Institution Type/Description: Firemen's Museum: housed in the former Narragansett Steam Fire Company Station Number 3.
Hours & Admission Prices: By appointment only. No charge.

MASSASOIT HISTORICAL ASSOCIATION, 59 Church St., Warren, RI 02885. Mailing Address: Massasoit Historical Association, P.O. Box 203, Warren, RI 02885. Tel.: 401-245-0392. Facebook: Massasoit Historical.
E-mail: kristin_read@yahoo.com
Web Site: www.massasoithistorical.org
Formerly: Maxwell House
Key Personnel: Pres., Debra Jobin.
Institution Type/Description: Historic House Museum: housed in the former home of Rev. Samuel Maxwell; built c.1752.
Hours & Admission Prices: Sat. 10-2; other times by appointment. No charge; donations accepted. Closed holidays.
Attendance: 250 (estimated)

TOUISSET MARSH WILDLIFE REFUGE, 107 Touisset Rd., Warren, RI 02885. Mailing Address: 12 Sanderson Rd., Smithfield, RI 02917-2606. Tel.: 508-761-8230.

E-mail: jhall@asri.org
Web Site: asri.org/hike/wild-life-refuges/touisset-marsh-wildlife-refuge.html
Institution Type/Description: Wildlife Refuge.
Hours & Admission Prices: Daily dawn-dusk. No charge; donations accepted.

Warwick

CLOUDS HILL VICTORIAN HOUSE MUSEUM, 4157 Post Rd., Warwick, RI 02886. Mailing Address: P.O. Box 522, East Greenwich, RI 02818-0522. Tel.: 401-884-9490.
E-mail: office@cloudshill.org
Web Site: www.cloudshill.org
Key Personnel: Dir., Wayne Cabral.
Institution Type/Description: Historic House Museum: built in 1872 by William Smith Slater for his daughter, Elizabeth Ives Slater.
Hours & Admission Prices: By appointment. Adults $15, seniors $10; discounts to groups.

GREENWOOD VOLUNTEER FIRE COMPANY AND MUSEUM, 45 Kernick St., Warwick, RI 02886. Mailing Address: P.O. Box 6057, Warwick, RI 02887-6057. Tel.: 401-736-8412 OR 401-302-1120.
E-mail: rcarlow00@gmail.com
Web Site: greenwoodfirecompany.webs.com
Key Personnel: Pres. (V), Robert Carlow; Museum Shop Mgr., Joan Lowder.
Institution Type/Description: Historic Building: housed in a former fire station; built in 1924.
Hours & Admission Prices: By appointment. No charge; donations accepted.
Attendance: 400 (estimated)

JOHN WATERMAN ARNOLD HOUSE - WARWICK HISTORICAL SOCIETY, 25 Roger Williams Circle, Warwick, RI 02888. Tel.: 401-467-7647. Facebook.
E-mail: fag311@cox.net
Web Site: www.whsri.org
Key Personnel: Dir., Felicia Gardella.
Institution Type/Description: Historic House Museum: built in 1786. Listed on the National Register of Historic Places.
Hours & Admission Prices: Wed. 11-3, 2nd Sat. each month 11-2. No charge; donations accepted.
Attendance: 600 (estimated)

STEAMSHIP HISTORICAL SOCIETY OF AMERICA, 2500 Post Rd., Warwick, RI 02886. Tel.: 401-463-3570. Fax: 401-463-3572.
E-mail: info@sshsa.org
Web Site: www.sshsa.org
Key Personnel: Exec. Dir. & Publr., Matthew S. Schulte; Editor, Jim Pennypacker; Membership Coord. & Editor, Alissa Cafferky; Research Asst., Astrid Drew; Office Admin, Karen Sylvia.
Institution Type/Description: Research Library.
Hours & Admission Prices: Mon.-Fri. 8:30-4:30. No charge. &

WARWICK MUSEUM OF ART, Kentish Artillery Armory, 3259 Post Rd., Warwick, RI 02886-7145. Tel.: 401-737-0010. Fax: 401-737-1796.
E-mail: info@warwickmuseum.org
Web Site: www.warwickmuseum.org
Key Personnel: Pres. Bd., Deborah Mercer; Program Dir., Simone Spruce-Torres.
Institution Type/Description: Art Gallery: housed in a former Armory; built in 1912.
Hours & Admission Prices: Mon.-Fri. 10-5, Sat. 10-3. No charge; donations accepted. Closed New Year's Day; Easter; Memorial Day; Independence Day; Labor Day; Rosh Hashanah; Thanksgiving; Christmas. &
Attendance: 9,000 (estimated)

West Kingston

BELL SCHOOL HOUSE, 5 Richmond Townhouse Rd., West Kingston, RI 02892. Mailing Address: c/o Richmond, R.I. Historical Society, P.O. Box 408, Wyoming, RI 02898. Tel.: 401-539-7676.
Institution Type/Description: Historic Building: housed in a former one room school; built in 1898.
Hours & Admission Prices: By appointment.

Westerly

BABCOCK-SMITH HOUSE MUSEUM, 124 Granite St., Westerly, RI 02891-2435. Tel.: 401-596-5704.
E-mail: bsh1734@verizon.net
Web Site: www.babcocksmithhouse.org
Key Personnel: Chm. (V), John B. Coduri.
Institution Type/Description: Historic House: housed in an early Georgian-style mansion, built c.1734. Listed on the National Register of Historic Places.
Hours & Admission Prices: May-June & Sept.-Oct. Sat. 2-5; July-Aug. Thurs.-Sun. 2-5; other times by appointment. Adults $5, children $1; members no charge.

WESTERLY ARMORY MUSEUM, 41 Railroad Ave., Westerly, RI 02891. Mailing Address: P.O. Box 641, Westerly, RI 02891. Tel.: 401-596-8554. Fax: 401-596-9529.
E-mail: westerlyarmory@aol.com
Web Site: www.westerlyarmory.org
Key Personnel: Operations Mgr., John G. Humble.
Institution Type/Description: History Museum.
Hours & Admission Prices: Mon. & Thurs. 9-4; other times by appointment. No charge; donations accepted.
Attendance: 2,500 (estimated)

WESTERLY PUBLIC LIBRARY, 44 Broad St., Westerly, RI 02891-1856. Tel.: 401-596-2877. Fax: 401-596-5600.
E-mail: bhopkins@westerlylibrary.org
Web Site: www.westerlylibrary.org
Key Personnel: Exec. Dir., Brigitte Hopkins.
Institution Type/Description: Art & History Museum: housed in Civil War Memorial building.
Hours & Admission Prices: Mon.-Wed. 9-8, Thurs.-Fri. 9-6, Sat. 9-4. No charge; donations accepted. Closed major holidays. &
Attendance: 280,000 (estimated)

Woonsocket

MUSEUM OF WORK & CULTURE, 42 S. Main St., Woonsocket, RI 02895-4274. Tel.: 401-769-9675.
E-mail: execdirector@rihs.org
Web Site: www.rihs.org/Museums.html
Institution Type/Description: History Museum.
Hours & Admission Prices: Tues.-Fri. 9:30-4, Sat. 10-4, Sun. 1-4. Adults $8, seniors & students $6; discounts to groups; members & children under 10 no charge.

SOUTH CAROLINA

(236 listings)

Abbeville

BURT-STARK MANSION, 400 N. Main St., Abbeville, SC 29620-1706. Mailing Address: P.O. Box 164, Abbeville, SC 29620-0164. Tel.: 864-366-0166.
E-mail: info@burt-stark.com
Web Site: www.burt-stark.com
Institution Type/Description: Historic House: built in 1830s. A National Historic Landmark.
Hours & Admission Prices: Feb.-Dec. Fri.-Sat. 1-5; other times by appointment. Adults $10. Closed major holidays.

DR. SAMUEL R. POLIAKOFF COLLECTION OF WESTERN ART - ABBEVILLE COUNTY LIBRARY, 201 S. Main St., Abbeville, SC 29620. Tel.: 864-459-4009. Fax: 864-459-4009.
Key Personnel: Dir., Mary Elizabeth Land.
Institution Type/Description: Library.
Hours & Admission Prices: Mon., Wed. & Fri. 9-5:30, Tues. & Thurs. 9-8, Sat. 9-3. No charge. Closed major holidays.

Aiken

AIKEN CENTER FOR THE ARTS, 122 Laurens St., S.W., Aiken, SC 29801-3888. Tel.: 803-641-9094. Fax: 803-641-2009. Facebook: Aiken Center for the arts.
E-mail: acaexecdir@bellsouth.net
Web Site: www.aikencenterforthearts.org
Key Personnel: Exec. Dir., Elizabeth Williamson; Pres., Skipper Perry; Treas., Janice Williams; Gallery Store Mgr., Michelle Petty.
Institution Type/Description: Art Museum.

Hours & Admission Prices: Mon.-Sat. 10-5. No charge. Closed Memorial Day; Independence Day; Labor Day; Thanksgiving; Christmas. &
Attendance: 25,000 (estimated)

AIKEN COUNTY HISTORICAL MUSEUM, 433 Newberry St., S. W., Aiken, SC 29801-4844. Tel.: 803-642-2017 & 2015. Fax: 803-642-2016. Facebook: Friends of Aiken County Historical Museum.
E-mail: bbaratto@aikencountysc.gov
Web Site: www.aikencountyhistoricalmuseum.org
Key Personnel: Dir., Brenda Baratto; Site & Event Mgr., Leah Walker; Chm. (V), Owen Clary; Collections Mgr., Lauren Virgo; Museum Shop Mgr., Nancy Goelz.
Institution Type/Description: History Museum: 1931 winter colony mansion.
Hours & Admission Prices: Tues.-Sat. 10-5, Sun. 2-5. No charge; donations accepted. Closed national holidays. &
Attendance: 20,778 (actual)

AIKEN THOROUGHBRED RACING HALL OF FAME AND MUSEUM, 135 Dupree Place, Aiken, SC 29801. Mailing Address: P.O. Box 1177, Aiken, SC 29802-1177. Tel.: 803-642-7631 & 643-2121. Fax: 803-643-4780.
E-mail: halloffame@cityofaikensc.gov
Web Site: www.aikenracinghalloffame.com
Key Personnel: C.E.O., Lisa J. Hall.
Institution Type/Description: Specialized Museum: housed in a restored carriage house.
Hours & Admission Prices: June-Aug. Sat.-Sun. 2-5; Sept.-May Tues.-Fri. & Sun. 2-5, Sat. 10-5. No charge; donations accepted. Closed New Year's Day; Martin Luther King Jr. Day; Good Friday; Easter; Memorial Day; Independence Day; Labor Day; Thanksgiving; Christmas. &
Attendance: 20,000 (estimated)

AIKEN VISITORS CENTER AND TRAIN MUSEUM, 406 Park Ave., S.E., Aiken, SC 29801. Mailing Address: City of Aiken Tourism Division, P.O. Box 1177, Aiken, SC 29802. Tel.: 803-293-7846, 888-245-3672.
E-mail: visitorscenter@cityofaikensc.gov
Web Site: aikenrailroaddepot.org
Institution Type/Description: Historic Building: housed in the former Aiken Railroad Depot.
Hours & Admission Prices: Wed.-Fri. 10-5, Sat. 9-2.

Anderson

ANDERSON CITY FIRE DEPARTMENT MUSEUM, 400 S. McDuffie, Anderson, SC 29624. Tel.: 864-231-2256.
Institution Type/Description: Firefighting History Museum.
Hours & Admission Prices: Mon.-Fri. 9-5; other times by appointment. No charge.

ANDERSON COUNTY ARTS CENTER, 110 Federal St., Anderson, SC 29625. Tel.: 864-222-2787. Fax: 864-224-8864.
E-mail: info@andersonartscenter.org
Web Site: www.andersonartscenter.org
Key Personnel: Exec. Dir., Kimberly Spears; Administrative Dir., Annette Buchanan; Pres., Dr. Bob Austin; Dir. Communications, Stacey McAdams.
Institution Type/Description: Arts Center: housed in 1908 Carnegie Library Building.
Hours & Admission Prices: Tues.-Fri. 9:30-5:30, Sat. open to groups by special request only. No charge; donations accepted. Closed Memorial Day; Labor Day; Thanksgiving & day after; Independence Day week.

ANDERSON COUNTY MUSEUM, 202 E. Greenville St., Anderson, SC 29621-5509. Tel.: 864-260-4737. Fax: 864-332-5320. Facebook: Anderson County Museum.
E-mail: bchilds@andersoncountymuseum.org
Web Site: www.andersoncountymuseum.org
Key Personnel: Exec. Dir., Beverly R. Childs; Cur. Collections, Dustin Norris.
Institution Type/Description: History Museum.
Hours & Admission Prices: Museum: Tues. 10-7, Wed.-Sat. 10-4. The Anderson County Roper Research Room: Tues. 1-7; other times by appointment. No charge; donations accepted. &
Attendance: 18,550 (actual)

Awendaw

CENTER FOR BIRDS OF PREY, 4719 N. Highway 17, Awendaw, SC 29429. Mailing Address: P.O. Box 1247, Charleston, SC 29402-1247. Tel.: 843-971-7474. Fax: 843-971-7029. Facebook: SC Birds of Prey.

E-mail: info@thecenterforbirdsofprey.org
Web Site: www.thecenterforbirdsofprey.org
Key Personnel: Dir., Jim Elliott, Jr.
Institution Type/Description: Nature Center.
Hours & Admission Prices: Guided Tours: Thurs.-Sat. 10:30 & 2. Flight Demonstrations: Thurs.-Sat. 11:30 & 3. Adults $18, youth $12; discounts for members depending on membership level & AAA members; children under 6 no charge. &
Attendance: 9,000 (estimated)

Barnwell

BARNWELL COUNTY MUSEUM, 9426 Marlboro Ave., Barnwell, SC 29812. Mailing Address: P.O. Box 422, Barnwell, SC 29812-0422. Tel.: 803-259-1916. Fax: 803-259-1916. Facebook.
E-mail: barnwellmuseum@gmail.com
Key Personnel: Chm. (V), H. Jerry Morris; Museum Shop Mgr., Marie Peeples.
Institution Type/Description: History Museum: housed in the Fuller House.
Hours & Admission Prices: Tues.-Thurs. & Sun. 3-5:30. No charge; donations accepted. Closed holidays. &
Attendance: 4,500 (estimated)

Beaufort

THE BEAUFORT ARSENAL, 713 Craven St., Beaufort, SC 29902-5571. Mailing Address: P.O. Box 11, Beaufort, SC 29901-0011. Tel.: 843-379-3331. Fax: 843-379-3371.
E-mail: eryan@historicbeaufort.org
Web Site: www.historic-beaufort.org
Formerly: Beaufort Museum at the Arsenal
Key Personnel: Dir. Museums, Elizabeth G. Ryan.
Institution Type/Description: History Museum: built in 1798.
Hours & Admission Prices: Mon.-Tues. & Thurs.-Sat. 10-5. Adults $3; children 6 & under and members no charge. Closed holidays.
Attendance: 12,000 (estimated)

THE KAZOO FACTORY, 12 John Galt Rd., Beaufort, SC 29906. Tel.: 843-982-6387; 800-326-0358.
Web Site: thekazoofactory.com
Institution Type/Description: Company Museum.
Hours & Admission Prices: Museum: Mon.-Fri. 9-4. No charge. Guided Tours: Mon.-Fri. 10 am, 11 am, 2 pm & 3 pm. Adults $7, children 4-11 $5; discounts to groups; children 3 & under no charge.

THE VERDIER HOUSE, 801 Bay St., Beaufort, SC 29902-5565. Mailing Address: Historic Beaufort Foundation, P.O. Box 11, Beaufort, SC 29901-0011. Tel.: 843-379-3331. Fax: 843-379-3371.
E-mail: director@historicbeaufort.org
Web Site: www.historicbeaufort.org
Key Personnel: Mgr., Sandy Patterson; Interim Exec. Dir., Maxine Lutz.
Institution Type/Description: Historic House: housed in the former home of John Mark Verdier; built c.1805.
Hours & Admission Prices: Mon.-Sat. 10-3:30; other times by appointment for groups of 8 or more. Verdier House: adults $10; students, children under 18, active military & foundation members no charge.
Attendance: 10,000

Beech Island

BEECH ISLAND HISTORICAL SOCIETY, 144 Old Jackson Hwy., Beech Island, SC 29842-4568. Tel.: 803-867-3600. Fax: 803-867-3600.
E-mail: bihs@comcast.net
Web Site: www.beechislandhistory.org
Key Personnel: Dir. & C.E.O., Jackie Bartley.
Institution Type/Description: History & Agricultural Museum.
Hours & Admission Prices: Wed.-Thurs. 11-1; other times by appointment. No charge; donations accepted. &
Attendance: 500 (actual)

REDCLIFFE PLANTATION STATE HISTORIC SITE, 181 Redcliffe Rd., Beech Island, SC 29842-9535. Tel.: 803-827-1473.
E-mail: redcliffe@scprt.com
Web Site: www.southcarolinaparks.com/redcliffe
Institution Type/Description: Historic House: housed in the home of South Carolina Sen. James Henry Hammond; built in 1859. Listed on the National Register of Historic Places.

Hours & Admission Prices: Tours: Thurs.-Mon. 11, 1, & 3. Adults 16 & over $5, children 6-15 $4, SC senior citizens $3.
Attendance: 5,000 (estimated)

Belton

BELTON CENTER FOR THE ARTS, 306 City Sq., Belton, SC 29627. Mailing Address: P.O. Box 368, Belton, SC 29627-0368. Tel.: 864-338-8556. Fax: 864-338-0280.
E-mail: betsy@beltonarts.org
Web Site: www.beltoncenterforthearts.org
Key Personnel: Dir., Betsy Chapman.
Institution Type/Description: Art Gallery.
Hours & Admission Prices: Tues.-Fri. 10-5:30, Sat. 10-2.

SOUTH CAROLINA TENNIS HALL OF FAME, 50 N. Main St., Belton, SC 29627. Mailing Address: P.O. Box 843, Belton, SC 29627-0843. Tel.: 864-338-7400. Fax: 864-338-4034.
E-mail: bama7400@aol.com
Web Site: www.beltonsc.com
Key Personnel: Historian, Rex Maynard; Chm. (V), Cam Littlejohn.
Institution Type/Description: Tennis Museum.
Hours & Admission Prices: Wed.-Fri. 10-4, Sat. 10-2. No charge. Closed holidays. &
Attendance: 2,500 (estimated)

Bennettsville

JENNINGS-BROWN HOUSE FEMALE ACADEMY, 121 S. Marlboro St., Bennettsville, SC 29512-4031. Mailing Address: P. O. Box 178, Bennettsville, SC 29512-0178. Tel.: 843-479-5624.
E-mail: marlborough@mecsc.net
Key Personnel: Bd. Pres. Historical Society (V), Marty Rankin; Exec. Dir. Museum, Lucille Carabo.
Institution Type/Description: Historic House: c.1826-27 Jennings-Brown House.
Hours & Admission Prices: Mon.-Thurs. 10-5, Fri. 10-1. Adults & students $2.
Attendance: 600 (estimated)

MARLBORO COUNTY HISTORICAL MUSEUM, 123 S. Marlboro St., Bennettsville, SC 29512-4031. Mailing Address: P. O. Box 178, Bennettsville, SC 29512. Tel.: 843-479-5624.
E-mail: marlborough@mecsc.net
Key Personnel: Exec. Dir. & Museum Shop Mgr., Susan Cloer.
Institution Type/Description: Historical & Preservation Society: housed in the former home of Dr. & Mrs. John Frank Kinney; built in 1902.
Hours & Admission Prices: Thurs.-Fri. 10-4. House: adults $2, children $1. Closed major holidays.
Attendance: 4,500 (estimated)

Bishopville

FRYAR TOPIARY GARDENS, 145 Broad Acres Rd., Bishopville, SC 29010-2819. Tel.: 803-484-5581.
E-mail: jeangrosser@gmail.com
Web Site: www.pearlfryar.com
Institution Type/Description: Garden.
Hours & Admission Prices: Tues.-Sat. 10-4. No charge; donations accepted.

LEE COUNTY VETERANS MUSEUM, 129 W. Cedar Lane, Bishopville, SC 29010. Mailing Address: 121 W. Cedar Lane, Bishopville, SC 29010. Tel.: 803-484-4497. Fax: 803-484-5203.
E-mail: sccottonmus@ftc-i.net
Web Site: www.sccotton.org
Key Personnel: Exec. Dir., J. Edward Grant.
Institution Type/Description: Military Museum.
Hours & Admission Prices: Mon.-Fri. 10-4:30, Sat. 10-4. Adult $6, senior 60 & up $4, student $3; discounts to AAA, AAM & ICOM members and Blue Star Museum participants; active duty military and children 5 & under no charge. &
Attendance: 10,281

SOUTH CAROLINA COTTON MUSEUM, 121 W. Cedar Ln., Bishopville, SC 29010-1454. Tel.: 803-484-4497. Fax: 803-484-5203.
E-mail: sccottonmus@ftc-i.net
Web Site: www.sccotton.org
Key Personnel: Exec. Dir., Janson L. Cox; Pres., Gail Player; Business Mgr., Melissa Brundage.
Institution Type/Description: History Museum.

Hours & Admission Prices: Mon.-Fri. 10-4:30, Sat. 10-4. Adults $6, senior citizens $4, students $3; discounts to AAA & ICOM members; active duty military, members, children 5 & under no charge. &
Attendance: 10,281 (actual)

Blacksburg

KINGS MOUNTAIN NATIONAL MILITARY PARK, 2625 Park Rd., Blacksburg, SC 29702-7325. Tel.: 864-936-7921. Fax: 864-936-9897. TDD: 864-936-7921.
E-mail: katherine_lynn@nps.gov
Web Site: www.nps.gov/kimo.htm
Key Personnel: Chief Interpretation & Resource Mgmt., Katherine Lynn; Bookstore Mgr., Wilma Scoggins.
Institution Type/Description: Military Park Museum.
Hours & Admission Prices: Daily 9-5. No charge; donations accepted. Closed New Year's Day; Martin Luther King Jr. Day; Columbus Day; Thanksgiving; Christmas. &
Attendance: 115,000 (actual)

Blackville

AGRICULTURAL HERITAGE CENTER, Clemson University's Edisto Research and Educ. Ctr., 64 Research Rd., Blackville, SC 29817. Tel.: 803-284-3343. Fax: 803-284-3684.
Institution Type/Description: History Museum.
Hours & Admission Prices: Mon.-Sat. 9-4. Tours: $2 per person; children K-12 no charge.

Branchville

BRANCHVILLE RAILROAD SHRINE AND MUSEUM, INC., 7504 Freedom Rd., Branchville, SC 29432-2310. Mailing Address: Town of Branchville, P.O. Box 85, Branchville, SC 29432-0085. Tel.: 803-274-8820. Fax: 803-274-8760.
E-mail: oldestjunction@gmail.com
Key Personnel: Pres., Johnny Norris; Vice Pres., Mike Norris.
Institution Type/Description: Transportation Museum: housed in 1877 Branchville Southern Railroad Depot at the site of the first railroad junction of the world.
Hours & Admission Prices: Fri.-Sat. 10-2, Sun. 2-5; other times by appointment. No charge; donations accepted. Closed major holidays. &

Camden

CAMDEN ARCHIVES & MUSEUM, 1314 Broad St., Camden, SC 29020-3535. Tel.: 803-425-6050. Fax: 803-424-4053.
E-mail: classicallycarolina@camdensc.org
Web Site: www.camdenarchives.org
Key Personnel: Dir., Howard Branham; Deputy Dir., Katherine Richardson; Chm. (V), Frank Goodale; Assoc. Archivist, Peggy Brakefield; Administrative Asst., Barbara Rogers.
Institution Type/Description: Archives & Local History Museum.
Hours & Admission Prices: Mon.-Fri. 8-5, Sat. 10-4, 1st Sun. each month 1-5. No charge; donations accepted. Closed city holidays. &
Attendance: 6,000 (estimated)

FINE ARTS CENTER OF KERSHAW COUNTY, INC., 810 Lyttleton St., Camden, SC 29020-4411. Mailing Address: P.O. Box 1498, Camden, SC 29021-8498. Tel.: 803-425-7676. Fax: 803-425-7679.
E-mail: kcobb@fineartscenter.org
Web Site: www.fineartscenter.org
Key Personnel: Exec. Dir., Kristin Cobb; Pres. Bd. Dir., Karen Eckford; Dir. Facility, Dianne Edwards; Dir. Finance, Daphne Cantey; Dir. Education, Steve LeVan; Dir. Mktg., Jane Peterson.
Institution Type/Description: Art Gallery: housed in Bassett Memorial Building.
Hours & Admission Prices: Winter: Mon.-Fri. 12-6, Sat. by appointment. Summer: Mon.-Fri. 9-5, Sat. by appointment. Gallery: no charge; donations accepted. Performance Series: call for admission fee. Closed New Year's Eve & Day; Easter; Memorial Day; Independence Day; Labor Day; Thanksgiving; Christmas Eve, Day & week. &
Attendance: 70,000 (actual)

HISTORIC CAMDEN REVOLUTIONARY WAR SITE, 222 Broad St., Camden, SC 29020. Mailing Address: P.O. Box 710, Camden, SC 29021-0710. Tel.: 803-432-9841.
E-mail: info@historiccamden.org
Web Site: historiccamden.org
Key Personnel: Chm., M. Trayser Dunaway; Vice Chm., Robert Giangiorgi; Exec. Dir., Halie Brazier.

Institution Type/Description: History Museum: housed in reconstructed 1777 Kershaw-Cornwallis House, located on 106 acre archeological park encompassing the colonial to late 18th-century village of Camden.
Hours & Admission Prices: Tues.-Sat. 10-5, Sun. 1-5. Self-Guided Tours & Site Admission: adults $5, children 6-15, seniors & military $4; discounts to members; children under 6 no charge. Guided Tours & Site Admission: adults $10, children 6-15, seniors & military $8; discounts to members; children under 6 no charge. Closed major holidays.
Attendance: 20,191 (estimated)

KERSHAW COUNTY HISTORICAL SOCIETY CAMDEN, SOUTH CAROLINA, 811 Fair St., Camden, SC 29020-4404. Mailing Address: P.O. Box 501, Camden, SC 29021-0501. Tel.: 803-425-1123.

E-mail: kershawcountyhistoricalsociety@gmail.com
Web Site: www.kershawcountyhistoricalsociety.org
Key Personnel: Pres., Julie Putnam; Dir., Kathleen P. Stahl.
Institution Type/Description: Historic House: housed in the Bonds Conway House; c.1812.
Hours & Admission Prices: Thurs. 1-5; other times by appointment. No charge; donations accepted. Closed holidays.
Attendance: 150 (estimated)

NATIONAL STEEPLECHASE MUSEUM, Springdale Race Course, 200 Knights Hill Rd., Camden, SC 29020-2154. Mailing Address: P.O. Box 2424, Camden, SC 29020-8008. Tel.: 803-432-6513, 800-780-8117. Fax: 803-432-4062.

E-mail: catherine@steeplechasemuseum.org
Web Site: www.steeplechasemuseum.org
Key Personnel: Exec. Dir., Catherine French; Chm. (V), Beverly Steinman.
Institution Type/Description: Steeplechase History Museum.
Hours & Admission Prices: Sept.-May Wed.-Sat. 10-4; other times by appointment. No charge; donations accepted. Closed major holidays. &
Attendance: 5,000 (estimated)

Cayce

CAYCE HISTORICAL MUSEUM, City of Cayce Municipal Complex, 1800 12th St., Cayce, SC 29033-2935. Tel.: 803-739-5385. Fax: 803-796-9072.

E-mail: caycemuseum@historysc.com
Key Personnel: Dir., Leo Redmond.
Institution Type/Description: History Museum.
Hours & Admission Prices: Tues.-Fri. 9-4, Sat.-Sun. 2-5. Adults $2, senior citizens & students $1; Sun. no charge. Closed city holidays.

Central

ASHTABULA HISTORIC HOUSE, 2725 Old Greenville Hwy., Central, SC 29630. Mailing Address: Pendleton Historic Foundation, P.O. Box 444, Pendleton, SC 29670-0444. Tel.: 864-646-7249.

E-mail: info@pendletonhistoricfoundation.org
Web Site: www.pendletonhistoricfoundation.org
Key Personnel: Pres., Carol Burdette.
Institution Type/Description: Historic House Museum.
Hours & Admission Prices: See website for hours & admission prices. &
Attendance: 4,383 (actual)

CENTRAL HERITAGE SOCIETY, 416 Church St., Central, SC 29630-9152. Mailing Address: P.O. Box 1162, Central, SC 29630-9152. Tel.: 864-639-2794 & 2156.

E-mail: heritage@innova.net
Institution Type/Description: History Museum.
Hours & Admission Prices: Sun. 2-4. Closed holidays.

Charleston

AIKEN-RHETT HOUSE, 48 Elizabeth St., Charleston, SC 29403-6250. Mailing Address: c/o Historic Charleston Foundation, 40 E. Bay St., Charleston, SC 29401. Tel.: 843-723-1623.

E-mail: vperry@historiccharleston.org
Web Site: www.historiccharleston.org
Key Personnel: Site Mgr., Valerie Perry.
Institution Type/Description: Historic House Museum: housed in the former home of Gov. William Aiken, Jr.; built in 1818. Listed on the National Register of Historic Places.
Hours & Admission Prices: Mon.-Sat. 10-5, Sun. 2-5. Adults $12, children 6-16 $10; children 5 & under no charge. Closed Thanksgiving; Christmas Eve & Day.

AVERY RESEARCH CENTER FOR AFRICAN AMERICAN HISTORY & CULTURE, 125 Bull St., College of Charleston, Charleston, SC 29424. Tel.: 843-953-7609, 843-953-7608. Fax: 843-953-7607. Facebook.

E-mail: averyadmin@cofc.edu
Web Site: avery.cofc.edu
Key Personnel: Exec. Dir., Patricia Williams Lessane, Ph.D.; Processing Archivist, Georgette Mayo; Cur., Coord. Public Programs & Facilities Mgr., Curtis J. Franks; Assoc. Dir., Deborah Wright.
Institution Type/Description: History Museum & Research Center.
Hours & Admission Prices: Museum Tours: Mon.-Fri. 10:30, 11:30, 1:30, 2:30 & 3:30; Reading Room: Mon.-Fri. 10-12:30 & 1:30-5. No charge; donations accepted. Closed university holidays. &
Attendance: 8,500 (estimated)

CALHOUN MANSION, 16 Meeting St., Charleston, SC 29401-2706. Tel.: 843-722-8205. Fax: 843-723-1147. Facebook: @calhounmansion.

E-mail: contact@calhounmansion.net
Web Site: www.calhounmansion.net
Institution Type/Description: Historic House: former home of George W. Williams, built in 1876.
Hours & Admission Prices: Tours: March-Nov. daily 11-5; Dec.-Feb. daily 11-4:30. Adults $16; children 11 & under no charge. Grand Tour: $75. Closed Thanksgiving; Christmas.

CHARLES TOWNE LANDING STATE HISTORIC SITE, 1500 Old Towne Rd., Charleston, SC 29407-6099. Tel.: 843-852-4200. Fax: 843-852-4205.

E-mail: ctlandingsp@scprt.com
Web Site: www.charlestownelanding.travel
Key Personnel: Park Mgr., Rob Powell.
Institution Type/Description: Historic Site: 1670 site of the first permanent European settlement in South Carolina.
Hours & Admission Prices: Daily 9-5. Adults $10, seniors $6.50, children 6-15 $6; children 5 & under no charge. Closed Christmas Eve & Day. &
Attendance: 135,000 (actual)

CHARLESTON LIBRARY SOCIETY, 164 King St., Charleston, SC 29401-2269. Tel.: 843-723-9912. Fax: 843-723-3500. Facebook & Twitter: @librarysociety.

E-mail: info@charlestonlibrarysociety.org
Web Site: www.charlestonlibrarysociety.org
Key Personnel: Exec. Dir., Anne W. Cleveland; Pres., Virginia A. Bush; Librarian/Archivist, Trisha Kometer.
Institution Type/Description: Historical & Cultural Library.
Hours & Admission Prices: Mon.-Fri. 9:30-5:30, Sat. 9:30-2. No charge. Closed holidays. &
Attendance: 11,500

THE CHARLESTON MUSEUM, 360 Meeting St., Charleston, SC 29403-6297. Tel.: 843-722-2996. Fax: 803-722-1784.

E-mail: cborick@charlestonmuseum.org
Web Site: www.charlestonmuseum.org
Key Personnel: Dir. & C.E.O., Carl P. Borick; Bd. Trustees Pres., Mrs. Douglas H. Sass; C.F.O., Marc Meech; Cur. Historical Archaeology, Martha Zierden; Chief Cur., J. Grahame Long; Chief of Education & Interpretation, Stephanie Thomas; Cur. of Textiles, Jan Z. Hiester; Archivist & Collections Mgr., Jennifer McCormick; Chief Museum Operations, Susan McKellar; Bldg. Maintenance Supvr., Marty Durham; Public Rels. & Events Coord., Suzanne Dibella-Olson.
Institution Type/Description: General Museum.
Hours & Admission Prices: Mon.-Sat. 9-5, Sun. 12-5. Adults $12, children $5; discounts to seniors, military & AAM members; museum members no charge. Closed Easter; Thanksgiving; Christmas. &
Attendance: 121,185 (actual)

CHARLESTON TEA PLANTATION & FACTORY TOUR, 6617 Maybank Hwy., Charleston, SC 29487. Tel.: 843-559-0383, ext. 4207.

E-mail: jknight@rcbigelow.com
Web Site: charlestonteaplantation.com
Institution Type/Description: Plantation Museum & Tour.
Hours & Admission Prices: Mon.-Sat. 10-4, Sun. 12-4. Factory Tour: no charge. Trolley Tour: adults $14, children under 12 $6. Closed New Year's Eve & Day; Easter; Independence Day; Thanksgiving; Christmas Eve & Day.

CHILDREN'S MUSEUM OF THE LOWCOUNTRY, 25 Ann St., Charleston, SC 29403-6213. Tel.: 843-853-8962. Fax: 843-853-1042. Facebook, Instagram & Twitter: @explorecml.

E-mail: info@explorecml.org
Web Site: explorecml.org
Key Personnel: Exec. Dir., Nichole A. Myles; Pres. (V), Anne P. Chastain; Dir. Education, Starr Jordan; Dir. Devel., Jacquie Berger; Dir. Mktg., McCown Griffin; Dir. Operations, Jason Dodd.
Institution Type/Description: Children's Museum.
Hours & Admission Prices: Tues.-Sat. 9-5, Sun. noon-5. Admission $12, SC residents $10; discounts to ACM, military & educators; members & children under one no charge. Closed Easter; Independence Day; Thanksgiving; Christmas Eve & Day. ♿
Attendance: 120,628 (actual)

THE CITADEL MUSEUM, 171 Moultrie St., Charleston, SC 29409-6141. Tel.: 843-953-2569. Fax: 843-953-8446.
E-mail: reference@citadel.edu
Web Site: library.citadel.edu/museum
Institution Type/Description: College History Museum.
Hours & Admission Prices: Daily 12-5. No charge; donations accepted. Closed college, religious & national holidays. ♿
Attendance: 8,378 (actual)

CITY HALL COUNCIL CHAMBER GALLERY, 80 Broad St., Charleston, SC 29401-2225. Tel.: 843-724-3729. Fax: 843-720-3959.
E-mail: maybankv@charleston-sc.gov
Web Site: www.charleston-sc.gov/index.aspx?NID=179
Key Personnel: Chief Tourism Official, Vanessa Turner Maybank.
Institution Type/Description: Art Gallery; housed in c.1801 1st U.S. Bank Building.
Hours & Admission Prices: Mon.-Fri. 9-5. No charge; donations accepted. Closed major holidays. ♿
Attendance: 20,000 (estimated)

CONFEDERATE MUSEUM, 188 Meeting St., Charleston, SC 29401. Mailing Address: P.O. Box 20997, Charleston, SC 29413-0997. Tel.: 843-723-1541. Facebook.
E-mail: confederatemuseum@gmail.com
Web Site: www.confederatemuseumcharlestonsc.com
Key Personnel: Dir., Jill Hunter Powell; Historian, June Wells.
Institution Type/Description: History Museum.
Hours & Admission Prices: Tues.-Sat. 11-3:30; group tours for 15 or more by appointment. Adults $5, children $3; active military & veterans no charge. Closed major holidays. ♿
Attendance: 18,000 (estimated)

DRAYTON HALL, 3380 Ashley River Rd., Charleston, SC 29414-7105. Tel.: 843-769-2600. Fax: 843-766-0878. Facebook, Instagram & Twitter: @draytonhall.
E-mail: info@draytonhall.org
Web Site: www.draytonhall.org
Key Personnel: Pres. & C.E.O., Carter C. Hudgins, Ph.D.; Chm. Bd. Trustees, Stephen F. Gates; Exec. Asst., Pamela Brown; C.F.O., Paula Marion; Dir. Communications, Kristine Morris; Dir. Philanthropy, Steve Mount; Dir. Visitor Svcs., Allison Jordan; Cur. Collections, Sarah Stroud Clarke; Cur. Education & Public Engagement, Shelia Harrell-Roye.
Institution Type/Description: Historic House Museum: housed in c.1738-42, Drayton Family Residence.
Hours & Admission Prices: Mon.-Sat. 9-5, Sun. 11-5. Tours: adults $22, youth 12-18 $10, children 6-11 $6; Grounds only $12; discounts to AAA members & military; children under 5 & National Trust members no charge. Closed New Year's Eve & Day; Thanksgiving; Christmas Eve & Day. ♿
Attendance: 53,000 (actual)

GIBBES MUSEUM OF ART, 135 Meeting St., Charleston, SC 29401-2297. Tel.: 843-722-2706. Fax: 843-720-1682. Facebook, Instagram & Twitter: @theGibbesmuseum.
E-mail: admack@gibbesmuseum.org
Web Site: www.gibbesmuseum.org
Key Personnel: Exec. Dir. & Chief Cur., Angela D. Mack; Dir. Devel., Jennifer Ross; Creative Dir., Erin Banks; Cur. Collections, Sara Arnold; Cur. Exhibitions, Pam Wall; Cur. Education, Rebecca Sailor; Dir. Collections & Operations, Zinnia Willits; Dir. Finance & Admin., Courtney Soler; Museum Store Coord., Lizzy Goodrich.
Institution Type/Description: Art Museum.
Hours & Admission Prices: Tues. & Thurs.-Sat. 10-5, Wed. 10-8, Sun. 1-5. Adults $12, seniors 62 & up, college students & military $10, youth 4-17 $6. Closed New Year's Day, Easter, Independence Day, Thanksgiving Day, Christmas Eve & Day. ♿
Attendance: 70,000 (estimated)

HALSEY INSTITUTE OF CONTEMPORARY ART AT THE COLLEGE OF CHARLESTON, 161 Calhoun St., Charleston, SC 29401. Tel.: 843-953-4422. Fax: 843-953-7890.
E-mail: sloanm@cofc.edu
Web Site: www.halsey.cofc.edu
Formerly: Halsey Gallery, School of the Arts, College of Charleston
Key Personnel: Dir., Mark Sloan; Chm. (V), Susan Bass.
Institution Type/Description: Art Gallery.
Hours & Admission Prices: Sept.-June Mon.-Sat. 11-4. No charge; donations accepted. ♿
Attendance: 20,000 (estimated)

HISTORIC CHARLESTON FOUNDATION, 40 E. Bay, Charleston, SC 29401-2547. Tel.: 843-723-1623. Fax: 843-577-2067. Facebook: @HistoricCharlestonFoundation; Twitter: @HistoricChas.
E-mail: krobinson@historiccharleston.org
Web Site: www.historiccharleston.org
Key Personnel: Pres. & C.E.O., Katharine S. Robinson; Chm. Bd. Trustees, Wilbur E. Johnson; C.F.O., Cynthia Ellis; Dir. Mktg., Holland Williams; C.O.O., Cynthia Wood; Chief Preservation Officer, Winslow Hastie; Dir. Museums, Lauren Northup; Chief Merchandising Officer, Rich Gaskalla.
Institution Type/Description: Foundation Operated House Museums: housed in the Captain James Missroon House; built in 1789.
Hours & Admission Prices: Nathaniel Russell House & Aiken-Rhett House Museums: Mon.-Sat. 10-5, Sun. 2-5. Admission to Single House: adults $12, youth 6-16 $5; Admission to Both Houses: adults $18, youth 6-16 $10; children 5 & under no charge. Closed Thanksgiving; Christmas Eve & Day. ♿
Attendance: 80,000 (actual)

MACAULAY MUSEUM OF DENTAL HISTORY, The Waring Historical Library, 175 Ashley Ave., Charleston, SC 29425. Mailing Address: 175 Ashley Ave., MSC 403, Charleston, SC 29425. Tel.: 843-792-2288. Fax: 843-792-8619.
E-mail: hoffius@musc.edu
Web Site: waring.library.musc.edu/macaulay.php
Key Personnel: Cur., Susan Hoffius.
Institution Type/Description: Dental Museum.
Hours & Admission Prices: Mon.-Fri. 8:30-5; by appointment. No charge; donations accepted. Closed holidays.
Attendance: 250

MAGNOLIA PLANTATION AND GARDENS, 3550 Ashley River Rd., Charleston, SC 29414-7127. Tel.: 843-571-1266. Facebook: Magnolia Plantation and Gardens.
E-mail: office@magnoliaplantation.com
Web Site: magnoliaplantation.com
Key Personnel: Exec. Dir., Tom Johnson.
Institution Type/Description: Historic House and Gardens: c.1680s Drayton family home & gardens.
Hours & Admission Prices: March 10-Oct. daily 8-5:30; Nov.-Feb. daily 8:30-4:30. Plantation: adults $15, children 6-12 $10; discounts to educational groups & groups of 15 or more; children under 6 no charge. House Museum: admission $8; children under 6 no charge. Audubon Swamp Garden: admission $8; children under 6 no charge. Nature Train Tour, Nature Boat Tour & Slavery to Freedom Tour $8.
Attendance: 135,500 (estimated)

MIDDLETON PLACE, 4300 Ashley River Rd., Charleston, SC 29414-7206. Tel.: 843-556-6020.
E-mail: ttodd@middletonplace.org
Web Site: middletonplace.org
Formerly: Middleton Place House Museum
Key Personnel: Pres. & C.E.O., Tracey Todd; Vice Pres. Horticulture & Maintenance, Sidney Frazier; Dir. Mktg. & Pub. Rels., Don Bussey.
Institution Type/Description: Historic House: restored 1755 structure.
Hours & Admission Prices: Garden & Plantation Stableyards: daily 9-5. House Museum: Mon. 12-4:30, Tues.-Sun. 10-4:30. House Guided Tour: $15, children 5 & under no charge. ♿
Attendance: 110,000 (estimated)

NATHANIEL RUSSELL HOUSE, 51 Meeting St., Charleston, SC 29401-2536. Mailing Address: c/o Historic Charleston Foundation, 40 E. Bay St., Charleston, SC 29401. Tel.: 843-724-8481.
E-mail: jdargan@historiccharleston.org
Web Site: www.historiccharleston.org
Key Personnel: Site Mgr., Julius Dargan.
Institution Type/Description: Historic House Museum: built in 1808. Listed on the National Register of Historic Places.

Hours & Admission Prices: Mon.-Sat. 10-5, Sun. 2-5. Adults $12, children 6-16 $10; children 5 & under no charge. Closed Thanksgiving; Christmas Eve & Day.

THE OLD EXCHANGE & PROVOST DUNGEON, 122 E. Bay St., Charleston, SC 29401-2103. Tel.: 843-727-2165, 888-763-0448. Fax: 843-727-2163. Facebook: @OldExchangeAndProvostDungeon.

E-mail: youmanst@charleston-sc.gov
Web Site: www.oldexchange.com
Key Personnel: Dir., Tony Youmans; Event Coord., Mrs. Kathryn Hernandez; Education Coord., Teresa Tabor; Gift Shop Supvr., Suzanne Houser.
Institution Type/Description: Historic Building; c.1771 The Old Exchange Building, based on its architectural distinction & its role in the formation of the United States, it is historically one of America's significant structures; an exchange & customs house, the building has maintained service to the people politically, socially, economically & educationally.
Hours & Admission Prices: Daily 9-5. Adults $8, children 7-12 $4; discounts to AAA & AARP members, seniors, groups, military & students; Friends of the Old Exchange members and children 6 & under no charge. Closed major holidays. ᕼ
Attendance: 56,242 (actual)

THE OLD SLAVE MART MUSEUM, 6 Chalmers St., Charleston, SC 29401-3005. Mailing Address: c/o City of Charleston Special Facilities Division, 135 Church St., Charleston, SC 29401. Tel.: 843-958-6467. Fax: 843-724-3734. Facebook: @OldSlaveMartMuseum.

E-mail: osmm@charleston-sc.gov
Web Site: www.oldslavemart.org
Key Personnel: Dir. Special Facilities, Cam Patterson.
Institution Type/Description: History Museum: housed in a former slave auction gallery; built in 1859.
Hours & Admission Prices: Mon.-Sat. 9-5. Closed New Year's Day; Thanksgiving; Christmas.

THE POWDER MAGAZINE, 79 Cumberland St., Charleston, SC 29401-3112. Tel.: 843-722-9350. Fax: 843-722-3711. Facebook: @PowderMagazineSC; Instagram: @powder_magazine; Twitter: @PowderMag.

E-mail: info@powdermag.org
Web Site: www.powdermag.org
Key Personnel: Dir., Alan Stello.
Institution Type/Description: History Museum: housed in c. 1713 Powder Magazine.
Hours & Admission Prices: Mon.-Sat. 10-4, Sun. 1-4. Adults $5, children $2; discounts for groups.
Attendance: 15,000 (estimated)

SOUTH CAROLINA AQUARIUM, 100 Aquarium Wharf, Charleston, SC 29401-6300. Tel.: 843-577-3474/800-722-6455. Fax: 843-720-3861. Facebook & Twitter: @scaquarium; Instagram: @southcarolinaaquarium.

E-mail: information@scaquarium.org
Web Site: www.scaquarium.org
Key Personnel: Pres. & C.E.O., Kevin Mills; Chm. (V), Jonathan Zucker; Exec. Vice Pres. & C.O.O., Jack Higgins; Dir. Husbandry, Rachel Kalisperis; Dir. Education, Brian Thill; Dir. Mktg. & Creative, Kevin Kampwerth; Dir. Human Resources, Paul Nunez; Dir. Finance, Mike Mistler; Dir. Advancement, Courtenay Lewandowski; Dir. Guest Svcs., Lauren McDaniel.
Institution Type/Description: Aquarium.
Hours & Admission Prices: March-Aug. daily 9-5, building closes at 6, Sept.-Feb. daily 9-4, building closes at 5. Adults $24.95, children 3-12 $17.95, 4-D theater $5; discounts to groups; children 2 & under and members no charge. Closed Thanksgiving; Christmas. ᕼ
Attendance: 427,101 (actual)

SOUTH CAROLINA HISTORICAL SOCIETY, 100 Meeting St., Charleston, SC 29401-2215. Tel.: 843-723-3225. Fax: 843-723-8584.

E-mail: faye.jensen@schsonline.org
Web Site: www.schistory.org
Key Personnel: Exec. Dir., Faye L. Jensen, Ph.D.; Chm. (V), William Cain, M.D.; C.O.O., John Tucker; Museum Dir. & Education, Heather A. Reed; Membership Coord., Selynne Ancheta; Dir. Archives & Research, Virginia Ellison; Publications, Matt Lockhart; Museum Curator & Programs Coord., Suzanne Dibella; Education & Volunteer Coord., Bailey Knight.
Institution Type/Description: Historical Society Library & Archives: housed in 1822 Robert Mills Building.

Hours & Admission Prices: Meeting St. location closed for renovations until 2018. Calhoun St. location: call for hours. ᕼ
Attendance: 3,500 (estimated)

WARING HISTORICAL LIBRARY, Medical University of South Carolina, 175 Ashley Ave., Charleston, SC 29425. Mailing Address: 175 Ashley Ave., MSC 403, Charleston, SC 29425. Tel.: 843-792-2288. Fax: 843-792-8619. Instagram & Twitter: @waringlibrary.

E-mail: hoffius@musc.edu
Web Site: waring.library.musc.edu
Key Personnel: Cur., Susan Hoffius; Digital Archivist, Tabitha Y. Samuel; Univ. Archivist, E. Brooke Fox.
Institution Type/Description: University Medical Museum & Library: housed in 1894 building designed by architect John Snook.
Hours & Admission Prices: Mon.-Fri. 10-4 by appointment. No charge; donations accepted. Closed state & federal holidays. ᕼ

Cheraw

CHERAW LYCEUM MUSEUM, 200 Market St., Cheraw, SC 29520-2414. Mailing Address: P.O. Box 219, Cheraw, SC 29520-0219. Tel.: 843-537-8401 & 8425. Fax: 843-537-8407.

E-mail: contact@cheraw.com
Web Site: www.cheraw.com
Key Personnel: C.E.O., J. William Taylor; Treas., Helen D. Funderburk; Cur., Sarah C. Spruill.
Institution Type/Description: History Museum: housed in a former court building; built in 1825
Hours & Admission Prices: Mon.-Fri. 9-5, Sat.-Sun. by appointment. No charge; donations accepted.
Attendance: 4,000 (estimated)

Chester

CHESTER COUNTY HISTORICAL SOCIETY MUSEUM, 107 McAliley St., Chester, SC 29706-1741. Mailing Address: P.O. Box 811, Chester, SC 29706-0811. Tel.: 803-385-2332. Facebook: Chester County, SC Historical Society.

E-mail: ccmuseum@truvista.net
Web Site: chesterschistory.org
Key Personnel: Museum Dir., Liz Anderson.
Institution Type/Description: Historical Society Museum: housed in 1914 Chester County Jail.
Hours & Admission Prices: Wed. & Fri.-Sat. 10-3. Adults $3; members no charge.
Attendance: 1,293 (actual)

CHESTER COUNTY TRANSPORTATION MUSEUM, 157 Wylie St., Chester, SC 29706. Mailing Address: c/o Chester County Historical Society, P.O. Box 811, Chester, SC 29706. Tel.: 803-385-2330.

E-mail: ccmuseum@truvista.net
Web Site: chesterhistory.org
Institution Type/Description: Transportation Museum: housed in the former Seaboard Railroad freight depot.
Hours & Admission Prices: Tues.-Sat. 11-2. Adults $3, students & senior citizens $2.

Clemson

BOB CAMPBELL GEOLOGY MUSEUM, 140 Discovery Lane, Clemson University, Clemson, SC 29634. Tel.: 864-656-4600. Fax: 864-656-4601.

E-mail: bcgm@clemson.edu
Web Site: www.clemson.edu/geomuseum
Key Personnel: Dir., Dr. Patrick McMillan; Cur., N. Adam Smith.
Institution Type/Description: Geology & Paleontology Museum.
Hours & Admission Prices: Daily 10-5. Closed on official Clemson University holidays. ᕼ
Attendance: 25,000 (estimated)

FORT HILL (THE JOHN C. CALHOUN HOUSE), Fort Hill St., Clemson University, Clemson, SC 29634-5615. Mailing Address: Trustee House, Clemson University, Box 345615, Clemson, SC 29634. Tel.: 864-656-2475. Fax: 864-656-1026.

E-mail: hiottw@clemson.edu
Web Site: www.clemson.edu/about/history/properties/fort-hill.html
Key Personnel: Dir., William D. Hiott, Sr.

Institution Type/Description: Historic House Museum: c.1803 home of John C. Calhoun, 1825-1850.
Hours & Admission Prices: Mon.-Sat. 10-12 & 1-4:30, Sun. 2-4:30. Suggested Donation: adults $5, senior & student $4, children $2; discounts to groups, AAM & ICOM members. Closed university holidays.
Attendance: 23,583 (actual)

HANOVER HOUSE, South Carolina Botanical Garden, Perimeter Rd., Clemson University, Clemson, SC 29634. Mailing Address: Box 345615, Historic Properties, Clemson University, Clemson, SC 29634-5615. Tel.: 864-656-2241 & 2475. Fax: 864-656-1026.
E-mail: hiottw@clemson.edu
Web Site: www.clemson.edu/about/history/properties/hanover-house.html
Key Personnel: Dir. & Cur., William D. Hiott, Sr.
Institution Type/Description: Historic House Museum: home built in 1716.
Hours & Admission Prices: Sat. 10-12 & 1-5, Sun. 2-4:30; groups & other times by appointment. Suggested Donations: adults $5, seniors $4, children $2; discounts for AAM & ICOM members; members no charge. Closed university holidays. &

RUDOLPH E. LEE GALLERY, G-50 Lee Hall, Clemson University, Clemson, SC 29634. Mailing Address: P.O. Box 340509, Clemson, SC 29634. Tel.: 864-656-3899. Fax: 864-656-7523.
E-mail: woodwaw@exchange.clemson.edu
Web Site: www.clemson.edu/caah/leegallery
Key Personnel: Dir., Denise Woodward-Detrich; Membership, Jennifer Staley; Volunteer Coord., Fleming Markel.
Institution Type/Description: Art Gallery.
Hours & Admission Prices: Mon.-Thurs. 9-4:30, Sun. 2-5. No charge. Closed university, state & national holidays.

THE SOUTH CAROLINA BOTANICAL GARDEN, 150 Discovery Lane, Clemson University, Clemson, SC 29634-0174. Tel.: 864-656-3405 & 2458. Fax: 864-656-6230.
E-mail: scbg@clemson.edu
Web Site: www.clemson.edu/scbg
Key Personnel: Dir., Patrick McMillan; Dir. Education, Lisa Wagner; Garden Mgr., James Arnold; Sr. Horticulturist, John Bodiford; Horticulturist, Kathy Bridges; Facilities Mgr., Eric Soto; Garden Rentals & Visitor Svcs. Mgr., Darlene Evand.
Institution Type/Description: Botanical Garden: located on part of the original John C. Calhoun Plantation Estate.
Hours & Admission Prices: Daily dawn-dusk. No charge; donations accepted. &
Attendance: 100,000 (estimated)

STROM THURMOND INSTITUTE, Clemson University, Silas Pearman Blvd., Clemson, SC 29634. Tel.: 864-656-4700. Fax: 864-656-4780.
E-mail: sti-web@strom.clemson.edu
Web Site: www.strom.clemson.edu
Key Personnel: Dir., Dr. Robert H. Becker.
Institution Type/Description: Archive.
Hours & Admission Prices: Mon.-Fri. 8-4:30. No charge. Closed university holidays & breaks; New Year's Day; Independence Day; Thanksgiving weekend; Christmas.

Clinton

MUSGROVE MILL STATE HISTORIC SITE VISITOR CENTER, 398 State Park Rd., Clinton, SC 29325. Tel.: 864-938-0100.
E-mail: musgrovemill@scprt.com
Institution Type/Description: Visitor Center: housed on the historic site of the Battle of Musgrove Mill in 1780.
Hours & Admission Prices: Call for hours. No charge; donations accepted.

Columbia

COLUMBIA FIRE DEPARTMENT MUSEUM, 1800 Laurel St., Columbia, SC 29201-2627. Tel.: 803-733-8350. Fax: 803-733-8311.
E-mail: cfdjreich@columbiasc.net
Web Site: www.columbiasouthcarolina.com/fire-museum.html
Key Personnel: Cur., John G. Reich.
Institution Type/Description: Fire-Fighting Museum.
Hours & Admission Prices: Mon.-Fri. 8:30-5, Sat.-Sun. by appointment. No charge; donations accepted. &
Attendance: 10,000 (estimated)

COLUMBIA MUSEUM OF ART, 1515 Main St., Columbia, SC 29201. Mailing Address: P.O. Box 2068, Columbia, SC 29202-2068. Tel.: 803-799-2810. Fax: 803-343-2150.
E-mail: ahorne@columbiamuseum.org
Web Site: www.columbiamuseum.org
Key Personnel: Interim Exec. Dir., Lynn Robertson; Chief Cur., Will South; Dir. Education & Engagement, Jackie Adams; Facility Project Advisor, Michael Roh; Chief Devel. Officer, Angi Fuller Wildt; Coord. Visitor & Group Svcs., Sherrie Belton; Museum Shop Mgr., Brantley Cox.
Institution Type/Description: Art Museum.
Hours & Admission Prices: Tues. Fri. 11-5, Sat. 10-5, 1st Fri. of month 11-8, Sun. 12-5. Adults $12, seniors 65 & over and military $10, students $5; discounts to AAM & ICOM members; children 5 & under, members and Sun. no charge. Closed major holidays. &
Attendance: 135,000 (actual)

EDVENTURE, INC., 211 Gervais St., Columbia, SC 29201-3067. Mailing Address: P.O. Box 1638, Columbia, SC 29202-1638. Tel.: 803-779-3100. Fax: 803-779-3144.
E-mail: info@edventure.org
Web Site: www.edventure.org
Key Personnel: C.E.O. & Pres., Karen S. Coltrane; Exec. Vice Pres., Nikki Williams; Exhibits Dir., Robert French; C.F.O., Tasha Derrick; Mktg. Coord., Kia Grant.
Institution Type/Description: Children's Museum.
Hours & Admission Prices: Summer: Mon.-Sat. 9-5, Sun. 12-5; Winter: Tues.-Sat. 9-5, Sun. 12-5. Adults & children $11.50; seniors 62 & over, military & educator $10.50, children 2 & under & members no charge. Closed Thanksgiving; Christmas Eve & Day. &
Attendance: 233,000 (estimated)

GOVERNOR'S MANSION, 800 Richland St., Columbia, SC 29201-2397. Tel.: 803-737-1710. Fax: 803-737-3860.
E-mail: nancybunch@gov.sc.gov
Web Site: www.scgovernorsmansion.org
Key Personnel: Cur. & Tour Dir., Nancy B. Bunch.
Institution Type/Description: Historic House: 1855 Governor's Residence.
Hours & Admission Prices: Tours: Summer: Tues.-Wed. 10, 10:30 & 11; Winter, Spring & Fall: Tues.-Thurs. 10, 10:30 & 11. No charge; donations accepted. &
Attendance: 15,000 (actual)

HISTORIC COLUMBIA FOUNDATION, 1601 Richland St., Columbia, SC 29201-2633. Tel.: 803-252-7742, ext. 14. Fax: 803-929-7695.
E-mail: rwaites@historiccolumbia.org
Web Site: www.historiccolumbia.org
Key Personnel: Exec. Dir., Robin Waites; Chmn. (V), Jenna Stephens; Dir. Cultural Resources, John Sherrer; Tour & Program Coord., Heather Bacon-Rogers.
Institution Type/Description: Historical Society Museum.
Hours & Admission Prices: Robert Mills, Hampton-Preston, Woodrow Wilson & Mann-Simions: Tues.-Sat. 10-4, Sun. 1-5. Houses: $6 each; discounts to AAM, AAA & SEMC members, senior citizens, teachers, students, military; members, Seibels House & Big Apple no charge.
Attendance: 35,000 (estimated)

THE MUSEUM OF EDUCATION, University of South Carolina, Wardlaw Hall, 820 Main St., Columbia, SC 29208. Tel.: 803-777-5741.
E-mail: museumofeducation@sc.edu
Web Site: www.ed.sc.edu/museum
Key Personnel: Cur., Dr. Craig Kridel.
Institution Type/Description: Education Museum.
Hours & Admission Prices: Mon.-Fri. 9-4. No charge. &

PONDER FINE ARTS GALLERY - BENEDICT COLLEGE, 1600 Harden St., Columbia, SC 29204. Tel.: 803-253-5000.
E-mail: pondergallery@benedict.edu
Web Site: www.benedict.edu/divisions/acadaf/sch-humanities/fine_arts/art/gallery/art-gallery.html
Institution Type/Description: Art Gallery.
Hours & Admission Prices: Mon.-Fri. 10-4. No charge.

RIVERBANKS ZOO & GARDEN, 500 Wildlife Pkwy., Columbia, SC 29210-8093. Mailing Address: P.O. Box 1060, Columbia, SC 29202-1060. Tel.: 803-779-8717. Fax: 803-253-6381.
E-mail: education@riverbanks.org
Web Site: www.riverbanks.org
Key Personnel: Pres. & C.E.O., Thomas Stringfellow; Financial Dir., George R. Davis; Dir. Animal Collections, Ed Diebold; Retail Sales Mgr., Jason Painter.
Institution Type/Description: Zoo & Botanical Garden.

Hours & Admission Prices: April 4-Oct. 4 Mon.-Fri. 9-5, Sat.-Sun. 9-6; Oct. 5-April 3 daily 9-5. Adults $13.95, military and seniors 62 & over $12.95, children 2-12 $11.50; discount to AZA members; AAZPA & AABGA members, reciprocal zoo societies, children under 2 & members no charge. Closed Thanksgiving; Christmas. &
Attendance: 872,000 (actual)

ROBERT MILLS HOUSE AND GARDENS, 1616 Blanding St., Columbia, SC 29201. Tel.: 803-252-7742.
Web Site: www.historiccolumbia.org/robert-mills-house-and-gardens
Institution Type/Description: Historic House Museum: built in c.1830.
Hours & Admission Prices: Tours: Tues.-Sat. 10am, 12 pm & 2pm, Sun. 1-3.

SOUTH CAROLINA CONFEDERATE RELIC ROOM AND MILITARY MUSEUM, 301 Gervais St., Ste. 1, Columbia, SC 29201-3073. Tel.: 803-737-8095. Fax: 803-737-8099. Facebook: @sccrrmm.
E-mail: jcassidy@crr.sc.gov
Web Site: www.crr.sc.gov.
Key Personnel: Dir., W. Allen Roberson; Admin. Coord. & Museum Shop Mgr., Shirley D. Schoonover; Cur. Education, William Joe Long; Cur. History, Kristina Dunn Johnson; Registrar, Rachel H. Cockrell; Cur. Exhibits & Design, Jami Cassidy.
Institution Type/Description: History Museum.
Hours & Admission Prices: Tues.-Sat. 10-5, 1st Sun. of month 1-5. Adults 18-61 $6, military & seniors $5, youth 10-17 $3; discounts 1st Sun. of month; members and children 12 & under no charge. Closed most state holidays. &
Attendance: 24,694 (actual)

SOUTH CAROLINA DEPARTMENT OF ARCHIVES & HISTORY, 8301 Parklane Rd., Columbia, SC 29223-4905. Tel.: 803-896-6196. Fax: 803-896-6186.
E-mail: gsalter@scdah.sc.gov
Web Site: scdah.sc.gov/
Key Personnel: Dir., W. Eric Emerson, Ph.D.; Chm. (V), A.V. Huff, Jr., Ph.D.; Deputy State Historic Preservation Officer, Elizabeth M. Johnson; Dir. Archives Svcs., Steve Tuttle.
Institution Type/Description: State Government Historical Agency.
Hours & Admission Prices: Tues.-Sat. 8:30-5. No charge. Reference Room: closed state holidays. &
Attendance: 5,947 (actual)

SOUTH CAROLINA DEPARTMENT OF PARKS, RECREATION AND TOURISM, 1205 Pendleton St., Columbia, SC 29201-3756. Tel.: 803-734-0156. Fax: 803-734-1017.
E-mail: gdavenport@scprt.com
Web Site: www.southcarolinaparks.com
Key Personnel: Dir. Parks, Phil Gaines; Chief Interpretation & Resource Mgmt., Terry Hurley.
Institution Type/Description: State Park & Museums.
Hours & Admission Prices: Contact individual park or site for hours & admissions.

SOUTH CAROLINA INSTITUTE OF ARCHAEOLOGY & ANTHROPOLOGY, 1321 Pendleton St., University of South Carolina, Columbia, SC 29208-4103. Tel.: 803-576-6573.
E-mail: nrice@sc.edu
Web Site: www.cas.sc.edu/sciaa
Key Personnel: Dir., Steven D. Smith; State Archaeologist, Jonathan M. Leader; Business Mgr., Susan M. Lowe; Cur., Sharon L. Pekrul.
Institution Type/Description: State Agency; Archaeology & Anthropology Research Institute.
Hours & Admission Prices: Mon.-Fri. 8:30-5. No charge. Closed state holidays. &

SOUTH CAROLINA LAW ENFORCEMENT OFFICERS HALL OF FAME, 5400 Broad River Rd., Columbia, SC 29212-3540. Tel.: 803-896-8756. Facebook: South Carolina Law Enforcement Officers Hall of Fame.
Web Site: www.scdps.gov/hof
Formerly: South Carolina Criminal Justice Hall of Fame
Key Personnel: Administrator, Marsha Ardila; Receptionist, Emily C. Harrison.
Institution Type/Description: Police Museum.
Hours & Admission Prices: Mon.-Fri. 8:30-5. No charge. Closed state holidays. &
Attendance: 7,000 (actual)

SOUTH CAROLINA MILITARY MUSEUM, One National Guard Rd., SM 23, Columbia, SC 29201-4752. Tel.: 803-806-4440. Fax: 803-806-4440.
Web Site: www.scmilitarymuseum.com

Key Personnel: Dir., Steven Jeffcoat; Chm. (V), LTG Stanhope S. Spears; Registar, Heather McPherson.
Institution Type/Description: Military Museum.
Hours & Admission Prices: Mon.-Sat. 10-4. No charge; donations accepted. &
Attendance: 10,000 (estimated)

SOUTH CAROLINA STATE HOUSE, 1100 Gervais St., Columbia, SC 29201. Tel.: 803-734-2430.
Institution Type/Description: Historic Building: built 1855-1907.
Hours & Admission Prices: Guided Tours: by appointment.

SOUTH CAROLINA STATE MUSEUM, 301 Gervais St., Columbia, SC 29201-3073. Mailing Address: 301 Gervais St., Loading Zone D, Columbia, SC 29201. Tel.: 803-898-4921. Fax: 803-898-4969.
E-mail: webmaster@scmuseum.org
Web Site: www.scmuseum.org
Key Personnel: Exec. Dir., William Calloway; Bd. Chair & Exec. Committee Chair, James Suddeth; Dir. Admin., Anita Anderson; Dir. Development, Karen Hall; Dir. Education, Tom Falvey; Dir. Collections, Paul Matheny; Dir. Opers., Doug Beerman; Dir. Mktg., Jennifer Thrailkill.
Institution Type/Description: General Museum: housed in former textile mill building.
Hours & Admission Prices: Mon. & Wed.-Fri. 10-5, Tues. 10-10, Sat. 10-6, Sun. 12-5. General Admission: adults 13 & over $8.95, senior citizens 62 & over $7.95, children 3-12 $6.95; members and children 2 & under no charge. Closed Easter; Thanksgiving; Christmas Eve & Day. &
Attendance: 182,000 (actual)

U.S. ARMY FINANCE CORPS MUSEUM, 4392 Magruder Ave., Columbia, SC 29207. Mailing Address: Commandant, U.S. Army Finance School, 10,000 Hampton Pkwy., Fort Jackson, SC 29207-7050. Tel.: 803-751-3771. Fax: 803-751-1749.
E-mail: atsg-fsa@jackson.army.mil
Key Personnel: Cur., Henry D. Howe, III.
Institution Type/Description: Military Museum.
Hours & Admission Prices: Tues.-Fri. 10-4. No charge. Closed federal holidays. &
Attendance: 12,000 (actual)

THE UNIVERSITY OF SOUTH CAROLINA MCKISSICK MUSEUM, 816 Bull St., Columbia, SC 29208. Tel.: 803-777-7251. Fax: 803-777-2829. Facebook.
E-mail: mckscal@mailbox.sc.edu
Web Site: artsandsciences.sc.edu/mckissickmuseum
Key Personnel: Exec. Dir., Jane Przybysz; Communications Mgr., Amanda Belue; Faculty Cur. & Museum Mngmnt. Program Dir., Lana Burgess; Cur. Natural Science, Christian Cicimurri; Cur. Exhibitions, Kate Crosby; Cur. Exhibition & Collection Mngmnt., Mark Smith; Chief Cur. Folklife & Fieldwork, Saddler Taylor.
Institution Type/Description: University Museum.
Hours & Admission Prices: Mon.-Fri. 8:30-5, Sat. 11-3. No charge; donations accepted. Closed New Year's Eve & Day; Independence Day; Labor Day; Thanksgiving; Christmas Eve, Day & week; University Holidays. &
Attendance: 35,000 (estimated)

Conway

HORRY COUNTY MUSEUM, 805 Main St., Conway, SC 29526-4343. Tel.: 843-915-5320. Fax: 843-248-1854.
E-mail: hcgmuseum@horrycounty.org
Web Site: www.horrycountymuseum.org
Key Personnel: Dir., R. Walter Hill, IV; Chm. (V), Jody Nyers; Education Specialist, Marion Haynes; Museum Shop Mgr., Julie Pinckney.
Institution Type/Description: Anthropology, History & Archaeology Museum.
Hours & Admission Prices: Tues.-Sat. 9-5. No charge; donations accepted. Closed county government holidays. &
Attendance: 40,000 (estimated)

REBECCA RANDALL BRYAN ART GALLERY, Edwards COHFA, Rm. 129, Conway, SC 29528. Mailing Address: P.O. Box 261954, Conway, SC 29528-6054. Tel.: 843-347-3161.
E-mail: marketing@coastal.edu
Web Site: www.coastal.edu
Key Personnel: Dir., Jim Arendt; Gallery Asst., Kendall Martin.
Institution Type/Description: Art Gallery.
Hours & Admission Prices: Mon.-Thurs. 9-5, Fri. 9-1. No charge. Closed university holidays.

Darlington

DARLINGTON RACEWAY STOCK CAR MUSEUM, NMPA HALL OF FAME, 1301 Harry Byrd Hwy., Darlington, SC 29532-3517. Mailing Address: P.O. Box 500, Darlington, SC 29540-0500. Tel.: 843-395-8900. Fax: 803-393-3911.
E-mail: dworden@darlingtonraceway.com
Web Site: www.darlingtonraceway.com
Formerly: NMPA Stock Car Hall of Fame, Joe Weatherly Museum
Key Personnel: Museum Shop Mgr., Vicki Sanders.
Institution Type/Description: Stock Car Museum.
Hours & Admission Prices: Mon.-Fri. 10-5, Sat. 10-4. Adults $5; children under 12 no charge. &
Attendance: 250,000 (estimated)

Dillon

JAMES W. DILLON HOUSE MUSEUM, 1302 W. Main St., Dillon, SC 29536. Mailing Address: Dillon County Historical Society, P.O. Box 1806, Dillon, SC 29536-1806. Tel.: 843-774-6122 & 441-5273. Fax: 843-774-5521.
E-mail: bbar830771@aol.com
Web Site: www.dillonmuseum.com
Key Personnel: Resource Mgr., Betty Barclay.
Institution Type/Description: Historic House.
Hours & Admission Prices: Tues.-Thurs. 2-4; other times by appointment. No charge; donations accepted. Closed Easter; Independence Day; Thanksgiving; Christmas. &
Attendance: 125 (estimated)

Due West

BOWIE ARTS CENTER, Erskine College, Two Washington St., Due West, SC 29639. Mailing Address: P.O. Box 338, Due West, SC 26939-0338. Tel.: 864-379-8867. Fax: 864-379-2167.
E-mail: burton@erskine.edu
Key Personnel: Dir., Jan B. Walker; Acting Cur., Ruth M. Burton.
Institution Type/Description: Art Gallery and Antiques Museum.
Hours & Admission Prices: Call for hours. No charge. Closed major holidays; college breaks.

Eastover

KENSINGTON MANSION/SCARBOROUGH-HAMER FOUNDATION, 4101 McCords Ferry Rd./ US 601, Eastover, SC 29044. Mailing Address: P.O. Box 237, Eastover, SC 29044-0237. Tel.: 803-353-0456.
E-mail: staff@kensingtonmansion.org
Web Site: www.kensingtonmansion.org
Key Personnel: Dir., Rickie Good; Chm. (V), Mary B. Waters.
Institution Type/Description: Historic House Museum: 1854 Italianate mansion built by Matthew Richard Singleton.
Hours & Admission Prices: Tours: March-July & Sept.-Dec. Thurs.-Sat. 9:30, 11, 1 & 2:30. Adults 13-59 $7, seniors 60 & over and active military $6, children 6-12 $5; children under 6 no charge. Closed major holidays.
Attendance: 3,000 (actual)

Edgefield

FRESHWATER COAST DISCOVERY CENTER, 405 Main St., Edgefield, SC 29824-1301. Mailing Address: South Carolina National Heritage Corridor, P.O. Box 477, Belton, SC 29627. Tel.: 803-637-0877. Fax: 803-637-6237.
E-mail: edgefielddc@scprt.com
Web Site: www.scnhc.org
Formerly: The Joanne T. Rainsford Heritage Discovery Center
Key Personnel: Pres. & C.E.O., Michelle McCollum.
Institution Type/Description: History Museum.
Hours & Admission Prices: Tues.-Sat. 10-5. No charge. Closed New Year's Day; Independence Day; Thanksgiving; Christmas.

OAKLEY PARK MUSEUM, 300 Columbia Rd., Edgefield, SC 29824-1224. Tel.: 803-637-4027.
E-mail: libby.ready1229@yahoo.com
Formerly: Oakley Park, UDC Shrine
Key Personnel: Pres. (V) & Dir. (V), Elizabeth Ready.
Institution Type/Description: Historic House: 1835 Oakley Park, where the Red Shirts of South Carolina were organized to ease reconstruction following the Civil War; ancestral home of Gen. Martin W. Gary & Gov. John Gary Evans.

Hours & Admission Prices: Thurs.-Sat. 10-4; other times by appointment. Adults $5, students $3; discount to senior, groups of 20 or more & AAM members with ID; children under 5 no charge. Closed New Year's Day; Thanksgiving; Christmas. &
Attendance: 4,000 (estimated)

WILD TURKEY CENTER AND WINCHESTER MUSEUM, 770 Augusta Rd., Edgefield, SC 29824-1573. Mailing Address: P.O. Box 530, Edgefield, SC 29824-0530. Tel.: 800-THE-NWTF & 637-7639.
E-mail: cboney@nwtf.net
Web Site: www.nwtf.org
Institution Type/Description: Wild Turkey History Museum.
Hours & Admission Prices: Mon.-Fri. 9-5. Adults $5, children $2; NWTF members no charge; donations accepted. Closed national holidays.
Attendance: 10,000 (estimated)

Edisto Island

EDISTO ISLAND HISTORIC PRESERVATION SOCIETY MUSEUM, 8123 Chisolm Plantation Rd., Edisto Island, SC 29438-6618. Tel.: 843-869-1954. Fax: 843-869-2754.
E-mail: gsmith@edistomuseum.org
Web Site: www.edistomuseum.org
Key Personnel: C.E.O. & Dir., Gretchen M. Smith; Pres. (V), Jane Darby.
Institution Type/Description: Historical & Preservation Society Museum.
Hours & Admission Prices: Jan.-Feb. Tues., Thurs. & Sat. 1-4; March-Oct. Tues.-Sat. 12-5; Nov.-Dec. Tues.-Sat. 11-4. Adult $4; discounts to AAM members; members and children 10 & under no charge. &
Attendance: 6,000 (estimated)

EDISTO ISLAND SERPENTARIUM, 1374 Hwy. 174, Edisto Island, SC 29438-6816. Tel.: 843-869-1171. Fax: 843-869-1959.
E-mail: info@edistoserpentarium.com
Web Site: www.edistoserpentarium.com
Institution Type/Description: Herpetology Museum.
Hours & Admission Prices: April 29-May 22 & Aug. 19-Sept. 4 Thurs.-Sat. 10-6; May 24-Aug. 14 Mon.-Sat. 10-6; call for additional hours. Adults 13 & over $12.95, seniors 65 & over $11.95, children 6-12 $9.95, children 4-5 $5.95; discounts to AAA members; children 3 & under no charge.

Ehrhardt

RIVERS BRIDGE STATE HISTORIC SITE, 325 State Park Rd., Ehrhardt, SC 29081-9157. Tel.: 803-267-3675. Fax: 803-267-3675.
E-mail: riversbridgesp@scprt.com
Web Site: scprt.com
Key Personnel: Park Mgr., John White.
Institution Type/Description: Historic Site: battle between the Confederacy & the Union army, Feb. 2-3, 1865. Listed on the National Register of Historic Places.
Hours & Admission Prices: Daily 9-6. No charge; donations accepted. Closed holidays. &
Attendance: 6,000 (estimated)

Elloree

ELLOREE HERITAGE MUSEUM & CULTURAL CENTER, INC., 2714 Cleveland St., Elloree, SC 29047. Mailing Address: P.O. Box 54, Elloree, SC 29047-0054. Tel.: 803-897-2225. Fax: 803-897-2809. Facebook.
E-mail: elloreemuseum@ntinet.com
Web Site: www.elloreemuseum.org
Key Personnel: Pres., Howard Shirer; Volunteer Coord., Jan Miller; Museum Shop Mgr., Jane Livingston.
Institution Type/Description: History Museum.
Hours & Admission Prices: Wed.-Sat. 10-5. Adults $5, seniors 60 & over $4, children 6-18 $3; discounts to groups; children under 6 no charge. &
Attendance: 1,450 (actual)

J'S TEA-RIFIC TEAPOT MUSEUM, 2732 Cleveland St., Elloree, SC 29047. Mailing Address: P.O. Box 157, Bowman, SC 29016-0157. Tel.: 803-829-2944; 803-707-2017.
Web Site: sites.google.com/site/jstearificmuseum
Key Personnel: Cur., Sybil Boland.
Institution Type/Description: Teapot Museum.
Hours & Admission Prices: Open by appointment only.

Florence

DOOLEY PLANETARIUM - FRANCIS MARION UNIVERSITY, Cauthen Educational Media Center, 2nd Fl., Florence, SC 29506. Mailing Address: P.O. Box 100547, Florence, SC 29502-0547. Tel.: 843-661-1381.
Institution Type/Description: Planetarium.
Hours & Admission Prices: By appointment.

FLORENCE COUNTY MUSEUM, 111 W. Cheves St., Florence, SC 29501. Tel.: 843-676-1200. Fax: 843-676-1203.
Web Site: www.florencemuseum.org
Formerly: Florence Museum of Art, Science & History and the Florence Railroad Museum
Key Personnel: Exec. Dir., Andrew Russel Stout; Cur., Interpretation & Collections, Stephen Motte; Cur., Education, Kim Groom.
Institution Type/Description: General Museum.
Hours & Admission Prices: Tues.-Sat. 10-5. No charge.
Attendance: 19,000 (estimated)

WAR BETWEEN THE STATES MUSEUM, 107 S. Guerry St., Florence, SC 29501-4328. Tel.: 843-669-1266.
Key Personnel: Dir., Carl Hill, Jr.
Institution Type/Description: History Museum.
Hours & Admission Prices: Wed. & Sat. 10-5. Adults $2, children $1. Closed Christmas.
Attendance: 2,000 (estimated)

Fort Jackson

FORT JACKSON MUSEUM, 4442 Jackson Blvd., Fort Jackson, SC 29207-5100. Mailing Address: 2179 Sumter St., Fort Jackson, SC 29207-6102. Tel.: 803-751-7419. Fax: 803-751-4434.
E-mail: williamsb1@jackson.army.mil
Web Site: www.jackson.army.mil/museum/index.htm
Institution Type/Description: Military Museum.
Hours & Admission Prices: Mon.-Fri. 9-4. No charge; donations accepted. Closed federal holidays. &
Attendance: 32,000

U.S. ARMY CHAPLAIN CORPS MUSEUM, USACHCS, 10100 Lee Rd., Fort Jackson, SC 29207-7000. Tel.: 803-751-8827 & 8079. Fax: 803-751-8890.
E-mail: marcia.g.mcmanus.civ@mail.mil
Web Site: usachcs.armylive.dodlive.mil
Key Personnel: Dir. & Cur., Marcia McManus; Museum Technician, Tim Taylor.
Institution Type/Description: Military History Museum.
Hours & Admission Prices: Mon.-Fri. 9-4. No charge. Closed federal holidays. &

Gaffney

CHEROKEE COUNTY HISTORY AND ARTS MUSEUM, 301 College Dr., Gaffney, SC 29340-3006. Tel.: 864-489-3988. Fax: 864-489-3988.
E-mail: chaps@cherokeecountyhistory.org
Web Site: www.cherokeecountyhistory.org
Key Personnel: Dir., Jane Waters; Pres. (V), Dinah Hamrick; Admin., Lisa Hissins.
Institution Type/Description: History Museum.
Hours & Admission Prices: Mon.-Fri. 10-4. Adults $5, children under 12 $3; members no charge. &
Attendance: 3,000 (estimated)

CHEROKEE COUNTY VETERANS MUSEUM, 200 S. Logan St., Gaffney, SC 29340. Mailing Address: P.O. Box 8001, Gaffney, SC 29340. Tel.: 864-812-4136. Fax: 864-487-6209.
E-mail: todd.humphries@cherokeecountysc.com
Key Personnel: Dir. & Museum Shop Mgr., Todd Humphries.
Institution Type/Description: Military History Museum.
Hours & Admission Prices: Mon. 1-3, Sat. 9am to noon, Sun. 2-4; groups by appointment. No charge. Closed holidays.
Attendance: 800 (estimated)

COWPENS NATIONAL BATTLEFIELD, Physical/Mailing Address: 338 New Pleasant Rd., Gaffney, SC 29341-4522. Tel.: 864-461-2828. Fax: 864-461-7795.
E-mail: cowp_interpretation@nps.gov
Web Site: www.nps.gov/cowp/
Key Personnel: Supt., Tim Stone; Administrative Officer, Michelle Lester; Chief Ranger, Kathy McKay.

Institution Type/Description: Military Museum: located on site of 1781 Battle of Cowpens.
Hours & Admission Prices: Daily 9-5. No charge; donations accepted. Closed New Year's Day; Thanksgiving; Christmas. &
Attendance: 208,566 (actual)

WINNIE DAVIS HALL OF HISTORY, Limestone College, 1115 College Dr., Gaffney, SC 29340-3778. Tel.: 864-488-4575.
E-mail: phoskins@limestone.edu
Web Site: www.limestone.edu
Key Personnel: College Historian, Patricia Hoskins.
Institution Type/Description: College Museum: housed in 1898-1901 Winnie Davis Hall of History, built to house Confederate records.
Hours & Admission Prices: By appointment only. No charge.

Georgetown

GEORGETOWN COUNTY MUSEUM, Georgetown County Historical Society, 120 Broad St., Georgetown, SC 29440-3630. Tel.: 843-545-7020. Fax: 843-545-7020.
E-mail: georgetownmuseum@gmail.com
Web Site: www.georgetowncountymuseum.com
Key Personnel: Museum Mgr., Susie Shoman.
Institution Type/Description: Historical Museum.
Hours & Admission Prices: Tues.-Fri. 11-4, Sat. 11-3. Adults $5, seniors 60 & over $4, children 7-18 $2; children under 6 & members no charge. &

HOBCAW BARONY DISCOVERY CENTER, 22 Hobcaw Rd., Georgetown, SC 29440-9500. Tel.: 843-546-4623. Fax: 843-545-7231.
E-mail: hobcaw@belle.baruch.sc.edu
Web Site: www.hobcawbarony.org
Formerly: Bellefield Nature Center
Institution Type/Description: History Museum.
Hours & Admission Prices: Center: Mon.-Fri. 9-5. No charge; donations accepted. Guided Tours: Tues.-Fri. by appointment. $20 per person.
Attendance: 12,000 (actual)

HOPSEWEE PLANTATION, 494 Hopsewee Rd., Georgetown, SC 29440-5598. Tel.: 843-546-7891. Fax: 843-546-3957.
E-mail: fdbeatie@gmail.com
Web Site: www.hopsewee.com
Key Personnel: Owner, Frank Beattie; Mgr. River Oaks Tea Room, Raejean Beattie; Docent, Jean Efird; Docent, Sara Morrison; Docent, Patricia Candale.
Institution Type/Description: Historic House: c.1735-40 birthplace of Thomas Lynch Jr., signer of the Declaration of Independence.
Hours & Admission Prices: House & Tea Room: Feb.-Nov. Tues.-Fri. 10-4, Sat. 12-4. Adults $17.50, children 5-17 $7.50; discounts to AAM members. Grounds: daily $5 per car. Closed Thanksgiving.
Attendance: 9,500 (estimated)

KAMINSKI HOUSE MUSEUM, 1003 Front St., Georgetown, SC 29440-3521. Tel.: 843-546-7706.
E-mail: rgabriel@kaminskimuseum.org
Web Site: www.kaminskimuseum.org
Key Personnel: Exec. Dir., Robin Gabriel; Museum Shop Mgr., Lisa Stalvey.
Institution Type/Description: Historic House: 1769 Harold Kaminski House.
Hours & Admission Prices: Mon.-Sat. 10-5; call for tour times. Adults $12, seniors $10, children 6-18 $3, discounts to ICOM, SEMC, AASLH, SCFM, AAM & active military; children under 6 & members no charge. &
Attendance: 13,000 (actual)

THE RICE MUSEUM, Lafayette Park, Front and Screven Sts., 633 Front St., Georgetown, SC 29440. Tel.: 843-546-7423. Facebook: The Rice Museum.
E-mail: thericemuseum@gmail.com
Web Site: www.ricemuseum.org
Key Personnel: Dir., James A. Fitch; Chm. (V), Frank Beatty.
Institution Type/Description: History Museum: housed in the 1842 Old Market Building located on the Old Market site.
Hours & Admission Prices: Mon.-Sat. 10-4:30. Adults $7, seniors $5, students 6-21 $3; discounts to groups; children under 6 no charge. Closed New Year's Day; Thanksgiving; Christmas. &
Attendance: 30,000 (estimated)

SOUTH CAROLINA MARITIME MUSEUM, 729 Front St., Georgetown, SC 29440. Mailing Address: P.O. Box 2228, Georgetown, SC 29440. Tel.: 843-520-0111. Facebook: SC Maritime Museum.

E-mail: info@sc-mm.org
Web Site: scmaritimemuseum.org
Institution Type/Description: Maritime History Museum.
Hours & Admission Prices: Mon.-Sat. 11-5. No charge; donations accepted.
Attendance: 21,000 (estimated)

Green Sea

COUNTRY FARM MUSEUM, 1991 Fair Bluff Hwy., Green Sea, SC 29545-4452. Tel.: 843-756-1682.
Institution Type/Description: Farm Museum.
Hours & Admission Prices: Call for hours.

Greenville

BOB JONES UNIVERSITY MUSEUM & GALLERY, INC., 1700 Wade Hampton Blvd., Greenville, SC 29614. Tel.: 864-770-1331. Fax: 864-770-1306. Facebook: Bob Jones University Museum & Gallery.
E-mail: contact@bjumg.org
Web Site: www.bjumg.org
Key Personnel: Dir., Erin Jones; Dir. Educations, Donnalynn Hess; Registrar, Barbara Sicko; Events Coord., Amy Basinger.
Institution Type/Description: Old Masters Museum.
Hours & Admission Prices: mid-Jan. to mid-Dec. Tues.-Sat. 2-5. Adults $7, senior citizens $6, students $5; members and children 12 & under no charge. Audio Tour: $5. North American, ROAM, and the Southeastern reciprocal membership programs. Closed Commencement Day; Independence Day; Thanksgiving weekend. M&G at Heritage Green: Tues.-Sat. 10-5. Adults $7, senior citizens $6, students $5; members & children 12 & under no charge. Closed New Year's Day; Thanksgiving; Christmas Eve & Day. &
Attendance: 21,743 (actual)

THE CHILDREN'S MUSEUM OF THE UPSTATE, 300 College St., Greenville, SC 29601. Tel.: 864-233-7755, 864-233-7790. Facebook: TCM Upstate.
E-mail: info@tcmgreenvillesc.org
Web Site: www.tcmupstate.org
Key Personnel: C.E.O. & Pres., Nancy Halverson; Pres. (V), Paul Sparks; Museum Shop Mgr., Charlie Bishop.
Institution Type/Description: Children's Museum.
Hours & Admission Prices: Memorial Day to Labor Day Mon.-Wed. & Fri.-Sat. 9-5, Thurs. 9-7; Sept.-May Tues.-Sat. 9-5, Sun. 11-5; groups by appointment. Adults $10, seniors & military $9.50, children 2-12 $9; members no charge. Closed New Year's Day; Easter; Thanksgiving; Christmas. &
Attendance: 150,000 (estimated)

GREENVILLE COUNTY MUSEUM OF ART, 420 College St., Greenville, SC 29601-2099. Tel.: 864-271-7570. Fax: 864-271-7579.
E-mail: info@gcma.org
Web Site: www.gcma.org
Key Personnel: Dir., Thomas W. Styron; Cur., Chesnee C.S. Klein; Head Devel., Stephanie Rainey; Communications, Paula Angermeier.
Institution Type/Description: Art Museum. American art from the 18th century to present.
Hours & Admission Prices: Wed.-Sat. 10-6, Sun. 1-5. No charge; donations accepted. Closed major holidays. &
Attendance: 125,000 (estimated)

GREENVILLE ZOO, 150 Cleveland Park Dr., Greenville, SC 29601-3147. Tel.: 864-467-4300.
E-mail: zooinfo@greenvillesc.gov
Web Site: www.greenvillezoo.com
Key Personnel: Foundation Exec. Dir., Lydia Thomas.
Institution Type/Description: Zoo.
Hours & Admission Prices: March-Sept. daily 9-5; Oct.-Feb. daily 10-5. Adults $9.75, active military & spouse and seniors 65 & over $8.75, children 3-15 $6.50, children of military $5.50; discounts to groups, children 2 & under no charge. Closed New Year's Day; Thanksgiving; Christmas. &
Attendance: 300,000 (estimated)

MUSEUM AND LIBRARY OF CONFEDERATE HISTORY, 15 Boyce Ave., Greenville, SC 29601-3109. Tel.: 864-421-9039. Fax: 864-421-9039.
E-mail: confedmuseum@att.net
Web Site: www.confederatemuseum.org
Formerly: South Carolina SCV Confederate Museum
Key Personnel: Dir., V. Michael Couch, Sr.; Chm. (V), Terry Lee Rude; Museum Shop Mgr., Greg Harrison.

Institution Type/Description: History Museum.
Hours & Admission Prices: Mon. & Wed. 10-3, Fri. 1-9, Sat. 10-5, Sun. 1-5; other times by appointment. No charge; donations accepted. Closed New Year's Day; Christmas. &
Attendance: 12,000 (estimated)

PARK CENTER - PARIS MOUNTAIN STATE PARK, 2401 State Park Rd., Greenville, SC 29609. Tel.: 864-244-5565.
E-mail: parismountain@scprt.com
Institution Type/Description: Park Museum: housed in a renovated bathhouse built by the Civilian Conservation Corps in the 1930s.
Hours & Admission Prices: Call for hours. Adults $2, senior citizens $1.25; children 15 & under no charge.

ROPER MOUNTAIN SCIENCE CENTER, 402 Roper Mountain Rd., Greenville, SC 29615-4298. Tel.: 864-355-8900. Fax: 864-355-8948.
E-mail: ropermtnsciencectr@greenville.k12.sc.us
Web Site: www.ropermountain.org
Key Personnel: Dir., Michael Weeks.
Institution Type/Description: Science Center.
Hours & Admission Prices: Mon.-Fri. 8:30-5. No charge. &
Attendance: 252,626 (actual)

SHOELESS JOE JACKSON MUSEUM AND BASEBALL LIBRARY, 356 Field St., Greenville, SC 29601-3541. Mailing Address: P.O. Box 4755, Greenville, SC 29608-4755. Tel.: 864-346-4867.
E-mail: info@shoelessjoejacksonmuseum.org
Web Site: www.shoelessjoejackson.org
Key Personnel: Pres., Cur. & Publicist, Arlene Marcley.
Institution Type/Description: History Museum: housed in the former home of Joe Jackson.
Hours & Admission Prices: Sat. 10-2; other times by appointment. No charge; donations accepted.

THOMPSON GALLERY - FURMAN UNIVERSITY, Art Dept., 3300 Poinsett Hwy., Greenville, SC 29613. Tel.: 864-294-2074.
E-mail: marta.lanier@furman.edu
Web Site: www2.furman.edu/academics/art/pages/default.aspx
Institution Type/Description: Art Gallery.
Hours & Admission Prices: Academic Year: Mon.-Fri. 9-5.

UPCOUNTRY HISTORY MUSEUM - FURMAN UNIVERSITY, 540 Buncombe St., Greenville, SC 29601-1906. Tel.: 864-467-3100. Fax: 864-467-3105. Facebook: Upcountry History Museum.
E-mail: info@upcountryhistory.org
Web Site: www.upcountryhistory.org
Key Personnel: Chm., Caroline Schroder; Exec. Dir., Dana L. Thorpe; Dir., Programs & Mktg., Elizabeth McSherry; Event Coord., Kimberly Adams; Dir., Opers., Ellen Hawkins; Information & Data Mgr., Kristen Pace; Cur., Katie Womble; Visitor Svcs. Coord., Jean Evans; Maintenance Supvr., Chad Coker; Finance Mgr., Tammy Burton.
Institution Type/Description: History Museum.
Hours & Admission Prices: Tues.-Sat. 10-5, Sun. 1-5. Adults $6, children $4; discounts to AAM, SEMC, NARM & Blue Star Museum members; members no charge. Closed major holidays. &
Attendance: 49,000 (estimated)

Greenwood

THE BENJAMIN E. MAYS MUSEUM AND HISTORIC SITE, 229 N. Hospital St., Greenwood, SC 29646. Mailing Address: P.O. Box 1326, Greenwood, SC 29648. Tel.: 864-229-8801 & 223-8434.
E-mail: lsartin@gleamns.org
Web Site: www.mayshousemuseum.org
Formerly: The Benjamin E. Mays Historic Site
Key Personnel: Dir. & Museum Shop Mgr., Loy E. Sartin.
Institution Type/Description: Historic House Museum: housed in the former home of Morehouse College President, Dr. Benjamin Mays.
Hours & Admission Prices: Mon.-Tues. & Thurs. 9-12, Wed. & Fri. 9-2:30; other times by appointment. No charge; donations accepted. Closed holidays. &
Attendance: 1,250 (actual)

THE MUSEUM AND RAILROAD HISTORICAL CENTER, 106 Main St., Greenwood, SC 29646-2763. Mailing Address: P.O. Box 3131, Greenwood, SC 29648. Tel.: 864-229-7093. Fax: 864-229-9317.

E-mail: greenwoodmuseumdirector@gmail.com
Web Site: www.greenwoodmuseum.org
Formerly: The Greenwood Museum
Key Personnel: Exec. Dir., Stacey Thompson; Pres. (V), Hannah Gantt; Dir. Programs, Bethany Wade.
Institution Type/Description: General Museum.
Hours & Admission Prices: Museum: Wed.-Sat. 10-5. No charge; donations accepted. &
Attendance: 10,000 (actual)

Greer

GREER HERITAGE MUSEUM, 106 S. Main St., Greer, SC 29651-3430. Mailing Address: P.O. Box 995, Greer, SC 29652-0995. Tel.: 864-877-3377.
E-mail: greerheritagemuseum@yahoo.com
Key Personnel: Dir., Cur. & Pres. (V), David V. Duncan; Founder, Carm Hudson.
Institution Type/Description: History Museum housed in the former City Hall & 1935 post office (WPA Building).
Hours & Admission Prices: Fri.-Sat. 10-4; groups of 10 or more by appointment. No charge; donations accepted. &
Attendance: 1,200 (actual)

ZENTRUM MUSEUM, 1400 Hwy. 101 S., Greer, SC 29651-6731. Tel.: 864-989-5528 & 6000.
E-mail: amber.scruggs@bmwmc.com
Web Site: www.bmwusfactory.com/#/zentrum/1248
Institution Type/Description: BMW History Museum.
Hours & Admission Prices: Museum: Mon.-Fri. 9:30-5;30; see website for holidays hours. No charge. Plant Tours: adults $10-$15, students 12 & over $5-$10.

Hampton

HAMPTON COUNTY MUSEUM AT THE OLD JAIL, 702 W. 1st St., Hampton, SC 29924. Mailing Address: P.O. Box 152, Hampton, SC 29924. Tel.: 803-943-5484. Facebook: Hampton County Museum.
E-mail: contact@hchssc.org
Formerly: Hampton County Historical Society Museum
Key Personnel: Pres. (V) Hampton County Historical Society, LaClaire W. Laffitte; Museum Dir., Mary Ann Sowell; Vice Pres., Steve Kemmerlin; Treas., Virginia Sinclair; Corresponding Sec., Iris Winn.
Institution Type/Description: History Museum: housed in c.1878 Old Jail. Listed on the National Register of Historic Places.
Hours & Admission Prices: Thurs. & Sun. 2-5; other times by appointment. No charge; donations accepted. &
Attendance: 500 (estimated)

Hartsville

CECELIA COKER BELL GALLERY, Coker College, Art Dept., 300 E. College Ave., Hartsville, SC 29550-3742. Tel.: 843-383-8156 & 8150, 843-858-7187. Fax: 843-383-8033. Facebook: Cecelia Coker Bell Gallery.
E-mail: artgallery@coker.edu
Web Site: www.ceceliacokerbellgallery.com
Key Personnel: Dir., Larry Merriman.
Institution Type/Description: Art Gallery & Teaching Gallery.
Hours & Admission Prices: Academic Year: Mon., Wed. & Fri. 10-4, Tues. & Thurs. 10-8; Summer: Mon.-Fri. 10-4. No charge. &
Attendance: 4,000 (estimated)

HARTSVILLE MUSEUM, 222 N. Fifth St., Hartsville, SC 29550-4136. Mailing Address: P.O. Box 431, Hartsville, SC 29551-0431. Tel.: 843-383-3005. Fax: 843-383-2477.
E-mail: info@hartsvillemuseum.org
Web Site: www.hartsvillemuseum.org
Key Personnel: C.E.O. & Dir., Kathy M. Dunlap; Chm., Glenn J. Lawhon, Jr.; City Mgr., James Pennington; Museum Shop Mgr., Penny Anthony.
Institution Type/Description: Local History Museum: housed in restored 1930 U.S. Post Office Building, changing gallery for Arts Programming.
Hours & Admission Prices: Mon.-Fri. 10-5, Sat. 10-2. No charge; donations accepted. Closed state holidays. &
Attendance: 12,500 (actual)

JACOB KELLEY HOUSE MUSEUM, 2585 Kellytown Rd., Hartsville, SC 29550. Mailing Address: 204 Hewitt St., Darlington, SC 29532-3214. Tel.: 843-332-6401 & 339-9093. Fax: 843-332-8017.
E-mail: dchc@darcosc.com

Key Personnel: Pres. (V), Jo Ann K. Lee; C.E.O. & Dir., Brian E. Gandy.
Institution Type/Description: Historic House: 1820 Federal style plantation house used as General Sherman's headquarters during Civil War.
Hours & Admission Prices: Feb.-Nov, first Sun. of the month 3-5. No charge; donations accepted.

KALMIA GARDENS, 1624 W. Carolina Ave., Hartsville, SC 29550-4906. Tel.: 843-383-8145. Fax: 843-383-8149.
E-mail: kalmia@coker.edu
Web Site: kalmiagardens.org
Key Personnel: Dir., Mary R. Ridgeway.
Institution Type/Description: Botanical Garden & Historic House Museum: home of Thomas E. Hart, built in 1820. Listed on the National Register of Historic Places.
Hours & Admission Prices: Daily. No charge.

Hilton Head Island

COASTAL DISCOVERY MUSEUM AT HONEY HORN, 70 Honey Horn Dr., Hilton Head Island, SC 29926. Tel.: 843-689-6767. Fax: 843-689-3035. Facebook.
E-mail: info@coastaldiscovery.org
Web Site: coastaldiscovery.org
Key Personnel: Pres. & C.E.O., Rex Garniewicz; Vice Pres. Finance & Administration, Jennifer Stupica; Vice Pres. Programs, Natalie Hefter; Vice Pres. Mktg. & Devel., Robin Swift; Mgr. Natural History, Carlos Chacon; Cur. Education, Dawn Brut.
Institution Type/Description: General Museum.
Hours & Admission Prices: Mon.-Sat. 9-4:30, Sun. 11-3. Suggested Donation: $5 per person. &
Attendance: 96,500 (actual)

HARBOUR TOWN LIGHTHOUSE MUSEUM, 149 Lighthouse Rd., Hilton Head Island, SC 29928. Tel.: 866-305-9814 (Toll Free), 843-671-2810.
E-mail: info@harbourtownlighthouse.com
Web Site: www.harbourtownlighthouse.com
Institution Type/Description: Lighthouse Museum.
Hours & Admission Prices: Call for hours.

THE SANDBOX, AN INTERACTIVE CHILDREN'S MUSEUM, 18A Pope Ave., Hilton Head Island, SC 29928-4708. Tel.: 843-842-7645.
E-mail: executivedirector@thesandbox.org
Web Site: www.thesandbox.org
Key Personnel: Exec. Dir., Steve Maglione; Operations Mgr., Caroline Rinehart.
Institution Type/Description: Children's Museum.
Hours & Admission Prices: April & June-Aug. Mon.-Sat. 10-5; May & Sept.-March Tues.-Sat. 10-5. Admission $6; members & children under one no charge. Closed Thanksgiving; Christmas. &
Attendance: 28,465 (actual)

Hopkins

CONGAREE NATIONAL PARK, 100 National Park Rd., Hopkins, SC 29061-8320. Tel.: 803-776-4396. Fax: 803-783-4241.
E-mail: gregory_cunningham@nps.gov
Web Site: www.nps.gov/cong
Formerly: Congaree Swamp National Monument
Key Personnel: Supt., K Lynn Berry; Chief Ranger, Jason Johnson; Chief of Interpretation, Greg Cunningham; Chief of Facilities, Charles Aznive; Chief of Resources, David Shelley.
Institution Type/Description: National Park & Preservation Project: 26,800-acre National Park.
Hours & Admission Prices: Visitor Center: Summer: daily 8:30-7; Winter: daily 8:30-5. No charge; donations accepted. Closed Christmas. &
Attendance: 134,000 (actual)

Hunting Island

HUNTING ISLAND NATURE CENTER, 2555 Sea Island Pkwy., Hunting Island, SC 29920. Tel.: 843-838-7437.
E-mail: huntingisland@scprt.com
Web Site: www.huntingisland.com
Institution Type/Description: Nature Center.
Hours & Admission Prices: Summer: daily 9-5; Winter: Tues.-Sat. 9-5.

Jackson

SILVER BLUFF AUDUBON CENTER, 4542 Silver Bluff Rd., Jackson, SC 29831. Tel.: 803-471-0291.
E-mail: pkoehler@audubon.org
Web Site: www.sc.audubon.org/Centers_SB.html
Institution Type/Description: Audubon Center.
Hours & Admission Prices: Call for hours.

Johnston

EDGEFIELD COUNTY PEACH MUSEUM, 416 Calhoun St., Johnston, SC 29832-1317. Tel.: 803-275-0010. Fax: 803-275-3586.
Institution Type/Description: History Museum.
Hours & Admission Prices: Mon.-Fri. 8:30-12:30; other times by appointment. Closed holidays.

Kingstree

THORNTREE PLANTATION, Nelson Blvd., Kingstree, SC 29556-3335. Mailing Address: Williamsburg Historical Society, 135 Hampton Ave., Kingstree, SC 29556-3423. Tel.: 843-355-3306.
Institution Type/Description: Historic House Museum: housed in the home of James Witherspoon; built in 1749.
Hours & Admission Prices: By appointment.

WILLIAMSBURGH HISTORICAL MUSEUM, 135 Hampton Ave., Kingstree, SC 29556-3423. Tel.: 843-355-3306.
E-mail: history1@ftc-i.net
Key Personnel: Dir., Joanne B. Brown.
Institution Type/Description: History Museum.
Hours & Admission Prices: Tues.-Thurs. 10-3. No charge; donations accepted. Closed major holidays.

Lake City

BROWNTOWN MUSEUM, Hwy. 341, Lake City, SC 29560. Mailing Address: 414 Main St., Hemingway, SC 29554-9190. Tel.: 843-558-2355.
E-mail: 3rivershs@ftc-i.net
Key Personnel: Dir. & Cur., Nell Morris; Pres., Kathy Loyd; Treas., Mona Prosser; Sec., Carol Cockfield.
Institution Type/Description: Historic Site & Preservation Project.
Hours & Admission Prices: Sat. 9-4; groups by appointment. Adults $5, children $2. ⅊
Attendance: 350 (estimated)

JONES-CARTER GALLERY, 105 Henry St., P.O. Box 943, Lake City, SC 29560-0943. Tel.: 843-374-1505.
Key Personnel: Gallery Mgr., Hannah Davis.
Institution Type/Description: Art Gallery.
Hours & Admission Prices: Tues.-Fri. 10-6, Sat. 11-5.

NATIONAL BEAN MARKET MUSEUM, 111 Henry St., Lake City, SC 29560. Mailing Address: P.O. Box 943, Lake City, SC 29560-0943. Tel.: 843-374-1500.
Institution Type/Description: Historic Building: built in 1936. Listed on the National Register of Historic Places.
Hours & Admission Prices: Mon.-Thurs 8-5, Fri. 8-4. No charge. Closed major holidays.

Lancaster

ANDREW JACKSON STATE PARK, 196 Andrew Jackson Park Rd., Lancaster, SC 29720-6404. Tel.: 803-285-3344.
E-mail: ajacksonsp@scprt.com
Web Site: southcarolinaparks.com/park-finder/state-park/1797.aspx
Key Personnel: Supt., Kirk Johnston.
Institution Type/Description: Park & History Museum: dedicated to Andrew Jackson, the 7th president of the United States.
Hours & Admission Prices: Park: Summer: daily 9-9; Winter: daily 8-6. Schoolhouse: mid-March to Nov. Sat. 1-5, Sun. 2-5. Museum: Sat.-Sun. 1-5; other times by appointment. Adults $2, seniors $1.25; children 15 & under no charge.
Attendance: 51,000 (estimated)

LANCASTER & CHESTER RAILWAY MUSEUM, 512 S. Main St., 2nd Fl., Lancaster, SC 29720-3622. Mailing Address: P.O. Box 1450, Lancaster, SC 29721-1450. Tel.: 803-286-2100 & 2102. Fax: 803-286-4158.
E-mail: jcc@gulfandohio.com
Web Site: landcrailroad.com
Institution Type/Description: Railway Museum.
Hours & Admission Prices: 1st & 3rd Sat. of the month 10-4. No charge.

Lando

LANDO MANETTA MILLS HISTORY CENTER, 3801 Lando Rd., Lando, SC 29729. Tel.: 803-789-6361. Facebook: Lando History Center.
E-mail: lmmhc3801@gmail.com
Web Site: landomanettamillshistorycenter.com
Institution Type/Description: Textile History Museum: housed in the former Manetta Mills Company office.
Hours & Admission Prices: Mon.-Fri. 9am to noon, Sun. 2-5. Closed major holidays.

Latta

DILLON COUNTY MUSEUM, 101 S. Marion St., Latta, SC 29565-1558. Mailing Address: Dillon County Historical Society, P. O. Box 1806, Dillon, SC 29536-1806. Tel.: 843-441-5273 & 774-6122.
E-mail: bbar830771@aol.com
Key Personnel: Dir., Betty L. Barclay.
Institution Type/Description: Historic Building: housed in the former office of Dr. Henry Edwards; built in 1925. Listed on the National Register of Historic Places.
Hours & Admission Prices: Tues.-Thurs. 2-4; other times by appointment. No charge; donations accepted. ⅊
Attendance: 500 (estimated)

Laurens

THE CHARLES H. DUCKETT HOUSE, 105 Downs St., Laurens, SC 29360. Mailing Address: c/o Laurens County African American Cultural Foundation, 109 Downs St., Laurens, SC 29360. Tel.: 803-896-6196.
Institution Type/Description: Historic House Museum: housed in the former home of prominent black businessman, Charlie Duckett; built c.1892. Listed on the National Register of Historic Places.
Hours & Admission Prices: Call for hours.

THE JAMES DUNKLIN HOUSE, 544 W. Main St., Laurens, SC 29360. Mailing Address: 2009 Lakeview Dr., Laurens, SC 29360-5132. Tel.: 864-984-4735 & 683-2432.
Key Personnel: Mgr., Shawn Brown.
Institution Type/Description: Historic Foundation: housed in 1812 The James Dunklin House. Listed on the National Register of Historic Places.
Hours & Admission Prices: 1st Sun. each month 2-5; other times by appointment. Adults $2, children 11 & under $1.
Attendance: 300 (actual)

Lexington

LEXINGTON COUNTY MUSEUM, 231 Fox St., Lexington, SC 29072-2654. Mailing Address: P.O. Box 637, Lexington, SC 29071-0637. Tel.: 803-359-8369. Fax: 803-808-2160. Facebook: Lexington County Museum.
E-mail: museum@lex-co.com
Web Site: www.lex-co.sc.gov/museum
Key Personnel: Chm. (V), Bill Kiesling; Dir., J.R. Fennell.
Institution Type/Description: History Museum.
Hours & Admission Prices: Tues.-Sat. 10-4, Sun. 1-4; last tour 3. Adults $5; members no charge. Closed major holidays.
Attendance: 20,000 (actual)

Manning

CLARENDON COUNTY ARCHIVES AND HISTORY CENTER, Old Manning Library, 211 N. Brooks St., Manning, SC 29103-3209. Tel.: 803-435-0328.
E-mail: clarendonarchives@clarendoncountygov.org
Web Site: www.clarendoncountyarchives.com
Institution Type/Description: History Museum.

Hours & Admission Prices: Mon.-Fri. 8:30-4.

Marion

MARION COUNTY MUSEUM, 101 Willcox Ave., Marion, SC 29571-2809. Mailing Address: P.O. Box 220, Marion, SC 29751-0220. Tel.: 843-423-8299.
E-mail: marioncountymuseum@att.net
Web Site: www.marionsc.org/museum
Key Personnel: Dir., Rosanne Black.
Institution Type/Description: Historic Building: housed in a former schoolhouse, c.1886. Listed on the National Register for Historic Sites.
Hours & Admission Prices: Tues.-Fri. 9-12 & 1-5; other times by appointment. No charge; donations accepted.

McClellanville

HAMPTON PLANTATION STATE HISTORIC SITE, 1950 Rutledge Rd., McClellanville, SC 29458-9588. Tel.: 843-546-9361. Fax: 843-527-4995.
E-mail: hampton@scprt.com
Web Site: www.southcarolinaparks.com
Formerly: Hampton Plantation State Park
Key Personnel: Rgnl. Chief, Ray Stevens; Park Mgr., Dale Purvis.
Institution Type/Description: Historic House: c.1750 Hampton House, former rice plantation.
Hours & Admission Prices: Park: daily 9-5. Mansion Tours: Sat.-Tues. 1pm, 2pm & 3pm. Adults $7.50, senior citizens $3.75, children $3.50. Closed Christmas. &
Attendance: 30,000 (actual)

THE VILLAGE MUSEUM, 401 Pinckney St., McClellanville, SC 29458. Mailing Address: P.O. Box 595, McClellanville, SC 29458. Tel.: 843-887-3030.
E-mail: villagemuseum@tds.net
Institution Type/Description: History Museum.
Hours & Admission Prices: Thurs.-Sat. 10-12 & 1-5. Adults $3; discounts to groups; members, children & students no charge.

McConnells

HISTORIC BRATTONSVILLE, 1444 Brattonsville Rd., McConnells, SC 29726-8768. Tel.: 803-684-2327. Fax: 803-684-0149.
E-mail: hbratton@chmuseums.org
Web Site: www.chmuseums.org
Key Personnel: Mgr., Kevin Lynch; Coord. Visitor Svcs., Denise Jensen; Mgr., School Programs, Karen Cox.
Institution Type/Description: Preservation Project: housed in 1823 federal style mansion located on the site of Huck's Defeat in battle during the Revolutionary War.
Hours & Admission Prices: Tues.-Sat. 10-5, Sun. 1-5; groups & Christmas tours by appointment. Adults $6, seniors 60 & over $5, youth 4-17 $3; members and children 3 & under no charge. Closed New Year's Day; Thanksgiving; Christmas. &
Attendance: 21,920 (actual)

McCormick

DORN MILL CENTER, 200 N. Main St., McCormick, SC 29835. Mailing Address: 300 Pineview, McCormick, SC 29835.
E-mail: mcparnell@wctel.net
Web Site: www.mccormickshistory.org
Key Personnel: Chm. (V), Marian Parnell.
Institution Type/Description: Interpretive Center.
Hours & Admission Prices: By appointment. No charge; donations accepted. &

Moncks Corner

BERKELEY COUNTY MUSEUM & HERITAGE CENTER, 950 Stony Landing Rd., Moncks Corner, SC 29461-2944. Tel.: 843-899-5101. Fax: 843-899-5101.
E-mail: berkmuseum@homesc.com
Formerly: Berkeley Museum, Inc.
Key Personnel: Chm. & Pres. (V), Willard Strong; Mgr., Carolyn Pilgrim.
Institution Type/Description: History Museum. Home of the Little David; birthplace of Francis Marion.
Hours & Admission Prices: Tues.-Sat. 9-4:30, Sun. 1-4:30. Adults $3, seniors $2; discounts to groups; children 6 & under no charge. Admission to Old Santee Canal Park includes entry to Berkeley Museum. Closed Easter; Thanksgiving; Christmas. &
Attendance: 10,000 (estimated)

CYPRESS GARDENS, 3030 Cypress Gardens Rd., Moncks Corner, SC 29461-6447. Tel.: 843-553-0515.
E-mail: tcook@berkeleycountysc.gov
Web Site: www.cypressgardens.info
Institution Type/Description: Gardens.
Hours & Admission Prices: Daily 9-5. Adults $10, seniors 65 & over $9, children 6-12 $5; children 5 & under no charge. Closed New Year's Day; Thanksgiving; Christmas Eve & Day.
Attendance: 45,000 (estimated)

OLD SANTEE CANAL PARK, 900 Stony Landing Rd., Moncks Corner, SC 29461-2944. Tel.: 843-899-5200. Fax: 843-761-7032.
E-mail: parkinfo@oldsanteecanalpark.org
Web Site: www.oldsanteecanalpark.org
Formerly: Old Santee Canal State Historic Site
Key Personnel: C.E.O., Lonnie N. Carter; Park Dir., Troy Diel; Museum Shop Mgr., Cindy Moyer.
Institution Type/Description: Park Museum: located on historic Stony Landing Plantation at southern terminus of the Santee Canal (1800-1850s), the first true canal constructed in the United States.
Hours & Admission Prices: Daily 9-5. Adults $3, senior citizens over 65, AAA members & military $2; children 6 & under no charge. Closed New Year's Day; Easter; Thanksgiving; Christmas Eve & Day. &
Attendance: 40,610 (actual)

Mount Pleasant

BOONE HALL PLANTATION & GARDENS, 1235 Long Point Rd., Mount Pleasant, SC 29464-9020. Tel.: 843-884-4371. Fax: 843-884-0475.
E-mail: info@boonehallplantation.com
Web Site: www.boonehallplanation.com
Institution Type/Description: History Museum: house built in 1936.
Hours & Admission Prices: late March to Labor Day Mon.-Sat. 8:30am-6:30pm, Sun. 1-5; Sept. to late March Mon.-Sat. 9-5, Sun. 1-4. Adults $19.50, children 6-12 $10; children 5 & under no charge.

CHARLES PINCKNEY NATIONAL HISTORIC SITE, 1254 Long Point Rd., Mount Pleasant, SC 29464. Mailing Address: 1214 Middle St., Sullivan's Island, SC 29482-9717. Tel.: 843-881-5516. Fax: 843-881-7070.
E-mail: shannon_woolfolk@nps.gov
Web Site: www.nps.gov/chpi
Key Personnel: Supt., Tim Stone; Chief Interpretation, Dawn Davis; Cur., Catherine Fowler; Museum Shop Mgr., Kevin Bates.
Institution Type/Description: Historic Site: located in a c.1828 plantation house.
Hours & Admission Prices: Daily 9-5. No charge; donations accepted. Closed New Year's Day; Thanksgiving; Christmas. &
Attendance: 35,000 (actual)

PATRIOTS POINT NAVAL AND MARITIME MUSEUM, 40 Patriots Point Rd., Mount Pleasant, SC 29464-4377. Tel.: 843-884-2727.
E-mail: info@patriotspoint.org
Web Site: www.patriotspoint.org
Key Personnel: Chm., Ray Chandler, Esq.; Exec. Dir., Mac Burdette; Dir. Operations, Bob Howard; Cur. Collections, Melissa Buchanan; Sr. Cur., David A. Clark; Museum Shop Mgr., Samuel Derrick.
Institution Type/Description: Maritime and Naval Museum: housed in the aircraft carrier USS Yorktown, destroyer USS Laffey, & submarine USS Clamagore located in Charleston Harbor; also houses Congressional Medal of Honor Museum & Carrier Aviation Hall of Fame.
Hours & Admission Prices: Daily 9-6:30. Adults $20, senior citizens & active military $17, children 6-11 $12; discounts to Historic Naval Ships Association; children under 6 with adult no charge. Closed Christmas. &
Attendance: 263,000 (actual)

Mullins

S.C. TOBACCO MUSEUM, 104 NE Front St., Mullins, SC 29574-2810. Tel.: 800-207-7967, 843-464-8194.
E-mail: cityofmullins@mullinssc.us
Web Site: www.mullinssc.us/sctobaccomuseumindex.html
Key Personnel: Dir., Reginald McDaniel.
Institution Type/Description: History Museum: housed in an historic train depot.
Hours & Admission Prices: Mon.-Fri. 9-5; groups by appointment. Adults $2, children & seniors $1. Closed holidays. &
Attendance: 2,000 (estimated)

Murrells Inlet

BROOKGREEN GARDENS, 1931 Brookgreen Dr., Murrells Inlet, SC 29576. Mailing Address: P.O. Box 3368, Pawleys Island, SC 29585-3368. Tel.: 843-235-6000, 800-849-1931. Fax: 843-235-6039.
E-mail: info@brookgreen.org
Web Site: www.brookgreen.org
Key Personnel: C.E.O. & Pres., Robert Jewell; Mgr., Jay Rowe; Vice Pres. Finance, Kathleen Zeiss; Vice Pres. & Cur. of Sculpture, Robin R. Salmon; Vice Pres. Horticulture & Conservation, Sara Millar; Vice Pres. Devel., Phillip A. Tukey; Vice Pres. Mktg., Helen Benso; Museum Shop Mgr., Ashley Gray.
Institution Type/Description: Art Museum & Botanical Garden.
Hours & Admission Prices: Daily 9:30-5. Adults $15, seniors $13, children 4-12 $7; children 3 & under no charge. Admission valid for 7 days. Closed Christmas. &
Attendance: 298,109 (actual)

Myrtle Beach

CHILDREN'S MUSEUM OF SOUTH CAROLINA, 2204 N. Oak St., Myrtle Beach, SC 29577-3054. Tel.: 843-946-9469. Fax: 843-946-7011.
E-mail: jessica@cmsckids.org
Web Site: www.cmsckids.org
Key Personnel: Gen. Mgr., Jessica Gregory.
Institution Type/Description: Children's Museum.
Hours & Admission Prices: Mon.-Sat. 9-5, Sun. 12-5. Admission $8; discounts to groups of 10 or more; children under 2 & members no charge. Closed Christmas. &
Attendance: 35,000 (actual)

FRANKLIN G. BURROUGHS-SIMEON B. CHAPIN ART MUSEUM, 3100 S. Ocean Blvd., Myrtle Beach, SC 29577-4858. Tel.: 843-238-2510. Fax: 843-238-2910. Facebook: Franklin G. Burroughs-Simeon B. Chapin Art Museum.
E-mail: pgoodwin@myrtlebeachartmuseum.org
Web Site: myrtlebeachartmuseum.org
Key Personnel: Dir., Patricia Goodwin; Chm., John C. Stewart; Treas., Bill Pritchard; Museum Shop Mgr., Casey Church.
Institution Type/Description: Art Museum.
Hours & Admission Prices: Tues.-Sat. 10-4, Sun. 1-4; call for holiday hours. No charge; donations accepted. &
Attendance: 26,000 (estimated)

FREEWOODS FARM, 9515 Freewoods Rd., Myrtle Beach, SC 29588. Tel.: 843-650-9139.
E-mail: oneal8072@yahoo.com
Web Site: www.freewoodsfarm.com
Institution Type/Description: African American Historical Farm Museum.
Hours & Admission Prices: Call for hours. No charge; donations accepted. &

MYRTLE BEACH STATE PARK NATURE CENTER, 4401 S. Kings Hwy., Myrtle Beach, SC 29575-4936. Tel.: 843-238-5325 & 0874. Fax: 843-238-9483.
E-mail: awilson@scprt.com
Web Site: www.southcarolinaparks.com
Key Personnel: Naturalist, Ann Malys Wilson.
Institution Type/Description: Nature Center.
Hours & Admission Prices: June-July Tues.-Sun. 11:30-4:30. Varied hours in off season. Park: adult $5, children 6-15 $3; children under 5 no charge. Nature Center: no charge. South Carolina State Park Passport: $75 annual pass. &
Attendance: 28,034 (actual)

RIPLEY'S AQUARIUM, 1110 Celebrity Circle, Myrtle Beach, SC 29577-7465. Tel.: 800-734-8888 (Toll Free), 843-916-0888.
E-mail: info@ripleysaquarium.com
Web Site: myrtlebeach.ripleyaquariums.com
Institution Type/Description: Aquarium.
Hours & Admission Prices: Daily 9-10. Adults 12 & over $18.99, children 6-11 $9.99, children 2-5 $3.99.

SOUTH CAROLINA CIVIL WAR MUSEUM, 4857 Hwy. 17 Bypass S., Myrtle Beach, SC 29577. Tel.: 843-293-3377. Facebook: South Carolina Civil War Museum.
E-mail: mbisr@mbisr.com
Web Site: mbisr.com/sccivilwarmuseum.html
Key Personnel: Dir., Connie B. Gragg.
Institution Type/Description: Military History Museum.

Hours & Admission Prices: Tues.-Sat. 10-6. Adults $4, seniors & veterans $3, students $2; discounts to AAM & ICOM members. &
Attendance: 5,234 (actual)

SOUTH CAROLINA HALL OF FAME, Myrtle Beach Convention Center, 2101 N. Oak St., Myrtle Beach, SC 29577. Mailing Address: P.O. Box 2115, Myrtle Beach, SC 29578-2115. Tel.: 843-626-7444. Fax: 843-448-3007.
E-mail: info@palmettoeventproductions.com
Web Site: southcarolinahalloffame.com
Key Personnel: Dir., Brad Dean; Chm. (V), Leo Twiggs.
Institution Type/Description: Hall of Fame.
Hours & Admission Prices: Daily 8:30-5. No charge.

WACCATEE ZOO, 8500 Enterprise Rd., Myrtle Beach, SC 29588-6626. Tel.: 843-650-8500.
E-mail: site_mgr@waccateezoo.com
Web Site: www.waccateezoo.com
Key Personnel: Owner, Kathleen Futrell.
Institution Type/Description: Zoo & antique barn.
Hours & Admission Prices: Daily 10-5. Adults 13 & over $10, children 1-12 $4; discounts to groups; children under one no charge.

Neeses

NEESES FARM MUSEUM, 6449 Savannah Hwy., Neeses, SC 29107. Mailing Address: P.O. Box 70, Neeses, SC 29107-0070. Tel.: 803-247-5811. Fax: 803-247-5811.
Key Personnel: Chm. (V) & Town Clerk, Sonja Gleaton.
Institution Type/Description: Agriculture Museum.
Hours & Admission Prices: By appointment. No charge; donations accepted. &
Attendance: 500 (estimated)

Newberry

NEWBERRY COUNTY HISTORICAL & MUSEUM SOCIETY, 1503 Nance St., Newberry, SC 29108-2740. Mailing Address: P.O. Box 186, Newberry, SC 29108-0186. Tel.: 803-276-8610. Facebook.
E-mail: eoshealy@newberry.net
Web Site: www.newberrycountyhistorical.com
Key Personnel: Dir., Ernest Shealy; Pres. (V), John Favors.
Institution Type/Description: History Museum.
Hours & Admission Prices: 1st & 3rd Sat. of each month 1-4; other times by appointment. No charge; donations accepted.

Ninety Six

NINETY SIX NATIONAL HISTORIC SITE, 1103 Hwy. 248 S., Ninety Six, SC 29666-8611. Tel.: 864-543-4068. Fax: 864-543-2058.
Web Site: www.NPS.gov/NISI
Key Personnel: Chief Ranger, Tim Cruze; Cur., Sarah Cunningham.
Institution Type/Description: History Museum & Site: commemorates community & village of the settlement of Ninety Six during the 18th-century & the siege of Ninety Six during the American Revolution interpreting the role of slavery.
Hours & Admission Prices: Visitor Center: daily 9-5. Cabin: open for special occasions & during Living History events. No charge; donations accepted. Closed New Year's Day; Thanksgiving; Christmas. &
Attendance: 50,000 (estimated)

North Charleston

HUNLEY SUBMARINE - WARREN LASCH CONSERVATION CENTER, 1250 Supply St., North Charleston, SC 29405-2219. Tel.: 843-743-4865, ext. 32. Fax: 843-744-1480.
E-mail: correia@hunley.org
Web Site: www.hunley.org
Institution Type/Description: History Museum.
Hours & Admission Prices: Sat. 10-5, Sun. 12-5. Adults $12; discounts to members, senior citizens & military.

NORTH CHARLESTON AND AMERICAN LAFRANCE FIRE MUSEUM AND EDUCATIONAL CENTER, 4975 Centre Pointe Dr., North Charleston, SC 29418-6945. Mailing Address: P. O. Box 190016, North Charleston, SC 29419-9016. Tel.: 843-740-5550. Fax: 843-740-5551.
E-mail: reneefryenc@yahoo.com

Web Site: www.northcharlestonfiremuseum.org
Key Personnel: Dir., Renee B. Frye.
Institution Type/Description: Fire Museum.
Hours & Admission Prices: Mon.-Sat. 10-5, Sun. 1-5. Adults 13 & over $6; discounts to groups of 15 or more; children 12 & under no charge. Closed New Year's Day; Thanksgiving; Christmas Eve & Day. &
Attendance: 32,000 (estimated)

North Myrtle Beach

NORTH MYRTLE BEACH AREA HISTORICAL MUSEUM, 799 2nd Ave. N., North Myrtle Beach, SC 29582. Tel.: 843-427-7668. Facebook.
E-mail: beachhistory@nmbmuseum.com
Web Site: www.nmbmuseum.com
Key Personnel: Dir., Jenean Neilsen Todd; Chm. (V), Bill Griste, Jr.
Institution Type/Description: History Museum.
Hours & Admission Prices: Wed.-Sun. 12-4. Adults $5, seniors 60 & over and students & military with ID $4, youth 5-17 $3; discounts to AAM & ICOM members; members no charge. Closed New Year's Day; Easter; Thanksgiving; Christmas. &
Attendance: 7,500 (estimated)

Orangeburg

I.P. STANBACK MUSEUM & PLANETARIUM, 300 College St., N.E., South Carolina State University, Orangeburg, SC 29117. Mailing Address: Stanback Planetarium & NASA ERC, P.O. Box 7636, South Carolina State Univ., Orangeburg, SC 29117. Tel.: 803-536-7174 & 8711. Fax: 803-536-8309.
E-mail: bmille26@scsu.edu
Web Site: www.scsucrash.blogspot.com
Key Personnel: Dir., Ellen Zisholtz.
Institution Type/Description: Planetarium & Art Museum.
Hours & Admission Prices: Museum: Mon.-Fri. 9-5. No charge. Planetarium Shows: Tues.-Fri. 4pm. No charge. &
Attendance: 30,000 (estimated)

Paris Island

PARRIS ISLAND MUSEUM, Bldg. 111 Panama St., MCRD, Paris Island, SC 29902-7607. Mailing Address: Commanding Gen., ATTN MUS, MCRD ERR, Box 5202, Parris Island, SC 29905-9001. Tel.: 843-228-2951. Fax: 843-228-3065.
E-mail: stephen.wise@usmc.mil
Key Personnel: Dir., Dr. Stephen R. Wise; Archaeologist, Kimberly Zawacki; Museum Shop Mgr., Rebecca Smith.
Institution Type/Description: Historic Site & Military Museum: located on the site of c.1566-1587, Spanish settlement, Santa Elena; later the 19th century Port Royal Navy Yard & Marine Corps Recruit Depot.
Hours & Admission Prices: Daily 10-4:30. No charge; donations accepted. Closed New Year's Day; Easter; Thanksgiving; Christmas. &
Attendance: 108,314 (actual)

Pendleton

BART GARRISON AGRICULTURAL MUSEUM OF SOUTH CAROLINA, 120 History Lane, Pendleton, SC 29670. Mailing Address: P.O. Box 565, Pendleton, SC 29670-0565. Tel.: 864-646-7271, 800-862-1795. Fax: 864-646-7768. Facebook: Bart Garrison Agricultural Museum of South Carolina.
E-mail: history@pendletondistrict.org
Web Site: www.bgamsc.org
Formerly: Pendleton District Agricultural Museum
Key Personnel: Dir., Les McCall; Chm., Sandra Powell; Asst. Coord. Education, Nikki Saylors.
Institution Type/Description: Agricultural Museum.
Hours & Admission Prices: Thurs.-Fri. 12-5, Sat. 10-3; groups by appointment. No charge; donations accepted. &
Attendance: 5,500 (actual)

PENDLETON DISTRICT HISTORICAL, RECREATIONAL AND TOURISM COMMISSION, 125 E. Queen St., Pendleton, SC 29670-1309. Mailing Address: P.O. Box 565, Pendleton, SC 29670-0565. Tel.: 864-646-3782 & 800-862-1795. Fax: 864-646-7768.
E-mail: les@pendletondistrick.org
Web Site: www.pendletondistrict.org

Key Personnel: Chm., Dr. Bill Steiser; Dir., Vicki B. Fletcher; Cur. Collections, Les McCall; Events & Tours Coord., Brook Havice.
Institution Type/Description: History Museum.
Hours & Admission Prices: April-Oct. Mon.-Fri. 9-4:30, Sat. 10-3; Nov.-March Mon.-Fri. 9-4:30. No charge; donations accepted. Closed state holidays. &
Attendance: 5,000 (estimated)

WOODBURN HISTORIC HOUSE, 130 History Lane, Pendleton, SC 29670-8700. Mailing Address: Pendleton Historic Foundation, P.O. Box 444, Pendleton, SC 29670. Tel.: 864-646-7249. Facebook; Twitter.
E-mail: info@pendletonhistoricfoundation.org
Web Site: www.pendletonhistoricfoundation.org
Formerly: Woodburn Plantation
Key Personnel: Pres. (V), Carol Burdette.
Institution Type/Description: Historic House: c.1830 four-story Greek Revival Plantation House.
Hours & Admission Prices: See website for hours & admission prices.
Attendance: 4,384 (actual)

Pickens

HAGOOD-MAULDIN HOUSE AND IRMA MORRIS MUSEUM OF FINE ARTS, 104 N. Lewis St., Pickens, SC 29671-2311. Mailing Address: P.O. Box 775, Pickens, SC 29671-0775. Tel.: 864-898-5963 & 878-1322.
E-mail: pickenscohistory@gmail.com
Web Site: pickenscountyhistoricalsociety.com
Key Personnel: Pres., Ken Nabors; Vice Pres., Wayne Kelley.
Institution Type/Description: Art Museum: housed in the former home of attorney James Hagood; built c.1856.
Hours & Admission Prices: April-Nov. 1st & 3rd Sat. 10-4; other times by appointment. Adults $5, students $1; members no charge. Closed Independence Day; Labor Day; Thanksgiving; Christmas.
Attendance: 350 (estimated)

PICKENS COUNTY MUSEUM OF ART & HISTORY, 307 Johnson St., Pickens, SC 29671-2463. Tel.: 864-898-5963. Fax: 864-898-5580.
E-mail: picmus@co.pickens.sc.us
Web Site: www.pickenscountymuseum.org
Key Personnel: Exec. Dir., C. Allen Coleman; Chm., Wayne Kelley; Cur., Dan Brennen; Preparator, Daniel James; Museum Shop Mgr., Katie Faulk.
Institution Type/Description: Art & History Museum.
Hours & Admission Prices: Tues.-Wed. & Fri. 9-5, Thurs. 9-7:30, Sat. 9-4:30. No charge; donations accepted. Closed major holidays. &
Attendance: 30,000 (estimated)

Ravenel

RAVENEL CAW CAW INTERPRETIVE CENTER, 5200 Savannah Hwy., Ravenel, SC 29470-5542. Tel.: 843-889-8898 & 795-4386.
E-mail: customerservice@ccprc.com
Institution Type/Description: Environmental Center.
Hours & Admission Prices: Wed.-Sun. 9-5. Admission $1 per person; children under 2 no charge.

Ridgeland

BLUE HERON NATURE CENTER, 321 Bailey Lane, Ridgeland, SC 29936-8597. Tel.: 843-726-7611. Fax: 843-726-3263.
Institution Type/Description: Nature Center.
Hours & Admission Prices: Call for hours.

PRATT MEMORIAL LIBRARY & WEBEL MUSEUM, 451A Wilson St., Ridgeland, SC 29936. Mailing Address: P.O. Drawer 1540, Ridgeland, SC 29936-1540. Tel.: 843-726-7744. Fax: 843-726-7813.
Key Personnel: Branch Mgr., Marcia Cleland.
Institution Type/Description: History Museum & Library.
Hours & Admission Prices: Library: Mon.-Thurs. 10:30-5:30, Fri. 10:30-4:30, Sat. 11-2. Museum: Mon. 10:30-6, Tues.-Thurs. 10:30-5:30, Fri. 10:30-4:30, Sat. 10-1. No charge. Closed holidays.

Rock Hill

CATAWBA CULTURAL PRESERVATION PROJECT, 1536 Tom Stevens Rd., Rock Hill, SC 29730. Tel.: 803-328-2427. Fax: 803-328-5791.
E-mail: wenonahh@ccppcrafts.com
Key Personnel: Dir., Wenonah G. Haire, D.M.D.; Museum Shop Mgr., Caitlin Totherow.
Institution Type/Description: Native American History Museum & Cultural Center.
Hours & Admission Prices: Mon.-Sat. 9-5. No charge; donations accepted. Closed New Year's Day; Indepedence Day; Thanksgiving; Christmas. &
Attendance: 12,000 (actual)

CENTER FOR THE ARTS - DALTON GALLERY, 121 E. Main St., Rock Hill, SC 29730-4539. Mailing Address: P.O. Box 2797, Rock Hill, SC 29732-4797. Tel.: 803-328-2787. Fax: 803-328-2165. Facebook: York County Arts.
E-mail: arts@yorkcountyarts.org
Web Site: www.yorkcountyarts.org
Key Personnel: Exec. Dir., Debra Heintz.
Institution Type/Description: Art Gallery.
Hours & Admission Prices: 2nd & 4th Sat. 10-2, Sun. 2-4 each month. No charge.

COMPORIUM TELEPHONE MUSEUM, 117 Elk Ave., Rock Hill, SC 29730. Mailing Address: P.O. Box 470, Rock Hill, SC 29731. Tel.: 803-324-4030.
Formerly: Rock Hill Telephone Company Museum
Institution Type/Description: Company History Museum.
Hours & Admission Prices: Mon., Wed. & Fri.-Sat. 10-2; groups by appointment.

MAIN STREET CHILDREN'S MUSEUM, 133 E. Main St., Rock Hill, SC 29730. Tel.: 803-684-2327.
E-mail: information@chmuseums.org
Institution Type/Description: Children's Museum.
Hours & Admission Prices: Tues.-Sat. 10-5, Sun. 12-5. Admission $5 per person; discounts to members & groups of 15 or more; children under one no charge. &

MUSEUM OF YORK COUNTY, 4621 Mount Gallant Rd., Rock Hill, SC 29732-9637. Tel.: 803-329-2121. Fax: 803-329-5249.
E-mail: info@chmuseums.org
Web Site: www.chmuseums.org
Key Personnel: Dir., Van W. Shields; Deputy Dir. Mktg. & Visitor Svcs., Jeannie Marion.
Institution Type/Description: General Museum.
Hours & Admission Prices: Mon.-Sat. 10-5, Sun. 1-5. Office: Mon.-Fri. 8:30-5:30. Adult $5, senior citizens 60 & over $4, children 4-17 $3; discount to AAM members; members & children 3 and under no charge. Closed New Year's Day; Thanksgiving; Christmas Eve & Day. &
Attendance: 60,000 (estimated)

WINTHROP UNIVERSITY GALLERIES, 701 Oakland Ave., Rock Hill, SC 29733. Mailing Address: 126 McLaurin Hall, Rock Hill, SC 29733. Tel.: 803-323-2493.
E-mail: derksenk@winthrop.edu
Web Site: www.winthrop.edu/galleries
Key Personnel: Dir., Karen Derksen.
Institution Type/Description: Art Galleries.
Hours & Admission Prices: Mon.-Fri. 9-5. No charge.

Roebuck

WALNUT GROVE PLANTATION, 1200 Otts Shoals Rd., Roebuck, SC 29376-3518. Tel.: 864-576-6546. Fax: 864-576-4058. Facebook: Walnut Grove Plantation.
E-mail: walnutgrove@spartanburghistory.org
Web Site: www.spartanburghistory.org
Key Personnel: C.E.O. & History Assoc., Jennifer Furrow; Exec. Dir., Becky Slayton; Dir., Zac Cunningham.
Institution Type/Description: Historic House Museum: c.1765 Walnut Grove Plantation, pre-Revolutionary manor house built on land grant from George III to Charles Moore.
Hours & Admission Prices: April-Oct. Tues.-Sat. 11-5, Sun. 2-5; Nov.-March Sat. 11-5; other times by appointment. Adults $6, seniors $5.50, children under 18 $3; discounts to AAA members; members no charge. Closed holidays. &
Attendance: 13,000 (actual)

Saint Helena Island

PENN CENTER, INC. NATIONAL HISTORIC LANDMARK/ YORK W. BAILEY MUSEUM, 16 Penn Center Cir., W., Saint Helena Island, SC 29920. Mailing Address: P.O. Box 126, Saint Helena Island, SC 29920-0126. Tel.: 843-838-2432. Fax: 843-838-8545.
E-mail: info@penncenter.com
Web Site: www.penncenter.com
Key Personnel: C.E.O. & Dir., Walter Mack; Chm. (V), John Smalls; Dir. History & Culture, Rosalyn Browne; Museum Shop Mgr., Karen Ward.
Institution Type/Description: History Museum.
Hours & Admission Prices: Mon.-Sat. 11-4; other times by appointment. Adults $5, children $3. Closed New Year's Day; Independence Day; Labor Day; Thanksgiving; Christmas. &
Attendance: 30,000 (estimated)

Saint Matthews

CALHOUN COUNTY MUSEUM & CULTURAL CENTER, 313 Butler St., Saint Matthews, SC 29135-1409. Tel.: 803-874-3964. Fax: 803-874-4790. Facebook: Calhoun County Museum Friends.
E-mail: calmus@oburg.net
Web Site: www.calhouncountymuseumandculturalcenter.org
Key Personnel: Dir., Debbie U. Roland; Chm. & Pres. (V), Sallie Porth.
Institution Type/Description: General Museum.
Hours & Admission Prices: Tues.-Fri. 9-4; groups of 10 or more & researchers by appointment. No charge; donations accepted. &
Attendance: 7,000 (estimated)

Saluda

SALUDA COUNTY HISTORICAL SOCIETY, 105 Law Range, Saluda, SC 29138-1701. Mailing Address: P.O. Box 22, Saluda, SC 29138. Tel.: 864-445-8550.
E-mail: info@saludacountyhistoricalsociety.org
Web Site: www.saludacountyhistoricalsociety.org
Formerly: Saluda County Historical Society Museum and Theater
Key Personnel: Dir., Meade Hendrix; Chm. (V), Bela Herlong; Pres. (V), Tommy Willis.
Institution Type/Description: Historical Society Museum: Flat Grove - birthplace of James Butler Bonham; Marsh-Johnson House. Listed on the National Register of Historical Places.
Hours & Admission Prices: Mon.-Fri. 10-4, Sat. 10-1. Theater, museum & both historic houses: $8, members, students & seniors $5; theater, museum & one historic house $5, members students & seniors $3. Closed major holidays.

Seneca

LUNNEY MUSEUM, 211 W. South 1st St., Seneca, SC 29678-3307. Tel.: 864-710-7494.
Key Personnel: Dir. & Cur., Dr. John Martin.
Institution Type/Description: Historic House: housed in a California-style bungalow, built in 1909 by Dr. & Mrs. W.J. Lunney. Listed on the National Register of Historic Places.
Hours & Admission Prices: Thurs.-Sun. 1-5. No charge; donations accepted. Closed major holidays.

THE WORLD OF ENERGY, 7812 Rochester Hwy., Seneca, SC 29672-0752. Tel.: 800-777-1004, ext. 1. Fax: 864-885-4605.
E-mail: worldofenergy@duke-energy.com
Web Site: www.duke-energy.com/worldofenergy
Formerly: World of Energy at Keowee-Toxaway
Key Personnel: Mgr. Community Rels., BJ Gatten.
Institution Type/Description: STEM (Science, Technology, Engineering & Math) Education Center: overlooking the Oconee Nuclear Station & the nearby lakes Keowee & Jocassee.
Hours & Admission Prices: Mon.-Fri. 9-5, Sat. 12-5. No charge. Closed some holidays. &
Attendance: 20,000 (estimated)

Spartanburg

HATCHER GARDEN AND WOODLAND PRESERVE, 820 John B. White Blvd., Spartanburg, SC 29306-4043. Mailing Address: P. O. Box 2337, Spartanburg, SC 29304. Tel.: 864-574-7724. Fax: 864-595-1195. Facebook.
E-mail: info@hatchergarden.org
Web Site: hatchergarden.org
Key Personnel: Dir., Robin Vollmer.

Institution Type/Description: Garden.
Hours & Admission Prices: Daily dawn to dusk. No charge. &
Attendance: 39,000 (actual)

MILLIKEN GALLERY, CONVERSE COLLEGE, 580 E. Main St., Spartanburg, SC 29302-0006. Tel.: 864-596-9214. Fax: 864-596-9606.

E-mail: kathryn.boucher@converse.edu
Web Site: www.converse.edu
Key Personnel: Dir., Kathryn Boucher.
Institution Type/Description: College Art Gallery.
Hours & Admission Prices: Mon.-Fri. 9-5, Sun. 2-5. No charge. Closed school holidays & breaks. &
Attendance: 1,700

THE SANDOR TESZLER LIBRARY, Wofford College, 429 N. Church St., Spartanburg, SC 29303-3663. Tel.: 864-597-4585. Fax: 864-597-4329.

E-mail: efurdyk@wofford.edu
Web Site: www.wofford.edu/library/
Key Personnel: Cur., Youmi Efurd.
Institution Type/Description: Art Gallery & College Museum: located on 1854 campus.
Hours & Admission Prices: Fall, Interim & Spring Semesters: Mon.-Thurs. 8am to midnight, Fri. 8-7, Sat. 10-5, Sun. 1pm to midnight. No charge. &

THE SEAY HOUSE, 106 Darby Rd., Spartanburg, SC 29306. Mailing Address: P.O. Box 887, Spartanburg, SC 29304-0887. Tel.: 864-596-3501. Fax: 864-596-2399.

E-mail: seayhouse@spartanburghistory.org
Web Site: www.spartanburghistory.org
Key Personnel: Dir., Caroline Sexton.
Institution Type/Description: Historic House: c.1890 home.
Hours & Admission Prices: April-Oct. 3rd Sat. of month 11-5; other times by appointment. No charge; donations accepted. Closed holidays. &
Attendance: 100 (estimated)

SPARTANBURG ART MUSEUM, 200 E. Saint John St., Spartanburg, SC 29306-5124. Tel.: 864-582-7616. Fax: 864-948-5353. TDD: 864-583-2776.

E-mail: museum@spartanarts.org
Web Site: www.spartanburgartmuseum.org
Formerly: Spartanburg County Museum of Art
Key Personnel: Exec. Dir., Elizabeth Goddard; Dir. Art School, Kathleen Digney; Dir. Colors Program, Kathy Wofford.
Institution Type/Description: Art Museum.
Hours & Admission Prices: Museum: Tues.-Sat. 10-5, Sun. 1-5. No charge. Artwalk: 3rd Thurs. each month 6pm-9pm. Closed New Year's Day; Veterans Day; Martin Luther King Jr. Day; Easter Monday; Memorial Day; Independence Day; Labor Day; Columbus Day; Presidents' Day; Thanksgiving; Christmas Eve & Day. &
Attendance: 12,000 (actual)

SPARTANBURG REGIONAL MUSEUM OF HISTORY, 200 E. St. John St., Spartanburg, SC 29306-5124. Mailing Address: P.O. Box 887, Spartanburg, SC 29304-0887. Tel.: 864-596-3501. Fax: 864-596-2399.

E-mail: regionalmuseum@spartanburghistory.org
Web Site: www.spartanburghistory.org
Formerly: Spartanburg County Regional Museum of History
Key Personnel: Dir., Caroline Sexton.
Institution Type/Description: Local History Museum.
Hours & Admission Prices: Tues.-Sat. 10-5. No charge; donations accepted. Closed major holidays. &
Attendance: 7,000 (actual)

SPARTANBURG SCIENCE CENTER, 200 E. Saint John St., Spartanburg, SC 29306-5124. Tel.: 864-583-2777. Fax: 864-948-5353.

E-mail: science@spartanarts.org
Web Site: spartanburgsciencecenter.org
Key Personnel: Exec. Dir., John F. Green.
Institution Type/Description: Science Museum & Center.
Hours & Admission Prices: Thurs.-Sat. 10-5, Sun. 1-5. Adults $4, seniors $3, college students $2.50, children 6-18 $2; children 5 & under and members no charge. &
Attendance: 25,000 (actual)

Sullivan's Island

FORT SUMTER NATIONAL MONUMENT, 1214 Middle St., Sullivan's Island, SC 29482-9748. Tel.: 843-883-3123, ext. 23 (chief ranger); ext. 22 (park historian). Fax: 843-883-3910.

E-mail: bill_martin@nps.gov
Web Site: www.nps.gov/fosu
Key Personnel: Supt., Tim Stone; Chief Interpretation, Dawn Davis; Historian, Richard Hatcher; Cur., Catherine Fowler; Museum Shop Mgr., Kevin Bates.
Institution Type/Description: Military Museums: housed in Fort Moultrie Visitor Center & 1829 Fort Sumter.
Hours & Admission Prices: Fort Sumter: call for hours. Accessible only by boat. Tour Boat: adults $17, seniors $15, children 6-11 $10; children 5 & under no charge. Fort Moultrie: daily 9-5. Families $5, adults $3, seniors 62 & over $1; children 16 & under no charge. Closed New Year's Day; Thanksgiving, Christmas. &
Attendance: 337,000 (estimated)

Summerton

SANTEE NATIONAL WILDLIFE REFUGE, 2125 Fort Watson Rd., Summerton, SC 29148-8638. Tel.: 803-478-2217. Fax: 803-478-2314.

E-mail: santee@fws.gov
Web Site: www.fws.gov/santee
Institution Type/Description: Wildlife Refuge: housed on Santee Indian Mound/ Fort Watson historic site.
Hours & Admission Prices: Center: Tues.-Sat. 8-4. Grounds: daily sunrise to sunset. No charge.
Attendance: 181,000 (estimated)

Summerville

OLD DORCHESTER STATE HISTORIC SITE, 300 State Park Rd., Summerville, SC 29485-8431. Tel.: 843-873-1740. Fax: 843-873-1740.

E-mail: colonialdorchester@scprt.com
Web Site: www.southcarolinaparks.com
Key Personnel: Park Mgr. & Archaeologist, Ashley Chapman.
Institution Type/Description: Preservation Project: archaeological site of the colonial Village of Dorchester founded in 1697 by Congregationalists from Massachusetts.
Hours & Admission Prices: Daily 9-6. Adult $2, seniors $1.25; children 15 & under no charge. &
Attendance: 118,300

SUMMERVILLE DORCHESTER MUSEUM, 100 E. Doty Ave., Summerville, SC 29483. Mailing Address: P.O. Box 1873, Summerville, SC 29484. Tel.: 843-875-9666.

E-mail: museumoffice@summervilledorchestermuseum.org
Web Site: www.summervilledorchestermuseum.org/
Institution Type/Description: History Museum: housed in the former Summerville Police Station.
Hours & Admission Prices: Mon.-Sat. 9-2. Closed Thanksgiving; Christmas.

Sumter

SUMTER COUNTY GALLERY OF ART, 200 Hasel St., Sumter, SC 29150-4506. Mailing Address: Box 1316, Sumter, SC 29151-1316. Tel.: 803-775-0543. Fax: 803-778-2787.

E-mail: director@sumtergallery.com
Web Site: www.sumtergallery.com
Key Personnel: Exec. Dir., Karen Watson; Dir. Art Education, Amanda Cox; Asst. Dir. & Cur., Frank McCauley.
Institution Type/Description: Art Museum.
Hours & Admission Prices: Tues.-Sat. 11-5, Sun. 1:30-5. No charge; donations accepted. Closed holidays. &
Attendance: 11,000 (estimated)

THE SUMTER COUNTY MUSEUM, 122 N. Washington St., Sumter, SC 29150-4920. Mailing Address: P.O. Box 1456, Sumter, SC 29151-1456. Tel.: 803-775-0908.

E-mail: rgood@sumtercountymuseum.org
Web Site: www.sumtercountymuseum.org
Key Personnel: Exec. Dir, Annie Rivers.
Institution Type/Description: Historic House: Williams-Brice House, a 1916 three story brick house; reconstructed homestead representing life in 1800.

Hours & Admission Prices: Museum: Thurs.-Sat. 10-5. Research Center: Tues.-Sat. 10-1 & 2-5. Museum: adults $3, children 6-17 $1. Research Center: $5 per day for non-members. &
Attendance: 9,000 (actual)

SWAN LAKE IRIS GARDENS, 822 W. Liberty St., Sumter, SC 29150. Mailing Address: P.O. Box 1449, 21 N. Main St., Sumter, SC 29150. Tel.: 803-436-2640. Fax: 803-436-2615.
E-mail: tourism@sumter.sc.com
Web Site: sumtertourism.com
Institution Type/Description: Garden.
Hours & Admission Prices: Daily 7:30 to dusk. No charge.

Sunset

JOCASSEE GORGES VISITOR CENTER, Keowee-Toxaway State Natural Area, 108 Residence Dr., Sunset, SC 29685-2128. Tel.: 864-868-2605.
E-mail: keoweetoxaway@scprt.com
Institution Type/Description: Natural History Museum: housed in the former Holly Springs Baptist Church.
Hours & Admission Prices: Daily 11am to noon & 4-5.

Union

CROSS KEYS PLANTATION, 163 Old Buncombe Rd., Union, SC 29379. Mailing Address: P.O. Box 220, Union, SC 29379-0220. Tel.: 864-429-5081.
E-mail: uncomus@bellsouth.net
Web Site: unioncountymuseum.com
Key Personnel: Pres. (V), Frank M. Hart.
Institution Type/Description: Historic House: housed in the former home of Barrum Bobo; built from 1812-1814.
Hours & Admission Prices: Sat. 12-5. No charge; donations accepted.
Attendance: 3,500 (estimated)

ROSE HILL PLANTATION STATE HISTORIC SITE, 2677 Sardis Rd., Union, SC 29379-7904. Tel.: 864-427-5966. Fax: 864-427-5966.
E-mail: rosehill@scprt.com
Web Site: www.southcarolinaparks.com
Key Personnel: Park Mgr., Trampas Alderman.
Institution Type/Description: State Park; housed in the former home of South Carolina Governor William Henry Gist; built in 1828.
Hours & Admission Prices: Mansion Tours: March-Oct. daily 1, 2 & 3; Nov.-Feb. Thurs.-Mon. 1, 2 & 3. Adults $5, students 6-16 $4, seniors $3. Park Grounds: daily 9-6. No charge. Closed Thanksgiving, Christmas Eve & Day.
Attendance: 3,500 (estimated)

UNION COUNTY MUSEUM, 127 W. Main St., Union, SC 29379. Mailing Address: P.O. Box 220, Union, SC 29379-0220. Tel.: 864-429-5081. Facebook: Union County Historical Society.
E-mail: uncomus@bellsouth.net
Web Site: unioncountymuseum.com
Key Personnel: Exec. Dir., Ola Jean Kelly; Pres. (V), Frank M. Hart.
Institution Type/Description: History Museum.
Hours & Admission Prices: Tues. & Thurs.-Fri. 9-4, Sat. 1-4; other times by appointment. No charge; donations accepted. Closed major holidays.
Attendance: 2,500 (actual)

Wagener

WAGENER MUSEUM, 12 Short St., Wagener, SC 29164. Mailing Address: P.O. Box 1004, Wagener, SC 29164-1004. Tel.: 803-564-3412 & 3507. Facebook: Wagener Museum.
E-mail: wagenermuseum@yahoo.com
Web Site: www.wagenersc.com
Key Personnel: Chm. (V), Cynthia R. Hardy.
Institution Type/Description: History Museum.
Hours & Admission Prices: Mon.-Tues. & Thurs.-Fri. 9-4, Sat. by appointment (through Town Hall entrance). No charge; donations accepted. Closed national holidays. &
Attendance: 90 (estimated)

Walhalla

OCONEE HERITAGE CENTER, 123 Brown Square Dr., Walhalla, SC 29691. Mailing Address: P.O. Box 395, Walhalla, SC 29691. Tel.: 864-638-2224.

E-mail: info@oconeeheritagecenter.org
Web Site: www.oconeeheritagecenter.org
Key Personnel: Dir., Leslie White; Asst. Cur., Jennifer Moss.
Institution Type/Description: History Museum.
Hours & Admission Prices: Thurs.-Fri. 12-6, Sat. 10-3; other times by appointment. No charge; donations requested. &
Attendance: 4,000 (actual)

OCONEE STATION STATE HISTORIC SITE, 500 Oconee Station Rd., Walhalla, SC 29691-3126. Tel.: 864-638-0079.
E-mail: rachenberg@scprt.com
Institution Type/Description: Historic Site: the area served as a military compound against attack from the Cherokee Indians.
Hours & Admission Prices: Sat.-Sun. 1-5; other times by appointment.

PATRIOT'S HALL-OCONEE VETERAN'S MUSEUM, 13 Short St., Walhalla, SC 29691-2229. Mailing Address: P.O. Box 591, Walhalla, SC 29691-0591. Tel.: 864-638-5455 & 972-8173.
E-mail: jkrautlarger42@gmail.com
Web Site: www.oconeeveteransmuseum.org
Key Personnel: Dir. & Chm. (V), A.J. Smith.
Institution Type/Description: Veterans Museum: housed in the Old Rock Building; built in 1933.
Hours & Admission Prices: Sat. 10-3; other times by appointment. No charge; donations accepted. &
Attendance: 1,900 (estimated)

Walterboro

COLLETON MUSEUM, FARMERS MARKET & COMMERICAL KITCHEN, 506 E. Washington St., Walterboro, SC 29488-4028. Tel.: 843-549-2303. Fax: 843-549-7215.
E-mail: mmardell@colletoncounty.org
Web Site: www.colletonmuseum.org
Key Personnel: Dir., Matt Mardell; Asst. Dir., Jill Chadwick; Prog. Coord., Jennie Meetze; Historical & Cultural Coord., Sean Demont-Devlin; Events Coord., Eartha Cunningham; Farmers Market Mgr., Robin Gunter; Volunteer & Greeter, Ann Bickley.
Institution Type/Description: History Museum, Farmers Market and Commerical Kitchen.
Hours & Admission Prices: Tues. 12-5, Wed.-Fri. 10-5, Sat. 10-2. No charge. &
Attendance: 19,000 (actual)

SLAVE RELICS MUSEUM, 208 Carn St., Walterboro, SC 29488-3965. Tel.: 843-549-9130.
Web Site: slaverelics.org
Institution Type/Description: History Museum.
Hours & Admission Prices: Tues.-Fri. 9:30-5, Sat. 10-3. Adults $6, children $5; discounts to groups.

SOUTH CAROLINA ARTISANS CENTER, 318 Wichman St., Walterboro, SC 29488-2921. Tel.: 843-549-0011. Fax: 843-549-7433.
E-mail: info@scartisanscenter.com
Web Site: scartisanscenter.com
Key Personnel: Pres., Chris Bickley; Exec. Dir., Gale M. Doggette; Treas., Dolly Droze.
Institution Type/Description: Arts & Crafts Museum: housed in a 1910 Victorian cottage in the Hickory Valley Historic District.
Hours & Admission Prices: Mon.-Sat. 9-5, Sun. 1-5. No charge. Closed New Year's Day; Easter; Independence Day; Thanksgiving; Christmas. &
Attendance: 125,000 (estimated)

Wellford

HOLLYWILD ANIMAL PARK, 2325 Hampton Rd., Wellford, SC 29385-9010. Mailing Address: P.O. Box 683, Inman, SC 29349-0683. Tel.: 864-472-2038.
E-mail: hollywildanimalpark@gmail.com
Web Site: www.hollywild.com
Institution Type/Description: Zoo.
Hours & Admission Prices: Call for hours and admissions.

Winnsboro

FAIRFIELD COUNTY MUSEUM, 231 S. Congress St., Winnsboro, SC 29180-1105. Mailing Address: P.O. Box 6, Winnsboro, SC 29180-0006. Tel.: 803-635-9811. Fax: 803-815-9811.

E-mail: fairfieldmus@truvista.net
Web Site: www.fairfieldsc.com/secondary.aspx?pageID=125
Key Personnel: Dir. & Museum Shop Mgr., Pelham Lyles.
Institution Type/Description: Historic Building & Site: housed in 1830 Cathcart-Ketchin, 3-story Federal brick structure.
Hours & Admission Prices: Tues.-Fri. 10-12 & 1-5, Sat. 10-3. No charge.
Attendance: 3,500 (estimated)

THE SOUTH CAROLINA RAILROAD MUSEUM, 110 Industrial Park Rd., Winnsboro, SC 29180-9113. Mailing Address: P.O. Box 7246, Columbia, SC 29202-7246. Tel.: 803-635-9893.
E-mail: info@scrm.org
Web Site: www.scrm.org
Key Personnel: Chm. (V), Kelvin Woods; Supt., Rodger Stroup; Museum Shop Mgr., Joe Palma.
Institution Type/Description: Railroad Museum.
Hours & Admission Prices: See website for hours and admissions. &
Attendance: 10,000 (actual)

Woodruff

HISTORIC PRICE HOUSE, 1200 Oak View Farms Rd., Woodruff, SC 29388-8313. Mailing Address: 1200 Otts Shoals Rd., Roebuck, SC 29376-3518. Tel.: 864-576-6546. Fax: 864-576-4058. Facebook: Historic Price House.
E-mail: pricehouse@spartanburghistory.org
Web Site: www.spartanburghistory.org
Key Personnel: Dir., Zac Cunningham.
Institution Type/Description: History Museum: housed in c.1795, three story brick structure, once located on 2,000 acres.
Hours & Admission Prices: May-Oct. Sat. 11-5, Sun. 2-5. Adults $5, children 6-17 $3; discount to groups; children under 6 no charge. Closed holidays.
Attendance: 400 (actual)

Yemassee

THE LOWCOUNTRY VISITORS CENTER & MUSEUM, 1 Lowcountry Lane, Yemassee, SC 29945. Mailing Address: P.O. Box 615, Yemassee, SC 29945-0615. Tel.: 843-717-3090, 800-528-6870. Fax: 843-717-2888. Facebook: SC Lowcountry Tourism Commission.
E-mail: peach@southcarolinalowcountry.com
Web Site: www.southcarolinalowcountry.com
Key Personnel: Exec. Dir., Peach Morrison.
Institution Type/Description: Historic House Museum: housed in the former home of the Frampton family; built in 1868.
Hours & Admission Prices: Daily 8:30-5. No charge. Closed federal & state holidays.

SOUTH DAKOTA

(139 listings)

Aberdeen

DACOTAH PRAIRIE MUSEUM, 21 S. Main St., Aberdeen, SD 57401-4218. Tel.: 605-626-7117.
E-mail: dacotahprairiemuseum@gmail.com
Web Site: brown.sd.us/dacotah-prairie-museum/home
Key Personnel: Dir., Sue Gates; Cur. Education, Sherri Rawstern; Cur. Exhibits, Lora Schaunaman; Cur. Collections, Jackie Ormand; Gift Shop Mgr., Patricia Kendall.
Institution Type/Description: General Museum: housed in 1889 bank.
Hours & Admission Prices: Tues.-Fri. 9-5, Sat.-Sun. 1-4. No charge; donations accepted. Closed national holidays. &
Attendance: 76,024 (actual)

NORTHERN GALLERIES, Northern State University, 1200 S. Jay St., Aberdeen, SD 57401-7198. Tel.: 605-626-7766 & 7762. Fax: 605-626-2263.
E-mail: kilianp@northern.edu
Key Personnel: Dir., Greg Blair.
Institution Type/Description: University Art Gallery.
Hours & Admission Prices: Sept.-May Mon.-Fri. 8-4:30. No charge.
Attendance: 4,700 (actual)

STORYBOOK LAND - TRAIN DEPOT MUSEUM, Wylie Park, N. Hwy 281, Aberdeen, SD 57401. Mailing Address: Aberdeen Parks, Recreation and Forestry Department, 225 SE 3rd Ave., Aberdeen, SD 57401-4245. Tel.: 605-626-7015. Fax: 605-626-7989.
E-mail: prf@aberdeen.sd.us
Web Site: www.aberdeen.sd.us/storybookland
Institution Type/Description: Park.
Hours & Admission Prices: Train Depot Museum: Memorial Day to Labor Day daily 10-9. No charge. Visitor Center: Memorial Day to Labor Day daily 10-9; call for additional hours & pricing. &
Attendance: 250,000 (estimated)

WEIN GALLERY, Presentation College, Southeast Nursing Bldg., 1500 N. Main St., Aberdeen, SD 57401-1280. Tel.: 605-229-8585.
E-mail: brad_tennant@presentation.edu
Key Personnel: Dir., Brad Tennant.
Institution Type/Description: Art Gallery.
Hours & Admission Prices: Mon.-Fri. 8-8, Sat. 1-7. No charge.

Armour

DOUGLAS COUNTY MUSEUM COMPLEX, Courthouse Grounds, Armour, SD 57313. Mailing Address: P.O. Box 638, Armour, SD 57313-0638. Tel.: 605-724-2129.
E-mail: jay.smith@state.sd.us
Key Personnel: Pres. & Cur., Sharon A. Wiese; Dir., Laverne Vanderwerff; Asst. Dir., Rebecca Thury.
Institution Type/Description: Historical Society Museum: housed in 1904 County Office Bldg.
Hours & Admission Prices: Tues., Fri. & holidays 1-5; other times by appointment. No charge; donations accepted.
Attendance: 600 (estimated)

Belle Fourche

TRI-STATE MUSEUM, 415 5th Ave., Belle Fourche, SD 57717-1435. Tel.: 605-723-1200. Facebook: Tri-State Museum.
E-mail: tristatemuseum@rushmore.com
Web Site: www.tristatemuseum.com
Key Personnel: Dir., Nancy Cole.
Institution Type/Description: History Museum.
Hours & Admission Prices: Summer: Mon.-Sat. 9-5, Sun. 12-4; Winter: Tues.-Sat. 10-4. No charge; donations accepted. &
Attendance: 14,000 (estimated)

Brookings

BROOKINGS ARTS COUNCIL, 524 Fourth St., Brookings, SD 57006-2045. Tel.: 605-692-4177. Fax: 605-692-8298.
E-mail: directorbac@swiftel.net
Web Site: www.brookingsartscouncil.org
Key Personnel: Pres., Jean Jostad; Dir., Heather Kallhoff; Gallery Asst., Ladan Bahmani; Gallery Asst., Julie Luke.
Institution Type/Description: Cultural Arts Center: housed in 1914 Carnegie Library Building.
Hours & Admission Prices: Tues.-Sat. 12-5. No charge; donations accepted. Closed national holidays. &
Attendance: 12,000 (estimated)

CHILDREN'S MUSEUM OF SOUTH DAKOTA, 521 4th St., Brookings, SD 57006. Tel.: 605-692-6700. Facebook: Children's Museum SD.
E-mail: info@prairieplay.org
Web Site: www.prairieplay.org
Key Personnel: Exec. Dir., Kate Treiber.
Institution Type/Description: Children's Museum.
Hours & Admission Prices: Tues.-Sat. 10-5, Sun. 12-5. Admission $7.50 per person; children under one & members no charge. Closed Easter; Independence Day; Thanksgiving; Christmas Eve & Day. &
Attendance: 120,000

MCCRORY GARDENS AT SOUTH DAKOTA STATE UNIVERSITY, 631 22nd Ave., Brookings, SD 57007. Tel.: 605-688-6707. Facebook.
E-mail: heather.costello@sdstate.edu
Web Site: www.mccrorygardens.com
Key Personnel: Dir., David F. Graper, Ph.D.; Opers. Mgr., Lisa Marotz.
Institution Type/Description: Arboretums.

Hours & Admission Prices: Dawn to dusk. Adults $6; discounts to American Horticulture Society Reciprocal Program members; members no charge. ♿
Attendance: 6,000 (estimated)

SOUTH DAKOTA AGRICULTURAL HERITAGE MUSEUM, South Dakota State University, 925 11th St., Brookings, SD 57007. Mailing Address: SDSU Box 601, Brookings, SD 57007. Tel.: 605-688-6226. Fax: 605-688-6303. Facebook: South Dakota Agricultural Museum.
E-mail: sdsu.agmuseum@sdstate.edu
Web Site: www.sdsu.edu/agmuseum
Formerly: State Agricultural Heritage Museum
Key Personnel: Dir., Gwen McCausland; Cur., Carrie Van Buren; Cur. & Museum Shop Mgr., Michelle Glanzer; Cur., Dawn Stephens.
Institution Type/Description: Agricultural Museum.
Hours & Admission Prices: Jan.-March Mon.-Sat. 10-5; April-Dec. Mon.-Sat. 10-5, Sun. 1-5. No charge; donations accepted. ♿
Attendance: 14,410 (actual)

SOUTH DAKOTA ART MUSEUM, Medary Ave. & Harvey Dunn, Brookings, SD 57007. Mailing Address: P.O. Box 2250, Brookings, SD 57007. Tel.: 605-688-5423, 866-805-7590. Facebook: SD Art Museum.
E-mail: sdsu.sdam@sdstate.edu
Web Site: www.southdakotaartmuseum.com
Key Personnel: Dir., Lynn Verschoor; Cur. Collections, Lisa Scholten; Cur. Exhibits, Jodi Lundgren; Museum Shop Mgr., Pam Adler.
Institution Type/Description: Art Museum.
Hours & Admission Prices: Jan.-March Mon.-Fri. 10-5, Sat. 10-4; April-Dec. Mon.-Fri. 10-5, Sat. 10-4, Sun. 12-4. No charge; donations accepted. Closed New Year's Day; Thanksgiving; Christmas; state holidays. ♿
Attendance: 150,000 (estimated)

Buffalo

BUFFALO HISTORICAL MUSEUM AND ONE-ROOM SCHOOLHOUSE, Hwy. 85, Buffalo, SD 57720. Mailing Address: P.O. Box 391, Buffalo, SD 57720. Tel.: 605-375-3800 & 3787.
E-mail: agreco@buffalohistory.org
Key Personnel: Pres. (V), Ray Anderson; Cur. & Museum Shop Mgr., Nora E. Boyer.
Institution Type/Description: History Museum.
Hours & Admission Prices: Memorial Day to Labor Day Mon.-Fri. 10:30-2:30; other times by appointment. No charge. ♿

Carthage

CAMPBELL ORIGINAL STRAW BALE BUILT MUSEUM, 206 Main St., E., Carthage, SD 57323. Mailing Address: P.O. Box 3, Carthage, SD 57323-0003. Tel.: 605-772-4166 & 5778.
E-mail: madfarms@alliancecom.net
Web Site: strawbalemus.com
Institution Type/Description: History Museum: housed in a museum insulated with home-grown straw.
Hours & Admission Prices: Call for hours.

Chamberlain

AKTA LAKOTA MUSEUM AND CULTURAL CENTER, 1301 N. Main St., Chamberlain, SD 57325-1656. Mailing Address: P.O. Box 89, Chamberlain, SD 57325-0089. Tel.: 605-234-3452 & 3300. Fax: 605-234-3388.
E-mail: aktalakota@stjo.org
Web Site: www.aktalakota.org
Key Personnel: C.E.O., Father Stephen Huffstetter, S.C.J.; Dir., Dixie Thompson; Cur., Sara A. Caspi; Museum Shop Mgr., Vickie Brennan.
Institution Type/Description: History Museum: Lakota culture & heritage.
Hours & Admission Prices: May-Oct. Mon.-Sat. 8-6, Sun. 9-5; Nov.-April Mon.-Fri. 8-5. No charge; donations accepted. Closed legal holidays. ♿
Attendance: 30,000 (estimated)

SOUTH DAKOTA HALL OF FAME, 1480 S. Main, Chamberlain, SD 57325. Mailing Address: 1485 Main St., Chamberlain, SD 57325. Tel.: 605-234-4216.
E-mail: info@sdhalloffame.com
Web Site: www.sdexcellence.org
Key Personnel: CEO, Greta Chapman; Visitor Svcs. & Programming Coord., Lori Platzer.

Institution Type/Description: Historic Research Institute & Heritage Center.
Hours & Admission Prices: Memorial Day to Labor Day Mon.-Sat. 9-5. Winter: Mon.-Fri. 9-5. No charge; donations accepted. Closed state holidays. ♿
Attendance: 4,000 (estimated)

Clark

BEAUVAIS HERITAGE COMPLEX, Hwy. 212, Clark, SD 57225. Mailing Address: c/o Clark Chamber of Commerce, P.O. Box 163, Clark, SD 57225. Tel.: 605-532-5772.
E-mail: clarksd@itctel.com
Web Site: www.clarksd.com/museum/museum.htm
Key Personnel: Pres., Clark County Historical Society, Greg Furness.
Institution Type/Description: Cultural & Historical Center.
Hours & Admission Prices: Tours by appointment. No charge; donations accepted. ♿
Attendance: 500 (estimated)

Crazy Horse

INDIAN MUSEUM OF NORTH AMERICA AT CRAZY HORSE MEMORIAL, 12151 Avenue of the Chiefs, Crazy Horse, SD 57730-8900. Tel.: 605-673-4681. Fax: 605-673-2185.
E-mail: memorial@crazyhorse.org
Web Site: www.crazyhorsememorial.org
Key Personnel: Chmn., Joe Dobbs.
Institution Type/Description: American Indian Museum.
Hours & Admission Prices: Daily dawn-dusk. Car $28, adults $11; discounts to senior citizens, Custer County residents, scouts & servicemen in uniform; members, children under 6 & American Indians no charge. ♿
Attendance: 1,000,000 (estimated)

Custer

CUSTER STATE PARK, 13329 US Hwy. 16A, Custer, SD 57730-8351. Tel.: 605-255-4464. Fax: 605-255-4460.
E-mail: custerstatepark@state.sd.us
Web Site: www.custerstatepark.com
Key Personnel: Mgr., Black Hills Region, Matt Snyder; Naturalist, Julie Brazell; Visitor Svcs. Coord., Craig Pugsley.
Institution Type/Description: Park & Visitor Center.
Hours & Admission Prices: Park: daily. Peter Norbeck Visitor Center: May-Oct. daily 8-8. Wildlife Station Visitor Center: late May-Sept. 10-4. Badger Hole Historical Site: May-Sept. 10-5. Entrance License: $15 vehicles ♿
Attendance: 1,800,000 (estimated)

1881 COURTHOUSE MUSEUM, 411 Mt. Rushmore Rd., Custer, SD 57730. Mailing Address: P.O. Box 826, Custer, SD 57730-0826. Tel.: 605-673-2443. Fax: 605-673-2443.
E-mail: cchstsoc@gwtc.net
Web Site: www.1881courthousemuseum.com
Key Personnel: Dir., Gary Enright; Chm. (V), Ralph Sowder; Museum Shop Mgr., Denny Hickok.
Institution Type/Description: Historical Society Museum: housed in 1881 County Court House. Western, pioneer, mining & lumbering, history of 1874 Black Hills Expedition.
Hours & Admission Prices: May & Sept. daily 10-4; Memorial Day-Labor Day Mon.-Sat. 10-7, Sun. 1-7. Adults $6, seniors $5, youth 12-18 yrs $2. ♿
Attendance: 5,600 (actual)

FOUR MILE OLD WEST TOWN, 11921 W. Hwy. 16, Custer, SD 57730-7114. Tel.: 605-673-3905.
E-mail: fourmile@gwtc.net
Web Site: www.fourmileoldwesttown.com
Formerly: Four Mile Ghost Town
Key Personnel: Dir., Mary Krogman.
Institution Type/Description: History Museum.
Hours & Admission Prices: May to early Oct. daily 8:30-7. Admission $6; discounts to groups, home schoolers, AAM, PBS & museum members; children 6 & under no charge. Pet friendly. ♿
Attendance: 18,000 (estimated)

JEWEL CAVE NATIONAL MONUMENT, 11149 US Hwy. 16, Bldg. B12, Custer, SD 57730-8166. Tel.: 605-673-8300. Fax: 605-673-8397. Facebook.
E-mail: jeca_interpretation@nps.gov
Web Site: www.nps.gov/jeca
Key Personnel: Supt., Bonnie Schwartz; Park Store Mgr., Patty Ressler.
Institution Type/Description: Visitor Center and Cave.

Hours & Admission Prices: Visitor Center: late May to mid-Sept. daily 9-5:30; late Sept. to mid-May daily 8:30-4:30. Scenic Tour: adults 17 & over $12, youth 6-16 $8; children under 5 no charge. Jewel Cave Discovery: adults 17 & over $4; youth & children 16 and under no charge. &
Attendance: 109,279 (actual)

De Smet

DE SMET DEPOT MUSEUM, 104 Calumet Ave., N.E., De Smet, SD 57231. Mailing Address: P.O. Drawer 70, De Smet, SD 57231-0007. Tel.: 605-854-3991 & 3731. Fax: 605-854-3731.
Key Personnel: C.E.O. & Mayor, Gary Wolkow; Finance Officer, Eileen Wolkow.
Institution Type/Description: History Museum; housed in Old Chicago Northwestern Depot & City Bldg.
Hours & Admission Prices: June-Aug. Mon.-Sat. 10-5. No charge; donations accepted. &
Attendance: 2,500 (estimated)

LAURA INGALLS WILDER MEMORIAL SOCIETY, INC., 105 Olivet Ave., S.E., De Smet, SD 57231. Mailing Address: P.O. Box 426, De Smet, SD 57231-0426. Tel.: 800-880-3383.
E-mail: laura@discoverlaura.org
Web Site: www.discoverlaura.org
Institution Type/Description: General Museum; housed in the original Surveyor's House from Laura's book By the Shores of Silver Lake.
Hours & Admission Prices: May & Sept. Mon.-Sat. 9-4; June-Aug. daily 9-5:50, Sun. 10-5:30; Oct.-April Mon.-Fri. 9-4. Adults $8, children 6-12 $4; children 5 & under no charge. &

Deadwood

DAYS OF '76 MUSEUM, 18 Seventy Six Dr., Deadwood, SD 57732-1527. Mailing Address: P.O. Box 252, Deadwood, SD 57732-0391. Tel.: 605-578-1657. Fax: 605-717-0052. Facebook: Deadwood History.
E-mail: carolyn@deadwoodhistory.com
Web Site: www.deadwoodhistory.com
Key Personnel: Exec. Dir., Carolyn Weber; Museum Shop Mgr., Michele Schulz.
Institution Type/Description: History Museum.
Hours & Admission Prices: Call for hours. Adults $5.50, children 7-13 $2.50; discounts to AAM members; children 6 & under and members no charge. &
Attendance: 15,000 (estimated)

DEADWOOD HISTORY, INC., 150 Sherman, Deadwood, SD 57732. Mailing Address: P.O. Box 252, Deadwood, SD 57732-0252. Tel.: 605-722-4800 & 578-1714. Fax: 605-717-0052. Facebook: Deadwood History.
E-mail: carolyn@deadwoodhistory.com
Web Site: www.deadwoodhistory.com
Formerly: Adams Museum & House
Key Personnel: Exec. Dir., Carolyn Weber; Dir. Communications, Rose Speirs; Finance Officer & Dir. Human Resources, April Hoover.
Institution Type/Description: History Museums.
Hours & Admission Prices: Research Center: Mon.-Fri. 10-4; other times by appointment. Adams Museum & Days of 76 Museum: May-Sept. daily 9-5; Oct.-April Tues.-Sun. 10-4. Historic Adams House: April & Oct. Tues.-Sun. 10-4; May-Sept. daily 9-5; other times by appointment. Adams Museum: Suggested Donation: adults $5, children $2. Days of 76 Museum: adults $5.50, children 7-13 $2.50; children 6 & under no charge. Adams House: adults $8, children 7-13 $3; children 6 & under no charge. &
Attendance: 100,000 (estimated)

Dell Rapids

DELL RAPIDS SOCIETY FOR HISTORICAL PRESERVATION, 407 E. 4th St., Dell Rapids, SD 57022-1927. Mailing Address: P.O. Box 143, Dell Rapids, SD 57022-0143. Tel.: 605-428-4821.
E-mail: achamley@goldenwest.net
Key Personnel: Pres. (V) & Museum Shop Mgr., Alice Chamley; Vice Pres., Jean Rave.
Institution Type/Description: History Museum.
Hours & Admission Prices: Memorial Day to Labor Day Tues.-Sat. 1-4. No charge.

LITTLE VILLAGE FARM MUSEUM, 47582 240th St., Dell Rapids, SD 57022-6113. Tel.: 605-428-5979. Fax: 605-428-4999.
Key Personnel: Chm. (V) & Museum Shop Mgr., Joan Redder-Lacey; Pres. (V), James Lacey.
Institution Type/Description: Pioneer History Museum.

Hours & Admission Prices: April-Oct. daily 8am to early evening by appointment. Adults $10, children $3. &
Attendance: 750 (estimated)

Elk Point

UNION COUNTY HISTORICAL SOCIETY, 707 W. Main, Elk Point, SD 57025. Mailing Address: P.O. Box 552, Elk Point, SD 57025-0552. Tel.: 605-356-3433. Facebook.
E-mail: mturner@cve.net
Key Personnel: Pres. (V). Mark Turner; Sec., Sondra Stickney.
Institution Type/Description: History Museum.
Hours & Admission Prices: Wed.-Sun. 1-4; other times by appointment. No charge; donations accepted. Closed holidays. &
Attendance: 600 (actual)

Elkton

ELKTON COMMUNITY MUSEUM AND HISTORICAL SOCIETY, 206 Elk St., Community Center, Elkton, SD 57026. Mailing Address: 21539 485th Ave., Elkton, SD 57026-8821. Tel.: 605-542-2451 & 3991, 605-542-5411.
E-mail: dikamp@itctel.com
Key Personnel: Pres. (V), Beverly Schwing.
Institution Type/Description: History Museum.
Hours & Admission Prices: By appointment. No charge; donations accepted. Closed holidays. &
Attendance: 100

Ellsworth AFB

SOUTH DAKOTA AIR AND SPACE MUSEUM, 2890 Davis Dr., Ellsworth AFB, SD 57706. Mailing Address: P.O. Box 871, Ellsworth Heritage Foundation, Inc., Box Elder, SD 57719-0871. Tel.: 605-385-5189. Fax: 605-385-6295.
E-mail: sdasm@midconetwork.com
Web Site: www.sdairandspacemuseum.com
Key Personnel: Exec. Dir., Dan Kuecker; Dir., Mark Wight.
Institution Type/Description: Military Museum.
Hours & Admission Prices: March-May & Sept.-Dec. daily 8:30-4:30; June to Labor Day daily 8:30-6. No charge. Closed Thanksgiving; Christmas. &
Attendance: 115,000 (actual)

Eureka

EUREKA PIONEER MUSEUM OF MCPHERSON COUNTY, INC., 1708 J Ave., Eureka, SD 57437. Mailing Address: P.O. Box 902, Eureka, SD 57437-0902. Tel.: 605-284-2331. eurekasd.com.
E-mail: jeanellenb@aol.com
Web Site: www.glpta.org/eurekamuseum.htm
Key Personnel: Chm. (V), Asst. Dir. & Cur., Bonnie Mehlhaff; Pres., Barry Lapp; Vice Pres., Don Fischer; Treas., Jean Bertsch; Dir. Public Rels. & Sec., Linda Bergman.
Institution Type/Description: History Museum with focus on the lives and work of pioneers.
Hours & Admission Prices: April 15-Nov. 1 Wed.-Fri. 1-5, Sat.-Sun. 2-5. No charge; donations accepted. &
Attendance: 2,500 (estimated)

Faulkton

FAULK COUNTY MUSEUM, 814 Court St., Faulkton, SD 57438. Mailing Address: c/o Faulkton Historical Society, P.O. Box 584, Faulkton, SD 57438-0584. Tel.: 605-598-4285.
E-mail: moritzcj@yahoo.com
Web Site: www.faulktoncity.org/historic_sites.htm
Key Personnel: Pres. (V), Jody Moritz; Dir., Janet G. Reed; Cur., Judy Dixon.
Institution Type/Description: History Museum.
Hours & Admission Prices: Summer: Wed. & Fri. 1-4. No charge; donations accepted.
Attendance: 50 (estimated)

PICKLER MANSION, 900 8th Ave., Faulkton, SD 57438. Mailing Address: c/o Faulkton Historical Society, P.O. Box 584, Faulkton, SD 57438-0584. Tel.: 605-598-4285.
E-mail: moritzcj@yahoo.com
Web Site: www.faulktoncity.org/historic-sites.htm
Key Personnel: Pres. & Chm. (V), Jody Moritz; Cur., Judy Dixon; Dir., Janet G. Reed.

Institution Type/Description: Historic House Museum: home of South Dakota's first U.S. Congressman & his wife, John & Alice Pickler.
Hours & Admission Prices: Memorial Day to Labor Day daily 1-4. Adults $8.
Attendance: 270 (actual)

Flandreau

MOODY COUNTY HISTORICAL SOCIETY MUSEUM & RESEARCH CENTER, 706 E. Pipestone Ave., Flandreau, SD 57028. Tel.: 605-997-3191.
E-mail: mchsmus1@vastbb.net
Web Site: www.moodycountymuseum.com
Key Personnel: Dir., Steve Stunes; Pres. (V), Bruce Porisch; Vice Pres., Roxee Johnson.
Institution Type/Description: History Museum.
Hours & Admission Prices: Tues.-Thurs. & Sat. 9-2; other times by appointment. No charge; donations accepted. Closed New Year's Eve & Day; Memorial Day; Thanksgiving weekend; Christmas Eve & Day.
Attendance: 1,500 (estimated)

Fort Meade

OLD FORT MEADE MUSEUM AND HISTORIC RESEARCH ASSOCIATION, Bldg. 55 Sheridan St., Fort Meade, SD 57741. Mailing Address: P.O. Box 164, Fort Meade, SD 57741-0164. Tel.: 605-347-9822.
E-mail: support@fortmeademuseum.org
Web Site: www.fortmeademuseum.org
Key Personnel: Pres. (V), Peg Aplan; Sec., Marshall Williams.
Institution Type/Description: Military Museum: U.S. Cavalry fort built in 1878 by Seventh Cavalry.
Hours & Admission Prices: May 15th & Sept. 15th 9-5; Memorial Day to Labor Day daily 9-5. Adults $5, groups $3; discounts to AAM members; children under 12, school groups & members no charge.
Attendance: 8,000 (estimated)

Fort Pierre

VERENDRYE MUSEUM, 115 Deadwood St., Fort Pierre, SD 57532. Mailing Address: PO Box 665, Fort Pierre, SD 57532-0665. Tel.: 605-223-7697.
E-mail: conniecarlisle@outlook.com
Web Site: www.fortpierce.com
Key Personnel: Pres. (V), Randy Seiler.
Institution Type/Description: History Museum.
Hours & Admission Prices: Memorial Day to Labor Day Mon.-Sat. 9-4, Sun. 11-4; other times by appointment. No charge; donations accepted.
Attendance: 600 (estimated)

Frankfort

FISHER GROVE COUNTRY SCHOOL/FISHER GROVE STATE PARK, 17290 Fishers Lane, Frankfort, SD 57440-6700. Tel.: 605-472-1212 & 1336.
E-mail: lake.louise@state.sd.us
Web Site: gfp.sd.gov/state-parks/directory/fisher-grove/
Key Personnel: Park Mgr., Charles Jones.
Institution Type/Description: Historic Building: 1884 Deiter School.
Hours & Admission Prices: Call for hours.

Freeman

HERITAGE HALL MUSEUM & ARCHIVES, 880 S. Cedar St., Freeman, SD 57029-2317. Mailing Address: P.O. Box 693, Freeman, SD 57029-1000. Tel.: 605-925-7545. Fax: 605-925-4271.
E-mail: heritagehallmuseum@gmail.com
Web Site: www.heritagehallmuseum.com
Key Personnel: Dir. & Archivist, Marnette Hofer; Chm. (V), Kevin Waltner; Cur., Roy Kaufman; Cur., Terry Quam.
Institution Type/Description: Ethnic Museum.
Hours & Admission Prices: May-Sept. Tues.-Sat. 10-4, Sun. 1-5; other times by appointment. Adults $5, students grades 1-12 $3; pre-school no charge.
Attendance: 4,000 (estimated)

Garretson

GARRETSON HISTORICAL SOCIETY MUSEUM, 609 Main St., Garretson, SD 57030. Mailing Address: P.O. Box 614, Garretson, SD 57030-0614. Tel.: 605-594-6694. Facebook.
E-mail: bgwhbarn@alliancecom.net

Key Personnel: Pres., Barbara Marsh; Chm. (V), Judy Hanson; Treas., Margie Martens.
Institution Type/Description: Historical Society Museum.
Hours & Admission Prices: April-Dec. Sat. 1-4; other times by appointment. No charge; donations accepted.
Attendance: 2,000 (estimated)

Geddes

GEDDES HISTORIC DISTRICT VILLAGE, 211 Main St., Geddes, SD 57342-0097. Mailing Address: P.O. Box 97, Geddes, SD 57342-0097. Tel.: 605-337-2501. Fax: 605-337-3535.
E-mail: dufsdfek@midstatesd.net
Web Site: www.geddes.org
Formerly: Charles Mix County Historical Restoration Society
Key Personnel: C.E.O., Chm. (V) & Sec., Ronald D. Dufek; Chm. (V) & Museum Shop Mgr., Irene Merkwan.
Institution Type/Description: History Museum.
Hours & Admission Prices: mid-May to mid-Sept. daily 9-7. No charge; donations requested.
Attendance: 400 (estimated)

Gettysburg

DAKOTA SUNSET MUSEUM, 205 W. Commercial Ave., Ste. 104, Gettysburg, SD 57442-1103. Tel.: 605-765-9480.
E-mail: dakotasunset@venturecomm.net
Web Site: www.dakotasunsetmuseum.com
Key Personnel: Pres. (V), Bob Potts; Dir., Cur. & Museum Shop Mgr., Kathleen Nagel; Archivist, Eileen Jost; Archivist, Mary Carol Potts.
Institution Type/Description: History Museum.
Hours & Admission Prices: Summer: Mon.-Sat. daily 1-5; Winter: Tues.-Sat. 1-5. No charge; donations accepted. Closed New Year's Day; Easter; Memorial Day; Independence Day; Labor Day; Thanksgiving; Christmas.
Attendance: 1,200 (estimated)

Groton

GRANARY RURAL CULTURAL CENTER, 40161 128th St., Groton, SD 57445-5405. Mailing Address: c/o Dacotah Prairie Museum, 21 S. Main St., Aberdeen, SD 57401. Tel.: 605-626-7117. Fax: 605-626-4026.
E-mail: sue.gates@browncounty.sd.gov
Web Site: www.granaryfinearts.org
Key Personnel: Chm. & Pres. (V), Sue Gates; Dir., Lora Schaunanman.
Institution Type/Description: Art Gallery.
Hours & Admission Prices: Call for hours. No charge; donations accepted.
Attendance: 3,500 (estimated)

Hermosa

HERMOSA ARTS AND HISTORY MUSEUM, 25 N. Second St., Hermosa, SD 57744. Mailing Address: P.O. Box 175, Hermosa, SD 57744-0175. Tel.: 605-431-0708.
E-mail: hermosamuseum@yahoo.com
Key Personnel: Dir., Doug Hesnard.
Institution Type/Description: History Museum: housed in the 1889 Hermosa school.
Hours & Admission Prices: By appointment. No charge.

Hill City

BLACK HILLS MUSEUM OF NATURAL HISTORY, 150 Deerfield Rd., Hill City, SD 57745-0614. Mailing Address: P.O. Box 614, Hill City, SD 57745-0614. Tel.: 605-574-9454.
E-mail: neal@bhmnh.org
Web Site: www.bhmnh.org
Key Personnel: Pres. (V), Rick Van Ness; Admin., Chris Van Ness; Sec., Neal Larson.
Institution Type/Description: Natural History Museum.
Hours & Admission Prices: Temporary closed. Collections can be viewed at the Black Hills Institute Museum.
Attendance: 76,465 (actual)

Hot Springs

BLACK HILLS WILD HORSE SANCTUARY & VISITORS CENTER, Highland Rd., Hot Springs, SD 57747. Mailing Address: P.O. Box 998, Hot Springs, SD 57747-0998. Tel.: 800-252-6652, 605-745-5955. Fax: 605-745-4339.
E-mail: iram@gwtc.net

Web Site: wildmustangs.com
Key Personnel: Program Mgr., Susan Watt.
Institution Type/Description: Wild Horse Sanctuary.
Hours & Admission Prices: Guided Tours: by appointment. 2 Hour Guided Tour: adults 19 & over $50, seniors 55 & over $45, youth 13-18 $15; children 5-12 $7.50; children 4 & under no charge. Additional tours available.

MAMMOTH SITE OF HOT SPRINGS, SOUTH DAKOTA, INC., 1800 US 18 Bypass, Hot Springs, SD 57747-9604. Mailing Address: P.O. Box 692, Hot Springs, SD 57747-0692. Tel.: 605-745-6017. Fax: 605-745-3038.
E-mail: joem@mammothsite.org
Web Site: mammothsite.com
Key Personnel: Chief Scientist & Site Dir., Dr. Jim Mead; C.O.O. & Business Mgr., Presstib Gabel; Accounting & Membership, Diana Turner; Collections Mgr., Olga Potapova; In-situ Bonebed Cur. & Educator, Justin Wilkins; Educator, Sharon McLain; Preparator, Monica Bugbee; Sec., Bethany Cook.
Institution Type/Description: Paleontology Museum.
Hours & Admission Prices: March to mid-May & Sept.-Oct. daily 9-5; mid-May to mid-Aug. daily 8-8; mid-Aug. to Aug. 31 daily 8-6; Nov.-Feb. Mon.-Sat. 9-3:30, Sun. 11-3:30. Adults $11, seniors 60 & over $9, children 4-12 $8; discounts to groups & AAM members; children 3 & under and members no charge. Closed New Year's Day; Easter; Thanksgiving; Christmas. &
Attendance: 90,847 (actual)

PIONEER MUSEUM IN HOT SPRINGS, 300 N. Chicago St., Hot Springs, SD 57747-1657. Mailing Address: P.O. Box 361, Hot Springs, SD 57747-0361. Tel.: 605-745-5147.
E-mail: pioneer@pioneer-museum.com
Formerly: Fall River County Historical Museum
Key Personnel: Dir., Wanda Aaberg; Pres., Carol Sides.
Institution Type/Description: Historical Society Museum: housed in 1893 schoolhouse.
Hours & Admission Prices: May 15-Oct. 15 Mon.-Sat. 9-5. Adults $5, seniors $4; discounts to families, school groups, bus tours & past military; children 12 & under, active military & members no charge. &
Attendance: 10,000 (estimated)

WIND CAVE NATIONAL PARK, Hot Springs, SD 57747. Mailing Address: 26611 U.S. Hwy. 385, Hot Springs, SD 57747-6027. Tel.: 605-745-4600. Fax: 605-745-4207.
E-mail: tom_farrell@nps.gov
Web Site: www.nps.gov/wica/
Key Personnel: Chief of Interpretation, Tom Farrell; Museum Technician, Randy Weiss.
Institution Type/Description: Natural History Museum.
Hours & Admission Prices: Winter: daily 8-4:30; Spring, Summer & Fall: call for expanded hours. Cave Tours: Natural Entrance Tour & Fair Grounds Tour: adults $12, children 6-16 & senior pass holders $6. Garden of Eden Tour: adults $10, children 6-16 $5; children under 5 no charge. Museum: no charge. Closed New Year's Day; Thanksgiving; Christmas. &
Attendance: 120,000 (estimated)

Howard

MINER COUNTY RURAL LIFE MUSEUM, 127 S. Main St., Howard, SD 57349. Mailing Address: P.O. Box 245, Howard, SD 57349-0245. Tel.: 605-772-5677. Facebook: Miner County Historical Society.
E-mail: mcrurallifemuseum@gmail.com
Key Personnel: Pres. (V), Mary E. Leary; Treas., Mary Holland; Sec., Patricia Winker; Bd. Member, Gloria Faye Truman; Bd. Member, Patricia Schneider; Bd. Member, Joyce Haak; Bd. Member, Dotty Hageman; Bd. Member, Kay Hageman.
Institution Type/Description: History Museum.
Hours & Admission Prices: Sun. 1-4. No charge; donations accepted. &
Attendance: 275 (actual)

Huron

DAKOTALAND MUSEUM, State Fair Grounds, 3rd St., Huron, SD 57350-1254. Mailing Address: P.O. Box 1254, Huron, SD 57350-1254. Tel.: 605-352-4626.
E-mail: rachelclenden@yahoo.com
Web Site: www.dakotalandmuseum.org
Key Personnel: Chm. (V), Peggy Gibson; Dir., Rachel Farrell.
Institution Type/Description: History Museum.
Hours & Admission Prices: Memorial Day-Labor Day Mon.-Fri. 10-6, Sat. 2-6, Sun. 1-3. Dakotaland Museum: adults $3, children 6-12 $1. &
Attendance: 1,300 (estimated)

PYLE HOUSE MUSEUM, 376 Idaho Ave., S.E., Huron, SD 57350-2527. Mailing Address: P.O. Box 1254, Huron, SD 57350-1254. Tel.: 605-352-2528.
E-mail: rachelclenden@yahoo.com
Web Site: www.thedakotalandmuseum.org
Key Personnel: Dir., Rachel Farrell; Chm. (V), Peggy Gibson.
Institution Type/Description: Historic House Museum: housed in the home of Gladys Pyle, the first elected woman U.S. senator, built in 1894.
Hours & Admission Prices: Summer: Mon.-Fri. 1-3:30; other times by appointment. Adults $3; children 12 & under no charge. Closed major holidays.
Attendance: 500 (estimated)

Interior

BADLANDS NATIONAL PARK, Physical/Mailing Address: 25216 Ben Reifel Rd., Interior, SD 57750. Tel.: 605-433-5361. Fax: 605-433-5404. TDD: 605-433-5361.
Web Site: www.nps.gov/badl
Institution Type/Description: Natural History Museum.
Hours & Admission Prices: Ben Reifel Visitor Center: mid-April to mid-May and early Sept. to late Oct. daily 8-5; Winter daily 8-4; Summer daily 8-7. Car $15, motorcycle $10, individual (hike, bicycle) $7. Closed New Year's Day; Thanksgiving; Christmas. &
Attendance: 906,868 (actual)

Ipswich

J.W. PARMLEY HISTORICAL HOME SOCIETY, 115 Main St., Ipswich, SD 57451. Mailing Address: P.O. Box 111, Ipswich, SD 57451-0111. Tel.: 605-426-6024 & 6949.
E-mail: Ipswichfo@valleytel.net
Web Site: www.ipswich-sd.com
Formerly: J.W. Parmley Historical Home Museum
Key Personnel: Cur., Ray Kub.
Institution Type/Description: Historic Building.
Hours & Admission Prices: Memorial Day to Labor Day Fri. & Sun. 2-5; other times by appointment. No charge; donations accepted.
Attendance: 500 (actual)

Kadoka

BADLANDS PETRIFIED GARDENS, Interstate 90, Exit 152, Kadoka, SD 57543. Mailing Address: P.O. Box 27, Kadoka, SD 57543-0027. Tel.: 605-837-2448.
Key Personnel: Pres. & Deputy Dir., Robert Fugate; Vice Pres., Cathy Fugate; Asst. Dir., Patty Ulman; Business Officer, Floy Fugate; Museum Shop Mgr., Bill Fugate.
Institution Type/Description: Natural History Museum.
Hours & Admission Prices: mid-April to Oct. daily 7-7. Adults $5, children 6-16 $2.50; discounts to groups. &
Attendance: 15,000 (estimated)

KADOKA DEPOT MUSEUM, S. Main St., Kadoka, SD 57543. Mailing Address: City of Kadoka, Box 58, Kadoka, SD 57543-0058. Tel.: 605-837-2229. Fax: 605-837-1262.
E-mail: kadokacity@wcenet.com
Web Site: www.kadokasd.com
Formerly: Jackson Washabaugh Historical Museum
Key Personnel: Financial Officer, Patty Ulmen.
Institution Type/Description: Historical Society Museum: housed in 1906 Chicago, Milwaukee, St. Paul Railroad Depot.
Hours & Admission Prices: Call for confirmation of hours.
Attendance: 500 (estimated)

Keystone

BIG THUNDER GOLD MINE, 604 Blair, Keystone, SD 57751. Mailing Address: Box 459, Keystone, SD 57751-0459. Tel.: 605-666-4847. Fax: 605-666-4566. Facebook.
E-mail: mclainsandra@aol.com
Web Site: www.bigthundermine.com
Key Personnel: Dir. & C.E.O., Sandra McLain; Museum Shop Mgr., Shae Hackett.
Institution Type/Description: Historic Site: 1890s gold mine.
Hours & Admission Prices: May-Sept. daily 8-8. Adults $9.95, children 6-12 $6.95; discounts to members, AAM & ICOM members. Gold Panning: $40 per half day; $9.95 without tour, $7.95 with tour. &
Attendance: 100,000 (estimated)

KEYSTONE AREA HISTORICAL SOCIETY, 410 3rd St., Keystone, SD 57751. Mailing Address: P.O. Box 177, Keystone, SD 57751-0177. Tel.: 605-666-4494. Fax: 605-666-4566. Facebook.
E-mail: mclainsandra@aol.com
Web Site: www.keystonehistory.com
Key Personnel: Pres. (V), Sandra McLain; Dir. & Museum Shop Mgr., Arlene Robinson; Dir. & Museum Shop Mgr., Jeanie Kirkpatrick; Treas., Wally Hunsacker.
Institution Type/Description: General Museum: housed in c.1900 three-story Victorian frame school house.
Hours & Admission Prices: May 15-Sept. 15 Mon.-Sat. 11-4. No charge; donations accepted. &
Attendance: 6,384 (actual)

MOUNT RUSHMORE NATIONAL MEMORIAL, 13000 Hwy. 244, Keystone, SD 57751-0268. Mailing Address: 13000 Hwy. 244, Bldg. 31, Ste. 1, Keystone, SD 57751-0268. Tel.: 605-574-3163. Fax: 605-574-2307.
E-mail: zane_martin@nps.gov
Web Site: www.nps.gov/moru/
Key Personnel: Supt., Cheryl A. Schreier.
Institution Type/Description: Park Museum: massive granite sculpture, carved into a mountainside, memorializing the likenesses of four American Presidents; Washington, Jefferson, Theodore Roosevelt & Lincoln.
Hours & Admission Prices: Information Center: late May to mid-Aug. daily 8am-10pm; mid-Aug. to Sept. daily 8am-9pm; Oct. to late May daily 8-5. Grounds: March 13-Sept. daily 5am-11pm; Oct.-March 12 daily 5am-9pm. Parking fee: $11 annual pass; $50 per bus per entry. &
Attendance: 2,754,261 (actual)

NATIONAL PRESIDENTIAL WAX MUSEUM, Hwy. 609 16-A, Keystone, SD 57751. Mailing Address: P.O. Box 238, Keystone, SD 57751-0238. Tel.: 605-666-4455. Fax: 605-666-4560. Facebook: National Presidential Wax Museum.
E-mail: info@presidentialwaxmuseum.com
Web Site: www.presidentialwaxmuseum.com
Key Personnel: Museum Shop Mgr., Clay King.
Institution Type/Description: Wax Museum.
Hours & Admission Prices: April-May & Sept.-Oct. 9-5; Memorial Day to Labor Day 9-8. Adults $10, senior citizens $8, children 6-12 $7; children under 6 no charge. &
Attendance: 28,000

RUSHMORE BORGLUM STORY, 342 Winter St., Keystone, SD 57751-2036. Tel.: 605-666-4448. Fax: 605-666-4482.
E-mail: borglum@gwtc.net
Web Site: www.rushmoreborglum.com
Institution Type/Description: History Museum.
Hours & Admission Prices: May & Sept. call for hours; June-Aug. daily 8:30-4:30. Adults $10. &

Kimball

SOUTH DAKOTA TRACTOR MUSEUM, 501 S. West St., Kimball, SD 57355. Mailing Address: P.O. Box 418, Kimball, SD 57355-0418. Tel.: 605-778-6513.
E-mail: rbickner@midstatesd.net
Web Site: sdtractormuseum.home.comcast.net
Key Personnel: Pres. (V), Maynard Konechne; Sec., Maxine Bickner; Museum Shop Mgr., Dale Stanek.
Institution Type/Description: Agriculture & Antiques Museum.
Hours & Admission Prices: Memorial Day to Oct. 1 Mon.-Fri. 9-5, Sat.-Sun. 12:30-5; other times by appointment. No charge; donations accepted. &
Attendance: 2,400 (actual)

Kyle

OGLALA LAKOTA COLLEGE HISTORICAL CENTER, 490 Piya Wiconi Rd, Kyle, SD 57752-0310. Mailing Address: P.O. Box 490, Kyle, SD 57752-0310. Tel.: 605-455-6000. Fax: 605-455-2787.
E-mail: mpourier@olc.edu
Web Site: www.olc.edu/about/historical_center
Institution Type/Description: Historical Center.
Hours & Admission Prices: June-Sept. Mon.- Fri. 9-5. No charge; donations accepted. &

Lake City

FORT SISSETON HISTORIC STATE PARK, 11907 434th Ave., Lake City, SD 57247-6153. Mailing Address: South Dakota Game Fish and Parks, 523 E. Capitol Ave., Pierre, SD 57501. Tel.: 605-448-5474. Fax: 605-448-5572. Facebook: Ft. Sisseton.
E-mail: fortsisseton@state.sd.us
Web Site: gfp.sd.gov/state-parks/directory/fort-sisseton/
Key Personnel: Park Mgr., Christopher Soukup.
Institution Type/Description: Historical Museum: located on site of c.1864 Ft. Wadsworth (Ft. Sisseton).
Hours & Admission Prices: Memorial Day-Labor Day daily 10-6; Sept. Mon.-Fri. 8-4:30; special group tours on request. Call for fees. &
Attendance: 65,000 (estimated)

Lake Norden

SOUTH DAKOTA AMATEUR BASEBALL HALL OF FAME, 519 Main Ave., Lake Norden, SD 57248. Mailing Address: P.O. Box 80, Lake Norden, SD 57248-0080. Tel.: 605-785-3553. Fax: 605-785-3315.
E-mail: rantonen@jrfeeds.com
Web Site: sdbaseballhalloffame.com
Key Personnel: Pres., Scott Fiedler; Vice Pres., Jerry Des Lauriers; Exec. Sec. & Cur., Rusty Antonen.
Institution Type/Description: Sports Museum.
Hours & Admission Prices: May to Sept. daily 9-7; other times by appointment. No charge; donations accepted. &

Lead

BLACK HILLS MINING MUSEUM, 323 W. Main, Lead, SD 57754-1604. Tel.: 605-584-1605.
E-mail: bhminingmuseum@rushmore.com
Web Site: www.mining-museum.blackhills.com
Key Personnel: Pres., Todd Duex; Dir., Mallory Everett.
Institution Type/Description: Mining History Museum.
Hours & Admission Prices: May-Sept. daily 9-5; Oct.-April call for hours. Call for admission prices. &
Attendance: 20,000 (estimated)

PRESIDENTS PARK SCULPTURE GARDEN, 11249 Presidents Park Loop, Lead, SD 57754-3846. Mailing Address: 104 S. Galena St., Lead, SD 57754-1674. Tel.: 605-584-9925.
Key Personnel: Mgr., Dave Olmstead.
Institution Type/Description: History Museum.
Hours & Admission Prices: Daily 9 to sunset; weather permitting. Adults $8, seniors 60 & over $6.50, children 5-15 $6; discounts to military & groups; children 5 & under no charge. &

SANFORD LAB HOMESTAKE VISITOR CENTER, 160 W. Main St., Lead, SD 57754-1362. Tel.: 605-584-3110. Facebook: Sanford Lab Homestake Visitor Center.
E-mail: bbierle@sanfordlab.org
Web Site: sanfordlabhomestake.com
Formerly: Homestake Gold Mine Visitor Center
Key Personnel: Exec. Dir., Billi Bierle.
Institution Type/Description: Mining History Museum.
Hours & Admission Prices: May-Sept. daily 8-6; groups by appointment. Tours: adults $7.50, seniors $6.75, students $6.50; discounts to groups of 10 or more and families with 4-6 members. &
Attendance: 35,000 (actual)

Lemmon

GRAND RIVER MUSEUM, 114 10th St. W., Lemmon, SD 57638-2202. Tel.: 605-374-3911, 605-374-7574.
E-mail: grmuseum@sdplains.com
Web Site: www.thegrandrivermuseum.com
Key Personnel: Pres. (V), Stuart T. Schmidt; Dir. & Museum Shop Mgr., Phyllis Schmidt.
Institution Type/Description: History Museum.
Hours & Admission Prices: May-Sept. Mon.-Sat. 9-6, Sun. 12-5. No charge; donations accepted. &
Attendance: 5,500 (estimated)

PETRIFIED WOOD PARK & MUSEUM, 500 Main St., Lemmon, SD 57638-1523. Tel.: 605-374-3964.
Key Personnel: Dir., Carolyn Penfield.
Institution Type/Description: Geological & Historical Museum.

Hours & Admission Prices: Museum: Memorial Day-Labor Day daily 8-6. No charge; donations accepted. &

Madison

KARL E. MUNDT HISTORICAL & EDUCATIONAL FOUNDATION, 820 N. Washington Ave., Madison, SD 57042. Tel.: 605-256-5211.
E-mail: archives@dsu.edu
Web Site: archives.dsu.edu
Institution Type/Description: History Museum.
Hours & Admission Prices: Research: Mon.-Fri. 8:30-4. No charge. Closed legal holidays. &

PRAIRIE VILLAGE, 45205 SD Hwy. 34, Madison, SD 57042. Mailing Address: P.O. Box 256, Madison, SD 57042-0256. Tel.: 605-256-3644, 800-693-3644. Facebook: Historic Prairie Village.
E-mail: info@prairievillage.org
Web Site: www.prairievillage.org
Key Personnel: Pres., George Lee; Vice Pres., Tim Ramstad; Museum Mgr., Stan Rauch.
Institution Type/Description: Village Museum.
Hours & Admission Prices: Village: Mother's Day weekend to Labor Day Mon.-Sat. 10-5, Sun. 11-5. Train Rides: Mother's Day to Labor Day Sat. 2 p.m. Adults $5; discounts for senior citizens, group tours. Season Pass: $30. &
Attendance: 40,000 (estimated)

SMITH-ZIMMERMANN HERITAGE MUSEUM, 221 N.E. 8th St., Madison, SD 57042-1639. Tel.: 605-256-5308.
E-mail: smith.zimmermann@dsu.edu
Web Site: www.smith-zimmermann.dsu.edu
Key Personnel: Pres., Susan Larsen; Coord., Cynthia Mallery.
Institution Type/Description: History Museum.
Hours & Admission Prices: Tues.-Fri. 1-4:30; tours by appointment. No charge; donations accepted. &
Attendance: 5,598 (actual)

McLaughlin

MAJOR JAMES MCLAUGHLIN HERITAGE CENTER, Main St., McLaughlin, SD 57642. Mailing Address: P.O. Box 228, McLaughlin, SD 57642-0642. Tel.: 605-823-4590.
Key Personnel: Pres. (V) & Museum Shop Mgr., Sharon Walker.
Institution Type/Description: History Museum.
Hours & Admission Prices: May-Sept. Mon.-Fri. 12-5. No charge; donations accepted. &
Attendance: 75 (estimated)

Midland

MIDLAND PIONEER MUSEUM, Main St., Midland, SD 57552. Mailing Address: 25135 Capa Rd., Midland, SD 57552-3201. Tel.: 605-843-2150.
E-mail: kry@gwtc.net
Web Site: www.gwtc.net/~kry
Key Personnel: C.E.O. & Dir., Janice D. Bierle.
Institution Type/Description: History Museum.
Hours & Admission Prices: June-Aug. Mon.-Tues. & Fri. 1:30-4; other times by appointment. No charge; donations accepted.

Milbank

GRANT COUNTY HISTORICAL MUSEUM, 211 S. 3rd St., Milbank, SD 57252. Mailing Address: P.O. Box 201, Milbank, SD 57252-0201. Tel.: 605-432-2351. Facebook.
E-mail: vcameron@itcmilbank.com
Web Site: www.history.sd.gov/aboutus/organizations/grant.aspx
Key Personnel: Cur., Bruce Johnson; Pres. (V), Arlo Levisen.
Institution Type/Description: Historical Museum. Listed on the National Register of Historic Buildings.
Hours & Admission Prices: Memorial Day-Labor Day Sun. 2-5. No charge; donations accepted.
Attendance: 400 (actual)

Mission

SICANGU HERITAGE CENTER, 2246 E. Industrial St., Sinte Gleska University, Antelope Lake Campus, Mission, SD 57555.

Mailing Address: P.O. Box 675, Mission, SD 57555-0675. Tel.: 605-856-8211.
E-mail: heritagecenter@sintegleska.edu
Web Site: www.sintegleska.edu/heritage-center.html
Key Personnel: Dir., Marcella Cash; Mgr. Museum Collections, Keli Herman; Gen. Asst., Terry Gray.
Institution Type/Description: Heritage Center.
Hours & Admission Prices: Mon.-Fri. 9-5. No charge; donations accepted. Closed holidays.

Mitchell

CARNEGIE RESOURCE CENTER, 119 W. 3rd Ave., Mitchell, SD 57301-3410. Tel.: 605-996-3209.
E-mail: rangep@mitchellcarnegie.org
Web Site: mitchellcarnegie.com
Formerly: Oscar Howe Art Center & YWCA
Key Personnel: Pres. (V), Lyle W. Swenson.
Institution Type/Description: History & Genealogy Research Center.
Hours & Admission Prices: Mon.-Sat. 1-5. No charge; donations accepted. Closed holidays.

DAKOTA DISCOVERY MUSEUM, 1300 McGovern Ave., Mitchell, SD 57301-7901. Mailing Address: P.O. Box 1071, Mitchell, SD 57301-7071. Tel.: 605-996-2122. Fax: 605-996-0323. Facebook: Dakota Discovery Museum.
E-mail: history@dakotadiscovery.com
Web Site: www.dakotadiscovery.com
Formerly: Middle Border Museum & Oscar Howe Art Center
Key Personnel: Exec. Dir., Lori Holmberg; Pres., Dianne Carr.
Institution Type/Description: Historic Village Museum and Art Center.
Hours & Admission Prices: May & Sept. Mon.-Tues. & Thurs.-Sat. 9-5; June-Aug. Mon.-Tues. & Thurs.-Sat. 9-7; Oct.-April Tues.-Fri. 10-4, Sat. 1-4. Adults $7, senior citizens $6, children 6-17 $3; discounts to groups, and AAM, ICOM & AAA members; members no charge. Closed New Year's Eve & Day; Easter Mon.; Thanksgiving; Christmas; Boxing Day. &
Attendance: 7,000 (actual)

MITCHELL PREHISTORIC INDIAN VILLAGE & MUSEUM, 3200 Indian Village Rd., Mitchell, SD 57301. Mailing Address: P.O. Box 621, Mitchell, SD 57301. Tel.: 605-996-5473.
E-mail: info@mitchellindianvillage.org
Web Site: www.mitchellindianvillage.org
Key Personnel: Exec. Dir., Cindy Gregg.
Institution Type/Description: Archaeological Site.
Hours & Admission Prices: April & Oct. Mon.-Fri. 9-4; May & Sept. daily 9-4; Memorial Day-Labor Day daily 8-6. Adults $6, seniors 60 & over $5, children 6-18 $4; children 5 & under no charge.

Mobridge

KLEIN MUSEUM, 1820 W. Grand Crossing, W. Hwy. 12, Mobridge, SD 57601-1114. Tel.: 605-845-7243.
E-mail: kleinmuseum@westriv.com
Web Site: mobridgekleinmuseum.com
Key Personnel: Chm. (V), Judy Curran; Pres. (V), Sally Perman; Museum Shop Mgr., Diane Kindt.
Institution Type/Description: General Museum.
Hours & Admission Prices: May-Oct. Mon.-Fri. 9-12 & 1-5, Sat.-Sun. 1-4. Adults $4, students $3; members no charge. &
Attendance: 4,000 (estimated)

Murdo

1880 TOWN, I-90 Exit 170, Murdo, SD 57559. Mailing Address: P.O. Box 507, Murdo, SD 57559-0507. Tel.: 605-344-2236. Fax: 605-344-2236.
E-mail: info@1880town.com
Web Site: www.1880town.com
Key Personnel: Mgr., Richard Hollinger.
Institution Type/Description: General Museum: built as a movie set but never used for filming.
Hours & Admission Prices: May-Oct. daily 8am to sunset. Adults $12, senior citizens $10, teens 13-18 $7, children 6-12 $5; discounts to groups; handicapped & children under 5 no charge. &
Attendance: 41,170 (actual)

PIONEER AUTO MUSEUM, 503 E. 5th St., Murdo, SD 57559. Mailing Address: P.O. Box 76, Murdo, SD 57559-0076. Tel.: 605-669-2691. Fax: 605-669-3217.

E-mail: pas@pioneerautoshow.com
Web Site: www.pioneerautoshow.com
Key Personnel: C.E.O., Dir. & Cur., Dave Geisler; Deputy Dir. & Cur., David M.
   Geisler; Dir. & Museum Shop Mgr., Vivian Sonder.
Institution Type/Description: Transportation Museum & Antique Town: located at
   the northern head of the Texas Cattle Trail.
Hours & Admission Prices: Memorial Day-Labor Day 7-10; Winter: 9-6. Adults
   $11.50, children 5-12 $5.75; discounts to groups, AAM, AAA & ICOM mem-
   bers. Closed New Year's Day; Easter; Thanksgiving; Christmas.
Attendance: 126,000 (estimated)

Newell

NEWELL MUSEUM, 108 3rd St., Newell, SD 57760. Mailing
   Address: P.O. Box 433, Newell, SD 57760-0433. Tel.: 605-456-
   1310. Fax: 605-456-9820. Facebook: Town of Newell.
E-mail: newellmuseum@yahoo.com
Web Site: www.cityofnewell.com
Key Personnel: Chm., David Morrel; Vice Chm., Douglas Parrow; Treas., Annitta
   Stolnack; Cur., Linda Velder; Archivist, Lynette Culver; Sec., Sharyl Scott.
Institution Type/Description: History Museum.
Hours & Admission Prices: May 30-Sept. Tues.-Sat. 1-5; other times by appoint-
   ment. No charge; donations accepted. &
Attendance: 670 (actual)

Oldham

LORIKS PETERSON HERITAGE HOUSE, 108 E. Williams St.,
   Oldham, SD 57051-7216. Mailing Address: 21617 443rd Ave.,
   Oldham, SD 57051-7216. Tel.: 605-482-8640.
E-mail: daniel.brosz@state.sd.us
Web Site: www.sdmuseums.org
Key Personnel: Vice Pres., Patricia Folsland.
Institution Type/Description: Historic House Museum.
Hours & Admission Prices: Memorial Day to Labor Day Sun. 1-4; other times by
   appointment. No charge; donations accepted. &
Attendance: 310 (estimated)

Philip

MINUTEMAN MISSILE NATIONAL HISTORIC SITE, 24545
   Cottonwood Rd., Philip, SD 57567-7002. Tel.: 605-433-5552. Fax:
   605-433-5558.
Web Site: www.nps.gov/mimi
Institution Type/Description: National Historic Site.
Hours & Admission Prices: Visitor Contact Station: Memorial Day to Labor Day
   Mon.-Sat. 8-4:30; Sept.-May Mon.-Fri. 8-4:30.

PRAIRIE HOMESTEAD, Exit 131 off Interstate 90 Hwy. 240,
   Philip, SD 57567-7007. Mailing Address: 21070 SD Hwy. 240,
   Philip, SD 57567-7007. Tel.: 605-433-5400.
Web Site: www.prairiehomestead.com
Key Personnel: Owner Operator, Grady Crew; Owner Operator, Bernice Crew;
   Museum Shop Mgr., Heidi Porch.
Institution Type/Description: Historic House: 1909 sod dugout, original home of
   Mr. & Mrs. Ed Brown.
Hours & Admission Prices: May-Oct. dawn to dusk. Adults $7, seniors $6.30, chil-
   dren 10-17 $6; discount to AAM & ICOM members; children under 10 no
   charge when accompanied by an adult. &
Attendance: 15,000 (estimated)

Piedmont

PETRIFIED FOREST OF THE BLACK HILLS, 8220 Elk Creek
   Rd., Piedmont, SD 57769-7208. Tel.: 605-787-4560, 800-846-
   2267. Fax: 605-787-6477.
E-mail: info@elkcreekresort.net
Web Site: www.elkcreekresort.net
Key Personnel: Dir. & Museum Shop Mgr., Arvid Scott; Museum Shop Mgr., Tim
   Scott.
Institution Type/Description: Natural History Museum.
Hours & Admission Prices: May & Oct. 15 daily 9-5; June-Aug. daily 8:30-6.
   Adults $6.50, senior citizens & youths 13-18 $5, children 6-12 $4; discounts to
   tour & group buses, AAM, AARP & ICOM members; children under 5 no
   charge. (prices include state sales tax) &
Attendance: 10,000 (actual)

Pierre

SOUTH DAKOTA DISCOVERY CENTER, 805 W. Sioux Ave.,
   Pierre, SD 57501-1858. Tel.: 605-224-8295. Fax: 605-224-2865.
   Facebook: South Dakota Discovery Center.
E-mail: kristiemaher@sd-discovery.com
Web Site: www.sd-discovery.com
Key Personnel: C.E.O., Kristie Maher; Pres. (V), Lynn Beck; Educational Dir., Sue
   Douglas; Special Programs, Anne Lewis; Museum Shop Mgr., Uncle Matt;
   Community Wellness Coord., Danette Jarzab.
Institution Type/Description: Science Museum.
Hours & Admission Prices: Memorial Day-Labor Day Mon.-Sat. 10-5, Sun. 1-5.
   Winter Sun.-Fri. 1-5, Sat. 10-5. Adults $4, children $3; discounts to AAA,
   ASTC members, museum members & groups. Closed New Year's Day; Good
   Friday; Easter; Thanksgiving; Christmas Eve & Day.
Attendance: 20,000 (actual)

SOUTH DAKOTA NATIONAL GUARD MUSEUM, 301 E.
   Dakota Ave., Pierre, SD 57501-3225. Tel.: 605-224-9991.
E-mail: sonja.johnson@state.sd.us
Web Site: ngmuseum.sd.gov
Key Personnel: Dir., Sonja Johnson; Cur., Seb Axtman.
Institution Type/Description: Military Museum.
Hours & Admission Prices: Mon.-Fri. 9-4; other times by appointment. No charge;
   donations accepted. &
Attendance: 3,000 (actual)

SOUTH DAKOTA STATE ARCHIVES, 900 Governors Dr.,
   Pierre, SD 57501-2200. Tel.: 605-773-3458 & 3804. Fax: 605-773-
   6041.
E-mail: Archref@state.sd.us
Web Site: history.sd.gov
Key Personnel: State Archivist, Chelle Somsen; Archivist, Virginia Hanson;
   Archivist, Sara Casper; Archivist, Matthew Reitzel; Microfilm Supvr., Marcia
   Wickett; Research Room Admin., Ken Stewart.
Institution Type/Description: State Archives.
Hours & Admission Prices: Mon.-Fri. & first Sat. of month 9-4:30. No charge; don-
   ations accepted. Closed national & state holidays. &
Attendance: 5,200 (actual)

SOUTH DAKOTA STATE CAPITOL, 500 E. Capitol, Pierre, SD
   57501. Tel.: 605-773-3688. Fax: 605-773-3887.
Institution Type/Description: Historic Building: built in 1910.
Hours & Admission Prices: Mon.-Fri. 8-7, Sat.-Sun. & holidays 8-5.

SOUTH DAKOTA STATE HISTORICAL SOCIETY, 900
   Governors Dr., Pierre, SD 57501-2200. Mailing Address: Cultural
   Heritage Center, 900 Governors Dr., Pierre, SD 57501-2217. Tel.:
   605-773-3458. Fax: 605-773-6041.
E-mail: Jay.Smith@state.sd.us
Web Site: history.sd.gov
Key Personnel: Museum Dir., Jay S. Smith.
Institution Type/Description: State Historical Society.
Hours & Admission Prices: Memorial Day to Labor Day Mon.-Sat. 9-6:30, Sun. 1-
   4:30; Sept.-May Mon.-Sat. 9-4:30, Sun. 1-4:30. Adults $4, senior citizens 60 &
   over $3; discounts to AAM members; members no charge. Closed New Year's
   Day; Easter; Thanksgiving; Christmas. &
Attendance: 19,899 (actual)

Pine Ridge

THE HERITAGE CENTER, 100 Mission Dr., Pine Ridge, SD
   57770-2100. Tel.: 605-867-5491. Fax: 605-867-1291.
E-mail: heritagecenter@redcloudschool.org
Web Site: www.redcloudschool.org
Key Personnel: Dir., Jose Rivera; Pres. (V), Rev. Peter Klink, S.J.; Cur., Mary
   Maxon; Museum Shop Mgr., James Star Comes Out.
Institution Type/Description: Native American Art Museum: housed in c.1888 Holy
   Rosary Mission, scene of battle the day after the Wounded Knee Massacre.
Hours & Admission Prices: Memorial Day to Labor Day Mon.-Sat. 8-6, Sun. & hol-
   idays 10-5; Sept.-May Tues.-Sat. 9-6. No charge; donations requested. &
Attendance: 12,000 (estimated)

Pollock

POLLOCK VISITORS/INTERPRETIVE CENTER, 110 Main
   St., Pollock, SD 57648. Mailing Address: P.O. Box 142, Pollock,
   SD 57648-0057. Tel.: 605-889-2450.
Key Personnel: Chm. (V), Delores Kluckman; Museum Shop Mgr., Vina LaFave.
Institution Type/Description: Interpretive Center.

Hours & Admission Prices: Mon.-Tues. & Fri. 9-4, Sat. 12:30-4. No charge; donations accepted. &
Attendance: 250 (estimated)

Rapid City

BEAR COUNTRY U.S.A., 13820 South Hwy. 16, Rapid City, SD 57702-6581. Tel.: 605-343-2290. Fax: 605-341-3206.
E-mail: pabear@bearcountryusa.com
Web Site: www.bearcountryusa.com
Key Personnel: Owner/Operator, Pauline Casey.
Institution Type/Description: Zoo. Drive-through Wildlife Park.
Hours & Admission Prices: May & Sept.-Oct. daily 9-4; June-Aug. daily 8-6; Nov. daily 9-3; groups of 15 or more by appointment. Adults $16, seniors 62 & over and military adult $13, children 5-12 $10, military child $7; discount to groups; children 4 & under no charge. &

BLACK HILLS REPTILE GARDENS, INC., 8955 S. Hwy. 16, Rapid City, SD 57702. Mailing Address: P.O. Box 620, Rapid City, SD 57709-0620. Tel.: 605-342-5873.
E-mail: joe-m@reptilegardens.com
Web Site: www.reptilegardens.com
Key Personnel: Pres. & C.E.O., Joe Maierhauser; Gen. Mgr. & Vice Pres., Tom Lang; Head Cur. Reptiles, Ken Earnest; Sales Mgr., Jeff Oldham; Public Rels. Dir., John Brockelsby.
Institution Type/Description: Reptile Museum.
Hours & Admission Prices: Spring & Fall: daily 9-4. Adults $12.50, senior citizens $11.50, children 5-12 $8.50. Summer: daily 8-6. Adults $17, senior citizens $15, children 5-12 $11. Winter: 9-3. Adults & seniors $9.50, children $6.50. Discount to groups; children 4 & under no charge. &
Attendance: 500,000

DAHL ARTS CENTER, 713 7th St., Rapid City, SD 57701-3695. Tel.: 605-394-4101. Fax: 605-394-6121.
E-mail: contact@thedahl.org
Web Site: www.thedahl.org
Key Personnel: Exec. Dir., Pepper S. Massey; Pres., RCAC Bd. Dirs. & Chm. (V), Debra Radley; Museum Shop Mgr., Kathi Maxson.
Institution Type/Description: Community Arts Center.
Hours & Admission Prices: Mon.-Fri. 10-6, Sat. 10-5. No charge; donations accepted. Closed major holidays. &
Attendance: 63,000 (estimated)

THE JOURNEY MUSEUM, 222 New York St., Rapid City, SD 57701-1199. Tel.: 605-394-1277. Fax: 605-394-6940.
E-mail: pchristie@journeymuseum.org
Web Site: www.journeymuseum.org
Key Personnel: Dir., Troy Kilpatrick; CEO & Facilities Mgr., Peg Christie; Chm. (V), Jim Green.
Institution Type/Description: Regional history museum with emphasis on Native Americans & pioneers.
Hours & Admission Prices: Summer: daily 9-5; Winter: Mon.-Sat. 10-5, Sun. 1-5. Adults $10, seniors 62 & over and college students and military with ID $8, students $7; children 5 & under and members no charge. &
Attendance: 31,896 (estimated)

MOTION UNLIMITED MUSEUM & CLASSIC CAR LOT, 6180 S. Hwy. 79, Rapid City, SD 57702-8467. Tel.: 605-348-7373.
E-mail: happymotoring@bluebottle.com
Web Site: www.motionunlimitedmuseum.com
Key Personnel: Owner, Bill Napoli; Owner, Peggy Napoli.
Institution Type/Description: Automobile, Motorcycle, & Toy Museum.
Hours & Admission Prices: May-Oct. Mon.-Fri. 9-6, Sat. 9-4, Sun. by appointment. Adults $5; discounts to members and AAM & ICOM members; active military and children 12 & under no charge. Closed New Year's Day; Easter; Independence Day; Thanksgiving; Christmas. &
Attendance: 1,500 (actual)

MUSEUM OF GEOLOGY, SOUTH DAKOTA SCHOOL OF MINES AND TECHNOLOGY, 501 E. St. Joseph, Rapid City, SD 57701-3901. Tel.: 605-394-2467. Facebook: @SDSMTGeoMuseum.
E-mail: museum@sdsmt.edu
Web Site: museum.sdsmt.edu
Key Personnel: Pres., Dr. James Rankin; Provost, Dr. Demitris Kouris; Dir., Dr. Laurie C. Anderson; Assoc. Dir., Sally Shelton; Asst. Dir., Danielle Serratos; Laboratory Mgr., Kelsie Abrams; Cur., Dr. Darrin Pagnac; Cur., Maribeth Price; Cur. Emeritus, James Fox; Program Asst., Samantha Hustoft.
Institution Type/Description: Science Museum.

Hours & Admission Prices: Summer (Memorial Day to Labor Day): Mon.-Sat. 9-6; Winter: Mon.-Sat. 9-4. No charge; donations accepted. Closed holidays. &
Attendance: 26,000 (actual)

SIOUX INDIAN MUSEUM, 222 New York St., Rapid City, SD 57701-1199. Tel.: 605-394-2381. Fax: 605-348-6182.
E-mail: sim@journeymuseum.org
Web Site: www.journeymuseum.org
Institution Type/Description: Indian Art Museum.
Hours & Admission Prices: mid-Jan. to May & Sept.-Dec. Mon.-Sat. 10-5, Sun. 1-5; Memorial Day-Labor Day daily 9-6. Museum: adults 18-61 $8, seniors 62 & over $6.90, students 11-17 & college students $5.75; discounts to groups. Planetarium: adults 18-61 $5.75, seniors 62 & over $4.60, students 11-17 $3.45, children 10 & under $2; discounts to school groups. Closed New Year's Day; Easter; Thanksgiving; Christmas. &
Attendance: 45,000 (estimated)

Redfield

REDFIELD'S HISTORIC CHICAGO AND NORTHWESTERN RR DEPOT, 715 3rd St. W., Redfield, SD 57469-1173. Tel.: 605-472-4566.
E-mail: cnwhistoricrrdepot@redfield.com
Key Personnel: Chm. (V), Pres. (V) & Museum Shop Mgr., Kathy Maddox.
Institution Type/Description: History Museum: housed in the restored C&NW Depot built in 1914.
Hours & Admission Prices: May 15-Nov. 1 Thurs.-Sun. 1-5; other times by appointment. No charge; donations accepted. &
Attendance: 1,115 (estimated)

SPINK COUNTY HISTORICAL SOCIETY, Courthouse Square, 225 E. 8th Ave., Redfield, SD 57469. Mailing Address: 213 E. 2nd St., Redfield, SD 57469. Tel.: 605-472-0758.
E-mail: info@spinkcountyhistory.com
Web Site: www.spinkcountysdhistory.com
Key Personnel: Treas., Jerry Hansen; Pres. (V), Clay Yeoman.
Institution Type/Description: History Museum.
Hours & Admission Prices: June-Aug. Thurs.-Sun. 1-5. No charge; donations accepted. &
Attendance: 300 (estimated)

Roslyn

INTERNATIONAL VINEGAR MUSEUM, 502 Main St., Roslyn, SD 57261. Mailing Address: P.O. Box 201, Roslyn, SD 57261-0201. Tel.: 605-486-0075. Facebook: International Vinegar Museum.
E-mail: museum@internationalvinegarmuseum.com
Web Site: internationalvinegarmuseum.com
Key Personnel: Chm. (V), Richard Snaza; Museum Shop Mgr., Mary Wagner.
Institution Type/Description: Vinegar Museum.
Hours & Admission Prices: June to Labor Day Thurs.-Sat. 10-6. Adults $2.
Attendance: 1,500 (estimated)

Saint Francis

BUECHEL MEMORIAL LAKOTA MUSEUM, St. Francis Mission, 350 S. Oak St. on Rosebud Reservation, Saint Francis, SD 57572. Mailing Address: P.O. Box 499, Saint Francis, SD 57572-0499. Tel.: 605-747-2745. Fax: 605-747-2361.
E-mail: museum@gwtc.net
Web Site: www.sfmission.org/museum
Key Personnel: Dir., Fr. John Hatcher, S.J.; Museum Shop Mgr., Marie Kills In Sight.
Institution Type/Description: Lakota Indian Museum.
Hours & Admission Prices: Memorial Day to Labor Day Mon.-Thurs. & Sat. 8-5, Fri. 8-2:30, Sun. 10-4. No charge; donations accepted. Closed holidays.
Attendance: 3,600 (actual)

Scotland

SCOTLAND HERITAGE CHAPEL & MUSEUM, 811 6th St., Scotland, SD 57059. Mailing Address: 351 4th St., Scotland, SD 57059-2112. Tel.: 605-583-4568, 2507 & 4144.
E-mail: tlkluthe@gwtc.net
Key Personnel: Dir., Marvin Thum; Pres. (V), Linda Kluthe; Vice Pres., Betty Woehl; Treas., Lori Schmidt; Sec., Theresa Sedlacek.
Institution Type/Description: Local History Museum: housed in c.1874 Methodist & Siemantal Churches.

Hours & Admission Prices: Summer: holidays & special occasions; other times by appointment. No charge; donations accepted. &
Attendance: 75 (estimated)

Sioux Falls

BATTLESHIP SOUTH DAKOTA MEMORIAL, Sherman Park, 12th St. & Kiwanis Ave., Sioux Falls, SD 57101. Mailing Address: Sioux Falls Parks & Recreation Dept., 100 E. 6th St., Sioux Falls, SD 57104. Tel.: 605-367-7141.
E-mail: info@usssouthdakota.com
Web Site: www.usssouthdakota.com
Key Personnel: Pres., Diane Diekman.
Institution Type/Description: Military & Nautical Museum.
Hours & Admission Prices: June-Sept. daily 9:30-5:30. No charge; donations accepted.
Attendance: 10,000 (estimated)

BUTTERFLY HOUSE & MARINE COVE, 4320 Oxbow Ave., Sioux Falls, SD 57106-4110. Tel.: 605-334-9466. Fax: 605-334-9662.
E-mail: audrey@marinecove.org
Web Site: butterflyhousemarinecove.org
Key Personnel: C.E.O., Audrey Willard.
Institution Type/Description: Butterfly House & Aquarium.
Hours & Admission Prices: Mon.-Sat. 10-5, Sun. 11-5. Adults 13-59 $10, seniors 60 & over $9, youth 3-12 $7; children 2 & under no charge. Closed Easter; Thanksgiving; Christmas. &

THE CENTER FOR WESTERN STUDIES, Augustana College, 2121 S. Summit, Sioux Falls, SD 57197. Mailing Address: 2001 S. Summit Ave., Sioux Falls, SD 57197. Tel.: 605-274-4007. Fax: 605-274-4999. Facebook: Center for Western Studies; Twitter: AugieCWS.
E-mail: cws@augie.edu
Web Site: www.augie.edu/cws/
Key Personnel: Exec. Dir., Dr. Harry F. Thompson; Office Coord., Kari Mahowald; Chm. (V), Stan Christopherson; Education Asst., Kristi Thomas; Collections Asst., Liz Cisar.
Institution Type/Description: Cultural, Research & Archival Agency.
Hours & Admission Prices: Mon.-Fri. 8-5, Sat. 10-2. No charge; donations accepted. Closed Independence Day; Christmas. &
Attendance: 7,000 (estimated)

EIDE-DALRYMPLE ART GALLERY, Augustana University, 30th St., & Grange Ave., Sioux Falls, SD 57197. Mailing Address: Augustana College, 2001 S. Summit Ave., Sioux Falls, SD 57197. Tel.: 605-274-4609. Fax: 605-274-5323.
E-mail: lindsay.twa@augie.edu
Web Site: www.augie.edu/gallery
Key Personnel: Dir., Lindsay Twa.
Institution Type/Description: Art Gallery.
Hours & Admission Prices: Mon.-Fri. 10-5, Sat. 12-5. No charge. Closed major holidays.
Attendance: 3,000 (estimated)

GREAT PLAINS ZOO & DELBRIDGE MUSEUM OF NATURAL HISTORY, 805 S. Kiwanis Ave., Sioux Falls, SD 57104-3798. Tel.: 605-367-7003. Fax: 605-367-8340.
E-mail: dsimon@gpzoo.org
Web Site: greatzoo.org
Key Personnel: C.E.O. & Pres., Elizabeth Whealy; Vice Pres. Operations, Dan Simon; Mgr. Guest Svcs., Bridget Nilges; Dir. Animal Programs, Lisa Smith.
Institution Type/Description: Zoo & Natural History Museum.
Hours & Admission Prices: April-Sept. daily 9-6; Oct.-March daily 10-4. Adults $11, seniors $10, youth $8; children under 2, zoo & museum members no charge. Closed New Year's Day; Thanksgiving; Christmas. &
Attendance: 286,337 (actual)

MUSEUM OF VISUAL MATERIALS, 500 N. Main Ave., Sioux Falls, SD 57104-5902. Tel.: 605-271-9500. Fax: 605-271-4793. Facebook; Twitter.
E-mail: miranda@sfmvm.com
Web Site: www.sfmvm.com
Key Personnel: Pres. (V), Keith Huber; Exec. Dir., Miranda Ochocki.
Institution Type/Description: Arts and Crafts Museum.
Hours & Admission Prices: Mon.-Wed. 9-4. No charge; donations accepted. &
Attendance: 16,000 (estimated)

OLD COURTHOUSE MUSEUM, 200 W. 6th St., Sioux Falls, SD 57104-6001. Tel.: 605-367-4210, ext. 0. Fax: 605-367-6004. Facebook: Old Courthouse Museum, Sioux Falls, SD.
E-mail: museum@minnehahacounty.org
Web Site: www.siouxlandmuseums.com
Formerly: Siouxland Heritage Museums
Key Personnel: Dir., William J. Hoskins; Mktg. Coord., Adam Nelson; Cur. Education, Kevin Gansz; Cur. Exhibits, Molly Engquist; Cur. Collections, Kari Kohlhoff; Events Coord., Accountant & Museum Shop Mgr., Staci Peters.
Institution Type/Description: General Museums: housed in 1889 The Pettigrew Home & Museum; housed in 1890 The Old Courthouse Museum.
Hours & Admission Prices: Old Courthouse Museum: Mon.-Wed. & Fri. 8-5, Thurs. 8-9, Sat. 9-5, Sun. 12-5. Pettigrew Home and Museum: May-Sept. Mon.-Wed. & Fri.-Sat. 9-5, Thurs, 9-9, Sun. 12-5; Oct.-April daily 12-5. No charge; donations accepted. Closed for major holidays. &
Attendance: 42,405 (actual)

PETTIGREW HOME AND MUSEUM, 131 N. Duluth, Sioux Falls, SD 57104. Mailing Address: 200 W. 6th St., Sioux Falls, SD 57104-6001. Tel.: 605-367-7097. Facebook: Pettigrew Home and Museum.
E-mail: museum@minnehahacounty.org
Web Site: www.siouxlandmuseums.com
Key Personnel: Dir., Bill Hoskins.
Institution Type/Description: Historic House Museum: c.1889 home of South Dakota's first senator, Richard Pettigrew.
Hours & Admission Prices: May-Sept. Mon.-Sat. 9-5, Sun. 12-5; Oct.-April daily 12-5. No charge; donations accepted. Closed major holidays. &
Attendance: 7,931 (actual)

SIOUX COUNCIL SCOUTERS ATTIC MUSEUM, 800 N. West Ave., Sioux Falls, SD 57104-5720. Tel.: 605-361-2697. Fax: 605-361-2381.
E-mail: sioux.council@scouting.org
Web Site: www.siouxbsa.org
Key Personnel: Pres., Kathy Thorson.
Institution Type/Description: History Museum.
Hours & Admission Prices: Mon. & Wed.-Fri. 9-6, Tues. 9-8, Sat. 9-3. No charge. &

SIOUX EMPIRE MEDICAL MUSEUM, 1305 W. 18th St., Sioux Falls, SD 57117-5039. Mailing Address: Box 5039, 1305 W. 18th St., Sioux Falls, SD 57117-5039. Tel.: 605-333-6397.
Key Personnel: Chm. History Museum Committee, Thenetta Nield; Co-Chm. (V), Carol Turgeon.
Institution Type/Description: Medical Museum.
Hours & Admission Prices: Mon.-Fri. 11-4. No charge. Closed major holidays. &
Attendance: 3,500 (actual)

WASHINGTON PAVILION OF ARTS AND SCIENCE, 301 S. Main Ave., Sioux Falls, SD 57104-6311. Tel.: 605-367-7397, ext. 2306. Fax: 605-367-7399.
E-mail: info@washingtonpavilion.org
Web Site: www.washingtonpavilion.org
Formerly: Visual Arts Center at the Washington Pavilion
Key Personnel: Pres., Darrin Smith; Dir., Visual Arts Center, Jason Folkerts; Dir. Community Learning Center, Rose Ann Hofland; Dir., Mktg. & Public Relations, Rebecca Sevening.
Institution Type/Description: Children's Museum.
Hours & Admission Prices: See website for hours & admission prices. &
Attendance: 41,392 (actual)

Spearfish

D.C. BOOTH HISTORIC NATIONAL FISH HATCHERY AND ARCHIVE, 423 Hatchery Circle, Spearfish, SD 57783-2643. Tel.: 605-642-7730, ext. 0. Fax: 605-642-2336.
E-mail: dcbooth@fws.gov
Web Site: dcbooth.fws.gov
Formerly: Spearfish Station, Spearfish National Fish Hatchery
Key Personnel: Exec. Dir., April Gregory; Asst. Dir., Anna Hanson.
Institution Type/Description: Historic Fisheries Museum: housed in a fish hatchery building; built in 1899. Listed on the National Register of Historic Places.
Hours & Admission Prices: Grounds: daily dawn to dusk. Fish Car Museum & Booth House & Fish Car: mid-May to Sept. 9-5. No charge; donations accepted. Group tour charge. &
Attendance: 150,000 (estimated)

DOLLS AT HOME MUSEUM, 435 Meier Ave., Spearfish, SD 57783-1977. Mailing Address: P.O. Box 987, Spearfish, SD 57783-0489. Tel.: 605-642-2471.
E-mail: bhpp@blackhills.com
Key Personnel: Dir. & Pres. (V), Johanna Della Vecchia; Cur. & Museum Shop Mgr., Sonya Albers.
Institution Type/Description: Doll Museum.
Hours & Admission Prices: Memorial Day to Labor Day by appointment. Season pass $10, adults $5, children $2.50; members no charge. &
Attendance: 500 (estimated)

HIGH PLAINS WESTERN HERITAGE CENTER, 825 Heritage Dr., Spearfish, SD 57783. Mailing Address: P.O. Box 524, Spearfish, SD 57783-0524. Tel.: 605-642-9378.
E-mail: info@westernheritagecenter.com
Web Site: www.westernheritagecenter.com
Key Personnel: Exec. Dir., Peggy Ables.
Institution Type/Description: History Museum.
Hours & Admission Prices: Daily 9-5. Adults 17-61 $7, seniors 62 & over $5, youth 6-16 $3.

Sturgis

BEAR BUTTE STATE PARK VISITORS CENTER, 20250 Hwy. 79, Sturgis, SD 57785. Mailing Address: P.O. Box 688, Sturgis, SD 57785-0688. Tel.: 605-347-5240. Fax: 605-347-7627.
E-mail: BearButte@state.sd.us
Web Site: gfp.sd.gov/state-parks/directory.bear-butte/
Key Personnel: Park Mgr., Jim Jandreau.
Institution Type/Description: State Park Visitors Center Museum: located on a Native American traditional religious site.
Hours & Admission Prices: Park: 8:30-5:30. Visitors Center: May to Sept. daily 9-6. Car $6, annual sticker $30. &
Attendance: 15,000

STURGIS MOTORCYCLE MUSEUM AND HALL OF FAME, 999 Main St., Sturgis, SD 57785-1620. Mailing Address: P.O. Box 602, Sturgis, SD 57785-0602. Tel.: 605-347-2001. Fax: 605-720-0632. Facebook: Sturgis Motorcycle Museum and Hall of Fame.
E-mail: info@sturgismuseum.com
Web Site: www.sturgismuseum.com
Key Personnel: Exec. Dir., Christine Paige Diers; Pres. (V), Craig Bailey; Museum Shop Mgr., Arlene Colaiacovo.
Institution Type/Description: Motorcycle Museum.
Hours & Admission Prices: Daily call for hours. One adult $10, 2 adults $15, discounts for seniors; members & children 12 & under no charge. Closed New Year's Day; Easter; Thanksgiving; Christmas. &
Attendance: 32,000 (actual)

Timber Lake

TIMBER LAKE AND AREA HISTORICAL SOCIETY, 800 Main St., Timber Lake, SD 57656. Mailing Address: P.O. Box 181, Timber Lake, SD 57656-0181. Tel.: 605-865-3553 & 3546.
E-mail: timberlakemuseum@yahoo.com
Web Site: www.timberlakehistory.org
Institution Type/Description: Historical Society Museum.
Hours & Admission Prices: By appointment.

Vermillion

AUSTIN-WHITTEMORE HOUSE MUSEUM, 15 Austin Ave., Vermillion, SD 57069-3055. Tel.: 605-624-8266.
E-mail: claycohistory@yahoo.com
Web Site: www.cchssd.org
Institution Type/Description: Historic House.
Hours & Admission Prices: Memorial Day to Labor Day Mon.-Fri. 10-4:30, Sat.-Sun. by appointment. No charge; donations accepted.

NATIONAL MUSIC MUSEUM, Clark & Yale Sts., Vermillion, SD 57069-2390. Mailing Address: 414 E. Clark St., Vermillion, SD 57069-2390. Tel.: 605-677-5306. Fax: 605-677-6995.
E-mail: nmm@usd.edu
Web Site: www.nmmusd.org
Formerly: Shrine To Music Museum
Key Personnel: Dir., Dr. Cleveland Johnson; Chm. (V), Tom Lillibridge; Conservator, John Koster; Sr. Cur., Dr. Margaret Downie Banks; Cur., Dr. Sabine Klaus; Cur., Arian Sheets; Cur. Education, Dr. Deborah Check Reeves;

Cur. Asst., Julie Boston; Cur. Asst., Micky Rasmussen; Collections Mgr., Rodger Kelly; Dir. Visitor Svcs., Vicky Lenz; Program Asst., Debra Schultz.
Institution Type/Description: Musical Instrument Museum.
Hours & Admission Prices: Mon.-Sat. 9-5, Sun. 2-5. Adults $10; discounts to AAM & ICOM members; members no charge. Closed New Year's Day; Easter; Thanksgiving; Christmas. &
Attendance: 12,803 (actual)

UNIVERSITY ART GALLERIES, Warren M. Lee Center, University of South Dakota, 414 E. Clark, Vermillion, SD 57069-2307. Tel.: 605-677-3177. Fax: 605-677-5988.
E-mail: alison.erazmus@usd.edu
Web Site: www.usd.edu/uag
Key Personnel: Dir., Alison Erazmus.
Institution Type/Description: Art Gallery.
Hours & Admission Prices: Main Gallery: Mon.-Fri. 8-5, Sat.-Sun. 1-5. Oscar Howe Gallery: Mon.-Sat. 1-5. No charge. Closed major holidays. &
Attendance: 20,000 (estimated)

W.H. OVER MUSEUM, 1110 University, Vermillion, SD 57069. Mailing Address: 414 E. Clark, Vermillion, SD 57069-2307. Tel.: 605-659-6151. Facebook.
E-mail: whover@usd.edu
Web Site: www.usd.edu/whover
Key Personnel: Pres. (V), Larry Bradley.
Institution Type/Description: Natural & Cultural History.
Hours & Admission Prices: Mon.-Sat. 10-4. No charge; donations accepted. Closed major holidays. &
Attendance: 12,416 (actual)

Volga

BROOKINGS COUNTY HISTORICAL SOCIETY MUSEUM, 207 Samara Ave., Volga, SD 57071. Mailing Address: P.O. Box 872, Brookings, SD 57006-0872. Tel.: 605-690-2140.
E-mail: wagner3540@brookings.net
Key Personnel: Chm. & Pres. (V), Harold Christianson; Vice Chm., Jerry Leslie; Bd. Member, Kristin Heismeyer; Sec., Robert Buchheim; Treas., Phillip Wagner; Bd. Member, Dorothy Husher; Bd. Member, Chuck Cecil; Bd. Member, Donald Kleinjan; Bd. Member, Lyle Strande; Bd. Member, Deanna Rude; Bd. Member, Grace Linn; Bd. Member, Dick Berreth; Bd. Member, Marvin Steinbeck; Bd. Member, Cynthia Jacobson; Bd. Member, Darla Strande.
Institution Type/Description: Local History Museum.
Hours & Admission Prices: Memorial Day to Labor Day daily 1-4 & by appointment. No charge; donations accepted. &
Attendance: 4,300 (estimated)

Wall

WOUNDED KNEE MUSEUM, 207 10th Ave., Wall, SD 57790. Mailing Address: PMB 348, Wall, SD 57790. Tel.: 605-279-2573.
E-mail: info@woundedkneemuseum.org
Web Site: www.woundedkneemuseum.org
Institution Type/Description: History Museum.
Hours & Admission Prices: May-Oct. 12 daily 9-5; groups by appointment. Adults $6; children under 12 no charge. &

Watertown

BRAMBLE PARK ZOO, 800 10th St., N.W., Watertown, SD 57201. Mailing Address: P.O. Box 910, Watertown, SD 57201-0910. Tel.: 605-882-6269. Fax: 605-882-5232.
E-mail: dmiller@watertownsd.us
Web Site: brambleparkzoo.com
Key Personnel: C.E.O. & Dir., Dan D. Miller; Pres., Will Morlock; Cur., Jim Lloyd; Education, Jaime Stricker; Museum Shop Mgr., Kim Konard.
Institution Type/Description: Zoo.
Hours & Admission Prices: Summer: daily 10-7; Winter: daily 10-4 (weather permitting). Adults $8, children 3-12 $6; discounts to AZA members; members & children under 3 no charge. Closed New Year's Day; Thanksgiving; Christmas. &
Attendance: 70,447 (actual)

CODINGTON COUNTY HERITAGE MUSEUM, 27 First Ave., S.E., Watertown, SD 57201-3612. Tel.: 605-886-7335. Facebook: Codington County Heritage Museum.
E-mail: christy@cchsmuseum.org
Web Site: www.cchsmuseum.org
Key Personnel: Exec. Dir., Christy Lickei; Pres., Roger Whittle.

Institution Type/Description: Local County History Museum: housed in c.1905-06 Carnegie Library Building.
Hours & Admission Prices: June-Aug. Mon.-Fri. 10-5, Sat. 1-5; Sept.-May Mon.-Fri. & 2nd Sun. each month 1-5. No charge; donations accepted. Closed holidays.
Attendance: 5,500 (estimated)

MELLETTE HOUSE, 421 Fifth Ave., N.W., Watertown, SD 57201. Mailing Address: 900 S. Lake Dr., Watertown, SD 57201-5460. Tel.: 605-886-4730.
E-mail: info@mellettehouse.org
Web Site: www.mellettehouse.org
Key Personnel: Pres. (V), Prudence K. Calvin; Treas. & Sec., Ann Edelman.
Institution Type/Description: Historic House: 1885 Mellette House, home of Arthur Calvin Mellette, first Governor of South Dakota.
Hours & Admission Prices: May-Oct. Tues.-Sun. 1-5. No charge; donations accepted.
Attendance: 2,750 (estimated)

REDLIN ART CENTER, 1200 Mickelson Dr., Ste. 314, Watertown, SD 57201-7261. Tel.: 605-882-3877. Fax: 605-882-3922.
E-mail: redlinac@redlinart.com
Web Site: www.redlinart.com
Key Personnel: Exec. Dir., Julie Ranum.
Institution Type/Description: Art Center.
Hours & Admission Prices: Mon.-Fri. 9-5, Sat. 10-4, Sun. 12-4. No charge. &

Webster

MUSEUM OF WILDLIFE, SCIENCE & INDUSTRY, 760 W. Hwy. 12, Webster, SD 57274-2212. Mailing Address: P.O. Box 235, Webster, SD 57274-0235. Tel.: 605-345-4751.
E-mail: info@sdmuseum.org
Web Site: www.sdmuseum.org
Key Personnel: Pres., Jim Rood; Cur., Elaine Gilbertson.
Institution Type/Description: General Museum.
Hours & Admission Prices: May 15-Labor Day Mon.-Sat. 10-5, Sun. 1-5; Labor Day-Oct. 15 daily 1-5; other times by appointment. Suggested donation $5.
Attendance: 1,600 (actual)

Wessington Springs

JERAULD COUNTY PIONEER MUSEUM, 105 Main St., Wessington Springs, SD 57382. Mailing Address: P.O. Box 363, Wessington Springs, SD 57382-0132. Tel.: 605-539-9211.
Key Personnel: Pres. (V), Judy Winegar.
Institution Type/Description: History Museum.
Hours & Admission Prices: April-Dec. Thurs. 9:30-12 & 1-4:30, Fri. 1-3:30; other times by appointment. No charge; donations accepted.
Attendance: 350 (estimated)

Winner

TRIPP COUNTY HISTORICAL SOCIETY MUSEUM, E. Hwy. 18, Winner, SD 57580. Mailing Address: P.O. Box 287, Winner, SD 57580-0287. Tel.: 605-842-0704 & 0647.
E-mail: gjbowar@gwtc.net
Key Personnel: Dir., Steve Davis.
Institution Type/Description: Historical Society Museum.
Hours & Admission Prices: Memorial Day to Labor Day Wed.-Sun. 2-5. No charge; donations accepted. &
Attendance: 500 (estimated)

Yankton

BEDE ART GALLERY, Mount Mary College, Art Office, 1105 W. 8th St., Yankton, SD 57078-3725. Tel.: 605-668-1574.
E-mail: dkahle@mtmc.edu
Web Site: www.mtmc.edu
Key Personnel: Dir., David Kahle.
Institution Type/Description: Art Gallery.
Hours & Admission Prices: Mon.-Fri. 8-8. No charge. &
Attendance: 10,000 (estimated)

DAKOTA TERRITORIAL MUSEUM, 82 Mickelson Dr., Yankton, SD 57078. Tel.: 605-665-3898. Facebook; Twitter.
E-mail: director@dakotaterritorialmuseum.org
Web Site: www.dakotaterritorialmuseum.org
Key Personnel: Dir., Crystal Nelson; Mktg., Laura Beall; Museum Shop Mgr., Heidi Henson.

Institution Type/Description: Historical Society Museum.
Hours & Admission Prices: May-Sept. Thurs.-Tues. 10-6; Oct.-April Mon.-Tues. & Thurs.-Fri. 10-4, Sat.-Sun. 1-5. Adults $8, seniors & children 5-18 $5. Closed New Year's Eve & Day; Good Friday; Easter; Thanksgiving; Christmas Eve & Day. &
Attendance: 5,780 (estimated)

GAVINS POINT NATIONAL FISH HATCHERY AND AQUARIUM, 31227 436th Ave., Yankton, SD 57078-6364. Tel.: 605-665-3352. Fax: 605-665-3360.
E-mail: r6ffa_gav@fws.gov
Web Site: www.fws.gov/gavinspoint
Key Personnel: Project Leader, Marc Jackson.
Institution Type/Description: Aquarium.
Hours & Admission Prices: Aquarium: April-Oct. daily 10-4. Hatchery: daily 8-4; guided group tours by appointment. No charge; donations accepted. &
Attendance: 110,000 (actual)

TENNESSEE

(316 listings)

Adamsville

BUFORD PUSSER HOME & MUSEUM, 342 Pusser St., Adamsville, TN 38310-2338. Mailing Address: P.O. Box 301, Adamsville, TN 38310. Tel.: 731-632-4080. Fax: 731-632-4085.
E-mail: info@bufordpussermuseum.com
Web Site: www.bufordpussermuseum.com
Key Personnel: Cur., Renee Moss.
Institution Type/Description: Historic House Museum.
Hours & Admission Prices: May-Oct. Mon.-Fri. 10-5, Sat. 9-5, Sun. 1-5; Nov.-April Mon.-Fri. 11-4, Sat. 9-4, Sun. 1-4.
Attendance: 4,680 (actual)

COON CREEK SCIENCE CENTER, 2985 Hardin Graveyard Rd., Adamsville, TN 38310. Tel.: 901-636-2320 & 2362. Fax: 731-632-4850.
Institution Type/Description: Science Center.
Hours & Admission Prices: By appointment to groups only.

Alamo

TENNESSEE SAFARI PARK, 618 Conley Rd., Alamo, TN 38001-4106. Tel.: 731-696-4423.
E-mail: info@tennesseesafaripark.com
Web Site: www.tennesseesafaripark.com
Key Personnel: Park Mgr., Claude Conley.
Institution Type/Description: Zoo.
Hours & Admission Prices: early Spring to late Fall Mon.-Sat. 10-4:30 (last car going through), Sun. 12-4:30 (last car going through); Winter: call for hours. Adults $16, children 2-12 $12; children one & under no charge.

Athens

MCMINN COUNTY LIVING HERITAGE MUSEUM, 522 W. Madison Ave., Athens, TN 37303. Mailing Address: P.O. Box 889, Athens, TN 37371-0889. Tel.: 423-745-0329 & 744-8100. Fax: 423-745-0329.
E-mail: livingheritagemuseum@livingheritagemuseum.com
Web Site: www.livingheritagemuseum.com
Key Personnel: Exec. Dir., Diane Hutsell; Museum Shop Mgr., Robin Muller.
Institution Type/Description: History Museum.
Hours & Admission Prices: Tues.-Fri. 10-5, Sat. 10-4. Adults $5, seniors & students $3; discounts to AAA & AAM members; members no charge. Closed New Year's Day; Easter; Memorial Day; Independence Day; Labor Day; Thanksgiving; Christmas. &
Attendance: 22,000 (actual)

SWIFT MUSEUM, McMinn County Airport, 223 County Rd. 552, Athens, TN 37303. Mailing Address: P.O. Box 644, Athens, TN 37371. Tel.: 423-745-9547. Fax: 423-745-9869.
E-mail: swiftmuseumfoundation@aol.com
Web Site: www.swiftmuseumfoundation.org
Key Personnel: Exec. Dir., Scott Anderson.
Institution Type/Description: History Museum.
Hours & Admission Prices: Mon.-Fri. 9-5 or by appointment. No charge; donations accepted.

Bartlett

DAVIES MANOR PLANTATION, 3570 Davieshire Dr., Bartlett, TN 38133. Tel.: 901-386-0715. Fax: 901-388-4677.
E-mail: daviesmanorassoc@bellsouth.net
Web Site: daviesmanorplantation.org
Key Personnel: Dir., Andrew Ross.
Institution Type/Description: Historic House: log cabin built c.1830. Listed on the National Register of Historic Places. Designation on TN Civil War Trail.
Hours & Admission Prices: April to mid-Dec. Tues.-Sat. 12-4. Adults $5, seniors $4, students $3; children under 6 and active military no charge.
Attendance: 1,000 (estimated)

Belvidere

MUSEUM OF POWER & INDUSTRY AT FALLS MILL, 134 Falls Mill Rd., Belvidere, TN 37306-2225. Tel.: 931-469-7161. Fax: 931-469-7161.
E-mail: fallsmill@tnco.net
Web Site: www.fallsmill.com
Key Personnel: Owner, John Lovett; Owner, Jane Lovett.
Institution Type/Description: Historic Building: an operating water-powered grain mill; built in 1873. Listed on the National Register of Historic Places.
Hours & Admission Prices: mid-Jan. to Dec. 23 Mon.-Tues. & Thurs.-Sat. 9-4, Sun. 12:30-4. Adults $5, senior citizens $4, children under 14 $3. Closed Thanksgiving.

Benton

NANCY WARD MUSEUM - POLK COUNTY HISTORICAL AND GENEALOGICAL SOCIETY, Commerce & Poplar Sts., Benton, TN 37307. Mailing Address: P.O. Box 636, Benton, TN 37307. Tel.: 423-338-1005.
E-mail: presswood@comcast.net
Web Site: www.pchgs.com
Institution Type/Description: Historical Society Museum.
Hours & Admission Prices: Call for hours.

Blountville

OLD DEERY INN AND MUSEUM, 3411 Hwy. 126, Blountville, TN 37617. Mailing Address: P.O. Box 3179, Blountville, TN 37617. Tel.: 423-323-4660.
E-mail: info@sullivancountytn.gov
Web Site: www.historicsullivan.com
Key Personnel: Dir., Shelia Hunt; Pres., Dennis Houser.
Institution Type/Description: Historic Building: built in c.1801 by William Deery.
Hours & Admission Prices: Mon.-Fri. 8-4:30. Adults $5, children $3.
Attendance: 2,000 (estimated)

Bristol

ERNIE FORD HOME & MUSEUM, 1223 Anderson St., Bristol, TN 37620. Mailing Address: P.O. Box 204, Bristol, TN 37621. Tel.: 423-989-4850.
E-mail: bha@bristolhistoricalassociation.com
Web Site: www.bristolhistoricalassociation
Key Personnel: Chm. (V), Brenda Otis; Museum Shop Mgr., Brenda Otis.
Institution Type/Description: Historic House Museum: housed in the birthplace of Ernie Ford; c.1900.
Hours & Admission Prices: By appointment. Adults $3.
Attendance: 100 (estimated)

NATURE CENTER AT STEELE CREEK PARK, 80 Lake Shore Dr., Bristol, TN 37620. Tel.: 423-989-5616.
E-mail: jstout@bristoltn.org
Web Site: www.bristoltn.org/540/steele-creek-nature-center
Institution Type/Description: Nature Center.
Hours & Admission Prices: Nature Center: Memorial Day to Labor Day Mon.-Sat. 11-6, Sun. 1-6; Sept.-May Mon.-Sat. 11-5, Sun. 1-5. Park: daily 9-9. Park Entrance: $1 per car.

Brownsville

JOHN ESTES HOUSE, 121 Sunny Hill Cove, Brownsville, TN 38012-8367. Tel.: 731-779-9000.
E-mail: info@westtnheritage.com
Web Site: www.westtnheritage.com
Institution Type/Description: Historic House Museum: housed in the former home of blues legend, John Adam Estes.

Hours & Admission Prices: Call for hours. No charge; donations accepted.
Attendance: 20,000 (actual)

Bulls Gap

ARCHIE CAMPBELL TOURISM COMPLEX AND MUSEUM, 139 S. Main St., Bulls Gap, TN 37711. Mailing Address: P.O. Box 181, Bulls Gap, TN 37711. Tel.: 423-235-5216.
Institution Type/Description: History Museum: housed in the childhood home of Hee-Haw star, Archie Campbell.
Hours & Admission Prices: By appointment.

Burns

CUMBERLAND PRESBYTERIAN CHURCH BIRTHPLACE SHRINE, Montgomery Bell State Park, Burns, TN 37029. Mailing Address: 8207 Traditional Place, Cordova, TN 38016-7414. Tel.: 901-276-8602. Fax: 901-272-3913.
E-mail: archives@cumberland.org
Web Site: www.cumberland.org/hfcpc/
Key Personnel: Dir. & C.E.O., Susan Knight Gore.
Institution Type/Description: Historic Shrine: located in Montgomery Bell State Park, Dickson, Tennessee.
Hours & Admission Prices: Daily 8-6. No charge.

Butler

BUTLER MUSEUM, 123 Selma Curtis Rd., Butler, TN 37640. Tel.: 423-768-3880.
E-mail: the@thehaleyenterprises.com
Web Site: www.thebutlermuseum.com
Institution Type/Description: History Museum.
Hours & Admission Prices: Memorial Day to Labor Day Sat.-Sun. 1-4; other times by appointment. Adults $3, children $2.

Byrdstown

BORDERLANDS EXHIBIT, 1005 Livingston Hwy., Byrdstown, TN 38549. Tel.: 931-864-7195, 888-406-4704.
E-mail: info@theborderlands.org
Key Personnel: Chm. (V), Billy Robbins.
Institution Type/Description: History Museum.
Hours & Admission Prices: Mon.-Fri. 8-4, Sat. 8-2. No charge; donations accepted.
Attendance: 850 (estimated)

CORDELL HULL BIRTHPLACE & MUSEUM STATE HISTORIC PARK, 1300 Cordell Hill Memorial Dr., Byrdstown, TN 38549-4627. Tel.: 931-864-3247.
E-mail: david.delk@tn.gov
Web Site: www.cordellhullmuseum.com
Institution Type/Description: History Museum: birthplace of Cordell Hull, appointed Secretary of State by President Franklin D. Roosevelt.
Hours & Admission Prices: Memorial Day to Labor Day daily 9-5; Sept.-May daily 9-4:30. No charge. Call the park for closings.
Attendance: 86,400 (actual)

Camden

TENNESSEE RIVER FRESHWATER PEARL MUSEUM FARM TOUR, Birdsong Resort, Marina & Campground, 255 Marina Rd., Camden, TN 38320-7832. Tel.: 731-584-7880, ext. 1 (Bookings). Fax: 731-584-3625.
E-mail: bob@birdsongresort.com
Web Site: www.tennesseeriverpearls.com
Formerly: A Pearl of a Tour
Key Personnel: Owner & Tour Guide, Bob Keast.
Institution Type/Description: General Museum.
Hours & Admission Prices: Museum: by appointment. Office: daily 9-6. Full Tour: adults $59.50. Mini Tour: adults $39.50.
Attendance: 250,000 (actual)

Carthage

SMITH COUNTY HERITAGE MUSEUM, 107 3rd St., Carthage, TN 37030-1472. Mailing Address: P.O. Box 195, Carthage, TN 37030. Tel.: 615-735-1104.
E-mail: heritagemuseum@dtccom.net
Web Site: www.smithcountyheritagemuseum.org

Institution Type/Description: History Museum.
Hours & Admission Prices: Fri.-Sat. 10-2. No charge.

Castalian Springs

CRAGFONT-HISTORIC CRAGFONT, INC., 200 Cragfont Rd., Castalian Springs, TN 37031-4743. Mailing Address: 1011 Durham Dr., Gallatin, TN 37066-3411. Tel.: 615-452-7070.
E-mail: carlene.fox.iflh@statefarm.com
Web Site: www.cragfont.net
Key Personnel: C.E.O., Mrs. Carlene Fox; Chm. Restoration, Mrs. James Gourley; Cur., Mr. Lowell Fayna.
Institution Type/Description: Historic House Museum: c.1798-1802 home of General James Winchester.
Hours & Admission Prices: April-Oct. Tues.-Sat. 10-4, Sun. 1-4; Nov.-March by appointment. Adults $5, children 6-12 $3; discounts to seniors & groups; members & children under 6 no charge. &
Attendance: 4,850 (estimated)

Celina

CLAY COUNTY MUSEUM, INC., 805 Brown St., Celina, TN 38551. Mailing Address: P.O. Box 684, Celina, TN 38551. Tel.: 931-243-4220.
Key Personnel: Pres., Mary Loyd Reneau.
Institution Type/Description: History Museum.
Hours & Admission Prices: Call for hours. No charge; donations accepted. &

Centerville

GRINDER'S SWITCH CENTER, 405 W. Public Sq., Centerville, TN 37033-1606. Mailing Address: c/o Hickman County Chamber of Commerce, P.O. Box 126, Centerville, TN 37033. Tel.: 931-729-5774.
Institution Type/Description: History Museum.
Hours & Admission Prices: Call for hours.

Chattanooga

BESSIE SMITH CULTURAL CENTER, 200 E. Martin Luther King Blvd., Chattanooga, TN 37403. Mailing Address: P.O. Box 11493, Chattanooga, TN 37401-2493. Tel.: 423-266-8658 & 267-1628. Fax: 423-267-1076.
E-mail: info@bessiesmithcc.org
Web Site: www.bessiesmithcc.org
Formerly: Chattanooga African Museum/Bessie Smith Hall
Key Personnel: Pres., Dionne Jennings; Dir. Operations, Paula Wilkes; Program Coord., Marty Mitchell.
Institution Type/Description: African-American History Museum.
Hours & Admission Prices: Mon.-Fri. 10-5, Sat. 12-4. Adults $7, seniors & students with I.D. $5, children 6-12 $3; discounts to groups, and AAM & NAAM members; children 5 & under no charge. Closed national & legal holidays. &
Attendance: 156,000 (actual)

CHATTANOOGA AFRICAN AMERICAN MUSEUM, 200 E. Martin Luther King Jr. Blvd., Chattanooga, TN 37403. Mailing Address: P.O. Box 11493, Chattanooga, TN 37401. Tel.: 423-266-8658.
Institution Type/Description: History Museum.
Hours & Admission Prices: Mon.-Fri. 10-5, Sat. 12-4.

CHATTANOOGA HISTORY CENTER CLOSED, 2 W. Aquarium Way, Ste. 200, Chattanooga, TN 37402. Mailing Address: P.O. Box 4464, Chattanooga, TN 37405-0464. Tel.: 423-265-3247. Fax: 423-266-9280.
E-mail: mp@chattanoogahistory.org
Web Site: www.chattanoogahistory.org
Institution Type/Description: Regional History Museum.
Hours & Admission Prices: Office: Mon.-Fri. 9-5. &

CHATTANOOGA ZOO, 301 N. Holtzclaw Ave., Chattanooga, TN 37404-2823. Tel.: 423-697-1322. Fax: 423-697-1329. Facebook: Chatt Zoo; Instagram & Twitter @chattanoogazoo.
E-mail: info@chattzoo.org
Web Site: www.chattzoo.org
Formerly: Warner Park Zoo
Key Personnel: C.E.O., Dardenelle Long.
Institution Type/Description: Zoo.

Hours & Admission Prices: Daily 9-5. Adults $12.95, seniors $10.95, children $9.95; discounts to military/veterans & AZA members; members and children 2 & under no charge. Closed New Year's Day; Thanksgiving; Christmas. &
Attendance: 207,000 (actual)

CREATIVE DISCOVERY MUSEUM, 321 Chestnut St., Chattanooga, TN 37402-4902. Mailing Address: P.O. Box 6339, Chattanooga, TN 37401-6339. Tel.: 423-756-2738. Fax: 423-267-9344.
E-mail: info@cdmfun.org
Web Site: www.cdmfun.org
Key Personnel: Exec. Dir., Henry H. Schulson; Exec. Asst., Sherri Hinton; Dir. Opers & Exhibits, Duane Rousseau; Dir. Education, Jayne Griffin.
Institution Type/Description: Children's Museum.
Hours & Admission Prices: Daily 10-5. Adults $15.95, military with ID $9.95; members no charge. Closed Thanksgiving; Christmas Eve & Day. &
Attendance: 206,323 (actual)

CRESS GALLERY OF ART, 752 Vine St., Chattanooga, TN 37403. Mailing Address: University of Tennessee at Chattanooga, 615 McCallie Ave., #1301, Chattanooga, TN 37403-2504. Tel.: 423-304-9789. Fax: 423-425-2101.
E-mail: ruth-grover@utc.edu
Web Site: www.cressgallery.org
Key Personnel: Dir. & Cur., Ruth Grover.
Institution Type/Description: Art Institute.
Hours & Admission Prices: Sept.-May Mon.-Fri. 9:30-7:30, Sat.-Sun. 1-4. No charge. Closed university holidays. &
Attendance: 6,500 (estimated)

HOUSTON MUSEUM OF DECORATIVE ARTS, 201 High St., Chattanooga, TN 37403-1185. Tel.: 423-267-7176.
E-mail: houstonmuseumchattanooga@gmail.com
Web Site: thehoustonmuseum.org
Key Personnel: Pres. (V), Clare Hetzler; Dir., Amy Autenreith.
Institution Type/Description: Antique Museum: housed in 1890 building. Decorative Arts Museum.
Hours & Admission Prices: Wed.-Sat. & first Sun of the month 12-4. Adults $9, children 4-17 $3.50; discounts to AAM members; children under 3 & members no charge. Closed major holidays.
Attendance: 10,000 (estimated)

HUNTER MUSEUM OF AMERICAN ART, 10 Bluff View, Chattanooga, TN 37403-1197. Tel.: 423-267-0968. Fax: 423-267-9844.
E-mail: membership@huntermuseum.org
Web Site: www.huntermuseum.org
Key Personnel: Exec. Dir., Virginia Anne Sharber.
Institution Type/Description: Art Museum: housed in a restored mansion.
Hours & Admission Prices: Mon.-Tues. & Fri.-Sat. 10-5, Wed. & Sun. 12-5, Thurs. 10-8. Adults $15, youth 3-17 $7.50; discounts to AAM & ICOM members; children under 3, members, military & their families, National Guard & Reserve no charge. North American reciprocal admission. &
Attendance: 57,182 (actual)

INTERNATIONAL TOWING & RECOVERY HALL OF FAME & MUSEUM, 3315 S. Broad St., Chattanooga, TN 37408-3052. Tel.: 423-267-3132.
E-mail: internationaltowingmuseum@comcast.net
Web Site: www.internationaltowingmuseum.org
Key Personnel: Pres., Bill Gratzianna.
Institution Type/Description: History Museum.
Hours & Admission Prices: March-Oct. Mon.-Sat. 9-5, Sun. 11-5; Nov.-Feb. Mon.-Sat. 10-4:30, Sun. 11-5. Adults $8, seniors 55 & over $7, children 6-18 $4; discounts to AAA members; children under 5 no charge. Closed major holidays.

NATIONAL MEDAL OF HONOR MUSEUM OF MILITARY HISTORY, 4900 Hixon Pike, Chattanooga, TN 37403. Mailing Address: P.O. Box 11467, Chattanooga, TN 37401-2467. Tel.: 423-877-2525 (museum) & 698-4511 (archives).
E-mail: info@mohm.org
Web Site: www.mohm.org
Formerly: Medal of Honor Museum
Key Personnel: Exec. Dir., Charles Googe; Chm. (V), Major General Bill Raines.
Institution Type/Description: History & Military Museum.
Hours & Admission Prices: Tues.-Fri. 11-5, Sat.-Sun. 1-5. No charge; donations accepted. Closed Easter; Independence Day; Thanksgiving; Christmas. &
Attendance: 6,500 (estimated)

REFLECTION RIDING ARBORETUM & NATURE CENTER,
400 Garden Rd., Chattanooga, TN 37419-1807. Tel.: 423-821-
1160, ext. 111. Fax: 423-821-1702.
E-mail: lazehnder@reflectionriding.org
Web Site: reflectionriding.org
Formerly: Chattanooga Arboretum & Nature Center
Key Personnel: Dir. Education, Corey Hagen; Educator & Facility Rentals, Susan
Russell; Dir. Wildlife, Tish Gailmard.
Institution Type/Description: Nature Center: located on Lookout Creek on the west-
ern side of Lookout Mountain, where the Battle of Lookout Mountain began;
now part of species survival program for endangered Red wolves & other ani-
mals indigenous to the southeast region.
Hours & Admission Prices: Tues.-Fri. 9:30-6:30, Sat.-Sun. 11-6:30. Adults $10,
children & senior citizens $7; members no charge. Closed New Year's Day;
Easter; Memorial Day; Independence Day; Labor Day; Thanksgiving;
Christmas. &
Attendance: 61,000 (estimated)

SISKIN MUSEUM OF RELIGIOUS AND CEREMONIAL ART,
1101 Carter St., Chattanooga, TN 37402-5017. Tel.: 423-648-1700.
Fax: 423-648-1749.
E-mail: linda.mcreynolds@siskin.org
Web Site: www.siskin.org/museum
Key Personnel: Chair, Mary Tanner; Dir. Devel. & Communications, Linda
McReynolds.
Institution Type/Description: Religious Museum.
Hours & Admission Prices: Mon.-Fri. 9-4; other times by appointment. No charge;
donations accepted. Closed New Year's Eve & Day; Christmas Eve, Day &
week; national holidays. &

TENNESSEE AQUARIUM, One Broad St., Chattanooga, TN
37402-1023. Tel.: 423-267-3474, 800-262-0695.
E-mail: webmaster@tnaqua.org
Web Site: www.tnaqua.org
Key Personnel: Pres. & C.E.O., Keith Sanford.
Institution Type/Description: Aquarium.
Hours & Admission Prices: Sun.-Thurs.: 9-5, Fri. & Sat. 9-6. Adults $34.95, chil-
dren 3-12 $21.95; children under 3 no charge. IMAX Theater: adults $11.95,
children 3-12 $9.95. Combination tickets available. Closed Thanksgiving;
Christmas. &
Attendance: 700,000 (estimated)

TENNESSEE VALLEY RAILROAD MUSEUM INC., 4119
Cromwell Rd., Chattanooga, TN 37421-2164. Tel.: 423-894-8028,
ext. 12. Fax: 423-894-8029. Facebook & Twitter: @tvrail.
E-mail: info@tvrail.com
Web Site: www.tvrail.com
Key Personnel: Gen. Mgr., George Walker; Museum Shop Mgr., Joyce Soule.
Institution Type/Description: Railroad Transportation Museum.
Hours & Admission Prices: Office: Mon.-Fri. 9-4:30. See Website for information
on excursions, events, exhibits and ticketing. &
Attendance: 80,000 (estimated)

Clarksville

**CLARKSVILLE-MONTGOMERY COUNTY MUSEUM DBA
CUSTOMS HOUSE MUSEUM & CULTURAL CENTER,** 200
S. Second St., Clarksville, TN 37040-3400. Mailing Address: P.O.
Box 383, Clarksville, TN 37041-0383. Tel.: 931-648-5780. Fax:
931-553-5179.
E-mail: info@customshousemuseum.org
Web Site: www.customshousemuseum.org
Key Personnel: Asst. Dir. & C.F.O., Linda Maki; Cur. Collections, Kali Mason;
Mktg. & Media Dir., Melinda Ludwig; Exhibit Preparator, Randall Spurgeon;
Cur. Education, Sue Lewis; Membership & Retail Sales Coord., Brittany
Morgan; Cur. Exhibits, Terri Jordan.
Institution Type/Description: General Museum: housed in c.1898 Post Office and
Customs House.
Hours & Admission Prices: Tues.-Sat. 10-5, Sun. 1-5. Adults $5, senior citizens $3,
college students $2, children 6-18 $1; discounts to AAM, ICOM, TAM, SEMC,
AAA & AARP members; members, children 5 and under & Sun. no charge.
Closed major holidays. &
Attendance: 35,000 (actual)

MARGARET FORT TRAHERN GALLERY, Dept of Art Austin
Peay State Univ., 601 College St., Clarksville, TN 37044. Tel.:
931-221-7333. Fax: 931-221-7432.
E-mail: dickinsm@apsu.edu
Web Site: www.apsu.edu/art/trahern-gallery
Key Personnel: Gallery Dir., Michael Dickens.

Institution Type/Description: University Art Gallery.
Hours & Admission Prices: Mon.-Fri. 9-4, Sat.-Sun. 1-4. No charge. Closed aca-
demic holidays. &
Attendance: 7,000

**SMITH TRAHERN MANSION HOME OF FAMILY AND
COMMUNITY EDUCATION,** 101 McClure St., Clarksville, TN
37040. Mailing Address: P.O. Box 852, Clarksville, TN 37041-
0852. Tel.: 931-648-9998.
E-mail: smithtrahern@hotmail.com
Institution Type/Description: Historic House Museum: housed in the home of tobac-
conist, Christopher Smith; built in 1858. Listed on the National Register of
Historic Places.
Hours & Admission Prices: Mon.-Fri. 9:30-2;30; other times by appointment.
Tours: $2.

Cleveland

MUSEUM CENTER AT 5IVE POINTS, 200 Inman St. E.,
Cleveland, TN 37311-6039. Tel.: 423-339-5745. Fax: 423-476-
7922.
E-mail: info@museumcenter.org
Web Site: www.museumcenter.org
Key Personnel: Janice Neyman; Creative Development, Mike Johnson; Curator of
Collections, Lindsay Shirkey; Curator of Education, Mitch Mizell; Museum
Shop Mgr., Katie Cortez.
Institution Type/Description: History Museum.
Hours & Admission Prices: Tues.-Fri. 10-5, Sat. 10-3. Adults $5; discounts to AAM
members; members no charge. &
Attendance: 25,000 (actual)

RED CLAY STATE HISTORIC PARK, 1140 Red Clay Park Rd.,
Cleveland, TN 37311. Tel.: 423-478-0339. Facebook: Red Clay
State Historic Park.
E-mail: erin.medley@tn.gov
Web Site: tnstateparks.com/parks/about/red-clay
Key Personnel: Park Mgr., Erin Medley.
Institution Type/Description: Historic Site Park: c.1832-38 seat of the Cherokee
government & site of eleven general councils national affairs.
Hours & Admission Prices: Daily 8-4:30. No charge; donations accepted. &
Attendance: 220,000 (actual)

Clifton

T.S. STRIBLING MUSEUM, 300 E. Water St., Clifton, TN 38425.
Mailing Address: c/o Clifton Library, P.O. Box 186, Clifton, TN
38425-0186. Tel.: 931-676-3678.
Web Site: www.cityofclifton.com
Institution Type/Description: Historic Site: housed in the former home of Pulitzer
Prize-winning author, T.S. Stribling.
Hours & Admission Prices: Tues.-Fri. 11:30-6.

Clinton

GREEN MCADOO CULTURAL CENTER & MUSEUM, 101
School St., Clinton, TN 37717. Mailing Address: P.O. Box 1214,
Clinton, TN 37717-1214. Tel.: 865-463-6500.
E-mail: marilynsue1@comcast.net
Web Site: www.greenmcadoo.org
Key Personnel: Dir., Marilyn Hayden.
Institution Type/Description: History Museum.
Hours & Admission Prices: Tues.-Sat. 10-5; groups by appointment.

MUSEUM OF APPALACHIA, 2819 Andersonville Hwy., Clinton,
TN 37716-6756. Mailing Address: P.O. Box 1189, Norris, TN
37828-1189. Tel.: 865-494-7680. Fax: 865-494-8957. Facebook:
Museum of Appalachia.
E-mail: museum@museumofappalachia.org
Web Site: www.museumofappalachia.org
Key Personnel: Pres., Elaine I. Meyer; Museum Shop Mgr., Samantha Kerley;
Chm. (V), Hon. Daryl Fansler.
Institution Type/Description: Historic Village and Folk Art Museum: village
includes over 30 restored pioneer log structures.
Hours & Admission Prices: Seasonal hours. Call for admission prices. &
Attendance: 100,000 (estimated)

Collegedale

LYNN H. WOOD ARCHAEOLOGICAL MUSEUM, Hackman Hall, 1st Fl., Southern Adventist Univ., Collegedale, TN 37315. Mailing Address: P.O. Box 370, Collegedale, TN 37315-0370. Tel.: 423-236-2030. Fax: 423-236-1977.
E-mail: museum@southern.edu
Institution Type/Description: Archaeological Museum.
Hours & Admission Prices: Sept.-April Mon.-Thurs. 9-12 & 1-5, Fri. 9-12, Sat.-Sun. 2-5. No charge. Closed university breaks & holidays.

Collierville

BIBLICAL RESOURCE CENTER & MUSEUM, 140 E. Mulberry St., Collierville, TN 38017-2675. Tel.: 901-854-9578. Fax: 901-854-9883. Facebook: Biblical Resource Center & Museum.
E-mail: info@biblical-museum.org
Web Site: www.biblical-museum.org
Key Personnel: Interim Dir., Don Bassett; Asst., Nancy Bassett; Dir. Education, Steve Truner.
Institution Type/Description: Religious & History Museum.
Hours & Admission Prices: Tues.-Sat. 10-5. Groups $3 per person; discounts to AAM & ICOM members. Closed major holidays. &
Attendance: 9,000 (actual)

MORTON MUSEUM OF COLLIERVILLE, 196 Main St., Collierville, TN 38017. Tel.: 901-457-2650. Fax: 901-457-2207. Facebook: Morton Museum of Collierville.
E-mail: museum@ci.collierville.tn.us
Web Site: colliervillemuseum.org
Key Personnel: Dir., Brooke Mundy.
Institution Type/Description: History Museum.
Hours & Admission Prices: Tues.-Sat. 10-4. No charge. Closed holidays. &
Attendance: 6,000 (actual)

Columbia

AMUSE'UM COLUMBIA CHILDREN'S MUSEUM, 123 W. 7th St., Columbia, TN 38401. Tel.: 931-223-6337. Facebook.
E-mail: columbiacm@hotmail.com
Web Site: amuseumcolumbia.org
Key Personnel: Exec. Dir., Maeghan Wall.
Institution Type/Description: Children's Museum.
Hours & Admission Prices: Mon.-Wed. & Fri. 9-2, Thurs. 9-6, Sat. 10-2. Admission $10 (includes one child & one adult, additional adult $5); children under one no charge.

PRESIDENT JAMES K. POLK HOME AND MUSEUM, 301 W. 7th St., Columbia, TN 38401-3132. Mailing Address: P.O. Box 741, Columbia, TN 38402-0741. Tel.: 931-388-2354. Fax: 931-388-5971.
E-mail: jameskpolk@bellsouth.net
Web Site: www.jameskpolk.com
Key Personnel: Dir., John C. Holtzapple; Pres. (V), Beth Sands.
Institution Type/Description: Historic House Museum: 1816 James K. Polk Ancestral Home.
Hours & Admission Prices: April-Oct. Mon.-Sat. 9-5, Sun. 1-5; Nov.-March Mon.-Sat. 9-4, Sun. 1-5. Adults $10, seniors 60 & up $8, youth 13-18 $7, childre 6-12 $5; discounts to groups & AAM members; members no charge. Closed New Year's Day; Thanksgiving; Christmas Eve & Day. &
Attendance: 11,937 (actual)

Cookeville

COOKEVILLE DEPOT MUSEUM, 116 N. Cedar Ave., Cookeville, TN 38501. Mailing Address: Dept. of Leisure Svcs., P. O. Box 998, Cookeville, TN 38503-0998. Tel.: 931-528-8570. Fax: 931-526-1167.
E-mail: depot@cookeville-tn.org
Web Site: www.cookevilledepot.com
Key Personnel: C.E.O. & Museums Admin., Judy Duke; Pres., John Buck.
Institution Type/Description: Transportation Museum: built in 1909 by the Tennessee Central Railroad, the Cookeville depot is highlighted by its unique pagoda roof line.
Hours & Admission Prices: Tues.-Sat. 10-4. No charge; donations accepted. Closed Good Friday; Memorial Day; Independence Day; Labor Day; Thanksgiving; Christmas Eve & Day. &
Attendance: 12,537 (estimated)

COOKEVILLE HISTORY MUSEUM, 40 E. Broad St., Cookeville, TN 38501-3210. Mailing Address: P.O. Box 998, Cookeville, 38503. Tel.: 931-520-5455.
E-mail: historymuseum@cookeville-tn.gov
Web Site: www.cookevillehistorymuseum.com
Institution Type/Description: History Museum.
Hours & Admission Prices: Wed.-Sat. 10-4. No charge; donations accepted. &
Attendance: 10,000 (estimated)

Cornersville

LAIRDLAND FARM HOUSE, 3238 Blackburn Hollow Rd., Cornersville, TN 37047-7001. Tel.: 931-363-2205.
E-mail: info@lairdlandfarmhouse.com
Web Site: www.lairdlandfarmhouse.com
Key Personnel: Dir., Bennita B. Rouleau; Chm. (V), Donald L. Rouleao.
Institution Type/Description: Historic House Museum: housed in the home of John Laird who received a 5,000 acre land grant from NC for his service during the Revolutionary War. Listed on the National Register of Historic Places.
Hours & Admission Prices: By appointment. Adults $12, students $5; children 8 & under no charge.
Attendance: 2,500 (estimated)

Covington

TIPTON COUNTY MUSEUM, VETERAN'S MEMORIAL & NATURE CENTER, 751 Bert Johnston Ave., Covington, TN 38019-2414. Mailing Address: P.O. Box 768, Covington, TN 38019-0768. Tel.: 901-476-0242. Fax: 901-476-0261. Facebook: Tipton County Museum.
E-mail: afisher@covingtontn.com
Web Site: www.tiptonco.com/museum.htm
Key Personnel: Dir., Barrie Foster; Program Coord., Elizabeth Newman.
Institution Type/Description: History Museum & Nature Center.
Hours & Admission Prices: Tues.-Fri. 9-5, Sat. 9-3. No charge. Closed major holidays. &
Attendance: 7,000 (actual)

Cowan

COWAN RAILROAD MUSEUM, 108 Front St., Cowan, TN 37318-0053. Mailing Address: P.O. Box 53, Cowan, TN 37318-0053. Tel.: 931-967-3078.
E-mail: secretary@cowanrailroadmuseum.org
Web Site: cowanrailroadmuseum.org
Institution Type/Description: Railroad Museum: housed in a former railroad depot, c.1904.
Hours & Admission Prices: May-Oct. Mon. & Thurs.-Sat. 10-4, Sun. 1-4; other times by appointment. No charge; donations accepted.

Cross Plains

CROSS PLAINS HERITAGE MUSEUM, LIBRARY & ARCHIVES, 7821 Hwy. 25 E., Cross Plains, TN 37049-4851. Tel.: 615-654-2228.
E-mail: nbellar@bellsouth.net
Institution Type/Description: History Museum.
Hours & Admission Prices: Thurs.-Fri. 10-2; other times by appointment. No charge.

Crossville

HOMESTEADS TOWER MUSEUM, 2611 Pigeon Ridge Rd., Crossville, TN 38555. Mailing Address: Cumberland Homesteads Tower Assoc., 96 Hwy. 68, Crossville, TN 38555. Tel.: 931-456-9663.
E-mail: kcox.tower@gmail.com
Web Site: www.cumberlandhomesteads.org
Institution Type/Description: Historic Building Museum: built in 1938.
Hours & Admission Prices: April-Oct. Mon.-Sat. 10-4. Adults $4, youth $2; children under 6 & members no charge.

MILITARY MEMORIAL MUSEUM, 20 S. Main St., Crossville, TN 38555-4518. Tel.: 931-456-5520.
E-mail: nitaboring@hotmail.com
Key Personnel: Dir., Nita M. Boring; Pres. (V), Sean A. Boring.
Institution Type/Description: Military History Museum.

Hours & Admission Prices: Mon.-Fri. 9-4; other times by appointment. No charge; donations accepted. &
Attendance: 2,473 (actual)

Cumberland Gap

LITTLE CONGRESS BICYCLE MUSEUM, 807 Llewellyn St., Cumberland Gap, TN 37724. Tel.: 423-869-9993. Facebook, Twitter.
Web Site: bicyclemuseum.net
Key Personnel: Cur., Judge R.E. McClanahan, II.
Institution Type/Description: Bicycle Museum
Hours & Admission Prices: Daily 8-8. No charge.

Dandridge

BUSH'S(R) VISITOR CENTER, 3901 US-411, Dandridge, TN 37725. Tel.: 865-509-3077. Facebook.
Web Site: bushbeans.com
Institution Type/Description: Company History Museum & Visitor Center.
Hours & Admission Prices: early April to early Nov. Mon.-Sat. 10-4; early Nov. to early April Mon.-Sat. 10-3. Closed New Year's Day; Memorial Day; Independence Day; Labor Day; Thanksgiving; Christmas Eve & Day.

JEFFERSON COUNTY MUSEUM & ARCHIVES, 202 W. Main St., Dandridge, TN 37725. Mailing Address: P.O. Box 1193, Dandrige, TN 37725. Tel.: 865-397-4904.
E-mail: archives@jeffersoncountytn.gov
Key Personnel: Museum Cur., Barbara Parsons.
Institution Type/Description: History Museum: housed in a courthouse; built in 1845.
Hours & Admission Prices: Call for hours. No charge.
Attendance: 1,000 (estimated)

Dickson

CLEMENT RAILROAD HOTEL MUSEUM, 100 Frank Clement Place, Dickson, TN 37055. Mailing Address: P.O. Box 306, Dickson, TN 37056-0306. Tel.: 615-446-0500. Facebook: com/crhmdickson.
E-mail: execdirector@clementrailroadmuseum.org
Web Site: clementrailroadmuseum.org
Key Personnel: Pres., Darrell James.
Institution Type/Description: Historic Building Museum: built in 1913. Listed on the National Register of Historic Places.
Hours & Admission Prices: Tues.-Fri. 9-5, Sat. 9-4. Adults $4, seniors 50 & over and students 15 & over $2; children 14 & under no charge. &
Attendance: 12,000 (estimated)

Dover

FORT DONELSON NATIONAL BATTLEFIELD, 120 Fort Donelson Rd., Dover, TN 37058. Mailing Address: P.O. Box 434, Dover, TN 37058-0434. Tel.: 931-232-5706 (Visitor Center) & 5348 (office). Fax: 931-232-6331.
E-mail: fodo_ranger_activities@nps.gov
Web Site: www.nps.gov/fodo
Key Personnel: Supt., Brian McCutchen; Chief Interpreter & Resource Mgr., Douglas J. Richardson.
Institution Type/Description: National Battlefield Museum.
Hours & Admission Prices: Office: Mon.-Fri. 8-4:30. Visitor Center: daily 8-4:30. No charge; donations accepted. Closed New Year's Day; Thanksgiving; Christmas. &
Attendance: 483,614 (actual)

Ducktown

DUCKTOWN BASIN MUSEUM, 212 Burra Burra St., Ducktown, TN 37326. Mailing Address: P.O. Box 458, Ducktown, TN 37326-0458. Tel.: 423-496-5778.
E-mail: burrahill@ellijay.com
Web Site: ducktownbasinmuseum.com/contact
Key Personnel: Dir., Ken Rush.
Institution Type/Description: History Museum: housed on the Burra Burra mine site. Listed on the National Register of Historic Places.
Hours & Admission Prices: Jan.-March Tues.-Sat. 9:30-4; April-Oct. Mon.-Sat. 10-4:30; Nov.-Dec. Mon.-Sat. 9:30-4. Adults $5, seniors $4, children 13-17 $2, children 12 & under $1. Closed Thanksgiving; Christmas. &

Dunlap

DUNLAP COKE OVENS PARK AND MUSEUM, 114 Walnut St., Dunlap, TN 37327. Tel.: 423-949-3483.
E-mail: LeavesAndAcorns@bledsoe.net
Institution Type/Description: History Museum.
Hours & Admission Prices: By appointment.

Dyersburg

DYERSBURG STATE COMMUNITY COLLEGE - WALTER E. DAVID WILDLIFE MUSEUM, 1501 Lake Rd., Dyersburg, TN 38024. Tel.: 731-286-3200.
E-mail: wells@dscc.edu
Key Personnel: Dir., Dr. Karen Bowyer; Cur., Dr. Brian Wells.
Institution Type/Description: Wildlife Museum.
Hours & Admission Prices: Mon.-Fri. 8 am-9 pm. No charge.
Attendance: 350 (estimated)

Elizabethton

JOHN & LANDON CARTER MANSION, 1013 Broad St., Elizabethton, TN 37643. Mailing Address: Sycamore Shoals Parks, 1651 W. Elk Ave., Elizabethton, TN 37643. Tel.: 423-543-5808. www.tnstateparks.com/sycamoreshoals.
E-mail: jennifer.bauer@tn.gov
Web Site: www.sycamoreshoalstn.org
Key Personnel: Park Manager, Jennifer Bauer.
Institution Type/Description: Historic House Museum: built c.1780.
Hours & Admission Prices: Tours: Memorial Day to mid-Aug. daily 2 pm. No charge; donations accepted.
Attendance: 13,000 (estimated)

SYCAMORE SHOALS STATE HISTORIC AREA, 1651 W. Elk Ave., Elizabethton, TN 37643. Tel.: 423-543-5808. Fax: 423-543-0078.
E-mail: ask.tnstateparks@tn.gov
Web Site: www.sycamoreshoalstn.org
Key Personnel: Park Mgr., Jennifer Bauer.
Institution Type/Description: Park & Visitor Center.
Hours & Admission Prices: Center: Mon.-Sat. 8-4:30, Sun. 1-4:30. Park: sunrise to sunset. No charge; donations accepted. &
Attendance: 305,000 (actual)

Elkton

MATT GARDNER HOMESTEAD MUSEUM, 110 Dixon Town Rd., Elkton, TN 38455. Mailing Address: P.O. Box 269356, Indianapolis, IN 46226. Tel.: 931-309-9695.
E-mail: info@mattgardnerhomestead.org
Web Site: www.mattgardnerhomestead.org
Key Personnel: Pres. (V), Carla Jones.
Institution Type/Description: History Museum.
Hours & Admission Prices: 1st & 3rd Sat. 10-3; call to confirm. Adults $5, students & children 5-12 $3; children under 5 no charge.

Englewood

ENGLEWOOD TEXTILE MUSEUM, 17 N. Niota St., Englewood, TN 37329-3245. Mailing Address: P.O. Box 253, Englewood, TN 37329. Tel.: 423-887-5455.
Key Personnel: Dir. & Chm. (V), Mark Cochran; Museum Shop Mgr., Gail Anderson.
Institution Type/Description: History Museum.
Hours & Admission Prices: Mon.-Sat. 10-5. No charge; donations accepted. Closed major holidays. &
Attendance: 1,000 (estimated)

Erwin

UNICOI COUNTY HERITAGE MUSEUM, 529 Federal Hatchery Rd., Erwin, TN 37650. Mailing Address: Unicoi County Chamber of Commerce, P.O. Box 713, Erwin, TN 37650. Tel.: 423-743-9449 & 8923.
E-mail: amanda@unicoicounty.org
Web Site: www.unicoicounty.org
Institution Type/Description: History Museum: housed in an early 1900s home.
Hours & Admission Prices: May-Oct. & Dec. daily 1-5; other times by appointment.

Eva

TENNESSEE RIVER FOLKLIFE INTERPRETIVE CENTER AND MUSEUM, Nathan Bedford Forrest State Park, 1825 Pilot Knob Rd., Eva, TN 38333. Tel.: 731-584-6356. Fax: 731-584-1841.
Institution Type/Description: History Museum.
Hours & Admission Prices: Daily 8-11 & 12-4:30.

Fairview

BOWIE PARK & NATURE CENTER, 7211 Bowie Lake Rd., Fairview, TN 37062. Tel.: 615-799-5544.
E-mail: bowiepark@fairview-tn.org
Web Site: www.fairview-tn.org/bowie-park
Institution Type/Description: Nature Center.
Hours & Admission Prices: Mon.-Sat. 9-4, Sun. 11-4.

Farragut

FARRAGUT MUSEUM, 11408 Municipal Center Dr., Farragut, TN 37934-2830. Tel.: 865-966-7057. Fax: 865-675-2096.
E-mail: jbarham@townoffarragut.org
Web Site: www.townoffarragut.org/index.aspx?nid=186
Key Personnel: Historic Resources Coord., Julia Barham; Museum Shop Mgr., Carolyn Sinclair.
Institution Type/Description: History Museum.
Hours & Admission Prices: Mon.-Fri. 10-4:30. No charge; donations accepted. Closed New Year's week; Martin Luther King Jr. Day; Good Friday; Memorial Day; Independence Day; Labor Day; Thanksgiving & day after; Christmas week. &
Attendance: 4,590 (actual)

Fayetteville

FAYETTEVILLE LINCOLN COUNTY MUSEUM AND CIVIC CENTER, 521 Main St., S., Fayetteville, TN 37334-3447. Mailing Address: 2270 Lewisburg Hwy., Fayetteville, TN 37334-6449. Tel.: 931-433-2921.
E-mail: flcmuseum@gmail.com
Web Site: www.flcmuseum.org
Key Personnel: Board Pres., Jim Harwell, DVM; Board Vice-Pres., Farris Beasley, DVM; Board Member/Lincoln County Historian, Delbert Wicks.
Institution Type/Description: History Museum.
Hours & Admission Prices: May-Nov. Thurs.-Sat. 12:30-4:30.

Franklin

CARNTON PLANTATION, 1345 Eastern Flank Cir., Franklin, TN 37064-3259. Tel.: 615-794-0903. Fax: 615-794-6563.
E-mail: info@battleoffranklintrust.org
Web Site: www.carnton.org
Key Personnel: C.O.O. & Historian, Eric Jacobson; Special Events Coord., Leigh Bawcom; Office & Membership Coord., Angell Wallace; Cur., Joanna Stephens.
Institution Type/Description: Historic Site: 1826 Federal House and Outbuildings.
Hours & Admission Prices: Mon.-Sat. 9-5, Sun. 12-5; last tour at 4. Adults $15, seniors 65 & up $12, children 6-12 $8; discount to groups of 10 or more; children under 5 no charge.
Attendance: 45,000 (actual)

THE CARTER HOUSE, 1140 Columbia Ave., Franklin, TN 37064-3617. Tel.: 615-791-1861. Fax: 615-794-6563. Facebook: Carter House.
E-mail: info@battleoffranklintrust.org
Web Site: www.battleoffranklintrust.org
Institution Type/Description: Historic house; battlefield & museum. Listed on the National Register of Historic Places.
Hours & Admission Prices: Mon.-Sat. 9-5, Sun. 12-5. Adults $15, seniors $12, children 6-12 $8. Closed New Year's Day; Easter; Thanksgiving; Christmas Eve & Day.
Attendance: 45,000 (actual)

LOTZ HOUSE MUSEUM, 1111 Columbia Ave., Franklin, TN 37064. Tel.: 615-790-7190. Fax: 615-790-7197.
E-mail: info@lotzhouse.com
Web Site: www.lotzhouse.com
Key Personnel: Dir., J.T. Thompson.
Institution Type/Description: Historic House Museum.

Hours & Admission Prices: Mon.-Sat. 9-5, Sun. 1-4; other times by appointment. Adults $10, seniors 65 & over $9, children 7-13 $5; discounts to groups and AAM & ICOM members; children 6 & under no charge.

WILLIAMSON COUNTY ARCHIVES MUSEUM, 611 W. Main St., Franklin, TN 37064. Mailing Address: P.O. Box 1066, Franklin, TN 37065-1066. Tel.: 615-790-5462.
Institution Type/Description: Archives.
Hours & Admission Prices: Mon.-Fri. 8-4:30. No charge.

Gainesboro

JACKSON COUNTY HISTORICAL MUSEUM, Fred Lucas Haile Bldg., 105 Montpelier St., Gainesboro, TN 38562. Mailing Address: c/o Jackson County Historical Society, P.O. Box 647, Gainesboro, TN 38562.
E-mail: snoll@jchs.org
Web Site: jchs.org/home
Key Personnel: Steve Knoll.
Institution Type/Description: History Museum.
Hours & Admission Prices: Call for hours. No charge.

Gallatin

HISTORIC ROSE MONT, 810 S. Water Ave., Gallatin, TN 37066-3735. Tel.: 615-451-2331, 888-451-2331.
E-mail: historicrosemont@att.net
Web Site: www.historicrosemont.com
Key Personnel: Pres. (V), Linda Webster; Museum Shop Mgr., Erleen Blurton.
Institution Type/Description: Historic House Museum: housed in the former home of Judge Walter Guild and his wife Bettie Alexander Guild; built in 1842.
Hours & Admission Prices: April 15 to Oct. Tues.-Sat. 10-4, Sun. 1-4. Adults $5, seniors over 55 $4, children 6-12 $3; discounts to groups; children under 6 no charge. Closed holidays. &
Attendance: 5,000 (estimated)

SUMNER COUNTY MUSEUM, 183 W. Main St., Gallatin, TN 37066-3252. Mailing Address: P.O. Box 1163, Gallatin, TN 37066. Tel.: 615-451-3738. Fax: 651-451-0878.
E-mail: contact@sumnercountymuseum.org
Web Site: www.sumnercountymuseum.org
Key Personnel: Dir. & Museum Shop Mgr., Juanita Frazor; Cur., Allen Haynes; Chmn. (V), Nathan Shadowens.
Institution Type/Description: History Museum.
Hours & Admission Prices: April-Oct. Wed.-Sat. 9-4:30, Sun. 1-4:30. Adults $5, children 6-12 $3; members & children under 6 no charge donations accepted.
Attendance: 600 (estimated)

TENNESSEE AVIATION HALL OF FAME, 395 Devon Chase Hill, #101, Gallatin, TN 37066. Tel.: 615-452-3696.
E-mail: info@tnaviationhof.org
Web Site: www.tnaviationhof.org
Institution Type/Description: History Museum.
Hours & Admission Prices: Call for hours.

Gatlinburg

ARROWMONT SCHOOL OF ARTS & CRAFTS, 556 Parkway, Gatlinburg, TN 37738-3202. Mailing Address: P.O. Box 567, Gatlinburg, TN 37738-0567. Tel.: 865-436-5860. Fax: 865-430-4101.
E-mail: info@arrowmont.org
Web Site: www.arrowmont.org
Key Personnel: Exec. Dir., Bill May; Gallery Mgr., Kelly Hider; Dir. Finance, Julia Clinton; Supply Store Mgr., Kelly Sullivan; Dir. Programs, Nick DeFord; Dir. Devel., Fran Day; Coord. Mktg. Support, Laura Tuttle; Coord., Anne May; Dir. Facilities, Jeff Webb.
Institution Type/Description: Art Gallery.
Hours & Admission Prices: Mon.-Fri. 8:30-5; call for holiday & weekend hours. No charge; donations accepted. &
Attendance: 11,500 (estimated)

COOTER'S PLACE GATLINBURG, 542 Pkwy., Gatlinburg, TN 37738-3202. Tel.: 865-430-9909.
E-mail: info@cootersplace.com
Web Site: www.cootersplace.com
Institution Type/Description: History Museum.
Hours & Admission Prices: Call for hours. No charge.

GREAT SMOKY MOUNTAINS, SUGARLANDS VISITOR CENTER, Great Smoky Mountains National Park, 107 Park Headquarters Rd., Gatlinburg, TN 37738-4102. Tel.: 865-436-1200. Fax: 865-436-1220.
Web Site: www.nps.gov/grsm
Key Personnel: Supt., Cassius Cash.
Institution Type/Description: Park Museum.
Hours & Admission Prices: March & Nov. daily 8-5; April-May daily 8-6; June-Aug. daily 8-7:30; Sept.-Oct. 8-6:30; Dec.-Feb. daily 8-4:30. No charge; donations accepted. Closed Christmas. ⑂
Attendance: 874,393 (actual)

GUINNESS WORLD RECORDS MUSEUM, Baskins Square Mall, 631 Pkwy., Ste. B-11, Gatlinburg, TN 37738-3258. Tel.: 865-436-9100 & 430-7800.
E-mail: gatlinburg@ripleys.com
Web Site: www.ripleys.com/gatlinburg/guinness-world-records
Institution Type/Description: World Record Museum.
Hours & Admission Prices: Jan.-Feb. daily 11-8; March-May & Sept.-Dec. daily 10-9; Memorial Day to Labor Day daily 10am-11pm. Adults 12 & over $12.99, children 6-11 $7.99; children 5 & under no charge.

HOLLYWOOD STAR CARS MUSEUM, 914 Pkwy., Gatlinburg, TN 37738-3104. Tel.: 865-430-2200.
Web Site: www.starcarstn.com
Key Personnel: Owner, Charles Moore.
Institution Type/Description: Car Museum.
Hours & Admission Prices: Daily 9am to 11pm. Adult $12.99, children 6-12 $6.99 children under 6 no charge.

RIPLEY'S AQUARIUM OF THE SMOKIES, 88 River Rd., Gatlinburg, TN 37738. Tel.: 865-430-8808; 888-240-1358. Facebook, Twitter.
E-mail: aquariumofthesmokies@ripleys.com
Web Site: ripleyaquariums.com
Institution Type/Description: Aquarium & Museum.
Hours & Admission Prices: Jan.-Feb. Mon.-Thurs. 9-8, Fri.-Sun. 9 am-10 pm; March to May & Sept.-Dec. Mon.-Thurs. 9-9, Fri.-Sun. 9 am-10 pm; Memorial Day to Labor Day Mon.-Thurs. 9 am-10 pm, Fri.-Sun. 9 am-11 pm. Basic: adult $44.99, youth 6-11 $29.99, children 2-5 $12.99; children under 2 no charge.

RIPLEY'S BELIEVE IT OR NOT! ODDITORIUM, 800 Parkway, Gatlinburg, TN 37738. Mailing Address: 88 River Rd., Gatlinburg, TN 37738. Tel.: 865-436-5096. Fax: 865-436-4145.
E-mail: gatlinburg@ripleys.com
Web Site: www.ripleysgatlinburg.com
Institution Type/Description: General Museum.
Hours & Admission Prices: Daily 10-9. Adults 12 & over $16.99, children 3-11 $9.99; discounts to groups; children 2 & under no charge. ⑂

SALT AND PEPPER SHAKER MUSEUM, 461 Brookside Village Way, Gatlinburg, TN 37738-4706. Tel.: 865-430-5515.
Web Site: www.thesaltandpeppershakermuseum.com
Key Personnel: Owner, Andrea Ludden; Owner, Rolf Ludden.
Institution Type/Description: General Museum.
Hours & Admission Prices: Daily 10-4. Adults $3; children 12 & under no charge.

Germantown

GERMANTOWN REGIONAL HISTORY AND GENEALOGY CENTER (GRHGC), 7779 Poplar Pike, Germantown, TN 38138-5952. Tel.: 901-757-8480.
E-mail: jbaker@germantown-tn.gov
Web Site: germantown-library.org
Key Personnel: Dir., Melody Pittman; Chm. (V), Byron Crain.
Institution Type/Description: Library.
Hours & Admission Prices: Mon. 10-2, Tues. & Thurs. 10-4, Sat. 9-5. No charge; donations accepted. Closed New Year's Day; Martin Luther King Jr. Day; Presidents' Day; Easter; Memorial Day; Independence Day; Labor Day; Thanksgiving & day after; Christmas Eve & Day.
Attendance: 2,400 (estimated)

PT BOATS MUSEUM & ARCHIVES, 1384 Cordova Rd., Ste. 2, Germantown, TN 38138-2219. Mailing Address: P.O. Box 38070, Germantown, TN 38183-0070. Tel.: 901-755-8440. Fax: 901-751-0522.
E-mail: ptboats@ptboats.org
Web Site: www.ptboats.org
Formerly: The P.T. Boat Museum & Library

Key Personnel: C.E.O., Dir. & Treas., Alyce N. Guthrie; Pres. (V), Charles B. Jones; P.T. Boat Cur., Don Shannon; Administrative Asst., Allyson Bethune; Museum Shop Mgr., Rick Bethune.
Institution Type/Description: Maritime, Naval Museum: located at Battleship Cove.
Hours & Admission Prices: Battle Ship Cove: Spring to May 23 daily 9-4:30; Summer daily 9-5. Adults $17, seniors, AAM members & U.S. military veterans with ID $15, children 6-12 $10.50; active military with ID $8.50; discounts to AAA & HNSA members; children under 6 & military in uniform no charge. Group: adults $13.60, children 6-12 $8.40. Germantown Headquarters: Mon.-Thur. 8-4, Fri. 8-noon. Closed New Year's Day; Thanksgiving; Christmas
Attendance: 100,000 (estimated)

Goodlettsville

MANSKER'S STATION & BOWEN PLANTATION HOUSE, 705 Caldwell Dr., Moss Wright Park, Goodlettsville, TN 37072. Tel.: 615-851-2241. Fax: 615-859-4563.
Web Site: www.manskersstation.org
Key Personnel: Dir., Allison Baker.
Institution Type/Description: Historic Sites & Preservation Societies.
Hours & Admission Prices: Tours: Mon.-Fri. 9-12 & 1-4:30, last tour at 3:30. Adults $8; discounts to seniors, children under 12, AAM members & groups of 15 or more. Closed New Year's Day; Thanksgiving & day after; Christmas Eve & Day. ⑂
Attendance: 8,000 (estimated)

Grand Junction

NATIONAL BIRD DOG MUSEUM, 505 Hwy. 57, Grand Junction, TN 38039-6059. Mailing Address: P.O. Box 774, Grand Junction, TN 38039-0774. Tel.: 731-764-2058. Fax: 731-764-3004.
E-mail: sportdog@bellsouth.net
Web Site: www.birddogfoundation.com
Key Personnel: Exec. Dir., Tonya Brotherton; Sec., Renee Houston; Education Coord. & Librarian, Lucy Cogbill; Pres. (V), Don Driggers; Museum Shop Mgr., Ruth Pierce.
Institution Type/Description: General Museum.
Hours & Admission Prices: Tues.-Fri. 9-2, Sat. 10-4, Sun. 1-4. No charge; donations accepted. ⑂
Attendance: 6,000 (estimated)

Granville

GRANVILLE MUSEUM, INC., Clover St., Granville, TN 38564. Mailing Address: P.O. Box 26, Granville, TN 38564-0026. Tel.: 931-653-4511 & 4151. Fax: 615-443-7117.
E-mail: rclemons@wilsonbank.com
Web Site: www.granvilletn.com
Key Personnel: Dir. & Pres. (V), Randall Clemons; Treas., Greg High; Sec., Kaye Loftis; Archivist, Liz Bennett; Museum Shop Mgr., Brenda Curtis.
Institution Type/Description: History Museum.
Hours & Admission Prices: Museum & Homestead: Wed.-Fri. 12-3, Sat. 12-5; other times by appointment. Museum: no charge. Homestead: adults $5, seniors 62 & over $4, children 6-12 $3; children under 6 no charge. ⑂
Attendance: 9,000 (estimated)

Gray

EAST TENNESSEE STATE UNIVERSITY & GENERAL SHALE NATURAL HISTORY MUSEUM AND GRAY FOSSIL SITE, 1212 Suncrest Dr., Gray, TN 37615-4114. Tel.: 423-439-3659, 866-202-6223. Fax: 423-439-3658.
E-mail: grayfossilinfo@etsu.edu
Web Site: www.etsu.edu/naturalhistorymuseum
Key Personnel: Dir., Dr. Blaine Schubert; Museum Operations Mgr., April Season Nye.
Institution Type/Description: Natural History Museum.
Hours & Admission Prices: Daily 8:30-5. Gray Fossil Site Walk-in Tour: adults 5, seniors 65 & over $4, children 5-12 $3. All access Pass: adults $10, seniors 65 & over $9, children 5-12 $7. Closed New Year's Day; Thanksgiving; Christmas. ⑂
Attendance: 53,798 (actual)

Greeneville

ANDREW JOHNSON NATIONAL HISTORIC SITE, 101 N. College St., Greeneville, TN 37743-5607. Mailing Address: 121 Monument Ave., Greeneville, TN 37743-5552. Tel.: 423-638-3551 (Visitor Center) & 639-3711 (Admin.). Fax: 423-638-9194 (Visitor Center) & 798-0754 (Admin.).
Web Site: www.nps.gov/anjo/

Key Personnel: Supt., David C. Foster.
Institution Type/Description: History Museum and Historic Houses.
Hours & Admission Prices: Daily 9-5. No charge; donations accepted. Closed New Year's Day; Thanksgiving; Christmas. &
Attendance: 48,553 (actual)

DICKSON-WILLIAMS MANSION, 108 N. Irish St., Greeneville, TN 37743. Mailing Address: Dickson-Williams Historical Association, 1241 Tanglewood Dr., Greeneville, TN 37743. Tel.: 423-787-0500.
E-mail: director@mainstreetgreeneville.com
Web Site: www.mainstreetgreeneville.com
Key Personnel: Chm., Sarah E.T. Webster.
Institution Type/Description: Historic House Museum: housed in the home built by Irish immigrant William Dickson for his daughter Catherine and her husband Dr. Alexander Williams; built in 1821. The mansion served as headquarters for both Union and Confederate armies during the Civil War.
Hours & Admission Prices: Tours: daily 1pm; groups of 12 or more by appointment. Adults $10. Closed holidays.

DOAK HOUSE MUSEUM, Tusculum College, 690 Erwin Hwy., Greeneville, TN 37743. Mailing Address: Tusculum College, Dept. of Museum Prog. & Studies, P.O. Box 5026, Greeneville, TN 37743. Tel.: 423-636-8554 & 7348. Fax: 423-638-7166.
E-mail: clucas@tusculum.edu
Web Site: www.doakhouse.tusculum.edu
Key Personnel: Dir., Dollie Boyd.
Institution Type/Description: College Museum; located in the former home of Samuel W. Doak, founder of Tusculum College. Listed on the National Register of Historic Places.
Hours & Admission Prices: Mon.-Fri. 9-5; other times by appointment. Adults $5, children $2; discounts to groups & AAM members. Closed New Year's Eve & Day; Good Friday; Memorial Day; Independence Day; Labor Day; Thanksgiving Day & day after; Christmas Eve, Day & week; college breaks.
Attendance: 6,509 (actual)

GREENEVILLE GREENE COUNTY HISTORY MUSEUM, 101 W. McKee St., Greeneville, TN 37743-4813. Tel.: 423-636-1558.
E-mail: betty@themuseum.us
Web Site: www.greenevillegreenecountyhistorymuseum.com
Formerly: Nathanael Greene Museum
Key Personnel: Dir., Betty L. Fletcher; Pres. (V), Carla Bewley; Chm. (V), Barbara , Lawrence.
Institution Type/Description: Heritage Museum.
Hours & Admission Prices: Feb.-Dec. Tues.-Sat. 11-4. No charge; donations accepted. Closed holidays.
Attendance: 9,000 (actual)

PRESIDENT ANDREW JOHNSON MUSEUM AND LIBRARY, 57 Gilland St., Greeneville, TN 37743. Mailing Address: Tusculum College, P.O. Box 5026, Greeneville, TN 37743. Tel.: 423-636-7348. Fax: 423-638-7166. Facebook: President Andrew Johnson Museum and Library.
E-mail: dboyd@tusculum.edu
Web Site: ajmuseum.tusculum.edu
Key Personnel: Dir., Dollie Boyd; Site & Events Mgr., Leah Walker; Archivist, Kathy Cuff.
Institution Type/Description: Presidential Library: housed in 1841 college building. Listed on the National Register of Historic Places.
Hours & Admission Prices: Mon.-Fri. 9-5. No charge. Closed all Tusculum College holidays. &
Attendance: 2,800 (actual)

Halls

THE VETERANS' MUSEUM, 100 Veterans' Dr., Halls, TN 38040-1342. Tel.: 731-836-7400. Fax: 731-836-7400. Facebook: The Veterans Museum.
E-mail: vetmuseumhalls2@bellsouth.net
Web Site: www.dyaab.us
Key Personnel: Dir., Chm. (V) & Pres. (V), Patricia M. Higdon; Asst. Dir. & Museum Shop Mgr., Nancy Holman.
Institution Type/Description: Military History Museum.
Hours & Admission Prices: Mon.-Fri. 10-4, Sat.-Sun. 2-5. Adults $5, veterans & children under 12 $2. Closed all holidays. &
Attendance: 9,273 (actual)

Harrogate

ABRAHAM LINCOLN LIBRARY & MUSEUM, LINCOLN MEMORIAL UNIVERSITY, 6965 Cumberland Gap Pkwy., Harrogate, TN 37752. Mailing Address: P.O. Box 2006, Harrogate, TN 37752. Tel.: 423-869-6235. Fax: 423-869-6350.
E-mail: thomas.mackie@lmunet.edu
Web Site: lmunet.edu/museum
Key Personnel: Dir., Thomas Mackie; Cur. & Asst. Dir., Steven Wilson; Education Coord., Program & Tourism Dir., Carol Campbell; Museum Archivist, Michelle Ganz; Guest Svcs., Jonathan Smallwood; Admin. Asst., Barbara Garman.
Institution Type/Description: History Museum.
Hours & Admission Prices: March to late Nov. Mon.-Fri. 10-5, Sat. 12-5, Sun. 1-5; late Nov.-Feb. Mon.-Fri. 10-5, Sat. 12-5. Adults $5, senior citizens $3.50, children 6-12 $3; discounts to groups & AAA members; Lincoln Memorial University staff, students and faculty & children under 6 no charge. Closed New Year's Day; Easter; Thanksgiving; Christmas.
Attendance: 13,500 (actual)

Hartsville

LIVING HISTORY MUSEUM, 101 White Oak St., Hartsville, TN 37074. Mailing Address: Chamber of Commerce, 240 Broadway, Hartsville, TN 37074-1336. Tel.: 615-374-9243. Fax: 615-374-0068.
Web Site: www.hartsvilletrousdale.com
Key Personnel: Dir. Chamber of Commerce, Natalie Knatson; Chm. (V), John Oliver.
Institution Type/Description: History Museum.
Hours & Admission Prices: By appointment. No charge; donations accepted.
Attendance: 250 (estimated)

Hendersonville

HENDERSONVILLE ARTS COUNCIL, 1017 Antebellum Circle, Hendersonville, TN 37075. Mailing Address: P.O. Box 64, Hendersonville, TN 37077-0764. Tel.: 615-822-0789.
E-mail: artscouncil@monthaven.org
Web Site: www.hendersonvillearts.org
Key Personnel: Exec. Dir., Alexander Brindley.
Institution Type/Description: Art Gallery.
Hours & Admission Prices: Mon.-Fri. 9-3. No charge; donations accepted.

HISTORIC ROCK CASTLE, 139 Rock Castle Lane, Hendersonville, TN 37075-4522. Tel.: 615-824-5081. Facebook: Historic Rock Castle.
E-mail: info@historicrockcastle.com
Web Site: www.historicrockcastle.com
Key Personnel: Dir., Sara Beth Gideon.
Institution Type/Description: Historic House Museum.
Hours & Admission Prices: Feb.-Dec. Tues.-Sat. 10-5, Sun. 1-5. Adults $7, seniors $6, children $5; members no charge. Closed TN state holidays. &
Attendance: 12,000 (estimated)

OLD HICKORY LAKE VISITOR CENTER, No. 5 Power Plant Rd., Hendersonville, TN 37075-3467. Tel.: 615-822-4846 & 847-2395. Fax: 615-822-2743.
Web Site: www.lrn.usace.army.mil/op/old/rec/
Institution Type/Description: History Museum & Visitor Center.
Hours & Admission Prices: Mon.-Fri. 7:30-4:30. No charge.
Attendance: 8,729,003 (actual)

Henning

ALEX HALEY MUSEUM AND INTERPRETIVE CENTER, 535 Haley Ave., Henning, TN 38041-7420. Tel.: 731-738-2240. Fax: 731-738-2585.
Web Site: www.alexhaleymuseum.org
Key Personnel: Dir., Richard Griffin; Chm. (V), Phillis Barlow.
Institution Type/Description: Historic House Museum: housed in the boyhood home of renowned author & Pulitzer Prize winner, Alex Haley. Listed on the National Register of Historic Places.
Hours & Admission Prices: Tues.-Sat. 10-5, Sun. by appointment. Adults $6; members no charge. &
Attendance: 4,000 (estimated)

FORT PILLOW STATE HISTORIC PARK, 3122 Park Rd., Henning, TN 38041-5210. Tel.: 731-738-5581 & 5731. Fax: 731-738-9117.

E-mail: ask.tnstateparks@tn.gov
Web Site: tnstateparks.com/parks/about/fort-pillow
Institution Type/Description: History Museum.
Hours & Admission Prices: Park: daily 8am to sunset. Museum: daily 8-11:30 & 12:30-4. No charge. Closed Thanksgiving; Christmas Eve & Day.

Hermitage

THE HERMITAGE: HOME OF PRESIDENT ANDREW JACKSON, 4580 Rachel's Lane, Hermitage, TN 37076-1331. Tel.: 615-889-2941. Fax: 615-889-9909.
E-mail: info@thehermitage.com
Web Site: www.thehermitage.com
Key Personnel: Dir. & C.E.O., Howard Kittell; Regent, Martha Cooper; Chief Cur. & Dir. Museum Svcs., Marsha A. Mullin; Dir. Finance, Kathy McCall; Dir. Mktg., Jason Nelson; Guest Svcs., Debbie Bourne; Exec. Asst. & Membership, Jane Maggard; Museum Shop Mgr., Amanda Millslagle.
Institution Type/Description: Historic House.
Hours & Admission Prices: April-Oct. 15 daily 8:30-5; Oct. 16-March daily 9-4:30. Adults $17, senior citizens $14, students 13-18 $11, children 6-12 $7; discounts to groups, AAA, AAM & ICOM members; children 5 & under and members no charge. Closed Thanksgiving; Christmas. &
Attendance: 235,603 (actual)

Hixson

HIXSON FLIGHT MUSEUM, 1824 E. Crabtree Rd., Hixson, TN 37343. Tel.: 423-228-2359.
E-mail: curator@hixsonflightmuseum.org
Web Site: www.hixsonflightmuseum.org
Institution Type/Description: Flight Museum.
Hours & Admission Prices: Wed.-Thurs. 9-3, Fri.-Sat. 9-4. Guided Tour: $5-$10.

Hohenwald

LEWIS COUNTY MUSEUM OF NATURAL HISTORY & HOHENWALD DISCOVERY CENTER, 108 E. Main St., Hohenwald, TN 38462. Tel.: 931-796-1550.
E-mail: questions@lewiscountymuseum.com
Web Site: www.lewiscountymuseum.com
Institution Type/Description: History Museum.
Hours & Admission Prices: Tues.-Sat. 10-4. Adults $5, seniors $4, students $2. Closed major holidays.

MERIWETHER LEWIS NATIONAL MONUMENT, 189 Meriwether Lewis Park, Hohenwald, TN 38462-5591. Mailing Address: National Park Service, Natchez Trace Pkwy., 2680 Natchez Trace Pkwy., Tupelo, MS 38804. Tel.: 800-305-7417. Fax: 662-680-4034.
Web Site: www.nps.gov/natr
Institution Type/Description: Historic Site Museum: 1809 death & burial site of Meriwether Lewis.
Hours & Admission Prices: Daily 8-5. No charge.
Attendance: 9,000 (estimated)

Humboldt

WEST TENNESSEE REGIONAL ART CENTER, 1200 Main St., Humboldt, TN 38343-3339. Mailing Address: P.O. Box 951, Humboldt, TN 38343-0951. Tel.: 731-784-1787. Fax: 901-784-1573.
E-mail: wtrac@aeneas.net
Web Site: www.wtrac.tn.org
Key Personnel: Chm. Bd., Charles Guy; Treas. Carolyn Barnett; Cur., Bill Hickerson.
Institution Type/Description: Art Center.
Hours & Admission Prices: Mon.-Fri. 9-4:30, Sat.-Sun. group tours by appointment. Upstairs Gallery: $2. Downstairs Gallery: no charge; donations accepted. Closed holidays. &
Attendance: 10,000 (estimated)

Huntsville

WORLD WAR II REMEMBRANCE MUSEUM, 400 Scott High Dr., Huntsville, TN 37756. Tel.: 423-663-2805.
E-mail: tennesseeman43@comcast.net
Institution Type/Description: Military History Museum.
Hours & Admission Prices: Call for hours.

Hurricane Mills

COAL MINER'S DAUGHTER MUSEUM, 1877 Hurricane Mills Rd., Hurricane Mills, TN 37078. Tel.: 931-296-1840. Fax: 931-296-1839.
E-mail: info@lorettalynnranch.net
Web Site: www.lorettalynn.com
Institution Type/Description: History Museum.
Hours & Admission Prices: Daily 9-5. Museum: adult $12.50, children under 10 no charge. Home Tour Package: $25, children under 10 no charge. &

Jackson

CASEY JONES HOME AND RAILROAD MUSEUM, Casey Jones Village, 30 Casey Jones Ln., Jackson, TN 38305. Tel.: 731-668-1222. Facebook.
E-mail: caseyjonesmuseum@gmail.com
Web Site: www.caseyjones.com
Key Personnel: Dir., Jimmy Bailey; C.E.O., T. Clark Shaw.
Institution Type/Description: Railroad Museum: housed in c.1900 home of Casey Jones.
Hours & Admission Prices: March-July Mon.-Sat. 9-5, Sun. 1-5; Aug.-Feb., Mon.-Sat. 10-5, Sun. 1-5. Adults $6.50, seniors $5.50, children 6-12 $4.50; discounts to groups, military, AAA & TAM members; children under 5 no charge. Closed Easter; Thanksgiving; Christmas. &
Attendance: 50,000 (estimated)

CYPRESS GROVE NATURE PARK - AERIE TRAIL RAPTOR CENTER, W. Airways Blvd., (Hwy. 70), Jackson, TN 38301. Mailing Address: 3 Westwood Gardens Dr., Jackson, TN 38301-4218. Tel.: 731-425-8316 & 8384.
E-mail: smacdiarmid@cityofjackson.net
Institution Type/Description: Nature Center.
Hours & Admission Prices: Park: daily 7:30 to dusk. Center: call for hours.

DISCOVERY MUSEUM OF WEST TENNESSEE, 305 E. College, Jackson, TN 38301-6215. Tel.: 731-410-8621. Fax: 731-410-8622.
E-mail: info@wtndiscovery.org
Web Site: wtndiscovery.org
Institution Type/Description: History Museum.
Hours & Admission Prices: Tues.-Sat. 9-4. &

HISTORIC DOWNTOWN N.C. & ST. L. DEPOT AND RAILROAD MUSEUM, 582 S. Royal St., Jackson, TN 38301. Tel.: 731-425-8223. Fax: 731-425-8682.
E-mail: thedepot@cityofjackson.net
Web Site: www.cityofjackson.net
Key Personnel: Dir., David Falk.
Institution Type/Description: Historic Building: built in 1907. Listed on the National Register of Historic Places.
Hours & Admission Prices: Mon.-Sat. 10-3. No charge. Closed city holidays. &
Attendance: 11,463 (actual)

INTERNATIONAL ROCK-A-BILLY HALL OF FAME MUSEUM, 105 N. Church St., Jackson, TN 38301-6213. Mailing Address: 314 Edenwood Dr., Jackson, TN 38301-3433. Tel.: 731-427-6262.
E-mail: rock@rockabillyhall.org
Web Site: www.rockabillyhall.org
Key Personnel: Dir. & Pres., Henry Harrison.
Institution Type/Description: History Museum.
Hours & Admission Prices: Mon.-Thurs. 10-5, Fri.-Sat. 10-2, Member adults $10. &

Jamestown

YE OLE JAIL MUSEUM, 114 Central Ave. W., Jamestown, TN 38556. Mailing Address: P.O. Box 1294, Jamestown, TN 38556. Tel.: 931-879-9948.
E-mail: leanns@jamestowntn.org
Web Site: jamestowntn.org
Institution Type/Description: Historic Building: housed in a former jail, used from 1900-1979.
Hours & Admission Prices: Call for hours. No charge; donations accepted. Closed federal holidays.
Attendance: 5,000 (estimated)

Jefferson City

GLENMORE MANSION, 1280 N. Chucky Pike, Jefferson City, TN 37760-4926. Mailing Address: P.O. Box 403, Jefferson City, TN 37760-0403.
E-mail: glenmorejeffcity@gmail.com
Web Site: glenmoremansion.com/contact
Formerly: The Oaks
Key Personnel: Pres. (V), Helen T. Gray; Museum Shop Mgr., Delene Wilson.
Institution Type/Description: Historic House: built in 1868. Listed on the National Register of Historic Places.
Hours & Admission Prices: May-Oct. Sat.-Sun. 1-5; other times by appointment. Adults $5, children under 12 $2.50; members no charge.
Attendance: 1,500 (estimated)

Johnson City

GENERAL SHALE MUSEUM OF ANCIENT BRICK, 3015 Bristol Hwy., Johnson City, TN 37602. Mailing Address: P.O. Box 3547, Johnson City, TN 37602. Tel.: 423-282-4661, 800-414-4661. Fax: 423-952-4103.
E-mail: dawn.henning@generalshale.com
Web Site: www.generalshale.com
Institution Type/Description: History Museum.
Hours & Admission Prices: Mon.-Fri. 8-5.

HANDS ON! REGIONAL MUSEUM, 315 E. Main St., Johnson City, TN 37601-5700. Tel.: 423-928-6508 & 6509. Fax: 423-928-6915.
E-mail: handson@handsonmuseum.org
Web Site: www.handsonmuseum.org
Key Personnel: Exec. Dir., Trish Patterson; Mktg. & Membership, Kristine Amerine Carter; Mgr. Finance, Kay Hobbs; Mgr. Education, Programs & Science Lab, April Bunch; Coord. Exhibits & Outreach, Franci Sloan; Reservations, Karen Deckard.
Institution Type/Description: Children's Museum.
Hours & Admission Prices: June-Aug. Mon.-Fri. 9-5, Sat. 10-5, Sun. 1-5; Sept.-May Tues.-Fri. 9-5, Sat. 10-5, Sun. 1-5. Adults $8; discounts to groups & ASTC members; members & children under 3 no charge. Closed New Year's Day; Martin Luther King Jr. Day; Easter; Memorial Day; Independence Day; Labor Day; Thanksgiving; Christmas Eve & Day.
Attendance: 70,013 (actual)

MUSEUM AT MOUNTAIN HOME - EAST TENNESSEE STATE UNIVERSITY, Dept. Learning Resources, Johnson City, TN 37614-1710. Mailing Address: P.O. Box 70579, Johnson City, TN 37614-1710. Tel.: 423-439-8069. Fax: 423-439-7025.
E-mail: whaleym@etsu.edu
Institution Type/Description: Medical & Military Museum.
Hours & Admission Prices: Temporarily closed. &

THE REECE MUSEUM, 363 Stout Dr., East Tennessee State University, Johnson City, TN 37614. Mailing Address: P.O. Box 70660, ETSU, Johnson City, TN 37614-1701. Tel.: 423-439-4392. Fax: 423-439-4283.
E-mail: sandersr@etsu.edu
Web Site: www.etsu.edu/reece
Key Personnel: Dir., Randall K. Sanders; Pres. ETSU, Dr. Brian Noland.
Institution Type/Description: History & Art Museum.
Hours & Admission Prices: Mon.-Fri. 9-4:30. Sat. hours for certain exhibitions. Suggested Donation: $5. Closed major holidays. &
Attendance: 7,089 (actual)

SLOCUMB GALLERIES, Ball Hall, Dept. of Art & Design, ETSU, Johnson City, TN 37614. Mailing Address: Box 70708 ETSU, Johnson City, TN 37614-1710. Tel.: 423-483-3179. Fax: 423-439-4393.
E-mail: contrera@etsu.edu
Web Site: art.etsu.edu/slocumb
Key Personnel: Dir., Karlota I. Contreras-Koterbay.
Institution Type/Description: Art Gallery.
Hours & Admission Prices: Mon.-Fri. 8:30-4. No charge. Closed university holidays. &
Attendance: 5,000 (estimated)

TIPTON-HAYNES STATE HISTORIC SITE, 2620 S. Roan St., Johnson City, TN 37601-7585. Tel.: 423-926-3631.
E-mail: tiptonhaynes@embarqmail.com
Web Site: tipton-haynes.org

Key Personnel: Exec. Dir., Penny McLaughlin; Chm. (V), Tony Galloway.
Institution Type/Description: Historic Home: c.1850 Tipton & Haynes House.
Hours & Admission Prices: April-Nov. Tues.-Sat. 9-4; Dec.-March call for hours. Adults $5, students 12 & under $2.50; discount AAA members, school & scout groups; members no charge. Closed New Year's Eve & Day; Thanksgiving & day after; Christmas week. &
Attendance: 9,000 (estimated)

Jonesborough

JONESBOROUGH-WASHINGTON COUNTY HISTORY MUSEUM, 117 Boone St., Historic Jonesborough Visitors Center, Jonesborough, TN 37659. Mailing Address: The Heritage Alliance, 212 E. Sabin Dr., Jonesborough, TN 37659-1306. Tel.: 423-753-9580. Fax: 423-753-5281.
E-mail: info@heritageall.org
Web Site: www.heritageall.org
Key Personnel: Museum Dir., Deborah Montanti.
Institution Type/Description: History Museum.
Hours & Admission Prices: Mon.-Fri. 9-5, Sat.-Sun. No charge; donations accepted. &
Attendance: 5,735 (actual)

Kingsport

BAYS MOUNTAIN PARK & PLANETARIUM, 853 Bays Mountain Park Rd., Kingsport, TN 37660. Tel.: 423-229-9447. Fax: 423-224-2589.
E-mail: willey@ci.kingsport.tn.us
Institution Type/Description: Nature Preserve & Planetarium.
Hours & Admission Prices: Nature Center: Mon.-Fri. 8:30-5, Sat.-Sun. 12-7. Park: March Mon.-Fri. 8:30-5, Sat. 8:30-8, Sun. 12-8; April-May & Sept.-Oct. Mon.-Tues. & Thurs.-Fri. 8:30-5, Wed. 8:30-7, Sat. 8:30-8, Sun. 12-8. Park: $4 per car. Planetarium Shows: adults & children 6 and over $4; children 5 & under no charge. Nature Programs: $2 per person.

EXCHANGE PLACE LIVING HISTORY FARM, 4812 Orebank Rd., Kingsport, TN 37664. Tel.: 423-288-6071. Facebook: Exchange Place Living History Farm.
E-mail: email@exchangeplace.info
Web Site: www.exchangeplace.info
Key Personnel: Chm. (V), Marshall Adesman; Museum Shop Mgr., Billee Moore.
Institution Type/Description: History Museum.
Hours & Admission Prices: May-Oct. Sat.-Sun. 2-4:30; groups by appointment. No charge; donations accepted.
Attendance: 6,000 (estimated)

NETHERLAND INN HOUSE MUSEUM & BOATYARD COMPLEX, 2144 Netherland Inn Rd., Kingsport, TN 37660-3052. Mailing Address: P.O. Box 293, Kingsport, TN 37660. Tel.: 423-335-5552.
E-mail: jgibson@naxs.net
Web Site: netherlandinn.com
Key Personnel: C.E.O. & Steering Committee Chm., Mrs. Dennis Phillips; Museum Dir., Furnishings Maintenance Chm. & Catalog Dept. Chm., Mrs. Jane Gibson; Guide Chm., Annette Pannell; Museum Shop Mgr., Mrs. Lib Findley.
Institution Type/Description: Historic House Museum: built in 1802.
Hours & Admission Prices: Guided Tours: May-Oct. Sat.-Sun. 2-4; groups & other times by appointment. Adults $4, children 6 & under $1; discount to groups; Tourism Bureau & museum members no charge. Additional fee for some special events. &
Attendance: 9,000 (estimated)

Kingston

ROANE COUNTY MUSEUM OF HISTORY & ART, 119 Court St., Kingston, TN 37763-2810. Mailing Address: P.O. Box 738, Kingston, TN 37763-0738. Tel.: 865-376-9211.
Web Site: www.roanetnheritage.com
Institution Type/Description: Art & History Museum: housed in former antebellum courthouse.
Hours & Admission Prices: Mon.-Fri. 8:30-12 & 1-4:30. No charge.

Knoxville

BECK CULTURAL EXCHANGE CENTER, INC., 1927 Dandridge Ave., Knoxville, TN 37915-1909. Tel.: 865-524-8461. Fax: 865-524-8462.
E-mail: beckcenter@beckcenter.net

Web Site: www.beckcenter.net
Key Personnel: 1st Vice Pres., Annazette Houston; 2nd Vice Pres., Arnold G. Cohen; Pres., Samuel P. Anderson; Archivist, Timothy Vasser.
Institution Type/Description: History Museum, Cultural Center & Local Black History.
Hours & Admission Prices: Tues.-Sat. 10-6. No charge; donations accepted. Closed holidays.
Attendance: 30,000 (actual)

BLOUNT MANSION, 200 W. Hill Ave., Knoxville, TN 37902-1812. Mailing Address: P.O. Box 1703, Knoxville, TN 37901-1703. Tel.: 865-525-2375, 888-654-0016 (toll free). Fax: 865-546-5315. Facebook: Blount Mansion.
E-mail: info@blountmansion.org
Web Site: www.blountmansion.org
Key Personnel: Exec. Dir., David Hearnes.
Institution Type/Description: Historic House Museum: 1792 home & office of William Blount, governor of the Territory of the United States South of the River Ohio (Southwest Territory).
Hours & Admission Prices: Tues.-Fri. 9:30-5, Sat. 10-2; tours at the top of the hour. Adults $7, senior citizens, veterans, CAA & AAA members $6, children 6-17 $5; discounts to groups; children under 5 and AASLH members no charge. Closed all major holidays; UT home football games.
Attendance: 6,000 (actual)

CONFEDERATE MEMORIAL HALL-BLEAK HOUSE, 3148 Kingston Pike, S.W., Knoxville, TN 37919-4627. Tel.: 865-522-2371.
E-mail: southerncheer61@aol.com
Web Site: www.knoxvillecmh.org
Key Personnel: Pres., Diane Wright-Green.
Institution Type/Description: General Museum: housed in 1858 Bleak House.
Hours & Admission Prices: Tues., Wed. & Fri. 1-4; other times by appointment, school & bus tours by appointment. Adults $5, senior citizens $4, students $3, children 7-12 $1.50; children 6 & under no charge.
Attendance: 1,300 (estimated)

CRESCENT BEND HOUSE & GARDENS, 2728 Kingston Pike, Knoxville, TN 37919-4600. Tel.: 865-637-3163 & 544-3000. Fax: 865-637-1709. Facebook: @crescent.bend.
E-mail: info@crescentbend.com
Web Site: www.crescentbend.com
Key Personnel: Chm., Ron Grimm; Communications Dir., Caroline Grimm.
Institution Type/Description: Decorative Arts Museum: housed in 1834 Armstrong-Lockett House.
Hours & Admission Prices: Wed.-Fri. 10-4, Sat. 10-2. Adults $7, students $5; discounts to AAA members & groups of 20 or more; children 12 & under no charge. Closed major holidays.
Attendance: 9,250 (actual)

EAST TENNESSEE HISTORICAL SOCIETY, 601 S. Gay St., Knoxville, TN 37902-1604. Mailing Address: P.O. Box 1629, Knoxville, TN 37901-1629. Tel.: 865-215-8824. Fax: 865-215-8819. Facebook: East Tennessee Historical Society.
E-mail: eths@eastTNhistory.org
Web Site: www.easttnhistory.org
Key Personnel: Dir., Cherel B. Henderson; Pres. (V), Joe Emert; Financial Mgr., Rudy McBee; Dir. Devel., Erica Sharber; Dir. Membership & Social Media, Lisa Belleman; Cur. Education, Lisa Oakley; Educ. & Vol. Coord., Hannah Rexrode; Cur. Collections, Michele MacDonald; Exec. Asst., Stephanie Henry; Admin. Asst., Carleigh Isbell; Museum Shop Mgr., Tim Yates; Visitor Svcs., Courtney Beard.
Institution Type/Description: Historical Society Museum: housed in the Old Customs House, which was built between 1870-1874.
Hours & Admission Prices: Mon.-Fri. 9-4, Sat. 10-4, Sun. 1-5. Adults $5, senior citizens 55 & over $4; members and children 16 & under no charge. Closed New Year's Day; Easter; Independence Day; Labor Day; Thanksgiving; Christmas Eve & Day.
Attendance: 50,778 (actual)

EWING GALLERY OF ART & ARCHITECTURE, University of Tennessee, 1715 Volunteer Blvd., Knoxville, TN 37996-2410. Tel.: 865-974-3200.
E-mail: ecagley@utk.edu
Web Site: www.ewing-gallery.utk.edu
Key Personnel: Dir., Sam Yates; Collections Mgr., Sarah McFalls; Registrar & Exhibitions Coord., Eric Cagley.
Institution Type/Description: Art & Architecture Museum.
Hours & Admission Prices: Mon. 10-5:30, Tues.-Fri. 10-5, Sun. 1-4. Closed national holidays.

HISTORIC RAMSEY HOUSE, 2614 Thorngrove Pike, Knoxville, TN 37914-9704. Tel.: 865-546-0745. Fax: 865-546-1851. TDD: 856-546-0745.
E-mail: info@ramseyhouse.org
Web Site: www.ramseyhouse.org
Formerly: Ramsey House Plantation
Key Personnel: Pres. Bd. Dir., Dr. Ted Lewis; Exec. Dir., Judy LaRose.
Institution Type/Description: Historical House Museum: c.1796-97 Ramsey House, formerly Swan Pond, restored; Heirloom Gardens.
Hours & Admission Prices: Wed.-Sat. 10-4. Adults $7, children 6-12 $5; discounts to seniors, AAA & National Trust members; Museums of Knoxville & Tennessee, Association of Museums members & children under 6 no charge. Closed major holidays.
Attendance: 11,382 (actual)

IJAMS NATURE CENTER, 2915 Island Home Ave., Knoxville, TN 37920. Tel.: 865-577-4717.
E-mail: lbales@ijams.org
Key Personnel: Exec. Dir., Amber Parker; Sr. Naturalist, Stephen Lyn Bales.
Institution Type/Description: Nature Center.
Hours & Admission Prices: Visitor Center: Tues.-Sat. 9-5, Sun. 1-5; other times by appointment. Trails: daily 8-6.

JOHN C. HODGES LIBRARY, 1015 Volunteer Blvd., Knoxville, TN 37996-1000. Tel.: 865-974-4351.
E-mail: utlibraries@utk.libanswers.com
Web Site: www.lib.utk.edu
Institution Type/Description: Library.
Hours & Admission Prices: Academic Year: call for hours; Summer: Mon.-Thurs. 7:30am-12am, Fri. 7:30-6, Sat. 10-6, Sun. 12pm-12am.

THE KNOXVILLE BOTANICAL GARDENS AND ARBORETUM, 2743 Wimpole Ave., Knoxville, TN 37914-5958. Tel.: 865-862-8717. Fax: 865-862-8721.
E-mail: info@knoxgarden.org
Web Site: www.knoxgarden.org
Key Personnel: Exec. Dir., Jim Richards; Dir. Horticulture, Brian Campbell.
Institution Type/Description: Botanical Garden & Arboretum.
Hours & Admission Prices: Daily sunrise-sunset. No charge.

KNOXVILLE MUSEUM OF ART, 1050 World's Fair Park Dr., Knoxville, TN 37916-1653. Tel.: 865-525-6101, ext. 0 & ext. 243. Fax: 865-546-3635.
E-mail: info@knoxart.org
Web Site: www.knoxart.org
Key Personnel: Chm. (V), Richard Jansen; Chm., Allison Lederer; Exec. Dir., David L. Butler; Cur., Stephen C. Wicks; Cur. Education, Rosalind Martin; Dir. Finance & Operations, Joyce Jones; Alive After Five Coord., Michael Gill; Dir. Devel., Mary Walker; Dir. Mktg., Angela Thomas; Dir. Memberships & Grants, Margo Clark; Dir. Administration, Denise DuBose; Mgr. Events & Special Projects, Carla Pare; Museum Shop Mgr., Susan Creswell; Curatorial Asst. & Registrar, Clark Gillespie.
Institution Type/Description: Art Museum: housed in an Edward Larrabee Barnes-designed facility.
Hours & Admission Prices: Tues.-Thurs. & Sat. 10-5, Fri. 10-8, Sun. 1-5. No charge; donations accepted. Closed New Year's Day; Martin Luther King Jr. Day; Easter; Memorial Day; Independence Day; Labor Day; Thanksgiving; Christmas.
Attendance: 49,352 (actual)

KNOXVILLE POLICE DEPARTMENT MUSEUM, 800 Howard Baker Jr. Ave., Knoxville, TN 37915. Tel.: 865-215-7000.
E-mail: chiefofpolice@knoxvilletn.gov
Institution Type/Description: History Museum.
Hours & Admission Prices: By appointment. No charges.

KNOXVILLE ZOOLOGICAL GARDENS, 3500 Knoxville Zoo Dr., Knoxville, TN 37914. Mailing Address: P.O. Box 6040, Knoxville, TN 37914-0040. Tel.: 865-637-5331. Fax: 865-637-1943.
E-mail: zooknox@zooknoxville.org
Web Site: www.knoxville-zoo.org
Key Personnel: Pres. & C.E.O., Lisa New.
Institution Type/Description: Zoo.
Hours & Admission Prices: Daily 10-4:30. Adults $19.95, senior citizens 65 & up and children 2-12 $16.95; discount to groups & AAM members; children under 2, members & AZA members no charge. Closed Christmas.
Attendance: 395,000 (actual)

MABRY-HAZEN HOUSE, 1711 Dandridge Ave., Knoxville, TN 37915-1905. Tel.: 865-522-8661. Fax: 865-522-8471.
E-mail: mabryhazenhouse@gmail.com
Web Site: mabryhazen.com
Key Personnel: Interim Dir., Patrick Hollis; Pres. (V), Bo Connor.
Institution Type/Description: Historic House: an 1858 Italianate four over four home, built by Joseph Alexander Mabry; used by the South and then the North during the Civil War.
Hours & Admission Prices: March-Dec. Wed.-Fri. 11-5, Sat. 10-3; Jan.-Feb. by appointment only. Adults $5, students K-12 $2.50; children 4 & under and members no charge. Closed New Year's Day; Independence Day; Thanksgiving; Christmas. &
Attendance: 2,000 (estimated)

MARBLE SPRINGS STATE HISTORIC SITE - GOVERNOR JOHN SEVIER MEMORIAL ASSOCIATION, 1220 W. Gov. John Sevier Hwy., Knoxville, TN 37920. Mailing Address: P.O. Box 20195, Knoxville, TN 37940-1195. Tel.: 865-573-5508.
E-mail: info@marblesprings.net
Web Site: www.marblesprings.net
Key Personnel: Exec. Dir., Anna Chappelle; Program Coord., Samantha Burleson; Grounds Mgr. & Youth Coord., John Gammon.
Institution Type/Description: Historic House: 1783-1815 Marble Springs plantation home of Tennessee's first governor, John Sevier.
Hours & Admission Prices: Jan.-Feb. Sat. 11-5, Sun. 1-5; March-Dec. Wed.-Sat. 10-5, Sun. 12-5; other times by appointment. Site: no charge. Guided Tours: adults $4; children 10 & under no charge. Closed New Year's Day; Easter; Thanksgiving; Christmas Eve & Day.
Attendance: 7,242 (actual)

MCCLUNG MUSEUM OF NATURAL HISTORY & CULTURE, University of Tennessee, 1327 Circle Park Dr., Knoxville, TN 37996-3200. Tel.: 865-974-2144. Fax: 865-974-3827.
E-mail: museum@utk.edu
Web Site: mcclungmuseum.utk.edu
Formerly: Frank H. McClung Museum
Key Personnel: Dir., Dr. Jefferson Chapman; Asst. Dir., Cur. & Social Media, Catherine Shteynbrg; Assoc. Dir. External Rels., Stacy Palado; Cur. Paleoethnobotany, Dr. Gary Crites; Cur. Archaeology, Dr. Timothy Baumann; Cur. Malacology, Gerald Dinkins; Registrar & Collections Mgr., Adriane Tafoya; Media Productions Coord., Lindsay Kromer; Exhibits Coord., Chris Weddig; Cur. Education, Leslie Chang Jantz; Asst. Museum Educator, Callie Bennett; Coord. Academic Programs, Lindsey Wainwright; Museum Shop Mgr., Lecy Campbell.
Institution Type/Description: General Museum.
Hours & Admission Prices: Mon.-Sat. 9-5, Sun. 1-5. No charge; donations accepted. Closed New Year's Day; Easter; Memorial Day; Independence Day; Labor Day; Thanksgiving; Christmas Eve & Day. &
Attendance: 63,460 (actual)

THE MUSE KNOXVILLE, 516 N. Beaman St., Chilhowee Park, Knoxville, TN 37914-4410. Mailing Address: P.O. Box 6204, Knoxville, TN 37914-0204. Tel.: 865-594-1494. Facebook: TheMuseKnoxville; Instagram: themuseknoxville; Twitter: MuseofKnoxville.
E-mail: info@themuseknoxville.org
Web Site: themuseknoxville.org
Formerly: Discovery Center (East Tennessee Discovery Center)
Key Personnel: Chm., Ameeta Lall; Exec. Dir., Ellie Kittrell; Office Mgr., Andrea Hudson; Visitors Svcs. Mgr., Bicki Rudd; Education Mgr., Nancy Laurence; Outreach Coord., Evelyn Napier; Gift Shop Coord., Elizabeth Gall.
Institution Type/Description: Science Museum & Planetarium.
Hours & Admission Prices: Mon. 9-12, Tues.-Fri. 9-5, Sat. 10-5, Sun. 1-5. Admission $7, Seniors (age 65+), children under 2, teachers with ID, military with ID no charge. Discounts to members of ACM and ASTC reciprocal programs. &
Attendance: 72,000 (actual)

UNIVERSITY OF TENNESSEE GARDENS, 2518 Jacob Dr., Knoxville, TN 37996. Mailing Address: 252 Ellington Plant Sciences Bldg., 2431 Joe Johnson Dr., Knoxville, TN 37996. Tel.: 865-974-8265. Fax: 865-974-1947.
E-mail: utgardens@utk.edu
Web Site: utgardens.tennessee.edu
Key Personnel: Dir., Dr. Susan Hamilton.
Institution Type/Description: Gardens.
Hours & Admission Prices: Daily. No charge.

WOMEN'S BASKETBALL HALL OF FAME, 700 Hall of Fame Dr., Knoxville, TN 37915. Tel.: 865-633-9000. Fax: 865-633-9294. Facebook.
E-mail: dhart@wbhof.com
Web Site: wbhof.com
Key Personnel: Pres. Bd., Danielle Donehew; Pres., Dana Hart; Dir. Basketball Operations, Josh Sullivan; Operations Mgr., Ashley Carter.
Institution Type/Description: Sports Museum.
Hours & Admission Prices: May-Sept. Mon.-Sat. 10-5; Labor Day to April Tues.-Fri. 11-5, Sat. 10-5. Adults $7.95, seniors 62 & over and children 6-15 $5.95; discounts to AAA & military members; members and children 5 & under no charge. &
Attendance: 20,236 (estimated)

Lafayette

GALEN SCHOOL MUSEUM, 6435 Galen Rd., Lafayette, TN 37083. Mailing Address: c/o Macon County Tennessee Historical Society, P.O. Box 231, Lafayette, TN 37083. Tel.: 615-666-2470.
Institution Type/Description: History Museum: built in 1929.
Hours & Admission Prices: Call for hours. No charge.

JOHNSTON CABIN AT KEY PARK, 208 Church St., Lafayette, TN 37083. Mailing Address: c/o Macon County Historical Society, P.O. Box 231, Lafayette, TN 37083. Tel.: 615-688-4247.
Key Personnel: Pres. (V), Teresa Whittemore; Museum Shop Mgr., Mickey Meador.
Institution Type/Description: Historic House Museum.
Hours & Admission Prices: Call for hours. No charge, donations accepted. &

Lake City

COAL MINER'S MUSEUM, 216 N. Main St., Lake City, TN 37769. Mailing Address: Coal Creek Watershed Foundation, Inc., 3502 Overlook Cir., Knoxville, TN 37909. Tel.: 865-426-7914.
E-mail: bthacker2@coalcreekaml.com
Institution Type/Description: History Museum.
Hours & Admission Prices: Call for hours. No charge.

Lawrenceburg

CHEROKEE MUSEUM AND CULTURAL CENTER, #1 Public Square, Lawrenceburg, TN 38464-3331. Mailing Address: 773 Powell Chapel Rd., Pulaski, TN 38478-6822. Tel.: 931-762-3733.
E-mail: centralbandofcherokee@gmail.com
Web Site: www.centralbandofcherokee.org
Institution Type/Description: Native American History Museum.
Hours & Admission Prices: Mon.-Sat. 9:30-4.

JAMES D. VAUGHN GOSPEL MUSIC MUSEUM, 25A Public Square, Lawrenceburg Municipal Complex, 3rd Fl., Lawrenceburg, TN 38464-3351. Mailing Address: c/o Mainstreet Lawrenceburg, 25A Public Square, Lawrenceburg, TN 38466. Tel.: 931-762-8991.
E-mail: director@mainstreetlawrenceburgtn.com
Key Personnel: Cur., Tom Crews.
Institution Type/Description: History Museum.
Hours & Admission Prices: Call for hours. No charge. &
Attendance: 5,000 (estimated)

LAWRENCE COUNTY HISTORICAL SOCIETY, Waterloo St., Lawrenceburg, TN 38468. Mailing Address: 1106 Hickory, Lawrenceburg, TN 38464-3921. Tel.: 931-762-4397.
E-mail: dtshaddix@yahoo.com
Institution Type/Description: Historical Society Museum: built in 1893.
Hours & Admission Prices: Tues.-Thurs. 10-2; other times by appointment.

Lebanon

FIDDLERS GROVE HISTORICAL VILLAGE, 945 E. Baddour Pkwy., Lebanon, TN 37087-4338. Tel.: 615-443-2626.
E-mail: info@fiddlersgrove.org
Web Site: www.fiddlersgrove.org
Institution Type/Description: Historic Village.
Hours & Admission Prices: By appointment. Tours: $4 per person; discounts to school groups.

LEBANON MUSEUM AND HISTORY CENTER, 200 N. Castle Heights Ave., Lebanon, TN 37087-2740. Tel.: 615-443-2839. Fax: 615-443-2851.
E-mail: info@lebanontn.org
Web Site: www.lebanontn.org
Institution Type/Description: History Museum.
Hours & Admission Prices: Mon.-Fri. 8-4; groups of 10 or more by appointment. No charge.
Attendance: 200

WILSON COUNTY MUSEUM AKA THE FESSENDEN HOUSE, 236 W. Main St., Lebanon, TN 37087. Mailing Address: 111 S. Greenwood St., Lebanon, TN 37087. Tel.: 615-444-9127.
Institution Type/Description: Historic House Museum.
Hours & Admission Prices: By appointment. No charge.

Lexington

BEECH RIVER CULTURAL CENTER & MUSEUM, 26 S. Broad St., Lexington, TN 38351-2002. Tel.: 731-967-0306.
E-mail: museum@netease.net
Institution Type/Description: History Museum.
Hours & Admission Prices: March 2-Dec. Wed. & Fri.-Sat. 10-3. No charge; donations accepted.

Limestone

DAVY CROCKETT BIRTHPLACE STATE PARK, 1245 Davy Crockett Park Rd., Limestone, TN 37681. Tel.: 423-257-2167.
E-mail: tnstateparks@tn.gov
Web Site: tnstateparks.com
Institution Type/Description: History Museum.
Hours & Admission Prices: Call for hours. No charge.

Livingston

OVERTON COUNTY HERITAGE MUSEUM, 318 W. Broad St., Livingston, TN 38570-1804. Tel.: 931-403-0909.
E-mail: pstover@twlakes.com
Web Site: www.overtonmuseum.com
Institution Type/Description: History Museum: housed in the former Livingston jail.
Hours & Admission Prices: Thurs.-Sat. 9-2; groups by appointment.

Lookout Mountain

BATTLES FOR CHATTANOOGA MUSEUM, 1110 E. Brow Rd., Lookout Mountain, TN 37350-1016.
E-mail: battle@seerockcity.com
Web Site: www.battlesforchattanooga.com
Institution Type/Description: History Museum.
Hours & Admission Prices: Summer: 9-6; Winter: daily 10-5. Adults $8, children 5-12 $6; children 4 & under no charge. ♿

CRAVENS HOUSE, Point Park Visitor Center, IN 148 Scenic Hwy., Lookout Mountain, TN 37350. Tel.: 423-821-7786. Fax: 423-825-5129.
Key Personnel: Supt., Cathleen Cook; Chief Interpretation, Kim Coons; District Interpreter, Anton J. Heinlein.
Institution Type/Description: Historic House: 1866 Cravens House, Post-Civil War home.
Hours & Admission Prices: Memorial Day to Labor Day Sat.-Sun. 1-5. No charge; donations accepted. Closed Christmas.
Attendance: 2,000 (actual)

Loretto

RALPH J. PASSARELLA MEMORIAL MUSEUM, 134 S. Main St., Loretto, TN 38469. Tel.: 931-853-4351. Fax: 931-853-4329.
E-mail: ralphallenmemorialmuseum@outlook.com
Key Personnel: Cur., Patty Brown.
Institution Type/Description: History Museum.
Hours & Admission Prices: Mon.-Tues. 9-4. No charge; donations accepted. ♿

Lynchburg

MOORE COUNTY JAIL MUSEUM, 231 Main St., Lynchburg, TN 37352-8300. Mailing Address: P.O. Box 231, Lynchburg, TN 37352-0421. Tel.: 931-759-4111.

E-mail: info@lynchburgtn.com
Web Site: www.lynchburgtn.com
Key Personnel: Cur., Bobby Fuller.
Institution Type/Description: Historic Building: housed in the county's first jail; built c.1893.
Hours & Admission Prices: Thurs.-Sat. 12-3. Adults $1; discounts to groups; children under 16 no charge. Closed holidays. ♿
Attendance: 5,000 (estimated)

TENNESSEE WALKING HORSE MUSEUM, 183 Main St., Lynchburg, TN 37352-8300. Mailing Address: P.O. Box 1010, Shelbyville, TN 37160. Tel.: 931-759-5747.
Institution Type/Description: History Museum.
Hours & Admission Prices: Tues.-Sat. 9-5. No charge. Closed major holidays.

Lynnville

LYNNVILLE RAILROAD MUSEUM, 162 Mill St., Lynnville, TN 38472. Mailing Address: P.O. Box 158, Lynnville, TN 38472. Tel.: 931-478-0880.
Web Site: www.lynnville.org/railroadmuseum.htm
Institution Type/Description: Railroad Museum.
Hours & Admission Prices: Mon.-Sat. 10-4, Sun. 12-4.

Madison

AMQUI STATION AND VISITORS CENTER - MUSIC AND THE RAILROAD MUSEUM, 301 B Madison St., Madison, TN 37115. Tel.: 615-891-1154.
E-mail: execdirector@amquistation.org
Web Site: www.amquistation.org
Key Personnel: Dir., Cate Hamilton; Chm. (V), Bill Beck; Pres. (V), Nathan Massey.
Institution Type/Description: History Museum & Visitors Center: housed in a former railroad switching and passenger depot; built in 1910.
Hours & Admission Prices: Mon.-Fri. 9-5.

Manchester

ARROWHEADS TO AEROSPACE MUSEUM, 24 Campground Rd., Manchester, TN 37355-6541. Tel.: 931-841-7738. Facebook: Coffee County/Manchester/Tullahoma Museum.
E-mail: jfworthington@bellsouth.net
Key Personnel: Dir. & Chm. (V), Judy Worthington; Museum Shop Mgr., Debbie Stribling.
Institution Type/Description: History Museum.
Hours & Admission Prices: Daily 10-2; other times by appointment. Adults $10, students 7-17 and seniors 65 & over $8, children 2-5 $4; discounts to groups, military, AAM, AAA & AARP members; members no charge. Closed New Year's Day; Christmas Eve & Day. ♿
Attendance: 5,000 (estimated)

Martin

J. HOUSTON GORDON MUSEUM, 10 Wayne Fisher Dr., The University of Tennessee at Martin, Martin, TN 38238. Tel.: 731-881-7094. Fax: 731-881-7074.
E-mail: museum@utm.edu
Formerly: University Museum.
Key Personnel: Dir., Samuel S. Richardson.
Institution Type/Description: General University Museum.
Hours & Admission Prices: Mon.-Fri. 8-4:30. No charge. Closed university holidays. ♿
Attendance: 1,000 (estimated)

Maryville

SAM HOUSTON MEMORIAL ASSOCIATION, 3650 Old Sam Houston School Rd., Maryville, TN 37804-5644. Tel.: 865-983-1550.
E-mail: samhoustonsch@aol.com
Web Site: samhoustonhistoricschoolhouse.org
Formerly: Sam Houston Historical Schoolhouse.
Key Personnel: Pres., Enoch B. Simerly; Vice Pres., Clara Peals; Treas., Charles England; Museum Shop Mgr., Mary Lynne Bell.
Institution Type/Description: Park Museum.
Hours & Admission Prices: Feb.-Dec. Tues.-Sat. 10-5, Sun. 1-5. Adults $3, children under 8 $1; members no charge. Closed New Year's Day; Easter; Thanksgiving; Christmas week. ♿
Attendance: 8,000 (estimated)

Maynardville

UNION COUNTY HERITAGE MUSEUM AND GENEALOGICAL LIBRARY, 3824 Maynardville Hwy., Maynardville, TN 37807. Mailing Address: P.O. Box 95, Maynardville, TN 37807. Tel.: 865-992-2136.
Formerly: Union County Heritage Museum and Library
Key Personnel: Chm. (V), James Meltabarger; Pres. (V), Wanda Cox Byerley.
Institution Type/Description: History Museum & Library (genealogy).
Hours & Admission Prices: Sun. 1-5, Mon.-Tues. 10-4. No charge; donations accepted. Closed Christmas. &
Attendance: 3,000 (estimated)

McKenzie

GORDON BROWNING MUSEUM & GENEALOGICAL LIBRARY, 640 Main St. N., McKenzie, TN 38201-1720. Tel.: 731-352-3510.
E-mail: gbmuseum640@gmail.com
Web Site: tn-roots.com/GordonBrowning
Key Personnel: Dir., Jere R. Cox; Pres., James E. Choate.
Institution Type/Description: History Museum.
Hours & Admission Prices: Mon.-Tues. & Thurs.-Fri. 9-4. No charge; donations accepted. Closed New Year's Day; Independence Day; Labor Day; Thanksgiving; Christmas. &
Attendance: 800 (estimated)

McMinnville

SOUTHERN MUSEUM & GALLERIES OF PHOTOGRAPHY, 210 E. Main St., McMinnville, TN 37110-2508. Tel.: 931-507-8102.
E-mail: artgallery@multipro.com
Institution Type/Description: Art Gallery.
Hours & Admission Prices: Wed. & Fri.-Sat. 10-4.

Memphis

ART MUSEUM OF THE UNIVERSITY OF MEMPHIS, 3750 Norriswood Ave., 142 CFA Building, Memphis, TN 38152. Mailing Address: 142 CFA Bldg., Memphis, TN 38152. Tel.: 901-678-2224. Fax: 901-678-5118.
E-mail: artmuseum@memphis.edu
Web Site: www.memphis.edu/amum
Key Personnel: Dir., Leslie Luebbers; Asst. Dir., Edmund Warren Perry; Administrative Asst., Anita Huggins; Museum Media Specialist, Jason N. Miller; Exhibit Specialist & Preparator, Neil O'Brien.
Institution Type/Description: Fine Arts Museum.
Hours & Admission Prices: Mon.-Sat. 9-5. No charge; suggested Donation: $2; discounts to AAM members. Closed New Year's Day; Martin Luther King Jr. Day; Memorial Day; Independence Day; Labor Day; Thanksgiving; Christmas. &
Attendance: 8,424 (actual)

BELZ MUSEUM OF ASIAN & JUDAIC ART, 119 S. Main St., Memphis, TN 38103-3647. Tel.: 901-523-2787. Fax: 901-523-8603.
E-mail: info@belzmuseum.org
Web Site: www.belzmuseum.org
Key Personnel: Dir., Belinda Fish; Guest Svcs. Admin., Wesley Paraham; Guest Svcs. Asst., Victoria Martin.
Institution Type/Description: Art Museum.
Hours & Admission Prices: Tues.-Fri. 10-5:30, Sat.-Sun. 12-5. Adults $6, seniors $5, students $4; children under 5 no charge. Closed New Year's Day; Easter; Independence Day; Thanksgiving; Christmas.

C.H. NASH MUSEUM AT CHUCALISSA, 1987 Indian Village Dr., Memphis, TN 38109-3005. Tel.: 901-785-3160. Fax: 901-785-0519.
E-mail: chucalissa@memphis.edu
Web Site: chucalissa.memphis.edu
Key Personnel: Mgr. & (V) Coord., Melissa Buchner; Admin. Asst., Emily Neal.
Institution Type/Description: Archaeology Museum: S.E. Native American, Choctaw & Pre-historic Native Mississippian culture.
Hours & Admission Prices: Tues.-Sat. 9-5, Sun. 1-5. Adults $6, children & senior citizens $4; discounts to AAA, groups of 10 or more, University of Memphis faculty & students; alumni association & museum members no charge. No admittance after 4:30. &
Attendance: 10,000 (actual)

CENTER FOR SOUTHERN FOLKLORE, 119 S. Main St., Memphis, TN 38103-3681. Tel.: 901-525-3655. Fax: 901-544-9965.
E-mail: info@southernfolklore.com
Web Site: www.southernfolklore.com
Key Personnel: Founder & Exec. Producer, Judy Peiser.
Institution Type/Description: Southern Performers History Museum.
Hours & Admission Prices: Mon.-Fri. 11-6, Sat. 2-11, Sun. 2-8. &

THE CHILDREN'S MUSEUM OF MEMPHIS, 2525 Central Ave., Memphis, TN 38104-5926. Tel.: 901-458-2678.
E-mail: info@cmom.com
Web Site: www.cmom.com
Key Personnel: Exec. Dir., Stephanie Butler.
Institution Type/Description: Children's Museum.
Hours & Admission Prices: Daily 9-5. Admission $15, carousel rides $3; discounts to ACM members; children under one & members no charge. Closed Easter; Thanksgiving; Christmas. &
Attendance: 367,505 (actual)

CLOUGH-HANSON GALLERY, RHODES COLLEGE, 2000 N. Parkway, Memphis, TN 38112-1690. Tel.: 901-843-3442. Fax: 901-843-3727.
E-mail: parsonsj@rhodes.edu
Web Site: www.rhodes.edu/content/clough-hanson-gallery
Key Personnel: Dir., Joel Parsons.
Institution Type/Description: College Art Gallery.
Hours & Admission Prices: Tues.-Sat. 11-5. No charge. Closed Martin Luther King Jr. Day; spring break; Good Friday; Easter; Memorial Day; Labor Day; fall break; Thanksgiving; Christmas. &
Attendance: 2,300 (estimated)

THE COTTON MUSEUM AT THE MEMPHIS COTTON EXCHANGE, 65 Union Ave., Memphis, TN 38103-5157. Tel.: 901-531-7826. Fax: 901-531-7827.
E-mail: info@memphiscottonmuseum.org
Web Site: www.memphiscottonmuseum.org
Key Personnel: Office Mgr., Matt Hicks.
Institution Type/Description: History Museum.
Hours & Admission Prices: Mon.-Sat. 10-5, Sun. 12-5. Adults $10, seniors & students $9, military $8, children 6-12 $7; discounts to AAM & ICOM members. children under 6 no charge, group rates also available. &

DIXON GALLERY AND GARDENS, 4339 Park Ave., Memphis, TN 38117-4698. Tel.: 901-761-5250. Fax: 901-682-0943.
E-mail: ntrenthem@dixon.org
Web Site: www.dixon.org
Key Personnel: Chm., C. Penn Owen, III; Dir., Kevin Sharp; Dir. Horticulture, Dale Skaggs; Dir. Devel., Elise Piper ; Registrar, Kristen Kimberling; Dir. Planned Giving, Susan Johnson; Dir. Education, Margarita Sandino; Cur., Julie Pierotti; Dir. Communications, Chantal Drake; Controller, Gail Hopper.
Institution Type/Description: Art Museum and Garden.
Hours & Admission Prices: Tues.-Sat. 10-5, 3rd Thurs. 10-8, Sun. 1-5. Adults $7, seniors 65 & over and students 18 & over $5, children 7-17 $3; discounts to AAM members & groups of 10 or more.; Sat. 10am-12pm, members and children 6 & under no charge. Closed New Year's Day; Independence Day; Thanksgiving; Christmas. &
Attendance: 103,294 (actual)

FIRE MUSEUM OF MEMPHIS, 118 Adams Ave., Memphis, TN 38103-2012. Tel.: 901-320-5650. Fax: 901-529-8422.
Web Site: www.firemuseum.com
Key Personnel: Mgr. Fire Prevention, Kelvin McGowan; Chm. (V), Bobby Wharton.
Institution Type/Description: Fire-Fighting Museum: housed in 1910 Fire Engine House No. 1, which served as a fire station until 1973. Listed on the National Register of Historic Places.
Hours & Admission Prices: Memorial Day to Labor Day Mon.-Sat. 9-6, Sun. 1-6; Sept.-May Mon.-Sat. 9-4:30. Adults $10, children 3-18, seniors 60 & over and military $8; discount to groups; members, children 2 & under no charge. &
Attendance: 33,000 (actual)

GRACELAND, 3764 Elvis Presley Blvd., Memphis, TN 38116-4198. Mailing Address: P.O. Box 16508, Memphis, TN 38186-0508. Tel.: 901-332-3322; 800-238-2000. Fax: 901-344-3116. Facebook: Graceland; TDD: 901-344-3146.
E-mail: graceland@elvis.com
Web Site: www.graceland.com

Key Personnel: C.E.O. & Pres., Jack Soden; Gen. Mgr. & Vice Pres. Operations, Regina Gambill; Exec. Vice Pres., Gary Hovey; Dir. Merchandising, Danny Hiltenbrand; Dir. Archives, Angela Marchese.
Institution Type/Description: Historic Home & Music Museum: housed in 1939 mansion occupied by singer/entertainer Elvis Presley from 1957 until his death in 1977.
Hours & Admission Prices: See website for hours. Mansion: adults $38.75, students and seniors 62 & over $34.90, children 7-12 $17; discounts to students, military & AAA members; teachers and children 6 & under no charge. Additional tour packages available. Closed New Year's Day; Thanksgiving; Christmas. &
Attendance: 650,000 (estimated)

LICHTERMAN NATURE CENTER, 5992 Quince Rd., Memphis, TN 38119-7257. Tel.: 901-636-2211. Fax: 901-682-3050.
E-mail: nature.reservations@memphistn.gov
Web Site: www.memphismuseums.org
Key Personnel: Mgr., Andy Williams; Chief Teacher & Naturalist, Dory Lerner.
Institution Type/Description: Environmental Education Center.
Hours & Admission Prices: Tues.-Thurs. 10-3, Fri.-Sat. 10-4. Adults $7, senior citizen $6, children 3-12 $5; discounts to ASTC members; members & children under 3 no charge. Closed New Year's Day; Thanksgiving; Christmas Eve & Day. &
Attendance: 40,000 (estimated)

MAGEVNEY HOUSE, 198 Adams Ave., Memphis, TN 38103. Mailing Address: 3050 Central Ave, Memphis, TN 38111-3316. Tel.: 901-523-1484. Fax: 901-320-6391.
Web Site: www.memphismuseums.org
Key Personnel: Dir., Steve Pike.
Institution Type/Description: Historic House: c.1836 Magevney House.
Hours & Admission Prices: 1st Sat. each month 1-4. No charge. Closed New Year's Day; Thanksgiving; Christmas.

MALLORY-NEELY HOUSE, 652 Adams Ave., Memphis, TN 38105. Mailing Address: 3050 Central Ave., Memphis, TN 38111-3316. Tel.: 901-523-1484. Fax: 901-636-6391.
Web Site: www.memphismuseums.org
Key Personnel: Dir., Steve Pike.
Institution Type/Description: Historic House.
Hours & Admission Prices: Fri.-Sat. 10-4; last tour 3pm. Adults $7, seniors 60 & over $6, youth 3-12 $5; discounts to groups; children under 3 no charge. &

MEMPHIS BOTANIC GARDEN, GOLDSMITH CIVIC GARDEN CENTER, 750 Cherry Rd., Memphis, TN 38117-4699. Tel.: 901-576-4100. Fax: 901-682-1561.
E-mail: info@memphisbotanicgarden.com
Web Site: www.memphisbotanicgarden.com
Key Personnel: Exec. Dir., Michael Allen; Bd. Pres., Vance Lewis; Dir., Administration, Mary Helen Butler; Dir., Finance, Walton Griffin; Dir., Mktg. & Public Rels., Jana Wilson.
Institution Type/Description: Botanic Garden: home of the Goldsmith Civic Garden Center.
Hours & Admission Prices: Summer: daily 9-6; Winter: daily 9-4:30. Adults $10, seniors 62 & over $8, children 2-12 $5; discounts to groups, and AHS & AABGA Reciprocal Gardens members; children under 2 & members no charge. Closed New Year's Day; Thanksgiving; Christmas. &
Attendance: 130,000 (actual)

MEMPHIS BROOKS MUSEUM OF ART, 1934 Poplar Ave., Overton Park, Memphis, TN 38104-2765. Tel.: 901-544-6200. Fax: 901-725-4071.
Web Site: www.brooksmuseum.org
Key Personnel: Exec. Dir., Emily Ballew Neff; Pres. (V), Deborah Craddock; C.F.O., Patty Burt; Chief Cur. American, Modern & Contemp. Art, Marina Pacini; Cur. European & Decorative Art, Stanton Thomas; Dir. Education, Kathy Dumlao; Collections Mgr., Kip Peterson; Registrar, Marilyn Masler; Dir. Devel., Kim Williams.
Institution Type/Description: Fine Arts Museum.
Hours & Admission Prices: Wed. 10-8, Thurs.-Fri. 10-4, Sat. 10-5, Sun. 11-5. Adults $7, seniors $6, students $3; discounts to AAM and ICOM members & scheduled groups; children under 6 & members no charge. Closed New Year's Day; Independence Day; Thanksgiving; Christmas. &
Attendance: 58,851 (actual)

MEMPHIS COLLEGE OF ART, 1930 Poplar Ave., Overton Park, Memphis, TN 38104-2756. Tel.: 901-272-5100, 800-727-1088, Fax: 901-272-5104. Facebook.
E-mail: info@mca.edu
Web Site: www.mca.edu

Key Personnel: Interim Pres., Laura Hine; Registrar, Erica Simpson; Coord. Galleries, Exhibitions & Lectures, Melissa Farris.
Institution Type/Description: Art College.
Hours & Admission Prices: Mon.-Fri. 8:30-5, Sat. 9-4, Sun. 12-4. No charge. Closed holidays. &
Attendance: 15,000 (estimated)

MEMPHIS ROCK 'N' SOUL MUSEUM, 191 Beale St., Ste. 100, Memphis, TN 38103-3715. Tel.: 901-205-2533. Fax: 901-205-2534.
Web Site: www.memphisrocknsoul.org
Key Personnel: Exec. Dir., John Doyle; Dir. Programming, Pam Hetsel.
Institution Type/Description: Music History Museum.
Hours & Admission Prices: Daily 10-7. Adults $12, youth 5-17 $9; discounts to AAA, AARP, & military. Closed New Year's Day; Thanksgiving; Christmas Eve & Day. &

MEMPHIS ZOO, 2000 Prentiss Place, Memphis, TN 38112-5033. Tel.: 901-333-6500. Fax: 901-333-6501.
E-mail: zooinfo@memphiszoo.org
Web Site: www.memphiszoo.org
Key Personnel: Dir. Animal Programs, Matt Thompson; Cur. Reptiles, Steve Reichling; Dir. Mktg., Angie Whitfield.
Institution Type/Description: Zoo.
Hours & Admission Prices: March-Oct. 16 daily 9-5; Oct. 17-Feb. daily 9-4. Adults 12 & over $15, senior citizens 60 & over $14, children 2-11 $10; discounts to military & groups; children under 2 & zoo members no charge. Closed Thanksgiving; Christmas Eve & Day. &
Attendance: 1,066,000 (estimated)

METAL MUSEUM, 374 Metal Museum Dr., Memphis, TN 38106-1514. Tel.: 901-774-6380. Fax: 901-774-6382.
E-mail: info@metalmuseum.org
Web Site: www.metalmuseum.org
Formerly: National Ornamental Metal Museum
Key Personnel: Exec. Dir., Carissa Hussong; Dir. Exhibitions & Collections, Grace Stewart; Exhibitions Coord., Nancy Cook; Museum Shop Mgr., Eva Langsdon.
Institution Type/Description: Metal Museum: historic & contemporary decorative & fine art metalwork.
Hours & Admission Prices: Tues.-Sat. 10-5, Sun. 12-5. Adults $6, senior citizens $5, students $4; members & children under 5 no charge. Closed New Year's Eve & Day; Easter; Independence Day; Thanksgiving; Christmas Eve, Day & day after; during exhibit changes. &
Attendance: 38,000 (estimated)

MISSISSIPPI RIVER MUSEUM AT MUD ISLAND RIVER PARK, 125 N. Front St., Memphis, TN 38103-1713. Tel.: 901-576-7241, 800-507-6507. Fax: 901-576-6666.
Web Site: www.mudisland.com
Key Personnel: General Mgr., Trey Giuntini; Museum & Park Operations Mgr., Alisa Bradley.
Institution Type/Description: History Museum Complex.
Hours & Admission Prices: April-Oct. Tues.-Sun. 10-5. Adults $10, senior $9, children 5-11 $7; discounts to groups; children 4 & under no charge. &
Attendance: 97,000 (estimated)

NATIONAL CIVIL RIGHTS MUSEUM AT THE LORRAINE MOTEL, 450 Mulberry St., Memphis, TN 38103-4214. Tel.: 901-521-9699. Fax: 901-521-9740. Facebook, Instagram, Twitter.
E-mail: cdyson@civilrightsmuseum.org
Web Site: www.civilrightsmuseum.org
Key Personnel: Pres., Terri Lee Freeman; Chm. Bd. Dirs., Herbert Hilliard; Chief Mktg. & External Affairs Officer, Faith Morris; Dir. Interpretation, Collections & Education, Noelle Trent; Chief Devel. Officer, Beverly Sakauye; Dir. Finance, Tsitsi Jones; Dir. Ops., Sherryl Tucker; Mng. Community Outreach, Veda Ajamu.
Institution Type/Description: History Museum: located at the Lorraine Motel, site of the assassination of Dr. Martin Luther King Jr.
Hours & Admission Prices: Mon. 9-6, Wed.-Sat. 9-5. Adults $17, senior citizens & students $15, children 5-17 $14; discounts to AAA, AAM & AARP members; members, active military and children 4 & under no charge. Closed New Year's Day; Easter; Thanksgiving; Christmas Eve & Day. &
Attendance: 200,000 (actual)

PINK PALACE FAMILY OF MUSEUMS, 3050 Central Ave., Memphis, TN 38111-3399. Tel.: 901-636-2362. Fax: 901-636-2391.
E-mail: steve.pike@memphistn.gov
Web Site: www.memphismuseums.org

Formerly: Memphis Pink Palace Museum & Sharpe Planetarium and IMAX Theater

Key Personnel: Dir., Steve Pike; Pres. (V), Mark Colombo; Admin. Program Affairs, Wesley S. Creel; Mgr. Collections, Louella Weaver; Mgr. Exhibits & Graphic Svcs., Steve Masler; Mgr. Education, Alice A. "Alex" Eilers; IMAX Dept. Mgr., Tony Hardy; Dir. Public Affairs, Richard Pugh; Mgr. Lichterman Nature Center, Andy Williams; Dir. Philanthropy, Cathi Johnson; Mgr. Business Affairs, Jerry Goudy.

Institution Type/Description: General, Natural History, Science & Cultural History Museum.

Hours & Admission Prices: Mon.-Sat. 9-5, Sun. 12-5. Exhibits: adults $12.75, senior citizens 60 & over $12.25, children 3-12 $7.25; discounts to ASTC & AAM members; museum on Tues. 1-5 no charge. Exhibits & Planetarium: adults $15.25, senior citizens $14.25, children 3-12 $9.25. Exhibits & Movie: adults $19.75, senior citizens $18.25, children $12.25. Closed New Year's Day; Thanksgiving; Christmas. &

Attendance: 520,113 (actual)

SLAVE HAVEN UNDERGROUND RAILROAD MUSEUM (BURKLE ESTATE), 826 N. Second St., Memphis, TN 38107-2302. Mailing Address: P.O. Box 3142, Memphis, TN 38173-0142. Tel.: 901-527-3427 & 7711.

E-mail: heritagetours@bellsouth.net

Web Site: www.slavehavenundergroundrailroadmuseum.org

Institution Type/Description: Historic House: former home of Jacob Burkle, built in 1849.

Hours & Admission Prices: June-August daily 10-5; Sept.-May: Mon.-Sat. 10-4. Adults $10, seniors $9, students 4-17 $8; discounts to groups.

STAX MUSEUM OF AMERICAN SOUL MUSIC, 926 E. McLemore Ave., Memphis, TN 38106-3338. Tel.: 901-942-7685; 888-942-7685. Fax: 901-507-1463.

E-mail: lisa.allen@soulsvillefoundation.org

Web Site: www.staxmuseum.com

Key Personnel: Exec. Dir., Jeff Kollath; Communications Dir., Tim Sampson.

Institution Type/Description: Soul Music Museum.

Hours & Admission Prices: Tues.-Sat. 10-5, Sun. 1-5. Adults $13, senior citizens 62 & over, students and military $12, children 9-12 $10; discounts to groups & AAA members; members and children 8 & under no charge. Closed Easter; Thanksgiving; Christmas. &

Attendance: 42,422 (actual)

W.C. HANDY HOUSE & MUSEUM, 352 Beale St., Memphis, TN 38103. Mailing Address: P.O. Box 3142, Memphis, TN 38173. Tel.: 901-527-3427; 901-522-1556. Fax: 901-527-8784.

E-mail: jshivers@bealestreet.com

Web Site: www.bealestreet.com/wc-handy-museum

Institution Type/Description: Historic House: housed in the former home of William Christopher Handy.

Hours & Admission Prices: Summer: Tues.-Sat. 10-5; Winter: Tues.-Sat. 11-4. Adults $6, children $4.

WOODRUFF-FONTAINE HOUSE MUSEUM, MEMPHIS CHAPTER APTA, 680 Adams Ave., Memphis, TN 38105-4902. Tel.: 901-526-1469. Facebook: @WoodruffFontaine; Instagram: @woodruff_fontaine_house_museum; Twitter: @fontainehouse.

E-mail: contact@woodruff-fontaine.org

Web Site: www.woodruff-fontaine.org

Key Personnel: Exec. Dir., Jennifer Cooper.

Institution Type/Description: Historic House: French Victorian mansion built in 1870 along "Millionaires Row."

Hours & Admission Prices: Wed.-Sun. 10-4. Adults $12, seniors over 65 $10, students $8; discounts to groups & military in uniform; members no charge. Closed holidays.

Milan

WEST TENNESSEE AGRICULTURAL MUSEUM, 3 Ledbetter Gate Rd., Milan, TN 38358-6543. Tel.: 731-686-8067.

E-mail: utagmuseum@utk.edu

Web Site: http://milan-tennessee.edu

Institution Type/Description: Agricultural Museum.

Hours & Admission Prices: Mon.-Fri. 8-4; Sat. & groups by appointment. No charge. Closed holidays. &

Monterey

MONTEREY DEPOT MUSEUM, 1 E. Depot St., Monterey, TN 38574. Tel.: 931-839-2111.

E-mail: depotadm@montereydepot.net

Web Site: montereytn.com

Key Personnel: Museum Admin., Ken Hall.

Institution Type/Description: Historic Building.

Hours & Admission Prices: Mon.-Sat. 10-4, Sun. 1-4.

Morristown

CROCKETT TAVERN MUSEUM, 2002 Morningside Dr., Morristown, TN 37814-5459. Tel.: 423-587-9900.

E-mail: info@crocketttavernmuseum.org

Web Site: www.crocketttavernmuseum.org

Key Personnel: Pres. (V) Hamblen County Chapter A.P.T.A. & Museum Shop Mgr., Sally A. Baker.

Institution Type/Description: History Museum: housed in 1794 replica of boyhood home of David Crockett.

Hours & Admission Prices: May-Oct. Tues.-Sat. 11-5. Adults $5, students 5-18 $1; discount to groups; members, children under 5, APTA members, and school & group trip chaperones no charge.

Attendance: 1,500 (estimated)

ROSE CENTER, 442 W. 2nd N. St., Morristown, TN 37814-4026. Mailing Address: P.O. Box 1976, Morristown, TN 37816-1976. Tel.: 423-581-4330. Fax: 423-581-4307.

E-mail: postmaster@rosecenter.org

Web Site: www.rosecenter.org

Key Personnel: Dir., Robert Lydick; Chm. (V), Pete Barile; Operations Coord., Patty Gracey; Coord. Education & Special Events, Beccy Hamm; Bldg. Mgr., Ray James.

Institution Type/Description: Civic Art & Cultural Center: housed in 1892 former high school.

Hours & Admission Prices: Mon.-Fri. 9:30-5, Sat. 9-1. No charge. Closed New Year's Day; Martin Luther King Day; Memorial Day; Independence Day; Labor Day; Thanksgiving; Christmas. &

Attendance: 65,000 (estimated)

Mount Pleasant

MT. PLEASANT - MAURY MUSEUM OF LOCAL HISTORY, 108 Public Sq., Mount Pleasant, TN 38474. Tel.: 931-379-9511.

E-mail: mtpleasantmuseum@gmail.com

Institution Type/Description: History Museum.

Hours & Admission Prices: Mon.-Sat. 9:30-4:30; other times by appointment.

Mountain City

JOHNSON COUNTY WELCOME CENTER & MUSEUM, 716 S. Shady St., Mountain City, TN 37683. Mailing Address: P.O. Box 1, Mountain City, TN 37683. Tel.: 423-727-5800. Fax: 423-727-4943. Facebook: Johnson County Welcome.

E-mail: johnsoncountywelcomecenter@centurylink.net

Institution Type/Description: History Museum.

Hours & Admission Prices: Jan.-May Mon.-Sat. 9-5; June-Dec. Mon.-Sat. 9-5, Sun. 1-5. No charge. &

Murfreesboro

BALDWIN PHOTOGRAPHIC GALLERY, Learning Resources Center, Murfreesboro, TN 37132. Mailing Address: MTSU, Box 305, Murfreesboro, TN 37132. Tel.: 615-898-2085 & 5628 (Off. of Secy.). Fax: 615-898-5682.

E-mail: tjimison@mtsu.edu

Key Personnel: Cur., Tom Jimison; Archivist, Valerie Menard.

Institution Type/Description: Photography Art Museum.

Hours & Admission Prices: Academic Year: Mon.-Fri. 8:30-4:30. Closed Labor Day. &

Attendance: 30,000 (estimated)

DISCOVERY CENTER AT MURFREE SPRING, 502 S.E. Broad St., Murfreesboro, TN 37130-4237. Tel.: 615-890-2300.

E-mail: info@explorethedc.org

Web Site: explorethedc.org

Key Personnel: C.E.O., Tara MacDougall; C.F.O. & Dir. Operations, Veronica Bosnak; Dir. Education, John Hawkins; Dir. Mktg. & Public Rels., Amy Stickel.

Institution Type/Description: Children's Museum.

Hours & Admission Prices: Mon.-Sat. 10-5, Sun. 1-5. Admission $8; children under 2 & members no charge. Closed major holidays. &

Attendance: 118,984

OAKLANDS HISTORIC HOUSE MUSEUM, 900 N. Maney Ave., Murfreesboro, TN 37130-2955. Mailing Address: P.O. Box 432, Murfreesboro, TN 37133-0432. Tel.: 615-893-0022. Fax: 615-893-0513. Facebook: Oaklands Historic House Museum.
E-mail: info@oaklandsmuseum.org
Web Site: www.oaklandsmuseum.org
Key Personnel: Exec. Dir., James W. Manning, Jr.; Pres. (V), Betty Hord; Dir. Education, Mary Beth Nevills; Museum Cur., Nila Gober; Special Events Coord., Raina van Setter.
Institution Type/Description: Historic House: 1818-1865 cotton plantation.
Hours & Admission Prices: Tues.-Sat. 10-4, Sun. 1-4; last tour starts at 3. Adults $10, senior citizens, AAA & military $7, college students & children 6-17 $5; discounts to groups of 10 or more; members & children under 5 no charge. Closed New Year's Day; Easter; Thanksgiving; Christmas. &
Attendance: 6,000 (estimated)

STONES RIVER NATIONAL BATTLEFIELD, 3501 Old Nashville Hwy., Murfreesboro, TN 37129-8621. Tel.: 615-893-9501. Fax: 615-893-9508. TDD: 615-893-9501.
E-mail: stri_administration@nps.gov
Web Site: www.nps.gov/stri
Key Personnel: Supt., Brenda Pennington; Chief of Interpretation, Education & Cultural Resource Mgmt., Jim Lewis.
Institution Type/Description: Park & Military Museum: adjacent to Stones River National Cemetery.
Hours & Admission Prices: Daily 8-5. No charge; donations accepted. Closed Thanksgiving; Christmas. &
Attendance: 228,000 (actual)

TODD ART GALLERY - MIDDLE TENNESSEE STATE UNIVERSITY, 1301 E. Main St., Box 25, Murfreesboro, TN 37132. Tel.: 615-898-5653.
E-mail: bjohnson@mtsu.edu
Web Site: www.mtsu.edu/art/
Key Personnel: Gallery Dir., Eric Snyder.
Institution Type/Description: Art Gallery.
Hours & Admission Prices: Mon.-Fri. 8-4:30. No charge. Closed state & university holidays. &

Nashville

ADVENTURE SCIENCE CENTER, 800 Fort Negley Blvd., Nashville, TN 37203-4833. Tel.: 615-862-5160. Fax: 615-862-5178.
E-mail: info@adventuresci.com
Web Site: www.adventuresci.com
Formerly: Cumberland Science Museum
Institution Type/Description: Science Center.
Hours & Admission Prices: Daily 10-5. Adults $14.95, youth 2-12 $10.95; discounts to ASTC members; members & children under 2 no charge. Shows: additional fee required. Closed Thanksgiving; Christmas Eve & Day. &
Attendance: 264,576 (actual)

ASSOCIATION FOR THE PRESERVATION OF TENNESSEE ANTIQUITIES, 110 Leake Ave., Nashville, TN 37205-3706. Tel.: 615-352-8247.
E-mail: info@theapta.org
Web Site: www.theapta.org
Key Personnel: Exec. Dir., Elliott W. McNiel, CAE.
Institution Type/Description: Historic Preservation Society: housed in c.1853 Belle Meade Plantation garden house.
Hours & Admission Prices: Call or write for information & details on chapter house museums. Closed New Year's Day; Thanksgiving; Christmas. &

BELLE MEADE PLANTATION, 110 Leake Ave., Nashville, TN 37205-2810. Tel.: 615-356-0501 & 800-270-3991. Fax: 615-356-2336.
E-mail: info@bellemeadeplantation.com
Web Site: www.bellemeadeplantation.com
Key Personnel: Exec. Dir., Alton W. Kelley; Museum Store Mgr., Joanne Tubb.
Institution Type/Description: Historic House: 1820 Belle Meade Mansion.
Hours & Admission Prices: Mon.-Sat. 9-5, Sun. 11-5. Adults $24, senior citizens 65 & over $20, children 6-18 $12; discount to groups; children 5 & under and members no charge. Closed New Year's Day; Easter; Thanksgiving; Christmas Eve & Day. &
Attendance: 360,000 (estimated)

BELMONT MANSION ASSOCIATION, 1700 Acklen Ave., Nashville, TN 37212. Mailing Address: 1900 Belmont Blvd., Nashville, TN 37212. Tel.: 615-460-5459. Fax: 615-460-5688. Facebook.
Web Site: www.belmontmansion.com
Key Personnel: Exec. Dir., Mark Brown; Pres. (V), Bonne Crigger.
Institution Type/Description: Historic House Museum.
Hours & Admission Prices: Mon.-Sat. 10-4, Sun. 12-4; groups by appointment. Adults $12, seniors 65 & over and military $11, children 6-12 $3; discounts to AAM & ICOM members & groups of 15 or more; members and children 5 & under no charge. Closed New Year's Day; Independence Day; Thanksgiving; Christmas.
Attendance: 25,000 (estimated)

CHEEKWOOD BOTANICAL GARDEN & MUSEUM OF ART, 1200 Forrest Park Dr., Nashville, TN 37205-4242. Tel.: 615-356-8000. Fax: 615-353-2731. Facebook.
E-mail: info@cheekwood.org
Web Site: cheekwood.org
Key Personnel: Pres. & C.E.O., Jane O. MacLeod; Chief Advancement Officer, Elizabeth Sheets; Vice Pres. Gardens & Horticulture, Peter Grimaldi; Vice Pres. Museum Affairs & Chief Cur., Gina Wouters; Chm. Bd., James V. Hunt, Sr.
Institution Type/Description: Art Museum & Botanical Garden: housed in a historic mansion built by the Cheek family between 1929-1932.
Hours & Admission Prices: Closed for construction. Reopening May 2018. Tues.-Sun. 9-5. Adults $20, seniors $18, college student $16, youth 3-17 $13; discounts to groups, military and AABGA & AAA members; children 2 & under and members no charge. Closed New Year's Day; June 2, 2018; Thanksgiving; Christmas. &
Attendance: 250,000 (estimated)

COOTER'S PLACE NASHVILLE, 2613 McGavock Pike, Nashville, TN 37214-1215. Tel.: 615-872-8358. Fax: 615-872-8359. Facebook: Cooter's Place Nashville.
E-mail: info@cootersplace.com
Web Site: cootersplace.ocm
Key Personnel: Museum Shop Mgr., Jaclyn Smith.
Institution Type/Description: History Museum.
Hours & Admission Prices: Sun.-Thurs. 8:30am-8pm, Fri.-Sat. 8:30am-9pm. No charge. Closed Thanksgiving; Christmas. &

COUNTRY MUSIC HALL OF FAME AND MUSEUM, COUNTRY MUSIC FOUNDATION, 222 5th Ave., S., Nashville, TN 37203-4206. Tel.: 615-416-2001. Fax: 615-255-2245. Facebook, Twitter & Snapchat: @countrymusichof; Instagram: @officialcmhof.
E-mail: info@countrymusichalloffame.org
Web Site: countrymusichalloffame.org
Key Personnel: C.E.O., Kyle Young; Chm. (V), Steve Turner; Sr. Vice Pres. Fin. Svcs. & Operations, Nina Burghard; Sr. Vice Pres. Museum Svcs., Carolyn Tate; Sr. Vice Pres. Sales & Mktg., Sharon Brawner; Vice Pres. Devel., Lisa Purcell; Vice Pres. Events & Mgmt., Jo Ellen Drennon McDowell.
Institution Type/Description: Country Music Museum & Historic Recording Studio and Historic Woodblock Print Shop.
Hours & Admission Prices: Daily 9-5. Adults $25.95, seniors 60 & over and students $23.95, military $22.95; children 6-12 $15.95; discounts to AAA & AAM members; children 5 & under and members no charge. Closed New Year's Day; Thanksgiving; Christmas. &
Attendance: 421,151 (actual)

DISCIPLES OF CHRIST HISTORICAL SOCIETY, 1101 19th Ave. S., Nashville, TN 37212-2196. Mailing Address: P.O. Box D, Bethany, WV 26032. Tel.: 615-327-1444. Fax: 615-327-1445.
E-mail: dchs1941@gmail.com
Web Site: www.discipleshistory.org
Key Personnel: Interim Exec. Dir., John M. Imbler; Archivist, Shelley L. Jacobs.
Institution Type/Description: Religious Museum.
Hours & Admission Prices: Tues.-Fri. 9-4. No charge. Closed national holidays. &
Attendance: 1,000 (estimated)

THE FISK UNIVERSITY GALLERIES, Fisk University, 1000 17th Ave., N., Nashville, TN 37208-3051. Tel.: 615-329-8720.
E-mail: galleries@fisk.edu
Web Site: www.fisk.edu/services-resources/fisk-university-galleries
Key Personnel: Dir. & Cur., Jamaal B. Sheets.
Institution Type/Description: Art Gallery & Museum: art galleries housed in 1888 Neo-Romanesque building & university library building.

Hours & Admission Prices: Van Vechten Gallery: Mon.-Wed. & Sat. 10-4, Thurs.-Fri. 10-7. Douglas Gallery: Academic Year: Mon.-Wed. & Sat. 10-4, Thurs.-Fri. 10-7. No charge. Closed university holidays. &
Attendance: 42,000 (actual)

FORT NASHBOROUGH, 170 1st Ave., N., Nashville, TN 37201-1924. Mailing Address: Centennial Park Office, Nashville, TN 37201. Tel.: 615-862-8400. Fax: 615-862-5493.
E-mail: jackie.jones@nashville.gov
Web Site: www.nashville.gov/parks
Key Personnel: Dir., Roy E. Wilson.
Institution Type/Description: Historic Building/Site Museum: 1780 site of Fort Nashborough, first settlement in Nashville.
Hours & Admission Prices: Temporarily closed for renovations. &

FRIST CENTER FOR THE VISUAL ARTS, 919 Broadway, Nashville, TN 37203-3822. Tel.: 615-244-3340. Fax: 615-244-3339. Facebook, Twitter & Instagram: @fristcenter; YouTube: FristCenter.
E-mail: mail@fristcenter.org
Web Site: www.fristcenter.org
Key Personnel: C.E.O., Susan Edwards; Chm. & Pres., Billy Frist; Dir. Education & Outreach, Anne Henderson; Registrar, Amie Geremia; Cur., Mark Scala.
Institution Type/Description: Art Museum.
Hours & Admission Prices: Mon.-Wed. & Sat. 10-5:30, Thurs.-Fri. 10-9, Sun. 1-5:30. Adults $12, senior citizens & college students $9, active military $7; discounts to groups of 10 or more and AAM & ICOM members; members, children 18 & under and college students Thurs.-Fri. 5pm-9pm no charge. Additional pricing for special exhibitions. Closed New Year's Day; Thanksgiving; Christmas. &
Attendance: 169,928 (actual)

HISTORIC TRAVELLERS REST PLANTATION, 636 Farrell Pkwy., Nashville, TN 37220-1218. Tel.: 615-832-8197. Fax: 615-832-8169. Facebook.
E-mail: director@travellersrestplantation.org
Web Site: www.travellersrestplantation.org
Formerly: Travellers Rest Plantation and Museum
Key Personnel: Exec. Dir., Mary Kerr; Dir. Education, Tonya Staggs.
Institution Type/Description: Historic House Museum: housed in 1799 home of Judge John Overton.
Hours & Admission Prices: Mon.-Sat. 10-4:30; call to confirm. Family $40, adults $12, seniors 65 & over and military $11, students 6-17 $10; children 5 & under no charge. Closed New Year's Eve & Day; Thanksgiving; Christmas Eve & Day. &
Attendance: 18,000 (estimated)

JOHN EARLY MUSEUM MAGNET MIDDLE SCHOOL, 1000 Cass St., Nashville, TN 37208. Tel.: 615-291-6369. Fax: 615-271-1782.
E-mail: communications@mnps.org
Web Site: johnearlyms.mnps.org/pages/johnearlymiddle
Institution Type/Description: History Museum.
Hours & Admission Prices: By appointment. No charge; donations accepted. &

LANE MOTOR MUSEUM, 702 Murfreesboro Pike, Nashville, TN 37210-4522. Tel.: 615-742-7445.
E-mail: info@lanemotormuseum.org
Web Site: www.lanemotormuseum.org
Key Personnel: Dir., Jeff Lane; Sec. & Bd. Member, David Yando.
Institution Type/Description: Transportation Museum.
Hours & Admission Prices: Thurs.-Mon. 10-5. Adults 18-64 $12, seniors 65 & over $8, youth 6-17 $3; members and children 5 & under no charge. Closed New Year's Day; Thanksgiving; Christmas. &
Attendance: 22,000

NASHVILLE ZOO AT GRASSMERE, 3777 Nolensville Pike, Nashville, TN 37211-3324. Tel.: 615-833-1534. Fax: 615-333-0728.
E-mail: pr@nashvillezoo.org
Web Site: www.nashvillezoo.org
Key Personnel: Pres., Rick Schwartz; Chm. (V), Julie W. Walker; C.F.O., Reagan Fairbairn; C.O.O., Andy Tillman; Ectotherm Cur., Dale McGinnity; Avian Cur., Joe deGraauw; Cur. Behavioral Husbandry, Jacqueline Menish; Sr. Zoo Veterinarian, Dr. Heather Robertson.
Institution Type/Description: Zoological Park.
Hours & Admission Prices: March 11-Oct. 12 daily 9-6; Oct. 13-March 10 daily 9-4. Adults $16, seniors $14, children 2-12 $11; discounts to groups & military; members & children under 2 no charge. &
Attendance: 648,034 (actual)

THE PARTHENON, Centennial Park, 2500 West End Ave., Nashville, TN 37203. Tel.: 615-862-8431. Fax: 615-880-2265. Facebook.
E-mail: info@parthenon.org
Web Site: www.parthenon.org
Key Personnel: Business Mgr., Andrea Gilbert Berger.
Institution Type/Description: Art Museum: housed in exact reproduction of Athenian Parthenon.
Hours & Admission Prices: Tues.-Sat. 9-4:30, Sun. 12:30-4:30; groups by appointment. Adults $6, seniors & children 4-17 $4; discounts to groups & AAM members; members & children under 4 no charge. Closed New Year's Day; Thanksgiving & day after; Christmas. &
Attendance: 150,000 (actual)

THE PUBLIC LIBRARY OF NASHVILLE AND DAVIDSON COUNTY, Nashville Room, Special Collections Div., 615 Church St., Nashville, TN 37219-2314. Tel.: 615-862-5800. Fax: 615-862-5838.
Web Site: www.library.nashville.org
Key Personnel: Library Mgr., Andrea Blackman.
Institution Type/Description: Local History Library.
Hours & Admission Prices: Tues.-Fri. 9-6, Sat. 9-5, Sun. 2-5. No charge. Closed Mondays & national holidays. &
Attendance: 48,162 (actual)

RYMAN AUDITORIUM, 116 Fifth Ave. N., Nashville, TN 37219. Tel.: 615-458-8700. Fax: 615-458-8701.
Web Site: www.ryman.com
Institution Type/Description: History Museum: housed in the home of the Grand Ole Opry from 1943-1974. A National Historic Landmark.
Hours & Admission Prices: Tours: daily 9-4. Closed New Year's Day; Thanksgiving; Christmas. &
Attendance: 150,000 (actual)

SARRATT GALLERY AT VANDERBILT, 207 Sarratt Student Center, Nashville, TN 37240. Tel.: 615-343-0491. Fax: 615-343-8081.
E-mail: david.f.heustess@vanderbilt.edu
Web Site: www.vanderbilt.edu/sarrattgallery
Key Personnel: Dir., David Heustess.
Institution Type/Description: Art Gallery.
Hours & Admission Prices: Academic Year: Mon.-Fri. 9-9, Sat.-Sun. 10-10; Summer: Mon.-Fri. 8:30-4:30. No charge.

SOUTHERN BAPTIST HISTORICAL LIBRARY AND ARCHIVES, 901 Commerce St., Ste. 400, Nashville, TN 37203-3628. Tel.: 615-244-0344. Fax: 615-782-4821.
E-mail: bill@sbhla.org
Web Site: www.sbhla.org
Key Personnel: Dir. & Archivist, Taffey Hall; Accountant, Teresa Scott; Librarian, Stephen Gateley; Library Clerk, Elyse Rives.
Institution Type/Description: Religious Museum.
Hours & Admission Prices: Mon.-Fri. 8-4; other times by appointment. No charge. Closed national holidays. &
Attendance: 1,100 (estimated)

TENNESSEE AGRICULTURAL MUSEUM, Ellington Agricultural Center, Nashville, TN 37204. Tel.: 615-837-5197. Facebook: Tennessee Agricultural Museum.
E-mail: tennessee.agricultural.museum@tn.gov
Web Site: tnagmuseum.org
Key Personnel: Greg Phillipy.
Institution Type/Description: Agriculture Museum: housed in a former horse barn which was once part of the Brentwood Hall estate of financier Rogers Caldwell.
Hours & Admission Prices: Mon.-Fri. 9-4; groups by appointment. Museum: no charge; donations accepted. Special Events: call for admission prices. Closed state holidays. &
Attendance: 22,203 (actual)

TENNESSEE CENTRAL RAILWAY MUSEUM, 220 Willow St., Nashville, TN 37210-2159. Tel.: 615-244-9001. Fax: 615-244-2120. Facebook: @TCRY.org.
E-mail: tbebout@nerr.com
Web Site: www.tcry.org
Key Personnel: C.E.O., Chm. (V) & Pres. (V), Terry L. Bebout; Public Rels., Robert E. Hultman; Museum Shop Mgr., Charles Owens.
Institution Type/Description: Railroad Museum.

Hours & Admission Prices: Office: Tues.-Fri. 9-4, Sat. 9-3. Hobby Shop: Tues. & Thurs. 12-4, Sat. 9-3. Museum: no charge; donations accepted. Model Train Shows: adults $4; discounts to active military & NRHS members.
Attendance: 50,000 (estimated)

TENNESSEE HISTORICAL COMMISSION, 2941 Lebanon Rd., Nashville, TN 37243-0442. Tel.: 615-532-1550. Fax: 615-532-1549.
E-mail: patrick.mcintyre@tn.gov
Web Site: www.tn.gov/environment/about-tdec/tennessee-historical-commission.html
Key Personnel: Exec. Dir., E. Patrick McIntyre, Jr.; Asst. Dir. State Programs, Linda T. Wynn; Deputy State Historic Preservation Officer, Claudette Stager; Historic Preservation Supvr., Holly M. Barnett; Historic Preservation Specialist, Claire Meyer; Historic Preservation Specialist, Rebecca Schmitt; Historic Preservation Specialist, Ms. Jane-Coleman Cottone; Historic Preservation Specialist, Mr. Christopher Kinder; Historic Preservation Specialist, Kerri Ross; Historic Preservation Specialist, Ms. Casey Lee; Historic Preservation Specialist, Ms. Peggy Nickell; Historic Preservation Specialist, Mr. Dan Brown; Historic Preservation Specialist, Ms. Nina Scall; Historic Preservation Specialist, Mr. Graham Perry; Historic Preservation Specialist, Ms. Susan McClamroch.
Institution Type/Description: State Historic Preservation Agency.
Hours & Admission Prices: Mon.-Fri. 8-4:30 by appointment. No charge. Closed holidays. &

TENNESSEE SPORTS HALL OF FAME MUSEUM, 501 Broadway, Nashville, TN 37203. Tel.: 615-242-4750. Fax: 615-242-4752. Facebook.
E-mail: tnsports@bellsouth.net
Web Site: www.tshf.net
Key Personnel: Exec. Dir., Dr. Bill Emendorfer.
Institution Type/Description: Sports Museum.
Hours & Admission Prices: Tues.-Sat. 10-5. Adults $3, seniors over 55 & children $2; discounts to groups of 10 or more. &

TENNESSEE STATE CAPITOL, 600 Charlotte Ave., Nashville, TN 37243-9034. Mailing Address: 505 Deaderich St., Nashville, TN 37243-1120. Tel.: 615-741-2692; 800-407-4324. Fax: 615-741-7231.
E-mail: museuminfo@tnmuseum.org
Web Site: www.tnmuseum.org/exhibits/tennessee_state_capitol
Key Personnel: Cur., James A. Hoobler.
Institution Type/Description: Historic Building: built in 1859. A National Historic Landmark.
Hours & Admission Prices: Mon.-Fri. 9-4. Guided Tours: Mon.-Fri. 9-11 & 1-3; groups of 10 or more by appointment. No charge.
Attendance: 30,000 (estimated)

TENNESSEE STATE LIBRARY AND ARCHIVES, 403 7th Ave. N., Nashville, TN 37243. Tel.: 615-741-2764. Facebook.
E-mail: reference.tsla@tn.gov
Web Site: www.tn.gov/tsla
Key Personnel: State Librarian & Archivist, Charles A. Sherrill.
Institution Type/Description: Library & Archives.
Hours & Admission Prices: Library Reading Room: Tues.-Sat. 8-4:30. Legislative History: Tues.-Fri. 8-4:30. Closed New Year's Day; Martin Luther King Jr. Day; Presidents' Day; Good Friday; Memorial Day; Independence Day; Labor Day; Columbus Day; Veterans Day; Thanksgiving; Christmas. &

TENNESSEE STATE MUSEUM, 600 James Robertson Pkwy., Nashville, TN 37243. Tel.: 615-741-5280. Facebook.
E-mail: info@tnmuseum.org
Web Site: tnmuseum.org
Key Personnel: Exec. Dir., Ashley Howell; Deputy Dir., Mary Jane Crockett-Green; Chief Cur. & Dir. Collections, Dan Pomeroy.
Institution Type/Description: History Museum.
Hours & Admission Prices: Temporarily closed for relocation. &
Attendance: 180,000 (estimated)

21C MUSEUM HOTEL NASHVILLE, 222 2nd Ave. N., Nashville, TN 37201. Tel.: 615-610-6400.
E-mail: BDowney@21cMuseum.org
Web Site: www.21cmuseumhotels.com/nashville/
Key Personnel: Museum Mgr., Brian Downey.
Institution Type/Description: Contemporary Art Gallery.
Hours & Admission Prices: See website for hours. No charge.

UPPER ROOM CHAPEL MUSEUM, 1908 Grand Ave., Nashville, TN 37212-2188. Tel.: 615-340-7207. Fax: 615-340-7293. Facebook.
E-mail: kkimball@upperroom.org
Web Site: www.upperroom.org
Key Personnel: Editor & Publisher, Stephen Bryant; Mgr. & Cur., Kathryn A. Kimball.
Institution Type/Description: Christian Art Museum.
Hours & Admission Prices: Mon.-Fri. 8-4:30, Suggested Donation: $5. Closed major holidays. &
Attendance: 8,500 (estimated)

VANDERBILT UNIVERSITY FINE ARTS GALLERY, 1220 21st Ave. S., Nashville, TN 37203. Mailing Address: PMB 273, 230 Appleton Place, Nashville, TN 37203-5721. Tel.: 615-322-0605 & 343-1704. Fax: 615-343-1382.
E-mail: joseph.mella@vanderbilt.edu
Web Site: www.vanderbilt.edu/gallery
Key Personnel: Dir., Joseph S. Mella.
Institution Type/Description: Art Gallery: housed in renovated 1928 building designed by McKim, Mead & White.
Hours & Admission Prices: School Year: Mon.-Fri. 11-4, Sat.-Sun. 1-5; Summer: Tues.-Fri. 12-4, Sat. 1-5. No charge. Closed school holidays. &
Attendance: 5,000 (estimated)

WARNER PARK NATURE CENTER, 7311 Hwy. 100, Nashville, TN 37221. Tel.: 615-352-6299. Fax: 615-880-2282.
E-mail: wpnc@nashville.gov
Institution Type/Description: Nature Center.
Hours & Admission Prices: Park: sunrise to sunset. Center: Tues.-Sat. 9-4. Closed major holidays.

WATKINS INSTITUTE - BROWNLEE O. CURRY JR. GALLERY, 2298 Rosa L. Parks Blvd., Nashville, TN 37228-1306. Tel.: 615-383-4848; 866-887-6395. Fax: 615-383-4849.
E-mail: info@watkins.edu
Web Site: watkins.edu
Institution Type/Description: Art Gallery with Art School.
Hours & Admission Prices: Mon.-Fri. 9-8, Sat. 10-4, Sun. 2-4. No charge. Closed New Year's Day; Independence Day; Labor Day; Thanksgiving; Christmas. &

WILLIE NELSON & FRIENDS GENERAL STORE & MUSEUM, 2613A McGavock Pike, Nashville, TN 37214-1215. Tel.: 615-885-1515. Fax: 888-517-6579. Facebook: @WillieNelsonMuseum.
E-mail: info@willienelsongeneralstore.com
Web Site: www.willienelsongeneralstore.com
Key Personnel: C.E.O., Mark Hughes.
Institution Type/Description: Country Music Stars Museum.
Hours & Admission Prices: Daily 8:30am-9pm. &
Attendance: 100,000 (estimated)

Newbern

NEWBERN DEPOT & RAILROAD MUSEUM, 108 Jefferson St., Newbern, TN 38059. Tel.: 731-627-3221.
Institution Type/Description: Railroad Museum.
Hours & Admission Prices: Call for hours.

Newport

NEWPORT - COCKE COUNTY MUSEUM, 433 Prospect Ave., Newport, TN 37821. Tel.: 423-623-7201.
E-mail: summers.pj@gmail.com
Web Site: www.tngenweb.org/cocke/countymuseum/museum.htm
Institution Type/Description: History Museum.
Hours & Admission Prices: Wed. 1-5. No charge.

Niota

NIOTA RAILROAD DEPOT, 201 E. Main St., Niota, TN 37826. Mailing Address: P.O. Box 515, Niota, TN 37826-0515. Tel.: 423-568-2584.
E-mail: cityofniota@gmail.com
Web Site: www.niota-tn.org
Institution Type/Description: Historic Building: housed in a former depot now serving as Niota City Hall; built in 1854. Listed on the National Register of Historic Places.
Hours & Admission Prices: By appointment.

Norris

NORRIS MUSEUM, Town Center, One Norris Sq., Norris, TN 37828. Mailing Address: P.O. Box 1110, Norris, TN 37828-1110. Tel.: 865-494-6800.
Key Personnel: Chm. (V), Ellalyn Crossno; Pres. (V), Jerry L. Crossno.
Institution Type/Description: History Museum.
Hours & Admission Prices: March-Dec. Tues. & Sun. 2-4; other times by appointment. No charge; donations accepted.

WILL G. AND HELEN H. LENOIR MUSEUM, 2121 Norris Frwy. (Hwy. 441), Norris, TN 37828. Mailing Address: P.O. Box 484, Norris, TN 37828. Tel.: 865-426-7461.
E-mail: Ask.TNStateParks@tn.gov
Web Site: tnstateparks.com/parks/about/norris-dam
Institution Type/Description: History Museum.
Hours & Admission Prices: Daily. No charge.

Oak Ridge

AMERICAN MUSEUM OF SCIENCE & ENERGY, 300 S. Tulane Ave., Oak Ridge, TN 37830-6726. Tel.: 865-576-3200. Fax: 865-241-8016.
E-mail: information@amse.org
Web Site: amse.org
Key Personnel: Exec. Dir., David L. Moore; Deputy Dir., Kenneth Mayes.
Institution Type/Description: Science & Technology Museum.
Hours & Admission Prices: Mon.-Sat. 9-5, Sun. 1-5. Adults 18-64 $5, seniors 65 & over $4, children 6-17 $3; ASTC Passport members, members & children under 6 no charge. Closed New Year's Day; Easter; Thanksgiving; Christmas Eve & Christmas. &
Attendance: 90,000 (actual)

CHILDREN'S MUSEUM OF OAK RIDGE, INC., 461 W. Outer Dr., Oak Ridge, TN 37830-3700. Tel.: 865-482-1074. Fax: 865-481-4889.
E-mail: chmor@childrensmuseumofoakridge.org
Web Site: www.childrensmuseumofoakridge.org
Key Personnel: Exec. Dir., Beth Shea; Business Mgr. & Museum Shop Mgr., Dawn Van Eek; Dir. Education, Lorraine Bowen; Program Dir. & Property Mgr., Bucky Smith.
Institution Type/Description: Children's Museum.
Hours & Admission Prices: June-Aug. Mon.-Fri. 9-5, Sat. 10-4, Sun. 1-4; Sept.-May Tues.-Fri. 9-5, Sat. 10-4, Sun. 1-4. Adults $8, senior citizens $7, children 3-18 $6; discounts to ACM Reciprocal Program & groups; children under 3 & members no charge. Closed New Year's Eve & Day; Memorial Day; Independence Day; Thanksgiving; Christmas Eve & Day.
Attendance: 150,000 (estimated)

OAK RIDGE ART CENTER, 201 Badger Ave., Oak Ridge, TN 37830-6216. Mailing Address: P.O. Box 7005, Oak Ridge, TN 37831-3305. Tel.: 865-482-1441. Fax: 865-482-9741.
E-mail: oakridgeartcenter@comcast.net
Web Site: oakridgeartcenter.org
Key Personnel: Dir., Leah Marcum-Estes; Pres. (V), Elizabeth Spooner.
Institution Type/Description: Art Center.
Hours & Admission Prices: Tues.-Fri. 9-5, Sat.-Mon. 1-4. No charge. Closed major holidays. &
Attendance: 50,000 (estimated)

UNIVERSITY OF TENNESSEE ARBORETUM, 901 S. Illinois Ave., Oak Ridge, TN 37830-8032. Tel.: 865-483-3571. Fax: 865-483-3572.
E-mail: utforest@utk.edu
Web Site: forestry.tennessee.edu/arboretum
Key Personnel: Dir., Kevin P. Hoyt; Sec., Lynne Lucas.
Institution Type/Description: Arboretum.
Hours & Admission Prices: Daily 8am-Sunset. Office: Mon.-Fri. 8-4:30. No charge; donations accepted. Closed national holidays.
Attendance: 35,000 (estimated)

Paris

PARIS-HENRY COUNTY HERITAGE CENTER, 614 N. Poplar St., Paris, TN 38242-3440. Mailing Address: P.O. Box 822, Paris, TN 38242-0822. Tel.: 731-642-1030.
E-mail: director@phchc.com
Web Site: www.phchc.com
Key Personnel: Chm., David Webb; Treas., Vicki Muzzall.

Institution Type/Description: History Museum.
Hours & Admission Prices: Tues.-Fri. 10-4, Sat. 10-2. No charge; donations accepted. Closed New Year's Eve & Day; Thanksgiving weekend; Christmas Eve, Day & week. &
Attendance: 2,500 (estimated)

Parsons

PARSONS AND GREATER AREA HISTORICAL MUSEUM, 535 Tennessee Ave., Municipal Bldg., Parsons, TN 38363. Mailing Address: P.O. Box 128, Parsons, TN 38363-0128. Tel.: 731-847-6358. Fax: 731-847-9272.
E-mail: coordinator@cityofparsons.com
Web Site: www.cityofparsons.com/museum.htm
Key Personnel: Chm. (V), Branson Townsend; Treas., Judy Daugherty.
Institution Type/Description: History Museum.
Hours & Admission Prices: Mon.-Tues. & Thurs.-Fri. 9-5, Wed. 9-2. Admission: $2; discounts to volunteers. &
Attendance: 1,000 (estimated)

Pigeon Forge

ELVIS & HOLLYWOOD LEGENDS MUSEUM, 2530 Parkway, Ste. 4, Pigeon Forge, TN 37863. Tel.: 865-428-2001.
E-mail: elvismuseumoftn@gmail.com
Web Site: www.elvispresleymuseum.com
Formerly: Elvis Presley Museum
Key Personnel: Asst. Mgr. & Mktg. Dir., Sunni McAllister; Mgr., Grace Savers; Elvis Tribute Artist, Doug Thompson; Dir. Operations, Owner, Lynn McAllister.
Institution Type/Description: History Museum.
Hours & Admission Prices: Mon.-Sat. 10-10, Sun. 10-6. Adults $14.99, seniors 55 & over & children 6-12 $10. Closed Thanksgiving; Christmas. &
Attendance: 13,000 (estimated)

PARROT MOUNTAIN & TROPICAL BIRD SANCTUARY, 1471 McCarter Hollow Rd., Pigeon Forge, TN 37862. Tel.: 417-823-0981, 800-987-9852. Fax: 865-428-7798.
Web Site: www.parrotmountainandgardens.com
Institution Type/Description: Bird Sanctuary.
Hours & Admission Prices: March-Nov. Mon.-Sat. 10-5. Adults 12 & over $17.95, seniors 65 & over $14.95, children 2-11 $7.95; discounts to groups of 10 or more. &

SMOKY MOUNTAIN CAR MUSEUM, 2970 Parkway, Pigeon Forge, TN 37863-3314. Mailing Address: P.O. Box 385, Pigeon Forge, TN 37868-0385. Tel.: 865-453-3433.
Institution Type/Description: Car Museum.
Hours & Admission Prices: April-June daily 10-6; July to Labor Day daily 10-7. Adults $7.50, children 3-10 $2.

SOUTHERN GOSPEL MUSIC HALL OF FAME & MUSEUM, Dollywood, 2700 Dollywood Park Blvd., Pigeon Forge, TN 37863. Mailing Address: Southern Gospel Music Assoc., P.O. Box 6729, Sevierville, TN 37864. Tel.: 865-908-4040.
E-mail: kim@sgma.org
Web Site: www.sgma.org/default.htm
Key Personnel: Exec. Dir., Charlie Waller.
Institution Type/Description: Music Museum.
Hours & Admission Prices: See Dollywood website for hours.

Piney Flats

ROCKY MOUNT MUSEUM, 200 Hyder Hill Rd., Piney Flats, TN 37686-4630. Mailing Address: P.O. Box 160, Piney Flats, TN 37686-0160. Tel.: 423-538-7396. Fax: 423-538-1086.
E-mail: info@rockymountmuseum.com
Web Site: www.rockymountmuseum.com
Key Personnel: C.E.O. & Exec. Dir., Gary Walrath; Pres. (V), James Kelly; Exec. Asst., Delores Miller; Museum Shop Mgr., Evelyn Hunt.
Institution Type/Description: Historic Site: 1790-92 original U.S. Territorial Capitol of Southwest Territory.
Hours & Admission Prices: Living History Tours: March to mid-Dec. Tues.-Sat. 11-5; other times by appointment. Adults $8, seniors $7, children 6-17 $5; discounts to groups, AAM, AAA & AARP members; members no charge. Office: Mon.-Fri. 9-5. Closed Thanksgiving. &
Attendance: 16,000 (estimated)

Pinson

PINSON MOUNDS STATE ARCHAEOLOGICAL AREA, 460 Ozier Rd., Pinson, TN 38366-9626. Tel.: 731-988-5614. Facebook: Pinson Mounds State Archaeological Park.
E-mail: wesley.williams@tn.gov
Web Site: tnstateparks.com/parks/about/pinson-mounds
Key Personnel: Park Mgr., Tim Poole; Park Ranger, Wes Williams.
Institution Type/Description: Archaeological Site: Middle Woodland Period ceremonial site, with mounds & earthworks.
Hours & Admission Prices: Daily 8-4:30. No charge. Closed state winter holidays.
Attendance: 110,000 (estimated)

Pleasant Hill

PIONEER HALL MUSEUM, 459 E. Main St., Pleasant Hill, TN 38578. Mailing Address: P.O. Box 264, Pleasant Hill, TN 38578. Tel.: 931-277-5313.
E-mail: kingsburymanor@frontiernet.net
Web Site: pioneerhallmuseum.net
Key Personnel: Pres. (V), Jeanne C. Kingsbury; Cur. & Museum Shop Mgr., Sharon Weible.
Institution Type/Description: History Museum: built in 1884. Listed on the National Register of Historic Places.
Hours & Admission Prices: Sun. 2-5, Wed. 10-4. No charge; donations accepted.
Attendance: 220 (estimated)

Portland

COLD SPRINGS SCHOOL AND MUSEUM, 303 Portland Blvd., Portland, TN 37148. Tel.: 615-325-2279.
Institution Type/Description: History Museum: housed in a former one-room schoolhouse.
Hours & Admission Prices: June-Sept. Sun. 1-4.

Pulaski

GILES COUNTY HISTORICAL SOCIETY & MUSEUM, 122 S. Second St., Pulaski, TN 38478-3219. Mailing Address: P.O. Box 693, Pulaski, TN 38478-0693. Tel.: 931-363-2720.
E-mail: newmangeorge@bellsouth.net
Key Personnel: Dir., George W. Newman.
Institution Type/Description: History Museum.
Hours & Admission Prices: Mon.-Wed. & Fri.-Sat. 10-4, Sun. 1-5. No charge; donations accepted. Closed holidays.
Attendance: 300 (estimated)

Red Boiling Springs

CYCLEMOS MOTORCYCLE MUSEUM, 319 E. Main St., Red Boiling Springs, TN 37150-2322. Tel.: 615-699-5049.
E-mail: cyclemos@nctc.com
Web Site: www.cyclemos.com
Institution Type/Description: Motorcycle Museum.
Hours & Admission Prices: Thurs.-Sun. 10-5.

HISTORIC RED BOILING SPRINGS - THE THOMAS HOUSE, 520 E. Main St., Red Boiling Springs, TN 37150. Mailing Address: P.O. Box 408, Red Boiling Springs, TN 37150. Tel.: 615-699-3006.
E-mail: thomashouse@nctc.com
Web Site: www.thethomashouse.com
Institution Type/Description: Historic House Museum.
Hours & Admission Prices: By appointment.

Ripley

LAUDERDALE COUNTY MUSEUM, 123 S. Jefferson St., Ripley, TN 38063-1553. Tel.: 731-635-9541. Fax: 731-635-9064.
E-mail: stodd@lauderdalecountytn.org
Web Site: www.lauderdalecountytn.org
Key Personnel: Dir., Susan Todd; Chm. (V), Keith Davidson; Treas., Maurice Gaines.
Institution Type/Description: Historic Building: housed in Sugar Hill Mansion; built in 1843.
Hours & Admission Prices: Mon.-Fri. 8-4:30; other times by appointment. No charge; donations accepted. Closed Independence Day; Thanksgiving; Christmas Eve & Day.
Attendance: 350 (estimated)

Rogersville

TENNESSEE NEWSPAPER & PRINTING MUSEUM, 415 S. Depot St., Rogersville, TN 37857-3331. Tel.: 423-272-1961. Fax: 423-272-1961.
Institution Type/Description: History Museum: housed in a restored 1890 Southern Railway depot. Listed on the National Register of Historic Places.
Hours & Admission Prices: Daily 10-4 by appointment. No charge; donations accepted.

Rugby

HISTORIC RUGBY, 1331 Rugby Pkwy., Rugby, TN 37733. Mailing Address: P.O. Box 8, Rugby, TN 37733-0008. Tel.: 423-628-2441. Fax: 423-628-2266. Facebook: Historic Rugby.
E-mail: historicrugby@highland.net
Web Site: www.historicrugby.org
Key Personnel: Site Mgr., Kelly McCauley; Pres., John Hicks; Museum Shop Mgr., Jesse Gully.
Institution Type/Description: Historic Site.
Hours & Admission Prices: See website for hours & admission prices.
Attendance: 15,000 (estimated)

Rutherford

DAVID CROCKETT CABIN, 219 N. Trenton St., Rutherford, TN 38369. Mailing Address: 945 S. Trenton, Rutherford, TN 38369-9670. Tel.: 731-665-7253.
E-mail: jobne@msn.com
Web Site: www.davycrockettcabin.org
Key Personnel: Mgr. & Treas., Joe Bone; Chm. (V), Tim Griggs.
Institution Type/Description: Historic Building: 1800s David Crockett Cabin.
Hours & Admission Prices: Memorial Day to Labor Day Tues.-Sat. 9:30-4:30, Sun. 1:30-4:30; other times by appointment. Requested Donations: family $7, adults $3, children 6 & over $1.50; discounts to students & seniors groups; children under 6 no charge.
Attendance: 1,500 (estimated)

Savannah

CHERRY MANSION, 265 Main St., Savannah, TN 38372. Tel.: 731-607-1208.
Institution Type/Description: Historic House: built in 1830, former home of W.H. Cherry & headquarters for General U.S. Grant in 1862.
Hours & Admission Prices: By appointment. Tours: adults $10, students $5.

TENNESSEE RIVER MUSEUM, 495 Main St., Savannah, TN 38372-2062. Tel.: 800-552-3866, 731-925-8181. Fax: 731-925-6987.
E-mail: beth@tourhardincounty.org
Web Site: www.tennesseerivermuseum.org
Key Personnel: Tourism Dir., Beth Pippin.
Institution Type/Description: History Museum.
Hours & Admission Prices: Mon.-Sat. 9-5, Sun. 1-5. Adults $3; children 18 & under no charge.
Attendance: 7,500 (actual)

Selmer

MCNAIRY COUNTY HISTORICAL MUSEUM, 114 N. Third St., Selmer, TN 38375-2112. Tel.: 731-646-0018.
Key Personnel: Dir., Judy Hammons.
Institution Type/Description: History Museum.
Hours & Admission Prices: Mon., Wed. & Fri. 12-3. No charge; donations accepted.
Attendance: 250 (estimated)

Sevierville

FLOYD GARRETT'S MUSCLE CAR MUSEUM, 320 Winfield Dunn Pkwy., Sevierville, TN 37876. Tel.: 865-908-0882.
E-mail: floydava@musclecarmuseum.com
Web Site: www.musclecarmuseum.com
Institution Type/Description: Car Museum.
Hours & Admission Prices: Jan.-March call or see website for hours. Adults $11, children 8-12 $5; children under 8 no charge. Closed Thanksgiving; Christmas.

NATIONAL KNIFE MUSEUM, INC., 2320 Winfield Dunn Pkwy., Sevierville, TN 37876-0557. Mailing Address: P.O. Box 8534, Chattanooga, TN 37414-0534. Tel.: 865-453-5871, ext. 259.
E-mail: nkmcurator@gmail.com
Web Site: www.nkcaknife.org
Key Personnel: On Site Mgr., Michael Zavasky; Staff, Ronald Ward.
Institution Type/Description: Knife and Cutlery Museum.
Hours & Admission Prices: Daily 10-9. No charge; donations requested. &
Attendance: 40,000 (actual)

RAINFOREST ADVENTURES DISCOVERY ZOO, 109 NASCAR Dr., Sevierville, TN 37862. Tel.: 865-428-4091. Fax: 865-908-5076.
E-mail: rainforest24@juno.com
Web Site: www.rfadventures.com
Institution Type/Description: Zoo.
Hours & Admission Prices: Daily 9-5. Adults $11.99, seniors 55 & over $9.99, youth 3-12 $6.99; children under 3 no charge. Closed Christmas.

SEVIER COUNTY HERITAGE MUSEUM, 167 Bruce St., Sevierville, TN 37862-3501. Tel.: 865-453-4058.
Institution Type/Description: History Museum: housed in the former post office. Listed on the National Register of Historic Places.
Hours & Admission Prices: Mon.-Tues. & Thurs.-Sat. call for hours. No charge.

SMOKY MOUNTAIN DEER FARM AND EXOTIC PETTING ZOO, 478 Happy Hollow Ln., Sevierville, TN 37876. Tel.: 865-428-3337. Fax: 865-429-2218. Facebook: Smoky Mountain Deer Farm and Exotic Petting Zoo.
E-mail: warden89@hotmail.com
Web Site: www.deerfarmzoo.com
Institution Type/Description: Zoo.
Hours & Admission Prices: Daily 10-5:30. Adults 13 & over $11.99, children 3-12 $7.99, children 1-2 $.99; children under one $.09; discounts to seniors, military & AAA members. Pony Ride: $7.99. Closed Thanksgiving; Christmas.

TENNESSEE MUSEUM OF AVIATION, 135 Air Museum Way, Sevierville, TN 37862-8703. Mailing Address: P.O. Box 5587, Sevierville, TN 37864. Tel.: 865-908-0171 & 0760. Fax: 865-908-8421.
E-mail: rmelton1@earthlink.net
Web Site: www.tnairmuseum.com
Key Personnel: Pres., C.E.O. & Chm, (V) R. Neal Melton; Membership Coord. & Education, Sandra Layman; Cur. & Archivist, Tom Walker; Museum Shop Mgr., Lana Johnson; Volunteer, Rhonda Melton.
Institution Type/Description: Aviation Museum: state's official Aviation Hall of Fame.
Hours & Admission Prices: Mon.-Sat. 10-6, Sun. 1-6. Adults $12.75, senior citizens $9.75, children 6-12 $6.75; discounts to AAM & ICOM members; members and children 5 & under no charge. &
Attendance: 50,000 (estimated)

Sewanee

UNIVERSITY ART GALLERY, UNIVERSITY OF THE SOUTH, Guerry Hall, Georgia Ave., Sewanee, TN 37383. Mailing Address: 735 University Ave., Sewanee, TN 37383-1000. Tel.: 931-598-1223. Fax: 931-598-3335.
E-mail: sjmaclar@sewanee.edu
Web Site: www.sewanee.edu/gallery
Key Personnel: Gallery Dir., Shelley MacLaren.
Institution Type/Description: University Art Gallery.
Hours & Admission Prices: Tues.-Fri. 10-5, Sat.-Sun. 12-4. No charge; donations accepted. Closed university holidays. &
Attendance: 6,000 (estimated)

Shiloh

SHILOH NATIONAL MILITARY PARK & CEMETERY, 1055 Pittsburg Landing Rd., Shiloh, TN 38376-4331. Tel.: 731-689-5275. Fax: 731-689-5450.
E-mail: shil_administration@nps.gov
Web Site: www.nps.gov/shil
Key Personnel: Supt., Dale Wilkerson.
Institution Type/Description: Military Museum.
Hours & Admission Prices: Shiloh Battlefield: daily dawn to dusk. Shiloh Battlefield Visitor Center & Corinth Civil War Interpretive Center: daily 8-5. No charge. Closed New Year's Day; Thanksgiving; Christmas. &
Attendance: 470,000 (estimated)

Smithville

APPALACHIAN CENTER FOR CRAFT, 1560 Craft Center Dr., Smithville, TN 37166-7352. Tel.: 615-597-6801. Fax: 615-597-6803.
E-mail: craftcenter@tntech.edu
Web Site: www.tntech.edu/craftcenter
Key Personnel: Dir., Ward Doubet; Gallery Mgr., Gail S. Looper.
Institution Type/Description: General Museum.
Hours & Admission Prices: Daily 9-5. No charge. Closed New Year's Eve & Day; Easter; Thanksgiving; Christmas Eve, Day & week. &
Attendance: 150,000 (estimated)

Smyrna

HISTORIC SAM DAVIS HOME & PLANTATION, 1399 Sam Davis Rd., Smyrna, TN 37167-2744. Tel.: 615-459-2341. Fax: 615-220-6053.
E-mail: director@samdavishome.org
Web Site: www.samdavishome.org
Formerly: Sam Davis Home
Key Personnel: Exec. Dir., Tiffany Johnson; Bd. Pres., Dr. Steve Murphree; Shop Mgr., Hewitt Spain.
Institution Type/Description: Historic House Museum.
Hours & Admission Prices: June-Aug. Mon.-Sat. 9-5; Sept.-May Mon.-Sat. 10-4; Jan. by 72-hour advance appointment. House & Museum: adults $12, seniors, veterans & active-duty military $10, college students & children 6-12 $6; children under 6 & members no charge; House or Museum only: adults $8, seniors/students $6, children 6-12 $4; children under 6 & members no charge.
Attendance: 22,000 (estimated)

Sneedville

VARDY COMMUNITY HISTORICAL CHURCH MUSEUM, Vardy Blackwater Rd., Sneedville, TN 37869. Mailing Address: Vardy Community Historical Society, P.O. Box 554, Sneedville, TN 37869. Tel.: 423-733-2305.
E-mail: claudefreeda@aol.com
Web Site: vardyhistoricalsociety.org
Key Personnel: Pres. (V), Charles Sizemore.
Institution Type/Description: Historical Society Museum: housed in a former Presbyterian Church built in 1889.
Hours & Admission Prices: By appointment. No charge; donations accepted. &
Attendance: 1,000 (estimated)

Southside

HISTORIC COLLINSVILLE, 4711 Weakley Rd., Southside, TN 37171. Tel.: 931-216-2911.
E-mail: frances@visitclarksvilletn.com
Web Site: www.historiccollinsville.com
Key Personnel: Dir., JoAnn B. Weakley; C.E.O., Glenn H. Weakley; Chair (V) & Pres. (V), Melissa Blocker; Museum Shop Mgr., Carolyn Gannaway.
Institution Type/Description: Historic Village.
Hours & Admission Prices: mid-May to mid-Oct. Thurs.-Sun. 1-5. Adults $5; school tours $7; guided tours $15. children under 5 no charge. &
Attendance: 4,500 (estimated)

Sparta

WHITE COUNTY HERITAGE MUSEUM, 144 S. Main St., Sparta, TN 38583-2215. Tel.: 931-837-3900.
E-mail: wcmuseum@blomand.net
Web Site: www.whitecountyheritagemuseum.org
Key Personnel: Dir. & Museum Shop Mgr., Peggie J. Hurteau; Asst. Dir., Brenda Templeton; C.E.O., Denny Wayne Robinson.
Institution Type/Description: Heritage Museum.
Hours & Admission Prices: Thurs. 10-4, Fri. 9-4, Sat. 9-2. No charge; donations accepted.
Attendance: 2,000 (estimated)

Spring Hill

RIPPAVILLA PLANTATION, 5700 Main St., Spring Hill, TN 37174-2408. Mailing Address: P.O. Box 1169, Spring Hill, TN 37174-1169. Tel.: 931-486-9037. Fax: 931-486-3175. Facebook: Rippavilla Plantation.
E-mail: rippavilla@bellsouth.net
Web Site: www.rippavilla.org
Key Personnel: Exec. Dir., Pam Perdue.

Institution Type/Description: Historic House Museum: c.1860.
Hours & Admission Prices: Tours: Mon.-Sat. 9:30-4:30, Sun. 1-4:30. House Tours: adults $10, senior citizens 62 & over $8, children 6-12 $5; discounts to groups; children 5 & under no charge. ⅋
Attendance: 15,000 (actual)

Springfield

ROBERTSON COUNTY HISTORY MUSEUM, 124 Sixth Ave. W., Springfield, TN 37172-2405. Mailing Address: P.O. Box 1022, Springfield, TN 37172-1022. Tel.: 615-382-7173.
E-mail: rchs@bellsouth.net
Web Site: rchsonline.org
Key Personnel: Dir., Linda D. Dean; Pres. (V), David C. Allen; Museum Shop Mgr., Charlotte E. Reedy.
Institution Type/Description: History Museum: housed in the former U.S. Post Office.
Hours & Admission Prices: Wed.-Fri. 10-4, Sat. by appointment. Adults $4, seniors $2, students $1; discounts to groups; members no charge. Closed most holidays. ⅋
Attendance: 800 (estimated)

Stanton

HATCHIE NATIONAL WILDLIFE REFUGE, 6772 Hwy. 76 S., Stanton, TN 38069-3648. Tel.: 731-772-0501. Fax: 731-772-7839.
E-mail: hatchie@fws.gov
Web Site: www.fws.gov/hatchie
Key Personnel: Refuge Mgr., Michael Chouinard.
Institution Type/Description: Wildlife Refuge.
Hours & Admission Prices: Call for hours.

Sweetwater

THE LOST SEA, 140 Lost Sea Rd., Sweetwater, TN 37874-6724. Tel.: 423-337-6616.
E-mail: thelostsea@gmail.com
Web Site: www.thelostsea.com
Institution Type/Description: Natural History Museum: a Registered National Landmark.
Hours & Admission Prices: March-April & Sept.-Oct. daily 9-6; May-June & Aug. daily 9-7; July daily 9-8; Nov.-Feb. daily 9-5. Adults $18.95, children 5-12 $9.95; discounts to groups of 15 or more by appointment; children 4 & under no charge. Closed Christmas.

SWEETWATER HERITAGE MUSEUM, North & High Sts., Sweetwater, TN 37874. Mailing Address: P.O. Box 143, Etowah, TN 37331.
Institution Type/Description: History Museum.
Hours & Admission Prices: March-Oct. Wed. & Sat.-Sun. 2-4.

Tellico Plains

CHARLES HALL MUSEUM, 229 Cherohala Skyway, Tellico Plains, TN 37385-5500. Tel.: 423-253-4369. Fax: 423-253-8000.
E-mail: charleshallmuseum@hotmail.com
Web Site: www.charleshallmuseum.com
Key Personnel: Dir., C.E.O. & Chm. (V), Charles Hall.
Institution Type/Description: History Museum.
Hours & Admission Prices: Daily. No charge; donations accepted. ⅋
Attendance: 30,000 (estimated)

Tiptonville

CARL PERKINS VISITOR CENTER, 230 Crl Perkins Pkwy., Tiptonville, TN 38079. Tel.: 731-253-9922.
E-mail: info@tiptonvillemainstreet.com
Web Site: www.tiptonville.org
Institution Type/Description: Visitor Center & Historic House Museum: housed in the boyhood home of singer, Carl Perkins.
Hours & Admission Prices: Call for hours.

Townsend

CADES COVE VISITOR CENTER AND OPEN-AIR MUSEUM, Great Smoky Mountains National Park, 10042 Campgrounds Dr., Townsend, TN 37882-5004. Mailing Address: Great Smoky Mountains National Park, 107 Park Headquarters Rd., Gatlinburg, TN 37738-4102. Tel.: 877-444-6777. Fax: 865-436-1220.

E-mail: grsm_smokies_information@nps.gov
Web Site: www.nps.gov/grsm
Key Personnel: Chief Resource Education, Cathleen Cook.
Institution Type/Description: Preservation Project: Cable Mill area & other historic structures typical of Southern Appalachia at turn of the 20th century.
Hours & Admission Prices: Museum: daily dawn to dusk. Visitor Center: Feb. & Nov. daily 9-5; March & Sept.-Oct. daily 9-6; April-Aug. daily 9-7; Dec.-Jan. daily 9-4:30. No charge. ⅋
Attendance: 1,000,000

GREAT SMOKY MOUNTAINS HERITAGE CENTER, 123 Cromwell Dr., Townsend, TN 37882-4323. Mailing Address: P.O. Box 268, Townsend, TN 37882-0268. Tel.: 865-448-0044. Fax: 865-448-6975. Facebook: Great Smoky Mountains Heritage Center.
E-mail: gsmhcevents@yahoo.com
Web Site: www.gsmheritagecenter.org
Key Personnel: Dir., Robert Patterson; Pres., James K. Leach; Treas., Carl Koella, III; Admin. Asst., Celeste Elias; Exhibit Technician, Bob Hood; Dir. Special Events, Rondi Smith; Dir. Mktg., Museum Shop Mgr. & Mgr. Cades Cove Heritage Tours, Don Alexander.
Institution Type/Description: History Museum.
Hours & Admission Prices: Jan.-March Mon.-Sat. 10-5; April-Dec. Mon.-Sat. 10-5, Sun. 12-5. Adults $8, senior citizens 60 & over $6; discounts to groups of 8 or more; members and children 5 & under no charge. Closed New Year's Day; Easter; Thanksgiving; Christmas Eve & Day. ⅋
Attendance: 37,000 (actual)

LITTLE RIVER RAILROAD AND LUMBER COMPANY MUSEUM, 7747 E. Lamar Alexander Pkwy., Townsend, TN 37882. Mailing Address: P.O. Box 211, Townsend, TN 37882. Tel.: 865-661-0170. Fax: 865-448-2312. Facebook: Little River Railroad & Lumber Company Museum.
E-mail: sandy@littleriverrailroad.org
Web Site: www.littleriverrailroad.org
Key Personnel: Pres. (V), Don Niday; Treas. & Museum Shop Mgr., Sandy Headrick.
Institution Type/Description: History Museum.
Hours & Admission Prices: April-May, Sept. & Nov. Sat. 10-5, Sun. 1-5; June-Aug. & Oct. Mon.-Sat. 10-5, Sun. 1-5; other times by appointment. No charge; donations accepted.
Attendance: 19,000 (estimated)

Trenton

TRENTON NIGHT LIGHT TEAPOT MUSEUM, Trenton City Hall, 309 College St., Trenton, TN 38382. Tel.: 731-855-2013. Fax: 731-855-1091.
Web Site: www.teapotcollection.com/285621.ihtml
Formerly: Porcelain Veilleuses-Theieres Museum
Institution Type/Description: Teapot Museum.
Hours & Admission Prices: Mon.-Fri. 9-5; groups by appointment. No charge; donations accepted.
Attendance: 5,000 (estimated)

Tullahoma

BEECHCRAFT HERITAGE MUSEUM, 570 Old Shelbyville Hwy., Tullahoma, TN 37388-4703. Mailing Address: P.O. Box 550, Tullahoma, TN 37388-0550. Tel.: 931-455-1974. Fax: 931-455-1994.
E-mail: sherry@beechcrafthm.org
Web Site: beechcrafthm.org
Key Personnel: Exec. Vice Pres., Charles L. Parish; Resident Dir., Sherry Roepke; Dir. Mktg. & Memberships, Jody Curtis.
Institution Type/Description: Aviation Museum.
Hours & Admission Prices: Tues.-Sat. 8:30-4:30. Adults $10, active & retired military & children 12-17 $5; members and children 11 & under no charge. ⅋
Attendance: 6,000 (estimated)

FLOYD AND MARGARET MITCHELL MUSEUM, South Jackson Civic Center, 404 S. Jackson St., Tullahoma, TN 37388. Mailing Address: P.O. Box 326, Tullahoma, TN 37388-0326. Tel.: 931-455-7239.
E-mail: museum@southjackson.org
Web Site: southjackson.org/museum.html
Institution Type/Description: History Museum.
Hours & Admission Prices: 1st Sun. each month 2-4; other times by appointment.

HANDS-ON SCIENCE CENTER, 101 Mitchell Blvd., Tullahoma, TN 37388. Tel.: 931-455-8387. Facebook: Hands-on Science Center.
E-mail: hosc@lighttube.net
Web Site: hosc.org
Key Personnel: Dir., Misty Marshall; Pres. (V), Sean Smith; Museum Shop Mgr., Jan Griffin.
Institution Type/Description: Children's Science Museum.
Hours & Admission Prices: Tues.-Sat. 10-5, Sun. 1-5. Admission $5; children 2 & under no charge. &
Attendance: 20,000 (estimated)

TULLAHOMA FINE ARTS CENTER REGIONAL MUSEUM OF ART, 401 S. Jackson St., Tullahoma, TN 37388-3469. Tel.: 931-455-1234. Fax: 931-455-1234.
E-mail: lucy@tullahomafinearts.org
Web Site: www.tullahomafinearts.org
Institution Type/Description: Art Museum.
Hours & Admission Prices: Call for hours.

Union City

DISCOVERY PARK OF AMERICA, 830 Everett Blvd., Union City, TN 38261. Mailing Address: P.O. Box 927, Union City, TN 38281. Tel.: 877-885-5455, 731-885-5455. Fax: 731-885-7276. Facebook; Twitter; Instagram.
E-mail: info@discoveryparkofamerica.com
Web Site: www.discoveryparkofamerica.com
Key Personnel: C.E.O., James L. Rippy, Jr.; C.F.O., Tammy Ursery; Dir. Exhibits, Jennifer Wildes; Museum Shop Mgr., Lauren Sims.
Institution Type/Description: General Museum.
Hours & Admission Prices: Tues.-Sun. 10-5. Adults $13.95, children 3-12 $10.95; discounts to seniors 65 & over, TAM, AAA, AARP, & military members; children under 3 no charge. Closed New Year's Day; Easter; Thanksgiving; Christmas Eve & Day. &
Attendance: 250,000 (actual)

DIXIE GUN WORKS' OLD CAR MUSEUM, 1412 W. Reelfoot Ave., Union City, TN 38261-5508. Tel.: 731-885-0561. Fax: 731-885-0440.
E-mail: dixiegun@earthlink.net
Web Site: www.dixiegunworks.com
Key Personnel: Pres., Lee Fry.
Institution Type/Description: Automobile Museum.
Hours & Admission Prices: Mon.-Fri. 8-5, Sat. 8-12. Adults $2, senior citizens & children $1. Closed New Year's Day; Memorial Day; Independence Day; Labor Day; Thanksgiving; Christmas.
Attendance: 3,000 (estimated)

OBION COUNTY MUSEUM, 1004 Edwards St., Union City, TN 38261-5316. Mailing Address: P.O. Box 323, Union City, TN 38281-0323. Tel.: 731-885-6774.
E-mail: adelledoss@gmail.com
Web Site: www.ocmuseum.com
Key Personnel: Chm. (V) & Treas., Larry Mink; Cur., Polly Brasher; Registrar, Jennifer Wildes.
Institution Type/Description: History Museum.
Hours & Admission Prices: Mon.-Fri. 10-4. Adults $2, children $1; discounts to groups and AAM & ICOM members; members no charge. Closed New Year's Day; Labor Day; Thanksgiving; Christmas. &
Attendance: 650 (estimated)

Vonore

FORT LOUDOUN STATE HISTORIC PARK, 338 Fort Loudoun Rd., Vonore, TN 37885-2704. Tel.: 423-884-6217. Fax: 423-884-2287.
E-mail: fortloudoun@tds.net
Web Site: www.fortloudoun.com
Institution Type/Description: Park Museum.
Hours & Admission Prices: Call for hours.

THE SEQUOYAH BIRTHPLACE MUSEUM, 576 Hwy. 360, Vonore, TN 37885-2816. Mailing Address: P.O. Box 69, Vonore, TN 37885-0069. Tel.: 423-884-6246. Fax: 423-884-2102.
E-mail: seqmus@tds.net
Web Site: www.sequoyahmuseum.org
Key Personnel: Dir., Charlie Rhodarmer; Chm. (V), Maxwell Ramsey; Museum Shop Mgr., Linda Bosket.

Institution Type/Description: Cultural History Museum.
Hours & Admission Prices: Mon.-Sat. 9-5, Sun. 12-5. Admission $3; members no charge. Closed New Year's Day; Thanksgiving; Christmas. &
Attendance: 17,500 (actual)

VONORE HERITAGE MUSEUM, 619 Church St., Vonore, TN 37885-2324. Tel.: 423-884-2989.
E-mail: vonoremuseum@yahoo.com
Key Personnel: Chm. (V), Violet K. Wolfe; Pres. (V), Cory Russell; Dir., Edna Blankenship.
Institution Type/Description: History Museum.
Hours & Admission Prices: Mon.-Thurs. 10-2, Sat. 1-3; other times by appointment. No charge; donations accepted. Closed New Year's Day; Labor Day; Good Friday; Thanksgiving & day after; Christmas. &
Attendance: 900 (estimated)

Waverly

HUMPHREYS COUNTY MUSEUM & CIVIL WAR FORT, 201 Fort Hill Dr., Waverly, TN 37185-2127. Tel.: 931-296-1099.
E-mail: sbrown@humphreystn.com
Web Site: www.humphreystn.com
Institution Type/Description: History Museum: housed in a 1922 mansion.
Hours & Admission Prices: Fri.-Sun. -4. No charge; donations accepted. Closed holidays.

1978 WAVERLY PROPANE EXPLOSION MUSEUM, W. Railroad St. & Richland Ave., Waverly, TN 37185. Mailing Address: City of Waverly, 101 E. Main St., Waverly, TN 37185-2143. Tel.: 931-296-2101. Fax: 931-296-1434.
E-mail: bfrazier@waverlytn.org
Web Site: waverlytn.org
Key Personnel: Dir., W.B. (Buddy) Frazier.
Institution Type/Description: History Museum: housed in a caboose on the site of the 1978 train derailment disaster.
Hours & Admission Prices: Daily 7:30 am-8:30 pm. No charge. &
Attendance: 1,000 (estimated)

White House

WHITE HOUSE INN LIBRARY & MUSEUM, 105B College St., White House, TN 37188-9086. Tel.: 615-672-0239. Fax: 615-672-9733.
Web Site: www.librarything.com/venue/22790/White-House-Inn-Library-Museum
Institution Type/Description: Library.
Hours & Admission Prices: Mon.-Wed. & Fri. 10-5:30, Thurs. 12-8, Sat. 10-4.

Winchester

FRANKLIN COUNTY OLD JAIL MUSEUM, 400 Dinah Shore Blvd., Winchester, TN 37398-1421. Tel.: 931-967-0524.
E-mail: kathyshowse@att.ney
Key Personnel: C.E.O., Pres. (V) Chm. Old Jail Museum Commission, Mrs. Kathryn Howse; Hostess, Mrs. Joyce Zingg; Treas., Annette B. Sisk; Sec., Dale Stewart.
Institution Type/Description: History of Franklin County.
Hours & Admission Prices: May 2-Oct. 30 Thurs.-Sat. 10-4. No charge; donations accepted
Attendance: 450 (estimated)

Woodbury

THE CANNON CULTURAL MUSEUM AND THE MARLEY BERGER GALLERY, Arts Center of Cannon County, 1424 John Bragg Hwy., Woodbury, TN 37190-6173. Tel.: 800-235-9073.
E-mail: artscenter@artscenterofcc.com
Web Site: www.artscenterofll.com
Key Personnel: Exec. Dir., Neal Appelabum.
Institution Type/Description: Art & History Museum.
Hours & Admission Prices: Call for hours. No charge; donations accepted. &

TEXAS

(679 listings)

Abilene

ABILENE ZOOLOGICAL GARDENS, 2070 Zoo Lane, Abilene, TX 79602-1996. Tel.: 325-676-6085. Fax: 325-676-6084.

E-mail: abilene.zoo@abilenetx.com
Web Site: www.abilenezoo.org
Key Personnel: Exec. Dir., William R. Gersonde; Pres. (V), John Pennington; Cur. Education, Joy Harsh; Museum Shop Mgr. & Admissions Mgr., John Black; Concessions Mgr., Vickey Byers; Admin. Coord., Sandra Turner; Mktg. & Devel. Coord., Keely Thompson.
Institution Type/Description: Zoo.
Hours & Admission Prices: June-Aug. Thurs. 9-9, Fri.-Wed. 9-5; Sept.-May daily 9-5. Adults $8, seniors 60 & over $7, children 3-12 $5.50; discounts to groups, AZS & AZA members; members & children under 3 no charge. Closed New Year's Day; Thanksgiving; Christmas. &
Attendance: 217,038 (actual)

CENTER FOR CONTEMPORARY ARTS, 220 Cypress St., Abilene, TX 79601. Tel.: 325-677-8389. Fax: 325-677-1171.
E-mail: info@center-arts.com
Web Site: www.center-arts.com
Key Personnel: Exec. Dir., Darla Harmon; Pres., Paul Bilberry; Pres.-Elect, Kevin Halliburton; Sec., Mary K. Huff; Treas., Jim Pizzorno; Past Pres., Phyllis Baum; Artist Member Pres., Patty Rae Wellborn; Artist Member Vice Pres., Chuck Roach.
Institution Type/Description: Art Gallery.
Hours & Admission Prices: Thurs. 11-9, Tues.-Wed. & Fri.-Sat. 11-5. No charge; donations accepted. &
Attendance: 50,000 (estimated)

FRONTIER TEXAS MUSEUM AND VISITOR CENTER, 625 N. First St., Abilene, TX 79601. Tel.: 325-437-2800. Fax: 325-437-2804.
E-mail: jeff@frontiertexas.com
Web Site: www.frontiertexas.com
Key Personnel: Exec. Dir., Jeff Salmon.
Institution Type/Description: History Museum & Visitor Center.
Hours & Admission Prices: Mon.-Sat. 9-6, Sun. 1-5. Adults $10, military, seniors (60 & over) $7, students & teachers $6; children 3-12 $5; children under 3 no charge. Closed New Year's Day; Thanksgiving; Christmas. &

THE GRACE MUSEUM, 102 Cypress St., Abilene, TX 79601-5817. Tel.: 325-673-4587. Fax: 325-675-5993. Facebook, Instagram, Twitter.
E-mail: info@thegracemuseum.org
Web Site: thegracemuseum.org
Key Personnel: Exec. Dir., Laura Moore; Chief Cur., Judy Deaton; Dir. Education, Kathryn Mitchell; Dir. Finance, & HR, Vicki Butts; Programming & Interpretation, Rebecca Bridges; Dir. Mktg. & Comm., Lori Thornton; Collecitons Mgr., Erika Aragon Parker; Dir. Events, Sheila Richardson.
Institution Type/Description: Art, History & Children's Participatory Museums.
Hours & Admission Prices: Tues.-Wed. & Fri.-Sat. 10-5, Thurs. 10-8. Adults $6, seniors, students & military $3; children 3 & under, members & Thurs. 5-8 no charge. &
Attendance: 70,678 (actual)

NATIONAL CENTER FOR CHILDREN'S ILLUSTRATED LITERATURE, 102 Cedar, Abilene, TX 79601-5718. Tel.: 325-673-4586. Fax: 325-673-0085. Facebook.
E-mail: info@nccil.org
Web Site: www.nccil.org
Key Personnel: Exec. Dir., Trish Dressen; Chm., Mike Warren; Venues & Touring Dir., Debbie Lillick; Business & Facilities Mgr., Rodney Goodman; School Tour Coord., Sandi Rainwater.
Institution Type/Description: Art Museum.
Hours & Admission Prices: Center: Tues.-Sat. 10-4. No charge; donations accepted. &
Attendance: 20,000 (estimated)

12TH ARMORED DIVISION MEMORIAL MUSEUM, 1289 N. 2nd St., Abilene, TX 79601. Tel.: 325-677-6515. Fax: 325-677-6515. Facebook: 12th Armored Division Memorial Museum.
E-mail: hellcatsmuseum@yahoo.com
Web Site: www.12tharmoredmuseum.com
Key Personnel: Bd. Chm., William J. McCarthy; Cur., William Lenches; Treas., Robert Hoeweler; Website Admin., Craig Miller.
Institution Type/Description: Military History Museum.
Hours & Admission Prices: Tues.-Sat. 10-5. Adults $5, seniors 60 & over, military and students $4, children 7-12 $2, children under 7, members & WWII veterans no charge. Closed federal holidays. &
Attendance: 3,000 (estimated)

Addison

CAVANAUGH FLIGHT MUSEUM, 4572 Claire Chennault, Addison, TX 75001. Tel.: 972-380-8800. Facebook: Cavanaugh Flight Museum.
E-mail: djeanes@cavflight.org
Web Site: www.cavanaughflightmuseum.com
Key Personnel: Museum Dir., Doug Jeanes; Asst. Museum Dir., Kevin Raulie; Finance Mgr., Martin Scott; Dir. of Maintenance, Russell Martin.
Institution Type/Description: History Museum.
Hours & Admission Prices: Mon.-Sat. 9-5, Sun. 11-5. Adults $12, seniors & military $8, children 4-12 $6; children 3 & under no charge.

MARY KAY MUSEUM, 16251 Dallas Pkwy., Addison, TX 75001. Tel.: 972-687-5720.
E-mail: askmarykay@mkcorp.com
Web Site: www.marykaymuseum.com
Key Personnel: Dir., Jennifer Cook; Chief Investment Officer, Ryan Rogers.
Institution Type/Description: Company Museum.
Hours & Admission Prices: Mon.-Fri. 9-4. No charge. Closed major holidays. &

Albany

THE OLD JAIL ART CENTER, 201 S. 2nd St., Albany, TX 76430-2503. Tel.: 325-762-2269. Fax: 325-762-2260. Facebook, Instagram, Twitter.
E-mail: info@theojac.org
Web Site: www.theoldjailartcenter.org
Key Personnel: Chair (V), Steve Waller; Exec. Dir. & Cur. of Exhibitions, Patrick Kelly; Registrar, Amy Kelly; Dir. Education, Erin Whitmore; Educ. Coord., Erin Whitmore; Archivist & Librarian, Molly Sauder.
Institution Type/Description: Art Museum: housed in c.1877 stone two-storied, Victorian classic-style jail building.
Hours & Admission Prices: Tues.-Sat. 10-5. No charge; donations accepted. Closed holidays. &
Attendance: 10,000 (estimated)

Alice

SOUTH TEXAS MUSEUM, 66 S. Wright St., Alice, TX 78332-4904. Mailing Address: P.O. Box 3232, Alice, TX 78333-3232. Tel.: 512-668-8891.
E-mail: stmuseum@sbcglobal.net
Key Personnel: Dir., Opal Hoy.
Institution Type/Description: History Museum: housed in c.1940 headquarters for the McGill Brothers ranching operations; Texas historic landmark.
Hours & Admission Prices: Tues.-Fri. 1-5, Sat. 10-2. No charge.
Attendance: 1,200 (estimated)

Alpine

HALLIE'S HALL OF FAME MUSEUM, 48421 FM 2627, Alpine, TX 79830-9752. Tel.: 432-376-2244.
E-mail: info@stillwellstore.com
Web Site: stillwellstore.com/hall-of-fame
Institution Type/Description: History Museum.
Hours & Admission Prices: Call for hours.

MUSEUM OF THE BIG BEND, Sul Ross State University, Alpine, TX 79832. Mailing Address: Box C-101, Alpine, TX 79832. Tel.: 432-837-8143. Fax: 432-837-8901.
E-mail: ejackson@sulross.edu
Web Site: www.sulross.edu/~museum/
Key Personnel: Dir., Mary Bones; Cur. of Temporary Exhibitions & Adult Programming, Maggie Rumbelow; Cur. of Collections & Youth Programming, MaryMatt Walter; Education Coord., Ginger Lemons.
Institution Type/Description: Regional History Museum.
Hours & Admission Prices: Tues.-Sat. 9-5, Sun. 1-5; guided tours by appointment. No charge; donations accepted. &
Attendance: 18,000 (estimated)

Alto

CADDO MOUNDS STATE HISTORIC SITE, 1649 State Hwy. 21 W., Alto, TX 75925-5739. Tel.: 936-858-3218.
E-mail: caddo-mounds@thc.texas.gov
Web Site: www.thc.texas.gov
Formerly: Caddoan Mounds State Historic Site

Institution Type/Description: State Historic Site: located on a former Caddo Village and Ceremonial Grounds, 750-1400 A.D. containing a Burial Mound, Ceremonial Mound and Temple Mound.
Hours & Admission Prices: Tues.-Sun. 8:30-4:30. Family $8; adults $4; Seniors, students (6-18) $3; school groups $1; children under 5 no charge. Closed New Year's Eve & Day, Thanksgiving, Christmas Eve and Day. ⅃
Attendance: 10,000 (estimated)

Alvin

ALVIN HISTORICAL MUSEUM, 300 W. Sealy, Alvin, TX 77511. Mailing Address: P.O. Box 1902, Alvin, TX 77512. Tel.: 281-331-4469. Facebook.
E-mail: alvinms@att.net
Web Site: www.alvinmuseum.org/AlvinHistoricalMuseum
Key Personnel: Pres., Barbara Passmore; Pres.-Elect, Charlie Goodson; Treas., Janie Lindsey; Past Pres., Katheryn Mattes; C.O.O., Tom Stansel.
Institution Type/Description: History Museum.
Hours & Admission Prices: Thurs.-Sat. 11-3. Adults $3; children under 12 no charge.
Attendance: 300 (estimated)

MARGUERITE ROGERS HOUSE MUSEUM, 113 E. Dumble, Alvin, TX 77511. Mailing Address: Alvin Museum Society, P.O. Box 1902, Alvin, TX 77512-1902. Tel.: 281-331-4469.
E-mail: alvinms@att.net
Key Personnel: Pres., Barbara Pasmore; Pres.-Elect, Charlie Goodson; Treas., Janie Lindsey; Past Pres., Katheryn Mattes; C.O.O., Tom Stansel.
Institution Type/Description: Historic House: built early 1900s.
Hours & Admission Prices: Tours are by appointment.
Attendance: 180 (estimated)

NOLAN RYAN CENTER, 2925 S. Bypass 35, Alvin, TX 77511. Tel.: 281-388-1134 & 888-350-7926. Fax: 281-388-1135.
E-mail: info@nolanryanfoundation.org
Web Site: nolanryanfoundation.org
Institution Type/Description: Sports History Museum.
Hours & Admission Prices: Mon.-Sat. 9-4.

Amarillo

AMARILLO BOTANICAL GARDENS, 1400 Streit Dr., Amarillo, TX 79106. Tel.: 806-352-6513. Facebook, Twitter, Instagram.
Web Site: www.amarillobotanicalgardens.org
Key Personnel: Pres., Ken Pirtle; Vice Pres., Cortney Reed; Sec., Lindsey Shelton; Treas., Jeff Sumpter; Exec. Dir., Jelaine Workman; Horticulturist/ Dir. of Gorunds, Greg Lusk.
Institution Type/Description: Botanical Gardens.
Hours & Admission Prices: Summer: Mon.-Fri. 9-7, Sat. 9-5, Sun. 1-5. Winter: Tues.-Fri. 9-5, Sat. 1-5. Memorial Day, Independence Day, Labor Day 9-5. Adults $5, seniors 60 & over $4, children through 8th grade $2, children 5 and under $2.

AMARILLO MUSEUM OF ART, 2200 S. Van Buren, Amarillo, TX 79109-2407. Mailing Address: P.O. Box 447, Amarillo, TX 79178. Tel.: 806-371-5050. Fax: 806-345-5682.
E-mail: amoa@actx.edu
Web Site: www.amarilloart.org
Key Personnel: Pres., Jack Craft; Pres.-Elect, Ellen Bivins; Treas., Jennie Knapp; Sec., Mike Ladd; Lilia Escajeda; Exec. Dir., Kim Mahan; Cur. of Art, Alex Gregory; Cur. of Education, Julie Talley; Dir. of Public Programs, Deana Craighead; Mktg. & Events Coord., Stephanie Bybee; Admin./ Advancement Asst., Taylor Willis.
Institution Type/Description: Art Museum.
Hours & Admission Prices: Tues.-Fri. 10-5, Sat.-Sun. 1-5. No charge; donations accepted. Closed major national holidays. ⅃
Attendance: 40,000

AMARILLO ZOO, 700 Comanchero Tr., Amarillo, TX 79107. Mailing Address: P.O. Box 1971, Amarillo, TX 79105. Tel.: 806-381-7911 & 5605. Fax: 806-381-7901.
E-mail: zoo@amarilloparks.org
Web Site: www.amarillozoo.org
Key Personnel: Zoo Cur., Rhonda Votino.
Institution Type/Description: Zoo.
Hours & Admission Prices: Daily 9:30-5. Adults 13-61 $4, seniors 62 & over $3, children 3-12 $1; children under 3 no charge, Mon. half price. Closed New Year's Day; Martin Luther King Jr. Day; Thanksgiving; Christmas.

AMERICAN QUARTER HORSE HALL OF FAME & MUSEUM, 1600 Quarter Horse Dr., Amarillo, TX 79104. Mailing Address: P.O. Box 200, Amarillo, TX 79168. Tel.: 806-376-4811. Fax: 806-349-6411. Facebook.
E-mail: museum@aqha.org
Web Site: www.aqha.com/museum
Formerly: American Quarter Horse Heritage Center & Museum
Key Personnel: Exec. Vice Pres., Craig Huffhines; Admin. Asst. to the Exec. Vice Pres., Robin Brooks; Chief Show Officer, Pete Kyle; Chief Publications Officer, Carl Mullins; Chief Racing Officer, Janet VanBebber; AQHA Gen. Counsel, Chad Pierce; Chief Intl. & Foundation Officer, Anna Morrison; Chief Information Officer, Barry Couper.
Institution Type/Description: Equine Hall of Fame & Museum.
Hours & Admission Prices: Mon.-Sat. 9-5. Adults $7, senior (55 and over) $6, children 6-18 $3; members, active duty military, children 5 & under no charge. Closed Independence Day. ⅃
Attendance: 30,000 (actual)

DON HARRINGTON DISCOVERY CENTER, 1200 Streit Dr., Amarillo, TX 79106-1759. Tel.: 806-355-9547.
Web Site: www.discoverycenteramarillo.org
Key Personnel: Exec. Dir., Dr. Aaron D. Pan; Dir. of Education & Exhibits, Kyle Hadley; Dir. of Devel., Regina Ralston; Dir. of Visitor Svcs., Mandi Ried.
Institution Type/Description: Science Museum & Planetarium.
Hours & Admission Prices: Tues.- Sat. 9:30-4:30, Sun. 12-4:30. Closed major holidays. Adults $11; seniors. military, children (3-12) $8; children (under 3) no charge. ⅃
Attendance: 143,000 (actual)

HARRINGTON HOUSE, 1600 S. Polk St., Amarillo, TX 79102. Tel.: 806-374-5490.
E-mail: harringtonhouse@att.net
Web Site: harringtonhousehistorichome.org
Key Personnel: Exec. Dir., Betty Howell.
Institution Type/Description: Historic House Museum: housed in the former home of Don & Sybil Harrington. Listed on the National Register of Historic Places.
Hours & Admission Prices: Tues. & Thurs. 10-12:30. No charge.

JULIAN BIVINS MUSEUM, Main & Hwy. 385, Amarillo, TX 79174. Mailing Address: P.O. Box 1890, Amarillo, TX 79174. Tel.: 806-372-2341 & 800-687-3722.
Institution Type/Description: History Museum.
Hours & Admission Prices: Daily 10-5. No charge. Closed major holidays.

KWAHADI MUSEUM OF THE AMERICAN INDIAN, 9151 I-40 E., Amarillo, TX 79120. Mailing Address: P.O. Box 32125, Amarillo, TX 79120-2125. Tel.: 806-335-3175.
Institution Type/Description: Native American History Museum.
Hours & Admission Prices: June-Aug. Wed.-Sun. 1-5; Sept.-May Sat.-Sun. 1-5. Adults $5, youth $3.

TEXAS AIR & SPACE MUSEUM, 10001 American Dr., Amarillo, TX 79111-1213. Mailing Address: P.O. Box 31535, Amarillo, TX 79120-1535. Tel.: 806-335-9159. Fax: 806-665-4627. Facebook.
E-mail: info@texasairandspacemuseum.org
Web Site: www.texasairandspacemuseum.org
Key Personnel: Dir., Ron Fernuik; Cur., Paul Devenney.
Institution Type/Description: History Museum.
Hours & Admission Prices: Mon.-Sat. 10-4; other times by appointment.

TEXAS PHARMACY MUSEUM, Texas Tech School of Pharmacy, 1300 S Coulter St., Amarillo, TX 79106-1712. Tel.: 806-414-9269. Fax: 806-356-4669.
E-mail: paul.katz@ttuhsc.edu
Web Site: www.ttuhsc.edu/sop/museum
Key Personnel: Cur., Susan Denney.
Institution Type/Description: Pharmacy Museum.
Hours & Admission Prices: Tues.-Thurs. 10-12 & 1:30-4. No charge. Closed New Year's Day; Thanksgiving; Christmas. ⅃
Attendance: 431 (actual)

WILDCAT BLUFF NATURE CENTER, 2301 N. Soncy Rd., Amarillo, TX 79124-5766. Tel.: 806-352-6007. Facebook, Instagram.
E-mail: info@wildcatbluff.org
Key Personnel: Dir., Vivien Young.
Institution Type/Description: Nature Center.
Hours & Admission Prices: Tues.-Sat. 9-4. Adults $4, children & seniors $3; children 3 & under no charge. Trail: sunrise to sunset. Closed holidays.

Angleton

BRAZORIA COUNTY HISTORICAL MUSEUM, 100 E. Cedar, Angleton, TX 77515-4602. Tel.: 979-864-1208. Fax: 979-864-1217. Facebook.
E-mail: office@bchm.org
Web Site: www.brazoriacountytx.gov/departments/museum
Institution Type/Description: History Museum: housed in 1897 Brazoria County Courthouse.
Hours & Admission Prices: Mon.-Fri. 8-5, Sat. 9-3. No charge; donations accepted. Closed major holidays. ♿
Attendance: 20,000 (estimated)

Anson

ANSON JONES MUSEUM, 1302 Ave. K, Anson, TX 79501. Tel.: 325-823-3096.
Web Site: www.traveltexas.com/attractions/anson-jones-museum
Institution Type/Description: History Museum.
Hours & Admission Prices: Sun. 2-4. No charge; donations accepted. Closed holidays.
Attendance: 377 (actual)

Aransas Pass

THIRD COAST SQUADRON CAF MUSEUM, 3201 FM3512, Hangar H11, Aransas Pass, TX 78336. Mailing Address: P.O. Box 8192, Corpus Christi, TX 78468-8192. Tel.: 361-356-4918.
E-mail: info.ThirdCoastCAF@gmail.com
Web Site: www.thirdcoastcaf.org/wordpress/
Key Personnel: Unit Leader, CAF Col. Troy Fitting; Exec. Officer, CAF Michael Riggins.
Institution Type/Description: Military History Museum.
Hours & Admission Prices: Thurs.-Sat. 10-4. Adults $5, children 3-12 $2, children 2 and under no charge.

Archer City

ARCHER COUNTY HISTORICAL MUSEUM, 400 W. Pecan St., Archer City, TX 76351. Mailing Address: P.O. Box 102, Archer City, TX 76351. Tel.: 940-257-4048.
Key Personnel: Cur., Mary Ann Levy.
Institution Type/Description: General Museum: housed in 1910 Old County Jail.
Hours & Admission Prices: May-Nov. Sat. 9-5, Sun. 1-5; other times by appointment. No charge; donations accepted.
Attendance: 500 (estimated)

Arlington

ARLINGTON MUSEUM OF ART, 201 W. Main St., Arlington, TX 76010. Tel.: 817-275-4600. Fax: 817-345-3567. Facebook, Twitter, Pintrest, Youtube.
E-mail: arlingtonmuseum@gmail.com
Web Site: www.arlingtonmuseum.org
Key Personnel: Exec. Dir., Chris Hightower.
Institution Type/Description: Art Museum & Gallery: located in a former 1950s storefront building on Main St. in downtown Arlington.
Hours & Admission Prices: Tues.-Sat. 10-5, Sun. 1-5. Adults $10, seniors/students $5, children (12 and under) no charge. Closed major holidays. ♿
Attendance: 18,000 (estimated)

THE GALLERY AT UTA, 502 S. Cooper St., Fine Arts Bldg., Arlington, TX 76019. Mailing Address: Box 19089, Arlington, TX 76019. Tel.: 817-272-3110.
E-mail: bhuerta@uta.edu
Web Site: www.uta.edu/gallery
Formerly: CRCA: The Gallery at UTA
Key Personnel: Dir., Benito Huerta; Asst. Dir., Patricia Healy.
Institution Type/Description: Art Museum.
Hours & Admission Prices: Mon.-Fri. 10-5, Sat. 12-5; Summer hours by appointment. No charge. Closed school holidays. ♿
Attendance: 7,400 (actual)

INTERNATIONAL BOWLING MUSEUM AND HALL OF FAME, 621 Six Flags Dr., Arlington, TX 76011-6305. Tel.: 817-385-8215. Facebook.
E-mail: info@bowlingmuseum.com
Web Site: www.bowlingmuseum.com
Key Personnel: Pres. & Chm., Mike Aulby; Business Dir., Tracy Ebarb; Cur., Jessica Bell; Dir. Tours & Events, Kari Smith.
Institution Type/Description: Sports Museum.
Hours & Admission Prices: Tues.-Sat. 9:30-5; Sun. 12-6. Adults $9.50; seniors & children $7.50; discounts to military, AAA, AARP, USBC, BPAA, & IBPSIA members; members no charge. ♿
Attendance: 5,300 (actual)

RIVER LEGACY LIVING SCIENCE CENTER, 703 N.W. Green Oaks Blvd., Arlington, TX 76006-2404. Tel.: 817-860-6752. Fax: 817-860-1595.
E-mail: reply@riverlegacy.org
Web Site: www.riverlegacy.org
Key Personnel: Exec. Dir., Jill Hill; Pres. Bd. (V), Larry Fowler; Dir. of Education, Debbie Vernon.
Institution Type/Description: Science & Nature Center.
Hours & Admission Prices: Mon.-Sat. 9-5. No charge; donations accepted. Closed New Year's Day; Easter; Independence Day; Labor Day; Thanksgiving; Christmas Eve & Day. ♿
Attendance: 75,000 (estimated)

Athens

EAST TEXAS ARBORETUM & BOTANICAL SOCIETY, 1601 Patterson Rd., Athens, TX 75751. Tel.: 903-675-5630. Facebook.
E-mail: etabsmary@gmail.com
Web Site: www.easttexasarboretum.org
Key Personnel: Exec. Dir., Mary Eggleston; Asst. Dir., Carolyn McClure Goodman; Pres., Hollis Driskell.
Institution Type/Description: History Museum.
Hours & Admission Prices: Spring & Summer: daily 7:30-7:30; Fall & Winter: daily 8-6. Suggested Donations: Adults $4, seniors & students $3, children (3 and over) $1, children (under 3) and members no charge. ♿
Attendance: 15,000 (estimated)

HENDERSON COUNTY HISTORICAL SOCIETY MUSEUM, 217 N. Prairieville, Athens, TX 75751-2042. Tel.: 903-677-3611.
Institution Type/Description: Historical Society Museum.
Hours & Admission Prices: Fri.-Sat. 10-3. No charge; donations accepted.

Austin

AUSTIN HISTORY CENTER, 810 Guadalupe St., Austin, TX 78701. Mailing Address: P.O. Box 2287, Austin, TX 78768-2287. Tel.: 512-974-7480. Facebook, Instagram.
E-mail: ahc_reference@austintexas.gov
Web Site: library.austintexas.gov/ahc/about-us
Key Personnel: Mng. Archivist, Mike Miller; Head Public Svcs., Nancy Toombs; Archives & Manuscripts Cur., Susan Rittereiser; Exhibits Coord., Steve Schwolert.
Institution Type/Description: Archives & Library: housed in 1933 former Austin Public Library building. A Texas Historic Landmark.
Hours & Admission Prices: Tues.-Sat. 10-6, Sun. 12-6. No charge; donations accepted. ♿
Attendance: 50,000 (actual)

AUSTIN NATURE & SCIENCE CENTER, 2389 Stratford Dr., Austin, TX 78746. Mailing Address: 301 Nature Center Dr., Austin, TX 78746. Tel.: 512-974-3888. Fax: 512-974-3885. Facebook: @ATXnaturecenter.
E-mail: ansc@austintexas.gov
Web Site: www.austintexas.gov/ansc
Key Personnel: Site Supvr., Kathy Maddox; Exhibit Coord., Josh Ransom.
Institution Type/Description: Nature Center.
Hours & Admission Prices: Mon.-Sat. 9-5, Sun. noon to 5. No charge; donations accepted. Check webpage for holidays. ♿
Attendance: 250,000 (actual)

AUSTIN ZOO, 10808 Rawhide Tr., Austin, TX 78736. Mailing Address: P.O. Box 91808, Austin, TX 78709. Tel.: 512-288-1490. Fax: 512-288-3972. Facebook, Twitter.
E-mail: info@austinzoo.org
Web Site: www.austinzoo.org
Formerly: Austin Zoo & Animal Sanctuary
Key Personnel: Dir. & Pres. (V), Patti R. Clark; Dir., Brian Falbo.
Institution Type/Description: Zoo.
Hours & Admission Prices: Feb.-Oct. daily 9:30-6; Nov.-Jan. daily 9:30-5:30. Adults $11.95, students, military & seniors $10.95, children 2-12 $8.95; Member guest $7.95. Closed Thanksgiving; Christmas. ♿
Attendance: 206,000 (actual)

BETTY AND EDWARD MARCUS SCULPTURE PARK AT LAGUNA GLORIA, 3809 W. 35th St., Austin, TX 78703-1001. Tel.: 512-458-8191.
Web Site: www.thecontemporaryaustin.org
Formerly: Austin Museum of Art Laguna Gloria
Institution Type/Description: Historic House & Art Museum: housed in the former home of author, playwright & politician Clara Driscoll and her husband Hal Sevier; built in 1916. Listed on the National Register of Historic Places.
Hours & Admission Prices: Grounds: Mon.-Sat. 9-5, Sun. 10-5. Driscoll Villa: Tues.-Sun. 10-4. Adults $5, seniors & students $3; youth under 18 & military no charge. Closed New Year's Day; Independence Day; Thanksgiving; Christmas Eve & Day.

BLANTON MUSEUM OF ART, 200 E. MLK Jr. Blvd., Austin, TX 78712. Mailing Address: University of Texas at Austin, 200 E. Martin Luther King Jr. Blvd., Stop D1303, Austin, TX 78712-1609. Tel.: 512-471-5482. Facebook, Instagram, Twitter.
E-mail: info@blantonmuseum.org
Web Site: www.blantonmuseum.org
Key Personnel: Dir., Simone Wicha; Deputy Dir. Curatorial Affairs & Cur. Prints & Drawings, Carter Foster; Cur. Modern & Contemporary Art, Veronica Roberts; Adjunct Cur. Latin American Art, Beverly Adams; Assoc. Cur. Carl & Marilynn Thoma Spanish Colonial Art, Rosario Granados-Salinas; Dir. Education & Academic Affairs, Ray Williams; Dir. Collections & Exhibitions, Gabriela Truly; Dir. Operations, Kim Theel; Dir. Devel., Anna Berns; Dir. Finance & Admin., Stacey Cilek.
Institution Type/Description: Art Museum.
Hours & Admission Prices: Tues.-Fri. 10-5, Sat. 11-5, Sun. 1-5, third Thurs. of every month 10-9. Adults $12, seniors $10, youth 13-21 & college students w/ ID $5; members, UT students, faculty & staff, children 12 & under, active military and every Thurs. no charge. Closed major holidays. &
Attendance: 158,000 (actual)

BRIG. GEN. JOHN C.L. SCRIBNER TEXAS MILITARY FORCES MUSEUM, 2200 W. 35th St., Austin, TX 78703-1222. Mailing Address: P.O. Box 5218, Austin, TX 78763-5218. Tel.: 512-782-5659. Facebook, Instagram.
E-mail: txmilmuseum@gmail.com
Web Site: www.texasmilitaryforcesmuseum.org
Institution Type/Description: Military Museum: housed at historic Camp Mabry.
Hours & Admission Prices: Tues.-Sun. 10-4. No charge; donations accepted. &
Attendance: 44,000 (actual)

BULLOCK TEXAS STATE HISTORY MUSEUM, 1800 N. Congress Ave., Austin, TX 78701-1342. Mailing Address: P.O. Box 12874, Austin, TX 78711-2874. Tel.: 512-936-8746. Facebook, Instagram, Twitter.
E-mail: contactus@thestoryoftexas.com
Web Site: www.thestoryoftexas.com
Key Personnel: Interim Dir., Margaret Koch; Head of Education, Kate Betz; Deputy Dir. Opers., Derek Lemons; Head of Exhibition Production, Toni Beldock; Dir. Creative Svcs., Gilbert Medina; Assoc. Dir. Membership, Leslie Adkins; Museum Store Mgr., Mike Byers; Head of Mktg., Emily Morris.
Institution Type/Description: History Museum.
Hours & Admission Prices: Mon.-Sat. 9-5, Sun. 12-5. Adults $13, seniors, military & college students $11, youth 4-17 $9; discounts to AAM & ICOM members; members and children 3 & under no charge. Closed New Year's Day; Thanksgiving; Christmas Eve & Day. &
Attendance: 485,085 (actual)

CAPITOL VISITORS CENTER, A DIVISION OF THE STATE PRESERVATION BOARD, Physical/Mailing Address: 112 E. Eleventh St., Austin, TX 78701-2403. Tel.: 512-305-8400. Fax: 512-305-8401.
E-mail: cvc.cvc@tspb.texas.gov
Web Site: www.tspb.texas.gov/prop/tcvc/cvc/cvc/html
Key Personnel: Exec. Dir., Rod Welsh; Dep. Exec. Dir., Bob Cash; C.F.O., Cynthia Provine, CPA; Capitol Cur., Ali James.
Institution Type/Description: Visitors Center: housed in the c.1856 Old General Land Office Building, designed by German architect C.C. Stremme. Oldest state office building in Texas.
Hours & Admission Prices: Mon.-Sat. 9-5, Sun. 12-5. No charge; donations accepted. Closed New Year's Day; Easter; Thanksgiving; Christmas Eve & Day. &
Attendance: 151,628 (actual)

THE CONTEMPORARY AUSTIN, The Jones Center, 700 Congress Ave., Austin, TX 78701-3217. Tel.: 512-453-5312. Fax: 512-459-4830. Facebook, Instagram, Twitter.
E-mail: info@thecontemporaryaustin.org

Web Site: thecontemporaryaustin.org
Formerly: Texas Fine Arts Association; Arthouse at the Jones Center
Key Personnel: Co-Chairperson, Jeanne Klein; Co-Chairperson, Richard Marcus; Pres., Kathleen Irvin Loughlin; Treas., James Dyess; Sec., Milam Newby.
Institution Type/Description: Art Museum.
Hours & Admission Prices: Tues.-Sat. 11-7, Sun. 12-5. Adults $5; seniors & students $3; members, under 18, military, Tuesdays no charge. &

ELISABET NEY MUSEUM, 304 E. 44th St., Austin, TX 78751-3813. Tel.: 512-974-1625 & 1628. Facebook, Instagram.
E-mail: enm@austintexas.gov
Web Site: www.austintexas.gov/Elisabetney
Key Personnel: Museum Site Coord., Oliver Franklin.
Institution Type/Description: Historic Site & Interpretive Center.
Hours & Admission Prices: Wed.-Sun. noon to 5. No charge; donations accepted.
Attendance: 13,000 (actual)

EMMA S. BARRIENTOS MEXICAN AMERICAN CULTURAL CENTER, 600 River St., Austin, TX 78701. Tel.: 512-974-3772. Fax: 512-974-3777. Facebook, Twitter.
E-mail: macc@austintexas.gov
Web Site: www.austintexas.gov/esbmacc
Key Personnel: Culture & Arts Education Mgr., Herlinda Zamora; Culture & Arts Education Coord., Marina Islas; Culture & Arts Education Specialist, Lori Navarrete; Gallery Specialist, Bob Jones; Media, Mktg. & Event Coord., Linda Crockett.
Institution Type/Description: Cultural Center.
Hours & Admission Prices: Mon.-Thurs. 10-6, Fri. 10-5:30, Sat. 10-4. No charge.

THE FRENCH LEGATION MUSEUM, 802 San Marcos St., Austin, TX 78702-2647. Tel.: 512-472-8180.
E-mail: info@earlyaustin.org
Web Site: frenchlegationmuseum.org
Key Personnel: Museum Coord., Mayra Vargas; Museum Coord., Rebecca Ramirez; Event Mgr., Denise Garza Steusloff, C.M.P.
Institution Type/Description: Historic Building Museum: housed in the former home of the French Charge d'Affaires to the Republic of Texas; built in 1841.
Hours & Admission Prices: Temporarily Closed &
Attendance: 20,000 (actual)

GEORGE WASHINGTON CARVER MUSEUM & CULTURAL CENTER, 1165 Angelina St., Austin, TX 78702-2034. Tel.: 512-974-4926. Facebook, Instagram, Twitter.
E-mail: carver.museum@austintexas.gov
Web Site: www.austintexas.gov
Key Personnel: Site Coord. & Theatre Mgr., Para Agboga; Culture & Arts Education Mgr., Bamidele Demerson; Culture & Arts Education Coord., Faith Weaver; Admin. Specialist, Arrietta Allen; Exhibit Coord., Carre Adams; Culture & Arts Education Specialist (Theatre Tech), Joyce Robinson; Collections Mgr., Shellie Eagan; Administrative Specialist (Rentals), Eric Jarmon; Museum Site Coord. (Genealogy), Cynthia Evans; Culture & Arts Education Specialist, Jennifer Rangubphai.
Institution Type/Description: African American History & Culture Museum.
Hours & Admission Prices: Mon.-Wed. & Fri. 10-6, Thurs. 10-9, Sat. 10-4. No charge. &
Attendance: 100,500 (actual)

HARRY RANSOM CENTER AT THE UNIVERSITY OF TEXAS AT AUSTIN, 300 W. 21st St., Austin, TX 78712. Mailing Address: P.O. Box 7219, Austin, TX 78713-7219. Tel.: 512-471-8944. Fax: 512-471-9646.
E-mail: webmail@hrc.utexas.edu
Web Site: www.hrc.utexas.edu
Key Personnel: Dir., Dr. Stephen Enniss; Assoc. Dir. for Acquisitions & Admin., Megan Barnard; Sr. Admin. Assoc., Cheryl McGrath; Admin. Asst., Melanie Zyck-Alberts.
Institution Type/Description: Humanities Research Library.
Hours & Admission Prices: Library Reading Room: Mon.-Sat. 9-5. Exhibits: Mon.-Wed. & Fri. 10-5, Thurs. 10-7, Sat.-Sun. 12-5. No charge; donations accepted. Closed university holidays. &
Attendance: 80,000 (actual)

LBJ PRESIDENTIAL LIBRARY, 2313 Red River St., Austin, TX 78705-5737. Tel.: 512-721-0200. Fax: 512-721-0171 & 0170. Facebook, Instagram, Twitter.
E-mail: johnson.library@nara.gov
Web Site: www.lbjlibrary.org
Formerly: Lyndon Baines Johnson Library and Museum
Key Personnel: Deputy Dir., Michael MacDonald; Dir. Public Programs, Sarah McCracken; Dir. Digital Strategy, Kassandra Navarro; Volunteer & Visitor

Svcs. Coord., Laura Eggert; Communications Dir., Anne Wheeler; Special Events Coord., Lisa Castro; Facility Mgr./IT, Darren Jernigan; Supervisory Archivist, Jennifer Cuddeback.
Institution Type/Description: Presidential Library.
Hours & Admission Prices: Daily 9-5. Adults $10, seniors $7, college students with ID & youth $3; children 12 & under, members, active-duty military, school groups with reservations, University of Texas faculty, staff & students, Martin Luther King Day, Presidents' Day, Memorial Day, Independence Day, LBJ's Birthday (Aug. 27th), Veterans Day, Austin Museum Day & Explore UT no charge. Closed New Year's Day; Thanksgiving; Christmas. &
Attendance: 130,576 (actual)

LADY BIRD JOHNSON WILDFLOWER CENTER, 4801 La Crosse Ave., Austin, TX 78739-1702. Tel.: 512-232-0100. Fax: 512-232-0156. Facebook.
E-mail: news@wildflower.org
Web Site: www.wildflower.org
Key Personnel: Exec. Dir., Patrick Newman; Dir. of Fin., Mike Abkowitz; Dir. Communications, Lee Clippard; Dir. Horticulture, Andrea DeLong-Amaya; Dir. Membership, Lori Bockstanz; Mgr. Volunteers, Carrie McDonald.
Institution Type/Description: Botanical Garden & Nature Center.
Hours & Admission Prices: Daily 9-5. Adults $10, seniors (65 and over) & students $8, youth (5-17) $4, children (under 4) no charge. Closed New Year's Eve & Day, Thanksgiving, Christmas Eve & Day. &
Attendance: 140,000 (actual)

MEXIC-ARTE MUSEUM, 419 Congress, Austin, TX 78701-3619. Tel.: 512-480-9373. Facebook, Instagram, Twitter.
E-mail: info@mexic-artemuseum.org
Web Site: www.mexic-artemuseum.org
Key Personnel: Exec. Dir., Sylvia Orozco; Pres. Bd., Michael Torres; Vice Pres., Devel., Elizabeth Caples Rogers; Vice Pres., Membership, Teresa C. Miller.
Institution Type/Description: Art Museum.
Hours & Admission Prices: Mon.-Thurs. 10-6, Fri.-Sat. 10-5, Sun. 12-5. Adults $5; seniors & students $4; children (12 and under) $1. &
Attendance: 50,000 (estimated)

MUSEUM OF THE WEIRD, 412 E. 6th St., Austin, TX 78701. Tel.: 512-476-5493. Facebook.
E-mail: info@museumoftheweird.com
Web Site: museumoftheweird.com
Institution Type/Description: General Museum.
Hours & Admission Prices: Daily 10 am to midnight. Adults $12, children (8 and under) $8.

NEILL-COCHRAN HOUSE MUSEUM, 2310 San Gabriel St., Austin, TX 78705-5014. Tel.: 512-478-2335. Fax: 512-478-1865. Facebook, Twitter.
E-mail: info@nchmuseum.org
Web Site: www.nchmuseum.org
Key Personnel: Exec. Dir., Rowena Houghton-Dasch, PhD; Museum Facilities Mgr., Gene E. Heard; Business & Programming Dir., Andrea Perry.
Institution Type/Description: Historic House: house in the Neill-Cochran House; built in 1855.
Hours & Admission Prices: Wed.-Sun. 1-4. Guided Tours: adults $5, seniors & students and children (12-18) $4; discounts to Time Travelers & school groups; members & children under 12 no charge. &
Attendance: 4,000 (estimated)

O. HENRY MUSEUM, 409 E. 5th St., Austin, TX 78701-3705. Tel.: 512-472-1903 & 974-1398. Fax: 512-472-7102. Facebook.
E-mail: Michael.Hoinski@Austintexas.gov
Web Site: www.austintexas.gove/department/o-henry-museum
Key Personnel: Site Coord., Melissa Parr; Culture & Arts Educ. Coord., Michael Hoinski; Culture & Arts Educ. Coord., Karlena Barbosa; Admin. Specialist, Katie Keckeisen; Arts Instructor, Grant Cross; Arts Instructor, Elyssa Browning.
Institution Type/Description: Historic House Museum: 1888 home of O. Henry.
Hours & Admission Prices: Wed.-Sun. 12-5. No charge; donations accepted. Closed New Year's Day; Independence Day; Labor Day; Thanksgiving; Christmas.
Attendance: 15,000 (estimated)

REPUBLIC OF TEXAS MUSEUM, 810 San Marcos St., Austin, TX 78702. Tel.: 512-339-1997. Facebook.
E-mail: headquarters@drtinfo.org
Web Site: www.drtinfo.org
Key Personnel: Museum Asst., Sharon Hill.
Institution Type/Description: History Museum.
Hours & Admission Prices: Closed for relocation. &

TEXAS GOVERNOR'S MANSION, 1010 Colorado St., Austin, TX 78701-2334. Mailing Address: P.O. Box 12428, Austin, TX 78711. Tel.: 512-305-8524 & 475-2324. Facebook, Twitter.
E-mail: mansion.tours@tspb.texas.gov
Web Site: gov.texas.gov/mansion
Key Personnel: Admin., Katie Taylor.
Institution Type/Description: Historic House & Site: designated as a National Historic Landmark in 1975.
Hours & Admission Prices: Tours: Wed.-Fri. 2-4, reservation required. &

TEXAS HISTORICAL COMMISSION, 1511 Colorado, Austin, TX 78701-1664. Mailing Address: P.O. Box 12276, Austin, TX 78711-2276. Tel.: 512-463-6100. Facebook, Twitter.
E-mail: historicsites@thc.state.tx.us
Web Site: www.thc.texas.gov
Key Personnel: Exec. Dir., Mark Wolfe; Deputy Exec. Dir. & Dir. Historic Sites, Joseph Bell; Dir. Historic Sites Opers. - Military & Archeological Sites, Brett Cruse; Dir. Historic Sites Opers. - House Museums, Ellen Cone Busch; Chief Architect, Glenn Reed; Chief Cur., Laura DeNormandie; Interpretive Specialist, Hal Simon-Hassell; Community Partnership Coord., Angela Reed; Exec. Asst. Historic Sites, Theresa Wenske; Div. Dir. History Programs, Charles Sadnick.
Institution Type/Description: Historic Sites.
Hours & Admission Prices: See individual listings. &

TEXAS MEMORIAL MUSEUM, 2400 Trinity St., Austin, TX 78705-5730. Mailing Address: 2400 Trinity St., Stop D1500, Austin, TX 78712-1621. Tel.: 512-471-1604. Fax: 512-471-4794. Facebook, Instagram, Twitter.
E-mail: tmminfo@austin.utexas.edu
Web Site: www.tnm.utexas.edu
Key Personnel: Dir., Edward C. Theriot; Assoc. Dir., Pamela R. Owen; Visitor Svcs. Mgr., Benjamin Grall; Sr. Admin. Assoc., Laura Naski Keffer; Security Guard, Michael R. Fallon.
Institution Type/Description: Natural Science Museum.
Hours & Admission Prices: Tues.-Sat. 9-5, Sun. 1-5. Ages 13 & up $7, Ages 2-12 $5, college students w/ID $4, active & retired military no charge; discounts to groups; UT-Austin faculty, staff & students and children under 2 no charge. Closed New Year's Eve & Day; Easter; Independence Day; Thanksgiving; Christmas Eve & Day. &
Attendance: 80,952 (actual)

TEXAS MUSIC MUSEUM, 1009 E. 11th St., Austin, TX 78702. Mailing Address: P.O. Box 16467, Austin, TX 78761-6467. Tel.: 512-203-4875 & 472-8891. Facebook.
E-mail: cshorkey@mail.utexas.edu
Web Site: www.texasmusicmuseum.org
Key Personnel: Pres. (V), Dr. Clayton Shorkey; Vice Pres., Rudy Martinez; Sec., Gina Bustos; Treas., Joyce Davids Christianson.
Institution Type/Description: Music Museum.
Hours & Admission Prices: Regular hours: Mon.-Fri. 8-5; summer hours: Tues.-Wed., Fri. 12-4, Thurs. hours vary. No charge; donations accepted. &
Attendance: 10,000 (estimated)

TEXAS PARKS AND WILDLIFE DEPARTMENT, 4200 Smith School Rd., Austin, TX 78744-3292. Tel.: 512-389-4800 & 800-792-1112.
E-mail: carter.smith@tpwd.texas.gov
Web Site: tpwd.texas.gov
Key Personnel: Exec. Dir., Carter Smith; Dir. State Parks, Brent Leisure; Dir. Cultural Resources Mgmt., Michael Strutt; Chief Cur., Sally Baulch; Dir. Natural Resources Management, David Riskind.
Institution Type/Description: Texas Parks & Wildlife Agency: administers over 95 state parks, historic sites & natural areas.
Hours & Admission Prices: Headquarters: Mon.-Fri. 8-5, call sites for hours. Fees vary. Annual Pass $70, adults $4-$7. &
Attendance: 8,000,000

TEXAS STATE LIBRARY AND ARCHIVES COMMISSION, 1201 Brazos St., Austin, TX 78701-1938. Mailing Address: Box 12927, Austin, TX 78711-2927. Tel.: 512-463-5455. Fax: 512-463-5436. Facebook; Twitter.
E-mail: info@tsl.texas.gov
Web Site: www.tsl.texas.gov
Key Personnel: Dir. & Librarian, Mark Smith; Chm. (V), Michael C. Waters.
Institution Type/Description: History Museum.
Hours & Admission Prices: Library: Mon.-Fri. 8-5. Genealogy Section: Mon.-Fri. 8-5. Sam Houston Center: Tues.-Fri. 8-5, 2nd Sat. each month 9-4. No charge. Closed major holidays. &
Attendance: 5,000

THINKERY, 1830 Simond Ave., Austin, TX 78723. Tel.: 512-469-6200. Facebook, Instagram, Twitter.
E-mail: info@thinkeryaustin.org
Web Site: www.thinkeryaustin.org
Formerly: Austin Children's Museum
Key Personnel: C.E.O., Patricia Young Brown; Dir. of Learning Experiences, Adrienne Barnett; Dir. Devel. & Mktg., Jessica Campos Hernandez; Dir. Finance, Devin Thomas.
Institution Type/Description: Children's Museum.
Hours & Admission Prices: Mon. 9-12, Tues.-Sun. 10-5. Visitors $12, children under 2 years no charge. ♿
Attendance: 425,000 (estimated)

UMLAUF SCULPTURE GARDEN & MUSEUM, 605 Azie Morton Rd., Austin, TX 78704-1453. Tel.: 512-445-5582. Facebook, Instagram, Twitter.
E-mail: director@umlaufsculpture.org
Web Site: umlaufsculpture.org
Key Personnel: Exec. Dir., Sarah Story; Museum Cur., Katie Robinson Edwards; Venue & Event Mgr., Amanda Valbracht; Dir. of Programs, Sara Athans; Membership & Devel. Mgr., Maryhelen Murray; Visitor Svcs. Assoc., Mary Cantrell; Collections Asst., Adrian Aguilera.
Institution Type/Description: Sculpture & Garden Museum.
Hours & Admission Prices: Tues.-Fri. 10-4, Sat.-Sun.12-4. Adults $5, senior citizens 60 & up $3, students $1; discounts for AAM, American Horticulture Society & Texas Association Museum members; members, active military personnel & family and children 12 & under no charge. Closed New Year's Eve & Day; Independence Day; Thanksgiving; Christmas Eve & Day. ♿
Attendance: 45,000 (actual)

WOMEN & THEIR WORK ART GALLERY, 1710 Lavaca St., Austin, TX 78701. Tel.: 512-477-1064. Facebook, Instagram, Twitter.
E-mail: info@womenandtheirwork.org
Web Site: www.womenandtheirwork.org
Key Personnel: Exec. Dir., Chris Cowden; Gallery Dir., Rachel Stuckey; Program Dir., Diane Sikes; Gift Shop, Lindsay Eyth.
Institution Type/Description: Art Gallery.
Hours & Admission Prices: Mon.-Fri. 10-6, Sat. 12-6. No charge; donations accepted. Closed major holidays. ♿

Austwell

ARANSAS NATIONAL WILDLIFE REFUGE & CLAUDE F. LARD VISITOR CENTER, 1 Wildlife Cir., Austwell, TX 77950. Mailing Address: P.O. Box 100, Austwell, TX 77950. Tel.: 361-286-3559. Fax: 361-286-3722.
E-mail: laura_bonneau@fws.gov
Web Site: www.fws.gov/refuge/Aransas
Institution Type/Description: Wildlife Refuge.
Hours & Admission Prices: Refuge: daily sunrise to sunset. Visitor Center: daily 8:30-4:30. Closed Thanksgiving; Christmas.

Baird

CALLAHAN COUNTY PIONEER MUSEUM, 100 W. 4th, #B1, Baird, TX 79504-5305. Tel.: 325-854-5875.
E-mail: library@callahancounty.org
Institution Type/Description: History Museum.
Hours & Admission Prices: Mon.-Fri. 1-5. No charge; donations accepted. Closed major holidays. ♿
Attendance: 372 (actual)

Bandera

FRONTIER TIMES MUSEUM, 510 13th St., Bandera, TX 78003. Mailing Address: P.O. Box 1918, Bandera, TX 78003-1918. Tel.: 830-796-3864.
E-mail: information@frontiertimesmuseum.org
Web Site: www.frontiertimesmuseum.org
Key Personnel: Pres., Kirk McMullan; Vice Pres., Anthony Ferragamo; Sec., Bill Pannebaker; Treas., Eddie Rowe; Exec. Dir., Rebecca Norton.
Institution Type/Description: Historic Building.
Hours & Admission Prices: Mon.-Sat. 10-4:30. Adults $6, seniors $4, children 6-17 $2; discounts to groups upon approval; children under 6 & members no charge. Closed New Year's Day; Easter; Thanksgiving; Christmas Eve & Day. ♿
Attendance: 10,000 (actual)

Bay City

MATAGORDA COUNTY MUSEUM, 2100 Ave. F, Bay City, TX 77414-0851. Tel.: 979-245-7502. Fax: 979-245-1233.
E-mail: mcma@matagordamuseum.com
Web Site: www.matagordamuseum.com
Key Personnel: Dir., Barbara Smith.
Institution Type/Description: Historical Society Museum: housed in c.1917 federal post office building.
Hours & Admission Prices: Wed.-Sun. 1-5. Adults $4, seniors $3, children $2; discounts to AAM, ICOM, TAM & SETMA members; members & children under 2 no charge. Closed New Year's Day; Memorial Day; Good Friday; Labor Day; Thanksgiving; Christmas. ♿
Attendance: 10,500 (actual)

Baytown

BAYTOWN HISTORICAL MUSEUM, 220 W. Defee St., Baytown, TX 77520-4010. Tel.: 281-427-8768.
E-mail: BHPA@BaytownHistory.org
Institution Type/Description: History Museum.
Hours & Admission Prices: Tues.-Sat. 10-2. No charge.

BAYTOWN NATURE CENTER, 6213 Bayway Dr., Baytown, TX 77520. Tel.: 281-932-1972. Facebook.
E-mail: Christina.Butcher@baytown.org
Key Personnel: Pres., Billy Barnett; Vice Pres., Larry Houston; Sec., Christine LaCoste; Treas., Dee Anne Navarre.
Institution Type/Description: Nature Center.
Hours & Admission Prices: Daily sunrise to sunset. Adults $4; children (5-12) and seniors $1; children (4 and under) no charge. Closed Thanksgiving & Christmas.

EDDIE V. GRAY WETLANDS CENTER, 1724 Market St., Baytown, TX 77520. Tel.: 281-420-7128. Fax: 281-420-7142.
E-mail: Tracey.Prothro@baytown.org
Institution Type/Description: Nature Center.
Hours & Admission Prices: Mon.-Fri. 8-4, Sat. 10-4; groups by appointment. No charge. Closed holidays.

Beaumont

ART MUSEUM OF SOUTHEAST TEXAS, 500 Main St., Beaumont, TX 77701. Tel.: 409-832-3432.
E-mail: info@amset.org
Web Site: www.amset.org
Key Personnel: Exec. Dir., Lynn P. Castle; Cur. Exhibitions & Collections, Sarah Beth Wilson; Pres., Albert Nolen; Pres. Elect, Sandra Clark; Administrator Finance & Personnel, Pam Bemis; Public Rels. Coord., Kara Timberlake; Admin. Asst., Kayleigh Thompson; Cur. Education, Christle Feagin.
Institution Type/Description: Art Museum.
Hours & Admission Prices: Mon.-Fri. 9-5, Sat. 10-5, Sun. 12-5. No charge; donations accepted. Closed major holidays ♿
Attendance: 36,000 (actual)

THE ART STUDIO, INC., 720 Franklin St., Beaumont, TX 77701-4424. Tel.: 409-838-5393. Facebook.
E-mail: artstudio@artstudio.org
Web Site: www.artstudio.org
Key Personnel: Exec. Dir. & Studio Res., Greg Busceme.
Institution Type/Description: Art Gallery with Exhibit Area.
Hours & Admission Prices: Tues.-Sat. 2-5; other times by appointment. No charge; donations accepted. Closed holidays. ♿
Attendance: 5,000 (estimated)

BABE DIDRIKSON ZAHARIAS MUSEUM, 1750 IH-10 E, Beaumont, TX 77704. Mailing Address: 2135 Brewton Cir., Beaumont, TX 77706. Tel.: 409-833-4622. Facebook: Babe Didrikson Zaharias Museum.
E-mail: klewis@ci.beaumont.tx.us
Web Site: www.babedidriksonzaharias.org
Key Personnel: Pres., W.L. Pate, Jr.
Institution Type/Description: Sports Museum.
Hours & Admission Prices: Mon.-Sat. 9-5. No charge; donations accepted. Closed Thanksgiving; Christmas. ♿
Attendance: 3,000 (estimated)

BEAUMONT ART LEAGUE, 2675 Gulf St., Beaumont, TX 77703-4417. Tel.: 409-833-4179. Facebook, Twitter, Google+, Youtube.
E-mail: info@beaumontartleague.org
Web Site: beaumontartleague.org

Key Personnel: Pres./Chm., Bridget M. Johnson; Vice Pres., Scot Meents; Sec., Nicole Cormier; Parliamentarian, Melinda McWhite.
Institution Type/Description: Art Museum & Gallery.
Hours & Admission Prices: Thurs.-Sat. 9-5. &
Attendance: 2,000 (estimated)

BEAUMONT ART LEAGUE, BROWN-SCURLOCK GALLERIES, 2675 Gulf St., Beaumont, TX 77703-4417. Tel.: 409-833-4179. Facebook.
E-mail: info@beaumontartleague.org
Web Site: www.beaumontartleague.org
Key Personnel: Pres./Chm., Bridget M. Johnson; Vice Pres., Scot Meents; Sec., Nicole Cormier; Parliamentarian, Melinda McWhite.
Institution Type/Description: Art Gallery.
Hours & Admission Prices: Thurs.-Sat. 9-5. No Charge. &
Attendance: 2,000 (estimated)

BEAUMONT BOTANICAL GARDENS, 6088 Babe Zaharias Dr., Beaumont, TX 77705-6747. Tel.: 409-842-3135. Fax: 409-840-6456.
E-mail: bcgc@beaumontbotanicalgardens.org
Formerly: Beaumont Council of Garden Clubs
Key Personnel: Bev Flosi; First Vice Pres., Jeanne Looney; Second Vice Pres., Melba Moses; Recording Sec., Mary Ellen Rinebold; Corresponding Sec., Kathryn Walker; Treas., Randy Hammerling.
Institution Type/Description: Botanical Garden.
Hours & Admission Prices: Daily 10-4. No charge, donations welcome. &
Attendance: 12,300 (estimated)

DISHMAN ART MUSEUM, 1030 E. Lavaca St., Beaumont, TX 77705. Mailing Address: P.O. Box 10027, Beaumont, TX 77710-0027. Tel.: 409-880-8959. Fax: 409-880-1799.
E-mail: dishmanart@lamar.edu
Web Site: www.lamar.edu/fine-arts-communication/dishman-art-museum/index
Key Personnel: Museum Dir., Dennis Kiel; Museum Asst., Alyssabeth Guerra.
Institution Type/Description: Art Museum.
Hours & Admission Prices: Mon.-Fri. 10-5. &
Attendance: 4,000 (estimated)

EDISON MUSEUM, 350 Pine St., Beaumont, TX 77701-2437. Tel.: 409-981-3089. Facebook: Edison Museum.
E-mail: director@edisonmuseum.org
Web Site: www.edisonmuseum.org
Formerly: Edison Plaza Museum
Institution Type/Description: History Museum: housed in the Travis Street substation; the first substation to distribute electric power in Southeast Texas.
Hours & Admission Prices: Tues.-Fri. 9-2, sat. 10-2. Closed major holidays. No charge. &
Attendance: 3,380 (actual)

FIRE MUSEUM OF TEXAS, 400 Walnut at Mulberry, Beaumont, TX 77701. Tel.: 409-880-3927.
E-mail: firemuseum@ci.beaumont.tx.us
Web Site: www.firemuseumoftexas.org
Key Personnel: Museum Mgr., Ami Kamara.
Institution Type/Description: Firefighting Museum: 1927 Beaumont Fire Department Firehouse; Texas Historical Landmark; Spanish Renaissance Revival.
Hours & Admission Prices: Mon.-Fri. 8-4:30, Sat.-Sun. by appointment. No charge; donations accepted. Closed New Year's Day; Martin Luther King Jr. Day; Good Friday; Memorial Day; Independence Day; Labor Day; Thanksgiving & day after; Christmas. &
Attendance: 23,478 (actual)

JOHN JAY FRENCH HOUSE, BEAUMONT HERITAGE SOCIETY, 3025 French Rd., Beaumont, TX 77706-7920. Mailing Address: Beaumont Heritage Society, 2240 Calder Ave., Beaumont, TX 77701. Tel.: 409-898-0348. Fax: 409-898-8487. Facebook.
E-mail: info@beaumontheritage.org
Web Site: beaumontheritage.org
Key Personnel: Pres., Christina Crawford; Vice Pres., Will Robbins.
Institution Type/Description: Historic House Museum: c.1845 Greek Revival house, John Jay French home.
Hours & Admission Prices: Tues.-Fri. 10-3, Sat. 10-2. Admission $5, school group tours $1 per student, children (4 and under) no charge. &
Attendance: 12,000 (estimated)

MCFADDIN-WARD HOUSE, Visitor Center, 1906 Calder Ave., Beaumont, TX 77701-1517. Mailing Address: 725 Third St., Beaumont, TX 77701-1629. Tel.: 409-832-1906 & 2134. Fax: 409-832-3483.
E-mail: alea@mcfaddin-ward.org
Web Site: www.mcfaddin-ward.org
Key Personnel: Dir., Allen Lea; Cur. Interpretation & Education, Judy Linsley; Cur., Sam Daleo, Jr.; Public Rels. Coord., Karen Chapman; Volunteer Coord., Becky Fertitta; Mgr. Facilities, Felix McFarland; Asst. Dir. & Admin., Arlene Christiansen.
Institution Type/Description: Historic House: 1906 Beaux Arts Colonial house built by early Texas oil & ranching family.
Hours & Admission Prices: Tues.-Sat. 10, 11, 1:30 & 2:30, Sun. 1-3. McFaddin-Ward House: children under 8 not admitted. Carriage House: Tues.-Sat. 10-4, Sun. 1-3. Reservations recommended. Adults $5; discounts to seniors, military, AAM, ICOM & TAM members; members no charge. Closed major holidays. &
Attendance: 10,387 (actual)

SPINDLETOP/GLADYS CITY BOOMTOWN MUSEUM, 5550 Jimmy Simmons Blvd., Beaumont, TX 77705. Mailing Address: P. O. Box 10070, Beaumont, TX 77710-0070. Tel.: 409-880-1750. Facebook, Twitter, Intagram.
E-mail: gladyscityinfo@gmail.com
Web Site: www.spindletop.org
Key Personnel: Dir., Troy Gray; Pres., Paula Bothe.
Institution Type/Description: Recreation of Oil Boomtown: located near the site of the Spindletop oilfield; discovered in 1901.
Hours & Admission Prices: Tues.-Sat. 10-5, Sun. 1-5; school groups by appointment. Adults $5, senior citizens 60 & over $3, children 6-12 $2; children 5 & under no charge. Closed all major holidays. &
Attendance: 25,000 (estimated)

TEXAS ENERGY MUSEUM, 600 Main St., Beaumont, TX 77701-3305. Tel.: 409-833-5100. Facebook: Texas Energy Museum.
E-mail: ryan@texasenergymuseum.org
Web Site: www.texasenergymuseum.org
Key Personnel: Dir. & C.E.O., D. Ryan Smith.
Institution Type/Description: Industry History Museum.
Hours & Admission Prices: Tues.-Sat. 9-5, Sun. 1-5. Adults $5, senior citizens & children 6-12 $3; AAM members, Lamar University students with valid I.D. & Texas Assoc. of Museums members no charge. &
Attendance: 16,000 (actual)

TYRRELL HISTORICAL LIBRARY, 695 Pearl St., Beaumont, TX 77701. Mailing Address: P.O. Box 3827, 695 Pearl St., Beaumont, TX 77704-3827. Tel.: 409-833-2759. Fax: 409-833-5828.
E-mail: wgrace@ci.beaumont.tx.us
Web Site: http://www.beaumontlibrary.org
Institution Type/Description: Historical Library: housed in a former Baptist Church; built in 1903. Listed on the National Register of Historic Places.
Hours & Admission Prices: Temporarily Closed &
Attendance: 5,257 (actual)

Beeville

BEEVILLE ART MUSEUM, 401 E. Fannin, Beeville, TX 78102-3515. Tel.: 361-358-8615. Facebook.
Key Personnel: Dir., Tracy Bell Saucier.
Institution Type/Description: Art Museum.
Hours & Admission Prices: Currently Closed.

Belton

BELL COUNTY MUSEUM, 201 N. Main St., Belton, TX 76513-3160. Tel.: 254-933-5243.
E-mail: info@bellcountymuseum.org
Web Site: www.bellcountymuseum.org
Key Personnel: Exec. Dir., Coleman Hampton; Curator of Collections, Mikaela Young; Education Coord., Kayte Ricketts; Office Mgr., Steven Rise.
Institution Type/Description: History Museum: housed in c.1904 Carnegie Library Building.
Hours & Admission Prices: Tues.-Fri. 12-5; Sat. 10-5. No charge; donations accepted. &
Attendance: 12,500 (estimated)

Benjamin

WICHITA - BRAZOS MUSEUM & CULTURAL CENTER, 200 E. Hayes St., Benjamin, TX 79505. Tel.: 940-459-2229. Facebook.

E-mail: kchc@srcaccess.net
Web Site: www.knoxcountytexas.com
Formerly: Knox County Museum
Key Personnel: C.E.O. & Chm. (V), Mary Jane Young.
Institution Type/Description: History Museum.
Hours & Admission Prices: Mon.-Fri. 1-5. No charge; donations accepted. Closed legal holidays. &
Attendance: 700 (actual)

Big Bend National Park

BIG BEND NATIONAL PARK, Science and Resource Management Center, 266 Tecolote Dr., Big Bend National Park, TX 79834. Mailing Address: Science and Resource Management Center, P.O. Box 129, Big Bend National Park, TX 79834-0129. Tel.: 432-477-2251. Fax: 432-477-1160 & 1176. Facebook, Twitter, Instagram.
E-mail: kate_hogue@nps.gov
Web Site: www.nps.gov/bibe
Key Personnel: Superintendent, Bob Krumenaker.
Institution Type/Description: National Park Visitor Centers.
Hours & Admission Prices: Daily 8-5. Annual Pass $40; autos $20 per week; bicycles, motorcycles & bus passengers $10 per week; Golden Age Passports: U.S. citizens 62 & over $10. &
Attendance: 360,000 (actual)

Big Lake

HICKMAN MUSEUM, 609 Main St., Big Lake, TX 76932. Tel.: 325-884-2082.
Institution Type/Description: Historic House Museum: housed in the former home of Gracie Hickman.
Hours & Admission Prices: Mon.-Fri. 9am to noon. No charge.
Attendance: 260 (estimated)

Big Spring

HANGAR 25 AIR MUSEUM, 1911 Apron Dr., Big Spring, TX 79720-7807. Mailing Address: P.O. Box 2925, Big Spring, TX 79721. Tel.: 432-264-1999.
E-mail: hangar25@crcom.net
Web Site: www.hangar25airmuseum.com
Key Personnel: Pres., Jim DePauw; Vice Pres., Emily McCann; Museum Admin., Amber Stokes; Museum Asst., Martha Vierra.
Institution Type/Description: Military History Museum.
Hours & Admission Prices: Tues.-Fri. 10-4, Sat. 10-2. No charge; donations accepted. &
Attendance: 5,000 (estimated)

HERITAGE MUSEUM & POTTON HOUSE, 510 Scurry, Big Spring, TX 79720-2736. Tel.: 432-267-8255.
E-mail: heritagemus@gmail.com
Web Site: www.heritagebigspring.com/index.php
Key Personnel: Pres., James Johnston.
Institution Type/Description: Historic Museum.
Hours & Admission Prices: Tues.-Fri. 8:30-4, Sat. 10-4 by appointment. Adults $2, students & seniors $1; members no charge. Closed national holidays. &
Attendance: 15,000 (actual)

Blanket

BLANKET HISTORICAL MUSEUM, 1200 S. Broadway, Blanket, TX 76432. Tel.: 325-748-2491.
E-mail: freda111@verizon.net
Key Personnel: Contact Person, Doris Teague.
Institution Type/Description: History Museum: housed in the former Blanket State Bank; built in 1901.
Hours & Admission Prices: Sat. afternoons & by appointment.
Attendance: 50

Boerne

AGRICULTURAL HERITAGE MUSEUM, Physical/Mailing Address: 102 City Park Rd., P.O. Box 1076, Boerne, TX 78006. Tel.: 830-249-6007.
E-mail: info@agmuseum.org
Web Site: www.agmuseum.us
Key Personnel: Pres., Kristy Watson; Acquisitions, Malcolm Homeier.
Institution Type/Description: Agriculture Museum.

Hours & Admission Prices: Feb. to Nov. Sat. 10-4; other times by appointment. Adults $5; children 12 & under no charge. Closed major holidays. &
Attendance: 4,000 (estimated)

KUHLMANN KING HISTORICAL HOUSE AND MUSEUM, 402 E. Blanco, Boerne, TX 78006-2008. Mailing Address: P.O. Box 178, Boerne, TX 78006-0178. Tel.: 830-249-7277.
Web Site: www.bahps.com
Formerly: Boerne Area Historical Preservation Society
Key Personnel: Pres., Peggy Cuny; Vice Pres., Martha Hawkins; Treas., Louise Davis; Sec., Mary Ann Ward.
Institution Type/Description: Historic House: c.1880, Kuhlmann-King Family Home. Historical Landmark Graham; historical business bldg. c.1850's.
Hours & Admission Prices: Appointment only. No charge; donations accepted. &
Attendance: 1,500 (estimated)

Bonham

FANNIN COUNTY MUSEUM OF HISTORY, One Main St., Bonham, TX 75418-4345. Tel.: 903-583-8042. Facebook.
E-mail: fcmuseum@hotmail.com
Web Site: www.fannincountymuseum.org
Key Personnel: Dir., Jean Dodson; Pres. (V), Glenn Taylor.
Institution Type/Description: History Museum: housed in the former Texas and Pacific Railway Depot; c.1900. Listed on the National Register of Historic Places.
Hours & Admission Prices: Tues.-Sat. 12-4. No charge; donations accepted.
Attendance: 3,500 (actual)

FORT INGLISH, 902 W. Sam Rayburn Dr., Bonham, TX 75418. Mailing Address: P.O. Box 395, Bonham, TX 75418-0395. Tel.: 903-583-3943.
E-mail: rick@forttours.com
Institution Type/Description: History Museum: housed in a replica of log fort used as protection against Indians, 1837-1843.
Hours & Admission Prices: April-Sept. 1 Thurs.-Sat. 11-3. No charge; donations accepted. &
Attendance: 3,500 (actual)

SAM RAYBURN HOUSE MUSEUM, 800 W. Sam Rayburn Dr., Bonham, TX 75418. Mailing Address: P.O. Box 309, Bonham, TX 75418-0308. Tel.: 903-583-2455. Fax: 903-583-7394. Facebook.
E-mail: srhm@thc.state.tx.us
Web Site: www.cah.utexas.edu/museums/rayburn_hours.php
Key Personnel: Admin. Asst., Kimberly Burpo; Research Assoc., Emma Trent.
Institution Type/Description: Historic House: 1916 two-story frame farmhouse with Colonial Revival facade, built by Sam Rayburn.
Hours & Admission Prices: Mon.-Fri. 9-4:30, Sat.10-2. No charge. &
Attendance: 7,500 (actual)

THE SAM RAYBURN MUSEUM, A DIVISION OF THE DOLPH BRISCOE CENTER FOR AMERICAN HISTORY, 800 W. Sam Rayburn Dr., Bonham, TX 75418-4103. Mailing Address: P.O. Box 309, Bonham, TX 75418-0309. Tel.: 903-583-2455. Fax: 903-583-7394.
E-mail: k.burpo@austin.utexas.edu
Web Site: www.cah.utexas.edu
Key Personnel: Admin. Asst., Kimberly Burpo; Research Assoc., Emma Trent.
Institution Type/Description: Biographical & Historical Museum.
Hours & Admission Prices: Mon.-Fri. 9-4:30, Sat. 10-2. No charge; donations accepted. &
Attendance: 7,500 (estimated)

Borger

HUTCHINSON COUNTY MUSEUM, 618 N. Main, Borger, TX 79007-3529. Tel.: 806-273-0130. Facebook.
E-mail: lynnhopkins@hutchinsoncnty.com
Web Site: www.hutchinsoncountymuseum.org
Key Personnel: Dir., Clay Renick; Admin., Lynn Hopkins; Registrar, Addison Killough.
Institution Type/Description: History Museum: housed in 1927 Grand Hardware, early store, located in 1926 Oil Boom Town.
Hours & Admission Prices: Tues.-Fri. 9-5, Sat. 1-4:30. No charge. Closed legal holidays. &
Attendance: 3,043 (actual)

Brady

HEART OF TEXAS COUNTRY MUSIC MUSEUM, 1701 S. Bridge, Brady, TX 76825. Tel.: 325-597-1895. Fax: 325-597-0515.
E-mail: tracy@hillbillyhits.com
Web Site: www.heartoftexascountry.com
Key Personnel: Dir., Mr. Tracy Pitcox; Chm. (V), Maxine Bradford; Museum Shop Mgr., Sharon Jackson.
Institution Type/Description: Music History Museum.
Hours & Admission Prices: Fri. 2-4, Sat. 10-4, Sun. 12-5. &
Attendance: 2,500 (estimated)

HEART OF TEXAS HISTORICAL MUSEUM, 117 N. High St., Brady, TX 76825. Mailing Address: P.O. Box 48, Brady, TX 76825. Tel.: 325-597-0526.
E-mail: hothistoricalmuseum@yahoo.com
Web Site: www.heartoftexashistoricalmuseum.com
Institution Type/Description: History Museum: housed in the former McCulloch County Jail; built in 1910. Listed on the National Register of Historic Places.
Hours & Admission Prices: Fri.-Sat. 1-5, Sun. 1-4; other times by appointment.

Breckenridge

BRECKENRIDGE AVIATION MUSEUM, Stephens County Airport, Breckenridge, TX 76424. Mailing Address: P.O. Box 388, Breckenridge, TX 76424. Tel.: 254-559-2515.
Web Site: www.breckenridgetexas.com
Institution Type/Description: Aviation Museum.
Hours & Admission Prices: By appointment.

BRECKENRIDGE FINE ARTS CENTER, 207 N. Breckenridge Ave., Breckenridge, TX 76424-3503. Tel.: 254-559-6602. Facebook.
E-mail: info@breckenridgefineart.org
Web Site: www.breckenridgefineart.org
Key Personnel: Dir., Victoria MacFarlane.
Institution Type/Description: Fine Art Gallery.
Hours & Admission Prices: Academic Year: Tues.-Fri. 10-5, Sat. 10-3; Summer: Tues.-Fri. 10-5. No charge; donations accepted. &
Attendance: 2,300 (estimated)

SWENSON MEMORIAL MUSEUM OF STEPHENS COUNTY, 116 W. Walker, Breckenridge, TX 76424-3530. Mailing Address: P.O. Box 350, Breckenridge, TX 76424-0350. Tel.: 254-559-8471.
Key Personnel: Cur., Freda Mitchell.
Institution Type/Description: History Museum: housed in 1920 bank building.
Hours & Admission Prices: Tues.-Fri. 10-5, Sat. 10-2. No charge; donations accepted. Closed Independence Day; Thanksgiving; Christmas. &
Attendance: 1,200 (actual)

Brenham

BLUE BELL CREAMERIES, 1101 S. Blue Bell Rd., Brenham, TX 77833. Tel.: 800-327-8135 & 979-836-7977.
Web Site: bluebell.com
Institution Type/Description: Company Museum.
Hours & Admission Prices: Visitor Center: Mon.-Fri. 8-5. Observation Deck: Mon.-Fri. 8-2; call to confirm.

BRENHAM HERITAGE MUSEUM, 105 S. Market, Brenham, TX 77833. Mailing Address: P.O. Box 1122, Brenham, TX 77834. Tel.: 979-830-8445.
E-mail: info@brenhamheritagemuseum.org
Web Site: www.brenhamheritagemuseum.org
Key Personnel: Exec. Dir., Douglas Price.
Institution Type/Description: History Museum.
Hours & Admission Prices: Closed for Renovations

TEXAS BAPTIST HISTORICAL MUSEUM, 10405 FM 50, Brenham, TX 77833-6424. Tel.: 979-836-5117.
E-mail: phillip.hassell@texasbaptists.org
Web Site: texasbaptisthistoricalmuseum.weebly.com
Key Personnel: Dir. & Cur., Phil Hassell.
Institution Type/Description: History Museum: housed in 1839 church, the original home of Baylor University.
Hours & Admission Prices: Tues.-Sat. 9-4. No charge; donations accepted. Closed New Year's Day; Easter; Independence Day; Christmas. &
Attendance: 10,000 (estimated)

Bronte

FORT CHADBOURNE VISITORS CENTER & MUSEUM, 651 Fort Chadbourne Rd., Bronte, TX 76933. Tel.: 325-743-2555 & 2556. Facebook, Twitter.
E-mail: ftchadbourne@taylortel.net
Key Personnel: Pres., Garland Richards; Sec. & Treas., Lana Richards.
Institution Type/Description: Visitor Center & History Museum.
Hours & Admission Prices: Tues.-Sat. 8-5. Donations requested.

Brookshire

WALLER COUNTY HISTORICAL MUSEUM, 906 Cooper St., Brookshire, TX 77423. Mailing Address: P.O. Box 438, Waller, TX 77484. Tel.: 281-934-2826.
E-mail: wlrctyhistsoc@gmail.com
Web Site: www.wallercountyhistory.org
Key Personnel: Pres. (V), Truett Bell.
Institution Type/Description: History Museum: housed in the former home of Dr. Paul Donigan; c.1910.
Hours & Admission Prices: Temporarily Closed.

Brownfield

TERRY COUNTY HERITAGE MUSEUM, 600 E. Cardwell, Brownfield, TX 79316. Mailing Address: P.O. Box 152, Brownfield, TX 79316-0152. Tel.: 806-637-2467.
Web Site: www.brownfieldchamber.com
Institution Type/Description: History Museum.
Hours & Admission Prices: Tues.-Sat. 10-12 & 1-3. Family $6, Adults $3, children $1. Closed major holidays.

Brownsville

BROWNSVILLE HERITAGE MUSEUM & STILLMAN HOUSE MUSEUM, 1325 E. Washington St., Brownsville, TX 78520-5705. Tel.: 956-541-5560. Fax: 956-435-0028.
E-mail: info@brownsvillehistory.org
Web Site: www.brownsvillehistory.org
Key Personnel: Exec. Dir., Tara Putegnat; Special Events & Program Coord., Ashley Guzman; Collections Mgr., Aubrey Nielsen; Museum Site Mgr., Eugene Fernandez.
Institution Type/Description: Museum Complex.
Hours & Admission Prices: Tues.-Sat. 10-4. Adults $6, seniors $4, students $2; members, veterans & children under 6 no charge. House & Museums: adults $10, seniors $6, students $3; veterans & children under 6 no charge.

BROWNSVILLE MUSEUM OF FINE ART, 660 E. Ringgold St., Brownsville, TX 78520. Tel.: 956-542-0941. Facebook.
Web Site: bmfa.us
Formerly: Brownsville Art League
Key Personnel: Pres., Gerardo Gonzalez; Vice Pres., Maria Luisa Diez; Treas., Norma Weaver.
Institution Type/Description: Art Museum.
Hours & Admission Prices: Mon.-Tues. & Thurs.-Sat. 10-4, Wed. 10-8. Adults $5, children 6-12, students, seniors, veterans & Wed. after 5 $2.50; discounts to groups; members, Wed. after 5pm and children under 6 no charge. &
Attendance: 25,000 (actual)

CHILDREN'S MUSEUM OF BROWNSVILLE, 501 Ringgold St., #5, Dean Porter Park, Brownsville, TX 78520. Tel.: 956-548-9300. Fax: 956-504-1348. Facebook: Brite Sun 5.
E-mail: guestrelations@cmofbrownsville.com
Web Site: www.cmofbrownsville.com
Institution Type/Description: Children's Museum.
Hours & Admission Prices: Tues.-Sat. 10-5, Sun. 12-5. Admission $8 per person; ACM members, members & children under one no charge. Closed New Year's Day, Easter, Memorial Day, Independence Day, Labor Day, Thanksgiving, Christmas Eve & Day. &

COSTUMES OF THE AMERICAS MUSEUM, #5 Dean Porter Park, 501 Ringgold St., Brownsville, TX 78520. Tel.: 956-547-6890.
E-mail: admin@costumesoftheamericasmuseum.net
Web Site: www.costumesoftheamericasmuseum.net
Institution Type/Description: Costume Museum.
Hours & Admission Prices: Tues.-Sat. 10-5, Sun. 12-4. Admission $2 per person; free admission once a month and children 10 & under no charge.
Attendance: 5,000 (estimated)

GLADYS PORTER ZOO, 500 Ringgold St., Brownsville, TX 78520-7998. Tel.: 956-546-7187 & 2177. Facebook, Instagram, Twitter.
E-mail: admin@gpz.org
Web Site: www.gpz.org
Key Personnel: Dir., Dr. Patrick M. Burchfield; Facilities Dir., Jerry Stone.
Institution Type/Description: Botanical Gardens & Zoo with Aquarium.
Hours & Admission Prices: Daily 9-5. Adults $12, seniors (65 and over) $10.50, children (2-13) $8, children (1 and under) no charge. &
Attendance: 500,000 (estimated)

HISTORIC BROWNSVILLE MUSEUM, 641 E. Madison St., Brownsville, TX 78520. Tel.: 956-548-1313.
E-mail: info@brownsvillehistory.org
Web Site: www.brownsvillehistory.org
Key Personnel: Exec. Dir., Tara Putegnat.
Institution Type/Description: History Museum: housed in the old Southern Pacific Railroad Depot; built in 1928. Listed on the National Register of Historic Places.
Hours & Admission Prices: Tues.-Sat. 10-4. Adults $6, seniors $4, students $2; discounts when visiting Historic Brownsville Museum & Brownsville Heritage Complex; veterans & children under 6 no charge.

PALO ALTO BATTLEFIELD NATIONAL HISTORICAL PARK, 7200 Paredes Line Rd., Brownsville, TX 78526. Mailing Address: 1623 Central Blvd., Ste. 213, Brownsville, TX 78520-8326. Tel.: 956-541-2785, ext. 333 & 221. Facebook, Instagram, Twitter.
Institution Type/Description: Historical Park & Visitor Center.
Hours & Admission Prices: Daily 8-5. No charge. Closed New Year's Day; Thanksgiving; Christmas. &

RIO GRANDE VALLEY WING C.A.F. MUSEUM, 955 S. Minnesota Ave., Brownsville, TX 78521. Tel.: 970-397-4604.
E-mail: wingleader@rgvcaf.org
Web Site: www.rgvcaf.org
Institution Type/Description: Air Museum.
Hours & Admission Prices: Temporarily Closed

Brownwood

BROWN COUNTY MUSEUM OF HISTORY, INC., 212 N. Broadway, Brownwood, TX 76801. Mailing Address: P.O. Box 2006, Brownwood, TX 76804-2006. Tel.: 325-641-1926. Facebook.
E-mail: wandaf@browncountymuseum.org
Web Site: www.browncountymuseum.org
Key Personnel: Dir., Wanda Furgason.
Institution Type/Description: History Museum: housed in the former Brown County Jail; built in 1902.
Hours & Admission Prices: Thurs.-Fri. 10-2, Sat. 10-4; other times by appointment. Admission $3; military w/ID $2; children 5 & under no charge. Closed Thanksgiving; Christmas. &
Attendance: 3,500 (estimated)

MARTIN & FRANCES LEHNIS RAILROAD MUSEUM, 700 E. Adams, Brownwood, TX 76801-7002. Tel.: 325-643-6376. Fax: 325-643-6376.
E-mail: kpeterson@ci.brownwood.tx.us
Web Site: www.ci.brownwood.tx.us/lrm
Key Personnel: Dir., Kim Peterson.
Institution Type/Description: Transportation Museum.
Hours & Admission Prices: Tues.-Sat. 10-4. Adults $3, seniors $2.50, children 5 & over $2; discounts to members, AAM & ICOM members, TAM, & active military. Closed holidays. &
Attendance: 3,500 (actual)

Bryan

BRAZOS VALLEY MUSEUM OF NATURAL HISTORY, 3232 Briarcrest Dr., Bryan, TX 77802-3015. Tel.: 979-776-2195. Fax: 979-774-0252. Facebook.
Web Site: www.brazosvalleymuseum.org
Key Personnel: Exec. Dir., Dr. Deborah F. Cowman; Pres. Bd. Trustees, Sue Lee; Cur. Collections & Exhibits, Rebecca Ingram; Assoc. Dir. & Education Coord., Maria Lazo.
Institution Type/Description: Natural History Museum.

Hours & Admission Prices: Tues.-Sat. 10-5. Adults $5, children (4-17), friends, seniors & students $4; first Tuesday $1; members and children 3 & under accompanied by parent no charge. &
Attendance: 30,000 (estimated)

THE CHILDREN'S MUSEUM OF THE BRAZOS VALLEY, 4001 E. 29th St., Ste. 80, Bryan, TX 77802-4211. Tel.: 979-779-5437. Facebook, Twitter.
E-mail: director@cmbv.org
Web Site: cmbv.org
Key Personnel: Pres., Lauren Hovde; Exec. Dir., Jabot Colvin; Asst. Dir., Jenna Dworkin; Mktg. Dir., Ashley Kortis.
Institution Type/Description: Children's Museum.
Hours & Admission Prices: Tues.-Sat. 10-5. Adults $7, children $6, senior $5.
Attendance: 40,000 (estimated)

Buffalo Gap

TAYLOR COUNTY HISTORY CENTER, 133 N. William, Buffalo Gap, TX 79508. Tel.: 325-572-3365 & 3974. Facebook, Twitter.
E-mail: taylorcountyhistorycenter@gmail.com
Web Site: taylorcountyhistorycenter.com/
Formerly: Buffalo Gap Historic Village
Institution Type/Description: Living History Museum.
Hours & Admission Prices: Summer hours: Tues.-Sat. 9-5, Sun. 1-5; regular hours Tues.-Sat. 10-5, Sun. 1-5. Adult $7; senior & military $6; group rate $5; students $4; children under 5, members, residents no charge.
Attendance: 15,000 (actual)

Burnet

FORT CROGHAN MUSEUM, 703 Buchanan Dr., Burnet, TX 78611. Mailing Address: P.O. Box 74, Burnet, TX 78611-0074. Tel.: 512-756-8281.
E-mail: ftcroghan.museum@gmail.com
Web Site: www.fortcroghan.org
Key Personnel: Pres., Buddy Inman.
Institution Type/Description: History Museum: located on the site of 1849 Fort Croghan.
Hours & Admission Prices: April-Aug. Thurs.-Sat. 10-5. No charge; donations requested. &
Attendance: 2,000 (estimated)

HIGHLAND LAKES SQUADRON COMMEMORATIVE AIR FORCE MUSEUM, Burnet Municipal Airport, Kate Craddock Field, U.S. Hwy. 281, Burnet, TX 78611. Tel.: 512-756-2226.
E-mail: caf@tstar.net
Key Personnel: Exec. Officer, Ed Holley.
Institution Type/Description: Air Force Museum.
Hours & Admission Prices: Wed. & Sun. 1-4, Sat. 10-4; other times by appointment. Discounts to active military & seniors. Closed New Year's Day; Christmas.

Burton

TEXAS COTTON GIN MUSEUM, 307 N. Main St., Burton, TX 77835. Mailing Address: P.O. Box 98, Burton, TX 77835-0098. Tel.: 979-289-3378. Fax: 979-289-5210. Facebook.
E-mail: burtoncottongin@earthlink.net
Web Site: www.cottonginmuseum.org
Formerly: Burton Cotton Gin & Museum
Key Personnel: Dir., Steph Jarvis; Pres., Tony Williams; Program Coord., VelAnne Clifton.
Institution Type/Description: History Museum.
Hours & Admission Prices: Tues.-Sat. 10-4. Gin Tours: Tues.-Sat. 10 & 2. Museum: no charge. Gin Tours: adults $6, students $4; discounts to groups of 10 or more & AAM members; members no charge. Closed major holidays. &
Attendance: 6,000 (estimated)

Caldwell

BURLESON COUNTY HISTORICAL MUSEUM, Burleson County Courthouse, 100 W. Buck, Caldwell, TX 77836. Tel.: 979-272-8407.
E-mail: contact@co.burleson.tx.us
Key Personnel: Chm. Burleson County Historical Commission, Tammy Kubecka; Pres., Melynda Giesenschlag.
Institution Type/Description: Local History Museum.

Hours & Admission Prices: Fri. 1:30-4:30; other times by appointment. No charge; donations accepted. &

Cameron

MILAM COUNTY MUSEUM, 201 E. Main St., Cameron, TX 76520. Mailing Address: P.O. Box 966, Cameron, TX 76520-0966. Tel.: 254-697-4770.
Web Site: www.milamcountyhistoricalcommission.org/
Key Personnel: Chm., Lynn Forney Young; Vice Chm., Denise Doss.
Institution Type/Description: History Museum.
Hours & Admission Prices: Tues.-Fri. 1-4, Sat. 10-2. No charge. &
Attendance: 4,500 (estimated)

Canadian

THE CITADELLE ART FOUNDATION, 520 Nelson Ave., Canadian, TX 79014. Tel.: 806-323-8899. Fax: 806-323-8122. Facebook, Twitter.
E-mail: info@thecitadelle.org
Web Site: www.thecitadelle.org
Key Personnel: Exec. Dir., Wendie Cook; Opers. & Preparator, Jon Long; Fin., Beth Briant.
Institution Type/Description: Historic Building: housed in the former First Baptist Church, built in 1910; converted into the Abraham family residence in 1977; later donated by family for use as public art museum.
Hours & Admission Prices: Tues.-Sat. 11-4; other times by appointment. Adults $10, seniors 65 & over $8; children under 18 no charge.

RIVER VALLEY PIONEER MUSEUM, 118 N. 2nd St., Canadian, TX 79014-2202. Mailing Address: P.O. Box 1201, Canadian, TX 79014-1201. Tel.: 806-323-6548. Fax: 806-323-8993. Facebook.
E-mail: Info@RiverValleyMuseum.org
Web Site: rivervalleymuseum.org
Key Personnel: Exec. Dir., Lisa Hanbury.
Institution Type/Description: History Museum.
Hours & Admission Prices: Tues.-Fri. 9-5, Sat. 1-2 (April-Oct.). No charge; donations accepted. &
Attendance: 3,000 (actual)

Canyon

PANHANDLE-PLAINS HISTORICAL MUSEUM, 2503 4th Ave., Canyon, TX 79015-4183. Tel.: 806-651-2244. Fax: 806-651-2250.
E-mail: administration@pphm.wtamu.edu
Web Site: www.panhandleplains.org
Key Personnel: Dir., Carol Lovelady; Cur. Western Art, Michael Grauer; Cur. Archeology, Miranda Bible; Mktg. & Communications Mgr., Stephanie Price.
Institution Type/Description: History Museum.
Hours & Admission Prices: June-Aug.: Mon.-Sat. 9-6, Sun. 1-6; Sept.-May: Tues.-Sat. 9-5. Adults $12.50, senior citizens (65 & over) $10, children (4-12) $6; discounts to groups; members & children under 4 no charge. Closed New Year's Day; Thanksgiving; Christmas Eve & Day. &
Attendance: 70,000 (estimated)

Canyon Lake

THE HERITAGE MUSEUM OF THE TEXAS HILL COUNTRY, 4831 FM 2673, Canyon Lake, TX 78133-0004. Mailing Address: P.O. Box 1598, Canyon Lake, TX 78133-0004. Tel.: 830-899-4542.
E-mail: museum@gvtc.com
Web Site: www.theheritagemuseum.com
Institution Type/Description: History Museum.
Hours & Admission Prices: June to mid-Aug. daily 10-4; mid-Aug to June daily 1-5. Adults $5, children 5-12 $4; discounts to active military personnel; children under 5 no charge. Closed New Year's Eve & Day; Easter; Thanksgiving; Christmas Eve & Day.

Carmine

TEXAS BASKETBALL MUSEUM, 107 Augsberg Ave., Carmine, TX 78932. Tel.: 713-898-7667.
E-mail: texasbkb@swbell.net
Web Site: www.texasbasketball.com
Key Personnel: Founder & Cur., Bob Springer.
Institution Type/Description: Sports Museum.
Hours & Admission Prices: By appointment. No charge; donations accepted.
Attendance: 350 (actual)

Carrollton

A. W. PERRY HOMESTEAD MUSEUM, 1509 N. Perry Rd., Carrollton, TX 75006-6122. Tel.: 972-466-6380 & 9816. Facebook: AW Perry Homestead Museum.
E-mail: parksadmin@cityofcarrollton.com
Web Site: cityofcarrollton.com/museum
Key Personnel: Cur., Cody Scallions.
Institution Type/Description: Historic House: housed in the former home of A.W. Perry; built in 1857, rebuilt in 1909 by his son using some of the lumber from the original house.
Hours & Admission Prices: Tours: Tues.-Thurs. & Sat. 11am & 1pm; other times by appointment. No charge; donations accepted. &
Attendance: 3,900 (estimated)

Castroville

STEINBACH HOUSE - CASTROVILLE AREA CHAMBER OF COMMERCE, 100 Karm St., Castroville, TX 78009. Mailing Address: P.O. Box 572, Castroville, TX 78009. Tel.: 830-538-9838. Fax: 830-538-3295. Facebook, Twitter.
E-mail: tourism@castrovilletx.gov
Web Site: http://www.steinbachhaus.com
Institution Type/Description: Historic House Museum: housed in a home originally built c.1618 in Wahlbach, France and relocated to Castroville in 1998.
Hours & Admission Prices: Mon.-Fri. 9-5, Sat. 10-4, Sun. 11-3. No charge.

Center

SHELBY COUNTY MUSEUM, 230 Pecan St., Center, TX 75935-3649. Mailing Address: P.O. Box 1542, Center, TX 75935-1542. Tel.: 936-598-3613.
E-mail: shelbymuseum@sbcglobal.net
Web Site: www.shelbycountytexashistory.net
Institution Type/Description: History Museum: housed in c.1900 Weaver-Oates House built by E.H. Barron.
Hours & Admission Prices: Mon.-Fri. 12-4; other times by appointment. No charge; donations accepted.

Chappell Hill

CHAPPELL HILL HISTORICAL SOCIETY MUSEUM, 9220 Poplar St., Chappell Hill, TX 77426-6312. Tel.: 979-836-6033. Facebook, Instagram, Twitter.
E-mail: chmuseum@chappellhillmuseum.org
Web Site: www.chappellhillmuseum.org
Key Personnel: Museum Site Mgr., Christine Hoffman.
Institution Type/Description: General Museum.
Hours & Admission Prices: Wed.-Sat. 10-4, Sun. 1-4; no charge donations accepted; groups by appointment. Tours: $40-$80. Closed New Year's Eve & Day; Thanksgiving; Christmas Eve & Day. &
Attendance: 3,500 (actual)

Childress

CHILDRESS COUNTY HERITAGE MUSEUM, 210 3rd St., N. W., Childress, TX 79201-4540. Tel.: 940-937-2261. Facebook.
E-mail: childressmuseum@sbcglobal.net
Key Personnel: Exec. Dir., Jo Ann De La Cruz.
Institution Type/Description: History Museum.
Hours & Admission Prices: Mon.-Fri. 10-5. No charge; donations accepted. Closed national holidays. &
Attendance: 7,000 (estimated)

Cisco

CONRAD HILTON CENTER & MUSEUM, 309 Conrad Hilton Ave., Cisco, TX 76437. Mailing Address: P.O. Box 350, Cisco, TX 76437. Tel.: 254-442-2537. Fax: 413-332-8592.
E-mail: Cisco.Hilton@gmail.com
Web Site: ciscochamber.com
Key Personnel: Exec. Dir., Dixon Seider.
Institution Type/Description: History Museum.
Hours & Admission Prices: Mon.-Fri. 9-12 & 1-5. No charge, donations accepted. Closed New Year's Day; Memorial Day; Independence Day; Labor Day; Thanksgiving; Christmas Eve, Day & week. &
Attendance: 300 (actual)

LELA LATCH LLOYD MUSEUM, Physical/Mailing Address: 116 W. 7th St., P.O. Box 62, Cisco, TX 76437. Tel.: 325-794-4400, ext. 4428, 254-442-2374.
E-mail: duane.hale@cisco.edu
Web Site: www.rcgates.com
Key Personnel: Pres., Dr. Duane Hale.
Institution Type/Description: History Museum.
Hours & Admission Prices: Sat. 9:30-4:30. No charge, donations are accepted.

Clarendon

SAINTS' ROOST MUSEUM, 610 E. Harrington St., Clarendon, TX 79226. Mailing Address: P.O. Box 781, Clarendon, TX 79226. Tel.: 806-874-2746.
E-mail: contact@saintsroostmuseum.com
Web Site: www.saintsroostmuseum.com
Key Personnel: Pres., Derlene Gray.
Institution Type/Description: History Museum: housed in the former Adair Hospital; built in 1910.
Hours & Admission Prices: Tues.-Sat. 10-5. or by appointment. Closed New Year's Day, Thanksgiving, Christmas.

Claude

ARMSTRONG COUNTY MUSEUM, CHARLES GOODNIGHT HISTORICAL CENTER AND GEM THEATRE, Physical/Mailing Address: 120 N. Trice, P.O. Box 450, Claude, TX 79019. Tel.: 806-226-2187 & 944-5591.
Web Site: www.charlesgoodnight.org
Formerly: Armstrong County Museum and Gem Theatre
Institution Type/Description: History Museum.
Hours & Admission Prices: March-Oct. Tues.-Sat. 10-5; Nov.-Feb. Thurs.-Sat. 10-5. Groups (20 or more) $28/person, adults $10, children (12 and under) $5. &

Cleburne

LAYLAND MUSEUM, 201 N. Caddo, Cleburne, TX 76031-4903. Tel.: 817-645-0940. Fax: 817-641-4161. Facebook, Instagram, Pinterest, Twitter.
E-mail: museum@cleburne.net
Key Personnel: Museum Mgr., Jessica Baber; Museum Asst., Leigh Naylor; Museum Educator, Stephanie Montero.
Institution Type/Description: History Museum: housed in 1905 Carnegie Library building.
Hours & Admission Prices: Tues.-Fri. 10-5, Sat. 10-4. No charge; donations accepted. Closed national holidays. &
Attendance: 8,000 (actual)

Clifton

BOSQUE MUSEUM, Physical/Mailing Address: 301 S. Ave. O, P. O. Box 345, Clifton, TX 76634. Tel.: 254-675-3845. Facebook, Instagram, Twitter, Youtube.
E-mail: info@bosquemuseum.org
Web Site: www.bosquemuseum.org
Formerly: Bosque Memorial Museum
Key Personnel: Pres., Dr. Mimi Wright; Vice Pres., Sue Megariety; Sec. & Treas., Linda Fehler; Program Chair, Shirley Dahl.
Institution Type/Description: History Museum.
Hours & Admission Prices: Tues.-Sat. 10-5. Adults $5; children under 10 & members no charge. &
Attendance: 2,487 (actual)

Clute

BRAZOSPORT MUSEUM OF NATURAL SCIENCE, 400 College Blvd., Clute, TX 77531-4778. Tel.: 979-265-7831. Fax: 979-265-6022.
E-mail: bmns@bcfas.org
Web Site: bmns.org
Key Personnel: Exec. Dir., Wes Copeland.
Institution Type/Description: Natural Science Museum.
Hours & Admission Prices: Tues.-Sat. 10-4, Sun. 2-5. No charge; donations accepted. &
Attendance: 14,021 (actual)

Coleman

HERITAGE HALL COLEMAN MUSEUM, 400 W. College Ave., Coleman, TX 76834. Tel.: 325-625-2000. Facebook.
E-mail: colemanmuseumandgallery@gmail.com
Web Site: colemanmuseumandgallery.com
Key Personnel: Pres., Josh Meadow; Vice Pres., Kathy Andrews.
Institution Type/Description: History Museum.
Hours & Admission Prices: Fri-Sat. 10-4. No charge; donations accepted.

College Station

FORSYTH GALLERIES, TEXAS A&M UNIVERSITY, 275 Joe Routt Blvd., Ste. 2440, College Station, TX 77843-4229. Tel.: 979-845-9251. Fax: 979-845-9252. Facebook.
E-mail: hbennett@uart.tamu.edu
Web Site: uart.tamu.edu
Formerly: MSC Forsyth Center Galleries,
Key Personnel: Dir., Catherine Hastedt; Asst. Dir. & Cur., Amanda Dyer; Collections Mgr., Heather Ann Bennett; Collections Mgr., Amanda Cagle; Cur. Education, Jenn Korolenko.
Institution Type/Description: Art Museum
Hours & Admission Prices: Tues.-Fri. 9-8, Sat.-Sun. 12-6; call to confirm hours. No charge. Closed university holidays. &
Attendance: 7,500 (actual)

GEORGE BUSH PRESIDENTIAL LIBRARY AND MUSEUM, Physical/Mailing Address: 1000 George Bush Dr. W., College Station, TX 77845. Tel.: 979-691-4000. Fax: 979-691-4050. Facebook, Twitter.
E-mail: info.bush@nara.gov
Web Site: bush41.org
Key Personnel: Pres., Alexander Ellis, III; Vice Pres., James W. Cicconi; Sec. & Treas., Terri Lacy; C.E.O., David B. Jones; C.F.O., Gary Booth; Sr. Dir. Devel., Stephanie Linder; Sr. Dir. of Programming and Communications, Christi Voelkel.
Institution Type/Description: Presidential Library.
Hours & Admission Prices: Mon.-Sat. 9:30-5, Sun. 12-5. Adults $9, seniors & retired military $7, youth and college students $3; discounts to groups; members and children 5 & under no charge. Closed New Year's Day; Thanksgiving; Christmas. &
Attendance: 138,252 (actual)

J. WAYNE STARK GALLERIES, Physical/Mailing Address: Texas A&M University Art Galleries Dept., 4229 TAMU, College Station, TX 77843-4229. Tel.: 979-845-6081 & 8501.
E-mail: uart@uart.tamu.edu
Web Site: uart.tamu.edu
Key Personnel: Dir. & Cur., Catherine Hastedt; Mgr. Collections, Amanda Cagle; Mktg., Molly Painter; Events Coord., Abigail Roy.
Institution Type/Description: University Art Gallery.
Hours & Admission Prices: Tues.-Fri. 9-8, Sat.-Sun. 12-6. No charge. Closed university holidays. &
Attendance: 18,035 (actual)

MUSEUM OF THE AMERICAN G.I., 19124 Highway 6 S., College Station, TX 77845. Mailing Address: P.O. Box 9599, College Station, TX 77845. Tel.: 979-690-0501.
E-mail: info@americangimuseum.org
Web Site: americangimuseum.org
Key Personnel: Pres. & C.E.O., Brent Mullins; Sec. & Treas., Leisha Mullins.
Institution Type/Description: Military History Museum.
Hours & Admission Prices: Summer hours Wed.-Sat. 10-5, Sun. 12-5, Mon. by appointment. Adults $6, seniors $5, active or retired US military $5, children (5-17) $4, school groups (10 or more) $3.50, children (4 and under) no charge.

Colorado City

HEART OF WEST TEXAS MUSEUM, 340 E. 3rd St., Colorado City, TX 79512-6408. Tel.: 325-728-8285. Fax: 325-728-8944.
E-mail: museum@cityofcoloradocity.org
Web Site: www.coloradocitytexas.org/museum
Key Personnel: Cur., Patty Pharis.
Institution Type/Description: History Museum.
Hours & Admission Prices: Tues.-Fri. 12-5. No charge; donations accepted. &
Attendance: 400 (actual)

Comanche

COMANCHE COUNTY HISTORICAL MUSEUM, 402 Moorman Rd., Comanche, TX 76442. Mailing Address: P.O. Box 22, Comanche, TX 76442. Tel.: 325-356-5115.
E-mail: onlymuseum1@verizon.net
Web Site: www.comanchecountytxmuseum.com
Key Personnel: Pres., Garry D. Steele; First Vice Pres., Cliff Conway; Second Vice Pres., David Gore.
Institution Type/Description: History Museum.
Hours & Admission Prices: Wed.-Sat. 10-4. No charge; donations accepted. Closed Thanksgiving; Christmas.
Attendance: 3,000 (estimated)

Comstock

SEMINOLE CANYON STATE PARK AND HISTORIC SITE, U.S. Hwy. 90 W., Comstock, TX 78837. Mailing Address: P.O. Box 820, U.S. Hwy. 90 West, Park Rd. 67, Comstock, TX 78837-0820. Tel.: 512-389-8900 & 432-292-4464.
E-mail: randy.rosales@tpwd.state.tx.us
Web Site: www.tpwd.state.tx.us
Formerly: Seminole Canyon State Historical Park
Key Personnel: Supt., Randy Rosales.
Institution Type/Description: Park & Archaeology Site.
Hours & Admission Prices: Daily 8-4:45. Adults $5; children under (12 and under) no charge. &
Attendance: 15,042 (actual)

Corpus Christi

ART MUSEUM OF SOUTH TEXAS, 1902 N. Shoreline Blvd., Corpus Christi, TX 78401-1164. Tel.: 361-825-3500. Facebook, Twitter.
E-mail: artmuseum@tamucc.edu
Web Site: artmuseumofsouthtexas.org
Key Personnel: Dir., Joseph B. Schenk; Asst. Dir., Sara Morgan; Devel. Officer, Sheri Emerick; Accountant, Susana DeVacque; Cur. Education, Linda Rodriguez; Cur., Deborah Fullerton; Coord. of Community Svcs., Karol Stewart.
Institution Type/Description: Art Museum.
Hours & Admission Prices: Tues.-Sat. 10-5, Sun. 1-5. Adults $8; Seniors (60 and over) & active military $6; Students (13 and over) $4; children 12 & under, TAMU-CC students and members no charge. &
Attendance: 115,000 (actual)

CORPUS CHRISTI MUSEUM OF SCIENCE AND HISTORY, 1900 N. Chaparral, Corpus Christi, TX 78401-1114. Tel.: 361-826-4667. Facebook: Corpus Christi Museum.
E-mail: ccmuseum@cctexas.com
Web Site: www.ccmuseum.com
Institution Type/Description: General Museum.
Hours & Admission Prices: Tues.-Sat. 10-5, Sun. 12-5. Adults $10.95, children 3-12 $8.95, senior citizens and military $7.95; members and children 2 & under no charge. Closed New Year's Day; Easter; Labor Day, Thanksgiving; Christmas Eve & Day. &
Attendance: 65,938 (actual)

PADRE ISLAND NATIONAL SEASHORE, 20420 Park Rd. 22, Corpus Christi, TX 78418. Mailing Address: P.O. Box 181300, Corpus Christi, TX 78480-1300. Tel.: 361-949-8068. Fax: 361-949-8023. Facebook, Instagram, Twitter.
E-mail: james_lindsay@nps.gov
Web Site: www.nps.gov/pais
Key Personnel: Supt., Mark Spier.
Institution Type/Description: National Park Visitor Center & Museum.
Hours & Admission Prices: Open 24 hours; visitor center: daily 9-5, closed christmas. No charge. &
Attendance: 60,888 (actual)

THE SELENA MUSEUM, 5410 Leopard St., Corpus Christi, TX 78408.
Web Site: www.selenaetc.com/museum
Institution Type/Description: History Museum.
Hours & Admission Prices: Mon.-Fri. 10-4. General admission $3.

SOUTH TEXAS BOTANICAL GARDENS & NATURE CENTER, 8545 S. Staples, Corpus Christi, TX 78413. Tel.: 361-852-2100.
E-mail: wmwomack@stxbot.org

Key Personnel: Exec. Dir., Michael Womack, Ed.D.; Dir. Mktg., Mary Jane Crull; Devel. Dir., Scott Simmonds; Office Mgr., Kathie Waid.
Institution Type/Description: Botanical Gardens & Nature Center.
Hours & Admission Prices: Daily 9-6. Adults $8, seniors, active military, college students $6, children 12 and under $4, children under 3 no charge.

TEXAS STATE AQUARIUM, 2710 N. Shoreline Blvd., Corpus Christi, TX 78402. Tel.: 361-881-1200, 800-477-4853. Fax: 361-881-1257. Facebook: Texas State Aquarium.
E-mail: mermaid@txstateaq.org
Web Site: www.texasstateaquarium.org
Institution Type/Description: Aquarium.
Hours & Admission Prices: Labor Day to Feb. daily 9-5; March to Sept. daily 9-6. Adults 13 & over $22.95, seniors & military $20.95, children 3-12 $16.95; children 2 & under no charge. Closed Thanksgiving; Christmas.
Attendance: 500,000 (actual)

TEXAS STATE MUSEUM OF ASIAN CULTURES & EDUCATIONAL CENTER, 1809 N. Champarral St., Corpus Christi, TX 78401-1111. Tel.: 361-881-8827.
E-mail: texasasianculturesmuseumcc@gmail.com
Web Site: www.asianculturesmuseum.org
Key Personnel: Pres. Bd., Julie Galbraith.
Institution Type/Description: Cultural Museum.
Hours & Admission Prices: Tues.-Sat. 12-5. Adults $6, seniors & military $5, students $4, children 4-12 $3; discounts to AAM members; members & law enforcement no charge. Closed New Year's Day; Easter; Thanksgiving; Christmas. &
Attendance: 15,000 (estimated)

TEXAS SURF MUSEUM, 309A N. Water St., Corpus Christi, TX 78401. Tel.: 361-882-2364. Fax: 361-887-7075. Facebook, Instagram, Twitter.
E-mail: info@texassurfmuseum.com
Web Site: www.texassurfmuseum.com
Institution Type/Description: Sports Museum.
Hours & Admission Prices: Mon.-Sat. 11-7, Sun. 11-5. No charge.

USS LEXINGTON MUSEUM ON THE BAY, 2914 N. Shoreline Blvd., Corpus Christi, TX 78402-1116. Mailing Address: P.O. Box 23076, Corpus Christi, TX 78403-3076. Tel.: 800-583-9539 & 361-888-4873. Fax: 361-883-8361. Facebook, Instagram, Twitter.
E-mail: debbie@usslexington.com
Web Site: www.usslexington.com
Key Personnel: Exec. Dir., Steve Banta; Operations, Security & Exhibits Dir., M. C. Reustle; Human Resources Mgr., Patti Gonzales; Historian Curatorial Research & Registrar, Cecil Johnson; Sr. Sales Mgr., Rebekah Everhart; Educ. Coord., Rene Moraida; Public Rels., Debbie Crites; Museum Shop Mgr., Maria Robles.
Institution Type/Description: Naval Military Museum: housed in the USS Lexington Aircraft Carrier.
Hours & Admission Prices: Memorial Day-Labor Day & Spring Break: 9-6; Labor day-Memorial Day: 9-5. Adults $16.95, seniors & military $14.95, children $11.95. Closed Thanksgiving & Christmas. &
Attendance: 340,000 (estimated)

Corsicana

CAPEHART COMMUNICATIONS COLLECTION, 409 S. 9th St., Corsicana, TX 75110-6502. Tel.: 903-872-0440. Fax: 903-872-0441. Facebook.
E-mail: ritaanddoncapehart@sbcglobal.net
Web Site: www.telcomhistory.org/vm/museumsCapehart.shtml
Institution Type/Description: Communications Museum.
Hours & Admission Prices: By appointment. No charge; donations accepted.
Attendance: 1,500 (estimated)

GLENN CUMBIE MUSEUM, 9000 Navarro Rd., Corsicana, TX 75109. Tel.: 903-654-4847. Facebook, Twitter.
E-mail: canifly@wifi45.com
Web Site: www.cfahf.org
Formerly: Corsicana Field Aviation Heritage Foundation
Key Personnel: Cur., Sarah Farley.
Institution Type/Description: Military History Museum.
Hours & Admission Prices: Mon.-Sat. 8-5. No charge, donations accepted. Closed Thanksgiving; Christmas. &
Attendance: 1,250 (estimated)

NAVARRO COUNTY HISTORICAL SOCIETY, PIONEER VILLAGE, 912 W. Park Ave., Corsicana, TX 75110-2931. Mailing Address: 301 S. Beaton St., Corsicana, TX 75110. Tel.: 903-654-4846 & 4850. Fax: 903-874-4441.
E-mail: byoung@ci.corsicana.tx.us
Key Personnel: Dir., Bobbie Young.
Institution Type/Description: Village Museum: eight log buildings constructed in Navarro County during 1838-1865, moved to City Park & restored.
Hours & Admission Prices: Mon.-Fri. 8-5, Sat. 9-5, Sun. 1-5.
Attendance: 2,620 (actual)

PEARCE MUSEUM, 3100 W. Collin St., Corsicana, TX 75110-3904. Tel.: 903-875-7642. Fax: 903-875-7473. Facebook, Instagram, Twitter.
E-mail: archives@navarrocollege.edu
Web Site: www.pearcemuseum.com
Formerly: Pearce Collections Museum
Key Personnel: Dir., Ann Steele Zembala; Cur. Exhibits & Collections, Christina Lucas; Education Specialist, Dr. Kaye Tindell; Education Tour & Volunteer Coord., Cindy Williams; Admin Asst., Jessica Martinez Kindon.
Institution Type/Description: Civil War & Western Art Museum.
Hours & Admission Prices: Mon.-Fri. 10-4, Sat. 12-4. Adults $8, seniors $6, children (3-18) & students (6-17) $4; discounts to groups. Closed New Year's Eve & Day; Thanksgiving; Christmas Eve & Day.
Attendance: 8,000 (estimated)

Cotulla

BRUSH COUNTRY MUSEUM, 201 S. Stewart, Cotulla, TX 78014-3070. Tel.: 830-879-2429. Facebook.
Institution Type/Description: History Museum.
Hours & Admission Prices: Tues. & Thurs. 10-12, 2-4; Wed., Fri., Sat. 1-4
Attendance: 600 (estimated)

Crane

MUSEUM OF THE DESERT SOUTHWEST, 409 S. Gaston, Crane, TX 79731-2621. Mailing Address: P.O. Box 398, Crane, TX 79731. Tel.: 432-558-2311.
E-mail: mtdsw@sbcglobal.net
Formerly: Crane County Museum
Institution Type/Description: History Museum.
Hours & Admission Prices: May-Sept. Sat. 9-12 & 1-5, Sun.-Fri. 1-4; Oct.-April Mon.-Fri. 1-4. No charge; donations accepted.

Crosbyton

CROSBY COUNTY PIONEER MEMORIAL MUSEUM, 101 W. Main, Crosbyton, TX 79322-2252. Tel.: 806-675-2331.
E-mail: ccpmm@door.net
Institution Type/Description: Local History Museum: partially housed in replica of Hank Smith rock house, original structure in 1876-77.
Hours & Admission Prices: Jan. to mid-Dec. Tues.-Sat. 9-12 & 1-5. No charge; donations accepted. Closed national holidays.
Attendance: 4,000 (estimated)

MT. BLANCO FOSSIL MUSEUM, 124 W. Main St., Crosbyton, TX 79322-2253. Mailing Address: P.O. Box 550, Crosbyton, TX 79322-0550. Tel.: 806-675-7777. Fax: 806-675-2421. Facebook: Mt. Blanco Fossil Museum.
E-mail: mtblanco1@aol.com
Web Site: www.mtblanco.com
Key Personnel: Dir., Joe Taylor.
Institution Type/Description: Paleontology Museum.
Hours & Admission Prices: Mon.-Fri. 9-5. Adults $5, children 6-12 $2; discounts to groups; children 5 & under no charge.
Attendance: 1,000 (estimated)

Cross Plains

ROBERT E. HOWARD MUSEUM, TX Hwy 36, Cross Plains, TX 76443. Tel.: 254-725-6114.
E-mail: jehanke@aol.com
Web Site: crossplainstx.com/howard-museum
Institution Type/Description: Historic House Museum: housed in the former home of Robert E. Howard, author of Conan the Barbarian.
Hours & Admission Prices: By appointment.

Crowell

FIREHALL MUSEUM, 116 N. Main St., Crowell, TX 79227. Tel.: 940-655-8818.
E-mail: donna_baize@yahoo.com
Institution Type/Description: History Museum.
Hours & Admission Prices: Mon.-Thurs. 10-3. No charge; donations accepted.
Attendance: 300 (estimated)

SANTA FE DEPOT MUSEUM & LIBRARY, 203 N. Main St., Crowell, TX 79227. Mailing Address: P.O. Box 317, Crowell, TX 79227.
Institution Type/Description: Library & History Museum: depot built c.1908.
Hours & Admission Prices: Mon.-Fri. 1:30-5.

Cuero

CHISHOLM TRAIL HERITAGE MUSEUM, 302 N. Esplanade, Cuero, TX 77954. Tel.: 361-277-2866.
E-mail: info@chisholmtrailmuseum.org
Web Site: www.chisholmtrailmuseum.org
Key Personnel: Exec. Dir., Sharon T. Weber.
Institution Type/Description: History Museum.
Hours & Admission Prices: Tues.-Sat. 10-4;30; other times by appointment. Adults $5, children 5-17 $3; discounts to groups; members, active military & children under 5 no charge.

DEWITT COUNTY HISTORICAL MUSEUM, Physical/Mailing Address: 312 E. Broadway, Cuero, TX 77954-2806. Tel.: 361-275-6322. Facebook.
E-mail: dewittcountyhistoricalmuseum@yahoo.com
Web Site: www.cityofcuero.com/444/DeWitt-County-Historical-Museum
Institution Type/Description: Local History Museum: housed in 1886 Bates-Sheppard home.
Hours & Admission Prices: Tues.-Fri. 10-12 & 1-4. No Charge.
Attendance: 3,000 (estimated)

Dalhart

XIT MUSEUM, 108 E. 5th St., Dalhart, TX 79022. Mailing Address: P.O. Box 730, Dalhart, TX 79022-0730. Tel.: 806-244-5390. Fax: 806-244-3031.
E-mail: curator@xitmuseum.com
Web Site: www.xitmuseum.com
Key Personnel: Dir. & Cur., Nicky Olson.
Institution Type/Description: Historical Society Museum: housed in a terra-cotta brick building.
Hours & Admission Prices: Tues.-Sat. 9-5. No charge; donations accepted.
Attendance: 5,000 (actual)

Dallas

AFRICAN AMERICAN MUSEUM, 3536 Grand Ave., Dallas, TX 75210-1005. Mailing Address: P.O. Box 150157, Dallas, TX 75315-0157. Tel.: 214-565-9026. Fax: 214-421-8204.
E-mail: info@aamdallas.org
Web Site: www.aamdallas.org
Key Personnel: Pres. & C.E.O., Dr. Harry Robinson, Jr.; Vice Pres. Institutional Advancement, Jane Jones; Exec. Asst. to Pres., Daphne Stephenson Baty; Mgr. Finance & Admin., Khaliq Bryant; Mgr. Programs & Graphic Design, Patrick Finnell.
Institution Type/Description: African American Culture Museum.
Hours & Admission Prices: Tues.-Fri. 11-5, Sat. 10-5. Self Guided Tours: adults $2, children 4-17 $1; children 3 & under no charge. Docent Guided Tours: adults $5, children 4-17 $3; children 3 & under no charge. Closed New Year's Day; Independence Day; Thanksgiving; Christmas Eve & Day.
Attendance: 201,000 (estimated)

CAF AIRPOWER MUSEUM, 5661 Mariner Dr., Dallas, TX 75237. Mailing Address: P.O. Box 764769, Dallas, TX 75376. Tel.: 432-567-3010. Facebook, Instagram, Twitter.
E-mail: visitorinfo@aahm.org
Web Site: www.airpowermuseum.org
Formerly: American Airpower Heritage Museum, Inc. & Commemorative Air Force Headquarters
Institution Type/Description: World War II, Military Aviation Museum.
Hours & Admission Prices: Tues.-Sat. 9-5. No Charge. Closed New Year's Eve & Day; Thanksgiving; Christmas Eve & Day.
Attendance: 35,000 (estimated)

CHILDREN'S AQUARIUM AT FAIR PARK, 1462 1st Ave., Dallas, TX 75210-1010. Tel.: 469-554-7340. Facebook, Instagram, Twitter.
E-mail: info@dallaszoo.com
Web Site: www.childrensaquariumfairpark.com
Formerly: The Dallas Aquarium at Fair Park
Key Personnel: Dir. of Communications and Social Media, Laurie Holloway; Aquarium Mgr., Ellen Zhao.
Institution Type/Description: Aquarium.
Hours & Admission Prices: Daily 9-4:30. Adults $8, seniors 65 & up and children 3-11 $6; school group $4; members and children 2 & under no charge. Closed Thanksgiving; Christmas. &
Attendance: 150,000 (estimated)

DALLAS ARBORETUM & BOTANICAL GARDEN, 8525 Garland Rd., Dallas, TX 75218-4335. Tel.: 214-515-6615 & 6500.
E-mail: customerservice@dallasarboretum.org
Web Site: www.dallasarboretum.org
Key Personnel: Chm., Mark Wolf; Vice Chm., Alan Walne; Sec., John Cuellar; Treas., Will McDaniel; Pres. & C.E.O., Mary Brinegar.
Institution Type/Description: Arboretum & Botanical Garden.
Hours & Admission Prices: Daily 9-5. Adults $17, seniors 65 & over $14, children 2-12 $12; members and children 2 & under no charge. Parking $15. Closed New Year's Day; Thanksgiving; Christmas. &
Attendance: 300,000 (actual)

DALLAS CONTEMPORARY, 161 Glass St., Dallas, TX 75207-6903. Tel.: 214-821-2522. Fax: 214-821-9103. Facebook.
E-mail: info@dallascontemporary.org
Web Site: www.dallascontemporary.org
Key Personnel: Pres., Maxine Trowbridge; Vice Pres., Laree Hulshoff; Sec., Rodger Kobes; Treas., John Clutts; Exec. Dir., Peter Doroshenko.
Institution Type/Description: Contemporary Art Museum.
Hours & Admission Prices: Tues.-Sat. 11-6, Sun. 12-5. No charge; donations accepted. Closed major holidays. &

DALLAS FIREFIGHTER'S MUSEUM, 3801 Parry Ave., Dallas, TX 75226. Tel.: 214-821-1500.
Web Site: www.texasfiremuseum.org
Formerly: Texas Fire Museum
Key Personnel: Pres. (V), Trixie Lohrke.
Institution Type/Description: Fire Museum.
Hours & Admission Prices: Wed.-Sat. 9-4. Adults $6, children $4. &
Attendance: 350 (estimated)

DALLAS FIREFIGHTERS MUSEUM, INC., 3801 Parry Ave., Dallas, TX 75226-1753. Tel.: 214-821-1500. Facebook.
E-mail: dallasfirefightermuseum@yahoo.com
Web Site: www.dallasfiremuseum.com
Key Personnel: Pres., Trixie Lohrke; Vice Pres., Daniel DeYear; Bd. Sec., Ray Cherry; Treas. & Capital Campaign Chair, Sherwood E. Blount, Jr.; Past Pres., Rett Blankenship.
Institution Type/Description: Firefighter's Museum.
Hours & Admission Prices: Wed.-Sat. 9-4. Adults $4, children $2. Closed New Year's Day; Thanksgiving; Christmas.
Attendance: 3,500 (estimated)

DALLAS HERITAGE VILLAGE AT OLD CITY PARK, 1515 S. Harwood St., Dallas, TX 75215. Tel.: 214-421-5141 & 413-3679. Fax: 214-428-6351.
E-mail: info@dallasheritagevillage.org
Web Site: www.dallasheritagevillage.org
Formerly: Old City Park: The Historical Village of Dallas
Key Personnel: Exec. Dir. & Pres., Melissa Prycer; Dir. of Curatorial Affairs, Evelyn Montgomery, PhD; Dir. of Education, Mandy Olsen; Dir. of Devel., Preston Cooley.
Institution Type/Description: Village Museum.
Hours & Admission Prices: Tues.-Sat. 10-4, Sun. 12-4, closed Jan.& Aug, New Year's Eve and Day, Thanksgiving, Christmas Eve and Day. Adult $9, senior (65 and over) $7, child (4-12) $5, special group pricing. &
Attendance: 55,000 (estimated)

DALLAS HISTORICAL SOCIETY, Hall of State at Fair Park, 3939 Grand Ave., Dallas, TX 75210. Mailing Address: P.O. Box 150038, Dallas, TX 75315-0038. Tel.: 214-421-4500. Fax: 214-421-7500. Facebook, Instagram, Twitter.
E-mail: research@dallashistory.org
Web Site: www.dallashistory.org
Key Personnel: Interim Dir., Molly Bogen; Exec. Asst., Kaitlyn Price; Dep. Dir., Alan Olson.

Institution Type/Description: History Museum.
Hours & Admission Prices: Tues.-Sat. 10-5, Sun. 1-5. No charge; donations accepted. Closed New Year's Day; Easter; Thanksgiving; Christmas. &
Attendance: 220,000 (estimated)

DALLAS HOLOCAUST AND HUMAN RIGHTS MUSEUM, 300 N. Houston St., Dallas, TX 75202. Tel.: 214-741-7500.
E-mail: info@dhhrorg
Web Site: www.dhhrm.org
Formerly: Dallas Holocaust Museum/Center for Education & Tolerance
Key Personnel: Pres. & C.E.O., Mary Pat Higgins; Chm., Frank Risch.
Institution Type/Description: History Museum.
Hours & Admission Prices: Mon.-Fri. 9:30-5, Sat.-Sun. 10-5; reservation recommended. Adults $16, seniors, educators & military $14, students $12; not recommended for children under 12. Closed New Year's Day; Rosh Hashanah; Yom Kippur; Thanksgiving; Christmas. &
Attendance: 86,000 (estimated)

DALLAS MUSEUM OF ART, 1717 N. Harwood St., Dallas, TX 75201-2398. Tel.: 214-922-1200. Facebook, Instagram, Twitter.
E-mail: members@DMA.org
Web Site: www.dma.org
Key Personnel: Pres., Catherine Marcus Rose; Chm. of the Bd., Melissa Foster Fetter; Vice Pres., A. Shonn Brown; Sec., Xuan-Thao Nguyen; Treas., Susan Byrne Montgomery.
Institution Type/Description: Art Museum.
Hours & Admission Prices: Tues.-Wed. & Fri.-Sun. 11-5, Thurs. 11-9. No charge for general admission. Special exhibition admission varies; members no charge. Closed Thanksgiving; Christmas. &
Attendance: 728,699 (actual)

THE DALLAS WORLD AQUARIUM, 1801 N. Griffin St., Dallas, TX 75202-1503. Tel.: 214-720-2224. Facebook.
E-mail: info@dwazoo.com
Web Site: www.dwazoo.com
Institution Type/Description: Aquarium.
Hours & Admission Prices: Daily 9-5. Adults $20.95, seniors 60 & over $16.95, children 2-12 $14.95; children under 2 no charge. Closed Thanksgiving; Christmas.

DALLAS ZOO, 650 S. R.L. Thornton Freeway, Dallas, TX 75203-3013. Tel.: 469-554-7500. Facebook.
E-mail: info@dalzoo.org
Web Site: www.dallaszoo.com
Key Personnel: Pres. & C.E.O., Gregg Hudson; C.F.O. & Vice Pres. Business Admin., Gayle Anderson; Vice Pres. Guest Experience, Sean Greene; Vice Pres. Animal Operations and Welfare, R. Harrison Edell; Vice Pres.Facilities & Sustainability Programs, Doug Dykman; Exec. Vice Pres. Advancement, Darryl Griffin; Special Counsel, Bill Evans.
Institution Type/Description: Zoo.
Hours & Admission Prices: March to Sep. 30 daily 9-5; Oct. to Feb. daily 9-4. Admission: March-Dec. adults $15, children 3-11 & seniors $12; children 2 & under and members no charge; Jan.-Feb. $7 per person; children 2 & under and members no charge. Parking: $10. Closed Christmas. &
Attendance: 1,020,000 (estimated)

FRONTIERS OF FLIGHT MUSEUM, 6911 Lemmon Ave., Dallas, TX 75209-3603. Tel.: 214-350-3600 & 1651. Fax: 214-351-0101.
E-mail: info@flightmuseum.com
Web Site: www.flightmuseum.com
Key Personnel: Pres. & C.E.O., Cheryl Sutterfield-Jones; Chm., David Norton.
Institution Type/Description: Aeronautical History Museum.
Hours & Admission Prices: Mon.-Sat. 10-5, Sun. 1-5. Adults $10, seniors (65 & over) $8, children (3-17) $7; discounts to groups, AAM, ICOM & TAM members; students, children under 3 & members no charge. Closed New Year's Eve & Day; Easter; Memorial Day; Independence Day; Labor Day; Thanksgiving; Christmas. &
Attendance: 100,000 (actual)

THE GEORGE W. BUSH PRESIDENTIAL LIBRARY AND MUSEUM, 2943 SMU Blvd., Dallas, TX 75205. Mailing Address: c/o George W. Bush Presidential Center, P.O. Box 259000, Dallas, TX 75225-9000. Tel.: 214-346-1650. Fax: 214-346-1699. Facebook, Instagram, Twitter.
E-mail: gwbush.library@nara.gov
Web Site: www.georgewbushlibrary.smu.edu
Key Personnel: Dir., Patrick X. Mordente.
Institution Type/Description: History Museum.

Hours & Admission Prices: Mon.-Sat. 9-5, Sun. 12-5. Adults $19, youth 13-17 $17, seniors 62 & over and college students $16, youth 5-12 & retired military $13; SMU students & staff, active military and children 4 & under no charge. Closed New Year's Day; Thanksgiving; Christmas. &

JESUIT DALLAS MUSEUM, 12345 Inwood Rd., Dallas, TX 75244. Tel.: 972-387-8700.
E-mail: connect@jesuitcp.org
Web Site: www.jesuitcp.org/museum
Key Personnel: Dir., Elizabeth Hunt Blanc; Pres. (V), Mike Earsing.
Institution Type/Description: Art Museum.
Hours & Admission Prices: Tours: Mon.-Fri. 9-4. No charge; donations accepted.
Attendance: 3,000 (estimated)

JUANITA J. CRAFT CIVIL RIGHTS HOUSE, 2618 Warren Ave., Dallas, TX 75215-2911. Tel.: 214-670-8637.
Institution Type/Description: Historic House Museum: housed in the former home of civil rights organizer, Juanita J. Craft; visited here by President Lyndon Johnson & Martin Luther King Jr. to discuss the future of the civil rights movement.
Hours & Admission Prices: Temporarily closed for renovations.

LATINO CULTURAL CENTER, 2600 Live Oak St., Dallas, TX 75204. Tel.: 214-671-0045. Fax: 214-670-0633. Facebook, Twitter.
E-mail: hortencia.rubalcava@dallascityhall.com
Web Site: www.dallasculture.org
Key Personnel: Gen. Mgr., Benjamin Espino; Cultural Programs Coord., Hortencia Rubalcava; Media & Mktg. Coord., Rosalinda Luna; Education & Outreach Coord., Jessica Trevizo; Technical Dir., Ryan Flores; Technician, Todd Dawson.
Institution Type/Description: Cultural Center.
Hours & Admission Prices: Tues.-Sat. 10-5. Center: no charge. Fee charged to some events.

THE MCKINNEY AVENUE CONTEMPORARY (THE MAC), 1601 S. Ervay St., Dallas, TX 75215. Mailing Address: 1501 S. Ervay St., Dallas, TX 75215. Tel.: 214-953-1212.
E-mail: macmembership@the-mac.org
Web Site: www.the-mac.org
Key Personnel: Exec. Dir., Rachel Rogerson; Facility Liaison, Leslie Connally.
Institution Type/Description: Art Gallery.
Hours & Admission Prices: Call for hours. No charge suggested donation $5. Closed major holidays. &
Attendance: 12,000 (estimated)

MEADOWS MUSEUM, Southern Methodist University, 5900 Bishop Blvd., Dallas, TX 75205. Mailing Address: P.O. Box 750357, Dallas, TX 75275-0357. Tel.: 214-768-2516. Fax: 214-768-1688. Facebook, Instagram, Twitter.
E-mail: meadowsmuseuminfo@smu.edu
Web Site: www.meadowsmuseumdallas.org
Key Personnel: Dir., Mark Roglan; Mktg. & Public Rels. Mgr., Carrie Sanger; Museum Accountant, Roni Arifin; Assoc. Dir. & Cur. Exhibitions, Bridget Marx.
Institution Type/Description: Art Museum.
Hours & Admission Prices: Tues.-Wed. & Fri.-Sat. 10-5, Thurs. 10-9, Sun. 1-5. Adults $12, seniors $8, students $4; members, children under 12, SMU faculty & staff no charge. Closed New Year's Day; Easter; Independence Day; Thanksgiving; Christmas. &
Attendance: 69,000 (actual)

MUSEUM OF BIBLICAL ART, 7500 Park Lane, Dallas, TX 75225-2025. Tel.: 214-368-4622. Fax: 214-361-1365.
E-mail: frontdesk@biblicalarts.org
Web Site: www.biblicalarts.org
Formerly: Biblical Arts Center
Key Personnel: Co Dir., R.J. Machacek; Co Dir., Scott Peck.
Institution Type/Description: Religious Art Museum.
Hours & Admission Prices: Wed.-Sat. 11-5, Sun. 1-5. Adults $12; senior citizens & students $10, children 6-12 $8; children 5 & under no charge. Closed New Year's Day; Independence Day; Thanksgiving; Christmas Eve & Day. &
Attendance: 70,000 (actual)

MUSEUM OF GEOMETRIC & MADI ART, 3109 Carlisle St., Dallas, TX 75204-1194. Tel.: 214-855-7802.
E-mail: info@geometricmadimuseum.org
Web Site: www.geometricmadimuseum.org
Formerly: MADI Museum
Key Personnel: Museum Dir., Dorothy Masterson.
Institution Type/Description: Art Museum.

Hours & Admission Prices: Tues.-Sat. 11-5, Sun. 1-5. No charge; donations accepted. Closed New Year's Day; Thanksgiving; Christmas. &
Attendance: 5,103 (actual)

NASHER SCULPTURE CENTER, 2001 Flora St., Dallas, TX 75201-2336. Tel.: 214-242-5100.
E-mail: info@nashersculpturecenter.org
Web Site: www.nashersculpturecenter.org
Key Personnel: Dir., Jeremy Strick; Pres., David Haemisegger; Chm., Stephen Stamas.
Institution Type/Description: Art Museum & Sculpture Garden.
Hours & Admission Prices: Tues.-Sun. 11-5. Adults $10, DART riders $8, senior citizens $7, educators & students $5; children under 12 & members no charge. Closed Independence Day; Thanksgiving; Christmas.
Attendance: 250,000 (estimated)

PEROT MUSEUM OF NATURE AND SCIENCE, 2201 N. Field St., Dallas, TX 75201. Tel.: 214-428-5555. Facebook.
E-mail: info@perotmuseum.org
Web Site: www.perotmuseum.org/
Formerly: Museum of Nature & Science, Southwest Museum of Science and Technology, The Science Place & TI Founders IMAX Theater, the Dallas Children's Museum
Key Personnel: Chief Experience Officer, Mary Baerg; Chief Advancement Officer, Julie Diaz; Chief Operating Officer, Dave Humphries; Chief Innovation Officer, Dan Kohl; Vice Pres. Research & Collections and Chief Cur., Dr. Anthony Fiorillo.
Institution Type/Description: Natural History, Science & Technology Museum.
Hours & Admission Prices: Memorial Day-Labor Day: Mon.-Sat. 10-6, Sun. 11-6; Regular hours: Mon.-Sat. 10-5, Sun. 11-5. Adult (13-64) $20, senior (65 and over) $14, youth (2-12) $13, discounts for educators, law enforcement, groups and more. See website for closures & holiday hours. &
Attendance: 1,300,000 (estimated)

THE SIXTH FLOOR MUSEUM AT DEALEY PLAZA, 411 Elm St., Dallas, TX 75202-3301. Tel.: 214-747-6660. Fax: 214-747-6662. Facebook, Instagram, Twitter.
E-mail: jfk@jfk.org
Web Site: www.jfk.org
Key Personnel: Exec. Dir., Nicola Longford; Chm. Bd., Victor Elmore; Dir. Collections & Intellectual Property, Megan Bryant; Collections Cataloguer, Jan Masterson.
Institution Type/Description: History Museum & Historical Site: the former Texas School Book Depository.
Hours & Admission Prices: Mon. 12-6, Tues.-Sun. 10-6. Adults $16, seniors 65 & up $14, youth 6-18 $13, children 5 & under with audio guide $4; discounts to groups, AAM & TAM members; children 5 & under without audio guide no charge. Audio Tour: available in six languages included with admission. Closed Thanksgiving; Christmas. &
Attendance: 400,000 (actual)

TEXAS DISCOVERY GARDENS, 3601 Martin Luther King Blvd., Gate 6 at Fair Park, Dallas, TX 75210. Mailing Address: P.O. Box 152537, Dallas, TX 75315-2537. Tel.: 214-428-7476. Fax: 214-428-5338. Facebook, Instagram, Twitter.
E-mail: tdg@texasdiscoverygardens.org
Web Site: www.texasdiscoverygardens.org
Formerly: Dallas Horticulture Center
Key Personnel: Exec. Dir., Dick Davis; Chm. (V), Michael Bosco; Mktg. Mgr., Haley Estrada; Rental Coord., Tammy Smith; Dir. Horticulture, Roger Sanderson.
Institution Type/Description: Arboretum & Botanical Garden Museum, Conservatory & Horticultural Resource Center: c.1936. A National Historic Landmark.
Hours & Admission Prices: Daily 10-5. Adults $10, seniors 60 & up $8, children 3-11 $5; discounts to groups; members, children under 3 no charge. Closed New Year's Day, Thanksgiving; Christmas Eve & Day. &
Attendance: 100,000 (actual)

THE TRAMMELL & MARGARET CROW COLLECTION OF ASIAN ART, 2010 Flora St., Dallas, TX 75201-2335. Tel.: 214-979-6430. Fax: 214-979-6439. Facebook, Instagram, Twitter.
E-mail: nhuffman@crowcollection.org
Web Site: www.crowcollection.org
Key Personnel: Dir., Amy Lewis Hofland; Pres., Trammell S. Crow; Dir. of Opers., Abraham Carrillo; C.F.O., Anne Woods; Dir. of Devel., Caroline Kim; Dir. of Content, Danny Skinner; Dir. of Educ. & Mindfulness, Elizabeth Reese, Ph.D.
Institution Type/Description: Art Museum.

Hours & Admission Prices: Tues.-Sun. 10-5. No charge; donations accepted. Closed New Year's Day, Independence Day, Thanksgiving, Christmas Eve & Day. &
Attendance: 80,000 (estimated)

Decatur

WISE COUNTY HERITAGE MUSEUM, 1602 S. Trinity, Decatur, TX 76234-2717. Tel.: 940-627-5586.
E-mail: wisemuseum@embarqmail.com
Web Site: www.wisehistory.com
Key Personnel: Pres., Kerry Clower; Dir., Rosalie Gregg; Vice Pres., Mary Hillard; Sec. & Trustee, Patti Gillispie.
Institution Type/Description: Local History Museum.
Hours & Admission Prices: Mon.-Sat. 10-3. Adults $2, children $1; members no charge. Closed major holidays. &
Attendance: 7,000 (estimated)

Del Rio

WHITEHEAD MEMORIAL MUSEUM, 1308 S. Main St., Del Rio, TX 78840-5998. Tel.: 830-774-7568. Facebook, Twitter.
E-mail: info@whiteheadmuseum.org
Web Site: www.whiteheadmuseum.org
Key Personnel: Dir., Michael Diaz; Pres. (V) Mike Parker.
Institution Type/Description: Historical Museum.
Hours & Admission Prices: Tues.-Sat. 10-6, Sun. 1-5; guided tours by appointment. Adults $8, seniors $6, children 6-17 $5; discount to TAM members; members and children 5 & under no charge. &
Attendance: 11,000 (estimated)

Denison

EISENHOWER BIRTHPLACE STATE HISTORIC SITE, 609 S. Lamar Ave., Denison, TX 75021-4821. Tel.: 903-465-8908. Facebook; Instagram.
E-mail: eisenhower-birthplace@thc.texas.gov
Web Site: www.visiteisenhowerbirthplace.com
Institution Type/Description: Historic House: 1877 house where Dwight D. Eisenhower was born.
Hours & Admission Prices: Tues.-Sat. 9-5, Sun. 1-5; last tour 4pm. Family (1 adult & 2 children) $8, each additional child $1; Adults $4, seniors 65 & over, children 6-18, students with ID & adult tour groups $3; school groups $1; children 5 & under no charge. Closed New Year's Eve & Day; Thanksgiving; Christmas Eve & Day. &
Attendance: 15,000 (estimated)

PERRIN AIR FORCE BASE HISTORICAL MUSEUM, 436 McCullum Ave., Denison, TX 75020. Tel.: 903-786-8741.
E-mail: airport@co.grayson.tx.us
Web Site: perrinafbhistoricalmuseum.org
Key Personnel: Dir. & Cur., John Elkins.
Institution Type/Description: Military History Museum.
Hours & Admission Prices: Tues.-Sat. 10-4. No charge; donations accepted. &
Attendance: 3,000 (actual)

RED RIVER RAILROAD MUSEUM, 101 E. Main St., Ste. 145, Denison, TX 75021-3001. Tel.: 903-463-5289.
E-mail: redriverrailmuseum@yahoo.com
Web Site: www.redriverrailmuseum.org
Key Personnel: Dir., Tina DiToma; Chm. (V), Doug Hoover; Membership Officer, Donald W. Scott.
Institution Type/Description: Railroad History Museum: housed in the former Katy Depot.
Hours & Admission Prices: Thurs.-Sat. 11-4, Sun. 1-4. No charge; donations accepted.

Denton

BAYLESS-SELBY HOUSE MUSEUM, 317 W. Mulberry St., Denton, TX 76201-6062. Mailing Address: 110 W. Hickory, Denton, TX 76201. Tel.: 940-349-2865 & 2852. Facebook, Twitter, Youtube.
E-mail: peggy.riddle@dentoncounty.com
Web Site: www.dentoncounty.com/bsh
Key Personnel: Museum Dir., Peggy Riddle.
Institution Type/Description: Historic House Museum.
Hours & Admission Prices: Summer Tues.-Sat. 10-2; Winter Wed.-Sat. 10-2. No Charge &

DAR MUSEUM FIRST LADIES OF TEXAS HISTORIC COSTUMES COLLECTION, 304 Administration Dr., Administration Conference Tower, 2nd Fl., Denton, TX 76204. Mailing Address: P.O. Box 425379, Denton, TX 76204-5379. Tel.: 940-898-3644. Fax: 940-898-3556. Facebook, Instagram, Twitter.
E-mail: webteam@twu.edu
Web Site: www.twu.edu
Institution Type/Description: Costume Museum.
Hours & Admission Prices: Mon.-Fri. 8-5; groups by appointment only. No charge. Closed national holidays; university holidays. &

DENTON COUNTY AFRICAN AMERICAN MUSEUM, 317 W. Mulberry St., Denton, TX 76201-6062. Tel.: 940-349-2865. Facebook, Instagram, Twitter.
E-mail: officeofhistoryandculture@dentoncounty.com
Web Site: www.dentoncounty.com/dcaam
Institution Type/Description: African American History Museum.
Hours & Admission Prices: Summer Tues.-Sat. 10-2, Winter Sat. 10-2; groups by appointment. No charge. Closed holidays. &

DENTON COUNTY OFFICE OF HISTORY AND CULTURE - COURTHOUSE-ON-THE-SQUARE MUSEUM, 110 W. Hickory, Denton, TX 76201-4116, Tel.: 940-349-2850.
E-mail: OfficeOfHistoryAndCulture@dentoncounty.com
Web Site: dentoncounty.com/chos
Key Personnel: Dir., Peggy Riddle; Asst. Dir., Roslyn Shelton; Cur. Collections, Kim Cupit; Cur. Exhibits, Joe Duncan; Education & Tourism Coord., Gretel L'Heureux; Museum Specialist, Kelsey Jistel.
Institution Type/Description: History Museum: housed in the former county courthouse; built in 1896. Listed on the National Register of Historic Places.
Hours & Admission Prices: Mon.-Fri. 10-4:30, Sat. 11-3, closed major holidays. No charge. &
Attendance: 86,000 (actual)

HANGAR 10 FLYING MUSEUM, 1945 Matt Wright Lane, Denton Municipal Airport, Denton, TX 76207-4537. Tel.: 940-565-1945.
Institution Type/Description: Aviation History Museum.
Hours & Admission Prices: Mon.-Sat. 8:30-3; other times by appointment. No charge; donations accepted.

TEXAS WOMAN'S UNIVERSITY ART GALLERIES, 302 Pioneer Cir., Visual Arts Bldg., Denton, TX 76204. Mailing Address: P.O. Box 425469, TWU Station, Denton, TX 76204-5469. Tel.: 940-898-2530. Fax: 940-898-2496. Facebook, Instagram, Twitter.
E-mail: visualarts@twu.edu
Web Site: www.twu.edu
Key Personnel: Gallery Coord., Danielle Avram.
Institution Type/Description: Art Museum.
Hours & Admission Prices: Mon.-Fri. 9-4. No charge. Closed national holidays. &

TEXAS WOMEN'S HALL OF FAME MUSEUM, Hubbard Hall, Texas Woman's Univ., Denton, TX 76204. Mailing Address: Texas Governor's Commission for Women, P.O. Box 12428, Austin, TX 78711. Tel.: 940-898-3644 & 512-475-2615.
E-mail: women@governor.state.tx.us
Web Site: www.twu.edu/twhf
Institution Type/Description: Hall of Fame Museum.
Hours & Admission Prices: Mon.-Fri. 8-5; other times by appointment. Closed university holidays & breaks.

UNIVERSITY OF NORTH TEXAS ART GALLERY, College of Visual Arts & Design, 1201 W. Mulberry, Denton, TX 76203. Mailing Address: 1155 Union Cir. #305100, Denton, TX 76203-5107. Tel.: 940-565-4005 & 4001. Fax: 940-565-4717.
E-mail: gallery@unt.edu
Web Site: gallery.unt.edu
Key Personnel: Dir., Tracee W. Robertson; Mgr. Programming, Katy Stewart; Asst. Dir. Exhibitions & Collections, Victoria Estrada Berg DeCuir.
Institution Type/Description: Art Gallery.
Hours & Admission Prices: Temporarily closed for construction. &
Attendance: 8,000 (actual)

Dickens

SPUR-DICKENS COUNTY MUSEUM, 609 Montgomery St., Dickens, TX 79370. Tel.: 806-294-5401.
E-mail: txcodickin@usgennet.org

Formerly: Dickens Historical Museum
Key Personnel: Dir., Harry Bob Martin.
Institution Type/Description: History Museum: housed in a former hardware store.
Hours & Admission Prices: Fri. & Sat. 1-5 and by appointment. No charge; donations accepted. Closed holidays. &

Dripping Springs

DR. POUND HISTORICAL FARMSTEAD MUSEUM, 570 Founders Park Rd., Dripping Springs, TX 78620. Mailing Address: Friends of the Pound House Foundation, P.O. Box 1150, Dripping Springs, TX 78620. Tel.: 512-858-2030. Facebook, Instagram, Twitter.
E-mail: poundhousefarmstead@gmail.com
Web Site: drpoundhistoricalfarmstead.org
Formerly: Dr. Pound Pioneer Farmstead Museum
Key Personnel: Exec. Dir., Andrea Larsen; Mktg. Dir., Jenny Pack.
Institution Type/Description: History Museum: housed on the farmstead built by one of the city's founding families; built in 1854.
Hours & Admission Prices: Wed.-Sat. 12-3; other times by appointment. Admission $5. &
Attendance: 3,200 (estimated)

Dublin

DUBLIN BOTTLING WORKS MUSEUM & WP KLOSTER MUSEUM ANNEX, 105 E. Elm, Dublin, TX 76446-2309. Tel.: 254-445-4210 & 888-398-1024. Facebook, Instagram, Twitter.
E-mail: lori@dublinbottlingworks.com
Web Site: www.dublinbottlingworks.com
Formerly: Dublin Dr Pepper Bottling Company Museum
Institution Type/Description: Company Museum.
Hours & Admission Prices: Tues.-Sat. 10-5, Sun. 1-5. Adult $5, children & seniors $4. Closed New Year's Day, Christmas Eve & Day. &
Attendance: 70,000 (estimated)

Dumas

MOORE COUNTY ART ASSOCIATION, The Art Center, 1810 S. Dumas Ave., Dumas, TX 79029-6002. Tel.: 806-935-5312.
E-mail: dumasmuseum@windstream.net
Web Site: www.dumasmuseumandartcenter.org
Key Personnel: Pres., Mary Ferris; Dir., Marti Christman; Treas., Glynda Pflug; Vice Pres., Mike DeBons; Office Asst., Risa Franco.
Institution Type/Description: Art Center.
Hours & Admission Prices: Mon.-Sat. 10-5. No charge; donations accepted. Closed New Year's Day; Thanksgiving; Christmas. &
Attendance: 6,600 (actual)

MOORE COUNTY HISTORICAL MUSEUM DBA WINDOW ON THE PLAINS, Window on the Plains, 1820 S. Dumas Ave., Dumas, TX 79029-6002. Tel.: 806-935-3113.
E-mail: dumasmuseum@windstream.net
Web Site: www.dumasmuseumandartcenter.org
Key Personnel: Dir. & Museum Shop Mgr., Terri George.
Institution Type/Description: History and Wildlife Museum.
Hours & Admission Prices: Mon.-Sat. 10-5. No charge; donations accepted. Closed New Year's Day; Thanksgiving; Christmas. &
Attendance: 5,930 (actual)

Duncanville

INTERNATIONAL MUSEUM OF CULTURES, 411 U.S. Hwy. 67, Duncanville, TX 75137. Tel.: 972-572-0462. Facebook.
E-mail: info@MICmuseum.org
Web Site: www.internationalmuseumofcultures.org
Key Personnel: Exec. Dir., Mary Fae Kamm; Chm. (V), Gwendolyn Brown.
Institution Type/Description: Anthropology Museum.
Hours & Admission Prices: Mon.-Fri. 10-4, Sat. by appointment. Adults $7.50, youth (under 18) & seniors (over 55) $5, children (under 4) and members no charge. &
Attendance: 13,500 (actual)

Eagle Lake

PRAIRIE EDGE MUSEUM, 408 E. Main St., Eagle Lake, TX 77434-2534. Tel.: 979-234-7442.
E-mail: prairieedgemuseum@yahoo.com
Web Site: www.prairieedgemuseum.com
Key Personnel: Dir., Christine Owen.

Institution Type/Description: History Museum.
Hours & Admission Prices: Mon.-Fri. 9-1; Sat.-Sun. 2-5. No charge; donations accepted. &

Eden

DON FREEMAN MEMORIAL MUSEUM, 120 Paint Rock St., Eden, TX 76837. Mailing Address: P.O. Box 915, Eden, TX 76837. Tel.: 325-869-2211 & 5074.
E-mail: cityadmin@edentexas.com
Web Site: www.edentexas.com
Key Personnel: Museum Cur., Carolyn Moody.
Institution Type/Description: History Museum.
Hours & Admission Prices: Sat. 10-5, Sun. 1-4. No charge; donations accepted.
Attendance: 267 (actual)

Edinburg

EDINBURG FIRE DEPARTMENT FIREFIGHTERS MUSEUM, 211 W. McIntyre, Edinburg, TX 78539. Tel.: 956-383-7691. Fax: 956-289-1853.
E-mail: ssnider@cityofedinburg.com
Key Personnel: Dir., Shawn M. Snider.
Institution Type/Description: Firefighting History Museum.
Hours & Admission Prices: Mon.-Fri. 8-5. No charge; donations accepted. Closed New Year's Day; Easter; Independence Day; Labor Day; Christmas. &
Attendance: 750

MUSEUM OF SOUTH TEXAS HISTORY, 200 N. Closner Blvd., Edinburg, TX 78541-3554. Tel.: 956-383-6911. Fax: 956-381-8518. Facebook, Twitter.
E-mail: info@mosthistory.org
Web Site: www.mosthistory.org
Formerly: Hidalgo County Historical Museum
Key Personnel: Exec. Dir., Shan Rankin; Cur. of Collections & Registrar, Lisa Kay Adam.
Institution Type/Description: History Museum: housed in the former county jail including hanging room & trap door; built in 1910.
Hours & Admission Prices: Tues.-Sat. 10-5, Sun. 1-5. Adults $7, senior citizens 62 & over, active military, and students 13 & over $5, children 4-12 $4; discounts to AAM members; Sat. before noon (excluding special events), children 3 & under and members no charge. Closed major holidays. &
Attendance: 32,000 (actual)

Edna

TEXANA MUSEUM AND LIBRARY ASSOCIATION, 403 N. Wells, Edna, TX 77957-2730. Tel.: 361-782-5431.
Key Personnel: C.E.O., Pres. (V) & Chm. (V), Harrison Stafford, II.
Institution Type/Description: History Museum.
Hours & Admission Prices: Tues.-Fri. 1-5. No charge. &
Attendance: 1,200 (estimated)

El Campo

EL CAMPO MUSEUM OF NATURAL HISTORY, 2350 N. Mechanic, El Campo, TX 77437-2343. Tel.: 979-543-6885. Facebook, Twitter.
E-mail: ask@elcampomuseum.org
Web Site: www.elcampomuseum.com
Formerly: El Campo Museum of Art, History and Natural Science
Key Personnel: Museum Dir., Cheri McGuirk.
Institution Type/Description: Natural History Museum.
Hours & Admission Prices: Tues.-Fri. 10-12 & 1-5; Sat. 10-3. &
Attendance: 7,000 (estimated)

El Paso

CENTENNIAL MUSEUM AND CHIHUAHUAN DESERT GARDENS, Physical/Mailing Address: 500 W. University Ave., El Paso, TX 79902. Tel.: 915-747-5565. Fax: 915-747-5411. Facebook, Instagram, Twitter.
E-mail: museum@utep.edu
Web Site: www.utep.edu/museum/
Key Personnel: Dir., Daniel Carey-Whalen; Museum Cur., Samantha Winer; Cur. Asst., Adam Presgraves; Admin. Asst., Lucero Duran; Education Cur., Kaye Mullins; Garden Cur., John White; Groundskeeper, Barb Bailey.
Institution Type/Description: Natural History Museum.

Hours & Admission Prices: Mon.-Sat. 10-4:30. No charge; donations accepted. Closed major holidays. &
Attendance: 15,000 (estimated)

CHAMIZAL NATIONAL MEMORIAL, Physical/Mailing Address: 800 S. San Marcial, El Paso, TX 79905-4123. Tel.: 915-532-7273. Fax: 915-532-7240. Facebook, Instagram, Twitter.
Web Site: www.nps.gov/cham
Key Personnel: Supt., Fernando "Gus" Sanchez.
Institution Type/Description: Park Museum: located on land acquired from Mexico through 1963 Treaty.
Hours & Admission Prices: Grounds: daily 7-10. Offices: daily 10-5. No charge. Call for theater information & pricing. &
Attendance: 226,353

EL PASO HOLOCAUST MUSEUM & STUDY CENTER, 715 N. Oregon, El Paso, TX 79902-3911. Tel.: 915-351-0048.
E-mail: info@elpasoholocaustmuseum.org
Web Site: elpasoholocaustmuseum.org
Key Personnel: Exec. Dir., Lori Shepherd; Programming and Education Dir., Jamie Flores; Volunteer Coord., Cynthia Serafin.
Institution Type/Description: History Museum.
Hours & Admission Prices: Tues.-Fri. 9-5, Sat.-Sun. 1-5. No charge; donations accepted. Closed major holidays. &
Attendance: 20,000 (estimated)

EL PASO MUSEUM OF ARCHAEOLOGY, 4301 Transmountain Rd., El Paso, TX 79924-3753. Tel.: 915-755-4332. Fax: 915-759-6824. Facebook.
E-mail: archaeologymuseum@elpasotexas.gov
Web Site: archaeology.elpasotexas.gov
Key Personnel: Dir., Jeff Romney; Cur., George Maloof; Store Sales Clerk, Armida Sosa.
Institution Type/Description: Archaeology Museum & Nature Center.
Hours & Admission Prices: Tues.-Sat. 9-5, Sun. 12-5. No charge; donations accepted. Closed New Year's Day; Martin Luther King Jr. Day; Memorial Day; Independence Day; Labor Day; Thanksgiving & day after; Christmas. &
Attendance: 22,000 (actual)

EL PASO MUSEUM OF ART, One Arts Festival Plaza, El Paso, TX 79901-1135. Tel.: 915-212-3064.
E-mail: EPMA-info@elpasotexas.gov
Web Site: www.epma.art
Key Personnel: Dir., Victoria Ramirez; Senior Cu., Patrick Shaw Cable; Cur., Kate Green.
Institution Type/Description: Art Museum.
Hours & Admission Prices: Tues.-Wed. & Fri.-Sat. 9-5, Thurs. 9-9, Sun. 12-5. No charge. Closed major holidays. &
Attendance: 100,000 (estimated)

EL PASO MUSEUM OF HISTORY, 510 N. Santa Fe St., El Paso, TX 79901-1145. Tel.: 915-212-0320. Fax: 915-212-0321. Facebook.
E-mail: cityhistorymuseum@elpasotexas.gov
Web Site: www.history.elpasotexas.gov
Key Personnel: Co-Chair, Rebeccas Whitaker; Co-Chair, David Saucedo.
Institution Type/Description: History Museum.
Hours & Admission Prices: Tues.-Wed. & Fri.-Sat. 9-5, Thurs. 9-9, Sun. 12-5. No charge; donations accepted. Closed city holidays. &
Attendance: 83,948 (actual)

EL PASO ZOO, 4001 E. Paisano, El Paso, TX 79905-4223. Tel.: 915-212-0966. Fax: 915-212-0252. Facebook, Twitter.
E-mail: elpasozoo@elpasotexas.gov
Web Site: www.elpasozoo.org
Key Personnel: Dir., Steve Marshall; Pres. & C.E.O., Jim Maddy; Media Contact, Karla Martinez.
Institution Type/Description: Zoo.
Hours & Admission Prices: Daily 9:30-4. Adults (18-59) $12, seniors (60 and over), active military & spouse, children (13-17) $9, children (3-12) $7.50. Closed New Year's Day, Thanksgiving, Christmas Day. &
Attendance: 285,971 (actual)

INSIGHTS-EL PASO SCIENCE MUSEUM, 521 Tays St., El Paso, TX 79901-1144. Mailing Address: P.O. Box 9248, El Paso, TX 79995-9248. Tel.: 915-534-0000. Facebook, Instagram, Twitter.
E-mail: info@insightselpaso.org
Web Site: www.insightselpaso.org
Key Personnel: Pres. (V), Ellen Esposito; Vice Pres., Carolyn Awalt; Museum Shop Mgr., Lourdes Ramirez.

Institution Type/Description: Science Center.
Hours & Admission Prices: See website for hours. Adults $5.50, military $4.50, children 4-12 $3.50; discounts to groups, ASTC, AAM & ICOM members; children under 3 & members no charge. Closed major holidays. &
Attendance: 7,500 (actual)

INTERNATIONAL MUSEUM OF ART, 1211 Montana Ave., El Paso, TX 79902-5511. Tel.: 915-543-6747. Facebook, Twitter.
E-mail: iavatx@aol.com
Web Site: www.internationalmuseumofart.net
Formerly: International Association for the Visual Arts
Key Personnel: Exec. Dir., Mitzi Quirarte.
Institution Type/Description: Art Museum: housed in the Turney Home.
Hours & Admission Prices: Wed.-Fri. 10-5, Sat.-Sun. 1-5. No charge.
Attendance: 18,960 (estimated)

MAGOFFIN HOME STATE HISTORIC SITE, 1120 Magoffin Ave., El Paso, TX 79901. Tel.: 915-533-5147. Fax: 915-544-4398.
E-mail: leslie.bergloff@thc.state.tx.us
Web Site: www.visitmagoffinhome.com
Key Personnel: Site Dir., Leslie Bergloff.
Institution Type/Description: Historic House Museum: 1875 territorial adobe house built by pioneer, businessman, and civic leader Joseph Magoffin. Listed on the National Register of Historic Places.
Hours & Admission Prices: Tues.-Sun. 9-5; tours on the hour; last tour begins at 4pm; school tours by appointment. Adults $7, seniors $6, children 6-18 & students $4; discounts to groups of 10 or more; children 5 & under no charge. Closed New Year's Eve & Day; Thanksgiving; Christmas Eve & Day. &
Attendance: 18,000 (actual)

THE NATIONAL BORDER PATROL MUSEUM AND MEMORIAL LIBRARY, 4315 Transmountain Rd., El Paso, TX 79924-3753. Tel.: 915-759-6060. Fax: 915-759-0992. Facebook, Twitter.
E-mail: nbpm@borderpatrolmuseum.com
Web Site: www.borderpatrolmuseum.com
Key Personnel: Pres. (V), David Ham; Museum Shop Mgr., David Apodaca; Archives Mgr., Annette Hekking.
Institution Type/Description: U.S. Border Patrol History Museum.
Hours & Admission Prices: Tues.-Sat. 9-5; guided tours by appointment. No charge; donations accepted. Parking: no charge. Closed major holidays. &
Attendance: 25,000 (actual)

STANLEE & GERALD RUBIN CENTER FOR THE VISUAL ARTS, UNIVERSITY OF TEXAS, EL PASO, Dawson Dr. at Sun Bowl Dr., El Paso, TX 79902. Mailing Address: 500 W. University Ave., El Paso, TX 79968-8900. Tel.: 915-747-6151. Fax: 915-747-6067. Facebook, Instagram, Twitter.
E-mail: rubincenter@utep.edu
Web Site: www.rubincenter.utep.edu
Key Personnel: Dir., Kerry Doyle; Asst. Dir., Melissa Barba; Registrar & Preparator, Daniel Szwaczkowski.
Institution Type/Description: Art Museum.
Hours & Admission Prices: Mon.-Wed. 10-5, Thurs. 10-7, Fri. 10-5, and by appointment. &
Attendance: 11,000 (estimated)

Eldorado

SCHLEICHER COUNTY HISTORICAL SOCIETY MUSEUM, 7 W. Murchison St., Eldorado, TX 76936. Tel.: 325-374-2554.
E-mail: judie.lipsett@gmail.com
Key Personnel: Pres., Judie Lipsett Stanford.
Institution Type/Description: Historical Society Museum.
Hours & Admission Prices: Tues. & Fri. 1-4. No charge.

Fairfield

FREESTONE COUNTY HISTORICAL MUSEUM, 302 E. Main St., P.O. Box 524, Fairfield, TX 75840-1530. Tel.: 903-389-3738.
E-mail: freestonecomuseum@windstream.net
Web Site: www.freestonecomuseum.com
Key Personnel: Pres., Linda Mullen; Vice Pres., Brad Pullin.
Institution Type/Description: Local History & Telephone Museum.
Hours & Admission Prices: Wed. & Fri.-Sat. 10-5; other times by appointment. Adults $3; children under 5 no charge. &
Attendance: 4,000 (actual)

Falfurrias

THE HERITAGE MUSEUM AT FALFURRIAS, INC., 415 N. St. Mary's, Falfurrias, TX 78355. Tel.: 361-325-2907.
E-mail: ltrevino_cantu@hotmail.com
Web Site: http://heritagemuseum-falfurrias.org/
Key Personnel: Vice Pres., Lourdes Cantu.
Institution Type/Description: History Museum.
Hours & Admission Prices: Tues.-Fri. 9-4, Sat. 9-1. No charge; donations accepted. &
Attendance: 1,000 (estimated)

Farmers Branch

FARMERS BRANCH HISTORICAL PARK, 2540 Farmers Branch Lane, Farmers Branch, TX 75234-6214. Tel.: 972-406-0184. Fax: 972-919-8733. Facebook, Instagram.
E-mail: historicalpark@farmersbranchtx.gov
Web Site: www.farmersbranch.info
Key Personnel: Museum Educator, Danielle Brissette; Museum Cur., Jamie Rigsby; Park Admin., Kim Jolly Chapman.
Institution Type/Description: Historical Park & Archives.
Hours & Admission Prices: Mon.-Fri. 8-6, Sat.-Sun. 12-6. Tours: by reservation. No charge; donations accepted. Closed New Year's Eve & Day; Easter; Thanksgiving; Christmas Eve and Day. &
Attendance: 50,000 (estimated)

Floydada

FLOYD COUNTY HISTORICAL MUSEUM, 105 E. Missouri St., Floydada, TX 79235. Tel.: 806-983-2415.
E-mail: fchmuseum@sbcglobal.net
Institution Type/Description: History Museum.
Hours & Admission Prices: Mon.-Fri. 1-5; other times by appointment. No charge; donations accepted. &
Attendance: 3,000 (actual)

Fort Bliss

FORT BLISS AND OLD IRONSIDE MUSEUMS, 1735 Marshall Rd., Fort Bliss, TX 79916. Tel.: 915-855-4677.
Formerly: U.S. Army Air Defense Artillery Museum & Fort Bliss Museum
Institution Type/Description: Military Museum.
Hours & Admission Prices: Mon.-Fri. 9-4, Sat. 10-3. No charge. Closed federal holidays. &
Attendance: 60,000 (actual)

Fort Davis

CHIHUAHUAN DESERT RESEARCH INSTITUTE, Physical/ Mailing Address: 43869 SH 118, P.O. Box 905, Fort Davis, TX 79734. Tel.: 432-364-2499. Facebook, Twitter.
Web Site: www.cdri.org
Key Personnel: Exec. Dir., Lisa Gordon; Dir. Operations & Finance., Rick Herrman; Gardener, Leslie Spicer; Site Mgr., Jason Tyree; Visitor Center Coord., Kay Plavidal; Visitor Svcs., Susie Liddell; Business Mgr., Laura Lannom.
Institution Type/Description: Arboretum & Visitor Center.
Hours & Admission Prices: Mon.-Sat. 9-5, Sun. 12:30-5:30. Adults $6; children 12 & under and members no charge. &
Attendance: 8,000 (estimated)

FORT DAVIS NATIONAL HISTORIC SITE, Physical/Mailing Address: P.O. Box 1379, 101 Lt. Flipper Dr. #1379, Fort Davis, TX 79734-0015. Tel.: 432-426-3224, ext. 220 (Historian Office). Fax: 432-426-3122.
Web Site: www.nps.gov/foda
Key Personnel: Pres. & Treas., Jerry Johnson; Vice Pres., Martha King.
Institution Type/Description: Military Museum: located on the site of 1854-1891 Fort Davis.
Hours & Admission Prices: Daily 8-5; research by appointment. No charge. Closed New Year's Day; Martin Luther King Jr. Day; Thanksgiving; Christmas. &
Attendance: 50,000 (actual)

Fort Hood

1ST CAVALRY DIVISION MUSEUM, Bldg. 2218, 56th & 761 Tank Bn. Ave., Fort Hood, TX 76545. Mailing Address: 1st Cavalry Div. Museum, P.O. Box 5187, Fort Hood, TX 76545. Tel.: 254-287-3626 & 737-3626. Fax: 254-287-6423 & 737-6423.
E-mail: steven.c.draper.civ@mail.mil
Web Site: www.hood.army.mil/1stcavdiv/1cdmuseum/index
Key Personnel: Dir., Steven C. Draper.
Institution Type/Description: Military Museum.
Hours & Admission Prices: Mon.-Fri. 9-4, Sat. 10-4, Sun. & Holidays 12-4.; No charge. &
Attendance: 50,000 (actual)

THIRD CAVALRY MUSEUM, Bldg. 409, 761st Tank BN Ave., Fort Hood, TX 76544. Tel.: 254-287-811. Fax: 254-287-3833. Facebook.
E-mail: braverifles1846@gmail.com
Key Personnel: Museum Dir., Ellis S. Hamric; Registrar, Sherri McDowney.
Institution Type/Description: Military Museum.
Hours & Admission Prices: Mon.-Fri. 9-4, Sat. 10-4, Sun. 12-4. No charge; donations accepted. Closed New Year's Day; Thanksgiving; Christmas. &
Attendance: 17,000 (actual)

Fort McKavett

FORT MCKAVETT STATE HISTORIC SITE, 7066 FM 864, Fort McKavett, TX 76841. Tel.: 325-396-2358. Fax: 325-396-2818.
E-mail: ft-mckavett@thc.texas.gov
Web Site: www.visitfortmckavett.com
Key Personnel: Site Mgr., Cody Mobley.
Institution Type/Description: Historic Site & Military Museum: 1852-1883 Fort McKavett, home to four Buffalo solder regiments.
Hours & Admission Prices: Daily 8-5. Adults $4, seniors, college students & children 6-18 $3; discounts to groups; children 5 & under no charge. Closed New Year's Eve & Day; Thanksgiving; Christmas Eve & Day. &
Attendance: 5,500 (estimated)

Fort Sam Houston

FORT SAM HOUSTON MUSEUM, 2400 Liscum Rd., Fort Sam Houston, TX 78234. Mailing Address: ARNO-CS-MU, 2108 Wilson Way, Fort Sam Houston, TX 78234. Tel.: 210-221-1886. Facebook.
E-mail: fshmuseum@gmail.com
Formerly: Fort Sam Houston Military Museum
Key Personnel: Dir., Jacqueline B. Davis; Cur., William Manchester.
Institution Type/Description: Military Historical Museum: located on Fort Sam Houston National Historic Landmark.
Hours & Admission Prices: Tues.-Fri. 10-4, Sat. 12-4. No charge. Closed federal holidays. &
Attendance: 30,000 (estimated)

U.S. ARMY MEDICAL DEPARTMENT MUSEUM, 3898 Stanley Rd. Building 1046, Fort Sam Houston, TX 78234. Mailing Address: P.O. Box 340244, Fort Sam Houston, TX 78234. Tel.: 210-221-6358. Fax: 210-221-6781. Facebook.
E-mail: scott.schoner@amedd.army.mil
Web Site: www.ameddmuseumfoundation.com
Key Personnel: Dir., George Wunderlich.
Institution Type/Description: Military Medical Museum.
Hours & Admission Prices: Tues.-Sat. 10-4. No charge; donations accepted. Closed federal holidays. &
Attendance: 34,876 (actual)

Fort Stockton

ANNIE RIGGS MEMORIAL MUSEUM, 301 S. Main St., Fort Stockton, TX 79735. Tel.: 432-336-2167. Fax: 432-336-7529.
E-mail: annieriggs@sbcglobal.net
Web Site: annieriggsmuseum.com
Key Personnel: Dir., Melba Montoya.
Institution Type/Description: General Museum: housed in 1899 Riggs Hotel.
Hours & Admission Prices: June-Aug. Mon.-Sat. 9-6; Sept.-May Mon.-Sat. 9-5. Adults $3, seniors 65 & over $2.50, children 6-12 $2, children under 6 no charge. &
Attendance: 4,000 (actual)

HISTORIC FORT STOCKTON, Physical/Mailing Address: 300 E. Third, Fort Stockton, TX 79735-5702. Tel.: 432-336-2400.
E-mail: historicfortstockonfort@gmail.com
Web Site: www.historicfortstockton.org
Key Personnel: Dir., Melba Montoya.
Institution Type/Description: Historic Site & Military Museum: 1867-1886 frontier fort during Indian Wars. Listed on National Register of Historic Places.

Hours & Admission Prices: June-Aug. Mon.-Sat. 9-6; Sept.-May Mon.-Sat. 9-5. Adults $3, senior citizens $2.50, children 6-12 $2; discounts to groups; TAM & AAM members and children under 6 no charge. Closed New Year's Day; Easter; Thanksgiving; Christmas. &
Attendance: 4,000 (estimated)

Fort Worth

AMERICAN AIRLINES C.R. SMITH MUSEUM, 4601 Texas Hwy. 360 at FAA Road, Fort Worth, TX 76155. Tel.: 817-967-1560. Facebook, Twitter.
E-mail: info.crsmithmuseum@aa.com
Web Site: www.crsmithmuseum.org
Key Personnel: Exec. Dir., Uli Sailer Das; Cur. & Head Interpretation & Education, Tim McElroy; Dir. of Devel. & Membership, Angie Gofredo; Museum Shop Mgr., Judith Clark; Marketing & Promotions, Latanne Steel ; Event Mgr., Shane Melvin; Dir. of Operations & Visitor Experience, Michael Sagar.
Institution Type/Description: Company Museum.
Hours & Admission Prices: Tues.-Sat. 9-5; see Web site for extended holiday hours. Adults $9, military, seniors 65 & up, students w/ID and children 2-17 $6; infants & members no charge.
Attendance: 50,000 (actual)

AMON CARTER MUSEUM OF AMERICAN ART, 3501 Camp Bowie Blvd., Fort Worth, TX 76107-2631. Tel.: 817-738-1933 & 989-5001. Facebook; Twitter; Instagram.
E-mail: visitors@cartermuseum.org
Web Site: www.cartermuseum.org
Key Personnel: Bd. Pres., Karen Johnson Hixon; C.O.O. & C.F.O., Scott Wilcox; Exec. Dir., Andrew J. Walker; Dir. Collections & Exhibitions, Brett Abbott; Dir. Devel. & Communications, Guy C. Vanderpool; Dir. Education & Library Svcs., Amanda Blake; Dir. Human Resources, Sherrie Fanning.
Institution Type/Description: Art Museum.
Hours & Admission Prices: Tues.-Wed. & Fri.-Sat. 10-5, Thurs. 10-8, Sun. 12-5. No charge; donations accepted. Closed major holidays. &
Attendance: 109,000 (actual)

THE ART GALLERIES AT TCU, 2900 W. Berry, Fort Worth, TX 76109. Tel.: 817-257-2588.
E-mail: theartgalleries@tcu.edu
Web Site: www.theartgalleries.tcu.edu
Formerly: Texas Christian University Moudy Gallery
Key Personnel: Dir. & Cur., Sara-Jayne Parsons.
Institution Type/Description: Art Galleries: Moudy Gallery & Fort Worth Contemporary Arts.
Hours & Admission Prices: Academic Year: Moudy: Mon.-Fri. 11-4, Sat. 1-4; other times by appointment. FWCA: Wed.-Sat. 12-5; other times by appointment. No charge. &

B-36 PEACEMAKER MUSEUM, 3300 Ross Ave., Fort Worth, TX 76121. Mailing Address: P.O. Box 121116, Fort Worth, TX 76121-1116. Tel.: 817-905-1889 & 855-733-8627. Facebook, Twitter, Instagram, Youtube.
E-mail: info@b-36peacemakermuseum.org
Web Site: www.b-36peacemakermuseum.org
Institution Type/Description: Military History Museum.
Hours & Admission Prices: Wed. 9-4, Sat. 9-5, Sun. 11-5. Adults $5; active military no charge. &

BUREAU OF ENGRAVING AND PRINTING - FORT WORTH, 9000 Blue Mound Rd., Fort Worth, TX 76131. Tel.: 866-865-1194 (Toll Free) & 817-231-4000.
Web Site: moneyfactory.gov
Institution Type/Description: History Museum.
Hours & Admission Prices: Office: Tues.-Fri. 8:30-5:30. Tours: Tues.-Fri. 8:30-4:30. No charge. Closed federal holidays.

CATTLE RAISERS MUSEUM, Physical/Mailing Address: 1600 Gendy St., Fort Worth, TX 76107. Tel.: 817-332-8551. Fax: 817-336-2470.
E-mail: cattleraisersmuseum@gmail.com
Web Site: www.cattleraisersmuseum.org
Key Personnel: Dir., Patricia W. Riley; Assoc. Dir., Sherry Flow; Membership Dir., Deanna Holderith; Collections Mgr., Hilary Baker; Museum Educator, Marta Torres.
Institution Type/Description: History Museum.
Hours & Admission Prices: Mon.-Sat. 10-5, Sun. noon-5. Admission to Fort Worth Museum of Science & History includes Cattle Raisers Museum. Adults $16,

children (2-12) $13; discounts to groups 15 or more. Closed Thanksgiving; Christmas Eve & Day. &
Attendance: 450,000 (estimated)

FORT WORTH AVIATION MUSEUM, 3300 Ross Ave., Fort Worth, TX 76106. Mailing Address: P.O. Box 161966, Fort Worth, TX 76161. Tel.: 855-733-8627. Facebook.
E-mail: info@ftwaviation.com
Web Site: www.fortworthaviationmuseum.com
Formerly: Veterans Memorial Air Park
Key Personnel: Chm. Bd., Chuck Burin; Exec. Dir., Jim Hodgson.
Institution Type/Description: Aviation History Museum.
Hours & Admission Prices: Wed. 9-4, Sat. 9-5, Sun. 11-5. Family $10, adults $5, youth (6-16) $1; museum & Blue Star Museum members, active duty military & children under 6 no charge. &
Attendance: 3,300 (actual)

FORT WORTH BOTANIC GARDEN, 3220 Botanic Garden Blvd., Fort Worth, TX 76107-3420. Tel.: 817-392-5510. Facebook, Instagram.
E-mail: BotanicGardenInfo@FortWorthTexas.gov
Web Site: www.fwbg.org
Key Personnel: Dir. of Volunteers & Public Engagement, Julie Donovan; Assoc. Dir. of Volunteers, Montana Williams.
Institution Type/Description: Botanical Garden.
Hours & Admission Prices: Garden: daily 8 am-6. No charge. Japanese Garden: daily 8-6. Adults $7, seniors (65 and over) $5, children (4-12) $4; members & children under 4 no charge. &
Attendance: 700,000 (estimated)

FORT WORTH MUSEUM OF SCIENCE AND HISTORY, 1600 Gendy St., Fort Worth, TX 76107-4062. Tel.: 817-255-9300. Fax: 817-732-7635. Facebook, Instagram, Twitter.
E-mail: webmaster@fwmsh.org
Web Site: www.fortworthmuseum.org
Key Personnel: Pres., Van A. Romans; Chm. Bd., Bill Pollard; Vice Chm., Dick Russack.
Institution Type/Description: General Museum.
Hours & Admission Prices: Mon.-Sat.10-5, Sun. 12-5. Exhibits: adults $16, junior $13, members no charge. &
Attendance: 792,581 (actual)

FORT WORTH NATURE CENTER AND REFUGE, 9601 Fossil Ridge Rd., Fort Worth, TX 76135-9148. Tel.: 817-392-7410. Facebook.
Web Site: www.fwnaturecenter.org
Key Personnel: Dir., Rob Denkhaus.
Institution Type/Description: Nature Center & Refuge.
Hours & Admission Prices: Mon.-Sun. 8-5. Adults $5, seniors (65 and over) $3, children (3-12) $2, children (under 3) free, military discount. &
Attendance: 37,730 (actual)

FORT WORTH ZOO, 1989 Colonial Pkwy., Fort Worth, TX 76110-6640. Tel.: 817-759-7555. Fax: 817-759-7501. Facebook, Instagram, Twitter.
E-mail: info@fortworthzoo.org
Web Site: www.fortworthzoo.org
Formerly: Fort Worth Zoological Park
Key Personnel: Dir., Michael Fouraker; Chm. (V), Ramona Bass.
Institution Type/Description: Zoo.
Hours & Admission Prices: July 2-Oct. 28 daily 10-5. Adults (13 and over) $14, seniors (65 and over) & children (3-12) $10, toddlers (2 and under) no charge. &
Attendance: 1,000,000 (estimated)

KIMBELL ART MUSEUM, 3333 Camp Bowie Blvd., Fort Worth, TX 76107-2792. Tel.: 817-332-8451. Fax: 817-877-1264. Facebook, Instagram, Twitter.
E-mail: pr@kimbellmuseum.org
Web Site: www.kimbellart.org
Key Personnel: Dir., Eric M. Lee; Pres., Mrs. Kimbell Fortson Wynne.
Institution Type/Description: Art Museum.
Hours & Admission Prices: Tues.-Thurs. & Sat. 10-5, Fri. 12-8, Sun. 12-5. Permanent Collection: No charge. Special Exhibitions: Adults $14, Seniors (60 and over) and students $12, children (6-11) $10, children (under 6), members & other museum employees no charge. Closed New Year's Day; Independence Day; Thanksgiving; Christmas. &
Attendance: 261,688 (estimated)

LOG CABIN VILLAGE, 2100 Log Cabin Village Lane, Fort Worth, TX 76109-1000. Tel.: 817-392-5881. Facebook, Twitter.
E-mail: logcabinvillage@fortworthtexas.gov
Web Site: logcabinvillage.org
Key Personnel: Historic Site Supvr., Kelli L. Pickard; Asst. Historic Site Supvr., Rena Lawrence.
Institution Type/Description: Village Museum.
Hours & Admission Prices: Tues.-Fri. 9-4, Sat.-Sun. 1-5. Adult $5.50, senior citizens & youth (4-17) $5; discounts to groups, AAM & Texas Association of Museums members; members no charge. &
Attendance: 28,736 (actual)

MODERN ART MUSEUM OF FORT WORTH, 3200 Darnell St., Fort Worth, TX 76107-2872. Tel.: 817-738-9215 & 866-824-5566. Facebook, Twitter.
E-mail: info@themodern.org
Web Site: www.themodern.org
Key Personnel: Dir., Dr. Marla Price.
Institution Type/Description: Art Museum.
Hours & Admission Prices: Tues.-Thurs. & Sat.-Sun. 10-5; Fri. 10-8. General $16, seniors (60 and over), active/retired military & first responders $12, students $10, children (under 18) no charge. &
Attendance: 180,000 (estimated)

NATIONAL COWGIRL MUSEUM AND HALL OF FAME, 1720 Gendy St., Fort Worth, TX 76107-4064. Tel.: 817-336-4475. Facebook, Instagram, Twitter.
E-mail: info@cowgirl.net
Web Site: www.cowgirl.net
Key Personnel: Exec. Dir., Pat Riley; Assoc. Exec. Dir., Diana Vela; Dir. of Finance, Shirley Baker; Dir. of Devel., Emmy Lou Prescott; Research & Education Mgr., Bethany Dodson; Museum Shop Mgr., Sarah Garrett.
Institution Type/Description: Research Center: emphasis on all aspects of Western American women.
Hours & Admission Prices: Tues.-Sat. 10-4. Adults, seniors (60 and over), military $5; children (4-12) $3.50; children (3 and under) no charge. &
Attendance: 35,089 (actual)

NATIONAL MULTICULTURAL WESTERN HERITAGE MUSEUM, 3400 Mount Vernon Ave., Fort Worth, TX 76103-2525. Mailing Address: 2401 Scott Ave., Fort Worth, TX 76103-2228. Tel.: 817-534-8801. Fax: 817-534-6277.
E-mail: info@cowboysofcolor.org
Web Site: www.cowboysofcolor.org
Formerly: National Cowboys of Color Museum and Hall of Fame
Key Personnel: Exec. Dir., Gloria R. Austin; Pres. Bd., James N. Austin, Jr.; Sec., Kyle B. Davie; Treas., Robert Holmes.
Institution Type/Description: History Museum.
Hours & Admission Prices: Wed.-Sat. 12-4. Adults $6, senior citizens $4, students $3; discounts to Blue Star Museum, AAM & ICOM members; members and children 5 & under no charge. &
Attendance: 10,000 (estimated)

OSCAR E. MONNIG METEORITE GALLERY, Texas Christian University, Sid Richardson Science Bldg., 2950 W. Bowie, Fort Worth, TX 76109. Tel.: 817-257-6277. Fax: 817-257-7789. Facebook.
E-mail: n.m.batiste@tcu.edu
Web Site: www.monnigmuseum.tcu.edu
Key Personnel: Cur., Dr. Rhiannon Mayne; Gallery Educator & Asst., Nona Batiste.
Institution Type/Description: Meteorite Gallery.
Hours & Admission Prices: Mon.-Fri. 1-4, Sat. 12-4. No charge. &
Attendance: 4,537 (actual)

SID RICHARDSON MUSEUM, 309 Main St., Fort Worth, TX 76102-4006. Tel.: 817-332-6554. Facebook, Instagram, Twitter.
E-mail: info@sidrichardsonmuseum.org
Web Site: www.sidrichardsonmuseum.org
Formerly: Sid Richardson Collection of Western Art
Key Personnel: Dir., Mary Burke; Dir. Adult Programs, Leslie Thompson; Dir. Education Resources, Betsy Thomas; Dir. of School & Family Programs, Shelby Orr; Museum Shop Mgr., Chris Gensheimer.
Institution Type/Description: Art Museum.
Hours & Admission Prices: Mon.-Thurs. 9-5, Fri.-Sat. 9-8, Sun. 12-5. No charge. Extended store hours. Closed major holidays. &
Attendance: 48,000 (actual)

STOCKYARDS MUSEUM, 131 E. Exchange Ave., Ste. 113, Fort Worth, TX 76164-8213. Tel.: 817-625-5082. Facebook.

E-mail: nfwhs@sbcglobal.net
Key Personnel: Dir., Teresa Burleson.
Institution Type/Description: History Museum.
Hours & Admission Prices: Mon.-Sat. 10-5; Memorial Day to Labor Day: Sun. 12-5.. Adults $2; veterans and children 12 & under no charge. &
Attendance: 15,000 (estimated)

TEXAS ASSOCIATION OF MUSEUMS, 101 Summit Ave., Ste. 802, Fort Worth, TX 76102-2615. Tel.: 817-332-1177. Fax: 817-332-1179. Facebook; Twitter.
E-mail: admin@texasmuseums.org
Web Site: www.texasmuseums.org
Key Personnel: Exec. Dir., Billy Fong; Admin. Coord., Jennifer Coleman; Dir. of Special Projects, Ruth Ann Rugg.
Institution Type/Description: State Museum Association.
Hours & Admission Prices: Call for hours.

TEXAS CIVIL WAR MUSEUM, 760 Jim Wright Freeway N., Fort Worth, TX 76108-1222. Tel.: 817-246-2323. Fax: 817-246-3951. Facebook.
E-mail: reservations@texascivilwarmuseum.com
Web Site: texascivilwarmuseum.com
Key Personnel: Pres. (V) & Cur., Ray Richey; Exec. Dir., Cynthia L. Harriman; Cur., Judy Richey; Dir. of Sales, John Bell; Reservations, Nancy Gentry; Facility & Operations Mgr., Marcus Richey.
Institution Type/Description: History Museum.
Hours & Admission Prices: Tues.-Sat. 10-5. Adults $6, children 7-12 $3; discounts to AAM members, groups & active military; children under 6 no charge. Closed major holidays. &
Attendance: 20,000 (estimated)

TEXAS COWBOY HALL OF FAME, 2515 Rodeo Plaza, Fort Worth, TX 76164-8210. Tel.: 817-626-7131. Fax: 817-626-7171. Facebook, Instagram.
E-mail: info@texascowboyhalloffame.org
Web Site: www.texascowboyhalloffame.org
Key Personnel: Exec. Dir., Julia Buswold.
Institution Type/Description: History Museum.
Hours & Admission Prices: Mon.-Thurs. 10-5, Fri.-Sat. 10-7, Sun. 11-5. Family $18, adult $6, senior 60 and up & students $5, children 5-12 $3. &
Attendance: 80,000

VINTAGE FLYING MUSEUM, Meacham International Airport, 505 N.W. 38th St., Hangar 33 S., Fort Worth, TX 76106-4386. Tel.: 817-624-1935. Fax: 817-624-2840. Facebook.
E-mail: info@vintageflyingmuseum.org
Web Site: www.vintageflyingmuseum.org
Formerly: B.C. Vintage Flying Machines
Key Personnel: C.E.O./Dir., Chuckie Hospers.
Institution Type/Description: Military Aircraft Museum.
Hours & Admission Prices: Fri. 10-5, Sat. 9-5, Sun. 12-5, Mon.-Thurs. by appointment, Adults $10, children 14-19 & seniors $8, children 6-12 $5; children under 6 no charge. &
Attendance: 5,000 (estimated)

Fredericksburg

GILLESPIE COUNTY HISTORICAL SOCIETY, 325 W. Main, Fredericksburg, TX 78624-3761. Tel.: 830-990-8441. Facebook.
E-mail: info@pioneermuseum.net
Web Site: pioneermuseum.net
Key Personnel: Pres., Annette Tilley; 1st Vice Pres., Crawford Guthrie; 2nd Vice Pres., Matt Seidenberger; Sec., Marcia Draper; Treas., Royce Hunter.
Institution Type/Description: Historical Society.
Hours & Admission Prices: Pioneer Museum: Mon.-Sat. 10-5. Vereins Kirche Museum: Mon-Tues., Thurs.-Sat. 10-4:30. Adults $7.50, children (6-17) $3; children (5 & under), AAM & ICOM mems. no charge. Closed major holidays. &
Attendance: 36,000 (actual)

NATIONAL MUSEUM OF THE PACIFIC WAR, 340 E. Main St., Fredericksburg, TX 78624-4612. Tel.: 830-997-8600. Facebook, Instagram, Twitter.
Web Site: www.pacificwarmuseum.org
Key Personnel: Pres. & C.E.O., Gen. Michael W. Hagee; Chm. Bd., Case D. Fischer; Vice Chm., Robert B. Phelps.
Institution Type/Description: History Museum: housed in 1850 Nimitz Hotel, a famous hostelry until about the turn of the century.
Hours & Admission Prices: Daily 9-5. Adults $15, seniors $12, active duty & retired military $10, children & students $7; discounts to TAM & AAM mem-

bers; World War II veterans, children 5 & under and members no charge. Closed Thanksgiving; Christmas Eve & Day. &
Attendance: 120,000 (estimated)

PIONEER MUSEUM AND VEREINS KIRCHE, 325 W. Main St., Fredericksburg, TX 78624-3711. Tel.: 830-990-8441. Fax: 830-990-2906. Facebook.
E-mail: info@pioneermuseum.net
Web Site: www.pioneermuseum.com
Key Personnel: Pres., Annette Tilley, .: 1st Vice Pers., Crawford Guthrie; 2nd Vice Pres., Matt Seidenberger; Sec., Marcia Draper; Treas., Royce Hunter.
Institution Type/Description: History Museum, House & Sites.
Hours & Admission Prices: Mon.-Sat. 10-5. &
Attendance: 36,000 (actual)

Frisco

THE FRISCO HERITAGE MUSEUM, 6101 Frisco Square Blvd., Frisco, TX 75034. Tel.: 972-292-5000.
E-mail: TPointer@FriscoTexas.gov
Key Personnel: Coord., Toyia Pointer.
Institution Type/Description: History Museum.
Hours & Admission Prices: Wed.-Sat. 10-5, Sun. 1-5. Family $8, adults $4, seniors $3, children 5-11 $2; children 4 & under, active military no charge. &
Attendance: 12,328 (actual)

MUSEUM OF THE AMERICAN RAILROAD, 8004 N. Dallas Pkwy., Frisco, TX 75034. Mailing Address: 6455 Page St., Frisco, TX 75034. Tel.: 214-428-0101. Facebook.
E-mail: info@historictrains.org
Web Site: www.historictrains.org
Formerly: Age of Steam Railroad Museum
Key Personnel: C.E.O., Robert LaPrelle; Chm., William Blaylock; Vice Chair, William Gibson; C.O.O., Kellie Murphy; Chief Mechanical Officer, Steven Wainscott; Dir. Programs & Svcs., John Garbutt; Education Coord., Rayna Alam; Gen. Counsel, William J. Brotherton.
Institution Type/Description: Railroad Museum.
Hours & Admission Prices: Museum: Wed.-Sat. 10-5, Sun. 1-5. Adults $8, children (3-12) $4; discounts to AAM members; members no charge.
Attendance: 32,000 (actual)

THE NATIONAL SOCCER HALL OF FAME, 9200 World Cup Way, Frisco, TX 75033. Tel.: 469-365-0208. Facebook, Instagram, Twitter.
E-mail: jillian.sweress@legends.net
Web Site: www.nationalsoccerhof.org
Key Personnel: Exec. Dir., Djorn Buchholz.
Institution Type/Description: Sports History Museum.
Hours & Admission Prices: Closed until 2019 for relocation. &

Fritch

LAKE MEREDITH AQUATIC AND WILDLIFE MUSEUM, 104 N. Robey, Fritch, TX 79036. Mailing Address: P.O. Box 758, Fritch, TX 79036-0758. Tel.: 806-857-2458. Fax: 806-857-3229.
E-mail: themuseum@fritchcityhall.com
Key Personnel: Dir., Stephanie Davidson.
Institution Type/Description: Natural History Museum.
Hours & Admission Prices: Tues.-Fri. 10-2. No charge; donations accepted. &
Attendance: 6,500 (estimated)

Gainesville

MORTON MUSEUM OF COOKE COUNTY, 210 S. Dixon St., Gainesville, TX 76240-4719. Mailing Address: P.O. Box 150, Gainesville, TX 76241-0150. Tel.: 940-668-8900.
E-mail: mortonmuseum@att.net
Web Site: www.mortonmuseum.org
Key Personnel: Museum Coord., Cathy Farquar.
Institution Type/Description: Historic Building, Historic Site & History Museum: housed in 1884 fire station, city hall & jail.
Hours & Admission Prices: Tues.-Fri. 10-5, Sat. 12-2. Adults $2, children (under 6) no charge. Closed New Year's Day; Thanksgiving; Christmas. &
Attendance: 5,000 (estimated)

Galveston

1892 BISHOP'S PALACE, 1402 Broadway, Galveston, TX 77550-2014. Tel.: 409-762-2475 & 765-3410.

E-mail: bp.user@galvestonhistory.org
Key Personnel: Exec. Dir., Dwayne Jones.
Institution Type/Description: Historic Building: 1886 Walter Gresham Home/Bishop's Palace.
Hours & Admission Prices: Sun.-Fri. 10-5, Sat. 10-6. Adults $14, youth 6-18 $9, children 5 and under no charge. Closed major holidays.
Attendance: 40,124 (actual)

GALVESTON ARTS CENTER, 2127 Strand St., Galveston, TX 77550-1632. Tel.: 409-763-2403.
E-mail: information@galvestonartscenter.org
Web Site: www.contemporaryartgalveston.org
Key Personnel: Exec. Dir., Lisa Shaw; Cur., Dennis Nance.
Institution Type/Description: Contemporary Art Museum: housed in the 1878 First National Bank building located in the Strand Historic District.
Hours & Admission Prices: Tues.-Sat. 11-5, Sun. 12-5. No charge. Closed New Year's Day, Easter, Independence Day, Thanksgiving, Christmas. &
Attendance: 12,000 (estimated)

GALVESTON COUNTY MUSEUM, Physical/Mailing Address: 722 Moody Ave., Galveston, TX 77550. Tel.: 409-766-2340.
Web Site: www.galvestoncountytx.gov
Key Personnel: Dir., Jennifer Wycoff.
Institution Type/Description: History Museum.
Hours & Admission Prices: Temporarily closed. &

GALVESTON HISTORICAL FOUNDATION, INC., 2228 Broadway St., Galveston, TX 77550-4640. Tel.: 409-765-7834. Fax: 409-765-6831.
E-mail: foundation@galvestonhistory.org
Web Site: www.galvestonhistory.org
Key Personnel: Exec. Dir. & C.E.O., Dwayne Jones; Pres., Alicia Cahill; Vice Pres., Kyle McFatridge.
Institution Type/Description: Preservation Project: housed in the U.S. Custom House; built in 1861.
Hours & Admission Prices: Call for hours. No charge; donations accepted. &
Attendance: 600,000 (actual)

GALVESTON RAILROAD MUSEUM, 2602 Santa Fe Place, Galveston, TX 77550-1493. Tel.: 409-765-5700. Fax: 409-765-5744. Facebook.
E-mail: galvrrmuseum@sbcglobal.net
Web Site: www.galvestonrrmuseum.com
Key Personnel: Exec. Dir., Morris S. Gould; Chm. (V), Dr. John E. Bertini; Mktg. Dir., Jennifer Keslo; Cur. & Collections Mgr., Sam Christensen; Museum Shop Mgr., Lanette Pacheco.
Institution Type/Description: Railroad Museum.
Hours & Admission Prices: Summer: daily 10-5; Winter: Mon.-Fri. 9-4, Sat.-Sun. 10-5. Adults $10, senior citizens 65 & over $8, children 4-12 $5; discounts to groups; military, members & children under 3 no charge. Train Rides: Sat. 11-2. Closed New Year's Day; Thanksgiving; Christmas Eve & Day. &

JOHN SYDNOR'S 1847 POWHATAN HOUSE - GALVESTON GARDEN CLUB, 3427 Avenue O, Galveston, TX 77550-6734. Tel.: 409-763-0077.
E-mail: evangelinewhorton@yahoo.com
Key Personnel: Pres. (V), Dwayne Johnson; Chm. (V), Evangeline Whorton.
Institution Type/Description: Historic Building & Site: c.1847 home of pioneer businessman & the first Mayor of Galveston, John Seabrook Sydnor; originally built for use as 24-room family dwelling and guest house; relocated in 1895. Listed on the National Register of Historic Places.
Hours & Admission Prices: Tours: by appointment.
Attendance: 2,000 (estimated)

THE MOODY MANSION MUSEUM, 2618 Broadway, Galveston, TX 77550-4427. Tel.: 409-762-7668. Fax: 409-762-7055. Facebook, Twitter.
E-mail: moodymansiongalveston@gmail.com
Web Site: www.moodymansion.com
Key Personnel: Exec. Dir., Betty Massey.
Institution Type/Description: Historic House Museum: built between 1893 & 1895 31-room mansion.
Hours & Admission Prices: Through Sept. 3 10-6; After Sept. 3 10-5. Adults $12, students 6 and over $6, tour pricing varies. &

OCEAN STAR OFFSHORE DRILLING RIG & MUSEUM, Pier 19 Harborside Dr., Galveston, TX 77550. Mailing Address: 200 N. Dairy Ashford Rd., #4119, Houston, TX 77079-1101. Tel.: 409-766-7827. Fax: 409-766-1242.

E-mail: osmuseum@oceanstaroec.com
Web Site: www.oceanstaroec.com
Key Personnel: Operations Mgr., Monica Crossno.
Institution Type/Description: Science & Technology Museum.
Hours & Admission Prices: Daily 10-5, summer hours 10-6. Family Package $30, Adults $10, Seniors (55 and over) & military $8, youth (7-18) $6, children (6 and under) no charge. ♿
Attendance: 36,000 (actual)

ROSENBERG LIBRARY MUSEUM, 2310 Sealy Ave., Galveston, TX 77550-2220. Tel.: 409-763-8854, ext. 125. Fax: 409-763-0275.
E-mail: ebarton@rosenberg-library.org
Web Site: www.rosenberg-library-museum.org
Key Personnel: Pres. (V), Mrs. Michael C. Doherty; C.E.O. & Exec. Dir., John Augelli; Museum Cur., Eleanor Barton; Special Collections Mgr., Lauren Martino.
Institution Type/Description: General Museum & Library.
Hours & Admission Prices: Mon.-Sat. 9-6. No charge; donations accepted. Closed national holidays. ♿
Attendance: 351,755 (estimated)

TEXAS SEAPORT MUSEUM, Pier 21, No. 8, Galveston, TX 77550. Tel.: 409-763-1877. Fax: 409-763-3037.
E-mail: elissa@galvestonhistory.org
Web Site: www.tsm-elissa.org
Key Personnel: Dir., James L. White; C.E.O. & Exec. Dir. Galveston Historical Foundation, Dwayne Jones; Chm. (V), Teresa Decker; Coord. Education, Susan Vanderford; Museum Shop Mgr., John Schaumburg.
Institution Type/Description: Maritime Museum.
Hours & Admission Prices: Daily 10-5. Adults $12, students & children 6-18 $9; members, children 5 & under and GHF members no charge. Closed Thanksgiving; Christmas. ♿
Attendance: 55,000 (estimated)

George West

GRACE ARMANTROUT MUSEUM, 1961 S. Hwy. 281, George West, TX 78022. Mailing Address: P.O. Box 1351, George West, TX 78022-0248. Tel.: 361-449-3325.
E-mail: gwmuseum@ymail.com
Key Personnel: Dir., Sallie Mackey.
Institution Type/Description: History Museum.
Hours & Admission Prices: Wed.-Fri. 1-5, Sat. 12-4. No charge; donations accepted.

Georgetown

WILLIAMSON MUSEUM, 716 S. Austin Ave., Georgetown, TX 78626. Tel.: 512-943-1670. Fax: 512-943-1672. Facebook, Twitter.
E-mail: mross@williamsonmuseum.org
Web Site: www.williamsonmuseum.org
Key Personnel: Exec. Dir., Mickie Ross; Museum Cur., Ann Evans.
Institution Type/Description: History Museum.
Hours & Admission Prices: Wed.-Fri. 12-5, Sat. 10-5. Closed major holidays.
Attendance: 15,000 (actual)

Gilmer

FLIGHT OF THE PHOENIX AVIATION MUSEUM, 43 Aviation Dr., Gilmer, TX 75645. Tel.: 903-790-7435. Facebook.
Key Personnel: Pres. & C.E.O., Stephen E. Dean.
Institution Type/Description: Aviation Museum.
Hours & Admission Prices: Mon.-Fri. 1-4, Sat.-Sun. by appointment. No charge.

HISTORIC UPSHUR MUSEUM, 119 Simpson St., Gilmer, TX 75644-2231. Tel.: 903-843-5483.
E-mail: hum1925@etex.net
Web Site: www.historicupshurmuseum.com/contact
Key Personnel: Pres., Carolyn Marshall; Vice Pres., Steve Stewart.
Institution Type/Description: History Museum.
Hours & Admission Prices: Thurs.-Fri. 10-4. Sat. 10-2. No charge; donations accepted.

LITERARY MUSEUM, 917 Madelaine St., Gilmer, TX 75644-3047. Tel.: 903-843-2282.
E-mail: english1@etex.net
Key Personnel: Contact Person, Larry W. Osborne.
Institution Type/Description: History Museum.
Hours & Admission Prices: By appointment. No charge.

Gladewater

GLADEWATER MUSEUM, 116 W. Pacific St., Gladewater, TX 75647. Mailing Address: P.O. Box 85, Gladewater, TX 75647. Tel.: 903-845-7608.
E-mail: info@gladewatermuseum.org
Web Site: gladewatermuseum.org
Key Personnel: Pres. & Dir., Elaine Roddy; Lois Reed.
Institution Type/Description: History Museum.
Hours & Admission Prices: Fri. & Sat. 10-4; other times by appointment.

Glen Rose

BARNARD'S MILL & ART MUSEUM, 307 S.W. Barnard St., P.O. Box 2537, Glen Rose, TX 76043. Tel.: 254-897-7494 & 888-346-6282. Facebook, Twitter.
E-mail: barnardsmill@barnardsmill.org
Web Site: www.barnardsmill.org
Key Personnel: Dir., Richard H. Moore.
Institution Type/Description: Art & History Museums; housed in historic Barnard's Mill built in 1860. Listed on the National Register of Historic Places.
Hours & Admission Prices: Sat. 10-5, Sun. 1-5; guided tours by appointment. No charge; donations accepted. Closed Christmas Eve & Day. ♿
Attendance: 3,000 (estimated)

CREATION EVIDENCE MUSEUM OF TEXAS, 3102 FM 205, Glen Rose, TX 76043-0309. Mailing Address: P.O. Box 309, Glen Rose, TX 76043-0309. Tel.: 254-897-3200.
E-mail: creation@creationevidence.org
Web Site: www.creationevidence.org
Key Personnel: Founder & Dir., Carl Baugh.
Institution Type/Description: Science Museum.
Hours & Admission Prices: Thurs.-Sat. 10-4. Admission $6; children 5 & under and active duty military no charge.

DINOSAUR VALLEY STATE PARK, 1629 Park Rd. 59, Glen Rose, TX 76043. Mailing Address: P.O. Box 396, Glen Rose, TX 76043-0396. Tel.: 254-897-4588 & 512-389-8900 (Reservations).
Web Site: www.tpwd.texas.gov/state-parks/dinosaur-valley
Institution Type/Description: Paleontological Site.
Hours & Admission Prices: Park: 7am-10pm. Headquarters: 8:30-4:30. Adults $7; children 12 & under no charge. ♿
Attendance: 400,000 (estimated)

DINOSAUR WORLD, 1058 Park Rd. 59, Glen Rose, TX 76043. Tel.: 254-898-1526. Facebook.
E-mail: texas@dinosaurworld.com
Web Site: www.dinosaurworld.com/dinosaur_world_glen_rose_texas/
Key Personnel: Owner, Christer Svensson.
Institution Type/Description: Natural History Museum.
Hours & Admission Prices: Mon.-Fri. 9-5, Sat. & Sun. 9-6. Daily: Adult $12.75, senior (60 and over) $10.75, child (3-12) $9.75, children (2 and under) no charge. Excavation Pass: Adult $18.95, child (3-12) $16.95.

FOSSIL RIM WILDLIFE CENTER, 2299 County Rd. 2008, Glen Rose, TX 76043. Mailing Address: 2155 County Rd. 2008, Glen Rose, TX 76043. Tel.: 254-897-2960. Fax: 254-897-3785.
E-mail: info@fossilrim.org
Web Site: www.fossilrim.org
Key Personnel: Exec. Dir., Mr. Kelley Snodgrass; C.F.O., Mr. Tom Clark.
Institution Type/Description: Wildlife Conservation Center.
Hours & Admission Prices: Winter (Nov. 1- March 10): 8:30-3:29; Rest of year (March 11-Oct. 31) 8:30-4:29. Weekday: Adults $21.95, child (3-11) $15.95; Weekend & Holidays: Adults $25.95, child (3-11) $19.95; seniors 10% off. ♿
Attendance: 135,000 (actual)

SOMERVELL COUNTY HISTORICAL MUSEUM, 101 SW Vernon St., Glen Rose, TX 76043. Mailing Address: Box 669, Glen Rose, TX 76043-0669. Tel.: 254-898-0640.
E-mail: grsloanb@gmail.com
Key Personnel: Chm. (V) & Museum Shop Mgr., Barbara Sloan.
Institution Type/Description: Historical Society Museum.
Hours & Admission Prices: Wed.-Sat. 11-4. No charge; donations accepted. Closed Thanksgiving; Christmas. ♿
Attendance: 5,000 (estimated)

Goliad

GOLIAD STATE PARK, 108 Park Rd. 6, Goliad, TX 77963-3206. Tel.: 361-645-3405. Fax: 361-645-8538.
E-mail: brenda.justice@tpwd.state.tx.us
Web Site: www.tpwd.state.tx.us
Key Personnel: Exec. Dir., Carter Smith; Supt., Brenda Justice.
Institution Type/Description: Historic Sites: 1749-1830 sites of Spanish mission Espiritu Santo de Zuniga.
Hours & Admission Prices: Daily 8-5. Adults $3, children (12 and under) no charge. Closed Christmas. &
Attendance: 150,000 (estimated)

PRESIDIO LA BAHIA, Refugio Hwy., 1 mile south of Goliad on Hwy. 183, Goliad, TX 77963. Mailing Address: P.O. Box 57, Goliad, TX 77963-0057. Tel.: 512-645-3752.
E-mail: presidiolabahia@goliad.net
Web Site: www.presidiolabahia.org
Key Personnel: Dir., Scott McMahon.
Institution Type/Description: Historic Site Museum: Spanish Fort on lower San Antonio River, part of the 1772 Presidio Line, scene of Goliad Massacre.
Hours & Admission Prices: Daily 9-4:45. Adults $4, senior citizens $3.50, children (6-12) $1; children (5 and under) & members no charge. Closed major holidays. &
Attendance: 27,000 (actual)

Gonzales

GONZALES MEMORIAL MUSEUM, 414 Smith, Gonzales, TX 78629. Tel.: 830-672-6350.
E-mail: curator@cityofgonzales.org
Web Site: www.cityofgonzales.org
Key Personnel: Cur., Gary Schurig.
Institution Type/Description: History Museum.
Hours & Admission Prices: Mon.-Sat. 10-5, Sun. 1-5. No charge; donations accepted. Closed Christmas. &
Attendance: 7,000 (actual)

Graham

OLD POST OFFICE MUSEUM & ART CENTER, 510 Third St., Graham, TX 76450. Tel.: 940-549-1470. Facebook.
E-mail: opomac@sbcglobal.net
Web Site: www.opomac.net
Key Personnel: Dir., Lynsey Browning.
Institution Type/Description: Historic Building & Art Center: housed in a former U.S. Post Office; built in 1937. Listed on the National Register of Historic Places.
Hours & Admission Prices: Wed.-Fri. 9-4, Sat. 10-3. No charge, donations accepted.

ROBERT E. RICHESON MEMORIAL MUSEUM, 1810 4th St., Graham, TX 76450. Tel.: 940-549-0401.
E-mail: cvb@grahamtexas.org
Web Site: www.visitgrahamtexas.com
Institution Type/Description: History Museum.
Hours & Admission Prices: By appointment only.

Grand Saline

SALT PALACE MUSEUM, 100 W. Garland Ave., Grand Saline, TX 75140. Tel.: 903-962-5631.
E-mail: saltpalacemuseum@yahoo.com
Web Site: www.grandsalinesaltpalace.com
Institution Type/Description: History Museum.
Hours & Admission Prices: Mon.-Sat. 9-4.

Grapevine

GRAPEVINE HISTORICAL MUSEUM, 206 W. Hudgins, Grapevine, TX 76051-5351. Mailing Address: Grapevine Historical Society, P.O. Box 995, Grapevine, TX 76099-0995. Tel.: 817-410-3526.
E-mail: grapevinehistory@gmail.com
Web Site: www.grapevinehistory.org
Key Personnel: Pres., Debi Meek; Museum Opers., Randy Barton; Program & Events, Margaret Hardin; Admin. Support, Joe Ann Standlee.
Institution Type/Description: History Museum.
Hours & Admission Prices: Tues.-Sat. 10-4, Sun. 11-4. No charge. &
Attendance: 24,000 (estimated)

Greenville

AUDIE MURPHY/AMERICAN COTTON MUSEUM, INC., 600 I-30, E., Greenville, TX 75401. Mailing Address: P.O. Box 347, Greenville, TX 75403-0347. Tel.: 903-450-4502. Facebook: Audie Murphy/American Cotton Museum.
E-mail: amacm@att.net
Web Site: www.cottonmuseum.com
Key Personnel: Exec. Dir., Susan Lanning; Asst. Dir., Kristen Still.
Institution Type/Description: Cotton & History Museum.
Hours & Admission Prices: Tues.-Sat. 10-5. Adults $6, senior citizens, veterans, & college students $4, youth 6-18 $2; discounts to AAM members; children (5 and under), active military & members no charge. Closed major holidays. &
Attendance: 8,443 (actual)

Harlingen

HARLINGEN ARTS AND HERITAGE MUSEUM, 2425 Boxwood St., Harlingen, TX 78550. Tel.: 956-216-4901. Fax: 956-430-8502.
E-mail: rgvmuse@hiline.net
Web Site: hiline.net/rgvmuse
Key Personnel: Dir. of Arts & Entertainment, Joel Humphries.
Institution Type/Description: History Museum.
Hours & Admission Prices: Tues.-Sat. 10-4, Sun. 1-4. Adults $2, children $1. Closed major holidays. &
Attendance: 15,500 (estimated)

IWO JIMA MEMORIAL MUSEUM, 320 Iwo Jima Blvd., Harlingen, TX 78550. Tel.: 956-423-6006.
Key Personnel: Dir., Gloria Boling.
Institution Type/Description: Military History Museum.
Hours & Admission Prices: Mon.-Sat. 1-4, Sun. 12-4. No charge; donations accepted.
Attendance: 10,000 (estimated)

Hempstead

LIENDO PLANTATION, 38653 Wyatt Chapel Rd., Hempstead, TX 77445. Tel.: 979-826-3126. Fax: 979-826-3244.
E-mail: info@liendoplantation.com
Web Site: liendoplantation.com
Institution Type/Description: Historic House: built in 1853 by Leonard Waller Groce. Listed on the National Register of Historic Places.
Hours & Admission Prices: 1st Sat. each month by appointment. Adults $10, seniors & students $7; discounts to groups.

Henderson

THE DEPOT MUSEUM COMPLEX, 514 N. High St., Henderson, TX 75652-5912. Tel.: 903-657-4303. Facebook.
E-mail: depot@depotmuseum.com
Web Site: www.depotmuseum.com
Key Personnel: Dir., Vickie Armstrong.
Institution Type/Description: History Museum.
Hours & Admission Prices: Mon.-Fri. 9-4, Sat. 9-12. Adults $3, seniors $2, children $1, school discounts, closed major holidays. &
Attendance: 33,234 (actual)

HOWARD-DICKINSON HOUSE MUSEUM, 501 S. Main St., Henderson, TX 75654-3544. Tel.: 903-657-5906 & 5528. Fax: 903-657-9283.
E-mail: lslov@suddenlink.net
Key Personnel: Pres., Art Rousseau; Treas., Louise Slover.
Institution Type/Description: Historic House Museum: 1855 restored Howard-Dickinson House with 1905 frame-wing authentically restored & furnished.
Hours & Admission Prices: By appointment only. Adults $10, children $1. Closed major holidays. &
Attendance: 1,479 (estimated)

Henrietta

CLAY COUNTY 1890 JAIL MUSEUM, Physical/Mailing Address: 116 N. Graham St., P.O. Box 483, Henrietta, TX 76365. Tel.: 940-524-3465 & 631-9506.
E-mail: 1890jailmuseum@gmail.com
Web Site: claycountyjailmuseum.com
Key Personnel: Pres. (V), Macon Boddy; Museum Shop Mgr., Judy Garner.
Institution Type/Description: History Museum.

Hours & Admission Prices: Thurs.-Fri. 10-2, Sat. 1-4. No charge; donations accepted. Closed major holidays.
Attendance: 1,033 (estimated)

Hereford

DEAF SMITH COUNTY MUSEUM, 400 Sampson, Hereford, TX 79045. Mailing Address: P.O. Box 1007, Hereford, TX 79045-1007. Tel.: 806-363-7070.
E-mail: deafsmithmuseum@wrt.net
Web Site: www.deafsmithcountymuseum.org
Institution Type/Description: History Museum.
Hours & Admission Prices: Mon.-Fri. 10-12 & 1-5, Sat. 10-12 & 1-3; Sun. by appointment only. No charge; donations accepted. Closed major holidays.
Attendance: 3,750 (estimated)

Hidalgo

OLD HIDALGO PUMPHOUSE, 902 S. Second St., Hidalgo, TX 78557-2703. Tel.: 956-843-8686. Fax: 956-843-6519.
E-mail: aflores@cityofhidalgo.net
Web Site: cityofhidalgo.net/pumphouse.html
Formerly: Hidalgo Pumphouse Heritage and Discovery Park
Key Personnel: Site Dir., Andres A. Flores; Administrative Asst., Melissa Sanchez.
Institution Type/Description: Agriculture Museum: housed in a restored pumphouse which operated from 1909 to 1983 pumping water from the Rio Grande for agricultural irrigation.
Hours & Admission Prices: Mon.-Fri. 8-6, Sat.-Sun. 9-6. No charge, tour prices may vary. &
Attendance: 3,000 (estimated)

Hillsboro

HILL COUNTY CELL BLOCK MUSEUM, 116 N. Waco St., Hillsboro, TX 76645-2140. Mailing Address: P.O. Box 555, Hillsboro, TX 76645-0555. Tel.: 254-582-8912.
Key Personnel: Chm. (V), Joyce Hollingsworth; Dir., Richard Johnson.
Institution Type/Description: History Museum: housed in the former county jail & sheriff's family home; built in 1893. Listed on the National Register of Historic Places.
Hours & Admission Prices: Sat. 10-4; other times by appointment. No charge; donations accepted.
Attendance: 300 (estimated)

TEXAS HERITAGE MUSEUM, 112 Lamar Dr., Hillsboro, TX 76645-2711. Tel.: 254-659-7750. Fax: 254-580-9529.
E-mail: jversluis@hillcollege.edu
Web Site: www.hillcollege.edu
Key Personnel: Dir., John Versluis.
Institution Type/Description: Military History Museum.
Hours & Admission Prices: Mon.-Thurs. 8-4:30, Fri. 8-4. No charge; donations accepted. Closed national holidays except Memorial Day. &
Attendance: 6,800 (actual)

Hondo

MEDINA COUNTY MUSEUM, 2202 18th St., Hondo, TX 78861. Mailing Address: P.O. Box 98, Hondo, TX 78861. Tel.: 830-426-3037.
Key Personnel: Bd. Pres., Frances Guinn.
Institution Type/Description: History Museum.
Hours & Admission Prices: Thurs.-Sat. 10-4, Sun. 1-4.

Houston

ART CAR MUSEUM, 140 Heights Blvd., Houston, TX 77007. Tel.: 713-861-5526. Fax: 713-529-6960. Facebook.
E-mail: info@artcarmuseum.com
Web Site: artcarmuseum.com
Key Personnel: Dir., Noah Edmundson.
Institution Type/Description: Art Museum.
Hours & Admission Prices: Wed.-Sun. 11-6. No charge.
Attendance: 14,500 (estimated)

ART LEAGUE OF HOUSTON, 1953 Montrose Blvd., Houston, TX 77006-1243. Tel.: 713-523-9530. Fax: 713-523-4053. Facebook, Twitter, Instagram.
E-mail: eepi@artleaguehouston.org
Web Site: www.artleaguehouston.org

Key Personnel: Pres. Bd. Dirs., Kristen Johnson; Exec. Dir., Jennifer Ash; Treas., Charlotte Conner; Sec., Susan Quarles; Finance Mgr., Janet Grantham.
Institution Type/Description: Art Gallery.
Hours & Admission Prices: Mon.-Thur. 9-9; Fri.-Sat. 9-5. No charge. &
Attendance: 10,000 (estimated)

ASIA SOCIETY TEXAS CENTER, 1370 Southmore Blvd., Houston, TX 77004. Tel.: 713-496-9901. Facebook; Twitter.
E-mail: txcenter@asiasociety.org
Web Site: asiasociety.org/texas
Key Personnel: Pres., Bonna Kol; Exec. Asst., Sofia Pasha; Vice Pres. Finance, Sophia Wong; Sr. Vice Pres. Comm. & Mktg., Joy Partain; Vice Pres. Operations, Michael H. Gillespie; Nancy C. Allen Cur. & Dir. Exhibitions, Bridget Bray; Dir. Education, Business & Policy, Saleena Jafry; Dir. Institutional Giving, Jenni Rebecca Stephenson; Events Mgr., Charles Gonzalez.
Institution Type/Description: Art Gallery.
Hours & Admission Prices: Tues.-Fri. 11-6, Sat. & Sun. 10-6. Sarofim Gallery: nonmembers $8; children 12 & under and members no charge. Closed major holidays. &

BAYOU BEND COLLECTION AND GARDENS, 6003 Memorial Dr., Houston, TX 77007. Mailing Address: P.O. Box 6826, Houston, TX 77265-6826. Tel.: 713-639-7750. Fax: 713-639-7770. Facebook: @mfah.org.
E-mail: bayoubend@mfah.org
Web Site: www.mfah.org/bayoubend
Key Personnel: Dir., Bonnie Campbell.
Institution Type/Description: Historic House & Site.
Hours & Admission Prices: Tues.-Sat. 10-5, Sun. 1-5. Visit Website for tour options and admissions.
Attendance: 80,000 (estimated)

BEER CAN HOUSE, 222 Malone St., Houston, TX 77023. Mailing Address: c/o Orange Show Center for Visionary Art, 2402 Munger St., Houston, TX 77023. Tel.: 713-926-6368. Facebook, Twitter.
E-mail: orange@orangeshow.org
Web Site: www.beercanhouse.org
Institution Type/Description: Historic House: housed in the former home of John Milkovisch.
Hours & Admission Prices: Memorial Day-Labor Day Wed.-Sun. 12-5. Sept.-May Sat.-Sun. 12-5. Adults $5; children 12 & under no charge.

BLAFFER ART MUSEUM, UNIVERSITY OF HOUSTON, 4173 Elgin St, Houston, TX 77004. Mailing Address: University of Houston, 120 Fine Arts Building, Houston, TX 77204. Tel.: 713-743-9521. Fax: 713-743-9525. Facebook, Instagram, Twitter, Youtube.
E-mail: kveneman@uh.edu
Web Site: blafferartmuseum.org
Key Personnel: Dir. & Chief Cur., Toby Kamps; Chief Registrar & Exhibitions Mgr., Youngmin Chung; Curatorial Fellow, Tyler Blackwell; Asst. Registrar & Installation Mgr., Teresa Munisteri; Sec. Coord., Colleen Maynard; Cur. Education, Katherine Veneman.
Institution Type/Description: Contemporary Art Museum.
Hours & Admission Prices: Tues.-Sat. 10-5. No charge; donations accepted. Closed university holidays. &
Attendance: 45,000 (actual)

BUFFALO SOLDIERS NATIONAL MUSEUM, 3816 Caroline St., Houston, TX 77004-5947. Tel.: 713-942-8920. Facebook, Twitter.
E-mail: info@buffalosoldiermuseum.com
Web Site: www.buffalosoldiermuseum.com
Key Personnel: Exec. Dir., Desmond Bertrand, M.B.A., M.Ed.; Admin. Asst., Mary Green.
Institution Type/Description: Military Museum.
Hours & Admission Prices: Mon.-Fri. 10-5, Sat. 10-4. Adults $10, students, seniors and active & retired military $5; members and children 5 & under no charge. &
Attendance: 20,000 (estimated)

THE CHILDREN'S MUSEUM OF HOUSTON, 1500 Binz St., Houston, TX 77004-7112. Tel.: 713-522-1138. Fax: 713-522-5747. Facebook, Instagram, Twitter.
E-mail: info@cmhouston.org
Web Site: www.cmhouston.org
Key Personnel: Exec. Dir., Tammie Kahn; Dir. Finance, Jana Gunter; Dir. Education, Cheryl McCallum; Dir. Business Devel., Alexandra Vasquez; Dir. Devel., Tracy Golden; Dir. HR, Rita Villanueva; Dir. Public Rels. & Promotions, Henry Yau; Membership Coord., Anna Nguyen.
Institution Type/Description: Children's Museum.

Hours & Admission Prices: Mon.-Wed. & Fri.-Sat. 10-6, Sun. 12-6, Thurs. 10-8. Adults & children $12. ♿
Attendance: 815,000 (actual)

CONTEMPORARY ARTS MUSEUM HOUSTON, 5216 Montrose Blvd., Houston, TX 77006-6547. Tel.: 713-284-8250. Fax: 713-284-8275. Facebook: @theCAMH; Twitter & Instagram: @camhouston.
E-mail: info@camh.org
Web Site: camh.org
Key Personnel: Dir., Bill Arning; Chair, Jereann Chaney; Pres., Dillon A. Kyle; Vice Pres., Howard Robinson; Deputy Dir., Christina Brungardt; Dir. Education & Public Programs, Felice Cleveland; Cur., Dean Daderko; Registrar, Tim Barkley; Retail Operations Dir., Sue Pruden; Asst. Dir. Facilities & Risk Management, Michael Reed; Controller, Monica Hoffman.
Institution Type/Description: Art Museum.
Hours & Admission Prices: Tues.-Wed. & Fri. 10-7, Thurs. 10-9, Sat. 10-6, Sun. 12-6. No charge; donations accepted. Closed New Year's Day; Thanksgiving; Christmas. ♿
Attendance: 66,586 (actual)

CY TWOMBLY GALLERY, 1515 Sul Ross St., Houston, TX 77006. Mailing Address: c/o The Menil Collection, 1533 Sul Ross St., Houston, TX 77006. Tel.: 713-525-9400.
E-mail: info@menil.org
Web Site: www.menil.org
Key Personnel: Dir., Rebecca Rabinow.
Institution Type/Description: Art Gallery.
Hours & Admission Prices: Wed.-Sun. 11-7. No charge. Closed major holidays. ♿
Attendance: 30,000 (actual)

CZECH CENTER MUSEUM HOUSTON, 4920 San Jacinto St., Houston, TX 77004. Tel.: 713-528-2060. Facebook, Instagram, Twitter.
E-mail: czech@czechcenter.org
Web Site: www.czechcenter.org
Key Personnel: C.E.O., Effie Rosene; Pres. of Admin., Bill Rosene; Treas., James E. Ermis.
Institution Type/Description: Cultural History Museum.
Hours & Admission Prices: Mon.-Sat. 10-4. Adult $6; youth (13-18) $3, children (12 and under) & members no charge.

DIVERSEWORKS, 3400 Main St. Ste. 292, Houston, TX 77002. Tel.: 713-223-8346.
E-mail: info@diverseworks.org
Web Site: www.diverseworks.org
Key Personnel: Exec. Dir. & Chief Cur., Xandra Eden.
Institution Type/Description: Art Gallery.
Hours & Admission Prices: Wed.-Sat. 12-6. No charge; donations accepted.
Attendance: 20,000 (estimated)

DOWNTOWN AQUARIUM, 410 Bagby St., Houston, TX 77002. Tel.: 713-223-3474. Facebook, Instagram, Twitter.
Web Site: www.aquariumrestaurants.com
Institution Type/Description: Aquarium.
Hours & Admission Prices: Sun.-Thurs. 10-8:30, Fri. & Sat. 10-10. Adults $12.99, seniors (65 and over) $10.99, children $9.99, children (under 2) no charge.

DUNHAM BIBLE MUSEUM, Morris Cultural Arts Ctr., Houston Baptist Univ., 7502 Fondren Rd., Houston, TX 77074-3298. Tel.: 281-649-3287. Facebook, Instagram, Twitter.
E-mail: dseverance@hbu.edu
Web Site: www.hbu.edu/biblemuseum
Formerly: Bible in America Museum
Key Personnel: Dir., Dr. Diana Severance.
Institution Type/Description: Religious Museum.
Hours & Admission Prices: Mon.-Sat. 10-4; groups by appointment. No charge; donations accepted. Closed university holidays & breaks. ♿
Attendance: 6,000 (actual)

THE HEALTH MUSEUM - JOHN P. MCGOVERN MUSEUM OF HEALTH & MEDICAL SCIENCE, 1515 Hermann Dr., Houston, TX 77004-7126. Tel.: 713-521-1515. Facebook, Instagram & Twitter.
E-mail: info@thehealthmuseum.org
Web Site: www.thehealthmuseum.org
Formerly: Museum of Health & Medical Science
Key Personnel: Pres. & C.E.O., John Arcidiacono; Controller, Bob Bright; Sr. Dir. HR, Mary Heartlein; Sr. Dir., Guest Experience, Becky Seabrook; Sr. Dir., Institutional Advancement, Kathryn Straw.
Institution Type/Description: Health Museum.
Hours & Admission Prices: Mon.-Wed. & Fri.-Sat. 9-5, Thurs. 9-7, Sun. 12-5. Adults $10, children 3-12 & seniors 65 and over $8, members & children 2 and under no charge. ♿
Attendance: 141,000 (actual)

THE HERITAGE SOCIETY, 1100 Bagby St., Houston, TX 77002-2504. Tel.: 713-655-1912. Fax: 713-655-9249. Facebook, Instagram, Twitter.
E-mail: info@heritagesociety.org
Web Site: www.heritagesociety.org
Key Personnel: Exec. Dir., Alison Ayres Bell; Pres., Jim Furr; Buildings Cur., Emily Ardoin; Collections Cur., Ginger Berni; Finance Dir., Emison Lewis; Registrar, David Thomas; Program Dir., Mike Vance.
Institution Type/Description: History Museum & Historic House Site.
Hours & Admission Prices: Tues.-Sat. 10-4. Historic Buildings Tours: Tues.-Sat. 10, 11:30, 1 & 2:30. Admission: adults $5; children 5-18 $2; Tours: Adults $15, senior citizens 65 & up $12, children 6-18 $6; discounts to members, Time Travelers, AAM, ICOM, AAA & TAM members; children 5 & under and members no charge. Closed major holidays. ♿
Attendance: 204,423 (actual)

HOLOCAUST MUSEUM HOUSTON, Physical/Mailing Address: Morgan Family Center, 9220 Kirby, Ste. 100, Houston, TX 77054-9220. Tel.: 713-942-8000. Fax: 713-942-7953. Facebook, Twitter.
E-mail: info@hmh.org
Web Site: www.hmh.org
Key Personnel: C.E.O., Kelly J. Zuniga, Ed.D.; Chm. (V), Benjamin Warren; Dir. Collections & Exhibitions, Carol Manley; Dir. Devel., Connie Boyd; Dir. Education, Mary Lee Webeck, Ph.D.; C.F.O., Kristin Albers Lamm, C.P.A.; Chief Mktg. Officer, Robin Cavanaugh; Mng. Dir./Dir. Public Programs, Tamara Savage; Dir. Visitor & Volunteer Svcs., Catherine Caverly; Security Officer & Maintenance Supvr., Roger Henderson.
Institution Type/Description: History Museum.
Hours & Admission Prices: Mon.-Fri. 9-5, Sat. 10-5, Sun. 12-5. Adults $12, AARP members & active-duty military $8; children, students & members no charge. Closed New Year's Day; 1st day of Rosh Hashana; Yom Kippur; Thanksgiving; Christmas. ♿
Attendance: 150,000 (actual)

HOUSTON ARBORETUM & NATURE CENTER, 4501 Woodway Dr., Houston, TX 77024-7708. Tel.: 713-681-8433. Fax: 713-681-1191. Facebook, Instagram, Twitter.
E-mail: arbor@houstonarboretum.org
Web Site: houstonarboretum.org
Key Personnel: Pres., Chad Hesters; Vice Pres., August Bering, V; Vice Pres., Nigel Curlet; Vice Pres., Ruth Flournoy; Vice Pres., Dr. Cullen Geiselman.
Institution Type/Description: Arboretum & Nature Center.
Hours & Admission Prices: Grounds & Trails: March to Sept. daily 7-7; Oct. to Feb. daily 7-6. Discovery Room: Tues.-Fri. 10-4. Closed Easter; Memorial Day; Independence Day; Labor Day Thanksgiving; Christmas Eve & Day; New Year's Eve.
Attendance: 200,000 (estimated)

HOUSTON BICYCLE MUSEUM, 1313 Binz St., Houston, TX 77004. Tel.: 713-459-4669. Facebook, Instagram, Twitter.
E-mail: info@houstonbicyclemuseum.org
Web Site: houstonbicyclemuseum.org
Key Personnel: Founder & Owner, Joy Boone.
Institution Type/Description: Bicycle Museum.
Hours & Admission Prices: Tues.-Wed. 10-5, Thurs. 10-7, Fri.-Sat. 10-6, Sun. 1-5. Adults $9; children 10 & under no charge.

HOUSTON CENTER FOR CONTEMPORARY CRAFT, 4848 Main St., Houston, TX 77002-9718. Tel.: 713-529-4848. Fax: 713-529-1288. Facebook, Instagram, Twitter.
E-mail: mheadrick@crafthouston.org
Web Site: www.crafthouston.org
Key Personnel: Exec. Dir., Perry Allen Price; Pres. Bd., Phyllis Childress; Deputy Dir., Mary Headrick; Special Projects Dir., Suzanne Sippel; Mktg. Dir., Jenny Lynn Weitz; Education Dir., Natalie Svacina; Curator, Kathryn Hall.
Institution Type/Description: Craft Museum.
Hours & Admission Prices: Wed.-Sat. 10-5, Sun. 12 to 5. No charge; donations accepted. Closed major holidays.
Attendance: 20,000 (actual)

HOUSTON CENTER FOR PHOTOGRAPHY, 1441 W. Alabama, Houston, TX 77006-4103. Tel.: 713-529-4755. Fax: 713-529-9248.
E-mail: info@hcponline.org
Web Site: www.hcponline.org
Key Personnel: Exec. Dir., Ashlyn Davis.
Institution Type/Description: Art Gallery.
Hours & Admission Prices: Wed.-Thurs. 11-9, Fri. 11-5, Sat.-Sun. 11-7. No charge; donations accepted. Closed New Year's Day; Thanksgiving & day after; Christmas; banking holidays. &
Attendance: 24,015 (actual)

HOUSTON FIRE MUSEUM, 2403 Milam St., Houston, TX 77006-2359. Tel.: 713-524-2526. Fax: 713-520-7566. Facebook.
E-mail: hfmi@houstonfiremuseum.org
Web Site: www.houstonfiremuseum.org
Key Personnel: Dir., Marina Shimer; Retail Mgr., Abigail Falk; Curriculum Devel. Lead, Denise Gomez; Designer & Print Production Artist, Julianne James; Pres., Tom McDonald.
Institution Type/Description: Fire-Fighting Museum: housed in 1899 Fire Station No. 7, active until 1969.
Hours & Admission Prices: Tues.-Sat. 10-4. Adults $5, senior citizens 65 & up $4, children 2-12 $3; discounts to AAM, ICOM & Texas Association of Museums members; members & children under 2 no charge. Closed holidays.
Attendance: 18,379 (actual)

HOUSTON MARITIME MUSEUM, 2311 Canal St, Ste. 100, Houston, TX 77030-3210. Tel.: 713-225-1688. Facebook, Instagram, Twitter.
E-mail: info@houstonmaritime.org
Web Site: www.houstonmaritime.org
Key Personnel: Dir., Leslie Bowlin; Pres. & C.E.O., Robert Fry; Asst. Museum Dir., Jenny Podoloff; Cur., Nathan Kyllonen; Social Media Asst., Natalia Kapacinskas; Curatorial Asst., Nathan Kyllonen.
Institution Type/Description: Maritime Museum.
Hours & Admission Prices: Tues.-Sat. 9-5. Admission $8, children 3-12 and seniors 65 & up $5; members, children under 3, active-duty military & veterans no charge. Closed New Year's Day; Independence Day; Thanksgiving; Christmas Eve & Day. &
Attendance: 3,000 (estimated)

HOUSTON MUSEUM OF NATURAL SCIENCE, 5555 Hermann Park Dr., Houston, TX 77030-1749. Tel.: 713-639-4629. Fax: 713-523-4125. Facebook, Instagram, Twitter.
E-mail: webmaster@hmns.org
Web Site: www.hmns.org
Key Personnel: Pres., Joel A. Bartsch; C.F.O., Stephen Sachnik; Vice Pres. Collections, Lisa Rebori; Vice Pres. Devel. & Membership, Barbara Hawthorn; Vice Pres. Astronomy & Physics, Dr. Carolyn Sumners; Vice Pres. Museum Facilities & Security, Oscar Ruiz; Vice Pres. Mktg. & Communications, Latha Thomas; Vice Pres. Film Programming & Distribution, Charlotte Brohi; Vice Pres. Youth Education, Nicole Temple; Dir. Adult Education, Amy Potts; Dir. Cockrell Butterfly Center, Nancy Greig; Dir. Membership, Shannon Jeffcoat; Dir. Exhibit Design & Graphics, Rodney Gentry; Dir. Exhibit Production & Maintenance, Victor Ticas; Dir. George Observatory, Joshua Rohn; Dir. Retail Opers., Becky Clark; Dir. & Chief Devel. Officer, HMNS at Sugar Land, Adrienne Barker; Dir. Visitor Services, Brad Levy; Dir. Volunteers, Lynn Wisda; Dir. Youth Education Sales, Amanda Norris.
Institution Type/Description: Natural Science Museum.
Hours & Admission Prices: HMNS at Hermann Park: daily 9-5, call for additional & holiday hours. Adults (12 & up) $25, seniors 62 & up, children 3-11 & college students w/ID $15; discounts for military w/ID & groups; children 2 & under and members no charge. Planetarium: daily 10-4. Adults $9, seniors 62 & up, children 3-11 & college students w/ID $7; discounts for military w/ID, groups & members. Butterfly Center: daily 9-5. Adults $9, seniors, children & college students w/ID $8; discounts for military w/ID, groups & members. Wortham Giant Screen Theatre: daily 10-4. Adults $12, seniors, children, seniors 62 & up & college students w/ID $10; discounts for military w/ID, groups & members. Special Exhibits: call for pricing. &
Attendance: 2,700,000 (actual)

HOUSTON POLICE MUSEUM, 1200 Travis, Houston, TX 77002. Tel.: 832-394-2360.
E-mail: hpd.museum@houstonpolice.org
Web Site: www.houstontx.gov/police/museum
Key Personnel: Dir., James Chapman.
Institution Type/Description: Police History Museum: located at the Houston Police Academy.
Hours & Admission Prices: Mon.-Fri. 9-9; guided tours by appointment. No charge. Closed city holidays.

HOUSTON ZOO, INC., 6200 Hermann Park Dr., Houston, TX 77030-1603. Mailing Address: 1513 Cambridge St., Houston, TX 77030-1603. Tel.: 713-533-6500. Facebook, Instagram, Twitter.
E-mail: education@houstonzoo.org
Web Site: www.houstonzoo.org
Formerly: Houston Zoological Gardens
Key Personnel: C.E.O., Lee Ehmke; Chm. Bd. Dirs., Stacy Methvin; C.F.O., Leslie Forestier; C.O.O., Sheryl Kolainski; Vice Pres. Animal Operations, Lisa Marie Avendano; Vice Pres. Wildlife Conservation, Peter Riger; Vice Pres. Devel., Nick Espinosa; Vice Pres. HR, Kristin Finney.
Institution Type/Description: Zoo.
Hours & Admission Prices: Winter: daily 9-6; Summer: daily 9-7. Adults 12-64 $19, children 2-11 $15, senior citizens 65 & over $12.50; discounts to school groups & military; children one & under and members no charge. Closed Christmas. &
Attendance: 2,155,095 (actual)

LAWNDALE ART CENTER, 4912 Main St., Houston, TX 77002. Tel.: 713-528-5858. Facebook, Instagram, Twitter.
E-mail: askus@lawndaleartcenter.org
Web Site: www.lawndaleartcenter.or
Key Personnel: Exec. Dir., Stephanie Mitchell; Public Program Coord., Emily Fens; Controller, Lisa Gertsch; Asst. Dir., Lauren Lohman.
Institution Type/Description: Contemporary Art Space.
Hours & Admission Prices: Wed.-Fri. 12-6, Sat. 11-5, Sun. 12 to 3. No charge. &
Attendance: 20,000 (estimated)

LONE STAR FLIGHT MUSEUM/TEXAS AVIATION HALL OF FAME, 11551 Aerospace Ave., Houston, TX 77034. Tel.: 346-708-2517.
E-mail: info@lonestarflight.org
Web Site: www.lsfm.org
Key Personnel: Pres. & C.E.O., Douglas Owens; C.O.O., Chris Richardson; C.M.O., Katie Jackman; C.F.O., Martha Mayberry Hoffman; Vice Pres. of Devel., Barabara Walker; Cur., Stewart W. Bailey; Dir. of Education & Outreach, Kenneth Morris.
Institution Type/Description: Aviation History & STEM Learning Facility.
Hours & Admission Prices: Memorial Day to Labor Day daily 9-5. Adults $12.95, youth (12-17) & senior citizens (65 & up) $10.95, children 4-11 $7.95; discounts to groups of 10 or more, active & retired military, veterans & for online ticket purchase; children under 4 no charge. Closed Thanksgiving; Christmas. &
Attendance: 75,000 (estimated)

THE MENIL COLLECTION, 1533 Sul Ross St., Houston, TX 77006. Tel.: 713-525-9400. Facebook, Instagram, Twitter.
E-mail: info@menil.org
Web Site: www.menil.org
Key Personnel: Chair, Janet M. Hobby; Pres., Douglas L. Lawing; Dir., Rebecca Rabinow; Deputy Dir & C.O.O., Sheryl Kolasinski; C.F.O., Michael Nicknish; Cur. Modern & Contemporary Art, Natalie Dupêcher; Chief Conservator, Brad Epley; Dir. Advancement, Karen Sumner; IT Mgr., Buck Bakke; Head Librarian, Lauren Gottlieb-Miller; Dir. Publishing, Joseph N. Newland; Dir. Facilities, Steve McConathy; Bookstore Mgr., Paul Forsythe.
Institution Type/Description: Art Museum.
Hours & Admission Prices: Wed.-Sun. 11-7. No charge; donations accepted. Closed major holidays. &
Attendance: 180,500 (actual)

MICHAEL E. DEBAKEY LIBRARY AND MUSEUM, Baylor College of Medicine, One Baylor Plaza, Houston, TX 77030-3411. Tel.: 713-798-4710.
E-mail: loriw@bcm.edu
Web Site: www.bcm.edu
Key Personnel: Cur., JoAnn Pospisil.
Institution Type/Description: Medical Museum.
Hours & Admission Prices: Mon.-Fri. 9-5. No charge. Closed holidays.

MOODY CENTER FOR THE ARTS AT RICE UNIVERSITY, 6100 Main St., Houston, TX 77005-1892. Tel.: 713-348-2787.
E-mail: moodyinfo@rice.edu
Web Site: moody.rice.edu
Formerly: Rice Gallery
Key Personnel: Exec. Dir., Alison Weaver; Chief Cur., Kimberly Davenport; Dir. of Devel., Katy Goodman; Dir. Mktg. and Communications, Connie McAllister.
Institution Type/Description: Art Gallery.
Hours & Admission Prices: Tues.-Sat. 10-5. No charge; donations accepted. Closed university holidays; between exhibits. &

MUSEUM OF AMERICAN ARCHITECTURE AND DECORATIVE ARTS, Houston Baptist University, 7502 Fondren Rd., Houston, TX 77074-3298. Tel.: 281-649-3997. Facebook.
E-mail: ssnoddy@hbu.edu
Web Site: www.hbu.edu
Key Personnel: Interim Dir., Suzy Snoddy.
Institution Type/Description: Social History & Doll Museum.
Hours & Admission Prices: Mon.-Sat. 10-4. Closed university holidays. &
Attendance: 7,000 (estimated)

THE MUSEUM OF FINE ARTS, HOUSTON, 1001 Bissonnet, Houston, TX 77005-1896. Tel.: 713-639-7300. Facebook, Twitter.
E-mail: guestservices@mfah.org
Web Site: www.mfah.org
Key Personnel: Dir., Gary Tinterow.
Institution Type/Description: Art Museum.
Hours & Admission Prices: Wed. 11-5, Thurs. 11-9, Fri.-Sat. 11-6, Sun. 12:30-6. Adults $19, seniors $16, youth 3-18 & college students w/ID $12; discounts to AAM & ICOM members; children, members, military, & Thurs. no charge. Closed Thanksgiving; Christmas Eve & Day. &

THE MUSEUM OF SOUTHERN HISTORY, Cultural Arts Center, Houston Baptist Univ., 7502 Fondren Rd., Houston, TX 77074-3298. Tel.: 281-649-3997. Facebook.
E-mail: mlbrown@hbu.edu
Web Site: www.hbu.edu
Key Personnel: Dir., Maggie Brown.
Institution Type/Description: Regional History Museum.
Hours & Admission Prices: Mon.-Sat. 10-4. Closed major holidays. &
Attendance: 7,500 (actual)

THE NATIONAL MUSEUM OF FUNERAL HISTORY, 415 Barren Springs Dr., Houston, TX 77090-5918. Tel.: 281-876-3063. Facebook, Twitter.
E-mail: contact@nmfh.org
Web Site: nmfh.org
Formerly: American Funeral Service Museum; Museum of Funeral History
Key Personnel: Founder & Chm. Emeritus, R. L. Waltrip; Chm., Robert M. Boetticher, Sr.; Pres., Genevieve Keeney; Dir., Lucy Gonzalez; Gift Shop Mgr., Ruby Rodriguez; Cremation Historian, Jason Engler; Museum Consultant, John Herzig.
Institution Type/Description: History Museum.
Hours & Admission Prices: Mon.-Fri. 10-4, Sat. 10-5, Sun. 12-5. Adults $10, veterans & senior citizens $9, children 6-11 $7; discount to groups; children 5 & under no charge. Closed New Year's Day; Easter; Thanksgiving; Christmas. &
Attendance: 7,000 (actual)

1940 AIR TERMINAL MUSEUM, 8325 Travelair St., Houston, TX 77061-4716. Tel.: 713-454-1940. Fax: 713-454-1930. Facebook: @1940atm.
E-mail: info@1940airterminal.org
Web Site: www.1940airterminal.org
Key Personnel: Mng. Dir., Amy Rogers.
Institution Type/Description: Aviation History Museum.
Hours & Admission Prices: Tues.-Sat. 10-5, Sun. 1-5. Adults $5, children $2; members, military, law enforcement, firefighters & their families no charge.
Attendance: 3,000 (estimated)

THE PRINTING MUSEUM, 1324 W. Clay, Houston, TX 77019-4036. Tel.: 713-522-4652. Fax: 713-522-5694. Facebook, Instagram, Twitter.
E-mail: info@printingmuseum.org
Web Site: printingmuseum.org
Formerly: The Museum of Printing History
Key Personnel: Exec. Dir., Jennifer C. Pearson; Chm. Bd., John Earles; Artist-in-Residence, Charles Criner.
Institution Type/Description: History & Art Museum.
Hours & Admission Prices: Wed.-Sat. 10-4. General admission $5; Guided tour prices: adults 13 and over $10, retired 55 and over, children 7-12, college students, active military and veterans $8; members $5. Closed major holidays. &
Attendance: 25,000 (estimated)

ROTHKO CHAPEL, 3900 Yupon St., Houston, TX 77006. Tel.: 713-524-9839. Facebook, Instagram, Twitter.
E-mail: info@rothkochapel.org
Web Site: www.rothkochapel.org
Key Personnel: Exec. Dir., David Leslie; Chair, Michael Piana; Dir. Programs & Engagement, Ashley Clemmer; Dir. Operations, Alison Pruitt; Dir. Advancement, Thuy M. Tran; Kim Ballesteros; Visitor Svcs. Coord., Caitlin

Ferrell; Volunteer & Program Coord., Kelly Johnson; Office Mgr., Chiquita Jones.
Institution Type/Description: Religious, Art & Architecture Museum.
Hours & Admission Prices: Daily 10-6; groups by appointment. No charge; donations accepted. &
Attendance: 84,542 (actual)

SHELDON LAKE STATE PARK & ENVIRONMENTAL LEARNING CENTER, 14140 Garrett Rd., Houston, TX 77044. Tel.: 281-456-2800. Facebook, Twitter.
E-mail: kelley.morris@tpwd.texas.gov
Web Site: tpwd.texas.gov/state-parks/sheldon-lake
Key Personnel: Park Supt., Kelley Morris.
Institution Type/Description: Science Museum.
Hours & Admission Prices: Park: daily 8-5; Office: Mon.-Fri. 8-5. No charge.

SPACE CENTER HOUSTON, 1601 NASA Pkwy., Houston, TX 77058-3199. Tel.: 281-244-2100. Facebook, Instagram, Twitter.
E-mail: schinfo@spacecenter.org
Web Site: spacecenter.org
Key Personnel: C.E.O., William T. Harris; Chair, Lon Miller; C.O.O., Tracy Lamm; Vice Pres. of Communications & External Relations, Gayden Cooper; Vice Pres. of Devel., Kim Parker; Vice Pres. of Education, Daniel Newmyer; Vice Pres. of Finance, Janet Brown.
Institution Type/Description: Space Museum.
Hours & Admission Prices: See website for hours. Adults $29.95, seniors $27.95, children 4-11 $24.95; discounts to active military & AAA; children under 4 no charge. Closed Christmas. &
Attendance: 1,000,000 (actual)

UNIVERSITY MUSEUM AT TEXAS SOUTHERN UNIVERSITY, 3100 Cleburne Ave., Houston, TX 77004. Tel.: 713-313-1164. Fax: 713-313-7342. Facebook, Instagram, Twitter.
E-mail: Bonita.Cutliff@tsu.edu
Web Site: www.umusetsu.org
Key Personnel: Dir., Dr. Alvia J. Wardlaw; Public Rels., Community Liaison & Graphic Design, Bonita Cutliff; Facilities Mgr. & Exhibition Coord., Samuel Blesson; Sr. Admin. Asst. & Volunteer Coord., Leola Marshall; Special Events & Accounts Specialist, Chrystal Robinson Davis.
Institution Type/Description: African American Art Museum.
Hours & Admission Prices: Tues.-Fri. 10-5, Sat.-Sun. 12-5. &

VIETNAM WAR FLIGHT MUSEUM, 8501 Telephone Rd., Houston, TX 77061. Tel.: 713-213-8454.
E-mail: resharpejr@aol.com
Web Site: www.vietnamwarflight.com
Formerly: Marine Aviation Museum
Institution Type/Description: Military History Museum.
Hours & Admission Prices: Call for hours. &

Hubbard

PELHAM COMMUNITY HISTORY MUSEUM, 22535 FM 744 Pelham Rd., Hubbard, TX 76648. Tel.: 254-678-1850. Fax: 254-678-1850.
E-mail: info@pelham-museum.org
Institution Type/Description: History Museum: housed in the former Pelham School; built in 1890.
Hours & Admission Prices: By appointment only. No charge.

Humble

HUMBLE MUSEUM, 219 E. Main St., Humble, TX 77338. Tel.: 281-446-2130.
E-mail: info@humblemuseum.com
Web Site: www.humblemuseum.com
Formerly: Humble Bicentennial Museum, Inc.
Institution Type/Description: History Museum.
Hours & Admission Prices: Closed until further notice. &
Attendance: 1,800 (estimated)

MCKAY CLINIC MEDICAL MUSEUM, 110 N. Ave. C, Humble, TX 77338. Mailing Address: c/o Humble Museum, 219 Main St., Humble, TX 77338. Tel.: 281-446-2130. Fax: 281-446-1964.
E-mail: humblemuseum@live.com
Web Site: www.humblemuseum.com
Institution Type/Description: History Museum: housed in the former clinic of Dr. McKay Sr. & Jr., used from 1938-1996.
Hours & Admission Prices: By appointment. No charge; donations accepted.

MERCER BOTANIC GARDENS, 22306 Aldine Westfield Rd., Humble, TX 77338-1071. Tel.: 713-274-4160. Fax: 713-437-8639. Facebook, Instagram, Twitter.
E-mail: mercerarboretum@hcp4.net
Web Site: www.hcp4.net/mercer
Formerly: Mercer Arboretum & Botanic Gardens
Key Personnel: Pres. (V), Maryanne Esser; Vice Pres., Catherine Powers.
Institution Type/Description: Arboretum & Botanic Gardens.
Hours & Admission Prices: Mid-March-Sept. 8-8, Oct.-Nov. 8-7:30, Nov.-Mid-March 8-5. No charge; donations accepted. Closed New Year's Day; Thanksgiving; Christmas Eve & Day.
Attendance: 200,000 (estimated)

Huntsville

H.E.A.R.T.S. VETERANS MUSEUM OF TEXAS, 463 State Hwy. 75 N., Huntsville, TX 77320-1119. Tel.: 936-295-5959.
E-mail: info@heartsmuseum.com
Web Site: www.heartsmuseum.com
Key Personnel: Exec. Dir., Tom Fordyce; Gift Shop Mgr., Teresa Lawson.
Institution Type/Description: Military History Museum.
Hours & Admission Prices: Mon.-Sat. 10-5. Adults $8, seniors $6, veterans $5, students $3; discounts to AAM, ICOM, VFW & American Legion members. Closed New Year's Day; Easter; Thanksgiving; Christmas. &
Attendance: 9,194 (actual)

SAM HOUSTON MEMORIAL MUSEUM, 1836 Sam Houston Ave., Huntsville, TX 77340. Mailing Address: Box 2057, SHSU, Huntsville, TX 77341-2057. Tel.: 936-294-1832 & 1831. Fax: 936-294-3670.
Web Site: www.samhoustonmemorialmuseum.com
Key Personnel: Dir., Mac Woodward; Cur. Collections, Michael Sproat; Cur. Exhibits, Casey Roon; Cur. Education, Cathy DeYoung; Registrar, Sandra Rogers; Coord. Mktg. & Museum Shop Mgr., Megan Buro; Administrative Asst., JoAnn Purvis.
Institution Type/Description: History Museum: 15-acre historical site.
Hours & Admission Prices: Tues.-Sat. 9-4:30, Sun. 12-4:30. Adults $5, seniors 65 & over $4, & children 6-18 $3; members no charge. Closed holidays. &
Attendance: 50,000 (estimated)

TEXAS PRISON MUSEUM, 491 State Hwy. 75 N., Huntsville, TX 77320-1119. Tel.: 936-295-2155. Fax: 936-295-0205. Facebook.
E-mail: david.stacks@txprisonmuseum.org
Web Site: www.txprisonmuseum.org
Key Personnel: Dir., David Stacks; Museum Shop Mgr., Riley Tilly; Cur., Joni White.
Institution Type/Description: Prison Museum.
Hours & Admission Prices: Mon.-Sat. 10-5, Sun. 12-5. Adults $7, seniors $5, children 6-17 $4; discounts to groups, active military, first responders & TDCJ employees; children under 6 no charge. &
Attendance: 33,000 (actual)

Iraan

ALLEY OOP MUSEUM & RV PARK, 9261 Alley Oop Lane, Iraan, TX 79744. Mailing Address: 501 W. 6th St., P.O. Box 153, Iraan, TX 79744. Tel.: 432-639-2301.
E-mail: iraanchamber@yahoo.com
Formerly: Iraan Museum
Key Personnel: Bd. Chair, Ellen Crossland.
Institution Type/Description: Archaeological & Historic Museum: located on what was once the San Antonio-San Diego Stage Line.
Hours & Admission Prices: Thurs.-Sun. 1-5. No charge &
Attendance: 800 (estimated)

Irving

IRVING ARTS CENTER, 3333 N. MacArthur Blvd., Ste. 300, Irving, TX 75062-4497. Tel.: 972-252-7558 & 2787. Fax: 972-570-4962. Facebook, Instagram, Twitter.
E-mail: minman@cityofirving.org
Web Site: www.irvingartscenter.com
Key Personnel: Exec. Dir., Todd Eric Hawkins; Chair, Judy Pierson.
Institution Type/Description: Art Museum & Center.
Hours & Admission Prices: Mon.-Wed. & Fri. 9-5, Thurs. 9-8, Sat. 10-5, Sun. 1-5. No charge. Closed New Year's Day; Thanksgiving; Christmas. &
Attendance: 48,000 (estimated)

IRVING HERITAGE HOUSE, 303 S. O'Connor, Irving, TX 75060-2949. Mailing Address: P.O. Box 171572, Irving, TX 75017-1572. Tel.: 972-252-3838. Facebook, Instagram, Twitter.
E-mail: irvingheritagesociety@yahoo.com
Web Site: www.irvingheritage.com
Key Personnel: Pres., Lea Bailey.
Institution Type/Description: Historic House Museum: housed in the former home of C.P. Schulze, brother of co-founder of Irving; built in 1912. A Texas State Historical Landmark.
Hours & Admission Prices: March-Dec. 1st Sun. each month 3pm-5pm. No charge; donations accepted.
Attendance: 385 (estimated)

THE NATIONAL MUSEUM OF COMMUNICATIONS, Physical/Mailing Address: 6305 N. O'Connor Rd. #123, Irving, TX 75039. Tel.: 972-869-7762.
E-mail: billbragg@mail.com
Web Site: www.yesterdayusa.com
Key Personnel: Founder & Exec. Cur., William J. Bragg; Exec. Producer, Ruth Bragg.
Institution Type/Description: Communications Museum.
Hours & Admission Prices: Call for information on hours. &
Attendance: 70,000 (estimated)

Jacksboro

FORT RICHARDSON STATE HISTORICAL PARK, 228 State Park Rd. 61, Jacksboro, TX 76458. Tel.: 940-567-3506. Fax: 940-567-5488.
Web Site: www.tpwd.texas.gov/state-parks/fort-richardson
Institution Type/Description: Park Museum: located on the site of 1867 Old Cavalry Fort.
Hours & Admission Prices: Open daily no gate. Adults $3; children under 12 no charge. Closed Christmas. &
Attendance: 65,000 (actual)

JACK COUNTY MUSEUM, 241 W. Belknap, Jacksboro, TX 76458. Tel.: 940-567-5410. Facebook.
E-mail: info@jackcountymuseum.com
Institution Type/Description: History Museum: housed in the former home of Mr. & Mrs. Stanley Cooper; built in 1882.
Hours & Admission Prices: Thurs.-Sat. 11-4; other times by appointment. No charge; donations accepted. &

Jefferson

EXCELSIOR HOUSE, 211 W. Austin St., Jefferson, TX 75657-2245. Tel.: 903-665-2513. Facebook, Instagram, Twitter.
E-mail: jgoulds@aol.com
Web Site: www.theexcelsiorhouse.com
Institution Type/Description: Historic Hotel.
Hours & Admission Prices: Daily 7-9. Adults $4; children under 10 no charge. Closed Christmas Eve & Day.

JEFFERSON HISTORICAL SOCIETY AND MUSEUM, 223 W. Austin, Jefferson, TX 75657-2253. Tel.: 903-665-2775.
E-mail: jeffersonmuseum@yahoo.com
Web Site: www.jeffersonmuseum.com
Institution Type/Description: Historical Society Museum: housed in 1888 old federal building.
Hours & Admission Prices: Daily 9:30-4:30. Adults 18-61 $7, senior over 62 $5, teens 13-17 $4, youth 6-12 $3; discounts to student groups; children under 5, military & veterans no charge. Closed New Year's Eve; Easter; Thanksgiving; Christmas Eve & Day.
Attendance: 19,500 (estimated)

Johnson City

THE EXOTIC RESORT ZOO, 235 Zoo Trail, Johnson City, TX 78636. Tel.: 830-868-4357. Fax: 830-868-7586. Facebook, Instagram.
E-mail: contact@zooexotics.com
Web Site: www.zooexotics.com
Institution Type/Description: Zoo.
Hours & Admission Prices: Daily 9-6. Adults $15.95, seniors $14.95, children 2-12 $13.95, military discount.

LYNDON B. JOHNSON NATIONAL HISTORICAL PARK, 100 Ladybird Lane, Johnson City, TX 78636. Mailing Address: P.O. Box 329, Johnson City, TX 78636-0329. Tel.: 830-868-7128. Fax: 830-868-0810 & 7863.
E-mail: lyjo_superintendent@nps.gov
Web Site: www.nps.gov/lyjo
Key Personnel: Supt., Russ Whitlock; Volunteer Coord., Elizabeth Lindig.
Institution Type/Description: Historic Site and Museum: 1901 Lyndon B. Johnson boyhood home, Johnson City, restored 1973-1974; 1867 Johnson Settlement, Johnson City, restored 1972-1974; 1888 Lyndon B. Johnson Birthplace, Stonewall, reconstructed 1964; Johnson Family Cemetery; 1894 Johnson Ranch, Stonewall.
Hours & Admission Prices: Visitor Center: daily 8-5. Johnson City District: daily 9-5. No charge. Minimal charge. Closed New Year's Day; Thanksgiving; Christmas. &
Attendance: 98,200 (actual)

Katy

JOHNNY NELSON KATY HERITAGE MUSEUM, 6002 George Bush Dr., Katy, TX 77493. Tel.: 281-574-8618.
Key Personnel: Dir. of Tourism, Kayce Reina.
Institution Type/Description: History Museum.
Hours & Admission Prices: Thurs.-Sun. 11-5. No charge.

KATY VETERANS MEMORIAL MUSEUM, 6206 George Bush Dr., Katy, TX 77493-1806. Tel.: 281-391-8387.
Web Site: www.museumsusa.org/museums/info/15789
Key Personnel: Dir. of Tourism, Kayce Reina.
Institution Type/Description: Military History & Memorial Museum.
Hours & Admission Prices: Mon.-Fri. 9-4. No charge.

Kerrville

THE MUSEUM OF WESTERN ART, 1550 Bandera Hwy., Kerrville, TX 78028-9547. Mailing Address: P.O. Box 294300, Kerrville, TX 78029-4300. Tel.: 830-896-2553. Fax: 830-257-5206. Facebook, Instagram, Twitter.
E-mail: sturnham@mowa.tx.com
Web Site: www.museumofwesternart.com
Formerly: National Center for American Western Art
Key Personnel: Chm. Bd., Pres. & C.E.O., Melissa Hoelscher; Dir., Stephanie Turnham.
Institution Type/Description: Art Museum.
Hours & Admission Prices: Tues.-Sat. 10-4. Adults $7, children 9-17 $5; discounts to groups; children 8 & under and members no charge. Closed New Year's Day; Easter; Memorial Day; Labor Day; Thanksgiving; Christmas Eve & Day. &
Attendance: 15,000 (estimated)

RIVERSIDE NATURE CENTER, 150 Francisco Lemos St., Kerrville, TX 78028-5211. Tel.: 830-257-4837. Fax: 830-257-4837. Facebook, Instagram.
E-mail: office@riversidenaturecenter.org
Web Site: www.riversidenaturecenter.org
Key Personnel: Exec. Dir., Becky Etzler; Exec. Asst., Lydia Jetson; Naturalist, Susan M. Sander; Operations Mgr., Jeanette Watson; Building & Grounds Asst., Matthew Thurlow.
Institution Type/Description: Herbarium.
Hours & Admission Prices: Mon.-Sat. 10-6. No charge. &
Attendance: 6,500 (estimated)

SCHREINER MANSION - HISTORICAL SITE AND EDUCATION CENTER, 912 Guadalupe St., Kerrville, TX 78028. Mailing Address: P.O. Box 291276, Kerrville, TX 78029. Tel.: 830-895-5222.
E-mail: info@caillouxfoundation.org
Web Site: www.caillouxfoundation.org
Formerly: The Hill Country Museum
Key Personnel: Exec. Dir., Sandra Cailloux.
Institution Type/Description: Historic House: 1870s home of Capt. Charles Schreiner.
Hours & Admission Prices: Closed for renovation.
Attendance: 10,600 (estimated)

Kilgore

EAST TEXAS OIL MUSEUM AT KILGORE COLLEGE, 1301 S. Henderson Blvd., Kilgore, TX 75662. Tel.: 903-983-8295. Fax: 903-983-8659.

E-mail: info@easttexasoilmuseum.com
Institution Type/Description: Oil Museum.
Hours & Admission Prices: April-Sept. Tues.-Sat. 9-5, Sun. 2-5; Oct.-March Tues.-Sat. 9-4, Sun. 2-5; call for special schedule Dec. 20-31. Adults $8, children 3-11 $5. Closed Easter; Thanksgiving; Christmas. &
Attendance: 40,000 (estimated)

Kingsbury

PIONEER FLIGHT MUSEUM, 190 Pershing Ln., Kingsbury, TX 78638. Tel.: 830-639-4162.
E-mail: info@pioneerflightmuseum.org
Web Site: pioneerflightmuseum.org
Key Personnel: Office Mgr., Charlotte Parker; Webmaster, Roger Ritter.
Institution Type/Description: Flight Museum.
Hours & Admission Prices: Mon.-Sat. 9-2. No charge. Closed New Year's Day, Memorial Day, Independence Day, Labor Day, Thanksgiving, Christmas.

Kingsville

JOHN E. CONNER MUSEUM, Texas A&M University-Kingsville, 905 W. Santa Gertrudis St., Kingsville, TX 78363. Tel.: 361-593-2810.
E-mail: connermuseum@tamuk.edu
Web Site: www.tamuk.edu/artsci/museum
Key Personnel: Dir., Jonathan Plant; Museum Cur., Ralph Cuevas; Educator, Sandra Allen; Administrative Asst., Cynthia F. Villalon.
Institution Type/Description: General Museum.
Hours & Admission Prices: Mon.-Fri. 8-5, Sat. 10-4. No charge. &
Attendance: 20,000 (estimated)

KING RANCH MUSEUM, 405 N. 6th St., Kingsville, TX 78363. Tel.: 361-595-1881.
E-mail: museum@king-ranch.com
Web Site: king-ranch.com/museum
Institution Type/Description: History Museum.
Hours & Admission Prices: Mon.-Sat. 10-4, Sun. 1-5. Closed Easter; Independence Day; Thanksgiving; Christmas Day. Adults $10, seniors (65 and over) $8, children (5-12) $4, children (4 and under) no charge.

KINGSVILLE TRAIN DEPOT MUSEUM, 1501 N. Hwy. 77, Kingsville, TX 78363. Mailing Address: c/o KCVB, 1501 Hwy. 77, Kingsville, TX 78363. Tel.: 361-592-8516 & 800-333-5032. Fax: 361-592-3227.
E-mail: howdy@cityofkingsville.com
Web Site: kingsvilletexas.com/1904-train-depot-museum
Key Personnel: Pres., Dr. Terisa Riley.
Institution Type/Description: Historic Building Museum: built in 1904.
Hours & Admission Prices: Mon.-Fri. 10-4, Sat. 11-2; groups by appointment. No charge.

Kountze

BIG THICKET NATIONAL PRESERVE, 6102 FM 420, Kountze, TX 77625-7841. Mailing Address: 6044 FM 420, Kountze, TX 77625. Tel.: 409-951-6700. Fax: 409-951-6714.
E-mail: bith_information@nps.gov
Web Site: www.nps.gov/bith/
Institution Type/Description: Biological Preserve.
Hours & Admission Prices: Visitor Center: daily 9-5. Headquarters: daily 24 hrs. No charge; donations accepted. &
Attendance: 115,000 (estimated)

Kyle

KATHERINE ANNE PORTER LITERARY CENTER, 508 Center St., Kyle, TX 78640. Tel.: 512-268-6637.
E-mail: kapliterarycenter@gmail.com
Institution Type/Description: History Museum.
Hours & Admission Prices: By appointment.

La Grange

FAYETTE HERITAGE MUSEUM & ARCHIVES, 855 S. Jefferson, La Grange, TX 78945-3230. Tel.: 979-968-3765 & 6418. Fax: 979-968-5357.
E-mail: archives@cityoflg.com
Web Site: www.cityoflg.com/library.html
Institution Type/Description: History Museum.

Hours & Admission Prices: Tues.-Fri. 10-6, Sat. 10-1. No charge. Closed major holidays. &
Attendance: 2,500 (estimated)

NATHANIEL W. FAISON HOME AND MUSEUM, 822 S. Jefferson St., State Hwy. 77, La Grange, TX 78945. Mailing Address: P.O. Box 681, La Grange, TX 78945. Tel.: 979-968-9416 & 713-628-9065. Facebook.
E-mail: marie.watts@faisonhouse.org
Web Site: www.faisonhouse.org
Key Personnel: Arnold Romberg; Marie Watts.
Institution Type/Description: Historic House: 1840-1855 Nathaniel W. Faison Home.
Hours & Admission Prices: 2nd Sat. each month 10-4; tours by appointment. Admission $3; children 11 & under no charge.
Attendance: 400 (estimated)

TEXAS QUILT MUSEUM, 140 W. Colorado St., La Grange, TX 78945. Tel.: 979-968-3104. Fax: 979-968-6010.
E-mail: projects@texasquiltmuseum.org
Web Site: www.texasquiltmuseum.org
Institution Type/Description: Quilt Museum: housed in two historic buildings; c.1890s.
Hours & Admission Prices: Thurs.-Sat. 10-4, Sun. 12-4. Adults $8; seniors & students $6; discounts to groups. Closed New Year's Day, Eve & week; Thanksgiving; Christmas Eve, Day & week.

La Porte

BATTLESHIP TEXAS STATE HISTORIC SITE, 3523 Independence Pkwy. S., La Porte, TX 77571. Tel.: 281-479-2431. Facebook, Twitter.
Web Site: tpwd.texas.gov/state-parks/battleship-texas
Formerly: Battleship Texas State Historical Park
Institution Type/Description: Historic Battleship.
Hours & Admission Prices: Daily 10-5. Tours: Adults $12; seniors $6; children (5-11) $3; children (4 and under) no charge. Closed Thanksgiving; Christmas Eve & Day.
Attendance: 111,000 (estimated)

SAN JACINTO MUSEUM OF HISTORY ASSOCIATION, One Monument Circle, La Porte, TX 77571-9585. Tel.: 281-479-2421. Fax: 281-479-2428.
E-mail: sjm@sanjacinto-museum.org
Web Site: sanjacinto-museum.org
Key Personnel: Pres., Larry Spasic; Chm., Mr. Townes Pressler, Jr.; Mktg. Coord., Dianne Powell.
Institution Type/Description: Historic Building: 1939 San Jacinto Monument.
Hours & Admission Prices: Daily 9-6. No charge. Three Venues pricing varies. &
Attendance: 450,000 (estimated)

Lackland Air Force Base

U.S.A.F. AIRMAN HERITAGE MUSEUM, 2051 George Ave., Bldg. 5206, Lackland Air Force Base, TX 78236-5218. Mailing Address: P.O. Box 761422, San Antonio, TX 78245-6422. Tel.: 210-671-3055. Facebook, Twitter.
E-mail: foundation@myairmanmuseum.org
Web Site: www.myairmanmuseum.org/the-museum/
Formerly: History and Traditions Museum
Key Personnel: Pres., Timmothy Dickens.
Institution Type/Description: Military Museum.
Hours & Admission Prices: Wed. & Fri. 9-3; Thurs. 10:30-5:30, Sat. 10-2. No charge; donation accepted. Closed federal holidays. &
Attendance: 30,000 (actual)

U.S.A.F. SECURITY FORCES MUSEUM, 1300 Femoyer St., Bldg. 10501, Lackland Air Force Base, TX 78236. Mailing Address: P.O. Box 276412, San Antonio, TX 78227-6412. Tel.: 210-671-3055.
Web Site: securityforcesmuseumfoundation.org/
Key Personnel: Dir., Bill Manchester.
Institution Type/Description: Military History Museum.
Hours & Admission Prices: Wed. & Fri. 9-3; Thurs. 10:30-5:30; Mon.-Tues. by appointment only. No charge. Closed federal holidays. &
Attendance: 16,885 (actual)

Lake Jackson

LAKE JACKSON HISTORICAL MUSEUM, 249 Circle Way, Lake Jackson, TX 77566-5232. Mailing Address: P.O. Box 242, Lake Jackson, TX 77566. Tel.: 979-297-1570. Fax: 888-247-0046.
E-mail: director@lakejacksonmuseum.org
Web Site: lakejacksonmuseum.org
Key Personnel: Pres., Vorin Dornan; Vice Pres., Joe Ripple.
Institution Type/Description: History Museum.
Hours & Admission Prices: Tues.-Sat. 10-4. No charge. &
Attendance: 6,000 (actual)

SEA CENTER TEXAS, 302 Medical Dr., Lake Jackson, TX 77566. Tel.: 979-292-0100. Facebook, Twitter.
E-mail: seacenter@tpwd.texas.gov
Web Site: tpwd.texas.gov/fishing/sea-center-texas
Key Personnel: Dir., David Abrego.
Institution Type/Description: Aquarium.
Hours & Admission Prices: Tues.-Sat. 9-4, Sun. 1-4. No charge; donations accepted. Closed New Year's Eve & Day, Easter, Thanksgiving, Christmas Eve & Day. &

Lamesa

DAL-PASO MUSEUM, 306 S. First St., Lamesa, TX 79331. Mailing Address: P.O. Box 1445, Lamesa, TX 79331. Tel.: 806-872-5007. Fax: 806-872-2181.
Key Personnel: C.E.O., Wayne C. Smith, Ed.D.
Institution Type/Description: General Museum: housed in 1925 restored Dal Paso Hotel.
Hours & Admission Prices: Mon., Thurs. & Sat. 2-5. No charge. &
Attendance: 1,000 (estimated)

Lampasas

LAMPASAS COUNTY MUSEUM, Physical/Mailing Address: 303 S. Western St., Lampasas, TX 76550. Tel.: 512-556-2224.
E-mail: lampasasmuseum@gmail.com
Web Site: business.lampasaschamber.org/list/member/lampasas-county-museum-lampasas-104
Formerly: Keystone Square Museum
Institution Type/Description: History Museum.
Hours & Admission Prices: Fri. & Sat. 10-4; other times by appointment. Closed Dec. 21-Feb. 1. &
Attendance: 1,100 (estimated)

Langtry

JUDGE ROY BEAN VISITOR CENTER, Hwy. 90, W., Loop 25, Langtry, TX 78871. Mailing Address: P.O. Box 160, Langtry, TX 78871-0160. Tel.: 800-452-9292 432-291-3340. Facebook.
E-mail: lytic@dot.state.tx.us
Web Site: www.dot.state.tx.us
Key Personnel: Supvr., Kenneth R. Fatheree.
Institution Type/Description: Historic Building Museum: c.1896 Judge Roy Bean Saloon.
Hours & Admission Prices: Daily 8-5. No charge. Closed New Year's Day; Easter; Thanksgiving; Christmas Eve & Day. &
Attendance: 70,000 (estimated)

Laredo

IMAGINARIUM OF SOUTH TEXAS, 5300 San Dario, Ste. 505, Mall del Norte, Laredo, TX 78041-3000. Tel.: 956-728-0404. Fax: 956-725-7776.
E-mail: info@imaginariumstx.org
Web Site: www.imaginariumstx.org
Formerly: Laredo Children's Museum
Key Personnel: Exec. Dir., Sandra Cavazos Ayala.
Institution Type/Description: Children's Museum: housed in c.1900 Fort McIntosh chapel & guardhouse.
Hours & Admission Prices: Wed.-Thurs. 10-7, Fri.-Sat. 10-8, Sun. 12-6. Children & adults $5; veterans $4; children under 1 and members no charge. Closed New Year's Day; Easter; Thanksgiving; Christmas Eve & Day. &
Attendance: 40,000 (actual)

LAREDO CENTER FOR THE ARTS, 500 San Agustin Ave., Laredo, TX 78040-8103. Tel.: 956-725-1715. Fax: 956-725-1741. Facebook, Instagram.
E-mail: info@laredoartcenter.org

Web Site: www.laredoartcenter.org
Key Personnel: Exec. Dir., Rosie Santos; Pres., Priscilla Beckelhymer; Vice Pres., Paty Figueroa.
Institution Type/Description: Art Museum.
Hours & Admission Prices: Tues.-Sat. 11-4. No charge.

League City

BUTLER LONGHORN MUSEUM AND HERITAGE PARK, Physical/Mailing Address: 1220 Coryell St., League City, TX 77573. Tel.: 281-332-1393. Facebook, Twitter.
E-mail: info@butlerlonghornmuseum.com
Web Site: www.butlerlonghornmuseum.com
Institution Type/Description: History Museum.
Hours & Admission Prices: Tues.-Wed. & Fri.-Sat. 10-4, Thurs. 10-7. Adults $10, seniors, military & children 6-12 $9; children under 6 no charge.
Attendance: 100,000 (actual)

WEST BAY COMMON SCHOOL CHILDREN'S MUSEUM, 210 N. Kansas Ave., League City, TX 77573-2466. Tel.: 281-554-2994. Facebook.
E-mail: rklewis45@gmail.com
Web Site: www.oneroomschoolhouse.org/
Key Personnel: Dir., Catharin Lewis.
Institution Type/Description: Children's Museum.
Hours & Admission Prices: Mon.-Thurs. 9-4, other times by appointment. Schoolhouse sessions: $5 per person. Docent Talk: no charge.

Leakey

REAL COUNTY HISTORICAL MUSEUM, Evergreen St., Leakey, TX 78873. Mailing Address: P.O. Box 852, Leakey, TX 78873. Tel.: 830-232-5330 & 6212.
E-mail: realmuseum@hctc.net
Web Site: www.realcountyhistoricalmuseum.com
Key Personnel: Pres., Norene La Baume; Vice Pres., Carol Ann Kolb; Sec., Pat Burrier; Treas., Susan Knight.
Institution Type/Description: History Museum.
Hours & Admission Prices: March-Dec. Fri.-Sat. 10-2. Adults $1, children (under 12) $.50.

Levelland

CHRISTINE DEVITT FINE ART CENTER, South Plains College, 1401 S. College Ave., Levelland, TX 79336. Tel.: 806-716-2261 & 2270.
E-mail: jwhiteside@southplainscollege.edu
Key Personnel: Cur., Julia Whiteside.
Institution Type/Description: Art Gallery.
Hours & Admission Prices: Call for hours. No charge. Closed school holidays.
Attendance: 1,000 (estimated)

Liberty

SAM HOUSTON REGIONAL LIBRARY & RESEARCH CENTER, 650 FM 1011, Liberty, TX 77575-6841. Mailing Address: P.O. Box 310, Liberty, TX 77575-0310. Tel.: 936-336-8821. Fax: 936-336-7049.
E-mail: samhoustoncenter@tsl.texas.gov
Web Site: www.tsl.texas.gov/shc/index.html
Key Personnel: Mgr., Alana Inman.
Institution Type/Description: Regional Museum & Archives.
Hours & Admission Prices: Tues.-Fri. 8-5, Sat. 9-4. No charge; donations accepted. Closed major holidays.
Attendance: 1,500 (actual)

Lipscomb

WOLF CREEK HERITAGE MUSEUM, 13310 Hwy. 305, Lipscomb, TX 79056. Mailing Address: P.O. Box 5, Lipscomb, TX 79056. Tel.: 806-852-2123 & 653-3321. Fax: 806-852-2172.
E-mail: staff@wolfcreekheritagemuseum.org
Web Site: www.wolfcreekheritagemuseum.org
Key Personnel: Dir., Virginia Scott.
Institution Type/Description: History Museum.
Hours & Admission Prices: Mon.-Fri. 10-4; other times by appointment. No charge; donations accepted.
Attendance: 1,686

Littlefield

DUGGAN HOUSE MUSEUM, 520 E. Waylon Jennings Blvd., Littlefield, TX 79339. Tel.: 806-385-9001.
E-mail: littlefieldmuseum@windstream.net
Institution Type/Description: History Museum.
Hours & Admission Prices: Call for hours. No charge; donations accepted.
Attendance: 250 (estimated)

Livingston

POLK COUNTY MEMORIAL MUSEUM, 514 W. Mill St., Livingston, TX 77351. Tel.: 936-327-8192. Fax: 936-327-8192.
E-mail: museum@livingston.net
Web Site: www.polkcountymemorialmuseum.com
Institution Type/Description: History Museum.
Hours & Admission Prices: Mon.-Fri. 9-5. No charge; donations accepted.
Attendance: 4,500 (actual)

Llano

LLANO COUNTY HISTORICAL MUSEUM, 310 Bessemer Ave., Llano, TX 78643. Tel.: 325-247-3026.
E-mail: llanomuseum@verizon.net
Key Personnel: Pres., Charles Wendt; Vice Pres., Marilyn Hale.
Institution Type/Description: History Museum: housed in the former Bruhl Drugstore building.
Hours & Admission Prices: Wed.-Sat. 11-5. No charge; donations accepted.

Longview

GREGG COUNTY HISTORICAL MUSEUM, 214 N. Fredonia St., Longview, TX 75601-7222. Tel.: 903-753-5840. Fax: 903-753-5854.
E-mail: director@gregghistorical.org
Web Site: gregghistorical.org
Key Personnel: Exec. Dir., Lindsay Luy; Pres. (V), Walter Northcutt.
Institution Type/Description: County Museum: housed in 1910 brick Everett bank building.
Hours & Admission Prices: Tues.-Fri. 10-4, Sat. 10-2. Adults $5, seniors $2, children under 18 $1; discount to AAA members; members no charge; Texas Association of Museums reciprocal admissions program. Closed major holidays.
Attendance: 12,000 (estimated)

LONGVIEW MUSEUM OF FINE ARTS, 215 E. Tyler St., Longview, TX 75601-7219. Mailing Address: P.O. Box 3484, Longview, TX 75606-3484. Tel.: 903-753-8103. Fax: 903-753-8217. Facebook, Instagram, Twitter.
E-mail: fineart@lmfa.org
Web Site: www.lmfa.org
Formerly: Longview Museum & Arts Center
Key Personnel: Exec. Dir., Tiffany Jehorek; Art Education Dir., Pilar McLemore.
Institution Type/Description: Art Museum.
Hours & Admission Prices: Tues, Wed. & Fri. 8-6, Thurs. 10-6, Sat. 10-2. Adults $5; discounts to NARM members; members no charge. Closed national holidays.
Attendance: 16,000 (estimated)

Los Fresnos

LAGUNA ATASCOSA NATIONAL WILDLIFE REFUGE, 22688 Buena Vista Rd., Los Fresnos, TX 78566. Mailing Address: 22817 Ocelot Rd., Los Fresnos, TX 78566. Tel.: 956-748-3607 & 244-2019. Fax: 956-748-3609. Facebook, Instagram, Twitter.
E-mail: marion_mason@fws.gov
Web Site: www.fws.gov/refuge/laguna_atascosa
Institution Type/Description: Wildlife Refuge.
Hours & Admission Prices: Refuge: daily sunrise to sunset. Visitor Center: Thurs.-Mon. Daily Permits: $3 per vehicle; discounts to groups; school groups & active military no charge. Annual Permit: $10.

Lubbock

AMERICAN WINDMILL MUSEUM INC., 1701 Canyon Lake Dr., Lubbock, TX 79403-4908. Tel.: 806-747-8734. Facebook, Twitter, Instagram, Youtube.
E-mail: sales@windmill.com
Web Site: windmill.com
Formerly: American Wind Power Center

Key Personnel: Exec. Dir., Coy Harris; Dir. of Mktg., Tanya Meadows; Media Dir., Tamara Hall.
Institution Type/Description: History Museum.
Hours & Admission Prices: Tues.-Sat. 10-5, Sun. 2-5. Adults $7.50, children (5-12) $5, family of four $20, seniors & veterans $6; active military & their families no charge. &

BAYER MUSEUM OF AGRICULTURE, 1121 Canyon Lake Dr., Lubbock, TX 79403-4911. Mailing Address: P.O. Box 505, Lubbock, TX 79408-0505. Tel.: 806-744-3786 & 1734. Facebook, Twitter.
E-mail: amadirector@agriculturehistory.org
Web Site: www.agriculturehistory.org
Formerly: American Museum of Agriculture
Key Personnel: Pres., Dan Taylor; Vice Pres., Patti Jones; Sec., Curtis Griffith; Treas., Stanley Young.
Institution Type/Description: Agriculture Museum.
Hours & Admission Prices: Tues.-Sat. 10-5. Adults $5, family of four $15.
Attendance: 21,000

BUDDY HOLLY CENTER, 1801 Crickets Ave., Lubbock, TX 79401-5128. Tel.: 806-775-3560. Fax: 806-767-0732. Facebook.
E-mail: museums@mylubbock.us
Web Site: www.buddyhollycenter.org
Key Personnel: Mng. Dir., Brooke Witcher; Cur., Jacqueline Bober; Media Inquiries, Briana Vela; Educational Outreach/Volunteering, Sebastian Forbush.
Institution Type/Description: History Museum.
Hours & Admission Prices: Tues.-Sat. 10-5, Sun. 1-5, closed holidays. &

LOUISE HOPKINS UNDERWOOD CENTER FOR THE ARTS, 511 Ave. K, Lubbock, TX 79401. Tel.: 806-762-8606. Facebook, Instagram, Twitter.
E-mail: contact@lhuca.org
Key Personnel: Pres., Andrea Tirey; Vice Pres., Ryan Henry; Mgr., Lindsey Maestri; Cur., Linda Cullum; Guest Svcs., Mica McGuire.
Institution Type/Description: Art Gallery.
Hours & Admission Prices: Tues.-Sat. 9-5.

MUSEUM OF TEXAS TECH UNIVERSITY, 3301 4th St., Lubbock, TX 79403-4613. Tel.: 806-742-2490. Facebook, Twitter.
E-mail: museum.texastech@ttu.edu
Web Site: www.depts.ttu.edu/museumttu
Key Personnel: Exec. Dir., Dr. Gary Morgan; Finance Specialist, Julie Flores; Asst. Dir. Academic Engagement, Nicky Ladkin; Asst. Dir. Museum Operations & Facilities, Dr. Cameron Saffell; Instructor, Dr. Jill Hoffman; Museum Registrar, Terri Carnes; Collections Mgr., Rachel Gruszka; Exhibits Mgr., Andrew Gedeon; Operations Mgr., Brad Johnson; Landmark Operations Mgr., Deborah Bigness; Landmark Education Program Mgr., Susan Rowe; Mgr. Administration & Finance, Jamie Looney; Cur. & Dir. Natural Science Research Lab., Dr. Robert Bradley; Cur. Paleontology, Dr. Sankar Chatterjee; Cur. History, Dr. Cameron Saffell; DeVitt Jones Cur. Art, Dr. Peter S. Briggs; Cur. Clothing & Textiles, Dr. Marian Ann Montgomery; Cur. Anthropology, Dr. Eileen Johnson.
Institution Type/Description: General Museum.
Hours & Admission Prices: Tues.-Sat. 10-5, Sun. 1-5. Main building: no charge; donations accepted. Closed Texas Tech University holidays. &
Attendance: 159,644 (actual)

NATIONAL RANCHING HERITAGE CENTER, Texas Tech University, 3121 Fourth St., Lubbock, TX 79409. Tel.: 806-742-0498.
E-mail: ranchhc@ttu.edu
Web Site: www.depts.ttu.edu/ranchhc
Key Personnel: Exec. Dir., Jim Bret Campbell.
Institution Type/Description: History Museum.
Hours & Admission Prices: Daily 10-5. No charge; donations accepted. Closed major holidays. &
Attendance: 55,671

SCIENCE SPECTRUM & OMNI THEATER, 2579 S. Loop 289 #250, Lubbock, TX 79423-1400. Tel.: 806-745-2525 & 1216. Fax: 806-745-1115.
E-mail: sandy@sciencespectrum.org
Web Site: sciencespectrum.org
Key Personnel: Dir., Cassandra L. Henry.
Institution Type/Description: Science Museum.
Hours & Admission Prices: Mon.-Fri. 10-5, Sat. 10-6, Sun. 1-5. Museum: adults $8, senior citizens 60 & over and children 3-12 $6.50; discounts to groups; members no charge. Omni Theater: adults $13.50, senior citizens 60 & over and children

3-12 $10.50; members $6; discounts to groups. Combination tickets available. Closed Thanksgiving; Christmas. &
Attendance: 200,000 (actual)

SILENT WINGS MUSEUM, 6202 N. Interstate 27, Ste. 2, Lubbock, TX 79403-7526. Tel.: 806-775-3049. Fax: 806-775-3337. Facebook, Instagram.
E-mail: museums@mylubbock.us
Web Site: www.silentwingsmuseum.com
Formerly: Military Glider Pilots Association, Silent Wings Museum
Key Personnel: Dir., Brooke Witcher; Asst. Dir., Eddy Grigsby; Cur., Donald Abbe.
Institution Type/Description: Military Museum.
Hours & Admission Prices: Tues.-Sat. 10-5, Sun. 1-5. Adults $8, seniors 60 & over $6, children 7-17 & students with college ID $5; members, children 6 & under accompanied by family member, WWII glider pilots & active duty military no charge. &
Attendance: 14,000 (actual)

Lufkin

ELLEN TROUT ZOO, 402 Zoo Circle, Lufkin, TX 75904-1345. Tel.: 936-633-0399. Facebook.
E-mail: gordon@ellentroutzoo.com
Web Site: www.cityoflufkin.com/zoo
Key Personnel: Zoo Dir., Gordon B. Henley, Jr.; Pres., Jamie Zayler; Dir. Educational Svcs., Charlotte Henley.
Institution Type/Description: Zoo.
Hours & Admission Prices: Daily 9-5. Adults $7; seniors (60 and over) $6; children (4-11) $3.50; children (under 4), museum, AZA & reciprocal members no charge. &
Attendance: 131,610 (actual)

MUSEUM OF EAST TEXAS, 503 N. Second St., Lufkin, TX 75901-3013. Tel.: 936-639-4434.
E-mail: jmcdonald@metlufkin.org
Web Site: www.metlufkin.org
Formerly: The Museum of East Texas
Key Personnel: Exec. Dir., J.P. McDonald; Cur. Education, Ann Reyes; Administrative Asst., Sherry Reinhardt.
Institution Type/Description: Museum of Art & History.
Hours & Admission Prices: Tues.-Fri. 10-5, Sat.-Sun. 1-5. No charge; donations accepted. Closed major holidays. &
Attendance: 15,000 (actual)

NARANJO MUSEUM OF NATURAL HISTORY, 5104 S. First St., Lufkin, TX 75901. Tel.: 936-639-3466. Facebook, Twitter.
E-mail: veronica@naranjomuseum.org
Web Site: naranjomuseum.org
Key Personnel: C.E.O. & Founder, Dr. Neal Naranjo; Museum Cur., Charlie Grumbles; Museum Mgr., Veronica Amoe; Guest Svcs., Donna Erdek.
Institution Type/Description: Natural History Museum.
Hours & Admission Prices: Mon.-Sat. 10-6, Sun. 1-6; groups by appointment. Adults $7.50, children 4-18 $5; children 3 & under no charge. Closed New Year's Day, Easter, Thanksgiving, Christmas Eve & Day.

TEXAS FORESTRY MUSEUM, 1905 Atkinson Dr., Lufkin, TX 75901-2505. Tel.: 936-632-9535.
E-mail: info@treetexas.com
Web Site: www.treetexas.com
Key Personnel: Museum Dir., Kendall Gay; Pres. Bd., Jennifer Smith; Educ. Coord., Kaitlin Wieseman; Museum Coord., Jessica Read; Educ. Asst., Grace Barnhill.
Institution Type/Description: Forestry Museum.
Hours & Admission Prices: Mon.-Sat. 10-5. No charge; donations accepted. Closed major holidays. &
Attendance: 10,000 (estimated)

Luling

CENTRAL TEXAS OIL PATCH MUSEUM, 421 E. Davis St., Luling, TX 78648. Tel.: 830-875-1922. Fax: 830-875-2082.
E-mail: info@lulingmuseum.org
Web Site: www.oilmuseum.org
Key Personnel: Dir., Carol Voigt.
Institution Type/Description: History Museum.
Hours & Admission Prices: Mon.-Fri. 9-12 & 1-4, Sat. 10-2. Requested $1 or donation. Closed most holidays.

Marble Falls

THE FALLS ON THE COLORADO MUSEUM, 2001 Broadway St., Marble Falls, TX 78654. Tel.: 830-798-2157. Facebook.
E-mail: focmuseum@gmail.com
Web Site: www.fallsmuseum.org
Key Personnel: Chmn. (V), Darlene Farmer Oostermeyer.
Institution Type/Description: History Museum.
Hours & Admission Prices: Thurs.-Sat. 10-4. No charge, donations accepted. &
Attendance: 1,240 (actual)

Marfa

CHINATI FOUNDATION, One Cavalry Row, Marfa, TX 79843. Mailing Address: P.O. Box 1135, Marfa, TX 79843-1135. Tel.: 432-729-4362. Fax: 432-729-4597.
E-mail: information@chinati.org
Web Site: www.chinati.org
Key Personnel: Dir., Jenny Moore.
Institution Type/Description: Art Museum: housed in c.1919 & 1938 buildings of former Fort D.A. Russell.
Hours & Admission Prices: Wed.-Sun. 9-5. Adults $25, students $10; discounts to AAM & ICOM members; members no charge. &
Attendance: 11,000 (estimated)

MARFA AND PRESIDIO COUNTY MUSEUM, 110 W. San Antonio St., Marfa, TX 79843. Mailing Address: P.O. Box 538, Marfa, TX 79843-0538. Tel.: 432-295-1023.
E-mail: marfapresidiocountymuseum@gmail.com
Key Personnel: Museum Bd. Pres., Maggie Marquez.
Institution Type/Description: History Museum.
Hours & Admission Prices: Mon. 1-5, Tues.-Sat. 2-5. No charge.
Attendance: 1,200 (actual)

Marshall

HARRISON COUNTY HISTORICAL MUSEUM, 1 Peter Whetstone Square, Marshall, TX 75670. Mailing Address: P.O. Box 1987, Marshall, TX 75671-1987. Tel.: 903-935-8417 Ext. 1.
E-mail: info@harrisoncountymuseum.org
Web Site: www.harrisoncountymuseum.org
Formerly: Old Courthouse Museum/Harrison County Historical Museum
Key Personnel: Dir., Janet Cook.
Institution Type/Description: Historical Museum: housed in the Harrison County Courthouse; built in 1901.
Hours & Admission Prices: Tues.-Sat. 10-4. Adults $6, seniors (60 and over) $5, students (16 and over) $1, students (under 16) & children no charge. &
Attendance: 600 (estimated)

MICHELSON MUSEUM OF ART, 216 N. Bolivar, Marshall, TX 75670-3307. Tel.: 903-935-9480. Facebook, Instagram.
E-mail: leomich@sbcglobal.net
Web Site: www.michelsonmuseum.org
Key Personnel: School Svcs. Coord., Willa Berryman; Dir., Susan Spears; Dir. Education, Bonnie Strauss; Dir. of Devel., Gayle Weinberg.
Institution Type/Description: Art Museum.
Hours & Admission Prices: Tues.-Fri. 10-4, Sat. 1-4. No charge; donations accepted. Closed Easter; Independence Day; Thanksgiving; Christmas. &
Attendance: 8,000 (estimated)

Mason

MASON COUNTY MUSEUM, 321 Moody St., Mason, TX 76856. Mailing Address: Mason County Museum, P.O. Box 1473, Mason, TX 76856. Tel.: 325-347-6681.
E-mail: janell@ctesc.net
Key Personnel: Pres. (V), Charles Davidartis; Vice Pres., Kathy Tallent; Chm., Nancy Jordan; Co-Chm., Dolores Keller; Sec., Lou Fleming; Treas., Joan Lindley.
Institution Type/Description: Local History Museum: housed in 1887 two-storied sandstone school building.
Hours & Admission Prices: March-Nov. 15 Thurs.-Sat. 11-4. No charge; donations requested.
Attendance: 1,350 (estimated)

MASON SQUARE MUSEUM, 103 Fort McKavitt, Mason, TX 76856. Mailing Address: P.O. Box 203, Mason, TX 76856. Tel.: 325-347-0507.
E-mail: info@masonsquaremuseum.org
Web Site: www.masonsquaremuseum.org

Key Personnel: Pres. Bd., Dennis Evans.
Institution Type/Description: History Museum.
Hours & Admission Prices: Thurs.-Sat. 10-4. No charge; donations accepted.
Attendance: 4,200 (actual)

Matador

MOTLEY COUNTY HISTORICAL MUSEUM, 828 Dundee St., Matador, TX 79244. Tel.: 806-347-2968.
Key Personnel: Chm. (V), Marisue Potts.
Institution Type/Description: History Museum: housed in the former Traweek Hospital; built in 1928.
Hours & Admission Prices: Wed. 1-5; other times by appointment. No charge; donations accepted.
Attendance: 400 (estimated)

McAllen

INTERNATIONAL MUSEUM OF ART AND SCIENCE, 1900 Nolana, McAllen, TX 78504-4199. Tel.: 956-681-2800. Fax: 956-686-1813. Facebook, Instagram, Twitter.
E-mail: info@imasonline.org
Web Site: www.imasonline.org
Formerly: McAllen International Museum
Key Personnel: Pres. & Exec. Dir., Serena Pandos; Dir. Finance, Adrian De Anda; Dir. Education, Claudia Martinez; Mgr. Visitor Svcs., Jessica Rodriguez.
Institution Type/Description: Arts & Sciences Museum.
Hours & Admission Prices: Tues.-Thurs. 9-3, Fri. 9-5, Sat. 10-5, Sun. 1-5. Adults $7, seniors & students $5, children 4-12 $4; children 3 & under no charge. Closed holidays. &
Attendance: 75,000 (estimated)

MCALLEN HERITAGE CENTER, INC., 301 S. Main St., McAllen, TX 78501-4806. Mailing Address: P.O. Box 1929, McAllen, TX 78505-1929. Tel.: 956-687-1904. Fax: 956-687-1906. Facebook.
E-mail: mcheritage@att.net
Web Site: www.mcallenheritagecenter.com
Key Personnel: Mng. Dir., Elva M. Cerda; Pres. (V), Nedra S. Kinerk; Museum Shop Mgr., Lily Hernandez.
Institution Type/Description: History Museum.
Hours & Admission Prices: Wed.-Fri. 1-5, Sat. 11-4. No charge; donations accepted. &
Attendance: 5,500 (estimated)

SOUTH TEXAS COLLEGE - LIBRARY ART GALLERY, 3201 W. Pecan, McAllen, TX 78501-6661. Tel.: 956-872-3488. Facebook.
Web Site: library.southtexascollege.edu/lag
Key Personnel: Gallery Assoc., Gina Otvos.
Institution Type/Description: Art Gallery.
Hours & Admission Prices: Call for hours. No charge. &

McCamey

MENDOZA TRAIL MUSEUM, Physical/Mailing Address: 207 E. 6th St., P.O. Box 1409, McCamey, TX 79752. Tel.: 432-652-3192 & 208-3243.
E-mail: info@texaspecostrail.com
Key Personnel: Museum Cur., Ellen Crossland.
Institution Type/Description: History Museum.
Hours & Admission Prices: Tues.-Fri. 1-5. No charge.

McKinney

CHESTNUT SQUARE HISTORIC VILLAGE - THE HERITAGE GUILD OF COLLIN COUNTY, 315 S. Chestnut St., McKinney, TX 75069-5607. Tel.: 972-562-8790. Facebook.
E-mail: info@chestnutsquare.org
Web Site: www.chestnutsquare.org
Key Personnel: Exec. Dir., Jaymie Pedigo.
Institution Type/Description: History Museum.
Hours & Admission Prices: Thurs. & Sat. 11. Tours: adults $7, seniors, military & children under 12 $5. &
Attendance: 50,000 (estimated)

COLLIN COUNTY FARM MUSEUM, 7117 County Rd. 166, McKinney, TX 75070. Tel.: 972-548-4792. Fax: 972-547-5743. Facebook: Collin County Farm Museum.

E-mail: ccfm@collincountytx.gov
Web Site: www.co.collin.tx.us/parks/myers/farm_museum.jsp
Key Personnel: Park Mgr., Judy Florence; Museum Coord., Jennifer Rogers.
Institution Type/Description: Farm Museum.
Hours & Admission Prices: Wed. & Sat. 10-3; other times by appointment. Group fee may apply. No charge; donations accepted. Closed major holidays. &
Attendance: 3,000 (estimated)

COLLIN COUNTY HISTORY MUSEUM, 300 E. Virginia St., McKinney, TX 75069-4325. Tel.: 972-542-9457. Facebook, Instagram, Twitter.
E-mail: info@collincountyhistoricalsociety.org
Web Site: collincountyhistoricalsociety.org
Formerly: North Texas History Center
Key Personnel: Dir., Bryan Lean.
Institution Type/Description: History Museum.
Hours & Admission Prices: Thurs., Fri. & Sat. 10-4. No charge.
Attendance: 10,000 (estimated)

HEARD-CRAIG CENTER FOR THE ARTS, 205 W. Hunt St., McKinney, TX 75069. Tel.: 972-569-6909. Fax: 972-542-5092. Facebook, Twitter.
E-mail: executivedirector@heardcraig.org
Web Site: heardcraig.org
Key Personnel: Exec. Dir., Karen Zupanic.
Institution Type/Description: Historic House Museum: built in 1900.
Hours & Admission Prices: Mon.-Fri. 8-4; other times by appointment. Tea & Tour: $10; discounts to AAM & ICOM members; members no charge.
Attendance: 30,000 (actual)

HEARD NATURAL SCIENCE MUSEUM & WILDLIFE SANCTUARY, 1 Nature Place, McKinney, TX 75069-8840. Tel.: 972-562-5566. Fax: 972-548-9119.
E-mail: info@heardmuseum.org
Web Site: www.heardmuseum.org
Key Personnel: Dir., Sy Shahid.
Institution Type/Description: Natural Science Museum & Wildlife Sanctuary.
Hours & Admission Prices: Tues.-Sat. 9-5, Sun. 1-5. Summer: Adults $9, seniors & children 3-12 $6; Fall/Winter: Adults: $12, seniors and children 3-12 $9; Spring: Adults $10, children 3-12 $7; discounts to AAM & ASTC members; members no charge. Closed New Year's Day; Thanksgiving; Christmas. &
Attendance: 100,000 (estimated)

McLean

DEVILS ROPE BARBED WIRE MUSEUM, 100 Kingsley St., McLean, TX 79057. Tel.: 806-779-2225. Facebook, Twitter, Instagram.
E-mail: barbwiremuseum@gmail.com
Web Site: www.barbwiremuseum.com
Institution Type/Description: History Museum.
Hours & Admission Prices: March-Nov. Mon.-Sat. 9-4. No charge; donations accepted.
Attendance: 6,418

MCLEAN-ALANREED AREA MUSEUM, 116 Main St., McLean, TX 79057. Mailing Address: P.O. Box 354, McLean, TX 79057-0354. Tel.: 806-779-2731.
E-mail: riemerkn@yahoo.com
Key Personnel: Cur., Charla Smith.
Institution Type/Description: Historical Society Museum.
Hours & Admission Prices: March-Dec. Tues.-Fri. 10-4. No charge; donation accepted. Closed holidays. &
Attendance: 1,125 (estimated)

Mertzon

IRION COUNTY MUSEUM, Physical/Mailing Address: 598 Lindell Ave., Mertzon, TX 76941. Tel.: 325-835-7771. Fax: 325-835-2195.
E-mail: grayins@aol.com
Web Site: www.museumsusa.org/museums/info/15883
Key Personnel: Museum Shop Mgr., Sylvia Martinez.
Institution Type/Description: History Museum.
Hours & Admission Prices: Tues.-Fri. 5pm-7pm, 2nd & 4th Sat. 9-2, Sun. 2-5. No charge; donations accepted. &
Attendance: 150 (actual)

Mesquite

FLORENCE RANCH HOMESTEAD, 1424 Barnes Bridge Rd., Mesquite, TX 75150-4206. Tel.: 972-204-4933 & 216-6468.
Web Site: www.cityofmesquite.com/200/Florence-Ranch-Homestead
Institution Type/Description: Historic Site.
Hours & Admission Prices: Thurs. & Fri. 10:30-3:30. Adults $4, children (3-12) $2, children (3 and under) no charge. &
Attendance: 1,100 (estimated)

Miami

ROBERTS COUNTY MUSEUM, 120 E. Commercial St., Miami, TX 79059. Mailing Address: P.O. Box 306, Miami, TX 79059-0306. Tel.: 806-868-3291. Fax: 806-868-3381.
E-mail: robertscomuseum@amaonline.com
Web Site: robertscountymuseum.org
Key Personnel: Exec. Dir., Emma Bowers.
Institution Type/Description: Historic Building & Museum: housed in c.1888 Santa Fe Depot.
Hours & Admission Prices: Tues.-Fri. 10-5, Sat.-Sun. call for hours. No charge; donations accepted. Closed major holidays. &
Attendance: 3,000 (estimated)

Midland

THE GEORGE W. BUSH CHILDHOOD HOME, 1412 W. Ohio Ave., Midland, TX 79701. Mailing Address: P.O. Box 8586, Midland, TX 79708-8586. Tel.: 432-685-1112 & 866-684-4380. Fax: 432-684-7012.
E-mail: gwbhome@bushchildhoodhome.org
Web Site: www.bushchildhoodhome.org
Key Personnel: Exec. Dir., Paul St. Hilaire.
Institution Type/Description: Historic Home: housed in the childhood home of former President George W. Bush.
Hours & Admission Prices: Tues.-Sat. 10-5, Sun. 2-5. &
Attendance: 6,500 (estimated)

MCCORMICK GALLERY, Midland College, Allison Fine Arts Bldg., 3600 N. Garfield, Midland, TX 79705. Tel.: 432-685-4770. Fax: 432-685-4721.
E-mail: mccormickgallery@midland.edu
Web Site: www.midland.edu/mccormick
Key Personnel: Dir., J. Don Wallace.
Institution Type/Description: Art Gallery.
Hours & Admission Prices: Mon.-Thurs. 8am-10pm, Fri. 8-5, Sat. 10-5, Sun. 1-5. No charge; donations accepted. Closed holidays. &
Attendance: 2,500 (actual)

MIDLAND COUNTY HISTORICAL MUSEUM, 301 W. Missouri, Midland, TX 79701-5108. Tel.: 915-688-8947.
Web Site: midlandhistoricalsociety.com
Key Personnel: Pres. & C.E.O., Midland Chamber of Commerce, Mrs. Bobby Burns.
Institution Type/Description: General Museum.
Hours & Admission Prices: Mon., Wed., Fri. 2-5. &
Attendance: 1,000 (estimated)

MUSEUM OF THE SOUTHWEST, 1705 W. Missouri Ave., Midland, TX 79701-6516. Tel.: 432-683-2882. Fax: 432-684-9151. Facebook.
E-mail: info@museumsw.org
Web Site: www.museumsw.org
Key Personnel: Exec. Dir., Daniel W. Eck; Pres. Bd. Trustees, Lori Wesley; Dir. Durham Children's Museum, Annelorre Robertson; Education Dir., Melissa Rowland; Program & Outreach Mgr., Samantha Voss; Dir. Devel., Megan Buck; Membership Mgr., Kristin Roberson; Chief of Security, Robin Pruett.
Institution Type/Description: Regional Art, Children's Museum & Planetarium.
Hours & Admission Prices: Tues.-Sat. 10-5, Sun. 2-5. Admission $5, seniors (over 65) & children (3-11) $3; discounts to seniors, active-duty military personnel & AAM members; children 2 & under and members no charge. &
Attendance: 111,110 (actual)

NITA STEWART HALEY MEMORIAL LIBRARY & J. EVETTS HALEY HISTORY CENTER, 1805 W. Indiana, Midland, TX 79701-6949. Tel.: 432-682-5785. Fax: 432-685-3512.
E-mail: info@haleylibrary.com
Web Site: www.haleylibrary.com
Key Personnel: Dir., J.P. "Pat" McDaniel.
Institution Type/Description: Research Library & History Center.

Hours & Admission Prices: Mon.-Fri. 10-5. No charge; donations accepted. &
Attendance: 2,000 (estimated)

PERMIAN BASIN PETROLEUM MUSEUM, 1500 Interstate 20
West, Midland, TX 79701-2041. Tel.: 432-683-4403.
E-mail: kshannon@petroleummuseum.org
Web Site: www.petroleummuseum.org
Key Personnel: Exec. Dir., Kathy Shannon; Devel. Dir., Luanne Thornton;
Education & Mktg. Dir., Stacie Hanna; Archives & Collections Mgr., Tiffany
Bradley; Finance Mgr., Lisa Worden; Programs & Rentals Dir., Carey
Behrends; Museum Shop Mgr., Channon Gregg.
Institution Type/Description: History & Technology Museum.
Hours & Admission Prices: Mon.-Sat. 10-5, Sun. 2-5. Adults $12, students &
seniors $8, children under 5 no charge. Closed New Year's Day; Easter;
Thanksgiving; Christmas Eve & Day. &
Attendance: 50,000 (estimated)

Z. TAYLOR BROWN-SARAH DORSEY HOUSE, 231 N.
Weatherford, Midland, TX 79701. Tel.: 432-682-2931.
E-mail: info@midlandtxchamber.com
Key Personnel: Pres. & C.E.O., Bobby Burns.
Institution Type/Description: Historic House: housed in c.1899 Z. Taylor Brown
House.
Hours & Admission Prices: Tours by appointment. No charge; donations accepted.
Attendance: 800 (estimated)

Mingus

**W.K. GORDON CENTER FOR INDUSTRIAL HISTORY OF
TEXAS,** 65258 I-20, Mingus, TX 76463. Mailing Address: P.O.
Box 218, Mingus, TX 76463-0218. Tel.: 254-968-1886. Fax: 254-
968-1903. Facebook, Instagram.
E-mail: mkadams@tarleton.edu
Web Site: www.tarleton.edu/gordoncenter
Key Personnel: Cur., Mary Adams.
Institution Type/Description: Industrial Museum.
Hours & Admission Prices: Tues.-Sat. 10-4, Sun. 1-4. Adults $5, seniors & military
$4, children $2.50; discounts to groups; AAM members no charge. Closed New
Year's Day; Easter; Thanksgiving; Christmas; university holidays. &
Attendance: 3,000 (estimated)

Mission

MISSION HISTORICAL MUSEUM, 900 Doherty Ave., Mission,
TX 78572-5812. Tel.: 956-580-8646.
E-mail: clopez@missiontexas.us
Web Site: www.missionmuseum.org
Key Personnel: Dir., Cynthia Lopez.
Institution Type/Description: History Museum.
Hours & Admission Prices: Tues.-Fri. 10-5, Sat. 10-2. No charge. Closed major hol-
idays. &
Attendance: 47,038 (actual)

Missouri City

DEWALT HERITAGE CENTER, Kitty Hollow Park, 9555 Hwy. 6
S., Missouri City, TX 77459. Mailing Address: P.O. Box 460,
Richmond, TX 77406-0012. Tel.: 281-342-1256.
Key Personnel: Exec. Dir., Claire Rogers; Chief Cur. of Collections, Chris
Godbold; Dir. of Devel., Zarinah K. Poole; Dir. of Mktg., Jennifer Farrell;
Admin. Svcs. Mgr., Daniela Abrego.
Institution Type/Description: Historic House Museum: built c.1900.
Hours & Admission Prices: Sun. 1-4. No charge. Closed holidays.

Monahans

WARD COUNTY MUSEUM COMPLEX, 400 Museum Blvd.,
Monahans, TX 79756. Tel.: 432-943-8401 & 2187.
E-mail: chamber@monahans.org
Web Site: monahans.org/chamber-of-commerce/museums
Formerly: Million Barrel Museum
Key Personnel: Bd. Pres., Jeppie Wilson.
Institution Type/Description: History Museum.
Hours & Admission Prices: Tues.-Sat. 10-6. No charge; donations accepted. Closed
most holidays. &
Attendance: 2,500 (estimated)

Mont Belviu

BARBERS HILL - MONT BELVIEU MUSEUM, 11607 Eagle
Dr., P.O. Box 1048, Mont Belviu, TX 77580. Tel.: 281-576-2213.
E-mail: wfarrell@montbelviu.net
Institution Type/Description: History Museum.
Hours & Admission Prices: Tues. & Thurs. 10-2, 2nd Sat. each month 10-2. No
charge.

Mount Vernon

FRANKLIN COUNTY HISTORICAL MUSEUM, 701 S.
Kaufman St., Mount Vernon, TX 75457. Tel.: 903-537-4760 &
7012. Facebook.
E-mail: fchadirector@mt-vernon.com
Web Site: www.fcha-online.org
Key Personnel: Pres. (V), B.F. Hicks.
Institution Type/Description: History Museum.
Hours & Admission Prices: Office: Tues.-Fri. 9-3. Museum: Thurs.-Sat. 10-2; other
times by appointment. No charge; donations accepted. &
Attendance: 2,500 (estimated)

Nacogdoches

DURST-TAYLOR HISTORIC HOUSE AND GARDENS, 304
North St., Nacogdoches, TX 75961-5002. Tel.: 936-560-4443 &
4441. Facebook, Instagram, Twitter.
E-mail: sowellj@ci.nacogdoches.tx.us
Web Site: www.ci.nacogdoches.tx.us
Key Personnel: Asst. Historic Sites Mgr., Jessica Sowell.
Institution Type/Description: Historic House Museum: former home of Bennet
Blake, delegate to the 1875 Constitutional Convention and later to Thomas J.
Rusk, a signer of the Texas Declaration of Independence; built c.1835. Listed on
the National Register of Historic Sites. Recorded Texas Historic Landmark &
State Archaeological Site.
Hours & Admission Prices: Tues.-Sat. 10-4. No charge; donations accepted. Closed
major holidays. &
Attendance: 2,100 (actual)

NACOGDOCHES FIRE MUSEUM, 214 E. Pillar St.,
Nacogdoches, TX 75961. Tel.: 936-559-2541.
Key Personnel: Fire Chief, Keith Kiplinger; Office Mgr., Terri Martin.
Institution Type/Description: Firefighting History Museum.
Hours & Admission Prices: By appointment. No charge.

STERNE-HOYA HOUSE MUSEUM AND LIBRARY, 211 S.
Lanana St., Nacogdoches, TX 75961-5148. Mailing Address: City
of Nacogdoches, Historic Sites Dept., P.O. Box 635030,
Nacogdoches, TX 75963-5030. Tel.: 936-560-5426. Fax: 936-569-
9813. Facebook, Instagram, Twitter.
E-mail: historicsites@ci.nacogdoches.tx.us
Web Site: ci.nacogdoches.tx.us
Key Personnel: Asst. Historic Sites Mgr., Jessica Sowell.
Institution Type/Description: History Museum: housed in Adolphus Sterne Home.
Hours & Admission Prices: Mon. group tours only, Tues.-Sat. 10-4. No charge;
donations accepted. Closed national holidays. &
Attendance: 3,700 (actual)

STONE FORT MUSEUM, 1808 Alumni Dr., N., Nacogdoches, TX
75962. Mailing Address: P.O. Box 6075, SFASU, Nacogdoches,
TX 75962. Tel.: 936-468-2408. Fax: 936-468-7084. Facebook.
E-mail: stonefort@sfasu.edu
Web Site: www.sfasu.edu/stonefort
Key Personnel: Dir., Carolyn Spears.
Institution Type/Description: Local History Museum: housed in 1936 reconstruction
of 1780s structure.
Hours & Admission Prices: Tues.-Sat. 9-5, Sun. 1-5. No charge; donations
accepted. Closed national & university holidays.
Attendance: 11,983 (actual)

Nederland

DUTCH WINDMILL MUSEUM, 1500 Boston Ave., Nederland,
TX 77627. Tel.: 409-723-1545 & 722-0279.
E-mail: nedcofc@nederlandtx.com
Web Site: www.nederlandtx.com
Institution Type/Description: History Museum: housed in a replica Dutch windmill.
Hours & Admission Prices: Until Sept. 1: Tue.-Sun. 1-5; After Sept. 1: Thur.-Sun.
1-5. No charge.

Needville

GEORGE OBSERVATORY AT BRAZOS BEND STATE PARK, 21901 FM 762, Needville, TX 77461. Tel.: 281-242-3055. Facebook, Instagram, Twitter.
Institution Type/Description: Observatory.
Hours & Admission Prices: Daylight Saving Time: Sat. 3pm-11pm; Nov. to early March Sat. 3pm-10pm. Observatory Planetarium: $3. George Observatory Telescopes: $7; children, military, teachers, seniors $6; members $4.

New Braunfels

MCKENNA CHILDREN'S MUSEUM, 801 W. San Antonio St., New Braunfels, TX 78130. Tel.: 830-606-9525. Fax: 830-606-9535.
E-mail: museum-info@mckenna.org
Web Site: www.mckennakids.org
Formerly: The Children's Museum in New Braunfels
Key Personnel: C.E.O., Alice Jewell.
Institution Type/Description: Children's Museum.
Hours & Admission Prices: Mon.-Sat. 10-5. Admission $7.50; members & children under one no charge. Closed New Year's Eve & Day; Easter; Memorial Day; Independence Day; Labor Day; Comal County Fair Day; Thanksgiving; Christmas Eve & Day. &
Attendance: 100,000 (actual)

NEW BRAUNFELS CONSERVATION SOCIETY, 1300 Church Hill Dr., New Braunfels, TX 78130-3205. Tel.: 210-629-2943. Facebook, Instagram, Twitter.
E-mail: lnbcs@att.net
Web Site: www.newbraunfelsbconservation.org
Key Personnel: Dir., Martha Rehler; Pres., Pam Brandt.
Institution Type/Description: Historical & Preservation Society: located on 3 sites, Conservation Plaza (15 buildings & Rose Conservatory over three and a half acres), Lindheimer Home & Buckhorn Barber Shop & Museum.
Hours & Admission Prices: Tues.-Fri. 9:30-11 & 1-2:30; Sat.-Sun. 1-2:30.
Attendance: 5,000 (estimated)

NEW BRAUNFELS RAILROAD MUSEUM, 302 W. San Antonio St., New Braunfels, TX 78131. Tel.: 830-627-8447.
E-mail: info@newbraunfelsrailroadmuseum.org
Web Site: www.newbraunfelsrailroadmuseum.org
Institution Type/Description: Railroad Museum.
Hours & Admission Prices: Winter hours: Mon., Thurs., Fri., Sun. 12-4; Sat. 10-4. Summer hours Mon.-Fri. 11-4; Sat. 10-4; Sun. 12-4. No charge.

SOPHIENBURG MUSEUM & ARCHIVES INC., 401 W. Coll St., New Braunfels, TX 78130-5618. Tel.: 830-629-1572. Fax: 830-629-3906. Facebook, Instagram, Twitter.
E-mail: director@sophienburg.com
Web Site: www.sophienburg.com
Key Personnel: Dir., Tara Kuhlenberg.
Institution Type/Description: History Museum: housed in fieldstone veneer building on site of the headquarters of original German colony founded in 1845 in Republic of Texas.
Hours & Admission Prices: Tues.-Sat. 10-4. Adults $8, groups (over 20, pre-booked) $7, students (13-18) $4, children (6-12) $2, members & children (under 6) no charge. Closed New Year's Day, Thanksgiving, Christmas Eve & Day. &
Attendance: 5,600 (estimated)

Newcastle

FORT BELKNAP MUSEUM AND ARCHIVES, INC., 135 Belknap Cir., Newcastle, TX 76372. Tel.: 940-846-3222.
E-mail: fortbelknap@youngcounty.org
Institution Type/Description: History & Military Museum.
Hours & Admission Prices: Museum: Mon.-Tues. & Thurs.-Sat. 9-12 & 1:30-5, Sun. 1:30-5. No charge; donations accepted. Archives: Sat. 8:30-5:30. Adults $10. &
Attendance: 30,000 (estimated)

Nocona

NORTH TEXAS SOCIETY OF HISTORY AND CULTURE DBA TALES 'N' TRAILS MUSEUM, 1522 E. Hwy. 82, Nocona, TX 76255. Tel.: 940-825-5330.
E-mail: contact@talesntrails.org
Web Site: talesntrails.org
Key Personnel: Pres., Tracy Mesler; Exec. Dir., Nell Ann McBroom; Vice Pres., Gale Cochran-Smith; Treas., Kim Combs; Sec., Melanie Howington.

Institution Type/Description: History Museum.
Hours & Admission Prices: Mon.-Sat. 10-5, Sun. by appointment. Adults $5; students & seniors (over 60) $3; preschoolers, veterans & active military no charge.

Odessa

ELLEN NOEL ART MUSEUM, 4909 E. University, Odessa, TX 79762-7960. Tel.: 432-550-9696. Facebook, Instagram, Twitter.
E-mail: info@noelartmuseum.org
Web Site: noelartmuseum.org
Key Personnel: Dir., Sheila Perry; Cur., Daniel Zies.
Institution Type/Description: Art Museum.
Hours & Admission Prices: Tues., Wed., Fri., Sat. 10-5; Thurs. 10-8; Sun. 2-5. No charge; donations accepted. Closed national holidays. &
Attendance: 22,000 (estimated)

THE ODESSA METEOR CRATER AND MUSEUM, 620 N. Grant Ave., Ste. 1204, Odessa, TX 79761-4549. Tel.: 432-381-0946.
E-mail: oliviam@odessacvb.com
Web Site: www.odessameteorcrater.com
Key Personnel: Museum Mgr., Douglas Neatherlin.
Institution Type/Description: Meteorite Museum.
Hours & Admission Prices: Tues.-Sat. 10-5, Sun. 1-5. No charge; donations accepted. &
Attendance: 15,000 (actual)

THE PRESIDENTIAL ARCHIVES AND LEADERSHIP LIBRARY, 4919 E. University Blvd., Odessa, TX 79762-8144. Mailing Address: 4901 E. University Blvd., Odessa, TX 79762. Tel.: 432-552-2850. Fax: 432-550-2851.
E-mail: jbs@utpb.edu
Web Site: shepperdinstitute.com/presidential-archives/
Key Personnel: Interim Exec. Dir., Tony Cucolo; Dir., Clay Finley.
Institution Type/Description: History Museum.
Hours & Admission Prices: Mon.-Fri. 8-5. No charge; donations accepted. &
Attendance: 5,210 (actual)

Olton

SAND CRAWL MUSEUM, Olton Library, 801 Main St., Olton, TX 79064. Tel.: 806-285-7772.
Institution Type/Description: History Museum.
Hours & Admission Prices: Mon. & Wed.-Fri. 9-12 & 1-5;30, Tues. 1-8.

Orange

HERITAGE HOUSE OF ORANGE COUNTY ASSOCIATION INC., 905 W. Division, Orange, TX 77630-6959. Tel.: 409-886-5385.
E-mail: hhmuseum@att.net
Web Site: www.heritagehouseoforangecounty.com
Key Personnel: Pres., Sue Denosowicz; Vice Pres., Peggy Wells.
Institution Type/Description: Historic House: housed in 1902 turn-of-the-century house.
Hours & Admission Prices: Mon.-Fri. 9-5. Adults $3, adults (50 and over) $2, students $1, children groups $.50, members no charge. &
Attendance: 1,800 (estimated)

SHANGRI LA BOTANICAL GARDENS, 2111 W. Park Ave., Orange, TX 77630. Mailing Address: P.O. Box 1044, Orange, TX 77631. Tel.: 409-670-9113. Fax: 409-670-9341.
E-mail: info@shangrilagardens.org
Web Site: www.shangrilagardens.org
Institution Type/Description: Botanical Gardens.
Hours & Admission Prices: Temporarily Closed

STARK MUSEUM OF ART, 712 Green Ave., Orange, TX 77630-5721. Tel.: 409-886-2787. Fax: 409-883-6361. Facebook: Stark Museum of Art.
E-mail: info@starkmuseum.org
Web Site: www.starkmuseum.org
Key Personnel: Dir. Stark Art & History Venues, Trina Nelson Thomas; Cur. Education, Jennifer Restauri; Cur., Dr. Sarah E. Boehme; Registrar, Katherine Barry; Mgr. Library & Archive, Jenniffer Hudson Connors.
Institution Type/Description: Art Museum.

Hours & Admission Prices: Tues.-Sat. 9-5. No charge; donations accepted. Closed New Year's Day; Easter; Independence Day; Thanksgiving; Christmas Eve & Day. &
Attendance: 14,247 (actual)

THE W.H. STARK HOUSE, 610 W. Main Ave., Orange, TX 77630-5704. Tel.: 409-883-0871. Facebook.
E-mail: info@whstarkhouse.org
Web Site: www.starkculturalvenues.org/whstarkhouse/
Key Personnel: Dir., Katrina Nelson Thomas; Educator & Asst. Site Mgr., Drew Whatley.
Institution Type/Description: Historic House: 1894 home of William H. Stark & Miriam Lutcher Stark.
Hours & Admission Prices: Call ahead for hours. No charge.
Attendance: 3,350 (actual)

Ozona

CROCKETT COUNTY MUSEUM, 408 11th St., Ozona, TX 76943. Mailing Address: P.O. Box 1444, Ozona, TX 76943-1444. Tel.: 325-392-2837.
E-mail: ccmuseum@wcc.net
Key Personnel: Pres. (V), Jan Van Schoubrouek; Vice Pres., Cathy Carson; Coord., Emily Guerra.
Institution Type/Description: History Museum.
Hours & Admission Prices: Mon.-Fri. 9-5, Sat. 10-3. Adults $3, children 5 & under no charge. Closed major holidays. &
Attendance: 2,100 (estimated)

Pampa

FREEDOM MUSEUM USA, 600 N. Hobart, Pampa, TX 79065-5235. Tel.: 806-669-6066.
E-mail: fusa@att.net
Web Site: freedommuseumusa.org
Key Personnel: Pres., John Tripplehorn; Vice Pres., Larry Stephens.
Institution Type/Description: Military History Museum.
Hours & Admission Prices: Tues.-Sat. 12-4. No charge; donations accepted.

WHITE DEER LAND MUSEUM, 116 S. Cuyler, Pampa, TX 79065. Tel.: 806-669-8041. Fax: 806-250-2185. Facebook.
E-mail: wdlmuseum@graycch.com
Web Site: www.pampamuseum.org
Key Personnel: Dir. & Cur., Kay Lard.
Institution Type/Description: General Museum: housed in 1916 White Deer Land Co. Building.
Hours & Admission Prices: Winter & Summer: Tues.-Fri. 1-4; group tours by appointment. No charge; donations accepted. Closed national holidays. &
Attendance: 2,000 (actual)

Panhandle

CARSON COUNTY SQUARE HOUSE MUSEUM, TX Hwy. 207 & Fifth St., Panhandle, TX 79068. Mailing Address: P.O. Box 276, Panhandle, TX 79068-0276. Tel.: 806-537-3524. Fax: 806-537-5628.
E-mail: shm@squarehousemuseum.org
Web Site: www.squarehousemuseum.org
Institution Type/Description: History Museum.
Hours & Admission Prices: Mon.-Sat. 9-5, Sun. 1-5. No charge; donations accepted. Closed New Year's Day; Easter; Thanksgiving; Christmas. &
Attendance: 21,275 (estimated)

Paris

SAM BELL MAXEY HOUSE STATE HISTORIC SITE, 812 S. Church St., Paris, TX 75460-7112. Tel.: 903-785-5716. Facebook, Instagram, Twitter.
E-mail: sam-bell-maxey@thc.texas.gov
Web Site: www.visitsbmh.com
Institution Type/Description: Historic House Museum: 1868 High Victorian Italianate style home belonging to Civil War Confederate Gen. & U.S. Senator, Sam Bell Maxey.
Hours & Admission Prices: Tues.-Sun. 9-4. Adults $4, seniors & college students & youth (6-18) $3, children (5 and under) no charge, special rates for groups. Closed New Year's Eve & Day, Thanksgiving, Christmas Eve & Day. &
Attendance: 2,250 (estimated)

Parker

SOUTHFORK RANCH & VISITOR CENTER, 3700 Hogge Rd., Parker, TX 75002. Tel.: 972-442-7800. Facebook.
E-mail: info@southforkranch.com
Web Site: www.southforkranch.com
Institution Type/Description: Historic Mansion: housed on the site of the filming for the television series "Dallas."
Hours & Admission Prices: Daily 10-5. Adults $15, seniors $13, children 6-12 $9; discounts to groups of 15 or more; children 4 & under no charge. Closed Thanksgiving; Christmas.

Pasadena

ARMAND BAYOU NATURE CENTER, 8500 Bay Area Blvd., Pasadena, TX 77507. Mailing Address: P.O. Box 58828, Houston, TX 77258-8828. Tel.: 281-474-2551. Fax: 281-474-2552.
E-mail: abnc@abnc.org
Web Site: www.abnc.org
Key Personnel: Exec. Dir., Timothy Pylate; Chief Naturalist and Dir. of Conservation, Mark Kramer; Education Dir., Heather Millar; Program Mgr., Kathy Gardner.
Institution Type/Description: Nature Center & Preserve: located on 2,500 acres of tallgrass prairie, forest and bayou including a demonstration turn-of-century farm, also includes several prehistoric archeological sites.
Hours & Admission Prices: Wed.-Sat. 9-5, Sun. 12-5. Adults (13-59) $4, children (4-12) & seniors 60 and over $2; children under 3 & members no charge. &
Attendance: 35,448 (actual)

POMEROY HOUSE AT PASADENA HERITAGE PARK, 204 Main, Pasadena, TX 77506. Tel.: 713-472-0565 & 0564.
E-mail: info@pasadenahistoricalsociety.org
Web Site: www.pasadenahistoricalsociety.org
Key Personnel: Pres. of Bd., Ray Morrison.
Institution Type/Description: History Museum: built in 1906.
Hours & Admission Prices: Tues.-Fri. 9:30-2:30, Sat. available by appointment.

Pecos

WEST OF THE PECOS MUSEUM, 120 E. Dot Stafford St., Pecos, TX 79772. Mailing Address: P.O. Box 1784, Pecos, TX 79772-1784. Tel.: 432-445-5076. Fax: 432-445-3149. Facebook.
E-mail: wpmuseum@windstream.net
Web Site: www.westofthepecosmuseum.com
Key Personnel: Pres. (V), Bill Oglesby; Cur., Dorinda Millan.
Institution Type/Description: History Museum: housed in 1896 two-story red sandstone saloon & c.1904 three-story concrete block Orient Hotel.
Hours & Admission Prices: Memorial Day-Labor Day: Mon.-Sat. 9-5, Sun. 1-4; Labor Day-Memorial Day: Tues.-Sat. 9-5. Closed Christmas week. &
Attendance: 10,000 (actual)

Perryton

MUSEUM OF THE PLAINS, 1200 N. Main, Perryton, TX 79070-2314. Tel.: 806-435-6400.
E-mail: MOTP@MUSEUMOFTHEPLAINS.COM
Web Site: www.museumoftheplains.com
Institution Type/Description: History Museum.
Hours & Admission Prices: Mon.-Fri. 9-5, Sat. 10-5. No charge; donations accepted. Closed New Year's Day; Thanksgiving; Christmas Eve & Day.

Pflugerville

HERITAGE HOUSE MUSEUM, 901 Old Austin Hutto Rd., Pflugerville, TX 78660. Tel.: 512-251-5082.
E-mail: heritagehouse@pflugervilletx.gov
Key Personnel: Pres., David Gebert; Vice Pres., Gloria Kuempel; Vice Pres., Gloria Wuthrich.
Institution Type/Description: History Museum.
Hours & Admission Prices: 1st Sun. each month 1-4; March-Oct.: Tues. 3-7.

Pittsburg

NORTHEAST TEXAS RURAL HERITAGE MUSEUM, 204 W. Marshall, Pittsburg, TX 75686-1312. Mailing Address: P.O. Box 157, Pittsburg, TX 75686-0157. Tel.: 903-856-1200 & 946-3243.
E-mail: campcountymuseum@aol.com
Web Site: www.pittsburgtexasmuseum.com
Key Personnel: Dir., Fanny Hively; Pres. (V), David Abernathy.
Institution Type/Description: History Museum.

Hours & Admission Prices: Thurs.-Sat. 10-4. Adults $4, senior citizens $3, students $2; discount to student groups; members no charge. &
Attendance: 3,164 (actual)

Plainview

MALOUF ABRAHAM FAMILY ARTS CENTER - WAYLAND BAPTIST UNIVERSITY AKA ABRAHAM ART GALLERY, Mabee Learning Resources, 1900 W. 7th St., CMB #1249, Plainview, TX 79072. Tel.: 806-291-1000 & 588-1928. Facebook.
E-mail: kellerc@wbu.edu
Key Personnel: Art Cur., Dr. Candace Keller.
Institution Type/Description: Art Gallery.
Hours & Admission Prices: Mon.-Thurs. 10-5, Fri. 10-4, Sat. 2-5. &
Attendance: 7,000 (estimated)

MUSEUM OF THE LLANO ESTACADO, Wayland University J. E. & L.E. Mabee Rgnl. Heritage Ctr., 1900 W. 8th St., Plainview, TX 79072. Mailing Address: 901 Broadway St., Plainview, TX 79072. Tel.: 806-291-3660. Fax: 806-291-1982.
E-mail: watsonr@wbu.edu
Web Site: www.wbu.edu/museum
Institution Type/Description: General Museum.
Hours & Admission Prices: Mon.-Thurs. 8-5, Fri. 8-4, Sat.-Sun. 1-5. No charge; donations accepted. Closed college holidays. &
Attendance: 6,200 (actual)

Plano

HERITAGE FARMSTEAD MUSEUM, 1900 W. 15th St., Plano, TX 75075-7329. Tel.: 972-881-0140. Fax: 972-422-6481.
E-mail: director@heritgefarmstead.org
Web Site: www.heritagefarmstead.org
Key Personnel: Exec. Dir., M'Lou Taylor Hyttinen; Dir. of Devel., Kathy Strobel; Educ. Dir., Lindsay Bradshaw.
Institution Type/Description: Historic House: 1891 Victorian farmhouse located on a 4-acre historic site.
Hours & Admission Prices: Grounds: Tues.-Sun. 10-4:30. Admission $3 per person; children 2 & under no charge. Docent Led House Tours: May 30-Sept. 3 Tues.-Sun. 10:30; Sept. 5-May 28 Sun. 1:30. Guided Tours: adults $7, students & children $5; children under 4 no charge. Closed holidays. &
Attendance: 32,612 (actual)

INTERURBAN RAILWAY MUSEUM, 901 E. 15th St., Plano, TX 75074-5807. Tel.: 972-941-2117. Facebook, Instagram, Twitter.
E-mail: info@interurbanrailwaymuseum.org
Web Site: www.interurbanrailwaymuseum.org
Formerly: Interurban Railway Station Museum
Key Personnel: Co-Dir., Russell C. Kissick; Co-Dir., Jeffrey Campbell.
Institution Type/Description: Transportation Museum.
Hours & Admission Prices: Mon.-Fri. 10-2, Sat. 1-5. No charge; donations accepted. &
Attendance: 20,000

Pleasanton

LONGHORN MUSEUM, 1959 Hwy. 97 E., Pleasanton, TX 78064-6500. Tel.: 830-569-6313.
E-mail: lhornmuseum@pleasantontx.gov
Web Site: www.pleasantontx.org/museum.html
Key Personnel: Dir., Valerie Purgason.
Institution Type/Description: History Museum.
Hours & Admission Prices: Mon.-Fri. 8-5; groups by appointment. No charge; donations accepted. Closed New Year's Day; Easter; Memorial Day; Independence Day; Labor Day; Thanksgiving; Christmas. &
Attendance: 2,500 (estimated)

Port Aransas

MARINE SCIENCE EDUCATION CENTER, 855 E. Cotter Ave., Port Aransas, TX 78373. Mailing Address: The University of Texas, 750 Channel View Dr., Port Aransas, TX 78373. Tel.: 361-749-6711. Fax: 361-749-6777.
E-mail: msi-edureserve@utlists.utexas.edu
Web Site: missionaransas.org
Key Personnel: Museum Shop Mgr., Lynn Ulch.
Institution Type/Description: Science Center.
Hours & Admission Prices: Currently closed. &

UNIVERSITY OF TEXAS MARINE SCIENCE INSTITUTE VISITOR CENTER, 750 Channel View Dr., Port Aransas, TX 78373. Tel.: 361-749-6711. Fax: 361-749-6777.
E-mail: msi-edureserve@utlists.utexas.edu
Key Personnel: Dir., Robert W. Dickey, Ph.D.
Institution Type/Description: Visitor Center.
Hours & Admission Prices: Mon.-Fri. 8-5, Sat. 10-3, Sun. 11-3.
Attendance: 40,000

WETLANDS EDUCATION CENTER - MARINE SCIENCE INSTITUTE, 750 Channel View Dr., Port Aransas, TX 78373. Tel.: 361-749-3153.
E-mail: robert.dickey@utexas.edu
Web Site: utmsi.utexas.edu/visit/public-programs/wetlands-education-center
Institution Type/Description: Science Center.
Hours & Admission Prices: Temporarily closed.

Port Arthur

MUSEUM OF THE GULF COAST, 700 Procter St., Port Arthur, TX 77640-6521. Mailing Address: P.O. Box 1374, Port Arthur, TX 77641-1374. Tel.: 409-982-7000. Fax: 409-982-9614.
E-mail: bearddv@lamarpa.edu
Web Site: www.museumofthegulfcoast.org
Key Personnel: Cur., Sarah Bellion.
Institution Type/Description: Regional History Museum.
Hours & Admission Prices: Mon.-Sat. 9-5. Adults $6, senior citizens over 62 & college students $5, students 4-18 $3; discounts to groups over 20; children 3 & under and members no charge. Closed major holidays. &
Attendance: 15,000 (actual)

TEXAS ARTISTS' MUSEUM, 3501 Cultural Center Dr., Port Arthur, TX 77642. Tel.: 409-983-4881. Facebook.
E-mail: texasartistmuseum@gmail.com
Web Site: www.texasartistmuseum.org
Key Personnel: Pres. (V), Nadine Kebodeaux.
Institution Type/Description: Art Museum.
Hours & Admission Prices: Tues.-Fri. 12-4, Sat. 11-4. No charge; donations accepted.
Attendance: 5,000 (estimated)

Port Isabel

PORT ISABEL HISTORICAL MUSEUM, 317 E. Railroad Ave., Port Isabel, TX 78578-4107. Tel.: 956-943-7602.
E-mail: museumdirector@copitx.com
Web Site: portisabelmuseums.com
Key Personnel: Dir. of Historical Preservation, Jeannie Marie Aby Flores.
Institution Type/Description: History Museum: housed in a building built by Charles Champion which served as a post office, US Customs house, railroad depot, general store, & restaurant with a residence upstairs; built in 1899.
Hours & Admission Prices: Tues.-Sat. 10-4. Adults $3, senior citizens $2, students $1; members and children 4 & under no charge. Combination tickets available.

PORT ISABEL LIGHTHOUSE & KEEPERS COTTAGE, 421 E. Queen Isabella Blvd., Port Isabel, TX 78578. Tel.: 956-943-2262.
E-mail: museumdirector@copitx.com
Web Site: portisabellighthouse.com
Key Personnel: Dir. of Historical Preservation, Jeannie Marie Aby Flores.
Institution Type/Description: Historic Buildings & Museum.
Hours & Admission Prices: Daily 9-5. Individual site ticket: adults $4, seniors $3, students $2, children (5 and under) & museum members no charge; combination site ticket: adults $9, seniors $7, children (5 and under) & members no charge.

TREASURES OF THE GULF MUSEUM, 317 E. Railroad Ave., Port Isabel, TX 78578. Tel.: 956-943-7602.
E-mail: info@portisabel-texas.com
Key Personnel: Museum Dir., Jeannie Flores.
Institution Type/Description: Maritime History Museum.
Hours & Admission Prices: Tues.-Sat. 10-4. Adults $4, senior citizens $3, students $2; members and children 4 & under no charge. Combination tickets available.

Port Lavaca

CALHOUN COUNTY MUSEUM, 301 S. Ann St., Port Lavaca, TX 77979-4205. Tel.: 361-553-4689.
E-mail: director@calhouncountymuseum.org
Web Site: www.calhouncountymuseum.org
Key Personnel: Dir., George Ann Cormier; Asst. to Dir., Vicki Cox.

Institution Type/Description: History Museum.
Hours & Admission Prices: Tues.-Wed. 10:30-4:30, Thurs.-Fri. 10:30-5, Sat. 10-3.
   No charge; donations accepted. Closed county holidays.
Attendance: 1,785 (actual)

Post

GARZA COUNTY HISTORICAL MUSEUM, 119 North Ave. N.,
   Post, TX 79356-3105. Tel.: 806-495-2207.
E-mail: lgpuckett@gmail.com
Web Site: garzacountymuseum.org
Key Personnel: Cur., Linda G. Puckett.
Institution Type/Description: History Museum.
Hours & Admission Prices: Tues.-Sat. 10-12 & 1-5. No charge; donations accepted.
   &
Attendance: 8,000 (actual)

OS MUSEUM, 201 E. Main St., Post, TX 79356. Mailing Address:
   P.O. Box 790, Post, TX 79356. Tel.: 806-495-3570. Fax: 806-495-
   2288. Facebook.
E-mail: os_museum@yahoo.com
Formerly: OS Ranch Museum
Key Personnel: Dir., Marie T. Neff.
Institution Type/Description: Fine Art Museum.
Hours & Admission Prices: Mon.-Fri. 10-12, 1-5; Sat. 10-2. No charge. Call for hol-
   iday hours. &

Presidio

FORT LEATON STATE HISTORICAL SITE, FM 170 E.,
   Presidio, TX 79845. Mailing Address: P.O. Box 2439, Presidio,
   TX 79845-2439. Tel.: 432-229-3613. Fax: 432-229-4814.
   Facebook, Twitter.
Web Site: www.tpwd.state.tx.us
Institution Type/Description: Historic Building & Museum: 1848 private 40-room
   adobe fortress built by Indian trader Benjamin Leaton, located on old Indianola-
   San Antonio-Chihuahua Trail & overlooking the Rio Grande.
Hours & Admission Prices: Daily 8-4:30. Adults $5; children under 12 no charge.
   Closed Christmas.
Attendance: 3,600 (actual)

Ralls

RALLS HISTORICAL MUSEUM, 801 Main St., Ralls, TX 79357.
   Mailing Address: P.O. Box 384, Ralls, TX 79357-0384. Tel.: 806-
   253-2425 & 454-0219.
E-mail: rallshistoricalmuseum@windstream.net
Key Personnel: Pres. (V), Dale Sedgwick; 1st Vice Pres., Bill Igal.
Institution Type/Description: General Museum: housed in 1918 First National
   Bank.
Hours & Admission Prices: Tues.-Fri. 10-12 & 1-3. No charge; donations accepted.
Attendance: 474 (actual)

Rankin

RANKIN MUSEUM, 101 W. Main St., Inside Yates Hotel, Rankin,
   TX 79778. Mailing Address: P.O. Box 22, Rankin, TX 79778-
   0022. Tel.: 915-693-2758.
Key Personnel: Pres. (V), Donna Bell.
Institution Type/Description: Local History Museum.
Hours & Admission Prices: Thurs.-Fri. 2-5, Sat. 1-5; other times by appointment.
   No charge; donations accepted. &
Attendance: 1,000 (estimated)

Refugio

REFUGIO COUNTY MUSEUM, 102 W. West St., Refugio, TX
   78377-2433. Tel.: 361-526-5555. Fax: 361-526-4943.
E-mail: brefugiomuseum@aol.com
Web Site: refugiocountytx.org/page/refugio-county-museum
Key Personnel: Dir., Bart Wales.
Institution Type/Description: Local History Museum.
Hours & Admission Prices: Tues.-Fri. 12-4, Sat. 1-5. No charge; donations
   accepted. Closed major holidays. &
Attendance: 2,500

Richmond

FORT BEND COUNTY MUSEUM ASSOCIATION, 500
   Houston, Richmond, TX 77469-3522. Tel.: 281-342-6478.
   Facebook.
E-mail: info@fortbendmuseum.org
Web Site: www.fortbendmuseum.org
Key Personnel: Site Mgr., Ana Alicia Estrada; Programs Coord., Jessica Avery;
   Texian Time Machine & Outreach Coord., Allison Harrell; Office Mgr., Connie
   Pike.
Institution Type/Description: Local History Museum.
Hours & Admission Prices: Tues.-Fri. 9-5, Sat. 10-5; Tours: 10 & 1. Adults $10;
   seniors (65 and over) $8; children (4-12) $5; children (3 and under), members,
   active-duty military no charge. &
Attendance: 14,852 (actual)

GEORGE RANCH HISTORICAL PARK, 10215 FM 762 Rd.,
   Richmond, TX 77469. Mailing Address: P.O. Box 1248,
   Richmond, TX 77406. Tel.: 281-343-0218. Facebook: George
   Ranch Historical Park.
E-mail: info@georgeranch.org
Web Site: www.georgeranch.org
Key Personnel: Exec. Dir., Claire Rogers; Pres., Tim Kaminski.
Institution Type/Description: Historic Ranch: housed on a 23,000 acre working
   ranch.
Hours & Admission Prices: Tues.-Sat. 9-5. Adults $15, seniors (62 & over) $12,
   children (4-12) $10; children (3 & under) and members no charge. Closed New
   Year's Day; Thanksgiving; Christmas Eve & Day. &
Attendance: 71,449 (actual)

Rockport

BAY EDUCATION CENTER, 121 Seabreeze Dr., Rockport, TX
   78382. Mailing Address: c/o Mission-Aransas Reserve, 750
   Channel View Dr., Port Aransas, TX 78373. Tel.: 361-749-3152.
E-mail: sarapel@utexas.edu
Web Site: missionaransas.org
Institution Type/Description: Science Center.
Hours & Admission Prices: Temporarily closed. &
Attendance: 7,000 (estimated)

FULTON MANSION STATE HISTORIC SITE, 317 S. Fulton
   Beach Rd., Rockport, TX 78382. Tel.: 361-729-0386.
E-mail: fulton-mansion@thc.state.tx.us
Web Site: www.visitfultonmansion.com
Key Personnel: Site Mgr., Marsha Hendrix.
Institution Type/Description: Historic House Museum: c.1877 French Second
   Empire style Mansion.
Hours & Admission Prices: Tues.-Sat. 10-4, Sun. 1-4. No charge; donations are
   accepted. &
Attendance: 20,100 (actual)

TEXAS MARITIME MUSEUM, 1202 Navigation Cir., Rockport,
   TX 78382-2773. Tel.: 361-729-1271. Fax: 361-729-9938.
   Facebook.
E-mail: klrd@pelicancoast.net
Web Site: www.texasmaritimemuseum.org
Key Personnel: C.E.O., Kathy Roberts-Douglass; Pres., Joanne Taylor; Exec. Asst.,
   Alisha Brundrett; Cur., Cassidy Mickelson; Educ. Dir., Aaron Martin.
Institution Type/Description: Texas Maritime Museum.
Hours & Admission Prices: Tues.-Sat. 10-4, Sun. 1-4. Adults $8, seniors & military
   $6, children 3-12 $3; discounts to AAM members w/ID and groups of 10 or
   more with 2 weeks notice; children 5 & under and members no charge. Closed
   New Year's Day; Easter; Memorial Day; Columbus Day; Labor Day;
   Thanksgiving; Christmas. &
Attendance: 16,232 (actual)

Rosenberg

ROSENBERG RAILROAD MUSEUM, 1921 Avenue F,
   Rosenberg, TX 77471. Mailing Address: P.O. Box 369, Rosenberg,
   TX 77471-0369. Tel.: 281-633-2846. Facebook.
E-mail: info@rosenbergrrmuseum.org
Web Site: www.rosenbergrrmuseum.org
Key Personnel: Pres., Greg Cauthen; Exec. Dir., Tracy Hobdy.
Institution Type/Description: Railroad Museum.
Hours & Admission Prices: Wed.-Sat. 10-5, Sun. 1-5. Adults $7.50, senior citizens
   55 & over, military, first responders $6, children 2-14 $5, children under 2 no

charge. Closed New Year's Eve & Day; Easter; Independence Day; Thanksgiving; Christmas Eve & Day.
Attendance: 17,500 (actual)

Round Mountain

WESTCAVE OUTDOOR DISCOVERY CENTER, 24814 Hamilton Pool Rd., Round Mountain, TX 78663. Tel.: 830-825-3442 & 512-276-2257. Facebook, Instagram, Twitter.
E-mail: info@westcave.org
Web Site: westcave.org
Key Personnel: Chair, William Steele.
Institution Type/Description: Geology Museum.
Hours & Admission Prices: Tues.-Fri. 10-2, Sat.-Sun. 9:30-4:30. Canyon Tours: adults $15, child 4-17 $7; Upland Trails: adults $7, child 4-17 $4.

Round Top

BRISCOE CENTER FOR AMERICAN HISTORY-WINEDALE HISTORICAL CENTER, UNIVERSITY OF TEXAS AT AUSTIN, 3738 FM Road 2714, Round Top, TX 78954. Mailing Address: P.O. Box 11, Round Top, TX 78954-0011. Tel.: 979-278-3530.
E-mail: winedale@austin.utexas.edu
Web Site: www.cah.utexas.edu/museums/winedale.php
Formerly: Winedale, Center for American History, University of Texas at Austin
Key Personnel: Winedale Admin. Program Coord., Toni Mason; Building Attendant, Natalie Schulle; Office Mgr., Beth Stewart; Security, Patrick Welch; Maintenance, David Chovanec.
Institution Type/Description: Historic House.
Hours & Admission Prices: Mon.-Fri. 8-5. Tours: by appointment. Adults $6. Closed holidays. &
Attendance: 9,862 (actual)

FESTIVAL-INSTITUTE, JAMES DICK FOUNDATION, 248 Jaster Rd., Round Top, TX 78954-5445. Mailing Address: P.O. Box 89, Round Top, TX 78954-0089. Tel.: 979-249-3129. Fax: 409-249-5078.
E-mail: info@festivalhill.org
Web Site: www.festivalhill.org
Key Personnel: Founder, Dir. & Pres., James Dick; Mng. Dir., Richard R. Royall; Dir. Museum & Library Collections, Lamar Lentz; Program Dir., Alain G. Declert.
Institution Type/Description: Architecture & Art Museum: historic restorations include 1883 Edythe Bates Old Chapel; 1884 William Lockhart Clayton House; 1902 C.A. Menke House.
Hours & Admission Prices: Mon.-Sat. by appointment. Tours: $5 per person; self-guided tours of grounds during day; discounts to AAM members. Closed Thanksgiving; Christmas. &
Attendance: 34,000 (estimated)

Salado

CENTRAL TEXAS AREA MUSEUM, INC., 423 S. Main St., Salado, TX 76571. Mailing Address: P.O. Box 36, Salado, TX 76571. Tel.: 254-947-5232. Fax: 254-947-5232.
E-mail: office@ctam-salado.org
Web Site: www.ctam-salado.org
Key Personnel: Pres., Sterling Ambrose; Exec. Dir./Cur., Madeleine Calcote; Sec., Beverly Turnbo; Treas., Pat Suggs; Museum Shop Mgr., Mary Mendez.
Institution Type/Description: General Museum: housed in an early Central Texas store building.
Hours & Admission Prices: Tues.-Sat. 10-4. No charge; donations accepted.
Attendance: (estimated)

Salt Flat

GUADALUPE MOUNTAINS NATIONAL PARK, 400 Pine Canyon Dr., Salt Flat, TX 79847-4755. Tel.: 915-828-3251. Fax: 915-828-3269.
E-mail: gumo_superintendent@nps.gov
Web Site: www.nps.gov/gumo
Key Personnel: Superintendent, Dennis Vasquez.
Institution Type/Description: National Park Museum.
Hours & Admission Prices: Park: open year-round; Visitor Center: daily 8-4:30. Daily individual fee $5. &
Attendance: 76,000 (actual)

San Angelo

ANGELO STATE UNIVERSITY PLANETARIUM, 2333 Vanderventer Ave., San Angelo, TX 76904. Tel.: 325-942-2188 & 2136.
E-mail: kcarrell@angelo.edu
Web Site: www.angelo.edu/dept/physics/planetarium.php
Key Personnel: Planetarium Dir., Kenneth Wayne Carrell.
Institution Type/Description: Planetarium.
Hours & Admission Prices: Call for hours. Adults $3, children, senior citizens & active military $2; ASU students, faculty & staff no charge.

FORT CONCHO NATIONAL HISTORIC LANDMARK, 630 S. Oakes St., San Angelo, TX 76903-7013. Tel.: 325-481-2646 & 657-4444. Facebook.
E-mail: admin@fortconcho.com
Web Site: fortconcho.com
Key Personnel: Pres., Kathy Keane; Vice Pres., Roger Banks; Sec., Sherley Spears; Treas., Darrin Fentress.
Institution Type/Description: Historic Landmark.
Hours & Admission Prices: Mon.-Sat. 9-5, Sun. 1-5. Adults $3; discounts for senior citizens, military, groups, Texas Forts Trail, NTHP, AAA & TAM members; members & children under 6 no charge. Closed New Year's Day; Thanksgiving; Christmas. &
Attendance: 60,000 (actual)

MISS HATTIE'S BORDELLO MUSEUM, 18 1/2 E. Concho Ave., San Angelo, TX 76903-6412. Tel.: 325-653-0112. Facebook, Youtube.
E-mail: info@misshatties.com
Web Site: www.misshatties.com
Institution Type/Description: History Museum.
Hours & Admission Prices: Tours: Tues.-Thurs. 2-4, Fri.-Sat. 1, 2, 3 & 4; groups of 10 or more by appointment. Adults $6, senior/military $5.

RAILWAY MUSEUM OF SAN ANGELO, 703 S. Chadbourne, San Angelo, TX 76903-6931. Tel.: 325-486-2140.
E-mail: railmuseum@gmail.com
Key Personnel: Pres. & Exec. Dir., Shannon Carpenter.
Institution Type/Description: Railway Museum: housed in the 1909 Orient-Santa Fe Passenger Depot built by the KCM&O.
Hours & Admission Prices: Sat. 10-4. Adults 12 & over $5, children 4-12 $3; discounts to seniors 65 & over and military; children under 4 no charge. &
Attendance: 8,560 (actual)

SAN ANGELO MUSEUM OF FINE ARTS, One Love St., San Angelo, TX 76903-6911. Tel.: 325-653-3333.
E-mail: museum@samfa.org
Web Site: www.samfa.org
Key Personnel: Dir., Howard Taylor; Pres., Dr. John Klingemann; Asst. Dir./Collections Mgr., Laura Romer Huckaby; Business Mgr., Jan Mulkey; Mktg. & Public Relations Mgr., Mary Claire Rizzardi; Graphic Designer, Blanca E. Hernandez; CASETA Admin., Valerie C. Bluthardt; Office Asst., Marsalis Mahome; Cultural District Mgr., Shaydee Watson; Curator of Educator, Rebekah Coleman; Weekend Supvr., Sylvia Grimaldo; Museum Shop Mgr., Andres Gonzales.
Institution Type/Description: Art Museum.
Hours & Admission Prices: Tues.-Sat. 10-4, Sun. 1-4. Adults $2, senior citizens $1; discounts to groups of 10 or more, Texas Assoc. of Museums, AAM & ICOM members; members, families with children, students & military no charge. Closed national holidays. &
Attendance: 60,000 (estimated)

SAN ANGELO NATURE CENTER, 7409 Knickerbocker Rd., San Angelo, TX 76904-7885. Tel.: 325-942-0121.
Key Personnel: Nature Center Coord., Selina McSherry.
Institution Type/Description: Nature Center.
Hours & Admission Prices: Tues.-Sat. 12-5. Adults $3, children (4-12) $2, children (3 and under) no charge.

San Antonio

THE ALAMO, 300 Alamo Plaza, San Antonio, TX 78205-2606. Tel.: 210-225-1391. Facebook, Instagram, Twitter.
E-mail: info@thealamo.org
Web Site: www.thealamo.org
Key Personnel: Dir., Douglass McDonald; Historian & Cur., Dr. Richard Bruce Winders.
Institution Type/Description: Historic Site & Complex: housed in the Colonial Spanish Mission, built in 1724; site of 1836 Battle of the Alamo.

Hours & Admission Prices: May 25 to Sept. 3 & Dec. 6-Jan. 5 daily 9-7; Sept.4-Dec. 5 & Jan. 6-May 24 daily 9-5:30. No charge; donations accepted. Closed Christmas Day. &
Attendance: 2,479,329 (actual)

ARTPACE SAN ANTONIO, 445 N. Main Ave., San Antonio, TX 78205-1441. Tel.: 210-212-4900. Fax: 210-212-4990. Facebook: Artpace San Antonio.
E-mail: info@artpace.org
Web Site: www.artpace.org
Key Personnel: Dir., Riley Robinson; Dir. Devel., Lisa Haiff; Dir., Residences & Exhibs., Erin Murphy.
Institution Type/Description: Art Museum.
Hours & Admission Prices: Tues.-Fri. 10-5, Sat. 10-5. No charge; donations accepted. &
Attendance: 72,000 (estimated)

BLUE STAR CONTEMPORARY ART CENTER, 116 Blue Star, San Antonio, TX 78204-1713. Tel.: 210-227-6960.
E-mail: bsc@bluestarcontemporary.org
Web Site: www.bluestarart.org
Key Personnel: Exec. Dir., Mary Heathcott; Cur. & Exhib. Mgr., Jacqueline Saragoza McGilvray; Education Mgr., Mari Hernandez; MOSAIC Artist-in-Residence, Alex Rubio.
Institution Type/Description: Contemporary Art Museum
Hours & Admission Prices: Thurs. 10-8, Fri.-Sun. 10-6, See website for admissions. &
Attendance: 150,000 (estimated)

BRISCOE WESTERN ART MUSEUM, 210 W. Market St., San Antonio, TX 78205. Tel.: 210-299-4499. Fax: 210-299-4118. Facebook, Twitter.
E-mail: info@briscoemuseum.org
Web Site: www.briscoemuseum.org
Key Personnel: Pres. & C.E.O., Michael Duchemin, Ph.D; Vice Pres., Liz Jackson; Head of Operations, Gracie Burciaga; Cur. Colls., Ryan Badger.
Institution Type/Description: Art Museum.
Hours & Admission Prices: Mon.-Sat. 10-5, Sun. 10-3. Adults $10; Seniors 65 and over & students $8, retired military, first responders, educators, firefighters & police with ID $5; members, children 12 & under, active military & family no charge. Holiday schedule see website. &

BUCKHORN SALOON & MUSEUM, 318 E. Houston St., San Antonio, TX 78205-1816. Tel.: 210-247-4000. Facebook, Instagram, Twitter.
E-mail: sales@buckhornmuseum.com
Web Site: www.buckhornmuseum.com
Institution Type/Description: Natural History Museum; Texas - San Antonio historic house site.
Hours & Admission Prices: Daily 10-closing times vary. Adults $19.99, children 3-11 $14.99. &
Attendance: 56,000 (actual)

CASA NAVARRO STATE HISTORIC SITE, 228 S. Laredo St., San Antonio, TX 78207. Tel.: 210-226-4801. Facebook, Instagram, Twitter.
E-mail: casa-navarro@thc.texas.gov
Web Site: www.thc.texas.gov/historic-sites/casa-navarro-state-historic-site
Key Personnel: Site Mgr., Georgia Ruiz Davis.
Institution Type/Description: Historic Site & House Museum: c.1850 home site of Texas patriot, Jose Antonio Navarro.
Hours & Admission Prices: Tues.-Sat. 10-5, Sun. 12-5. Adults $4, seniors & college students, children 6-18, adult tour groups $3; discounts to school & adult tour groups; children 5 & under no charge. Closed New Year's Eve & Day, Thanksgiving, Christmas Eve & Day. &
Attendance: 4,277 (actual)

CENTRO DE ARTES, 101 S. Santa Rosa Ave., San Antonio, TX 78207. Mailing Address: P.O. Box 839966, San Antonio, TX 78283-3966. Tel.: 210-206-2787(ARTS). Fax: 210-207-4526. Facebook, Twitter.
E-mail: arts@sanantonio.gov
Web Site: www.getcreativesanantonio.com
Formerly: The Alameda National Center for Latino Arts and Culture
Key Personnel: Dir., San Antonio Dept. Arts & Culture, Debbie Racca-Sittre.
Institution Type/Description: Latino Arts & Culture.
Hours & Admission Prices: Tues.-Sun. 11-6. No charge.

THE DOSEUM, 2800 Broadway St., San Antonio, TX 78209-7034. Tel.: 210-212-4453. Facebook, Instagram, Twitter.
E-mail: info@thedoseum.org
Web Site: www.thedoseum.org
Formerly: San Antonio Children's Museum
Key Personnel: C.E.O., Daniel Menelly; Sr. Vice Pres. Finance & Administration, Dee-Ann Calderon; Vice Pres. Education, Richard A. Kissel; Vice Pres. of Exhibits, Meredith Doby; Vice Pres. of Mktg., Sandra Garcia; Vice Pres. Devel., Sara Pfeifer.
Institution Type/Description: Children's Museum.
Hours & Admission Prices: Mon.-Fri. 9-6, Sat. 12-5. Members: Sun. 11-12. . &
Attendance: 540,000 (actual)

GUINNESS WORLD RECORDS MUSEUM, 329 Alamo Plaza, San Antonio, TX 78205-2667. Tel.: 210-226-2828.
E-mail: info@phillipsentertainmentinc.com
Web Site: www.ripleys.com/phillips/
Key Personnel: Pres. & C.E.O., Davis Phillips.
Institution Type/Description: World Records Museum.
Hours & Admission Prices: See website for hours. Adults: One Attraction $21.99, Two Attractions $24.99, Three Attractions $29.99; Children 3-11: One Attraction $13.99, Two Attractions $16.99, Three Attractions $19.99. &

MCNAY ART MUSEUM, 6000 N. New Braunfels Ave., San Antonio, TX 78209. Tel.: 210-824-5368. Facebook, Instagram, Twitter.
E-mail: info@mcnayart.org
Web Site: www.mcnayart.org
Formerly: Marion Koogler McNay Art Museum
Key Personnel: Dir., Richard Aste; Head, Curatorial Affairs, Rene Paul Barilleaux; Dir. Education, Katharine E. Carey; HR Sr. Mgr., Lisa R. Penn; Head Opers., Luis Barthel; Cur. Collections, Lyle W. Williams; Cur. Tobin Collection of Theatre Arts, R. Scott Blackshire; Cur. Prints & Drawings, Lyle Williams; Museum Store & Visitor Svcs. Mgr., Janet D. Goddard.
Institution Type/Description: Fine Arts Museum.
Hours & Admission Prices: Wed. & Fri. 10-6, Thurs. 10-9, Sat. 10-5, Sun. 12-5. Adults $20; students, seniors (65 & over) $15, teens 13-19 $10; members, children 12 and under, active military WIC, SNAP & MAP recipients no charge. Closed New Year's Day; Independence Day; Thanksgiving; Christmas. &
Attendance: 134,000 (estimated)

NSSA-NSCA MUSEUM & HALL OF FAME, 5931 Roft Rd., San Antonio, TX 78253. Tel.: 210-688-3371. Fax: 210-688-3014. Facebook, Instagram.
E-mail: museum@nssa-nsca.com
Web Site: www.nssa-nsca.org
Key Personnel: Cur., Mike Brazzell; Asst. Cur., Jim Harris.
Institution Type/Description: National Shooting Museum
Hours & Admission Prices: Complex: Mon.-Fri. 8-5. Call for museum hours.

SAN ANTONIO ART LEAGUE MUSEUM, 130 King William St., San Antonio, TX 78204-1311. Tel.: 210-223-1140.
E-mail: saalm@att.net
Web Site: www.saalm.org
Key Personnel: Pres., Dona Belisle LeCrone Walston.
Institution Type/Description: Art Museum.
Hours & Admission Prices: Tues.-Sat. 10-3. No charge; donations accepted. &
Attendance: 500

SAN ANTONIO BOTANICAL GARDEN, 555 Funston Place, San Antonio, TX 78209-6631. Tel.: 210-536-1400. TDD: 210-207-3255.
E-mail: info@sabot.org
Web Site: www.sabot.org
Key Personnel: C.E.O., Sabina Carr; Chief Financial Officer, Cindy Campbell; Dir. Progs., Katie Erickson; Dir. Opers., Sam Hogg; Dir. Mktg., Eliana Rodriguez.
Institution Type/Description: Botanical Garden.
Hours & Admission Prices: March-Oct. Mon.-Fri. 9-7, Sat.-Sun. 9-5; Nov.-Feb. Mon.-Sun. 9-5. Adults $15, students & military $13, children 3-13 $12; children under 3 no charge. &
Attendance: 100,000 (estimated)

SAN ANTONIO CONSERVATION SOCIETY, 107 King William St., San Antonio, TX 78204-1312. Tel.: 210-224-6163. Fax: 210-224-6168.
E-mail: conserve@saconservation.org
Web Site: www.saconservation.org
Key Personnel: Exec. Dir., Vincent Michael; Pres. (V), Patti Zaiontz.

Institution Type/Description: Historic House Museums: Wulff House (library only; no tours); 1840-1860 Yturri-Edmunds Historic Site; 1876 Steves Homestead House Museum.
Hours & Admission Prices: Call for hours & admissions. &

Attendance: 11,000 (actual)

SAN ANTONIO MISSIONS NATIONAL HISTORICAL PARK, Visitor Center, 6701 San Jose Dr., San Antonio, TX 78210. Mailing Address: 2202 Roosevelt Ave., San Antonio, TX 78210. Tel.: 210-932-1001. Fax: 210-534-1106. Facebook, Instagram, Twitter.
E-mail: saan_interpretation@nps.gov
Web Site: www.nps.gov/saan
Key Personnel: Park Supt., Mardi Arce.
Institution Type/Description: National Historic Park: comprised of the following four Spanish missions: 1720 San Jose Y San Miguel de Aguayo; 1731 La Purisima Concepcion; 1731 San Juan Capistrano; 1731 San Francisco de la Espada.
Hours & Admission Prices: Daily sunrise-sunset. No charge; donations accepted. Closed New Year's Day; Thanksgiving; Christmas. &
Attendance: 1,400,000 (estimated)

SAN ANTONIO MUSEUM OF ART, 200 W. Jones Ave., San Antonio, TX 78215-1402. Tel.: 210-978-8100. Facebook, Instagram, Twitter.
E-mail: info@samuseum.org
Web Site: www.samuseum.org
Key Personnel: Co-Interim Dir., Emily Sano; Cur. Emeritus of Latin American Art, Marion Oettinger, Jr.; Cur. of Art of the Ancient Mediterranean World, Jessica Powers; Cur. of Modern & Contemporary Art, Suzanne Weaver.
Institution Type/Description: Art Museum: housed in restored turn-of-the-century Lone Star Brewing Company.
Hours & Admission Prices: Tues. & Fri. 10-7, Wed.-Thurs., Sat.-Sun. 10-5. Adults $20, seniors $17, students & military $12, youth 13-18 $10; children 12 and under & members no charge. &
Attendance: 162,000 (estimated)

SAN ANTONIO ZOOLOGICAL SOCIETY, 3903 N. Saint Mary's St., San Antonio, TX 78212-7183. Tel.: 210-734-7184. Fax: 210-734-7291. Facebook. Instagram, Twitter.
E-mail: information@sazoo.org
Web Site: www.sazoo.org
Key Personnel: C.E.O. & Exec. Dir., Tim Morrow; Bd. Pres., Chris Bathie.
Institution Type/Description: Zoo.
Hours & Admission Prices: Sun. 9-6, Mon.-Fri. 9-5, Sat. 9-9. Adults $21.99, child $18.99; discounts to military personnel, persons with disabilities & school groups; children 2 & under & members no charge. &
Attendance: 1,000,000 (estimated)

SOUTHWEST SCHOOL OF ART, 300 Augusta St., San Antonio, TX 78205-1216. Tel.: 210-200-8200. Fax: 210-224-9337.
E-mail: information@swschool.org
Web Site: www.swschool.org
Key Personnel: Pres., Paula Owen; Vice Pres., Kevin Conlon.
Institution Type/Description: Contemporary Art Center & History Museum.
Hours & Admission Prices: Exhibitions: Mon.-Sat. 9-5. Museum Shop: Mon.-Sat. 10-5. No charge; donations accepted. Closed major holidays. &
Attendance: 250,000 (estimated)

SPANISH GOVERNOR'S PALACE, 105 Plaza de Armas, San Antonio, TX 78205-2412. Tel.: 210-207-2111.
E-mail: spanishgovpalace@sanantonio.gov
Web Site: www.spanishgovernorspalace.org
Key Personnel: Dir., World Heritage Office, Colleen Swain; Museum Asst., Charlotte Boord.
Institution Type/Description: Historic Building: 1722 Spanish Governor's Palace.
Hours & Admission Prices: Tues.-Sat. 9-5, Sun. 10-5. Adults $5, military/ seniors $3, children 7 to 13 $3, children under 7 no charge. &
Attendance: 22,092 (actual)

STEVES HOMESTEAD, 509 King William St., San Antonio, TX 78204-1411. Tel.: 210-225-5924 & 227-9160. Fax: 210-223-9014.
E-mail: homestead@saconservation.org
Web Site: www.saconservation.org
Key Personnel: Exec. Dir., Bruce MacDougal.
Institution Type/Description: History Museum.
Hours & Admission Prices: Steves Homestead: daily 10-3:30. Adults $7.50, seniors 65 & over, military and students $5; children under 12 & members no charge. Wulff House: no tours; research library only. Mon.-Thurs. 10-3. Call for infor-

mation for other sites. Yturri-Edmunds by appointment only. Closed most major holidays.
Attendance: 10,154 (actual)

TEXAS AIR MUSEUM, Stinson Field, 1234 99th St., San Antonio, TX 78214. Tel.: 210-977-9885.
E-mail: info@texasairmuseum.org
Web Site: www.texasairmuseum.org
Key Personnel: Founder & Dir., John D. Tosh.
Institution Type/Description: Military Aviation History Museum.
Hours & Admission Prices: Tues.-Sat. 9-4. Adults $6, seniors 55 & over $5, military $4, youth $3, children $2; discounts to school groups. Closed New Year's Eve & Day; Thanksgiving; Christmas Eve & Day. &
Attendance: 4,000 (estimated)

TEXAS TRANSPORTATION MUSEUM, 11731 Wetmore Rd., San Antonio, TX 78247-3606. Tel.: 210-490-3554. Facebook.
E-mail: hugh@txtransportationmuseum.org
Web Site: www.txtransportationmuseum.org
Key Personnel: Mgr., Hugh Hemphill; Chm. (V), David W. Cenova.
Institution Type/Description: Transportation Museum.
Hours & Admission Prices: Fri. 9-3, Sat.-Sun. 9-4. Adult $10, child 4-12 $8; children under 4 no charge. &
Attendance: 10,000 (actual)

TOILET SEAT ART MUSEUM, 239 Abiso Ave., San Antonio, TX 78209-5103. Tel.: 210-824-7791.
E-mail: colonyevents@texastruckyard.com
Web Site: truckyardthecolony.com/museum
Key Personnel: Owner, Barney Smith.
Institution Type/Description: Art Museum.
Hours & Admission Prices: Daily 11-2. No charge.

UTSA INSTITUTE OF TEXAN CULTURES, 801 E. Cesar E. Chavez Blvd., San Antonio, TX 78205-3296. Tel.: 210-458-2300. Facebook, Instagram, Twitter.
E-mail: christian.clark@utsa.edu
Web Site: www.texancultures.com
Formerly: Institute of Texan Cultures
Key Personnel: Exec. Dir., Angelica Docog; Dir. of Public Engagement, Christian Clark; Dir. Special Events & Festivals, Jo Ann Andera; Dir. of Advancement, Amber Phifer-Forrest.
Institution Type/Description: Educational center for the history & diverse cultures of Texas.
Hours & Admission Prices: Mon.-Sat. 9-5, Sun. 12-5. Adults $12, seniors over 65, military & children 6-17, college students $9; discounts to tours & school groups; USTA & Alamo Colleges students, faculty and staff, children 5 & under & members no charge. Closed New Year's Day; Easter; Thanksgiving; Christmas. &
Attendance: 150,000 (estimated)

THE UNIVERSITY OF TEXAS AT SAN ANTONIO, ART GALLERY, 1604 Campus Art Building, 2nd Floor, San Antonio, TX 78249-1130. Tel.: 210-458-4391.
E-mail: art.events@utsa.edu
Web Site: art.utsa.edu/galleries.art-gallery/
Key Personnel: Cur., Scott Sherer.
Institution Type/Description: University Art Gallery.
Hours & Admission Prices: Tues.-Fri. 10-4, Sat. 1-4. No charge; donations accepted. Closed university holidays. &
Attendance: 3,000 (estimated)

VILLA FINALE MUSEUM & GARDENS, 401 King William St., San Antonio, TX 78204. Tel.: 210-223-9800.
E-mail: villafinale@villafinale.org
Web Site: villafinale.org
Key Personnel: Exec. Dir., Jane Lewis; Chm. (V), Nancy H. Avellar.
Institution Type/Description: Historic House Museum: housed in the former home of preservationist & civic leader, Walter Mathis; c.1876.
Hours & Admission Prices: Tues.-Sat. 10-1. Self-guided tours: Adults $10, seniors, students & military with ID $8. Guided tours: adults $12, seniors, students & military with ID $10; discounts to members & National Trust members. Admission tickets sold at Carriage House. &
Attendance: 8,500 (estimated)

WITTE MUSEUM, 3801 Broadway, San Antonio, TX 78209-6396. Tel.: 210-357-1900. Facebook, Instagram, Twitter.
E-mail: info@wittemuseum.org
Web Site: www.wittemuseum.org

Key Personnel: Pres. & C.E.O., Marise McDermott; Chief Admin. Officer, Bea Abercrombie; Chief Advancement, Heather Welder Russo; Chief Business Officer, Kim Biffle; Chief Cur., Amy Fulkerson; Chief Strategic Initiatives, Michelle Everidge; Chief Opers., Brady Haynes.
Institution Type/Description: History Museum: located in Brackenridge Park.
Hours & Admission Prices: Mon. & Wed.-Sat. 10-5, Tues. 10-6, Sun. 12-5. Adults $14, military with ID & senior citizens 65 & over $13, children 4-11 $10; children 3 & under & members no charge. Closed Easter; 3rd Mon. in Oct.; Thanksgiving; Christmas. &
Attendance: 200,000 (actual)

WOODEN NICKEL HISTORICAL MUSEUM, 345 Old Austin Rd., San Antonio, TX 78209-6933. Tel.: 800-750-9915. Fax: 210-829-1303. Facebook, Instagram, Twitter.
E-mail: wninfo@wooden-nickel.com
Web Site: www.ot-wooden-nickel.com
Institution Type/Description: Virtual Museum.
Attendance: 400 (estimated)

San Augustine

MISSION DOLORES STATE HISTORIC SITE, 701 S. Broadway St., San Augustine, TX 75972. Tel.: 936-275-3815.
E-mail: missiondolores@thc.texas.gov
Web Site: visitmissiondolores.com
Key Personnel: Site Mgr., Michael Haven.
Institution Type/Description: Historic Site: housed on the site of an 18th century Spanish Mission.
Hours & Admission Prices: Tues.-Sun. 8-5. No charge; donations accepted. Closed New Year's Eve & Day; Thanksgiving; Christmas Eve & Day. &
Attendance: 2,000 (estimated)

San Benito

LOS EBANOS PRESERVE AND CASA LOS EBANOS, 27715 Hwy. 100, San Benito, TX 78586. Tel.: 956-399-9097.
E-mail: casalosebanos@aol.com
Web Site: www.casalosebanos.com
Institution Type/Description: Nature Preserve & Historic House: housed on an 82-acre site.
Hours & Admission Prices: By appointment.

San Elizario

LOS PORTALES MUSEUM & INFORMATION CENTER, 1521 San Elizario Rd., San Elizario, TX 78949. Mailing Address: P.O. Box 1090, San Elizario, TX 79849. Tel.: 915-851-1682. Fax: 915-851-0045.
E-mail: saneligenealogy@att.net
Web Site: sanelizariogenealogy.com
Key Personnel: Pres., Mary Alice Garcia; 1st Vice Pres., Erasmo Payan; 2nd Vice Pres., Ray Borrego.
Institution Type/Description: History Museum.
Hours & Admission Prices: Tues.-Sat. 10-2, Sun. 12-4. No charge; donations accepted. Closed major holidays. &
Attendance: 9,000 (actual)

San Marcos

CALABOOSE AFRICAN AMERICAN HISTORY MUSEUM, 200 W. Martin Luther King Jr. Dr., San Marcos, TX 78666-5522. Tel.: 512-393-8421. Facebook.
Web Site: www.sanmarcosarts.com/mcal.htm
Institution Type/Description: History Museum.
Hours & Admission Prices: Sat. 10-2; other times by appointment. Suggested Donation: $3.

COMMEMORATIVE AIR FORCE CENTRAL TEXAS WING, San Marcos Municipal Airport, 1814 Airport Dr., Bldg. 2249, San Marcos, TX 78666. Tel.: 512-396-1943. Fax: 512-396-1992.
E-mail: contact@cafcentex.com
Web Site: www.cafcentex.com
Key Personnel: Exec. Officer, James Wyatt Ellis.
Institution Type/Description: Military History Museum.
Hours & Admission Prices: Mon., Wed. & Fri.-Sat. 9-4. Suggested Donation: $3 per person.
Attendance: 7,000 (estimated)

DICK'S CLASSIC GARAGE, 120 Stagecoach Trail, San Marcos, TX 78666. Tel.: 512-878-2406.
E-mail: info@dicksclassicgarage.org
Web Site: www.dicksclassicgarage.org
Formerly: CTMAH
Key Personnel: Museum Founder & Pres., Dick Burdick; Museum Cur., Thom Fortney; Rentals & Special Events, Kathleen Cheatham; Chief Mechanic, Ray Terry.
Institution Type/Description: Automotive Museum.
Hours & Admission Prices: Mon.-Sat. 10-5, Sun. 12-5. Adults $10, senior citizens & students, military $8, children (6-12) $5, children (5 and under) no charge. Closed New Year's Day; Easter; Thanksgiving; Christmas Eve & Day.
Attendance: 26,000 (estimated)

LBJ MUSEUM OF SAN MARCOS, 131 N. Guadalupe, San Marcos, TX 78666-5606. Mailing Address: P.O. Box 3, San Marcos, TX 78667-0003. Tel.: 512-353-3300. Fax: 512-353-3305.
E-mail: director@lbjmuseum.com
Web Site: www.lbjmuseum.com/contactus.htm
Key Personnel: Pres. (V), Ed Michalkanin.
Institution Type/Description: History Museum.
Hours & Admission Prices: Thurs.-Sat. 10-5, Sun. 10-3. No charge; donations accepted. &
Attendance: 1,716 (actual)

MEADOWS CENTER FOR WATER AND THE ENVIRONMENT, 201 San Marcos Springs Dr, San Marcos, TX 78666. Mailing Address: 601 University Dr., San Marcos, TX 78666. Tel.: 512-245-9200. Facebook, Instagram, Twitter.
E-mail: meadowscenter@txstate.edu
Web Site: www.meadowscenter.txstate.edu
Key Personnel: Exec. Dir., Andrew Sansom, PhD; Dep. Exec. Dir., Robert Mace, PhD.
Institution Type/Description: Natural Science Museum.
Hours & Admission Prices: Daily 9:30-6:30. No charge.

THE WITTLIFF COLLECTIONS - TEXAS STATE UNIVERSITY-SAN MARCOS, 601 University Dr., Alkek Library, 7th Fl., San Marcos, TX 78666-4604. Mailing Address: Alkek Library, 601 University Dr., San Marcos, TX 78666-4604. Tel.: 512-245-2313. Fax: 512-245-7431. Facebook, Instagram, Twitter.
E-mail: thewittliffcollections@txstate.edu
Web Site: www.thewittliffcollections.txstate.edu
Key Personnel: Dir., David Coleman; Cur., Steve Davis.
Institution Type/Description: History Museum.
Hours & Admission Prices: Exhibition hours: Mon.-Fri. 8:30-4:30, Sat. 11-5, Sun. 12-5; Research hours: Mon.-Fri. 8:30-12 & 1-4:30. No charge.

San Saba

SAN SABA COUNTY HISTORICAL MUSEUM, Mill Pond Park, San Saba, TX 76877. Mailing Address: 500 E. Wallace St., San Saba, TX 76877.
E-mail: sansabamuseum@yahoo.com
Web Site: www.sansabamuseum.org
Key Personnel: Pres., Lynn Blankenship; Vice Pres., Clione Rochat; Sec., Pat Johnson; Treas., David Williams.
Institution Type/Description: History Museum.
Hours & Admission Prices: April-Oct. Sat.-Sun. 1:30-4. No charge; donations accepted. &

Sanderson

TERRELL COUNTY MEMORIAL MUSEUM, 203 E. Mansfield St., Sanderson, TX 79848. Mailing Address: P.O. Box 7, Sanderson, TX 79848-0702. Tel.: 432-345-2936 & 2324.
E-mail: katiedroberts@hotmail.com
Web Site: http://www.terrellmuseum.info/
Key Personnel: Cur., Bill Smith.
Institution Type/Description: History Museum: former home of the Lemmons family.
Hours & Admission Prices: Mon.-Fri. 10-12 & 2-4. No charge, donations accepted.

Sarita

KENEDY RANCH MUSEUM OF SOUTH TEXAS, 200 E. La Parra Ave., Sarita, TX 78385. Mailing Address: P.O. Box 70, Sarita, TX 78385. Tel.: 361-294-5751. Fax: 361-294-5228.

E-mail: hsv@kenedy.org
Web Site: kenedyranchmuseum.org
Key Personnel: Coord., Homero S. Vera.
Institution Type/Description: History Museum.
Hours & Admission Prices: Tues.-Sat. 10-4, Sun. 12-4. Adults $3, seniors & children (13-18) $2. Closed New Year's Day; Good Friday; Easter; Independence Day; Thanksgiving; Christmas. ♿

Schulenburg

STANZEL MODEL AIRCRAFT MUSEUM, 311 Baumgarten St., Schulenburg, TX 78956-2101. Mailing Address: P.O. Box 6, Schulenburg, TX 78956-0006. Tel.: 979-743-6559.
E-mail: museum@stanzelmuseum.org
Web Site: www.stanzelmuseum.org
Key Personnel: Pres., Robert Stanzel; Vice Pres., Theodore Stanzel.
Institution Type/Description: Aircraft Museum.
Hours & Admission Prices: Mon., Wed. & Fri.-Sat. 10:30-4:30. Adults $4, senior citizens $2; school groups & children under 12 no charge. Closed New Year's Day; Martin Luther King Jr. Day; Presidents' Day; Good Friday; Mother's Day; Memorial Day; Independence Day; Labor Day; Veterans Day; Thanksgiving; Christmas Eve & Day. ♿
Attendance: 4,099 (actual)

Seabrook

BAY AREA MUSEUM, 5000 Nasa Rd. I, Seabrook, TX 77586. Tel.: 281-326-5950. Fax: 281-326-5950.
E-mail: bayarea_museum@yahoo.com
Web Site: www.museumbayarea.org/index.html
Key Personnel: Pres., Sharon Dillard.
Institution Type/Description: General Museum: housed in the church which Buzz Aldrin celebrated communion from the surface of the moon in 1969.
Hours & Admission Prices: Sat. 10-4, Sun. 1-5. No Charge. ♿

Seagraves

SEAGRAVES-LOOP MUSEUM AND ART CENTER INC., Seagraves-Loop Div., 201 Main St., Seagraves, TX 79359. Tel.: 806-546-2810. Fax: 806-546-2810. Facebook.
Key Personnel: Dir., Treas. & Museum Shop Mgr., Leslie McConal.
Institution Type/Description: Historic Building: built in 1926; survived town fire.
Hours & Admission Prices: Mon.-Fri. 9-12 & 1-5. No charge; donations accepted. ♿
Attendance: 500 (estimated)

Seguin

LOS NOGALES MUSEUM, 415 S. River, Seguin, TX 78155. Mailing Address: P.O. Box 245, Seguin, TX 78156-0245. Tel.: 830-401-0586. Fax: 830-379-4685.
Web Site: www.seguinconservation.org
Key Personnel: Pres. (V), Kay Martin; Vice Pres., Norma Colunga.
Institution Type/Description: Conservation Society Museum: housed in 1849 building.
Hours & Admission Prices: May-Sept. Sun. 2-5; other times by appointment. No charge; donations accepted.
Attendance: 2,000 (estimated)

Seminole

GAINES COUNTY MUSEUM, SEMINOLE DIVISION, 700 Hobbs Hwy., Seminole, TX 79360. Tel.: 432-758-4016. Facebook.
E-mail: seminolemuseum@co.gaines.tx.us
Web Site: www.gainescountymuseum.org
Key Personnel: Dir., Sally Davis; Pres., Paul Elam; Vice Pres., Kristi Duncan; Museum Asst., Vicki Smith.
Institution Type/Description: History Museum.
Hours & Admission Prices: Mon.-Fri. 9-12 & 1-5. No charge; donations accepted.
Attendance: 4,000 (estimated)

Seymour

BAYLOR COUNTY MUSEUM, 116 N. Washington St., Seymour, TX 76380-2557. Tel.: 940-889-6780.
E-mail: baylorcomuseum@srcaccess.net
Institution Type/Description: History Museum.
Hours & Admission Prices: Mon.-Fri. call for hours.

Shamrock

PIONEER WEST MUSEUM, 204 N. Madden, Shamrock, TX 79079-2340. Tel.: 806-256-3941.
Institution Type/Description: History Museum: housed in the former Reynolds Hotel; built in 1925.
Hours & Admission Prices: Mon.-Fri. 9-12 & 1-5. No charge.

Sheffield

FORT LANCASTER STATE HISTORIC SITE, Mailing Address: 629 Fort Lancaster Rd., Sheffield, TX 79781. Tel.: 432-836-4391. Fax: 432-836-4552. Facebook, Instagram, Twitter.
E-mail: ft-lancaster@thc.texas.gov
Web Site: www.thc.texas.gov/historic-sites/fort-lancaster-state-historic-site
Key Personnel: Site Mgr., Jefferson Spilman.
Institution Type/Description: Historic Site & Military Museum: housed on the grounds of Fort Lancaster, 1855-1870s and the 1867 battle site.
Hours & Admission Prices: Daily 9-5. Adults $4, seniors, children & college students $3; discounts to groups; children 5 & under no charge. Closed New Year's Eve & Day; Thanksgiving; Christmas Eve & Day. ♿
Attendance: 4,000 (estimated)

Sherman

C.S. ROBERTS HOUSE MUSEUM, 915 S. Crockett, Sherman, TX 75090. Tel.: 903-893-4067.
E-mail: info@shermantx.org
Institution Type/Description: Historic House Museum: built in 1896.
Hours & Admission Prices: Sun. 1-4; other times by appointment. No charge.

THE SHERMAN MUSEUM, 301 S. Walnut, Sherman, TX 75090-7152. Tel.: 903-893-7623.
E-mail: theshermanmuseum@verizon.net
Web Site: www.theshermanmuseum.org
Formerly: Red River Historical Museum
Key Personnel: Pres., Dickie Gerig; 1st Vice-Pres., Bea Herod Harmon; 2nd Vice-Pres., Jeannie Duarte; Treas., Susan Stephens; Sec., Dorothy McKee.
Institution Type/Description: Museum: housed in 1914 Andrew Carnegie Library building.
Hours & Admission Prices: Thurs.-Sat. 10-4. Adults $5, seniors 60 and over $3, students $2; children 5 and under & members no charge.
Attendance: 3,000 (actual)

Shiner

EDWIN WOLTERS MEMORIAL MUSEUM, 306 S. Ave. I, Shiner, TX 77984. Tel.: 512-594-3774.
Key Personnel: Cur., Bernard Siegel; Asst. Cur., Mamie Murphy.
Institution Type/Description: General Museum: housed in 1900 home of Edwin Wolters, founder of museum.
Hours & Admission Prices: Mon.-Fri. 8-12 & 1-5; every second and fourth Sun. 2-5; groups by appointment. No charge; donations accepted. ♿
Attendance: 741 (actual)

Sinton

WELDER WILDLIFE FOUNDATION & REFUGE, 10620 Hwy. 77 N., Sinton, TX 78387. Mailing Address: P.O. Box 1400, Sinton, TX 78387-1400. Tel.: 361-364-2643. Fax: 361-364-2650.
E-mail: welderfoundation@welderwildlife.org
Web Site: www.welderwildlife.org
Key Personnel: Dir., Dr. Terry L. Blankenship; Asst. Dir., Dr. Selma N. Glasscock.
Institution Type/Description: Wildlife Refuge.
Hours & Admission Prices: Thurs. 3-5. No charge; donations accepted.
Attendance: 2,900 (actual)

Slaton

TEXAS AIR MUSEUM, 12102 FM 400, Slaton, TX 79364. Mailing Address: P.O. Box 36, Slaton, TX 79364-4192. Tel.: 806-796-7618.
E-mail: info@texasairmuseum.org
Web Site: www.thetexasairmuseum.org
Key Personnel: Pres., Mike Delano.
Institution Type/Description: Aeronautics Museum.
Hours & Admission Prices: Sat. 8:30-5. Adults $5, senior citizens $4, youth 12-16 $3, children 11 & under $2; discounts for groups, AAM & ICOM members; members no charge. Closed New Year's Day; Thanksgiving; Christmas. ♿
Attendance: 6,324 (actual)

Snyder

SCURRY COUNTY MUSEUM, Western Texas College, 6200 College Ave., Snyder, TX 79549-6105. Tel.: 325-573-6107. Facebook.
E-mail: scm@snydertex.com
Web Site: www.scurrycountymuseum.org
Key Personnel: Exec. Dir., Nicole DeGuzman; Pres. (V), Lynn Fuller; Cur., Laurel Lamb; Photographer & Asst. Cur., Gerald Corkran; Educator, Erika Jayne Christian; Arthouse Mgr., Laura Greenwood; Office Mgr., Brenda Tovar.
Institution Type/Description: History Museum.
Hours & Admission Prices: Mon. by appointment, Tues.-Fri. 9-5:30, Sat. 10-2. No charge. &
Attendance: 9,000 (actual)

Sonora

OLD ICE HOUSE RANCH MUSEUM, 206 S. Water Ave., Sonora, TX 76950. Tel.: 325-387-3754.
E-mail: icehousemuseum1@yahoo.com
Web Site: old-ice-house-ranch-museum.com
Formerly: Sutton County Historical Society - Miers Home Museum, Cauthorn Memorial Depot and Old Ice House Ranch Museum
Key Personnel: Dir., Joyce Raska.
Institution Type/Description: History Museum.
Hours & Admission Prices: Wed.-Sat. 10-6, Sun. 1-6. Guided Downtown Tour $10, Museum only $4. &
Attendance: 876 (actual)

VETERANS OF ALL WARS & PIONEER RANCH WOMEN MUSEUM, 105 Concho St., Sonora, TX 76950. Tel.: 325-387-2248. Fax: 325-387-3198.
E-mail: fhsmainstreet@verizon.net
Institution Type/Description: History Museum.
Hours & Admission Prices: Mon.-Fri. 10-4; other times by appointment. No charge.

South Padre Island

COASTAL STUDIES LABORATORY - THE UNIVERSITY OF TEXAS-PAN AMERICAN, 100 Marine Lab Dr., South Padre Island, TX 78597. Tel.: 956-761-2644. Fax: 956-761-2913.
E-mail: coastal@utpa.edu
Web Site: www.utpa.edu/csl
Institution Type/Description: Marine Science Museum.
Hours & Admission Prices: Mon.-Fri. 1:30-4:30. Closed major holidays. Lab: no charge; donations accepted. Park: $4 per car, $10-$15 per bus.

Spearman

STATIONMASTER'S HOUSE MUSEUM, 30 S. Townsend, Spearman, TX 79081-2644. Tel.: 806-659-3008.
Key Personnel: Pres., Helen Boyd; Sec., Joanne Eaton; Historical & Museum Treas., Rubyjo Wilbanks; Sec. to Museum, Cindy Blackman.
Institution Type/Description: Historic House Museum: housed in the former station master's house; built in 1920.
Hours & Admission Prices: Tues.-Sat. 1-5; other times by appointment. No charge.

Spring

PEARL FINCHER MUSEUM OF FINE ARTS, 6815 Cypresswood Dr., Spring, TX 77379-7705. Tel.: 281-376-6322. Fax: 281-376-2944. Facebook, Instagram, Twitter.
E-mail: development@pearlmfa.org
Web Site: www.pearlmfa.org
Key Personnel: Museum Dir., Ani Boyajian; Operations Mgr., Kayla Osby; Community Engagement Dir., Emily Guerra; Admin. Asst., Shannon Jacobson; Dir. of Devel., Clara Lewis; Facilities Mgr., Henry Griffin; Art Instructor, Joella Wheeler; Museum Operations Asst., David Remley; Cur., Terry Capps.
Institution Type/Description: Art Museum.
Hours & Admission Prices: Tues.-Sat. 10-5. No charge; donation accepted. &
Attendance: 25,000 (estimated)

Stamford

COWBOY COUNTRY MUSEUM, 113 S. Wetherbee St., Stamford, TX 79553. Tel.: 325-773-2500.
E-mail: cowboymuseum1977@att.net
Institution Type/Description: History Museum.

Hours & Admission Prices: Mon.-Thur. 9-12 & 1-3:30; other times by appointment. No charge; donations accepted. &
Attendance: 700 (estimated)

Stanton

MARTIN COUNTY HISTORICAL MUSEUM, 207 E. Broadway, Stanton, TX 79782. Mailing Address: P.O. Box 929, Stanton, TX 79782-0929. Tel.: 432-756-2722.
E-mail: martincountymuseum@gmail.com
Key Personnel: Dir., Elodia Bravo; Pres., Randy Turner.
Institution Type/Description: County History Museum: includes old jail & Connell House.
Hours & Admission Prices: Mon.-Fri. 9-11:30 & 12:30-5:30; other times by appointment. No charge; donations accepted. Closed major holidays. &
Attendance: 1,000 (estimated)

Star

STAR HISTORICAL MUSEUM, 44 S. FM 1047, Star, TX 76880. Mailing Address: P.O. Box 356, Star, TX 76880. Tel.: 325-648-2356.
E-mail: jm23hm@hotmail.com
Web Site: www.startexasmuseum.org
Institution Type/Description: History Museum.
Hours & Admission Prices: By appointment.

Stephenville

STEPHENVILLE MUSEUM, 525 E. Washington, Stephenville, TX 76401-4439. Mailing Address: P.O. Box 899, Buffalo Gap, TX 79508-0899. Tel.: 254-965-5880.
E-mail: svillemuseum@embarqmail.com
Formerly: Stephenville Historical House Museum
Key Personnel: Pres., Dianne Wilson; Vice Pres., Dorothy Farrar; Treas., Tessa Harrison; Sec., Dana Adams.
Institution Type/Description: General Museum: housed in 1869 Berry House; blacksmith shop.
Hours & Admission Prices: Tues.-Sat. 10-5, Sun. 1-5. No charge; donations accepted.
Attendance: 5,000 (estimated)

Sugar Land

HOUSTON MUSEUM OF NATURAL SCIENCE AT SUGAR LAND, 13016 University Blvd., Sugar Land, TX 77479. Tel.: 281-313-2277.
E-mail: sugarlandprograms@hmns.org
Web Site: www.hmns.org/hmns-at-sugar-land/
Key Personnel: Pres., Joel A. Bartsch.
Institution Type/Description: Science Museum.
Hours & Admission Prices: Thurs.-Fri. 9-3, Sat. 9-5, Sun. 12-5. Adult $12, child & senior $9.

Sulphur Springs

SOUTHWEST DAIRY MUSEUM, 1210 Houston, Sulphur Springs, TX 75482-2310. Mailing Address: Southwest Dairy Farmers, P.O. Box 936, Sulphur Springs, TX 75483. Tel.: 903-439-6455. Fax: 903-439-1125. Facebook: Southwest Dairy Museum.
E-mail: cmckinney@southwestdairyfarmers.com
Web Site: www.southwestdairyfarmers.com
Key Personnel: C.E.O. & Gen. Mgr., Jim Hill; Dir. of Admin., Carolyn McKinney; Dir. of Events & Exhibits, Jay Crawford.
Institution Type/Description: Dairy Museum.
Hours & Admission Prices: Museum: Mon.-Fri. 9-4. Office: Mon.-Fri. 8-5. No charge; donations accepted. &
Attendance: 11,150 (actual)

Sweetwater

CITY COUNTY PIONEER MUSEUM, 610 E. Third, Sweetwater, TX 79556. Tel.: 325-235-8547. Facebook, Instagram, Twitter.
Key Personnel: Chm. Bd., Jerry Byrd; Exec. Dir., Melonnie Hicks.
Institution Type/Description: Local History Museum.
Hours & Admission Prices: Wed. quiet hours 1-3; Tues.-Fri. 1-4; Sat. 10-3; other times by appointment. No charge; donations accepted. Closed holidays. &
Attendance: 3,500 (estimated)

THE NATIONAL WASP WWII MUSEUM, 210 Avenger Field Rd., Sweetwater, TX 79556. Tel.: 325-235-0099. Facebook, Instagram.
E-mail: waspmuseum@yahoo.com
Key Personnel: Exec. Dir., Ann Hobing; Assoc. Dir., Carol Cain; Head Archivist/ Collections Mgr., Ann Haub; Bd. Pres., Sandra Spears; Vice Pres., Larry Ludlum.
Institution Type/Description: Military History Museum.
Hours & Admission Prices: Tues.-Sat. 10-5, Sun. 1-5. No charge; donations accepted.
Attendance: 4,800 (estimated)

Taft

BLACKLAND MUSEUM, 301 Green Ave., Taft, TX 78390. Tel.: 361-528-2206. Facebook, Twitter.
E-mail: blacklandmuseum@aol.com
Web Site: www.blacklandmuseum.com
Institution Type/Description: History Museum.
Hours & Admission Prices: Thurs.-Fri. 10-4, Sat. 10-2, Sun. 2-5. No charge; donations accepted.

Taylor

GOV. DAN MOODY MUSEUM, 114 W. Ninth St., Taylor, TX 76574. Mailing Address: P.O. Box 669, Taylor, TX 76574. Tel.: 512-352-5990 & 365-7396. Facebook: Moody Museum.
E-mail: moodymuseum@gmail.com
Web Site: moodymuseum.com
Key Personnel: Chm. (V), Susan Komandosky.
Institution Type/Description: History Museum: housed in the boyhood home of Texas Governor, Dan Moody; served from 1927-1931.
Hours & Admission Prices: Sun.-Sun. 2-5; other times by appointment. No charge; donations accepted. &
Attendance: 400 (estimated)

Teague

BURLINGTON-ROCK ISLAND RAILROAD AND HISTORICAL MUSEUM, 208 S. 3rd Ave., Teague, TX 75860-1645. Tel.: 254-739-2145.
E-mail: adladyginny@gmail.com
Web Site: therailroadmuseum.com
Key Personnel: Pres. (V), Benny Walker; Contact Person, Ginny Folsom.
Institution Type/Description: History Museum: housed in 1906 former Trinity & Brazos Valley Railway Depot, listed on National Register of Historic Places.
Hours & Admission Prices: Sat.-Sun. 1-5; group tours by appointment. Adults $2, children $1; discounts to groups; members & school group tours no charge. &
Attendance: 2,000 (estimated)

Temple

CZECH HERITAGE MUSEUM & GENEALOGY CENTER, 119 W. French Ave., Corner of Third St. and French Ave., Temple, TX 76501. Tel.: 254-899-2935.
E-mail: czechheritagemuseum@gmail.com
Web Site: www.czechmuseum.org
Formerly: SPJST Library Archives & Museum
Key Personnel: Museum Dir., Susan Chandler.
Institution Type/Description: Library & Museum of Czech History, Culture & Genealogy.
Hours & Admission Prices: Tues.-Sat. 10-4. Adult $4, seniors (60 and over) $3; children (12 and under) $2. &
Attendance: 3,500 (estimated)

TEMPLE RAILROAD & HERITAGE MUSEUM, 315 W Ave. B, Temple, TX 76501-4226. Tel.: 254-298-5172 & 5190. Fax: 254-298-5171. Facebook.
E-mail: rrhm@templetx.gov
Web Site: www.rrhm.org
Formerly: Railroad Pioneer Museum
Key Personnel: Dir., Stephanie Long.
Institution Type/Description: Transportation & History Museum.
Hours & Admission Prices: Tues.-Sat. 10-4. Adults $4, senior citizens $3, children 5-12 $2; active military & children under 5 no charge. NARM reciprocal admissions. &
Attendance: 15,000 (actual)

Terrell

NO. 1 BRITISH FLYING TRAINING SCHOOL MUSEUM, INC., 119 Silent Wings Blvd., Terrell, TX 75160. Tel.: 972-551-1122. Facebook.
E-mail: info@bftsmuseum.org
Web Site: www.bftsmuseum.org
Key Personnel: Pres., Rudy Bowling; Treas., Nancy Pope; Sec., Mike Grout.
Institution Type/Description: Military History Museum.
Hours & Admission Prices: Wed.-Sat. 10-4; other times by appointment. No charge; donations accepted. Closed New Year's Day; Christmas. &
Attendance: 4,000 (estimated)

TERRELL HERITAGE SOCIETY MUSEUM, 207 N. Frances, Terrell, TX 75160. Tel.: 972-524-6082.
E-mail: terrellheritage@sbcglobal.net
Web Site: terrellheritagemuseum.org
Key Personnel: Museum Dir., James McCord.
Institution Type/Description: Historical Society Museum.
Hours & Admission Prices: Wed. 10-4, Sat. & Sun. 1-4. No charge.

Texarkana

ACE OF CLUBS HOUSE, 420 Pine St., Texarkana, TX 75501-5513. Tel.: 903-793-4831. Facebook.
E-mail: aceofclubs@texarkanamuseums.org
Web Site: www.texarkanamuseum.org/ace-of-clubs
Key Personnel: Pres., Velvet Hall Cool.
Institution Type/Description: Historic House: 1885 Italianate house in form of rectangle with three octagonal bays, club shape & surrounded by dry moat.
Hours & Admission Prices: Tues.-Sat. 10am, 1pm & 3:30, Sun. 1pm & 3:30pm. Admission 3 & over $5, seniors & military, AA $4; children under 3 no charge. &
Attendance: 1,033 (actual)

TEXARKANA MUSEUMS SYSTEM, 219 N. State Line Ave., Texarkana, TX 75501-5606. Mailing Address: P.O. Box 2343, Texarkana, TX 75504-2343. Tel.: 903-793-4831. Fax: 903-793-7108. Facebook.
E-mail: curator@texarkanamuseums.org
Web Site: www.texarkanamuseums.org
Key Personnel: Bd. Pres., Velvet Hall Cool.
Institution Type/Description: History & Science Museum.
Hours & Admission Prices: Tues.-Sat. 10-5, Sun. 1-5. Admission $5 per site; discounts to seniors, AAA & veterans; children under 3 no charge. Closed legal holidays. &
Attendance: 1,442 (actual)

Texas City

TEXAS CITY MUSEUM, 409 6th St. N., Texas City, TX 77590-7854. Tel.: 409-229-1660. Fax: 409-229-1636. Facebook.
E-mail: avance@texas-city-tx.org
Web Site: www.texas-city-tx.org/page.rec.museum
Key Personnel: Cur., Amanda Vance.
Institution Type/Description: History Museum.
Hours & Admission Prices: Tues.-Sat. 10-4. Adults $7, seniors $5, students $4; children under 6 no charge. Railroad Club: Sat. 10-4. Closed Easter; Thanksgiving; Christmas Eve & Day. &
Attendance: 7,000 (estimated)

The Woodlands

THE WOODLANDS CHILDREN'S MUSEUM, 4775 W. Panther Creek Dr. #280, The Woodlands, TX 77381. Tel.: 281-465-0955. Facebook, Instagram, Twitter.
E-mail: museum@woodlandschildrensmuseum.org
Web Site: www.woodlandschildrenmuseum.org
Key Personnel: Exec. Dir., Angela Colton.
Institution Type/Description: Children's Museum.
Hours & Admission Prices: Tues.-Sat. 10-5, Sun. 12-5; Memorial Day-Labor Day: daily. Admission $6. Closed New Year's Day, Easter, Independence Day, Thanksgiving, Christmas Eve & Day.

Tulia

SWISHER COUNTY ARCHIVES AND MUSEUM, 127 S.W. 2nd St., Tulia, TX 79088-2700. Tel.: 806-995-2819. Facebook.
E-mail: swishercountymuseums@hotmail.com
Key Personnel: Dir., Sally Murrell.

Institution Type/Description: History Museum & Archives; housed in community building.
Hours & Admission Prices: Tues.-Thurs. 9-11 & 12-4, other times by appointment. No charge.
Attendance: 2,000 (estimated)

Tyler

CALDWELL ZOO, 2203 W. Martin Luther King, Tyler, TX 75702-2954. Mailing Address: P.O. Box 4785, Tyler, TX 75712-4785. Tel.: 903-593-0121. Facebook, Instagram, Twitter.
E-mail: info@caldwellzoo.org
Web Site: www.caldwellzoo.org
Institution Type/Description: Zoo.
Hours & Admission Prices: March to Labor Day daily 9-5; after Labor Day-Feb. daily 9-4. Adults 13-54 $14.95, senior 55 & up $12.50, children 3-12 $10.50; children 2 & under no charge. Closed New Year's Day; Thanksgiving; Christmas. ♿
Attendance: 600,000 (estimated)

DISCOVERY SCIENCE PLACE, 308 N. Broadway Ave., Tyler, TX 75702-5711. Tel.: 903-533-8011. Facebook, Twitter.
Web Site: www.discoveryscienceplace.org
Key Personnel: Bd. Chair, Diane Kavanaugh; Immediate Past Chairman, Leah Wansley; Treas., Craig Wheeler; Sec., Clint James.
Institution Type/Description: Children's Museum.
Hours & Admission Prices: Tues.-Sat. 10-5; Sun. 1-5. Adults $8, chldren & seniors (65 and over) &6, active military $5, children (under 2) and members no charge. Closed Major Holidays. ♿
Attendance: 60,000 (estimated)

GOODMAN MUSEUM, 624 N. Broadway Ave., Tyler, TX 75702-5344. Tel.: 903-531-1286.
E-mail: gmuseum@tylertexas.com
Key Personnel: Cur., Patricia J. Heaton.
Institution Type/Description: Historic House: 1859 4-room cottage remodeled in 1880 into 2-story Texas Colonial by Dr. William J. Goodman, remodeled in 1924 into a Greek Revival Mansion by Dr. Goodman's daughter, Sallie Goodman LeGrand.
Hours & Admission Prices: Tues.-Sat. 10-4. Suggested Donation: $2 per person. Closed national holidays. ♿
Attendance: 6,000 (estimated)

HISTORIC AVIATION MEMORIAL MUSEUM, Tyler Pounds Airport, 150 Airport Dr., Tyler, TX 75704-6642. Mailing Address: 150 Airport Dr., Box 2-7, Tyler, TX 75704-6600. Tel.: 903-526-1945. Fax: 903-526-0946.
E-mail: cjverver@aol.com
Web Site: www.tylerhamm.org
Key Personnel: Pres., Louis Thomas; Events & Media Coord., Carolyn Verver; Finance Mgr., Karon Gilmore.
Institution Type/Description: Aviation Museum.
Hours & Admission Prices: Spring/Summer: Tues.-Sat. 10-4; Fall/Winter: Tues.-Sat. 10-4. Adults $6, seniors $5, teens (13-17) $3, children (6-12) $2, active military and children (5 and under) no charge. ♿
Attendance: 6,000 (actual)

SMITH COUNTY HISTORICAL SOCIETY, 125 S. College Ave., Tyler, TX 75702-7216. Tel.: 903-592-5993. Fax: 903-526-0924. Facebook, Instagram.
E-mail: info@smithcountyhistoricalsociety.org
Web Site: www.smithcountyhistoricalsociety.org
Key Personnel: Pres., Carol Kehl; Vice Pres., Scott Fitzgerald.
Institution Type/Description: History Museum: housed in c.1904 Carnegie Library.
Hours & Admission Prices: Tues.-Fri. 10-4, Sat. 12-4; archives by appointment. No charge; donations accepted. Closed New Year's Day; Independence Day; Thanksgiving; Christmas. ♿
Attendance: 3,600 (estimated)

TYLER MUSEUM OF ART, 1300 S. Mahon Ave., Tyler, TX 75701-3438. Tel.: 903-595-1001. Facebook, Instagram, Twitter.
E-mail: info@tylermuseum.org
Web Site: www.tylermuseum.org
Key Personnel: Exec. Dir., Christopher M. Leahy; Cur., Caleb Bell; Registrar & Collections Mgr., Elizabeth Bradshaw Hyatt; Accountant & Human Resources Mgr., Kerry Moses; Facility Mgr., Robert Owen; Communications & Membership Coord., Jon Perry.
Institution Type/Description: Art Museum.
Hours & Admission Prices: Tues.-Sat. 10-5, Sun. 1-5. Closed national holidays. ♿
Attendance: 25,000 (estimated)

TYLER ROSE MUSEUM, 420 Rose Park Dr., Tyler, TX 75702-6859. Tel.: 903-597-1212. Facebook, Twitter.
E-mail: info@texasrosefestival.com
Web Site: texasrosefestival.com
Key Personnel: Exec. Dir. & Cur., Liz Ballard.
Institution Type/Description: Rose Museum.
Hours & Admission Prices: Mon.-Fri. 9-4:30, Sat. 10-4:30, Sun. 1:30-4:30. Adults $3.50, children 2-11 $2. ♿
Attendance: 100,000 (estimated)

Uvalde

AVIATION MUSEUM AT GARNER FIELD, 201 Sul Ross Dr., Uvalde, TX 78801. Tel.: 830-278-2552.
E-mail: avmusgarner@yahoo.com
Institution Type/Description: Aviation History Museum.
Hours & Admission Prices: Tues. & Fri. 9-4. No charge; donations accepted.
Attendance: 500 (estimated)

BRISCOE-GARNER MUSEUM, 333 N. Park St., Uvalde, TX 78801-4658. Tel.: 830-278-5018. Fax: 830-279-0512. Facebook, Twitter.
E-mail: m.lara@austin.utexas.edu
Web Site: www.cah.utexas.edu/museums/garner.php
Formerly: John Nance Garner Museum
Key Personnel: Office Asst., Maria Lara.
Institution Type/Description: Historic House: 1920 Home of Vice President John N. Garner.
Hours & Admission Prices: Tues.-Sat. 9-4. No charge.
Attendance: 3,500 (actual)

DOLPH BRISCOE CENTER FOR AMERICAN HISTORY, Physical/Mailing Address: 333 N. Park St., Uvalde, TX 78801-4658. Tel.: 830-278-5018. Fax: 830-279-0512. Facebook, Twitter.
E-mail: m.lara@austin.utexas.edu
Web Site: www.cah.utexas.edu
Formerly: Center for American History
Key Personnel: Exec. Dir., Dr. Don Carleton; Dir. for Devel., Lisa Avra; Dir. Special Projects, Alison M. Beck; Dir. of Research & Collections, Stephanie Malmros.
Institution Type/Description: History Museum.
Hours & Admission Prices: Tues.-Sat. 9-4. No charge. ♿
Attendance: 39,000 (estimated)

Van Horn

CLARK HOTEL HISTORICAL MUSEUM, 112 W. Broadway, Van Horn, TX 79855-0231. Mailing Address: P.O. Box 231, Van Horn, TX 79855. Tel.: 432-283-8028.
E-mail: clarkhotelmuseum@yahoo.com
Web Site: clarkhotelmuseum.com
Formerly: Culberson County Historical Museum
Institution Type/Description: General Museum: housed in 1906 two-story adobe & cement block, Clark Hotel Building.
Hours & Admission Prices: Mon.-Fri. 8-4; No charge; donations accepted. ♿
Attendance: 1,200 (estimated)

Vanderpool

LONE STAR MOTORCYCLE MUSEUM, 36517 Hwy. 187 N., Vanderpool, TX 78885. Tel.: 830-966-6103.
E-mail: awjohncock@swtexas.net
Web Site: lonestarmotorcyclemuseum.com
Key Personnel: Museum Dir., Alan Johncock.
Institution Type/Description: Motorcycle Museum.
Hours & Admission Prices: March-Nov. Fri.-Sun. 10-5. Adults $7, seniors 65 & over, groups of 10 or more $6; children under 15 no charge.

Vernon

RED RIVER VALLEY MUSEUM, 4600 College Dr., Vernon, TX 76384-4052. Tel.: 940-553-1848. Fax: 940-553-1849. Facebook.
E-mail: rrvm1@yahoo.com
Web Site: www.rrvm.net
Key Personnel: Pres. Bd. Dir., Staley Heatly.
Institution Type/Description: History, Science & Fine Arts Museum.
Hours & Admission Prices: Tues.-Fri. 10:30-5, Sat. 10:30-2:30; other times by appointment. Adults $5, children $3. Closed major holidays. ♿
Attendance: 8,000 (estimated)

Victoria

MUSEUM OF THE COASTAL BEND, The Victoria College, 2200 E. Red River, Victoria, TX 77901-4442. Tel.: 361-582-2511. Fax: 361-582-2437.
E-mail: sue.prudhomme@victoriacollege.edu
Web Site: www.museumofthecoastalbend.org
Key Personnel: Dir., Sue Prudhomme; Exhibit & Collections Mgr., Elizabeth Neucere; Education Coord., Amanda Lanum; Admin. Asst., Cheryl Beran.
Institution Type/Description: Heritage Museum.
Hours & Admission Prices: Tues.-Sat. 10-4. No charge; donations accepted. Closed major holidays. 🚹
Attendance: 4,900 (actual)

NAVE MUSEUM, 306 W. Commercial, Victoria, TX 77901. Mailing Address: P.O. Box 1776, Victoria, TX 77902. Tel.: 361-575-8228. Facebook.
E-mail: info@navemuseum.com
Web Site: www.navemuseum.com
Key Personnel: Operations Mgr., Diana Kallus; Cur., Justine Ochoa.
Institution Type/Description: Art Museum.
Hours & Admission Prices: Tues.-Fri. 12-5, Sat.-Sun. 12-4. Admission no charge. 🚹
Attendance: 7,500 (estimated)

THE TEXAS ZOO, 110 Memorial Dr., Victoria, TX 77901-6334. Tel.: 361-573-7681. Fax: 361-576-1094.
E-mail: contactus@texaszoo.org
Web Site: www.texaszoo.org
Key Personnel: Exec. Dir., Liz Jensen; Cur. Animals, Michael Magaw.
Institution Type/Description: Zoo.
Hours & Admission Prices: Daily 9-4:30. Adults $8, children 3-12 $7, seniors 55 & over $5.50, active/retired military $4.50; discounts to reciprocal members; members & children 2 & under no charge. Closed New Year's Day; Thanksgiving; Christmas Eve & Day. 🚹
Attendance: 50,000 (estimated)

Waco

ARMSTRONG BROWNING LIBRARY, Armstrong Browning Library, 710 Speight Ave., Waco, TX 76706. Mailing Address: One Bear Place, #97152, Waco, TX 76798-7152. Tel.: 254-710-3322. Facebook, Instagram, Twitter.
E-mail: office@baylor.edu
Web Site: www.browninglibrary.org
Key Personnel: Dir., Jennifer Borderud; Scholar in Residence, Josh King; Cur., Laura J. French.
Institution Type/Description: Library of Browningiana.
Hours & Admission Prices: Mon.-Fri. 9-5, Sat. 10-2. No charge; donations accepted. Closed University holidays. 🚹
Attendance: 30,000 (estimated)

THE ART CENTER OF WACO, 712 Austin Ave., Waco, TX 76701. Tel.: 254-752-4371. Facebook, Instagram, Twitter.
E-mail: artcenterwaco1300@gmail.com
Web Site: www.artcenterwaco.org
Key Personnel: Exec. Dir., Claire Sexton; Program Coord., Meg Gilbert; Education Coord., Karen Alleman.
Institution Type/Description: Art Center.
Hours & Admission Prices: Tues.-Sat. 10-5. No charge; donations accepted. Closed New Year's Day; Martin Luther King Jr. Day; Memorial Day; Independence Day; Labor Day; Thanksgiving; Christmas. 🚹
Attendance: 7,300 (actual)

CAMERON PARK ZOO, 1701 N. 4th St., Waco, TX 76707-2463. Tel.: 254-750-8400.
Web Site: www.cameronparkzoo.com
Institution Type/Description: General Museum.
Hours & Admission Prices: Mon.-Sat. 9-5, Sun. 11-5. Adults $10, senior citizens $9, children 4-12 $7; discount to groups & AZA members; members & children under 3 no charge. Closed New Year's Day; Thanksgiving; Christmas. 🚹
Attendance: 231,893 (actual)

DR PEPPER MUSEUM AND FREE ENTERPRISE INSTITUTE, 300 S. 5th St., Waco, TX 76701-2115. Tel.: 254-757-1025. Facebook, Instagram, Twitter.
E-mail: pr@drpeppermuseum.com
Web Site: www.drpeppermuseum.com
Key Personnel: Pres. & C.E.O., Chris Dyer; Assoc. Dir., Joy Summar-Smith; Dir. of Fin., Daniel Reyna; Dir. of Operations, Gabe Schooley.
Institution Type/Description: History Museum: housed in a 3-story, 18,000 sq. ft. 1906 building, which was the home of Dr Pepper. Structure is of architectural significance to Waco, reflecting the popularity of Richardsonian Romanesque architecture in Texas.
Hours & Admission Prices: Mon.-Sat. 10-5:30, Sun. 12-5:30; Adults $10, seniors & military $8, students & children $6; children (4 and under) and members no charge. Closed New Year's Day; Easter; Thanksgiving; Christmas. 🚹
Attendance: 58,089 (actual)

THE EARLE-HARRISON HOUSE & PAPE GARDENS, 1901 N. 5th St., Waco, TX 76708-3603. Tel.: 254-753-2032. Facebook.
E-mail: earleharrisonpapegardens@gmail.com
Web Site: www.earleharrison.com
Formerly: The Earle-Harrison House and Gardens on 5th Street
Key Personnel: Property Mgr., Kathy Riggs.
Institution Type/Description: Historic House: 1858-1859 Greek Revival antebellum house.
Hours & Admission Prices: By appointment. Admission $5. 🚹
Attendance: 19,100 (actual)

HISTORIC WACO FOUNDATION, 810 S. Fourth St., Waco, TX 76706-1036. Tel.: 254-753-5166. Fax: 254-714-1242.
E-mail: hwf@hot.rr.com
Web Site: www.historicwaco.org
Key Personnel: Exec. Dir., Jill Barrow; Office Admin., Valerie Williams.
Institution Type/Description: Historic Foundation & Historic Houses.
Hours & Admission Prices: Earle-Napier-Kinnard: Tues.-Sat. 10-4, Sun. 1-4. East Terrace Tues.-Sat. 10-4, Sun. 1-4. McCulloch House & Fort House Sat. 10-4, Sun. 1-4. Adults $5, seniors & students $4. 🚹
Attendance: 20,292 (actual)

MARTIN MUSEUM - BAYLOR UNIVERSITY, 60 Baylor Ave., Waco, TX 76706. Tel.: 254-710-6371. Fax: 254-710-1566.
E-mail: martin_museum@baylor.edu
Key Personnel: Dir., Allison Chew; Collections Mgr., Chani Jones; Education Coord., Krista Latendresse.
Institution Type/Description: Art Gallery.
Hours & Admission Prices: Tues.-Fri. 10-6, Sat. 10-4, Sun. 1-4. No charge.

MASONIC GRAND LODGE LIBRARY AND MUSEUM OF TEXAS, 715 Columbus, Waco, TX 76701-1349. Mailing Address: P.O. Box 446, Waco, TX 76703-0446. Tel.: 254-753-7395. Fax: 254-753-2944.
E-mail: gs@grandsecretaryoftx.org
Web Site: grandlodgeoftexas.org
Key Personnel: Cur. & Librarian, Barbara Mechell; Grand Librarian, Orville L. O'Neill.
Institution Type/Description: History Museum: Educational Masonic Library.
Hours & Admission Prices: Jan. 3-Dec. 22 Mon.-Fri. 8:30-4. No charge; donations accepted. Closed national holidays. 🚹
Attendance: 10,000 (estimated)

MAYBORN MUSEUM COMPLEX, 1300 S. University Parks Dr., Baylor University, Waco, TX 76706-1221. Mailing Address: One Bear Place #97154, Baylor Univ., Waco, TX 76798-7154. Tel.: 254-710-1110. Fax: 254-710-1173. Facebook: Mayborn Museum Complex.
E-mail: patricia_pack@baylor.edu
Web Site: www.baylor.edu/mayborn/
Formerly: Strecker Museum Complex
Key Personnel: Dir., Charles Walter; Asst. Dir. Visitor Experience, Lesa Bush; Mgr. Museum Operations, Patricia Pack; Asst. Dir. Facilities, Tom Haddad; Asst. Dir. Communications, Rebecca Tucker Nall; Collections Mgr., Anita Benedict.
Institution Type/Description: Natural Science & History Museum.
Hours & Admission Prices: Mon.-Wed. & Fri.-Sat. 10-5, Thurs. 10-8, Sun. 1-5. Adults $8, seniors 65 & over $7, children 2-12 yrs. $6. Closed New Year's Day; Easter weekend; Thanksgiving; Christmas; all Baylor University home football games. 🚹
Attendance: 145,000 (actual)

TEXAS RANGER HALL OF FAME AND MUSEUM, 100 Texas Ranger Trail, Waco, TX 76706-1209. Mailing Address: P.O. Box 2570, Waco, TX 76702-2570. Tel.: 254-750-8631. Fax: 254-750-8629.
E-mail: info@texasranger.org
Web Site: www.texasranger.org
Key Personnel: Dir. & CEO, Byron A. Johnson; Museum Shop Mgr., Lisa Daniel.
Institution Type/Description: Western History Museum: specializing in Texas Ranger History.

Hours & Admission Prices: Daily 9-5; guided tours by appointment. Adults $7, seniors & military $6, children 6-12 $3; discounts to AAM & ICOM members, groups, & law enforcement personnel; children 5 & under no charge. Closed New Year's Day; Thanksgiving; Christmas. &
Attendance: 80,000 (actual)

TEXAS SPORTS HALL OF FAME, 1108 S. University Parks Dr., Waco, TX 76706-1223. Tel.: 254-756-1633, 800-567-9561. Fax: 254-756-2384. Facebook: Texas Sports Hall of Fame.
E-mail: phyllis.trice@tshof.org
Web Site: www.tshof.org
Key Personnel: Exec. Dir., C.E.O. & Pres., Jared Mosley; Vice Pres. Operations, Jay Black; Mgr. Operations and Coord. Sales & Mktg., Phyllis Trice; Dir. Collections & Exhibits, Ryan Sprayberry; Museum Shop Mgr., Kalynne Allen.
Institution Type/Description: Sports Museum.
Hours & Admission Prices: Mon.-Sat. 9-5. Adults $7, seniors 60 & over $6, students & children over 5 $3; discounts to groups of 10 or more; members, active military & children under 6 no charge. Closed New Year's Day; Easter; Thanksgiving; Christmas. &
Attendance: 30,000 (actual)

Washington

BARRINGTON LIVING HISTORY FARM, Washington-on-the-Brazos State Historic Site, 23400 Park Rd. 12, Washington, TX 77880. Tel.: 936-878-2213 & 2214. Facebook.
E-mail: office@wheretexasbecametexas.org
Web Site: www.birthplaceoftexas.com
Institution Type/Description: Historic House: 1844-57 Barrington, home of Anson Jones, fourth & last president of the Republic of Texas; house was moved to Washington State Park, site of the signing of the Texas Declaration of Independence.
Hours & Admission Prices: Daily 10-4:30. Single site ticket: Adults $5, students & children (over age 6) $3, family $15; Brazos Pass (unlimited admission) Adults $9, students $6, family $27, children (under 6) no charge. &
Attendance: 265,000 (estimated)

STAR OF THE REPUBLIC MUSEUM, 23200 Park Rd. 12, Washington, TX 77880. Mailing Address: P.O. Box 317, Washington, TX 77880-0317. Tel.: 936-878-2461. Fax: 936-878-2462. Facebook.
E-mail: star@blinn.edu
Web Site: www.starmuseum.org
Key Personnel: Dir., Houston McGaugh; Cur. Education, Lisa Berg; Coord. Visitor Svcs., Donna Barker; Office Mgr., Effie Wellmann.
Institution Type/Description: History Museum: located on the site of the signing of the Texas Declaration of Independence, twice the capital of the Republic of Texas.
Hours & Admission Prices: Daily 10-5. Family $15, adults $5, students $3; discounts to AAM & Texas Assoc. of Museums members. Closed New Year's Eve & Day; Thanksgiving; Christmas Eve, Day & week. &
Attendance: 35,000 (actual)

Waxahachie

ELLIS COUNTY MUSEUM, INC., 201 S. College, Waxahachie, TX 75165-3711. Mailing Address: P.O. Box 706, Waxahachie, TX 75168-0706. Tel.: 972-937-0681.
E-mail: ecmuseum@sbcglobal.net
Web Site: elliscountymuseum.org
Key Personnel: Dir. & Cur., Shannon Simpson.
Institution Type/Description: History Museum: housed in 1889 Masonic Lodge Hall Bldg.
Hours & Admission Prices: Mon.-Sat. 10-5. No charge; donations accepted.
Attendance: 9,000 (actual)

Weatherford

CLARK GARDENS BOTANICAL PARK, 567 Maddux Rd., Weatherford, TX 76088. Mailing Address: P.O. Box 276, Mineral Wells, TX 76068. Tel.: 940-682-4856. Fax: 940-682-4078. Facebook, Instagram, Twitter.
E-mail: info@clarkgardens.org
Web Site: www.clarkgardens.org
Institution Type/Description: Botanical Gardens.
Hours & Admission Prices: Mon.-Sat. 8-6, Sun. 10-5. Adults $9, seniors 65 & over $7, children 4-12 $5; discounts to groups of 25 or more; children 4 & under no charge. &

DOSS HERITAGE AND CULTURE CENTER, 1400 Texas Dr., Weatherford, TX 76086. Mailing Address: P.O. Box 215, Weatherford, TX 76086-0215. Tel.: 817-599-6168. Fax: 817-599-6193.
E-mail: info@dosscenter.org
Web Site: www.dosscenter.org
Key Personnel: Pres. & Mng. Dir., Dean Hungate.
Institution Type/Description: History Museum.
Hours & Admission Prices: Tues., Wed., Fri., Sat. 10-5; Thurs. 10-8. No charge. &

MUSEUM OF THE AMERICAS, 216 Fort Worth Hwy., Weatherford, TX 76086. Tel.: 817-341-8668.
E-mail: museumam@sbcglobal.net
Web Site: www.museumoftheamericas.com
Institution Type/Description: History Museum; Ethnographic Museum.
Hours & Admission Prices: Tues.-Fri. 10-5, Sat. 11-4; tours by appointment. Suggested Donation: $2 per person. Closed Aug. 1-31 & Dec. 24- Jan. 31.

THE NATIONAL VIETNAM WAR MUSEUM, 12685 Mineral Wells Hwy., Weatherford, TX 76088. Mailing Address: P.O. Box 1779, Weatherford, TX 76086. Tel.: 940-325-4003 & 452-1470. Facebook.
E-mail: info@nationalvnwarmuseum.org
Web Site: nationalvnwarmuseum.org
Key Personnel: Pres., Gerald Brazell; Vice Pres., Edward T. Luttenberger; Treas., Jim Messinger; Sec., Rowena Ash.
Institution Type/Description: Military Museum.
Hours & Admission Prices: Memorial Gardens: daily dawn to dusk. Visitor Center: Sun.-Mon. & Wed.-Sat. 9-1, Tues. 9-5. No charge; donations accepted. Closed New Year's Day; Thanksgiving; Christmas. &
Attendance: 20,000 (estimated)

Wellington

COLLINGSWORTH COUNTY MUSEUM, Physical/Mailing Address: 824 East Ave., P.O. Box 495, Wellington, TX 79095. Tel.: 806-447-5327.
E-mail: collingsworthmuseum@windstream.net
Web Site: www.collingsworthcountymuseum.org
Key Personnel: Pres., Rudolph Tate; Dir., W. Doris Stallings.
Institution Type/Description: Historic Buildings.
Hours & Admission Prices: Mon.-Fri. 9-5; other times by appointment. No charge; donations accepted. Closed holidays. &
Attendance: 353 (actual)

Weslaco

FRONTERA AUDUBON SOCIETY, 1101 S. Texas Blvd., Weslaco, TX 78596-7001. Tel.: 956-968-3275. Fax: 956-968-1388.
E-mail: fronteraaudubon@gmail.com
Web Site: www.fronteraaudubon.org
Key Personnel: Dir., Sarah Williams.
Institution Type/Description: Wildlife Refuge.
Hours & Admission Prices: Tues.-Sat. 8-4, Sun. 12-4. Adults $5, seniors $4; students (13 and over) $3; members & children (12 and under) no charge. &
Attendance: 2,351 (actual)

LOWER RIO GRANDE VALLEY NATURE CENTER, 301 S. Border Ave., P.O. Box 8125, Weslaco, TX 78599-8125. Tel.: 956-969-2475. Fax: 956-969-9915.
E-mail: info@valleynaturecenter.org
Web Site: www.valleynaturecenter.org
Key Personnel: Exec. Dir., Lydia Cavazos Guerra; Pres., Mark Gibbs.
Institution Type/Description: Nature Center.
Hours & Admission Prices: Tues.-Fri. 9-5, Sat. 8-5, Sun. 1-5. Adults $5, seniors 55 & over $3, children 12 & under $2; members no charge. Closed major holidays.
Attendance: 10,000 (actual)

WESLACO MUSEUM, 500 S. Texas, Weslaco, TX 78596-6202. Mailing Address: P.O. Box 8062, Weslaco, TX 78599-8062. Tel.: 956-968-9142. Fax: 956-447-0955. Facebook, Instagram, Twitter.
E-mail: info@weslacomuseum.org
Web Site: weslacomuseum.org
Formerly: Weslaco Bicultural Museum
Key Personnel: Dir., Sara Walker; Pres., Vicki Payne Rainwater.
Institution Type/Description: Local History & Cultural Art Museum.
Hours & Admission Prices: Tues.-Sat. 10-4. Adults $4, seniors $3, students, & veterans $2; members & children under 5 no charge. Closed New Year's Day; Good

Friday; Memorial Day; Independence Day; Labor Day; Thanksgiving; Christmas. &
Attendance: 5,000 (actual)

West Columbia

COLUMBIA HISTORICAL MUSEUM, Physical/Mailing Address: 247 E. Brazos Ave., P.O. Box 867, West Columbia, TX 77486. Tel.: 979-345-6125 & 3123.
Key Personnel: Cur., Margaret Willke.
Institution Type/Description: History Museum.
Hours & Admission Prices: Thurs.-Sat. 10-2; other times by appointment. No charge; donations accepted. Groups will be charged a nominal fee. &

VARNER-HOGG PLANTATION STATE HISTORIC SITE, 1702 N. 13th St., West Columbia, TX 77486. Tel.: 979-345-4656. Fax: 979-345-4412.
E-mail: susan.miller@thc.state.tx.us
Key Personnel: Exec. Dir. THC, Mark Wolfe; Site Mgr., Sue Miller; Pres. (V), Janet Dahse.
Institution Type/Description: State Historic Site.
Hours & Admission Prices: Mansion: Tues.-Sun; 9-4:30. Mansion Tours: Tues.-Sun. 11-2:30; Visitors center exhibits & museum store: Tues.-Sun. 8-5. Adults $7, seniors $6, children 6-18 & college students $4, children 5 and under no charge, special group rates. Closed New Year's Eve & Day, Thanksgiving, Christmas Eve & Day.
Attendance: 8,000 (actual)

Wharton

WHARTON COUNTY HISTORICAL MUSEUM, 3615 N. Richmond Rd., Wharton, TX 77488-2022. Mailing Address: P.O. Box 349, Wharton, TX 77488-0349. Tel.: 979-532-2600. Fax: 979-532-0871.
E-mail: wchm@awesomenet.net
Web Site: www.whartoncountymuseum.org
Key Personnel: C.E.O. & Museum Shop Mgr., Marvin Albrecht; Pres. (V), Linda Joy Stovall.
Institution Type/Description: History Museum: housed in former Marshall & Lillie A. Johnson residence.
Hours & Admission Prices: Closed temporarily. &
Attendance: 6,000 (estimated)

White Settlement

WHITE SETTLEMENT HISTORICAL MUSEUM, INC., 8320 Hanon Dr., White Settlement, TX 76108-2317. Tel.: 817-246-9719.
E-mail: wshm@sbcglobal.net; hanontx@lycos.com
Web Site: www.wsmuseum.com
Key Personnel: Pres., Jim Weaver.
Institution Type/Description: History Museum.
Hours & Admission Prices: Tues.-Sat. 10-3. No charge; donations accepted. Closed New Year's Eve & Day; Independence Day; Thanksgiving & day after; Christmas; Boxing Day. &
Attendance: 1,200 (estimated)

Wichita Falls

THE JUANITA HARVEY ART GALLERY - MIDWESTERN STATE UNIVERSITY, 3410 Taft Blvd., Wichita Falls, TX 76308-2099. Tel.: 940-397-4264.
E-mail: nicolette.daubert@mwsu.edu
Web Site: mwsu.edu/academics/finearts/art/gallery/index
Key Personnel: Gallery Dir., Gary Goldberg; Sec., Nicolette Daubert.
Institution Type/Description: Art Gallery.
Hours & Admission Prices: Mon.-Fri. 9-12 & 2-5.

KELL HOUSE MUSEUM, 900 Bluff St., Wichita Falls, TX 76301-3203. Tel.: 940-723-2712. Fax: 940-723-6592. Facebook: Kell House; Twitter: @WichitaHeritage.
E-mail: kellhouse1909@yahoo.com
Web Site: www.wichita-heritage.org
Key Personnel: Exec. Dir., Delores Culley; Cur., Stacie Crosetto Flood.
Institution Type/Description: Historic House: 1909 home of Frank Kell.
Hours & Admission Prices: Undergoing extensive renovation project, call ahead for tour hours.
Attendance: 6,885 (estimated)

KEMP CENTER FOR THE ARTS, 1300 Lamar, Wichita Falls, TX 76301-7031. Tel.: 940-767-2787. Fax: 940-767-3956. Facebook, Instagram, Twitter.
E-mail: info@kempcenter.org
Web Site: www.kempcenter.org
Formerly: Arts Council Wichita Falls Area
Key Personnel: C.E.O., Carol Sales; Chair, Britt Milstead.
Institution Type/Description: Community Art Center.
Hours & Admission Prices: Mon.-Fri. 9-5, Sat. 10-4, Sun. 12:30-4. No charge; donations accepted. Closed New Year's Day; Good Friday; Memorial Day; Independence Day; Labor Day; Thanksgiving; Christmas. &
Attendance: 32,000 (estimated)

MUSEUM OF NORTH TEXAS HISTORY, 720 Indiana St., Wichita Falls, TX 76301-6512. Mailing Address: P.O. Box 1619, Wichita Falls, TX 76307-1619. Tel.: 940-322-7628.
E-mail: month@sbcglobal.net
Web Site: www.museumofnorthtexashistory.org
Institution Type/Description: History Museum.
Hours & Admission Prices: Tues.-Sat. 10-4. No charge. &
Attendance: 6,137 (actual)

WICHITA FALLS MUSEUM OF ART, Two Eureka Cir., Wichita Falls, TX 76308-2998. Tel.: 940-397-8900.
E-mail: wfma@mwsu.edu
Web Site: www.wfmamsu.org
Key Personnel: Pres., Lola Pitzer; Museum Dir., Dr. Francine Carraro, Ph.D.
Institution Type/Description: General Museum.
Hours & Admission Prices: Tues.-Sat. 10-5. No charge; donations accepted. Closed university holidays. &
Attendance: 20,000 (estimated)

Wimberley

JACK GLOVER'S COWBOY MUSEUM, 333 Wayside Dr., Wimberley, TX 78676-5117. Tel.: 512-847-3338.
E-mail: cowboymuseum@earthlink.net
Formerly: Old West Museum
Key Personnel: Owner & Cur., Jack N. Glover; Co-Owner, Cherie Glover.
Institution Type/Description: General Museum.
Hours & Admission Prices: Call ahead for hours. No charge. &
Attendance: 2,500 (estimated)

PIONEER TOWN, 333 Wayside Dr., Wimberley, TX 78676-5117. Tel.: 512-847-2517. Fax: 512-847-6705. Facebook, Instagram, Twitter.
E-mail: information@7aresort.com
Web Site: www.7aranch.co
Key Personnel: Sec. & Treas., John D. White.
Institution Type/Description: Village Museum: authentic reproduction of c.1880 old West Town.
Hours & Admission Prices: By appointment. No charge; donations accepted.
Attendance: 35,000 (estimated)

WIMBERLEY VALLEY ART LEAGUE AND GALLERY, 14068 Ranch Rd. 12, Wimberley, TX 78676. Mailing Address: P. O. Box 1652, Wimberley, TX 78676. Tel.: 512-826-4286.
E-mail: lynncmyers@live.com
Web Site: www.visitwimberley.com/artleague
Key Personnel: Pres., Jan Fitzhugh; Vice Pres. & Pres. Elect, Jack Krietzburg.
Institution Type/Description: Art Gallery.
Hours & Admission Prices: Mon. 10-2, Tues.-Thurs. 9-4, Fri. 9-12.

Wink

ROY ORBISON MUSEUM, 205 E. Hendricks Blvd., Wink, TX 79789. Mailing Address: P.O. Box 431, Wink, TX 79789. Tel.: 432-527-3743.
Key Personnel: Cur., Edith Jones.
Institution Type/Description: History Museum.
Hours & Admission Prices: By appointment only. No charge; donations accepted.
Attendance: 300 (estimated)

Woodville

ALLAN SHIVERS MUSEUM, 302 N. Charlton, Woodville, TX 75979-4806. Tel.: 409-283-3709.
E-mail: ashivers.library@yahoo.com
Key Personnel: Dir., Rosemary Bunch.

Institution Type/Description: Historic House Museum: 1881 restored building.
Hours & Admission Prices: Mon.-Fri. 9-11:30, Sat & 1-2:30. Adults $5, seniors & children under 14 $2. Closed major holidays.
Attendance: 185 (actual)

HERITAGE VILLAGE MUSEUM, Physical/Mailing Address: Hwy. 190 W., P.O. Box 888, Woodville, TX 75979. Tel.: 409-283-2272, 800-323-0389. Fax: 409-283-2194.
E-mail: hvillagemuseum@att.net
Web Site: www.heritage-village.org
Key Personnel: Dir. & Museum Shop Mgr., Ofeira Gazzaway; Pres., Keelin Parker; Vice Pres., Charles Smith.
Institution Type/Description: Pioneer Village Museum.
Hours & Admission Prices: Mon.-Fri. 9-3, Sat.-Sun. 9-5. Adults $5, children under 12 $3; members no charge. Closed New Year's Eve & Day; Easter, Thanksgiving; Christmas. &
Attendance: 15,000 (estimated)

Woodway

CARLEEN BRIGHT ARBORETUM, Physical/Mailing Address: 1 Pavilion Way, Woodway, TX 76712. Tel.: 254-399-9204.
E-mail: jschaffer@woodwaymail.org
Web Site: www.woodway-texas.com/carleen-bright-arboretum/
Key Personnel: Dir., Janet Schaffer.
Institution Type/Description: Arboretum.
Hours & Admission Prices: Daily dawn to dusk. No charge; donations accepted.

Yorktown

YORKTOWN HISTORICAL MUSEUM, 144 W. Main St., Yorktown, TX 78164. Tel.: 361-564-9115 & 935-5243. Facebook.
E-mail: bcbruns@wildblue.net
Key Personnel: Chm. (V) & Pres. (V), Beverly Bruns.
Institution Type/Description: Historical & Preservation Society; housed in 1876 C. Eckhardt & Sons Store.
Hours & Admission Prices: Sat. 1-4, Sun. 2-5. No charge; donations accepted. &
Attendance: 700 (actual)

UTAH

(123 listings)

Alpine

ALPINE ART CENTER, 450 S, Alpine Hwy., Alpine, UT 84004-1508. Tel.: 801-763-7173. Fax: 801-763-9799.
E-mail: steves@alpineartcenter.com
Web Site: alpineartcenter.com
Key Personnel: Event Dir., Steve Streadbeck.
Institution Type/Description: Art Center.
Hours & Admission Prices: Art Center: Mon.-Fri. 10-5. Sculpture Park & Gardens: daily.

American Fork

TIMPANOGOS CAVE NATIONAL MONUMENT, Alpine Loop, Hwy. 92, American Fork, UT 84003-9803. Mailing Address: R.R. 3, Box 200, American Fork, UT 84003-9803. Tel.: 801-756-5239. Fax: 801-756-5661.
Web Site: www.nps.gov/tica/
Key Personnel: Supt., Jim Ireland; Administrative Officer, Shannon Stephens.
Institution Type/Description: Park Museum.
Hours & Admission Prices: May to Sept. daily. Cave Tours: adults $7, junior 6-15 $5, child 3-5 $3; discounts to seniors; infants under 2 no charge. &
Attendance: 12 (actual)

Blanding

THE DINOSAUR MUSEUM, 754 S. 200 W., Blanding, UT 84511-3909. Tel.: 435-678-3454.
E-mail: dinos@dinosaur-museum.org
Web Site: www.dinosaur-museum.org
Institution Type/Description: Dinosaur History Museum.
Hours & Admission Prices: April 15-Oct. 15 Mon.-Sat. 9-5. Adults $3.50, senior citizens $2.50, children $2; discounts to AAA & AAM members & groups of 10 or more; members no charge. &

EDGE OF THE CEDARS STATE PARK MUSEUM, 660 West, 400 N., Blanding, UT 84511. Tel.: 435-678-2238. Fax: 435-678-3348.
E-mail: edgeofthecedars@utah.gov
Web Site: parks.state.ut.us/parks/www1/edge.htm
Key Personnel: Museum Dir., Teri Paul; Museum Shop Mgr., Kathrina Perkins; Cur. Collections, Deborah Westfall; Maintenance & Historic Replication, Andrew Goodwin; Cur. Education, Rebecca Stoneman.
Institution Type/Description: Native American Cultural Museum: site of ancestral Puebloan village occupied A.D. 700-1220.
Hours & Admission Prices: mid-April to mid-Sept. daily 9-6; mid-Sept. to mid-April daily 9-5. Adults $5; discounts to Fun Tag members 65 & over; children no charge. Closed New Year's Day; Thanksgiving; Christmas. &
Attendance: 19,777 (actual)

HUCK'S MUSEUM AND TRADING POST, 1243 S. Main St., Blanding, UT 84511-3204. Mailing Address: 1387 S. Main St., Blanding, UT 84511. Tel.: 435-678-2329.
Institution Type/Description: History Museum.
Hours & Admission Prices: Daily 8-5. Adults $10.

Boulder

ANASAZI STATE PARK MUSEUM, 460 N. Hwy. 12, Boulder, UT 84716. Mailing Address: P.O. Box 1429, Boulder, UT 84716-1429. Tel.: 435-335-7308. Fax: 435-335-7352.
E-mail: nrdpr.ansp@state.ut.us
Web Site: www.stateparks.utah.gov/parks/anasazi
Key Personnel: Park Supt., Mike Nelson; Div. Dir., Mary Tullis; Cur., Bill Latady; Cur., Don Montoya; Museum Shop Mgr., Brenda Woolsey.
Institution Type/Description: Historic Site: 1050-1200 A.D., excavated Anasazi Indian Village.
Hours & Admission Prices: Memorial Day-Labor Day daily 8-6; Sept.-May daily 9-5. Admission: $3 per person; $5 per car; discount to groups; children under 6 & senior citizens from State of Utah no charge. Closed New Year's Day; Thanksgiving; Christmas. &
Attendance: 35,000 (actual)

Bountiful

BOUNTIFUL DAVIS ART CENTER, 90 N. Main St., Bountiful, UT 84010-6132. Tel.: 801-451-3660. Fax: 855-385-9988.
E-mail: info@bdac.org
Web Site: www.bdac.org
Key Personnel: Exec. Dir., Emma J. Dugal; Chm. (V), Jon Bouwhuis; Museum Shop Mgr., Elizabeth B. Barbano.
Institution Type/Description: Art Center.
Hours & Admission Prices: Tues.-Fri. 10-6, Sat. 2-5. No charge; donations accepted. Closed holidays. &
Attendance: 35,000 (estimated)

BOUNTIFUL HISTORICAL MUSEUM, 845 S. Main St., Ste. B5, Bountiful, UT 84010-6482. Tel.: 801-296-2060.
E-mail: tomsgrafix@aol.com
Web Site: legacy.bountifulutah.gov/HistoricalCommission/A_index01.html
Institution Type/Description: History Museum.
Hours & Admission Prices: Wed. 2-4, Sat. 1-3.

Brigham City

BRIGHAM CITY MUSEUM OF ART AND HISTORY, 24 N. 300 W., Brigham City, UT 84302-2030. Mailing Address: P.O. Box 583, Brigham City, UT 84302-0583. Tel.: 435-226-1439. Facebook: Brigham City Museum.
E-mail: bcmuseum@brighamcity.utah.gov
Web Site: www.brighamcitymuseum.org
Key Personnel: Dir., Kaia Landon; Dir. Research, Mary Alice Hobbs.
Institution Type/Description: Art Gallery & History Museum: collections span Box Elder County history from 1851-present.
Hours & Admission Prices: Tues.-Fri. 11-6, Sat. 1-5. No charge; donations accepted. &
Attendance: 10,000 (estimated)

Bryce

BRYCE WILDLIFE ADVENTURE - BRYCE CANYON MUSEUM, 1945 W. Utah State Hwy. 12, Bryce, UT 84764. Mailing Address: P.O. Box 640049, Bryce, UT 84764-0049. Tel.: 435-834-5555.

E-mail: terri@brycewildlifeadventure.com
Web Site: www.brycewildlifeadventure.com
Formerly: Paunsaugunt Wildlife Museum
Key Personnel: Owner & Cur., Robert Driedonks; Owner & Cur., Terri Driedonks.
Institution Type/Description: History Museum.
Hours & Admission Prices: April-Nov. 15 daily 9-9. Adults $8, children 6-12 $5; discounts to AAM members; children under 3 no charge. &

Bryce Canyon

BRYCE CANYON NATIONAL PARK VISITOR CENTER, Bryce Canyon National Park, Hwy. 63 Bryce #1, Bryce Canyon, UT 84717. Mailing Address: P.O. Box 640201, Bryce Canyon, UT 84764. Tel.: 435-834-5322. Fax: 435-834-4107. TDD: 435-834-5322.
E-mail: brca_reception_area@nps.gov
Web Site: www.nps.gov/brca
Key Personnel: Supt., Lisa Eckert.
Institution Type/Description: Natural History Museum.
Hours & Admission Prices: Park: daily. Visitors Center: April & Oct. daily 8-6; May-Sept. daily 8-8; Nov.-March daily 8-4:30. Park: $30 per car; $15 per individual on foot, motorcycle, bicycle or non-commercial group. Visitors Center: closed New Year's Day; Thanksgiving; Christmas. &
Attendance: 1,600,000 (estimated)

Castle Dale

MUSEUM OF THE SAN RAFAEL, 70 N. 100 E., Castle Dale, UT 84513. Mailing Address: P.O. Box 1088, Castle Dale, UT 84513. Tel.: 435-381-5252. Fax: 435-381-2863. Facebook: Museum of the San Rafael.
E-mail: museum@co.emery.ut.us
Web Site: museumsanrafael.org
Formerly: Emery County Pioneer Museum
Institution Type/Description: Pioneer Museum.
Hours & Admission Prices: Mon.-Fri. 10-4, Sat. 12-4.Donations Accepted

Cedar City

CEDAR BREAKS NATIONAL MONUMENT, 4730 S Hwy 148, Cedar City, UT 84719. Mailing Address: 2390 W Hwy 56 Ste #11, Cedar City, UT 84720. Tel.: 435-586-9451 & 0787. Fax: 435-586-3813. Facebook: Cedar Breaks National Monument.
Web Site: www.nps.gov/cebr
Key Personnel: Supt., Paul Roelandt; Chief Park Ranger, Matthew Harrison.
Institution Type/Description: Park Museum.
Hours & Admission Prices: Visitor Center: late May to mid-Oct. daily 9-6. 7-day individual fee $4; children 15 & under no charge. &
Attendance: 60,000 (estimated)

FRONTIER HOMESTEAD STATE PARK & MUSEUM, 635 N. Main, Cedar City, UT 84721-6179. Tel.: 435-586-9290. Facebook; Twitter; Instagram.
E-mail: frontierhomestead@utah.gov
Web Site: www.stateparks.utah.gov
Formerly: Iron Mission State Park & Museum
Key Personnel: Park Manager, Todd Prince; Cur., Ryan Paul.
Institution Type/Description: Pioneer History Museum.
Hours & Admission Prices: June-Aug. Mon.-Sun. 9-6; Sept.-May Mon.-Sat. 9-5. Adults $4, members $2; children under 6 no charge. Closed New Year's Day; Thanksgiving; Christmas. &
Attendance: 25,000 (actual)

SOUTHERN UTAH MUSEUM OF ART, 351 W. University Blvd., Cedar City, UT 84720-2470. Tel.: 435-586-5432. Fax: 435-865-8012. Facebook: @SUMACC; Instagram: @suma_museum.
E-mail: suma@suu.edu
Web Site: www.suu.edu/suma
Formerly: Braithwaite Fine Arts Gallery
Key Personnel: Dir., Jessica Farling.
Institution Type/Description: College Art Museum.
Hours & Admission Prices: Tues.-Sat. 11-5, open until 8 on Thurs. No charge; donations accepted. Closed major holidays; campus holidays. &
Attendance: 18,700 (estimated)

Coalville

SUMMIT COUNTY HISTORICAL MUSEUM, 60 N. Main St., Coalville, UT 84017-9809. Mailing Address: P.O. Box 128, Coalville, UT 84017-0128. Tel.: 435-336-3200 & 3015.
E-mail: nvernon@summitcounty.org
Web Site: summitcounty.org
Key Personnel: Dir., NaVee Vernon; Chm. (V), Russell Judd.
Institution Type/Description: History Museum.
Hours & Admission Prices: Mon.-Fri. 8-5; other times by appointment. No charge; donations accepted. &
Attendance: 1,000 (estimated)

Delta

GREAT BASIN HISTORICAL SOCIETY & MUSEUM, 45 W. Main St., Delta, UT 84624. Mailing Address: P.O. Box 550, Delta, UT 84624-0550. Tel.: 435-864-5013. Fax: 435-864-2446.
E-mail: gbm@frontiernet.net
Web Site: www.greatbasinmuseum.com
Key Personnel: Dir. & Pres., Owen Neilsen; Treas. & Devel., Linda Neilsen; Cur. & Sec., Janeal Young.
Institution Type/Description: Historical Society Museum.
Hours & Admission Prices: Mon.-Sat. 10-5, call for additional hours. No charge; donations accepted. &
Attendance: 3,500 (actual)

Draper

LIVING PLANET AQUARIUM, 12033 S. Lone Peak Pkwy., Draper, UT 84020. Tel.: 801-355-3474.
E-mail: info@thelivingplanet.com
Web Site: www.thelivingplanet.com
Institution Type/Description: Aquarium.
Hours & Admission Prices: Summer: Fri.-Sat. 10-8, Sun.-Thurs. 10-7; Winter: Fri.-Sat. 11-7, Sun.-Thurs. 11-6. Adults $8, seniors, military & students $7, children $6; children 2 & under no charge.

Ephraim

SNOW COLLEGE ART GALLERY, 150 E. College Ave., Ephraim, UT 84627-1550. Tel.: 435-283-7416.
E-mail: adam.larsen@snow.edu
Web Site: www.snow.edu/art/gallery/index.html
Institution Type/Description: Art Gallery.
Hours & Admission Prices: Mon.-Fri. 9-5; other times by appointment.

Eureka

TINTIC MINING MUSEUM, 241 Main St., Eureka, UT 84628. Mailing Address: P.O. Box 325, Eureka, UT 84628-0325. Tel.: 435-433-2054; 433-6649. Fax: 435-433-6891. Facebook.
E-mail: kayfun333@yahoo.com
Key Personnel: C.E.O., Dir. & Registrar, Kathleen Fulton; Vice Pres. (V), Ferrel Thomas; Treas., Warren Homan.
Institution Type/Description: Mining Museum: housed in 1899 Eureka City Hall.
Hours & Admission Prices: May-Sept. Sat.-Sun. 3-5; other times by appointment. No charge; donations accepted. &
Attendance: 1,500 (estimated)

Fairfield

CAMP FLOYD/STAGECOACH INN STATE PARK, 18035 W. 1540 N., Fairfield, UT 84013-9612. Tel.: 801-768-8932.
E-mail: marktrotter@utah.gov
Web Site: campfloyd.utah.gov
Key Personnel: Park Supt., Mark A. Trotter.
Institution Type/Description: Historic Site: 1858 site of Camp Floyd, former army camp of Utah.
Hours & Admission Prices: Mon.-Sat. 9-5. Family $9, adults $3; children 5 & under no charge. Closed New Year's Day; Thanksgiving; Christmas. &
Attendance: 16,000 (actual)

Fairview

FAIRVIEW MUSEUM OF HISTORY & ART, 85 N. 100 E., Fairview, UT 84629. Mailing Address: P.O. Box 157, Fairview, UT 84629-0157. Tel.: 435-427-9216. Fax: 435-427-3329.
E-mail: fvmuseum@cut.net
Web Site: www.sanpete.com

Key Personnel: Dir., Erma Lee Hansen; Pres. (V), Branch Cox.
Institution Type/Description: General Museum & Pioneer Park.
Hours & Admission Prices: Summer: Mon.-Sat. 10-6; Winter: Mon.-Sat. 10-5; other times by appointment. No charge; donations accepted. ⅃
Attendance: 20,000 (actual)

Farmington

PIONEER VILLAGE, 375 N. Lagoon Lane, Farmington, UT 84025-2502. Mailing Address: P.O. Box 696, Farmington, UT 84025-0696. Tel.: 801-451-8000. Fax: 801-451-8015.
E-mail: info@lagoonpark.com
Key Personnel: Dir., Peter Freed.
Institution Type/Description: History Museum.
Hours & Admission Prices: April-May & Sept.-Oct. Sat.-Sun. 9-4:30; June-Aug. daily 9-6. Admission $10; seniors no charge. ⅃
Attendance: 500,000 (actual)

Fillmore

TERRITORIAL STATEHOUSE STATE PARK & MUSEUM, 50 W. Capitol Ave., Fillmore, UT 84631-5556. Tel.: 435-743-5316. Fax: 435-743-4723. Facebook: Territorial Statehouse State Park & Museum.
E-mail: caldrich@utah.gov
Web Site: stateparks.utah.gov/parks/territorial-statehouse/
Key Personnel: Dir., Carl Camp; Cur. & Museum Shop Mgr., Carl J. Aldrich.
Institution Type/Description: Regional History Museum: housed in Utah's first territorial Capitol 1855-1858.
Hours & Admission Prices: Mon.-Sat. 9-5; other times by appointment. Family $6, adults 12 & over $2, children 6-11 $1; members & children under 6 no charge. Closed New Year's Day; Thanksgiving; Christmas. ⅃
Attendance: 45,000 (estimated)

Fort Douglas

FORT DOUGLAS MILITARY MUSEUM, 32 Potter St., Fort Douglas, UT 84113-5046. Tel.: 801-581-1251. Fax: 801-581-9846.
E-mail: admin@fortdouglas.org
Web Site: www.fortdouglas.org
Key Personnel: C.E.O. & Dir., Robert S. Voyles; Pres. (V), Brent Ashworth; Cur., Beau Burgess; Historian/Visitor Svcs. Mgr., Su Richards.
Institution Type/Description: Military Museum: housed in 1875 Quartermaster Victorian Infantry Barracks Building, located in Fort Douglas, founded in 1862 by California Volunteers to protect the Overland Mail & Telegraph lines.
Hours & Admission Prices: Tues.-Sat. 12-5. No charge; donations accepted. Closed federal holiday weekends. ⅃
Attendance: 6,000 (actual)

Fort Duchesne

CULTURAL RIGHTS AND PROTECTION DEPARTMENT -UTE INDIAN TRIBE, 910 South 7500 East, Fort Duchesne, UT 84026. Mailing Address: P.O. Box 190, Fort Duchesne, UT 84026-0190. Tel.: 435-722-5141. Fax: 435-722-2083.
Web Site: www.utetribe.com
Key Personnel: Dir., Betsy Chapoose.
Institution Type/Description: Indian Museum: located on site related to the era of U.S. Cavalry and Old Fort Duchesne.
Hours & Admission Prices: Mon.-Thurs. 8-4:30.

Grantsville

DONNER-REED PIONEER MUSEUM, 90 N. Cooley, Grantsville, UT 84029. Tel.: 435-884-3767 & 3411.
Web Site: www.donner-reed-museum.org
Institution Type/Description: History Museum.
Hours & Admission Prices: By appointment.

UTAH FIREFIGHTERS MUSEUM, 37 N. Church, Grantsville, UT 84029. Mailing Address: P.O. Box 1128, Grantsville, UT 84029-1128. Tel.: 435-884-6680.
Institution Type/Description: Fire Museum.
Hours & Admission Prices: Fri.-Sat. 11-3; other times by appointment.

Green River

JOHN WESLEY POWELL MUSEUM, 1765 E. Main St., Green River, UT 84525. Mailing Address: P.O. Box 387, Green River, UT 84525-0387. Tel.: 435-564-3427. Fax: 435-564-3526.
E-mail: museum@johnwesleypowell.com
Web Site: www.jwprhm.com
Key Personnel: Dir., Tim Glenn; Chm. (V), Penney Riches; Museum Shop Mgr., JoAnn Wetherington.
Institution Type/Description: River History Museum.
Hours & Admission Prices: Call for hours & admission prices. ⅃
Attendance: 30,000

Heber City

COMMEMORATIVE AIR FORCE UTAH WING MUSEUM, CAF Hangar - Russ McDonald Field, 2365 S. Airport Rd., Heber City, UT 84068. Mailing Address: P.O. Box 507, Heber City, UT 84032. Tel.: 435-709-7269. Facebook: Utah Wing Commemorative Air Force.
E-mail: caf.utah@gmail.com
Web Site: www.cafutahwing.org
Key Personnel: Wing Leader, Steve Guenard; Officer, D.K. Gorrell; Officer, Matt McNamara.
Institution Type/Description: Military History Museum.
Hours & Admission Prices: May-Oct. Thurs.-Sun. 10-5. No charge; donations requested. ⅃
Attendance: 5,000 (estimated)

Helper

WESTERN MINING + RAILROAD MUSEUM, 294 S. Main St., Helper, UT 84526. Mailing Address: P.O. Box 221, Helper, UT 84526-0221. Tel.: 435-472-3009.
E-mail: helpermuseum@helpercity.net
Web Site: www.wmrrm.com
Key Personnel: Dir. & Museum Shop Mgr., James Boyd; Chm. (V), Pat Kokal.
Institution Type/Description: History Museum: housed in the Old Helper Hotel, built c.1913.
Hours & Admission Prices: May. 15-Sept. 14 Mon.-Sat. 10-5; Sept. 15-May 14 Tues.-Sat. 11-4. No charge; donations accepted. ⅃
Attendance: 5,000 (estimated)

Hill Air Force Base

HILL AEROSPACE MUSEUM, 7961 Wardleigh Rd., Hill Air Force Base, UT 84056-5842. Tel.: 801-825-5817. Fax: 801-777-6386.
E-mail: calendar@aerospaceutah.org
Web Site: www.aerospaceutah.org
Key Personnel: Dir., Scott Wirz; Chm. (V), Marc Reynolds; Museum Shop Mgr., Lorrie Slade.
Institution Type/Description: Aerospace Museum.
Hours & Admission Prices: Mon.-Sat. 9-4:30. No charge; donations accepted. Closed New Year's Day; Thanksgiving; Christmas. ⅃
Attendance: 180,000 (actual)

Hurricane

HURRICANE VALLEY HERITAGE PARK MUSEUM, 35 W. State, Hurricane, UT 84737-1961. Mailing Address: P.O. Box 91, Hurricane, UT 84737-0091. Tel.: 435-635-3245. Fax: 435-635-4696.
E-mail: hurricanemuseum@hotmail.com
Web Site: www.hurricane-pioneer.org
Key Personnel: C.E.O. & Pres. (V), Gregory Lawton; Treas., Verlin Leavett; Cur., Phyllis Lawton; Registrar, Lee Beaty.
Institution Type/Description: General Museum.
Hours & Admission Prices: Mon.-Sat. 9-5. No charge; donations accepted. Closed New Year's Day; Thanksgiving; Christmas. ⅃
Attendance: 10,000 (estimated)

Hyrum

HYRUM CITY MUSEUM, 50 W. Main St., Hyrum, UT 84319-1297. Tel.: 435-245-0208.
E-mail: museum@hyrumcity.com
Key Personnel: Dir., Jami J. Van Huss.
Institution Type/Description: History Museum.

Hours & Admission Prices: Tues.-Thurs. 12-6, Sat. 10-3. No charge. &
Attendance: 3,314 (actual)

Kanab

KANAB HERITAGE MUSEUM & JUNIPER FINE ARTS GALLERY, 13 S. 100 E., Kanab, UT 84741. Mailing Address: City Office, 76 N. Main, Kanab, UT 84741. Tel.: 435-644-3966.
Institution Type/Description: History Museum & Art Gallery.
Hours & Admission Prices: Summer: Mon.-Fri. 1-5. No charge; donations accepted.

Kaysville

KAYSVILLE LECONTE STEWART GALLERY OF ART, 44 N. Main, Kaysville, UT 84037-1949. Tel.: 801-544-2826. Fax: 801-544-5646.
E-mail: admin@kaysvillecity.com
Institution Type/Description: Art Gallery.
Hours & Admission Prices: Call for hours.

Layton

HERITAGE MUSEUM OF LAYTON, 403 N. Wasatch Dr., Layton, UT 84041-3238. Tel.: 801-336-3930.
E-mail: bsanders@laytoncity.org
Web Site: www.laytoncity.org/public/museum/default.aspx
Key Personnel: Cur., Bill Sanders.
Institution Type/Description: History Museum.
Hours & Admission Prices: Tues.-Fri. 11-6, Sat. 1-5. No charge. Closed holidays. &
Attendance: 6,500 (actual)

Lehi

JOHN HUTCHINGS MUSEUM OF NATURAL & CULTURAL HISTORY, 55 N. Center St., Lehi, UT 84043-1826. Tel.: 385-201-1020. Fax: 385-201-1021. Facebook: Hutchings Museum in Lehi.
E-mail: hmuseum@lehi-ut.gov
Web Site: www.lehi-ut.gov/discover/hutchings-museum
Key Personnel: Dir., Ben Woodruff.
Institution Type/Description: Natural & Cultural History Museum.
Hours & Admission Prices: Tues.-Sat. 11-5. Adults $4, senior citizens, children & students $3; discount to groups; children under 2 no charge. Closed national holidays. &
Attendance: 10,000 (estimated)

NORTH AMERICAN MUSEUM OF ANCIENT LIFE, 2929 Thanksgiving Way, Lehi, UT 84043-3740. Tel.: 801-766-5000.
E-mail: membership@thanksgivingpoint.org
Web Site: www.thanksgivingpoint.com
Institution Type/Description: Paleontology Museum.
Hours & Admission Prices: Mon.-Sat. 10-8. Exhibits: adults $15, senior citizens 65 & over and children 3-12 $12; discounts to military; members and children 2 & under no charge. Exhibits & Movie: adults $20, senior citizens 65 & over and children 3-12 $17. Closed Thanksgiving; Christmas.

Logan

INTERMOUNTAIN HERBARIUM, UTAH STATE UNIVERSITY, Dept. of Biology, Utah State Univ., Logan, UT 84322. Mailing Address: 5305 Old Main Hill, Utah State University, Logan, UT 84322-5305. Tel.: 435-797-4034. Fax: 435-797-1575.
E-mail: paul.wolf@usu.edu
Web Site: herbarium.usu.edu/
Key Personnel: Dir., Paul G. Wolf.
Institution Type/Description: Herbarium.
Hours & Admission Prices: Mon.-Fri. 8-5. No charge; donations accepted. Closed state & national holidays.
Attendance: 300 (actual)

NORA ECCLES HARRISON MUSEUM OF ART, Utah State University, 650 N. 1100 E., Logan, UT 84322. Mailing Address: 4020 Old Main Hill, Logan, UT 84322-4020. Tel.: 435-797-0163. Fax: 435-797-3423. Facebook: Nora Eccles Harrison Museum of Art.
E-mail: nehma@usu.edu
Web Site: www.artmuseum.usu.edu

Key Personnel: Exec. Dir., Katie Lee Koven; Registrar, Casey Allen; Cur. Education, Nadra E. Haffar; Cur. Collections & Exhibitions, Rebecca Dunham; Administrative Coord., Andrea DeHaan; Coord. & Exhibitions, Zoira Arredando.
Institution Type/Description: Art Museum.
Hours & Admission Prices: Closed for expansion in 2017. &
Attendance: 12,695 (actual)

STOKES NATURE CENTER, 2696 E. Hwy. 89, Logan, UT 84323. Mailing Address: P.O. Box 4204, Logan, UT 84323-4204. Tel.: 435-755-3239. Fax: 435-755-6586.
E-mail: nature@logannature.org
Web Site: www.logannature.org
Key Personnel: Exec. Dir., Jennifer Hamilton; Dir. Education, Sasha Broadstone; Dir. Operations, Ru Mahoney.
Institution Type/Description: Nature Center.
Hours & Admission Prices: Wed.-Fri. 10-4; call to confirm. No charge; donations accepted. &
Attendance: 11,000

UTAH STATE UNIVERSITY'S MUSEUM OF ANTHROPOLOGY, 730 Old Main Hill, Logan, UT 84322-0730. Tel.: 435-797-7545. Fax: 435-797-1240.
E-mail: anthro.museum@usu.edu
Web Site: www.usu.edu/anthro/museum
Key Personnel: Dir., Dr. Patricia Lambert; Deputy Dir. & Cur., Molly Boeka Cannon.
Institution Type/Description: Anthropology Museum.
Hours & Admission Prices: Tues.-Fri. 9-5, 1st Sat. of the month 10-2. No charge; donations accepted. Closed university holidays; federal holidays. &
Attendance: 7,000 (estimated)

ZOOTAH, 419 W. 700 S., Logan, UT 84321-5599. Tel.: 435-750-9894. Facebook.
E-mail: community@zootah.org
Web Site: zootah.org
Formerly: Willow Park Zoo
Key Personnel: Dir., Troy Cooper.
Institution Type/Description: Zoo.
Hours & Admission Prices: March-April & Sept.-Oct. Fri.-Sat. 1-5; May-Aug. Mon.-Sat. 11-5. Adults $4, children 2-11 $3. Closed New Year's Day; Thanksgiving; Christmas.
Attendance: 125,000 (estimated)

Magna

MAGNA ETHNIC AND MINING MUSEUM, 9056 W. Magna Main St., Magna, UT 84044-1149. Mailing Address: P.O. Box 742, Magna, UT 84044-0324. Tel.: 801-250-5656.
E-mail: noel@magnadesigns.com
Web Site: utahethnicandminingmuseumofmagna.com
Institution Type/Description: Mining Museum.
Hours & Admission Prices: Tues. & Thurs.-Fri. 11-3, Wed. 11-5; other times by appointment.

Midvale

MIDVALE HISTORICAL SOCIETY MUSEUM, 7697 S. Main St., Midvale, UT 84047-7107. Tel.: 801-569-8040.
E-mail: mid_museum@xmission.com
Key Personnel: Chmn. (V), Bill Miller; Pres. (V), Don Rogers.
Institution Type/Description: History Museum.
Hours & Admission Prices: Tues.-Wed. & Sat. 12-4. No charge; donations accepted. &
Attendance: 580 (actual)

Moab

ARCHES NATIONAL PARK VISITOR CENTER, N. Hwy. 191, Moab, UT 84532. Mailing Address: P.O. Box 907, Moab, UT 84532-0907. Tel.: 435-719-2100 & 2299. Fax: 435-719-2305. TDD: 435-719-2319.
E-mail: archinfo@nps.gov
Web Site: www.nps.gov/arch
Key Personnel: Park Supt., Kate Cannon.
Institution Type/Description: Natural History Museum.
Hours & Admission Prices: Park: daily 24 hours a day. Visitor Center: daily 9-4. 7-day vehicle $25, 7-day individual $10. Closed Christmas. &
Attendance: 733,000 (actual)

DAN O'LAURIE MUSEUM OF MOAB, 118 E. Center St., Moab, UT 84532-2430. Tel.: 435-259-7985.
E-mail: moabmuseum@frontiernet.net
Web Site: www.moabmuseum.org
Formerly: Dan O'Laurie Canyon Country Museum
Key Personnel: Dir., Travis Schenck; Pres. (V), Lloyd Holyoak.
Institution Type/Description: General Museum.
Hours & Admission Prices: March-Oct. Mon.-Fri. 10-5, Sat.-Sun. 12-5; Nov.-Feb. Mon.-Sat. 12-5. Family $10, adult $5; children under 17 with adult & members no charge. Closed New Year's Day; Memorial Day; Independence Day; Labor Day; Thanksgiving; Christmas. ᘎ
Attendance: 7,000 (actual)

DEAD HORSE POINT STATE PARK, Hwy. 313, Moab, UT 84532. Mailing Address: P.O. Box 609, Moab, UT 84532-0609. Tel.: 435-259-2614. Fax: 435-259-2615. Facebook: Dead Horse Point State Park.
E-mail: deadhorsepoint@utah.gov
Web Site: www.stateparks.utah.gov
Key Personnel: Park Mgr., Megan Blackwelder; Asst. Mgr., Crystal White.
Institution Type/Description: State Park Visitor Center.
Hours & Admission Prices: Visitor Center: mid-March to mid-Oct. 8-6; mid-Oct. to mid-March 9-5. Park: daily. Daytime: $10 per car; Camping: $30 per night; Yurts: $99 per night; call for campground reservations. Visitor Center: closed New Year's Day; Thanksgiving; Christmas. ᘎ
Attendance: 403,737 (estimated)

HOLE N' THE ROCK, 11037 S. Hwy. 191, Moab, UT 84532-3969. Tel.: 435-686-2250. Fax: 435-686-9959.
E-mail: hnrock@citlink.net
Web Site: www.theholeintherock.com
Key Personnel: Dir., Wyndee Hansen; Pres., Erik Hansen; Museum Shop Mgr., Malaine Wareham.
Institution Type/Description: Historic Home: housed in the home, carved out of rock by Albert and Gladys Christenson.
Hours & Admission Prices: Daily 9-5. Tours: adults $5, children 5-10 $3.50; children under 5 no charge. ᘎ
Attendance: 50,000 (estimated)

MOAB MUSEUM OF FILM & WESTERN HERITAGE, Red Cliffs Lodge, Mile Post 14., Hwy. 128, Moab, UT 84532-9618. Tel.: 435-259-2002, 866-812-2002. Fax: 435-259-5050.
Web Site: www.redcliffslodge.com/museum
Institution Type/Description: History & Film Museum.
Hours & Admission Prices: Daily 7am-9pm. No charge. ᘎ
Attendance: 15,000 (estimated)

Monticello

FRONTIER MUSEUM, 216 S. Main, Monticello, UT 84535. Mailing Address: P.O. Box 763, Monticello, UT 84535-0763. Tel.: 435-587-3401.
E-mail: ging0209@gmail.com
Web Site: www.utahscanyoncountry.com/en/entities/226/
Institution Type/Description: History Museum.
Hours & Admission Prices: Winter: Oct.-March Fri.-Sun. 10-6. No charge, donations accepted. ᘎ

Mount Carmel

THUNDERBIRD FOUNDATION FOR THE ARTS, 2200 S. State St., Mount Carmel, UT 84755. Mailing Address: P.O. Box 5555, Mount Carmel, UT 84755-5555. Tel.: 435-648-2653.
E-mail: sdb_611@yahoo.com
Web Site: www.thunderbirdfoundation.com
Key Personnel: Dir., Susan Bingham; Chm. (V), Paul Bingham; Pres. (V), Daniel Shea; Treas., Emily Hollingshead; Devel., Bruce Bell; Security, Richard Anderson.
Institution Type/Description: Art Museum: housed in the summer home of American painter, Maynard Dixon.
Hours & Admission Prices: March-Oct. daily 10-5; other times by appointment. Self-guided Tour: $10 per person. Guided Tour: $20 per person; discounts to large groups. ᘎ
Attendance: 3,000 (estimated)

Mount Pleasant

MT. PLEASANT PIONEER MUSEUM, 146 S. State St., Mount Pleasant, UT 84647. Tel.: 435-462-2456. Fax: 435-462-2581.
E-mail: pandk@cut.net

Institution Type/Description: Historic House Museum.
Hours & Admission Prices: Mon.-Tues. 10-2, Wed.-Sat. 10-6. No charge; donations accepted.

Ogden

ECCLES COMMUNITY ARTS CENTER, 2580 Jefferson, Ogden, UT 84401-2411. Tel.: 801-392-6935. Fax: 801-392-5295. Facebook: Eccles Community Arts Center.
E-mail: eccles@ogden4arts.org
Web Site: www.ogden4arts.org
Key Personnel: C.E.O., Pat Poce; Chm. (V), Steve Kaufman.
Institution Type/Description: Art Center: housed in c.1893 David Eccles Home.
Hours & Admission Prices: Mon.-Fri. 9-5, Sat. 9-3. No charge; donations accepted. Closed national holidays. ᘎ
Attendance: 30,000 (estimated)

FORT BUENAVENTURA, 2450 A Ave., Ogden, UT 84401. Mailing Address: 1181 N. Fairgrounds, Ogden, UT 84404-3100. Tel.: 801-399-8099.
E-mail: jcarter@co.weber.ut.us
Web Site: www.co.weber.ut.us/parks/fortb
Key Personnel: Park Mgr., Jim Carter.
Institution Type/Description: Historic Site: housed in an 1846 fort & 1874 Browning home.
Hours & Admission Prices: Easter to Oct. daily 8-8. Admission $2 per person with education program, $1 per person without education program; discounts to family & school groups; children under 5 no charge. Season Pass: family $100, individual $30. ᘎ
Attendance: 14,700 (estimated)

THE MARY ELIZABETH DEE SHAW GALLERY, Kimball Visual Arts Ctr., 2001 University Cir., Ogden, UT 84408. Tel.: 801-626-6420. Fax: 801-626-6976.
E-mail: katherinelee@weber.edu
Web Site: www.weber.edu/shawgallery
Formerly: Weber State University Art Gallery
Key Personnel: Gallery Dir., Katie Lee Koven.
Institution Type/Description: Art Gallery.
Hours & Admission Prices: Mon.-Fri. 11-5, 1st Fri. of month 11-9, Sat. 12-5. No charge. ᘎ
Attendance: 4,000 (estimated)

MUSEUM OF NATURAL SCIENCE, Weber State University, 3848 Harrison Blvd., Ogden, UT 84408-2509. Tel.: 801-626-6160.
E-mail: ajohnston@weber.edu
Web Site: www.community.weber.edu/sciencemuseum
Institution Type/Description: Natural Science Museum.
Hours & Admission Prices: Mon.-Fri. 8-5. No changes.
Attendance: 18,000 (estimated)

OGDEN NATURE CENTER, 966 W. 12th St., Ogden, UT 84404-5410. Tel.: 801-621-7595. Fax: 801-621-1867. Facebook.
E-mail: info@ogdennaturecenter.org
Web Site: www.ogdennaturecenter.org
Key Personnel: Dir., Brandi Bosworth; Chm. (V), Chris Hoagstrom; Museum Shop Mgr., Jennifer Callaway.
Institution Type/Description: Nature Center.
Hours & Admission Prices: Mon.-Fri. 9-5, Sat. 9-4. Adults 12-64 $5, seniors 65 & over $4, children 2-11 $3; members no charge. Closed major holidays.
Attendance: 38,000 (actual)

OGDEN UNION STATION MUSEUMS, 25th & Wall Ave., Union Station, Ogden, UT 84401. Mailing Address: 2501 Wall Ave., Ogden, UT 84401-1359. Tel.: 801-393-9886. Fax: 801-621-0230. Facebook: Ogden Union Station Museums.
E-mail: museums@theunionstation.org
Web Site: www.theunionstation.org
Key Personnel: Dir., Elizabeth Sutton; C.E.O., Leon Jones; Pres. (V), Julie Lewis.
Institution Type/Description: History Museum: housed in 1924 Ogden Union Depot.
Hours & Admission Prices: Mon.-Sat. 10-5. Adults $5, seniors $4, children 2-12 $3; discounts to groups with reservations. Closed New Year's Day; Thanksgiving; Christmas Eve & Day. ᘎ
Attendance: 60,000 (estimated)

OGDEN'S GEORGE S. ECCLES DINOSAUR PARK, 1544 E. Park Blvd., Ogden, UT 84401-0803. Tel.: 801-393-3466. Fax: 801-399-0895. Facebook: Ogden's George S. Eccles Dinosaur Park.

E-mail: info@dinosaurpark.org
Web Site: www.dinosaurpark.org
Key Personnel: Park Dir., Casey Allen; Bd. Chair, John Peterson; Museum Shop Mgr., Samantha Taylor.
Institution Type/Description: Dinosaur Park & Museum.
Hours & Admission Prices: Memorial Day to Labor Day Mon.-Sat. 10-8, Sun. 10-6; Sept.-May Mon.-Sat. 10-6. Adults $7, senior citizens 62 & over and students $6, children 2-12 $5; discounts to groups of 15 or more with reservation; children one & under no charge. Closed New Year's Eve & Day; Thanksgiving & day after; Christmas Eve & Day. &
Attendance: 125,000 (actual)

OTT PLANETARIUM, Weber State University, 3750 Harrison Blvd., Ogden, UT 84408. Mailing Address: 2508 University Circle, Ogden, UT 84408-2508. Tel.: 801-626-6163.
E-mail: planetarium@weber.edu
Web Site: ottplanetarium.org
Key Personnel: Dir., Dr. Stacy Palen.
Institution Type/Description: Planetarium.
Hours & Admission Prices: By appointment. Call or see website for admission prices.

TREEHOUSE MUSEUM, 347 22nd St., Ogden, UT 84401. Tel.: 801-394-9663.
E-mail: treehouse@treehousemuseum.org
Web Site: www.treehousemuseum.org
Key Personnel: exec. Dir., Lynne H. Goodwin.
Institution Type/Description: Children's Museum.
Hours & Admission Prices: June-Aug. Mon.-Thurs. & Sat. 10-5, Fri. 10-8; Sept.-May Mon. 10-3, Tues.-Thurs. & Sat. 10-5, Fri. 10-8. Children 1-12 $6, 13 & up $5; discounts to scheduled groups; children under one & members no charge. Closed New Year's Day; Independence Day; Thanksgiving; Christmas. &
Attendance: 169,621 (actual)

Orem

WOODBURY ART MUSEUM, 575 E. University Pkwy., #250, Orem, UT 84097-7400. Tel.: 801-863-4200. Fax: 801-426-6218.
E-mail: uvmuseum@uvu.edu
Web Site: www.uvu.edu/museum
Key Personnel: Interim Dir., Melissa Hempel; Registrar, Rebekah Monahan; Graphic Designer, Amanda Luker; Preparator, Chris Juber; Visitor Svcs., Katherine Hall; Museum Asst., Tia Mickelson.
Institution Type/Description: Art Museum.
Hours & Admission Prices: Tues. 11-8, Wed.-Sat. 11-5. No charge.
Attendance: 5,670 (actual)

Park City

ALF ENGEN SKI MUSEUM, 3419 Olympic Pkwy., Park City, UT 84098. Mailing Address: P.O. Box 980187, Park City, UT 84098. Tel.: 435-658-4240. Fax: 435-658-4258.
Key Personnel: Exec. Dir., Connie Nelson.
Institution Type/Description: History Museum.
Hours & Admission Prices: Daily 9-6. Adults $7, seniors & youth 3-17 $5.

JOE QUINNEY WINTER SPORTS CENTER, Olympic Legacy Plaza, Olympic Pkwy., Park City, UT 84098. Mailing Address: P. O. Box 980187, Park City, UT 84098. Tel.: 435-658-4233.
Institution Type/Description: Sports Museum.
Hours & Admission Prices: Daily 10-6. Closed New Year's Day; Easter; Thanksgiving; Christmas.

KIMBALL ART CENTER, 1401 Kearns Blvd., Park City, UT 84060-5106. Mailing Address: P.O. Box 1478, Park City, UT 84060-1478. Tel.: 435-649-8882. Fax: 435-649-8889. Facebook: Kimball Art Center.
E-mail: director@kimballartcenter.org
Web Site: www.kimballartcenter.org
Key Personnel: Dir., Robin Marrouche; Chm. (V), Matt Mullin.
Institution Type/Description: Art Center.
Hours & Admission Prices: Mon.-Thurs. 10-5, Fri. 10-7, Sat. 12-7, Sun. 12-5. No charge; donations accepted. Closed major holidays. &
Attendance: 118,000 (estimated)

PARK CITY MUSEUM, 528 Main St., Park City, UT 84060. Mailing Address: P.O. Box 555, Park City, UT 84060-0555. Tel.: 435-649-7457. Fax: 435-649-7384.
E-mail: info@parkcityhistory.org

Web Site: parkcityhistory.org
Formerly: Park City Historical Society & Museum
Key Personnel: Exec. Dir., Sandra Morrison; Pres., Ron Butkovich; Cur. Collections & Exhibits, Courtney Titus; Dir. Education, Jenette Purdy.
Institution Type/Description: History Museum.
Hours & Admission Prices: Mon.-Sat. 10-7, Sun. 12-6. Adults $10, seniors, students & military $8, children 7-17 $5; discounts to AAM members; children 6 & under & members no charge. Closed Thanksgiving; Christmas. &
Attendance: 73,505 (actual)

Parowan

PAROWAN OLD ROCK CHURCH MUSEUM, 90 S. Main, Parowan, UT 84761. Mailing Address: P.O. Box 576, Parowan, UT 84761-0576. Tel.: 435-477-3549.
Institution Type/Description: Historic Church: housed in a church built by hand by early pioneers in 1865.
Hours & Admission Prices: Memorial Day to Labor Day Mon.-Sat. 1-5; other times by appointment. No charge.

Payson

HISTORIC PETEETNEET MUSEUM, CULTURAL ARTS AND SOCIAL CENTER, 10 N. 600 E., Payson, UT 84651-2359. Mailing Address: P.O. Box 603, Payson, UT 84651-0603. Tel.: 801-465-5265. Fax: 801-465-9427. Facebook: Historic Peteetneet Museum.
E-mail: sdee41@comcast.net
Web Site: peteetneetmuseum.org
Institution Type/Description: Historic Building: housed in a Victorian school building built in 1901.
Hours & Admission Prices: Mon.-Fri. 10-4. No charge; donations accepted. &
Attendance: 12,500 (estimated)

Price

COLLEGE OF EASTERN UTAH ART GALLERY, GALLERY EAST, 451 E. 400 North, Price, UT 84501-2699. Tel.: 435-613-5241. Fax: 435-613-4102.
E-mail: communications_office@ceu.edu
Web Site: www.ceu.edu
Key Personnel: Dir., Nole Carmack.
Institution Type/Description: Art Gallery.
Hours & Admission Prices: mid-Sept. to May Mon.-Fri. 8:30-5; other times by appointment. No charge. Closed major holidays. &
Attendance: 10,000 (estimated)

UTAH STATE UNIVERSITY - COLLEGE OF EASTERN UTAH PREHISTORIC MUSEUM, 155 E. Main St., Price, UT 84501-3033. Mailing Address: 451 E. 400, N., Price, UT 84501-2699. Tel.: 435-613-5060, 800-817-9949. Fax: 435-637-2514.
E-mail: ken.carpenter@ceu.edu
Web Site: www.ceu.edu/museum
Key Personnel: Dir. & Cur. Paleontology, Dr. Kenneth Carpenter; Chm. (V), Michael Fleck; Museum Shop Mgr., Christine Trease.
Institution Type/Description: Anthropology, Paleontology & Geology Museum.
Hours & Admission Prices: April-Sept. daily 9-5; Oct.-March Mon.-Sat. 9-5. Family $15, adult $5, seniors $4, children 2-12 $2; members no charge. &
Attendance: 40,000 (actual)

Promontory

GOLDEN SPIKE NATIONAL HISTORIC SITE, 6200 N. 22300 W., Promontory, UT 84307. Mailing Address: P.O. Box 897, Brigham City, UT 84302-0897. Tel.: 435-471-2209, ext. 29. Fax: 435-471-2341.
E-mail: gosp_interpretation@nps.gov
Web Site: www.nps.gov/gosp
Key Personnel: Supt., Leslie Crossland; Chief Interpretation, Justin Glasgow; Museum Shop Mgr., Gary Willden.
Institution Type/Description: Golden Spike National Historic Site: first transcontinental railroad was completed here on May 10, 1869.
Hours & Admission Prices: Daily 9-5. May to Columbus Day: $7 per vehicle. mid-Oct. to April $5 per vehicle. Federal Interagency passes honored. Closed New Year's Day; Thanksgiving; Christmas. &
Attendance: 47,500 (actual)

Provo

BRIGHAM YOUNG UNIVERSITY MUSEUM OF ART, N. Campus Dr., Provo, UT 84602-1400. Mailing Address: 490 MOA, N. Campus Dr., Provo, UT 84602-1400. Tel.: 801-422-8257. Fax: 801-422-0530.
E-mail: moa@byu.edu
Web Site: moa.byu.edu
Key Personnel: Dir., Dr. Mark A. Magleby; Assoc. Dir., Ed Lind; Cur., Dr. Marian Wardle; Exhibition Design, Jeff Barney; Head Education, Janalee Emmer; Educator, Kalisha Grimsman; Educator, Lynda Palma; Cur., Jeff Lambson; Mgr. Exhibition Fabrication, John Adams; Head Security, Jeffrey Strong; Museum Shop Mgr., Cheri Koford; Exec. Asst. & Event Scheduler, Romy Cotten; Registrar, Trevor Weight; Mktg. & Communications Mgr., Hilarie Ashton; Collection Mgr., Clyda Ludlow; Custodial Supvr., Suzanne Barney; Grounds Supvr., Steven Roylance; Business Mgr., Teresa Taylor; Project Mgr., Ann Lambson.
Institution Type/Description: Art Museum.
Hours & Admission Prices: Mon.-Tues. & Sat. 10-6, Wed.-Fri. 10-9. No charge; donations accepted. Closed New Year's Day; Independence Day; Thanksgiving; Christmas. &
Attendance: 327,000 (actual)

BRIGHAM YOUNG UNIVERSITY MUSEUM OF PALEONTOLOGY, 1683 N. Canyon Rd., Provo, UT 84602. Mailing Address: 140 ESM, BYU, P.O. Box 23300, Provo, UT 84602-3300. Tel.: 801-422-3939. Fax: 801-378-7919.
E-mail: rod_scheetz@byu.edu
Web Site: geology.byu.edu/museum/
Formerly: Brigham Young University Earth Science Museum
Key Personnel: C.E.O. Brigham Young Univ., Thomas S. Monson; Pres. Brigham Young Univ., Kevin J. Worthen; Mgr. & Cur., Rod Scheetz, Ph.D.; Vertebrate Paleontologist, Brooks Britt, Ph.D.
Institution Type/Description: Paleontology Museum.
Hours & Admission Prices: Mon.-Fri. 9-5. No charge; donations accepted. Closed state holidays. &
Attendance: 25,000 (estimated)

THE CRANDALL HISTORICAL PRINTING MUSEUM, 275 E. Center St., Provo, UT 84606-3133. Tel.: 801-377-7777. Fax: 801-375-5555.
E-mail: lou_crandall@yahoo.com
Web Site: crandallprintingmuseum.org
Key Personnel: Pres. (V), Louis E. Crandall; Chm. (V), Brent Ashford; Museum Shop Mgr., Wallace Saling.
Institution Type/Description: Writing & Printing History Museum.
Hours & Admission Prices: Mon.-Fri. 9-2. Adults $2; discount to Boy Scouts working on certificate or patch. Closed major holidays.
Attendance: 6,000 (estimated)

MONTE L. BEAN LIFE SCIENCE MUSEUM, 645 E. 1430 N., Brigham Young University, Provo, UT 84602. Tel.: 801-422-5052. Fax: 801-422-0093.
E-mail: secretary@museum.byu.edu
Web Site: mlbean.byu.edu/
Key Personnel: Dir., Larry L. St. Clair; Assoc. Dir., Dr. Leigh Johnson; Asst. Dir., Marta Adair; Asst. Store Mgr., Perry Chee.
Institution Type/Description: Life Science Museum.
Hours & Admission Prices: Mon.-Fri. 10-9, Sat. 10-5. No charge. Closed New Year's Day; Independence Day; Pioneer Day; Thanksgiving; Christmas Eve & Day. &
Attendance: 210,000 (estimated)

MUSEUM OF PEOPLES AND CULTURES, 2201 N. Canyon Rd., Provo, UT 84602. Mailing Address: B-67, Rm. 126, Provo, UT 84602. Tel.: 801-422-0020. Fax: 801-422-0026.
E-mail: mpc_programs@byu.edu
Web Site: mpc.byu.edu
Key Personnel: Dir., Paul Stavast; Cur. Education, Kari Nelson.
Institution Type/Description: Anthropology and Ethnology Museum.
Hours & Admission Prices: Mon. & Wed.-Fri. 9-5, Tues. 9-7. No charge. Closed New Year's Day; Presidents' Day; Civil Rights Day; Memorial Day; Independence Day; Labor Day; Thanksgiving; Christmas. &
Attendance: 26,765 (actual)

Saint George

BRIGHAM YOUNG'S WINTER HOME, 67 West 200 North, Saint George, UT 84770. Mailing Address: St. George Temple Visitor's Center & Historic Sites, 490 S. 300 E., Saint George, UT 84770-3665. Tel.: 435-673-5181.
E-mail: vcsgeorge@ldschurch.org
Web Site: www.stgeorgetemplevisitorcenter.org/byounghome.html
Key Personnel: Dir. Exhibits & Visitors' Centers, LDS Church, Tom Peterson; Cur. Exhibits & Historic Sites, Don Enders; Cur. Art & Artifacts, Richard G. Oman; Registrar, T. Michael Smith.
Institution Type/Description: Historic House: 1869-70 Brigham Young Winter Home.
Hours & Admission Prices: Winter: daily 9-5. Summer: daily 9-7. No charge.
Attendance: 39,746 (actual)

ROSENBRUCH WILDLIFE MUSEUM, 1835 Convention Center Dr., Ste. B, Saint George, UT 84790-5843. Tel.: 435-656-0033 & 986-6697. Fax: 435-986-6694.
E-mail: angieh@rosenbruch.org
Web Site: www.rosenbruch.org
Key Personnel: Exec. Dir. Museum & Foundation, Angie Rosenbruch-Hammer; Pres. (V), Jimmie C. Rosenbruch; Cur., Dustin Hammer; Dir. Mktg., Melissa Young.
Institution Type/Description: Wildlife Museum.
Hours & Admission Prices: Mon. 10-8, Tues.-Sat. 10-6. Adults $8, senior citizens $6, children 3-12 $4; discounts to Utah Museum Assoc. members. Annual Pass available. Closed New Year's Day; Thanksgiving; Christmas. &
Attendance: 40,500 (actual)

ST. GEORGE ART MUSEUM, 47 E. 200 N., Saint George, UT 84770-2843. Tel.: 435-627-4525.
E-mail: museum@sgcity.org
Web Site: www.sgartmuseum.org
Key Personnel: Dir., Deborah Reeder; Chm. (V), Joe Viers; Museum Shop Mgr., Valerie Sullivan; Museum Asst., April Cummings.
Institution Type/Description: Art Museum.
Hours & Admission Prices: Mon.-Sat. 10-5. Adults $3, children 3-11 $1; discounts to AAM & ICOM members; museum professionals, children under 3 & members no charge. &
Attendance: 8,908 (actual)

ST. GEORGE DINOSAUR DISCOVERY SITE AT JOHNSON FARM, 2180 E. Riverside, Saint George, UT 84790-2483. Tel.: 435-574-3466. Fax: 435-627-0340.
E-mail: tracksofdinos@gmail.com
Web Site: www.utahdinosaurs.com
Key Personnel: Dir., Diana Azevedo; Pres. (V), Gary Watts; Cur., Andrew R. C. Milner.
Institution Type/Description: Natural History Museum.
Hours & Admission Prices: Daily 10-6. Adults $6, children 4-11 $3; members & children under 3 no charge. Closed New Year's Day; Easter; Thanksgiving; Christmas. &
Attendance: 48,800 (actual)

WESTERN SKY AVIATION WARBIRD MUSEUM, 4196 S. Airport Pkwy., Saint George, UT 84790. Mailing Address: 2050 W. Canyon View Dr. #2, Saint George, UT 84770. Tel.: 435-669-0655. Facebook: Western Warbirds.
E-mail: jhunter88@msn.com
Web Site: www.westernskywarbirds.org
Institution Type/Description: Military Aviation Museum.
Hours & Admission Prices: Fri.-Sat. 10-4. No charge; donations accepted. &
Attendance: 14,000 (estimated)

Salt Lake City

CHASE HOME MUSEUM OF UTAH FOLK ARTS, 1150 S. Constitution Dr., Salt Lake City, UT 84105. Mailing Address: c/o Utah Div. of Arts & Museums, 617 E. South Temple, Salt Lake City, UT 84102-1101. Tel.: 801-533-5760. Fax: 801-533-4202. Facebook: @chasehomemuseum.
E-mail: chasemuseum@utah.gov
Web Site: heritage.utah.gov/arts-and-museums/chasehome
Key Personnel: Mgr. Museum Svcs., Jennifer Ortiz; Folk Arts Specialist, Adrienne Decker; Admin., Sabrina Sanders.
Institution Type/Description: Folk Arts Museum: 1853 two-story adobe structure built by Isaac Chase and Mormon leader Brigham Young, sold to city in 1880, renovated in 2000.

Hours & Admission Prices: Memorial Day to Labor Day: Tues., Thurs.-Sat. 11-4, Wed. 11-8; Labor Day to Memorial Day Tues.-Fri. 11-4. No charge.
Attendance: 9,300 (actual)

CHURCH HISTORY MUSEUM, 45 N. West Temple St., Salt Lake City, UT 84150-0902. Tel.: 801-240-3310. Fax: 801-240-5342. Facebook: @churchhistorymuseum.
E-mail: history@ldschurch.org
Web Site: history.lds.org/section/museum
Formerly: Museum of Church History and Art
Key Personnel: Dir., Alan Johnson.
Institution Type/Description: History & Art Museum.
Hours & Admission Prices: Mon.-Fri. 9-9, Sat. 10-5. No charge. Closed New Year's Day; Easter; Thanksgiving; Christmas Eve & Day.
Attendance: 250,000 (estimated)

CHURCH OF JESUS CHRIST OF LATTER-DAY SAINTS - BEEHIVE HOUSE, 67 E. South Temple, Salt Lake City, UT 84150-9719. Tel.: 801-240-2681. Fax: 801-240-2695. TDD: 801-240-2672.
Web Site: www.lds.org/locations/historic-beehive-house
Key Personnel: Dir., Alan Johnson.
Institution Type/Description: Historic House: 1854-1877 Brigham Young's residence & office.
Hours & Admission Prices: Daily 9:30-8:30. No charge. Closed New Year's Day; Thanksgiving; Christmas.
Attendance: 3,000,000 (estimated)

CLARK PLANETARIUM, 110 S. 400 W., Salt Lake City, UT 84101-1145. Tel.: 385-468-7827. Facebook: @ClarkPlanetarium; Twitter: @ClarkPlanet.
E-mail: sjarvis@slco.org
Web Site: clarkplanetarium.org
Formerly: Hansen Planetarium
Key Personnel: C.E.O. & Dir., Seth Jarvis; Assoc. Dir. Devel & Mktg. Mgr., Lindsie Smith; Programs Mgr., Ron Proctor; Education & Exhibits Mgr., Duke Johnson; Fiscal Mgr., Anna Marie Tueller; Operations Mgr., Rob Morris; Facilities Mgr., Brad Rich; Planet Fun Store Mgr., Mike Sheehan.
Institution Type/Description: Planetarium, Space Science Museum.
Hours & Admission Prices: Sun.-Wed. 10:30-7, Thurs. 10:30-10, Fri.-Sat. 10:30-11. Star Show: adults $9, children 12 & under $7; discounts to shows before 5pm; ASTC reciprocal admission; members no charge. Call 801-456-7827 for current showtimes & prices. Closed Christmas; Thanksgiving.
Attendance: 350,000 (actual)

CLASSIC CARS INTERNATIONAL MUSEUM, 355 W. 700 South St., Salt Lake City, UT 84101-2609. Tel.: 801-201-1683. Fax: 801-322-5586.
E-mail: classiccarsintl@hotmail.com
Web Site: www.classiccarsintl.net
Key Personnel: C.E.O., Stacy Williams.
Institution Type/Description: Automobile Museum.
Hours & Admission Prices: Open by appointment. Adults $6, senior citizens & children $4; discounts to AAA, AAM & ICOM members. Closed New Year's Eve & Day; Christmas Eve, Day & week.
Attendance: 1,000 (estimated)

DISCOVERY GATEWAY CHILDREN'S MUSEUM, 444 W. 100 S., Salt Lake City, UT 84101-1195. Tel.: 801-456-5437. Fax: 801-456-5440. Facebook & Instagram: @discoverygateway; Twitter: @DGchildmuseum.
E-mail: info@discoverygateway.org
Web Site: www.discoverygateway.org
Formerly: The Children's Museum of Utah
Key Personnel: Exec. Dir., Laurie Hopkins; Chm. (V), Timothy J. Dance; Dir. Opers., Tammy Spicer; Sr. Devel. Mgr., Rachel Tibolla; Mktg. Mgr., Shanna Sheline.
Institution Type/Description: Children's Museum & Discovery Center.
Hours & Admission Prices: Mon.-Thurs. 10-6, Fri.-Sat. 10-7, Sun. noon to 6. Admission $9.50, seniors $7; discounts on Sundays; members & children under 2 no charge. Closed Easter; Independence Day; Thanksgiving; Christmas.
Attendance: 285,000 (estimated)

FINCH LANE GALLERY, 54 Finch Lane, Salt Lake City, UT 84102-1809. Tel.: 801-596-5000. Fax: 801-530-0547. Facebook: @SLCartscouncil; Instagram: @slc_artscouncil; Twitter: @SLArtsCouncil;.
E-mail: info@saltlakearts.org
Web Site: saltlakearts.org

Key Personnel: Asst. Dir., Kelsey Ellis; Gallery Asst., Deanne Coles.
Institution Type/Description: Art Gallery.
Hours & Admission Prices: Mon.-Fri. 8-5. No charge. Closed holidays; between scheduled exhibits.

HELLENIC CULTURAL MUSEUM, The Greek Orthodox Cathedral of the Holy Trinity, 279 S. 300 W., Salt Lake City, UT 84101-1703. Tel.: 801-328-9681.
E-mail: jpezely@gmail.com
Web Site: www.pahh.com/hca/museum.html
Key Personnel: Dir. & C.E.O., Jon Pezely.
Institution Type/Description: Greek Heritage Museum.
Hours & Admission Prices: Wed. 9-12, Sun. after church services; groups of 30 or more by appointment. No charge; donations accepted.
Attendance: 223 (actual)

THE LEONARDO, 209 E. 500 S., Salt Lake City, UT 84111. Tel.: 801-531-9800. Facebook: The Leonardo.
E-mail: info@theleonardo.org
Web Site: www.theleonardo.org
Key Personnel: Exec. Dir., Alexandra Hesse; Chm., Dinesh Patel, Ph.D.; Dir. Devel., Katie Smith; Mktg. Dir., Andrew Parker.
Institution Type/Description: Art Museum.
Hours & Admission Prices: Fri. 10-10, Sat.-Thurs. 10-5. Adults $12.95, seniors 65 & over, military with valid ID and students with valid ID $9.95, children 3-12 & member guest $8.95; members, children 3 & under and ASTC members no charge
Attendance: 160,000 (actual)

NATURAL HISTORY MUSEUM OF UTAH, 301 Wakara Way, Salt Lake City, UT 84108. Tel.: 801-581-6927 & 4303. Fax: 801-585-3684. Facebook: @naturalhistorymuseumofutah; Instagram & Twitter: @NHMU.
E-mail: info@nhmu.utah.edu
Web Site: nhmu.utah.edu
Formerly: Utah Museum of Natural History
Key Personnel: Exec. Dir., Sarah B. George; C.F.O., Tony Millet; Dir. Mktg., Jim Breitinger; Dir. Public Rels., Patti Carpenter; Dir. Philanthropy, Chris Eisenberg; Chief Cur., Cur. Anthropology, Duncan Metcalfe; Cur. Paleontology, Randall Irmis; Cur. Vertebrate Zoology, Eric Rickart; Cur. Botany, Mitchell Power; Mgr. School Programs, Tracey Collins; Assoc. Dir. Community & Govt. Rels., Ann Hannibal; Assoc. Dir. Visitor Experience, Becky Menlove; Museum Shop Mgr., Suzanne Ruhlman.
Institution Type/Description: Natural History Museum.
Hours & Admission Prices: Thurs.-Tues. 10-5, Wed. 10-9. Adults $14.95, senior citizens 65 & over and young adults 13-24 $12.95, children 3-12 $9.95; University of Utah faculty, staff & students, children under 3 and members no charge. Closed Thanksgiving; Christmas.
Attendance: 262,000 (estimated)

PIONEER MEMORIAL MUSEUM, 300 N. Main St., Salt Lake City, UT 84103-1699. Tel.: 801-532-6479. Fax: 801-532-4436.
E-mail: info@isdup.org
Web Site: isdup.org
Key Personnel: Pres. & Museum Dir., Maurine P. Smith; 1st Vice Pres., Cheryl Searle; Artifacts Office, Kari Main; Historian, Cathy Tingey; Librarian, Phyllis Griffiths.
Institution Type/Description: Pioneer History Museum.
Hours & Admission Prices: Mon., Tues., Thurs.-Sat. 9-5, Wed. 9-8; No charge; donations accepted. Closed national holidays.
Attendance: 36,263 (actual)

PRICE FAMILY HOLOCAUST MEMORIAL, I.J. and Jeanne Wagner Jewish Community Center, 2 N. Medical Dr., Salt Lake City, UT 84113-1101. Tel.: 801-581-0098. Fax: 801-581-0718.
E-mail: info@slcjcc.org
Web Site: www.slcjcc.org
Key Personnel: Exec. Dir., Andrea Alcabes.
Institution Type/Description: History Museum.
Hours & Admission Prices: Call for hours. No charge.

RED BUTTE GARDEN & ARBORETUM, University of Utah, 300 Wakara Way, Salt Lake City, UT 84108. Tel.: 801-585-0556.
E-mail: information@redbutte.utah.edu
Web Site: www.redbuttegarden.edu
Key Personnel: Exec. Dir., Gregory Lee; Chm. (V), Tom Ramsey; Dir. Devel., Wendy Loyning; Volunteer Coord., Lauren Miller; Mktg. & Public Rels., Bryn Ramjoue; Visitor Svcs. Dir. & Museum Shop Mgr., Derrek Hanson; Horticulture Education Dir., Sara Sorenson; Museum Shop Mgr., Dianne Crosby.
Institution Type/Description: Botanical Garden & Arboretum.

Hours & Admission Prices: April & Sept. daily 9-7:30; May-Aug. daily 9-9; Oct.-March daily 9-5; garden closed at 5pm on concert days. Adults $12, students & seniors $10; discounts to APGA & AHS reciprocal garden program; children under 3 & members no charge. Closed New Year's Eve & Day; Thanksgiving; Christmas Eve, Day & week. &
Attendance: 200,000 (actual)

THIS IS THE PLACE HERITAGE PARK, 2601 E. Sunnyside Ave., Salt Lake City, UT 84108-1453. Tel.: 801-582-1847. Fax: 801-583-1869. Facebook & Instagram: @thisistheplaceheritage-park; Twitter: @Thisistheplace1.
E-mail: cservice@thisistheplace.org
Web Site: www.thisistheplace.org
Key Personnel: Exec. Dir., Ellis Ivory; Finance & HR Dir., Lorin Cummings; Programming Dir., Cliff Harris; Public Rels. & Customer Rels. Dir., Tresha Kramer; Facilities Dir., Steve Hirschi; Programming Dir., Cliff Harris; Mktg. Dir., Anna Hirschi; Programming Mgr. & Volunteer Dir., Holly Curtis.
Institution Type/Description: Park Visitor Center, Monument & Living History Museum.
Hours & Admission Prices: Winter: Nov.-March daily 10-5. Adults $5-$6.95, children 3-11 & seniors $3-$3.95; children 2 & under no charge. Summer: April-Oct. daily 10-5. Adults $12.95, children 3-11 & seniors $8.95; discounts on Sun.; children 2 & under no charge. Closed New Year's Day; Thanksgiving; Christmas. &
Attendance: 300,000 (estimated)

TRACY AVIARY, 589 E. 1300 S., Salt Lake City, UT 84105-1111. Tel.: 801-596-8500. Fax: 801-596-7325. Facebook, Instagram & Twitter: @tracyaviary.
E-mail: info@tracyaviary.org
Web Site: tracyaviary.org
Key Personnel: C.E.O. & Exec. Dir., Tim Brown.
Institution Type/Description: Aviary.
Hours & Admission Prices: Daily 9-4. Memorial Day to Labor Day: adults $9.95, seniors, students, & military $6.95, children 3-12 $5.95; Sept.-May: adults $7.95, seniors, students & military $6.95, children 3-12 $4.95; discount to groups, AZA, AAA, & AHS members; members & children 2 & under no charge. Reciprocal admission with other participating facilities. Closed Thanksgiving; Christmas. &
Attendance: 135,000 (estimated)

UTAH MUSEUM OF CONTEMPORARY ART, 20 S. West Temple, Salt Lake City, UT 84101-1406. Tel.: 801-328-4201. Facebook & Twitter: @UtahMoCA.
E-mail: michelle.sulley@utahmoca.org
Web Site: www.utahmoca.org
Formerly: Salt Lake Art Center
Key Personnel: Controller, Lori Johnson; Devel. Coord., Michelle Sulley; Cur. Exhibitions, Jared Steffensen; Visitor Svcs. Coord. & Art Shop, Jessica Simpson.
Institution Type/Description: Contemporary Art Museum.
Hours & Admission Prices: Tues.-Thurs. & Sat. 11-6, Fri. 11-9. Suggested donation $5. Closed holidays. &
Attendance: 28,000 (estimated)

UTAH MUSEUM OF FINE ARTS, Marcia and John Price Museum Bldg., University of Utah, 410 Campus Center Dr., Salt Lake City, UT 84112-0360. Tel.: 801-581-7332. Fax: 801-585-5198. Facebook & Instagram: @utahmuseumfinearts; Twitter: @umfa.
Web Site: umfa.utah.edu
Key Personnel: Exec. Dir., Gretchen Dietrich; Deputy Dir. Finance & Operations, George Lindsey; Deputy Dir. Planning & Program, Sonja Lunde; Dir. Collections & Exhibits, David Carroll; Preparator, David Hardy; Dir. Education & Engagement, Jorge Rojas; Dir. Mktg. & Communications, Mindy Wilson; Dir. Devel., Johann Jacobs; Museum Store Supvr., Carol Bigelow.
Institution Type/Description: Art Museum.
Hours & Admission Prices: Tues. & Thurs.-Fri. 10-5, Wed. 10-8, Sat.-Sun. 11-5. Museum: adults $14, youth 6-18, seniors & out of state college students $12; members, Utah higher education students, staff & faculty, NARM members, military families and children 5 & under no charge. Closed major holidays. &
Attendance: 131,190 (estimated)

UTAH STATE CAPITOL, 350 N. State St., 120 State Capitol, Salt Lake City, UT 84114. Tel.: 801-538-1800. Facebook & Twitter: @UTStateCapitol.
E-mail: capitoltours@utah.gov
Web Site: utahstatecapitol.utah.gov
Key Personnel: Exec. Dir., Allyson Gamble; Operations Mgr., Dana Jones; Inventory & Collections Mgr., Stephanie Angelides; Visitor Svcs. Mgr., Rachel Parkinson.

Institution Type/Description: Historic Building: built in 1916.
Hours & Admission Prices: Mon.-Fri. 7am-8pm, Sat.-Sun. & holidays 8-6.
Attendance: 200,000 (estimated)

UTAH STATE HISTORICAL SOCIETY, 300 S. Rio Grande St., (450 West), Salt Lake City, UT 84101-1182. Tel.: 801-245-7225. Fax: 801-533-0587. TDD: 801-533-3502.
E-mail: lbuckmiller@utah.gov
Web Site: heritage.utah.gov
Key Personnel: Dir. & State Historic Preservation Officer (SHPO), P. Brad Westwood; Chm. (V), Dina Blaes; Research Center Mgr., Greg Walz; Archaeology Record Mgr., Arie Leeflang; Research/Collections Coord., Doug Misner; Historical Architect, Don Hartley; Program Specialist, Alycia Rowley; Historical Collections Cur., Melissa Coy; SHPO Compliance, Preservation, Chris Hansen; National Register, Cory Jensen.
Institution Type/Description: Historical Society Museum.
Hours & Admission Prices: Office: Mon.-Fri. 8-5, Research Center: Mon.-Fri. 9-4. No charge; donations accepted. Closed national & state holidays. &
Attendance: 75,000 (estimated)

UTAH'S HOGLE ZOO, 2600 E. Sunnyside Ave., (840 South), Salt Lake City, UT 84108-1454. Tel.: 801-584-1700. Fax: 801-584-1770. Facebook, Instagram & Twitter: @HogleZoo.
Web Site: www.hoglezoo.org
Key Personnel: Exec. Dir., Craig Dinsmore; Chm. Bd. Dirs., Paul M. Dougan; Dir. Devel., Eve Mary Verde; Dir. Animal Care, Michele Stancer.
Institution Type/Description: Zoo.
Hours & Admission Prices: March-Oct. daily 9-6; Nov.-Feb. daily 9-5. May-Sept. adults $16.95, senior citizens 65 & over $14.95, children 3-12 $12.95; Oct.-April adults $14.95, senior citizens $12.95, children 3-12 $10.95; discounts to groups of 20 or more; children under 2 no charge. Closed New Year's Day; Christmas. &
Attendance: 847,831 (actual)

WHEELER HISTORIC FARM, 6351 South 900 E., Salt Lake City, UT 84121-2438. Tel.: 385-468-1755. Fax: 385-468-1754. Facebook: Wheeler Historic Farm.
E-mail: wheeler1@slco.org
Web Site: www.wheelerfarm.com
Key Personnel: Facility Mgr., Kathleen Bailey; Communications & Pub. Rels. Mgr., Callie Birdsall; Program Coord., Raegan Scharman; Office Coord., Randi Morishita; Historic Mgr., Sara Roach; Head Farmer, Richard Snow; Agricultural Specialist, Liz Hamilton.
Institution Type/Description: Preservation Project: 1898 Wheeler Farm House, representing the initial statehood period & typical of Utah agriculture in 1898.
Hours & Admission Prices: Daily dawn-dusk. No charge. Wagon Rides: youth 13 & up $3, children 2 & up $2. Historic Farm House Tours: adults $4, children 3-12 $2. Cow Milking: $1. Closed New Year's Day; Christmas. &
Attendance: 395,735 (actual)

Sandy

HILL GALLERY & SCULPTURE PARK, 8847 South 360 East, Sandy, UT 84070. Tel.: 801-562-9242.
E-mail: dchill35@outlook.com
Web Site: www.danhillsculpture.com
Institution Type/Description: Gallery and Sculpture Park.
Hours & Admission Prices: Tues.-Fri. 12-5; other times by appointment.

SANDY MUSEUM, 8744 S. Center St., Sandy, UT 84070-1404. Tel.: 801-566-0878.
E-mail: sandymuseum@hotmail.com
Key Personnel: Dir., Sherry Slaugh; C.E.O. & Pres. (V), Frank Slaugh.
Institution Type/Description: History Museum: built 1890.
Hours & Admission Prices: Tues.-Thurs. & Sat. 1-5; other times by appointment. No charge; donations accepted. Closed Independence Day; Thanksgiving; Christmas Eve & Day. &
Attendance: 2,000 (actual)

Santa Clara

JACOB HAMBLIN HOME, 3325 Hamlin Dr., Santa Clara, UT 84770. Mailing Address: St. George Temple Visitor's Center & Historic Sites, 490 S. 300 E., Saint George, UT 84770-3665. Tel.: 435-673-5181. Fax: 435-652-9589.
E-mail: vcsgeorge@ldschurch.org
Key Personnel: Cur. Exhibits & Historic Sites, Don Enders; Cur. Art & Artifacts, Richard G. Oman; Registrar, T. Michael Smith.
Institution Type/Description: Historic House: 1862-64 Jacob Hamblin Home, church leader & pioneer of the area.

Hours & Admission Prices: Winter: daily 9-5; Summer: daily 9-7. No charge. &
Attendance: 22,592 (actual)

Sevier

FREMONT INDIAN STATE PARK AND MUSEUM, 3820 W. Clear Creek Canyon Rd., Sevier, UT 84766-6058. Tel.: 435-527-4631. Fax: 435-527-4735. Facebook: @fremontindian.
E-mail: fremontindian@utah.gov
Web Site: stateparks.utah.gov/parks/fremont-indian/
Institution Type/Description: Park Museum.
Hours & Admission Prices: Visitor Center & Museum: Summer: daily 9-6; Winter: Mon.-Sat. 9-5; individual $4, for a vehicle up to 8 people $8; discounts to seniors. Closed Thanksgiving; Christmas; New Year's Day. &
Attendance: 80,000 (estimated)

Springdale

ZION NATIONAL PARK, ZION HUMAN HISTORY MUSEUM, SR 9, Springdale, UT 84767-1099. Tel.: 435-772-3256. Fax: 435-772-3426.
E-mail: zion_park_information@nps.gov
Web Site: www.nps.gov/zion
Formerly: Zion National Park Museum
Key Personnel: Supt., Jeff Bradybaugh; Chief Park Ranger, Cindy Purcell.
Institution Type/Description: Natural History and Human History Museum.
Hours & Admission Prices: National Park: 24 hours a day. Human History Museum: March-Nov. Daily 10-5. 7-day vehicle entrance fee $30, 7-day motorcycle $25, individual entrance fee $15. Martin Luther King, Jr. Day, National Park Week, National Park Service Day, National Public Lands Day & Veterans Day Weekend no charge. &
Attendance: 4,300,000 (estimated)

Springville

SPRINGVILLE MUSEUM OF ART, 126 E. 400 S., Springville, UT 84663-1953. Tel.: 801-489-2727. Fax: 801-489-2739. Facebook; Twitter; Instagram; Pinterest.
E-mail: npetersen@springville.org
Web Site: www.smofa.org
Key Personnel: Dir., Dr. Rita Wright, PhD; Assoc. Dir., Natalie Petersen; Head Education, Jessica R. Weiss, MA.
Institution Type/Description: State Museum of Utah Art.
Hours & Admission Prices: Tue. & Thurs.-Sat. 10-5, Wed. 10-9. No charge; donations accepted. Closed holidays. &
Attendance: 110,000 (estimated)

Stansbury Park

BENSON GRIST MILL, 325 State Rd. 138, Stansbury Park, UT 84074. Mailing Address: 2930 W. Hwy. 112, Tooele, UT 84074. Tel.: 435-882-7678. Fax: 435-882-6003.
E-mail: bensonmill@trilobyte.net
Web Site: www.bensonmill.org
Key Personnel: Mill Dir., Jodi Brunson.
Institution Type/Description: History Museum: listed on the National Register of Historic Sites.
Hours & Admission Prices: May-Oct. Thurs.-Sat. 10-6. &
Attendance: 12,000 (estimated)

Syracuse

SYRACUSE MUSEUM & CULTURAL CENTER, 1891 West 1700 South, Syracuse, UT 84075. Tel.: 801-825-3633. Fax: 801-825-3001.
Institution Type/Description: History Museum.
Hours & Admission Prices: Tues.-Thurs. 2-5, Fri. 1-4.

Tooele

OQUIRRH MOUNTAIN MINING MUSEUM, 47 S. Maine, Tooele, UT 84074-2148. Tel.: 435-843-4000.
E-mail: chamber@tooelechamber.com
Institution Type/Description: Mining Museum.
Hours & Admission Prices: Call for hours. No charge.

TOOELE PIONEER MUSEUM, 47 E. Vine St., Tooele, UT 84074-2133. Tel.: 435-843-0771 & 882-1092.
E-mail: pioneer@getbeehive.net

Web Site: tooelepioneermuseum.com
Key Personnel: Dir. & Chm. (V), Tim Booth; Museum Shop Mgr., John Cluff.
Institution Type/Description: History Museum.
Hours & Admission Prices: May-Sept. Tues. 10-1; other times by appointment. No Charge. &
Attendance: 2,500 (actual)

TOOELE VALLEY RAILROAD MUSEUM, 35 N. Broadway, Tooele, UT 84074. Mailing Address: 90 N. Main St., Tooele, UT 84074-2139. Tel.: 435-882-2836. Fax: 435-643-7888.
E-mail: brianr@tooelecity.org
Web Site: www.tooelecity.org/parks&recreation/railroadmuseum.asp
Key Personnel: Chm., Larry Deppe, Ph.D.; Dir. & Chm. (V), Jean Mogus; Pres., Bruce Grim.
Institution Type/Description: History Museum.
Hours & Admission Prices: Memorial Day to Labor Day Tues.-Sat. 1-4. No charge; donations accepted. Closed Independence Day. &
Attendance: 3,000 (actual)

UTAH STATE FIREFIGHTERS MUSEUM, Deseret Peak Complex, 2930 W. Hwy. 112, Tooele, UT 84074. Mailing Address: P.O. Box 1128, Grantsville, UT 84029. Tel.: 435-843-4040. Fax: 435-830-6556.
E-mail: curator@utahfiremuseum.com
Web Site: www.utahfiremuseum.com
Key Personnel: Cur., Dave Hammond.
Institution Type/Description: Fire-Fighting Museum.
Hours & Admission Prices: Call for hours.

Torrey

CAPITOL REEF NATIONAL PARK VISITOR CENTER, 52 W Headquarters Dr, Torrey, UT 84775. Mailing Address: Capitol Reef National Park, HC 70 Box 15, Torrey, UT 84775. Tel.: 435-425-3791, ext. 4111. Fax: 435-425-3026.
E-mail: care_information@nps.gov
Web Site: www.nps.gov/care
Key Personnel: Supt., Leah McGinnis.
Institution Type/Description: Natural History & Native American Ethnology Museum.
Hours & Admission Prices: Summer season daily 8-6; winter season daily 8-4:30. Park: 7-day vehicle pass $10, 7-day individual pass $7. Closed some holidays. &
Attendance: 750,000 (estimated)

Tremonton

TREMONTON FIREFIGHTERS MUSEUM, 102 S. Tremont St., Tremonton, UT 84337-1636. Tel.: 435-257-2625.
Institution Type/Description: Firefighting History Museum.
Hours & Admission Prices: By appointment.

Vernal

UINTAH COUNTY HERITAGE MUSEUM, 155 E. Main St., Vernal, UT 84078. Tel.: 435-789-7399. Fax: 435-789-9798. Facebook.
E-mail: lwilson@uintah.utah.gov
Web Site: www.uintahmuseum.org
Formerly: Western Heritage Museum
Key Personnel: Dir., Samuel Passey.
Institution Type/Description: History Museum.
Hours & Admission Prices: Memorial Day to Labor Day Mon.-Fri. 9-6, Sat. 10-4; Sept.-May Mon.-Fri. 9-5, Sat. 10-2. No charge. Closed New Year's Day; Human Rights Day; Presidents' Day; Memorial Day; Independence Day; Pioneer Day; Labor Day; Columbus Day; Veterans Day; Thanksgiving; Christmas. &
Attendance: 7,744 (actual)

UTAH FIELD HOUSE OF NATURAL HISTORY STATE PARK, 496 E. Main St., Vernal, UT 84078-2610. Tel.: 435-789-3799. Fax: 435-789-4883.
E-mail: parkcomment@utah.gov
Web Site: www.stateparks.utah.gov
Key Personnel: Park Mgr., Steven D. Sroka; Cur. Education, Mary Beth Bennis-Smith; Cur. Collections, Heather Finlayson; Museum Maintenance, Craig Gerber; Retail Sales Mgr., Colleen Lawson.
Institution Type/Description: Natural History Museum.
Hours & Admission Prices: April-Sept. daily 9-5; Oct.-March Mon.-Sat. 9-5. Adults $6, children 6-12 $3; children 5 & under no charge. Closed New Year's Day; Thanksgiving; Christmas. &
Attendance: 45,000 (actual)

Wellsville

AMERICAN WEST HERITAGE CENTER, 4025 S. Hwy., 89-91, Wellsville, UT 84339. Tel.: 435-245-6050, 800-225-3378. Fax: 435-245-6052.
E-mail: info@awhc.org
Web Site: www.awhc.org
Formerly: Ronald V. Jensen Living Historical Farm
Key Personnel: Exec. Dir., Steve Delong; Chm. (V), Gary Anderson; Cur., Reece Summers; Program Admin., Lorraine Bowen.
Institution Type/Description: Living Historical Farm: 1917 farm based on operations of Scandinavian & British emigrants influenced by extension programs of Utah Agricultural College.
Hours & Admission Prices: Jan.-May & Sept.-Oct. Mon.-Fri. 10-4; Memorial Day-Labor Day Tues.-Sat. 10-4. Adults $7, senior citizens & students $6, children $5; discounts to members. Closed New Year's Eve & Day; Christmas Eve, Day & week. &
Attendance: 60,000 (actual)

Wendover

BONNEVILLE SPEEDWAY MUSEUM, 900 E. Wendover Blvd., Wendover, UT 84083. Tel.: 775-664-4400. Facebook: Bonneville Speedway Museum.
Web Site: bonnevillespeedmuseum.com
Institution Type/Description: Racing Museum.
Hours & Admission Prices: Closed for renovation of new site.

HISTORIC WENDOVER AIRFIELD MUSEUM, 345 S. Airport Apron, Wendover, UT 84083. Tel.: 435-665-2308.
Web Site: www.wendoverairbase.com
Institution Type/Description: Military Museum.
Hours & Admission Prices: Daily 8-6. No charge; donations accepted. &
Attendance: 12,000

VERMONT

(168 listings)

Addison

CHIMNEY POINT STATE HISTORIC SITE, 8149 VT Rte. 17W., Addison, VT 05491-8751. Tel.: 802-759-2412. Fax: 802-759-2547. Facebook: Vermont State Historic Sites.
E-mail: elsa.gilbertson@vermont.gov
Web Site: www.historicsites.vermont.gov/chimneypoint
Key Personnel: Historic Site Operations Chief, Tracy Martin; Site Admin. & Museum Shop Mgr., Elsa Gilbertson.
Institution Type/Description: Historic Building: late 18th-century tavern.
Hours & Admission Prices: late May to mid-Oct. Wed.-Sun. & Mon. holidays 10-5. Adults $5; discounts to AAM members. &
Attendance: 2,300 (actual)

Barnard

BARNARD HISTORICAL SOCIETY, Village School, VT Rte. 12, Barnard, VT 05031. Mailing Address: P.O. Box 234, Barnard, VT 05031-0234. Tel.: 802-457-3020. Fax: 802-234-9080.
E-mail: babrdh@gmail.com
Web Site: www.barnardacademy.org
Key Personnel: Pres., Caz Rozonewski.
Institution Type/Description: Historical Society Museum: housed in the former Village School; c.1850.
Hours & Admission Prices: Memorial Day to Oct. Sat. 12-3; other times by appointment.

Barnet

BARNET HISTORICAL SOCIETY, 26 Goodwillie Rd., Barnet, VT 05821-9555. Mailing Address: P.O. Box 34, Barnet, VT 05821. Tel.: 802-633-3831.
E-mail: barneths@yahoo.com
Key Personnel: Pres., Dylan Ford; Treas., Ruth Anderson; Sec., Alan Boye.
Institution Type/Description: Historical Society Museum: housed in c.1790 Goodwillie House.
Hours & Admission Prices: July-Sept. 10-4; tours by appointment. No charge; donations accepted. &
Attendance: 200 (estimated)

Barre

STUDIO PLACE ARTS, 201 N. Main St., Barre, VT 05641-4125. Tel.: 802-479-7069. Facebook: Studio Place Arts.
E-mail: info@studioplacearts.org
Web Site: www.studioplacearts.com
Key Personnel: Exec. Dir., Sue Higby.
Institution Type/Description: Visual Arts Center.
Hours & Admission Prices: Tues.-Fri. 11-5, Sat. 12-4. No charge; donations accepted. &
Attendance: 12,000 (estimated)

VERMONT GRANITE MUSEUM & STONE ARTS SCHOOL, 7 Jones Brothers Way, Barre, VT 05641. Mailing Address: P.O. Box 282, Barre, VT 05641-0282. Tel.: 802-476-4605. Fax: 802-476-6866. Facebook: Vermont Granite Museum.
E-mail: info@vtgranitemuseum.org
Web Site: www.vtgranitemuseum.org
Key Personnel: Chm. (V), Patricia L. Meriam; Dir., Scott A. McLaughlin; Treas., Paul Hutchins.
Institution Type/Description: Cultural Heritage Museum.
Hours & Admission Prices: May-Oct. by appointment. Family $10, adults $5, seniors $4, children $3. &
Attendance: 1,500 (estimated)

VERMONT HISTORICAL SOCIETY MUSEUM, 60 Washington St., Ste. 1, Barre, VT 05641. Mailing Address: 109 State St., Montpelier, VT 05609-0002. Tel.: 802-479-8500. Fax: 802-828-1415.
E-mail: info@vermonthistory.org
Web Site: www.vermonthistory.org
Key Personnel: Exec. Dir., Steve Perkins; Dir. Development, Tori Hart; Librarian, Paul Carnahan; Dir. Fin. & Opers., John Grosvenor.
Institution Type/Description: History Museum.
Hours & Admission Prices: Museum: Mon.-Fri. 9-4. Family $20, adults $7, students, children 6-17 & seniors $5; members & children under 6 no charge. Library: Tues. & Thurs.-Fri. 9-4, Wed. 9-8, 2nd Sat. each month 9-4. Adults $7; discounts to AAM & ICOM members; members & students no charge. Closed major holidays. &
Attendance: 18,000 (estimated)

Barton

CRYSTAL LAKE FALLS HISTORICAL ASSOCIATION, 97 Water St., Barton, VT 05822. Mailing Address: 536 Breezy Hill Rd., Barton, VT 05822-8641. Tel.: 802-525-3084.
E-mail: bartonclfha@gmail.com
Web Site: sites.google.com/site/bartonmuseum
Formerly: Barton Museum
Key Personnel: Pres., Earle Randall; Vice Pres., Patti Bondor; Treas., Bill May; Sec., Dorothy Hathaway.
Institution Type/Description: Historical and Industrial Museum: housed in a c.1820 structure.
Hours & Admission Prices: June-Aug. Sun. 1-4; other times by appointment. No charge; donations accepted. &
Attendance: 146 (actual)

Bellows Falls

ADAMS OLD STONE GRIST MILL, Mill St., Bellows Falls, VT 05101. Mailing Address: 47 Atkinson, Bellows Falls, VT 05101-1675. Tel.: 802-463-3706.
E-mail: ourtown@sover.net
Key Personnel: Pres. Historical Society, Dennis Ladd.
Institution Type/Description: Historical Society Museum.
Hours & Admission Prices: By appointment. No charge; donations accepted.
Attendance: 340

Belmont

MOUNT HOLLY COMMUNITY HISTORICAL MUSEUM, Tarbellville Rd., Belmont, VT 05730. Mailing Address: P.O. Box 17, Belmont, VT 05730-0017. Tel.: 802-259-2460. Facebook: Mount Holly Community Historical Museum.
E-mail: mounthollymuseum@gmail.com
Web Site: www.mounthollyvtmuseum.org
Formerly: Community Historical Museum of Mount Holly
Key Personnel: Chm. (V), Dennis J. Devereux; Cur., Robin Eatmon.
Institution Type/Description: General & Historical Society Museum: housed in 1834 blacksmith shop.

Hours & Admission Prices: July-Aug. Sat.-Sun. 2-4. No charge; donations accepted. ♿
Attendance: 550 (estimated)

Bennington

BENNINGTON CENTER FOR THE ARTS, 44 Gypsy Ln., Bennington, VT 05201-9692. Tel.: 802-442-7158.
E-mail: shirley@thebennington.org
Web Site: www.thebennington.org
Formerly: Laumeister Center for the Arts
Key Personnel: Dir., Shirley Hutchins; C.E.O., Bruce Laumeister; Pres. (V) & Museum Shop Mgr., Elizabeth Small.
Institution Type/Description: Art & Culture Center.
Hours & Admission Prices: Call for hours. Adults $9, seniors & students $8; discounts to Mass. teachers; children under 12 no charge. ♿
Attendance: 48,000 (estimated)

THE BENNINGTON MUSEUM, 75 Main St., Bennington, VT 05201-2885. Tel.: 802-447-1571. Fax: 802-442-8305.
E-mail: administration@benningtonmuseum.org
Web Site: www.benningtonmuseum.org
Key Personnel: Exec. Dir. & Dir. Public Programs, Deana Mallory; Chm. Bd., Raymond Bolton; Cur., Jamie Franklin; Devel. Assoc., Joy Danila; Public Rels., Susan Strano; Mgr. Collections, Callie Stewart; Visitor Svcs., Karen Harrington; Museum Educator, Elizabeth Kane; Mgr. Devel., Denise Lariscy.
Institution Type/Description: Art, Decorative Arts & History Museum.
Hours & Admission Prices: Feb.-June & Nov.-Dec. Thurs.-Tues. 10-5; July -Oct. daily 10-5. Adults $10, senior citizen & students $9, groups of 10 or more $8:50 per person; discounts to NARM & Consortium of New England Art Museums; members & children under 18 no charge. Closed New Year's Day; Thanksgiving Day; Christmas. ♿
Attendance: 34,752 (actual)

THE BURGHDORF GALLERY AT SOUTHERN VERMONT COLLEGE, 982 Mansion Dr., Bennington, VT 05201-9269. Tel.: 802-442-5427. Fax: 802-447-4695.
E-mail: gwinter@svc.edu
Web Site: https://svc.edu
Formerly: Southern Vermont College Art Gallery
Key Personnel: Dir., Greg Winterhalter.
Institution Type/Description: College Art Gallery: housed in 1910 Everett Estate, built in the style of a 14th century English-Norman castle. Listed on the National Register of Historic Places.
Hours & Admission Prices: Mon.-Fri. 9-6. No charge; donations accepted. Closed major holidays. ♿
Attendance: 5,000

SUZANNE LEMBERG USDAN GALLERY, Bennington College, 1 College Dr., Bennington, VT 05201-6003. Tel.: 802-442-5401.
Web Site: http://usdan.bennington.edu
Key Personnel: Mgr., Elizabeth Pellerin.
Institution Type/Description: Art Gallery.
Hours & Admission Prices: Tues.-Sat. 1-5 during exhibitions. No charge.

VERMONT COVERED BRIDGE MUSEUM, 44 Gypsy Ln., Bennington, VT 05201-9692. Tel.: 802-442-7158.
E-mail: shirley@thebennington.org
Web Site: www.thebennington.org/covered-bridge/
Key Personnel: Gallery Dir., Shirley Hutchins; Dir. Opers., Jana Lillie.
Institution Type/Description: History Museum.
Hours & Admission Prices: Wed.-Mon. 10-5. Families $20, adults $9, students & seniors $8; discounts to Mass. teachers; children under 12 no charge. ♿
Attendance: 12,255 (actual)

Bethel

BETHEL HISTORICAL SOCIETY, 40 Main St., Bethel, VT 05032. Mailing Address: P.O. Box 25, Bethel, VT 05032. Tel.: 802-234-7258. Facebook: Bethel Historical Society.
E-mail: gjfedak@gmail.com
Institution Type/Description: Historical Society Museum: housed in the former Town Hall; built in 1892.
Hours & Admission Prices: July-Aug. Sat. 10-2; other times by appointment. No charge; donations accepted. ♿
Attendance: 300 (estimated)

Bradford

BRADFORD HISTORICAL SOCIETY INC., Bradford Academy Bldg., Main St., Bradford, VT 05033. Mailing Address: P.O. Box 424, Bradford, VT 05033-9142. Tel.: 802-222-4423.
E-mail: lccoffin@charter.net
Key Personnel: Pres., Lawrence Coffin; Vice Pres., Meroa Benjamin; Sec., Jeanette Nordham; Treas., Diane Smarro.
Institution Type/Description: Historical Society Museum: housed in 1894 Woods School.
Hours & Admission Prices: March-Dec. Fri. 10-12; other times by appointment. No charge; donations accepted. Closed holidays. ♿
Attendance: 300 (estimated)

Brandon

BRANDON MUSEUM & VISITOR CENTER AT THE S.A. DOUGLAS BIRTHPLACE, 4 Grove St., Brandon, VT 05733. Tel.: 802-247-6401.
E-mail: info@brandon.org
Web Site: www.brandon.org/the-brandon-museum
Key Personnel: Pres. (V), John Dilts.
Institution Type/Description: History Museum: housed in the birthplace of statesman, Stephen A. Douglas; built in 1802.
Hours & Admission Prices: Museum: mid-May to mid-Oct. daily 11-4. Visitor Center: daily 8-6. No charge. ♿
Attendance: 1,000 (estimated)

Brattleboro

BRATTLEBORO HISTORICAL SOCIETY, 230 Main St., Ste. 301, Brattleboro, VT 05301-2880. Tel.: 802-258-4957.
E-mail: histsoc@sover.net
Web Site: www.brattleborohistoricalsociety.org
Institution Type/Description: Local History Museum.
Hours & Admission Prices: Research Room & Office, 230 Main St., Thurs. 2-4, Sat. 10 to noon, other times by appointment. History Center & Museum, 196 Main St., Fri. 2-4, Sat. 11-2.

BRATTLEBORO MUSEUM & ART CENTER, 10 Vernon St., Brattleboro, VT 05301-3390. Tel.: 802-257-0124.
E-mail: info@brattleboromuseum.org
Web Site: www.brattleboromuseum.org
Key Personnel: Dir., Danny Lichtenfeld; Chief Cur., Mara Williams; Operations Mgr., Erin Jenkins.
Institution Type/Description: Visual Art Center: housed in 1915 former Union Railroad Station.
Hours & Admission Prices: Sun.-Mon. & Wed.-Thurs. 11-5; Fri. 11-7; Sat. 10-5. Adults $8, senior citizens $6, students $4; children under 6 & members no charge. Closed New Year's Day; Independence Day; Thanksgiving; Christmas. ♿
Attendance: 23,421 (estimated)

ESTEY ORGAN MUSEUM, 108 Birge St., Brattleboro, VT 05301-6460.
E-mail: info@esteyorganmuseum.org
Web Site: www.esteyorganmuseum.org
Institution Type/Description: Organ Museum.
Hours & Admission Prices: Summer: Sat.-Sun. 2-4; other times by appointment. Admission $5; members no charge. ♿

Brookfield Center

HISTORICAL SOCIETY OF BROOKFIELD-MARVIN NEWTON HOUSE, 1133 Ridge Rd., Brookfield Center, VT 05036. Mailing Address: P.O. Box 447, Brookfield, VT 05036-0447. Tel.: 802-276-3959 & 3497. Fax: 802-276-3023.
E-mail: glord@norwich.edu
Web Site: brookfieldhistoricalsociety.wordpress.com
Key Personnel: Pres., Michael Dempsey; Treas., Mary Waldo; Trustee, Linda Runnion; Trustee, Gary Lord; Trustee & News Editor, Greg Sauer; Trustee, Bonnie Fallon; Trustee, Joanna Boden Weber; Cur., Jacalin Wilder; Historian & Genealogist, Elinor Gray.
Institution Type/Description: Historic House: 1835, Marvin Newton house.
Hours & Admission Prices: July-Aug. Sun. 2-5; other times by appointment. Adults $2.
Attendance: 135 (estimated)

Brownington

ORLEANS COUNTY HISTORICAL SOCIETY & THE OLD STONE HOUSE MUSEUM, 109 Old Stone House Rd., Brownington, VT 05860-4420. Tel.: 802-754-2022. Fax: 802-754-9336. Facebook: Old Stone House Museum.
E-mail: information@oldstonehousemuseum.org
Web Site: oldstonehousemuseum.org
Key Personnel: Dir., Peggy Day Gibson; OCHS Pres. Bd., Courtney Mead; OCHS Vice Pres., Sara McKenny; Museum Shop Mgr. & Admin. Asst., Dayna Drake.
Institution Type/Description: Local History Museum: housed in 1836 Old Stone House built by Rev. Alexander Twilight, originally used as school dormitory.
Hours & Admission Prices: May 15-Oct. 15 Wed.-Sun. 11-5. Adults $8, Orleans County Residents & AAM members $7, students $5; discount to groups and NEMA, VMGA & AAA members; active military & members no charge. &
Attendance: 3,000 (estimated)

Brownsville

WEST WINDSOR HISTORICAL SOCIETY, The Grange Hall, Rte. 44, Brownsville, VT 05037. Mailing Address: P.O. Box 12, Brownsville, VT 05037-0012. Tel.: 802-484-7474.
E-mail: town.of.west.windsor@valley.net
Web Site: www.westwindsorvt.govoffice2.com
Key Personnel: Pres., Genevieve Lemire.
Institution Type/Description: Historical Society Museum.
Hours & Admission Prices: Call for hours. No charge.

Burlington

BCA CENTER, 135 Church St., Firehouse Center for the Visual Arts, Ground Fl., Burlington, VT 05401-8415. Tel.: 802-865-7166. Fax: 802-865-5839.
E-mail: ajimenez@burlingtoncityarts.org
Web Site: www.burlingtoncityarts.org/BCAcenter
Formerly: The Firehouse Gallery
Key Personnel: Exec. Dir., Doreen Kraft; Cur. & Dir. Exhibits, Heather Ferrell.
Institution Type/Description: Art Museum.
Hours & Admission Prices: Call for hours. No charge; donations accepted. &
Attendance: 60,000 (actual)

ECHO, LEAHY CENTER FOR LAKE CHAMPLAIN, One College St., Leahy Center for Lake Champlain, Burlington, VT 05401-5215. Tel.: 802-864-1848, 877-ECHOFUN. Fax: 802-864-6832. Facebook: ECHO Vermont.
E-mail: info@echovermont.org
Web Site: www.echovermont.org
Formerly: ECHO Lake Aquarium and Science Center/Leahy Center for Lake Champlain
Key Personnel: Chm. (V), Tim Volk; Exec. Dir., Dr. Phelan R. Fretz; Dir. Devel. & Communications, Erik Oliver; Dir. Programs & Exhibits, Nina Ridhibhinyo; Dir. Finance & Admin., David Bardaglio; Dir. Guest Svcs. & Events, Tina Lecours; Animal Care & Facilities Mgmt., Steve Smith.
Institution Type/Description: Lake Aquarium & Science Center
Hours & Admission Prices: Daily 10-5. Adult $14.50, seniors 60 & over and college students with ID $12.50, children 3-17 $11.50; theater film showings additional admission; discount to military & ASTC members; children under 3 & members no charge. Closed Thanksgiving; Christmas Eve & Day. &
Attendance: 150,000 (actual)

ETHAN ALLEN HOMESTEAD MUSEUM & HISTORIC SITE, 1 Ethan Allen Homestead, Burlington, VT 05408-1141. Tel.: 802-865-4556. Fax: 802-865-0661.
E-mail: info@ethanallenhomestead.org
Web Site: www.ethanallenhomestead.org
Key Personnel: Exec. Dir., Corbett Torrence; Pres. (V), Phyllis Drury.
Institution Type/Description: Historic Site.
Hours & Admission Prices: May-Oct. daily 10-4; groups by appointment. Adults $8, seniors, students & VT residents $7, children 4-12 $5; children under 4 & members no charge. &
Attendance: 4,000 (actual)

FRANCIS COLBURN GALLERY, University of Vermont, Dept. of Art & Art History, Williams Hall, 72 University Pl., Burlington, VT 05405-0168. Tel.: 802-656-2014. Fax: 802-656-2064.
E-mail: artdept@uvm.edu
Web Site: www.uvm.edu/~artdept
Key Personnel: Administrative Asst., Simone Blaise.
Institution Type/Description: University Art Gallery: housed in 1896 campus building.

Hours & Admission Prices: Sept.-May Mon.-Fri. 9-4:30. No charge. &

FROG HOLLOW GALLERIES, 85 Church St., Burlington, VT 05401-4420. Tel.: 802-863-6458. Fax: 802-860-6506.
E-mail: rhunter@froghollow.org
Web Site: www.froghollow.org
Key Personnel: Dir., Rob Hunter.
Institution Type/Description: Art Gallery.
Hours & Admission Prices: Winter: Mon.-Sat. 10-6, Sun. 12-5; Summer & Fall: Mon.-Wed. 10-6, Thurs.-Sat. 10-8, Sun. 11-7.

OLD SPOKES HOME, 322 N. Winooski Ave., Burlington, VT 05401. Tel.: 802-863-4475. Facebook.
Web Site: oldspokeshome.com
Key Personnel: Owner, Glenn Eames.
Institution Type/Description: Bicycle Museum.
Hours & Admission Prices: Mon.-Sat. 10-6, Sun. 12-5.

PERKINS GEOLOGY MUSEUM AT THE UNIVERSITY OF VERMONT, Delehanty Hall - Trinity Campus, 180 Colchester Ave., Burlington, VT 05405-1758. Tel.: 802-656-8694.
E-mail: geology@uvm.edu
Web Site: www.uvm.edu/perkins/
Key Personnel: Chm., Dept. of Geology, Andrea Lini.
Institution Type/Description: Geology Museum.
Hours & Admission Prices: Academic Year: Mon.-Fri. 9-6, Sat.-Sun. 11-6; Call for summer hours. No charge. &

ROBERT HULL FLEMING MUSEUM, Univ. of Vermont, 61 Colchester Ave., Burlington, VT 05405. Tel.: 802-656-0750. Fax: 802-656-8059.
E-mail: fleming@uvm.edu
Web Site: www.flemingmuseum.org
Key Personnel: Dir., Janie Cohen; Cur., Andrea P. Rosen; Education & Public Programs Cur., Christina Fearon; Public Rels. & Mktg. Mgr., Chris Dissinger; Mgr. Collections & Exhibitions, Margaret Tamulonis; Exhibition Designer & Preparator, Jeff Falsgraf; Financial Mgr., Stephanie Glock.
Institution Type/Description: Art & Anthropology Museum.
Hours & Admission Prices: May to Labor Day, Tues.-Fri. 12-4, Sat.-Sun. 1-5; Sept.-April Tues. & Thurs.-Fri. 9-4, Wed. 9-8. Adults $5, seniors & students $3; discounts to AAM members; members no charge. Closed major holidays. &
Attendance: 25,000 (estimated)

Cabot

CABOT HISTORICAL SOCIETY, 3216 Main St., Cabot, VT 05647-9755. Mailing Address: P.O. Box 275, Cabot, VT 05647-0275.
E-mail: cabothistorical@gmail.com
Web Site: sites.google.com/site/histsocorg1/home
Key Personnel: Pres., Bonnie S. Dannenberg; Cur., Eric Ginette.
Institution Type/Description: Historical & Preservation Society: housed in 1845 schoolhouse in Cabot Village.
Hours & Admission Prices: Special local holidays & by appointment. No charge; donations accepted.
Attendance: 500 (estimated)

Castleton

CASTLETON HISTORICAL SOCIETY, The Higley Homestead, 407 Main St., Castleton, VT 05735-0219. Mailing Address: P.O. Box 219, Castleton, VT 05735-0219. Tel.: 802-468-5105.
E-mail: blueshoehh@hotmail.com
Web Site: www.castletonvermont.org
Key Personnel: Pres. (V) & Museum Shop Mgr., Holly Hitchcock.
Institution Type/Description: Village Museum: main office housed in 1811 Federal-style Georgian house, The Higley Homestead, listed on National Register of Historic Places; Buel Block, 556 Main St., Castleton, VT.
Hours & Admission Prices: May-Dec. by appointment. No charge; donations accepted. &
Attendance: 150 (estimated)

CHRISTINE PRICE GALLERY, Castleton State College, Fine Arts Ctr., 45 Alumni Dr., Castleton, VT 05735. Tel.: 802-468-5611. Fax: 802-468-1440.
E-mail: richard.cowden@castleton.edu
Web Site: www.castleton.edu/arts/art-galleries
Institution Type/Description: Art Gallery.
Hours & Admission Prices: Academic Year: Mon.-Fri. 8-4:30.

Cavendish

CAVENDISH HISTORICAL SOCIETY MUSEUM, 1958 Main St., Rte. 131, Cavendish, VT 05142. Mailing Address: P.O. Box 472, Cavendish, VT 05142-9647. Tel.: 802-226-7807.
E-mail: margoc@tds.net
Key Personnel: Coord., Margo Caulfield.
Institution Type/Description: Historical Society Museum: housed in a former 19th-century town hall.
Hours & Admission Prices: late June to mid-Oct. Sun. 2-4; other times by appointment. No charge.

Colchester

COLCHESTER HISTORICAL SOCIETY - LOG SCHOOLHOUSE MUSEUM, Airport Park, 488 Colchester Point Rd., Colchester, VT 05446. Tel.: 802-879-0042.
E-mail: tmulcahyvt@comcast.net
Web Site: colchestervt.gov/422/Colchester-Historical-Society
Key Personnel: Dir., Carol Reichard; Pres. (V), Dr. H. Clinton Reichard.
Institution Type/Description: Historical Society Museum: housed in a log school-house; c.1815.
Hours & Admission Prices: Memorial Day to Labor Day Fri.-Mon. 11-3. No charge; donations accepted.
Attendance: 1,750 (estimated)

MCCARTHY ARTS CENTER GALLERY, Saint Michael's College, One Winooski Park, Colchester, VT 05439. Tel.: 802.654.2000.
E-mail: bcollier@smcvt.edu
Web Site: www.smcvt.edu/academics/finearts
Institution Type/Description: Art Gallery.
Hours & Admission Prices: Mon.-Fri. 9-5. No charge.

Concord

CONCORD HISTORICAL SOCIETY MUSEUM, Concord Town Hall, Concord, VT 05824. Mailing Address: P.O. Box 301, Concord, VT 08524-0301. Tel.: 802-695-2288.
E-mail: info@concordhistorical.org
Key Personnel: Pres. (V), Kathleen Fisher.
Institution Type/Description: Historical Society Museum.
Hours & Admission Prices: Sept. last Sat.-Sun.; other times by appointment. No charge; donations accepted.

Cuttingsville

SHREWSBURY HISTORICAL SOCIETY, INC., 5419 Rte. 103, Cuttingsville, VT 05738. Tel.: 802-492-3324.
E-mail: ruth@shrewsburyhistoricalsociety.com
Web Site: shrewsburyhistoricalsociety.com
Key Personnel: Pres., Grace Brigham; Sec., Ruth A. Winkler.
Institution Type/Description: Historical Society Museum.
Hours & Admission Prices: July-Oct. Sun. 1-3. No charge; donations accepted.
Attendance: 75 (estimated)

Danville

DANVILLE HISTORICAL SOCIETY, 121 Hill St., Danville, VT 05828. Mailing Address: P.O. Box 274, Danville, VT 05828-0274. Tel.: 802 684 2055.
E-mail: historicalsociety.director.dan@gmail.com
Web Site: danvillevthistorical.org
Key Personnel: Pres., Mary Pryor.
Institution Type/Description: Library & Archives.
Hours & Admission Prices: Mon., Wed. & Fri. 2-4; other times by appointment.

Dorset

DORSET HISTORICAL SOCIETY, Rte. 30 at Kent Hill Rd., Dorset, VT 05251. Mailing Address: P.O. Box 52, Dorset, VT 05251-0052. Tel.: 802-867-0331. Fax: 802-867-0412.
E-mail: info@dorsetvthistory.org
Web Site: www.dorsetvthistory.org
Key Personnel: Chm. (V) & Pres. (V), Richard Hittle.
Institution Type/Description: Historical Society Museum: housed in Bley House.
Hours & Admission Prices: April 15-Nov. Wed. 10-12, Thurs.-Sat. 10-4; Dec.-April 14 Wed.-Sat. 10-2; other times by appointment. No charge; donations accepted. Closed Christmas.
Attendance: 1,000 (actual)

East Montpelier

BRAGG FARM SUGAR HOUSE, 1005 VT Rte. 14 N., East Montpelier, VT 05651. Tel.: 802-223-5757, 800-376-5757.
E-mail: braggfarmmaple@aol.com
Web Site: www.braggfarm.com
Institution Type/Description: Farm History Museum.
Hours & Admission Prices: June-Aug. daily 8:30-8; Sept.-May daily 8:30-6.

East Poultney

POULTNEY HISTORICAL SOCIETY MUSEUM, On-the-Green, East Poultney, VT 05741. Mailing Address: P.O. Box 605, East Poultney, VT 05741-0605. Tel.: 802-287-5252.
E-mail: info@poultneyhistoricalsociety.org
Web Site: poultneyhistoricalsociety.org
Key Personnel: Pres., Ina Smith.
Institution Type/Description: Antiques Museum: housed in 1800 Old Blacksmith Shop & Melodeon Factory; 1791 brick schoolhouse; 1895 Victorian school-house.
Hours & Admission Prices: Memorial Day to Labor Day Sun. 1-4; other times by appointment. No charge; donations accepted.
Attendance: 350 (estimated)

Fairfield

PRESIDENT CHESTER A. ARTHUR HISTORIC SITE, 4588 Chester Arthur Road, Fairfield, VT 05455. Mailing Address: Historic Preservation, National Life Bldg., 6th Fl., Montpelier, VT 05633. Tel.: 802-828-3051. Fax: 802-828-3206.
E-mail: tracy.martin@vermont.gov
Web Site: www.historicsites.vermont.gov/directory/arthur
Key Personnel: Historic Sites Section Chief, Tracy N. Martin.
Institution Type/Description: Historic Houses: Chester A. Arthur childhood home (recreation); 1820 Brick Church.
Hours & Admission Prices: July 4 to mid-Oct. Sat.-Sun. & Mon. holidays 11-5. No charge; donations accepted.
Attendance: 3,000 (estimated)

Ferrisburgh

ROKEBY MUSEUM, 4334 Rte. 7, Ferrisburgh, VT 05456-9779. Tel.: 802-877-3406. Fax: 802-877-3406.
E-mail: rokeby@comcast.net
Web Site: www.rokeby.org
Formerly: Rokeby (Ancestral Estate of Rowland Evans Robinson)
Key Personnel: Pres. (V), Catherin Brooks; Dir., Jane Williamson.
Institution Type/Description: Historic House: c.1784 Rokeby.
Hours & Admission Prices: May-Oct. daily 10-5. Guided House Tours: Fri.-Mon. 11 & 2. Adults $10, seniors $9, students $8; discounts to AAM members, groups & Vermont museum employees; members & children under 5 no charge.
Attendance: 4,000 (actual)

Glover

BREAD & PUPPET MUSEUM, 753 Heights Rd., Rte. 122, Glover, VT 05839-9637. Tel.: 802-525-6972 & 3031.
E-mail: breadpuppetlinda@gmail.com
Web Site: www.breadandpuppet.org
Key Personnel: Dir., Peter Schumann; Sec. & Museum Shop Mgr., Elka Schumann.
Institution Type/Description: Puppet Theater & Museum: housed in a 100 year old barn.
Hours & Admission Prices: June-Nov. 1 daily 10-6; other times by appointment. No charge; donations accepted.
Attendance: 20,000 (estimated)

Grafton

GRAFTON HISTORICAL SOCIETY, 147 Main St., Grafton, VT 05146. Mailing Address: P.O. Box 202, Grafton, VT 05146-0202. Tel.: 802-843-2584.
E-mail: grafhist@vermontel.net
Web Site: www.graftonhistoricalsociety.com
Key Personnel: Pres., Harold Tincher.
Institution Type/Description: Local History Museum.
Hours & Admission Prices: Memorial Day to Columbus Day Mon. & Thurs.-Sun. 10-4; Oct.-May Mon. & Thurs.-Fri. 10-4; other times by appointment. No charge; donations accepted.
Attendance: 1,700 (actual)

THE NATURE MUSEUM, 186 Townshend Rd., Grafton, VT 05146. Mailing Address: P.O. Box 38, Grafton, VT 05146-0038. Tel.: 802-843-2111.
E-mail: info@nature-museum.org
Web Site: www.nature-museum.org
Key Personnel: Pres. (V), Laurie Danforth; Exec. Dir. & Museum Shop Mgr., Carrie King; Treas., Steven Davis
Institution Type/Description: Natural History Museum.
Hours & Admission Prices: Memorial Day to Columbus Day Thurs. & Sat.-Sun. 10-4; Oct.-May Thurs. 10-4. Call for additional hours. no charge. Closed major holidays.
Attendance: 4,550 (actual)

Grand Isle

GRAND ISLE HISTORICAL SOCIETY, 228/230 U.S. Rte. 2, P. O. Box 23, Grand Isle, VT 05458. Tel.: 802-372-4024.
E-mail: hatchhillfarm@myfairpoint.net
Formerly: Grand Isle County Historical Society
Key Personnel: Pres. (V), Jean B. Prouty.
Institution Type/Description: Historical Society Museum.
Hours & Admission Prices: Memorial Day to Columbus Day Fri.-Sun. 11-5. Adults $3; children under 14 no charge. &

Graniteville

ROCK OF AGES VISITOR CENTER, 558 Graniteville Rd., Graniteville, VT 05654. Mailing Address: P.O. Box 482, Barre, VT 05641-0482. Tel.: 802-476-3119; 866-748-6877 (Toll Free). Fax: 802-476-0329.
E-mail: visitor@rockofages.com
Web Site: www.rockofages.com
Key Personnel: Dir., Todd Paton.
Institution Type/Description: Granite Industry Museum.
Hours & Admission Prices: Visitors Center: mid-May to mid-Oct. Mon.-Sat. 9-4. Quarry Tours: Fri. of Memorial Day Weekend to mid-Oct. Mon.-Sat. 10:30-2:50. Closed Independence Day. &

Guilford

GUILFORD HISTORICAL SOCIETY, Guilford Center Rd., Guilford, VT 05301. Mailing Address: 236 School Rd., Guilford, VT 05301. Tel.: 802-254-5910; 251-5154.
E-mail: robin@frehseecarpentry.com
Key Personnel: Chm. (V) & Cur., Ann Bonneville; Pres. (V), Richard A. Austin; Asst. Cur., Michelle Frehsee.
Institution Type/Description: Historical Society Museum: housed in the Town Hall building; built in 1822.
Hours & Admission Prices: June-Sept. Tues.-Sat. 10-2. No charge; donations accepted. &
Attendance: 200 (actual)

Hardwick

GRACE - GRASS ROOTS ART AND COMMUNITY EFFORT, 59 Mill St., Hardwick, VT 05843. Mailing Address: P.O. Box 960, Hardwick, VT 05843. Tel.: 802-472-6857. Fax: 802-472-9578.
E-mail: grace@vtlink.net
Web Site: www.graceart.org
Key Personnel: Dir., Carol Putnam; Chm. (V), Stephen Farber.
Institution Type/Description: Art Gallery: housed in the Old Firehouse; built in 1885. Listed on the National Register of Historic Sites.
Hours & Admission Prices: Tues.-Thurs. 10-4. No charge; donations accepted. &
Attendance: 1,200 (estimated)

Hartford

HARTFORD HISTORICAL SOCIETY - GARIPAY HOUSE MUSEUM, 1461 Maple St., Hartford, VT 05047. Mailing Address: P.O. Box 547, Hartford, VT 05047-0547. Tel.: 802-296-3132. Facebook: Hartford Historical Society.
E-mail: info@hartfordhistoricalsociety.com
Web Site: www.hartfordhistory.org
Key Personnel: Chm. (V), Mary Nadeau; Pres. (V), Susanne Abetti.
Institution Type/Description: Historical Society Museum: housed in Dr. Garipay's home.
Hours & Admission Prices: May-Sept. Mon.-Fri. 9-1, 1st Tues. each month 6-8, 2nd Sun. each month 2-4; Oct.-April Mon.-Fri. 9-1; other times by appointment. No charge; donations accepted.
Attendance: 200 (estimated)

Hartland

HARTLAND HISTORICAL SOCIETY, Rte. 12, Hartland, VT 05048. Mailing Address: P.O. Box 198, Hartland, VT 05048-0198. Tel.: 802-436-1703.
E-mail: info@hartlandhistory.org
Web Site: www.hartlandhistory.org
Key Personnel: Pres., Carol Mowry.
Institution Type/Description: Historical Society Museum
Hours & Admission Prices: Mon. 1-4, Fri. 9-11am; other times by appointment. No charge; donations accepted. Closed holidays.
Attendance: 100 (estimated)

Holland

HOLLAND HISTORICAL SOCIETY MUSEUM, INC., Gore Rd., Holland, VT 05830. Mailing Address: 120 School Rd., Derby Line, VT 05830. Tel.: 802-766-5375.
Key Personnel: Dir., Harvey McDonald; Dir., Martha Judd; Dir., Albert Hauver; Dir., Laurel Mosher; Pres. (V), Diane Judd; Vice Pres., Melody Ricard; Sec., Bea Nelson.
Institution Type/Description: Historical Society Museum: housed in c.1848 Congregational Church, birth town of Horace Tabor, the Silver king of Colorado.
Hours & Admission Prices: Aug. 1st Sun.; other times by appointment. No charge; donations accepted.
Attendance: 175 (estimated)

Hubbardton

HUBBARDTON BATTLEFIELD STATE HISTORIC SITE, 5696 Monument Hill Rd., Hubbardton, VT 05749. Mailing Address: Historic Preservation, National Life Bldg., 6th Fl., Montpelier, VT 05620. Tel.: 802-759-2412 & 273-2282. Fax: 802-828-3206.
E-mail: elsa.gilbertson@vermont.gov
Web Site: www.historicsites.vermont.gov/directory/hubbardton
Key Personnel: Historic Sites Section Chief, Tracy N. Martin; Site Admin., Elsa Gilbertson.
Institution Type/Description: State Historic Site: Hubbardton Battlefield.
Hours & Admission Prices: late May to mid-Oct. Wed.-Sun. & Mon. holidays 10-5. Adults $3; discounts to AAM members; registered school groups & children under 14 no charge. &
Attendance: 5,000 (estimated)

Huntington

BIRDS OF VERMONT MUSEUM, 900 Sherman Hollow Rd., Huntington, VT 05462-9420. Tel.: 802-434-2167.
E-mail: museum@birdsofvermont.org
Web Site: www.birdsofvermont.org
Key Personnel: Dir., Erin Talmage; Chm. (V), William Mayville.
Institution Type/Description: Woodcarving Bird Museum.
Hours & Admission Prices: May-Oct. daily 10-4; Nov.-April by appointment. Adults $7, seniors $6, children 3-17 $3.50; discounts to AAA members; members no charge. &
Attendance: 4,500 (actual)

Isle La Motte

ISLE LA MOTTE HISTORICAL SOCIETY, Main St. & Quarry Rd., Isle La Motte, VT 05463-9808. Mailing Address: P.O. Box 18, Isle La Motte, VT 05463-0018. Tel.: 802-928-3077.
E-mail: gloilm@yahoo.com
Key Personnel: Cur., Gloria McEwen.
Institution Type/Description: Local History Museum.
Hours & Admission Prices: July-Aug. Sat. 1-4; other times by appointment. No charge, donations accepted.
Attendance: 500 (estimated)

Jacksonville

WHITINGHAM HISTORICAL MUSEUM, 669 Reed Hill Rd., Jacksonville, VT 05342-9733. Mailing Address: P.O. Box 125, Jacksonville, VT 05342-0125. Tel.: 802-368-2448.
E-mail: chelsea22@myfairpoint.net
Key Personnel: Pres., Stella Stevens; Sec., Cindy Bernard.
Institution Type/Description: History Museum.

Hours & Admission Prices: June-Oct. Sun. 2-4; school groups & other times by appointment. No charge; donations accepted. &
Attendance: 375 (estimated)

Jeffersonville

BRYAN MEMORIAL GALLERY, 180 Main St., Jeffersonville, VT 05464. Mailing Address: P.O. Box 340, Jeffersonville, VT 05464-0340. Tel.: 802-644-5100. Fax: 802-644-8342. Facebook.
E-mail: info@bryangallery.org
Web Site: www.bryangallery.org
Key Personnel: Exec. Dir., Mickey Myers; Pres. (V), Susan Lassiter; Mgr., Tom Waters.
Institution Type/Description: Art Gallery.
Hours & Admission Prices: Spring & Fall: Thurs.-Sun. 11-4; Summer: daily 11-5; other times by appointment. No charge; donations accepted. &
Attendance: 4,000 (estimated)

Jericho

EMILE A. GRUPPE GALLERY, 22 Barber Farm Rd., Jericho, VT 05465-9795. Tel.: 802-899-3211.
Web Site: www.emilegruppegallery.com
Institution Type/Description: Art Gallery: housed in an 1860s English Sheep barn at the home of Emile's daughter, Emilie Gruppe Alexander & her husband.
Hours & Admission Prices: Thurs.-Sun. 10-3; other times by appointment.

JERICHO HISTORICAL SOCIETY, 4A Red Mill Dr., Jericho, VT 05465. Mailing Address: P.O. Box 35, Jericho, VT 05465-0035. Tel.: 802-899-3225.
Web Site: jerichohistoricalsociety.org
Key Personnel: Pres. (V), Ann Squires; Archives Chm., Susan Richardson; Sales Shop Mgr., Gail Prior.
Institution Type/Description: Historical Society Museum: housed in 1885 Chittenden Mills, five-story building once used as a grist mill.
Hours & Admission Prices: Jan.-March Wed. & Sat. 10-5, Sun. 11:30-4; April-Dec. Mon.-Sat. 10-5, Sun. 11:30-4. Call to confirm summer hours. No charge. Closed Easter; Independence Day; Thanksgiving; Christmas. &
Attendance: 14,000 (estimated)

Johnson

JULIAN SCOTT MEMORIAL GALLERY, Johnson State College, Dibden Center, 337 College Hill, Johnson, VT 06565. Tel.: 800-635-2356, 802-635-1469.
E-mail: Phillip.Robertson@ccv.edu
Web Site: www.jsc.edu
Key Personnel: Dir., Leila Bandar.
Institution Type/Description: Art Gallery.
Hours & Admission Prices: Tues.-Fri. 10-6, Sat. 10-4.

RED MILL GALLERY - VERMONT STUDIO CENTER, 80 Pearl St., Johnson, VT 05656. Mailing Address: P.O. Box 613, Johnson, VT 05656-0613. Tel.: 802-635-2727.
E-mail: info@vermontstudiocenter.org
Web Site: vermontstudiocenter.org
Key Personnel: Gallery Mgr., G. Todd Haun.
Institution Type/Description: Art Gallery.
Hours & Admission Prices: Call for hours. No charge.
Attendance: 1,000 (estimated)

Lincoln

LINCOLN HISTORICAL SOCIETY, 88 Quaker St., Lincoln, VT 05443-9253. Tel.: 802-453-7502; 802-453-3371.
E-mail: rhutster@gmail.net
Key Personnel: Dir., Sandra Rhodes; Pres., Rhonda Hutchins; Vice Pres., Eleanor Menzer; Treas., Larry Masterson.
Institution Type/Description: Historical Society Museum.
Hours & Admission Prices: Memorial Day to mid-Oct. 2nd & 4th Sun. 1-5; other times by appointment. No charge; donations accepted. &
Attendance: 100 (estimated)

Ludlow

BLACK RIVER ACADEMY MUSEUM, 14 High St., Ludlow, VT 05149. Mailing Address: P.O. Box 73, Ludlow, VT 05149-0073. Tel.: 802-228-5050.
E-mail: glbrehm@tds.net

Web Site: bramvt.org
Key Personnel: Pres. (V), Susan Pollender; Dir., Georgia Brehm.
Institution Type/Description: Historical Society Museum: housed in Black River Academy, from which Pres. Calvin Coolidge, 30th president, graduated in 1890.
Hours & Admission Prices: June to Labor Day Tues.-Sat. 12-4; Sept. to Columbus Day Sat.-Sun. 12-4. Adults $2; children under 2 no charge. &
Attendance: 1,100

Lyndon Center

SHORES MEMORIAL MUSEUM, 202 Center St., Lyndon Center, VT 05850. Mailing Address: P.O. Box 85, Lyndon Center, VT 05850-0085. Tel.: 802-626-9321.
E-mail: warden960a@charter.net
Web Site: www.shoresmuseum.org
Key Personnel: Chm. (V), Pres. (V) & Museum Shop Mgr., Eric Paris; Cur., Chris Raymond.
Institution Type/Description: History Museum: housed in 1896 Queen Anne style home built by James Shores.
Hours & Admission Prices: By appointment. Donations requested.

Lyndonville

QUIMBY GALLERY, 1001 College Rd., Lyndonville, VT 05851. Mailing Address: P.O. Box 919, Lyndonville, VT 05851. Tel.: 802-626-6487.
E-mail: barclay.tucker@lyndonstate.edu
Web Site: lyndon-visualarts.net/?page_id=160
Institution Type/Description: Art Gallery.
Hours & Admission Prices: Academic Year: Mon.-Fri. 8-4. No charge.

Manchester

THE AMERICAN MUSEUM OF FLY FISHING, 4070 Main St., Manchester, VT 05254. Mailing Address: P.O. Box 42, Manchester, VT 05254-0042. Tel.: 802-362-3300. Fax: 802-362-3308. Facebook; Twitter.
E-mail: sfoster@amff.org
Web Site: www.amff.org
Key Personnel: Pres. (V), Karen Kaplan; Deputy Dir., Yoshi Akiyama; Coord. Memberships & Events, Samantha Pitcher; Exec. Dir., Sarah Foster; Dir. Visual Communications, Sara Wilcox; Editor, Kathleen Achor; Accounts Mgr., M. Patricia Russell; Administrative Asst., Kelsey McBride.
Institution Type/Description: Sports Museum.
Hours & Admission Prices: June-Oct. Tues.-Sun. 10-4; Nov.-May Tues.-Sat. 10-4 Family $10, adults $5, children $3; discounts to NARM, AAM & ICOM members; members no charge. Closed major holidays. &
Attendance: 3,000 (estimated)

HILDENE, THE LINCOLN FAMILY HOME, 1005 Hildene Rd., Manchester, VT 05254. Mailing Address: P.O. Box 377, Manchester, VT 05254-0377. Tel.: 802-362-1788; 800 578-1788. Fax: 802-362-1564.
E-mail: info@hildene.org
Web Site: www.hildene.org
Key Personnel: Chm. (V), Kenneth Moriarty; Exec. Dir., Seth B. Bongartz; Dir. Education, Diane Newton; Deputy Dir., Laine Dunham; Volunteer Coord., Paula Maynard; Accountant, Ann Dailey; Farm Mgr., Peggy Galloup; Grounds Maintenance, Cary Lewis; Buildings Maintenance, T.J. Lillie; Dir. Private Functions, Sheila Burks; Museum Shop Mgr., Carol Korzelius.
Institution Type/Description: Historic House: 1905 Robert Todd Lincoln Home.
Hours & Admission Prices: Daily 9:30-4:30. Adults $16, children 6-14 $5; discounts to groups with reservation and AAM & AAA members; children under 6 & members no charge. Closed Easter; Thanksgiving; Christmas. &
Attendance: 35,000 (estimated)

MANCHESTER HISTORICAL SOCIETY, Cemetery Ave., Manchester, VT 05255. Mailing Address: P.O. Box 363, Manchester, VT 05254-0363. Tel.: (802) 549-4582. Facebook: Manchester Historical Society.
E-mail: info@manchesterhistoricalsocietyvt.org
Web Site: www.manchesterhistoricalsocietyvt.org
Institution Type/Description: Historical Society Museum.
Hours & Admission Prices: Thurs. 1-3; other times by appointment.

SOUTHERN VERMONT ARTS CENTER, 930 Southern Vermont Arts Center Dr., Manchester, VT 05254. Mailing Address: P.O. Box 617, Manchester, VT 05254-0617. Tel.: 802-362-1405.
E-mail: info@svac.org

Web Site: www.svac.org
Key Personnel: Exec. Dir., Elizabeth Paxson; Programs & Gallery Dir., Samantha Melton; Devel. & Volunteer Coord., Hannah Evans; Pres. Bd. & Chm., Judi McCormick.
Institution Type/Description: Art Center.
Hours & Admission Prices: Tues.-Sat. 10-5, Sun. 12-5. &
Attendance: 20,000 (estimated)

Marlboro

MARLBORO HISTORICAL SOCIETY, 364 South Rd., Marlboro, VT 05344. Mailing Address: P.O. Box 242, Marlboro, VT 05344-0242. Tel.: 802-258-2568.
E-mail: forrest810@gmail.com
Web Site: https://digitalmarlboro.omeka.net
Key Personnel: Pres., Forrest Holzapfel; Vice Pres., Donald Sherefkin; Treas., Jill Golden; Clerk, Augusta Bartlett.
Institution Type/Description: Local History Museum, Historical & Preservation Society; housed in 1814 Rev. Ephraim Holland Newton House & 1895 Houghton Schoolhouse.
Hours & Admission Prices: June to Labor Day Sat. 2-5. Research: by appointment, call 802-254-2172. No charge; donations accepted.
Attendance: 100 (estimated)

Middlebury

HENRY SHELDON MUSEUM OF VERMONT HISTORY, One Park St., Middlebury, VT 05753-1101. Tel.: 802-388-2117. Fax: 802-388-2112.
E-mail: info@henrysheldonmuseum.org
Web Site: henrysheldonmuseum.org
Key Personnel: Exec. Dir., William F. Brooks, Jr.; Pres., Marnie Wood; Vice Pres., Lyn DeGrass; Assoc. Dir., Mary Ward Manley; Archivist, Eva Garcelon Hart; Bookkeeper, Judi Loewer.
Institution Type/Description: History Museum: housed in 1829 Judd-Harris House.
Hours & Admission Prices: Tues.-Sat. 10-5. Families $12, adults $5, senior citizens $4.50; discounts to AAM & NEMA members; children 6 & under and members no charge. Closed New Year's Day; Independence Day; Thanksgiving; Christmas. &
Attendance: 10,000 (estimated)

MIDDLEBURY COLLEGE MUSEUM OF ART, Mahaney Center for the Arts, Route 30, Middlebury, VT 05753-6177. Tel.: 802-443-5235 & 5007. Fax: 802-443-2069.
E-mail: rsaunder@middlebury.edu
Web Site: museum.middlebury.edu
Key Personnel: Dir., Richard H. Saunders; Cur. Modern & Contemporary Art, Emmie Donadio; Chm. Friends of Art, Mary Jo Champlin; Exhibit Designer, Kenneth Pohlman; Registrar, Margaret Wallace; Cur. Education, Jason Vrooman; Admin. Operations Mgr., Douglas Perkins; Museum Preparator, Thatcher Littlefield; Museum Preparator, Chris Murray; Bookstore & Receptionist Coord., Mikki Lane.
Institution Type/Description: Art Museum.
Hours & Admission Prices: Sept. to mid-Aug. Tues.-Fri. 10-5, Sat.-Sun. 12-5. No charge. Closed New Year's Eve & Day; Christmas Day & week. &
Attendance: 15,000 (estimated)

VERMONT FOLKLIFE CENTER, 88 Main St., Middlebury, VT 05753-1425. Tel.: 802-388-4964. Fax: 802-388-1844.
E-mail: info@vermontfolklifecenter.org
Web Site: www.vermontfolklifecenter.org
Key Personnel: Co Dir., Greg Sharrow; Co Dir., Andy Kolovos; Chm. (V), Melinda Moulton; Dir. Education, Kathleen Haughey; Operations, Bob Hooker.
Institution Type/Description: Folk Life Center & Archive.
Hours & Admission Prices: Gallery & Shop: Mon.-Sat. 10-5. Archive & Research Center: Mon.-Fri. 10-4. No charge; donations accepted. Closed New Year's Eve, Day & week; Christmas Day & week.
Attendance: 12,000 (actual)

VERMONT SOAPWORKS DISCOUNT FACTORY OUTLET AND SOAP MUSEUM, 616 Exchange St., Middlebury, VT 05753-1181. Mailing Address: 183 Industrial Ave., Middlebury, VT 05753. Tel.: 802-388-4302, 866-762-7482 (toll free). Fax: 802-388-7471.
E-mail: info@vermontsoap.com
Web Site: www.vermontsoap.com
Key Personnel: C.O.O., Hilde Whalley; C.E.O. & Shop Mgr., Larry Plesent.
Institution Type/Description: Soap Museum.
Hours & Admission Prices: Tues.-Sat. 10-4. No charge. Closed most holidays. &
Attendance: 10,000 (estimated)

Milton

MILTON HISTORICAL MUSEUM, 13 School St., Milton, VT 05468-3632. Tel.: 802-893-1604.
E-mail: miltonhistorical@yahoo.com
Formerly: Milton Museum
Key Personnel: Museum Dir. (V), Lorinda Henry; Pres. (V) Milton Historical Society, Bill Kaigle.
Institution Type/Description: Local History Museum.
Hours & Admission Prices: Call for hours & admission prices. &
Attendance: 750 (estimated)

Montpelier

MORSE FARM MAPLE SUGARWORKS & OUTDOOR FARM LIFE MUSEUM, 1168 County Rd., Montpelier, VT 05602-8135. Tel.: 800-242-2740.
E-mail: maple@morsefarm.com
Web Site: www.morsefarm.com
Institution Type/Description: History Museum.
Hours & Admission Prices: Call for hours.

T.W. WOOD GALLERY & ARTS CENTER, 46 Barre St., Montpelier, VT 05602. Tel.: 802-262-6035. Facebook: TW Wood Gallery.
E-mail: twwoodgallery@gmail.com
Web Site: twwoodgallery.org
Key Personnel: Exec. Dir., Ginny Callan; Education Dir., Binta Colley.
Institution Type/Description: Art Gallery.
Hours & Admission Prices: Tues.-Sat. 12-4. No charge; donations accepted. Closed major holidays.
Attendance: 5,000 (estimated)

USS MONTPELIER MUSEUM, 39 Main St., 2nd Fl., Montpelier, VT 05602-3064. Mailing Address: 11 Greenfield Terr., Montpelier, VT 05602. Tel.: 802-223-9502. Fax: 802-223-9519.
E-mail: wfraser@montpelier-vt.org
Web Site: www.montpelier-vt.org/community/367.html
Key Personnel: City Mgr., William J. Fraser.
Institution Type/Description: Naval History Museum.
Hours & Admission Prices: Call for hours. No charge. Closed holidays. &
Attendance: 200 (estimated)

THE VERMONT STATE HOUSE, 115 State St., Montpelier, VT 05633-0004. Tel.: 802-828-2228. Fax: 802-828-2424.
E-mail: sgtatarms@leg.state.vt.us
Web Site: www.leg.state.vt.us
Key Personnel: Cur., David Schutz; Chief of Capitol Police, Matthew Romei.
Institution Type/Description: Historic Building.
Hours & Admission Prices: July 11-Oct. 17 Mon.-Fri. 7:45-4:15, Sat. 11-3; Oct. 18-July 10 Mon.-Fri. 7:45-4:15. No charge; donations accepted. Closed state holidays. &
Attendance: 100,000 (estimated)

Morrisville

NOYES HOUSE MUSEUM, 122 Lower Main St., Morrisville, VT 05661. Mailing Address: Morristown Historical Society, P.O. Box 1299, Morrisville, VT 05661-1299. Tel.: 802-888-7617. Facebook: @NoyesHouseMuseum; Twitter: @HouseNoyes.
E-mail: noyeshousemuseum@gmail.com
Web Site: noyeshousemuseum.org
Key Personnel: Dir., Tracy Haerther; Pres., Jill Mudgett.
Institution Type/Description: Historic House Museum: built in the early 19th-century by the Safford family.
Hours & Admission Prices: June-Aug. Thurs. 12-4, Fri.-Sat. 10-4; Sept.-Oct. Fri. 12-4, Sat. 10-4; other times by appointment. No charge; donations accepted. &
Attendance: 500 (estimated)

Moscow

LITTLE RIVER HOTGLASS STUDIO & GALLERY, 593 Moscow Rd., Moscow, VT 05672. Mailing Address: P.O. Box 1504, Stowe, VT 05672-1504. Tel.: 802-253-0889. Fax: 802-253-4128.
E-mail: info@littleriverhotglass.com
Web Site: littleriverhotglass.com
Institution Type/Description: Art Gallery.
Hours & Admission Prices: Thurs.-Mon. 10-5; other times by appointment.

Newfane

HISTORICAL SOCIETY OF WINDHAM COUNTY, Rte. 30, Main St., Newfane, VT 05345. Mailing Address: P.O. Box 246, Newfane, VT 05345-0246. Tel.: 802-365-4148.
E-mail: info@historicalsocietyofwindhamcounty.org
Web Site: www.historicalsocietyofwindhamcounty.org
Institution Type/Description: Historical Society County Museum & West River Railroad Museum.
Hours & Admission Prices: Memorial Day to Columbus Day Wed. & Sat.-Sun. 12-5. No charge; donations accepted.
Attendance: 500 (estimated)

Newport

MEMPHREMAGOG HISTORICAL SOCIETY OF NEWPORT, Emory Hebard State Office Bldg., 2nd Fl., 100 Main St., Newport, VT 05855-5543. Mailing Address: 96 Stagecoach Dr., Newport, VT 05855-9153. Tel.: 802-334-6195.
Institution Type/Description: Historical Society Museum.
Hours & Admission Prices: Mon.-Fri. 9-5; other times by appointment. No charge.
&

North Bennington

HISTORIC PARK-MCCULLOUGH, One Park St., North Bennington, VT 05257. Mailing Address: P.O. Box 388, North Bennington, VT 05257-0388. Tel.: 802-442-5441. Fax: 802-442-5442.
E-mail: info@parkmccullough.org
Web Site: www.parkmccullough.org
Key Personnel: Pres. (V), Katherine Traver; Bookkeeper, David Adams.
Institution Type/Description: Historic House Museum: housed in 1865 Second Empire mansion built for Trenor & Laura Hall Park which was also the home of two Vermont Governors.
Hours & Admission Prices: Hourly Tours: mid-May to Oct. daily 9-5. Adults $10, senior citizens $9, students $7; discounts to groups, AAM, VMGA, AAA & NEMA members; children under 12 & members no charge. &
Attendance: 6,500 (estimated)

North Springfield

SPRINGFIELD ART & HISTORICAL SOCIETY - MILLER ART CENTER, 65 Route 106, North Springfield, VT 05150. Mailing Address: P.O. Box 336, North Springfield, VT 05150. Tel.: 802-886-7935.
E-mail: sahs@vermontel.net
Web Site: www.springfieldartandhistorical.org
Key Personnel: Dir., Maureen Bolduc; Bd. Pres., Leonard Bolduc.
Institution Type/Description: Art Museum: housed in 1865 house last occupied by Edward W. Miller & family.
Hours & Admission Prices: Thurs.-Fri. 11-5, Sat. 11-4. Adults $3; members no charge. &
Attendance: 1,500 (estimated)

North Troy

MISSISQUOI VALLEY HISTORICAL SOCIETY, Main St., North Troy, VT 05859. Mailing Address: P.O. Box 237, North Troy, VT 05859-0237. Tel.: 802-988-4656.
E-mail: missisco@hotmail.com
Key Personnel: Dir. & Pres. (V), Nancy L. Allen; Vice Pres., John Starr; Treas., Roy Barnett.
Institution Type/Description: Historical Society Museum: housed in 1883 former St. Augustine Church.
Hours & Admission Prices: Memorial Day, Labor Day & Alumni Weekend; other times by appointment. Donations accepted. &
Attendance: 20 (estimated)

Northfield

NORTHFIELD FIRE DEPARTMENT MUSEUM, 128 Wall St., Northfield, VT 05663. Mailing Address: Northfield Municipal Bldg., 51 S. Main St., Northfield, VT 05663. Tel.: 802-485-6121; 485-8443.
E-mail: catmanl@aol.com
Institution Type/Description: Firefighting History.
Hours & Admission Prices: By appointment.

SULLIVAN MUSEUM AND HISTORY CENTER, 158 Harmon Dr., Northfield, VT 05663-1000. Tel.: 802-485-2183.
E-mail: smhc@norwich.edu
Web Site: www.norwich.edu/museum
Formerly: Norwich University Museum
Key Personnel: Dir., Sarah E. Henrich; Chm. (V), Robert Guptill; Museum Registrar, John T. Hart; University Historian, Gary T. Lord; Exhibitions Assoc., Katherine Taylor-McBroom; Museum Asst., Heather Cipolla; Oral History Coord., Joseph Cates.
Institution Type/Description: University Museum.
Hours & Admission Prices: Mon.-Fri. 8-4, Sat. 11-4; other times by appointment. No charge; donations accepted. Closed holidays. &
Attendance: 22,010 (actual)

Norwich

MONTSHIRE MUSEUM OF SCIENCE, INC., 1 Montshire Rd., Norwich, VT 05055-9334. Tel.: 802-649-2200. Fax: 802-649-3637.
E-mail: montshire@montshire.org
Web Site: www.montshire.org
Key Personnel: Dir., Marcos Stafne; Chm. (V), Ginny Bensen; Dir. Education, Greg DeFrancis; Dir. Mktg. & Communications, Beth Krusi; Dir. Devel., Jennifer Rickards; Museum Shop Mgr., Barbara Mathewson.
Institution Type/Description: Science Museum.
Hours & Admission Prices: Daily 10-5. See website for seasonal fees. Closed Thanksgiving; Christmas. &
Attendance: 137,000 (actual)

NORWICH HISTORICAL SOCIETY, 277 Main St., Norwich, VT 05055. Mailing Address: P.O. Box 1680, Norwich, VT 05055-1680. Tel.: 802-649-0124.
E-mail: info@norwichhistory.org
Web Site: www.norwichhistory.org
Key Personnel: Dir., Sarah Rooker.
Institution Type/Description: Historical Society Museum: located in Lewis House. Listed on the National Register of Historic Places.
Hours & Admission Prices: Memorial Day to Oct. Wed. 10-4, Sat. 10am to noon; other times by appointment. No charge. &
Attendance: 1,000 (estimated)

Old Bennington

BENNINGTON BATTLE MONUMENT, 15 Monument Cir., Old Bennington, VT 05201-2134. Mailing Address: Historic Preservation, National Life Bldg., 6th Fl., Montpelier, VT 05620. Tel.: 802-447-0550. Fax: 802-447-6421.
E-mail: tracy.martin@vermont.gov
Web Site: www.historicsite.vermont.gov/directory/bennington
Key Personnel: Historic Sites Section Chief, Tracy N. Martin; Site Admin., Marylou Chicote.
Institution Type/Description: State Historic Site: located near the site of the Bennington Battle of the Revolutionary War.
Hours & Admission Prices: Mid-April-Oct. daily 9-5. Adults $5, children 6-14 $1; discounts to AAM members; registered school groups no charge. &
Attendance: 30,000 (estimated)

Orwell

MOUNT INDEPENDENCE STATE HISTORIC SITE, Mount Independence Rd., Orwell, VT 05760. Mailing Address: Historic Preservation, National Life Bldg., 6th Fl., Montpelier, VT 05620. Tel.: 802-828-3051. Fax: 802-828-3206.
E-mail: tracy.martin@vermont.gov
Web Site: www.historicsites.vermont.gov/directory/mount_independence
Key Personnel: State Historic Sites Section Chief, Tracy N. Martin; Site Admin., Elsa Gilbertson.
Institution Type/Description: Historic Site: site of major Revolutionary War fort.
Hours & Admission Prices: late May to mid-Oct. daily 10-5. Adults & children 15 & over $5; discounts to AAM members; children 14 & under no charge. &
Attendance: 8,000 (actual)

Peacham

PEACHAM HISTORICAL ASSOCIATION, 145 Church St., Peacham, VT 05862. Mailing Address: P.O. Box 101, Peacham, VT 05862-0101. Tel.: 802-592-3049.
E-mail: historic@peacham.net
Web Site: peachamhistorical.org
Key Personnel: Pres. (V), Johanna Branson; Cur., Lorna Quimby.

Institution Type/Description: Historical Society Museum.
Hours & Admission Prices: House: late June to Sept. Sun. 2-4; other times by appointment. Archives: May-Sept. Mon. 10 am to noon. No charge; donations accepted. &
Attendance: 400 (estimated)

Pittsford

NEW ENGLAND MAPLE MUSEUM, 4578 Rt. 7, Pittsford, VT 05763. Mailing Address: P.O. Box 131, Pittsford, VT 05763-0131. Tel.: 802-483-9414; 800-639-4280. Fax: 802-483-2101.
E-mail: info@maplemuseum.com
Web Site: www.maplemuseum.com
Key Personnel: Pres., Michael Blanchard; Dir. & Museum Shop Mgr., Mary Blanchard.
Institution Type/Description: History Museum.
Hours & Admission Prices: mid-March to Dec. daily 10-4. Adults $5, tours & children 12 and under $1; discounts to members. &
Attendance: 35,000 (estimated)

PITTSFORD HISTORICAL SOCIETY MUSEUM, U.S. Rte. 7 #3399, Pittsford, VT 05763. Mailing Address: P.O. Box 423, Pittsford, VT 05763-9774. Tel.: 802-483-2040.
E-mail: peggy.armitage@gmail.com
Web Site: www.pittsfordhistorical.com
Institution Type/Description: Historical Society Museum; located in Eaton Hall, former Masonic Hall.
Hours & Admission Prices: April-June Tues. 9-4; July-Oct. Tues. 9-4, Sun. 1-4. No charge; donations accepted. &
Attendance: 275 (actual)

Plymouth

THE CALVIN COOLIDGE PRESIDENTIAL FOUNDATION, INC., 3780 Rte. 100A, Plymouth, VT 05056. Mailing Address: Box 97, Plymouth, VT 05056-0097. Tel.: 802-672-3389.
E-mail: info@coolidgefoundation.org
Web Site: www.coolidgefoundation.org
Key Personnel: Exec. Dir., Matthew Denhart; Chm., Amity Shlaes.
Institution Type/Description: Historic Foundation.
Hours & Admission Prices: Mon.-Fri. 9-4:30. No charge; donations accepted. Closed federal holidays except Independence Day. &
Attendance: 25,000 (estimated)

Plymouth Notch

CALVIN COOLIDGE STATE HISTORIC SITE, 3780 Rte. 100A, Plymouth Notch, VT 05056. Mailing Address: Historic Preservation, National Life Bldg., 6th Fl., Montpelier, VT 05620. Tel.: 802-828-3051& 672-3773. Fax: 802-828-3206.
E-mail: william.jenney@vermont.gov
Web Site: www.historicsites.vermont.gov/directory/coolidge
Key Personnel: Historic Sites Section Chief, Tracy N. Martin.
Institution Type/Description: Historic House Museum: Calvin Coolidge birthplace & homestead.
Hours & Admission Prices: late May to mid-Oct. daily 9:30-5:30. Adults over 13 $9, children 6-14 $2; discounts to AAM members; registered school groups & children under 6 no charge. &
Attendance: 40,000 (estimated)

Proctor

VERMONT MARBLE MUSEUM, 52 Main St., Proctor, VT 05765-1177. Mailing Address: P.O. Box 607, 52 Main St., Proctor, VT 05765-0607. Tel.: 802-459-2300, 800-427-1396. Fax: 802-459-2948.
E-mail: info@vermontmarblemuseum.org
Web Site: www.vermontmarblemuseum.org
Key Personnel: C.E.O., Marsha Hemm; Mgr., Robert Pye; Museum Shop Mgr., Cathy Miglorle.
Institution Type/Description: Mining & Geology Museum.
Hours & Admission Prices: mid-May to Oct. daily 9-5:30. Adults $7, senior citizens $5, teens 15-18 $4, groups $3.50 per person; children 12 & under with parent no charge. &
Attendance: 45,000 (estimated)

WILSON CASTLE, 2970 W. Proctor Rd, Proctor, VT 05765. Mailing Address: P.O. Box 290, Center Rutland, VT 05736-0290. Tel.: 802-773-3284. Fax: 802-773-3284.
E-mail: wilsoncastle@aol.com

Web Site: www.wilsoncastle.com
Key Personnel: Dir., Denise Davine; Entertainment Dir., Rusty Trombley.
Institution Type/Description: Historic Building: 1867 Wilson Castle. Victorian Building.
Hours & Admission Prices: Memorial Day to late Oct. daily 9-5. Adults $10, children 6-12 $6; discounts to AAA, AAM & ICOM members; children 5 & under no charge. &
Attendance: 75,000

Putney

PUTNEY HISTORICAL SOCIETY, 15 Kimball Hill, Putney, VT 05346. Mailing Address: P.O. Box 260, Putney, VT 05346-0260. Tel.: 802-387-4411.
E-mail: putneyhistory@gmail.com
Web Site: www.putneyhistory.us
Key Personnel: Cur., Laura Heller; Cur., Barbara A. Taylor.
Institution Type/Description: History Museum: housed in 1871 Town Hall.
Hours & Admission Prices: June-Aug. Tues. & Sat. 10-2; other times by appointment. No charge; donations accepted. &
Attendance: 250 (estimated)

Quechee

VERMONT INSTITUTE OF NATURAL SCIENCE, Mailing Address: 149 Natures Way, P.O. Box 1281, Quechee, VT 05059. Tel.: 802-359-5000. Fax: 802-359-5001.
E-mail: info@vinsweb.org
Web Site: www.vinsweb.org
Key Personnel: Exec. Dir., Charles Rattigan; Asst. Exec. Dir., Mary Davidson Graham; Finance & Human Resources, Jennifer Speckert; Mgr. Nature Center Programs, Chris Collier; Welcome Center, Amy Givent.
Institution Type/Description: Nature Center.
Hours & Admission Prices: mid-April through Oct. daily 10-5; Nov. to mid-April daily 10-4. Adults $14.50, students and seniors 62 & over $13.50, youth 3-18 $12.50; discounts to groups, educators, veterans, EBT for NH & VT, and AAA, & ICOM members; children under 4 & members no charge. Closed Thanksgiving; Christmas. &
Attendance: 45,000 (estimated)

VERMONT TOY & TRAIN MUSEUM, 5573 Woodstock Rd., Quechee, VT 05059. Mailing Address: P.O. Box 730, Quechee, VT 05059-0730. Tel.: 802-295-1550, ext. 102. Fax: 802-295-6759. Facebook: Vermont Toy & Train Museum.
E-mail: quechee@quecheegorge.com
Web Site: www.quecheegorge.com
Key Personnel: Dir., Gary Neil; Museum Shop Mgr., Robin Neil.
Institution Type/Description: Toy Museum.
Hours & Admission Prices: Daily 10-5. No charge; donations accepted.
Attendance: 35,000 (estimated)

Randolph

RANDOLPH HISTORICAL SOCIETY, INC., 6 Salisbury St., Randolph, VT 05060. Mailing Address: 31 Beacon Hill,, Chester, VT 05038. Tel.: 802-728-9780.
E-mail: randolph.vt.history@gmail.com
Web Site: www.randolphvthistoricalsociety.wordpress.com
Key Personnel: C.E.O., Laurence Leonard; Cur. & Museum Shop Mgr., Harriet Chase.
Institution Type/Description: History Museum.
Hours & Admission Prices: May-Sept. 3rd Sun. each month 2-4; July 4 call for hours; other times by appointment. No charge; donations accepted.
Attendance: 550 (estimated)

Reading

READING HISTORICAL SOCIETY, Main St., Rte. 106, Reading, VT 05062. Mailing Address: P.O. Box 252, Reading, VT 05062-0252.
E-mail: jebart2@myfairpoint.net
Institution Type/Description: General Museum.
Hours & Admission Prices: By appointment only. No charge; donations accepted.

Readsboro

READSBORO HISTORICAL SOCIETY, Main St., Readsboro, VT 05350. Mailing Address: P.O. Box 16, Readsboro, VT 05350. Tel.: 802-423-5432.
E-mail: skybart@att.net

Web Site: www.readsborohistoricalsociety.org
Key Personnel: Pres. (V), Alfred Scaia; Vice Pres., Jim Franzinelli; Sec. & Treas., Rhonda Smith; Dir., Mitchell Holland.
Institution Type/Description: Historical Society Museum: housed in 1840 frame structured church.
Hours & Admission Prices: June-Oct. Sun. 1-3; other times by appointment. No charge; donations accepted.
Attendance: 100 (actual)

Richmond

OLD ROUND CHURCH - RICHMOND HISTORICAL SOCIETY, 25 Round Church Rd., Richmond, VT 05477. Mailing Address: P.O. Box 453, Richmond, VT 05477-0453. Tel.: 802-434-3654. Facebook: Old Round Church.
E-mail: rhs@oldroundchurch.com
Web Site: www.oldroundchurch.com
Key Personnel: Pres. (V), Frances Thomas.
Institution Type/Description: Historic Building: housed in a 16-sided church built in 1812. A National Historic Landmark.
Hours & Admission Prices: Summer & Fall daily 10-4. No charge; donations accepted. &
Attendance: 2,000 (estimated)

Rochester

ROCHESTER HISTORICAL SOCIETY, Rochester Library, 2nd Fl., Main St., Rochester, VT 05767. Mailing Address: P.O. Box 428, Rochester, VT 05767-0428. Tel.: 802-767-4453.
E-mail: admin@rochesterhistorical.org
Web Site: www.rochesterhistorical.org
Institution Type/Description: Historical Society Museum.
Hours & Admission Prices: By appointment.

Royalton

ROYALTON HISTORICAL SOCIETY, 15 Rte. 110, Royalton, VT 05068-5084. Mailing Address: P.O. Box 11, S. Royalton, VT 05068-0011. Tel.: 802-763-8567.
E-mail: jpdumville@yahoo.com
Key Personnel: Pres., John P. Dumville; Asst. Dir., Ralph Eddy; Business Officer & Publications Dir., Richard L. McGovern.
Institution Type/Description: Historical Society Museum: housed in 1840 Royalton Town House located on Town Common.
Hours & Admission Prices: Summer by appointment. No charge; donations accepted.
Attendance: 1,000 (estimated)

Rutland

NORMAN ROCKWELL MUSEUM OF VERMONT, 654 Rte. 4 E., Rutland, VT 05701. Tel.: 877-773-6095 (toll free). Fax: 802-775-2440.
E-mail: sales@normanrockwellvt.com
Web Site: www.normanrockwellvt.com
Key Personnel: Mng. Cur., Rachel Lynes-Bells.
Institution Type/Description: Art Museum.
Hours & Admission Prices: Daily 9-4. Adults $5.50, seniors 62 & above $5, children $2.50; discount to AAA members & groups 10 and over.

RUTLAND AREA ART ASSOCIATION DBA CHAFFEE ART CENTER & CHAFFEE DOWNTOWN, 16 S. Main St., Rutland, VT 05701. Mailing Address: 16 S. Main St., Rutland, VT 05702. Tel.: 802-775-0356. Facebook: Chaffee Art Center.
E-mail: info@chaffeeartcenter.org
Web Site: www.chaffeeartcenter.org
Formerly: Chaffee Center for the Visual Arts
Key Personnel: Exec. Dir., Margaret Barros; Gallery Coord., Richelle Franzoni; Asst. Gallery Coord., Beth Seck; Pres. (V), W. Tracy Carris, Esq.
Institution Type/Description: Art Center: built from 1892-94.
Hours & Admission Prices: Downtown Gallery: Tues.-Thurs. 11-6, Fri.-Sat. 11:30-7. Art Center: March-Nov. Thurs.-Sat. 12-6. No charge; donations accepted. &
Attendance: 23,000 (estimated)

RUTLAND HISTORICAL SOCIETY, 96 Center St., Rutland, VT 05701-4023. Tel.: 802-775-2006. Facebook: Rutland Historical Society.
E-mail: president@rutlandhistory.com
Web Site: rutlandhistory.com
Key Personnel: Chm. (V), Tom Carpenter; Pres. (V), Pam Johnson.

Institution Type/Description: Historical Society: housed in the former Nickwackett Firehouse, built in 1860.
Hours & Admission Prices: Mon. 6-9pm, Sat. 1-4pm; other times by appointment. No charge; donations accepted. &
Attendance: 200 (estimated)

Saint Albans

ST. ALBANS HISTORICAL MUSEUM, 9 Church St., Saint Albans, VT 05478-1675. Mailing Address: P.O. Box 722, Saint Albans, VT 05478-0722. Tel.: 802-527-7933.
E-mail: museum@stamuseum.org
Web Site: www.stamuseum.org
Key Personnel: Dir., Alex Lehning.
Institution Type/Description: Historical Society Museum: housed in 1861 three-story brick Franklin County Grammar School.
Hours & Admission Prices: June-Oct. Wed.-Fri. 11-4, Sat. 10-2; other times by appointment. Adults $6, children 6-14 $2; members & children under 6 no charge. Closed holidays. &
Attendance: 2,000 (actual)

Saint Johnsbury

FAIRBANKS MUSEUM AND PLANETARIUM, 1302 Main St., Saint Johnsbury, VT 05819-2224. Tel.: 802-748-2372. Fax: 802-748-1893. Facebook.
E-mail: info@fairbanksmuseum.org
Web Site: www.fairbanksmuseum.org
Key Personnel: Exec. Dir., Adam Kane; Chm. (V), Tracy Zschau; Museum Shop Mgr., Virginia Platt.
Institution Type/Description: General Museum & Planetarium.
Hours & Admission Prices: Museum: Wed. 10-5. Adults $9, senior citizens & children 5-17 $7; discounts to groups & AAM members; members and children 4 & under no charge. Planetarium: daily. Admission $3-$5 per person; discounts to groups, AAM, ASTC & NEMA members. Closed New Year's Day; Easter; Thanksgiving; Christmas. &
Attendance: 36,000 (actual)

MAPLE GROVE SUGARHOUSE MUSEUM AND GIFT SHOP, 1052 Portland St., Saint Johnsbury, VT 05819-2041. Tel.: 802-748-5141; 800-525-2540 ext 5547 (Toll Free). Fax: 802-748-0844.
E-mail: maple@maplegrove.com
Web Site: www.maplegrove.com
Formerly: Maple Grove Museum and Factory
Institution Type/Description: Historic Building: housed in a former sugarhouse.
Hours & Admission Prices: March 15 to May Mon.-Fri. 8-5; June to Jan. 10 Mon.-Fri. 8-5, Sat.-Sun. 9-5. No charge. Closed Thanksgiving; Christmas.

NORTHEAST KINGDOM ARTISANS GUILD, 430 Railroad St., #2, Saint Johnsbury, VT 05819-1727. Tel.: 802-748-0158.
E-mail: nekguild@gmail.com
Web Site: www.nekartisansguild.com
Institution Type/Description: Art Gallery.
Hours & Admission Prices: Mon.-Sat. 10:30-5:30.

ST. JOHNSBURY ATHENAEUM, 1171 Main St., Saint Johnsbury, VT 05819-2289. Tel.: 802-748-8291. Fax: 802-748-8086.
E-mail: inform@stjathenaeum.org
Web Site: www.stjathenaeum.org
Key Personnel: Exec. Dir., Matthew Powers; Head Librarian, Lisa Von Kann; Chm. (V), William Marshall.
Institution Type/Description: Art Museum and National Historic Landmark.
Hours & Admission Prices: Mon.-Fri. 10-5:30, Sat. 9:30-5. Art Gallery: adults $8; members no charge. Closed national holidays. &
Attendance: 70,000 (estimated)

STEPHEN HUNECK GALLERY AT DOG MOUNTAIN, 143 Parks Rd., Saint Johnsbury, VT 05819-8907. Tel.: 800-449-2580, 802-748-2700. Fax: 802-748-3075.
E-mail: contact@dogmt.com
Web Site: www.dogmt.com
Key Personnel: Dir. & C.E.O., Gwendolyn Huneck; Chm. (V) & Pres. (V), Lisa Nelson; Museum Shop Mgr., Amanda McDermott.
Institution Type/Description: Art Gallery.
Hours & Admission Prices: Mon.-Sat. 10-5, Sun. 11-4. No charge; donations accepted. &
Attendance: 10,000 (estimated)

Saxtons River

SAXTONS RIVER HISTORICAL SOCIETY, Main St., Saxtons River, VT 05154. Mailing Address: P.O. Box 18, Saxtons River, VT 05154-0018. Tel.: 802-869-2566.
E-mail: luring@vermontel.net
Institution Type/Description: Historical Society Museum: housed in the former Congregational Church, built in 1836.
Hours & Admission Prices: Summer: Sun. 2-4:30; other times by appointment. No charge.

Shaftsbury

ROBERT FROST STONE HOUSE MUSEUM, 121 Historic Rte. 7A, Shaftsbury, VT 05262. Tel.: 802-447-6200.
E-mail: frostnow@sover.net
Web Site: www.frostfriends.org
Institution Type/Description: Historic House Museum: housed in the former home of American poet, Robert Frost.
Hours & Admission Prices: May-Nov. daily 10-5; Adults $6, seniors 60 & over $5, students under 18 $3, children under 10 no charge.

SHAFTSBURY HISTORICAL SOCIETY, 3542 VT Rte. 7A, Shaftsbury, VT 05262. Mailing Address: P.O. Box 401, Shaftsbury, VT 05262-0401. Tel.: 802-375-6376.
E-mail: gronning@sover.net
Web Site: www.shaftsburyhistoricalsociety.org
Key Personnel: Pres. (V), Mitchell Race; Vice Pres., Norman D. Gronning; Treas., David Rekas; Sec., Kathy Cardiff.
Institution Type/Description: Historical Society Museum: housed in 1846 Meeting House, oldest Baptist Church in Vermont.
Hours & Admission Prices: Tues., Thurs. & Sat.-Sun. by appointment. No charge; donations accepted.
Attendance: 200 (estimated)

Shelburne

FURCHGOTT SOURDIFFE GALLERY, 86 Falls Rd., Shelburne, VT 05482-6208. Tel.: 802-985-3848.
E-mail: mail@fsgallery.com
Web Site: www.fsgallery.com
Institution Type/Description: Art Gallery.
Hours & Admission Prices: Tues.-Fri. 9:30-5:30, Sat. 10-5.

NATIONAL MUSEUM OF THE MORGAN HORSE, 4066 Shelburne Rd. Ste. 5, Shelburne, VT 05482. Mailing Address: P.O. Box 101, Middlebury, VT 05753. Tel.: 802-985-4944. Fax: 802-985-8897.
E-mail: morganmuseum@gmail.com
Web Site: www.morganhorse.com
Key Personnel: Dir., Amy Mincher.
Institution Type/Description: Equine Museum.
Hours & Admission Prices: Tues.-Fri. 1-5, Sat. 10-5; other times by appointment. Donation Requested. Closed major holidays.
Attendance: 4,500 (estimated)

SHELBURNE FARMS, 1611 Harbor Rd., Shelburne, VT 05482. Tel.: 802-985-8686.
E-mail: info@shelburnefarms.org
Web Site: www.shelburnefarms.org
Key Personnel: Pres., Alec Webb; Cur. Colls., Julie Eldridge Edwards.
Institution Type/Description: Historic Farm.
Hours & Admission Prices: mid-May to mid-Oct. daily 9-5:30; mid-Oct. to mid-May daily 10-5. Adults $8, seniors $6, children 3-17 $5; children under 3 & Shelburne residents no charge. Closed Thanksgiving; Christmas.

SHELBURNE MUSEUM, INC., 6000 Shelburne Rd., Shelburne, VT 05482-7491. Mailing Address: P.O. Box 10, Shelburne, VT 05482-0010. Tel.: 802-985-3346. Fax: 802-985-2331. Facebook; Twitter.
E-mail: info@shelburnemuseum.org
Web Site: www.shelburnemuseum.org
Key Personnel: Chm., Peter Martin; Vice Chm., Frances von Stade Downing; Vice Chm., Charles Granquist; Sec., Alice Cooney Frelinghausen; Treas., David Starr; Asst. Sec., Caroline Almy Gerry; Dir., Thomas Denenberg; Dir. Devel., Mike Smiles; Deputy Dir., Berenice Sarafzade; Dir. Visitor Experience, Karen Petersen; Dir. Preservation of Landscape, Chip Stulen; Dir. Protection Svcs., Stephen Boudah; Mgr. Landscape & Gardens, Jessica Gallas; Merchandising Mgr., Lee Wheeler; Mgr. Communications, Geeda Searfoorce.
Institution Type/Description: Art & Design Museum.

Hours & Admission Prices: Jan.-April Wed.-Sun. 10-5; May-Dec. daily 10-5. Jan.-April: adults $10; May-Dec.: adults $24. Closed New Year's Day; Thanksgiving; Christmas.
Attendance: 100,000 (estimated)

VERMONT TEDDY BEAR COMPANY, 6655 Shelburne Rd., Shelburne, VT 05482. Tel.: 802-985-1319. Facebook; Twitter..
Web Site: vermontteddybear.com
Institution Type/Description: Company Museum.
Hours & Admission Prices: Office: daily 9-5. Tours: daily seasonal hours. Adults $4, seniors $3; children 12 & under no charge. Closed New Year's Eve & Day; Easter; Independence Day; Thanksgiving; Christmas Eve & Day.

Shoreham

SHOREHAM HISTORICAL SOCIETY, Rte. 22-A, Old Stone Schoolhouse, Shoreham, VT 05770. Mailing Address: P.O. Box 156, Shoreham, VT 05770-0235. Tel.: 802-897-2580.
E-mail: shorehamtreasurer@shoreham.net
Key Personnel: Pres., Dale Birdsall; Cur., Ginny Spadaccini.
Institution Type/Description: Historical Society Museum.
Hours & Admission Prices: By appointment. No charge.

South Hero

SOUTH HERO BICENTENNIAL MUSEUM, Rte. 2, South Hero, VT 05486. Mailing Address: P.O. Box 49, South Hero, VT 05486-4802. Tel.: 802-372-7811.
E-mail: southherohistoricalsociety@gmail.com
Key Personnel: Chm. (V), Hazel Quelch; Pres. (V), Lorraine Janick; Pres., Teresa Robinson; Vice Pres., Ron Phelps; Treas., Cathie Merrihew; Sec., Marty Sherman; Archivist, Alice Wells.
Institution Type/Description: Local History Museum.
Hours & Admission Prices: June-Aug. Mon. & Thurs. 1:30-3:30. No charge.
Attendance: 30 (estimated)

South Royalton

JOSEPH SMITH BIRTHPLACE MEMORIAL & VISITORS CENTER, 357 LDS Lane, South Royalton, VT 05068. Tel.: 802-763-7742.
E-mail: hsjsmemorial@ldschurch.org
Institution Type/Description: History Museum: the birthplace of Joseph Smith, the first president & prophet of The Church of Jesus Christ of Latter-day Saints.
Hours & Admission Prices: May-Oct. Mon.-Sat. 9-7, Sun. 1:30-7; Nov.-April Mon.-Sat. 9-5, Sun. 1:30-5. No charge.
Attendance: 25,000 (estimated)

South Woodstock

GREEN MOUNTAIN PERKINS ACADEMY & HISTORICAL ASSOCIATION, 32 Academy Circle, VT Rte. 106, South Woodstock, VT 05071. Mailing Address: P.O. Box 143, South Woodstock, VT 05071-0143. Tel.: 802-457-3779.
E-mail: marymaple13@gmail.com
Web Site: www.greenmountainperkinsacademy.org
Key Personnel: Pres., Mary McCuaig.
Institution Type/Description: Historic House Museum: housed in a building that served as a private high school until 1898; built in 1848.
Hours & Admission Prices: July-Aug. Sat. 2-5; other times by appointment.
Attendance: 300 (estimated)

Springfield

EUREKA SCHOOL HOUSE, 470 Charlestown Rd., Rte. 11, Springfield, VT 05156. Mailing Address: Historic Preservation, National Life Bldg., 6th Fl., Montpelier, VT 05620. Tel.: 802-828-3051. Fax: 802-828-3206.
E-mail: tracy.martin@vermont.gov
Web Site: www.historicsites.vermont.gov/vt_history/eureka_schoolhouse
Key Personnel: Historic Sites Section Chief, Tracy N. Martin.
Institution Type/Description: Historic Buildings: school built in 1785.
Hours & Admission Prices: Late May to mid-Oct. Sat.-Sun. 10-4. No charge; donations accepted.
Attendance: 3,000 (estimated)

JAMES HARTNESS-RUSSELL PORTER ASTRONOMY MUSEUM, 30 Orchard St., Springfield, VT 05156-2612. P.O. Box 601, Springfield, VT 05156. Tel.: 802-885-2115.

E-mail: vtsteampunksociety@gmail.com
Web Site: stellafane.org/history/early/museum-home.html
Institution Type/Description: Astronomy Museum.
Hours & Admission Prices: Call for hours.

Stannard

STANNARD HISTORICAL SOCIETY, Old Methodist Church, 621 Stannard Mountain Rd., Stannard, VT 05842. Mailing Address: 92 Old Pasture Rd., Greensboro Bend, VT 05842-2100. Tel.: 802-533-2561.
Key Personnel: Pres., Jan Lewandoski.
Institution Type/Description: Historical Society Museum: housed in an 1888 church. Listed on the National Register of Historic Sites.
Hours & Admission Prices: By appointment.

Stowe

GREEN MOUNTAIN FINE ART GALLERY, 64 S. Main St., Stowe, VT 05672. Mailing Address: P.O. Box 1384, Stowe, VT 05672-1384. Tel.: 802-253-1818. Fax: 802-253-6837.
E-mail: scott@greenmountainfineart.com
Web Site: www.greenmountainfineart.com
Institution Type/Description: Art Gallery.
Hours & Admission Prices: Daily 11-6.

HELEN DAY ART CENTER, 90 Pond St., Stowe, VT 05672. Mailing Address: P.O. Box 411, Stowe, VT 05672-0411. Tel.: 802-253-8358.
E-mail: mail@helenday.com
Web Site: www.helenday.com
Key Personnel: Exec. Dir., Rachel Moore; Dir. Education, Susan Holliday; Deputy Dir., Jennifer Schoeberlein; Operations Mgr. & Program Asst., Chiyomi McKibbin; Gallery Mgr. & Mktg. Asst., Amanda Marquis.
Institution Type/Description: Art Center: housed in 1863 Greek Revival building used as a school for 100 years.
Hours & Admission Prices: Tues.-Sat. 12-5; other times by appointment. No charge; donations accepted. Closed New Year's Day; Presidents' Day; Easter; Memorial Day; Independence Day; Thanksgiving; Christmas. &
Attendance: 15,000

ROBERT PAUL GALLERY, 394 Mountain Rd., Stowe, VT 05672. Mailing Address: P.O. Box 1413, Stowe, VT 05672-1413. Tel.: 802-253-7282.
E-mail: robertpaulgalleries@aol.com
Web Site: www.robertpaulgalleries.com
Institution Type/Description: Art Gallery.
Hours & Admission Prices: Mon.-Sat. 10-6, Sun. 10-5.

STOWE HISTORICAL SOCIETY MUSEUM, 90 School St., Stowe, VT 05672. Mailing Address: P.O. Box 730, Stowe, VT 05672-0730. Tel.: 802-253-1518.
E-mail: info@stowehistoricalsociety.org
Web Site: www.stowehistoricalsociety.org
Key Personnel: Pres., Barbara Baraw; Vice Pres., Chuck Dudley.
Institution Type/Description: Historical Society Museum: housed in 2 school-houses.
Hours & Admission Prices: Tues., Thurs. & Sat. 12-3; other times by appointment. No charge; donations accepted. Closed New Year's Eve & Day; Christmas Eve, Day & week; state holidays. &
Attendance: 400 (estimated)

VERMONT SKI AND SNOWBOARD MUSEUM, The Perkins Bldg., One S. Main St., Stowe, VT 05672. Mailing Address: The Perkins Bldg., P.O. Box 1511, Stowe, VT 05672-1511. Tel.: 802-253-9911. Fax: 802-253-2616.
E-mail: info@vtssm.com
Web Site: www.vtssm.com
Key Personnel: Dir. & Cur., Meredith Scott; Chm., Rick Hamlin; Museum Shop Mgr., Susi Clark.
Institution Type/Description: History Museum.
Hours & Admission Prices: June-Oct. 30 & Dec.-March Wed.-Mon. 12-5. Suggested Donations: family $5, individual $3; discounts to groups; members no charge. &
Attendance: 8,000 (estimated)

WEST BRANCH GALLERY & SCULPTURE PARK, 17 Towne Farm Lane, Stowe, VT 05672-4138. Mailing Address: P.O. Box 250, Stowe, VT 05672-0250. Tel.: 802-253-8943.

E-mail: art@westbranchgallery.com
Web Site: www.westbranchgallery.com
Institution Type/Description: Art Gallery.
Hours & Admission Prices: Tues.-Sun. 9-5; other times by appointment.

Strafford

JUSTIN SMITH MORRILL STATE HISTORIC SITE, 214 Justin Morrill Memorial Hwy., Strafford, VT 05072. Mailing Address: Historic Preservation, National Life Bldg., 6th Fl., Montpelier, VT 05620. Tel.: 802-828-3051 & 765-4484. Fax: 802-828-3206.
E-mail: tracy.martin@vermont.gov
Web Site: www.historicsites.vermont..gov/directory/morrill
Key Personnel: Historic Site Section Chief, Tracy Martin.
Institution Type/Description: Historic House Museum: c.1849 Justin Smith Morrill Homestead, Gothic Revival Homestead with seven Agricultural Buildings.
Hours & Admission Prices: late May to mid-Oct. Wed.-Sun. 11-5. Adults $6; discounts to AAM members; registered school groups no charge. &
Attendance: 2,000 (estimated)

Swanton

ABENAKI CULTURAL CENTER, 49 Church St., Swanton, VT 05488. Tel.: 802-868-2559.
Formerly: Abenaki Tribal Museum & Cultural Center
Institution Type/Description: Native American Museum.
Hours & Admission Prices: Call for hours.

Thetford

HUGHES BARN MUSEUM, 2274 Rte. 113, Thetford, VT 05074. Mailing Address: Thetford Historical Society, P.O. Box 33, Thetford, VT 05074. Tel.: 802-785-2068.
E-mail: info@thetfordhistoricalsociety.org
Web Site: www.thetfordhistoricalsociety.org
Institution Type/Description: History Museum.
Hours & Admission Prices: Aug. to Labor Day Sun. 2-5. No charge.

THETFORD HISTORICAL SOCIETY LIBRARY AND MUSEUM, Bicentennial Bldg., 16 Library Rd., Thetford, VT 05074. Mailing Address: P.O. Box 33, Thetford, VT 05074-0033. Tel.: 802-785-2068.
E-mail: info@thetfordhistoricalsociety.org
Web Site: www.thetfordhistoricalsociety.org
Key Personnel: Pres. (V) & Librarian, Charles Latham; Asst. Dir., Martha Howard.
Institution Type/Description: Library & Agriculture Museum.
Hours & Admission Prices: Library: Mon. & Thurs. 2-4, Tues. 10-12. Barn Museum: Aug. Sun. 2-5. No charge; donations accepted.
Attendance: 300 (estimated)

Vergennes

BIXBY MEMORIAL LIBRARY, 258 Main St., Vergennes, VT 05491-1056. Tel.: 802-877-2211. Fax: 802-877-2411.
E-mail: jane.spencer@bixbylibrary.org
Web Site: www.bixbylibrary.org
Key Personnel: Dir., Jane Spencer; Bd. Chm., Derek Cohen; Youth Svcs. Librarian, Rachel Plant; Adult Svc. Librarian, Muir Haman.
Institution Type/Description: Library & History Museum.
Hours & Admission Prices: Mon. 12:30-7, Tues. & Fri. 12:30-5, Wed. 10-5, Thurs. 10-7, Sat. 9-2. No charge; donations accepted.

LAKE CHAMPLAIN MARITIME MUSEUM, 4472 Basin Harbor Rd., Vergennes, VT 05491-9192. Tel.: 802-475-2022. Fax: 802-475-2953.
E-mail: info@lcmm.org
Web Site: lcmm.org
Key Personnel: Exec. Dir., Susan Evans McClure; Dir. Archaeological Projects, Chris Sabick; Dir. Exhibits & Collections, Eloise Beil; Dir. Boat-building & Outdoor Education, Nick Patch; Museum Shop Mgr., Lisa Percival.
Institution Type/Description: Maritime & Nautical Archaeology Museum.
Hours & Admission Prices: late May to mid-Oct. daily 10-4. Adults $14, senior citizens $12, students 6-18 $8; discounts to military veterans, AAM, AAA & VT museum & Gallery Alliance members; Council of American Maritime Museums, children 5 & under and members no charge. &
Attendance: 14,800 (actual)

Vernon

VERNON HISTORIANS, INC., Vernon Historical Museum, 567 Governor Hunt Rd., Vernon, VT 05354-9484. Tel.: 802-257-0292.
Key Personnel: Pres., Dale Gassett.
Institution Type/Description: Historical Museum & Chapel.
Hours & Admission Prices: Museum: June-Sept. Sun. 2-4. Pond Road Chapel: by appointment. No charge; donations accepted.
Attendance: 200 (estimated)

Waitsfield

WAITSFIELD HISTORICAL SOCIETY AT GENERAL WAIT HOUSE, 4061 Main St., Waitsfield, VT 05673. Mailing Address: P.O. Box 816, Waitsfield, VT 05673-0816. Tel.: 802-496-2027.
E-mail: stepback@gmavt.net
Web Site: www.waitsfieldhistoricalsociety.com
Key Personnel: Pres. & Treas., Lois De Heer; Vice Pres., Peter Laskowsky; Sec., Barbara Mansfield; Archivist, Judy Dodds.
Institution Type/Description: Historic Site: housed in the former home of General Wait; built c.1793.
Hours & Admission Prices: Daily 9-5. No charge; donations accepted.
Attendance: 1,500 (estimated)

Waterbury

BEN & JERRY'S FACTORY TOUR, 1281 Waterbury-Stowe Rd., Waterbury, VT 05676. Tel.: 802-882-2047 & 2040. Facebook; Twitter..
Web Site: benjerry.com
Institution Type/Description: Company Museum & Factory Tour.
Hours & Admission Prices: Jan.-May 18 & Oct. 21-Dec. daily 10-6; May 19-June daily 10-7; July-Aug. 18 daily 9-9; Aug. 19-Oct. 20 daily 9-7; groups of 10 or more by appointment. Adults $4, senior $3, children 12 & under no charge. Flavor Fanatic Experience: Sat. 9:45, 11:45, & 2:15. $175 per person. Closed New Year's Day; Thanksgiving; Christmas.

GREEN MOUNTAIN COFFEE VISITOR CENTER, 1 Rotarian Place, Waterbury, VT 05676-1582. Tel.: 877-879-2326.
Institution Type/Description: Visitor Center: housed in an 1867 Amtrak station.
Hours & Admission Prices: Memorial Day to Labor Day daily 7-7; Winter: daily 7-6; groups by appointment. Suggested Donation: $1. Closed New Year's Day; Thanksgiving; Christmas.

Waterbury Center

GREEN MOUNTAIN CLUB, INC., 4711 Waterbury Stowe Rd., Waterbury Center, VT 05677-8325. Tel.: 802-244-7037. Fax: 802-244-5867.
E-mail: gmc@greenmountainclub.org
Web Site: greenmountainclub.org
Key Personnel: Pres. (V), Richard Windish; Dir. Devel., Shawn Keeley, Jr.; Dir. Finance, Jason Buss.
Institution Type/Description: History Museum.
Hours & Admission Prices: Memorial Day-Oct. Mon.-Fri. 9-5, Sat.-Sun. 8-4; Nov.-May Mon.-Sat. 10-5. No charge; donations accepted. Closed federal holidays; Christmas Eve.
Attendance: 5,000 (estimated)

Weathersfield

REVEREND DAN FOSTER HOUSE, MUSEUM OF THE WEATHERSFIELD HISTORICAL SOCIETY, 2656 Weathersfield Center Rd., Weathersfield, VT 05156. Mailing Address: P.O. Box 126, Perkinsville, VT 05151-0126. Tel.: 802-263-5230. Fax: 802-263-9263.
E-mail: ellen.clattenburg@dresden.us
Key Personnel: Pres., Ginger Wimberg; Cur., Ellen F. Clattenburg.
Institution Type/Description: Local History Museum.
Hours & Admission Prices: June-Oct. by appointment. No charge; donations accepted.
Attendance: 200 (estimated)

West Addison

DAR JOHN STRONG MANSION MUSEUM, 6656 VT Rte. 17 W., West Addison, VT 05491-8893. Tel.: 802-759-2309.
E-mail: sferland@comcast.net
Web Site: www.johnstrongmansion.org
Key Personnel: Cur., Maureen Labenski.

Institution Type/Description: Historic House.
Hours & Admission Prices: Memorial Day weekend to Labor Day weekend. Sat.-Sun. 10-5. Family $10, adults $5, seniors & students $3; discount to groups, AAM, ICOM & VMGA members; members no charge.
Attendance: 500 (actual)

West Brattleboro

TASHA TUDOR MUSEUM, 974 Western Ave., West Brattleboro, VT 05301. Mailing Address: P.O. Box 2546, Brattleboro, VT 05301. Tel.: 802-258-6564; 257-4444. Fax: 802-257-1805.
E-mail: info@tashatudormuseum.org
Web Site: www.tashatudorandfamily.com
Key Personnel: Dir., Amy Tudor.
Institution Type/Description: Art Museum: housed in the historic Jeremiah Beal House.
Hours & Admission Prices: Museum: May 2-Oct. 18 Wed.-Sat. 10-4; call to confirm. Adults $6, seniors over 65 & children 3-12 $4; children under 3, members & active military no charge. Corgi Cottage: limited tours by appointment. Adults $165, children 12 & under $65.

West Halifax

HALIFAX HISTORICAL SOCIETY MUSEUM, Mailing Address: P.O. Box 94, West Halifax, VT 05358. Tel.: 802-368-7490.
E-mail: dpark127@aol.com
Key Personnel: Pres. (V), Arthur Copeland; Museum Shop Mgr., Doug Parkhurst.
Institution Type/Description: Historical Society Museum: housed in a former two-room schoolhouse.
Hours & Admission Prices: Summer: Sat. 2-4; other times by appointment. No charge.
Attendance: 40 (estimated)

West Marlboro

SOUTHERN VERMONT NATURAL HISTORY MUSEUM, Hogback Mt. Overlook, 7599 Vermont Rte. 9, West Marlboro, VT 05363. Tel.: 802-464-0048. Fax: 802-464-6249.
E-mail: museum@sover.net
Web Site: www.vermontmuseum.org
Key Personnel: Pres. (V) & Exec. Dir., Edward C. Metcalfe.
Institution Type/Description: Natural History Museum.
Hours & Admission Prices: Daily 10-4. Winter: call ahead in inclement weather. Adults 13 & over $5, senior citizens $3, children 5-12 $2; children under 5, NEMA, UMGA, SPNHC, AAM & ICOM members no charge. Closed Thanksgiving; Christmas.
Attendance: 15,000 (estimated)

West Rutland

CARVING STUDIO & SCULPTURE CENTER, 636 Marble St., West Rutland, VT 05777. Mailing Address: P.O. Box 495, West Rutland, VT 05777-0495. Tel.: 802-438-2097. Fax: 802-438-2020.
E-mail: info@carvingstudio.org
Web Site: www.carvingstudio.org
Institution Type/Description: Sculpture Center.
Hours & Admission Prices: Call for hours.

Westminster

WESTMINSTER HISTORICAL SOCIETY, 3651 U.S. Route 5, Westminster, VT 05158. Mailing Address: P.O. Box 2, Westminster, VT 05158-0002.
Web Site: www.westminsterVThistory.org
Key Personnel: C.E.O. & Pres. (V), Ruth Grandy; Vice Pres., Pat Haas; Treas., Dan Axtell; Sec., Barbara Greenough; Dir., Racheal Scott; Dir., Virginia Lisai; Dir., Bob Haas; Dir., Pat Haas; Dir., Barbara Taylor; Dir., Karen Larsen.
Institution Type/Description: Historical Society Museum: housed in c.1890 Old Town Hall.
Hours & Admission Prices: July-Sept. Sun. 2-4. No charge; donations accepted.
Attendance: 100 (estimated)

Weston

FARRAR-MANSUR HOUSE & OLD MILL MUSEUM, Main St., Weston, VT 05161. Mailing Address: P.O. Box 247, Weston, VT 05161-0247. Tel.: 802-824-5294.
Key Personnel: Dir., Jean Lindman.
Institution Type/Description: Historic House Museum.

Hours & Admission Prices: July-Aug. Wed. & Sun. 1-4, Sat. 10-4; Sept. Sat. 10-4. No charge; donations accepted.
Attendance: 2,000 (estimated)

White River Junction

THE MAIN STREET MUSEUM, 58 Bridge St., Studio 6, White River Junction, VT 05001-7040. Tel.: 802-356-2776.
E-mail: info@mainstreetmuseum.org
Web Site: www.mainstreetmuseum.org
Key Personnel: Dir., David Fairbanks Ford; Pres. (V), Bunny Harvey; Museum Shop Mgr., Christopher W. Comperry.
Institution Type/Description: General Museum.
Hours & Admission Prices: Thurs.-Sun. 1-6. Suggested Donation: $3-$5; discounts to groups; members no charge. &
Attendance: 5,000 (actual)

Williamstown

WEATHERED BARN DOLL MUSEUM, 452 George Rd., Williamstown, VT 05679-9403. Tel.: 802-433-6077.
Institution Type/Description: Doll Museum.
Hours & Admission Prices: May-Dec. call for hours.

Windsor

AMERICAN PRECISION MUSEUM, INC., 196 Main St., Windsor, VT 05089-1312. Mailing Address: P.O. Box 679, Windsor, VT 05089-0679. Tel.: 802-674-5781. Fax: 802-674-2524.
E-mail: info@americanprecision.org
Web Site: www.americanprecision.org
Key Personnel: C.E.O., Ann Lawless; Chm. (V), Gilbert Whittemore.
Institution Type/Description: Industrial History Museum: housed in 1846 Robbins & Lawrence Armory. National Historic Landmark.
Hours & Admission Prices: Memorial Day-Oct. daily 10-5. Family $18, adults $6, students $4; members & Sun. no charge. New England Museum Association reciprocal admissions program. &
Attendance: 4,597 (actual)

OLD CONSTITUTION HOUSE - STATE HISTORIC SITE, 16 N. Main St., Windsor, VT 05089-1307. Mailing Address: Historic Preservation, National Life Bldg., 6th Fl., Montpelier, VT 05620. Tel.: 802-672-3773. Fax: 802-828-3206.
E-mail: william.jenney@vermont.gov
Web Site: www.historicsites.vermont.gov/directory/old_constitution
Key Personnel: Historic Sites Operations Chief, John P. Dumville.
Institution Type/Description: Historic House Museum: 1777 Old Constitution House.
Hours & Admission Prices: late May to mid-Oct. Sat.-Sun. & Mon. holidays 11-5. Adults $3; discounts to AAM members; registered school groups no charge. &
Attendance: 2,000 (estimated)

Winooski

HERITAGE WINOOSKI MILL MUSEUM, Champlain Mill, 20 Winooski Falls Way, Winooski, VT 05404. Mailing Address: 20 Winooski Falls Way, Ste. 302, Winooski, VT 05404. Tel.: 802-355-9937. Facebook.
E-mail: info@themillmuseum.org
Web Site: www.themillmuseum.org
Key Personnel: Dir. & C.E.O., Miriam Block.
Institution Type/Description: History Museum: mill listed on the National Historic Register.
Hours & Admission Prices: Mon.-Fri. 9-5. No charge; donations accepted. Closed holidays.
Attendance: 600 (estimated)

MCCARTHY GALLERY, McCarthy Arts Center, St. Michael's College, Winooski, VT 05404. Tel.: 802-654-2246.
E-mail: bcollier@smcvt.edu
Institution Type/Description: Art Gallery.
Hours & Admission Prices: Mon.-Fri. 3-5 & 7:30-9:30, Sat.-Sun. 1-5.

Woodstock

BILLINGS FARM & MUSEUM, 69 Old River Rd., Woodstock, VT 05091. Mailing Address: P.O. Box 489, Woodstock, VT 05091-0489. Tel.: 802-457-2355. Fax: 802-457-4663.
E-mail: info@billingsfarm.org

Web Site: www.billingsfarm.org
Key Personnel: Pres., David A. Donath; Sr. Vice Pres., Darlyne S. Franzen; Dir., David M. Simmons; Admin. Officer, Marian E. Koetsier; Facilities Mgr., David V. Ferrero; Sec., Marjorie Wakefield; Curatorial & Facilities Asst., Emily Koetsier; Asst. Farm Mgr., Alayna Perkins; Farm Worker, Michael Birkett; Farm Worker, Charlie Ferrero; Farm Worker, Paul Brock.
Institution Type/Description: History Museum: housed on a 320 acre dairy farm.
Hours & Admission Prices: May-Oct. daily 10-5; Nov.-Feb. Sat.-Sun. 10-4, call for additional hours. Adults $14, seniors $13, children 5-15 $8, children 3-4 $4; discounts to AAM & ICOM members; members & children 2 & under no charge. &
Attendance: 54,858 (actual)

WOODSTOCK HISTORICAL SOCIETY, INC., 26 Elm St., Woodstock, VT 05091-1024. Tel.: 802-457-1822. Fax: 802-457-2811.
E-mail: info@woodstockhistorical.org
Web Site: www.woodstockhistorical.org
Key Personnel: Dir., Matthew Powers; Chm., Chuck Wise; Pres. (V), Heidi Lang; Collections Mgr., Rebecca Talcott; Guide Admin., Gina Moore; Coord. Education, Jennie Shurtleff.
Institution Type/Description: History Museum: housed in 1807 Federal style house with brick gables, designed by Nathaniel Smith.
Hours & Admission Prices: Office: Mon.-Fri. 9-5. Library: by appointment. Museums: Wed.-Sat. 1-4, Sun. 11-3. No charge; donations accepted. &
Attendance: 4,450 (actual)

VIRGINIA

(396 listings)

Abingdon

HISTORICAL SOCIETY OF WASHINGTON COUNTY, VIRGINIA, 306 Depot Square, Abingdon, VA 24210-3102. Mailing Address: P.O. Box 484, Abingdon, VA 24212-0484. Tel.: 276-623-8337.
E-mail: office@hswcv.org
Web Site: hswcv.org
Key Personnel: Pres. & Bulletin Editor, Eleanor Grasselli; Treas., Mike Shaffer; Recording Sec., Doris Wells; Corresponding Sec., Ina Stephenson-Marbury; Membership, Riley Clark; Local History, Joella Barbour; Newsletter Editor, Greg McMillian; Database Mgr., Jack Niemann; Photo Digitization, Jane Oakes; Library Mgr., Melissa Watson.
Institution Type/Description: Historical Society Library.
Hours & Admission Prices: Jan. 15-March & Dec. 1-Dec. 15 Mon.-Fri. 10-4; April-Nov. Mon.-Fri. 10-4 & 1st and 3rd Sat. 11-4. No charge; donations accepted.
Attendance: 2,500 (estimated)

WILLIAM KING MUSEUM CENTER FOR ART AND CULTURAL HERITAGE, 415 Academy Dr., Abingdon, VA 24210-2617. Mailing Address: P.O. Box 2256, Abingdon, VA 24212-2256. Tel.: 276-628-5005. Fax: 276-628-3922.
E-mail: mmiller@wkmuseum.org
Web Site: www.williamkingmuseum.org
Formerly: William King Regional Arts Center
Key Personnel: Exec. Dir., Marcy Miller; Pres. Bd. (V), Evelyn Goldston; Vice Pres., Joe Lyle; Treas., John Jeter; Treas, Doris Shuman; Sec., Pam Kramer; Cur., Leila Cartier.
Institution Type/Description: Art Museum: housed in 1913 school building.
Hours & Admission Prices: Tues.-Wed. & Fri. 10-5, Thurs. 10-9, Sat.-Sun. 1-5. Adults $5; members no charge. Closed New Year's Eve & Day; Easter; Memorial Day; Independence Day; Labor Day; Thanksgiving; Christmas Eve & Day. &
Attendance: 20,000 (actual)

Alexandria

ALEXANDRIA ARCHAEOLOGY MUSEUM, 105 N. Union St., # 327, Alexandria, VA 22314-3217. Tel.: 709-746-4399. Fax: 703-838-6491. Facebook: Alexandria Archaeology Museum; Twitter: @AlexArchaeology.
E-mail: archaeology@alexandriava.gov
Web Site: www.alexandriava.gov/archaeology
Key Personnel: Acting City Archaeologist, Eleanor Breen; Museum Education Specialist, Emma Richardson; Archaeologist, Garrett Fesler; Archaeologist, Benjamin Skolnik; Museum Technician, Tatiana Niculescu; Admin. Support, Jennifer Barker.
Institution Type/Description: Archaeology Museum.

Hours & Admission Prices: Tues.-Fri. 10-3, Sat. 10-5, Sun. 1-5. No charge; donations accepted. &
Attendance: 54,833 (actual)

ALEXANDRIA BLACK HISTORY MUSEUM, 902 Wythe St., Alexandria, VA 22314-1839. Tel.: 703-838-4356. Fax: 703-706-3999.
E-mail: blackhistory@alexandriava.gov
Web Site: www.alexblackhistory.org
Formerly: Alexandria Black History Resource Center
Key Personnel: Dir., Louis Hicks; Asst. Dir & Cur., Audrey P. Davis; Cur., Lillian Patterson; Sec., Jewel Plummer.
Institution Type/Description: History Museum: located in former public library.
Hours & Admission Prices: Tues.-Sat. 10-4. Admission $2. Closed New Year's Day; Martin Luther King Jr. Day; Easter; Independence Day; Thanksgiving; Christmas. &
Attendance: 10,300 (estimated)

ALEXANDRIA LIBRARY - LOCAL HISTORY & SPECIAL COLLECTIONS, 717 Queen St., Alexandria, VA 22314-2420. Tel.: 703-838-4577. Fax: 703-706-3912.
E-mail: gkcombs@alexandria.lib.va.us
Web Site: www.alexandria.lib.va.us/branches/lhsc.html
Institution Type/Description: Library.
Hours & Admission Prices: Mon. 1-9, Tues. 2-7, Wed. & Fri. 10-7, 1st Sat. of month 10-5. No charge.
Attendance: 14,865 (actual)

ARCHIVES & RECORDS CENTER, 801 S. Payne St., Alexandria, VA 22314. Tel.: 703-746-4591. Fax: 703-519-3326.
E-mail: jackie.cohan@alexandriava.gov
Institution Type/Description: Archives.
Hours & Admission Prices: Mon.-Fri. by appointment.

CARLYLE HOUSE HISTORIC PARK, 121 N. Fairfax St., Alexandria, VA 22314-3229. Tel.: 703-549-2997. Fax: 703-549-5738.
E-mail: carlyle@NVRPA.org
Web Site: www.carlylehouse.org
Key Personnel: Dir., Susan Hellman; Cur., Helen Wirka; Educator, Vanessa Herndon.
Institution Type/Description: Historic House: 1753 Carlyle House, Georgian style, used by General Braddock as headquarters for planning early campaigns of French & Indian War.
Hours & Admission Prices: Tues.-Sat. 10-4, Sun. 12-4. Adults $5, children 11-17 $3; discount to AAM members; members & children 10 & under no charge. Closed New Year's Day; Thanksgiving; Christmas Eve & Day. &
Attendance: 22,000 (actual)

COLLINGWOOD LIBRARY AND MUSEUM ON AMERICANISM, 8301 E. Boulevard Dr., Alexandria, VA 22308-1399. Mailing Address: 3609 Sanders Ln., Catharpin, VA 20143-1037. Tel.: 703-765-1652. Fax: 703-765-8213.
E-mail: pfrank@collingwoodlibrary.org
Web Site: collingwoodlibrary.org
Key Personnel: Exec. Dir. & C.E.O., Paul A. Frank, CFRE; Pres. (V), Kent S. Webber.
Institution Type/Description: American History Museum: housed in 1785 structure used as overseer's house for George Washington's River Farm.
Hours & Admission Prices: Mon.-Fri. 10-4 appointment suggested. No charge; donations accepted. &
Attendance: 9,000 (estimated)

FORT WARD MUSEUM AND HISTORIC SITE, 4301 W. Braddock Rd., Alexandria, VA 22304-1007. Tel.: 703-746-4848. Fax: 703-671-7350.
E-mail: fort.ward@alexandriava.gov
Web Site: oha.alexandriava.gov/fortward/
Key Personnel: Dir., Susan G. Cumbey.
Institution Type/Description: Military Museum: located on the site of 1861-65 Fort Ward, built to protect Washington DC during the Civil War.
Hours & Admission Prices: Museum: Tues.-Sat. 10-5, Sun. 12-5. Park: daily 9-sunset. Office: Tues.-Sat. 9-5. No charge; donations accepted. Closed New Year's Day; Thanksgiving; Christmas. &
Attendance: 40,000 (estimated)

FRANK LLOYD WRIGHT'S POPE-LEIGHEY HOUSE, 9000 Richmond Hwy., Alexandria, VA 22309. Tel.: 703-780-4000. Fax: 703-780-8509. Facebook: Woodlawn & Pope Leighey House;

Instagram: @woodlawnandpopeleighey; Twitter: @woodlawnpopel.
E-mail: woodlawn@savingplaces.org
Web Site: www.woodlawnpopeleighey.org
Key Personnel: Coun. Chm., Peter Christensen; Dir. Site Interpretation & Partnerships, Amanda Phillips; Program Asst. for Events & Fundraising, Jackie Devine.
Institution Type/Description: Historic House: 1940 Frank Lloyd Wright Usonian house, located on the grounds of Woodlawn.
Hours & Admission Prices: March-Nov. Fri.-Mon. 12-4. Adults $10, seniors & active-duty military $8, students K-12 $5; discounts to NTHP members.
Attendance: 10,500 (actual)

FRIENDSHIP FIREHOUSE MUSEUM, 107 S. Alfred St., Alexandria, VA 22314-3001. Tel.: 703-746-3891 & 4994. Fax: 703-838-4997.
E-mail: friendship@alexandriava.gov
Web Site: www.friendshipfirehouse.org
Formerly: Friendship Firehouse
Key Personnel: Lyceum Dir., Jim Mackay; Chmn. (V), Joe Shumard.
Institution Type/Description: Firehouse Museum: housed in c.1855 Italianate-style brick building which has a first-floor engine room for storing apparatus & a second-floor meeting room for social & ceremonial activities.
Hours & Admission Prices: Sat.-Sun. 1-4. Adults $2; discounts to AAM & ICOM members. Closed New Year's Day; Thanksgiving; Christmas. &
Attendance: 3,896 (actual)

GADSBY'S TAVERN MUSEUM, 134 N. Royal St., Alexandria, VA 22314-3226. Tel.: 703-746-4242. Fax: 703-838-4270.
E-mail: gadsbys.tavern@alexandriava.gov
Web Site: gadsbystavern.org
Key Personnel: Dir., Gretchen M. Bulova; Asst. Dir., Lizabeth Williams; Cur. Collections, Callie Stapp; Cur. Education, Michele Longo; Museum Shop Mgr., Sue Walker.
Institution Type/Description: Historic Buildings: c.1785 tavern; 1792 Federal style City Hotel.
Hours & Admission Prices: April-Oct. Sun.-Mon. 1-5, Tues.-Sat. 10-5; Nov.-March Wed.-Sat. 11-4, Sun. 1-4. Adults $5, children 5-12 $3; discounts to groups, and AAM, VAM, HHMC & ICOM members; children under 5 no charge. Closed major holidays.
Attendance: 25,000 (actual)

GEORGE WASHINGTON MASONIC NATIONAL MEMORIAL, 101 Callahan Dr., Alexandria, VA 22301-2751. Tel.: 703-683-2007. Fax: 703-519-9270.
E-mail: gseghers@gwmemorial.org
Web Site: www.gwmemorial.org
Formerly: George Washington Masonic Memorial
Key Personnel: Exec. Dir., George D. Seghers; Chm. (V), Ridgely H. Gilmour; Dir. Collections, Mark A. Tabbert; Dir. Communications, Shawn E. Eyer; Special Events Administration, Radka Mavrova.
Institution Type/Description: History Museum.
Hours & Admission Prices: Daily 9-5. General Admission $15; children 12 & under no charge. Closed New Year's Day; Veterans Day; Memorial Day; Independence Day; Labor Day; Thanksgiving; Christmas. &
Attendance: 35,000 (estimated)

JEROME "BUDDIE" FORD NATURE CENTER, 5750 Sanger Ave., Alexandria, VA 22311-5602. Tel.: 703-838-4829; 746-5559.
E-mail: mark.kelly@alexandriava.gov
Web Site: alexandriava.gov/recreation/info/default.aspx?id=12362
Key Personnel: Dir., Mark S. Kelly.
Institution Type/Description: Nature Center.
Hours & Admission Prices: April-Nov. Wed.-Sat. 10-5, Sun. 1-5; Dec.-March Wed.-Sat. 10-5. No charge; donations accepted. Closed holidays. &
Attendance: 23,500 (actual)

LEE-FENDALL HOUSE MUSEUM AND GARDEN, 614 Oronoco St., Alexandria, VA 22314-2308. Tel.: 703-548-1789. Fax: 703-229-6350. Facebook: Lee Fendall House Museum & Garden.
E-mail: contact@leefendallhouse.org
Web Site: www.leefendallhouse.org
Key Personnel: Exec. Dir., Erin Adams.
Institution Type/Description: Historic House: 1785 Lee-Fendall House, Lee family home & former home of labor leader John L. Lewis, located in Alexandria's Old Town Historic District.
Hours & Admission Prices: Feb. to mid-Dec. Wed.-Sat. 10-3, Sun. 1-3. Adults $5, children 5-17 $3; discounts to NTHP, AAM & ICOM members; children 4 & under no charge. Closed major holidays; private events.
Attendance: 9,500 (actual)

THE LYCEUM, ALEXANDRIA'S HISTORY MUSEUM, 201 S. Washington St., Alexandria, VA 22314-3697. Tel.: 703-746-4994. Fax: 703-838-4997. Facebook: The Lyceum Alexandria's History Museum.
E-mail: lyceum@alexandriava.gov
Web Site: www.alexandriahistory.org
Key Personnel: Dir., James C. Mackay; Asst. Dir., Kristin B. Lloyd; Visitor Svcs., Pamela Budde.
Institution Type/Description: History Museum; housed in 1839 The Lyceum.
Hours & Admission Prices: Mon.-Sat. 10-5, Sun. 1-5. Adults $2; discounts to AAM members. Closed New Year's Day; Thanksgiving; Christmas Eve & Day. &
Attendance: 27,902 (estimated)

NATIONAL INVENTORS HALL OF FAME, 600 Dulany St. Madison W., Alexandria, VA 22314. Mailing Address: 3701 Highland Park, N.W., North Canton, OH 44720. Tel.: 571-272-0095. Fax: 703-706-0484.
E-mail: museum@invent.org
Web Site: www.invent.org
Key Personnel: Exec. Dir., Rini Paiva; Dir. Merchandising & Store Operations, Mitch Scott.
Institution Type/Description: Science & History Museum.
Hours & Admission Prices: Mon.-Fri. 9-5, Sat. 12-5. No charge. Closed federal holidays. &
Attendance: 70,000 (estimated)

THE NORTHERN VIRGINIA FINE ARTS ASSOCIATION AT THE ATHENAEUM, 201 Prince St., Alexandria, VA 22314-3313. Tel.: 703-548-0035.
E-mail: admin@nvfaa.org
Web Site: www.nvfaa.org
Key Personnel: Exec. Dir., Veronica Szalus; Opers. Dir., Thomas Schultz; Pres., Amy Heiden.
Institution Type/Description: Art Gallery; housed in 1851, restored Greek Revival Building.
Hours & Admission Prices: Thurs.-Fri. & Sun. 12-4, Sat. 1-4. Athenaeum: no charge. Lecture & performance fees discounted for members. Closed major holidays.
Attendance: 41,000 (estimated)

OFFICE OF HISTORIC ALEXANDRIA, 220 N. Washington St., Alexandria, VA 22314-2521. Tel.: 703-746-4554. Fax: 703-838-6451. Facebook.
E-mail: historicalexandria@alexandriava.gov
Web Site: historicalexandria.org
Key Personnel: Dir. Office of Historic Alexandria, J. Lance Mallamo; Deputy Dir. Office of Historic Alexandria & Dir. Stabler-Leadbeater Apothecary Museum, Gretchen Bulova; Dir. The Lyceum, Alexandria's History Museum & Dir. Friendship Firehouse, James C. Mackay, III; Dir. Alexandria Archaeology, Francine Bromberg; Dir. Alexandria Black History Museum, Audrey P. Davis; Dir. Fort Ward Museum & Historic Site, Susan G. Cumbey; Gadsby's Tavern Museum, Liz Williams.
Institution Type/Description: Historical Agency.
Hours & Admission Prices: Office: Mon.-Fri. 8-5. For times & admissions see individual listings. &
Attendance: 175,000 (actual)

RAMSAY HOUSE VISITORS CENTER, 221 King St., Alexandria, VA 22314-3209. Tel.: 703-746-3301. TDD: 703-838-6494.
Web Site: visitalexandriava.com/
Key Personnel: Pres. & C.E.O., Stephanie Brown; Mgr., Renee Cardone.
Institution Type/Description: Historic House & Visitor Center: c.1724 home of William Ramsay, First Lord Mayor, first postmaster.
Hours & Admission Prices: Daily 10-8. No charge; donations accepted. Closed New Year's Day; Thanksgiving; Christmas. &
Attendance: 194,256

STABLER-LEADBEATER APOTHECARY MUSEUM, 105-107 S. Fairfax St., Alexandria, VA 22314. Tel.: 703-746-3852. Fax: 703-838-4270.
E-mail: apothecary.museum@alexandriava.gov
Web Site: www.apothecarymuseum.org
Key Personnel: Site Mgr., Lauren Gleason.
Institution Type/Description: Pharmaceutical Museum; housed in 1796 drugstore building.
Hours & Admission Prices: April-Oct. Sun.-Mon. 1-5, Tues.-Sat. 10-5; Nov.-March Wed.-Sat. 11-4, Sun. 1-4. Adults $5, children 5-12 $3; discounts to AAM, VAM & HHMC members; members no charge. Closed Thanksgiving; Christmas.
Attendance: 10,000 (estimated)

TORPEDO FACTORY ART CENTER, 105 N. Union St., Alexandria, VA 22314-3217. Tel.: 703-838-4565. Fax: 888-882-7695. Facebook: Torpedo Factory Art Center.
E-mail: marketing@torpedofactory.org
Web Site: www.torpedofactory.org
Key Personnel: Pres., Mike Detomo.
Institution Type/Description: Art Center & Archaeology Museum: housed in World War II torpedo factory.
Hours & Admission Prices: Thurs. 10-9, Fri.-Wed. 10-6. No charge. Closed New Year's Day; Easter; Independence Day; Thanksgiving; Christmas. &
Attendance: 500,000 (estimated)

WOODLAWN, 9000 Richmond Hwy., Alexandria, VA 22309. Tel.: 703-780-4000. Fax: 703-780-8509. Facebook: Woodlawn & Pope Leighey House; Instagram: @woodlawnandpopeleighey; Twitter: @woodlawnpopel.
E-mail: woodlawn@savingplaces.org
Web Site: www.woodlawnpopeleighey.org
Key Personnel: Chm. Council, Peter Christensen; Dir. Site Interpretation & Partnerships, Amanda Phillips; Program Asst. for Events & Fundraising, Jackie Devine.
Institution Type/Description: Historic House: 1800-1805 Woodlawn Home of Maj. Lawrence & Eleanor Parke Custis Lewis, nephew and granddaughter of George & Martha Washington.
Hours & Admission Prices: March-Nov. Fri.-Mon. 12-4. Adults $10, seniors & active-duty military $8, students K-12 $5; discounts to NTHP members.
Attendance: 10,500 (actual)

Altavista

AVOCA MUSEUM, 1514 Main St., Altavista, VA 24517-1161. Tel.: 434-369-1076. Fax: 434-369-1077 (call first).
E-mail: avocamuseums@embarqmail.com
Web Site: www.avocamuseum.org
Key Personnel: Dir., Michael Hudson.
Institution Type/Description: History Museum.
Hours & Admission Prices: mid-April to Oct. Thurs.-Sat. 11-3, Sun. 1:30-4:30; call to confirm hours. Adults $5, seniors $4; members no charge. &

Amherst

AMHERST COUNTY MUSEUM & HISTORICAL SOCIETY, 154 S. Main St., Amherst, VA 24521. Mailing Address: P.O. Box 741, Amherst, VA 24521-0741. Tel.: 434-946-9068.
E-mail: staff@amherstcountymuseum.org
Web Site: www.amherstcountymuseum.org/
Key Personnel: Dir., Octavia Starbuck; Genealogist, Midge Elliott.
Institution Type/Description: County History Museum: housed in 1907 Georgian Revival house; reconstructed one-room schoolhouse.
Hours & Admission Prices: Tues.-Fri. 10-4. No charge; donations accepted. Closed major holidays. &
Attendance: 1,500 (actual)

Appomattox

APPOMATTOX COURT HOUSE NATIONAL HISTORICAL PARK, VA Rte. 24, Appomattox, VA 24522. Mailing Address: P. O. Box 218, Appomattox, VA 24522-0218. Tel.: 434-352-8987, ext. 26. Fax: 434-352-8330.
E-mail: joe_williams@nps.gov
Web Site: www.nps.gov/apco
Key Personnel: Supt., Robin Snyder; Historian, Patrick Schroeder; Chief Museum Svcs., Ann Roos; Admin. Officer, David Richardson; Chief Education & Visitor Svcs., Beth Parnicza; Chief Natural Resources, Brian Eick.
Institution Type/Description: Historic Village Museum: located on the site where General Lee surrendered to General Grant to end the Civil War.
Hours & Admission Prices: Visitor Center: daily 8:30-5. Call for admission prices. Closed New Year's Day; Martin Luther King Jr. Day; Presidents' Day; Thanksgiving; Christmas. &
Attendance: 200,000 (actual)

Arlington

ARLINGTON ARTS CENTER, 3550 Wilson Blvd., Arlington, VA 22201-2348. Tel.: 703-248-6800. Fax: 703-248-6849.
E-mail: information@arlingtonartscenter.org
Web Site: www.arlingtonartscenter.org
Key Personnel: Exec. Dir., Stefanie Fedor; Pres., Jerrie Bethel; Dir. Education, Penelope Nunes; Exhibitions Coord., Catherine Satterlee; Administrative & Mktg. Coord., Samantha Marques-Moudkofsky.

Institution Type/Description: Art Center: housed in 1910 Matthew F. Maury School.
Hours & Admission Prices: Wed.-Fri. 1-7, Sat.-Sun. 12-5. No charge; donations accepted. ♿
Attendance: 30,000 (estimated)

ARLINGTON HISTORICAL MUSEUM & SOCIETY, INC., 1805 S. Arlington Ridge Rd., Arlington, VA 22202-1628. Mailing Address: P.O. Box 100402, Arlington, VA 22210-3402. Tel.: 703-892-4204. Facebook: Arlington Historical Society.
E-mail: info@arlingtonhistoricalsociety.org
Web Site: www.arlingtonhistoricalsociety.org
Key Personnel: Dir., Dr. Mark Benbow; Pres. (V), John P. Richardson; Museum Shop Mgr., Eleanor Pourron.
Institution Type/Description: Historical Society & Museum: housed in the former Hume School; built in 1891.
Hours & Admission Prices: Sat.-Sun. 1-4; other times by appointment. No charge; donations accepted.
Attendance: 1,000 (estimated)

ARLINGTON HOUSE, THE ROBERT E. LEE MEMORIAL, Arlington National Cemetery, Arlington, VA 22211. Mailing Address: George Washington Memorial Pkwy., c/o Turkey Run Park, McLean, VA 22101. Tel.: 703-289-2500. Fax: 703-235-1546.
E-mail: gwmp-arlingtonhouse@nps.gov
Web Site: www.nps.gov/arho
Key Personnel: Park Supt., Alex Romero; Site Mgr., Brandon Bies.
Institution Type/Description: Historic House Museum: residence of Gen. Robert E. Lee, built by George Washington Parke Custis, foster son of George Washington, restored to 1861 appearance as a national memorial to General Lee.
Hours & Admission Prices: March-May & Sept. daily 9-5; June-Aug. daily 9-5:30; Oct.-Feb. daily 9:30-4:30. No charge. Closed New Year's Day; Christmas. ♿
Attendance: 500,000 (actual)

BALL-SELLERS HOUSE, 5620 Third St. S., Arlington, VA 22204-1118. Mailing Address: P.O. Box 100402, Arlington, VA 22210-3402. Tel.: 703-892-4204. Facebook: Ball-Sellers House.
E-mail: info@arlingtonhistoricalsociety.org
Web Site: www.arlingtonhistoricalsociety.org
Key Personnel: Chm. (V), Annette Benbow.
Institution Type/Description: Historic House Museum: housed in the log cabin built by John Ball c.1750s; addition built in 1880.
Hours & Admission Prices: April-Oct. Sat. 1-4. No charge; donations accepted.
Attendance: 250 (estimated)

BLUEMONT HISTORICAL RAILROAD JUNCTION, 601 N. Manchester St., Arlington, VA 22205. Mailing Address: 2100 Clarendon Blvd., Ste. 414, Arlington, VA 22201. Tel.: 703-525-0294.
Key Personnel: Ranger, Sedgewick Moss; Ranger Coord., Lynne Everly.
Institution Type/Description: Transportation Museum: housed in former Southern Railway Caboose X-441, built in 1972, on the W&OD trail.
Hours & Admission Prices: May-Sept. Sat. & holidays 10-6, Sun. 1-5. No charge; donations accepted.
Attendance: 5,000 (estimated)

GULF BRANCH NATURE CENTER, 3608 N. Military Rd., Arlington, VA 22207-4830. Tel.: 703-228-3403.
E-mail: gulfbranchnaturectr@arlingtonva.us
Web Site: www.arlingtonva.us
Key Personnel: Dir., Denise Chauvette.
Institution Type/Description: Nature Center.
Hours & Admission Prices: Tues.-Sat. 10-5, Sun. 1-5. No charge.

LEE ARTS CENTER, 5722 Lee Hwy., Arlington, VA 22207. Tel.: 703-228-0560. Fax: 703-228-0559.
E-mail: leearts@arlingtonva.us
Web Site: www.arlingtonarts.org
Key Personnel: Dir., Steven Munoz.
Institution Type/Description: Art Gallery.
Hours & Admission Prices: Mon. & Fri. 9:30-6, Tues.-Thurs. 9:30-9, Sat. 9:30-5.

LONG BRANCH NATURE CENTER, 625 S. Carlin Springs Rd., Arlington, VA 22204-1000. Tel.: 703-228-6535. Fax: 703-845-2654.
E-mail: aabugattas@arlingtonva.us
Key Personnel: Acting Dir., Alonso Abugattas.
Institution Type/Description: Nature Center.
Hours & Admission Prices: Tues.-Sat. 10-5, Sun. 1-5. No charge. ♿

THE NATURE CONSERVANCY, 4245 N. Fairfax Dr., Ste. 100, Arlington, VA 22203-1606. Tel.: 703-841-5300. Fax: 703-841-1283.
E-mail: member@tnc.org
Web Site: www.nature.org
Key Personnel: Pres. & C.E.O., Mark R. Tercek; Coord., Maria Fisher.
Institution Type/Description: Conservation Area: educational & passive recreational opportunities on largest private nature preserve system in country.
Hours & Admission Prices: Mon.-Fri. 9-5. No charge; donations accepted. Closed federal holidays.
Attendance: 200,500 (estimated)

Ashland

FLIPPO GALLERY, Randolph-Macon College, Pace-Armistead Hall, 211 N. Center St., Ashland, VA 23005. Tel.: 804-752-4707.
E-mail: kimberlyberry@rmc.edu
Web Site: www.rmc.edu/departments/studio-arts/flippo-gallery
Key Personnel: Cur., Kimberly Berry.
Institution Type/Description: Art Gallery: housed in Pace-Armistead Hall, c.1876. Listed on the National Register of Historic Places.
Hours & Admission Prices: Mon.-Fri. 10-4; other times by appointment.

Bastian

WOLF CREEK INDIAN VILLAGE & MUSEUM, 6394 N. Scenic Hwy., Bastian, VA 24314-5202. Tel.: 276-688-3438. Fax: 276-688-2496.
E-mail: jwilliams@indianvillage.org
Web Site: indianvillage.org
Key Personnel: General Mgr., Jaime K. Williams; Museum Program Coord, WCIV, Jaime Williams.
Institution Type/Description: American Indian History Museum.
Hours & Admission Prices: Tues.-Sat. 9-5. Adults $10, children 6-12 $6; discounts to AAA, AAM, & ICOM members & groups of 10 or more; children 5 & under and members no charge. Closed Thanksgiving; Christmas Eve & Day. ♿
Attendance: 30,000 (estimated)

Beaverdam

PATRICK HENRY'S SCOTCHTOWN, 16120 Chiswell Lane, Beaverdam, VA 23015-1726. Mailing Address: 204 W. Franklin St., Richmond, VA 23220. Tel.: 804-227-3500. Fax: 804-227-3559.
E-mail: scotchtown@preservationvirginia.org
Web Site: www.preservationvirginia.org/scotchtown
Key Personnel: Site Mgr., Ann Reid; C.E.O., Elizabeth Kostelny; Dir. Properties, Louis J. Malon; Dir. Museum Operations & Education, Jennifer Hurst-Wender; Coord. Digital Communications, Krysha Snyder.
Institution Type/Description: Historic House Museum: housed in the home of Patrick Henry, 1771-1778, the first elected governor of Virginia and the residence from where he rode to St. John's Church to give his Give Me Liberty or Give Me Death speech.
Hours & Admission Prices: March-Dec. Fri. 10-5, Sun. 12-5; other times by appointment. Adults $8, AAA members $7, seniors $6, students $5; preservation members & children under 6 no charge. Closed Easter; Christmas Eve & Day.
Attendance: 2,308 (actual)

Bedford

BEDFORD MUSEUM AND GENEALOGICAL LIBRARY, 201 E. Main St., Bedford, VA 24523-2012. Tel.: 540-586-4520.
E-mail: bccm-info@bedfordvamuseum.org
Web Site: www.bedfordvamuseum.org
Formerly: Bedford City/County Museum
Key Personnel: Dir., Doug Cooper; Chm. (V) & Cur., Annie Polland; Aide, Grace Peterson; Museum Shop Mgr., Shirley Wheeler.
Institution Type/Description: History Museum & Historic Building: c.1895 three-story Masonic building.
Hours & Admission Prices: June-Sept. Mon.-Sat. 10-5. No charge; donations accepted. ♿
Attendance: 8,725 (actual)

NATIONAL D-DAY MEMORIAL, 3 Overlord Cir., Bedford, VA 24523. Mailing Address: P.O. Box 77, Bedford, VA 24523. Tel.: 540-587-3619.
E-mail: dday@dday.org
Web Site: www.dday.org
Institution Type/Description: Military Memorial: honoring the Allied forces that participated in the invasion of Normandy on June 6, 1944 during World War II.

Hours & Admission Prices: March-Nov. daily 10-5; Dec.-Feb. Tues.-Sun.10-5. Purchase tickets at the Bedford Area Welcome Center: adults $10, veterans & active military $8, students 6-18 $6; children under 6 no charge. Closed New Year's Day; Thanksgiving; Christmas. &
Attendance: 50,000 (actual)

PEAKS OF OTTER VISITOR CENTER, 85919 Blue Ridge Pkwy., Bedford, VA 24523-3795. Tel.: 540-586-4357. Fax: 540-586-9445.
Web Site: www.nps.gov/blri
Key Personnel: District Ranger, Paulette Mullinox; Interpretive Specialist, Randy Sutton; Park Ranger, Bobby Miller.
Institution Type/Description: Natural History & Cultural Museum.
Hours & Admission Prices: late April to May Fri.-Tues. 9-5; Memorial Day to Oct. daily 9-5. No charge.

Berryville

CLARKE COUNTY HISTORICAL ASSOCIATION, INC., 32 E. Main St., Berryville, VA 22611-1338. Mailing Address: P.O. Box 306, Berryville, VA 22611-0306. Tel.: 540-955-2600. Fax: 540-955-0285.
E-mail: admin@clarkehistory.org
Web Site: www.clarkehistory.org
Key Personnel: Dir., Laura Christiansen; Pres. (V), Howard Means; Treas., Lucia Henderson; Archivist, Mary T. Morris.
Institution Type/Description: Historical Society Museum: housed in 19th-century home.
Hours & Admission Prices: Museum: call for hours. Archives: Mon.-Fri. 10-5. Museum: no charge; donations accepted. Archives: adults $5; members & locals no charge. Closed New Year's Eve, Day & day after; Christmas Eve, Day & week. &
Attendance: 1,000 (estimated)

Big Stone Gap

HARRY W. MEADOR, JR. COAL MUSEUM, E. Third and Shawnee Ave., Big Stone Gap, VA 24219. Mailing Address: 505 E. 5th St. S., Big Stone Gap, VA 24219-3050. Tel.: 276-523-9209.
E-mail: tfranklin@bigstonegap.org
Web Site: www.bigstonegap.org/attract/coal.htm
Key Personnel: Dir., Tammy Franklin.
Institution Type/Description: Coal Mining Museum.
Hours & Admission Prices: Wed.-Sat. 10-5, Sun. 1-5; other times by appointment. No charge.

SOUTHWEST VIRGINIA MUSEUM HISTORICAL STATE PARK, 10 W. 1st St. N., Big Stone Gap, VA 24219-2528. Mailing Address: c/o Friends of the SW Virginia Museum, 106 W. 1st St. N, Big Stone Gap, VA 24219-2530. Tel.: 276-523-1322.
E-mail: resvs@dcr.virginia.gov
Web Site: www.swvamuseum.org
Key Personnel: Dir., Sharon B. Ewing.
Institution Type/Description: State Park & Historic House: 1888-95 Ayers Mansion.
Hours & Admission Prices: March-May & Sept.-Dec. Tues.-Thurs. 10-4, Fri. 9-4, Sat. 10-5, Sun. 1-5; Memorial Day-Labor Day Mon.-Thurs. 10-4, Fri. 9-4, Sat. 10-5, Sun. 1-5. Adults $4, children 6-12 $2; discounts to groups, AAM & ICOM members; children under 6 no charge. Closed Thanksgiving; Christmas.
Attendance: 19,984 (actual)

Blacksburg

BLACKSBURG CHILDREN'S MUSEUM, 1470 S. Main St., Ste. 106, Blacksburg, VA 24060. Tel.: 540-953-0103.
E-mail: info@blacksburgchildrensmuseum.org
Web Site: childrensmuseumofblacksburg.org
Key Personnel: Coord. Operations & Special Programs, Julene Rice; Coord. Exhibits, Candace Willis; Coord. Exhibits, Tess Brooke; Coord. Events, Jana Cranwell; Mktg., Melissa Richards; Mktg., Janet Novoselich.
Institution Type/Description: Children's Museum.
Hours & Admission Prices: Sat.-Sun. 10-5. Admission $5; members no charge.

HISTORIC SMITHFIELD PLANTATION, 1000 Smithfield Plantation Rd., Blacksburg, VA 24060. Tel.: 540-231-3947. Fax: 540-231-3006.
E-mail: info@smithfieldplantation.org
Web Site: smithfieldplantation.org
Key Personnel: Dir. Bd., Joann Sutphin; Administrative Dir., Douglas W. Anderson; Museum Shop Mgr., Judy Foster.

Institution Type/Description: Historic House: 1774 Smithfield Plantation built by Revolutionary War hero, William Preston & later the home of three Virginia Governors.
Hours & Admission Prices: March to 1st weekend in Dec. Mon.-Tues. & Thurs.-Sat. 10-5, Sun. 1-5; special tours by appointment. Adults $8, students $5, children 5-11 $3; discounts to military, AAA members & groups.
Attendance: 5,500 (estimated)

MUSEUM OF GEOSCIENCES, Virginia Tech, 2062 Derring Hall, 926 W. Campus Dr., Blacksburg, VA 24061. Tel.: 540-231-6894. Fax: 540-231-3386.
E-mail: mogs@vt.edu
Web Site: www.geos.vt.edu/museum-of-geosciences
Formerly: Museum of the Geological Sciences
Key Personnel: Dir., Dr. Robert J. Tracy; Coord., Llyn Sharp.
Institution Type/Description: Geology & Mineralogy Museum.
Hours & Admission Prices: During academic semesters Mon.-Fri. 8-5; call to confirm. No charge; donations accepted. Closed holidays; university breaks. &
Attendance: 8,000 (actual)

PERSPECTIVE GALLERY, Virginia Tech/Aquires Student Center, Blacksburg, VA 24061. Tel.: 540-231-4053. Fax: 540-231-5430.
E-mail: squiresgallery@ut.edu
Web Site: www.studentcenters.vt.edu/perspectivegallery/index.php
Key Personnel: Art Dir., Robin Scully Boucher.
Institution Type/Description: Art Gallery.
Hours & Admission Prices: Academic Year: Tues.-Sat. 12-9, Sun. 1-5. No charge. Closed during academic breaks. &
Attendance: 6,785 (actual)

Boyce

ORLAND E. WHITE ARBORETUM, Blandy Experimental Farm, 400 Blandy Farm Lane, Boyce, VA 22620-2117. Tel.: 540-837-1758. Fax: 540-837-1523.
E-mail: blandy@virginia.edu
Web Site: blandy.virginia.edu
Key Personnel: Dir., Dr. David E. Carr; Cur., Dr. T'ai H. Roulston; Dir., Foundation of State Arboretum, Martha Bjelland; Pres., Foundation of State Arboretum, Bruce Downing; Arborist, Robert D. Arnold; Public Rels. Coord., Tim Farmer; Dir. Education, Candace Lutzow-Felling; Dir. Pub. Programs, Dr. Steven B. Carroll; Landscape Architect, Nancy Takahashi; Bldg. Supt., Dennis Heflin.
Institution Type/Description: Arboretum.
Hours & Admission Prices: Daily dawn to dusk; tours by appointment. Office: Mon.-Fri. 9-4. No charge; donations accepted.
Attendance: 150,000 (estimated)

Bridgewater

REUEL B. PRITCHETT MUSEUM, Bridgewater College, 402 E. College St., Bridgewater, VA 22812. Tel.: 540-828-5462. Fax: 540-828-5482.
E-mail: sgardner@bridgewater.edu
Web Site: www.bridgewater.edu
Key Personnel: Dir. Library & Museum, Andrew Pearson; Cur., Stephanie Gardner.
Institution Type/Description: College Museum.
Hours & Admission Prices: Temporary closed. &

Bristol

BIRTHPLACE OF COUNTRY MUSIC MUSEUM, 520 Birthplace of Country Music Way, Bristol, VA 24201. Mailing Address: P.O. Box 1927, Bristol, VA 24203. Tel.: 423-573-1927. Fax: 423-573-4877.
E-mail: info@birthplaceofcountrymusic.org
Web Site: www.birthplaceofcountrymusic.org
Key Personnel: Dir., Dr. Jessica Turner; C.E.O., Leah Ross; Museum Shop Mgr., Landy Mathes.
Institution Type/Description: Music Museum.
Hours & Admission Prices: Tues.-Sat. 10-6, Sun. 1-5. Adults $13, seniors, students, military & children 6-17 $11; children 5 & under no charge. Closed major holidays. &

Brookneal

RED HILL-PATRICK HENRY NATIONAL MEMORIAL, 1250 Red Hill Rd., Brookneal, VA 24528-3302. Tel.: 434-376-2044. Fax: 434-376-2647. Facebook: Patrick Henry's Red Hill.
E-mail: redhill@redhill.org
Web Site: www.redhill.org

Key Personnel: Chm., Mark Holman; C.O,O,, Hope Marstin; C.E.O., Scott Brown; Museum Shop Mgr., Bonnie George.
Institution Type/Description: Historic Site: Last home & burial place of Patrick Henry.
Hours & Admission Prices: April-Oct. Mon.-Sat. 9-5, Sun. 1-5; Nov.-March Mon.-Sat. 9-4, Sun. 1-4. Adults $8, students $4; discounts to groups, seniors, AAA, military & NPS. Closed New Year's Day; Thanksgiving; Christmas. craft
Attendance: 9,289 (actual)

Cape Charles

CAPE CHARLES MUSEUM AND WELCOME CENTER, 814 Randolph Ave., Cape Charles, VA 23310. Mailing Address: The Cape Charles Historical Society, P.O. Box 11, Cape Charles, VA 23310-0011. Tel.: 757-331-1008.
E-mail: ccmuseum@hughes.net
Web Site: www.smallmuseum.org/capechas.html
Key Personnel: Pres. (V), Marion Naar; Museum Shop Mgr., Mary Morris.
Institution Type/Description: History Museum.
Hours & Admission Prices: April-Nov. Mon.-Fri. 10-2, Sat. 10-5, Sun. 1-5. No charge; donations accepted. craft
Attendance: 3,033 (actual)

Chantilly

NATIONAL AIR AND SPACE MUSEUM - STEVEN F. UDVAR-HAZY CENTER, SMITHSONIAN INSTITUTION, 14390 Air & Space Museum Pkwy., Chantilly, VA 20151. Mailing Address: P.O. Box 37012, Washington, DC 20013-7012. Tel.: 703-572-4118.
E-mail: nasm-visitorservices@si.edu
Web Site: airandspace.si.edu/udvarhazy
Key Personnel: John & Adrienne Mars Dir., Ellen Stofan; Deputy Dir., Christopher Browne; Assoc. Dir. External Affairs, Meg Caulk; Broh-Kahn Weil Dir. Ed., Beth Crownover; Assoc Dir. Collections, Archives, & Logistics, Rick Flansburg; Dir. Advancement, Laura Gleason; Chief Cur., Peter L. Jakab; Asst. Dir. Business Opers. & Tech., Stephanie A. Brinley; Asst. Dir. Exhibits, Francisco Torres.
Institution Type/Description: Aviation & Space Museum.
Hours & Admission Prices: Daily 10-5:30. (All visitors screened upon entry). Center: no charge. Parking: $15. Closed Christmas. craft
Attendance: 1,600,000 (actual)

WALNEY VISITOR CENTER-AT ELLANOR C. LAWRENCE PARK, 5040 Walney Rd., Chantilly, VA 20151-2306. Tel.: 703-631-0013. Fax: 703-653-6604.
Web Site: www.fairfaxcounty.gov/parks/eclawrence
Key Personnel: Park & Visitor Center Mgr. and Naturalist, John Shafer.
Institution Type/Description: Visitor Center: housed in 1780 structure, located on 650-acre park.
Hours & Admission Prices: Jan.-Feb. Wed.-Mon. 12-5; March-Dec. Mon. & Wed.-Fri. 9-5, Sat.-Sun. 12-5. No charge; donations accepted. Closed New Year's Day; Thanksgiving; Christmas. craft
Attendance: 47,830 (actual)

Charles City

BERKELEY PLANTATION, 12602 Harrison Landing Rd., Charles City, VA 23030-3339. Tel.: 804-829-6018, 888-466-6018. Fax: 804-829-6757.
E-mail: info@berkeleyplantation.com
Web Site: www.berkeleyplantation.com
Key Personnel: Owner & Operator, Malcolm E. Jamieson.
Institution Type/Description: Historic House: 1726 Berkeley Plantation.
Hours & Admission Prices: Tours daily 9:30-4:30. Adults $11, students 13-16 $7.50, children 6-12 $6; discounts to groups, senior citizens, military & AAA members. Closed Thanksgiving; Christmas.

NORTH BEND PLANTATION, 12200 Weyanoke Rd., Charles City, VA 23030. Tel.: 804-829-5176.
Institution Type/Description: Historic House Museum: built in 1801. Listed on the National Register of Historic Places.
Hours & Admission Prices: House Tours: by appointment only, Adults $10; Grounds: daily 9-5, Adults $3.

SHERWOOD FOREST PLANTATION, 14501 John Tyler Memorial Hwy., Charles City, VA 23030. Mailing Address: P.O. Box 104, Charles City, VA 23030-0008. Tel.: 804-829-5377.
E-mail: annique@sherwoodforest.org
Web Site: www.sherwoodforest.org

Key Personnel: Exec. Dir., Annique Dunning.
Institution Type/Description: Historic House: c.1730, home of Pres. John Tyler.
Hours & Admission Prices: Grounds: daily 9-5. Adults $10; children under 15 no charge. House Tours: by appointment. Adults $35. Closed Thanksgiving; Christmas. craft
Attendance: 5,000 (estimated)

SHIRLEY PLANTATION FOUNDATION, 501 Shirley Plantation Rd., Charles City, VA 23030-2907. Tel.: 804-829-5121. Fax: 888-600-6308.
E-mail: info@shirleyplantation.com
Web Site: www.shirleyplantation.com
Key Personnel: Gen. Mgr., Lauren Carter.
Institution Type/Description: Historic Site: Virginia's first plantation, 1613.
Hours & Admission Prices: Daily 9:30-4. Adults $12.50, senior 60 & over $11.50, youth 7-16 $8.50; discounts to AAA & AAM members, groups of 10 or more, & military w/ID; children 6 & under no charge. Closed Thanksgiving; Christmas Eve & Day.
Attendance: 35,000 (actual)

Charlottesville

ALBEMARLE CHARLOTTESVILLE HISTORICAL SOCIETY, McIntire Bldg., 200 Second St., NE, Charlottesville, VA 22902-5245. Tel.: 434-296-1492. Fax: 434-296-4576.
E-mail: info@albemarlehistory.org
Web Site: albemarlehistory.org
Formerly: The Albemarle County Historical Society
Key Personnel: Pres., Steven G. Meeks; Librarian, Margaret M. O'Bryant; Communications & Collections Mgr., Keri Matthews.
Institution Type/Description: Historical Society Museum.
Hours & Admission Prices: Library: Mon.-Fri. 9-5, Sat. 10-1. No charge; donations accepted. Closed holidays. craft

ASH LAWN-HIGHLAND, 2050 James Monroe Pkwy., Charlottesville, VA 22902-7505. Tel.: 434-293-8000. Fax: 434-979-9181.
E-mail: info@ashlawnhighland.org
Web Site: ashlawnhighland.org
Key Personnel: Exec. Dir., Sara Bon-Harper; Mktg., Communications & Events Mgr., Katie Falcone; Business Mgr., Nancy Stahon; Education Programs Mgr., Nancy Stetz; Museum Shop Mgr., Barbara Hensley.
Institution Type/Description: Historic House: 1799 Ash Lawn-Highland house built by James Monroe with 535-acre working plantation.
Hours & Admission Prices: April-Oct. Mon.-Fri. 9-6, Sat.-Sun. 9-5:30; Nov.-March Mon.-Fri. 11-5, Sat.-Sun. 11-4:30. Adults $14, seniors $12, children 6-11 $8; discounts to groups, military, AAM, ICOM & AAA members; members & children under 6 no charge. Closed New Year's Day; Thanksgiving; Christmas. craft
Attendance: 68,000 (actual)

THE FRALIN MUSEUM OF ART AT THE UNIVERSITY OF VIRGINIA, 155 Rugby Rd., Charlottesville, VA 22904-4119. Mailing Address: P.O. Box 400119, Charlottesville, VA 22904-4119. Tel.: 434-924-3592. Fax: 434-924-6321. Facebook.
E-mail: mmp4pe@virginia.edu
Web Site: www.virginia.edu/artmuseum
Formerly: Bayly Art Museum of the University of Virginia; University of Virginia Art Museum
Key Personnel: Dir. & Chief Cur., Matthew McLendon; Academic Cur., Education Dept., M. Jordan Love; Dir. Devel., Elizabeth Wright; Exhibitions Coord., Patrick Burton.
Institution Type/Description: Art Museum.
Hours & Admission Prices: Tues.-Thurs. & Sat. 10-5, Fri. 10-8, Sun. 12-5. No charge; donations accepted. Closed New Year's Day; Independence Day; Thanksgiving; Christmas. craft
Attendance: 25,000 (estimated)

KLUGE-RUHE ABORIGINAL ART COLLECTION, U. VA, 400 Worrell Dr., Pantops, Peter Jefferson Pl., Charlottesville, VA 22911-8691. Tel.: 434-244-0234. Fax: 434-244-0235.
E-mail: kluge-ruhe@virginia.edu
Web Site: www.kluge-ruhe.org
Key Personnel: Dir. & Cur., Margo Smith; Mgr. Collections & Registrar, Nicole Wade; Adjunct Cur., Howard Morphy; Education & Program Coord., Lauren Maupin.
Institution Type/Description: Art & Culture Museum.
Hours & Admission Prices: Tues.-Sat. 10-4, Sun. 1-5. Guided Tour: Sat. 10:30. No charge; donations accepted. craft

LEANDER J. MCCORMICK OBSERVATORY, Dept. of Astronomy, 530 McCormick Rd., The University of Virginia, Charlottesville, VA 22904. Mailing Address: P.O. Box 400325, Charlottesville, VA 22904-4325. Tel.: 434-924-7494. Fax: 434-924-3104. TDD: 434-982-4327; Facebook.
E-mail: dept@mail.astro.virginia.edu
Web Site: astronomy.as.virginia.edu
Key Personnel: Dir., Ed Murphy.
Institution Type/Description: Observatory.
Hours & Admission Prices: April-Oct. 1st & 3rd Fri. each month 9pm-11pm; Nov.-March 1st & 3rd Fri. each month 7pm-9pm. No charge.
Attendance: 4,000 (estimated)

MCGUFFEY ART CENTER, 201 Second St., N.W., Charlottesville, VA 22902-5012. Tel.: 434-295-7973. Fax: 434-295-0322.
E-mail: mcguffey@mcguffeyartcenter.com
Web Site: www.mcguffeyartcenter.com
Institution Type/Description: Art Center.
Hours & Admission Prices: Tues.-Sat. 10-6, Sun. 1-5. No charge. Closed New Year's Day; Independence Day; Thanksgiving; Christmas.

MICHIE TAVERN CA. 1784, 683 Thomas Jefferson Pkwy., Rt. 53, Charlottesville, VA 22902-7145. Tel.: 434-977-1234. Fax: 434-296-7203.
E-mail: info@michietavern.com
Web Site: www.michietavern.com
Key Personnel: Gen. Mgr., Gregory L. MacDonald; Asst. Mgr., Sam Morris; Cur., Cynthia Conte; Museum Shop Mgr., Wendy Pugh.
Institution Type/Description: Historic Tavern: housed in c.1784 structure, relocated to present site in 1927 at the height of the Colonial Revival era; grist mill c.1797, Piney River Cabin c.1790, Sowell House c. 1820; 1784 tavern; 1822 rural Virginia house.
Hours & Admission Prices: Daily 9-5. Adults $9, senior citizens $8, children 6-11 $4.50; children under 6 & members no charge. Closed New Year's Day; Christmas. &

MONTICELLO, HOME OF THOMAS JEFFERSON, THOMAS JEFFERSON FOUNDATION, INC., 931 Thomas Jefferson Pkwy., Charlottesville, VA 22902-7148. Mailing Address: P.O. Box 316, Charlottesville, VA 22902-0316. Tel.: 434-984-9800. Fax: 434-977-7751.
Web Site: www.monticello.org
Formerly: Thomas Jefferson Memorial Foundation
Key Personnel: Pres., Leslie Greene Bowman; Exec. Vice Pres., Ann H. Taylor; Vice Pres. & C.F.O., Laura Terry; Dir. Archaeology, Fraser D. Neiman; Richard Gilder Sr. Cur. & Vice Pres. Museum Programs, Susan R. Stein; Foundation Librarian, Jack Robertson; Robert H. Smith Dir. Restoration, Gardiner Hallock; Dir. Devel., Joshua Scott; Dir. Gardens & Grounds, Gabriele Rausse; Vice Pres. Thomas Jefferson Foundation, Saunders Dir. Robert H. Smith Intl. Ctr. for Jefferson Studies, Andrew O'Shaughnessy.
Institution Type/Description: Historic House Museum and Plantation: 1769-1826 Monticello, designed by Thomas Jefferson.
Hours & Admission Prices: March-Oct. daily 8:30-5; Nov.-Feb. daily 10-5. Adults $20-$25, children 5-11 $9; discounts to groups; children under 5 no charge. Closed Christmas. &
Attendance: 433,221 (actual)

THE ROTUNDA, UNIVERSITY OF VIRGINIA, 1826 University Ave., Charlottesville, VA 22904-0305. Mailing Address: P.O. Box 400305, Charlottesville, VA 22904-4305. Tel.: 434-924-7969 & 1019. Fax: 434-924-3817.
E-mail: rotunda@virginia.edu
Web Site: www.virginia.edu/~urelat/Tours/rotunda/rotunda.html
Key Personnel: C.E.O., Michael Strine; Admin., Leslie M. Comstock; Pres., Teresa Sullivan.
Institution Type/Description: Historic Buildings: site of Thomas Jefferson's original academic village, which includes the Rotunda, pavilions, student rooms & the lawn (1817-1826).
Hours & Admission Prices: mid-Jan. to mid-Dec. daily 9-4:45. Historical Tours: daily 10, 11, 2, 3, 4. No charge. &
Attendance: 135,000 (actual)

SECOND STREET GALLERY, 115 Second St., S.E., Charlottesville, VA 22902-5270. Tel.: 434-977-7284. Fax: 434-979-9793.
E-mail: members@secondstreetgallery.org
Web Site: www.secondstreetgallery.org

Key Personnel: Exec. Dir., Warren Craghead; Chm., Charlotte Dammann; Chm., Claire Holmann Thompson; Asst. Dir., Erica Barnes.
Institution Type/Description: Contemporary Art Gallery.
Hours & Admission Prices: Tues.-Sat. 11-6. Suggested Donation: $3. &
Attendance: 15,000 (estimated)

THE VIRGINIA DISCOVERY MUSEUM, 524 E. Main St., East End of the Downtown Mall, Charlottesville, VA 22902. Mailing Address: P.O. Box 1128, Charlottesville, VA 22902-1128. Tel.: 434-977-1025. Fax: 434-977-9681.
E-mail: vadm@vadm.org
Web Site: www.vadm.org
Key Personnel: Exec. Dir., Janine Dozier; Exec. Dir., Beth Solak; Bd. Chair, Michael Phillips; Dir. Operations, Lindsay Jones; Mgr. Education, Kaitlin Clear; Mktg. Mgr., Matt Berman; Visitor Svcs. Mgr., Madeline Hermsmeier.
Institution Type/Description: Children's Museum.
Hours & Admission Prices: Mon.-Sat. 9:30-5. Private rentals available on Sun. Admission $8; discounts to AAA, AARP, military, ACM & ASTC members and groups. Pay what you wish the 1st Wed. each month. Closed major holidays; New Year's Day; Memorial Day; Independence Day; Labor Day; Thanksgiving & day before; Christmas Eve & Day. &
Attendance: 73,864 (actual)

Chase City

MACCALLUM MORE MUSEUM AND GARDENS, 603 Hudgins St., Chase City, VA 23924-1237. Mailing Address: P.O. Box 104, Chase City, VA 23924-0104. Tel.: 434-372-0502. Fax: 434-372-3483.
E-mail: mmmg@verizon.net
Web Site: www.mmmg.org
Key Personnel: Exec. Dir., Amber Bradford; Pres. (V), Diana Ramsey; Treas., Dr. Earle Moore; Public Rels., Joe Epps.
Institution Type/Description: General Museum & Botanical Garden.
Hours & Admission Prices: Museum, Office & Gift Shop: Mon.-Fri. 10-5, Sat. 10-1. Gardens: daily 10-5. Museum & Gardens: adults $5, children under 12 $2.50; discounts to military, AAA, AAM & ICOM members; members no charge. Gardens (after hours): $2 donation. &
Attendance: 6,500 (estimated)

Chesapeake

CHESAPEAKE PLANETARIUM, 310 Shea Dr., Chesapeake, VA 23328. Mailing Address: 312 Cedar Rd., Chesapeake, VA 23328-6496. Tel.: 757-547-0153, ext. 208.
E-mail: hittrja@cps.k12.va.us
Key Personnel: C.E.O., Dr. Robert J. Hitt.
Institution Type/Description: Planetarium & Space Science Museum.
Hours & Admission Prices: Winter: Mon.-Wed. & Fri. 10:30-4:30, Thurs. 10:30-4:30 & 8 p.m.; June & Aug. Thurs. 8pm; other times by appointment. Group lectures or demonstrations $45; Chesapeake school groups no charge. &
Attendance: 40,000 (estimated)

PORTLOCK GALLERIES AT SONO, 3815 Bainbridge Blvd., Chesapeake, VA 23324-1607. Tel.: 727-502-4901.
E-mail: nbenson@cityofchesapeake.net
Institution Type/Description: Art Gallery: housed in a 1908 four-room schoolhouse.
Hours & Admission Prices: Tues.-Fri. 10-5, Sat.-Sun. 12-4. No charge. Closed holidays. &

Chesterfield

CHESTERFIELD HISTORICAL SOCIETY OF VIRGINIA - CHESTERFIELD COUNTY MUSEUM COMPLEX, 6813 Mimms Loop, Chesterfield, VA 23832. Mailing Address: P.O. Box 40, Chesterfield, VA 23832-0040. Tel.: 804-768-7311. Fax: 804-777-9643.
E-mail: admin@chesterfieldhistory.com
Web Site: www.chesterfieldhistory.com
Key Personnel: Admin., Diane Dallmeyer; Pres. (V), Therese Wagenknecht; Historic Sites Specialist, Bryan Truzzie; Cur. Magnolia Grange House & Museum Shop Mgr., Tamara Evans; Cur. County Museum, Pat Roble.
Institution Type/Description: Historical Society Museum.
Hours & Admission Prices: Tues.-Fri. 10-4, Sat. 10-2. Magnolia Grange: adults $5, seniors $4, students $2; members no charge. County Museum: Suggested Donation: adults $2; discounts to AAA members; members no charge. Historic Jail: $1. Closed Chesterfield holidays.
Attendance: 10,517 (actual)

Chincoteague

MUSEUM OF CHINCOTEAGUE ISLAND, 7125 Maddox Blvd., Chincoteague, VA 23336. Mailing Address: P.O. Box 352, Chincoteague, VA 23336-0352. Tel.: 757-336-6117.
E-mail: chincoteaguemuseum@verizon.net
Formerly: The Oyster and Maritime Museum of Chincoteague
Key Personnel: Dir., William Borges; Pres., John Jester; Officer, Kelly Conklin; Officer, William Spann; Officer, Christian Young.
Institution Type/Description: Local History Museum.
Hours & Admission Prices: Tues.-Sun. 10-5. Adults $3; children 12 & under no charge. &
Attendance: 13,000 (actual)

Christiansburg

CAMBRIA DEPOT MUSEUM, 630 Depot St., N.E., Christiansburg, VA 24073. Tel.: 540-382-6431.
E-mail: historiccambria@gmail.com
Institution Type/Description: Historic Building: built in 1868. Listed on the National Register of Historic Places.
Hours & Admission Prices: Fri.-Sat. 10-5, Sun. 1-5; other times by appointment.

MONTGOMERY MUSEUM & LEWIS MILLER REGIONAL ART CENTER, 300 S. Pepper St., Christiansburg, VA 24073-3537. Tel.: 540-382-5644. Facebook: Montgomery Museum and Lewis Miller Regional Art Center.
E-mail: director@montgomerymuseum.org
Web Site: www.montgomerymuseum.org
Key Personnel: Exec. Dir., Sue Farrar; Chm. (V) & Pres. (V), Kim Harich; Mgr. Collections, Sherry Wyatt; Treas., Nancy Miller; Museum Shop Mgr., Susan Keith.
Institution Type/Description: Historic House: 1850 Presbyterian Manse.
Hours & Admission Prices: Tues.-Sat. 10:30-4:30. Tours: adults $2, children under 12 $1; members no charge. Closed New Year's Eve & Day; Thanksgiving & two days after; Christmas Eve, Day & day after. &
Attendance: 875 (actual)

Clarksville

OCCONEECHEE STATE PARK, 1192 Occoneechee Park Rd., Clarksville, VA 23927-2946. Tel.: 434-374-2210.
E-mail: occoneechee@dcr.virginia.gov
Web Site: www.dcr.virginia.gov/state_parks/occ.shtml
Key Personnel: VA State Parks Dir., Joe Elton.
Institution Type/Description: Native American History Museum.
Hours & Admission Prices: Parking: Mon.-Fri. $2, Sat.-Sun. $3. &
Attendance: 202,000 (actual)

PRESTWOULD FOUNDATION, 429 Prestwould Dr., Clarksville, VA 23927. Mailing Address: P.O. Box 872, Clarksville, VA 23927-0872. Tel.: 434-374-8672. Fax: 434-374-3060.
Web Site: sovahomefront.org/_site_prestwould.php
Key Personnel: C.E.O., Dr. Julian D. Hudson.
Institution Type/Description: Local History Museum: house built in 1795 Prestwould House.
Hours & Admission Prices: April 15-Oct. Thurs.-Sat. 12:30-3, Sun. 1:30-3. Adults $10, seniors over 65 $8, children 6-12 $4; discounts to groups of 15 or more. Grounds only $4.
Attendance: 7,000 (actual)

Clifton Forge

ALLEGHANY HIGHLANDS ARTS & CRAFTS CENTER, INC., 439 E. Ridgeway St., Clifton Forge, VA 24422-1326. Mailing Address: P.O. Box 273, Clifton Forge, VA 24422-0273. Tel.: 540-862-4447.
E-mail: info@HighlandsArtsandCrafts.com
Web Site: highlandsartsandcrafts.com
Key Personnel: Exec. Dir., Nancy Newhard-Farrar; Pres. (V), Carolyn O. Conner; Museum Shop Mgr., Madelyn Miller.
Institution Type/Description: Arts & Crafts Center: housed in early 1900s building.
Hours & Admission Prices: Jan.-April Tues.-Sat. 10-4:30; May-Dec. Mon.-Sat. 10-4:30; groups by appointment. No charge; donations accepted. Closed Thanksgiving; Christmas Eve & Day. &
Attendance: 13,928 (actual)

Clintwood

RALPH STANLEY MUSEUM, 249 Main St., Clintwood, VA 24228. Mailing Address: P.O. Box 456, Clintwood, VA 24228-0456. Tel.: 276-926-8550 & 5591. Fax: 276-926-8693.
E-mail: tammy@ralphstanleymuseum.com
Web Site: www.ralphstanleymuseum.com
Key Personnel: Dir., Tammy Hill.
Institution Type/Description: History Museum.
Hours & Admission Prices: March-Dec. Tues.-Sat. 10-5. Adults $5; children 12 & under no charge. Closed New Year's Day; Memorial Day; Independence Day; Thanksgiving; Christmas. &

Colonial Beach

GEORGE WASHINGTON BIRTHPLACE NATIONAL MONUMENT, 1732 Popes Creek Rd., Colonial Beach, VA 22443-5115. Tel.: 804-224-1732. Fax: 804-224-2142.
E-mail: melissa_cobern@nps.gov
Web Site: www.nps.gov/gewa
Key Personnel: Supt., Tarona Armstrong; Administrative Officer, John Storke.
Institution Type/Description: Historic Site: birthplace of George Washington, 1730-1750.
Hours & Admission Prices: Daily 9-5. No charge. Closed New Year's Day; Thanksgiving; Christmas. &
Attendance: 131,000 (actual)

Colonial Heights

VIOLET BANK MUSEUM, 303 Virginia Ave., Colonial Heights, VA 23834. Tel.: 804-520-9395.
E-mail: woodburnr@colonialheightsva.gov
Web Site: www.colonial-heights.com
Institution Type/Description: History Museum: housed in a manor house, built in 1815. Former headquarters of Gen. Robert E. Lee.
Hours & Admission Prices: Tues.-Sat. 10-5, Sun. 1-6. No charge; donations accepted.

Courtland

RAWLS MUSEUM ARTS, 22376 Linden St., Courtland, VA 23837-1143. Tel.: 757-653-0754. Fax: 757-653-0341.
E-mail: leighanne@rawlsart.com
Web Site: www.rawlsarts.com
Key Personnel: Pres. Bd., Pat Hartman; Exec. Dir., Leigh Anne Chambers.
Institution Type/Description: Art Museum & Visual Arts Center.
Hours & Admission Prices: Tues. & Sat.-Sun. 1-5, Wed.-Fri. 10-5. No charge; donations accepted. &
Attendance: 6,749 (estimated)

Critz

REYNOLDS HOMESTEAD, 463 Homestead Lane, Critz, VA 24082-3044. Tel.: 276-694-7181. Fax: 276-694-7183.
E-mail: jws@vt.edu
Web Site: www.reynoldshomestead.vt.edu
Key Personnel: Dir., Julie Walters Steele; Sr. Program Coord., Lisa Martin; Asst. Program Coord., Sarah Wray; Historical Svcs. Asst., Beth Ford; Admin. Asst., Terri Leviner.
Institution Type/Description: Historic House: 1843 boyhood home of R.J. Reynolds, founder of Reynolds Tobacco.
Hours & Admission Prices: April-Oct. Sat.-Sun. 1-4pm. Adults $5, students $3; RJR Tobacco Inc. employees & former employees no charge. Group tours scheduled. Closed New Year's Day; Thanksgiving; Christmas. &
Attendance: 1,500 (estimated)

Culpeper

THE MUSEUM OF CULPEPER HISTORY, 113 S. Commerce St., Culpeper, VA 22701. Tel.: 540-829-1749. Fax: 540-829-9698.
E-mail: director@culpepermuseum.com
Web Site: www.culpepermuseum.com
Formerly: Culpeper Cavalry Museum
Key Personnel: Bd. Trustees Pres. (V), C. Dale Duvall; Museum Coord., Gloria Cooper; Museum Shop Mgr., Karen Quaintance.
Institution Type/Description: History Museum.
Hours & Admission Prices: Mon.-Sat. 10-5, Sun. 1-5; tours by appointment. Adults $4; discounts to museum professionals with ID, AAM, AARP, VAM, AAA, AASLH & Small Museum Assn. members; children, members, and town & county residents no charge. &
Attendance: 15,000 (actual)

Danville

AAF TANK MUSEUM, 3401 U.S. Hwy. 29B, Danville, VA 24540-1429. Tel.: 434-836-5323. Fax: 434-836-3532. Facebook: AAF Tank Museum.
E-mail: aaftank@gamewood.net
Web Site: www.aaftankmuseum.com
Institution Type/Description: Military Museum.
Hours & Admission Prices: Jan.-March Sat. 10-4; April-Dec. Fri.-Sat. 10-4. Adults $12, seniors over 60 & children under 12 $10; members no charge. Closed Thanksgiving; Christmas.
Attendance: 22,000 (actual)

DANVILLE MUSEUM OF FINE ARTS & HISTORY, 975 Main St., Danville, VA 24541-1822. Tel.: 434-793-5644.
E-mail: info@danvillemuseum.org
Web Site: danvillemuseum.org
Key Personnel: Exec. Dir., Ricahrd A. Loveland; Education Coord., Cynthia Hubbard; Office Mgr., Gerry Scearce; Visitor Svcs., C.B. Maddox.
Institution Type/Description: Art & History Museum: located in the Sutherlin Mansion where confederate President Jefferson Davis stayed when the confederacy fled Richmond in 1865 and issued the last proclamation of the confederacy.
Hours & Admission Prices: Tues.-Sat. 10-5, Sun. 2-5. Adults $8, senior citizens 62 & over $7, students $4; children 6 & under and members no charge.
Attendance: 14,264 (estimated)

DANVILLE SCIENCE CENTER, 677 Craghead St., Danville, VA 24541-1503. Tel.: 434-791-5160. Fax: 434-791-5168.
E-mail: dscstaff@smv.org
Web Site: www.dsc.smv.org
Key Personnel: Chm. Trustees, Robert O. Satterfield; Pres. DSC, Inc. Directors, Margie E. Wilkinson; Exec. Dir., Jeff Liverman; Asst. Dir., Sonya Wolen; Education Coord., Robin H. Bailey; Exec. Dir. DSC, Inc., Deborah L. Anderson.
Institution Type/Description: Science Museum.
Hours & Admission Prices: Tues.-Sat. & holiday Mon. 9:30-5, Sun. 1-5. Adults $7, seniors 60 & over, college students and active military $6, youth 4-18 $5; discounts to groups & AAA; members, ASTC members and children 3 & under no charge. Closed Thanksgiving; Christmas.
Attendance: 44,432 (estimated)

Dayton

HARRISONBURG-ROCKINGHAM HISTORICAL SOCIETY, 382 High St., Dayton, VA 22821. Mailing Address: P.O. Box 716, Dayton, VA 22821-0716. Tel.: 540-879-2616 & 2681. Fax: 540-879-2616.
E-mail: heritage@heritagecenter.com
Web Site: www.heritagecenter.com
Formerly: Shenandoah Valley Folk Art and Heritage Center
Key Personnel: Pres. (V) & C.E.O., Dale MacAllister; Admin., Mary Nelson.
Institution Type/Description: Historical Society Museum.
Hours & Admission Prices: April-Nov. Tues.-Sat. 10-5, Sun. 1-5; Dec.-March Tues.-Sat. 10-5. Adults $5; youth under 18 & members no charge.
Attendance: 7,493 (actual)

Deltaville

DELTAVILLE MARITIME MUSEUM & HOLLY POINT NATURE PARK, 287 Jackson Creek Rd., Deltaville, VA 23043. Mailing Address: P.O. Box 466, Deltaville, VA 23043-0466. Tel.: 804-776-7200.
E-mail: museumpark@verizon.net
Web Site: deltavillemuseum.com
Key Personnel: Dir. & Museum Shop Mgr., Bob LeBoeuf; Dir., Chuck McGhinnis; Pres. (V), William Powell; Museum Shop Mgr., Kristen DeGraw.
Institution Type/Description: Maritime Museum.
Hours & Admission Prices: Call for hours. Adults $15; discounts to retired & active duty military; members no charge.
Attendance: 20,000 (actual)

Duffield

NATURAL TUNNEL STATE PARK, 1420 Natural Tunnel Pkwy., Duffield, VA 24244-3672. Tel.: 276-940-1643. Fax: 276-940-2029.
E-mail: megan.france@dcr.virginia.gov
Web Site: www.virginiastateparks.gov
Institution Type/Description: State Park.

Hours & Admission Prices: Visitor Center: April-May & mid-Sept.-Oct. Sat.-Sun. 10-6; Memorial Day-Labor Day Thurs.-Mon. 10-6. The Blockhouse: May-Oct. Sat.-Sun. 2-4. No charge.

Fairfax

CHILDREN'S SCIENCE CENTER LAB, 11948L Fair Oaks Mall, Fairfax, VA 22033. Mailing Address: 2214 Rock Hill Rd., Ste. 380, Herndon, VA 20170. Tel.: 703-648-3130.
E-mail: info@childsci.org
Web Site: childsci.org
Institution Type/Description: Science Center.
Hours & Admission Prices: Call for hours.

FAIRFAX COUNTY PARK AUTHORITY, RESOURCE MANAGEMENT DIVISION, 12055 Government Center Pkwy., #927, Fairfax, VA 22035-1118. Tel.: 703-324-8702. Fax: 703-324-3996.
E-mail: parkmail@fairfaxcounty.gov
Web Site: www.fairfaxcounty.gov/parks
Key Personnel: Div. Dir., Cindy Walsh; Mgr. Cultural Resources Protection, Liz Crowell; Mgr. Colvin Run Mill, Mike Henry; Mgr. Sully, Carol McDonnell; Site Operations Branch Mgr., Todd Brown; Mgr. Green Spring Gardens, Mary Olien; Mgr. Ellanor C. Lawrence Park, Leon Nawojchik; Mgr. Huntley Meadows Park, Kevin Munroe; Mgr. Hidden Oaks Nature Center, Michael McDonnell; Mgr. Hidden Pond Nature Center, Jim Pomeroy; Mgr. Riverbend, Marty Smith.
Institution Type/Description: Historic Sites & House Museums.
Hours & Admission Prices: Call for hours. Grounds: no charge. Closed New Year's Day; Thanksgiving; Christmas.
Attendance: 403,939 (actual)

FAIRFAX MUSEUM & VISITOR CENTER, 10209 Main St., Fairfax, VA 22030-2403. Tel.: 703-385-8414 & 8415. Fax: 703-385-8692.
E-mail: sgray@fairfaxva.gov
Web Site: www.fairfaxva.gov
Key Personnel: Cur. & Visitor Svcs. Mgr., Susan Inskeep Gray.
Institution Type/Description: History Museum & Historic Site: housed in 1873 historic Fairfax elementary school, the first brick public school in Fairfax County.
Hours & Admission Prices: Daily 9-5. No charge; donations accepted. Closed New Year's Day; Easter; Thanksgiving; Christmas.
Attendance: 10,200 (actual)

GALLERY 123 - GEORGE MASON UNIVERSITY FINE ARTS GALLERY, Rm. 123, Johnson Center, Fairfax, VA 22030. Tel.: 703-993-8888.
E-mail: avt@gmu.edu
Key Personnel: Dir., Walter Kravitz.
Institution Type/Description: Art Gallery.
Hours & Admission Prices: Mon.-Fri. 9-9; other times by appointment.

NATIONAL FIREARMS MUSEUM, 11250 Waples Mill Rd., Fairfax, VA 22030-7400. Tel.: 703-267-1600. Fax: 703-267-3913.
E-mail: nfmstaff@nrahq.org
Web Site: nramuseum.com
Key Personnel: Pres., Allan D. Cors.; Exec. Vice Pres., Wayne LaPierre; Museum Dir., Jim Supica; Museum Cur., Doug Wicklund; Museum Cur., Phil Schreier; Museum Shop Mgr., Benjamin Van Scoyoc.
Institution Type/Description: Firearms Museum focus on American society from 1350 to present.
Hours & Admission Prices: Daily 9:30-5. No charge; donations accepted. Closed Christmas Day.

Falls Church

CHERRY HILL FARMHOUSE & BARN, 312 Park Ave., Falls Church, VA 22046-3301. Tel.: 703-248-5171. Fax: 703-536-8150.
E-mail: recreation@fallschurchva.gov
Web Site: www.fallschurchva.gov
Key Personnel: Dir., Rachel Crichton; Chmn. (V), Diane Morse.
Institution Type/Description: Historic Site: listed on the National Register of Historic Places, built in 1845.
Hours & Admission Prices: April-Oct. Sat. 10-1; Nov.-March Mon.-Thurs. 10-3. No charge; donations accepted.
Attendance: 5,000 (estimated)

Farmville

LONGWOOD CENTER FOR THE VISUAL ARTS, 129 N. Main St., Farmville, VA 23901-1305. Tel.: 434-395-2206. Fax: 434-392-6441. TDD: 800-828-1120.
E-mail: robertsbm@longwood.edu
Web Site: www.longwood.edu/lcva/
Key Personnel: Dir., Scott Habes; Chm. (V), Julie K. Heyn.
Institution Type/Description: College Art Museum.
Hours & Admission Prices: Galleries: Mon.-Sat. 11-5. Administrative: Mon.-Fri. 8:30-5. No charge; donations accepted. Closed college holidays; Thanksgiving; Christmas. &
Attendance: 39,000 (actual)

ROBERT RUSSA MOTON MUSEUM, 900 Griffin Blvd., Farmville, VA 23901-2236. Mailing Address: P.O. Box 908, Farmville, VA 23901-0908. Tel.: 434-315-8775. Fax: 434-392-8568.
E-mail: info@motonmuseum.org
Institution Type/Description: History Museum.
Hours & Admission Prices: By appointment. No charge.

Ferrum

BLUE RIDGE INSTITUTE AND MUSEUM, 20 Museum Dr., Ferrum College, Ferrum, VA 24088. Mailing Address: P.O. Box 1000, Ferrum, VA 24088-9001. Tel.: 540-365-4412. Fax: 540-365-4419.
E-mail: bri@ferrum.edu
Web Site: www.blueridgeinstitute.org
Key Personnel: Coord. Special Pojects, Bethany Worley; Co Dir., J. Roderick Moore; Co Dir., Vaughan Webb; Office Mgr., Jenny Rorrer; Head Interpreter, Rebecca Austin.
Institution Type/Description: History Museum.
Hours & Admission Prices: BRI Museum & Blue Ridge Heritage Archive: daily 10-4. Closed holidays. Farm Museum: May-Aug. Sat. 10-5, Sun. 1-5. Farm tour $5, special tours, senior citizens & children 6-15 $4; discount to ICOM, AAM & VA Assoc. of Museums members; children under 6 no charge. &
Attendance: 15,000 (estimated)

Fincastle

BOTETOURT COUNTY HISTORICAL SOCIETY, 3 W. Main St., Fincastle, VA 24090. Mailing Address: P.O. Box 468, Fincastle, VA 24090-0468. Tel.: 540-473-8394.
E-mail: info@bothistsoc.org
Web Site: www.bothistsoc.org
Key Personnel: Exec. Dir., Weldon L. Martin.
Institution Type/Description: Historical Society Museum.
Hours & Admission Prices: Mon.-Sat. 10-2, Sun. 2-4. No charge; donations accepted.

Floyd

FLOYD COUNTY HISTORICAL SOCIETY, 217 N. Locust St., Floyd, VA 24091. Mailing Address: P.O. Box 292, Floyd, VA 24091-0292. Tel.: 540-745-3247.
E-mail: floydhistoricalsociety@gmail.com
Web Site: www.floydhistoricalsociety.org
Key Personnel: Museum Shop Mgr., Rhonda F. Smith.
Institution Type/Description: Historical Society Museum: housed in a former hospital built by Lather Hylton for Dr. Martin L. Dalton who practiced there from 1914-1923.
Hours & Admission Prices: Thurs.-Fri. 12-4, Sat. 11-3. No charge; donations accepted. &
Attendance: 500 (estimated)

Forest

THOMAS JEFFERSON'S POPLAR FOREST, 1542 Bateman Bridge Rd., Forest, VA 24551. Mailing Address: P.O. Box 419, Forest, VA 24551-0419. Tel.: 434-525-1806. Fax: 434-525-7252.
E-mail: media@poplarforest.org
Web Site: www.poplarforest.org
Key Personnel: Pres. & C.E.O., Jeffrey L. Nichols; Chm. Bd. Directors, Madeline Miller; Dir. Communications, Kelcey Thurman; Dir. Interpretation & Education, Octavia Starbuck; Mgr. Visitor Svcs. & Volunteers, Dianne Kinney; Dir. Archaeology & Landscapes, Jack Gary; Assoc. Archaeologist, Eric Proebsting; Dir. Architectural Restoration, Travis C. McDonald; Museum Shop Mgr., Kyle

Tello; Dir. Devel., Alyson Ramsey; Dir. Institutional Advancement, Wayne Gannaway.
Institution Type/Description: Historic House: 1806 octagon house Thomas Jefferson designed & used as his personal retreat; architectural restoration in progress.
Hours & Admission Prices: March 15-Dec. 15 daily 10-4; groups by appointment. Adults $14, military & senior citizens $12, youth & students 12-18 $6, children 6-11 $2; discount to groups & AAA members; children 5 & under no charge. Closed Easter; Thanksgiving. &
Attendance: 22,473 (actual)

Fort Defiance

THE AUGUSTA MILITARY ACADEMY MUSEUM, 1640 Lee Hwy., Fort Defiance, VA 24437. Mailing Address: P.O. Box 100, Fort Defiance, VA 24437-0100. Tel.: 540-248-3007. Fax: 540-248-4533.
E-mail: augustamilitaryacademy@verizon.net
Web Site: www.amaalumni.org
Key Personnel: Exec. Dir., Crysta Stephenson; Chm. (V), Frank Williamson; Pres. (V), Jorge Rovirosa.
Institution Type/Description: Military History Museum: housed in Roller-Robinson House.
Hours & Admission Prices: Tues.-Sun. 10-4; other times by appointment. No charge; donations accepted. Closed major holidays. &
Attendance: 2,000 (estimated)

Fort Eustis

U.S. ARMY TRANSPORTATION MUSEUM, 300 Washington Blvd., Besson Hall, Fort Eustis, VA 23604-5260. Tel.: 757-878-1115. Fax: 757-878-5656. Facebook: US Army Transportation Museum.
E-mail: david.s.hanselman.civ@mail.mil
Web Site: www.transportation.army.mil/museum/transportation museum/museum.htm
Key Personnel: Dir., David S. Hanselman; Pres., Col. John C. Race, Jr., (Ret.); Cur., Marc W. Sammis; Education Coord., Matthew Fraas.
Institution Type/Description: Military Transportation Museum.
Hours & Admission Prices: Tues.-Sun. 9-4:30. No charge; donations accepted. Closed federal holidays; Easter. &
Attendance: 78,000 (actual)

Fort Lee

U.S. ARMY ORDNANCE TRAINING & HERITAGE CENTER, 2221 Adams Ave., Bldg. 5020, Fort Lee, VA 23801. Tel.: 804-734-4878.
E-mail: usarmy.lee.tradoc.mbx.ordnance-museum@mail.mil
Web Site: www.goordnance.apg.army.mil/museum
Institution Type/Description: History & Military Museum.
Hours & Admission Prices: Closed for relocation. &
Attendance: 75,000 (estimated)

U.S. ARMY WOMEN'S MUSEUM, 2100 A Ave., Fort Lee, VA 23801-2100. Tel.: 804-734-4327. Fax: 804-734-4337. Facebook: U.S. Army Women's Museum.
E-mail: usarmy.lee.tradoc.mbx.leee-awmweb@mail.mil
Web Site: www.awm.lee.army.mil
Key Personnel: Pres. Bd., Lt. Col. Pat Sigle; Museum Dir., Dr. Francoise Bonnell.
Institution Type/Description: Military History Museum.
Hours & Admission Prices: Gallery: Tues.-Fri. 10-5, Sat. 11-5; call to confirm; other times by appointment. No charge; donations accepted. Closed New Year's Day; Thanksgiving; Christmas; Federal holidays. Administrative Hours: Mon.-Sat. 8-5. &
Attendance: 40,000 (estimated)

THE UNITED STATES ARMY QUARTERMASTER MUSEUM, 2220 Adams Ave., Bldg 5218, Fort Lee, VA 23801-1601. Tel.: 804-734-4203. Fax: 804-734-4359.
E-mail: luther.d.hanson.civ@mail.mil
Web Site: www.qmmuseum.lee.army.mil
Key Personnel: Cur., Luther D. Hanson; Exhibits Technician, Patrick Fisher; Cur. Education, Laura Baghetti; Office Svcs. Asst., Susan Tatum; Museum Shop Mgr., Paulette Bordwell.
Institution Type/Description: Military & History Museum.
Hours & Admission Prices: Tues.-Fri. 10-5, Sat.-Sun. & holidays 11-5. No charge; donations accepted. Closed New Year's; Thanksgiving; Christmas. &
Attendance: 50,000 (estimated)

Fort Monroe

CASEMATE MUSEUM, 20 Bernard Rd., Fort Monroe, VA 23651-1004. Mailing Address: P.O. Box 3308, Hampton, VA 23663-0308. Tel.: 757-788-3391. Fax: 757-788-3886.
E-mail: claire.samuelson@us.army.mil
Key Personnel: Pres. Foundation, Robert Wood; Coord., Earle Richards; Cur., Claire Samuelson; Museum Specialist, David J. Johnson; Museum Shop Mgr., Rosalinda Watson.
Institution Type/Description: Military Museum: built in 1826 casemates in Fort Monroe, VA.
Hours & Admission Prices: Daily 10:30-4:30. No charge; donations accepted. Closed New Year's Day; Thanksgiving; Christmas. &
Attendance: 37,747 (actual)

Fort Myer

THE OLD GUARD MUSEUM, 201 Lee Ave., Fort Myer, VA 22211-1203. Mailing Address: c/o The Old Guard Assn., P.O. Box 1785, Fort Meyer, VA 22211-1785. Tel.: 703-696-6670. Fax: 703-696-4256. Facebook: Old Guard Museum.
Web Site: oldguardhistory.blogspot.com
Key Personnel: Dir., Kirk Heflin.
Institution Type/Description: Military Museum: housed in late 19th-century building originally used as barracks.
Hours & Admission Prices: Temporarily closed for renovations & relocation.
Attendance: 8,000 (estimated)

Fredericksburg

CENTRAL RAPPAHANNOCK HERITAGE CENTER, 900 Barton St., Unit 111, Fredericksburg, VA 22401-5784. Tel.: 540-373-3704.
E-mail: crhc@verizon.net
Web Site: www.crhcarchives.org
Key Personnel: Dir., Barbara Barrett.
Institution Type/Description: History Museum.
Hours & Admission Prices: Tues.-Thurs. 10-4, 1st Sat. of each month 10-1; other times by appointment. No charge; donations accepted. &

FREDERICKSBURG & SPOTSYLVANIA NATIONAL MILITARY PARK, 120 Chatham Lane, Fredericksburg, VA 22405-2508. Tel.: 540-371-0802; 373-6122 (visitor's center). Fax: 540-371-1907.
Web Site: www.nps.gov/ffrsp
Key Personnel: Supt., Russell P. Smith; Chief Historian, Robert K. Krick; Staff Historian, Donald C. Pfanz.
Institution Type/Description: Military Park Museum: located on the site of the Battlefields of Fredericksburg, Chancellorsville, Wilderness & Spotsylvania.
Hours & Admission Prices: Fredericksburg Battlefield Visitor Center, Chancellorsville Visitor Center: Mon.-Fri. 9-5, Sat.-Sun. 9-6. Chatham Manor: daily 9-4:30. Jackson Shrine: daily 9-5. Adults $3; children 16 & under no charge. Closed New Year's Day; Christmas. &
Attendance: 230,000 (actual)

FREDERICKSBURG AREA MUSEUM & CULTURAL CENTER, INC., 907 Princess Anne St., Fredericksburg, VA 22401. Mailing Address: P.O. Box 922, Fredericksburg, VA 22404-0922. Tel.: 540-371-3037. Fax: 540-371-1001.
E-mail: mjohnson@famcc.org
Web Site: www.famcc.org
Key Personnel: Dir., Pres. & C.E.O., Sara Poore, Ph.D.; Sr. Devel. Officer, Melanie Johnson; Office Mgr., Darlene Davis.
Institution Type/Description: History Museum.
Hours & Admission Prices: Please call or visit website before visiting. &
Attendance: 22,900 (actual)

GARI MELCHERS HOME AND STUDIO, 224 Washington St., Fredericksburg, VA 22405-2360. Tel.: 540-654-1015. Fax: 540-654-1785.
E-mail: belmont@umw.edu
Web Site: www.garimelchers.org
Formerly: Belmont, The Gari Melchers Estate and Memorial Gallery
Key Personnel: Dir., David S. Berreth; Cur., Joanna D. Catron; Mktg. & Museum Shop Mgr., Susan Taylor-Schran; Mgr. Education & Communications, Michelle Dolby; Mgr. Site Preservation, Beate Jensen; Mgr. Special Events, Betsy Labar.
Institution Type/Description: Art Museum: housed in 18th-century Belmont, the home & studio of the American artist Gari Melchers, 1860-1932.
Hours & Admission Prices: Thurs.-Tues. 10-5. Adults $10; discounts to museum, ICOM, & AAM members; children 18 & under, other museum staff, volunteers,

students, faculty & staff of University of Mary Washington no charge. Closed New Year's Eve & Day; Easter; Independence Day; Thanksgiving; Christmas Eve & Day. &
Attendance: 18,000 (actual)

THE GEORGE WASHINGTON FOUNDATION, HISTORIC KENMORE & GEORGE WASHINGTON'S BOYHOOD HOME AT FERRY FARM, 1201 Washington Ave., Fredericksburg, VA 22401-3747. Tel.: 540-373-3381. Fax: 540-371-6066.
E-mail: mailroom@kenmore.org
Web Site: www.kenmore.org
Formerly: George Washington's Fredericksburg Foundation
Key Personnel: Dir. & C.E.O., William E. Garner; Chm. (V), Fielding L. Cocke; Vice Chm., Samuel C. Harding, Jr.; Museum Shop Mgr., Susan Bailey.
Institution Type/Description: Historic Houses: Kenmore, the 18th century home of Revolutionary War patriot Fielding Lewis and his wife, Betty, sister of George Washington. Ferry Farm: George Washington's boyhood home from 6 to 20 years old.
Hours & Admission Prices: March-Oct. daily 10-5; Nov.-Dec. daily 10-4. Kenmore: adults $10, seniors 60 & over $9, children 6-17 $5; discounts to groups, trolley passengers, Time Travelers, AAA, DAR members & active military; children under 6 no charge. Ferry Farm: adults $8, seniors 60 & over $7, children 6-17 $4; discounts to groups, trolley passengers, Time Travelers, AAA, DAR members & active military; children under 6 no charge. Closed New Year's Eve & Day; Easter; Thanksgiving; Christmas Eve & Day. &
Attendance: 28,791 (actual)

HUGH MERCER APOTHECARY SHOP, 1020 Caroline St., Fredericksburg, VA 22401-3814. Mailing Address: 1300 Charles St., Fredericksburg, VA 22401. Tel.: 540-373-3362. Facebook: Hugh Mercer Apothecary Shop.
E-mail: hmas@washingtonheritagemuseums.org
Web Site: www.washingtonheritagemuseums.org
Key Personnel: Exec Dir., Anne Darron; Mgr., Genevieve Bugay; Chm. (V), Michael Spencer.
Institution Type/Description: Historic Building: 1761 Hugh Mercer Apothecary Shop.
Hours & Admission Prices: Call for hours. Adults $7, children $3; discount to members, AAA members, military families & groups; active military & WHM members no charge. Closed New Year's Eve & Day; Thanksgiving; Christmas Eve & Day.
Attendance: 12,000 (actual)

JAMES MONROE MUSEUM, 908 Charles St., Fredericksburg, VA 22401-5801. Tel.: 540-654-1043; 800-828-1120 (TTY). Fax: 540-654-1106.
E-mail: sharris4@umw.edu
Web Site: www.jamesmonroemuseum.org
Formerly: James Monroe Museum and Memorial Library
Key Personnel: Dir., Scott H. Harris; Cur., Jarod Kearney; Membership & Events Coord., Adele Uphaus-Conner; Office Mgr., Lynda Allen.
Institution Type/Description: Presidential Historical Museum.
Hours & Admission Prices: March-Nov. Mon.-Sat. 10-5, Sun. 1-5; Dec.-Feb. daily 10-4. Adults $6, youth 6-17 $2; discounts to senior citizens, groups, AAM, AAA, ICOM, VAM & Timeless Ticket to Fredericksburg members; UMW students, children 5 & under and museum members no charge. Closed New Year's Eve & Day; Thanksgiving; Christmas Eve & Day. &
Attendance: 10,000 (estimated)

MARY WASHINGTON HOUSE, 1200 Charles St., Fredericksburg, VA 22401-3706. Tel.: 540-373-1569. Fax: 540-373-1569. Facebook: Mary Washington House.
E-mail: mwhouse@washingtonheritagemuseums.org
Web Site: www.washingtonheritagemuseums.org
Key Personnel: Exec. Dir., Anne Darron; Mgr. Mary Washington House, Michelle Hamilton; Chm. (V), James Branscome; Museum Shop Mgr., Jan Swager.
Institution Type/Description: History Museum: 1772-1789 home of Mary Ball Washington.
Hours & Admission Prices: Call for hours. Adults $5, children $2; discounts to AAA members, military families, and groups of 10 & over; active military & WHM members no charge. Closed New Year's Eve & Day; Thanksgiving; Christmas Eve & Day.
Attendance: 10,000 (actual)

RISING SUN TAVERN, 1304 Caroline St., Fredericksburg, VA 22401-3704. Mailing Address: 1300 Charles St., Fredericksburg, VA 22401. Tel.: 540-371-1494. Fax: 540-373-5630. Facebook: Rising Sun Tavern.
E-mail: rst@washingtonheritagemuseums.org

Web Site: www.washingtonheritagemuseums.org
Key Personnel: Exec. Dir., Anne Darron; Chm. (V), James Branscome; Mgr., Jo Atkins.
Institution Type/Description: Historic House Museum: c.1760 built by Charles Washington as his home; later used as tavern.
Hours & Admission Prices: Call for hours. Adults $5, children $2; discounts to AAA members, military families & groups of 10 or more; active military & WHM members no charge. Closed New Year's Eve & Day; Thanksgiving; Christmas Eve & Day.
Attendance: 10,000 (actual)

ST. JAMES' HOUSE, 1300 Charles St., Fredericksburg, VA 22401-3708. Mailing Address: 1200 Charles St., Fredericksburg, VA 22401. Tel.: 540-373-5630. Facebook: St. James' House.
E-mail: office@washingtonheritagemuseums.org
Web Site: www.washingtonheritagemuseums.org
Key Personnel: Exec. Dir., Anne Darron; Chm., Michael Spencer.
Institution Type/Description: Historic House: c.1770 home of Hon. James Mercer.
Hours & Admission Prices: Garden Week: April & 1st week Oct.; 1-4 on dates listed; other times by appointment. Adults $5, children 6-18 $2; discount to groups; WHM members no charge.
Attendance: 175 (estimated)

UNIVERSITY OF MARY WASHINGTON GALLERIES, 1301 College Ave. at Seacobeck St., Fredericksburg, VA 22401-5358. Tel.: 540-654-1013. Fax: 540-654-1171.
E-mail: wordpress@umwgalleries.org
Web Site: galleries.umw.edu
Key Personnel: Dir., Rosemary Jesionowski; Mgr. Collections, Ashley Holdsworth; Coord. Exhibitions, Rachel Hutcheson.
Institution Type/Description: College Art Galleries.
Hours & Admission Prices: Sept.-April Tues.-Fri. 10-4, Sat.-Sun. 1-4; May-Aug. Tues.-Thurs 10-4. No charge. Closed university holidays & breaks. &
Attendance: 7,000 (actual)

Front Royal

WARREN RIFLES CONFEDERATE MUSEUM, 95 Chester St., Front Royal, VA 22630-3368. Mailing Address: P.O. Box 1304, Front Royal, VA 22630-0027. Tel.: 540-636-6982 & 660-0941.
E-mail: warrenriflescmm@gmail.com
Key Personnel: Dir. & Pres. (V), Suzanne W. Silek; Museum Shop Mgr., Frances Woodward.
Institution Type/Description: History & Military Museum: located on one of oldest streets in Front Royal.
Hours & Admission Prices: mid-April to Nov. Mon.-Sat. 9-4, Sun. 12-4; other times by appointment. Groups: call for admission prices; discounts to members, AAA, AAM & AARP members; students no charge. &
Attendance: 1,000 (estimated)

Galax

JEFF MATTHEWS MEMORIAL MUSEUM, 606 W. Stuart Dr., Galax, VA 24333-2718. Tel.: 276-236-7874.
E-mail: info@jeffmatthewsmuseum.org
Web Site: www.jeffmatthewsmuseum.org
Key Personnel: Chm. (V), Bobby Thomson, Jr.; Cur., Tony Burcham.
Institution Type/Description: History Museum.
Hours & Admission Prices: Wed.-Sat. 11-4; other times by appointment. No charge; donations accepted. Closed New Year's Day; Easter; Thanksgiving; Christmas. &
Attendance: 4,253 (actual)

Glen Allen

THE CULTURAL ARTS CENTER AT GLEN ALLEN, 2880 Mountain Rd., Glen Allen, VA 23060-2121. Mailing Address: P.O. Box 1249, Glen Allen, VA 23060-1249. Tel.: 804-261-2787.
E-mail: info@artsglenallen.com
Web Site: www.artsglenallen.com
Key Personnel: Pres., K. Alferio; Performing Arts Mgr. & Technical Dir., Richard Koch; Visual Arts Mgr., Lauren Hall; Dir. Mktg. & Public Rels., Christopher Murphy.
Institution Type/Description: Cultural Arts Center.
Hours & Admission Prices: Call for hours.
Attendance: 100,000 (estimated)

THE MUSEUM IN MEMORY OF VIRGINIA E. RANDOLPH, 2200 Mountain Rd., Glen Allen, VA 33060-2232. Mailing

Address: P.O. Box 90775, Henrico, VA 23273-0775. Tel.: 804-360-2071.
E-mail: loglesby@vahistorical.org
Institution Type/Description: Historic Building: housed in the former office of vocation school teacher, Virginia Randolph; built in 1937. A National Register Landmark.
Hours & Admission Prices: Call for hours. No charge.

Gloucester

GLOUCESTER MUSEUM OF HISTORY, 6539 Main St., Gloucester, VA 23061. Mailing Address: P.O. Box 5, White Marsh, VA 23183-0005. Tel.: 804-693-1234. Fax: 804-693-1234.
E-mail: bdeal@gloucesterva.info
Web Site: www.gloucesterva.info/museum/historyhome.htm
Key Personnel: Dir., Betty Jean Deal.
Institution Type/Description: History Museum: built ca 1770.
Hours & Admission Prices: Mon.-Sat. 10-3; tours by appointment. No charge; donations accepted. Closed holidays.
Attendance: 3,000 (actual)

THE ROSEWELL PLANTATION RUINS, 5113 Old Rosewell Lane, Gloucester, VA 23061. Mailing Address: P.O. Box 1456, Gloucester, VA 23061. Tel.: 804-693-2585. Facebook: The Rosewell Foundation.
E-mail: rosewell@rosewell.org
Web Site: www.rosewell.org
Key Personnel: Pres. (V) & C.E.O., Lawrence Henry; Opers. Officer, Katrina White-Brown.
Institution Type/Description: Historic House Museum: the ruins of the Page family mansion; built in 1725.
Hours & Admission Prices: Summer: Tues.-Sat. 10-4, Sun. 1-4; Winter: call for hours; groups by appointment. Adults $5, students $3, children 6-12 $2; discount to Student Time Travelers; children 5 & under & members no charge. &
Attendance: 1,600 (actual)

WALTER REED BIRTHPLACE, 4021 Hickory Fork Rd., Gloucester, VA 23061. Mailing Address: 204 W. Franklin St., Richmond, VA 23220-5012. Tel.: 804-693-6688.
E-mail: info@gloucesterpreservationfoundation.org
Institution Type/Description: Historic House: three-room frame house, the birthplace of Walter Reed, September, 1851, a Major in the U.S. Army & the surgeon who is known as the conqueror of yellow fever.
Hours & Admission Prices: May-Oct. 2nd Sat. each month 1-4; other times by appointment.
Attendance: 50 (actual)

WARNER HALL GRAVEYARD, 4750 Warner Hall Rd, Gloucester, VA 23061-4507. Tel.: 804-648-1889.
E-mail: info@preservationvirginia.org
Web Site: www.apva.org/warnergraveyard
Key Personnel: Exec. Dir., Elizabeth Kostelny.
Institution Type/Description: Historic Site: graveyard containing the tombs of the Warner & Lewis Families; including that of Augustine Warner, the first Warner to settle in Gloucester County & the forefather of George Washington.
Hours & Admission Prices: Daily 10-4. No charge. &
Attendance: 500 (estimated)

Gloucester Point

VIRGINIA INSTITUTE OF MARINE SCIENCE, Rte. 1208, Greate Rd., Gloucester Point, VA 23062. Mailing Address: P.O. Box 1346, Gloucester Point, VA 23062-1346. Tel.: 804-684-7000 & 7285. Fax: 804-684-7097.
E-mail: jmusick@vims.edu
Web Site: www.vims.edu
Key Personnel: Dean & Dir., John Wells; Chief Administrative Officer, Jennifer LaTour; Dir. Communications, Dave Malmquist; Dir. Library, Carl Coughlin; Bibliographic Svcs. Librarian, Marilyn Lewis; Cur., Paul Gerdes.
Institution Type/Description: Marine Research Institute: located on Colonial Village archaeological site.
Hours & Admission Prices: Mon.-Fri. 9-4:30. Open to qualified professional scientists. No charge. &

Goldvein

THE GOLD MINING CAMP MUSEUM, 14421 Gold Dust Pkwy., Goldvein, VA 22720. Tel.: 540-422-8170. Fax: 540-422-8171.
E-mail: monroepark@fauquiercounty.gov
Web Site: www.goldvein.com

Institution Type/Description: History Museum.
Hours & Admission Prices: Wed.-Sat. 9:30-5, Sun. 12-4. No charge; donations accepted. Closed New Year's Day; Easter; Independence Day; Thanksgiving; Christmas. &
Attendance: 10,000 (estimated)

Goochland

GOOCHLAND COUNTY MUSEUM & HISTORICAL CENTER, 2875 River Rd. W., Rte. 6, Goochland, VA 23063. Mailing Address: P.O. Box 602, Goochland, VA 23063-0602. Tel.: 804-556-3966. Fax: 804-556-3966. TDD: 804-556-5300.
E-mail: goochlandhistory@verizon.net
Web Site: www.goochlandhistory.org
Key Personnel: Pres. (V), Scott Johnson; Exec. Dir., Phyllis Silber.
Institution Type/Description: Local History Center; housed in 1836 old jail.
Hours & Admission Prices: Historical Center: Wed.-Fri. 10-3. Jail Museum: by appointment. No charge; donations accepted. Closed legal holidays. &
Attendance: 500 (actual)

Gordonsville

THE EXCHANGE HOTEL CIVIL WAR MEDICAL MUSEUM, 400 S. Main St., Gordonsville, VA 22942. Mailing Address: P.O. Box 542, Gordonsville, VA 22942-0542. Tel.: 540-832-2944.
E-mail: hgiexchangehotel@gmail.com
Web Site: www.hgievchange.com
Formerly: Civil War Museum at the Exchange Hotel
Key Personnel: Dir. & Museum Shop Mgr., Angel May; Pres. (V), Christopher Stephens.
Institution Type/Description: Civil War Museum; built in 1860 railroad hotel used as a Confederate receiving hospital during the Civil War & as a Freedmans Bureau at the end of the Civil War until Dec. 1868.
Hours & Admission Prices: Mon.-Thurs. & Sat. 10-4, Fri. 12-4, Sun. 1-4. Adults $10, children 8-12 $3; children 7 & under no charge.
Attendance: 5,100 (actual)

Gum Springs

GUM SPRINGS MUSEUM & CULTURAL CENTER, 8100 Fordson Rd., Gum Springs, VA 22306. Tel.: 703-375-9825.
Web Site: www.gshsfcva.org/gshs05.htm
Key Personnel: Pres., Ron Chase.
Institution Type/Description: History Museum.
Hours & Admission Prices: Call for hours.

Gwynn's Island

GWYNN'S ISLAND MUSEUM, Old Ferry Rd., Gwynn's Island, VA 23066. Tel.: 804-725-7949.
E-mail: tdedwards141@yahoo.com
Web Site: www.gwynnsislandmuseum.org
Institution Type/Description: History Museum.
Hours & Admission Prices: April-Oct. Fri.-Sun. 1-5; other times by appointment. No charge; donations accepted.

Hampden-Sydney

THE ESTHER THOMAS ATKINSON MUSEUM, College Rd., Hampden-Sydney, VA 23943. Mailing Address: P.O. Box 745, Hampden-Sydney, VA 23943-0745. Tel.: 434-223-6134. Fax: 434-223-6344.
E-mail: away@hsc.edu
Web Site: www.hsc.edu/Museum/
Key Personnel: Chm. Program Bd., Frank B. Atkinson; Dir. & Cur., Angela Way.
Institution Type/Description: College Museum.
Hours & Admission Prices: Tues.-Fri. 10-12 & 1-5; other times by appointment. No charge; donations accepted. Closed school holidays. &
Attendance: 3,100 (estimated)

Hampton

CHARLES H. TAYLOR ARTS CENTER, 4205 Victoria Blvd., Hampton, VA 23669-4243. Tel.: 757-727-1490. Fax: 757-727-1167.
E-mail: artscom@hampton.gov
Web Site: www.hamptonarts.net
Key Personnel: Dir., Michael P. Curry; Gallery Mgr., James Warwick Jones; Chm. (V), Ross A. Mugler.
Institution Type/Description: Visual Arts Center.

Hours & Admission Prices: Tues.-Fri. 10-6, Sat.-Sun. 1-5. No charge; donations accepted. Closed New Year's Day; Presidents' Day; Memorial Day; Independence Day; Labor Day; Thanksgiving; Christmas; city holidays. &
Attendance: 10,348 (actual)

HAMPTON HISTORY MUSEUM, 120 Old Hampton Lane, Hampton, VA 23669-4096. Tel.: 757-727-1610. Fax: 757-727-6712.
E-mail: gdrummond@hampton.gov
Web Site: www.hampton1610.com
Key Personnel: Operations Mgr. & Grants Admin., Gaynell Drummond; Museum Assn. Pres., Tim Smith; Museum Assn. Treas., Robert Allsbrook; Museum Educator & Public Rels., Winette Jeffery; Registrar, Bethany Austin; Cur., Michael Cobb; Museum Shop Mgr., Vivian Tanzer; Administrative Asst., Gloria Jones.
Institution Type/Description: History Museum.
Hours & Admission Prices: Mon.-Sat. 10-5, Sun. 1-5. Adults $5, senior citizens, students & children $4; discount to groups & AAM members; members no charge. Closed New Year's Day; Thanksgiving; Christmas. &

HAMPTON UNIVERSITY MUSEUM, Hampton University, Hampton, VA 23668. Tel.: 757-727-5308. Fax: 757-727-5170.
E-mail: museumeducation@hamptonu.edu
Web Site: museum.hamptonu.edu
Key Personnel: C.E.O., William R. Harvey; Dir., Nashid Madyun; Cur. Collections, Vanessa Thaxton-Ward; Office Mgr., Brenda Carpenter; Visitor Svcs., Robert Jondreau; Editor International Review of African American Art, Juliette Harris; Asst. to the Archivist, Donzella Maupin; Archivist Staff, Cynthia Poston; Archivist Staff, Andreese Scott.
Institution Type/Description: General Museum.
Hours & Admission Prices: Mon.-Fri. 8-5, Sat. 12-4. No charge; donations accepted. Closed national holidays; campus holidays. &
Attendance: 30,000 (estimated)

ST. JOHN'S CHURCH AND PARISH MUSEUM, 100 W. Queens Way, Hampton, VA 23669-4014. Tel.: 757-722-2567. Fax: 757-722-0641.
E-mail: office@stjohnshampton.org
Web Site: www.stjohnshampton.org
Key Personnel: Parish Historian & Cur., Beverly F. Gundry.
Institution Type/Description: Historic Buildings; c.1728 church, fourth site of worship in Elizabeth City Parish, established in 1610. Museum housed in 1889, Parish Hall.
Hours & Admission Prices: Mon.-Fri. 9-3:30, Sat. 9-12. No charge; donations accepted. Closed holidays. &
Attendance: 1,969 (estimated)

VIRGINIA AIR & SPACE CENTER, 600 Settlers Landing Rd., Hampton, VA 23669-4033. Tel.: 757-727-0900. Fax: 757-727-0898. Facebook: Virginia Air & Space Center.
E-mail: rgriesmer@vasc.org
Web Site: www.vasc.org
Formerly: Virginia Air and Space Center and Hampton Roads History Center
Key Personnel: Exec. Dir. & C.E.O., Robert R. Griesmer; Pres. (V), James A. Firth; Dir. Programs, Danelle Price; Dir. Administrative Svcs., Jenny Kelly; Cur. & Dir. of Exhibits & Collections, Allen Hoilman; Museum Shop Mgr., Helena Brice; Dir. Visitor Svcs., Pearl Osby.
Institution Type/Description: Air, space, science & technology museum.
Hours & Admission Prices: Jan. 2-May 18 & Sept. 6-Dec. Tues.-Sat. 10-5, Sun. 12-5, call for Mon. holiday hours; May 19-Sept. 5 Mon.-Wed. 10-5, Thurs.-Sat. 10-6, Sun. 12-5. Exhibits & one educational IMAX film: adults $18, senior citizens $16, military & NASA $15, children (3-18) $14.50; discounts for some ASTC members. Closed Thanksgiving; Christmas. &
Attendance: 272,379 (actual)

Hanover

HANOVER HISTORICAL SOCIETY MUSEUM - OLD STONE JAIL, Hwy. 301, Court Green, Hanover, VA 23069. Mailing Address: c/o Hanover County Historical Society, P.O. Box 91, Hanover, VA 23069-0091. Tel.: 804-537-6262.
Institution Type/Description: Historical Society Museum.
Hours & Admission Prices: By appointment. No charge; donations accepted.
Attendance: 8,042 (estimated)

Hardy

BOOKER T. WASHINGTON NATIONAL MONUMENT, 12130 Booker T. Washington Hwy., Hardy, VA 24101-3968. Tel.: 540-721-2094. Fax: 540-721-8311. Facebook.

E-mail: betsy_haynes@nps.gov
Web Site: www.nps.gov/bowa
Key Personnel: C.E.O., Carla Whitfield; Bookstore Mgr., L. Betsy G. Haynes;
Volunteer Coord., Janet Blanchard.
Institution Type/Description: National Monument: located on the site of Burroughs
Plantation, birthplace & early home of Booker T. Washington.
Hours & Admission Prices: Daily 9-5. No charge; donations accepted. Closed New
Year's Day; Thanksgiving; Christmas. &
Attendance: 20,000 (estimated)

Harrisonburg

D. RALPH HOSTETTER MUSEUM OF NATURAL HISTORY,
Eastern Mennonite University, 1200 Park Rd., Harrisonburg, VA
22802-2462. Tel.: 540-432-4400 & 4000. Fax: 540-432-4488.
E-mail: dossc@emu.edu
Web Site: http://www.emu.edu/sciencecenter
Key Personnel: Museum Educator, Christine C. Hill; Educational Dir., Maureen
Gallon; Cur., James Yoder.
Institution Type/Description: Natural History Museum.
Hours & Admission Prices: Academic Year: Sun. 2-4; groups by appointment. &
Attendance: 6,000 (actual)

**DUKE HALL GALLERY OF FINE ART, JAMES MADISON
UNIVERSITY,** Main & Grace Sts., Duke Hall, Rm. 101,
Harrisonburg, VA 22807. Mailing Address: MSC 7101, Duke Hall,
Harrisonburg, VA 22807. Tel.: 540-568-6407. Fax: 540-568-5862.
E-mail: freebugl@jmu.edu
Formerly: Sawhill Gallery, James Madison University
Key Personnel: Dir., Gary L. Freeburg.
Institution Type/Description: Art Gallery.
Hours & Admission Prices: Academic Year: Mon.-Fri. 10-5, Sat. 12-5; Summer:
call for hours. No charge. Closed university holidays. &
Attendance: 10,000 (estimated)

EXPLORE MORE DISCOVERY MUSEUM, 150 S. Main St.,
Harrisonburg, VA 22803. Mailing Address: P.O. Box 957,
Harrisonburg, VA 22803. Tel.: 540-442-8900.
E-mail: info@iexploremore.com
Institution Type/Description: Children's Museum.
Hours & Admission Prices: Tues.-Sat. 9:30-5. Admission $5 per person; children
under one no charge.

JOHN C. WELLS PLANETARIUM, James Madison University, c/
o Physics Dept., Harrisonburg, VA 22807. Mailing Address: James
Madison University, Miller Hall Rm 102, MSC-4502,
Harrisonburg, VA 22807. Tel.: 540-568-2312. Fax: 540-568-2800.
Facebook: JMU Planetarium.
E-mail: planetarium@jmu.edu
Web Site: www.jmu.edu/planetarium
Key Personnel: Dir., Shanil N. Virani.
Institution Type/Description: Planetarium.
Hours & Admission Prices: Visit website for hours. No charge; donations accepted.
&
Attendance: 20,000 (actual)

VIRGINIA QUILT MUSEUM, 301 S. Main St., Harrisonburg, VA
22801-2606. Tel.: 540-433-3818. Fax: 540-433-3818.
E-mail: info@vaquiltmuseum.org
Web Site: www.vaquiltmuseum.org
Key Personnel: Dir., Kimberly L. McCray.
Institution Type/Description: Quilt Museum: housed in an antebellum home; built
in 1856.
Hours & Admission Prices: Feb.-Dec. Tues.-Sat. 10-4. Adults $7, students 5-18 $5;
children under 5 no charge. Closed major holidays; between exhibits. &
Attendance: 5,962 (actual)

Heathsville

NORTHERN NECK FARM MUSEUM, 12705 Northumberland
Hwy., Heathsville, VA 22473. Mailing Address: P.O. Box 365,
Heathsville, VA 22473-0365. Tel.: 804-443-1118.
Web Site: thefarmmuseum.org
Institution Type/Description: Farm Museum.
Hours & Admission Prices: May-Oct. Sat. 10-2, Sun. 1-4. Adults $2, children $1;
children under 6 no charge.

Henrico

**ARMOUR HOUSE AND GARDENS AT MEADOWVIEW
PARK,** 4001 Clarendon Rd., Henrico, VA 23223. Mailing
Address: Henrico County Historical Society, P.O. Box 90775,
Henrico, VA 23273-0775. Tel.: 804-343-3506.
E-mail: ola@co.henrico.va.us
Institution Type/Description: Historic House Museum: built in 1915.
Hours & Admission Prices: Mon.-Fri. 9-4:30. &

Herndon

KIDWELL FARM AT FRYING PAN PARK, 2709 W. Ox Rd.,
Herndon, VA 20171-3807. Tel.: 703-437-9101.
E-mail: friends@fryingpanpark.org
Web Site: www.fairfaxcounty.gov/parks/fryingpanpark/kidwell.htm
Institution Type/Description: Living History Museum & Zoological Park: depicting
a family dairy farm from 1920-1950.
Hours & Admission Prices: Park: daily dawn to dusk. Farm: daily 9-5.

Hood

ROARING TWENTIES ANTIQUE CAR MUSEUM, Rte. 230,
W., Hood, VA 22723. Mailing Address: 1445 Wolftown-Hood Rd.,
Hood, VA 22723-9802. Tel.: 540-948-6290. Fax: 540-948-6290.
Facebook: Roaring Twenties Antique Car Museum.
E-mail: oldautoz@gmail.com
Key Personnel: C.E.O. & Owner, Clarissa Dudley; Cur. & Museum Shop Mgr.,
Martha Dudley.
Institution Type/Description: Transportation Museum.
Hours & Admission Prices: By appointment only, please call 540-948-6290. Adults
& students $10, children 6-12 $3; discounts to AAM, ICOM, AACA & car club
members and groups of 2 or more; children under 6 no charge.
Attendance: 225 (estimated)

Independence

**GRAYSON CROSSROADS MUSEUM AND CULTURAL
EXHIBITS,** 107 E. Main St., Independence, VA 24348. Mailing
Address: P.O. Box 336, Independence, VA 24348-0336. Tel.: 276-
773-3711.
E-mail: 1908courthouse@gmail.com
Key Personnel: Bd. Pres., Laura Bryant.
Institution Type/Description: Local History Museum: housed in the former county
courthouse, 1908.
Hours & Admission Prices: Mon.-Fri. 10-5, Sat. 10-4. No charge; donations
accepted. Closed holidays. &
Attendance: 3,000 (estimated)

Irvington

STEAMBOAT ERA MUSEUM, 156 King Carter Dr., Irvington,
VA 22480. Mailing Address: P.O. Box 132, Irvington, VA 22480-
0132. Tel.: 804-438-6888.
E-mail: director@steamboatmuseum.org
Web Site: www.steamboateramuseum.org
Key Personnel: Exec. Dir., Barbara Brecher; Pres., Eric Nost.
Institution Type/Description: Steamboat Era Museum.
Hours & Admission Prices: Spring & Fall: Fri.-Sat. 10-4; Summer: Tues.-Sat. 10-4.
Adults $5. &
Attendance: 2,000 (actual)

Isle of Wight

BOYKIN'S TAVERN MUSEUM, 17146 Monument Cir., Isle of
Wight, VA 23397. Tel.: 757-357-5182.
E-mail: jengland@smithfieldva.com
Web Site: www.historicisleofwight.com
Institution Type/Description: Historic Building: built in 1762. Listed on the
National Register of Historic Places.
Hours & Admission Prices: Wed.-Fri. 11-4, Sat. by appointment. Guided Tours: $5
per person. Closed Easter; Thanksgiving; Christmas Eve, Day & week.

Jamestown

HISTORIC JAMESTOWNE, 1368 Colonial Pkwy., Jamestown,
VA 23081. Tel.: 757-856-1250. Fax: 757-564-3844.
E-mail: hjvcservices@preservationvirginia.org
Web Site: www.historicjamestowne.org

Formerly: Jamestown National Historic Site
Key Personnel: Exec. Dir. Preservation Virginia, Elizabeth Kostelny; Pres. & Chief Historian, Dr. James Horn; Dir. Research & Interpretation, Preservation Virginia, Dr. William Kelso; Supt., CNHP, Kym Hall; Cur. Archaeology, Preservation Virginia, Merry Outlaw; Information Officer, CNHP, James Perry; Retail Mgr., Historic Jamestowne, Carrie Wiggins.
Institution Type/Description: Historic Site & Preservation Project: first permanent English settlement in North America.
Hours & Admission Prices: Daily 8:30-4:30. Admission $14; discounts to Preservation Virginia & National Park Service members; children under 15 no charge. Closed New Year's Day; Thanksgiving; Christmas. &
Attendance: 220,000 (actual)

Kilmarnock

KILMARNOCK MUSEUM, 76 N. Main St., Kilmarnock, VA 22482. Mailing Address: P.O. Box 1371, Kilmarnock, VA 22482. Tel.: 804-436-9100.
E-mail: contact@kilmarnockva.com
Institution Type/Description: History Museum.
Hours & Admission Prices: Thurs.-Sat. 11-3.

King George

KING GEORGE MUSEUM AND RESEARCH CENTER, 9483 Kings Hwy., King George County Courthouse, King George, VA 22485. Mailing Address: P.O. Box 424, King George, VA 22485-0424. Tel.: 540-775-9477.
Web Site: www.kghistory.org
Institution Type/Description: Historical Society Museum.
Hours & Admission Prices: March-Oct. Thurs. & Sat. 10-2; Nov.-Feb. Sat. 10-2; other times by appointment. Closed New Year's Eve & Day; Easter; Memorial Day; Independence Day; Labor Day; Thanksgiving weekend; Christmas Eve, Day & week.

King William

KING WILLIAM HISTORICAL MUSEUM, 227 Horse Landing Rd., King William, VA 23086. Mailing Address: P.O. Box 233, King William, VA 23086-0233. Tel.: 804-769-9619.
E-mail: kwits@kingwilliamhistory.org
Web Site: www.kingwilliamcounty.us
Key Personnel: Chm. (V) & Museum Shop Mgr., Rebecca Townsend; Society Pres., David Brown.
Institution Type/Description: History Museum.
Hours & Admission Prices: Sat.-Sun. 1-5; other times by appointment. No charge; donations accepted.
Attendance: 500 (estimated)

PAMUNKEY INDIAN MUSEUM, 175 Lay Landing Rd., King William, VA 23086-2126. Tel.: 804-843-4792.
Key Personnel: Mgr., Joyce Krigsvold.
Institution Type/Description: American Indian Museum.
Hours & Admission Prices: Tues.-Sat. 10-4, Sun. 1-4. Adults $2.50, seniors $1.75, children 6-12 $1.25; children under 6 no charge.

Kinsale

KINSALE FOUNDATION AND MUSEUM, 447 Kinsale Rd., Kinsale, VA 22488. Mailing Address: P.O. Box 307, Kinsale, VA 22488-0307. Tel.: 804-472-3001.
E-mail: museumdirector@gmail.com
Key Personnel: Dir., Lynn Norris.
Institution Type/Description: History Museum.
Hours & Admission Prices: May-Sept. Fri.-Sat. 10-5, Sun. 2-5; Oct.-April Fri.-Sat. 10-5. No charge.

Lancaster

MARY BALL WASHINGTON MUSEUM & LIBRARY, INC., 8346 Mary Ball Rd., Lancaster, VA 22503. Mailing Address: P.O. Box 97, Lancaster, VA 22503-0097. Tel.: 804-462-7280. Fax: 804-462-6107.
E-mail: history@mbwm.org
Web Site: www.MBWM.org
Key Personnel: C.E.O., Karen Hart.
Institution Type/Description: Historical Society Museum.
Hours & Admission Prices: Call for hours. Requested Donation: $5; additional fee for research & special programs.
Attendance: 1,000 (actual)

Lawrenceville

BRUNSWICK COUNTY MUSEUM, 228 N. Main St., Lawrenceville, VA 23868-1823. Mailing Address: 234 N. Main St., Lawrenceville, VA 23868. Tel.: 434-848-6773, 866-783-9768 (Toll Free). Fax: 434-848-8553.
Web Site: www.brunswickco.com
Institution Type/Description: History Museum.
Hours & Admission Prices: Tues. & Thurs. 10:30-1, Sat. 1:30-4; other times by appointment.

Leesburg

LOUDOUN MUSEUM, INC., 16 Loudoun St., S.W., Leesburg, VA 20175-2907. Tel.: 703-777-7427. Fax: 703-777-8873.
E-mail: info@loudounmuseum.org
Web Site: www.loudounmuseum.org
Key Personnel: Pres. (V), Elizabeth Whiting; Cur., Alana Blumenthal.
Institution Type/Description: Local History Museum: housed in mid-19th century buildings.
Hours & Admission Prices: Fri.-Sat. 10-5, Sun. 1-5. Adults & students $1; discounts to military; children under 4, military & members no charge. Closed New Year's Day; Thanksgiving; Christmas Eve & Day. &
Attendance: 35,500 (estimated)

THE MARSHALL HOUSE, 217 Edwards Ferry Rd., Leesburg, VA 20176-4173. Mailing Address: 312 E. Market St., #C, Leesburg, VA 20176. Tel.: 703-777-1880 & 1301. Fax: 703-777-1889.
E-mail: info@georgecmarshall.org
Web Site: www.georgecmarshall.org
Formerly: Dodona Manor
Key Personnel: Pres. & C.E.O., Patricia Magee Daly; Chm., Dr. Edgar B. Hatrick, III; Vice Pres. Museum Operations & History Programs, Dr. Laurie West Van Hook; Docent Dir., Tom Bowers.
Institution Type/Description: Historic House Museum: housed in the former residence of General & Mrs. George C. Marshall. A National Historic Landmark.
Hours & Admission Prices: Tours: March-Dec. Sat. 10-5, Sun. and Memorial Day & Labor Day 1-5; groups by appointment. Adults $10; seniors & groups $8; students with ID & children 9-17 $5.
Attendance: 4,000 (estimated)

MORVEN PARK, 17263 Southern Planter Lane, Leesburg, VA 20176-7131. Mailing Address: P.O. Box 6228, Leesburg, VA 20178-7433. Tel.: 703-777-6034. Fax: 703-771-9211.
E-mail: jshafagoj@morvenpark.org
Web Site: www.morvenpark.org
Key Personnel: Exec. Dir., Frank Milligan.
Institution Type/Description: Historic House Museum.
Hours & Admission Prices: Daily. Closed New Year's Day; Thanksgiving; Christmas. &
Attendance: 20,000 (actual)

OATLANDS, 20850 Oatlands Plantation Lane, Leesburg, VA 20175-6572. Tel.: 703-777-3174. Fax: 703-777-4427.
E-mail: oatlands@erols.com
Web Site: www.oatlands.org
Key Personnel: Exec. Dir., Andrea McGimsey; Chm., Mike O'Conner; Dir. Operations, Carolyn McCarthy; Museum Shop Mgr., Carolyn Barnett.
Institution Type/Description: Historic House Museum: 1804 Oatlands mansion with English walled garden, built by George Carter; a portico with Corinthian capitals, carved by Henry Farnham, was added in 1827.
Hours & Admission Prices: April-Dec. Mon.-Sat. 10-5, Sun. 1-5. Adults $12, senior citizens $10; discounts to groups, National Trust for Historic Preservation members; members no charge. &
Attendance: 40,000 (estimated)

Lexington

GEORGE C. MARSHALL MUSEUM CLOSED, 1600 VMI Parade Ground, Lexington, VA 24450. Mailing Address: P.O. Drawer 1600, Lexington, VA 24450-1600. Tel.: 540-463-7103, ext. 125. Fax: 540-464-5229.
E-mail: marshallfoundation@marshallfoundation.org
Web Site: www.marshallfoundation.org
Formerly: George C. Marshall Research Foundation
Key Personnel: Pres., Brian D. Shaw; Assoc. Dir. Leadership Programs, Marti Bissell; Dir. Admin., Carol E. Wheeler; Dir. Library & Archives, Paul B. Barron.
Institution Type/Description: Library and History Museum.

Hours & Admission Prices: Tues.-Sat. 11-4, Sun. 1-5. Adults $5, senior citizens $3, students $2; discounts to groups of 10 or more; children & active military no charge. Closed New Year's Eve & Day; Christmas Eve, Day & week, Easter. &
Attendance: 18,000 (estimated)

LEE CHAPEL & MUSEUM, Washington & Lee University, Lexington, VA 24450-2116. Mailing Address: 11 University Place, Lexington, VA 24450-2116. Tel.: 540-458-8768. Fax: 540-458-5804.
E-mail: leechapel@wlu.edu
Web Site: leechapel.wlu.edu
Key Personnel: Mgr., Lucy Wilkins.
Institution Type/Description: History Museum: housed in 1868 historic building constructed under the direction of R.E. Lee.
Hours & Admission Prices: April-Oct. Mon.-Sat. 9-5, Sun. 1-5; Nov.-March Mon.-Sat. 9-4, Sun.1-4; call to verify. Suggested Donation: adults $5, children under 12 $3. Closed New Year's Eve & Day; Easter; Independence Day; Thanksgiving & weekend after; Christmas Eve, Day & week; university holidays. &
Attendance: 45,000 (estimated)

THE REEVES CENTER, WASHINGTON AND LEE UNIVERSITY, 204 W. Washington St., Lexington, VA 24450. Tel.: 540-458-8034 & 8476. Fax: 540-458-8741.
E-mail: pgrover@wlu.edu
Key Personnel: Dir., Peter Dun Grover; Assoc. Dir. & Cur. Collections, Patricia Hobbs; Mgr. & Cur., Ronald W. Fuchs; Coord. Collections, Kyra Swanson.
Institution Type/Description: Art Museum: housed in two buildings - 1840 Greek Revival house on the front campus & a Palladian-style pavilion with two galleries.
Hours & Admission Prices: Mon.-Fri. 9-4:30, Sat.-Sun. by appointment. No charge. Closed New Year's Eve & Day; Memorial Day; Independence Day; Thanksgiving; Christmas Day & week. &
Attendance: 5,000 (estimated)

ROCKBRIDGE HISTORICAL SOCIETY, 101 E. Washington St., Lexington, VA 24450. Mailing Address: P.O. Box 1409, Lexington, VA 24450-1409. Tel.: 540-464-1058.
E-mail: rochist@hotmail.com
Web Site: rockhist.org
Key Personnel: Exec. Dir., Eric Wilson; Pres., Dr. Steve Beck.
Institution Type/Description: General Museum: housed in c.1844 Campbell House, a 3-story brick home.
Hours & Admission Prices: mid-April to mid-Oct. Wed.-Fri. 10-3, Sat. 1-3; mid-Oct. to mid-April Mon.-Sat. 10-1, Sun. 1-4. No charge; donations accepted. Closed New Year's Eve & Day; Christmas Eve, Day & week. &
Attendance: 2,000 (estimated)

STANIAR GALLERY, Wilson Hall, 100 Glasgow St., Washington & Lee University, Lexington, VA 24450-2116. Tel.: 540-458-8861 & 8860. Fax: 540-458-8112.
E-mail: archerc@wlu.edu
Web Site: www.wlu.edu
Formerly: Dupont Gallery
Key Personnel: Dir., Clover Archer Lyle.
Institution Type/Description: University Art Gallery.
Hours & Admission Prices: Sept.-May Mon.-Fri. 9-5. No charge. &

STONEWALL JACKSON HOUSE, 8 E. Washington St., Lexington, VA 24450-2529. Tel.: 540-464-7704. Fax: 540-463-4088. Facebook.
E-mail: stonewalljacksonhouse@vmi.edu
Web Site: www.stonewalljackson.org
Key Personnel: Supvr. Interpretation, Grace Abele; Supvr. Visitor Svcs. & Museum Shop Mgr., Tracey Lackey.
Institution Type/Description: Historic House Museum: 1859-1861 Stonewall Jackson Home.
Hours & Admission Prices: March-Dec. Mon.-Sat. 9-5. Adults $8, youth 6-17 $6; discounts to groups, and AAM, CAA, VAM & SEMC members. Closed New Year's Day; Easter; Thanksgiving; Christmas.
Attendance: 20,709 (actual)

VIRGINIA MILITARY INSTITUTE MUSEUM, Virginia Military Institute, Jackson Memorial Hall, 415 Letcher Ave., Lexington, VA 24450-2194. Tel.: 540-464-7334. Fax: 540-464-7112. TDD: 540-464-7616.
E-mail: gibsonke@vmi.edu
Web Site: www.vmi.edu/museum
Key Personnel: Exec. Dir., Keith E. Gibson; Registrar, Barbara J. Blakey; Museum Shop Mgr., Betty E. Skillman.

Institution Type/Description: Military, National Historic District and General Museum: located on Virginia Military Institute campus.
Hours & Admission Prices: Daily 9-5. No charge; donations accepted. Closed New Year's Eve, Day & day after; Thanksgiving; Christmas Eve, Day & week. &
Attendance: 40,000 (actual)

Lorton

POHICK EPISCOPAL CHURCH, 9301 Richmond Hwy., Lorton, VA 22079-1519. Tel.: 703-339-6572. Fax: 703-339-9884.
E-mail: troknya@pohick.org
Web Site: www.pohick.org
Key Personnel: Rector, Rev. Donald D. Binder.
Institution Type/Description: Active Church: housed in 1774 parish church of George Washington & George Mason.
Hours & Admission Prices: Mon.-Sat. 9-4:30, Sun. 8-4:30. No charge; donations accepted. &

WORKHOUSE PRISON MUSEUM AT LORTON, 9518 Workhouse Way, Lorton, VA 22079. Tel.: 703-584-2917. Fax: 703-690-1880.
E-mail: info@workhousearts.org
Web Site: www.workhousemuseum.org
Formerly: Lorton Arts Center
Key Personnel: C.E.O., John Mason; Chm. (V), Fred Bollerer.
Institution Type/Description: Art Galleries & Historic Prison Museum.
Hours & Admission Prices: Wed.-Fri. 12-3, Sat.-Sun. 12-4. No charge; donations accepted. Closed New Year's Day; Easter; Independence Day; Labor Day; Thanksgiving; Christmas. &
Attendance: 75,000 (estimated)

Louisa

LOUISA COUNTY HISTORICAL SOCIETY, 214 Fredericksburg Ave., Louisa, VA 23093-6531. Mailing Address: P.O. Box 1172, Louisa, VA 23093-1172. Tel.: 540-967-5975. Facebook: Louisa County Historical Society.
E-mail: louisahistory@verizon.net
Web Site: www.louisahistory.org
Key Personnel: Pres. (V), Maren Smith.
Institution Type/Description: Historical Society Museum: housed in 1868 jail.
Hours & Admission Prices: Jail Museum: April-Sept. Fri.-Sat. 10am-12pm. Sargeant Museum: Mon.-Sat. 10-4, call to confirm. No charge; donations accepted. &
Attendance: 950 (actual)

Lovettsville

LOVETTSVILLE HISTORICAL SOCIETY INCORPORATED, 4 E. Pennsylvania Ave., Lovettsville, VA 20180. Mailing Address: P.O. Box 5, Lovettsville, VA 20180-0005. Tel.: 540-822-5499. Fax: 540-822-9797.
E-mail: info@lovettsvillehistoricalsociety.org
Web Site: lovettsvillehistoricalsociety.org
Key Personnel: Chm. (V), Thomas Bullock.
Institution Type/Description: Historical Society Museum.
Hours & Admission Prices: May-Dec. Sat. 1-4; other times by appointment. No charge; donations accepted.
Attendance: 890 (estimated)

Luray

SHENANDOAH NATIONAL PARK, 3655 U.S. Hwy. 211 E., Luray, VA 22835-4702. Tel.: 540-999-3500. Fax: 540-999-3601.
E-mail: shen_superintendent@nps.gov
Web Site: www.nps.gov/shen
Key Personnel: Supt., Jim Northup.
Institution Type/Description: Park Museum & Visitor Center.
Hours & Admission Prices: Park: daily 24 hours. $20 per car, $15 for motorcycles, $15-20 per night for campers, $10 per person. Park Visitor & Information Centers: call or visit website for hours. &
Attendance: 1,200,000 (estimated)

Lynchburg

AMAZEMENT SQUARE, 27 Ninth St., Lynchburg, VA 24504-1422. Tel.: 434-845-1888. Fax: 434-845-5221. Facebook: Amazement Square.
E-mail: visitus@amazementsquare.org
Web Site: www.amazementsquare.org

Key Personnel: Pres. & C.E.O., Mort Sajadian, Ph.D.; Chm. (V), Hylan T. Hubbard, III; Dir. Mktg., Ashleigh Karol; Dir. Operations, Amanda Fortner; Dir. Exhibitions & Programs, Emily Joseph; Deputy Dir. Devel., Michelle Bergman; Fiscal Officer, Aileen Hull; Exhibit Fabricator, John Kastner.
Institution Type/Description: Children's Science Museum.
Hours & Admission Prices: Tues.-Sat. 10-5, Sun. 1-5; call for Mon. holiday hours. Offices: Mon.-Fri. 9-5. Admission 2-59 $9, senior citizens 60 & over $6; discounts to groups of 10 or more by appointment; members & children under one no charge. ♿
Attendance: 77,644 (actual)

THE ANNE SPENCER MEMORIAL FOUNDATION, INC., 1313 Pierce St., Lynchburg, VA 24501-1935. Tel.: 434-845-1313.
Key Personnel: Chm., Hugh R. Jones; Chm. Tours, Liz Lovern.
Institution Type/Description: Historic House & Garden: housed in the former home of poet, Anne Spencer; built in 1903. Listed on the National Register of Historic Places.
Hours & Admission Prices: By appointment only. Adults $10, seniors & college students $5, children under 12 $3; discounts to groups.
Attendance: 1,000 (estimated)

CREATION HALL MUSEUM, 1971 University Blvd., Lynchburg, VA 24502. Tel.: 434-582-2209. Fax: 434-582-2488.
E-mail: dadewitt@liberty.edu
Web Site: www.liberty.edu
Formerly: Museum of Earth and Life History
Key Personnel: Dir., David A. DeWitt, Ph.D.
Institution Type/Description: Natural History Museum.
Hours & Admission Prices: Mon.-Tues. & Thurs.-Fri. 8-8, Wed. 8-4, Sat. 9-6, Sun. 1-4. No charge. ♿
Attendance: 4,000 (estimated)

DAURA GALLERY, Lynchburg College, 1501 Lakeside Dr., Lynchburg, VA 24501-3199. Tel.: 434-544-8343 & 8349. Fax: 804-544-8277. Facebook.
E-mail: rothermel@lynchburg.edu
Web Site: www.lynchburg.edu/daura
Key Personnel: Dir., Barbara Rothermel, PhD; Asst. Dir., Steve Riffee, MFA; Chmn. (V), Beverly Shorter Baker; Staff, Laurie Cassidy.
Institution Type/Description: Art Gallery.
Hours & Admission Prices: Aug.-May Mon.-Fri. 9-4, Sun. call for hours; June-July by appointment. No charge; donations accepted. Closed college holidays; New Year's Day; Thanksgiving; Christmas. ♿
Attendance: 6,000 (estimated)

LEGACY MUSEUM OF AFRICAN-AMERICAN HISTORY, 403 Monroe St., Lynchburg, VA 24504-2808. Mailing Address: P. O. Box 308, Lynchburg, VA 24505-0308. Tel.: 434-845-3455. Fax: 434-845-9809.
E-mail: legacymuseum@ntelos.net
Web Site: www.legacymuseum.org
Key Personnel: Museum Admin., Cheryl Robinson.
Institution Type/Description: History Museum.
Hours & Admission Prices: Wed.-Sat. 12-4, Sun. 2-4; other times by appointment. Adults $5, seniors $3, youth $2; children under 6 no charge. Closed major holidays. ♿

LYNCHBURG MUSEUM SYSTEM - LYNCHBURG MUSEUM, 901 Court St., Lynchburg, VA 24504-1603. Mailing Address: P.O. Box 529, Lynchburg, VA 24505-0529. Tel.: 434-455-6226. Fax: 434-528-0162. Facebook; Twitter; Instagram.
E-mail: museum@lynchburgva.gov
Web Site: www.lynchburgmuseum.org; www.pointofhonor.org
Key Personnel: Dir., Ted Delaney; Pres. (V) & Museum Shop Mgr., Laura Crumbley; Bd. Chm., Charlotte Fischer; Cur., Laura Wilson; Educator & Volunteer Coord., Whitney Roberts.
Institution Type/Description: History Museum.
Hours & Admission Prices: Mon.-Sat. 10-4, Sun. 12-4. Museum: no charge; donations accepted. Closed New Year's Day; Thanksgiving; Christmas Eve & Day. ♿
Attendance: 24,628 (actual)

MAIER MUSEUM OF ART AT RANDOLPH COLLEGE, One Quinlan St., Lynchburg, VA 24503-1519. Mailing Address: 2500 Rivermont Ave., Lynchburg, VA 24503-1526. Tel.: 434-947-8136 & 8000. Fax: 434-947-8726. Facebook: Maier Museum.
E-mail: museum@randolphcollege.edu
Web Site: maiermuseum.org
Formerly: Maier Museum of Art, Randolph-Macon Woman's College
Key Personnel: Dir., Martha Kjeseth Johnson; Cur. Education, Laura McManus; Registrar, Deborah Spanich; Office Mgr. & Public Engagement Coord., Danni Schreffler; Preparator & Security Guard, John Spanich; Gallery Monitor, Anne McDaniel.
Institution Type/Description: Art.
Hours & Admission Prices: mid-May to late Aug. Wed.-Sun. 1-4; late Aug. to mid-May Tues.-Sun. 1-5. No charge; donations accepted. Closed academic holidays, New Year's Day; Easter; Independence Day; Thanksgiving; Christmas.
Attendance: 7,200 (estimated)

OLD CITY CEMETERY MUSEUMS & ARBORETUM, 401 Taylor St., Lynchburg, VA 24501-1245. Tel.: 434-847-1465. Fax: 434-856-2004.
E-mail: occ@gravegarden.org
Web Site: www.gravegarden.org
Key Personnel: Dir., D. Bruce Christian; Pres. (V), Betty Brown; Museum Shop Mgr., Kathy Wise.
Institution Type/Description: Historic Landmark: listed on the National Register of Historic Places.
Hours & Admission Prices: Cemetery: daily dawn to dusk. Visitor Center & Victorian Mourning Exhibit: May & Oct. daily 10-3; June-Sept. & Nov.-April Mon.-Sat. 10-3. No charge; donations accepted.
Attendance: 30,844 (actual)

POINT OF HONOR, 112 Cabell St., Lynchburg, VA 24504-1211. Mailing Address: Lynchburg Museum System, P.O. Box 529, Lynchburg, VA 24505-0529. Tel.: 434-455-6226. Fax: 434-528-0162. Facebook & Twitter: Lynchburg Museum System.
E-mail: museum@lynchburgva.gov
Web Site: www.pointofhonor.org
Key Personnel: Admin., Douglas K. Harvey; Chm. (V), Rob Craighill; Pres. (V), Tom Smith; Museum Shop Mgr., Laura Crumbley.
Institution Type/Description: Historic House: home of Dr. George Cabell, physician to Patrick Henry.
Hours & Admission Prices: Mon.-Sat. 10-4, Sun. 12-4. Adults $6, seniors 60 & over $5, youth 6-17 $3; discounts to AAM & ICOM members; museum professionals, members & children under 6 no charge. Closed New Year's Day; Thanksgiving; Christmas Eve & Day.
Attendance: 9,232 (actual)

SOUTH RIVER MEETING HOUSE, 5810 Fort Ave., Lynchburg, VA 24502-1928. Tel.: 434-239-2548. Fax: 434-239-6071.
E-mail: lnorment@virginia.org
Web Site: qmpc.org/contents/meetinghousehistory.shtml
Key Personnel: Dir., Diane Baldwin.
Institution Type/Description: Historic Site: a restored Society of Friends meeting house, c.1791. Listed on the National Register of Historic Places.
Hours & Admission Prices: Mon.-Fri. 9-2; guided tours by appointment. No charge; donations accepted. Closed major holidays. ♿
Attendance: 350

Machipongo

EASTERN SHORE OF VIRGINIA BARRIER ISLANDS CENTER, 7295 Young St., Machipongo, VA 23405. Mailing Address: P.O. Box 206, Machipongo, VA 23405-0206. Tel.: 757-678-5550. Fax: 888-315-8780.
E-mail: barrierislandscenter@live.com
Web Site: www.barrierislandscenter.com
Institution Type/Description: History Museum.
Hours & Admission Prices: Tues.-Sat. 10-4. No charge; donations accepted. ♿

Manassas

MANASSAS MUSEUM SYSTEM, 9101 Prince William St., Manassas, VA 20110-5615. Tel.: 703-368-1873. Fax: 703-257-8406. TDD: 703-257-8255.
E-mail: egossman@ci.manassas.va.us
Web Site: www.manassasmuseum.org
Key Personnel: Dir., Elizabeth S. Via-Gossman; Chm. (V), Keith Mueller; Museum Shop Mgr., Jane Riley.
Institution Type/Description: History Museum.
Hours & Admission Prices: Memorial Day to Labor Day daily dawn to dusk; Sept.-May Tues.-Sun. dawn to dusk. Adults $5, seniors & students $4; children under 6 no charge. Closed New Year's Day; Thanksgiving; Christmas. ♿
Attendance: 17,571 (actual)

MANASSAS NATIONAL BATTLEFIELD PARK, 6511 Sudley Rd., (Rt. 234), Manassas, VA 20109-2358. Mailing Address: 12521 Lee Hwy., Manassas, VA 20109. Tel.: 703-361-1339. Fax: 703-361-7106. TDD: 703-361-7075.
E-mail: jon_james@nps.gov

Web Site: www.nps.gov/mana
Key Personnel: Supt., Jon G. James; Chm. (V), Henry Elliott; Museum Shop Mgr., Janda Sample.
Institution Type/Description: Park Museum & Visitor Center
Hours & Admission Prices: Visitor Center: daily 8:30-5. No charge; donations accepted. Closed Thanksgiving; Christmas. &
Attendance: 502,525 (actual)

Marion

SMYTH COUNTY MUSEUM, 123 E. Main St., Marion, VA 24354-2707. Mailing Address: P.O. Box 710, Marion, VA 24354-0710. Tel.: 276-783-7286.
E-mail: webadmin@smythcountymuseum.org
Web Site: smythcountymuseum.org
Key Personnel: Pres. (V), Anna Leigh DeBord.
Institution Type/Description: History Museum.
Hours & Admission Prices: April-Oct. Mon.-Thurs. 11-4, Fri. 11-8, Sat. 10-2. No charge; donations accepted. &
Attendance: 3,000 (estimated)

Martinsville

PIEDMONT ARTS, 215 Starling Ave., Martinsville, VA 24112-3832. Tel.: 276-632-3221.
E-mail: kathyrogers@piedmontarts.org
Web Site: www.piedmontarts.org
Key Personnel: Exec. Dir., Kathy Rogers; Mgr. Finance, Pam Allen; Dir. Mktg. Communications & Design, Bernadette Moore; Dir. Exhibitions, Heidi Pinkston; Education Coord., Becki Williams Vasquez.
Institution Type/Description: Arts Center: housed in c.1900 M.R. Schottland Estate.
Hours & Admission Prices: Mon.-Fri. 10-5, Sat. 10-3. No charge; donations accepted. Closed holidays. &
Attendance: 36,000 (estimated)

VIRGINIA MUSEUM OF NATURAL HISTORY, 21 Starling Ave., Martinsville, VA 24112-2921. Tel.: 276-634-4141. Fax: 276-634-4199. TDD: 276-634-4149.
E-mail: information@vmnh.virginia.gov
Web Site: www.vmnh.net
Key Personnel: Chm. Bd. Trustees, James W. Severt, II; Pres. VMNH Foundation, Manly Boyd; Exec. Dir., Joe B. Keiper, Ph.D.; Dir. Education & Public Programs, Dennis A. Casey, Ph.D.; Dep. Dir., Ryan L. Barber; Dir. Research & Collections, Cur. Earth Sciences, James S. Beard, Ph.D.; Cur. Archaeology, Elizabeth A. Moore, Ph.D.; Asst. Cur. Paleontology, Alexander K. Hastings, Ph. D.; Asst. Cur. Recent Invertebrates, Kaloyan Y. Ivanov, Ph.D.; Visitor Svcs. Mgr., Diane Clark.
Institution Type/Description: Natural History Museum.
Hours & Admission Prices: Mon.-Sat. 9-5; Adults $7, children 3-18 and seniors 65 & over $5; children under 3 & members no charge. Closed New Year's Day; Thanksgiving; Christmas. &
Attendance: 33,109 (actual)

Mason Neck

GUNSTON HALL PLANTATION, 10709 Gunston Rd., Mason Neck, VA 22079-3901. Tel.: 703-550-9220. Fax: 703-550-9480.
E-mail: Historic@GunstonHall.org
Web Site: www.gunstonhall.org
Key Personnel: First Regent (V), Mrs. Wylie G. Raab; Devel. Coord., Susan Blankenship; Administrative Asst., Lena McAllister; Education Asst., Frank Barker; Librarian & Archivist, Mark Whatford; Docent Chm., Mary Kay Ruwe; Archaeologist, David Shonyo; Museum Shop Mgr., Karen E. Bazzle.
Institution Type/Description: Historic House: 1755 Gunston Hall, plantation home of George Mason.
Hours & Admission Prices: Daily 9:30-5. Adults $10, senior citizens 60 & over $8, children 6-18 $5; discount to AAM members; members and children under 6 no charge. Closed New Year's Day; Thanksgiving; Christmas. &
Attendance: 25,000 (actual)

Mathews

MATHEWS COUNTY HISTORICAL SOCIETY, INC., Headquarters at Tompkins Cottage, 27 Brickbat Rd., Mathews, VA 23109. Mailing Address: P.O. Box 855, Mathews, VA 23109-0855.
Web Site: www.rootsweb.com/~vamchs/index.html
Key Personnel: Pres. (V), Reed B. Lawson; Museum Shop Mgr., Martha Ellen Traband.
Institution Type/Description: Historic House: housed in a former mercantile store owned by Christopher Tompkins, father of Captain Sally Tompkins, the first

female commissioned officer in the U.S. military; built in 1815. Historic Store c. 1820 named Old James Store.
Hours & Admission Prices: Spring & Summer Fri.-Sat. 10-1. No charge; donations accepted.

McDowell

HIGHLAND COUNTY MUSEUM, 161 Mansion House Rd., McDowell, VA 24458. Mailing Address: P.O. Box 63, McDowell, VA 24458-0063. Tel.: 540-396-4478. Fax: 540-396-4478.
E-mail: highlandhist@mgwnet.com
Web Site: www.highlandcountyhistory.com
Key Personnel: Exec. Dir., Lorraine White; Chm., Sarah Samples; Vice Chm., Christopher Scott; Treas., James Blagg.
Institution Type/Description: History Museum: housed in an 1851 former hospital used during the Civil War which later became a hotel & stagecoach stop on the Staunton to Parkersburg Turnpike.
Hours & Admission Prices: Fri.-Sat. 11-4, Sun. 1-4. No charge; donations accepted.
Attendance: 1,935 (actual)

McLean

NATIONAL PARK SERVICE-GREAT FALLS PARK, 9200 Old Dominion Dr., McLean, VA 22102. Mailing Address: 700 George Washington Memorial Pkwy., McLean, VA 22101. Tel.: 703-285-2966. Fax: 703-285-2223. Facebook: National Park Service-Great Falls Park.
Web Site: www.nps.gov/grfa
Key Personnel: Park Supt., Alexcy Romero; Site Mgr. & Museum Shop Mgr., Brent O'Neill.
Institution Type/Description: Park Museum: site of the 1785 Patowmack Canal developed by George Washington.
Hours & Admission Prices: Mon.-Fri. 10-5, Sat.-Sun. 10-6; seasonal hours vary. $10 per vehicle, $3 per person; discounts to seniors 62 & over and disabled. Annual passes available. &
Attendance: 600,000 (estimated)

Middleburg

NATIONAL SPORTING LIBRARY & MUSEUM, 102 The Plains Rd., Middleburg, VA 20117. Mailing Address: P.O. Box 1335, Middleburg, VA 20118-1335. Tel.: 540-687-6542. Fax: 540-687-8540.
E-mail: museum@nsl.org
Web Site: www.nsl.org
Key Personnel: Exec. Dir., Melanie Mathewes; Librarian, John Connolly; Cur., Claudia Pfeiffer; Cur. Permanent Collection, Nicole Stribling; Coord. Membership, Diana Kingsbury-Smith; Mgr. Membership & Devel., Alexandra McKay; Bookkeeper, Mary Deppa; Accountant, Jo Wolford.
Institution Type/Description: Library & Art Museum.
Hours & Admission Prices: Wed.-Sat. 10-5, Sun. 1-5. Adults $10; seniors 65 & over and youth 13-18 $8; discounts to AAM, SERM & NARM members; members and children 12 & under no charge. Closed federal holidays. &
Attendance: 7,431 (actual)

Middletown

BELLE GROVE PLANTATION, 336 Belle Grove Rd., Middletown, VA 22645. Mailing Address: P.O. Box 537, Middletown, VA 22645-0537. Tel.: 540-869-2028. Fax: 540-869-9638. Facebook: Belle Grove Plantation.
E-mail: info@bellegrove.org
Web Site: www.bellegrove.org
Key Personnel: Exec. Dir., Kristen Laise; Coord. Programs & Events, Rich Coyle; Outrerach & Coord. (V), Karen Haizlett; Supt. Bldgs. & Grounds, Dennis Campbell; Chm. (V) Belle Grove, Inc., Suzanne Conrad; Housekeeper, Dorothy Fletcher; Museum Shop Mgr., Karen Schmedding.
Institution Type/Description: Historic House: 1797 Belle Grove home of Revolutionary War officer Maj. Isaac Hite, Jr., brother-in-law of President James Madison, & 1864 Civil War headquarters of Gen. Philip Sheridan, Civil War Battle of Cedar Creek was fought on Belle Grove's grounds. Thomas Jefferson assisted on design.
Hours & Admission Prices: April-Oct. Mon.-Sat. 10-4 (last tour 3:15). Sun. 1-5 (last tour 4:15); Nov.-Dec. call for hours. Adults $12, senior citizens $11, students 6-12 $6; discounts to groups, AAA, National Park, Mobile Travel, National Trust; members no charge. Closed Easter; Memorial Day; Independence Day; Labor Day; Columbus Day; Thanksgiving; Christmas Eve & Day.
Attendance: 14,000 (actual)

Millwood

BURWELL-MORGAN MILL, 15 Tannery Ln., Millwood, VA 22646. Mailing Address: P.O. Box 306, Berryville, VA 22611-0306. Tel.: 540-837-1799. Fax: 540-955-0285.
E-mail: bmmill@clarkehistory.org
Web Site: www.clarkehistory.org/themill.htm
Key Personnel: Dir., Laura Christiansen; Pres. (V), Howard Means; Archivist, Mary Morris.
Institution Type/Description: History Museum: 1782-85, operating, water-powered Merchant Grist & Flour Mill.
Hours & Admission Prices: May-Nov. Sat. 10-5, Sun. 12-5. No charge.
Attendance: 10,000 (estimated)

Mineral

NORTH ANNA NUCLEAR INFORMATION CENTER, Rte. 700, 1022 Haley Dr., Mineral, VA 23117. Mailing Address: 1022 Haley Dr., Mineral, VA 23117-4527. Tel.: 540-894-2029.
E-mail: mike.duffey@dominionenergy.com
Web Site: www.dominionenergy.com
Key Personnel: Communications Specialist, Michael Duffey; Sr. Communications Specialist, Scott Miller.
Institution Type/Description: Nuclear Energy Museum.
Hours & Admission Prices: Mon.-Fri. 9-4. No charge. Closed major holidays. &
Attendance: 3,000 (actual)

Monterey

HIGHLAND MAPLE MUSEUM, 61 Highland Center Rd., Monterey, VA 24465. Mailing Address: P.O. Box 223, Monterey, VA 24465-0223. Tel.: 540-468-2550. Fax: 540-468-2551.
E-mail: highcc@cfw.com
Web Site: www.highlandcounty.org
Key Personnel: C.E.O., Carolyn Pohowsky.
Institution Type/Description: Agriculture Museum.
Hours & Admission Prices: Daily. No charge; donations accepted. &
Attendance: 3,000 (estimated)

Montross

ARMSTEAD TASKER JOHNSON HIGH SCHOOL MUSEUM, 18849 King's Hwy., Montross, VA 22520. Mailing Address: P.O. Box 1149, Montross, VA 22520-1000. Tel.: 804-493-7070.
E-mail: atjohnsonmuseum1@verizon.net
Key Personnel: Chm. (V), Marian Veney Ashton; Pres. (V), Dr. Lois Harrison-Jones.
Institution Type/Description: History Museum: housed in the first high school in the Northern Neck for African American students.
Hours & Admission Prices: May-Sept. Wed.-Thurs. & Sat. 1-4; Sept.-Nov. Sat. 1-4; other times by appointment. No charge; donations accepted. &
Attendance: 300 (estimated)

WESTMORELAND COUNTY MUSEUM AND LIBRARY, INC., 43 Court Square, Montross, VA 22520. Mailing Address: P. O. Box 247, Montross, VA 22520-0247. Tel.: 804-493-8440. Fax: 804-493-1312.
E-mail: wcmuseum@verizon.net
Web Site: www.westmoreland-county.org
Institution Type/Description: History Museum.
Hours & Admission Prices: Mon.-Sat. 10-4. No charge; donations accepted. Closed county holidays.

Morattico

MORATTICO WATERFRONT MUSEUM, Morattico Rd., Morattico, VA 22523. Mailing Address: P.O. Box 80, Morattico, VA 22523-0080. Tel.: 804-462-0532.
E-mail: moratticowaterfrontmuseum@yahoo.com
Institution Type/Description: History Museum: housed in the former Morattico General Store; built in 1901.
Hours & Admission Prices: May-Oct. Sat. 12-4, Sun. 1-4. &

Mount Vernon

GEORGE WASHINGTON'S MOUNT VERNON, 3200 Mount Vernon Memorial Hwy., Mount Vernon, VA 22309. Mailing Address: P.O. Box 110, Mount Vernon, VA 22121-0110. Tel.: 703-780-2000. Fax: 703-799-8654. TDD: 703-799-8121.
E-mail: info@mountvernon.org
Web Site: www.mountvernon.org
Formerly: Mount Vernon: George Washington's Estate & Gardens
Key Personnel: Regent, Barbara Lucas; Pres. & C.E.O., Curtis Viebranz; C.F.O., Philip Manno; Sr. Vice Pres. Visitor Engagement, Robert Shenk; Chief of Staff, Megan Dunn; Vice Pres. Mktg., Rebecca Aloisi; Sr. Vice Pres. Historic Preservation & Collections, Carol Cadou; Vice Pres. Operations & Mgmt., Joe Sliger; Dir. Retail, Julia Mosley; Dir. Human Resources, Sara Walker; Dir. Horticulture, Dean Norton; Mount Vernon Inn Mgr., Jay Quander; Founding Dir. FWS Natl. Library for the Study of George Washington, Doug Bradburn.
Institution Type/Description: Historic Plantation: 1735-1799 Mount Vernon, home of George Washington.
Hours & Admission Prices: March & Sept.-Oct. daily 9-5; April-Aug. daily 8-5; Nov.-Feb. daily 9-4. Adults $20, senior citizens $19, youth 6-11 $10; discount to groups of 20 or more; children 5 & under and scout groups in uniform no charge. &
Attendance: 1,136,793 (actual)

Natural Bridge

NATURAL BRIDGE ZOOLOGICAL PARK, 5784 S. Lee Hwy., Natural Bridge, VA 24578. Mailing Address: P.O. Box 88, Natural Bridge, VA 24578-0088. Tel.: 540-291-2420. Fax: 540-291-1891.
E-mail: naturalbridgezoo@hotmail.com
Web Site: www.naturalbridgezoo.com
Institution Type/Description: Zoo.
Hours & Admission Prices: Spring & Summer: Mon.-Fri. 9-6, Sat.-Sun. 9-7; Fall & Winter: daily 9-5. Adults $12, senior citizens $10, children 3-12 $8; children 2 & under no charge.

New Market

VIRGINIA MUSEUM OF THE CIVIL WAR, 8895 George Collins Dr., New Market, VA 22844. Mailing Address: P.O. Box 1864, New Market, VA 22844-1864. Tel.: 540-740-3101, 866-515-1864 (toll free). Fax: 540-740-3033. TDD: 703-464-7616.
E-mail: nmbshp@vmi.edu
Web Site: www.vmi.edu/newmarket
Formerly: New Market Battlefield State Historical Park
Key Personnel: Exec. Dir., Col. Keith E. Gibson; Dir., Major Troy D. Marshall; Visitor Svcs. Supvr., Judith Drury; Supvr. Historical Interpretation, Stacey R. Nadeau; Office Mgr., Brittney Phillips.
Institution Type/Description: Military History Museum: located on the site of the 1864 Battle of New Market.
Hours & Admission Prices: Daily 9-5. Adults $10, seniors $9, children 6-12 $6; discounts to groups, seniors, military, VAM & AAM members. Closed New Year's Day; Thanksgiving; Christmas Eve and Day. &
Attendance: 41,258 (actual)

Newbern

WILDERNESS ROAD REGIONAL MUSEUM, State Rt. 611, 5240 Wilderness Rd., Newbern, VA 24126. Mailing Address: P.O. Box 373, Newbern, VA 24126-0373. Tel.: 540-674-4835. Facebook: Wilderness Road Regional Museum.
Web Site: www.wildernessroadregionalmuseum.org
Key Personnel: C.E.O. & Pres. (V), Carolyn Mathews; Dir., Chm. (V), Dir. Public Rels. & Museum Shop Mgr., Andrew M. Hamblin; Librarian & Genealogy Researcher, Elinor Farmer; Treas., Barbara Duncan; Administrative Asst., Rebecca Gunn; Collections Admin., Kasey Campbell.
Institution Type/Description: Historical Society Museum: housed in c.1810 2-story frame/log building located in Old Newbern National Historic District.
Hours & Admission Prices: mid-March to mid-Dec. Tues.-Sat. 10:30-4:30; mid-Dec. to mid-March by appointment only. No charge; donations accepted. Closed New Year's Day; Easter; Mother's Day; Labor Day; Thanksgiving; Christmas. &
Attendance: 20,000 (estimated)

Newport News

ENDVIEW PLANTATION, 362 Yorktown Rd., Newport News, VA 23603-1017. Tel.: 757-887-1862. Fax: 757-888-3869.
E-mail: endview@nnva.gov
Web Site: www.endview.org
Key Personnel: Site Coord., Laura Willoughby; Education Coord., Tim Greene.
Institution Type/Description: Historic House Museum: plantation built c.1769.
Hours & Admission Prices: Jan.-March Thurs.-Sat. 10-4, Sun. 1-5; April-Dec. Mon. & Thurs.-Fri. 10-4, Sat. 10-5, Sun. 12-5. Adults $8, seniors 62 & over $7, children 7-18 $6; children under 7 no charge.
Attendance: 2,700 (actual)

GOLF MUSEUM, James River Country Club, 1500 Country Club Rd., Newport News, VA 23606-2840. Tel.: 757-595-3327, Fax: 757-596-4807.
E-mail: info@jamesrivercountryclub.com
Key Personnel: Dir. & C.E.O., William S. Hargette.
Institution Type/Description: Sports Museum.
Hours & Admission Prices: By appointment. No charge. Closed holidays. &
Attendance: 1,000 (estimated)

JAMES A. FIELDS HOUSE, 617 27th St., Newport News, VA 23607-4033. Tel.: 757-245-1991.
E-mail: jafieldshouse@hotmail.com
Key Personnel: Dir., Saundra N. Cherry.
Institution Type/Description: Historic House Museum: housed in the former home & law office of James A. Fields. Listed on the National Register of Historic Places.
Hours & Admission Prices: Tues.-Sat. 11-4. Admission $3.
Attendance: 250 (estimated)

LEE HALL MANSION, 163 Yorktown Rd., Newport News, VA 23603-1127. Tel.: 757-888-3371. Fax: 757-888-3373.
E-mail: leehallmansion@nnva.com
Web Site: www.leehall.org
Key Personnel: Site Coord., Laura Willoughby.
Institution Type/Description: Historic House Museum: housed in the former home of Richard Decauter Lee, built in 1859.
Hours & Admission Prices: Jan.-March Thurs.-Sat. 10-4, Sun. 1-5; April-Dec. Mon. & Thurs.-Fri. 10-4, Sat. 10-5, Sun. 12-5; research library by appointment. Adults $8, seniors 62 & up $7, children 7-18 $6; children under 7 no charge. Closed New Year's Day; Easter; Thanksgiving; Christmas. &
Attendance: 3,700 (actual)

THE MARINERS' MUSEUM, 100 Museum Dr., Newport News, VA 23606-3759. Tel.: 757-596-2222, 800-581-7245. Fax: 757-591-7311.
E-mail: info@marinersmuseum.org
Web Site: www.marinersmuseum.org
Key Personnel: Pres. & C.E.O., Howard H. Hoege, III; Chm. (V), Anne C.H. Conner; Devel. & External Rels., Anna Norville; Vice Pres. Collections & Chief Cur., Lyles Forbes; Museum Shop Mgr. & Dir. Visitor Svcs., Cassi LeDuc.
Institution Type/Description: International & National Maritime History Museum.
Hours & Admission Prices: Memorial Day to Labor Day daily 9-5; Sept.-May Mon.-Sat. 9-5, Sun. 11-5. Adults 13 & up 13.95, seniors 65 & up $12.95, children 4-12 $8.95; discounts to active duty military, AAA & AAM, members; members and children 3 & under no charge. Closed Thanksgiving; Christmas. &
Attendance: 69,732 (actual)

THE NEWSOME HOUSE MUSEUM & CULTURAL CENTER, 2803 Oak Ave., Newport News, VA 23607-3713. Tel.: 757-247-2360. Fax: 757-928-6754.
E-mail: ddavis@nngov.com
Web Site: www.newsomehouse.org
Key Personnel: Historic Site Mgr., Mary Kayaselcuk.
Institution Type/Description: Historic House: built in 1899 The Newsome House is a modified Queen Anne structure, which was home to the Joseph Thomas Newsome family from 1906-1977.
Hours & Admission Prices: Thurs.-Sat. 10-5. Suggested Donation: adults $2. Closed New Year's Day; Easter; Thanksgiving; Christmas Eve & Day. &
Attendance: 5,000 (estimated)

PENINSULA FINE ARTS CENTER, 101 Museum Dr., Newport News, VA 23606-3758. Tel.: 757-596-8175. Fax: 757-596-0807. Facebook: Peninsula Fine Arts Center.
E-mail: info@pfac-va.org
Web Site: www.pfac-va.org
Key Personnel: Exec. Dir., Courtney Gardner; Pres. & Chm. (v), Chris Stewart; Dir. Programs, Michael Preble; Staff Accountant & Personnel Mgr., Debbie Hill; Dir. Mktg., Michael McGrann; Mgr. Exhibitions & Facilities, Fred Rich.
Institution Type/Description: Arts Center.
Hours & Admission Prices: Tues.-Sat. 10-5, Sun. 1-5. Adults $7.50, students, military and seniors 65 & over $6, children 6-12 $4; discounts to AAA members; members and children 5 & under no charge. Call for special exhibition charges. Closed New Year's Day; Thanksgiving; Christmas. &
Attendance: 40,000 (estimated)

VIRGINIA LIVING MUSEUM, 524 J. Clyde Morris Blvd., Newport News, VA 23601-1999. Tel.: 757-595-1900. Fax: 757-599-4897. TDD: 757-595-1900.
E-mail: webmaster@thevlm.org
Web Site: www.thevlm.org

Key Personnel: Interim Exec. Dir. & Devel. Dir., Rebecca Kleinhampler; Deputy Dir., Fred Farris; Pres. (V), Alonzo R. Bell, Jr.; Curatorial Dir., George K. Mathews, Jr.; Dir. Education, Dan Summers; Deputy Dir. Administration, Dave Osman; Dir. Mktg., Virginia Gabriele; Dir. Volunteer Svcs., Shandran J. Thornburgh; Museum Shop Mgr., Sarah Wilcox.
Institution Type/Description: Specialized Natural Center.
Hours & Admission Prices: Summer: daily 9-5; Winter: Mon.-Sat. 9-5, Sun. 12-5. Museum: adults $20, children 3-12 $15; discounts for senior citizens, groups & ASTC (restrictions apply) members; members & children under 3 no charge. Planetarium $4 additional fee; members no charge. Closed New Year's Day; Thanksgiving; Christmas Eve & Day. &
Attendance: 197,894 (actual)

THE VIRGINIA WAR MUSEUM, 9285 Warwick Blvd., Huntington Park, Newport News, VA 23607-1537. Tel.: 757-247-8523. Fax: 757-247-8627. Facebook: Virginia War Museum.
E-mail: virginiawarmuseum@nnva.gov
Web Site: www.warmuseum.org
Key Personnel: Cur., G. Richard Hoffeditz; Registrar, Jerry Coggeshall.
Institution Type/Description: Military Museum.
Hours & Admission Prices: Mon.-Sat. 9-5, Sun. 12-5. Adults $7, active military & senior citizens $6, children 7-18 $5; discounts to AAA members; members no charge. Closed New Year's Day; Easter; Thanksgiving; Christmas Eve & Day. &
Attendance: 50,000 (estimated)

Norfolk

AFRICAN ART GALLERY, Norfolk State University, 700 Park Ave., Norfolk, VA 23504-8050. Tel.: 757-823-2002. Fax: 757-823-2005.
E-mail: amontgomery@nsu.edu
Web Site: www.nsu.edu/provost/archives/art-gallery
Formerly: Lois E. Woods Museum
Key Personnel: Dir., Dr. Tommy L. Bogger; Asst. Dir., Annette Montgomery.
Institution Type/Description: African Museum.
Hours & Admission Prices: Mon.-Fri. 9-5. No charge; donations accepted. Closed holidays. &
Attendance: 1,300 (estimated)

BARON & ELLIN GORDON ART GALLERIES, OLD DOMINION UNIVERSITY, 4509 Monarch Way, Norfolk, VA 23529. Mailing Address: 9000 Batten Arts and Letters, Norfolk, VA 23529. Tel.: 757-683-6271. Fax: 757-683-6776.
E-mail: raustin@odu.edu
Web Site: al.odu.edu/art/gallery/about.shtml
Key Personnel: Sr. Cur., Ramona M. Austin; Collections Mgr. & Prep., Christopher M. Norton.
Institution Type/Description: University Art Gallery
Hours & Admission Prices: Jan. 7-Dec. 19 Tues.-Sat. 11-5, Sun. 1-5. No charge. &
Attendance: 7,743 (estimated)

CHRYSLER MUSEUM OF ART, One Memorial Place, Norfolk, VA 23510-1587. Tel.: 757-664-6200. Fax: 757-664-6201. Facebook: Chrysler Museum of Art and Chrysler Museum Glass Studio.
E-mail: info@chrysler.org
Web Site: www.chrysler.org
Key Personnel: Dir., Erik H. Neil; Chm. Bd., Thomas L. Stokes, Jr.; Dir. Operations & C.F.O., Dana Fuqua; Dir. Devel., Kate Wilson; Dir. Education & Public Programs, Anne Corso; Dir. Visitor Svcs., Colleen Higginbotham; Dir. Communications, Meridith Gray; Deputy Dir. Collections, Susan Leidy.
Institution Type/Description: Art Museum.
Hours & Admission Prices: Museum & Glass Studio: Tues.-Sat. 10-5, Sun. 12-5. No charge; donations accepted. Fee charged for some special exhibitions. Historic Houses: Sat.-Sun. 12-5. No charge. Closed New Year's Day; Independence Day; Thanksgiving; Christmas. &
Attendance: 212,730 (actual)

GENERAL DOUGLAS MACARTHUR MEMORIAL, 198 Bank St., Norfolk, VA 23510-2382. Tel.: 757-441-2965. Fax: 757-441-5389.
E-mail: macarthurmemorial@norfolk.gov
Web Site: www.macarthurmemorial.org
Key Personnel: Dir., Christopher Kolakowski; Administrative Asst., Janice S. Dudley; Archivist, James W. Zobel; Cur., Corey Thornton; Museum Shop Mgr., Ruby Papa.
Institution Type/Description: Military Museum: housed in 1850 courthouse building.

Hours & Admission Prices: Tues.-Sat. 10-5, Sun. 11-5. No charge; donations accepted. Closed New Year's Day; Thanksgiving; Christmas. &
Attendance: 35,378 (actual)

HAMPTON ROADS NAVAL MUSEUM, Physical/Mailing Address: One Waterside Dr., Ste. 248, Norfolk, VA 23510-1607. Tel.: 757-322-2987 & 444-8971. Fax: 757-445-1867. Facebook: @HRNavalMuseum.
E-mail: hrnavalmuseum@navy.mil
Web Site: www.hrnm.navy.mil
Key Personnel: Foundation Pres., John Griffing; Public Information Officer, Susanne Greene; Cur., Joseph M. Judge; Volunteer Coord., Thomas M. Dandes; Exhibits Specialist, Donald Darcy; Educator, Joseph Miechle; Administrative Officer, Michele J. Levesque; Registrar, Katherine Renfrew; Historian, Clay Farrington; Deputy Dir. Education, Laura Orr.
Institution Type/Description: Naval History Museum: housed on the second floor of NAUTICUS.
Hours & Admission Prices: Memorial Day to Labor Day daily 10-5; Sept.-May Tues.-Sat. 10-5, Sun. 12-5. No charge. Closed Thanksgiving; Christmas Eve & Day. &
Attendance: 446,312 (actual)

HERMITAGE MUSEUM AND GARDENS, 7637 North Shore Rd., Norfolk, VA 23505-1730. Tel.: 757-423-2052. Fax: 757-423-2410.
E-mail: info@thehermitagemuseum.org
Web Site: www.thehermitagemuseum.org
Key Personnel: Chm., Olin Walden; Exec. Dir., Jen Duncan; Public Programs Mgr., Melissa Ball; Weddings, Events & Tours Mgr., Lil Acosta; Cur. Gardens & Grounds, Yolima Carr; Mktg. Mgr., Jennifer Lucy; Mgr. Membership & Devel., Julie Morgan; Cur. Collections, Lindsay Neal; Cur. Contemporary Art & Education, Carrie Spencer.
Institution Type/Description: Art Museum.
Hours & Admission Prices: Tues.-Fri. 10-5, Sun. 1-5. Adults $5.50, college students w/ID $3.30, children 6-18 $2.20; discounts to AAM, SERM & NARM members; children under 6, active military & members no charge. Closed New Year's Day; Memorial Day; Independence Day; Labor Day; Columbus Day; Veterans Day; Thanksgiving; Christmas. &
Attendance: 75,000 (actual)

HUNTER HOUSE VICTORIAN MUSEUM, 240 W. Freemason St., Norfolk, VA 23510-1221. Tel.: 757-623-9814. Facebook; Twitter; Instagram.
E-mail: hhvm1894@gmail.com
Web Site: www.hunterhousemuseum.org
Key Personnel: Dir., Jackie Spainhour.
Institution Type/Description: Historic House Museum.
Hours & Admission Prices: April-Dec. Wed.-Sat. 10:30-3:30, Sun. 12:30-3:30; other times by appointment. Adults $5, senior citizens $4, children $1.

MOSES MYERS HOUSE, 323 E. Freemason St., Norfolk, VA 23510. Mailing Address: Chrysler Museum of Art, 245 W. Olney Rd., Norfolk, VA 23510-1587. Tel.: 757-333-1087. Fax: 757-333-1089.
E-mail: info@chrysler.org
Web Site: www.chrysler.org
Key Personnel: Dir., Dr. William Hennessey; Historic House Mgr., John Christiansen.
Institution Type/Description: Historic House: c.1792 late Georgian, early Federal brick 2-story townhouse.
Hours & Admission Prices: Sat.-Sun. 12-5. No charge; donations accepted. Closed New Year's Day; Independence Day; Thanksgiving; Christmas.
Attendance: 7,500 (actual)

NAUTICUS, One Waterside Dr., Ste. 100, Norfolk, VA 23510-1737. Tel.: 757-664-1000, 800-664-1080. Fax: 757-623-1287.
E-mail: info@nauticus.org
Web Site: www.nauticus.org
Formerly: Nauticus, The National Maritime Center
Key Personnel: Exec. Dir., Stephen Kirkland; Chm. (V), Maryellen Baldwin; C.F.O., Raymond McEvoy; Dir. Devel. & External Affairs, Joy Eyrolles; Dir. Mktg., Shelia Harrison; Museum Shop Mgr., Elizabeth Joseph; Dir. Visitor Opers., Christine Arrasate.
Institution Type/Description: Maritime Museum.
Hours & Admission Prices: Memorial Day to Labor Day daily 9-5; Sept.-May Tues.-Sat. 10-5, Sun. 12-5. Adults $10.95, senior citizens $9.95, children $8.50; discount to AAA members, active military & groups; members and children 3 & under no charge. Closed New Year's Day; Thanksgiving; Christmas. &
Attendance: 320,000 (actual)

NORFOLK BOTANICAL GARDEN, 6700 Azalea Garden Rd., Norfolk, VA 23518-5337. Tel.: 757-441-5830. Fax: 757-853-8294.
E-mail: michael.desplaines@nbgs.org
Web Site: www.norfolkbotanicalgarden.org
Key Personnel: Exec. Dir., Michael P. Deplaines; Chm. (V) & C.E.O., Ryan W. Snow; Retail Mgr., Jo Hartsook.
Institution Type/Description: Botanical Garden.
Hours & Admission Prices: Gardens: April-Oct. 20 daily 9-7; Oct. 21-March daily 9-5. Children's Garden: April-Oct. 15 daily 9:30-6:30; Oct. 16-March daily 9:30-4:30. Butterfly House: Father's Day through Sept. daily 10-7. Adults $12, children 3-17 $10; discounts to groups & AAA members; children 2 & under and members no charge. Closed New Year's Day; Thanksgiving; Christmas. &
Attendance: 356,207 (actual)

NORFOLK HISTORICAL SOCIETY, 810 Front St., Norfolk, VA 23510. Mailing Address: P.O. Box 6367, Norfolk, VA 23508-0367. Tel.: 757-640-1720.
E-mail: info@norfolkhistorical.org
Web Site: www.norfolkhistorical.org
Key Personnel: Pres. (V), Barry Weber.
Institution Type/Description: Historic Site: 1810 fort.
Hours & Admission Prices: Self-Guided Tours: Mon.-Fri. call for hours. No charge; donations accepted.
Attendance: 500 (estimated)

OHEF SHOLOM TEMPLE ARCHIVES, 530 Raleigh Ave., Norfolk, VA 23507-2199. Tel.: 757-625-4295. Fax: 757-625-3762.
E-mail: information@ohefsholom.org
Web Site: www.ohefsholom.org
Key Personnel: Chm. (V), Mark Friedman; Exec. Dir., Linda Peck.
Institution Type/Description: Religious Museum.
Hours & Admission Prices: Mon.-Fri. 9-5. No charge; donations accepted. &
Attendance: 2,000 (estimated)

PRETLOW PLANETARIUM, Old Dominion University, Dept. of Physics, OCNPS Bldg., Rm. 306, 4600 Elkhorn Ave., Norfolk, VA 23529. Tel.: 757-683-3865.
E-mail: planetarium@odu.edu
Web Site: www.odu.edu/planetarium
Key Personnel: Dir., Justin Mason.
Institution Type/Description: Planetarium.
Hours & Admission Prices: Call for hours; groups by appointment. No charge; donations accepted.
Attendance: 3,000 (estimated)

VIRGINIA ZOOLOGICAL PARK, 3500 Granby St., Norfolk, VA 23504-1329. Tel.: 757-441-5227 & 2374. Fax: 757-441-5408.
E-mail: virginiazoo@norfolk.gov
Web Site: www.virginiazoo.org
Key Personnel: Exec. Dir., Greg Bockheim.
Institution Type/Description: Zoology Museum.
Hours & Admission Prices: Daily 10-5. Adults $14.95, senior citizens $12.95, children $11.95; members & children under 2 no charge. Closed New Year's Day; Thanksgiving; Christmas Eve & Day. &
Attendance: 285,000 (estimated)

WILLOUGHBY-BAYLOR HOUSE, 601 E. Freemason St., Norfolk, VA 23510-2404. Mailing Address: Chrysler Museum of Art, 245 W. Olney Rd., Norfolk, VA 23510-1587. Tel.: 757-441-1526. Fax: 757-333-1089.
E-mail: museum@chrysler.org
Web Site: www.chrysler.org
Formerly: Norfolk History Museum
Key Personnel: Dir., Erik Neil.
Institution Type/Description: History Museum: housed in former home of Captain William Willoughby; built in 1794.
Hours & Admission Prices: Sat.-Sun. 12-5. No charge; donations accepted. Closed New Year's Day; Independence Day; Thanksgiving; Christmas.
Attendance: 4,000 (actual)

Occoquan

MILL HOUSE MUSEUM, 413 Mill St., Occoquan, VA 22125. Mailing Address: P.O. Box 65, Occoquan, VA 22125-0065. Tel.: 703-491-7525. Facebook: Occoquan Historical Society.
E-mail: president@occoquanhistoricalsociety.org
Web Site: www.occoquanhistoricalsociety.org
Institution Type/Description: General Museum: housed in 1790 Miller's Cottage of Grist Mill.

Hours & Admission Prices: Daily 11-4. No charge; donations accepted. Closed New Year's Day; Thanksgiving; Christmas. &
Attendance: 14,000 (actual)

Onancock

EASTERN SHORE OF VIRGINIA HISTORICAL SOCIETY (ESVHS) - KER PLACE, 69 Market St., Onancock, VA 23417-4223. Mailing Address: P.O. Box 179, Onancock, VA 23417-0179. Tel.: 757-787-8012. Fax: 757-787-4271. Facebook.
E-mail: executivedirector@shorehistory.org
Web Site: www.shorehistory.org
Key Personnel: Exec. Dir., Hilary Hartnett-Wilson; Pres., Caleb Fowler; Treas., Ridgway Dunton.
Institution Type/Description: Historical Society Museum: housed in Ker Place, a c.1799 federal period 2-story building.
Hours & Admission Prices: March 15-Dec. 15 Tues.-Sat. 11-3. No charge; donations accepted. Groups of 5 or more $3 per person. Closed national holidays. &
Attendance: 3,000 (estimated)

Orange

THE ARTS CENTER IN ORANGE, 129 E. Main St., Orange, VA 22960. Mailing Address: P.O. Box 13, Orange, VA 22960-0011. Tel.: 540-672-7311.
E-mail: theartsorange@aol.com
Web Site: www.artscenterorange.org
Key Personnel: Exec. Dir., Laura Thompson; Pres., Ed Harvey.
Institution Type/Description: Art Museum.
Hours & Admission Prices: Mon.-Sat. 10-5.

THE JAMES MADISON MUSEUM OF ORANGE COUNTY HERITAGE, 129 Caroline St., Orange, VA 22960-1532. Tel.: 540-672-1776. Facebook.
E-mail: jamesmadisonmuseuminfo@gmail.com
Web Site: www.thejamesmadisonmuseum.net
Key Personnel: Pres. (V), Tom Matthes; Vice Pres. (V), Patty Parmer; Dir., Bethany W. Sullivan.
Institution Type/Description: History Museum.
Hours & Admission Prices: Tues.-Sat. 11-5. Adults $5.50, children 6-17 $2.50. &
Attendance: 2,200 (actual)

JAMES MADISON'S MONTPELIER - THE MONTPELIER FOUNDATION, 11395 Constitution Hwy., Orange, VA 22957. Mailing Address: P.O. Box 911, Orange, VA 22960-0551. Tel.: 540-672-2728. Fax: 540-301-2776.
E-mail: ewessel@montpelier.org
Web Site: www.montpelier.org
Key Personnel: Exec. Vice Pres. & C.O.O., Sean T. O'Brien; Montpelier Foundation Chm. (V), Greg May; Dir. Archaeology, Dr. Matthew Reeves; Dir. Finance & Administration, Sherida Hawthorne; Acting Cur., Meg Kennedy; Horticulturist, Sandy Mudrinich; Vice Pres. & C.O.O., Sean O'Brien; Dir. Restoration & Facilities, John Jeanes; Dir. Education & Visitor Engagement, Christian Cotz; Dir. Retail & Special Events, Rick Payne.
Institution Type/Description: Historic House: lifelong home of President James Madison (1751-1836); 20th century home of William duPont family.
Hours & Admission Prices: House: April-Oct. Tues.-Sun. & Mon. federal holidays 9:30-5:30, Nov.-March Wed.-Sun. & Mon.-Tues. federal holidays 10:30-4:30. Adults $18, National Trust members $9, children 6-14 $7; children under 6 & Friends of Montpelier no charge. Closed Thanksgiving; Christmas. &
Attendance: 125,000 (estimated)

Palmyra

THE FLUVANNA COUNTY HISTORICAL SOCIETY OLD STONE JAIL MUSEUM, 14 Stone Jail St., Palmyra, VA 22963. Mailing Address: P.O. Box 8, Palmyra, VA 22963-0008. Tel.: 434-589-7910. Fax: 434-589-7910 (call first).
E-mail: info@fluvannahistory.org
Web Site: www.fluvannahistory.org
Key Personnel: Pres., Marvin Moss; Dir., Judith Mickelson.
Institution Type/Description: Historical Society Museum.
Hours & Admission Prices: Archives: Tues.-Wed. 1-4, Museum: June-Oct. Wed. 1-4, Sun. 2-5; other times by appointment. No charge; donations accepted.
Attendance: 500 (estimated)

Parksley

EASTERN SHORE RAILROAD MUSEUM, INC., 18468 Dunne Ave., Parksley, VA 23421. Mailing Address: P.O. Box 135, Parksley, VA 23421. Tel.: 757-665-7245.
E-mail: kparksley@aol.com
Web Site: easternshorerailwaymuseum.org
Key Personnel: Pres. (V), Helena T. Killian.
Institution Type/Description: Historic Building: housed in a former railroad station.
Hours & Admission Prices: March-Oct. Thurs.-Sat 12-4; other times by appointment. No charge; donations accepted.
Attendance: 1,500 (estimated)

Pearisburg

GILES COUNTY HISTORICAL SOCIETY, 208 N. Main St., Pearisburg, VA 24134-1626. Tel.: 540-921-1050. Facebook: Giles County Historical Society.
E-mail: info@gilescountyhistorical.org
Web Site: www.gilescountyhistorical.org
Key Personnel: Exec. Dir., Joseph R. Yost; Pres. (V), Doug Martin.
Institution Type/Description: Historical Society Museum.
Hours & Admission Prices: March-Dec. Wed.-Fri. 12-5, Sat.-Sun. 2-5. No charge; donations accepted. &
Attendance: 1,500 (estimated)

Petersburg

BLANDFORD CHURCH & RECEPTION CTR. (THE PETERSBURG MUSEUMS), 321 S. Crater Rd., Petersburg, VA 23803-3213. Mailing Address: Petersburg Museums, 15 W. Bank St., Petersburg, VA 23803-3213. Tel.: 804-733-2396. Fax: 804-863-0837.
E-mail: matkinson@petersburg-va.org
Web Site: www.petersburg-va.org
Key Personnel: Site Coord., Martha Atkinson; Acting Museum Mgr. & Cur. Collections, Laura Willoughby.
Institution Type/Description: Historic Building: 1735 Colonial Church of Bristol Parish, located in Blandford Cemetery, containing graves of 30,000 Confederate soldiers.
Hours & Admission Prices: Call for hours. Adults $5, senior citizens, active duty military & children 7-12 $4. Closed New Year's Eve, Day & day after; Thanksgiving; Christmas Eve, Day & day after. &
Attendance: 10,000 (estimated)

CENTRE HILL MUSEUM (THE PETERSBURG MUSEUMS), 1 Centre Hill Ave., Petersburg, VA 23803-3213. Mailing Address: Petersburg Museums, 15 W. Bank St., Petersburg, VA 23803-3213. Tel.: 804-733-2401. Fax: 804-863-0837.
E-mail: lwilloughby@petersburg.va.org
Web Site: www.petersburg-va.org
Key Personnel: Acting Museum Mgr. & Cur. Collections, Laura Willoughby.
Institution Type/Description: Historic House: c.1823 Centre Hill Mansion.
Hours & Admission Prices: Call for hours. Adults $5, Block Ticket to 3 Museums: Adults $11; discounts to seniors, children & military; Petersburg residents no charge. Closed New Year's Day; Thanksgiving; Christmas Eve & Day.
Attendance: 4,000 (estimated)

FARMERS BANK, 19 Bollingbrook St., Petersburg, VA 23803-4548. Mailing Address: Preservation Virginia, 204 W. Franklin St., Richmond, VA 23220-5012. Tel.: 804-733-2400.
E-mail: info@preservationvirginia.org
Web Site: preservationvirginia.org
Key Personnel: Sr. Interpreter, Dawn Holmes.
Institution Type/Description: Bank Museum & City of Petersburg Visitor Center.
Hours & Admission Prices: Sat. 10am-12pm. Adults $5, senior citizens, active duty military & children 7-12 $4; block tickets available; discounts to AAM & ICOM members. Closed New Year's Day; Thanksgiving; Christmas Eve & Day.

PAMPLIN HISTORICAL PARK AND THE NATIONAL MUSEUM OF THE CIVIL WAR SOLDIER, 6125 Boydton Plank Rd., Petersburg, VA 23803-7494. Tel.: 804-861-2408. Fax: 804-861-2820.
E-mail: generalmailbox@pamplinpark.org
Web Site: www.pamplinpark.org
Key Personnel: Exec. Dir., Jerry Desmond; Pres. (V), Dr. Robert B. Pamplin, Jr.; Dir. Mktg. & Devel., Colin Romanick; Dir. Operations, Patrick A. Olienyk.
Institution Type/Description: Military History Museum: Park includes The National Museum of the Civil War Soldier; Tudor Hall Plantation & Field Quarter; The Banks House; re-created Military Encampment; Battlefield Center; The

Breakthrough Battlefield, a National Historic Landmark; Civil War Adventure Camp; Hart Farm.
Hours & Admission Prices: March-Nov. daily 9-5; Dec.-Feb. open by appointment. Adults $13, children $8; discounts to AAM members, schools & groups, seniors and military; members & children under 6 no charge. Closed New Year's Day; Thanksgiving; Christmas. &

PETERSBURG AREA ART LEAGUE, 7 E. Old St., Petersburg, VA 23803-4558. Tel.: 804-861-4611.
E-mail: galleryadmin@paalart.org
Web Site: www.paalart.org
Key Personnel: Pres. (V), Ellen Ende; Membership & Corresponding Sec., Walt Smith.
Institution Type/Description: Art Gallery: housed in c.1700 granary where Indians came to trade goods.
Hours & Admission Prices: Tues.-Fri. 12-6, Sat. 10-4. No charge; donations accepted. Closed major holidays. &
Attendance: 4,300

PETERSBURG NATIONAL BATTLEFIELD, 1539 Hickory Hill Rd., Petersburg, VA 23803-4721. Tel.: 804-732-3531. Fax: 804-732-3615.
Web Site: www.nps.gov/pete
Key Personnel: Supt., Lewis Rogers.
Institution Type/Description: Military Museum: located on Petersburg Battlefield.
Hours & Admission Prices: Battlefield: daily 8:30-dusk. Visitor Center: daily 9-5. Vehicle $5, individual $3. Closed New Year's Day; Thanksgiving; Christmas. &

SIEGE MUSEUM (THE PETERSBURG MUSEUMS), 15 W. Bank St., Petersburg, VA 23803-3213. Tel.: 804-733-2403. Fax: 804-863-0837.
E-mail: lwilloughby@petersburg.va.org
Web Site: www.petersburg.va.org
Key Personnel: Cur. Collections, Laura Willoughby.
Institution Type/Description: Historic Museum: housed in an 1839 Greek revival style agricultural exchange.
Hours & Admission Prices: Call or visit website for hours. Adults $5; discounts to seniors, children, military; Petersburg residents no charge. Closed New Year's Day; Thanksgiving; Christmas Eve & Day. &
Attendance: 6,000 (estimated)

THE WARD CENTER FOR CONTEMPORARY ART, 132-A N. Sycamore St., Petersburg, VA 23803. Tel.: 804-793-8300.
E-mail: noelle@thewardcenter.org
Web Site: www.thewardcenter.org
Formerly: Petersburg Regional Arts Center
Key Personnel: Co Founder SBAC, Rusty Davis; Co Founder SBAC, Deanna Thomas; Dir., Donna Jacobs; Asst. Dir., Angela Long.
Institution Type/Description: Art Center.
Hours & Admission Prices: Call for hours. &

Pocahontas

POCAHONTAS MINE & MUSEUM, 11 Centre St., Pocahontas, VA 24635. Mailing Address: P.O. Box 128, Pocahontas, VA 24635-0128. Tel.: 276-945-2134 & 9522. Fax: 276-945-9904.
E-mail: pocahontas@comcast.net
Institution Type/Description: History Museum: designated as a national historic landmark.
Hours & Admission Prices: April to Oct. Mon.-Sat. 10-5, Sun. 1-5. Adults $7, children 6-12 $4.50; discounts to AAA members & groups; children under 6 no charge.

Portsmouth

CHILDREN'S MUSEUM OF VIRGINIA, 221 High St., Portsmouth, VA 23704. Mailing Address: 521 Middle St., Portsmouth, VA 23704. Tel.: 757-393-5258.
E-mail: schweize@portsmouthva.gov
Web Site: childrensmuseumva.com
Key Personnel: Dir., Nancy S. Perry.
Institution Type/Description: Children's Museum.
Hours & Admission Prices: Mon.-Sat. 9-5, Sun. 11-5. Adults 18 & over $11, children 2-17 $10; military & seniors $9; discounts to VAM & AAM members; members & children under 2 no charge. &
Attendance: 143,690 (actual)

THE HILL HOUSE, 221 North St., Portsmouth, VA 23704. Tel.: 757-393-0241.
E-mail: info@thehillhousemuseum.org

Web Site: thehillhousemuseum.org
Institution Type/Description: Historic House Museum.
Hours & Admission Prices: April-Dec. Sat. 11-3.

PORTSMOUTH ART & CULTURAL CENTER, 400 High St., Portsmouth, VA 23704. Mailing Address: 521 Middle St., Portsmouth, VA 23704. Tel.: 757-393-8543.
E-mail: paulg@portsmouth.gov
Web Site: www.portsmouthartcenter.com
Formerly: Courthouse Galleries Art Museum
Key Personnel: Dir., Nancy Perry; Cur., Gayle Paul; Museum Shop Mgr., Liona Bourgeault.
Institution Type/Description: Art Museum.
Hours & Admission Prices: Memorial Day to Labor Day Mon.-Sat. 10-5, Sun. 1-5; Sept.-May Tues.-Sat. 10-5, Sun. 1-5. Adults $3; discounts to AAA & AAM members, senior citizens & military.
Attendance: 27,816 (actual)

PORTSMOUTH HISTORICAL ASSOCIATION, 221 North St., Portsmouth, VA 23704-2601. Tel.: 757-393-0241.
Institution Type/Description: Historical House: c.1830 Hill House.
Hours & Admission Prices: April-Dec. Sat. 11-3; tour groups & other times by appointment. Adults $3, children 6-12 $1; children under 6 with adult & members with dues card no charge.
Attendance: 601 (actual)

PORTSMOUTH MUSEUMS, 521 Middle St., Portsmouth, VA 23704-3708. Tel.: 757-393-8983. Fax: 757-393-5228.
E-mail: perryn@portsmouthva.gov
Web Site: www.portsmouthva.gov
Key Personnel: Dir., Nancy Perry; Site Mgr. Children's Museum of Virginia, Al Schweizer; Cur. Portsmouth Art & Cultural Center, Gayle Paul; Naval Shipyards & Lightship Museum Cur., Diane Cripps; Exhibit Supvr., Tim Michalski; Portsmouth Community Colored Library Museum Supvr., Linda Holmes; Education Coord., Christine Matyseck.
Institution Type/Description: General Museum.
Hours & Admission Prices: Portsmouth Art & Cultural Center: Wed.-Sat. 10-5, Sun. 1-5. Admission $3. Children's Museum of Virginia: Tues.-Sat. 9-5, Sun. 11-5. Adults $11, children $10; children under 2 no charge. Portsmouth Naval Shipyard Museum: Wed.-Sat. 10-5, Sun. 1-5. Lightship Museum: Memorial Day to Labor Day Fri.-Sat. 10-5, Sun. 1-5; Sept.-May Sat. 10-5, Sun. 1-5. Admission $4; Portsmouth Community Library Museum: May-Sept. Fri.-Sat. 10-noon & 1-4, other times by appointment. No charge; donations accepted. Discounts to AAM & VAM members; members no charge. Combination tickets available.
Attendance: 230,836 (actual)

PORTSMOUTH NAVAL SHIPYARD MUSEUM, 2 High St., Portsmouth, VA 23704. Tel.: 757-393-8591.
E-mail: contact@portsmouthnavalshipyardmuseum.com
Web Site: www.portsmouthnavalshipyardmuseum.com
Institution Type/Description: Naval History Museum.
Hours & Admission Prices: Tues.-Sat. 10-5, Sun. 1-5. Tues.-Thurs. adults $2, seniors 62 & over and military $1.50, students 2-17 $1; children under 2 no charge. Fri.-Sun. (includes admission to the Lightship Portsmouth Museum): adults $4, seniors 62 & over and military $3, students 2-17 $2; children under 2 no charge.

VIRGINIA SPORTS HALL OF FAME & MUSEUM, 206 High St., Portsmouth, VA 23704-3720. Mailing Address: P.O. Box 370, Portsmouth, VA 23705-0370. Tel.: 757-393-8031. Fax: 757-393-8288. Facebook: VSHFM.
E-mail: info@vshfm.com
Web Site: www.vshfm.com
Key Personnel: Pres., Eddie Webb; Chm. (V), Joel Rubin; Bookkeeper, Salima Ramos; Dir. Operations, Elizabeth Goodwin; Education Coord., Elaina Trafny.
Institution Type/Description: Sports Museum: located in Historic Olde Towne Portsmouth.
Hours & Admission Prices: Summer: Mon.-Sat. 10-5, Sun. 1-5; Fall & Spring Tues.-Fri. 10-2, Sat. 10-5, Sun. 1-5. Adults $7; discounts to AAA members & military; members no charge. Closed New Year's Day; Thanksgiving; Christmas. &
Attendance: 70,000 (estimated)

Pulaski

FINE ARTS CENTER FOR NEW RIVER VALLEY, 21 W. Main St., Pulaski, VA 24301-5015. Mailing Address: P.O. Box 309, Pulaski, VA 24301-0309. Tel.: 540-980-7363. Fax: 540-980-7363. Facebook: Fine Arts Center for New River Valley.
E-mail: info@facnrv.org

Web Site: www.facnrv.org
Key Personnel: Dir., Judy C. Ison; Pres. (V), Beckie Cox; Asst., Donna Rorrer.
Institution Type/Description: Art Museum: housed in 1898 Victorian Commercial structure.
Hours & Admission Prices: Mon.-Fri. 10-4:30, Sat. 11-3. No charge; donations accepted. Closed federal holidays. &

Attendance: 20,000 (estimated)

RAYMOND F. RATCLIFFE MEMORIAL MUSEUM, Pulaski Railroad Station, 124 S. Washington Ave., Pulaski, VA 24301. Mailing Address: P.O. Box 269, Pulaski, VA 24301. Tel.: 540-980-2055.
Institution Type/Description: History Museum: housed in the historic Pulaski Train Depot; built in 1886.
Hours & Admission Prices: Call for hours.

Radford

GLENCOE MUSEUM, 600 Unruh Dr., Radford, VA 24141-1501. Mailing Address: P.O. Box 3339, Radford, VA 24143-3339. Tel.: 540-731-5031.
E-mail: info@glencoemuseum.org
Web Site: www.glencoemuseum.org
Key Personnel: Dir., Scott L. Gardner; Chm. (V), Margaret Sproule.
Institution Type/Description: History Museum: housed in c.1870 home built by Gen. Gabriel Colvin Wharton.
Hours & Admission Prices: Tues.-Sat. 10-4, Sun. 1-4. No charge; donations accepted. Closed national holidays. &

Attendance: 2,271 (actual)

RADFORD UNIVERSITY ART MUSEUM, Corner of Jefferson & Downey Sts., Radford, VA 24142. Mailing Address: P.O. Box 6965, Radford, VA 24142-6965. Tel.: 540-831-5754. Fax: 540-831-6799.
E-mail: ruartmuseum@radford.edu
Web Site: www.radford.edu/rumuseum
Key Personnel: Dir., Steve Arbury; Registrar, Kim Cochran.
Institution Type/Description: University Art Museum.
Hours & Admission Prices: May-July Mon.-Fri. 10-4, Sat.-Sun. 12-4; Sept.-April Mon.-Fri. 10-5, Sat.-Sun. 12-4. No charge. Closed national holidays & school vacations. &

Attendance: 17,400 (actual)

Raphine

MCCORMICK MEMORIAL MUSEUM, 128 McCormick Farm Circle, Raphine, VA 24472. Tel.: 540-377-2255. Fax: 540-377-5850.
E-mail: dafiske@vt.edu
Web Site: www.vaes.vt.edu/steeles/history.html
Key Personnel: Supt., David A. Fiske.
Institution Type/Description: Agricultural History Museum.
Hours & Admission Prices: Daily 8-5. No charge; donations accepted. Closed during inclement weather; major holidays.
Attendance: 8,000 (estimated)

Reedville

REEDVILLE FISHERMEN'S MUSEUM, 504 Main St., Reedville, VA 22539-4401. Mailing Address: P.O. Box 306, Reedville, VA 22539-0306. Tel.: 804-453-6529. Fax: 804-453-7159.
E-mail: office@rfmuseum.org
Web Site: www.rfmuseum.org
Key Personnel: Dir., Janet Ridgely; Pres. (V), Bill Brent; Museum Shop Mgr., Jeri Brewer.
Institution Type/Description: Regional Maritime Museum.
Hours & Admission Prices: March-April Sat.-Sun. 10:30-4:30; May-Oct. daily 10:30-4:30; Nov.-Jan. Fri.-Mon. 10-30-4:30. Adults $5, senior citizens over 60 $3; discounts to CAMM & AAM members; children under 12 & members no charge. &

Attendance: 14,500 (estimated)

Reston

THE GREATER RESTON ARTS CENTER (GRACE), 12001 Market St., Ste. 103, Reston, VA 20190-6244, Tel.: 703-471-9242. Fax: 703-471-0952.
E-mail: info@restonarts.org
Web Site: www.restonarts.org
Key Personnel: Dir., Damion Sinclair; Exhibitions Dir., Holly Koons McCullough.

Institution Type/Description: Civic Art & Cultural Center.
Hours & Admission Prices: Tues.-Sat. 11-5. No charge. Closed New Year's Day; Easter; Christmas. &

Attendance: 20,000

RESTON MUSEUM, 1639 Washington Plaza, Reston, VA 20190-4305. Tel.: 703-709-7700. Fax: 703-709-6668.
E-mail: restonmuseum@gmail.com
Web Site: www.restonmuseum.org
Key Personnel: Chair, Shelley Mastran.
Institution Type/Description: History Museum.
Hours & Admission Prices: Mon.-Sat. 11-4. No charge; donations accepted. &

Attendance: 6,913 (actual)

Richmond

AGECROFT HALL, 4305 Sulgrave Rd., Richmond, VA 23221-3256. Tel.: 804-353-4241. Fax: 804-353-2151.
E-mail: kreynolds@agecrofthall.com
Web Site: www.agecrofthall.com
Key Personnel: Exec. Dir., Anne Kenny-Urban; Business Officer & Museum Shop Mgr., Sieglinde F. Nix; Cur. Education, Jill Pesesky; Mgr. Tour Svcs., Katie Reynolds.
Institution Type/Description: Historic House: 15th-century English Country Manor House disassembled in 1926, brought over & rebuilt; formerly located at Lancashire, England.
Hours & Admission Prices: Tues.-Sat. 10-4, Sun. 12:30-5. Adults $8, senior citizens $7, students $5; discounts to AAA & active military; children 5 & under no charge. Closed legal holidays. &

Attendance: 18,654 (actual)

THE AMERICAN CIVIL WAR MUSEUM AT HISTORIC TREDEGAR, 500 Tredegar St., Richmond, VA 23219-4328. Tel.: 804-649-1861. Fax: 804-780-0264.
E-mail: info@tredegar.org
Web Site: www.tredegar.org
Formerly: Tredegar National Civil War Center Foundation
Key Personnel: C.E.O., Christy S. Coleman; Dir. Strategic Initiatives, Christie Ann Bieber; Interpretation & Programs Specialist, Sean Kane; Cur., Cathy Wright.
Institution Type/Description: History Museum.
Hours & Admission Prices: Daily 9-5. Adults $8, seniors 62 & up $6, children 6-17 $4; discounts to AAM members; groups and children 5 & under no charge. Closed New Year's Day; Thanksgiving; Christmas. &

Attendance: 116,244 (actual)

ARTSPACE GALLERY, 31 E. 3rd St., Richmond, VA 23224. Mailing Address: Zero E. 4th St., Richmond, VA 23224-4202. Tel.: 804-232-6464. Facebook.
E-mail: artspaceorg@gmail.com
Web Site: artspacegallery.org
Key Personnel: Pres., Dana Frostick.
Institution Type/Description: Art Gallery.
Hours & Admission Prices: Tues.-Sun. 12-4; other times by appointment. No charge; donations accepted. &

Attendance: 4,925 (actual)

BETH AHABAH MUSEUM & ARCHIVES, 1109 W. Franklin St., Richmond, VA 23220-3700. Tel.: 804-353-2668. Fax: 804-358-3451. Facebook: Beth Ahabah Museum.
E-mail: bama@bethahabah.org
Web Site: www.bethahabah.org
Key Personnel: Exec. Dir., David Farris; Docent & Administrative Asst., Amy Roberts; Admin., Bonnie Eisenman.
Institution Type/Description: Jewish History Museum.
Hours & Admission Prices: Sun.-Thurs. 10-3; call to confirm. No charge; donations accepted. Closed Jewish & national holidays.

Attendance: 1,500 (actual)

BLACK HISTORY MUSEUM & CULTURAL CENTER OF VIRGINIA, 122 W. Leigh St., Richmond, VA 23220. Mailing Address: P.O. Box 61052, Richmond, VA 23261-1052. Tel.: 804-780-9093. Fax: 804-780-9107.
E-mail: information@blackhistorymuseum.org
Web Site: blackhistorymuseum.org
Key Personnel: Dir., Adele Johnson.
Institution Type/Description: History Museum.
Hours & Admission Prices: Tues.-Sat. 10-5; other times by appointment. Adults $10, seniors & students $8, children 3-12 $6; discounts to military; children under 3 no charge.

THE BRANCH MUSEUM OF ARCHITECTURE AND DESIGN, 2501 Monument Ave., Richmond, VA 23220-2618. Tel.: 804-644-3041. Fax: 804-643-4607.
E-mail: info@aiava.org
Web Site: www.branchmuseum.org
Formerly: Virginia Center for Architecture
Key Personnel: Dir., Penelope C. Fletcher.
Institution Type/Description: Architecture & Design Museum.
Hours & Admission Prices: Tues.-Fri. 10-5, Sat.-Sun. 1-5; groups by appointment. No charge; donations accepted. Closed New Year's Day; Easter; Thanksgiving; Christmas. &
Attendance: 8,600

CHASEN GALLERIES OF FINE ART, 3554 W. Cary St., Richmond, VA 23221-2729. Tel.: 804-204-1048. Fax: 804-204-1049.
E-mail: art@chasengalleries.com
Web Site: www.chasengalleries.com
Key Personnel: Dir., Jeff Timlin; Pres., Andrew Chasen.
Institution Type/Description: Art Gallery.
Hours & Admission Prices: Mon.-Sat. 10-6; other times by appointment. No charge. Closed holidays.
Attendance: 2,000 (actual)

CHILDREN'S MUSEUM OF RICHMOND CLOSED, 2626 W. Broad St., Richmond, VA 23220-1904. Tel.: 804-474-7000 & 7062. Fax: 804-474-7099.
E-mail: info@c-mor.org
Web Site: www.c-mor.org
Key Personnel: Pres. & C.E.O., Shannon Venable.
Institution Type/Description: Children's Museum.
Hours & Admission Prices: Memorial Day-Labor Day: daily 9:30-7; Sept.-May: daily 9:30-5. Adults & children $9, seniors $8; discounts to groups & military, children under one & members no charge. Closed New Year's Day; Easter; Thanksgiving; Christmas. &
Attendance: 360,000 (actual)

CROSSROADS ART CENTER GALLERY, 2016 Staples Mill Rd., Richmond, VA 23230-3109. Tel.: 804-278-8950.
Key Personnel: Owner & Dir. Exhibitions, Jenni Kirby.
Institution Type/Description: Art Gallery.
Hours & Admission Prices: Mon.-Sat. 10-6, Sun. 12-4.

DABBS HOUSE MUSEUM, 3812 Nine Mile Rd., Richmond, VA 23223-4848. Mailing Address: c/o Henrico Co. Recreation & Parks, P.O. Box 90775, Henrico, VA 23273-0775. Tel.: 804-652-3406.
E-mail: dabbshouse@henrico.us
Web Site: henrico.us/rec/places/dabbs-house
Key Personnel: Dir. Recreation & Parks, Neil Luther.
Institution Type/Description: Historic House Museum: housed in the former field headquarters of General Lee during the summer of 1862.
Hours & Admission Prices: Tours: Wed.-Sun. 9-5; other times by appointment. No charge.

EDGAR ALLAN POE MUSEUM, 1914-16 E. Main St., Richmond, VA 23223-6964. Tel.: 804-648-5523. Fax: 804-648-8729.
E-mail: info@poemuseum.org
Web Site: www.poemuseum.org
Key Personnel: Pres. (V), Annemarie Beebe; Exec. Dir., Jaime Robinson Fawcett.
Institution Type/Description: Literary Museum.
Hours & Admission Prices: Tues.-Sat. 10-5, Sun. 11-5; tours on the hour. Adults $8, senior citizens 60 & over and youth 7-17 $6; discounts to AAA members; AAM members, children under 7 & members no charge. Group tours available, email tours@poemuseum.org or call 804-648-5523 x221. Closed New Year's Day; Thanksgiving; Christmas.
Attendance: 25,000 (estimated)

ELEGBA FOLKLORE SOCIETY'S CULTURAL CENTER, 101 E. Broad St., Richmond, VA 23219-1733. Tel.: 804-644-3900. Fax: 804-644-3919.
E-mail: gallery@efsinc.org
Web Site: www.efsinc.org
Key Personnel: Found Pres. & Artistic Dir., Janine Bell.
Institution Type/Description: Art Museum.
Hours & Admission Prices: Mon.-Fri. 10-6, Sat. 12-4; other times by appointment. No charge; donations accepted.

GRAND LODGE AF & AM LIBRARY, MUSEUM AND HISTORICAL FOUNDATION - ALLEN E. ROBERTS MASONIC LIBRARY AND MUSEUM, 4115 Nine Mile Rd., Richmond, VA 23223-4926. Tel.: 804-222-3110. Fax: 804-222-4253.
E-mail: library@grandlodgeofvirginia.org
Web Site: grandlodgeofvirginia.org/library-museum
Key Personnel: Pres. (V), John R. Quinley.
Institution Type/Description: Fraternal Museum & Freemasonry.
Hours & Admission Prices: Mon., Wed. & Fri. 9-12:30 & 1:30-4. No charge; donations accepted. Closed Presidents' Day; Easter Mon.; Memorial Day; Labor Day; Thanksgiving; Christmas.
Attendance: 300 (estimated)

HENRICO COUNTY HISTORIC PRESERVATION & MUSEUM SERVICES, 8600 Dixon Powers Dr., Richmond, VA 23228-2735. Mailing Address: P.O. Box 27032, Richmond, VA 23273. Tel.: 804-501-5736 & 7275. Fax: 804-501-5284.
E-mail: gre26@co.henrico.va.us
Web Site: www.co.henrico.va.us/rec
Key Personnel: History Supvr., Christopher M. Gregson; Cur., Kimberly Sicola; Site Mgr., Anna Truong; Asst. Site Mgr., Linda Eikmeier.
Institution Type/Description: History Museum: housed in c.1810 Meadow Farm, depicting mid-19th century rural life in southeastern Virginia.
Hours & Admission Prices: March to mid-Dec. Tues.-Sun. 12-4. No charge. &
Attendance: 60,000 (estimated)

HISTORIC ST. JOHN'S CHURCH, 2401 E. Broad St., Richmond, VA 23223-7128. Tel.: 804-648-5015 & 877-915-1775.
E-mail: info@historicstjohnschurch.org
Web Site: www.historicstjohnschurch.org
Key Personnel: Exec. Dir., Sarah F. Whiting.
Institution Type/Description: Historic Building & Site: 1741 church, location of the 2nd Virginia Convention where Patrick Henry addressed the Convention on March 23, 1775 with his famous, Give me liberty or give me death speech.
Hours & Admission Prices: Mon.-Sat. 10-4, Sun. 1-4, last tour 3:30; see website to confirm hours. Adults $8, senior citizens 62 & over $7, students $6; discounts to groups of 10 or more; children under 7 no charge. Closed New Year's Eve & Day; Easter; Thanksgiving; Christmas Eve & Day. &
Attendance: 40,000 (actual)

THE JOHN MARSHALL HOUSE, 818 E. Marshall St., Richmond, VA 23219-1917. Mailing Address: P.O. Box 1098, Richmond, VA 23218-1098. Tel.: 804-648-7998. Fax: 804-648-5880.
E-mail: johnmarshallhouse@preservationvirginia.org
Web Site: www.preservationvirginia.org
Key Personnel: Exec. Dir. APVA, Elizabeth Kostelny; Cur., Catherine Dean; Dir. Museum Operations, Jennifer Hurst Wender; Museum Operations Asst., Krysha Snyder.
Institution Type/Description: Historic Site & Historic House: 1790 home of U.S. Chief Justice John Marshall & only surviving 18th-century brick Federal house in Richmond.
Hours & Admission Prices: March-Dec. Fri.-Sat. 10-5, Sun. 12-5. Adults $8, AAA members $7, seniors 55 & over $6, students $5; discounts to National Trust members; preservation members & children under 6 no charge.
Attendance: 3,354 (actual)

LEWIS GINTER BOTANICAL GARDEN, 1800 Lakeside Ave., Richmond, VA 23228-4700. Tel.: 804-262-9887. Fax: 804-262-9934.
E-mail: contactus@lewisginter.org
Web Site: www.lewisginter.org
Key Personnel: Interim Exec. Dir., Kim Dove; Dir. Horticulture, John Morse; Dir. Education & Exhibitions, Kristin Thoroman; Dir. Public Rels. & Mktg., Beth Monroe; Dir. Advancement, Alice Baker; Pres. Emeritus, Frank Robinson.
Institution Type/Description: Botanical Garden & Historic House: c.1888.
Hours & Admission Prices: Daily 9-5; call for extended summer hours. Adults $14, seniors $11, military with ID $10, children 3-12 $8; children under 3 & members no charge. Closed Thanksgiving; Christmas Eve & Day. &
Attendance: 175,000 (actual)

THE LIBRARY OF VIRGINIA, 800 E. Broad St., Richmond, VA 23219-8000. Tel.: 804-692-3535. Fax: 804-692-3556.
E-mail: sandra.treadway@lva.virginia.gov
Web Site: www.lva.virginia.gov
Key Personnel: Dir. & State Librarian, Sandra G. Treadway; Chm. Library Bd. (V), R. Chambliss Light, Jr.; Deputy Administration, Connie Warne; Deputy Collections & Programs, John Metz; Public Information & Policy Coord., Janice M. Hathcock; Dir. Public Svcs. & Outreach, Gregg Kimball; Museum Shop Mgr., Jennifer Blessman.

Institution Type/Description: State Library & Archives.
Hours & Admission Prices: Mon.-Sat. 9-5. No charge; donations accepted. Closed most state holidays. ♿
Attendance: 244,457 (estimated)

MAGGIE L. WALKER NATIONAL HISTORIC SITE, 600 N. 2nd St., Richmond, VA 23219. Mailing Address: 3215 E. Broad St., Richmond, VA 23223-7517. Tel.: 804-771-2017. Fax: 804-771-2226.
E-mail: dave_ruth@nps.gov
Web Site: www.nps.gov/mawa
Key Personnel: Supt., David R. Ruth; Chief Interpreter, Beth Stern; Cur., Ethan P. Bullard; Supvr. Park Rangers, Ajena Rogers; Park Guide, Melissa Weissert.
Institution Type/Description: Historic House: Victorian-Italianate home of Maggie Lena Walker, first woman founder & president of an African American bank, newspaper editor & African-American community leader; African-American & women's history.
Hours & Admission Prices: March-Oct. Mon.-Sat. 9-5; Nov.-Feb. Mon.-Sat. 9-4:30. No charge; donations accepted. Closed New Year's Day; Thanksgiving; Christmas. ♿
Attendance: 12,000 (actual)

MAYMONT, 1700 Hampton St., Richmond, VA 23220-6899. Tel.: 804-358-7166, ext. 310. Fax: 804-358-9994.
E-mail: info@maymont.org
Web Site: www.maymont.org
Key Personnel: Assoc. Exec. Dir., C. Fred Murray; Dir. Historical Collections & Programs, Dale C. Wheary; Dir. Nature Center, Henry Bireline; Mgr. Zoology, Joe Neel; Carriage Collections Mgr., Armistead Wellford; Mgr. Historical Programs, Nancy Lowden; Dir. Finance, Ron Thompson; Dir. Administration, Ann Voss; Mgr. Environmental Education, Krista Westherford; Dir. Advancement & Devel., Anne Du Bois; Dir. Mktg. & Public Rels., Cathie Rosenberg; Asst. Dir. Mktg. & Public Rels., Carla Murray; Mgr. Historical Collections, Kathy Garrett-Cox; Dir. Horticulture, Peggy M. Singlemann; Dir. Special Events, Kim Arnold; Mgr. Membership, Megan Senske.
Institution Type/Description: Historic House & Gardens: housed in c.1890s estate of James H. Dooley.
Hours & Admission Prices: Maymont Mansion: Tues.-Sun. 12-5. Suggested Donation: $5. Grounds & Gardens: April-Sept. daily 10-7; Oct.-March 10-5; No charge. Nature & Visitor Center: Tues.-Sun. 10-5. Admission $4, children 4-12 and seniors 60 & over $3; members & children under 4 no charge. Children's Farm & Barn: daily 10-5. Suggested Donation: $5 per person. Carriage House: Tues.-Sun. 12-5. Closed New Year's Day; Thanksgiving; Christmas. ♿
Attendance: 500,000 (estimated)

MUSEUM OF VIRGINIA CATHOLIC HISTORY, Cathedral of the Sacred Heart, 18 N. Laurel St., Richmond, VA 23220. Mailing Address: 7800 Carousel Ln., Richmond, VA 23294. Tel.: 804-359-5661.
E-mail: ejeter@richmonddiocese.org
Web Site: http://richmonddiocese.org
Key Personnel: Dir. Archives Office, Edie Jeter; Cur., Katie Lemza.
Institution Type/Description: Religious Museum.
Hours & Admission Prices: By appointment. No charge; donations accepted. ♿
Attendance: 1,500 (estimated)

PRESERVATION VIRGINIA, 204 W. Franklin St., Richmond, VA 23220-5012. Tel.: 804-648-1889. Fax: 804-775-0802.
E-mail: ekostelny@preservationvirginia.org
Web Site: www.preservationvirginia.org
Formerly: Association for the Preservation of Virginia Antiquities
Key Personnel: C.E.O., Elizabeth Kostelny; Devel. Coord., Alexis Feria; Dir. Preservation Svcs., Louis J. Malon; Dir. Finance, Cheryl Greenday; Dir. Museum Operations & Education, Jennifer Hurst-Wender; Coord. Digital Communications, Krysha Snyder.
Institution Type/Description: Historic Building & Site; Preservation Project.
Hours & Admission Prices: For hours & admission prices of House Museums see separate listings or web site.
Attendance: 400,000 (estimated)

RICHMOND NATIONAL BATTLEFIELD PARK, Chimborazo Medical Museum, 3215 E. Broad St., Richmond, VA 23223-7517. Tel.: 804-226-1981, ext. 3. Fax: 804-771-8522. Facebook: Richmond National Battlefield Park.
Web Site: www.nps.gov/rich
Key Personnel: Supt., Dave Ruth; Chief Interpretation, Elizabeth Stern; Chief Ranger, Timothy Mauch; Cur., Ethan P. Bullard.
Institution Type/Description: Civil War Military Museum.
Hours & Admission Prices: Tredegar Iron Works, Cold Harbor Visitor Center, & Chimborazo Medical Museum: daily 9-5. Glendale/Malvern Hill Visitor Center

& Fort Harrison Visitor Center; seasonal. No charge; donations accepted. Closed New Year's Day; Thanksgiving; Christmas. ♿
Attendance: 245,504

RICHMOND RAILROAD MUSEUM, 102 Hull St., Richmond, VA 23224-4240. Mailing Address: P.O. Box 8583, Richmond, VA 23226-0583. Tel.: 804-231-4324.
E-mail: jdemajo@demajo.net
Web Site: www.odcnrhs.org
Formerly: Old Dominion Railway Museum
Key Personnel: Pres., John G. DeMajo; 1st Vice Pres. (V), Kevin Frick; Cur., Calvin Boles; Archivist, Bob Dickinson.
Institution Type/Description: Railroad History Museum: housed at site of 1915-1957 Southern Railway depot.
Hours & Admission Prices: Sat. 11-4, Sun. 1-4. Adults 14 & over $5; children no charge. Closed Christmas Eve & Day. ♿
Attendance: 4,078 (actual)

SCIENCE MUSEUM OF VIRGINIA, 2500 W. Broad St., Richmond, VA 23220-2057. Tel.: 804-864-1400. Fax: 804-864-1560.
E-mail: info@smv.org
Web Site: www.smv.org
Key Personnel: Chm., David Botkins; Dir. & Chief Wonder Officer, Richard C. Conti; Dir. Playful Learning & Inquiry, Charles English; Dir. Technology & Innovation, Jim Peck.
Institution Type/Description: Science Museum.
Hours & Admission Prices: Memorial Day to Labor Day Mon.-Sat. 9:30-5, Sun. 11:30-5; Sept.-May Tues.-Sat. 9:30-5, Sun. 11:30-5; call for additional school holiday hours. Exhibits only: adults 13-59 $14, senior citizens 60 & over and youth 4-12 $13; ASTC & museum members and children 3 & under no charge. Exhibits & DOME: adults $18, youth 4-12 and seniors 60 & over $17; discounts to groups & members; children 3 & under no charge. Closed Thanksgiving; Christmas Eve & Day. ♿
Attendance: 343,429 (actual)

1708 GALLERY, 319 W. Broad St., Richmond, VA 23220-4218. Mailing Address: P.O. Box 12520, Richmond, VA 23241-0520. Tel.: 804-643-1708. Fax: 804-643-7839. Facebook: 1708 Gallery.
E-mail: info@1708gallery.org
Web Site: 1708gallery.org
Key Personnel: Exec. Dir., Emily Smith; Gallery Coord. & Operations Mgr., Erin Willett; Pres. (V), Lucy Meade.
Institution Type/Description: Art Gallery.
Hours & Admission Prices: Tues.-Fri. 11-5, Sat. 11-4; other times by appointment. No charge. ♿
Attendance: 21,173 (actual)

UNIVERSITY OF RICHMOND MUSEUMS, 28 Westhampton Way, Richmond, VA 23173-. Tel.: 804-289-8276. Fax: 804-287-1894.
E-mail: museums@richmond.edu
Web Site: museums.richmond.edu
Formerly: Marsh Art Gallery, University of Richmond
Key Personnel: Exec. Dir., Richard Waller; Deputy Dir. & Cur. Exhibitions, Elizabeth Schlatter; Museum Preparator, Stephen Duggins; Museum Preparator, Henley Guild; Cur. Museum Programs, Heather Campbell; Coord. Museum Visitor & Tour Svcs., Martha Wright; Mgr. Museum Operations, Katreena Clark; Asst. Collections Mgr., David Hershey.
Institution Type/Description: University Museums.
Hours & Admission Prices: University Museums; mid-Aug.-Mid-May, Sun.-Fri. 1-5 No charge. Closed spring break; fall break; Thanksgiving week; Easter weekend; semester breaks. ♿
Attendance: 15,223 (actual)

THE VALENTINE, 1015 E. Clay St., Richmond, VA 23219-1527. Tel.: 804-649-0711. Fax: 804-643-3510. Facebook.
E-mail: info@thevalentine.org
Web Site: www.thevalentine.org
Formerly: Valentine Museum/Richmond History Center
Key Personnel: Dir., William J. Martin; Deputy Dir., Sarah M. Kim; Dir. Pub. Rels. & Mktg., Domenick Casuccio; E. Claiborne Robins, Jr. Dir. Pub. Progs., Jeff Aronowitz; Student Progs. & Tours Mgr., Marisa Day; Adult Progs. & tours Mgr., Liz Reilly-Brown; Cur. Archives, Meg Huges; Elise H. Wright Cur. General Collections, David Voelkel; Dir. Collections, The Nathalie L. Klaus Cur. Costume & Textiles, Kristen Stewart; Latino Project Cur., Wanda Hernandez; Collection Project Mgr. & Registrar, Alicia Guillama; Dir. Retail & Visitor Svcs., Caitlin Orrison; Visitor Svcs. Mgr., Stephanie Saavedra; Dir. Devel., Haley McCall McLaren; Devel. Coord., Ashley Burch; Dir. Opers. & Capital Projects; Facility Rentals, Ken Myers; Wedding Coord., Peggy Hudert;

Dir. Finance & H.R., Donna Kolba; Chm. (V), Charles N. Whitaker; Vice Chm., Marjorie N. Grier.
Institution Type/Description: Urban History Museum.
Hours & Admission Prices: Tues.-Sat. 10-5, Sun. 12-5. Adults $10, senior citizens 55 & over, students & groups $8; discounts to AAM & ICOM members; military with ID, children & members no charge. Court End Passport $10. Closed New Year's Day; Thanksgiving; Christmas Eve & Day. ♿
Attendance: 43,000 (actual)

VIRGINIA ASSOCIATION OF MUSEUMS, 301 N. Sheppard St., Richmond, VA 23221. Mailing Address: 3126 W. Cary St. #447, Richmond, VA 23221-3504. Tel.: 804-358-3171. Fax: 804-358-3174.
Web Site: vamuseums.org
Key Personnel: Exec. Dir., Jennifer Thomas.
Institution Type/Description: State Association: service organization to museum professionals throughout Virginia.
Hours & Admission Prices: Mon.-Fri. 9-5. ♿

VIRGINIA DEPARTMENT OF CONSERVATION AND RECREATION, 600 E. Main St., 24th Fl., Richmond, VA 23219. Tel.: 804-786-1712. Fax: 804-786-9294. TDD: 804-786-2121.
E-mail: pco@dcr.virginia.gov
Web Site: dcr.virginia.gov
Key Personnel: Dir., Clyde Cristman.
Institution Type/Description: State Parks & Historic Sites.
Hours & Admission Prices: Call for hours & admission fees, information differs for separate locations. ♿

VIRGINIA DEPARTMENT OF HISTORIC RESOURCES, 2801 Kensington Ave., Richmond, VA 23221-2470. Tel.: 804-482-6446. Fax: 804-367-2391. TDD: 804-367-2386.
E-mail: dee.deroche@dhr.virginia.gov
Web Site: www.dhr.virginia.gov
Key Personnel: State Archaeologist, Michael B. Barber; Chief Cur., Dee DeRoche.
Institution Type/Description: Preservation Agency.
Hours & Admission Prices: Mon.-Fri. 8:15-5. No charge. Closed state holidays. ♿
Attendance: 2,000 (estimated)

VIRGINIA HISTORICAL SOCIETY, 428 North Blvd., Richmond, VA 23220-3307. Mailing Address: P.O. Box 7311, Richmond, VA 23221-0311. Tel.: 804-358-4901. Fax: 804-342-9647. Facebook.
E-mail: jguild@vahistorical.org
Web Site: www.virginiahistory.org
Key Personnel: Pres. & C.E.O., Jamie O. Bosket; Dir. HR, Paula Davis; Vice Pres. Advancement, Anna E. von Gehr; Vice Pres. Collections & Exhibitions, Adam E. Scher; Dir. Collections Cataloging, Eileen L. Parris; Sr. Dir. Curatorial Affairs, Andrew Talkov; Dir. Research & Publications, John McClure; Sr. Vice Pres. Operations & C.F.O., Richard S.V. Heiman; Dir. Collections Mgmt., Rebecca A. Rose; Vice Pres. Guest Engagement, Michael Plumb; Vice Pres. Mktg. & Comms., Tracy D. Schneider.
Institution Type/Description: Virginia History Museum: Virginia House.
Hours & Admission Prices: Galleries: daily 10-5. Library: Mon.-Sat. 10-5. Adults $10, seniors 65 & over $8, youth 6-17 $5; discounts to groups & military. Closed New Year's Day; Thanksgiving; Christmas. ♿
Attendance: 60,000 (estimated)

VIRGINIA HOLOCAUST MUSEUM, 2000 E. Cary St., Richmond, VA 23223-7032. Tel.: 804-257-5400. Fax: 804-257-4314. Facebook.
E-mail: mferenczy@vaholocaust.com
Web Site: www.vaholocaust.org
Key Personnel: Chm., Marcus M. Weinstein; Education, Megan Ferenczy.
Institution Type/Description: History Museum.
Hours & Admission Prices: Mon.-Fri. 9-5, Sat.-Sun. 11-5; groups of 10 or more by appointment. No charge; donations accepted. Closed New Year's Eve & Day; Easter; First Day of Rosh Hashanah; Yom Kippur; Thanksgiving; Christmas Eve & Day. ♿
Attendance: 40,000 (actual)

VIRGINIA MUSEUM OF FINE ARTS, 200 N. Boulevard, Richmond, VA 23220-4007. Tel.: 804-340-1400 & 1401, 800-943-8632. Fax: 804-340-1548. TDD: 804-340-1401.
E-mail: visitorservices@vmfa.museum
Web Site: www.vmfa.museum
Key Personnel: Pres., Kelly B. Armstrong; Dir. & C.E.O., Alex Nyerges; Deputy Dir. Collections & Facilities Management, Stephen Bonadies; C.F.O., Hossein Sadid.
Institution Type/Description: Art Museum.
Hours & Admission Prices: Thurs.-Fri. 10-9, Sat.-Wed. 10-5; Holidays: 12-5. No charge. ♿
Attendance: 534,252 (actual)

VIRGINIA STATE CAPITOL, 1000 Bank St., Richmond, VA 23219. Tel.: 804-698-1788. Fax: 804-698-1906.
E-mail: capitoltourguides@house.virginia.gov
Institution Type/Description: Historic Building.
Hours & Admission Prices: Self-Guided Tours: Mon.-Sat. 8-5, Sun. 1-5. Guided Tours: Mon.-Sat. 9-4, Sun. 1-4; groups of 10 or more by appointment.

VIRGINIA WAR MEMORIAL, 621 S. Belvidere St., Richmond, VA 23220-6504. Tel.: 804-786-2060. Fax: 804-786-6652. Facebook; Twitter.
E-mail: info@vawarmemorial.org
Web Site: www.vawarmemorial.org
Key Personnel: Education Specialist, Candice L. Shelton; Museum Shop Mgr., Martha Schley Smith.
Institution Type/Description: Military Memorial.
Hours & Admission Prices: Shrine of Memory: 5 am to midnight. Visitor Center: Mon.-Sat. 9-4, Sun. 12-4. No charge; donations accepted. Closed New Year's Day; Easter; Thanksgiving; Christmas. ♿
Attendance: 68,000 (actual)

THE VISUAL ARTS CENTER OF RICHMOND, 1812 W. Main St., Richmond, VA 23220. Tel.: 804-353-0094. Facebook: Visual Arts Center of Richmond.
E-mail: info@visarts.org
Web Site: visarts.org
Formerly: The Hand Workshop
Key Personnel: Dir., Caroline Wright.
Institution Type/Description: Art Gallery.
Hours & Admission Prices: True F. Luck Gallery: Mon.-Fri. 9-9, Sat. 10-4, Sun. 1-4. No charge; donations accepted.
Attendance: 20,000 (actual)

WHITE HOUSE OF THE CONFEDERACY, 1201 E. Clay St., Richmond, VA 23219-1615. Tel.: 804-649-1861.
E-mail: info@acwm.org
Web Site: www.acwm.org
Formerly: The Museum of the Confederacy
Key Personnel: C.E.O., Christy S. Coleman; Dir. ACWM Foundation, S. Waite Rawls, III; Chm. (V), Dr. Edward L. Ayers; Sr. Cur. & Dir. Collections, Robert Hancock; Cur., Cathy Wright; Dir. Museum Operations, Eric D. App; Historian, Dr. John M. Coski; Dir. Mktg. & Public Rels., Patrick Saylor; Dir. Retail & Visitor Services, Bob Sayre.
Institution Type/Description: History Museum: historic site.
Hours & Admission Prices: Museum & White House: daily 10-5. White House or Museum: $10; discounts to AAM members. Combination Ticket: $15; discounts to AAM members. Closed New Year's Day; Thanksgiving; Christmas. ♿
Attendance: 65,009 (actual)

WILTON HOUSE MUSEUM, 215 S. Wilton Rd., Richmond, VA 23226-2212. Tel.: 804-282-5936. Fax: 804-288-9805.
E-mail: wiltonmuseum@comcast.net
Web Site: www.wiltonhousemuseum.org
Key Personnel: Dir., Keith D. MacKay; Dir. Education & Public Rels., William Strollo; Mgr. Devel., Andrew Lunney; Operations & Rental Mgr., Elizabeth Gosack-Fleming; Mgr. Collections, Erica L. Borey.
Institution Type/Description: Historic House: 1753 Georgian brick mansion, home of William Randolph, III & moved to present James River location in 1935.
Hours & Admission Prices: Tues.-Sat. 10-4:30. Adults $10, seniors $8, students $6; discounts to groups, National Trust for Historic Preservation, AASLH, AAA, VAM, ICOM & AAM members; Colonial Dames, members, active military & children under 6 no charge. Closed national holidays.
Attendance: 10,000 (actual)

Roanoke

CATHOLIC HISTORICAL MUSEUM OF THE ROANOKE VALLEY, 400 Campbell Ave., S.W., Roanoke, VA 24016-3627. Tel.: 540-982-0152. Fax: 540-982-0152.
Web Site: chsrova.org
Institution Type/Description: History Museum.
Hours & Admission Prices: Tues. 10-2; other times by appointment. No charge; donations accepted. ♿
Attendance: 500 (estimated)

ELEANOR D. WILSON MUSEUM AT HOLLINS UNIVERSITY, 8009 Fishburn Dr., Roanoke, VA 24020-1679. Mailing Address: P.O. Box 9679, Roanoke, VA 24020-1679. Tel.: 540-362-6532. Fax: 540-362-6694. Facebook: Siddy Wilson.
E-mail: wilsonmuseum@hollins.edu
Web Site: www.hollins.edu/museum
Key Personnel: Mgr. Museum Operations, Laura Jane Ramsburg; Exhibitions Coord., Janet Carty; Museum Coord., Karyn McAden.
Institution Type/Description: Art Museum.
Hours & Admission Prices: Tues.-Fri. 10-4, Sat. 1-5. No charge; donations accepted. Closed university breaks. ♿
Attendance: 10,000 (estimated)

HARRISON MUSEUM OF AFRICAN-AMERICAN CULTURE, 1 Market Sq., S.E., 2nd Fl., Roanoke, VA 24011. Mailing Address: P.O. Box 12544, Roanoke, VA 24026-2544. Tel.: 540-857-4395. Fax: 540-224-1238.
E-mail: info@harrisonmuseum.com
Web Site: harrisonmuseum.com
Key Personnel: Exec. Dir., Aletha Bolden; Exec. Asst., Donna Davis.
Institution Type/Description: History Museum.
Hours & Admission Prices: Mon.-Sat. 10-5, Sun. 1-5. Adults $7, children 5-17 $4.75; children 4 & under no charge.

HISTORY MUSEUM OF WESTERN VIRGINIA, 101 Shenandoah Ave., NE, Roanoke, VA 24016. Tel.: 540-982-5465. Fax: 540-982-5683.
E-mail: info@vahistorymuseum.org
Web Site: www.roanokehistory.org
Formerly: History Museum and Historical Society of Western Virginia
Key Personnel: Pres., Stephen Warren; Museum Mgr., Lynsey Allie; Cur., Ashley Webb.
Institution Type/Description: History Museum.
Hours & Admission Prices: Tues.-Sat. 10-5. Adults $6,seniors, students & military $5.50, children $5; children under 3 no charge. Closed New Year's Day; Martin Luther King Jr. Day; Memorial Day; Independence Day; Labor Day; Thanksgiving; Christmas. ♿
Attendance: 23,300 (actual)

MILL MOUNTAIN ZOO, Pkwy. Spur Rd., Roanoke, VA 24034. Mailing Address: P.O. Box 8159, Roanoke, VA 24014-0159. Tel.: 540-343-3241. Fax: 540-343-8111.
E-mail: info@mmzoo.org
Web Site: www.mmzoo.org
Key Personnel: Exec. Dir., Sean Greene; Administration Mgr., Michaela Pace-Wilson.
Institution Type/Description: Zoo.
Hours & Admission Prices: Winter: Thurs.-Sun. 10-4:30; Summer: daily 10-5. Adults $7.50, children 3-11 $5; children under 2 and members no charge. Closed Christmas. ♿
Attendance: 18,679 (actual)

O. WINSTON LINK MUSEUM, 101 Shenandoah Ave., N.E., Roanoke, VA 24016-2044. Tel.: 540-982-5465. Fax: 540-982-5683.
E-mail: info@vahistorymuseum.org
Web Site: www.linkmuseum.org
Key Personnel: Dir., Kimberly Parker; Interim Chm. (V), Tucker Lemon; Pres. (V), David Helmer; Exec. Dir., Jeanne M. Bollendorf; Coord. Education, Shannon Lugar; Treas., Ron Sink; Devel. Officer, Monica Johnson; Security, Jack Stilton; Museum Shop Mgr., Jennifer Miller.
Institution Type/Description: Photography Museum.
Hours & Admission Prices: Mon.-Sat. 10-5, Sun. 1-5. Adults $5, senior citizens $4.50, children $4; discounts to groups; members no charge. Closed New Year's Day; Easter; Thanksgiving; Christmas. ♿
Attendance: 18,679 (actual)

SCIENCE MUSEUM OF WESTERN VIRGINIA, 1 Market Sq., Roanoke, VA 24011. Tel.: 540-342-5710. Fax: 540-224-1240.
E-mail: frontdesk@smwv.org
Web Site: www.smwv.org
Key Personnel: Chm. (V), Tom Roller; Dir., Rachel Hopkins; Dir. Devel. & Mktg., Sarah Van Zele; Dir. Operations, Becky Lattuca.
Institution Type/Description: Science Museum.
Hours & Admission Prices: Call for hours. Museum: adults 18-59 $15.50, seniors 60 & up, military, youth 6-17 and students $13.50, children 3-5 $7.50; discounts to ASTC members; infants & toddlers and members no charge. Butterfly Garden: admission $7.60; discounts to ASTC members; infants & toddlers no charge. ♿
Attendance: 90,000 (estimated)

TAUBMAN MUSEUM OF ART, 110 Salem Ave., S.E., Roanoke, VA 24011-1410. Tel.: 540-342-5760. Fax: 540-342-5798.
Web Site: taubmanmuseum.org
Formerly: Art Museum of Western Virginia
Key Personnel: Exec. Dir., Della Watkins; Deputy Dir., Devel., Holly DiGangi; Deputy Dir., Finance, Opers. & H.R., Cheri Warren; Deputy Dir., Exhibitions & Collections, Amy Moorefield; Deputy Dir., Educ. & Visitor Svcs., Cindy Petersen.
Institution Type/Description: Art Museum.
Hours & Admission Prices: Wed.-Sat. 10-5, Sun. 12-5, 3rd Thurs & 1st Fri. each month 10-9. General gallery admission: no charge. Closed holidays. ♿
Attendance: 97,000 (actual)

VIRGINIA MUSEUM OF TRANSPORTATION, INC., 303 Norfolk Ave., S.W., Roanoke, VA 24016-3620. Tel.: 540-342-5670. Fax: 540-342-6898. Facebook: Virginia Museum of Transportation Inc.
E-mail: info@vmt.org
Web Site: www.vmt.org
Key Personnel: Dir., Beverly T. Fitzpatrick, Jr.; Museum Shop Mgr., Susan Loveman.
Institution Type/Description: Transportation Museum.
Hours & Admission Prices: Mon.-Sat. 10-5, Sun. 1-5. Adults $8, senior citizens $7, children 3-11 $6; discounts to AAA members; children under 3 & members no charge. Closed New Year's Eve & Day; Easter; Thanksgiving; Christmas Eve & Day. ♿
Attendance: 52,000 (actual)

Salem

THE SALEM MUSEUM, 801 E. Main St., Salem, VA 24153-4312. Tel.: 540-389-6760. Fax: 540-387-3724.
E-mail: info@salemmuseum.org
Web Site: www.salemmuseum.org
Key Personnel: Dir., Peggy Shifflett; Pres., William Robertson.
Institution Type/Description: History Museum: located in the c.1845 Williams-Brown House-Store.
Hours & Admission Prices: Tues.-Fri. 10-4, Sat. 10-3. No charge; donations accepted. Closed New Year's Eve, Day & weekend; Independence Day; Thanksgiving; Christmas. ♿
Attendance: 12,000 (estimated)

Saltville

MUSEUM OF THE MIDDLE APPALACHIANS, 123 Palmer Ave., Saltville, VA 24370. Mailing Address: P.O. Box 910, Saltville, VA 24370-0910. Tel.: 276-496-3633. Fax: 276-496-7033.
E-mail: museumoma@embarqmail.com
Web Site: www.museum-mid-app.org
Key Personnel: Pres., James Hatfield; Pres., Mamie Maule; Treas., Carl Rickman; Devel., Christine Helton; Museum Shop Mgr., Harry R. Haynes; Coord., Janice Orr.
Institution Type/Description: Natural History Museum.
Hours & Admission Prices: Mon.-Sat. 10-4, Sun. 1-4. Adults $3, senior citizens & children 6-12 $2, senior & student groups $1; members & children under 6 no charge. Closed New Year's Day; Easter; Thanksgiving; Christmas. ♿
Attendance: 10,000 (actual)

Scottsville

SCOTTSVILLE MUSEUM, 290 Main St., Scottsville, VA 24590. Mailing Address: 290 Main St., P.O. Box 101, Scottsville, VA 24590-0101. Tel.: 434-286-2247.
E-mail: smuseum@avenue.org
Key Personnel: Pres. (V), Evelyn Edson.
Institution Type/Description: History Museum.
Hours & Admission Prices: April-Oct. Sat. 10-5, Sun. 1-5; other times by appointment. No charge; donations accepted.
Attendance: 2,000 (estimated)

Smithfield

ISLE OF WIGHT COURTHOUSE, 130 Main St., Smithfield, VA 23430-1323. Tel.: 757-757-9016. Fax: 757-357-3191.
E-mail: dhaynes@isleofwightus.net
Institution Type/Description: Historic Building: restored Courthouse; built in 1750.
Hours & Admission Prices: Call for hours.
Attendance: 5,000 (estimated)

THE SCHOOLHOUSE MUSEUM, 516 Main St., Smithfield, VA 23430. Mailing Address: P.O. Box 1113, Smithfield, VA 23431. Tel.: 757-365-4789.
E-mail: hrw624@icloud.com
Web Site: www.theschoolhousemuseum.com
Key Personnel: Pres. (V), Marion Wrenn; Docent, Gina Blount-Jones.
Institution Type/Description: Historic Building: housed in a former one-room schoolhouse built to educate county African American children.
Hours & Admission Prices: Mon.-Thurs. & Sun. 1-4 other times by appointment. No charge. &
Attendance: 450 (estimated)

South Boston

SOUTH BOSTON-HALIFAX COUNTY MUSEUM OF FINE ARTS & HISTORY, 1540 Wilborn Ave., South Boston, VA 24592-2400. Mailing Address: P.O. Box 383, South Boston, VA 24592-0383. Tel.: 434-572-9200. Fax: 434-572-8996. Facebook: South Boston Halifax County Museum of Fine Arts and History.
E-mail: sbhcm1@centurylink.net
Web Site: sbhcmuseum.org
Key Personnel: Pres., Paul Smith; Vice Pres., Linda Mercer; Dir., Beth Coates; Treas., Jane Jones; Sec., Louise Sheppard.
Institution Type/Description: History Museum.
Hours & Admission Prices: Wed.-Sat. 10-4. No charge; donations accepted. Closed New Year's Day; Thanksgiving; Christmas. &
Attendance: 3,300 (estimated)

Spotsylvania

SPOTSYLVANIA HISTORICAL ASSOCIATION AND MUSEUM, 9019 Old Battlefield Blvd., Spotsylvania, VA 22553. Mailing Address: P.O. Box 64, Spotsylvania, VA 22553-0064. Tel.: 540-507-7278.
E-mail: shainc@verizon.net
Key Personnel: Dir., Treas. & Cur., Jo Harding; Pres., John E. Pruitt, Jr.; Vice Pres., Stephen P. Lampert.
Institution Type/Description: General Museum.
Hours & Admission Prices: Daily 9-5. No charge; donations accepted. Closed New Year's Day; Thanksgiving; Christmas Eve & Day. &
Attendance: 5,000 (estimated)

Springfield

DEA MUSEUM & VISITORS CENTER, 8701 Morrissette Dr., Springfield, VA 22152. Tel.: 202-307-3463. Fax: 202-307-8956.
Web Site: www.deamuseum.org
Key Personnel: Dir., Sean T. Fearns; Pres. (V), William Alden; Museum Shop Mgr., Jim Lumsden.
Institution Type/Description: History Museum.
Hours & Admission Prices: Tues.-Fri. 10-4; groups by appointment. No charge. &

Staunton

AUGUSTA COUNTY HISTORICAL SOCIETY, 20 S. New St., 3rd Fl., Staunton, VA 24401. Mailing Address: P.O. Box 686, Staunton, VA 24402-0686. Tel.: 540-248-4151.
E-mail: augustachs@ntelos.net
Web Site: www.augustacountyhs.org
Institution Type/Description: Historical Society Museum.
Hours & Admission Prices: Tues. & Thurs.-Fri. 9-12; other times by appointment.

CAMERA HERITAGE MUSEUM, 1 W. Beverley St., Staunton, VA 24401. Tel.: 540-886-8535.
E-mail: info@cameraheritagemuseum.com
Web Site: www.cameraheritagemuseum.com/index.html
Institution Type/Description: Camera History Museum.
Hours & Admission Prices: Mon.-Fri. 9-5, Sat. 9-2. Admission $5; donations accepted.

FRONTIER CULTURE MUSEUM OF VIRGINIA, 1290 Richmond Rd., Staunton, VA 24401. Mailing Address: P.O. Box 810, Staunton, VA 24402-0810. Tel.: 540-332-7850. Fax: 540-332-9989. TDD: 540-332-7850.
E-mail: visitors.center@frontiermuseum.org
Web Site: www.frontiermuseum.org
Formerly: Museum of American Frontier Culture
Key Personnel: Exec. Dir., John Avoli; Deputy Dir., Eric Bryan; Fiscal Officer, Merritt Schoonover; Mktg. Dir., Joe Herget; Buildings & Grounds Supt., Cliff Edwards; Operations & HR Mgr., Lydia Volskis; Education Dir., Andrew Richardson.
Institution Type/Description: Outdoor Living History Museum.
Hours & Admission Prices: early-March to Nov. daily 9-5; Dec. to early-March daily 10-4; group & educational tours available. Adults $10, seniors $9.50, students $9, children 6-12 $6; discounts to AAM members; children under 6 & members no charge. Closed New Year's Day; Thanksgiving; Christmas. &
Attendance: 78,000 (actual)

MARY BALDWIN COLLEGE/HUNT GALLERY, Market & Vine, Staunton, VA 24401. Mailing Address: Dept. of Art & Art History, Deming Hall, Mary Baldwin College, Staunton, VA 24401-3610. Tel.: 540-887-7196. Fax: 540-887-7139.
E-mail: pryan@mbc.edu
Web Site: www.mbc.edu/college/events/huntgallery.asp
Key Personnel: Dir., Paul Ryan.
Institution Type/Description: College Art Gallery & Museum.
Hours & Admission Prices: Sept.-May Mon.-Fri. 9-5. No charge. &
Attendance: 1,200 (estimated)

MUSEUM OF BANK HISTORY AT SUNTRUST BANK, 2-14 W. Beverley St., Staunton, VA 24401. Tel.: 540-887-0174.
Institution Type/Description: History Museum.
Hours & Admission Prices: Mon.-Thurs. 9-5, Fri. 9-6. No charge.

STAUNTON AUGUSTA ART CENTER, 20 S. New St., Staunton, VA 24401-4308. Tel.: 540-885-2028. Facebook: Staunton Augusta Art Center.
E-mail: info@saartcenter.org
Web Site: www.saartcenter.org
Key Personnel: Exec. Dir., Beth Hodge; Pres. (V), David Bottenfield; Cur., Hannah Scott.
Institution Type/Description: Art Association: housed in 19th-century pump house which once supplied water for the city of Staunton.
Hours & Admission Prices: Mon.-Fri. 10-5, Sat. 10-4. No charge; donations accepted. Closed major holidays; between exhibitions. &
Attendance: 14,000 (estimated)

STAUNTON MILITARY ACADEMY MUSEUM & VIRGINIA WOMEN'S INSTITUTE FOR LEADERSHIP MUSEUM, Mary Baldwin College, 227 Kable St., Staunton, VA 24402. Mailing Address: SMA Alumni Assoc., P.O. Box 958, Staunton, VA 24402-0958. Tel.: 540-885-1309.
E-mail: smaoffice@sma-alumni.org
Web Site: www.sma-alumni.org/museum.htm
Institution Type/Description: History Museum.
Hours & Admission Prices: Wed. & Sat.-Sun. 1-4. No charge.

WOODROW WILSON PRESIDENTIAL LIBRARY, 20 N. Coalter St., Staunton, VA 24401-4332. Mailing Address: P.O. Box 24, Staunton, VA 24402-0024. Tel.: 540-885-0897. Fax: 540-886-9874.
E-mail: info@woodrowwilson.org
Web Site: www.woodrowwilson.org
Formerly: Woodrow Wilson Birthplace & Museum
Key Personnel: Pres. & C.E.O., Robin von Seldeneck; Chm. (V), Brig. Gen. Theodore Shuey, Jr.; Administrative Officer, Karen Dodson; Head Archivist, Mark Peterson; Cur., Andrew Phillips; Coord. Visitor Svcs., Cynthia Polhill.
Institution Type/Description: Historic House: 1846 former Presbyterian Manse & birthplace of Woodrow Wilson, 28th President of the U.S.
Hours & Admission Prices: Hours vary by season; see website for hours. Adults $14, AAA members, seniors & active military $12, students 13 & over $7, children 6-12 $5; discounts to groups; members & children under 6 no charge. Closed New Year's Day; Easter; Thanksgiving; Christmas Eve & Day. &
Attendance: 21,500 (actual)

Stephens City

NEWTOWN HISTORY CENTER, 5408 Main St., Stephens City, VA 22655-2829. Mailing Address: P.O. Box 143, Stephens City, VA 22655-0143. Tel.: 540-869-1700. Fax: 540-869-0400. Facebook: Newtown History Center.
E-mail: info@newtownhistorycenter.org
Web Site: newtownhistorycenter.org
Formerly: Historic Stephensburg Museums
Key Personnel: Pres. (V), Linden A. Fravel; Dir. & Cur., Byron C. Smith; Treas., Mary S. Dyke; Mgr. Collections & Programs, Wayne A. Eldred.
Institution Type/Description: History Museum.

Hours & Admission Prices: June-Aug. Tues.-Sat. 10-4, Sun. 1-5; Sept.-Nov. Wed.-Sat. 10-4, Sun. 1-5; Dec.-May by appointment. Family $5, adults $2, children 6-18 $1; AASLH members and military & their family no charge. Closed New Year's Day; Martin Luther King Jr. Day; Presidents' Day; Good Friday; Labor Day; Columbus Day; Thanksgiving & day after; Christmas Eve & Day.
Attendance: 276 (actual)

Sterling

LOUDOUN HERITAGE FARM MUSEUM, 21668 Heritage Farm Lane, Sterling, VA 20164-9207. Tel.: 571-258-3800. Fax: 571-258-3801.
E-mail: nursydal@aol.com
Web Site: www.heritagefarmmuseum.org
Formerly: Heritage Farm Museum of Loudoun County
Key Personnel: Pres. (V), Su Webb; Co Dir., Katie Eichler Jones; Co Dir., Christie Love.
Institution Type/Description: History Museum.
Hours & Admission Prices: Tues.-Sat. 9:30-4:30, Sun. 11:30-4:30. Adults $5, senior citizens $4, children $3.
Attendance: 16,400 (actual)

Strasburg

STRASBURG MUSEUM, 440 E. King St., Strasburg, VA 22657-2433. Mailing Address: P.O. Box 333, Strasburg, VA 22657-0333. Tel.: 540-465-3175 & 3728.
E-mail: gastick@shentel.net
Web Site: strasburgmuseum.org
Key Personnel: Pres. (V), Gloria Stickley; Vice Pres., John Adamson; Treas., Philip Loving; Sec., Tina Crabill; Museum Shop Mgr., Margo Hammock.
Institution Type/Description: History Museum: housed in 1891 pottery factory, later converted to train station.
Hours & Admission Prices: May-Oct. daily 10-4. Adults $5.
Attendance: 3,500 (estimated)

Stratford

STRATFORD HALL, ROBERT E. LEE MEMORIAL ASSOCIATION, INC., 483 Great House Rd., Stratford, VA 22558. Tel.: 804-493-8038. Fax: 804-493-0333.
E-mail: info@stratfordhall.org
Web Site: www.stratfordhall.org
Formerly: Stratford, Robert E. Lee Memorial Foundation, Inc.
Key Personnel: Pres., John S. Bacon; Chm. (V), Mary H. Wilson; Dir. Research & Library Collections, Judith S. Hynson; Dir. Education & Interpretation, Abby Newkirk; Dir. Mktg., Jim Schepmoes; Cur., Gretchen Goodell Pendleton; Plantation Store Mgr., Janet Branson; Editor, Lee Family Archive, Colin Woodward.
Institution Type/Description: Historic Site & General Museum: housed in 1738 Stratford Hall with operating plantation.
Hours & Admission Prices: Daily 9:30-4. Adults $12, National Trust for Historical Preservation members $9, senior citizens 60 & over, AAA members, groups of 20 or more, active duty military $11, children 6-11 $7; children under 6 no charge. Grounds pass: adults $7, children $5. Closed New Year's Eve & Day; Christmas Eve & Day.
Attendance: 28,000 (estimated)

Stuart

WOOD BROTHERS RACING MUSEUM, 21 Performance Dr., Stuart, VA 24171. Tel.: 276-694-2121.
E-mail: 21team@woodbrothersracing.com
Web Site: woodbrothersracing.com
Institution Type/Description: Racing Company.
Hours & Admission Prices: Call for hours. No charge.

Suffolk

RIDDICK'S FOLLY HOUSE MUSEUM, 510 N. Main St., Suffolk, VA 23434. Tel.: 757-934-0822. Fax: 757-934-0411. Facebook: Riddick's Folly House Museum.
E-mail: rfcurator@verizon.net
Web Site: www.riddicksfolly.org
Formerly: Riddick's Folly
Key Personnel: Pres., Larry W. Riddick; Dir., Cur. & Museum Shop Mgr., Edward L. King.
Institution Type/Description: Historic House Museum: built in 1837 Greek revival home of the Riddick family which was commandeered by the Union army as a headquarters during the occupation of Suffolk.

Hours & Admission Prices: Wed.-Fri. 10-5, Sat. 10-4, Sun. 1-5; groups by appointment. Adults $5, seniors 55 & over and active military $4, children 3-12 $3. Closed New Year's Day; Easter; Independence Day; Thanksgiving; Christmas.
Attendance: 4,000 (estimated)

THE SUFFOLK MUSEUM, 118 Bosley Ave., Suffolk, VA 23434-5755. Tel.: 757-514-7284. Fax: 757-538-0833.
E-mail: nkinzinger@city.suffolk.va.us
Institution Type/Description: Art Museum.
Hours & Admission Prices: Tues.-Sat. 10-5, Sun. 1-5. No charge. Closed New Year's Day; Lee-Jackson-King Day; Washington's Birthday; Easter; Memorial Day; Independence Day; Labor Day; Veterans Day; Thanksgiving; Christmas.
Attendance: 18,000 (actual)

SUFFOLK SEABOARD STATION RAILROAD MUSEUM, 326 N. Main St., Suffolk, VA 23434. Mailing Address: P.O. Box 1255, Suffolk, VA 23439-1255. Tel.: 757-923-4750. Fax: 757-923-4751. Facebook: Suffolk Seaboard Station Railroad Museum.
E-mail: info@suffolktrainstation.org
Web Site: www.suffolktrainstation.org
Institution Type/Description: Historic Building: housed in a former railroad station; built in 1885.
Hours & Admission Prices: Thurs.-Sat. 10-4, Sun. 1-4.

Surry

CHIPPOKES FARM & FORESTRY MUSEUM, 695 Chippokes Park Rd., Surry, VA 23883-2406. Tel.: 757-294-3439. Fax: 757-294-3550.
E-mail: chippokes@dcr.virginia.gov
Key Personnel: Pres. (V), Sen. Frederick M. Quayle; Exec. Dir., Linda Guntharp; Museum Shop Mgr., Sarah Cosby.
Institution Type/Description: Farm & Forestry Museum: housed in series of buildings, two of which are historically significant, at Chippokes Plantation State Park.
Hours & Admission Prices: April-Oct. Mon. & Wed.-Fri. 10-3, Sat. 10-5, Sun. 12-5. No charge. Fee for special events.
Attendance: 8,408 (actual)

SMITH'S FORT PLANTATION, 217 Smith's Fort Lane, Surry, VA 23883. Mailing Address: P.O. Box 240, Surry, VA 23883-0240. Tel.: 757-294-3872. TDD: 757-294-3872.
E-mail: smithsfortplantation@preservationvirginia.org
Web Site: preservationvirginia.org/visit/historic-properties/smiths-fort-plantation
Key Personnel: C.E.O., Elizabeth Kostelny; Dir., A. Kent Harrell; Mgr., Thomas Forehand.
Institution Type/Description: Historic House Museum: 17th-century fort site; earthworks remain of fort started in 1609 by Capt. John Smith; property a dower gift in 1614 from Powhatan to John Rolfe & Pocahontas; 18th-century brick dwelling a Faulcon family property 1754-1835.
Hours & Admission Prices: Memorial Day to Labor Day Mon. & Fri.-Sat. 10-5, Sun. 12-5; Sept.-May Fri.-Sat. 10-5, Sun. 12-5; other times by appointment. Adults $8, senior citizens $6, students $5; discounts to AAM members & groups; children under 6 & APVA members no charge.
Attendance: 3,000 (estimated)

SURRY NUCLEAR INFORMATION CENTER, 5570 Hog Island Rd., Surry, VA 23883. Tel.: 757-357-5410. Fax: 757-357-4711.
Web Site: www.dom.com
Institution Type/Description: Science Museum.
Hours & Admission Prices: Mon.-Fri. 9-4. Closed major holidays.

Surry County

BACON'S CASTLE, 465 Bacon's Castle Trail, Surry, VA 23883-2213. Mailing Address: 204 W. Franklin St., Richmond, VA 23220. Tel.: 757-357-5976, 804-648-1889. Fax: 804-775-0802.
E-mail: baconscastle@preservationvirginia.org
Web Site: www.preservationvirginia.org/baconscastle
Key Personnel: C.E.O., Elizabeth Kostelny; Site Coord., Carol Wiedel; Dir. Preservation Svcs., Louis J. Malon; Dir. Museum Operations & Education, Jennifer Hurst-Wender; Dir. Finance, Cheryl Greenday; Digital Communications Coord., Krysha Snyder.
Institution Type/Description: Historic Site & Historic House: 1665 Jacobean manor house used by Nathaniel Bacon's troops as a fortress during the rebellion against Royal Governor William Berkeley in 1676.
Hours & Admission Prices: Memorial Day to Labor Day Mon. & Fri.-Sat. 10-5, Sun. 12-5; March-Dec. Fri.-Sat. 10-5, Sun. 12-5. Adults $8, AAA members $7,

seniors $6, students $5; children under 6 & members no charge. Block Tickets (Smith's Fort Plantation): General $12, senior $10. Closed Independence Day. &
Attendance: 5,726 (actual)

Sweet Briar

SWEET BRIAR COLLEGE ART COLLECTION AND GALLERIES, Sweet Briar College, 134 Chapel Rd., Sweet Briar, VA 24595-1115. Tel.: 434-381-6248.
E-mail: klawson@sbc.edu
Web Site: sbc.edu/art-galleries
Key Personnel: Dir., Karol A. Lawson, Ph.D.; Chm. (V), Nancy Dobbs Loftin; Registrarial Asst., Nancy McDearmon.
Institution Type/Description: College Art Gallery: housed in 1906 historic landmark building.
Hours & Admission Prices: Sept.-May Mon.-Thurs. 10-5, Fri. 10-2. Sun. 1-4; Summer by appointment. No charge; donations accepted. Closed college breaks; reading days; exams. &
Attendance: 2,500 (estimated)

SWEET BRIAR MUSEUM, Sweet Briar College, 134 Chapel Rd., Boxwood Alumnae House, Sweet Briar, VA 24595. Mailing Address: Sweet Briar College, Sweet Briar, VA 24595-1056. Tel.: 434-381-6246.
E-mail: museum@sbc.edu
Web Site: sbc.edu/museum
Key Personnel: Dir., Karol A. Lawson.
Institution Type/Description: College History Museum: housed in renovated c.1929 college building.
Hours & Admission Prices: Academic Year: Tues.-Thurs. 1-4. No charge. Closed college breaks, reading days, exams. &
Attendance: 500 (estimated)

Tangier Island

TANGIER HISTORY MUSEUM & INTERPRETIVE CULTURAL CENTER, 16215 Main Ridge Rd., Tangier Island, VA 23440. Mailing Address: P.O. Box 182, Tangier, VA 23440-0182. Tel.: 757-891-2374.
E-mail: thmicc@aol.com
Web Site: tangierhistorymuseum.org
Key Personnel: Dir., Henrietta Dise; C.E.O., Chm. (V) & Pres. (V), Edward V. Parks.
Institution Type/Description: History Museum.
Hours & Admission Prices: late April to late Oct. 11-4; other times by appointment. Adults $3; school groups & military no charge. &
Attendance: 15,000 (actual)

Tappahannock

ESSEX COUNTY MUSEUM & HISTORICAL SOCIETY, 218 Water Lane, Tappahannock, VA 22560. Mailing Address: P.O. Box 404, Tappahannock, VA 22560-0404. Tel.: 804-443-4690.
E-mail: info@ccmhs.org
Web Site: www.essexmuseum.org
Key Personnel: Pres. (V), Suzanne Derieux; Museum Shop Mgr., Priscilla Vaughan.
Institution Type/Description: Historical Society Museum.
Hours & Admission Prices: Mon.-Tues. 10-3, Thurs.-Sat. 10-3. No charge; donations accepted. &

Tazewell

HISTORIC CRAB ORCHARD MUSEUM & PIONEER PARK, INC., Rts.19 & 460 at Crab Orchard Rd., 3663 Crab Orchard Rd., Tazewell, VA 24651-9200. Tel.: 276-988-6755. Fax: 276-988-9400. Facebook: Historic Crab Orchard Museum & Pioneer Park Inc.
E-mail: info@craborchardmuseum.com
Web Site: www.craborchardmuseum.com
Key Personnel: C.E.O. & Dir., Charlotte G. Whitted; Chm. (V), Martha Hurst; Dir. Museum Programs, I. Joan Yates; Museum Shop Mgr., Cindy Ringstaff; Cur., Elisabeth Hemsworth.
Institution Type/Description: Historic Houses & Site: located on Big Crab Orchard Archaeological & Historic Site.
Hours & Admission Prices: Nov. to Memorial Day Tues.-Sat. 9-5; day after Memorial Day to last Sun in Oct. Tues.-Sat. 9-5, Sun. 1-5. Adults $4, senior citizens over 60 $3, children 6-12 $2; discounts to AAM, AAA & AARP; children

under 6 & members no charge. Closed New Year's Day; Thanksgiving; Christmas. &
Attendance: 25,000 (actual)

The Plains

AFRO AMERICAN HISTORICAL ASSOCIATION OF FAUQUIER COUNTY, 4243 Loudoun Ave., The Plains, VA 20198-0340. Mailing Address: P.O. Box 340, The Plains, VA 20198-0340. Tel.: 540-253-7488. Fax: 540-253-5126.
E-mail: info@aahafauquier.org
Web Site: aahafauquier.org
Key Personnel: Pres., Karen Hughes White; Vice Pres., Karen King Lavore.
Institution Type/Description: History Museum.
Hours & Admission Prices: Tues.-Wed. 10-3; other times by appointment. No charge; donations accepted. Closed holidays.
Attendance: 2,188 (actual)

Triangle

NATIONAL MUSEUM OF THE MARINE CORPS, 18900 Jefferson Davis Hwy., Suite 100, Triangle, VA 22172-1938. Tel.: 877-653-1775. Fax: 703-221-2988.
E-mail: info@usmcmuseum.org
Web Site: www.usmcmuseum.org
Key Personnel: Dir., Lin Ezell.
Institution Type/Description: Military Museum.
Hours & Admission Prices: Daily 9-5. No charge; donations accepted. Closed Christmas. &
Attendance: 534,966 (actual)

PRINCE WILLIAM FOREST PARK VISITOR CENTER, 18100 Park Headquarters Rd., Triangle, VA 22172-1644. Tel.: 703-221-7181 & 4706. Fax: 703-221-3258. TDD: 703-221-7181.
E-mail: prwi_info@nps.gov
Web Site: www.nps.gov/prwi
Key Personnel: Asst. Supt., George Liffert; Chief Interpretation, Laura Cohen.
Institution Type/Description: Park Museum.
Hours & Admission Prices: March to mid-Dec. daily 9-5; mid-Dec. to March 1 Fri.-Mon. 9-5. Seven Day Pass: $5 per vehicle, $3 per person; children under 16 & permanently disabled or blind persons no charge. Closed New Year's Day; Thanksgiving; Christmas. &
Attendance: 30,000

University of Richmond

VIRGINIA BAPTIST HISTORICAL SOCIETY, Boatwright Library, University of Richmond, VA 23173. Mailing Address: P. O. Box 34, University of Richmond, VA 23173. Tel.: 804-289-8434. Fax: 804-289-8953.
E-mail: fred.anderson@bgav.org
Web Site: www.baptistheritage.org
Key Personnel: C.E.O., Fred Anderson; Pres. (V), Frank G. Schwall, Jr.
Institution Type/Description: Historical Society Museum.
Hours & Admission Prices: Mon.-Fri. 9-12 & 1-4:30. No charge; donations accepted. Closed legal holidays.
Attendance: 5,000 (estimated)

Vienna

MEADOWLARK BOTANICAL GARDENS, 9750 Meadowlark Gardens Ct., Vienna, VA 22182. Tel.: 703-255-3631. Fax: 703-255-2392.
E-mail: ktomlinson@nvrpa.org
Web Site: www.nvrpa.org
Institution Type/Description: Botanical Gardens.
Hours & Admission Prices: March & Oct. daily 10-6; April & Sept. daily 10-7; May daily 10-7:30; June-Aug. daily 10-8; Nov.-Feb. daily 10-5. Adults $5; discounts to APGA; members no charge. Closed New Year's Day; Thanksgiving; Christmas.
Attendance: 50,000 (actual)

Virginia Beach

ATLANTIC WILDFOWL HERITAGE MUSEUM, 1113 Atlantic Ave., Virginia Beach, VA 23451-3503. Tel.: 757-437-8432. Fax: 757-437-9055.
E-mail: director@atwildfowl.org
Web Site: www.awhm.org

Key Personnel: Dir., Charles L. (Lynn) Hightower; Pres. (V), Albert Henley; Museum Shop Mgr., Ann Smith.
Institution Type/Description: Wildfowl Museum: located in an 1895 three-story beach house on the Atlantic Ocean; an example of Queen Anne architecture.
Hours & Admission Prices: Memorial Day-Oct. 1 Mon.-Sat. 10-5, Sun. 12-5; Oct. 2-May Tues.-Sat. 10-5. Adults 16 & over $2. Closed New Year's Eve & Day; Easter; Thanksgiving; Christmas Eve & Day.
Attendance: 15,000 (actual)

BACK BAY NATIONAL WILDLIFE REFUGE, 4005 Sandpiper Rd., Virginia Beach, VA 23456. Mailing Address: 1324 Sandbridge Rd., Virginia Beach, VA 23456-4023. Tel.: 757-301-7329.
E-mail: Erica_Ryder@fws.gov
Web Site: www.fws.gov/refuge/back_bay
Institution Type/Description: National Wildlife Refuge.
Hours & Admission Prices: Refuge: daily dawn to dusk. Visitor Center: Memorial Day to Labor Day Tues.-Fri. 8-4, Sat.-Sun. 9-4; Labor Day to Memorial Day Tues.-Fri. 8-4, Sat. 9-4.

CAPE HENRY LIGHTHOUSE, 583 Atlantic Ave., Fort Story, VA 23459-1048. Mailing Address: 204 W. Franklin St., Richmond, VA 23220-5012. Tel.: 757-422-9421. Facebook: Cape Henry Lighthouse.
E-mail: capehenry@preservationvirginia.org
Web Site: www.preservationvirginia.org/capehenry
Formerly: Old Cape Henry Lighthouse
Key Personnel: C.E.O., Elizabeth Kostelny; Pres. (V), Mrs. William E. Loughridge; Site Coord., Jessica Kinder; Dir. Operations & Education, Jennifer Hurst-Wender.
Institution Type/Description: Historic Building: 1791 first commissioned public works building in the United States, built near the monument marking the first landing of the Jamestown colonists.
Hours & Admission Prices: March 16-Oct. daily 10-5; Nov.-March 15 daily 10-4. Adults $8, youth 12 & under $6; discounts to groups; members & children under 3 no charge. Closed New Year's Eve & Day; Thanksgiving; Christmas Eve, Day & week after.
Attendance: 55,802 (actual)

FIRST LANDING STATE PARK, 2500 Shore Dr., Virginia Beach, VA 23451-1415. Tel.: 757-412-2300. Fax: 757-412-2315.
E-mail: firstlanding@dcr.virginia.gov
Web Site: www.virginiastateparks.gov
Key Personnel: Park Mgr., Bruce Widener.
Institution Type/Description: Park Museum.
Hours & Admission Prices: Daily 8-dusk. No charge. Parking: Mon.-Fri. $4, Sat.-Sun. $5. Annual parking passes available. Closed New Year's Day; Thanksgiving; Christmas.
Attendance: 1,500,000 (estimated)

MILITARY AVIATION MUSEUM, 1341 Princess Anne Rd., Virginia Beach, VA 23457-1542. Tel.: 757-721-7767. Fax: 757-497-8083.
E-mail: director@aviationmuseum.us
Web Site: www.militaryaviationmuseum.org
Key Personnel: Dir., Jarod Hoogland; Gift Shop Mgr., Tammy Taylor.
Institution Type/Description: Military Aviation Museum.
Hours & Admission Prices: Daily 9-5. Adults $10; discounts to seniors & active military & groups; WWII veterans & members & children 5 & under no charge. Closed Thanksgiving; Christmas.
Attendance: 50,000 (estimated)

VIRGINIA AQUARIUM & MARINE SCIENCE CENTER, 717 General Booth Blvd., Virginia Beach, VA 23451-4811. Tel.: 757-385-FISH (24 hour recording) & 385-7777 (office). Fax: 757-437-4976.
E-mail: fish@virginiaaquarium.com
Web Site: www.virginiaaquarium.com
Key Personnel: Deputy Dir., Stanley Burchfield; Dir. Finance, Donna Ellis; Dir. Devel., Russell Turner; Dir. Research & Conservation, Mark Swingle; Dir. Education, Chris Witherspoon; Mgr. Volunteer Resources, Kathleen Reed.
Institution Type/Description: Marine Science Center & Aquarium.
Hours & Admission Prices: Memorial Day to Labor Day daily 9-6; Sept.-May daily 9-5. Aquarium: adults $22, senior citizens 62 & over $20, children 3-11 $15; children 2 & under no charge. IMAX Film: $8 per person. Closed Thanksgiving; Christmas.
Attendance: 622,000 (estimated)

VIRGINIA BEACH HISTORY MUSEUMS - ADAM THOROUGHGOOD HOUSE, 1636 Parish Rd., Virginia Beach, VA 23455-4401. Mailing Address: Francis Land House, 3131 Virginia Beach Blvd., Virginia Beach, VA 23452-6923. Tel.: 757-385-5100. Fax: 757-460-7644. Facebook: VB History Museums.
E-mail: vbhistory@vbgov.com
Web Site: www.museumsvb.org
Key Personnel: History Museums Coord., Anne Miller; Educator II, Sarah Linden-Brooks; Educator, Kimberly Schmidtmann.
Institution Type/Description: Historic House: c.1719 Southern modified hall & parlor, one & one-half story brick structure located on the Grand Patent of 1636 which is part of the original land grant given to Adam Thoroughgood.
Hours & Admission Prices: Tues.-Sat. 10-4, Sun. 12-4; extended hours for special events. Adults $5, seniors $4, children 6-18 $3; discounts to groups; children under 5 no charge.
Attendance: 6,899 (actual)

VIRGINIA BEACH HISTORY MUSEUMS - FRANCIS LAND HOUSE, 3131 Virginia Beach Blvd., Virginia Beach, VA 23452-6923. Tel.: 757-385-5100. Fax: 757-431-3733. Facebook: VB History Museums.
E-mail: vbhistory@vbgov.com
Web Site: www.museumsvb.org
Key Personnel: History Museums Coord., Anne Miller; Educator II, Sarah Linden-Brooks; Educator, Kimberly Schmidtmann.
Institution Type/Description: Historic Site & House: late 18th-early 19th century brick plantation home of gentry-class planters, built by later generation of Land family.
Hours & Admission Prices: Thurs.-Sat. 10-4, Sun. 12-4. Adults $5, senior citizens $4, students 6 & over $3; children under 6 no charge. Closed most major holidays.
Attendance: 13,807 (actual)

VIRGINIA BEACH HISTORY MUSEUMS - LYNNHAVEN HOUSE, 4409 Wishart Rd., Virginia Beach, VA 23455. Mailing Address: 3131 Virginia Beach Blvd., Virginia Beach, VA 23452. Tel.: 757-385-5100. Fax: 757-460-7537. Facebook: VB History Museums.
E-mail: vbhistory@vbgov.com
Web Site: www.museumsvb.org
Key Personnel: History Museums Coord., Anne Miller; Educator II, Sarah Linden-Brooks; Educator, Kimberly Schmidtmann.
Institution Type/Description: Historic House: preserved c.1725 brick dwelling, that is an example of early 18th-century eastern Virginia vernacular architecture.
Hours & Admission Prices: Thurs.-Sat. 10-4, Sun. 12-4; extended hours for special events. Adults $5, seniors $4, children 6-18 $3; discount to groups; children under 5 no charge.
Attendance: 3,510 (actual)

VIRGINIA BEACH SURF & RESCUE MUSEUM, 2401 Atlantic Ave., Virginia Beach, VA 23451. Mailing Address: P.O. Box 1035, Virginia Beach, VA 23451-0035. Tel.: 757-422-1587. Fax: 757-491-8609. Facebook & Instagram: @VBSRM; Twitter: @VBSRMuseum.
E-mail: william@vbsrm.org
Web Site: vbsurfrescuemuseum.org
Formerly: Virginia Beach Maritime Museum, Inc./The Old Coast Guard Station
Key Personnel: Exec. Dir., Kathryn A. Fisher; Admin. Dir., William Hazel.
Institution Type/Description: Maritime Museum: housed in 1903 former United States Life-Saving & Coast Guard Station.
Hours & Admission Prices: May-Sept. Mon.-Sat. 10-5, Sun. 12-5; Oct.-April Tues.-Sat. 10-5, Sun. 12-5. Adults $8, senior citizens, active military & children 6-15 $5; discounts to AAM members; members & children under 6 no charge. Closed New Year's Day; Thanksgiving; Christmas Eve & Day.
Attendance: 15,000 (estimated)

VIRGINIA MUSEUM OF CONTEMPORARY ART, 2200 Parks Ave., Virginia Beach, VA 23451-4062. Tel.: 757-425-0000. Fax: 757-425-8186. Facebook: Virginia MOCA.
E-mail: info@virginiamoca.org
Web Site: www.virginiamoca.org
Formerly: Contemporary Art Center of Virginia
Key Personnel: Exec. Dir., Debi Gray; Chm. Bd. Trustees, Andrew Hodge; Dir. Devel., Emily Barnhill; Dir. Operations & Facility Mgmt., Andrew Coulomb; Dir. Exhibitions & Education, Alison Byrne; Asst. Dir. Devel., Jennifer Golden; Facilities Mktg., Kay Barbini; Devel. Coord., Ashley Lambert; Administrative Asst., Rita Utz; Accounting & Human Resources, Jane Cullipher; Mgr. School & Educator Programs, Rebecca Davidson; Registrar & Preparator, Monee Bengtson; Cur., Heather Hakimzadeh; Assoc. Cur. Education, Truly Matthews.
Institution Type/Description: Art Museum, Center & School.

Hours & Admission Prices: Tues. 10-9, Wed.-Fri. 10-5, Sat.-Sun. 10-4. Adults $7.70, students 5 & over, seniors, military and AAA members $5.50; discounts to AAM, ICOM & VAM members; members and children 4 & under no charge. Closed New Year's Day; Martin Luther King Jr. Day; Presidents' Day; Independence Day; Labor Day; Thanksgiving & day after; Christmas Eve & Day. &

Attendance: 525,555 (estimated)

Wallops Island

NASA WALLOPS FLIGHT FACILITY VISITOR CENTER, Bldg. J-17, Rte. 175, Wallops Island, VA 23337. Tel.: 757-824-1344.

E-mail: Kim.A.Check@nasa.gov
Institution Type/Description: Science Museum.
Hours & Admission Prices: Visitor Center: July-Aug. daily 10-4; Sept.-June Tues.-Sat. 10-4; during launch operations. Gift Shop: March-May & Sept.-Nov. Tues.-Sat. 10-4; July-Aug. daily 10-4. No charge. Closed most federal holidays &

Warm Springs

BATH COUNTY HISTORICAL SOCIETY, 99 Courthouse Hill Rd., Warm Springs, VA 24484. Mailing Address: P.O. Box 212, Warm Springs, VA 24484-0212. Tel.: 540-839-2543. Fax: 540-839-2566. Facebook: Bath County Historical Society.

E-mail: bathcountyhistory@tds.net
Web Site: www.bathcountyhistory.org
Key Personnel: Pres. (V), Richard Armstrong; Vice Pres., Murphy Wilson.
Institution Type/Description: Historical Society Museum.
Hours & Admission Prices: April-Dec. Wed.-Sat. 10-4; other times by appointment. No charge; donations accepted. &
Attendance: 300 (estimated)

Warrenton

THE COLD WAR MUSEUM, 7142 Lineweaver Rd., Warrenton, VA 20187. Mailing Address: P.O. Box 861526, Vint Hill, VA 20187. Tel.: 540-341-2008.

E-mail: museum@coldwar.org
Web Site: www.coldwar.org
Key Personnel: Exec. Dir., Jason Hall.
Institution Type/Description: History Museum: housed in one of the former Vint Hill Farm Station buildings used during the Cold War by the US Army, the National Security Agency, and the CIA to intercept and interpret coded messages.
Hours & Admission Prices: Sat. 11-4, Sun. 1-4; other times by appointment. No charge; donations accepted.

THE FAUQUIER HISTORY MUSEUM AT THE OLD JAIL, 10 Ashby St. Courthouse Sq., Warrenton, VA 20186. Mailing Address: P.O. Box 675, Warrenton, VA 20188-0675. Tel.: 540-347-5525. Facebook.

E-mail: fhsoldjailmuseum@gmail.com
Web Site: www.fauquierhistory.org
Formerly: The Old Jail Museum
Key Personnel: Dir., Elizabeth Ryan; Pres. (V), Yakir Lubowsky; Cur., Margaret Lovitt.
Institution Type/Description: Local History Museum: housed in two buildings, 1808 jail and 1823 jail, the town's only existing jail until 1966.
Hours & Admission Prices: Wed.-Mon. 10-4; guided tours by appointment. Adults $2, youth 10-18 $1; children under 10 no charge. Closed New Year's Day; Easter; Thanksgiving; Christmas.
Attendance: 12,408 (actual)

MOSBY MUSEUM, 173 Main St., Warrenton, VA 20186. Mailing Address: P.O. Box 3528, Warrenton, VA 20188. Tel.: 540-349-8606. Fax: 540-349-9299.

E-mail: jennifer@partnershipforwarrenton.org
Web Site: mosbymuseum.org
Formerly: Brentmoor: The Spilman-Mosby House
Institution Type/Description: Historic House Museum: housed in the former home of Judge Edward Spilman, Judge James Keith, Colonel John Singleton Mosby, & U.S. Senator Eppa Hunton; 1859-1902. Listed on the National Register of Historic Places.
Hours & Admission Prices: Mon.-Fri. 9-5.

Warsaw

RICHMOND COUNTY MUSEUM, 5874 Richmond Rd., Warsaw, VA 22572. Mailing Address: P.O. Box 884, Warsaw, VA 22572. Tel.: 804-333-3607. Fax: 804-333-3408.

E-mail: museum@co.richmond.va.us
Institution Type/Description: History Museum: housed in a two-story brick county jail; built in 1872.
Hours & Admission Prices: Feb. to mid-Dec. Wed.-Sat. 11-3; other times by appointment. No charge. Closed holidays.

Waverly

MILES B. CARPENTER MUSEUM, 201 Hunter St., Waverly, VA 23890-2631. Mailing Address: 201 Hunter St., P.O. Box 1376, Waverly, VA 23890-1376. Tel.: 804-834-2151 & 3327. Fax: 804-834-3327.

E-mail: hollandshe@msn.com
Web Site: www.milesbcarpentermuseum.com
Key Personnel: Dir., Shirley Eley; Financial Dir., Thelma Wyatt; Cur., Shirley S. Yancey; Public Rels., Carolyn Cooper Wright; Sec., Doretha Johnson.
Institution Type/Description: Wood Products Museums.
Hours & Admission Prices: Thurs.-Mon. 2-5. No charge; donations accepted. Closed New Year's Day; Easter; Thanksgiving; Christmas. &
Attendance: 1,000 (estimated)

Waynesboro

HUMPBACK ROCKS MOUNTAIN FARM & VISITOR CENTER, Blue Ridge Pkwy., Mile Post 5.9, Waynesboro, VA 24483. Mailing Address: 133 Whetstone Ridge Rd., Vesuvius, VA 24483-2113. Tel.: 540-377-2377 (Montebello Ranger Station). Fax: 540-377-6758.

Web Site: www.nps.gov/blri
Key Personnel: District Ranger, Bruce Bytnar; Interpretive Specialist, Randy Sutton; Supt. Blue Ridge Pkwy., Phil Francis; Admin. Tech., Susan Bryant.
Institution Type/Description: Park Museum: 1880-1900 pioneer mountain farm.
Hours & Admission Prices: late April to Nov. 1 daily 10-5. No charge. &
Attendance: 150,000

P. BUCKLEY MOSS MUSEUM, 329 W. Main St., Waynesboro, VA 22980-4508. Tel.: 540-949-6476, 800-343-8643.

E-mail: mossmuseum@aol.com
Web Site: pbuckleymoss.com
Key Personnel: Dir., Corrado Gabellieri; Pres., Jake Henderson; Museum Shop Mgr., Jo Cowherd.
Institution Type/Description: Art Museum.
Hours & Admission Prices: Summer: Mon.-Sat. 10-5, Sun. 12:30-5. Winter: call for hours. No charge. Closed holidays. &
Attendance: 19,056 (actual)

Weems

FOUNDATION FOR HISTORIC CHRIST CHURCH, INC., 420 Christ Church Rd., Weems, VA 22576. Mailing Address: P.O. Box 24, Irvington, VA 22480-0024. Tel.: 804-438-6855. Fax: 804-438-5186.

E-mail: info@christchurch1735.org
Web Site: www.christchurch1735.org
Key Personnel: Exec. Dir., Camille E. Bennett; Pres. (V), Rev. Hugh C. White, III; Office Mgr., Trish Geeson.
Institution Type/Description: Historic Foundation.
Hours & Admission Prices: Historic Christ Church: April-Nov. Mon.-Sat. 10-4, Sun. 2-5; Dec.-March Mon.-Fri. 8:30-4:30. Carter Reception Center: April-Nov. Mon.-Sat. 10-4, Sun. 2-5; other times by appointment. Adults $5, senior citizens $4; active military & their families no charge. Closed New Year's Eve & Day; Thanksgiving; Christmas Eve, Day & week. &
Attendance: 13,000 (estimated)

West Point

CHELSEA PLANTATION, 874 Chelsea Plantation Lane, West Point, VA 23181. Tel.: 804-843-2386. Fax: 804-843-2386 (call first).

E-mail: donmasterson2@gmail.com
Institution Type/Description: Historic House Museum: built in 1709.
Hours & Admission Prices: Thurs.-Sun. 10-4:30; other times by appointment. Adults $15.

MATTAPONI INDIAN MUSEUM, 1271 Mattaponi Reservation Cir., West Point, VA 23181. Tel.: 804-769-2229 & 2194.
E-mail: uppermattaponipowwow@gmail.com
Key Personnel: Dir., Gertrude Custalow.
Institution Type/Description: Native American Museum.
Hours & Admission Prices: Sat.-Sun. 2-5. Admission $2.

Williamsburg

ABBY ALDRICH ROCKEFELLER FOLK ART MUSEUM, 326 W. Francis St., Williamsburg, VA 23185. Mailing Address: P.O. Box 1776, Williamsburg, VA 23187-1776. Tel.: 757-220-7554. Fax: 757-565-8804. Facebook: Art Museums of Colonial Williamsburg.
E-mail: museums@cwf.org
Web Site: www.colonialwilliamsburg.com/do/art-museums
Key Personnel: Pres. & C.E.O., Mitchell B. Reiss; Senior Vice Pres. Core Experience, Ghislain D'humieres; Vice Pres. Conservation, Collections & Museums, Ronald Hurst; Dir. Museum Design & Operations, Richard Hadley; Education & Programs, Patricia Balderson; Mgr. Museum Operations, Mary Cottrill; Mgr. Exhibits, Jan Gilliam; Registrar, Virginia Foster; Museum Shop Mgr., Joanna Heitz; Public Security, Donia Fowler.
Institution Type/Description: Art Museum.
Hours & Admission Prices: Jan. to mid-March Sun.-Thurs. 10-5, Fri.-Sat. 10-7; mid-March to Dec. daily 10-7. Museum: adults $12.99, youth 6-12 $6.49; children under 6 no charge. Annual Museum Pass: adults $22.99; youth 6-12 $11.49. Admission also included in any Colonial Williamsburg pass. ᪥
Attendance: 200,000 (actual)

BASSETT HALL, 522 E. Francis St., Williamsburg, VA 23185-4207. Mailing Address: c/o Colonial Williamsburg Foundation, P. O. Box 1776, Williamsburg, VA 23187-1776. Tel.: 757-220-7453. Fax: 757-220-7173.
E-mail: museums@cwf.org
Web Site: www.colonialwilliamsburg.com/do/art-museums/bassett-hall
Key Personnel: Pres. & C.E.O., Mitchell B. Reiss; Senior Vice Pres. Core Experience, Ghislain D'humieres; Vice Pres. Museums & Collections, Ron Hurst; Site Mgr., Virginia Kauffman; Dir. Collections Programs & Operations, Virginia Foster.
Institution Type/Description: Historic House Museum & Grounds: built in c.1753, purchased in 1800 by Burwell Bassett, nephew of Martha Washington, and acquired by the Rockefellers in the 1920s.
Hours & Admission Prices: Jan. to mid-March Wed.-Thurs. & Sat. 9:30-4:30; mid-March to Dec. Wed.-Thurs. & Sat. 9-5. Adults $12.99, youth 6-12 $6.49; children under 6 no charge. Annual Pass: adults $22.99, youth $11.49. Admission also included in any Colonial Williamsburg pass. ᪥
Attendance: 21,000 (actual)

THE COLONIAL WILLIAMSBURG FOUNDATION, 101 Visitor Center Dr., Williamsburg, VA 23185-4138. Mailing Address: P.O. Box 1776, Williamsburg, VA 23187-1776. Tel.: 888-965-7254.
Web Site: www.colonialwilliamsburg.com
Key Personnel: C.E.O. & Pres., Mitchell Reiss; Sr. Vice Pres. Core Admin., Ghislain d'Humieres; Exec. Dir., Strategic Communications, Kevin Crossett; Public Rels. Mgr., Joe Straw.
Institution Type/Description: Foundation: preserves, restores & operates Virginia's 18th-century capital of Williamsburg.
Hours & Admission Prices: Visitor Center: daily 8:45-5. Single Day: adults $40.99, children 6-12 $20.49. Multi Day: adults $50.99, children 6-12 $25.49. Annual: adults $66.99, children 6-12 $33.49. ᪥
Attendance: (actual)

DEWITT WALLACE DECORATIVE ARTS MUSEUM, 326 W. Francis St., Williamsburg, VA 23185. Mailing Address: P.O. Box 1776, Williamsburg, VA 23187-1776. Tel.: 757-220-7554. Fax: 757-565-8804. Facebook: Art Museums of Colonial Williamsburg.
E-mail: museums@cwf.org
Web Site: www.colonialwilliamsburg.com/do/art-museums
Key Personnel: Pres. & C.E.O., Mitchell B. Reiss; Sr. Vice Pres. Core Experience, Ghislain D'humieres; Vice Pres. Conservation, Collections & Museum, Ronald Hurst; Dir. Museum Design & Operations, Richard Hadley; Education & Programs, Patricia Balderson; Exhibition Planning, Jan Gilliam; Exhibition Conservation, Patty Silence; Registrar, Virginia Foster; Public Security, Donia Fowler; Mgr. Museum Operations, Mary Cottrill; Museum Shop Mgr., Joanna Heitz.
Institution Type/Description: Decorative Arts Museum.
Hours & Admission Prices: Jan. to mid-March Sun.-Thurs. 10-5, Fri.-Sat. 10-7; mid-March to Dec. daily 10-7. Museum: adult $12.99, youth 6-12 $6.49; chil-

dren under 6 no charge. Annual Museum Pass: adult $22.99, youth 6-12 $11.49. Admission also included in any Colonial Williamsburg pass. ᪥
Attendance: 200,000 (actual)

JAMESTOWN-YORKTOWN FOUNDATION, JAMESTOWN SETTLEMENT, AMERICAN REVOLUTION MUSEUM AT YORKTOWN, Rte. 31 S., 2110 Jamestown Rd. (GPS), Williamsburg, VA 23185. Mailing Address: P.O. Box 1607, Williamsburg, VA 23187-1607. Tel.: 757-253-4838. Fax: 757-253-5299. TDD: 757-253-5110.
E-mail: laura.bailey@jyf.virginia.gov
Web Site: www.historyisfun.org
Key Personnel: Exec. Dir., Philip G. Emerson; Exec. Asst. to Bd., Laura W. Bailey; Deputy Exec. Dir. Administration, J. Jeffrey Lunsford; Sr. Dir. Museum Operations & Education, Peter J. Armstrong; Dir. Education, Mark Howell; Sr. Dir. Mktg. & Retail Operations, Susan K. Bak; Dir. Programs & Partnerships, Pamela J. Pettengell; Sr. Dir. Devel., Julie W. Basic; Curatorial Svcs. Mgr., Dr. Thomas E. Davidson; Mgr. Human Resources, Carole Moore; Sr. Retail Operations Mgr., Janet Kane.
Institution Type/Description: History Museum.
Hours & Admission Prices: Jamestown Settlement & American Revolution Museum at Yorktown: June 15-Aug. 15 daily 9-6; Aug. 16-June 14 daily 9-5. Settlement: adults $17, children 6-12 $8; children 5 & under no charge. Yorktown: adults $12, children 6-12 $7; children 5 & under and AAM members no charge. Combination: adults $23, children 6-12 $12; children 5 & under and AAM members . American Heritage Annual Pass: adults $35, children 6-12 $17.50; children 5 & under and AAM members no charge. Closed New Year's Day; Christmas. ᪥
Attendance: 610,092 (actual)

MUSCARELLE MUSEUM OF ART, Lamberson Hall, College of William and Mary, 603 Jamestown Rd., Rm. 1, Williamsburg, VA 23185. Mailing Address: Lamberson Hall, College of William and Mary, P.O. Box 8795, Williamsburg, VA 23187-8795. Tel.: 757-221-2710. Fax: 757-221-2711. Facebook: Muscarelle Museum of Art.
E-mail: museum@wm.edu
Web Site: muscarelle.org
Key Personnel: Chm. Bd. Directors, Ray C. Stoner, Esq.; Dir. & C.E.O., Aaron H. De Groft, Ph.D.; Senior Assoc. Dir., Christina M. Carroll, Esq.; Asst. to Dir., Cindy Lucas; Head Collections & Exhibitions Mgmt., Melissa M. Parris; Facilities & Exhibitions Mgr., Kevin Gilliam; Chief Cur. & Distinguished Scholar-in-Residence, John T. Spike, Ph.D.; Dir. Security, Larry Wright.
Institution Type/Description: Art Museum.
Hours & Admission Prices: Tues.-Fri. 10-5, Sat.-Sun. 12-4. Special Exhibitions: adults $15; members no charge. Closed all major holidays; New Year's Eve & Day; Christmas Eve, Day & week. ᪥
Attendance: 160,000 (estimated)

WILLIAMSBURG CONTEMPORARY ART CENTER, 110 Westover Ave., Williamsburg, VA 23185. Tel.: 757-229-4949.
E-mail: visitWCAC@gmail.com
Web Site: visitwcac.org
Formerly: The Twentieth Century Gallery
Key Personnel: Exec. Dir., Kerry Mellette; Pres. (V), Michael Kirby; Vice Pres., Linda Caviness; Artistic Dir., Apryl Altman; Sec., Sharon Parker; Treas., Greg Spryn; Business Mgr., Charlene Zolad; Office Mgr., Mav Reyes.
Institution Type/Description: Art Center.
Hours & Admission Prices: Tues.-Sat. 11-3, Sun. 12-4. No charge; donations accepted. ᪥
Attendance: 4,800 (estimated)

Winchester

THE MUSEUM OF THE SHENANDOAH VALLEY, 901 Amherst St., Winchester, VA 22601. Tel.: 540-662-1473, 888-556-5799.
E-mail: visit@themsv.org
Web Site: themsv.org
Key Personnel: Dir. & C.E.O., Dana Hand Evans; Chm. (V), Calvin Allen, Ph.D.; Museum Shop Mgr., Bonnie Barr.
Institution Type/Description: History Museum.
Hours & Admission Prices: Tues.-Sun. call for hours. Adults $10; seniors & youth 13-18 $8; discounts to groups; children 12 & under and members no charge. Blue Star Museum. Closed New Year's Day; Thanksgiving; Christmas Eve & Day. ᪥
Attendance: 46,000

SHENANDOAH VALLEY DISCOVERY MUSEUM, 19 W. Cork St., Winchester, VA 22601. Tel.: 540-722-2020. Fax: 540-722-2189. Facebook.
E-mail: business@discoverymuseum.net
Web Site: www.discoverymuseum.net
Key Personnel: Exec. Dir., Mary Braun; Chm., Neile Martin; Dir. Programs, Jan Kirby; Business & Retail Mgr., Pamela Lam; Gallery Mgr., Mark Lawson.
Institution Type/Description: Children's Discovery Museum.
Hours & Admission Prices: Mon.-Sat. 9-5, Sun. 1-5. Adults $6; discounts to ASTC, ACM, & AAA members; members no charge. Closed Federal holidays. &
Attendance: 72,000 (actual)

WINCHESTER-FREDERICK COUNTY HISTORICAL SOCIETY, INC., 1360 S. Pleasant Valley Rd., Winchester, VA 22601-4447. Mailing Address: 1340 S. Pleasant Valley Rd., Winchester, VA 22601. Tel.: 540-662-6550.
E-mail: cshull@wincesterhistory.org
Web Site: www.winchesterhistory.org
Key Personnel: Dir., Cissy Shull.
Institution Type/Description: History Museum Complex.
Hours & Admission Prices: April-Oct. daily 10-4, Sun. 12-4. Abrams's Delight & Stonewall Jackson's Headquarters: adults $5, senior citizens $4.50, children $2.50. George Washington's Office: adults $5, children $1.75. Block Tickets: adults $12; members & children under 6 no charge.
Attendance: 15,000 (estimated)

Wise

WISE COUNTY HISTORICAL SOCIETY, Wise County Courthouse, Rm. 250, Wise, VA 24293. Mailing Address: 238 Grandview Dr., S.E., Wise, VA 24293-5300. Tel.: 276-328-6451 & 6569.
E-mail: wchs_133@yahoo.com
Web Site: www.wisevahistoricalsoc.org
Key Personnel: Pres. (V), William C. Gobble; Vice Pres., Denver J, Osborne; Treas., Wanda Rose; Archivist, Fannie Steele; Museum Shop Mgr., Bill Porter.
Institution Type/Description: Historical Society.
Hours & Admission Prices: Mon.-Thurs. 9-4, Fri. 9-12. No charge; donations accepted.
Attendance: 12 (estimated)

Woodstock

WOODSTOCK MUSEUM OF SHENANDOAH COUNTY, INC., 104 S. Muhlenberg St., Woodstock, VA 22664. Mailing Address: P.O. Box 741, Woodstock, VA 22664-0741. Tel.: 540-459-5518.
E-mail: info@woodstockmuseumva.org
Web Site: woodstockmuseumva.org
Key Personnel: Pres., Jean Martin.
Institution Type/Description: Local History Museum.
Hours & Admission Prices: May-Oct. Thurs.-Sat. 1-4. No charge; donations accepted. &
Attendance: 400 (estimated)

Wytheville

THE EDITH BOLLING WILSON BIRTHPLACE, 145 E. Main St., Wytheville, VA 24382-2319. Tel.: 276-223-3484 & 228-8474. Fax: 276-228-5987.
E-mail: info@edithbollingwilson.org
Web Site: www.edithbollingwilson.org
Key Personnel: Dir., Leslie King; Chm. (V), William Smith.
Institution Type/Description: Historic House Museum: housed in the birthplace of First Lady Edith Bolling Wilson, the second wife of the 28th President of the United States, Woodrow Wilson.
Hours & Admission Prices: Tues.-Sat. 10-5. Season House Tour: adults $5, seniors $4, students $2. Closed Thanksgiving; Christmas. &

HALLER - GIBBONEY ROCK HOUSE MUSEUM, 205 Tazwell St., Wytheville, VA 24382-2313. Mailing Address: 115 W. Spiller St., Wytheville, VA 24382. Tel.: 276-223-3330. Fax: 276-223-3455. Facebook: Wytheville Museums.
E-mail: museum@wytheville.org
Web Site: museums.wytheville.org/museums.htm
Key Personnel: Museum Dir., Frances Emerson.
Institution Type/Description: Historic House: 1823 home of Dr. John Haller, the first resident physician of Wytheville.
Hours & Admission Prices: Tues.-Fri. 10-5 (last tour 3:30), 3rd Sat. each month 10-5 (last tour 3:30). Adults $4, children 6-12 $2.
Attendance: 3,000 (estimated)

THE THOMAS J. BOYD, 295 Tazwell St., Wytheville, VA 24382. Mailing Address: 115 W. Spiller St., Wytheville, VA 24382. Tel.: 276-223-3330. Fax: 276-223-3315. Facebook: Wytheville Museum.
E-mail: museum@wytheville.org
Web Site: museums.wytheville.org
Key Personnel: Museum Dir., Frances Emerson.
Institution Type/Description: General History Museum.
Hours & Admission Prices: Tues.-Fri. 10-5, 3rd Sat. each month 10-5, last tour 3:30, Adults $4, children 6-12 $2.
Attendance: 3,000 (estimated)

Yorktown

COLONIAL NATIONAL HISTORICAL PARK: JAMESTOWN & YORKTOWN, 1000 Colonial Pkwy., Yorktown, VA 23690. Mailing Address: P.O. Box 210, Yorktown, VA 23690. Tel.: 757-898-2410. Fax: 757-898-6346.
E-mail: colo_interpretation@nps.gov
Web Site: www.nps.gov/colo/
Key Personnel: Supt., Kim Hall; Museum Shop Mgr., Vicki Nickels.
Institution Type/Description: Historical Park: *1607-1781, first permanent English settlement at Jamestown Island & last major battle of American Revolution at Yorktown, VA.
Hours & Admission Prices: Jamestown & Yorktown: daily 9-5. Jamestown: adult $14; Yorktown: adult $7; children 16 & under no charge. Senior Interagency, Access Interagency & America The Beautiful passes honored. Closed New Year's Day; Thanksgiving; Christmas. &
Attendance: 3,100,000 (estimated)

GALLERY ON THE YORK - YORKTOWN ARTS FOUNDATION, 7907 George Washington Memorial Hwy., Yorktown, VA 23692-4857. Mailing Address: P.O. Box 657, Yorktown, VA 23690-0657. Tel.: 757-898-3076.
Web Site: www.galleryontheyork.com
Formerly: On the Hill Cultural Arts Center
Key Personnel: Chm. & Pres. (V), Gary Hess; Gallery Mgr., Brian Lobarr; Museum Shop Mgr., Helen C. Hughes.
Institution Type/Description: Art Center & Gallery.
Hours & Admission Prices: Tues.-Sat. 10-5, Sun. 1-4. No charge; donations accepted. Closed New Year's Day; Mother's Day; Thanksgiving; Christmas. &
Attendance: 8,000 (estimated)

WATERMEN'S MUSEUM, 309 Water St., Yorktown, VA 23690. Mailing Address: P.O. Box 519, Yorktown, VA 23690-0519. Tel.: 757-887-2641. Fax: 757-888-2089.
E-mail: admin@watermens.hrcoxmail.com
Web Site: watermens.org
Key Personnel: Pres., John Hanna; Mng. Dir., David Niebuhr; Vice Pres., Dick Lane; Sec., Jim Smith; Treas., Fred Malvin; Founder, Marian Hornsby Bowditch; Coord. Education, Kathryn Hanna; Public Rels., Jim Baumgardner; Asst. to Dir., Linda Myers; Museum Shop Mgr., Joan Karafa; Gift Shop Mgr., Tina McManus.
Institution Type/Description: Seafood Industry Museum: housed in 1935 Colonial Revival house & outbuildings.
Hours & Admission Prices: April to late Nov. Tues.-Sat. 10-5, Sun. 1-5; late Nov. to March Sat. 10-5, Sun. 1-5. Adults $4, students $1; discounts for pre-arranged groups of 20 or more; members no charge. &
Attendance: 7,572 (actual)

YORK COUNTY HISTORICAL MUSEUM, 301 Main St., Yorktown, VA 23692-5431. Mailing Address: P.O. Box 2431, Yorktown, VA 23692-5431. Tel.: 757-890-3508.
E-mail: meredith@yorkcounty.gov
Key Personnel: Pres. (V), Jim Funk.
Institution Type/Description: History Museum.
Hours & Admission Prices: Tues.-Sun. 1-3:30. No charge.
Attendance: 3,000 (actual)

WASHINGTON

(275 listings)

Aberdeen

ABERDEEN MUSEUM OF HISTORY, 111 E. Third St., Aberdeen, WA 98520-4002. Tel.: 360-533-1976. Facebook: Aberdeen Museum of History.
E-mail: dannsears@aberdeen-museum.org

Web Site: www.aberdeen-museum.org
Key Personnel: Dir. & Cur., Dann Sears; Pres. (V), Lisa Scott; Museum Shop Mgr., Barbara Caskey.
Institution Type/Description: History Museum.
Hours & Admission Prices: Tues.-Sat. 10-5, Sun. 12-4. Suggested Donations: family $5, adults $2, students & seniors $1. &
Attendance: 6,000 (actual)

Anacortes

ANACORTES MUSEUM & MARITIME HERITAGE CENTER, 1305 8th, Anacortes, WA 98221-1833. Tel.: 360-293-1915.
E-mail: coa.museum@cityofanacortes.org
Web Site: museum.cityofanacortes.org
Key Personnel: Dir., Steve Oakley; Administrative Asst., Elaine Walker; Educator, Bret Lunsford; Cur. Collections, Judy Hakins; Museum Shop Mgr., Pam Bagnall.
Institution Type/Description: History Museum: housed in 1910 Carnegie Library Building.
Hours & Admission Prices: Gallery: Tues.-Sat. 10-4, Sun. 1-4. No charge; donations accepted. Vessel: April-May & Sept.-Oct. Sat. 10-4, Sun. 11-4; June-Aug. Tues.-Sat. 10-4, Sun. 11-4. Adults $3, seniors 65 & over $2, children 8-16 $1; children under 8 no charge. Closed New Year's Day; Easter; Thanksgiving; Christmas Eve & Day. &
Attendance: 5,278 (estimated)

Anderson Island

ANDERSON ISLAND HISTORICAL SOCIETY, 9306 Otso Point Rd., Anderson Island, WA 98303-9653.
E-mail: support@anderson-island.org
Web Site: www.andersonislandhs.org
Key Personnel: Pres. (V), Ed Stephenson; Museum Shop Mgr., Jeanne Ditmore.
Institution Type/Description: Historical Society Museum.
Hours & Admission Prices: Call for hours. No charge; donations accepted.
Attendance: 5,000 (estimated)

Arlington

STILLAGUAMISH VALLEY PIONEER MUSEUM, 20722 67th Ave., N.E., Arlington, WA 98223. Tel.: 360-435-7289.
E-mail: stillypioneers@frontier.com
Web Site: www.stillymuseum.org
Key Personnel: Pres. (V), Myrtle Rausch.
Institution Type/Description: History Museum.
Hours & Admission Prices: March-Oct. Wed. & Sat.-Sun. 1-4; other times by appointment. Adults $5, children 12 & under $2. Closed Easter; Mother's Day; Father's Day; Independence Day. &
Attendance: 1,000 (estimated)

Ashford

MT. RAINIER NATIONAL PARK CLOSED, 55210 238th Ave. E., Ashford, WA 98304. Tel.: 360-569-2211. Fax: 360-569-2169.
Web Site: www.nps.gov/mora/
Key Personnel: Supt., Randy King.
Institution Type/Description: Natural History Museum.
Hours & Admission Prices: Park: daily. Park Visitor & Information Centers: call or visit website for hours. Park: $20 per automobile, $5 per person, good for seven days. Annual Pass: $40. &
Attendance: 2,000,000 (actual)

Auburn

NEELY MANSION, 12303 Auburn-Black Diamond Rd., Auburn, WA 98092. Mailing Address: P.O. Box 738, Auburn, WA 98071-0738. Tel.: 253-833-9404. Facebook: Neely Mansion Association.
E-mail: neelymansionassociation@gmail.com
Web Site: www.neelymansion.org
Institution Type/Description: Historic House Museum: built in 1894 by Aaron & David Neely.
Hours & Admission Prices: Summer: Sat. 1-4; other times by appointment. No charge; donations requested. &

WHITE RIVER VALLEY MUSEUM, 918 H St., S.E., Auburn Community Campus, Auburn, WA 98002-6112. Tel.: 253-288-7433. Fax: 253-931-3098.
E-mail: pcosgrove@auburnwa.gov
Web Site: www.wrvmuseum.org
Key Personnel: C.E.O., Patricia Cosgrove; Chm. (V), Ronnie Beyersdorf.
Institution Type/Description: Historical Museum.

Hours & Admission Prices: Jan. 5-Dec. 20 Wed.-Sun. 12-4 by appointment for group tours & research. Adults $2, seniors & children $1; Wed. no charge. &
Attendance: 15,000 (actual)

Bainbridge Island

BAINBRIDGE ARTS AND CRAFTS GALLERY, 151 Winslow Way E., Bainbridge Island, WA 98110. Tel.: 206-842-3132. Fax: 206-780-8149.
E-mail: gallery@bacart.org
Web Site: www.bacart.org
Key Personnel: Dir., Lindsay Masters.
Institution Type/Description: Art Gallery.
Hours & Admission Prices: Mon.-Sat. 10-6, Sun. 11-5.
Attendance: 41,500 (actual)

BAINBRIDGE ISLAND HISTORICAL MUSEUM, 215 Ericksen Ave., N.E., Bainbridge Island, WA 98110-1855. Tel.: 206-842-2773.
E-mail: info@bainbridgehistory.org
Web Site: www.bainbridgehistory.org
Institution Type/Description: Historical Society Museum.
Hours & Admission Prices: Daily 10-4. Adults $4, seniors & students $3; discounts to NARM members; members no charge. Closed New Year's Day; Easter; Thanksgiving; Christmas. &
Attendance: 15,000 (actual)

BAINBRIDGE ISLAND MUSEUM OF ART, 550 Winslow Way E., Bainbridge Island, WA 98110. Mailing Address: P.O. Box 11413, Bainbridge Island, WA 98110. Tel.: 206-842-4451, 855-613-1342 (Toll Free).
E-mail: info@biartmuseum.org
Web Site: www.biartmuseum.org
Institution Type/Description: Art Museum.
Hours & Admission Prices: Daily 10-6. No charge. Closed Thanksgiving; Christmas.

THE BLOEDEL RESERVE, 7571 N.E. Dolphin Dr., Bainbridge Island, WA 98110-1097. Tel.: 206-842-7631. Fax: 206-842-8970.
E-mail: email@bloedelreserve.org
Web Site: www.bloedelreserve.org
Key Personnel: Exec. Dir., Ed Moydell; Pres. (V), Suzanne Kelly; Museum Shop Mgr., Andrea Mercado.
Institution Type/Description: arboretum botanical gardens.
Hours & Admission Prices: Tues.-Sun. 10-4. Adults $13, seniors 65 & over $9, children 13 & over and college students $5; discounts to groups; children 12 & under no charge. Closed New Year's Day; Thanksgiving; Christmas.
Attendance: 47,500 (estimated)

CLASSIC CYCLE MUSEUM, 740 Winslow Way N.E., Bainbridge Island, WA 98110. Tel.: 206-842-9191.
Web Site: classiccycleus.com
Institution Type/Description: Bicycle Museum.
Hours & Admission Prices: Tues.-Fri. 10-6:30, Sat. 10-5, Sun. 12-4; other times by appointment. No charge.

Bellevue

BELLEVUE ARTS MUSEUM, 510 Bellevue Way, N.E., Bellevue, WA 98004-5014. Tel.: 425-519-0770. Fax: 425-637-1799. Facebook: Bellevue Arts Museum.
E-mail: info@bellevuearts.org
Web Site: www.bellevuearts.org
Key Personnel: Exec. Dir., Linda Pawson; Dir. Mktg. & Communications, Karin Kidder; Dir. Devel., Sonia Doughty.
Institution Type/Description: Art Museum.
Hours & Admission Prices: Tues.-Sun. 11-5. Family $30, adults $12, students & senior citizens $10; discounts to AAM members; first Fri. 11-8; children under 6 & members no charge. Closed New Year's Day; Martin Luther King Jr, Day; Easter; Independence Day; Labor Day; Thanksgiving; Christmas. &
Attendance: 80,000 (actual)

THE BELLEVUE BOTANICAL GARDEN, 12001 Main St., Bellevue, WA 98005-3522. Tel.: 425-452-2750.
E-mail: nkartes@bellevuewa.gov
Web Site: www.bellevuebotanical.org
Institution Type/Description: Botanical Garden.

Hours & Admission Prices: Garden: daily dawn to dusk. Visitor Center: daily 9-4. No charge; donations accepted. &
Attendance: 300,000 (estimated)

EASTSIDE HERITAGE CENTER, 11660 Main St., Bellevue, WA 98005. Mailing Address: P.O. Box 40535, Bellevue, WA 98015. Tel.: 425-450-1049. Fax: 425-450-1050.
E-mail: director@eastsideheritagecenter.org
Web Site: www.eastsideheritagecenter.org
Key Personnel: Bd. Pres., Kim Radcliffe; Dir., Heather Trescases; Education Coord., Jane Morton; Collections Mgr., Sarah Fredcerick.
Institution Type/Description: Historical Society Museum.
Hours & Admission Prices: McDowell House at 11660 Main St.: Mon.-Fri. 10-4; Winters House at 2102 Bellevue Way, S.E.: Tues. 10-4, Thurs.-Sat. 10-2. No charge; donations accepted. &
Attendance: 10,040 (actual)

KIDSQUEST CHILDREN'S MUSEUM, 1116 108th Ave., N.E., Bellevue, WA 98004. Tel.: 425-637-8100. Facebook: Kidsquest Children's Museum.
E-mail: info@kidsquestmuseum.org
Web Site: www.kidsquestmuseum.org
Formerly: iQuest Children's Museum
Key Personnel: Pres. & C.E.O., Putter Bert; Co Chm., Tom Gilchrist; Co Chm., Janet Kelly; Dir. Advancement, Shelley Saunders; Dir. Education, Jamie Bonnett.
Institution Type/Description: Children's Museum.
Hours & Admission Prices: Call for hours. Ages 1 & up $12.50, ages 60 & up $11.50; discounts to ACM, ASTC & NWAYM members; members no charge. &
Attendance: 194,000 (actual)

Bellingham

BELLINGHAM RAILWAY MUSEUM CLOSED, 1320 Commercial St., Bellingham, WA 98225. Tel.: 360-393-7540. Facebook; Twitter; Blog.
E-mail: bellinghamrailwaymuseum@gmail.com
Web Site: www.bellinghamrailwaymuseum.org
Key Personnel: Exec. Dir. & Museum Shop Mgr., Shelissa Griffin; Pres. (V), Michael G. Lower; Chm. (V) & Vice Pres. (V), Mike Pagano.
Institution Type/Description: Railway Museum.
Hours & Admission Prices: Tues.-Sat. 12-5; other times by appointment. Family $10, adults $5, children 2-17 $3; Fri. & children under 2 no charge. Closed New Year's Day; Thanksgiving; Christmas & day after. &
Attendance: 10,000

SPARK MUSEUM OF ELECTRICAL INVENTION, 1312 Bay St., Bellingham, WA 98225-4322. Tel.: 360-738-3886. Fax: 360-733-2532.
E-mail: tana@sparkmuseum.org
Web Site: www.sparkmuseum.org
Formerly: American Museum of Radio and Electricity
Key Personnel: Dir., Tana Granack; C.E.O., John D. Jenkins.
Institution Type/Description: Science Museum.
Hours & Admission Prices: Wed.-Sun. 11-5; other times by appointment. Adults $5, children 12 & under $2; members no charge. Closed national holidays. &
Attendance: 12,000 (estimated)

VIKING UNION GALLERY, 516 High St., Western Washington University, Bellingham, WA 98225-5946. Tel.: 360-650-6534. Fax: 360-650-7736.
E-mail: asp.vu.gallery@wwu.edu
Web Site: gallery.as.wwu.edu
Formerly: Viking Union Satellite Gallery
Key Personnel: Dir. & Coord., Allie Paul.
Institution Type/Description: University Art Gallery.
Hours & Admission Prices: Mon.-Fri. 11-5. No charge. Closed national holidays. &
Attendance: 10,000 (estimated)

WESTERN GALLERY, WESTERN WASHINGTON UNIVERSITY, Fine Arts Complex, Bellingham, WA 98225-9068. Tel.: 360-650-3900 & 3963. Fax: 360-650-6878.
E-mail: sarah.clarklangager@wwu.edu
Web Site: www.westerngallery.wwu.edu
Key Personnel: Dir. & C.E.O., Hafthor Yngvason; Museum Preservation Specialist II, Paul Brower.
Institution Type/Description: University Art Gallery.

Hours & Admission Prices: Academic Year: Mon.-Tues. & Thurs.-Fri. 10-4, Wed. 10-8, Sat. 12-4. No charge; donations accepted. &
Attendance: 55,000 (estimated)

WHATCOM MUSEUM, 121 Prospect St., Bellingham, WA 98225-4497. Tel.: 360-778-8930. Fax: 360-778-8931. Facebook; Twitter; Instagram.
E-mail: info@whatcommuseum.org
Web Site: www.whatcommuseum.org
Formerly: Whatcom Museum of History and Art
Key Personnel: Dir., Patricia Leach; C.F.O., Charles Marcks; Mktg. & Public Rels. Mgr., Christina Claassen; Cur. Art, Barbara Matilsky; Cur. Collections, Rebecca Hutchins; Archivist & Historian, Jeff Jewell; Exhibitions Designer, Scott Wallin; Public Programs Coord. & Educator, Chris Brewer; Public Programs Coord. & Educator, Mary Jo Maute; Museum Store & Visitor Rels. Mgr., Ann Kelly.
Institution Type/Description: Art, History & Children's Museum: housed in three buildings including the 1892 Old City Hall.
Hours & Admission Prices: Lightcatcher & Old City Hall: Wed.-Sun. 12-5. Photo Archives: Wed.-Fri. 1-5. Family Interactive Gallery: Wed.-Sat. 10-5, Sun. 12-5. Admission $10, youth 6-17, students, military & seniors $8, children 2-5 $5; children under 2, NARM members & members no charge. Closed New Year's Day, Thanksgiving & Christmas Eve & Day. &
Attendance: 90,000 (estimated)

Beverly

WANAPUM HERITAGE CENTER, 15655 Wanapum Village Lane, S.W., Beverly, WA 99321-9705. Mailing Address: P.O. Box 878, Ephrata, WA 98823-0878. Tel.: 509-754-5088, ext. 2571. Fax: 509-766-2522 & 5020.
E-mail: wanapum@grantpud.org
Web Site: www.wanapum.org
Formerly: Wanapum Dam Heritage Center
Key Personnel: Museum Dir., Angela Buck.
Institution Type/Description: General Museum.
Hours & Admission Prices: Mon.-Fri. 8:30-4:30, Sat.-Sun. 9-5. No charge. &
Attendance: 13,780 (actual)

Bingen

WEST KLICKITAT COUNTY HISTORICAL SOCIETY - GORGE HERITAGE MUSEUM, 202 E. Humboldt, Bingen, WA 98605. Mailing Address: P.O. Box 394, Bingen, WA 98605-0394. Tel.: 509-493-3228.
E-mail: ghm@gorge.net
Web Site: community.gorge.net/ghmuseum/About.htm
Key Personnel: Pres. (V), Etta Hepner.
Institution Type/Description: Historic Building Museum: housed in the former Bingen Congregational Church; c.1912.
Hours & Admission Prices: Late May to late Sept. Fri.-Sun. 12-5; other times by appointment. Adults 16 & over $5; members no charge.
Attendance: 250 (estimated)

Black Diamond

BLACK DIAMOND MUSEUM & HISTORICAL SOCIETY, 32626 Railroad Ave., Black Diamond, WA 98010. Mailing Address: P.O. Box 232, Black Diamond, WA 98010-0232. Tel.: 360-886-2142.
E-mail: museum@blackdiamondmuseum.org
Web Site: www.blackdiamondmuseum.org
Key Personnel: Pres., Keith Watson; Vice Pres., Ken Jensen.
Institution Type/Description: Historic Building Museum: housed in the former train depot.
Hours & Admission Prices: Summer: Thurs. 9-4, Sat.-Sun. 12-4; Winter: Thurs. 9-4, Sat.-Sun. 12-3.

Bremerton

KITSAP COUNTY HISTORICAL SOCIETY MUSEUM, 280 4th St., Bremerton, WA 98337-1813. Tel.: 360-479-6226. Fax: 360-415-9294.
E-mail: info@kitsaphistory.org
Web Site: www.kitsaphistory.org
Key Personnel: Dir., Dean Tingey; Pres. (V), Scott Nelson; Vice Pres., John Sledd; Exec. Asst., Juahela Leiter.
Institution Type/Description: History Museum: housed in a former bank building.
Hours & Admission Prices: Tues.-Sat. 10-4, 1st Fri. Artwalk 5-8. Adults $4, seniors 65 & up, military with ID & children 6-17 $3; children under 6 & members no

charge. Closed New Year's Day; Independence Day; Thanksgiving; Christmas.
♿
Attendance: 6,000 (actual)

PUGET SOUND NAVY MUSEUM, 251 First St., Bremerton, WA
98337-5612. Tel.: 360-627-2275. Fax: 360-627-2273.
E-mail: danell.eaton@navy.mil
Web Site: www.pugetsoundnavymuseum.org
Formerly: Bremerton Naval Museum
Key Personnel: Dir., Lindy Dosher; Deputy Dir., Danelle Feddes; Cur., Megan
 Churchwell; Educator, Carolyn Lane; Mgr. Collections, Kathrine Young; Mgr.
 Colls., Megan Jablonski; Vol. & Visitor Svcs. Coord, Alexander Hostettler.
Institution Type/Description: Naval History Museum.
Hours & Admission Prices: May-Sept. daily 10-4; Oct.-April Wed.-Mon. 10-4. No
 charge; donations accepted. Closed New Year's Day; Easter; Thanksgiving;
 Christmas. ♿
Attendance: 100,000 (actual)

USS TURNER JOY MUSEUM SHIP, 300 Washington Beach Ave.,
Bremerton, WA 98337-5668. Tel.: 360-792-2457. Fax: 360-377-
1020.
E-mail: dd951@sinclair.net
Web Site: ussturnerjoy.org
Key Personnel: Dir., Jack James; Chm. (V), John Hanson.
Institution Type/Description: Military Ship Museum: housed on a Navy destroyer
 from the Vietnam War.
Hours & Admission Prices: March to late Oct. daily 10-5; Winter: Wed.-Sun. 10-
 3:30 (weathering permitting). Adults $12, seniors 62 & over $10, children 5-12
 $7; children under 5 no charge. Closed New Year's Day; Easter; Thanksgiving;
 Christmas.

Brewster

FORT OKANOGAN INTERPRETIVE CENTER, 14379 Hwy. 17,
Brewster, WA 98812. Mailing Address: Alta Lake State Park, 1 B
Otto Rd., Pateros, WA 98846-9618. Tel.: 509-689-6665. Fax: 509-
923-2980.
Web Site: www.parks.wa.gov
Key Personnel: Dir., Rex Derr; Park Mgr., Sharon Soelter.
Institution Type/Description: Historic Building & Site: history of fur trade & Indian
 Interpretive Center.
Hours & Admission Prices: May 14-Aug. Wed.-Sun. 9-5; other times by appoint-
 ment only. No charge; donations accepted. ♿
Attendance: 9,000 (estimated)

Buckley

FOOTHILLS HISTORICAL SOCIETY & MUSEUM, 130 River
Ave., Buckley, WA 98321. Mailing Address: P.O. Box 530,
Buckley, WA 98321-0530. Tel.: 360-829-1291.
E-mail: foothillsmuseum@cityofbuckley.com
Key Personnel: Pres. (V), Martha Olsen; Museum Shop Mgr., Ann Gibson.
Institution Type/Description: Historical Museum.
Hours & Admission Prices: Tues.-Thurs. 12-4, Sun. 1-4. No charge. ♿
Attendance: 2,000 (estimated)

Burlington

CHILDREN'S MUSEUM OF SKAGIT COUNTY, 550 Cascade
Mall Dr., Burlington, WA 98233. Tel.: 360-757-8888.
E-mail: INFO@SKAGITCM.ORG
Key Personnel: Exec. Dir., Cate Melcher.
Institution Type/Description: Children's Museum.
Hours & Admission Prices: Mon.-Sat. 10-6, Sun. 12-6. Toddler Tuesdays: 8:30am-
 10am. Admission $5 per person; children under one no charge. Closed Easter;
 Memorial Day; Independence Day; Thanksgiving; Christmas.

HERITAGE FLIGHT MUSEUM, 15053 Crosswind Dr.,
Burlington, WA 98233. Tel.: 360-733-4422. Fax: 360-733-4423.
E-mail: admin@heritageflight.org
Web Site: www.heritageflight.org
Institution Type/Description: Military Aircraft Museum.
Hours & Admission Prices: Call for hours.

Cashmere

**CHELAN COUNTY HISTORICAL SOCIETY - CASHMERE
MUSEUM & PIONEER VILLAGE,** 600 Cotlets Way,
Cashmere, WA 98815-1602. Mailing Address: P.O. Box 22,

Cashmere, WA 98815-0022. Tel.: 509-782-3230. Facebook:
Chelan County Historical Society -Cashmere Museum & Pioneer
Village.
E-mail: info@cashmeremuseum.org
Web Site: cashmeremuseum.org
Key Personnel: Pres. (V), James Wonn; Museum Shop Mgr., ReBecca Peyton;
 Mgr. Bldg. & Grounds, Fred Harvey.
Institution Type/Description: History Museum & Village.
Hours & Admission Prices: March-Nov. 1. daily 10:30-4:30. Adults $7, seniors 62
 & over $6, students 13 & up $4.50; discounts to AAA members, military &
 school groups; children under 6 & members no charge. Closed Easter. ♿
Attendance: 8,500 (estimated)

Castle Rock

MOUNT ST. HELENS VISITOR CENTER AT SILVER LAKE,
3029 Spirit Lake Hwy., Castle Rock, WA 98611-8706. Tel.: 360-
274-0962.
E-mail: silver.lake@parks.wa.gov
Web Site: parks.state.wa.us
Institution Type/Description: Visitor Center.
Hours & Admission Prices: Summer: daily 9-5. Adults $5, youth 7-17 $2.50.
 Closed New Year's Day; Thanksgiving; Christmas.

Cathlamet

WAHKIAKUM COUNTY HISTORICAL SOCIETY MUSEUM,
65 River St. & Division, Cathlamet, WA 98612. Tel.: 360-846-
1604. Facebook.
E-mail: wahkiakumhistory@gmail.com
Key Personnel: Cur., Kari Kandoll.
Institution Type/Description: Natural History Museum & Historic Site: housed in
 the former homestead of Judge William Strong, the first Territorial Judge in the
 Oregon Territory.
Hours & Admission Prices: May-Oct. Sat.-Sun. 1-4; other times by appointment.
 Adults $5, seniors $2.50; children, military & members no charge. ♿
Attendance: 1,000 (estimated)

Chehalis

LEWIS COUNTY HISTORICAL MUSEUM, 599 N.W. Front
Way, Chehalis, WA 98532-2048. Tel.: 360-748-0831. Fax: 360-
740-5646.
E-mail: director@lewiscountymuseum.org
Web Site: www.lewiscountymuseum.org
Key Personnel: Pres., Peter Lahmann; Dir. & Museum Shop Mgr., Steven (Andy)
 Skinner.
Institution Type/Description: Local History Museum.
Hours & Admission Prices: Tues.-Fri. 10-4, Sat. 10-2. Adults $5; members no
 charge. Closed major holidays. ♿
Attendance: 5,836 (actual)

VETERANS MEMORIAL MUSEUM, 100 S. W. Veterans Way,
Chehalis, WA 98532-1100. Tel.: 360-740-8875.
E-mail: vmm@compprime.com
Web Site: www.veteransmuseum.org
Key Personnel: Dir., Lee T. Grimes; Pres. (V), Ernest Graichen.
Institution Type/Description: Military Museum.
Hours & Admission Prices: June-Sept. Tues.-Sat. 10-5, Sun. 1-5; Oct.-May Tues.-
 Sat. 10-5. Adults $6, veterans & seniors $5, children 6-18 $3; members & active
 duty military no charge. ♿
Attendance: 20,000 (actual)

Chelan

CHELAN MUSEUM, 204 E. Woodin Ave., Chelan, WA 98816.
Mailing Address: P.O. Box 1948, Chelan, WA 98816. Tel.: 509-
682-5644.
E-mail: museum@chelanmuseum.com
Web Site: chelanmuseum.com
Key Personnel: Dir., Samantha Lagge.
Institution Type/Description: Historical Society Museum: housed in the former
 Miners & Merchants Bank; built in 1907.
Hours & Admission Prices: Winter: Mon.-Fri. 10-12 & 1-4; Summer: Mon.-Fri. 10-
 4, Sat. 10-3; other times by appointment. Adults $2; members no charge.
Attendance: 4,750 (actual)

Chinook

FORT COLUMBIA HOUSE MUSEUM, Fort Columbia State Park, Hwy. 101, Chinook, WA 98614. Mailing Address: P.O. Box 488, Ilwaco, WA 98624-0488. Tel.: 360-777-8221. Fax: 360-642-4216.
E-mail: lcic@parks.wa.gov
Institution Type/Description: Historic House: 1902 Commanding Officer's house at Fort Columbia State Park.
Hours & Admission Prices: Summer: daily 6:30 a.m.-9:30 p.m. Winter: daily 8-5. No charge; donations appreciated.

Clarkston

VALLEY ART CENTER, INC., 842-6th St., Clarkston, WA 99403-2013. Tel.: 509-758-8331. Facebook: Valley Art Center.
E-mail: artcenter@cableone.net
Key Personnel: Dir. & Pres. (V), Robin Harvey; Museum Shop Mgr., Shar Schenk.
Institution Type/Description: Art Center.
Hours & Admission Prices: Tues.-Thurs. & Sat. 9-3, Fri. 12-6; other times for tours by appointment. No charge; donations accepted. Closed New Year's Eve & Day; Christmas Eve, Day & week. &
Attendance: 6,800 (estimated)

Cle Elum

CLE ELUM TELEPHONE MUSEUM, 221 E. 1st St., Cle Elum, WA 98922-1103. Mailing Address: 302 W. 3rd, Cle Elum, WA 98922. Tel.: 509-649-2880.
E-mail: info@highcountryartists.com
Web Site: www.nkcmuseums.org
Key Personnel: Pres., Bonnie Hawk.
Institution Type/Description: Communications Museum: housed in a former Bell Telephone building.
Hours & Admission Prices: Memorial Day-Labor Day Sat.-Sun. 12-4 by appointment. Suggested Donation: $1 per person.
Attendance: 1,301 (actual)

Coulee City

DRY FALLS INTERPRETIVE CENTER, 34875 Park Lake Rd., N.E., Coulee City, WA 99115-9607. Tel.: 509-632-5214. Fax: 509-632-5971.
E-mail: dry.falls@parks.wa.gov
Web Site: www.parks.wa.gov
Key Personnel: Park Mgr., Denis Felton.
Institution Type/Description: Natural Science Museum.
Hours & Admission Prices: April-Oct. daily 9-5; Nov.-March Fri.-Wed. 9-4. Donation: $1. Closed holidays. &
Attendance: 350,000 (estimated)

Coupeville

ADMIRALTY HEAD LIGHTHOUSE INTERPRETIVE CENTER, 1280 Engle Rd., Coupeville, WA 98239. Mailing Address: P.O. Box 5000, Coupeville, WA 98239-5000. Tel.: 360-240-5584. Fax: 360-678-4120.
E-mail: admiraltyheadlighthouse@gmail.com
Web Site: admiraltyhead.wsu.edu
Formerly: Fort Casey Interpretive Center
Key Personnel: Park Mgr., Jon Crimmins; Program Coord., Julie Pigott; Ranger II, Brett Bayne; Museum Shop Mgr., Cheryl Thomas.
Institution Type/Description: Military/Lighthouse Museum: housed in late 1890s masonry lighthouse located within the former boundaries of Fort Casey, an Endicott period coastal fortification.
Hours & Admission Prices: March Sat.-Sun. 11-5; April & Sept. Fri.-Mon. 11-5; May Thurs.-Mon. 11-5; June daily 11-5; Oct.-Dec. Sat.-Sun. 11-4. No charge; donations accepted. Closed Christmas Eve & Day.
Attendance: 55,000 (actual)

ISLAND COUNTY HISTORICAL SOCIETY MUSEUM, 908 N. W. Alexander St., Coupeville, WA 98239. Mailing Address: P.O. Box 305, Coupeville, WA 98239-0305. Tel.: 360-678-3310. Fax: 360-678-1702.
E-mail: ed-ichs@whidbey.net
Web Site: wp.islandhistory.org
Key Personnel: Exec. Dir., Richard Castellano.
Institution Type/Description: Local History Museum: located in the historic town of Coupeville, founded in 1853.

Hours & Admission Prices: May-Sept. Mon.-Sat. 10-5, Sun. 11-5; Oct.-April Mon.-Sat. 10-4. Family $6, adults $3, military, students & senior citizens $2.50; children under 5 & members no charge. &
Attendance: 12,000 (estimated)

PACIFIC NORTH WEST ART SCHOOL GALLERY, 15 N.W. Birch St., Coupeville, WA 98239. Tel.: 360-678-3396, 866-678-3396.
E-mail: info@pacificnorthwestartschool.org
Web Site: www.pacificnorthwestartschool.com
Institution Type/Description: Art Gallery.
Hours & Admission Prices: Call for hours.

Davenport

FORT SPOKANE VISITOR CENTER: NPS (NATIONAL PARK SERVICE), 44150 District Office Lane N., Davenport, WA 99122-9338. Tel.: 509-754-7893. Facebook: Lake Roosevelt NRA.
E-mail: denise_bausch@nps.gov
Web Site: www.nps.gov/laro/index.htm
Key Personnel: Chief, Interpretation & Education, Denise Bausch.
Institution Type/Description: Military Museum: housed in 1892 guardhouse located on the site of Fort Spokane, former army reservation 1880-99 & Indian agency headquarters, school & hospital 1899-1929.
Hours & Admission Prices: Memorial Day to Labor Day call for hours. No charge; donations accepted. &
Attendance: 5,000 (actual)

LINCOLN COUNTY HISTORICAL MUSEUM, 7th & Park, Davenport, WA 99122. Mailing Address: P.O. Box 585, Davenport, WA 99122-0585. Tel.: 509-725-6711.
E-mail: patrick_katz@hotmail.com
Web Site: www.davenportwa.org
Key Personnel: Pres. (V), John Coley; Treas., Nancy Ellis; Dir. Visitors Information Center & Sec., Tannis Jeschke.
Institution Type/Description: General Museum: located on the site of an early Indian campsite along Cottonwood Springs Crossroads for early pioneer trails.
Hours & Admission Prices: May-Sept. Mon.-Sat. 9-5. No charge; donations accepted.
Attendance: 1,500 (estimated)

Dayton

BOLDMAN HOUSE MUSEUM, 410 N. Frist St., Dayton, WA 99328. Mailing Address: 222 E. Commercial, Dayton, 99328. Tel.: 509-382-1548. Facebook.
E-mail: boldmanhousemuseum@gmail.com
Web Site: www.daytonhistoricdepot.org
Key Personnel: Dir., Tamara Fritze.
Institution Type/Description: Historic House Museum: built in 1880.
Hours & Admission Prices: May-Sept. Wed.-Sat. 11-4; Oct.-April Thurs.-Sat. 1-4; other times by appointment. No charge; donations accepted.
Attendance: 1,300 (actual)

DAYTON HISTORICAL DEPOT SOCIETY, 222 E. Commercial St., Dayton, WA 99328-1313. Tel.: 509-382-2026. Facebook.
E-mail: info@daytonhistoricdepot.org
Web Site: daytonhistoricdepot.org
Key Personnel: Pres. (V), Cathy Lee-Haight; Dir. & Museum Shop Mgr., Tamara Fritze; Treas., Jennie Dickinson.
Institution Type/Description: Historic House Museum: historic train depot.
Hours & Admission Prices: Summer: Wed.-Sat. 10-5; Winter: Wed.-Sat. 11-4. No charge; donations accepted. Closed New Year's Day; Thanksgiving; Christmas. &
Attendance: 3,650 (actual)

DuPont

DUPONT HISTORICAL SOCIETY, 207 Barksdale Ave., DuPont, WA 98327-9001. Tel.: 253-964-2399. Fax: 253-964-3554. Facebook: Dupont Historical Museum.
E-mail: info@dupontmuseum.com
Web Site: www.dupontmuseum.com
Formerly: Dupont Historical Museum
Key Personnel: Pres. (V), Carol Estep.
Institution Type/Description: Historical Society Museum: housed in 1910 building constructed by DuPont Co. as part of a company town.
Hours & Admission Prices: Wed.-Fri. & Sun. 1-4; other times by appointment. No charge; donations accepted. Closed holidays. &
Attendance: 1,000 (estimated)

Eatonville

NORTHWEST TREK WILDLIFE PARK, 11610 Trek Dr. E., Eatonville, WA 98328-9502. Mailing Address: Metro Parks Tacoma, 4702 S. 19th St., Tacoma, WA 98405. Tel.: 360-832-6117. Fax: 360-832-6118.
E-mail: whitney.dalbalcon@pdza.org
Web Site: www.nwtrek.org
Key Personnel: Dir., Gary Geddes; Mktg. & Public Rels. Mgr., Whitney DalBalcon.
Institution Type/Description: Wildlife Park.
Hours & Admission Prices: Seasonal hours, please call or check website to confirm. Adults 13-64 $18.25, senior citizens 65 & over $16.75, youth 5-12 $12.95, tots 3 & 4 $9.25; discounts for Pierce County residents & military personnel; children 2 & under and members no charge. Closed Thanksgiving; Christmas. &
Attendance: 182,000 (actual)

PIONEER FARM MUSEUM AND OHOP INDIAN VILLAGE, 7716 Ohop Valley Rd. E., Eatonville, WA 98328-9342. Tel.: 360-832-6300. Fax: 360-832-4533. Facebook: Pioneer Farm Museum.
E-mail: pioneer@mashell.com
Web Site: www.pioneerfarmmuseum.org
Key Personnel: Bd. Pres. (V), Merrilee McBride; Museum Mgr., Valerie Sivertson; Sec. & Treas., Lori Ramsey; Museum Shop Mgr., Nora Cady.
Institution Type/Description: History Museum: hands-on living history c.1880 farm.
Hours & Admission Prices: Public Tours: March-May & Sept. to mid-Nov. Sat.-Sun. 11-4; Father's Day-Labor Day daily 11-4. Group Tours: mid-March to Thanksgiving by reservation only. Adults $9, children $8; discounts to AAA & museum members. Native American Seasons Tour: Father's Day to Labor Day Fri.-Sun. 1 & 2:30. Adults $8.50, children $7.50; members no charge. &
Attendance: 26,000 (estimated)

Edmonds

EDMONDS ART FESTIVAL FOUNDATION, Frances Anderson Center, 700 Main St., Edmonds, WA 98020-3032. Mailing Address: Edmonds Arts Festival Foundation, P.O. Box 699, Edmonds, WA 98020-0699. Tel.: 425-771-1984.
E-mail: hardarmc@verizon.net
Web Site: www.eaffoundation.org
Key Personnel: Pres. (V), Dir. & Cur., Darlene McLelland.
Institution Type/Description: Art Museum: located in Frances Anderson Center.
Hours & Admission Prices: Mon.-Fri. 9-9, Sat. 10-3. No charge. Closed federal holidays. &
Attendance: 250,000 (estimated)

EDMONDS SOUTH SNOHOMISH COUNTY HISTORICAL SOCIETY, INC., 118 Fifth Ave., N., Edmonds, WA 98020-3145. Mailing Address: P.O. Box 52, Edmonds, WA 98020-0052. Tel.: 425-774-0900. Fax: 425-774-6507.
E-mail: edmondsmuseum118@gmail.com
Web Site: www.historicedmonds.org
Key Personnel: Museum Dir., Peter Bojakowski; Pres., Bill Lambert.
Institution Type/Description: Historical Society Museum: housed in 1910 Carnegie Library.
Hours & Admission Prices: Wed.-Sun. 1-4. Suggested Donation: adults $5, children & students $2. Closed holidays. &
Attendance: 4,700 (estimated)

Elbe

THE LITTLE WHITE CHURCH OF ELBE, 54206 Mountain Hwy. E., Elbe, WA 98330. Tel.: 360-832-4922.
E-mail: twothechutes@comcast.net
Web Site: www.elbehistoricchurch.com/index.php
Institution Type/Description: Historic Building: housed in a Lutheran church; built in 1906. Listed on the National Register of Historic Places.
Hours & Admission Prices: Worship Services: 3rd Sun. each month 2:30. Tours: May-Sept. call for hours.

Ellensburg

CLYMER MUSEUM & GALLERY, 416 N. Pearl St., Ellensburg, WA 98926-3112. Tel.: 509-962-6416. Fax: 509-962-6424.
E-mail: support@clymermuseum.org
Web Site: www.clymermuseum.org
Formerly: Clymer Museum of Art
Key Personnel: Dir., Jami-Lynn Tate; Pres. (V), Phil Backman; Museum Shop Mgr., Edie Roulean.
Institution Type/Description: Art Museum: honoring John F. Clymer housed in 1901 building in historic downtown Ellensburg.

Hours & Admission Prices: Mon.-Fri. 10-5, Sat. 10-4. No charge; donations accepted. Closed major holidays. &
Attendance: 40,000 (actual)

KITTITAS COUNTY HISTORICAL MUSEUM, 114 E. Third Ave., Ellensburg, WA 98926-3346. Tel.: 509-925-3778. Facebook.
E-mail: kchm@kchm.org
Web Site: www.kchm.org
Key Personnel: Dir., Sadie Thayer.
Institution Type/Description: History Museum.
Hours & Admission Prices: Mon.-Sat. 10-4. No charge; donations accepted. &
Attendance: 8,301 (actual)

MUSEUM OF CULTURE & ENVIRONMENT, 400 E. University Way, Ellensburg, WA 98926-7544. Tel.: 509-963-2313. Fax: 509-963-3215.
E-mail: museum@cwu.edu
Web Site: www.cwu.edu/~museum/
Formerly: Museum of Man, Anthropology Museum
Key Personnel: Dir., Kathleen Barlow.
Institution Type/Description: University Anthropology Museum.
Hours & Admission Prices: Mon.-Fri. 8-5 by appointment only. No charge; donations accepted. &
Attendance: 3,242 (actual)

OLMSTEAD PLACE STATE PARK, 921 N. Ferguson Rd., Ellensburg, WA 98926-8109. Tel.: 509-925-1943. Fax: 509-925-1955.
E-mail: olmstead.place@parks.wa.gov
Web Site: www.parks.wa.gov/556/Olmstead-Place
Key Personnel: Park Ranger, Brandon Holkstra.
Institution Type/Description: Historic Site: 160-acre 1875 homestead.
Hours & Admission Prices: Summer: 6:30am to dusk; Winter: 8am to dusk. No charge; donations accepted.
Attendance: 43,000

Enumclaw

ENUMCLAW PLATEAU HISTORICAL SOCIETY, 1837 Marion St., Enumclaw, WA 98022. Tel.: 360-825-3356. Facebook.
E-mail: enumclawmuseum@gmail.com
Web Site: enumclawhistorymuseum.com
Key Personnel: Dir. & Pres. (V), Patricia Shepherd; Treas., Merilyn Tyler.
Institution Type/Description: Historical Society Museum: housed in a former Masonic Hall, c.1909.
Hours & Admission Prices: Thurs. & Sun. 1-4. No charge; donations accepted. Closed most holidays. &
Attendance: 1,300 (actual)

Ephrata

GRANT COUNTY HISTORICAL MUSEUM, 742 Basin St., N. W., Ephrata, WA 98823-1635. Mailing Address: P.O. Box 1141, Ephrata, WA 98823-1141. Tel.: 509-754-3334. Fax: 509-754-2148.
E-mail: grantcomuseum@mail.com
Web Site: www.tourgrantcounty.com/ephrata
Key Personnel: Pres. (V), Rita Mayrant; Dir. & Museum Shop Mgr., Pat Witham.
Institution Type/Description: Local History Museum: 38 building village.
Hours & Admission Prices: May-Sept. Mon.-Tues. & Thurs.-Sat. 10-5, Sun. 1-4. Adults $3.50, students 5-15 $2.50; members & children under 5 no charge. &
Attendance: 7,500 (estimated)

Everett

FLYING HERITAGE COLLECTION, 3407 109th St., S.W., Everett, WA 98204-1351. Tel.: 206-342-4242. Fax: 206-342-4235.
E-mail: michelled@flyingheritage.com
Web Site: www.flyingheritage.com
Key Personnel: Exec. Dir., Adrian Hunt; Museum Shop Mgr., Liz Davidson.
Institution Type/Description: Military Aviation History.
Hours & Admission Prices: Memorial Day to Labor Day daily 10-5; Sept.-May Tues.-Sun. 10-5. Adults $12, military & seniors $10, youth 6-15 $8; discounts to groups of 15 or more; children 5 & under no charge. &

IMAGINE CHILDREN'S MUSEUM, 1502 Wall St., Everett, WA 98201-4008. Tel.: 425-258-1006. Fax: 425-258-5406.
E-mail: info@imaginecm.org
Web Site: www.imaginecm.org
Key Personnel: Exec. Dir., Nancy Johnson; Museum Shop Mgr., Lynndee Blair.
Institution Type/Description: Children's Museum.

Hours & Admission Prices: Tues.-Wed. 9-5, Thurs.-Sat. 10-5, Sun. 11-5. Admission $7.75; discounts Thurs. 3:30-5; children one & under no charge. Closed New Year's Day; Easter; Memorial Day; Labor Day; Thanksgiving; Christmas.

RUSSELL DAY GALLERY, Everett Community College, Parks Student Union Bldg., Rm. 219, 2000 Tower St., Everett, WA 98201-1352. Tel.: 425-388-9036.
E-mail: slepper@everettcc.edu
Web Site: www.everettcc.edu/russelldaygallery
Key Personnel: Dir., Sandra Lepper.
Institution Type/Description: Art Gallery.
Hours & Admission Prices: Mon. & Wed. 10-4, Tues. & Thurs. 12-4, Fri. 10-2.

Federal Way

PACIFIC BONSAI MUSEUM, 2515 S. 336th St., Federal Way, WA 98003. Mailing Address: P.O. Box 6108, Federal Way, WA 98063-6108. Tel.: 253-353-7345. Facebook & Instagram: @pacificbonsaimuseum.
E-mail: info@pacificbonsaimuseum.org
Web Site: pacificbonsaimuseum.org
Formerly: Pacific Rim Bonsai Collection
Key Personnel: Dir., Kathy McCabe; Cur., Aarin Packard; Museum Coord., Liz Sullivan.
Institution Type/Description: Art Conservatory.
Hours & Admission Prices: March-Sept. Tues.-Sun. 10-4; 3rd Thurs. 10-7; Oct.-Feb. Tues.-Sun. 10-4. No charge; donations accepted. Closed New Year's Day; Thanksgiving; Christmas Eve & Day. &
Attendance: 32,000 (actual)

RHODODENDRON SPECIES BOTANICAL GARDEN, 2525 S. 336th St., Federal Way, WA 98003-7825. Mailing Address: P.O. Box 3798, Federal Way, WA 98063-3798. Tel.: 253-838-4646. Fax: 253-838-4686. Facebook: Rhododendron Species Botanical Garden.
E-mail: info@rhodygarden.org
Web Site: www.rhodygarden.org
Key Personnel: Exec. Dir & Cur., Steve Hootman; Program Mgr., Katie Swickard; Museum Shop Mgr., Pat Whempner.
Institution Type/Description: Botanical Garden.
Hours & Admission Prices: Tues.-Sun. 10-4. Adults $8, seniors & students $5; Weyerhaeuser employees, children under 12 & military no charge. &
Attendance: 14,712 (actual)

Fife

FIFE HISTORY MUSEUM, 2820 54th Ave. E., Fife, WA 98424-2140. Tel.: 253-896-4710. Facebook: FHM Fife.
E-mail: fifehistorymuseum1957@gmail.com
Web Site: www.fifehistorymuseum.org
Key Personnel: Pres. (V), Connie Cook; Mng. Dir., Jocelyn Goldschmidt.
Institution Type/Description: History Museum: housed in the former home of Louis Dacca, a member of the original Fife City Council.
Hours & Admission Prices: Wed. 12-4:30, Fri. 9-4:30, Sat. 9-1; other times by appointment. No charge; donations accepted. &
Attendance: 1,000 (estimated)

Forks

FORKS TIMBER MUSEUM, 1421 S. Forks Ave., Forks, WA 98331-9383. Mailing Address: P.O. Box 873, Forks, WA 98331-0873. Tel.: 360-374-9663.
E-mail: info@forkstimbermuseum.org
Key Personnel: Mgr., Linda Offutt; Pres. Bd. Dirs., Tom Rosmond.
Institution Type/Description: Logging History Museum.
Hours & Admission Prices: Daily 10-4. Admission 3 & over $3.
Attendance: 3,600 (estimated)

Fox Island

FOX ISLAND HISTORICAL SOCIETY, 1017 Ninth Ave., Fox Island, WA 98333. Mailing Address: P.O. Box 242, Fox Island, WA 98333-0242. Tel.: 253-549-2835. Facebook: Fox Island Historical Society Museum.
E-mail: foxislandmuseum@centurytel.net
Web Site: www.foxislandmuseum.org
Key Personnel: Pres. & Acting Dir., Marie Weis; Treas., Vera Hackett.
Institution Type/Description: Historical Society Museum.

Hours & Admission Prices: Wed. & Sat.-Sun. 1-4. No charge; donations accepted. Closed New Year's Day; Easter; Christmas. &
Attendance: 1,000 (estimated)

Friday Harbor

SAN JUAN HISTORICAL SOCIETY, 323 & 405 Price St., Friday Harbor, WA 98250. Mailing Address: P.O. Box 441, Friday Harbor, WA 98250-0441. Tel.: 360-378-3949. Fax: 360-378-3949 (call first). Facebook: San Juan Historical Society.
E-mail: museum_admin@sjmuseum.org
Web Site: www.sjmuseum.org
Key Personnel: Pres., Mary Jean Cahail; Exec. Dir., Kevin Loftus.
Institution Type/Description: Historical Society Museum: housed in turn-of-the-century farmhouse.
Hours & Admission Prices: April & Oct. Sat. 1-4; May-Sept. Wed.-Sat. 10-4, Sun. 1-4; other times by appointment. Adults $5, seniors 60 & over $4, youth under 18 $3; members & children under 5 no charge.
Attendance: 6,500 (estimated)

SAN JUAN ISLAND NATIONAL HISTORICAL PARK, 650 Mullis St., Ste. 100, Friday Harbor, WA 98250-7951. Mailing Address: P.O. Box 429, Friday Harbor, WA 98250-0429. Tel.: 360-378-2240, ext. 2233. Fax: 360-378-2615.
E-mail: sajh_interpretation@nps.gov
Web Site: www.nps.gov/sajh
Key Personnel: Supt., Steve Gibbons; Chief Ranger, Barry Lewis.
Institution Type/Description: Park Museum: area includes American & English camps. Joint occupation of San Juan Island by British & Americans occurred until the final settlement of the water boundary dispute & the Pig War in 1872.
Hours & Admission Prices: June-Sept. 3 daily 8:30-5; Sept. 4-May Wed.-Sun. 8:30-4:30. No charge. Closed federal holidays in winter. &
Attendance: 274,000 (estimated)

SAN JUAN ISLANDS MUSEUM OF ART, 540 Spring St., Friday Harbor, WA 98250. Mailing Address: IMA, P.O. Box 339, Friday Harbor, WA 98250-0339. Tel.: 360-370-5050. Fax: 360-370-5805. Facebook: San Juan Islands Museum of Art.
E-mail: info@sjima.org
Web Site: www.sjima.org
Formerly: Island Museum of Art, Westcott Bay Institute
Key Personnel: Dir., Jennifer Elise.
Institution Type/Description: Art Museum.
Hours & Admission Prices: Thurs.-Sat. 11-5, Sun. 1-4. No charge; donations accepted. &
Attendance: 20,000 (estimated)

THE WHALE MUSEUM, 62 1st St. N., Friday Harbor, WA 98250. Mailing Address: P.O. Box 945, Friday Harbor, WA 98250-0945. Tel.: 360-378-4710, 800-946-7227, ext. 30. Fax: 360-378-5790. Facebook: The Whale Museum.
E-mail: info@whalemuseum.org
Web Site: www.whalemuseum.org
Key Personnel: Dir., Jenny L. Atkinson; Bd. Pres., Richard Day; Finance Mgr., Elli Gull; Collections Cur., Jennifer Olson; Education Cur., Cindy Hansen; Museum Shop Mgr., Rena Eubanks.
Institution Type/Description: Natural History Museum.
Hours & Admission Prices: June-Sept. daily 9-6; Oct.-May daily 10-5. Adults $6, senior citizens $5, college student & children $3; children under 5 & members no charge. Closed New Year's Day; Thanksgiving; Christmas.
Attendance: 28,000 (actual)

Gig Harbor

HARBOR HISTORY MUSEUM, 4121 Harborview Dr., Gig Harbor, WA 98332. Mailing Address: P.O. Box 744, Gig Harbor, WA 98335-0744. Tel.: 253-858-6722. Fax: 253-853-4211.
E-mail: info@harborhistorymuseum.org
Web Site: www.harborhistorymuseum.org
Formerly: Gig Harbor Peninsula History Museum
Key Personnel: Exec. Dir., John Ross.
Institution Type/Description: Historical Society Museum; history museum.
Hours & Admission Prices: Museum: Tues.-Sun. 10-5. Research: by appointment. Adults $7, seniors 65 & over and military $6, youth 7-17 $5; discounts to NARM members; members no charge. Closed Martin Luther King Jr. Day; Independence Day; Labor Day; Thanksgiving; Christmas. &
Attendance: 14,000 (actual)

Goldendale

GOLDENDALE OBSERVATORY, 1602 Observatory Dr., Goldendale, WA 98620-3315. Tel.: 509-773-3141. Fax: 509-773-6929.
E-mail: goldendale.observatory@parks.wa.gov
Web Site: www.perr.com/gosp.html
Key Personnel: Area Mgr., Lem Pratt; Museum Mgr., Troy Carpenter.
Institution Type/Description: Observatory.
Hours & Admission Prices: April-Sept. Wed.-Sun. 10am-11:30pm; Oct.-March Mon.-Fri. 10-4. Access by Washington State Parks Discover Pass: One Day Pass $10 per vehicle; Annual Pass $30 per vehicle. ⑆
Attendance: 25,000 (estimated)

KLICKITAT COUNTY HISTORICAL SOCIETY, 127 W. Broadway, Goldendale, WA 98620. Mailing Address: P.O. Box 86, Goldendale, WA 98620-0086. Tel.: 509-773-4303.
E-mail: presbymuseum@gorge.net
Web Site: www.presbymuseum.com
Key Personnel: Pres. (V), Bonnie Beeks; Sec., Mary Evans Childs; Treas., Dennis Birney; Museum Shop Mgr., Marilyn Enwards.
Institution Type/Description: History Museum: housed in 1903 W.B. Presby Mansion.
Hours & Admission Prices: May-Oct. 15 daily 10-4; other times by appointment. Adults $5, students $1; members no charge. ⑆
Attendance: 968 (actual)

MARYHILL MUSEUM OF ART, 35 Maryhill Museum Dr., Goldendale, WA 98620-4601. Tel.: 509-773-3733. Fax: 509-773-6138.
E-mail: maryhill@maryhillmuseum.org
Web Site: www.maryhillmuseum.org
Key Personnel: C.E.O. & Dir., Colleen Schafroth; Pres. (V), David Savinar; Cur. Art, Steven Grafe; Cur. Education, Carrie Clark-Peck; Collections Mgr., Anna Berg; Museum Shop Mgr., Jacque Francois; Operations & Finance Mgr., Leslie Wetherell.
Institution Type/Description: Art Museum: housed in a beaux-arts style concrete mansion; built in 1914. Listed on the National Register of Historic Places.
Hours & Admission Prices: mid-March to mid-Nov. daily 10-5. Adults $9, senior citizens 65 & over $8, children 7-18 $3; discounts to AAM & ICOM members; members no charge. ⑆
Attendance: 46,712 (actual)

Granite Falls

GRANITE FALLS HISTORICAL MUSEUM, 109 E. Union St., Granite Falls, WA 98252. Mailing Address: P.O. Box 1414, Granite Falls, WA 98252-1414. Tel.: 360-691-2603.
E-mail: info@gfhistory.org
Web Site: www.gfhistory.org
Institution Type/Description: History Museum.
Hours & Admission Prices: Sun. 12-5; other times by appointment. No charge; donations accepted. ⑆
Attendance: 2,000 (estimated)

Greenbank

MEERKERK RHODODENDRON GARDENS, 3531 Meerkerk Lane, Greenbank, WA 98253. Mailing Address: P.O. Box 154, Greenbank, WA 98253-0154. Tel.: 360-678-1912.
E-mail: meerkerk@whidbey.net
Web Site: www.meerkerk gardens.org
Key Personnel: Dir., Joan Bell; Pres. (V), Don Lee.
Institution Type/Description: Garden.
Hours & Admission Prices: Daily 9-4. Adults $5; members & children under 16 no charge. ⑆
Attendance: 6,000 (estimated)

Greenwater

CATHERINE MONTGOMERY INTERPRETIVE CENTER, Federation Forest State Park, 49201 Hwy. 410, Greenwater, WA 98022-8015. Tel.: 360-663-2207. Fax: 360-663-0172.
Web Site: www.parks.wa.gov
Key Personnel: Park Mgr., Eric Lewis.
Institution Type/Description: Nature Center.
Hours & Admission Prices: April-Oct. 8 a.m to dusk. ⑆
Attendance: 75,000 (estimated)

Hoquiam

POLSON MUSEUM, 1611 Riverside Ave., Hoquiam, WA 98550-2739. Mailing Address: P.O. Box 432, Hoquiam, WA 98550-0432. Tel.: 360-533-5862.
E-mail: jbl@polsonmuseum.org
Web Site: www.polsonmuseum.org
Key Personnel: Dir., John Larson; Pres. (V), Bill Wieland.
Institution Type/Description: History Museum: 1924 mansion located on 1884 homestead site of timber pioneer Alex Polson.
Hours & Admission Prices: Wed.-Sat. 11-4, Sun. 12-4. Families $10, adults $4, students $2, children $1; discounts to AASLH & AAM members; members no charge. Closed major holidays.
Attendance: 4,000 (estimated)

Ilwaco

COLUMBIA PACIFIC HERITAGE MUSEUM, 115 S.E. Lake St., Ilwaco, WA 98624. Mailing Address: P.O. Box 153, Ilwaco, WA 98624-0153. Tel.: 360-642-3446. Fax: 360-642-4615. Facebook: Columbia Pacific Heritage Museum.
E-mail: infocphm@centurytel.net
Web Site: columbiapacificheritagemuseum.org
Formerly: Ilwaco Heritage Museum
Key Personnel: Exec. Dir., Betsy Millard; Chm. Bd. & Pres. (V), Bill Garvin; Librarian, Carol Bell; Collections Mgr., Barbara Minard; Museum Shop Mgr., Rosemary Hickman.
Institution Type/Description: History Museum.
Hours & Admission Prices: Tues.-Sat. 10-4, Sun. 12-4. Adults $5, seniors $4, youths 12-17 $2.50; discounts to AAM & ICOM members; Thurs. & members no charge. Closed Thanksgiving; Christmas. ⑆
Attendance: 13,500 (actual)

LEWIS & CLARK INTERPRETIVE CENTER, Cape Disappointment State Park, Ilwaco, WA 98624. Mailing Address: P.O. Box 488, Ilwaco, WA 98624-0488. Tel.: 360-642-3078. Fax: 360-642-4216.
E-mail: lcic@parks.wa.gov
Web Site: www.capedisappointment.org
Key Personnel: Mgr., Aaron Webster.
Institution Type/Description: Interpretive Center.
Hours & Admission Prices: Daily 10-5. Adults $5, children 7-17 $2.50; children 6 & under no charge. Closed Thanksgiving; Christmas. ⑆
Attendance: 48,000 (estimated)

Issaquah

ISSAQUAH HISTORY MUSEUMS, 165 S.E. Andrews & 150 First Ave., N.E., Issaquah, WA 98027. Mailing Address: P.O. Box 695, Issaquah, WA 98027-0026. Tel.: 425-392-3500. Fax: 425-392-4236.
E-mail: info@issaquahhistory.org
Web Site: www.issaquahhistory.org
Formerly: Gilman Town Hall Museum
Key Personnel: Pres., Bob Brock; Dir., Erica S. Maniez; Volunteer Coord., Dorota Rchn; Administrative Coord., Polly Good; Mgr. Collections, Julie Hunter; Archival Specialist, Julia Belgrave.
Institution Type/Description: Historical Society/Gilman Town Hall Museum & Train Depot.
Hours & Admission Prices: Depot: Fri.-Sun. 11-3. Town Hall: Thurs.-Sat. 11-3. Admission $2 per person; members no charge. Closed holidays & holiday weekends. ⑆
Attendance: 7,000 (actual)

Joint Base Lewis-McChord

LEWIS ARMY MUSEUM, 4320 Main St., Bldg. 4320, Joint Base Lewis-McChord, WA 98433-1001. Mailing Address: P.O. Box 331001, Joint Base Lewis-McChord, WA 98433-1001. Tel.: 253-967-7206. Fax: 253-966-3029. Facebook.
E-mail: usarmy.jblm.incom.list.museum@mail.mil
Web Site: lewisarmymuseum.com
Formerly: Fort Lewis Military Museum
Institution Type/Description: Military Museum.
Hours & Admission Prices: Wed.-Sun. 11-5. No charge; donations accepted. Closed legal holidays. ⑆
Attendance: 15,000 (estimated)

Kelso

COWLITZ COUNTY HISTORICAL MUSEUM, 405 Allen St., Kelso, WA 98626-4103. Tel.: 360-577-3119. Fax: 360-423-9987. Facebook: Cowlitz County Historical Museum.
E-mail: freeced@co.cowlitz.wa.us
Web Site: www.co.cowlitz.wa.us/museum
Key Personnel: Pres. (V), Maryanne Wainwright; Exec. Dir., David W. Freece; Cur., Bill Watson; Education Coord., Danielle Robbins; Administrative Asst., Jim Elliott.
Institution Type/Description: History Museum.
Hours & Admission Prices: Tues.-Sat. 10-4. No charge; donations accepted. Closed holidays. &
Attendance: 12,000 (estimated)

Kennewick

EAST BENTON COUNTY HISTORICAL MUSEUM, 205 Keewaydin Dr., Kennewick, WA 99336-0602. Tel.: 509-582-7704. Facebook; Twitter.
E-mail: ebchs@frontier.com
Web Site: ebchs.org
Key Personnel: Dir., Stephanie Button.
Institution Type/Description: History Museum.
Hours & Admission Prices: Tues.-Sat. 12-4. Adults $5, seniors $4, veterans & children 5-17 $1; active military & members no charge. &
Attendance: 2,000 (estimated)

Kent

GREATER KENT HISTORICAL SOCIETY MUSEUM, 855 E. Smith St., Kent, WA 98030-4623. Tel.: 253-854-4330. Facebook: Greater Kent Historical Society and Museum.
E-mail: ctyofkent@msn.com
Web Site: www.gkhs.org
Key Personnel: Dir., Zachary E. Van Tassel; Pres. (V) Jon Johnson.
Institution Type/Description: Historical Society Museum; housed in Bereiter's home; built in 1907. A National Historic Landmark.
Hours & Admission Prices: Wed.-Sat. 12-4. No charge; donations accepted. &
Attendance: 1,750 (estimated)

HYDROPLANE & RACEBOAT MUSEUM, 5917 S. 196th St., Kent, WA 98032-2132. Tel.: 206-764-9453. Fax: 206-766-9620. Facebook: Thunderboats.
E-mail: ddw@thunderboats.org
Web Site: www.hydromuseum.org
Key Personnel: Dir., David D. Williams; Museum Shop Mgr., Glenn Raymond; Pres. (V), Rick Lentz; Museum Shop Mgr., Ken Strong.
Institution Type/Description: Sport Museum.
Hours & Admission Prices: Tues. & Thurs. 10-8, Wed. & Fri.-Sat. 10-4. Adults $10, seniors & students $5; discounts to groups; members no charge. Closed holidays. &
Attendance: 3,000 (estimated)

Kettle Falls

KETTLE FALLS HISTORICAL CENTER, 1188 Portage Rd., Kettle Falls, WA 99141. Mailing Address: P.O. Box 498, Kettle Falls, WA 99141. Tel.: 509-738-6964.
E-mail: meclaywoman@gmail.com
Web Site: sites.google.com/site/kettlefallshistoricalcenter
Institution Type/Description: History Museum.
Hours & Admission Prices: May-Sept. Wed.-Sat. 11-5.

Keyport

NAVAL UNDERSEA MUSEUM, 1 Garnett Way, Keyport, WA 98345-7600. Mailing Address: Navy Region Northwest, 1103 Hunley Rd., Silverdale, WA 98315-1103. Tel.: 360-396-4148.
E-mail: NUM_curator@navy.mil
Web Site: www.navalunderseamuseum.org
Key Personnel: Dir., Bill Galvani; Cur., Mary Ryan; Educator, John Buchinger; Exhibits, Ron Roehmholdt; Mgr. Collections, Jennifer Heinzelman; Mgr. Collections, Lorraine Scott; Mgr. Operations, Olivia Wilson; Museum Shop Mgr., Daina Birnbaums.
Institution Type/Description: Military Museum.
Hours & Admission Prices: June-Sept. daily 10-4; Oct.-May Wed.-Mon. 10-4. No charge; donations accepted. Closed New Year's Day; Easter; Thanksgiving; Christmas. &
Attendance: 56,000 (actual)

Kirkland

KIRKLAND ARTS CENTER, 620 Market St., Kirkland, WA 98033-5421. Tel.: 425-822-7161.
E-mail: info@kirklandartscenter.org
Web Site: www.kirklandartscenter.org
Key Personnel: Exec. Dir., Kelly Dylla.
Institution Type/Description: Art Museum.
Hours & Admission Prices: Mon.-Fri. 11-6, Sat. 11-5. No charge; donations accepted. Closed national holidays.

La Conner

MUSEUM OF NORTHWEST ART, 121 S. First St., La Conner, WA 98257. Mailing Address: P.O. Box 969, La Conner, WA 98257-0969. Tel.: 360-466-4446, ext. 109. Fax: 360-466-7431.
E-mail: timd@museumofnwart.org
Web Site: www.museumofnwart.org
Key Personnel: C.E.O. & Pres. (V), Jessica Pavish; Exec. Dir., Tim Detweiler; Cur., Kathleen Moles; Museum Shop Mgr., Jacque Chase.
Institution Type/Description: Art Museum.
Hours & Admission Prices: Sun.-Mon. 12-5, Tues.-Sat. 10-5. Adults $8, seniors $4, student $3; members & youth under 12 no charge. Closed Thanksgiving; Christmas. &
Attendance: 14,291 (actual)

PACIFIC NORTHWEST QUILT & FIBER ARTS MUSEUM, Mailing Address: 703 S. 2nd St., P.O. Box 1270, La Conner, WA 98257-1270. Tel.: 360-466-4288.
E-mail: info@qfamuseum.org
Web Site: www.qfamuseum.org
Formerly: La Conner Quilt & Textile Museum
Key Personnel: Dir., Amy Green.
Institution Type/Description: Quilt & Fiber Arts Museum.
Hours & Admission Prices: Wed.-Sun. 11-5; other times by appointment. Adults $7, students & military $5; members & children under 12 no charge. Closed Thanksgiving; Christmas.
Attendance: 10,000 (estimated)

SKAGIT COUNTY HISTORICAL MUSEUM, 501 S. 4th St., La Conner, WA 98257-0818. Mailing Address: P.O. Box 818, La Conner, WA 98257-0818. Tel.: 360-466-3365. Fax: 360-466-1611.
E-mail: museum@co.skagit.wa.us
Web Site: www.skagitcounty.net/museum
Key Personnel: Exec. Dir., Jesse Kennedy, III, Ph.D.; Pres. (V), Kelley Moldstad; Cur., Karen Summers; Tour Coord., Eileen Barnes; Librarian, Mari C. Anderson-Densmore; Dir. Devel., Jo Wolfe; Maintenance & Security, Bob Skeele; Business Mgr., Kathy Pace.
Institution Type/Description: History Museum.
Hours & Admission Prices: Tues.-Sun. 11-5. Family $10, adults $5, seniors & children 6-12 $4; discounts to AAM & ICOM members; historical society members and children 5 & under no charge. &
Attendance: 10,000 (estimated)

Lacey

LACEY MUSEUM, 829 Lacey St., S.E., Lacey, WA 98503. Mailing Address: 420 College St., S.E., Lacey, WA 98503. Tel.: 360-438-0209.
E-mail: museum@ci.lacey.wa.us
Web Site: www.laceymuseum.org
Key Personnel: Cur., Erin Quinn Valcho; Educator, Marisa Merkel.
Institution Type/Description: History Museum.
Hours & Admission Prices: Thurs.-Fri. 11-3, Sat. 10-4; other times by appointment. No charge; donations accepted.
Attendance: 915 (actual)

Lakewood

HISTORIC FORT STEILACOOM, 9601 Steilacoom Blvd. S.W. (on Western State Hospital grounds), Lakewood, WA 98498-7213. Mailing Address: P.O. Box 88447, Steilacoom, WA 98388-0447. Tel.: 253-582-5838.
E-mail: info@historicfortsteilacoom.org
Web Site: www.historicfortsteilacoom.org
Key Personnel: Pres., Carol Stout; Dir. & Sec., Joseph W. Lewis; Treas., Michael McGuire.
Institution Type/Description: Historic Site: four original buildings remaining on the site of Fort Steilacoom.

Hours & Admission Prices: Jan.-May & Sept.-Dec. first Sun. each month 1-4; June-Aug. Sun. 1-4. No charge; donations accepted. Docent-led tours: Adults $5, Children $3, Family $10.

LAKEWOLD GARDENS, 12317 Gravelly Lake Dr., S.W., Lakewood, WA 98499. Mailing Address: P.O. Box 39780, Lakewood, WA 98496. Tel.: 253-584-4106, 888-858-4106. Fax: 253-584-3021.
E-mail: swalsh@lakewoldgardens.org
Web Site: www.lakewoldgardens.org
Key Personnel: Exec. Dir., Stephanie Walsh; Mgr. Administrative Svcs., Irene Russo; Mgr. Volunteer Svcs., Cora Wells; Mgr. Visitor Svcs., Diane Thomas; Special Projects & Youth Program Mgr., Pam Felts; Mgr. Horticulture, Mark Lyke.
Institution Type/Description: Gardens: housed on 10 acres, landscape architecture by Thomas Church.
Hours & Admission Prices: April-Sept. Wed.-Sun. 10-4; winter hours vary, call ahead; docent & group tours by appointment. Adults $9, seniors 62 & over, students and military $7; discounts to groups; children under 12 & members no charge. Closed Independence Day; Thanksgiving & weekend after.
Attendance: 11,000 (actual)

LAKEWOOD COLONIAL CENTER, 6211 Mt. Tacoma Dr., S.W., Lakewood, WA 98499. Tel.: 253-682-3480.
Institution Type/Description: History Museum.
Hours & Admission Prices: Wed.-Sat. 12-4. No charge; donations accepted. Closed major holidays.

Langley

ROB SCHOUTEN GALLERY, 101 Anthes Ave., Langley, WA 98260. Mailing Address: P.O. Box 1596, Langley, WA 98260. Tel.: 360-222-3070.
E-mail: info@robschoutengallery.com
Institution Type/Description: Art Gallery.
Hours & Admission Prices: Summer: daily 10-5; Winter: daily 11-4.

SOUTH WHIDBEY HISTORICAL SOCIETY, 312 Second St., Langley, WA 98260. Mailing Address: P.O. Box 612, Langley, WA 98260. Tel.: 360-221-2101.
E-mail: wharolds@whidbey.com
Web Site: www.southwhidbeyhistory.org
Key Personnel: Pres. (V), Bill Haroldson.
Institution Type/Description: Historical Society Museum.
Hours & Admission Prices: Feb.-May & Sept.-Nov. Sat.-Sun. 1-4; June-Aug. Fri.-Sun. 1-4; other times by appointment.
Attendance: 1,500 (estimated)

Leavenworth

LEAVENWORTH NUTCRACKER MUSEUM, 735 Front St., Leavenworth, WA 98826. Mailing Address: P.O. Box 129, Leavenworth, WA 98826. Tel.: 509-548-4573.
E-mail: curator@nutcrackermuseum.com
Web Site: www.nutcrackermuseum.com
Institution Type/Description: Nutcracker Museum.
Hours & Admission Prices: Jan.-March Sat.-Sun. 2-5, call for additional hours; April-Dec. daily 2-5; other times by appointment. Adults $5, seniors 65 & over $3.50, students 6-16 $2; discounts to groups; active military & their families and children 5 & under no charge.
Attendance: 10,000 (estimated)

Lind

ADAMS COUNTY HISTORICAL SOCIETY MUSEUM, First St., Lind, WA 99341. Mailing Address: P.O. Box 526, Lind, WA 99341-0526. Tel.: 509-659-4202.
E-mail: info@adamscountyhistoricalsociety.com
Web Site: www.adamscountyhistoricalsociety.com
Institution Type/Description: Local History Museum.
Hours & Admission Prices: By appointment only. No charge; donations accepted.
Attendance: 400 (estimated)

Long Beach

PACIFIC COAST CRANBERRY RESEARCH FOUNDATION MUSEUM & GIFT SHOP, 2907 Pioneer Rd., Long Beach, WA 98631-5011. Tel.: 360-642-5553.

E-mail: cranberries@willapabay.org
Web Site: www.cranberrymuseum.com
Institution Type/Description: Cranberry Farm Museum.
Hours & Admission Prices: April-Dec. 15 daily 10-5; other times by appointment.

WORLD KITE MUSEUM & HALL OF FAME, 303 Sid Snyder Dr., Long Beach, WA 98631-3725. Mailing Address: P.O. Box 964, Long Beach, WA 98631-0964. Tel.: 360-642-4020. Facebook.
E-mail: info@worldkitemuseum.com
Web Site: www.worldkitemuseum.com
Key Personnel: Dir., Holli Friddle-Kemmer; Chm. (V), Blaine Walker.
Institution Type/Description: Hobby Museum: promote fun, art & science of kiting by telling the history of kites, recording the present & honoring the people involved.
Hours & Admission Prices: April-Sept. daily 11-5; Winter Fri.-Tues. 11-5. Adults $5, senior citizens $4, children $3; discounts to groups of 10 or more & AAM members. Closed New Year's Day; Thanksgiving; Christmas.
Attendance: 11,000 (estimated)

Longview

THE ART GALLERY, LOWER COLUMBIA COLLEGE FINE ARTS GALLERY, 1600 Maple St., Longview, WA 98632-3907. Mailing Address: P.O. Box 3010, Longview, WA 98632-0310. Tel.: 360-442-2510. Fax: 360-577-6620.
E-mail: dbartlett@lowercolumbia.edu
Web Site: lowercolumbia.edu/gallery
Key Personnel: Dir., Diane Bartlett.
Institution Type/Description: College Art Gallery.
Hours & Admission Prices: Mon.-Tues. & Fri. 10-4, Wed.-Thurs. 10-7. No charge. Closed legal holidays.
Attendance: 5,437 (actual)

Lopez Island

LOPEZ ISLAND HISTORICAL MUSEUM, 28 Washburn Pl., Lopez Village, Lopez Island, WA 98261. Mailing Address: P.O. Box 163, Lopez Island, WA 98261-0163. Tel.: 360-468-2049.
E-mail: lopezmuseum@rockisland.com
Web Site: www.lopezmuseum.org
Key Personnel: Exec. Dir., Mark Thompson-Klein; Pres. (V), Karen Alexander.
Institution Type/Description: Historical Society & Museum.
Hours & Admission Prices: May-Sept. Wed.-Sun. 12-4. Adults $2; members no charge. Closed Memorial Day Sun.; Independence Day.
Attendance: 2,500 (actual)

Lynden

LYNDEN PIONEER MUSEUM, 217 W. Front St., Lynden, WA 98264-1418. Tel.: 360-354-3675. Facebook: Lynden Pioneer Museum.
E-mail: lyndenpioneermuseum@gmail.com
Web Site: www.lyndenpioneermuseum.com
Key Personnel: Dir. & Cur., Troy Luginbill; Pres. (V), Clarence Zylstra; Treas., David Vos; Volunteer & Membership Mgr., Tammi Rylaarsdam.
Institution Type/Description: History Museum.
Hours & Admission Prices: Mon.-Sat. 10-4. Adults $7, senior citizens & students $4; discounts to groups, Washington Museum Association members, AAM & ICOM members; members, children 6 & under no charge.
Attendance: 28,000 (estimated)

Lynnwood

GENEALOGY RESEARCH LIBRARY, 19827 Poplar Way, Lynnwood, WA 98036-6940. Tel.: 425-775-6267.
Web Site: www.grlresearch.com
Institution Type/Description: Library: housed in the Humble House.
Hours & Admission Prices: Tues. 10-2, Thurs. 10-8, Sat. 10-3.

HERITAGE PARK MUSEUM AND INTERURBAN CAR 55, 19921 Poplar Way, Lynnwood, WA 98036-6940. Mailing Address: P.O. Box 5008, Lynnwood, WA 98046-5008. Tel.: 425-776-3977.
E-mail: solson@lynnwoodwa.gov
Web Site: www.playlynnwood.com
Key Personnel: Dir., Parks Recreation & Cultural Arts, Lynn Sordel; Deputy Dir. Parks, Recreation & Cultural Arts, Sarah Olson.
Institution Type/Description: Transportation History Museum.
Hours & Admission Prices: Park Museum: Mon.-Tues. & Thurs.-Fri. 9-5, Wed. & Sat.-Sun. 9-3. Trolley Tours: June-Sept. 2nd Sat. each month 11-3. No charge.
Attendance: 3,000 (estimated)

HERITAGE RESOURCE CENTER, 19903 Poplar Way, Lynnwood, WA 98036-6940. Mailing Address: Alderwood Manor Heritage Assoc., P.O. Box 2206, Lynnwood, WA 98036-2206. Tel.: 425-775-4694.
E-mail: info@alderwood.org
Institution Type/Description: Heritage Center: housed in the Alderwood Manor Heritage Cottage.
Hours & Admission Prices: Tues., Thurs. & Sat. 11-3.

SNOHOMISH COUNTY VISITOR INFORMATION CENTER, 19921 Poplar Way, Lynnwood, WA 98036-6940. Tel.: 425-776-3977.
E-mail: visitor@snohomish.org
Institution Type/Description: Visitor Center.
Hours & Admission Prices: Sun., Tues. & Thurs. 9-3, Mon., Wed. & Fri.-Sat. 9-5.

TRANSPORTATION MUSEUM, 19921 Poplar Way, Lynnwood, WA 98036-6940. Tel.: 425-774-6478.
Institution Type/Description: Transportation Museum.
Hours & Admission Prices: Sun., Tues. & Thurs. 9-3, Mon., Wed., & Fri.-Sat. 9-5.

Maple Valley

MAPLE VALLEY HISTORICAL SOCIETY, 23015 S.E. 216th Way, Maple Valley, WA 98038-8412. Mailing Address: P.O. Box 123, Maple Valley, WA 98038-0123. Tel.: 425-432-3470.
E-mail: thepavos@hotmail.com
Web Site: www.maplevalleyhistorical.com
Key Personnel: Pres. & Museum Shop Mgr., Dick Peacock.
Institution Type/Description: Historical Society Museum.
Hours & Admission Prices: 1st Sat. of each month 10-2; other times by appointment. No charge; donations accepted.
Attendance: 1,323 (actual)

Marysville

MARYSVILLE HISTORICAL SOCIETY, 6805 Armar Rd., Marysville, WA 98270. Mailing Address: P.O. Box 41, Marysville, WA 98270. Tel.: 360-659-3090.
E-mail: info@marysvillehistory.org
Web Site: marysvillehistory.org
Key Personnel: Pres. (V), Ken Cage.
Institution Type/Description: Historical Society Museum.
Hours & Admission Prices: Mon.-Sat. 10-3. No charge; donations accepted. &
Attendance: 2,000 (estimated)

McChord Field

MCCHORD AIR MUSEUM, Air Force Base, 100 Main St., McChord Field, WA 98438. Mailing Address: McChord Air Museum Foundation, P.O. Box 4205, Tacoma, WA 98438-0205. Tel.: 253-982-2419. Fax: 253-982-9560.
E-mail: raymond.jordan@mcchord.af.mil
Web Site: www.mcchordmuseum.org
Key Personnel: Vice Pres., Randy Getz; Pres. (V), Tom Hansen; Museum Shop Mgr., Ernie White, II.
Institution Type/Description: Military Museum.
Hours & Admission Prices: Wed.-Fri. 12-4; military ID required for entry. No charge; donations accepted.
Attendance: 5,000 (actual)

Moclips

MUSEUM OF THE NORTH BEACH, 4658 State Rte. 109, Moclips, WA 98562. Mailing Address: P.O. Box 231, Moclips, WA 98562-0231. Tel.: 360-276-4441.
E-mail: kelly@moclips.org
Web Site: www.moclips.org
Key Personnel: Pres. Bd. Dirs., Kelly Calhoun.
Institution Type/Description: History Museum.
Hours & Admission Prices: May-Oct. Thurs.-Mon. 11-4; Nov.-April Sat.-Sun. 11-4.

Monroe

MONROE HISTORICAL MUSEUM, 207 E. Main St., Monroe, WA 98272. Mailing Address: P.O. Box 1044, Monroe, WA 98272-4044. Tel.: 360-217-7223.
E-mail: info@monroehistoricalsociety.comcastbiz.net

Web Site: monroehistoricalsociety.org
Formerly: Monroe Historical Society Museum
Key Personnel: Pres. (V) Tami Kinney; Dir., Chris Bee.
Institution Type/Description: Historical Society Museum.
Hours & Admission Prices: Mon., Wed. & Sat. 12-3. No charge; donations accepted.
Attendance: 914 (actual)

Moses Lake

MOSES LAKE MUSEUM & ART CENTER, 401 S. Balsam, Moses Lake, WA 98837-1933. Mailing Address: P.O. Box 1579, Moses Lake, WA 98837. Tel.: 509-764-3830. Fax: 509-764-3709.
E-mail: fliggett@cityofml.com
Web Site: www.moseslakemuseum.com
Formerly: Adam East Museum
Key Personnel: Dir. & C.E.O., Freya K. Liggett; Cur., Ann Schempp.
Institution Type/Description: History Museum & Art Center.
Hours & Admission Prices: Mon.-Sat. 11-5. No charge. Closed major holidays. &
Attendance: 12,000 (estimated)

Mukilteo

FUTURE OF FLIGHT AVIATION CENTER & BOEING TOUR, 8415 Paine Field Blvd., Mukilteo, WA 98275-3239. Tel.: 425-438-8100, ext. 224. Fax: 425-265-9808.
E-mail: info@futureofflight.org
Web Site: www.futureofflightfoundation.org
Key Personnel: Dir. & C.E.O., Bonnie Hicory; Pres. (V), Louise Stanton-Masten; Museum Shop Mgr., Peter Bro.
Institution Type/Description: Aviation Center.
Hours & Admission Prices: Daily 8:30-5:30. Adults $20, children 5-15 $14, children under 5 no charge; discounts for online tickets. Closed New Year's Day, Thanksgiving; Christmas. &
Attendance: 300,000 (estimated)

HISTORIC FLIGHT FOUNDATION, 10719 Bernie Webber Dr., Mukilteo, WA 98275. Tel.: 425-348-3200. Facebook: Historic Flight.
E-mail: airborne@historicflight.org
Web Site: historicflight.org
Institution Type/Description: Aviation History Museum.
Hours & Admission Prices: Tues.-Sun. 10-5. Adults $15; discounts to seniors, military & AAA members; members no charge. Closed Thanksgiving; Christmas. &
Attendance: 25,000 (actual)

MUKILTEO LIGHT STATION & INTERPRETIVE CENTER, 608 Front St., Mukilteo, WA 98275. Mailing Address: Mukilteo Historical Society, 304 Lincoln Ave., Ste. 101, Mukilteo, WA 98275.
E-mail: info@mukilteohistorical.org
Web Site: mukilteohistorical.org
Institution Type/Description: Light Station Museum.
Hours & Admission Prices: Grounds: daily. Lighthouse & Center: April-Sept. Sat.-Sun. & holidays 12-5; other times by appointment. No charge.

Neah Bay

MAKAH CULTURAL AND RESEARCH CENTER, 1880 Bayview Ave., Neah Bay, WA 98357. Mailing Address: P.O. Box 160, Neah Bay, WA 98357. Tel.: 360-645-2711. Fax: 360-645-2656.
E-mail: makahmuseum@centurytel.net
Web Site: makahmuseum.com
Institution Type/Description: Native American History Museum.
Hours & Admission Prices: Daily 10-5. Adults $5, students, military & seniors $4; discounts to groups; children & under no charge.

Nine Mile Falls

SPOKANE HOUSE INTERPRETIVE CENTER, 9711 W. Charles, Nine Mile Falls, WA 99026-8648. Tel.: 509-465-5064 & 466-4747. Fax: 509-465-5571.
E-mail: riverside@parks.wa.gov
Web Site: www.riversidestatepark.org
Key Personnel: Chief Interpretive Svcs., Steve Wang; Agency Dir., Rex Derr; Park Mgr., Rene Wiley.
Institution Type/Description: Historic Site Museum: 1810, trading post used as a fur trading post & operated at various times by British, Canadian & American interests.

Hours & Admission Prices: Memorial Day to Labor Day Sat.-Sun. 10-4. No charge; donations accepted. &

Attendance: 7,000 (actual)

North Bend

SNOQUALMIE VALLEY HISTORICAL MUSEUM, 320 Bendigo Ave., S., North Bend, WA 98045-8260. Mailing Address: P.O. Box 179, North Bend, WA 98045-0179. Tel.: 425-888-3200. Fax: 425-888-3200. Facebook: Snoqualmie Valley Historical Museum.

E-mail: info@snoqualmievalleymuseum.org
Web Site: www.snoqualmievalleymuseum.org
Key Personnel: Pres. (V), Gardiner Vinnedge; Treas., Vicki Bettes; Asst. Dir., Cristy Lake.
Institution Type/Description: Local Historical Museum.
Hours & Admission Prices: April-Oct. Sat.-Tues. 1-5; Nov.-March Mon.-Tues. 1-5; other times by appointment. Admission by donation. Closed national holidays. &

Attendance: 4,000

Oak Harbor

PBY NAVAL HERITAGE CENTER, NAS Whidbey Island - Seaplane Base, Simard Hall Bldg. 12, 315 W. Pioneer Way, Oak Harbor, WA 98278. Mailing Address: P.O. Box 941, Oak Harbor, WA 98277-0941. Tel.: 360-240-9500.

E-mail: directorops@pbymf.org
Web Site: www.pbymf.org
Key Personnel: Dir., Will Stein; Chm. (V)., Richard Rezabek; Pres. (V), Win Stites; Museum Shop Mgr., George Love.
Institution Type/Description: Military History Museum; Heritage Center.
Hours & Admission Prices: Wed.-Sat. 11-5. (Photo ID, car registration & insurance papers required for entry). No charge; donations accepted. &

Attendance: 1,790 (actual)

Okanogan

OKANOGAN COUNTY HISTORICAL SOCIETY & FIRE HALL MUSEUM, 1410 2nd Ave. N., Okanogan, WA 98840-1129. Tel.: 509-422-4272.

E-mail: ochs@ncidata.com
Web Site: www.okanoganhistory.org
Institution Type/Description: History Museum.
Hours & Admission Prices: Daily 10-4.

Olympia

BIGELOW HOUSE MUSEUM, 918 Glass Ave., N.E., Olympia, WA 98506-3976. Mailing Address: P.O. Box 1821, Olympia, WA 98507-1821. Tel.: 360-753-1215.

E-mail: bigelowhousemuseum@gmail.com
Web Site: www.bigelowhouse.org
Key Personnel: Pres. (V), Mark Foutch.
Institution Type/Description: Historic House Museum: ca. 1860 Bigelow House.
Hours & Admission Prices: Check website for scheduled tours. Adults $5, students & seniors $3, children 12 & under $1; members no charge. &

Attendance: 930 (actual)

EVERGREEN GALLERY, The Evergreen State College, 2700 Evergreen Pkwy., N.W., Olympia, WA 98505. Tel.: 360-867-5125. Fax: 360-867-6794. Facebook: Evergreen Gallery Olympia WA.

E-mail: gallery@evergreen.edu
Web Site: www.evergreen.edu/gallery
Key Personnel: Dir., Ann Friedman.
Institution Type/Description: College Art Gallery.
Hours & Admission Prices: Oct.-May Mon.-Thurs. 12-4. No charge. Closed national holidays. &

HANDS ON CHILDREN'S MUSEUM, 414 Jefferson St., N.E., Olympia, WA 98501. Tel.: 360-956-0818, ext. 0. Fax: 360-754-8626. Facebook: Hands On Children's Museum.

E-mail: hocm@hocm.org
Web Site: www.hocm.org
Key Personnel: C.E.O. & Dir., Patty Belmonte; Pres. Elect, Carrie Bell; Financial Dir., Jamin May; Dir. Exhibits & Facilities, Kathy Irwin.
Institution Type/Description: Children's Museum.

Hours & Admission Prices: Sun.-Mon. 11-5, Tues.-Sat. 10-5. Adults $9.95, seniors $7.95, toddlers $6.95; babies no charge. Closed New Year's Day; Easter; Independence Day; Thanksgiving; Christmas. &

Attendance: 260,000 (estimated)

MONARCH CONTEMPORARY ART CENTER AND SCULPTURE PARK, 8431 Waldrick Rd., S.E., Olympia, WA 98501. Mailing Address: P.O. Box 1125, Tenino, WA 98589-1125. Tel.: 360-264-2408.

E-mail: sculpturepark@monarchartcenter.org
Web Site: monarchartcenter.org
Key Personnel: Founder, Dir. & Cur., Myrna Orsini.
Institution Type/Description: Art Center.
Hours & Admission Prices: Outdoor Gallery: dawn to dusk. Indoor Gallery: June-Oct. 1 by appointment. No charge; donations accepted. &

Attendance: 5,000 (estimated)

OLYMPIC FLIGHT MUSEUM, 7637 A Old Hwy. 99, S.E., Olympia, WA 98501-5728. Tel.: 360-705-3925. Fax: 360-236-9839.

E-mail: info@olympicflightmuseum.com
Web Site: www.olympicflightmuseum.com/
Key Personnel: Pres. & Founder, Brian Reynolds; Dir., Teri Thorning.
Institution Type/Description: Aviation History Museum.
Hours & Admission Prices: Summer: daily 11-5; Winter: Tues.-Sun. 11-5. Adults $7, children 7-12 $5; discounts to AAA members; members and children 6 & under no charge. Closed Thanksgiving; Christmas. &

Attendance: 20,000 (actual)

Orcas Island

ORCAS ISLAND HISTORICAL MUSEUMS, 181 N. Beach Rd., Orcas Island, WA 98245. Mailing Address: P.O. Box 134, Eastsound, WA 98245-0134. Tel.: 360-376-4849. Fax: 360-376-4869.

E-mail: info@orcasmuseums.org
Key Personnel: Pres., James Biddick; Administrative Asst., Jesse Clark McAbee.
Institution Type/Description: General Museum: housed in six original homestead cabins built between the 1880s & 1890s.
Hours & Admission Prices: School: Memorial Day to Labor Day Wed.-Sat. 11-4. Pioneer Museum: May-Sept. Wed.-Sat. 11-4, Sun. 12-3; Oct.-April Wed.-Sat. 12-3. Adults $5; discounts to AAM; members no charge.

Attendance: 8,500 (actual)

Pasco

FRANKLIN COUNTY HISTORICAL MUSEUM, 305 N. 4th Ave., Pasco, WA 99301-5324. Tel.: 509-547-3714. Fax: 509-545-2168.

Key Personnel: Pres., Anne Hayden; Treas., Hazel Hanson; Museum Shop Mgr., Gracie Cooper; Admin., Sherel Webb.
Institution Type/Description: Historical Society Museum: housed in 1911 Andrew Carnegie library building.
Hours & Admission Prices: Tues.-Fri. 12-4; other times by appointment. No charge; donations accepted. Society members 10% off gift shop purchases. Closed national holidays. &

Attendance: 6,280 (actual)

SACAJAWEA INTERPRETIVE CENTER, Sacajawea State Park, 2503 Sacajawea Park Rd., Pasco, WA 99301-6413. Tel.: 509-545-2361.

E-mail: reade.obern@parks.wa.gov
Web Site: www.park.wa.gov/stewardship/sacajawea
Key Personnel: Park Mgr., Reade Obern.
Institution Type/Description: Interpretive Center.
Hours & Admission Prices: April-Nov. 1 daily 10-5. Suggested Donation: $1. &

Attendance: 650 (estimated)

WASHINGTON STATE RAILROADS HISTORICAL SOCIETY MUSEUM, 122 N. Tacoma Ave., Pasco, WA 99301. Mailing Address: P.O. Box 552, Pasco, WA 99301-0552. Tel.: 509-543-4159.

E-mail: email@wsrhs.org
Web Site: www.wsrhs.org
Key Personnel: Pres. (V), Tom Gronewald; Museum Shop Mgr., James M Bowers.
Institution Type/Description: Railroad Museum.
Hours & Admission Prices: May to mid-Dec. Thurs.-Fri. 12-4, Sat. 9-3. Adults $2, teens & seniors $1; children & members no charge. &

Port Angeles

CLALLAM COUNTY HISTORICAL SOCIETY, Museum at the Carnegie, 207 S. Lincoln St., Port Angeles, WA 98362. Mailing Address: P.O. Box 1327, Port Angeles, WA 98362-0244. Tel.: 360-452-2662. Fax: 360-452-2662. Facebook: Clallam County Historical Society.
E-mail: artifact@olypen.com
Web Site: clallamhistoricalsociety.org
Formerly: The Museum of Clallam Historical Society
Key Personnel: Pres. (V), John Hubbard; Exec. Dir., Kathryn M. Monds.
Institution Type/Description: History Museum.
Hours & Admission Prices: Wed.-Sat. 1-4. Suggested donation: Family $5, adults $2. &
Attendance: 8,000 (estimated)

FEIRO MARINE LIFE CENTER, 315 N. Lincoln St., Port Angeles, WA 98362. Mailing Address: P.O. Box 625, Port Angeles, WA 98362-0112. Tel.: 360-417-6254. Facebook: Feiro Marine Life Center.
E-mail: deborahm@feiromarinelifecenter.org
Web Site: www.feiromarinelifecenter.org
Formerly: Arthur D. Feiro Marine Life Center c/o Peninsula College
Key Personnel: Pres., Betsy Wharton; Dir., Deborah Moriarty; Coord., Robert Campbell.
Institution Type/Description: Marine Life Center.
Hours & Admission Prices: Memorial Day to Labor Day daily 10-5; Sept.-May daily 12-4; other times by appointment. Adults $4, youth 4-17 $1; children 3 & under no charge. &
Attendance: 20,000 (estimated)

OLYMPIC NATIONAL PARK VISITOR CENTER, 3002 Mt. Angeles Rd., Port Angeles, WA 98362-6775. Mailing Address: 600 E. Park Ave., Port Angeles, WA 98362. Tel.: 360-565-3130 & 3000. Fax: 360-565-3147. Facebook: Olympic National Park.
E-mail: olym_interpretation@nps.gov
Web Site: www.nps.gov/olym
Key Personnel: Supt., Sarah Creachbaum; Museum Shop Mgr., David Sheriff.
Institution Type/Description: Visitor Center for National Park.
Hours & Admission Prices: Daily seasonal hours. No charge. Closed Thanksgiving; Christmas. &
Attendance: 160,000 (actual)

PORT ANGELES FINE ARTS CENTER & WEBSTER'S WOODS ART PARK, 1203 E. Lauridsen Blvd., Port Angeles, WA 98362-6630. Tel.: 360-457-3532.
E-mail: pafac@olypen.com
Web Site: www.pafac.org
Key Personnel: Exec. Dir., Jessica Elliott; Administrative Coord., Lindsay Smithberg.
Institution Type/Description: Art Museum.
Hours & Admission Prices: See website for hours & admissions. &
Attendance: 18,000 (estimated)

Port Gamble

PORT GAMBLE HISTORIC MUSEUM, 32400 Rainier Ave., N. E., Port Gamble, WA 98364. Mailing Address: P.O. Box 85, Port Gamble, WA 98364-0085. Tel.: 360-297-8078. Fax: 360-297-5616.
E-mail: tcaswell@orminc.com
Web Site: www.portgamble.com
Key Personnel: C.E.O., Tom Ringo; Museum Mgr., Tonya Caswell.
Institution Type/Description: History Museum: housed in 1853 Port Gamble General Store.
Hours & Admission Prices: May-Sept. daily 10-5; Oct.-April Fri.-Sun. 11-5. Adults $4, students & senior citizens $3; children 5 & under no charge. &
Attendance: 7,800 (actual)

Port Townsend

JEFFERSON MUSEUM OF ART AND HISTORY, 540 Water St., Port Townsend, WA 98368-5725. Tel.: 360-385-1003.
E-mail: billtennent@jchswa.org
Web Site: www.jchsmuseum.org
Formerly: Jefferson County Historical Society Museum
Key Personnel: Pres. (V), Chris Prescott; Dir., William Tennent; Museum Coord., Kris Lawson; Archivist, Marsha Moratti.

Institution Type/Description: Art & History Museum: housed in 1892 City Hall focusing on Jefferson County history & prehistory (Native American & European).
Hours & Admission Prices: Daily 11-4; special tours available. Adults $4, children under 12 $1; members no charge. Closed New Year's Day; Thanksgiving; Christmas. &
Attendance: 20,000 (estimated)

KELLY ART DECO LIGHT MUSEUM, Vintage Hardware, 2000 Sims Way, Port Townsend, WA 98368-2229. Tel.: 360-379-9030. Fax: 360-379-9029.
E-mail: vhprs@earthlink.net
Web Site: www.thedecomuseum.com
Key Personnel: Dir., Chm. & Founder, Ken Kelly.
Institution Type/Description: Decorative Art Museum.
Hours & Admission Prices: Daily 10-5. No charge; donations accepted.

NORTHWIND ARTS CENTER, 701 Water St., Port Townsend, WA 98368-5728. Tel.: 360-379-1086.
E-mail: info@northwindarts.org
Web Site: northwindarts.org
Institution Type/Description: Art Center.
Hours & Admission Prices: Thurs.-Mon. 12-5. No charge; donations accepted.
Attendance: 5,000

PORT TOWNSEND AERO MUSEUM, 105 Airport Rd., Port Townsend, WA 98368. Tel.: 360-379-5244.
E-mail: ptam@olypen.com
Web Site: www.ptaeromuseum.com
Key Personnel: Dir., Michael Payne.
Institution Type/Description: Aviation Museum.
Hours & Admission Prices: Wed.-Sun. 9-4; groups by appointment. Adults $10, senior & military $9; members no charge. Closed Thanksgiving; Christmas &
Attendance: 5,000 (actual)

PORT TOWNSEND MARINE SCIENCE CENTER, Fort Worden State Park, 532 Battery Way, Port Townsend, WA 98368-3431. Tel.: 360-385-5582. Fax: 360-385-7248.
E-mail: info@ptmsc.org
Web Site: www.ptmsc.org
Key Personnel: Dir., Anne Murphy.
Institution Type/Description: Marine & Natural History Museum: housed at c.1900 Fort Worden.
Hours & Admission Prices: Summer, Spring & Fall: Two Exhibits. Adults $5; youth & members no charge. Winter: One Exhibit. Adults $3, youth $2; members no charge. &
Attendance: 20,000 (actual)

PUGET SOUND COAST ARTILLERY MUSEUM AT FORT WORDEN, Bldg. 201, Fort Worden State Park, Port Townsend, WA 98368. Mailing Address: 200 Battery Way, Port Townsend, WA 98368-3621. Tel.: 360-385-0373.
E-mail: coastartillery@gmail.com
Web Site: pscoastartillerymuseum.org
Key Personnel: Treas. & Museum Shop Mgr., Mike Cornforth.
Institution Type/Description: Military Museum: housed in 1904, Enlisted Barracks, Bldg. 201 of the Harbor Defense of Puget Sound.
Hours & Admission Prices: July-Aug. Sun.-Thurs. 11-4, Fri.-Sat. 10-5; Sept.-June daily 11-4. Adults $3, children $2; active military no charge. &

ROTHSCHILD HOUSE STATE PARK, Franklin St., Port Townsend, WA 98368. Mailing Address: Fort Worden State Park, 200 Battery Way, Port Townsend, WA 98368-3621. Tel.: 360-385-1003 & 344-4400. Fax: 360-385-7248.
E-mail: kate.burke@parks.wa.gov
Web Site: www.fortworden.net
Key Personnel: Park Mgr. Fort Worden, Kate Burke; Museum Mgr., Phyllis Snyder.
Institution Type/Description: Historic House Museum: 1868 Rothschild House, built by the merchant D.C.H. Rothschild.
Hours & Admission Prices: May-Sept. daily 11-4. Adults $4, children $1; discounts to JCHS members.
Attendance: 3,225 (actual)

Poulsbo

POULSBO MARINE SCIENCE CENTER, 18743 Front St., N.E., Poulsbo, WA 98370. Mailing Address: P.O. Box 408, Keyport, WA 98345-0408. Tel.: 360-598-4460.

E-mail: info@poulsbomsc.org
Web Site: www.poulsbomsc.org
Key Personnel: Dir. Aquarium, Patrick Mus; Dir. Education, Bruce Claiborne; Chm. (V), Bruce Harlow.
Institution Type/Description: Marine Science Center.
Hours & Admission Prices: Thurs.-Sun. 11-4. No charge; donations accepted. &
Attendance: 10,500 (estimated)

SUQUAMISH MUSEUM, 15838 Sandy Hook Rd., Poulsbo, WA 98370-7867. Mailing Address: P.O. Box 498, Suquamish, WA 98392-0498. Tel.: 360-394-8496.
E-mail: jsmoak@suquamish.nsn.us
Web Site: www.suquamish.nsn.us
Key Personnel: Tribal Chm., Leonard Forsman; Tribal Council Sec., Nigel Lawrence; Dir., Marilyn Jones; Cur., Lydia Woods.
Institution Type/Description: Native American Museum: located on the Port Madison Indian Reservation.
Hours & Admission Prices: Daily 10-5. Call for pricing. Closed major holidays. &
Attendance: 10,000 (estimated)

Prosser

BENTON COUNTY HISTORICAL MUSEUM, 1000 Paterson Rd. (located in the city park), Prosser, WA 99350. Mailing Address: P. O. Box 1407, Prosser, WA 99350-0800. Tel.: 509-786-3842.
E-mail: prossermuseum@hotmail.com
Key Personnel: Pres. (V), Dick Sampson; Cur., Frankie Wallace.
Institution Type/Description: General Museum.
Hours & Admission Prices: Tues.-Sat. 11-4, Sun. call for hours. Adults $3, children $1; students no charge. Closed New Year's Day; Easter; Thanksgiving; Christmas. &
Attendance: 2,400 (estimated)

Pullman

CHARLES R. CONNER MUSEUM, Washington State University, Pullman, WA 99164. Tel.: 509-335-3515. Fax: 509-335-3184.
E-mail: connermuseum@wsu.edu
Web Site: sbs.wsu.edu/connermuseum
Key Personnel: Dir., Larry Hufford; Cur., Dr. Kelly M. Cassidy.
Institution Type/Description: Zoology Museum; Natural History Museum.
Hours & Admission Prices: Daily 8-5. No charge; donations accepted. &
Attendance: 23,000 (estimated)

MUSEUM OF ANTHROPOLOGY, Department of Anthropology, Washington State University, College Hall, Pullman, WA 99164. Tel.: 509-335-3441. Fax: 509-335-3999.
E-mail: collinsm@wsu.edu
Key Personnel: Dir., Mary Collins.
Institution Type/Description: Anthropology Museum.
Hours & Admission Prices: Academic Year: Mon.-Fri. 9-4; other times by appointment. No charge; donations accepted. Closed school holidays & vacations. &
Attendance: 4,000 (estimated)

MUSEUM OF ART, 6077 Wilson Rd., Fine Arts Center, Pullman, WA 99164-7460. Mailing Address: P.O. Box 647460, Pullman, WA 99164-7460. Tel.: 509-335-1910. Fax: 509-335-1908.
E-mail: artmuse@wsu.edu
Web Site: museum.wsu.edu
Key Personnel: Dir., Chris Bruce; Assoc. Dir., Anna-Maria Shannon; Cur. Arts & Exhibitions, Ryan Hardesty; Cur. Education & Collections, Zach Mazur; Public Rels. & Media Mgr., Debby Stinson; Dir. Devel., Jill Aesoph.
Institution Type/Description: University Art Museum.
Hours & Admission Prices: June-July. Tues.-Sat. 12-4; Aug.-May Mon.-Wed. & Fri.-Sat. 10-4, Thurs.10-7. No charge. Closed during semester breaks; between exhibition installations. &
Attendance: 30,000 (estimated)

PALOUSE DISCOVERY SCIENCE CENTER, 950 N.E. Nelson Ct., Pullman, WA 99163. Tel.: 509-332-6869.
E-mail: director@palousescience.org
Web Site: www.palousescience.org
Key Personnel: Exec. Dir., Victoria Scalise.
Institution Type/Description: Science Center.
Hours & Admission Prices: Tues. 10-5, Wed.-Sat. 10-3. Adults $7.50, seniors 55 & over $6, children 2-14 $5; children under 2 no charge.

Puyallup

THE FRED OLDFIELD WESTERN HERITAGE & ART CENTER, 110 9th S.W., Puyallup, WA 98371. Mailing Address: P.O. Box 1539, Puyallup, WA 98371-0216. Tel.: 253-752-9708, 866-445-9175 (Toll Free). Fax: 253-752-9708.
E-mail: foldfield@comcast.net
Key Personnel: Dir., Joella Oldfield; Chm. (V), Glennis Golden.
Institution Type/Description: Heritage Center.
Hours & Admission Prices: Sat. 12-4; other times by appointment. No charge; donations accepted. &
Attendance: 30,000 (estimated)

PAUL H. KARSHNER MEMORIAL MUSEUM, 309 Fourth St., N.E., Puyallup, WA 98372-3062. Tel.: 253-841-8748. Fax: 253-840-8951.
E-mail: curator@karshnermuseum.org
Web Site: www.karshnermuseum.org
Key Personnel: Cur., Beth Bestrom.
Institution Type/Description: Children's History Museum: housed in c.1920 school building.
Hours & Admission Prices: Call for appointment. No charge; donations accepted. Closed national holidays. &
Attendance: 12,000 (estimated)

PUYALLUP HISTORICAL SOCIETY AT MEEKER MANSION, 312 Spring St., Puyallup, WA 98372. Mailing Address: P.O. Box 103, Puyallup, WA 98371-0011. Tel.: 253-848-1770.
E-mail: ezra@meekermansion.org
Web Site: www.meekermansion.org
Key Personnel: Historian, Andy Anderson; Dir. & Museum Shop Mgr., Sue Fass; Pres. (V), Robert Minnich.
Institution Type/Description: Historic House Museum: 1890 Ezra Meeker Home, a Victorian mansion located at end of the Oregon Trail.
Hours & Admission Prices: March to mid-Dec. Wed.-Sun. 12-4; other times for special events. Adults $4, senior citizens & students $3, children $2; members no charge. Closed Easter; Thanksgiving. &
Attendance: 10,000 (actual)

Quilcene

QUILCENE HISTORICAL MUSEUM, 151 E. Columbia St., Quilcene, WA 98376. Mailing Address: P.O. Box 574, Quilcene, WA 98376-0574. Tel.: 360-765-4848.
E-mail: quilcenemuseum@olypen.com
Web Site: quilcenemuseum.org & worthingtonparkquilcene.org
Key Personnel: Chm. (V), Mari Phillips; Museum Shop Mgr., Larry McKeehan.
Institution Type/Description: History Museum.
Hours & Admission Prices: March-Sept. Fri.-Mon. 1-5. No charge; donations accepted. &
Attendance: 2,100 (estimated)

Raymond

THE NORTHWEST CARRIAGE MUSEUM, 314 Alder St., Raymond, WA 98577-2434. Mailing Address: P.O. Box 534, Raymond, WA 98577. Tel.: 360-942-4150. Facebook: Northwest Carriage Museum.
E-mail: laurieb@nwcarriagemuseum.org
Web Site: www.nwcarriagemuseum.org
Key Personnel: Dir., Laurie Bowman.
Institution Type/Description: Transportation History Museum.
Hours & Admission Prices: Daily 10-4. Adults $8, children 6-18 $5, family $20; discounts to seniors, military & AAA members; members no charge. &
Attendance: 7,000 (actual)

WILLAPA SEAPORT MUSEUM, 1 Ocean Ave., Raymond, WA 98335. Tel.: 360-942-4149 & 2855.
E-mail: info@willapaharbor.org
Web Site: willapaharbor.org
Formerly: Puget Sound Maritime Museum
Key Personnel: Dir., Pete Darrah; Pres. (V), Bill Coomer.
Institution Type/Description: Maritime Museum.
Hours & Admission Prices: March-Dec. Wed.-Sun. 12-4; special tours or after hours admissions by calling Capt. Pete: 360-589-3964. Adults $5; children no charge. &
Attendance: 1,500 (actual)

Renton

RENTON HISTORICAL SOCIETY AND MUSEUM, 235 Mill Ave. S., Renton, WA 98057-2133. Tel.: 425-255-2330. Fax: 425-255-1570. Facebook: Renton History Museum.
E-mail: estewart@rentonwa.gov
Key Personnel: Dir., Elizabeth P. Stewart; Pres., Theresa Clymer; Treas., Phyllis Hunt; Collection Mgr., Sarah Samson; Volunteer Coord., Dorota Rahn.
Institution Type/Description: Historic Fire Station: 1942 art deco building.
Hours & Admission Prices: Tues.-Sat. 10-4. Adults: non-city residents $3, city residents $2, children ages 8-16 $1; discounts to AAM & ICOM members; members no charge. &
Attendance: 4,000 (actual)

Republic

STONEROSE INTERPRETIVE CENTER, 15-1 N. Kean St., Republic, WA 99166. Mailing Address: P.O. Box 987, Republic, WA 99166-0987. Tel.: 509-775-2295.
E-mail: stonerose@frontier.com
Web Site: www.stonerosefossil.org
Key Personnel: Dir., Katherine Meade.
Institution Type/Description: Paleontology Museum.
Hours & Admission Prices: May & Sept.-Oct. Wed.-Sun. 8-5; Memorial Day to Labor Day daily 8-5. Site Admission Sticker: adults $10, senior citizens & student $5; discounts to Burke Museum members; members no charge. &
Attendance: 8,000 (actual)

Richland

HANFORD REACH INTERPRETIVE CENTER, 1766 Fowler St., Richland, WA 99352-4843. Mailing Address: P.O. Box 1160, Richland, WA 99352-1160. Tel.: 509-943-4100. Fax: 509-943-4133.
E-mail: reach@visitthereach.org
Web Site: www.visitthereach.org
Formerly: Hanford Reach National Monument Heritage & Visitor Center (The Reach)
Key Personnel: C.E.O., Lisa Toomey; Finance Dir., Amy Viggiano; Operations Mgr., Dianna Millisap; Cur. Programs & Education, Stephanie Button.
Institution Type/Description: History Museum.
Hours & Admission Prices: Tues.-Sat. 10-4, Sun. 12-4. Adults $8, students 6-18 & seniors 65 & up $6; children 5 & under & members no charge. &

Seattle

BURKE MUSEUM OF NATURAL HISTORY AND CULTURE, University of Washington Campus, 17th Ave. N.E. & N.E. 45th St., Seattle, WA 98195. Mailing Address: Burke Museum of Natural History and Culture, University of Washington, Box 353010, Seattle, WA 98195. Tel.: 206-616-3962 & 543-7907. Fax: 206-685-3039.
E-mail: theburke@uw.edu
Web Site: www.burkemuseum.org
Key Personnel: Exec. Dir., Dr. Julie K. Stein.
Institution Type/Description: Anthropology & Natural History Museum.
Hours & Admission Prices: Daily 10-5, 1st Thurs. each month 10-8. Adults $10, senior citizens $8, students and youth 5-18 $7.50; UW students, faculty & staff, members, 1st Thurs. of month and children 4 & under no charge. Closed New Year's Day; Independence Day; Thanksgiving; Christmas. &
Attendance: 96,000 (actual)

CARL S. ENGLISH JR. BOTANICAL GARDENS, 3015 N.W. 54th St., Seattle, WA 98107-4213. Tel.: 206-789-2622. Fax: 206-782-3192.
E-mail: paoteam@nws02.usace.army.mil
Web Site: www.nws.usace.army.mil
Institution Type/Description: Botanical Gardens.
Hours & Admission Prices: Grounds: daily 7am-9pm. Visitor Center: May-Sept. daily 10-6; Oct.-April Thurs.-Mon. 10-4. No charge. &

CENTER FOR WOODEN BOATS, 1010 Valley St., Seattle, WA 98109-4444. Tel.: 206-382-2628. Fax: 206-382-2699.
E-mail: info@cwb.org
Web Site: www.cwb.org
Institution Type/Description: Operational Maritime Museum.
Hours & Admission Prices: See website for seasonal hours. Fees for use of boats & maritime skills workshops. Closed Thanksgiving; Christmas. &
Attendance: 60,000 (estimated)

CENTER ON CONTEMPORARY ART, Seattle Design Center, Ste. 258, 5701 6th Ave. S., Seattle, WA 98108. Mailing Address: 114 3rd Ave. S., Seattle, WA 98104. Tel.: 206-728-1980. Fax: 206-728-1980.
E-mail: info@cocaseattle.org
Web Site: www.cocaseattle.org
Key Personnel: Vice Pres. & Chm., Sara Everett; Dir. Talent & Mktg., Lauren Collins.
Institution Type/Description: Art Museum.
Hours & Admission Prices: Winter: Thurs.-Sat. 10:30-4:30; Summer: Mon.-Fri. 10-5. No charge; donations accepted. Closed Independence Day; Thanksgiving; Christmas. &
Attendance: 15,000 (estimated)

CONNECTIONS MUSEUM SEATTLE, 7000 E. Marginal Way S., Seattle, WA 98108-3411. Mailing Address: P.O. Box 8719, Denver, CO 80201-8719. Tel.: 206-767-3012. Facebook; Twitter.
E-mail: info@connectionsmuseum.org
Web Site: www.connectionsmuseum.org
Formerly: The Herbert H. Warrick, Jr. Museum of Communications
Key Personnel: Dir., Lisa Berquist.
Institution Type/Description: Communications Museum.
Hours & Admission Prices: Sun. 10-3; groups of 8 or more by appointment. Suggested Donation: adults $5, youth 12-18 $2. &
Attendance: 875 (estimated)

DAYBREAK STAR INDIAN CULTURAL CENTER - SACRED CIRCLE GALLERY, Discovery Park on Magnolia Hill, 5011 Bernie Whitebear Way, Seattle, WA 98199. Mailing Address: United Indians of All Tribes Foundation - Discovery Park, P.O. Box 99100, Seattle, WA 98139-0100. Tel.: 206-285-4425. Fax: 206-282-3640. Faceboo.
E-mail: info@unitedindians.org
Web Site: www.unitedindians.org
Institution Type/Description: Art Gallery.
Hours & Admission Prices: Call for hours.

DES MOINES HISTORICAL SOCIETY MUSEUM, 730 S. 225th St., Seattle, WA 98198-6824. Mailing Address: P.O. Box 98055, Des Moines, WA 98198-0055. Tel.: 206-824-5226.
E-mail: info@dmhs.org
Web Site: dmhs.org
Institution Type/Description: History Museum.
Hours & Admission Prices: Memorial Day to Labor Day Sat. 1-4; other times by appointment. No charge; donations accepted.

FRYE ART MUSEUM, 704 Terry Ave., Seattle, WA 98104-2019. Tel.: 206-622-9250. Fax: 206-223-1707.
E-mail: info@fryemuseum.org
Web Site: www.fryemuseum.org
Key Personnel: Dir./C.E.O., Joseph Rosa; Communications & Press, Ingrid Langston; Sr. Deputy Dir., Jill Rullkoetter; Public Progs., Negarra A. Kudumu; Creative Aging Progs., Mary Jane Knecht; Museum Shop Mgr., Rachael Lang.
Institution Type/Description: Art Museum.
Hours & Admission Prices: Tues.-Wed. & Fri.-Sun. 11-5, Thurs. 11-7. No charge; donations accepted. Closed New Year's Day; Independence Day; Thanksgiving; Christmas. &
Attendance: 100,000 (estimated)

GATES FOUNDATION VISITOR CENTER, 440 Fifth Ave. N., Seattle, WA 98109. Mailing Address: P.O. Box 23350, Seattle, WA 98102-0650. Tel.: 206-709-3100, ext. 7100.
E-mail: visitorcenterstaff@gatesfoundation.org
Web Site: www.gatesfoundation.org
Institution Type/Description: Visitor Center.
Hours & Admission Prices: June-Aug. Tues.-Sat. 10-6; Sept.-May Tues.-Sat. 10-5; other times by appointment. No charge. Closed New Year's Day; Independence Day; Thanksgiving; Christmas Eve & Day. &

HENRY ART GALLERY, 15th Ave. N.E. & N.E. 41st St., University of Washington, Seattle, WA 98195-1410. Mailing Address: U.W. Box 351410, Seattle, WA 98195. Tel.: 206-543-2280. Fax: 206-685-3123.
E-mail: info@henryart.org
Web Site: www.henryart.org
Key Personnel: Dir., Sylvia Wolf; Pres. (V), Lisa Simonson; Chm. (V), Steve Hoedemaker; Deputy Dir. External Rels., Jill Leininger; Dir. Finance & Administration, Daren Hekcer; Exhibitions, Collections, and Programs Asst., Emily Schmierer; Assoc. Dir. Mktg., Communications & Public Rels., Dana

Van Nest; Cur. Collections, Judy Sourakli; Exhibitions Mgr. & Registration, Susan Lewandowski; Exhibition Designer & Lead Preparator, Jes Gettler; Exec. Asst. to Dir., Dustin Engstrom.
Institution Type/Description: Art Museum.
Hours & Admission Prices: Wed. & Fri.-Sun. 11-4, Thurs. 11-9, Adults $10, senior citizens 62 & over $6; discounts to AAM, AAA & ICOM members; members, students & children no charge. Closed New Year's Day; Independence Day; Veterans Day; Thanksgiving; Christmas. &
Attendance: 39,070 (actual)

HIRAM M. CHITTENDEN LOCKS VISITOR CENTER, 3015 N.W. 54th St., Seattle, WA 98107-4213. Tel.: 206-780-2500.
Web Site: www.ballardlocks.org
Institution Type/Description: History Museum.
Hours & Admission Prices: May-Sept. daily 10-6; Oct.-April Thurs.-Mon. 10-4.

KLONDIKE GOLD RUSH NATIONAL HISTORICAL PARK, 319 Second Ave. S., Seattle, WA 98104-2618. Tel.: 206-220-4240. Facebook: Klondike Gold Rush National Historical Park.
E-mail: klse_Ranger_Activities@nps.gov
Web Site: www.nps.gov/klse
Key Personnel: Supt., Jacqueline L. Ashwell; Cur. Record, Brooke Childrey.
Institution Type/Description: Historic Building & Museum: housed in Seattle's Pioneer Square Historical District.
Hours & Admission Prices: Memorial Day-Labor Day daily 9-5; Sept.-May daily 10-5. No charge; donations accepted. Closed New Year's Day; Thanksgiving; Christmas. &
Attendance: 70,000 (estimated)

LAST RESORT FIRE DEPARTMENT MUSEUM, 301 2nd Ave. S., Seattle, WA 98107. Tel.: 206-783-4474. Fax: 206-784-1485.
E-mail: lastresortfd@hotmail.com
Web Site: www.lastresortfd.org/museum.htm
Key Personnel: Owner, Galen Thomaier.
Institution Type/Description: Firefighting History Museum.
Hours & Admission Prices: Summer: Wed.-Thurs. 11-3; Winter: Wed. 11-3. No charge.

LIVING COMPUTER MUSEUM CLOSED, 2245 First Ave. S., Seattle, WA 98134. Tel.: 206-342-2020.
Web Site: www.livingcomputermuseum.org
Institution Type/Description: History Museum.
Hours & Admission Prices: Wed.-Sun. 10-5, 1st Thurs. each month 10-8. Admission $12; 1st Thurs. 5pm-8pm and children 5 & under no charge. Closed Thanksgiving; Christmas. &

THE MUSEUM OF FLIGHT, 9404 E. Marginal Way S., Seattle, WA 98108-4097. Tel.: 206-764-5700. Fax: 206-764-5707. Facebook.
E-mail: info@museumofflight.org
Web Site: www.museumofflight.org
Key Personnel: Pres. & C.E.O., Matt Hayes; C.O.O., Laurie Haag; Vice Pres. Education, Reba Gilman; Vice Pres. Devel., Trip Switzer; Vice Pres. Mktg., Erica Callahan; Dir. Sales, Rich Rime; Dir. Aircraft Collections, Tom Cathcart; Controller, Lynda King; Sr. Public Rels. Mgr., Ted Huetter; Museum Shop Mgr., Mary Christensen; Dir. Facilities, Clark Miller.
Institution Type/Description: Aeronautics & Space Museum: c.1910 the first aircraft manufacturing facility in the region
Hours & Admission Prices: Daily 10-5, first Thurs. each month 10-9. Adults $21, seniors $18, children 5-17 $13; discount to groups and Boeing employees, active military & AAM members; members and children 4 & under no charge. Closed Thanksgiving; Christmas. &
Attendance: 527,396 (actual)

MUSEUM OF HISTORY & INDUSTRY (MOHAI), 860 Terry Ave. N., Seattle, WA 98109. Tel.: 206-324-1126. Fax: 206-324-1346. Facebook: @seattlehistory; Instagram: @mohaiseattle; Twitter @mohai.
E-mail: information@mohai.org
Web Site: www.mohai.org
Key Personnel: Exec. Dir., Leonard Garfield; Pres. (V), Chuck Nordhoff; Collections Specialist, Clara Berg; Collections Mgr., Betsy Bruemmer; C.F.O. & C.O.O., Donna DiFiore; Dir. Mktg. & Communications, Jackie Durban; Cur. Photography, Howard Giske; Exhibits Mgr., Mark Gleason; Registrar, Kristin Halunen; Archivist, Jody Hendrickson; Mgr. Volunteer Resources & Curatorial Projs., Kimberly Jacobsen; Visitor Services Mgr., Melanna Kallionakis; Events Mgr., Christine Kolodge; Art Dir., Beth Koutsky; Public Rels. Mgr., Wendy Malloy; Dir. Devel., Lynne Marvet; Librarian, Carolyn Marr; Public Programs Mgr., Karin Moughamer; Exec. Assoc. & Bd. Rels. Mgr., Alice Stenstrom; Dir. Curatorial Services, Dave Unger; Digital Media Specialist, Lauren Valone; Sr.

Mgr. Facilities & Security, Jason Young; Mgr. Corp. & Foundation Rels., Amy Zarlengo.
Institution Type/Description: History & Industry Museum: housed in renovated historic landmark Naval Reserve Armory in Lake Union Park.
Hours & Admission Prices: Daily 10-5. Adults $19.95, seniors 62 & over $15.95, students and military w/ID $13.95; youth 14 & under & members no charge. Closed Thanksgiving; Christmas. &
Attendance: 193,718 (actual)

MUSEUM OF POP CULTURE (MOPOP), 325 5th Ave. N., Seattle, WA 98109-4630. Mailing Address: 120 6th Ave. N. #100, Seattle, WA 98109-5002. Tel.: 206-770-2700. Fax: 206-770-2727. Facebook, Twitter, Instagram.
E-mail: experience@empmuseum.org
Web Site: www.mopop.org
Formerly: Experience Music Project, EMP Museum
Key Personnel: Vice Pres. & Gen. Mgr., Alexis Lee; Artistic Dir., Jasen Emmons; Dir. Finance, Jon Eastlake; Dir. Mktg., Ivan Figueroa; Museum Shop Mgr., Chris Maresca.
Institution Type/Description: Pop Culture, Music & Science Fiction Museum.
Hours & Admission Prices: Memorial Day to Labor Day daily 10-7; Sept.-May daily 10-5. Adults $28, seniors & students $25, military $22, youth $19; AAM and children 4 & under no charge. Closed Thanksgiving; Christmas. &
Attendance: 743,533 (actual)

NORDIC MUSEUM, 2655 N.W. Market St., Seattle, WA 98107. Tel.: 206-789-5707. Fax: 206-789-3271. Facebook.
E-mail: nordic@nordicmuseum.org
Web Site: www.nordicmuseum.org
Key Personnel: C.E.O., Eric Nelson; Mgr. Collections, Fred Poyner, IV; Coord. Children Education, Alison Church.
Institution Type/Description: Heritage Museum: housed in 1907 Daniel Webster School.
Hours & Admission Prices: Tues.-Wed. & Fri.-Sun. 10-5, Thurs. 10-8. Adults $15, senior citizens $12, college students & children $10; members, children 4 & under and 1st Thurs. each month no charge. Closed New Year's Eve & Day; Easter; Thanksgiving; Christmas Eve & Day. &
Attendance: 65,000 (estimated)

NORTH SEATTLE COMMUNITY COLLEGE ART GALLERY, 9600 College Way N., Instruction Building IB 1430, Seattle, WA 98103-3599. Tel.: 206-528-4557.
E-mail: nscartgallery@seattlecolleges.edu
Web Site: artgallery.northseattle.edu
Key Personnel: Coord. & Cur., Amanda Knowles.
Institution Type/Description: Art Gallery.
Hours & Admission Prices: During Exhibitions: Mon.-Tues. & Fri. 11-3, Wed.-Thurs. 11-3 & 6-8.

NORTHWEST AFRICAN AMERICAN MUSEUM, 2300 S. Massachusetts St., Seattle, WA 98144-3821. Tel.: 206-518-6000. Fax: 206-518-5665.
E-mail: info@naamnw.org
Web Site: www.naamnw.org
Key Personnel: Exec. Dir., LaNesha DeBardelaben.
Institution Type/Description: African American Museum.
Hours & Admission Prices: Wed. & Fri.-Sun. 11-5, Thurs. 11-7. Adults $7, children 4-12, students and seniors 62 & over $5; discounts to AAM & ICOM members; children 3 & under, NAAM members, and 1st Thurs. each month no charge. Closed New Year's Eve, Day & day after; Independence Day; Thanksgiving & weekend after; Christmas Eve, Day & week. &
Attendance: 20,500 (actual)

NORTHWEST KIDNEY CENTERS - DIALYSIS MUSEUM, 700 Broadway, Seattle, WA 98122. Tel.: 206-720-3713. Facebook; Twitter.
E-mail: museum@nwkidney.org
Web Site: nwkidney.org/about-us/dialysis-museum
Institution Type/Description: Medical Museum.
Hours & Admission Prices: By appointment. No charge.

NORTHWEST MUSEUM OF LEGENDS AND LORE, Seattle, WA 98134. Mailing Address: P.O. Box 12213, Seattle, WA 98102-0213. Tel.: 206-523-6348 & 465-9601.
E-mail: seattlemysterymuseum@gmail.com
Web Site: www.nwlegendsmuseum.com
Formerly: Seattle Museum of the Mysteries
Key Personnel: Dir., Charlette LeFevre; Librarian, Philip Lipson.
Institution Type/Description: Paranormal Science Museum.

Hours & Admission Prices: Online Museum only with occasional tours & events. Ᏸ
Attendance: 5,000

OLYMPIC SCULPTURE PARK, 2901 Western Ave., Seattle, WA 98121-1025. Mailing Address: 1300 First Ave., Seattle, WA 98101-2003. Tel.: 206-654-3100 & 3137. TDD: 206-441-4261.
E-mail: groups@seattleartmuseum.org
Web Site: www.seattleartmuseum.org/visit/olympic-sculpture-park
Key Personnel: Illsley Ball Nordstrom Dir. & CEO, Kimerly Rorschach; Dir. Human Resources, Elizabeth Detels; Chief Conservator, Nicholas Dorman; COO, Richard Beckerman.
Institution Type/Description: Sculpture Park Museum.
Hours & Admission Prices: Sculpture Park: daily 30 minutes prior to sunrise to 30 minutes after sunset. Pavilion: March-Oct. Tues.-Sun. 10-5; Nov.-Feb. Sat. -Sun. 10-4. No charge. Closed New Year's Eve & Day; Thanksgiving; Christmas Eve & Day.

PACIFIC SCIENCE CENTER, 200 2nd Ave. N., Seattle, WA 98109-4895. Tel.: 206-443-2001. Fax: 206-443-3631. TDD: 206-443-2887.
E-mail: cwheaton@pacsci.org
Web Site: pacificsciencecenter.org
Key Personnel: Pres. & C.E.O., Will Daughterty; C.O.O. & C.F.O., Chris Wheaton; Guest Svcs. Dir., Jennifer Tucker; Theater Operations Mgr., Elizabeth Calhoun; Sr. Vice Pres. Develop., April Collier; Vice Pres. Science Engagement & Outreach, Keni Sturgeon; Vice Pres. Exhibits & Life Sciences, Diana Johns; Dir. Mktg. & Sales, Elin Waldman.
Institution Type/Description: Science & Technology Museum.
Hours & Admission Prices: Mon.-Fri. 10-5, Sat.-Sun. & Holidays 10-6. Exhibits & IMAX: adults $25.75, seniors $22.75, youth 6-15 $18.75, children 3-5 $13.75. Exhibits: adults $19.75, senior citizens 65 & over $17.75, youth 6-15 $14.75, children 3-5 $11.75; members no charge. IMAX: adults $10, seniors $9, youth 6-15 $8; children 3-5 $6. Closed Thanksgiving; Christmas. Ᏸ
Attendance: 937,000 (actual)

PHOTO CENTER NW, 900 Twelfth Ave., Seattle, WA 98122. Tel.: 206-720-7222. Fax: 206-720-0306.
E-mail: pcnw@pcnw.org
Web Site: pcnw.org/gallery
Key Personnel: Exec. Dir. & Cur., Michelle Dunn Marsh.
Institution Type/Description: Art Gallery.
Hours & Admission Prices: Mon.-Thurs. 12-9, Sat.-Sun. 12-6. No charge; donations accepted. Closed New Year's Day; Memorial Day; Independence Day; Labor Day; Thanksgiving; Christmas. Ᏸ

PRATT FINE ARTS CENTER, 1902 S. Main St., Seattle, WA 98144-2206. Tel.: 206-328-2200. Fax: 206-328-1260.
E-mail: info@pratt.org
Web Site: www.pratt.org
Key Personnel: Exec. Dir., Steve Galatro.
Institution Type/Description: Art Gallery.
Hours & Admission Prices: Daily 8:30am-10pm. Closed New Year's Day; Memorial Day; Independence Day; Labor Day; Thanksgiving; Christmas.

SEATTLE AQUARIUM, 1483 Alaskan Way, Pier 59, Seattle, WA 98101-2015. Tel.: 206-386-4300. Fax: 206-386-4328.
E-mail: info@seattleaquarium.org
Web Site: www.seattleaquarium.org
Key Personnel: Dir. Public Affairs, Tim Kuniholm; Interim Dir. Finance & Admin., April Henderson; Mktg. & Creative Dir., Marsha Savery; Dir. Devel., Rachael Weakland; Dir. Human Resources, Veronica Smolen; Dir. Life Sciences, C.J. Casson; Dir. Conservation & Education, Jim Wharton.
Institution Type/Description: Aquarium and Marine Museum: located on downtown waterfront.
Hours & Admission Prices: Daily 9:30-5. Adults $24.95, youth 4-12 $16.95; children 3 & under and members no charge. Closed Christmas. Ᏸ
Attendance: 829,668 (actual)

SEATTLE ART MUSEUM, 1300 First Ave., Seattle, WA 98101-2003. Tel.: 206-654-3100. Fax: 206-654-3135. TDD: 206-654-3137; Facebook: @seattleartmuseum.
E-mail: pr@seattleartmuseum.org
Web Site: www.seattleartmuseum.org
Key Personnel: Illsley Ball Nordstrom Dir., Kimerly Rorschach; Dir. Communications, Domenic Morea; Mgr. Public Rels., Rachel Eggers.
Institution Type/Description: Art Museum.
Hours & Admission Prices: Wed. & Fri.-Sun. 10-5, Thurs. 10-9. Suggested Admissions: adults $19.95, seniors 62 & over and military with ID $17.95; students with ID & teen 13-19 $12.95; discounts to groups, AAM, ICOM, AAA & Entertainment members; members, children 12 & under, 1st Thurs. each month

& SAM collection galleries and no charge; special exhibition prices may apply. Ᏸ
Attendance: 500,000 (estimated)

SEATTLE ASIAN ART MUSEUM, 1400 E. Prospect, Volunteer Park, Seattle, WA 98112-3303. Tel.: 206-654-3100; 206-344-5267 (TTY). Fax: 206-654-3135.
E-mail: pr@seattleartmuseum.org
Web Site: www.seattleartmuseum.org
Key Personnel: Illsley Ball Nordstrom Dir. & C.E.O., Kimerly Rorschach; C.O.O., Richard Beckerman.
Institution Type/Description: Art Museum.
Hours & Admission Prices: Wed. & Fri.-Sun. 10-5, Thurs. 10-9. Adults $9, seniors 62 & up & military w/I.D. $6, students w/I.D & youth 13-19 $5; discounts to AAM & ICOM members; children 12 7 under, members and first Thurs. each month no charge. Closed Thanksgiving; Christmas. Ᏸ
Attendance: 74,878 (actual)

SEATTLE CHILDREN'S MUSEUM, 305 Harrison St., Seattle, WA 98109-4623. Tel.: 206-441-1768. Fax: 206-448-0910. Facebook: Seattle Children's Museum.
E-mail: infoplease@thechildrensmuseum.org
Web Site: www.thechildrensmuseum.org
Formerly: The Children's Museum, Seattle
Key Personnel: Exec. Dir., Christi Stapleton; Acting Dir. Operations, Crystal Dean; Dir. Education & Volunteers, Amy Hale.
Institution Type/Description: Children's Museum.
Hours & Admission Prices: Mon.-Fri. 10-5, Sat.-Sun. 10-6. Admission $8.25, seniors $7.25; discounts to groups of 10 or more; children under one no charge. Closed New Year's Day; Labor Day weekend; Thanksgiving; Christmas. Ᏸ
Attendance: 187,250 (actual)

SOUTHWEST SEATTLE HISTORICAL SOCIETY - LOG HOUSE MUSEUM, 3003 61st Ave., S.W., Seattle, WA 98116-2810. Tel.: 206-938-5293. Facebook: Log House Museum.
E-mail: loghousemuseum@comcast.net
Web Site: www.loghousemuseum.info
Key Personnel: Pres., Karen Sisson; Cur., Lissa Kramer.
Institution Type/Description: History Museum: log house; built in 1904.
Hours & Admission Prices: Thurs.-Sun. 12-4. Suggested Donation: adults $3, children $1. Closed holidays. Ᏸ
Attendance: 2,000 (estimated)

SUYAMA SPACE, 2324 Second Ave., Seattle, WA 98121. Tel.: 206-256-0809. Fax: 206-256-0810. Facebook: Suyama Space.
E-mail: info@suyamaspace.org
Web Site: www.suyamaspace.org
Key Personnel: Dir. & Cur., Beth Sellars; Dir., George Suyama; Chm. (V), Richard Andrews.
Institution Type/Description: Art Gallery.
Hours & Admission Prices: Mon.-Fri. 9-5. No charge; donations accepted. Ᏸ
Attendance: 10,000 (estimated)

SWEDISH FINN HISTORICAL SOCIETY ARCHIVES AND LIBRARY, 1920 Dexter Ave. N., Seattle, WA 98109-2718. Tel.: 206-706-0738. Fax: 206-782-5813.
E-mail: info@swedishfinnhistoricalsociety.org
Web Site: www.swedishfinnhistoricalsociety.org
Institution Type/Description: Historical Society Museum.
Hours & Admission Prices: Mon. & Thurs. 9:30-12:30, Wed. 2-5; 1st Sun. each month 1-3.

UNIVERSITY OF WASHINGTON BOTANIC GARDEN, 3501 N.E. 41st St., Seattle, WA 98105. Mailing Address: Box 354115, Seattle, WA 98195-4115. Tel.: 206-543-8616. Fax: 206-685-2692. Facebook: UW Botanic Gardens.
E-mail: uwbg@uw.edu
Web Site: depts.washington.edu/uwbg/index.php
Formerly: Washington Park Arboretum
Institution Type/Description: Arboretum & Botanical Garden.
Hours & Admission Prices: Arboretum: daily dawn-dusk. No charge. Visitors' Center: daily 9-5. Japanese Garden: visit website for information. Closed New Year's Day; Thanksgiving; Christmas.
Attendance: 400,000 (estimated)

WING LUKE MUSEUM OF THE ASIAN PACIFIC AMERICAN EXPERIENCE, 719 S. King St., Seattle, WA 98104-3035. Tel.: 206-623-5124. Fax: 206-623-4559. Facebook: Wing Luke Museum.

E-mail: visit@wingluke.org
Web Site: www.wingluke.org
Key Personnel: Exec. Dir., Beth Takekawa; Deputy Exec. Dir., Cassie Chinn; Deputy Dir. Finance & Operations, Gary Yamamoto; Deputy Dir. Mktg., Margaret Su; Sr. Community Programs Specialist, Charlene Mano-Shen; Dir. Facilities Operations, John Hom; Mgr. Devel., Josie Baltan; Mgr. Community Programs, Vivian Chan; Mgr. Collections, Robert Fisher; Dir. Exhibits, Michelle Kumata; Education & Tour Dir., Rahul Gupta; Sr. Front of House Mgr., Rayann Onzuka; Exhibit Devel. & Oral History Mgr., Mikala Woodward; Sr. Accountant, Troy Tsuchikawa; Education Specialist & YouthCAN Mgr., Roldy Ablao; Information Technology Specialist, Alex Plemitscher.
Institution Type/Description: Asian Pacific American History, Art & Culture Museum.
Hours & Admission Prices: Tues.-Sun. 10-5, 1st Thurs. each month 10-8. Adults $14.95, seniors $11.95, students13-18 $10.95, children 5-12 $9.95; discounts to AAM & ICOM members; members & children under 5 no charge. Closed New Year's Day; Independence Day; Thanksgiving; Christmas Eve & Day. &
Attendance: 45,000 (estimated)

WOODLAND PARK ZOO, 5500 Phinney Ave. N., Seattle, WA 98103-5897. Tel.: 206-548-2500; 206-548-2599 (TTY). Fax: 206-548-1536.
E-mail: zooinfo@zoo.org
Web Site: www.zoo.org
Key Personnel: Pres. & C.E.O., Alejandro Grajal, Ph.D.; Vice Pres. Human Resources, Dana Keeler; Vice Pres. Public Affairs & Communications, Lauri Hennessey; Dir. Animal Health, Dr. Darin Collins; Vice Pres. Education, Wei Ying Wong.
Institution Type/Description: Zoo.
Hours & Admission Prices: May-Sept. daily 9:30-6; Oct.-April daily 9:30-4. Summer: adults $20.95, children 3-12 $12.95; children 2 & under no charge. Winter: adults $14.95, children 3-12 $9.95; children 2 & under no charge. Closed Christmas. &
Attendance: 1,094,514 (actual)

Sedro-Woolley

NORTH CASCADES NATIONAL PARK SERVICE COMPLEX, 810 State Route 20, Sedro-Woolley, WA 98284-1239. Tel.: 360-854-7200. Fax: 360-856-1934.
E-mail: noca_interpretation@nps.gov
Web Site: www.nps.gov/noca
Key Personnel: Supt., Karen Taylor-Goodrich.
Institution Type/Description: Park & Visitor Centers: Newhalem Visitor Center, Newhalem, WA; Golden West Visitor Center, Stehekin, WA.
Hours & Admission Prices: Visitor's Center: May-June & Sept.-Oct. daily 9-5, July-Sept. 9-6. &
Attendance: 10,000 (estimated)

SEDRO-WOOLLEY MUSEUM, 725 Murdock St., Sedro-Woolley, WA 98284-1450. Tel.: 360-855-2390.
Web Site: sedro-woolleymuseum.com
Key Personnel: Pres. (V) & Museum Shop Mgr., Carolyn Freeman; Vice Pres., Dale Robertson.
Institution Type/Description: History Museum.
Hours & Admission Prices: Wed. 12-4, Thurs. 11:30-3:30, Sat. 9-4, Sun. 1-4; other times by appointment. Suggested Donation: adults $1.50, seniors & children $1; members no charge. &
Attendance: 3,750 (actual)

Sequim

DUNGENESS RIVER AUDUBON CENTER AT RAILROAD BRIDGE PARK, 2151 Hendrickson Rd., Sequim, WA 98382. Mailing Address: P.O. Box 2450, Sequim, WA 98382-2450. Tel.: 360-681-4076. Fax: 360-681-8060.
E-mail: rivercenter@olympus.net
Web Site: www.dungenessrivercenter.org
Formerly: Dungeness River Audubon Center
Key Personnel: Dir., Bob Boekelheide.
Institution Type/Description: Audubon Center.
Hours & Admission Prices: April-Oct. Tues.-Sat. 10-4, Sun. 12-4; Nov.-March Tues.-Fri. 10-4, Sat. 12-4. No charge; donations accepted. &
Attendance: 21,500 (actual)

MUSEUM AND ARTS CENTER IN THE SEQUIM DUNGENESS VALLEY, 175 W. Cedar St., Sequim, WA 98382-3318. Tel.: 360-681-2257. Facebook: Museum Arts Center in the Sequim Dungeness Valley.
E-mail: sequimmuseum@olypen.com
Web Site: sequimmuseum.com

Key Personnel: Exec. Dir., Judy Stipe.
Institution Type/Description: General Museum.
Hours & Admission Prices: Wed.-Sat. 11-3. No charge; donations accepted. Closed holidays. &
Attendance: 4,000 (estimated)

Shaw Island

SHAW ISLAND LIBRARY & HISTORICAL SOCIETY, Blind Bay Rd., Shaw Island, WA 98286. Mailing Address: P.O. Box 844, Shaw Island, WA 98286-0844. Tel.: 360-468-4068.
E-mail: rkg@rockisland.com
Web Site: www.shawislanders.org/others/library/library.htm
Key Personnel: Pres., Jennifer Swanson; Cur., Alex McCloud; Historian, Sheri Christiansen; Head Librarian, Jeb Nichols.
Institution Type/Description: Local History Museum: housed in c.1870 one room log cabin.
Hours & Admission Prices: Tues. 2-4, Thurs. 11-1, Sat. 10-12 & 2-4; other times by appointment. No charge.

Shoreline

SHORELINE HISTORICAL MUSEUM, 18501 Linden Ave., N., Shoreline, WA 98133-4801. Mailing Address: P.O. Box 55594, Shoreline, WA 98155-0594. Tel.: 206-542-7111.
E-mail: shm@shorelinehistoricalmuseum.org
Web Site: shorelinehistoricalmuseum.org
Key Personnel: Exec. Dir. & C.E.O., Victoria Stiles; Pres. (V), Barrett Monsaas.
Institution Type/Description: Historical Museum.
Hours & Admission Prices: Tues.-Sat. 10-4. No charge; donations accepted. Closed New Year's Day; Independence Day; Thanksgiving; Christmas. &
Attendance: 8,000 (estimated)

Snohomish

BLACKMAN HOUSE MUSEUM, 118 Ave. B, Snohomish, WA 98290. Mailing Address: P.O. Box 174, Snohomish, WA 98291-0174. Tel.: 360-568-5235.
E-mail: visitor@snohomish.org
Web Site: www.snohomishhistoricalsociety.org
Key Personnel: Pres. (V), Chris Gee; Archivist, Middy Ruthruff.
Institution Type/Description: Historical Society Museum: 1878 Blackman House, home of town's first mayor.
Hours & Admission Prices: April to mid-Dec. Sat.-Sun. 11-3. Donation requested. Closed Mother's Day.
Attendance: 1,000 (estimated)

Snoqualmie

NORTHWEST RAILWAY MUSEUM, 38625 S.E. King St., Snoqualmie, WA 98065. Mailing Address: P.O. Box 459, Snoqualmie, WA 98065-0459. Tel.: 425-888-3030, ext. 7201. Fax: 425-888-9311. Facebook: Northwest Railway Museum.
E-mail: info@trainmuseum.org
Web Site: www.trainmuseum.org
Key Personnel: Exec. Dir., Richard R. Anderson; Pres., Dennis Snook; Vice Pres., Mary Nelson; Sec., Cindy Walker; Treas., Jon Beveridge; Deputy Dir., Jessie E. Cunningham; Museum Shop Mgr., James Sackey.
Institution Type/Description: Railroad Museum & Historic Building: c.1890 railroad depot.
Hours & Admission Prices: Snoqualmie Depot: daily 10-5. No charge. Railway Excursion: April-Oct. Sat.-Sun., occasional weekdays & holidays. April-June 28 & Sept. 12-Oct. 18 adults $18, seniors 62 & over $16, children 2-12 $10. Steam Train: Memorial Day weekend, Independence Day, July 25-Sept. 7, Oct. 24-25 & 31 adults $20, seniors $18, children $12; discounts to groups & AAM members; children under 2 no charge. &
Attendance: 89,571 (actual)

South Bend

PACIFIC COUNTY HISTORICAL SOCIETY & MUSEUM (PCHS), 1008 W. Robert Bush Dr., South Bend, WA 98586-0039. Mailing Address: P.O. Box P, South Bend, WA 98586-0039. Tel.: 360-875-5224. Fax: 360-875-5224 (call first).
E-mail: museum@willapabay.org
Web Site: www.pacificcohistory.org
Key Personnel: Pres. (V), Steve Rogers; Mgr., Patricia Neve.
Institution Type/Description: Local History Museum.

Hours & Admission Prices: Daily 11-4. No charge; donations accepted. Closed Easter; Independence Day; Thanksgiving; Christmas. &
Attendance: 4,028 (actual)

South Cle Elum

DEPOT INTERPRETIVE CENTER/CASCADE RAIL FOUNDATION, 801 Milwaukee Rd., South Cle Elum, WA 98943. Mailing Address: P.O. Box 462, South Cle Elum, WA 98943-0462. Tel.: 509-656-4352. Facebook.
E-mail: mapndug@gmail.com
Web Site: www.milwelectric.org
Formerly: Depot Museum/Cascade Rail Foundation
Key Personnel: Pres. (V), Paul Krueger; Vice Pres., Mark Borleske; Treas., Mary Pittis; Sec., Wayne Monger.
Institution Type/Description: Railroad Museum.
Hours & Admission Prices: May-Oct. Sat.-Sun. 12-4. No charge; donations accepted. &
Attendance: 652 (actual)

Spokane

CHASE GALLERY AT CITY HALL, Spokane City Hall, 808 W. Spokane Falls Blvd., Spokane, WA 99201-3301. Mailing Address: P.O. Box 978, Spokane, WA 99210. Tel.: 509-321-9614.
E-mail: info@spokanearts.com
Web Site: www.visitspokane.com/art/
Key Personnel: Exec. Co-Dir., Shannon Halberstadt; Co-Dir., Luke Baumgarten.
Institution Type/Description: Art Gallery.
Hours & Admission Prices: Mon.-Fri. 8-5. No charge. &
Attendance: 24,000 (estimated)

CORBIN ART CENTER, 507 W. 7th Ave., Spokane, WA 99204-2709. Mailing Address: 808 W. Spokane Falls Blvd., 5th Fl. City Hall, Spokane, WA 99201-3301. Tel.: 509-625-6677.
E-mail: spokaneparks@spokanecity.org
Web Site: www.spokaneparks.org/recreation/CAC.htm
Institution Type/Description: Art Gallery: housed in D.C. Corbin house, built in 1898. Listed on the National Register of Historic Places.
Hours & Admission Prices: Mon.-Thurs. 9-4. No charge.

JOHN A. FINCH ARBORETUM, 3404 W. Woodland Blvd., Spokane, WA 99224-2240. Mailing Address: Park Operations, 2304 E. Mallon, Spokane, WA 99202. Tel.: 509-363-5455. Fax: 509-363-5454. snittalo@spokanecity.org.
E-mail: ssullivan@spokanecity.org
Web Site: www.spokanecity.org/parks
Key Personnel: Park Div. Mgr., Tony Madunich.
Institution Type/Description: Arboretum.
Hours & Admission Prices: Mon.-Fri. 7:30-3:30 & 1-4. No charge; donations accepted.

JUNDT ART MUSEUM, 502 E. Boone Ave., Spokane, WA 99258. Tel.: 509-313-6843. Fax: 509-313-5525. Facebook.
E-mail: manoguerra@gonzaga.edu
Web Site: www.gonzaga.edu/jundt
Key Personnel: Dir. & Cur., Dr. Paul A. Manoguerra; Cur. Education, Karen Kaiser; Preparator/Art Handler, Robin Dare; Program Coord., Anita Martello.
Institution Type/Description: Art Museum/Center.
Hours & Admission Prices: Mon.-Sat. 10-4. No charge. Closed university holidays. &
Attendance: 25,000

MOBIUS CHILDREN'S MUSEUM, 808 W. Main, Lower Level, Spokane, WA 99201. Tel.: 509-624-5437. Fax: 509-624-6453.
E-mail: info@mobiusspokane.org
Web Site: www.mobiusspokane.org
Formerly: Children's Museum of Spokane
Key Personnel: C.O.O., Karen Hudson; Pres., Amaile Day; C.E.O., Phil Lindsey.
Institution Type/Description: Children's Museum.
Hours & Admission Prices: Tues.-Sat. 10-5, Sun. 11-5. Adults & children $8; seniors & military $7; members & children under one no charge. Closed New Year's Day; Easter; Thanksgiving; Christmas. &
Attendance: 85,000 (estimated)

MOBIUS SCIENCE CENTER, 313 N. Post St., Spokane, WA 99201. Mailing Address: 808 W. Main Ave., LL015, Spokane, WA 99201. Tel.: 509-321-7133.
E-mail: info@mobiusspokane.org

Web Site: mobiusspokane.org
Key Personnel: CEO, Phil Lindsey; Pres., Amalie Day; COO, Karen Hudson.
Institution Type/Description: Science Center.
Hours & Admission Prices: Tues.-Sat. 10-5, Sun. 11-5. Adults & children $8, seniors & military $7; members and children under 12 months under no charge. &
Attendance: 50,000 (estimated)

NORTHWEST MUSEUM OF ARTS & CULTURE (EASTERN WASHINGTON STATE HISTORICAL SOCIETY), W. 2316 First Ave., Spokane, WA 99201-5906. Tel.: 509-456-3931. Fax: 509-363-5303.
E-mail: betsy.godlewski@northwestmuseum.org
Web Site: www.northwestmuseum.org
Formerly: Eastern Washington State Historical Society, Cheney Cowles Museum
Key Personnel: Exec. Dir., Forrest B. Rodgers; Communications & Public Rels., Reebcca Bishop.
Institution Type/Description: General Museum.
Hours & Admission Prices: Wed.-Sun. 10-5. Adults $10, senior 65 & over $7.50, college students with ID & children 6-18 $5; discount to National Trust for Historic Preservation members; reciprocal with NARM & Time Travelers; first Fri. of month 5-8pm by donation; members & children 5 & under no charge. Closed major holidays. &
Attendance: 140,000 (estimated)

SPOKANE FALLS COMMUNITY COLLEGE FINE ART GALLERY, Fine Arts Bldg., Bldg. 6, 3410 W. Fort George Wright Dr., Spokane, WA 99224-5288. Tel.: 509-533-3710. Fax: 509-533-3484.
E-mail: tomo@spokanefalls.edu
Institution Type/Description: College Art Gallery.
Hours & Admission Prices: Sept.-May Mon.-Fri. 8-4, Sat. 11-2. No charge. Closed college holidays & breaks.

SPOKANE FIRE DEPARTMENT MUSEUM, 1618 N. Rebecca, Spokane, WA 99207. Tel.: 509-625-7062.
E-mail: tommyhmuseumguy@aol.com
Institution Type/Description: Firefighting History Museum.
Hours & Admission Prices: Call for hours.

WASHINGTON FIRE LOOKOUT MUSEUM, 123 W. Westview, Spokane, WA 99218-2226. Tel.: 509-466-9171.
E-mail: rkresek@webtv.net
Web Site: www.firelookouts.com/museum.html
Institution Type/Description: History Museum.
Hours & Admission Prices: March-Nov. by appointment. No charge.

Stanwood

STANWOOD AREA HISTORY MUSEUM & D. O. PEARSON HOUSE MUSEUM, 27108 102nd Ave., N.W., Stanwood, WA 98292. Mailing Address: P.O. Box 69, Stanwood, WA 98292-0069. Tel.: 360-629-6110.
Web Site: www.sahs-fncc.org
Institution Type/Description: History Museum.
Hours & Admission Prices: Wed., Fri. & Sun. 1-4. No charge; donations accepted. &

Steilacoom

NATIONAL ORR HOME AND ORCHARD, 1811 Rainier St., Steilacoom, WA 98388. Mailing Address: P.O. Box 88016, Steilacoom, WA 98388. Tel.: 253-584-4133. Facebook.
E-mail: steilacoomhistorical@gmail.com
Web Site: www.steilacoomhistorical.com
Institution Type/Description: Historic House Museum: built in 1857.
Hours & Admission Prices: April-May & Sept.-Oct. Sat.-Sun. 1-5; June-Aug. Wed. 2-5, Sat.-Sun. 1-5. Suggested Donation: $2.

STEILACOOM HISTORICAL MUSEUM, Rainier & Main, Steilacoom, WA 98388. Mailing Address: P.O. Box 88016, Steilacoom, WA 98388-0016. Tel.: 253-584-4133. Facebook: Steilacoom Historical Museum Association.
E-mail: steilacoomhistorical@gmail.com
Web Site: www.steilacoomhistorical.org
Key Personnel: Dir., French Wetmore; Pres. (V), Jan Lucas; Museum Shop Mgr. & Office Mgr., Marianne Bull; Cur., Joan Curtis.
Institution Type/Description: Local History.

Hours & Admission Prices: April-Oct. Sat.-Sun. 1-5. Suggested Donation: $2; Blue Star Museum participant. &

Attendance: 4,800 (estimated)

STEILACOOM TRIBAL MUSEUM & CULTURAL CENTER,
1515 Lafayette St., Steilacoom, WA 98388. Tel.: 253-584-6308.
E-mail: steilacoomtribe@msn.com
Institution Type/Description: Native American Museum.
Hours & Admission Prices: Sat. 10-4. Adults $4. Closed major holidays. &

Stevenson

COLUMBIA GORGE INTERPRETIVE CENTER MUSEUM,
990 S.W. Rock Creek Dr., Stevenson, WA 98648. Mailing Address: P.O. Box 396, Stevenson, WA 98648-0396. Tel.: 509-427-8211. Fax: 509-427-7429. Facebook: Columbia Gorge Interpretive Center Museum.
E-mail: info@columbiagorge.org
Web Site: www.columbiagorge.org
Key Personnel: Dir., Robert Peterson; Pres. (V), Ken Cole.
Institution Type/Description: Local History Museum.
Hours & Admission Prices: Daily 9-5. Family $30, adults $10, students & senior citizens $8, children 6-12 $6; discounts to AAM, ICOM, AAA, media & tourism industry members; county residents on 1st Sat. of month, members, children 5 & under, and during the anniversary celebration no charge. Closed New Year's Day; Thanksgiving; Christmas. &
Attendance: 21,410 (actual)

Sumner

HERITAGE QUEST RESEARCH LIBRARY,
1007 Main St., Sumner, WA 98390. Tel.: 253-863-1806.
E-mail: research@hqrl.com
Web Site: www.hqrl.com
Institution Type/Description: Genealogy Library.
Hours & Admission Prices: Mon.-Sat. 10-4. Closed New Year's Eve & Day; Memorial Day; Independence Day; Labor Day; Thanksgiving; Christmas Eve & Day.

RYAN HOUSE MUSEUM - SUMNER HISTORICAL SOCIETY,
1228 Main St., Sumner, WA 98390. Tel.: 253-863-2670.
E-mail: sumnermuseum@comcast.net
Web Site: sumnerhistoricalsociety.com
Key Personnel: Cur., Vicki Connor.
Institution Type/Description: Historic House Museum: built in 1860.
Hours & Admission Prices: April-Aug. Sat.-Sun. 1-4. Closed Mother's Day; Memorial Day; Father's Day.

Sunnyside

SUNNYSIDE HISTORICAL MUSEUM,
704 S. 4th St., Sunnyside, WA 98944-2162. Mailing Address: Box 782, Sunnyside, WA 98944-0782. Tel.: 509-837-6010 & 2105.
E-mail: ssmuseum@bentonrea.com
Key Personnel: Pres., John Saras; Vice Pres. & Cur., Don Wade.
Institution Type/Description: Early Pioneer Museum.
Hours & Admission Prices: Thurs.-Sun. 1-4. No charge; donations accepted. &
Attendance: 1,000 (estimated)

Tacoma

BROWNS POINT LIGHTHOUSE PARK - COTTAGE MUSEUM,
201 Tulalip St., N.E., Tacoma, WA 98422. Mailing Address: 6716 Eastside Dr., N.E., Ste. 1 PMB 35, Tacoma, WA 98422. Tel.: 253-927-2536.
E-mail: pointsnortheast@comcast.net
Web Site: www.pointsnortheast.org
Institution Type/Description: History Museum.
Hours & Admission Prices: April-Nov. Sat. 1-4.

CHILDREN'S MUSEUM OF TACOMA,
1501 Pacific Ave., Ste. 202, Tacoma, WA 98402. Tel.: 253-627-6031. Fax: 253-627-2436.
E-mail: tandrews@playtacoma.org
Web Site: www.playtacoma.org
Key Personnel: Exec. Dir., Tanya Andrews; Pres. Bd., Dave Edwards; Dir. Communications & Operations, Brenda Morrison; Mgr. Experience, Deean Marsh; Mgr. Research & Assessment, Kimberly McKenney.
Institution Type/Description: Children's Museum.

Hours & Admission Prices: Wed.-Sun. 10-5. Pay As You Will. Closed New Year's Day; Easter; Independence Day; Labor Day; Thanksgiving; Christmas Eve & Day. &
Attendance: 120,169 (actual)

FORT NISQUALLY LIVING HISTORY MUSEUM,
5400 N. Pearl St., #11, Tacoma, WA 98407-3224. Tel.: 253-591-5339. Fax: 253-759-6184.
E-mail: fortnisqually@tacomaparks.com
Web Site: www.fortnisqually.org
Formerly: Fort Nisqually Historic Site
Key Personnel: Fort Nisqually Foundation Chm. (V), Gail Cram; Museum Supvr., Jim Lauderdale; Metro Parks Tacoma Exec. Dir., Jack Wilson; Cur. Education, Lane Sample; Cur., Claire Keller-Scholz; Events & Volunteers, Allison Campbell; Museum Shop Mgr., Jill Stephenson; Education Specialist, Lane Sample; Special Projects, Peggy Barchi.
Institution Type/Description: Historic Site & History Museum Complex.
Hours & Admission Prices: May-Sept. daily 11-5; Oct.-April Wed.-Sun. 11-4. Family $22, adults $8, seniors $7, students $6; discount to AAA members; members no charge. Closed New Year's Day; Thanksgiving; Christmas. &
Attendance: 30,000 (actual)

FOSS WATERWAY SEAPORT,
705 Dock St., Tacoma, WA 98402-4625. Tel.: 253-272-2750.
E-mail: info@fosswaterwayseaport.org
Web Site: www.fosswaterwayseaport.org
Formerly: Working Waterfront Maritime Museum
Key Personnel: Exec. Dir., Wesley Wenhardt; Administrative Asst., Vickie Glastetter; Dir. Education, Kaddee Lawrence.
Institution Type/Description: Maritime Museum.
Hours & Admission Prices: Wed.-Sat. 10-4, Sun. 12-4. Adults $10, senior citizens 62 & over, students, children 5 & over, and military $8; discounts to groups of 10 or more; members no charge. Closed New Year's Day; Easter; Independence Day; Memorial Day; Thanksgiving; Christmas.

JAMES R. SLATER MUSEUM OF NATURAL HISTORY,
University of Puget Sound, 1500 N. Warner St., #1088, Tacoma, WA 98416. Tel.: 253-879-2798.
E-mail: slatermuseum@pugetsound.edu
Web Site: www.ups.edu/slatermuseum.xml
Formerly: Puget Sound Museum
Key Personnel: Dir., Dr. Peter Wimberger; Mgr. Collections, Dr. Gary Shugart; Dir. Emeritus, Dr. Dennis R. Paulson.
Institution Type/Description: Natural History Museum.
Hours & Admission Prices: By appointment. No charge. Closed holidays. &

JOB CARR CABIN MUSEUM,
2350 N. 30th St., Tacoma, WA 98403-3323. Mailing Address: P.O. Box 7609, Tacoma, WA 98417-0609. Tel.: 253-627-5405.
E-mail: mbowlby@jobcarrmuseum.org
Web Site: www.jobcarrmuseum.org
Key Personnel: Exec. Dir., Mary Bowlby; Program Mgr., Holly Stewart.
Institution Type/Description: History Museum: housed in a replica of Job Carr's home built in 1865. He was Tacoma's first settler, Postmaster and Mayor.
Hours & Admission Prices: Jan. by appointment; Feb.-May & Oct.-Dec. Wed.-Sat. 1-4; June-Sept. Wed.-Sat. 12-4. No charge; donations accepted. &
Attendance: 4,500 (actual)

THE KARPELES MANUSCRIPT LIBRARY MUSEUM,
407 S. "G" St., Tacoma, WA 98405-4711. Tel.: 253-383-2575.
E-mail: kmuseumtaq@aol.com
Web Site: www.rain.org/~karpeles/taqfrm.html
Key Personnel: Dir., Thomas M. Jutila.
Institution Type/Description: History Museum.
Hours & Admission Prices: Tues.-Fri. 10-4. No charge.

KITTREDGE GALLERY, UNIVERSITY OF PUGET SOUND ART DEPT.,
1500 N. Warner St., CMB 1072, Tacoma, WA 98416-0005. Tel.: 253-879-3701. Fax: 253-879-3500.
E-mail: communications@pugetsound.edu
Web Site: www.pugetsound.edu/kittredge
Institution Type/Description: Art Gallery.
Hours & Admission Prices: Sept. to mid-May Mon.-Fri. 10-5, Sat. 12-5. No charge. Closed holidays; semester breaks. &
Attendance: 4,000 (actual)

LEMAY AMERICA'S CAR MUSEUM,
2702 E. D St., Tacoma, WA 98421. Tel.: 253-779-8490. Fax: 253-779-8499.
E-mail: info@americascarmuseum.org
Web Site: www.lemaymuseum.org

Formerly: Harold E. LeMay Museum
Institution Type/Description: Transportation Museum.
Hours & Admission Prices: Guided Tours: Tues.-Sun. 10-5 by appointment. Guided Tours: adults $16, seniors 65 & over and military $14, students $12, children 6-12 $8; children 5 & under and members no charge. Closed major holidays.
Attendance: 400,000 (estimated)

MUSEUM OF GLASS, 1801 Dock St., Tacoma, WA 98402-3217. Tel.: 253-284-4750 & 4719, 866-468-7386. Fax: 253-396-1769. Facebook: www.facebook.com/museumofglass.
E-mail: info@museumofglass.org
Web Site: www.museumofglass.org
Key Personnel: Exec. Dir., Debbie Lenk; Chm. (V), Gail T. Weyerhaeuser; Dir. Operations & Finance, Jeff Ganung; Dir. Visitor Svcs., Tom Findlay; Artistic Dir., Susan Warner.
Institution Type/Description: Art Museum.
Hours & Admission Prices: Memorial Day to Labor Day daily; Sept.-May Wed.-Sun. Adults $15; discounts to children, seniors, students, military, AAA members & EBT cardholders; members no charge. Closed New Year's Day; Thanksgiving; Christmas. &
Attendance: 130,000 (estimated)

PACIFIC LUTHERAN UNIVERSITY GALLERY, Dept. of Art & Design, Ingram Hall, Tacoma, WA 98447. Tel.: 253-535-7150. Fax: 253-536-5063.
E-mail: soac@plu.edu
Web Site: www.plu.edu/gallery
Key Personnel: Prof. Heather Mathews.
Institution Type/Description: University Art Gallery.
Hours & Admission Prices: Mon.-Fri. 9-4. No charge.

POINT DEFIANCE ZOO & AQUARIUM, 5400 N. Pearl St., Tacoma, WA 98407-3224. Tel.: 253-404-3800.
E-mail: comments@pdza.org
Web Site: www.pdza.org
Key Personnel: Dir., Alan Varsik; Deputy Dir., Sarah Oliver.
Institution Type/Description: Zoo & Aquarium.
Hours & Admission Prices: Hours vary throughout the year, call or visit Web site for detailed information. Adults $17, senior citizens 65 & up $16, youth 5-12 $11, tots 3-4 $6.75; discounts to military & Pierce County residents; children under 2 no charge. Closed Thanksgiving; Christmas. &
Attendance: 500,000 (actual)

SHANAMAN SPORTS MUSEUM, 2727 E. "D" St. (Tacoma Dome), Tacoma, WA 98421-1216. Mailing Address: 9908-63rd Ave. Ct. E., Puyallup, WA 98373-1170. Tel.: 253-627-5857.
E-mail: marc@tacomasportsmuseum.com
Web Site: www.tacomasportsmuseum.com
Key Personnel: Pres., Marc Blau.
Institution Type/Description: Sports Museum.
Hours & Admission Prices: Open during sporting events & trade shows; other times by appointment. No charge when attending sporting event; donations accepted.
Attendance: 4,376

SPANAWAY HISTORICAL SOCIETY & PRAIRIE HOUSE MUSEUM, 812 E. 176th St. E., Tacoma, WA 98387. Mailing Address: Spanaway Historical Society, P.O. Box 1238, Spanaway, WA 98387. Tel.: 253-536-6655. Facebook:.
E-mail: celebratespanaway@earthlink.net
Web Site: www.celebratespanaway.com/PrairieHouse.htm
Institution Type/Description: Historical Society Museum: housed in an 1880s farm house.
Hours & Admission Prices: Wed. 11-2, 3rd Sun. each month 2-4. No charge; donations accepted.

TACOMA ART MUSEUM, 1701 Pacific Ave., Tacoma, WA 98402-3214. Tel.: 253-272-4258. Fax: 253-627-1898.
E-mail: info@tacomaartmuseum.org
Web Site: www.tacomaartmuseum.org
Key Personnel: Dir., Mark Holcomb; Pres. (V), Steve Harlow; Deputy Dir., Teresa Macaluso; Chief Cur., Rock Hushka; Dir. Education, Samantha Kelly; Dir. Devel., Tobin Eckholt; Dir. Mktg. & Communications, Alyce McNeil.
Institution Type/Description: Art Museum.
Hours & Admission Prices: Tues.-Sun. 10-5. Adults $15, student, military and seniors 65 & over $13; discounts to families, AAM members; third Thurs. of the month, members, and children 5 & under no charge. Closed New Year's Day; Independence Day; Labor Day; Thanksgiving; Christmas. &
Attendance: 80,000 (actual)

TACOMA HISTORICAL SOCIETY, 919 Pacific Ave., Tacoma, WA 98401. Mailing Address: P.O. Box 1865, Tacoma, WA 98401-1865. Tel.: 253-472-3738. Facebook: Tacoma Historical Society.
E-mail: info@tacomahistory.org
Web Site: www.tacomahistory.org
Key Personnel: Pres., Bill Baarsma; Museum Shop Mgr., Debby Freedman.
Institution Type/Description: Historical Society.
Hours & Admission Prices: Wed.-Sat. 12-5. No charge, donations accepted. discounts to WMA members. &
Attendance: 2,000 (estimated)

TACOMA PUBLIC LIBRARY/THOMAS HANDFORTH GALLERY, 1102 Tacoma Ave., S., Tacoma, WA 98402-2098. Tel.: 253-292-2001 ext. 1111.
E-mail: ddomkoski@tacomapubliclibrary.org
Web Site: www.tpl.lib.wa.us
Key Personnel: Library Dir., Susan Odencrantz; Media Rels. Officer, David Domkoski.
Institution Type/Description: Public Library & Art Gallery: housed in 1903 Carnegie Building.
Hours & Admission Prices: Tues.-Wed. 11-8, Thurs.-Sat. 9-6. No charge. &
Attendance: 1,600,000

W.W. SEYMOUR BOTANICAL CONSERVATORY, 316 South G St., Tacoma, WA 98405-4733. Tel.: 253-591-5330. Fax: 253-627-2192.
E-mail: wwseymour@tacomaparks.com
Web Site: www.metroparkstacoma.org/conservatory/
Key Personnel: Natural Resources Supvr., Mary Anderson; Horticulture Technician, Tyra Shenaurlt; Natural Resources Mgr., Joe Brady.
Institution Type/Description: Botanical Garden: museum housed in Victorian styled conservatory with twelve-sided central dome containing two side wings & an entry wing.
Hours & Admission Prices: Tues.-Sun. 10-4:30. Suggested Donation: $3. Closed New Year's Day; Thanksgiving; Christmas. &
Attendance: 78,000

WASHINGTON STATE HISTORICAL SOCIETY & HISTORY MUSEUM, 1911 Pacific Ave., Tacoma, WA 98402-3109. Tel.: 253-272-3500; 888-BE-THERE. Fax: 253-272-9518. Facebook; Twitter.
E-mail: receptionist@wshs.wa.gov
Web Site: www.washingtonhistory.org
Key Personnel: Dir., Jennifer Kilmer; Financial Svcs. Dir., Teresa Mattson; Human Resources Mgr., Kathy Tarli; Mktg. & Communications Dir., Julianna Verboort; Dir. Philanthropy, Camille Perezselsky; Heritage Capital Projects Mgr., Lissa Kramer; Editor Columbia Magazine, Feliks Banel.
Institution Type/Description: History Museum.
Hours & Admission Prices: Tues.-Sun. 10-5, 3rd Thurs. each month 10-8. Adults $14, seniors, students 6-17 & active duty military $11; discounts to AAA members; children 5 & under, members & third Thurs. of month 2-8 no charge. Closed Memorial Day; Independence Day; Labor Day; Thanksgiving Day; Christmas Eve & Day. &
Attendance: 81,670 (actual)

Tenino

TENINO DEPOT MUSEUM, 399 W. Park, Tenino, WA 98589. Mailing Address: P.O. Box 339, Tenino, WA 98589-0339. Tel.: 360-264-4321.
Web Site: www.teninodepotmuseum.org
Key Personnel: Pres., Bob Hill.
Institution Type/Description: Local History Museum.
Hours & Admission Prices: mid-April to mid-Oct. Sat.-Sun. 12-4. No charge; donations accepted. &
Attendance: 1,800 (estimated)

Toppenish

MARY L. GOODRICH LIBRARY & TOPPENISH HISTORICAL MUSEUM, One S. Elm, Toppenish, WA 98948-1574. Tel.: 509-865-3600.
E-mail: kcorbray@yvl.org
Web Site: www.yvl.org
Formerly: Toppenish Museum
Key Personnel: Mng. Librarian, Krystal Corbray.
Institution Type/Description: History Museum: housed in 1923 first Agency Building for the Yakima Indian Nation.
Hours & Admission Prices: Mon.-Thurs. 10-7, Fri.-Sat. 10-5.

NORTHERN PACIFIC RAILWAY MUSEUM, 10 Asotin Ave., Toppenish, WA 98948-0889. Mailing Address: P.O. Box 889, Toppenish, WA 98948-0889. Tel.: 509-930-7210 (Curator).
E-mail: srmeodell@gmail.com
Web Site: www.nprymuseum.org
Formerly: Yakima Valley Rail & Steam Museum
Key Personnel: Cur. & Archivist, Larry Rice; Treas., Dennis Lee; Gift Shop Mgr., Roger O'Dell; Gift Shop Mgr., Mary O'Dell.
Institution Type/Description: Railway Museum.
Hours & Admission Prices: May-Oct. 15 Tues.-Sat. 10-4, Sun. 12-4. Adults $5, children 12 & under $3; discount to groups & Northern Pacific Railway Historical Association members; members no charge. &
Attendance: 4,700 (actual)

YAKAMA NATION MUSEUM, 118 Spiel-yi Loop, Toppenish, WA 98948. Mailing Address: P.O. Box 151, Toppenish, WA 98948-0151. Tel.: 509-865-2800. Fax: 509-865-5749. Facebook: Yakama Nation Cultural Center.
E-mail: heather@yakama.com
Web Site: www.yakamamuseum.com
Key Personnel: Tribal Chm., Jo De Goudy; Photograph Collection, Liz Antelope; Mgr. Collections, Heather Hull.
Institution Type/Description: Tribal Museum: located on the Yakama Indian Reservation.
Hours & Admission Prices: Daily 8-5. Family $15, adults $6, senior citizens 55 & up, active military, & children 11-18 $4, children 10 & under $2. Guided Tours: $25. Closed New Year's Day; Thanksgiving; Christmas. &
Attendance: 70,000 (estimated)

Union Gap

CENTRAL WASHINGTON AGRICULTURAL MUSEUM, 4508 Main St., Union Gap, WA 98903-2138. Tel.: 509-457-8735. Facebook: Central Washington Agricultural Museum.
E-mail: info@centralwaagmuseum.org
Web Site: centralwaagmuseum.org
Key Personnel: Pres. (V), Nick Schultz; Vice Pres., Wally Moen; Treas., Dick Drew; Sec., Marty Humphrey.
Institution Type/Description: Agricultural Museum.
Hours & Admission Prices: Museum: April-Oct. Tues.-Sat. 10-4, Sun. 1-4. Grounds: dawn to dusk. No charge; donations accepted. Host lives on grounds. &
Attendance: 8,500 (estimated)

Vancouver

THE ARCHER GALLERY, Clark College, Penguin Student Union Bldg., 1933 Fort Vancouver Way, Vancouver, WA 98663-3501. Tel.: 360-992-2246. Fax: 360-992-2888.
E-mail: mhirsch@clark.edu
Web Site: www.clark.edu
Key Personnel: Dir., Marjorie Hirsch.
Institution Type/Description: Art Gallery.
Hours & Admission Prices: Tues.-Thurs. 10-7, Fri.-Sat. 12-5. No charge; donations accepted. &
Attendance: 5,000 (estimated)

CLARK COUNTY HISTORICAL SOCIETY & MUSEUM, 1511 Main St., Vancouver, WA 98660-2945. Mailing Address: P.O. Box 61916, Vancouver, WA 98666. Tel.: 360-993-5679. Fax: 360-993-5683.
E-mail: cchm@pacifier.com
Web Site: www.cchmuseum.org
Key Personnel: Exec. Dir., Katie Anderson.
Institution Type/Description: General Museum.
Hours & Admission Prices: Tues.-Sat. 11-4, 1st Thurs. of month call for additional hours. Adults $4, seniors & students $3, children 6-18 $2; discounts to WMA, AAM & ICOM members; members, active military and children 5 & under no charge. Closed major holidays. &
Attendance: 15,000 (estimated)

FORT VANCOUVER NATIONAL HISTORIC SITE, 612 E. Reserve St., Vancouver, WA 98661-3897. Tel.: 360-816-6200. Fax: 360-816-6363.
E-mail: FOVA_superintendent@nps.gov
Web Site: www.nps.gov/fova
Key Personnel: Park Supt., Tracy Fortmann; Cur. Park, Theresa Langford; Chief Ranger, Greg Shine; Museum Shop Mgr., Mike true.
Institution Type/Description: Historic Site: site of Old Fort Vancouver, administrative headquarters & supply depot for the Hudson's Bay Company 1829-1860.

Hours & Admission Prices: Call for hours & admission prices. Closed Thanksgiving; Christmas Eve & Day. &
Attendance: 1,000,000 (estimated)

PEARSON AIR MUSEUM, 1115 E. 5th St., Vancouver, WA 98661-3802. Tel.: 360-816-6232. Fax: 360-816-6363. Facebook: Pearson Air Museum.
E-mail: bob_cromwell@nps.gov
Web Site: www.nps.gov/fova/learn/historyculture/pearson.htm
Key Personnel: Mgr., Robert Cromwell; Coord. Special Park Uses, Eva Dodd.
Institution Type/Description: Aeronautics Museum: located on the Army Air Corps CA 1921-1941 Pearson Field.
Hours & Admission Prices: Tues.-Sat. 9-5. No charge; donations accepted. Closed New Year's Day; Thanksgiving; Christmas. &
Attendance: 51,686 (actual)

Vantage

GINKGO PETRIFIED FOREST STATE PARK, Interstate 90, Exit 136, Vantage, WA 98950. Mailing Address: P.O. Box 1203, Vantage, WA 98950-1203. Tel.: 509-856-2700. Fax: 509-856-2294.
Web Site: parks.wa.gov
Key Personnel: Area Mgr., Jim Mitchell.
Institution Type/Description: State Park Museum.
Hours & Admission Prices: Summer: daily 6:30am to dusk. Winter: Sat.-Sun. 8am to dusk. Suggested Donation $1.
Attendance: 35,000 (actual)

Vashon

VASHON-MAURY ISLAND HERITAGE MUSEUM, 10105 S.W. Bank Rd., Vashon, WA 98070-4645. Mailing Address: P.O. Box 723, Vashon, WA 98070-0723. Tel.: 206-463-7808.
E-mail: admin@vashonheritage.org
Web Site: www.vashonheritage.org
Key Personnel: Pres., Deb Dammann; Vice Pres., Brian Breeno; Treas., Steve Church; Sec., Katherine Golding; Corresponding Sec., Hunter Davis; Museum Shop Mgr., Barbara Cooper.
Institution Type/Description: History Museum.
Hours & Admission Prices: Wed.-Sun. 1-4. No charge; donations accepted. &
Attendance: 2,300 (estimated)

Vaughn

KEY PENINSULA HISTORICAL SOCIETY, 17010 S. Vaughn Rd., Vaughn, WA 98394. Tel.: 253-888-3246.
E-mail: kphsmuseum@gmail.com
Web Site: www.keypeninsulamuseum.org
Key Personnel: President, Judy A. Mills.
Institution Type/Description: Historical Society and Museum.
Hours & Admission Prices: Tues. & Sat. 1-4; call to confirm. No charge; donations accepted.

Walla Walla

FORT WALLA WALLA MUSEUM, 755 Myra Rd., Walla Walla, WA 99362-8035. Tel.: 509-525-7703. Fax: 509-525-7798. Facebook: Fort Walla Walla Museum.
E-mail: info@fwwm.org
Web Site: fwwm.org
Key Personnel: Exec. Dir., James Payne; Pres., Linda Emmerson; Bookkeeper, Carolyn Burdine; Collection Mgr., Laura Schulz; Tour Coord., Bill Lake; Programs, Abigaill Scholar; Mgr. Bldgs. & Grounds, James Klees; Museum Shop Mgr., Kt Sharkey; Exec. Asst., Carolyn Keyes.
Institution Type/Description: Pioneer Settlement & Agricultural Museum: housed on the 1858 military reservation of Old Ft. Walla Walla. General history.
Hours & Admission Prices: March-Oct. daily 10-5; Nov.-Feb. daily 10-4; tours by appointment. Adults $8, senior citizens & students $7, children 6-12 $3; discounts to AAA members & Time Travelers; members and children 5 & under no charge. &
Attendance: 25,100 (actual)

KIRKMAN HOUSE MUSEUM, 214 N. Colville St., Walla Walla, WA 99362-1917. Tel.: 509-529-4373. Fax: 509-529-4373.
E-mail: khm@kirkmanhousemuseum.org
Web Site: www.kirkmanhousemuseum.org
Key Personnel: Pres. (V), Kent Settle.
Institution Type/Description: Historic House Museum: built in 1880. Listed on the National Register of Historic Places.

Hours & Admission Prices: Wed.-Sat. 10-4, Sun. 10-2. Adults $7; members no charge.
Attendance: 3,072

SHEEHAN GALLERY AT WHITMAN COLLEGE, Olin Hall, 814 Isaacs, Walla Walla, WA 99362. Mailing Address: 345 Boyer Ave., Walla Walla, WA 99362-2083. Tel.: 509-527-5249. Fax: 509-527-5039.
E-mail: forbesdm@whitman.edu
Web Site: www.whitman.edu/sheehan/sheehan_mission.html
Key Personnel: Interim Dir., Dawn Forbes; Pres. Whitman College. Thomas E. Cronin; Pres. Bd. Trustees, Charles E. Anderson; Dean Faculty, Patrick Keef, Ph.D.; Treas., Peter Harvey; Collections & Exhibitions Mgr., Kynde Kiefel.
Institution Type/Description: Art Museum/Center.
Hours & Admission Prices: Sept.-May Mon.-Fri. 12-5, Sat.-Sun. 12-4. No charge; donations accepted. Closed spring breaks; Christmas. &
Attendance: 12,000 (estimated)

WHITMAN MISSION NATIONAL HISTORIC SITE, 328 Whitman Mission Rd., Walla Walla, WA 99362-7299. Tel.: 509-522-6360. Fax: 509-522-6355. TDD: 509-522-6357.
E-mail: stephanie_martin@nps.gov
Web Site: www.nps.gov/whmi
Institution Type/Description: Park Museum.
Hours & Admission Prices: Historic Site: daily 8-4:30; Visitor Center: Spring to Fall Wed.-Sun. 9-4. No charge; donations accepted. Historic Site & Visitor Center closed federal holidays. &
Attendance: 70,000 (actual)

Washougal

TWO RIVERS HERITAGE MUSEUM, 1 Durgan St., Washougal, WA 98671. Mailing Address: P.O. Box 204, Washougal, WA 98671-0204. Tel.: 360-835-8742. Facebook.
E-mail: referenceroom@trhm.comcastbiz.net
Web Site: www.2rhm.com
Key Personnel: Pres., James Cobb; Chm. (V), Lois Cobb.
Institution Type/Description: History Museum.
Hours & Admission Prices: Thurs.-Sat. 11-3. Adults $5, seniors 60 & over $4, students $2; discounts to AAA members; members & children under 5 no charge. &
Attendance: 1,000 (estimated)

Wenatchee

ROBERT GRAVES GALLERY, Wenatchee Valley College, 1300 5th St., Wenatchee, WA 98801-1741. Tel.: 509-682-6776.
E-mail: robertgravesgallery@wvc.edu
Web Site: www.wvc.edu
Formerly: Gallery '76
Key Personnel: Bd. Pres. (V) & Acting Coord., John Crew.
Institution Type/Description: Art Gallery.
Hours & Admission Prices: Mon. 8-8, Tues.-Thurs. 9-1; other times by appointment. No charge; donations accepted. Closed holidays. &
Attendance: 4,500 (actual)

ROCKY REACH DAM, 5000 State Hwy. 97A N., Wenatchee, WA 98801-2011. Mailing Address: P.O. Box 1231, Wenatchee, WA 98807-1231. Tel.: 509-663-7522. Fax: 509-661-8149. Facebook.
E-mail: debbie.gallaher@chelanpud.org
Web Site: www.chelanpud.org
Key Personnel: C.E.O., Steve Wright; Museum Shop Mgr., Debbie Gallaher.
Institution Type/Description: General Interpretive Museum.
Hours & Admission Prices: March-Oct. daily 9-4. No charge. &
Attendance: 62,000 (actual)

WENATCHEE VALLEY MUSEUM AND CULTURAL CENTER, 127 S. Mission St., Wenatchee, WA 98801-3039. Tel.: 509-888-6240. Fax: 509-888-6256. Facebook: Wenatchee Museum.
E-mail: info@wvmcc.org
Web Site: www.wvmcc.org
Formerly: North Central Washington Museum
Key Personnel: Dir., Sandy Cohen; Pres. (V), Jewl Cripe; Deputy Dir., Marriah Thornock; Cur. Exhibits & Programs, Kasey Koski; Education Coord., Selina Danko; Administrative Svcs. Mgr., Anna Spencer; Museum Shop Mgr., Carol Hofmann; Cur. Collections, Melanie Wachholder; Mktg. Dir., Lyn Kelley; Development Dir., Nicolle LaFleur.
Institution Type/Description: General Museum.

Hours & Admission Prices: Tues.-Sat. 10-4. Adults $5, seniors $4, children 6-12 $2; members & children under 6 no charge. Closed major holidays. &
Attendance: 36,156 (estimated)

West Seattle

SOUTH SEATTLE COMMUNITY COLLEGE ART GALLERY, South Seattle Community College, Jerry Brockey Student Center, West Seattle, WA 98106. Mailing Address: 6000 16th Ave., S.W., Seattle, WA 98106-1499. Tel.: 206-934-5337. Fax: 206-934-5807.
E-mail: mktko.masker@seattlecolleges.edu
Web Site: www.southseattle.edu/student-life/art-gallery/
Key Personnel: Gallery Coord., Jessica Heide.
Institution Type/Description: Art Gallery.
Hours & Admission Prices: Mon.-Fri. 9-3. No charge. Closed school holidays & breaks.
Attendance: 4 (actual)

Westport

WESTPORT MARITIME MUSEUM, 2201 Westhaven Dr., Westport, WA 98595. Mailing Address: P.O. Box 1074, Westport, WA 98595-1074. Tel.: 360-268-0078. Facebook: Westport Maritime Museum.
E-mail: operations@westportmaritimemuseum.com
Web Site: www.westportmaritimemuseum.com
Key Personnel: Exec. Dir., John Shaw; Opers. Mgr. & Education Coord., Julie Smith.
Institution Type/Description: Maritime Museum.
Hours & Admission Prices: Memorial Day to Labor Day Thurs.-Mon. 10-4; Labor Day to Memorial Day Thurs.-Mon. 12-4.
Attendance: 18,000 (actual)

White Swan

FORT SIMCOE STATE PARK, 5150 Fort Simcoe Rd., White Swan, WA 98952-9745. Tel.: 509-874-2372. Fax: 509-874-2351.
E-mail: infocent@parks.wa.gov
Formerly: Fort Simcoe Interpretive Center
Key Personnel: Park Mgr., Jim Mitchell.
Institution Type/Description: Military Museum: housed in 1856-59 military outpost.
Hours & Admission Prices: Summer: 6:30am to dusk. No charge.

Winlock

JOHN R. JACKSON HOUSE, Lewis & Clark State Park, Winlock, WA 98596. Mailing Address: 4583 Jackson Hwy., Winlock, WA 98596-9646. Tel.: 360-864-2643.
Key Personnel: Dir., Rex Derr; Chief Interpretive Svcs., Steve Wang.
Institution Type/Description: Historic House Museum: 1850 John R. Jackson Home.
Hours & Admission Prices: House: April-Sept. 8am to dusk; tours by appointment. No charge; donations accepted. &

Winthrop

SHAFER HISTORICAL MUSEUM, 285 Castle Ave., Winthrop, WA 98862. Mailing Address: P.O. Box 46, Winthrop, WA 98862-0046. Tel.: 509-996-2712.
E-mail: staff@shafermuseum.com
Web Site: shafermuseum.com
Institution Type/Description: Historic Buildings: listed in the National Register of Historical Places.
Hours & Admission Prices: Memorial Day to Labor Day Thurs.-Mon. 10-5. Adults $2; members no charge.
Attendance: 20,000 (estimated)

Yakima

LARSON GALLERY, 1015 S. 16th Ave., Yakima Valley College, Yakima, WA 98902. Mailing Address: P.O. Box 22520, Yakima, WA 98907-2520. Tel.: 509-574-4875. Fax: 509-574-6826. TDD: 509-574-4600; Facebook: Larson Gallery; Instagram: @larsongallery; Twitter: @larsongalleryg.
E-mail: gallery@yvcc.edu
Web Site: www.larsongallery.org
Key Personnel: Dir., David Lynx; Pres. (V), Teresa Pritchard; Project Mgr., Randy La Pierre; Registrar, Haylee Olsen.
Institution Type/Description: Art Gallery.

Hours & Admission Prices: Sept.-July 14 Tues.-Sat. 10-5. No charge, donations accepted. &
Attendance: 10,000 (actual)

MCALLISTER MUSEUM OF AVIATION, 2008 S. 16th Ave., Yakima, WA 98903. Tel.: 509-457-4933.
E-mail: mcallister@nwinfo.net
Web Site: mcallistermuseum.org
Institution Type/Description: Aviation Museum: housed in a former flight school owned by Charlie & Alister McAllister.
Hours & Admission Prices: Thurs.-Fri. 10-4, Sat. 9-4.

YAKIMA AREA ARBORETUM & BOTANICAL GARDEN, 1401 Arboretum Dr., Yakima, WA 98901. Tel.: 509-248-7337. Fax: 509-248-8197. Facebook: Yakima Area Arboretum.
E-mail: info@ahtrees.org
Web Site: www.ahtrees.org
Key Personnel: Co-Exec. Dir., Colleen Adams-Schuppe; Co-Exec. Dir., Jheri Ketcham; Pres. (V), Leslie Wahl; Groundkeeper, Jeff Neal; Nature Science Dir., Jacob Belsher; Care Taker, Joy Howell; Care Taker, Bob Howell; Facility Mgr., Gaye McCarthy.
Institution Type/Description: Arboretum & Botanical Garden.
Hours & Admission Prices: Daily dawn to dusk. Visitor Center: Mon.-Sat. 9-5. No charge; donations accepted. &
Attendance: 10,000 (estimated)

YAKIMA VALLEY MUSEUM AND HISTORICAL ASSOCIATION, 2105 Tieton Dr., Yakima, WA 98902-3766. Tel.: 509-248-0747. Fax: 509-453-4890.
E-mail: info@yakimavalleymuseum.org
Web Site: www.yakimavalleymuseum.org
Key Personnel: Exec. Dir., Peter Arnold; Pres. (V), Juana Rezaie; Cur. Collections, Michael Siebol; Guest Svcs. Mgr., Cheryl Thyken.
Institution Type/Description: Historical Museum.
Hours & Admission Prices: Mon.-Sat. 10-5. Families $12, adults $5, students & senior citizens $3; discounts to AASLH, AAA, ICOM & AAM members; members & children under 6 no charge. &
Attendance: 27,000 (estimated)

WEST VIRGINIA

(136 listings)

Anstead

AFRICAN AMERICAN HERITAGE FAMILY TREE MUSEUM, Logtown Rd., Anstead, WV 25812. Mailing Address: P.O. Box 369, Amsted, WV 25812. Tel.: 304-658-5528.
E-mail: normanjordan@pocketmail.com
Institution Type/Description: History Museum.
Hours & Admission Prices: Summer: by appointment.

Ansted

CONTENTMENT, Rte. 60, Ansted, WV 25812. Mailing Address: HC 66 Box 94B, Hico, WV 25854-7468.
Institution Type/Description: Historic House Museum: housed in the former home of Civil War Col. George Imboden.
Hours & Admission Prices: June-Aug. Mon.-Sat. 10-4.

Arthurdale

ARTHURDALE HERITAGE, INC., Q & A Rds., Arthurdale, WV 26520. Mailing Address: P.O. Box 850, Arthurdale, WV 26520-0850. Tel.: 304-864-3959. Fax: 304-864-4602. Facebook: Arthurdale Heritage, Inc.
E-mail: ahi@arthurdaleheritage.org
Web Site: www.arthurdaleheritage.org
Key Personnel: Dir., Jeanne Goodman; Pres. (V), Randy Weaver; Museum Shop Mgr., Theresa Marthey.
Institution Type/Description: Historic Site: housed in several buildings constructed in 1930s when Arthurdale became the first New Deal homestead.
Hours & Admission Prices: May-Oct. Tues.-Sat. 11-3, Sun. 1-5; Nov.-April Tues.-Fri. 11-3; other times by appointment. Adults $10, seniors $9, children $3; discounts to groups of 10 or more & AAA members; members and children 5 & under no charge. Closed holidays. &
Attendance: 5,000 (estimated)

Athens

CONCORD COLLEGE ARTHUR BUTCHER ART GALLERY, Alexander Fine Arts Center, Athens, WV 24712. Mailing Address: P.O. Box 1000, Athens, WV 24712-1000. Tel.: 304-384-3115.
Institution Type/Description: Art Gallery.
Hours & Admission Prices: Mon.-Thurs. 9-4.

Aurora

AURORA AREA HISTORICAL SOCIETY, 23976 George Washington Hwy., Aurora, WV 26705. Mailing Address: P.O. Box 100, Aurora, WV 26705. Tel.: 304-288-6850.
E-mail: jadams2823@aol.com
Institution Type/Description: Historical Society Museum: housed in a former general store; built c.1850.
Hours & Admission Prices: Call for hours.

Barboursville

DAUGHTERS OF THE AMERICAN REVOLUTION TOLL HOUSE MUSEUM, 731 Main St., Barboursville, WV 25705. Mailing Address: 214 Forestview Dr, Huntington, WV 25705. Tel.: 304-652-2922.
Institution Type/Description: Historic House Museum: housed in a former toll house originally located on the Guyan River bank to collect tolls from ferry riders; built in 1837.
Hours & Admission Prices: By appointment.

Beckley

EXHIBITION COAL MINE & YOUTH MUSEUM, 513 Ewart Ave., Beckley, WV 25801. Tel.: 304-256-1747 & 252-3730.
E-mail: lgbharley@beckleymine.com
Web Site: beckley.org/entertainment
Institution Type/Description: Mining Museum.
Hours & Admission Prices: April-Nov. 1 daily 10-6.

RALEIGH COUNTY VETERANS MUSEUM, 1557 Harper Rd., Beckley, WV 25801-3307. Mailing Address: P.O. Box 3165, Beckley, WV 25801-1945. Tel.: 304-253-1775.
Web Site: rcvm.org
Institution Type/Description: Veterans Museum.
Hours & Admission Prices: April-Oct. Fri.-Sat. 1-7, Sun. 1-5; other times by appointment. Adults $2, children 12 & under $.50.

WILDWOOD HOUSE MUSEUM, 121 Laurel Ter., Beckley, WV 25801-4217. Mailing Address: P.O. Box 2514, Beckley, WV 25802-2514. Tel.: 304-252-3730. Fax: 304-252-3764.
E-mail: info@beckleymine.com
Web Site: beckley.org
Key Personnel: Dir. & C.E.O., Leslie Baker.
Institution Type/Description: Historic House: housed in the former home of General Alfred Beckley; built in 1836. Listed on the National Register of Historic Places.
Hours & Admission Prices: April-Nov. Sat.-Sun. 10-6 Adults $5.
Attendance: 1,000 (estimated)

YOUTH MUSEUM OF SOUTHERN WEST VIRGINIA, 509 Ewart Ave., Beckley, WV 25802. Mailing Address: P.O. Box 2514, Beckley, WV 25802-2514. Tel.: 304-252-3730. Fax: 304-252-3764. Facebook: Youth Museum of SWV.
E-mail: info@beckleymine.com
Web Site: beckley.org
Key Personnel: Exec. Dir. & C.E.O., Leslie Gray Baker; Museum Shop Mgr., Donna Clark Totten.
Institution Type/Description: Youth Museum.
Hours & Admission Prices: April-Nov. 1 daily 10-6; Nov. 2-March Tues.-Sat. 10-5. Call for rate schedule. Adults $5. Closed New Year's Day; Christmas. &
Attendance: 50,000 (estimated)

Berkeley Springs

MUSEUM OF THE BERKELEY SPRINGS, Fairfax & Wilkes St., Berkeley Springs, WV 25411. Mailing Address: P.O. Box 99, Berkeley Springs, WV 25411-0099. Tel.: 800-447-8797.
E-mail: history@museumoftheberkeleysprings.com
Web Site: www.museumoftheberkeleysprings.com

Key Personnel: Pres., David Milburn; Vice Pres., Betty Lou Harmison; Treas., Susan Winkeler-Milburn; Exec. Dir. & Museum Shop Mgr., Tamme Marggraf.

Institution Type/Description: History Museum: housed in the c.1820 Roman Bath building in Berkeley Springs State Park.

Hours & Admission Prices: Feb.-Dec. Sat.-Sun. 11-4; call for additional hours. No charge; donations accepted.

Attendance: 8,476 (actual)

Bethany

HISTORIC BETHANY - ALEXANDER CAMPBELL MANSION, Bethany College, Rte. 67 E., Bethany, WV 26032. Mailing Address: HIstoric Bethany, 31 E Campus Dr., Bethany, WV 26032-3002. Tel.: 304-829-4258. Fax: 304-829-4258.

E-mail: historic@bethanywv.edu

Key Personnel: Program Dir. & Archivist, Sharon Monigold.

Institution Type/Description: Historic Mansion: housed in the former home of Bethany College founder, Alexander Campbell; built c.1794. Listed on the National Register of Historic Places.

Hours & Admission Prices: April-Oct. Tues.-Fri. 10-12 & 1-4; other times by appointment. Adults $4; youth 1-12 grade $2; discounts to AAM & AAA members. Closed holidays. &

Attendance: 3,500 (estimated)

Beverly

BEVERLY HERITAGE CENTER, One Court St., Beverly, WV 26253. Tel.: 304-637-7424.

E-mail: info@beverlyheritagecenter.org

Web Site: www.historicbeverly.org/bevhcent.htm

Institution Type/Description: Heritage Center.

Hours & Admission Prices: Call for hours.

RANDOLPH COUNTY MUSEUM (AT BEVERLY), Main St., Beverly, WV 26253. Mailing Address: P.O. Box 342, Elkins, WV 26241-1164. Tel.: 304-636-0841, 304-334-2125 (Pres.).

E-mail: dlrice@suddenlink.net

Key Personnel: C.E.O. (V) & Pres. (V), Donald Teter; Acting Cur. & Archivist, Donald Rice.

Institution Type/Description: History Museum: housed in the Blackman-Bosworth Store building.

Hours & Admission Prices: Museum late-May to early-Oct. Thurs.-Sat. 11-4; openings for special events; other times by appointment. No charge; donations requested.

Attendance: 700 (estimated)

Bluefield

EASTERN REGIONAL COAL ARCHIVES & CRAFT MEMORIAL LIBRARY, 600 Commerce St., Bluefield, WV 24701. Tel.: 304-325-3943. Fax: 304-325-3702.

E-mail: cml@mail.mln.lib.wv.us

Web Site: craftmemorial.lib.wv.us

Key Personnel: Library Dir., Eva H. McGuire.

Institution Type/Description: History Museum.

Hours & Admission Prices: Archives: by appointment. Library: Mon.-Thurs. 9:30-7, Fri.-Sat. 9:30-5. No charge; donations accepted. Closed holidays.

Attendance: 237 (estimated)

THE SCIENCE CENTER OF WEST VIRGINIA, 500 Bland St., Bluefield, WV 24701-4257. Tel.: 304-325-8855. Fax: 304-324-0513.

E-mail: svanzele@smwv.org

Key Personnel: Chm. (V) & Pres. (V), Patty Wilkinson; Dir., Thomas Willmiten; Museum Shop Mgr. & Administrative Asst., Pam R. Lester.

Institution Type/Description: Science Center/Museum.

Hours & Admission Prices: June-Aug. Tues.-Sat. 10-5; Sept.-May Tues.-Thurs. 9-3, Sat. 10-4. Adults $5; discounts to groups & ASTC members; children under 2 & members no charge. Closed holidays. &

Attendance: 20,000 (estimated)

Bramwell

COAL HERITAGE TRAIL INTERPRETIVE CENTER, 100 Station Sq., Bramwell, WV 24715. Mailing Address: P.O. Box 103, Bramwell, WV 24715. Tel.: 304-248-8595.

E-mail: info@coalheritage.org

Web Site: www.coalheritage.org

Key Personnel: Dir., Richard Bullins.

Institution Type/Description: Mining Museum: housed in a former train depot.

Hours & Admission Prices: Mon.-Sat. 10-4, Sun. 11-4. No charge; donations accepted. &

Capon Bridge

CAPON BRIDGE MUSEUM, Rte. 50, Capon Bridge, WV 26711. Tel.: 304-856-2661.

Institution Type/Description: History Museum: housed in the former dental office of Dr. Gardner.

Hours & Admission Prices: Call for hours.

Ceredo

CEREDO MUSEUM, 501 Main St., Ceredo, WV 25507. Mailing Address: P.O. Box 691, Ceredo, WV 25507. Tel.: 304-453-3025.

Institution Type/Description: History Museum.

Hours & Admission Prices: Tues. & Thurs. 9-4. &

RAMSDELL HOUSE, 1108 B St., Ceredo, WV 25507. Mailing Address: P.O. Box 446, Ceredo, WV 25507-0446. Tel.: 304-453-2482.

Institution Type/Description: Historic House: housed in the home of Union Capt. Z. D. Ramsdell; built in 1858.

Hours & Admission Prices: By appointment. &

Charleston

CLAY CENTER FOR ARTS & SCIENCES WEST VIRGINIA, One Clay Sq., Charleston, WV 25301-2424. Tel.: 304-561-3570. Fax: 304-561-3598.

E-mail: info@avampatodiscoverymuseum.org

Web Site: www.theclaycenter.org

Formerly: Avampato Discovery Museum

Key Personnel: Pres. & C.E.O., Al Najjar; Vice Pres. Devel., Kathy Bush-Morris; C.F.O., Rebecca Gillespie.

Institution Type/Description: Performing & Visual Arts & Science Museum.

Hours & Admission Prices: Mon-Fri. 8:30-6, Sat. 9:30-5, Sun. 11:30-5. groups by appointment. Adults $7.50, senior citizens, teachers & children $6; discounts to groups & AAM members; museum members, children under 3 & members no charge. Closed national holidays. &

Attendance: 180,000 (actual)

CRAIK-PATTON HOUSE, 2809 Kanawha Blvd. E., Charleston, WV 25311-1727. Mailing Address: P.O. Box 175, Charleston, WV 25321. Tel.: 304-925-5341. Facebook: Craik-Patton House.

E-mail: info@craik-patton.org

Web Site: www.craik-patton.org

Key Personnel: Dir., Brianne Jackson; Dir., Paul Zuros; Pres. (V) Jessica Graney.

Institution Type/Description: Historic House Museum: built by James Craik in 1834; owned by George Smith Patton, a leader in the Confederate Army & grandfather of General George S. Patton.

Hours & Admission Prices: Mon.-Fri. 10-4, Sat.-Sun. by appointment. No charge; donations accepted.

Attendance: 1,000 (actual)

WEST VIRGINIA STATE CAPITOL, 1900 Kanawha Blvd. E., Charleston, WV 25305. Tel.: 304-558-4839.

Institution Type/Description: Historic Building: built 1924-1932. Listed on the National Register of Historic Places.

Hours & Admission Prices: Mon.-Fri. 9-6, Sat. 12-6. Closed holidays.

WEST VIRGINIA STATE MUSEUM, 1900 Kanawha Blvd., E., Charleston, WV 25305-0009. Tel.: 304-558-0220. Fax: 304-558-2779. TDD: 304-558-3562.

E-mail: charles.w.morris@wv.gov

Web Site: www.wvculture.org

Key Personnel: Commissioner, Randall Reid-Smith; Dir. West Virginia State Museum, Charles Morris, III; Coord. Exhibits, Cailin A. Howe; Dir. West Virginia Independence Hall, Deborah Jones; Dir. Grave Creek Mound Historic Site, Jeremy A. Kohus; Site Mgr. Camp Washington Carver, James Hess; Cur., James Mitchell.

Institution Type/Description: Cultural Center; History Museum.

Hours & Admission Prices: Tues.-Sat. 9-5. No charge. Closed Christmas; most holidays. &

Attendance: 120,000 (actual)

Clifftop

WEST VIRGINIA CAMP WASHINGTON-CARVER, Rte. 41 S., Clifftop, WV 25831. Mailing Address: HC 35, Box 5, Clifftop, WV 25831-9601. Tel.: 304-438-3005. Fax: 304-438-3006.
E-mail: campwashingtoncarver@wvculture.org
Web Site: www.wvculture.org/sites/carver.html
Key Personnel: Facility Mgr., George Sheaves.
Institution Type/Description: Historic Site: Park Museum/Visitor Center; camp built as first 4-H Camp for blacks in U.S.
Hours & Admission Prices: June-Oct. Mon.-Fri. call for appointment. No charge. ♿
Attendance: 10,000 (estimated)

Elizabeth

BEAUCHAMP NEWMAN MUSEUM, Court St., Elizabeth, WV 26143. Mailing Address: P.O. Box 621, Elizabeth, WV 26143-0621. Tel.: 304-275-3569.
E-mail: cmommene2@aol.com
Key Personnel: Regent, Carole Menefee.
Institution Type/Description: Historic House.
Hours & Admission Prices: Holidays & by appointment. No charge; donations accepted.

Elkins

STIRRUP GALLERY, Davis and Elkins College, Myles Center for the Arts, Elkins, WV 26241-3971. Tel.: 304-637-1341. Fax: 304-637-1238.
E-mail: morganw@elkins.edu
Web Site: www.davisandelkins.edu
Formerly: Darby's Prehistoric and Early Pioneer's Art Museum
Key Personnel: Coord., Mark Lanham.
Institution Type/Description: History Museum.
Hours & Admission Prices: Mon.-Fri. 9-5; other times by appointment. ♿

Fairmont

FRANK & JANE GABOR WEST VIRGINIA FOLKLIFE CENTER, Squibb Wilson Blvd., Fairmont, WV 26555. Mailing Address: 1201 Locust Ave., Fairmont, WV 26554. Tel.: 304-367-4403. Fax: 304-333-3604. Facebook.
E-mail: wvfolklife@fairmontstate.edu
Web Site: www.fairmontstate.edu/folklife
Formerly: Fairmont State University One Room Schoolhouse Museum
Key Personnel: Interim Dir., Patricia Musick.
Institution Type/Description: History & Folklife Museum: repurposed historic buildings.
Hours & Admission Prices: Center: Mon.-Fri. 9-3; Special Events: evenings & weekends; One-Room Schoolhouse: open by appointment. No charge. ♿
Attendance: 1,500 (estimated)

MARION COUNTY HISTORICAL SOCIETY MUSEUM, INC., 210 Adams St., Fairmont, WV 26554-2826. Mailing Address: P.O. Box 1636, Fairmont, WV 26555-1636. Tel.: 304-367-5398. Facebook: Marion County Historical Society.
E-mail: marionhistorical@yahoo.com
Web Site: www.marionhistorical.org
Key Personnel: Pres. (V), Dora Kay Grubb; Museum Shop Mgr., Betty Andrews.
Institution Type/Description: Historical Society Museum: housed in the Marion County Sheriffs' home from 1913-1985. Listed on the National Historic Register of Landmarks.
Hours & Admission Prices: Mon.-Sat. 10-2; tours by appointment. No charge; donations accepted.
Attendance: 2,000 (actual)

PRICKETTS FORT, Rte. 3, Fairmont, WV 26554-9470. Mailing Address: c/o Pricketts Fort Memorial Foundation, 88 State Park Rd., Fairmont, WV 26554. Tel.: 304-363-3030. Fax: 304-363-3857.
E-mail: info@prickettsfort.org
Web Site: www.prickettsfort.org
Key Personnel: Exec. Dir., Greg Bray; Asst. Dir., Jessica Kittle.
Institution Type/Description: Historic Site & House: c.1859 Job Prickett House & 18th century civilian refuge fort.
Hours & Admission Prices: mid-April to May & Sept.-Oct. Wed.-Sat. 10-5, Sun. 12-5; Memorial Day to Labor Day Mon.-Sat. 10-5, Sun. 12-5. Adults $8, senior citizens $6, children 6-12 $4; discounts to Frontiers to Mountaineers, tour groups, AAA & CAA members; members & children under 6 no charge. ♿
Attendance: 13,652 (actual)

French Creek

WEST VIRGINIA STATE WILDLIFE CENTER, 163 Wildlife Rd., French Creek, WV 26218-1400. Tel.: 304-924-6211. Fax: 304-924-6781.
E-mail: eugene.r.thorn@wv.gov
Web Site: www.dnr.state.wv.us/wvwildlife/wildlifectr.htm
Key Personnel: Dir. WV Div. Natural Resources, Frank Jezioro; Biologist, Eugene Thorn; Museum Shop Mgr., Joann Kruk.
Institution Type/Description: Zoo.
Hours & Admission Prices: April & Sept.-Oct. daily 9-5; May-Aug. daily 9-6; Nov.-March daily 9-3. Adults $3, children 3-15 $1.50; discounts to groups & Golden Mountaineer members; children under 3 no charge. Annual passes also available. ♿
Attendance: 40,000 (estimated)

Grafton

ANNA JARVIS BIRTHPLACE MUSEUM, Rte. 119/250 S., Grafton, WV 26354. Mailing Address: 3576 Webster Pike, Grafton, WV 26354-9643. Tel.: 304-265-5549.
E-mail: ajhouse26354@yahoo.com
Web Site: ww.annajarvismuseum.com
Key Personnel: Dir., Olive Ricketts.
Institution Type/Description: Historic House Museum: housed in the birthplace of Anna Jarvis, the founder of Mother's Day.
Hours & Admission Prices: April-Dec. Tues.-Sat. 10-2. Adults $5; discounts to AAA & AAM members; children under 6 no charge.
Attendance: 500 (estimated)

INTERNATIONAL MOTHERS DAY SHRINE AND MUSEUM, 11 E. Main St., Grafton, WV 26354-1322. Mailing Address: P.O. Box 513, Grafton, WV 26354-0513. Tel.: 304-265-1589.
E-mail: info@mothersdayshrine.com
Institution Type/Description: Historic Church: built in 1873. Listed on the National Register of Historic Places.
Hours & Admission Prices: April 15-Oct. 15 Fri.-Sat. 10-4, Sun. 12-4; groups & other times by appointment. No charge; donations accepted. Closed holidays.

Green Bank

NATIONAL RADIO ASTRONOMY OBSERVATORY - GREEN BANK SCIENCE CENTER, Rte. 28/92, Green Bank, WV 24944-0002. Mailing Address: P.O. Box 2, Green Bank, WV 24944-0002. Tel.: 304-456-2011. Fax: 304-456-2229.
Institution Type/Description: Science Center.
Hours & Admission Prices: Memorial Day to Labor Day daily 8:30-7; Sept.-Oct. Thurs.-Mon. 8:30-7. Closed New Year's Eve & Day; Easter; Thanksgiving; Christmas Eve & Day.

Harpers Ferry

THE APPALACHIAN TRAIL CONSERVANCY, 799 Washington St., Harpers Ferry, WV 25425-6587. Mailing Address: P.O. Box 807, Harpers Ferry, WV 25425-0807. Tel.: 304-535-6331. Fax: 304-535-2667.
E-mail: info@appalachiantrail.org
Web Site: www.appalachiantrail.org
Key Personnel: Exec. Dir., David N. Startzell; Chm. (V), Bob Almand; Treas., Kennard Honick; Dir. Devel., Royce Gibson; Foundation & Corp. Rels. Mgr., Amy McCormick; Gift Shop Mgr., Laurie Potteiger.
Institution Type/Description: Appalachian Trail Maintenance Association: housed in 1892 building.
Hours & Admission Prices: Daily 9-5. No charge; donations accepted. Closed New Year's Day; Washington's Birthday; Columbus Day; Thanksgiving & day after; Christmas. ♿
Attendance: 29,000 (estimated)

HARPERS FERRY NATIONAL HISTORICAL PARK, Fillmore St., Harpers Ferry, WV 25425. Mailing Address: P.O. Box 65, Harpers Ferry, WV 25425-0065. Tel.: 304-535-6224. Fax: 304-535-6244.
E-mail: hfha@earthlink.net
Web Site: www.nps.gov/hafe
Key Personnel: Rgnl. Dir., Robert Vogel; Supt., Rebecca L. Harriett; Chief Ranger, Ryan Levins; Cultural Resources Mgr., Mia Parsons; Museum Shop Mgr., Cathy Baldau; Lands Management Asst., Andrew Lee; Education Specialist, Stan McGee; Visitor Svcs., Todd P.H. Bolton; Volunteers & Outreach, Samantha Zurbuch.

Institution Type/Description: National Historic Park: approx. 56 restored buildings & Civil War fortifications.

Hours & Admission Prices: Summer: daily 8-6; Winter: daily 8-5. Admission: $10 per car or $5 per person 17-62 (7 day pass); seniors, children 16 & under and Interagency Pass holders no charge. Annual Pass: $30. &

Attendance: 350,000 (estimated)

JOHN BROWN WAX MUSEUM INC., 168 High St., Harpers Ferry, WV 25425. Tel.: 304-535-6342.
E-mail: info@johnbrownwaxmuseum.com
Web Site: www.johnbrownwaxmuseum.com
Formerly: National Historical John Brown Wax Museum
Key Personnel: Mgr., Ann Fern.
Institution Type/Description: Wax Museum: housed in c.1820 historic town building.
Hours & Admission Prices: March 15-March 31 & Dec. 1-Dec. 15 Sat.-Sun. 9-4:30; Spring & Fall daily 9-4:40; Summer daily 10-5:30; call to confirm. Adults $7, senior citizens 60 & up $6, child 6-12 $5; discounts to groups of 10 or more; children under 6 no charge.

Helvetia

HELVETIA MUSEUM, Historic Sq., Helvetia, WV 26224-9999. Mailing Address: 120 Betler Ridge, Helvetia, WV 26224-0042. Tel.: 304-924-5455.
Key Personnel: Pres. & Chm. (V), Eleanor L. Betler; Mgr., Bruce Cressler.
Institution Type/Description: Historical & Preservation Society: housed in 1871 Betler Cabin.
Hours & Admission Prices: May-Sept. Sat.-Sun. 12-4; other times by special arrangement. No charge; donations accepted.
Attendance: 500 (estimated)

Hillsboro

PEARL S. BUCK BIRTHPLACE FOUNDATION, 8129 Seneca Trail, Hillsboro, WV 24946. Tel.: 304-653-4430.
E-mail: info@pearlsbuckbirthplace.com
Web Site: www.pearlsbuckbirthplace.com
Key Personnel: Gen. Mgr., Phyllis Lubin-Tyler; Pres. (V), Kirk Judd; Vice Pres. (V), Cara Rose.
Institution Type/Description: Historic House: Stulting House built by maternal ancestors; Sydenstricker house built by paternal ancestors.
Hours & Admission Prices: late May to Oct. Mon. & Fri.-Sat. 10-4, Sun. 1-4; group tours 10 & over by appointment. Adults $6, senior citizens $5, students $3; children under 6 no charge. &
Attendance: 2,000 (estimated)

Hinton

CAMPBELL FLANNAGAN MURRELL HOUSE, INC., 422 Summer St., Hinton, WV 25951-2221. Tel.: 304-445-5769. Facebook: Campbell Flannagan Murrell House, Inc..
E-mail: cfm_fmh@yahoo.com
Web Site: cfm-fmh.org
Formerly: Campbell Flannagan Murrell House
Key Personnel: Pres. (V), Dwight Emrich.
Institution Type/Description: Historic House Museum: built in 1875. Listed on the National Register of Historic Places.
Hours & Admission Prices: Call for hours. No charge; donations accepted.
Attendance: 234 (actual)

HINTON RAILROAD MUSEUM, 206 Temple St., Hinton, WV 25951-2331. Tel.: 304-466-5420. Fax: 304-466-5420.
Key Personnel: Dir., Dorothy Jean Boley.
Institution Type/Description: Railroad Museum.
Hours & Admission Prices: Summer: Mon.-Sat. 10-4. Winter: Mon.-Sat. 10-2. No charge; donations accepted. &

VETERANS MEMORIAL MUSEUM, 419 Ballengee St., Hinton, WV 25951. Mailing Address: P.O. Box 694, Hinton, WV 25951-0694. Tel.: 304-466-4443.
Institution Type/Description: Military History Museum.
Hours & Admission Prices: May-Nov. Fri.-Sat. 12-4; other times by appointment.

Huntington

BENJY'S HARLEY-DAVIDSON, 408 4th St., Huntington, WV 25701-1315. Tel.: 304-523-1340. Fax: 304-523-5474.
E-mail: info@benjyshd.com
Institution Type/Description: Motorcycle Museum.

Hours & Admission Prices: Mon.-Thurs. 10-6, Fri. 10-9, Sat. 10-2:30. No charge.

BIRKE ART GALLERY - MARSHALL UNIVERSITY, Dept. of Art & Design, One John Marshall Dr., Huntington, WV 25755. Tel.: 304-696-2296.
E-mail: galleries@marshall.edu
Web Site: www.marshall.edu/art/birke-art-gallery
Institution Type/Description: University Art Gallery.
Hours & Admission Prices: Mon.-Fri. 10-4. No charge. Closed during summer. &

CHARLES W. AND NORMA C. CARROLL GALLERY-MARSHALL UNIVERSITY, Visual Arts Center, 927 Third Ave., Huntington, WV 25701. Tel.: 304-696-7299.
E-mail: galleries@marshall.edu
Web Site: www.marshall.edu/art/vac
Institution Type/Description: University Art Gallery.
Hours & Admission Prices: Mon.-Fri. 10-4. No charge. Closed during the summer. &

COLLIS P. HUNTINGTON RAILROAD HISTORICAL SOCIETY, INC., 1323 8th Ave., Huntington, WV 25701-2919. Mailing Address: P.O. Box 393, Huntington, WV 25708-0393. Tel.: 866-639-7487, 304-523-0364. Fax: 304-523-0366. Facebook: New River Train.
E-mail: newrivertrain@aol.com
Web Site: www.newrivertrain.com
Formerly: Huntington Railroad Museum
Key Personnel: Pres., Duane Legg; Vice Pres., Brian Cavender; Dir., Chris Lockwood; Dir., David Webb; Dir., Eugene Bosh; Dir., Skip Reinhard; Dir., Ernie Clay.
Institution Type/Description: Transportation Museum.
Hours & Admission Prices: Call for hours. No charge; donations accepted.
Attendance: 6,800 (estimated)

GEOLOGY MUSEUM, Marshall University, One John Marshall Dr., Huntington, WV 25755. Mailing Address: Dept. of Geology, 176 Science Bldg., Huntington, WV 25755. Tel.: 304-696-6720. Fax: 304-696-3243.
E-mail: martinor@marshall.edu
Web Site: www.marshall.edu/geology
Key Personnel: Chm., Dr. William Niemann; Geology Dept., Dr. Ronald L. Martino; Geology Dept., Dr. Aley El-Shazly.
Institution Type/Description: Geology Museum.
Hours & Admission Prices: Mon.-Fri. 8-4:30. No charge. Closed university holidays. &

HERITAGE FARM MUSEUM & VILLAGE, 3300 Harvey Rd., Huntington, WV 25704-9112. Tel.: 304-522-1244. Fax: 304-523-6115.
E-mail: hfmv@comcast.net
Web Site: www.heritagefarmmuseum.com
Key Personnel: Chm. (V), A. Michael Perry; Pres. (V), Henriella Perry.
Institution Type/Description: History Museum.
Hours & Admission Prices: March-Nov. Mon.-Sat. 10-3. Guided Tours: adults 13-64 $8, senior citizens 65 & over $7, children 3-12 $6; discounts to groups of 15 or more; children 2 & under no charge. Closed holidays. &
Attendance: 5,000 (estimated)

HUNTINGTON MUSEUM OF ART, INC., 2033 McCoy Rd., Huntington, WV 25701-4999. Tel.: 304-529-2701. Fax: 304-529-7447.
Web Site: www.hmoa.org
Key Personnel: Exec. Dir., Margaret Mary Layne.
Institution Type/Description: Art Museum & Conservatory Gardens: includes 50 acres of woodlands & the C. Fred Edwards Conservatory.
Hours & Admission Prices: Tues. 10-9, Wed.-Sat. 10-5, Sun. 12-5. Adults $5; discounts to SEMC & AAM members; members, children under 18, military & Tues. no charge. Closed New Year's Eve & Day; Independence Day; Thanksgiving; Christmas Eve & Day. &
Attendance: 45,448 (actual)

MADIE CARROLL HOUSE PRESERVATION SOCIETY, INC., 234 Guyan St., Huntington, WV 25702-1526. Mailing Address: P. O. Box 3266, Huntington, WV 25702-0266. Tel.: 304-736-1655.
E-mail: knnance@comcast.net
Web Site: www.madiecarrollhouse.org

Key Personnel: Pres. (V), Johnny Nance; Vice Pres., Mary Jo Martin; Recording Sec., Karen N. Nance; Cur., Greg Miller; Corresponding Sec., Easter Miller; Treas., Robert Edmunds.
Institution Type/Description: Historic House Museum: built c.1810.
Hours & Admission Prices: By appointment. No charge; donations accepted.
Attendance: 2,000 (estimated)

MUSEUM OF RADIO & TECHNOLOGY, INC., 1640 Florence Ave., Huntington, WV 25701-4546. Tel.: 304-525-8890.
E-mail: wvradiomuseum@gmail.com
Web Site: www.mrtwv.org
Key Personnel: Pres., Geoffrey Bourne; Vice Pres., Dave Bond; Treas., Judy Taylor; Sec., David Spears; Librarian, Bill Reich; Education, Fred Crews; Public Rels., Garry Ritchie; Public Rels., Jack Woodrum.
Institution Type/Description: Technology Museum: housed in c.1931 school building.
Hours & Admission Prices: Jan.-April call for hours; May-Dec. Fri.-Sat. 10-4, Sun. 1-4. No charge; donations accepted. &
Attendance: 5,000 (estimated)

Lesage

JENKINS PLANTATION MUSEUM, 8814 Ohio River Rd., Lesage, WV 25537. Mailing Address: c/o West Virginia Division of Culture and History, 1900 Kanawha Blvd. E., Charleston, WV 25305-0300. Tel.: 304-762-1059.
E-mail: Jeremy.A.Kohus@wv.gov
Institution Type/Description: History Museum: housed in the former home of Captain William Jenkins and General Albert Gallatin Jenkins; built in 1863.
Hours & Admission Prices: Temporarily closed.

Lewisburg

CARNEGIE HALL MUSEUM, 116 Church St., Lewisburg, WV 24901-1303. Tel.: 304-645-7917. Fax: 304-645-5228.
E-mail: info@carnegiehallwv.com
Web Site: www.carnegiehallwv.com
Key Personnel: Exec. Dir., Sara Crickenberger; Artistic Dir., Lynn Creamer.
Institution Type/Description: Art Museum.
Hours & Admission Prices: Mon.-Fri. 9-4:30, Sat. 10-1. No charge. &

GREENBRIER HISTORICAL SOCIETY, INC. - NORTH HOUSE MUSEUM, 301 W. Washington St., Lewisburg, WV 24901-1324. Tel.: 304-645-3398. Fax: 304-645-5201. Facebook: Greenbrier Historical Society.
E-mail: info@greenbrierhistorical.org
Web Site: www.greenbrierhistorical.org
Key Personnel: Dir., Nick LaCasse; Pres. (V), Margaret Hambrick; Treas., John B. Arbuckle, Jr.; Museum Coord., Toni Ogden; Archivist, James Talbert.
Institution Type/Description: Historic House Museum: built c.1820.
Hours & Admission Prices: Mon.-Sat. 10-4. No charge; donations accepted. Closed most major holidays. &
Attendance: 5,000 (estimated)

GREENBRIER MILITARY SCHOOL MEMORIAL MUSEUM, 400 N. Lee St., Lewisburg, WV 24901-1128. Mailing Address: P. O. Box 922, Lewisburg, WV 24901-0922. Tel.: 304-645-3247.
E-mail: gmsmary@yahoo.com
Web Site: www.gmsaa.org
Key Personnel: Cur., Mary Essig-Beatty.
Institution Type/Description: Historical Museum.
Hours & Admission Prices: Mon.-Fri. No charge. Closed holidays. &
Attendance: 450 (estimated)

LOST WORLD CAVERNS VISITOR CENTER AND NATURAL HISTORY MUSEUM, 308 HC 34, Lewisburg, WV 24901. Mailing Address: 907 Lost World Rd., Lewisburg, WV 24901. Tel.: 304-645-6677, 866-228-3778.
Web Site: www.lostworldcaverns.com
Institution Type/Description: Natural History Museum & Visitor's Center.
Hours & Admission Prices: Jan.-March 1 Sat.-Sun. 10-4; March to May daily 10-5; Memorial Day to Labor Day daily 9-7; Sept.-Nov. 23 daily 9-5; Nov. 24-Dec. daily 10-4. Adults 13 & over $12, children 6-12 $6; discounts to groups; children under 6 no charge. Closed Thanksgiving; Christmas.

Logan

MUSEUM IN THE PARK, Chief Logan State Park, 376 Little Buffalo Creek Rd., Logan, WV 25601. Tel.: 304-792-7229.

E-mail: chieflogansp@wv.gov
Web Site: www.chiefloganstatepark.com/activities.html
Institution Type/Description: Park Museum.
Hours & Admission Prices: Jan. to late Nov. Wed.-Sat. 10-6, Sun. 1-6; late Nov. to Dec. call for hours. No charge. &

Lost Creek

WATTERS SMITH MEMORIAL STATE PARK & LIVING HISTORY MUSEUM, Duck Creek Rd., Lost Creek, WV 26385. Mailing Address: P.O. Box 296, Lost Creek, WV 26385-0296. Tel.: 304-745-3081. Fax: 304-745-3631.
E-mail: watterssmithsp@wv.gov
Web Site: www.watterssmithstatepark.com
Key Personnel: Supt., Larry A. Jones.
Institution Type/Description: Historic House & State Park: located on site of 1876 Watters Smith Farm.
Hours & Admission Prices: Memorial Day-Labor Day daily 11-7. No charge; donations accepted. &

Lost River

LOST RIVER MUSEUM, Harper Barn, Rte. 259, Lost River, WV 26810. Mailing Address: P.O. Box 26, Lost River, WV 26810-0026. Tel.: 304-897-7242.
E-mail: lrac@hardynet.com
Key Personnel: Dir., Dan W. Blumhagen, Ph.D.; C.E.O., Timothy Wheeler.
Institution Type/Description: History Museum.
Hours & Admission Prices: Call for hours. No charge; donations accepted. &
Attendance: 400 (estimated)

Madison

BITUMINOUS COAL HERITAGE FOUNDATION MUSEUM, 347 Main St., Madison, WV 25130-1221. Tel.: 304-369-5180 & 9118. Fax: 304-369-9130.
E-mail: boonedevcorp@yahoo.com
Web Site: wvcoalmuseum.org
Key Personnel: Pres., Joy Underwood; Sec. & Treas., Larry V. Lodato.
Institution Type/Description: History Museum.
Hours & Admission Prices: Mon.-Fri. 12-4.

Mannington

WEST AUGUSTA HISTORICAL SOCIETY MUSEUM, 917 E. Main St., Mannington, WV 26582. Mailing Address: P.O. Box 414, Mannington, WV 26582. Tel.: 304-986-1252, 1298 & 2636.
Key Personnel: Dir., Nany Ult; Chm. (V), Normz Wilcox; Pres. (V), Beverly Jones; Museum Shop Mgr., Esther Sturm.
Institution Type/Description: Historical Society Museum: housed in the former Wilson School, built in 1912.
Hours & Admission Prices: May-Sept. Mon.-Fri. 9-2, Sun. 1-4; other times by appointment. No charges; donations accepted. &
Attendance: 230 (actual)

Marlinton

POCAHONTAS COUNTY MUSEUM, 17890 Seneca Trail, Marlinton, WV 24954. Mailing Address: P.O. Box 453, Marlinton, WV 24954. Tel.: 304-799-4369. Fax: 304-799-6466. Facebook.
E-mail: wpmcneel@gmail.com
Web Site: www.pocahontashistorical.org
Key Personnel: Pres. (V), Joseph Smith; Librarian & Historian, William P. McNeel.
Institution Type/Description: Local History & Historical Society Museum: housed in the Frank & Anna Hunter Home.
Hours & Admission Prices: Memorial Day-Labor Day Mon.-Sat. & holidays 11-5, Sun. 1-5. Families $10, adults $4, children 12-17 $2; discounts to groups; members & children under 12 no charge.
Attendance: 660 (actual)

Martinsburg

THE ARTS CENTRE, INC., 300 W. King St., Martinsburg, WV 25401-3202. Tel.: 304-263-0224. Fax: 304-263-0857.
Web Site: www.theartcentre.org
Key Personnel: Pres., Mary Lewis; Prog. Coord., Justis Saradji.
Institution Type/Description: Art Museum.
Hours & Admission Prices: Call for hours.

BERKELEY COUNTY MUSEUM - BERKELEY COUNTY HISTORICAL SOCIETY, 136 E. Race St., Martinsburg, WV 25401-4310. Mailing Address: P.O. Box 1624, Martinsburg, WV 25401. Tel.: 304-267-4713.
E-mail: bchs@bchs.org
Web Site: bchs.org
Formerly: Belle Boyd House Museum - Berkeley County Historical Society
Key Personnel: Pres. (V), Todd Funkhouser.
Institution Type/Description: Historical Society Museum.
Hours & Admission Prices: Open Mon.-Sun. 9-5. No charge, donations accepted. Closed all major holidays.
Attendance: 1,546 (actual)

GENERAL ADAM STEPHEN HOUSE, 309 E. John St., Martinsburg, WV 25402. Mailing Address: General Adam Stephen Memorial Association, P.O. Box 1496, Martinsburg, WV 25402-1496. Tel.: 304-267-4434.
Web Site: www.orgsites.com/wv/adam-stephen
Key Personnel: Pres. (V), Martin Keesecker; Cur., Keith E. Hammersla.
Institution Type/Description: Historic House: 1772-1789 Gen. Adam Stephen House.
Hours & Admission Prices: May-Oct. Sat.-Sun. 2-5; other times by appointment. No charge; donations accepted. &
Attendance: 2,500 (estimated)

TRIPLE BRICK MUSEUM, 313 E. John St., Martinsburg, WV 25401. Mailing Address: c/o General Adam Stephen Memorial Association, P.O. Box 1496, Martinsburg, WV 25402. Tel.: 304-267-4434.
E-mail: adamstephenhouse@gmail.com
Web Site: www.orgsites.com/wv/adam-stephen
Institution Type/Description: History Museum: housed in a former apartment building; built c.1874.
Hours & Admission Prices: Call for hours.

Mathias

LOST RIVER STATE PARK, 321 Park Dr., Mathias, WV 26812-8088. Tel.: 304-897-5372. Fax: 304-897-5325.
E-mail: lostriversp@wv.gov
Web Site: www.lostriversp.com
Key Personnel: Park Supt., Mike Foster; Asst. Supt., Colby Caldwell.
Institution Type/Description: Park Museum & Historic House: housed in Lee House Museum; built by Charles Carter Lee, as a summer retreat for son of Henry (Light Horse Harry) Lee; built in 1800.
Hours & Admission Prices: Memorial Day-Labor Day Sat. 11-4, Sun.11-3. Office: Mon.-Fri. 8-4, Sat.-Sun. 10-3; other times by appointment. No charge.

Middlebourne

TYLER COUNTY HERITAGE & HISTORICAL SOCIETY, Dodd St., Middlebourne, WV 26149. Mailing Address: P.O. Box 317, Middlebourne, WV 26149-0317. Tel.: 304-758-2100 & 4288.
E-mail: tchandhs@verizon.net
Key Personnel: Pres. (V), Ruth Moore; Chm. (V), Peggy Shields; Museum Shop Mgr., Lonnie Doak.
Institution Type/Description: Historic Building: housed in the former Tyler County High School; built in 1908.
Hours & Admission Prices: May-Oct. Sun., Tues. & Thurs. 1-4; tours by appointment. No charge; donations accepted. &
Attendance: 1,200 (estimated)

Mineral Wells

NEW ERA ONE-ROOM SCHOOL - LIVING HERITAGE MUSEUM, 1838 Elizabeth Pike, Mineral Wells, WV 26150. Mailing Address: P.O. Box 340, Mineral Wells, WV 26150-0340. Tel.: 304-863-3583. Facebook: New Era One Room School.
E-mail: esthercarroll@casinternet.net
Web Site: www.neweraoneroomschool.com
Institution Type/Description: History Museum: housed in one-room school built in 1884.
Hours & Admission Prices: May-Oct. Tues. 1-3; other times by appointment. No charge; donations accepted.

Morgantown

COOK-HAYMAN PHARMACY MUSEUM, 1132 Health Sciences North, 1st Fl., Morgantown, WV 26506. Mailing Address: P.O. Box 9500, Morgantown, WV 26506-9500. Tel.: 304-293-7806.
E-mail: wvusoppr@hsc.wvu.edu
Web Site: pharmacy.hsc.wvu.edu
Institution Type/Description: Pharmacy Museum.
Hours & Admission Prices: By appointment; No charge; donations accepted. &
Attendance: 50 (estimated)

CORE ARBORETUM, Monongahela Blvd., Rte. 7, WVU Evansdale Campus, Morgantown, WV 26506. Mailing Address: Dept. of Biology, P.O. Box 6057, Morgantown, WV 26506-6057. Tel.: 304-293-6670. Fax: 304-293-6363.
E-mail: jweems@wvu.edu
Web Site: www.wvu.edu/biology/facility/arboretum.html
Key Personnel: Arboretum Specialist, Jonathan Weems.
Institution Type/Description: Arboretum & Botanical Gardens.
Hours & Admission Prices: Daily dawn-dusk. No charge.
Attendance: 30,000 (estimated)

EASTON ROLLER MILL, Easton Mill Rd., Morgantown, WV 26507-0127. Mailing Address: P.O. Box 127, Morgantown, WV 26507-0127. Tel.: 304-594-2290.
Key Personnel: Chm. (V), Richard Walters.
Institution Type/Description: History Museum: mill built in 1867 Listed on the National Register of Historic Places.
Hours & Admission Prices: Call for hours. No charge; donations accepted.
Attendance: 250 (estimated)

MONONGALIA ARTS CENTER, 107 High St., Morgantown, WV 26505-5412. Mailing Address: P.O. Box 239, Morgantown, WV 26507-0239. Tel.: 304-292-3325. Fax: 304-292-3326.
E-mail: info@monartscenter.com
Web Site: www.monartscenter.com
Key Personnel: Exec. Dir., Ro Brooks; Gen. Admin. & Cur., Clint Fisher; Media & Adv. Coord., Lauren Riviello; Theatre Coord., Roger Banks; Museum Lobby Mgr., Danny Gibbons.
Institution Type/Description: Arts & Culture Center.
Hours & Admission Prices: Mon.-Fri. 11-7, Sat. 11-4, Sun. by appointment. Closed major holidays. &

MORGANTOWN HISTORY MUSEUM, 175 Kirk St., Morgantown, WV 26505. Tel.: 304-319-1800. Facebook; Twitter.
E-mail: info@morgantownhistorymuseum.org
Web Site: www.morgantownhistorymuseum.org
Key Personnel: Chm. (V), Pamela A. Ball.
Institution Type/Description: History Museum.
Hours & Admission Prices: Tues.-Sat. 10-4. No charge; donations accepted. Closed New Year's Day; Memorial Day; Independence Day; Veterans Day; Thanksgiving; Christmas. &
Attendance: 3,450 (estimated)

THE ROYCE J. & CAROLINE B. WATTS MUSEUM, 334 Mineral Resources Bldg., Morgantown, WV 26506. Mailing Address: West Virginia University, Box 6070, Morgantown, WV 26506-6070. Tel.: 304-293-4609. Fax: 304-293-5708.
E-mail: wattsmuseum@mail.wvu.edu
Web Site: www.cemr.wvu.edu/wattsmuseum
Formerly: Comer Museum
Key Personnel: Dir., Danielle M. Petrak; C.E.O., Royce J. Watts.
Institution Type/Description: Industrial History Museum.
Hours & Admission Prices: Mon., Wed. & Fri. 1-4; other times by appointment. No charge. &
Attendance: 2,000 (estimated)

SPARK! IMAGINATION AND SCIENCE CENTER, Mountaineer Mall, Ste. #G-12, 5000 Greenbag Rd., Morgantown, WV 26501. Mailing Address: P.O. Box 104, Morgantown, WV 26507. Tel.: 304-292-4646, 309-287-6271.
E-mail: info@sparkwv.org
Formerly: Children's Discovery Museum of West Virginia
Key Personnel: Exec. Dir., Julie Bryan; Education Coord., Tiffany Martin; Coord. Operations, Christy Thompson.
Institution Type/Description: Children's Museum.
Hours & Admission Prices: Tues.-Sat. 10-1. Admission $3.50; children under one no charge.

WEST VIRGINIA UNIVERSITY-MESAROS GALLERIES, Creative Arts Center, Evansdale Campus, West Virginia University, Douglas O. Blaney Lobby, Morgantown, WV 26506-6111. Mailing Address: P.O. Box 6111, Div. of Art, Morgantown, WV 26506-6111. Tel.: 304-293-4841, ext. 3210. Fax: 304-293-5731.
E-mail: bob.bridges@mail.wvu.edu
Web Site: artanddesign.wvu.edu/mesaros_galleries
Key Personnel: Dean & Dir., Bernard Schultz; Chm., Paul Krainik; Cur., Robert Bridges.
Institution Type/Description: College Art Gallery.
Hours & Admission Prices: Mon.-Sat. 12-9:30. No charge. Closed university holidays. &
Attendance: 20,000 (actual)

Moundsville

FOSTORIA GLASS MUSEUM, 511 Tomlinson Ave., Moundsville, WV 26041. Mailing Address: P.O. Box 826, Moundsville, WV 26041-0826. Tel.: 304-845-9188. Fax: 304-845-9188.
E-mail: fostoriaglassmuseum@frontier.com
Web Site: www.fostoriaglass.org
Key Personnel: Dir. & Pres. (V), Jim Davis; Chm. & Museum Shop Mgr., Ralph C. Clark.
Institution Type/Description: Glass Museum.
Hours & Admission Prices: March-Nov. Wed.-Sat. 1-4. Suggested Donation: adults $6; members no charge. Closed holidays. &
Attendance: 1,000 (estimated)

GRAVE CREEK MOUND ARCHAEOLOGICAL COMPLEX, 801 Jefferson Ave., Moundsville, WV 26041-2241. Mailing Address: P.O. Box 527, Moundsville, WV 26041-0527. Tel.: 304-843-4128. Fax: 304-843-4131.
E-mail: david.e.rotenizer@wv.gov
Web Site: www.wvculture.org/museum/GraveCreekmod.html
Formerly: Grave Creek Mound Historic Site
Key Personnel: Site Mgr., David E. Rotenizer.
Institution Type/Description: Adena Culture Mound, Interpretive Museum, & State Cultural Facility.
Hours & Admission Prices: Museum: Tues.-Sat. 9-5, Sun. 12-5. Mound & Gift Shop: Tues.-Sat. 9-4:30, Sun. 12-4:30. No charge; donations accepted. Closed holidays. &
Attendance: 30,000 (actual)

MARX TOY MUSEUM, 915 2nd St., Moundsville, WV 26041-1422. Tel.: 304-845-6022.
E-mail: museum@marxtoymuseum.com
Web Site: www.marxtoymuseum.com
Key Personnel: Owner, Francis Turner.
Institution Type/Description: Toy Museum.
Hours & Admission Prices: April-Dec. Tues.-Sat. 11-5; other times by appointment. Adults $8.50, seniors $7.50, students $5; discounts to groups; children under 6 no charge. &

WEST VIRGINIA PENITENTIARY, 818 Jefferson Ave., Moundsville, WV 26041-2235. Tel.: 304-845-6200. Fax: 304-843-4146.
E-mail: cas@wvpentours.com
Web Site: www.wvpentours.com
Key Personnel: Pres. (V), Sid Grisell; Dir., Paul Kirby; Museum Shop Mgr., Tom Stiles.
Institution Type/Description: Penitentiary Museum.
Hours & Admission Prices: April-Nov. Tues.-Sun. 11-4. Adults $10; discounts to senior citizens, school & church groups and U.S. military. Closed holidays.
Attendance: 30,000 (actual)

Mullens

TWIN FALLS STATE PARK & MUSEUM, RR 97, Mullens, WV 25882. Mailing Address: P.O. Box 667, Mullens, WV 25882-0667. Tel.: 304-294-4000. Fax: 304-294-5000.
E-mail: twinfallsinfo@wv.gov
Web Site: www.twinfallsresort.com
Key Personnel: Supt., A. Scott Durham.
Institution Type/Description: State Park & Historic House: 1920 Old Severt Home.
Hours & Admission Prices: Memorial Day-Labor Day daily 10-6. No charge; donations accepted.

New Cumberland

HANCOCK COUNTY MUSEUM, 1008 Ridge Ave., New Cumberland, WV 26047-9501. Mailing Address: P.O. Box 672, New Cumberland, WV 26047-0672. Tel.: 304-564-4800 & 374-4884. Fax: 304-387-1427. Facebook: Hancock County Museum.
E-mail: vivianweigel@hotmail.com
Web Site: hancockcountymuseum.com
Key Personnel: Dir. & Pres. (V), Vivian Weigel; Treas., Robert McNeil.
Institution Type/Description: Historic House Museum: housed in the Victorian home of Oliver Sheridan Marshall, past president of the WV State Senate; built in 1887.
Hours & Admission Prices: Sun. 12:30-4; other times by appointment. No charge; donations accepted. &
Attendance: 500 (estimated)

Nitro

NITRO WORLD WAR I BOOMTOWN MUSEUM, 302 21st St., Nitro, WV 25143-1738. Mailing Address: P.O. Box 308, Nitro, WV 25143-0308. Tel.: 304-546-4460 & 755-1405.
E-mail: nitrowarmuseum@yahoo.com
Web Site: nitrowarmuseum.com
Institution Type/Description: Military Museum.
Hours & Admission Prices: Fri. 9-2, Sat. 9 to noon.

Oceana

WYOMING COUNTY HISTORICAL MUSEUM, Cook Pkwy. & Logan St., Oceana, WV 24870. Mailing Address: P.O. Box 2041, Oceana, WV 24870. Tel.: 304-682-5096.
E-mail: jimcook@jetbroadband.com
Web Site: wyomingcountymuseum.webs.com
Key Personnel: Dir., Jim Cook.
Institution Type/Description: Historical Society Museum.
Hours & Admission Prices: Mon. & Fri. 9-3, Sat. 10-4; other times by appointment. No charge; donations accepted. &
Attendance: 315 (actual)

Parkersburg

THE BLENNERHASSETT MUSEUM OF REGIONAL HISTORY, 137 Juliana St., Parkersburg, WV 26101-5331. Tel.: 304-420-4800.
Web Site: www.blennerhassettislandstatepark.com/museum.html
Institution Type/Description: History Museum.
Hours & Admission Prices: Call for hours. Adults $3. &
Attendance: 30,000 (estimated)

HENRY COOPER CENTENNIAL CABIN MUSEUM, 2522 Grand Ave., Parkersburg, WV 26101. Mailing Address: P.O. Box 4589, Morgantown, WV 26504-4589.
Institution Type/Description: Historic Building Museum: housed in a two-story log house built by early settler, Henry Cooper; c.1805. Listed on the National Register of Historic Places.
Hours & Admission Prices: Memorial Day to Labor Day Sun. 1:30-4:30.

OIL & GAS MUSEUM, 119 Third St., Parkersburg, WV 26101-5310. Mailing Address: P.O. Box 1685, Parkersburg, WV 26102-1685. Tel.: 304-485-5446.
E-mail: pchob3@gmail.com
Web Site: oilandgasmuseum.org
Key Personnel: Pres., Paul C. Hoblitzell, III.
Institution Type/Description: History Museum.
Hours & Admission Prices: Mon.-Sat. 11-5, Sun. 12-5. Adults $7, children $4.
Attendance: 4,000 (estimated)

PARKERSBURG ART CENTER, 725 Market St., Parkersburg, WV 26101-4628. Tel.: 304-485-3859. Fax: 304-485-3850. Facebook: The Parkersburg Art Center.
E-mail: info@parkersburgartcenter.org
Web Site: parkersburgartcenter.org
Formerly: The Cultural Center of Fine Arts
Key Personnel: Exec. Dir., Abby Hayhurst; Education & Membership Dir., Jessie Siefert; Event Coord., M.J. Ayson; Facility Coord., Dwain Hartley.
Institution Type/Description: Arts Center.

Hours & Admission Prices: Wed.-Sat. 10-5, Sun. 1-5; groups by appointment. Admission $2; discounts for AAM members; members & children under 12 no charge. Closed national holidays. &
Attendance: 18,000 (estimated)

SUMNERITE AFRICAN AMERICAN HISTORY MUSEUM, 1016 Avery St., Parkersburg, WV 26101-4727. Mailing Address: P.O. Box 4426, Parkersburg, WV 26104-4426. Tel.: 304-485-1152 & 422-0985.
Institution Type/Description: African American History Museum.
Hours & Admission Prices: By appointment.

VETERANS MUSEUM OF MID-OHIO VALLEY, 1829 7th St., Parkersburg, WV 26101-4250. Tel.: 304-420-0332 & 0337. Fax: 304-420-0337.
E-mail: veteransmuseum@hotmail.com
Web Site: veteransmuseumofmidohiovalley.com
Key Personnel: Dir., Gary Farris; Pres. (V), Ron Salter; Administrative Asst., Angela Shoemaker.
Institution Type/Description: Veterans Museum.
Hours & Admission Prices: Mon.-Sat. 10-5. Adults $3; children 12 & under $1; veterans & members no charge. Closed New Year's Day; Christmas. &
Attendance: 1,025 (estimated)

Pence Springs

GRAHAM HOUSE, Rte 3 & 12 at Lowell, Pence Springs, WV 24962. Mailing Address: 2108 Lowell Rd., Pence Springs, WV 24962-9700. Tel.: 304-466-3321 & 716-6430.
E-mail: jbowling44@yahoo.com
Web Site: www.grahamhouse.org
Key Personnel: Pres. (V), Roberta Song.
Institution Type/Description: Historic House Museum: housed in the 2 story log home of Colonel James Graham; built in 1770.
Hours & Admission Prices: Memorial Day to Labor Day Sat. 11-5, Sun. 1-5; Sept.-May by appointment only. Adults $2, children $.50; discounts to school children. &
Attendance: 1,642 (estimated)

Pennsboro

OLD STONE HOUSE MUSEUM, 310 Myles Ave., Pennsboro, WV 26415-1329. Tel.: 304-643-2738.
E-mail: info@ritchiehistoricalsociety.com
Key Personnel: Pres., David Scott.
Institution Type/Description: Historic House Museum: built c.1810. Listed on the National Register of Historic Places.
Hours & Admission Prices: By appointment.

Petersburg

TOP KICK'S MILITARY MUSEUM, 149 Army Ln., Petersburg, WV 26847. Mailing Address: P.O. Box 152, Petersburg, WV 26847-0152. Tel.: 304-257-1392.
E-mail: topkicks@hardynet.com
Web Site: www.topkicksmilitarymuseum.com
Key Personnel: Owner & Cur., Gerald W. Bland.
Institution Type/Description: Military Museum.
Hours & Admission Prices: March-Nov. Mon.-Sat. 9 am to dusk, Sun. 12 to dusk; other times by appointment. Adults $5; discounts to groups; children under 12 no charge. &
Attendance: 1,000 (estimated)

Philippi

ADALAND MANSION AND HISTORIC BARN, 324 Mansion Dr., Philippi, WV 26416. Mailing Address: P.O. Box 74, Philippi, WV 26416-0074. Tel.: 304-457-1587 & 2415. Fax: 304-457-2703.
E-mail: info1@adaland.org
Web Site: adaland.org
Key Personnel: Chm. (V), Dr. Ann Serafin; Pres. (V), Okey F. Gallien, Jr.
Institution Type/Description: Historic House Museum: housed in the former home of an early county sheriff & bank president. Listed on the National Register of Historic Places.
Hours & Admission Prices: May-Dec. Wed.-Thurs. & Sat. 11-5, Sun. 1-4. Adults $10; discounts to AAA, AAM & ICOM members; children under 12 no charge. &
Attendance: 3,485 (actual)

BARBOUR COUNTY HISTORICAL SOCIETY MUSEUM, 13 Museum St., Philippi, WV 26416-1100. Tel.: 304-457-4846.
Key Personnel: Pres. (V), Edgar Brown; Sec., Treas. & Museum Shop Mgr., Doretta Brown.
Institution Type/Description: Historical Society Museum: housed in a renovated railway station.
Hours & Admission Prices: May-Oct. Fri.-Sat. 11-4, Sun. 1-4; other times by appointment. No charge; donations accepted.
Attendance: 4,000 (actual)

ONE ROOM CAMPBELL SCHOOL, Alderson Broaddus University, 101 College Hill Dr., Box 2154, Philippi, WV 26416. Tel.: 304-457-6322. Fax: 304-457-6239.
E-mail: mcconnelljs@ab.edu
Web Site: www.ab.edu
Institution Type/Description: Historic Building: c.1865.
Hours & Admission Prices: Call for hours. No charge.
Attendance: 150 (estimated)

Point Pleasant

MOTHMAN MUSEUM, 400 Main St., Point Pleasant, WV 25550. Tel.: 304-812-5211. Facebook; Twitter.
E-mail: mothmanmuseum@gmail.com
Web Site: mothmanmuseum.com
Institution Type/Description: History Museum.
Hours & Admission Prices: Mon.-Thurs. 10-5, Fri.-Sat. 10-6, Sun. 12-5. Adults $4.50, children 10 & under $1.50. Closed New Year's Day; Easter; Thanksgiving; Christmas.

POINT PLEASANT RIVER MUSEUM, 28 Main St., Point Pleasant, WV 25550-1026. Mailing Address: P.O. Box 412, Point Pleasant, WV 25550-0412. Tel.: 304-674-0144.
E-mail: museum@pprivermuseum.com
Web Site: www.pprivermuseum.com/
Key Personnel: Exec. Dir., Jack Fowler; Pres., Clifford "Butch" Leport.
Institution Type/Description: History Museum.
Hours & Admission Prices: Tues.-Fri. 10-3, Sat. 11-4, Sun. 1-5. Adults $5, children $2; Life members no charge.

TU-ENDIE-WEI STATE PARK, 1 Main St., Point Pleasant, WV 25550-1025. Mailing Address: P.O. Box 486, Point Pleasant, WV 25550-0486. Tel.: 304-675-0869. Fax: 304-674-6162.
E-mail: tuendieweisp@wv.gov
Web Site: wvstateparks.com/park/tu-endie-wei-state-park/
Formerly: Point Pleasant Battle Monument State Park
Key Personnel: Park Supt., Doug Wiant.
Institution Type/Description: Historic House & Site: 1796, The Mansion House, built by Walter Newman, first hand-hewn log house built in Kanawha Valley, where the first battle of the Revolution was fought.
Hours & Admission Prices: May-Oct. Mon.-Sat. 10-4:30, Sun. 1-4:30; tour groups by appointment. No charge; donations accepted. &
Attendance: 40,000 (estimated)

WEST VIRGINIA STATE FARM MUSEUM, 1458 Fairground Rd., Point Pleasant, WV 25550-3421. Tel.: 304-675-5737. Fax: 304-675-5430.
E-mail: wvsfm@wvfarmmuseum.org
Web Site: www.wvfarmmuseum.org
Key Personnel: Acting Dir., Lloyd Akers; Financial Dir. & Treas., Dennis Brumfield.
Institution Type/Description: Agriculture Museum & Historic Village: over 31 buildings; largest historical farm museum east of the Mississippi River.
Hours & Admission Prices: April-Nov. 15 Tues.-Sat. 9-5, Sun. 1-5. No charge; donations accepted. Closed major holidays. &
Attendance: 100,000 (estimated)

Princeton

DR. ROBERT B. MCNUTT HOUSE MUSEUM, 1522 N. Walker St., Princeton, WV 24740. Tel.: 304-487-1502. Fax: 304-425-0227.
E-mail: pmccc@frontiernet.net
Web Site: www.pmccc.com/mcnutt_history.htm
Institution Type/Description: History Museum: housed in the former home & office of Dr. McNutt; built in 1840. Later served as a hospital and headquarters for Lt. Col. Rutherford B. Hayes and Sgt. William McKinley in May 1862. Listed on the National Register of Historic Places.
Hours & Admission Prices: Mon.-Fri. 8-5. No charge.

PRINCETON RAILROAD MUSEUM, 99 Mercer St., Princeton, WV 24740. Mailing Address: c/o Mercer County Historical Society, P.O. Box 5012, Princeton, WV 24740. Tel.: 304-487-5060.
E-mail: princetonrailroadmuseum@aol.com
Web Site: www.princetonrailroadmuseum.com
Institution Type/Description: Railroad Museum.
Hours & Admission Prices: May-Aug. Wed.-Sat. 11-4, Sun. 2-5; Sept.-April Thurs.-Sat. 11-4, Sun. 2-5; call to confirm. No charge.

THOSE WHO SERVED WAR MUSEUM, 1500 W. Main St., Princeton, WV 24740-2627. Tel.: 304-487-3670. Facebook: Those Who Served War Museum.
E-mail: mc.war.museum@gmail.com
Web Site: thosewhoseserved.shutterfly.com
Key Personnel: Pres., Michael W. Kessinger; Sec. & Treas., Rose Kessinger.
Institution Type/Description: Military History Museum.
Hours & Admission Prices: March-Nov. Mon.-Fri. 10-4. No charge; donations accepted.

Ravenswood

WASHINGTON'S WESTERN LANDS MUSEUM & SAYRE LOG HOUSE, 220 Riverfront Park, Ravenswood, WV 26164. Mailing Address: P.O. Box 324, Ravenswood, WV 26164. Tel.: 304-273-3316.
E-mail: russ2245@suddenlink.net
Key Personnel: Pres., Jackson County Historical Society, Bryan Thompson; Dir. & Sec., Jackson County Historical Society, Nancy Burford.
Institution Type/Description: Historical Society Museum: located on site of Ravenswood Land, once owned by George Washington.
Hours & Admission Prices: May-Oct. Sat.-Sun. 1-5; other dates & times by appointment. No charge; donations accepted.
Attendance: 468 (actual)

Romney

TAGGART HALL CIVIL WAR MUSEUM & VISITOR'S CENTER, 91 S. High St., Romney, WV 26757. Tel.: 304-822-4320.
Institution Type/Description: History Museum.
Hours & Admission Prices: Call for hours.

Rowlesburg

ROWLESBURG AREA HISTORICAL SOCIETY, Buffalo St., Rowlesburg, WV 26425. Mailing Address: P.O. Box 605, Rowlesburg, WV 26425-0605. Tel.: 304-454-9303.
Key Personnel: Dir. & Pres. (V), Robert Ayersman.
Institution Type/Description: Historical Society Museum.
Hours & Admission Prices: By appointment. No charge.
Attendance: 50 (estimated)

Saint Albans

C & O DEPOT MUSEUM, 404 Fourth Ave., Saint Albans, WV 25177. Mailing Address: 69 Central Ave., Saint Albans, WV 25177-2411. Tel.: 304-727-4439.
Institution Type/Description: Railroad Depot Museum: housed in the Chesapeake & Ohio Railroad Depot.
Hours & Admission Prices: By appointment only.

MORGAN'S KITCHEN PLANTATION MUSEUM, Rte. 60 MacCorkle Ave., Saint Albans, WV 25177. Mailing Address: 404 4th Ave., Saint Albans, WV 25177-2829. Tel.: 304-727-2654.
E-mail: drdallied@aol.com
Web Site: stalbanshistory.com
Key Personnel: Pres. (V), Bill Dean.
Institution Type/Description: Plantation Museum: built in 1846.
Hours & Admission Prices: Memorial Day to Labor Day Sun. 2-4; other times by appointment. No charge.
Attendance: 300 (estimated)

Scarbro

WHIPPLE COMPANY STORE & APPALACHIAN HERITAGE EDUCATIONAL MUSEUM, 7485 Okey L. Patterson Rd., Scarbro, WV 25917. Mailing Address: P.O. Box 150, Scarbro, WV 25917-0150. Tel.: 304-465-0331.
E-mail: whipple@whipplecompanystore.com
Web Site: www.whipplecompanystore.com
Institution Type/Description: Company History Museum.
Hours & Admission Prices: May-Oct. Wed.-Mon. 11-6. Tours: adults $10; children under 3 no charge.

Shepherdstown

HISTORIC SHEPHERDSTOWN MUSEUM, 129 E. German St., Shepherdstown, WV 25443. Mailing Address: P.O. Box 1786, Shepherdstown, WV 25443-1786. Tel.: 304-876-0910. Facebook: Historic Shepherdstown Museum.
E-mail: hsc1786@gmail.com
Web Site: www.historicshepherdstown.com
Key Personnel: Board Pres., Jerry Bock; HSC Admin., Teresa McLaughlin.
Institution Type/Description: Historic Building: housed in the 1786 Entler Hotel.
Hours & Admission Prices: April-Oct. Sat. 11-5, Sun. 1-4. Suggested Donation $4; discounts to students; members no charge.
Attendance: 2,637 (actual)

Shinnston

BICE-FERGUSON MEMORIAL MUSEUM, 400 Pike St., Shinnston, WV 26431-1406. Mailing Address: 40 Main St., Shinnston, WV 26431-1199. Tel.: 304-627-7876. Fax: 304-592-1597. Facebook: @bicefergusonmuseum.
E-mail: shinnstonmuseum@yahoo.com
Web Site: bice-fergusonmuseum.com
Key Personnel: Dir., Braden Noon; Chm. (V), Woody Maley.
Institution Type/Description: History Museum.
Hours & Admission Prices: April-Oct. Fri. 4-8, Sat.-Sun. 12-4; additional hours for special programs. No charge; donations accepted. Closed holidays.
Attendance: 1,200 (actual)

LEVI SHINN LOG HOUSE MUSEUM, US Rte. 19, Shinnston, WV 26431. Mailing Address: 602 Highland Ave., Shinnston, WV 26431-1026. Tel.: 304-592-5631.
Institution Type/Description: Historic House: built in 1778.
Hours & Admission Prices: Wed. by appointment.

South Charleston

GORBY'S MUSEUM OF MUSIC, 214 Seventh Ave., South Charleston, WV 25303. Tel.: 304-744-9452, 800-642-3070.
E-mail: info@gorbysmusic.com
Web Site: www.gorbysmusic.com
Institution Type/Description: Musical Instrument Museum.
Hours & Admission Prices: By appointment.

SOUTH CHARLESTON MUSEUM FOUNDATION, 311 D St., South Charleston, WV 25303-3105. Mailing Address: P.O. Box 18226, South Charleston, WV 25303. Tel.: 304-744-9711. Fax: 304-720-3769. Facebook: South Charleston Museum Foundation, Inc..
E-mail: museum@cityofsouthcharleston.com
Web Site: cityofsouthcharleston.com/attractions
Key Personnel: Dir., C.E.O. & Chm. (V), Peggy Thompson; Corresponding Sec. & Museum Shop Mgr., Judy Romano; Treas., Bill Breese; Asst. Treas., Lindell Griffith.
Institution Type/Description: History Museum.
Hours & Admission Prices: Mon.-Fri. 9-4; groups by appointment. Archives by appointment. No charge. Special events: adults $5; discounts to members. Closed major holidays.
Attendance: 5,000 (estimated)

Summersville

CARNIFEX FERRY BATTLEFIELD STATE PARK & MUSEUM, 1194 Carnifex Ferry Rd., Summersville, WV 26651-4911. Tel.: 304-872-0825, 800-225-5982. Fax: 304-872-3820.
E-mail: carnifexferrysp@wv.gov
Web Site: www.carnifexferrybattlefieldstatepark.com
Key Personnel: Supt., Samuel Cowell.

Institution Type/Description: State Park & History Museum: housed in c.1855 frame house, built by Henry Patterson.
Hours & Admission Prices: Memorial Day to Labor Day Sat.-Sun. 10-5. No charge.

Terra Alta

HISTORY HOUSE - PRESTON COUNTY HISTORICAL SOCIETY, 109 E. Washington Ave., Terra Alta, WV 26764-1203. Mailing Address: 100 Richfield Lane, Terra Alta, WV 26764. Tel.: 304-379-6612.
Key Personnel: Pres. (V), Dave Thomas; Vice Pres. & Cur., Edna Britton.
Institution Type/Description: Historical Society Museum.
Hours & Admission Prices: June-Sept. Sun.; other times by appointment. No charge; donations accepted.

RECKART'S MILL, 17 Reckart Mill Rd., RR 2, Terra Alta, WV 26764. Mailing Address: RR2 Box 31, Terra Alta, WV 26764. Tel.: 304-789-2225.
Web Site: reckart.net/r-mill.html
Key Personnel: Owner, Glenn Hardesty; Owner, Terri Hardesty.
Institution Type/Description: Historic Building: grist mill powered by a 20 ft. Filz water wheel; built in 1865.
Hours & Admission Prices: April-Oct. Sun.-Thurs. by appointment; Fri.-Sat. 10-4. &

Union

REHOBOTH CHURCH AND MUSEUM, Rte. 3, Union, WV 24983. Mailing Address: H.C. 83, P.O. Box 154, Union, WV 24983. Tel.: 304-772-3518.
Web Site: www.gcah.org
Institution Type/Description: Historic Church: built in 1786.
Hours & Admission Prices: April-Oct. Thurs.-Sat. 11-5, Sun. 1-5.

Wellsburg

BROOKE COUNTY HISTORICAL MUSEUM & CULTURE CENTER, 704 Charles St., Wellsburg, WV 26070. Tel.: 304-737-4060.
E-mail: bchmcc2012@gmail.com
Web Site: sites.google.com/site/bchmcc2012/
Key Personnel: Pres. (V), Vickey Gallagher.
Institution Type/Description: History Museum: housed in the former G.C. Murphy 5 & 10 from 1920 to 1991.
Hours & Admission Prices: April-Oct. Thurs.-Fri. & Sun. 1-5; other times by appointment. No charge; donations accepted. &

BROOKE COUNTY PUBLIC LIBRARY MUSEUM BRANCH, 945 Main St., Wellsburg, WV 26070. Tel.: 304-737-1551. Fax: 304-737-1010.
E-mail: bcpl@lycos.com
Web Site: wellsburg.lib.wv.us
Key Personnel: Chm., David Hubbard; Devel. & Public Rels., George Wallace; Education, Kimberly Harless; Treas., Edward Jackfert; Registrar, Doris Tennant; Cur., Mary Kay Wallace; Security, Jeff Cionni; Archivist, Jane Kraina; Museum Shop Mgr., Dorothy Craig.
Institution Type/Description: History Museum.
Hours & Admission Prices: Mon.-Thurs. 10-7, Fri. 10-5, Sat. 10-4. No charge; donations accepted. Closed New Year's Day; Easter; Thanksgiving; Christmas. &
Attendance: 635 (actual)

Weston

THE MOUNTAINEER MILITARY MUSEUM, Mailing Address: 345 Center Ave., Weston, WV 26452-2030. Tel.: 304-472-3943 & 516-0800.
E-mail: mountaineermilitarymuseum@yahoo.com
Web Site: mountaineermilitarymuseum.com
Key Personnel: Dir., Ron McVaney; C.E.O., Barbara McVaney.
Institution Type/Description: Military Museum: housed in the historic Colored School of Weston.
Hours & Admission Prices: Memorial Day to Oct. Fri.-Sat. 10-5; Fall & Winter: Sat. 10-5; other times by appointment. No charge; donations accepted. &
Attendance: 1,500 (estimated)

MUSEUM OF AMERICAN GLASS IN WEST VIRGINIA, 230 Main Ave., Weston, WV 26452. Mailing Address: P.O. Box 574, Weston, WV 26452-0574. Tel.: 304-269-5006. Fax: 304-269-5006.
E-mail: wvmuseumofglass@aol.com

Web Site: wvmag.bglances.com
Key Personnel: C.E.O., Dean Six; Pres. (V), Helen S. Jones.
Institution Type/Description: Glass Museum.
Hours & Admission Prices: Mon.-Tues. & Thurs.-Sat. 12-4. No charge; donations accepted.
Attendance: 2,000 (estimated)

WVU JACKSON'S MILL FARMSTEAD, WVU Jackson's Mill State 4-H Camp, 160 WVU Jackson Mill, Weston, WV 26452-8011. Tel.: 800-287-8206, ext. 7012. Fax: 304-269-3409.
E-mail: jacksons.mill@mail.wvu.edu
Web Site: www.jacksonsmill.wvu.edu
Formerly: Jackson's Mill Historic Area
Key Personnel: Heritage Program Specialist, Dean Hardman.
Institution Type/Description: Historic Building: housed on the historic site and former boyhood home of Stonewall Jackson.
Hours & Admission Prices: April to Nov. 1 Wed.-Sun. 10-5. Call for admission prices. &
Attendance: 60,000 (estimated)

Wheeling

CHILDREN'S MUSEUM OF THE OHIO VALLEY, 1000 Main St., Wheeling, WV 26003. Tel.: 304-214-5437. Fax: 304-214-5437.
E-mail: cmovkids@gmail.com
Web Site: www.cmovkids.org
Key Personnel: Pres., Amelia Parsons.
Institution Type/Description: Children's Museum.
Hours & Admission Prices: Tues.-Sat. 10-5, Sun. 12-5. Child $4, adult $2; discounts to ACM members & groups of 10 or more; members no charge. &
Attendance: 7,500 (estimated)

THE ECKHART HOUSE, 810 Main St., Wheeling, WV 26003-2530. Tel.: 304-232-5439.
E-mail: gfigaretti@gmail.com
Web Site: www.eckharthouse.com
Institution Type/Description: Historic House Museum: housed in the former home of banker, George W. Eckhart, Jr.; built in 1892. Listed on the National Register of Historic Places.
Hours & Admission Prices: Guided Tours: April-Dec. Sat. 2pm; other times by appointment. Tea Luncheons & Afternoon Tea by appointment. Closed major holidays.

GOOD ZOO AT OGLEBAY, Oglebay Park, 465 Lodge Dr., Wheeling, WV 26003-9361. Tel.: 304-243-4030. Facebook: @OglebayGoodZoo.
Web Site: www.oglebay.com
Key Personnel: C.E.O., Wheeling Park Commission, Stephen Hilliard; Zoo Dir., Joe Greathouse; Cur. Education, Vickie Markey-Tekely.
Institution Type/Description: Zoo.
Hours & Admission Prices: Daily 11-4. Adults $9.95, children 3-12 $5.95; children 2 & under and members no charge. &
Attendance: 124,575 (actual)

KRUGER STREET TOY & TRAIN MUSEUM, 144 Kruger St., Wheeling, WV 26003-5158. Tel.: 304-242-8133, 877-242-8133 (Toll Free). Fax: 304-242-1925. Facebook: @ToyandTrain.
E-mail: museum@toyandtrain.com
Web Site: www.toyandtrain.com
Key Personnel: Cur. Emeritus, Allan R. Miller; Cur., James M. Schulte; Museum Shop Mgr., Liz Hastings.
Institution Type/Description: Toy & Model Train Museum: housed in a Victorian-era schoolhouse.
Hours & Admission Prices: Jan.-May Fri.-Sun. 9-4; Memorial Day to New Year's Eve daily 9-4. Adults $10, senior citizens 65 & over $7.50, children 4-17 $5; discounts to AAA & active military; children 3 & under & members no charge. Closed New Year's Day, Easter, Thanksgiving, Christmas. &
Attendance: 20,000 (estimated)

THE MUSEUMS OF OGLEBAY INSTITUTE - MANSION MUSEUM & GLASS MUSEUM, The Burton Center, Rte. 88, Oglebay Resort, Wheeling, WV 26003. Mailing Address: 1330 National Rd., Wheeling, WV 26003-5706. Tel.: 304-242-7272. Fax: 304-242-7287.
E-mail: cbyrum@oionline.com
Web Site: www.oionline.com
Key Personnel: Dir., Christin Stein Byrum; Asst. Dir., Mary Coffman; Cur., Kara Yenkevich; Cur. Glass, Holly McCluskey.

Institution Type/Description: Decorative Arts & History Museum: housed in 1846 brick farm house renovated to be a mansion at the turn of the century.
Hours & Admission Prices: Feb.-March Sat.-Sun. 10-5; April-Oct. daily 10-5; Nov.-Dec. daily call for extended hours. One Museum: adults $7. Two Museums: adults $10; discounts to AAM & ICOM members; members and children 12 & under no charge. Closed New Year's Day; Thanksgiving; Christmas.
Attendance: 32,377 (actual)

POINT OVERLOOK MUSEUM, 989 Grandview St., Wheeling, WV 26003-3048. Tel.: 304-232-3010.
Institution Type/Description: Tourist Center & Museum.
Hours & Admission Prices: Daily 10-3. Adults $3, senior $2; children 12 & under no charge.

SCHRADER ENVIRONMENTAL EDUCATION CENTER, 1330 National Rd., Wheeling, WV 26003. Tel.: 304-242-6855. Fax: 304-242-5197.
Web Site: www.oionline.com
Key Personnel: Dir., Molly Check; Pres., Danielle McCracken.
Institution Type/Description: Nature Center.
Hours & Admission Prices: Jan.-March daily 12-5; April-Dec. Mon.-Sat. 10-5, Sun. 12-5. No charge; donations accepted.
Attendance: 45,000 (actual)

WEST VIRGINIA INDEPENDENCE HALL, 1528 Market St., Wheeling, WV 26003-3532. Tel.: 304-238-1300. Fax: 304-238-1302. Facebook: @WestVirginiaIndependenceHall.
E-mail: deborah.j.jones@wv.gov
Web Site: www.wvculture.org
Key Personnel: Site Mgr., Debbie Jones.
Institution Type/Description: History Museum & Historic Site.
Hours & Admission Prices: Tues.-Sat. 9-5; call ahead for groups & tours. No charge; donations accepted. Closed major & state holidays.
Attendance: 8,000 (estimated)

WEST VIRGINIA NORTHERN COMMUNITY COLLEGE ALUMNI ASSOCIATION MUSEUM, 1704 Market St., Wheeling, WV 26003-3643. Tel.: 304-233-5900 ext. 8817. Fax: 304-232-0965.
Web Site: www.wvncc.edu
Key Personnel: Sec. & Treas., Joan Weiskircher.
Institution Type/Description: History Museum.
Hours & Admission Prices: Call for confirmation of hours.
Attendance: 92,000 (actual)

White Sulphur Springs

PRESIDENT'S COTTAGE MUSEUM-THE GREENBRIER, 300 W. Main St., White Sulphur Springs, WV 24986-2414. Tel.: 304-536-1110, ext. 7314 & 7198. Fax: 304-536-7854.
E-mail: the_greenbrier@greenbrier.com
Web Site: www.greenbrier.com
Key Personnel: Cur., Dr. Robert S. Conte.
Institution Type/Description: History Museum: housed in 1835-1858 summer cottage used as the vacation home & resort of Presidents Van Buren, Tyler, Pierce, Fillmore & Buchanan.
Hours & Admission Prices: April-Nov. Mon.-Sat. 10-5, Sun. 10-3; other times by appointment. Adults $30, children 10-17 $15.
Attendance: 15,000 (estimated)

Williamson

WILLIAMSON AREA RAILROAD MUSEUM, INC., 100 Prichard St., Williamson, WV 25661. Mailing Address: P.O. Box 466, Williamson, WV 25661-0466. Tel.: 304-235-0105. Fax: 304-235-4910.
E-mail: museumsofwv@gmail.com
Key Personnel: Pres. (V), R. Doyle Van Meter, II.
Institution Type/Description: Railroad Museum.
Hours & Admission Prices: Fri.-Sat. 10-4. No charge; donations accepted.

Williamstown

HENDERSON HALL, 517 River Rd., Williamstown, WV 26187. Mailing Address: P.O. Box 1685, Parkersburg, WV 26102-1685. Tel.: 304-375-2129.
E-mail: visit@hendersonhall.com
Institution Type/Description: Historic House Museum.

Hours & Admission Prices: Daily call for hours.

WISCONSIN
(327 listings)

Albany

ALBANY HISTORICAL SOCIETY MUSEUM, 117-119 N. Water St., Albany, WI 53502. Tel.: 608-862-3423.
E-mail: villageclerk@albanywi.org
Key Personnel: Cur., Dorothy Peterson.
Institution Type/Description: History Museum.
Hours & Admission Prices: Memorial Day to Aug. Sat.-Sun. 1-4.

Alma

THE ALMA AREA MUSEUM, 505 S. 2nd St., Alma, WI 54610. Mailing Address: P.O. Box 473, Alma, WI 54610. Tel.: 608-685-3554. info@almahistory.org.
E-mail: info@almahistory.org
Web Site: www.almahistory.org/almaareamuseum.html
Institution Type/Description: History Museum: housed in the former Buffalo County Training School & Teachers College; built in 1902.
Hours & Admission Prices: Memorial Day to early Oct. Sat.-Sun. 1-4. No charge; donations accepted.

WINGS OVER ALMA NATURE & ART CENTER, 110 N. Main St., Alma, WI 54610. Mailing Address: P.O. Box 191, Alma, WI 54610. Tel.: 608-685-3303.
E-mail: center@wingsoveralma.org
Web Site: www.wingsoveralma.org
Key Personnel: Coord., Julene Rohrer.
Institution Type/Description: Nature & Art Center.
Hours & Admission Prices: June-Oct. Thurs.-Mon. 11-4; Nov.-May Thurs.-Sun. 11-4. Closed Easter, Thanksgiving; Christmas.

Almond

ALMOND HISTORICAL SOCIETY - OLD BANK BUILDING MUSEUM, Main St., Almond, WI 54909. Mailing Address: P.O. Box 74, Almond, WI 54909. Tel.: 715-366-8571. Fax: 715-366-4558.
E-mail: valmond@uniontel.net
Key Personnel: Pres. (V), Arthur Pagel; Vice Pres., Dianne Trebiatowski.
Institution Type/Description: Historical Society Museum: housed in a former bank building.
Hours & Admission Prices: May-Sept. Tues. 1:30-4; other times by appointment. No charge; donations accepted.
Attendance: 200 (estimated)

Amberg

AMBERG MUSEUM, N15065 Grant St., Amberg, WI 54102. Mailing Address: P.O. Box 22, Amberg, WI 54102. Tel.: 715-759-5372.
E-mail: society@amberghistory.org
Web Site: www.amberghistory.org
Institution Type/Description: History Museum.
Hours & Admission Prices: Memorial Day to Labor Day Fri. 1-4, Sat. 10-4. No charge; donations accepted.

Antigo

LANGLADE COUNTY HISTORICAL SOCIETY MUSEUM, 404 Superior St., Antigo, WI 54409-1855. Tel.: 715-627-4464.
E-mail: lchs@dwave.net
Web Site: langladehistory.com
Key Personnel: Pres. (V), Joe Hermolin; Cur., Mary Kay Wolf.
Institution Type/Description: Historic Building & Museum.
Hours & Admission Prices: Thurs.-Sat. 10-4. Suggested donation: adults $5, children over 6 $2; children under 6 no charge.
Attendance: 16,000 (estimated)

Appleton

THE BUILDING FOR KIDS CHILDREN'S MUSEUM, 100 W. College Ave., Appleton, WI 54911-5749. Tel.: 920-734-3226.
Web Site: www.buildingforkids.org

Formerly: Fox Cities Children's Museum
Key Personnel: Exec. Dir., Oliver Zornow.
Institution Type/Description: Children's Museum.
Hours & Admission Prices: Tues.-Sat. 9-5, Sun. 12-5. Call to confirm. Adults & children $7.50, seniors 65 & over $6.50, military with valid ID $5.50; children under 1 no charge. Closed New Year's Day; Easter; Memorial Day; Independence Day; Labor Day; Thanksgiving; Christmas. &
Attendance: 109,000 (actual)

HEARTHSTONE HISTORIC HOUSE MUSEUM, 625 W. Prospect Ave., Appleton, WI 54911-6042. Tel.: 920-730-8204.
E-mail: gschroeder@hearthstonemuseum.org
Web Site: www.hearthstonemuseum.org
Key Personnel: Dir., George Schroder.
Institution Type/Description: Historic House Museum: first residence in the world to be lighted from a central hydroelectric power plant using the Edison system in 1882.
Hours & Admission Prices: Tours: Thurs.-Sat. 10-3:30, Sun. 1-3:30. Adults $8, children $5.
Attendance: 5,500 (estimated)

THE HISTORY MUSEUM AT THE CASTLE, 330 E. College Ave., Appleton, WI 54911-5715. Tel.: 920-735-9370.
E-mail: matt@myhistorymuseum.org
Web Site: www.myhistorymuseum.org
Formerly: Outagamie Museum
Key Personnel: Exec. Dir., Matthew J. Carpenter; Chief Cur., Dustin Mack; Business Mgr., Sheila Ploeckelman; Mgr. Education & Collections, Erin Comer.
Institution Type/Description: Regional History Museum.
Hours & Admission Prices: Memorial Day to Labor Day Fri.-Sun. 10-4; Winter: Tues.-Sun. 10-4. Adults $10, children 5-17 $7.50; children under 5 & members no charge. Closed New Year's Day, Easter, Independence Day, Thanksgiving, Christmas Eve & Day. &
Attendance: 19,019 (actual)

PAPER DISCOVERY CENTER, 425 W. Water St., Appleton, WI 54911-6058. Tel.: 920-380-7491. Facebook: Paper Discovery Center.
E-mail: maria@paperdiscoverycenter.org
Web Site: www.paperdiscoverycenter.org
Key Personnel: Exec. Dir., Maria B. Costello; Lead Educator, Michael Breza.
Institution Type/Description: Paper Museum.
Hours & Admission Prices: Mon.-Sat. 10-4. Adults $7, seniors & child 3-18 $5; members no charge. Closed holidays. &
Attendance: 10,000 (actual)

THE TROUT MUSEUM OF ART, 111 W. College Ave., Appleton, WI 54911. Tel.: 920-733-4089. Facebook; Twitter; Instagram.
E-mail: info@troutmuseum.org
Web Site: www.troutmuseum.org
Formerly: Appleton Art Center
Key Personnel: Dir. Financial Opers., Meg O'Brien; Mktg. Mgr., Melissa Haen; Education Coord., Marci Hoffman.
Institution Type/Description: Art Museum.
Hours & Admission Prices: Tues.-Wed. & Fri.-Sat. 10-4, Thurs. 10-8, Sun. 12-4. &
Attendance: 30,000 (estimated)

WRISTON ART CENTER GALLERIES, Lawrence University, 613 E. College Ave., Appleton, WI 54912-0599. Mailing Address: 711 E. Boldt Way, Appleton, WI 54911. Tel.: 920-832-6890.
E-mail: beth.a.zinsli@lawrence.edu
Web Site: www.lawrence.edu/dept/wriston
Key Personnel: Cur. & Galleries Dir., Beth A. Zinsli; Collections & Gallery Asst., Elizabeth Larew.
Institution Type/Description: Art Gallery.
Hours & Admission Prices: Tues.-Fri. 10-4, Sat.-Sun. 12-4. No charge. &
Attendance: 7,472 (actual)

Ashippun

HONEY OF A MUSEUM, N. 1557 Hwy. 67, Ashippun, WI 53003. Tel.: 800-558-7745; 920-474-4411.
E-mail: info@honeyacres.com
Web Site: www.honeyacres.com
Institution Type/Description: Honey Bee History Museum.
Hours & Admission Prices: June-Oct. Mon.-Fri. 8-3:30, Sat. 10-4; Nov.-April Mon.-Fri. 9-3:30. No charge.

Ashland

ASHLAND HISTORICAL SOCIETY MUSEUM, 216 W. Main St., Ashland, WI 54806-1513. Tel.: 715-682-4911. Facebook: Ashland Historical Society Museum.
E-mail: museum@ashlandwihistory.com
Web Site: www.ashlandwihistory.com
Institution Type/Description: General Museum.
Hours & Admission Prices: June to mid-Oct. Mon.-Sat. 10-3; mid-Oct. to May Mon.-Fri. 10-3. No charge; donations accepted. Closed major holidays. &
Attendance: 3,611 (actual)

Ashwaubenon

ASHWAUBENON HISTORICAL SOCIETY, 936 Anderson Dr., Ashwaubenon, WI 54304. Tel.: 920-429-2863.
E-mail: ahshistory@att.net
Web Site: ashhs.com
Key Personnel: Pres. (V), Annette Aubinger.
Institution Type/Description: Historical Society Museum.
Hours & Admission Prices: March-Dec. Wed. & Sat. 1-4; other times by appointment. No charge; donations accepted.
Attendance: 600 (estimated)

Augusta

1864 DELLS MILL HISTORICAL LANDMARK & MUSEUM, E18855 County Rd. V, Augusta, WI 54722. Tel.: 715-286-2714.
Web Site: www.dellsmill.com
Institution Type/Description: Historic Building: mill built in 1864. Listed on the National Register of Historic Places.
Hours & Admission Prices: May-Oct. call for hours.

Baileys Harbor

THE RIDGES SANCTUARY, INC., 8166 Hwy. 57, Baileys Harbor, WI 54202. Mailing Address: P.O. Box 152, Baileys Harbor, WI 54202-0152. Tel.: 920-839-2802.
E-mail: info@ridgessanctuary.org
Web Site: www.ridgessanctuary.org
Key Personnel: Exec. Dir., Steve Leonard; Devel. Dir., Drew Richmond; Prog. Coord., Kate LeRoy.
Institution Type/Description: Nature Center.
Hours & Admission Prices: Nature Center: daily 9-5. Trails: daily dawn to dusk. Adults $5; members & children under 18 no charge.
Attendance: 17,500 (estimated)

Balsam Lake

POLK COUNTY MUSEUM, 120 Main St., Balsam Lake, WI 54810. Mailing Address: P.O. Box 41, Balsam Lake, WI 54810-0041. Tel.: 715-485-9269.
E-mail: info@polkcountymuseum.org
Web Site: www.polkcountymuseum.com
Key Personnel: Pres. (V), Greta Palmberg.
Institution Type/Description: General Museum.
Hours & Admission Prices: Memorial Day to Labor Day Thurs.-Mon. 12-4. No charge; donations accepted. &
Attendance: 2,500 (actual)

Baraboo

CIRCUS WORLD MUSEUM, 550 Water St., Baraboo, WI 53913-2578. Tel.: 608-356-8341. Fax: 608-356-1800. Facebook.
E-mail: ringmaster@circusworldbaraboo.org
Web Site: www.circusworldbaraboo.org
Institution Type/Description: Circus Museum: site of 1884-1918 original winter quarters of Ringling Bros. Circus.
Hours & Admission Prices: Mon.-Fri. 10-4. See website for seasonal admission prices. &
Attendance: 71,106 (actual)

THE INTERNATIONAL CLOWN HALL OF FAME & RESEARCH CENTER, INC., 102 4th Ave., Baraboo, WI 53913. Tel.: 608-852-6767.
E-mail: gkdesanto@aol.com
Web Site: www.theclownmuseum.com
Key Personnel: Dir., Greg DeSanto.
Institution Type/Description: Clown Museum.

Hours & Admission Prices: Sept.-May by appointment. Adults $8, children under
  12 $5. &
Attendance: 25,000 (estimated)

INTERNATIONAL CRANE FOUNDATION, E. 11376 Shady
  Lane Rd., Baraboo, WI 53913-0447. Mailing Address: P.O. Box
  447, Baraboo, WI 53913-0447. Tel.: 608-356-9462, ext. 118.
E-mail: info@savingcranes.org
Web Site: www.savingcranes.org
Key Personnel: Co-Founder & Sr. Conservationist, George Archibald; C.E.O. &
  Pres., Richard Beilfuss; Vice Pres. & CFO, Charles Gibbons.
Institution Type/Description: Aviary & Ornithology Museum.
Hours & Admission Prices: April 15-Oct. daily 9-5. Adults $12.50, senior citizens
  62 & over $10, children 6-17 $6; children 5 & under and members no charge. &
Attendance: 24,500 (actual)

SAUK COUNTY HISTORICAL SOCIETY AND MUSEUM, 531
  4th Ave., Baraboo, WI 53913-2034. Mailing Address: P.O. Box
  651, Baraboo, WI 53913-0651. Tel.: 608-356-1001.
E-mail: history@saukcountyhistory.org
Web Site: www.saukcountyhistory.org
Key Personnel: Exec. Dir., Paul Wolter; Office & Research Mgr., Linda
  Levenhagen; Cur., Rebecca DuBey.
Institution Type/Description: General Museum.
Hours & Admission Prices: Museum: Fri.-Sat. 12-4. No charge; donations accepted.
  Closed major holidays. &
Attendance: 2,000 (estimated)

Bayfield

BAYFIELD HERITAGE CENTER, 30 N. Broad St., Bayfield, WI
  54814. Mailing Address: P.O. Box 137, Bayfield, WI 54814. Tel.:
  715-779-5958.
E-mail: bayfieldheritage@centurytel.net
Web Site: www.bayfieldheritage.org/index.html
Key Personnel: Exec. Dir., Megan Boyle.
Institution Type/Description: History Museum.
Hours & Admission Prices: See website for hours. No charge; donations accepted.

Beaver Dam

**BEAVER DAM AREA ARTS ASSOCIATION AT THE
  SEIPPEL HOMESTEAD AND CENTER FOR THE ARTS,**
  305 S.. Spring St., Beaver Dam, WI 53916-1103. Mailing Address:
  P.O. Box 442, Beaver Dam, WI 53916-0442. Tel.: 920-885-3635.
E-mail: info@bdaaa.org
Web Site: www.bdaaa.org
Key Personnel: Exec. Dir., Jessalyn Braun.
Institution Type/Description: Art Museum.
Hours & Admission Prices: Call for hours.
Attendance: 3,500 (estimated)

DODGE COUNTY HISTORICAL SOCIETY MUSEUM, 105
  Park Ave., Beaver Dam, WI 53916-2107. Tel.: 920-887-1266.
E-mail: kurtsampson1968@gmail.com
Web Site: www.dodgecountyhistory.com
Formerly: Williams Free Library
Key Personnel: Cur., Kurt Sampson.
Institution Type/Description: General Museum.
Hours & Admission Prices: Wed.-Sat. 1-4; tours by appointment. No charge; dona-
  tions accepted. Closed holidays.
Attendance: 1,800 (estimated)

Belmont

FIRST CAPITOL - WISCONSIN HISTORICAL SOCIETY,
  18904 Cty. Hwy. G, Belmont, WI 53510. Mailing Address: P.O.
  Box 270, Mineral Point, WI 53565. Tel.: 608-987-2122.
E-mail: firstcapitol@wisconsinhistory.org
Web Site: www.firstcapitol.org
Key Personnel: Site Mgr., Bethany Brander.
Institution Type/Description: History Museum.
Hours & Admission Prices: See website for hours. No charge; donations accepted.
  &
Attendance: 1,000 (estimated)

Beloit

BELOIT ART CENTER, 520 E. Grand Ave., Beloit, WI 53511-
  6314. Tel.: 608-313-9083.
E-mail: info@beloitartcenter.com
Web Site: beloitartcenter.com
Formerly: Beloit Fine Arts Incubator
Institution Type/Description: Art Gallery.
Hours & Admission Prices: Mon. 10-2, Tues.-Fri. 10-5, Sat. 10-3. No charge.
  Closed holidays.
Attendance: 4,500 (estimated)

BELOIT HISTORICAL SOCIETY, 845 Hackett St., Beloit, WI
  53511-5227. Tel.: 608-365-7835.
E-mail: info@beloithistoricalsociety.com
Web Site: www.beloithistory.com
Formerly: Hanchett Bartlett Homestead
Key Personnel: Exec. Dir., Donna Langford; Dir. Programming & Office Mgr.,
  Kelly Washburn; Devel. Dir., Tim McKearn.
Institution Type/Description: Historic Site & History Museum: housed in 1857
  restored homestead.
Hours & Admission Prices: Hanchett-Bartlett Homestead: by appointment. Office:
  Mon.-Fri. 12-4. No charge; donations accepted. &
Attendance: 1,500 (estimated)

LOGAN MUSEUM OF ANTHROPOLOGY, 700 College St.,
  Beloit, WI 53511-5509. Tel.: 608-363-2677. Facebook: Logan
  Museum.
E-mail: meistern@beloit.edu
Web Site: www.beloit.edu/logan
Key Personnel: Dir., Nicolette Blum Meister; Cur. Collections, Manuel Ferreira.
Institution Type/Description: Anthropology Museum.
Hours & Admission Prices: Tues.-Sat. 11-4. No charge; donations accepted. Closed
  college holidays. &
Attendance: 5,900 (actual)

WRIGHT MUSEUM OF ART, BELOIT COLLEGE, 700 College
  St., Beloit, WI 53511-5595. Tel.: 608-363-2079. Facebook.
E-mail: wrightmuseum@beloit.edu
Web Site: www.beloit.edu/wright/
Key Personnel: Dir. & Parker Chair in Art History, Joy Elizabeth Beckman;
  Collections Mgr., Christa Story.
Institution Type/Description: Art Museum.
Hours & Admission Prices: Tues.-Sat. 11-4. No charge; donations accepted. Closed
  college holidays. &
Attendance: 5,000 (estimated)

Berlin

**BERLIN AREA HISTORICAL SOCIETY MUSEUM OF
  LOCAL HISTORY,** 111 S. Adams Ave., Berlin, WI 54923-2023.
  Mailing Address: P.O. Box 83, Berlin, WI 54923-0083. Tel.: 920-
  361-2460.
E-mail: contact@berlinareahistoricalsociety.com
Web Site: www.berlinareahistoricalsociety.com
Institution Type/Description: Historical Society Museum.
Hours & Admission Prices: Memorial Day to Labor Day 2nd & 4th Sun. 1-4; other
  times by appointment. No charge; donations accepted.
Attendance: 450 (estimated)

Birchwood

**BIRCHWOOD AREA HISTORICAL SOCIETY LOG
  MUSEUM,** Main St., Birchwood, WI 54817. Mailing Address: c/o
  Birchwood Area Historical Society, 2823 27th St., Birchwood, WI
  54817. Tel.: 715-354-3879.
Institution Type/Description: Historical Society Museum.
Hours & Admission Prices: June-Aug. 1st & 3rd Sat. 11-4. No charge.

HOWARD MOREY HOUSE, Park Ave., Birchwood, WI 54817.
  Mailing Address: 2823 27th St., Birchwood, WI 54817. Tel.: 715-
  354-3115.
E-mail: kathy@birchwoodvillagewi.com
Institution Type/Description: Historic House Museum: housed in the boyhood home
  of Howard Morey; built in 1901.
Hours & Admission Prices: June-Aug. 1st & 3rd Sat. 11-4; other times by appoint-
  ment. No charge.

Black Earth

BLACK EARTH DEPOT MUSEUM, 934 Mills St., Black Earth, WI 53515. Mailing Address: P.O. Box 214, Black Earth, WI 53515. Tel.: 608-767-2307.
E-mail: behistoricalsoc@gmail.com
Web Site: ww.blackearthhistory.org
Institution Type/Description: Historic Depot: c.1857.
Hours & Admission Prices: Memorial Day to Oct. Sun. 1-4.
Attendance: 125 (estimated)

Black River Falls

JACKSON COUNTY HISTORICAL SOCIETY, 321 Main St., Black River Falls, WI 54615-0037. Mailing Address: P.O. Box 37, Black River Falls, WI 54615-0037. Tel.: 715-284-5314. Facebook.
E-mail: jacksoncohistory@gmail.com
Web Site: www.blackriverfalls.com
Institution Type/Description: Historical Society Museum: housed in the former 1915 Carnegie Library.
Hours & Admission Prices: April-Oct. 12-4

Blanchardville

BLANCHARDVILLE HISTORICAL SOCIETY & MUSEUM, 101 S. Main St., Blanchardville, WI 53516. Mailing Address: P.O. Box 62, Blanchardville, WI 53516. Tel.: 608-523-1220.
E-mail: blanchardvillehistorical@gmail.com
Web Site: www.blanchardville.com
Institution Type/Description: History Museum: housed in the former hydrostatic station used to help generate power for the city.
Hours & Admission Prices: April-Oct. Sat. 9-12.

Blue Mounds

CAVE OF THE MOUNDS -NATIONAL NATURAL LANDMARK, 2975 Cave of the Mounds Rd., Blue Mounds, WI 53517-0148. Mailing Address: P.O. Box 148, Blue Mounds, WI 53517-0148. Tel.: 608-437-3038.
E-mail: info@caveofthemounds.com
Web Site: www.caveofthemounds.com/contact/contact-us/
Institution Type/Description: Natural History Museum.
Hours & Admission Prices: mid-March to May & Sept. to mid-Nov. Mon.-Fri. 9-5, Sat.-Sun. 9-6; Memorial Day to Labor Day daily 9-7; mid-Nov. to mid-March Mon.-Fri. 11 & 2 by appointment, Sat.-Sun. hourly 10-5. Adults $18.95, children 4-12 $10.95; children 3 & under no charge.

Boscobel

BOSCOBEL DEPOT MUSEUM, 800 Wisconsin Ave., Boscobel, WI 53805. Tel.: 608-375-2672.
Web Site: www.visitboscobel.com/directory/listing/boscobel-depot-museum
Institution Type/Description: Historic Building: housed in a former depot; built in 1857.
Hours & Admission Prices: May-Oct. Sat. 8-2. No charge.

GRAND ARMY OF THE REPUBLIC MUSEUM, 102 Mary St., Boscobel, WI 53805. Mailing Address: 1004 Chestnut St., Boscobel, WI 53805. Tel.: 608-375-5693 & 2672.
Web Site: www.visitboscobel.com/directory/listing/g-a-r-hall-grand-army-of-the-republic
Institution Type/Description: Historic Building: built in 1896. Listed on the National Register of Historic Places.
Hours & Admission Prices: June-Aug. open by appointment. &
Attendance: 104 (actual)

Bowler

ARVID E. MILLER MEMORIAL LIBRARY/MUSEUM OF THE STOCKBRIDGE MUNSEE TRIBE, N8510 Moh-He-Con-Nuck Rd., Bowler, WI 54416. Mailing Address: P.O. Box 70, Bowler, WI 54416. Tel.: 715-793-4270.
E-mail: yvette.malone@mohican-nsn.gov
Web Site: www.mohican.com/librarymuseum/
Key Personnel: Library & Museum Specialist, Yvette Malone.
Institution Type/Description: Research Library & Historic Museum.
Hours & Admission Prices: Mon.-Fri. 8-4:30. No charge; donations accepted.
Attendance: 700 (estimated)

Brandon

BRANDON HISTORICAL SOCIETY & MUSEUM, 102 E. Main St., Brandon, WI 53919. Mailing Address: P.O. Box 344, Brandon, WI 53919. Tel.: 920-346-2962. Facebook.
Institution Type/Description: Historical Society Museum.
Hours & Admission Prices: Sat. 2-4; other times by appointment.

Brillion

ARIENS(R) COMPANY MUSEUM, 109 Calumet St., Brillion, WI 54110-0157. Mailing Address: 655 W. Ryan St., Brillion, WI 54110. Tel.: 920-756-4273.
Web Site: www.ariens.com/en-us/company/museum
Institution Type/Description: Company Museum.
Hours & Admission Prices: Mon.-Fri. 9-5 by reservation only. &

BRILLION HISTORY HOUSE AND MUSEUM, 110 N. Francis St., Brillion, WI 54110. Mailing Address: P.O. Box 35, Brillion, WI 54110. Tel.: 920-756-9294.
E-mail: omafuhrmann@yahoo.com
Institution Type/Description: History Museum: housed in the former Green Hotel; built in 1872.
Hours & Admission Prices: By appointment. No charge; donations accepted. &
Attendance: 500 (actual)

Brodhead

BRODHEAD HISTORICAL SOCIETY & DEPOT MUSEUM, 1108 1st Center Ave., Brodhead, WI 53520. Mailing Address: 707 9th St., Brodhead, WI 53520. Tel.: 608-897-4150.
E-mail: info@brodheadhistory.org
Web Site: www.brodheadhistory.org/depot.html
Institution Type/Description: Historical Society Museum: housed in the former Milwaukee Road Depot; built in 1881.
Hours & Admission Prices: Memorial Day to Labor Day Wed. & Sat.-Sun. 1-4; other times by appointment.

Brookfield

DOUSMAN STAGECOACH INN MUSEUM, 1075 Pilgrim Pkwy., Brookfield, WI 53005. Mailing Address: Elmbrook Historical Society, P.O. Box 292, Brookfield, WI 53008. Tel.: 262-782-4057.
E-mail: elmbrookhistoricalsociety@gmail.com
Web Site: www.elmbrookhistoricalsociety.org
Institution Type/Description: History Museum: housed in a former stagecoach inn; built in 1857.
Hours & Admission Prices: Tours: May-Oct. 1st & 3rd Sun. 1-4. Adults Closed federal holidays.$6, children 3-12 $3; children 2 & under no charge.
Attendance: 5,000 (estimated)

PLOCH ART GALLERY AT THE WILSON CENTER, Brookfield's Mitchell Park, 19805 W. Capitol Dr., Brookfield, WI 53045. Tel.: 262-373-5022.
E-mail: rsvp@wilson-center.com
Web Site: www.wilson-center.com
Institution Type/Description: Art Gallery.
Hours & Admission Prices: Call for hours. No charge.

Browntown

BROWNTOWN HISTORICAL MUSEUM, 110 S. Mill St., Browntown, WI 53520. Tel.: 608-966-3514.
E-mail: rsmith97@sbcglobal.net
Institution Type/Description: History Museum.
Hours & Admission Prices: 2nd & 4th Sun. 1-4.

Burlington

BURLINGTON HISTORICAL SOCIETY, 232 N. Perkins Blvd., Burlington, WI 53105. Tel.: 262-767-2884.
E-mail: burlingtonhistory@gmail.com
Web Site: www.burlingtonhistory.org
Institution Type/Description: Historical Society Museum.
Hours & Admission Prices: Sun. 1-4; other times by appointment. No charge; donations accepted. &

BURLINGTON HISTORICAL SOCIETY PIONEER - LOG CABIN MUSEUM, Wehmhoff Sq., 416 N. Perkins Blvd., Burlington, WI 53105. Mailing Address: 232 N. Perkins Blvd., Burlington, WI 53105. Tel.: 262-767-2884.
E-mail: burlingtonhistory@gmail.com
Web Site: www.burlingtonhistory.org
Institution Type/Description: Historical Society Museum: housed in an 1850 log cabin.
Hours & Admission Prices: Sun. 1-4; other times by appointment.

BURLINGTON HISTORICAL SOCIETY - WHITMAN SCHOOL, 401 W. Beloit St., Burlington, WI 53105. Mailing Address: 232 N. Perkins Blvd., Burlington, WI 53105. Tel.: 262-767-2884.
E-mail: burlingtonhistory@gmail.com
Web Site: www.burlingtonhistory.org
Institution Type/Description: Historic Building: built in 1840.
Hours & Admission Prices: By appointment. No charge; donations accepted.

CHOCOLATE EXPERIENCE MUSEUM, 113 E. Chestnut St., Ste. B, Burlington, WI 53105. Tel.: 262-763-6044.
E-mail: info@burlingtonchamber.org
Web Site: chocolateexperiencemuseum.org
Institution Type/Description: History Museum.
Hours & Admission Prices: Mon.-Fri. 9-5, Sat. 10-2. No charge; donations accepted. Closed federal holidays.

LOGIC PUZZLE MUSEUM, 533 Milwaukee Ave., Burlington, WI 53105. Tel.: 262-763-3946. Facebook.
E-mail: logicpuzzlemuseum@hotmail.com
Web Site: www.logicpuzzlemuseum.com
Key Personnel: Dir., Judith Schulz.
Institution Type/Description: Toy Museum; hands-on.
Hours & Admission Prices: Call for hours. Admission $10.

SPINNING TOP & YO-YO MUSEUM, 533 Milwaukee Ave., Burlington, WI 53105. Tel.: 262-763-3946. Facebook.
E-mail: thetopmuseum@hotmail.com
Web Site: www.topmuseum.org
Institution Type/Description: Toy Museum.
Hours & Admission Prices: By appointment; see website for hours & admission prices, tours & programs.

Cable

CABLE NATURAL HISTORY MUSEUM, 13470 County Hwy. M, Cable, WI 54821. Mailing Address: P.O. Box 416, Cable, WI 54821-0416. Tel.: 715-798-3890.
E-mail: info@cablemuseum.org
Web Site: cablemuseum.org
Key Personnel: Dir., Deb Nelson.
Institution Type/Description: Natural History Museum.
Hours & Admission Prices: Tues.-Sat. 10-4, Sun.-Mon. 10-2. Adults $5; members & children no charge.
Attendance: 25,000 (estimated)

Cambridge

CAMBRIDGE HISTORIC SCHOOL MUSEUM, 213 South St., Cambridge, WI 53523-9617. Tel.: 608-423-2630.
Web Site: www.cambridgehistoricmuseum.org
Key Personnel: Dir., Jeff Veesenmeyer; Vice Pres., Peg Sullivan; Treas., Patricia Strohbusch; Cur., Russ Amacher.
Institution Type/Description: Historic Building: housed in the former Cambridge school building built in 1906.
Hours & Admission Prices: mid-May to mid-Oct. Wed. & Sat. 12:30-3; other times by appointment.

Cameron

BARRON COUNTY HISTORICAL SOCIETY'S PIONEER VILLAGE MUSEUM, 1866 13 1/2 - 14th Ave., Cameron, WI 54822. Mailing Address: P.O. Box 242, Cameron, WI 54822-0242. Tel.: 715-458-2080.
E-mail: museum1@chibardun.net
Web Site: www.pioneervillagemuseum.org
Key Personnel: Dir., Tamera Schutz.
Institution Type/Description: state and local history.

Hours & Admission Prices: June to early Sept. Fri. & Sun. 1-5, Sat. 10-5. Adults $10, children 5-12 $5; discounts to groups of 25 or more; children under 5 no charge.
Attendance: 5,000 (estimated)

Camp Douglas

WISCONSIN NATIONAL GUARD MUSEUM, 101 Independence Dr., Volk Field, Camp Douglas, WI 54618. Tel.: 608-427-1280. Facebook.
E-mail: wngmuseum@gmail.com
Key Personnel: Cur., Eric Lent.
Institution Type/Description: Military Museum: housed in 1896 rustic lodge made of white pine logs.
Hours & Admission Prices: Wed.-Sat. 9-4, Sun. 10-2; call to confirm hours. No charge.
Attendance: 18,500 (actual)

Campbellsport

HENRY S. REUSS ICE AGE VISITOR CENTER, DNR, Kettle Moraine State Forest - Northern Unit, N2875 Hwy. 67, Campbellsport, WI 53010. Mailing Address: N1765 County Hwy. G, Campbellsport, WI 53010. Tel.: 920-533-8322.
E-mail: jackie.scharfenberg@wisconsin.gov
Web Site: dnr.wi.gov/topic/parks/name/kmn/naturecenter.html
Key Personnel: NR Educator, Jackie Scharfenberg.
Institution Type/Description: Park & Geology Museum.
Hours & Admission Prices: April-Oct. Mon.-Fri. 8:30-4, Sat.-Sun. 9:30-5; Nov.-March call for hours. No charge; donations accepted.
Attendance: 28,000 (estimated)

Cassville

STONEFIELD HISTORIC SITE, 12195 County Rd. V V, Cassville, WI 53806-9775. Tel.: 608-725-5210.
E-mail: stonefield@wisconsinhistory.org
Web Site: stonefield.wisconsinhistory.org
Key Personnel: Dir., Allen Schroeder.
Institution Type/Description: State Agricultural Museum: housed in a re-created 1890 village located on the 1868 estate of Wisconsin's first state governor, Nelson Dewey. An Historic Site.
Hours & Admission Prices: See website for hours. Adults $10, students & senior citizens $9, children 5-17 $6; children 4 & under & Wisconsin Historical Society members no charge.
Attendance: 7,200 (actual)

Cedarburg

GENERAL STORE MUSEUM, W61 N480 Washington Ave., Cedarburg, WI 53012-2426. Tel.: 262-377-5856.
E-mail: stephanie@artmusichistory.org
Web Site: www.cedarburgculturalcenter.org
Key Personnel: Exec. Dir., Stephanie Hayes.
Institution Type/Description: History Museum: housed in a restored 1860's era frame building.
Hours & Admission Prices: Call for hours.

KUHEFUSS HOUSE MUSEUM, W63 N627 Washington Ave., Cedarburg, WI 53012-1945. Mailing Address: W62 N546 Washington Ave., Cedarburg, WI 53012-0084. Tel.: 262-375-3676.
E-mail: cccmail@artmusichistory.org
Web Site: www.cedarburgculturalcenter.org
Key Personnel: Exec. Dir., Stephanie Hayes.
Institution Type/Description: Historic House.
Hours & Admission Prices: Call for hours.

OZAUKEE ART CENTER, W 62 N718 Riveredge Dr., Cedarburg, WI 53012-1337. Tel.: 262-377-8230.
E-mail: pjyank@pauljyank.com
Key Personnel: Dir., Paul Yank.
Institution Type/Description: Art Gallery: housed in 1843 Cedarburg brewery.
Hours & Admission Prices: Wed.-Sun. 1-4.
Attendance: 10,000 (estimated)

WISCONSIN MUSEUM OF QUILTS & FIBER ART, N50 W5050 Portland Rd., Cedarburg, WI 53012-2158. Tel.: 262-546-0300.

E-mail: info@wiquiltmuseum.com
Web Site: www.wiquiltmuseum.com
Key Personnel: Exec. Dir., Melissa Wraalstad; Collections Dir., Carol Butzke; Volunteer Dir., Linda Vargo; Gift Shop Mgr., Sharon Hartley Iverson.
Institution Type/Description: History Museum.
Hours & Admission Prices: Wed.-Sat. 10-4, Sun. 12-4. ✦
Attendance: 2,000 (actual)

Chilton

CALUMET COUNTY HISTORICAL SOCIETY, INC., 3324 Irish Rd., Chilton, WI 53014. Mailing Address: 928 Wieting Ct., Chilton, WI 53014. Tel.: 920-849-4042. Facebook: Calumet County Historical Society.
E-mail: Info@CalumetCountyHistoricalSociety.org
Web Site: calumetcountyhistoricalsociety.org
Key Personnel: Pres., Terry Friederichs; Vice Pres., Chuck Schuknecht; Treas., Karen Gerhartz; Historian & Sec., Doris Zarling.
Institution Type/Description: Farm Museum.
Hours & Admission Prices: June-Sept. Sun. 1-4; other times by appointment. No charge; donations accepted. ✦
Attendance: 200 (estimated)

Chippewa Falls

CHIPPEWA COUNTY HISTORICAL SOCIETY, 123 Allen St., Chippewa Falls, WI 54729. Tel.: 715-723-4399.
E-mail: cchs123@att.net
Web Site: www.chippewacountywihistoricalsociety.org/
Key Personnel: Pres. (V), Dave Gordon.
Institution Type/Description: Historical Society Museum: housed in the former Notre Dame Convent; built in 1883.
Hours & Admission Prices: Tues. 9-4. No charge donations accepted.
Attendance: 510 (actual)

CHIPPEWA FALLS MUSEUM OF INDUSTRY AND TECHNOLOGY, 21 E. Grand Ave., Chippewa Falls, WI 54729-2560. Tel.: 715-720-9206.
E-mail: info.cfmit@gmail.com
Web Site: www.cfmit.org
Key Personnel: Museum Coordr., Alitia Kerr; Bd. Pres., Bill Quirk.
Institution Type/Description: Industry & Technology Museum.
Hours & Admission Prices: Thurs.-Sat. 10-3; other times by appointment. Adults 18 & over $5, children 13-17 $3; children under 12 $1.
Attendance: 1,200 (estimated)

COOK-RUTLEDGE MANSION, 505 W. Grand Ave., Chippewa Falls, WI 54729. Tel.: 715-723-7181.
E-mail: info@cookrutledgemansion.com
Web Site: www.cookrutledgemansion.com
Institution Type/Description: Historic House Museum: housed in the former home of Wisconsin Lt. Governor James Bingham; built in 1873.
Hours & Admission Prices: Tours: June-Aug. Thurs.-Sun. 2pm; Dec. call for hours. Adults $8, children $1.

Clear Lake

CLEAR LAKE AREA HISTORICAL MUSEUM, 450 Fifth Ave., Clear Lake, WI 54005. Mailing Address: P.O. Box 242, Clear Lake, WI 54005-0242. Tel.: 715-263-3050 & 2042.
Key Personnel: Pres. (V) & Cur., Charles T. Clark; Vice Pres., Tim Wyss; Treas. & Sec., Ardeth Clark.
Institution Type/Description: Historical Society Museum: housed in 1912 Old Brick Elementary School.
Hours & Admission Prices: Memorial Day to Labor Day Tues. & Fri. 11-4, Sun. 1:30-4:30; other times by appointment. No charge; donations accepted.
Attendance: 1,200 (estimated)

Clintonville

FOUR WHEEL DRIVE FOUNDATION, Mailing Address: 79 8th St., Clintonville, WI 54929. Tel.: 715-823-4552.
Web Site: www.fourwheeldrivefoundation.com
Key Personnel: Sec., Treas, John Rosenheim.
Institution Type/Description: Company Museum: housed in 1906, Zachow-Besserdick Machine Shop.
Hours & Admission Prices: June-Sept. Sat. 1-4 by appointment only. No charge; donations accepted. ✦
Attendance: 500

WISCONSIN BOWHUNTING HERITAGE FOUNDATION INC. MUSEUM, Mailing Address: P.O. Box 240, Clintonville, WI 54929. Tel.: 715-823-4670.
E-mail: office@wisconsinbowhunters.org
Web Site: www.wisconsinbowhunters.org
Key Personnel: Pres. (V), Brian Tessmann; Vice Pres. (V), Kaleb Case.
Institution Type/Description: Wisconsin Bowhunting History Museum.
Hours & Admission Prices: Mon.-Fri. 8-4:30, Sat.-Sun. by appointment. Call ahead to verify hours. No charge; donations accepted. Closed holidays. ✦
Attendance: 400 (estimated)

Colfax

COLFAX RAILROAD MUSEUM, 500 E. Railroad Ave., Colfax, WI 54730. Tel.: 715-962-2076.
E-mail: colfaxrr@wwt.net
Web Site: www.colfaxrrmuseum.org
Key Personnel: Chm. (V), Herbert Sakalaucks.
Institution Type/Description: History Museum.
Hours & Admission Prices: May-Oct. Wed.-Sun. 11-4; other times by appointment. Adults $8, youth 7-14 $4; children under 7 no charge. ✦
Attendance: 1,800 (estimated)

Coon Valley

NORSKEDALEN NATURE & HERITAGE CENTER, INC., N455 O. Ophus Rd., Coon Valley, WI 54623. Mailing Address: P. O. Box 235, Coon Valley, WI 54623-0235. Tel.: 608-452-3424. Fax: 608-452-3424.
E-mail: info@norskedalen.org
Web Site: www.norskedalen.org
Key Personnel: Exec. Dir., Lori Dubczak.
Institution Type/Description: Nature & Heritage Center, Inc.
Hours & Admission Prices: May-Oct. Mon-Fri. 9-5, Sat. 10-5, Sun. 11-4. Nov.-April Mon.-Fri. 8-4, Sat 10-3, Sun. 11-3. Families $15, adults $6; children K-12 $3; members & preK children no charge. Closed New Year's Eve & Day; Good Friday; Easter; Thanksgiving & day After; Christmas Eve & Day. ✦
Attendance: 14,000 (estimated)

Crandon

FOREST COUNTY POTAWATOMI CULTURAL CENTER AND MUSEUM, 5460 Everybody's Rd., Crandon, WI 54520. Tel.: 715-478-4841.
Web Site: www.fcpotawatomi.com/culture-and-history/
Institution Type/Description: Cultural Center & Museum.
Hours & Admission Prices: Call for hours.

Danbury

FORTS FOLLE AVOINE HISTORIC PARK, 8500 County Rd. U, Danbury, WI 54830-9351. Tel.: 715-866-8890. Facebook: Forts Folle Avoine Historic Park.
E-mail: fahp@centurytel.net
Web Site: www.theforts.org
Institution Type/Description: Fur Trade Museum.
Hours & Admission Prices: Memorial Day weekend - Sept Wed.-Sun. 10-4. Adults $10, past or active military & seniors 65 & over $8, children 6-17 $6; children 5 & under and members no charge. ✦
Attendance: 12,000 (estimated)

De Pere

ONEIDA NATION MUSEUM, W892 County Hwy. EE, De Pere, WI 54115. Mailing Address: P.O. Box 365, Oneida, WI 54155-0365. Tel.: 920-869-2768. Fax: 920-869-2959.
E-mail: rlara@oneidanation.org
Web Site: www.oneidanation.org/museum
Key Personnel: Dir., Rita Lara; Asst. Dir., Stacy S. Coon.
Institution Type/Description: History & Cultural Museum: located on site of original Wisconsin reservation land.
Hours & Admission Prices: Sept.-May Tues.-Fri. 9-5; June-Aug. Tues.-Fri. 9-5, Sat. 9-1 Nov.-Dec. Tues. & Thurs.-Fri. 9-5, Wed. 9-7. Adults $4, seniors 55 & over & children under 18 $2; Oneida Tribal members no charge. ✦
Attendance: 12,472 (actual)

Delafield

HAWKS INN HISTORICAL SOCIETY, INC., 426 Wells St., Delafield, WI 53018-1419. Mailing Address: P.O. Box 180104, Delafield, WI 53018-0104. Tel.: 262-646-4794.
E-mail: hawksinn@wi.rr.com
Web Site: www.hawksinn.org
Key Personnel: Pres. (V), Mary Daniel.
Institution Type/Description: Historic Building Museum: 1846, restored stage coach inn.
Hours & Admission Prices: May-Oct. Sat. 1-4; tours by appointment. No charge, donations accepted. &
Attendance: 1,100 (estimated)

ST. JOHN'S NORTHWESTERN MILITARY ACADEMY ARCHIVES & MUSEUM, 1101 Genesee St., Delafield, WI 53018-1411. Tel.: 262-646-7119.
Web Site: www.sjnma.org
Institution Type/Description: History Museum: housed in 1884 military school.
Hours & Admission Prices: By appointment. No charge; donations accepted.

Delavan

COOKIE JAR HEAVEN MUSEUM, 313 E. Walworth Ave., 2nd Fl., Delavan, WI 53115. Tel.: 262-728-8670.
E-mail: remwhen1998@sbcglobal.net
Web Site: rememberwhenllc.com
Institution Type/Description: Cookie Jar Museum.
Hours & Admission Prices: Mon. & Fri.-Sat. 9:30-5:30, Tues. 11-4.

Dodgeville

IOWA COUNTY HISTORICAL SOCIETY MUSEUM, 1301 N. Bequette St., P.O. Box 44, Dodgeville, WI 53533-0044. Tel.: 608-935-7694.
E-mail: ichistory@mhtc.net
Web Site: iowacountyhistoricalsociety.org
Key Personnel: Pres. (V), John Hess.
Institution Type/Description: Historical Society Museum.
Hours & Admission Prices: Tues.-Fri. 1-4; other times by appointment. No charge; donations accepted. &
Attendance: 500 (estimated)

Eagle

OLD WORLD WISCONSIN, W372 S9727 Hwy. 67, Eagle, WI 53119-2004. Mailing Address: P.O. Box 69, Eagle, WI 53119-0069. Tel.: 262-594-6301. Fax: 262-594-6342.
E-mail: oww@wisconsinhistory.org
Web Site: oldworldwisconsin.wisconsinhistory.org
Key Personnel: Dir., Dan Freas; Asst. Dir.- Guest Experience, Anna Altschwager.
Institution Type/Description: Ethnic Museum & Historic Village.
Hours & Admission Prices: Spring: Sat.-Sun. 10-5; Summer: daily 10-5; Fall: Thurs.-Sun. 10-5. Adults $19, senior citizens 65 & over $16, children 5-17 $10; WHS members and children 4 & under no charge. &
Attendance: 75,000 (estimated)

Eagle River

NORTHWOODS CHILDREN'S MUSEUM, 346 W. Division St., Eagle River, WI 54521. Mailing Address: P.O. Box 216, Eagle River, WI 54521-0216. Tel.: 715-479-4623.
Web Site: www.northwoodschildrensmuseum.com
Key Personnel: Dir., Rouleen Gartner.
Institution Type/Description: Children's Museum.
Hours & Admission Prices: Mon.-Sun. 10-5. Admission $8.50 per person. Closed Thanksgiving, Christmas Eve & Day, New Year's Eve and Day. &
Attendance: 25,000 (actual)

East Troy

EAST TROY RAILROAD MUSEUM, 2002 Church St., East Troy, WI 53120-1302. Mailing Address: P.O. Box 943, East Troy, WI 53120-0943. Tel.: 262-642-3263.
E-mail: info@easttroyrr.org
Web Site: www.easttroyrr.org
Formerly: Wisconsin Trolley Museum, Inc.
Key Personnel: Exec. Dir., Charles Kaiser.
Institution Type/Description: Transportation Museum.

Hours & Admission Prices: April-May Sat.-Sun. 10-4; June-Oct. Fri.-Sun. 10-4.. Adults $12.50, seniors $10.50, children $8; children under 3 & members no charge.
Attendance: 25,000 (estimated)

Eau Claire

CHILDREN'S MUSEUM OF EAU CLAIRE, 220 S. Barstow St., Eau Claire, WI 54701. Tel.: 715-832-5437. Facebook.
E-mail: info@childrensmuseumec.com
Web Site: www.childrensmuseumec.com
Key Personnel: Exec. Dir., Mike McHomey; Pres. (V), James Lahti.
Institution Type/Description: Children's Museum.
Hours & Admission Prices: Tues.-Wed. & Fri.-Sat. 9-5, Thurs. 9-7, Sun. 12-5. Admissions $7 per person; members & children under one no charge. &
Attendance: 70,000 (estimated)

CHIPPEWA VALLEY MUSEUM, INC., 1204 Half Moon Dr., Eau Claire, WI 54703. Mailing Address: P.O. Box 1204, Eau Claire, WI 54702-1204. Tel.: 715-834-7871.
E-mail: info@cvmuseum.com
Web Site: www.cvmuseum.com
Key Personnel: Dir. & Cur., Carrie Ronnander; Asst. Cur., Kathie Roy; Archivist, Liz Reuter; Educator, Karen Jacobson; Prog. Coord., Angela Allred; Finance Mgr., Dorie Boetcher; Opers. Mgr., Jill York; Facilities Mgr., Dondi Hayden; Communications Specialist, Olaf Lind.
Institution Type/Description: Regional Historical Museum.
Hours & Admission Prices: Memorial Day-Labor Day Mon. & Wed.-Sat. 10-5, Tues. 10-8, Sun. 1-5; Sept.-May Tues. 1-8, Wed.-Fri. & Sun. 1-5, Sat. 10-5. Adults $7, children 4-17 & students $4; children under 4 & members no charge. &
Attendance: 22,012 (actual)

FOSTER GALLERY, UNIVERSITY OF WISCONSIN-EAU CLAIRE, 121 Water St., Eau Claire, WI 54702-4004. Mailing Address: P.O. Box 4004, Eau Claire, WI 54702-4004. Tel.: 715-836-2328.
E-mail: fostergallery@uwec.edu
Web Site: www.uwec.edu/academics/college-arts-sciences/departments-programs/art-design/foster-gallery/
Key Personnel: Dept. Chair, Christos Theo.
Institution Type/Description: University Gallery.
Hours & Admission Prices: Mon.-Wed. & Fri. 10-4:30, Thurs. 10-4:30 & 6pm-8pm, Sat.-Sun. 1-4:30. No charge. Closed academic holidays. &
Attendance: 6,500 (actual)

PAUL BUNYAN LOGGING CAMP MUSEUM, 1110 Half Moon Dr., Eau Claire, WI 54703. Tel.: 715-835-6200.
E-mail: info@paulbunyancamp.org
Web Site: www.paulbunyancamp.org
Key Personnel: Exec. Dir., Diana Peterson.
Institution Type/Description: Logging & Lumbering Museum.
Hours & Admission Prices: May-Sept. Mon.-Sat. 10-4:30, Sun. 1-4:30. Adults $7, children $4. &
Attendance: 12,000 (actual)

Edgerton

ALBION ACADEMY HISTORICAL MUSEUM, 605 Campus Ln., Edgerton, WI 53534. Tel.: 608-884-9206.
E-mail: nancydurgin@yahoo.com
Web Site: www.aahs50.wordpress.com
Key Personnel: Pres., Gary Durgin; Vice Pres., Thad Andrews; Treas., Eric Baker; Sec., Nancy Durgin.
Institution Type/Description: Historical Society Museum: located on site of 1853, rebuilt Albion Academy, first coeducational institution of higher learning in the state of Wisconsin.
Hours & Admission Prices: June-Aug. Sun. 1-4; other times by appointment. No charge; donations accepted.
Attendance: 174 (actual)

Egg Harbor

CHIEF OSHKOSH NATIVE AMERICAN ARTS, 7631 State Hwy. 42, Egg Harbor, WI 54209-9548. Tel.: 920-868-3240. Facebook: Chief Oshkosh Native American Arts.
E-mail: chiefoshkosh97@yahoo.com
Institution Type/Description: Native American Art Gallery.
Hours & Admission Prices: Daily 10-5. No charge; donations accepted. Closed most holidays.

CUPOLA HOUSE, 7836 Hwy. 42, Egg Harbor, WI 54209-9564. Tel.: 920-868-3941. Facebook: Cupola House.
E-mail: cupolahouse@gmail.com
Key Personnel: C.E.O., Gloria Hansen.
Institution Type/Description: Historic House: 1871 house built by Levi Thorp, located on the Door County Peninsula.
Hours & Admission Prices: Daily 10-6. No charge; donations accepted. &
Attendance: 100,000 (estimated)

Elkhart Lake

ELKHART LAKE HISTORIC DEPOT MUSEUM, 80 Square St., Elkhart Lake, WI 53020. Mailing Address: c/o Elkhart Lake Tourism, 41 E. Rhine St., Elkhart Lake, WI 53020. Tel.: 920-627-3767.
Web Site: www.elkhartlake.com
Institution Type/Description: Historic Building Museum.
Hours & Admission Prices: Memorial Day to Labor Day Fri. 1-4, Sat. 8:30-12:30, Sun. 11-1.

HENSCHEL'S INDIAN MUSEUM & TROUT FARM, N8661 Holstein Rd., Elkhart Lake, WI 53020. Tel.: 920-876-3193.
Web Site: www.henschelsindianmuseumandtroutfarm.com
Institution Type/Description: History Museum.
Hours & Admission Prices: Memorial Day to Labor Day Tues.-Sat. 1-5; other times by appointment. Adults $6, children $3. &

Elkhorn

WEBSTER HOUSE MUSEUM, 9 E. Rockwell, Elkhorn, WI 53121-1728. Mailing Address: P.O. Box 273, Elkhorn, WI 53121-0273. Tel.: 262-723-4248.
E-mail: walcohistory@tds.net
Web Site: walcohistory.org
Key Personnel: Pres., James Boardman.
Institution Type/Description: Historic House: 1830s Webster House.
Hours & Admission Prices: May to mid-Oct. Wed.-Fri. 1-5. &
Attendance: 6,000 (estimated)

Ellison Bay

DEATH'S DOOR MARITIME MUSEUM (GILLS ROCK), 12724 Wisconsin Bay Rd., Ellison Bay, WI 54210-9796. Mailing Address: 120 N. Madison Ave., Sturgeon Bay, WI 54235-3416. Tel.: 920-743-5958. Fax: 920-743-9483. Facebook: Door County Maritime Museum; Cana Island Lighthouse.
E-mail: info@dcmm.org
Web Site: www.dcmm.org
Formerly: Door County Maritime Museum (at Gills Rock)
Key Personnel: Exec. Dir., Mktg. & Communications, Amy Paul; Pres., Bill Harder; Vice Pres., Terry Connelly; Treas., Frank Forkert; Museum Shop Mgr., Cassie Buntin.
Institution Type/Description: Maritime Museum.
Hours & Admission Prices: May-Oct. daily 10-5. Adults $6, youth 5-17 $3; children 4 & under, active military & members no charge. &
Attendance: 3,758 (actual)

NEWPORT STATE PARK, 475 Cty. Hwy. NP, Ellison Bay, WI 54210. Tel.: 920-854-2500. Fax: 920-854-1914.
E-mail: Michelle.Hefty@wisconsin.gov
Web Site: https://dnr.wi.gov/topic/parks/name/newport/
Key Personnel: Park Mgr., Michelle M. Hefty.
Institution Type/Description: State Park: located on the Door County Peninsula.
Hours & Admission Prices: Daily 6am-11pm. Call for entrance & camping fees. &

Ephraim

EPHRAIM HISTORICAL FOUNDATION, 3060 Anderson Ln., Ephraim, WI 54211. Mailing Address: P.O. Box 165, Ephraim, WI 54211-0165. Tel.: 920-854-9688. Facebook: Ephraim Historical Foundation.
E-mail: info@ephraim.org
Web Site: ephraim.org
Key Personnel: Exec. Dir., Thea S. Thompson; Outreach Dir. & Cur., Emily Irwin; Dir. Opers., John M. Grochowski.
Institution Type/Description: Historic Buildings.
Hours & Admission Prices: mid-June to Labor Day Tues.-Sat. 11-4; Sept. to mid-Oct. Fri.-Sat. 11-4. No charge; donations accepted. &
Attendance: 5,100 (estimated)

Fennimore

FENNIMORE DOLL & TOY MUSEUM, 1135 6th St., Fennimore, WI 53809. Tel.: 608-822-4100.
E-mail: dolltoy@fennimore.com
Web Site: www.dollandtoymuseum.com
Key Personnel: Dir., Connie Neal.
Institution Type/Description: Doll & Toy Museum.
Hours & Admission Prices: Memorial Day to Labor Day daily 10-4; mid-Sept.-Oct. Sat.-Sun. 10:30-4; Nov.-May by appointment. Adults $3, children 5-12 $1.50; children under 5 no charge. &

FENNIMORE RAILROAD HISTORICAL SOCIETY MUSEUM, 610 Lincoln Ave., Fennimore, WI 53809-1559. Tel.: 608-822-6144.
Web Site: https://www.fennimore.com/community-life/museums/railroad-and-historical-society-museum/
Institution Type/Description: History Museum: housed in the former city power house and utility building.
Hours & Admission Prices: Memorial Day to Labor Day daily 10-4; Sept.-Oct. Sat.-Sun. 10-4; other times by appointment.

Fifield

OLD TOWN HALL MUSEUM, W7213 Pine St., Fifield, WI 54524-0156. Mailing Address: P.O. Box 156, Fifield, WI 54524-0156. Tel.: 715-339-2254.
E-mail: dabkbrayton03@pctcnet.net
Web Site: www.pricecountyhistoricalsociety.org
Key Personnel: Pres. (V), Etola Foytek.
Institution Type/Description: History Museum: housed in 1894 Old Town Hall.
Hours & Admission Prices: June to Labor Day Fri. & Sun. 1-3. No charge; donations accepted. &
Attendance: 714 (actual)

Fish Creek

EAGLE BLUFF LIGHTHOUSE MUSEUM, 9462 Shore Rd., Peninsula State Park, Fish Creek, WI 54212. Mailing Address: P.O. Box 71, Sturgeon Bay, WI 54235. Tel.: 920-421-3636.
E-mail: info@doorcountyhistoricalsociety.org
Web Site: www.eagleblufflighthouse.org
Key Personnel: Exec. Dir., Trudy Herbst; Site Mgr., Linda Faust.
Institution Type/Description: Historic House: 1868 Eagle Bluff Lighthouse located on the Door County Peninsula.
Hours & Admission Prices: mid-May to late Oct. daily 10-3:30. Adults $8.50, students 13-17 $5.50, youth 6-12 $3.50; children 5 & under no charge. &
Attendance: 16,000 (actual)

FRANCIS HARDY GALLERY, 3038 Anderson Ln., Fish Creek, WI 54212. Mailing Address: P.O. Box 394, Ephraim, WI 54211. Tel.: 920-854-5535.
E-mail: info@thehardy.org
Web Site: www.thehardy.org
Key Personnel: Exec. Dir., ElizabethSarah Zamecnik.
Institution Type/Description: Art Gallery.
Hours & Admission Prices: mid-May to mid-Oct. Mon.-Sat. 10-5; call for additional hours. Closed Independence Day. &

PENINSULA STATE PARK, 9462 Shore Rd., Fish Creek, WI 54212-9696. Tel.: 920-868-3258.
E-mail: kathleen.harris@wisconsin.gov
Web Site: dnr.wi.gov/topic/parks/name/peninsula/
Key Personnel: NR Educator, Kathleen Harris.
Institution Type/Description: State Park: located on the Door County Peninsula.
Hours & Admission Prices: Daily 6am-11pm; call for reservations. See website for admissions. Nature Center: Memorial Day to Labor Day daily 10-2; Sept.-May call for hours.

Fond du Lac

CHILDREN'S MUSEUM OF FOND DU LAC, 75 W. Scott St., Fond du Lac, WI 54935. Tel.: 920-929-0707.
E-mail: info@cmfdl.org
Web Site: www.cmfdl.org
Key Personnel: Dir., Andrea Welsch.
Institution Type/Description: Children's Museum.
Hours & Admission Prices: Tues.-Thurs. 9-5, Fri. 9-7, Sat.-Sun. 10-4. Adults & children $8, seniors $7; children under one & members no charge. &
Attendance: 46,000 (actual)

GALLOWAY HOUSE AND VILLAGE - BLAKELY MUSEUM, 336 Old Pioneer Rd., Fond du Lac, WI 54935-6126. Mailing Address: P.O. Box 1284, Fond du Lac, WI 54936-1284. Tel.: 920-922-1166. Facebook: Fond du Lac Historical Society.
E-mail: info@fdlhistory.com
Web Site: www.fdlhistory.com
Key Personnel: Pres., Mat Mueller; Treas., Linda Evans; Sec., Marianne Geiger.
Institution Type/Description: Historic House & Village Museum: 30 historic buildings including Galloway house built in 1868.
Hours & Admission Prices: Memorial Day-Labor Day Wed.-Sat. 11-4, Sun. 1-3. Family $30, adults $9, children 7-17 & seniors $8; children 6 & under and members no charge. &
Attendance: 7,000 (estimated)

THELMA SADOFF CENTER FOR THE ARTS, 51 Sheboygan St., Fond du Lac, WI 54935-4219. Tel.: 920-921-5410. Facebook: Thelma Sadoff Center for the Arts.
E-mail: info@thelmaarts.org
Web Site: www.thelmaarts.org
Formerly: Windhover Center for the Arts
Key Personnel: Exec. Dir., Jacqui Corsi; Cur. & Arts Education Coord., Michael Wartgow.
Institution Type/Description: Art Gallery.
Hours & Admission Prices: Mon.-Fri. 10-5, Sat. 11-3. No charge. &
Attendance: 50,000 (estimated)

Fort Atkinson

HOARD HISTORICAL MUSEUM'S NATIONAL DAIRY SHRINE MUSEUM, 401 Whitewater Ave., Fort Atkinson, WI 53538-2255. Tel.: 920-563-7769.
E-mail: info@hoardmuseum.org
Web Site: www.hoardmuseum.org
Formerly: Hoard Historical Museum and National Dairy Shrine's Visitors Center
Key Personnel: Dir., Merrilee Lee; Asst. Dir., Dana Bertelsen; Volunteer Coord., Tammy Doellstedt.
Institution Type/Description: Local History Museum.
Hours & Admission Prices: Tues.-Sat. 9:30-4:30. No charge; donations accepted. &
Attendance: 20,000 (actual)

Fountain City

ELMER'S AUTO & TOY MUSEUM, W903 Elmers Rd., Fountain City, WI 54629. Tel.: 608-687-7221.
E-mail: elmerstoys@yahoo.com
Web Site: www.elmersautoandtoymuseum.com
Institution Type/Description: Auto & Toy Museum.
Hours & Admission Prices: See website for hours. Adults $10, seniors 65 & over $8, students 6-17 $5; children under 6 no charge.

Fox Lake

FOX LAKE HISTORICAL MUSEUM, INC., 211 Cordelia St. & S. College Ave., Fox Lake, WI 53933. Tel.: 920-296-0254. Facebook.
Web Site: www.foxlakehistoricalsociety.com/museum
Institution Type/Description: Railroad Museum.
Hours & Admission Prices: June-Oct. 1st & 3rd Sun. 1-4; other times by appointment. No charge; donations accepted. &
Attendance: 250 (estimated)

Genesee Depot

TEN CHIMNEYS FOUNDATION, S43 W31575 Depot Rd., Genesee Depot, WI 53127. Mailing Address: P.O. Box 225, Genesee Depot, WI 53127-0225. Tel.: 262-968-4110. Facebook.
E-mail: info@tenchimneys.org
Web Site: www.tenchimneys.org
Key Personnel: Pres. & C.E.O., Randy Bryant; Experience Mgr. & Museum Shop Mgr., Janis Foll.
Institution Type/Description: Historic House: housed in the estate of theatre legends, Alfred Lunt and Lynn Fontanne. Listed on the National Registry of Historic Places.
Hours & Admission Prices: Tours: mid-May to early Dec. Tues.-Sat. 10-2:30, Sun. 12-2:30; reservations recommended. Adults $28-$50; children under 12 not admitted.
Attendance: 12,000 (estimated)

Germantown

SILA LYDIA BAST BELL MUSEUM & FIRE HALL, N128 W18780 Holy Hill Rd., Germantown, WI 53022. Mailing Address: P.O. Box 31, Germantown, WI 53022. Tel.: 262-628-3170.
E-mail: germantownhistoricalsociety@gmail.com
Web Site: www.germantownhistoricalsociety.org
Institution Type/Description: History Museum.
Hours & Admission Prices: June-Nov. 1 Fri.-Sun. 1-4; other times by appointment. &

Gordon

GORDON-WASCOTT HISTORICAL MUSEUM, 9672 E. County Rd. Y, Gordon, WI 54838. Mailing Address: P.O. Box 222, Gordon, WI 54838. Tel.: 715-376-4234.
Web Site: www.townofwascott.org/history.shtml
Key Personnel: Chm. (V), Nancy Hasbrouck.
Institution Type/Description: Historical Society Museum.
Hours & Admission Prices: Memorial Day-Labor Day Fri.-Mon. 10-4.

Green Bay

GREEN BAY BOTANICAL GARDEN, 2600 Larsen Rd., Green Bay, WI 54303-4841. Tel.: 920-490-9457. Facebook: Green Bay Botanical Garden.
E-mail: info@gbbg.org
Web Site: www.gbbg.org
Key Personnel: Exec. Dir., Susan Garot; Dir. Horticulture, Mark A. Konlock.
Institution Type/Description: Botanical Garden.
Hours & Admission Prices: Jan.-March Mon.-Sat. 9-5; April & Oct.-mid-Nov. daily 9-5; May & Sept. daily 9-7; June-Aug. daily 9-8; mid.-Nov.-Dec. Mon.-Fri. 9-5. Adults $10, seniors, military, students, AAA & AARP members $8 children 13-17 $5; children 2, & under and NWTC faculty & students no charge. &
Attendance: 125,000 (actual)

GREEN BAY PACKERS HALL OF FAME, 1265 Lombardi Ave., Green Bay, WI 54304-3997. Mailing Address: P.O. Box 10628, Green Bay, WI 54307-0628. Tel.: 920-569-7512.
E-mail: zegersk@packers.com
Web Site: www.packers.com/lambeau-field/hall-of-fame/visit
Key Personnel: Cur., Brent Hensel; Hall of Fame & Stadium Tour Mgr., Krissy Zegers.
Institution Type/Description: Sports Museum & Hall of Fame.
Hours & Admission Prices: Mon.-Sat. 9-6, Sun. 10-5. Adults $15, seniors 62 & over, youth 12-17, military & college students $12, children 6-11 $9; children 5 & under no charge. &
Attendance: 100,000 (estimated)

HAZELWOOD HISTORIC HOME MUSEUM, Physical/Mailing Address: 1008 S. Monroe Ave., P.O. Box 1411, Green Bay, WI 54301. Tel.: 920-437-1840. Fax: 920-455-4518.
E-mail: bchs@netnet.net
Web Site: www.browncohistoricalsoc.org
Key Personnel: Exec. Dir., Christine Dunbar; Prog. Mgr. & Vol. Coord., Brooke Uhl.
Institution Type/Description: Historic House Museum: built in 1837.
Hours & Admission Prices: June-Aug. Thurs.-Sun. 12-4; Dec. see website for hours. Adults $4, seniors $3.50, students 5-17 $2.50; members no charge.
Attendance: 1,500 (estimated)

HERITAGE HILL STATE HISTORICAL PARK, 2640 S. Webster Ave., Green Bay, WI 54301-2997. Tel.: 920-448-5150. Fax: 920-448-5147.
E-mail: info@heritagehillgb.org
Web Site: www.heritagehillgb.org
Key Personnel: CEO, Margaret Karius; Finance & Admin. Mgr., Kristine Auguston; Dir. Sls & Mktg., Rebecca Lom; Dir. Education, Erin Comer; Dir. Opers., Nik Backhaus.
Institution Type/Description: Village & Park Museum: located on the site of 1820s Camp Smith, former army outpost.
Hours & Admission Prices: Memorial Day to Labor Day Tues.-Fri. 10-4:30, Sun. 12-4:30; Sept. to late May Tues.-Fri. 10-4:30. General admission: adults $8, seniors 62 & over and veterans $5, children 3-15 & students $5. &
Attendance: 56,000 (actual)

LAWTON GALLERY, UNIVERSITY OF WISCONSIN-GREEN BAY, 2420 Nicolet Dr. (TH 230), Green Bay, WI 54311-7003. Tel.: 920-465-2916. Facebook.

E-mail: hitzmane@uwgb.edu
Web Site: www.uwgb.edu/lawton
Key Personnel: Cur. Art, Emma Hitzman.
Institution Type/Description: Art Gallery.
Hours & Admission Prices: Sept.-May Tues.-Sat. 10-3. No charge. &
Attendance: 3,000 (actual)

NATIONAL RAILROAD MUSEUM, 2285 S. Broadway, Green Bay, WI 54304-4832. Tel.: 920-437-7623. Facebook: Friends of the National Railroad Museum.
Web Site: www.nationalrrmuseum.org
Key Personnel: Exec. Dir., Jacqueline D. Frank; Mgr. Operations & Cur., Daniel Liedtke; C.F.O., Robert Bloedorn; Dir. Education, Bob Lettenberger; Museum Shop Mgr., Chris Gustofson; Mktg. & Communs. Dir., Jan Padron.
Institution Type/Description: Railroad Museum.
Hours & Admission Prices: Jan.-March Tues.-Sat. 9-5, Sun. 11-5; April-Dec. Mon.-Sat. 9-5, Sun. 11-5. Adults $10, senior citizens $9, children 2-12 $7.50; children under 2 no charge. Closed New Year's Day; Easter; Thanksgiving; Christmas Eve & Day. &
Attendance: 86,000 (actual)

NEVILLE PUBLIC MUSEUM OF BROWN COUNTY, 210 Museum Pl., Green Bay, WI 54303-2780. Tel.: 920-448-4460. Fax: 920-448-4458.
E-mail: bc_museum@co.brown.wi.us
Web Site: www.nevillepublicmuseum.org
Key Personnel: Exec. Dir., Beth Lemke; Deputy Dir., Kevin Cullen; Cur., Lisa Cain; Collections Mgr., Louise Pfotenhauer.
Institution Type/Description: General Museum.
Hours & Admission Prices: Sun. 12-5, Tues. 12-8, Wed.-Sat. 9-5. Adult $7, children 6-15 $3; discounts to school & youth groups; members and children 5 & under no charge. &
Attendance: 64,508 (actual)

NEW ZOO & ADVENTURE PARK, 4378 Reforestation Rd., Green Bay, WI 54313. Tel.: 920-434-7841.
E-mail: info@newzoo.org
Web Site: www.newzoo.org
Institution Type/Description: Zoo and Adventure Park.
Hours & Admission Prices: April-May & Sept.-Oct. daily 9-6; June-Aug. daily 9-8; Nov.-March 9-4; see website to confirm hours. Adults 16 & over $9, seniors 62 & over and children 3-15 $6; members and children 2 & under no charge. Adventure Park: see website for hours and admissions.

Green Lake

DARTFORD DEPOT MUSEUM, 554 Mill St., Green Lake, WI 54941. Mailing Address: P.O. Box 638, Green Lake, WI 54941. Tel.: 920-294-6194.
E-mail: info@dartfordhistorical.org
Web Site: www.dartfordhistorical.org
Institution Type/Description: History Museum: housed in a former railroad depot; built in 1870s.
Hours & Admission Prices: Memorial Day to Labor Day Sat. 10-1. No charge; donations accepted.
Attendance: 400 (estimated)

DARTFORD HISTORICAL SOCIETY, 501 Mill St., Green Lake, WI 54941. Mailing Address: P.O. Box 638, Green Lake, WI 54941. Tel.: 920-294-6194.
E-mail: info@dartfordhistorical.org
Web Site: www.dartfordhistorical.org
Institution Type/Description: Historical Society Museum: housed in the former public library.
Hours & Admission Prices: Open by appointment. No charge; donations accepted. &
Attendance: 300 (estimated)

Greenbush

WADE HOUSE HISTORIC SITE, W 7965 Hwy. 23, Greenbush, WI 53026. Mailing Address: P.O. Box 34, Greenbush, WI 53026-0034. Tel.: 920-526-3271.
E-mail: wadehouse@wisconsinhistory.org
Web Site: www.wadehouse.org
Formerly: Wade House Stagecoach Inn & Wesley Jung Carriage Museum State Historic Site
Key Personnel: Dir., David Warner; Cur. Interpretation, James Willaert.
Institution Type/Description: Historic Site & Transportation Museum.

Hours & Admission Prices: See website for hours & admission prices. &
Attendance: 28,651 (actual)

Greenfield

GREENFIELD HISTORICAL SOCIETY, 5601 W. Layton Ave., Greenfield, WI 53220. Tel.: 414-327-8321. Facebook.
E-mail: greenhistory@outlook.com
Web Site: greenfieldhistoricalsocietywi.org/index.html
Institution Type/Description: Historical Society Museum.
Hours & Admission Prices: Open during major events occurring at the civic facility. No charge; donations accepted.
Attendance: 200 (estimated)

Hales Corners

FRIENDS OF BOERNER BOTANICAL GARDEN, INC., 9400 Boerner Dr., Hales Corners, WI 53130-2273. Tel.: 414-525-5653. Facebook.
E-mail: ehayward@fbbg.org
Web Site: www.boernerbotanicalgardens.org
Key Personnel: Pres. & C.E.O., Ellen Hayward; Education Mgr., Paul Vandermeuse; Mktg. & Events Coord., Sarah Warran; Gift Shop Mgr., Nancy Roeglin.
Institution Type/Description: Botanical Gardens.
Hours & Admission Prices: Garden: late April to late Sept. daily 8-6; late Sept.-Oct. call for hours. Education & Visitor Center: April-Sept. daily 8-6; Oct.-April Mon.-Fri. 9-4, Sun. 10-2. Adults $6.50, seniors, disabled & students $5, juniors 6-17 $4.50. &
Attendance: 100,000 (estimated)

Hartford

WISCONSIN AUTOMOTIVE MUSEUM, 147 N. Rural St., Hartford, WI 53027-1407. Tel.: 262-673-7999. Facebook: Wisconsin Auto Museum.
E-mail: info@wisconsinautomuseum.com
Web Site: www.wisconsinautomuseum.com
Formerly: Hartford Heritage Auto Museum
Key Personnel: Exec. Dir., Dawn Bondhus.
Institution Type/Description: Transportation Museum.
Hours & Admission Prices: May-Sept. Mon.-Sat. 10-5, Sun. 12-5; Oct.-April Wed.-Sat. 10-5, Sun. 12-5. Adults $10, seniors over 62 $9, students 6-16 $6; children 5 & under no charge. &
Attendance: 10,000 (estimated)

Hayward

NATIONAL FRESH WATER FISHING HALL OF FAME, 10360 Hall of Fame Dr., Hayward, WI 54843. Mailing Address: P.O. Box 690, Hayward, WI 54843-0690. Tel.: 715-634-4440.
E-mail: fishhall@chegnet.net
Web Site: www.freshwater-fishing.org
Key Personnel: Exec. Dir., Emmett A. Brown, Jr.
Institution Type/Description: Freshwater & Marine Museum.
Hours & Admission Prices: mid-April-May & Sept.-Oct. daily 9:30-4; June-Aug. daily 9:30-4:30. Adults $8.25, children 4-17 $6.25, children 3 & under and active military no charge. &
Attendance: 40,000 (estimated)

Hillsboro

HILLSBORO AREA HISTORICAL SOCIETY, 678 Maple St., Hillsboro, WI 54634. Tel.: 608-489-3594.
E-mail: hillsborohistory@gmail.com
Institution Type/Description: General Museum.
Hours & Admission Prices: June-Labor Day Sun. 1-3; other times by appointment. No charge; donations accepted.
Attendance: 385 (actual)

Horicon

SATTERLEE CLARK HOUSE, 322 Winter St., Horicon, WI 53032-1035. Tel.: 920-485-0483.
E-mail: horiconhistoricalsociety@yahoo.com
Institution Type/Description: Historical Society Museum: housed in c.1863, Satterlee Clark Home.
Hours & Admission Prices: May-Oct. 4th Sun. each month 1-4; Dec. 1st Sun. 1-4; other times by appointment. No charge; donations accepted.
Attendance: 1,000 (estimated)

Hudson

THE OCTAGON HOUSE, 1004 Third St., Hudson, WI 54016-1219. Tel.: 715-386-2654. Facebook: St. Croix County Historical Society.
E-mail: octagon@stcroixcountyhistory.org
Web Site: www.stcroixcountyhistory.org
Key Personnel: Dir., Leila Albert; Asst. Dir., Mary Lesher.
Institution Type/Description: Victorian Museum: housed in 1855 Octagonal House; carriage house & garden house.
Hours & Admission Prices: May-late Oct. Fri.-Sun. 11-4; early to mid-Dec. Sat.-Sun. 11-4. Adults $10, seniors, active military, AAM members 7 groups of 10 or more $8, students 6-18 $3, children 5 & under no charge.
Attendance: 3,000 (estimated)

THE PHIPPS CENTER FOR THE ARTS GALLERIES, 109 Locust St., Hudson, WI 54016. Tel.: 715-386-8409.
E-mail: info@thephipps.org
Web Site: www.thephipps.org
Key Personnel: Pres. (V), Roger Olson.
Institution Type/Description: Art Gallery.
Hours & Admission Prices: Mon.-Fri. 9-4, Sat. 9-12.

Hurley

IRON COUNTY HISTORICAL MUSEUM, 303 Iron St., Hurley, WI 54534-1356. Tel.: 715-561-2244.
E-mail: genec@chartermi.net
Formerly: Old Iron County Courthouse Museum
Key Personnel: C.E.O., Chm. & Museum Shop Mgr., Gene Cisewski; Pres. (V), Nick L. Zuvich; Treas., Minerva Stefani; Sec., Helen Zuvich.
Institution Type/Description: General Museum: housed in 1893 Old Iron County Courthouse.
Hours & Admission Prices: Mon., Wed. & Fri.-Sat. 10-2; other times by appointment. No charge. Closed holidays. &
Attendance: 5,200 (estimated)

Janesville

THE LINCOLN-TALLMAN RESTORATIONS, 440 N. Jackson St., Janesville, WI 53548. Tel.: 608-756-4509.
E-mail: officemgr@rchs.us
Web Site: www.rchs.us
Key Personnel: Interim Exec. Dir., Tim Maahs; Opers. Mgr., Keighton Klos; Archives Mgr., Kristin Arnold; Education Cur., Nathan Fuller.
Institution Type/Description: Historic House.
Hours & Admission Prices: See website for hours. Adults $10, seniors 62 & over and college students $9, children 6-17 $6; discounts to groups; AMM, AAM, AASLH, WFH, RCHS members, veterans and children 5& under no charge. &
Attendance: 4,480 (actual)

ROCK COUNTY HISTORICAL SOCIETY, 426 N. Jackson St., Janesville, WI 53548. Tel.: 608-756-4509. Facebook, Twitter, Pinterest & Instagram: rockctyhistory.
E-mail: kklos@rchs.us
Web Site: www.rchs.us
Key Personnel: Exec. Dir., Michael Reuter; Pres. (V), Rich Gruber; Operations Mgr., Keighton Klos; Cur. & Collections Mgr., Laurel Fant; Education Cur., Nathan Fuller; Volunteer & Intern Program Mgr., Amanda Strobel Wise.
Institution Type/Description: Historical Society Museum.
Hours & Admission Prices: Archives: March-Dec. Wed.-Fri. 10-4. Museum: Feb.-May Mon.-Fri. 10-4; June-Dec. 30 daily 10-4. Lincoln-Tallman House: Feb.-May tours by appointment; June-Dec. 30 daily 10-4. Adults $8; AAA, AMM, WFM, U.S. veterans & members no charge. &
Attendance: 11,000 (estimated)

Jefferson

AZTALAN MUSEUM, N6284 Hwy. Q, Jefferson, WI 53549. Mailing Address: P.O. Box 122, Lake Mills, WI 53551-0122. Tel.: 920-648-4632. Facebook: Lake Mills Aztalan.
E-mail: lakemillsaztalanhistorical@gmail.com
Web Site: www.lakemillsaztalanhistory.com
Key Personnel: Pres. (V), Robin Untz.
Institution Type/Description: General Museum.
Hours & Admission Prices: May & Sept. Sat.-Sun. 12-4; June-Aug. Fri.-Sun. 12-4. Adults $5, seniors & students $3; children 5 & under no charge.
Attendance: 2,000 (estimated)

Kaukauna

CHARLES A. GRIGNON MANSION, 1313 Augustine St., Kaukauna, WI 54130-1613. Mailing Address: P.O. Box 341, Kaukauna, WI 54130. Tel.: 920-766-6106.
E-mail: info@grignonmansion.org
Web Site: www.myhistorymuseum.org
Institution Type/Description: Historic House: housed in the former home of Charles A. Grignon Mansion; built in 1837.
Hours & Admission Prices: May to Labor Day Sat.-Sun. 12-4; other times by appointment. Adults $6, seniors 62 & over $5, children 6-17 $3; children under 5 no charge.
Attendance: 6,000 (actual)

Kenosha

ANDERSON ARTS CENTER, 6603 Third Ave., Kenosha, WI 53143. Tel.: 262-653-0481. Facebook: Anderson Arts Center.
E-mail: carolina@andersonartscenter.com
Web Site: www.andersonartscenter.com
Key Personnel: Admin., Carolina Curi-Bado; Cur., Candace Hoffmann; Education Dir., June Ristau; Special Events Coord., Flora Doody; Volunteer Coord., Robin Ingrouille.
Institution Type/Description: Arts Center.
Hours & Admission Prices: Tues.-Sun. 1-4. No charge; donations accepted.
Attendance: 6,304 (actual)

CIVIL WAR MUSEUM, 5400 First Ave., Kenosha, WI 53140-6508. Tel.: 262-653-4141. Facebook.
E-mail: thaase@kenosha.org
Web Site: museums.kenosha.org/civilwar/
Key Personnel: Dir., Dan Joyce; Deputy Dir., Peggy Gregorski; Education Mgr., Doug Dammann; Devel. Mgr., Lisa Dretske; Exhibits & Collections Mgr., Gina Radandt.
Institution Type/Description: Military History Museum.
Hours & Admission Prices: Mon.-Sat. 10-5, Sun. noon-5. Admission $9; discounts to Kenosha/Somers residents; members and children 15 & under no charge. Closed Martin Luther King, Jr. Day; Good Friday; Easter; Memorial Day; Labor Day; Thanksgiving; Christmas Eve & Day; New Year's Eve & Day &
Attendance: 74,557 (actual)

DINOSAUR DISCOVERY MUSEUM, 5608 Tenth Ave., Kenosha, WI 53140. Tel.: 262-653-4450. Facebook: Dinosaur Discovery Museum.
E-mail: djoyce@kenosha.org
Web Site: museums.kenosha.org/dinosaur/
Key Personnel: Dir., Dan Joyce; Deputy Dir., Peggy Gregorski; Devel. Mgr., Lisa Dretske; Education Mgr., Doug Dammann.
Institution Type/Description: Dinosaur Museum.
Hours & Admission Prices: Tues.-Sun. 12-5. No charge; donations accepted. Closed New Year's Eve & Day; Martin Luther King Jr. Day; Good Friday; Easter; Memorial Day; Independence Day; Labor Day; Thanksgiving; Christmas Eve & Day. &
Attendance: 42,699 (actual)

KENOSHA COUNTY HISTORICAL SOCIETY AND MUSEUM, INC., 220 51st Place, Kenosha, WI 53140-2909. Tel.: 262-654-5770. Fax: 262-654-1730.
E-mail: kchs@kenoshahistorycenter.org
Web Site: www.kenoshahistorycenter.org
Key Personnel: Exec. Dir., Chris Allen; Cur. Collections, Archivist & Educator, Cynthia Nelson.
Institution Type/Description: Local History Museum.
Hours & Admission Prices: History Center: Tues.-Fri. 10-4:30, Sat. 10-4, Sun. 12-4. Light Station & Museum: May 3-Oct. Thurs.-Sat. 10-4, Sun. 12-4. No charge. Closed holidays. &
Attendance: 18,000 (actual)

KENOSHA PUBLIC MUSEUM, 5500 First Ave., Kenosha, WI 53140-3778. Tel.: 262-653-4140. Facebook: Kenosha Public Museum.
E-mail: djoyce@kenosha.org
Web Site: museums.kenosha.org/public
Key Personnel: Dir., Dan Joyce; Deputy Dir., Peggy Gregorski; Devel. Dir., Lisa Dretske; Education Mgr., Doug Dammann; Exhibits & Collection Mgr., Gina Radandt.
Institution Type/Description: Natural Science & Fine Arts Museum.
Hours & Admission Prices: Mon.-Sat. 10-5, Sun. 12-5. No charge; donations accepted. New Year's Eve & Day; Martin Luther King Jr. Day; Good Friday; Easter; Memorial Day; Labor Day; Thanksgiving; Christmas Eve & Day. &
Attendance: 130,151 (actual)

Kewaunee

KEWAUNEE COUNTY HISTORICAL JAIL MUSEUM, Court House Sq., Kewaunee, WI 54216. Mailing Address: 217 Ellis St., Kewaunee, WI 54216. Tel.: 920-388-0369.
E-mail: gandolfoo@hotmail.com
Web Site: www.kewauneecountyhistory.com/
Key Personnel: Pres. (V), Thomas Schuller; Vice Pres., Richard Dorner; Treas., Arletta Bertrand; Sec., Gloria Peterson.
Institution Type/Description: General Museum: housed in 1876 sheriff's residence & adjoining dungeon type jail cells.
Hours & Admission Prices: Memorial Day-Labor Day Thurs.-Sun. 12-4. Suggested Donation: adults $2, students $1.
Attendance: 356 (actual)

La Crosse

CHILDREN'S MUSEUM OF LA CROSSE, 207 Fifth Ave. S., La Crosse, WI 54601. Tel.: 608-784-2652. Facebook: Funmuseum.
E-mail: info@funmuseum.org
Web Site: funmuseum.org
Key Personnel: Exec. Dir., Anne Snow; Mktg. & Devel. Dir., Leanne Poellinger.
Institution Type/Description: Children's Museum.
Hours & Admission Prices: Tues.-Sat. 10-5, Sun. 12-5. Admission $7; discounts to ACM & ASTC members & Sun.; children under one & members no charge. Closed major holidays. &
Attendance: 72,980 (actual)

HIXON HOUSE, 429 N. 7th St., La Crosse, WI 54601-3301. Mailing Address: La Crosse County Historical Society, 145 West Ave. S., La Crosse, WI 54601-4382. Tel.: 608-782-1980.
E-mail: admin@lchshistory.org
Web Site: www.lchshistory.org/hixon-house/
Key Personnel: Exec. Dir., Peggy Derrick; Collections Mgr., Amy Vach.
Institution Type/Description: Period Home: housed in c.1859 Hixon House.
Hours & Admission Prices: Memorial Day to Labor Day Tues.-Sat. 10-2; group tours by appointment. Adults $10, seniors 62 & over $8, students $6. &
Attendance: 8,000 (estimated)

PUMP HOUSE REGIONAL ARTS CENTER, 119 King St., La Crosse, WI 54601. Tel.: 608-785-1434. Facebook; Twitter;.
E-mail: contact@thepumphouse.org
Web Site: www.thepumphouse.org
Key Personnel: Exec. Dir., Toni Asher; Arts Admin., Shelby Phillips; Arts Admin. & Facility Mgr., Ken MacKenzie.
Institution Type/Description: Arts Center: housed in 1880 brick Romanesque revival water pumping building. Listed on National Register of Historic Buildings.
Hours & Admission Prices: Tues.-Fri. 11-7, Sat. 12-4. &
Attendance: 31,250 (estimated)

RIVERSIDE MUSEUM, 410 E. Veterans Memorial Dr., La Crosse, WI 54601-4490. Mailing Address: 145 West Ave. S., La Crosse, WI 54601-4382. Tel.: 608-782-1980.
E-mail: admin@lchshistory.org
Web Site: www.lchshistory.org/riverside-museum/
Key Personnel: Exec. Dir. & Cur., Peggy Derrick; Collections Mgr., Amy Vach.
Institution Type/Description: History Museum: housed in an old fish hatchery building. Listed on the National Register of Historic Sites.
Hours & Admission Prices: Memorial Day-Labor Day Mon.-Fri. 9:30-4:30, Sat.-Sun. 10-4; Sept.-May Mon.-Fri. 9:30-4:30. Families $12, adults $4. &
Attendance: 12,000 (actual)

La Pointe

MADELINE ISLAND MUSEUM, 226 Colonel Woods Ave., La Pointe, WI 54850. Mailing Address: P.O. Box 9, La Pointe, WI 54850-0009. Tel.: 715-747-2415.
E-mail: madeline@wisconsinhistory.org
Web Site: www.madelineislandmuseum.org
Key Personnel: Site Dir., Keldi Merton; Supt. Bldgs. & Grounds, Tim Eldred.
Institution Type/Description: Historic Site & Museum.
Hours & Admission Prices: Late May to late June daily 10-4; Late June to early Sept. daily 10-5; early Sept. to late Oct. Tues.-Sun. 10-4. Adults 19-64 $8, seniors 65 & over & students $7; children 17 & under and members no charge. &
Attendance: 12,192 (actual)

Lac du Flambeau

OJIBWE MUSEUM AND CULTURAL CENTER, 603 Peace Pipe Rd., Lac du Flambeau, WI 54538. Mailing Address: P.O. Box 804, Lac du Flambeau, WI 54538. Tel.: 715-588-3333. Facebook.
E-mail: tmitchell@ldftribe.com
Web Site: www.ldfmuseum.com
Key Personnel: Dir., Teresa Mitchell.
Institution Type/Description: Native American History Museum.
Hours & Admission Prices: See website for hours. Adults $4, seniors 65 & over & children 6-17 $3. &
Attendance: 2,500 (estimated)

Ladysmith

RUSK COUNTY HISTORICAL SOCIETY, 998 E. 3rd St. N., Ladysmith, WI 54848. Tel.: 715-415-5615; 415-3114. Facebook: Rusk Co. Historical Museum.
Web Site: ruskcountymuseum.com/
Institution Type/Description: Historical Museum.
Hours & Admission Prices: Memorial Day-Labor Day, Sat.-Sun. 12:30-4:30; other times by appointment. No charge; donations accepted. &
Attendance: 2,067 (estimated)

Lake Geneva

GENEVA LAKE MUSEUM, 255 Mill St., Lake Geneva, WI 53147-1927. Tel.: 262-248-6060. Pintrest: Geneva Lake Museum.
E-mail: staff@genevalakemuseum.org
Web Site: www.genevalakemuseum.org
Formerly: Geneva Lake History Buffs, Inc.
Key Personnel: Dir. Admin., Janet Ewing; Dir. Opers., Dale Buelter; Cur., Helen Brandt.
Institution Type/Description: History Museum: located in the 1929 Wisconsin Power and Light Building.
Hours & Admission Prices: Jan.-March & Nov.-Dec. Tues. & Fri.-Sun. 11-3; April Tues. & Fri.-Sat. 10-4, Sun. 11-3; May Mon.-Tues. & Sat. 10-4, Fri. & Sun. 11-3; June-Oct. Mon.-Sat. 10-4, Sun. 11-3. Adults $7, seniors & college students with ID $6; children through high school age, active military with ID & up to 5 family members, members with ID no charge. &
Attendance: 19,234 (actual)

Lake Tomahawk

LAKE TOMAHAWK HISTORICAL SOCIETY, 7247 Kelly Dr., Lake Tomahawk, WI 54539. Tel.: 715-277-2080.
E-mail: beverlyfagan@frontier.com
Formerly: Northland Historical Society, Inc.
Institution Type/Description: Historical Society Museum.
Hours & Admission Prices: Sat. 1-3; other times by appointment. No charge; donations accepted. &
Attendance: 50 (estimated)

Lancaster

CUNNINGHAM MUSEUM, 129 E. Maple St., Lancaster, WI 53813. Tel.: 608-723-4925.
Web Site: grantcountyhistory.org
Institution Type/Description: History Museum.
Hours & Admission Prices: Mon.-Fri. 1-4:30; other times by appointment. No charge; donations accepted.

Laona

CAMP FIVE MUSEUM FOUNDATION, INC., 5480 Connor Farm Rd., Laona, WI 54541-9201. Mailing Address: P.O. Box 5, Laona, WI 54541-0005. Tel.: 715-674-3414. Fax: 715-674-7400.
E-mail: info@lumberjacksteamtrain.com
Web Site: www.lumberjacksteamtrain.com
Institution Type/Description: Logging Museum & Ecology Complex: operates Laona & Northern Railway's Lumberjack Special steam train.
Hours & Admission Prices: mid-June to late Aug. Thurs.-Mon. Trains at 11, 12, 1 & 2 to Camp Five Logging Museum Complex. Adults $20, children 4-16 $8; discounts to active military & families, groups & seniors; children under 3 no charge. &
Attendance: 13,918 (actual)

Madison

CHAZEN MUSEUM OF ART, 750 University Ave., Madison, WI 53706-1479. Tel.: 608-263-2246.
E-mail: reception@chazen.wisc.edu
Web Site: chazen.wisc.edu
Formerly: Elvehjem Museum of Art
Key Personnel: Dir., Amy Gilman; Asst. Dir. Admin., Kristine Zickuhr; Cur. Paintings, Sculpture & Decorative Arts, Maria Saffiotti Dale; Cur. Education, Candie Waterloo; Distinguished Cur. Prints, Drawings & Photographs, Andrew Stevens; Registrar, Andrea Selbig; Exhibition Mgr. & Registrar, Ann Sinfield; Dir. Devel., Ale Nicolet; Devel. Specialist, Amy Guthier; Editor, Kirstin Pires; Communications Designer, Jeff Weyer.
Institution Type/Description: Art Museum.
Hours & Admission Prices: Tues.-Wed. & Fri. 9-5, Thurs. 9-9, Sat.-Sun. 11-5. No charge; donations accepted. Closed New Year's Day; Thanksgiving; Christmas Eve & Day. ♿
Attendance: 105,750 (actual)

HELEN LOUISE ALLEN TEXTILE COLLECTION, 1300 Linden Dr., Univ. of Wisconsin, 1235 Nancy Nicholas Hall, Madison, WI 53706-1524. Tel.: 608-262-1162.
E-mail: hlatc@sohe.wisc.edu
Web Site: textilecollection.wisc.edu
Key Personnel: Dir., Sherry Harlacher; Cur. Collections, Carolyn Jenkinson.
Institution Type/Description: Textile & Costume Collection.
Hours & Admission Prices: Mon.-Fri. 10-4. ♿

HENRY VILAS PARK ZOO, 702 S. Randall Ave., Madison, WI 53715-1600. Tel.: 608-266-4732.
E-mail: zoo@countyofdane.com
Web Site: www.vilaszoo.org
Key Personnel: Dir., Ronda Schwetz; Deputy Dir., Jeff Halter; Cur., Greg Peccie.
Institution Type/Description: Zoo.
Hours & Admission Prices: Buildings: daily 10-4. Grounds: daily 9:30-5. Call for holiday hours. No charge; donations accepted. ♿
Attendance: 700,000 (estimated)

JAMES WATROUS GALLERY OF THE WISCONSIN ACADEMY OF SCIENCES, ARTS AND LETTERS, Overture Center for the Arts, 201 State St., 3rd Fl., Madison, WI 53703. Tel.: 608-265-2500. Facebook: Wisconsin Academy.
E-mail: contact@wisconsinacademy.org
Web Site: www.wisconsinacademy.org/gallery
Key Personnel: Exec. Dir., Jane Elder; Dir., Jody Clowes.
Institution Type/Description: Art Gallery.
Hours & Admission Prices: Wed.-Thurs. & Sun. 12-5, Fri.-Sat. 12-8; other times by appointment. No charge; donations accepted. ♿
Attendance: 10,000 (estimated)

MADISON CHILDREN'S MUSEUM, INC., 100 N. Hamilton St., Madison, WI 53703-2116. Tel.: 608-256-6445.
E-mail: fedwardsmiller@madisonchildrensmuseum.org
Web Site: madisonchildrensmuseum.org
Key Personnel: Pres. & C.E.O., Deborah Gilpin; Dir. Exhibitions, Brenda Baker; Dir. Mktg. & Communs., Jonathan Zarov; Dir. Education, Kia Karlen; Dir. Devel, Dani Luckett; Dir. Facilities, Luke Schultz.
Institution Type/Description: Children's Museum.
Hours & Admission Prices: May-Sept. daily 9:30-5; Labor Day to Memorial Day Tues.-Sun. 9:30-5. Admission $9, seniors & grandparents $8; children under one & members no charge. Closed some national holidays. ♿
Attendance: 200,000 (estimated)

MADISON MUSEUM OF CONTEMPORARY ART, 227 State St., Madison, WI 53703-2214. Tel.: 608-257-0158. Fax: 608-257-5722.
E-mail: info@mmoca.org
Web Site: www.mmoca.org
Formerly: Madison Art Center
Key Personnel: Dir., Stephen Fleischman; Devel. Officer, Kaitlin Kropp; Cur. Exhibitions, Leah Kolb; Cur. Permanent Collection, Mel Becker Colomon; Cur. Education, Sheri Castelnuovo; Business Mgr., Michael Paggie; Head Registrar, Marilyn Sohi; Dir. Devel., Elizabeth Tucker; Dir. Events & Volunteers, Annik Dupaty; Dir. Communications, Erika Monroe-Kane; Dir. Retail Operations, Leslie Genszler; Dir. Installations & Facilities, Brian Bartlett; Dir. Public Opers., Bob Sylvester.
Institution Type/Description: Art Museum.
Hours & Admission Prices: Tues.-Thurs. & Sun. 12-5, Fri. 12-8, Sat. 10-8. No charge; donations accepted. Closed major holidays. ♿
Attendance: 200,000 (estimated)

OLBRICH BOTANICAL GARDENS, 3330 Atwood Ave., Madison, WI 53704-5808. Tel.: 608-246-4550. Fax: 608-246-4719. Facebook.
E-mail: olbrichinformation@cityofmadison.com
Web Site: www.olbrich.org
Key Personnel: Dir., Roberta Sladky; Dir. Horticulture, Jeff Epping; Conservatory Cur., Colten Blackburn.
Institution Type/Description: Botanical Garden.
Hours & Admission Prices: Lobby & Garden: April-Aug. daily 9-8; Sept.-Oct. daily 9-6; Nov.-March daily 9-4. Bolz Conservatory: daily 10-4. Outdoor Gardens: no charge; donations accepted. Conservatory: $2; children 5 & under, members, Wed. & Sat. mornings no charge. Closed New Year's Day; Third Sat. in June; Thanksgiving; Christmas. ♿
Attendance: 325,530 (actual)

STEENBOCK GALLERY, Wisconsin Academy of Sciences, Arts and Letters, 1922 University Ave., Madison, WI 53726. Tel.: 608-263-1692. Fax: 608-265-3039.
E-mail: contact@wisconsinacademy.org
Web Site: www.wisconsinacademy.org
Key Personnel: Dir., James Watrous Gallery, Jody Clowes.
Institution Type/Description: Art Gallery.
Hours & Admission Prices: Mon.-Fri. 8:30-4:30.

UNIVERSITY OF WISCONSIN-MADISON ARBORETUM, 1207 Seminole Hwy., Madison, WI 53711-3726. Tel.: 608-263-7888. Fax: 608-262-5209.
E-mail: info@arboretum.wisc.edu
Web Site: arboretum.wisc.edu
Key Personnel: Dir., Karen Oberhauser.
Institution Type/Description: Arboretum.
Hours & Admission Prices: Trails: daily 7am-10pm. Visitor Center: Mon.-Fri. 9:30-4, Sat.-Sun. 12:30-4. No charge; donations accepted. ♿
Attendance: 650,000 (actual)

UNIVERSITY OF WISCONSIN - MADISON GEOLOGY MUSEUM, 1215 W. Dayton St., Weeks Hall, Madison, WI 53706. Tel.: 608-262-1412. Fax: 608-262-0693.
E-mail: museum@geology.wisc.edu
Web Site: www.geology.wisc.edu/museum
Key Personnel: Dir., Richard Slaughter; Cur., Carrie Eaton.
Institution Type/Description: Geology Museum.
Hours & Admission Prices: Mon.-Fri. 8:30-4:30, Sat. 9-1. No charge. ♿
Attendance: 50,000 (estimated)

UNIVERSITY OF WISCONSIN ZOOLOGICAL MUSEUM, 250 N. Mills St., Lowell E. Noland Zoology Bldg., Madison, WI 53706-1708. Tel.: 608-262-3766.
E-mail: uwzm@mailplus.wisc.edu
Web Site: uwzm.integrativebiology.wisc.edu
Key Personnel: Cur. Collections, Laura A. Monahan; Cur. Mammalogy & Birds, Paul M. Holahan; Registrar, Emily Halverson.
Institution Type/Description: Zoology Museum.
Hours & Admission Prices: By appointment. ♿
Attendance: 3,500 (estimated)

WISCONSIN HISTORICAL MUSEUM, 30 N. Carroll St., Madison, WI 53703-2707. Tel.: 608-264-6555.
E-mail: museum@wisconsinhistory.org
Web Site: historicalmuseum.wisconsinhistory.org
Formerly: State Historical Museum of Wisconsin
Key Personnel: Museum Deputy Dir., Mike Hollander; Exhibits Designer, Doug Griffin; Mus. Shop Mgr., Anna Lange.
Institution Type/Description: History Museum.
Hours & Admission Prices: Tues.-Sat. 9-4. Adults $5, children 5-17 $3; children 4 & under no charge. Closed national holidays. ♿
Attendance: 72,500 (actual)

WISCONSIN STATE CAPITOL, 2 E. Main St., Madison, WI 53702. Tel.: 608-266-0382.
Web Site: tours.wisconsin.gov/
Institution Type/Description: Historic Building: built in 1906.
Hours & Admission Prices: Mon.-Fri. 8-6, Sat.-Sun. 8-4.

THE WISCONSIN UNION GALLERIES, UNIVERSITY OF WISCONSIN-MADISON, 1308 W. Dayton St., Madison, WI 53715. Tel.: 608-262-7592. Fax: 608-890-4411. Facebook; Twitter; Instagram.
E-mail: art@union.wisc.edu

Web Site: union.wisc.edu/get-involved/wud/art/
Key Personnel: Dir., Brandon Phouybanhdyt Liu; Installation Assoc. Dir., Sophie Plzak; Installation Assoc. Dir., Ellie Braun; Assoc. Dir. Mktg., Celia Glime; Assoc. Dir. Devel., Lily Miller; Graphic Design Assoc. Dir., Emma Waldinger; Deputy Installation Assoc. Dir., Abi Case.
Institution Type/Description: Art Gallery.
Hours & Admission Prices: See website for hours. Closed holidays & during school breaks. &
Attendance: 300,000 (estimated)

WISCONSIN VETERANS MUSEUM, 30 W. Mifflin St., Suite 200, Madison, WI 53703-2589. Tel.: 608-267-1799. Facebook: Wisconsin Veterans Museum.
E-mail: veterans.museum@dva.wisconsin.gov
Web Site: wisvetsmuseum.com
Key Personnel: Dir., Michael Telzrow; Asst. Dir., Jennifer Van Haaften; Reference Archivist, Russell Horton; Sr. Mktg. Specialist, Karen Burch; Collections Mgr., Andrea Hoffman; Registrar, Sarah Kapellusch; Cur. Exhibits, Gregory Krueger; Cur. History, Kevin Hampton; Oral Historian, Ellen Brooks; Gift Store Mgr., Gregory Lawson.
Institution Type/Description: State Military History Museum: located downtown Madison.
Hours & Admission Prices: April-Sept. Tues.-Sat. 9-4:30. Sun. 12-4; Oct.-March Tues.-Sat. 9-4:30. Research Center: Tues.-Fri. by appointment. No charge. Closed holidays. &
Attendance: 110,064 (actual)

Manitowoc

LINCOLN PARK ZOO, 1215 N. 8th, Manitowoc, WI 54220. Tel.: 920-683-4685 (Zoo) & 686-3060 (Office).
E-mail: zoo@manitowoc.org
Web Site: www.manitowoc.org/766/Lincoln-Park-Zoo
Key Personnel: Recreation Div. Mgr., Denise Larson.
Institution Type/Description: Zoo.
Hours & Admission Prices: April to late May & early Sept.-Oct. Mon.-Sat. 9-5; Memorial Day to Labor Day daily 7-7; Nov.-March Mon.-Sat. 7-3. No charge; donations accepted. &
Attendance: 55,584 (estimated)

MANITOWOC COUNTY HISTORICAL SOCIETY, 924 Pinecrest Rd., Manitowoc, WI 54220. Tel.: 920-684-4445.
E-mail: info@manitowoccountyhistory.org
Web Site: www.manitowoccountyhistory.org
Key Personnel: Exec. Dir., Amy Meyer.
Institution Type/Description: History Museum.
Hours & Admission Prices: Pinecrest Historical Village: May-Oct. 24 Tues.-Sun. 10-4. Adults $10, children 5-17 $7; discounts to seniors; members & children under 5 no charge.
Attendance: 7,000 (estimated)

RAHR WEST ART MUSEUM, 610 N. 8th St., Manitowoc, WI 54220-3998. Tel.: 920-686-3090.
E-mail: rahrwest@manitowoc.org
Web Site: www.rahrwestartmuseum.org
Key Personnel: Exec. Dir., Greg Vadney; Asst. Dir. & Cur., Diana Bolander.
Institution Type/Description: Art Museum.
Hours & Admission Prices: Tues.-Fri. 10-4, Sat.-Sun. 11-4. Suggestion donation: adults $5, children $2. &
Attendance: 25,612 (actual)

WISCONSIN MARITIME MUSEUM, 75 Maritime Dr., Manitowoc, WI 54220-6823. Tel.: 920-684-0218. Fax: 920-684-0219.
E-mail: museum@wisconsinmaritime.org
Web Site: www.wisconsinmaritime.org
Key Personnel: CEO, Rolf E. Johnson; Deputy Dir. & Chief Cur., Cathy Green; Financial Svcs. Mgr., Tom Smith; Educator, Abbie Diaz; Dir. Collections, Tiffany Charles.
Institution Type/Description: Maritime Museum.
Hours & Admission Prices: Museum & Submarine: Mid-March-June & Sept.-Oct. daily 9-5; July-Aug. daily 9-6; Nov.-mid-March Mon. & Thurs.-Fri. 10-4, Sat.-Sun. 9-4. Adults $15, seniors & veterans $12, youth 4-12 $8; children 3 & under and active military with current ID no charge. Closed New Year's Day; Easter; Thanksgiving; Christmas Eve & Day. &
Attendance: 46,525 (actual)

Marinette

MARINETTE HISTORICAL MUSEUM, 1650 Bridge St., Marinette, WI 54143. Tel.: 715-732-0831.

E-mail: flauerman@new.rr.com
Web Site: www.marinettemuseum.com
Institution Type/Description: History Museum: building & c.1895 log cabin.
Hours & Admission Prices: Memorial Day to Labor Day Mon. 12-4 & Tues.-Fri. 10-4. Adults $3, teens $1; children 12 & under no charge. &
Attendance: 2,000 (estimated)

Marshfield

NEW VISIONS GALLERY, INC., 1000 N. Oak Ave., Marshfield, WI 54449-5703. Tel.: 715-387-5562. Facebook: New Visions Gallery, Inc..
E-mail: nvgallery@marshfieldclinic.org
Web Site: www.newvisionsgallery.org
Key Personnel: C.E.O. & Dir., Bobbie Erwin.
Institution Type/Description: Art Museum.
Hours & Admission Prices: Call for hours. &
Attendance: 25,000 (estimated)

UPHAM MANSION - NORTH WOOD COUNTY HISTORICAL SOCIETY, 212 W. 3rd St., Marshfield, WI 54449-2706. Mailing Address: P.O. Box 142, Marshfield, WI 54449-0142. Tel.: 715-387-3322. Facebook.
E-mail: nwchs@uphammansion.com
Web Site: www.uphammansion.com
Key Personnel: Pres. (V), Brad Allen; Coord., Kim Krueger.
Institution Type/Description: Historic Building/Site: Italianate-Victorian style home, built in 1880 by William Henry Upham, leading businessman of Marshfield till his death in 1924; governor of WI 1895-96.
Hours & Admission Prices: Mansion: Wed. & Sat. 1:30-4; groups by appointment. Adults $2; children 12 & under and members no charge. Office: Mon. & Thurs. 9-1, Wed. 10-4.
Attendance: 1,800 (actual)

Mauston

THE BOORMAN HOUSE - THE JUNEAU COUNTY HISTORICAL SOCIETY, 211 N. Union St., Mauston, WI 53948-1418. Mailing Address: P.O. Box 321, Mauston, WI 53948-0321. Tel.: 608-847-3294. Facebook: Boorman House.
E-mail: rclarkjco@gmail.com
Key Personnel: Historiographer & Museum Shop Mgr., Rose Clark.
Institution Type/Description: Historical Site & Building. Listed on the National Register of Historic Places and on the Wisconsin Register of Historic Homes.
Hours & Admission Prices: Call for hours.
Attendance: 2,090 (estimated)

Mayville

MAYVILLE HISTORICAL SOCIETY, INC., 1 N. German St., Mayville, WI 53050. Mailing Address: P. O. Box 82, Mayville, WI 53050. Tel.: 920-344-6736 (Tours). Facebook.
E-mail: barlarsen@att.net
Web Site: mayvillehistoricalsociety.org
Key Personnel: Tours, Barbara Larsen.
Institution Type/Description: Historical Society Museum.
Hours & Admission Prices: May-Oct. 2nd & 4th Sun. 1:30-4:30. No charge; donations accepted. &
Attendance: 385 (actual)

Mazomanie

MAZOMANIE HISTORICAL SOCIETY, 118 Brodhead St., Mazomanie, WI 53560. Mailing Address: Box 248, Mazomanie, WI 53560-0248. Tel.: 608-795-2992.
E-mail: rita42@centurytel.net
Web Site: www.mazomaniehistory.org
Key Personnel: Mgr., Andrew Szudy.
Institution Type/Description: General Museum.
Hours & Admission Prices: May-Sept. Sun. 1-4, call to confirm. Suggested Donation: adults $3. &
Attendance: 334 (actual)

McFarland

MCFARLAND HISTORICAL SOCIETY, 5814 Main St., McFarland, WI 53558. Tel.: 608-838-3992.
E-mail: bluebee@madtown.net
Web Site: www.mcfarlandhistorical.org
Key Personnel: Pres. (V), Dale Marsden.

Institution Type/Description: Historical Society Museum: housed in a log cabin.
Hours & Admission Prices: Memorial Day to late Sept. Sun. 1-4; tours by appointment. No charge; donations accepted.
Attendance: 2,000 (estimated)

Menasha

WEIS EARTH SCIENCE MUSEUM, University of Wisconsin-Fox Valley, 1478 Midway Rd., Menasha, WI 54952-1224. Tel.: 920-832-2925. Facebook.
E-mail: scott.mikulic@uwc.edu
Web Site: www.weismuseum.org/index.html
Key Personnel: Dir., Scott Mikulic.
Institution Type/Description: Earth Science Museum.
Hours & Admission Prices: Mon.-Fri. 12-3, Sat. 10-5, Sun. 1-5. Adults $3, seniors 60 & over and teens 13-17 $2, children 3-12 $1; children under 3, UW Fox students, faculty & staff with ID no charge. Closed national holidays.

Menomonee Falls

HARLEY-DAVIDSON - POWERTRAIN OPERATIONS TOUR CENTER, W156 N9000 Pilgrim Rd., Menomonee Falls, WI 53051. Tel.: 877-883-1450.
Web Site: harley-davidson.com
Institution Type/Description: Company History Museum.
Hours & Admission Prices: Steel Toe Tour: Mon.-Fri. 10 am & 12 pm. Adults $38; discounts to groups of 15 or more. Classic Factory Tour: Mon.-Fri. 9 am, 10:30 am, 11:45, 12:45, & 1:30 pm. Adults $10; discount to groups of 10 or more. Freedom Factory Tour: Mon.-Fri. 8:30 am. No charge.

OLD FALLS VILLAGE, Hwy. Q & Pilgrim Rd., Menomonee Falls, WI 53052. Mailing Address: P.O. Box 91, Menomonee Falls, WI 53051-0091. Tel.: 262-250-3901.
E-mail: mfhistory@yahoo.com
Web Site: www.oldfallsvillage.com/
Key Personnel: Pres. (V), Rev. Nancy Greifenhagen.
Institution Type/Description: Historic Houses.
Hours & Admission Prices: Call for hours.
Attendance: 6,000 (estimated)

Menomonie

DUNN COUNTY HISTORICAL SOCIETY, 1820 Wakanda St., Menomonie, WI 54751-1631. Mailing Address: P.O. Box 437, Menomonie, WI 54751-0437. Tel.: 715-232-8685. Facebook: Dunn County Historical Society.
E-mail: dchs@dunnhistory.org
Web Site: www.dunnhistory.org
Key Personnel: Exec. Dir., Frank Smoot; Cur. Emeritus, John Russell; Registrar, Sofi Doane; Education, Melissa Kneeland.
Institution Type/Description: Historical Society Museum.
Hours & Admission Prices: Heritage Museum: May-Sept. Wed.-Sun. 10-5; Oct.-April Wed.-Sun. 12-4. Families $12, adults $5, youth 13-18 $3, children 6-12 $1, children 5 & under and DCHS members no charge. &
Attendance: 5,000 (actual)

JOHN FURLONG GALLERY, Micheels Hall, 415 13th Ave. E., Menomonie, WI 54751-3279. Mailing Address: University of Wisconsin-Stout, 712 S. Broadway St., 309C Applied Arts Bldg., Menomonie, WI 54751. Tel.: 715-232-2261 & 1097. Fax: 715-232-1669.
E-mail: furlong@uwstout.edu
Web Site: www.uwstout.edu/academics/colleges-schools/school-art-design/furlong-gallery
Key Personnel: Dir., Robert Atwell.
Institution Type/Description: University Art Gallery.
Hours & Admission Prices: Mon.-Thurs. 10-5, Fri. 10-2, Sat. 12-4. No charge; donations accepted. &
Attendance: 7,000 (estimated)

WILSON PLACE MANSION, 101 Wilson Cir., Menomonie, WI 54751-1860. Mailing Address: P.O. Box 437, Menomonie, WI 54751. Tel.: 715-235-2283. Facebook: Wilson Place Mansion.
E-mail: wilsonplacemansion@gmail.com
Web Site: www.dunnhistory.org/history/exwp.html
Formerly: Wilson Place Museum
Key Personnel: Exec. Dir., Frank Smoot.
Institution Type/Description: History Museum.

Hours & Admission Prices: mid-Nov. to mid.-Dec. daily 1-5. Adults $5, seniors, students & children $3.

Mequon

CONCORDIA UNIVERSITY-WISCONSIN, ART GALLERY, 12800 N. Lake Shore Dr., Barth 109, Mequon, WI 53097-2418. Tel.: 262-243-4470.
E-mail: Theresa.Kenney@cuw.edu
Web Site: www.cuw.edu/life/involvement-and-activities/fine-arts/art-gallery/index.html
Key Personnel: Dir., Theresa Ann Kenney.
Institution Type/Description: Art Gallery.
Hours & Admission Prices: Mon.-Thurs. 4-8, Fri.-Sat. 12-4. &
Attendance: 600 (estimated)

Merrill

MERRILL HISTORICAL SOCIETY, 100 E. Third St., Merrill, WI 54452-2321. Tel.: 715-536-5652.
E-mail: merrillhs@frontier.com
Web Site: merrillhistory.org
Key Personnel: Pres., Beatrice Lebal; Treas., Patricia Burg; Collections Admin., Beverly King.
Institution Type/Description: Historic Society Museum.
Hours & Admission Prices: Tues.-Tues. & Thurs.-Fri. 9-1, Wed. 9-3, Sat. 10-1; other times by appointment.
Attendance: 6,915 (actual)

Middleton

NATIONAL MUSTARD MUSEUM, 7477 Hubbard Ave., Middleton, WI 53562-3117. Tel.: 800-438-6878.
E-mail: customerservice@mustardmuseum.com
Web Site: www.mustardmuseum.com
Formerly: Mount Horeb Mustard Museum
Key Personnel: Cur., Barry Levenson.
Institution Type/Description: Food Museum.
Hours & Admission Prices: Daily 10-5. No charge; donations accepted. Closed New Year's Day; Easter; Thanksgiving; Christmas. &
Attendance: 30,000 (estimated)

Milton

MILTON HOUSE MUSEUM HISTORIC SITE, 18 S. Janesville St., Milton, WI 53563-1527. Tel.: 608-868-7772.
E-mail: kklebba@miltonhouse.org
Web Site: www.miltonhouse.org
Key Personnel: Exec. Dir., Kari Klebba; Asst. Dir., Doug Welch.
Institution Type/Description: History Museum: housed in a stagecoach inn used as a stop on the Underground Railroad.
Hours & Admission Prices: Memorial Day-Labor Day daily 10-4; other times by appointment. Adults $8, seniors $6, youth $4; children under 5 no charge. Closed Fathers' Day. &
Attendance: 10,000 (estimated)

Milwaukee

BETTY BRINN CHILDREN'S MUSEUM, 929 E. Wisconsin Ave., Milwaukee, WI 53202-5406. Tel.: 414-390-5437. Fax: 414-291-0906.
E-mail: questions@bbcmkids.org
Web Site: www.bbcmkids.org
Key Personnel: Pres., Jessica Lochmann Allen; Vice Pres., Admin., Matt D'Attilio; Vice Pres., Education, Victoria Teerlink; Vice Pres., Exhibitions, Melissa Nelsen; Vice Pres., Finance, Stephanie Lyons; Vice Pres., Friends, Maggie Hammes; Vice Pres., Mktg., April Dunn; Vice Pres., Nominating & Develop., Erik Zipp; Vice Pres., Product Develop., Joan Phillips.
Institution Type/Description: Children's Museum.
Hours & Admission Prices: Mon.-Sat. 9-5, Sun. 12-5. Adults & children 1 & over $8; seniors 55 & over $7; discounts to Association of Children's museum & military; members, 3rd Thurs. of month 5-8, children under one no charge. &
Attendance: 160,000 (estimated)

THE CAPTAIN FREDERICK PABST MANSION, 2000 W. Wisconsin Ave., Milwaukee, WI 53233-2004. Tel.: 414-931-0808.
E-mail: info@pabstmansion.com
Web Site: pabstmansion.com
Key Personnel: Pres., Pamela Williams-Lime; Exec. Dir., John C. Eastberg; Cur., Jodi Rich-Bartz; Dir. Guest Experience, Gary Strothmann; Archivist, Jocelyn Slocum.

Institution Type/Description: Historic House: former home of Captain Frederick Pabst, built in 1892.
Hours & Admission Prices: See website for hours and admissions. &

Attendance: 25,000 (estimated)

CHARLES ALLIS ART MUSEUM, 1801 N. Prospect Ave., Milwaukee, WI 53202-1933. Tel.: 414-278-8295.
E-mail: info@cavtmuseums.org
Web Site: www.cavtmuseums.org
Key Personnel: Exec. Dir., John Sterr; Sr. Cur., Shana McCaw; Asst. Cur. & Collections Mgr., Jenille Junco; Mktg. Mgr., Kayle Karbowski; Events Mgr., Michael Keiley; Membership Mgr., Matt Pappas; Rentals Mgr., Robyn Erickson; Beverage Mgr., Samantha Joseph.
Institution Type/Description: Art Museum: housed in 1909 Tudor style mansion designed by Alexander Eschweiler.
Hours & Admission Prices: Wed. & Fri.-Sun. 1-5, Thurs. 1-8. Adults $7, seniors over 65, military & students $5; 1st Wed. of the month, children 12 & under & members no charge. Closed New Year's Eve & Day; Thanksgiving; Christmas Eve & Day. &
Attendance: 1,657 (actual)

DISCOVERY WORLD, 500 N. Harbor Dr., Milwaukee, WI 53202-5601. Tel.: 414-765-9966.
E-mail: info@discoveryworld.org
Web Site: www.discoveryworld.org
Formerly: Discovery World - The James Lovell Museum of Science, Economics and Technology
Key Personnel: Pres. & C.E.O., Joel Brennan; C.O.O., Carl Schoettel; CFO, Kate Halfwassen.
Institution Type/Description: Science, Economics & Technology Museum.
Hours & Admission Prices: Tues.-Fri. 9-4, Sat.-Sun. 10-5. Adults $19, seniors 60 & over & children 3-17 $16, college students, veterans & active military $14; children 2 & under no charge. &
Attendance: 400,000 (estimated)

THOMAS A. GREENE GEOLOGICAL MUSEUM, UNIVERSITY OF WISCONSIN-MILWAUKEE, 3367 N. Downer Ave., Milwaukee, WI 53211-3102. Mailing Address: P.O. Box 413, Milwaukee, WI 53201-0413. Tel.: 414-229-5067.
E-mail: sdornbos@uwm.edu
Web Site: uwm.edu/geosciences/research/greene-museum/
Key Personnel: Cur., Stephen Dornbos.
Institution Type/Description: Geology Museum.
Hours & Admission Prices: See website for hours. No charge; donations accepted. Closed major holidays & university breaks.

GROHMANN MUSEUM, 1000 N. Broadway, Milwaukee, WI 53202. Mailing Address: 1025 N. Broadway, Milwaukee, WI 53202-3109. Tel.: 414-277-2300. Facebook.
E-mail: grohmannmuseum@msoe.edu
Web Site: www.msoe.edu/museum
Key Personnel: Dir., James Kieselburg; Collections & Exhibition Mgr., Russ Piant; Visitor Svcs. Coord., Ann Rice.
Institution Type/Description: Art Gallery.
Hours & Admission Prices: Mon.-Fri. 9-5, Sat. 12-6, Sun. 1-4. Adults $5, students & seniors $3; MSOE students, alumni, faculty & staff, & children under 12 no charge. &
Attendance: 22,000 (estimated)

HARLEY-DAVIDSON MUSEUM, 400 W. Canal St., Milwaukee, WI 53203-3208. Tel.: 414-287-2789.
Web Site: www.harley-davidson.com/us/en/museum.html
Institution Type/Description: Motorcycle Museum.
Hours & Admission Prices: See website for hours. Adults $20, senior citizens 65 & over, US military with ID and students with ID $14, children 5-17 $10; members & children under 5 with adult no charge.

JEWISH MUSEUM MILWAUKEE, 1360 N. Prospect Ave., Milwaukee, WI 53202. Tel.: 414-390-5730.
E-mail: info@jewishmuseummilwaukee.org
Web Site: www.jewishmuseummilwaukee.org
Key Personnel: Exec. Dir., Patti Sherman-Cisler; Cur., Molly Dubin; Education Dir., Elli Gettinger; Archives Dir., Jay Hyland; Special Events and Programs Coord., Cassie Sacotte.
Institution Type/Description: Jewish History Museum.
Hours & Admission Prices: Mon.-Thurs. 10-5, 3rd Thurs. each month 10-7, Fri. 10-3, Sun. 12-4. Adults $7, seniors $6, students $4; active military & children 6 & under no charge. Closed New Year's Day, Memorial Day, Independence Day, Labor Day, Thanksgiving & Jewish holidays.
Attendance: 5,500 (estimated)

LYNDEN SCULPTURE GARDEN, 2145 W. Brown Deer Rd., Milwaukee, WI 53217. Tel.: 414-446-8794. Fax: 414-446-8492.
E-mail: info@lyndensculpturegarden.org
Web Site: www.lyndensculpturegarden.org
Key Personnel: Exec. Dir., Polly Morris; Mgr. Collections, Bruce Knackert; Dir. Education, Jeremy Stepien.
Institution Type/Description: Sculpture Garden.
Hours & Admission Prices: Winter, Spring & Fall: Fri.-Wed. 10-5; Summer: Wed. 10-7:30, Fri.-Tues. 10-5. Adults $9, seniors, students & children $7; children under 6 no charge. &
Attendance: 17,000 (estimated)

MILWAUKEE ART MUSEUM, 700 N. Art Museum Dr., Milwaukee, WI 53202-4098. Tel.: 414-224-3200.
E-mail: mam@mam.org
Web Site: www.mam.org
Key Personnel: Dir., Marcelle Polednik.
Institution Type/Description: Art Museum.
Hours & Admission Prices: Tues.-Wed. & Fri.-Sun. 10-5, Thurs. 10-8. Adults $19, military, senior citizens 65 & over & students with ID $17; 1st Thurs. of month, WI K-12 teachers with ID, members & children 12 and under no charge. Closed Thanksgiving; Christmas. &
Attendance: 400,000 (estimated)

MILWAUKEE COUNTY HISTORICAL SOCIETY, 910 N. Old World Third St., Milwaukee, WI 53203-1591. Tel.: 414-273-8288.
E-mail: info@milwaukeehistory.net
Web Site: www.milwaukeehistory.net
Key Personnel: Exec. Dir., Mame Croze McCully; Cur., Ben Barbera.
Institution Type/Description: History Museum: housed in 1913 bank.
Hours & Admission Prices: Mon.-Sat. 9:30-5. Closed Martin Luther King, Jr. Day; Memorial Day; Independence Day; Labor Day; Thanksgiving Day & day after; Christmas Eve & Day; New Year's Eve & Day. &
Attendance: 65,000 (estimated)

MILWAUKEE COUNTY ZOOLOGICAL GARDENS, 10001 W. Blue Mound Rd., Milwaukee, WI 53226-4384. Tel.: 414-771-3040. Fax: 414-256-5410.
Web Site: www.milwaukeezoo.org
Key Personnel: Exec. Dir., Charles Wikenhauser; Deputy Zoo Dir. Animal Mgmt. & Health, Beth Rich; Deputy Zoo Dir. Admin. & Finance, Vera Westphal; Mktg. & Communications Dir., Laura Pedriani.
Institution Type/Description: Zoo.
Hours & Admission Prices: March-late May & Sept.-Oct. daily 9-4:30; late May-early Sept. daily 9-5; Nov.-Feb. Mon.-Fri. 9:30-2:30, Sat.-Sun. 9:30-4:30. Jan.-March adults $11;75, seniors $10.25, children 3-12 $8.75. April-Oct. adults $15.50, seniors $14.50, children 3-12 $12.50. Nov.-Dec. adults $13, seniors $11.50, children 3-12 $10; children 2 & under no charge. &
Attendance: 1,300,000 (actual)

MILWAUKEE FIRE HISTORICAL SOCIETY, LTD., Mailing Address: 1615 W. Oklahoma Ave., Milwaukee, WI 53215. Tel.: 414-286-5272. Facebook.
E-mail: milwfiremuseum@gmail.com
Institution Type/Description: Fire Museum & Educational Center: housed in the former headquarters of Engine 23; built in 1927.
Hours & Admission Prices: April-Dec. 1st Sun. each month 12-3 (excluding holidays). &

MILWAUKEE PUBLIC MUSEUM, 800 W. Wells St., Milwaukee, WI 53233-1478. Tel.: 414-278-2702.
E-mail: hillary.olson@mpm.edu
Web Site: www.mpm.edu
Key Personnel: Interim Pres. & CEO, Ellen Censky, Ph.D.; Sr. Vice Pres. Opers. & Finance, Ryan O'Desky; Sr. Vice Pres., Devel., Julie Quinlan Brame; Vice Pres. Audience & Community Engagement, Hillary Olson.
Institution Type/Description: Natural & Human History Museum.
Hours & Admission Prices: Mon.-Fri. 10-5, Sat. 9-5, Sun. 11-5; 1st Thurs. each month 9-8. Adults $18, senior citizens 65 & over, students & active military $14, youth 4-13 $12; discounts to groups & Milwaukee County residents; children 3 & under, members & 1st Thurs. of the month no charge. &
Attendance: 411,000 (estimated)

MITCHELL GALLERY OF FLIGHT, General Mitchell International Airport, c/o Milwaukee County Airport Div., 5300 S. Howell Ave., Milwaukee, WI 53207-6156. Tel.: 414-747-4503. Facebook.
E-mail: flymitchell@mitchellgallery.org
Web Site: www.mitchellgallery.org
Key Personnel: Pres. (V) & Dir., Bill Streicher.

Institution Type/Description: Aviation Museum.
Hours & Admission Prices: Open during normal airport hours. No charge; donations accepted. &
Attendance: 200,000 (estimated)

MITCHELL PARK HORTICULTURAL CONSERVATORY (THE DOMES), 524 S. Layton Blvd., Milwaukee, WI 53215-1236. Tel.: 414-257-5611.

E-mail: sandy.folaron@milwaukeecountywi.gov
Web Site: county.milwaukee.gov/EN/Parks/Explore/The-Domes
Key Personnel: Dir. of The Domes, Sandy Folaron.
Institution Type/Description: Botanical Garden & Conservatory: housed on site of the Jacques Vieau settlement, one of the first permanent buildings built in the Milwaukee area.
Hours & Admission Prices: Mon.-Fri. 9-5, Sat., Sun. & major holidays 9-4. Adults $8, students, juniors 6-17 & handicapped $6; senior citizens 60 & over $5; discounts to groups of 20 or more & residents; children 5 & under, members, Friends of Domes & Mon. 9-12 for Milwaukee County residents no charge. &
Attendance: 200,000 (actual)

THE PATRICK & BEATRICE HAGGERTY MUSEUM OF ART, Marquette University, 13th & Clybourn, Milwaukee, WI 53233. Mailing Address: P.O. Box 1881, Milwaukee, WI 53201-1881. Tel.: 414-288-1669.

E-mail: haggertym@marquette.edu
Web Site: www.marquette.edu/haggerty
Key Personnel: Dir. & Chief Cur., Susan Longhenry; Cur., Collections & Exhibition, Emilia Layden; Cur. Academic Engagement, Lynne Shumow; Registrar, Michelle Burton; Head Designer & Preparator, Daniel Herro; Mgr., Mus. Admin., Rachel Kieselburg; Visitor Experience Coord., Wiliam Farr; Mgr. Community Engagement, Mary Ann Bonet.
Institution Type/Description: Art Museum.
Hours & Admission Prices: Mon.-Wed. & Fri.-Sat. 10-4:30, Thurs. 10-8, Sun. 12-5; call to confirm. No charge; donations accepted. Closed some holidays. &
Attendance: 16,000

PECK SCHOOL OF THE ARTS, UNIVERSITY OF WISCONSIN-MILWAUKEE, 2155 N. Prospect Ave., Milwaukee, WI 53202. Tel.: 414-229-5070. Facebook.

E-mail: uwmpsoa@uwm.edu
Web Site: uwm.edu/arts/
Institution Type/Description: Art Museum.
Hours & Admission Prices: See website for hours. &
Attendance: 18,000 (actual)

UWM UNION-ART GALLERY, UWM Student Union Room W199, Campus Level, 2200 E. Kenwood Blvd., Milwaukee, WI 53211-3361. Tel.: 414-229-6310. Fax: 414-229-6709. Facebook.

E-mail: agallery@uwm.edu
Web Site: uwm.edu/studentinvolvement/arts-and-entertainment/union-art-gallery
Key Personnel: Gallery Mgr., Madison Auten; Asst. Mgr., Danielle Paswaters; Heah Gallery Asst., Leah Schretenthaler; Mktg. Coord., Grace Winter; Gallery Asst., Emily Hankins; Gallery Asst., Bailey Danz.
Institution Type/Description: Art Gallery.
Hours & Admission Prices: Sept.-May Mon.-Wed. & Fri. 12-5, Thurs. 12-7. No charge. Closed holidays; university breaks. &
Attendance: 13,000

VILLA TERRACE DECORATIVE ARTS MUSEUM, 2220 N. Terrace Ave., Milwaukee, WI 53202-1216. Tel.: 414-271-3656. Facebook, Twitter, Instagram.

E-mail: jsterr@cavtmuseums.org
Web Site: www.cavtmuseums.org
Key Personnel: Exec. Dir., John Sterr; Sr. Cur., Shana McCaw; Asst. Cur. & Collections Mgr., Jenille Junco; Events Mgr., Michael Keiley; Membership Mgr., Matt Pappas; Rentals Mgr., Megan Maikowski; Visitor Experience & Beverage Mgr., Taytum Markee.
Institution Type/Description: Italian style villa designed by David Adler in 1923 for Lloyd & Agnes Smith of the A.O. Smith Co.; European & fine decorative arts.
Hours & Admission Prices: Wed. & Fri.-Sun. 1-5., Thurs. 1-8 Adults $7, seniors, active military & students $5; 1st Wed. of the month, children under 13 & members no charge. Closed major federal holidays. &
Attendance: 4,465 (actual)

WALKER'S POINT CENTER FOR THE ARTS, 839 S. 5th St., Milwaukee, WI 53204-1730. Tel.: 414-672-2787.

E-mail: xela@wpca-milwaukee.org
Web Site: www.wpca-milwaukee.org
Key Personnel: Exec. Dir., Marcela Garcia; Program Coord., Cyndi Bergloff; Art Educator, Oscar Quinto Zamudio, Jr.

Institution Type/Description: Art Gallery.
Hours & Admission Prices: Tues.-Sat. 12-5. &
Attendance: 8,000 (actual)

WISCONSIN BLACK HISTORICAL SOCIETY/MUSEUM, 2620 W. Center St., Milwaukee, WI 53206-1155. Tel.: 414-372-7677. Facebook.

E-mail: info@wbhsm.org
Web Site: www.wbhsm.org
Key Personnel: Exec. Dir., Clayborn Benson.
Institution Type/Description: Historical Society Museum.
Hours & Admission Prices: Mon.-Fri. 11-4, Sat. 10-12:30. Call to confirm hours. General admission $5. Closed major holidays

WISCONSIN MARINE HISTORICAL SOCIETY, 814 W. Wisconsin Ave., Milwaukee, WI 53233-2385. Tel.: 414-286-3074. Fax: 414-286-2137. Facebook; Twitter.

E-mail: info@wmhs.org
Web Site: www.wmhs.org
Key Personnel: Exec. Dir., Suzette J. Lopez.
Institution Type/Description: Marine Historical Society.
Hours & Admission Prices: Call for hours. No charge. &

Mineral Point

PENDARVIS HISTORIC SITE, 114 Shake Rag St., Mineral Point, WI 53565-1063. Tel.: 608-987-2122. Facebook; Instagram; Pinterest; YouTube.

E-mail: pendarvis@wisconsinhistory.org
Web Site: www.pendarvishistoricsite.org
Key Personnel: Site Mgr., Bethany Brander.
Institution Type/Description: Historic House: 1841-1852 miners' cottages built by immigrants from Cornwall, England.
Hours & Admission Prices: late May to late Oct. Tues.-Sun. 10-4. Adults $10, groups & members $9, children 5-17 $6,WHS members no charge.
Attendance: 8,000 (actual)

Mishicot

MISHICOT HISTORICAL MUSEUM, 411 Buchanan, Mishicot, WI 54228. Tel.: 920-755-2525 & 3317.

E-mail: magic@mishicot.org
Web Site: www.mishicothistoricalmuseum.org
Institution Type/Description: History Museum: housed in a former two-room schoolhouse, built in 1874.
Hours & Admission Prices: May-Oct. Sat.-Sun. 1-4; other times by appointment.

Monroe

MONROE ARTS CENTER, 1315 11th St., Monroe, WI 53566. Mailing Address: P.O. Box 472, Monroe, WI 53566-0472. Tel.: 608-325-5700. Fax: 608-325-5701.

E-mail: info@monroeartscenter.com
Web Site: monroeartscenter.com
Key Personnel: Exec. Dir., Kathy Hennessy.
Institution Type/Description: Art Gallery.
Hours & Admission Prices: Tues.-Sat. 10-5.

NATIONAL HISTORIC CHEESEMAKING CENTER MUSEUM, 2108 6th Ave., Monroe, WI 53566-2768. Mailing Address: P.O. Box 516, Monroe, WI 53566. Tel.: 608-325-4636.

E-mail: info@greencountywelcomecenter.org
Web Site: nationalhistoriccheesemakingcenter.org
Institution Type/Description: History Museum.
Hours & Admission Prices: May-Oct. Tues.-Sat. 9-4, Sun. 11-4. Adults $5; children under 16 no charge.

Mount Horeb

MT. HOREB AREA MUSEUM, 100 S. Second St., Mount Horeb, WI 53572-2106. Tel.: 608-437-6486. Facebook: Mt. Horeb History.

E-mail: mthorebmuseum@mhtc.net
Web Site: www.mthorebhistory.org
Key Personnel: Dir., Destinee Udelhoven.
Institution Type/Description: History Museum.
Hours & Admission Prices: Daily 10-4. Families !0, adults $4, seniors 55 & over $3, children 12 & under $2; active duly military & veterans no charge. &
Attendance: 3,000 (actual)

Neenah

BERGSTROM-MAHLER MUSEUM OF GLASS, 165 N. Park Ave., Neenah, WI 54956-2956. Tel.: 920-751-4658. Facebook; Twitter; Instagram.
E-mail: answers@bmmglass.com
Web Site: bmmglass.com
Formerly: Bergstrom-Mahler Museum
Key Personnel: Exec. Dir., Jan Mirenda Smith; Mktg. & Communications Dir., Jennifer Stevenson; Asst. Cur., Casey Eichhorn; Museum Shop Mgr., Laureen Endter; Glass Studio Mgr., Taylor Moeller-Roy; Visitor Svcs. Coord., Kathy Ziminski.
Institution Type/Description: Art Museum.
Hours & Admission Prices: Tues.-Sat. 10-4:30, Sun. 1-4:30; 3rd Thurs. 10-7. No charge; donations accepted. Closed legal holidays. &
Attendance: 22,698 (actual)

NEENAH HISTORICAL SOCIETY, HIRAM SMITH, NEENAH'S HERITAGE PARK, OCTAGON HOUSE & WARD HOUSE, 343 Smith St., Neenah, WI 54956-2434. Mailing Address: P.O. Box 343, Neenah, WI 54957-0343. Tel.: 920-729-0244.
E-mail: neenahhistoricalsociety@gmail.com
Web Site: neenahhistoricalsociety.com
Key Personnel: Exec. Dir., Jane Lang; Asst. Exec. Dir., Becky Heidke Kwiatkowski.
Institution Type/Description: General Museum: housed in 1850s octagon house.
Hours & Admission Prices: By appointment. No charge; donations accepted. &
Attendance: 3,000 (estimated)

New Berlin

THE NEW BERLIN HISTORICAL SOCIETY, 19885 W. National Ave., New Berlin, WI 53146. Tel.: 262-643-8855.
E-mail: djtotten@earthlink.net
Web Site: newberlinhistoricalsociety.org
Key Personnel: Pres. (V), Dave Totten; Cur., Carol Gorichanaz.
Institution Type/Description: Historical Society Museum.
Hours & Admission Prices: Call for hours; group tours by appointment. No charge; donations accepted.
Attendance: 1,200 (estimated)

New Glarus

CHALET OF THE GOLDEN FLEECE, 618 2nd St., New Glarus, WI 53574. Mailing Address: c/o Village of New Glarus, P.O. Box 399, New Glarus, WI 53574. Tel.: 608-527-2614. Facebook.
E-mail: nggoldenfleece@gmail.com
Institution Type/Description: Historic House Museum: Swiss chalet.
Hours & Admission Prices: Memorial Day weekend to Oct. Sat. 10-3. Call for admissions.
Attendance: 4,000 (estimated)

SWISS HISTORICAL VILLAGE, 612 7th Ave., New Glarus, WI 53574. Tel.: 608-527-6838. Facebook.
E-mail: info@swisstown.com
Web Site: www.swisshistoricalvillage.org
Key Personnel: Pres., John Colstad.
Institution Type/Description: Historic Village.
Hours & Admission Prices: Late-May to mid-Oct. daily 10-4. Adults $9, children 6-13 $3. &
Attendance: 10,000 (estimated)

New Holstein

TIMM HOUSE HISTORIC SITE, 1600 Wisconsin Ave., New Holstein, WI 53061-1340. Tel.: 920-948-7748. Facebook.
E-mail: newholsteinhistory@gmail.com
Web Site: www.newholsteinhistory.info
Formerly: Pioneer Corner Museum
Key Personnel: Cur., Terry Thiessen.
Institution Type/Description: Historical Society Museum: built in the 1870s with an addition added in 1892.
Hours & Admission Prices: Timm House Historic Site: May-Oct. & Dec. Sat.-Sun. 1-4; other times by appointment. Pioneer Corner Museum: May-Oct. Sat.-Sun. 1-4; other times by appointment. Combo ticket (both museums) $10, adults $7, combo ticket children 12 & under $5. &
Attendance: 825 (estimated)

New London

NEW LONDON PUBLIC MUSEUM, 406 S. Pearl St., New London, WI 54961-1441. Tel.: 920-982-8520. Fax: 920-982-8617. Facebook.
E-mail: museum@newlondonwi.org
Web Site: www.newlondonwi.org/museum
Key Personnel: Dir., Christine Cross; Asst. Dir., Alice Gilman.
Institution Type/Description: General Museum.
Hours & Admission Prices: Memorial Day to Labor Day Mon.-Fri. 10-5; Sept.-May Mon.-Fri. 10-5, Sat. 10-1. No charge; donations accepted. &
Attendance: 3,800 (actual)

New Richmond

NEW RICHMOND HERITAGE CENTER, 1100 Heritage Dr., New Richmond, WI 54017-1741. Tel.: 715-246-3276.
E-mail: info@nrheritagecenter.org
Web Site: nrheritagecenter.org
Formerly: New Richmond Preservation Society
Key Personnel: Dir., Irv Sather; Bd. Asst., Rachel Starbuck; Pres., Cheryl Emerson; Treas., Gary Knutson; Cur., Mary Sather.
Institution Type/Description: Heritage Center.
Hours & Admission Prices: Mon.-Fri. 10-4. Adults $5, children $1; members no charge. Closed New Year's Day; Memorial Day; Independence Day; Labor Day; Thanksgiving; Christmas. &
Attendance: 10,000 (estimated)

North Freedom

MID-CONTINENT RAILWAY MUSEUM, E8948 Diamond Hill Road, North Freedom, WI 53951-9699. Mailing Address: P.O. Box 358, North Freedom, WI 53951-0358. Tel.: 608-522-4261. Fax: 608-522-4490.
E-mail: jeff@midcontinent.org
Web Site: www.midcontinent.org
Key Personnel: C.E.O., Chm. (V) & Pres. (V), Jeffrey B. Bloohm; Museum Shop Mgr. (V), Jeffrey Haertlien.
Institution Type/Description: Railway Museum.
Hours & Admission Prices: mid-May to Labor Day daily 9:30-5; day after Labor Day to mid-Oct. Sat.-Sun. 9:30-5. Adults $11, senior citizens $10, children $6; discounts to groups & AAA members; members no charge. &
Attendance: 29,329 (actual)

Oak Creek

OAK CREEK HISTORICAL SOCIETY-PIONEER VILLAGE, S. 15th Ave. & E. Forest Hill Ave., Oak Creek, WI 53154. Mailing Address: P.O. Box 243, Oak Creek, WI 53154-0243. Tel.: 414-529-0196.
E-mail: roweworld@att.net
Web Site: plschu.wixsite.com/ochistorical
Key Personnel: Pres., Lawrence Rowe; Vice Pres., Peter Schumacher; Treas., Beverly Zehren; Cur., Marge Berres; Archivist & Genealogist, Henry Kohler.
Institution Type/Description: History Museum.
Hours & Admission Prices: Memorial Day-Labor Day Sun. 2-4. No charge; donations accepted.
Attendance: 750 (estimated)

Oconomowoc

OCONOMOWOC AREA HISTORICAL SOCIETY & MUSEUM, 103 W. Jefferson St., Oconomowoc, WI 53066-3633. Mailing Address: P.O. Box 245, Oconomowoc, WI 53066-0245. Tel.: 262-569-0740.
E-mail: oahs-m@att.net
Web Site: www.oconomowochistoricalsociety.com
Key Personnel: Pres., Rod Bluhm; Admin., Nancy Lins.
Institution Type/Description: Historical Society Museum.
Hours & Admission Prices: Jan.-April by appointment; May-Nov. Thurs.-Sun. 1-4.

Oconto

BEYER HOME, OCONTO COUNTY HISTORICAL SOCIETY MUSEUM, 917 Park Ave., Oconto, WI 54153-1641. Mailing Address: Box 272, Oconto, WI 54153-0272. Tel.: 920-835-5733.
E-mail: ocrl@bayland.net
Web Site: ocontocountyhistsoc.org
Key Personnel: Pres., Peter Stark.

Institution Type/Description: Historic House Museum: 1868 Beyer Home, Victorian brick mansion, carriage house & G.E. Hall Annex.
Hours & Admission Prices: Beyer Home & Museum Annex: June-Labor Day Mon.-Fri. & Sun. 12-4. Family $10, adults $4, students 6-18 $2; discount to groups & AAA members; members & children under 6 no charge.
Attendance: 1,000 (estimated)

COPPER CULTURE MUSEUM, Mill St., Oconto, WI 54153. Mailing Address: Oconto Historical Society, 917 Park Ave., Oconto, WI 54153-1641. Tel.: 920-834-6206.
E-mail: ocm@bayland.net
Institution Type/Description: Historic Site: listed on the National Registry of Historic Places.
Hours & Admission Prices: June to Labor Day Sat.-Sun. & holidays 10-3. No charge.

Oshkosh

EAA AVIATION MUSEUM, 3000 Poberezny Rd., Oshkosh, WI 54902-8900. Mailing Address: EAA Aviation Center, P.O. Box 3086, Oshkosh, WI 54903-3086. Tel.: 920-426-4800. Fax: 920-426-6765.
E-mail: museum@eaa.org
Web Site: www.airventuremuseum.org
Formerly: EAA AirVenture Museum
Key Personnel: Dir., Bob Campbell; Cur. Collections, Zack Baughman; Museum Program Coord., Chris Henry; Museum Educator, Tara Parkhurst.
Institution Type/Description: Aviation Museum.
Hours & Admission Prices: Daily 10-5. Family $31, adults $12.50, senior citizens 62 & over $10.50, students 6-17 $9.50; discounts to groups & AAM members; children under 6 & EAA members no charge. Closed New Year's Day; Easter; Thanksgiving; Christmas Eve & Day. ⅁
Attendance: 100,000 (estimated)

MILITARY VETERANS MUSEUM, INC., 4300 Poberezny Rd., Oshkosh, WI 54902. Mailing Address: P.O. Box 2194, Oshkosh, WI 54903-2194. Tel.: 920-426-8615. Fax: 920-426-1828.
E-mail: mvm@athenet.net
Web Site: www.mvmwisconsin.com
Key Personnel: Pres. & Special Projects, Dave Kerstyn; Vice Pres., Ron Twellman; Sec., Terri Schlack; Treas., George Egner.
Institution Type/Description: Military Museum.
Hours & Admission Prices: Fri.-Sun. 10-5. No charge; donations accepted.

MORGAN HOUSE - WINNEBAGO COUNTY HISTORICAL AND ARCHAEOLOGICAL SOCIETY, 234 Church Ave., Oshkosh, WI 54901. Tel.: 920-232-0260.
E-mail: julieandvictor@tds.net
Web Site: www.winnebagocountyhistoricalsociety.com
Key Personnel: Pres. (V), Julie Johnson.
Institution Type/Description: Historic House Museum: built in 1884. Listed on the National Register of Historic Places.
Hours & Admission Prices: Sat. 9-1; other times by appointment. Adults $5; children no charge.

OSHKOSH PUBLIC MUSEUM, 1331 Algoma Blvd., Oshkosh, WI 54901-2799. Tel.: 920-236-5799.
E-mail: museum@ci.oshkosh.wi.us
Web Site: www.oshkoshmuseum.org
Key Personnel: Dir., Bradley Larson; Pres. (V), Richard Rego; Cur., Anna Cannizzo; Registrar, Joan Lloyd; Mktg. & Membership, Karla Szekeres; Archivist, Scott Cross.
Institution Type/Description: General Museum.
Hours & Admission Prices: Tues.-Sat. 10-4:30, Sun. 1-4:30. Adults $7, seniors & students $5, children 6 & over $3.50; children under 6 & members no charge. Closed national holidays. ⅁
Attendance: 28,233 (actual)

PAINE ART CENTER AND GARDENS, 1410 Algoma Blvd., Oshkosh, WI 54901-7708. Tel.: 920-235-6903. Fax: 920-235-6303.
E-mail: info@thepaine.org
Web Site: www.thepaine.org
Key Personnel: Exec. Dir., Aaron Sherer.
Institution Type/Description: Art Museum & Arboretum: housed in 19th-century Tudor Revival Manor house.
Hours & Admission Prices: Tues.-Sun. 11-4. Adults $9, youth 5-17, senior citizens 65 & over on Wed. and students with ID $5; children 4 & under and members no charge. Closed national holidays. ⅁
Attendance: 55,915 (actual)

Peshtigo

PESHTIGO FIRE MUSEUM, 400 Oconto Ave., Peshtigo, WI 54157-1299. Mailing Address: P.O. Box 26, Peshtigo, WI 54157. Tel.: 715-582-3244.
E-mail: contact@peshtigo.info
Web Site: www.peshtigofire.info/museum.htm
Key Personnel: Pres. (V) & Cur., Ronald Strojny; Sec. & Cur., Mary Hahn; Treas. & Cur., Pat Roland; Cur., Sally Kahl; Cur., Margaret Wood; Cur., Sharon Schounard; Cur., Rosemary Leslie; Cur., Joan Berth; Cur., Pauline King.
Institution Type/Description: History Museum: Housed in 1878 Old Church located on the 1871 site of the worst forest fire in U.S. history.
Hours & Admission Prices: May 17-Oct. 8 daily 10-4:30. No charge; donations accepted.
Attendance: 7,500 (actual)

Pewaukee

CLARK HOUSE MUSEUM, 206 E. Wisconsin Ave., Pewaukee, WI 53072. Tel.: 262-691-0233.
Web Site: clarkehousemuseum@cityofchicago.org.
Institution Type/Description: History Museum.
Hours & Admission Prices: Memorial Day to Oct. Sun. 1-4, Wed. 1-4 & 7-9; other times by appointment.

Phillips

JUMP RIVER VALLEY HISTORICAL SOCIETY & MUSEUM, N6882 The Loop, Phillips, WI 54555. Tel.: 715-339-2642 & 474-6775.
E-mail: koerner2@pctcnet.net
Institution Type/Description: Historical Society Museum.
Hours & Admission Prices: June-Sept. 2nd & 4th Sat. 10-3. No charge. ⅁

Platteville

PLATTEVILLE MINING MUSEUM, 385 E. Main St., Platteville, WI 53818-3204. Mailing Address: P.O. Box 780, Platteville, WI 53818-0780. Tel.: 608-348-3301. Fax: 608-348-4640.
E-mail: museums@platteville.org
Web Site: www.mining.jamison.museum
Key Personnel: Dir., Diana Bolander; Pres., Tracey Roberts; Cur., Stephanie Saager-Bourret; Education Coord., Mary Huck.
Institution Type/Description: Mining Museum: housed in 1863 schoolhouse & 1845 lead mine.
Hours & Admission Prices: May-Oct. daily 9-5; Nov.- April Mon.-Fri. 9-4; group tours by appointment. May-Oct. family $27, adults $10, senior citizens $8.50, children $5; discount to groups, AAM & ICOM members; members no charge. Nov.-April adults $4, children $2. Closed New Year's Day; Veterans Day; Thanksgiving & day after; Christmas. ⅁
Attendance: 9,068 (actual)

ROLLO JAMISON MUSEUM, 405 E. Main St., Platteville, WI 53818-2834. Mailing Address: P.O. Box 780, Platteville, WI 53818-0780. Tel.: 608-348-3301. Fax: 608-348-4640.
E-mail: museums@platteville.org
Web Site: www.mining.jamison.museum
Key Personnel: Dir., Diana Bolander; Pres. (V), Tracey Roberts; Cur., Stephanie Saager-Bourret; Education Coord., Mary C. Huck.
Institution Type/Description: History Museum.
Hours & Admission Prices: May-Oct. daily 9-5; Nov.-April Mon.-Fri. 9-4; group tours by appointment. May-Oct. family $27, adults $10, senior citizens $8.50, children $5; discount to groups, AAM & ICOM members; members no charge. Nov.-April adults $4, children $2. Closed New Year's Day; Thanksgiving & day after; Christmas. ⅁
Attendance: 9,068 (actual)

Pleasant Prairie

JELLY BELLY COMPANY WAREHOUSE TOURS, 10100 Jelly Belly Ln., Pleasant Prairie, WI 53158. Tel.: 866-868-7522.
Web Site: jellybelly.com
Institution Type/Description: Company History & Tour.
Hours & Admission Prices: Store: daily 9-5. Tours: daily 9-4. No charge. Closed New Year's Day; Easter; Thanksgiving; Christmas. ⅁

Plymouth

BRADLEY GALLERY OF ART, W. 3718 South Dr., Plymouth, WI 53073. Mailing Address: P.O. Box 359, Sheboygan, WI 53082-0359. Tel.: 920-565-2111 & 1280. Fax: 920-565-1206.
E-mail: brickhamm@lakeland.edu
Web Site: www.lakeland.edu
Key Personnel: Co-Dir., Monique Brickham; Co-Dir., William R. Weidner.
Institution Type/Description: Art Gallery.
Hours & Admission Prices: Sept.-May Mon.-Fri. 9-5. No charge. Closed school holidays; semester breaks. &
Attendance: 3,000 (estimated)

JOHN G. VOIGT HOUSE, W 5639 Anokijig Lane, Plymouth, WI 53073. Tel.: 920-893-0782. Fax: 920-893-0873.
Key Personnel: Camp Dir., Jim Scherer.
Institution Type/Description: Historic House: 1850 Log Cabin.
Hours & Admission Prices: By appointment only. No charge; donations accepted.

Port Edwards

ALEXANDER HOUSE, 1131 Wisconsin River Dr., Port Edwards, WI 54469-1039. Tel.: 715-887-3442. Facebook: Alexander House Center for Art & History.
E-mail: crlhenke5921@gmail.com
Web Site: www.alexanderhouseonline.org
Key Personnel: Dir., Connie Henke; Dir., Dave Thiel; Dir., Karen Thiel; Dir., Joan Palen.
Institution Type/Description: Art & History Museum.
Hours & Admission Prices: Tues., Thurs. & Sun. 1-4; other times by appointment. No charge. &
Attendance: 3,000 (estimated)

Port Washington

JUDGE EGHART HOUSE, 302 W. Grand Ave., Port Washington, WI 53074. Mailing Address: P.O. Box 87, Port Washington, WI 53074. Tel.: 262-284-2584.
E-mail: info@egharthouse.org
Web Site: www.egharthouse.org
Institution Type/Description: Historic House Museum: built in 1872.
Hours & Admission Prices: Memorial Day to Labor Day Sun. 1-4. Adults $3, children $1.

Portage

FORT WINNEBAGO SURGEONS QUARTERS, 1824 E. State Rd. 33, Portage, WI 53901-1466. Tel.: 608-742-2949.
E-mail: fortwinnebagosurgeonsquarters@gmail.com
Key Personnel: State Cur., Nancy Burns; Dir., Paul Nelson.
Institution Type/Description: History Museum: housed in 1828 surgeons quarters.
Hours & Admission Prices: May 15-Oct. 15 Wed.-Sun. 10-4; tours by appointment. Family $18, adults $7.50, senior citizens $6, children 6-18 & college students $3; discounts to AAA & AAM members; active & retired military, life members & children 5 & under no charge.
Attendance: 5,000 (estimated)

HISTORIC INDIAN AGENCY HOUSE, 1490 Agency House Rd., Portage, WI 53901-0084. Mailing Address: P.O. Box 84, Portage, WI 53901-0084. Tel.: 608-742-6362. Facebook: Historic Indian Agency House.
E-mail: historicindianagencyhouse@gmail.com
Web Site: www.agencyhouse.org
Formerly: Old Indian Agency House
Key Personnel: Chm., Barbara Meyer; Pres., Dr. Anne Vrarick; Dir., Destinee Udelhoven.
Institution Type/Description: Historic House: 1832 Historic Indian Agency House.
Hours & Admission Prices: May 15 to Oct. 15 daily 10-4; other times by appointment. Family $18, adults $7.50, senior citizens & AAA members $6, students 5-18 $3; discounts to National Trust for Historic Preservation members; veterans, military & members no charge.
Attendance: 3,000 (estimated)

Potosi

NATIONAL BREWERY MUSEUM, 209 S. Main St., Potosi, WI 53820. Mailing Address: P.O. Box 177, Potosi, WI 53820. Tel.: 608-763-4002, ext. 109.
E-mail: info@potosibrewery.com
Web Site: www.potosibrewery.com

Institution Type/Description: Company History Museum.
Hours & Admission Prices: Call for hours. Adults $5, seniors 60 & over $3; children 17 & under no charge.

PASSAGE THRU TIME MUSEUM, 104 N. Main St., Potosi, WI 53820. Tel.: 608-763-2745.
Institution Type/Description: History Museum.
Hours & Admission Prices: Call for hours.

POTOSI BREWING COMPANY TRANSPORTATION MUSEUM, 209 S. Main St., Potosi, WI 53820. Mailing Address: P.O. Box 177, Potosi, WI 53820. Tel.: 608-763-4002, ext. 106.
E-mail: info@potosibrewery.com
Institution Type/Description: Transportation Museum.
Hours & Admission Prices: Call for hours.

Poynette

MACKENZIE ENVIRONMENTAL EDUCATION CENTER, W7303 County Rd. CS & Q, Poynette, WI 53955-9690. Tel.: 608-635-8105. Fax: 608-635-2743.
E-mail: friendsofmackenzie@gmail.com
Key Personnel: Dir., Ruth Ann Lee; Pres. Friends of Mackenzie (V), Reggie Finn; Animal Keeper, Anna Lynn Hammond; Maintenance Foreman, Dan Lee.
Institution Type/Description: Natural History Museum.
Hours & Admission Prices: Exhibits & Zoo: May-Nov. 1 daily 8-4; Nov.-April Mon.-Fri. 8-4; guided tours by appointment. Grounds: daily dawn-dusk. No charge; donations accepted. &
Attendance: 46,000 (estimated)

Prairie du Chien

FORT CRAWFORD MUSEUM, c/o Prairie du Chien Historical Society Inc., 717 S. Beaumont Rd., Prairie du Chien, WI 53821. Mailing Address: P.O. Box 298, Prairie du Chien, WI 53821-0298. Tel.: 608-326-6960.
E-mail: ftcrawmu@mhtc.net
Web Site: www.fortcrawfordmuseum.com
Formerly: Prairie du Chien Museum at Fort Crawford
Key Personnel: Pres. Historical Society (V), Mary Antoine; Sec. Historical Society, Janet Finn.
Institution Type/Description: History Museum: a National Historical Landmark.
Hours & Admission Prices: May-Oct. daily 9-4. Family $15, adults $5, seniors $4, children 12 & under $3; discounts to tour groups; members no charge. &
Attendance: 6,000 (actual)

VILLA LOUIS HISTORIC SITE, 521 Villa Louis Rd., Prairie du Chien, WI 53821-1333. Mailing Address: P.O. Box 65, Prairie du Chien, WI 53821-0065. Tel.: 608-326-2721. Fax: 608-326-5507.
E-mail: villalouis@wisconsinhistory.org
Web Site: villalouis.wisconsinhistory.org
Key Personnel: Site Dir., Susan Caya-Slusser; Facilities Mgr., Jacob Koresh; Program Asst., M. Susan Witters.
Institution Type/Description: History Museum: housed in 1870 Villa Louis, home of family of fur trader Hercules Dousman, on the site of 1814 Fort Shelby & 1816-1829 Fort Crawford.
Hours & Admission Prices: Tours: Winter by appointment only; Spring Wed.-Sun. 11, 1 & 3; Summer & Fall daily on the hour 10-4. Adults $10, seniors 65 and over & students $8.50, children 5-17 $5; discounts to groups; Wisconsin Historical Society members no charge. Closed New Year's Day; Easter; Christmas Eve & Day. &
Attendance: 16,000 (actual)

Prairie du Sac

SAUK PRAIRIE AREA HISTORICAL SOCIETY, INC., 565 Water St., Prairie du Sac, WI 53578-1128. Tel.: 608-644-8444. Fax: 680-644-8444.
E-mail: spahs@frontier.com
Web Site: www.saukprairiehistory.org
Key Personnel: Pres., Jody Kapp; Mgr. & Correspondence Sec., Jack Berndt; Sec., Barb Wolfe; Treas., Marie Goddard.
Institution Type/Description: Historical Society Museum.
Hours & Admission Prices: Fri.-Sat. 9-1; other times by appointment. No charge; donations accepted.
Attendance: 3,500 (estimated)

Racine

FIREHOUSE NO. 3 MUSEUM, 700 Sixth St., Racine, WI 53403. Mailing Address: P.O. Box 081042, Racine, WI 53408. Tel.: 262-886-6603.
E-mail: tgavahan@sbcglobal.net
Key Personnel: Dir., Judy Jones.
Institution Type/Description: Firefighting History Museum: housed in the former fire station; built in 1882.
Hours & Admission Prices: By appointment.

RACINE ART MUSEUM (RAM), 441 Main St., Racine, WI 53403-1030. Mailing Address: P.O. Box 187, Racine, WI 53401-0187. Tel.: 262-638-8300. Fax: 262-898-1045. Facebook: Racine Art Museum.
E-mail: raminfo@ramart.org
Web Site: www.ramart.org
Formerly: Charles A Wustum Museum of Fine Arts
Key Personnel: C.E.O., Bruce W. Pepich; Pres. (V), James Walker; Facilities Mgr., Jim Sheppard; Accountant, Carol Rannow; Dir., Opers. & Devel., Laura D'Amato; Cur. Education, Tricia Blasko; Principal Guest Experience & Retail Division, Lisa Englander; Devel. Coord., Susan K. Buhler-Maki; Wustum Bldg. & Grounds Supvr., Dennis Kennow; Curatorial Asst., Liz Siercks; Education Asst., Maureen Fritchen; Education Asst., Veronica Averkamp; Registrar, Adam Hutler; Mktg. & Publications Mgr., Jessica Z. Schafer; Mktg. Asst., Laura Gillespie; Librarian, Nancy Elsmo; Exhibition Preparator, Janelle Cairo; Exhibition Preparator II, Chelsea Kaufman; Vol. Coord., Michelle Ortwein.
Institution Type/Description: Arts Center.
Hours & Admission Prices: RAM: Tues.-Sat. 10-5, Sun. 12-5. Wustum: Tues.-Sat. 10-5. Adults $5; discounts to NARM members; members no charge. NARM reciprocal membership over $100. Closed federal holidays; Easter. &
Attendance: 56,617 (actual)

RACINE HERITAGE MUSEUM, 701 S. Main St., Racine, WI 53403-1211. Tel.: 262-636-3926. Fax: 262-636-3940. Facebook: Racine Heritage Museum.
E-mail: inquire@racineheritagemuseum.org
Web Site: www.racineheritagemuseum.org
Key Personnel: Exec. Dir., Christopher Paulson; Cur. & Asst. Dir., Karen Braun; Archivist, Mary Kay Nelson; Dir. Mktg. & Programs, Sally Orth; Cur. Educator, Kari DeBerg; Office Mgr., Crystiana Schlitz.
Institution Type/Description: Southeast Wisconsin Industrial, Cultural, Invention & Product History: housed in 1904 Carnegie Library building.
Hours & Admission Prices: Tues.-Fri. 9-5, Sat. 10-3, Sun. 12-4. No charge; donations accepted. Closed national holidays.
Attendance: 30,000 (actual)

RACINE ZOOLOGICAL SOCIETY, 2131 N. Main St., Racine, WI 53402-4795. Mailing Address: 200 Goold St., Racine, WI 53402-4795. Tel.: 262-636-9189. Fax: 262-636-9307.
E-mail: info@racinezoo.org
Web Site: www.racinezoo.org
Key Personnel: Exec. Dir., Elizabeth Heidorn.
Institution Type/Description: Zoo.
Hours & Admission Prices: Memorial Day to Labor Day daily 9-6; Sept.-May daily 9-4:30. Adults $8, seniors $7, children $6; discounts to Association of Zoo & Aquarium members; reciprocating AZA institutions; members no charge. &
Attendance: 100,000 (estimated)

THE SOUTHEAST WISCONSIN AVIATION MUSEUM, EAA Chapter 838 Batten International Airport, 3333 N. Green Bay Rd., Racine, WI 53404. Tel.: 262-634-7575.
Web Site: www.eaa838.org/museum.asp
Institution Type/Description: Aviation Museum.
Hours & Admission Prices: May-Oct. 2nd Sat. each month 8:30am-12pm; other times by appointment.

Rhinelander

PIONEER PARK HISTORICAL COMPLEX, Kemp St., Rhinelander, WI 54501. Mailing Address: c/o City of Rhinelander Pioneer Park Museum Advisory Committee, 135 S. Stevens St., Rhinelander, WI 54501. Tel.: 715-369-5004.
Formerly: Rhinelander Logging Museum
Key Personnel: PPHC Coord., Aprelle Rawski.
Institution Type/Description: Pioneer Logging Industry Museum.
Hours & Admission Prices: Memorial Day to Labor Day Tues.-Sun. 10-5; Sept. Fri.-Sat. 10-5. No charge; donations accepted. &
Attendance: 14,378 (actual)

Ripon

LITTLE WHITE SCHOOLHOUSE, BIRTHPLACE OF THE REPUBLICAN PARTY NATIONAL HISTORIC SITE, 305 Blackburn St., Ripon, WI 54971-1524. Mailing Address: P.O. Box 305, Ripon, WI 54971-0305. Tel.: 920-748-6764. Fax: 920-748-6784.
E-mail: chamber@ripon-wi.com
Web Site: www.ripon1854.com
Key Personnel: Exec. Dir., Jason Mansmith; Pres., John Rockwood.
Institution Type/Description: Historic Building: c.1854 Little White Schoolhouse, birthplace of Republican Party.
Hours & Admission Prices: May & Sept.-Oct. Sat.-Sun. 10-4; June to Labor Day daily 10-4; other times by appointment. Adults $2. &
Attendance: 3,500 (actual)

River Falls

GALLERY 101, University of Wisconsin-River Falls, Fine Arts, 410 S. Third St., River Falls, WI 54022-5010. Tel.: 715-425-3266. Fax: 715-425-0657.
E-mail: susan.m.zimmeer@uwrf.edu
Web Site: www.uwrf.edu/art
Key Personnel: Chm. Art Dept., Randy Johnson.
Institution Type/Description: Art Gallery.
Hours & Admission Prices: Sept.-May Mon.-Fri. 9-5 & 7-9, Sun. 2-4. No charge. &

Saint Croix Falls

ST. CROIX NATIONAL SCENIC RIVERWAY, 401 N. Hamilton St., Saint Croix Falls, WI 54024-9214. Tel.: 715-483-2274. Fax: 715-483-3288.
E-mail: chris_stein@nps.gov
Web Site: www.nps.gov/sacn
Key Personnel: Supt., Chris Stein.
Institution Type/Description: National Park & Museum.
Hours & Admission Prices: mid-April to late Oct. daily 9-5. No charge. &
Attendance: 17,700 (actual)

Saint Germain

SNOWMOBILE HALL OF FAME AND MUSEUM, 8481 W. Hwy. 70, Saint Germain, WI 54558. Mailing Address: P.O. Box 720, Saint Germain, WI 54558-0720. Tel.: 715-542-4463. Fax: 715-542-4260.
E-mail: info@snowmobilehalloffame.com
Web Site: www.snowmobilehalloffame.com
Institution Type/Description: History Museum.
Hours & Admission Prices: Off Season: Thurs.-Fri. 10-5, Sat. 10-3; Winter: call for hours.

Saukville

OZAUKEE COUNTY PIONEER VILLAGE, 4880 County Hwy. I, Saukville, WI 53080. Mailing Address: P.O. Box 206, Cedarburg, WI 53012-0206. Tel.: 262-377-4510. Fax: 262-377-4510.
E-mail: jean.steinke@gmail.com
Web Site: www.co.ozaukee.wi.us/ochs
Formerly: Ozaukee County Historical Society Pioneer Village
Key Personnel: Pres. (V), Jean Steinke; Volunteer Coord., Tom Oliver; 1st Vice Pres., Curt Gruenwald; 2nd Vice Pres., Allen Buchholz; Archivist, Dr. Nina Look; Sec., Trevor Weis; Treas., Tom Hogan.
Institution Type/Description: Pioneer Village: over 20 buildings ranging from mid-1840 to 1907.
Hours & Admission Prices: Memorial Day to 2nd Sun. in Oct. Sat.-Sun. 12-5; other times groups by appointment. Family $16, adults $6, senior citizens & students 12-18 $4, children 6-12 $3; children 5 & under and members no charge. Additional charge for special events. &
Attendance: 4,500 (actual)

SAUKVILLE AREA HISTORICAL SOCIETY - SAUKVILLE CROSSROADS MUSEUM, 200 N. Mill St., Saukville, WI 53080. Tel.: 262-692-9425.
Institution Type/Description: History Museum: housed in the former Saukville Firehouse Station; built in 1912.
Hours & Admission Prices: Call for hours.

Seymour

SEYMOUR COMMUNITY MUSEUM, 133 Depot St., Seymour, WI 54165. Mailing Address: P.O. Box 237, Seymour, WI 54165-1331. Tel.: 920-833-2868.
E-mail: pma@billcollar.com
Web Site: www.seymourhistory.org
Key Personnel: Pres. (V), Bill Collar; Vice Pres., Lois Dalke; Historian, Marge Coenen; Business Officer, Janice Eick; Asst., Mike Keyzers.
Institution Type/Description: Historic Building & Site: housed in 1879 Lumber Sales Building.
Hours & Admission Prices: Summer: Tues.-Sat. No charge; donations accepted. ⅄
Attendance: 3,512 (actual)

Shawano

SHAWANO COUNTY HISTORICAL SOCIETY, INC., 524 N. Franklin St., Shawano, WI 54166-1933. Tel.: 715-526-3323.
E-mail: schsociety@granitewave.com
Key Personnel: Pres., Ron Schumacher.
Institution Type/Description: General Museum: located in Heritage Park on the site where the first white man in Shawano County settled in 1848.
Hours & Admission Prices: Mon.-Thurs. 9-4, call to confirm. Tours: Thurs. 1:30-4, Sat. 9:30 am to noon; other times by appointment. Adults $3.
Attendance: 1,000 (estimated)

Sheboygan

ABOVE & BEYOND CHILDREN'S MUSEUM, 902 N. 8th St., Sheboygan, WI 53081-4005. Tel.: 920-458-4263. Fax: 920-458-3402. Facebook.
E-mail: abcm@abkids.org
Web Site: www.abkids.org
Key Personnel: Exec. Dir., Jeff Mehn.
Institution Type/Description: Children's Museum.
Hours & Admission Prices: Tues.-Sun. 10-6. Admission $6; members & children one & under no charge. ⅄
Attendance: 30,000 (estimated)

GREAT LAKES AEROSPACE SCIENCE AND EDUCATION CENTER, 802 Blue Harbor Dr., Sheboygan, WI 53081-4989. Tel.: 920-889-7148.
E-mail: danielb@spacesheboygan.com
Web Site: www.spacesheboygan.com
Institution Type/Description: Science Center.
Hours & Admission Prices: June 9-Aug. 10 Tues.-Sat. 11-5. Planetarium Shows: daily 1 & 3. Adults 12 & over $5, children 5-12 $2; children under 5 no charge.

JOHN MICHAEL KOHLER ARTS CENTER, 608 New York Ave., Sheboygan, WI 53081-4507. Tel.: 920-458-6144. Fax: 920-458-4473. Facebook: JMKAC.
E-mail: rkohler@jmkac.org
Web Site: www.jmkac.org
Key Personnel: Dir. Strategic Initiatives, Ruth DeYoung Kohler; Pres. Bd., Sandra Sachse; Pres., Friends of Art Council, Kristi Richerson; Deputy Dir. Operations, Kelley Renzelmann; Deputy Dir. Programming, Amy Horst; Cur., Karen Patterson; Asst. Cur., Emily Schlemowitz; Librarian & Archivist, Alison Lowen; Registrar, Larry Donoval; Assoc. Registrar, Emily Bianchi; Assoc. Registrar, Lenny Cicero; Exhibitions Mgr., Jo Bjorkman; Arts Industry Coord., Kristin Plucar; Retail Mgr., Mary Kopp; Sr. Mgr. Public Programs, Ann Brusky; Advancement Mgr., Marlene Yang; Human Resources Mgr., Anne Stauber Tritz.
Institution Type/Description: Visual & Performing Arts Center.
Hours & Admission Prices: Mon., Wed. & Fri. 10-5, Tues. & Thurs. 10-8, Sat.-Sun. 10-4. No charge; donations accepted. ⅄
Attendance: 200,000 (estimated)

SHEBOYGAN COUNTY HISTORICAL MUSEUM, 3110 Erie Ave., Sheboygan, WI 53081-3660. Tel.: 920-458-1103. Facebook.
E-mail: museum@sheboygancounty.com
Web Site: www.sheboyganmuseum.org
Key Personnel: Exec. Dir. & C.E.O., Travis Gross; Pres. (V), Paul Rudnick.
Institution Type/Description: History Museum.
Hours & Admission Prices: Feb.-Oct. Mon.-Fri. 10-5, Sat. 10-3; day after Thanksgiving-Dec. 30 Mon. & Tues. 12-7, Wed.-Sun. 12-5. Adults $6, seniors & active military $5, youth 6-17 $3; members and children 5 & under no charge. Closed Memorial Day; Independence Day; Labor Day; Christmas Eve & Day. ⅄
Attendance: 12,000 (estimated)

Sheboygan Falls

AVIATION HERITAGE CENTER OF WISCONSIN, N6191 Resource Dr., Sheboygan Falls, WI 53085. Tel.: 920-467-2043. Facebook.
E-mail: takeflight@ahcw.org
Web Site: www.ahcw.org
Key Personnel: Dir., Jon Helminiak; Pres. (V), Paul Walter; Museum Shop Mgr., Kris Krentz.
Institution Type/Description: Aviation History Museum.
Hours & Admission Prices: Summer: Wed.-Sun. 10-5; Winter: Wed.-Sun. 11-4; other times by appointment. No charge; donations accepted. ⅄
Attendance: 6,000 (estimated)

Shell Lake

MUSEUM OF WOODCARVING, 539 Hwy. 63 N., Shell Lake, WI 54871-4438. Mailing Address: P.O. Box 371, Shell Lake, WI 54871-0371. Tel.: 715-468-7100.
Web Site: www.roadsideamerica.com/attract/WISHEwood.html
Key Personnel: Owner, Cur. & Museum Shop Mgr., Maria McKay.
Institution Type/Description: Woodcarving Museum.
Hours & Admission Prices: May-Oct. daily 9-6. Adults $6.75, children under 12 $4.75; discounts to groups of 20 or more, AARP, AAA & AAM members. ⅄
Attendance: 25,000 (estimated)

WASHBURN COUNTY HISTORICAL SOCIETY MUSEUM, 102 W. 2nd Ave., Shell Lake, WI 54871. Mailing Address: P.O. Box 366, Shell Lake, WI 54871-0366. Tel.: 715-468-2982.
E-mail: wchs54871@gmail.com
Web Site: www.rootsweb.com/~wiwashbu
Key Personnel: Pres., Cathy Wahlstrom.
Institution Type/Description: Historic Society Museum: housed in six buildings.
Hours & Admission Prices: Memorial Day-Labor Day Fri.-Sat. 11-4. No charge; donations accepted. ⅄
Attendance: 615 (estimated)

Shullsburg

BADGER MINE AND MUSEUM, 279 W. Estey St., Shullsburg, WI 53586. Mailing Address: P.O. Box 580, Shullsburg, WI 53586. Tel.: 608-965-4860.
Institution Type/Description: General Museum.
Hours & Admission Prices: Memorial Day-Labor Day Wed.-Thurs. 12-4, Fri.-Sun. 11-4. Museum: adults $3, seniors over 65 $2, children under 10 $1.50. Mine & Museum: adults $5, seniors over 65 $4, children under 10 $3. ⅄
Attendance: 2,300 (actual)

South Milwaukee

SOUTH MILWAUKEE HISTORICAL SOCIETY MUSEUM, 717 Milwaukee Ave., South Milwaukee, WI 53172-2113. Tel.: 414-762-5214.
E-mail: lasplant@gmail.com
Web Site: www.southmilwaukee.org
Key Personnel: Pres. & C.E.O., Lois L. Schreiter; Sec., Sue Ziarek; Treas., Judy Balestrieri.
Institution Type/Description: Historical Society Museum: housed in Victorian home.
Hours & Admission Prices: Memorial Day-Labor Day first Thurs. of the month 1-3; other times by appointment. No charge.
Attendance: 600 (estimated)

Sparta

THE DEKE SLAYTON MEMORIAL SPACE & BICYCLE MUSEUM, 200 W. Main St., Sparta, WI 54656. Tel.: 608-269-0033.
E-mail: dekeslayton@centurytel.net
Web Site: www.dekeslaytonmuseum.com
Institution Type/Description: Transportation Museum.
Hours & Admission Prices: Mon.-Sat. 10-4:30.

MONROE COUNTY LOCAL HISTORY ROOM & LIBRARY, 200 W. Main St., Sparta, WI 54656-2141. Tel.: 608-269-8680. Fax: 608-269-8921. Facebook: @mclhr.
E-mail: mclhr@centurytel.net
Web Site: www.mclhr.org
Key Personnel: Chm. Bd. Trustees, Carolyn Habelman; Dir., Jarrod Roll.

Institution Type/Description: Historical Society Museum: located in the former Masonic Temple, Monroe County, Sparta, WI.
Hours & Admission Prices: Mon.-Sat. 9-4:30. No charge; donations accepted. Closed Memorial Day; Independence Day; Labor Day; Thanksgiving; Christmas. ♿
Attendance: 8,500 (estimated)

Spooner

WISCONSIN CANOE HERITAGE MUSEUM, 312 N. Front St., Spooner, WI 54801. Mailing Address: P.O. Box 365, Spooner, WI 54801. Tel.: 715-635-5002.
E-mail: info@wisconsincanoeheritagemuseum.com
Web Site: www.wisconsincanoeheritagemuseum.com
Key Personnel: Exec. Dir., Jed Malischke; Cur., Mike Johnson.
Institution Type/Description: Heritage Museum: housed in the former Baker Grain Elevator company building; built c.1912.
Hours & Admission Prices: Summer: Wed.-Sat. 10-4, Sun. 11-3; Sept. Sat.-Sun. 11-3; other times by appointment. Suggested Donations: adults $4, youth 13-18 $2; children 12 & under no charge. ♿
Attendance: 1,500 (estimated)

Spring Green

THE HOUSE ON THE ROCK, 5754 State Rd. 23, Spring Green, WI 53588-8912. Tel.: 608-935-3639. Fax: 608-935-9472.
E-mail: information@thehouseontherock.com
Web Site: www.thehouseontherock.com
Key Personnel: Owner, Art Donaldson; Pres., Susan Donaldson; Asst. Mgr., Paula Widdish; Mktg. Mgr., Betty Smith.
Institution Type/Description: Historical House Museum & Complex: original structure rests on a 60 foot chimney of rock jutting high above Wyoming Valley of Southwestern Wisconsin; multi-building complex on different levels & various outbuildings.
Hours & Admission Prices: May-Aug. daily 9-6; Sept.-April daily 9-5. One Tour: adults $12.50, children $7.50. Additional tour packages available. ♿
Attendance: 500,000

Stevens Point

CENTRAL WISCONSIN CHILDREN'S MUSEUM, 1100 Main St., Stevens Point, WI 54481. Tel.: 715-344-2003.
E-mail: cwcm@cwchildrensmuseum.org
Web Site: cwchildrensmuseum.org
Key Personnel: Dir., Katy Matthai.
Institution Type/Description: Children's Museum.
Hours & Admission Prices: Tues.-Wed. & Fri. 9-4, Thurs. 9-8, Sat. 10-4, Sun. 12-4. Adults $5; children under one & members no charge. ♿
Attendance: 21,000 (actual)

PORTAGE COUNTY HISTORICAL SOCIETY, 1475 Water St., Stevens Point, WI 54481-2920. Mailing Address: P.O. Box 672, Stevens Point, WI 54481-0672.
E-mail: pchswi@gmail.com
Web Site: www.pchswi.org
Key Personnel: Pres., Tim Siebert; Vice Pres., David Simonis; Treas., Jeanne Regnier; Sec., Karen J. Zinda.
Institution Type/Description: History Museum.
Hours & Admission Prices: Memorial Day to Labor Day Sat.-Sun. 1-4. Admission $2.
Attendance: 3,000 (estimated)

THE UWSP MUSEUM OF NATURAL HISTORY, 900 Reserve St., University of Wisconsin, Stevens Point, WI 54481-1962. Tel.: 715-346-2858 & 2821. Fax: 715-346-2367.
E-mail: rreser@uwsp.edu
Web Site: www.uwsp.edu/museum/
Key Personnel: Dir., Ray P. Reser; C.E.O., Chris cirmo; Museum Shop Mgr., Lisa Viegut.
Institution Type/Description: Natural History Museum.
Hours & Admission Prices: Academic Year: Mon.-Thurs. 7:45am-12am, Fri. 7:45am-9pm, Sat. 9-9, Sun., 11-4. No charge; donations accepted. ♿
Attendance: 12,000 (estimated)

Stoughton

STOUGHTON HISTORICAL SOCIETY, 324 S. Page St., Stoughton, WI 53589-2166. Mailing Address: 901 U.S. Hwy. 51, Stoughton, WI 53589-3874. Tel.: 608-873-8005.
E-mail: catherine_haynes@sbcglobal.net
Web Site: stoughtonhistoricalsociety.com
Key Personnel: Pres. (V), David Kalland.
Institution Type/Description: Historical Society Museum: housed in 1858 Universalist Church.
Hours & Admission Prices: mid-May to Sept. Sat. 11-3. Requested Donation: $2.
Attendance: 1,500 (estimated)

Sturgeon Bay

DOOR COUNTY HISTORICAL MUSEUM, 18 N. 4th Ave., Sturgeon Bay, WI 54235-2423. Tel.: 920-743-5809. Facebook: Door County Historical Museum.
E-mail: dcmuseum@co.door.wi.us
Web Site: www.doorcountyhistoricalmuseum.com
Key Personnel: Cur., Margaret S. Weir; Asst. Cur., Ginny Haen; Asst. Cur., Nyla Small; Asst. Cur., William Rice.
Institution Type/Description: Historical Museum.
Hours & Admission Prices: May-Oct. daily 10-4:30. No charge; donations accepted. ♿
Attendance: 10,000 (estimated)

DOOR COUNTY MARITIME MUSEUM & LIGHTHOUSE PRESERVATION SOCIETY (AT STURGEON BAY), 120 N. Madison Ave., Sturgeon Bay, WI 54235-3416. Tel.: 920-743-5958. Fax: 920-743-9483. Facebook: Door County Maritime Museum; Cana Island Lighthouse.
E-mail: info@dcmm.org
Web Site: www.dcmm.org
Key Personnel: Exec. Dir., Mktg. & Communication, Amy Paul; Museum Shop Mgr., Cassie Buntin.
Institution Type/Description: Maritime Museum.
Hours & Admission Prices: Jan.-March daily 10-4; April-June & Sept.-Dec. daily 10-5; July to Labor Day daily 9-5. Adults $15, youth 5-17 $10; children 4 & under, active military & members no charge. ♿
Attendance: 57,195 (actual)

THE FARM, 4285 Hwy. 57, Sturgeon Bay, WI 54235. Mailing Address: P.O. Box 44, Sturgeon Bay, WI 54235-0044. Tel.: 920-743-6666. Fax: 920-743-2266.
E-mail: info@thefarmindoorcounty.com
Web Site: www.thefarmindoorcounty.com
Key Personnel: Owner, David Tanck; Vice Pres., Jeff Tanck; Museum Shop Mgr., Jenny Tanck; Museum Shop Mgr., Shirley Tanck.
Institution Type/Description: Historical Farm Museum.
Hours & Admission Prices: Memorial Day to mid-Oct. daily 9-5. Adults $8, children 4-12 $4; discounts to AAA members, senior citizens & groups; children under 3 no charge. ♿
Attendance: 35,000 (estimated)

HERITAGE VILLAGE AT BIG CREEK, 2041 Michigan St., Sturgeon Bay, WI 54235. Mailing Address: P.O. Box 71, Sturgeon Bay, WI 54235. Tel.: 920-421-2332.
E-mail: director.dchistoricalsociety@gmail.com
Web Site: doorcountyhistoricalsociety.com
Key Personnel: C.E.O., Trudy Herbst; Chm. (V), Jay Zahn.
Institution Type/Description: Historical Society Museum: village consists of 9 restored buildings.
Hours & Admission Prices: June-Sept. Tues.-Sat. 10-3. Adults $5; members no charge. Closed holidays.
Attendance: 5,000 (estimated)

MILLER ART MUSEUM, 107 S. 4th Ave., Sturgeon Bay, WI 54235-2203. Tel.: 920-746-0707 (Offices). Facebook: Miller Art Museum.
E-mail: emam@dcwis.com
Web Site: millerartmuseum.org
Key Personnel: Dir. & Museum Shop Mgr., Elizabeth Meissner-Gigstead; Chm. (V), Sharon Virlee; Pres. (V), Kristi Roenning; Cur. Exhibits & Permanent Collections, Deborah Rosenthal.
Institution Type/Description: Art Museum: housed in Door County Library.
Hours & Admission Prices: Mon. 10-8, Tues.-Sat. 10-5. No charge; donations accepted. Closed major holidays & 3 days preceding each exhibit. ♿
Attendance: 19,000 (actual)

POTAWATOMI STATE PARK, 3740 County PD, Sturgeon Bay, WI 54235. Tel.: 920-746-2890. Fax: 920-746-2896.
E-mail: erin.brownstender@wisconsin.gov
Web Site: www.wiparks.net
Key Personnel: Park Supvr., Erin Brown-Stender.
Institution Type/Description: State Park: located on the Door County Peninsula.

Hours & Admission Prices: Daily 6am-11pm. Entrance fee & camping fee. Reservations accepted.

WHITEFISH DUNES STATE PARK, 3725 Clark Lake Rd., Sturgeon Bay, WI 54235. Tel.: 920-823-2400. Fax: 920-823-2640.
E-mail: wiparks@dnr.state.wi.us
Web Site: www.dnr.state.wi.us
Key Personnel: Park Ranger, Tony Knipfer; Naturalist, Carolyn Rock; Pres. Friends Group (V), Dick Weidman.
Institution Type/Description: Nature Center.
Hours & Admission Prices: Daily 8-8. State Park admission sticker required, fees apply. Closed winter holidays.
Attendance: 250,000 (estimated)

Sun Prairie

CITY OF SUN PRAIRIES HISTORICAL LIBRARY & MUSEUM, 115 E. Main St., Sun Prairie, WI 53590-2222. Mailing Address: 300 E. Main St., Sun Prairie, WI 53590-2222. Tel.: 608-837-2915. Fax: 608-825-6879. Facebook: Sun Prairie Historical Museum.
E-mail: derickson@cityofsunprairie.com
Web Site: www.sunprairie.com/museum
Key Personnel: Chm. Bd., Joe Chase; Dir. & Cur., Dennis Erickson; Museum Asst., Bernice Brown; Registrar, Mary Peck; Chm. Dept. Economic Growth & Devel., Neil Stechschulte; Recreation, Jana Stephens.
Institution Type/Description: History Museum.
Hours & Admission Prices: May-Oct. Mon., Wed. & Fri.-Sat. 3-5; private tours & research by appointment. No charge; donations accepted.
Attendance: 9,526 (actual)

Superior

A WORLD OF ACCORDIONS MUSEUM, 1401 Belknap, Superior, WI 54880. Tel.: 218-393-0245.
E-mail: accordion@sprynet.com
Web Site: worldofaccordions.org
Key Personnel: Cur., Helmi Strahl Harrington, Ph.D.
Institution Type/Description: Musical Instrument Museum.
Hours & Admission Prices: Sun.-Mon. 10-6, Sat. 3-6; tours by appointment. Self-Guided Tours: adults $10. Curator-Narrated Tour: adults $20. Instrument Demo Tour: adults $20. Discounts for groups of 10 or more.

DOUGLAS COUNTY HISTORICAL SOCIETY, 1101 John Ave., Superior, WI 54880-1640. Tel.: 715-392-8449. Facebook: Douglas County Historical Society.
E-mail: dchs@douglashistory.org
Web Site: www.douglashistory.org
Key Personnel: Pres., Doug Dalager; Exec. Dir., Tony D. Tracy.
Institution Type/Description: County Historical Society Museum.
Hours & Admission Prices: Tues.-Fri. 11-5. No charge.
Attendance: 835 (estimated)

FAIRLAWN MANSION & MUSEUM, 906 E. 2nd St., Superior, WI 54880-3245. Tel.: 715-394-5712. Fax: 715-394-2043.
E-mail: info@superiorpublicmuseums.org
Web Site: www.superiorpublicmuseums.org
Key Personnel: Dir., Sara Blanck; Museums Coord., Stacie Buchanan.
Institution Type/Description: Historic House Museum: housed in 42 room Queen Anne Victorian style mansion, c.1891; home of Martin & Grace Pattison until 1918 when it was donated to be used as a home & refuge for children and young women.
Hours & Admission Prices: mid-May to mid-Oct. Mon.-Sat. 9-4, Sun. 11-4; Winter: Sun.-Fri. 12-3, Sat. 10-3. Adults $10, college students with ID and senior citizens 62 & over $8, children 6-17 $5; children 5 & under no charge.
Attendance: 8,000 (actual)

OLD FIREHOUSE AND POLICE MUSEUM, 402 23rd Ave. E., Superior, WI 54880. Mailing Address: 906 E. 2nd St., Superior, WI 54880-3245. Tel.: 715-394-5712.
E-mail: info@superiorpublicmuseums.org
Web Site: www.superiorpublicmuseums.org
Key Personnel: Dir., Sara Blanck; Museum Coord., Stacie Buchanan.
Institution Type/Description: History Museum: housed in Superior's former firehouse, Station No. 4; built in 1898.
Hours & Admission Prices: mid-May to Aug. Thurs.-Sat. 10-5, Sun. 11-5; Sept. to mid-Oct. Sat. 10-5, Sun. 12-5. No charge; donations accepted.

RICHARD I. BONG VETERANS HISTORICAL CENTER, 305 Harbor View Pkwy., Superior, WI 54880-6845. Tel.: 715-392-7151. Fax: 715-395-5526.
E-mail: fuhrman@bvhcenter.org
Web Site: www.bvhcenter.org
Formerly: Richard I. Bong WWII Heritage Center
Key Personnel: Exec. Dir., Robert B. Fuhrman; Chm. (V), Terry Lunberg; Museum Shop Mgr., Sandy Harty.
Institution Type/Description: History Museum.
Hours & Admission Prices: May-Oct. Mon.-Sat. 9-5, Sun. 12-5; Winter: Tues.-Sat. 9-5. Adults $9, senior citizens & students $8, children $7; discounts to groups; veterans on designated days, active military & members no charge. Closed New Year's Day; Easter; Thanksgiving; Christmas.
Attendance: 13,910 (actual)

S.S. METEOR MARITIME MUSEUM, 300 Marina Dr., Barker's Island, Superior, WI 54880-3287. Mailing Address: 906 E. 2nd St., Superior, WI 54880-3245. Tel.: 715-394-5712. Fax: 715-394-2043.
E-mail: info@superiorpublicmuseums.org
Web Site: www.superiorpublicmuseums.org
Key Personnel: Dir., Sara Blanck; Museums Coord., Stacie Buchanan.
Institution Type/Description: Historic Ship Museum: housed in the hull & quarters of the 1896 S.S. Meteor, last of the whalebacks.
Hours & Admission Prices: Mid-May-Sept. Mon.-Sat. 10-4, Sun. 11-4. Adults $8, college students w/ID and senior citizens 62 & up $7, kids 6-17 $5; discount to groups; children 5 & under no charge.
Attendance: 6,000 (estimated)

Two Rivers

HAMILTON WOOD TYPE & PRINTING MUSEUM, 1816 10th St., Two Rivers, WI 54241-3066. Tel.: 920-794-6272. Facebook: Hamilton Wood Type Printing Museum.
E-mail: info@woodtype.org
Web Site: www.woodtype.org
Key Personnel: Museum Dir., Jim Moran, Sr.
Institution Type/Description: Printing History Museum.
Hours & Admission Prices: May-Oct. Tues.-Sat. 10-5, Sun. 1-5; Nov.-April Tues.-Sat. 10-5. Adults $5, senior citizens, military veterans & children 12 & under $3.

Viroqua

VERNON COUNTY MUSEUM, 410 S. Center Ave., Viroqua, WI 54665-2001. Mailing Address: P.O. Box 444, Viroqua, WI 54665-0444. Tel.: 608-637-7396. Facebook: Vernon County Historical Society.
E-mail: museum@vernoncountyhistory.org
Web Site: www.vernoncountyhistory.org
Key Personnel: Pres. (V), Marcia Andrew; Cur., Kristen Parrott; Asst. Cur., Carol Krogan.
Institution Type/Description: Local History Museum: housed in Vernon County Normal School.
Hours & Admission Prices: Museum: April-May & Sept.-Oct. Mon.-Fri. 12-4; June-Aug. Mon.-Fri. 12-4, Sat. 10-2; Nov.-March Tues.-Thurs. 12-4; other times by appointment. No charge; donations accepted. Sherry-Butt House: Memorial Day to Labor Day Sat.-Sun. 1-5. Adults $5; members no charge. Closed holidays.
Attendance: 3,600 (actual)

Warrens

WISCONSIN CRANBERRY DISCOVERY CENTER, 204 Main St., Warrens, WI 54666. Mailing Address: P.O. Box 187, Warrens, WI 54666-0187. Tel.: 608-378-4878. Facebook: Wisconsin Cranberry Discovery Center.
E-mail: director@discovercranberries.com
Web Site: www.discovercranberries.com
Key Personnel: Exec. Dir., Kelly Murray; Pres. (V), Jerry Bach; Museum Coord., Deb Pearson.
Institution Type/Description: History Center.
Hours & Admission Prices: Mon.-Fri. 10-4, Sat.-Sun. see website for hours. Adults $5, seniors & military $4, students $3.

Washburn

WASHBURN HISTORICAL MUSEUM & CULTURAL CENTER, INC. AKA WASHBURN CULTURAL CENTER, 1 E. Bayfield St., Washburn, WI 54891-4401. Mailing Address: P.O. Box 725, Washburn, WI 54891-0725. Tel.: 715-373-5591.
E-mail: washburnw@centurytel.net

Web Site: washburnculturalcenter.com
Key Personnel: C.E.O. & Chm. (V), Richard Olson; Dir., Steve Cotherman.
Institution Type/Description: Historical Museum & Cultural Arts Center.
Hours & Admission Prices: Jan.-April Mon.-Sat. 12-4; May-Dec. Mon.-Sat. 10-4. No charge. Closed New Year's Day; Thanksgiving; Christmas. &
Attendance: 4,000 (estimated)

Washington Island

ROCK ISLAND STATE PARK, 1924 Indian Point Rd., Washington Island, WI 54246-9078. Tel.: 920-847-2235.
Web Site: www.dnr.state.wi.us/parks/
Key Personnel: Supt., Kirby Foss.
Institution Type/Description: State Park: located on the Door County Peninsula.
Hours & Admission Prices: Memorial Day-Columbus Day daily. Park: No charge; donations accepted. Camping fee, camping reservations recommended, to reserve a campsite, call Reserve America at 888-947-2747.
Attendance: 30,000

Watertown

OCTAGON HOUSE-FIRST KINDERGARTEN IN AMERICA, 919 Charles St., Watertown, WI 53094-5001. Tel.: 920-261-2796.
E-mail: whs@watertownhistory.org
Web Site: www.watertownhistory.org
Key Personnel: C.E.O. & Museum Shop Mgr., Linda Werth; Pres., Melissa Lampe.
Institution Type/Description: History Museum: housed in 1854 Victorian Octagon House belonging to John & Eliza Richards and family; 1856 first kindergarten building in America.
Hours & Admission Prices: May & Sept.-Oct. daily 11-3; Memorial Day to Labor Day 10-4. Adults $9, senior citizens & AAA members $8, students 6-17 $5; discounts to AAM & AAA members.
Attendance: 5,000 (estimated)

Waukesha

WAUKESHA COUNTY MUSEUM, 101 W. Main St., Waukesha, WI 53186-4811. Tel.: 262-521-2859. Fax: 262-521-2865.
E-mail: info@wchsm.org
Web Site: www.waukeshacountymuseum.org
Formerly: Waukesha County Historical Society & Museum
Key Personnel: Exec. Dir., Dennis Cerreta.
Institution Type/Description: History Museum: housed in 1893 Waukesha County Courthouse.
Hours & Admission Prices: Thurs. 1-4. No charge, donations appreciated. Closed major holidays. &
Attendance: 16,683 (actual)

Waupaca

WAUPACA HISTORICAL SOCIETY: HOLLY HISTORY & GENEALOGY CENTER & HUTCHINSON HOUSE MUSEUM & WAUPACA RAILROAD DEPOT, 321 S. Main St., Waupaca, WI 54981-1745. Tel.: 715-258-5958 (museum) & 256-9980 (history center).
E-mail: wauphistsoc@waupacaonline.net
Web Site: www.waupacahistoricalsociety.org
Formerly: Holly History Center & Hutchinson House Museum
Key Personnel: Pres., Dennis Lear; Vice Pres., Mike Kirk; Treas., Robert Kessler; Sec., Betty Stewart.
Institution Type/Description: Historic House & Preservation Project: 1854 Hutchinson House.
Hours & Admission Prices: History Center: Summer: Wed. & Fri. 12-4, Sat. 9-12; Winter: Wed. & Fri. 12-3. No charge; donations accepted. Museum: Memorial Day-Labor Day Sat.-Sun. & holidays 1-4; special group tours by appointment. No charge; donations accepted. &
Attendance: 1,200 (estimated)

Wausau

CENTER FOR THE VISUAL ARTS GALLERY, 427 N. 4th St., Wausau, WI 54403. Tel.: 715-842-4545.
E-mail: cvawausau@gmail.com
Web Site: www.cvawausau.org
Institution Type/Description: Art Gallery.
Hours & Admission Prices: Tues.-Fri. 10-5, Sat. 10-4. No charge; donations accepted. Closed holidays. &

LEIGH YAWKEY WOODSON ART MUSEUM, 700 N. 12th St., Wausau, WI 54403-5007. Tel.: 715-845-7010. Fax: 715-845-7103.

E-mail: museum@lywam.org
Web Site: www.lywam.org
Key Personnel: Dir., Kathy Kelsey Foley; Cur. Exhibitions, Andrew J. McGivern; Cur. Collections, Jane Weinke; Cur. Education, Lisa Hoffman; Cur. Education, Catie Anderson; Administrative Svcs. Mgr., Shari Schroeder; Facilities Mgr., Dave Jones; Business Mgr., Diane Wendt; Mgr. Mktg. & Communications, Amy Beck.
Institution Type/Description: Art Museum.
Hours & Admission Prices: Tues.-Fri. 9-4, 1st Thurs. each month 9-7:30, Sat.-Sun. 12-5. No charge; donations accepted. Closed national holidays. &
Attendance: 58,000 (estimated)

MARATHON COUNTY HISTORICAL SOCIETY, 410 McIndoe St., Wausau, WI 54403-4745. Tel.: 715-842-5750. Fax: 715-848-0576.
E-mail: director@marathoncountyhistory.org
Web Site: www.marathoncountyhistory.org
Key Personnel: Dir., Mary Forer; Cur. Events & Public Rels., Sara Goetsch; Librarian, Gary Gisselman; Cur. Education, Anna Straub; Yawkey House Attendant, Gary Walters.
Institution Type/Description: History Museum.
Hours & Admission Prices: Tues.-Fri. 9-4:30, Sat.-Sun. 1-4:30. Woodson History Center, Exhibits & Library: no charge. Yawkey House Museum: adults $7, seniors $6, students $5; members no charge. Closed national holidays. &
Attendance: 20,000 (estimated)

Wauwatosa

LOWELL DAMON HOUSE, 2107 Wauwatosa Ave., Wauwatosa, WI 53213-1730. Mailing Address: 910 N. Old World 3rd St., Milwaukee, WI 53203-1591. Tel.: 414-273-8288.
E-mail: info@milwaukeehistory.net
Web Site: www.milwaukeehistory.net
Institution Type/Description: Historic House.
Hours & Admission Prices: March-Nov. Sun. 12-5. Admission $2 per person. Closed major holidays.

West Allis

WEST ALLIS HISTORICAL SOCIETY MUSEUM, 8405 W. National Ave., West Allis, WI 53227-1733. Tel.: 414-541-6970.
E-mail: wahs8405@gmail.com
Web Site: www.westallishistory.org
Institution Type/Description: General Museum: housed in 1887 cream city brick Romanesque style school building.
Hours & Admission Prices: Tues. 7pm-9pm, Sun. 2-4; groups by appointment. No charge; donations accepted. Closed New Year's Eve & Day; Memorial Day; Independence Day; Thanksgiving; Christmas. &
Attendance: 831 (actual)

West Bend

MUSEUM OF WISCONSIN ART, 205 Veterans Ave., West Bend, WI 53095-3413. Tel.: 262-334-9638. Fax: 262-334-8080.
E-mail: lwinters@wisconsinart.org
Web Site: www.wisconsinart.org
Formerly: West Bend Art Museum
Key Personnel: Exec. Dir. & C.E.O., Laurie Winters; Dir. Collections & Exhibitions, Graeme Reid; Registrar, Andrea Waala; Dir. Devel., Heidi Wirth; Dir. Cultural Rels., Miranda Levy; Museum Shop Mgr., Julia Jackson.
Institution Type/Description: Art Museum.
Hours & Admission Prices: Tues.-Wed. & Fri.-Sun. 10-5, Thurs. 10-8. Closed New Year's Day; Independence Day; Thanksgiving; Christmas Eve & Day. &
Attendance: 35,000 (actual)

WASHINGTON COUNTY HISTORICAL SOCIETY, 320 S. 5th Ave., West Bend, WI 53095-3333. Tel.: 262-335-4678. Fax: 262-335-4612.
E-mail: wchs@historyisfun.com
Web Site: www.historyisfun.com
Key Personnel: Exec. Dir., Patricia Lutz; Pres. (V), John Best; Cur., Janean Mollet Van Beckum; Cur. Education, Jessica Sawinski; Research Supvr., Heather Przybylski.
Institution Type/Description: History Museum: housed in 1889 County Courthouse; 1886 Old County Jailhouse Museum.
Hours & Admission Prices: Wed.-Fri. 11-5, Sat. 9-5, Sun. 1-4:30. Jailhouse Tour: adults 17-61 $5, children 6-16 $4; children under 6 & members no charge. Closed New Year's Eve & Day; Easter; Independence Day; Labor Day; Christmas Eve & Day. &
Attendance: 9,300 (estimated)

West Salem

HAMLIN GARLAND HOMESTEAD, 357 W. Garland St., West Salem, WI 54669-1146. Mailing Address: P.O. Box 884, West Salem, WI 54669-0884. Tel.: 608-786-1399.
Web Site: www.westsalemhistoricalsociety.org
Key Personnel: C.E.O. & Pres., Errol Kindschy.
Institution Type/Description: Historic House: 1857-60 Hamlin Garland Homestead.
Hours & Admission Prices: Memorial Day to Labor Day Mon.-Sat. 10-4, Sun. 1-4; other times by appointment. Family $2.50, adults $1, students $.50; members no charge. Discounts to AAA members.
Attendance: 649 (actual)

PALMER/GULLICKSON OCTAGON HOME, 360 N. Leonard, West Salem, WI 54669-1238. Mailing Address: P.O. Box 884, West Salem, WI 54669-0884. Tel.: 608-786-1399.
Key Personnel: C.E.O. & Pres., Errol Kindschy.
Institution Type/Description: Historical Society Museum.
Hours & Admission Prices: Memorial Day-Labor Day Mon.-Sat. 10-4, Sun. 1-4; other times by appointment. Family $2.50, adults $1, students $.50; discounts to AAA members; members no charge.
Attendance: 510 (actual)

Westfield

MARQUETTE COUNTY HISTORICAL SOCIETY, 125 Lawrence St., Westfield, WI 53964-9030. Mailing Address: P.O. Box 172, Westfield, WI 53964-0172. Tel.: 608-296-4700.
E-mail: mcgwin@frontier.com
Web Site: www.marqcohistorical.org
Formerly: Cochrane-Nelson House
Key Personnel: Pres., LeRoy Stublaski; Vice Pres., Ed Thalacker; Sec. & Cur., Carol Claesges; Treas. & Cur., Joannie Ingraham.
Institution Type/Description: Historical Society Museum.
Hours & Admission Prices: Wed. 1-4; other times by appointment. No charge; donations accepted. &
Attendance: 1,500 (estimated)

Weyauwega

LITTLE RED SCHOOL HOUSE MUSEUM, Weyauwega Community Park, 411 W. High St., Weyauwega, WI 54983. Mailing Address: P.O. Box 294, Weyauwega, WI 54983-0294. Tel.: 920-867-2500 & 2630.
E-mail: weyauwegaareahistoricalsociety@yahoo.com
Web Site: www.cityofweyauwega-wi.gov
Key Personnel: Caretaker, Suzanne Dyer.
Institution Type/Description: Historic Building: housed in 1861 Old Wood School House.
Hours & Admission Prices: Memorial Day-Labor Day Sun. 1-4; other times by appointment. No charge; donations accepted.
Attendance: 100 (estimated)

Whitewater

CROSSMAN GALLERY, UW-WHITEWATER, 950 W. Main St., Whitewater, WI 53190. Mailing Address: 800 W. Main Street, Whitewater, WI 53190-1705. Tel.: 262-472-5708 & 1207. Fax: 262-472-2808. Facebook.
E-mail: flanagam@uww.edu
Web Site: www.uww.edu
Key Personnel: Dir., Michael Flanagan.
Institution Type/Description: University Art Gallery.
Hours & Admission Prices: Academic Year: Mon.-Thurs. 10-5 & 6-8, Fri. 10-5, Sat. 1-4; Summer: call for hours. No charge. Closed Easter; Christmas. &
Attendance: 9,500 (actual)

WHITEWATER HISTORICAL MUSEUM, 301 W. Whitewater St., Whitewater, WI 53190. Mailing Address: P.O. Box 149, Whitewater, WI 53190. Tel.: 262-473-6820.
E-mail: whitewaterwihistoricalsociety@gmail.com
Institution Type/Description: History Museum: housed in 1890 Chicago, Milwaukee & St. Paul Railroad depot.
Hours & Admission Prices: Memorial Day-Labor Day Thurs. 5:30pm-7:30pm, Sun. 1-4; Fall: Tues. 3-7, Thurs. 6pm-8pm, Fri. 10-1, Sat.-Sun. 1-4; other times by appointment. No charge; donations accepted. &
Attendance: 400 (estimated)

Wild Rose

PIONEER MUSEUM & WILD ROSE HISTORICAL SOCIETY, 477 & 479 Main St., Wild Rose, WI 54984. Mailing Address: P.O. Box 63, Wild Rose, WI 54984-0063.
E-mail: waushara@yahoo.com
Key Personnel: Pres. & Cur., Pam Anderson; Vice Pres., Joe Smith; Treas., Helen Cox; Museum Shop Mgr., Mary Ann Erdman.
Institution Type/Description: Pioneer Museum.
Hours & Admission Prices: mid-June to Labor Day Wed. & Sat. 10-1. No charge; donations accepted. Closed Independence Day.
Attendance: 350 (estimated)

Wisconsin Dells

BEAVER SPRINGS PUBLIC AQUARIUM, 600 Trout Rd., Wisconsin Dells, WI 53965. Mailing Address: P.O. Box 1, Wisconsin Dells, WI 53965. Tel.: 608-254-2735. Fax: 608-253-9446.
E-mail: beaversprings@dellsnet.com
Institution Type/Description: Aquarium.
Hours & Admission Prices: April-May & Sept.-Oct. daily 10-5; June-Aug. daily 9-7; Nov.-March daily 10-4. Adults $7.99, children $5.99.

H.H. BENNETT STUDIO, 215 Broadway, Wisconsin Dells, WI 53965. Mailing Address: P.O. Box 147, Wisconsin Dells, WI 53965. Tel.: 608-253-3523. Fax: 608-253-4635.
E-mail: hhbennett@wisconsinhistory.org
Web Site: www.hhbennettstudio.org
Key Personnel: Site Dir., Alan Hanson.
Institution Type/Description: Photography Museum.
Hours & Admission Prices: Adults $7, students and seniors 65 & over $6, children 5-17 $3.50; discounts to AAM members; children under 5 no charge. &

PARSON'S INDIAN TRADING POST & MUSEUM, 370 Wisconsin Dells Pkwy., Wisconsin Dells, WI 53965. Tel.: 608-254-8533, 866-281-8704. Fax: 608-253-6766.
E-mail: parsonitp@hotmail.com
Institution Type/Description: Native American History Museum.
Hours & Admission Prices: Summer: daily 9-9; Winter: daily 9-5. &

RIVERSIDE & GREAT NORTHERN RAILWAY, N115 County Rd. N., Wisconsin Dells, WI 53965-9124. Tel.: 608-254-6367. Fax: 608-254-5628.
E-mail: dellstrain@gmail.com
Web Site: dellstrain.com
Key Personnel: Dir., Gary Gleason; Chm. (V) & Pres. (V), Steve Bradly; Museum Shop Mgr., Mary Simerson.
Institution Type/Description: Railway History Museum.
Hours & Admission Prices: Call for hours. No charge; donations accepted. &
Attendance: 12,000 (estimated)

TIMBAVATI WILDLIFE PARK, 2220 Wisconsin Dells Pkwy., Wisconsin Dells, WI 53965. Tel.: 608-253-2391.
E-mail: info@timbavatiwildlifepark.com
Web Site: www.timbavatiwildlifepark.com
Key Personnel: Owner, Mark Schoebel.
Institution Type/Description: Wildlife Park.
Hours & Admission Prices: Memorial Day to Labor Day daily 9-8. Adults $18.95; children 2-12 $12.95; military & children under 2 no charge.

TOMMY BARTLETT EXPLORATORY - INTERACTIVE SCIENCE CENTER, 560 Wisconsin Dells Pkwy., Wisconsin Dells, WI 53965. Tel.: 608-254-2525.
E-mail: bartlett@tommybartlett.com
Web Site: www.tommybartlett.com
Formerly: Exploratory Interactive Science Center
Institution Type/Description: Science Center.
Hours & Admission Prices: Summer: daily 9-9; Spring, Fall, & Winter: daily 10-4. Adults $15, seniors 65 & over $12, children 5-11 $12; discounts to groups of 20 or more; children 4 & under no charge. &

WISCONSIN DEER PARK, 583 Wisconsin Dells Pkwy., Wisconsin Dells, WI 53965. Tel.: 608-253-2041.
Web Site: wisdeerpark.com/park.htm
Institution Type/Description: Nature Center.
Hours & Admission Prices: May & Sept.-Oct. daily 10-4; Memorial Day to Labor Day daily 9-7. Adults 12 & over $12, children 3-11 $8; children 2 & under no charge. &

Wisconsin Rapids

SOUTH WOOD COUNTY HISTORICAL CORP., 540 Third St. S., Wisconsin Rapids, WI 54494-4352. Tel.: 715-423-1580.
E-mail: lori@swch-museum.com
Web Site: www.swch-museum.com
Key Personnel: Pres., Philip M. Brown; Dir., Dave Engel; Admin., Lori Brost.
Institution Type/Description: Historical Society Museum: housed in 1907 mansion.
Hours & Admission Prices: Memorial Day to Labor Day Sun. & Tues.-Thurs. 1-4. No charge; donations accepted.
Attendance: 1,300 (estimated)

WYOMING

(126 listings)

Afton

CALLAIR MUSEUM, 150 S. Washington St., Afton, WY 83110. Mailing Address: Call Air Foundation, P.O. Box 1491, Afton, WY 83110. Tel.: 307-885-3995.
E-mail: info@starvalleychamber.com
Web Site: callairmuseum.org
Institution Type/Description: Company History Museum.
Hours & Admission Prices: Memorial Day to Labor Day Mon.-Fri. 1-5; other times by appointment. No charge.

STAR VALLEY HISTORICAL SOCIETY, 138 S. Washington, Afton, WY 83110. Mailing Address: P.O. Box 1212, Afton, WY 83110. Tel.: 307-885-9648 * 883-0993.
E-mail: svhs@silverstar.com
Web Site: starvalleyhs.lincolncountywy.org
Formerly: Daughters of Utah Pioneers, Lincoln Company
Key Personnel: Museum Dir., Carlie C. Jensen; Asst. Museum Dir., Ruth H. Petersen.
Institution Type/Description: History Museum.
Hours & Admission Prices: June-Aug. Fri. & Sat. 1-5; May & Sept. by appointment. No charge; donations accepted. ⅋
Attendance: 793 (actual)

Banner

FORT PHIL KEARNY, 528 Wagon Box Rd., Banner, WY 82832-9604. Tel.: 307-684-7629.
E-mail: misty.stoll@wyo.gov
Web Site: www.fortphilkearny.com
Key Personnel: Site Supt., Misty Stoll; Cur., Sonny Reisch.
Institution Type/Description: Historic Site & Visitor Center: Fort Phil Kearny, the Wagon Box Fight site & the Fetterman Fight site.
Hours & Admission Prices: May-Sept. daily 8-6; Oct.-Nov. Wed.-Sun. 12-4; Dec.-April by appt. Adults $2 (residents), $4 (non-residents); children 17 & under no charge. ⅋
Attendance: 24,000 (actual)

Big Horn

BOZEMAN TRAIL MUSEUM, 335 Johnson St., Big Horn, WY 82833. Mailing Address: P.O. Box 566, Big Horn, WY 82833. Tel.: 307-674-6363.
E-mail: info@sheridanmedia.com
Key Personnel: Dir. & Museum Shop Mgr., Kevin Knapp; Chm. (V), Judy Slack; Pres. (V), Mike Kuzara.
Institution Type/Description: Historic Building Museum: housed in a former blacksmith shop; built in 1879.
Hours & Admission Prices: Memorial Day to Labor Day Sat.-Sun. 11-4; other times by appointment. No charge; donations accepted. ⅋
Attendance: 400 (estimated)

THE BRINTON MUSEUM, 239 Brinton Rd., Big Horn, WY 82833. Mailing Address: P.O. Box 460, Big Horn, WY 82833-0460. Tel.: 307-672-3173. Fax: 307-672-3258. Facebook: @TheBrinton.
E-mail: kschuster@thebrintonmuseum.org
Web Site: www.thebrintonmuseum.org
Formerly: Bradford Brinton Memorial & Museum
Key Personnel: Dir. & Chief Cur., Kenneth L. Schuster; COO, Joel Wardell; Asst. Dir. Devel., Barbara Schuster; Cur. Exhibitions & Educ., Barbara McNab; Registrar, Lisa Ranallo; Accountant & Human Resources, Emily Wardell; Mktg. & Membership, Tod Windsor; Mus. Store, Michele Folster.
Institution Type/Description: Historic House and Art Museum: on a gentleman's working ranch established in 1892.

Hours & Admission Prices: May 15 to Labor Day daily 9:30-5; Sept.-Dec. 23 Wed.-Sun. 9:30-5. Adults $10, seniors & students over 13 $8; discounts to AAA members; children 12 & under, active military & families, veterans (Blue Star Museums program), Sheridan and Johnson County students, school groups & museum, ROAM & NARM members no charge. Closed New Year's Day; Christmas. ⅋
Attendance: 22,000 (estimated)

Big Piney

GREEN RIVER VALLEY MUSEUM, 206 N. Front St., Big Piney, WY 83113. Mailing Address: P.O. Box 12, Big Piney, WY 83113-0012. Tel.: 307-276-5343. Facebook.
E-mail: grvmuseum@gmail.com
Web Site: www.grvm.com
Key Personnel: Dir., Clarica Pinkerton; Astt. Dir., Jeff Bell; Bookkeeper, Karen Taylor.
Institution Type/Description: History Museum.
Hours & Admission Prices: June-Oct. 15 Tues.-Sat. 11-5. No charge; donations accepted.
Attendance: 600 (estimated)

Buffalo

JIM GATCHELL MEMORIAL MUSEUM, 100 Fort St., Buffalo, WY 82834. Mailing Address: P.O. Box 596, Buffalo, WY 82834-0596. Tel.: 307-684-9331.
E-mail: director@jimgatchell.com
Web Site: www.jimgatchell.com
Key Personnel: Dir., Sylvia Bruner; Mus. Asst., DavKelseyd McDonnell; Museum Educator, Jennifer Romanoski.
Institution Type/Description: History Museum.
Hours & Admission Prices: Memorial Day to Labor Day Mon.-Sat. 9-6; Sept.-May Mon.-Sat. 9-4. Adults $7, seniors, retired military & teens (12-18) $5, youth 6-11 $3; active military, members & children under 5 no charge. ⅋
Attendance: 7,500 (actual)

MUSEUM OF THE OCCIDENTAL, 10 N. Main St., Buffalo, WY 82834-1815. Tel.: 307-684-0451.
E-mail: info@occidentalwyoming.com
Web Site: www.occidentalwyoming.com
Institution Type/Description: History Museum.
Hours & Admission Prices: Daily 10-6. No charge.

Casper

CASPER PLANETARIUM, 904 N. Poplar St., Casper, WY 82601-1348. Tel.: 307-577-0310. Facebook.
E-mail: casperplanetarium@gmail.com
Web Site: www.casperplanetarium.com
Key Personnel: Supvr., Michelle Wistisen.
Institution Type/Description: Planetarium.
Hours & Admission Prices: Office: Mon.-Fri. 9-5; public shows Tues-Fri. 4:15; Sat. 7 & 8.. Admission $2.50. Closed major holidays.

CRIMSON DAWN MUSEUM & PARK, 1620 E. Crimson Dawn Rd., Casper, WY 82601-9740. Mailing Address: P.O. Box 2578, Mills, WY 82644. Tel.: 307-235-1303. Facebook.
E-mail: contact@crimsondawnpark.org
Institution Type/Description: History Museum.
Hours & Admission Prices: mid-June to mid-Sept. Sat.-Sun. 10-7. No charge; donations accepted.
Attendance: 2,000 (estimated)

FORT CASPAR MUSEUM, 4001 Fort Caspar Rd., Casper, WY 82604-2923. Tel.: 307-235-8462.
E-mail: ryoung@casperwy.gov
Web Site: www.fortcasparwyoming.com
Key Personnel: C.E.O., Richard L. Young; Cur., Michelle Bahe; Administrative Support Tech, Anne Holman.
Institution Type/Description: Social History Museum: Listed on the National Register of Historic Places.
Hours & Admission Prices: Museum: May-Sept. daily 8-5; Oct.-April Tues.-Sat. 8-5. Fort Buildings: May-Sept. daily 8:30-4:30. ⅋
Attendance: 35,000 (estimated)

IDA GOODSTEIN VISUAL ARTS CENTER, Casper College, 125 College Dr., Casper, WY 82601-4612. Tel.: 307-268-2060.
E-mail: vinnella@caspercollege.edu
Web Site: www.caspercollege.edu

Key Personnel: Dir., Valerie Innella Maiers.
Institution Type/Description: Art Museum.
Hours & Admission Prices: Mon.-Thurs. 9-4. No charge. Closed holidays.

NATIONAL HISTORIC TRAILS INTERPRETIVE CENTER,
1501 N. Poplar St., Casper, WY 82601-1375. Mailing Address: P.
O. Box 397, Casper, WY 82602. Tel.: 307-265-8030. Fax: 307-
265-0986.
E-mail: nhtcf@hotmail.com
Web Site: nhtcf.org
Key Personnel: Exec. Dir., Carrie O. Reece.
Institution Type/Description: History Museum.
Hours & Admission Prices: Memorial Day to Labor Day Tues.-Sun 8-5; Sept.-April
Tues.-Sat. 9-4:30. See website for admissions. Closed New Year's Day; Easter;
Thanksgiving; Christmas. &
Attendance: 25,000 (actual)

NICOLAYSEN ART MUSEUM AND DISCOVERY CENTER,
400 E. Collins St., Casper, WY 82601-2815. Tel.: 307-235-5247.
E-mail: info@thenic.org
Web Site: thenic.org
Key Personnel: Exec. Dir., Ann Ruble; Chief Cur., Eric Wimmer.
Institution Type/Description: Art Museum.
Hours & Admission Prices: Wed.-Sat. 10-5, Sun. 12-4. Adults $5, seniors, students
with valid ID & children 3-17 $3; Sun., military, children under 2 & members
no charge. &
Attendance: 50,000 (actual)

THE SCIENCE ZONE, INC., 111 W. Midwest Ave., Casper, WY
82601. Tel.: 307-473-9663.
E-mail: steven.schnell@thesciencezone.org
Web Site: www.thesciencezone.org
Key Personnel: Exec. Dir., Steven Schnell; Dir. Education, Leah Ritz; Opers. Mgr.,
Kathy Nickerson.
Institution Type/Description: Science Center.
Hours & Admission Prices: Mon.-Sat. 10-5, 1st Thurs. each month 10-7. Adults $4,
children $3; members & children under 2 no charge. &
Attendance: 25,000 (actual)

TATE GEOLOGICAL MUSEUM, Casper College, 125 College
Dr., Casper, WY 82601-4612. Tel.: 307-268-2447.
E-mail: pfinkle@caspercollege.edu
Web Site: www.caspercollege.edu/tate
Key Personnel: Dir., Patti Wood Finkle; Cur., Dr. Kent Sundell; Cur., Melissa
Connely.
Institution Type/Description: Geology Museum.
Hours & Admission Prices: Mon.-Fri. 9-5, Sat. 10-4. No charge; donations
accepted. &
Attendance: 19,000 (actual)

WERNER WILDLIFE MUSEUM, 405 E. 15th St, Casper, WY
82601-4612. Mailing Address: Casper College, 125 College Dr.,
Casper, WY 82601. Tel.: 307-235-2108. Facebook: Werner
Wildlife Museum.
E-mail: indiahayford@caspercollege.edu
Web Site: www.caspercollege.edu/werner-wildlife-museum
Key Personnel: Dir., Patti Wood Finkle; Museum Asst., India Hayford.
Institution Type/Description: Wildlife Museum.
Hours & Admission Prices: Mon.-Fri. 9-4:30; call for holiday hours. No charge;
donations accepted. &
Attendance: 6,000 (estimated)

WYOMING VETERANS MEMORIAL MUSEUM, 3740
Jourgensen Ave., Casper, WY 82604. Tel.: 307-472-1857.
Facebook: Wyoming Veterans Museum.
E-mail: douglas.cubbison@wyo.gov
Web Site: wyomilitary.wyo.gov/veteransmuseums/vets-museum/
Key Personnel: Dir., John Woodward; Cur., Douglas Cubbison.
Institution Type/Description: Military History Museum.
Hours & Admission Prices: Summer: Tues.-Sat. 9-4. No charge; donations
accepted. &
Attendance: 3,000 (actual)

Centennial

NICI SELF HISTORICAL MUSEUM, 2734 Hwy. 130, Centennial,
WY 82055. Tel.: 307-742-7763 & 307-745-3108. Facebook: Nici
Self Historical Museum.
E-mail: cvha@live.com

Web Site: www.niciselfmuseum.org
Institution Type/Description: History Museum: housed in 1907 Railroad Depot
located at the base of the Medicine Bow Mountains.
Hours & Admission Prices: Memorial Day to Labor Day Thurs.-Mon. 12-4; Sept.
Sat.-Sun. 12-4; other times by appt. No charge; donations accepted.
Attendance: 1,450 (estimated)

Cheyenne

CHEYENNE BOTANIC GARDENS, 710 S. Lions Park Dr.,
Cheyenne, WY 82001-7503. Tel.: 307-637-6458.
E-mail: info@botanic.org
Web Site: www.botanic.org
Key Personnel: Dir., Tina Worthman; Children's Village Mgr., Aaron Sommers;
Exterior Horticulture, Jacob Mares; Interior Horticulturist, Isaiah Smith;
Education & Outreach Horticulturist, Nettie Eakes.
Institution Type/Description: Botanical Garden.
Hours & Admission Prices: Grounds: daily dawn-dusk. Conservatory: Wed.-Sun.
10-6. Children's Village: Tues.-Sun 10-5. No charge; donations accepted. Closed
New Year's Day; Easter; Thanksgiving; Christmas. &
Attendance: 42,525 (actual)

CHEYENNE DEPOT MUSEUM, 121 W. 15th St. Ste. 300,
Cheyenne, WY 82001. Tel.: 307-632-3905. Fax: 307-632-0614.
E-mail: info@cheyennedepotmuseum.org
Web Site: www.cheyennedepotmuseum.org
Formerly: Wyoming Transportation Museum
Key Personnel: Exec. Dir., Christy McCarthy; Cur., Sarah Gadd.
Institution Type/Description: Railroad History Museum.
Hours & Admission Prices: June-Aug. Mon.-Fri. 9-6:30, Sat. 9-5, Sun. 11-3; Jan-
May & Sept.-Dec. Mon.-Fri. 9-5, Sat. 9-3, Sun. 11-3. Adults $8; seniors & mili-
tary $7; children 12 & under no charge. &
Attendance: 120,000 (estimated)

CHEYENNE FRONTIER DAYS OLD WEST MUSEUM, 4610 N.
Carey Ave., Cheyenne, WY 82001-7505. Mailing Address: P.O.
Box 2720, Cheyenne, WY 82003-2720. Tel.: 307-778-7290.
Facebook.
E-mail: info@oldwestmuseum.org
Web Site: oldwestmuseum.org
Key Personnel: Exec. Dir., Amiee Reese; Assoc. Dir. & Cur., Mike Kassel; Cur.
Exhibits, Brian Briggs; Facilities, CJ McCutchen; Arts Education Coord.,
Megan Hesser; Volunteer & Rental Coord., Janet Wampler; Outreach & Mktg.
Dir., Morgan Marks.
Institution Type/Description: History Museum.
Hours & Admission Prices: Daily 9-5. Adults $10, seniors & military $9; children
12 & under & members no charge. Closed New Year's Day; Easter;
Thanksgiving; Christmas. &
Attendance: 45,000 (estimated)

COWGIRLS OF THE WEST, 203-205 W. 17th St., Cheyenne, WY
82001-4411. Mailing Address: P.O. Box 525, Cheyenne, WY
82003. Tel.: 307-638-4994.
Web Site: www.cowgirlsofthewestmuseum.com
Key Personnel: Museum Shop Mgr., Pam Cooper.
Institution Type/Description: History Museum.
Hours & Admission Prices: Jan. 16-Dec. Tues.-Fri. 11-4, Sat. 11-3. No charge; don-
ations accepted.
Attendance: 4,000 (actual)

THE ESTHER AND JOHN CLAY FINE ARTS GALLERY,
Laramie County Community College, Fine Arts Bldg., 1400 E.
College Dr., Cheyenne, WY 82007-3204. Tel.: 307-778-1285.
E-mail: events@artscheyenne.com
Web Site: lccc.wy.edu
Institution Type/Description: Art Gallery.
Hours & Admission Prices: Mon.-Fri. 8-5. No charge.

HISTORIC GOVERNORS' MANSION, 300 E. 21st. St.,
Cheyenne, WY 82001-3712. Mailing Address: Dept. of State Parks
& Cultural Resources, Barrett Bldg., Cheyenne, WY 82002. Tel.:
307-777-7878.
E-mail: sphs@state.wy.us
Web Site: www.cheyenne.org
Key Personnel: Dir. Div. Parks, Domenic Bravo.
Institution Type/Description: Historic Building: 1904 Colonial Revival Mansion &
Carriage House.

Hours & Admission Prices: June-Aug. Mon.-Sat. 9-5, Sun. 1-5; Sept.-May Wed.-Sat. 9-5; groups by appointment. No charge; donations accepted. Closed most holidays. ♿
Attendance: 10,189 (actual)

NELSON MUSEUM OF THE WEST, 1714 Carey Ave., Cheyenne, WY 82001-4420. Tel.: 307-635-7670.
E-mail: office.nelsonmuseum@gmail.com
Web Site: www.nelsonmuseum.com
Key Personnel: Dir., Robert Nelson.
Institution Type/Description: History Museum.
Hours & Admission Prices: May & Sept.-Oct. Mon.-Fri. 9-4:30; June-Aug. Mon.-Sat. 9-4:30; other times by appointment. Adults $5, seniors 65 & over $4; discounts to groups; children under 12 no charge. ♿
Attendance: 5,000 (actual)

WYOMING ARTS COUNCIL, 2301 Capitol Ave., Cheyenne, WY 82002. Tel.: 307-777-7742.
E-mail: brittany.perez@wyo.gov
Web Site: www.wyomingartscouncil.org
Key Personnel: Exec. Dir., Michael Lange; Office Mgr., Brittany Perez.
Institution Type/Description: State Agency.
Hours & Admission Prices: Mon.-Fri. 8-5. ♿
Attendance: 600 (estimated)

WYOMING NATIONAL GUARD MUSEUM, 624 E. Pershing Blvd., Cheyenne, WY 82001. Tel.: 307-432-0057.
E-mail: wyoguard@gmail.com
Web Site: wyomilitary.wyo.gov/veterans/museum/guard-museum/
Institution Type/Description: Military History Museum: housed in the former Armory for the Wyoming Army National Guard.
Hours & Admission Prices: Wed.-Sat. 9-4, Thurs. by appointment. No charge.
Attendance: 1,200 (actual)

WYOMING STATE CAPITOL, 200 W. 24th St., Cheyenne, WY 82002. Tel.: 307-777-7220.
E-mail: capitoltours@wyo.gov
Web Site: ai.wyo.gov/capitol-tours-home-page
Institution Type/Description: Historic Building: built in 1890. A National Historic Landmark.
Hours & Admission Prices: Closed for renovations until July 2019.

WYOMING STATE MUSEUM, 2301 Central Ave., Barrett Bldg., Cheyenne, WY 82001-3110. Tel.: 307-777-7022. Facebook.
E-mail: mark.brammer@wyo.gov
Web Site: wyomuseum.state.wy.us
Key Personnel: Museum Dir., Mark Brammer; Pres. (V), Pete Hutchinson; Supvr. Collections, Jennifer Alexander; Supvr. Collections, Jim Allison; Cur. Education, Jeremy Thornbrugh; Cur. Collections, Mandy Langfald; Cur. Collections, Mariah Emmons; Cur. Exhibits, Carlos Santos; Cur. Interpretation, Megan Reel; Registrar, Kristy Griffin; Museum Preparator, Matthew Wilson; Supervisor Museum Programs & Exhibits, Kevin Ramler.
Institution Type/Description: State History Museum.
Hours & Admission Prices: Mon.-Sat. 9-4:30. No charge; donations accepted. Closed state & federal holidays. ♿
Attendance: 45,000 (estimated)

Chugwater

CHUGWATER MUSEUM, Main St., Chugwater, WY 82210. Tel.: 307-422-3509.
Key Personnel: Dir., Ruth Vaughn.
Institution Type/Description: History Museum.
Hours & Admission Prices: Memorial Day to Labor Day Sat.-Sun. & holidays 1-4; other times by appointment. No charge; donations accepted.
Attendance: 400 (estimated)

Clearmont

UCROSS FOUNDATION ART GALLERY, 30 Big Red Lane, Clearmont, WY 82835-9723. Tel.: 307-737-2291.
E-mail: info@ucross.org
Web Site: www.ucrossfoundation.org/art-gallery/
Key Personnel: Pres., Sharon Dynak.
Institution Type/Description: Art Gallery.
Hours & Admission Prices: Oct.-June Mon.-Fri. 8:30-4; July-Sept. Mon.-Fri. 8:30-4, Sat. 10-4. No charge; donations accepted. Closed major holidays.

Cody

BIG HORN GALLERIES, 1167 Sheridan Ave., Cody, WY 82414-3627. Tel.: 307-527-7587. Fax: 307-527-7586.
E-mail: bhgcody@aol.com
Web Site: www.bighorngalleries.com
Institution Type/Description: Art Gallery.
Hours & Admission Prices: Call for hours.

BUFFALO BILL CENTER OF THE WEST, 720 Sheridan Ave., Cody, WY 82414-3428. Tel.: 307-587-4771.
E-mail: info@centerofthewest.org
Web Site: centerofthewest.org
Formerly: Buffalo Bill Historical Center
Key Personnel: Exec. Dir., Bruce Eldredge; Cur. Buffalo Bill Museum, Jeremy Johnston; Scarlett Cur. of Western American Art, Karen McWhorter; Cur. Plains Indian Culture, Rebecca West; Willis McDonald IV Sr. Cur. of Natural Science,, Dr. Charles Preston; Housel Dir., Mary Robinson; Dir. Devel., Kelly Jensen; Robert W. Woodruff Cur., Ashley Hlebinsky.
Institution Type/Description: Art, History, & Natural Science Museum.
Hours & Admission Prices: March-April & Nov. daily 10-5; May-Sept. 15 daily 8-6; Sept. 16-Oct. daily 8-5; Dec.-Feb. Thurs.-Sun. 10-5. Adults $19.50, seniors $18.50, students with valid ID $18; youth 6-17 $13; children 5 & under no charge. Closed New Year's Day; Thanksgiving; Christmas. ♿
Attendance: 175,000 (actual)

BUFFALO BILL DAM VISITOR CENTER, 4808 N. Fork Hwy., Cody, WY 82414. Mailing Address: 1002 Sheridan Ave., #109, Cody, WY 82414. Tel.: 307-527-6076.
E-mail: manager@bbdvc.com
Web Site: www.bbdvc.com
Key Personnel: Mgr., Brad Constantine.
Institution Type/Description: History Museum.
Hours & Admission Prices: May & Sept. Mon.-Fri. 8-6, Sat.-Sun. 9-5; June-Aug. Mon.-Fri. 8-7, Sat.-Sun. 9-5. No charge; donations accepted.

THE CODY DUG UP GUN MUSEUM, 1020 12th St., Cody, WY 82414. Tel.: 307-587-3344.
E-mail: codydugupgunmuseum@hotmail.com
Web Site: www.codydugupgunmuseum.com
Key Personnel: Dir., Hans Kurth; C.E.O., Eva Kurth.
Institution Type/Description: History Museum.
Hours & Admission Prices: May-Sept. daily 9-9. No charge; donations accepted.
Attendance: 17,500 (estimated)

MUSEUM OF THE OLD WEST & OLD TRAIL TOWN, 1831 DeMaris Dr., Cody, WY 82414. Mailing Address: P.O. Box 546, Cody, WY 82414-0546. Tel.: 307-587-5302.
E-mail: visitus@oldtrailtown.org
Web Site: www.oldtrailtown.org
Institution Type/Description: Historic Buildings: 26 buildings built 1879-1901.
Hours & Admission Prices: mid-May to Sept. daily 8-7. Adults $9, seniors 65 & over $8, children 6-12 $5; discounts to groups; children 5 & under no charge.

SIMPSON GALLAGHER GALLERY, 1161 Sheridan Ave., Cody, WY 82414-3627. Tel.: 307-587-4022.
E-mail: sue@simpsongallaghergallery.com
Web Site: www.simpsongallaghergallery.com
Institution Type/Description: Art Gallery.
Hours & Admission Prices: Call for hours. ♿

Colter Bay Village

GRAND TETON NATIONAL PARK, COLTER BAY VISITOR CENTER, Colter Bay Visitor Center, Grand Teton National Park, Colter Bay Village, WY 83012. Mailing Address: P.O. Box 170, Moose, WY 83012-0170. Tel.: 307-739-3594. Fax: 307-739-3504.
E-mail: grte_info@nps.gov
Web Site: www.nps.gov/grte/
Formerly: Grand Teton National Park, Colter Bay Indian Arts Museum
Key Personnel: Supt., David Vela.
Institution Type/Description: National Park.
Hours & Admission Prices: See website for hours & admissions. ♿

Devils Tower

DEVILS TOWER VISITOR CENTER, Devils Tower National Monument, State Hwy. 110, Bldg. 170, Devils Tower, WY 82714.

Mailing Address: P.O. Box 10, Devils Tower, WY 82714-0010. Tel.: 307-467-5283.
E-mail: deto_interpretation@nps.gov
Web Site: www.nps.gov/deto
Key Personnel: Chief Interpretation & Education, Nancy Stimson.
Institution Type/Description: National Monument Museum; 1930s CCC/WPA log building.
Hours & Admission Prices: Visitor Center: Summer: daily 8-7; Winter: daily 9-4. Monument: daily 24 hrs. $10 per vehicle. Closed New Year's Day; Christmas. &
Attendance: 358,000 (estimated)

Douglas

DOUGLAS RAILROAD INTERPRETIVE MUSEUM, 121 Brownfield Rd., Douglas, WY 82633-2558. Tel.: 307-358-2950. Facebook.
E-mail: chamber@jackalope.org
Web Site: www.cityofdouglas.org/Facilities/Facility/Details/Locomotive-Park-4
Institution Type/Description: Historic Building: housed in the former Fremont, Elkhorn and Missouri Valley Railroad depot; built in 1886.
Hours & Admission Prices: Summer: Mon.-Fri. 9-5, Sat.-Sun. 10-4; Winter: Mon.-Thurs. 9-5, Fri. 9-4. No charge; donations accepted. &
Attendance: 9,000 (estimated)

FORT FETTERMAN STATE HISTORIC SITE, 752 Hwy. 93, Douglas, WY 82633-9267. Mailing Address: P.O. Box 911, Douglas, WY 82633-0911. Tel.: 307-358-9288.
E-mail: mel.glover@wyo.gov
Web Site: www.wyoparks.state.wy.us
Formerly: Fort Fetterman State Museum
Key Personnel: C.E.O., Dominic Bravo; Site Supvr., Mel Glover.
Institution Type/Description: Military Museum: housed in 1867-1882 historic Fort Fetterman Officer's Quarters & ordnance building on original site.
Hours & Admission Prices: Memorial Day to Labor Day daily 9-5. See website for admissions. &
Attendance: 10,000 (actual)

WYOMING PIONEER MEMORIAL MUSEUM, Wyoming State Fairgrounds, 400 W. Center St., Douglas, WY 82633. Mailing Address: P.O. Box 911, Douglas, WY 82633-0911. Tel.: 307-358-9288.
E-mail: mel.glover@wyo.gov
Web Site: wyoparks.state.wy.us/index.php/places-to-go/wyoming-pioneer-museum
Key Personnel: Supt., Mel Glover.
Institution Type/Description: General Museum.
Hours & Admission Prices: Summer: Mon.-Sat. 8-5; Winter: Tues.-Sat. 8-4. No charge; donations accepted. Closed national holidays. &
Attendance: 20,000 (actual)

Dubois

DUBOIS MUSEUM: WIND RIVER HISTORICAL CENTER, 909 W. Ramshorn St, Dubois, WY 82513. Mailing Address: P.O. Box 896, Dubois, WY 82513-0896. Tel.: 307-455-2284.
E-mail: duboismuseum@gmail.com
Web Site: fremontcountymuseums.com/dubois
Formerly: Wind River Historical Center Dubois Museum
Key Personnel: Dir., Johanna Thompson.
Institution Type/Description: Local History & Natural History Museum and Interpretive Center.
Hours & Admission Prices: Mon.-Sat. 9-5. Adults $5, students and seniors $4; children no charge.
Attendance: 5,000 (actual)

NATIONAL BIGHORN SHEEP INTERPRETIVE CENTER, 10 Bighorn Ln., Dubois, WY 82513. Mailing Address: P.O. Box 1435, Dubois, WY 82513-1435. Tel.: 307-455-3429 or 888-209-2795. Facebook: National Bighorn Sheep Interpretive Center.
E-mail: info@bighorn.org
Web Site: www.bighorn.org
Key Personnel: Exec. Dir., Sara Domek; Education Mgr., Karen Sullivan; Devel. Mgr., Trudy Trevarthen.
Institution Type/Description: Nature Center.
Hours & Admission Prices: Memorial Day to Labor Day daily 9-6; Sept.-Dec. & April-May Mon.-Sat. 10-4; Dec. 26-March Tues.-Sat. 10-4. Adults $6, seniors & military $5, youth 8-17 $3; discounts to groups; children under 8 and members no charge.
Attendance: 10,000 (estimated)

Encampment

GRAND ENCAMPMENT MUSEUM, INC., 807 Barnett Ave., Encampment, WY 82325. Tel.: 307-327-5308. Facebook.
E-mail: gemdirector@gemuseum.com
Web Site: www.gemuseum.com
Key Personnel: Dir., Tim Nicklas.
Institution Type/Description: Regional Museum.
Hours & Admission Prices: Summer: Tues.-Sun. 9-5; Winter: Call for hours. No charge; donations accepted. &
Attendance: 6,000 (estimated)

Evanston

CHINESE JOSS HOUSE MUSEUM, Depot Square, 10th and Front Streets, Evanston, WY 82930-3464. Mailing Address: 1200 Main St., Evanston, WY 82930-3316. Tel.: 307-783-6320.
E-mail: museum@nglconnection.net
Web Site: www.uintacounty.com/index.asp?NID=195
Institution Type/Description: Chinese History Museum: housed in a replica of the 19th century Chinese temple that stood in Evanston's Chinatown.
Hours & Admission Prices: Mon.-Fri. 9-5, Sat. 10-4. No charge; donations accepted. &
Attendance: 1,500 (estimated)

UINTA COUNTY MUSEUM, 1020 Front St., Evanston, WY 82930-3437. Tel.: 307-789-8248.
E-mail: museum@nglconnection.net
Web Site: www.uintacounty.com
Key Personnel: Exec. Dir. & Cur., Kay Rossiter.
Institution Type/Description: History Museum.
Hours & Admission Prices: Mon.-Fri. 9-5, Sat. 10-4. No charge; donations accepted. &
Attendance: 8,000 (actual)

Evansville

RESHAW EXHIBIT, Evansville Community Center, 71 Curtis St., Evansville, WY 82636. Tel.: 307-234-6530.
Institution Type/Description: History Museum.
Hours & Admission Prices: Mon.-Fri. 11-1; other times by appointment. No charge. Closed holidays. &
Attendance: 225 (estimated)

Fort Bridger

FORT BRIDGER STATE MUSEUM, 37,000 Business Loop I-80, Fort Bridger, WY 82933. Mailing Address: P.O. Box 35, Fort Bridger, WY 82933-0035. Tel.: 307-782-3842.
Web Site: wyoparks.state.wy.us/index.php/about-fort-bridger
Key Personnel: Admin., Domenic Bravo.
Institution Type/Description: General Museum: housed in 1888-1890 enlisted men's barracks located at historic Fort Bridger.
Hours & Admission Prices: April & Oct. Fri.-Sun. 9-5; May-Sept. daily 9-5. &
Attendance: 97,000 (actual)

Fort Laramie

FORT LARAMIE NATIONAL HISTORIC SITE, 965 Gray Rocks Rd., Fort Laramie, WY 82212-7625. Tel.: 307-837-2221.
Web Site: www.nps.gov/fola
Institution Type/Description: Historic Site.
Hours & Admission Prices: Labor Day to Memorial Day daily 8-4:30; Summer daily 8-7. No charge. Closed New Year's Day; Thanksgiving; Christmas. &
Attendance: 50,820 (actual)

Frances E. Warren Air Force Base

WARREN ICBM & HERITAGE MUSEUM, 7405 Barnes Loop, 90th SW/MU, Bldg. 210, Frances E. Warren Air Force Base, WY 82005-2865. Mailing Address: 90 SW/MU, Francis E. Warren Air Force Base, WY 82005. Tel.: 307-773-2980.
E-mail: paula.taylor@warren.af.mil
Institution Type/Description: Military Museum: housed in c.1900 Military Post Headquarters Building located on the site of 1867 Fort D. A. Russell.
Hours & Admission Prices: Call for hours. &
Attendance: 31,000 (estimated)

Gillette

CAMPBELL COUNTY ROCKPILE MUSEUM, 900 W. 2nd St., Gillette, WY 82716-3405. Tel.: 307-682-5723. Fax: 307-686-8528.
E-mail: rockpile@vcn.com
Web Site: www.rockpilemuseum.com
Key Personnel: Dir., Robert Henning; Registrar, Angela Beenken; Museum Educator & Museum Shop Mgr., Penny Schroder; Collections Asst., Cara Reeves.
Institution Type/Description: History Museum.
Hours & Admission Prices: Mon.-Sat. 9-5. No charge; donations accepted. Closed holidays except Memorial Day, Independence Day & Labor Day. &
Attendance: 13,500 (actual)

FRONTIER AUTO MUSEUM LLC, 211 W. 2nd St., Gillette, WY 82716. Tel.: 307-686-5667.
E-mail: fbarnett@frontierauto.net
Web Site: www.frontierautomuseum.com
Key Personnel: Dir., Jeff Wandler; Museum Shop Mgr., Briana Brewer.
Institution Type/Description: Transportation Museum.
Hours & Admission Prices: Summer: Mon.-Sat. 10-5; Winter: Mon. & Thurs.-Sat. 10-5. Adults $5; discounts to groups; senior citizens over 80 and children 7 & under no charge.
Attendance: 5,000 (estimated)

Glendo

GLENDO HISTORICAL MUSEUM, Town Hall on Yellowstone Ave., Glendo, WY 82213. Tel.: 307-735-4242.
E-mail: townofglendo@yahoo.com
Institution Type/Description: History Museum.
Hours & Admission Prices: Call for hours. &

Glenrock

GLENROCK DEER CREEK MUSEUM, 935 W. Birch St., Glenrock, WY 82637. Mailing Address: P.O. Box 417, Glenrock, WY 82637-0417. Tel.: 307-436-2810.
Web Site: glenrock.org
Institution Type/Description: History Museum.
Hours & Admission Prices: Memorial Day to Labor Day Tues.-Sat. 10-4; other times by appointment. No charge; donations accepted. &
Attendance: 300 (estimated)

GLENROCK PALEONTOLOGICAL MUSEUM, 506 W. Birch St., Glenrock, WY 82637. Tel.: 307-436-2667.
E-mail: hello@dinosaurswyoming.com
Web Site: www.dinosaurswyoming.com
Key Personnel: Dir., Stuart I. McCrary; Cur., Sean Smith.
Institution Type/Description: Paleontology Museum.
Hours & Admission Prices: Thurs.-Sat. 11-4. Adults 13 & over $5; children 12 & under no charge.

Green River

SEEDSKADEE NATIONAL WILDLIFE REFUGE, Hwy. 372, Green River, WY 82935. Mailing Address: P.O. Box 700, Green River, WY 82935. Tel.: 307-875-2187. Fax: 307-875-4425.
E-mail: seedskadee@fws.gov
Web Site: www.fws.gov/refuge/Seedskadee
Key Personnel: Project Leader, Tom Koerner.
Institution Type/Description: Wildlife Refuge.
Hours & Admission Prices: Refuge: daily 30 minutes before sunrise to 30 minutes before sunset. Office & Visitors' Center: Mon.-Fri. 7:30-4:30. No charge. &
Attendance: 8,000 (estimated)

SWEETWATER COUNTY HISTORICAL MUSEUM, 3 E. Flaming Gorge Way, Green River, WY 82935-4239. Tel.: 307-872-6435. Fax: 307-872-3234.
E-mail: info@sweetwatermuseum.org
Web Site: sweetwatermuseum.org
Key Personnel: Dir., Brigida Blasi; Cur., Amanda Benson; Exhibits Coord., David Mead.
Institution Type/Description: History Museum.
Hours & Admission Prices: Mon.-Sat. 10-6. No charge; donations accepted. Closed holidays. &
Attendance: 5,034 (actual)

Greybull

GREYBULL MUSEUM, 325 Greybull Ave., Greybull, WY 82426-2049. Mailing Address: Box 348, Greybull, WY 82426-0348. Tel.: 307-765-2444. Facebook.
Web Site: www.greybull.com
Institution Type/Description: General Museum.
Hours & Admission Prices: Call for hours. &
Attendance: 7,000 (actual)

GREYBULL MUSEUM OF FLIGHT AND AERIAL FIREFIGHTING, 2534 Hiller Ln., Greybull, WY 82426. Tel.: 307-272-1247.
E-mail: museumofflight15@gmail.com
Web Site: museumofflight.us
Key Personnel: Dir., Bob Hawkins.
Institution Type/Description: Aviation Museum.
Hours & Admission Prices: mid-May to Sept. Mon.-Fri. 9-5, Sat. 10-5. No charge; donations accepted.
Attendance: 7,000 (estimated)

Guernsey

LAKE GUERNSEY MUSEUM-GUERNSEY STATE PARK, Interstate 25, exit 92 to U.S. 26 to State Rte. 270, Guernsey, WY 82214. Mailing Address: P.O. Box 429, Guernsey, WY 82214-0429. Tel.: 307-836-2334 (office) & 2900 (museum). Fax: 307-836-3088.
E-mail: state.parks.parks@wyo.gov
Web Site: wyoparks.state.wy.us/index.php/activities-amenities-guernsey/museum-guernsey
Key Personnel: Parks Supt., Todd Stevenson.
Institution Type/Description: Historical Museum: housed in 1930s building constructed by the CCC.
Hours & Admission Prices: May-Sept. daily 9-5. &
Attendance: 5,000 (estimated)

Hanna

HANNA BASIN MUSEUM, 502 Front Street, Hanna, WY 82327. Tel.: 307-325-6465.
E-mail: hannabasinmuseum@gmail.com
Web Site: www.hannabasinmuseum.com
Key Personnel: Dir., Sarah Jones.
Institution Type/Description: History Museum.
Hours & Admission Prices: Memorial Day to Labor Day: Fri.-Sun. 1-5; Winter: Fri. 1-5; other times by appointment. No charge; donations accepted.

Jackson

JACKSON HOLE CHILDREN'S MUSEUM, 174 N. King St., Jackson, WY 83001. Mailing Address: P.O. Box 995, Jackson, WY 83001. Tel.: 307-733-3996.
E-mail: info@jhchildrensmuseum.org
Web Site: www.jhchildrensmuseum.org
Key Personnel: Founder & C.F.O., Craig Morris; Founder & Dir., K.J. Morris; Exec. Dir., Jean Lewis; Dir. Opers., Sara Fagan; Education Dir. & Lead Teacher, Hatilie Anderson Lemke.
Institution Type/Description: Children's Museum.
Hours & Admission Prices: Summer: Mon.-Fri. 10-3. Admission $8; children under 2 & Blue Star families no charge.

JACKSON HOLE HISTORICAL SOCIETY AND MUSEUM, 225 N. Cache St., Jackson, WY 83001. Mailing Address: P.O. Box 1005, Jackson, WY 83001-1005. Tel.: 307-733-2414.
E-mail: info@jacksonholehistory.org
Web Site: www.jacksonholehistory.org
Key Personnel: Exec. Dir., Morgan Albertson Jaouen; Dir. Devel., Becky Kimmel; Research & Collections Coord., Nora DeWitt-Hoeger; Opers. & Mktg. Coord., Quinn Feller; Education & Progs. Coord., Frances Ritchie.
Institution Type/Description: History Museum & Research Center.
Hours & Admission Prices: Tues.-Sat. 10-5. Walking Tours: call for information. Adults $6, seniors & students $4; children 6 & under & members no charge. &
Attendance: 16,000 (actual)

NATIONAL MUSEUM OF WILDLIFE ART, 2820 Rungius Rd., Jackson, WY 83001. Mailing Address: P.O. Box 6825, Jackson, WY 83002-6825. Tel.: 307-733-5771.
Web Site: www.wildlifeart.org

Formerly: Wildlife of the American West
Key Personnel: Museum Dir., Steve Seamons; CFO, Lisa Holmes; Sugden Chief Cur. Education, Jane Lavino; Joffa Kerr Chief Cur. Art, Adam Duncan Harris, Ph.D.; Dir. Opers., Mike Hofhiens; Dir. Progs. & Events, Amy Colcoechea; Mgr. Retail Opers., Debra Ross Vassar.
Institution Type/Description: Art Museum.
Hours & Admission Prices: May-Oct. daily 9-5; Nov.-April Tues.-Sat. 9-5, Sun. 11-5. Adults $14, seniors $12, 1st child 5-18 $6, additional children $2; discounts to military; children under 5, members, AAM & Museums West no charge. &
Attendance: 75,000 (estimated)

Kaycee

HOOFPRINTS OF THE PAST MUSEUM, 344 Nolan Ave., Kaycee, WY 82639. Mailing Address: P.O. Box 114, Kaycee, WY 82639-0042. Tel.: 307-738-2381.
E-mail: hoofprintsofthepast@outlook.com
Web Site: www.hoofprintsofthepast.org
Key Personnel: Dir., Keri Malson; Cur., Laurel Foster.
Institution Type/Description: History Museum.
Hours & Admission Prices: May 15 -Oct. Mon.-Sat. 10-5, Sun. 1-5. No charge; donations accepted. &
Attendance: 3,500 (actual)

Kelly

THE MURIE MUSEUM, 1 Ditch Creek Rd., Kelly, WY 83011. Tel.: 307-733-1313.
E-mail: info@tetonscience.org
Web Site: www.tetonscience.org
Key Personnel: C.E.O., John Shea.
Institution Type/Description: Natural History Museum.
Hours & Admission Prices: Call for hours. No charge; donations accepted.
Attendance: 2,500 (estimated)

Kemmerer

FOSSIL BUTTE NATIONAL MONUMENT VISITOR CENTER, 864 Chicken Creek Rd., Kemmerer, WY 83101. Mailing Address: P.O. Box 592, Kemmerer, WY 83101. Tel.: 307-877-4455. Fax: 307-877-4457.
Web Site: www.nps.gov/fobu
Key Personnel: Supt., Angela Wetz.
Institution Type/Description: Paleontology Museum.
Hours & Admission Prices: See website for seasonal hours. No charge; donations accepted. &
Attendance: 16,000 (actual)

FOSSIL COUNTRY MUSEUM, 400 Pine, Kemmerer, WY 83101. Tel.: 307-877-6551. Facebook.
Web Site: www.hamsfork.net/~museum/
Institution Type/Description: History Museum.
Hours & Admission Prices: Call for hours. &
Attendance: 3,000 (actual)

J.C. PENNEY HOMESTEAD & HISTORICAL FOUNDATION, 109 J.C. Penney Dr., Kemmerer, WY 83101-2941. Tel.: 307-877-3164.
E-mail: swchm@sweetwater.net
Institution Type/Description: History Museum: housed in the Penney's first home & the site of the first J.C. Penney store which is still in operation today. Cottage is a National Historic Landmark.
Hours & Admission Prices: Memorial Day to Labor Day Mon.-Sat. 9-6, Sun. 1-6. No charge; donations accepted.

ULRICH'S FOSSIL GALLERY, 4400 Fossil Butte County Rd., Kemmerer, WY 83101. Tel.: 307-877-6466.
E-mail: ulrichsfossilgallery@gmail.com
Web Site: www.ulrichsfossilgallery.com
Institution Type/Description: Eocene Fossil Gallery.
Hours & Admission Prices: Summer: daily 8:30-5; Winter: Mon.-Fri. 9-4. No charge. Fossil Digs: by appointment. &
Attendance: 400 (estimated)

Lander

EVANS/DAHL MEMORIAL MUSEUM, 545 Main St., Lander, WY 82520-3075. Tel.: 307-332-8190.
Institution Type/Description: History Museum.
Hours & Admission Prices: Call for hours.

FREMONT COUNTY PIONEER MUSEUM, 1443 Main St., Lander, WY 82520-2649. Tel.: 307-332-3339. Facebook: Pioneer Museum Lander County.
E-mail: a.teamfcpm@gmail.com
Web Site: www.fremontcountymuseums.com
Key Personnel: Site Mgr., Randall Wise; Colls. Mgr., Robin Allison.
Institution Type/Description: History Museum.
Hours & Admission Prices: Mon.-Sat. 9-5. Adults $5, seniors & students $4; children no charge. &
Attendance: 10,000 (estimated)

LANDER ART CENTER, 224 Main St., Lander, WY 82520. Tel.: 307-332-5772.
E-mail: frontdesk@landerartcenter.com
Web Site: www.landerartcenter.com
Key Personnel: Exec. Dir., Stacy Stebner; Gallery Dir., Maggie Godwin-Bell; Education Coord., Samantha Gale.
Institution Type/Description: Art Gallery.
Hours & Admission Prices: Tues.-Thurs. 10-6, Fri.-Sat. 10-4. &
Attendance: 4,000 (estimated)

LANDER CHILDREN'S MUSEUM, 465 Lincoln Ave., Lander, WY 82520-2831. Tel.: 307-332-1341.
Web Site: www.landerchildrensmuseum.org
Key Personnel: Exec. Dir., Brian Reisig.
Institution Type/Description: Children's Museum.
Hours & Admission Prices: Tues.-Fri. 10-5, Sat. 1-4. Adults $3; children under 2 no charge.
Attendance: 3,500 (actual)

MUSEUM OF THE AMERICAN WEST, 1445 W. Main St., Lander, WY 82520. Tel.: 307-335-8778.
E-mail: amwest@wyoming.com
Web Site: museumoftheamericanwest.com
Institution Type/Description: History Museum.
Hours & Admission Prices: Village: Mon.-Fri. 9-4. Office: Mon.-Sat. 9-4. No charge; donations accepted.

Laramie

LARAMIE PLAINS MUSEUM, 603 E. Ivinson Ave., Laramie, WY 82070-3243. Tel.: 307-742-4448.
E-mail: lpmdirector@laramiemuseum.org
Web Site: www.laramiemuseum.org
Key Personnel: C.E.O., Dir., Mary Mountain; Cur., Konnie Cronk; Colls. Mgr. & Specialty Grants, Judy Knight.
Institution Type/Description: Historical House Museum: housed in 1892 Victorian Mansion built by early pioneer banker, Edward Ivinson.
Hours & Admission Prices: Tues.-Sat. 9-5, Sun. 1-4. Families $25, adults $10, senior citizens $7, students $5; discounts to military & AAA members; children under 6 no charge. Closed major holidays. &
Attendance: 28,000 (estimated)

ROCKY MOUNTAIN HERBARIUM, Aven Nelson Bldg., Rm. 114, UW Campus, Laramie, WY 82071-3165. Mailing Address: University of Wyoming-Department of Botany, Dept. 3165, 1000 E. University Ave., Laramie, WY 82071-2000. Tel.: 307-766-4158. Fax: 307-766-2851.
E-mail: thanse23@uwyo.edu
Web Site: www.uwyo.edu/botany/rocky-mountain-herbarium/
Key Personnel: Cur., Burrell E. Nelson.
Institution Type/Description: Herbarium.
Hours & Admission Prices: Academic Year: Mon.-Fri. 7:30-4:30. No charge; donations accepted. &
Attendance: 200 (estimated)

UNIVERSITY OF WYOMING, AMERICAN HERITAGE CENTER, 2111 Willett Dr., Centennial Complex, Laramie, WY 82071. Mailing Address: 1000 E. University Ave., Dept. 3924, Laramie, WY 82071-2000. Tel.: 307-766-4114. Fax: 307-766-5511.
E-mail: ahc@uwyo.edu
Web Site: ahc.uwyo.edu
Key Personnel: Interim Dir. & Dean, UW Libraries, Ivan Gaetz.
Institution Type/Description: History Museum.
Hours & Admission Prices: Mon. 8 am-9 pm, Tues.-Fri. 8-5.

UNIVERSITY OF WYOMING ANTHROPOLOGY MUSEUM,
12th & Lewis, Laramie, WY 82071. Mailing Address: 1000 E.
University Ave., Dept. 3431 - Anthropology, Laramie, WY 82071-
2000. Tel.: 307-766-5136.
E-mail: anthropology@uwyo.edu
Web Site: www.uwyo.edu/anthropology/museum.html
Key Personnel: Dir., Dr. Mary Lou Larson.
Institution Type/Description: Anthropology Museum.
Hours & Admission Prices: mid-May to Aug. Mon.-Fri. 7:30-4:30; Sept. to mid-
May Mon.-Fri. 8-5. No charge. Closed school vacations & holidays. &
Attendance: 10,000 (estimated)

UNIVERSITY OF WYOMING ART MUSEUM, 2111 Willett Dr.,
Laramie, WY 82071. Mailing Address: 1000 E. University Ave.,
Dept. 3807, Laramie, WY 82071-2000. Tel.: 307-766-6622.
E-mail: uwartmus@uwyo.edu
Web Site: www.uwyo.edu/artmuseum
Key Personnel: Dir., Marianne E. Wardle; Chief Cur., Nicole Crawford; Cur.
Education & Statewide Engagement, Katie Christensen; Chief Preparator,
Sterling Smith.
Institution Type/Description: Art Museum.
Hours & Admission Prices: Feb.-April & Sept.- Nov. Mon. 10-7, Tues.-Sat. 10-5;
Jan, May-Aug. & Dec. Mon.-Sat. 10-5. No charge; donations accepted. &
Attendance: 118,755 (actual)

UNIVERSITY OF WYOMING GEOLOGICAL MUSEUM,
Department of Geology and Geophysics, 1000 E. University Ave.,
Laramie, WY 82071-2000. Tel.: 307-766-2646.
E-mail: geolmus@uwyo.edu
Web Site: www.uwyo.edu/geomuseum
Institution Type/Description: Geology Museum.
Hours & Admission Prices: Mon.-Sat. 10-4. No charge, donations accepted. Closed
university holidays. &
Attendance: 17,000 (estimated)

UNIVERSITY OF WYOMING INSECT MUSEUM, Dept. of
Renewable Resources, 100 E. University, Laramie, WY 82071-
3354. Mailing Address: Department of Renewable Resources, P.O.
Box 3354, Laramie, WY 82071-3354. Tel.: 307-766-5338.
Web Site: www.uwho.edu
Key Personnel: Cur., Scott Shaw.
Institution Type/Description: Insect Museum.
Hours & Admission Prices: By appointment. No charge.

WYOMING TERRITORIAL PRISON STATE HISTORIC SITE,
975 Snowy Range Rd., Laramie, WY 82070-6719. Tel.: 307-745-
3733.
Web Site: wyoparks.state.wy.us/index.php/places-to-go/wyoming-territorial-prison
Formerly: Wyoming Territorial Park
Key Personnel: Contact, Deborah Amend.
Institution Type/Description: Historic Site: 1872-1903 Wyoming Territorial Prison;
only prison in North America to hold Butch Cassidy.
Hours & Admission Prices: May-Sept. daily 8-7; April & Oct. 8-5. Adults $5, stu-
dents 12-17 $2.50; children 11 & under no charge. &
Attendance: 47,000 (actual)

Lingle

WESTERN HISTORY CENTER, 2308 U.S. Hwy. 26, Lingle, WY
82223-8527. Tel.: 307-837-3052. Facebook.
E-mail: ggzzk@embarqmail.com
Institution Type/Description: History Museum.
Hours & Admission Prices: Call for hours. &
Attendance: 10,000 (estimated)

Lovell

BIGHORN CANYON NRA VISITOR CENTER, 20 Hwy. 14A E.,
Lovell, WY 82431. Mailing Address: Bighorn Canyon National
Recreation Area Headquarters Office, P.O. Box 7458, Fort Smith,
MT 59035. Tel.: 406-666-2412. Fax: 406-666-2415. Facebook:
Bighorn Canyon NRA.
Web Site: www.nps.gov/bica
Key Personnel: Supt., John Bundy.
Institution Type/Description: Visitor Center.
Hours & Admission Prices: See website for hours & admissions. &
Attendance: 185,000 (estimated)

Lusk

NIOBRARA HISTORICAL SOCIETY, 322 S. Main, Lusk, WY
82225. Mailing Address: P.O. Box 367, Lusk, WY 82225-0367.
Tel.: 307-334-3444.
E-mail: stagecoachmuseumlusk@gmail.com
Web Site: niobraracountylibrary.org/museum
Formerly: Cheyenne-Black Hills Stagecoach
Institution Type/Description: History Museum: stagecoach used on the Cheyenne-
Black Hills Stage and Express Line; built in 1860s by Abbott & Downing at
Concord, NH.
Hours & Admission Prices: May-Oct. Mon.-Fri. 10-4:30, Sat.-Sun by appointment.
Adults $2; members no charge. &

Lyman

BRIDGER VALLEY HERITAGE MUSEUM, 100 E. Sage-Lyman
Town Hall 2 Fl., Lyman, WY 82937. Tel.: 307-787-3525.
Facebook.
Formerly: Trona Mining Museum of Bridger Valley
Institution Type/Description: History Museum.
Hours & Admission Prices: Summer: Mon.-Fri. 10-4. &
Attendance: 800 (actual)

Medicine Bow

MEDICINE BOW MUSEUM, 405 Lincoln Hwy., Medicine Bow,
WY 82329. Tel.: 307-379-2383.
E-mail: medbowmuseum@outlook.com
Web Site: medbowmuseum.com
Institution Type/Description: History Museum: housed in the former old railroad
depot, built in 1913. Listed on the National Register of Historical Places.
Hours & Admission Prices: Memorial Day to Labor Day Mon.-Fri. 10-5, Sat.-Sun.
9-3.

Meeteetse

MEETEETSE BANK MUSEUM, 1033 Park Ave., Meeteetse, WY
82433. Mailing Address: P.O. Box 248, Meeteetse, WY 82433.
Tel.: 307-868-2423.
E-mail: info@meeteetsemuseums.org
Web Site: www.meeteetsemuseums.org
Key Personnel: Dir., David Cunningham.
Institution Type/Description: Historic Building Museum: housed in a former bank
building; built in 1900. Listed on the National Register of Historic Places.
Hours & Admission Prices: Feb.-April & Oct.-Dec. Tues.-Sat. 10-4; May-Sept.
Tues.-Sat, 10-5.
Attendance: 2,270 (actual)

MEETEETSE MUSEUMS, 1947 State St., Meeteetse, WY 82433.
Mailing Address: P.O. Box 248, Meeteetse, WY 82433. Tel.: 307-
868-2423.
E-mail: info@meeteetsemuseums.org
Web Site: www.meeteetsemuseums.org
Formerly: Meeteetse Museum Inc. & Charles J. Belden Museum of Western
Photography
Key Personnel: Dir., David Cunningham.
Institution Type/Description: History Museum.
Hours & Admission Prices: Feb.-April & Oct.-Dec. Tues.-Sat. 10-4; May-Sept.
Tues.-Sat. 10-5, Sun. 12-4. Closed Thanksgiving. &
Attendance: 7,000 (actual)

Midwest

SALT CREEK MUSEUM, 531 Peake St., Midwest, WY 82643.
Mailing Address: P.O. Box 190, Midwest, WY 82643-0190. Tel.:
307-437-6513. Facebook.
Web Site: www.midwest.govoffice.com
Key Personnel: Cur., Sandra Schutte.
Institution Type/Description: History Museum.
Hours & Admission Prices: By appointment. No charge; donations accepted. &
Attendance: 500 (estimated)

Moorcroft

WEST TEXAS TRAIL MUSEUM, 100 E. Weston St., Moorcroft,
WY 82721. Mailing Address: P.O. Box 497, Moorcroft, WY
82721. Tel.: 307-756-9300. Facebook: West Texas Trail Museum.
E-mail: wttmdirector@rtconnect.net
Web Site: www.westtexastrailmuseum.com

Key Personnel: Dir., Cynthia Clonch.
Institution Type/Description: History Museum.
Hours & Admission Prices: Mon.-Fri. 9-5. No charge; donations accepted. &
Attendance: 2,700 (actual)

Pine Bluffs

HIGH PLAINS ARCHAEOLOGY MUSEUM, 211 Elm St., Pine Bluffs, WY 82082. Tel.: 307-245-9372.
Institution Type/Description: History Museum.
Hours & Admission Prices: Call for hours.

TEXAS TRAIL MUSEUM, 201 W. 3rd St., Pine Bluffs, WY 82082. Mailing Address: P.O. Box 545, Pine Bluffs, WY 82082-0545. Tel.: 307-245-3713. Facebook.
E-mail: texastrailmuseum@aol.com
Institution Type/Description: History Museum.
Hours & Admission Prices: Call for hours. &
Attendance: 600 (actual)

Pinedale

MUSEUM OF THE MOUNTAIN MAN, 700 E. Hennick, Pinedale, WY 82941. Mailing Address: P.O. Box 909, Pinedale, WY 82941-0909. Tel.: 307-367-4101 or 1-877-686-6266.
E-mail: director@mmmuseum.com
Web Site: www.museumofthemountainman.com
Key Personnel: Exec. Dir., Clint Gilchrist; Asst. Dir., Laurie Hartwig.
Institution Type/Description: History Museum.
Hours & Admission Prices: May-Oct. daily 9-5; Nov.-April by appointment. Adults $10, seniors $8; children 12 & under no charge. &
Attendance: 12,000 (estimated)

Powell

HOMESTEADER MUSEUM, 324 E. 1st St., Powell, WY 82435. Mailing Address: P.O. Box 54, Powell, WY 82435-0054. Tel.: 307-754-9481.
E-mail: homesteader@bresnan.net
Web Site: www.homesteadermuseum.com
Key Personnel: Dir., Rowene Weems; Registrar Collections, Brandi Wright.
Institution Type/Description: History Museum.
Hours & Admission Prices: April to Memorial Day Tues.-Fri. 10-4; June-Sept. Tues.-Fri. 10-5, Sat. 10-2; Oct.-Dec. Tues.-Fri. 10-5. No charge; donations accepted. &
Attendance: 5,000 (estimated)

Ranchester

T-REX NATURAL HISTORY MUSEUM, 1116 Big Horn Dr., Ranchester, WY 82839. Tel.: 307-655-3359. Facebook.
E-mail: info@sheridanwyoming.org
Institution Type/Description: History Museum.
Hours & Admission Prices: Call for hours.

Rawlins

CARBON COUNTY MUSEUM, 904 W. Walnut St., Rawlins, WY 82301-6556. Tel.: 307-328-2740. Facebook: Carbon County Museum.
E-mail: info@carboncountymuseum.org
Web Site: www.carboncountymuseum.org
Key Personnel: Dir., Dr. Steven Dinero.
Institution Type/Description: History Museum.
Hours & Admission Prices: Tues.-Sat. 10-6. &
Attendance: 3,785 (actual)

WYOMING FRONTIER PRISON MUSEUM, 500 W. Walnut St., Rawlins, WY 82301-4768. Tel.: 307-324-4422. Facebook: Wyoming Frontier Prison Museum.
E-mail: wyomingfrontierprison@gmail.com
Web Site: wyomingfrontierprison.org
Institution Type/Description: Prison Museum: housed in the Wyoming Frontier Prison which operated from 1901 to 1981. Site for the filming of the 1987 movie, Prison.
Hours & Admission Prices: Museum: daily 8-5. Guided Tours: daily 8:30-4:30. Guided Tours: adults $10, seniors 60 & over and children 6-12 $8. Museum: no charge.
Attendance: 15,000

Riverton

RIVERTON MUSEUM, 700 E. Park Ave., Riverton, WY 82501-3657. Tel.: 307-856-2665. Facebook.
E-mail: rivertonwymuseum@gmail.com
Web Site: www.fremontcountymuseums.com
Key Personnel: Central Dir., Scott Goetz.
Institution Type/Description: Local History Museum.
Hours & Admission Prices: Mon.-Sat. 9-5. Adults $5, seniors & students $4; children no charge. &
Attendance: 1,707 (estimated)

ROBERT A. PECK ART CENTER, 2660 Peck Ave., Riverton, WY 82501-2215. Tel.: 307-855-2000, 800-735-8418.
E-mail: gallery@cwc.edu
Web Site: www.cwc.edu/artscenter
Institution Type/Description: Art Center.
Hours & Admission Prices: Mon.-Thurs. 7am-10pm, Fri. 7-5.
Attendance: 5,000 (estimated)

WIND RIVER HERITAGE CENTER, 1075 S. Federal Blvd., Riverton, WY 82501-4407. Mailing Address: P.O. Box 206, Riverton, WY 82501-0039. Tel.: 307-856-0706.
E-mail: windriverheritagecenter@gmail.com
Web Site: windriverheritagecenter.com
Institution Type/Description: Heritage Center.
Hours & Admission Prices: Summer: Mon.-Sat. 10-2. No charge; donations accepted. &
Attendance: 10,000 (estimated)

Rock Springs

COMMUNITY FINE ARTS CENTER, 400 C St., Rock Springs, WY 82901-6225. Tel.: 307-362-6212. Fax: 307-352-6657.
E-mail: cfac@sweetwaterlibraries.com
Web Site: www.cfac4art.com
Key Personnel: Dir., Debora Thaxton Soule.
Institution Type/Description: Arts Center.
Hours & Admission Prices: Mon.-Thurs. 10-6, Fri.-Sat. 12-5. No charge; donations accepted. &
Attendance: 9,978 (actual)

ROCK SPRINGS HISTORICAL MUSEUM, 201 "B" St., Rock Springs, WY 82901-6250. Tel.: 307-362-3138.
E-mail: jennifer_messer@rswy.net
Web Site: www.rswy.net/department/index.php?structureid=15
Key Personnel: Museum Coord., Jennifer Messer; Museum Tech, Janice Brown.
Institution Type/Description: History Museum: 1894 Rock Springs City Hall, listed on the National Register of Historic Places, houses 1894 Rock Springs fire station & jail, stable & jail additions. A two-story sandstone structure, the building features two turreted bays, council chambers & mayor's balcony.
Hours & Admission Prices: Mon.-Sat. 10-5. No charge; donations accepted. Closed Independence Day; major holidays. &
Attendance: 11,000 (actual)

WEIDNER WILDLIFE MUSEUM, Western Wyoming Community College, 2500 College Dr., Rock Springs, WY 82901-5802. Tel.: 301-382-1600.
Web Site: www.westernwyoming.edu
Institution Type/Description: Wildlife Museum.
Hours & Admission Prices: Mon. & Wed. 10-1, Tues. & Thurs. 1-4. No charge; donations accepted. Closed WWCC holidays.

WESTERN WYOMING COMMUNITY COLLEGE ART GALLERY, 2500 College Dr., Rock Springs, WY 82901-5802. Mailing Address: P.O. Box 428, Rock Springs, WY 82902-0428. Tel.: 307-382-1723.
E-mail: fmcewin@wwcc.wt.edu
Web Site: www.wwcc.wy.edu
Key Personnel: Dir., Florence Alfano McEwin, Ph.D.
Institution Type/Description: Art Gallery.
Hours & Admission Prices: Call for hours. No charge. &
Attendance: 2,000 (estimated)

Saratoga

SARATOGA MUSEUM, 104 E Constitution Ave., Saratoga, WY 82331. Mailing Address: P.O. Box 1131, Saratoga, WY 82331-

1131. Tel.: 307-326-5511. Facebook: Saratoga Historical & Cultural Association.
E-mail: saratogamuseum@gmail.com
Web Site: www.saratoga-museum.com
Key Personnel: Dir., Mikayla Larrow.
Institution Type/Description: Historical Society Museum: housed in c.1890 Union Pacific Depot.
Hours & Admission Prices: Memorial Day to Sept. Wed.-Sat. 10-4, Sun. 12-4. Adults $5, youth 13-17 $3; children 12 & under no charge. &
Attendance: 1,800 (estimated)

Savery

LITTLE SNAKE RIVER MUSEUM, 13 CR 561 N., Savery, WY 82332. Mailing Address: P.O. Box 13, Savery, WY 82332-0013. Tel.: 307-383-7262.
E-mail: lsrmuseum@dteworld.com
Web Site: www.littlesnakerivermuseum.com
Key Personnel: Dir., Lela Emmons; Pres. (V), Joe Jussila; Asst. Dir. & Museum Shop Mgr., Beth Shorma.
Institution Type/Description: History Museum.
Hours & Admission Prices: Memorial Day to Oct. daily 10-5. No charge; donations accepted. &

Sheridan

CUSTOM GROUP PROPERTIES LLC DBA HISTORIC SHERIDAN INN, 856 Broadway St., Sheridan, WY 82801-3623. Mailing Address: 901 S. 9th St., Broken Arrow, OK 74012. Tel.: 307-655-7462. Facebook: Historic Sheridan Inn.
E-mail: info@sheridaninn.com
Web Site: www.sheridaninn.com
Formerly: Historic Sheridan Inn
Institution Type/Description: Historic Building: Sheridan Inn built c.1892.
Hours & Admission Prices: Daily 10-8. Tours: daily 11-3. No Charge &

KING SADDLERY MUSEUM, 184 N. Main, Sheridan, WY 82801-3906. Tel.: 307-672-2702, 800-443-8919. Fax: 307-672-5235.
E-mail: kingropes@fiberpipe.net
Web Site: www.kingssaddlery.com/museum.htm
Key Personnel: Cur., Jean King.
Institution Type/Description: Western History Museum.
Hours & Admission Prices: Mon.-Sat. 8-5. No charge; donations accepted.

SHERIDAN COUNTY HISTORICAL SOCIETY & MUSEUM, 850 Sibley Cir., Sheridan, WY 82801-9626. Tel.: 307-675-1150.
E-mail: info@sheridanmuseum.org
Web Site: www.sheridanmuseum.org
Formerly: Sheridan County Museum
Key Personnel: Dir., John P. Woodward; Educator, Erin Schock; Colls. Asst., Peg Cullen; Mercantile Mgr., Ariel Downing.
Institution Type/Description: History Museum.
Hours & Admission Prices: Thurs.-Mon. 9-5. Adults $6, seniors 60 & over $5, students & youth $3; children 12 & under no charge. &
Attendance: 4,500 (actual)

TRAIL END STATE HISTORIC SITE, 400 Clarendon Ave., Sheridan, WY 82801-4053. Tel.: 307-674-4589.
E-mail: teguilds@gmail.com
Web Site: www.trailend.org
Institution Type/Description: Historic House.
Hours & Admission Prices: April-May & Sept.-Dec. 14 daily 1-4; June-Aug. daily 9-6. Nonresident adults $4, resident adults $2; children 17 & under no charge. &
Attendance: 14,000 (actual)

Sinclair

PARCO SINCLAIR MUSEUM, 300 E. Lincoln Ave., Sinclair, WY 82334. Mailing Address: P.O. Box 247, Sinclair, WY 82334-0247. Tel.: 307-324-3058.
E-mail: sinclr@tribcsp.com
Web Site: www.sinclairwyoming.com/museum.aspx
Institution Type/Description: History Museum: housed in the former First National Bank; built in 1924.
Hours & Admission Prices: Call for hours. No charge.

South Pass City

SOUTH PASS CITY STATE HISTORIC SITE, 125 South Pass Main, South Pass City, WY 82520-8703. Tel.: 307-332-3684.
E-mail: info@southpasscity.com
Web Site: www.southpasscity.com
Institution Type/Description: Historic Building & Site: c.1867-1910 gold-mining town consisting of 25 furnished buildings.
Hours & Admission Prices: mid-May to Sept. daily 9-6. Adults: nonresident $4, resident $2; children under 18 no charge. &
Attendance: 20,000 (actual)

Sundance

CROOK COUNTY MUSEUM & ART GALLERY, 309 Cleveland St., Sundance, WY 82729. Mailing Address: P.O. Box 63, Sundance, WY 82729-0063. Tel.: 307-283-3666. Facebook.
E-mail: ccmuseum@rangeweb.net
Key Personnel: Chm., Rocky Courchaine.
Institution Type/Description: History Museum.
Hours & Admission Prices: See website for hours. &
Attendance: 7,000 (estimated)

Ten Sleep

TEN SLEEP PIONEER MUSEUM, 500 Second St., Ten Sleep, WY 82442. Mailing Address: P.O. Box 93, Ten Sleep, WY 82442-0093. Tel.: 307-366-2759.
E-mail: tsmuseum@tctwest.net
Institution Type/Description: History Museum.
Hours & Admission Prices: Call for hours. No charge; donations accepted.

Thermopolis

HOT SPRINGS COUNTY MUSEUM AND CULTURAL CENTER, 700 Broadway, Thermopolis, WY 82443-2722. Tel.: 307-864-5183. Fax: 307-864-2974.
E-mail: hschistory@rtconnect.net
Web Site: hschistory.org
Key Personnel: Dir., Pete Coggi; Cur., Mike Cavin; Cur. & Gift Shop Mgr., Racine Morgan; Cur., Simian Osteology, Barbara Roach.
Institution Type/Description: History Museum.
Hours & Admission Prices: May-Sept. Mon.-Sat. 8-5; Oct.-April Tues.-Sat. 9-4. Adults $5, senior citizens & children 6-17 $3; discounts to locals; active duty & families, veterans & children 5 & under no charge. &
Attendance: 4,630 (actual)

THE WYOMING DINOSAUR CENTER, 110 Carter Ranch Rd., Thermopolis, WY 82443-2457. Mailing Address: P.O. Box 868, Thermopolis, WY 82443-0868. Tel.: 307-864-2997, 800-455-3466. Fax: 307-864-5762.
E-mail: wdinoc@wyodino.org
Web Site: www.wyodino.org
Key Personnel: Gen. Mgr., Angie Guyon.
Institution Type/Description: Paleontology (Science) Museum.
Hours & Admission Prices: mid-May to mid-Sept. daily 8-6; mid-Sept. to mid-May daily 10-5. Adults $10, senior citizens 60 and over, children 4-12 & veterans $8; discounts to groups; children 3 & under no charge. Closed New Year's Day; Thanksgiving; Christmas. &
Attendance: 32,000 (estimated)

Torrington

HOMESTEADERS MUSEUM, 495 Main St., Torrington, WY 82240. Mailing Address: P.O. Box 250, Torrington, WY 82240-0250. Tel.: 307-532-5612. Fax: 307-532-3731. Facebook: Homesteaders Museum.
E-mail: schaires@torringtonwy.gov
Web Site: torringtonwy.gov/departments/museum
Key Personnel: Dir., Sarah Chaires.
Institution Type/Description: Local History Museum: housed in a historic 1926 Union Pacific depot.
Hours & Admission Prices: Mon.-Fri. 9:30-4. No charge; donations accepted.
Attendance: 2,800 (actual)

Upton

UPTON RED ONION MUSEUM, 729 Birch St., Upton, WY 82730. Tel.: 307-468-2672.

E-mail: urom@rtconnect.net
Web Site: www.uptonwy.com/upton-chamber/town-of-upton/attractions/?item=904
Institution Type/Description: History Museum.
Hours & Admission Prices: Mon.-Fri. 9-5. No charge.

Wheatland

LARAMIE PEAK MUSEUM, 1601 16th St., Wheatland, WY 82201. Tel.: 307-331-3765. Facebook.
Institution Type/Description: History Museum.
Hours & Admission Prices: Mid-May to Mid.-Sept. Mon.-Fri. 10-5, Sat. 10-3. No charge; donations accepted. Closed holidays.
Attendance: 641 (actual)

WYOMING TRAILS GALLERY, 1004 16th St., Wheatland, WY 82201-2530. Tel.: 307-322-3300.
E-mail: barbara@wyomingtrailsgallery.com
Web Site: www.wyomingtrailsgallery.com
Institution Type/Description: Art Gallery.
Hours & Admission Prices: Call for hours.

Worland

WASHAKIE MUSEUM, 2200 Big Horn Ave., Worland, WY 82401-2932. Tel.: 307-347-4102.
E-mail: creichelt@washakiemuseum.org
Web Site: www.washakiemuseum.org
Key Personnel: Exec. Dir., Cheryl Reichelt; Cur., Rebecca Brower; Asst. Cur., Temporary & Traveling Exhibits, Victoria Frisbee; Museum Educator, Becca Ward.
Institution Type/Description: General Museum.
Hours & Admission Prices: May 15 to Sept. 15 Mon.-Fri. 9-5:30, Sat. 9-5, Sun. 1-4; Sept. 16 to May 14 Tues.-Sat. 9-4. Families $25, adults $8, seniors 62 & over $7, children 7-12 $6; discount to AAA members; children 6 & under no charge. &
Attendance: 14,088 (actual)

Wright

WRIGHT CENTENNIAL MUSEUM, 104 Ranch Court, Wright, WY 82732. Tel.: 307-464-1222.
E-mail: WrightMuseum@vcn.com
Web Site: www.wrightcentennialmuseum.org/
Key Personnel: Dir., Nolene Wright.
Institution Type/Description: History Museum.
Hours & Admission Prices: Mid-May to early Oct. 15 Mon.-Fri. 10-5, Sat. 10-2. No charge; donations accepted. &
Attendance: 700 (estimated)

(U.S. TERRITORIES)
AMERICAN SAMOA

(1 listings)

Pago Pago

JEAN P. HAYDON MUSEUM, Fagatogo, Pago Pago, AS 96799. Mailing Address: Fagatogo, P.O. Box 1540, Pago Pago, AS 96799-1540. Tel.: 684-633-4347. Fax: 684-633-2059.
E-mail: ascach07@gmail.com
Key Personnel: Museum Shop Mgr., Johnston Yardall.
Institution Type/Description: Historic Building & Site, General Museum & Art Museum: housed in 1900s old Post Office Building.
Hours & Admission Prices: Mon.-Fri. 7:30-4. Special Programs: Sat. by appointment. No charge; donations accepted. &
Attendance: 30,000 (estimated)

GUAM

(3 listings)

Hagatna

FANINADAHEN KOSAS GUAHAN-GUAM MUSEUM, 193 Chalan Santo Papa, Juan Pablo Dos, Hagatna, GU 96910. Mailing Address: P.O. Box 2950, Hagatna, GU 96932-2950. Tel.: 671-989-4455. Fax: 671-989-5566.
E-mail: info@guammuseum.org
Web Site: guammuseum.org

Institution Type/Description: General Museum: housed in 1776 Garden House.
Hours & Admission Prices: Daily 11-6. No charge; donations accepted. Closed holidays &
Attendance: 60,000 (actual)

Mangilao

ISLA CENTER FOR THE ARTS AT THE UNIVERSITY OF GUAM, #15 Dean's Circle, Mangilao, GU 96923. Mailing Address: UOG Station, Mangilao, GU 96923. Tel.: 671-735-2965 & 2966. Fax: 671-735-2967.
E-mail: islacenter@gmail.com
Web Site: www.uog.edu/dynamicdata/classislacenterarts.aspx?siteid+1&p=191
Key Personnel: Dir., Velma Yamashita; Extension Assoc., Gi Young Hwang.
Institution Type/Description: Art Museum.
Hours & Admission Prices: Mon.-Fri. 10-5, Sat. 10-2. No charge; donations accepted. Closed federal & government of Guam holidays. &
Attendance: 5,000 (estimated)

Piti

WAR IN THE PACIFIC NATIONAL HISTORICAL PARK, 460 N. Marine Dr., Piti, GU 96922. Mailing Address: 135 Murray Blvd., Ste. 100, Hagatna, GU 96910-5104, Tel.: 671-477-7278, ext. 1001. Fax: 671-477-7281.
E-mail: wapa_administration@nps.gov
Web Site: www.nps.gov/wapa
Key Personnel: Supt., Jim Richardson.
Institution Type/Description: World War II Military Museum: located on the site of the American recapture of Guam.
Hours & Admission Prices: Daily 9-4:30. No charge; donations accepted. Closed New Year's Day; Thanksgiving; Christmas. &
Attendance: 45,000 (actual)

MARIANA ISLANDS

(1 listings)

Saipan

THE NORTHERN MARIANA ISLANDS MUSEUM OF HISTORY AND CULTURE, Chalan Pale Arnold Rd., Garapan, Saipan, MP 96950. Mailing Address: P.O. Box 504570, Saipan, MP 96950-4305. Tel.: 670-664-2164.
E-mail: cnmimuseum@gmail.com
Web Site: cnmimuseum.wix.com/welcome#!
Institution Type/Description: History & Archaeology Museum: housed in historic Japanese hospital.
Hours & Admission Prices: Mon.-Fri. 9-4. Off-island visitors 6 & up $2, CNMI residents with I.D. $1; discounts to groups; children under 6 no charge. Closed holidays & designated austerity Fridays. &
Attendance: 8,600 (estimated)

PUERTO RICO

(20 listings)

Aguadilla

RAMEY AIR FORCE BASE HISTORICAL ASSOCIATION & MUSEUM, 572 Hangar Rd., Aguadilla, PR 00604. Mailing Address: P.O. Box 250165, Aguadilla, PR 00604.
E-mail: rameymuseum@gmail.com
Web Site: www.rameyafb.net
Institution Type/Description: Military History Museum.
Hours & Admission Prices: Sun.-Fri. by appointment. No charge; donations accepted. &

Arecibo

ARECIBO OBSERVATORY, 53995 Caja, Arecibo, PR 00612. Tel.: 787-878-2612.
Institution Type/Description: Observatory.
Hours & Admission Prices: Call for hours.

Barranquitas

LUIS MUNOZ RIVERA MUSEUM, 10 Munoz Rivera St., Barranquitas, PR 00794-1607. Tel.: 787-857-0230. Fax: 787-857-0230.
E-mail: mgomez@icp.gobierno.pr
Web Site: www.icp.gobierno.pr
Key Personnel: Exec. Dir., Mercedes Gomez Marrero; Dir., Nicole Pietri.
Institution Type/Description: History Museum: housed in the birthplace of patriot, Luis Munoz Rivera.
Hours & Admission Prices: Wed.-Sun. 8-4. No charge. &
Attendance: 5,000 (estimated)

Bayamon

DR. JOSE CELSO BARBOSA HOUSE MUSEUM, Calle Barbosa No. 16, Bayamon, PR 00961-6346. Mailing Address: Instituto de Cultura Puertorriquena, Apartado 9024184, San Juan, PR 00902-4184.
E-mail: mgomez@icp.gobierno.pr
Web Site: www.icp.gobierno.pr
Key Personnel: C.E.O., Prof. Mercedes Gomez; Dir., Nicole Pietri.
Institution Type/Description: Historic House.
Hours & Admission Prices: Tues.-Sat. 8:30-12 & 1-4:30. No charge.
Attendance: 1,534 (actual)

Cayey

DR. PIO LOPEZ MARTINEZ ART MUSEUM, University of Puerto Rico, Cayey Campus, 205 Antonio R. Barcelo Ave., Cayey, PR 00736-4127. Tel.: 787-738-2161, ext. 2209 & 2191. Fax: 787-738-0650.
E-mail: museo.cayey@upr.edu
Web Site: www.cayey.upr.edu
Key Personnel: Dir., Prof. Humberto Figueroa.
Institution Type/Description: Art & History Museum.
Hours & Admission Prices: Mon.-Fri. 8-4:30, Sat.-Sun. 11-5. No charge. &
Attendance: 4,360 (actual)

Fajardo

LAS CABEZAS DE SAN JUAN NATURE RESERVE (EL FARO), Rte. 987, Km 5.9, Fajardo, PR 00738. Mailing Address: The Conservation Trust of Puerto Rico, P.O. Box 9023554, San Juan, PR 00902-3554. Tel.: 787-860-2560. Fax: 787-722-5872 & 860-1451.
E-mail: fideicomiso@fideicomiso.org
Web Site: www.fideicomiso.org
Key Personnel: Exec. Dir., Fernando Lloveras San Miguel, Esq.; Archivist, Rafael Lebron; Supt., Elizabeth Padilla.
Institution Type/Description: Nature Reserve: 316-acre reserve on northeastern tip of Puerto Rico includes 1880 lighthouse (El Faro), second oldest of Puerto Rico's 14 lighthouses.
Hours & Admission Prices: Oct. to mid-Aug. Wed.-Sun. by reservation only. Tours: 9:30, 10, 10:30 & 2. Adults $10, senior citizens & students $7; discounts to groups of 20 or more; children under 4 no charge. Closed New Year's Day; Epiphany; Good Friday; Mother's Day; Father's Day; Independence Day; Thanksgiving; Christmas.
Attendance: 43,830 (actual)

Guaynabo

CAPARRA MUSEUM AND HISTORIC PARK, Villa Caparra, 212 Carretera No. 2, Guaynabo, PR 00966-1718. Mailing Address: Instituto de Cultura Puertorriquena, Apartado 9024184, San Juan, PR 00902-4184. Tel.: 787-781-4795. Fax: 787-723-7837.
E-mail: mgomez@icp.gobierno.pr
Web Site: www.icp.gobierno.pr
Key Personnel: Exec. Dir., Mercedes Gomez Morrero.
Institution Type/Description: Historic Site: ruins of Caparra was the first spot of colonization in Puerto Rico founded by Ponce de Leon in 1508.
Hours & Admission Prices: Mon.-Fri. 8-12 & 1-4:30, Sat.-Sun. by appointment. No charge. &
Attendance: 1,876 (actual)

Gurabo

TURABO UNIVERSITY, Carr. 189, Km. 3.1, Gurabo, PR 00778. Mailing Address: P.O. Box 3030, Gurabo, PR 00778-3030. Tel.: 787-743-7979, ext. 4135. Fax: 787-743-7979, ext. 4149.
E-mail: admisiones-ut@suagm.edu
Web Site: ut.suagm.edu
Institution Type/Description: Archaeology Museum.
Hours & Admission Prices: Aug.-May daily 8-12 & 1-5. No charge; donations accepted.
Attendance: 3,500

Mayaguez

UNIVERSITY OF PUERTO RICO DEPARTMENT OF MARINE SCIENCES MUSEUM, Dept. of Marine Sciences, Univ. of Puerto Rico, Mayaguez, PR 00681. Mailing Address: Call Box 9000, Mayaguez, PR 00681. Tel.: 787-832-4040, exts. 3443, 3447 & 3838. Fax: 787-899-5500 & 265-5408 & 832-3432.
E-mail: cima@uprm.edu
Web Site: uprm.edu/cima
Key Personnel: Dir., Dr. Ernesto Otero; Cur. Marine Invertebrates, Dr. Nikolaos Schizas; Cur. Fish, Dr. Richard Appeldoorn.
Institution Type/Description: Marine Museum.
Hours & Admission Prices: Call 787-899-2048 for appointment. No charge. &

Old San Juan

LA CASA DEL LIBRO, 255-257 Calle del Santo Cristo, Old San Juan, PR 00902. Mailing Address: P.O. Box 9023544, San Juan, PR 00902-3544. Tel.: 787-723-0354. Fax: 787-723-0354. Facebook.
E-mail: info@lacasadellibro.org
Web Site: www.lacasadellibro.org
Key Personnel: Dir. & CEO, Karen Cana-Cruz; Registrar, Rafael Linares.
Institution Type/Description: Book Museum & Library: housed in an 18th century Spanish colonial house.
Hours & Admission Prices: Tues.-Sat. 11-5. Adults $4.50, children $2.50.
Attendance: 3,000 (estimated)

Ponce

HACIENDA BUENA VISTA, Rte. 123, Km. 16.8, Ponce, PR 00731. Mailing Address: The Conservation Trust of Puerto Rico, P.O. Box 9023554, San Juan, PR 00902-3554. Tel.: 787-722-5882. Fax: 787-841-5997.
E-mail: fideicomiso@fideicomiso.org
Web Site: www.fideicomiso.org
Key Personnel: Exec. Dir., Fernando Lloveras San Miguel, Esq.; Chm., Jorge San Miguel, Esq.; Visitor Svcs. Mgr., Sandra Franqui.
Institution Type/Description: Historic Site: reconstructed 1833 coffee plantation & corn mill in southern Puerto Rico.
Hours & Admission Prices: Wed.-Sun. by appointment. Adults $8, senior citizens & students $5; discounts to groups of 20 or more; children 4 & under no charge. Closed New Year's Day; Epiphany; Good Friday; Independence Day; Thanksgiving; Christmas.
Attendance: 25,130 (actual)

MUSEO DE ARTE DE PONCE, 2325 Blvd. Luis A. Ferre-Aguayo, Ponce, PR 00717-0776. Mailing Address: P.O. Box 9027, Ponce, PR 00732-9027. Tel.: 787-840-1510 & 848-0074. Fax: 787-841-7309. Facebook: Museo de Arte de Ponce.
E-mail: info@museoarteponce.org
Web Site: www.museoarteponce.org
Key Personnel: Exec. Dir. & C.E.O., Alejandra Pena; Volunteer Coord., Mariela Vera; Financial & Administration Dir., Floribeth Anciani; Chief Educator, Ana Margarita Hernandez; Assoc. Cur., Pablo Perez; Registrar, Soraya Serra; Dir. Conservation Laboratory, Lidia Aravena; Human Resources Mgr., Nancy Colon; Museum Shop Asst., Luis Torres.
Institution Type/Description: Art Museum.
Hours & Admission Prices: Mon. & Wed.-Sat. 10-5, Sun. 12-5. Adults $6, children under 12 $3; discounts to groups & AAM members; members no charge. Closed New Year's Day; Three Kings Day; Good Friday; Thanksgiving; Christmas. &
Attendance: 48,582 (actual)

San Juan

CASA BLANCA MUSEUM, Calle San Sebastian No. 1, San Juan, PR 00901-1156. Mailing Address: Instituto de Cultura Puertorriquena, Apartado 9024184, San Juan, PR 00902-4184. Tel.: 787-725-1454. Fax: 787-723-7837.
E-mail: mgomez@icp.gobierno.pr
Web Site: www.icp.gobierno.pr
Key Personnel: Exec. Dir., Mercedes Gomez Marrero.
Institution Type/Description: Historic House: c.1521 building constructed for the sons of Juan Ponce de Leon & inhabited by their descendants until mid-18th century.
Hours & Admission Prices: Wed.-Sun. 8:30-12 & 1-4:30. Adults $2, children $1; seniors no charge. ♿
Attendance: 12,300 (actual)

LUIS TORRES DIAZ PHARMACY MUSEUM, Pharmacy and Deanship of Students Bldg., Medical Sciences Campus, University of Puerto Rico, San Juan, PR 00936. Mailing Address: P.O. Box 365067, San Juan, PR 00936-5067. Tel.: 787-758-2525. Fax: 787-751-5680.
E-mail: farma@rcm.upr.edu
Web Site: farmacia.rcm.upr.edu
Institution Type/Description: Pharmacy Museum.
Hours & Admission Prices: Tues.-Fri. 1-4.

MUSEO DE LAS AMERICAS, Cuartel de Ballaja, at the entrance of El Morro, 2nd Fl., San Juan, PR 00901. Mailing Address: P.O. Box 9023634, San Juan, PR 00902-3634. Tel.: 787-724-5052. Fax: 787-722-2848. Facebook: @museolasamericas; Instagram @museodelasamericas_pr.
E-mail: correo.mla@museolasamericas.org
Web Site: www.museolasamericas.org
Key Personnel: Dir., Maria Angela Lopez-Vilella; Museum Shop Mgr., Walleska Rivera.
Institution Type/Description: Folk Art Museum: housed in the 19th-century Ballaja Barracks.
Hours & Admission Prices: Tues.-Fri. 9-12 & 1-4, Sat. 10-5, Sun. 12-5. Adults $6, children, students, teachers & seniors $4. Closed New Year's Eve & Day; 3 Kings Eve & Day; Good Friday; Mother's Day; Father's Day; Thanksgiving; Christmas Eve & Day. ♿
Attendance: 50,000 (estimated)

MUSEUM OF HISTORY, ANTHROPOLOGY AND ART, University of Puerto Rico, San Juan, PR 00931. Mailing Address: P.O. Box 21908 UPR, San Juan, PR 00931-1908. Tel.: 787-764-0000, ext. 83080, 83083, 83082 & 763-3939. Fax: 787-763-4799. Facebook, Instagram & Twitter.
E-mail: museo.universidad@upr.edu
Key Personnel: Dir. & Cur. Art Collections, Flavia Marichal Lugo; Cur. Archaeological Collections, Ivan Mendez; Designer, Lionel Ortiz-Melendez; Educator, Lisa Ortega; Art Photographer, Jesus E. Marrero; Registrar, Chakira Santiago; Administrative Sec., Yolanda Vasquez; Admin., Maritza Rodriguez.
Institution Type/Description: Art, History & Archaeology Museum.
Hours & Admission Prices: Sun. 11-5, Mon.-Tues. & Fri. 9-4:30, Wed. 9-8:30. No charge. Closed holidays; university recesses. ♿
Attendance: 20,000

PUERTO RICO MUSEUM OF CONTEMPORARY ART, Rafael M. Labra Bldg., Ponce de Leon Ave., Corner of Roberto H. Todd (Stop 18), San Juan, PR 00909. Mailing Address: P.O. Box 362377, San Juan, PR 00936-2377. Tel.: 787-977-4030. Fax: 787-977-4036.
E-mail: administracion@mac-pr.org
Web Site: www.mac-pr.org
Key Personnel: Exec. Dir., Marianne Ramirez Aponte; Pres. Bd., Ruben Mendez Benabe; Vice Pres., Rafael Flores; Registrar, Lourdes Ranero; Admin., Michelle Dilan; Education Coord., Rafael Vargas Bernard; Museum Shop Mgr., Jorge L. Pardo.
Institution Type/Description: Art Museum.
Hours & Admission Prices: Tues.-Fri. 10-4, Sat. 11-5, Sun. 1-5. Suggested Donations: adults $5, students with ID, children 5 & over, seniors 60-75 and persons with disabilities $3; discount to AAM & ICOM members; museum members and seniors 75 & over no charge. Closed New Year's Eve & Day; Three Kings Day; Good Friday; Independence Day; Constitution Day; Discovery of America Day; Thanksgiving; Christmas. ♿
Attendance: 30,000 (estimated)

SAN JUAN NATIONAL HISTORIC SITE, 501 Norzagaray St., San Juan, PR 00901-1213. Tel.: 787-729-6777. Fax: 787-405-8712.
Web Site: www.nps.gov/saju/
Key Personnel: Supt., Walter Chavez.
Institution Type/Description: Historic Buildings: 16th to 19th-century Spanish fort located in Old San Juan, 3 miles of city walls.
Hours & Admission Prices: Daily 9-6. Admission $5, children 15 & under and seniors 65 & over with Golden Age Pass no charge. Closed New Year's Day; Thanksgiving; Christmas. ♿
Attendance: 1,300,000 (actual)

Santurce

MUSEO DE ARTE DE PUERTO RICO, 299 De Diego Ave., Stop 22, Santurce, PR 00909-1766. Mailing Address: P.O. Box 41209, San Juan, PR 00940-1209. Tel.: 787-977-6277. Fax: 787-977-4444. Facebook Museo de Arte PR; Twitter & Instagram: Museo MAPR.
E-mail: info@mapr.org
Web Site: www.mapr.org
Key Personnel: Exec. Dir., Ms. Lourdes Ramos Rivas, Ph.D.
Institution Type/Description: Art Museum.
Hours & Admission Prices: Tues. & Thurs.-Sat. 10-5, Wed. 10-8, Sun. 11-6. Adults $6, senior citizens, children & students $3; Wed. 2-8 & members no charge. Closed New Year's Day; Good Friday; Election Day; Thanksgiving; Christmas. ♿
Attendance: 125,923 (actual)

Vieques

MUSEO FUERTE CONDE DE MIRASOL DE VIEQUES, Isabel Segunda, Vieques, PR 00765-0071. Mailing Address: P.O. Box 71, Vieques, PR 00765-0071. Tel.: 787-741-1717.
E-mail: bieke@prdigital.com
Web Site: www.icp.gobierno.pr/
Key Personnel: Dir., Roberto L. Rabin.
Institution Type/Description: History Museum: housed in a two-story 19th-century Spanish fortress constructed of brick & local wood.
Hours & Admission Prices: Museum: Wed.-Sun. 9-5:30. Historic Archives: Mon.-Fri. by appointment. Closed Good Friday; Mother's Day; Father's Day.
Attendance: 15,000 (estimated)

U.S. VIRGIN ISLANDS

(4 listings)

Saint Croix

CHRISTIANSTED NATIONAL HISTORIC SITE, Mailing Address: 2100 Church St. #100, Danish Custom House, Christiansted, Saint Croix, VI 00820-5402. Tel.: 340-773-1460. Fax: 340-719-1791.
E-mail: CHRI_superintendent@nps.gov
Web Site: www.nps.gov/chri
Key Personnel: Chief Resource Management, Zandy Hillis-Starr; Park Supt., Joel A. Tutein; Chief Interpretation, David J. Goldstein.
Institution Type/Description: Historic Site & Historic Houses: depicts Danish Colonial development in the West Indies.
Hours & Admission Prices: Mon.-Fri. 8-5, Sat.-Sun. 9-5. Adult $3; senior citizens with Golden Age Pass & youth under 16 no charge. Closed Thanksgiving; Christmas.
Attendance: 100,000 (actual)

WHIM PLANTATION MUSEUM, 52 Estate Whim, Frederiksted, Saint Croix, VI 00840-3744. Tel.: 340-772-0598. Fax: 340-772-9446.
E-mail: info@stcroixlandmarks.org
Web Site: www.stcroixlandmarks.org
Institution Type/Description: History Museum: located on a former 18th century sugar plantation.
Hours & Admission Prices: Wed.-Sat. 10-3. Adults & children 13 and over $10, groups of 10 or more adults $8, senior citizens 65 & over $6, children 7-12 $5; St. Croix Landmarks Society member & active duty or retired U.S. military personnel no charge; U.S. Virgin Islands resident no charge on Sat. ♿

Saint John

VIRGIN ISLANDS NATIONAL PARK, 1300 Cruz Bay Creek, Saint John, VI 00830-6108. Tel.: 340-776-6201, ext. 238.
E-mail: ken_wild@nps.gov
Web Site: www.nps.gov/viis

Key Personnel: Supt., Btion FitzGerald; Chief Interpretive Ranger, Dave Worthington; Dir., Ken Wild.
Institution Type/Description: National Park Museum & Visitor Center.
Hours & Admission Prices: Visitor Center: daily 8:30-4:30. No charge. Closed Independence Day; Thanksgiving; Christmas. &
Attendance: 250,000 (estimated)

Saint Thomas

SEVEN ARCHES MUSEUM, Off Kongens Gade, Government Hill, Saint Thomas, VI 00802. Mailing Address: P.O. Box 6456, Saint Thomas, VI 00804-6456. Tel.: 340-774-9295.

E-mail: sevenarchesmuseum@yahoo.com
Web Site: www.sevenarchesmuseum.com
Key Personnel: Dir. & Cur., Barbara Demaras.
Institution Type/Description: History Museum.
Hours & Admission Prices: By appointment. Tours: $7 donation; school groups no charge.
Attendance: 1,000 (estimated)

Index to
Institutions

Additional data elements available online at: www.officialmuseumdirectory.com/OMD/login

G

S

V

Additional data elements available online at: www.officialmuseumdirectory.com/OMD/login

Index to
Institutions by Category

List of Categories

ART

Arts and Crafts Museums

Civic Art and Cultural Centers–Continued

The Greater Reston Arts Center (GRACE), Reston, VA.............1139

Hana Cultural Center, Hana, Maui, HI.............277

Hattiesburg Arts Council Gallery, Hattiesburg, MS.............587

Hennepin History Museum, Minneapolis, MN.............571

Henry County Museum and Cultural Arts Center, Clinton, MO.............599

Hiwan Homestead Museum, Evergreen, CO.......157

Holocaust Memorial and Tolerance Center, Glen Cove, NY.............748

Hot Springs County Museum and Cultural Center, Thermopolis, WY.............1217

Icehouse Gallery, Mayfield, KY.............425

Ida B. Wells-Barnett Museum, Holly Springs, MS.............587

Imperial Centre for the Arts & Sciences, Rocky Mount, NC.............828

Indian Pueblo Cultural Center, Albuquerque, NM.............706

Irving Arts Center, Irving, TX.............1070

Jacqueline Casey Hudgens Center for the Arts, Duluth, GA.............259

Jaffrey Civic Center, Jaffrey, NH.............667

James A. Michener Art Museum, Doylestown, PA.............938

James & Meryl Hearst Center for the Arts and Hearst Sculpture Garden, Cedar Falls, IA.............361

Janice Mason Art Museum, Cadiz, KY.............414

Kennedy-Douglass Center for the Arts, Florence, AL.............8

Kentuck Museum Association, Inc., Northport, AL.............15

Kinston Community Council for the Arts, Kinston, NC.............818

Lac Qui Parle County Historical Society, Madison, MN.............570

LaGrange Art Museum, LaGrange, GA.............263

Lesbian Herstory Educational Foundation, Inc. aka Lesbian Herstory Archives, Brooklyn, NY.............732

The Log House Museum of the Historical Society of Columbiana-Fairfield Township, Columbiana, OH.............860

Los Angeles Municipal Art Gallery - Barnsdall Art Park, Los Angeles, CA.............93

Lou Holtz/Upper Ohio Valley Hall of Fame, East Liverpool, OH.............864

Loveland Museum Gallery, Loveland, CO.............164

Lubeznik Center for the Arts, Michigan City, IN.............347

Lyndon House Arts Center, Athens, GA.............250

Madison-Morgan Cultural Center, Madison, GA.............265

The Main Street Museum, White River Junction, VT.............1116

Mary G. Hardin Center for Cultural Arts, Gadsden, AL.............9

Mayslake Peabody Estate, Oak Brook, IL.............319

McAllen Heritage Center, Inc., McAllen, TX...1075

Memphis Botanic Garden, Goldsmith Civic Garden Center, Memphis, TN.............1031

Milliken Museum, Los Banos, CA.............95

Miners Foundry Cultural Center, Nevada City, CA.............100

Mission Cultural Center for Latino Arts, San Francisco, CA.............123

Mount Dora Center for the Arts, Mount Dora, FL.............231

Muckenthaler Cultural Center and Mansion Museum, Fullerton, CA.............79

Museo Italo Americano, San Francisco, CA.......124

Museum at Eldridge Street, New York, NY.......768

National Hellenic Museum, Chicago, IL.............303

Nevada County Depot and Museum, Prescott, AR.............56

New Americans Museum CLOSED, San Diego, CA.............119

New Museum Los Gatos (NUMU), Los Gatos, CA.............95

North Central Arkansas Art Gallery, Fairfield Bay, AR.............47

North Shore Arts Association, Gloucester, MA.............509

Oceanside Museum of Art, Oceanside, CA.............103

Octagon Center for the Arts, Ames, IA.............358

OZ Mueseum/Columbian Theatre Foundation, Inc., Wamego, KS.............410

Pelham Art Center, Pelham, NY.............778

Pittsburgh Filmmakers/Pittsburgh Center for the Arts, Pittsburgh, PA.............967

Pontiac Creative Arts Center, Pontiac, MI.............556

Prince George's African American Museum & Cultural Center (PGAAMCC), North Brentwood, MD.............486

Rahr West Art Museum, Manitowoc, WI.............1196

Rialto Historical Society, Rialto, CA.............113

Rice Interpretive Center, J.D. Miller Music Recording Studio Museum and Ford Automotive Museum, Crowley, LA.............434

River Edge Cultural Center, River Edge, NJ.......698

Romanian Ethnic Art Museum, Cleveland, OH.............860

Rose Center, Morristown, TN.............1032

Rutland Area Art Association dba Chaffee Art Center & Chaffee Downtown, Rutland, VT.............1112

San Francisco African American Historical and Cultural Society, Inc., San Francisco, CA.............124

Schweinfurth Memorial Art Center, Auburn, NY.............725

Sedona Arts Center, Inc., Sedona, AZ.............36

Show Low Historical Society Museum, Show Low, AZ.............36

Snake River Heritage Center, Weiser, ID.............293

Snug Harbor Cultural Center & Botanical Garden, Staten Island, NY.............790

South Arkansas Arts Center, El Dorado, AR.........46

Southdown Plantation House/The Terrebonne Museum, Houma, LA.............436

Southern Ohio Museum, Portsmouth, OH.............879

Southern Vermont Arts Center, Manchester, VT.............1108

Sparks Heritage Foundation & Museum, Sparks, NV.............661

Stauth Memorial Museum, Montezuma, KS.......403

Stephen Foster Folk Culture Center State Park, White Springs, FL.............248

SullivanMunce Cultural Center, Zionsville, IN.............357

Tangier History Museum & Interpretive Cultural Center, Tangier Island, VA.............1146

Tarpon Springs Cultural Center, Tarpon Springs, FL.............246

Tennessee State Museum, Nashville, TN.............1035

Tennessee Valley Art Center, Tuscumbia, AL.......18

Thelma Sadoff Center for the Arts, Fond du Lac, WI.............1191

Thomasville Cultural Center, Inc., Thomasville, GA.............274

Thornhill Gallery at Avila University, Kansas City, MO.............607

The Toledo Museum of Art, Toledo, OH.............883

Torpedo Factory Art Center, Alexandria, VA...1118

Troy-Hayner Cultural Center, Troy, OH.............883

UTSA Institute of Texan Cultures, San Antonio, TX.............1084

Union County Heritage Museum and Genealogical Library, Maynardville, TN.....1030

Union Street Gallery, Chicago Heights, IL.............305

Urban Institute for Contemporary Arts, Grand Rapids, MI.............546

Vermont Folklife Center, Middlebury, VT.......1109

Vilna Shul Boston's Center for Jewish Culture, Boston, MA.............501

Virginia Museum of Fine Arts, Richmond, VA.............1142

Volcano Art Center Gallery, Volcano, HI.............283

The Walker African American Museum & Research Center, Las Vegas, NV.............659

WaterWorks Art Museum, Miles City, MT.......632

Watts Towers Arts Center & Charles Mingus Youth Arts Center, Los Angeles, CA.............95

Western Folklife Center, Elko, NV.............656

William Bonifas Fine Arts Center, Escanaba, MI.............543

William King Museum Center for Art and Cultural Heritage, Abingdon, VA.............1116

Worcester Center for Crafts, Worcester, MA.......531

Decorative Arts Museums

Adsmore Museum, Princeton, KY.............428

African Art Museum of the S.M.A. Fathers, Tenafly, NJ.............700

Alleghany Highlands Arts & Crafts Center, Inc., Clifton Forge, VA.............1123

American Folk Art Museum, New York, NY.......762

American Museum of Ceramic Art, Pomona, CA.............110

American Museum of Straw Art, Long Beach, CA.............88

American Sign Museum, Cincinnati, OH.............855

Appalachian Center For Craft, Smithville, TN..1038

Ash Lawn-Highland, Charlottesville, VA.............1121

Atlantic Wildfowl Heritage Museum, Virginia Beach, VA.............1146

Banning Museum, Wilmington, CA.............145

Bard Graduate Center: Decorative Arts, Design History, Material Culture, New York, NY.............763

Batsto Village, Hammonton, NJ.............684

Bayou Bend Collection and Gardens, Houston, TX.............1066

Beauport, Sleeper-McCann House, Gloucester, MA.............509

Bellamy Mansion Museum of History and Design Arts, Wilmington, NC.............834

Bellport-Brookhaven Historical Society and Museum, Bellport, NY.............727

The Bennington Museum, Bennington, VT.......1104

Bergstrom-Mahler Museum of Glass, Neenah, WI.............1200

Bernard Judaica Museum, Congregation Emanu-El of the City of New York, New York, NY.............763

Blair Museum of Lithophanes, Toledo, OH.............882

Boscobel House & Gardens, Garrison, NY.............747

Brunnier Art Museum, Ames, IA.............358

Burlington County Historical Society, Burlington, NJ.............677

California Heritage Museum, Santa Monica, CA.............134

Campbell House Museum, Saint Louis, MO.......616

Caramoor Center for Music & the Arts, Inc., Katonah, NY.............754

Catskill Fly Fishing Center & Museum, Livingston Manor, NY.............757

Central Connecticut State University Art Galleries, New Britain, CT.............182

Cogswell's Grant, Essex, MA.............508

The Colonial Williamsburg Foundation, Williamsburg, VA.............1149

Colorado Springs Museum, Colorado Springs, CO.............150

Concord Museum, Concord, MA.............505

Cooper Hewitt, Smithsonian Design Museum, New York, NY.............764

Crescent Bend House & Gardens, Knoxville, TN.............1027

COLLEGE AND UNIVERSITY MUSEUMS

COLLEGE AND UNIVERSITY MUSEUMS–Continued

COMPANY MUSEUMS

EXHIBIT AREAS

GENERAL MUSEUMS–Continued

GENERAL MUSEUMS–Continued

Historic Houses and Historic Buildings

Historic Houses and Historic Buildings—Continued

Historic Sites

Historic Sites—Continued

Historic Sites–Continued

Historical and Preservation Societies

History Museums

History Museums—Continued

Additional data elements available online at: www.officialmuseumdirectory.com/OMD/login

History Museums–Continued

Maritime, Naval Museums and Historic Ships

Military Museums–Continued

LIBRARIES HAVING COLLECTIONS OF BOOKS

LIBRARIES HAVING COLLECTIONS OTHER THAN BOOKS

NATIONAL AND STATE AGENCIES, COUNCILS AND COMMISSIONS

NATURE CENTERS

PARK MUSEUMS AND VISITOR CENTERS

SCIENCE

Academies, Associations, Institutes and Foundations

Aeronautics and Space Museums

Anthropology and Ethnology Museums

Arboretums

Archaeology Museums and Archaeological Sites

Entomology Museums

Herbaria

William & Joan Soderlund Pharmacy
Museum, Saint Peter, MN.....................579
Wood Library-Museum of Anesthesiology,
Schaumburg, IL.....................325
Woodson County Historical Society, Yates
Center, KS.....................412
World AIDS Museum and Educational
Center, Wilton Manors, FL.....................248

Natural History and Natural Science Museums

The Academy of Natural Sciences of Drexel
University, Philadelphia, PA.....................956
Agate Fossil Beds National Monument,
Harrison, NE.....................643
Aiken County Historical Museum, Aiken, SC.....987
Alabama Museum of Natural History,
Tuscaloosa, AL.....................16
Alaska Museum of Science & Nature,
Anchorage, AK.....................19
Alley Pond Environmental Center, Inc.,
Douglaston, NY.....................741
American Bald Eagle Foundation, Haines,
AK.....................21
American Cave Museum & Hidden River
Cave, Horse Cave, KY.....................420
American Museum of Natural History, New
York, NY.....................762
Amherst College Museum of Natural History,
Amherst, MA.....................494
Anadarko Basin Museum of Natural History,
Elk City, OK.....................895
Angel Island State Park, Tiburon, CA.....................140
Angel Mounds State Historic Site, Evansville,
IN.....................338
Anniston Museum of Natural History,
Anniston, AL.....................3
Annmarie Sculpture Garden & Art Center,
Solomons, MD.....................491
Anza-Borrego Desert State Park, Borrego
Springs, CA.....................64
Arches National Park Visitor Center, Moab,
UT.....................1096
Arizona Museum of Natural History, Mesa,
AZ.....................30
Arizona-Sonora Desert Museum, Tucson, AZ.....39
Arizona State Parks Board, Phoenix, AZ.....................32
Arkansas State University Museum,
Jonesboro, AR.....................51
Arthur F. McClure II Archives and University
Museum, Warrensburg, MO.....................622
Ash Hollow State Historical Park, Lewellen,
NE.....................645
Asheville Museum of Science, Asheville, NC.....797
Ataloa Lodge Museum, Muskogee, OK.....................901
Audubon Insectarium, New Orleans, LA.....................441
Audubon National Wildlife Refuge,
Coleharbor, ND.....................839
Audubon Society of New Hampshire,
Concord, NH.....................664
Audubon Society of Rhode Island
Environmental Education Center, Bristol,
RI.....................977
Aurora Fossil Museum Foundation, Inc.,
Aurora, NC.....................798
Austin Nature & Science Center, Austin, TX.....1043

Badlands National Park, Interior, SD.....................1009
Badlands Petrified Gardens, Kadoka, SD.....................1009
The Bailey-Matthews National Shell
Museum, Sanibel, FL.....................242
Bandon Historical Society Museum, Bandon,
OR.....................914
Bartels Museum - Concordia University,
Seward, NE.....................652
The Bartlett Museum, Amesbury, MA.....................494
Bear Mountain Trailside Museums and Zoo,
Bear Mountain, NY.....................727
Becker County Historical Society, Detroit
Lakes, MN.....................564
Bell Museum + Planetarium, Saint Paul, MN.....577
Berkshire Museum, Pittsfield, MA.....................521

Big Basin Redwoods State Park, Boulder
Creek, CA.....................64
Big Bend National Park, Big Bend National
Park, TX.....................1048
Big Bone Lick State Historic Site, Union, KY.....430
Big Cypress National Preserve, Ochopee, FL.....234
Big Thicket National Preserve, Kountze, TX.....1071
Big Thunder Gold Mine, Keystone, SD.....................1009
Billings Curation Center, Billings, MT.....................624
Birds of Vermont Museum, Huntington, VT.....1107
Birmingham Botanical Gardens,
Birmingham, AL.....................4
Biscayne National Park, Homestead, FL.....................223
Bishop Museum, Honolulu, HI.....................278
Black Hills Museum of Natural History, Hill
City, SD.....................1008
Blackwater Draw Museum, Portales, NM.....................715
Blue Hills Trailside Museum, Milton, MA.....................516
Bollinger County Museum of Natural
History, Marble Hill, MO.....................611
Boone County Historical Center, Boone, IA.....360
Boone County Historical Museum, Belvidere,
IL.....................296
Boone's Lick State Historic Site, Boonesboro,
MO.....................596
Boonshoft Museum of Discovery, Dayton,
OH.....................863
Boyce Thompson Arboretum, Superior, AZ.....................37
Bramble Park Zoo, Watertown, SD.....................1015
Brazos Valley Museum of Natural History,
Bryan, TX.....................1050
Brazosport Museum of Natural Science,
Clute, TX.....................1052
Brevard Museum of History and Natural
Science, Cocoa, FL.....................215
Briar Bush Nature Center, Abington, PA.....................929
Brigham City Museum of Art and History,
Brigham City, UT.....................1093
Brown County History Center, Nashville, IN.....349
Bruce Museum, Greenwich, CT.....................176
Bryce Canyon National Park Visitor Center,
Bryce Canyon, UT.....................1094
Buckhorn Saloon & Museum, San Antonio,
TX.....................1083
Buena Vista Museum of Natural History,
Bakersfield, CA.....................61
Buffalo Bill Center of the West, Cody, WY.....1211
Buffalo Museum of Science, Buffalo, NY.....................734
Buffalo National River, Harrison, AR.....................49
Buffalo Trails Museum, Epping, ND.....................840
Burke Museum of Natural History and
Culture, Seattle, WA.....................1164
Burpee Museum of Natural History,
Rockford, IL.....................324
Burritt on the Mountain - A Living Museum,
Huntsville, AL.....................10

C.E. Smith Museum of Anthropology,
Hayward, CA.....................81
C.H. Nash Museum at Chucalissa, Memphis,
TN.....................1030
Cable Natural History Museum, Cable, WI.....1187
Cabrillo National Monument, San Diego, CA.....117
California Academy of Sciences, San
Francisco, CA.....................122
Calkins Nature Area/Field Museum, Iowa
Falls, IA.....................372
Call of the Wild Museum, Gaylord, MI.....................544
Calvert Marine Museum, Solomons, MD.....................491
Cape Cod Museum of Natural History, Inc.,
Brewster, MA.....................501
Cape Cod National Seashore, Wellfleet, MA.....529
Cape Fear Museum of History and Science,
Wilmington, NC.....................834
Capitol Reef National Park Visitor Center,
Torrey, UT.....................1102
Capulin Volcano National Monument,
Capulin, NM.....................709
Carl G. Fenner Nature Center, Lansing, MI.....549
Carlsbad Caverns National Park, Carlsbad,
NM.....................709

Carlsbad Museum & Art Center, Carlsbad,
NM.....................709
Carnegie Museum of Natural History,
Pittsburgh, PA.....................965
Carnegie Museums of Pittsburgh (Carnegie
Institute), Pittsburgh, PA.....................965
Carolina Raptor Center, Huntersville, NC.....................816
Catherine Montgomery Interpretive Center,
Greenwater, WA.....................1157
Cave of the Mounds -National Natural
Landmark, Blue Mounds, WI.....................1186
Cave of the Winds, Manitou Springs, CO.....................164
Cedar Bog Nature Preserve, Urbana, OH.....................884
Cedar Breaks National Monument, Cedar
City, UT.....................1094
Cedar Key Museum State Park, Cedar Key,
FL.....................214
Centennial Museum and Chihuahuan Desert
Gardens, El Paso, TX.....................1058
Center for American Archeology,
Kampsville, IL.....................314
Center for Meteorite Studies - Arizona State
University, Tempe, AZ.....................38
Champaign County Historical Museum,
Urbana, OH.....................884
Channel Islands National Park, Robert J.
Lagomarsino Visitor Center, Ventura, CA.....143
Charles R. Conner Museum, Pullman, WA.....1163
Charlotte County Historical Center, Punta
Gorda, FL.....................238
Chattahoochee Nature Center, Roswell, GA.....269
Chelan County Historical Society - Cashmere
Museum & Pioneer Village, Cashmere,
WA.....................1153
Cheraw Lyceum Museum, Cheraw, SC.....................991
Chesapeake Bay Environmental Center,
Grasonville, MD.....................482
Chesapeake Biological Laboratory Visitors
Center, Solomons, MD.....................491
The Chicago Academy of Sciences/Peggy
Notebaert Nature Museum, Chicago, IL.....299
Chickasaw National Recreation Area,
Sulphur, OK.....................909
Chief Plenty Coups Museum, Pryor, MT.....................634
The Children's Museum of Indianapolis,
Indianapolis, IN.....................342
Chippewa Nature Center, Midland, MI.....................552
Chiricahua National Monument, Willcox, AZ.....42
Cincinnati Museum Center at Union
Terminal, Cincinnati, OH.....................856
Cleveland Metroparks Outdoor Education
Division, Cleveland, OH.....................858
The Cleveland Museum of Natural History,
Cleveland, OH.....................858
Cliff Dwellings Museum, Manitou Springs,
CO.....................164
Cliffs of the Neuse State Park, Seven Springs,
NC.....................829
Coal Heritage Trail Interpretive Center,
Bramwell, WV.....................1174
Coastal Discovery Museum at Honey Horn,
Hilton Head Island, SC.....................997
Coastal Studies Laboratory - The University
of Texas-Pan American, South Padre
Island, TX.....................1087
Coke Hallowell Center for River Studies,
Fresno, CA.....................78
Colleton Museum, Farmers Market &
Commerical Kitchen, Walterboro, SC.....................1004
Colorado National Monument, Fruita, CO.....158
Colorado Plateau Biodiversity Center,
Flagstaff, AZ.....................27
Columbia Gorge Discovery Center and
Wasco County Museum, The Dalles, OR.....927
Columbia Gorge Interpretive Center
Museum, Stevenson, WA.....................1169
The Community Historical Society, Maxwell,
IA.....................376
Congaree National Park, Hopkins, SC.....................997
Connecticut Audubon Birdcraft Museum,
Fairfield, CT.....................174

Planetariums, Observatories and Astronomy Museums

SPECIALIZED

Agriculture Museums

Antiques Museums

Architecture Museums

Crime Museums

Lapidary Arts Museums

Logging and Lumber Museums

Money and Numismatics Museums

Musical Instruments Museums

Philatelic Museums

Scouting Museums

Technology Museums

Typography Museums

Village Museums